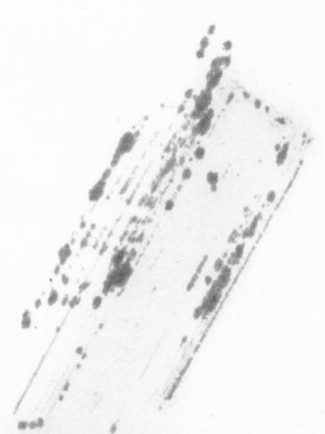

A DICTIONARY OF
SLANG AND UNCONVENTIONAL
ENGLISH

ERIC PARTRIDGE

A DICTIONARY OF SLANG AND UNCONVENTIONAL ENGLISH

Colloquialisms and Catch-phrases
Solecisms and Catachreses
Nicknames
Vulgarisms
and
such Americanisms as have been naturalized

SEVENTH EDITION

Two volumes in one
VOLUME I: THE DICTIONARY
VOLUME II: THE SUPPLEMENT

69364

MACMILLAN PUBLISHING CO., INC.

NEW YORK

To the memory of

THE LATE

ALFRED SUTRO

(OF SAN FRANCISCO)

LOVER OF LOVELY THINGS

IN ART AND LITERATURE

DEVOTEE TO KNOWLEDGE

AND

TRUE FRIEND

MACMILLAN PUBLISHING CO., INC.
866 THIRD AVENUE, NEW YORK, N.Y. 10022

Printed in the United States of America
Library of Congress catalog card number: 79-136481

Originally published in two volumes
VOLUME I: THE DICTIONARY
VOLUME II: THE SUPPLEMENT

1st edition, 1937
2nd edition, enlarged, 1938
3rd edition, much enlarged, 1949
4th edition, revised, 1951
reprinted 1953, 1956
5th edition
supplement much enlarged, 1961
6th edition
supplement revised and enlarged, 1967
7th edition
supplement revised and enlarged, 1970
reprinted 1972, 1974

PREFACE

THIS dictionary, at which I have worked harder than (I hope, but should not swear) I shall ever work again and which incorporates the results of a close observation of colloquial speech for many years, is designed to form a humble companion to the monumental *Oxford English Dictionary*, from which I am proud to have learnt a very great amount.

A Dictionary of Slang and Unconventional English, i.e. of linguistically unconventional English, should be of interest to word-lovers; but it should also be useful to the general as well as the cultured reader, to the scholar and the linguist, to the foreigner and the American. I have, in fact, kept the foreigner as well as the English-speaker in mind; and I have often compared British with American usage. In short, the field is of all English other than standard and other than dialectal.

Although I have not worked out the proportions, I should say that, merely approximately, they are:

Slang and Cant	50%
Colloquialisms	35%
Solecisms and Catachreses	6½%
Catch-phrases	6½%
Nicknames*	1½%
Vulgarisms	½%

(By the last, I understand words and phrases that, in no way slangy, are avoided in polite society.) For the interrelations of these classes, I must refer the reader to my *Slang To-day and Yesterday: a Study and a History*, where these interrelations are treated in some detail.

The degree of comprehensiveness? This may best be gauged by comparing the relevant terms in any one letter (I suggest a 'short' one like *o* or *v*) of either *The Oxford English Dictionary* and its *Supplement* or Farmer and Henley's *Slang and its Analogues* with the terms in the same letter here (including the inevitable Addenda). On this point, again, I have not worked out the proportions, but I should guess that whereas the *O.E.D.* contains † roughly 30% more than *F. & H.*, and *F. & H.* has some 20% not in the *O.E.D.*, the present dictionary contains approximately 35% more than the other two taken together and, except accidentally, has missed nothing included in those two works. Nor are my additions confined to the period since ca. 1800, a period for which—owing to the partial neglect of Vaux, Egan, 'Jon Bee', Brandon,

'Ducange Anglicus', Hotten, Ware, and Collinson, to the literally complete neglect of Baumann and Lyell, and the virtually complete neglect of Manchon, not to mention the incomplete use made of the glossaries of military and naval unconventional terms—the lexicography of slang and other unconventional English is gravely inadequate: even such 17th-18th century dictionaries as Coles's, B.E.'s, and Grose's have been only culled, not used thoroughly. Nor has proper attention been given, in the matter of dates, to the various editions of Grose (1785, 1788, 1796, 1811, 1823) and Hotten (1859, 1860, 1864, 1872, 1874): collation has been sporadic.

For Farmer & Henley there was only the excuse (which I hasten to make for my own shortcomings) that certain sources were not examined; the *O.E.D.* is differently placed, its aim, for unconventional English, being selective—it has omitted what it deemed ephemeral. In the vast majority of instances, the omissions from, e.g., B.E., Grose, Hotten, Farmer & Henley, Ware, and others, were deliberate: yet, with all due respect, I submit that if Harman was incorporated almost *in toto*, so should B.E. and Grose (to take but two examples) have been. The *O.E.D.*, moreover, has omitted certain vulgarisms and included others. Should a lexicographer, if he includes *any* vulgarisms (in any sense of that term), omit the others? I have given them all. (My rule, in the matter of unpleasant terms, has been to deal with them as briefly, as astringently, as aseptically as was consistent with clarity and adequacy; in a few instances, I had to force myself to overcome an instinctive repugnance; for these I ask the indulgence of my readers.)

It must not, however, be thought that I am in the least ungrateful to either the *O.E.D.* or *F. & H.* I have noted *every* debt* to the former, not merely for the sake of its authority but to indicate my profound admiration for its work; to the latter, I have made few references—for the simple reason that the publishers have given me *carte blanche* permission to use it. But it may be assumed that, for the period up to 1904, and where *no* author or dictionary is quoted, the debt is, in most instances, to Farmer & Henley—who, by the way, have never received their dues.

It has, I think, been made clear that I also owe a very great deal to such dictionaries and glossaries as those of Weekley, Apperson; Coles, B.E.,

---

*I am keenly aware that, in these, the Dictionary is woefully defective.

†For the period up to 1904, when *F. & H.* was completed.

*Often, indeed, I have preferred its evidence to that on which I came independently.

Grose; 'Jon Bee', Hotten; Baumann, Ware; Manchon, Collinson,* Lyell; Fraser & Gibbons, and Bowen.

Yet, as a detailed examination of these pages will show, I have added considerably from my own knowledge of language-byways and from my own reading, much of the latter having been undertaken with this specific end in view.

But also I am fully aware that there must be errors, both typographical and other, and that, inevitably, there are numerous omissions. Here and now, may I say that I shall be deeply grateful for notification (and note) of errors and for words and phrases that, through ignorance, I have omitted.†

Finally, it is a pleasure to thank, for terms§ that I might well have failed to encounter, the following lady and gentlemen:

Mr J. J. W. Pollard, Mr G. D. Nicolson, Mr G. Ramsay, Mr K. G. Wyness-Mitchell, Mr G. G. M. Mitchell, Mr A. E. Strong, Mr Robert E. Brown (of Hamilton), all of New Zealand; Mr John Beames, of Canada; Mr Stanley Deegan, Mrs J. Litchfield, Mr H. C. McKay, of Australia; Dr Jean

---

*Professor W. E. Collinson's admirable *Contemporary English. A personal speech record,* 1927 (Leipzig and Berlin), is mentioned here for convenience' sake.

†With information on their *milieu* and period, please! This applies also to omitted senses of terms and phrases that are already represented in this work.

§The number of terms so gleaned is approximately one-eighth of the number found in the course of 'ad hoc' reading (outside the dictionaries and glossaries, *bien entendu*).

Bordeaux, of Los Angeles. From Great Britain: Mr John Gibbons (most unselfishly), Mr Alastair Baxter (a long, valuable list), Mr Julian Franklyn (author of *This Gutter Life*), Mr John Brophy, Professor J. R. Sutherland, Mr J. Hodgson Lobley, R.B.A., Mr Alfred Atkins, the actor, Major-General A. P. Wavell, C.M.G., Commander W. M. Ross, Major A. J. Dawson, Mr R. A. Auty, Mr Allan M. Laing, Mr R. A. Walker, Mr G. W. Pirie, Mr D. E. Yates, Mr Joe Mourant, Mr Hugh Milner, Sgt T. Waterman, the Rev. A. K. Chignell, the Rev. A. Trevellick Cape, Mr Henry Gray, Mr E. Unné, Mr Malcolm McDougall, Mr R. B. Oram, Mr L. S. Tugwell, Mr V. C. Brodie, Mr Douglas Buchanan, Mr Will T. Fleet, Mr Fred Burton, Mr Alfred T. Chenhalls, Mr Digby A. Smith, Mr George S. Robinson (London), Mr Arthur W. Allen, Mr Frank Dean, Mr M. C. Way, Mr David MacGibbon, Mr A. Jameson, Mr Jack Lindsay, Mr 'David Hume' (of 'thriller' fame), Mr J. G. Considine, the Rev. M. Summers, Mr C. H. Davis, Mr H. E. A. Richardson, Mr J. Hall Richardson, Mr R. Ellis Roberts, Mr George Baker (who has a notable knowledge of unconventional English and no selfishness), Mr F. R. Jelley, Mr Barry Moore, Mr H. C. Cardew-Rendle, Mr Norman T. McMurdo, Mr R. H. Parrott, Mr F. Willis (Sheffield), Mr E. C. Pattison (of *A Martial Medley*), and, for introducing me to the work of Clarence Rook and the early work of Edwin Pugh, Mr Wilson Benington.

E. P.

LONDON; *November* 11, 1936.

PREFACE TO THE FIFTH EDITION

THE new matter, which runs to some 100,000 words, has been incorporated with the Addenda of the second, third, fourth editions to form one vocabulary—a Supplement to the first edition, published in February, 1937. The earlier matter (first-fourth editions) has been revised; the corrections, when not mere 'literals' (duly listed before the dictionary proper), are included in the Supplement which now comprises Volume II.

The Supplement consists mainly of new words and phrases. Of these the most important section is the slang of World War II; next in importance, however, comes the slang first recorded in this, the fifth, edition.

The first-recorded matter covers many centuries and countries. Besides indicating many earlier datings and a few old terms, gathered by my generous correspondents from all over the world and by myself from extensive reading done during the past ten or eleven years, it is (I like to think) notable in two fields: that of the Dominions, whence various good fellows have largely enriched my own researches; and the fascinating area of

catch-phrases, in which—although aided by others —I have undertaken much *ad hoc* work, for I felt that the earlier editions were deficient. My readings of catch-phrases are still necessarily incomplete, but no longer are they grossly inadequate.

Among my numerous helpers, all of whom I warmly thank for their patience and generosity, there are a few whose names could not be omitted from even the most cavalier and perfunctory list: Sidney J. Baker, author of *The Australian Language* and *The Drum*; Harold Griffiths, of New Zealand; Mr Douglas Leechman and Professor F. E. L. Priestley, of Canada; Colonel Albert F. Moe, of Arlington, Virginia; and, in Britain, Laurie Atkinson (well-informed and scholarly)— Julian Franklyn, author of *The Cockney* and *A Dictionary of Rhyming Slang*—Wilfred Granville, whose *Sea Slang of the Twentieth Century* is so very unfortunately out of print—and Albert Petch of Bournemouth, tireless gleaner and tenacious rememberer.

March 30, 1960.

E. P.

CONTENTS

NOTE TO SECOND EDITION

HEARTY thanks must be—and readily are—given to the following gentlemen for notice of errors and omissions:—Dr W. P. Barrett; Colonel Bates; Mr Wilson Benington; Mr John Brophy; Lieut.-General Sir J. R. E. Charles, K.C.B.; Dr M. Clement, M.D.; 'Mr J. J. Connington', very generously; Mr B. Crocker; Mr James Curtis, author of that masterly underworld novel, *The Gilt Kid*; Mr Brian Frith; M. François Fosca; Mr Julian Franklyn (a very valuable list); Mr David Garnett; Mr G. W. Gough; Mr Robert Graves; illegible signature (Jewish terms); Mr Harold James; Mr Gershon Legman; Mr J. Langley Levy; Mr Jack Lindsay; Dr E. V. Lucas; Mr David MacGibbon; Mr H. L. Menchen; Mr Hamish Miles; Mr George Milne; Mr Raymond Mortimer; Mr Robert Nott; Dr C. T. Onions, C.B.E.; Mr H. D. Poole; Mr Vernon Rendall (notably); Mr Basil de Sélincourt; Mr Kazim Raza Siddiqui (Lucknow); Mr G. W. Stonier, most generously; Professor J. R. Sutherland; the leader-writer in *The Times* (Feb. 15, 1937) and the reviewer in *The Times Literary Supplement*; Mr Evelyn Waugh; Major-General A. P. Wavell, C.M.G. (extensively); Professor Ernest Weekley; Mr Wilfred Whitten. These gentlemen have, in the aggregate, contributed about one-third of the new terms (and senses) incorporated, in this new edition, into the already existing Addenda: and it is more by good luck than by good management that my own contribution amounts to so much as two-thirds; I admit, however, that I looked hard for the luck.

E. P.

July 9, 1937.

NOTE TO THIRD EDITION

AFTER an interval of eleven years, with the fertilizing influence of the war, there has been a considerable increase of material, especially in the combatant services. Both the new words, and the additional matter affecting the older material, have been incorporated into the Addenda—a supplement that brings together, in this one section, not only the Addenda of the second edition (1938) but also the entirety of the later, and of the later-discovered, material. To mention every single person that has helped me, in one degree or another, would be almost impossible, but I must particularize the kindness of Mr Sidney J. Baker and Lieut. Wilfred Granville, R.N.V.R., without whose published and unpublished works these Addenda would be so very much poorer; for the new South African matter, I am indebted to the four correspondents that supplied me with South African cant for *A Dictionary of the Underworld*, where, by the way, the curious will find a much fuller treatment of such cant terms as are included in *A Dictionary of Slang* and many not there included, this applying especially to terms of American origin. Of Service contributors, one of the most valuable has been Sgt-Pilot F. Rhodes (to quote his rank in September, 1942); Sgt Gerald Emanuel (letter of March 29, 1945) vies with him; and Flying-Officer Robert Hinde and Wing-Commander Robin McDouall have been most helpful. My best Army contributor has been Lieut. Frank Roberts, R.A., now a master at Cotton College. Nor may I, without the grossest discourtesy, omit the names of Mr F. W. Thomas (of *The Star*); the late Professor A. W. Stewart (widely known as 'J. J. Connington', writer of detective novels); and, above all, Mr Albert Petch (of Bournemouth)—three loyal helpers. Also, at the eleventh hour, I have received a valuable set of pellucid and scholarly notes from Mr Laurie Atkinson.

July 31, 1948.

E. P.

NOTE TO FOURTH EDITION

A few corrections have been made.   *June 14, 1950.*   E. P.

A NOTE ON ARRANGEMENT

There are two main systems of arranging words in a dictionary. The strictly alphabetical; the 'something before nothing'. No system is wholly satisfactory; the arrangements* in the 'O.E.D.', in 'Webster' and, to compare small things with great, the present dictionary are open to severe criticism —severe but unreasonable. No arrangement is, for no arrangement can be, perfect.

Here, the 'something before nothing' system has been adopted—for the simple reason that it is the most suitable to a dictionary of this kind. Thus *A.B.* precedes *abaddon*, but it also precedes *Aaron*. Perhaps an example is more illuminating: *a; A.A. of the G.G.; A.B.; A.B.C.; A.B.C., as easy as; a-cockbill a-crash of, go; A.D.; a-doing of; a.f.; A from a windmill; A1; Aaron; abaa; abaddon; abaht.* Further, all *come* (or *come-*) terms, beginning with *come*, including *come it, come out, come the . . .*, and ending with *come Yorkshire*, precede *comedy-merchant*. Terms that are spelt both as two words (e.g. *cock-tail*) and as one (*cocktail*) present a difficulty. I give them as, e.g., *cock-tail*, and at, e.g., *cocktail* insert a cross-reference: to scholars, some of these precautions may seem mere foolishness, but there are others to be considered.

---

*An examination of any ten consecutive pages in these three works will show the recalcitrance of the English (and American) vocabulary—with its 'analytical' phrases—to the rigidity, and the desirability, of lexicographical principles, however sound those principles may be.

ABBREVIATIONS AND SIGNS

abbr. . . .	abbreviation, or shortening; abbreviated, abridged
adj. . . .	adjective
adv.. . . .	adverb
after . . .	after the fashion of; on the analogy of
anon. . . .	anonymous
app.. . .	apparently
Apperson . .	G. L. Apperson, *English Proverbs and Proverbial Phrases*, 1929
B. & P. . . .	Brophy & Partridge, *Songs and Slang of the British Soldier, 1914–1918* (3rd ed. 1931)
Barrère & Leland .	Barrère & Leland, *A Dictionary of Slang, Jargon, and Cant*, 1889–90
Baumann . .	Heinrich Baumann's *Londonismen*, 1887
B.E. . .	B.E.'s *Dictionary of the Canting Crew*, ca. 1690. (Better dated 1698–99)
Bee . . .	'Jon Bee', *Dictionary*, 1823.
Bowen . .	F. Bowen's *Sea Slang*, 1929
Brandon . .	Brandon's Glossary of Cant in 'Ducange Anglicus'
c. . . .	cant, i.e. language of the underworld
C. . . .	century; as C. 18, the 18th century
c. and low . .	cant and low slang
ca.. . .	about (the year . . .)
cf. . . .	compare
C.O.D. . .	*Concise Oxford Dictionary*
Coles. . .	E. Coles, *Dictionary*, 1676
coll. . . .	colloquial(ism)
Collinson . .	W. E. Collinson, *Contemporary English*, 1927
c.p.. . .	a catch-phrase
d. . . .	died
Dawson . .	L. Dawson's *Nicknames and Pseudonyms*, 1908
dial.. . .	dialect; dialectal(ly)
Dict. . .	Dictionary
D.N.B. . .	*Dictionary of National Biography*
'Ducange Anglicus' .	his *The Vulgar Tongue*, 1857
ed. . . .	edition
E.D.D. . .	*The English Dialect Dictionary*, by Joseph Wright
e.g. . . .	for example
Egan's Grose .	See 'Grose' below.
Eng.. . .	English
esp. . . .	especially
ex . . .	from; derived from
F. & Gibbons .	Fraser & Gibbons, *Soldier and Sailor Words and Phrases*, 1925
F. & H. . .	Farmer & Henley's *Slang and its Analogues*, 7 vols., 1890–1904
fig. . . .	figurative(ly)
fl. . . .	flourished (*floruit*)
Fowler . .	H. W. Fowler's *Modern English Usage*, 1926
Fr. . . .	French
gen.. . .	general(ly); usual(ly)
Ger.. . .	German
Gr. . . .	Greek
Grose . .	Grose's *Dictionary of the Vulgar Tongue* (1785, 1788, 1796, 1811, 1823). Hence, Egan's Grose = Egan's ed. of Grose, 1823. Grose, P. = my annotated reprint of the 3rd ed.
G.W. . .	The War of 1914–18
H. . .	J. C. Hotten, *The Slang Dictionary*, 1859, 1860, etc.
ibid.. . .	in the same authority or book
id. . . .	the same
i.e. . . .	that is

imm..	immediately
Irwin	Godfrey Irwin, *American Tramp and Underworld Slang*, 1931
It.	Italian
j.	jargon, i.e. technical(ity)
Jice Doone	Jice Doone, *Timely Tips to New Australians*, 1926
L.	Latin
Lewis	W. J. Lewis, *The Language of Cricket*, 1934
Lex. Bal.	*The Lexicon Balatronicum*, or 4th ed. of Grose, 1811
lit.	literal(ly)
literary	literary English, i.e. unused in ordinary speech
Lyell.	T. Lyell's *Slang, Phrase and Idiom in Colloquial English*, 1931
Manchon	J. Manchon's *Le Slang*, 1923
M.E.	Middle English
mod.	modern
Morris	E. E. Morris, *Austral English*, 1898
n.	noun
n.b.	note carefully
ob.	obsolescent; cf. †
occ.	occasional(ly)
O.E.	Old English; i.e. before ca. 1150
O.E.D. (Sup.)	*The Oxford English Dictionary* (Supplement)
on	on the analogy of
Onions	C. T. Onions, *A Shakespeare Glossary*, ed. of 1919
opp.	opposite; as opposed to
orig.	original(ly)
Pettman	C. Pettman, *Africanderisms*, 1913
pl.	plural; in the plural
Port.	Portuguese
ppl.	participle; participial
prob.	probable, probably
pron.	pronounced; pronunciation
pub..	published
q.v.	which see!
resp.	respective(ly)
s.	slang
sc.	supply!; understand!
S.E.	Standard English
Slang	My *Slang To-Day and Yesterday*, revised ed., 1935
Smart & Crofton	B. C. Smart & H. T. Crofton, *The Dialect of the English Gypsies*, revised ed., 1875
S.O.D.	*The Shorter Oxford Dictionary*
sol.	solecism; solecistic
Sp.	Spanish
s.v.	see at
temp.	in or at the time of
Thornton	R. H. Thornton's *American Glossary*, 1912
U.S.	The United States of America; American
v.	verb. Hence, *v.i.*, intransitive; *v.t.*, transitive
Vaux	J. H. Vaux's 'Glossary of Cant, 1812', in his *Memoirs*, 1819
vbl.n.	verbal noun
vulg.	vulgar(ism). See Preface
W.	Ernest Weekley's *Etymological Dictionary of Modern English*
Ware	J. Redding Ware's *Passing English*, 1909
Words	My *Words, Words, Words!*, 1933
Yule & Burnell	Yule & Burnell, *Hobson-Jobson*, revised ed., 1903

— (before a date)	.	known to exist then and presumably used some years earlier[1]
+ (after a date)	.	in significant first use then, but still extant
† . . .	.	obsolete; cf. ob.
= . . .	.	equal(s); equal to; equivalent to
> . . .	.	become(s); became
* before a word	.	a cant term

[1] A date, unpreceded by ' ca.', signifies that this is the earliest discovered record; it is well to bear in mind, however, that in slang, cant, colloquialism, catch-phrase, and solecism, the first *use* goes back, generally a few, occasionally many, years earlier.

ABBREVIATIONS, Supplement

Cross-references (unless specifically to *Dict.*) are to terms within this volume.

Atkinson	= Laurie Atkinson, typescript glossary mostly of Forces' slang, received June 1, 1948. And, 1959, a glossary of general slang, received in March.
B., 1941, 1942, 1943, 1945, 1953	= Sidney J. Baker, *New Zealand Slang*, 1941; *Australian Slang*, 1942; *Australian Slang*, 3rd ed., 1943; *The Australian Language*, 1945; *Australia Speaks*, 1953.
B. & L.	= Barrère & Leland's *A Dictionary of Slang, Jargon and Cant*, 1889 (A–K)–1890 (L–Z).
Bebbington (, John)	= letter, March 12, 1949.
Berrey	= Lester V. Berrey, 'English War Slang', in *The Nation* (U.S.A.) of Nov. 9, 1940.
Blaker	= Richard Blaker, *Medal without Bar*, 1930.
Boxiana	= Pierce Egan, *Boxiana*, 4 vols., 1818–24.
Franklyn (, Julian)	= various communications (1945–59);
Franklyn, *Rhyming*	= his *Dictionary of Rhyming Slang*, 1960.
Gilderdale	= Michael Gilderdale, 'A Glossary for Our Times', in *The News Chronicle*, May 22 and (= Gilderdale, 2) May 23, 1958.
Granville	= Wilfred Granville, *A Dictionary of Naval Slang*, typescript, 1945 (invaluable). And many later communications.
H. & P.	= J. L. Hunt & A. G. Pringle, *Service Slang*, 1943.
Jackson	= C. H. Ward Jackson, *It's a Piece of Cake*, 1943.
Leechman	= Douglas Leechman, numerous communications, especially in 1959.
MacArthur & Long	= Alex. MacArthur & H. Kingsley Long, *No Mean City*, 1935.
Marples	= Morris Marples, *Public School Slang*, 1940.
Marples (2)	= Morris Marples, *University Slang*, 1950.
Matthews	= W. Matthews, 'London Slang at the Beginning of the XVIII Century' in *Notes and Queries*, June 15, 22, 29, 1935.
Mayhew	= Henry Mayhew, *London Labour and the London Poor*, 3 vols., 1851.
Moe	= Albert F. Moe, Colonel (ret'd) U.S. Marine Corps, communication of April 26, 1959.
Nevinson, 1895	= H. W. Nevinson, *Neighbours of Ours*, 1895.
Norman	= Frank Norman, *Bang to Rights*, 1958. The richest non-lexical source-book since James Curtis's *The Gilt Kid*, 1936.
P-G-R.	= Partridge, Wilfred Granville, Frank Roberts, *A Dictionary of Forces' Slang: 1939–1945*, published in 1948.
Partridge, 1945	= Eric Partridge, *A Dictionary of R.A.F. Slang*, 1945 (Jan.).
Petch	= Albert B. Petch, numerous communications made during 1945–57.
Pugh	= Edwin Pugh, *The Cockney at Home*, 1914.
Pugh (2)	= Edwin Pugh, *The Spoilers*, 1906.
Richards	= Frank Richards, *Old-Soldier Sahib*, 1936.
Sessions	= *Session Paper of the Central Criminal Court*, 1729–1913.
Shaw	= Frank Shaw, many notes.
Sinks	= Anon., *Sinks of London Laid Open*, 1848.
Spy	= C. E. Westmacott, *The English Spy*, 1825; vol. II, 1826.
'Taffrail'	= 'Taffail', *Carry On*, 1916; esp. the article entitled 'The Language of the Navy', orig. published not later than 1915.
The Pawnshop Murder	= John G. Brandon, *The Pawnshop Murder*, 1936.
Underworld	= Eric Partridge, *A Dictionary of the Underworld* (British & American), 1949.

To several other correspondents, I owe much; their material being, in the main, corrective or modificatory or supplementary, they are not mentioned above. Especially, Dr David Aitken, Mr N. T. Gridgeman, Professor F. E. L. Priestley, Dr D. Pechtold and Mr C. A. Roy.

CORRIGENDA

(*Pages* 1–974)

2, **abo.** Read ' mid C. 19–20 ' and ' Australian coll.'

18, **article of virtue.** For ' virgins ' read ' virgin '.

19, **aste.** For second line read ' Perhaps ex It. *asta*, auction '.—**atcha !** For ' C. 20 ' read ' from ca. 1860 '. Ex Hindustani *accha*, good.—**Atkins.** Read : ' See **tommy, 4** '

24, **back of Bourke.** In line 3, read ' north-western N.S.W.'.

26, **bag of rations.** Read ' domineer-ing '.

27, **baked.** For ' 1850 ' read ' 1910 '.

28, **balaam.** For ' 1826 ' read ' 1818 '.

31, **bang goes saxpence !:** see Addenda, s.v. **saxpence . . .**

38, **batty.** ' Batta ' should be ' bhatta '. 45, **bell, ring the,** line 2: read ' strength-testing '.

49, **Bess o' Bedlam.** The period should be ' C. 17—early 19 '. See esp. Jack Lindsay's *Tom o' Bedlam*.

50, **bevie, bevry.** Read **bevie, bevvy.**

54, **bint.** In Arabic *bint* has no lit. meaning other than ' daughter '.

56, **bit of cavalry.** For ' 1825–80 ' read ' 1825–1915 '.—**bit of sticks.** For ' corpse ' read ' copse '.

59, **Black Hole, the,** sense 2, line 2. The date, obviously, should be 1757 !

75, **boiled.** For ' C.20 ' read ' from ca. 1875; orig. among Australian gold-diggers '.

76, **bolo.** In Hindustani *bolo the bat* would rather mean ' speak the matter (or words) '.

79, **bookmaker's pocket** should be **book-maker's . . .**

81, **booze the jib** should read ' **booze one's** (or the) **jib** or **tip**; also **booze up the jib** '.

91, **break the neck of.** For ' 1860 ' read ' 1810 '. 98, **brunch.** Current at Cambridge in 1893: Arnold Wall.

102, **bug, v. 3.** For ' bug over ' read ' *bug over* '.

106, **bum, adj.** See Addenda.

107, **bum-fodder.** Sense 1 goes back to ca. 1700.

108, **bundabust.** ' A tying, a binding ' should be ' a tying and binding '. The word also means ' revenue settlement '; often spelt *bundobust*.

110, **buoy, round the.** Read **buoy, go round the.**

115, **buttered bun.** In sense 2, read ' mid-C. 17–20 '.

132, **cat, v.,** line 1. Read ' C. 18 '.

137, **chai.** In line 3, read ' *char* '.

140, **charwallah** should have been printed **char-wallah.**

145, **cheesy-hammy . . .** Read **. . . topsides.**

150, **chootah.** Ex Urdu *chota*, small.—**chop.** Ex Hindi *chhap*, lit. a print, hence a seal or band.

153, **chuck a dummy,** line 1. ' To ', not ' A '.

169, **cold tea.** The later limit should be 1910.

180, **coppers, hot.** Ignore both the entries and see **hot coppers.**

183, **cottage, 2.** For ' ca. 1900–12 ' read ' from ca. 1900; slightly ob '.

189, **crate.** Read ' 1914 '.

191, col. 1, line 1. For ' dia.' read ' dial '.

206, **dance, v. 2.** The date should be ' ca. 1650 '. The term appears in Randle Holme's *Armory*, 1688.

220, **Digby duck** should come between **dig up** and **digger; dig out after** should follow **dig out.**

221, **dime museum.** Obviously Ware meant ' tenth '.—222, **dip, v.,** l. 3. Read ' thy lands '.

223, **dipped in wing** should be **dipped in the wing.**

227, **do it.** Add ' : C. 19–20 '.

233, **domino-thumper.** For ' Barrière ' read ' Barrère '.—**donkey ?, who stole the.** The period should be ' ca. 1835–1910 '.

235, **doolally . . . ,** line 5. Read ' See also . . . '

238, **down on, put a.** For ' 1840 ' read ' 1800 '.

248, **dumpling-depôt.** For ' Conington ' read ' Connington '. 254, **eclipse.** Read ' manipulation '.

258, **equality Jack.** For dating, read ' since ca. 1810 '.

276, **fine ham . . .** For ' (–1934) ' read ' : C. 20 '.

277, **finnif.** B. & L. defines *finnup ready* as ' a five-pound note '.

287, **flip, n., 3.** Read ' A (short) '.

29z, **flying dustman.** Read : see Addenda.—296, **forget,** l. 2. Read ' lapse '.

304, **frosty face.** For ' 1890 ' read ' 1910 '.

313, **gamaliel,** lines 2–4. Read ' Ex the name of several rabbis famous in the first two or three Christian centuries '. (There was a confusion with Gallio.)—327, **gibber,** l. 2. Read ' Pron. *ghibbher* '.

332, **glass-work.** For ' 1880 ' read ' 1905 '.—**Glesca Kulies** should be **Glesca Keelies.**

358, **grubby.** The later limit should be 1920.

363, **gutsy.** For ' courage ' read ' courageous '.

364, **guy, n., 6.** See Addenda.

xii

365, **h.o.p., on the.**   Add ' From ca. 1880 '.
367, **Hairyfordshire.**   In l. 2, the *f* is missing.
372, **hang it out,** line 4.   For ' 2 ' read ' 3 '.
373, **hanky-spanky.**   Supply a period after ' 1880 '.—For ' **Hans Corvel's ring** ' read ' . . . **Carvel's** . . .'
383, **hearty,** line 5.   For ' 1920 ' read ' 1910 '.
386, **hell and high water** should immediately precede **hell and spots.**—389, Read **hey-gammer-cock** . . .
390, first line.   For ' late ' read ' mid ': the term occurs in *Verdant Green.*—**high-flyer,** 5. the later date should
     be 1910.
394, **Hobson Jobson.**   For ' Mohammedan wailing cry ' read ' Shia (or Shia-Mohammedan) wailing cry '.
     ' Wailing cries are forbidden in Muslim religion ' (Kazim Raza Siddiqui).—398, col. 2, l. 1: ' (low) '.
412, **how's your poor feet** dates from the Great Exhibition of 1851: witness J. Leech's sketches.
415, **hunger.**   The period, obviously, should be C. 14–15.
421, **impot.**   Change ' 1890 ' to ' 1880 '.
426, **invade.**   Read *intercrural.*
433, col. 2, **jan.**   ' *Murk-All* ' should be ' *Mark-All* '.
435, **jay,** last line.   Read ' easy '.
436, **jerk the cat.**   The references should be to **cat, shoot the.**
436, **jerry,** n., 4.   The period should be: ca. 1840–1900.
438, **Jew's harp,** l. 2.   For ' blowing ' read ' humming '.
444, **Jollies, the.**   Extant in war of 1939–45.
447, **jumboism.**   Delete last sentence.
448, **jungli.**   Ex Urdu; *jungli* means, lit., ' belonging to jungle ', hence uncouth or uncultured.
448, **juwaub.**   In Hindustani also does it mean ' refusal ' and ' dismissal '.—449, **kath,** line 4, read ' Alpers '.
458, **klep,** v.   Delete the period after ' Ex '.
456, **king.**   For second ' 2 ', read ' 3 '.
463, **knuckled.**   For ' handsome ' read ' hand-sewn '.
471, **lattice.**   Delete this reference.
476, **left, be** or **get.**   Read ' 1890 '.—**leg on.**   ' Burns ', not ' Bruns '.
477, **length of one's foot.**   The reference should be to **foot, know the length of one's.**
480, **lie nailed to the counter.**   The reference should be to the entry at ' [**nab,** to bite gently ', p. 548.
491, **long lie** (following **long,** adv.) should follow **long legs,** p. 492.
503, **madam.**   For ' 4 ' read ' 3 '.
505, **main-brace, splice the.**   See Addenda.
506, **make, on the.**   ' Adopted '.
512, line 1: insert comma after ' horse-dealer '.
513, **May.**   For ' Occ. *Mays* ' read ' In C. 20, always *Mays* '.
529, **monkey-coat.**   Insert hyphen before **jacket.**
539, **muck-train.**   The date should be 1850–90.—In col. 2, both at head of page and at entry, **mug-fog**
     should be **mud-fog.**
     muckin.   Not *makkhn* but *makkhan.*
540, **mud-picker,** l. 1: the earlier date should be 1885.—**mud-pipes:** see Addenda.
543, **mumming-booth.**   For ' late C. 19– ' read ' mid-C. 18– '.
567, **noffgur.**   Not ' Keltner ' but ' Kettner '.—572, **nothing to write home about,** l. 2: read ' usual '.
580, **oh.**   Not in *Dict.* but in Addenda are the following to be found:—**oh, after you !** ; **oh, dummy !** ; **oh,**
     swallow yourself !—Read **ogging ot** (not **of**) **tekram.**
586, **old tots** should be **Old Tots.**
590, 3rd entry should read ' **ooja-ka-piv** or **ooja-ka** (or **cum**)**-pivvy** '.
601, **pal,** n.   In line 9, for ' ex ' read ' cf.'
606, **parentheses** is out of position: it should come on p. 605, between **Paree** and **parenthesis.**
606, **Parlyaree,** l. 10: read *parlare.*
609, **pastry.**   For ' 1917 ' read ' 1885 '; before ' Manchon ' insert ' Barrère & Leland; '.
610, **Paul's pigeon.**   For ca. ' 1550–1750 ' read ' from ca. 1550 '.
616, **pen,** 3.   The earlier date should be 1870.
617, **penny loaf,** l. 2.   Read ' prefer '.
622, **phenomenon.**   ' Crumbles ' should be ' Crummles '.
630, **pill,** v., 2.   Earlier date: 1885.
632, **pink,** adj., 3: ' Bloody '.—**pints round:** this should be on p. 633, between **pintle-smith** and **pinurt pots.**
635, **Piss-Pot Hall.**   Read ' Clapton '.   At end of page, read ' *King Henry the Fifth,* II, ii '.
643, **poddy,** fat; delete this line.
649, **poot.**   ' I cannot find any such Hindustani word.   Probably it is Oriental beggars' version of some
     European word ' (K. R. Siddiqui).
661, **proggins.**   See Addenda.
665, **puckerow.**   Properly the Hindustani word (which means ' seize ' or ' hold ') cannot be compared with
     the Maori (which means ' broken ' or ' crushed ').
671, **pusserpock,** 2.   See Addenda.
685, **Ralph,** 2.   The date should be 1810.
688, **rat-trap.**   Sense 1 survived until the end of the century.
692, **red face, have a.**   Also *take a r.f. to oneself* and dating from before the G.W.
701, **rivets.**   The earlier date should be 1875.   Extant: in, e.g., J. Curtis, *You're in the Racket Too,* 1937.
705, **roosting-key** should be **roosting-ken.**
708, **roughing.**   For ' scragging ' read ' ragging '.   See Addenda.
712, ' Rugby School slang ': insert bracket at end of entry and see the note at **Oxford -er** in Addenda.

721, **sahib.** ' In Arabic and Urdu " sahib " is a respectful address to all and not confined to Europeans only, though always used for Europeans ' (Siddiqui).

724, **sam !, upon my.** For ' See preceding entry ' read ' See **sam, stand** '.

725, **sandbag,** n. In line 3, 1820 should obviously be 1920.

727, **sargentlemanly.** Read ' So gentlemanly '.—738, **screw-thread** . . . For ' spiral ' read ' helical '.

749, **shakes, the.** Sense 3 goes back to ca. 1880.

772, **sitting-room,** l. 2. Read ' slightly '.

776, **skitting-dealer.** For ' C. 19 ' read ' C. 18 '.—**skittles.** In last line, read, ' Pagett '.

779, **slant,** v. In line 1, ' 1899 ' should read ' 1890 '.

780, **slater,** line 2. Read ' less '.

791, **snarl.** The dating should read: from ca. 1860.—791, **snavel,** 2. Read: since ca. 1810.

792, **sneezes.** In line 4, for ' —ins.—' read ' quite '. Something very odd happened here !

794, **snooty.** In line 4, read ' that ' for ' preceding '.

795, col. 1, l. 3. Read ' arm-chair '.

803, **sowcar.** Ex Hindustani *sahukar*, a native banker, esp. one doing business on a large scale. Most Hindu bankers are misers, hence the meaning of *sowcar*.

806, **spec,** 4. Alter date to ' mid-C. 18–20 '.

807, col. 2, **spirrib** should be **sperrib.**—**spess:** remembered in 1879 (Professor Arnold Wall).

809, **spill the beans,** line 4. Read *Bellona.*

811, **splice,** v., 3. For ' 1903 ' read ' 1897 '.

813, **spoffy.** In line 2, for ' 3 ' read ' 2 '.

824, **standing bridge** should be **standing budge.**

827, **steaming.** For ' 1903 ' read ' 1897 '.

837, **straight-up.** Also as exclamation. Dating since ca. 1905. Elaboration of synonymous **straight.**

838, **strawer,** 2. For ' 1903 ' read ' 1890 '.

839, **strides.** In line 1, read ' 1890 ' for ' 1904 '.

840, **strike-me-blind.** For ' 1904 ' read ' 1890 '.—**stringer.** Ditto.

842, **stuff,** n., 5. For ' C. 20 ' read ' late C. 19–20 ', and for ' 1904 ' read ' 1890 '.

847, **Sunday clothes.** Add: From ca. 1880.

851, **swan-slinger.** For ' 1904 ' read ' 1890 '.

853, **sweat one's guts out.** For ' Lyell ' read ' Barrère & Leland '.

862, **take the biscuit.** For ' 1923 ' read ' 1890 '.—**take care of dowb** should be . . . **Dowb.**

869, In col. 1, line 3, for *teeg* read *tayg.*

870, ***tekelite,** 2. For ' Robert ' read ' Roger '.

883, **tickler,** 6, l. 3. Read ' 1903–ca. 1910 '.

898, **too many for.** For ' Juggers ' read ' Jaggers '.—For **tools, fixed** . . . read **tools, fined** . . .

899, **top, over the.** Read ' See **top, go over the** '.

906, **trampler.** The dating should be 1605–50.

907, **traverse.** For ' **cart, traverse the** ' read ' **cart, walk the** '.

910, **triple tree.** Randolph, 1634.

915, **tumbler,** 4. For ' 1904 ' read ' 1890 '.—**tug,** line 5. Read ' work '.

924, **ultray.** See Addenda.

931, **very.** Read ' sentence '.

933, **voker.** In line 2, for ' the orig.' read ' a debased '. Perhaps *voker* is a mere misapprehension for *rokker* (**rocker**).

937, **waltz Matilda.** Prob. since 1880; song ex phrase.—**wanky.** See Addenda.

941, **waunds !** Type adrift !

943, **weenie.** In line 4, for ' C. 20. F. & H., 1904 ' read ' late C. 19–20. Barrère & Leland '.

945, **Westphalia.** ' 1904 ' read ' 1890 '.

951, **whip,** n., 2. For ' (—1904). F. & H.' read ' (—1890), Barrère & Leland '. And for **whip-sticks,** ditto.

952, **whisky jack,** l. 3. Read ' grey jay '.

953, **whistle and ride:** For ' (—1904). F. & H.' read ' (—1890), Barrère & Leland '.

954, **white-horsed in:** ditto.—**white stuff** is earlier recorded in Barrère & Leland.

974, col. 1, line 4. The semi-colon should be a colon.

A GHOST WORD

At end of **F**, on p. 309, I list **fye-buck** (cf.—on p. 99—**buck,** n., 6: *fyebuck* should read *syebuck*) with meaning ' sixpence '. But Parker has *syebuck*, with the long *s*, which I genuinely misread, not misapprehended, as *fyebuck*; F. & H.'s error may also have arisen from poor reading and not from ignorance. For this, I have to thank the erudite ' wordman ', the late Gerald Hatchman.

A DICTIONARY OF SLANG AND UNCONVENTIONAL ENGLISH

a, 'a. Sol. and dial. for *has, have* (e.g. " I would a done it, if . . .") : C. 18–20 ; earlier S.E. By way of *ha'*, which in C. 15–17 was S.E., coll. or dial. thereafter.—2. Of : esp. in *kinda, sorta* : see **kinder, sorter.**—3. An : sol. mostly London (— 1887). Baumann.—4. Superfluous, therefore catachrestic, of C. 19–20, as in ' No more signal a defeat was ever inflicted '. Fowler.—5. ' *a-, an-*, not or without, should be prefixed only to Greek stems . . . [*amoral*], being literary is inexcusable, and *non-moral* should be used instead,' Fowler.—6. Superfluous or, rather, intrusive in vv. : sol. : C. 19–20. ' He's the party as had a done it.' Cf. *of*, v. Esp. with present pcpp. : see, e.g., quotation at *a-doing of.*

A.A. of the G.G. (or **Gee-Gee**). The Institute of the Horse and Pony Club, which was founded in 1930. Sir Frederick Hobday, in *The Saturday Review*, May 19, 1934. Lit., the Automobile Association of the Gee-Gee (or horse).

A.B. An able-bodied seaman (— 1875) ; coll. by 1900. *Chambers's Journal*, No. 627, 1875.

A.B.C. An Aerated Bread Company's tea-shop : from ca. 1880 ; coll. by 1914.—2. At Christ's Hospital, C. 19, ale, bread and cheese on ' going-home night '.

A B C, (as) easy as. Extremely easy or simple to do : C. 19–20. Adumbrated in 1595 by Shakespeare's ' then comes answer like an Absey booke '. Always coll.

a-cockbill. Free ; dangling free ; nautical coll. (— 1887). Baumann ; Bowen.

a-crash of, go. To assault (a person) : low coll. (— 1923). Manchon.

A.D. A drink : male dancers' coll. (— 1909) inscribed on dance-programmes ; ob. Ware.

a-doing of. Doing : sol. : mid-C. 19–20. (D. Sayers, 1933, ' I arst you wot you was a-doin' of.')

a.f. Having met with (come across) a ' flat ', who has, to the speaker's advantage, laid his bets all wrong : the turf (— 1823) ; † by 1870. ' Jon Bee.'

A from a windmill or the gable-end, not to know. To be very ignorant, or illiterate : coll. : resp. C. 15, C. 19–20 (ob.). See also **B from** . . .

A1. Excellent, first-class : first of ships (Lloyd's Register) ; then of persons and things, Dickens, 1837. U.S. form : *A No. 1*. Variants, *A1 copper-bottomed* (Charles Hindley, 1876), now ob. ; *A1 at Lloyd's* (from ca. 1850) ; *first-class, letter A, No. 1* (— 1860). H., 2nd ed.—2. A commander of 900 men : Fenian coll. > j. : ca. 1865–90. Erroneously *No. 1.* (A lower officer was known as *B.*)

*Aaron, in c., a cadger ; *the Aaron*, a captain of thieves. ? C. 17–19. Cf. *abandannad*, a pickpocket.

abaa. A non-unionist ; hence, adj. : silly. Proletarian (— 1903). F. & H., revised.

*abaddon. A thief turned informer : c. : late C. 19–20 ; ob. ? a pun on *a bad 'un* and the angel *Abaddon.*

abaht. Cockney for *about* : sol. : C. 19 (? earlier)–20. See **-ah-.**

*abandannad. A thief specializing in *bandanna* handkerchiefs : c. (— 1864). H., 3rd ed. There is perhaps a pun on *abandoned*—2. Hence, any petty thief : c. : late C. 19–20 ; virtually † .

abandoned habits. The riding dresses of demimondaines in Hyde Park : ca. 1870–1900.

abber. At Harrow School, an abstract or an absit : from 1890's. Oxford **-er.**

abbess (1782 +), **Lady Abbess** (— 1785). The keeper of a brothel : late C. 18–19. A procuress : C. 19. Ex Fr. *abbesse*, a female brothel-keeper. Cf. *abbot* and see esp. F. & H. *Peter Pindar*, John Wolcot (d. 1819) :

> So an old abbess, for the rattling rakes,
> A tempting dish of human nature makes,
> And dresses up a luscious maid.

abbey lubber. A lazy monk : ca. 1538–1750 : coll. >, by 1600, S.E.—2. A lazy, thriftless person : nautical, ca. 1750–1900.

abbot. The husband, or the preferred male, of a brothel-keeper (see **abbess**) : C. 19. Cf. the old S.E. terms, *abbot of misrule*, *abbot of unreason*, a leader in a disorderly festivity.

Abbott's Priory. The King's Bench Prison : ca. 1820–80 ; ? ex Sir Charles Abbott, Lord Chief Justice, 1818. Likewise, *Abbott's Park*, the rules thereof. ' Jon Bee.'

abdominal. An abdominal case : medical coll. : C. 20. (A. P. Herbert, *Holy Deadlock*, 1934.)

abdominal crash. An aeroplane smash ; a heavy fall : Air Force : from 1916. F. C. Gibbons. On *gutser.*

Abdul. A Turkish soldier ; collectively, the Turks : military coll. : from 1915. B. & P. Ex frequency of Abdul as a Turkish name.

abear. Except in dial., it is, in C. 19–20, a sol. or perhaps only a low coll. for ' tolerate ', ' endure ', after being S.E. Ex O.E sense, to carry.

abel-w(h)ackets. See **able-w(h)ackets.**

Aberdeen cutlet. A dried haddock : from ca. 1870. By F. & H. denoted familiar, but definitely s. Ob. Cf. *Billingsgate pheasant* and *Yarmouth capon.*

aberuncator. Incorrect for *averruncator* (instrument for lopping) : from ca. 1860. O.E.D.

abide. To abye (pay, atone for) : catachrestic : ca. 1585–1720. O.E.D. By confusion of form and sense. Cf. the C. 15 *abite* for *abye.*

Abigail. A lady's-maid : from ca. 1616, though not recorded fig. till 47 years later : coll. >, by 1800, S.E. Ex the Bible. In Beaumont &

Fletcher, Fielding, Smollett; coll. from ca. 1700. Now outmoded literary.

[-able, -ible : when to use which. See Fowler.]

able-w(h)ackets, wrongly *abel-w(h)ackets*. A nautical card-game in which every lost point—or game—entails a whack with a knotted handkerchief (Grose, Smyth) : coll. : from ca. 1780 ; † by 1883 : witness Clark Russell's nautical dictionary.

Abney Park, to have gone to. To be dead : proletarian London (— 1909) ; very ob. Ware. Ex Abney Park Cemetery.

abnoxious. Incorrect for *obnoxious* : mid C. 17 (? -18). O.E.D.

abo, Abo. An aboriginal : Australian : late C. 19–20, orig. journalistic. Jice Doone. Cf. *aboliar*, q.v.

aboard of, fall. To meet (a person) : nautical coll. (— 1887). Baumann.

aboliar (or A-) ; properly abo-liar. A regular writer on Aborigine lore or of Aborigine stories : s. (from ca. 1910) >, by 1925 coll. and by 1936 virtually j. It is a coinage of *The Sydney Bulletin*, which, by the way, also coined *Billjim* and *Maoriland*. Cognate, and from the same mint, is *aboriginality*, a (preferably *original*) contribution to *Aborigine* lore : Australian coll. : C. 20. Gen. in pl., in which shape it heads a column in *The Bulletin*.

abominable. A late C. 19–20 sol., or jocular coll., for *abdominal* ; esp. in *abominable pains*.—2. Very unpleasant : coll., from ca. 1860 : the same with the adv. (-bly). Cf. the S.E. senses and :

abominate. To dislike 'intensely', i.e. very much : from ca. 1875. Coll.

aboriginality. See aboliar.

about, the other way. (Fig.) precisely the contrary : gen. in reference to a statement just made. Coll., from ca. 1860.

about one, have something. 'To show character or ability' ; to be, in some undefined or intangible way, charming or, perhaps because of some mystery, fascinating : coll. (and dial.) : from ca. 1890 (? earlier). E.D.D. (Sup.), 'That fellow has something about him, I must admit.' Cf. the analogous use of *there's something to* (a person or a thing).

about proper. An illiterate variant of *proper*, adv. : q.v.

about right. Correct ; adequate. Frank Smedley, 1850. Coll. ; post-G.W. prefers *about it*.

[about that, approximately that, is S.E. verging on coll.]

about the size of it. Approximately (right) : from ca. 1870, coll. ; ? orig. U.S.

About Turn. Hébuterne, a village in France : Western-Front military : G.W. F. & Gibbons.

above board. Openly ; without artifice or dishonesty. Coll. verging on, and occ. achieving, S.E. Ex position of hands in card-playing for money. Earliest record, 1608 (Apperson).

above oneself. Too ambitious or confident, not by nature but momentarily : C. 20.

above par. In excellent health, spirits, money in hand, mild drunkenness. All from ca. 1870, ex stocks and shares at a premium. Cf. *below par*.

abrac ; Abrac. Learning : ca. 1820–50. 'Jon Bee', 1823. Corruption of *Arabic* or abbr. of *abracadabra*.

Abraham. "A clothier's shop of the lowest description" : chiefly East End of London and ex Jewish name ; ca. 1870–1920.—2. The penis : low : late C. 19–20 ; ob. Whence *Abraham's bosom*, the female pudend.

Abra(ha)m, sham. See Abra(ha)m-sham.

*Abra(ha)m-cove or -man. A pseudo-madman seeking alms ; a genuine lunatic allowed on certain days to leave Bethlehem Hospital (whence *bedlam beggar*) to beg. The term flourished most ca. 1550–1700, *A. cove* being, however, unrecorded in C. 16 ; this sense > archaic only ca. 1830 ; ex Luke xvii (Lazarus) ; described by Awdelay, Harman, Shakespeare, Massinger, B.E., Grose.---2. Also, in late C. 18–19, a mendicant pretending to be an old naval rating cast on the streets. Cf. *abram*, q.v.—3. (Only Abram man.) A thief of pocket-books : c. (— 1823) ; † by 1870. 'Jon Bee.'

Abra(ha)m-sham. A feigned illness or destitution : C. 19. Ex *sham Abra(ha)m*, to pretend sickness (— 1759), in C. 19 mostly nautical and often *do Abra(ha)m* ; also—see **Abraham Newland**—to forge banknotes, † by 1840.

*Abraham Grains (or g-). A publican brewing his own beer : c. : late C. 19–20.

Abraham Newland. A banknote, ex the Bank of England's chief cashier of 1778–1807 : ca. 1780–1830 ; Scott uses it in 1829. H., 2nd ed. (1860), records the c.p. (? orig. the words of a song), *sham Abraham you may, but you mustn't sham Abraham Newland*. Cf. a *bradbury*, q.v.

abraham (or abram) work. Any sham or swindle, esp. if commercial : mid-C. 19–20 ; ob. As adj. *abra(ha)m* = spurious, as in c. *abraham suit*, false pretences or representations : C. 19.

Abrahamer. A vagrant : low (— 1823) ; † by 1900. 'Jon Bee', who defines *Abrahamers* as 'a lot, or receptacle full of beggars, half naked, ragged, and dirty' : an ambiguous set of words.

Abraham's balsam. Death by hanging : C. 18 low. Punning S.E. *Abraham's balm* (tree).

Abraham's willing. A shilling : rhyming s. (— 1859). H., 1st ed.

abram. A malingerer : C. 19–20 nautical ; ob. —2. As adj., c. : mad, C. 16–17 ; naked, C. 17–18, this latter developing ex *auburn* corrupted, for (as in Shakespeare) *abra(ha)m*, later *abram-coloured*, = auburn, hence fair. Cf. the *abrannoi* (naked) of Hungarian Gypsy (V. Sackville-West, *Knole and the Sackvilles*, 1922).—3. For sham Abram, see Abra(ha)m-sham.

*abram cove. 'A Naked or poor Man, also a lusty strong Rogue', B.E. ; the latter being of the 17th Order of the Canting Crew : c. : C. 17–early 19. Cf. *abram*, 2.

*Abram man. See Abraham-man.—Abramsham. See Abraham-sham.—abram work. See abraham work.

abridgements. Knee-breeches. ? Nonce word : Bulwer Lytton's play, *Money*, 1840.

abroad. In error, wide of the mark (Dickens) ; earlier (Pierce Egan, 1821), *all abroad*, with additional sense of 'confused' ; *all abroad* is, in the former sense, now ob. From ca. 1860 ; both coll. —2. Also, (of convicts) transported : ca. 1830–90. —3. At Winchester College, C. 19, *(come) abroad* meant to return to work after being ill.

abroaded. Living on the Continent as a defaulter from England : Society, 1860–90.—2. Sent to a penal settlement whether at home or in the Colonies : police, ca. 1840–80. Cf. *abroad*.—3. In c., imprisoned anywhere : ca. 1870–1920.

abs. At Winchester College in C. 19, now ob. : absent ; to take away ; to depart (quickly). Ca. 1840, *abs a tolly*, to put out a candle ; late C. 19–20, to extinguish a candle demands the 'notion' *dump* it. To *have one's wind absed*, is to get a 'breather' or 'winder'.

*****abscotchalater.** See absquatulate.

[absence in its Eton sense (a roll-call) is now j., but it may orig. have been s. : see esp. 'Eton slang', § 1.]

absent without leave. (Of one) having absconded : from ca. 1860.—2. In c., escaped from prison : id.

absence without leave, give (one). To discharge (one) suddenly from employment : from ca. 1820 ; ob. 'Jon Bee.'

absent-minded beggar. A soldier : semi-jocular coll. : 1899–1902. Ex Kipling's poem.

absentee. A convict : semi-euphemistic coll. : ca. 1810–60.

abso-bloody-lutely. The most frequent of the *bloody* interpolations, as *not fucking likely* is of the *fucking* interpolations : C. 20.

absolute, on the. On the granting of the decree absolute : divorce-agency coll. : C. 20. (A. P. Herbert, *Holy Deadlock*, 1934.)

absolutely ! Certainly ! Coll. intensification of 'yes' : C. 20.

absolutely true. Utterly false : Society : ca. 1880. Ware. Ex title of book.

absorb. To drink (liquor) : v.t. and i. : C. 20, as in 'He absorbs a lot, you know ! '

absquatulate. To depart, gen. hastily or in disgrace. Anglicized ca. 1860, ob. by 1900 ; orig. U.S. (1837). Thornton ; H., 1st ed. An artificial word : perhaps on *abscond* and *squat*, with a L. ending. Hence *absquatulating, -ize, -ation, -ator*, not very gen. ; and **abscotchalater*, one in hiding from the police.—2. V.t., rare : to cause to do so : 1844 (O.E.D.).

abstropelous. A C. 18–mid-19 variant of *obstropolous*.

absurd is coll. in its loose, Society usage : from ca. 1920. D. Mackail, *Greenery Street*, 1925, 'Besides, *caveat emptor* and—generally speaking—don't be absurd.'

abthain, abthane. A superior thane : catachrestic : C. 16–20. (Correctly, an abbey.) O.E.D.

Abyssinian medal. A button showing in the fly : military : ca. 1896–1914. Ware. Ex the Abyssinian War (1893–6). Cf. *Star of the East*.

Ac, the. The Royal Academy : artists' : from ca. 1870 ; slightly ob. Ware.

academic nudity. 'Appearance in public without cap or gown', Ware : Oxford University (— 1909) ; † by 1921.

academician. A harlot : ca. 1760–1820. Ex *academy*, a brothel : c. of late C. 17–18. B.E., Grose. In C. 19, *academy* = a thieves' school : cf. Fagan in *Oliver Twist*. But in late C. 19–20, *academy* is also a hard-labour prison and (— 1823) its inmates are *academicians*. Bee.

academics. (University) cap and gown : from ca. 1820 ; ob. Coll. rather than s. ; the j. would be *academicals*.

Academite. 'A graduate of the old Royal Naval Academy at Portsmouth' : nautical coll. : from ca. 1870 ; ob. Bowen.

*****Academy.** See academician.—2. (Academy.) Abbr. *Academy-figure*, a 'half-life' drawing from the nude : artists', C. 20.—3. A billiard-room : ca. 1885–1910. Ware, 'Imported from Paris '.

Academy, the. Platonism and Platonists : from the 1630's : academic s. >, in G. 18 university coll. >, by 1830, philosophic j. The other four of the chief schools of Greek philosophy are *The Garden*

(Epicureanism), *The Lyceum* (Aristotelianism), *The Porch* (Stoicism), and *The Tub* (Cynicism) : same period and changes of status. Fowler.

acater. A ship chandler : nautical coll. C. 19–20 ; ob. Bowen. A survival of † S.E. *acatur*, a purveyor : ex Fr. *acheteur*, a buyer.

acause. A sol. for *because* ; now rare except in dial. : C. 18–20.

accedence, accidence. Occ. confused : C. 16–20. O.E.D.

access. A C. 19–20 sol. for *excess*. Pronunciation often *ax-sess*.

accessary, -ory. Often confused : C. 19–20. Fowler.

accident. An untimely, or accidental, call of nature : coll. : 1899. O.E.D.

accident-maker. A report dealing with accidents and disasters : London journalists' (— 1887) : † by 1920. Baumann.

accidentally on purpose. With purpose veiled : c.p. : C. 20.

accidently. Accidentally : sol. : late C. 19–20.

accommodation house. A brothel ; a disorderly house ; from ca. 1820, now ob. Coll. 'Jon Bee.'

according, adv. A C. 20 sol. (earlier, S.E.) for *accordingly*. Esp. in *and the rest according*. Cf. :

according, that's. A coll. abbr. of the cautious *that's according to*, i.e. dependent on, *the circumstances*. (Not in the sense, in accordance *with*.)

according to Cocker. Properly, correctly. From ca. 1760, ex Edward Cocker (d. 1675). The U.S. phrase (partly acclimatized in England by 1909 : Ware) is *according to Gunter*, a famous mathematician : the C. 19 nautical, *according to John Norie*, the editor of a much-consulted Navigator's Manual.

account, go on the. To turn pirate, or buccaneer (— 1812). Coll., †. Scott.

account for. To kill : from ca. 1840 (Thackeray, 1842). Sporting coll. >, by 1890, S.E.

accounts, cast up one's. To vomit : C. 17–19. In C. 20, rare ; by 1930, †. Dekker ; Grose. A nautical variant, C. 19–20 : *audit one's accounts at the court of Neptune*.—2. In c., to turn King's evidence : mid-C. 19–20 ; ob.

accrue chocolate. 'To make oneself popular with the officers' : naval : C. 20 ; ob. Bowen.

accumulator. (Racing) a better carrying forward a win to the next event : from ca. 1870.

accur(re), occur. Often confused : mid-C. 16–18. O.E.D. (Properly, *accur* = to meet.)

ace. A variant of *ace of spades*, 1.—2. A showy airman : Air Force coll., 1918 ; ob. F. & Gibbons. Ex the lit. S.E. sense, a crack airman.

ace of spades. A widow : C. 19.—2. The female pudend : low : mid-C. 19–20. F. & H., 'Hence, *to play one's ace and take the Jack* (q.v.) = *to receive a man*'.—3. A widow : low (— 1811) ; † by 1890. Lex. Bal.—4. A black-haired woman : proletarian (— 1903). F. & H., revised ed.

ace of, within an. Almost : C. 18–20 : coll. >, by 1800, S.E. 'Facetious' Tom Brown, 1704. Orig. *ambs-* or *ames-ace*.

achage. Jocularly coll. : an aching state : C. 20. After *breakage* (S.O.D.).

achronical, -ycal, and derivative adv. Incorrect for *acronyc(h)al, -ly* : C. 17–20. O.E.D.

acid, come the. To exaggerate : exaggerate one's authority ; make oneself unpleasant ; endeavour to shift one's duty on to another : military : from ca. 1910. F. & Gibbons.

Acid Drop, the. Mr. Justice Avory : legal nick-name : C. 20. (*The Saturday Review*, March 9, 1935.)

acid on, put the. To ask for a loan : Australia, New Zealand : C. 20. Jice Doone. Punning S.E. *acid test.*

ack ! No !, as the refusal of a request : Christ's Hospital, C. 19. Cf. Romany *ac !*, stuff !

Ack ; Beer ; Don.—A, B, D Company : military coll. : from 1914. Ex signalese. Cf. :

ack emma. A.m. : military : from 1915. Ex signalese for these two letters.

ack over tock. See **arse over turkey.**

'ackin' corf. A hacking cough : 'pseudo-vulgarly in jest ' (— 1927) ; i.e. coll. when jocular, illiterate when serious. Collinson.

*****ackman**, c., is a fresh-water thief : mid-C. 18–19. Corruption of *arkman*, q.v. F. & H. adduces also *ack-pirate* and *ack-riff.*

acknowledge the corn, v.i. Admit, acknowledge (Sala, 1883) ; ob. Ex U.S. (— 1840), to admit failure or outwitting. See esp. Thornton.

*****acorn, a horse foaled by an.** The gallows ; gen. as *ride a horse . . .*, to be hanged : c. : late C. 17–mid-19. Motteux, Ainsworth. Cf. *three-legged* or *wooden mare*, qq.v.

acquaintance, scrape (an). To make acquaint-ance. Coll. : Farquhar, 1698, ' no scraping acquaint-ance, for Heaven's sake '.

acquire. To steal : coll. : C. 20. Not a euphem-ism, for it is used jocularly.—2. Occ. confused with (*en*- or) *inquire* and *require* : C. 17–20. O.E.D.

acre, knave's. A mid-C. 16–early 17 variant of *weeping cross*, q.v. See also **beggar's bush** for a very pertinent quotation.

Acres, Bob Acres. A coward, esp. if boastful. Ex a character in Sheridan's *Rivals*, 1775. Coll., †.

acrobat. A drinking-glass : music-hall (— 1903). F. & H., revised. Punning *tumbler.*

acromatic. Incorrect for *achromatic* (late C. 18–20) and *acroamatic* (C. 17–20). O.E.D.

across, come. To meet with accidentally : mid. C. 19–20 : coll., > S.E., not literary, in C. 20.—2. *come across (with it) !* Confess !, speak out ! ; hand it over ! : post-G.W. Ex U.S.. See also **come across, 1.**

across, get, v.t. Irritate or offend (a person) : C. 20 ; coll.

across, put it. See **put it across.**

acrost. Across : sol., mostly London (— 1887) ; also dial. Baumann.

act of parliament. (Military) small beer perforce supplied free to a soldier : late C. 18–early 19. Grose.

Acteon. A cuckold : C. 17–18. B.E., Grose.—2. To cuckold : late C. 17–early 18. B.E. Coll. Ex legend of Diana and Acteon.

acting dicky. A temporary appointment : naval (— 1903) ; ob. F. & H., revised. On *acting-order.*—2. (Often *a.D.*) A man acting in the name of an enrolled solicitor : legal (— 1903). Ibid.

acting dish. A dish resembling an old favourite ; *acting rabbit-pie* is made of beef : naval : C. 20. Bowen. Ex *acting officer.*

acting lady. An inferior actress : ironic theat-rical coll. : 1883, *Entr'acte* (February) ; † by 1920. Ware. Mrs. Langtry's social-cum-theat-rical success in 1882 caused many society women to try their luck on the stage ; mostly with deplorable results.

acting rabbit-pie. See **acting dish.**

acting the deceitful. (Theatrical.) Acting : C. 19. Duncombe.

acting the maggot, vbl. n. and ppl. adj. Shirking work : (mostly Anglo-Irish) bank-clerks' (— 1935).

active citizen. A louse : low (— 1811) ; † by 1890. *Lex. Bal.* Cf. *bosom friend.*

actor's Bible, the. The *Era* : theatrical coll. : ca. 1860–1918. Ware. A fling at sacred matters prompted by the sensation caused by *Essays and Reviews.*

actressy. Characteristic of an actress ; theat-rical or somewhat melodramatic in manner : coll. : late C. 19–20. (Edward Shanks, *The Enchanted Village*, 1933.)

actual, the. Money, collectively, esp. if in cash : mid-C. 19–20. At this word, F. & H. has an admir-able essayette on, and list of English and foreign synonyms for, money. In 1890 there were at least 130 English, 50 French synonyms.

ad. An advertisement : printers' coll. : 1854 (Dickens) ; in C. 20, gen. Occ. *ádvert*, rarely *adver.*

ad lib. A coll. abbr. of *ad libitum*, as much as one likes : C. 19–20.

adad ! An expletive : coll. : ca. 1660–1770. Prob. ex *egad !*

Adam. A bailiff, a police sergeant : C. 16–17. Shakespeare.—2. In mid-C. 17–19 c., an accom-plice : with *tiler* following, a pickpocket's assistant. Coles, 1676 ; B.E. ; Grose.—3. A foreman : work-men's (— 1903) ; ob. F. & H., revised.

Adam ; adam. (Gen. in passive.) To marry : c. : 1781, G. Parker, ' " What, are you and Moll *adamed* ? " " Yes . . . and by a rum Tom Pat too " ' ; † by 1850. Ex Adam and Eve.

Adam and Eve. To believe : rhyming s. (— 1914). F. & Gibbons.

Adam and Eve on a raft. Eggs on toast : mostly military : C. 20. Ibid. Cf. :

Adam and Eve wrecked. Scrambled eggs : id. : id. : Ibid.

Adam and Eve's togs. Nudity : proletarian London (— 1909) ; slightly ob. Ware. Cf. *birth-day suit.*

Adam tiler. See **Adam,** n., 2.

Adam's ale. Water. Coll. C. 17–18 ; jocular S.E. in C. 19–20, but now outworn. Prynne. The Scottish equivalent is *Adam's wine* (— 1859) : H., 1st ed.

adaption. Adaptation : C. 19–20 : S.E. until C. 20, when gen. considered sol.

add. To come to the correct or wished-for total : coll. : 1850, Dickens. O.E.D. Sup.

added to the list. I.e. of geldings in training ; hence, castrated. Racing s. (— 1874). H., 5th ed. Orig. a euphemism.

addel. See **addle.**

Adders. Addison's Walk : Oxford University : late C. 19–20. By ' the Oxford *-er* '.

addition. Paint or rouge or powder for the face : ca. 1690–1770. Mrs. Centlivre : ' Addition is only paint, madam.' Society s.

addle ; often spelt **addel.** Putrid drinking water : nautical : late C. 19–20. Bowen. Ex *addled.*

addle cove. A fool ; a facile dupe : late C. 18–19. On *addle-head* or *-pate.*

Addle (or Addled) Parliament. The Parliament of 1614 : coll. nickname. O.E.D.

addle-plot. " A Martin Mar-all ", B.E. ; a spoil-sport : coll. : late C. 17–18.

addlings. ' Pay accumulated on a voyage or

during a commission ' : nautical, esp. naval : late C. 19–20. Bowen.

addressed to. (Of a missile, esp. a shell) aimed at : military : 1915 ; ob. F. & Gibbons.

a-deary me ! Dear me ! : lower-class coll. (— 1896) and dial. (— 1865). E.D.D.

adjective-jerker. A journalist : literary : late C. 19–20 ; ob. Cf. *ink-slinger.*

[Adjectives used as advv. unrecognized in S.E. are, according to the extent of the offence, either sol. or coll. In the approximate period 1670–1820 they were undoubtedly coll. : e.g. *mighty, monstrous, tolerable.*]

adjoin. A sol. for *enjoin* : C. 19–20.

adjutant's gig. (Military) a roller, esp. that of the barracks : ca. 1870–1914.

adjutant's nightmare. ' A confidential Army Telephone Book : Army Officers ' : 1916–18. B. & P., ' Very complicated and frequently revised '.

***Adkins's Academy.** A certain London house of correction : c. (— 1823) ; † by 1860. ' Jon Bee.'

administer (a rebuke or blow). To give, deal : mid-C. 19–20 : jocular coll. >, by 1900, S.E.

admiral. In C. 17–early 18, a S.E. variant of *admirable* : in C. 19–20 a sol. Occ. *ammiral,* which is also a sol. for *admirable.*

admiral, tap the. (Nautical) to drink illicitly : mid-C. 19–20 ; ob. H., 3rd ed. (at *tap*). Cf. *suck the monkey.*

admiral of the blue. A publican ; a tapster : ca. 1730–1860. (In C. 17, the British Fleet was divided into the red, white, and blue squadrons, a division that held until late in C. 19.)

admiral of the narrow seas. A drunk man vomiting into another's lap : nautical : late C. 18–mid-19. Grose, 2nd ed.

admiral of the red. A wine-bibber : C. 19, mainly nautical. Cf. :

admiral of the white. A coward : mid-C. 19–20 ; ob. Never very much used.

admirals of the red, white, and blue. Bedizened beadles or bumbles : C. 19.

Admiral's Regiment, the. The Royal Marines : military : mid-C. 19–20 ; ob. Also *Globe-Rangers, Jollies, Little Grenadiers.*

Admiralty ham. Any tinned meat : naval : late C. 19–20. Bowen.

admiration. Abbr. *note of admiration, admiration-mark* (written !) : coll. : C. 20, mainly printers', publishers', authors' : rare.

ado, dead for. Dead and done with : C. 16–17 ; coll. > S.E.

ado, once for. Once for all : C. 17 ; coll. > S.E. (Like preceding, S.O.D.)

adod ! A C. 17 oath : coll. Cf. *bedad, egad.*

adonis. A kind of wig : ca. 1760–1800 : coll. bordering on S.E. Cf. **Adonis** (1765 +), a beau. (O.E.D.)

adonize. (Of men) to adorn one's person : C. 17–19. Society s. that > Society j.

adorable, said H. A. Vachell late in 1933, ' is a much debased word ; a diabolical twin of " deavie " ' : upper and upper-middle class : from ca. 1925.

adore. To like (very much) : mid-C. 19–20 ; (mostly Society) coll.

adrift. Harmless (C. 17) ; discharged (C. 18–19) ; temporarily missing or absent without leave (mid-C. 19–20) ; wide of the mark, confused (C. 20 : coll.). Nautical. B.E. has ' *I'll turn ye adrift,* a Tar-phrase, I'll prevent ye doing me any harm ' ; Bowen records the third sense.

'Ads. God's : **a** coll. minced oath occurring in combination (*Adsbody, adsheart*) : late C. 17–early 19. Congreve, Smollett, O.E.D.

Adullamites. As a political nickname, recorded as early as 1834, but made current in 1866 for **a** group of seceding Liberals ; by 1870, any obstructionists of their own party. Soon coll., now historical. (Cf. *cave,* q.v.) Ex a reference by Bright to 1 Samuel xxii. 1, 2. O.E.D., W.

adventure(s), at (all). At random, wholly at risk : coll. >, by 1600, S.E. ; late C. 15–18. Caxton, Berners, Locke. (O.E.D.)

Adversity Hume. Joseph Hume, politician (1777–1855). ' Owing to his predictions of national disaster ' in the 1820's. Dawson.

advert. See **ad.**

advertisement conveyancers. Sandwich men : London society : ca. 1883–5. Ware. Coined by Gladstone and ridiculed by Society.

advertising. Given to seeking publicity—and using it. C. 20 ; coll. As in ' He's an advertising (sort of) blighter.' Abbr. *self-advertising.*

Adzooks ! A coll. expletive or oath : mid-C. 18–mid-C. 19. I.e. *God's hooks* > '*d's hooks* > *adshooks* > *Adzooks.* Cf. **'Ads,** q.v.

æger. A medical certificate ; a degree taken by one excused for illness (1865) : coll. >, by 1890, **j.** Ex *ægrotat* (— 1794), the same—though always j.

ærate is incorrect for *aerate* : late C. 19 -20. Fowler.

aerioplane. See *areoplane.*

afeard. Afraid : C. 16–20 : S.E. until early C. 18, then dial. and coll. ; in C. 20, sol. Lit., *afeared,* terrified, ex † *afear.* Also *'feard.*

affair. Of things, esp. buildings, machines : coll. from ca. 1800, C. 20 S.E. Gen. with a preceding adj. or a sequent adj. phrase. E.g. ' The house was a crazy affair of old corrugated iron '.

affair of honour. A duel resulting in an innocent man's death : ca. 1800–70. Coll.

affect and **effect** are often confused : mid-C. 17–20. Rarely *affective, effective* : C. 20. Occ., however, *affection*—even *infection*—was, in late C. 14–mid-C. 16, confused with † *effection.* (O.E.D.)

affidavit men. Professional witnesses ready to swear to anything : late C. 17–18. (Cf. *knights of the post,* q.v.) B.E., Grose.

affigraphy. See **affygraphy.**

***afflicke,** a thief, is either c. or low : C. 17. Rowlands, in *Martin Mark-all.* But see **flick.**

afflicted. See **inflicted.**

afflicted. Tipsy : coll. : mid-C. 19–20 ; ob. Orig. euphemistic.

afflictions. Mourning clothes and accessories : chiefly drapers', mid-C. 19–20 ; ob. Hence, *mitigated afflictions,* half-mourning.

affygraphy, to an. Exactly ; precisely. *In an affygraphy,* immediately. Mid-C. 19–early 20. Sol. H., 3rd ed. ; 1864 ; Ware. Perhaps a confusion of *affidavit* and *autobiography.*

afloat ; with back teeth well afloat. Drunk : from late 1880's ; ob.

afore and **ahind (ahint),** before and behind resp., have, since ca. 1880, been either low coll. or perhaps rather sol. when they are not dial.

after-dinner, or **afternoon('s), man.** An afternoon tippler : resp. : C. 19–20, C. 17–19 : coll. verging on S.E. Overbury, Earle, Smythe-Palmer.

after four, after twelve. 4–5 p.m., 12–2 p.m. : C. 19 Eton ; the latter is in Whyte Melville's *Good for Nothing.* Perhaps rather j. than coll.

after the Lord Mayor's show (comes the shit-cart). A G.W. military c.p. addressed to a man just back from leave, esp. if in time for an imminent ' show '. B. & P.

after you, partner ! After you ! : a coll. c.p. (— 1927). Collinson. Ex cards, esp. bridge.

after you with the push ! A London street c.p. addressed with ironic politeness to one who has roughly brushed past : ca. 1900–14. Ware.

afternoon ! Good afternoon ! : coll. : mid-C. 19–20. Cf. *day !* and *morning !*

afternoon buyer. One on the look-out for bargains : provincial coll. (— 1903). F. & H., revised.

afternoon farmer. A procrastinator : s. only in non-farming uses. Mid-C. 19–20, ob. H., 3rd ed.

afternoon man. See after-dinner man.

afternoon tea. Detention after 3 p.m. : Royal High School, Edinburgh (— 1903).

afternoonified. Smart : Society, esp. in London : 1897–ca. 1914. Ware quotes an anecdote.

afters. The second course, if any ; thus ' Any afters ? ' = ' Any pudding ? ' : military : C. 20. F. & Gibbons.

against. Against (i.e. for) the time when : low coll. when not dial. : mid-C. 19–20. J. Greenwood, ' If I don't get the breakfuss ready against Jim comes in ' (Baumann).

against (the) collar. In difficulties ; at a disadvantage : ca. 1850–1900.

against the grain. Unwilling(ly), unpleasant(ly) : mid-C. 17–19, coll. ; in C. 20, S.E. Ray, Swift, Dickens. (Apperson.)

Agamemnons, the Old. The 69th Foot Regiment, now the Welch : military : C. 19–20 ; ob. F. & Gibbons, ' From their service with Nelson on board H.M.S. *Agamemnon*, 1793–5 '.

agardente. ' Fiery spirits . . . smuggled on board in the Mediterranean ' : naval coll. : mid-C. 19–20. Bowen. Ex Sp. *agua ardiente*, brandy.

agate. A very small person : late C. 16–17 ; coll. > S.E. Ex the tiny figures cut on agate seals.

agen ; agin (esp. *the government*). Against ; in late C. 19–20, sol. ; earlier, S.E. These are Southern forms of the † *again*, against. (W.)

agent. One in charge of the job ; esp. an ' outside ' (not an office) man : Public Works' coll. (— 1935).

-agger. Mostly in Charterhouse words. E.g. *combinaggers*, a combination suit (esp. of football attire). From ca. 1890. A. H. Tod, 1900. On ' -er, the Oxford ', q.v. This prefix is very common in Oxford *-er* words, e.g. *Jaggers*. See also ' Harrow Slang ' and cf. *-ugger*, q.v.

aggerawator, rarely *agg(e)ravator* ; occ. *hagrerwa(i)ter* or *-or*. A well-greased lock of hair twisted spirally, on the temple, towards either the ear or the outer corner of the eye ; esp. among costermongers : ca. 1830–1910. For a very early mention, see Dickens's *Sketches by Boz* ; Ware. Cf. *beaucatchers, Newgate knockers*.

Aggie. Any ship named *Agamemnon* : naval : C. 19–20. Bowen.—2. Miss Agnes Weston, the philanthropist : nautical : late C. 19–20 ; ob. Ibid.

Aggie, see. To visit the w.c. : schools' : mid-C. 19–20.

aggravate, to annoy, verges on catachresis : mid-C. 19–20. Fowler.

aggravation. A station : rhyming s. : C. 20. F. & G.

aggregate, v.t. to amount, in aggregate, to : 1865 (O.E.D.) : coll. >, by 1920, S.E.

agility, show one's. (Of women) in crossing a stile, in being swung, to show much of the person : ca. 1870–1914. Perhaps a pun on *virility*.

agin. See agen.

agitate, v.t. To ring (a bell) : jocular coll. ; from ca. 1830.

agitator. A bell-rope ; a knocker : ca. 1860–1900. Ex preceding.

agolopise. See ajolopise.

*agony. Difficulty, problem ; story one has to tell : c. : from ca. 1930. James Curtis, *The Gilt Kid*, 1936. Ex *Conway* Training Ship s. : late C. 19–20. Masefield.—2. A newly joined young officer nervous or confused in command : military (not officers') : 1915 ; ob. F. & Gibbons.

Agony. Agny, near Arras : military in G.W. Richard Blaker, *Medal without Bar*, 1930. This, like many other G.W. place-names, will eventually disappear.

agony, pile up (or on) the. To exaggerate. Ex U.S. (Haliburton, 1835 : O.E.D.) ; anglicised ca. 1855. In C. 20, coll. ; the former, now rare.

agony-bags. Scottish bagpipes : English (not Scottish) Army officers' : from ca. 1912.

agony column. The personal column in a newspaper's advertisements (first in *The Times*). Laurence Oliphant, in *Piccadilly*, 1870 ; W. Black, 1873. Coll. by 1880.

agony in red. A vermilion costume : London society : ca. 1879–81. Ware. Ex Aestheticism.

agony-piler. (Theatrical) an actor of sensational parts : ca. 1870–1910.

agony-waggon. A medical trolley : military : 1916–18.

agree like bells. Explained by the fuller form, *a.l.b., they want nothing but hanging* : coll. verging on (proverbial) S.E. : 1630, T. Adams ; 1732, Fuller ; ob. in C. 20. Apperson. Cf. the C. 18–20 (ob.) *agree like pickpockets in a fair*.

agreeable ruts of life, the. The female pudend : low ' superior ' (— 1903) ; ob.

agricultural. See cow-shot. Prob. influenced also by *mow*, n. and v., in cricket j.

aground. At a loss ; ruined : C. 18–20. Coll. > in C. 19, S.E.

ah for ou, ow, is typical of Cockney, as in *tahn* for *town* ; also Cockney for *aw* as in *brahn* for *brawn*. See the quotation at bruvver and the entries at i, ' v for th ', ' v for w ', and ' w for v '.

ah, que je can be bete ! How stupid I am : ' half-society ' (Ware) : ca. 1899–1912. Macaronic with Fr. *je*, I, and *bête*, stupid.

ahind, ahint. See afore.

Aiglers, the. The 87th Foot Regiment ; from ca. 1881, the 1st Battalion of the Royal Irish Fusiliers : military : from early C. 19 ; ob. At Barossa, in the Peninsular War, they captured the eagle (Fr. *aigle*) of a French Regiment.

Ailsa. Glasgow & South-Western [Railway] Deferred Ordinary Stock (A. J. Wilson) : Stock Exchange (— 1895). *Ailsa* being a Scottish Christian name.

aim. The person that aims : coll. : from ca. 1880. Cf. S.E. *shot*.

ain't. Sol. for *am*, or *is* or *are*, *not*. Swift, 1710. As = *are not*, also dial. ; as = *am* or *is not*, mainly Cockney. Cf. *a'n't*, q.v.—2. Sol. for *has not*, *have not* : C. 19–20 ; esp. London. ' I ain't done nothing to speak on,' Baumann.

air, give the. See give the air.

air, go (straight) up in the. ' To get angry, excited ' (Lyell) : col. : C. 20.

air, hot. See **hot air.**

air, in the. (Of news, rumours) generally known or suspected, but not yet in print : C. 19 coll., C. 20 S.E. ; likely to happen : 1920 +, coll. ; uncertain, problematic, remote or fanciful : C. 19 coll., C. 20 S.E.

air, on the. (Wireless telegraphy) on the ' wireless ' programme ; if applied to a person, it often connotes that he—or she—is important, or notorious, as news or publicity. Resp. 1927 (O.E.D.) and 1930 : coll. ; by 1935, verging on S.E.

air, take the. To go for a walk : coll. > S.E. : C. 19–20. Also, make oneself scarce : coll. ; from ca. 1880.

*air and exercise. A flogging at the cart's tail : c. : late C. 18–early 19. Grose.—2. In C. 19 c., penal servitude.—3. Ca. 1820–40, ' the pillory, revolving ', Bee.

air-flapper. A signaller : military : C. 20. F. & Gibbons.

air-hole. ' A small public garden, gen. a dismally converted graveyard ' : London society : 1885–95. Ware ascribes it to the Metropolitan Public Gardens Association.

air-pill. A bomb dropped from an aeroplane : military : 1916 ; ob. F. & Gibbons.

air-man-chair. A chairman : music-halls' : ca. 1880–1900. Ware. By transposition of *ch* and the duplication of *air* ; a variation on central s.

air-merchant. A balloon-officer ; a flying man : military : 1917 : F. P. H. Prick van Wely, ' War Words and Peace Pipings ' in *English Studies*, 1922.

air one's heels. To loiter, dawdle about : mid-C. 19–20 : s. >, by 1900, coll.

air one's pores. To be naked : C. 20. Cecil Barr, *Amour* French for Love, 1933.

air one's vocabulary. To talk for the sake of talking or for that of effect : coll. : from ca. 1820. Ob

airey. See **airy.**

airing. (The turf) a race run with no intention of winning : ca. 1870–1914.

airing, give it an. An imperative = take it away ! ; coll. ; from ca. 1890. Also, be quiet ! : C. 20.

airoplane, occ. **aerioplane.** Aeroplane : sol. spelling : from ca. 1910. Cf. *airyplane* and *areoplane*.

airs, give oneself. To put on ' side ' or ' swank ' : coll. in C. 18, then S.E. Fielding.

airs and graces. Faces (cf. C. 19 ' rhymed ' *Epsom races*) : rhyming s. : C. 20.

airy, occ. **airey.** The *area* of a building : sol. : 1694, *The London Gazette* (O.E.D.).

airy-fairy. As light or dainty as a fairy : coll., now verging on S.E. : 1869, W. S. Gilbert. Ex Tennyson's *airy, fairy Lilian.* O.E.D. (Sup.).

airyplane. Aeroplane : sol. : from ca. 1912. Cf. *areoplane*, q.v.

airyvated, ppl.adj. Excited ; worked-up : low : from ca. 1931. J. Curtis, *The Gilt Kid*, 1936. Ex :—2. Aerated : sol. : C. 20.

Ajax. A jakes, a water-closet : late C. 16–18. A spate of cloacal wit was loosed by Harington's tract. *The Metamorphosis of Ajax*, 1596.

ajolopise ; more correctly **agolopise.** To apologise : non-aristocratic, jocular perversion : C. 20.

Ak. A variant of *Ack*, q.v. (Philip Macdonald, *Rope to Spare*, 1932.)

ak dum. At once : military : late C. 19–20. F. & Gibbons. Ex Hindustani *ek dam.*—2. A

German notice-board : 1916–18. Ibid. Ex the caption *Achtung !*, beware.

ak dum and viggery ! At once ! : rare : from 1919. A combination of *ak dum*, 1, and (corrupted) *iggri.* I.e. ex two Army phrases, the former from Hindustani, the latter from Arabic !

Akerman's hotel. Newgate prison. ' In 1787,' says Grose, ' a person of that name was the gaoler, or keeper.' † by 1850.

Akeybo. As in ' He beats Akeybo, and Akeybo beats the devil ' : proletarian (— 1874) ; ob. H., 5th ed. Cf. *Banaghan, Banagher*, q.v. *Akeybo*, however, remains an etymological puzzle. Is there a connexion with Welsh Gypsy *ake tu !*, here thou art ! (a toast : cf. *here's to you !*) : Sampson.

akka. An Egyptian piastre : Regular Army's : from ca. 1920. Ex the slang of Egyptian beggars : *piastre* corrupted.

alacompain. Rain : rhyming s. (— 1859) ; ob. H., 1st ed. Also *alla-, ali, eli-.* Cf. *France and Spain.*

alas, my poor brother ! A coll. c.p. of the 1920's. Collinson. Ex a famous Bovril advertisement.

Albany beef. North American sturgeon : nautical : mid-C. 19–20. Bowen. Ex that town.

albert. Abbr. *Albert chain* : from ca. 1884 ; coll. till ca. 1901, then S.E. Ex the name of the Prince Consort of Queen Victoria.

Albertine. ' An adroit, calculating, business-like mistress ' : aristocratic : ca. 1860–80. Ware. Ex the character so named in Dumas the Younger's *Le Père Prodigue.*

Albertopolis. Kensington Gore, London : Londoners' : the 1860's. Yates, 1864 ; H., 1874, notes it as †. Ex Albert Prince Consort, intimately associated with this district.

albonized. Whitened : pugilistic, ca. 1855–1900. ' Ducange Anglicus ', 1857. Ex L. *albus*, white. Cf. *ebony optic*, q.v.

alcalde and **alcayde** are sometimes confused mid-C. 18–20. O.E.D.

*alderman. A half-crown : c. : from 1830's ; ob. Ex its size. ' Ducange Anglicus ', 1857 : Brandon, 1839.—2. A long pipe (= *churchwarden*) : ca. 1800–50.—3. A turkey, esp. if roasted and garnished with sausages : late C. 18–early 20 ; variant *alderman in chains.* George Parker, ca. 1782, says it is c.—4. Late C. 19 c., precisely a ' jemmy ' : see *citizen. The Daily Telegraph*, May 14, 1883.—5. A qualified swimmer : Felsted School : ca. 1870–90. Ex the *Alders*, a deep pool in the Chelmer.

alderman, vote for the. To indulge in drink : ca. 1810–50. Cf. *Lushington*, q.v., and :

alderman in chains. See **alderman, 3.**

Alderman Lushington. Intoxicants : Australian, ca. 1850–1900. Ex *Alderman Lushington is concerned*, He is drunk : a c.p. of ca. 1810–50. Vaux.

aldermanity. The quality of being an alderman ; a body of aldermen. From ca. 1625 ; in C. 19–20, S.E. *Aldermanship* is the regular form, *aldermanity* a jocular variant, a cultured coll. after *humanity.*

alderman's pace. A gait slow and solemn : C. 17 coll. > S.E. Cotgrave ; Ray.

Aldgate, a draught or **bill on the pump at.** A bad bill of exchange : late C. 18–19 commercial. Grose, 1st ed. (at *draught*).

ale-draper. An ale-house keeper (implied in 1592) : jocular coll. >, by 1750, S.E. † by 1850.

This jocular term actually occurs in the burial-entry of a Lincolnshire parish register of the C. 18.

ale-head wind, beatin(g) up against an. Drunk : nautical : late C. 19–20. I.e. ' tacking all over the place ', esp. the pavement.

ale-knight. A drunkard ; a boon companion (1575) : C. 16–17 : coll. > S.E.

ale-spinner. A brewer ; a publican. C. 19.

ale-stake. A tippler : coll., C. 17–18. In S.E. *ale-stake* = *ale-pole*, a pole serving as an ale-house sign.

Alec. See **smart Alec.**

alecie, alecy. Lunacy ; intoxication : Lyly, 1598. Cited as an example of pedantic nonce-words, it may be considered s. because of its derivation, after *lunacy*, from *ale* + *cy*. (N.B. : despite a subconscious belief to the contrary, culture and/or pedantry do not prevent a word from being s. or coll. ; indeed, culture and pedantry have their own unconventionalisms.)

ales. (Stock Exchange) the shares of Messrs S. Allsopp & Sons : from ca. 1880. Also *slops*. (A. J. Wilson.)

ales, in his. In his cups, or rather his tankards of ale (*ale* orig. synonymous with *beer*) : C. 16–17 ; coll. Shakespeare.

Alex. Alexandria (in Egypt) : military (1915) ex Anglo-Egyptian (late C. 19–20). E.g. in F. Brett Young, *Jim Redlake*, 1930.

Alexander. To hang (a person) : Anglo-Irish coll. : ca. 1670–1800. Ex the merciless way in which Sir Jerome Alexander, an Irish judge in 1660–74, carried out the duties of his office. F. & H., revised.

Alexandra limp. The limp affected, as a compliment to the Princess of Wales, by Society ca. 1865–80. Coll. *Chamber's Journal*, 1876. Cf. *Grecian bend*, q.v.

'alf a mo'. A tooth-brush moustache : Australian military : 1916–18.

'alf a mo', Kaiser ! A c.p. of 1916–18. F. & Gibbons. Ex a recruiting poster thus headed.

Alfred David, Affidavy. Affidavit : sol. resp. 1865, Dickens (and again, ca. 1880, Harry Adams in a music-hall song), and C. 19–20. Occ. mid-C. 19–20, *after Davy*. Cf. *david* and *davy*, qq.v.

Algerine. (Theatrical) one who, when salaries are not paid, reproaches the manager. Also, an impecunious borrower of small sums. Ca. 1850–1900. Perhaps ex the U.S. sense : a pirate (1844).

Algie, -y. Generic for a young male aristocrat (esp. if English) : coll. : from ca. 1895. See my *Name This Child*, 1936.

alias and **alibi** are, in late C. 18–20, occ. confused. —2. *alias* = otherwise (not in the legal sense) is a loose, coll. deviation from the S.E. sense : C. 19–20.

Alice. An imitation tree (serving as an observation-post) in the Fauquissart sector : G.W. military. F. & Gibbons.

alike . . . or. Alike . . . and : catachrestic : C. 19–20. See quotation at *dry smoke*.

alive, look. (Gen. in imperative.) To make haste : coll. : 1858, T. Hughes, ' [He] . . . told [them] to look alive and get their job done ', O.E.D.

alive and kicking ; all alivo. Very alert and active. Coll. : from ca. 1852 : see *all serene*.

aliveo. Lively ; sprightly : (low) coll. : late C. 19–20. Ex *all alivo*. J. Storer Clouston, 1932, ' Mrs. Morgan considered herself quite as aliveo and beanful as these young chits with no figures.'

all, and. See **and all.**

all a-cock. ' Overthrown, vanquished ', Ware : proletarian (— 1909). Ware thinks that it derives either ex *knocked into a cocked hat* or ex cock-fighting.

all a treat. ' Perfection of enjoyment, sometimes used satirically to depict mild catastrophe ', Ware : London street coll. (— 1909).

all abroad. See **abroad.**

all afloat. A coat : rhyming **s.** (— 1859). H., 1st ed.

all alive. (Tailors') ill-fitting : ca. 1850–1910.

all alivo. See **alive and kicking.**

All-Aloney, the. The Cunard liner *Alaunia* : nautical : C. 20. Bowen.

(all) along of. Sol. for ' solely because of ' : C. 19–20. Cf. *along of*.

all arms and legs. See **arms and legs.**

all at sea. At a loss ; confused : C. 19–20 ; coll. from ca. 1890. Cf. *abroad*, q.v.

all brandy. (Of things) excellent, commendable : non-aristocratic : ca. 1870–1910.

all callao (or **-io**). Quite happy : nautical : late C. 19–20 ; ob. Bowen. Prob. ex *Callao*, the Peruvian sea-port, to reach which must be a comfort and a relief.

all cando. All right : naval : late C. 19–20. Ibid. ? *all canned-o*.

all-clear. An all-clear signal : coll. : from 1918. Often fig. ; orig. in respect of hostile air-craft.

all cut. Confused ; upset ; excited : military : C. 20. F. & Gibbons.

all dick(e)y with. See **dicky,** adj.

all dressed-up and nowhere to go ! A c.p. : from ca. 1915 ; ob. Collinson. Ex ' a song by Raymond Hitchcock, an American comedian '.

all-fired. Infernal ; cursèd. Orig. (1835) U.S. ; anglicised ca. 1860. Thornton. Euphemises *hell-fired*.—2. Hence the adv. *all-firedly* : U.S. (1860), anglicised ca. 1870 ; ob.

all fours, be or go on. To proceed evenly. C. 19–20 coll.

*****all gay !** The coast is clear : C. 19 c. Cf. *bob*, adj.

*****All Hallows.** The ' tolling place ' (? scene of robbery), in Prigging Law (lay) : c. of ca. 1580–1630). Greene, 1592.

all hands and the cook. Everybody on the ship : nautical coll. : mid-C. 19–20. Bowen. The cook being called on only in emergency.

all-hands ship. A ship on which all hands are employed continuously : nautical coll. : mid-C. 19–20. Bowen.

all hands to the pump. A concentration of effort : C. 18–19 ; ob. by 1890. Coll. rather than s.

all harbour light. All right : orig. (1897) and mostly cabbies' rhyming s. ; ob.

all his buttons on, have. To be shrewd, alert, and/or active : London proletariat : ca. 1880–1915. Ware.

all holiday at Peckham. A mid-C. 18–19 proverbial saying = no work and no food (pun on *peck*) ; doomed, ruined. Grose, 3rd ed.

all-hot. A hot potato : low (— 1857) ; † by 1900. ' Ducange Anglicus ', 1st ed.

all-in. An all-in assurance policy : insurance-world coll. : from ca. 1927.

all in, adj. (Stock Exchange) depressed (of the market) : coll. : mid-C. 19–20 ; opp. *all out*. These are also terms shouted by dealers when prices are, esp., falling or rising.—2. Hence, in C. 20, *all in* (of persons, occ. of animals) = exhausted.—3. ' Without limit or restriction ', C. J. Dennis :

Australian coll. : C. 20. Cf. S.E. nuance, 'inclusive of all '.

all in a bust. See **bust, all in a.**

all in fits. (Of clothes) ill-made : mid-C. 19–20 : tailors'.

all in the seven. See **seven, all in the.**

all jaw (like a sheep's head). Excessively talkative ; eloquent. From ca. 1870 ; ob. Variant, *all mouth* : ca. 1880–1910.

all kiff. All right, all correct : military (— 1914) >, by 1920, fairly gen. F. & Gibbons ; Manchon. Perhaps ex *all k'rect* = *O.K.* ; prob. ex Fr. s. *kif-kif*.

all legs and wings. (Of a sailing vessel) overmasted : nautical : late C. 19–20 ; ob. Bowen.

all Lombard Street to ninepence, to a china orange. Heavy odds : coll. : 1819 +, — 1880 respectively. The former is † ; the latter slightly ob. Cf. *bet you a million to a bit of dirt !*, q.v.

all my eye (and Betty Martin.) Nonsense ! ' *All my eye* is perhaps the earliest form (Goldsmith has it in 1768), although it is clear that Grose's version '—*that's my eye, Betty Martin*—' was already familiar in 1785. . . . Cf. the Fr. *mon œil !*,' Grose, P. The *Betty Martin* part, despite ingenious, too ingenious, hypotheses (esp. that sponsored by ' Jon Bee ' and silently borrowed by H. : ' a corruption . . . of . . . *Oh, mihi, beate Martine*'), remains a mystery. It is, however, interesting to note that Moore the poet has, in 1819, *all my eye, Betty*, and Poole, in *Hamlet Travestied*, 1811, has *that's all my eye and Tommy* ; this problematic *tommy* recurs in *like Hell and Tommy* (W.) Cf. the next two entries.

all my eye and (my) elbow. A London elaboration of the preceding : 1882 ; † by 1920. Ware, ' One can wink with the eye and nudge with the elbow at once ' ; he also points to the possibility of mere alliteration. Cf. :

all my eye and my grandmother. A London variant (— 1887) of the preceding ; ob. Baumann. Cf. *so's your grandmother !*, which, in late C. 19–20, expresses incredulity : gen. throughout England.

all nations. A mixture of drinks from all the unfinished bottles : late C. 18–early 19. Grose, 1st ed.—2. A coat many-coloured or much-patched : C. 19.

all-night man. A body-snatcher : ca. 1800–50. See esp. Ramsay, *Reminiscences*, 1861.

all of a dither. Trembling, shivering, esp. with fear. A phrase app. first recorded, as ' unconventional', in 1917, but existing in Lancashire dial. at least as early as 1817.

all of a doodah. Nervous : C. 20. See *doodah*. —2. Hence, esp. ' of an aeroplane pilot getting nervous in mid-air ' : Air Force : from 1915. F. & Gibbons.

all of a heap. Astounded ; nonplussed : C. 18–20 ; coll. by 1800. In Shakespeare, *all on a heap*.

all of a piece. ' Awkward, without proper distribution or relation of parts ' : low coll. (— 1909) ; slightly ob. Ware.

all of a hough, or **huh.** Clumsy ; unworkmanlike : tailors', ca. 1870–1914.—2. Lopsided : ex Somerset dial., from ca. 1855. H., 1st ed.

all one's own. One's own master : London apprentices' : ca. 1850–1905. Ware.

all out. Completely : from ca. 1620 ; coll. > S.E. by ca. 1750.—2. Of a big drink, ex *drink all out*, **to** empty a glass, C. 17–19, coll.—3. In error : C. 19–20.—4. (The turf) unsuccessful : ca. 1870–1900.—5. (Stock Exchange) improving, cf. *all*

in, q.v. for period and status.—6. Exhausted : athletics, ca. 1880–1900 ; then gen.—7. In post-G.W. athletics coll. it also means exerting every effort, as indeed it has done in gen. use since the early 1890's ; by 1930, S.E. (O.E.D.).

all over, adj. Feeling ill or sore all over the body : coll. : 1851, Mayhew, who affords also the earliest English instance of *all-overish*.

all over grumble. Inferior ; very unsatisfactory : London proletarian : 1886, *The Referee*, March 28, ' It has been a case of all over grumble, but Thursday's show was all over approval ' ; ob. (Ware.)

all over oneself. Very pleased ; over-confident : C. 20, esp. in the Army. Lyell.

all over red. Dangerous : ca. 1860–1920. Ware. Ex the railway signal.

all-over pattern. A pattern that is either very intricate or non-recurrent or formed of units unseparated by the ' ground ' : coll. from ca. 1880.

all over the shop. Ubiquitous (G. R. Sims, 1883) ; disconcerted (1887) ; confused, untidy (C. 20).

all over with, it is. (Of persons) ruined ; disgraced ; fatally ill or mortally wounded : from ca. 1860 ; coll. soon S.E. Cf. the L. *actum est de.* (S.O.D.)

all-overish. Having an indefinite feeling of general indisposition or unease : from ca. 1840 : coll. Perhaps ex U.S., where it is recorded as early as 1833 (Thornton).

all-overishness. The state of feeling ' all-overish ' (q.v.) : from ca. 1840 ; coll. Early examples in Harrison Ainsworth (1854) and John Mills (1841).

all present and correct. See **correct, all . . .**

all poshed up. See **all spruced up.**

all profit. See **profit, all.**

all right ! Yes !, agreed ! ; you needn't worry ! C. 19–20 ; coll. As adj. and rare adv., *all right* is S.E.

all right, a bit of. See **bit of all right.**

all right, all right. A coll. emphasising of *all right* : C. 20. (D. Sayers, *Murder Must Advertise*, 1933, ' She's a smart jane all right, all right.')

all right up to now. Serene, smiling : a c.p., mainly women's : 1878–ca. 1915. ' Used by Herbert Campbell . . . in Covent Garden Theatre Pantomime, 1878 ', Ware, who adds that it is derived ex ' *enceinte* women making the remark as to their condition '.

[**all round.** Versatile ; adaptable, whether at sport or in life (James Payn, 1881) ; of things, or rents, average (1869 : O.E.D.). S.E. bordering on coll.]

all round my hat. Indisposed : ca. 1850–1900. As an exclamation (1834–ca. 1890) = nonsense ! Hence, *spicy as all round my hat* (ca. 1870–1900), sensational : 1882, *Punch*.

all-rounder. A versatile or adaptable person, esp. at sport (— 1887) ; coll. >, by 1910, S.E.—2. A collar of equal height all round and meeting in front (Trollope, 1857), unfashionable by ca. 1885, rarely worn after 1890.

all saints. See **mother of all saints** (Bridges, 1772).

all serene. Correct ; safe ; favourable : c.p., now ob. Dickens, 1853 : ' An audience will sit in a theatre and listen to a string of brilliant witticisms, with perfect immobility ; but let some fellow . . . roar out " It's all serene ", or " Catch 'em all alive, oh ! " (this last is sure to take), pit, boxes, and gallery roar with laughter.' In 1901, Fergus Hume used the rare variant, *all sereno* (O.E.D.)

all-set. (Of a rogue, a desperate character) 'ready to start upon any kind of robbery, or other mischief', Bee, 1823 : low or perhaps c.—2. Ready ; arranged in order ; comfortable : coll. : from ca. 1870. Ex the *all set ?—ready !—go* used in starting those athletic races in which the starter does not employ a pistol.

all Sir Garnet. See **Sir Garnet.**

all smoke, gammon and pickles or **spinach.** All nothing, i.e. all nonsense : ca. 1870–1900.

all sorts. Tap-droppings ('Jon Bee ', 1823) ; cf. *alls, all nations.*

all souls. See **mother of all souls.**

all spice, all-spice. A grocer : mid-C. 19–20 ; ob. The S.E. sense, aromatic herb, goes back to the early C. 17.

all spruced up—poshed up—togged up. Smartened up, esp. to meet someone : C. 20 : resp. coll., s. (not before 1915), and s. (late C. 19–20) ; the second was orig. military. (F. & Gibbons.)

all-standing, sleep, or, gen., *turn in.* ' To turn in with one's clothes on ' : nautical coll. : late C. 19–20. Bowen ; Lyell.

all t.h. Good ; correct. Tailors' *A1, all right* : ca. 1860–1910.

all that, and. See **and all that** and cf. :

all that sort of thing, which has long been S.E., was regarded by 'Jon Bee ' (see at *warblers*), 1823, as coll.

all the go. Genuine ; thoroughly satisfactory ; esp. in demand, fashionable (see **go**) : C. 19–20 ; ob.

all the way down. Completely suitable or suited : coll., ca. 1850–1910. Lit., from top to toe.—2. Hence, as adv. : excellently. A coll. of late C. 19–20. Manchon.

all the way there. A variant, ca. 1860–90, of *all there*, q.v. H., 3rd ed.

all the world and his wife. See **wife, all the . . .**

all there. Honest, reliable (— 1860) ; ready-witted (1880) ; sane (late C. 19–20). H., 2nd ed. ; Lyell.

all to pieces. Collapsed, ruined : C. 17–20 coll.—2. Out of form or condition : C. 19–20, ob.—3. (Of a woman) confined : mid-C. 19–20. All three esp. with *go.*

all to smash. Utterly (Cuthbert Bede, 1861) ; ob.—2. Ruined, bankrupt, mid-C. 19–20. H., 1st ed. Perhaps ex Somersetshire dial.

all togged up. See **all spruced up.**

all up (with). Of things, projects : fruitless, ruined : late C. 18–20. Of persons : bankrupt, utterly foiled, doomed to die : C. 19–20, as in Dickens's ' all up with Squeers '. Rarely *up* alone.

all-up. An ' easy ' ; a rest : Public Schools' : C. 20. Desmond Coke, *The School Across the Road,* 1910.

all upon. See **upon,** 2.

All Very Cushy. The (now Royal) Army Veterinary Corps : military : 1915 ; ob. F. & Gibbons. See **cushy,** comfortable.

all very large and fine. A c.p. indicative of ironic approval : coll. : 1886 ; slightly ob. Ex ' the refrain of a song sung by Mr. Herbert Campbell ' (Ware) : cf. *all right up to now.*

allacompain. See **alacompain.**

allee samee. All the same : ' pidgin ' (— 1883). Ware.

allegiance. See **alliance.**

alleluia lass. A Salvation Army girl : London proletarian : 1886 ; ob. Ware.

alleviator. A drink. Coined by Mark Lemon in the 1840's. Ob.

all(e)y. A marble of medium size : C. 18–20 schoolboys' coll. > S.E. Defoe has it. Perhaps ex *alabaster.*—2. A go-between : proletarian (— 1909) ; virtually †. Ware derives ex Fr. *aller,* to go.

alley ! See **ally !**

Alley, the. Coll. abbr. of *Change Alley,* London, ' the scene of the gambling in South Sea stocks ', early C. 18.

alley, toss in the. To die : Australian (— 1916). C. J. Dennis. Ex marbles.

alleyed. Gone away ; dead : military : 1915 ; ob. See **ally !**

Alleyman. A German : military : late 1914–15. B. & P. Ex Fr. *Allemand.* See **Fritz** and **Jerry.**

alliance, allegiance. Occ. confused : from late C. 16. Cf. *allegation, alligation* : C. 17–20. O.E.D.

allicholly. Melancholy : jocular coll. or deliberate s. in Shakespeare's *Two Gentlemen of Verona* : punning *ale* + *melancholy.*

alligator. See **halligator.**—2. One who, singing, opens his mouth wide : ca. 1820–50. Bee.

alligator pear. An avocado pear : South African coll. (— 1892). By corruption. Pettman.

allow. Weekly pocket-money : Harrow School, C. 19–20 ; ob.

alls. Short for *all nations* (tap-droppings), q.v. ; ca. 1840–1914.—2. Also, ca. 1850–1900, a workman's term—the American equivalent is, or used to be, *bens*—for his tools.

Allslops. Allsopp & Sons' ale : not upper-classes' : from ca. 1900. It had a slump in quality at one time ; the name has unjustly stuck.

allus. Sol. for *always* : mostly London : C. 18–20.

ally or **alley !** Go away ! ; clear off ! : military : from 1915. Fr. *allez(-vous en).* Often *ally at the toot,* be off quickly. (F. & Gibbons.)

Ally Slopers' Cavalry. The Army Service Corps : military : from 1914. Ex *Ally Sloper,* that buffoon who named a pre-War comic paper. Also, occ., *Army Safety Corps,* also ex the initials : 1915–18. F. & Gibbons ; B. & P.

almanach. The female pudend : low : late C. 19–early 20.

almighty. Great(ly), might(il)y. A U.S. coll. never properly acclimatised in Great Britain and now ob. De Quincey, 1824 : ' Such rubbish, such almighty nonsense (to speak *transatlanticé*) . . .'

almighty dollar, the. Wealth : coll. (— 1876) ex U.S. (1836). Probably coined by Washington Irving, after Ben Jonson's *almighty gold,* though the first printed record does not occur in Irving's work. In England the phrase is always satirical, nor is it yet S.E. : and frequently it connotes the (supposed) American devotion to and absorption in money-making.

almond rocks. Socks : rhyming s. : late C. 19–20. Since 1914 among soldiers : *Army rocks.* B. & P.

almonds. Abbr. of **almond rocks.** P. P. *Rhyming Slang,* 1932.

aloft. Dead : C. 18–20 ; ob. Also coll. is *go aloft,* to die : Dibdin's *Tom Bowling,* 1790, contains the verses,

> Faithful below, **Tom** did his duty,
> And now he's gone aloft.

At *aloft,* F. & H. has a fascinating synonymy for ' to die ' ; see too the essay on euphemisms in *Words !* Cf. *alow and aloft,* q.v.

alone, go. To be experienced, wary, and alert: ca. 1800- 25.

along, get. An imperative = go away ! : coll.; C. 19–20. Ordinarily, *get along* is S.E. and = get on, move along.

along of. Owing to. In C. 19–20, except in dial., it is sol., but in C. 16–17 it was indubitably S.E.—2. With, as in 'Being friendly along o' you': sol.: mid-C. 19–20. Baumann. Ex dial.

along-shore boys. Landsmen: nautical coll. (— 1823); † by 1910. Egan's Grose.

along with. A coll. weakening of *with*: late C. 19–20. C. Williams, *The Greater Trumps*, 1932, 'Her engagement to—her understanding with—whatever . . . she had along with this young Henry Lee fellow—had hardened her.'

alonger. Along of: sol. form (— 1887), mostly London. Baumann.

aloud, used fig., is coll.: mid-C. 19–20. (The O.E.D. record: 1872.)

alow and aloft. 'Below decks and aloft'; nautical coll.: mid-C. 19–20. Bowen.—2. Hence, 'dead and alive', i.e. lethargic, dull: nautical: late C. 19–20; ob. Ibid.

*Alps, over the. See **over the Alps**.

alright. An erroneous form of *all right*: late C. 19–20. Fowler.

*Alsatia (the Higher). Whitefriars. **Alsatia the Lower,** the Mint in Southwark, London. C. of ca. 1680–1800; afterwards, historical. From early in C. 17 until 1697, when both liberties or asylums or sanctuaries were suppressed, these were the haunts of bankrupts, fleeing debtors, gamesters and sharks. In Shadwell's comedy, *The Squire of Alsatia*—the first record of the term—occurs the illuminating: 'Who are these ? Some inhabitants of White-fryers; some bullies of Alsatia.' *Alsatia* = Alsace, a 'debateable ground' province. In C. 18–19 *Alsatia* meant any asylum for criminals, any low quarter, while *squire of Alsatia* synonymised a sharper or a 'shady' spendthrift. Besides Shadwell's play, consult Scott's *Fortunes of Nigel*, Macaulay's *History* at I, iii, E. Beresford Chancellor's *Annals of Fleet Street*, and M. Melville Balfour's historical novel, *The Long Robe*.

Alsatia phrase. A term in s. or, esp., in c.: Swift, 1704; † by 1750. Coll. very soon S.E.

*Alsatian. Pertaining to 'Alsatia'; criminal; debauched: c. of late C. 17–18; then historical. Whence the n.—2. Abbr. *Alsatian wolf-dog*: from 1925; coll. almost imm. S.E. (*A. wolf-dog* itself—see the S.O.D.—dates only from 1924.)

also ran, an. A nonentity: mostly Australian (— 1916) >, by 1918, gen. C. J. Dennis; Collinson. Ex horse-racing.

alt, in. Haughty: coll.: 1748, Richardson; † by 1820. (Apperson). Ex *altitude*.

alta(or **e** or **u**)**ma**(or **e**)**l**(**l**). All together; altogether (adv.): late C. 17–18. N., the total of a bill, an account: C. 18. Adj., nautical, esp. of s. and j.: C. 18. Since the adv. and the n. are always, so far as I can discover, spelt *alta*(or *e*)*me*(or *a*)*l*(*l*) and F. & H. derives them from Dutch *altemal* (modern Dutch *allemaal*)—Hexham, 1658, 'Al-te-mael, Wholly, or All at once', and since the O.E.D. derives the adj., always spelt *altumal*, from *altum* (*mare*) + *al*, the two forms and derivations suggest, indeed they almost necessitate, two distinct origins.

altar. 'Master's desk in old Lower Senior Room': Bootham School: late C. 19–20. Anon., *Dict. of Bootham Slang*, 1925. **Ex the shape.**

alter. Unpleasant; e.g. 'We had an alter parade this morning': military (not officers'): from ca. 1930. Perhaps ex (— 1898) Hampshire dial. *alteration* and (— 1898) Berkshire dial. *altery*, (of weather that is) uncertain, tending to rain. (E.D.D.)

alter the jeff's click. To make a garment regardless of the cutter's chalkings or instructions: tailors' (— 1903). F. & H., revised.

*altham, C. 16 c., a wife; a mistress. Whence(?) the c. adj. *autem*, q.v.

altifrontal, adj. High-brow: 1932; somewhat pejorative, 'Is he intelligent ?—Oh, very altifrontal, I'd say.' London authors', reviewers', and publishers'.

altitude, grabbing for. (Occ. in other tenses.) Becoming very angry: aircraft engineers': from ca. 1932. *The Daily Herald*, Aug. 1, 1936.

altitudes, in the (or *his, my*, etc). In elevated mood (coll.: Jonson, 1630); drunk (ca. 1700). Both were † by 1840. Cf. *elevated*.

altocad. An oldish paid member that in the choir takes alto: Winchester College, from ca. 1850.

altogether and **all together** are often confused: mid-C. 19–20. The former = entirely, on the whole. Fowler.

altogether, the. The nude: coll.: 1894, Du Maurier (Ware). I.e. *the altogether* (wholly) *naked*.

altogethery. Drunk: Society: 1816, Byron; † by 1930. Ware. Ex *altogether drunk*.

'Am and Tripe, the. H.M.S. *Amphritite*: naval: C. 20. Bowen.

amachoor. A coll. written form of *amateur*, which, after all, is thus pronounced by the majority. (D. Sayers, *Murder Must Advertise*, 1933.)

amazingly. Very: coll.: from ca. 1790. Maria Edgeworth, 'She speaks English amazingly well for a Frenchwoman.' O.E.D.

ambassador. A sailors' trick upon new hands: mid-C. 18–19. Grose, 1st ed. In a King-Neptune form, *King Arthur*.—2. See:

ambassador of commerce. A commercial traveller: coll.: late C. 19–20; ob. Baumann. In C. 20, often *ambassador*.

Ambassador of Morocco. A shoemaker: ca. 1810–30. *Lex. Bal*. Punning *morocco* (leather).

amber, shoot the. See **shoot the amber**.

ambi, ambitious. 'Zealous, with a view to personal advantage; also foolishly zealous, asking for more work, etc., etc.', John Masefield, in the *Conway*, 1933. Conway Training Ship s., from ca. 1880.

ambi(or **o**)**dexter.** A double-dealing witness, lawyer or juror: C. 16–19; coll.; S.E. after 1800. —2. Any double-dealer: from ca. 1550, coll.; by 1880 S.E.

ambish. Ambition: from ca. 1925. E.g. Garnett Radcliffe in *The Passing Show*, Jan. 27, 1934.

ambrol. A naval corruption of *admiral*: late C. 17–18. B.E.

ambs-ace, ames ace. Bad luck: M.E.–C. 19. —2. Next to nothing: C. 17–18. Lit. the double ace; and soon coll.—3. *Within ambs-ace*, almost: late C. 17–early 19, coll. in C. 18–19.

amen-chapel. 'The service used in Winchester School [*sic*] upon Founder's Commemorations, and certain other occasions, in which the responses and Amens are accompanied on the organ', E.D.D., 1896.

amen-curler. A parish clerk: late C. 18–19. Grose, 1st ed. A C. 18 variant: *amen-clerk*. A mid-C. 19–20 variant, *amen-bawler* (Mayhew, 1851). Cf. *amen-snorter* and *amen-wallah*.

amen-snorter. A parson. Rare in England, frequent in Australia (ca. 1880–1900).

' amen ' to everything, say ' yes ' and. To agree to everything : coll. : late C. 18–mid–19. Grose, 3rd ed. Cf. *amener*, q.v.

amen wallah. A chaplain's clerk : C. 19–20. In G.W. occ. the chaplain himself. Cf. *amen-curler*, q.v.

amener. An assiduous assenter : C. 19–20 ; ob. (*Amen*, the concluding word.)

[**amercy** for *God have mercy* was orig. coll. and is still far from ' literary '.]

American shoulders. A coat cut square to give the appearance of broadness. From ca. 1870 ; at first, tailors' j., but s. by 1890.

*American tweezers. A burglar's instrument for opening doors : from ca. 1870 ; orig. c. H., 5th ed.

Americans. American stocks and shares : Stock Exchange coll. (mid-1880's) >, by 1910, j. (O.E.D.)

amidships. On the solar plexus ; in or on the belly. Nautical : C. 18–20.

Aminidab, Aminadab. A Quaker : C. 18–early 19 ; derisive. Ned Ward, 1709 ; Grose.

ammedown. Hand me down (v.), or hand-me-down (adj.) : poorest London low coll. (– 1909). Ware.

ammo. Ammunition (n. and adj.) : military : C. 20.—2. Hence, *ammos*, ammunition boots, the ordinary Army boots : from 1915. F. & Gibbons.

ammunition. Toilet paper : C. 19–20 ; ob. Cf. *bum-fodder*, q.v.

ammunition leg. A wooden leg : military : C. 19. (*Ammunition* = munition.)

ammunition wife. (Gen. pl.) A harlot : nautical : ca. 1820–70. Egan's Grose ; Bowen. Cf. *gunpowder* and *hot stuff*.

among(st) other things or **among(st) others** is gen. illogical for ' along with, *or* in addition to, other things '. This catachresis, however, seems to have been consecrated by long usage.

amorosa. A wanton : ca. 1630–1720 : Society, mainly. It. word, never acclimatised.

amoroso. A (male) lover : ca. 1615–1770 ; chiefly Society. An It. word never properly anglicised.

amost, a'most. Almost : London sol. (– 1887). Baumann.

amourette. A trifling love affair or, esp., amour : ca. 1860–1914 : Society coll. Directly ex Fr. ; cf. C. 17 S.E. *amorets*, dalliance.

amours, in. In love : gen. followed by *with* (some person) : ca. 1725–1800 : Society s. > coll. > S.E.

amp. An amputation : medical students' (– 1933). *Slang*, p. 190.

ampersand. The posterior(s). ' & ' used to come at the end of nursery-book alphabets : hence the hinder parts. Ca. 1885–1914. The lit. sense is about a century old. Ex *and per se—and*, i.e. ' & by itself = and '.

amputate one's mahogany or **timber.** To ' cut one's stick ', to depart, esp. depart quickly : from the 1850's ; ob. ' Ducange Anglicus ', 1857. There is a rich synonymy for rapid departure ; see F. & H., also my *Slang*.

*amuse, in late C. 17–18 c., is to throw dust, pepper, snuff, etc., in the eyes of the person to be robbed ; an *amuser* is one who does this. B.E.

amy. ' A friendly alien serving in a man-of-war ' : naval : ca. 1800–60. Bowen notes that in the old days there were many foreigners serving in the British Navy. ? a mutilated blend of *enemy man* or simply an adoption of Fr *ami*, a friend.

an'. A sol. pronunciation of *and* ; it is also dial. C. 15–20.—2. See **a**, 4.

anabaptist. A pickpocket that, caught in the act, is ducked in pond or at pump : late C. 18–early 19. Grose, 1st ed.

anagogical, applied to persons, is catachrestic : from ca. 1840. O.E.D.

anan. ' What do you say, Sir ? ' in reply to an order or remark not understood : naval : C. 18. Bowen. Perhaps *anon* corrupted.

anatomical. Bawdy : sexual : artists' : from ca. 1920. E.g. ' anatomical stories, jokes, humour, wit '.

anatomy. An extremely emaciated—or skinny—person : late C. 16–20. (Low) coll. Cf. *atomy*, q.v.

ancestral home. Merely home : jocular coll. : C. 20 : university and Society.

anchor, swallow the. To settle down—above all, to loaf—on shore, esp. if one is still active : nautical : late C. 19–20. Ware.—2. To surrender or yield : c. : from ca. 1919. George Ingram, *Stir*, 1933.

anchor, bring one's arse to an. To sit down : nautical : late C. 18–mid 19. Grose, 2nd ed. Cf. :

anchor (oneself), come to an anchor. To halt ; sit down, rest ; sojourn. Coll., C. 18–20.—2. Hence *anchor*, an abode or a place of residence : C. 19–20 coll. At first nautical, both v. and n. soon > gen.

anchor to the windward of the law, let go an. To keep within the letter of the law : nautical : late C. 18–mid 19. Grose, 3rd ed.

anchors. Brakes : busmen's : from ca. 1929. *The Daily Herald*, Aug. 5, 1936.

ancient mariner. A sea-gull : nautical : C. 19–20. Sea-gulls are ' supposed to possess the souls of dead sailormen ', Bowen. Cf. Coleridge's *Ancient Mariner*.

ancient mariners. At Oxford, an occasionally-rowing group or crew of dons ; at Cambridge, any graduates that, still associated with the university, continue to row. From ca. 1880 ; ob. Ware quotes *The Daily News* of Nov. 7, 1884.

-and. In coll. names of drinks, of which *cider-and*, 1742, is the earliest.

— and —. Between adjj., *and* either is intensive, as in *hot and hot* (very hot), in the † *pure and —*, and in *rare and* some other adj. (very —) ; or it gives a familiar tang, as in *nice and hot* (nicely hot, hence pleasantly hot) : both usages are coll., the former of C. 19–20, the latter of C. 18–20.—2. The familiar note occurs also in adv. phrases, as (*I hit him*) *good and hard* : coll. : mid-C. 18–20.—3. Of its coll. presence between two vv., there are two examples : *try and* (e.g. *do something*) ; *go and* (*do something*) : see these two phrases.

and all. As well : lower-class coll. tag implying a grumble : from ca. 1860. Cf. S.E. usage.

and all that. And all the rest of it : S.E. in ordinary usage : since 1929, however, it has had a coll. connotation owing, in part, to such book-titles as *Good-Bye to All That, 1066 and All That*.

(and) don't you forget it ! A c.p. orig. U.S. (– 1888) adopted in England ca. 1890. An almost pointless intensive.

and he didn't ! A tailors' c.p. implying a discreditable action : ca. 1870–1920.

and how ! ' Rather ! ' : an American c.p. anglicised by 1933. *The Western People* (Balling), Nov. 11, 1933.

and no error or **mistake !** See **mistake, and no.**

and no mogue ! A tailors' implication of slight incredulity = 'that's true ?' From ca. 1880. *Mogue* is an etymological puzzle, as are so many s. terms.

and no whistle. Another tailors' implication: that the speaker is actually, though ostensibly not, speaking of himself. Ca. 1860–1900.

and so forth and so fifth. See **fifth.**

and so he died ; and then she died. These Restoration-drama tags verge on c.pp. : See Dryden, ed. Summers, I, 419.

and so she prayed me to tell ye. An almost meaningless c.p. (with slight variations) rounding off a sentence : ca. 1670–90. E.g. in Duffett's burlesque, 'The Mock-Tempest,' 1675.

and the rest ! A sarcastic retort or comment : from ca. 1860. The implication is that something has been omitted.

and things. See **things, and.**

and welcome ! And you're welcome to it ; I'm glad (to let you have it, etc.) : coll., non-aristocratic : late C. 19–20. Manchon.

and which. See **which.**

Andrew. A gentleman's servant : coll. > S.E. : 1698, Congreve ; † by 1800. Because a very common name.—2. In full, *Andrew Millar.* A ship, esp. *of war* : rhyming s. (— 1864) ; ob.—3. Hence, a revenue cutter ; Australian smugglers' : ca. 1870–1900. But this, like sense 2, may abbr. *Andrew Miller's* (or *-ar's*) *lugger,* 'a king's ship and vessel', 1813 (sea cant), a phrase † by 1880.—4. Abbr. *Andrew Millar,* 2 ; always *the Andrew.*

Andrew Mack. H.M.S. *Andromache*: naval : C. 20. Bowen.

Andrew Makins, (stop your). (Stop your) goings-on or fooling : Anglo-Irish : C. 20. Is there an allusion to merry Andrews ? : cf. the Essex and Sussex *Andrew,* a clown.

Andrew Millar. See **Andrew,** 2.—2. The Royal Navy : hence, any Government department : naval : mid-C. 19–20 ; ob. Bowen.

Andy Cain. Rain : rhyming s. : late C. 19–20. P. P., *Rhyming Slang,* 1932.

Angel. A harlot plying near the Angel at Islington : low Cockney (— 1909). Ware. Cf. *Sluker.*

***angel.** A sandwich-man ; C. 20 c. Ex *wings,* the boards. Jennings, *Tramping with Tramps,* 1932.—2. In C. 20 theatrical s., *angel* is any outsider that finances the production of a play.—3. (Gen. pl.) A wireless rating in the Royal Navy : naval : from ca. 1923. Ex wings on badge. (Bowen.)—4. The ' boy who fetches Reeve's meat at breakfast ' : Bootham School : C. 20. Anon., *Dict. of Bootham Slang,* 1925.

angel, flying angel. A ride astride a person's shoulder (James Greenwood, 1880) : ca. 1860–1900.

angel altogether. A confirmed drunkard. Mainly West Indian : ca. 1876–1914.

angel face. A boyish(-looking) probationary flight-officer : Air Force : 1915 ; ob. F. & Gibbons.

angel-maker. A baby-farmer : proletarian : 1889 ; ob. Ware, ' Because so many of the farmed babies die'. Probably ex the Fr. *faiseuse des anges.*

angelic, Angelica. An unmarried girl. The former ca. 1810–50, the latter ca. 1850–1900. Moncrieff in *Tom and Jerry,* 1821, speaks of ' the angelics at Almack's '.

angel's food. Strong ale : ca. 1575–1620. Harrison's *England,* II, viii.

angel's foot-stool. A sail carried over the moon-

sail by American clippers : nautical coll : mid-C. 19–20 ; ob. Bowen.

angel's gear. Women's clothes : nautical : mid-C. 19–20 ; ob. Baumann.

Angels of Christ. The Army Ordnance Corps : military : G.W. (B. & P.)

angel's oil. Money employed in bribery. Variant, *oil of angels.* C. 17. Punning *angel,* the small gold coin struck in 1465.

angel's suit. Coat and waistcoat made in one, with trousers buttoned thereto. Tailors', ca. 1870–1885. ' Neither garment nor name was extensively adopted,' F. & H.

angel's whisper. See **whisper, angel's.**

***angler.** A pilferer that, with a hooked stick, steals from open windows and doors : mid-C. 16–early 19. Harman, B.E., Grose. Cf. *area sneak, hooker, starrer.*—2. A hook : c. of ca. 1580–1620. Greene.

Anglican inch. ' The short square whisker . . . so much affected by the Broad Church party ' : ritualistic clergy's : 1870 ; very ob. Ware.

***angling cove.** A receiver of stolen goods : C. 19 c. In C. 18–early 19 c., *angling for farthings* is begging, with cap and string, from a prison window. Grose.

Anglos. The shares of the Anglo-American United, with which ' the dogs ' (q.v.) were amalgamated : from ca. 1890 ; Stock Exchange. A. J. Wilson, *Stock Exchange Glossary,* 1895, defines it, however, as ' Anglo-American Telegraph Company [shares] '.

angry boy. A blood : late C. 16–17. Greene ; Beaumont & Fletcher.

Angry Cat, the. The French battleship *Henri IV* at the Dardanelles in : 1915 : naval. Bowen.

Anguagela. Language : central s. (— 1909) ; ob., as all central s. is. Ware.

angular party. A gathering or social group odd in number : coll., from ca. 1870 ; ob.

Animal. The Elephant and Castle Station : London Railway passengers' : ca. 1860–1910. Ware.—2. *The Animal.* ' A disguised, or flippant, reference amongst boon companions to the tavern, used in common when the sign is zoological . . . but more esp. referring to the Elephant and Castle . . . ; until (1882) this place was exceptionally dubbed "Jumbo",' Ware.

animal, go the whole. A U.S. phrase adapted by Dickens as *go the extreme animal,* by Sala as . . . *entire* . . . A C. 19 variant on the U.S. *go the whole hog.*

animal, mere. ' A very silly fellow ', B.E. : late C. 17–18 coll. Wycherley.

animal spirits. Liveliness of character, (gen. considerable) vivacity of manner and action, a healthy animalism : coll. ; from ca. 1810. Jane Austen.

ankle, have sprained one's. To have been seduced (cf. Fr. *avoir mal aux genoux*) : late C. 18–20 ; ob. Grose, 1st ed.

ankle-biters. Trousers hussar-fashion : lower classes' (— 1923). Manchon.

ankle-bone. A crawfish : nautical : late C. 19–20 ; ob. Bowen.

ankle-beater. A boy specialising (ca. 1820–80) in driving, to the slaughter-yard, the animals purchased by the butcher. To avoid the damaging of flesh, only the beasts' ankles were touched. Also known as a *penny-boy.*

***ankle-spring warehouse.** The stocks : Anglo-Irish c. : ca. 1780–1830.

Annie Laurie. A lorry: rhyming s. (of an unusual kind): military: G.W. (B. & P.)

Anna Maria. A fire: rhyming s.: 1892, 'Pomes' Marshall, *Sporting Times*, Oct. 29.

annas of dark blood, have at least two. To be of mixed parentage: Anglo-Indian coll. (— 1886). Yule & Burnell. Cf. *coffee-colour*, q.v.

Anne's fan, properly *Queen Anne's fan.* Thumb to nose and fingers outspread; intensified by twiddled fingers or by addition of other hand similarly outspread: late C. 18–19. Now *cock a snook* at a person.

Annie. See **Asiatic Annie.**

Annie's Bar. 'A place of comfort and refreshment leading off the Members' Lobby' (in the House of Commons): Parliamentary coll.: C. 20. *Time and Tide*, June 1, 1935.

Annie's room (up) in. A military c.p. reply to a query concerning someone's whereabouts: military, slightly pre-G.W. The original implication being that he was 'a bit of a lad'. Cf. *hanging on the barbed wire.*

annihilate. To direct a withering glance at; reprimand severely: coll.; C. 20.

anno domini. Late middle, or old, age (1885); old ('extremely old' is *B.C.*); the passage of the years (however young one is after early adulthood): from ca. 1910. Coll. Ware, 1909, '" He must be very anno domini, mustn't he?" "A.D.? my dear fellow, say B.C."'; *B.C.* is virtually †. Cf. *anno domini ship,* an old-fashioned whaler: whaling: from ca. 1880; ob.

annual. A holiday taken once a year: coll. (— 1903). F. & H., revised.

anodyne necklace. A halter: mid-C. 18–early 19. Goldsmith, 1766; Grose, 2nd ed. (In C. 17 simply *necklace*). One of numerous synonyms. In C. 18 also a supposedly medicinal amulet.

anoint. To beat well, to thrash: C. 17–20; ob. Adumbrated in M.E.

anoint a (or the) palm. To bribe: C. 16–18. Cf. *grease the palm.*

anointed. Depraved, worthless, pejoratively ulter: late C. 18–19; ? mainly Anglo-Irish. H., 3rd ed. Prob. ex *anoint,* q.v.

anonyma. A demi-mondaine, esp. if a high-flyer. Ca. 1860–79, then less common; rare in C. 20. Sala, 1864, 'Bah! There are so many anonymas nowadays.'

another, you're. See **you're another.**

another acrobat. Another drink: punning *tumbler.* Ca. 1870–1900.

another guess; another guess sort of man. (A) 'fly' (man): C. 19. Perhaps ex *another gates,* but prob. direct from U.S.

another point(, steward)! Make that drink stronger!: nautical: from ca. 1860. *The Glasgow Herald,* Nov. 9, 1864. Cf. the *north* drinking-terms.

anser. See goose.—**answer is a lemon.** See **lemon, the answer is a.**

a'n't. Am not: coll.; C. 19–20.—2. Sol., when not dial., for 'is not', 'are not', or, as occ., 'has not': C. 18–20. Cf. *ain't.*

antagonise, v.i. To compete; strive to win: sporting coll. (— 1887); † by 1920. Baumann.

ante up. To hand over, surrender (a thing): military: from not later than 1915. F. & Gibbons. Ex U.S. poker j.

*antem. Prob. a misprint for *autem,* q.v.

Ant(h)ony, cuff or **knock.** To knock one's knees together in walking: late C. 18–19. Grose, 1st ed. Variant, *cuff Jonas.*—2. **Ant(h)ony Cuffin,** a knock-kneed man: C. 19.

Anthony; St. Anthony's pig; antony pig. The smallest pig in a litter: late C. 16–20; ob. Coll. by 1750. St. Anthony the hermit was the patron of swineherds. Apperson.

anti. Erroneous for **ante** (before): mod. English.—2. A person opposed to a given opinion or party; one by nature a rebel, an objector: coll. (1889) >, by 1920, S.E. Ex the adj. (O.E.D.)

anti-guggler. 'A straw or tube . . . for sucking liquor out of casks or bottles': nautical coll.: C. 20. Bowen.

Anti-Hope, the. The clipper *Antiope,* 'a very unlucky ship': nautical: late C. 19–early 20. Bowen.

anti-tempus. Anti-tetanus; anti-tetanus serum: military sol.: from 1916. (Van Wely.)

antics. Tactical exercises: naval coll.: C. 20. Bowen. Also steam *antics.*

antidote. 'A very homely woman', B.E.: jocular: late C. 17–mid 18. Against lust.

antimony. Type: printers' (— 1890). F. & H. 'Antimony is a constituent part' of the metal.

antipodean. With everything topsy-turvy: from ca. 1850. Orig. jocularly pedantic S.E., then jocularly coll.

Antipodes, the or **her.** The female pudend: late C. 19–20.

antiquarianise. To play at being an antiquary: C. 20; coll.

antiquated rogue. An ex-thief; an out-of-date thief: ca. 1660–1730. At the angle formed by three linguistic regions: c., j., and S.E. Only in B.E.

Antonio. A Portuguese soldier: military: G.W. Also *Tony.* (B. & P.)

Antony. See **Anthony.**

anty. Sugar: military: C. 20. F. & Gibbons. Possibly ex the sweetness of gifts from Anty or Auntie.

any. At all: s. (and dial.): late C. 19–20. Kipling, 1890, 'You don't want bein' made more drunk any' (E.D.D.).

any, I'm not taking (— 1903) or **having** (from ca. 1895). Not for me!; 'not for Joe!': c.p. Hence in ordinary constructions. The earlier form occurs in J. Milne, *Epistles of Atkins,* 1902.

Any Bloody (occ. **Blooming) How, the.** H.M.S. *Howe,* 'which alway steered like a dray': naval: C. 20. Bowen. Ex:

any how, anyhow. Indifferently; badly: coll. (— 1859).

any of these men here? A military c.p. (from ca. 1910) by a wag that, imitating a sergeant-major at a kit-inspection, continues, 'Knife, fork, spoon . . . ?' B. & P., 'Sometimes the reply would be given: " Yes, he is,"' whereupon the wag or a third party would ask, 'Who is?' to which the retort was 'A*se-holes.'

any old (e.g. **thing).** Any . . . whatsoever: U.S. (ca. 1910) anglicised ca. 1914. W. J. Locke, 1918, 'Mate, Bill, Joe—any old name.' O.E.D.

anyhows. Anyhow: sol., esp. London (— 1887). Baumann.

anyone is incorrect for either *any one (of . . .)* or *any* (pronoun): C. 20. E.g. E. Phillips Oppenheim, *The Bank Manager,* 1934, 'Mr. Huitt . . . did not . . . summon anyone of the clients who were waiting to see him?'

any more for any more ? Does anyone desire a second helping ? : military mess-orderlies' c.p. : 1915 ; ob.

any racket. A penny faggot : rhyming s., ca. 1855–1910. H., 1st ed.

any road. See road, any.

anything, as or like. Very ; much. The *as* form, C. 16–20 ; ob. ; the *like*, C. 19–20. Coll.

anything ! so help me. God help me ! : euphemistic coll., non-aristocratic (— 1923). Manchon.

anything else but. See nothing but.

anythingarian. A person of no fixed or decided views : from ca. 1707, when coined by Swift ; whence *anythingarianism*, defined by Kingsley in 1851 as ' modern Neo-Platonism '. Coll., soon S.E. ; ob.

anythink. Anything : sol., as are *nothink, somethink.* C. 16–20.

anyways. In any case : dial. and sol. : 1865, Dickens (O.E.D.) Ex *anyway.*

anywhere down there ! A tailors' c.p. when something is dropped on the floor : ca. 1860–1910.

anywheres. Anywhere : sol. : late C. 19–20. Cf. *anyways*, q.v., and *somewheres.*

Anzac. A member of the Australian and New Zealand Army Corps on Gallipoli : military coll. (April 26, 1915—the day after the landing) >, by 1919, S.E.—2. Loosely, any Australian or New Zealand soldier serving in the G.W. : coll. : from late 1918.

Anzac poker. See kangaroo poker.

Anzac shandy. Beer and champagne : New Zealand soldiers' : 1915–18.

Anzac wafer. A large (hard) Army biscuit : New Zealand soldiers' : 1915–18.

apartments to let. (With *have*) brainless ; silly : from early 1860's. H., 3rd ed. ; ob.—2. In C. 18, descriptive of a widow.

ape, if applied pejoratively to a person, tends in C. 20 to rank as a low coll. Cf. *baboon.*

ape, make anyone his. To befool : C. 17–19 coll. Variant, *put an ape into one's hood or cap.*

'apenny bumper. ' A two-farthing omnibus ride ' : London streets' : ca. 1870–1900. Ware.

'apenny-lot day. ' A bad time for business ' : costers' (— 1909) ; ob. Ware. Because on such a day, the sales total ½*d.*

apes in hell, lead. To be an old maid : C. 16–20 ; ob. ' Euphues ' Lyly was one of the first to record the phrase ; Gascoigne was app. the first. Apperson.—Whence, *ape-leader,* an old maid : mid-C. 17–early 19. Brome : Grose. (O.E.D.)

ape's paternoster, say an. To chatter with cold. Recorded by Cotgrave in 1611. For the quaint proverbs and proverbial sayings connected with the ape, see esp. G. L. Apperson's *English Proverbs,* 1929.

apes. First mortgage bonds of the Atlantic and North-Western Railway : Stock Exchange, ca. 1870–1914.

apiary and **aviary** are occ. confused : late C. 17–20.

apiece. For each person : coll. ; C. 19–20. (S.E. when applied to things.)

apoplectic. Choleric ; violent-tempered. C. 20 ; coll.

apostles. ' The knight-heads, bollards and bitts of a sailing-ship ' : nautical : mid-C.19–20 ; ob. Bowen. Why ?

apostles, manœuvre the. To rob Peter to pay Paul : mid-C. 18–20 ; ob. Grose, 2nd ed.

Apostles, the (Twelve). The last twelve on the

degree list : Cambridge University : late C. 18–19. Ex *post alios,* after the others, is H.'s suggestion. Variant, *the chosen twelve.*

Apostle's Grove, the. St. John's Wood district, London : 1864. H., 3rd ed. Variant, *the Grove of the Evangelist* : H., 5th ed., 1874. Ex the numerous demi-mondaines living there ca. 1860–1910. Ob.

apostle's pinch. A pinch of a very indelicate nature : low : C. 20.

apothecaries' Latin. Law Latin, dog Latin : late C. 18–early 19 coll. Grose, 1st ed.

apothecary, talk like an. To talk nonsense : mid-C. 18–early 19 : coll. Grose, 1st ed.

apothecary's bill. A long bill : mid-C. 18–early 19. Grose, 1st ed.

appalling. Objectionable ; ugly ; noticeable, marked : coll. (Society and middle class) ; C. 20.

appallingly. Very : C. 20 ; coll.

Appii, the. The Three Tuns, a noted Durham inn : Durham University (— 1903). F. & H., revised. By a misreading of Acts xxviii. 15.

apple and pears. An early form of *apples and pears,* q.v. ' Ducange Anglicus ', 1857.

apple-cart. The human body. Grose, 2nd ed., 1788, has ' down with his apple-cart ; knock or throw him down ' : cf. H., 1st ed., 1859, ' " down with his applecart," i.e. upset him. *North*[ern].' In *upset the apple-cart* there seems to be a merging of two senses : body and, in dialect, plan ; originating app. ca. 1800, this phrase > coll. ca. 1850. In 1931, thanks largely to G. B. Shaw's play, *The Apple Cart,* it was admitted into S.E. though not into literary English. For fuller information, see F. & H., O.E.D., W., and Apperson.

apple-cart, upset the old woman's ; upset the apple-cart and spill the gooseberries (or peaches). Variants, dating from ca. 1880, of *upset the apple-cart* : see preceding entry. F. & H.

apple-dumpling shop. A woman's bosom : late C. 18–19. Grose, 2nd ed. Cf. :

apple-monger, apple-squire ; apron-squire. A harlot's bully. Coll., respectively C. 18, C. 16–early 19, late C. 16–19. Perhaps ex *apple,* a woman's breast. Cf. preceding entry.

apple-pie bed. A bed short-sheeted : late C. 18–20 ; coll. by 1830 ; S.E. by 1880. Grose, 2nd ed., defines it as ' A bed made apple-pye fashion, like what is termed a turnover apple-pye '.

Apple-Pie Day. That day on which, at Winchester College, six-and-six was, C. 19, played. On this day, the Thursday after the first Tuesday in December, apple-pies were served on ' gomers ', in College, for dinner. F. & H.

apple-pie order. Perfect order, impeccable precision (Scott, 1813) : coll. >, by 1900, S.E.

apple-squire. A male bawd : orig. (— 1591), c. Greene. See also apple-monger.

Appleby ?, who has any lands in. A c.p. addressed to ' The Man at whose Door the Glass stands Long ' (B.E. at *landlord*) : late C. 17–mid 18. (Cf. *parson Mallum* and *parson Palmer.*) Perhaps orig. of cider.

apples. Testicles : low : C. 19–20. Cf. *nutmegs.* —2. See apples and pears.

apples and pears. Stairs (— 1859). ' Ducange Anglicus,' 1st ed., and H., 1st ed., have *apple and pears.* Ware records, for 1882, the abbr. *apples,* which has never > gen.

apples swim, how we ! What a good time we have ! C. 17–20 ; ob. Clarke, 1639 ; Ray, 1678 ;

FitzGerald, 1852. (Apperson.) Another unsolved etymological conundrum.

appro, on. Coll.: abbr. *on approbation* or *approval* (things), from ca. 1870 (H., 5th ed.); *on approbation* (persons): from ca. 1900.

apree la gare ; appray la guerre. Sometime, or never : military c.p.: 1916–18. Ex Fr. *après la guerre*, after the war.

April gentleman. A man newly married : coll.; C. 16–17. Greene. Ex the popularity of marriages in April.

apron and gaiters. A bishop ; a dean : coll. (— 1913). Arthur H. Dawson's *Dict. of Slang.*

apron-rogue. A labourer, an artisan : C. 17 coll. (In C. 17 S.E., *apron-man*.)

apron-squire. See **apple-monger.**

apron-string hold or **tenure.** An estate held only during a wife's life : late C. 17–19 coll. Ray, 1678, ' To hold by the apron-strings, i.e. in right of his wife ' (Apperson).

apron-strings, tied to (or always at) the (or a woman's). Dangling after a woman, C. 18 ; under petticoat government, C. 18–20.

apron-up. Pregnant : lower and lower-middle class coll. : C. 19–20 ; ob. Because modest women tend, in pregnancy, to use their aprons as ' disguise '.

apron-washings. Porter : proletarian (— 1903) ; ob. F. & H., revised. Ex brewers' *porters*' aprons.

aproneer. A shopkeeper : ca. 1650–1720 ; coll. During the Civil War, a Roundhead. On the other hand, *aproner* (ca. 1600–40) = a barman, a waiter.

'appy dosser. See **dosser.**

aqua pompaginis (or pump-). Apothecaries' Latin for water from the well : C. 18–early 19. Harrison Ainsworth, drawing heavily on Egan's Grose, uses the term several times.

aquarius. ' Controller of evening bath "set"'': Bootham School s. (late C. 19–20) verging on **j.** Anon., *Dict. of Bootham Slang*, 1925.

aquatics. A game of cricket played by the oarsmen ; the playing-field used by them : Eton ; mid C. 19–20.

ar ! Ah ! : low coll. : C. 19–20. Manchon. I.e. *ah* with ' r ' rasped.

Arab, city Arab, street Arab. A young vagrant ; a poor boy playing much in the streets. Coll >, by 1910, S.E. : respectively — 1872, 1848, ca. 1855.

Arabs ; Arab merchants. ' The Indian merchants and shopkeepers in Natal are locally, but erroneously known by these designations. They are chiefly Mohammedans and are also known as "Bombay merchants",' Pettman : from early 1890's.

arbor vitæ. Lit., the tree of life, i.e. the penis : late C. 18–20 ; ob. Grose, 3rd ed. Pedantic.

'Arbour !, our. A Melbourne c.p. at Sydney's expense : C. 20. Sydneyites being apt to boast about their very beautiful harbour ; in retaliation they gibe at Melbourne's rather smelly river, the Yarra : see **Yarra.**

Arbroath ! A Scottish sporting c.p. (from Sept. 6, 1885) to anyone boasting. Because on Sept. 5, 1885, Dundee Harp defeated Aberdeen Rovers by 35–0 and sent a telegram to their great rivals Arbroath, ' You can't beat this ', to which Arbroath, having the same day defeated Bon Accord, in a Scottish Cup Tie, by 36–0, replied, 'Can't we ?' *Athletic News Football Annual,* 1935–6.

*arch-cove or **rogue.** As c., the leader of a gang of thieves : from ca. 1600 to 1800. · The latter as s.,

a confirmed rogue, from **ca.** 1650 ; playfully, C. 18–19. In c., *arch* = principal ; confirmed ; extremely adept. *Arch-doll* or *doxy*, however, is the wife of an *arch-cove* : Grose, 2nd ed.

archdeacon. Merton ale, stronger brew : Oxford University, C. 19–20 ; ob.—2. **The Archdeacon,** H.M.S. *Venerable* : naval : C. 20 ; Bowen. Ex that dignitary's ' style '.

archduke. A comical or an eccentric man : late C. 17–18. Grose, 3rd ed. Perhaps suggested by the Duke in *Measure for Measure.*

Archer up ! (He, etc., is) safe ; or, bound to win : London c.p.: 1881–6. Ex the famous jockey, Fred Archer, who (d. 1886) sprang into fame in 1881.

archideclyne ; archiemander. Incorrect for *architricline* (C. 15), *archimandrite* (late C. 16–20). O.E.D.

Archibald. The air-bump over the corner of the Brooklands aerodrome next to the sewage-farm : aviation : ca. 1910–14. Ex youth's fondness for bestowing proper names on inanimate objects. W. Whence perhaps *Archie*, v.

Archibald, certainly not ! No ! : c.p. of ca. 1913–20. Ex a music-hall song having this refrain. (F. & Gibbons.)

Archie. An anti-aircraft gun : occ., such **a** gunner : military : from 1915. Perhaps ex *Archibald*, but cf. :

Archie ; gen. *archie*, v.t., gen. in passive. To shell (an aviator and his 'plane when they are) in the air : military aviation : from 1915. Prob. ex *Archibald*, q.v. W.

archiemander. See **archideclyne.**

*ard. Hot, both of objects and of persons or passions : C. 17–early 19 c. Ex Fr. *ardent.*

ardelio(n). A busybody : C. 17 ; coll. Never properly acclimatised. Florio ; Burton. Ex L. *ardelio* ex *ardere*, to be zealous.

ardent. Spirituous liquor : Society : 1870 ; † by 1920. Ware. Abbr. *ardent spirits.*

are we down-hearted ? A military c.p. of the G.W. (for variant and elaboration, see B. & P., p. 194) ; orig (ca. 1906) political but soon gen.

area-sneak. A sneak haunting areas in order to thieve (Vaux, 1812 ; Dickens, 1838). Coll.; S.E. by 1880 at latest. For a lengthy list of English and Continental synonyms for a thief see F. & H.

aren't ; arnt. Resp. coll. and sol. for *are not*: C. 18–20.—2. Sol. for *am not, is not.*—3. Have not : sol. : C. 19–20. I.e., *'an't* = *han't* = *haven't.*

areoplane. An aeroplane : sol. : from ca. 1912. By *-ero- > -reo.* Cf. *airoplane* and *airyplane.*

arer. A Cockney term of ca. 1900–15, as in Ware's quotation, ' We *are*, and what's more, we can't be any arer ', i.e. more so.

'arf. 'Alf, i.e. half : Cockney sol.: C. 19–20. Esp. in *'arf a mo* (or *tick*) : late C. 19–20. Ware.

'arf-and-'arf. Ale and porter mixed equally : Cockney ; from ca. 1830. Cf :

arfarfanarf. Drunk : Cockney (— 1909) ; **ob.** Ware. Lit., half, half, and half ; applied orig. to one who has had many an *arf-and-arf*, q.v. .

arg. To argue : low (— 1903). F. & H., revised.

argal ; argol-bargol. In Shakespeare, *argal* = therefore : obviously corrupted from *ergo. Argol-bargol,* unsound reasoning, cavilling,—as v., to bandy words,—is of the C. 19–20 (ob.) and seems to be echoically rhyming after *willy-nilly, hocus-pocus,* etc. Moreover, *The Times*, in 1863, used *argal* as = quibble, and Galt, forty years earlier, employed the adj. *argol-bargolous*, quarrelsome; *argy-bargy* (− 1887) is mostly Scottish. Note, however, that *argle*, to dispute about, dates from ca. 1589.

argol. Incorrect for botanic *archil* or *orchil*: mid-C. 18–20; ob. O.E.D.

*argot. 'A term used amongst London thieves for their secret . . . language', H.: c. (− 1859); † by 1920. The Fr. *argot*, properly cant, loosely slang.—2. For its misuse as = 'slang', see introductory chapter of *Slang*: 1843, *The Quarterly Review*, 'Some modern argot or vulgarism'.

argue the leg off an iron pot. To be, on one occasion or many, extremely argumentative: coll.: from ca. 1880. Also *argue a dog's tail off*: coll. (− 1903). F. & H., revised.

argue the toss. 'To dispute loudly and long': low: from ca. 1910. B. & P.

argufy. To signify: mid-C. 18–20: low coll. and dial. Smollett, 1751. Ex *argue* on *speechify.*— 2. Hence, to pester with argument: id.: 1771, Smollett; ob.—3. Hence, v.i., to argue, wrangle: id.: 1800, Maria Edgeworth. The commonest sense.

argy-bargy. See **argal.**

arico vein. A varicose vein: C. 19–20 sol.; ob. Ware. Influenced by *haricot (beans).*

Aristippus. Canary wine: C. 17: Middleton, 'rich Aristippus, sparkling sherry'. Ex the hedonistic Greek philosopher.

aristo. An aristocrat: dated by the O.E.D. Sup. at 1864, but perhaps rather from ca. 1790 and perhaps influenced by Fr. s.

aristocrat. A 'swell', a 'toff': C. 19–20; coll., but at no time at all gen.

aristocratic vein. (Gen. pl.) A blue vein: theatrical coll. (− 1909); ob. Ware. Cf. S.E. *blue blood.*

Aristotle. A bottle: rhyming s.: late C. 19–20; ob. *The Evening News*, Aug. 19, 1931.

*ark. See **arkman.**—2. A barrack-room chest: military coll. (− 1903); ob. A survival ex S.E.

ark, be (or have come) out of the. To be very old or very stale: coll.: C. 20. Lyell, 'Good Heavens! This cheese must have *come out of the Ark!*'

*ark and win(n)s. A sculler; a row-boat; c.: late C. 18–mid 19. Grose, 1st ed. See **arkman.**

ark-floater. An aged actor: C. 19. Ex *Noah's ark + floats*, the footlights.

*ark-pirate. A thief 'working' navigable rivers: nautical c. (− 1823); † by 1900. Egan's Grose.

*arkman. A Thames waterman: C. 18–19; c. or low. *Ark*, a boat, is not c. except perhaps ca. 1750–1850. Thence *ark-ruff(ian)*, a fresh-water thief: c.; C. 18–mid 19. *A New Canting Dict.*, 1725.

arks. A sol. pronunciation (− 1874) of *ask*. H., 5th ed. Cf. *arst, ax*.

Arleens. Orleans plums: Cockney coll. Recorded by Baumann, 1887.

arm, as long as one's. Very long: coll.; late C .19–20.

arm, chance one's. See **chance your arm !**

arm, make a long. To stretch one's arm after something: from ca. 1880; coll.

arm, under the. (Of a job) additional: tailors' (− 1903). F. & H., revised.—2. No good: tramps' c. (− 1935). Also *under the crutch*.

Arm-in-Tears; Arminteers. Armentières: military: from late 1914. Immortalised in that lengthy, scabrous, humorous song, *Mademoiselle from Arminteers* (for which, see esp. B. & P.).

*arm-pits, work under the. To avoid being hanged, to commit only petty larcenies: c.: C. 19. Vaux, 1812.

arm-props. Crutches: coll.: from ca. 1820; † by 1910. Moncrieff, 1821.

arm the lead. 'To fill a small cavity with tallow to bring up a sample of the bottom' when sounding the depth: nautical: mid-C. 19–20: coll. >, by 1900, j. Bowen.

armadillo scout. An aeroplane introduced by Armstrong-Whitworth in 1918: Air Force s. verging on j.; † by 1925. F. & Gibbons.

armado. Incorrect for *armada*: C. 16–17. Shakespeare, *Comedy of Errors*, III, ii.

Arminteers. See **Arm-in-Tears.**

armour, be in. To be pot-valiant: late C. 17–18. B.E. Cf. *Dutch courage* and perhaps the C. 17 proverbial *armour is light at table* (Apperson).

armour, fight in. To use a 'French letter': ca. 1780–1840. Grose, 1st ed.

arms and legs (,all). Weak beer: without *body*. C. 19–20.—2. Hence, weak tea: military: C. 20. F. & Gibbons.

arm's length, work at. To work at a disadvantage; clumsily: coll. > S.E.; C. 19–20; ob.

arms of Murphy, in the. Asleep: low (− 1903). F. & H., revised. I.e. *Morpheus*.

Army rocks. See **almond rocks.**

Army Safety Corps. See **Ally Sloper's Cavalry.**

Army Service Cunts. The A.S.C.: infantrymen's pejorative: G.W.

arnt. See **aren't.**

arra. See **arrow.**

arrah ! An Anglo-Irish expletive of emotion, excitement: coll.: late C. 17–20.

array. To thrash, flog; afflict; disfigure, befoul: ironically or jocularly coll.: late C. 14–16. Cf. *dress down, dressing down*.

arrect. Sol. for *aret*, to impute (C. 14–17): C. 15–16. (O.E.D.)

arrest. Either sol. or catachrestic for *wrest*: late C. 16–20.

arri ! An exclamation of astonishment or vexation: Midland Districts of South Africa: coll.: from early 1880's. Ex Hottentot *aré*, Pettman.

arrival. An enemy shell arriving—and bursting —in the English lines: military coll.: from 1915. B. & P. Cf. *theirs.*—2. A landing of the completest mediocrity: Royal Air Force's: from 1932.

arrow. Sol. for *ever a, any*: mid-C. 18–20; slightly ob. Fielding; Smollett, 1771, 'I now carries my head higher than arrow private gentlewoman of Vales.' Occ. *arra*: C. 19–20.

'Arry and 'Arriet. A typical costermonger and his, or any, coster lass; hence, any low-bred and lively (esp. if not old) man and woman. Popularised by Milliken. From ca. 1870; coll. Whence *'Arryish*, 'costermongerish', vulgarly jovial: coll.; from ca. 1880. Also, *'Arry's worrier*, a concertina: Cockney: 1885; ob. Ware.

ars musica. The 'musical arse', i.e. the podex: late C. 18–19. Grose, 1st ed. Punning the L. for musical art.

arse. Posterior; buttocks. Until ca. 1660, S.E.; then a vulg. Ca. 1700–1930, rarely printed in full: even B.E. (1690) on one occasion prints as 'ar—', and Grose often omits the *r*, while Frederic Manning (d. Feb., 1935) was in Jan., 1930, considered extremely daring to give its four letters in his magnificent War-novel, *Her Privates We.*

arse, v.t. To kick (C. 19–20), to dismiss, esp.

from a job (G.W.); s.—2. **arse off**, v.i., to depart, late C. 19–20 s.

arse, anchor one's. A C. 19–20 variant of *anchor, bring . . .*, q.v.

arse !, ask my. I don't know ! : low : mid-C. 19–20. Manchon. See also **ask mine . . .**

arse, grease a fat sow in the. See **grease . . .**

arse, hang an or **the.** To hold or hang back ; to hesitate timorously : C. 17–20 coll. ; ob.

arse !, so is my († *mine*). A low c.p. of incredulity or contempt : C. 17–20. Jonson.—Also *kiss* † *mine* or *my arse !* : C. 18–20. Swift.

arse, thickest part of his thigh is nearest his. See **hamdudgeon.**

arse about, v.i. To fool about, waste time : C. 20 s. In late C. 18–19, (v.i.) to turn round : a vulgarism.

arse and shite through his ribs, he would lend his. A c.p. applied to ' anyone who lends his money inconsiderately ', Grose, 2nd ed. : ca. 1780–1860.

arse-cooler. (Women's dress, C. 19) a bustle.

arse-crawler or **-creeper.** A sycophant : low coll. : late C. 19–20.

arse-foot. A penguin : (nautical) coll. (— 1598) ; Florio, Goldsmith ; † by 1880. Because its feet are placed so far back.

arse from one's elbow, not to know one's. To be very ignorant : lower-classes' : late C. 19–20.

arse-holes (to you) ! A low contemptuous interjection : late C. 19–20. Ex *arse-hole*, a vulgarism for the anus : C. 19–20.

arse if it was loose, he would lose his. A c.p. ' said of a careless person ', Grose, 2nd ed. : ca. 1780–1860 ; but in a more gen. form C. 16. Nowadays we say . . . *head* . . .

arse off. See **arse**, v.

arse off, tear one's. To work furiously : low (— 1923). Manchon.

arse on . . . See **bandbox.**

arse over turkey. Head over heels : low : late C. 19–20. In military s., esp. officers', it >, in 1916, **ack over tock** : which suggests an original *arse over top*.

Arse-ups, the. The 4th Battalion of the N.Z. Rifle Brigade : New Zealand military in G.W. Ex the shape of the battalion shoulder-patch.

arse upwards. In good luck ; luckily ; coll. : C. 17–20. Esp. *rise with one's . . .* (Ray.)

arse-worm. ' A little diminutive Fellow ', B.E. : late C. 17–18.

-arsed. Having a — arse : C. 16–20 ; see *arse*, n., for status. Heywood, 1562 (*bare-arst*) ; Cotgrave. O.E.D.

arser. A fall on one's behind : mostly hunting and turf : C. 20. E.g. Evelyn Waugh, *A Handful of Dust*, 1934, ' You just opened your bloody legs and took an arser.'

arsmetry. A late C. 16–early 17 sol. (after *geometry*) for † *arsmetik, arsmetric* or *-ck*, arithmetic. (O.E.D.).

arst. Asked : a C. 18–20 sol. Cf. *arks* and *ax*, qq.v.

arsty ! Slowly ! ; slow down ! : Regular Army : late C. 19–20. (B. & P.) Ex Hindustani *ahisti*. Opp. *jildy*.

arsy-varsy, adv. Head over heels, esp. with *fall*, C. 18–20 ; adj., preposterous, topsy-turvy, mid-C. 17–19. Ex *varsy*, a rhyming addition, properly *versy*, L. *versus* (turned), and coll.

arter. After : a C. 17–20 sol. Cf. *arst.*

arterial. Abbr. *arterial road* : 1931 : coll.—soon, prob., to be S.E.

artesian. Beer made in Australia : Australian : ca. 1880–1914.

artful dodger. A lodger : rhyming s. (— 1857). ' Ducange Anglicus.'—2. An expert thief : ca. 1864–1900, perhaps ex the character in *Oliver Twist*.

artful fox. A box : music-hall rhyming s. : 1882 ; † by 1916. Ware.

Arthur, King. See **ambassador.** Grose, 1st ed.

artic. Arctic : sol. : late C. 19–20.

artichoke. See **hearty choke.**

artichoke ripe. To smoke a pipe ; rhyming s. : ca. 1855–80. H., 1st ed.

article. A girl, a woman : ca. 1810–70. *Lex. Bal.*—2. Contemptuous of any person : from ca. 1856 ; coll. ' Ducange Anglicus ', 1st ed. Ex ' its common use in trade for an item of commodity, as in the phr[ase] " What's the next article ? " of the mod. shopkeeper ', E.D.D.

article, the (very). The precise thing ; the thing (or person) most needed. Coll. From ca. 1850. Trollope.

article of virtue. Virgins : ca. 1850–1914. Punning *virtue*, (*objets de*) *vertu*.

articles. Breeches, trousers ; C. 18–19. Grose, 2nd ed.—2. In c. of 1780–1830, a suit of clothes.

artillery, esp. the heavy. ' Big wigs ' ; convincing or very important reasons : coll. ; from late 1916 ; ob.

artilleryman. A drunkard : low (— 1903) ; † by 1919. F. & H., revised. Ex noisiness.

artist. A person ; ' chap ', ' fellow ' : from ca. 1905. Cf. *merchant, chap, customer*.—2. **the Artists.** The Artists' Rifles : military coll. : C. 20.

arty. Artistic ; esp. spuriously or affectedly artistic in practice, theory, or manners : coll. : C. 20. Cf. :

arty-and-crafty ; arty-crafty. Artistic but not notably useful or comfortable : coll. : resp. 1902 and ca. 1920. (O.E.D.)

-arv- for *-ath-*, as in *farver* (father) and *rarver*, and for *-arth*, as in *farver* (farther), is typical of Cockney.

Arvernus. A frequent error for *Avernus*, esp. in C. 20. (Virgil, *facilis descensus Averno*.)

ary. Ever a (of which it is a corruption) ; any . . . whatsoever : a C. 19–20 sol. Perhaps imm. ex *arrow*, q.v.

as. Relative pronoun = that ; who, which. In C. 18–20, sol. ; previously, M.E. onwards, S.E. (It survives also in dial.)—2. As conjunction = *that.* (Variant *as how.*) See *how, as.*

— as —. Very — ; e.g. *drunk as drunk*, very drunk : coll. : mid-C. 19–20. Perhaps ex — *as can be.*

as . . . as they make 'em. Utterly ; very. Esp. with *bad, drunk, fast, mad.* From ca. 1880. Coll.

as ever is. A (mostly lower classes') coll. c.p.-tag, emphasising the preceding statement : C. 20. D. Sayers, *Unnatural Death*, 1927, ' This very Whitsuntide as ever is '. Ex dial. (— 1898) : E.D.D.

as how. See **how, as.**

as such. See **such, as.—as that.** See **that, as.** Cf. *as how* (at *how, as*).

as (he, I, etc.) used to was. As (he, I, etc.) used to be : c.p. : C. 20. Somerset Maugham, *Cakes and Ale*, 1930, ' I'm not so young as I used to was.'

as why ? Why is that ? Why ? : sol. : **1742**, Fielding. (O.E.D.)

as you were. ' Used . . . **to** one who is going too fast in his assertions ' (— 1864) ; post-War, ' Sorry ! my mistake.' Coll. Ex Army.

ash-cat. A fireman in the Merchant Service : nautical, esp. naval : late C. 19–20. Bowen.

ash cookie. A ne'er-do-well : South African coll. (— 1913). Ex *ash cookie*, a dough cake ' roasted in the ashes of a wood fire ' (Pettman), itself ex Dutch *koek*, a cake.

ash-plant. A light cane carried by subalterns : military coll. : 1870 ; ob. Ware. Ex its material.

Ashes, the. ' The symbolical remains of English cricket taken back to Australia ' (S.O.D.) : 1882. Also *win, regain* or *recover*, or *lose the Ashes*, to win or lose a series of test matches (from the English point of view) : 1883 (W. J. Lewis). Coll. ; in C. 20 S.E.

Asia Minor. Kensington and Bayswater (London, W.8 and W.2), ex the large number of retired Indian-Civil servants there resident ca. 1860–1910 : London : ca. 1880–1915.

(Asiatic) Annie. ' A Turkish heavy gun at the Dardanelles ' : military : 1915. F. & Gibbons.

asinego, occ. **assinego.** A little ass : C. 17.—2. A fool : C. 17–18. Shakespeare has ' An Asinico may tutor thee ; Thou . . . Asse.' Ex Sp. (O.E.D.)

ask another ! Don't be silly ! : Cockney c.p. addressed to one who asks a stale riddle : 1896 ; ob. Ware.

ask bogy. An evasive reply : nautical mid-C. 18–19. Sea-wit, says Grose, for ' ask mine a–se '. Cf. *Bogy*, q.v.

ask for it. To incur foolishly ; be fooled unnecessarily, ludicrously : coll : C. 20 ; the O.E.D. (Sup.) dates it at 1909, but it is at least four years older. Cf. *buy it*.

ask mine, (in C. 19–20) **my, arse !** A low coll. evasive reply : mid-C. 18–20 ; orig. nautical. Grose, 2nd ed. Cf. the C. 20, ' God knows, (for) *I* don't.'

ask out. To invite to (an) entertainment : coll. : from late 1880's. O.E.D. (Sup.)

asker. A beggar : euphemistic s. : 1858, Reade ; ob. E.D.D.

*askew. A cup : c. of ca. 1550–1650. Harman. ? etymology. Prob. an error for *a skew*.

asking, not you by your. A c.p. reply (late C. 18–early 19) to ' Who owns this ? ' Cf. the late C. 19–20 *none the better for your asking* (health).

asking !, that's. I.e. when you shouldn't, or when I shouldn't reply : coll. c.p. : late C. 19–20.

aspect. (A look of) ardour ; hence, impudence : Hatton Garden district (London) : C. 20. Ware. Ex It. *aspetto !*

aspidestr(i)a. Incorrect for *aspidistra* : mid-C. 19–20. (O.E.D.)

Aspinall. Enamel : coll. (— 1909). Ware. Ex the inventor of an oxidised enamel paint. The **v.** is S.E.

aspro, take the. See **take the aspro.**

Asquith. A French match : military of G.W. Ex Asquith's too-famous ' Wait and see ' : such matches often failed to light.

ass. A compositor : journalists', ca. 1850–1900. Variant, *donkey*.—2. A very stupid or ignorant person : formerly S.E. ; in C. 20, coll. (N.B., *make an ass of* is going the same way.)—3. Arse : dial. and late coll. : C. 19–20. This is the gen. U.S. pronunciation, as in Tess Slesinger's *The Unpossessed*, 1934 (London, 1935).

ass about. To fool about : schoolboys' (— 1899) >, by 1910, gen. (O.E.D.) Cf. *ass*, 3 : q.v.

assassin. An ornamental bow worn on **the** female breast : ca. 1900–14. Very ' killing '.

Assayes, the. The 74th Foot Regiment ; from ca. 1881, the 2nd Battalion of the Highland Light Infantry : military coll. : from 1803 (Battle of Assaye), for them a notable year.

assig. An assignation, an appointment : ca. 1680–1830. B.E.

assinego. See **asinego.**

assinuate. To insinuate : sol. : 1742, Fielding (O.E.D.). Rare in late C. 19–20.

assoil, assoilment. Catachrestic for *soil* (to sully ; defilement) : C. 19–20. (O.E.D.)

assy. Asphalt : schoolboys' : C. 20.

ast. To ask : sol. : C. 19–20.

astard-ba. Bastard : low : C. 20. James Curtis, *The Gilt Kid*, 1936. By transposition.

astarrakan. Astrachan (fur) : jocular Cockney : late C. 19–20. Ware.

aste. Rare c. for money : early C. 17. Nares. Ex *asti*, old It. c. for the same.

astonish me !, you. Well, that's pretty obvious, isn't it ! : ironic c.p. : from ca. 1920.

astonisher. An exclamation mark : bookworld's : from ca. 1925.

astrologer. See **conjuror.**

astronomer. A horse that carries its head high : C. 19. In C. 18 called a *star-gazer*.

'at. That (chiefly as pronoun) : sol. : C. 19–20. Francis D. Grierson, *Murder at Lancaster Gate*, 1934, ' " Mr. Croggs ? " . . . " 'At's my name, Guv'ner." '

at that. See **that, at.**

at the high port. At once ; vigorously ; unhesitatingly ; very much : military ; from ca. 1925. I.e. in fine style.

*atch. To arrest ; tramps' c. (— 1923). Manchon. Ex Romany (?) : but it may abbr. *atchker*, q.v.

atcha ! All right ! : military : C. 20.

atchker. To arrest : central s. (— 1923) on *catch*. Manchon.

ate. Sol., esp. Cockney, for *eaten :* C. 19–20. ' He's ate it all,' Baumann.

atfler. See **hatfler.**

Athanasian wench. ' A forward girl, ready to oblige every man that shall ask her ', Grose. Ca. 1700–1830. Variant, *quicunque vult* (whosoever desires)—the opening words of the Athanasian Creed.

Athenæum ; gen. **the A.** The penis : cultured (— 1903) ; very ob. F. & H., revised. Perhaps ex *Athenæum*, an association of persons meeting for mutual improvement.

Athie. *The Athenæum* ; printers' (— 1887) ; † by 1920. Baumann.

-ation, as used in humorous neologisms, verges on the coll. E.g. *hissation*, a hissing.

Atkins. See **Thomas Atkins.**

Atlantic ranger. A herring : coll. : from ca. 1880 ; ob. Variant, *sea-rover*.

atmospherics. A coll. abbr. of *atmospheric disturbances* (' wireless ') : 1928 + ; by 1935, almost S.E. Hence, fig., an irritable or quarrelsome or highly strung atmosphere : 1932 +.

atomy. A very small, a small thin, a small deformed person : late C. 16–19. Coll. by 1700 ; from mid-C. 19, S.E. ; slightly ob. Ex *anatomy*, **q.v.** (variant *ot(t)omy*)—confused prob. **by** *atom*

(W). Shakespeare: 'Thou atomy, thou! . . . you thin thing.' Sala: 'A miserable little atomy, more deformed, more diminutive, more mutilated than any beggar in a bowl.'

atrocious. Very bad; execrable; very noticeable: coll.; from ca. 1830.—2. Adv. in *-ly*: 1831, Alford, 'The letter had an atrociously long sentence in it', F. & H., revised.

atrocity. A bad blunder; an offence against good taste, manners, or morals. 1878. (O.E.D.)

attaboy! Go it!: U.S. (— 1917); anglicised in 1918. F. & Gibbons. The O.E.D. and Collinson derive it from *that's the boy !*, but possibly it represents *at her, boy !*, where *her* is sexless; prob., however, it is a corruption of the exclamatory U.S. *staboy* recorded by Thornton.—2. Hence, an approbatory exclamation, from ca. 1931, as in D. Sayers, *Murder Must Advertise*, 1933, ' " Picture of nice girl bending down to put the cushion in the corner of the [railway] carriage. And the headline [of the advertisement] ? ' *Don't let them pinch your seat.*' " "Attaboy!" said Mr. Bredon [Lord Peter Wimsey].'

attache case. Incorrect for *attaché case*: C. 20. E.g. frequently in Miles Burton's thriller, *To Catch a Thief*, 1934.

attack. To address oneself to; commence. From ca. 1820, coll.; after ca. 1860, S.E. due to Gallic influence.

attackted. Attacked: sol.: C. 19 (prob. earlier)–20. Rarely written. Cf. *drowned*.

attend to. To thrash: coll.; from ca. 1800. Cf. L. *animadvertere*.

attest. See **detest.**

attic. occ., not before ca. 1850, and now ob., **attic-storey.** The head: pugilistic (— 1823). ' Jon Bee '; H., 1st ed. By 1870 (Dean Alford), gen. Cf. *upper storey*, q.v.—2. Esp. (*be*) *queer in the attic*, weak-minded; rarely, mad: from ca. 1870. H., 5th ed. In C. 20, occ. (*have*) *rats in the attic* (Lyell). Ex.—3. Orig. (— 1859), *queer in the attic* = intoxicated: pugilistic; † by 1890. H., 1st ed.—4. The female pudend (*attic* only): low (— 1903); ob. F. & H., revised.—5. Top deck of a bus: busmen's: from ca. 1920. *The Daily Herald*, Aug. 5, 1936.

attorney. A goose or turkey drumstick, grilled and devilled: punning *devil*, a lawyer working for another: 1829, Griffin, ' I love a plain beef steak before a grilled attorney '; ob. (*Attorney* as a legal title was abolished in England in 1873.)—2. In c., a legal adviser to criminals: late C. 19–20, ob.

Attorney-General's devil. A barrister doing a K.C.'s heavy work: ca. 1860–1920. Ware.

atween, atwixt. Between, betwixt: sol., mostly London (— 1887). Baumann.

au reservoir! Au revoir. Orig. U.S., adopted ca. 1880. In C. 20 often *au rev*.

auctioneer, deliver or **give** or **tip** (one) **the.** To knock a person down: ca. 1860–1930. Sala, 1863 (*deliver*); H., 5th ed. (*tip*). ' Tom Sayers's right hand was known to pugilistic fame as the *auctioneer* ' (Sayers, d. 1865, fought from 1849 to 1860, in which latter year he drew, miraculously, with Heenan); Manchon.

audit. Abbr. *audit ale*, a brew peculiar to Trinity College, Cambridge, and several other Cambridge and Oxford colleges; made orig. for drinking on audit days: mid-C. 19–20; coll. verging on S.E. Ouida, 1872.

audit one's accounts. See **accounts.**

Aug. See **Feb.**

aught. Nought—the cypher: C. 18–20 sol. Cf. *ought*.

aujence. Audience: sol., esp. Cockney: late C. 19–20. G. R. Sims, *Anna of the Underworld*, 1916, ' The sportin' gents in the aujence '.

auld case or **gib.** An elderly man: Glasgow coll. (— 1934). Ex *gib*, a tom-cat.

Auld Hornie. The Devil. Mainly Scottish: C. 18–20, ob. Ex his horn. For accounts of the Devil's names, see Weekley's *Word and Names*, 1932, and *Words !*, 1933.—2. The penis: Scots (— 1903) A pun on *horn*, a priapism.

Auld Reekie. Orig. the old-town part of Edinburgh: late C. 18–ca. 1860. Then the whole city. Lit., ' Old Smoky '; cf. *the Great Smoke*, London. Coll. from ca. 1890.

auly-auly. (Winchester College) a game played ca. 1700–1840 in Grass Court after Saturday afternoon chapel. A collective game with an india-rubber ball. Supposedly ex *haul ye, call ye*, but, in view of Winchester's fame in Classics, prob. ex Gk. αὐλή, a court or a quadrangle.

aunt. A procuress, a concubine, a prostitute: C. 17–ca. 1830. *Mine* (or *my*) *aunt*, as in Grose, 1st ed. Shakespeare,

> Summer songs for me and my aunts,
> While we lie tumbling in the hay.

2. Also, at Oxford and Cambridge Universities, a students' name for ' the sister university ': C. 17–18. Fuller, 1755.—3. A children's coll. for a non-related woman (cf. *uncle*): C. 19–20. Cf. the U.S. usage (an aged negress as addressed by a child) and see **auntie.**

aunt, or **auntie, go to see one's.** To visit the w.c.: euphemistic, mostly women's: from ca. 1850. Cf. *Mrs. Jones*, which is occ. *Aunt Jones* (H., 5th ed.).

aunt, my. See **my aunt.**

aunt !, my ; my sainted aunt ! A mild exclamation: coll.: resp. from late 1880's and ca. 1920. O.E.D. (Sup.)

aunt had been my uncle, if my. See **uncle.**

Aunt Maria. The female pudend: low (— 1903). F. & H., revised.

Aunt Sally. A wicket-keeper: cricketers' jocular coll.: 1898. (W. J. Lewis.)

aunt's sisters. Ancestors: London middle-class (— 1909); virtually †. Ware. By pun.

Aunt Voss. The *Vossische Zeitung* (famous Ger. newspaper): 1915, *The Daily Mail*, Dec. 22. (Van Wely.)

auntie, aunty. Coll. form of *aunt*: from ca. 1790. Also, like *uncle*, used by children for a friend of the house: C. 19–20.—2. A 12-inch gun: military: 1915; ob.—3. See **aunt, go to see one's.**

aurev! Au revoir: from ca. 1920. Galsworthy, *The White Monkey*, 1924. Cf. *au reservoir*.

Aussie, occ. **Aussey.** Australia: from ca. 1895. An Australian: from ca. 1905. Both coll. and orig. Australian; popularised by G.W. In 1914 +, also adj. Cf. *digger*, *dinkum*.

Aussieland. An occ. variant, C. 20, of *Aussie*, sense 1. Rare among Australians.

Austin Reed service, I suppose ?,—just a part of the. Included in the service, I presume ?; all free ?: a c.p. of 1936 based on a slogan (1935–) of the well-known men's clothiers.

Australasian, n. and adj. (An inhabitant) belonging to Australasia: no longer—since ca. 1925—used of either an Australian or a New Zealander. Cf. the fate of *Anglo-Indian*.

Australian flag. A shirt-tail rucked up between trousers and waistcoat : Australian, ca. 1870–1910.

Australian grip. A hearty hand-shake : Australian, ca. 1885–1914 ; coll.

*__autem__, a church, mid-C. 16–18 c., is the parent of many other c. terms, e.g. *autem bawler*, a parson ; *autem cackler*, a Dissenter or a married woman ; *autem-cackle tub*, a Dissenters' meeting-house or a pulpit ; *autem dipper* or *diver*, a Baptist or a pickpocket specialising in churches ; *autem gog(g)ler*, a pretended prophet, or a conjuror ; *autem jet*, a parson ; *autem prickear*, see *autem cackler* ; *autem quaver*, a Quaker ; and *autem-quaver tub*, a Quakers' meeting-house or a desk therein. Perhaps via *antem*, an anthem.

autem, adj. Married, esp. in the two c. terms, *autem cove*, a married man, and *autem mort*, a married woman : C. 17–18. Perhaps ex *altham* (q.v.), a wife.

author-baiting. Summoning an unsuccessful dramatist before the curtain : theatrical, ca. 1870–1900.

authordox ; unauthordox. Such occ. errors for *orthodox, unorthodox*, as would be impossible to anyone with an elementary knowledge of Greek or with even a moderately sensitive ear.

auto. Abbr. *automobile* : 1899 ; coll. ; S.E. by 1910 but never gen. Ex Fr. (S.O.D.)

*__autom, autum.__ Variants of *autem*, q.v.

automatic. Abbr. *automatic revolver* : C. 20 ; coll. > S.E. Esp. in G.W.

autumn. (The season or time of) an execution by hanging : low : mid-C. 19–20 ; ob. H., 2nd ed.

avadavat. Incorrect for *amadavat* : 1777, Sheridan. Yule & Burnell.

avast ! Hold on ! Be quiet ! Stop ! Nautical : C. 17–20 ; coll. >, by late C. 19, S.E. Prob. ex Dutch *hou'vast*, hold fast.

avaunt, give the. To dismiss (a person) : late C. 16–early 17. Shakespeare. Ex *avaunt !*, be off ! (C. 15 +).

avec. Spirits : Western Front military : 1917–18. F. & Gibbons. Ex Fr. *café avec* (coffee with—gen., rum).

avenue. Possibility, as in *explore every avenue*, to try all possible means : C. 20 ; mainly political, journalistic, and commercial : soon > coll. ; perhaps soon to > S.E.

average man, the. The ordinary person : C. 19–20 ; coll. > S.E. Cf. *the man in the street* (s.v. *street*).

*__avering.__ A boy's begging naked to arouse compassion : c. : late C. 17–early 18. Kennett, 1695, has also *go a-avering*. ? ex *aver*, to declare (it) true.

avert, evert, revert. Occ. confused : C. 16–20. (O.E.D.)

aviary. See **apiary**.

avoirdupois. Obesity : jocular coll. ; late C. 19–20.

*__avoirdupois lay.__ The thieving of brass weights from shop counters : late C. 18–mid 19 c. Grose, 2nd ed.

avuncular relation or **relative.** A pawnbroker : facetiously coll., ca. 1860–1900. Sala, in 1859, speaks of pawnbroking as *avuncular life*.

awake. To inform, let know : from mid-1850's ; ob. ' Ducange Anglicus ', 1st ed.

*__awaste.__ A c. form of *avast* as in *bing avast*, q.v.

away. Erroneous for *way* : C. 17–18. Hakluyt, Smollett. O.E.D.—2. In imperatives, e.g. *say away*, it gives to the phrase a coll. tinge : C. 17 (? earlier)–20. Galsworthy, 1924, ' *Baise* [kiss] away ! '—3. To depart : theatrical : ca. 1905–14.

Ware. Ex melodramatic *away !*—4. In prison : low London (— 1909). Ware. By euphemism.

aweer. Aware : London sol. or, rather, Cockney low coll. (— 1887). Baumann.

awful, esp. *a penny awful*. A ' penny dreadful ', a blood-and-thunder tale. Ca. 1860–1900.—2. **(awful.)** Offal : Cockney sol. (— 1887). Baumann.

awful, adj. A catch-intensive. Apparently C. 18 Scottish, then U.S. (see Bartlett), and ca. 1840 adopted in England. Lamb, 1834 : ' She is indeed, as the Americans would express it, something awful.' Coll., as is the adv. *awful(ly)* = very : mid-C. 19–20. In 1859 occurs *awfully clever* ; *Punch* satirised it in 1877 in the phrase, ' it's too awfully nice ' ; P. G. Wodehouse, 1907 (see **frightfully**) ; Lyell, 1931, ' We had awful fun at my brother's party.' Cf. Society's post-G.W. use of *grim* for ' unpleasant '. F. & H. : O.E.D.

*__awful place, the.__ Dartmoor Prison : c. dating from the late 1890's.

awfully. See **awful**, adj.

awright. See **orright**.

awhile for *a while* is catachrestic when *while* is purely a n.

'Awkins. A severe man ; one not to be trifled with : Cockney : ca. 1880–1900. Ware. Ex Judge Sir Frederic Hawkins, reputed to be a ' hanging ' judge.

awkward. Pregnant : euphemistic : late C. 19–20 ; ob. F. & G., revised. Cf. *bumpy*.

awkward squad. Recruits, esp. a segregated group of recruits, commencing to learn to drill or having their drill improved : naval and military, from ca. 1870 ; coll. by 1890 ; j. by G.W.

awls and be gone, pack up one's. To depart for good : (low) coll. (— 1756). Prob. *awls* is a corruption of *all*, as Manchon suggests.

awry, tread the shoe. To fall from virtue : C. 16–20, ob. ; coll. ; then, in C. 18–20, S.E. Cf. in S.E. *take* or *make a false step*.

ax(e). To ask. Down to ca. 1600, S.E. ; since then, sol. (Cf. *arks, arst*, qq.v.) Chaucer : ' If any fellow have neede of sapiens [= wisdom], axe it of God.'—2. To reduce (expenses) by means of ' the axe ' : 1923. Coll. ; S.E. by 1925. (S.O.D.) Cf. :

axe, the. Reduction of expenses, mainly in personnel, in the public services : 1922.—2. A body of officials (*quis custodiet ipsos custodes*) effecting these reductions : 1922. Coll. ; both S.E. by 1925. See :

axe, the Geddes. That reduction of public-service expenses which was recommended in 1922 by Sir Eric Geddes, who aimed at the *size* of the various staffs. Recorded in 1923 : coll. : by 1925, S.E. and historical.

axe, where the chicken got the. See **chicken got** . . .

axe after the helve, send the. (Better, *send the helve after the hatchet*.) To take a further useless step ; send good money after bad. Coll. ; from C. 16 ; in C. 19–20, rare but S.E.

axe in the helve, put the. To solve a doubt. Coll. ; from C. 16 ; ob. Like the preceding, proverbial.

axe (or axes) to grind. An ulterior motive, gen. selfish. Coll., orig. (— 1815) U.S., adopted ca. 1840. At first of politics, it soon widened in applicability ; by 1850, moreover, it had > S.E.

ax(e)-my-eye, an. A very alert fellow : cheapjack's, ca. 1850–1910. Hindley.

axle-grease. See **grease**, n., 5.

Ayrshires. Glasgow and South-Western Railway shares : Stock Exchange from ca. 1880.

B

b. A bug: coll.; from ca. 1860. Also *b flat*: 1836 (F. & H., revised). Ex the insect's initial letter and appearance.—2. In c., abbr. *blue*, q.v.—3. See ' **A1** ', 2.

b. and s. ; **B. and S.** Brandy and soda: Whyte-Melville, 1868: s. >, ca. 1890, coll. The *b* is occ. separable, as in ' Give me some B in my S ', Baumann, 1887.

B.A. Buenos Aires: nautical coll.: late C. 19–20. W. McFee, *The Beachcomber*, 1935.

B.B. Gen. pl. **B.B.'s.** A bluejacket: naval: C. 20. F. & Gibbons. Ex ' British **B**lue ', with a non-drawing-room pun.—2. Bloody bastard: C. 20.

B.B.A. Born **B**efore **A**rrival: medical students': C. 20. (*Slang*, p. 189.)

B.B.C. The British Broadcasting Corporation (founded ca. 1924): coll.; by 1933, S.E.—2. Any broadcasting corporation: 1933 (*The Daily Telegraph*, early Aug.); coll.

B.B.C., the. The 2.10 a.m. freight express train from London to Wolverhampton: railwaymen's: from ca. 1929. *The Daily Telegraph*, Aug. 15, 1936. It passes through **B**asingstoke, **B**irmingham and **C**rewe. Cf. *the Bacca*, q.v.

***b.c.** A person bringing a wholly inadequate action for libel: from ca. 1870. Ex the *bloody cat* of an actual lawsuit. †.

B.C. See **anno domini**.

B.C. play. A Classical drama: theatrical: 1885; very ob. Ware. I.e. before Christ.

b.f. A frequent C. 20 coll. (rare before G.W.) euphemising of *bloody fool*. Lyell.

b flat. See **b**, 1.

B from a battledore, or, rarely, **from a broomstick** or, very gen., **from a bull's foot, not to know.** To be illiterate, extremely ignorant: resp. mid-C. 16–17, C. 19, C. 15–20. A battledore was an alphabet-hornbook. For the first phrase and the third, see esp. Apperson's *English Proverbs and Proverbial Phrases.* Also *not to know great A from a battledore* or (*great*) *A from a bull's foot.*

B.H. A bank holiday: non-aristocratic coll.: 1880; ob.—2. Bloody hell: 1928 (O.E.D. Sup.). Also *bee aitch.*

B.I.D. **B**rought **I**n **D**ead (to the hospital): medical students': C. 20. Cf. *B.B.A.*

b.k.'s. ' Military officers in *mufti*, when out on the spree, and not wishing their profession to be known, speak of their barracks as the B.K.'s ', H., 3rd ed: military (— 1864); ob.

b.n. Bloody nuisance. C. 20.

B.N.C. **B**rasenose **C**ollege, Oxford: from ca. 1840: coll. >, by 1900, j. Cf. *Brazen Nose College, you were bred in*, q.v.

B.P. The British Public: theatrical (1867) >, by 1910, gen. coll. Ware.—2. See *Bups.*

B.P.N. A **B**loody **P**ublic **N**uisance: C. 20. Cf. *B.F.*

b.r. or B.R. A bedroom steward, in the First Class: nautical: C. 20. Bowen.

b.s. A euphemism for *bull-shit*, q.v.: from ca. 1910.

b.t.m. A coll. domestic euphemism for *bottom* (posterior): late C. 19–20.

ba-ha. Bronchitis: tailors': from the 1890's; slightly ob. By deliberate slurring.

baa-baa. A sheep: nursery coll.: C. 19–20.

Ex the sheep's bleat. Cf. *bow-wow, cock-a-doodle* (*-doo*), *moo-cow, quack-quack.*

baa-baa (black sheep), go. To *bar* the favourite: race-course s. (— 1932). *Slang*, pp. 242, 246. There is, further, an allusion to the nursery rhyme.

Baa-Baas, the. The Barbarian Rugby Football team: sporting: from ca. 1924.

***baa cheat.** A sheep: c.: C. 18. Anon., *Street-Robberies Consider'd* (*ba cheat*), 1728. Lit., ' baa '-thing.

baa-lamb. A lamb (cf. *baa-baa*, q.v.): nursery coll.: C. 19–20.—2. (with capitals) H.M.S. *Barham*: naval: C. 20.

baal ! See **bale !**

baas. A master, a manager, a head man of any sort: South African coll.: 1785, Sparrman, *A Voyage to the Cape of Good Hope . . . from 1772 to 1776.* Ex Dutch *baas*, master, foreman. Pettmann.—2. The term of address to the skipper of a Dutch ship: nautical coll.: C. 19–20. Bowen.

Bab, the. The Straits of **Bab**-el-Mandeb: nautical: C. 17–18. W.

baba. A coll., gen. a child's, variant of *papa*: C. 19–20. In late C. 16–17, *bab*.—2. In Anglo-Indian coll., a child. Ex Turki *baba* influenced by our *baby*. Yule & Burnell.

babbie, babby, vocative. Baby: coll.: late C. 19–20. Ex C. 16–20 dial.

babbler ; babbling brook. A cook: C. 20: resp. military, ex the latter; and gen. rhyming s. B. & P.

babe. The latest-elected member of the House of Commons: opp. *father of the house.* Parliamentary coll.: from ca. 1870.

babe, kiss the. See **kiss the babe.**

babe in the wood. A criminal in the stocks or the pillory: late C. 18–early 19. Grose, 1st ed.—2. In C. 20, the pl. = dice.

babe of grace. Bee defines the pl. as ' sanctified-looking persons, not so ': fast society: ca. 1820–40.

babes. A gang of disreputables that, at an auction, forbear to bid against the bigger dealers; their reward, drinks and/or cash. From ca. 1860 ob. H., 2nd ed. Cf. *knock-outs*, q.v.

Babies ; Baby Wee-Wees. **B**uenos **A**ires **W**ater **W**orks shares: Stock Exchange: from ca. 1870. The shorter ex the longer, which combines an acrostic with a pun on *Water Works* and *wee-wee* (urination).

babies' cries. A variant of *baby's cries*, q.v.

baboon. Fig. for a person: like *ape*, this is in C. 20 considered low coll.

Babsky. A wind-swept part of Liverpool: Liverpool: 1886. Ware. I.e. *Bay o' Biscay.*

baby. A twopenny bottle of soda-water: public-house: ca. 1875–1900. Ware.—2. A girl; sweetheart: U.S. (ca. 1910), adopted ca. 1930.—3. ' The R.N.A.S. small Sopwith aeroplane in the early days of the War ': naval: 1914–16. Bowen.

baby, the. A diamond-mining sifting machine: Vaal River coll. (— 1886); ob. Ex *Babe*, its American inventor. Pettmann, who notes *baby*, to sift ground with this machine: from mid-1880's.

Baby Act, plead the. To excuse oneself as too inexperienced: from ca. 1900; ob. Ex.—2. ' To plead minority as voiding a contract ': coll. :

from late 1890's. Ex the plea of *infancy* in its legal sense.

baby and nurse. 'A small bottle of soda-water and two-pennyworth of spirit in it': public-house: ca. 1876–1900. Ware. Cf. *baby*, q.v.

baby bunting. See bunting.

baby crying, the. The bugle-call to defaulters: military: late C. 19–20; ob. F. & Gibbons. Cf. *angel's whisper*, 1.

baby-farmer or **-stealer.** A male or a female courter or lover of one much younger, very young: C. 20.

baby-maker. The penis: euphemistically jocular: late C. 19–20; ob.

baby- or **baby's-pap.** A cap: (mostly underworld) rhyming slang: ca. 1855–1900. 'Ducange Anglicus', 1857.

baby-snatcher. One who marries a person much younger: jocular coll. (— 1927). Collinson.

baby spot. See Moving-Picture Slang, §3.

Baby Wee-Wees. See Babies.

babylon(it)ish. C. 19 Winchester College for a dressing-gown: ex *Babylon(it)ish garment*.

baby's cries. Eyes: rhyming s.: from ca. 1920. A. Hyder, *Black Girl, White Lady*, 1934.

baby's head. Meat pudding: naval: C. 20. F. & Gibbons, 'Suggested by its smooth, round appearance.'

baby's public-house. The female breast: proletarian: 1884, *The Referee*, Oct. 5. Ware.

Bacca, the. The express goods-train carrying tobacco (including cigarettes) from Bristol to London: railwaymen's: from ca. 1910. *The Daily Telegraph*, Aug. 15, 1936. Cf. *the Biscuit, the Flying Pig, the Leek, the Magic Carpet, the Sparagras, the Spud*; also *the Early Bird, the Early Riser, the Farmer's Boy, the Feeder*, and *the Mopper Up*. These railwaymen's nicknames were recognised as official in the G.W.R.'s *Guide to Economical Transport*, issued in August, 1936.

bacca, bacco, baccy. Tobacco: low coll.: 1858; 1860; 1833, Marryat. (O.E.D.) Cf. *backer.*—2. Hence *bacca-*, more gen. *baccy-box*, the mouth; the nose: low (— 1923). Manchon.

bacca-pipes. Whiskers curled in ringlets (—1880; † by 1890).

baccare !; backare ! Go back, retire ! Ca. 1540–1680. Heywood; Udall; Lyly; Shakespeare, 'Baccare ! you are marvellous forward'; Howell, 1659. (Apperson.) Jocular on *back*: perhaps Latinised or Italianised *back there*. (O.E.D.)

Bacchus. A set of Latin verses written on Shrove Tuesday at Eton : ? C. 18–early 19 : coll. at Eton College. Ex the verses there written, on that day, in praise or dispraise of Bacchus. Anon., *Etoniana*, 1865.

bacco, baccy, baccy-box. See bacca.

bach. A bachelor: in U.S. in 1850's; anglicised ca. 1900. Ware prefers *bache*. Cf.:

bach, occ. **batch,** v. To live by oneself, doing one's own work; orig. like a bachelor. Ex U.S.; anglicised ca. 1890. Cf. the n.

bachelor !, then the town bull is a. A semi-proverbial c.p. retort incredulous on a woman's alleged chastity: mid-C. 17–18. Ray, 1678; he does not, however, restrict it to either women or chastity.

bachelor's baby. An illegitimate child: coll., mid-C. 19–20. Whiteing, 1899, Ray, ca. 1670, and Grose, 1788, have *bachelor's* (or *batchelor's*) *son*.

bachelor's fare. Bread, cheese, and kisses:

C. 18–19. Swift, ca. 1708 (published 30 years later). '*Lady*. . . . Some ladies . . . have promised to breakfast with you . . .; what will you give us ? *Colonel*. Why, faith, madam, bachelor's fare, bread and cheese and kisses'; Grose, 3rd ed.

[**back.** To support by a bet, was perhaps orig. (C. 17) coll., but O.E.D. and S.O.D.—rightly, one suspects—treat it as always S.E.]

back, on one's. Penniless; utterly puzzled: late C. 19–20. Nautically, *on the bones of one's back*: Bowen.

back, ride on one's. To fool or deceive a person, esp. successfully: coll.: C. 18–19.

back and belly. All over: C. 18–19 familiar coll. *Keep one b. and b.*, C. 18–19 coll.; adumbrated in C. 16.

back and fill. See backing and filling.

back-biters, his bosom friends are become his. A punning c.p. (cf. *bosom friend*, q.v.) of ca. 1700–1840. Swift, ca. 1708; Grose, 1st ed.

back-breaker. A person setting, or a thing being, a task beyond normal endurance : C. 18–20 coll. The adj., *back-breaking*, gen. goes with *job* or *work*.

back-breakers. 'Old-fashioned ship's pumps': nautical: late C. 19–20. Bowen. A special application of the preceding.

back-chat. A variant of *back-talk*, q.v.: 'A slang term applied to saucy or impertinent replies', Pettman : South African (— 1901) and (? hence) Australian.

***back-cheat.** A cloak: C. 18–early 19 : c.

back-cloth star. An actor or actress that plays up-stage, thus forcing the others to turn their backs to the audience : theatrical (— 1935).

back door, a gentleman or an usher of the. A sodomist: mid-C. 18–20, ob. Grose, 1st ed. Hence *back-door work*, sodomy. Cf. *backgammon-player*.

back-door trot. Diarrhœa: from ca. 1870; orig. dial. Cf. *Jerry-go-nimble*.

back-door trumpet. A mid-C. 19–20 variant of *ars musica*, q.v.

back down, often a *square-back-down*. An utter collapse ; complete surrender of claims : from early 1880's : coll. >, by 1920, S.E.—2. A severe rebuff: from ca. 1890.

back down. To yield, to retire : from ca. 1880 : coll. >, by 1910, S.E. Ex U.S. (1849 : O.E.D.).

back-ender. 'A horse entered for a race late in the season', F. & H.: racing coll.: ca. 1889. Ex *back-end*, the last two months of the horse-racing season.

back-hair part. A role ' in which the agony of the performance at one point in the drama admits of the feminine tresses in question floating over the shoulders': theatrical: 1884; ob. by 1920, † by 1930. Ware.

back-hairing. 'Feminine fighting, in which the occipital locks suffer severely', Ware: London streets' (— 1909).

back-hand. To drink more than one's share: ca. 1850–1910. In G. A. Lawrence's best novel, *Guy Livingstone*, 1857, it occurs as a vbl. n., *back-handing*.—2. **back-hand !** Get out of the way: ships' stokers' c.p.: C. 20.

back-handed. Indirect ; unfair : from ca. 1815 : coll. >, by 1880, S.E. Dickens, 1865, has *a back-handed reminder*. Cf. *back-hander*, 3, q.v.

back-handed turn. An unprofitable transaction : Stock Exchange, ca. 1870–1914.

back-hander. A drink either additional or out of

turn : coll. : ca. 1850–1900. Ex :—2. A blow with the back of the hand : coll. >, by 1870, S.E. : 1836, Marryat ; Farrar.—3. Hence, a rebuke : ca. 1860–1900 (e.g. in Whyte-Melville) : coll. >, by 1900, S.E. Cf. *back-handed*, q.v.

back is up,—Sir, I see somebody has offended you, for your. A jeering c.p. addressed to a hump-backed man : ca. 1780–1850. Grose, 1st ed. See **back up**, adj.

*back-jump. To enter (e.g. a house) by a back door or window : c. from ca. 1855. H., 1st ed. Ex :—2. A back window : c. (— 1812). Vaux. Because one jumps from it in escape.

back-mark. See **back-marked**.—2. Hence, to outdistance (easily) : sporting : 1928 (O.E.D., Sup.).

back-marked, be. To have one's athletic handicap reduced : late C. 19–20 coll., ob. Rare in active voice.

back number. (Of a person) a 'has been' : coll. : U.S. (1890 : O.E.D. (Sup.)) anglicised ca. 1905 ; by 1935, S.E. Prob. ex the back numbers of periodicals.

Back Numbers, the. The 28th Foot, in late C. 19–20 the Gloucestershire Regiment : military : C. 19–20. Ex the sphinx worn, as distinction for services at the Battle of Alexandria, 1801, on both the back and the front of the helmet until 1881. F. & Gibbons.

back of, break the. See **break the neck** or **back of.**

back o' the green. Behind the scenes : theatrical and music-halls' : ca. 1880–1910. Ware, with reference to the green curtain and in imperfect rhyme on *scenes.*

back of Bourke. The farthest distance known : Australian c.p. : C. 20. Bourke being a town in south-western New South Wales.

back of one's neck, talk through (rarely **out of) the.** To talk nonsense : from ca. 1920. Ex *talk through one's hat.*

back of the hand down. Bribery : from ca. 1890 ; ob. (J. Milne, *The Epistles of Atkins*, 1902.)

back out. To retreat from a difficulty or unpleasantness : 1818, Scott : coll. >, by 1860, S.E. Ex lit. sense.

back pedal ! Steady ! ; tell that to the marines ! : c.p. : from ca. 1910. Collinson. Ex cycling.

back-racket. A *tu-quoque* : coll. ; C. 17–18. Ex the S.E. sense, 'the return of a ball in tennis', S.O.D.

back-row hopper. A sponger affecting taverns haunted by actors : theatrical (— 1909) : virtually †. Ware.

back-scratching. (A) flogging : naval : late C. 19–early 20. Bowen. (As sycophantic flattery, it is S.E.)

*back-scuttle. Same as *back-slang it*, q.v. : c. of C. 19.—*do* or *have a back-scuttle*, to possess a woman *a retro* : low : mid-C. 19–20.

back-seam, be (down) on one's. To be out of luck, unfortunate. Tailors' (— 1887). Baumann ; Whiteing, 1899. Cf. *back, on one's*, q.v.

back seat, take a. To retire ; yield ; fail. Orig. (1863) U.S. ; anglicised ca. 1880 : coll. >, by 1920, S.E. (Thornton.)

[Back-slang dates from ca. 1850. *Slang*, pp. 276–7.]

*back-slang it. To go out the back way : ca. 1810–1910 : low ; prob. orig. c. Vaux ; H., 1st ed. Cf. *back slum.*—2. In Australia, ca. 1850–1905, to seek unoffered lodging in the country.

Morris. Perhaps ex Vaux's second sense :—3. To go a circuitous or private way through the streets in order to avoid meeting certain persons : c. of ca. 1810–50. Vaux.

*back slum. A back room ; the back-entrance of a building. 'Thus, we'll *give it* 'em *on the back slum*, means, we'll get in at the back door', Vaux, 1812 : c. >, ca. 1870, low. Cf. *back-jump* and *back-slang it.*

back slums. In C. 20, S.E. for very poor urban districts, but orig. (— 1821) s. for residential area of criminals and near-criminals.

back-staircase. A woman's bustle : ca. 1850–1900. (*Bustle* occurs in 1788 : S.O.D.)

*back-stall. In C. 19–20 ob. c., an accomplice covering a thief. Cf. *stall*, q.v.

back-strapped. (Of a ship or a boat) 'carried back into an awkward position by the tide and held there' : nautical coll. : mid-C. 19–20.

back-talk. Impudence ; verbal recalcitrance. Esp. as *no back-talk !* From ca. 1870 ; coll. Cf. *back-chat.* Ex dial.

back teeth underground, have one's. To have eaten one's fill ; to have them *awash* or *under water* = to be drunk. Both are jocular (— 1913) and ob. A. H. Dawson.

back the barrer (i.e. **barrow).** To intervene unasked : low Australian (— 1916). C. J. Dennis.

back-timber. Clothing : C. 17–18 ; coll.

back-to-backs, the. Mean, small, thickly set, parallel-ranged houses in slums and mining towns. C. 20 ; coll.

back-tommy. Cloth covering the stays at the waist : tailors' : late C. 19–20.

back or backs to the wall. Hard pressed : C. 19 coll., C. 20 S.E. In C. 16–18 with *at* for *to.*

back up. To be ready to help, chiefly in games : coll. (in C. 20, S.E.) : from ca. 1860.—2. Winchester College, from ca. 1870 : to call out, e.g. for help.

back up, adj. Annoyed, aroused. *One's back to be up*, to be annoyed, C. 18–19 coll. ; *put* or *set one's back up*, to be, or to make, annoyed, C. 18–20 coll. : from ca. 1800 both phrases tended to be considered as S.E. though not literary. Since ca. 1870, *get one's back up*, to become or to make annoyed, is the gen. form : this, however, has always been coll. Cf. *back is up*, q.v.

backare ! See **baccare !**

backed. Dead : late C. 17–early 19. Perhaps = set on one's back ; B.E. and Grose, however, explain as 'on six men's shoulders', i.e. carried to the grave.

backer, back(e)y. Tobacco : low coll. : 1848, Dickens (*backer*). E.D.D. Cf. *bacca.*

backgammon-player. A sodomist : mid-C. 18–early 19 ; cf. *back door, gentleman of the.*

backgammoner. The same : ca. 1820–80. 'Jon Bee.'

background. Retiring ; modest : coll. : 1896, 'A reticent, background kind of lover', O.E.D. I.e. keeping in the background.

backhanding, n. Giving gratuities : lower classes' : C. 20. Ex the motion of the donor.

backing and filling, vbl. n. and adj. Irresolute, dilatory, shifty ; shiftiness, irresolution : coll. : from ca. 1840. Ex nautical j. In Barham's use, 'moving zigzag', the orig. sense lingers. Bowen adds the sense, 'lazy' : nautical : ca. 1850–1900.

backings-up. The ends of half-burnt faggots : Winchester College, C. 19.

backs to the wall. See **back to the wall.**

backsheesh, -shish ; baksheesh, ba(c)kshee. See **bakshee** (the latest form).

backside. The posteriors : C. 16–20. Always S.E., but ca. 1870–1914 a vulgarism. See *Slang*, p. 138.

backward, ring the bells. To give the alarm : ca. 1500–1890 ; coll. > S.E. Cleveland, Scott. Ex the practice of beginning with the bass when the bells were rung.

backward in coming forward. Shy ; modest : jocular coll. (semi-c.p.) : C. 20.

backward station. 'In the old Coastguard Service one that was considered most undesirable, frequently on account of its distance from a school' : coastguardsmen's coll. : C. 19. Bowen.

backwards, go. To go to the w.c. : C. 20 ; very ob. F. & H., revised.

backwards, piss. To defecate : low : late C. 19–20 ; ob. Ibid.

backy. A shop-mate working behind another : tailors', from ca. 1870 ; ob.—2. See **backer.**

backyard, two feet one. See **two feet one backyard** and cf. *boats.*

***bacon.** See **bacon, save one's.**

bacon, a good voice to beg. A c.p. derisive of an ill voice : late C. 17–18. B.E.

bacon, bring home the. See **bring home** . . .

bacon, pull. To put one's fingers derisively **to** one's nose : mid-C. 19–20.

bacon, save one's. To escape narrowly : late C. 17–20 ; coll. from ca. 1750. A. Behn, 1682, ' I go [to church] to save my bacon as they say, once **a** month ' (Apperson). Perhaps from the days of heretics burnt at the stake ; *A New Canting Dict.* (1725), however, says that in this phrase, *bacon* ' in the Canting Sense, is the Prize, of whatever kind, which Robbers make in their Enterprizes '. (Cf. the 1934 advertisement slogan, ' Breakfast on *Shredded Wheat* and save your bacon.')

bacon-faced. Full-faced : late C. 17–19. Recorded first in Otway.

bacon-fed. Fat ; greasy : coll. : late C. 16–19. Occurring in Shakespeare.

bacon-slicer. A rustic : coll. : mid C. 17–early 19. Urquhart, 1653.

bad. Difficult ; esp. in *bad to beat,* as in Hawley Smart's *Post to Finish,* 1884 : coll. Ob.

bad, adv. Badly : sol. : C. 18 (? earlier)–20. Cf. *badder,* q.v.

bad, go to the. To be ruined ; become depraved. From ca. 1860 ; coll. >, ca. 1910, S.E. Early users are Miss Braddon and ' Dagonet ' Sims. Ex *to the bad,* in deficit.

bad, not. Rather or (patronisingly) quite good : upper (hence, derivatively, middle) classes' coll. : from ca. 1860 (Ware) ; the O.E.D. (Sup.) example at 1835 is prob. isolated and perhaps inoperative.

bad, not half. Fairly good : coll. : from late 1890's. Cf. *not half.*

bad, taken. Taken ill : (low) coll. : late C. 19–20. On *taken short.*

bad, to the. In deficit. The O.E.D. quotes an example in 1816. Coll.

bad bargain. A worthless soldier (gen. preceded by *King's* or *Queen's*) : C. 18–20 ; coll. from 1800. Grose, 1st ed.—2. Hence, since ca. 1860 (without *King's* or *Queen's*), any worthless person : coll.

bad cess to ! Evil befall . . . ! Anglo-Irish coll. ; from ca. 1850 (S.O.D. records it at 1859). Prob. ex *cess* = assessment, levy, rate(s) ; but perhaps abbr. *success.*

bad egg. A rascal ; a scoundrel ; worthless fellow. Orig. (1853) U.S. ; anglicised ca. 1860. Thornton, '. . . The κάκου κόρακος κακὸν ὠὸν of the Greeks.'

bad form. Vulgar ; rude ; unaccepted of Society : Society s. : from ca. 1860, according to Ware. Ob., *not done* superseding it. In C. 20, *b.f.* > coll. *Punch,* 1882 (an Eton boy to his hale old uncle) : '. . . Energy's such awful bad form, you know ! ', F. & H. Ex horse-racing.

bad ha(lf)penny. A ne'er-do-well : from ca. 1850. Ex the c.p., *it is a bad halfpenny,* said by one who, having failed, returns as he went : ca. 1810–50 : Vaux.

bad hat. A rascal : from ca. 1880. Besant, 1883 ; Galsworthy, 1924, ' If that young man's story's true, we're in the hands of a bad hat.' In *The Daily Telegraph* of July 28, 1894, G. A. Sala, citing Sir William Fraser's *Words on Wellington,* suggests that the phrase *what a-shocking bad hat,* which > a c.p., was coined by the Duke in the 1830's : this rests on hearsay. Sala continues, ' The catchword soon lost its political associations, and after a few years, was merged in the purely imbecile query, " Who's your hatter ? " ' which was † by 1900. Ware thinks that *bad hat* was, prob., Irish in origin, ' the worst Hibernian characters always wearing bad high hats (caps are not recognised in kingly Ireland) '. Cf. *bad lot* and see **hat !, what a shocking bad** and, **for** an anticipation, see **queer nob.**

bad job. See **job.**

bad lot. A person of—often worse than—indifferent morals : coll. : Thackeray, 1849. Ex auctioneering. Cf. *bad egg, bad hat, bad 'un,* qq.v.

bad mark. See ' **mark, bad** or **good** '.

bad match twist. Red hair and black whiskers : hairdresser's, from ca. 1870 ; †.

bad shilling, a. One's last shilling : proletarian (— 1909) ; slightly ob. Ware.

bad shot. A poor guess (— 1844 ; Kinglake in *Eothen*). In C. 20, coll.

bad slang. Spurious curiosities : circus, from ca. 1870. Hindley, 1876.

***bad smash.** Counterfeit coin : c. : C. 20. David Hume.

bad 'un. Same as *bad hat,* q.v. : mid-C. 19–20.

bad young man. See **good young man.**

badder, baddest. Once S.E., but in C. 18–20 sol., for *worse, worst.*

badders. Something (event, news, etc.) bad or unpleasant : from ca. 1925. (Evelyn Waugh, *A Handful of Dust,* 1934.) ' The Oxford *-er.*'

Baden-Powell. A trowel : workmen's rhyming s. : late C. 19–20. *John o' London's Weekly,* June 9, 1934.

***badge.** A brand in the hand : C. 18 c.

***badge, he has got his.** He has been branded on the hand : c. of ca. 1720–1840. *A New Canting Dict.,* 1725.

***badge-cove.** A parish-pensioner : C. 18–early 19. *A New Canting Dict.,* 1725.—2. In C. 16–18, a licensed beggar. Both low ; prob. c.—at first at any rate.

badger. Nautical (occ. with *-bag*) : Neptune in equatorial ceremonies : C. 19.—2. Schoolboys' : a red-headed person : C. 19–20, ob. ; at Wellington, late C. 19, a 2nd XV Rugby player.—3. In c., a river-thief that, after robbing, murders and throws his victim into the river : ca. 1720–1830. *A New Canting Dict.,* 1725. Hence perhaps :—**4, in**

C. 19 c., a common harlot.—5. A brush: artists':
late C 19–20.—6. In Australia often, though ever
less, used catachrestically for a bandicoot, rock-
wallaby, or, esp. in Tasmania, a wombat: C. 19–20.
Morris.

badger. To tease; persecute. Perhaps s. when
used by the dramatist O'Keeffe in 1794, but very
soon coll.; S.E. by 1860. Perhaps ex lit. *draw the
badger*; cf.:

badger, overdraw the. To overdraw one's banking account: ca. 1840–1914. Hood.

badger-bag. 'Neptune and his court in the ceremony of crossing the Line': nautical: mid-C. 19–
20. Bowen. See **badger**, n., 1.

badger-box. A very small dwelling, like an inverted V in section: Tasmanian coll.: ca. 1870–
1915. *Proceedings of the Royal Society of Tasmania*,
Sept., 1875. Ex badgers' 'dwellings'. Morris.

badger-legged. With one leg shorter than the
other: coll.: from ca. 1700; ob. Cf. the earlier
semi-proverbial *badger-like, one leg shorter than the
other* (Howell, 1659). Ex the erroneous belief that a
badger has legs of unequal length.

badges and bull's eyes. Badges and medals:
military: Oct., 1899; † by 1915. Applied (says
The Daily Telegraph, Dec. 21, 1899) by General
Gatacre to the officers' badges, etc., because they
offered so splendid a mark for Boer bullets. (Ware.)

badgy. An enlisted boy; **badgy fiddler**, a boy
trumpeter: military: ca. 1850–1905. F. & Gibbons. Either because he was a nuisance or because
he was bullied or persecuted.

Badian. A Barbadian: ca. 1860 + in the West
Indies. Cf. *Bim*.

badly. Much; greatly: with such vv. as *need,
want, require, miss*: coll.; from ca. 1850.

badminton. A cooling drink, esp. a claret-cup:
Disraeli (1845), Whyte-Melville (1853), Ouida
(1868). Coll. >, by 1870, S.E.; ob.—2. In boxing
slang, ca. 1860–90, blood. H., 3rd ed. Cf. *claret*.
Ex the Duke of Beaufort's seat of that name. The
former sense has suggested the latter.

baffaty. Calico: drapery-trade s. (— 1864); ob.
H., 3rd ed. Ex S.E. *baft, bafta(h), baffeta*.

bag. Milk: Westminster School, C. 19–20.—2.
See **bags**, 1.—3. A pot of beer: printers' (— 1887).
Cf. *bag, get one's head in a*, q.v.

bag. To obtain for oneself, esp. anything advantageous: Mortimer Collins, 1880, but also for at
least a decade earlier.—2. To catch, take, or steal
(1818): a common school term, Farrar using it in
1862.—3. To beget or to conceive: C. 15–17. All
three senses, coll.

bag, empty the. To tell everything; close a discussion: coll., C. 18–19.

bag, get or **put one's head in a** or **the.** To drink:
printers' and sailors': from middle 1880's. *The
Saturday Review*, May 14, 1887. See **bag**, n., 3.

bag, give the. To deceive: C. 16–17, coll., as
are the senses, to give (a master) warning, to abandon (a thing): late C. 16–17; in C. 18, *give* (one)
the bag often = to slip away from (a person), while in
late C. 18–19 the phrase came to mean dismiss (cf.
give the sack). In C. 17–18 *receive the bag* = get the
sack, be dismissed; coll. But *give the bag to hold*
= to engage one's attention with a view to deceive:
late C. 17–19: coll. >, by 1800, S.E.

bag, in the bottom of the. In reserve; as a last
resource: mid-C. 17–18: coll. >, by 1750, S.E.
Cf. C. 20 *out of the bag*.

bag, let the cat out of the. To disclose a secret

or a trick: from ca. 1750: coll. >, by 1840, S.E.
Wolcot, Mrs. Gaskell.

bag, put one in a. To have the upper hand of:
C. 17–18 coll. Fuller.

bag, put one's head in a. See **bag, get one's head**.

bag a brace. See **brace**.

bag and baggage. Entirely; leaving nothing.
Esp. of departure. Coll. >, by 1800, S.E. C.
16–20. Orig. dignified military j.

bag and bottle. Food and drink: mid-C. 17–18
coll. Eachard's *Observations*, 1671.

bag and wallet, turn to. To become a beggar:
late C. 16–17 coll. Hakluyt.

bag of, a. Enough; plenty of: military: C. 20.
F. & Gibbons. Possibly suggested by the next.
Cf. *bags of*.

bag o(f) beer. A quart of beer: proletarian
(— 1909); † by 1930; ob., indeed, by 1916. Ware,
'This once stood for "pot o' four 'arf an' 'arf",
reduced to "[pot o'] four 'arf", and thence to,
"bag o' beer".'

bag of bones. A very thin person: Dickens,
1838: coll.: in C. 20, S.E.

bag o(f) moonshine. Nonsense: C. 19–20; ob.
Lower-class coll. Cf. *moonshine*.

bag of mystery. See **bags of mystery**.

bag of nails, squint like a. To squint very badly
late C. 18–mid-19. Grose, 2nd ed., 'I.e. his eyes are
directed as many ways as the points of a bag of
nails.'

Bag of Nails, the. The Bacchanals: a tavern in
Pimlico (London): ca. 1770–1830. Grose, 3rd ed.
(Folk etymology.)

bag of rations. A fussy, too zealous, or domineer-
in superior: military: 1915–18. F. & Gibbons.
Ex the noise it made when agitated.

bag of tricks, the; or the whole b. of t. Every
expedient: C. 19–20. Ex the fable of the Fox and
the Cat (O.E.D.)—2. Penis and testicles: low:
mid-19-20.

bag on the bowline. To drift off a course:
nautical coll.: mid-C. 19–20. Bowen. Cf. **baggy**,
adj.

*****bag-thief.** See **bagger**.

baggage. A saucy young woman: Davenant,
1672; coll. by 1700. A worthless man: C. 16–17.
A harlot or a loose woman: Shakespeare, 1596;
coll. by 1660; † by 1800. Rubbish, nonsense:
C. 16, e.g. in Gascoigne.

baggage, heavy. Women and children: late
C. 18–19 (Grose, 2nd ed., records it); cf. Fr. *pas de
bagage en train de plaisir*.

*****bagger, bag-thief.** One who, in stealing rings,
seizes the victim's hand: late C. 19–early 20 c. Ex
Fr. *bague*, a ring.

bagging. Food taken between meals: provincial s. rather than dial., C. 18–19. In Lancashire dial., from ca. 1880, high tea.

baggonet. See **bagonet**.

baggy. (Gen. pl.) A rating in the old naval
troopers: military: ca. 1860–1900. Bowen, 'On
account of their uniform trousers.'

baggy, adj. (Of clothes, esp. trousers at the knee)
unduly stretched: coll. (1858) >, by 1910, S.E.

bagman. A commercial traveller: S.E. in C. 18
(— 1765) and until ca. 1850, when it > pejorative
and coll.—2. A bag-fox: sporting (1875). O.E.D.

[**bagnio.** A brothel: C. 17–18: coll., or perhaps
rather S.E. (See O.E.D.)]

bagonet; also **baggonet**, rarely **bagnet**. In
C. 19–20, sol. (but in C. 17–18, S.E.) for *bayonet*; it

was often heard among the Tommies in 1914–18. In late C. 17–early 18 s., however, it meant, B.E. tells us, a dagger.

bagpipe. A long-winded talker : C. 17–19 ; Carlyle has it. Coll.—2. As v., to indulge in a sexual practice that even F. & H. says is 'too indecent for explanation' : late C. 18–19. Grose, 1st ed., has recorded the synonymous *huffle* : neither word occurs in later edd.

bags. Trousers : 'Cuthbert Bede', in *Verdant Green*, 1853. A low variant, from ca. 1860 but ob., is *bum-bags. Oxford bags*, very wide-legged : from 1922. Ca. 1870–1910, *go-to-meeting bags*, (a man's) best clothes, and 1850–90, *howling bags* (H., 1st ed., Introduction) : trousers very 'loud' in pattern or colour(s).—2. **B**uenos **A**ires **G**reat **S**outhern Railway Bonds : Stock Exchange : from ca. 1885.—3. See **bags of.**—4. See **bags, mount the.**

bags ! ; bags I ! That's mine ! Schoolboys' from ca. 1860. Cf. *bar, fain, pike.* On illiterate *says I.*—2. Hence, *I bags first go* (innings) : from not later than 1897, likewise schoolboys'. Collinson.

bags, have the. To be of age ; have plenty of money : mid-C. 19–20 : coll. ; ob. Variant, *have the bags off* : H., 1st ed.

bags, mount the ; over the bags. (To climb) over the trench parapet—made of sandbags—in order to attack the enemy : military s. (1915) >, by 1917, coll. Cf. *over the top.*

bags, rough as. Extremely uncouth ; very 'tough' : Australian, G.W. +. Jice Doone.

bags, take the. To be hare in hare-and-hounds : athletic, coll. : from ca. 1870.

bags I ! See **bags !**

bags of. Much, plenty ; many. E.g. 'bags of time'. C. 20. B. & P.; Lyell. Cecil Litchfield entitled his first, and wittily funny, novel : *Bags of Blackmail.* Cf. *bag of, a.*

bags off, have the. See **bags, have the.**

bags of mystery. Sausages and saveloys : from ca. 1850, says Ware. H., 3rd ed. ; Whiteing, *No. 5, John Street*, 1899. Rare in the singular.

bagsy. Unshapely : Glasgow coll. (– 1934). I.e. with as much delicacy of shape as a bag.

bail ! See **bale !**

bail, to give leg. To run away from : coll. : from ca. 1770 ; ob. Scott in *Guy Mannering.* Occ. varied in C. 19 as *take leg bail and give land security.*

bail up. To demand payment, money, or other settlement from : Australian, from ca. 1878. Esp. Morris. Ex earlier lit. use : (of a bushranger) to hold up,—which (– 1864) was, by Cockneys, adopted, in the imperative, to mean 'Stop !' : H., 3rd ed.

bailed man. (Gen. pl.) One who had bribed the Press Gang for his immunity : nautical coll. : mid-C. 18–mid 19. Bowen.

bailer. A ball that, on being bowled, hits the bails : cricket ; the O.E.D. records it for 1881. Coll. >, by 1900, S.E.

bait ; esp. *a rousing bait* or *bate*, a great rage (Eton). Anger ; rage : from mid-1850's. Mayhew, 1857 (E.D.D.) ; Anstey's *Vice Versa*, 1882. University and esp. Public School. Perhaps a back-formation ex *baited*, harassed or tormented.—2. See **Scotch bait, Welsh bait.**—3. Food : railwaymen's, esp. of those on a Pullman-provided train : from ca. 1920. *The Daily Herald*, Aug. 5, 1936. Ex *fish-bait.*

bait-land. A port where refreshments can be procured : C. 18–19, nautical, † by 1867.

bak. See **buck,** n., 11 ; also v., 2.

bake. The head : a C. 20 military corruption of *boco*, 1. F. & Gibbons.—2. A fiasco ; a useless act : low and military : C. 20. Frank Richards, *Old Soldiers Never Die*, 1933, 'I found a stretcher-bearer already attending to Smith . . . and he informed me that it was a bloody bake, as Smith had stopped it through the pound.' With *bake*, cf. Fr. *four*, an utter failure theatrically ; *pound* is *pound of lead*, rhyming s. for 'head' : late C. 19–20 (cf. *lump of lead*).

bake, v. To rest, lie down : Winchester College, C. 19. Whence († by 1890), *bakester*, a sluggard. Cf. also *baker* and *baking-leave*, qq.v.

bake it. To refrain from visiting the w.c. when one should go there to ease the major need : low : late C. 19–20.

bake one's bread. To kill (a person) : C. 14–19 ; coll. > S.E.

*bake-out. The disinfection of clothes in an oven : c. : from ca. 1920. Michael Harrison, *Weep for Lycidas*, 1934. Sc. : *of lice.*

baked. (Of persons) exhausted : ca. 1790–1850, coll.—2. **only half baked**, half-witted : coll. : from ca. 1860 ; ob. H., 2nd ed.

*baked dinner. Bread—which is baked : c. : from ca. 1860 ; virtually †. Ex a joke played on new-comers to prison.

baker. A cushion ; any seat. Winchester College, C. 19. Whence († by 1890) *baker-layer*, a fag carrying from hall a prefect's cushion.

baker (or **Baker**) **!, not to-day.** A lower-classes' c.p. addressed to a man paying unwelcome attentions (to a woman) : 1885–ca. 1915. Ware. Ex housewives' reply to a baker and also ex a soldier named Baker paying undesired court to a young lady : see **Baker's Light Bobs.**

baker, spell. To attempt something difficult : C. 18–19 coll. From old spelling books, where *baker* was gen. the first dissyllabic word.

baker-legged, baker-kneed. C. 17–18, C. 18–19 coll. : knock-kneed.—2. Effeminate : C. 17–18.

baker's dozen. Thirteen counted as twelve ; loosely, fourteen so counted : late C. 16–20 : coll. >, by 1800, S.E. Florio, Fielding, Scott, *et alii.* Cf. *devil's dozen*, q.v.—2. 'Grimly used for a family of twelve and another', Ware : proletarian coll. (– 1909). ? 'another on the way'.—3. **The Baker's Dozen.** The 13th Hussars : military : mid-C. 19–20. F. & Gibbons.

baker's dozen, give one a. To thrash vigorously : mid-C. 19–20 ; ob. H., 2nd ed. ; Manchon. Cf. *what for*, q.v.

Baker's Light Bobs. The 10th Hussars : military : from ca. 1870 ; ob. The reference is to Valentine Baker (1827–87), who commanded them —and developed their efficiency to an extraordinary degree—in 1860–72. He was both a practical and a theoretical authority on cavalry tactics. (D.N.B.)

baking. Very hot : with *weather* or *day.* Coll. : from ca. 1850.

baking leave. Permission to sit in another's study : from ca. 1885, Winchester College. Prior to this date : permission to rest. **baking place :** a sofa. Ex *bake*, v : q.v.

bakshee (C. 20 only), **backshee ; ba(c)ksheesh** (most gen. form), **buckshee, bucksheesh, buckshish.** A tip ; gratuity. Near-Eastern and Anglo-Indian ; from ca. 1750. Popularised by the British Army in India and Egypt, esp. in G.W., though it was fairly gen. even by 1800. The forms in *-ee* are the more coll. Ex the Persian (thence Arabic, Urdu and Turkish) word for a present. See esp. the O.E.D. and Yule & Burnell.—2. Occ. as v.t. and v.i. : coll. : from ca. 1880. (O.E.D.)—3. (Likewise ex sense 1.) Adj. and adv., free, costing nothing : late C. 19–20 : orig. and mainly military.—4. Hence additional ; unexpected : military : C. 20. For senses 3, 4, see esp. F. & Gibbons ; B. & P.—5. A light wound : military, esp. New Zealanders' : in G.W.

bakshee (gen. **buckshee**) **king.** A paymaster : military : C. 20. F. & Gibbons. Ex the preceding.

bakshee lance-Jack. A lance-corporal : military (esp. Australians' and New Zealanders') : in G.W.

bala. ' Low, mean, or senseless talk ', Bee : rare London : ca. 1820–50. Cf. Cornish *bal*, loud talking.

balaam. (Journalistic) ' padding ' kept in standing type : Scott, 1826 ; slightly ob. A strange perversion of the Biblical Balaam and his ass.

balaam-basket. (Journalistic) the receptacle for type representing padding. Also, the basket for rejected contributions (1827). Both senses are slightly ob. Ex preceding.

balaclava. ' A full beard ' : ca. 1856–70. Ex the beards worn by those soldiers who were lucky enough to return from the Crimea. Ware.

Balaclava day. (Military) a pay-day. ' Balaclava, in the Crimean War (1854–6) was the base of supply for the English troops ; and, as pay was drawn, the men went . . . to make their purchases ', F. & H. † by 1914.

balance. The remainder : in England, orig. (ca. 1864) a sol. ex U.S. (1819 : Thornton), but accepted by English business men ca. 1870 and > very gen. s. by 1880 ; not yet acceptable to culture—though it might, in 1937, be considered as having attained the rank of coll. *Blackwood's Magazine*, April, 1875, ' *Balance*, long familiar to American ears, is becoming so to ours.' See esp. O.E.D., F. & H., Thornton, and S.O.D.

balb. To manœuvre (an enemy 'plane) into a bad position : Air Force : 1918. F. & Gibbons. Ex U.S. *balb*, to ' get round ' a person. Possibly connected with Balbus, who ' was building a wall ' (cf. next).

Balbus. A Latin prose-composition (book) : school coll. From the textbook of Dr. Arnold (d. 1842) : recorded in 1870, † by 1920. Cf. the preceding.

bald. See **bladder of lard.** Cf. *bald as a coot* : coll. : late C. 13–20. Apperson.

bald-coot. An elderly or old man that, in gambling, is plucked : fast life (— 1823) ; † by 1890. ' Jon Bee ', *Dictionary of the Turf*.

bald-faced stag. A bald-headed man : from ca. 1860 ; ob. H., 3rd ed. Cf. *stag*.

bald-headed. (Of a ship in square-rig) ' with nothing over her top-gallants ' ; (of a schooner) ' without top-masts ' : nautical : mid-C. 19–20 ; ob. Bowen.

bald-headed, go (at) it. To be impetuous or whole-hearted in an action. Orig. (— 1850) U.S. ; anglicised ca. 1900. Perhaps a perversion of Dutch *balddadig*, audacious (W.).

bald-headed butter. Butter without hairs : trade (— 1909) ; ob. Ware.

bald-headed hermit. The penis : ' cultured ' : late C. 19–20 ; ob.

bald-headedly. The coll. ad**v.** (1920, W. J. Locke : witness O.E.D. Sup.) corresponding to *bald-headed, go at it*, q.v.

bald-rib. A thin bony person : jocularly coll. ; from ca. 1620. Ex S.E. sense, ' a joint of pork cut nearer the rump than the spare-rib ', S.O.D.

balderdash. A nonsensical farrago of words : from ca. 1660 ; coll. by 1700 ; S.E. by ca. 1730. Prob. ex earlier (late C. 16–17) sense, ' froth '.—2. As adulterated wine, late C. 17–18, the term presumably never rose above coll. See O.E.D. and Grose, P., for other, i.e. S.E., senses.

*****baldober, baldower.** A leader ; a spokesman : C. 19–20, ob., c. Ex German c.

balductum. Nonsense ; verbal farrago : late C. 16–17. Orig. (and S.E.) a posset.

bale ; baal ; bail. No ! : Australian ' pidgin ' (— 1870). Ex Aborigine. Cf. *cabon*. Morris.

bale up. See **bail up.**

Balfour's maiden. A battering ram : Parliamentary, 1889 ; † by 1920. Ex the Irish elections of 1888–9, when Mr. Balfour was Secretary. Coined by Sir Wm. Harcourt.

balk. See **baulk** and **baulk, in ;** also **miss, give a.**

Balkan tap is a Salonican Front variant (1915–18) of *doolally tap* (q.v.). B. & P.

*****ball.** A prison ration of food, esp. the six ounces of meat ; also, a drink. Both are mid-C. 19–20 c. ; the former occurs in Brandon, 1839.

ball, open the. To begin : from ca. 1810 : coll. ; in C. 20, S.E. Byron ; *The Eton Chronicle*, July 20, 1876. (O.E.D.)

ball, take up the. To take one's due turn in conversation, work, etc. : coll. >, by 1900, S.E. ; from ca. 1840. (O.E.D.)

ball and bat. A hat : rhyming s. (— 1914). F. & Gibbons.

ball at one's feet, have the. To have something in one's power : coll. >, by 1880, S.E. ; from ca. 1800. Occ. and earlier, *before one*.

ball before the bound, catch or **take the.** To forestall, anticipate opportunity : coll. >, by 1800, S.E. ; from ca. 1640. (O.E.D.)

ball is with you, the. It is your turn ; it is ' up to ' you : coll. >, by 1910, S.E. ; from ca. 1850 ; slightly ob. (O.E.D.)

ball-keeper. A fag looking after cricket-, footballs : C. 19, Winchester College.

ball of fire. A glass of brandy : ca. 1820–60. Egan's Grose. Ex sensation in throat : for semantics, cf. *fire a slug*, q.v.

ball of lead. Head : rhyming s., mostly and orig. (— 1914) military. F. & Gibbons.

ball o(f) wax. A shoemaker : C. 19. Ex the wax used in shoemaking.

ball rolling, or up, keep the. To keep an activity, a conversation, going : coll. >, by 1840, S.E. ; from ca. 1780. (O.E.D.) *Set the ball rolling* therefore = to begin, start a thing going : same period. Cf. *open the ball*, where however the *ball* = a dance.

ball under the line, strike the. To fail : coll. : mid-C. 16–17. Ex (royal) tennis. Apperson.

ball-up. A kick-about at Association football : Charterhouse : C. 20.

ballad-basket. A street singer : C. 19. In C. 19, a street singer sang mostly ballads, which, now, are much less popular ; *basket* has perhaps been suggested by the synonymous ' street *pitcher* '.

ballast. Money : from ca. 1850, orig. nautical. Whence (— 1890 ; now ob.) *well ballasted*, rich.

ballast-shooting. ' The strictly prohibited sailing-ship practice of dumping ballast overboard at the end of a voyage, to the detriment of the fairway ' : nautical coll. : late C. 19–20 ; ob. Bowen.

ballahou. 'A term of derision applied to an ill-conditioned slovenly ship', *The Century Dict.*: nautical: from ca. 1885. ? etymology: not impossibly ex *ballyhooly*, q.v.

Ballambangjang, Straits of. Straits as imaginary as they are narrow: nautical coll. (— 1864); slightly ob. H., 3rd ed.

Ballarat lantern. See **lantern, Ballarat.**

balley. See **bally,** v.

ballock ; now gen. **bollock.** A testicle ; gen. in pl. A very old word, S.E. until ca. 1840, then **a** vulg. Cf. :

ballocks. A parson: late C. 18–early 19. Grose, 2nd ed. Often as *ballocks the rector.*—2. Nonsense: late C. 19–20. Now gen. *bollocks.* Cf. *balls, all,* and *cods,* qq.v.; very rarely with *all.* Cf. also *boloney.*

ballocky. A bluejacket: naval: C. 20. F. & Gibbons. Ex:

Ballocky Bill the Sailor. A mythical person commemorated in a late C. 19–20 low ballad and often mentioned, by way of evasion (cf. *up in Annie's room*), by the soldiers in the G.W.; he is reputed to have been most generously testicled. Pronounced and occ. spelt *bollicky.* Cf., as perhaps partially operative, dial. *ballocky, bollocky,* left-handed, or, hence, clumsy.

Balloo ; Ballyhooly. Bailleul : Western Front military coll. and s.: late 1914–18. It was an attractive town. Cf. *Pop.*—2. Whence, *a trip to Balloo,* a pleasure trip : military coll. : 1916–early 18. F. & Gibbons.

balloon. 'A week's enforced idleness from want of work', Ware : tailors' (— 1909); ob. Ex Fr. *bilan.*

balloon go up ?, when does the ; also **the balloon goes up at** (such a time). When does it happen ? ; it happens at: 1915, orig. military ; slightly ob. Cf. *zero hour,* q.v. (B. & P.)

balloonatic. A man handling a naval kite-balloon : naval: 1915 ; ob. Punning *lunatic.* (Bowen.)

balloon - juice. Soda - water : 'public-house, 1883', Ware ; † by 1930. Ex gaseousness.—2. Whence *balloon-juice lowerer,* a total abstainer : ca. 1884–1920. Ware.

ballooning. Jockeying of the prices of stocks: Stock Exchange (— 1890, ob.).

balls ; all balls. Nonsense (— 1890). In Feb., 1929, it was held to be obscene ; by 1931 it had > permissible in print. Low coll. For semantics, cf. *ballocks,* 2, and *boloney* (orig. U.S.), qq.v., also the U.S. *nerts* (as an interjection). See esp. Allen Walker Read, *Lexical Evidence from Folk Epigraphy,* 1935 (Paris ; privately printed).

balls, bring through. To collect footballs to be blown up : Winchester College, from ca. 1850.

balls of, make (a). To spoil ; do wrongly — 1890). Low.

balls on. See **do one's balls on.**

balls to you ! Rats to you ! : low : late C. 19–20. (Cf. *balls,* q.v.) Manchon.

balls-up. To make a mess or a blunder of ; to confuse inextricably ; misunderstand wholly ; do altogether wrongly : low : C. 20. Cf. U.S. *ball-up* and (also for *balls-up*) the somewhat rare *ball,* to clog, gen. of a horse getting its feet clogged with balls of clay or snow.

ballum rancum. A dance at which all the women are harlots ; Grose, 2nd ed., adds, 'N.B. The company dance in their birthday suits' : from ca. 1780 (Grose, 1st); † by 1900. Cf. *buff ball,* q.v. Ex *ball,* a testicle.

bally ; gen. balley. To depart (speedily): London traders' (— 1909); virtually †. Ware. Cf. *hop it, polka, skip, waltz,* qq.v.

bally, adj. A euphemism for *bloody.* From 1884, says Ware (1909) who classifies it as sporting s. and quotes from *The Sporting Times,* April 11, 1885. W., after F. & H. (revised), suggests ex *Ballyhooly truth*; cf. *blighter, blinking, blooming.* See my *Words !*

ballyhoo. An abbr. (orig.—ca. 1913—U.S.) of, and from ca. 1925 more gen. than, *ballyhooly* (though cf. next entry): s. >, by 1930, coll.; now verging on S.E. 'The now recognised term for eloquence aimed at the pocket-book', *The Times Literary Supplement,* July 19, 1934.

ballyhoo of blazes. 'The last word of contempt for a slovenly ship': nautical : C. 20. Bowen. Perhaps ex *ballahou,* 'a West Indian schooner with foremast raking forward and mainmast aft' (Bowen).

ballyhooly. Copy-writers' or politicians' exaggeration ; 'advance publicity of a vulgar or misleading kind' (H. G. Le Mesurier): from ca. 1910, coll. by 1925. Abbr. *Ballyhooly truth,* a ca. 1880–85 music-hall tag perhaps ex *whole bloody truth* (W.). —2. See **Balloo.**

Ballylana, drunk as. Very drunk : Anglo-Irish coll. : late C. 19–20. Perhaps rather *Ballylannan.*

Ballymena(s). Belfast and Northern Counties Railway shares : Stock Exchange (— 1895). A. J. Wilson, *Stock Exchange Glossary.* Ex Ballymena, the urban district and market town 11½ miles north of Antrim (*Bartholomew's Gazetteer*).

bally-rag. See **bully-rag.**

balm. A lie (— 1820 ; † by 1900). Duncombe. Variant of *bam,* n. : q.v.

balmedest balm. 'Balm in the extreme', Ware : proletarian London (— 1909); virtually †.

balmy. (Always *the b.*) Sleep. Dickens in *The Old Curiosity Shop,* 1840 : 'As it's rather late, I'll try and get a wink or two of the balmy.' Prob. suggested by *balmy slumbers* (Shakespeare), *balmy sleep* (Young): F. & H., revised.—2. An idiot: low : C. 20. Ex :

balmy ; perhaps more correctly **barmy.** Adj. : anything from stolid to manifestly insane ; gen., just a little mad. Henry Mayhew, 1851. Whence *balmy cove,* a weak-minded man. Perhaps ex S.E. *balmy,* soft, but see also **barmy :** the latter form prob. suggested the former.

balmy stick, put on the. To simulate madness : low (— 1923). Manchon. Ex preceding.

baloney, or **-ie.** See **bolon(e)y.—Baloo.** See **Berloo.**

*balsam. Money : late C. 17–18, c. ; C. 19–early 20, s. B.E. ; Grose ; Ware, prob. wrong in stating that it was 'orig. confined to dispensing chemists'. Ex its healing properties.

Baltic Fleet. 'The Fourth Division of the Home Fleet for some years before the War, when the smallness of the nucleus crews reminded seamen of Rozhdestvensky's ill-fated squadron', Bowen.

balum rancum. See **ballum rancum.** (The spelling in 4th, 5th edd. of Grose.)

bam ; bamb (C. 18). A hoax ; an imposition: *Dyche's Dictionary* (5th ed.), 1748. Ex :—2. As v.i., to sham, be in jest (— 1754); v.t., hoax (in print, 1738), a sense that was current as early as 1707. Abbr. *bamboozle,* q.v.

bamblusterate. Noisily to hoax or to confuse: rare : C. 19. Ex *bam* + *bluster.*

bamboo backsheesh. A blow evoked by importunate begging for money : Anglo-Indian : from ca. 1850 ; ob. See **bakshee.**

bamboozle. To hoax, deceive, impose upon (both v.t. and v.i.) : Cibber, 1703. To mystify (1712). Swift in 1710 : 'The third refinement . . . consists in the choice of certain words invented by some pretty fellows, such as banter, bamboozle, country-put, and kidney, some of which are now struggling for the vogue, and others are in possession of it.' In late C. 18–mid 19 naval s., it meant ' to deceive an enemy by hoisting false colours ' (Bowen). As n., Cibber, 1703 ; **bamboozling** (1709) is much more frequent and occurs also as adj. (— 1731). **bamboozable,** easily deceivable, is a late (1886) development, and so is **bamboozlement** (1855) : these two were never s. but have never quite risen to S.E. Etymology still a mystery ; prob. ex a c. word of which no record is extant ; perhaps ex *banter* corrupted, or rather, perverted ; W., however, suggests an interesting alternative.

bamboozler. A hoaxer, an imposer on others (1712).

bambosh. Humbug ; a hoax(ing) : 1865 : rare and ob. Prob. ex *bam + bosh*, qq.v.

ban. A Lord-Lieutenant of Ireland : Irish : C. 18–20 ; ob. Ware, ' Bedad, one ban or anoder, 'tis the same man.' Perhaps punning *ban*, a curse or edict, and *banshee*, the precursor of sorrow, as Ware suggests.

Banaghan, beat. To tell a (too) marvellous story : orig. and mostly Anglo-Irish coll. : late C. 18–20. Grose, 1st ed. ; *The Passing Show*, Jan. 21, 1933, has the variant, *beat banagher*.

banagher. To bang. I find no record earlier than F. & H. (1890), which says ' old '. App. † by 1900. Prob. a word heard by Farmer in his youth and possibly a reduction from *beat Banaghan* or, from ca. 1840, *Banagher* (or *banagher*) : this phrase, however, suggests that *banagher* may be a development of *bang*, to strike violently, a view supported by the fact that the most usual form is *this bangs Ban(n)agher*, an Irish proverbial saying, with which cf. *beat creation*, for *Banagher* is a village in King's County (W.).

banana !, have a. A low c.p., expressive of contempt : C. 20 ; ob. Ex a popular song (Collinson). —2. Perhaps ex the popular song, ' I had a banana With Lady Diana,' the phrase *to have a banana with* meant, ca. 1905–30, to coït with (a woman).

Bananaland ; Bananalander. Queensland ; a native of. Australian coll. (— 1887) ; slightly ob.

bananas !, yes, we have no. See **yes, we . . .**

Banbury. A loose woman : low London : 1894, *The People*, Feb. 4 ; † by 1920. Ware. By association with hot-cross buns and ' (jam-)tarts '.

Banbury story (of a cock and bull). ' Silly chat ', B.E. : late C. 17–early 19. Cf. the C. 19 dial. *Banbury tale* and see Grose, P.

banchoot, beteechoot. A coarse Anglo-Indian term of abuse : late C. 18–20 ; ob. Lit., pudend. Yule & Burnell. In late C. 19–20, gen. **barnshoot,** q.v.

banco. Evening preparation, superintended by a monitor : Charterhouse : from ca. 1832. Tod, *Charterhouse*, 1900, p. 81. Cf. *toy-time* and, for origin, the legal *in banco*.

band, beat the. See **beat the band.—band, follow the.** See **follow the band.** Cf. :

band-party, the. Members of the Church of England : military : late C. 19–20 ; ob. F. & Gibbons. See also **follow the band.**

band played !, and then the. The fat is in the fire : c.p. ; ca. 1880–1910. Cf. *good night !* and Kipling's ' It's " Thank you, Mister Atkins ", when the band begins to play ' (1892). Also *then the band began* (*to play*) : C. 20 ; ob. D. Coke, *Wilson's*, 1911.

bandage-roller. A sick-bay rating : naval : late C. 19–20. Bowen. Cf. *Linseed Lancers*.

Bandagehem, Dosinghem, Mendinghem ; or **Bandage-'em,** etc. Jocular names for three hospital stations in Flanders : military : 1915–18. F. & Gibbons. On such names as Ebblinghem.

bandan(n)a. A silk (in C. 20, also cotton) handkerchief, with white or yellow spots left in the coloured base : coll. in C. 18 India, but there accepted ca. 1800, in England in 1854 (Thackeray), as S.E.

bandbox, (orig. that is) my or **mine arse on (Bee, in) a !** That won't do ! : a late C. 18–mid 19 c.p. Grose, 1st ed. Ex the inadequacy of bandbox as a seat.

bandboxical. Like, or of the size of, a bandbox : coll. : 1787, Beckford, ' Cooped up in a close, bandboxical apartment ', O.E.D. ; slightly ob. On *paradoxical*.

banded. Hungry : c. or low : 1812, Vaux ; H., 1st ed. Cf. *bands, wear the*, q.v. (With band or belt tightened round one's middle.)

bandicoot, miserable as a. See **miserable . . .**

bando ! Make (the rope) fast : coll., Anglo-Indian ; whence London docks (— 1886). Direct ex Hindustani *bandho*. Yule & Burnell.

bandog. A bailiff or his assistant : late C. 17–18. B.E. Ex lit. sense, a fierce mastiff watch-dog : ex *band*, a fastening.—2. Also late C. 18–early 19, a bandbox : either sol. or jocular.

bandog and Bedlam, speak. To speak in a rage, like a madman : late C. 16–17 coll. Dekker. Cf. preceding entry, 1.

bandok. See **bundook.**

Bandons. Shares in the Cork, Bandon and South Coast Railway : Stock Exchange coll. (— 1895). A. J. Wilson in his *Stock Exchange Glossary*.

bandore. A widow's head-dress (the Fr. *bandeau* corrupted) : ca. 1690–1750 : orig., perhaps S.E. ; by 1785 (Grose) coll. if not s. Note that the O.E.D.'s two examples occur in very light works and that B.E. has it. (The other sense, a banjo (itself a corruption of *bandore*), has a different etymology and was always S.E.)

*bands, wear the. To be hungry. C. 19 : c. or low. Vaux. Cf. *banded*.

bandstand. ' A circular gun-platform on a warship ' : naval : late C. 19–20. Bowen.—2. A cruet : naval and military : C. 20. F. & Gibbons, ' From its shape.'

bandy. A sixpence : mid-C. 19–20 (ob.) ; c. and low s. H., 1st ed. Because easily bent : cf. *bender* and *cripple*.

bandy. To band together : ' — 1818 ', says O.E.D. ; but B.E. (? 1690) has it = ' follow a faction ' : so that, in C. 18, it was probably—until ca. 1760, at any rate (for Grose does not give it) — either s. or coll.

bang. A blow (— 1550). If on a thing, S.E. ; if on a person, still coll. (as in *a bang on the nose*).—2. A sudden movement, (unexpected) impetus, as in C. 18–20 *with a bang*. Coll.—3. ' The front hair cut square across the forehead ' (1880), ex U.S.

(O.E.D.) : a sense that rapidly > S.E., though the **v.** (1882) is even yet hardly S.E.—4. A lie : **s.** (1879, Meredith) >, by 1910, coll. ; ob. Cf. *bang-word*, a swear-word : coll. : C. 20. O.E.D.—5. A piece of sexual intercourse ; whence a female in the act : *have a bang, be a good bang* : low : C. 20. Cf. etymology of *fuck*.

bang, v. To strike. If the object is a thing, it is S.E. ; if a person, coll. (— 1550).—2. To outdo : from ca. 1805 : coll.—3. (Rare) to have sexual intercourse (v.t. and with a woman) : C. 20.—4. Loudly or recklessly to offer stock in the open market, with the intention of lowering the price if necessary : Stock Exchange : from ca. 1880. Often as vbl. n., *banging*.

bang, adj. Afraid, frightened : Midland and Western Districts of South Africa : coll. (— 1899). Ex Dutch *bang*, afraid. Pettman.

bang, go full. To go at full speed or as quickly as possible : coll. (— 1923). Manchon.

bang alley ; bangalay. The timber of *Eucalyptus botrioides* : Sydney workmen's : late C. 19–20. Morris. Ex Aborigine.

bang Banagher. See **Banagher.**

bang-beggar. A constable (— 1865) : orig. and mainly Scots. E.D.D. Ex Northern dial.

bang goes saxpence ! A jocular c.p. applied to any small expense incurred, esp. if on entertainment or with a light heart : from ca. 1880. Popularized by Sir Harry Lauder ; obviously Scottish in origin. Here, *bang* suggests abruptness : W.

bang-Mary. A ' bain Marie ' : kitchen sol. (— 1909) verging on coll. Ware. Cf. *bummaree*, n., 2.

bang-off. Immediately : coll. : C. 19–20. Ex detonation.

bang-out, v. To depart hurriedly and noisily : C. 19–20, ob. Adv., entirely and suddenly : C. 19–20.

bang-pitcher. A drunkard : C. 17–18 ; coll. Clarke, 1639. Cf. *toss-pot*.

bang-straw. A thresher : ? orig. and mainly dial. : late C. 19–20, ob. Grose, 1785, adds : ' Applied to all the servants of a farmer '.

bang-tailed. (Esp. of horse) short-tailed : T. Hughes, 1861. Coll. rising to S.E. The n., *bang-tail*, is recorded for 1870 by the O.E.D., which considers it S.E.

bang through the elephant, have been. To be thoroughly experienced in dissipation : low London (— 1909) ; virtually †. Ware refers it to *elephant = elephant's trunk*, drunk ; but cf. rather *elephant, see the*, and *bang up to the Elephant*, qq.v.

bang-up. A dandy : in fast life (— 1811) ; † by 1920. *Lex. Bal.* ; 1882 in *Punch.* Ex the adj. :— 2. First-rate : *Lex. Bal.*, 1811 ; Vaux, 1812, implies that it may, slightly earlier, have been (the certainly synonymous) *bang-up to the mark* ; the Smiths in *Rejected Addresses*, 1812 : † by 1910, except in U.S. Cf. *slap-up*, q.v. Prob. echoic ; but perhaps, as Ware suggests, influenced by Fr. *bien* used exclamatorily. The form *banged-up* was later and less used.—3. V.t., make smart, as, passively, in the third of William Combe's *Tours*.

bang-up prime. An intensive of *bang-up*, **2 :** 1811, *Lex. Bal.* ; † by 1890.

bang-word. See **bang**, n., 4.

bang up to the Elephant. ' Perfect, complete, unapproachable ', Ware : London : 1882–ca. 1910. With reference to the Elephant and Castle Tavern, long the centre of South London public-house life.

bangalay. See **bang alley.—banged-up.** See **bang-up.**

banged up to the eyes. Drunk : mid-C. 19–20, ob.

*banged to rights, be. To be caught ' on the job ' or in possession of stolen property : c. : C. 20. (David Hume.) Lit., defeated utterly. Cf. *dead to rights*, 2.

banger. A notable lie : from ca. 1810 ; † by 1900. Cf. *thumper*, q.v.—2. One who ' bangs ' : Stock Exchange (— 1895). A. J. Wilson's *Glossary.* Ex *bang*, v., 4.—3. See **stick and bangers.**

Bangers, the. The 1st Life Guards : military C. 19–20 ; ob.

bangies. See **bangy.—banging.** See **bang**, v., 4.

banging, adj. Great : coll. : Grose, 2nd ed. (1788), has *a fine banging boy*, but the O.E.D.'s quotation from Nashe (1596) may be a genuine anticipation of both the ' great ' and the ' overwhelming ' sense. One of the many percussive adjj. that are coll. Cf. *thumping.*—2. In C. 19, *a banging lie.*—3. Also, C. 19 coll., overwhelming, as in *a banging majority.*

bangle. (Gen. pl.) A hoop round a made mast : nautical : late C. 19–20 ; ob. Bowen.

bangs Ban(n)agher and Ban(n)agher bangs the world, that. A mid-C. 19–20 variant of *this bangs Ban(n)agher, beat Banaghan* (etc.) : see **banagher.**

bangster. A braggart : mid-C. 16–18 coll. verging on S.E.—2. Whence, victor : id. : Scott, 1820 ; now † except in dial. (mostly Scottish).

bangy. Brown sugar : Winchester College, C. 19 ; ex *Bangalore*. Adj., brown, whence *bangies*, brown trousers : both, from ca. 1855, Winchester College ; *Bangy Gate*, that gate ' by Racquet Court, into Kingsgate Street ' and ' a brown gate from Grass Court to Sick House Meads ' (F. & H.) : id. ; ibid.

banian or banyan. The skin : nautical : late C. 19–20 ; ob. Ware.—2. A lounging-jacket or short dressing-gown : at the R.M.A., Woolwich, in the 1860's. E.D.D. Ex S.E. sense.

banian- or banyan-days. Days on which sailors eat no flesh : nautical : indirectly in Purchas, 1609 ; directly in Ovington, 1690. In C. 19 (now rare), the term > fairly gen., e.g. in Lamb and Thackeray. Ex the Banians, a Hindu caste or class of traders, who eat not of flesh.

banian (or banyan)-party. ' A picnic party from a man-of-war ' : naval : mid-C. 19–20. Bowen. Ex preceding. Cf. *banzai party*, q.v.

banister ; bannister. A baluster : 1667 (O.E.D.) : sol. until mid-C. 18, then S.E. By a corruption of the earlier *baluster* : see W.

banjo. A bed-pan : ca. 1850–1910. Like the next sense, ex the shape.—2. In Australia, C. 20 : a shovel ; hence, in G.W., an entrenching tool. —3. **Banjo.** See **ring**, v., 6. Hence, in Australia, all Pat(t)ersons are *Banjo* : C. 20.

banjoey. A banjoist : London society : 1890's. Ex *banjoist + joey*, a clown. Ware, ' Said to be a trouvaille by the Prince of Wales [King Edward VII], who brought banjo orchestras into fashion, being a banjoey himself.'

bank. A lump sum ; one's fortune : C. 19–20 coll., ob. An extension of C. 16–18 S.E. *bank*, a sum or amount of money.—2. **The Bank**, in C. 19 c., is Millbank Prison.

*bank, v. In C. 19–20 c. : to purloin ; put in a safe place ; go equal or fair shares.

bank-note. A piece of toilet paper : Bootham School (— 1925). Anon., *Dict. of Bootham Slang.*

bank, go to the. To go to the Labour Exchange : workmen's : from ca. 1924.

Bank of England Team. Aston Villa Football Club : Northern sporting : from mid-Dec. 1935. Ex the very large fees paid out by this club to get such players as might save it from relegation.

bank on. To anticipate as certain : from ca. 1880 : coll. >, by 1910, S.E. To consider as safe as money in the bank : cf. *safe as the Bank of England.*

bank up, v.i. and t. To complete, almost to excess : North Country coal districts' coll. (— 1896). Ware. Ex ' building up a huge fire '.

banker. A river running flush—or almost flush— with the top of its banks : Australian (— 1888). Coll. by 1890 and ' accepted ' by 1900—if not before.—2. See **bawker.**

Banker Chapel Ho. Whitechapel ; hence, vulgar language : East London (— 1909) ; virtually †. Ware, ' A ludicrous Italian translation—*Bianca*, white ; *cappella*, chapel . . . Anglicisation entering in, the first word got into " Banker " and the second back into " Chapel ", with the addition of the rousing and cheery " oh ! " '

bankers. Clumsy boots or shoes : C. 19, † by 1890.

Bankers' Battalion, the. ' The 26th (Service) Battalion of the Royal Fusiliers, raised early in 1915 mainly from Bank Clerks and Accountants ' : military coll. : 1915–18. F. & Gibbons.

bankrupt cart. A one-horse chaise : ca. 1785–95 and very sectional. Grose, 2nd ed., ' Said to be so called by a Lord Chief Justice, from their being so frequently used on Sunday jaunts by extravagant shopkeepers and tradesmen.'

bankruptcy list, to be put on the. To be completely knocked out : pugilistic : ca. 1820–60. Egan, *Randall's Diary*, 1823.

Bankside ladies. Harlots, esp. of the theatrical quarter : coll. : C. 17. Randolph, 1638. In 1721, Strype ' explains ' : ' The Bank-Side where the Stews were ' (O.E.D.).

bannister. See **banister.**

bannock. A hard ship's-biscuit : nautical catachresis : late C. 19–20. Bowen.

bant. To follow a special dietary for the reduction of obesity : from 1865 ; soon coll. Ex *banting*, such a dietary (1863), devised by W. Banting, a London cabinet-maker : a word coll. by the next year, S.E. by 1870, but now slightly ob.

[**Bantams, the,** as a military term, is S.E. ; not, as so often asserted, s. nor even coll.]

banter. Ridicule, esp. if wantonly merry or supposedly humorous. B.E., 1690 : ' a pleasant way of prating, which seems in earnest, but is in jest, a sort of ridicule '. In 1688 it was s., but in C. 18 it came gradually to mean harmless raillery and by 1800 it attained S.E. Ex :

banter, v. Ridicule, make fun of (1667, Pepys) ; in C. 18, prob. ca. 1750, it lost both its sting and its s. associations and > S.E.—2. As = to cheat, deceive, impose on, it was current only ca. 1685–1820. B.E. Etymology problematic ; but if—as Swift, in 1710, says—it ' was first borrowed from the bullies in White Friars ', then it is perhaps a perversion of † S.E. *ban*, to chide.

banterer, bantering. The agent and action of *banter*, v. : q.v.

bantling. A bastard, lit. a child conceived on a *bench* and not in the marriage-bed : late C. 16–17 and, in this sense, certainly not lower than coll. But = a child, a brat, it was (see B.E. and Grose) s. in late C. 17–18.

banyan. See **banian.**—**banyan-days** and **-party.** See **banian-days** and **-party.**

banzai party. Naval men going ashore on a spree. The same as a *hurrah-party*, for *banzai* is Japanese for *hurrah*, ' the phrase dating from the British Navy's enthusiasm for anything Japanese during the Russian war ' (1904–5) ; ob. Bowen.

baptise. Esp. of wine, to dilute : C. 17–early 19. Healey, *Theophrastus*, 1636. Cf. *christen.*

baptist. ' A pickpocket caught and ducked ', Bee : ca. 1820–50. Ex *anabaptist*, q.v.

bar. A slice of bread : Bootham School : C. 20. Anon., *Dict. of Bootham Slang*, 1925.—2. One pound sterling ; orig., a sovereign : c. : late C. 19–20. (Edwin Pugh, *The Cockney at Home*, 1914.) Direct ex Romany ; the gypsies' *bar* prob. derives ex Romany *bauro*, big or heavy—cf. Gr. βαρύς.

[**bar**, to exclude, prohibit, object to, and **bar**, prep. = except, have always (from C. 16, C. 18 resp.) been S.E., though not quite literary since ca. 1880 : they are idiomatic, not pedantic, and here they are noted only as a corrective to F. & H. Note, however, that W. considers *bar*, to coldshoulder, to be university s. ; also, the Public Schools' sense, ' to dislike (intensely) ', may be s. : late C. 19–20 : see quotation at **rag**, v.t.]

Bar, the. Marble Bar, a township in N.W. Australia : Australian coll. : from ca. 1910. Ion L. Idriess, *Flynn of the Inland*, 1932.

bar-keep. A bar-keeper : coll. : late C. 19–20. Abbr. *bar-keeper.*

bar-rabble. A pre-arranged ' famine ', **q.v.** : Bootham School : late C. 19–20.

[**bar sinister.** See Fowler.]

bar-stock, be on the. To carry ' the daily supply of liquor from the store-room to the bar ' : (liners') nautical coll. : C. 20. Bowen.

baragan tailor. A rough-working tailor : tailors', ca. 1870–1914. Ex *barragan*, a kind of fustian.

*barb, v.t. To clip or shave gold. Ben Jonson in *The Alchemist.* C. 17 c. Ex *to barber.*

Barbados. To transport to (formerly, the) Barbados : coll. >, by 1700, S.E. : ca. 1650–1850.

barbar. A scholarship candidate from another school : Durham School : late C. 19–20. Ex L. *barbarus*, a stranger, a barbarian. Cf. *ski*, q.v.

barbed wire, hanging on the (old). See **hanging . . .**

barber. A thick faggot ; any large piece of timber : Winchester College, C. 19–20.

barber, v. See **barberise.**

barber, that's the. A street saying of ca. 1760–1825 signifying approbation. Grose, 1st ed. Cf. such almost meaningless c.pp. as *all serene, get your hair cut, how's your poor feet, have a banana.*

barber-monger. A fop : coll., C. 17–18. Shakespeare. Frequently visiting the barber.

barberise ; also **barber.** Act as a deputy in the writing of (a task or an imposition) : University and Public School : ca. 1850–80. ' Cuthbert Bede ', 1853. Ex tradition of a learned barber so employed.

barberiser. A deck-planing machine : nautical : C. 20. Bowen. Because it ' shaves ' so delicately.

barber's block. See **block, barber's.**

barber's cat. A weak, sickly-looking, esp. if thin, person : from ca. 1860 ; ob. H., 3rd ed. Ware suggests that it is a corruption of *bare brisket*, q.v. at *bare-bones.*—2. A loquacious, gossipy, or tale-bearing person : mostly military : late C. 19–20. F. & Gibbons.

barber's chair. A harlot, 'as common as a barber's chair' (Grose). From ca. 1570; † by 1890. See e.g. Burton's *Anatomy* and Motteux's translation of *Pantagruel*. (The whole phrase = very common, fit for general use.)

barber's clerk. A person overdressed : from ca. 1830 (ob.), esp. among mechanics and artisans. The term occurs in Dickens. Cf. *barber-monger*, q.v.—2. Hence, A well-groomed seaman not much use at his job : nautical : mid-C. 19–20 ; ob. Bowen.

barber's knife. A razor : C. 18–early 19 : coll. verging on (? achieving) S.E.

barber's knock. 'A double knock, the first hard and the second soft as if by accident', F. & H. revised : ca. 1820–60. Bee.

barber's music. Harsh, discordant music (— 1660) ; † by 1800. Coll. bordering on S.E. (A cittern was provided by the barber for his waiting customers.)

barber's sign. Penis and testicles : low : late C. 18–19. Grose, 2nd ed., explains this scabrous pun : see Grose, P.

Barclay Perkins. Stout : Cockney (— 1909) ; virtually †. Ware. Ex the brewers, *Barclay, Perkins & Co.*

***bard** (or **bar'd**) **dice.** See **barred dice.**

bare-bone(s). A skinny person : coll. ; late C. 16–early 19.

bare-brisket. The same : proletarian : C. 19–20 ; ob. Suggested by preceding.

bare-bum. A dinner-jacket, as opp. to *tails*, the full-dress evening coat. Australia : C. 20 ; low.

bare navy (or **N.**). The rigid scale of preserved rations, without fresh meat or supplementaries : naval : late C. 19–20. Bowen.

Barebone's Parliament. The Little Parliament (120 members nominated by Cromwell and sitting July–Dec. 1653) : coll. nickname. Ex Praise-God Barbon, one of its members. (O.E.D.)

bargain, beat a or **the.** To haggle : ca. 1660–1700. Coll. >, almost imm., S.E. Killigrew, Pepys. O.E.D.

bargain, Dutch. See **Dutch bargain.**

bargain, make the best of a bad. To combat a misfortune : from ca. 1790 ; coll. till ca. 1840, then S.E. Boswell, 'According to the vulgar phrase, "making the best of a bad bargain"', O.E.D. But the phrase is found as early as 1663 (Pepys) with *market* († by 1850), as 1680 (L'Estrange) with the rarer *game* († by 1800) ; in C. 20, we often say *best of a bad job.* Apperson.

bargain, sell a. To befool ; as in Shakespeare and Swift, who, however, uses it of a specific "sell" practised at Court. † by ca. 1750. Coll. See esp. Onions's *Shakespeare Glossary*, Grose, 2nd ed., and F. & H. revised.

barge. Printers' : either a ' case ' in which there is a dearth of the most useful letters or a receptacle for ' spaces ' if formes are being corrected away from ' case '. Perhaps j. rather than s. : from ca. 1870 ; ob. H., 5th ed.—2. Little cricket : Sherborne School : late C. 19–20. Prob. ex clumsiness of the stump used as a bat.—3. See **barges.**—4. A dispute : low : late C. 19–20. Ex *barge*, v., 1.—5. A crowd, a mellay : Scottish Public Schools' : C. 20. Ian Miller, *School Tie*, 1935.

barge, v. Speak roughly or abusively to : ca. 1850–1920. Albert Smith, 1861, 'Whereupon they all began to barge the master at once '. Prob. ex *bargee*.—2. Whence, at Charterhouse and Upping-

ham, to hustle (a person) : late C. 19–20.—3. Hence (?), gen. *barge about* : to move, or rush, heavily (about) : late C. 19–20. W. Ex a barge's clumsy motion. Cf. the next three entries.—3. To push or knock : Public Schools' : late C. 19–20. P. G. Wodehouse, *Tales of St. Austin's*, 1903, ' To him there was something wonderfully entertaining in the process of " bargeing " the end man off the edge of the form into space, and upsetting his books over him.'

barge-arse. A person with a rotund behind : low : ca. 1870–1910. Whence *barge-arsed*, which Mr. Aldous Huxley would prob. define as *cacopygous.*

barge in, v.i. To intrude ; to interfere, esp. if rudely or clumsily : C. 20. Manchon. Cf. :

barge into. To collide with : orig. Uppingham School (— 1890). In C. 20, gen., and often = meet, encounter esp. if unexpectedly. Cf. *barge* (v., 2), *barge in.*

barge-man. (Gen. pl.) A large, black-headed maggot of the kind that, formerly, infested ship's biscuits : nautical : mid-C. 19–20 ; ob. Bowen.

barge-mate. The officer taking command of a ship when notabilities visited it : naval : ca. 1880–1920. Bowen.

barge-pole. The largest stick in a faggot ; hence any large piece of wood. Winchester College, from ca. 1850 ; †. Cf. *barber*, n.—2. A window-pole : Bootham School : C. 20. Anon., *Dict. of Bootham Slang*, 1925.

barge-pole, wouldn't touch with (the end of) a. One person thus indicates that he will have nothing to do with either another person or, it may be, a project : coll. : late C. 19–20. Cf. *not touch with a pair of tongs.*

bargee. A lout ; an uncultivated person : Public Schools' coll. : 1909, P. G. Wodehouse, *Mike.*

barges. Imitation breasts : proletarian : ca. 1884–90. Ware adds : ' Which arrived from France, and prevailed for about four years . . . From their likeness to the wide prow of canal-barges '.

barishnya. ' An unmarried girl, character not guaranteed. A Murmansk Expeditionary Force term ' : 1919. F. & Gibbons. Ex Russian.

bark. An Irish person : C. 19. See **Barks.**—2. The human skin : from ca. 1750 ; in C. 18, dial.—3. A cough : from ca. 1870 ; coll., as is the vbl.n., *barking*, (a fit of) coughing (— 1788 : see Grose at **Barkshire**).

bark, v.t. Scrape the skin off : from ca. 1850, e.g. in *Tom Brown's Schooldays.*—2. V.i. To cough : from ca. 1880.—3. ' To sit up at night to watch the fire when camping out in the open veld ', Pettman : South African : 1873, Boyle, *To the Cape for Diamonds.* Ex a dog's barking.

bark at the moon. To agitate, or to clamour, uselessly : C. 17–20. Coll. ; S.E. in C. 19–20. With *against* for *at*, C. 15–17 ; S.E. after 1550, having been coll.

bark off, take the. To reduce in value ; as in Dickens, 1849. (Take the skin off.)

bark up the wrong tree. To be at fault in an attempt, an aim, a method ; follow a false scent ; deal with the wrong person. Orig. U.S. (— 1833) ; anglicised ca. 1890, but less in Britain than in Australia and New Zealand. Coll. rather than s. Ex a dog hunting a racoon.

barker. A pistol : Scott (1815), Dickens, Charles

Kingsley. Variation of c., and earlier, *barking iron.*—2. (Nautical) a lower-deck gun on a ship of war : ca. 1840–90. (O.E.D.)—3. One who, standing in front of shops or shows, attracts the attention of passers-by (there are still several in the Strand) : B.E., 1690 ; *Dyche's Dictionary*, 1748, and Grose, 1785 ; coll. by 1800, S.E. by 1850. Cf. *bow-wow shop*, q.v.—4. A noisy brawler : Caxton, 1483 ; † by 1660 in England, but extant in U.S. in C. 19. —5. (University) a noisy, assertive man ; also, favourably, a great swell : C. 19.—6. A sheep-drover's assistant, deputising a dog : Greenwood, *Outcasts of London*, 1879.—7. A person with a nasty cough : from ca. 1880.—8. One who ' barks ' as at **bark**, v., 3, q.v. : 1873. Pettman.—9. A sausage : lower classes' and soldiers' : C. 20. Ex that once excessively popular song, ' Oh vare, and oh vare, is my leedle vee dog ? Oh vare, oh vare, is he gone ? ' F. & Gibbons.

barkey. A little bark : coll. : from ca. 1840, Barham (O.E.D.).—2. Hence, a vessel well liked by its crew : as expressed by that crew : mid-C. 19–20, ob. Bowen.

Barking Creek, have been to. To have a bad cough : a ca. 1820–50 variant of *Barkshire*, 2, q.v. Bee.

*barking irons. Pistols : late C. 18–early C. 19 c. ; recorded by Grose, 1785.—2. In the Navy, ca. 1830–70, large duelling pistols.

Barkis is willin(g). An indication of a man's willingness to marry ; later, to do anything. Coll. Ex the character in *David Copperfield*, 1849–50.

Barks. The Irish : either low or c. To judge by the anon. *No. 747*, in use ca. 1845, but prob. much earlier. Cf. :

Barkshire. Ireland : C. 19.—2. Also, late C. 18–19, as in Grose, 2nd ed., ' A member or candidate for Barkshire ; said of one troubled with a cough, vulgarly styled barking ' ; ob.

barley broth. ' Oil of barley ', i.e. strong beer : 1785, Grose ; † by 1860.

barley-bun gentleman. A rich gentleman eating poorly and otherwise living in a miserly way : coll. : C. 17. Minsheu.

barley-cap. A tippler : late C. 16–17. E. Gilpin, 1598.—2. *Have on*, or *wear, a barley-cap*, to be drunk, a drunkard : late C. 16–17 coll.

barmy. Very eccentric ; mad : mid-C. 19–20. Ex *barmy*, full of barm, i.e. yeast. Cf. the (mainly Yorkshire) proverbial saying, *his brains will work without barm*, Ray, 1670 ; Burns, 1785, ' My barmish noddle's working fine ' (O.E.D.) ; Ware, 1909, notes the variant *barmy in the crumpet.* The E.D.D. remarks, ' frothing like barm [yeast], hence, full of ferment, flighty, empty-headed '. Cf. *balmy*, q.v.—2. Hence, a mad or a very eccentric person : non-cultured : from ca. 1880. Also in dial. (E.D.D.)

barn. A public ball-room : London : ca. 1892–1915. Ware derives ex *Highbury Barn*, a ' garden ball-room ' ; possibly ex *barn dance*. Cf. *Barner*, q.v.

barn, a parson's. ' Never so full but there is still room for more ', Grose, 2nd ed. : C. 18–early 19 coll. whence the C. 19 Dorsetshire *big as a parson's barn.*

barn-door. A target too big to be missed ; coll. : late C. 17–20 ; hence *barn-door practice*, battues in which the game can hardly escape.—2. A batsman that blocks every ball : from ca. 1880 ; ob. Cf. *stonewaller.*

barn-door savage. A yokel : ca. 1880–1910. F. & H., revised. Ex dial.

barn-mouse, bitten by a. Tipsy : late C. 18–early 19. Grose, 2nd ed.

barn-stormer. A strolling player : theatrical (— 1859). H., 1st ed. Coll. by 1884 (O.E.D.'s date), S.E. by 1900.—2. *barn-storming*, ranting acting, must also have long preceded the earliest O.E.D. record (1884). They frequently performed and stormed in barns : see, e.g., Hugh Walpole's *Rogue Herries.*

Barnaby dance. To move quickly or unevenly : C. 18–19 coll. Ex ' *Barnaby*, an old dance to a quick movement ' (Grose, 2nd ed.) popular in C. 17. Barnaby, it seems, was a dancing jester.

barnacle. A too constant attendant ; an acquaintance keeping uncomfortably close to one : from ca. 1600 ; coll.—2. One who speaks through his nose : ca. 1550–1660.—3, 4, 5, 6. In † c., there are at least four senses :—A pickpocket : (? C. 18–) C. 19 ; a good job easily got : late C. 17–18 (B.E.) ; a gratuity given, at horse-sales, to grooms : late C. 17–18 ; a decoy swindler : late C. 16–early 17 : Greene, Dekker.—7. ' A senior officer who hangs on to the job to which his juniors hope to be appointed ' : naval : late C. 19–20. Bowen.

barnacled, ppl. adj. Wearing spectacles : from ca. 1690 ; coll.

barnacles. Spectacles : in mid-C. 16–17, gen. coloured ; in C. 18–19, any spectacles : coll. Prob. ex *barnacle*, a powerful bit for horse or ass (as in Wyclif, 1382), for these old spectacles pinched the nose considerably.—2. In c. (late C. 17–18 : B.E.), fetters.

*barnard. The (gen. drunken) man acting as a decoy in Barnard's Law (lay) : c. : ca. 1530–1630. Anon., *Dice Play*, 1532 ; Greene ; Dekker. Occ. *bernard.*

*barnard's law. ' A drunken cosinage by cards ', Greene : c. : ca. 1530–1630.

barndook. See **bundook.**

Barner, barner. ' A " roaring " blade, a fast man of North London ', Ware, who derives it ex ' Highbury Barn, one of those rustic London gardens which became common casinos ' : North London : ca. 1860–80. Cf. *barn*, q.v.

Barneries. The Adelphi Stores, The Strand, London : London : 1887, *The Referee*, Feb. 20 ; † by 1910. Ex *Miss Barnes*, the proprietress. Ware.

barnet ! Nonsense : ca. 1800–80, Christ's Hospital. ? cf. *barney*, 3.

Barnet Fair. The hair : rhyming s., orig. (— 1857) thieves'. ' Ducange Anglicus.' In C. 20, often *Barnet.*

Barney. The invariable Australian nickname (C. 20) of men surnamed Allen. Ex Barney Allen, a famous and very wealthy Australian bookmaker.

barney. A jollification, esp. if rowdy ; an outing : from late 1850's ; ob. H., 1st ed. ? ex *Barney*, typical of a noisy Irishman (cf. *paddy*, anger : W.). —2. ? hence, crowd : low s. or c. (— 1859). Ibid. —3. Humbug, cheating : low (1864). H., 3rd ed. This sense may have a different origin : cf. ' *come ! come ! that's Barney Castle !* . . . an expression often uttered when a person is heard making a bad excuse in a still worse cause ', recorded in the *Denham Tracts*, 1846–59, Apperson, whose other two *Barney* proverbs suggest that the ultimate reference is to ' the holding of Barnard Castle by Sir George Bowes during the Rising of the North in 1569 ', E. M. Wright, *Rustic Speech*, 1913.—

4. Hence, an unfair sporting event, esp. a boxing match (— 1882); ob.—5. 'Eyewash' (1884 +).— 6. A quarrel; a fight; grafters' (— 1934). Philip Allingham. Prob. ex sense 1.

barney, adj. Unfair, pre-arranged : *Bell's Life*, Jan. 3, 1885, '. . . barney contests have been plentiful '. Ex the n., 4 and 5.

Barney Dillon. A shillin(g): Scots rhyming **s.**: C. 20. (*The Daily Telegraph*, March 8, 1935.)

Barney's. 'St. Barnabas, a noted "high" church ': Oxford University : late C. 19–20. Collinson.

Barney's bull, like. Extremely fatigued or (physically) distressed : a low c.p. of late C. 19–20, esp. among Australians. Often was added either *bitched, buggered, and bewildered* or *well fucked and far from home* : these two phrases occ. stand by themselves.

barnshoot. 'A corruption of the Hindustani word *bahinchut*. A vile and unforgivable insult in India, this word is a piece of gentle badinage in England,' George Orwell, *Down and Out in Paris and London*, 1933. Earlier *banchoot*, q.v.

Barnwell ague. Venereal disease : ca. 1670–1850. Ray, 1678. Apperson.

baron. An Army commander ; military : 1915; ob. F. & Gibbons. Ex his power and importance.

Baron George. A stout man : South London : ca. 1882–1915. Ware derives it ex 'a Mr. George Parkes, a portly theatrical lessee in S. London, who came to be called Baron George ; e.g. "He's quite the Baron George !"'

baronet. A sirloin of beef: Fielding, *Tom Jones*, 1749. Ex earlier *baron of beef*. This *baronet*, jocular, was never much used ; † by 1800.

barpoo, go. To lose one's nerve or even one's head ; **to crash** : Air Force : 1916. F. & Gibbons. Perhaps a blend of ' barmy ', ' potty ', and ' loopy '.

barrack. See **barracking.**—**Barrack.** Berwick : nautical coll. : C. 18–20. E.g., a *Barrack master* was the captain of a Berwick smack carrying ' passengers ' down the East Coast before the days of steam ' (Bowen).

barrack-hack. A woman attending garrison balls year after year : from ca. 1860 ; ob.—2. A soldier's trull : from ca. 1850 ; coll. At this word, F. & H. has a long list of English, French, Italian and Spanish synonyms for a prostitute.

barracking. Banter, chaff ; noisy jeering at either visiting or native cricket or football teams that offend the spectators, esp. at Sydney and Melbourne ; not, as the S.O.D. says, ' so as to disconcert players ', but merely to demonstrate and emphasise the spectators' displeasure ; Australian (— 1890), coll. by 1897. The v., jeer at, interrupt clamorously, appears to have arisen ca. 1880 as a football term, which, in its sporting sense, it remained until ca. 1896 ; *barrack for*, however, has always (— 1890) meant to support, esp. to support enthusiastically. A *barracker*, noisy interrupter. is not recorded before 1893 ; as a supporter, not before 1894. The various words were adopted in England ca. 1920, though they were known there as early as 1900. Either ex Aboriginal *borak* (n., chaff, fun), as the author of *Austral English* and the S.O.D. editors contend, or ex costermonger Cockney *barrakin, barrikin*, gibberish, a jumble of words (— 1851), as W. suggests, or else, as I hold, from *barrikin* influenced by *borak*.

barracks. The marines' quarters aboard : naval coll. : mid-C. 19–20. Bowen.

barracoota, -couta. An inhabitant of Hobart, Tasmania : Australian nickname (— 1898) ; ob. Ex the name of an edible fish. Morris.

barrage. An excessive number or quantity : military : 1917 ; ob. Ex the myriad shells fired during a barrage.

barrakin. See **barrikin.**

***barred cater tra(y) or trey.** (Gen. pl.) False dice so made that the four (*quatre*) and the three (*trois*) were seldom cast : c. of ca. 1600–50. Dekker ; Taylor (1630).

***barred dice.** Card-sharpers' tampered dice : late C. 16–17 c. Greene (*barddice*).

barrel. A nickname for a round-bellied male : coll. : C. 20.

barrel-fever. Ill health, disease, caused by excessive drinking : late C. 18–20 ; ob. Grose, 3rd ed., ' He died of the barrel fever '.

barrel of treacle. Love : low London : 1883 ; † by 1920. Ware. Ex its sweetness.

barrel the better herring, never a. Nothing to choose between them : coll. : from 1530's ; slightly ob. Bale, ca. 1540 ; Jonson, 1633 ; Fielding, 1736 ; FitzGerald, 1852. Apperson. Obviously ex the fish-markets.

barrel tinter. Beer : Yorkshire **s.**, not dial. : 1851, Tom Treddlehoyle, *Trip ta Lunnan*. E.D.D.

Barrell's Blues. (Military) the Fourth Foot Regiment ; since ca. 1881, the King's Own Royal Regiment (Lancaster). From its blue facings and its colonel of 1734–49, the celebrated General Wm. Barrell.

barrener. A cow not calving for a given season, i.e. for a year : farming coll. : > S.E. : from ca. 1870.

***barrer.** To convey (a ' drunk ') home on a barrow : either low Cockney or c. : ca. 1870–1915. Ware.

barres. (Gaming) money lost but not yet paid : C. 17–early 19. Ex *bar*.

barrikin ; occ. **barrakin.** Gibberish ; a farrago of words ; jargon : Cockney's : Henry Mayhew, 1851 ; ob. Of the prob. Fr. original (*baragouin*) H., 1st ed., rather aptly remarks that ' *Miège* calls it " a sort of stuff " ,' for Frenchmen still say *Je ne puis rien comprendre à ce baragouin.* Cf. *barracking*, q.v.

barring. For sure, certainly, indubitably : tailors' : C. 20. *The Tailor and Cutter*, Nov. 29, 1928, ' A powerful shiner, barring '. Abbr. *barring none.*

barring-out. (Schools) the shutting of the door against a master : from ca. 1700 ; coll. ; S.E. by ca. 1840. Notable instances in Swift and Tennyson.

***barrister's.** A coffee-house affected by thieves : c. : late C. 19– early 20. Ex ' a celebrated host of this name ', Ware.

barrow-bunter. A female costermonger : coll. : mid-C. 18–19 ; ob. by 1890. Smollett, 1771.

barrow-man. A costermonger : C. 17–19 ; S.E. by 1700.—2. A man under sentence of transportation : ca. 1810–50. *Lex. Bal.*, ' Alluding to the convicts at Woolwich, who are principally employed in wheeling barrows full of brick or dirt '.

barrow-tram. An ungainly person : C. 19. Lit., *b.-t.* = the shaft of a barrow (C. 16–19).

barrow wallah. A big man (occ., thing); **chota wallah,** a little man (loosely, thing) : Regular Army coll. : late C. 19–20. B. & P. Direct ex Hindustani.

bart. A harpoon : C. 19. Bowen, ' More used by the sword-fishermen than the whalers '. Per-

haps an abbr. of the † Westmorland *bartle*, the large
pin in the game of ninepins (E.D.D.).—2. Jocular
coll., esp. in address (as in Galsworthy, *The White
Monkey*, 1924), for a *baronet*, which it abbr. in
superscriptions, *Bart* being much more frequent,
formal and polite than *Bt*.

barter. A half-volley at cricket : Winchester
College, from ca. 1835 ; there too, the v. = to
swipe (1836) and *hitting barters* (— 1890), practice
at catching. All, orig. coll., soon > S.E. See
F. & H., as well as Mansfield's and Adams's books
on the College (1870, 1878 resp.) ; also W. J.
Lewis, who, in his admirable lexicon, *The Language
of Cricket*, 1934, derives it from Robert Barter :
' He entered Winchester College in 1803, and held
the post of Warden from 1832 till 1861 ' ; ' He was
renowned for his half-volley hits '.

Bartholomew baby. A gaudily dressed doll
(1670), a tawdrily dressed woman (1682) : the
former, coll., soon S.E., the latter always s. Both
† by 1850 or so.

Bartholomew(-Boar-)Pig. A fat man : late
C. 16–17. Roasted pigs were a great attraction at
Bartholomew Fair (West Smithfield, London,
1133–1855) : see esp. Jonson's Rabelaisian comedy,
Bartholomew Fair, 1614.

Bart's. St. Bartholomew's Hospital, London :
orig. (from ca. 1880) medical students'.

base Trojan. A term of abuse : late C. 16–
early 17. Shakespeare, *Henry V*.

base wallah. A soldier employed behind the
lines ; orig. and esp. at a Base : military coll. :
1915–18. F. & Gibbons. See **wallah** : and C. E.
Montague's *Honours Easy*. The New Zealanders
preferred *base-walloper*.

baseball. ' Small, insignificant. [Orig. and
mainly U.S., " 1880 on ".] Sometimes heard in
Liverpool. Suggested by the small size of the ball
in question ', Ware : as Liverpool s., it dates ca.
1890–1915.

*basengro. A shepherd : tramps' c. (— 1923).
Manchon. Ex Romany, in which -*engro* (man) is
a frequent suffix.

bash, to strike with a crushing blow (— 1790), is
S.E. in the North, only just S.E.—if not, rather,
coll.—in the South. The same is true of the n.
(from ca. 1800) ; certainly neither is dignified.
In c., however, it = to beat heavily with the fists
only : C. 19–20. Vbl.n., *bashing*. The origin is
obscure : but prob. it is either echoic or, as W.
suggests, a blend of *bang + smash*, or, again, a
thickening of *pash*. Whence :

bash, be on the. To be a prostitute : c. : C. 20.
Prob. suggested by *batter, on the* : q.v.

bash into. To meet (a person) by chance : low :
from ca. 1920. James Curtis, *The Gilt Kid*, 1936.
Cf. S.E. *strike*.

basher. A prize-fighter : low. Also, but in c.,
a professional thug. From ca. 1860.—2. A tin
receptacle holding treacle : naval : ca. 1850–1900.
Bowen.—3. A boater (hat) : Bedford School :
C. 20. Cf. *hard-hitter*.

Bashi-Bazouk. A ruffian ; mildly, a rascal :
from ca. 1870 ; ob. Orig. a Turkish irregular
soldier (from ca. 1850).—2. A Royal Marine, ' a
name that appears to have been bestowed when
Phipps Hornby took the Fleet up the Dardanelles
in 1877 ', Bowen ; virtually †.

basil. A C. 18–20 sol. for *bezel*, esp. in jewellery.
—2. A fetter on one leg only : c. : late C. 16–18.
Greene.

Basing, that's. A card-playing c.p., of mid-
C. 17–18, applied when clubs are turned up trumps.
Ex Basing House, captured in the Civil War while
the inmates were playing cards. By a pun : ' Clubs
were trumps when Basing was taken.' F. & H.
revised.

basinite. A hot-water fag : Charterhouse : C. 19,
A. H. Tod.

basket ! A cry directed, in cock-pits, at persons
unable, or unwilling, to pay their debts : C. 18.
Such persons were suspended in a basket over the
cock-pits (Grose.)—2. Hence *basketed*, left out in
the cold, misunderstood, nonplussed : late C. 18–
19.—3. Stale news : tailors' : late C. 19–20.
Perhaps ex *waste-basket*.—4. Occ. used jocularly as
a euphemism for *bastard* (in the vocative) : from
ca. 1930.

basket, be brought or **go, to the.** To be imprisoned : C. 17–18 coll.

basket, left in the. Rejected ; abandoned :
mid-C. 19–20 : coll. >, by 1890, S.E. Barham
(O.E.D.). Like the worst fruit.

basket, pick of the. The best : from ca. 1870 ;
coll. >, by 1910, S.E.

basket, pin the. To conclude, settle : mid-
C. 17–18 coll. Osborn, ca. 1659.

basket-making. Sexual intercourse : mid-C. 18–
early 19. Grose, 1st ed.

basket of chips, grin like a. To grin broadly :
late C. 18–mid-19, coll. Grose, 2nd ed. Cf.
smile like . . . chips, an old Shropshire saying.

basket of oranges. A pretty woman : ' Australian, passing to England ', says Ware : late
C. 19–early 20. Ex *basket of oranges*, ' a discovery
of nuggets of gold in the gold fields ' : Australian
miners' coll. : late C. 19–20 ; ob.

basket-scrambler. One who lives on charity :
C. 17–18 ; coll.

basketed. See **basket !**

Bass. Bass's ale (1849) ; almost imm. coll. ; in
C. 20 S.E. ' Cuthbert Bede.'

basset, make a. To blunder : racing (— 1932).
Slang, p. 245.

basso. A shoal : nautical coll. : C. 19. Bowen.
Perhaps ex Staffordshire *bassiloe*, the mound of
earth at or near the edge of a pit (E.D.D.).

bastard. A fellow, chap, man, with no pejorative connotation : coll. : C. 20, chiefly Australian,
perhaps ex U.S. ; see esp. Grose, P., and cf. the
colourless use of *bugger*, q.v.—2. Fig of a thing, an
incident, a situation : low coll. : C. 20. James
Curtis.

bastardly gullion. A bastard's bastard : (Lancashire dial. and) low coll. : late C. 18–early 19.
Grose, 2nd ed. Cf. *bell-bastard*, q.v.

baste. To thrash : from ca. 1530. In C. 16,
coll. ; thereafter, S.E., though far from dignified.

baste-up. A half-wit ; an objectionable fellow :
tailors' : C. 20. E.g. in *The Tailor and Cutter*,
Nov. 29, 1928. Ex tailors' j., wherein it = half-
made.

*Bastile. A workhouse : low (mostly vagrants),
from ca. 1860 ; esp. in the North. H., 3rd ed.
Ex its short-lived S.E. sense (a prison) comes
steel, q.v.—2. Early in C. 19, among criminals,
Bastile was applied as a nickname to Coldbath
Fields Prison, demolished ca. 1890. (Ware.)

basting. A thrashing : in Shakespeare and till
ca. 1660, coll. ; then virtually S.E. Grose records
it as *give* (a person) *his basting(s)*.

bat. A prostitute favouring the night : C. 17–

early 19.—2. Pace : from ca. 1800 ; dial. >, **ca.** 1870, s. Prob. ex dial. *bat*, a stroke.—3. A spoken language (orig. that of India) : military : late C. 19–20. Ex Hindustani for speech, word. Only in *bolo* or *sling* or *spin the bat*, q.v.—4. A batman : military : C. 20 ; but it > gen. military only in G.W.—5. A drinking bout ; esp. *go on the bat*, on the spree : Canadian (ex U.S.) : late C. 19–20.— 6. Price ; *come the bat*, to mention the price : grafters' (— 1934). Philip Allingham. Perhaps ex senses 2 and 3.

bat, carry (out)—occ. **bring out**—**one's.** To outlast others ; finally to succeed : coll. : from ca. 1870. Ex a batsman not out at cricket ; the lit. sense ' goes back to the less luxurious days when the man " out " left the bat for the next comer ', W.

bat, off (rarely **on**) **one's own.** Without assistance ; independently : coll. >, by 1880, S.E. (Sydney Smith, 1845.) Also ex cricket.

bat, sling or **spin the.** See **sling the bat.**

bat and wicket. A ticket : rhyming s. : C. 20. B. & P.

bat-boat. ' An unusual type of Sopwith seaplane ' : naval : 1915–18. Bowen. Cf. *batman*.

*bat-fowl, v.t. and i. To swindle ; victimise the simple or the inexperienced : from ca. 1585. Greene. Very little later were its pure derivatives, *bat-fowler*, a swindler, confidence trickster, and the vbl.n., *bat-fowling*. All † by 1840. Ex the nocturnal catching of birds by dazzling them and then batting them with a stick.

bat-mugger. An instrument for rubbing oil into cricket bats : Winchester College, ca. 1860–1910.

bat out of hell, go like a. To go, esp. fly, extremely fast : Air Force coll. : from 1915. F. & Gibbons.

batch. A dose or bout of liquor : late C. 18– early 19. Grose, 2nd ed. Prob. ex dial. : ? cf. *batch*, a quantity of things (e.g. bottles).

batch, v. See **bach,** v.—**batchelor's fare.** See **bachelor's fare.**

batchy. Silly ; mad : military : late C. 19–20. Lyell. Perhaps ex Hindustani.

bate. See **bait.**

*Bate's Farm or **Garden,** occ. preceded by **Charley.** Coldbath Fields Prison : C. 19 c. Partly ex a warder's name. Whence ?

*Bates' farm, feed the chickens on Charley. To be put to the treadmill : c. of ca. 1860–90. Ex preceding.

Bath, give the Order of the. To duck : from ca. 1890. Punning ; cf. *give the Order of the Boot.*— see **order.**

Bath, go to. To become a beggar : mid-C. 17–19. Bath, being fashionable, attracted many vagrants. As, ca. 1830–1930, an injunction, often with addition of *and get your head shaved* : stop !, go away !, ' dry up, you're cracked ! ' In addition to beggars, Bath drew lunatics, who were ' supposed to benefit from the waters ' of this noted spa (W.).

bath-mat. (Gen. pl.) ' The flooring of wooden battens laid over the mud of trenches ' : military : 1915 ; slightly ob. F. & Gibbons.

bathing machine. A 10-ton brig : sailors', ca. 1850–1900.—2. Whence, a four-wheeled cab : London busmen's : ca. 1890–1915.

Bathing Towel. Lord (earlier, General) Baden-Powell : from ca. 1875. Also, from 1900, *B.P.*

batman. In S.E., a ' muleteer ' of bat-horses ; hence, a cavalry officer's servant. In G.W. it was

applied to any Army officer's servant (the practice has survived) : a coll. that had by 1932 attained unto S.E.—2. A third-term cadet avoiding duty by acting as personal servant to a petty officer : Worcester Training-Ship coll. : C. 20. Bowen. —3. A sycophantic private : military coll. : 1915 ; ob. B. & P.

*batner. See **battener.**

*bats. A pair of bad boots : c. or low s. : ca. 1855–1930. H., 1st ed. ; Manchon.

bats, adj. Very eccentric ; mad, to any degree : C. 20. Ex *bats in the belfry*.

Bats, Captain. George Ransley, notable Kentish smuggler of the 1820's : ca. 1820–40, then historic. Bowen, ' From his readiness to employ batmen, or armed bullies, to protect his runs from the Coast Blockade men '.

bats in the belfry, have. To be very eccentric ; mad, to any degree : late C. 19–20.

batt. A battalion : military coll. : late C. 19–20. B. & P.

batta. See **batty,** n.

*battalion. A gang of criminals : C. 18 c.

[**battels.** Account(s) for provisions : j. ; not s. nor coll. as implied by F. & H.]

*batt(e)ner. An ox : mid-C. 17–18 c. Coles, 1676 ; B.E. Beef tending to *batten* (fatten).

batter. Wear and tear : C. 19–20 coll. ' He can't stand the batter," H., 1864.—2. A variant of *butter*, n., sense 2.—3. See **batters.**

batter, (go) on the. (To walk the streets) as a harlot, to be debauched ; to be on a riotous spree : from late 1830's ; ob. H. Rodger, 1839 (O.E.D.) ; H., 1st ed. ; Whiteing, 1899. Presumably cognate with U.S. *bat* (1848) ; cf. *bait*, q.v.

batter through. To struggle through (e.g. a part) : proletarian : C. 19–20 ; ob. Ware. Abbr. *batter one's way through.*

battered. Given up to debauchery : from ca. 1860 : †. Cf. *go on the batter.*

battered bully. A late C. 17–early 18 term combining two senses of *battered*, thus : ' an old well cudgell'd and bruis'd huffing fellow ', B.E. : low coll.

batterfang, battyfang. (Lit. and fig.) to batter, maul : ca. 1630–1830, then dial. The former was S.E., the latter (C. 18–20) is a sol.

batters. Defective type : printers' : 1880 (O.E.D.) coll. >, by 1910, j. Ex *batter*, ' a bruise on the face of printing type '.

Battersea. See **simples, go to Battersea to be cut for the.**

Battle-Axe Company, the. The ' J ' Coast Battery of the Royal Artillery : military coll. : from 1809, when its predecessors (the 43rd Company, 7th Battalion, R.A.) received, for services at the capture of Martinique, a trophy consisting of a French battle-axe. F. & Gibbons.

battle-bag. A big rigid airship designed to operate with the Fleet : naval : 1915 ; ob. Bowen.

battle-bowler. A steel shrapnel-helmet : military : 1915. F. & Gibbons.

Battle of the Nile. A ' tile ', a hat : rhyming s. (— 1859) ; ob. H., 1st ed. Occ. *battle* (— 1874).

battle-royal. A vehement quarrel, a vigorous fight : from ca. 1690 ; coll. >, by 1840, S.E. Ex medieval jousting between two sides each commanded by a king (S.E.) ; also cock-pit j.

battle the watch. ' To do one's best against difficulty. To depend on one's own exertions ' : nautical coll. : mid-C. 19–20 ; slightly ob. Bowen battledore. See **B from a battledore, not to know.**—Cf. *battledore-boy*, one learning his alphabet : late C. 17–mid-18 : coll. or, rather, S.E. Here, however, *battledore* is abbr. *battledore-book*, a horn-book.

Battling 'Ells (or L's), the. The "L" Class of destroyers : naval coll. : G.W. (F. & Gibbons.)

Battling Third. The 3rd Destroyer Flotilla of the Harwich Force : naval coll. : G.W. F. & Gibbons, 'Noted for its part in the action off Heligoland, in August, 1914 '.

battlings. (Public schools') a weekly allowance of money (— 1864). Either coll. or j. Mostly at Winchester, where used from before 1859 : E.D.D.

*****battner.** See **battener.** (Coles spells it *batner*.)

batty. Wages, perquisites : coll. : orig. (Hook, 1824), *batta*, ex Hindustani ; in India it properly meant (late C. 17–20) subsistence money, extra pay on campaign, then pay for Indian service. Yule & Burnell.

batty, adj. Mad : C. 20, esp. among soldiers. Cf.—perhaps ex—*bats in the belfry*.

batty-fang. To beat : coll. : C. 19–20, ob. Also, in C. 17–19, *batter-fang*. Prob., to hit and bite ; Ware's ' evidently *battre à fin* ' is presumably a joke.

baub. See **bob, s'help me.—baubee.** See **bawbees. —baubles.** See **bawbles.—baudye.** See **bawdy.**

baulk. (Winchester College) a false report : from ca. 1850. Hence *sport a baulk*, to circulate one.—2. (Gen.) a mistake : mid-C. 19–20, ob. A survival of *balk, baulk*, C. 15–18 S.E. for a mistake or blunder.

baulk, give the miss in. See **miss in baulk.**

baulk (balk), at. To avoid : coll. : 1908 (O.E.D. Sup.). Semantics : ' jib at '.

baulk (or balk), in. Checked ; **at a loss** : coll. ; from ca. 1880. Ex billiards.

*****baulker.** Frequently spelt *bawker*, q.v.

' baw-baw ', quoth Bagshaw. You're a liar : semi-proverbial c.p. (— 1570) ; † by 1700. Levins ; Nashe. Ex *baw-baw !*, indicating contempt or derision ; *Bagshaw*, prob. for the jingle. F. & H. revised.

bawbees. Money ; cash. C. 19–20. In singular, coll. for a halfpenny, a ' copper ' : late C. 17–20, as in B.E.

bawbles. (Properly but rarely **baubles.**) Human testicles : late C. 18–early 19. Grose, 3rd. Earlier, e.g. in Shakespeare, *bauble* = the penis ; this is prob. S.E.

bawbard. Larboard : nautical coll. : C. 18–19. A corruption of *larboard* (Bowen) ; prob. influenced by Fr. *babord*.

bawcock. A fine fellow, gen. derisively : Shakespeare's *Henry V* ; † by 1700, though resuscitated by Ainsworth in 1862. Coll. ; ex Fr. *beau coq*.

bawd. A procurer or—as always after 1700—a procuress. In C. 14–16, S.E. ; in C. 17–18, coll. ; in C. 19–20, literary. In C. 18–19 occ. a female brothel-keeper. Prob. abbr. *bawdstrot* (O.E.D.).

bawdy bachelor. A ' confirmed ' bachelor : late C.17–19, low coll. B.E. (But how hard he falls !)

bawdy banquet. Whoremongering : C. 16 ; not recorded before Harman, 1567. ? c.

*****bawdy basket.** In mid-C. 16–17, c. ; in C. 18, ob. s. ; † by 1840. A seller—gen. female—of obscene literature, ballads, pins, tape, but living mostly by theft. Harman, B.E., Grose. Ex the bawdy books carried in the basket.—2. A harlot : this rarer sense (late C. 16–17) is indubitably s.

bawdy-house bottle. A very small one : late C. 17–18 : low coll. B.E., Grose.

*****bawdy-ken.** A brothel : c. or low s. : ca. 1810–60. Bee (at *bodikin*).

bawd(y) physic. A saucy fellow : ca. 1560–90 : c. or low. Awdeley.

*****bawker.** A cheater at bowls : late C. 16–early 17 c. Greene. (= *baulker*.) At least once it is misspelt *banker* (Greene, at beginning of 2nd Cony-Catching).

*****bawl.** ' To suck or swallow ' : East End of London c. (— 1933). George Orwell, *Down and Out*.

bawl out. A C. 20 and perhaps catachrestic variant of *bowl out*, q.v.

Bawra. The British Australian Wool Realisation Association : Australian coll. : from 1922. See the editor's *Australia and New Guinea*, 1937, at ' Commerce ', § 12.

Bay, the. Port Elizabeth : South African coll. : from ca. 1870. Ex *Algoa Bay*, on which the town stands. Pettman.

Bay fever. ' A term of ridicule applied to convicts, who sham illness, to avoid being sent to Botany Bay ', *Lex. Bal.* : coll. : ca. 1810–60. Cf. :

Bay of Condolence. ' Where we console our friends, if plucked, and left at a nonplus ', Egan's Grose, 1823 : Oxford University : ca. 1820–40.

baywindow. A belly protuberant through either pregnancy or obesity : mid-C. 19–20.—2. Hence, and ex the baywindows of clubs : talk imitative of that of clubmen : artisans' (— 1935).

Bayard of ten toes. One's feet. Esp. *ride B. . . . toes*, to walk. Coll. in late C. 16–early 18, then dial. (ob.). Breton, Fuller, Grose. Breton's use in *Good and Bad*, 1616, tends to show that the phrase had been current long before that. Ex *Bayard*, a horse famous in medieval romance. Apperson.

Bays. Shares in the Hudson's Bay Company : Stock Exchange coll. (— 1895). A. J. Wilson, *Stock Exchange Glossary*.

Bays, the. The 2nd Dragoon Guards : military coll. : ' from 1767 when the regiment was first mounted on bay horses ', F. & Gibbons.

Bayswater captain. A sponger : ca. 1879–1910 ; mostly London. Because so many of these club parasites resided in Bayswater, W.2. Cf. *turnpike sailor*.

*****bazaar.** A shop ; a counter : c. : ca. 1830–80. ' Ducange Anglicus.'· Ex (and cf.) S.E. sense ex Hindi—ultimately Persian *bazar*, a market.

bazaar, v.t. To rob ; gen. as *bazaar'd* : Society : 1882–ca. 1915. Ware derives it ex ' the extortion practised by remorseless, smiling English ladies at bazaars '.

bazaar (or B.), in the. In the (money-)market ; to be bought ; procurable : Anglo-Indian coll. of late C. 19–20. Thus, in Richard Blaker, *Here Lies a Most Beautiful Lady*, 1935, an Indian Army officer says, ' Garstein seems to think that Johnnie's oil shares are as good as anything in the Bazaar at the moment.' Ex the importance that the bazaars have in life in India.

Bazaar Motor-Vans. The French village, Autos Bazars : military : G.W. (F. & Gibbons.)

[**bazaar rumour,** doubtful news, is Army coll. (1882 ; † by 1920) that imm. > S.E. ; but perhaps it was always S.E.]

bazooker. A thing, esp. if mechanical (e.g. a motor-car) : low : C. 20. (R. Blaker, *Night-Shift*, 1934.) An artificial word : cf. *ooja-ka-piv*.

be. Am: when not dial., it is sol.: C. 18–20. Dibdin, 'I be one of they sailors' (Baumann).—2. By (prep'n): low coll. verging on sol.: mid-C. 19–20. Ex dial.

be damned. See **damned, be.**

be good! A c.p. 'au revoir': from ca. 1912. B. & P. Often *be good and, if you can't be good, be careful!*

be gorra! See **begorra!—be jabers!** See **jabers!, be.—be there.** See **there, be.—be yourself!** See **yourself!, be.**

beach, be or **go on the.** To be or become a beach-comber: coll.: late C. 19–20. Cf.:

beach, on the. Ashore, whether on leave or having retired from the sea: nautical: mid-C. 19–20. Bowen. Also **be beached**, to be 'put out of employment': naval: late C. 19–20. [F. & Gibbons.

beach-cadger. A beggar favouring seaside resorts: ca. 1860–1910: coll.

beach-comber. A (disreputable) fellow haunting the sea-shore for odd jobs (*Blackwood's Magazine*, 1847). Coll.; from ca. 1870, S.E.; perhaps, as Thornton implies, orig. U.S.—2. A river boatman: nautical: from ca. 1860; ob.—3. A sea-shore thief: ? c.: from ca. 1865.—4. 'A yachting tourist', Ware: nautical: ca. 1890–1915.

beach-men. 'West African surf men and interpreters': nautical coll. verging on S.E.: late C. 19–20. Bowen.

beach-tramper. A coastguardsman: nautical: ca. 1880–1910. Baumann.

bead-counter. A cleric, religious recluse, or worshipper: coll.: C. 19. Malkin, 1809. Ex the use of the rosary in the Roman Catholic communion.

beached, be. See **beach, on the.**

Beachy Bill. A Turkish heavy gun at Gallipoli: military: 1915. B. & P.

*****beadle.** A blue roquelaure; esp. to *fly* or *sport a beadle*, to wear one: c.: ca. 1820–50. Egan's Grose. Prob. because beadles often wore a blue jacket.

[**beagle.** A spy, man-hunter: despite F. & H., it is S.E.]

beagle-ball. (Gen. pl.) A meat rissole served in the Royal Naval College, Dartmouth: there: late C. 19–20. Bowen.

*****beak.** A magistrate: C. 18–20. In C. 16–17, the form was *beck*, the meaning a constable (a sense lingering till ca. 1860); also it was c., as *beak* itself was until ca. 1850, since when the most frequent use has been *up before the beak*, on trial by a magistrate; in the G.W. this phrase = before the orderly officer. See esp. Grose, P.—Hence, 2, in schools (esp. Eton and Marlborough), from ca. 1880, an assistant master.—3. The nose: Thackeray, *The Newcomes*, 1854. (Very much earlier in dial.: see the E.D.D.) See esp. Grose, P.: Manchon, 1923, notes *keep your beak up!*, don't lose heart!: lower classes'. All senses prob. ex Fr. *bec*, a beak.—4. See **beaker.**

*****beak, v.** Late C. 16–early 17 c. as in Rowlands, 1610, 'What maund doe you beake, what kind of begging use you?' (O.E.D.).—2. To bring (a malefactor) before a magistrate: low (— 1887). Baumann, who rightly implies that it is used mostly in the passive. Ex *beak*, n., 1.

beak, strop one's. (Of the male) to coït: low: late C. 19–20; ob.

beak-gander. A judge in the higher courts: from ca. 1870; ob. (*Gander* = old man.)

*****beaker,** occ. abbr. to **beak.** A fowl. C. 19–20 c. as is (— 1839: Brandon) the derivative *beak(er)-hunter*, a poultry-yard thief.

*****beaksman.** A constable: C. 18–19 c. Ex *beak*, 1, q.v. Cf. *beck*.

beam, broad in the. (Of a person) broad-seated: C. 19–20; orig. nautical.

beam-ends. The buttocks: Marryat, 1830; *Cuthbert Bede*, 1853. Cf. next.

beam-ends, on one's. Utterly exhausted: nautical: ca. 1830–80. Marryat.—2. In a difficulty (Dickens, 1844); short of money (H. Mayhew). Coll. Ex a vessel in imminent danger of capsizing.

beamy old buss. Any very broad ship: nautical coll.: mid-C. 19–20. Bowen. Ex the broad herring buss or smack; cf. *broad in the beam*.

bean or **bien.** A guinea coin: prob. c.: ca. 1800–40; a sovereign: low: ca. 1840–1900. (The guinea coin ceased in 1813 to be struck.) In pl., money, esp. cash: from late 1850's. H., 1st ed. ? ex Fr. *bien*, something good.—2. The head: late C. 19–20. Ex shape (very approximate!). Whence:—3. (Gen. *old bean*, q.v.) A man, chap, fellow: C. 20. Manchon.—4. A 'beano' (sense 2): rather rare (— 1923). Manchon.

bean, not have a. Esp. *I haven't a bean*, I'm penniless: late C. 19–20. (C.O.D., 1934 Sup.) Cf.:

bean, not worth a. Of very little value: from C. 13; coll. since ca. 1400.

bean, old. See **old bean.**

bean-belly. A Leicestershire man: mid-C. 17–19. Adumbrated in C. 15. Leicestershire has for centuries produced an abundance of beans.

bean-cod. 'The Iberian type of small craft with sharp lines and a stream raking aft from the waterline': nautical: C. 19–20; virtually †. Bowen. Ex shape.

bean-feast. A jollification: C. 20. Orig. (1806) an annual feast given to workmen by their employers. (Tailors as early as 1890 applied *bean-feast* to any good meal.) Hence *bean-feaster*, ca. 1883–1900, a participator in such an annual feast. —2. The act of kind: low: C. 20; ob.

bean-pole or **-stick.** A tall thin man: coll. (? ex dial.) > almost S.E.: from ca. 1830.

bean-tosser. The penis: low: late C. 19–20; ob.

beaner. A chastisement: proletarian, mostly London (— 1909); ob. Ware. Ex *beans, give*, q.v.

beano. Orig. (— 1898) an annual feast: printers'. —2. From ca. 1897 (see Ware), a jollification. Ex *bean-feast*, perhaps (via lingua franca) influenced by Sp. *bueno* or It. *buono*, good. Cf. *bingo*, q.v.

beanpea. An effeminate youth: ca. 1875–1915. Ware. Ex a case of two youths, *B.* and *P.*, tried by Lord Cockburn (d. 1880).

beans. See **bean.**

beans, abstain from. To take no part in politics: not very gen. (— 1923); ob. Manchon.

beans, full of. Vigorous; energetic; in high spirits: from ca. 1870. H., 5th ed. (at *full of beans*). Cf. *beany*, q.v.

beans, give. To chastise; defeat severely (— 1890). Kipling.—2. *get beans*, be chastised.

beans, like. Excellently; forcibly: from ca 1860; ob.

beans, spill the. See **spill the beans.**

beans make five (white ones), know how many. To be alert : Galt, 1830 ; adumbrated in Shelton's *know how many numbers are five*, 1612. Apperson.

beans in a or **one blue bladder, three blue.** Noisy and empty talk : late C. 16–18. Origin obscure : even Nares failed to discover it.

beany. Vigorous ; spirited : from ca. 1850. Cf. *full of beans* (see **beans**) : beans being great energy-makers.—2. Hence, in good humour : from ca. 1860.

bear. At first (ca. 1700), stock sold in the hope of a fall : either S.E. or j. Then (− 1744) the speculator for a fall, as in Foote, Colman, Scott ; the term > coll. only ca. 1900, Peacock having, in 1860, written : ' In Stock Exchange slang, bulls are speculators for a rise, bears for a fall.' See the chapter on commercial slang in my *Slang*. The orig. phrase was prob. *sell the bear-skin*, such bargainers being called *bear-skin jobbers*, in reference to the proverb, ' to sell the bear's skin before one has caught the bear'. Hence, *sell a bear*, to sell what one does not possess : C. 18 coll.—2. The pupil of a private tutor : late C. 18–mid-C. 19. See **bear-leader.**—Also, 3, a very gruff person : C. 18–20 coll. Notably used by Lord Chesterfield. —4. ' A matted stone or shot, or a coir mat filled with sand, dragged over the deck to clean it after the fashion of a holystone ' (Bowen) : nautical coll. : mid-C. 19–20 ; ob. Ex ob. S.E. *bear* (*bere*), a pillow-case.

bear, v.i. To speculate for a fall in prices : Stock Exchange, from ca. 1840, as is the v.t. sense, to effect or manœuvre a fall in the price of (a stock or commodity). This term > j., and by 1930 it was considered S.E.

bear, play the. To behave rudely and roughly : late C. 16–17 : coll. >, by 1600, S.E.

bear a bob. To lend a hand : nautical and gen. : C. 19–20 ; ob. Imperative : look alive ! : nautical, C. 19–20.

bear-garden discourse (or language) or **jaw.** ' Rude, vulgar language ', Grose, 1st ed. : late C. 17–early 19. With *discourse* or *language*, coll. ; with *jaw*, s. Ray, 1678, has ' He speaks Beargarden '. Apperson.

bear, it would bite or **have bit you, if it were or had been a.** A semi-proverbial c.p. applied, as B.E. phrases it, to ' him that makes a close search after what lies just under his Nose ' : C. 17–18. Draxe, 1633 ; Swift. (Apperson.)

Bear-Leader, the. Boswell (1740–95), because he ' led ' Johnson (*Ursa Major*) : late C. 18.—2. Wm. Gifford, the ' *bearish* ' critic (1757–1826) : early C. 19. (Dawson.)

bear-leader. A travelling tutor in the days of the Grand Tour : Walpole, 1749 ; Thackeray, 1848 ; H., 1874. Coll. in C. 19 ; † by 1880. He licks ' cubs ' into shape : W.

bear one's blushing honours . . . See **thick upon one.**

bear-pits, the. The empty and barred yards outside the ' zeros ' [w.c.'s] : Bootham School : C. 20. Anon., *Dict. of Bootham Slang*, 1925.

bear-play. Rough and noisy behaviour : apparently not recorded before 1883. Coll., soon S.E.

bear-up. The act of pursuing a woman : coll. : U.S. >, by 1900, Australian ; rare. H. Lawson (O.E.D. Sup.).

bear to the stake, go like a. To ' hang an Arse ', B.E. : coll. : C. 15–early 19. Lydgate, ca. 1430 ; Florio ; Defoe ; Scott. (Apperson.)

bear up, v. To support in a swindle (− 1828) ; ob. by 1900. Hence *bearer-up*, such a supporter.—Hence, 2, v.i., to ' log-roll ' : 1883, *The Referee*, Dec. 2.—3. Have courage : coll., C. 17 ; S.E. thereafter, though the imperative, *bear up !*, has a coll. tang.

bear with, play the. To play the deuce with : dial. (− 1881) >, by 1889, coll. ; ob. O.E.D. (Sup.).

beard, make a man's. To outwit or trick him : coll. : C. 15–16.

beard, to one's. To a person's face ; frankly ; openly : coll. (in C. 20 S.E. and archaic) ; from ca. 1780.

beard-splitter. A frequenter of prostitutes, an enjoyer of women : late C. 17–early 18 ; B.E. and Grose. Cf. U.S. low s. or c. *beard-jammer*.—2. Also, the penis : C. 18–19.

bearded cad. A College porter conveying luggage from station to school : Winchester College, ca. 1850–1910.

beard without a razor, make a man's. To behead : coll. : ca. 1520–1700.

beardie, -y (or **B.**). A Christian Israelite : a Victorian (Australia) nickname : 1875. O.E.D. (Sup.). A sect that let its hair grow.

beärgered. Drunk : low coll. (− 1859) ; ob. by 1910. H., 1st ed. ; Ware.

bearing, vbl.n. Acting as a speculating ' bear ' : from ca. 1860, Stock Exchange.

bearings, bring one to one's. To cause to see reason : late C. 18–20 coll., orig. (− 1785) nautical, as Grose, 1st ed., indicates.

bearish. Indicative of, natural to, or tending to, a fall in prices : Stock Exchange ; from ca. 1880.

bears ?, are you there with your. There you are again ! ; so soon ? James Howell, 1642 ; Richardson, 1740 ; Scott, 1820. †.

bear's paw. A saw : rhyming s., mostly workmen's : late C. 19–20. *John o' London's Weekly*, June 9, 1934.

bearskin-jobber. A seller of ' bear ' stock (− 1726) ; money market ; ob. by 1750. See **bear.**

beast. Anything naturally unpleasant or momentarily displeasing, as *a beast of a day* (Baumann, 1887) : coll. : from ca. 1860.—2. A youth that, having left school, goes to Cambridge to study before entering the University : Cambridge University ; from ca. 1820 ; very ob.—3. A bicycle : youths' : ca. 1870–90. Ware.

beast, drink like a. To drink only when thirsty : late C. 18–19. Grose, 2nd ed. Contrast S.E. *drink like a fish.*

beast with two backs. ' A man and woman in the act of copulation ', Grose ; gen. with *make* (*the*), as in Shakespeare's *Othello*. † by 1830 and prob. never gen. s.

beastie. A coll. and endearing form, orig. Scottish, of *beast* : gen. only since ca. 1890.

beastly. Unpleasant ; bad (however slightly) : coll. ; in C. 20, the adj. verges on S.E., while the adv. has definitely remained coll. Cf. *awful, terrible.* From ca. 1850, as is the adv., which = very. Anstey, 1882, has *feeling beastly* ; *The Daily Telegraph*, 1865, ' he was in good health . . . looked almost " beastly well " ' : but adumbrations appear in Barclay, 1509, Dekker in 1611, in Johnson, 1778, and in Dickens, 1844.

beasty. See **bheestie.**

beat. A normal round (as of prostitute or policeman) : G. A. Stevens, 1788 ; sphere of influence :

The Saturday Review, 1862. In both senses, coll. for some forty years, then S.E. but not literary. —2. Hence, one's 'lady friend': naval seamen's: late C. 19–20. Bowen.—3. A newspaper 'scoop': journalistic: from ca. 1925. (Richard Keverne, *The Man in the Red Hat*, 1930.)

beat. Exhausted: from ca. 1830. Often *dead beat.*—2. Baffled, defeated: coll.: from ca. 1840.

beat, get a. (Constructed with *on*.) To obtain an advantage (over): from ca. 1850; ob. In c., the term implies secret, shady, or illicit means.

beat, have (a person). To be superior to, to have the better of: from ca. 1910.

beat, off the. Out of the usual routine: Australian coll. (— 1916). C. J. Dennis. See **beat, n.**

beat a carpet, couldn't. Ineffective; weak; or of a very 'poor' boxer: late C. 19–20; coll.

beat daddy-mammy. To practise the elements of drum-beating: C. 18 military.

beat goose or (nautical) **the booby.** To strike the hands across the chest and under the armpits to warm one's chilled fingers: coll.: from ca. 1880. (O.E.D.) Earlier, *cuff* or *beat Jonas*. Jocularly varying *beat oneself*.

beat it. (Of criminals) to run away: mostly New Zealand: C. 20. Ex U.S. coll. *beat it* (to depart). Cf. the coll. *beat the hoof* of C. 17–18.

beat it ? !, can you. Well, I'm dashed ! damned ! etc. Coll.: C. 20.

beat it while the beating's or **going's good.** To depart at ease or without trouble: C. 20 coll.: ? ex U.S.

beat one's way through the world. To push oneself ahead: from ca. 1860: coll.

beat the band. To be remarkable, superior, startling: C. 20. Esp., *That beats the band.*—2. Whence, *to beat the band*, greatly, excessively, utterly, as in the Tommies' translation of the Hymn of Hate: ''Ate of the 'art and 'ate of the 'and,|'Ate by water and 'ate by land,|'Oo do we 'ate to beat the band ?|England !' (W.). Cf. the prototype, *to bang banagher* (see **banagher**).

beat the hoof. To walk: late C. 17–18. In Anthony Wood's *Athenæ Oxonienses*, 1691.

beat the road. To travel by rail without paying: low, mostly U.S. (— 1890).

beat the streets. To walk up and down: C. 19–20: coll. till ca. 1890, then S.E.

beat up the quarters of. To visit unexpectedly, very informally: coll.: 1741, Richardson (O.E.D.); Ware (the shorter form). From ca. 1891, gen. just *beat up*. Ex S.E. sense, 'to disturb'.

beaten out. Impoverished: in very severe straits: H. Mayhew, 1851; coll.; ob.

beater. The decoy in a swindle: c. of ca. 1585–1620. Greene. Ex fowling.—2. A foot: low: late C. 19–20; ob. Manchon. Cf. :

beater-cases. Boots: in late C. 18–early 19, c.; then low s. Nearly † in 1859, quite † by 1890. Grose, 2nd ed. Succeeded, in mid-C. 19, by *trotter-cases.*

beating the bush. The inveigling of a prospective victim: c. of ca. 1585–95. Greene.

beau-catcher. See **bow-catcher.**

beau-nasty. 'One finely dressed, but dirty', Grose, 2nd ed.: late C. 18–early 19.

beau-trap. A sharper, neatly dressed: late C. 17–18. B.E.—2. A loose pavement-stone, over-lying water: late C. 18–early 19. Grose.—3. A fop outwardly well dressed but of unclean linen, body, habits: late C. 18–early 19.

beaucoup ; often spelt **bokoo.** Plenty of; many: military: late 1914–18, then as survival. E.g. *beaucoup beer* or *cigarettes*. Direct ex Fr. (B. & P.)

beaut. (Rarely of persons.) A 'beauty': non-aristocratic: C. 20. Ex U.S.

beautiful. An adj. applied coll. by a person to anything that he likes very much: mid-C. 19–20. Cf. *sweet.*

beautify. To beatify: catachrestic: C. 17–20; rare after 1800. (O.E.D.)

beauty, be a. Gen. *he's a beauty !, you're a beauty*, i.e. a person very clumsy or not to be trusted or relied on: coll.: from ca. 1880. Baumann. Ex ironic use of lit. sense.

beauty, it was a great. It was a fine sight: coll.: ca. 1520–1600. Berners, 1523 (O.E.D.) Cf. :

beauty of it, that's—occ. **that was—the.** That is the feature affording the greatest pleasure or keenest satisfaction: coll.: 1754, Richardson, 'That's the beauty of it ; to offend and make up at pleasure', O.E.D.

beauty sleep. Sleep before midnight, supposedly conducive to good looks and health : Frank Smedley's first notable novel, *Frank Fairleigh*, 1850 : coll. >, by 1910, S.E.

beaver. In the sense of hat, always—despite F. & H.—S.E.—2. As a beard, hence a bearded man, decidedly s.: a passing term and pastime of the middle 1920's. Collinson.—3. Hence, a no-score at skittles: from ca. 1926; ob. 'When the nought is chalked up, people sometimes draw a face in the circle and attach a beard or " beaver " to it,' Brian Frith in a letter to myself, Feb. 24, 1935.— 4. As 'snack', see **bever.**—5. A warning: military: from ca. 1910. B. & P.

beaver, cock one's. To assume a swaggering air: C. 17, as in that strange Cambridge Platonist, Henry More, in 1642. Coll.

beaver, in. In tall hat and non-academical attire: ca. 1820–60: university.

beaver-tail. 'A feminine mode of wearing the back-hair . . . loose in a . . . net . . . which fell . . . on to the shoulders.' Ex resemblance to 'a beaver's flat and comparatively shapeless tail', Ware, who classifies it as middle-class of ca. 1860–70.

bebee ; beebee. A lady: Anglo-Indian coll. (— 1864). H., 3rd ed. By 1886 (Yule & Burnell), no longer applied to ladies: in fact, in late C. 19–20 military, it = a bed-mate (Manchon). Ex Hindustani *bibi*, a lady.

becalmed, the sail sticks to the mast,—I am. 'My shirt sticks to my back,' Grose, 1st ed., adding: 'A piece of sea wit sported in hot weather': a nautical c.p. of mid-C. 18–mid-19.

beck. A constable; a beadle: c.: mid-C. 16–17. Harman. See **beak, 1.**

beck, v. To imprison: (? C. 18–)C. 19 c.; rare. Reade in his greatest novel, 1861.

beckets !, hands out. Hands out of your pockets !: nautical: C. 19–20; ob. Bowen. A becket is a nautical loop or bracket.

Becky. Mary Wells, actress (fl. 1780–1810) Ex her part in O'Keeffe's comedy, *The Agreeable Surprise.* (Dawson.)

become to be + p.ppl. To become: catachrestic: C. 20. E.g. ' He became to be known as a most reliable person.' By confusion of *become* (e.g. known) and *come to be* (e.g. known).

[**becos** is a foolish spelling employed by those who

think it represents a sol. : *becos* is a S.E. pronunciation ; one of two that are recognised to be equally
correct. In short, it rivals *offen* in ineptitude.]

bed, get up on the wrong side of the. See **wrong
side.**—**bed, more belongs to marriage than . . .** See
legs in a bed.

bed, go up a ladder to. To be hanged : mid-
C. 18–early 19 : low s. verging on c. ' In many
country places ', says Grose, 1st ed., ' persons
hanged are made to mount up a ladder, which is
afterwards turned round or taken away ; whence
the term, " turned off ".'

[**bed-bug.** The entry in the first edition was
based on my foolish misapprehension of two passages in James Curtis's *The Gilt Kid*, 1936.]

bed of guns. A ship over-gunned : jocular
naval coll. : C. 19–20 ; ob. Bowen.

bed one has made, lie or **sleep in the.** To abide
(patiently) by one's actions : from ca. 1850 ; coll. >
proverbial >, by 1850, S.E. Hanway, 1753
(O.E.D.). By fig. extension of *make a bed*, to put it
in order.

bed with a mattock, put to, often amplified with
and tucked up with a spade. Dead and buried :
C. 18–early 19. From ca. 1830, the form was gen.
put to bed with a pickaxe and shovel, while C. 19–20
dial. prefers *put to bed with a shovel.*

bed-fag(g)ot. A hussy ; a harlot : coll. : C. 19–
20 ; ob. (Not a Society term.) H., 3rd ed. Ex
fagot as part of firewood. Cf. *warming-pan,* q.v.
But *bed-sister, -piece,* and *-presser* may be S.E.

bed-house. A house of assignation where beds
may be had for any period desired : C. 19 coll.

bed in one's boots, go to. To be very drunk : low
coll. : late C. 19–20.

bed-post, between you and me and the. Between
ourselves : coll. : 1830 (O.E.D. Sup.) ; Bulwer
Lytton, 1832. Variants with *post,* as in Dickens,
1838—*door-post,* from ca. 1860—*gate-post,* id.,—
gate, C. 20.

bed-post or **-staff, in the twinkling of a.** Immediately : resp. from ca. 1830 (ob.), and ca. 1670–
1850 (Shadwell, 1676). Prob. ex its well-known use
as a ready and handy weapon : O.E.D.

bed-presser. See **bed-fag(g)ot.**—2. A dull, heavy
fellow : coll. : late C. 19–20 ; ob.

bed-sitter. A bed-sitting room : s. (from ca.
1890) >, ca. 1930, coll. Collinson. Oxford *-er.*

bed-staff, in the twinkling of a. See **bed-post,
in . . .**

bed-work. Lit., work that can be done in bed ;
hence, very easy work : coll. : late C. 16–18.
Shakespeare, in *Troilus and Cressida.*

bedad ! An Anglo-Irish coll. asseveration : 1710,
Swift ; 1848, Thackeray, ' " Bedad it's him," said
Mrs. O'Dowd,' O.E.D Lit., *by dad* or (cf. *begad,*
q.v.) *by God.*

bedaubed all over with lace. A ' vulgar saying of
any one dressed in clothes richly laced ', Grose,
1st ed. : mid-C. 18–mid-19.

bedder. A college servant : Cambridge University ; from ca. 1870.—2. A bed-room : Oxford
University (1897) ; ob. O.E.D. (Sup.). Cf. *bed-
sitter,* q.v. Also, in C.20, at certain Public Schools :
witness Desmond Coke, *The House Prefect,* 1908.

Bedford go. A rich chuckle : taverns' : ca.
1835–60. Ex Paul Bedford, the actor. Ware.

Bedfordshire. Bed : C. 17–20, ob. ; coll.
Middleton, 1608, ' You come rather out of Bedford-
shire ; we cannot lie quiet in our beds for you ' ;
Cotton ; Swift ; Hood E. V. Lucas, 1927.

(Apperson.) Cf. *blanket fair, cloth market, land of
nod, sheet alley.* These simple witticisms (cf. *Gutter
Lane*) are mostly old.

Bedlam, like. Confused, noisy, unreasonable, all
to a ' mad ' extent : coll. ; late C. 18–20. Ex the
famous London lunatic asylum.

*****bee, put on the ;** v.t., **put the bee on.** To ask for
a loan or a gift of money : c. : from ca. 1930.
James Curtis, *The Gilt Kid,* 1936. For semantics,
cf. the corresponding v., *sting.*

bee aitch. See **b.h.**

bee fool. A b— fool (see **b.f.**) : 1926, Galsworthy, *The Silver Spoon.*

bee in a treacle-pot. See **busy as . . .**

bee in one's or **the head** or **bonnet, have a.** To
have queer ideas, be eccentric : C. 17–20 ; adumbrated in 1553 (Apperson) ; ob. Have an obsession : C. 20. A variant : *one's head is full of bees,*
C. 16–20 : this, however, also = one is (very)
' anxious ' or ' restless ' (Heywood ; Franklin, 1745) ;
† by 1900. Apperson.

bee-line, make or **take a.** To go direct : coll. ;
orig. (— 1830) U.S. ; anglicised ca. 1870 ; in C. 20,
S.E.

beebee. See **bebee.**

*****Beecham's (pills).** Bills, placards, etc., showing
that one is an ex-soldier : tramps' c. (— 1935).
Rhyming s. on *bills.*

beef. Human flesh, as in *put on beef,* put on
weight : from ca. 1860. Coll.—2. Hence, in
pejorative address, e.g. *you great beef, you !* : coll. :
late C. 19–20 ; ob.—3. Strength ; effort : nautical
(— 1863) : whence *beef up !,* try harder,—also coll.
—4. The male member : C. 19–20 ; ob.—5. Cat's
meat : Clare Market, London : ca. 1870–1900.
Ware.—6. A shout ; a yell : theatrical : from ca.
1880 ; ob. Ware suggests, as genesis : *bull—
bellow—beef.* Cf., however, *beef !,* q.v.—7. See **beefs.**

beef, v.t. To shout, yell : theatrical : from ca.
1880 ; ob. Ware. Cf. *beef,* n., 6, and *beef !*—2.
Hence, v.i., to ' grouse ' : military : C. 20. Manchon.—3. V.t. To hit, punch : low : C. 20.
(A. Hyder, *Black Girl, White Lady,* 1934).—4. See
beef it.

beef ! Stop thief : c. >, by 1870, low s. : ca.
1810–1910. Vaux, 1812. (See esp. Grose, P.)

beef, be dressed like Christmas. Dressed in one's
best : from ca. 1870 ; ob. Ex a butcher's shop on
Christmas Eve.

beef, be in a man's. To wound him with a
sword : late C. 18–early 19. Grose, 1st ed. Cf. :

beef, be in a woman's. To have intercourse with
a woman : late C. 18–mid-19 (Grose, 2nd ed.).
Contrast preceding entry and cf. *do* or *have a bit
of beef, take in beef,* low for women *in coïtu* : C.
19–20.

*****beef** or **hot beef, cry** or **give.** To set up a hue and
cry : c. : C. 18–20, ob. Grose, 1st ed. Occ.
whiddle beef.

beef, dressed like Christmas. Clad in one's best :
proletarian : from ca. 1860.

*****beef, make.** To decamp : C. 19 c. Cf. *ampu-
tate,* q.v., and *beef, cry.*

beef !, more. Work harder : nautical coll. : mid-
C. 19–20. Cf. *beef up !*

beef, take in. See **beef, be in a woman's.**

*****beef, whiddle.** See **beef, cry.**

beef a bravo. To lead the applause : music-
halls' : from ca. 1880 ; ob. Ware. Ex *beef,* v. : q.v.

beef à-la-mode. Stewed beef : commercial London (— 1909) ; ob. by 1915, † by 1920. Ware.

beef-boat. See **beef-trip**.

beef-brained. Dull-witted : **C. 17**, coll. Feltham, 1627. Cf. *beef-witted*.

beef-head. A blockhead : coll., C. 18–early 19. Unrecorded before 1775. Whence *beef-headed* (– 1864) : H., 3rd ed.

beef-heart. (Gen. pl.) A bean : low : late C. 19–20. B. & P. Rhyming on *fart* : ex the effect of (peas and) beans.

beef into it, put some. (Gen., imperative.) To try or work hard : coll. : C. 20. Cf. *more beef !* and *beef up !*, q.v.

beef (it), v. To eat heartily : C. 19 coll. ; orig. dial., then East End Cockney.

beef it out. To declaim vociferously : Australian (– 1916). C. J. Dennis.

beef one's way (through). To force one's way (through) : Rugby football coll. : C. 20.

beef-stick. The bone in a joint of beef : military : ca. 1870–1910.

beef-trip ; beef-boat. ' The service of supplying the Fleet with food ' ; the ships therein engaged : naval coll. : G.W. Bowen.

beef to the heels (or, in C. 20, **knees**), **like a Mullingar heifer.** (Of a man) stalwart, (of a woman) ' fine ' : mostly Anglo-Irish : mid-C. 19–20.

beef-tugging. ' Eating cook-shop meat, not too tender, at lunch-time ', Ware : City, of London, mostly clerks' (– 1909) ; ob.

beef up. See **beef**, n., 3.

beef up ! Pull especially hard !, ' put some beef into it ' : nautical (– 1903).

beef-witted. Doltish : coll. verging on S.E. : late C. 16–20 ; ob. (Cf. *beef-brained*.) As in Shakespeare's *Troilus and Cressida*. Whence *beef-wittedness* (– 1863).

Beefeaters. The Yeomen of the Guard : from ca. 1670. Also of the Warders of the Tower of London : C. 18–20. Coll. ex S.E. *beef-eater*, a well-fed servant.

beefiness. Solid physique : coll., orig. (– 1859) at Oxford.

*beefment, on the. On the alert : c. (– 1903). F. & H. Cf. *beef !*, q.v.

beefs. Ordinary Shares in the Eastman Company : Stock Exchange (– 1895). A. J. Wilson, *Stock Exchange Glossary*.

beefy. Thick, esp. of hands or ankles (– 1859) ; obese, fleshy (– 1860) ; stolid (1859) : coll., all three senses.—2. Lucky (– 1874). H., 5th ed.

Beelzebub's Paradise. Hell : C. 19–20 literary coll. ; ob. Ex St. Matthew x. 25 and xii. 27 (F. & H.). Heywood, in his *Proverbs*, 1546, had used *Beelzebub's bower*.

been. Sol. for *has* (or *have*) *been* ; *was*, *were* ; *went*. C. 17–20.—2. See **bene**.

been and (done). A tautological elaboration, indicative of surprise or annoyance, of the second participle : illiterate coll. : 1837, Dickens, ' See what you've been and done,' O.E.D. Cf. :

been and gone and done it, I (etc. **have** or **he** (etc.) **has.** A jocularly coll. emphasised form of *I have* (etc.) *done it*, with esp. reference to marriage. C. 20. Ware. Ex illiterate speech (*gorn and done it* or as in preceding entry) : cf. P. G. Wodehouse, *Tales of St. Austin's*, 1903, ' Captain Kettle had, in the expressive language of the man in the street, been and gone and done it.' This elaboration is peculiarly reminiscent of *veni, vidi, vici*, which is a rhetorical amplification of *vici*.

been in the sun. Drunk. Variant *been standing too long in the sun* ; cf. *have the sun in one's eyes*, be tipsy. Of these the first is C. 18–20 and recorded in Grose, the other two are C. 19–20.

been there. (Of women) having sexual experience : C. 19–20. (Of men) experienced ; shrewd : anglicised ca. 1900 ex (– 1888) U.S. Both senses are coll., and rare except when preceded by *has* or *have*.

*beenship. See **beneship**.

Beer. See **Ack**.—2. See :

Beer. Burton-on-Trent : railwaymen's : from ca. 1920. *The Daily Herald*, Aug. 5, 1936. So much beer is brewed there.

beer, v. To drink beer ; to become intoxicated : coll. ; ca. 1780–1850, as in *Peter Pindar*.

beer, do a. To take a drink of beer : coll. (– 1880). See **do a beer, a bitter**.

beer, in. Drunk : C. 19–20. A coll. that, ca. 1880, > S.E. Cf. *in liquor*.

beer, on the. On a bout of drinking : lower-class coll. (– 1909). Ware. More gen., *on the booze*.

beer, small, n. and adj. (Something) unimportant, trifling : C. 17–20, coll. Shakespeare in *Othello* : ' To suckle fools, and chronicle small beer '. Hence *think no small beer of oneself*, have a good opinion of oneself, as in De Quincey (? earliest record), 1840.

Beer and Bible Association. Licensed victuallers' leaders (' many of whom were strong High Churchmen ', Dawson) and Conservatives leagued to resist a measure introduced by moderate Liberals in 1873. *The Morning Advertiser*, earlier known as *The Gin and Gospel Gazette* (it artfully backed beer as well as the Bible), was thereupon called *The Beer and Bible Gazette*. The *B. and B.* terms were ob. by 1882.

beer and skittles, not all. Not wholly pleasant : coll. from ca. 1860 ; by 1930 almost S.E.

beer-barrel. The human body : C. 19–20, coll. ; ob. Cf. *bacon* and :

beer-bottle. ' A stout, red-faced man ' : London streets' (– 1909) ; ob. Ware.

beer-drink. A gathering of aborigines to drink ' Kaffir beer ' : South African coll. : from the 1890's. Pettman.

beer-eater. A mighty drinker of beer : 1887, *The Referee*, Aug. 21 ; ob., except in the Army. Ware.

beer o(h). A c.p. cry among artisans exacting a fine for some breach or omission : ca. 1850–1900. Ware.

beer-slinger. A drinker, esp. if frequent, of beer : from ca. 1870.

Beer Street (or **beer street**). The throat : low (– 1909) ; ob. Cf. *Gutter Lane*.

beerage. See **beerocracy**. (Ca. 1880–1900.)

beeriness. Near-intoxication : coll. from ca. 1865. Ex S.E. *beery* (1859 : H., 1st ed.).

beerocracy. Brewers and publicans : coined in either 1880 or 1881. This might be described as pedantic coll. ; the likewise coll. *beerage*, which, esp. as *beerage and peerage*, was much neater and much more viable, had app. > † by 1909 if not, indeed, by 1900 (Ware's testimony being ambiguous).

beery buff. A fool : rhyming s. on *muff* : C. 20.

Bees (the B.). The Brentford ' soccer ' team : sporting : C. 20.—2. **bees.** See **be in** . . .

bees and honey. Money : rhyming s. : from not later than 1892. E.D.D.

bees, his head is full of. To be very anxious, fanciful, restless : coll. : ca. 1540–1850. Apperson.

bee's knee, not as big as a. Very small ; gen.

applied to a tiny piece of anything : late C. 18–20 : coll. (ob.) and dial. verging on S.E. Locker-Lampson, 1896. Apperson.

bee's knees, the. The acme of perfection, beauty, attractiveness, skill, desirability, etc. : from ca. 1930. Only this year (1936) I heard a girl described as ' a screamer, a smasher, a—oh ! the bee's knees '. Cf. *the cat's pyjamas*.

*****bees-wax.** Soft, inferior cheese : c. or low s. : Moncrieff, in *Tom and Jerry*, 1821 ; ob.—2. Whence (?), a bore : gen. as *old bees-wax* : ca. 1850–1900.

bees-waxers. Football-boots : Winchester College, from ca. 1840.

bees-wing, old. A nickname for a genial drinker : from ca. 1870 ; gen. in address. Ex the film in long-kept port wine.

beestie. See **bheestie.**

beetle, as deaf or **dull** or **dumb as a.** Extremely deaf, dull, or dumb : coll. verging on S.E. : resp. C. 18–19, C. 16–17, and C. 17–18. This may refer to the implement, not the insect.

beetle-case. A large boot or shoe : ca. 1850–1900.

beetle-crusher. A large, esp. if flat, foot : from ca. 1840 and popularised by Leech in *Punch*. In this sense, no longer gen. after 1880, *beetle-squasher* was an occ. variant.—2. A large boot or shoe (– 1869) : in G.W. an Army boot. ' The bluejacket's name for a Marine's boots, never his own ', Bowen.—3. (Military) an infantryman : from ca. 1885 ; cf. the more usual *mud-crusher*.

beetle-crushing. Solid of tread : coll., from ca. 1870. Anon., *Anteros*, 1871.

beetle off. To fly straight in departure : Air Force : 1915. F. & Gibbons, ' As a beetle flies '. Since the War, *beetle about*, to wander about actively, as frequently in John Brandon's *The One-Minute Murder*, 1934, and *beetle off*, to depart, as in Denis Mackail's *Summer Leaves*, 1934.

beetle-squasher. See **beetle-crusher.**

beetle-sticker. An entomologist : from ca. 1870 ; perhaps coll. rather than s., H., 5th ed.

beetles. Colorado mine stocks : Stock Exchange (– 1887).

beetle's (or beetles') blood. Stout (the drink) : Anglo-Irish (– 1935). Ex the colour and the consistency.

beetroot mug. A red face : London streets' : ca. 1870–1915. Prob. coined by Charles Ross, that creator of Ally Sloper, who was ' a humorist of the more popular kind ' (Ware).

beezer. A nose : from late 1920's ; ? orig. U.S. C.O.D., 1934 Sup. Perhaps ex *boco* + *sneezer*.

before for **until** is catachrestic : throughout Mod. E.

before the wind. Well-placed, prospering, fortunate : coll. : from ca. 1840 ; orig. nautical.

before you bought your shovel ! A tailors' c.p. implying that something has been done, or thought of, before : C. 20. Cf. :

before you came (or **come**) **up !** See **came up** . . . Elaborations were '*fore you listed, before you had a regimental number* or *your number was dry* (or *up*) or *you knew what a button-stick was* or *you was breeched* or *you nipped*, also *before your bollocks dropped* or *you lost the cradle-marks off your arse* ; or *when your mother was cutting bread on you* or *while you were clapping your hands at Charlie* (Chaplin) or *when you were off to school* (with tags) ; or *I was cutting barbed wire while you was* or *were cutting your teeth*. B. & P. The prototype is the proverbial saying (Fuller,

1732), *your mamma's milk is scarce out of your nose yet* : Apperson. There is also a Shakespearian anticipation : see at *nails on one's toes*.

beforehand with the world. Having a reserve of money : from ca. 1640 ; coll. ; in C. 19 S.E. ; C. 20, archaic.

beg (a person) **for a fool, an idiot** or **an innocent.** To consider, set down as a fool ; from ca. 1580 : coll. >, ca. 1700, S.E. ; in C. 19–20, archaic. (O.E.D.)

begad ! An exclamation, gen. in support : coll. : 1742, Fielding (O.E.D.). Ex *by God !*

begarra ! An occ. variant of *begorra(h) !*, q.v.

beggar. A euphemism for *bugger* : whether n. or v. E.g. in *I'll be beggared if . . . !*, I swear I won't . . . : C. 19–20.—2. (N. only.) Playfully coll. : from ca. 1830 ; cf. *scamp*.—3. A man, chap, fellow : from ca. 1850.

beggar boy's ass. Bass (the drink) : rhyming s. : late C. 19–20. P. P., *Rhyming Slang*, 1932. Often abbr. to *beggar boy's*. (There is a curious connexion between P.P.'s volume of rhyming s. and that dict. which had been published only the year before : J. Phillips's *Dict. of Rhyming Slang*.)

beggar on the gentleman, put the. To drink beer after spirits : mid-C. 19–20, ob. H., 5th ed. A variant of *churl (up)on the gentleman*.

beggar-maker. A publican : late C. 18–early 19, coll. Grose, 1st ed., where also *beggar-makers*, an ale-house : an entry that should, I think, read *beggar-maker*, etc., for the singular is all that is necessary.

beggared if. See **beggar, 1.**

beggarly. Mere : coll. ; C. 19–20. E.g. ' He gave the rescuer a beggarly fiver.'

beggars. Cards of denomination 2 to 10 : coll., C. 19–20 ; ob.

beggar's benison. ' May your prick and (your) purse never fail you ' : low : C. 18–early 19. Grose, 1st ed. Cf. *best in Christendom, both ends of the busk*, and *the sailor's farewell*, qq.v.

beggars' bolts or **bullets.** Stones : coll., resp. late C. 16–17, late C. 18–early 19 (as in Grose, 1st ed.).

beggar's brown. Scotch snuff : coll. : C. 19–20 ; ob. Orig. and mainly Scottish. It is light brown in colour.

beggar's bush, go (home) by. To be ruined : late C. 16–19 ; in 1564, Bullein has a rare variant, thus : ' In the ende thei go home . . . by weepyng cross, by beggers barne, and by knave's acre,' Apperson. Beggars have always, in summer, slept under trees and bushes ; in winter, if possible, they naturally seek a barn.

beggar's plush. Corduroy or perhaps cotton velvet : late C. 17–18 coll. *The London Gazette*, 1688.

beggar's velvet. Downy matter accumulating under furniture : C. 19–20, ob. ; coll. Cf. *sluts' wool*.

begin to, not to. ' Not to (do something) ' emphasised ; to be in no way ; fall short of being or doing : coll. : U.S. (1842 : Thornton), anglicised ca. 1860. E.g. an ill-disposed person might say, ' This does not begin to be a dictionary.'

begin (up)on. To attack, either physically or verbally : coll. : ca. 1825, Mrs. Sherwood, ' All the company began upon her, and bade her mind her own affairs.'

begorra(h) ! By God : Anglo-Irish coll. : C. 19–20. By corruption. Cf. *be jabers !*

[**begun** (in the preterite). Began : sol., in gen. opinion. This *begun*, though objectionable, **is not strictly incorrect.**]

behalf of, on. In behalf of, i.e. in the interest of : catachrestic : late C. 18–20. As the O.E.D. remarks, ' to the loss of an important distinction ' ; see also Fowler.

behave oneself. To behave with propriety : coll. : mid-C. 19–20. (O.E.D.)

Behemoths, the. The 3rd Battle Squadron of the Grand Fleet : naval coll. : 1914–18. F. & Gibbons. Orig. it comprised eight battleships of the King Edward VII Class. Cf. *Wobbly Eight.*

behind. The posterior ; the rear part of a garment. The first record is of 1786. The O.E.D. and the S.O.D. designate it as coll. and low : in 1933, however, was it not on the borderline between coll. and S.E., and nearer the latter ? Certainly it was no longer low : it lost that stigma ca. 1930. See *Slang.*—2. At Eton and Winchester Colleges, ca. 1850–1914, a back at ' soccer ' : coll. > j.

behind chests. ' Dark nooks on the orlop deck ' : *The Conway* : from ca. 1875. Masefield's history of that training-ship.

behind oneself, be. To be late, a long way behind, far from ' up to the minute ' : non-aristocratic coll. : 1896 ; slightly ob. Ware.

behindativeness, have (e.g. **a deal of**). To have a (big) dress-pannier : Society : 1888–ca. 1905. Ware.

behove. Incorrect for *behote* : ca. 1470–1550. Malory. (O.E.D.)

***Beilby's ball** (where the sheriff plays the music* is added in Grose, 3rd ed.), **dance at.** To be hanged : late C. 18–early 19 : prob. orig. c. Grose, 1st ed. It is not known who Mr. Beilby was ; perhaps a notable London sheriff. But *Beilby's* is more prob. a personified and punning perversion of *bilboes*, fetters ; F. & H. infers that it implied an Old *Bailey* hanging.

bejan, occ. **baijan.** A freshman at the Universities of Edinburgh (where † by 1880), Aberdeen, St. Andrew's. From ca. 1640 : s. only in C. 17, then j. Ex the *bec jaune* of the Sorbonne, where the term was certainly s.

bekos. A variant of *becos*, q.v.

***bel-shangle.** (Perhaps) a buffoon : prob. c. : late C. 16–early 17. Kemp, 1600. ? *bell-jangler.*

belay. To speak, esp. if vigorously : nautical : from ca. 1790 ; ob. Dibdin, ' My timbers ! what lingo he'd coil and belay.' (O.E.D.)—2. To stop, gen. *belay that yarn !,* we've had enough of that story : nautical (— 1823). Egan's Grose ; Smyth. Cf. :

belay there ! Stop ! Nautical : from ca. 1860. Cf. :

belaying-pin soup. Rough treatment of seamen by officers, esp. in sailing-ships : nautical : late C. 19–20 ; ob. Bowen.

belch. Beer, esp. if inferior and therefore apt to cause belching : from ca. 1690 ; ob. B.E. One recalls Sir Toby Belch, a jolly blade, but he, I surmise, avoided poor beer. Cf. *swipes.*

belch, v.i. To eructate : C. 11–20 : S.E. until mid-C. 19, then a vulgarism.

belcher. A blue handkerchief white- or, occ., yellow-spotted (*Lex. Bal.*, 1811) ; from ca. 1860, loosely, a handkerchief of any base with spots of another colour. Soon > coll., and from ca. 1875 it has been S.E. Ex the boxer Jim Belcher (d. 1811).—2. A (gen. hard) drinker of beer : C. Hindley, 1876, but prob. in use at least twenty years earlier : circus and showmen's s., which is nearer c. than to s.—3. A thick ring : 1851, Mayhew ; ob. c.

belfry, the. The head : see **bats in the belfry.**

Belgeek. A Belgian : military coll. : late 1914–18. F. & Gibbons. Ex Fr. *Belgique,* Belgium.

Belgians !, give it to the. C.p. advice to a man complaining about his food or clothing or inquiring what to do with some superfluity : New Zealand soldiers' : 1916–18.

Belial. *Balliol* College : Oxford, ca. 1870–1914.

believe, you wouldn't. You would not, or you would hardly, believe it : low coll. : mid-C. 19–20. Dorothy Sayers, *Murder Must Advertise,* 1932, ' The edges of the steps get that polished you wouldn't believe.'

believe you, I. Yes ! Coll. (—1835, when employed by Dickens) ; ob. Cf. the much later c.p., *I believe you, my boy !,* q.v.

***bell.** A song : C. 19 tramps' c. (— 1859). H. 1st ed. Abbr. *bellow.*

bell, v. To run away with (a marble) : schoolboys', ca. 1850–1910.

bell, ring one's own. To blow one's own trumpet : coll. verging on S.E. : C. 19–20 ; ob. Cf. *who pulled your chain ?,* q.v. at **chain.**

bell, ring the. To win (v.i.), be the best : coll. : 1928 (O.E.D. Sup.). Either ex a weight-testing machine (O.E.D.) or ex the bell rung by a shot hitting the bull's-eye at a shooting-gallery.

bell, sound as a. In excellent health, of unimpaired physique : coll., C. 19–20.

bell-bastard. The bastard child of a bastard mother : C. 19 West Country. Why the *bell ?* Cf. *bastardly gullion.*

bell, book and candle. Jocular coll. for the accessories of a religious ceremony : C. 19–20 ; coll. > S.E. Ex a medieval form of excommunication, these nn. occurring in the final sentence.

bells go rotten. See **rotten, bells go.**

bell-rope. A man's curl in front of the ear ; cf. *aggravator.* Punning *bell* and *bells.* Low (— 1868) ; ob.

bell-shangle. See **bel-shangle.**

bell the cat. To undertake something dangerous : from ca. 1720, coll. ; S.E. by 1800.

bell-tongue. See **beltong.**

bell-top. A *membrum virile* unusually large-headed ; gen. as adj., *bell-topped,* occ. *-knobbed.* C. 19 (?–C. 20). F. & H. designate it as ' harlotry '.

bell-topper. A silk hat : W. Kelly, *Life in Victoria* (Australia, 1859) ; G. A. Sala, 1885 : coll. by 1900.

bell-wether. Leader of a mob : C. 15–20 ; coll. >, by 1750, S.E. Ex ' a flock of sheep, where the wether has a bell about its neck ', Grose.—2. ' A clamorous noisy man ', B.E. : s. in C. 17–early 19, coll. in C. 15–16.

beller-croaker. Ravishingly beautiful : non-educated : ca. 1860–85. A corruption of Fr. *belle à croquer,* which ' lasted into 1883, in English Society ', Ware.

bellering cake. ' Cake in which the plums are so far apart that they have to beller (bellow) when they wish to converse ', Ware : schools' (— 1909) ; ob

bellers. See **bellows.**

bellibone. A smartly dressed girl : low (— 1923). Manchon derives it ex Fr. *belle et bonne.*

bellied. Stuck fast : Tank Corps coll., applied to a tank under-caught by, e.g., a tree-stump : 1917–18. F. & Gibbons.

bellower. A town crier : late C. 18–early 19. Grose, 2nd ed.

bellows ; illiterately, **bellers.** The lungs. Recorded for 1615, but that was a fig. use; as s., C. 18–20. Cf.:

bellows away!; bellows him well! An adjuration to a boxer not to spare his opponent, i.e. to make him pant for wind: boxing: ca. 1820–70. 'Jon Bee', 1823.

bellows to mend, have. (Of a horse) to be broken-winded; hence, of a man: mid-C. 19–20. 'Cuthbert Bede' in *Verdant Green*.

*bellowsed. Transported as a convict: ca. 1820–60. Cf. (*to*) *lag*, q.v.

bellowser. A blow in 'the wind': boxing, from ca. 1810; ob.—Hence, 2, a sentence of transportation for life: c. of ca. 1810–60. *Lex. Bal.*, 1811; Vaux, *knap* (i.e. nap) *a bellowser*.

bells down. The last peal of chapel-warning: Winchester College, ca. 1840–1900. *Bells go single* was the second of the warning-notices. See the works of Mansfield and Adams.

belly, his eye was bigger than his. 'A saying of a person at table, who takes more on his plate than he can eat', Grose, 2nd ed.: mid-C. 18–mid-19.

belly-ache. A pain in the bowels. Since ca. 1840 it has been considered both coll. and low, but orig. (— 1552), and until ca. 1800, it was S.E.

belly-ache, v. Grumble, complain, esp. querulously or unreasonably: ex U.S. (— 1881), anglicised ca. 1900: coll., somewhat low.

belly and wipe my eyes with it, I could take up the slack of my. I am very hungry: a nautical c.p. frequent on ships where rations are inadequate: late C. 19–20.

belly-band. A cholera belt: military: from 1915. F. & Gibbons.

belly-bound. Costive: coll.: from ca. 1660 and gen. of horses.

belly-bumper or **-buster, get a.** To be got with child; whence *belly-bump*, to coït. Low: C. 19–20.

belly-can. A tin vessel that, shaped like a saddle, is easily secreted about the body: used for the illicit conveyance of beer and holding about four quarts: political, 1889 +, but ob. by 1900.

*belly-cheat. An apron: ca. 1600–1830: c. or low s. Compounds with *cheat*, earlier *chete*, a thing, an article, are all either low s. or c.—2. Also: food: c.: C. 17. Fletcher, 1622.—3. (Cf. sense 1.) A pad designed to produce a semblance of pregnancy: c. (— 1823); † by 1900. 'Jon Bee.'

belly-cheer. Food: late C. 16–early 19; slightly earlier (— 1549), gratification of the belly. V., to feast heartily or luxuriously: C. 16–17. Orig. these terms were S.E., but in the later C. 17 the v., in C.18–19 the n., were coll. The vbl.n., *belly-cheering*, meant eating and drinking: C. 18–19 coll.

belly-flop, do a. See the next.—2. To drop down as a shell approaches: military: 1916; ob. B. & P.

belly-flopping. Sectional rushes by attacking troops advancing at the crouch and flopping down at intervals: military coll.: 1916–18. F. & Gibbons.

belly-friend. A hanger-on: C. 17–18, coll. verging on S.E.

belly-full, bellyful. A thrashing: late C. 16–19; e.g. in Nashe, Chapman, Pepys. In the sense of a sufficiency, the word has, since ca. 1840, > coll. simply because it is considered coarse.—(Of a woman) *have a*—or *have got her*—*bellyful*, to be with child: low: late C. 18–mid-19. Grose, 3rd ed.

belly-furniture. Food: C. 17 coll., as in Urquhart's *Rabelais*; cf. *belly-timber*.

belly-go-firster. (Boxing) an initial blow, given—as such a blow was once so often given—in the belly. C. 19. 'Jon Bee', 1823.

belly-gut. A greedy, lazy person; gen. of a man: coll.: C. 16–18.

belly-hedge. (Shrewsbury School) a steeplechase obstruction belly-high and therefore easily jumped: from ca. 1850.

belly-paunch. A glutton: mid-C. 16–17, coll. verging on S.E.; cf. *belly-gut*.

belly-piece. A concubine, a mistress, a harlot: coll.: C. 17.—2. Also, an apron (cf. *belly-cheat*): late C. 17–18; coll. It occurs in that lively, slangy play, Shadwell's *Bury Fair*.

belly-plea. An excuse of pregnancy, esp. among female prisoners. C. 18–early 19, coll. Defoe, in *Moll Flanders*, 1721: 'My mother pleaded her belly, and being found quick with child, she was respited for about seven months'; Gay, in *The Beggar's Opera*; Grose.

belly-ruffian. The penis: ? C. 17–19: low (? coll. rather than s.). F. & H.

belly thinks . . . See **throat is cut, my belly thinks my.**

belly-timber. Food: from ca. 1600. In C. 17, S.E.; then coll. In C. 19 s.; in C. 20, an archaism. Butler's use tended to make it ludicrous. (O.E.D.)

belly-up, adj. and **adv.** Of a pregnant woman: C. 17–18, low.

belly-vengeance. Sour beer: C. 19. Since ca. 1870, it is mainly dial. Cf.:

belly-wash. Thin liquor, rinsings: coll.: late C. 19–20. Manchon.

bellyful, fight for a. I.e. 'without stakes, wager, or payment', Bee: pugilistic: mid C. 18–20; very ob.

belong. To 'be rightly a member of (club, coterie, household, grade of society, etc.)': U.S. coll., partly anglicised by 1935. C.O.D., 1934 Sup.

belongings. Goods, possessions: coll., from ca. 1800.—2. Relatives: Dickens, 1852; coll.; ob.

below the belt, adv. and adj. Unfair(ly): from ca. 1870; coll., in C. 20 S.E.

below the waist. Too bad; esp. *nothing below the waist*, good or shrewd: tailors': C. 20. E.g. *The Tailor and Cutter*, Nov. 29, 1928.

belsh. Incorrect spelling of *belch*, n., q.v. B.E.

belswagger. A bully; blustering fellow: coll.: Greene, 1592; Dryden, 1680; Grose. † by 1830.—2. A womaniser; a pimp: C. 18. Ash's Dictionary distinguishes by spelling the former *bellyswagger*, the latter as *belswagger*.

belt. A hit, blow, punch. 'He caught me an awful belt on the ear.' From ca. 1895. Ex the v.: cf. *belting*, q.v.

belt, give (a person) **the.** To dismiss or reject: low: from ca. 1925. James Curtis, *The Gilt Kid*, 1936.

belter. A harlot: 'old', says F. & H. (revised): but when? She 'punishes' one's purse. Cf. *beltinker*, q.v.

belting. A thrashing, whether punitive or pugilistic: mid-C. 19–20: coll. verging on S.E.—2. A busy period: busmen's: from ca. 1930. *The Daily Herald*, Aug. 5, 1936. Opp. *convalescence*, q.v.

beltinker, n. and v. A thrashing, to thrash. Coll.: ? C. 19. F. & H. Perhaps a pun on *belt*, thrash with a belt.

beltong, bell-tongue. Incorrect for *biltong*: C. 19–20. O.E.D.

bemean (oneself). To lower oneself: sol: mid-C. 17–20. Ex *demean + mean*. O.E.D.; W.

bemused (with beer). In C. 18–mid-19, S.E., as in its originator, Pope ; ca. 1860 it > a fashionable phrase and genuinely s. ; ob. in C. 20.

ben. A coat, C. 19, ex *benjamin* ; a waistcoat (− 1846), ex *benjy*. Both ob.—2. (Theatrical) a benefit performance : from ca. 1850. H., 1st ed. Cf. *stand ben*, to stand treat (− 1823) ; † by 1900. Bee.—3. In c., a fool : late C. 17–18. B.E., Grose. ? 'a good fellow' : see **bene.**—4. A 'tara-diddle' : Society : ca. 1880–1914. Ware : *ben* ex *Ben* ex *Ben Tro* ex *Ben Trovato* ex *Benjamin Trovato* ex *se non è vero—è Benjamin* (for *ben*) *trovato*, if it isn't true it's nonetheless felicitous.

*****ben**, adj. ; gen. **bene** ; often **bien.** Good : c. : mid-C. 16–early 19. Ex L. *bene*, well (adv.), or Fr. *bien.* Harman, B.E., Grose. Cf. at **bene.**

ben, stand. See **ben**, n., 2.

*****ben-** or **bene-bowsie.** Drunk (esp. with good wine) : c. : C. 17–18. Jonson. Ex *bene bowse* (see **bene**).

*****ben cull**, C. 19 ; **ben cove**, C. 17–18. Both c. : for a friend or a companion. See **ben** and **bene**, *bene* also being found, in same sense, with *cove* and, less often, *cull*.

*****Ben Flake** or **ben-flake.** A steak : thieves' rhyming s. : from ca. 1855. 'Ducange Anglicus', 1st ed. (Rhyming s. may have been invented by criminals.)

Ben Tro and **Ben Trovato.** See **ben**, n., 4.

*****benar.** Better. *Benat* : best. The former in Coles, but prob. both are C. 17–18 ; c. See **bene.**

bench-winner. A dog successful at many dog-shows : Society : 1897, *The Daily Telegraph*, Feb. 11 ; ob. Ex the exhibits being placed on benches.

bench-points. 'Classified physical advantages' : London : ca. 1900–15. Ware. Ex show animals. Cf. preceding.

[**bencher.** A frequenter of public-houses : despite F. & H., it is S.E.]

bend (mid-C. 18–20) ; **bend to** (mid-C. 19–20). To drink hard : Scots ; ob. Alan Ramsay ; lexicographer Jamieson ; memoirist Ramsay. O.E.D., 'Perhaps "to pull, strain" in reference to pulling or straining a bow . . . ; or "to ply, apply oneself to".'

bend, above one's. Beyond one's ability : coll. from ca. 1860 ; ob. H., 3rd ed. Earlier U.S. (1848, Cooper). Perhaps *above one's bent*.

bend, Grecian. The body bent forward in walking : a Society vogue of ca. 1872–80. The term long outlasted the craze and is now but moribund.

bend, on a. A-drinking ; on a spree : U.S. (1887) anglicised ca. 1890. Also **on the bend** ; see sense 2 of :

bend, on the. Crooked, underhand : coll. from ca. 1850 ; ob. Cf. *crooked*.—2. The same as the preceding entry : 1891, Kipling (O.E.D. Sup.). Prob. ex *on a bender* : see **bender**, 4.

bend, round the. See **round the bend.**

bend o(f) the filbert. A bow, a nod : low London : ca. 1860–1900. Ware. See **filbert.**

bender. A sixpence : late C. 18–20, ob. : c. >, by 1820, low s. Parker, *Life's Painter of Variegated Characters*, 1789 ; Dickens, 1836 ; Whyte-Melville, 1869. (Because easily bent.) 'Ducange Anglicus', 1857, defines it as a shilling : prob. in error.—2. The arm : C. 19–20, ob. : cf. the C. 17–18 medical use of the term for a flexor muscle.—3. Hence, the elbow : late C. 19–20 ; ob. Ware.—4. A drinking spree : orig. (1827), U.S. ; anglicised ca. 1895. Cf.

bend, on a (q.v.), and Ramsay's and Tannahill's *bender*, a hard drinker. Thornton.—5. In certain Public Schools, a stroke of the cane administered to a boy bending his back : from ca. 1870.—6. General schoolboys', ca. 1870–1910 : 'the bow-shaped segment of a paper kite'. Blackley, *Hay Fever*, 1873.—7. A 'tall' story : nautical : late C. 19–20. Cf. the next two entries.

*****bender !** I don't believe it ! ; as a c.p. tag, I'll do no such thing : c. (− 1812) ; † by 1890. Vaux. Cf. :

bender, over the. Exaggerated, untrue ; often as an exclamation of incredulity. Cf. *over the left* (shoulder). C. 19–20, ob.—2. (Of a partridge) before Sept. 1st ; (of a pheasant) before Oct. 1st : poachers' (− 1909). Ware.

bendigo. A rough fur cap : ca. 1845–1900. Ex the Nottingham prize-fighter, Wm. Thompson (1811–89), *nom-de-guerre*'d Bendigo, whose first challenge dates 1835 and who afterwards turned evangelist : see Weekley's *Romance of Words*.

bending. See **catch one bending**.—2. A severe parade conducted by a N.C.O. to tire out the men : military : from ca. 1920. Also a *sweating*.

bends, the. Diver's paralysis or, more accurately, cramp : pearl-fishers' : C. 20.

*****bene, bien.** In c. as n., tongue : C. 16–18, prob. by transference ex the adj. :—2. Good, with *benar*, better, and *benat*, best : mid-C. 16–early 19. Variant *ben*, q.v., and even *bien*. E.g. *ben(e)*, *bowse, booze*, etc., excellent liquor.

*****bene** (or **bien**), **on the.** Well : expeditiously. As in B.E.'s *pike on the bene* (there spelt *bien*), run away quickly. C. of late C. 17–18.

*****bene darkmans !** Good night ! Mid-C. 16–18 : c. See **darkmans** ; contrast *lightmans*, q.v.

*****bene feaker.** A counterfeiter of bills : late C. 17–18 : c. *Bene* here = skilful. See **feaker.**

*****bene feaker of gybes.** A counterfeiter of passes : late C. 17–18 : c. B.E. See **gybe.**

*****bene**, or **bien**, **mort.** A fine woman or pretty girl ; hence, a hostess. C. 16–18 : c. Revived by e.g. Scott. See **mort, mot**, a woman, a girl.

benedick. Sol. (? : for see Fowler) for *benedict*, a newly married man : C. 17–20.—2. Also, C. 19, sol. for a bachelor.

Benedict, benedict. Any married man : catachrestic : mid-C. 19–20. In New Zealand, contests between married and single men are described as being between *bachelors and benedicts*. (Properly, a newly married man, esp. if a 'confirmed' bachelor).

beneficience, -ficiency, -ficient. Erroneous for *beneficence, -ficency, -ficent* : mid-C. 16–20. O.E.D.

benefit. A fine job or a fine time : coll. (− 1933). O.E.D. (Sup.)

benefit, take the. I.e. of the insolvent debtor's Act : coll. (− 1823) ; † by 1890. Bee.

*****ben(e)ship.** Profitable : worshipful : mid-C. 16–18 c. Harman.—2. Hence adv., *beneshiply*, worshipfully : C. 17–18. Ex *bene*, 2, q.v.

benevolence. 'Ostentation and fear united, with hopes of retaliation in kind *hereafter*', Bee, 1823 : Society : ca. 1820–40.

*****benfeaker.** A variant of *bene feaker*, q.v.

Bengal blanket. The sun ; a blue sky : soldiers in India : mid-C. 19–20 ; very ob. Cf. *blue blanket*, q.v. (Ware.)

Bengal light. (Gen. pl.) An Indian soldier in France : military : 1915–18. B. & P.

Bengal Tigers. The Seventeenth Foot Regiment,

from ca. 1881 the Leicestershires: military, from ca. 1825. Ex ' badge of a royal tiger, granted for services in India from 1804–23 ', F. & H. They were also, from the facings, called The Lily-Whites.

bengi. An onion: military, from ca. 1860. Perhaps cognate with Somerset *benge*, to drink to excess ; cf. *binge*.

bengy. See **benjy.**

*benish, occ. **bennish.** Foolish: late C. 17–18 c. B.E. See **ben.**

benison, beggar's. See **beggar's benison.**

benjamin or **Benjamin.** A coat (from ca. 1815), whence *upper benjamin* (1817), a greatcoat. Peacock in *Nightmare Abbey* : ' His heart is seen to beat through his upper Benjamin.' Borrow in *Lavengro* : ' The coachman . . . with . . . fashionable Benjamin '. The word may have begun as c. ; in C. 20, ob. Perhaps, as Brewer suggests, ex the name of a tailor ; more prob. on *joseph*, q.v.—2. At Winchester College, from ca. 1860, a small ruler. I.e. *Benjamin* small in comparison with *Joseph*.—3. A husband : Australian pidgin-English (— 1870). Chas. H. Allen, *A Visit to Queensland*, 1870. Morris. Cf. *Mary*, q.v.

Benjamin Trovato. See **ben**, n., 4.

benjo. A riotous holiday : nautical : late C. 19–20 ; ob. Perhaps ex *beano* + *bender*, 4 ; Ware suggests derivation ex *buen giorno* (? via Lingua Franca).

*benjy. A waistcoat : c. > low (— 1821) ; ob. Haggart. Ex *benjamin*, 1.—2. Hence, a waistcoat-maker : tailors' : mid-C. 19–20.—3. Nautical (perhaps ex dial. : see E.D.D.), C. 19 : a straw hat, low-crowned and broad-brimmed.

*benly, rare adv. Well : c. : ? mid-C. 18–early 19. Baumann. Perhaps abbr. *beneshiply.*

*bennish. See **benish.**

bens. Tools : workmen's : late C. 19–20. ? ex **ben**, n., 2, q.v.

*benship. See **beneship.**

bent. Broken (esp. if fig.) : C. 20. Either dysphemistic ex such phrases as (e.g. I) *bend but do not break* or evolutionary ex any bent object, esp. a coin. B. & P.

bent on a splice, be. To be on the look-out for a wife : nautical : from ca. 1860 ; ob. Smyth. Perhaps punning *spliced*, married.

beong ; occ. **beonck.** (Costers') a shilling : mid-C. 19–20. H., 1st ed. Ex *bianco* (lit. white), a silver coin. It. via Lingua Franca. Whence *bimp*, q.v.

[**beray,** wrongly **bewray.** To defile, befoul : C. 16–20, ob. ' Old cant ', says F. & H. ; it is merely old S.E.]

*bereavement lurk. The pretended loss of a wife as a pretext for begging : c. (— 1875). Ribton-Turner, *Vagrants and Vagrancy*. See **lurk** and contrast **dead lurk.** O.E.D.

*berk. A fool : c. : from ca. 1930. J. Curtis, *The Gilt Kid*, 1936. By abbr. ex :

Berkeley. The *pudendum muliebre* : C. 20. Abbr. *Berkeley Hunt*, a cunt.—2. In the pl., and from ca. 1875,—never, obviously, with *Hunt*—it denotes a woman's breasts ; F. & H. adduce Romany *berk* (or *burk*), breast, pl. *berkia.*

Berloo or **Baloo.** Bailleul : military : G.W. ; ob. (B. & P.)

Bermondsey banger. A man prominent in the society of the South London tanneries : Cockney (— 1909) ; † by 1930. Ware, ' He must . . . be prepared . . . to fight at all times for his social belt.'

Bermoothes. See **Bermudas.**

Bermuda Exiles, the. The Grenadier Guards : ca. 1895–1914. In 189-, a portion of this regiment was, to expiate insubordination, sent to the West Indies. F. & H. revised.

Bermudas, Bermoothes. A London district (cf. *Alsatia*, q.v.) privileged against arrest : certain alleys and passages contiguous to Drury Lane, near Covent Garden, and north of the Strand : Jonson, *The Devil's an Ass* (1616) : ' Keeps he still your quarter in the Bermudas.' Grose and Ainsworth are almost certainly in error in referring the term to the Mint in Southwark. In C. 17, certain notable debtors fled to the Bermuda Islands, says Nares.

Bermudian. A wet ship : naval coll. : C. 19. Ex ' the Bermudian-built 3-masted schooners in the Napoleonic wars ' : they ' went through the waves instead of rising to them ' (Bowen).

*bernard. See **barnard.**

berry. (Gen. pl.) £1 (note) : from ca. 1931. K. G. R. Browne in *The Humorist*, May 26, 1934. Prob. ex U.S. monetary sense.

berry, get the. (Of an action) to be hissed : theatrical : C. 20. Collinson. Like synonymous *get the rasp*, it obviously derives ex *get the raspberry.*

Bert. Albert on the Western Front : military : late 1914–18. F. & Gibbons.

Bertha (bertha) ; also **big Bertha.** Nicknames of any one of the long-range German guns that, in the summer of 1917, shelled the back areas on the Western Front and, in 1918, Paris : mid-1917–18 : military > gen. In Ger., *die dicke Bertha.* Ex *Bertha* Krupp of Essen. W. ; B. & P.

Berthas. Ordinary stock of the London, Brighton and South Coast Railway Company : Stock Exchange from ca. 1885. *The Rialto*, March 23, 1889.

Berwicks. The ordinary stock of the North Eastern Railway : Stock Exchange (— 1890).

beside the lighter. In a bad condition : late C. 17–18. B.E. Perhaps the lighter going out to a ship proceeding to the convict plantations. Cf. *book, beside the.*

besognio. A low, worthless fellow : coll. : ca. 1620–1840. Pronounced and often spelt *besonio.* Ex It. *bisogna* via S.E. *beso(g)nio*, a raw soldier.

besom, jump the. To go through a mock marriage : ca. 1700–1820. Manchon implies its survival into C. 20. Cf. *broomstick (jump the)*, q.v.

bespattered. A coll. euphemism, ca. 1918–30, of *bloody.* Manchon.

bespeak-night. (Theatrical) a benefit performance : from the mid-1830's ; ob. Ex *bespeak*, to choose, arrange, the actor's friends choosing the play. Often abbr. to *bespeak* (as in Ware).

*bess. A burglar's tool : see **betty.**—See **brown bess** (or **Bess**).

Bess o' Bedlam. An insane beggar : C. 18–early 19. Scott in *Kenilworth* : ' Why, what Bess of Bedlam is this, would ask to see my lord on such a day as the present ? '

best. To worst ; get the better of : coll. (— 1859), as in H., 1st ed., and in Charles Hindley's best-known book, *A Cheap Jack.*—2. Hence, to cheat, as in Hindley, ' His game was besting everybody, whether it was for pounds, shillings, or pence,' 1876. Cf. *bester*, q.v.—3. Hence as in *best the pistol*, to get away before the pistol is fired : athletics : 1889, *The Polytechnic Magazine*, July 7.

*best, get one's money at the. ' To live by dishonest or fraudulent practices ' : c. (— 1812) ; † by 1890. Vaux.

*best, give. See give best.

best, not in the. Not in the best of tempers : coll. : from ca. 1890.

best, — of the. Of £1 notes ; thus, *five of the best*, £5 : C. 20. Collinson.

best, one of the. A 'good fellow', i.e. a good companion : Society : from ca. 1920.

best bib and tucker, gen. one's, occ. the. (Rarely of children's and only loosely of men's) best clothes : U.S. (1793 : O.E.D. Sup.), anglicised in Lancashire dial. ca. 1870, in coll. ca. 1880 ; ob.

best foot or leg foremost, put one's. To try hard : coll. >, by 1850, S.E. : *foot* from late C. 16, *leg* from late C. 15 ; ob. Apperson.

best in Christendom, to the. A toast very popular ca. 1750–80 (cf. *beggar's benison* and *both ends of the busk*, qq.v.). Grose, 1st ed. Sc. *cunt.*

best leg of three, the. The penis : low : late C. 19–20 ; ob.

*best mog. The cat-skin or coney fur worn by a bookie's wife when he has been very successful : C. 20 racing c.

best of a bad bargain (etc.). See bargain, best . . .

best of a Charley, the. 'Upsetting a watchman in his box', Egan's Grose : ca. 1820–40.

best part, best thing, etc. The best part, thing, etc. : coll. : late C. 19–20. (R. Knox, 1933, 'He'd been here best part of three weeks.')

best the pistol. See best, 3.

*bester. A swindler ; a 'smart Alec' criminally or illicitly : orig. (— 1859), c. ; then low. H., 1st ed. ; Mayhew. Ex *best*, q.v.

bestest, adj. Best : sol. (and dial.) : C. 19–20. E.D.D. Cf. *betterer*, q.v.

bestial. 'Beastly', objectionable, disappointing : from ca. 1910 ; slightly ob. Ernest Raymond, *A Family That Was*, 1929.

bet !, you. Certainly : ? orig. (ca. 1870) U.S., anglicised ca. 1890.—2. *You betcha* (or *betcher*), *you bet your* (e.g. *boots*) : U.S. phrases anglicised ca. 1905.

bet levels, you devils ! A bookmakers' c.p. (— 1932). See *Slang*, p. 241.

*bet on top. A bogus bet laid, *pour encourager les autres*, by a pal of the bookie. The bookie's clerk places the bet 'on top', not in the body of the betting book. Often abbr. to *on top*. C. 20 racing c.

bet you a million to a bit of dirt ! A sporting c.p. indicative of 'the betting man's Ultima Thule of confidence', Ware : ca. 1880–1914. Cf. *all Lombard Street to a China orange.*

bet your boots or life or bottom dollar ! Orig. (resp. 1868, 1852, and 1882) U.S. ; anglicised ca. 1910, 1880, 1890 resp., largely owing to the writings of Bret Harte and Mark Twain. Thornton ; Ware.

betcha, betcher ; you betcha (or betcher). See bet, you, 2.

bête noir. A common error (mid-C. 19–20) for *bête noire*, pet aversion.

beteechoot. See banchoot.

bethel the city. To refrain from keeping an hospitable table ; to eat at chop-houses : C. 18. Ex Bethel, one of the two Sheriffs of London elected in 1680.

*Bethlehemites. Christmas carol-singers : late C. 18–early 19 c. Grose, 3rd ed. Ex *Bethlehem*, frequent in carols.

betide. To betoken or bode : catachrestic : late C. 18–20. Cowper. (O.E.D.)

Betsy. The inevitable nickname of anyone sur-

named Gay : late C. 19–20. Ex the old song. Bowen considers it to have been orig. naval. Cf. *Dusty.*

better. More : a sol. in C. 19–20, though S.E. in C. 16–18. E.g. Dickens, 1857 : 'Rather better than twelve years ago.'—2. With *had* omitted, as in 'You better mind what you say !' : coll., orig. (1845) U.S., anglicised ca. 1910. O.E.D. (Sup.).

better half. A wife : coll. from ca. 1570. In C. 16–18, *my better half* and seriously, in C. 19–20, *a*, or *anyone's, b. h.*, and jocularly.

better hole or 'ole. See hole, better.

better never than come in rags ! I.e. in poverty (see *rag*, a farthing) : a c.p. retort to *better late than never* : ca. 1820–50. 'Jon Bee.'

better than a dig in the eye with a blunt stick or than a kick in the pants (or up the arse). Better than nothing ; by meiosis, very much better than nothing or than a set-back : resp. mid-C. 19–20 (ob.) coll., C. 20 s., and C. 20 low s. Contrast :

better than a drowned policeman. (Of a person) very pleasant, attractive, good or expert : c.p. : ca. 1900–15. (J. B. Priestley, *Faraway*, 1932.)

betterer. Better : sol. : C. 19–20. Cf. *worserer*, q.v.

betterish. Somewhat better or superior : coll. (— 1888) ; verging on S.E.—but ugly !

bettermost. Best : (somewhat low) coll. (— 1887). Baumann.

betting, often corrupted to getting, round. The laying of odds on all the likely horses : from ca. 1860 ; ob. H., 3rd ed. Whence *bettor round*, such a better, as in 'Thormanby', *Famous Racing Men*, 1882.

betting lay, the. Betting on horses : turf (— 1887). Baumann.

betty, occ. bess. A picklock (instrument) : mid-C. 17–19. Orig. c. ; the form *bess* († by 1880) remained c. For *betty*, much the commoner, see Head's *English Rogue*, Coles, B.E., Ned Ward, Grose, and Henry Mayhew ; for *bess*, B.E. and Grose. Cf. *jemmy* and *jenny*, qq.v., and see esp. Grose, P.—2. Also (cf. *molly*), a man assuming a woman's domestic duties : C. 19–20 ; coll. Cf. *betty*, v.—3. Miss, as a title : Bootham School : late C. 19–20. Anon., *Dict. of Bootham Slang*, 1925.

betty, v. Fuss, or potter, *about* : coll. : from ca. 1850 ; slightly ob.

*betty !, all. It's all up ! C. 19 c. ; opp. *it's all bob*, see bob. (This kind of pun (*Betty* and *Bob*) is not rare in c.)

Betty Martin. See all my eye (and Betty Martin).

betwattled. Astounded, bewildered ; berayed : late C. 18–early 19. Grose, 1st ed.

between. For a catachrestic usage, common in late C. 19–20, see the quotation at *Trades Union*.

between hell and high water. See hell and high water, between.

between the flags. On the actual race-course : sporting (— 1865) ; ob.

between wind and water. See water, between wind and.—between you and me (and . . .). See bed-post.

betwixt and between. Intermediate(ly) ; indecisive(ly) ; neither one thing nor the other : adv. and adj. Coll. : from ca. 1830. 'A betwixt and between fashionable street', Marryat. (O.E.D.)

bever ; often beaver ; occ. bevir, etc. etc. Orig. S.E. and in C. 19–20 mainly dial., but as used at Eton and as *bevers* at Winchester College for after-

noon tea—a sense recorded by B.E.—it is s. See
in my *Words!* the essay entitled 'The Art of
Lightening Work'. Ex L. *bibere*, to drink, in the
Old Fr. form, *beivre*, this is one of the most interesting words in the language. Cf. *bivvy* and *beverage*,
qq.v.—2. Hence, as v. : C. 17–early 19.

beverage. 'A Garnish money, for any thing',
B.E. ; Grose adds that it is drink-money—cf. the
Fr. *pourboire*—demanded of any person wearing a
new suit ; in gen., a tip. Coll. : late C. 17–20 ;
† by ca. 1820, except in dial.

bevie, v. ; gen. **bevvy.** To drink : Parlyaree, esp.
among grafters : late C. 19–20. (Philip Allingham,
Cheapjack, 1934.) Ex :

bevie, bevry. A public-house : mid-C. 19–20
Parlyaree. Seago, *Circus Folk,* 1933.—2. Beer ;
loosely, any drink : military and theatrical : late
C. 19–20. F. & Gibbons. Either ex sense 1 or ex
beverage.

bevie-homey. A drunken actor : theatrical :
C. 20. Ex *bevie,* 2.—2. Any drunkard : grafters' :
C. 20. Philip Allingham (*bevvy omee*).

bevir. See **bever.**

beware. Any drinkable : low s., from ca. 1840.
Mayhew in that mine of Cockney and low s.,
London Labour and the London Poor, 4 vols., 1851–
61, says in vol. iii : 'We [strolling actors] call
breakfast, dinner, tea, supper, all of them "numyare" ; and all beer, brandy, water, or soup, are
"beware"'. *Numyare* (? a corruption of It.
mangiare, to eat) and *beware* (cf. *bever, beverage,* and
bivvy) are Lingua Franca words employed in
Parlyaree, the s. of circuses, showmen, and strolling
actors : see *Slang,* section on the circus.

*bewer. A girl : (– 1845) : rare and ob.
See *No. 747,* p. 416. ? Ex. Romany or dial.—2.
Hence, a tramp's woman : tramps' c. (—1935).

bewray. Incorrect for *beray,* to disfigure, befoul :
C. 17–20. So *bewrayer.* O.E.D.

bexandebs. Easy-going young Jewesses in the
Wentworth Street district : East London : late
C. 18–20 ; ob. Ware. Ex *Beck* (Rebecca) + *Deb*
(Deborah).

beyind. Behind : sol. (– 1909). Ware (at *bad
shilling*).

beyond, be (a person). To pass the comprehension of : coll. ; from ca. 1800. Jane Austen.

beyond the beyonds. 'The absolute outside
edge', 'the limit' : Anglo-Irish : from ca. 1910.

bheestie, -y. A water-bearer : from ca. 1780 :
Anglo-Indian coll. >, by 1850, j. Ex Urdu *bhisti,*
but prob. by a pun on Scots *beastie,* a little beast.
(In C. 18, often spelt *beasty* ; in C. 19 *beestie.*)
Yule & Burnell.

b'hoy. 'A town rowdy ; a gay fellow', Thornton : ex U.S. (1846), anglicised—almost wholly in
the latter sense—ca. 1865. (Cf. *g'hal.*) Ex Irish
pronunciation. (O.E.D.)

bi-cennoctury. The 200th performance : theatrical catachresis : ca. 1870–1915. Ware.

bianc. A shilling : c. and Parlyaree : late
C. 19.–20. It. *bianco,* white.

Bianca Capella. (Gen. pl.) A 'White Chapeller'
(cigar) : East London : 1886, *The Referee,* June 6 ;
† by 1920. Cf. *Banker Chapel Ho,* q.v.

bias, on the. Illicit : dishonourable ; dishonest :
dressmakers' (– 1909). Cf. *on the cross* (at *cross*).

*bib, nap a or **one's.** To weep : c. or low s. ; late
C. 18–20 ; ob. G. Parker, 1789 ; Vaux ; Egan.
Lit., to take one's bib in order to wipe away one's
tears.

bib-all-night. A toper : C. 17, coll. (*Bib,* to
tipple.)

bib and tucker, best. See **best bib** . . .

bibe. A bringer of bad luck : Anglo-Irish
(– 1935). Corruption of an Irish word.

bible. Nautical : 'a hand-axe ; a small holystone [sandstone employed in the cleaning of
decks], so called from seamen using them kneeling' :
Admiral Smyth in his valuable *Sailors' Word Book,*
1867. C. 18–20 ; ob. The holystones were also
named *prayer-books.* For nautical s. in gen., see
Slang.—2. Lead wrapped round the body by those
who 'fly the blue pigeon' ; what they stow in
their pockets is a *testament* : c. : late C. 18–mid-19.
G. Parker, 1789.—3. ? hence : in mid-C. 19–20 c.
(vagrants'), a pedlar's box of pins, needles, laces,
etc.

bible, v. Implied in *bibler, bibling.*

bible, that's. That's true ; that's excellent :
C. 19–20 (ob.), coll. Cf. S.E. *Bible oath.*

Bible-banger. A pious, esp. if ranting person :
late C. 19–20. Cf. *Bible-pounder.*

*bible-carrier. One who sells songs without
singing them : c. (vagrants') : ca. 1850–1915.
H., 1st ed.

Bible class, been to a. 'With two black eyes,
got in a fight' : printers' (– 1909). Ware. Prob.
suggested by the noise and excitement common at
printers' *chapels.*

Bible-clerk. (Winchester College) a prefect appointed to full power for one week ; he reads the
lessons in chapel. From ca. 1850 : see esp. Mansfield and Adams : coll. soon > j. (In S.E., an
Oxford term.)

bible (or **B.**) **leaf.** (Gen. pl.) A thin strip of
blubber ready for the fry-pot : whalers' : coll. :
late C. 19–20. Bowen. Ex leaves preserved by
being kept in the family Bible.

Bible-mill. A public-house ; esp., noisy talking
there : London proletarians' : ca. 1850–1910.
Ware, 'An attack upon Bible classes.'

Bible-pounder. A clergyman, esp. if excitable :
coll., C. 19–20. Cf. *bible-banger* and the next two
terms :

Bible-punching. A sermon ; religious talk :
C. 20. (E.g. in Michael Harrison, *Spring in
Tartarus,* 1935.) Cf. :

Bible-thumper. A pious seaman : nautical coll. :
mid.-C. 19–20. Bowen. Cf. *Bible-banger.*

bibler, bibling. Six cuts on the back : the former
ca. 1830–60, the latter from ca. 1860. Winchester
College : see Adams, Mansfield, and *Blackwood's
Magazine,* 1864, vol. xcv. A *bibler,* later *bibling,
under nail* : a pillory-process before the cuts were
administered. The *bibling-rod,* a handle with four
apple-twigs twisted together at the end : invented
by Warden Baker in 1454 ; † by 1890.

*bice and a roht or **a half.** Odds of 2½, i.e. 5 to 2:
C. 20 racing c. John Morris.

bid stand, bid-stand, bidstand. A highwayman:
coll. : late C. 16– ? 18. Ben Jonson. For the
philology of highwaymen, see *Words !*

biddy. A chicken : coll. : late C. 16–early 19 ;
then dial. Occ. *chick-a-biddy.*—2. A young woman
(ex *Bridget*) : C. 18–early 19, as in Grose, 1st ed.
—3. Any woman : C. 19, as in O. W. Holmes,
Guardian Angel, 1869.—4. At Winchester College,
see :

bidet or **biddy.** A bath. Also, though this is
S.E. as *bidet,* coll. as *biddy,* defined thus by Grose :
'A kind of tub, contrived for ladies to wash them-

selves, for which purpose they bestride it like a little French pony or post horse, called in French bidets', as also is this toilet accessory.—2. See :

biddy-biddy ; biddybid. The burr named in Maori *piripiri* : New Zealand coll. (— 1880). By the process of Hobson-Jobson.—2. Hence, gen. as *biddy*, to rid of burrs : 1880. Morris.

'Bidgee, the. The Murrumbidgee River : Australian coll. : mid-C. 19–20.

*bien. See **bean, ben** and **bene.**

*bienly. Excellently : c. : late C. 18–early 19. Grose, 2nd ed. See **bene.**

biff. A blow ; (? orig. U.S., anglicised) ca. 1895. Prob. an abbr. and emaciated form of *buffet* (W.). —2. Slightly earlier as v., gen. v.t. : to hit resoundingly, sharply, abruptly, or crisply. E.g., ' I'll biff him one if he's not careful.' Echoic or as in sense 1.—3. Gen. *biff round*, to go round : from ca. 1930. E.g., Will Scott in *The Humorist*, 1934.

biffin. An intimate friend : from ca. 1840 ; virtually †. Ex a kind of apple. Cf. *ribstone* and *pippin*, qq.v., and the C. 20 *old fruit*.

big. Great ; important : coll. ; from ca. 1570. On the verge of S.E. is this humorous substitute for *great* as in Shakespeare's ' I Pompey am, Pompey surnam'd the big', O.E.D.

big, go ; go over big. See **go big.**

big, look. To attempt an impressive manner : coll., C. 16–19. E.g. in Shakespeare's *Winter's Tale.*

big, talk. To boast, talk pretentiously : from ca. 1650 ; coll. verging on S.E. Smollett, 1771 : ' The squire affected . . . to talk big.'

big as bull-beef. See **bull-beef, big as.**

big-bellied. Far gone in pregnancy : Addison, 1711. Coll. : ob.

Big Ben. The clock in the tower of the Houses of Parliament, Westminster : coll. (— 1869). Ex Sir Benjamin Hall, under whose Commissionership of Works it was constructed in 1856–7.

big Bertha. See **Bertha.**

big bird, get or give the. To be hissed ; to hiss. Theatrical ; cf. *give the goose* and *be goosed*. From ca. 1860. H., 3rd ed. See **goose** and **bird, n.,** 5. —2. Ware, however, notes that ca. 1860–1910, the phrase also = ' to be appreciatively hissed for one's performance in the role of villain '.

big bug. An important person : orig. (1830 : O.E.D. Sup.) U.S. ; anglicised ca. 1880. Prob. ultimately ex C. 18 *bug*, a person of considerable importance (?).

big country. Open country : hunting coll. (— 1890). F. & H.

big dig. A reprimand made by a C.O. : military coll. : from ca. 1920.

big digger. At cards, the ace of spades (cf. *diggers*) : from ca. 1850 ; ob.

big dog. A chucker-out : coll. : from ca. 1870. ' He was " big-dog " to a disorderly house ', *Good Words*, June 1884. O.E.D.

big drink. The ocean, esp. the Atlantic : Miss Braddon, 1882. (In U.S., from 1846, the Mississippi.)

big, or long, drink. Liquor from a long glass : C. 19–20, coll. ; in C. 20, indeed, almost S.E.

*big getter. A ' teller of the tale ' in a grand and genteel manner : C. 20 c. ' Stuart Wood ', *Shades of the Prison House*, 1932.

big gun. A person of note : orig. (— 1900) U.S. ; anglicised ca. 1910.

big head. The morning-after feeling (— 1880) :

coll. Get a or *the b.h.,* to become intoxicated : from ca. 1870.

big, or large, house. The workhouse : among the indigent (— 1851). Mayhew. In the U.S., a prison.

Big Lizzie. H.M.S. *Queen Elizabeth* : naval : C. 20. Bowen.

big loaf and little loaf. A political c.p. used by Liberals during the fiscal controversy ca. 1906. Collinson.

big mouth. A tale-teller ; an informer : low Glasgow (— 1934).

big noise. An important person : from ca. 1907 (in U.S.). Popularised in England in G.W.

big number. (Gen. pl.) A brothel : Parisian Englishmen's : ca. 1820–1910. Ex ' the huge size of the number on the swinging door, never shut, never more than two or three inches open ', Ware. Possibly in part, also, a pun on *bagnio*.

big one or **un.** A notable person : coll., ca. 1800–50 ; cf. *big gun* and *pot* and *wig*.

big people. Important people : coll. : from ca. 1855 ; slightly ob. Trollope.

big pond. The Atlantic : (prob. ex U.S. and anglicised) ca. 1880 ; cf. *big drink*.

big pot. A person of consequence ; a don : Oxford, ca. 1850–60. Thence, solely the former and in gen. use. Perhaps *pot*, abbr. *potentate*. Ware implies that, ca. 1878–82, it had, in the music-halls, the special sense of ' a leader, supreme personage '.

big shot. A gang-leader ; a notorious gangster : U.S., anglicised as coll. in C. 20. Prob. on *big gun* and *big noise*.

big side. (Rugby and other Public Schools') the bigger boys combining in one game or sport ; the ground used therefor. Whence *b.-s. run*, a paper chase in which all houses take part. C. 19–20 ; ob.

big smoke (or **B.S.**), **the.** See **Smoke, Big.**

big stuff. Heavy shells : military coll. : late 1914–18, and after. F. & Gibbons.

big talk. Pompous, or sesquipedalian, speech : (— 1874) coll.

big triangle, the. ' The old sailing-ship tramping route—from U.K. to Australia with general cargo, on to the West Coast of S. America with coal from Newcastle, N.S.W., and then home with nitrates ' : from ca. 1860 (now ob.) : nautical coll. >, by 1880, j.

big wig. A person of high rank or position or money. It occurs in Ned Ward early in C. 18, but it > gen. only ca. 1840. Whence *big-wigged*, consequential (Carlyle, 1851), *big-wiggery*, a display of pompousness or importance (Thackeray, 1848),— and *big-wiggism*, pomposity, pretentiousness (George Eliot) : all three being coll. at first, then soon S.E.—though seldom employed.

big Willie. See **Willie.**

big word. A word of many syllables or much pretentiousness : coll. (— 1879) rising to S.E. In the pl., pomposity : from ca. 1850 ; in C. 20 almost S.E., though rarely used.

bigger and better. A jocular coll., as in *bigger and better babies* : from ca. 1924. Ex the Coué vogue of 1923 with its self-adjurations to grow ' better and stronger ', etc.

biggin. A woman's coif : a late C. 17–18 catachresis recorded by B.E. Properly a serjeant-at-law's coif (also a night-cap, a hood for the head).

bike. Abbr. *bicycle* : from ca. 1890. Since G.W., coll. Cf. *trike*.

*bil. A late C. 17–mid-18 c. abbr., recorded by B.E., of *bilboa*.

bilayutee pawnee. Soda-water : Anglo-Indian coll. (— 1886). See **parnee.**

bilbo(a). In C. 16–17, S.E. : a sword noted for the excellence of its temper and made orig. at Bilbao in Spain. Hence, in late C. 17–18 (in C. 19, archaic), coll. : the sword of a bully. Congreve in the *Old Bachelor* : 'Tell them . . . he must refund—or bilbo's the word, and slaughter will ensue.'

Bilboy's ball. See **Beilby's ball.** (Grose, 1st ed.)

bile. The pudenda muliebria : so says F. & H., but I suspect that there is a confusion with *bite*, q.v. —2. A C. 19–20 sol. for *boil*, n. and v., though for the n. *bile* was once S.E.

bile yer can ! A sarcastic c.p. retort : proletarian Glasgow (— 1934).

bilge. Nonsense ; empty talk : Public Schools' (from ca. 1906) >, in 1919, gen. Desmond Coke, *The House Prefect*, 1908, ' Let's go . . . This is awful bilge ' ; Lyell ; R. Blaker, *Night-Shift*, 1934, referring to 1920, ' " Bilge " was the polite word, current in those days for the later " tripe ".' Ex *bilge-water*.

bilge-cod. Fish served at dinner on Fridays : *Conway* s. : from ca. 1890. Masefield.

bilge-water. Bad beer : coll. : C. 19–20. Ex the bad water collecting at the bottom of a ship.

bilin', biling. Boiling : sol. Esp. in *the whole bilin'* or *biling*. See **boiling, the whole.** Baumann.

bilious. Bad, ' rotten ', as e.g. ' in bilious form ' : Society : from 1930. (Graham Shepard, *Tea-Tray in the Sky*, 1934.)

biliously. The corresponding adv. : id. : id. (Ibid.)

bilk. A statement or a reply devoid of truth or sense : ca. 1630–1800. Perhaps a thinned form of *balk*.—2. A hoax, humbug, or imposition (— 1664) ; ob.—Hence, 3. A swindler or a cheat, as in Sheridan, ' Johnny W[i]lks, Johnny W[i]lks, thou greatest of bilks ', 1790. Adj., wrong, misleading, senseless : C. 18. Ex cribbage and = *balk*.

bilk, v. To deceive, cheat ; defraud, fail to pay ; elude, evade : all these coll. senses (B.E. is prob. wrong in considering the word to be c.) arose in Restoration days and all had > S.E. by 1750. Grose, 1st ed., 'Bilking a coachman, a box keeper, or a poor whore, was formerly among men of the town thought a gallant action.' Cf. the n.

*bilk the blues. To evade the police : c. or low s. : from ca. 1845 ; ob.

bilk the schoolmaster. To gain knowledge—esp. by experience—without paying for it : 1821, Moncrieff's *Tom and Jerry* : coll. ; ob.

bilker. A cheat(er), swindler : s. (1717 : O.E.D. Sup.) >, ca. 1800, coll. ; now almost S.E. Likewise *bilking*, vbl.n. (— 1750), was almost S.E. by 1850 ; *bilker* is now, except in its abbr. form *bilk*, rather ob.

Bill. See **Billy.**

bill. A list of boys due to see the headmaster at noon, as in Brinsley Richards, *Seven Years at Eton*, 1876 ; also of those excused from ' absence '. At Harrow School, names-calling : from ca. 1850. —2. In c., a term of imprisonment : from ca. 1830. Always with *long* or *short*.—3. A variant of *bil*, q.v. (*A New Canting Dict.*, 1725.)

Bill Adams. Euphemistic for *b****r all*, nothing or extremely little : military : G.W. Cf. *Fanny Adams*. **(B. & P.)**

bill at sight, pay a. To be, by nature, apt to enter into sexual intercourse : ca. 1820–1910. Egan's Grose, 1823.

Bill Bailey. A jocular c.p. form of address : ca. 1900–12. Collinson. Cf. *would you* . . .

bill brighter. A small faggot used for lighting coal fires : from ca. 1840 ex Bill Bright, a servant extant at least as late as 1830 : Winchester College (see Mansfield).

Bill Harris. Bilharziasis (or -osis) : Australian military : late 1914–16. By ' Hobson-Jobson '.

bill in the water, hold one with (his). To keep (him) in suspense : ca. 1570–1700. Coll.

Bill Jim ; occ. **Billjim.** An Australian : Australian : from ca. 1912. Ex the frequency of those two hypocoristic forms of *William* and *James*.

Bill Massey's. N.Z. army-boots : New Zealand soldiers' : in G.W. Ex the late Wm. Massey, who was the N.Z. War Minister.

bill on the pump at Aldgate. See **Aldgate.**

bill of sale. Widow's mourning clothes, esp. her hat : late C. 17–19 († by 1890) B.E. Cf. *house* (or *tenement*) *to let*.

bill up. To confine (a soldier) to barracks : military coll. (— 1890). Esp. as :

billed up. Confined to barracks : in the Guards' regiments, ca. 1860–1915.

biller, billing-boy. A boy distributing advertisements (*bills*) : commercial coll. (— 1887). Baumann.

billet. A post, a job : from ca. 1880 ; coll. In c., *get a billet* = to get a soft job in prison : late C. 19–20.

billet, every bullet has its. Every bullet must land somewhere, and only those die in battle who are marked by fate for such a death. Coll. from ca. 1695. Wesley in his *Journal*, June 6, 1765—I quote the O.E.D.—' He never received one wound. So true is the odd saying of King William, that " every bullet has its billet ".' The phrase is anticipated by Gascoigne, 1575, ' Every bullet hath a lighting place ' ; cf. Smollett's ' Every shot has its commission, d'ye see ' (Apperson). In the G.W. many soldiers pessimistically assumed that the phrase implied a loading of the dice against them.

billiard-block. One who, for ulterior motives, suffers fools and other disagreeables with apparent gladness : Mrs. Gore, *Mothers and Daughters*, 1831. † Society s.

*billiard slum. In Australian c. of ca. 1870–1910, false pretences. Here, *slum* = trick, dodge, game. *Go on the b.s.*, to practise such trickery. Ex :—*give it* (*to*) '*em on the billiard slum*, to impose on them with that swindle which is termed a ' mace ' (q.v.) : c. of ca. 1810–70. Vaux, 1812.

billicock. See **billycock.**

billieo !, go to. Go to blazes ! : New Zealanders' (—' 1935). Cf. *billy-o*.

billikin. A small tin can used as a kettle : coll. : 1926 (O.E.D. Sup.). Ex *billy-can*.

billing-boy. See **biller.**

Billingsgate. Foul language ; vituperation : Commonwealth period ; coll. > S.E. by 1800. Gayton, 1654, ' Most bitter Billingsgate rhetorick ' (Apperson). The language used at the Billingsgate fish-market was certainly ' strong '. See esp. O.E.D. and F. & H.—2. Whence, a person foulmouthed or vituperative : ca. 1680–1830.

Billingsgate (it). To talk coarsely ; to vituperate (a person) : (— 1678) coll. ; † by 1850. In C. 19–20, *talk Billingsgate*, also coll.

Billingsgate fish-fag, no better than a. Rude; uncouth : C. 19–20 coll. ; ob.

Billingsgate pheasant. A red herring : from ca. 1830 ; ob. Cf. *Atlantic ranger*.

Billio. See billy-o.—**Billjim.** See Bill Jim.

Bill(y). Shakespeare ; esp. *spout Bill(y)* : (low) coll. (— 1887). Baumann. Ex *William* Shakespeare.—2. (**Billy.**) Abbr. *silly Billy* : coll. : late C. 19–20.

billy. A silk pocket-handkerchief : ca. 1820–1900 : c. (Scottish says ' Ducange Anglicus ', citing Brandon, 1839) or low. Other C. 19 styles and fancies in handkerchiefs—several of the terms survive—were the *belcher, bird's-eye wipe, blood-red fancy, blue billy, cream fancy, king's man, Randal's man, Water's man, yellow fancy, yellow man* : qq.v. —2. A truncheon (— 1874). H., 5th ed. Ex U.S. —3. In Australia and derivatively, but less, in New Zealand, the can that serves the bushman as both kettle and tea-pot : s. (ca. 1850) >, by 1880, coll. ; *billy-can* (— 1892) is rarer and more an urban than a rural term. Morris.—4. In c., *billy* is stolen metal : mid-C. 19–20. Implied in H., 1st ed. Cf. *billy-hunting*.—5. The removal or shifting of a marble : schoolboys' : late C. 19–20.—6. Abbr. *billycock* (*hat*) : coll. (— 1887). Baumann.—7. Abbr. *billy-goat* : coll. : C. 20.—8. See **billy with, play.**

Billy, Our. The Duke of Clarence, son of George IV : ca. 1820–40. *The Creevey Papers.*

billy (or **B.**), whistling. A locomotive : coll. : late C. 19–20. Manchon. Cf. *puffing billy*, q.v.

Billy Barlow. A street clown, a mountebank : from ca. 1840 ; † by 1920. Ex an actual character, the hero of a slang song. Such a clown is also called a *Jim Crow* (by rhyming s. with *saltimbanco*) or a *saltimbanco*.

Billy Blue. Admiral Cornwallis (1744–1819) : naval nickname : late C. 18–early 19. He ' always kept the Blue Peter flying when weather drove him to shelter from the blockade of Brest ' (Bowen) in 1795. ' His various nicknames among the sailors, " Billy go tight ", given on account of his rubicund complexion, " Billy Blue ", " Coachee ", and " Mr. Whip ", seem to show that he was regarded with more of affection than reverence ' (*Encyclopædia Britannica*).—2. Unless the usually dependable Dawson errs, also Lord Admiral St. Vincent (1735–1823) : from ca. 1790 ; long †.

Billy Bluegum. A native bear (coala or koala): Australian coll. : C. 20.

Billy born drunk. ' A drunkard beyond the memory of his neighbours ', Ware : low London : 1895, *The People*, Jan. 6 ; very ob.

billy-boy. (Sailors') a two-masted vessel resembling a galliot, the fore-mast square-rigged. Coming mostly from Goole, they are also called *Humber keels*. From ca. 1850 ; coll.

billy-button. A journeyman tailor : from ca. 1840.—2. In rhyming s., mutton (— 1857). ' Ducange Anglicus.'

*billy buz(z)man. A thief specialising in silk pocket- and necker-chiefs : ca. 1830–1900 c. See **billy,** sense 1, and **buzman.**

billy-can. See **billy,** 3.

billy-cock. A low-crowned, wide-brimmed felt hat : coll. (— 1862). In Australia, the hat so named is made of hard, not soft felt, and its brim is turned up : coll. (— 1880). The word may be a phonetic development from the C. 18 *bully-cocked* (Amherst's *Terræ Filius*, 1721) ; but the hats were,

in precisely this style, made first for *Billy Coke*, a Melton Mowbray sportsman, ca. 1842—though admittedly this derivation smacks of folk-etymology.

billy-doo. A *billet-doux*, a love-letter : C. 18–20 ; coll.

*billy-fencer. A marine-store dealer : c. ; from ca. 1840 ; ob. See the two words.

*billy-fencing shop. A shop receiving stolen precious metal : c. (— 1845) ; ob.

Billy-go-tight. See **Billy Blue.**

billy-goat. A male goat : coll. : 1861, Peacock (O.E.D.).—2. Hence (— 1882) the s. sense, a tufted beard.

billy-goat in stays. An effeminate officer : naval : ca. 1870–85, when many young ' swells ' wore stays. Ware.

billy-ho. See **billy-o.**

*billy-hunting. Post-1820, ob. c. for collecting and buying old metal : ex *billy*, sense 4. Also, going out to steal silk handkerchiefs : same period : ex *billy*, sense 1.

billy-o (or **oh**) or occ. **billy-ho, like.** With great vigour or speed : mid-C. 19–20. *The Referee,* Aug. 9, 1885, ' It'll rain like *billy-ho* ! ' Perhaps ex the name used euphemistically for *the devil*.

Billy Puffer or **B.p.** or **b.p.** A name given to the early steamers by seamen : ca. 1840–1920. Bowen, ' Compare Puffing Billies on land.'

billy-roller. ' A long stout stick . . . used . . . to beat the little ones employed in the mills when their strength fails ', Mrs. Trollope, *Michael Armstrong,* 1840. (The O.E.D. records at 1834.) See, too, Ure's *Dict. of the Arts*, vol. iii, 1875. Coll., †. Cf. *billy*, a truncheon.

Billy Ruffian. H.M.S. *Bellerophon* : naval : C. 20. Bowen. By ' Hobson-Jobson '.

Billy the Butcher. The Duke of Cumberland (1721–65). Ex his cruelty when suppressing the Jacobite rising after the battle of Culloden, 1746. His sobriquets were *the Bloody Butcher* and *the Butcher of Culloden.* Dawson.

Billy Turniptop. An agricultural labourer : from ca. 1890 ; virtually †. *The Daily Telegraph,* July 10, 1895. (Ware.)

Billy Wells. A big gun or its shell : military : late 1914–18. F. & Gibbons. Ex Bombardier Wells, the English heavy-weight boxer. Cf. *Jack Johnson,* q.v.

billy with, play. To play the deuce with : coll. : late C. 19–20. (R. Knox, *The Body in the Silo,* 1933.) See also **billy-o.**

Bim (or **Bimm**) ; **Bimshire.** A Barbadian (cf. *Badian*) ; the island of Barbados, which is also (— 1890) called *Little England* : coll. : mid-C. 19–20. Perhaps ex *vim*, as suggested in Paton's *Down the Islands,* 1887.

bime-by. By-and-by : dial. (— 1839 and) Cockney sol. (— 1887). Ex U.S., where recorded in 1824 (O.E.D. Sup.). Baumann.

Bimm. See **Bim.**

*bimp. A shilling : C. 20 vagrants' c. See **beong.**

bimster. ' A rope's end used in the training ships for punishment purposes ' : naval : late C. 19–20. Bowen. Perhaps *beamster*, something applied to the ' beam ' or rump : but cf. **bim** (Addenda).

bin. Been : in C. 19–20, sol. except in dial. Earlier, a S.E. variant.

*bin. A trousers-pocket : c., and low : from ca. 1920. J. Curtis, *The Gilt Kid,* 1936. One dips thereinto.

bind. A depressing or very dull person, task or duty : Royal Air Force : from ca. 1920. (Cf. *binder*, 4.) Ex :

bind, v. To weary, bore a person : Royal Air Force : from ca. 1920. Cf. *binder*, 4. ' Jack ? Oh, he binds me solid ! '

*****binder.** An egg : late C. 19–20 c. >, by 1910, low. Ware. Cf. the † S.E. medical sense of *binder* : Anything causing constipation.—2. A meal, esp. a good, satisfying one : New Zealanders' : C. 20.—3. See **tiddley and binder.**—4. A bore (person) : Royal Air Force : from ca. 1920. Ex *bind*, v. Cf. *bind*, n.

binder, go a. To eat a meal : New Zealanders' (esp. tramps') : from before 1932. See **binder**, 2.

bindle. A notable ' howler ' : Dulwich College (— 1907). Collinson. Origin ? Perhaps a blend : ? *bungle* + *swindle*.

bing or **byng.** Gen. *bing a-vast*. To go : c. of mid-C. 16–early 19. Scott has *b. out*, in *Guy Mannering*, and *b. avast*, in *Nigel*. Perhaps of Romany origin.

bing-bang. Echoic for a repeated heavy impact or a continued banging : coll. : from ca. 1910. (O.E.D. Sup.) Prob. at first a nursery word evoked by the excitement arising from ' playing soldiers '.

binge. A drinking bout : Oxford University (— 1889). Barrère & Leland. Hence, in G.W., ' an expedition, deliberately undertaken in company for the purpose of relieving depression, celebrating an occasion or a spasm of high spirits, by becoming intoxicated ' (B. & P.) ; also as v. Food often, music and singing sometimes, form part of a ' binge '. More an officers' than a private soldiers' word. Perhaps ex *bingo*, q.v. ; or ex dial. v. *binge* influenced by *bingo*, the latter being the more prob., for *binge*, a heavy drinking-bout, exists in dial. as early as 1854 (O.E.D.).—2. See :

binge, have a ; haul off and take a binge. To (go away) get a sleep : nautical : ca. 1880–1910.

binge a cask. ' To get the remaining liquor from the wood by rinsing it with water ' : nautical coll. : C. 19–20. Bowen. Ex *binge*, to drench : see **binge.** Also *bull the* (or *a*) *cask*, q.v.

bingey. See **bingy.**

Bingham's Dandies. (Military) the 17th Lancers : from ca. 1830 ; slightly ob. Its colonel of 1826–37, Lord Bingham, insisted on well-fitting uniforms. Earlier, the 17th Lancers were called *the Horse Marines*, q.v., and from ca. 1870 *the Death or Glory Boys*.

binghi. See **bingy.**

bingling. A combination, barberly and verbal, of *bobbing* and *shingling* : coll. : middle 1920's. Collinson.

*****bingo.** In late C. 17 (as in B.E.) and in C. 18, c. ; in C. 19 (as in *Tom Brown at Oxford*), s. ; ob. Spirituous liquor, esp. brandy. Perhaps *b*, (cf. *b. and s.*) + *stingo*, q.v., or ex *binge*, to soak, steep, after *stingo* (see Grose, P.). The word occurs notably in *Fighting Attie's Song*, in Lytton's *Paul Clifford*. The O.E.D. dates it at 1861.—2. Whence *bingo boy* and *mort*, male and female dram-drinker : c. of late C. 17–early 19.

*****bingo club.** ' A set of Rakes, Lovers of that Liquor ' (brandy), B.E. : late C. 17–18 c.

*****bingo mort.** See **bingo**, 2.

bingy ; bingey ; or, as *The Sydney Bulletin*, keeping closer to the Aboriginal, spells it, **binghi.** Stomach, belly : Australian : C. 20. Dictionaried in Webster, 1926.

bingy, adj. (Of butter) bad, ropy ; cf. *vinnied*. Largely dial. (— 1857) ; as s., ob.

binnacle word. An affected, a too literary word, which, says Grose (1785), the sailors jeeringly offer to chalk up on the binnacle. † by 1890.

binned, be. To be hanged : London : 1883–ca. 1910. Ware, ' Referring to Bartholomew Binns, a hangman appointed in 1883.'

bint. A girl or woman ; a prostitute,—in which role the female was often called *saida* [sah-eeda] *bint*, lit. ' a " Good-day ! " girl ' : among soldiers in Egypt : late C. 19–20, but esp. in G.W. Direct ex Arabic.—2. Hence, *the bint*, the man playing ' a female part in a Divisional Concert Party or Troupe ' : military : 1916–18. F. & Gibbons.

biockey. Money : Anglo-Italian, esp. in London : mid-C. 19–20. Ex It. *baiocchi*, ' browns '.

bionet. B.E.'s variant of *bagonet*, q.v.

bioscope. (A drink of) brandy : ca. 1910–14. The more a man drinks, the more ' moving pictures ' he sees.

birch broom. A room : rhyming s. (— 1857). ' Ducange Anglicus '.

birch-broom in a fit, like a. (Of a head) rough, tously, tousled : C. 19 ; e.g. in Hindley's *Cheap Jack*, 1876.

Birchen or **Birchin(g) Lane, send one to.** To flog ; ex *birch*, to thrash : coll. : ? C 17–18. An allusion to Birchin Lane, London. Cf. :

birchen salve, anoint with. To cane ; thrash : C. 16–17 coll. Tyndale. (O.E.D.)

Bird : always **the Bird.** The Eagle Tavern : theatrical : ca. 1840–85. Ware, ' General Booth of the Salvation Army bought it up (1882).'

*****bird.** ' The foole that is caught ', Greene : c. of ca. 1585–1600.—2. A prisoner : New Zealand military : 1915–18. Ex *cage*, a detention-camp. Prob. ex earlier *cage*, a prison, is :—3. Prison. Rare except as *do bird*, to ' do time ', and *in bird*, in prison. C. 20 c. Edgar Wallace in *The Mind of Mr. J. G. Reader* ; David Hume.—4. Collectively, previous convictions : c. (— 1935). David Hume. —5. As **the bird**, a hissing of an actor : theatrical (1883 ; ob.) ; cf. *big bird*, *goose*, qq.v. Actors used to say ' The bird's there.' Ware. Ex the hissing of a goose.—6. A man, a chap ; esp. in *old bird* (1853). O.E.D. (Sup.). Cf. *downy bird*, q.v.— 7. A troublesome seaman : nautical : late C. 19–20. Bowen.—8. (A) **bird**, a girl : from ca. 1880. A sweetheart : military : from ca. 1890. A harlot : from ca. 1900. The last two nuances may represent a survival ex early S.E., but more prob. they have arisen independently.—9. See **bird, give the.**

bird, v. To thieve, steal, seek for plunder : late C. 16–17. Cf. *black-birding*.

bird, big. See **big bird.**

bird, funny. An occ. variant of *bird*, *queer*, q.v. : late C. 19–20. Baumann.

bird, give (one) or, hence, **get the.** To dismiss (a person), send him about his business ; to be so treated : late C. 19–20. Ex the theatre : see **bird**, n., 5.—2. In Australia, *give the bird* is to treat with derision : from before 1916. C. J. Dennis.

bird, like a. See the **like a . . .** entry.

bird, little. An unnamed informant or, rarely, informer : (— 1833) coll. >, by 1890, S.E.— though far from literary.

bird, old. See **bird**, n., 6.

bird, queer. A strange fellow : C. 19–20 ; coll. See **queer, quire bird.**

Bird and Baby, the. A mid-C. 18–early 19

facetious version of the Eagle and Child (inn). Grose, 1st ed.

bird-cage. (Women's dress) a bustle : ca. 1850–1900.—2. A four-wheeled cab : ca. 1850–1910.—3. (Racing) The Newmarket race-course paddock where the saddling is done (— 1884) ; ob.—4. In G.W., a compound for prisoners ; cf. *cage.*—5. A point occupied by a sniper : military : G.W. (B. & P.)—6. **The Birdcage,** 'the elaborately entrenched position, north of Salonika, constructed in 1916 to serve as a final stronghold ' : Eastern troops' for rest of the War. F. & Gibbons.

Bird-Catchers, the. The Royal Irish Fusiliers, since 1811 ; the 1st Royal Dragoons and the Scots Greys, since 1815 (Waterloo) : military. F. & Gibbons. Ex the capture of French eagles : cf., therefore, *Aiglers.*

bird-lime. A thief : C. 18, e.g. in Vanbrugh. —2. Time : rhyming s. (— 1857). ' Ducange Anglicus ', 1st ed.—3. In G.W. : a recruiting sergeant ; ob.

bird-lime !, come off the. Tell that to the marines ! : low (— 1923). Manchon.

bird-man. An aviator : coll. : ca. 1908–18. O.E.D. (Sup.).

bird-mouthed. Apt to mince matters : from ca. 1600 ; coll. > S.E. by 1700 ; ob.

bird of passage. A person never long in one place : C. 19–20 : coll. ; in C. 20, S.E.

bird-seed. Sweets ; chocolates : military : C. 20. F. & Gibbons, ' Something nice for the " Bird " ' : see bird, n., 8, 2nd nuance.

bird-spit. A rapier : coll : ca. 1600–1820.

bird-witted. Wild-headed, inattentive ; inconsiderate ; gullible : ca. 1600–1890 ; coll. till ca. 1800, then S.E. B.E., Grose. (O.E.D.)

birdie. A hole done in one under the bogey figure : golfing coll. : from ca. 1920. O.E.D. (Sup.). Cf. *eagle.*

bird's-eye. Baumann, 1887, records it as a variant of :

bird's-eye wipe. A silk handkerchief with eye-like spots : from ca. 1820 ; ob. Also *bird's-eye fogle* : low. Adumbrated in Pepys's *Diary* (*bird's-eye hood*) ; app. first in Egan's Grose, 1823.

birds of a feather. Rogues of the same gang : late C. 17–18 ; e.g. in B.E. Ex late C. 16–20 S.E. sense, persons of like character, mainly in the proverb *birds of a feather fly* (1578 ; long †) or *flock* (1607) *together,* as esp. in Apperson.

birds with one stone, kill two. To manage to do two things where one expects, or has a right to expect, to do only one : from ca. 1600 ; coll. till ca. 1700, when it > S.E.

birk. A house ; back s. on *crib,* q.v. H., 1st ed., 1859.

Birreligion. The (political) import of Augustine Birrell's Educational Bill of 1906 : political ; now only historical. Collinson.

birthday suit, in one's. Naked. Smollett, *Humphry Clinker,* 1771 : ' I went in the morning to a private place, along with the housemaid, and we bathed in our birth-day soot.' Increasingly less used in C. 20 owing to the supremacy of *in the altogether.* Prob. suggested by Swift's *birthday gear,* 1731—cf. the rare *birthday attire* (1860) : both of which are prob. to be accounted as s. O.E.D. (Sup.).

Biscuit, the. The 10.30 p.m. express goods-train carrying biscuits from Reading to London : railwaymen's : from ca. 1910. *The Daily Telegraph,* Aug. 15, 1936. Cf. *the Bacca,* q.v.

biscuit ; occ. a **dog-biscuit.** A brown mattress or palliasse : military : 1909. Collinson ; B. & P. Ex shape, colour, and hardness.

biscuit, take the. See **take the biscuit.**

biscuit and beer. To subject to a *biscuit and beer bet,* a swindling bet of a biscuit against a glass of beer : low London : ca. 1850–1910. Ware.

*****Biscuit Factory, the.** The Reading Gaol (closed down a few years ago) : early C. 20 c. (It adjoined Huntley & Palmer's factory.) Cf. :

Biscuit Men, the. Reading Football Club (' soccer ') : sporting : C. 20. See preceding ; cf. *Toffee Men.*

bish. A bishop : C. 20 ; rare before G.W.—2. A mistake : Seaford Preparatory School : from ca. 1925.

bishop. A fly burnt at a candle : late C. 16–mid-17. Florio. Cf. *bishop,* v., 1.—Cf. 1, *b,* ' a mushroom growth in the wick of a burning candle ' : late C. 16–19.—2. A warm drink of wine, with sugar and either oranges or lemons : Ned Ward in *The English Spy,* that work which, at the beginning of C. 18, held an unflattering but realistically witty mirror up to London. Ob. by 1890 after being coll. by 1750, S.E. by 1800.—3. ' One of the largest of Mrs. Philips's purses [cundums], used to contain the others ', Grose, 1st ed. : low : late C. 18–early 19.—4. A chamber-pot : C. 19–20, ob.—5. At Winchester College, ca. 1820–1900, the sapling that binds a large faggot together ; cf. *dean,* q.v.

bishop, v. Burn, let burn : coll., C. 18–20. Ex the C. 16–20 (ob.) proverbial sayings, ' The bishop has put his foot into the pot ' or ' The bishop hath played the cook ', both recorded in Tyndale.—2. To use deception, esp. the burning of marks into the teeth, to make a horse look young (— 1727, R. Bradley, *The Family Dict.*) : v.t. ex a man so named, and often as vbl.n., *bishoping.* Coll. by ca. 1780, S.E. by ca. 1820.—3. To murder by drowning : from 1836, when one Bishop drowned a boy in order to sell the body for dissecting purposes : the irrepressible Barham, ' I burk'd the papa, now I'll bishop the son.' F. & H. describes it as † in 1890, but the S.O.D. allows it currency in 1933.—4. In printing, *bishop the balls,* to water the balls : 1811, *Lex. Bal.* ; ob.

bishop ! (rarely) ; **oh bishop !** A c.p. used in derision on the announcement of stale news : the 1890's : *Conway* Training Ship. Masefield.

bishop, do a. See **do a bishop.**

bishop hath blessed it !, the. A c.p. of C. 16 applied ' when a thing speedeth not well ' (Tyndale, 1528).

bishoping. The performing of a bishop's duties : coll. : 1857, Trollope. (O.E.D.)—2. See **bishop,** v., 2.

Bishops, the. The Bishop Auckland ' soccer ' team : sporting : C. 20.

bishop's finger. A guide-post : C. 19. Halliwell. Cf. *finger-post,* a parson.

bishop's sister's son, he is the. He has a big ' pull ' (much influence) : ecclesiastical c.p. : C. 16. Tyndale, 1528.

bishop's wife, as in *what, a bishop's wife ? eat and drink in your gloves ?* A semi-proverbial c.p. of mid-C. 17–early 18. Ray, 1678. ' This is a cryptic saying ', remarks Apperson ; prob. it = ' You're quite the fine lady (now) ! '

biskiwits, biskiwitz. Prisoners of war in Germany : military : 1915–18. B. & P. Ex the Ger. for the maize biscuits sometimes obtainable from the canteen in prison camps

Bismarcker, bismarquer, to. Cheat, esp. at cards or billiards : ca. 1866–1900. In 1865–6, Bismarck, the German Chancellor, pursued a foreign policy that rendered indignant a large section of European thought. The *bismarquer* form shows Fr. influence.

bisque, give (someone) **fifteen,** etc., **and a.** To defeat very easily ; ' leave standing '. Coll. : from ca. 1880 ; ob. Ex tennis.

bit. In C. 16–early 19 c., with variant *bite*, money ; in C. 19 c., *bit* also = a purse.—2. The silver piece of lowest denomination in almost any country : C. 18–19.—3. Any small piece of money : coll., C. 19–20, ob.—4. A fourpenny-bit (1829) : still so called in 1890, though *joey* was much commoner.—5. The smallest coin in Jamaica : Dyche, 1748.—6. A term of imprisonment : c. (— 1869) > low.—7. A girl, a young woman, esp. regarded sexually : low coll. : C. 19–20. Cf. *piece*, q.v.— 8. In such phrases as *a bit of a fool*, rather or somewhat of a fool, the word is coll. ; from ca. 1880. Baumann.—9. Coll. also in the adv. phrases *a bit*, a little or a whit, late C. 17–20 ; *not a bit*, not at all, from ca. 1749 (Fielding) ; and *every bit*, entirely (— 1719).—10. Likewise coll. when it = a short while, either as *for*, or *in*, *a bit* or simply as *a bit* : from ca. 1650. Walton ; Wm. Godwin, in his best work (*Caleb Williams*), ' I think we may as well stop here a bit.' (O.E.D.)

*****bit,** past ppl. of **bite,** v., 1 : q.v. ' Robb'd, Cheated or Out-witted ', B.E.

bit, do a. See **do a bit.**

bit, do one's. See **do one's bit.**

*****bit-faker** or **bit-turner-out.** A coiner of bad money : C. 19–20 c. ; the latter †. Vaux. Whence *bit-faking*, vbl.n., counterfeiting. See **bit,** n., 1.

bit his grannam. See **bite his grannam.**

bit-maker. A counterfeiter (— 1857), ob. : low, perhaps even c.

bit of all right, a (**little**). Something excellent ; a pretty or an obliging female : C. 20. Manchon ; Freeman Wills Crofts, *Mystery in the Channel*, 1931, ' This looked a bit of all right.' Cf. *bit of ' tout droit '*, q.v.

bit o(f) beef. ' A quid of tobacco ; less than a pipeful. A . . . reference to tobacco-chewing staying hunger ', Ware : low : ca. 1850–1910.

bit of ; bits of. (Cf. *bit*, n., 8.) When used affectionately or depreciatively, it is a coll., dating from late C. 18. Anderson, *Ballads*, 1808, ' Oor bits o' bairns ' (E.D.D.).

bit o(f) blink. A drink : tavern rhyming s. (— 1909) : ob. Ware.

bit of blood. A high-spirited or a thoroughbred horse : 1819, Tom Moore ; slightly ob.

bit o(f) bull. Beef : C. 19. Like the preceding entry, s. verging on coll.

bit of cavalry. A horse : ca. 1825–80. Moncrieff, 1821.

bit o(f) crumb. ' A pretty plump girl—one of the series of words designating woman imm. following the introduction of " jam " as the fashionable term (in unfashionable quarters) for lovely woman ', Ware : from ca. 1880 ; ob. Cf. *crummy*, 1, q.v., and *bit of grease*.

*****bit o(f) dirt.** A hill : tramps' c. (— 1935).

bit of doing, take a. To be difficult to do : coll. : late C. 19–20.

bit of ebony. A negro or a negress : C. 19–20, coll.

bit of fat. An unexpected advantage, esp. (cf.

bunce) if pecuniary : C. 19–20 ; cf. *fat*, n.—2. Whence *have a bit of fat from the eye*, to eat ' the orbits ' of a sheep's eyes—a delicacy (Ware, 1909).

bit of fluff. The same as *bit of muslin*, q.v. : C. 20.

*****bit of gig.** Fun ; a spree : c. (— 1823) ; very ob. Egan's Grose.

bit o(f) grease. (Not derogatory.) A stout and smiling Hindu woman : Anglo-Indian military (— 1909). Ware. Cf. *bit of crumb*, q.v.

bit of grey. ' An elderly person at a ball or a marriage . . . to give an air of staid dignity ' : Society : ca. 1880–1910. Ware. Ex grey hair.

bit of haw-haw. A fop ; London taverns' : ca. 1860–1914. Ware. Ex *haw ! haw !*

bit of hard (or **stiff**). A *penis* (*erectus*) : low: C. 19–20.

bit of it !, not a. No ; not at all ; you're wrong: coll. : late C. 19–20.

bit o(f) jam. Something easy ; a pretty, esp. if accessible, girl ; prob. from ca. 1850, though Ware dates it at 1879. Cf. *tart*, *jam* ; and see **bit of crumb.**

*****bit of leaf.** Tobacco : mid-C. 19–20 c. ; ob. J. Greenwood, 1876.

bit of (**one's**) **mind.** Gen. with *give*. One's candid, unfavourable opinion : coll. ; from ca. 1860.

bit o(f) muslin. A (young) girl, esp. if a prostitute : ca. 1873 ; ob. H., 5th ed. (a *bit of stuff*) ; Whiteing, 1899, ' She's a neat little bit o' muslin, ain't she now ? ' Cf. *skirt* and *bit of fluff*.

bit of mutton. A woman ; gen. a harlot : C. 19–20, ob. ; perhaps coll. rather than s.

bit o(f) pooh. Flattery, ' blarney ' ; courtship: workmen's (— 1909) ; almost †. Ware. Ex *pooh !*, nonsense !

bit o(f) prairie. ' A momentary lull in the traffic at any point in the Strand . . . From the bareness of the road for a mere moment, e.g. " A bit o' prairie—go ",' Ware : London : ca. 1850–1914. Cf. S.E. *island*.

bit o(f) raspberry. An attractive girl : from ca. 1880 ; very ob. Ware. On *bit of jam*, q.v.

bit o(f) red. A soldier : coll. : late C. 18–19. Ware. Ex colour of jacket.

bit of skirt. A girl ; a woman : coll. : from ca. 1900 ; esp. military, Australian, New Zealand.

bit of snug. The act of kind : low : late C. 19– 20 ; ? ob.—2. The penis : id. : id.

bit o(f) soap. A charming girl—though frail : low London : 1883–ca. 1914. Ware.

bit of sticks. A corpse : sporting, from ca. 1860 ; ob.

bit of stiff. Money not in specie ; a bank or a currency note ; a bill of exchange : from ca. 1850. Lever. Whence *do a bit of stiff*, to accept a bill of exchange or a post-dated cheque.—2. See **bit of hard.**

bit o(f) stuff. An overdressed man : low (— 1874). H., 5th ed.—2. A (young) woman ; mid-C. 19–20 ; ob. Cf. Marryat's *piece of stuff*, 1834, and *bit of muslin*, q.v.

bit of ' tout droit ', a. A ' bit of all right ', q.v. : Anglo-French (— 1923) ; ob. Manchon. Ex the bogus Fr. *un petit morceau de tout droit*.

bit o(f) tripe. A wife : rhyming (!) s. (— 1909) ; virtually †. Ware. Cf. *trouble and strife*.

bit off, a. See **off, a bit.**

bit on, (have) a. (To lay) a stake : racing : 1894, George Moore.—2. As adj., *a bit on* = drunk : low : C. 19–20 ; ob. ? cf. *bite one's grannam*, q.v.

*bit the blow. See **bite the blow.**

bit of wood in the hole, put a. See **wood in it !**

bit you ?, what's. See **what's bit you ?**

bitch. A lewd woman : S.E. from origin (— 1400) to ca. 1660, when it > coll. ; since ca. 1837 it has been a vulg. rather than a coll. (In C. 20 low London it = a fast young woman.) As coll. : e.g. in Arbuthnot's *John Bull* and Fielding's *Tom Jones.* —2. Opprobriously of a man : in C. 16, S.E. ; in C. 17–18, coll., as in Hobbes and Fielding.—3. Tea : Cambridge University, ca. 1820–1914. E.D.D. Prob. ex *stand bitch.*—4. The queen in playing-cards, mainly public-house ; from ca. 1840. Cf. *butcher.*—5. A male harlot : c. : C. 20. James Curtis, *The Gilt Kid*, 1936.

bitch, v. Go whoring ; frequent harlots : from Restoration times to ca. 1830 : coll. Ex *bitch*, n., 1. —2. To yield, cry off, from fear : coll. verging on S.E. : C. 18–early 19. Ex a bitch's yielding.— 3. V.t., to spoil or bungle : from ca. 1820 : coll. ' Jon Bee ', 1823. Prob. a thinned form of *botch* : W.

bitch !, I may be a whore but can't be a. A low London woman's c.p. reply on being called *a bitch* : late C. 18–mid-19. Grose (1st ed.), who prefaces it with : ' The most offensive appellation that can be given to an English woman, even more provoking than that of whore, as may be gathered from the regular Billingsgate or St. Giles answer ', etc. Cf. the C. 18 proverbial saying, *the bitch that I mean is not a dog* (Apperson).

bitch, stand. To preside at tea or perform some other female part : late C. 18–early 19. Grose, 1st ed.

bitch booby. A rustic lass : mid-C. 18–early 19 ; military (Grose, 1st ed.). Cf. *dog booby*, q.v.

bitch of, make a. A variant of *bitch*, v. 3 : low : C. 20.

bitch party. A party composed of women : from ca. 1880. Orig. (ca. 1850) a tea-party : Cambridge and Oxford. Ex *bitch*, n., 3.

bitch-pie !, go to hell (where you belong) **and help your mother to make a.** A c.p. elaboration of *go to hell !* : mid-C. 18–20 ; ob. Grose, 2nd ed., 1788 ; Manchon.

bitch the pot. To pour out the tea : under-graduates' : late C. 18–mid-19. Ware.

bitched, buggered, and bewildered. See **Barney's bull.**

bitches' wine. Champagne : from ca. 1850. Cf. *cat's water.*

*bite. The female pudend : (prob.) c. : late C. 17–early 19, as in B.E. (' *The Cull wapt the Mort's bite*, i.e. the Fellow enjoyed the Whore briskly ') and Grose ; perhaps ex A.-S. *byht*, the fork of the legs, a sense recurring in *Sir Gawayn*, vv. 1340, 1349.—2. A deception, from harmless to criminal : Steele, 1711 ; ob. by 1890, † by 1920.— Hence, 3. A sharper ; trickster : c. or low s. > gen. s. : late C. 17–early 19, as in B.E., Fielding, Smollett.—Hence, 4. A hard bargainer : C. 19.— ? hence, 5. Any person or thing suspected of being different from, not necessarily worse than, what appearances indicate : C. 19–20 coll., ob.—6. (Cf. sense 4.) A Yorkshireman : from late 1850's, though recorded in Cumberland dialect as early as 1805 ; ob. ; at first, pejorative. H., 1st ed.—7. In c., C. 16–early 19 : money ; cash. It occurs as late as John Davis's novel, *The Post Captain*, 1805. Cf. *bit*, 1, q.v.

*bite, v. To steal ; rob : late C. 17–early 19 c. B.E.—2. Deceive, swindle : orig. (— 1669) c., but

by 1709, when Steele employs it in the *Tatler*, it is clearly s. ; except in the passive, † by ca. 1870.— 3. To ' take the bait ' : C. 17–20 coll.—4. To drive a hard bargain with : C. 19–20 coll. Implied in ' Jon Bee ', 1823.—5. (Of a book, a MS.) to impress or appeal to : publishers' : from 1935. Thus a publisher might say to his ' reader ' : ' So it didn't bite you, after all ? '

bite ! Sold ! done ! tricked you ! Only ca. 1700–60. Swift makes a male character, in reply to a young woman's ' I'm sure the gallows groans for you ', exclaim, ' Bite, Miss ; I was but in jest.' 2. At Charterhouse, C. 19–20 : cave !—3. At the Blue-Coat School : give it to me ! : 1887, Baumann.

*bite a blow ; gen. **to have bit the blow.** To have ' accomplish'd the Theft, plaied the Cheat, or done the Feat ', B.E. : c. of late C. 17–18.

bite in the collar or the cod-piece ?, do they. A c.p. of late C. 18–early 19. ' Water wit to anglers ', says Grose, 3rd ed.

bite me !, frost ; (dog) bite my ear ! A lower-classes' cry of astonishment (— 1923). Manchon.

bite (up)on the bit or the bridle. To be reduced in circumstances : C. 14–20 : coll. verging on S.E. ; in C. 19–20, mainly dial. Gower, ca. 1390 ; Latimer ; Smollett. (Apperson.)

bite one's, or the, ear. To borrow money from : since ca. 1850. In C. 19, c. : in C. 20, low.

bite one's grannam, gen. as **to have bit one's grannam.** To be very drunk : late C. 17–18. B.E.

bite one's hips. To regret something : tailors', ca. 1850–1910.

bite one's name in. To drink heavily ; tipple : low : C. 19–20 ; very ob.

bite one's, or the, thumb. To make a contemp-tuous gesture ; v.t. with *at*. Coll. : C. 16–18. Shakespeare, in *Romeo and Juliet* : ' I will bite my thumb at them : which is a disgrace to them if they bear it.'

*bite the tooth. To be successful : c. : late C. 19–20. Ware, ' Origin unknown.'

bite up, n. A disagreeable altercation : tailors', ca. 1840–1920 ; as is *biting up*, grief, bitter regret.— 2. (bite-up.) A meal ; refreshments. Also v., to eat, occ. as *bite up a hole*. Tailors' : C. 20. E.g. in *The Tailor and Cutter*, Nov. 29, 1928.—3. V.i., to grumble ; a grumbling or a complaint : id. : id.

biteëtite. See **bitytite.**

biter. A sharper ; late C. 17–18 c. Cotton.— 2. A hoaxer : from late C. 17 coll. passing to S.E. ; except in *the biter bit*, † by ca. 1870.—3. In mid-C. 18–early 19 low s., ' a lascivious, rampant wench ', Grose (q.v.).

bites, when the maggot. At one's own sweet will : coll. ; from late C. 17 ; very ob. L'Estrange.

biting you. See **what's bit you ?**

biting up. See **bite up, 1.**

bits of. See **bit of.**

*bitt. A variant of *bit*, 1.

bitten. See **bite, v.**

bitter. (A glass of) bitter beer : coll. : ' Cuthbert Bede ', 1856, ' . . . to do bitters, . . . the act of drinking bitter beer '. After ca. 1880, coll.

bitter-ender. One who resists or fights to the bitter end : coll. : mid-C. 19–20. O.E.D. (Sup.).

bitter oath, e.g. **take one's.** To swear solemnly : low : ca. 1850–1910. Ware. Corruption of *better oath* (as e.g., *by God !* is ' better ' than *by hell !, the devil !*, etc.).

bittock. A distance or a period of uncertain

length ; properly, a little bit. Orig. (— 1802), dial. ; but from ca. 1860, also coll.

bitwise. Little by little : coll. : from the 1890's ; very ob.

*****bitty.** A skeleton key : c. : late C. 19–20. Ex *bit*, a piece of mechanism.

bitytite ; biteëtite (or bite-etite). Hunger : (low) East London : ca. 1890–1915. Ware. Ex *bite* on *appetite*. Cf. *drinkitite*, q.v.

bivvy. Dial. and Cockney (? ex L. *bibere* via Lingua Franca) for : beer, esp. in *shant o(f) bivvy*, a pot or a quart of beer. In Cockney since ca. 1840.— 2. (Occ. *bivy*.) A temporary shelter : military : 1915. Ex :—3. A bivouac : military : from ca. 1900.

bivvy, v. To halt for the night : military : from ca. 1910. Ex n., 3.—2. Hence, to put up any-where : military : from 1916. F. & Gibbons.

bivvy-sheet. A waterproof sheet : military : from 1914. F. & Gibbons.

biz. Business. Orig. (1865) U.S. ; anglicised ca. 1880 : it appears in *The Saturday Review*, Jan. 5, 1884, in Baumann, and in the 'comic strip', *Ally Sloper*, on Aug. 17, 1889.

biz, good ! Excellent ! : C. 20. Lyell. Ex *good biz*, profitable business or transaction (— 1889).

Bizzy ; Busy. Bismarck : from ca. 1880 ; ob. Baumann. On *Dizzy*.

blab, a ; blab, to. An indiscreet talker ; to talk indiscreetly, also v.t. C. 16–20. Until ca. 1660, S.E. ; thereafter, the v. is coll., the n. (see esp. Grose, P.) is almost s. Likewise *blabber* and † *blabberer*, in the same senses, were orig. S.E., but from ca. 1750 coll. *Blabbing*, tale-telling, indiscreet talk, has always been coll. rather than S.E., except perhaps in C. 20 : from ca. 1600. Wesley.—2. A synonym of *juice-meeting* (q.v.), but † by 1925. Anon., *Dict. of Bootham Slang*, 1925.

black. A poacher working with a blackened face : s. or coll. : C. 18. F. & H.—2. A black-mailer : c. : C. 20. Cf. :

*****black, v.** In C. 20 c., to blackmail. Whence *the black*, blackmail ; *at the black*, on the blackmail 'lay' ; *put the black on*, to blackmail ; *pay black*, to pay blackmail ; and *blacking*, vbl.n., blackmail-(ing) :—Edgar Wallace, *passim*.

black, adj. See **table-cloth.**

Black Agnes. Agnes, the heroic Countess of Dunbar (ca. 1312–69). Ex her dark complexion. Dawson.

black-a-moor, black Moor. (Gen. unhyphenated.) Recorded in 1547 ; † in S.E. senses. In C. 19–20 used as a nickname and as a playful endearment (cf. *Turk*) : essentially coll. Also adj. As in *black-avised*, the *a* is prob. euphonic and to be compared with the nonsensical but metrically useful -*a* in jog-trot verses.

black and tam. An Oxford undergraduette : Oxford University : late 1921–ca. 1925. Ex the *black* gown and the *tam* o'shanter affected at that period, with a pun on the *Black and Tans* (q.v.). W.

*****black and tan.** Porter (or stout) mixed equally with ale : from ca. 1850 : c. (vagrants') >, by 1900, gen. low s. Ex resp. colours.

Black and Tans. The men who, in 1921, assisted the Royal Irish Constabulary. Ex their khaki coats and black caps, the nickname coming the more readily that, near Limerick, is the famous Black and Tan Hunt. (Weekley, *More Words Ancient and Modern*.)

*****black and white.** Night ; to-night : c. rhyming

s. : late C. 19–20.—2. As in *a pennyworth of b. and w.*, of tea and sugar : Glasgow lower classes' : from ca. 1920. MacArthur & Long, *No Mean City*, 1935.

black and white, in. Written or printed ; hence, binding. Late C. 16–20, coll. Cf. *black on white*, which, C. 19–20, only very rarely applies to writing and tends to denote the printing of illustrations, hence printed illustrations.

black army, the. The female underworld : low (— 1923). Manchon.

black arse. A kettle ; a pot : late C. 17–early 19. B.E. ; Grose, 2nd ed. From the proverb, ' the pot calls the kettle black arse ', the last word has disappeared (*pudoris causa*).

black art. An undertaker's business : from ca. 1850 ; undertakers'.—2. In late C. 16–19 c., lock-picking. Greene ; Grose.

black as the Earl of Hell's riding-boots or **waist-coat.** (Of a night) pitch-dark : resp. naval and nautical : resp. ca. 1900–25 and 1880–1910. Bowen.

black-bagging. ' Dynamitarding ' : journalistic coll. : 1884–ca. 1910. Ware. Ex the black bags in which the explosive so often was carried.

black-ball. To exclude (a person) from a club : late C. 18–20 : coll. >, ca. 1830, S.E. Ex the black ball indicative of rejection.

black-balling. Vbl.n. of preceding term.—2. Stealing, pilfering : nautical : ca. 1850–1910. It originated on the old Black Ball line of steamers between Liverpool and New York : a line infamous for the cruelty of its officers, the pilfering of its sailors.

black beetles. The lower classes : coll. : ca. 1810–50. Moncrieff, 1821.

black bird. An African captive aboard a slaver : nautical (— 1864) : this sense is rare.—2. Gen., a Polynesian indentured labourer, virtually a slave : nautical (— 1871) ; soon coll. See esp. the anon. pamphlet entitled *Narrative of the Voyage of the Brig 'Carl '*, 1871.

black-bird, v. To capture Negroes and esp. Polynesians : nautical (— 1885). The term > S.E. soon after this branch of kidnapping ceased. Whence *black-birding*, vbl.n., such kidnapping (— 1871), and adj. (— 1883).

blackbird and thrush. To clean (one's boots) : rhyming s. (on *brush*) : 1884, Barrett, *Navvies*. E.D.D.

black(-)bird catching. The slave-trade : nautical (— 1864). Displaced by *black-birding* (1871).

black-birders. Kidnappers of Polynesians for labour (— 1880) ; quickly coll. ; by 1900, S.E.

black-birding. See **black-bird, v.,** and **black-bird catching.**

black books, in one's. Out of favour. Late C. 16–20 coll. In C. 19–20 gen. regarded as S.E.

*****black box.** A lawyer : either c. or low s. : ca. 1690–1860. B.E. ; Grose ; Duncombe's *Sinks of London*, 1848. Ex the black boxes in which he deposits clients' papers.

black boy. A parson : C. 17–early 19. Cf. *black-coat*.

black bracelets. Handcuffs : (? late C. 18–19.) E.g. in Harrison Ainsworth's *Jack Sheppard*.

black cattle. Parsons : mid-C. 18–20 ; ob. Whence *black-cattle show*, a gathering of clergymen : C. 18–19.—2. Lice : C. 19–20 ; ob.

Black Charlie. Sir Charles Napier (1786–1860), British admiral. Dawson.

black (or scab) coal. ' Coal imported from abroad

or dug by blacklegs during the stoppage ' caused by the General Strike of May 1926 : Trade Unions' coll., often revived. Collinson.

black coat. A parson : from ca. 1600 ; coll. ; ob.

Black Cuffs, the. (Military) the Fifty-Eighth Foot, from ca. 1881 the 2nd Battalion of the Northamptonshires : C. 19–20. Ex the facings, which have been black since 1767.

black cutter. A service cutter for the use of Dartmouth naval cadets : naval coll. verging on j. : late C. 19–20. Bowen.

black diamond. A rough person that is nevertheless very good or very clever : ca. 1800–75. Displaced by *rough diamond*, q.v.—2. **The Black Diamond.** Tom Cribb (1781–1848), the great boxer. Dawson, ' From his occupation as a coalporter.'

black diamonds. Coals : from ca. 1810 : c. until ca. 1840, then s. ; by 1870, coll. Vaux, 1812 ; Various, *Gavarni in London*, 1848 ; H., 3rd ed.—2. ' Talented persons of dingy or unpolished exterior ' : ca. 1860–1900. H., 3rd ed. Superseded by *rough diamond*.

Black Dick. Admiral Howe (1726–99), who, tradition says, smiled only when a battle was imminent : naval : ca. 1770–1820. Bowen.

black dog. A counterfeit silver coin, esp. a shilling : ca. 1705–30. (*Black* had long before been applied to base coins.)—2. Ill-humour : coll., from ca. 1825 ; ob. Scott.

black—occ. **blue** (— C. 18)—**dog, blush like a.** I.e. not at all : hence, to be shameless : mid-C. 16–18 ; coll. Gosson, Swift.

black dog (sitting) on one's back, have (got) a. To be depressed : coll. : late C. 19–20 ; ob. Lyell.

black doll. The sign outside a *dolly shop*, q.v. Dickens, *Sketches by Boz*, 1835. Ob. if not †.

black donkey, ride the. To cheat in weight : *sosters* ' : late C. 19–20.—2. To sulk, be illhumoured or obstinate : mid-C. 19–20 ; ob. Ex a donkey's obstinacy ; *black* merely intensifies.

black eye, give a bottle a. To empty a bottle (of spirits) : late C. 18–mid. 19. Grose, 2nd ed.

***black-faced mob.** A gang of burglars who, blackening their faces as a disguise, trust to violence rather than skill : c. (— 1845) ; ob.

black fly. Pejorative for a clergyman : ca. 1780–1850. Grose, 2nd ed. Esp. in relation to farmers, who, on account of the tithes, dislike clergymen more than they do insect pests.

***black friars ! ; Blackfriars !** Beware ! look out ! : mid-C. 19–20 c. ' Ducange Anglicus ', 1st ed.

Black Friday. A gen. examination : schoolboys' : C. 17. Cf. *Black Monday*.—2. May 10, 1886, when Overend, Gurney & Co.'s bank suspended payment ; ob.

black gentleman, the. The devil : C. 17–mid-19 : coll. verging on familiar S.E. Dekker. Also *the black man* : mid-C. 19–20 ; ob. Meredith.

black gown. A learned person : C. 18 ; coll.

black guard, later **blackguard.** A scoundrel, esp. if unprincipled : from ca. 1730 ; > coll. ca. 1770, S.E. ca. 1830. At first this was a collective n. : in C. 16–17, the scullions of a great house ; in late C. 16–17, the Devil's body-guard ; in C. 17, the camp-followers ; in C. 18, a body of attendants of black dress, race, or character, or the underworld, esp. the shoe-blacking portion thereof. A collective adumbration of the sense, ' a criminal, a scoundrel ',

occurs in a MS. of 1683 : ' . . . of late a sort of vicious, idle, and masterless boys and rogues, commonly called the black-guard . . .' Two notable derivatives are :—*blackguard*, v. To act the blackguard (— 1786) ; S.E. by 1800, but long †. Treat as a blackguard, revile (1823 +) ; S.E. by 1850. (S.O.D.) And : *blackguard*, adj., blackguardly ; vile. From ca. 1750 ; S.E. by 1800. Smollett, 1760 : ' He is become a blackguard gaol-bird ' ; Byron, ' I have heard him use language as blackguard as his action.' For this interesting word—the early senses are all coll. rather than s., and all became S.E. thirty to fifty years after their birth—see an admirable summary in the S.O.D., a storehouse in the O.E.D., a most informative paragraph in Weekley's *More Words Ancient and Modern*, and a commentary-lexicon in F. & H.

black-hand gang. A forlorn-hope party ; a party of trench-raiders : military : 1916–18.—2. Hence, bombers or stretcher-bearers : military : 1917–18. (Cf. *suicide club*.) F. & Gibbons.

black hat. A new immigrant : Australian : ca. 1885–1905. Morris. Perhaps ex the bowler so common among Englishmen, so rare among Australians. Cf. *pommy*, q.v.

Black Hole, the. Cheltenham : from ca. 1870 ; ob. Ex the number of former residents of India, esp. officers and civil servants, who go to live there. —2. A place of imprisonment, 1831, whence the famous Black Hole of Calcutta (1856).—3. Whence, from ca. 1870, a punishment cell, and from ca. 1890, the guard-room : military.

Black Horse, the. The Seventh Dragoon Guards, ex the regimental facings and their (at one time) black horses ; occ. abbr. to *The Blacks* : from ca. 1720 ; slightly ob. Temp. George II, *The Virgin Mary's Guard* ; from ca. 1880, *Strawboots*.

blackhouse. A business house of long hours and miserable wages : ca. 1820–1900, trade.

black incher. A black bull-ant : Australian children's : C. 20. Opp. *red incher*, q.v.

Black Indies. Newcastle : from ca. 1690–1830 ; in B.E. and Grose. But in C. 19–20 (ob.), among seamen, it means Shields and Sunderland as well (Bowen).

black is . . . See **black's my eye.**

black jack. A leathern drinking-jug : late C. 16– 20, ob. ; > coll. ca. 1700, S.E. ca. 1800.—2. **Black Jack.** The Recorder of London : c. of ca. 1810–30. *Lex. Bal.*, 1811.—3. **Black Jack.** John Philip Kemble (1757–1823), English tragedian : late C. 18– early 19. Ex his black hair, worn long, and his dark complexion. (Dawson.)—4. At Winchester College, C. 19, a leathern beer-jug holding two gallons.—5. A (small) black portmanteau : London bag-makers' and -sellers' : mid-C. 19–early 20. Ware.

black job. A funeral ; also adj. Ca. 1850– 1920. Yates, 1866. Cf. *black art*, 1.

black joke. The female pudend : late C. 18– early 19. Grose, 2nd ed.

black-leg, usually as one word. A turf swindler : Parsons, *Newmarket*, vol. ii, 1771. ' So called perhaps from their appearing generally in boots, or else from game cocks, whose legs are always black ', Grose, 1st ed. ; W., however, suggests—more pertinently—that it is ' a description of the *rook* '. —2. Whence, any sharper : 1774. Colman, *Man of Business*. Perhaps ex *black-leg*(*s*), a disease affecting the legs of sheep and cattle (1722, S.O.D.). —3. (Ex 1 and 2.) Pejorative for a workman willing to continue when his companions have gone on strike (1865) : S.E. by 1900.—4. Hence, fig., any non-participator (1889) ; coll. by 1920. (All senses : partly O.E.D.)

black-leg, v. (Tailors') to boycott a fellow-tailor : ca. 1870–1910.—2. V.i., or as *black-leg it,* to return to work before a strike has been settled : from ca. 1885 ; coll. ; S.E. by 1920.

black-leggery. Swindling : Maginn, 1832 ; coll. ; S.E. by 1850, but never very common.

black man, the. The Devil. See **black gentleman.**

black man choke, enough to make a. See **choke.**

*****black man's, blackmans.** The dark ; night : a C. 17–18 c. variant of *darkmans,* q.v. Jonson.

*****black Maria.** A prison van, for the conveyance of prisoners. From ca. 1870 : orig. c. ; by 1902, s. ; by 1930, coll. H., 5th ed. ; Ware. Occ. *sable Maria* († by 1920). By personification.—2. A gun that ejects a shell emitting a dense cloud of smoke (1915) ; the shell or its burst (Oct. 1914) : military. Ex sense 1. F. & Gibbons, ' The Germans, curiously, had a similar term, " Schwarze Maria ", for our heavy shells.'

black (or B—) Monday. The Monday on which, after the (esp. summer) holidays, school re-opens : from ca. 1730 : ' What is called by school-boys Black Monday ', Fielding, *Tom Jones* ; P. G. Wode-house, *A Prefect's Uncle,* 1903, ' There is nothing of Black Monday about the first day of term at a public school. Black Monday is essentially a private school institution.' Contrast *bloody Monday,* q.v.—2. The Monday—it often is a Monday—on which the death-sentence is executed : from ca. 1840.

black mouth. A slanderer : from ca. 1640 ; ob. Coll., passing in C. 19–20 to S.E. B.E. has it as the corresponding adj.

black mummer. An actor habitually unkempt and unclean : ca. 1820–90. Bee.

black muns. Late C. 17–18 : ' hoods and scarves of alamode lutestring ', Grose. B.E. gives as c., which it may be ; *muns* = face.

black neb. A person with democratic sym-pathies, orig. and esp. with France : ca. 1790–1800.

black nob. A non-unionist ; a blackleg : from ca. 1870 ; ob. Punning *blackleg.* (Trade.)

black pan. Remains of cabin food, ' in certain steamers regarded as the perquisite of the firemen who come off watch at 8 p.m.' : nautical : C. 20. Bowen. Because gathered together into a large black pan.

black pope (or B.P.), the. The Superior-General of the Jesuits : Roman Catholics' nickname (— 1877). O.E.D. (Sup.).

black pot. A toper : late C. 16–19. Ex *black pot,* a beer mug. (The S.O.D. is, I think, wrong to ignore F. & H.'s pre-1818 (= Scott) examples, indecisive though they be.)—2. A Eurasian apothe-cary in an Army hospital in India : Indian Army (not officers') : from ca. 1890. Frank Richards, *Old-Soldier Sahib,* 1936.

Black Prince. The devil : ca. 1590–1700, coll. The eldest son of Edward III was so named in 1563, for reasons as yet undiscovered.

black psalm, sing the. To weep : mid-C. 18–early 19. Grose, 1st ed., ' A saying used to children.' Cf. *neck-verse.*

Black Rod. Gentleman Usher of the Black Rod : C. 17–20, coll.

black Sal or Suke(y). A kettle : low : mid-C. 19–20 ; ob.

black Saturday. A Saturday on which, because of advances received, there is no wage to take : mid-C. 19–20, workmen's. Cf. *dead horse,* q.v.

Black Sea Cat, the. ' H.M. paddle frigate *Terrible,* on account of her activity during the Crimean War ' : naval : ca. 1855–80. Bowen.

black shark. An attorney : mostly naval : ca. 1820–60. ' Jon Bee.'

black sheep. Mild for a scapegrace, a ' bad lot ' : from ca. 1790 ; coll. ; in C. 20, S.E. though not literary. Perhaps (W.) ex ' *Ba! Ba! black sheep'.*—2. A workman refusing to join in a strike : ca. 1860–1900. H., 2nd ed.—3. As v., Winchester College, to ' jockey ', get above : C. 19.

black ship. One of the ' teak-built ships from Indian yards in the days of the East India Com-pany ' : nautical : mid-C. 18–mid-19. Bowen.

Black Shirt. A Fascist : 1923 +. Coll. passing rapidly into S.E. Orig. a translation of the It. (S.O.D.)

black-silk barge. A stout woman that, frequent-ing dances, dresses thus to minimise her ampli-tude : ball-room (— 1909) ; † by 1920. Ware. Cf. *barges.*

*****black-spice racket.** The stealing of tools, bag and soot from chimney-sweepers : c. : (? C. 18–) early C. 19. *Lex. Bal.*

*****black spy.** The devil : late C. 17–18 c. and low. B.E.

black squad. A stokehold crew : nautical coll. : late C. 19–20. Bowen.

black strap. Pejorative for thick, sweet port : coll. : late C. 18–19 ; variant, *black stripe.* Ex *strap,* wine, C. 16.—2. A task imposed as punish-ment on soldiers at Gibraltar, late C. 18–early 19 : military (Grose, 1st ed.).—3. Molasses : C. 19–20 (ob.) : naval. Bowen. Ex sense 1.—4. The hospital in a ship of war : naval : late C. 18–mid-19. Bowen. Cf. sense 2.—5. (Gen. pl.) One of ' the specially made strong bags used for removing pilfered cargo from a ship ' ; nautical (either low or c.) : mid-C. 19–20. Bowen.

black teapot. A negro footman : lower class : C. 19–20 ; ob.

Black Tom. Thomas, Lord Fairfax (1612–71) : mostly military, he being a notable general. Dawson.

Black Tom Tyrant. Sir Thomas Wentworth (1593–1641) : nickname given by the Scots in 1740. Ibid.

black velvet. Stout and champagne mixed : public-house s., mostly Anglo-Irish : C. 20. Ex its colour and its smoothness.

Black Watch, the. The Royal Highlanders : military : from ca. 1725 : s. >, by 1800, coll. >, by 1881, S.E. Ex their dark tartan.

black whale. An Antarctic right-whale : nau-tical coll. : mid-C. 19–20. Bowen.

black-work. Funeral-undertaking (1859, G. A. Sala, *Gaslight and Daylight*). Cf. *black art,* 1, and *black job.*

blackamoor's teeth. Cowrie shells : C. 18, coll.

blackberry swagger. A hawker of tapes, shoe-laces, etc. : c. or low s. : ca. 1850–1910. H., 1st ed.

Blackbirdy. J. M. W. Turner (1775–1851), the artist. Dawson.

blackee, blackey. See **blacky.**

Blackford-block, -swell, -toff. A person (gen. male) well-dressed on occasion : London : ca. 1890–1910. ' Blackford's is a well-known . . . tailors' and outfitting establishment which also lets out evening and other garments on hire ', F. & H. (revised).

Blackfriars ! See **black friars !**

Blackfriars Buccaneers. ' The London division of the Royal Naval Volunteer Reserve, whose headquarters have been at Blackfriars for many years past ', Bowen, 1929 : naval : C. 20.

blackguard. See **black guard.**

blacklead. A blacklead pencil : coll. (— 1927), not very gen. Collinson.

blackleg. See **black-leg.**—*blackmans.** See **black man's.**

Blacks. See **Black Horse.**

black's his, my or **your eye, say.** To accuse ; reprimand : C. 15–20, ob. ; coll. A mid-C. 18–19 variant was *say black is the white of your eye*, as in Smollett (Apperson). Note, however, that *black's the white of my eye* is ' an old-time sea protestation of innocence ' (Bowen).

blacksmith's daughter. A key (— 1859) ; esp. in .lial. (which has also *blacksmith's wife*), lock and key, padlock.

blacksmith's shop. ' The apron of the unpopular Cunningham's patent reefing topsails in the mid-19th century ', Bowen : nautical : at that period.

Blackwall, have been to. To have a black eye : Cockney : ca. 1865–85.

Blackwall fashion. (To conduct a sailing-ship) ' with all the smartness and ceremony of the old Blackwall Frigates. On the other hand it was frequently applied to a seaman who did not exert himself unduly ' : nautical : C. 19. Bowen.

Blackwall navy (or **N.**). Ships of the Union Castle Line : late C. 19–20 : nautical. Bowen. Ex London as base and the ships' grey hulls.

blacky ; occ. **blackey, blackee, blackie.** A black man : from ca. 1810 ; coll. ; occ. as a nickname. Moore, 1815 ; Thackeray, 1864. Cf. *darky*. (O.E.D.)

blad. A sheaf of specimen pages or other illustrative matter : booksellers' and publishers' (— 1933). *Slang*, p. 181. Ex S.E. *blad*, a fragment.

bladder. A very talkative, long-winded person : from ca. 1578 ; coll. >, by 1800, S.E. ; ob. by 1900.

bladder of fat. A hat : rhyming s. : C. 20. B. & P.

bladder of lard. A bald-headed person (— 1864) ; low. H., 3rd ed. Ex *bladdered lard*. Cf. the app. later semi-proverbial *bald as a bladder of lard* (Apperson).

bladderdash. Nonsense : low : late C. 19–20 ; slightly ob. Corrupted *balderdash*.

blade. A ' good fellow ', or simply a man : from ca. 1859 (H., 1st ed.). Ca. 1750–1860, a sharp fellow : coll. Late C. 16–early 18, a roisterer, a gallant : S.E. The earliest sense appears in Shakespeare, the second in Goldsmith, and the latest in Dickens. Cf. Fr. *une bonne épée*, a noted swordsman : W.

Blades, the. Sheffield Football Club : sporting : from ca. 1920. Ex the knife-factories of Sheffield.

***blag.** To snatch a watch-chain right off : C. 20 c. Charles E. Leach. Perhaps ex Yorkshire dial. *blag*, to gather blackberries, itself ex Yorkshire *blag*, a blackberry.

blag. To wheedle ; persuade into spending money : low, esp. among grafters : C. 20. Philip Allingham, *Cheapjack*, 1934. Perhaps cognate with *blah*.

blah, n. and adj. Nonsense ; silly or empty

(talk) ; deliberately wordy, insincere, window-dressing (matter) : 1927, esp. among publishers and journalists. From U.S., where it existed in 1925. Cf. *blurb*, q.v. Perhaps ex Fr. *blague*, but more prob. ex Ger. s. *Blech*, nonsense, there being millions of Germans in ' the States '. More prob. still is derivation ex Scottish and Irish *blaflum*, nonsense, idle talk ; Ulster has the variant *blah flah*.

blah. Mad : 1928, A. E. W. Mason, *The Prisoner in the Opal*. By confusion of *gaga* and the preceding ; but see *go blah*.

blah-blah. An occ. form of *blah*, n.

blame it ! Euphemistic for *damn it !* : coll. Cf. *blamenation*, damnation. C. 19–20 ; ob.

blamed. A coll. pejorative (= ' blinking ', ' blanky ') : non-aristocratic : late C. 19–20. Ex U.S.

Blanco. The inevitable nickname of all men surnamed White : naval and military : C. 20. F. & Gibbons. Not ex Blanco White, poet and theologian (d. 1841), but ex ' Blanco ', that white accoutrement-cleanser which came on the market in 1895.

blandander. To tempt blandishingly, to cajole : coll. : 1888, Kipling ; ob. By rhyming reduplication on the stem of *blandish*. O.E.D. (Sup.).

blandander. To blether ; talk nonsense : low : from ca. 1930. James Curtis, *The Gilt Kid*, 1936. Perhaps ex *blather* and *blarney*.

blandiloquence. Smooth or flattering speech or talk : mid-C. 17–20 ; ob. The O.E.D. considers it S.E. ; W., s. ; perhaps it is a pedantic coll. Blount, 1656. Ex L. for ' bland speech '.

blank, blanked. Damn ; damned. From ca. 1850. ' Cuthbert Bede.' Most euphemisms are neither s. nor coll., but *blamenation* and *blank(ed)* are resp. s. and coll. ; cf. the remark at *blast !* and see **blankety.**—2. See **blinkers !, blank your.**

blanked. Tipsy : military : 1915 ; ob. F. & Gibbons. Ex Fr. *vin blanc*, white wine. Also *blonked*.

blanker. A discharge-certificate with one corner removed to indicate bad conduct : naval : late C. 19–20. Bowen.

blanket. The coating of blubber in a whale : nautical coll. : mid-C. 19–20. Bowen.—2. See **blankets.**

blanket, (born) on the wrong side of the. Illegitimate : from ca. 1770 ; coll. ; from ca. 1850, S.E. Smollett.

blanket, lawful. A wife : from ca. 1800 ; coll.

blanket, wet. A spoil-sport : coll. (— 1830) ; in C. 20, almost S.E. Spencer.

Blanket Bay. The nautical form (late C. 19–20 : Manchon) of *blanket fair*. Cf. :

blanket-drill. An afternoon siesta : Regular Army : late C. 19–20. B. & P.

blanket fair. Bed : coll. : C. 19–20, ob. Cf. *Bedfordshire, sheet alley, cloth market.*

blanket hornpipe. Sexual intercourse : from ca. 1810 ; ob. *Lex. Bal.* Cf. the C. 17 S.E. *blanket-love*, illicit amours.

***blanket stiff.** A tramp that never utilises the casual wards : C. 20 c. ? ex U.S.

blanketeer. See **hot blanketeer.**

blankets. (Extremely rare in singular.) The 10's in a pack of cards : military : from 1915. F. & Gibbons. Ex the rolling of blankets in tens for convenience of transport.

blankety ; blanky. Damned ; accursed : coll. (mostly and prob. orig. American) : from ca. 1880.

Ex *blank*, q.v., the ' blank ' being the dash (' — ') beloved of prudes and printers.

blarm me ! Blimey ! : Cockney (— 1887). Baumann. Cf. :

blarmed, adj. ' Blamed ', confounded (e.g. thing) : Cockney (— 1887). Baumann.

blarney. Honeyed flattery, smooth cajolery (— 1819) ; coll. Grose, 1785, records a sense rather more grave : ' He has licked the Blarney stone ; he deals in the wonderful, or tips us the traveller ' ; ibid, ' To tip the Blarney, is figuratively used for telling a marvellous story, or falsity.' In the 3rd ed. he adds : ' Also sometimes to express flattery.' Ex a stone in the wall of Castle Blarney, Ireland, the kissing of which—' a gymnastic operation ', W.—is reputed to ensure a gift of cajolery and unblushing effrontery. Cf. :

blarney, v.i. and v.t. To cajole ; flatter grossly : coll., ex the n. Southey in 1803 (O.E.D.). The vbl.n. *blarneying* is fairly common, *blarneyer* much less so.

blarneyfied. Adj., blarneyed : 1830, *Fraser's Magazine*, ' No balderdash of blarneyfied botheration ' (O.E.D.).

blarsted. See **blasted.**

blasé. Satiated with pleasure. From 1819 until ca. 1860, s., but ca. 1860–1900 coll. ; thereafter S.E. Byron uses the term, but its popularity came ca. 1840–4, when two versions of the Fr. farce, *L'Homme Blasé*, were played on the London stage. —2. Hence, conceited ; pretentious : Charterhouse : from ca. 1910.

blase. A conceited or pretentious person : Charterhouse : from ca. 1910. Ex *blasé*, 2. Hence :

blase, v. To be conceited ; put on ' side ' : Charterhouse : from ca. 1910.

blashy. Esp. *a blashy day*, wretched weather : nautical coll. (— 1887) ex dial. *blashy*, gusty, rainy (1788). Baumann.

blast. To curse and swear (intransitively) : coll. >, in late C. 19, S.E. : from ca. 1850, in gen. use (orig. military) ; foreshadowed in C. 17.

[**blast !** A curse. Oaths, unless they consist of words already s. or coll., are often neither s. nor coll. though they verge on the latter.]

blast, at (or **in**) **full.** (Hard) at work : coll. ; from ca. 1860 ; now bordering on S.E. Ex the lit. sense (— 1800).

blasted. As a euphemism for *bloody*, it has no place here, but as a low expletive adj., violently coll. and = ' execrable ', it is in point. From ca. 1740. (Cf. the ensuing pair of entries.) The spelling *blarsted* is superfluous : nobody except a rustic, i.e. in dial., so draws out the *a*—and even then the spelling should be, not *blarsted* but *blaasted*.

blasted brimstone. A harlot : ca. 1780–1830. Grose, 1st ed. Cf. :

blasted fellow. An abandoned rogue : ca. 1760–1830 ; cf. Chesterfield's ' the most notorious blasted rascal in the world ', in a letter of Jan. 8, 1750.

blat. To talk much : s. (— 1923) ex C. 18–20 dial. *blate*, *bleet*, to roar, to talk wildly. Manchon.

*blater. A sheep : C. 18–mid-19 c. Lytton. A corruption of *bleater*. See **bleating.**—2. A calf : c. : mid-C. 18–19. Grose, 2nd ed.

blather. See **blether.—blatherskite.** See **bletherskate.**

blatter. (Gen. in passive.) To strike, assault : Glasgow : C. 20. Prob. ex dial. *blatter* (gen. *blather*), to splash or befoul.

Blayney's Bloodhounds. (Military) the Eighty-Ninth Foot, from ca. 1881 the 2nd Battalion of the Royal Irish Fusiliers : from 1798, during the Irish Rebellion. Blayney was their colonel : and they excelled in tracking the rebels. Also known as *The Rollickers*, for they bore themselves jovially, swaggeringly.

blaze a trail. Lit., S.E. and orig. (— 1737) U.S. Fig., C. 19–20 : coll. at first but soon S.E. and soon anglicised.

(**blaze away** and) **blaze away !** Look sharp ! Work hard ! Later (cf. *fire away !*) go ahead ! Coll. : from ca. 1825 in the indicative and from ca. 1850 as an adjuration. Ex the rapid firing of cannons and rifles.

blazer. A (light) sports jacket : 1880. Orig. the bright scarlet jacket of the Lady Margaret Boat Club of St. John's College, Cambridge. Coll. ; in C. 20, S.E. *Punch* in 1885 : ' Harkaway turns up clad in what he calls a blazer, which makes him look like a nigger minstrel out for a holiday.'—2. A bombketch ; a mortar-boat : naval : C. 19. Bowen.

blazers. Spectacles : Cockney (— 1887) ; ob. Baumann. Ex the sun therefrom reflected.

blazes. The bright clothes of flunkeys : ex the episode of Sam Weller and the ' swarry ' in Dickens's *Pickwick Papers*. Ob. Cf. :

blazes ! A forcible exclamation : from the 1830's. Ex the flames of hell.

blazes, drunk as. Exceedingly drunk : from ca. 1860. Perhaps not from *blazes !* (q.v.) but a folk-etymology corruption of *drunk as blaizers*, ca. 1830–60, a phrase arising from a feast held in honour of St. Blaize, *blaizers* being the participants. See F. & H.

blazes, go to. To depart hastily ; to disappear melodramatically : cf. the adjuration, *go to blazes !* and **to** († **the**) **blazes** (e.g. **with it**) ! From the mid-1830's. Also in such phrases as that in ' He consigned me to blazes.' See **blazes !**

blazes, how or **what** or **who the ?** ! An intensive coll. interrogation ; e.g. in Dickens, 1838, ' What the blazes is in the wind now ? ' (O.E.D.), and ibid, 1836, ' How the blazes you can stand the head-work you do, is a mystery to me.' See **blazes !**

blazes, like. Vehemently ; with ardour. From ca. 1840 ; coll. As in Disraeli's *Sybil*, ' They . . . cheered the red-coats like blazes.' See **blazes !**

Blazes, Old. The devil : from ca. 1845 ; ob. Cf. *blazes !*, q.v.

blazing. A coll. intensive adj. (gen. euphemistic ; e.g. for *bloody*), as in *a blazing shame* : from ca. 1880.—2. Hence, (of a money-market that is) exceptionally active and good : Stock Exchange coll. : C. 20.

*bleached mort. A very fair-complexioned girl : mid-C. 18–early 19 c. Grose, 1st ed. (Cf. the C. 20 *peroxide blonde*.) Prob. ex *the mort lay last night a-bleaching*, ' the wench looks very fair to Day ', *A New Canting Dict.*, 1725.

bleacher. A maid-servant : Glasgow (— 1934).

blear the eyes of. To hoodwink, deceive, trick : C. 14–19 ; coll. > S.E. by C. 16. Chaucer, Shakespeare, Scott. Cf. *throw dust in the eyes.* (O.E.D.)

bleat. A grumble : naval : late C. 19–20. Bowen. Cf. :

bleat. To complain, grumble ; to lay information : from ca. 1560. This pejorative implies either feebleness or cowardice or an unpleasant readiness to blab.

*bleater. A victim of sharp or rook : c. : C. 17–

early 19. Dekker. Grose.—2. A sheep: c.:
C. 17–early 19. Brome. Cf.:

*bleating, in C. 17–early 19 c., is an adj.: sheep;
as in *bleating cull*, a sheep-stealer; *bleating prig* or
rig, sheep-stealing; *bleating cheat* = a sheep.—2.
Among the lower classes, a euphemism for *bloody*:
C. 20. Manchon.

bleed. Blood, 'as "She'll have his bleed"—
usually said of a woman who is rating her husband',
Ware: proletarian (mostly London): from ca.
1890. Cf. *bleeding*, q.v.

bleed, v. To extort, overtly or covertly, money
from: late C. 17–20, coll. V.i. part (freely) with
money: from ca. 1660, coll. in C. 19; ob.; little
used since ca. 1850. Dryden, 1668, 'He is vehement, and bleeds on to fourscore or an hundred;
and I, not willing to tempt fortune, come away a
moderate winner of two hundred pistoles.'—3. In
printing, a book *bleeds* when the margin is so cut
away that portions of the printed matter are also
removed: from ca. 1870: s. > coll. > j. But
since ca. 1920 (also *bleed off*), one *bleeds* a book-
jacket when the colours are made to run over, i.e.
appear to continue beyond the edges.—4. To let out
water: nautical: late C. 19–20. F. & H., revised.
—5. Hence, to let (cask, etc., of e.g. wine) fall in
order to steal the escaping liquor: c.: C. 20.
Manchon.

bleed a buoy. 'To let the water out': nautical
coll. (now verging on j.): mid-C. 19–20. Bowen.

bleed off. See bleed, v., 3.

bleed the monkey. (Naval) to steal rum from the
mess tub or *monkey*. C. 19. Cf. *suck the monkey*
and *tap the admiral*.

bleeder. A spur: low: C. 19–20; ob. Vaux.—
2. A sovereign: C. 19–20 sporting, ob.—3. A
notable duffer: university s., ca. 1870–1910.
Hence, gen., = a bloody fool, ca. 1880–1914.—
4. Hence (owing to the influence of *silly bleeder*), a
fellow, a man: from ca. 1890; mainly Cockney.
Clarence Rook, *The Hooligan Nights*, 1899.
See essay, 'The Word *Bloody*', in *Words*! Cf.
bleeding, q.v.—5. A person whose blood does not
coagulate properly: medical coll.: C. 20. (As a
person suffering from hæmophilia, *bleeder* is S.E.)

bleeding. A low coll. intensive adj. of little
meaning: its import is emotional, not mental.
(Rarely used as a euphemism for *bloody*.) From
ca. 1857 (O.E.D. Sup.). Besant & Rice in *Son of
Vulcan*, 1877, 'When he isn't up to one dodge he is
up to another. You make no bleeding error.' Cf.
bleed (n.) and *bleeder*, qq.v.

*bleeding cully. An easy victim; a ready parter
with money: late C. 17–late 19 c. Grose, 1st ed.
Ex. *bleed*, v., 2.

bleeding new. Quite new; fresh: mid-C. 18–20,
ob.; coll. Grose, 3rd ed. Ex fish, which do not
bleed when stale.

[Blends. See *Slang*, pp. 279–80.]

Blenheim Pippin, the. Lord Randolph Churchill:
political nickname: 1883, *Entr'acte*, April 7.
Punning that variety of apple; Lord Randolph, a
son of the Duke of Marlborough (whose family seat is
Blenheim, near Oxford), was 'diminutive' (Ware).

bless my (or me) soul! See soul!, bless my.

bless oneself. Ironical for curse: from ca. 1600;
coll. After ca. 1800, S.E. 'How my Lord Treasurer
did bless himself', Pepys in his diary, April 1, 1665.
Also, *to bless* another: to reprimand, scold, curse,
curse at, sweat at him: coll. > S.E.; C. 19–20.

bless oneself with, not a (penny, shilling, etc.) to.

Penniless: from ca. 1550: coll. till ca. 1800, then S.E.
Dickens has it. 'In allusion to the cross on the
silver penny . . . or to the practice of crossing the
palm with a piece of silver', S.O.D. In fact a
proverbial phrase, recorded in 1540, runs: *not a
cross* [coin] *to bless oneself with* (Apperson).

bless one's stars. To consider oneself lucky:
coll. (— 1845). Hood.

blessed, blest. As euphemism, S.E.; as irony,
coll.: C. 19–20. Cf. *bless oneself*. But *blessed if I
do* = I certainly won't, is 'pure' coll.; from ca.
1880.

blessing. A small surplus of goods given by a
huckster: late C. 18–19; coll. Grose, 2nd ed.
Extant in dial.—2. A bottle of whisky given to the
pilot as he left a ship: nautical coll.: C. 19.
Bowen.

blether, occ. blather. Vapid or noisy talk;
voluble nonsense: coll. from ca. 1840. The term is
ex Scottish and Northern dial. and was orig. (M.E.)
—and still is—a v. *Blather* is the earlier form, but
its use in coll. English is owing to U.S. influence.
Edward Yates, in *Broken to Harness*, 1864:
'There's a letter . . . from Sir Mordaunt . . .
promisin' all sorts of things; but I'm sick of him
and his blather.' W. Clark Russell, 1884: 'Mrs.
O'Brien was blathering about the pedigree of the
O'Briens.' *The Pall Mall Gazette*, May 3, 1886:
'Havelock's florid adjurations to his men, the grim
veterans of the 78th, bluntly characterised as
blether.' Hence *blethering*, vbl.n. and adj., in exactly corresponding senses: dial. >, ca. 1860, coll.

blethering. A variant of *blithering*, q.v.: coll.:
from ca. 1914. O.E.D. (Sup.).

bletherskate, occ. blatherskite. The former is the
Scottish, the latter the American form: orig. (C. 17),
Scottish dial.; > popular in U.S. in 1860's and
coll. in England ca. 1870.

blew. To inform on, expose: mid-C. 19–20, ob.
H., 1st ed. Cf. *blow upon*.—2. To cause to disappear; spend, waste: from ca. 1850: gen. of
money, as in *blew one's screw*, squander one's wages
or salary. ? ex idea of sending into the sky (W.).
The Sporting Times, better known as *The Pink Un*,
June 29, 1889:

'Isabel and Maudie knew the Turf and all its arts—
They had often blewed a dollar on a wrong 'un—
And Isabel one evening met a mug from rural parts,
An attenuated Juggins, and a long 'un.'

blew, adj. An † form of *blue*, q.v.

*blew it. To inform to the police: c. (— 1839);
ob. Brandon.

blewed. See blued.

blick. See 'Westminster School slang'.

bli'me! See blimy! (C. J. Dennis.)

blig. A town boy: schoolboys': C. 20. Ex
Northern dial. Ex dial. blig, a blackguard, a cad
(E.D.D.).

bliged. Obliged: Cockney coll. (— 1887). Baumann.

blighted. Euphemistic for *bloody*: coll.: C. 20.
Manchon.

blighter. A contemptible person (rarely of a
woman): from ca. 1896. A euphemism (perhaps
on *blithering*) for b*gger*: W.—2. A 'Jonah'
actor: theatrical (1898); ob. Ware.—3. A chap,
fellow: C. 20; ex jocular use of primary sense.

Blighty. England; home: military: recorded
by O.E.D. (Sup.) for 1915, but in use in India for
at least five years earlier. Ex Hindustani *bilayati*

(Arabic *wilayati*), foreign, esp. European.—2. Hence, a wound taking one home : military : from 1915. Occ. *blighty boy* (1916).—3. Adj., as in *Blighty leave*, furlough to England : military : from 1916. See esp. O.E.D. (Sup.), B. & P., and Yule & Burnell (at *blatty*, an early form).

Blighty !, roll on. 'When this bloody war is over, | Oh ! how happy I shall be' : a military c.p. of 1916–18. (Manchon.)

Blighty bag. A small stuff-bag issued at the Casualty Clearing Stations, where soldiers were deprived of their kit and so had nothing in which to carry personal belongings : military : 1915–18. F. & Gibbons. Ex their 'manufacture' in *Blighty*.

Blighty hut. (One's) home : military : 1917–18. Cf. *Blighty*, 2.

Blighty touch, have the. To be lucky : military : 1916–19. Cf. *Blighty*, 3.

blim(e)y, occ. **blymy !** Abbr. *Gorblimy* (God blind me) ! : mostly Cockney : late C. 19–20. Barrère & Leland.

blimey, adj. Sentimental ; (likewise esp. of songs) sentimental and popular : theatrical, music-halls' : from ca. 1920. Maurice Lincoln, *Oh ! Definitely*, 1933.

blimp. 'A small non-rigid dirigible airship' : 1915 : military s. rapidly > coll., then j. Invented by Horace Shortt (O.E.D. Sup. ; B. & P.).

blind. The night time : C. 19 coll.—2. A pre-text : from ca. 1660. In C. 18, coll. ; thereafter, S.E.—3. Among printers, from ca. 1870, a paragraph mark, ¶ : ex the filling-up of the 'eye' of the reversed *P*.—4. A (very) drunken bout : from ca. 1912. Ex *blind drunk*.—5. See **blind baggage** (Addenda).

blind. To curse : soldiers' > gen. : from the late 1880's. Kipling :

'If you're cast for fatigue by a sergeant unkind,
Don't grouse like a woman, nor crack on, nor blind.'

Ex such curses as *blind your eyes !*—2. To go heedlessly, esp. of a motorist recklessly speeding : 1923 (O.E.D. Sup.).—3. To cheat (a person) : c. or low : ca. 1815–40. (O.E.D. at *nail*, v., § 8, c.)

blind, adj. In liquor ; tipsy : C. 17–18 c. (Cf. the S.E. *blind-drunk*.) The c. term has, in C. 20, > slang, popularised during the G.W.—2. See **table-cloth**.—3. See **blind ten**.

blind, go (it). To enter uninformed or rashly into an undertaking : U.S. (1848) anglicised ca. 1900. Prob. ex poker.

blind, when the devil is. Never : from ca. 1650, ob. ; coll. Howell, Scott.

blind alley. The *pudendum muliebre* : low : C. 19–20.

blind as a brickbat. Lit. and fig., exceedingly blind : coll. verging on S.E. : Dickens, 1850. Ex the C. 17–20 S.E. *blind as a bat*. Cf. the idiomatic *blind as a beetle, as a buzzard, as a mole*.

blind buckler. A wooden plug that, for use with hawse-pipes, has no passage for the cable : nautical coll. verging on j. : late C. 19–20. Bowen.

blind cheeks. The posteriors : late C. 17–20, ob. ; after ca. 1800, coll. Recorded first in B.E., who adds '*Kiss my Blind-cheeks*, Kiss my Ar—' ; Grose, 2nd ed., has '*Buss blind cheeks* ; kiss mine a-se.' Cf. :—*blind Cupid*. The same : low : ca. 1810–60. *Lex. Bal.*

blind drunk. Very drunk : from ca. 1830 : coll. >, ca. 1890, S.E. Disraeli in *Sybil*, 1845 : ' Hang me if I wasn't blind drunk at the end of it.' Cf. *blind*, n., 4.

blind eye. The podex : low : C. 18–20 ; ob. Cf. *blind cheeks*.

blind guard. A guard-post invisible from the central watch-house (and therefore popular) : coastguardsmen's coll. : C. 19. Bowen.

Blind Half Hundred (occ. **Hundredth**), **the.** The Fiftieth Regiment of Foot : from ca. 1881 the 1st Battalion of the Royal West Kents. H., 3rd. ed., says ex the ophthalmia common in the Egyptian campaign, 1801. Hence, from ca. 1890 in the game of house, ' 50 '. The regiment was also known as *The Dirty Half-Hundred*, q.v., and *The Gallant Fiftieth*, q.v.

*****blind harper.** A beggar that, counterfeiting blindness, plays the harp or the fiddle : late C. 17–18 c. B.E. ; Grose.

blind Hookey. A great risk : non-aristocratic (– 1909) ; ob. Ware, ' " Oh, it's Blind Hookey to attempt it." From a card game.'

blind man (occ. **officer, reader**). One who deals with 'blind', i.e. imperfectly or indistinctly addressed, letters : from ca. 1864. S. > coll. > j. (S.O.D.)

blind man's holiday. Night, darkness : late C. 16–17. From 1690, the gloaming : early examples occur in B.E. and Swift. Coll. ; in late C. 19–20, S.E.

blind monkeys to evacuate, lead the. A C. 19–20 (ob.) coll., implicative of a person's inability to do any worth-while job. Apparently from ca. 1840 and in reference to the Zoological Gardens : see H.

blind roller. A single, unexpected big sea in calm weather : nautical coll. : mid-C. 19–20. Bowen.

blind side. The weakest, most assailable side : Chapman, 1606. Coll. ; S.E. in C. 19–20.

blind swiping. See **swiping**.

blind ten, twenty, thirty. 10, 20, 30 (etc.) in the game of house : military : C. 20. B. & P. Ex the noughts : having only one ' 0 ' or eye.

blinded with science. A c.p. applied to brawn defeated by brains : Australian and New Zealand : C. 20.

blinder. 'A huge, curling wave' before the pre-1913 deepening of the channel at Durban : mostly Durban : late C. 19–early 20. Pettman. —2. See **poodler**.

*****blinder, take a.** To die : mid-C. 19–20 c. ; ob. I.e. take a blind leap in, or into, the dark.

blindo. A drunken spree or bout : low : ca. 1860–1910. Cf. *vido*.—2. Hence, tipsy : military : C. 20. F. & Gibbons.—3. A sixpenny piece : C. 20 vagrants' c. Cf. *broad*, n.

blindo. To die : ca. 1860–1910. Military : perhaps on *dekko*, q.v., and cf. *blinder, take a*.

*****blink.** A light : c. of ca. 1820–70. Egan's Grose.—2. See **bit of blink**.—3. A cigarette-stump : military : C. 20. F. & Gibbons. It caused one to do so in smoking it.

blink, like a. Immediately ; in but a moment : coll. : C. 20. E. Phillips Oppenheim, *The Strange Boarders of Palace Crescent*, 1935, ' Must have died like a blink.' Prob. on *like winking* or *in a flash*.

*****blink-fencer.** A seller of spectacles : mid-C. 19–20 (ob.) c.—2. Hence, tipsy : military : C. 20. F. & Gibbons. Ex *blinks* = blinkers ; see **blinks**, 1, and **fence(r)**.

blinker. The eye (1816, ob.) ; pl., spectacles : coll. > S.E. : from ca. 1730.—2. A hard blow in the eye : C. 19.—3. A blackened eye : Norwich s.

(— 1860); †. H., 2nd ed.—4. A chap, fellow : late C. 19–20 dial. > C. 20 s. Cf. *blighter, bleeder,* and *blinking,* prob. its effective origin.

blinkers !, blank your. Damn your eyes ! : jocularly euphemistic (— 1890); ob. See **blinker, 1.**

blinking. A verbal counter, indicating mild reprobation or mere excitement : from ca. 1890. ' Prob. for *blanking,* euphemism for *bleeding,* with vowel thinned as in *bilk* ', W.

Blinking Sam. Dr. Samuel Johnson (1709–84). Dawson.

*****blinko.** An amateur entertainment—gen. held at a ' pub '. C. : from ca. 1870 ; ob. Perhaps because it makes one *blink* ; in form, cf. *blindo.*

*****blinks.** A pair of spectacles : c. (— 1845); ob.—2. One who blinks : a coll. nickname : C. 17–20.

blip. ' To switch an aeroplane engine on and off ' : Air Force : from 1915. F. & Gibbons. Blend ex *blink up* ; or a perversion of *flip.*

blip-o ! A derisive cry at a boat's coxswain colliding with anything : *Worcester* training-ship : late C. 19–20. Bowen.

blister. ' The anti-torpedo bulge in a man-of-war ' : naval : C. 20. Bowen.—2. An objectionable person : Public Schools' : C. 20. Ian Hay, *The Lighter Side of School Life,* 1914. Prob. ex Northern Ireland, where it has been in use from before 1898 (E.D.D.). Semantically it is to be compared with *blistering,* q.v.

blister, v. To punish moderately ; to fine : proletarian : from 1890 ; ob. Ware.—2. To thrash : C. 20 ; ob. A. H. Dawson.

blister it, them, etc. Blast it, them ! : euphemistic coll. : 1840, H. Cockton.

blistering. A euphemism for *bloody* : coll. : C. 20. Manchon.

blitherer. A silly fool : coll. : C. 20. (P. G. Wodehouse, *Mike,* 1909.) Ex :

blithering (gen. with **idiot**). Volubly nonsensical ; hence merely ' arrant ' : coll. (1889) >, by 1930, S.E. (O.E.D. Sup.) ' Thinned form of . . . *blether,* with vowel perhaps suggested by *drivelling* ', W.

blizzard. A sharp or stunning blow ; an overwhelming argument, a severe reprimand. Coll. : orig. (— 1830), U.S. ; anglicised ca. 1875, but ob. by 1930. See esp. F. & H.

blizzard collar. A woman's high stand-up collar : Society : 1897, *The Daily Telegraph,* Jan. 16 ; † by 1920. Ware, ' Suggestive of cold weather '.

*****bloak.** See **bloke.**

bloat. ' A drowned body. (2) A drunkard. (3) A contemptuous term applied indiscriminately to anybody ', A. H. Dawson : ? error for *bloater.* Late C. 19–20.

bloated. A lower-classes' euphemism for *bloody* : C. 20. Manchon.

bloated aristocrat. Any man of rank and wealth : coll. ; from ca. 1850, though adumbrated in 1731. Thackeray, 1861 : ' What a bloated aristocrat Thingamy has become since he got his place ! ' In C. 20 the term is *bloated plutocrat,* which when used seriously is S.E. ; when jocularly, coll.

bloater. A B.E.8 aeroplane : Air Force : late 1914–15. F. & Gibbons.

bloater, mild. A little dandy, a dandy of no account : low : C. 20. Manchon.

bloater, my. My darling ; my man : low : C. 20. Ibid.

blob. A ' duck's egg ' : cricket : coll. : 1898, says Ware ; 1934, W. J. Lewis, ' From the cipher 0 placed against his name on the score-sheet ' ; ultimately ex *blob,* a blot, a shapeless mass.—2. A glass of beer : military ; C. 20. F. & Gibbons.—3. Patter or beggars' tales : vagrants' c. (— 1861). Mayhew. Cf.

*****blob,** v. To talk, esp. if indiscreetly ; **to** ' patter ' : from ca. 1850 ; c. Same period : *on the blob,* by talking (Mayhew, 1851). Ex *blab.*

blob, get a. To make no score : cricketers' coll. : 1905, Norman Gale (W. J. Lewis). Ex the n. Also *make a blob,* 1903 (O.E.D. Sup.) ; used fig., to make nothing, it is likewise coll. : from ca. 1905.

blob, on the. See **blob, v.**

block. A person either stupid or hard-hearted : C. 16–20 ; coll. until ca. 1660, then S.E. Early examples are offered by Udall (in *Ralph Roister Doister*), Shakespeare, Jonson. Cf. *deaf, dull,* etc., as a *block.*—2. The head : C. 17–20. Shirley, ca. 1637. See also **block, lose the.**—3. In Scottish c., a policeman : recorded for 1868 (Ware), but prob. from ca. 1860.—4. ' The young lady of fine shape who in the mantle department tries on for the judgment of the lady customer ', Ware : linen-drapers' coll. : C. 20.

block, v.t. Have intercourse with a woman : C. 20, low.—2. See **blocking.**—3. See **block a hat.** —4. (Usually **block a pub.**) To occupy, or remain, long in : non-aristocratic (— 1909). Ware, ' Gen. said of a sot '.

block, a chip of the same or (same) old. Of the same character ; with inherited characteristics. Coll. : C. 17–20. In a sermon, Sanderson, 1627 : ' Am I not a child of the same Adam, a vessel of the same clay, a chip of the same block with him ? ' (O.E.D.)

block, barber's. The head : from ca. 1820 ; in Scott.—2. Also, an over-dressed man (— 1876, ob.). Both ex the wooden block on which barbers displayed a wig.

block, do in the ; occ. **do one's block.** See **block, lose the.**

block, do the. To promenade : 1869, Marcus Clarke : Melbourne s. >, by 1890, gen. Australian coll. Ex the fashionable block of buildings in Collins Street between Swanston and Elizabeth Streets. Morris.—2. Hence, *on the block,* promenading thus : Australian coll. : 1896, *The Argus,* July 17.

block, lose (or do in) the ; occ. **do one's block.** To become angry, excited, diffident : Australian (— 1916). C. J. Dennis, who has also *keep the block,* to remain dispassionate.

block, off one's. Panicky ; crazy ; occ., angry : late C. 19–20. F. & Gibbons. See **block, n., 2.**

block a hat. ' To knock a man's hat down over his eyes ', H., 3rd ed. : from ca. 1860. Perhaps ex *block,* the head.

block and fall. Irritably drunk : Anglo-Irish : C. 20.

block-house. A prison : ca. 1620–1840, but not gen. before late C. 18. (B.E. considers it to be c.) Earlier, S.E. : a fort ; cf. G.W. usage.

block-ornament, blocker. A small piece of inferior meat displayed on a butcher's *block* : coll. : from ca. 1845 ; slightly ob.—2. A queer-looking person : from ca. 1860 ; †.

block with a razor, cut a. (Often *blocks* for *a block.*) To try in a futile or incongruous way : coll. Goldsmith, 1774. Ob.

blocker. A bowler hat : mainly stores and hatters' : C. 20. (John Brophy, *Waterfront,* 1934.) —2. See **block-ornament.**

blocking. (Parliamentary) the preventing or postponing of a bill being passed, esp. of its being voted-on after 12.30 at night : 1884 ; coll. > j. > S.E. (S.O.D.)

*bloke ; in mid-C. 19, occ. **bloak.** Occ. contemptuous ; occ. a term of address among sailors. A man ; a chap, fellow (— 1839). Until ca. 1860, c. ; until ca. 1900, low. Pre-1870 examples : Brandon (in ' Ducange Anglicus '), Mayhew, Sala, Kingsley, Ouida, Miss Braddon, James Greenwood. Also, 2, a lover (' Sally and her bloke ', Ware) : from ca. 1880. And, 3, in C. 20 Navy, a man's (passive) male ; 4, in late C. 19–early 20 universities, an ' outsider ', a book-grubber, as Ware notes. Perhaps ex Dutch *blok*, a fool, or (via Romany) ex Hindustani, *loke*, a man ; Weekley thinks that it derives ex Shelta (Irish tinkers' c.). Note, however, the slightly earlier *gloak*, q.v. : though, of course, *gloak* may well derive ex Shelta.

bloke, the. The commander of one's man-of-war : naval : late C. 19–20. Bowen.

*bloke with the jasey, the. The judge : c. or low s. (— 1874). H., 5th ed. Ex *bloke*, 1.

blondie or **-y.** A blonde girl : non-aristocratic and non-cultured coll. : from ca. 1925.

*blone. A corruption of *blowen*, q.v. (Egan's Grose.)

blonked. See **blanked.**

[**blood,** by itself or in combination with *God's, Christ's,* in oaths : all † by 1900.]

blood. A fast or a foppish man : C. 16–early 19, coll. Now literary and archaic.—2. University and Public Schools' : a senior held to be a setter of fashion and manners : from ca. 1880.—3. Hence, a passenger favourably regarded : ships' stewards' : C. 20. Bowen.—4. Money : coll. : C. 18–19.—5. A wall-flower : low, mostly London : late C. 19–20 ; slightly ob. Ware. Cf. *bug*, n., 3 : likewise ex the colour.—6. A ' penny dreadful ' : naval (— 1909). Ware.—7. Hence, any ' thriller ' : gen. public : from ca. 1918.—8. A third-class shot : military : late C. 19–20 ; ob. F. & Gibbons.—9. A blood orange : fruiterers' and grocers' coll. : late C. 19–20.

blood, v. Deprive of money : ca. 1860–1910. Hawley Smart, 1884. Cf. *bleed.*

blood, adj. Fashionable ; distinguished : Public Schools' : late C. 19–20. P. G. Wodehouse, *Mike*, 1909, ' You might think it was the blood thing to do to imitate him.' Ex *blood*, n., 2.

blood, in and **out of.** Vigorous, weak. C. 19–20 hunting s. ex hunting j.

blood, young. (C. 20 political.) A youthful and vigorous member of a party.

blood and entrails (more gen., **guts**). The red ensign : nautical : late C. 19–20. Bowen.

blood and guts alderman. A pompous man ; a man with a large ' corporation ' : C. 19.

Blood-and-Iron. Bismarck : a coll., journalistic nickname (— 1887) ; virtually †. Baumann. Ex his doctrine.

blood and 'ouns ! I.e. God's blood and wounds : C. 18–19.

blood and thunder. A mixture of port wine and brandy : ca. 1860–1910. Ex colour and effect, resp. (The phrase was orig. an oath.)

blood and thunder tales. Low-class, sensational, over-adventurous fiction : ? orig. U.S. ; in England from ca. 1885. Coll. Cf. *awfuls, penny dreadfuls, shilling shockers.*

blood ball. ' The butchers' annual hopser [*sic*],

a very lusty and fierce-eyed function ' : London trade : late C. 19–20 ; virtually †. Ware. Cf. *bung ball*, q.v.

blood-boat. A tally-boat : naval : late C. 19–20. Ex high prices charged.—2. A particularly hard sailing ship with a brutal afterguard : nautical coll. : mid-C. 19–20. Bowen.

blood-curdler or **-freezer.** A thrilling, esp. a ' creepy ' narration or incident : coll., from ca. 1870. Cf. *blood-and-thunder tales, shilling shocker, thriller,* and *blood,* n., 6 and 7.

blood for blood. In kind : tradesmen's, esp. in purchase and payment ; from ca. 1780 ; ob. Grose, 2nd ed. (With *deal.*)

blood for breakfast ! (, there's). A naval c.p. (late C. 19–20) in reference to the admiral's or captain's morning temper if it is bad. Bowen.

Blood-Hole, the. A Poplar theatre specialising in melodrama : East London : ca. 1880–1914. Ware.

blood on the bullet. A musketry-instructors' c.p. intimating that a bullet should, if possible, have a fleshy billet : 1915 ; ob. F. & Gibbons.

blood or beer ? A London streets' jocular c.p. = fight or pay for such refreshment ! : ca. 1900–15. Ware.

blood-red fancy. A red silk handkerchief (— 1839, ob.) : boxing world. Brandon.

blood-stained. A C. 20 (mainly post-G.W.) facetious alternative, rarely euphemistic, for *bloody,* adj.

blood-sucker. A lazy fellow involving his shipmates in additional work : nautical coll. (— 1867). Smyth.

Blood-Suckers. The Sixty-Third Regiment of Foot, now—and since ca. 1881—the 1st Battalion of the Manchester Regiment : military : from ca. 1860 ; ob.

blood-worm. A sausage ; esp. a black pudding : proletarian London : ca. 1850–1910. Ware.

bloody, adj. A low coll. intensive, orig., and still occ., connoting detestation : from ca. 1810. *Lex. Bal.,* 1811, ' A favourite word used by the thieves in swearing, as bloody eyes, bloody rascal ' ; Egan, 1823, added : ' *Irish* '. During the G.W., an adj. of all work, often used with a splendid disregard for congruity. Ex and cf. :

bloody, adv. (In mid-C. 17–18, gen. *bloody drunk.*) Also a low coll. intensive ; = very. C. 17–20, but respectable till ca. 1750. In C. 17, there was an undertone of violence, in early C. 18 (cf. *blood,* n., q.v.) of high but roistering birth : from ca. 1750, neutral ethically and socially, but (until ca. 1920, at least) objectionable æsthetically. Only since the G.W. has it, in post-1800 days, been at all gen. written in full. There is no need for ingenious etymologies : the idea of blood suffices. For both adj. and adv., see F. & H., O.E.D., Weekley's *Adjectives* and his *Words Ancient and Modern,* Robert Graves's *Lars Porsena* in the revised ed., and esp. my *Words !* ; the last contains a 2,000-word essay on the subject.—2. It is often inserted, as in *abso-bloody-lutely, hoo-bloody-rah, not bloody likely* : C. 20. Manchon.

bloody back. A soldier : pejorative : late C. 18–early 19. Grose, 1st ed. Ex the scarlet uniform.

bloody carpet bags of, make. To mutilate, e.g. with a razor : imported (— 1909) into Liverpool from U.S. ; ob. Ware. Many carpet bags are red.

Bloody Claverse. Graham of Claverhouse, Viscount Dundee (1643–89). Dawson.

Bloody Eleventh. The Eleventh Regiment of

Foot, now—and since ca. 1881—the Devonshire Regiment : military : C. 19–20, ob. Ex. the bloody battle of Salamanca in the Peninsular War ; they had already suffered heavily at Fontenoy. Dawson.

*bloody end to me ! ; I wish my bloody eyes may drop out if it is not true ! ; God strike me blind ! Thieves' oaths recorded in Egan's Grose, 1823.

bloody flag. That single red flag which is the signal for close action : naval : C. 19–20 ; ob. Bowen.

Bloody Forty (or **b.f.**), **the.** A criminal gang infesting the Liverpool Docks in the 1850's : nautical coll. It was ' broken up by Captain Samuels of the *Dreadnought* ' (Bowen).

bloody jemmy. An uncooked sheep's head : ca. 1810–1914. Vaux, 1812 ; H., 1st ed. Also known as a *sanguinary James* and a *mountain pecker.*

Bloody King's. That red-brick church (St. Mary's the Less) in Barnwell which resembles King's College Chapel in architecture : Cambridge University : late C. 19–20. Cf. *Bloody Mary's.*

Bloody Mackenzie. Sir G. Mackenzie (1636–91), a lawyer bitter against the Covenanters. Dawson.

Bloody Mary. Queen Mary of England (d. 1558). Ex the persecutions she allowed. (This nickname soon > an historical and theological counter, a mere sobriquet of ' the Swan of Avon ' type.)

Bloody Mary's. ' The red-brick church, St. Paul's, resembling St. Mary's in Cambridge, the University church ', F. & H. revised : Cambridge University : late C. 19–20.

bloody (or **B.**) **Monday.** The first day of vacation, set aside for the detention and punishment of offenders : schoolboys' (orig. Winchester) : **ca.** 1670–1770. O.E.D. Contrast *black Monday.*

Bloody Pirates. A good-natured South-Seas nickname for Burns, Philp & Co., the big steamship firm of the Pacific : C. 20. Punning *B.P.'s,* as they are also called.

bloomer. A mistake : Australian and English (— 1889). Barrère & Leland. Perhaps a ' blend ' of *blooming error.*

bloomeration. Illumination : London illiterate : 1897 ; ob. and, prob., never gen. Ware.

blooming. (Occ. euphemistic—cf. *bleeding*—for *bloody.*) A mild intensive adj. and adv. ; cf. *bally, blinking.* The S.O.D. dates the earliest instance at 1882 ; the usage was foreshadowed early in C. 18. Its popularity in the 1880's was owing largely to Alfred G. Vance, the comic singer.

Bloomsbury Birds. ' Hot-spirited recusants ', the disciples of ' corner-miching priests ' : London ecclesiastical circles : ca. 1630–90. Hacket (whose phrases they are).

*bloss, blowse. A wench ; a low harlot : the former certainly c. always, the latter prob. a c. word at one period. These senses date from late C. 17. Prob. ex *blowse,* 2, q.v., but not impossibly abbr. *blossom.* Cf. *blower,* q.v.—2. ' A Thief or Shop-lift ', B.E. : c. of late C. 17–early 19. Prob. an extension of sense 1.

blossom-faced, bloated ; **blossom-nose,** a tippler : lower classes' : mid-C. 19–20 ; ob.

blot one's copy book. A C. 20 coll. : to make a mistake, a *faux pas,* a bad impression. Ex elementary school.

*blot the scrip. To put in writing : mid-C. 17–18 ; prob. c. Hence *blot the scrip and jark it,* to stand engaged ; be bound for anyone : late C. 17–18 c. *Jark* = a, or to, seal.

blotto. Drunk : from ca. 1905. P. G. Wodehouse, of a drunken man, ' He was oiled, boiled, fried, plastered, whiffled, sozzled, and blotto.' Ex the porousness of blotting-paper, possibly suggested or influenced by Romany *motto,* intoxicated.

blouser. ' To cover up, to hide, to render nugatory ', to mislead : ca. 1880–1914. Ex the Fr. workman's *blouse.* Ware, ' Probably in an anti-Gallican spirit '.

blow. In c., goods, esp. in *bite the blow* : late C. 17–18. B.E., Grose.—2. A shilling : ca. 1870–1910, low.—3. A spree, drunken frolic : Oxford and Cambridge, ca. 1800–70.—4. A breathing-space : coll., C. 19–20. Cf. *get a blow,* to get a breath of fresh air, or a considerable exposure to wind : from ca. 1890 ; coll.—5. A copulation : from the man's standpoint : C. 20. Perhaps ex :—6. A harlot : c. or low s. (— 1823) ; † by 1890. Egan's Grose. Abbr. *blowen.*—7. A warning . secret information : c. (— 1926). O.E.D. (Sup.). Ex *blow,* v., 2.—8. (Also *cold blow* if esp. windy.) A taxi-cab rank : taxi-drivers' : from ca. 1925. Ex the food or the rest one can get there.—9. A smoke ; esp., a cigarette : c. : from ca. 1920. James Curtis, *The Gilt Kid,* 1936.

blow, v. To fume, storm, speak angrily : C. 16–20, coll. (O.E.D.) In later C. 19–20 the term, in its first two nuances, has, after nearly a century of obsolescence, been revived by contact with Australia and America, where, as ' to boast ', it had—and has—a second life.—2. To inform, give information (v.t. absolute, in B.E., but gen. with *up* or *upon,* later *on*) : from ca. 1570 ; S.E. till ca. 1660, coll. till C. 19, then s. ' D—n me, if I don't blow . . . I'll tell Tom Neville,' Leigh Hunt. (S.O.D.) —3. The euphemistic *blow* (*me !*) is also used as a low jocular coll. = to curse, swear at (often with past tense *blowed*), v.i. and v.t. : 1835, Marryat, ' If I do, blow me ! ' (O.E.D.). Occ. *blow me tight !,* † by 1920 ; *blow me up !,* current ca. 1780–1830 (George Parker), *blow it ! :* mid-C. 19–20 (cf. *blast it !*).—4. Spend, lose money : see **blew.** —5. University, occ. as *go on the blow* : to indulge in a spree : C. 19.—6. Winchester College, C. 19–20 : to blush (a corruption or a variant of *blue,* q.v.).—7. In C. 20 c., to go away, esp. if quietly and quickly.—8. Also, v.i., to ' blow the gaff ' (v.t. with *to*) : c. : C. 20. Wallace, *Room 13.* Cf. sense 2.—9. To open (a safe) by the use of powder : c. : late C. 19–20. James Spenser, 1934.

blow ! Go away ! : lower classes' (— 1935). Ex *blow.* v., 7.

blow a cloud. To smoke a cigar or a pipe : coll., verging on S.E. : late C. 18–19. Tom Moore, 1819. (In late C. 17–18, *raise a cloud* = to smoke a pipe.)

*blow a tank. To dynamite a safe : post-G.W. New Zealand c.

blow-along, roll-along tub. A full-lined sailing. ship : clipper-ship sailors' coll. : mid-C. 19–20 ob. Bowen.

blow-book. A book containing indelicate pictures : C. 18, coll. *The Post Man,* June 8, 1708.

blow great guns. To blow a violent gale : from ca. 1840 ; coll. Hugh Miller. Occ. *b.g.g. and small arms,* †.

blow hot and cold. To vacillate ; be treacherous : mid-C. 16–20 ; coll. till ca. 1800, then S.E.

blow-in. To arrive ; enter (v.i.) ; come. *blow-in on* (a person), to visit. Coll. ; C. 20. From U.S.A.

blow (in) a bowl. To ɒe a confirmed drunkard: C. 16 (? early 17); coll. Barclay, 1515. (O.E.D.)

blow in one's pipe. To spend money: low: ca. 1870–1920. Cf. *blow*, v., 4.

blow it !; blow me (tight) !; blow me up ! See **blow**, v., 3; for 1st, see also **blew it.**

blow off my last limb (or wind) ! I swear that's true: nautical (— 1923). Manchon.

blow off steam. To work, talk, swear, etc., hard, as a 'safety-valve': from ca. 1830; coll. Marryat.

blow off the line. To lose in a contest: military: G.W. (F. & Gibbons.)

*****blow off the loose corns.** 'To Lie now and then with a Woman', B.E.: late C. 17–mid-18; c. Cf. *blow the groundsels*, q.v.

blow one's bazoo. To boast, 'show off': ca. 1870–1910. Ex Dutch *bazu = bazuin*, trumpet.

blow one's hide out. To eat heavily: low coll. (— 1857); ob. 'Ducange Anglicus.'

blow-out. A heavy meal: from ca. 1820. Bee, 1823; Scott, 1824.—2. V., *blow oneself out*: Barham, 1837; H., 1874, 'Sometimes the expression is, "*blow out* your bags".'—2. In c., to steal (something): late C. 19–20; ob.

blow sky high. To scold, or blame, most vehemently: ? orig. U.S. and anglicised ca. 1900.

*****blow the gab** or **gaff.** To reveal a secret: in C. 18, c. (as in Grose, 1st ed.); then, always with *gaff*, low s., as in Marryat.

blow the grampus. (Nautical) to throw cold water on a man asleep on duty: C. 19–20; ob.

*****blow the groundsels.** To 'lie with' a woman on the floor: C. 17–18; c. In B.E. *blow-off on . . .*

blow-through, have a. (Of a man) to coït: low: C. 20.

blow together. To make in a slovenly way: tailors': from ca. 1850; ob.

blow-up. A discovery, disclosure: coll.: late C. 18–early 19. Grose, 2nd ed.—2. A scolding: from ca. 1839. More gen. (1839) **blowing-up.** Ex:— 3. V., to scold: 1827, Lytton, but prob. earlier. —4. A quarrel (temporary): from ca. 1880.—5. To accost (a person): New Zealanders': C. 20. Ex sense 3.

blow upon. To betray: C. 15–19, coll. To make public: C. 17–19. To discredit: C. 17–19, coll.

blowed, be. Euphemistic when *blowed* = damned; otherwise, low coll. From the mid-1830's. Dickens, 1836, 'You be blowed.' Cf. *blow*, v., 3: q.v. N.B.: in late C. 19–20, *blowed* is, except in this phrase, considered sol. for *blown*.

*****blowen ; blowing(g).** A woman, esp. a harlot: c.: resp. late C. 18–19 (Grose, 2nd ed.) and late C. 17–early 19 (B.E.). Borrow, in his *Romano Lavo-Lil*, says : 'Signifying a sister in debauchery . . . the Beluñi of the Spanish Gypsies'.

blower. A boaster; a very talkative person. Australian (and U.S.): from ca. 1860; ob.—2. In late C. 17–18 c., a mistress; a whore, as in Coles, 1676. In C. 19 c., a girl: pejoratively opp. to *jomer*, q.v. A variant of *blowen*, q.v. Brandon. —3. A pipe: low (— 1811); † by 1890. *Lex. Bal.*—4. **The Blower**, the Dolphin (public-house): low: ca. 1820–50. Bee.—5. In C. 20 c., a telephone. Charles E. Leach.—6. Hence, a telephone or a telegraph for the transmission of racing news: low (— 1935).

blower and striker. A hard officer; esp., a 'bucko' mate: nautical: late C. 19–20. Bowen.

blowhard. A boaster: Australian: 1880. In U.S. (1855; ob.), an adj., whence prob. the n. —2. Whence, a blustering officer, of no use with his fists: sailing-ship seamen's: from ca. 1885. Bowen.

blowing, vbl.n. Boasting: from ca. 1860. Trollope in Australia and New Zealand, 1873, 'A fine art much cultivated in the colonies, for which the colonial phrase of "blowing" has been created'. —2. See **blowen.**

blowing marlin-spikes(, it's). (It is) a full gale: nautical coll.: mid-C. 19–20. Bowen. I.e. the gale is strong enough to lift a marlin-spike (or almost).

blowing of a match, in the. In a moment: coll., mostly London (— 1887); ob. Baumann.

blowing-up. See **blow-up,** 2.

blown in !, look (or see) what the wind has. See who has arrived !: jocular coll.: C. 20.

blowsabella. A country wench: C. 18; coll. Suggested by the character in Gay's poem, *The Shepherd's Week*. Cf. *blousalinda*, which likewise has a coll. savour.

blowse, blowze. A beggar's trull; a wench: late C. 16–18: either c. or low s. Chapman in *All Fools*. Cf. *bloss*, q.v.—Cf. 2, a slatternly woman: C. 16–18.

blub. To weep, esp. of children: mid-C. 19–20. Ex *to blubber*.—2. Also, to wet with weeping: coll.: 1804, Tarras (O.E.D.). Ex equivalent *blubber*.

*****blubber.** The mouth: in C. 18–early 19, c.; then (but in C. 20 ob.), s. *A New Canting Dict.,* 1725; Grose, 1st ed.—2. A woman's breasts: low: late C. 18–20, esp. in *sport blubber*, to expose the breasts. Grose, 2nd ed.

blubber, v. To weep effusively, noisily: C. 15– 20. Until ca. 1800, S.E.; then coll. Smollett, Scott. (Gen. pejorative.)

blubber and guts. Obesity: C. 19–20, ob.; low. Cf. :

blubber-belly. A fat person: C. 19–20, low coll.; ob. Cf. preceding entry.

blubber-head(ed). (A) foolish (person): C. 19– 20, ob. Mostly nautical.

blubber-hunter. A whaling-ship: pejorative nautical coll.: mid-C. 19–20. Bowen.

blucher. Winchester College: a prefect in half power: ca. 1830–1915. Also, a non-privileged cab plying at railway stations: ca. 1850–1900. Ex the Prussian field-marshal, who arrived somewhat late at the Battle ɔf Waterloo.

bludge. To use a bludgeon: 1924, Galsworthy, *The White Monkey.*

*****bludgeon business.** See **swinging the stick.**

*****bludgeoner.** A harlot's bully; a bawdy-house chucker-out: c. (— 1852); ob. Also, in late C. 19–20, *bludger.*

*****bludger.** A thief apt to use a bludgeon, i.e. violence: c.; from ca. 1850. H., 1st ed.—2. See **bludgeoner.**

[**blue.** This word, in the S.E., coll., and s. of C. 18–20—it is rare before ca. 1700—plays a protean and almost intangible part, for it expresses a gamut of opinions and emotions. For an excellent gen. introduction on the subject, see F. & H. at *blue*.]

blue. The Blue Squadron: from ca. 1700; orig. naval and coll.; in C. 19, gen. and S.E. See the note at *admiral of the blue.*—2. A 'blue stocking': 1788, Mme. D'Arblay; after ca. 1800, coll. Byron, in *Don Juan*: 'The Blues, that tender tribe, who sigh o'er sonnets '; ' Cuthbert Bede ' : ' Elizabeth, the very Virgin Queen of Blues '. Hence *blue* = female learning ; † by 1900 : Byron, 'a twilight tinge of blue '.—3. A scholar of Christ's Hospital : abbr. *blue-coat boy* : from ca. 1820 ; †.—4. A policeman : from ca. 1835. Cf. *blue bottle* and *boy, man in blue*, etc.—5. A compromise between the half-pint and the pint pot : public-house, ca. 1870–1900.—6. Gen. *get Don's blue*. Fig. for election to an Oxford or Cambridge team in a major inter-university sport or competition : mid-C. 19–20 : soon coll. ; in C. 20, S.E. The Oxford colours are dark, the Cambridge light, blue.—7. (Gen. pl.) A bluejacket : nautical coll. : mid-C. 19–20 ; ob. Bowen.

blue, v. Blush : early C. 18. At Winchester College in C. 19. Swift, in *The Tatler*, ' If a Virgin blushes, we no longer cry she blues.'—2. To spend, waste : mid-C. 19–20, see **blew**.—3. Pawn, pledge : ca. 1850–1920. H., 1st ed.—4. To miscalculate ; bungle ; ruin : 1880 (O.E.D.).—5. Cf. the C. 20 racing c. use of *blue* as v.i. to mean : lose on a race. The bookie's clerk accordingly marks the book B. (John Morris). Cf. *cop*.—6. In mid-C. 19 gen. c., to steal ; plunder.

blue, adj. (Of women) learned, literary : from ca. 1780 ; coll. In C. 19–20 (ob.), S.E. Lever, in *Harry Lorrequer*, ' She was a . . . very little blue— rather a dabbler in the " ‘ologies " than a real disciple.'—2. Obscene : from late 1830's (cf. *blueness*) : coll. by 1900. Perhaps ex the blue dress of harlots (F. & H.), perhaps ex *La Bibliothèque Bleue*, a series of French books (H), perhaps simply in contrast to *brown*.—3. Gloomy, low-spirited : from ca. 1850, coll. : cf. *look blue, in a blue funk*.— 4. Drunk : Australian : from ca. 1920. Perhaps ex the resultant ' blue devils '.

blue, a bolt from the. Something (gen. un-pleasant) wholly unexpected (— 1888) ; coll. till C. 20, when S.E.

blue, burn it. See **burn it blue**.

blue, by all that's. Decidedly ! Gen., however, a euphemism for ' by God ! ' : coll. : from 1830's ; ob. ? ex *parbleu* = *par Dieu*.

blue, in the. Gone astray, gone wrong ; having failed, a failure : military : C. 20. F. & Gibbons. Perhaps = ' gone off into the blue haze of the horizon '.—2. Hence, in a ' deserted place far away and difficult of access ' : coll. (— 1931). Lyell.— 3. (Also ex sense 1.) In debt ; in a ' fix ' : Aus-tralian : from ca. 1927.

blue, look. To be confounded, astonished, dis-appointed : coll. : late C. 16–20, coll.—2. See **blue, till all look**, 2.

blue, make the air. To curse ; to use obscene or blasphemous language : mid-C. 19–20.

blue, men in. (Singular rare.) The police : coll. : from ca. 1870 ; ob. Cf. :

Blue, Royal Regiment of Foot-Guards. See **blues**, 4.

blue, till all is. To the utmost, the limit ; for an indefinite time : perhaps orig. U.S. (1806) ; ob. Admiral Smyth refers to a ship reaching deep, i.e. blue, water.—2. In drinking : till one becomes drunk, as in Barham ; *till all look* or *seem blue* is a C. 17 (?–18) variant.

blue, true. Faithful(ness) : C. 17–20, coll. Foreshadowed by 1500. In C. 17, of Scottish Whigs ; in C. 19–20, of strong Tories.

Blue and Buff. A literary nickname, ca. 1880 + for *The Edinburgh Review* (d. 1929).

Blue and Orange. The nickname of the Loyal and Friendly London club of the 1740's. Grose.

blue and white, gentleman in. A policeman : coll. : ca. 1860–1900.

blue-apron. A tradesman : C. 18–19, coll. > S.E. Amherst, *Terræ Filius*, 1726.

blue as a razor. Extremely blue : late C. 18–early 19. Grose, 2nd ed., pertinently suggests *blue as azure*.

blue-back. One of the old privately prepared charts : nautical coll. : C. 19–20 ; ob. Bowen. Contrast :

blue-backs. Orange Free State paper money : ca. 1860–1900. Thus F. & H.

blue-backs. See, however, **bluebacks**.

*blue-belly. A policeman : c. (— 1909). Ware. Cf. *blue*, n., 4.

blue bill. Winchester College : a tradesman's bill sent to the pupil's home : C. 19–20, ob. Ex the colour of the envelopes gen. used.

blue billy. A blue handkerchief white-spotted : low ; boxing : from the 1830's ; ob. Brandon, 1839.

blue-book. See ' Westminster School slang '.

blue blanket. The sky : C. 18–20 coll. ; ob. Defoe in his *History of the Devil*. Cf. *Bengal blanket*, q.v.—2. ' A rough overcoat made of coarse pilot cloth ', H., 2nd ed. : coll. : ca. 1860–90.

blue boar. A venereal chancre : late C. 18–19, low. Grose, 2nd ed. Perhaps ex the Blue Boar Tavern, in the ' Latin Quarter ' of the London of ca. 1750–1850.

blue board. A C. 20 variant of the preceding.

blue boat. (Gen. pl.) A skiff for the use of cadets at Dartmouth : naval coll. : late C. 19–20. Bowen. Cf. *black cutter*, q.v.

blue bottle. A beadle, a policeman : coll. : 1597, Shakespeare. Little used in late C. 17–18, but re-popularised ca. 1850.—2. A serving man : coll. : C. 19. Scott, G. P. R. James. Cf. *blue-apron*.

blue boy. A chancre : C. 18–19, low. Cf. *blue boar*.

blue boys. (Rare in singular.) The police : James Greenwood, 1883. Ob.

blue breeches !,—by my eyes, limbs, and. See **Eyes and Limbs, the**.

blue butter. Mercurial ointment, against para-sites : (Cockney) coll. : from ca. 1870 ; ob. H., 5th ed.

Blue Cap. A Scotsman : ca. 1590–1800 ; coll. > S.E. Cf. the S.E. *blue bonnet* and contrast :

Blue Caps, the. The Dublin Fusiliers : military : 1857 (Indian Mutiny) ; slightly ob. Ware. Occ. *Neill's Blue Caps*, ex their gallant colonel killed at Lucknow. (F. & Gibbons.)

blue coat. A blue-coated soldier : C. 16–17. In C. 19, occ. for a sailor. Coll. usages.—2. A police-man : C. 17–20, ob. ; And—3. Also, a serving man : C. 17–18.

blue-cross gas. German sneezing-gas : military coll. : 1917–18. B. & P. Ex the mark on the shell.

blue dahlia. Something rare or unheard of : coll. (— 1888) >, almost imm., S.E. Cf. Robert Hichens's *The Green Carnation*, 1894, and *blue roses*, 1885 (*The Daily News*, June 25).

blue damn, (I don't care a). A slightly evasive curse : coll. (— 1909) ; ob. Ware's semantics are rather far-fetched : prob. ex *blue*, adj., 2.

blue devils. Low spirits : from ca. 1780 : coll. >, by 1850, S.E. Grose, 1st ed. ; Cowper has *Mr. Blue Devil*. Ex *blue devil*, a baleful demon.—Hence 2, delirium tremens : from ca. 1822 : coll. >, by 1880, S.E. Scott and Cobbett. Cf. *blues*, 3.—3. The police : ca. 1845–1905. Cf. *blues*, 4.—4. *the Blue Devils*, the French Chasseurs Alpins : military coll. : 1915–18. F. & Gibbons. Ex their blue uniforms.

blue duck. A rumour, esp. if baseless : New Zealand soldiers' : in G.W. Semantics : *quack ! quack !*

blue-eyed boy. A pet, a favourite : coll. (— 1914) >, by 1930, S.E. F. & Gibbons. The allusion is to innocence : cf. (*mother's*) *white-haired boy*, q.v.

blue fear. Extreme fright : ca. 1870–1900 ; coll., rare. R. L. Stevenson. Cf. *blue funk*, q.v.

blue fire. Adj., sensational : from ca. 1870 ; mainly theatrical. Post-1920, however, it is fairly usual and, in its gen. use, coll. > S.E. Ex a blue light used on the stage to create a weird effect ; cf. S.E. *blue light*.

blue flag. A publican : mid-C. 18–early 19. Grose, 1st ed. Esp. in *hoist the b.f.*, become a publican.

blue funk. Extreme fear (— 1856). Thomas Hughes popularised it.

blue-funk school. A coll. form of *the blue-water school*, q.v. : its opponents' : from ca. 1906. Collinson.

Blue-Funneller (or **b.-f.**). An Alfred Holt steamer : nautical coll. : C. 20. Bowen.

blue glasses, see through. ' To see things from a wrong—generally depressed—point of view ' : coll. (— 1931). Lyell.

blue-handled rake. ' The railing and steps leading to the platform of a fair-booth stage ' : late C. 19–20. Ware.

Blue Horse, the. The Fourth Dragoon Horse : military : late C. 18–20 ; ob. Ex its facings of 1746–88.

*****blue it.** See **blew it.**

blue jack (or **Jack**). Cholera morbus : nautical (— 1909). Ex colour of skin (Ware). On *yellow jack*.

blue light. An order for money (during a temporary shortage) on the N.A.A.F.I. issued by a military unit : from 1924 or 1925. (With thanks to Major-General A. P. Wavell, C.M.G.).—2. A sanctimonious seaman : nautical : late C. 19–20. Bowen. Contrast :

blue lights. A naval gunner : naval : late C. 19–20. Bowen.

blue marines (or **B.M.**), **the.** The Royal Marine Artillery before they were amalgamated with the Light Infantry : naval coll. : C. 19. Bowen.

blue Monday. A Monday spent, away from work, in dissipation : from ca. 1880 ; ob.

blue moon. A rarely-recurrent (event or) period : coll. (— 1859). H., 1st ed. Ex :

blue moon, once in a. Extremely seldom : coll. : C. 17–20. *Till a blue moon* occurs in 1860, and the phrase is adumbrated as early as 1528 (Roy & Barlowe). Apperson.

blue murder, cry. See **blue murders.**

blue murder, like. With great rapidity, esp. if hastily or in a panic : 1914 (O.E.D. Sup.). Ex :

blue murder(s). Cries of terror or alarm : a great noise, horrible din : from late 1850's ; coll. H., 1st ed. Gen. as *cry b. m.* Cf. the Fr. *morbleu*, which, however, = *mort* (*de*) *Dieu*.

Blue Nose. A Nova Scotian : coll. ; orig. (1830) U.S., anglicised ca. 1840. Thornton. Ex the extreme cold of the Nova Scotian winter.

blue o'clock in the morning, at. ' Pre-dawn,

when black sky gives way to purple ' : London streets' : 1886, *The Daily News*, Oct. 12, ; ob. Rhyming on *two o'clock* (Ware).

blue paper, fly. See **fly blue paper.**

blue peter. (Cards) the signal for trumps at whist : coll. > j. : ca. 1860–1905.—2. Also fig. in its coll. use, as in Byron, for immediate departure.

blue pigeon. (Nautical) the sounding-lead : from ca. 1820.—2. In mid-C. 18–19 c., *blue pigeon* is roofing-lead ; hence, *b.-p. flyer* is a stealer of lead from houses and churches. Grose, 1st ed.

*****blue pigeon, fly the.** To steal roof-lead and lead pipes from house and church exteriors : mid-C. 18–19 c. Cf. *blue pigeon*, 2, q.v.

blue pill. A bullet : C. 19. Cf. the American *blue whistler* and *blue plum*.—2. A mercury pill against syphilis : c. (— 1887) ; ob. Baumann.

*****blue plum(b).** A mid-C. 18–19 c. term for a bullet. Grose, 1st ed. ; Harrison Ainsworth, 1834. Grose has the following phrases : *surfeited with a blue plumb*, ' wounded with a bullet ', and *a sortment* (i.e. an assortment) *of George R—'s* (i.e. Rex's) *blue plumbs*, ' a volley of ball, shot from soldiers' firelocks '.

blue ribbon. Gin : low : mid-C. 19–20 ; ob. Cf. *satin*, q.v.

blue-ribbon faker. A blatant upholder of abstinence from liquor : London streets' : 1882–ca. 1914. Ware.

blue pugaree. (Gen. pl.) A military policeman : New Zealander soldiers' : 1915–18. Ex the distinctive colour of their hat-bands.

blue-ribboner or **-ribbonite.** A teetotaller : coll. verging on S.E. : from ca. 1880. Ware. The blue ribbon worn by certain teetotallers is recorded in 1878 (S.O.D.).

blue ruin. Gin ; esp., bad gin : from ca. 1810 ; ob. *Lex. Bal.*, Keats, T. Moore, Lytton, Sala. Cf. (its prob. ' offspring ') *blue ribbon* and *blue tape*.

blue shirt at the mast-head, (there's) a. (There is) a call for assistance : nautical : late C. 19–20. Bowen. Ex the blue flag then flown.

blue skin. A Presbyterian : C. 18–early 19. Blue is the Presbyterian colour ; ' Hudibras ' Butler speaks of ' Presbyterian true blue '.—2. In the West Indies : a half-breed of black and white : C. 19–20, ob.—3. In late C. 18–early 19, any ' person begotten on a black woman by a white man ', Grose, 2nd ed. Cf. :

blue squadron, (belonging to the). (Of) mixed blood, white with Hindu : India, C. 19. In late C. 18–early 19, of anyone with ' a lick of the tar brush ', Grose, 3rd ed. See the note appended to *admiral of the blue*.

blue stocking. A literary or a learned lady (— 1790). The adj. began to be applied in the 1750's to the frequenters of Montagu House, London, where literary and cognate talk replaced cards. Both n. and adj. were coll. by 1810, S.E. by 1820 ; both are ob. Ex the blue worsted stockings affected by Benjamin Stillingfleet, a near-poet, who was a shining light of the Montagu House assemblies—by Admiral Boscawen dubbed the Blue Stocking Society. See esp. the O.E.D.

Blue Stocking Parliament. The ' Little Parliament ' of 1653 : coll., ca. 1653–1700. Ex their puritanically plain clothes.

blue stone. Gin or whisky so inferior that it resembles vitriol, which in Scottish and Northern dial. is called ' blue stone '. Ca. 1850–1900.

blue tape. Gin : ca. 1780–1850 ; perhaps c.

Grose, 2nd ed. Cf. *blue ruin* and *sky blue*, the latter in Grose, 3rd ed.

Blue Un, The. *The Winning Post*: sporting (— 1909); ob. Ware. Ex its colour, adopted to distinguish it from *The Pink Un's*.

blue unction. A blue ointment used to exterminate body-lice: military: from 1915. B. & P. Ex *unguent*.

blue-water school. Those who believe that naval offence is Britain's best defence: 1905. S. > coll. >, by 1914, S.E.

bluebacks. 'The notes of the Transvaal Government issued in 1865. The impecunious condition of the Transvaal at the time made these notes very much less than their face value. Cf. the American term "Greenbacks",' Pettman. (These notes lapsed before 1884, the term was ob. by 1900.) Ex their colour. Occ. *blue-backs*.

blued, occ. **blewed.** Drunk: low: C. 19–20; ob. This word perhaps influenced *screwed* and *slewed*.

bluely, come off. To have ill success, bad luck: coll.; ca. 1650–1840. Urquhart.

blueness. Indecency: literary s.; not much used. Carlyle, 1840. Ex *blue*, adj., 2.

bluer. See 'Harrow slang'.

blues, the. See **blue**, n., 2 and 7.—2. Despondency; low spirits. Apparently Washington Irving was, in 1807, the first to abbr. *blue devils*, q.v.— 3. Delirium tremens : from ca. 1850 but never very gen.—4. The police : see **blue,** n., 4 : from ca. 1835. 'Sometimes called the Royal Regiment of Footguards *Blue*,' H., 5th ed.: ca. 1870–90.—5. The Royal Horse-Guards : C. 17–20. Ca. 1690–1780, gen. *the Oxford Blues*, to distinguish them from King William the III's Dutch troops, also called *the Blues*.

*bluey. In mid-C. 19–20 c., lead : ex *blue pigeon*, q.v. H., 1st ed.—2. In New Zealand C. 20 c., a summons. Ex the blue paper on which it comes.— 3. A bushman's, esp. a sundowner's, bundle, usually wrapped in a blue blanket: Australian (— 1888); in C. 20, coll. Esp. in *hump bluey*, in C. 20 often *hump one's bluey*, to go on the tramp (— 1890). Morris. Cf. *swag*.—4. In Tasmania, a 'smock-coat' shirt or blouse worn in wet districts (1891, ob.). Ibid.—5. A nickname for a red-headed man : from ca. 1890, esp. in Australia and New Zealand.

*bluey-cracking. The stealing of lead from building-exteriors : c. (— 1845); ob.

bluey-hunter. An habitual stealer of lead roofing and piping : mid-C. 19–20 c. Cf. *blue-pigeon flyer*, s.v. *blue-pigeon*.

bluff. A considerable assurance adopted to impress an opponent : orig. (— 1848) U.S., anglicised ca. 1870 : cf. the v. Coll.; in C. 20, S.E.—2. In low s., an excuse : a sense firmly grounded in England—see Mayhew's *London Labour*—as early as 1851 : this sense may, perhaps, not come from the U.S.

bluff, v.i. and v.t. To impress, intimidate, make an excuse ; *bluff off*, to frighten away by bluffing ; *bluff out of*, to frighten out of. Orig. (1850) : (Thornton), U.S. ; anglicised as a coll., in the early 1860's or even the late 1850's, for H., 1859, makes no comment on the American origin of either n. or v.; in C. 20, S.E. The American usage, for both n. and v., perhaps derives from the Restoration senses, *bluff*, to blindfold (as in Ray) and *look bluff*, look big (as in B.E.); but see **bluffing** and W. at *bluff*.

bluff, call one's. To challenge a person, with

implication of showing up his weakness : coll. : C. 20. From U.S.A.

bluff the rats. To spread panic : low (— 1923). Manchon.

*bluffer. In c. of mid-C. 17–early 19, 'a Host, Inn-keeper or Victualler ', B.E. ; Coles, 1676. Prob. ex dial. *bluff*, to hoodwink.—2. An imposer that relies on an assumed appearance and speech : from ca. 1885 ; coll.—3. A bosun : nautical : ca. 1840–1914.

bluffing. Vbl.n., 'imposing on another with a show of force, where no real force exists : a phrase taken from the game of poker ', Thornton, who records it for U.S. at 1850. Anglicised, as coll., ca. 1880.

blug. An earlier form († by 1925) of *oickman*, q.v. : Bootham School. Anon., *Dict. of Bootham Slang*.

bluggy. A jocular, therefore s., not—except among purists or prudes—a euphemistic twisting of *bloody* : 1877. The O.E.D. (Sup.) remarks : '[A] pretended infantile pronunciation of *bloody* '. Hence, *blugginess* (1894 : ibid.).

blunderbuss. A stupid, or ignorant, clumsy fellow : from ca. 1690 ; coll. verging on, perhaps achieving, S.E. ; ob. Ex the weapon's unwieldiness.—2. Also, ca. 1680–1800, a noisy and truculent talker : coll. Ex the noise of its report.

blunk. A squall ; a period of squally weather : dial. (— 1790) >, by 1820, nautical coll. Bowen. Dial. has a v. *blunk*, which is cognate with *blench* (E.D.D.).

*blunt. Money, esp. cash (— 1714); orig. c. ; ob., except among tramps as *the blunt*. John Hall ; Grose (2nd ed.), Moncrieff, Dickens (in *Oliver Twist*), *Punch* (1882). Etymology doubtful : perhaps, indeed prob., ex the blunt rim of coins ; perhaps, however, ex John Blunt, chairman of the South Sea Company ; or perhaps, despite its surface improbability, ex the Fr. *blond* (cf. *brown*, a halfpenny), as H. and F. & H. maintain.—2. Whence *in blunt*, *out of blunt*, rich, poor : C. 19. Bee.

Blunt Magazine. A bank ; esp. the Bank of England : low : ca. 1820–60. Bee. Ex *blunt*, 1.

blunted. In possession of money : rare ; ca. 1850–90. Gen. *well-blunted*. Ex *blunt*, q.v.

blunty. A variant of the preceding. 'Jon Bee ', 1823.

blurb. A publishers' recommendation of a book : on the jacket, or in the front, of the book itself. Orig. U.S. (? 1923), anglicised in 1924. Coll. ; after 1933, S.E., but rarely heard beyond the world of books. Perhaps ex *blurred effect* ; perhaps a corruption of *splurge*. Cf. *blah*, q.v.

blurry. A slurring, gen. euphemistic, of *bloody* : from not later than 1910. B. & P.

blurt ! Pooh ! A fig. for ! : late C. 16–(? only early) 17 : coll. Lyly. Cf. the derisive c.p., *blurt, master constable !* : C. 17. Middleton. O.E.D. ; Apperson.

blurt, v. To let or cause an escape of anal wind : C. 20 ; low coll.

blush. See **black dog**.

blushing. Bloody : euphemistic coll.: C. 20. Manchon.

blushing honours. See **thick upon one**.

blusteration. Bluster ; a blustering : dial. (— 1803) >, ca. 1860, coll. (O.E.D.)

*bly. 'A burglar's oxy-acetylene blow lamp': c. (— 1933). George Orwell, *Down and Out in Paris and London*. By telescoping *blow* and *oxy*.

bly ! ; **bly me.** Reduced forms of *God blimey, Godblimey* : low : late C. 19–20. Ware.

*bly-hunker. A horse : vagrants' c. (– 1845) ; †. ? ex *blinker*.

Blyti. See **Blighty.**

bo. (In vocative) mate : U.S. (– 1905), partly anglicised ca. 1918. Perhaps ex (*you*) *hobo*, but see esp. Irwin.

bo or **boo to a goose, say** or **cry ;** occ. **to a battle-dore.** To open one's mouth ; to talk, speak : gen. in negative. Coll. ; from ca. 1580

bo-peep. Sleep : rhyming s. : C. 20. B. & P.—2. (**Bo-Peep.**) Boescheppe on the Western Front : military in G.W. W. H. L. Watson, *Adventures of a Despatch Rider*, 1915.

*bo-peep, play at. In turn to hide and appear in public ; to keep watch : late C. 18–early 19. Grose, 2nd ed. Ex the game.

boa-constrictor. An instructor : naval : late C. 19–20 ; virtually †. F. & Gibbons. Ex his ' fascinating ' eye.

board. A picture sold in the streets : C. 20 vagrants' c.—2. A sideboard : furniture-dealers' coll. : late C. 19–20. *The Spectator*, June 7, 1935.—3. A railway signal : railwaymen's : from the 1880's. *Tit-Bits*, Nov. 1, 1890, notes the synonymous **stick.**

board, v. To accost : C. 16–20. In Surrey and Shakespeare, S.E. ; but from ca. 1660, coll., as in Vanbrugh's *False Friend*, ' What do you expect from boarding a woman . . . already heart and soul engaged to another ? ' In C. 19–20, much more definitely nautical in flavour : before 1800, the Fr. *aborder*, to approach, accost, impressed rather by its Gallicism than by its nauticism.—2. ? hence, to borrow money from (a person) : military (– 1890) ; ob. F. & H.

board, above. See **above board.**

board, get the. To receive the right-away signal : railwaymen's : from ca. 1927. *The Daily Herald*, Aug. 5, 1936.

board, keep one's name on the. To remain a member of one's College : Cambridge coll. : from ca. 1850. In C. 20, S.E.

board, on the. (Tailoring) enjoying all the privileges and perquisites of a competent workman : ca. 1850–1920. Perhaps j. rather than s.

board, sail on another. To behave differently : C. 16–early 17 ; coll.

board, sweep the. To win all the prizes ; obtain every honour : coll. : from ca. 1830. Ex the card-game senses, take all the cards, win all the stakes : S.E., C. 17–20.

board, under. Deceptively : C. 17–18 ; coll. Cf. *above board*, q.v.

board in the smoke. (Nautical) to take by surprise : C. 19. Ex the lit. usage of boarding a ship under cover of broadside-smoke.

*board job. A sandwich-man's job : C. 20 c. Ex the board he carries.

Board-man. See **boardman, 2.**

board of green cloth. A card table : C. 19–20 ; a billiard-table : C. 18–20. Coll. ; ob.

board-work. See **boardman.**

boarder-bug. A boarder at school : schoolboys' : from late C. 19. Collinson. Opp. *day-bug*, same period.

*boarding house or **school.** A prison ; house of correction : c. ; ca. 1690–1840. B.E. ; Grose. Hence, *boarding scholars*, ' Bridewell-birds ', B.E.

*boardman. A standing patterer, who often carried a board with coloured pictures : c. (vagrants') : ca. 1840–1900. The practice was, by Cockneys, called *board-work.*—2. (Or **Board-man.**) A school-attendance inspector : London coll. (– 1887) ; ob. Baumann.

*boards. Playing cards : C. 20 c. Edgar Wallace in *The Mixer*, 1927.

boards, the. The stage ; theatre : from ca. 1770 : coll. till ca. 1880, then S.E.

*boat, always **the boat.** The hulks ; or any public works or prison : c. ; ca. 1810–95. Mayhew. Ex convict-hulks.

*boat, v. To transport (convicts) : ca. 1800–60.—2. To sentence to penal servitude : ca. 1870–1910. Both are c. In the latter sense, *get the boat* or *be boated* = to receive a severe sentence : H., 5th ed.

boat, be in the same. I.e. in the same position or circumstance(s) : coll., from ca. 1850, though anticipated in late C. 16 ; in C. 20, S.E.

boat, good. A soldier spending freely among poorer comrades : military : ca. 1890–1915.

boat, have an oar in another's or **every.** To meddle, be a busybody : from mid-C. 16 ; ob. Coll. till ca. 1600, then S.E.

boat, miss the. To be too late : nautical coll. : C. 20. Bowen.

boat, push out the. To pay for a round of drinks : naval : late C. 19–20. Bowen. Contrast *push the boat out*, q.v., at *push.*

boat, put on the. To deport ; as adj., deported : low : late C. 19–20.

boat, sail in the same. To act together : coll. ; from late C. 16 ; in C. 19–20, S.E.

boats. Large boots : middle-class jocular : C. 20. Cf. *carts* and *two feet* . . .

boatswain-captain. A naval captain thoroughly competent as a seaman : naval coll., contemptuously used by the envious : C. 19. Bowen.

boaty. Fond of, addicted to, boating : coll. : 1886 (O.E.D.). Cf. *horsey.*

bob. A man, a fellow : coll. : from ca. 1700 : ob. Cf. *Jack* and *Tom, Dick and Harry*, the commonness of the name giving rise to a generic sense. Cf. sense 3, where, however, the idea may be that of *bobbing* in, out, and up ; also *dry* and *wet bob* (see **bob, dry**).—2. A shilling : from ca. 1810. In 1812 Vaux records it in his *Flash Dict.* Origin obscure : perhaps abbr. *bobstick*, q.v. ; Weekley suggests ex *Robert*, cf. *joey*, q.v.—3. In c., a shoplifter's assistant : late C. 17–19. Cf. sense 1.—4. Gin : C. 18.—5. At Winchester College, C. 19 : a large white beer-jug, holding about a gallon.—6. See **bob, s'help me.**

*bob, v. ; occ. as **bob out of.** To cheat, trick. Late C. 17–19 c. C. 14–16, S.E. ; C. 17, coll. Ex Old Fr. *bober*, to befool.

bob, adj. Lively, pleasant, ' nice ' : C. 18–20 ; ob. Cibber, 1721. Coll.—2. In c., safe ; esp. in *all is bob* ; late C. 17–early 19. Cf. *betty, all* : q.v.

bob ! Stop ! Enough ! : Society, ca. 1880–1900. Ex gen. *bob it !*, drop it ! (– 1864).

bob !, all is. See **bob,** adj., 2.

bob !, bear a. Be quick ! Look lively : coll., from ca. 1860 ; ob. Ex *bear a bob* (lit., a refrain), join in the chorus.

bob, dry. Incomplete coïtion : applied to the man : ca. 1660–1930. Rochester ; Grose ; F. & H. (revised). Ex *dry bob*, a blow that leaves the skin intact.—2. See :

bob, dry and wet. At Eton College, one who concentrates resp. on land games and sports and on boating, swimming, (recently) water-polo. *Dry bob* occurs in Disraeli's *Coningsby*: the terms would therefore seem to date from ca. 1835; they were coll. by 1875, S.E. by 1900.

bob, give the. To dismiss: C. 17, coll. (In S.E., *give the bob* = to befool, impose on.)

bob, light. A soldier in the light infantry, artillery, etc.; coll.; from ca. 1840. Here, as in *dry* and *wet bob, bob* abbr. *Robert*, so common a name that it > generic for a man, a fellow; cf. *Jack, Joe, Dick,* etc.

bob (or, in Ware, **baub**)**!, s'help me.** As an oath, euphemistic (*bob* = God). It is s. only when, as in 'Jon Bee' 1823, in Barham, 1837, and in James Payn, 1880, it is virtually or actually an asseveration (= 'you may be sure') made jocularly. 'The word . . . comes from Catholic England, and is " babe "—meaning the infant Saviour,' Ware. Now *s'help, s'elp,* is often, deliberately or otherwise, pronounced *swelp* (q.v.) and among the middle and upper classes, after ca. 1890, it is always spoken in jest.

hob, shift one's. To move, go away: mid-C. 18–20; ob. Grose.

bob, wet. See **bob, dry.**

bob-a-day gunner or **guns.** A temporary gunnery-officer: naval: C. 20. F. & Gibbons; Bowen. He draws an additional shilling a day.

bob a nob. Almost a c.p.: a shilling a head. Ca. 1820–1910. Bee; H., 3rd ed., records in this form, which is correct; F. & H. as *bob a nod,* which I believe to be an error.

bob around. To go quickly from place to place: coll.; from ca. 1860. Cf. *bob, shift one's.*

***bob cull.** A 'good fellow', pleasant companion: late C. 18–19 c. See **bob,** adj., and **cull.**

bob-down man. An anti-aircraft sentry: military coll.: 1915–18. F. & Gibbons. His warning caused men to take cover.

***bob groin.** See **groin.**

Bob, Harry, and Dick. Sick, esp. after drink: rhyming s.: 1868; virtually †. Ware.

***bob ken; bowman ken.** 'A good or well Furnished House, full of Booty, worth Robbing; also a House that Harbours Rogues and Thievs', B.E.: c.: late C. 17–early 19.

bob (or **Bob**) **my pal.** A girl: rhyming s. on *gal.* From ca. 1855; ob. 'Ducange Anglicus', 1857.

bob-tack. Cleaning-wherewithal; brass polish: military: C. 20. F. & Gibbons. Perhaps ironically ex *bob,* adj., 1; see also **tack.**

bob-tailor. 'A cruiser-sterned merchant ship': nautical: late C. 19–20. Bowen.

bob up. To appear; to return, as in 'he's always bobbing up'. C. 20, coll.

bob(b)ajee. A cook: Regular Army coll.: mid-C. 19–20; ob. F. & Gibbons. Ex Hindustani *bawachi.*

bobber. A fellow-workman; mate, chum: dial. (— 1860) >, by 1870, coll. and by 1885, s. Ex lit. sense.—2. A spurious pl. of *bob,* a shilling, as in *two bobber,* a two-shilling piece, though this (ca. 1880–1910) may conceivably be due to the Oxford *-er.*— 3. A tale-bearer: military: C. 20. F. & Gibbons. Ex bobbing along to become one.

bobbery. A noise; disturbance; squabble. From ca. 1800: Kenney has it in his comedy, *Raising the Wind,* 1803 ; *Punch* honoured it in 1879. Ex Hindi *Bap re !,* Oh, father: often employed to express grief or surprise. Since ca. 1890 it has been little used except among soldiers and others with

experience of India; current among the Tommies in the G.W. See also **bubbery.**

bobbery-pack. A heterogeneous squadron: naval: ca. 1820–90. Bowen, 'Borrowed from the sportsmen ashore'.

bobbing-bastard. A disappearing-' man ' target: marksmen's: C. 20.

bobbing-drill. Target practice: military: C. 20. F. & Gibbons. Orig. and esp. at a disappearing target.

Bobbing John. The Earl of Mar: a nickname: 1715. Ex political behaviour. O.E.D.

bobbing on. Anticipating, expecting (something unpleasant): military: C. 20. F. & Gibbons. E.g. 'He's bobbing on a court martial'.

bobbish. 'Clever, smart, spruce ', Grose, 2nd ed.: ca. 1785–1820. Ex *bob,* 'a light, rebounding movement'.—2. Hence, in good health and/or spirits: implied in 1813; ob. except as *pretty bobbish.—* Adv., *bobbishly* : 1813, Scott (O.E.D.); ob.

bobble. A confused movement of water: nautical coll.: from the 1870's. Ex:

bobble, v.i. To move with frequent or continual bobbing: coll.: 1812, W. Tennant (O.E.D.). A frequentative of *bob.*

bobbles. Testicles, gen. a man's: sol. for *baubles* (but cf. *bobble*): C. 19–20; ob.

bobbly. Jerky, jumpy: coll.: 1909 (O.E.D. Sup.). Ex *bobble,* q.v.—2. (Esp. of trousers) 'loose and undulating'; baggy: coll.: 1921 (ibid.).

bobby. A policeman (— 1851). Ex Mr., later Sir, *Robert* Peel (cf. *peeler*), mainly responsible for the Metropolitan Police Act of 1828. F. & H. points out that, long before 1828, *Bobby the beadle* = 'a guardian of a public square or other open space '. —2. Hence, at Oxford and Cambridge, ca. 1860–90, the proctors were called *bobbies.*

Bobby Atkins. An occ., coll. variant of *Tommy Atkins*: ca. 1900–14. Ware.

bobby-dazzler. 'A top much longer and narrower than the ordinary kind ': Midlands': C. 20. R. Aubrey Thompson in *The Observer,* March 3, 1935. A s. elaboration of *bobby dazzler,* a dazzling thing or person : dial. (— 1866): E.D.D. Perhaps euphemistic for *bloody dazzler.*

***bobby(-)horse.** A chink-backed horse: vagrants' c. (— 1845); ob.

***bobby-twister.** A burglar or thief that, on being pursued or seized, uses violence: mid-C. 19–20 (ob.): c. Ex *bobby,* a policeman.

bobby's labourer. A special constable: such constables in 1868. Ware. See **bobby,** 1.

bobby's job. A safe job; an easy one: military coll.: 1915–18. F. & Gibbons. A hit at the military police.

Bobs. Lord (General) Roberts: Society (1900) > gen. (late 1900); ob. As *Bob* for *Robert,* so *Bobs* for *Roberts.* (Ware.)

Bob's horse, with nobody to pay the reckoning,— off, like. To decamp with all money, furniture and personal effects: nautical: from 1830's; ob. Dana.

bobstay. 'The frenum of a man's yard ', Grose, 2nd ed.: mid-C. 18–20 (ob.); low coll.

***bobstick.** A shilling's worth (— 1789). Orig. c., then low s.; † by 1860. George Parker; Moncrieff, 1821. Whence perhaps *bob,* n., 2, q.v.,— but then what is the origin of *bobstick* ?

bobtail, bob-tail, bob tail. A lewd woman, lit. one with a lively pudend: coll.: C. 17–18. B.E.,

Grose. Cf. *wag-tail.*—2. A contemptible fellow : C. 17, perhaps coll.—Cf. 3. A eunuch ; an impotent man : C. 17–18 ; ex *bob* = cut short (cf. *a bobtail horse*) and *tail* = male member.—4. A partridge : vendors of game : late C. 18–early 19. Grose, 3rd ed. Ex its short tail.—5. A dandy wearing a pointed tail-coat : early C. 19 : mostly proletarian. Ware.

bobtail, -tag, rag and ; or tag-rag and bob-tail. The rabble (— 1659) ; coll. in C. 18, S.E. thereafter : the common herd (of any social class) : C. 19–20. Pepys has it first, but it was doubtless used earlier.

Boche. N., then also adj. : German, esp. a German soldier : from 1914 ; not much used by the British soldiers. Direct ex Fr. slang, where the word (from ca. 1870) is of uncertain origin : see esp. *Words !*, p. 221.

boco, boko. The nose. Orig. (ca. 1820) pugilistic, but gen. by 1873. Prob. ex *beak* ; but if *coconut* (also, in U.S., simply *coco* or, erroneously, *cocoa*) existed some years before its earliest record, then perhaps *boco* derives ex *beak + coco*. Ware thinks that it may derive ex Grimaldi's tapping his nose and exclaiming *c'est beaucoup* : cf. sense 3.—2. Nonsense : ca. 1870–1910 ; etymology uncertain. *Punch*, Sept. 25, 1886 : 'Lopsided Free Trade is all boko.'—3. (G.W. +, chiefly military.) Much : Tommy's version of Fr. *beaucoup.* Cf. Sussex dial. sense, a good haul of fish.

boco-smasher. A rough : low London : late C. 19–early 20. Ware. Ex *boco*, 1.

Bodder. The Bodleian Library : Oxford University : from the late 1890's. Dorothy Sayers in *The Passing Show*, March 25, 1933. Ex *Bodley*, q.v. : see '-er, the Oxford '.

bod(d)eration. An early C. 19 form of *botheration* (see bother).

Bodger. The inevitable nickname of all men surnamed Lees : late C. 19–20 : mostly naval and military. F. & Gibbons.

bodier. (Boxing) a blow on the side ; loosely, on breast or belly : ca. 1820–1914. Bee.

bodies. 'The foot guards, or king's body guards', Grose, 1785 ; † by 1890.

*****bodikin.** A contraction of *bawdy ken*, a brothel : c. : ca. 1820–50. Bee.

Bodikin(s). See [body].

bodkin. (Sporting) one who sleeps in a bed only on alternate nights : ca. 1850–1900. Ex the next entry.—2. A midshipman's dirk : jocular naval coll. : C. 19–20 ; ob. Bowen.

bodkin, ride or sit. C. 19–20 ; adumbrated in Ford, 1638, and occurring in 1798 as to *bodkin* alone ; ob. To be wedged between two others when there is, altogether, room for only two. Coll. Ex *bodkin*, to make, as it were, a bodkin of.

Bodley, the. The Oxford University Library : from ca. 1870 ; coll. Cf. *Bodder*, q.v.

[body appears, from ca. 1530, as part of many ancient oaths. E.g. *Bod(i)kin(s)*, a little body.]

body. A person : in C. 19–20, either a sol. or a facetious coll. In dial., however, its usage is serious and respectable.

body-line work. Unfair or dishonest work or play : coll. : 1933. Ex the body-line cricket controversy, which began in Dec., 1932. See esp. *Slang*, p. 234.

body-lining. Bread : drapers' (— 1909). Ware. Ex their trade.

body-louse, brag or brisk or busy as a. Very brisk or busy : coll. ; resp. late C. 16–17, (the gen. form) mid-C. 17–20, mid-C. 17–19.

*****body-slangs.** Fetters : C. 19 c. (See slang.) Vaux, 1812.

body of divinity bound in black calf. A parson : mid-C. 18–early 19. Grose, 2nd ed.

body-snatcher. A bailiff : mid-C. 18–early 19 : perhaps c. Grose, 1st ed.—2. A member of a ship's police force : nautical : mid-C. 19–20 ; ob. Bowen. —3. A policeman : ca. 1840–1900, low.—4. A resurrectionist (— 1812), ob. : coll. ; after ca. 1850, S.E. Vaux, 1812. Body-snatching > a trade ca. 1827.—5. An undertaker : from ca. 1820 ; ob. Bee, 1823.—6. A cat-stealer (— 1859), † by 1900.— 7. A cabman : London streets' : ca. 1840–60. Ware. Ex his habits.—8. A stretcher-bearer : military : C. 20. F. & Gibbons. Also in pl., the Army Medical Corps.—9. Occ., a sniper : military : G.W. (Ibid.)

Boers. A coll. form of *Boer brandy*, i.e. brandy manufactured in South Africa : 1884, *The Queenstown Free Press*, June 22 (Pettman). Cf. *Cape smoke*, q.v.

bog, often bogs. Abbr. *bog-house*, q.v., a privy : from ca. 1840 ; orig. either printers' or Public Schoolboys' s. ; in C. 20, coll.—2. In c. (? ever in the singular), the land-reclaiming works at Dartmoor : from ca. 1860 ; ob.

bog, v. To ease oneself, evacuate : from ca. 1870 : s. >, ca. 1920, low coll. Baumann. Ex preceding or possibly ex :

bog, go to. 'To go to stool', *Lex. Bal.*, 1811 : low.

bog-house. A privy : from ca. 1670 ; low coll. Head in *The English Rogue* ; B.E. ; Ned Ward ; Grose. Ex the ca. 1550–1660 S.E. *boggard.*

Bog-land. Ireland : late C. 17–20, ob. Coll., orig. and mainly jocular. Cf. :

Bog-Lander. An Irishman : coll. : from ca. 1690 ; ob. B.E., Grose. Ireland is famous for rain : cf. *bog-trotter* and *Urinal of the Planets.*

bog-Latin. Spurious Latin : late C. 18–20, ob. ; coll. Grose, 1st ed. ? an Irish perversion of *dog Latin.*

bog-orange. A potato : C. 18–20, ob. ; coll. So many potatoes come from Ireland.

bog-shop. A ca. 1840–1910 low variant of *bog-house* (q.v.).

Bog-Trotter. A wild Irishman (cf. *Bog-Lander*) : coll. : from ca. 1680. Ex the numerous bogs in Ireland : cf. *bog-lander*, q.v.—2. Earlier, ca. 1660–90, 'Scotch or North Country Moss-troopers or High-way Men', B.E. : coll. (cf. Camden) : coll.—3. From ca. 1720, however, the term > a nickname for any Irish person whatsoever. Bailey's Dictionary.— 3. (b.-t.). One who goes often to 'the bogs' : C. 20. Manchon.

bog-trotting. A pejorative adj. applied to Irishmen, esp. if uncouth : from ca. 1750 ; coll. Employed by Goldsmith and Thackeray.

bogee or bougie. To force (a mixture of cement and water) into the required position by means of compressed air : Public Works' (— 1935). Ex the medical sense of *bougie.*

bogey. See bogy.

boggle-de-botch, boggledybotch. A bungling ; a 'mess' : coll. (— 1834) ; ob. Maria Edgeworth, 1834. Ex *boggle*, a, or to, bungle, and *botch*, to do, or make, clumsily.

boggy. (Gen. of a child) diarrhœa : schoolboys' : late C. 19–20. Ex *bog*, n., 1.

boguer. A clumsy sailing-ship : nautical coll. : mid-C. 19–20. Bowen. ? *bogger.*

bogus. Sham ; spurious ; illicit. Orig. (— 1840) U.S. and = counterfeit (ex instrument, thus named, for the uttering of base coin). Acclimatised ca. 1860 in England, where it > coll. ca. 1900, S.E. ca. 1930. As W. remarks, ' *calibogus,* " rum and spruce beer, an American beverage " (Grose [1st ed.]) suggests a parallel to *balderdash* ' ; but, as F. & H. (revised) remarks, *bogus* may be cognate with *bogy* ; the editor proposes derivation ex *bogy* on *hocus-pocus.* See esp. the O.E.D., F. & H., and Thornton. Cf. *scamp, snide,* qq.v.—2. Hence, unpleasant ; dull ; silly : Society : from ca. 1929. Evelyn Waugh, *Vile Bodies,* 1930, ' " Oh, dear," she said, " this really is all too bogus." '

bogy. See **ask bog(e)y.**—2. A landlord : from ca. 1860 ; ob. Perhaps orig. *bogy-man.* Ex *Bogy, Old,* q.v.—3. In C. 20 c., a detective or a policeman (Charles E. Leach) ; also, 4, a stove for heating.— 5. A mistake, a blunder : military : C. 20. F. & Gibbons.—6. **Bog(e)y.** The inevitable nickname of men surnamed Harris : (naval and) military : late C. 19–20. Ibid.—7. A bath : Queensland and Northern Territory coll. (C. 20.) An Aboriginal word.—8. ' One who spoils one's game or interferes with one's pitch ' : grafters' : C. 20. P. Allingham, *Cheapjack,* 1934. Also known as a *nark.*

bogy, adj. Sombre of tint or colour : studio s., ca. 1870–1910.

bogy (or bogey), go. To become prophetic ; be or become gifted with second sight : actors' and music-hall performers' : C. 20. E.g. Christine Jope-Slade in *The Passing Show,* Feb. 24, 1934.

Bogy (or Bogey), Old. The devil : from ca. 1820. Soon coll. ; now ob. Barham. Occ. without *old.* But a comparison with *ask bogy,* q.v., suggests that this sense, which precedes by thirty years that of a goblin, a person to be dreaded, may be fifty years earlier than 1820. It is true that *bogle,* the presumed and prob. orig. of *bogy,* antedates *bog-house* by 150 years or so, yet the indelicate sense of *ask bogy* provides a not-to-be-ridiculed possibility both of *ask bogy's* derivation from *bog-house* and even of an esoteric connexion between *ask bogy, bog-house,* and *Bogy.*

*boil. To betray : ca. 1600–50 ; ? orig. c. Rowlands ; Middleton & Dekker. (O.E.D.)

boil down. To condense : orig. (— 1880) journalistic coll. ; but S.E. in C. 20.

boil one's lobster. To leave the Church for the Army : mid-C. 18–early 19 : military. (*Lobster :* a soldier.)

boil over. To fly into a rage : coll., from ca. 1850 ; in C. 20, S.E.

boil your head !, go and. A proletarian injunction not to be silly : C. 20. (Compton MacKenzie, *Water on the Brain,* 1933). Occ. *go away and boil yourself !*

boiled. Boiled beef or mutton : coll., since ca. 1840. Dickens, 1848, ' A great piece of cold boiled ' (O.E.D.).

Boiled Bell (or b.-b.). Port Glasgow : nautical, esp. by Greenock men : mid-C. 19–20. Bowen, ' The reference is to a traditional bell . . . painted so much that it would not ring ' ; the paint had to be boiled off. Cf. *Gilted Gabbar.*

boiled dog. ' Side ' : New Zealanders' : from ca. 1910. Perhaps on *boiled shirt.*

boiled lobster. See **lobster, boiled.**

boiled over, ppl. adj. (Of a market) that has

been good but has had a set-back : Stock Exchange : C. 20. Ex a kettle that has boiled over.

boiled owl, drunk as a. Extremely drunk : from the early 1880's. Why ? Ware thinks that it may be a corruption of *drunk as Abel Boyle.*

boiled rag, feel like a. ' To feel excessively limp ', or unwell : coll. : C. 20. Lyell. Also . . . (*piece of*) *chewed rag* or *string,* which is less respectable.

boiled shirt. A dress-suit shirt : C. 20, coll. Ex U.S., where it orig. (— 1854) signified any white linen shirt. (Uncultured Americans rather like the pronunciation, and spelling, *biled.*)

boiled stuff. Collectively for harlots : ca. 1580–1630 ; as in Shakespeare's *Cymbeline.* Prob. extremely rare outside of *Cymbeline.*

boiler. Abbr. *pot-boiler,* q.v.—2. At Winchester College, until ca. 1910, a *four and sixpenny boiler* was actually a large, plain coffee-pot used for heating water, from, not the price but the amount of milk they held ; and a τὸ πᾶν *boiler*—lit. a whole-lot boiler—was a large saucepan-like vessel in which water for bidets (q.v.) was heated.

Boilers or Brompton Boilers. The name given orig.,—since ca. 1873 it has been applied to the Bethnal Green Museum (likewise in London),—to the Kensington Museum and School of Art (now the Victoria and Albert Museum), because of the peculiar form of the buildings and also because of their sheet-iron roofs. H., 2nd ed., 1860.—2. (Only as *boilers.*) At the Royal Military Academy, from ca. 1880, boiled potatoes, *greasers* being fried potatoes : the Oxford *-er.*

*boiling. A discovery, a betrayal : c. of ca. 1600–59. Ex *boil,* q.v.

boiling, the whole. The whole lot : 1837, Marryat. Common also in U.S. (*the boiling,* 1796 : O.E.D. Sup.). Ex *boiling,* a quantity of food boiled at the one time : cf. S.E. *batch* (W.). Also cf. *the whole shoot.*

boiling point, at (the). About to fly into a rage : from ca. 1880 ; coll. Adumbrated by Emerson.

bokay. Bouquet : a sol. spelling and pronunciation, esp. Australian (— 1916). C. J. Dennis.

*boke. The nose : a late C. 19–20 c. variant of *boco,* q.v.

boko. See **boco.**—**boko-smasher.** See **boco-smasher.**—**bokoo.** A variant of **boco,** 3.

bold as a miller's shirt. Explained by its frequent appendage, *which every day takes a rogue by the collar.* Coll. : C. 18–early 19.

bold as brass. Presumptuous ; shameless : from ca. 1780 ; coll. George Parker ; Thackeray, 1846, ' He came in as bold as brass ' ; Weyman, 1922. Apperson. Cf. *brass,* 2.

bold boat. A seaworthy ship : nautical coll. : mid-C. 19–20. Bowen has also *a bold hawse,* ' said of a ship when her hawse pipes are well out of the water '. Both phrases verge on j.

Bold Fifteenth, the. The 15th Hussars : military coll. now verging on S.E. : C. 19–20. F. & Gibbons.

boler. See **bowler.**

boldrumptious. Presumptuous : late C. 19–early 20. Ex *bold* + *rumpus* + the *-tuous* of *presumptuous* : E.D.D.

bollicky. See **ballocky** (n.).—**Bollicky Bill.** See **Ballocky Bill the Sailor.**—**bollocks.** See **ballock** and **ballocks,** 2.

bolly. At Marlborough College : pudding, esp. if boiled ; from ca. 1860 ; ob. Cf. the North Country *boily,* gruel. Both, prob., **ex Fr.** *bouillie.*

Bolo. A Bolshevist: military (North Russian campaign, 1918). ? partly on *Bolo* Pasha, shot in April, 1918, for carrying out, in France (bold fellow !), 'pacifist propaganda financed from Germany', W. Cf.:—2. A spy: id., id. Same origin. F. & Gibbons.

bolo, v. To speak; esp. *bolo the bat*, to speak the language, and therefore = *sling* (or *spin*) *the bat*: Regular Army: late C. 19–20. F. & Gibbons. Ex Hindustani.

Bolo House. The Air Ministry's Headquarters at the Hotel Cecil: Air Force: 1918. Ibid. Ex *Bolo Pasha*: see **Bolo**, 1.

boloney; incorrectly **baloney.** Nonsense; 'eyewash'. Of this U.S. word, anglicised by 1931 (thanks to the 'talkies'), Dr. Jean Bordeaux—in a private letter —writes thus : ' Used since at least 1900 in U.S.A., especially around New York, to mean "buncombe" or "a poppycock story". It appears in songs of 1900, and [the word *boloney* as a corruption of *Bologna sausage*] probably dates back twenty years earlier because there was a music-hall song, " I Ate the Boloney " popular in the late 70's, early 80's. . . . There is much to uphold belief that the sausage origin has merit, on analogy that it's a mixture of ground-up meat and then you *stuff* the casing. Hence, mix up a tale and stuff the auditor.' Yet, at the risk of appearing too sceptical, I must declare my disbelief in that origin and my opinion that ' It's (or that's) all boloney '— the usual form—is exactly synonymous with ' That's all balls,' the etymology of *boloney* being the Gipsy *peloné*, testicles : cf. the U.S. *nerts !* and *ballocks*, 2 (q.v.), and see **balls.**

Bolshie; **Bolshy.** (All senses are coll.) A Bolshevik: 1920. Any revolutionary: 1933. Jocularly of an unconventional person : 1924 or 1925. Also adj.: same dates for the corresponding senses. The word *Bolshevik* (a majority socialist) seems to have been first used in 1903. See the S.O.D. for an admirable summary. Cf. *Bolo*, q.v.

bolster-pudding. A roly-poly pudding: non-aristocratic : late C. 19–20. Ex shape.

bolt. The throat: early C. 19 ; mainly Cockney. Moncrieff in *Tom and Jerry*. Perhaps ex † *bo(u)lt*, a flour-sieve.—2. A rupture, gen. incompletely honourable, with a political party: coll.: orig. (— 1840) U.S.; accepted in England as a coll., ca. 1860.

bolt, v. To escape; depart hastily: C. 17–20. In C. 17 S.E.; ca. 1710–80, coll. ; ca. 1780–1870, s. ; then coll., then in C. 20, again S.E. In Moncrieff and Barham it is wholly s.; the latter having ' Jessy ransack'd the house, popp'd her breeks on, and when so | Disguis'd, bolted off with her beau— one Lorenzo.'—2. V.t., to eat hurriedly, without chewing; gulp down: coll. : from ca. 1780. Grose, 1785 ; Wolcot, 1794 ; Dickens, 1843. With the speed of a bolt.—3. To break with a political party (*bolt from*): orig. (1813) U.S., anglicised ca. 1860 as a coll. and in C. 20 considered S.E. Thornton.

bolt, butcher and. A political c.p. applied contemporaneously to the Egyptian policy of 1884–5. Baumann.

*****bolt, get the.** To be sentenced to penal servitude : c.; from ca. 1840. Influenced by *boat*, n. and v.

Bolt-Hole, the. The Channel Islands, where the income-tax is low : political coll. : from ca. 1920. Collinson. Ex a rabbit's bolt-hole.

*****Bolt-in-Tun, go to the.** To bolt, run away : c. ; from ca. 1810 ; †. Vaux. Ex a famous London inn. A play on the v. *bolt*, q.v. Also, as c.p., *the Bolt-in-Tun is concerned* (Vaux) : † by 1890.

bolt of it, make a shaft or a ; gen. **a bolt or a shaft.** To risk this or that issue ; accept a risk : ca. 1590– 1750 ; coll. >, by 1660, S.E. Shakespeare ; Fuller. (Apperson.)

Bolt Street, turn the corner of. To run away : low coll. : from ca. 1880 ; ob. Baumann. Ex *make a bolt for it.*

bolt the moon. To depart with one's goods without paying the rent : C. 19–20 ; ob.

bolter. In c., one who, for fear of arrest, hides in his own house : C. 18. Dyche, 1748.—2. One restive under authority : coll. : from ca. 1850 ; ob. Cf. Fr. *rouspéteur.*—3. One who leaves his political party : coll. : orig. (1812 : Thornton) U.S.; anglicised ca. 1870 as a coll. ; in C. 20 almost S.E.

bolter of the Mint, or of White Friars. One who may peep out but does not, for fear of arrest, venture abroad. Prob. orig. c. : ca. 1690–1800. B.E., Grose.

boltsprit, bowsprit. Late C. 17–18, C. 19–20 (ob.) resp. : the nose. Until ca. 1770, low. Shadwell ; B.E., ' *He has broke his Boltsprit*, he has lost his Nose with the Pox.'

bolus. An apothecary ; a physician : late C. 18– 20, ob. Ex *bolus*, a large pill. Grose, 2nd ed.

*****boman.** A gallant fellow : c. : C. 17–18. See quotation at *pop*, n., 3. Prob. ex *beau man.* Also as adj.

*****boman ken.** A variant of *bowman ken* : see **bob ken.**

*****boman prig.** An expert thief: c. : late C. 17– early 19.

bomb, drop a. Cause a very unpleasant or painful surprise : 1919 + ; coll. Ex bomb-dropping in G.W.

bomb-dodger. One who, during the G.W., lived out of London to escape the air-raids : coll. : 1916– 18. F. & Gibbons.

bomb-proof job. A safe job, i.e. one at the Base : military : 1916–18. B. & P. Hence, *bomb-proofer*, a man holding such a job. Cf. U.S. *bomb-proof*, a Southerner who did not join the Confederate Army (Thornton).

bomb-proofer. ' A man given to scheming methods of evading duty on dangerous occasions ' : military : 1916–18, hence as a survival. F. & Gibbons. Ex *bomb-proof*, q.v. for 2.

Bomb-Proofs, the. The 14th Foot, since 1881 the Prince of Wales's Own West Yorkshire Regiment : military : mid-C. 19–20 ; ob. F. & Gibbons, ' From the immunity from casualties when in the trenches before Sebastopol '.

Bomb Shop, the. The (formerly Hendersons') very interesting bookshop at 66, Charing Cross Road, London, W.C.2 : it offers a notable display of advanced belles-lettres and, esp., political writings. G. H. Bosworth's novel, *Prelude*, 1932, at p. 227. I myself first heard it so described by the proprietor early in 1928, but it has enjoyed this distinction since ca. 1924.

bomb the chat, gen. as vbl.n. To practise trickery or plausible deception ; to ' tell the tale ' ; to exaggerate : military : C. 20. F. & Gibbons. Origin ? Prob. supplied by the variant *bum the chat* (B. & P.). Also *bum one's load.*

Bombardier Fritz ; occ. **pom(me) Fritz.** Fried potatoes : military : G.W. A corruption, by ' Hobson-Jobson ', of the Fr. *pommes de terre frites.*

Bombay duck. That Indian fish which, alive, **is** called the *bummalo*, whence, by the Law of Hobson-Jobson, the present anomaly (cf. *Welsh rabbit*) : at first (C. 18) coll. ; by 1890 S.E. Cordiner in his C. 18 *Voyage to India*. W.

Bombay Ducks. The Bombay regiments of the East India Company's forces : C. 18–early 19.

Bombay merchant. See **Arabs.—Bombay Toughs.** See **Old Toughs.**

Bombay oyster. A glass of milk containing a double dose of castor-oil : training-ships' : late C. 19–20. Bowen.

Bombay Rock. Bombareck in India : nautical : 1812, Morier. Yule & Burnell.

bombing the chat. See **bomb the chat.**

bombo. See **bumbo.**

bom'deer. A bombardier : military **coll.** (— 1887) ; † by 1920. Baumann.

bomp on. To get one's unemployment-card stamped : dockers' : from ca. 1930. *The Daily Herald*, late July or early Aug., 1936. Prob. echoic : *bomp* = bump.

bon. Good ; excellent ; very acceptable : military coll. : G.W., and after. Also *tray bon* (Fr. *très bon*).—2. Hence, *bon drop*, a goodly portion (of, e.g., sleep) ; *bon for the bust*, good to eat ; *bon sonty* (Fr. *bonne santé !*), good health, good luck ! F. & Gibbons ; B. & P. The reverse was *no bon.*

bona. A girl ; a belle : C. 19–20, ob. ; low, prob. a reminiscence of *bona-roba*. Cf. *dona(h)*.

bona, adj. Good ; pleasant, agreeable : theatre and circus s., from ca. 1850. E.g. in Thomas Frost's *Circus Life*, 1875, and Edward Seago's *Circus Company*, 1933. Cf. *bono.*

bona roba, bona-roba. A harlot, esp. a showy one : late C. 16–early 19 ; in C. 18–19, archaic and S.E. Shakespeare, Jonson, Cowley, Scott. Ex It. *buona roba*, lit. a fine dress.

bonable. Abominable : a C. 16 (? later) sol. O.E.D.

bonanza. A stroke of fortune ; a prosperous enterprise. Orig. (1847) U.S., a rich mine—perhaps ex an actual Nevada mine. Accepted in England as a coll., ca. 1895, and as S.E., ca. 1910. Ultimately, via the Sp. *bonanza*, prosperity, ex L. *bonus*, good.—2. Hence, in Glasgow (— 1934), money very easily obtained.

bonce ; occ. **bonse.** The head : schoolboys' : from ca. 1870. Ex *bonce* (— 1862), a large marble. Ware.—2. Hence, a hat : Cockney's : C. 20 ; ob. Edwin Pugh, *The Cockney at Home*, 1914.

bone. A subscriber's ticket for the Opera : London : C. 19 ; † by 1887 (Baumann). Ex Fr. *abonnement*, subscription.—2. (Always *the bone*.) The thin man : London : 1882–ca. 1910. Ware.

*bone, v. To seize, arrest ; rob, thieve ; make off with. From ca. 1690 ; until ca. 1830 (witness B.E., Dyche, Grose (2nd ed.)**,** Vaux), c. As s., it appears in Dickens, 1838, and Miss Braddon, 1861, and it had a great life in the G.W. : see *Words !* and cf. *make, nab, win.* ' Perhaps from the dog making off with the bone ', W.

*bone, adj. Good ; excellent : c. ; from ca. 1850 ; ob. Mayhew, 1851. Ex Fr. *bon* or It. *buono.* Opp. *gammy*, q.v. Cf. *bona* and *bono.*

bone, dry or **hard as a.** Free from moisture : coll. (— 1833) >, by 1890, S.E.

bone-ache. Venereal disease, esp. in men : late C. 16–17 ; coll. verging on S.E. Nashe, Shakespeare.

bone-baster. A staff **or** cudgel : coll. : late C. 16–mid-17.

bone-box. The mouth : late C. 18–20, low. Grose, 1st ed. Contrast *bone-house.*

bone-breaker. Fever and ague : lower classes' : late C. 19–20 ; ob.

bone-cleaner. A servant : late C. 19–20 ; ob. Cf. *bone-picker*, 1.

bone-crusher. A large-calibre rifle : sporting ; from ca. 1850 ; ob. Stanley's *Livingstone*, 1872.

bone-grubber. A scavenger and seller of bones from refuse-heaps and -tins : coll. ; from ca. 1850, the word occurring in Henry Mayhew. Cf. the C. 18 *grubber.*—2. A resurrectionist : ca. 1820–60.—3. Hence, anyone having to do with funerals : esp. a mute : from ca. 1860 ; ob. Sala, 1863.

bone-house. The human body : coll., from ca. 1860 ; ob.—2. A charnel-house : from ca. 1820 ; ob.—3. A coffin : coll. : from the 1790's ; † by 1890.

bone in any one's hood, put a. To cut off his head : C. 16–early 17 ; facetious coll.

bone in the mouth, carry a. (Of a ship) to make the water foam before her, ' cut a feather ' : nautical coll. : C. 19–20 ; ob. Bowen prefers *bone in her teeth.*

bone in the throat, have a ; occ. **leg, arm,** etc. C. 16–20, coll., the *throat* form (app. † by 1800) occurring in Udall, 1542, the *arm* in Torriano, 1666, the *leg* in Swift, ca. 1708 (printed 1738) : a humorous excuse ; a feigned obstacle. Apperson.

bone-lazy. Extremely indolent : coll. : from 1890's. Ex *lazy-bones* on S.E. *bone-idle.*

bone-orchard. A cemetery : lower classes' : C. 20. B. & P. Cf. *bone-yard.*

bone-picker. A footman : late C. 18–19, coll. in the latter. Grose, 3rd ed. Because frequently he has to eat leavings.—2. A collector and seller of bones, rags, and other refuse from the streets and garbage-tins : from ca. 1850 : coll > , by 1910, S.E. Ruskin, *Crown of Wild Olives*, 1866.

bone-polisher. A cat-o'-nine tails (1848) ; its wielder (1857) : nautical. (O.E.D.)

bone-setter. A horse hard in the riding ; a rickety conveyance : mid-C. 18–early 19. Grose, 1st ed. ; Moncrieff. Ironical pun on *bone-setter*, a surgeon. Cf. *bone-shaker.*

bone-shake. To ride one of the early bicycles : ca. 1867–1910.

bone-shaker. The early bicycle : from 1865 or 1866. The first bicycle to be cranked and pedalled was ridden in Paris in 1864 ; England followed suit most enthusiastically. These old bicycles lacked indiarubber tyres and were very heavy ; as late as 1889 a ' safety roadster ' weighed 36 pounds, but as early as 1870–1 ' the low, long bone-shaker began to fall in public esteem '. Cf. *bone-setter*, q.v.

bone-shop. A workhouse : lower classes' (— 1909) ; slightly ob. Ware.

bone-sore or **-tired.** Very idle : coll., now verging on S.E. : from 1880's. Ex dial. Cf. *bone-lazy*, q.v.

bone the sweeter the meat, the nearer the. See **meat, the nearer.**

bone with, pick a. (Occ. *bones.*) To have an unpleasant matter to settle with someone : coll. : mid-C. 16–20.

bone-yard. A cemetery : Canadian : late C. 19–20. B. & P. Cf. *bone-orchard.*

boner. A sharp blow on the spine : Winchester College, mid-C. 19–20 ; ob. Adams, *Wyke-*

hamica.—2. Hence, a bad mistake : C. 20. (*The Passing Show*, Dec. 9, 1933, ' Poor Carol . . . She made a boner to-night . . . Ronnie was simply livid.')—3. See **boners.**

boner nochy ! Good night ! : Clerkenwell (London), which contains many Italians : late C. 19–20. Ex the It. for ' good-night ! ', though *nochy* more closely resembles Sp. *noche.* Ware.

boners. A form of punishment : Charterhouse : † before 1900. A. H. Tod, *Charterhouse*, 1900. Cf. *boner,* 1.

bones. Dice : C. 14–20 ; coll. in C. 14–15, thereafter S.E.—2. Bones played castanet-wise (—1590) : coll., but very soon S.E.—3. A player of the bones : from ca. 1840 ; coll.—4. The human teeth : C. 19–20 ; ob.—5. A surgeon : C. 19 ; abbr. *sawbones.*—6. The examination in osteology : medical students' (— 1923). Manchon.—7. (Stock Exchange) the shares of Wickens, Pease & Co., also the First Preference shares of North British 4% : ca. 1880–1914 ; cf. *bonettas.*—8. Something very good, orig. tasty ; almost an adj. : from ca. 1880 ; ob. Coll. Tupper. (O.E.D.) Prob. = L. *bonus,* good.

bones, be on one's. To be (almost) destitute : non-aristocratic : C. 20. Galsworthy, *The White Monkey*, 1924, ' Give us a chance, constable ; I'm right on my bones.' Ex emaciation. Cf. *ribs, on the,* 2.

bones !, by these ten. A coll. asseveration : late C. 15–early 17. Shakespeare. An allusion to one's fingers (cf. *by this hand I witness*). Cf. the late C. 16 exclamation *bones a* (or *of*) *me* (or *you*) *!*

bones, feel a thing in one's. To have an idea ; feel sure : coll. ; 1875 (O.E.D. Sup.) ; by 1910, S.E. Ex *be in one's bones,* to be felt as certain : itself S.E. verging on coll.

bones, make no. To hesitate not ; make no scruple : C. 16–20 ; coll. Udall, Greene, Wycherley, Thackeray. In C. 15–16 the more gen. phrase was *find no bones* (*in the matter*) : this,—along with *without more bones,* without further obstacle, delay, discussion (late C. 16–19),—would indicate that the reference is to bones in soup or stew.

bones, sleep on. See **sleep on bones.**

bones of, be upon the. To attack : late C. 17–18, low. L'Estrange (d. 1704) : ' Puss had a month's mind to be upon the bones of him, but was not willing to pick a quarrel.'

bonettas. (Stock Exchange) the 4% Second North British 2nd Preference stock : ca. 1880–1914.

Boney. Bonaparte : ca. 1800–21 ; before, ' the Corsican Ogre ' ; after, historical, then legendary. Most British people still know whom *Boney* nicknames. Sidney Rogerson, in Introduction to his notable War book, *Twelve Days*, 1933.

Boney Cobbett. Wm. Cobbett (d. 1835), from bringing back to England the bones of Thomas Paine (d. 1809). Dawson.

boney-fide. See **bonyfide.**

*bongy, drunk, in the anon. *Street-Robberies Consider'd*, 1728, is prob. a misprint for *bousy,* ' boozy' .

bonfire. A cigarette : military : G.W. (F. & Gibbons.)

bong. A variant of *bon,* q.v.

bong-tong, adj. Patrician : sol., esp. Australian (— 1916). C. J. Dennis. I.e. *bon-ton.*

bongo-boosh. ' A tasty morsel ' (of anything) : military on Western Front : 1915–18. F. & Gibbons, ' A perversion of the Fr. *bonne bouche* '.

Boniface. The landlord of an inn or a country tavern : C. 18–20, ex the bonny-faced, jovial inn-

keeper in Farquhar's lively comedy, *The Beaux Stratagem*, 1707. The first record, however, of the generic use is not until 1803, and by 1850 the term was considered S.E.

bonjer. A ' duck ' : cricketers' : 1934, ' Patsy' Hendren, *Big Cricket*, ' If I had landed a bonjer '. Perhaps ex *bon jour !*—but prob. not. (*Notes and Queries*, Oct. 13, 1934.)

bonk. A short, steep hill : circus s. ; from ca. 1840 ; ob. C. Hindley, *Adventures of a Cheap Jack*, 1876. Adopted from dial. (In S.E., † form.)

bonk, v. To shell : military : 1915–18. Gen. in passive ; prob. ex *plonk,* q.v. (B. & P.)

bonner. A bonfire : Oxford undergraduates' : from late 1890's. ' Oxford -*er.*' Perhaps in allusion to ' Bishop Bonner, who certainly lit up many bonfires—Smithfield way ', Ware.

*bonnet, bonneter. — 1812, — 1841 resp., both c. in origin : a gambling cheat or decoy ; a decoy at auctions. Possibly ' a reminiscence of Fr. *deux têtes dans un bonnet,* hand and glove ', W.—Cf. 2, a pretext or a pretence : Vaux, *Flash Dict.*, 1812 ; orig. c. ; † by 1890.—3. A woman (cf. *petticoat, skirt*) : ca. 1870–1900 ; coll.

bonnet, v. Act as a decoy (see the n.) ; cheat ; illicitly puff : C. 19–20, low ; ob.—2. To crush a man's hat over his eyes : coll. (1837 ; ob.) ; Dickens often uses the word ; vbl.n. not uncommon either.—3. See **bonnet for.**

bonnet, have a bee in one's. See **bee in** . . .

bonnet, have a green. To go bankrupt : C. 18–19 ; coll. Ramsay,—in fact it is mainly Scottish. Ex the green cap formerly worn by bankrupts.

bonnet-builder. A milliner : coll. (— 1839) ; ob. Jocular.

*bonnet for. To corroborate the assertions of, put a favourable construction on the actions of : c. of ca. 1810–70. Vaux. Cf. *bonnet,* v., 1.

bonnet-laird. A petty proprietor : Scots coll. : ca. 1810–60. ' As wearing a bonnet, like humbler folk ', F. & H. (revised).

bonnet-man. A Highlander : coll. verging on S.E. : C. 19. Cf. *kiltie.*

bonneter. A decoy (see *bonnet,* n.).—2. A crushing blow on the hat : ca. 1840–1910.

bonnets so blue. Irish stew : rhyming s. (— 1859) ; ob. H., 1st ed.

bonny-clabber, -clapper, -clatter, -clab(b)o(r)e. Sour butter-milk : coll. : C. 17–18. Jonson, 1630 ; B.E. Ex Irish *baine,* milk + *claba,* thick : E.D.D.

bono. Adj., good : Parlyaree : from ca. 1840. Via Lingua Franca. Cf. *bona.*

bono-Johnny. An Englishman : London's East End (— 1890) and ' pidgin ' English (— 1909). Barrère & Leland ; Ware. Ex preceding. As it were ' honest John (Bull) '.

bonse. See **bonce.—bonser.** See **bonza.**

bonus. An additional dividend (— 1808) ; money received unexpectedly or additionally : from ca. 1770. Both senses were orig. money-market s. ; by 1830, coll. ; by 1860, S.E. *Bonus* is mock-Latin for *bonum,* a good thing. Cf. *bunce,* q.v.

bony. See **boney.**

bonyfide, boney-fide. Bona-fide : sol., or low coll., mostly Cockney (— 1887). Baumann.

bonza ; occ. bonser or bonzer ; loosely, bonzo. Anything excellent, delightful : Australian : C. 20. Perhaps ex *bonanza.* Also adj. Cf. *boshta.*

boo to a goose. See **bo to a goose.**

boobies' hutch. More gen. *booby's hutch,* q.v.

boob. A booby, a fool, a ' soft ' fellow ; hence

loosely, a fellow : U.S. (— 1912), anglicised in 1918. Collinson. (O.E.D. Sup.).—2. (the b.) A detention-cell ; prison : military, G.W. +. Ex *booby-hutch*.

booby, beat the. See beat the booby.

booby-ack. A bivouac : military : **C. 20. B. & P.**

booby-hutch. A dug-out : military : G.W. +. Ex :—2. In late C. 19–early 20 c. or low, a police station, a cell.—3. In late C. 18–early 19, it meant a one-horse chaise or a buggy. Also a leather bottle. (Grose, 2nd ed.)

booby-trap. A practical joke of the jug-of-water-on-top-of-door kind : coll. (— 1850) ; after ca. 1890, S.E.—2. Hence, a bomb left behind by the Germans to catch the unwary : military coll. : 1917–18. See esp. F. & Gibbons.

booby's hutch. A barracks' drinking-point open after the canteen closes : military : ca. 1860–1910. Ware, ' Satire . . . upon the fools who have never had enough '. Cf. *booby-hutch*, 1.

boodle. Bribe(ry), illicit spoils, political perquisites, profits quietly appropriated, party funds,— all these are *boodle*. Orig. (1858 : Thornton) U.S. ; anglicised ca. 1890 ; in C. 20, coll. Hence, money in general, with no reference to the illicit : coll. ; orig. (— 1888) U.S. ; > gen. in England ca. 1900, but this sense has remained s. Etymology obscure : W. suggests Dutch *boedel*, estates, effects.—2. A stupid noodle : ca. 1860–90. Kingsley, 1862 (O.E.D.). Perhaps a corruption of *noodle*.

*booget. An itinerant tinker's basket : c. of ca. 1560–1640. Harman. Perversion of † S.E. *budget*, a bag or wallet.

boohoo ; boo-hoo. To weep noisily : coll. : from 1830's. Barham. Echoic.

book. (Sporting.) A bookmaker's arrangement of his bets on a given day's racing or other ' bookmaker-able ' competition. (The bookmaker tries so to arrange his bets that he will be unlikely to lose.) Coll. : from ca. 1830 ; in *Henrietta Temple*, 1837, Disraeli, ' Am I to be branded because I have made half a million by a good book ? ' Hence, a betting-book : from ca. 1850 ; coll. Both senses have, since 1900, been j.—2. A libretto : C. 18–20, coll. ; the words of a play : from ca. 1850 ; coll.— 3. The first six tricks at whist (— 1890), at bridge (— 1910) : these coll. terms soon > j.—4. A bookmaker : Australian (— 1916). C. J. Dennis. Abbr. *bookie*, q.v.

book, v. Engage (a person) as a guest : coll. (1872 : O.E.D.)—2. To pelt with books : schoolboys' (— 1909). Ware.—3. To catch (a person) wrong-doing : Public Schools' : from ca. 1895. P. G. Wodehouse, *The Pothunters*, 1902, ' If he books a chap out of bounds it keeps him happy for a week.'—4. To understand, ' get the hang of ' : Public Schools' : from late 1890's. Ibid, ' There's a pane taken clean out. I booked it in a second as I was going past to the track.'

book, beside the. (Utterly) mistaken : from ca. 1670 ; ob. Coll. >, by 1700, S.E. Walker, 1672 (Apperson). Cf. *beside the lighter*, q.v.

book, bring to. Cause to show authority, genuineness ; investigate ; hence, detect : coll. : C. 19–20. Orig., to ask chapter and verse for a statement.

book, by (the). In set phrases : late C. 16–20 ; brig. coll. but soon S.E. Shakespeare, ' You kisse by th' booke.'

book, drive to the. To make (someone) give

sworn evidence : C. 15–18 ; coll. soon S.E. ; cf. *book, bring to*, q.v.

book, know one's. To come to a decision ; see one's potential advantage : coll. ; from ca. 1880 ; ob.

book, let run for the. (Of a bookmaker) not to bet against a horse : from ca. 1870. H., 5th ed.

book, out of one's. Mistaken(ly) : C. 16–17 ; coll. soon S.E. Latimer.

book, speak like a. To talk excellent sense : informatively, accurately : coll. ; from ca. 1840 ; prob. from U.S., where ' *talk* like a book ' occurs as early as 1829.

book, suit one's. To be opportune, very suitable : coll. (— 1851) >, by 1890, S.E. Prob. ex betting.

book, take a leaf out of a person's. To follow his (gen. his good) example : C. 18–20 ; coll. till C. 20, when S.E.

book, without. Late C. 17–20 ; occ. *without his book*. Without authority ; from memory. Orig. coll., soon S.E.

book-boy. A native ' shipped in certain ships on the West African trade to help the officers tally cargo ' : nautical coll. verging on j. : late C. 19–20. Bowen.

book-chambers. See books, 2.

book-form. Theoretical form, at first of horses ; coll. (— 1880) ; in C. 20, j. in racing, S.E. elsewhere.

book-holder. A prompter : theatrical (— 1864) ; ob. by 1890, † by 1920.

book-keeper. ' One who never returns borrowed books ', Grose (2nd ed.), who speaks feelingly : coll. ; late C. 18–early 19. Punning one who keeps accounts.

book-maker, bookmaker. A professional taker of the odds at races of any sort. (Contrast with the professional *punter*, who deposits money, i.e. backs a horse, with the bookmaker and who bets only on certain races.) He keeps a book (lays the odds) and operates from a stand on the course or from an office. (— 1862) coll. ; by 1880, S.E. See esp. O.E.D. and F. & H.—Hence a *bookmaker's pocket* (a sporting coll.), a breast-pocket, inside the waistcoat, for notes of high denomination : from ca. 1850.

bookmaker's pocket. See book-maker (at end).

book-pad, v.t. and i. To plagiarize : pedantic after *foot-pad* : ca. 1680–1730. (O.E.D.)

book-work. Oxford and Cambridge : memorisable matter in mathematics : ca. 1845–90 as s. ; then coll., by 1910 S.E., for any ' swottable ' learning.

booka. Hungry : Regular Army : late C. 19–20. F. & Gibbons. Ex Hindustani *bhukha*.

booked, ppl. adj. Destined ; caught ; disposed of. Coll. (— 1839), orig. low. Brandon, Hood, Jas. Payn. Cf. *book*, v.—2. Hence, in for trouble : coll. : C. 20. Lyell, ' Third time you've been late this week. *You're booked* all right, my boy, when the Manager comes in.'

bookie. See booky.

bookri. Out of line, crooked ; wrong : military : C. 20. F. & Gibbons. Perhaps a perversion of *crooked*.

books. A pack of cards : C. 18–20. Mrs. Centlivre ; H. Cf. *devil's books*.—2. Winchester College usages :—The prizes presented, C. 19, to the ' Senior ' in each division at the end of ' half ' : *sixth book, fifth book*, and—ceasing to exist ca. 1865 —*fourth book* ; *up at books*, from ca. 1880 *up to books*, in class ; *book-chambers*, a short lesson without a master ; *get* or *make books*, to make the highest score at any game.

books, get or **make.** To make the highest score : coll. (— 1890) ; slightly ob.

books (or **cards**), **get one's.** To be paid off : Public Works' coll. : from ca. 1924. On being paid off, a workman receives his insurance-card.

books, in a person's good or **bad.** In favour, or disfavour, with him : coll. ; C. 19–20. In C. 16–18, the phrase was *in* or *out of a person's books* : coll. > S.E., though Grose has it.

*****books, plant the.** ' To place the cards in the pack in an unfair manner ', *Lex. Bal.* : c. of ca. 1810–70.

books, shut the. To cease from business operations : coll. (— 1858) ; ob.

Booksellers' Row. Holywell Street : book-world coll. : ca. 1850–80. See also **Row, the.**

booky, often **bookie.** (In all such words, the *-y* form is preferable.) A bookmaker : sporting s. : 1881, says Ware ; in C. 20, coll. See *Slang* at pp. 241–7 for a dialogue in bookies' s.—2. A bouquet : low coll., mostly Cockney (— 1887). Baumann.

booky, adj. Bookish : from ca. 1880 ; coll. Presumably from U.S., where used as early as 1833 : Thornton.

boom. A rush of (esp. commercial) activity ; effective launching of any goods or stocks ; vigorous support of a person. Orig. (— 1875) U.S. ; anglicised as a coll. ca. 1883, S.E. in C. 20. Baumann. Ex :

boom, v.i. and t. To go, set, off with a rush, at first of a ship, then in commerce, then in publicity. In its fig. and mod. senses, orig. (1850) U.S. ; accepted as coll. in England ca. 1885, in C. 20 S.E. Perhaps ex some such phrase as ' *a ship comes booming,* "she comes with all the sail she can make " (*Sea Dict.*, 1708) ' : W. On this word n. and v. see esp. F. & H. and Thornton.

boom off, top one's. To start : nautical (— 1860) ; ob. H., 2nd ed., has—erroneously, I believe—*tip one's boom off.* (In Marryat, 1840, *boom off* is v.t., to push off with a pole.)—2. **top your boom !** See **top . . .**

boom-passenger. A convict on board ship : nautical, ca. 1830–60. Convicts were chained to, or took exercise on, the booms.

boom the census. To get a woman with child : jocular coll. : C. 20 ; ob.

boomer. A propagandist : C. 20 coll. One who booms an enterprise : coll., from ca. 1890. Orig. U.S. (— 1885).—2. In Australia, a very large kangaroo, esp. if a male ; in its earliest spelling (1830), *boomah.* Soon > coll. Ex *boom,* v.—3. Whence, anything very large : coll. : 1885 ; slightly ob. Morris.

booming. Flourishing ; successful. Coll., in England from ca. 1890 ; orig. (— 1879) U.S. Cf. :

boomlet. A little boom : Stock Exchange coll. : from mid-1890's ; Ware dates it at 1896. (By 1920, S.E., as the O.E.D. (Sup.) shows.) Cf. :

boomster. One who booms stock : money-market coll. (1898) >, by 1930, S.E. Ware. Ex U.S.

boon-companion. A drinking(-bout) companion ; ' a good fellow ' : 1566, Drant : coll. >, by C. 18, S.E. Whence *boon-companionship*, Nashe, 1592 ; in C. 18–20, S.E.

boorish, the. Illiterate speech : **C. 17.** Shakespeare.

boord(e). See **borde. — boose.** See **booze. — boos(e)y.** See **boozy.**

boost. Vigorous support ; ' push up '. Orig. (1825) U.S., anglicised ca. 1865 ; in C. 20, coll. Ex the v.—2. Hence, in G.W. military : an attack (cf. *push*), a raid, a heavy bombardment. F. & Gibbons.

boost, v. To support vigorously ; ' push ' enthusiastically, significantly. Orig. (1825), U.S. ; anglicised ca. 1860. In C. 20, coll. and, like the n., applied, since 1929, chiefly to publishing—and authorship. Thornton. Origin obscure : ? ex *boot* + *hoist.*—2. Hence, to support without reason : naval : C. 20. · F. & Gibbons.

booster. One who ' boosts ' (see **boost,** v.) : U.S. coll. (— 1909) >, by 1912, English coll. verging now on S.E.—2. Hence, ' one who by false or misleading statements bolsters up a case ' : naval : C. 20. F. & Gibbons. (O.E.D. Sup.)

boot. Money ; an advance on wages : tailors' and shoemakers' ; late C. 19–20. Ware ; *The Tailor and Cutter*, Nov. 29, 1928.—2. (Gen. pl.) The float of a sea-plane : aviators' : from 1933. *The Daily Telegraph*, Feb. 19, 1935.

boot, v. To thrash ; punish with a strap : military, C. 19–20 ; ob. At first with a jack-boot. —2. To kick, e.g. ' I booted him good and hard ' · coll. : from ca. 1880.—3. Hence (gen. *boot out*), to dismiss, get rid of : 1902 (O.E.D. Sup.).—4. To kick (the ball) exceedingly hard : football coll. (1914 : O.E.D. Sup.). (Vbl.n., *booting*, in all four senses.)—5. V.i. and t, to borrow (money) on account : tailors' : C. 20. Ex *boot,* n., 1.

boot, give or **get the.** To dismiss ; be dismissed : s. (1888, Rider Haggard) >, by 1920, coll. (O.E.D. Sup.). Cf. :

boot, give or **get the order of the.** To dismiss or to expel ; be dismissed : C. 20 : s. >, by 1930, coll. An elaboration of the preceding ; cf. *the order of the bath.*

boot, put in the. ' To kick a prostrate foe ', C. J. Dennis : mostly Australian (— 1916). See also **boot in.**—2. To shoot : military rhyming s. : from ca. 1915.

boot-brush. A rough beard : jocular (— 1927). Collinson.

boot-catch(er). An inn servant that pulls off guests' boots : C. 18–early 19. The longer form, the more gen., is in Swift and Grose.

boot-eater. A juror who would rather ' eat his boots ' than find a person guilty : 1880 ; ob. Coll.

boot in, put the. A variant (likewise v.i.) of *boot, put in the.* Both > v.t. with *into* for *in.*

boot is on the other leg, the. The case is altered ; the responsibility is another's : coll. ; C. 19–20, ob.

boot-jack. A general-utility actor : theatrical (— 1895). Ex a boot-jack's usefulness. (O.E.D. Sup.)

boot-joe. Musketry drill : military : mid-C. 19–early 20. Why ?

boot-legger. A dealer in and distributor of contraband liquor in the U.S. ; orig. (— 1919) U.S., anglicised ca. 1927 as coll. ; 1932 +, S.E. From the old days when spirits, in flat bottles, was carried on the leg to the Red Indians : in this connexion, the word appears in U.S. as early as 1890 (O.E.D. Sup.). Whence *boot-legging*, the sale and distribution of illicit liquor in the U.S. See, e.g. James Spenser's *Limey*, 1933, and Godfrey Irwin's *American Tramp and Underworld Slang*, 1931.

boot-lick. To toady (to) ; undertake ' dirty ' work (for) : coll. Ex U.S. (1845), anglicised in the 1880's.

boot-licker. A toady ; a doer of 'dirty' work : coll. (— 1890). The U.S. form is *boot-lick.*

boot-neck. A Royal Marine : naval : mid-C. 19–20 ; ob. Bowen ; F. & Gibbons, 'From the tab closing the tunic collar'. Cf. *leather-neck.*

boot out. See boot, v., 3.

boot serve for either leg, make one. To speak, rarely to act, ambiguously : C. 16–17 ; coll. > S.E.

*booth. A house, as in *heave a booth*, rob a house : mid-C. 16–19 c.

booth-burster. A noisy actor : from ca. 1870 ; ob. Cf. *barn-stormer* and :

booth-star. A leading actor (or actress) in a booth or a minor theatre : theatrical coll. (— 1909) ; ob. Ware.

booting. See boot, v.

boots. The youngest officer in a mess : military : late C. 18–20. Grose, 1st ed.—2. A servant, gen. a youth, affected to the cleaning of boots : late C. 18–20 ; from ca. 1820, coll. ; post-1850, S.E.— 3. See lazy, smooth and sly boots, where *boots* = a fellow.—4. See boot, n., 2.

boots !, bet your. See bet your boots.

boots, buy old. To marry, or keep, another's cast-off mistress : C. 18–19 ; coll. Cf. *boots, ride in a person's old*, q.v.

boots, go to bed in one's. See bed in . . .

boots, have one's heart in one's. To be much afraid : C. 19–20, coll. In C. 17–18, *wish one's heart* . . .

boots, in one's. At work ; still working ; not in bed. Gen. with *die*. Coll. mid-C. 19–20. In S.E., *die in one's boots* or *shoes* is to be hanged.—2. Very drunk : late C. 19–20 ; ob.

boots, like old. Vigorously, thoroughgoingly : coll., C. 19–20. Lit., like the devil. Variant with *as* : Miss Bridgman, 1870, 'She's as tough as old boots' (O.E.D.).

boots !, not in these ; not in these (trousers) ! Certainly not ! : c.pp., resp. of ca. 1867–1900 and C. 20 (ob.). *Quotations* Benham ; Collinson.

boots,—over shoes, over. Adj. and adv. : recklessly persistent : coll., ca. 1640–1820.

boots, ride in (a person's) **old.** 'To marry or keep his cast-off mistress', Grose, 2nd : late C. 18– mid-19. Cf. *boots, buy old*, q.v.

boots to, put the. To leap on (a person) with one's spiked boots : Canadian lumbermen's : C. 20. (John Beames.) Cf. *put in the boot.*

booty. Playing booty : C. 17–18. See :

booty, play. To play falsely ; covertly to help one's apparent opponent : C. 16–19. Until ca. 1660, c. ; then s. merging into coll. ; from ca. 1790, S.E. As in Dekker, Fielding, Scott, Disraeli.

booty-fellow. A sharer in plunder : see preceding entry. C. 17–early 19. Coll.

*booze (C. 18–20), rarely **booz** (late C. 17–18) ; **boose** (C. 18–20) ; **bouze** (C. 16–20, as is, also, **bouse**) ; **bowse** (C. 16–20) ; **bowze** (C. 18). (The O.E.D.'s quotation of ca. 1300 prob. refers to a drinking vessel.) Drink, liquor : c. (— 1567) until C. 19, then low s. ; in C. 20, coll. Harman, B.E., Bailey, Grose. Ex v., 1, q.v.—2. Hence, a draught of liquor : late C. 17–20. Implied in B.E.—3. (Also ex sense 1.) A drinking-bout : 1786, Burns : low s. >, by ca. 1850, gen. s. > by 1900, coll.

*booze, etc., v. To drink, esp. heavily ; tipple : (in C. 14, S.E., ; it reappears as c. in mid-) C. 16–20 ; status thenceforth as for n. Harman, Nashe, B.E., Colman, Grose, Thackeray. Perhaps ex Dutch *buizen* (low Ger. *busen*) to drink to excess : W.—

2. Hence *booze* (etc.) *it*, mostly C. 17, always c., and v.t., C. 17–20, e.g. in Harington.—3. V.t. To spend or dissipate in liquor : mid-C. 19–20. Often *booze away* (e.g. a fortune).

booze, on the. On a prolonged drinking bout : low (— 1889) >, by 1910, coll. (O.E.D. Sup.)

booze-fencer or **-pusher.** A licensed victualler : low London : from ca. 1880 ; ob. Ware.

booze-fighter. A notable drinker ; a drunkard : Australian (— 1915) and American (— 1916).

booze-shunter. A beer drinker : orig. (— 1870), railwaymen's : from ca. 1870, gen. public-house ; slightly ob. Ware.

booze the jib. (Nautical) to drink heavily ; tipple : 1837, Marryat (O.E.D.) ; ob.

boozed, etc., ppl. adj. Drunk : C. 19–20, low. P. Crook, in *The War of Hats*, 1850, 'Boozed in their tavern dens, | The scurril press drove all their dirty pens.'

boozed-up. A C. 20 variant of the preceding.

boozer, etc. A drunkard (— 1611) : low. Cotgrave, Wolcot, Thackeray.—2. A public-house : chiefly Australian and New Zealand (— 1914) ; also (1895) English c. and low s. *The People*, Jan. 6, 1895 ; Charles E. Leach, in *On Top of the Underworld*, 1933, 'Guv'nor, the "diddikayes" are "ramping" a "tit" in the "spruce" there ; they're "three-handed" ; a "nose" told me in the "boozer" ; there's nobody "screwing", as they don't think the "busies" are "wise" ; come along quick with the "mittens".'

boozing, etc., vbl.n. Heavy drinking ; guzzling : C. 16–20, low. Until ca. 1660, c. Harman, Nashe, Head, G. Eliot.—2. Also, adj. : C. 16–20 : same remarks. Addicted to drink.

*boozing cheat. A bottle : c. ; C. 17–18 (? earlier). See cheat.

*boozing-glass. A wine-glass ; a tumbler : c. ; C. 17–early 19. Baumann.

*boozing ken. A drinking den ; an ale-house : c. ; mid-C. 16–mid-19.

*boozington ; or, in derisive address, **Mr. Boozington.** A drunkard : Australian c. ; ca. 1860– 1910. Prob. after *lushington*.

boozy, etc. Drunken, esp. if mildly ; showing the marks of drink : C. 16–20, ob. ; low. Skelton, in his famous poem of the drunken Eleanor, 'Droupy and drowsie, | Scurvy and lousie, | Her face all bowsie' ; Dryden, in his *Juvenal*, 'Which in his cups the bowsy poet sings' ; Thackeray, in *The Book of Snobs*, 'The boozy unshorn wretch'. (The earliest spellings of the *booze* group are in *-use*, *-uze* ; the *-oze* form seems not to occur before C. 18.)

bor, gen. in vocative. Mate, friend : on the borders of dial. (Eastern counties of England), Romany (properly *ba*), and provincial s. : C. 19–20. E.D.D. ; Smart & Crofton ; Sampson. Cf. Middle High Ger. *bur.*

borachio. A drunkard : coll. : late C. 17–early 19. B.E. (as *boracho*) ; Grose. Also, perhaps earlier, as noted by B.E., a skin for holding wine : coll. Ex It. or Sp. The Parlyaree form is *borarco.*

borak. See '2' in :

borak, poke. To impart fictitious news to a credulous person ; to jeer. V.t. with *at*. Australian (— 1885), ex a New South Wales Aborigine word ; it had, by 1923, so spread that Manchon classifies it simply as military and nautical. (Perhaps, though not prob., the origin of *to barrack*, *barracker*, qq.v.) In G.W. +, *borak* was occ. corrupted, jocularly, to *borax.*—2. **borak**, banter, fun, occurs independently in 1845. Morris.

borarco. See **borachio.**—**borax.** See **borak.**—**bord.** See **borde.**

bord you ! (Properly, no doubt, *board you.*) C. 19. Nautical, in drinking : my turn next !

*****bord(e).** In c. of mid-C. 16–18, a shilling. Harman. Perhaps ex *bord*, a shield.—2. Whence *half borde*, a sixpence.

bordeaux. Blood : boxing, ca. 1850–1910. Cf. *badminton* and esp. *claret*, q.v.

bordello. A brothel : late C. 16–18 ; coll. (*bordel* is S.E.) Grose, P.

bore. Ennui (1766) ; 2, a boring thing, an annoyance (1778). Prob. ex next entry.—3. A wearying, an uncongenial, person (— 1785) : Grose. Until ca. 1820, the second and third senses were coll., thereafter S.E. ; the first hardly outlived the C. 18 ; the rare sense, 4, a bored, a listless person, arose in 1766 and soon died (O.E.D.). Of the third, Grose remarks that it was ' much in fashion about the years 1780 and 1781 ' ; it again > fashionable ca. 1810.

bore, v. To weary a person (1768) ; coll. In C. 19–20, S.E. Perhaps ex *bore*, an instrument for boring ; cf. A.-S. *borian*, to pierce. (Its athletic sense is j.)—2. To annoy : Bootham School coll. (— 1925). Anon., *Dict. of Bootham Slang*, 1925.

Borealis. Abbr. *Aurora Borealis* : late C. 18–20 : coll. >, by 1850, S.E.

born call. Sound reason : Australian coll. (now rare) : 1890, Mrs Campbell Praed, *The Romance of a Station.* E.D.D.

born days, in (all) **one's.** In one's lifetime ; ever : coll. : 1742, Richardson.

born in a mill. Deaf : coll. : ca. 1570–1700. Whetstone, 1578 ; Ray, 1678. (Apperson.) I.e. deafened by the noise of a mill working at top speed.

born under a threepenny halfpenny planet (**, never to be worth a groat**). Extremely unsuccessful : C. 17–19 ; coll.

born weak. Nautical, of a vessel : weakly built. From ca. 1850 ; ob.

born with a silver spoon in one's mouth. Born wealthy or very lucky : coll. >, by 1840, S.E. : C. 18–20. In C. 17, *penny.*

borned. Born : sol. : C. 19–20.

Boro-Onions. ' Boronians ', i.e. the people of the Borough of Southwark : ca. 1820–40. Bee.

borough-monger. A rabbit : rare Scottish : C. 19. E.D.D.

borrow. To steal : jocularly coll. : from ca. 1880.

borrow, on the, adj., adv. Cadging. C. 20 ; coll.

borrow trouble. To seek trouble ; to anticipate it unnecessarily or very unwisely : coll. : from the 1890's.

Bos. Bosanquet (see **bosie**) : cricketers' nickname : 1900. Lewis.

*****bos-ken.** A farm-house : mid-C. 19–20 vagrants' c. Mayhew, 1851. Ex L. *bos*, an ox ; *ken*, a place or house. Cf. :

*****bos-man.** A farmer : mid-C. 19–20 c. (vagrants'). Ex Dutch. Etymology disputable, but cf. *bos-ken.*

bosky. See ' Westminster School slang '.

Bosch(e). See **Boche**, for which these two forms are erroneous.

bose. Abbr. *bo'sun*, itself an eligible slurring of *boatswain.* Both are nautical, the former dating from (?) the late C. 19, the latter from (?) the late

C. 18. The former is often used in addressing that link between officers and deck-hands.

Bosey. See **bosie, Bosie.**

bosh. Trash ; nonsense : 1834. Coll. after ca. 1860. Ex Turkish (for ' empty ', ' worthless ') ; popularised by Morier's *Ayesha* and later novels.— 2. Hence, as interjection : nonsense ! : 1852 ; coll. after ca. 1870. Dickens in *Bleak House.*—3. In vagrants' c., a fiddle : see **bosh-faker.**—4. Butterine ; oleomargarine ; similar substitutes for butter : lower official English (— 1909) ; ob. Ex sense 1.—5. **Wabash** Railroad preferred shares : Stock Exchange (— 1895). A. J. Wilson, *Stock Exchange Glossary.*

bosh, v. To spoil ; mar : 1870 ; ob. Ex *bosh*, n., 1.—2. Hence, to humbug, make fun of (—1883), as in Miss Braddon's *Golden Calf.*—3. Cut a dash : coll. ; from ca. 1709 ; †. Ex Fr. *ébauche*, via English *bosh*, an outline or rough sketch (— 1751) ; †). S.O.D., O.E.D.

bosh, adj. Inferior ; ' wretched ' (e.g. *bosh boots*) : from ca. 1880 ; ob. Baumann. Ex n., 1. Cf. *boshy.*

*****bosh-faker.** A violin-player : vagrants' c. ; from ca. 1850. In Romany, *bosh* is a violin ; the use of *faker* as = *maker* is unusual.

bosh up. To go bankrupt : C. 20. Manchon. Ex *bosh*, v., 1.

boshman. The same as *bosh-faker* : low or c. (— 1865). O.E.D. (Sup.)

boshta, boshter. Like *bosker*, a variant of *bonza*, q.v. C. J. Dennis.

boshy, adj. Trashy ; nonsensical : coll. (—1882 ; slightly ob.) Anstey in *Vice Versa.* Cf. *bosh*, n., 1.

bosie, Bosie ; bosey (or **B.**). A ' googly ' (ball or bowler) : Australian cricketers' coll. : 1912–ca. 1921. Ex B. J. T. Bosanquet, who demonstrated the googly in Australia early in 1903 (W. J. Lewis), in which year *googlie* (or -*y*) first occurs : s. >, by 1910, coll. >, by 1930, S.E.

bosken. Incorrect for *bos-ken*, q.v., as *bosman* perhaps is for *bos-man.*

bosker. A variant of *bonza*, q.v. C. J. Dennis.

boskiness. Fuddlement ; state of intoxication : from ca. 1880 ; ob. Coll. Ex :

bosky. Dazed or fuddled ; mildly drunk : 1730, Bailey ; F. & Gibbons ; ob. Possibly dial., and perhaps ex *bosky*, wooded, bushy ; though it ' may be perverted from Sp. *boquiseco*, dry mouthed ', W., who, however, acutely adds that ' adjs. expressive of drunkenness seem to be created spontaneously '.—2. Thorough, as in *a bosky beano* : low : C. 20. Manchon.

bosom friend. A body-louse : C. 18–20. In proverbial form as *no friend like to a bosom friend, as the man said when he pulled out a louse*, Fuller, 1732 (Apperson). Cf. *back-biters*, q.v. An alternative form is *bosom chum* : military : late C. 19–20. F. & Gibbons.

Bosphorescence. ' The dazzling rather than sound finance of European banks in Turkey,' ca. 1900–7 : journalistic of that period. Sir Harry Luke, *An Eastern Chequerboard*, 1934. A blend of *Bosphorus* + *phosphorescence.*

boss. A fat woman : ca. 1575–1650 :· coll. Lyly. Ex *boss*, a protuberance.—2. A master, owner, manager ; leader ; a ' swell ' : in these senses, orig. (1806), U.S. ; anglicised ca. 1850. In England the term has a jocular undertone ; in Australia and New Zealand, it lacks that undertone. Ex Dutch *baas*, master.—3. (Gen. with *political.*)

'The leader of a corrupt following', Thornton: coll., orig. (— 1908) U.S. and still applied rarely to politics outside of the U.S.—4. A short-sighted person; one who squints: mid-C. 19–20, ob. ? ex Scots *boss*, hollow, powerless.—5. Hence (?), a miss, mistake, blunder: C. 19–20, ob. Cf. *boss*, v., 2.

boss, v. To be the master or the manager of; control, direct. Orig. (1856) U.S.; anglicised ca. 1870, as in *The Athenæum*, March 9, 1872, 'A child wishing to charge his sister with being the aggressor in a quarrel for which he was punished, exclaimed, "I did not boss the job; it was sister ".'—2. To miss, v.t. and i.; to bungle; to fail in an examination: schoolboys' s. in the main: from ca. 1870. Baumann; Manchon. Perhaps ex *boss-eyed* (W.); cf. *boss*, adj., 3.

boss, adj. Chief, principal: orig. (1840) U.S.; anglicised ca. 1875.—2. Pleasant; excellent; champion. Orig. (— 1888) U.S.; anglicised ca. 1895, but never very gen.—3. Short-sighted: Christ's Hospital (— 1887). Baumann. Abbr. *boss-eyed*. Cf. *boss*, v., 2.

boss, have a. To have a look: schoolboys': from ca. 1899. Collinson. Cf. *boss-eye(d)*.

boss-cockie. A farmer employing labour and himself working: Australian (— 1898). Ex and opp. *cockatoo*, q.v. Morris.

boss-eye. One who squints or has an injured eye: from ca. 1880; ob. In a broadside ballad of ? 1884. Cf. *boss*, n., 4. Imm. ex:

boss-eyed, adj. With one eye injured; with a squint: from ca. 1860. H., 2nd ed.; Baumann, 1887, notes the variant *bos-eyed*. Perhaps on † *boss-backed*, hump-backed: W.—2. Hence, lop-sided; crooked: C. 20. C.O.D., 1934 Sup.

boss-shot. A bad aim: see **boss**, n. and v., (to) miss. Ca. 1870–1914; extant in dial. Cf. *boss*, n., 4, and *boss-eyed*.

boss up. To manage or run (a house, its servants); to keep in order; act as the 'boss' over: servants' coll.: C. 20. E.g. in F. Brett Young's *The Cage Bird and Other Stories*, 1933.

boss up! Take care!: South African coll.: from ca. 1890. Ex Cape Dutch *pas op !*, look out. Pettman aligns Ger. *passen sie auf !*

bossers. Spectacles: ca. 1870–1910. Prob. ex *boss-eyed*, q.v.

bosso. A look or glance: low: C. 20. Margery Allingham, *Look to the Lady*, 1931. Perhaps orig. a squint; if so, then prob. ex *boss-eyed* on *dekko*.

bossy, adj. Over-fond of acting as leader or of giving orders: late C. 19–20. Ex (— 1882) U.S.: cf. *boss*, n., 2, and v., 1, qq.v.

Boston Tea-Party. The throwing of (chests of) tea into Boston (Mass.) harbour by American patriots—the 'casus belli' of the War of American Independence: s. soon > coll.; in C. 19–20, historical S.E. See esp. *A Covey of Partridge*, 1937.

Boston wait. (Gen. in pl.) A frog: jocular coll. (— 1769); † by 1850, except in dial.—and even there, now virtually †. (O.E.D.)

bostruchizer; occ. **-yzer.** A small comb for curling the whiskers: Oxford University: ca. 1870–80. H., 5th ed. Prob. ex Gr. βόστρυχος, a ringlet.

bo'sun. See **bose**.

bot. See **bot-fly.**—2. A germ: New Zealand medical: from ca. 1928. Perhaps ex the *bot*(-*fly*), which, in horses, lays eggs that are said to penetrate into the animal when they hatch.—3. Hence, a tubercular patient: id.: from ca. 1929. Cf. *bots biting*, q.v.

bot-fly. A troublesome, interfering person: Australian: C. 20. In G.W. +, often abbr. to *bot*. Ex the bot-fly, which in hot weather greatly troubles horses. Cf. *botty*, q.v.

***botanical excursion.** Transportation, orig. and properly to Botany Bay, Australia: c.; ca. 1820–70. 'Jon Bee.' Cf. sense 3 of:

Botany Bay. 1, Worcester College, Oxford (1853); 2, a portion of Trinity College, Dublin (1841). The former in 'Cuthbert Bede', *Verdant Green*, the latter in Lever, *Charles O'Malley*. Because of their distance from (*a*) other colleges, (*b*) the rest of the college, the reference being to Botany Bay in New South Wales—so far from England.—3. In c., penal servitude: ca. 1790–1900. Ex the famous penal settlement (1787–1867) at that place. Cf. *botanical excursion* and next two entries.—4. 'The Rotunda of *the Bank*; the Jobbers and Brokers there being for the most part those who have been absolved from *the house* opposite', Bee: London commercial: ca. 1820–50.

Botany Bay, go to. To be transported as a convict: euphemistic coll.: ca. 1810–60. Baumann.

Botany Bay fever. Transportation; penal servitude. Ca. 1815–60. (Egan's Grose.)

Botany-beer party. 'A meeting where no intoxicants are drunk': Society: ca. 1882–1910. Ware.

botch. A tailor: mid-C. 18–19. Grose, 2nd ed. Abbr. *botcher*. Cf. *snip*, q.v. (In Whitby dial., a cobbler.)

both ends of the busk ! A late C. 18–early 19 toast. Grose, 3rd ed. Ex the piece of whalebone stiffening the front of women's stays. Cf. *best in Christendom*, q.v.

both sheets aft. With both hands in his pockets: nautical: late C. 19–20. Bowen.

bother, v. (The n. is gen. considered as S.E.) To bewilder (with noise); confuse, fluster: mostly Anglo-Irish: ca. 1715–1850. Perhaps ex *pother*, but perhaps ex Gaelic (see J. J. Hogan, *An Outline of English Philology*, 1935.)—2. Hence, to pester, worry: from ca. 1740. V.i., to give trouble, make a fuss: from ca. 1770. All senses are coll., as is *botheration* (1800), the act of bothering, a petty annoyance. Both *bother* and *botheration* are used as exclamations. O.E.D.—3. *I'm* or *I'll be bothered* is a disguised form of swearing (see **bugger**, v., 1): coll.: prob. from the 1860's.

Bother, General. Botha, the Boer general: from late 1899; ob. He made himself a general nuisance, though he was an excellent general.

Botherams (-ums). The nickname of a latter-C. 18 convivial society. Grose (*Botherams*).—2. (Rare in singular.) Yellow marigolds: agricultural (— 1909); ob. except in a few localities. Ware. They are 'difficult to get rid of'.

botheration. See **bother**, 2.—**botherment.** Variation of *botheration*: coll.: mid-C. 19–20; ob. (O.E.D.)

bothered !, I'm or I'll be. See **bother**, 3.

bots, botts, the. Colic; belly-ache. From ca. 1770; coll. when not, as usually, dial. Orig., an animal disease caused by maggots.

bots biting ?, how are the. How are you ?: New Zealand medical: from ca. 1929. See **bot**, 2, 3.

bottle, v.i. To collect money for, e.g., a 'chanter': vagrants' c.: C. 20.—2. V.t., to fail: Public Schools': C. 20. Alec Waugh, *Public School Life*, 1922.

bottle, not much. Not much good: grafters'

c.p.: from ca. 1910. Philip Allingham, *Cheapjack*, 1934. Ex *bottles, no*, q.v.

bottle, on the. (Reared) by means of the feeding-bottle : coll. in C. 19 ; S.E. in C. 20.

bottle, over a. In a sociable way : from ca. 1770 : coll. ; in late C. 19–20, S.E.

bottle, turn out no. To fail : sporting : from ca. 1870 ; ob. Baumann.

bottle-ache. Drunkenness ; delirium tremens : mid-C. 19–20 ; ob. F. & H.

bottle and glass. The posterior : low rhyming on *arse* : C. 20. B. & P.

bottle-arse ; bottle-arsed. (A person) ' broad in the beam ' : low coll. : late C. 19–20 ; ob.—2. (*bottle-arsed* only.) See :

bottle-arsed, adj. (Printers' concerning type) thicker at one end than at the other : coll. : ca. 1760–1910 ; in C. 20, of type wider at the bottom than at the top.—2. See preceding.

bottle-boy. An apothecary's assistant ; a doctor's page : coll. : from ca. 1855 ; slightly ob.

bottle-head, n. and adj. (A) stupid (fellow) : the n., ca. 1654 ; the adj. (variant, as in Grose, *bottle-headed*), ca. 1690. Coll. ; in C. 19–20, S.E. but archaic.

bottle-holder. A second at a boxing-match (1753 ; in C. 20, ob.) : coll. Smollett in *Count Fathom*, ' An old bruiser makes a good bottle-holder.'—2. Hence, a second, backer, supporter, adviser (— 1851) : coll. *Punch* in 1851 had a cartoon of Palmerston as the ' judicious bottle-holder ', for he gave much help to oppressed states ; *bottle-holder* > his nickname. Whence *bottle-holding* : journalistic, ca. 1860–1900, for support, backing.

bottle-nose. A person with a large nose : (low) coll. : late C. 19–20.

bottle of brandy in a glass. A glass of beer : ca. 1885–1905. It didn't deserve a longer life.

bottle of cheese. A drink of Guinness : public-houses' (— 1935).

bottle of smoke, pass the. To countenance a white lie : coll. : Dickens, 1855 : ob. (O.E.D.)

bottle of spruce. Twopence : rhyming s. on *deuce*, two. (— 1859 ; ob.) H., 1st ed.—2. Nothing ; almost nothing ; (almost) valueless : non-aristocratic : late C. 18–mid-19. Ware. Ex *spruce beer*, which was inferior.

bottle of water. A daughter : rhyming s. (— 1931).

bottle-screws. Stiff, formal curls : coll., ca. 1800–40. Succeeded by *corkscrews*.

bottle-sucker. Nautical, ca. 1850–1914 : an able-bodied seaman, *b.s.* being humorously expanded.

bottle-tit or **-tom.** The long-tailed tit, from the shape of its nest : coll., from ca. 1845.

bottle-up. To keep, hold back : C. 17–20, coll. ; restrain (feelings) : C. 19–20, also coll. (Military) enclose, shut up : C. 19–20 ; coll., but S.E. in C. 20.

bottle-washer. Often *head cook and b.-w.* A factotum : jocular coll. : 1876, C. Hindley, ' Fred Jolly being the head-cook and bottle-washer '.

bottled. ' Arrested, stopped, glued in one place ' : low coll. : 1898 ; ob. Ware, who considers that it partly arises from the bottling-up, in Santiago, of the Spanish fleet by the U.S. squadron.

Bottled Beer. Alex. Nowell (ca. 1507–1602), English ecclesiastic. Dawson.

*bottled belly-ache. Cheap beer : C. 20 : tramps' c.

bottled-up, be. To be fully engaged and therefore

unable to accept any further engagements : low (— 1887) ; ob. Baumann.

*bottler. A collector of money for a band, a singer, an instrumentalist on the street : tramps' c. (— 1935). Cf. *nobber*.

bottles. Barrett's Brewery and Bottling Co.'s shares : Stock Exchange, ca. 1880–1914.

bottles, no. No good ; useless : low (— 1923). Manchon. Prob. ex *bottle, not much*, q.v.

bottling, n. Persuading onlookers to put money in the hat : showmen's : C. 20. P. Allingham, in *The Evening News*, July 9, 1934. Cf. *bottler*, q.v.

bottom. The posteriors : 1794, Dr. Darwin : coll. See *Slang*, p. 138. Ex lit. sense, as prob. is :—2. Capital, property : C. 17, coll.—3. Stamina, ' grit ' : 1747 ; ob. Captain Godfrey, in *The Science of Defence*, was apparently the first to use the term in print, thus : '. . . Bottom, that is, wind and spirit, or heart, or wherever you can fix the residence of courage '. Little used after 1855, *pluck* taking its place. Semantically : that on which a thing rests, or that which is at the base, is dependable.—4. Spirit poured into a glass before water is added : coll. ; from ca. 1850, Trollope having it in 1857, Theodore Martin as a v. in 1854.

bottom, at (the). In reality : coll. in C. 18, S.E. in C. 19–20.

bottom, stand on one's own. To be independent : C. 17–20 ; coll. till ca. 1800, then S.E. ; cf. the proverbial *let every tub stand on its own bottom* : C. 17–20.

bottom dollar. See *bet your boots*.

bottom drawer(, get together one's). Of a girl, (to prepare her) trousseau : coll. (— 1927). Collinson.

bottom facts. The precise truth : coll., from ca. 1890, but not much used. Orig. (— 1877) U.S. (Thornton).

bottom of, be at the. To be the actual, not merely the supposed, author or source of : coll. in C. 18, S.E. in C. 19–20. Steele has the equivalent *be at the bottom on't.*

bottom of a woman's ' tu quoque ', the. ' The crown of her head ', Grose, 3rd ed. : late C. 18–early 19. See *tu quoque*.

bottom on to (gold). To strike : Australian coll. (— 1926). Jice Doone.

bottom out, tale of a tub with the. ' A sleeveless frivolous Tale ', B.E. : coll. : late C. 17–mid-18. Cf. the title of Swift's masterpiece.

bottom out of, knock the. To overcome, defeat ; expose (the fallacy of). Orig. (— 1900) U.S. ; anglicised ca. 1905 as a coll.

bottom-wetter. See *wet bottom*.

bottomer. In drinking, a draught or a gulp that empties the glass or tankard : C. 19–20 ; coll.

bottomless pit. The female pudend : late C. 18–early 19. Grose, 2nd ed. (In S.E., hell : cf. Boccaccio's story about ' putting the devil in hell '.) —2. **Bottomless Pit.** Pitt the Younger (d. 1806). Dawson, ' In allusion to his remarkable thinness '.

Bottomley's Own. The 12th Londons : 1916–17. Because this regiment, which had been in camp for some time at Sutton Veny and Longbridge Deverill, was suddenly despatched to the front as the result of Horatio Bottomley's article (in *John Bull*) on Armies Rotting in England. By the way, they pronounced it *Bumley's*, in accordance with a very famous and presumably apocryphal story about Bottomley calling on a Cholmondeley (pronounced *Chumley*).

botty. An infant's posteriors : orig. and mainly

nursery. Mid-C. 19–20 ; coll. H., 5th ed. Ex *bottom.*

botty, adj. Conceited, swaggering : at first, and still chiefly, racing s. (— 1860) and dial. (see the E.D.D.). H., 2nd ed. Lit., troubled with the botts (parasitic worms). Cf. *bot-fly*, q.v.

Bouguereau quality. Risky effeminacy : art-world coll. (1884) >, by 1910, j. ; ob. Ware notes that this Fr. painter (1825–1905) excelled in delicate presentation of the—mostly feminine—nude.

[**bough.** A gallows, despite F. & H., is S.E.— 2. See **heave.**]

boughs, up in the. Much excited ; in a passion. Coll. ; late C. 17–early 19. B.E., Grose ; the former has the variant *a-top of the house.* (Extant in dial.)

boughs, wide in the. See **bows.**—**bougie.** See **bogee.**

boufer. A C. 18 variant of *buffer*, a dog. C. Hitchin, *The Regulator*, 1718.

boule. 'A conversation in which anyone may join ' ; Charterhouse : ca. 1860–1910. A. H. Tod. Ex Gr. βουλή, a council.

Boulognie. A wounded man, desirous of getting to England but going no farther than Boulogne : military coll. : 1916–18. B. & P.

bouman. A companion or friend, a ' pal ' ; also as term of address : Dublin lower classes' : from ca. 1910. Perhaps cf. *bowman*, 2.

bounce. A boastful lie, a pretentious swagger : coll. >, by 1800, S.E. (archaic in C. 20) : Steele, 1714, ' This is supposed to be only a bounce.' Ex † *bounce*, the loud noise of an explosion.—2. Hence, an exaggeration : coll (— 1765) ; as in Goldsmith, Whyte-Melville.—3. Impudence : coll. ; from ca. 1850 : as in *Blackwood's Magazine*, May, 1880, ' The whole heroic adventure was the veriest bounce, the merest bunkum ! ' Adumbrated in Ned Ward in 1703 (Matthews). Ex senses 1, 2.—4. A boaster, swaggerer : from ca. 1690 ; as in B.E.—5. Hence, a flashily dressed swindler : from ca. 1800 : low. Vaux. All these five senses are practically † ; the only operative extant one being that wholly C. 20 *bounce* = a bluffer, esp. if constitutional, regular, or persistent.—6. Cherry brandy : low : from the 1890's. Prob. ex its exhilarating effect.—7. A big dog-fish : nautical : late C. 19–20. Bowen. Ex its bounding ways.—8. A perquisite, an illicit surplus : military : C. 20. F. & Gibbons.—9. Dismissal ; esp. *get* or *give the bounce* : mostly military : from ca. 1910. Ibid.

bounce, v.i. and t. To bluster, hector ; boast ; bully ; scold : C. 17–20 ; ob. Coll. ; but all except the last > S.E. ca. 1750.—2. V.i. and (with *out of*) t., to lie (†), cheat, swindle : from ca. 1750. Foote, 1762, ' If it had come to an oath, I don't think he would have bounced.' Cf. the n., senses 4, 5, qq.v. —3. To scold severely : coll. (— 1888). Cf. sense 1 of the n. : semantically, ' blow up '. O.E.D.— 4. To bluff (a person) : military : late C. 19–20. F. & Gibbons.—5. To coït with (a woman) : low : late C. 19–20. F. & H. (revised).

bounce, give it to 'em upon the. To escape from the police, even to extract an apology from them, by assuming an appearance of respectability and importance : c. of ca. 1810–60. Vaux.

bounce, on the. (' In continual spasmodic movement ' : S.E. : C. 18–19. Hence :) Lively :, ca. 1850–1900 ; coll.—2. Hence, since ca. 1850 : as a, by attempting a, bluff ; by rushing one.—3. Hence, ' on the spur of the moment. At the critical moment ' : military : 1914 ; ob. F. & Gibbons.

bounceable, bouncible. Prone to boast ; bumptious : ca. 1825–1910 ; coll. Samuel Warren, 1830 ; 1849, Charles Dickens, who, eleven years earlier, uses the coll. adv. *bounceably.* Cf. n., 1, and v., 1.

bouncer. A bully, swaggerer, blusterer : late C. 17–19 ; coll. B.E., Dyche. Ex *bounce*, v., 1.— 2. A cheat, swindler ; also (— 1839), a thief operating while bargaining with a bouncer (Brandon) : from ca. 1770 ; † ; perhaps orig. c. Extant, however, is the nuance, a professional beggar : Cockneys' : 1851, Mayhew ; ob. E.D.D.—3. A liar : coll. ; ca. 1755–1900, as in Foote's comedy, *The Liar.* Hence, a lie, esp. a big lie : from ca. 1800 ; coll. ; ob.—4. Anything large (cf. *bouncing*) : coll. : late C. 16–20 ; ob. Nashe, 1596, ' My Book will grow such a bouncer, that those which buy it must be faine to hire a porter to carry it after them in a basket.'—5. Naval, ca. 1860–1914 : a gun that ' kicks ' when fired.—6. In c., a harlot's bully : C. 19–20, ob.—7. A ' chucker-out ' : public-house s. (1883, *The Daily News*, July 26) >, by 1910, coll. Ware. Perhaps orig. U.S.

bounceful. Arrogant ; domineering : Cockney coll. : ca. 1850–90. Mayhew. Ex *bounce*, n., 1, 3.

bouncible. See **bounceable.**

bouncing. N., a good scolding (— 1885) : coll. O.E.D. Cf. *bounce*, v., 3.

bouncing, adj. Big rather than elegant ; lusty, vigorous ; mid-C. 16–20 ; coll., but after ca. 1700, S.E.—2. Of a lie : C. 19, coll. Cf. *a thumping lie.*

bouncing ben. A learned man : c. (— 1864) ; †. H., 3rd ed.

bouncing buffer. A beggar : c. of ca. 1820–60. Ainsworth, 1834 (E.D.D.).

bouncing cheat. A bottle : c. of ca. 1720–1830. *A New Canting Dict.*, 1725 ; Grose, 1st ed. Ex the noise of drawn corks.

bound, I dare or will be. I feel certain : certainly : coll. ; from ca. 1530 ; the *dare* form being rare after ca. 1800.

bounded, ppl. passive. Catachrestic for *bound*, *bounden* : late C. 16–20. O.E.D.

bounder. A four-wheeler cab, a ' growler ' : ca. 1855–1900.—2. (University) a dog-cart : ca. 1840– 1900.—3. One whose manners or company are unacceptable : Cambridge University, from ca. 1883. Lit., one who bounds ' offensively ' about.—4. Hence, a vulgar though well-dressed man, an unwelcome pretender to Society, a vulgarly irrepressible person—gen. a man—within Society : from ca. 1885.

bounetter. A fortune-telling cheat : C. 19 c., mostly vagrants'. Brandon, 1839. Prob. a Gypsy corruption of *bonneter.*

boung. See **bung,** n., sense 3.—**boung-nipper.** See **bung-nipper.**

bourn(e). A realm, domain : catachrestic : C. 19–20. O.E.D.

Bournemouth. The Gaiety Theatre : theatrical : late 1882–mid-1883. Ware. That theatre was icy that winter ; Bournemouth is much affected by the weak-chested.

bous(e), bouz(e) ; bousy, etc. See **booze.**

'bout. A coll. abbr. of *about* : almost S.E. in C. 13–18 ; but, esp. in words of command, e.g. *'bout turn*, it is mainly naval and military : C. 19–20.

bouz. A variant of *boozy*, q.v.

bow. (Boating, competitive or otherwise) the rower sitting nearest to the bow : coll. : from ca. 1830.

bow, by the string rather than by the. By the most direct way: late C. 17–18; coll. > S.E. (O.E.D.)

bow, draw the long. To exaggerate; lie. From ca. 1820; coll. Byron.

bow, shoot in another's. To practise an art not one's own: C. 17–18: coll. soon > S.E.

bow, two or **many strings to one's.** With more resources than one, with an alternative: coll. > S.E.; from ca. 1550. In C. 19–20, gen. in reference to suitors or sweethearts. Ex archery.

bow and arrow. A sparrow: rhyming s.: late C. 19–20. B. & P.

bow-catcher. A kiss curl: ca. 1854–1900. H., 2nd ed; Ware. Corruption of *beau-catcher*, which is a variant form.

bow-hand, (wide) on the, adv. and adj. Wide of the mark; inaccurate: C. 17–18; coll. soon > S.E.

Bow Street. The orderly room: military: from ca. 1910. B. & P. Ex the famous London police-station.

bow up to the ear, draw the. To act with alacrity; exert oneself: coll.; from ca. 1850; ob.

bow-window. A big belly. From the 1830's. Marryat, 1840. Ex shape.

bow-windowed. Big-bellied: from the 1840's. Thackeray in *Pendennis*. Ex preceding.

bow-wow. A dog: jocular and nursery coll.: from ca. 1780. Grose, 1st ed.; 1800, Cowper, 'Your aggrieved bow-wow'. Ex the bark. Cf. *moo-cow*, etc.—2. A lover, a 'dangler': mainly in India; from ca. 1850. Ex his 'yapping'.

bow-wow! You gay dog!: coll.: C. 20. Manchon.—2. See **wow-wow!**

bow-wow mutton. Dog's flesh: ca. 1780–1890. Grose, 1st ed. Ware, 1909, '(Naval) [Mutton] so bad that it might be dog-flesh'.

bow-wow shop. A salesman's shop in, e.g. Monmouth Street: late C. 18–early 19. Grose, 2nd ed., 'So called because the servant [at the door] barks and the master bites'.

bow-wow word. An echoic word: from ca. 1860. Academic coll. (coined by Max Müller) >, by 1890, S.E. The (always S.E.) *bow-wow theory* is that of human speech imitating animal sounds.

bow-wows, go to the. To go to 'the dogs'; jocular coll.: 1838, Dickens. (O.E.D. Sup.)

bowd-eaten. (Of biscuits) eaten by weevils: dial. (where gen. *boud*) and nautical coll.: mid-C. 19–20. Bowen.

*bowl; gen. **bowl-out.** A discovery, disclosure: c.: C. 19. Ex cricket.

bowl a gallon. To do the hat-trick: cricketers' at Eton: ca. 1860–90. Lewis. Thus, the bowler earned a gallon of beer.

bowl (or try) for timber. To propel the ball at the batsmen's legs: cricketers' coll.: ca. 1890–1914. Ware, 1909, remarks, 'Discountenanced in later years—rather as a waste of time than with any view of repression of personal injury'. An interesting sidelight for the great cricket controversy begun late in 1932.

bowl out. To overcome, defeat, get the better of: from ca. 1810. Ex cricket.—2. In c., gen. in passive, to arrest, try, and convict: C. 19–20. Vaux.—3. For the n., see **bowl**.

bowl over. To defeat, worst; dumbfound (—1862). Ex skittles. Another variant (Dickens's) is *bowl down*, 1865.

bowl the hoop. Soup: rhyming s. (—1859); ob. H., 1st ed.

bowla, but gen. in pl. (**bowlas**) or in pl. used as singular. A round tart made of sugar, apple, and bread: ca. 1820–1900; coll. Mayhew, 1851 ? ex the Anglo-Indian *bowla*, a portmanteau.

bowled. (Winchester College) 'ploughed' in an examination. C. 19–20, †. Cf. *croppled*.

bowler (1882); **bowler-hat** (1861); occ. **boler** (— 1890). A stiff felt hat; fairly low in the crown and gen. black: coll. In its etymology, it was long regarded as a *bowl*-shaped hat, but it almost certainly derives ex the name of a London hatter (W.: *Words and Names*). Dates: O.E.D.

bowler, be given one's. To be demobilised: military: late 1918–19. F. & Gibbons. I.e. a civilian bowler in exchange for one's 'battle-bowler'.

bowler hat, be given a. To be sent home or 'sacked': military: 1915–18. B. & P.

bowles. Shoes: ca. 1850–1910. H., 1st ed. ? ex *bowl-shaped*.

*bowman, excellent, adept; mostly *bowman prig*, 'an eminent Thief . . .; a dexterous Cheat', *A New Canting Dict.*, 1725: c. of ca. 1720–1840. ? *beau* (fine).—2. Whence *bowman*, n., a thief: c. (—1823); † by 1890. Egan's Grose. Perhaps cf. *bouman*.

bowman, all's. All's safe: c.; from ca. 1820; † by 1890. Cf. *bob*.

*bowman ken. See **bob ken.**

bows, wide in the. 'With wide hips and posteriors', *Lex. Bal.*, where, as in Egan's Grose, *bows* is spelt *boughs*: nautical coll.: ca. 1810–70.

bows under(, with). Having too much work to do: nautical coll.: late C. 19–20. Bowen. Ex a ship labouring in a heavy sea.

bowse, bowser, bowsy, etc. See **booze,** etc.; but——

bowse, v. To haul hard, is nautical coll.: C. 19–20. Bowen. Perhaps cognate with dial. *bowse,* to rush, as the wind.

bowse, in. In trouble: nautical coll.: mid-C. 19–20. Bowen. Perhaps cf. dial. *bowse,* the recoil of a gust of wind against a wall (E.D.D.).

bowsprit. The nose: see **boltsprit.** *Bowsprit in parenthesis, have one's,* to have one's nose pulled: C. 19, orig. nautical (officers').

bowyer. (Lit., a bowman: C. 15 +.) An exaggerator; a liar: mid-C. 18–early 19. Grose, 1st ed. Cf. *bow, draw the long.*

bowze, etc. See **booze,** etc.

box. A small drinking-place: late C. 17–18: coll. B.E. Cf. the mod. Fr. *boîte.*—2. In C. 19 c., a prison cell.—3. (*the box.*) 'A fielding position between point and the slips': cricketers' s. (1913) >, by 1920, coll. >, by 1930, S.E.—but ob., for *the gully* is much more gen. Lewis.—4. (*the box.*) A coffin; esp. *put in the box*: military coll.: late C. 19–20. F. & Gibbons.—5. 'A safe of the old-fashioned kind': c.: late C. 19–20. James Spenser, *Limey Breaks In*, 1934, 'It is easy to rip off the back.'

box, v. To take possession of, 'bag': Winchester School, from ca. 1850; ob.—2. Overturn in one's box, in reference to a watchman or a sentry (— 1851, ob.); esp. *box a charley*, cf. *charley.*—3. To give a Christmas box: coll.: from ca. 1845; ob.—4. In C. 19 racing c., esp. as *box carefully*: (of a bookie) to see that one's betting liabilities do not exceed one's cash in hand.—5. V.t., 'to manipulate the figures of returns, esp. musketry returns, for purposes of deception': military: C. 20. F. & Gibbons.—6. To mix (two flocks or herds): Australian pastoral coll.: from ca. 1870. (R. D. Barton, *Reminiscences of an Australian Pioneer*, 1917.)

box, be in a. To be cornered; in a fix: coll., C. 19–20, ob. Prob. ex:

box, in a or **the wrong.** Out of one's element, in a false position, in error. Coll.; mid-C. 16–20. In C. 16, Ridley, Udall (J. not N.); later, Smollett, Marryat. 'The original allusion appears to be lost; was it to the boxes of an apothecary ?', O.E.D.

box, on the. On strike and receiving strike pay: workmen's, mainly in North England: ca. 1880–1910.

box !, the. Prepare for battle: naval coll. (— 1823); † by 1870. Egan's Grose.

box about, box it about. To drink briskly: C. 17–18. B.E. Cf. the C. 19–20 S.E.

*****box-getter, -getting.** A stealer, stealing, from tills: C. 20 c. Charles E. Leach.

box Harry. To take lunch and afternoon-tea together: commercial travellers'; ca. 1850–1910. H., 1st ed. Ex:—2. To do without a meal: from ca. 1820. 'Jon Bee', 1823.

box-hat. A tall silk hat: lower class s. (—1890) verging on coll.

*****box-irons.** Shoes: ca. 1780–1830; c. George Parker, 1789.

box-lobby loungers. A 'fast' London coll. of ca. 1820–60; thus in Bee, 1823, 'The ante-room at the Theatres is frequented by persons *on the Town* of both sexes, who meet there to make appointments, lounging about.'

box of dominoes. The mouth: mid-C. 19–20.

box of minutes. A watch; a watchmaker's shop: ca. 1860–80. H., 3rd ed.

box on. To keep fighting; hence, to continue doing anything important or strenuous: Australian: C. 20.

box open, box shut ! A soldier's c.p. indicating that though he was offering cigarettes, 'the donor's generosity was limited by hard circumstance' (B. & P.): G.W.

box the compass. To answer all questions; to adapt oneself to circumstances: orig. and mainly nautical; coll.; mid-C. 18–20. Smollett, 1751, 'A light, good-humoured, sensible wench, who knows very well how to box her compass'. Ex the nautical feat of naming, in order, backwards, or irregularly, the thirty-two points of the compass.

box the Jesuit and get cockroaches. To masturbate: mid-C. 18–19. Grose, 1st ed., 'a sea term'. An unsavoury pun on *cock* and a too true criticism of nautical and cloistered life.

box-up. A mix-up; confusion; muddle: mostly military: C. 20. Coll. Sidney Rogerson, 1933. Perhaps on *mix-up.*

box-wallah. A native pedlar, gen. itinerant: Anglo-Indian coll.; from ca. 1820.—2. Hence, pejoratively, a European commercial man: Anglo-Indian (— 1934). C.O.D., 1934 Sup.

boxed. (Of a book) impounded by Library Committee: Charterhouse: late C. 19–20. A. H. Tod.

boxer. A gratuity; esp., to the 'ringie' (in two-up) from the winning betters: New Zealand and Australian (— G.W. +). ? ex *Christmas box.* 2. Earlier, a stiff, low-crowned felt hat: Australian (— 1897). *The Argus*, Jan. 9, 1897. Morris. Cf. *hard-hitter.*—3. A tall hat: ca. 1880–1910. E.D.D.

boxing-out. A bout of boxing: U.S. >, before 1909, Australian coll.; † by 1920. Ware.

boy. A hump on a man's back: lower class,

from ca. 1800. Whence *him and his boy*, a hunchback (H., 5th ed.).—2. In India, hence South Africa and Australia: a native servant: C. 17–20; coll. 'Influenced by Telugu *bōyi*, Tamil *bōvi*, a caste who were usually palankeen bearers', W.—3. (Often *the boy*.) Champagne: from ca. 1880; ob. *Punch*, 1882, 'Beastly dinner, but very good boy. Had two magnums of it.'—4. See b'hoy.—5. In C. 20 c., and gen. in pl.: a prisoner. Cf. *boys*, q.v.—6. (Also **the boyo.**) Always **the boy**, the penis: late C. 19–20.

boy, my or **old.** A term of address: coll., though sometimes it is, clearly, familiar S.E.: C. 17–20. Shakespeare, Richardson.

boy, old (with the). One's father: late C. 19–20. One's business chief, 'governor': C. 20. The devil: C. 19–20, jocular. All now coll., though **s.** at their inception.

boy, yellow. See **yellow boy.**

boy Jones, the. A secret, or unnamed, informant: a virtual c.p., mostly London: mid-C. 19. Ex an inquisitive boy that wormed his way several times into Buckingham Palace. See esp. Horace Wyndham, *Victorian Sensations*, 1933.

boy with the boots, the ; the nailer ; Old Nick. The joker in a pack of cards: Anglo-Irish: late C. 19–20. Ex his effectiveness.

boyno ! A friendly valediction or, occ., greeting: nautical (— 1909); slightly ob. Ware. Ex or via Lingua Franca for 'good'.

boyo. (Gen. vocative.) Boy: late C. 19–20. This -*o* is an endearment-suffix. Ex Anglo-Irish *boyo*, 'lad, chap, boy' (E.D.D.).—2. See **boy**, 6.

boys; always **the boys.** The fraternity of bookmakers and their associates: racing: from ca. 1850. —2. The lively young fellows of any locality: from ca. 1860; coll. Cf. *lads of the village.*

Boys, Angry or **Roaring.** A set of young bloods, noisy-mannered, delighting to commit outrages and enter into quarrels, in late Elizabethan and in Jacobean days. Greene, *Tu Quoque*, 'This is no angry, nor no roaring boy, but a blustering boy'. Coll.; since ca. 1660, S.E. and merely historical. Cf. *Mohawks.*

Boys of the Holy Ground. Bands of roughs frequenting the less reputable parts of St. Giles, London, ca. 1800–25. Moore, *Tom Crib's Memorial*, 1819.

boysie. A term of address to a boy or, rarely by father, to son of any age whatsoever: coll., mostly Australian: C. 20. Isabel Cameron, *Boysie*, 1929; Christina Stead, *Seven Poor Men of Sydney*, 1934. Cf. *boyo*, 1, and dial. *boykin.*

Bozzy. Boswell: from ca. 1780. See **Bear-leader, the.** For the form, cf. **Dizzy.**

brace. Two 'noughts' in a match: 1912. But *bag a brace*, to be twice dismissed for 0, occurs as early as 1867; the ob. *brace of ducks* in 1891. All are s. >, by 1920 at latest, coll.

brace, face and. To bluster, domineer; be defiant: C. 16: coll. Skelton; Latimer, 'Men . . . woulde face it and brace it and make a shewe of upryght dealynge,' O.E.D. Cf. *brace* (*up*), *brace oneself.*

brace—or couple—of shakes, in a. In a moment; almost immediately: from ca. 1830. Barham, Ouida. Egan's Grose, 1823, has '[*in a*] *brace of snaps.* Instantly' and classifies it as nautical.

brace tavern, the. Late C. 18–early 19 only: low: 'a room in the S.E. corner of the King's Bench, where, for the convenience of prisoners residing thereabouts, beer purchased at the tap-house was retailed at a halfpenny per pot advance. It was kept by two brothers of the name of Partridge, and thence called the *Brace*,' Grose, 2nd ed.

*brace up. To pawn stolen goods, esp. at a good price : C. 19–20 c. ; ob. Vaux. Ware suggests that it may derive from Fr. c. *braser* as in *braser des faffes*, to fabricate false papers.

bracelet. A handcuff : from ca. 1660. Always low ; in C. 17–18, prob. c. ; ob.

bracer. A tonic : C. 18–19. ' What you need is a bracer.' The medical sense, which was S.E., has long been † ; as another word for a strong drink (cf. *tonic*, q.v.), a coll., from ca. 1860 : ex U.S. (1825 : O.E.D. Sup.).

brack. A mackerel : nautical : late C. 19–20. Bowen. Ex Isle of Man dial.

bracket-face(d). Ugly : late C. 17–early 19. B.E. ; Grose. Whence :

bracket-mug. An ugly face : C. 19.

brad. See bradbury.

brad-faking. A mid-C. 19 corruption of *broad-faking*, q.v. H., 1st–3rd edd.

bradbury, occ. abbr. to brad. A Treasury note ; esp. a £1 note : 1915 ; ob. (These notes, by the way, were hardly artistic.) Ex Sir John Bradbury, the Secretary of the Treasury, which circulated the 10s. and £1 notes from late 1914 until November, 1928, when the nation's note issue was consolidated in the Bank of England ; the Treasury's notes ceased to be legal tender on July 31, 1933. See the third leader and the City Editor's note, *The Daily Telegraph*, Aug. 1, 1933. Cf. *Fisher*, q.v.

brads. Money ; copper coins. From ca. 1810 (Vaux recording it in 1812) ; low until ca. 1860, by which date the ' copper ' sense was †. Prob. ex the shoemakers' rivets so named.—2. Cigarettes : military : C. 20. F. & Gibbons. For semantics, cf. *coffin-nail*.

brads, tip the. To be generous with money ; hence, be a gentleman : ca. 1810–40 ; low.

bradshaw. The complete time-table to the trains of Great Britain : from ca. 1845 ; soon coll. ; in C. 20 S.E. Abbr. *Bradshaw's Railway Guide*.— 2. Hence, a person very good at figures : middle-class coll. (— 1909) ; almost †. Ware. Ex that Manchester printer who in 1839 published the first railway time-table, in 1841 issued the first monthly railway-guide. (W.) ' O mighty Bradshaw, speaker of the thunderous line ' : from an un-published and unpublishable ode.

brag. A braggart ; ' A vapouring, swaggering, bullying Fellow ', B.E. : late C. 17–20. After ca. 1800, S.E.—2. In c., a money-lender ; a Jew : C. 19–20. Ex his exorbitant demands.

*braggadocia, -io. Three months' imprisonment to reputed thieves, who prob. boast that they can do it ' on their heads ' : c. ; ca. 1850–70. Dickens in *Reprinted Pieces*, 1857.

Braggs. See Old Braggs.

Brahma. ' Something good. Also a flashily dressed girl ' : Regular Army : late C. 19–20. F. & Gibbons. Ex *Brahma*, the Hindu deity : the idols being often bejewelled. Hence *brama*, q.v.— 2. See Bramah knows.

brain, bear a. To be cautious ; have a brain, i.e. some intelligence : C. 16–early 19 ; coll. soon > S.E. Skelton.

brain, have on the. Be obsessed by, crazy about : mid-C. 19–20. Coll. in C. 19, then S.E.

brain-canister. The head : pugilistic : ca. 1850–85. H., 3rd ed. On :

brain-pan. (As skull, S.E.) The head : C. 17–20, ob. ; after ca. 1730, coll. Skelton, Dekker, Scott.

brain-storm. The same as *brain-wave* but with the connotation of a more sustained mental effort : from ca. 1925 ; now verging on coll. Ex the S.E. sense, ' a succession of sudden and severe paroxysms of cerebral disturbance ' (Dorland, 1901 : O.E.D. Sup.).

brain-wave. A sudden, esp. if a brilliant, idea : from ca. 1914 ; since 1933, coll. Ex telepathy.

brains. The paste with which a sub-editor sticks his scissors-cuttings together : printers' (— 1887) ; slightly ob. Baumann.

brains, beat, break, cudgel ; drag ; busy, puzzle one's. To think hard, in order to understand or to contrive : C. 16–20, except *break* († by 1800) : all coll. ; but all, since ca. 1860, S.E.

brains, have some guts in one's. To be knowledgeable : late C. 18–early 19 : coll. Grose, 3rd ed.

brains, pick or suck someone's. To elicit information, knowledge, ' brain-wave ', and utilise it (without permission). Coll. (— 1838), very soon S.E. Lytton.

brains as guts, if you had as much. (Gen. followed by *what a clever fellow you would be !*) A c.p. addressed to a person fat and stupid : ca. 1780–1820. Grose, 2nd ed.

brains on ice. See have one's brains on ice.

brainy. Clever : coll. ; late C. 19–20 ; now verging on S.E. Ex U.S. (— 1873) and, even now, more typically U.S. than English.

brake. A tutor : Public Schoolboys' (— 1933). Perhaps suggested by *coach*.

brake, set one's face in a. To assume a ' poker ' face : coll. ; C. 17. Ex *brake*, ' a framework intended to hold anything steady ' (O.E.D.). Variants with *looks*, *vizard*, etc. Chapman in that fine, ranting tragedy, *Bussy D'Amboise*, 1607, ' O (like a Strumpet) learn to set thy looks | In an eternal Brake.'

*brama. A pretty girl : c. : from ca. 1922. James Curtis, *The Gilt Kid*, 1936. Ex *Brahma*, q.v.

Bramah knows : *I* don't. A euphemism (!) for *God knows ! I don't !* : ca. 1880–1910. More correctly *Brahma*.

bramble. A lawyer : mainly Kentish, hence and partly Cockney, s. : ca. 1850–1914.

bramble-gelder. An agriculturist : chiefly Suffolk, but occ. heard elsewhere : mid-C. 19–20 ; ob. H., 3rd ed.

bran. A loaf : coll., ca. 1830–1910. Dickens in *Oliver Twist*. Ex *bran-loaf*.

bran-faced. Freckled : mid-C. 18–early 19 : coll. Grose, 2nd ed. Cf. *christened by a baker*.

bran mash, bran-mash. Bread soaked in tea or coffee : military, from ca. 1870 ; ob.

bran-new. I.e. *brand-new* (earlier, *fire-new*) : a C. 19–20 sol., heard on the lips of those who persist in saying *Welsh rarebit*.

brancho- is incorrect for *branchio*- : mid-C. 19–20. O.E.D.

branded ticket. A discharge-ticket recording a crime, esp. a serious one : nautical coll. : ca. 1830–1925. Cf. *blanker*.

brandy, all. See all brandy.

brandy and Fashoda. Brandy and soda : Society : Oct. 1898–early 99. Ware. Ex ' the discovery of the Fr. captain, Marchand, at Fashoda '.

brandy blossom. A red-pimpled nose : coll. (— 1887). Baumann. Ex *b.b.*, a pimple that, on the nose, is caused by drink, esp. by brandy.

brandy-face. A drunkard : late C. 17–early 19. Cotton, ca. 1687, ' You goodman brandy-face '. Whence :

brandy-faced. Red-faced, esp. from liquor : from ca. 1700. Grose ; Sala, ' brandy-faced viragos '.

brandy is Latin for (a) goose, later **fish.** The former (ob.), from late C. 16 ; the latter (†), from ca. 1850. Coll. Mar-Prelate's *Epitome*, 1588 ; Swift ; Marryat. (Apperson.) Brewer has thus neatly stated the semantic equation : ' *What is the Latin for goose ?* (Answer) *Brandy.* The pun is on the word answer. *Anser* is the Latin for goose, which brandy follows as surely and quickly as an answer follows a question.' Concerning *fish*, Mayhew tells us that the richer kinds of fish produce a queasy stomach, restored only by a drink of brandy. Cf. :

brandy is Latin for pig and goose. Halliwell, 1847 : ' An apology for drinking a dram after either '. Coll. ; extremely ob. A variant on the preceding entry.

Brandy Nan. Queen Anne of England : early C. 18. Dawson, ' From her fondness for spirits '.

brandy pawnee (occ. **pahnee**). Brandy and water. India and the Army : coll. From ca. 1810. Thackeray, 1848, ' The refreshment of brandy-pawnee which he was forced to take '. See **pawnee.**

brandy-shunter. A too frequent imbiber of brandy : non-aristocratic : from ca. 1880 ; ob. Ware. On *booze-shunter*, q.v.

brass. Money. In late C. 16–17, S.E. ; in C. 18, coll. ; thereafter, s. Mrs. Gaskell ; Miss Braddon, ' Steeve's a little too fond of the brass to murder you for nothing.' H., 5th ed., ' " Tin " is also used, and so are most forms of metal.' Cf. *brass up.*—2. Impudence ; effrontery. Adumbrated by Shakespeare, but popularised by Defoe in *The True Born Englishman*, ' a needful competence of English brass '. Also in Farquhar, North, Goldsmith, T. Moore, Dickens. Coll. ; in C. 19–20, S.E. Prob. suggested by slightly earlier *brazen-face.*—3. A confidence-trick betting-system : c. C. 20. Charles E. Leach, in *On Top of the Underworld*, 1933.—4. Abbr. of **brass-nail**, q.v. : from ca. 1920. Philip Allingham, *Cheapjack*, 1934.

brass along. To go gaily and/or impudently ahead : from ca. 1918. (R. Blaker, *Night-Shift*, 1934.) Ex *brass*, 2.

Brass Before and Brass Behind. The Gloucestershire Regiment : military : late C. 19–20. F. & Gibbons. By a pun on *Back Numbers*, q.v.

brass-bound and copper-fastened. (Of a lad) dressed in a midshipman's uniform : nautical ; mid-C. 19–20 ; ob.

brass-bounder. A midshipman ; a premium apprentice : nautical : late C. 19–20. Bowen. Ex preceding.

brass-face. An impudent person : coll. : ca. 1820–60. ' Jon Bee.' Ex *brass*, 2.

brass farthing. A farthing—or less. Coll. : mid-C. 17–20 ; S.E. after ca. 1850.

brass-hat. A high-ranked officer : military and, in C. 20, naval : 1893, Kipling. Ex ' gilt ornamentation of his cap ' (O.E.D. Sup.). See esp. B. & P.

Brass Heads, the. The 3rd Bombay European—now the Leinster—Regiment : military : 1858,

when they excellently endured the sun in Sir Hugh Rose's campaign in Central India. F. & Gibbons.

*brass-knocker. Broken victuals : scraps of food : vagrants' c. (— 1874) ; ob. H., 5th ed. ? ex the hardness, or possibly, via India, ex Hindustani *basi khana*, stale food ; it affords an interesting comment on Yule & Burnell's *brass-knocker.*

brass monkey. See **monkey, cold enough . . .**

*brass-nail. A prostitute : c. : C. 20. Rhyming s. on *tail.* (Also among grafters : Philip Allingham.)

brass-neck. Impudent : military : C. 20. F. & Gibbons, ' A brass-neck lie '.

brass off, v.i. To grumble : military : C. 20. F. & Gibbons. Perhaps ex *part brass-rags.*

brass-plate merchant. An inferior middleman in coal : ca. 1840–1920 ; mainly London. Mayhew.

brass-plater. ' A man of the merchant class ' : from ca. 1920. (O.E.D. Sup.) Ex preceding.— 2. (**brass-** or **door-plater.**) A doctor : C. 20. Manchon. Ex the brass name-plate at his door.

brass-rags. See **part brass-rags.**

brass tacks, get down to. To come to, to face, realities ; to consider the practical aspect : coll. : U.S. (1903), anglicised by 1910 : O.E.D. (Sup.). (In U.S., there is the variant . . . *brass nails*.) I suspect, however, that **brass tacks** may have arisen before C. 20 and be rhyming s. for *facts*.

brass up. To pay (up), gen. v.i. : C. 20. In Feb., 1917, subscriptions to the War Loan were solicited in Nottingham (and elsewhere) by *brass up* legending the tramcars (W.). The term is more gen. in the North and the Midlands than in the South.

brasser. A bully : Christ's Hospital, C. 19–20 ; ob. Ex *brass*, 2.

brassy. Impudent ; shameless : coll. (— 1576) ; S.E. after 1800 ; in C. 20, ob. Wolcot, i.e. *Peter Pindar*, ' Betty was too brassy.' Cf. the S.E. usages.

brat. Brother ; ' one behaving in a manner not befitting his years ' : Bootham School : late C. 19–20. Anon., *Dict. of Bootham Slang*, 1925.

bratchet. A little brat : endearing or pejorative coll. : from ca. 1600 ; ob. by 1900.

brattery. A nursery : pejorative coll. : from ca. 1780. Beckford, 1834, ' The apartment above my head proves a squalling brattery.' (O.E.D.)

brave. A bully ; assassin : late C. 16–17, coll. ; thereafter S.E. ; ob. by 1850, † by 1890.

Brave Fifteenth, the. The 15th Hussars : C. 19–20 : military coll. now verging on j. and obsolescence. F. & Gibbons, ' From an old regimental song—" The Brave Fifteenth " '.

bravo. ' A mercenary Murderer, that will kill any body,' B.E. ; Steele, ' dogged by bravoes '. Late C. 16–18, coll. ; thereafter S.E. ; by 1930 slightly ob.

brawn. Strength as opp. to brains : coll., C. 19–20.

brawn, hawk one's. (See the quotation at *bruvver*.) To be a male prostitute (i.e. a man offering his ' charms ' to women) ; to be a passive homosexual for money : low (esp. Cockneys') : C. 20.

brayvo, Hicks ! Splendid ! : music-halls' and minor theatres' : from ca. 1830 ; ob. by 1910 ; † by 1930. Ware, ' In approbation of muscular demonstration. . . From Hicks, a celebrated . . . actor . . ., more esp. " upon the Surrey side " . . . [In late C. 19–early 20] applied in S. London widely ; e.g. " Brayvo Hicks—into 'er again." ' Cf :

brayvo, Rouse. Splendid ! ; well done ! : East London c.p. (— 1909) ; † by 1914. Ware. Ex ' the name of an enterprising proprietor of "The Eagle " . . . ; a theatre . . . in the City Road '. A very successful, though unauthorised, presenter of Fr. light opera, esp. ' all the best of Auber's work ' (Ware).

brazen-face. A brazen-faced person : late C. 16–20, ob. ; coll. till ca. 1800, then S.E.

[**brazen-faced,** impudent. Given by B.E. as either s. or coll., and by F. & H. as coll. It is, however, doubtful if this C. 16–20 word has ever been other than S.E.]

Brazen Nose College, you were bred in. You are impudent : c.p. : C. 18. Fuller. A pun on *brazen-face* and Brasenose College, Oxford.

brazil, as hard as. Extremely hard : from ca. 1635. Coll. till 1700, then S.E. ; ob. Either ex *Brazil-wood* or, much less prob., ex *brazil,* iron pyrites. (S.O.D.)

breach. A breach of promise : 1840, Dickens : coll. now verging on S.E. (O.E.D. Sup.)

bread !, as I live by. As true (or sure) as I stand here ! : coll. : late C. 19–20. Manchon.

bread, in bad. In a disagreeable situation : mid-C. 18–mid-19 : coll. Grose, 3rd ed. Here, *bread* = employment. Cf. :

bread, out of. Out of work : coll., mid-C. 18–early 19. Grose, 3rd ed.

bread and boo. Bread-and-scrape : nursery coll. (— 1923). Manchon.

bread and butter. A livelihood : coll., from ca. 1840. Ex U.S. (1820 : Thornton).—2. A gutter : rhyming s. : late C. 19–20. (*The Evening Standard,* Aug. 19, 1931.)—3. An app. cryptic term that resolves itself into an abbr. of *bread and butter letter,* q.v. Such shortenings are beloved of Society.

bread-and-butter, adj. Boyish, girlish, esp. schoolgirlish, as in *a bread-and-butter miss* : coll. ; from ca. 1860.

bread and butter letter. A letter thanking one's recent hostess : Society : anglicised, as a coll., ca. 1905 ex U.S. Occ. abbr. to *bread and butter* : from ca. 1925.

bread and butter of mine, no. No business of mine ; no potential profit for me : coll. : from ca. 1760 ; ob.

bread and butter squadron (or with capitals). The Mediterranean Squadron : naval : late C. 19–20. Bowen. Because it is ' cushy '.

Bread and Butter Warehouse. The Ranelagh Gardens of C. 18–early 19. In reference to their debauchery,—cf. Joseph Warton's *Ranelagh House,* 1747,—*bread-and-butter fashion* being a mid-C. 18–20 c.p. descriptive of human coïtion. Grose, 3rd ed.

bread and butter wicket. A wicket extremely easy for batsmen : cricketers' coll. : 1887. Lewis.

bread and cheese. Adj., ordinary ; inferior ; stingy : coll. : late C. 17–19. B.E.—N., plain fare or living : late C. 16–20, coll. > S.E. by 1700.

bread and cheese in one's head, have (got). To be drunk : mid-C. 17–mid-18 ; coll. and proverbial. Ray, 1678. (Apperson.)

bread and jam. A tram : rhyming s. : C. 20. B. & P.

bread and meat. The commissariat : military, from ca. 1850 ; ob. in G.W. ; †.—2. Hence, *bread-and-meat man,* an officer in the A.S.C. : military (— 1909) ; † by 1920. Ware.

bread and pullet. Just bread : jocular (— 1913). A. H. Dawson. With pun on *pull it.*

bread and salt, take. To curse and swear : C. 20. Manchon.

bread-artist. An artist working merely for a living : art : from 1890's ; very ob. A variation of *pot-boiler* with a pun on *bred.*

bread-bags. Anyone in the victualling department : Army, Navy : mid-C. 19–20 ; ob. H., 3rd ed.

bread-barge. The distributing tray or basket of biscuits : nautical, C. 19–20 ; ob.

bread-basket. The stomach : from ca. 1750. Foote, 1753, ' I let drive . . ., made the soup-maigre rumble in his bread-basket, and laid him sprawling.' Cf. *bread-room, dumpling-depôt, porridge-bowl,* and *victualling-office* : all pugilistic.

bread buttered on both sides. Great or unexpected good fortune : coll. ; mid-C. 17–20. Ray, 1678 ; Lockhart. (Apperson.)

bread-crumbs ! A naval c.p. (C. 20) uttered by the senior subaltern officer in the gun-room : an ' order for all junior midshipmen to put their fingers in their ears to avoid conversation unfitted for their youth ' (Bowen).

bread is buttered, know on which side one's. To seek one's own advantage : C. 16–20 : coll. ; in C. 19–20, S.E. Heywood, Cibber, Scott, Vachell. (Apperson.)

bread out of one's mouth, take the. To spoil or destroy a person's livelihood ; to remove what another is on the point of enjoying. From ca. 1700 ; coll. till C. 19, then S.E.

bread-picker. A junior's nominal office at Winchester College : C. 19. Evidently ex some old fagging-duty connected with bread.

bread-room. The stomach : 1761, Smollett ; † by 1860. Cf. *bread-basket* and *victualling-office.*

bread-room Jack. A purser's servant : nautical : mid-C. 19–20 ; ob.

breads. Portions or helpings of bread : coll. : ca. 1860–1910.—2. (**Breads.**) Shares in the Aerated Bread Company : Stock Exchange (— 1895). A. J. Wilson, *Stock Exchange Glossary.*

*break. Money collected by friends for a prisoner's defence or for his assistance when he leaves prison : c. : from ca. 1870 ; ob. J. W. Horsley.—2. (Gen. *bad break.*) A mistake, blunder, *faux pas.* C. 20, coll. Ex U.S. By itself, *break,* esp. in U.S. (— 1827), usually means a piece of good luck : cf., however, Thornton.—3. A continuous or an unbroken run or journey : railwaymen's coll. : 1898. O.E.D. (Sup.). Prob. ex a break at billiards.

break, v. To ' cut ' (a person) : middle-class (— 1909) ; † by 1920. Ware. Abbr. *break away from.*—2. To leave the employment of (a person) ; to discharge (an employee) : tailors' : C. 20. E.g. *The Tailor and Cutter,* Nov. 29, 1928, both senses.

break, do a. To depart hastily : Australian (— 1916). C. J. Dennis. Cf. S.E. *break-away.*

break a lance with. To enjoy a woman : C. 19–20. Coll. Eligible only when jocular, otherwise a mere S.E. euphemism. Ex S.E. sense : to enter the lists against.

break a straw with. To quarrel with : jocular coll. : C. 17–18. Florio's *Montaigne.* (O.E.D.)

break-bulk. A captain that appropriates a portion of his cargo : C. 17–20, ob. ; coll. till ca. 1700, then S.E. Ex S.E. *to break bulk,* to begin to unload.

break-down. A measure of liquor : Australian, ca. 1850–1910.—2. A noisy dance : coll., orig. U.S., anglicised in Edmund Yates, 1864 ; from ca. 1880, also coll., a convivial gathering : in C. 20, both senses are S.E. and, by 1930, ob. Also, from ca. 1870, as v., to dance riotously, be boisterously convivial, and adj., riotously dancing, noisily convivial.

*break down, v. To make lighter : C. 20. New Zealand c.—2. See n., 2.

break (e.g. it) down to. To tell (a person) something : tailors' : C. 20. E.g. *The Tailor and Cutter*, Nov. 29, 1928.

break-necker. A ball that, with a very big break, takes a wicket : cricketers' : ca. 1850–80. Lewis.

break one's back. To become bankrupt : coll., C. 17–18, as in Shakespeare's *Henry VIII*. To cause to go bankrupt : C. 17–20, coll., as in Rowley, 1632 ; and in H., 3rd ed. ; and in Baring-Gould's *The Gamecocks*, 1887. (Apperson.)

break one's duck. See duck, the cricketing n.

break one's leg. See broken-legged.—break one's shins against. See Covent Garden rails.

break out again. To do again something that is unpleasant or ridiculous : C. 20, coll. Perhaps a development ex :

break out in a fresh place. To commence a new undertaking ; assume (lit. or fig.) a different position : ? orig. U.S. and anglicised ca. 1905.

break-pulpit. A noisy, vigorous preacher : late C. 16–17 ; coll.

*break shins. To borrow money : C. 17–20 ; ob. In C. 17–18, c. (as in B.E.). Cf. *bite the ear.*

break square(s). To depart from or to interrupt the usual order ; do harm. *It breaks no square*, it does not matter, was proverbial. From ca. 1560 ; coll. till ca. 1620, then S.E. The proverb is ob., the phrase †. Apperson.

break-teeth words. Words hard to pronounce : late C. 18–early 19 : coll. Grose, 2nd ed. Cf. *jaw-breaker*, q.v.

break the balls. To begin : sporting, from ca. 1870 ; ob. In billiards j., the phrase = to commence playing.

break the ice. To begin ; get to know a person. From ca. 1590. Coll. ; by 1800, S.E. Nashe, Shirley, Dickens. (Apperson.)

break the back of. See break the neck of.

break the neck, occ. the back, of. To have almost completed ; to accomplish the major, or the most difficult, part of any undertaking. From ca. 1860 ; in C. 19, coll. ; in C. 20, S.E.

break up, break-up. (As v., idiomatic S.E.) The end of a school-term, or of any performance. From ca. 1840 : coll. soon > S.E.

breakfast, think about. To be absorbed in thought : coll. : late C. 19–20 ; ob. E. C. Bentley, *Trent's Last Case*, 1913, ' He was thinking about breakfast. In his case the colloquialism must be taken literally : he really was thinking about breakfast.'

breakfuss. Breakfast : London low coll. : mid-C. 19–20. See quotation at *against*.

breaking one's neck for a (drink, etc.), be. To long for a (drink, etc.) : coll. : late C. 19–20. Perhaps ex *to (be willing to) break one's neck for the sake of* . . .

*breaking-up of the spell. ' The nightly termination of performance at the Theatres Royal, which is regularly attended by pickpockets of the lower order ', Vaux : c. of ca. 1810–80. Here, *spell* = *spell-ken*, a theatre.

breaky-leg. A shilling : ca. 1835–70. Brandon, 1839.—2. Strong drink : from ca. 1860 ; ob. H., 2nd ed. Ex its effects.

breamy !, that's. That's bad ! : a military c.p. of C. 20. F. & Gibbons. ? = ' That's fishy.'

breast fleet, belong to the. To be a Roman Catholic : late C. 18–early 19. Grose, 1st ed. Ex the crossing or beating of hands on the breast.

breast of, make a clean. To confess in full. From ca. 1750 : coll. till ca. 1800, then S.E.

breast up to. To accost : (low) Australian (— 1916). C. J. Dennis.

breast work. The caressing of a woman's breasts : C. 20, somewhat pedantic and seldom heard. Punning *breastwork*, a defensive fieldwork breast-high.

breath strong enough to carry (the) coal, with a. Drunk : U.S., anglicised ca. 1905 ; virtually †. Ware.

breathe again. To be and feel relieved in mind : C. 19–20, anticipated by Shakespeare ; coll. > S.E. ' Phew ! we breathe again.'

breather. A breathing-space : a short rest : C. 20 : coll., now verging on S.E.—2. A tropical squall : nautical : late C. 19–20. Bowen.

breech, gen. in passive. To flog, be flogged on the breech : in C. 16–18, coll. if not S.E. ; in C. 19–20, schoolboys' s., ob. Tusser, ' Maides, up I beseech yee | Least Mistres doe breech yee ' ; Massinger, ' How he looks ! like a school-boy that . . . went to be breech'd.'—2. In C. 20 c., to steal from the back trouser-pocket.

breech makes buttons, one's. See buttons, one's . . .

*breeched. Rich ; in good case : c. : from ca. 1810 ; ob. Vaux. Cf. *bags (off)*, *have the*, q.v., and Fr. *déculotté*, bankrupt.

breeches. Trousers : coll. and jocular (also in dial.) : from ca. 1850. In S.E., breeches come no farther than just below the knee.

breeches, wear the. (Of women) to usurp a husband's authority, be ' boss '. From ca. 1550, though the idea is clearly indicated in C. 15. Coll. until ca. 1700, when it > S.E. Nashe, 1591, ' Diverse great stormes are this yere to be feared, especially in houses where the wives weare the breeches.'

Breeches Martyrs. W. O'Brien and several other Irish M.P.s, imprisoned in 1889. Dawson adduces that they ' refused to put on the prison dress '.

breeches-part. A role in which an actress wears male attire : theatrical (— 1865) ; ob.

breeching. A flogging : in C. 16–18, S.E. ; in C. 19–20 (ob.), schoolboys' s.

breed-bate. A causer or fomenter of bate, i.e. strife : late C. 16–20 ; ob. Coll. >, by 1620, S.E. Shakespeare, ' No tel-tale, nor no breede-bate ', 1598.

breeding. Parentage : low coll. : ca. 1597–1620. Shakespeare. Ex primary S.E. sense. O.E.D.

breeding-cage. A bed : low : ca. 1860–1920. W. E. Henley, in an unpublished ballad written in 1875, ' In the breeding cage I cops her, | With her stays off, all a-blowin' ! | Three parts sprung . . .'

breef. See brief, sense 3.—breefs. See briefs.

breeks. Orig. dial. (esp. Scottish) form of *breeches*. Since ca. 1860, coll. for trousers, very rarely for breeches. Baumann.

breeze. A disturbance, row, quarrel, tiff : coll., from ca. 1780. Grose, 1st ed. ; T. Moore.—2. A rumour ; a gossipy whisper : coll. : 1879, Stevenson (O.E.D.) ; ob.—3. See breeze up.

breeze. To boast : military : mid-C. 19–early 20. F. & Gibbons. Cf. *blow* in same sense.

breeze (along). To move or go quickly: from ca. 1920. Cf. :

breeze in. To arrive unexpectedly: from ca. 1920. On *blow in.*

breeze in one's breech, have a. To be perturbed: coll.: C. 17. Beaumont & Fletchér; Ray. A breeze is a gadfly. Apperson. Whence *breeze*, n., 1, q.v.

breeze up or **vertical, have the.** To ' have the wind up ', which it deliberately varies: 1916: orig. and mainly military. Whence:

breezer. A rest: military: C. 20. F. & Gibbons. Cf. *breather*, 1, q.v.

*breezy. Afraid: c.: from ca. 1918. Charles E. Leach. Ex G.W. soldiers' s.—2. Short-tempered: s. (— 1931) verging on coll. Lyell. Apt to ' blow up '.

breffus, brekfus(s). Breakfast: sol., esp. Cockney (— 1887). Baumann. Cf. :

brekker. Breakfast. From late 1880's. By elision of *fast* and collision of *break* and the Oxford -*er*, though—admittedly—it looks rather like a child's slurring of *breakfast* : cf. preceding entry.

brevet-wife. ' A woman who, without being married to a man, lives with him, takes his name, and enjoys all the privileges of a wife ', F. & H. Coll.: ca. 1870–1914.

brew, n. See **buroo.**—2. ' Drink made on the spot ': Bootham School: late C. 19–20. Anon., *Dict. of Bootham Slang*, 1925. Ex :—3. A study-tea : certain Public Schools': mid-C. 19–20. Cf. :

brew, v.i. To make afternoon tea : Marlborough and hence other Public Schools : mid-C. 19–20, ob. Hence *brewing*, the making thereof. —2. V.i., to have afternoon tea : at certain other Public Schools : late C. 19–20.

brewer, fetch the. To become intoxicated : from ca. 1840 ; ob. Cf. :

brewer's fizzle. Beer ; ale : 1714, Ned Ward, *The Republican Procession* ; † by 1800, and never common. (W. Matthews.)

brewer's horse. A drunkard. Late C. 16–20 ; ob. Shakespeare, 1597, Falstaff speaking, ' I am a peppercorn, a brewer's horse ' ; Halliwell, 1847. In late C. 19–20, mainly dial. Often in semi-proverbial form, *one whom (a) brewer's horse hath* (or *has*) *bit.* Cf. :

brewery, cop the. To get drunk : low : from ca. 1860 ; ob. Ware.

brewising. See **bruising the bed.**

Brian o' Lynn, occ. **o' Linn.** Gin : rhyming s. (— 1857, ob.). ' Ducange Anglicus.'

briar, properly **brier.** A brier-wood pipe : coll., from ca. 1870 ; now virtually S.E. Ware.

briar-root. ' A corrugated, badly-shaped nose ' : proletarian (— 1909) ; ob. Ware. Ex a briar-root pipe.

brick. A loyal, dependable person (orig. only of men) ; ' a good fellow ' : 1840 : s. >, ca. 1890, coll. Barham, ' a regular brick ' ; Thackeray, 1855, ' a dear little brick ' ; George Eliot, 1876, ' a fellow like nobody else, and, in fine, a brick '. Prob. ex the solidity of a brick ; a fanciful etymology is Aristotle's τετράγωνος ἀνήρ, a man worthy of commemoration on a monumental stone.—2. A misfortune, piece of hard luck : Public Schools' : 1909, P. G. Wodehouse, *Mike.* Cf. v., 1.—3. A piece of bread ; bread : Charterhouse : late C. 19–20.—4. A mellay ; a ' terrific ' scrum : ibid. : C. 20.

brick, v. Gen. *that's bricked it*, that's spoilt it,

that's the end of it : 1923, Manchon ; slightly ob. Ex next entry.—2. V.t., to push, ' barge into ' (a person) : Charterhouse : C. 20. Cf. n., 4.

brick, drop a. Make a *faux pas*, esp. of tact or speech : (— 1923), now verging on coll. Manchon. Perhaps ex dropping a brick on someone's toes.

brick, like a ; like bricks ; like a thousand (of) bricks. The second seems to be the oldest form (Dickens, 1836 ; Barham) ; the third to have been orig. (1842) U.S. Vigorously, energetically, thoroughly, very quickly, with a good will. Coll. >, by 1890, S.E.—2. But *swim like a brick* is the coll. opp. (— 1927) of S.E. *swim like a fish.* Collinson.

brick walls, make. To eat one's food without masticating it : lower classes' : late C. 19–20.

brickduster. A dust-storm : Sydney (— 1880) ; coll. See **brickfielder.**

Brickdusts, the. (Military) the Fifty-Third Regiment of Foot, which, from ca. 1881, has been the King's Shropshire Light Infantry. Ex its brick-red facings. Also called *The Old Five-and-Three-pennies* (ex its number and the daily pay of an ensign).

bricked. Smartly or fashionably dressed : late C. 16–mid-17 : ? orig. c. Greene.

brickfielder. (Less often *brickduster* ; cf. *(southerly) buster*.) A Sydney coll. for a cold dust- or sand-storm brought by southerly winds from nearby brickfields and sand-hills. Ca. 1830–90. But from ca. 1860, and predominantly from ca. 1890, the word has meant a severe hot wind, with dust or without. The change in meaning was caused largely by the disappearance, ca. 1870, of the brick-fields themselves. Morris's *Austral English* gives an excellent account of the word.

brickish. Excellent ; ' fine ', ' jolly ' : 1856, A. Smith (O.E.D.). Ex *brick*, n., 1 : q.v.

bricklayer. A clergyman. From ca. 1850 ; ob. Perhaps ex the part played by ecclesiastics in architecture. For interesting suppositions, see F. & H.

bricklayer's clerk. A lubberly sailor : nautical : ca. 1820–1925. Cf. *strawyarder.*

bricks. A sort of pudding : Wellington College, from ca. 1870 ; ob.—2. See **brick, like a.**

bricks and mortar. A heavy style of acting : theatrical (— 1935).

bricky. A bricklayer or his assistant ; coll. (1883). O.E.D.—2. Hence, a low fellow : schoolboys' : from ca. 1895. Collinson.

bricky, adj. Fearless ; adroit ; like a ' brick ' (q.v.) : 1864 ; perhaps orig. schoolboys' ; slightly ob. (O.E.D. Sup.) Cf. *brickish.*

bride and groom. A broom : rhyming s. : late C. 19–20. B. & P.

bridge. (Cards) a cheating trick by which a particular card is located, and made operative in the cut, by previously imparting to it a slight curve ; that curve produces an almost imperceptible gap in the resultant pack. From ca. 1850 ; after ca. 1870, j. Mayhew, Lever, Yates. Vbl.n., *bridging.*—2. Hence (?) an absentee from a meeting : printers' : from ca. 1880 ; very ob. Ware.—3. In New Zealand post-G.W. c., a look, a glance.

*bridge, v. To betray the confidence of. Variant : *throw over the bridge* : c. or low s. (— 1812) ; † by 1900. Vaux.

bridge, a gold or **a silver.** An easy and attractive means of escape : late C. 16–20 ; ob. Coll. > S.E. in C. 17.

bridge, beside the. Astray ; off the track : C. 17–18 ; coll. Culpepper, 1652. (O.E.D.)

bridge of anyone's nose, make a. To push the bottle past him, so that he misses a drink. Coll. : mid-C. 18–early 19 ; then dial. Grose, 2nd ed.

bridge-ornament. (Gen. pl.) An executive officer : nautical engineers' : late C. 19–20. Bowen. Opp. *educated trimmer*, q.v.

bridge-telegraph. A boy standing at the engine-room sky-light and repeating the captain's orders : London river-steamers' : ca. 1850–1910. Bowen.

bridges and no grasses. (A meeting, a pact, that is) secret : printers' : from ca. 1880 ; ob. Ware.

bridges, bridges ! 'A cry to arrest a long-winded story' : printers' : from ca. 1880 ; ob. Ware. 'Prob. corruption of [Fr.] " abrégeons—abrégeons " . . . Anglicised '.

bridgeting. The plausible acquisition of money from Irish servant girls, for political—or allegedly political—purposes : 1866 ; ob. Ware. *Bridget* (*Biddy*), a Christian name very gen. in Ireland.

bridle-cull. A highwayman : low or c. : ca. 1740–1800. Fielding. See **cull.**

Bridport or **Brydport dagger, stabbed with a.** Hanged. The *Bridport dagger* is a hangman's rope, much hemp being grown round Bridport. Mid-C. 17–early 19 ; coll. Fuller ; Grose's *Provincial Glossary* ; Southey.

brief. A ticket of any kind ; a pocket-book : from ca. 1850. In C. 19, c. ; in C. 20, low s. (In the late C. 19–20 Army, it signifies a discharge certificate ; and in C. 20 c., a convict-licence.) Ex its shortness. Hence *briefless, ticketless.*—2. In late C. 19–20 c., a false reference or recommendation.—3. Often spelt *breef* and always preceded by *the* : a cheating-device at cards : late C. 17–18.—4. (Cf. sense 2.) A letter : proletarian : mid-C. 19–20. Ware.—5. A furlough-pass : military : C. 20. B. & P.—6. A bank- or currency-note : bank-clerks', mostly Anglo-Irish : C. 20.—7. Hence (?), a cheque : c. (— 1933). George Ingram. —8. A fig. bias : c. (— 1933). Ibid.

*brief, get one's. To obtain one's ticket-of-leave : c. : late C. 19–20.

brief for, hold no. Not to support, defend, actively sympathise with (a person) : coll. : from ca. 1910. (O.E.D. Sup.)

*brief-jigger. A ticket-office, esp. at a railway-station : c. (— 1850).

*brief-snatcher. A pocket-book thief : c. : mid-C. 19–20. See **brief,** 1.—2. Also, vbl.n., *brief-snatching.*

briefless. Ticketless : from ca. 1870. Low in C. 20 ; earlier, c.

Briefless, Mr. An advocate without brief : coll., mostly London (— 1887) ; ob. Baumann.

*briefs. 'Jockeyed' playing-cards : C. 18–20 ; low, if not indeed c. Occ. *breefs.* Cf. *brief,* 3.— 2. Very short women's-knickers : feminine coll. : from 1932 or 1933. In *Books of To-Day,* Nov., 1934, C. G. T. writes feelingly, in the poem entitled *Too Much of Too Little* : " I'm bored to tears with ' scanties ', | I'm sick to death of ' briefs ', | Of specialists in ' panties ', | And combination chiefs.' " Cf. *neathie-set,* q.v.

brier. See **briar.**

briers, in the. In trouble : C. 16–18 ; coll. *Briers,* vexation(s), is S.E., C. 16–20, ob.

brieze. A sol. spelling of *breeze* : from before 1887. Baumann.

brig, the. Punishment-cells : naval, mostly

American : mid-C. 19–20. Bowen. Often *in the Dutch brig.*—2. **The Brig.** The pilot-steamer at the mouth of the Hughly : nautical coll. : late C. 19–20. Ibid.—3. As in *brig's po-juggler.* In military s., *the Brig,* one's or the Brigadier-General, dates from late C. 19.

brigdie. A basking shark : C. 19 nautical coll. ex Scots dial. (— 1810). Bowen ; E.D.D.

*brigh. A pocket, esp. a trousers-pocket : c. (— 1879) ; ob. *? ex breeks.*

Brigham. Inevitable nickname for anyone surnamed Young : late C. 19–20. Bowen. Ex the Mormonite.

bright. A dandy, fop, finical fellow : Society : ca. 1760–80. O.E.D. Cf. *smart.*

bright in the eye. Slightly drunk : from ca. 1870 : s. till C. 20, then coll. ; ob. (Lyell).

bright specimen, a. A silly, foolish, rash, stupid, bungling person. (Always complementary to the verb *to be.*) Coll. (— 1888).

bright-work juice. Liquid metal-polish : *Conway* cadets' : from ca. 1895. John Masefield, *The Conway,* 1933.

Brighton A's. Deferred ordinary shares in the London, Brighton & South Coast Railway : Stock Exchange coll. (— 1895) >, by 1910, j. (A. J. Wilson, *Stock Exchange Glossary.*)

Brighton bitter. A mixture of mild and bitter beer sold as bitter : public-houses' (— 1909) ; ob. Ware. Cf. :

Brighton tipper. 'The celebrated staggering ale', Dickens, 1843. Coll., ca. 1830–70.

Brightons. Shares in the London, Brighton & South Coast Railway : Stock Exchange coll. (— 1895) >, by 1910, j. A. J. Wilson's glossary.

brig's po-juggler. A brigade (lit., the Brigadier's) orderly officer : Australian military : 1915–18.

brim. A harlot : late C. 17–mid-19. B.E. ; Bailey. Cf. sense 3.—2. A termagant ; an angry, violent woman : from ca. 1780.—3. In late C. 19–20 c., a fearless harlot. Abbr. *brimstone.*

brim, v. (Of a man) to have intercourse ; v.t. **with.** C. 17–18, sporting. B.E. Ex the copulation of boar with sow.

brimmer. A hat with a brim, esp. if big : mid-C. 17–early 18 ; coll. at first, then S.E.—2. A variant of *brim,* 1, q.v. : c. of ca. 1820–50. Bee.

brimstone. A virago, a spitfire : from ca. 1700 ; coll. verging on S.E. ; ob. by 1890. ' " Oh, madam," said the bishop, " do you not know what a brimstone of a wife he had ? " ', Bishop Burnet, 1712.—2. Also, a harlot : from ca. 1690. B.E. Both ex *brimstone,* sulphur, which is notably inflammable.

Brimstone ; Brimstone Spurgeon. Charles Haddon Spurgeon, the great preacher (1834–92) ; ob. Baumann. Because he spoke so eloquently of the fires of Hell.

brimstone and treacle. Flowers of sulphur and dark treacle : domestic coll. : from ca. 1880. Collinson.

briney or **briny, the.** The sea : coll. (1856). Whyte-Melville in *Kate Coventry.* Cf. Dick Swiveller's use of *the mazy* and *the rosy* : W.— 2. Hence, *do the briny,* to weep : low : mid-C. 19–20 ; ob. 'Cuthbert Bede' ; Baumann. See **main, turn on the.**

bring. To steal : ca. 1820–60. Bee, who cites a v.i. sense : ' Dogs are said " to *bring* well ", when they run off with goods for their masters.'

bring down the house, bring the house down. To

be heartily applauded (— 1754). Coll. until ca. 1895, then S.E. 'His apprehension that your statues will bring the house down', *The World*, 1754; 'Why, it would . . . bring down the house,' 'Cuthbert Bede', 1853.

bring-'em near. A telescope: nautical: late C. 19–20. Bowen.

bring home the bacon. To succeed in a given undertaking: 1924, P. G. Wodehouse (O.E.D. Sup.).

bring in. (Of a jury) to find, e.g. guilty. Coll. (— 1888). 'The jury brought her in not guilty.'

bring up, v.i. and t. To vomit: coll.; from ca. 1830.

briny, the. See briney.

bris-à-bris, brise-à-bise. Incorrect for *brise-bise*, a net or lace curtain for the lower part of a window: from 1920. O.E.D. (Sup.).

brisby. A coll. form (1923) of *brise-bise*: see bris-à-bris. Ibid.

brisk as a bee or as a bee in a tar-pot. (C. 18–20, latterly dial.), as in Fielding, and *brisk as bottled ale* (C. 18), as in Gay. Very lively: coll. Apperson. Cf. *body-louse*, q.v.

brisk up (occ. about) To enliven or animate: coll.: 1864. Dickens. O.E.D.

brisket. The chest: low Australian (— 1916). C. J. Dennis. Significantly cf.:

brisket-beater. A Roman Catholic: late C. 18–19. Grose, 1st ed.; H., 2nd–5th edd. Cf. *breast fleet, craw-thumper*, and *brisket*, q.v.

brisket-cut. A punch on the breast or collarbone: pugilistic: ca. 1820–50. Bee.

bristler; gen. pl. A (better-class) motor-car commandeered, in that Spanish civil war which commenced in July, 1936, by the combatants, who therein rush about the streets and shoot indiscriminately all such persons as come within range: among the English colony in Spain: 1936, *The Times*, Aug. 6.

bristles, bristle dice. C. 19, C. 16–19 resp.; perhaps c. Dice falsified by the insertion of bristles. *Bristles* occurs in Scott's novel of the underworld, *The Fortunes of Nigel*.

Bristol. A visiting-card: Society: ca. 1830–1914. Ware, 'From the date when these articles were printed upon Bristol—i.e. cardboard'.

Bristol man. 'The son of an Irish thief and a Welch whore', *Lex. Bal.*: low: ca. 1810–50. Because both of those worthies would geographically tend to drift to Bristol.

Bristol milk. Sherry; esp. rich sherry: from ca. 1660; coll. till ca. 1800, then S.E. Prynne, Fuller, Grose, Macaulay. Ex the large quantities of sherry imported, in C. 17–18, into England by way of Bristol.

Bristol stone. Sham diamond(s): C. 17–18. In S.E., to this day, the term *Bristol diamond* or *gem* or *stone* denotes a transparent rock-crystal found in the limestone at Clifton, that beautiful outer suburb of Bristol.

Brit. See Britt, 2.

britches. Breeches: sol. (mostly U.S.): mid-C. 19–20. Ex careless pronunciation.

British. Shares in the North British Railway: Stock Exchange coll. (— 1895) soon > j.; now only historical. A. J. Wilson's glossary.

British champa(i)gne. Porter: ca. 1810–40. *Lex. Bal.* Cf. *English burgundy*.

British constitution, unable to say. Drunk: coll.: late C. 19–20; ob.

British Museum religion. Anglican cere-

monialists advocating the precise following of medieval uses: ecclesiastical pejorative coll.: ca. 1899–1902.

British official, n. and adj. Unreliable (news): military coll.: Oct. 1915–June 1918. Before and after these dates, official communications were trustworthy and regarded as such. See esp. B. & P.; cf. *bulletin*, q.v.

British roarer. The heraldic lion: non-aristocratic: from ca. 1880; ob. Ware.

British treasury note. A blanket: New Zealand soldiers': in G.W. Ex thinness of many Army blankets.

Briton, a. A good fellow; a staunch friend; a loyal, helpful person. Coll.: from ca. 1890.

Brits's violets. See violets, Brits's.

Brit(t), the. The Britannia Theatre: Cockney: ca. 1860–1910.—2. (As *Brit.*) A Briton: coll.: C. 20.

Brittania is a frequent error for *Britannia*: C. 18–20.

bro. Brother: Charterhouse: C. 20. Cf. the Yorkshire and Lancashire *broo*.

broach claret. To draw blood: boxing: from ca. 1820; ob.

broad. A 20-shilling piece: low: C. 19. Manchon. Whence, prob., *broads*, 2, q.v.—2. See 'Moving-Picture English', § 3.

broad, adj. Alert; 'knowing': late C. 19–20; ob. Suggested by *wide*, q.v.

Broad, the. Broad Street, Oxford: Oxford undergraduates': from the 1890's. Collinson.

broad and shallow. adj. Middle-way: applied to the 'Broad' Church, as opp. to the 'High' and 'Low' Churches: coll.: ca. 1854; ob. Cf. *high and dry* and *low and slow*.

broad-arse(d). (A person) 'broad in the beam': low coll.: late C. 19–20.

broad as it's long (or long as it's broad), it's as. It makes no difference; it comes to the same thing either way. From the 1670's; in C. 19–20, S.E. Ray, 1678; 'Hudibras' Butler. (Apperson.)

Broad-bottoms. The coalition ministry of 1741 was called the *Broad Bottom*: '. . . the reigning cant [i.e. vogue] word, . . . the taking all parties and people, indifferently, into the ministry', Walpole. A similar ministry in 1807 was described as *the Broad Bottoms*. Both were coll.; in histories, however, they are S.E.: cf. *Rump, the*.

broad-brim. A Quaker: 1712, ob.; coll. *The Spectator*, Fielding. Ex the Quakers' broad-brimmed hats.—2. Ca. 1840–90, any quiet, sedate old man. H.—3. Hence *broad-brimmed*, Quakerish; sedate: from ca. 1700; coll.; ob.

broad-brimmer. A broad-brimmed hat: coll.: ca. 1855–1900.

broad-cooper. A brewers' negotiator with publicans; he is an aristocrat among 'commercials'. Brewers, ca. 1850–1914. H., 3rd ed.

*****broad cove.** A card-sharper (— 1821; † by 1920): c. See broads.

*****broad-faker.** A card-player; esp., a cardsharper: C. 19–20 c.

broad-faking. Card-playing, esp. if shady; also three-card trickery: c.; from ca. 1855. H., 2nd ed., erroneously gives it as *brad-*.

*****broad-fencer.** A 'correct card' seller at horseraces: c.: from ca. 1850. H., 1st ed.

broad-gauge lady. A large-hipped woman: railway officials' (ca. 1880) >, by 1884, gen.; † by 1900. Ware.

broad in the beam. See beam, broad in the.

*broad-man. A card-sharper : C. 20 c. Edgar Wallace, *Again the Ringer*, 1929. Ex *broadsman*.

*broad mob, the. ' Broadsmen ' : c. : late C. 19–20. David Hume.

*broad-player. An expert card-player, not necessarily a sharper ; c. (— 1812) ; ob. Vaux.

*broad-pitcher. A man with a three-card-trick ' outfit ' : c. : from the 1860's. B. Hemyng, *Out of the Ring*, 1870.

Broad-Stripers. Royal Marine Artillery : naval : C. 19. Bowen. Opp. *Narrow-Stripers*.

broadcast is incorrect as the past tense of (*to*) *broadcast* on the wireless ; the past ppl. is either *broadcast* or *broadcasted*.

*broads. Playing cards : c. from ca. 1780 ; ob. George Parker, Vaux, Ainsworth, Charles E. Leach. Whence *broadsman*.—2. Money in coin : c. or low (— 1923). Manchon.

*broads, fake the ; work the broads. To issue counterfeit coin ; to play dishonestly at cards : both low verging on c. (— 1923). Manchon.

*broads, fake the. See also fake the broads.

*broadsman. A card-sharper : from ca. 1850 : c. H., 2nd ed., Charles E. Leach. Ex *broads*, q.v. Cf. *broad-man*.

broady. Cloth : coll., somewhat low : from ca. 1850. Mayhew. Ex *broadcloth*.—2. Hence, in c., anything worth stealing : from before 1890.

*broady-worker. A seller of vile shoddy as excellent and, esp., stolen material : ca. 1845–1914 ; c.

Brobdignag(ian). Sol. for *Brobdingnag(ian)*, as in Swift, 1726 : from ca. 1730. Disraeli.

brock. Catachrestically for a beaver : late C. 14–early 17. O.E.D.—2. A dirty fellow, a ' skunk ' : late C. 16–19 ; coll. verging on S.E. Ex *brock*, a badger.

brock, v. To bully ; tease : Winchester College : mid-C. 19–20, ob. Ex :—2. To taunt ; to chaff : ibid. : ca. 1800–1850. Wrench. Perhaps ex Ger. *brocken*.

Brock's benefit. Very lights, star-shells, etc., over the front line : military : 1915–18. F. & Gibbons, ' From the annual firework display at the Crystal Palace '.

brockster. (Winchester College) : a bully : a persistent teaser : mid-C. 19–20.

brodrick. The peaked cap worn by the British soldier : from ca. 1902 : military s. >, by 1925, coll. >, by 1930, j. Ex St. John *Brodrick*, Secretary for War (1900–3). W.—2. *Brodrick* or *little Brodrick*, a soldier of inferior physique : military coll. : 1903–ca. 1914. Ex his lowering of the standard. (O.E.D. Sup.)

broganeer, broganier. ' One who has a strong Irish pronunciation or accent ', Grose, 1st ed. : coll. : latish C. 18–early 19. Ex *brogue*.

brogues. Breeches : Christ's Hospital, C. 19–20 ; ob. Coll. rather than s., for in mid-C. 19 S.E. it meant either hose or trousers.

broiler. A very hot day : from ca. 1815 : in C. 20, S.E. Cf. *roaster, scorcher*.

broke. Bankrupt ; very short of money. Often —e.g. in N. Kingsley, 1851—*dead* or—e.g. in G. R. Sims, 1887—*stone broke*. Coll. ; from ca. 1820. (In S.E., C. 15–18.) A form of *broken* now † in S.E. but gen. enough as a sol. Cf. :

broke to the world. Penniless : from ca. 1915. An elaboration of the preceding.

broken feather in one's wing, have a. To have a

stain on one's character : C. 19–20, ob. ; coll. verging on S.E. Mrs. Oliphant in *Phœbe*, 1880.

broken her leg at the church-door, she hath. From a hard-working girl she has, on being married, become a slattern : coll. and (mainly Cheshire) dial. Apperson. Contrast the phrases at *broken-legged*.

broken-kneed. Of a girl or woman seduced : C. 18–20 ; ob. ; coll. Ex farriery. Cf. *ankle* (*sprain one's*) and :

broken-legged, ppl. adj. Seduced : C. 17–20 ; ob. Coll. More gen. is the semi-proverbial coll. form, *she hath broken her leg* (occ. *elbow*) *above the knee*. Beaumont & Fletcher, Cibber, Grose. Cf. the C. 19–20 Craven dial. *he hath broken his leg*, of ' a dissolute person on whom a child has been filiated ', and contrast *broken her leg* (as above).

broker. A pedlar or monger : pejorative : late C. 14–18 ; S.E. till C. 17, when it > coll.—2. In late C. 16–early 17 c., a receiver of stolen goods. Greene in 2nd *Cony-Catching*.—3. broker ; gen. dead-broker ; occ. stony-broker.. A person either ruined or penniless : coll. : from ca. 1890.

brokered, be. ' To suffer a visitation by the brokers : lower classes' : from 1897 ; ob. Ware.

brolly. An umbrella : from ca. 1873 ; in C. 20, coll. H., 5th ed., 1874 ; *Punch*, June 6, 1885. F. & H. : ' First used at Winchester, being subsequently adopted at both Oxford and Cambridge Universities '.

brolly-hop. A parachute jump : Royal Air Force's (— 1932). *Slang*, p. 259. Also as v., with frequent vbl.n., *brolly-hopping*, 1934, *The Daily Express*, June 27.

bromide. A commonplace person or saying ; a cliché : U.S. (1906), anglicised by 1909 ; by 1930, coll. E.g. C. E. Bechofer Roberts, in *The Passing Show*, June 16, 1934, ' Bassett occasionally put in a booming bromide.' Ex *bromide*, ' a dose of bromide of potassium taken as a sedative ' (O.E.D. Sup.).

bromidic. Of the nature of a ' bromide ' (q.v.) : U.S. (1906) anglicised ca. 1910 ; now coll. (Ibid.)

Brompton Boilers. See Boilers.

Bronc(h)o. The inevitable nickname of men surnamed Rider (Ryder) : military : C. 20. Cf. *Buck* q.v., and :

bronco-buster. A breaker-in of broncos, coll., U.S. (1880's) anglicised by 1897. O.E.D. (Sup.).

bronze. A cheat, deception, humbug : ca. 1815–60. *Blackwood's*, No. 1, 1817. Cf. *brass*, impudence.—2. Also as v.t. : same period. Likewise O.E.D.

broody. Very thoughtful and taciturn ; sullenly silent, with the implication of hatching a plan ; in the Army, lethargic, slack, sleepy : coll. : C. 20. F. & Gibbons. Ex fowls inclined to sit, a C. 16–20 S.E. sense. (Earlier in dial.)

brooks. (A pair of) trousers : South African coll. (— 1913). Ex Dutch. (Pettman.)

Brooks of Sheffield. This conveys a warning to be careful as to names : middle classes' c.p. : ca. 1850–1910. Ware. Ex *David Copperfield*, where David is thus referred to by Mr. Murdstone.

broom. A warrant : C. 18–19, coll. ; mainly dial. Also, the *pudenda muliebria* : C. 19–20, low ; whence *broomstick*, the male member. Cf. C. 19–20 Scottish *besom*, a low woman.

broom, v. (gen. broom it). To depart ; run away : low : late C. 18–19. Moncrieff, 1821. Suggested by *sweep away*.

broom-squires. Mainly Gypsy squatters that, esp. in the New Forest, earn a living by making brooms out of heath : C. 19–20 ; after ca. 1900, S.E.

broom up (at the mast-head), she carries the. She's a whore : a seaport c.p. of ca. 1820–90. Bee. Ex that broom which, attached to the mast-head, signified that a ship was sold.

broombee. See **brumbie.**

broomstick. A rough cricket bat, of one piece of wood. Coll. ; from ca. 1870 ; ob.—2. A worthless bail : C. 19 low. Vaux.—3. See **broom,** n.—4. A rifle or shot-gun : Canadian (— 1909) ; ob. Ware.

broomstick, enough to charm the heart of a. Very charming : ironic coll. (— 1887) ; ob. Baumann.

broomstick, jump (over) the ; hop the broom-(stick) ; marry over the broomstick. The first, C. 18–20 ; the second and third, C. 19–20 : all coll. and ob. Though unmarried, to live as man and wife : in reference to the pretence-marriage ceremony performed by both parties jumping over a stick. The ceremony itself = *a broomstick wedding.* Cf. *besom, jump the,* and *Westminster wedding.*

broseley. A pipe, esp. in *cock a broseley,* smoke a pipe. Ca. 1850–80. Broseley, in Shropshire, is—or was—famous for its ' churchwardens '.

brosier, brozier. A boy with no more pocketmoney : Eton College : from ca. 1830 ; ob. Ex Cheshire *brozier,* a bankrupt. Cf. gen. coll. *broziered,* ruined, penniless, bankrupt : late C. 18–early 19.

brosier, brozier, v. To clear the table or the larder of : Eton : mid-C. 19–20, ob. Rev. W. Rogers, *Reminiscences,* 1888. Ex *brosier,* n. ; cf. :

brosier- or **brozier-my-dame,** v. and n. (To make) a clearance of the housekeeper's larder : Eton College : from ca. 1835.

broth. Breath : low : late C. 19–20.

broth, in lunatic's. Drunk : 1902, *The Daily Telegraph,* June 20 ; ob. Cf. :

broth, take one's. To drink (liquor) : mid-C. 18–mid-19 nautical. Grose, 3rd ed. (s.v. *capsize*). Cf. preceding entry.

broth of a boy, a. A real, an essential boy : coll. ; Byron in *Don Juan,* 1822. Orig. and mainly Anglo-Irish. Ex the effervescence of broth ; or perhaps rather ' the essence of manhood, as broth is the essence of meat ', P. W. Joyce.

brother blade. A fellow-soldier ; one of the same trade or profession (cf. *brother chip*) : coll. : C. 19–20, ob.—2. In mid-C. 17–18, *brother of the blade,* a swordsman, hence a soldier. Coll. B.E., Grose, Ainsworth.

brother bung. A fellow-publican : London taverns' : from ca. 1880. Ware.

brother chip. A fellow-carpenter : C. 18. In C. 19–20, one of the same calling or trade : as in Clare's *Poems of Rural Life,* 1820. Mainly provincial. Coll.

brother of the angle. A fellow-angler ; an angler : from ca. 1650 ; ob. Coll. > S.E. Walton.

brother of the blade. See·**brother blade,** 2.

brother of the brush. An artist : coll. : late C. 17–20.—2. A house-painter : C. 19–20.

brother of the bung. A brewer ; a fellow-brewer. Coll. : late C. 18–20, ob. Grose, 1st ed. Cf. *bung,* n., and *brother bung.*

brother of the buskin. A (fellow-)player ; actor : late C. 18–20 coll., ob. Grose, 1st ed.

brother of the coif. A serjeant-at-law : C. 18–19 coll. Addison, Grose. Ex *coif,* a close-fitting white cap formerly worn by lawyers, esp. serjeants-at-law.

brother of the gusset. A pimp, a procurer, a whoremaster : late C. 17–19 ; coll. B.E., Grose. Cf. *placket.*

brother of the quill. An author : late C. 17–20 coll. B.E. ; Martin's Dict. (2nd ed.), 1754.

brother of the string. A fiddler ; a musician : coll., late C. 17–20, ob. B.E.

brother of the whip. A coachman : coll., mid-C. 18–20. *The World,* 1756.

brother smut. Gen. in *ditto, brother* (rarely *sister*) *smut* : the same to you ! ; you too : mid-C. 19–20 coll. H., 5th ed. Cf. *pot calling the kettle black.*

brother starling. A man sharing another's mistress : late C. 17–early 19. B.E., Grose.

brother-where-art-thou. A drunk man : late C. 19–20. Manchon, ' . . . Qui cherche toujours son camarade en lui demandant où es-tu ? '

Broughtonian. A boxer : coll. : ca. 1750–1800. Grose, 1st ed. Ex Broughton, the champion of England ca. 1730–5.

Broughton's mark. See **mark,** n., 7.

brown. A halfpenny ; a ' copper ' : from ca. 1810 ; low until ca. 1830. Vaux, 1812 ; Barham, ' The magic effect of . . . crowns Upon people whose pockets boast nothing but browns '.—2. Porter, whereas *heavy brown* = stout : Corcoran's *The Fancy,* 1820. Both, C. 19.—3. Twopenn'orth of whiskey : Mooney's, The Strand, London (— 1909) ; † by 1920. Ware.

brown, v. To do perfectly ; hence, to worst : from ca. 1870, †. Abbr. *do brown.*—2. Understand : from ca. 1830 ; ob.—3. To fire indiscriminately at : 1873 : coll. >, by 1910, S.E. Ex *brown, into the* ; see sense 2. (O.E.D. Sup.)

brown, adj. Alert (to), familiar (with). From ca. 1820 ; J. Bee, *Picture of London,* 1828.

brown, do. To do thoroughly ; hence, to worst ; to cheat. From ca. 1830 ; gen. as *done brown,* completely swindled. Barham, ' We are all of us done so uncommonly brown.' There is an anticipation in ' Ha ! browne done ! ' in the anon. *John Bon,* ca. 1600. In U.S., *do up brown* : see Thornton.—2. *do it brown,* to prolong a frolic or a spree, to exceed sensible bounds : from ca. 1850 ; ob.

brown, into the. (Shooting) at the brown stripe on the side of an antelope ; *the brown* is also applied to a moving herd of springbucks. South African coll. : 1898, G. Nicholson, *Fifty Years in South Africa.* (Pettman.) Ex :—2. *fire into the brown,* i.e. ' into the midst of a covey instead of singling out a bird ' : coll. (1871) >, by 1910, S.E.—3. Hence, fig. : 1885 : coll. >, by 1910, S.E. (Likewise O.E.D. Sup.)

*****brown, roast.** See **roast brown.**

brown Bess. A harlot : C. 17, coll.—2. The old regulation flint-lock musket : coll., C. 18–19. Recorded first in Grose, 1st ed., but prob. used much earlier ; *brown musquet* occurs in 1708. Ex the brown stock, the frequent browning of the barrel, and the soldier's devotion to the weapon : cf. the G.W. *soldier's best friend,* a rifle, and the Ger. *Braut,* the soldier's bride.—3. In rhyming s. : yes (— 1859) ; ob. H., 1st ed.

brown Bess, hug. To serve as a private soldier : ca. 1780–1850 ; coll. Grose, 1st ed. See **brown Bess,** 2.

brown cow. A barrel of beer : C. 18–early 19 : coll.

brown creatures. Bronchitis : lower classes' (— 1923). Manchon.

brown George. A loaf of coarse brown bread

prob. munition-bread : late C. 17–early 19 : orig. naval and military s., then gen. coll. Randle Holme ; Grose.—2. Also, a hard, coarse biscuit : late C. 18–19 : coll. Smyth.—3. Hence, ca. 1780–1850, a brown wig : coll. in C. 19.—4. Hence also, an earthenware jug, orig. and gen. brown : from ca. 1860 ; soon coll. and, in C. 20, S.E. Hughes, *Tom Brown at Oxford.* (The O.E.D. gives all four senses as always S.E., but the very name almost proves a s. or coll. birth.)

brown hat. A cat : rhyming s. : late C. 19–20. B. & P.

brown Janet. A knapsack : nautical : mid-C. 19–20, ob. In dial. as early as 1788 (E.D.D.).

brown Joe. Rhyming s. for 'no ! ' (Cf. *brown Bess*, yes !) From ca. 1855 ; ob. H., 1st ed.

brown madam. (Variant *Miss Brown.*) The monosyllable : late C. 18–early 19 ; low. Grose, 2nd ed.

brown off. To become tired of : Royal Air Force : from ca. 1920 ; slightly ob. Perhaps = S.E. *get rusty.*

***brown-paper men.** Low gamblers : c. of ca. 1850–1900. H., 1st ed. They play for pence or 'browns'.

brown-paper warrant. A warrant for boatswains, carpenters, etc., granted and cancellable by the captain : naval : C. 19. Bowen. Ex colour thereof and in allusion to the uses to which brown paper is put.

brown polish. A mulatto : late C. 19–20 ; ob. Ware. Cf. *Day and Martin*, q.v.

brown salve ! A term indicative of surprise coupled with understanding : ca. 1850–70. H., 1st ed.

brown talk. Very ' proper ' conversation : coll., from ca. 1700 ; ob. Cf. *brown study*, C. 16–20, serious thoughts, in C. 20 an idle reverie,—B.E., by the way, considered it as either s. or coll. for ' a deep Thought or Speculation '. Contrast *blue*, immoral.

brown to, v.t. To understand, to ' twig ' : low (— 1909) ; ob. Ware, ' Prob. from a keen man of this name ' ; H., 2nd ed., records it as an Americanism.

Brown Un, The. *The Sporting Times* : sporting : ca. 1870, when its colour was brown. See **Pink Un.**

browned-off. Depressed ; disgusted ; having given up hope : Royal Air Force : from ca. 1920 ; slightly ob. Ex *brown off*, q.v.

brownie, browny. The polar bear : nautical : coll. : mid-C. 19–20.—2. An Australian coll., dating from the 1880's : ' Cake made of flour, fat and sugar, commonly known as " Browny " ', E. D. Cleland, *The White Kangaroo*, 1890. Morris.—3. A copper coin : ca. 1820–1910. ' John Bee ', 1823. Ex *brown*, n., 1.—4. (Gen. pl.) A cheap cigarette—three for a ' brown ' or halfpenny : ' lower London ' (Ware) : ca. 1896–1915.—5. A trout : anglers' coll. : from ca. 1925. O.E.D. (Sup.).—6. (Gen. pl.) A Land Army girl worker : coll. : 1916–18. F. & Gibbons, ' From their being garbed in brown.'—7. Hence (likewise gen. pl.), a girl-messenger in a Government office : coll. : 1919. Ibid., ' From the brown overalls when on duty.'

browse. To idle ; take things easily : Marlborough and Royal Military Academy, C. 19–20 ; ob. Whence :

browse, adj. Idle ; with little work. Marlborough and R.M.A. ; C. 19–20 ; ob.

Broy hounds. Irish Free State special tax-collecting police : I.F.S. : from ca. 1925. On *bloodhounds* ex the name of their first Chief.

brozier. See **brosier.**

bruffam. A brougham : society : ca. 1860–1910. Ware. A pronunciation-pun, for whereas *brougham* is pronounced *broom*, the surname *Brough* is pronounced *Bruff.*

bruise, v. To fight ; box : pugilists', C. 19–20, ob. Anticipated in Fletcher, 1625, ' He shall bruise three a month.'

bruise along. To pound along : hunting : from ca. 1860. Cf. (hunting) *bruiser.*

bruise-water. A broad-bowed ship : nautical coll. : mid-C. 19–20 ; ob. Bowen.

bruiser. A prize-fighter ; 1744 (Walpole). In C. 19–20, coll., as in S. Warren, 1830, ' a scientific . . . thorough-bred bruiser '.—Hence, 2, any person fond of fighting with the fists ; a chucker-out : C. 19–20, coll.,—a sense implicit in Walpole's use of the term.—3. A reckless rider : hunting : 1830 ; cf. *bruise along* and *bruising*, adj.—4. In c., a harlot's ' fancy man ' or bully : mid-C. 19. Cf. *bouncer.*—5. ' An inferior workman among chasers' (of metal) : trade coll. (— 1788) ; ob. Grose, 2nd ed. Ex his rough workmanship.

bruising. Fighting with the fists : C. 19–20, coll. Ex C. 18–20 (coll. after 1800) sense : boxing, as in Smollett, 1751, and Thackeray, 1855, ' bruising . . . a fine manly old English custom '. Ca. 1800–30, boxing was not only popular but fashionable.

bruising, ppl. adj. (Given to) pounding along or reckless riding. Hunting : from ca. 1870. Ex *bruise along*, q.v. Cf. *bruiser*, 3.

bruising-match. A boxing-match : from ca. 1790 ; coll. till ca. 1850, when it > S.E.

bruising or **brewising the bed.** Fouling the bed : low : late C. 18–early 19. Grose, 1st ed., ' From *brewes*, or *browes*, oatmeal boiled in the pot with salt beef.'

brum. A counterfeit coin : C. 18–20 ; in late C. 17, counterfeit groats. Abbr. *Brummagem*, q.v.—2. A spur : coll., 1834 + but now †.—3. Almost anything, but esp. jewellery, that is counterfeit or worthless : from ca. 1870 ; e.g. in *The Daily Telegraph*, July 9, 1883.—4. Copper coins minted by Boulton & Watt, at their Birmingham works (— 1787) ; †, except historically.—5. (**Brum.**) A native of *Brummagem*, Birmingham : from ca. 1870.—6. (**Brum.**) Birmingham itself : from ca. 1860.—7. See **Brums.**

brum, adj. Not genuine ; counterfeit ; trashy : from ca. 1880 ; rather rare. Lit., made at *Brum* (Birmingham).—2. Hence, at Winchester College : mean ; poor ; stingy : 1883 (E.D.D.). Ex *Brum-(magem)*, or ex L. *bruma*, winter, or—the traditional College explanation—ex L. *brevissimum,* the shortest (thing). Wrench, however, adduces Kentish dial. *brumpt*, bankrupt, penniless.

brumbie or **brumby ;** occ. **broombee, brumbee.** A wild horse : Australian coll. Orig. (ca. 1864) in Queensland, but gen. by 1888 as we see by Cassell's *Picturesque Australasia*, of that date. The word appears in Kipling's *Plain Tales from the Hills.* Perhaps ex Aborigine *booramby*, wild. Morris, thus : *The Illustrated Tasmanian*, June 13, 1935, however, in a convincing article on ' Wild " Brumbies " ', states that the term arose in the second decade of C. 19 in New South Wales and that the term derives ex Major Wm. Brumby, who, from Richmond, went to Australia early in C. 19 ; he was a keen breeder of horses, and many of his young horses ran more or less, finally quite, wild. (The Brumby family now lives in Tasmania.)

Brummagem. Birmingham : from ca. 1860 ; except as dial., low coll.—2. Base money : in late C. 17–early 18, counterfeit groats ; C. 18–20, any counterfeit money, esp. of copper, as in Martin's Dict., 1754, and in Southey's fascinating farrago-'omnibus', *The Doctor.* Ex the local spelling, which was—and still often is—phonetic of the local pronunciation. *Brummagem = Bromwicham* (after *Bromwich*) a corruption of *Brimidgeham*, the old form of *Birmingham.* (W.) Faked antiques, etc., are still made at Birmingham.—3. Hence, a spur : from ca. 1830 ; ob.

Brummagem, adj. Counterfeit ; cheap and pretentious : coll. ; 1637, ' Bromedgham blades ' = inferior swords. Ca. 1690, B.E., ' *Bromigham-conscience,* very bad [one], *Bromigham-protestants,* Dissenters or Whiggs [see the O.E.D.], *Bromigham-wine,* Balderdash, Sophisticate Taplash.' The C. 20 connotation is that of shoddiness or of showy inferiority : as such, it is coll. See the n.

Brummagem buttons. Counterfeit coin, esp. of copper (— 1836) ; ob. Cf. *Brummagem.*

Brummagem Joe. Joseph Chamberlain (1836–1914). Ex his adopted city. Dawson.

Brummagem Johnson. Dr. Samuel Parr (1747–1825). Dawson, ' He imitated the manner of Dr. Johnson.' Perhaps rather a sobriquet than a nickname.

brummish. Counterfeit ; doubtful ; inferior : coll. : from ca. 1800 ; slightly ob. Cf. *brum.*

Brums. London and North Western—formerly London and Birmingham—Railway stock. Stock Exchange : from ca. 1880. Cf. *brum,* n., 5, 6.—2. Tawdry finery : Australian (— 1916). C. J. Dennis. Ex *brum,* n., 3, q.v.—3. **the Brums.** The Birmingham Football Club (' soccer ') : sporting : late C. 19–20.

brunch. Breakfast and lunch in one : university s. >, ca. 1930, gen. coll. : C. 20. Cf. *tinner.*

brush. A hasty departure : coll. : C. 18–19 ; in the latter, coll. Fielding in *Tom Jones.*—2. He who departs hastily : c. (— 1748) ; † by 1850. Dyche.—3. A house-painter : mid-C. 19–20 ; ob. H., 3rd ed. Cf. *brother of the brush,* q.v.—4. A small dram-drinking glass : public-houses' (—1909) ; slightly ob. Ex resemblance of its outline to that of a house-painter's brush (Ware).—5. A generic term for women : Australian c. (— 1935). Ex the pubic hair.

brush, v. To depart hastily ; run away. Late C. 17–20, ob. In C. 17, c. or low ; in C. 18, s. then coll. Post-1800, coll. and then S.E. ' Sergeant Matcham had brush'd with the dibs', Barham. Also *brush along* or *off* : C. 19 (Bee).—2. To flog : Christ's Hospital, C. 19–20.

brush, at a or **at the first.** At first ; immediately : coll. : C. 15–18.

brush, brother of the. See **brother of the brush.**

***brush, buy a.** To run away : c. of ca. 1670–1830. Also, C. 19–20 (s., not c.), *show one's brush* (Manchon). Cf. *brush,* n. and v.

***brush and lope.** To depart hastily, to decamp : late C. 18–mid-19 : c. Grose, 1st ed. Lit., to depart and run. See **brush,** v., 1.

brush one's coat for him. To thrash (cf. *dust one's jacket*) : coll. : ca. 1660–1820. Bunyan.

brush up. To revive one's knowledge of : coll. : C. 20 ; by 1933, thanks to the Brush Up Your (e.g.) French series of books, S.E.

brush up a flat. To flatter, ' soft-soap ' a person : C. 19–20, low.

brush with, have a. To fight with a man, lie with a woman : mid-C. 18–20, ob. Grose, 1st ed.

brusher. A full glass : ca. 1690–1830. B.E., Grose.—2. A schoolmaster : C. 19–20. Prob. abbr. *bum-brusher,* q.v. ; cf. *brush,* v., 2.

brusher, give. To depart with debts unpaid ; e.g. ' He gave them brusher ' : Australian-bush s. (— 1898). Ex *brusher,* a small and lively wallaby. Morris.

Brussel sprouts. Brussels sprouts : sol. contemporaneous with the correct term.

***Brussels.** A variant (from ca. 1920) of, and ex, *carpet,* n. (I.e. Brussels carpet.)

brute. One who has not matriculated : Cambridge University, C. 19. Prob. ex S.E. *brute.*—2. A term of reprobation : coll., from ca. 1660. ' The brute of a cigar required relighting ', G. Eliot.

bruvver. See **-uvver.** A little-known Army song (1914–18, and after) runs : ' Why should we be pore ? | My bruvver 'awks 'is brahn ; | Why should we be pore ? | My sister walks the tahn. | Farver's a bit of a tea-leaf, | Muvver's a West-End 'ore, | An' I'm a bit of a ponce meself— | Why should we be pore ? ' which is reminiscent of Villon.

bry or **Bry.** Abbr. *Brian o' Lynn,* q.v. : 1868, says Ware.

Bryant and Mays. Stays : rhyming s. : C. 20. B. & P. Cf. :

Bryant & May's chuckaway. (Gen. pl.) A girl working in that firm's match-factory : East London : 1876 ; ob. by 1910, † by 1920. A *chuckaway* is a lucifer match ; such match-making used to be unhealthy.

Brydport. See **Bridport dagger.**—**Bryan o' Lynn.** See **Brian o' Lynn.**

B's. Members of the Patriotic Brotherhood, or Irish Invincibles : Fenian : 1883 ; † by 1920. Ware.

***bub.** Strong drink, esp. malt liquor : from ca. 1670 ; ob. C. until ca. 1820, then low. Head. Often as *bub and grub,* food and (strong) drink. Either echoic or ex L. *bibere,* to drink ; Dr. Wm. Matthews says : abbr. of *bubble.*—2. A brother, rare, C. 18 ; C. 19–20, (mostly U.S.) a little boy. Perhaps ex Ger. *bube,* boy (w.).—3. A woman's breast, C. 19–20 ; rare in singular and not very frequent in this abbr. form : see **bubby.**—4. ' One that is cheated ; an easy, soft Fellow ', B.E. : late C. 17–19 ; c. until ca. 1810. Abbr. *bubble,* q.v.

bub, v. To drink : C. 18–19 ; c. until ca. 1820, then low. Prob. ex *bub,* n., 1.—2. To bribe ; cheat : C. 18–early 19 ; rare ; low, as in D'Urfey, 1719, ' Another makes racing a Trade . . . And many a Crimp match has made, | By bubbing another Man's Groom.' Ex *bubble,* v. Cf. *bub,* n., 4.

bub, humming. Strong beer or ale : ca. 1820–90. Bee. See **bub,** n., 1.

***bubber.** A hard drinker ; a toper. C. 17–late 18 : c. in C. 17, then low. Middleton, B.E., Grose. Cf. *bub,* n., 1, and v., 1.—2. A drinking-bowl : c. : late C. 17–early 19. B.E., Grose.—3. A stealer of plate from taverns and inns : c. of ca. 1670–1830. Head, Grose. Cf. sense 1.

bubbery. Senseless clamour ; ' a wordy noise in the street ' : low (— 1823) ; † by 1900. Bee. A corruption of *bobbery,* q.v.

bubbing. Drinking, tippling : ca. 1670–1830 : low. Cf. *bub* and *bubber.*

bubble. A dupe; a gullible person: ca. 1668–1840. Sedley, Shadwell, Swift (' We are thus become the dupes and bubbles of Europe '), Fielding, George Barrington (who left England ' for his country's good '). Coll. >, ca. 1800, S.E. Cf. and presumably ex:

bubble, v. To cheat, swindle; delude, humbug; overreach: coll., but S.E. after ca. 1800: 1664, Etherege; Dryden; Fielding, ' He . . . actually bubbled several of their money '; Sheridan; McCarthy the historian, 1880, ' the French Emperor had bubbled [Cobden] '. Also *bubble* (a person) *of*, *out of*, or *into*: 1675, Wycherley. Perhaps ex *bubble*, ' to cover or spread with bubbles ' (O.E.D.); more prob. via ' delude with *bubbles* ' or unrealities, as W. proposes.

bubble, bar the. ' To except against the general rule, that he who lays the odds must always be adjudged the loser; this is restricted to betts laid for liquor ', Grose, 2nd ed.: drinking: late C. 18–early 19. Punning *bubble*, a deception, + *bib* (or *bibber*) as a drinking term.

bubble and squeak. Cold meat fried with potatoes and greens, or with cabbage alone. Coll. From ca. 1770: Grose, 1st ed., being the first to record it in a dictionary; it occurs, however, in Bridges's *Homer*, 1772. After ca. 1830, S.E.; Lytton has it in *My Novel*. Ex the sound emitted by this dish when cooking. Cf. *bubbling squeak*, q.v.

Bubble and Squeak. Sir Walter Wynne, 5th baronet (fl. 1793). Dawson.—2. Thos. Sheridan, scholar. Ibid.

bubble and squeak, v. To speak: rhyming s.: (?) mid-C. 19–20. *Everyman*, March 26, 1931.

bubble-bow or **-boy.** A lady's tweezer case: ca. 1704–60: s. > coll. Pope. (= beau-befooler.) O.E.D.

bubble buff. A bailiff: C. 17. Rowlands.

bubble company. A dishonest firm: coll. passing to S.E., C. 19–20. Adumbrated in C. 18: see Martin's Dict., 2nd ed., 1754. ' *Bubble* . . . a name given to certain projects for raising money on imaginary grounds ': the South Sea Bubble was semantically responsible.

bubbleable. Gullible: *temp*. Restoration. Rare: coll.

bubbled, ppl. adj. Gulled, befooled, deluded. Coll., late C. 17–20; ob. Defoe:

> Who shall this bubbled nation disabuse,
> While they, their own felicities refuse ?

bubbler. A swindler: ca. 1720–1830: coll. > S.E. by 1770. Pope. (O.E.D.)

bubbling, adj. Cheating: ca. 1675–1750. Wycherley. (The n. is late—1730—and S.E.)

bubbling squeak. Hot soup: military: mid-C. 19–20; ob. Cf. *bubble and squeak*.

bubbly, often **the bubbly.** Champagne: from ca. 1895. Also *bubbly water*: C. 20.—2. Grog: naval: C. 20. Bowen.—3. A look-out posted by those playing Crown and Anchor (etc.): naval: C. 20. Ibid.

bubbly Jock. A turkey cock. Orig. (— 1785) Scottish; but well acclimatised in England by 1840; Thackeray and Besant & Rice use it. Grose, 1st ed. Either it is ex the turkey's ' bubbly ' cry or it is an early rhyming synonym (see *Slang*, p. 274).—2. Hence, a stupid boaster: C. 19.—3. Hence, a conceited, pragmatical fellow; a prig; a cad: from ca. 1860; ob. G. A. Sala, 1883.

Bubbly Jocks, the. Some Scottish regiment that

F. & H. (revised) does not name: military: late C. 19–early 20. F. & Gibbons, however, defines it as the Scots Greys and derives it from *bubbly Jock*, 1, ex the colour.

bubbly water. See **bubbly.**

bubby. A woman's breast. Rare in singular. Late C. 17–20; S.E. till late C. 18, then dial. and low. D'Urfey, in 1686, ' The Ladies here may without Scandal shew | Face or white Bubbies, to each ogling Beau.' Congreve, in the *Old Bachelor*, ' Did not her eyes twinkle, and her mouth water ? Did she not pull up her little bubbies ? ' Either ex *bub*, to drink, or semantically ex a milk-needing babe's *bu bu !*; for the latter possibility, see the congruous matter in Weekley's delightful baby-talk essay in *Adjectives and Other Words*.

*****bube.** Syphilis: late C. 17–early 19 c. B.E. Ex S.E. *bubo*, which Coles, 1676, perhaps wrongly classifies as c. even though he applies his c. *bubo* to ' pox ', his S.E. *bubo* to ' a large fiery pimple '.

Buck. A nickname for all men surnamed Taylor: orig. nautical: late C. 19–20. Bowen. Prob. ex ' Buck ' Taylor, a popular member of Buffalo Bill's cowboy team visiting England in 1887.

buck. A forward, daring woman: rare, perhaps only c.: ca. 1720–30.—2. Likewise coll., a man of spirit and gay conduct: ca. 1700–1805. Grose, 2nd ed., has *buck of the first head*, ' a blood or choice spirit ', a notable debauchee; prob. ex *like a buck of the first head*, which, in Ray, 1678, means little more than pert or brisk (Apperson). ' A large assembly of young fellows, whom they call bucks ', Fielding, 1752.—3. A dandy: from ca. 1805, ob. by 1887, now merely archaic: coll. > S.E. Thackeray in *Vanity Fair*, ' A most tremendous buck.' Cf. *masher, dude, swell*.—4. A cuckold: ca. 1770–1820. Abbr. *buck('s) face*, q.v.—5. An unlicensed cabdriver: ca. 1850–1905. Also, same period, a sham fare, a hanger-about at omnibus-stands.—6. A sixpence: C. 19–20, ob.; gen. with a preceding sum in shillings, as *three and a buck*. Prob. abbr. *fyebuck*, q.v.—7. A large marble: schoolboys', ca. 1870–1910.—8. In British Guiana (1869), a native Indian of South America: coll. rather than s. (Cf. the U.S. usage.) Australians apply *buck nigger* to any big man of very dark race: C. 20.—9. Grose, 1st ed., 1785, has ' *buck*, a blind horse ': this is rare, but hardly disputable: presumably s.: late C. 18–early 19.—10. A small dealer in the service of a greater (a ' stock-master '): Cockney (— 1887). Baumann.—11. Conversation: 1895, Mrs. Croker. Ex Hindustani *bak*. Also *bukh* (O.E.D. Sup.)—12. Hence, tall talk, boasting, excessive talk: military: C. 20. F. & Gibbons.—13. Hence, impertinence, impudence: Bootham School (— 1925). Anon, *Dict. of Bootham Slang*.

buck, v. To falsify—an account or balance-sheet: commercial, from ca. 1870; ob. Cf. *cook*, sense 4.—2. (Also *bukh, bukk*; Manchon spells it *bak*.) To chatter; talk with egotistical superabundance: Anglo-Indian coll.: 1880. Ex Hindustani *bakna*. Yule & Burnell. (Cf. *buck*, n., 11.) Whence *buck-stick*, a chatterer (— 1888).—3. Also, v.i., to object, be reluctant (v.t. with *at*): coll., from ca. 1890; mainly Australia and New Zealand.—4. In C. 20 c., to fight against, withstand. Perhaps ex S.E. *buck off*.

buck, adj. Handsome: Winchester College; C. 19. Wrench. Ex *buck*, a dandy.

buck, go to. A low coll. of C. 18, as in *A New Canting Dict.*, 1725, ' *She wants to go to buck, . . .*

of a wanton Woman, who is desirous of Male-Conversation.'

buck, old. A term of address : from ca. 1830 ; ob. by 1915 but not yet quite †. Cf. *old horse.*

buck, run a. To poll an invalid vote : late C. 18–early 19 ; orig. and mainly Anglo-Irish. Grose, 2nd ed. Cf. *buck,* n., 9 ; perhaps, however, a pun on *run amuck.*

buck a (blessed) hurricane or **a town down.** Resp. — 1870, — 1881, both ob., Australian coll.: (of a horse) to buck furiously. A. C. Grant : *Bush Life in Queensland,* 1881, at I, 131, for both.

buck against. To oppose violently : coll. (— 1909). Ex U.S. Cf. *buck,* v., 3.

*buck bail. ' Bail given by a sharper for one of the gang ', Grose, 2nd ed. : late C. 18–early 19 ; c. and low. In F. & H., misprinted *b.-bait.*

Buck Brummell. The beau : Eton nickname. Dawson.

buck-doctor. A Government veterinary surgeon : coll. of South African Midlands : late C. 19–20. Ex early attention to lung-diseased goats. Pettman.

buck down. To be sorry ; unhappy. Winchester College, from ca. 1860 ; ob. Cf. *bucked.*

buck face, buck's face. A cuckold : late C. 17–early 19. B.E.

buck-fat. Goat-lard : Cape Colony coll. (—1902). Pettman. Cf. *buck-doctor.*

buck-fever. The nervous excitement of a young sportsman when out shooting : South African coll. : 1892, Nicolls & Eglinton, *The Sportsman in South Africa.* Pettman.

buck fitch. An old lecher or roué : late C. 17–early 19. B.E., Grose. *Fitch = fitchew* = polecat.

[**buck-jump,** in its various senses and forms, is S.E. There is a tendency to regard it as coll. or even s., perhaps because of its Australian or, less prob., American origin. See Morris.]

buck of the first head. See **buck,** n., 2.

buck one's stumps. To get a move on (lit., stir one's legs): *Conway* Training Ship (— 1891). Masefield.

buck-shot. A settlers' term for granulated lava (always imbedded in a sandy alluvium) : New Zealand s. (— 1851) > coll. Morris.

*buck the horse. To make trouble in prison by resisting warders, etc. : C. 20 c.

buck the tiger. To gamble heavily : U.S. (from ca. 1862), anglicised before 1909 ; ob. Ware.

buck tooth. A large tooth that projects : from ca. 1750 ; in C. 18–19, S.E. ; in C. 20, coll.

buck up. Orig. (— 1854), v.i. and t., to dress up. Ex *buck,* a dandy. Then, 2, from ca. 1860, to make haste, or—esp. in the imperative—to become energetic, cheerful. Also, 3, from ca. 1895, to encourage, cheer up, or refresh (' A spot of b. and s. bucked him up no end ') ; and as v.i., to be encouraged ; esp. in *buck up !*

bucked. Tired : Uppingham, from ca. 1860 ; ob. Contrast *buck up.*—2. Encouraged, elated ; cheered, cheerful : from ca. 1905. Cf. *buck up,* 3.

buckee. A variant of *buckie.* (*The Tailor and Cutter,* Nov. 29, 1928.)

buckeen. A bully : coll., Anglo-Irish : late C. 18–early 19. In S.E., ' a younger son '. Ex *buck* after *squireen.*

bucker. A porpoise : nautical : mid-C. 19–20. Bowen. Ex its jumps into the air.

*bucket, v. To deceive, cheat, swindle, ruin : from ca. 1810 ; until ca. 1830, c. or low. Vaux, Scott.—2. To ride (a horse) hard : from ca. 1850 :

coll. ; in C. 20 j. Often as vbl.n., *bucketing* (Whyte-Melville, 1856).—3. In rowing : to take the water with a scoop ; swing the body ; hurry unduly the body's forward swing : from ca. 1869 ; coll. ; in C. 20 rather j. than coll. (Besant & Rice, 1876.)

bucket. A glass of spirits : low Ayrshire : 1870, John Kelso Hunter, *Life Studies of Character,* ' A rest for twa-three minutes, and a bucket the piece wad be acceptable.' In the E.D.D. (Sup.), it is classified as c. : but I doubt this.

bucket, give the. (With indirect object.) To dismiss from one's employment : coll. (— 1863). Cf. (*give the*) *sack.*

bucket, kick the. To die : late C. 18–20. Grose, 1785 ; Wolcot, ' Pitt has kicked the bucket ', 1796. Prob. ex the beam or yoke from which, as in Norfolk, pigs are hung ; *bucket* in this sense is C. 16–20 S.E.

bucket, passive. A patient listener : C. 20. Manchon. Making no complaint as bilge and slush are poured into it.

bucket about. To oscillate : coll. (— 1923). Manchon. Prob. ex rowing j.

bucket afloat. A coat : rhyming s. (— 1874) ; †. H., 5th ed. Often contracted to *bucket,* now †. The term current in C. 20 is *I'm afloat,* q.v. Soldiers use *bucket and float* (B. & P.).

bucket of beer. A pint of beer : public-house s., mostly Anglo-Irish : C. 20.

bucket shop. An unauthorised office for the sale of stocks : orig. (? 1881), U.S., anglicised ca. 1887 ; Ware prob. errs when he dates its English use as early as 1870. In C. 19, coll. ; C. 20, S.E. Ex *bucket,* ' the vessel in which water is drawn out of a well ' (Johnson) or ex *bucket,* to swindle, or ex the bucket into which falls the recording-tape or ' ticker '.

*bucketing concern. The vbl.n. of *bucket,* v., 1, q.v. : c. of ca. 1810–80. Vaux.

bucketsful, coming down. Raining heavily : coll. : late C. 19–20.

buckhorse. A blow, or a smart box, on the ear : coll. ; from ca. 1850, ex Buckhorse, actually John Smith, a celebrated pugilist, who would, for a small sum, allow one to strike him severely on the side of the head. Often as vbl.n., *buckhorsing* : see *Blackwood's Magazine,* 1864, vol. II, the Public Schools' Report—Westminster.

buckie. A refractory person : coll., when not, as gen., Scottish : C. 18–19 ; ob., except among tailors, who, in late C. 19–20, use it also of a bad tailor or of a shoemaker.

bucking. Washing sails : nautical coll. : mid-C. 19–20. Bowen. Ex a technical process in bleaching.

Buckinger's boot. The monosyllable : ca. 1740–95. Ex Matthew Buckinger, a daft limbless fellow married to ' a tall handsome woman ', Grose, 3rd ed.

buckish. Foppish, dandyish : from ca. 1780. Until ca. 1870, S.E. ; then coll. ; ob. *Mme D'Arblay's Diary,* at 1782 ; Wolcot ; George Parker ; Combe ; George Eliot.—2. (Of persons) in good spirits, in excellent fettle : from ca. 1912. Ex *buckish,* (of horses) inclined to buck. O.E.D. (Sup.).

buckle. A fetter ; gen. in pl. : coll., C. 17–early 18. E.g. in Egan's Grose.—2. **buckle (my shoe).** A Jew : rhyming s. : C. 20. B. & P.

buckle, v. To be married : late C. 17–19, extant as vbl.n., *buckling.* Marry, v.t. : C. 18–20. Both are coll. ; the former in Dryden, ' Is this an age to buckle with a bride ? ', the latter in, e.g.

Scott, 'Dr. R., who buckles beggars for a tester and a dram of Geneva.'—2. In c. and low s., v.t., to arrest: mid-C. 19–20 (ob.); gen. in past ppl. passive. H., 5th ed.

buckle and bare thong, come (or **be brought**) **to.** To be stripped of—to lose—everything: coll.: ca. 1550–1850, though extant in dial. Apperson.

buckle(-)beggar. A celebrator of prison, hence of irregular, marriages; a hedge-priest. Coll. Late C. 17–early 19. Orig. and mainly Scottish. Cf. *couple-beggar.*

buckle-bosom. A constable: C. 17: coll. Mabbe's trans. of *Guzman d'Alfarache.* (O.E.D.)

buckle down. To settle down: mid-C. 19–20: coll.

buckle-hammed. Crooked-legged: C. 17: coll. Gaule, 1629, 'Buckle-hamm'd, Stump-legg'd, Splay-footed'. (O.E.D.)

buckle-hole (of one's belt), be reduced or starved to the last. To be near death by starvation: Cockney coll. (— 1887). Baumann.

buckle my shoe. See **buckle, n., 2.**

buckle of the girdle (or, C. 19, **belt**), **turn the.** To prepare to fight: coll. (Cromwell, 1656, 'an homely expression') : late C. 16–19; extant in dial. Ex the turning of the buckle to the back, so that the belly be not injured thereby.

buckle to, v.i. Set to with a will, apply oneself energetically (1712). Coll. A development from *buckle,* v.i., to grapple, as in Butler, 'He with the foe began to buckle', 1663.—2. V.t., understand: C. 19.

Bucklebury. Euphemistic (— 1923) for *buggery.* Manchon. Ex the Berkshire locality.

Buckley, who struck ? A c.p. used, in C. 19, to irritate Irishmen. Origin obscure—though H., 5th ed., offers a plausible and amusing story.

*Buckley's (chance). A forlorn hope: Australian: from ca. 1875. C. J. Dennis. 'Buckley was a declared outlaw whose chance of escape was made hopeless', Jice Doone. (There have been many other explanations.)

bucko. (Pl. **-oes.**) A swashbuckling, domineering, or blustering man; occ. as term of address; swagger or bluster: nautical (— 1909). Ex *buck,* n., 2, + *o.* O.E.D. (Sup.).—2. Hence, corresponding adj.: nautical (— 1924). Ibid.

buckra. A white man: orig. (1794) in *negro* talk; then, since ca. 1860, among those Britons who live in the wilder parts of the British Empire. Coll. ex Calabar *backra,* master. (W.)

buckra, adj. (ex the preceding). Genuine: West Indies coll.: C. 20. A. Hyder, *Black Girl,* 1934.

buck's face. See **buck face.—buckshee.** See **bakshee(sh).**

buckshot rule. A political coll. for the upholding of government only, or chiefly, by a constabulary armed with rifles. Orig. applied to the Ireland of 1881. *Buck(-)shot* is large shot.

buckskin. An American soldier during the Revolutionary war; also, ca. 1820–60, a native American. Ex U.S. sense (1755 +): a Virginian.

bucksome. Happy; in good spirits: a C. 19 survival, at Winchester College, of C. 17–18 'buck-som, wanton, merry', B.E. *Bucksome* is from *buck* (up), q.v., and influenced by *buxom,* of which, need I say ?, B.E.'s *bucksome* is merely a variant spelling and nowise related to *buck.*

buckstick. A braggart: Anglo-Indian coll. (— 1924). O.E.D. (Sup.). See **buck, n., 12.—2.** See **buck, v., 2.**

bud. A débutante: society (— 1913); † by 1930. A. H. Dawson.

bud, nip in the. To check or ruin a project in its beginnings: from ca. 1840; coll. passing, in late C. 19, into S.E. The † *crush in the bud* occurs as early as 1746.

[**bud sallogh** in Grose, 1st ed., is ineligible.]

Buddoo. An Arab: Eastern Fronts: military in G.W. (B. & P.) Cf. *Abdul,* a Turk.

buddy. An American term of address (lit., brother): mid-C. 19–20; partially anglicised by 1914.—2. A chum; a recruit: military: from ca. 1914. F. & Gibbons. Ex sense 1.

*budge: 'or **sneaking budge**', Grose, 1st ed. A sneaking thief: c. or low s.: from ca. 1670. Head; Coles, esp. of cloaks; Fielding, in *Amelia.* † by 1850.—2. A thief's accomplice, esp. one who hides in a house to open the door later: c.: C. 18.—3. Liquor: c. (— 1821); †. A perversion of *bub,* n., 1, or *booze.*

budge, v. To depart: low: mid-C. 18–19. Grose, 1st ed. Cf. S.E. *budge,* to move however slightly.—2. To inform; 'split': low (— 1859); ob. by 1890; † by 1920.

*budge, sneaking or **standing.** A thief's scout or spy: c.: late C. 18–19.

*budge a beak(e). To decamp; to flee from justice: C. 17 (early): c. *Beak* = a constable.

*budge and snudge. A housebreaker and his assistant; such burglary: ca. 1670–1800; c.

*budge kain. A public-house: Scottish c. (— 1823); † by 1900. Egan's Grose. Cf. *budge,* n., 3. Presumably *kain* = *ken.*

*budger. A drunkard: C. 19 c. Ex *budge,* n., 3, q.v.

budgeree. Good; excellent. Australian, from ca. 1800. Recorded as early as 1793 and 'dictionaried' in 1796. Ex Port Jackson Aborigine dial. Morris.

budget, open one's. To speak one's mind: C. 17–early 18: coll.

*budging ken. A public-house: C. 19 c. Hence, *cove of the b.-k., a publican.* Ex *budge,* n., last sense.

budgy. Drunk: low (— 1874). H., 5th ed. Ex *budge,* n., 3.

budmash. A rascal; a thief: Regular Army: late C. 19–20. F. & Gibbons. Ex Hindustani *badmash.*

Buenos Aires. The Royal Crescent at Margate: the 1880's.

Buenos Aires, go or take the road to. To become a prostitute, esp. by way of a procurer's offices: coll. rather than merely euphemistic: C. 20. Ex the Fr.

bufa. See **buffer, 1.**

*bufe. A dog: mid-C. 16–18 c. Harman. Ex its bark. Cf. *buffer,* 1, q.v., and *bugher,* an 'anglicised' representation of the Scottish *bugher* pronounced properly *bu'ha,* loosely *buffer* : cf. the correct pronunciation of Scottish words like *Benachie* (approximately *Ben-a-he*).

*bufe-nabber, -napper. Mid-C. 17–early 19, C. 19 c.: a dog-stealer. B.E.; Grose.

*bufe's nob. A dog's head: c. (— 1785); † by 1900. Grose, 1st ed.

buff. The bare skin: coll., C. 17–20; ob. except in *stripped to the buff* (C. 19–20). Chapman, 1654, 'Then for accoutrements you wear the buff.' Ex the colour.—2. A man; a fellow; often as a term of address (*A New Canting Dict.,* 1725): coll.: ca. 1700–1830. Kersey's Dict., 1708; Smollett, in

Roderick Random, 1748. Cf. *buffer*; sense 2.—3. A variant of *bufe*, q.v. : C. 18. Cf. *buff-knapper*.— 4. (**Buff.**) A member of the Royal Antediluvian Order of Buffaloes, which, founded in or about 1875, aims at promoting universal brotherhood : 1879 : coll. >, by 1910, S.E. (O.E.D. Sup.)

buff, v. To strip oneself, often as *buff it*. From ca. 1850 ; ob. Mayhew. Ex *buff*, n., 1 ; perhaps imm. ex *buffing the dog*.—2. To maintain a statement ; swear to a person's identity (*buff to*) ; inform on. If absolutely, *buff it* : ' Do you buff it ?' From ca. 1880. Vaux. (Cf. U.S. sense : Thornton.) Perhaps ex *to buffet* or *to bluff*.—3. To polish with a buff : coll. in metal trades from ca. 1880. O.E.D.—4. See **buffing the dog.**

buff, in. Naked : C. 17–20. At first s., then coll. Dekker, ' I go . . . in buff.' Already ob. by 1890. See **buff, n.**

buff, stand. To bear the brunt ; endure without flinching. V.t. with *to* or *against*. Coll. ; from *temp*. Restoration ; ob. by 1850, † by 1890. Cf. *buff*, v., and S.E. *be a buffer, buffer state*. Butler, in *Hudibras's Epitaph*, ca. 1680 : ' And for the good old cause stood buff | 'Gainst many a bitter kick and cuff' ; Fielding ; Dyche's Dict. ; Scott.

buff and blue, or **blue and buff.** The Whig party : ca. 1690–1830 : political coll. Ex its former colours.

*buff-ball. C. 19–20 ; ob. ; c. and low. Greenwood, *In Strange Company*, 1880 : ' The most favourite entertainment at this place is known as buff-ball, in which both sexes—innocent of clothing —madly join.' Cf. *ballum rancum* and *buttock-ball*.

buff-coat. A soldier : ca. 1660–1900 : coll. >, by 1700, S.E. Cf. *Buffs*.

Buff Howards, the. The 3rd Foot—from 1881 the East Kent—Regiment : military s. (ca. 1740) >, by 1800, coll. F. & Gibbons. Ex its colonel of 1738–49 (Thomas Howard) and the colour of its facings. Contrast *Green Howards*.

*buff-(k)napper. A dog-stealer : c. : C. 18– early 19. *A New Canting Dict.*, 1725.

buff nor baff, say neither. To say nothing at all : coll. : late C. 15–17. A C. 16–19 variant is *not to say buff to a wolf's shadow*. Here, *buff*, like *baff*, is prob. echoic. (O.E.D.)

buff-stick. An orderly man : Regular Army : C. 20. F. & Gibbons. Ex the polishing instrument so named.

*buff to the stuff. To claim stolen property : late C. 19–20 c. Ware. See **buff,** v., 2.

buffalo. A buffalo-robe : Canadian and U.S. coll. : 1856 (O.E.D.).

Buffalo Bill. W. F. Cody (1845–1917), American scout and showman popular in England ca. 1885– 1900. Ex his exploits in killing buffaloes for the Government. (Dawson.)

buffalo boy. A negro comic : music-halls' (— 1909) ; ob. by 1920, † by 1930. Ware.

*buffer. A dog : in mid-C. 16–early 19 c. ; after ca. 1830, low ; ob. The C. 16–17, occ. the C. 18, spellings are *bufe* (q.v.), *bufa*, *buffa*. Lover, in *Handy Andy*, 1840 : ' It is not every day we get a badger . . . I'll send for my " buffer " . . . spanking sport.'—2. In late C. 17–18 c., ' a Rogue that kills good sound Horses only for their Skins ', B.E.—3. A man, in C. 19 often, in C. 20 gen., as *old buffer*. Recorded in 1749 ; Barham ; Anstey, ' an old yellow buffer '. Perhaps ex *buff*, the bare skin, but cf. dial. sense, a foolish fellow.—4. One who, for money, takes a false oath : C. 19. Cf. *to buff*, 2nd

sense.—5. A boxer : mostly Anglo-Irish : ca. 1810– 50. *Lex. Bal.*, 1811 ; Tom Moore in *Tom Crib's Memorial*, 1819, ' Sprightly *to the Scratch* both Buffers came.' Cf. S.E. *buffet*.—6. A boatswain's mate : naval : mid-C. 19–20. H., 3rd ed. It was he who, in the old days, administered the ' cat '.— 7. A pistol : early C. 19. Scott, 1824. Cf. *barker*. —8. An innkeeper, says Grose, 1st ed. Perhaps an error, perhaps a variant of *bluffer*, 1, q.v. If authentic, then it is prob. c. of ca. 1780–1830.

*buffer-lurking. Dog-stealing : C. 19 c.

*buffer-nabber. A dog-stealer : c. (— 1823) ; ob. Egan's Grose. See **buffer,** n., 1.

*buffer's nab. A false seal, shaped like a dog's head (*nab* = nob), to a false pass. Late C. 17– 18 c. B.E. Cf. *bufe's nob*.

*buffing the dog. The practice of killing such stolen dogs as are not advertised for, stripping them of their skins (cf. *buff*, n., 1 and v., 1), which they sell, and giving the flesh to other dogs : c. (— 1781) ; app. † by 1860 or so. G. Parker, 1781. Prob. ex *buff*, n., 1.

buffle. A fool : mid-C. 16–18 ; coll. >, by 1720, S.E. Ex Fr. *buffle*, a buffalo, and abbr. :

buffle-head. A fool ; an ignorant fellow : mid-C. 17–18 ; coll. till ca. 1700, then S.E. Whence :

buffle-headed. Foolish : stupid : late C. 17–19 ; coll. until ca. 1750, then S.E.

Buffs. The Third Regiment of Foot (now, and since 1881, the East Kent Regiment). Also *the old Buffs* (— 1806), the *young Buffs* being the 31st Regiment, raised in 1702. From ca. 1740, ex its 1737–49 colonel, it was called the *Buff Howards*, a name that, in C. 19, yielded to the old name, the *Buffs*. The regimental facings were buff-coloured. See *Tinsley's Magazine*, April, 1886. N.b., *the Ross-shire Buffs* = the old 78th Regiment (now, and from 1881, the 2nd Battalion of Seaforth Highlanders).

buffy. Drunk : from ca. 1859 ; ob. H., 1st ed. ; Yates, 1866, ' Flexor was fine and buffy when he came home last night.' Perhaps a corruption of *budgy*, q.v., or ex *bevvy*, q.v.

*buft. Either a decoy (*buffet*) or a bully : late C. 16 c. Greene.

bug. Anglo-Irish, mid-C. 18–19 : an Englishman. Grose, 1st ed. Ex bugs, introduced, Irishmen say, into Ireland by Englishmen.—2. In c., a breast-pin : mid-C. 19–20 ; ob.—3. (Gen. pl.) A wall-flower : low London (— 1909). Ware. Cf. *blood*, n., 4.—4. See **big bug.**—5. An electric-light bulb : Bootham School (— 1925). Anon., *Dict. of Bootham Slang*, 1925.—6. A school ' blood ' : certain Public Schools' : late C. 19–20. Ian Hay, ' *Pip* ', 1907.

bug, v. To exchange ' some of the dearest materials of which a hat is made for others of less value ', Grose, 1st ed. : late C. 18–early 19 : hatters'.—2. To bribe : late C. 17–19 c. ; cf. *bug the writ*, q.v. Whence vbl.n., *bugging*, the police's taking of bribes not to arrest : late C. 17–19 c. B.E.—3. Also, to give ; hand over (bug over) : c. (— 1812) : †. Vaux.—4. To obtain shadily from : c. or low : C. 20. John G. Brandon, *Th' Big City*, 1931, ' Supposin' one of them [harlots] bugs a bloke for a few Brads in a taxi . . .' Semantics : *sting* as an insect does.

bug-blinding. A bout of whitewashing : military, from ca. 1870 ; ob.

bug-hunter. An upholsterer : late C. 18–19. Grose, 2nd ed.—2. A robber of the dead : mid-

C. 19–20 : c. or low s. H., 1st ed.—3. One who collects as an entomologist : coll. : 1889 (O.E.D.). —4. A robber of drunken men's breast-pins : c. : from ca. 1860.

bug-hutch. 'A small hut or sleeping place' : military : 1915 ; ob. F. & Gibbons. Cf. *booby-hutch.*

bug in a rug, snug as a. See **snug as . . .**

bug-juice. Treacle : at the Borstal Institution at Portland : C. 20.—2. See **juice, bright-work** entry. —3. Ginger ale : ca. 1870–1910, low.—4. Whiskey : Canadian (and U.S.) : C. 20. (John Beames.)

bug-letter. A letter in stereotyped form : typists' (— 1935).

bug-shooter. A volunteer (soldier) : schools' and universities' : ca. 1898–1914. Ware.

*bug the writ. (Of bailiffs) to refrain from, or postpone, serving a writ, money having passed : c. : late C. 18–early 19. Grose, 1st ed.

bug-trap. A small vessel ; a bunk : nautical : from ca. 1890. Because easily overrun with cockroaches. (O.E.D. Sup.)

bug-walk. A bed : low ; ca. 1850–1930. H., 3rd ed.

*bugaboo. A sheriff's officer ; a weekly creditor : C. 19 c. Egan's Grose. Ex lit. sense.

buggah. A variant, rare in C. 20, of sense 2 of :

bugger. In c., a stealer of breast-pins from drunks : C. 19. Ex *bug*, n., 2.—2. A man : fellow ; chap : low coll. ; 1719, D'Urfey. In S.E. (C. 16–20), a sodomite. In low coll. and in dial., as in the U.S., the word has no offensive connotation whatsoever : cf. the remark at *pakeha*, q.v., and the gradual and complete decolorisation of *bastard*, q.v., and of Fr. *bougre*, as in C. 19–20 *un bon bougre*, a good chap. But also as a pejorative : disagreeable person of either sex ; an unpleasant, very difficult, or dangerous thing, project, episode, circumstance, as in G.W. 'It's a bugger making a raid on a wet night.' In 1929, still an actionable word if printed (Norah James : *Sleeveless Errand*) ; in 1934, no longer so (R. Blaker : *Night-Shift* ; Geoffrey Dennis : *Bloody Mary's*). See also **bugger, not a.** Ex L. *Bulgarus*, a Bulgarian : the Albigensian heretics were often perverts. O.E.D. ; E.D.D. ; and the introduction to B. & P.

bugger, v. To spoil ; ruin ; check or change drastically : from ca. 1880 ; in 1914 +, badly wounded, done for. In the G.W. the Tommy and his Colonial peers were often heard to say, 'Well, *that's* buggered it.' Doubtless a development from the S.E. sense, to commit sodomy with. The past ppl. passive, *buggered*, occurs in expletive phrases, e.g. 'Well, I'm buggered !', damned ; 'you be buggered !' (cf. ' bugger you ! '), go to the devil !— 2. V.i. and t., to cheat at cards : c. or low : late C. 19–20 ; ob.—3. See **bugger about.**

bugger ! A strong expletive : latish C. 19–20. Manchon.

bugger, not a. Not at all, as in *not care a bugger* : low coll. : C. 20. Geoffrey Dennis, 1934.

bugger about, v. Potter about ; fuss ; act ineffectually ; waste time on a thing, with a person. Hence, *bugger about with*, to caress intimately ; interfere with (person or thing). C. 20 : coll. rather than s. ; in Australia more than in Britain.

bugger all. A low variant of *damn all*, q.v

bugger up. To spoil, ruin ; nullify : low : late C. 19–20. Cf. *bugger*, v., 1.

bugger you ! A strong expletive : low (— 1887). Baumann.

buggered. See **bugger,** v., 1, latter part.

buggerlugs. An offensive term of address : mainly nautical : late C. 19–20. (J. Brophy, *Waterfront*, 1934.)

buggery. (In S.E., sodomy : like *bugger* and *to bugger*, it is the correct legal term : see O.E.D. and S.O.D.) In unconventional English, in two phrases : *(all) to buggery*, completely, destructively, ruinously : C. 20. In G.W., ' Our batteries shelled poor old Jerry to buggery ' ; Manchon.—2. **like buggery** : either vigorously, cruelly, vindictively ; or, as an expletive, certainly not ! From ca. 1890.

buggly, v.t. To exchange, to swap : military : C. 20. F. & Gibbons. ? ex Hindustani.

*bugher ; occ. as in Coles, 1676, *bughar.* A dog, esp. if a mongrel or given to yelping or barking : ca. 1670–1820 : orig. c., then low. Cf. *buffer*, 1, and see **bufe.**

bugs. A dirty seaman : nautical : late C. 19–20. Bowen. Cf. *bug-trap.*—2. Bacteria ; bacteriology : medical students' (— 1933). *Slang*, p. 191.

build. (Of clothes) make, cut, tailoring : coll. : from ca. 1840. ' Cuthbert Bede ', *Verdant Green*, 1853 ; *Punch*, Jan. 10, 1880, in the delightful contribution on *The Spread of Education*. Cf. *build up*, q.v.

build a chapel. To steer badly : nautical : C. 19–20, ob.

*build up. ' To array in good clothes, for trade purposes ' : c. : late C. 19–20. Ware. Cf. *build*, q.v.

built by the mile . . . See **cotton-box.**

built that way. (Gen. in negative.) Like, such a person as, that ; of such a nature or character. Orig. (— 1890), U.S. ; anglicised ca. 1900 as a coll.

bukh. See **buck,** n., 11, and v., 2.—**bukk.** See **buck,** v., 2.

bukra, adv. To-morrow : mostly New Zealanders' : in G.W. ; and diminishingly afterwards. Ex Arabic for ' to-morrow '.

bulchin. Lit., a bull-calf. A term of contempt or endearment to boy, youth, or man : coll., ca. 1615–1830.—2. B.E. has it for a chubby boy or lad : coll., C. 17–18. Also as *bulkin* (late C. 16–17) and, in Grose, *bull chin.*

Bulgarian atrocities. Varna and Rutschuk Railway 3% obligations : ca. 1885–1914 : Stock Exchange.

bulge. ' Bilge ', q.v. : from ca. 1922. Manchon. Cf. Austin Reed's clever advertisement, 1935, of a waistcoat that doesn't bunch up (*Talking bulge*). Prob. of jocular origin via nautical j.

bulge (on a person), get the. To obtain an advantage : U.S. (1860), partly anglicised ca. 1890 ; ob. Ware ; Manchon ; O.E.D. (Sup.). Whence :

bulge on, have (got) the. To have the advantage of : 1903, P. G. Wodehouse, *Tales of St. Austin's*, 1903.

bulger, n. and adj. (Anything) large. Coll. (— 1859) ; ob. H., 1st ed.

bulgine. An engine : nautical : mid-C. 19–20 ; ob. An old shanty has : ' Clear the track, let the bulgine run.' Bowen.

*bulk, a thief's assistant, late C. 17–mid-19, is certainly c. as is *bulk and file* (pickpocket and his jostling accomplice) : Coles, 1676.—2. *bulker*, the same and of same period, is prob. c. : but *bulker*, a low harlot, if c. in late C. 17, > low s. in mid-C. 18. Lit., one who sleeps on a *bulk* or heap.

*bulker. See preceding entry. B.E.—**bulkin.** See **bulchin.**

*bulky. A police constable : Northern c. or low : C. 19–20 ; ob. *The Edinburgh Magazine*, Aug., 1821.

bulky, adj. Rich, generous ; generously rich. Winchester College, C. 19–20. Opp. *brum*.

bull. False hair worn by women, ca. 1690–1770. B.E.—2. Abbr. *bull's-eye*, a crown piece : c. : late C. 18–19.—3. C. also (— 1860 : H., 2nd ed.) is the sense : a ration of beef ; and (3, *a*), the C. 20 one, ex U.S. : a policeman.—4. In † S.E., a ludicrous jest, a self-contradictory statement. But in C. 19–20, a ludicrous inconsistency unnoticed by its perpetrator and often producing an unintentional pun. *Irish* was not added until ca. 1850, about which time the coll. > S.E. Henry Kingsley, in one of his two best novels, *Geoffrey Hamlyn*, 1859 : ' the most outrageous of Irish bulls '. ? suggested by *cock and bull story.*—5. In the money market (opp. to *bear*), a speculator for a rise : from ca. 1840. Orig. (1714) a speculation for a rise. At first, in either sense, s. ; but by 1880, 1740 resp., coll. In C. 20, the more modern sense is S.E.—6. Coll., lower classes, from ca. 1850, ' a " bull " is a teapot with the leaves left in for a second brew ', G. R. Sims, in *How the Poor Live*, 1887.—7. At Winchester College, from ca. 1873 but now ob., cold beef, esp. at breakfast (cf. sense 3.).—8. Abbr. *John Bull* : ca. 1825–1900, coll.—9. Abbr. *bull's-eye*, the centre of the target ; hence, a hit there. From ca. 1870 ; in C. 20, coll. Military and marksmen's.—10. A broken-winded horse : low : late C. 19–20.—11. A small keg : nautical : C. 19–20.—12. Abbr. *bull-shit*, q.v.— 13. **the Bull.** Lord Allenby : military nickname : G.W. (F. & Gibbons). Ex his physique and his blunt simplicity.—14. Milk : Bootham School : C. 20. Anon., *Dict. of Bootham Slang*, 1925.

bull, v. To have intercourse with a woman (cf. the C. 17–early 19 proverb, ' who bulls the cow must keep the calf ') : low coll., C. 18–20.—2. To befool, mock : C. 16–17. To cheat : C. 17–18. Both nuances coll.—3. (Stock Exchange) v.i. and t., try to raise the price (of) : from ca. 1840 ; coll. after 1880 ; in C. 20, S.E.—4. V.i., to toil ; to struggle : Canadian, esp. lumbermen's : C. 20. John Beames. —5. See **bull the cask.**

bull-a-bull ; bullybul. *Poroporo* (a flowering shrub) : New Zealand : 1845 (Morris).

bull and cow. A ' row ', disturbance : rhyming s. (— 1859). H., 1st ed. Recorded also in that excellent modern glossary of rhyming s. : ' *Rhyming Slang* ' . . . *An authentic compilation by P.P.*, 1932.

bull at a (five-barred) gate, like a. Furiously ; impetuously ; clumsily : coll. : late C. 19–20, coll.

bull-bait. To bully ; hector. Dickens in *Great Expectations*, 1860. ? a nonce-word.

bull-beef ; occ. **bull's-beef.** Meat, esp. if beef : C. 16–20, ob. ; low coll. Adj., fierce, haughty, intolerant : C. 18, coll.

bull-beef, big as. Stout and hearty ; very big ; big and grim : coll. : late C. 17–18 ; thereafter, dial. W. Robertson, 1681 ; Motteux, 1712. Apperson. Cf. :

bull-beef, eat. To become strong ; fierce, presumptuous : late C. 16–19. Gosson, 1579.

bull-beef, like. Big and grim, esp. with *bluster* and *look*. C. 17–19 ; coll. B.E., Wolcot. See **bull-beef, big as.**

bull-beef !, sell yourself for. Often preceded by *go and*. A C. 19 coll. : run away ! ; don't be silly ! H., 3rd ed.

bull-beef, ugly as. Very ugly indeed. C. 18–19 coll. Ex *bull-beef, big as*.

bull by the tail, trust one as far as one could fling a. I.e. not at all : coll. : 1853, Reade ; ob.

bull-calf. A big hulking or clumsy fellow : mid-C. 18–early 19 ; coll. Grose, 1st ed.

bull chin. See **bulchin.**

bull-dance. A dance with men only : nautical : mid-C. 19–20 ; ob. Smyth. Cf. *bull-party*, *stag-dance*.

bull-dog. A sheriff's officer : late C. 17–early 19 : coll. Farquhar, 1698.—2. A pistol : late C. 17–19 : coll. Cf. *barker* and *buffer*. Farquhar, 1700, ' He whips out his stiletto, and I whips out my bull-dog ' ; Scott, 1825.—3. (Naval) a main-deck gun, C. 19–20 ; ob. If housed or covered, it is a *muzzled b.-d.*— 4. A sugar-loaf : early C. 19 ; low, perhaps c.— 5. A university (Oxford or Cambridge) proctor's assistant : from ca. 1810 ; coll. Lockhart, in 1823, ' Long-forgotten stories of proctors bit and bull-dogs baffled.' See also **proctor's dogs.** Cf. *buller*.—6. A member of Trinity College, Cambridge : C. 19 ; † by 1890.

Bull Dog Corps, the. The 6th Army Corps : occ. military nickname : 1915–18. F. & Gibbons. Ex the Corps sign : a bull-dog.

bull-dose or **-doze.** A severe flogging, as is *bull-dozing*, which also = violent, esp. if political, coercion. Orig. (— 1876), U.S., anglicised ca. 1881 as a coll. Ex :

bull-doze, v. To flog severely ; hence coerce by violent methods, esp. in politics. Orig. U.S., anglicised ca. 1880 as a coll. Hence *bull-dozer*, an applier of violent coercion. Lit., to give a dose strong enough for a bull ; W., however, thinks there may be some connexion with † Dutch *doesen*, to strike violently and resoundingly.

bull(-)finch. A fool ; a stupid fellow : coll., C. 17–18.—2. In hunting, a high quickset hedge that, with a ditch on one side, is too—or almost too —difficult for a horse to jump. From ca. 1830 ; by 1890, S.E. G. Lawrence in *Guy Livingstone*, ' an ugly black bull-finch '. Perhaps a perversion of *bull-fence*. Whence :

bull-finch, v.i. To leap a horse *through* such a hedge : from ca. 1840 ; coll.—2. Hence **bull-fincher**, a horseman that does, or is fond of doing, this : coll., from ca. 1850. Also, such a hedge : coll. (1862).

bull-flesh. Boastfulness ; swagger : coll. : 1820 ; † by 1890. F. & H.

bull-head. A stupid fellow : C. 17–18 ; coll. Cf. S.E. *bull-headed*, impetuously.

bull in a china shop, like a. Clumsily : coll. (— 1841), verging, in C. 20, on S.E. Marryat. Perhaps suggested by *cow in a cage*, q.v.

*bull in trouble. A bull in the pound : c. (— 1823) ; † by 1890. Egan's Grose.

bull-jine. A locomotive : nautical ; from ca. 1850 ; ob. Perhaps ex U.S. Punning *engine* : *hengine*, *hen-gine* or *-jine*. Also *bulgine*, q.v.

bull money. ' Money extorted from or given by those who in places of public resort have been detected *in flagrante delicto* with a woman, as a bribe to silence ', F. & H. ; low coll., from ca. 1870 ; ob.

bull-nurse. A male attendant on the sick : nautical : ca. 1840–1900. *The Graphic*, April 4, 1885, ' Years ago (it may be so still) it was the sailors' phrase . . .'

bull-party. A party of men only : C. 19–20 ; ob. C. 19. Cf. *bull-dance*.

bull-point. An advantage ; a (point of) superiority : coll. : C. 20. O.E.D. (Sup.) Why ?

bull-puncher. Both a variant of *cow-puncher* and an abbr. of *bullock-puncher*. Australian : from ca. 1870 ; ob. C. H. Eden, *My Wife and I in Queensland*, 1872.

bull-ring. A training-ground, at a base, notorious for severity of the drill and surly insensibility of the instructors : military : from 1915. B. & P., ' From Spanish bull-fights . . . The most notorious was at Etaples.'

bull-shit. Nonsense ; empty talk ; humbug-(ging) : mostly Australian, C. 20 ; ? ex U.S. Often abbr. to *bullsh* or *bulsh* (mostly Australian and New Zealand) and *bull* (naval : C. 20. Bowen).

bull the (or a) barrel or cask. To pour water into an empty rum cask and, after a sensible interval, to drink the intoxicating resultant : nautical (— 1824) ; ob. If the officers, to keep the wood moist, used salt water, even the ensuing *salt-water bull* was sometimes drunk. One speaks also of *bulling a teapot* ; cf. **bull**, n., 6.

*bull-tit. A horse with broken wind : c., mostly vagrants' : ca. 1830–80. Cf. *roarer*.

buller. An Oxford *bull-dog* (q.v.) : C. 20. Manchon. Oxford *-er*.

bullet. A ' small aeroplane, introduced in 1915 by Vickers ' : Air Force coll. nickname ; † by 1919. F. & Gibbons.

bullet, get and give the. To be dismissed and to dismiss, resp. *Get the b.* seems to be the earlier : from ca. 1840 and recorded in Savage's *Dict. of Printing*, 1841 ; *get the instant bullet* is to be discharged on the spot. *Shake the bullet at one* (from ca. 1850) : to threaten with dismissal. Ex the effectiveness of a bullet.

bullet has its billet, every. See **billet, every bullet has its**.

bullet-head(ed), n. and adj. Dull or foolish (person) : coll. : C. 17–18. Cf. the S.E. and the U.S. senses.

bullet with (e.g. my) name on it, there is (was, etc.) a. A military c.p. in reference to chances of death in action : 1915–18.

bulletin, false as a. Inaccurate ; false : coll. ca. 1795–1820, when, according to Carlyle, it was a proverbial saying : cf. *British Official* in the G.W.

bulley. See **bully**, n., 6.

bullfincher. See **bull-finch**, v.

bullish. (Stock Exchange) aiming at or tending to a rise in prices : from ca. 1880 ; coll. ; in C. 20, S.E. ' Bullish about cotton ', 1884 (S.O.D.). Ex *bull*, n., 5.

bullock. A cheat at marbles : schoolboys', ca. 1840–1910. *Notes and Queries*, Nov. 3, 1855.—2. A Royal Marine artilleryman : ca. 1820–90.—3. Hence, any Royal Marine : likewise naval : late C. 19–20. Bowen.—4. A bushman : Australian : ca. 1870–1900 ; very rarely, *bullock-puncher*, from ca. 1870, being much commoner : a bullock-driver.

bullock, v. To bully, intimidate : coll., from ca. 1715. M. Davies, 1716 ; Fielding ; Foote ; Grose. Since ca. 1900, dial. only.—2. See **bullock's horn**.

*bullock-and-file. A ' buttock-and-file ' (see at **buttock and tongue**) : c. : late C. 18–mid-19. Baumann. A fusion of *bulk-and-file* and *buttock-and-file*. More prob. Baumann's misreading.

bullock-puncher. A bullock-driver : Australian, from ca. 1870 ; coll. Cf. *bull-puncher*.

bullock's heart. A fart : rhyming s. (— 1890).—2. ' A single . . . order to print, of two hundred and

fifty copies only, the lowest paying number in the scale of prices . . . Not a " fat " but a " lean " job, hence the comparison to a bullock's heart, which, unless suffering from " fatty degeneration ", is the essence of leanness ', Jacobi in Barrère & Leland, 1890 : printers' : from the 1880's.

bullock's horn. To pawn : rhyming s. (—1874) ; often abbr. to *bullock*. H., 5th ed.—2. Also = in pawn, ca. 1870–1910 ; occ. abbr. to *bullocks*, which is extant.

bullock's liver. A river : rhyming s. : late C. 19–20. B. & P.

bullocky. A bullock-driver : Australian, from ca. 1888. At first s., then coll. Also, as in Boldrewood's *Colonial Reformer*, 1890, an adj. Cf. *bullock*, n., 4.

bulls. Counterfeit coin : low or perhaps c. (— 1923). Manchon. Cf. *bull*, n., 2.

bull's-eye. A crown piece : late C. 17–early 19 : c. B.E. ; Grose. Cf. *bull*, n., 2.—2. A globular sweetmeat of peppermint : from ca. 1820 ; coll. until ca. 1850, when it > S.E. Hone's *Every-Day Book*, 1825.—3. A bull's-eye lantern : (—1851) ; in C. 20, S.E.—4. (South Africa) a small dark cloud, red-hearted, frequently seen about the Cape of Good Hope and supposed to foretell a storm ; the storm so portended. Recorded, the cloud in 1753, the storm in 1849 : coll. by 1870, S.E. by 1900. O.E.D.—5. A small, thick, old-fashioned watch : C. 19. F. & H. (Smaller than a ' turnip ', q.v.)—6. See **badges** and **bull's-eyes**.

bull's-eye villas. The small open tents used by the Volunteers at their annual gathering : ca. 1870–1914.

bull's feather, give or get the. To cuckold or be cuckolded : C. 17–early 19 ; coll. Nares quotes a C. 17 song entitled *The Bull's Feather*, and Richardson uses it in *Clarissa Harlowe*. Cf. the Fr. *se planter des plumes de bœuf* and the C. 16–early 19 variant *wear the bull's feather* (as in Grose, 1st ed.).

bull's foot. See **B from a battledore**.

bull's noon. Midnight : low : 1839 ; very ob. and mainly provincial.

bull's-wool. The dry, tenuously fibrous ' inner portion of the covering of the stringy-bark tree ', Morris : Australian, esp. Tasmanian : (— 1898) : coll.—2. Hence, esp. in Tasmania, a youth with a mop of bushy hair : C. 20.

bullsh. See **bull-shit**.

bully. A protector and exploiter of prostitutes : from ca. 1690 ; coll. until ca. 1750, then S.E. B.E. ; Defoe in his *Jure Divino*, 1706, ' Mars the celestial bully they adore, | And Venus for an everlasting whore.' Ex the S.E. C. 16–17 sense of sweetheart.—2. Companion, mate : from ca. 1820 : nautical (and dial.).—3. In Eton football, a scrimmage (cf. Winchester College *hot*) : recorded in 1865, it has since ca. 1890 ranked as a coll. and it may now be considered S.E.—4. Abbr. *bully-beef* or corruption of Fr. *bouilli* : pickled or tinned beef : 1883 : coll. in C. 19, S.E. in C. 20.—5. A C. 20 South African juvenile coll. name for the bird more properly known as a yellow seed-eater (*serinus sulphuratus*). Pettman.—6. ' The lappet of a King's scholar's gown ', Ware : Westminster School : late C. 19–20. Ex its wearer, a good fellow.

bully, adj. First-rate, ' champion', splendid : Canada, Australia, and New Zealand, from ca. 1860, ex U.S. ' The roof fell in, there was a " bully " blaze ', Meade's *New Zealand*, 1870. Ex the late C. 17–18 S.E. *bully*, worthy, admirable, applied only to persons.

bully about the muzzle. 'Too thick and large in the mouth', Ware : dog-fanciers' : 1883, Miss Braddon.

bully-back. A brothel's bully and chucker-out ; a bully supporting another person : C. 18–early 19. Amherst, 1726, ' old lecherous bully-backs ', and Grose, who describes some of this scoundrel's wiles and duties. Occ. *bully-buck*. Also as v.

bully-beef. (Cf. *bully*, n., fourth sense.) In the Navy, boiled salt beef ; in the Army, tinned beef. *Bully* may be the earlier form, *bully-beef* an elaboration after *bull-beef*. From ca. 1884. Coll. till ca. 1900, then S.E.

bully-beggar. A sol. form of *bull-beggar*, which may itself be a corruption of *bugbear*. C. 18–early 19.

bullybul. See **bull-a-bull.**

*****bully-cock.** One who foments quarrels in order to rob the quarrellers : c. or low s. : late C. 18–early 19. Grose, 1st ed.—2. A low, round, broad-brimmed hat : see **billy-cock.**

bully fake. A piece of luck : low London : ca. 1882–1915. Ware. Ex *bully*, adj. (q.v.) + *fake*, an action.

bully fop. A brainless, silly, talkative fellow, apt to hector : ca. 1680–1800. B.E. describes as c., but I very much doubt it.

bully for you !, capital !, reached England ca. 1870 after having, in 1864–6, enjoyed a phenomenal vogue in the U.S. It has seldom been heard since the G.W.

bully huff-cap. A boasting bully, a hector : coll. : C. 18. More gen. : *bully-huff*, late C. 17–18, as in Cotton and B.E.

bully-rag, occ. **bally-rag.** To intimidate ; revile ; scold vehemently : from late 1750's, Thomas Warton employing it in his *Oxford Newsman's Verses*, 1760. Coll. (and dial.), as is the derivative vbl.n., *bully-*, occ. *bally-*, *ragging*, recorded first in 1863 but doubtless used a century earlier. Etymology obscure : perhaps, semantically, to ' make a bully's rag of ' (a person).

bully-rock or -rook. A boon companion : late C. 16–early 18 : coll., as in Shakespeare.—2. Ca. 1650–1720, c., then low s. for a hired ruffian or ' a boisterous, hectoring fellow ', Martin's Dict., 1754. The *rock* form is not recorded before 1653 and may be in error for *rook*. B.E. has *-rock*, but B.E. contains a few misprints—some of which have been solemnly reproduced by other writers.

bully ruffian. A highwayman that, in attacking, uses many oaths and imprecations : late C. 17–18. B.E., Grose.

bully the troops !, don't. A military c.p. ' rebuke to anyone talking too loudly or too much ' : from ca. 1910. F. & Gibbons.

bully-trap. A mild-looking man the match of any ruffian : mid-C. 18–early 19. Grose, 1st ed.—2. In late C. 17–early 18 c., a sharper, a cheat. B.E.

bully up. To hurry, gen. in imperative : Uppingham School : mid-C. 19–20 ; ob.

bulrush, seek or **find a knot in a.** To look for—or find—difficulties where there are none : late C. 16–18 ; coll. till ca. 1700, then S.E.

bulsh. See **bull-shit.**

bum. The posteriors : dating from M.E. ; not abbr. *bottom*, which, in this sense, dates only from C. 18 ; prob. echoic : cf. It. *bum*, the sound of an explosion. Shakespeare, Jonson, Swift. This good English word began to lose caste ca. 1790, and ca. 1840 it > a vulg. and has been eschewed.—2. Abbr.

bum-bailiff : ca. 1660–1880 (but extant in Anglo-Irish for a sheriff's assistant) : coll. Butler, 1663, ' Sergeant Bum ' ; Ned Ward, in *The London Spy*, ' The Vermin of the Law, the Bum.'—3. A child's, and a childish word, for a drink, drink ! : coll., C. 16–17.—4. A birching : public schools' : C. 19 ; cf. the C. 17–18 v., to strike, thump.—5. A beggar ; a cadger : C. 20 ; ex U.S. See **hobo** ; cf. v., 3.—6. See **bum ball.**

bum, v. To arrest : late C. 17–18. Ex *bum*, n., 2.—2. To serve with a county-court summons. C. 19–20 ; ob.—3. To beg (v.t. and i.), esp. as a tramp : low coll. : C. 20 ; ex U.S.—4. To boast : low (esp. in Glasgow) : C. 20. Cf. *bum the chat*, lit. to boast about the thing.

bum, adj. Inferior, bad ; reprehensible ; dishonest : from ca. 1917 : s. >, by 1930, coll. ; orig. (1880's), U.S. Ex *bum*, n., 5.

bum. A coll. contraction of *by my* : ca. 1570–90. Edwards, 1571, ' Bum broth, but few such roisters come to my years.' O.E.D.

bum, on the. A-begging : C. 20. Ex U.S. See **bum,** n., 5.

bum, toe—occ. **hoof**—**one's.** To kick one's behind ; ' chuck out '. Low coll. : from ca. 1870.

bum-bags. Trousers : low ; from ca. 1855. See **bags,** n., 1. Prob. ex Warwickshire dial. (1840 : E.D.D.).

bum-bailiff or baily. ' A bailiff of the meanest kind ', Johnson. Recorded in 1601 (Shakespeare), it was coll. in C. 17, S.E. in C. 18–19 ; in C. 20, archaic. Blackstone considered it a corruption of *bound bailiff*, but prob. the term comes ex the constant and touching proximity of bailiff to victim.

bum ball (1870) ; less gen. **bum** (1867). A cricketers' catachresis for a *bump(-)ball*. Lewis.

bum-bass. A violoncello : low coll. : late C. 18–19. Samuel Pegge in *Anonymiana*, 1809.

bum-baste. To beat hard on the posteriors : mid-C. 16–17. In C. 18–19 coll., to beat, thrash From ca. 1860, dial. only. Cf. *baste*, q.v.

bum-beating, vbl.n. Jostling : C. 17 ; coll. Beaumont & Fletcher in *Wit without Malice.*

bum-boat. A scavenger's boat : C. 17–early 18 : coll.—2. A boat carrying provisions or merchandise to ships lying in port or at some distance from the shore : s. (— 1769) > coll. >, by 1880, S.E.

bum boozer. A desperate drinker : theatrical (— 1909) ; ob. Ware.

bum-boy. A catamite : low coll. : late (? mid-) C. 19–20.

bum-brusher. A schoolmaster ; an usher. From ca. 1700. Tom Brown, 1704 ; *The New London Magazine*, 1788, '. . . that great nursery of bum-brushers, Appleby School ' ; *Blackwood's Magazine*, Oct., 1832. Cf. *flay-bottom.*

*****bum card.** A marked playing-card : ca. 1570–1620 : gaming c., revived in C. 20. Northbrook, *Treatise against Dicing*, 1577 ; Rowlands, 1608.

*****bum-charter.** Prison bread steeped in hot water : c. of ca. 1810–50. Vaux, 1812.

bum clink. Inferior beer : Midland Counties s., from ca. 1830 ; ob. (*Clink*, a ringing sound.) Cf. *clink*.

Bum Court. The Ecclesiastical Court : a low nickname : ca. 1540–90. O.E.D. Perhaps ex the members' long sessions on their backsides (see **bum,** n., 1.)

bum-creeper. ' One who walks bent almost double ', F. & H. revised : low : late C. 19–20.

bum-curtain. (Cambridge University) a very short gown : 1835 ; †. Esp., until 1835, the Caius College gown ; after that date, esp. the St. John's gown. See Charles Whibley's delightful *Three Centuries of Cambridge Wit*, 1889.

bum-feag(u)e, -feagle, -feg. To thrash, esp. on the posteriors : jocular coll. : late C. 16–early 17.

bum-fiddle. The posteriors : late C. 17–early 19, low. Cotton, Grose, Southey. For the pun, cf. *ars musica*. Fletcher, 1620, has ' bum-fiddled with a bastard ', i.e. saddled with one : but *bum-fiddle*, v., is also used to mean : use as toilet paper : and dates from ca. 1550. The derivative *bum-fiddler*, ? a fornicator, is C. 17 and rare. O.E.D.

bum-fidget. A restless person : C. 18–19, low coll.

bum-fighter ; -fighting. A whoremonger ; coïtion : low coll. : C. 18. D'Urfey, 1719.

bum-fodder. Trashy literature : from ca. 1720 ; S.E. till ca. 1800, then coll. ; † by 1890. *The Scots' Magazine*, April, 1753.—2. Toilet paper : from ca. 1659 ; recorded by B.E. and Grose. Often, in C. 19–20, abbr. to *bumf*, q.v.

bum-freezer. An Eton jacket : C. 19–20, low. Cf. *bum-perisher*, q.v.

bum-jerker. A schoolmaster : low : C. 19–20 ; very ob. Malkin, 1809.

bum one's load. To lounge in the canteen while one waits for a comrade to come and pay for one's drink : military (– 1923). Manchon.

bum-perisher and -shaver. A short-tailed coat ; a jacket. Cf. *bare-bum, bum-curtain*.

bum-roll. The C. 17 coll. equivalent of a bustle or dress-improver. Jonson in the *Poetaster*. Cf. *bird-cage* and *cork rump*.

bum-shop. A brothel ; the *pudendum muliebre* : low : mid-C. 19–20 ; ob.

bum-suck ; often **bumsuck.** V.i., to toady : coll. : late C. 19–20. Ernest Raymond, *The Jesting Army*, 1930.

bum-sucker. A toady, lick-spittle ; a sponger, hanger-on. C. 19–20, low coll.

bum the chat. See **bomb the chat** and **bum,** v., 4.

bum-trap. A bailiff : mid-C. 18–early 19. Fielding in *Tom Jones*. Perhaps the origin of *traps*, police. Ex *bum*, n., 2, q.v.

bum up. To compliment (a person) : military : from ca. 1925.

bumble ; bumbler. A blunderer ; an idler : resp. late C. 18–mid-19, mid-C. 19–20.—2. (Only *bumble*.) Hence, a beadle : first in Dickens's *Oliver Twist*, as a person's name, and then, 1856, any beadle : coll., soon S.E., as was *bumbledom*, stupid and pompous officiousness, 1856 +.

bumble. To fornicate : Restoration period. E.g. in Dryden's *The Kind Keeper*. Cf. *bum-shop*.

bumble and buck. The game of crown and anchor : military : 1915 ; ob. B. & P. (For an excellent and very interesting account of this game, see Stephen Graham, *A Private in the Guards*, 1919.)

bumble-crew. Corporations, vestries, and other official bodies : from ca. 1860 ; coll.

bumble-jar. A harmonium : naval : C. 20. Bowen. Cf. *hum-box*, q.v.

bumble-puppy. Family, i.e. inexpert, whist (– 1884) : coll. ; ob.—2. Also, ca. 1800–80, a public-house version of the ancient game of troule-in-madame : coll. H.

bumbles. Horses' blinkers : Northern coll., C. 19–20.

bumbo ; occ. **bombo.** The female pudend : mid-C. 18–19, West Indian ; orig. a negroes' word. Grose, 1st ed.—2. A drink composed of rum, sugar, water, and nutmeg (Smollett, 1748 : earliest record), or of brandy, water, and sugar. (Grose.) A Northern variation was made with gin. † by 1920 ; coll. passing to S.E. Cf. It. *bombo*, a child's word for a drink (S.O.D.), but prob. ex *bum*, childish for drink, after *rumbo*, q.v. (W.) N.B. : in America, it was occ. called *mimbo* and was there made of rum, hot water, and sugar (see W. E. Woodward, *Washington*, 1928) ; the same drink is served to-day as *grog américain* in certain cafés in Paris.

bumf. A schoolboys' and soldiers' abbr. of *bum-fodder*, toilet paper : mid-C. 19–20. Hence, from ca. 1870, paper : hence, the Wellington College *bumf-hunt*, a paper-chase. In G.W. +, chiefly among officers : ' orders, instructions, memoranda, etc., especially if of a routine nature, e.g. " snowed under with bumf from the Division " ', B. & P.

bumf, v.i. and t. To crib by copying another's work : Charterhouse : late C. 19–20. Ex *bumf*, paper.—2. Hence, v.i., to listen to or butt in on the conversation of others : Charterhouse : C. 20.

bumfer. A boy given to cribbing from another's work : Charterhouse : late C. 19–20. Ex *bumf*, v., 1.

bumkin. 'A burlesque term for the posteriors.' C. 17. Nares, well-read lexicographer. Lit., a little bum : see **bum,** n., 1.

bummaree. A Billingsgate fishmarket middle-man (– 1786) : coll. till ca. 1800, when it > S.E. Etymology obscure ; perhaps ex S.E. *bottomry* (1622) : cf. Fr. *bomerie*, bottomry. Cf. the v.—2. A *bain-marie* : cooks' (– 1909). Ware. Cf. *bang-Mary*, q.v.

bummaree, v.i. and t. To retail fish on a large scale : mid-C. 19–20, coll. >, by 1900, S.E. Hence, vbl.n., *bummareeing (it)*, such retailing : G. A. Sala, 1859. Ex preceding.—2. ' To run up a score at a newly opened public-house ' : ca. 1820–80. (E.D.D.)

bummer. A bum-bailiff : ca. 1670–1810.—2. A severe pecuniary loss : racing : ca. 1870–1914.—3. A beggar, a sponger, a loafer : orig. (1856), U.S. ; anglicised ca. 1870. ? ex Ger. *bummler*, an idler ; a tramp ; esp. in C. 20, a beggar tramp.—4. A bombardier : military : C. 20 ; ob. F. & Gibbons. —5. An officer's batman : military : from 1916. Ibid.

bumming. A thrashing : schools, esp. Wellington College, C. 19–20 ; ob.—2. Vbl.n., loafing, sponging : from ca. 1895, orig. U.S.

bumming the chat. A variant of *bombing the chat* (see **bomb . . .**). F. & Gibbons.

bummy. (Cf. *bummer*.) A corruption of *bum-bailiff*, q.v. : C. 18–19.

bump. A human faculty : coll. : from ca. 1820. Ex *bump*, a cranial prominence as in phrenology : (1815) likewise coll., though in C. 20 almost S.E.

bump, v. To touch an opposing boat and thus win the race : Oxford and Cambridge. The intransitive is *make a bump*. From 1826. At first coll., but by 1870 both forms were S.E. The vbl.n., *bumping* (Thackeray, 1849) soon > S.E. ; cf. *bumping race*, S.E., †.—2. A c. variant (from ca. 1915) of U.S. *bump off*, to murder (1910 : O.E.D. Sup.). Wallace.—3. To meet ; to accost aggressively : low Australian (– 1916). C. J. Dennis.—4. To shell (v.i. and t.) : military : 1915 ; ob. F. & Gibbons. Ex the noise and the impact.

bump, feel (a person's). To know what he is thinking : coll. (– 1923). Manchon.

bump !, give your head a. Pull yourself together !; look lively ! : military : C. 20. F. & Gibbons.

bump off. To kill, destroy, criminally : an Americanism anglicised by 1933. See, e.g. David Esdaile's article in *The Daily Mirror*, Nov. 18 of that year.

bump-supper. A supper to celebrate a college boat's success in Sloggers or Toggers, Mays or Eights : Cambridge, Oxford. From ca. 1860 ; coll. until C. 20, then S.E.

bumper. A full glass : from ca. 1660 : in C. 18, coll. ; thereafter S.E.—2. A crowded house : theatrical (1839, Dickens).—3. Anything very large : coll. : from ca. 1859. Cf. *corker, thumper, whacker, whopper*. (O.E.D.)—4. A bumping race : Oxford and Cambridge Universities' : 1910. O.E.D. (Sup.). Perhaps ex :

Bumpers, the. The Bumping Races at : Shrewsbury School : late C. 19–20. Desmond Coke, *The Bending of a Twig*, 1906. On *Sloggers* and *Toggers*, qq.v.

bumping. Large : coll. : from ca. 1860 ; somewhat ob. Cf. *bumper*, 3.

bumping on the bottom. (Of market prices) that have reached their lowest level : Stock Exchange (— 1935). Ex boating.

bum(p)kin. See **bumkin.**

bumpology, bumposopher. The 'science' of cranial 'bumps' ; one learned therein : jocular coll. : 1834, 1836. O.E.D.

bumps !, now she ; what ho, she bumps ! Excellent ! ; splendid ! : coll. : resp. ca. 1895–1910, from ca. 1905. The former in F. & H. revised. Prob. ex boating.

bumpsie, -sy. Drunk : coll. : C. 17. *Tarleton's Jests*, 1611 (Halliwell). 'Apt to bump into people' is a possible suggestion as to origin.

bum's rush, get or give the. To be kicked out, or to kick out : low : C. 20. E.g. in John G. Brandon, *The One-Minute Murder*, 1934.

bumptious. Self-assertive : coll. ; from ca. 1800. Mme. D'Arblay, Dickens. Other senses, S.E. : the same applies to *bumptiousness* (Hughes, 1857) and *bumptiously* (M. Collins, 1871). Prob. ex *bump*, a sudden collision or a dull heavy blow, on some such word as *fractious*. (O.E.D.)

Bums, Cherry. (Military) the 11th Hussars. C. 19–early 20. Ex their cerise trousers ; but cf. *cherubim*.

bumsuck. See **bum-suck.**

bun. A familiar coll. for the squirrel : from late C. 16.—Perhaps hence, 2, a coll. endearment : C. 17–19. Cf. *bunny*, 3,—3. In C. 17–19, the *pudendum muliebre* (cf. Grose, 2nd ed., 'To touch bun for luck ; a practice observed among sailors going on a cruize '), ex the Scottish and Northern dial. sense the tail of a hare, hence, in Scottish, the 'tail' of a person.—4. A familiar name for a rabbit : coll. : late C. 18–20. Grose, 3rd ed. (Not merely dial. as the O.E.D. implies.) Abbr. *bunny*.—5. A harlot : Glasgow (— 1934). Prob. ex sense 3.

bun or cake, take the. To obtain first honours ; 'beat the band'. While *cake* is orig. U.S. ; anglicised ca. 1885, *take the bun* is an English derivative : from the early 1890's. Also *take the biscuit*, hence *take the Huntley and Palmer*. In Australia, ca. 1895–1905, *capture the pickled biscuit*.

bun-feast or -fight. A tea-party : late C. 19–20 coll. Cf. *crumpet-scramble, muffin-worry.*

bun-house, over the. On public assistance : dockers' : from ca. 1930. *The Daily Herald*, late July or early Aug., 1936. As if getting food from the bakery.

bun for luck, touch. The C. 18–19 (? †) nautical practice of effecting an intimate caress (*bun*, 3) before going on a (long) voyage.

bun-puncher or -strangler. A teetotaller : military : late C. 19–20 ; ob. Resp. Frank Richards and F. & Gibbons. Ex preference of buns to beer.

bun-struggle or -worry. A tea-party for sailors or soldiers : military and naval : from ca. 1870. In C. 20, the *struggle* form is ob. Cf. *tea-fight*.

bun-wallah. A variant of *bun-puncher*. F. & Gibbons. Cf. *char-wallah.*

bunce (the predominant C. 19–20 spelling), **bunse**, **bunt(s).** Money : C. 18–early 19. D'Urfey spells it *buns*. In mid-C. 19–20 it = (costermongers') perquisites ; profit ; commission ; Mayhew spells it *bunse* and *bunts*. In C. 20, almost coll. and still = profit, but more esp. and gen. an unexpected profit or commission or receipt of money. Mayhew pertinently proposes derivation ex sham L. *bonus*, q.v.—2. At Edinburgh High School (— 1879), he who, when another finds anything, cries *bunce* ! has a traditional, though ob., claim to the half of it : whence *stick up for your bunce* = claim one's share, stand up for oneself.

buncer. A seller on commission : from ca. 1860. † by 1930.

bunch. A group or gang of persons : from ca. 1905 : s. >, by 1936, coll. (C.O.D., 1934 Sup.)

bunch. To abandon (esp. a job) : Canadian : from ca. 1910. Perhaps orig. of a group of men leaving in a bunch : cf., however, Warwickshire dial. *bunch*, v.i., to hurry away (E.D.D.).

bunch, best of the. The best of them all, 'the lot' : C. 20 ; coll.

bunch of fives. The hand ; fist : pugilistic (— 1823). Egan's Grose ; Lytton, 1847 ; Charles Reade ; *Punch*, 1882, 'his dexter bunch of fives'. Cf. *fives*.

bunch of snarls. See **snarls.**

bunco. See **bunko.—buncombe.** See **bunkum.**

bund. A dam ; a dyke : Anglo-Indian coll. ; from ca. 1810.—2. An embanked (sea-shore) quay : Anglo-Chinese (— 1875). Ex Persian.

bundabust. Preparations ; preliminary arrangements : Regular Army : late C. 19–20. F. & Gibbons. Ex Hindustani *band-o-bast*, a tying, a binding.

bunder-boat. A boat used either for communicating with ships at anchor or for purely coastal trade : on the Bombay and Madras coast. Anglo-Indian coll. (— 1825). Ex Hindi *bandar*, a harbour, ex Persian. As for *bund*, see Yule & Burnell.

bundle. A considerable sum of money : racing coll. : C. 20. Cf. *packet*. O.E.D. (Sup.).—2 A wife : naval. See **bundle-man.**—3. A fight : workmen's (— 1935) and criminals (— 1936).

[**bundle**, v., and **bundling**, vbl.n., in reference to the semi-sexual sleeping custom, long †, of Wales and New England, first recorded in 1781, are, despite H. and F. & H., clearly S.E.]

bundle, drop one's or **the.** To surrender ; abandon hope ; become frightened : Australian (— 1914). C. J. Dennis. Prob. abbr. *drop one's bundle and run.*

bundle-man. A married seaman : lower-deck : nautical : from ca. 1890. Frazer & Gibbons. ' Apparently suggested by the small bundle tied up with a blue handkerchief which married seamen in a Home Port usually take ashore with them when going on leave.'

bundle of ten. Army blankets, because rolled in tens : military : late C. 19–20. F. & Gibbons.—2. A packet of ten cigarettes : id. : C. 20. Ibid. Cf. *blankets*, q.v.—3. The tens in a pack of cards : id. : id. Ibid.

bundle off. To send away hurriedly : from ca. 1820 ; coll. ; from 1880, S.E.

bundle-tail. A short lass either fat or squat : late C. 17–18. B.E.

bundook ; occ. **bandook** or **barndook** ; even, says Manchon, **bundoop.** A rifle ; earlier, a musket ; earlier still, cross-bow. Ultimately ex the Arabic *banadik*, Venice, where cross-bows were made. (Native Egyptians still call Venice *Bundookia*.) The Regular Army stationed in India used the term as early as C. 18, and in the G.W. it > fairly common. In the Navy, a big gun (C. 20. Bowen). Yule & Burnell ; B. & P. Whence :

bundook and spike. A Regular Army term, from ca. 1850, for rifle and bayonet. See the preceding entry.

bung. A brewer ; a landlord of a ' pub ', esp. in sporting circles ; (nautical) a master's assistant superintending the serving of grog. From ca. 1850 ; all senses ob. Hence, *bung-ball*, the annual dance held by the brewers : London trade (— 1909). Ware.—2. In c. of mid-C. 16–early 19, a purse. Harman, Greene, Grose. Cf. A.-S. and Frisian *pung*, a purse (O.E.D.).—3. Hence, in c. or low s. of late C. 16–17, e.g. in Shakespeare, a cutpurse. Hence *bung-knife*, late C. 16, is either a knife for purse-slitting or one kept in a purse.—4. (Also *bung-hole*.) The anus : low : late C. 18–20.—5. Only in *tell a bung*, to tell a lie : schoolboys' (— 1887) ; ob. Baumann. Perhaps the corruption of a noted liar's surname.—6. Cheese : military : C. 20 : military. Ex its costiveness. Also *bung-hole* and *bungy*. F. & Gibbons.

bung, v. Gen. as *bung up*, to close up the eyes with a blow : C. 19–20 coll., esp. among boxers. But in C. 16–early 18, S.E., and applicable to mouth, ears, etc., and fig.—2. Often as *bung over*, to pass, hand (over), give ; (not before C. 20) to send (a person, e.g. into the Navy ; or a thing, e.g. a letter to the post) : coll. Shakespeare, Beaumont & Fletcher.—3. To throw forcibly : dial. (— 1825) >, ca. 1890, s. Echoic : O.E.D. (Sup.).—4. To deceive with a lie : C. 19. Cf. *cram*, *stuff*.

bung, adj. Drunk ; fuddled : a Scottish low coll. : C. 18–20 ; ob. Ramsay. ? ' bung-full '.

bung, adv. Heavily ; ' smack ' : coll. : late C. 19–20. Esp. (*go*, etc.) *bung into*. Kipling.—2. Precisely, absolutely : coll : C. 20. Manchon, ' He's bung in the fairway.'

bung, go. To explode, go to smash : from ca. 1860 ; ob.—2. Hence, mainly in Australia, slightly in New Zealand, to fail, esp. to go bankrupt : from ca. 1880 : prob. influenced by *go bong* or *bung*, to die, a ' pidgin ' phrase (— 1881) ex East Australian aborigine adj. *bong*, *bung*, dead : cf. *Humpy*(·)*Bong*, lit. the dead houses, a suburb of Brisbane. Morris.

bung-ball. See bung, n., 1.

bung-eyed. Drunk ; fuddled : low : mid-C. 19–20, ob. Mayhew. Ex Scottish *bung*, tipsy.—2. Hence, cross-eyed : low : from ca. 1860 ; slightly ob.

bung-ho ! Au revoir ! ; occ., good-bye ! : from ca. 1925. (D. Sayers, 1933, ' Cheerio, Mary dear.

Bung-ho, Peter.') Perhaps on *cheer-ho*.—2. Also as an upper-class toast : 1928, D. Sayers, *The Unpleasantness at the Bellona Club*. Perhaps with a reference to the bung of liquored casks.

bung in it, put a. See put a bung in it.—**bunghole.** See bung, n., 4 and 6.

*bung-juice. Beer ; porter. C. 19–20 (ob.) c. Ex *bung*, a stopper for casks.

*bung-nipper. A cutpurse. In mid-C. 17–18, c. ; in C. 19 low s. Ex *bung*, n., 2.

bung off. To depart : from ca. 1905. John G. Brandon, 1931, ' He . . . bunged off, respected by everyone.' Cf. *pop off*.

bung one's eye. To drink heartily : mid-C. 18–early 19. Hence, to drink a dram : late C. 18–early 19. Grose, 2nd ed. I.e. till one's eyes close.

bung-starter. Nautical : (*a*) the captain of the hold ; (*b*) an apprentice serving in the hold. Both (— 1867) are ob.

bung up and bilge free. Everything aboard in excellent order : nautical : late C. 19–20. Bowen. Ex proper storing of barrels.

bung upwards, adv. On his face ; prone : late C. 18–19 (orig. brewers'). Grose, 2nd ed. Suggested by *arse upwards*, q.v., or by *bung-hole*, the anus.

bunga, bungy. Punga (the stem of the black fern) : New Zealand coll. : mid-C. 19–20. Morris.

bungaloid, adj. Infested with bungalows ; esp. in *bungaloid growth* after *fungoid growth*. Coll. quickly promoted to S.E. ; from ca. 1926.

bungalow, top of the bleeding. See top of the house.

bungaree or **-rie.** A public-house : low : ca. 1870–1920. Ware. Ex *bung*, n., 1.

Bungay !, go to. Go to hell ! C. 19 ; mostly dial. Bungay is a township in East Suffolk ; it has vestiges of a castle built by that aristocratic family, the *Bigods*.

Bungay fair and broke(n) both his legs, he's been to. He's drunk ; he got drunk : C. 19 coll. Cf. preceding entry and *breaky-leg*.

bungery. A tavern : mostly London (— 1909) ; ob. Ware. Cf. *bung*, n., 1. Also *bungaree*, q.v.

bungie ; **bungy.** A typist's eraser : typists' (— 1935). Cf. dial. *bungy*, anything short and thick.

bungie-bird. Pejorative for a friar : late C. 16–early 17. Cf. Greene's Friar Bacon and Friar Bungay. (O.E.D.)

bungler. ' An unperforming Husband ', B.E. : C. 17–18 ; coll.

bungole. A frequent New Zealand military corruption of *bung-hole* : in G.W.

bungs. A ship's cooper : mid-C. 19–20 nautical. Bowen. Also *Jimmy Bungs*.

bungy. See bung, n., 6, **bunga** and **bungie.**

bungy man. A physical-training instructor ; naval : C. 20. Bowen. Ex *india-rubber man*.

buniony. Lumpy in outline : art : 1880 ; ob. Ware. Ex ' a bunion breaking up the " drawing " of a foot '.

bunjie or **-jee.** An officer instructor of physical training : naval : C. 20. F. & Gibbons.

bunk. Nonsense : abbr. *bunkum*, q.v. C. 20, ex U.S.—2. The sisters' sitting-room at the end-entrance to a hospital ward : nurses' : late C. 19–20.

bunk, v. To decamp : from early 1890's : orig. low ; in C. 20, near-coll. *The Referee*, Feb. 16, 1885.—2. Hence, to absent *oneself from* : from ca. 1890. R. H. Mottram, 1934, ' I'll bunk my class and take you for a walk.'—3. At Wellington College : to expel ; ca. 1870–1915.—4. **bunk (it),** to sleep in a bunk : coll. Orig. and mainly U.S. : anglicised ca. 1886.

bunk, do a. To depart hastily : from ca. 1865. Cf. *bunk,* v., 1.

bunk, do a. See also **do a bunk.**

Bunk, the. Head Office : busmen's, esp. in London : from ca. 1930. *The Daily Herald,* Aug. 5, 1936. A comfortable billet.

bunk in with. To ' share a bivvy or a funk-hole ' with (another soldier) : Canadian military coll. : from 1914. B. & P. Ex *bunk,* v., 4.

bunked, be or get. To be expelled : Shrewsbury School : late C. 19–20. Desmond Coke,'*The Bending of a Twig,* 1906. Ex *bunk,* to depart. Cf. *bunk,* v., 3.

bunker. Beer : ca. 1850–1910. H., 3rd ed. ? ex *bona aqua* or ex *coal-bunker,* from which one ' coals up '.—2. A feast in a low lodging-house : low (— 1887). Baumann. Perhaps ex sense 1.

bunker-cat. A low-class fireman : Canadian nautical : late C. 19–20. Bowen.

bunker-plate with spanner. A tin of sardines with patent opener : naval : C. 20. F. & Gibbons.

bunkered, be. To be in a situation difficult of escape : coll. : 1890 (O.E.D. Sup.) Ex golf. Cf. *stymied.*

Bunkey Boo. General Sir J. M. S. Bunker : military : C. 20. F. & Gibbons. Anecdotal.

bunko. (Of persons) shifty ; disreputable : seaports' (esp. Liverpool), from ca. 1905, ex U.S. Cf. :

bunko-steerer. A swindler, esp. at cards : orig. (— 1876), U.S. ; anglicised ca. 1895, but never at all gen. Ex *bunko,* occ. *bunco,* a swindling card-game or lottery.

bunkum or buncombe. In England from ca. 1856 ; ex U.S. (— 1827). In C. 19, coll. ; in C. 20, S.E. and rarely spelt *buncombe.* Talk, empty or ' tall ' ; humbug ; claptrap ; insincere eloquence. G. A. Sala, 1859 : ' . . . " bunkum " (an Americanism I feel constrained to use, as signifying nothingness, ineffably inept and irremediably fire-perforated windbaggery, and sublimated cucumber sunbeams . . .) '. Ex *Buncombe* County, North Carolina. See esp. Thornton, O.E.D., S.O.D.

bunky. Awkward ; badly finished : Christ's Hospital, C. 19–20 ; ob.

bunnick (up). To settle ; dispose of ; thrash : Cockney : ca. 1880–1914. *Punch,* July 17, 1886, ' We've bunnicked up Gladsting ' (Gladstone) ; Baumann. Perhaps cognate with *bunker* (in *bunkered,* q.v.).

bunny. A rabbit : in C. 17 s., then coll. The S.O.D. records at 1606 ; B.E. has it.—2. In C. 20, an occ. variant of *rabbit,* a very poor player of any given game.—3. Also, C. 19–20, a nickname, as for H. W. Austin, England's most classical lawn tennis player since the Dohertys.—4. The female pudend : C. 18–20. D'Urfey, 1719. Diminutive of *bun,* 3, q.v.

bunny-grub. Green vegetables : Cheltenham College : mid-C. 19–20. Cf. *grass* and :

bunny's meat. The same : nautical : late C. 19–20. Bowen.

buns, bunse. See **bunce.**

bunt. An apron : late C. 18–early 19. Grose, 2nd ed. Ex the S.E. *bunt,* the bag- or pouch-shaped part of a net or a sail.—2. See **bunce.** Ca. 1850–1900. Mayhew.

bunt, v. Knock ; butt ; ' to run against or jostle ', Grose, 2nd ed. Except when used of

animals, this (— 1788) is coll. and dial. Perhaps ex *butt* + *bounce* (or *bunch*), as the O.E.D. suggests.

bunt fair. Before the wind : nautical coll. : late C. 19–20. Bowen.

bunter. A low, esp. a low thieving, harlot : from ca. 1700. Ned Ward, 1707, ' Punks, Strolers, Market Dames, and Bunters ' ; Goldsmith, 1765. In this sense until ca. 1900. Perhaps ex *bunt* ; i.e. a sifter of men, not of meal.—2. Derivatively, ca. 1730–1900, any low woman. Attributively in Walpole's *Parish Register,* 1759, ' Here Fielding met his bunter Muse.'—3. (Semantically, cf. sense 1.) A gatherer of rags, bones, etc. : from ca. 1745. Dyche's Dict., 1748 ; Mayhew.—4. A woman that, after a brief sojourn, departs from her lodgings without paying : ca. 1830–1900. Mayhew. Too early to be ex *bunk,* to depart ; cf. senses 1 and 3.

bunting. A coll. endearment, esp. as *baby bunting* : from ca. 1660. Perhaps ex Scottish *buntin.*

bunting time. Late C. 17–mid-18, coll. : ' when the Grass is high enough to hide the young Men and Maids ', B.E. Cf. *bunt,* v., q.v.

bunting-tosser ; occ. **bunts** or **buntin(g).** A signaller : naval (1905) ; ob. (O.E.D. Sup.) Ware, ' Signals are small flags made of bunting.'

***buntling.** (Gen. pl.) A petticoat : late C. 17–early 19 c. B.E. Ex *bunt,* n., q.v.

bunts. See **bunce** and **bunting-tosser.**

buntuck. A New Zealand soldiers' variant of *bundook* (q.v.) : in G.W.

Bunty. The inevitable nickname of any short man : military : late C. 19–20. F. & Gibbons. Ex dial. (and U.S.) *bunty,* short and stout.

buoy, round the. (To have) two helpings from a dish : nautical : C. 20.

bup. See :

bupper. Bread and butter : children's, whence lower classes' : C. 19–20. By ' infantile reduction ', says Ware, who notes the occ. abbr. *bup.*

Bups ; B.P. (General) Baden-Powell : 1900 (Ware).

Burberry or -bury. Burbure in France : military in G.W. (F. & Gibbons.)

burble. To talk continuously with little pertinence or sense : C. 20. Cf. the C. 16–17 S.E. *burble,* to make a bubbling sound.

***Burdon's Hotel.** Whitecross Street Prison : o. ca. 1850–1910. Ex a Governor named Burdon.

burerk. See **burick.**

***Burford bait.** See **take a Burford bait.**

burg. A town ; a city : coll., U.S. partly anglicised (thanks to the ' talkies ') by 1932. C.O.D., 1934 Sup. Ex Ger.

Burglar. (Gen. pl.) A Bulgarian : military : in G.W. (F. & Gibbons.)

burgoo, burgue. Oatmeal porridge : from ca. 1740 ; in C. 19, coll. ; in G.W., military s. Marryat, Sala. In G.W., the Tommy preferred the latter pronunciation, the Australians the former : the ' Aussies ', moreover—prob. on a rhyming-s. basis— occ. used it loosely for stew (*stoo*). Ex *burghul,* Turkish for wheat porridge. Whence :

burgoo-eater. A Scottish seaman : nautical : late C. 19–20. Bowen.

***burick,** occ. **burerk.** At first (— 1812), a prostitute, a low woman : c. Vaux. From ca. 1850, a lady, esp. if showily dressed : low. Mayhew, 1851. From ca. 1890 the word has increasingly meant, chiefly among Cockneys, a wife, ' old woman '. The etymology is obscure ; but *burick* may perhaps be found to derive•ex the Romany *burk*, a breast, pl. *burkaari*, or to be a corruption of Scots *bure*, a loose woman, recorded by E.D.D. for 1807.

burke. To dye one's moustaches : military, ca. 1870–80. Dyed for uniformity, the semantic key being *burke*, to smother, as did the celebrated criminal executed in 1829. (*Burke*, to hush up, from ca. 1840, was at first a coll. development from its natural meaning, to strangle or suffocate, which arose in 1829.)

*****burn**, in c., = to cheat, swindle : C. 17–18. (Extant in dial.) Cf. *burn the ken*, q.v.

burn, one's ears. To feel that somebody is speaking of one : coll. ; from ca. 1750, but in other forms from C. 14 (e.g. Chaucer).

burn (a hole) in one's pocket. Of money and gen. preceded by *money* : to be eager to spend one's money, a definite sum often being mentioned. Coll. ; 1768, Tucker, concerning children, 'As we say, it [money] burns in their pockets', O.E.D.

burn-crust. A baker : mid-C. 18–20 ; jocular, coll. rather than s. Grose, 1st ed.

burn daylight. Lit., have a light burning in the daytime, hence to waste the daylight. At first (ca. 1587), coll. ; soon S.E. Shakespeare, in *Romeo*, ' Come, we burn daylight.' Apperson.

burn-fire. A C. 18–19 corruption, either sol. or catachrestic or dial. : a bonfire.

burn it blue. To act outrageously (?) : C. 18. Swift in *Stephen and Chloe*. (O.E.D.)

burn my breeches, like *dash my wig !*, is a jocular oath. Both are in Moore's *Tom Crib*.

burn one's or **the candle at both ends.** To work early and late, or to work early and pursue pleasure till late, in the day. From ca. 1650. Coll. > S.E. by 1800. Ex the Fr. phrase recorded in England as early as Cotgrave.—2. (Only . . . *the* . . .) To be very wasteful : coll. : mid-C. 18–20. Smollett. (Apperson.)

burn one's fingers. To incur harm, damage by meddling. From ca. 1700. Coll. > S.E.

burn oneself out. To work too hard and die early. C. 19–20 coll. > S.E. by 1900.

*****burn the ken.** To live at an inn or lodging-house without paying one's quarters : C. 18–early 19 : c.. *A New Canting Dict.*, 1725 ; Grose, 1st ed. Cf. *burn the town*.

burn the parade. To warn for guard more men than are necessary and then excuse the supernumeraries for money—ostensibly to buy coal and candles for the guard : mid-C. 18–early 19, military. Grose (Captain and Adjutant of Militia), 1st ed.

burn the planks. To remain long seated. Coll. verging on S.E. : from ca. 1840 ; ob. Carlyle. (O.E.D.)

burn the Thames. To do something very remarkable : coll. : Wolcot, 1787 ; ob. A jocular variation of *set the Thames on fire*.

burn the town. (Of soldiers and sailors) to leave a place without paying for one's quarters : late C. 17–18. B.E. Cf. *burn the ken*, q.v.

burn the water. To spear salmon by torchlight. From ca. 1800 ; s. > coll. by 1850, S.E. by 1890.

burn you ! Go to hell ! : (low) coll. (— 1887) ; ob. Baumann. Ex dial., where it occurs as early as 1760 (E.D.D.).

burned, burnt, ppl. adj. Infected with venereal disease. Late C. 16–20, ob. ; coll. Shakespeare's pun in *Lear*, ' No heretics burned, but wenches' suitors' ; B.E., ' Poxt, or swingingly Clapt '. Cf.

the mid-C. 18–early 19 sailors' 'be sent out a sacrifice and come home a burnt offering', of catching a venereal disease abroad (Grose, 1st ed.).

*****burner.** A card-sharper : C. 18 (? earlier) c. Ex *burn*, q.v.—2. A sharp blow or punch : c. : C. 19. Baumann. Ex the tingle it causes.—3. See :

burner, burning. A venereal disease : the latter (coll. > S.E.) from c.a. 1750 ; the former (s. > coll.) from ca. 1810 (*Lex. Bal.*) and ob.

burner of navigable rivers, be no. To be a simple or a quite ordinary person : mid-C. 18–early 19. Grose, 2nd ed. Cf. *burn the Thames*.

burning, vbl.n. Smoking : training-ships' : late C. 19–20. Bowen.

burning, adj. A coll. euphemism (— 1923) for *bloody* ; ob. Manchon.

burning shame. ' A lighted candle stuck into the private parts of a woman', Grose, 1st ed. : low : mid-C. 18–early 19. Punning the stock phrase.—2. ' Having a watchman placed at the door of a bawdy-house, with a lantern on his staff, in the day-time, to deter persons from going in and out ', Egan's Grose : low : ca. 1820–40.

burnt, n. See **spots on burnt.**—2. Adj. See **burned.**

burnt cinder. A window : rhyming s. (— 1914) on *winder*.

burnt offering. See **burned.**—2. Food, esp. meat, that has been allowed to burn : jocular coll. : late C. 19–20.—2. Roast meat : naval : C. 20. Bowen.

buroo or **brew.** An employment-exchange : Public Works' coll. : from ca. 1924. I.e. *bureau.*

bur(r). A hanger-on, a persistent ' clinger ' : late C. 16–20 ; until ca. 1750 (B.E. has it) it was coll., then it > S.E. ; slightly ob.

bur(r), v. To fight ; scrimmage ; ' rag '. Marlborough College : mid-C. 19–20, ob.

burr-pump. The old manual bilge-pump : nautical coll. : mid-C. 19–20 ; ob. Bowen. Because it so often ' stuck '.

burra, adj. Great, big ; important, as *burra sahib.* Chiefly in India : from ca. 1800.

burra beebee. A lady claiming, or very apt to claim, precedence at a party : Anglo-Indian : recorded in 1807 ; ob. In Hindi, lit. great lady. Yule & Burnell.

burra khana. Lit., big dinner, it = a great, gen. a solemn, banquet : Anglo-Indian (— 1880).

burra mem. The chief lady at a station : Anglo-Indian (— 1903). Lit. *burra*, great, + *mem*, white lady. See **mem** and **mem-sahib** ; cf. *burra beebee*.

burrow. To hide ; live secretly or quietly. From ca. 1750. Coll. in C. 18, then S.E. The S.O.D. quotes ' to burrow in mean lodgings', Marryat.

*****burst.** A burglary : c. (— 1857) ; ob. ' Ducange Anglicus.'—2. A ' spree ' ; a hearty meal. Esp. *on the burst*, on the spree : *Blackwood's*, 1880 ; Praed, 1881, in *Policy and Passion.* Coll.—3. (Sporting) a spurt (— 1862) : coll. >, by 1900, S.E.—4. Hence (?), the ' outpour of theatrical audiences about [11 p.m.] into the Strand ' : London police : 1879 ; ob. Ware.

burst, v. To drink, v.t. with *pot, cup, bottle*, etc. : coll. : from ca. 1850 ; ↑.—2. To spend extravagantly : from ca. 1890. See **bust**, v., 3.

burst at the broadside. To break wind : drinkers' : ca. 1670–1850. Ray. (Apperson.)

burst him (her, etc.**) !** Confound him : low coll. (— 1887) ; ob. Baumann.

burst one's crust. To break one's skin : boxers' : ca. 1800–80. Ware.

burst up. To be greatly perturbed, angered, excited : coll. ; late C. 19–20 ; ob.

bursted. Burst (past tense and ppl.) : since ca. 1800, dial. and, other 'ise, sol.

burster. Bread : low (— 1857) ; † by 1920. 'Ducange Anglicus.'—2. An exhausting physical effort : coll. ; rather rare. Recorded in 1851. O.E.D.—3. (Racing) a heavy fall, ' cropper ' : from ca. 1860 ; ob.—4. (Australia) a violent gale from the south, esp. at Sydney : from ca. 1870 ; coll. ; rare for (*southerly*) *buster*.—5. See **buster**.

Burton-on-Trent. The rent one pays : rhyming s. : from ca. 1880. P. P., *Rhyming Slang*, 1932. Often abbr. to *Burton*.

*****bury a moll.** C. and low : to run away from a mistress : from ca. 1850. H., 1st ed. Perhaps suggested by dial. (— 1847) *burying-a-wife*, ' a feast given by an apprentice at the expiration of his articles ', Halliwell.

bury a Quaker. To defecate, evacuate : orig. and mainly Anglo-Irish : from ca. 1800. F. & H., at *bury*, gives a long list of synonyms.

bury the hatchet. (In C. 14–18, *hang up the hatchet.*) To swear peace, become friendly again. Ex U.S. (ca. 1784), anglicised ca. 1790 as a coll. that, in C. 20, has > S.E. ; Wolcot uses it in 1794. Ex a Red Indian custom. (Apperson.)

bus. Abbr. *business* : in the theatrical sense. From ca. 1850. (Pronounced *biz*.)—2. Abbr. *omnibus* : from 1832. In C. 20, coll. On March 13, 1935, by the edict of the London Transport Board, *bus* > the standard word (to the exclusion of *omnibus*) ; pl. *buses*. (Fowler considered *busses* ' sure to come '.) Harriet Martineau, Dickens, Thackeray, Black the novelist.—3. (A) dowdy dress : society : 1881 ; † by 1920. Ware. I.e. a dress suited only to that conveyance.—4. Enough ! stop ! : Anglo-Indian coll. (— 1853). Ex Hindi *bas*. Yule & Burnell.—5. An aeroplane : 1913 (O.E.D. Sup.).— 6. A motor-car (or even a motor-bike : Lyell) : not among mechanics, says Richard Blaker : from ca. 1920. Cf. sense 2.

bus, v. Also *bus it*. To go by bus : coll. ; 1838 (O.E.D.).

bus ! See **bus,** n., 4.

bus, miss the. To lose one's opportunity : coll. : from ca. 1915. C. J. Dennis.

bus-bellied Ben. An alderman : East London : ca. 1840–1910. Ware. Ex tendency to corpulence.

*****bus-napper** and **b.-n.'s kinchin.** See **buzznapper.**

*****bush.** Either any or some special so-named tavern where a ' pigeon ' is plucked : c. of ca. 1585–95. Greene.—2. The cat-o'-nine-tails : c. : from ca. 1890. O.E.D. (Sup.).

bush or **bush it.** To camp in the bush : from ca. 1885 ; not much used.—2. *be bushed*, be lost in the bush (— 1856) ; hence, 3, to be lost, at a loss : from ca. 1870 ; all three are Australian coll. Both voices occur in B. L. Farjeon's *In Australian Wilds*, 1889. With sense 3, cf. the early C. 19 c. *bushed*, penniless, destitute.

bush, beat or **go about the.** To go deviously (fig.) : coll., from ca. 1550 ; the latter † by 1850 ; the latter S.E. in C. 20.

bush, go. To go wild : Australian coll. : C. 20. Ion L. Idriess, *Lasseter's Last Ride*, 1931, ' Most of their camels " had gone bush ".'

bush, take to the. To become a bushranger : Australian coll. : ca. 1835–90.

bush baptist. A person of uncertain religion : Australian and New Zealand (— 1910) mostly ; but orig. English, it being used by soldiers in the Boer War—witness J. Milne, *The Epistles of Atkins*, 1902.

*****bush-cove.** A gypsy : c. (— 1823) ; † by 1900. ' John Bee ', 1823, says, ' From their lodging under hedges, etc.'

bush lawyer. A layman fancying he knows all about the law—and given to laying it down : Australian coll. : from early 1890's. H. G. Turner, 1896 (Morris). See also **lawyer.**

bush-ranger. A convict, later anyone, living on plunder in the Australian bush : recorded in 1806 : coll. soon > S.E. Now usually *bushranger*.

bush-scrubber. ' A bushman's word for a boor, bumpkin, or slatternly person ' : Australian coll. : 1896. Morris. Ex the *scrub*, whence such a person may be presumed to have come.

bush-whacker. Australian, ex U.S. : an axeman, feller of trees, opener of new country ; hence, in C. 20, one who lives in the (more remote) country districts. The orig. sense has > S.E., the latter remains Australian coll.

*****bushed.** See **bush,** v., 2. Cf. *Bushy Park, at.*

bushed on, vbl. adj. Pleased ; delighted with. C. 19.

bushel and peck. The neck : rhyming s. : late C. 19–20. B. & P.

bushel bubby. A woman with large, full breasts : low : mid-C. 18–19. Grose, 1st ed. Ex *bushel*, a large quantity, + *bubby*, a woman's breast.

bushy. A dweller in ' the bush ' or remoter country districts : Australian coll. : from late 1890's.

Bushy Park. A lark (lit. and fig.) : rhyming s. (— 1859). H., 1st ed.—2. The female pubic hair : low : from ca. 1860. Hence, *take a turn in Bushy Park*, to possess a woman.

*****Bushy Park, at ; in the park.** Poor : c. : from ca. 1810 ; virtually †. Vaux.

Business. Busnes in France : Western Front military in G.W. (F. & Gibbons.)

business. Sexual intercourse : C. 17–18, coll. Taylor the Water Poet, 1630, ' Laïs . . . asked Demosthenes one hundred crownes for one night's businesse.'—2. (Theatrical) dialogue as opp. to action : S.E., late C. 17–early 18 ; but from ca. 1750, as in *The World*, 1753, and Scott, in 1820, it has meant by-play and as such it is coll.—3. A matter in which one may intervene or meddle : late C. 17–20 ; coll.—4. In deliberately vague reference to material objects : coll. : 1654, Evelyn ; 1847, Leigh Hunt, ' A business of screws and iron wheels '. Cf. *affair*. O.E.D.—5. A difficult matter : coll. ; from ca. 1840. Carlyle, ' If he had known what a business it was to govern the Abbey . . .', 1843.

business, do one's (for one), v.i. and t. To kill ; cause death of. From ca. 1660 ; S.E. until ca. 1800, then coll.

business, mean. To be in earnest : coll. : 1857, Hughes (O.E.D.).

business, mind one's own. To abstain from meddling in what does not concern one. Coll. From ca. 1860 ; earlier, S.E. (O.E.D.)

business, send about one's. To dismiss, send packing, just as *go about one's business* = to depart. In C. 17–18, the latter, S.E. ; in C. 19, both coll. ; in C. 20, both S.E.

business end, the. The commercial part of a firm's activities : coll. : late C. 19–20. From ᴜᴀ.

1910, this use of *end* has been extended : thus one can speak of *the selling* and *the buying end* of a retail business.—2. The part that matters : coll. : C. 20. E.g. the business end of a sword is the point or the blade. Ex :

business end of a tin tack, the. The point of a tack : U.S. (− 1882), anglicised in 1883 (*The Daily News*, March 27). Ware. Cf. *get down to brass tacks*.

*busk. To sell obscene songs and books in public-houses ; whence *busking*, such occupation, and *busker*, such vendor. Orig.—prob. the 1840's, though not recorded till the '50's—vagrants' and always low. Mayhew, *London Labour and the London Poor*, vols. I and III. Prob. ex C. 18–20 S.E. *busk*, to go about seeking, influenced by a corset-*busk* ; cf. nautical *busk*, to cruise as a pirate. —2. Hence, ' to perform in the street ' : grafters' : C. 20. P. Allingham, *Cheapjack*, 1934.

busk !, both ends of the. See **both ends . . .**

*busker. A man that sings or performs in a public-house : c. (− 1859). H., 1st ed. Cf. *busk* q.v.—2. Hence, an itinerant : c. or low s. (− 1874). H., 5th ed.

Busky. A frequent nickname of men surnamed Smith : naval and military : late C. 19–20. F. & Gibbons.

busnack ; gen. as vbl. n. To pry ; to interfere unduly, be fussy : naval : late C. 19–20 ; ob. Prob. ex the *buzz* of a fly. Whence *buzz-nagger*, q.v.

buss. A variant of *bus*, n., 2. H., 1st ed.

buss. A scholarship or bursary : Aberdeenshire s., not dial. : 1851, Wm. Anderson, *Rhymes, Reveries and Reminiscences*. E.D.D. (Sup.). Perhaps because as pleasant as a kiss.

buss-beggar. A harlot, old and of the lowest : low coll. : C. 17–19.—2. Specifically, ' an old super-annuated fumbler, whom none but ' beggar-women ' will suffer to kiss them ', Grose, 1st ed. : low coll. : C. 18–early 19.

bust. Sol. for *burst*, n. and v. Apparently un-recorded in England before 1830, Dickens being one of the earliest sources : *Oliver Twist* (*busting*, adj.) ; *Nicholas Nickleby*, ' His genius would have busted ' ; *Martin Chuzzlewit*, ' Keep cool, Jefferson . . . don't bust ' ; *Two Cities*, ' Bust me if I don't think he'd been a drinking ! '

bust, n. A frolic, spree, drinking-bout : esp. as *go on the bust*, orig. (− 1860) U.S., acclimatised ca. 1880. Cf. *burst*.—2. In c., a burglary : ca. 1850–1910. See also *burst*, n., 1.

bust, v. To bust ; explode : sol. except when jocularly deliberate. Dickens, 1838.—2. To put out of breath : from ca. 1870. E.g. in *Taking Out the Baby*, a broadside ballad of ca. 1880.—3. In c. (occ. as *burst*), to rob a house, v.t., rarely v.i. ; also, v.i., to inform to the police, whence the vbl. n., *busting*. Both C. 19–20, the latter ob.—4. To de-grade a non-commissioned officer : military coll. : late C. 19–20.

bust ! Dash it ! : New Zealanders' : C. 20. Also *bust it !* Cf. *bust me*, q.v.

bust, all in a. Very excited : lower classes' (− 1923). Manchon.

*bust, do a. To break into a place : C. 20 c. Charles E. Leach. Cf. *bust*, v., 3.

bust-maker. A womaniser ; a seducer. Low coll. : C. 19. Ex the bosom's enlargement in pregnancy and punning the S.E. sense.

bust me ! A mild oath : non-aristocratic : 1859, Dickens. Also *bust it !*, *bust you* (or *yer*) *!*

bust up. (Or hyphenated.) A great quarrel, ' row ', or excitement : 1899, Kipling : coll. now on verge of S.E. (O.E.D. Sup.)

busted, or **gone bust.** Ruined : coll. : late C. 19–20. Lyell.

buster, burster. A small new loaf ; a large bun. Until ca. 1850, the form is gen. *burster* ; after, *buster*. *Burster* occurs in Moncrieff's *Tom and Jerry*, *buster* in H., 1st ed., and Hindley's *Cheap Jack*. Ob.—2. (*Buster* only :—) Anything of su-perior size or astounding nature : orig. (− 1850), U.S., anglicised ca. 1859 (witness H., 1st ed.), e.g. in Dickens's *Great Expectations*.—3. In c., a burglar : ca. 1845–1910.—4. A spree, rarely except in *in for a buster*, determined on or ready for a spree : orig. U.S. ; from ca. 1858 in England (cf. *bust*, n.) ; ob.— 5. Hence, a dashing fellow : low : from ca. 1860 ; ob.—6. (Australian) a southerly gale with much sand or dust, esp. at Sydney : coll., from ca. 1880. Much earlier and more gen. as *southerly buster*. Cf. *brickfielder*.—7. A piece of bread and butter : schoolboys' : C. 20. Cf. sense 1. Gen. in pl.—8. (Gen. *burster*.) ' A very successful day or season ' : grafters' : from ca. 1880. Philip Allingham, *Cheap-jack*, 1934. Ex sense 2.

buster, a. Adv. Hollow ; utterly : low : ca. 1885–1910. See quotation at *molrowing*.

buster, come a. To fall, or be thrown, heavily from a horse : coll. : Australian (− 1888).

buster, old. See **old buster.—busters.** See **buster, 7.**

bustle. A dress-improver. Recorded in 1788 and presumably coll. for a few years before becom-ing S.E., as in Dickens, Miss Mitford, Trollope.— 2. Money : from ca. 1810. At first c., but fairly gen., low s. by ca. 1860 ; ob. Vaux, Hotten.

bustle, v. To confuse ; perplex : coll., from ca. 1850. Cf. the transitive S.E. senses.

Busy. See **Bizzy.**

*busy, occ. **busy fellow.** A detective : c. : C. 20 ; mostly American. Edgar Wallace's crime stories ; Charles E. Leach.

busy, get. To become active : coll. : U.S. (1905), anglicised by 1910. O.E.D. (Sup.).

busy as a bee in a treacle-pot. Very busy : coll. (− 1923). Manchon.

busy as a hen with one chick. Anxious ; fussy ; ludicrously proud : C. 17–20 (ob.) ; proverbial coll. Shirley, 1632 ; Grose.

busy as the devil in a high (in mid-C. 19–20, often **in a gale of**) **wind.** In a great flurry : low coll. : from ca. 1780 ; ob. Grose, 2nd ed.

busy-sack. A carpet-bag : coll. : from ca. 1860 ; ob. H., 3rd ed. Cf. American *grip-sack*.

but, for that, after **it is not unlikely, impossible,** etc., is sol. : from ca. 1660.—2. *but*, expressing ' mere surprise or recognition of something unex-pected ', as in ' I say ! but you had a narrow escape,' ' Excuse me ! but you have smut on your nose,' is coll. : from ca. 1850.—3. For the conjunctive *but* that generates a redundant negative (for *but* properly = *that . . . not*), see Fowler.—4. When placed at the end of a sentence, as *however* often is, *but* is coll. verging on sol. : C. 20. E.g. ' I didn't do it but ! '

but . . . however, where either *but* or *however* (not both) is needed, is catachrestic : mid-C. 19–20. Fowler.

but what. In e.g. ' I don't know but what . . .', = *but that*. Coll. : C. 19–20 ; earlier, S.E. (Fowler.)

butch. To be a butcher, act as or like a butcher. In late C. 18–early 19, S.E.; thereafter, and still, dial.; but in non-dial. circumstances it is, from ca. 1900, coll. (cf. *buttle*, q.v.): so too with the vbl.n. *butching*.

butcha. A baby, a young child: Anglo-Indian (— 1864). H., 3rd ed.; Manchon. Ex Hindustani.

butcher. The king in playing-cards. Orig., ca. 1850, and, though ob., still mainly public-house s. Cf. *bitch*, n., 4.—2. Stout (the drink): public-houses': from ca. 1890. Ware. Butchers are often fat.—3. In G.W., ex C. 19 c.: a medical officer.—4. A slop-master: artisans': ca. 1850–1900. Mayhew.

butcher ! Mid-C. 18–early 19, nautical and military: a jocular comment (on need of bleeding) when a comrade falls down. Grose, 1st ed.

butcher about. To make a din; humbug or fool about. Wellington College: late C. 19–20, ob. Perhaps a euphemism for *bugger about*.

butcher and bolt. See bolt, butcher and.

butchering, adj. and adv. Far; much; great(ly); low: from ca. 1870; ob. E.g. 'a butchering sight too forward ' (J. Greenwood). Cf. *bloody* and other violences. Baumann.

butcher's. See butcher's hook.

butcher's bill. The casualty list of a battle, esp. of those killed: coll. (— 1881). Occ. for the monetary cost of a war: coll. (— 1887). If this term, in either sense, is employed sarcastically and indignantly, it is then, for all its cynicism, rather S.E. than coll.

butcher's dog, be or lie like a. To ' lie by the beef without touching it; a simile often applicable to married men ', Grose, 2nd ed. Low coll.: late C. 18–early 19.

butcher's (hook). A look: rhyming s.: late C. 19–20. B. & P.—2. (Adj.) Angry: Australian rhyming s.: C. 20. On *crook* and gen., as sense 1, in abbr. form.

butcher's horse by his carrying a calf so well, that must have been a. A c.p. jest at the expense of an awkward rider. So Grose, 2nd ed.; Ray, in *English Proverbs*, 2nd ed., 1678, gives it in a slightly different form. Coll.: C. 17–20; ob.

butcher's jelly. Injured meat: lower classes': 1887, *The Standard*, Sept. 24 (E.D.D.).

butcher's meat. Meat had on credit and not yet paid for: late C. 18–19 jocular punning the S.E. sense of the phrase. Grose, 3rd ed.

butcher's mourning. A white hat with a black mourning hat-band: from ca. 1860; ob. H., 3rd ed. Apparently ex butchers' distaste for black hats.

[**butler-English.** ' The broken English spoken by native servants in the Madras Presidency . . . thus *I telling* = " I will tell "; *I done tell* = " I have told; *done come* = " actually arrived " . . .' Masters as well as servants used it: C. 18–20; ob. by 1903. Yule & Burnell.]

butler's grace. A ' thank-you ' but no money: coll.: 1609, Melton; † by 1700. Apperson.

butt. A buttock; also the buttocks: low coll. in C. 19–20 after being, in C. 15–17, S.E. (Also dial. and U.S. coll.)

butt in. To interfere; interrupt: v.i. V.t., *butt into*, rare. From ca. 1895; coll. >, by 1920, S.E.

butt-notcher. A sniper: military: 1915–18. F. & Gibbons. Ex the tally of his victims kept by notches on his rifle-butt.

butteker. A shop: late C. 18–19. Prob. ex Fr. *boutique* or Sp. *bodega*. Cf. *buttiken*, q.v.

butter. An inch of butter: C. 18–19 Cambridge. E.g. in pl., ' Send me a roll and two butters.' Grose who, in 2nd ed., corrects the *Oxford* of the 1st. —2. Fulsome flattery, unctuous praise, ' soft soap '. From ca. 1820; coll. *Blackwood's Magazine*, 1823, ' You have been daubed over by the dirty butter of his applause.' Cf. the slightly earlier *buttering-up*.

butter, v. In c. and low, to increase the stakes at every game or, in dicing, at every throw: ca. 1690–1840. B.E.; Grose.—2. Flatter, or praise, unctuously or fulsomely. Coll.; from late C. 19. Congreve, in the *Way of the World*, 1700: ' The squire that's buttered still is sure to be undone.' Coll.; S.E. by 1850.—3. ' To cheat or defraud in a smooth or plausible manner ', *A New Canting Dict.*, 1725: c.: C. 18.—4. To whip; from ca. 1820; ob. Gen. as *buttered*, past ppl. passive.—5. To miss (a catch): cricket: 1891. Lewis. Ex *butter-fingers*.

butter and cheese of, make. To humbug; bewilder: C. 17; coll. Cf. Gr. τυρεύειν. (O.E.D.)

butter-and-eggs. ' The feat of butter-and-eggs consists in going down the [frozen] slide on one foot and beating with the heel and toe of the other at short intervals,' *Macmillan's Magazine*, Jan., 1862. Coll. Cf. *knocking at the cobbler's door*, q.v.—2. A popular, i.e. (when not sol.) coll., name for flowers of two shades of yellow, esp. toadflax and narcissus: from ca. 1770. (S.O.D.)

butter-and-eggs trot. A short jig-trot: coll.; mid-C. 18–early 19. Ex market women's gait. Grose, 3rd ed.

butter-bag or -box. A Dutchman: C. 17–early 19. Dekker and B.E. have the latter, Howell the former. ? ex Holland as a formerly important butter-producing country, or rather ex ' the great quantity of butter eaten by people of that country ', Grose, 1st ed.

butter-boat, empty the. To lavish compliments; also, to battle. Coll.; from early 1860's. A butter-boat is a table vessel in which one serves melted butter.

butter-box. A full-lined coasting brig: nautical coll., orig. (— 1840) U.S.; anglicised ca. 1850; ob. Bowen.—2. A Dutch ship or seaman: nautical coll.: C. 19–20; ob. Ibid. Cf. *butter-bag*, q.v.— 3. See ' Fops ' in Addenda.—4. See ' Regional names ' in Addenda.

butter-churn. A turn (on the stage): music-halls' rhyming s. (— 1909). Ware.

butter-coloured beauties. ' A dozen or so pale yellow motor-cabs ' appearing in 1897: London: 1897. Ware. Cf. *margarine messes*.

butter dear, don't make. A jape addressed to patient anglers: mid-C. 18–early 19. Grose. The origin of the phrase is (fortunately, I suspect) obscure.

butter-fingered. Apt to let things, esp. (1841) a ball, slip from one's hand: coll. Meredith in *Evan Harrington*. Ex:

butter-fingers. One who lets things, esp. a ball, slip from his grasp. Coll.; Dickens, 1837; Hood, 1857, ' He was a slovenly player, and went among the cricket lovers by the sobriquet of butter-fingers.'

butter-flap. A trap, i.e. a light carriage: rhyming s. (— 1873). Ob.—Also (— 1859), but † by 1870, a cap. H., 1st ed. Cf. *baby pap*.

butter-mouth. A Dutchman: pejorative coll.: mid-C. 16–19. Cf. *butter-bag*, q.v.

Butter-Nut. A soldier in the Southern Army in the American Civil War : 1863 and soon anglicised. Ex the brownish-grey uniform.

butter one's bread on both sides. To be wasteful. Coll. ; from ca. 1660.

butter-print. A child, esp. if illegitimate : Fletcher, 1616; † by 1800. Cf. *buttercup.* (O.E.D.)

butter-queen and **-whore.** A scolding butter-woman : coll. ; resp. C. 17 (H. More), late C. 16–18 (Nashe, T. Brydges).

butter-slide. A very slippery ice-slide : children's coll. : late C. 19–20. Collinson.

butter the fish. To win at cards : from ca. 1920. Manchon.

butter upon bacon. Extravagance; extravagant ; domestic coll. (— 1909). Ware.

butter-weight. Good measure : ca. 1730–1900. Coll. Swift, 1733, ' Yet why should we be lac'd so strait ? | I'll give my monarch butter-weight.' (O.E.D.) Ex *b.-w.,* formerly 18 (or more) ounces to the pound.

butter when it's hot, it will cut. Of a knife that is blunt. Coll. from ca. 1860.

butter will stick on his bread, no. He is always unlucky : C. 17–19 ; coll. B.E. ; Scott. With *cleave* : C. 16–17.

butter would not melt in one's mouth, (look) as if. (To seem) demure. Coll. from the 1530's ; Palsgrave (O.E.D.), Latimer, Sedley, Swift, Scott, Thackeray. In reference to women, Swift and Grose add : *yet, I warrant you, cheese would not choke her,* the meaning of which must be left to the reader who will look at **cheese.**

buttercup. A child. A pet name : coll. Mrs. Lynn Linton, 1877. From ca. 1865 ; ob.

buttered bun(s). A mistress : ca. 1670–90, as in W. Cullen, 1679, in reference to Louise de Quérouaille.—2. (In C. 19–20 only **buttered bun.**) A harlot submitting sexually to several, or more, men in quick succession : late C. 17–20 ; slightly ob. B.E. ; Grose, 1st ed., ' One lying with a woman that has just lain with another man, is said to have a buttered bun.'—3. (**buttered bun.**) ' A Man pretty much in Liquor ', *A New Canting Dict.,* 1725 : low : ca. 1720–60.—4. See ' Dupes ' in Addenda. Matthews, however, may err in distinguishing it from sense 3.

butterfly. A river barge : nautical ; from ca. 1870 ; ob. Ironical.—2. The reins-guard affixed to the top of a hansom cab : cabmen's, from ca. 1870 ; ob. Coll. ; in C. 20, S.E.

butterfly boat. A paddle (esp. if excursion) steamer : nautical : mid-C. 19–20. Bowen. Ex the ' wings '.—2. Hence, a cross-Channel leave boat (esp. Southampton–Le Havre) : military : 1915–18. F. & Gibbons.

buttering-up. Fulsome flattery or praise : coll., ca. 1815–60. Tom Moore, 1819, ' This buttering-up against the grain '.

buttery. Addicted to excessive flattery : from ca. 1840 ; coll. passing to S.E. Cf. *butter,* v., 2.— 2. The adj. to *butter-fingers,* q.v. : cricketers' coll. : 1864. Lewis.

buttery Benjie. A Scottish Universities **s.** synonym for *bejan,* q.v. : from ca. 1840 ; ob.

*buttiken. A shop : c. (— 1857) ; † by 1890. 'Ducange Anglicus.' While *ken* = a place, *butti* prob. = Fr. *boutique.*

[**buttie** in Collinson is Northern dial. rather than coll. (A piece of bread and butter.)]

butting. An obscure C. 16 endearment : coll. Sketon. Perhaps cognate with *bunting.*

buttinski. An inquisitive person : Australian (— 1926) and English (— 1933). Jice Doone. Ex U.S. pun on *butt in.*

buttinski, v.i. To interrupt, esp. when one's presence is undesired : New Zealand soldiers' : 1915.

buttle. To act or serve as a *butler* : in C. 20 coll. Earlier, dial. Cf. † *suttle* ex *sutler.*

*buttock. A low whore : ca. 1660–1830 : c. Head, Shadwell, B.E., Grose.

buttock and tongue. A shrew. C. 18–19. ? punning c. *buttock and twang* (late C. 17–early 19), a common prostitute but no thief (also a *down buttock and sham file,* Grose, 1st ed.) and perhaps glancing at c. *buttock and file* (late C. 17–early 19 : B.E.), a prostitute that is also a pickpocket ; if in the latter c. phrase *sham* is inserted before *file,* the sense of c. phrase is obtained.

buttock and trimmings. See **rump and dozen.**

buttock-ball. A dance attended by prostitutes. Low coll. : late C. 17–early 19. Tom Brown, 1687. Cf. *ballum-rancum.* See **buttock.**—2. Human coïtion : late C. 18–early 19. Grose, 1st ed. Here the reference is doubly anatomical.

buttock-banqueting. Harlotry : coll. : C. 16– early 17.

buttock-broker. A procuress ; the proprietress or manager of a brothel ; a match-maker. Late C. 17– early 19 ; low. B.E., Grose. In the first two senses, *buttock* == a harlot, in the third a cheek of the posteriors.

buttock-mail. A fine imposed for fornication : Scottish pejorative coll. : C. 16–19. Lyndesay, Scott.

buttocking-shop. A low brothel : low : C. 19. *Lex. Bal.* Also *buttocking-ken* : c. : C. 19.

*button. A shilling : good, ca. 1840–1900 ; counterfeit, from ca. 1780 ; orig. c., then low ; †. Grose, 1st ed. Cf. *Brummagem buttons.*—2. An illicit decoy of any kind : from ca. 1840 ; c. and low. Mayhew.—3. A baby's penis : low. C. 19–20.

*button, v. Decoy, v.t. : v.i., act as an enticer in swindles. From ca. 1840 ; ob. C. and low. Cf. *button,* n., 2.

button, have lost a ; be a button short. To be slightly crazy : proletarian : late C. 19–20 ; ob. F. & H., revised.

button, not to care a (brass). Not to care at all. Coll. : C. 15–20. Cf. *rap.*

button, take by the. To button-hold. C.19–20. Coll., soon S.E.

button-boy. A page : coll. ; from ca. 1875. Cf. *boy in buttons.*

button-bung. A button thief : ' old ', says F. & H. ; prob. C. 17.

button-bu(r)ster. A low comedian : theatrical, from ca. 1870 ; ob. It is the audience that suffers.

button-catcher. A tailor : mostly nautical : from ca. 1870 ; ob. Cf. *snip.*

button-hole. Abbr. *button-hole flower(s)* or *bouquet.* Recorded in 1879. Coll.—2. The female pudend : low : mid-C. 19–20. Hence *button-hole worker, working,* penis, coïtion, and *button-hole factory,* a brothel, a bed.

button-hole, v. To button-hold, i.e. to catch hold of a person by a button and detain him, unwilling, in conversation. Orig. (— 1862) coll., in C. 20 S.E. and displacing *button-hold.*

button-hole, take one down a ; occ. take a b.-h. lower. To humiliate ; to de-conceit : coll. : from late C. 16. Shakespeare.

button-holer. A tedious detainer in conversation : C. 20 ; coll., soon to > S.E.—2. A button-hole flower : coll. App. first in *Punch*, Nov. 29, 1884 (O.E.D.).

button loose, (have) a. (To be) silly, crazy, slightly mad : military : C. 20. F. & Gibbons. Ex *buttons on one*, q.v.

Button-Maker, the. King George III : London nickname : ca. 1765–1800. Ware.

button on, have a. To be despondent ; temporarily depressed. Tailors', from ca. 1860 ; ob.

button on to. To get hold of (a person), to button-hole (him) ; to cultivate (his) company : 1904, Charles Turley. Perhaps ex *buttonhole* (v.) + *cotton on to*.

button-pound. Money, esp. cash : provincial s., ca. 1840–1900. Extant in dial., whence prob. it came.

button short, be a. See **button, have lost a.**

button up. To refrain from admitting a loss or disappointment : coll. ; from ca. 1890. Ex U.S. stock-broking (1841).

*buttoner. A decoy (see **button, v.**) : c. >, ca. 1870, low ; from ca. 1839. Ob. Brandon ; *Blackwood's Magazine*, 1841 ; *Cornhill Magazine*, 1862.

buttons. A page : coll. : 1848, Thackeray. Ex numerous jacket-buttons. Cf. *boots*.—2. The warden or superintendent : work-houses' (— 1887). Baumann.

buttons, boy in. A page : from ca. 1855 ; coll. until C. 20, when S.E.

buttons !, dash my. A coll. and often jocular exclamation of surprise or vexation : ca. 1840–1914. (O.E.D.)

buttons, have a soul above. To be, actually or in presumption only, superior to one's position : coll. : C. 19–20. Adumbrated in Colman, 1795, luminous in Marryat and Thackeray.

buttons, it is in one's. One is bound to succeed : coll. : late C. 16–18. Shakespeare, 1598, ''Tis in his buttons, he will carry 't.' O.E.D.

buttons, one's arse or breech makes. Also *make buttons* (C. 17–19). To look or be sorry, sad, in great fear : coll. ; mid-C. 16–early 19. Gabriel Harvey, captious critic, laborious versifier, and patterning prosateur ; playwright Middleton ; Grose, 3rd ed., ' His a–se makes buttons,' he is ready to befoul himself through fear ; in Ainsworth's *Latin Dict.*, 1808, we find *his tail maketh buttons* (O.E.D.). Apperson. Ex *buttons*, the excreta of sheep.

buttons (on or on one), not to have all one's. To be slightly mad ; weak-minded. Mid-C. 19–20 ; ob. H., 2nd ed. In dial. the affirmative form, indicative of great shrewdness, is common.

buttons on, put one's. To ' bet one's shirt ' on ; hence, to trust absolutely in : military (— 1923). Manchon.

butty. A comrade, a mate ; a policeman's assistant (†). Coll. and dial. : from ca. 1850. Henry Kingsley, 1859. Either from mining, where *butty* = a middleman, or from Romany *booty-pal*, a fellow workman, or, most prob., ex Warwickshire *butty*, a fellow servant or labourer (Rev. A. Macaulay, *History of Claybrook*, 1791). See esp. O.E.D., F. & H., and *Words !* at ' Terms of Address ' ; also Irwin.

buvare. Any drinkable : Parlyaree and low : from ca. 1840. Cf. *beware*, q.v.

buxie. An occ. variant of *baksheesh*, q.v.

Buxton limp. ' The hobbling walk of invalids taking the waters ' : Society, esp. at Buxton : 1883–ca. 1890. Ware. On *Alexandra limp*, q.v.

buy. A purchase ; an opportunity to purchase : Stock Exchange coll. : from ca. 1925. In *Time and Tide*, Sept. 8, 1934, ' Securitas ' writes thus : ' [Anglo-Dutch rubber] looks . . . one of the soundest of the solid buys, as opposed to the exciting gambles, in the market.'

buy, v. To incur, hear, receive, be ' landed with ' (something unpleasant) with one's eyes open or very credulously : C. 20. Cf. *ask for it*.—2. To wangle (something) : military : 1915 ; ob. F. & Gibbons.

*buy a brush. See **brush, buy a.**

buy a prop ! The market is flat (with no support) : Stock Exchange, ca. 1880–1900.

buy a pup. See **pup, buy a.**

buy a white horse. To squander money : nautical : late C. 19–20. Bowen. Ex the fleeting splendour of a ' white horse ' wave.

buy and sell. To betray for a bribe : coll. verging on S.E. : C. 18–19.—2. To be far too clever for (a person) : coll. : C. 20.

buy, on the. Actively buying : commercial coll. : 1929 ; earlier in U.S.A. (O.E.D. Sup.)

buy it !, I'll. Tell me the answer or catch : c.p. : from ca. 1905. Ex *buy*, v., 1, q.v.

buy money. To bet heavily on a favourite : racing : C. 20. Ex the short odds. (O.E.D. Sup.)

buy one's boots in Crooked Lane and one's stockings in Bandy-Legged Walk. To have crooked or bandy legs : a mid-C. 18–early 19 c.p. Grose, 3rd ed.

buy one's thirst. To pay for a drink : U.S., anglicised in 1884 ; virtually † by 1909. Ware.

*buy oneself out. To get oneself discharged : Australian c. : 1932, *The Melbourne Age*, April 29. Ironic.

*buyer. A ' fence ', a receiver : C. 20 c. Charles E. Leach.

buz(z). A parlour and a public-house game, in which the players count 1, 2, 3, 4, etc., with *buz(z)* substituted for seven and any multiple thereof : coll., then, by 1900, S.E. From ca. 1860 ; ob. Miss Allcott, *Little Women*, 1868.—2. (Gen. the **buzz.**) In c., the picking of pockets : late C. 18–early 19. Cf. *buzz*, v., 2.—3. A rumour : naval coll. : late C. 19–20. Bowen. Ex ob. S.E. *buzz*, a busy or persistent rumour.

buz(z), v.t. Drain (a bottle or decanter) to the last drop. Coll. : late C. 18–19. Germ in Grose, 1785 ; clearly in *The Gentleman's Magazine*, 1795 ; Moncrieff ; Thackeray. ? *booze*, corrupted. See **buzza.** In C. 19, to share equally the last of a bottle of wine, when there is not a full glass for each person.—2. V.i. and t., to pick pockets : from ca. 1800 : c., then—ca. 1860—low. Whence the late C. 18–19 c. terms, *buz(z)-man*, *buz(z)-gloak*, *buzz-bloke* or *-cove*, and *buzz-napper*, a pickpocket.— [*buzz*, v.] 3. To cast forcibly, throw swiftly : coll. : 1893, Kipling, ' Dennis buzzed his carbine after him, and it caught him on the back of his head ' (O.E.D. Sup.).—4. To pass by, esp. *buzz the bottle* : University : C. 20.—5. Often *buzz off*. To depart ; esp. to depart quickly : from ca. 1905. Edwin Pugh, *The Cockney at Home*, 1914.

buzz-box. A motor-car : from ca. 1930. (*The Passing Show*, May 12, 1934.)

*buz(z)-faking. Pocket-picking. C. 19 c. Ware has *buz-faker*.

*buz(z)-gloak. See **buzz, v., 2.**

*buz(z)-man. See buzz, v., 2.—2. More gen., however, an informer: c. (— 1864). H., 3rd ed.

buzz-nagger. A too talkative person: military: C. 20. F. & Gibbons.

*buz(z)-nappers' academy. A school for the training of thieves: late C. 18–mid-19 c. George Parker, 1781; see, e.g., *Oliver Twist*.

*buz(z)-napper's kinchin. A watchman: late C. 18–early 19 c. Grose, 2nd ed.

buzz off. See buzz, v., 5. An occ. variant is *buzz away*.

buzz-wag(g)on. A hydro-glider, 'attaining a high speed with an aeroplane engine and propeller': naval: 1916. Bowen.—2. A motor-car: 1923, Manchon.

buzza. An early form of *to buzz*, sense 1: late C. 18 only. Grose, 1st ed.: 'To *buzza* one is to challenge him to pour out all the wine in the bottle into his glass, undertaking to drink it', i.e. the whole of the wine, 'should it prove more than the glass would hold; commonly said to one who hesitates to drink a bottle that is nearly out'. In the 3rd ed. he adds: ' Some derive it from *bouze all*, i.e. drink it all.'

buzzard. A stupid, ignorant, foolish, gullible person: C. 14–19, extant in dial. B.E. gives as s., S.O.D. as S.E.; prob. it wavered between coll. and S.E. before it > dial. Often, in C. 18–20, in form *blind buzzard*. Ex *buzzard*, a useless hawk.

buzzed, be. To be killed: military: late 1914; ob., F. & Gibbons. Ex the buzz of a bullet.

buzzer. A whisperer of scandal and gossip: C. 17–18; coll. Shakespeare.—2. A pickpocket: from ca. 1850; c. and low; ob. Cf. *buz-napper*. Ex *buzz*, v., 2.—3. A motor-car: non-aristocratic: 1898 (Ware); † by 1920.—4. A signaller by Morse: military coll.: from ca. 1910. F. & Gibbons.—5. A wireless rating: naval: from ca. 1922. Bowen.

*buzzing. Pocket-picking: c. (— 1812). Vaux. See buzz, v., 2.

buzzy. Crazy: ca. 1880–1914. F. Brett Young, in *Jim Redlake*, 1930, ' Ladylike poses and high-class music and scenery that sends you buzzy' (a description of Russian ballet). Lit., making one's head buzz.

[by occurs in many oaths, strong or (e.g. *by golly*) mild, blasphemous or ludicrous or innocuously senseless. Although many of these are neither s. nor coll., some of the funny or witty ones are coll. or s: e.g. *by the jumping Moses, by the living jingo, by my bootlaces*. The psychology of oaths is akin to that of s., but that fact does not make an oath necessarily s. See *Words !*; also *Slang*; also, esp., Robert Graves, *Lars Porsena*, 1927.]

by (properly agential) is in C. 20 used more and more for the merely instrumental *with*; it is a pity that this useful distinction—L. a(b) and cum—is disappearing.—2. In South African coll.: late C. 19–20. E.g. 'He is by', he is in, 'the house.' Ex Dutch *bij*, by, with, in. Pettman.

by and by. Presently; soon. C. 16–20; coll. but S.E. (though not dignified) after ca. 1700.

by the by(e). Incidentally. In conversation only. C. 18–20; coll. > S.E. So, too, *by the way*.

by the wind. In difficulties; short of money: C. 19–20 (ob.), nautical.

by-blow. A bastard: late C. 16–20; coll. till ca. 1800, then S.E. Robert Browning, ' A drab's brat, a beggar's bye-blow '. Cf.:

by-chop. A bastard: C. 17–18; coll. Ben Jonson. Cf.:

by-scape. A bastard: mid-C. 17; coll. verging on S.E. Cf.:

by-slip. A bastard: late C. 17–18; coll. soon > S.E. ' Ungracious by-slips ', Hacket, 1693, in the *Life of Williams*, one of the great biographies.

bye ! or 'bye ! Good-bye !: C. 20 coll. Henry Handel Richardson, in *The New Statesman and Nation*, March 31, 1934.

bye-bye. A sound made to induce sleep in a child: coll.: C. 17–20. Hence *go to bye-bye*, orig. an imperative, > go to sleep, fall asleep; go to bed: C. 19–20; coll. In C. 20, often *go (to) bye-byes*.

bye-bye ! Good-bye ! C. 18–20; coll. Recorded in 1709.

bye-byes ! Good-bye ! But *go to bye-byes* is to go to sleep. C. 20. Both occur, e.g., in H. A. Vachell, *Martha Penny*, 1934.

bye-commoner. One who mistakenly thinks he can box: pugilistic: ca. 1820–50. ' Jon Bee ', 1823. Ex *commoner*, 2.

by(e)-drink or -drinking. A drink, gen. stronger than tea, at other than meal-times. From ca. 1760; coll., but S.E. in C. 19–20; ob.

bymeby. See bimeby.

Byng boys, the. The Canadian troops: Canadian military: 1917–18. Ex Lord Byng, commanding them in 1917, and ' The Bing Boys Are Here ', a very popular revue. F. & Gibbons; B. & P.

byte. See bite, of which it is a frequent C. 17–18 spelling.

C

*C or c. Abbr. of racing c. *cop*, v., q.v.—2. But with the c is put against that horse of which, besides the favourite, bookies should be careful: C. 20.

C.B. A confinement to barracks: military j.: >, in C. 20, also coll. Ex Confined to Barracks.

C.H. A conquering hero: coll.: Nov., 1882; † by 1915. Ware. Ex the frequent playing, to soldiers returned from the Egyptian War, of ' See the Conquering Hero Comes.' (Like *hero* in the G.W., *C.H.* soon > derisive among the soldiers.)

C.M.A.R. (, the). The Royal Army Medical Corps, the reversed initials representing ' can't manage a rifle ': a jocular c.p. of 1915–18. F. & Gibbons.

c.o.d. (or C.O.D.), a or that's a. A military c.p. applied to a heavy gun just fired: 1915–18. F. & Gibbons. I.e. ' there would be the deuce to pay '—cash on delivery—when the shell landed.

c.p. or C.P. A euphemistic abbr. (— 1923) of *cunt-pensioner*, q.v. Manchon.

C.-T. See cock-teaser.

C.T.A. The police: circus and showmen's: from ca. 1860. Origin ?

C3. Inferior; highly unfit: coll.: 1915 +. Ex the G.W. classification of physical fitness, C3 being the lowest.—2. A ' bradbury ' (q.v.): military (esp.

Australian) in G.W. Ex the emaciated figure of St. George.

ca'-canny. Adj., applied to an employee's policy of working slowly, ' going slow '. Coll., recorded in 1896 and, since 1918, considered as S.E. Ex Scottish ; lit., call shrewdly, i.e. go cautiously.

ca sa or **ca-sa.** See *casa*, 1.

cab. Abbr. *cavalier* influenced by Sp. *caballero* : ca. 1650–1710. Coll. (S.O.D.).—2. Abbr. *cabriolet*, a public carriage, two- or four-wheeled, seating two or four persons, and drawn by one horse, introduced into England in 1820, the term appearing seven years later, at first s., then soon coll., then by 1860 S.E. Occ., a cab-driver (1850, Thackeray : O.E.D.). Also, from ca. 1910, an abbr. of *taxi-cab* : coll. ; comparatively rare.—3. A brothel : ca. 1800–50. *Lex. Bal.* : ' How many tails have you in your cab ? i.e. how many girls have you in your bawdy house ? ' Prob. ex *cabin*.—4. (Universities' and Public Schools') from ca. 1850 as in ' Cuthbert Bede ', *Verdant Green*, 1853 : ' Those who can't afford a coach get a cab,'—one of this author's best puns—' *alias* a crib, *alias* a translation '. Ex *cabbage*, n., 5, q.v.—5. The second gig of the *Conway* : *Conway* Training Ship s., in the 1890's. Masefield.

cab ; gen. **cab it**, v. To go by cab : coll. ; from ca. 1830 ; Dickens has it in *Pickwick Papers* ; ob.— 2. (Schoolboys') to use a crib : from ca. 1855. Like the corresponding n., ob. by 1930. Ex *cabbage*, v., 2.—3. To pilfer : schoolboys' (— 1891) ; ob. Perhaps ex Scots : see E.D.D.

cab-moll. A harlot professionally fond of cabs and trains : low ; ca. 1840–1900.

Cabal. The English ministry of 1672 : **C**lifford, **A**rlington, **B**uckingham, **A**shley, and **L**auderdale ; coll. nickname. Ex *Cabal* as applied by Pepys in 1665 to the junto of the Privy Council : itself ex *cabal*, intrigue : ex Hebrew. W.

cabbage. Pieces of material filched by tailors ; small profits in the shape of material. After ca. 1660, coll. ; by 1800, S.E. Randolph, 1638 ; Dyche, 1748 ; Grose, 1st ed. ; Cobbett, 1821. Perhaps ex *garbage* : see O.E.D. and F. & H. Cf. *hell.*—2. A tailor : late C. 17–early 19. B.E.—3. A late C. 17 mode of dressing the hair similar to the chignon : coll., ca. 1680–1720, as in the anon. *Mundus Muliebris*, ' Behind the noddle every baggage | Wears bundle " choux ", in English cabbage.'—4. A cigar, esp. if inferior : coll. : from ca. 1840, ob. *Punch's Almanack*, Aug. 12, 1843, punningly : ' The cigar dealers, objecting to their lands being cribbed, have made us pay for the cabbage ever since.'—5. A translation or ' crib ' : from ca. 1850 ; schoolboys' ; ob.—6. The female pudend : C. 19–20, ob. Cf. *greens.*—7. **(The Cabbage.)** The *Savoy* Theatre : 1881 ; slightly ob. Ware.—8. A ' chap ' or ' fellow ' : ca. 1750–70. Johnson, 1756, in the *Connoisseur* (quoted by O.E.D.), ' Those who . . . call a man a cabbage, an odd fish, and an unaccountable muskin, should never come into company without an interpreter.' Suggested by the Fr. *mon chou* (as endearment).

cabbage, v. To purloin : orig. and mainly of tailors : from ca. 1700 ; soon coll. and by 1800 S.E. ; Arbuthnot, in *John Bull*, 1712.—2. (Schoolboys') to ' crib ', from ca. 1830, recorded 1837 : this precedes the n. *cabbage*, whence *cab*, a ' crib '. Vbl.n., *cabbaging* : pilfering ; cribbing : C. 19–20 ; ob.

cabbage-contractor. A tailor : low (perhaps c.) : C. 19. Ex *cabbage*, n., 1.

cabbage-garden patriot. A coward : political coll. : 1848–ca. 1910. Ware. William Smith O'Brien (1803–64) led, in the summer of 1848, a pitiable insurrection in Ireland ; his followers having fled, he successfully hid for several days in a cabbage-patch.

Cabbage Gardens, the. Victoria (Australia) : Australian nickname : from ca. 1920.

cabbage-gelder. A market gardener ; a greengrocer : late C. 19–20 ; ob.

cabbage-head. A fool : coll. : from ca. 1660. A broadside ballad of ca. 1880 : ' I ought to call him cabbage-head, | He is so very green.' In F. & H., a synonymy.

cabbage-leaf. An inferior cigar : from ca. 1840 ; ob. Cf. *cabbage*, n., 4.

cabbage-looking. See **green as I'm cabbage-looking, not so.**

***Cabbage Patch, the.** ' That little triangle of grass behind the Admiralty Arch which they call the Cabbage Patch ' : London vagrants' : C. 20. James Curtis, *The Gilt Kid*, 1936.

***cabbage-plant.** An umbrella : c. : ca. 1820–60, Egan's Grose, where also *summer cabbage*.

cabbage-stump. A leg : C. 19–20 ; gen. in pl. Cf. *drumstick.*

cabbage-tree. A hat, large, low-crowned, broad-brimmed, made from cabbage-tree leaves : Australia : from ca. 1850 ; †. Morris.

cabbage-tree mob ; cabbagites. Roughs : Australian, ca. 1850–80. Ex their cabbage-palm hats. This word gave way to *larrikin(s)*, q.v. Lt.-Col. G. C. Mundy's *Our Antipodes*, 1852. Morris.

cabbager. A tailor : C. 19–20 ; ob. See *cabbage*, n., 1 and 2.

cabbagites. See **cabbage-tree mob.**

cabber. A cab-horse : 1884 ; coll. *The Times*, Oct. 27, 1884. (O.E.D.)

cabbie, cabby. A cab-driver : coll. ; from ca. 1850. Smedley, 1852, in *Lewis Arundel* ; Yates, in *Broken to Harness*. Ex *cab*, n., 2.

cabbing. (Vbl.n. ex *cab*, v., 2.) The use of a crib : esp. at Shrewsbury School. See notably Desmond Coke's wholly admirable school-story, *The Bending of a Twig*, 1906.

cabin-cracker, -cracking. A thief breaking into a ship's cabins ; the act or action : nautical (— 1887). Baumann.

cabin-window, through the. (Of an officer obtaining his position) entirely through influence : naval officers' : late C. 19–20. Bowen. Opp. *hawse-pipe*, q.v.

Cabinetable. Fit to belong to the Cabinet : political and journalistic coll. : 1896 (O.E.D. Sup.).

cable. Abbr. *cablegram* : coll. : 1883 ; in C. 20 virtually S.E.—2. V.i., seldom t., to send a telegram by cable : recorded for 1871 : coll., but almost imm. S.E. (S.O.D.)

cable, slip one's. See **slip one's cable.**

cable-hanger. An illicit catcher of oysters : C. 18–20 ; coll. ; ob. Defoe in his *Tour Through Great Britain.*

cable has parted, one's. One dies : nautical coll. (— 1887). Baumann.

cable home about, nothing to. Unimportant, ordinary, unexciting : Australian coll., G.W. +. Cf. *nothing to write home about*, the more gen. locution.

cabman's rest. A female breast ; gen. in pl. : rhyming s., from ca. 1870.

cabobbled, ppl. adj. Perplexed ; confused : nautical, C. 19–20, ob. Perhaps an intensive (see **ker-**) of *bubble*, to deceive ; the word occurs also in dial. which has *bobble*, a ground swell of the sea (E.D.D.).

cabon. Much : Australian (orig. and mainly Queensland) ' pidgin ' (— 1872). Chas. H. Allen, *A Visit to Queensland and her Goldfields,* 1872. Morris. Ex Aborigine.

caboodle, the whole. The whole lot (persons or things) : orig. (1848), U.S., anglicised ca. 1895. Prob. via U.S. *the whole kit and boodle* (*kit and* being slurred to *ca*), ex English *kit* (see sense 2) and U.S. *boodle,* ' a crowd ' (Thornton), itself perhaps ex Portuguese *cabedal,* ' a stock, what a man is worth ' : W.

*caboose. A kitchen : tramps' c. : mid-C. 19–20. Ex *caboose,* a ship's galley.—2. A small dwelling : Australian (— 1916). C. J. Dennis.—3. A prison ashore : nautical : late C. 19–20 ; ob. Bowen.

cacafuego. A spitfire ; braggart ; bully : C. 17–early 19. Until ca. 1680, S.E. ; ca. 1680–1750, coll. ; then s. Fletcher ; Phillips's Dict. ; B.E. ; Grose. Its descent in the wordy world was due to its lit. meaning, shit-fire, for ca. 1750 it began to be considered vulgar.

cacagogue. Incorrect for *caccagogue* (an ointment) : C. 19–20. O.E.D.

caccle. Jon Bee's spelling of *cackle.*

cack, n. and (rare) v. (To void) excrement. Orig. S.E. ; in late C. 19–20 dial. and low coll. Among children, often as a semi-interjection, *cacky.* Ex L. *cacare* ; prob. echoic.

cack-handed. Left-handed ; hence, clumsy : C. 20. ? ex preceding term ; perhaps rather a corruption of Scottish *car-hand.*

cackle. Idle talk. Without *the* it is S.E. ; with inseparable *the,* it is coll., as in *Punch,* Sept. 10, 1887, ' If a feller would tackle | A feminine fair up to Dick, | He 'as got to be dabs at the cackle.' C. 19–20. Ex :—2. (As for sense 3 : *cackle.*) The patter of clowns : from ca. 1840.—3. Hence, the dialogue of a play : from ca. 1870. Cf. v., 2.

cackle, v.i. To reveal secrets by indiscreet or otherwise foolish talk : late C. 17–20 c. and low ; ob. B.E.—2. The v. corresponding to n., 2 and 3 : theatrical : same periods.

cackle !, cut the. ' Shut up ! ' : late C. 19–20. Occ. in other moods} esp. in *cut the cackle and come to the 'osses,* which, however, = to get down to business (e.g. D. Sayers, *Unnatural Death,* 1927).

cackle, up to the. See **up to the cackle.**

cackle-berry. (Gen. pl.) An egg : Canadian : late C. 19–20. Ex U.S. Cf. *hen-fruit.*

cackle-chucker. (Theatrical) a prompter : from ca. 1860 ; ob.

cackle-merchant. (Theatrical) a dramatic author : from ca. 1860 ; ob.

*cackle-tub. A pulpit : c. > low ; from ca. 1850. H., 3rd ed. ; Musgrave, *Savage London,* 1888. Cf. *tub-thumper.*

cackler. A blabber : coll., C. 18–20. Other senses, S.E. Bailey's Dict.—2. A showman with a speaking part : from ca. 1840. In C. 20, loosely, an actor. Dickens.—3. A fowl (— 1673) ; orig. c. ; by 1730, low ; in C. 20, almost coll. and certainly ob. Hence, *cackler's ken,* a hen-roost ; a fowlhouse : 1788, Grose, 2nd ed.

*cackling cheat or **chete.** A fowl : c. : ca. 1550–1830. Harman, Grose.

cackling-cove. An actor : theatrical : from ca. 1830. H., 3rd ed. Lit., talking or talkative man. Also called a *mummery-cove.*

*cackling fart. An egg : c. : late C. 17–18. Coles, 1676 ; B.E. *Cackling* here = *cackler's.*

*cacks. Children's shoes : c. (— 1923). Manchon. Ex dial. (— 1897 : E.D.D.).

cad. At Oxford and certain Public Schools (esp. Eton), from ca. 1820, a townsman : pejoratively. † by 1918. Hone. Abbr. *caddie, cadee* (i.e. cadet) : W.—Hence, 2, an ill-bred, esp. if vulgar, fellow : from ca. 1835 ; ob. Since ca. 1900, a man devoid of fine instincts or delicate feelings. Coll. Kingsley, Thackeray, Anstey.—3. A passenger taken up by a coachman for his own profit : coll., from ca. 1790 ; † by 1870.—4. An omnibus conductor : coll., ca. 1832–70. Hood, Dickens, Mayhew.—5. An inferior assistant or an assistant in a low association : coll., ca. 1834–1900. Theodore Hook.—6. A messenger, errand-boy : coll., ca. 1835–1914, as in Hood, ' Not to forget that saucy lad | (Ostentation's favourite cad), | The page, who looked so splendidly clad '.—7. A familiar friend ; a chum : ca. 1840–1900 ; coll.

cad-catcher. A picture ' painted to attract the undiscriminating ', *The Artist,* Feb. 1, 1882 (O.E.D.): art s. >, by 1890, coll ; ob. Cf. *pot-boiler,* q.v.

cadator. A beggar pretending to be a decayed gentleman : low or c. : late C. 17–early 18. Not in O.E.D., but in Ned Ward and Tom Brown. Ex L. *cadere,* to fall.

cadaver. A bankrupt ; a bankruptcy : U.S. (— 1900) anglicised, in commerce, ca. 1905 : coll. Ware.

[**caddee.** A thief's assistant or abettor : c. according to Baumann, but S.E. according to O.E.D.]

caddie, caddy. ' A bush name for a slouch hat ' : Australian (— 1898). Morris. Perhaps a corruption of *cady,* q.v.—2. (**Caddie.**) *The Academy* literary weekly : printers' (— 1887) ; † by 1920. Baumann. Cf. *Athie,* q.v.

caddish. Offensively ill-bred : from ca. 1860 (recorded, 1868) ; coll. Shirley Brooks in *Sooner or Later,* Mrs. Lynn Linton in *Patricia Kemball.* In C. 20 it tends to mean glaringly deficient in moral and/or aesthetic delicacy.

Cade, the. Burlington Arcade : Society, from ca. 1870 ; ob.

cadey. See **cady.**

cadge. The act or the practice of begging : low coll., from ca. 1810. Vaux. ? ex *catch.*—2. A message : low Glasgow (— 1934).

cadge, v. To go about begging : from ca. 1810.—2. V.t., to beg from (a person) : low (— 1811). *Lex. Bal.*—Also, 3, beg, obtain by begging : recorded in 1848. Low coll. N. and v. are recorded in Vaux's *Flash Dict.,* 1812, and since ca. 1880 the words have occ. been used jocularly and inoffensively. Perhaps imm. ex Dutch, ultimately ex Fr. *cage,* a wicker basket carried on back of cadger (pedlar) or his pony : W. For a synonymy, see F. & H.

cadge, do a. See **do a cadge.**

*cadge-cloak or **-gloak.** A beggar : C. 18–early 19. Bamfylde-Moore Carew. See **gloak.**

cadger. A beggar, esp. if whining : from ca. 1820 ; low coll. (But in Scots as early as 1737 : see E.D.D.) Egan's Grose, where wrongly classified as c.—2. Whence, a genteel, despicable ' sponger ' : coll. ; from ca. 1880. A transitional use occurs in James Greenwood's *The Little Ragamuffins,* 1884. For synonymy, see F. & H.

cadging. Esp. *cadging-bag* and *cadging-face.* Vbl.n., abject begging ; ' sponging '. Coll. ; **re-**

corded in 1839 (Brandon), but prob. much earlier. Henry Kingsley, James Greenwood.—2. Applied esp. to 'cabmen when they are off the ranks, and soliciting a fare': ca. 1855–1900. 'Ducange Anglicus.'

cadi. An occ. and, by 1930, † variant of *cady*.

cads on castors. Bicyclists: ca. 1880–5. *The Daily News*, Sept. 10, 1885. (Ware.)

cady; occ. **cadey** or **kadi.** A hat. From ca. 1885. (Recorded in Lancashire dial. in 1869: see E.D.D.) Walford's *Antiquarian*, April, 1887: 'Sixpence I gave for my cady, | A penny I gave for my stick.' Perhaps ex Yiddish; perhaps, however, a corruption of Romany *stadi*, a hat, itself prob. ex Modern Gr. σκιάδι (Sampson). Cf. *caddie*, q.v.— 2. Hence, a Kilmarnock or Balmoral cap worn by Scottish regiments: military: C. 20; esp. in G.W. (F. & Gibbons).—3. Hence also, a straw hat: New Zealanders': from ca. 1920.

caff. A café: low: from ca. 1920. James Curtis, *The Gilt Kid*, 1936.

[**caffan** is erroneous in B.E. and repeated by Grose and Egan, for *cassam, cassan*, i.e. cheese. Owing to the old-fashioned long *s*.]

Caffre's lightener. See **Kaffir's lightener.**

cag. A quarrelsome argument; gossip: nautical: from ca. 1870, slightly ob. Bowen; F. & Gibbons. Ex.

cag, v. 'To irritate, affront, anger': schoolboys': 1801, Southey (E.D.D.)—2. And as early as 1811 (*Lex. Bal.*) it = to render sulky, ill humoured. Prob. ex dial.

cag, carry the. To be vexed or sullen: low: 1811, *Lex. Bal.* Cf. preceding.

cag-mag. See **cagmag.**

cage. In C. 16–17, S.E. (as in Shakespeare) and = a prison. In C. 17–19, low if not indeed c., in C. 20 low and ob., for a lock-up. In G.W., esp. as *bird-cage*, a compound for prisoners. At *cage*, F. & H. has a list of synonyms, English, French, German, Spanish, and Italian, for a prison.—2. A dress-improver ⊾ coll.; from ca. 1850; †. Cf. *bird-cage*.—3. A bed: ca. 1860–1900. Abbr. *breeding-cage*, q.v.—4. (**The Cage.**) the Ladies' Gallery in the House of Commons (– 1870). *London Figaro*, June 10, 1870.—5. (**cage.**) A military tender covered with netting against bombs: Anglo-Irish: from 1916; ob.

cagg, n. and v. reflexive. (A vow) to abstain from liquor for a certain period: mid-C. 18–early 19 military. Grose, 1st ed. Perhaps cognate with *cag*, v.: thus, to vex or mortify oneself by abstention from liquor.

caggy. Unfit to eat: dial. and low coll., now † as latter: 1848, Marryat. O.E.D. Ex:

cagmag; **cag-mag.** (Of food, esp. meat) odds and ends, scraps, refuse. From ca. 1810; ob. Coll. ex dial. *Lex. Bal.*, 1811. Mayhew, *London Labour*, 'Do I ever eat my own game if it's high ? No, sir, never, I couldn't stand such cag-mag.' Also as adj., tainted, inferior (– 1860); ob. Origin obscure: but prob. the term derives ex *cag(g)-mag(g)*, an old goose (see Grose, 2nd ed.).— 2. Hence, gossip, idle talk: Cockney coll.: from ca. 1880. Manchon. (Also in dial.)

cagnas. Barracks: Canadian military: G.W. Ex a Fr. Army term via the French Canadians; orig. an Annamite word. F. & Gibbons; B. & P.

Cain, raise. To make a disturbance, a din; to quarrel noisily. Orig. (ca. 1840), U.S., anglicised

ca. 1870. App. euphemistic for *raise the devil* (W.). Cf. *raise hell and Tommy* and *cane upon Abel*.

Cain and Abel. A table: rhyming s. (– 1857). 'Ducange Anglicus', 1st ed., classifies it as c., but it very soon > gen. Cockney.

Cainsham smoke. The tears of a wife-beaten husband: C. 17–18; coll. Dunton's Dict. Etymology obscure: presumably topographically proverbial.

cairn, add a stone to someone's. To honour a person as much as possible after his death: coll.; C. 18–19. Ex a Celtic proverbial saying, recorded by traveller Pennant in 1772.

cake, cakey. A fool, gull, or blockhead: late C. 18–20, ob. In C. 19–20, coll. Grose, 1785; J. R. Planché, 'Your resignation proves that you must be | The greatest cake he in his land could see !'; Mrs. Henry Wood. From either the softness of some cakes or the flatness of others: in either case, a pun.—2. At Christ's Hospital (*cake* only), C. 19–20, ob., a stroke with a cane.—3. (*cakey* only.) Half-witted: Glasgow (– 1934). Ex Northern and Midland dial. (– 1897: E.D.D.). Cf. *batchy* for the semantics.

cake, v. (Christ's Hospital) to cane: C. 19–20, ob.

cake, get one's share of the. To succeed: coll., C. 17–18. Cf.:

cake, take the. To carry off the honours; be the best; (theatrical) 'fill the bill': coll., from ca. 1880. Ex U.S. In C. 20, also = be impudent, a piece of impudence: coll. 'The allusion is not to a cake walk', as Thornton suggests, for *cake-walk* is later; perhaps 'a jocular allusion to Gr. πυραμοῦς, prize of victory, orig. cake of roasted wheat and honey awarded to person of greatest vigilance in night-watch', W. See also **bun, take the,** and **biscuit, take the.**

cake and has paid (her) a loaf, the devil owed (her) a. A great instead of a small misfortune has befallen her. Coll.: C. 17–19. B.E.

cake is dough, one's. One's project, or one's business, has failed: mid-C. 16–20: coll. Becon, 1559; Shakespeare; B.E.; Hardy. The S.O.D., app. misled by Nares, says †, but this is incorrect, though the phrase may—only *may*—be ob. A Scottish variant (Ramsay, 1737) is *one's meal is dough* (E.D.D.).

cake-walk. 'A raid or attack that turns out to be unexpectedly easy': military coll.: 1914; ob. B. & P. Ex that easy-motioned pre-War dance.— 2. Money very easily obtained: Glasgow coll. (– 1934).

Cakes, Land of. Scotland: C. 18–20; coll.

cakes, like hot. Very quickly, promptly; esp. *sell* or *go like* . . . Orig. U.S., anglicised ca. 1888.

cakes and ale. Pleasant food; good living: coll., from ca. 1570. Shakespeare, 1601, 'Dost thou think, because thou art vertuous, there shall be no more Cakes and Ale ?'

cakey. See **cake,** n., 1.

*****cakey-pannum fencer.** A street seller of pastry: C. 19 c. See **pannam.**

Cal. Abbr. *Calcraft*, the common hangman: ca. 1860–70.

calaboose, n. and (rarely) v. Prison, esp. a common gaol. Nautical ex Spanish ex (1797) U.S. Dana, 1840, has the Sp. form, *calabozo.*

calcography. Incorrect for *chalcography*: late C. 17–20. O.E.D.

calculate, v. Think, believe, expect, suppose; intend. Coll., anglicised ca. 1870 ex U.S. (−1812) usage. John Galt in *Lawrie*. (Thornton.)

Caleb Quotem. A parish clerk; jack of all trades. Coll., ca. 1860–80. From a character in *The Wags of Windsor*.

calendars, give out. To issue unemployment cards prior to dismissing employees: workmen's (− 1935).

caleys. Ordinary stock(s) of the Caledonian Railway: Stock Exchange, from ca. 1880.

calf. A meek, harmless, (and occ.) brainless person: C. 16–20. S.O.D. gives as S.E., but it is surely coll. ? ! Hamilton Aïdé, *Morals and Mysteries*, 1872, ' She had a girlish fancy for the good-looking young calf.'

calf, slip or **cast the** or **one's.** (Of women) to have a miscarriage; to suffer abortion: C. 17–18: facetiously coll. Pepys.

calf !, you are a. You *do* weep a lot, don't you ! : c.p. (− 1923). Manchon. Perhaps influenced by the Fr. *tu pleures comme un veau.*

calf-bed. Bovine parturition: jocular after *child-bed* : Southey, 1822. Rare.

calf-clingers. Very close-fitting trousers, i.e. pantaloons: ca. 1830–1914. James Greenwood, *The Little Ragamuffins*, 1884.

calf in the cow's beily, eat the. To anticipate unduly: mid-C. 17–20 proverbial coll.; ob. Fuller; Richardson in *Clarissa Harlowe*. (Apperson.)

calf-lolly. An idle simpleton: coll., mid-C. 17–18. Urquhart. Cf. *calf* and *lo(blo)lly.*

calf-love. A youthful and romantic attachment: coll.; from ca. 1820; in C. 20, S.E.

***calf-sticking.** The selling of worthless, on the pretence that they are smuggled, goods: c.; ca. 1850–1920.

calf-, cow-, and **bull-week.** Coll., ca. 1830–80. The 1st, 2nd, and 3rd week before Christmas: among operatives, who, during this period, worked hours increasing in length in each successive week, until in *bull-week* they had extremely little time free. *The Echo*, Dec. 4, 1871.

calf's head. A very stupid fellow: late C. 16–early 19; coll.

calfskin, smack. To swear on the Bible: low: mid-C. 19–20; ob. Baumann.

calfskin fiddle. A drum: late C. 18–early 19. Grose, 1st ed.

calibash. A New South Wales farmers' term (ca. 1860–1900), thus in R. D. Barton's *Reminiscences of an Australian Pioneer*, 1917: ' In those days . . . everyone [on the station] was paid by orders, " calibashes " we used to call them, drawn on himself by the person paying. The townships all followed the same system.' Prob. ex some Aborigine word.

calicate is incorrect for *calycate*. O.E.D.

calico. Thin, attenuated; wasted. Coll.: C. 18–20; ob. N. Bailey, *Colloquies of Erasmus*, 1725; Sala, 1861.

calico ball. A cheap public dance: ca. 1860–1915; coll. The rare adj. *calico-bally*, derivatively = somewhat fast, occurs in a ca. 1890 ballad, *The Flipperty-Flop Young Man. Calico hop*, heard occ. in England, is the U.S. version.

calicot. A ' cad ' (sense 2): trade: ca. 1885–1910. Ware. Ex coll. Fr. *calicot*, a counterjumper.

calidity. Incorrect for *callidity* : C. 17. O.E.D.

California or Californian. Gen. in (*-ns*) pl. A gold piece: from ca. 1860; ob. by 1915; now almost †. H., 3rd ed. Ex the gold-fields rush (1849) and wealth of California.

Californian. A red, a hard-dried, herring: from ca. 1850; ob. Actually, Scottish herrings, the name coming from the Californian gold-discoveries. Cf. *Atlantic ranger.*

calix, calyx. ' Distinct (but cognate) words, though now usually confused by writers on botany ', W.

calk. See **caulk.**—2. To throw: Eton College, C. 19–20, ob.

calkes. ' Illiterate spelling of calx ', O.E.D.

call, n. The time when the masters do not call ' absence ': Eton coll.: C. 19–20.

call, v. To beg through (e.g. a street): c.: mid-C. 18–20. Bamfylde-Moore Carew, ' I called a whole street.' Ex the v.i., *to call*, to call at a house to beg: which is S.E.—2. (Nearly always in passive.) Abbr. *call to the bar* : legal: from ca. 1830. Dickens in *Sketches by Boz.*—3. To blame: lower classes' coll.: late C. 19–20. ' Don't call me, sir, if I'm a bit clumsy at first.' Ex *call down*, q.v., or *call names.*

call, have the. To be in the most demand: from ca. 1840; coll.; by 1880, S.E.

call a go. See **call it a day.**

call down. To reprimand: late C. 19–20; coll. Cf. † S.E. *call down*, to denounce.

call in. (*At* makes it v.t.) To visit a place incidentally: coll.: from ca. 1700.

call it a day. To state one's decision to go no further, do no more; rest content, e.g. with one's gain or loss. Occ. *call it a night*, if *night* lends point to the locution, as in James Spenser, *Limey Breaks In*, 1934, ' There were at least sixty pounds [£60] there, and I quickly collared the lot and called it a night.' C. 20; coll. Perhaps ex low *call a go*, to change one's stand, alter one's tactics, give in: mid-C. 19–20. H., 1st ed.: itself prob. ex cribbage.

call it eight bells ! A nautical c.p. serving as an excuse for a drink before noon, before which hour it is not etiquette to take liquor: C. 20. Ware.

call of, within. Near. From ca. 1700: coll. soon S.E.

call one for everything under the sun. To abuse thoroughly, vilify vigorously: coll.: late C. 19–20. Cf. the C. 17–early 19 (then dial.) *call*, to abuse, vilify.

call one's bluff. See **bluff, call one's.**

call sir and something else. To address as *sirrah*; hence, to speak contemptuously to: coll.: ca. 1660–1800.

call the game in. To cease doing something; to admit one has had enough: New Zealand coll.: from ca. 1912.

call upon, have a. To have the first chance of or with. Orig. (− 1888) U.S.; anglicised ca. 1895, but never very gen. Coll.

calla. Incorrect for the white arum (Ethiopian lily): 1870. O.E.D.

Callao painter. An evil-smelling gas arising from sea at that port: nautical coll.: late C. 19–20. Bowen.

***calle.** A cloak; a gown: c. of ca. 1670–1840. Coles; B.E. Ex ?

callindger. A calendar: sol.: C. 19–20.

***calling.** Begging, esp. as a tramp: tramps' c. (− 1935). Ex *calling at houses*. Cf. *call*, v., 1.

[**calloh.** The correct form of *kollah*.]

callous. Incorrect for *callus*: mid-C. 17–20. O.E.D.

Calm-Laylas, the. The Egyptian Labour Corps: military: 1914–18. Ex *kam laya, kam yom !* (how many nights, how many days), ' the droning chant of the men leading camels on the march' (F. & Gibbons).

*****calp** (C. 19) or **kelp** (C. 18–19). A hat: ca. 1750–1850. John Poulter. Cf. *calpac(k)*, a Turkish and Tartar felt cap (recorded 1813); any oriental or exotic cap. (S.O.D.)

Calvert's Entire. The Fourteenth Foot: from ca. 1835 to ca. 1880. Sir Harry Calvert was its Colonel in 1806–26 and, when Adjutant General, he had three entire battalions maintained. The name was suggested by the earlier (from ca. 1770) *Calvert's entire*, which, as in Tomlinson's *Slang Pastoral*, 1780, meant liquor, esp. if malt, Calvert being a maker of malt liquors.

calves gone to grass. Spindle shanks, meagre calves. Late C. 17–20 (ob.); coll. Ray, 1678, ' His calves are gone down to grass.' A late C. 18–19 variant is *veal will be cheap, calves fall* (Grose, 2nd ed.).

calves' heads, there are many ways of dressing. I.e. of doing any, but esp. a foolish, thing. C. 19–20; ob.

calves' heads are best hot. A jeering apology for one who sits down to eat with his hat on: coll.; C. 19–20.

calves' (or even **calves**) **liver.** Calf's liver: a frequent eating-house catachresis: mid-C. 19–20.

calx. (Eton College) the goal line in football. Not recorded before 1864. Ex the L. word.

calyciform. Incorrect for *caliciform*, as *calycle* is for *calicle*: late C. 18–20. O.E.D.

cam. A camisole: C. 20. Also *cami, cammy*. Cf. *com*, 3, q.v.

Cam roads. ' Retreat to Cambridge by way of a change,' Egan's Grose: Oxford University: ca. 1820–40.

Camarhas, the. The 79th—from 1881 the Cameron—Highlanders: military: C. 19–20. Ex *Old Cia Ma Tha* (lit., old how-are-you), the nickname of its first colonel, Sir Alan Cameron. F. & Gibbons.

Camberwell Death-trap, the. The Surrey Canal: Camberwell (London): ca. 1870–1900. Ware. Ex the number of children that, playing on its crumbling banks, were drowned there.

Cambridge fortune. A woman without substance: late C. 17–early 19. B.E. Like *Whitechapel fortune*, it is scabrous, Grose defining: ' A wind-mill and a water-mill'. These objects, here indelicately punned, being in the C. 18 very common in Cambridgeshire.

Cambridge (occ. **Cambridgeshire**) **oak.** A willow: mid-C. 18–20 coll.; ob. Grose, 1st ed. Willows abound in the Fen district.

Cambridgeshire camel. A native of, one long resident in, Cambridgeshire: mid-C. 17–mid-19. Fuller, 1662; Grose in his *Provincial Glossary*. Ex stilt-walking in the Fens. Apperson.

Cambridgeshire, or **fen, nightingale.** A frog: C. 19–20. Ex the dykes and canals so common in that county. Cf. *Cape nightingale*.

Cambridgeshire oak. See **Cambridge oak.**

Camden Town. A ' brown', i.e. a halfpenny: rhyming s. (— 1859). H., 1st ed.

came up ! Come up !: London cabmen to their horses: ca. 1890–1915. Ware.

came (often **come**) **up, before you.** Before you joined up: military c.p. by an experienced to bumptious young soldier: 1916–18. B. & P. See also at **before you came up.**

camel. A giraffe: South African coll., esp. among hunters: mid-C. 19–20. Pettman.—2. See **camels.**

Camel Corps, the. The infantry: jocular military of 1915–18. Because they were so heavily laden. B. & P.

camel night. Guest night on a warship: naval: late C. 19–20. Bowen. Why ? Perhaps because, on that night, one did not ' get the hump', for *lucus a non lucendo* etymologies are fairly common in s.

camel wallah. A native camel-driver: military coll.: G.W. (F. & Gibbons.) See **wallah.**

cameleon. See *chameleon* (B.E.).

cameleopard. A giraffe: a South African sol. (— 1913). Pettman. Cf. *camel*, q.v.

camelia. A frequent mistake (C. 18–20) for *camellia*: cf. *fuschia* for *fuchsia.*

camelier. A member of the Camel Corps proper: Australian military: 1916–18. On *muleteer*. But also *camellia*, ex the flower.

camel's complaint. The ' hump', low spirits. From ca. 1870; ob.

camels. (Very rare in singular.) Sopwith scouting aeroplanes used at sea: naval: 1915. Bowen. —2. Turkish, or Egyptian, cigarettes: New Zealand soldiers': in G.W. Ex their odour.

camera obscura. The posterior (— 1900): facetious. Perhaps ex U.S.

Cameronians. The 26th Regiment of Foot, British Army (now the 1st Battalion of Scottish Rifles). C. 18–20 military coll.: ? ob. Ex Richard Cameron, whose religious followers espoused the cause of William the Third.

*****camesa, camisa, camiscia, camise, kemesa.** A shirt or a shift: c.; ca. 1660–1880. Ex Sp. *camisa.* Cf. *commission.*

cami. Abbr. *camisole*: from ca. 1900; shop and women's. Also *cammy* and *cam.* Cf. :

cami-knicks. Abbr. *cami-knickers* (1915): from ca. 1917; shop and women's.

camisa, camiscia. See **camesa.**

*****camister.** A clergyman: c. (— 1851). Ex L. *camisia*, an alb, after *minister*; cf., however, *canister*, 3.

camouflage. Disguise; pretence, ' eye-wash ': ex military j., itself ex Parisian s. *camoufle*, a person's description by the police (i.e. standard-French *signalement*), and *camoufler*, to disguise. Also as v. ' Naturalised with amazing rapidity early in 1917 ', W. G. B. Shaw, ' I was in khaki by way of camouflage,' *The Daily Chronicle*, March 5, 1917 (W.). For its military senses, see, e.g., B. & P.

camp. To sleep or rest in an unusual place or at an unusual time (— 1893): Australian coll.—2. Hence, ' to stop for a rest in the middle of the day', Morris: idem: 1891. Occ. as a n.—3. To prove superior to: Australian: 1886, C. H. Kendall; very ob. Morris. Perhaps ex † S.E. *camp*, to contend, and *camping*, warfare.

camp, adj. Addicted to ' actions and gestures of exaggerated emphasis . . . Prob. from the Fr.', Ware; pleasantly ostentatious or, in manner, affected: London streets' (— 1909) >, by 1920, Uranian. (Perhaps rather ex the C. 19–20 dial. *camp* or *kemp*, uncouth, rough: see esp. the E.D.D.—2. Whence, objectionable; (slightly) disreputable; bogus: Society: from ca. 1930.—

3. Effeminate : theatrical (— 1935) and Society (— 1933). M. Lincoln, *Oh ! Definitely*, 1933. Ex sense 1.

Camp, the. Sydney : ca. 1790–1830.—2. Hobart : ca. 1830–50. Both Australian coll.

camp, go to. To go to bed ; lie down to rest : Australian coll., from ca. 1880. Also *have a camp*, to rest for a while. Cf. *camp*, v., 2.

camp, take into. To kill. From ca. 1880, orig. U.S. ; ob. (Mark Twain.)

camp-candlestick. An empty bottle ; a bayonet : late C. 18–early 19. Military. Grose, 2nd ed.

camp-stool brigade. The early waiters outside a theatre, etc. : coll., from ca. 1880.

campaign coat. A late C. 17 mode in men's dress ; orig. military and S.E. ; then loosely and coll. ; the word > † ca. 1750.—2. In C. 18 c., a tattered cloak worn to move compassion. *A New Canting Dict.*, 1725.

campaniloger. Incorrect for *campanologer* : C. 19–20. O.E.D.

*****Campbell's academy.** The hulks. Ca. 1770–1820 ; c., then low. A Mr. Campbell was the first director. George Parker, 1781 ; Grose.

campo. A playground or playing field : schools' : C. 17. O.E.D. Ex *in campo*.

can back, take the. See take the can back.

Can (the C.). H.M.S. *Canopus* : naval : early C. 20. Ware.—2. **(can.)** A reprimand : nautical : late C. 19–20. Bowen. See **carry the can.**—3. **(can.)** A barman : a Lambeth term, dating from ca. 1890. Clarence Rook, *The Hooligan Nights*, 1899.

can, in the. See ' Moving-Picture Slang ', § 6.

can do. I can (do it) ; can you (do it) ? : ' pidgin ' : mid-C. 19–20.—2. Hence, all right ! : military : late C. 19–20.

can I help you with that ? A non-aristocratic c.p. (1895 ; ob.) implying ' I'd like some of that.' Ware, ' When said to the fairer sex the import is different.'

can it ! Be quiet ! Stop talking : from ca. 1918 ; ex U.S.

can you say uncle to that ? A dustmen's c.p. (— 1909), in which *say uncle* = ' reply '. Ware notes that the c.p. answer is *yes—I can*. Perhaps there is a pun on dust-bins.

Canack. See **Canuck.**

canader. A Canadian canoe : Oxford undergraduates' (— 1909) ; ob. Ware. By ' Oxford -*er* '.

canadoe. A drink from a can : rare : C. 17 jocular coll. *Histrio-Mastix*, 1610, ' And now, my maisters, in this bravadoe, | I can read no more without Canadoe. | *Omnes.* What ho ! some Canadoe quickly ! ' (O.E.D.) ? *can* + *d'eau*, macaronic for a can of water, the water being *eau de vie*.

Canady. Canada : sol. : C. 19–20.

canaller. One who works or lives on a canal-boat (1864) ; a canal-boat (1887) : coll. : mostly U.S. (O.E.D.)

*****canakin.** A variant of *canniken, -kin*, q.v. Coles's spelling.

Canaries, the. Norwich City ' soccer ' team : sporting : late C. 19–20. Ex yellow jerseys.

canary ; occ. in senses 1–4, **canary-bird.** An arch knavish boy, a young wag : late C. 17–18. B.E.—2. A gaol-bird : c. and low : mid-C. 17–20 ; ob. Head. Recorded in Australia, 1827–90, of a convict. Peter Cunningham, 1827, says : ex the yellow clothes they wear on landing : Morris.—3. A

mistress : C. 18–early 19, ex c. sense, a harlot.—4. A guinea : C. 18–early 19 ; from ca. 1830, a sovereign : ob. Ex its yellow colour : cf. *yellow boy*, q.v.—5. A written promise of a donation or a subscription : Salvation Army : 1882. Coined by General Booth ex the colour of the demand-slips. (The semantics of the senses 1–5 : resp. liveliness, cage, nos. 3–5 colour.)—6. Also a sol., orig. malapropistic as in Shakespeare's *Merry Wives of Windsor*, for *quandary*.—7. In c. (— 1862), a thief's female assistant. Cf. *crow*, q.v.—8. A ' chorus-singer amongst the public—gen. in gallery ' : music-halls' : 1870 ; ob. Ware.—9. ' An ideal hip-adornment ', actually a modified cod-piece : costermongers' dress and term : 1876. Ware notes that it has some connexion with the ' nightingale ' of Boccaccio's sprightly story.—10. ' Any soldier wearing a yellow brassard ' (e.g. a gas-instructor) : military : 1915–18. F. & Gibbons.

canary-bird. See preceding, senses 1–4.

cancer, catch or **capture a.** (Rowing, university) ' catch a crab '. Coll., ca. 1850–1900. Hood in *Pen and Pencil Pictures*, 1857. Ex L. *cancer*, a crab.

candidate. To stand as a candidate. (Vbl.n. and adj., *candidating*.) Coll. : from ca. 1880. Not common.

candle, not able or **fit to hold a,** followed by **to.** Not fit to be compared with ; ' not in the same street ' (q.v.). From ca. 1640 ; a coll. that was S.E. by 1800. Developed from the affirmative form of the phrase (to help as a subordinate) : C. 15–18 and S.E.

candle, sell or **let by inch of.** To sell or let, hence to do anything, under fantastic or trivially precise conditions. Coll. : from ca. 1650 ; S.E. after ca. 1750. Ex an auction at which bids are received only while a small piece of candle remains burning. (Variant : *by the candle*.)

candle, the game is not worth the. Of any activity not worth the cost or the trouble : coll., from ca. 1550 ; in C. 18–20, S.E. Ex the playing of cards.

candle at both ends, burn one's or **the.** See **burn one's candle.**

candle-ends, drink off or **eat.** Lit. and fig., thus to express devotion while drinking a lady's health : ca. 1590–1640. The O.E.D. gives as S.E., but this is prob. because its users are Shakespeare, Fletcher, Ben Jonson : orig., it was prob. coll.

candle-keeper. (Winchester College) A privileged senior not a prefect : C. 19–20, ob.

candle-shop. ' A Roman Catholic chapel, or Ritualistic church—from the plenitude of lights ', Ware ; Low Churchmen's (— 1909).

candle-stick. A candidate : Winchester College, from ca. 1840. Ob. For this and for *candle-keeper*, see Mansfield's and Adams's books on the College.—2. Gen. in pl., a fountain in Trafalgar Square, London, W.C.2 : from ca. 1840 ; ob. Mayhew.—3. In pl., bad, small, or untunable bells : ' Hark ! how the candlesticks rattle,' Grose, 1st ed. : mid-C. 18–early 19.

candle to the devil, hold or **set a.** To be actively evil : C. 19–20, coll. ; the earlier sense (mid-C. 15–18), with *before* instead of *to*, is to placate with a candle, i.e. to treat the devil as a saint. The two senses tend to overlap.

candle-waster. One who studies, one who dissipates, late at night : coll. : late C. 16–20 ; rare after C. 17. Shakespeare in *Much Ado about Nothing*.

candles, see. See **see stars.**

candy. Drunk : mid.-C 18–early 19. Rare out-side of Ireland. Grose, 1st ed.

candy(-)man. A bailiff, process-server : North-ern, from 1844 ; ob. Ex an 1844 army of ejectors among whom were a few 'candymen' or hawkers of sweets ; the term spread rapidly.

candy-slinger. A vendor of toffee that he has pulled into wisps : grafters' : C. 20. Philip Allingham, *Cheapjack*, 1934.

*cane. A thieves' 'jemmy', q.v. : C. 20 c. Charles E. Leach.

cane, v. (Gen. in passive.) To punish (e.g. with C.B.) : military : G.W. (F. & Gibbons.)—2. To damage considerably, to shell heavily : id. : id. (Ibid.)—3. Hence, to treat badly, e.g. a motor-car : from 1918.

cane upon Abel. A stout stick stoutly laid about a man's shoulders : late C. 17–early 19 coll. B.E. Cf. *raise Cain* and *Cain and Abel*.

caniculars. Doggerel verses : jocularly pedantic coll. : 1872. Ex L. *canis*, a dog. O.E.D.

canine. A dog : jocular coll. : from 1869 ; ob.

canister. The head : from ca. 1790 ; mainly pugilistic ; ob. Moncrieff, 1821, 'I've nobb'd him on the canister.'—2. See canister-cup.—3. A clergy-man ; a preacher : London streets' (— 1909). Ware proposes derivation ex a preacher surnamed *Kynaster* (or even *Kynaston* ?) ; more prob. a corruption of *camister*, q.v.

canister-cap. A hat : from ca. 1820. Ca. 1870 it was abbr. to *canister*.

*canned. Tipsy : C. 20 c. and low s. Charles E. Leach. A G.W. military variant was *canned up* (F. & Gibbons).

*cank ; in C. 17, occ. *canke*. Dumb : from ca. 1670 : c. >, in C. 18, s. ; >, in early C. 19, dial. ; † by 1885. Coles, 1676 ; B.E. ; Grose. Extant in dial. is *cank*, to gabble, chatter, gossip.

*cannaken, -kin. An occ. variant of *canniken*, *-kin*, q.v.

cannibal. C. 17–18 coll. : 'a cruel rigid Fellow in dealing', B.E. Ex lit. S.E. sense.—2. (Cam-bridge University) a College's second boat that beats, i.e. 'bumps', its first, or a third that beats its second : from ca. 1880. Earlier (— 1864), a train-ing boat for freshmen, i.e. a boat racing in 'sloggers' ; also its rowers. In the former sense, cannibalism is punned-on, while in the latter *cannot-pull* is jocularly corrupted.

*canniken, cannikin. The plague : c. of ca. 1670–1820. Coles, 1676 ; Holme ; B.E. ? ety-mology : perhaps cognate with S.E. *canker*.

` cannon. A round beef-steak pudding : low (— 1909). Ware. Ex resemblance to small can-non ball.

*can(n)on, adj. Drunk : c. (— 1879). ? abbr. *cannoned*, mod. s. 'shot'. Cf. Ger. *er ist geschos-sen*.

cannon ball. A nickname (1852–ca. 1880) for an irreconcilable opponent of free trade. Gen. in pl. *The Saturday Review*, Oct. 30, 1858.—2. A human testicle : likewise gen. in pl. : from ca. 1885.

cannot (gen. can't) seem to. Seem (to be) unable to ; be apparently unable to ; cannot, apparently : coll. (and catachresis) : C. 20. Thus Kathleen Norris in *The Passing Show*, Dec. 6, 1933, 'I must be nervous this afternoon. I can't seem to settle down to anything.' Careless thinking, perhaps via *I cannot, it seems, do* (something or other) and *I don't seem to be able to*.

canoe, paddle one's own. To be independent.

Orig. (1828) U.S., anglicised ca. 1875 : coll. (O.E.D. Sup.)

canoe it. To travel, or go, in a canoe : coll. : from ca. 1880 in U.S., soon adopted in England.

canoer. A canoe : Oxford undergraduates' (— 1909). Ware. By 'Oxford -er'. Cf. *canader*, q.v.

canœuvre. 'A low manœuvre or essay at decep-tion', Bee : rare London : ca. 1820–50.

canoneer. One skilled in *canon* law, i.e. a canonist. Ca. 1640–1800 : jocular coll. after *cannoneer*. Baxter, 1659, 'We turn this Canon against the Canoneers.' (O.E.D.)

canoodle, v.t. and i. Fondle ; bill and coo. Coll. Orig. (— 1859) U.S., thoroughly anglicised by G. A. Sala in 1864. Perhaps ex *canny*, gentle, on *firkytoodle* ; but cf. the Somersetshire *canoodle*, a donkey, which may be noodle (fool) intensified.—2. Also as n., though *canoodling* (Sala, 1859) is more gen.—3. To coax : from ca. 1870 ; ob.—4. At Oxford University, ca. 1860–70, to propel a canoe. By a pun on *canoe*.—4. To make off : C. 20 ; ob. Manchon.

canoodler. A persistent biller and cooer. From ca. 1860. See canoodle, 1.

canooser, -zer. Sol. (— 1887) for *connoisseur*. Baumann.

canpacs (or C-.). Shares in the Canadian Pacific Railroad : Stock Exchange (— 1895). A. J. Wilson, *Stock Exchange Glossary*.

[Cant is the 'secret' speech of the underworld. This word *cant* dates from ca. 1700—*canting* is much earlier—and was long contemptuous and almost coll., as is the v., which dates from ca. 1600 ; like-wise *canter, canting*. See my *Slang*; Grose, P. ; O.E.D.; F. & H.; and Weekley.]

*cant. In c. (vagrants'), both food (— 1860) and (— 1839) a gift (see cant of togs).—2. (Pugilistic) a blow : coll. ; from ca. 1750. Ex S.E. sense : a toss, a throw.

*cant, v. In c., v.i. and t. : to speak ; to talk : mid-C. 16–19. Harman.

can't. Abbr. *cannot*, the C. 20 form of *can not* : coll. ; C. 18–20.

cant a slug into your bread(-)room ! Drink a dram ! Nautical : mid-C. 18–early 19. Grose, 2nd ed.

can't be did ! See did, 3.

*cant of dobbin. A roll of ribbon : c. : ca. 1810–60. Vaux. See Dobbin.

*cant of togs. A gift of clothes : beggars' c. (— 1839). Brandon. Ware shrewdly remarks, 'The mode of begging for clothes affords a word to describe the present or benefit gained by canting.'

can't see a hole in or through a ladder. Of a person very drunk. From ca. 1855. 'Ducange Anglicus', 1st ed. Sometimes, and at least as early as 1882, ... *a forty-foot ladder* (Ware).

can't see it ! I don't see why I should ! ; no ! : non-aristocratic coll. (— 1909). Ware.

can't show itself (or oneself) to. To be inferior to : lower classes' : 1880 ; ob. Ibid.

can't you feel the shrimps ? Don't you smell the sea ? : Cockney c.p. : 1876 ; ob. Ib.

Cantab. A member of the University of Cam-bridge : coll., first in Coventry's amusing novel, *Pompey the Little*, 1750. Abbr. *Cantabrigian*.

cantabank. A common or inferior singer of ballads : from ca. 1840 ; coll. Earlier, S.E. for a singer upon a platform. Ex It. *cantambanco*.

cantankerous. Cross-grained, ill-humoured ; acridly self-willed ; quarrelsome. Coll. : ? coined by Goldsmith in *She Stoops to Conquer*, 1772 ; Sheridan, *The Rivals*. Perhaps, says O.E.D., ex M.E. *contak*, contention, after *cankerous* ; H., 3rd ed., suggests a corruption of *contentious* ; W. thinks that the word may be of Irish formation (as suggested by O.E.D.).—2. Also, adv. with -*ly*, abstract n. with -*ness*.

canteen. A public-house : South African coll., prob. at first military : from ca. 1830. Pettman.— 2. Hence, *canteen-keeper*, the proprietor of one : 1832.

canteen eggs. A gas attack : military : 1917–18. ' The age of eggs used at the canteen was not guaranteed ' (F. & Gibbons).

canteen-keeper. See **canteen**.

canteen medal. A beer stain on one's tunic : military : from ca. 1875.—2. A good-conduct medal : military : late C. 19–20. F. & Gibbons. Many of those who wore it were hard drinkers—but they had even harder heads.

canteen merchant. One who serves in the ship's canteen : C. 20 : *Conway* Training Ship. Masefield.

canteen rat. ' An old soldier who constantly hangs about by the canteen, in order to be treated ' : military coll. : C. 20. B. & P.

canteen stinker. A cheap cigarette : military : 1915–18. F. & Gibbons.

canteen wallah. A man addicted to beer : military coll. : late C. 19–20. B. & P.

canter. See **canting crew**.

Canterbury. ' A sort of a short or Hand-gallop ', B.E. : C. 17–18. Abbr. *Canterbury gallop*, cf. *C. pace, trot, rate*, etc. [Whence *canter*, v. recorded in 1706, n. (an easy gallop) in 1755. S.O.D.]

Canterbury tale or occ. **story**. A story long and tedious : from ca. 1540 ; at first coll., but soon S.E. Latimer, 1549 ; Turberville, 1579 ; Grose, 1st ed. (Apperson.) Ex the long stories told by pilgrims proceeding to Canterbury.

canticle. A parish clerk : mid-C. 18–early 19. Grose, 1st ed. The parish clerk led the congregation's singing. Cf. *amen-curler*.

canting crew, the. Criminals and vagabonds, the *canters* (C. 17–18) : C. 17–19 : coll. In B.E.'s title, 1690 ; Hindley's *James Catnach*, 1878.

Canuck, occ. **Canack, K(a)nuck**. A Canadian : in England, from ca. 1915. Orig. (1855) a Canadian and American term for a French Canadian, which, inside Canada, it still means. Etymology obscure : perhaps *Canada* + *uc* (**uq**), the Algonquin n.- ending ; W., however, proposes, I think rightly, ex *Canada* after *Chinook*.—2. Hence, a Canadian horse (or pony) : coll. : U.S. (1860) >, ca. 1920 anglicised. (O.E.D. Sup.)

canvas, receive the. To be dismissed : C. 17, coll. Shirley in *The Brothers*. Cf. *get* and *give the bag* or *the sack*, qq.v.

canvas-climber. A sailor : coll. : late C. 16–17. Shakespeare in *Pericles*.

canvas town. A mushroom town : coll., from ca. 1850 ; Dickens, 1853.—Hence, 2, the Volunteer Encampment at Wimbledon (not since ca. 1905) or Bisley where the National Rifle Association meets.

canvass, cold. See **cold-canvass**.

canvas(s)eens. (Nautical) a sailor's canvas trousers : coll., C. 19–20, ob.

cap. The proceeds from an improvised collection (*cf. to send round the cap* or *hat*, C. 19–20 coll.), esp. for a huntsman on the death of the fox : ca. 1850– 1914. Abbr. *cap-money*, S.E. and extant.—2. At Westminster School, the amount collected at ' play and ' election ' dinners.—3. (Gen. in pl.) Abbr *capital letter* : coll., orig. printers' (— 1900), then publishers' and authors'.—4. In c., a false cover to a ' cover-down ' or tossing-coin : ca. 1840–80. H., 3rd ed.—5. A synonym for c. sense of *bonnet*, n. (q.v.) : c. : ca. 1810–50. Vaux.—6. (Only in vocative.) Captain : coll. : late C. 19–20. Ware, 1909, ' Common in America—gaining ground in England '.

cap, v. (University and Public School) to take off one's cap or hat in salutation of : late C. 16–20, ob. Coll., S.E. by 1700. ' . . . To cap a fellow ', *Gradus ad Cantabrigiam*, 1803.—2. In c., to take an oath : late C. 17–early 19. B.E. ; Grose.

cap, not to have come back for one's. (Of an aviator) to have been killed : military : 1918. Manchon.

cap, put on one's considering or **thinking. To** think, take time to think : coll., from ca. 1650.

cap acquaintance. Persons only slightly acquainted : C. 18–early 19 ; coll. Grose.

cap after it, fling or **throw one's.** To do something that is no longer of use, esp. when a project or a business is past hope. Coll. : late C. 17–19. B.E.

cap at, cast one's. ' To show indifference to, give up for lost ' : C. 16–17 ; coll. In proverbial form : *cast one's cap into the wind*.

cap at, set one's. (Of women only) to try, and keep trying, to gain a man's heart—or hand. Coll., from ca. 1770. Goldsmith, Thackeray. Ex navigation : cf. Fr. *mettre le cap sur* (W.).

cap-badge. A piece of bone (in, e.g., a stew) : military : from ca. 1910. F. & Gibbons.

cap be made of wool, if his or **your.** As sure as his cap is made of wool, i.e. indubitably : C. 17–18 ; coll.

*****cap for.** See **bonnet for** : c. : ca. 1810–40. Vaux.

cap on nine hairs(, with his). Jaunty or jovial, the cap being worn at an extreme angle : naval : late C. 19–20. Bowen.

*****cap, or cast, one's skin.** To strip naked : C. 19–20 (ob.) c.

cap set, have one's. Variant : **have (enough) under one's cap.** To be drunk : coll. : C. 17–18. Cf. :

cap-sick. Intoxicated : coll. : C. 17 (? 18). H. Hutton's anatomisation of folly, 1619. (O.E.D.)

cap the quadrangle. C. 18 university : (of undergraduates) ' to cross the area of the college cap in hand, in reverence to the Fellows who sometimes walk there ', Grose, 2nd ed.

capabarre. ' The looting of naval stores, mentioned in Marryat ' (Bowen) : naval coll. : C. 19. Semantics : ' by curtailment '.

cape. To keep a course : nautical coll. : C. 19– 20. Bowen.

Cape, the. The Cape of Good Hope : coll. > S.E. ; from ca. 1660.—2. Hence, Cape Town : 1828 (Pettman) ; † by 1850.—3. And Cape Colony : coll. ; from ca. 1845.—4. And even, likewise coll. (— 1913), South Africa in gen. Pettman.

Cape Cod turkey. Salt fish : ? mainly nautical (— 1874). H., 5th ed. On *Bombay duck*, q.v.

Cape doctor, the. A strong S.E. wind : Cape Colony coll. : C. 19–20. ' In the earlier days . . . when the Cape was used by Anglo-Indians as a sanatorium, they were wont to term these winds the *Cape Doctor* and they still retain the name,' Pettman, 1913.

Cape Flyaway. Imaginary land on the horizon : nautical coll. : C. 19–20. Bowen.

Cape Horn, double. See **double Cape Horn.**

Cape Horn fever. Malingering in bad weather : sailing-ship seamen's : mid-C. 19–20. Bowen.

Cape Horn rainwater. Rum : nautical : late C. 19–20 ; slightly ob. Bowen.

Cape nightingale. A frog : South African coll. : from ca. 1880. H. A. Bryden, *Kloof and Karoo*, 1889. Cf. *Cambridgeshire nightingale.*

Cape of Good Hope. Soap : rhyming s. (— 1914). F. & Gibbons.

Cape smoke. ' A brandy manufactured in nearly all the vine-growing districts of the Colony ', Pettman : South African coll. : 1848, H. H. Methuen, *Life in the Wilderness.* Described in 1879 as ' a poison calculated to burn the inside of a rhinoceros '. Pettman. It is of a cloudy colour.

Cape Stiff. Cape Horn : nautical : mid-C. 19–20. Bowen. Because, to a sailing ship, it was stiff work to beat round it.

Cape Turk, not to have rounded. See **Turk, not to . . .**

capella. A coat : theatrical, C. 19–20, ob. Direct ex It.

capeovi. Sick, ill : costermongers', from ca. 1860 ; ob. Cf. *capivvy.*

caper. A dodge, device, performance : coll., orig. (— 1851) low. *The London Herald*, March 23, 1867, ' " He'll get five years penal for this little caper," said the policeman.' Ex the S.E. senses and cf. *play the giddy goat,* for ultimately *caper* is the L. *caper,* a goat.—2. Whence, a chorister boy ; a ballet-girl : low : mid-C. 19–20 ; ob. Mayhew (O.E.D.).

caper, v.i. To be hanged : late C. 18–mid 19. Wolcot (E.D.D.). Prob. ex *cut a caper upon nothing,* q.v.

*****caper, flying.** An escape from prison : c. (— 1923). Manchon.

caper-corner-ways. Diagonally : nautical coll. : C. 19–20. Bowen. Presumably *caper* is a corruption of *cater,* four.

caper-cousin. Incorrect for *cater-cousin* : C. 17–20. O.E.D.

caper-merchant. A dancing master : mid-C. 18–19. Grose, 1st ed. ; H., 5th ed. Cf. *hop-merchant.*

caper (up)on nothing, cut a ; occ. **cut capers . . .** Like **cut caper sauce,** = to be hanged : low coll., C. 18–19. Hanging has many synonyms, some much grimmer than these.

caperdewsie, occ. **caperdochy** (as in Heywood, 1600) or **cappadochio.** Stocks ; a prison. Low : late C. 16–17.

capital. Excellent : coll., from ca. 1760 ; S.E. after ca. 1820. Often as exclamation. Ex *capital,* important. Cf. the tendency of *awful.*

capital, work. To commit a capital offence : c. or low ; from ca. 1830 ; † by 1920.

capital out of, make. To turn to account. From ca. 1850 ; coll. almost imm. S.E.

capitation drugget. Cheap and inferior drugget : coll., late C. 17–18. Ex the capitation tax on this clothing-material. B.E.

capivi, capivvy. Sol. for *balsam copaiba,* a popular remedy for gonorrhœa. From ca. 1850.

capivvy, cry. To be persecuted to death, or near to it : sporting s., from ca. 1840 ; ob. Orig. a hunting term, as in Surtees, *Handley Cross,* 1843.

cap'n. Captain : coll. : mid-C. 19–20. Baumann. Cf. *capting.*

capon. A red herring : from ca. 1640. Orig. jocular S.E., it > coll. ca. 1700. Cf. *Yarmouth capon,* q.v.

capot me ! A coll. imprecation : mid-C. 18–early 19. Foote. Ex *capot,* to ' score off '. O.E.D.

cappadochio. See **caperdewsie.**

capped, be. ' To be checked by strong currents ' : nautical coll. : mid-C. 19–20. Bowen.

capper. (Auctioneers') a dummy bidder at an auction : from ca. 1870.

capricornified. ' Hornified ', cuckolded : mid-C. 18–early 19. Grose, 1st ed.

caprification. Artificial fertilisation : catachrestic : from 1830's. O.E.D.

capron hardy. An impudent fellow : coll. ; ca. 1450–1630. Awdelay.

caps. Capitals (letters of alphabet) : printers' j. >, by 1920, authors' and typists' coll. Manchon.

caps, pull. (Only of women) to wrangle in unseemly fashion : from ca. 1750 ; ob. if not † ; coll. Colman, 1763, ' A man that half the women in town would pull caps for ' ; Scott, 1825, ' Well, dearest Rachel, we will not pull caps about this man.'

capsize, v.t. To overturn, upset : orig. nautical s. (witness use by Dibdin and Grose, 2nd ed.), prob. ex Sp. *cabezar* (— 1788) ; S.E. by 1820.

capstan, the. A punishment whereby the arms were outstretched on a capstan-bar and a weight suspended from the neck : naval coll. : C. 17–early 18. Bowen.

capstan-step. The time or beat kept by the old ship's fiddler for capstan work : nautical : C. 19. Bowen.

captain. A familiar and/or jesting term of address : coll. ; C. 17–20. Shakespeare. Cf. U.S. *judge.*—2. In C. 18, a prosperous highwayman, a gaming or a bawdy-house bully : both low, the latter perhaps c.—3. Money, esp. in *the captain is not at home,* I have no money : C. 18–early 19. Dyche. —4. A glandered horse : knackers' s., from ca. 1830.

Captain Armstrong. A dishonest jockey : from ca. 1860. More gen. in phrase, *come Captain Armstrong,* to ' pull ' a horse and thus prevent him from winning : from ca. 1850. Turf. *Sporting Life,* Nov. 5, 1864.

*****Captain Bates ?, been to see.** A ' how-d'ye-do ' to one recently released from gaol : c., then Cockney : late C. 19–20. ' Captain Bates was a well-known metropolitan prison-governor,' Ware.

Captain Bow-Wow. A famous Clyde passenger-boat skipper : C. 19. Bowen. He used a dog as a makeshift fender.

Captain Cook ; Cooker or **cooker.** Orig. (—1879), a wild pig ; hence (— 1894), ' a gaunt, ill-shaped, or sorry-looking pig ', E. Wakefield : New Zealand ; slightly ob. Morris. Pigs were introduced into New Zealand by Captain Cook.—2. (*Captain Cook.*) A book : rhyming s. : late C. 19–20. B. & P.

Captain Copperthorn's crew. All officers ; a crew in which everyone wishes to be captain : mid-C. 18–19 ; nautical. Grose, 1st ed.

Captain Cork. A man slow in passing the bottle : C. 19–20, ob. ; military.

Captain Crank. The leader of a group of highwaymen : C. 18–early 19.

Captain Grand. A haughty, blustering man : C. 18–19 ; coll. Cf. *furioso.*

Captain Hackum. (**Hack 'em.**) A fighting, blustering bully. Ca. 1600–1850. B.E., Grose.

captain is at home or **come, the.** Menstruation proceeds : late C. 18–early 19 ; low. Grose, 3rd ed. Punning *catamenia*.

captain lieutenant. Meat half-way between veal and beef : military : late C. 18–19. Grose, 2nd ed. Ex the brevet officer, who, receiving lieutenant's pay, ranks as a captain. (The rank was abolished before 1893.)

Captain MacFluffer, as in **take C.M. badly.** (To have a bad bout of) loss of memory on the stage : theatrical (— 1909) ; ob. Ware. An elaboration of *fluff*, n., 2, and v., 3, qq.v. ; the *Mac* may pun the Scottish *mak'*, to make,—whence *MacFluffer* is, lit., a ' fluff '-maker.

Captain Podd. An C. 18 nickname for a puppet-showman. Grose, 3rd ed.

Captain Queernabs. An ill-dressed or shabby man : late C. 17–early 19. In C. 17–mid-18, either c. or low s. B.E.

Captain Quiz. A mocker : C. 18 ; coll. Amplifying *quiz*.

Captain Rag. Edmund Smith, the English poet (1672–1710), now completely forgotten. Dawson.

Captain Sharp. An arrant cheat ; a huffing, sneaking, cowardly bully : late C. 17–early 19. B.E.—2. Hence, a gamesters' bully : mid-C. 18–early 19. Grose, 1st ed.

Captain Swosser. A blustering naval officer : non-aristocratic coll. (— 1882) ; ob. Ware. Ex ' a character of Marryat's '.

Captain Tom. The leader of a mob ; the mob itself : late C. 17–early 19. B.E., Grose.

captain's cloak, the. The 36th Article of War : naval : C. 20. Bowen. It relates to powers of punishment.

capting. Captain : low coll. : C. 19–20. Bäumann. Cf. *cap'n*.

capture the pickled biscuit. See **bun, take the.**

captured a sugar-boat !, they (occ. we) **must have.** A c.p. explaining the issue of a liberal ration of sugar : New Zealanders' : in G.W.

caput. The monitors' big study in a School house : Sherborne : mid-C. 19–20. Desmond Coke, *Wilson's*, 1922. Ex L. *caput*, head : cf. the relationship of *block*, head, to *block-house*.—2. (Also *kaput, kapout*.) Finished ; no more : military : 1915 ; ob. Ex Ger. *kaputt*, done for, ruined, insolvent. Used similarly to *napoo*, q.v. F. & Gibbons ; my *Words !*

car it. To go by car (of whatever sort the context indicates) : coll. : from ca. 1860.

carachou. Good : among prisoners of war in Germany : 1914–18. Direct ex Russian. (B. & P.)

***caravan.** A dupe ; a man swindled : late C. 17–18. C. and low. Etherege, in *The Man of Mode*, ' What spruce prig is that ? A caravan, lately come from Paris.' Perhaps ex caravans frequently robbed.—2. ? hence, a large sum of money : late C. 17–18 c. B.E. Cf. *cargo*, 2.—3. A railway train carrying people to a prize-fight : from ca. 1845 ; boxing. Prob. ex its length : cf., however, Blount, 1674, ' Of late corruptly used with us for a kind of waggon to carry passengers to and from London ' (W.).

caravan, v. To have or hold a picnic : prob. sol. (— 1923) for or ex *carnival*. Manchon.

caravansera. A railway station : ca. 1845–1900 ; boxing. Ex *caravan*, 3.

carbon. A carbon copy (opp. to *the top*) of a typewritten MS. or sheet thereof : coll. : C. 20 : authors' and typists'.

carbonado. To cut, hack : late C. 16–17. Coll. soon S.E. Shakespeare.

carbuncle face. A red, large-pimpled face : coll. : late C. 17–18. B.E., Grose.

card. A device ; expedient : from ca. 1700 (but cf. *card, that's a sure*) ; ob. by 1900. Frances Brooke, in *Lady Julia Mandeville*.—2. A ' character ', an odd fellow : from ca. 1835. Dickens, 1836 ; *The Card*, a novel (1911) by Arnold Bennett. ' It may be an extension of the metaphorical *good card, sure card*, etc., or . . . an anglicised form of Scottish *caird*, tinker (cf. *artful beggar*, etc.) ' : W. Often with *downy, knowing, queer*.—3. **(the card.)** The correct number, price, or thing, the ' ticket ' : from ca. 1850, coll. Mayhew. Perhaps ex *the correct card* of racing.—4. A troublesome rating : naval : late C. 19–20. Bowen. Ex sense 2.

card, v. To torture with a loom-card : from ca. 1550 ; coll., passing to S.E. In C. 19, an Irish political diversion. *The Scots Observer*, 1889, ' to card a woman's hide '. Ob. The n. is *carding*.—2. To fix on a card : trade coll. : from ca. 1880. O.E.D.

card, a cooling. Anything that cools enthusiasm : ca. 1570–1750 ; coll. Ex an obscure card-game.

card, a leading. An example or precedent : coll. ; C. 17–19. B.E.

card, one's best. A last resort ; more gen., one's best plan or action. Coll. : C. 19–20.

card, speak by the. To speak precisely, most accurately. Coll. : C. 17–20 ; S.E. in C. 19–20. Shakespeare in *Hamlet*, ' We must speak by the card, or equivocation will undo us.'

card, that's a sure. That's a safe device or expedient, or one likely to bring success ; also of such a person. C. 16–20 ; coll. *Thersites, an Interlude*, ca. 1537 ; B.E.

***card-con(e)y-catching.** Swindling : c. : late C. 16. Greene. (O.E.D.) See **cony-catching.**

card of ten, brag or **face it out with a.** To assume a bold front : ca. 1540–1700 ; coll. Ex cards ; a card of ten pips being none too high.

cardiagraphy. Cardiography : incorrect : from ca. 1870. O.E.D.

cardinal. Mulled red wine : from ca. 1860. In *Tom Brown at Oxford*.—2. Gen. in pl., a shoeblack. From ca. 1880 ; † by 1915. Cf. *city red*.

cardinal, adj. Carnal, esp. in *cardinal sin* : mid-C. 16–20 sol. Shakespeare jocularly uses *cardinally* for *carnally*. Vice versa, *carnal* is sol. for cardinal, esp. in *the carnal points* : C. 16–20.

cardinal is come, the. A variant of *captain is . . .*, q.v. Grose, 3rd.

Cards. Adrian Quist, the Australian lawn-tennis player (fl. 1932–), who is very fond of bridge.

cards, a house of. An unsafe project or circumstance : from ca. 1800 ; coll. soon S.E.

cards, get one's. To be dismissed : busmen's : from ca. 1925. James Curtis, *The Gilt Kid*, 1936. I.e. one's employment-card.

cards, get one's. See also **books, get one's.**

cards, have or **go in with good.** Reasonably to expect success : late C. 16–18 : coll., > S.E. in C. 17.

cards, on the. Possible ; almost probable. Coll. >, by 1850, S.E. ; gen. from 1849, when popularised by Dickens ; in use earlier, being adumbrated by Smollett in 1749. Opp. to *out of the cards*, which lasted only ca. 1810–70. Perhaps ex cartomancy (O.E.D.).

cards . . ., play one's. With *badly, well*, etc. To act clumsily, cleverly, etc. From ca. 1640 ; coll., soon S.E.

cards, show one's. To disclose one's power or plans : from ca. 1580 ; coll. soon S.E.

cards, throw up (or down) one's. To abandon a project, a career, etc. From late C. 17 ; coll.

Cardwell's men. Ca. 1869–90, military coll.: officers promoted not by purchase but on merit (and still, inevitably, by influence). Edward, Viscount Cardwell (1813–86) was in 1868 appointed Secretary for War ; he thereupon reorganised the British Army. (D.N.B.)

care a pin, farthing, rap, a damn, three damns, a tinker's curse, a fig—not to. These phrases are all coll., resp. — 1633, 1709, 1800, 1785, 1760, 1830, 1850 ; in C. 20, the first three and the last one are all S.E. There are others : e.g. . . . *a button, a chip, a cent* (mostly U.S.).

***care-grinder,** gen. preceded by *vertical*. The treadmill : c. ; ca. 1860–1900.

care if I . . ., I don't. I am disposed to . . . From ca. 1840 ; coll., now on verge of S.E.

care if I do, I don't. Yes, all right. Orig. (— 1870), U.S., anglicised ca. 1900. (Gen. in acceptance of a drink.)

careening ; careened. Physic-taking ; forced to take physic : naval : ca. 1820–60. Bee. Ex lit. S.E. sense.

careful. Mean in money matters : coll. : from ca. 1890.

carfindo. A ship's carpenter : naval : C. 19. F. & Gibbons. Perhaps a corruption of *carpenter* influenced by dial. *carf*, a notch in wood.

cargo. Contemptuous for a person : C. 17 ; coll. Ben Jonson. Perhaps ex Sp. *cargo* (S.O.D.).—2. Money : c. and low, late C. 17–18. B.E. For semantics, cf. *caravan*, 2, q.v.—3. (Winchester College) a hamper from home : from ca. 1840 ; ob.

cargo, despatch one's. To ease oneself (of the major need) : euphemistic, yet rather objectionable (— 1923). Manchon.

cargo (or C.) Bill. A R.N. Reserve officer serving in the Navy : naval : ca. 1870–1914. Bowen. Before the G.W. he used to be considered a ' passenger '.

Carl the caretaker's in charge ! This is a quiet sector (of the line) !: military c.p. : 1915–18 (Western Front). This imaginary German was occ. called *Minnie's husband* (see **minnie**) or *Hans the grenadier* (ex the bombing-parties). F. & Gibbons.

Carlo Khan. Charles James Fox. Ex his magnificence. (Dawson.) Cf. *Young Cub*.

Carmagnole. A French soldier : ca. 1790–1800. Burns uses it of Satan. Ex the Fr. revolutionary song. (S.O.D.)

carmine. Blood : sporting (— 1860) ; † by 1900. *Chambers's Journal*, 1860. Cf. *ruby* and *claret*.

carnal. Sol. for *cardinal* : mid-C. 16–20. See also **cardinal**.

carnardine. Incorrect for *carnadine* : C. 17–20. O.E.D.

carney, carny. Seductive flattery ; suave hypocrisy. From ca. 1820 ; coll. (See **carneying**.) More common as v.t. and i. :

carn(e)y, v. To coax, wheedle insinuatingly : coll. (— 1811) and dial. ? ex It. *carne*, flesh. Cf. the n. and the next two entries.

carn(e)y. Sly ; cunning, artful : low and military (— 1914). F. & Gibbons. Ex the n. ; cf. :

carney, come the. To speak or act flatteringly : low (— 1923). Manchon. Ex *carney*, n.

carneying, ppl. adj. Wheedling, coaxing, insinuating, seductively flattering, suavely hypocritical : from ca. 1830. Coll. Mayhew ; R. L. Stevenson, 1884, ' the female dog, that mass of carneying affectations '. This and its radical prob. come ex L. *caro, carnis*, flesh (cf. S.E. *carnal* and c. *carnish*, meat), via It. *carne* and after *blarney*.

***carnish.** Meat : C. 19–20 c. Ex Lingua Franca ex It. Hence *carnish-ken*, a thieves' eating-house or ' prog-shop '. North Country.

carny. See **carney**.

caroon. In low Cockney and Parlyaree : a crown(piece). Ca. 1845–1915 ; surviving in *medza caroon*, half a crown. Perhaps ex It. *corona*, perhaps merely *crown* mispronounced ; Sampson's note at *kuruna* suggests a Gypsy origin (cf. Romany *koórona*).

carousel. Incorrect for *carousal* : C. 18–20. (O.E.D.)

carpenter scene. Comic dialogue, in front of the curtain, while elaborate sets are being erected : theatrical : ca. 1860–95. Ware.—2. The raising of the curtain : theatrical (— 1923). Manchon.

carpenter's herb. ' Erroneously, bungle and yarrow ' : C. 18–20. O.E.D. Properly, self-heal.

***carpet.** A prison sentence or term of three months : C. 20 c. Charles E. Leach ; *Slang*, p. 243.

carpet, v. To reprimand : coll. : recorded in 1840, H. Cockton's once famous novel, *Valentine Vox*. Ex *carpet, walk the*, q.v.

carpet, bring on the. To bring (a matter) up or forward for discussion : from ca. 1720 ; coll. till C. 19, when S.E. Lit., bring on the table (before the council, etc.), for carpets ' covered tables and beds before they were used for floors ' : W.

carpet, walk the. To be reprimanded : from ca. 1820 ; coll. John Galt. Ex ' servants . . . summoned into the " parlour " for a wigging ', W.

carpet-bag recruit. (Military) a recruit worth more than what he stands up in : from ca. 1875. Cf. the U.S. adj., *carpet-bag*, and n., *carpet-bagger* : see Thornton.

carpet-dance. An (informal) drawing - room dance : Society coll. (1877) ; ob. Ware.

carpet-knight. Prior to 1800 the stress is on the boudoir ; after, on the drawing-room (see **carpet-man**). A stay-at-home soldier : from ca. 1570 ; coll. ; in C. 19–20, S.E. Etymologically, ' one knighted at court, kneeling on the carpet before the throne, instead of on the battlefield ', W.

carpet-man or **-monger.** A frequenter of ladies' boudoirs and carpeted chambers : late C. 16–17 ; coll. The occupation is *carpet-trade* : late C. 16–17, coll.—2. (*Carpet-man* only.) A naval officer promoted by influence : naval : late C. 19–20. Bowen.

carpet-road. A level, well-kept road : coll. : late C. 17–18. B.E.

carpet-slippered bugger. ' A heavy shell passing far overhead, therefore with but a faint noise ' : military : 1915 ; ob. B. & P. Also *carpet slipper*, a shell passing silently, esp. if of the naval high-explosive type : the two words, therefore, are virtually synonymous.

carpet-swab. A carpet bag : from ca. 1835 ; coll. Barham in his poem, *Misadventure at Margate*.

carpeting. A scolding : coll. : from ca. 1870 ; ob. Ex *carpet*, v., q.v.

carping. Carking : catachrestic : late C. 16–20. O.E.D.

carriage, Her Majesty's. See Queen's bus.

carriage-company. People—orig. merchants and tradesmen—having their own carriages : coll. > S.E. ; from ca. 1830 ; ob. Thackeray, 1855, ' No phrase more elegant . . . than . . . " seeing a great deal of carriage-company " '. (O.E.D.)

carried. Married : rhyming s. (— 1909) ; ob. Ware.

*carrier, in (? late C. 17–)C. 18–early 19 c., is a criminal band's spy or look-out. *A New Canting Dict.*, 1725.

carrier pigeon. (Racing) a person running hither and thither with ' commissions '. From ca. 1850. In C. 20, however, it is also racing s. for a thief, according to Manchon : but I suspect an error here. —2. In c., a victimiser of lottery-office keepers : mid-C. 18–early 19. G. Parker, 1781.

carrion. A harlot : C. 18–19.—2. The human body : C. 19–20 ; pejoratively indicated in C. 17, = low coll.

carrion-case. A shirt ; a chemise. Low : C. 19–20 ; ob.

carrion-hunter. An undertaker : ca. 1780–1850. Grose, 1st ed. *Carrion* = corpse was S.E. of ca. 1760–1900. Cf. cold cook.

carrion-row. A place where inferior meat is sold : ca. 1720–1800. Swift.

carrogh. Incorrect for *curragh*, coracle. O.E.D.

carrot !, take a. A low and insulting c.p. (— 1874) ; ob. H., 5th ed. Orig. said to women only and of a scabrous implication : contrast *have a banana !*, the C. 20 innocent phrase that soon came, in certain circles, to be used obscenely. Cf. the ob. French *Et ta sœur, aime-t-elle les radis ?*

carrot-nob. See carrots. — carrot-pated. See carroty.

carrots. Red hair : coll. : Wesley *père* seems to have been, in 1685, the first to print the term, as B.E. was the first to record it of a red-haired person ; as the latter, a rather uncouth nickname, with the C. 20 variant, *carrot-nob* (Manchon).

carroty. Having red hair : from ca. 1740 ; coll. >, by 1880, S.E. Smollett in *Roderick Random*, Thackeray in the *Newcomes*. Mark Lemon, the mid-Victorian humorist, noted of the Greeks that all the Graces were Χάριται. Earlier was *carrot-pated* (B.E.), likewise coll. (Often misspelt *carrotty*.)

carry. The distance for which an occupied stretcher is, or has, to be carried : Royal Army Medical Corps coll. in G.W.—and since. Philip Gosse, *Memoirs of a Camp-Follower*, 1934.

carry a (great) stroke. To have, wield much influence : ca. 1640–1800 ; coll. > S.E.

carry an M under one's girdle. See girdle, ne'er an . . .

carry coals. To endure, put up with an insult or an injury : late C. 16–17 : coll. >, by 1620, S.E. Shakespeare, in *Romeo and Juliet*, ' Gregory, o' my word, we'll not carry coals.'

carry corn. To behave well in success : mid-C.19–20, gen. as ' . . . doesn't carry corn well '. Ex the behaviour of corn-fed horses. Doubtless adopted from dial. (E.D.D. records it for 1845) and at first mainly rural.

carry dog. See dog, put on.

carry-knave. A low harlot : C. 17–18 ; coll. Taylor the Water Poet.

carry Matilda. See Matilda.

carry me out and bury me decent(ly) ! An exclamation indicative of the auditor's incredulity or, occ., displeasure : coll. ; from ca. 1780. After

ca. 1870, gen. abbr. to *carry me out !* Post-1850 variants, all † by 1930, were *carry me out and leave me in the gutter, carry me upstairs, carry me home,* and *whoa, carry me out* : cf. *let me die* and *good night !,* qq.v. (Ware.)

carry on. To behave conspicuously ; frolic ; flirt. Coll. : from ca. 1850. Whyte-Melville, 1856, ' Lady Carmine's eldest girl is carrying on with young Thriftless.' Prob. nautical in origin : ex *carrying on sail*. See carryings-on.—2. To endure hardship ; show quiet and constant fortitude : a C. 20 coll. popularised by the G.W. An imperative, orig. a military order, then (1917) = go ahead !, continue !, esp. continue as you are now doing. Cf.:

carry on or carry under. A c.p. slogan employed by old sailing-ship captains, ' whose creed was to clap on sail regardless of risk ' (Bowen) : C. 19–20 ; ob. Cf. :

carry on, Sergeant-Major ! Go ahead ; Oh, *you* do that ! ; I've finished, you can do as you like : military (rarely among officers) c.p. : from 1915. B. & P., ' Often a lazy or incompetent officer's evasion, [it] was originally the Company Commander's order to his S.M.'

carry out one's bat. See bat.

carry-tale. A tale-bearer : ca. 1570–1840 ; coll. in C. 16, then S.E.

*carry the banner. To tramp the road ; be a tramp : vagrants' c., C. 20.

carry the can. To be reprimanded : naval : late C. 19–20. Bowen. Prob. suggested by *carry the keg,* q.v. In the form *carry the can back* it means, since ca. 1920 in the R.A.F. : to be made the scape-goat ; to do the dirty work while another person gets the credit.

*carry the keg. A c. pun on *cag, carry the,* q.v. : 1812, Vaux ; † by 1890. Whence *distiller, walking,* q.v.

*carry the stick. Applied to the operation whereby a woman, in conversation, robs a well-dressed elderly, or drunk, man, and her male associate, masquerading as a detective, makes a fuss and enables her to depart. Scottish thieves' : ca. 1860–1920. The London equivalent, same period, is *to trip up.*

carrying three red lights. Drunk : nautical : C. 20. Bowen, ' From the " Not under Control " signal '.

carryings-on. Conspicuous behaviour ; frolics ; flirtation : from ca. 1840 ; coll. G. A. Sala, 1859. A much earlier coll. sense is : questionable proceed-ings, as in Butler, *Hudibras,* ' Is this the end | To which these Carryings-on did tend ? ' Cf. *goings-on.*

*carsey. A C. 19–20 c. variant of *case* (q.v.), a house, a den, a brothel.—2. A place : grafters' : C. 20. Philip Allingham.

cart. A race-course : racing-men's : ca. 1855–70. ' Ducange Anglicus ', 1st ed. ? connected with *correct card,* q.v.—2. The upper shell of a crab : coll. and dial. (— 1850). H., 2nd ed.—3. A bed : Regular Army's : mid-C. 19–20 ; ob. F. & Gibbons.—4. Hence, a bunk : ships' stewards' : from ca. 1919.—5. See carts.

cart, v.t. To defeat, surpass, do better than : Oxford and Cambridge University : from ca. 1850 ; † by 1934. Esp. as *we carted them home,* defeated them badly. Cf. the next entry.—2. To arrest : low Glasgow (—1934). Alastair Baxter ; Alex. MacArthur & Kingsley Long. Gen. in the passive. —3. To hit vigorously at cricket : Public Schools' :

from ca. 1890. V.i. in P.G. Wodehouse, *A Prefect's Uncle*, 1903 : v.t. in Id., *Tales of St. Austin's*, 1903.

cart, in the. Wrong ; in the wrong ; in a ' fix '. Esp. as *put in the cart*, to deceive, trick, embarrass, incommode seriously, as a jockey his owner. Racing and gen. from ca. 1865. Occ. as *carted* or as *in the box*. ' Perhaps goes back to the cart in which criminals were taken to execution ', W.—2. In the know : from ca. 1870. *The Referee*, April 1, 1883. —3. (Occ. as *on the tail-board*), it is applied to the lowest scorer : gaming, mid-C. 19–20. Cf. sense 1.

cart, walk the. To walk over the course : racing, from ca. 1870. In ' Ducange Anglicus ', 1857, the form is *traverse the cart*.

cart away, occ. **off** or **out.** To remove : coll., C. 19–20.

cart before the horse, set or **put.** To reverse the usual order, whether of things or of ideas. From ca. 1500 ; a coll. that, in C. 17, > S.E.

cart-grease. Bad butter, then any butter : from ca. 1875. Cf. *cow-grease*.

cart-wheel. Variant *coach-wheel*. Both gen. abbr. to *wheel*. A crown piece : low : from ca. 1855. ' Ducange Anglicus ', 1st ed.—2. A broad hint : C. 19.—3. **turn cart-wheels,** to execute a series of lateral somersaults (the arms and legs resembling wheel-spokes) : from ca. 1860 ; coll. ; in C. 20, S.E. Earlier (ca. 1840–75), *do a Catharine wheel*, q.v.

Cartholic. See **Catholic**.

carts. A pair of shoes : mid-C. 19–20 ; ob. Hotten explains by Norfolk *cart*, a crab's shell ; Ware refers it to the noise made by a labourer walking heavily. Cf. *boats* and *two feet . . .*, qq.v.

carty. Of the build and/or breed of a cart-horse : 1863 ; coll. (O.E.D.) In C. 20, rare.

*carve up. To swindle an accomplice out of his share : C. 20 c. Charles E. Leach.—2. Hence, a *carve-up* is any swindle : lower classes' (— 1935).— 3. The amount of money left by a will : C. 20. (M. Harrison, *Spring in Tartarus*, 1935.) Cf. *cut up rich* (or *warm*).

Carvel's ring. The *pudendum muliebre* : mid-C. 18–early 19 : low coll. Ex a scabrous anecdote, for which see the (sometimes legally) inimitable Grose (1st ed.).

carver and gilder. A match-maker : from ca. 1820 ; ob. Egan's Grose.

carving knife. A wife : military rhyming s. (— 1914). F. & Gibbons. Much more gen. is *trouble and strife*.

casa, ca-sa, or **ca. sa.** A writ of *capias ad satisfaciendum*. Legal coll. : late C. 18–20 ; ob.—2.

casa, case. A house, a brothel, c., C. 17–20, leads to C. 19–20 c. and low s. *case-house*, a brothel, and late C. 18–18 c. and low s. *case vrow*, a harlot attached to a particular bawdy-house.—3. The *case* form, in C. 19, also means a water-closet. Ex It. *casa*.

casabianc. The last of anything, esp. of cigarettes : naval and military. Mid C. 19–20. Bowen ; B. & P. Ex *Casabianca*, the boy hero of Mrs. Hemans.

casalty (boy). See **casualty**, n. and adj. It is a sol. form.

cascade. A trundling and gymnastic performance : theatrical, from ca. 1840 ; ob.—2. Beer : in Tasmania, then slightly on the Australian continent : from ca. 1880. Ex the cascade water from which it was made : the firm that, at Hobart, makes it is known as the Cascade Brewery Company.

cascade, v. To vomit : low coll., from ca. 1780. Smollett's ' She cascaded in his urn ', 1771, is only analogous ; Grose, however, has it (2nd ed.).

*case. A bad crown-piece : c. and low, ca. 1835–1900. Brandon. Hence, the sum of five shillings : C. 20 low. Prob. ex Yiddish *caser*.—2. An eccentric person, a ' character ', a ' cure '. Orig. (— 1833) U.S., anglicised ca. 1850. H., 1st ed.—3. The female pudend : C. 17 (e.g. in Fletcher's *The Chances*).—4. An unfortunate matter, end, as in ' I fear it's a case with him ' : from ca. 1864.—5. The certainty to fall in love : from ca. 1870, as ' it's a case with them.' Miss Braddon, in *To the Bitter End*, 1872.—6. A love-affair : schoolgirls', from ca. 1860 ; ob. H., 2nd ed.—7. A ' love-affair ' between two boys : Public Schools' : C. 20.—8. Case *casa*, 2.—9. Hence, occ., a water-closet : c. or low s. (— 1864). H., 3rd ed.—10. In C. 20 racing c., a fool, a ' mug '. Wallace in *The Twister*.—11. (Westminster School) the discussion by ' seniors ' and ' upper election ' of a thrashing, likewise the tanning itself : from ca. 1860 ; ob.—12. That which is, in the circumstances, to be expected : coll. (— 1924). O.E.D. (Sup.).—13. Often very loosely and unnecessarily used : C. 19–20. (See esp. Fowler ; Sir Arthur Quiller-Couch also has written with effective and, one hopes, effectual causticity on the subject.)

*case, v. In C. 20 c., to report (a prisoner) for slackness ; punish with solitary confinement.—2. To spoil ; delay inevitably : c. (— 1934). James Spenser, 1934, ' Well, this cases things for a while. We'll have to lie low.'

'case. Abbr. *in case* (= to ensure against the possibility, or the fact, that) : coll. : from ca. 1890.

*cased up with, be. To live with (a woman, esp. one's mistress) : c. : C. 20. James Curtis, *The Gilt Kid*, 1936.

*case-fro. Variant for *case-vrow*. B.E.

case-hardened. ' Tough ' ; of one who is *a hard case* : both coll., the latter (orig. U.S.) from ca. 1860, the former from ca. 1700 and S.E. by 1800.

*case-keeper. The keeper of a brothel : (? C. 19,) C. 20 c. See *casa*, 2.

*caseo. A C. 20 variant, in c., of *casa*, n., 2. J. Curtis, *The Gilt Kid*, 1936.

case of crabs. A failure : coll., ca. 1870–1920. ? ex *catch a crab*.

case of pickles. An incident, esp. if untoward ; a break-down, -up. Coll. ; from ca. 1870. † by 1920.

case of stump, a. (E.g. he is) penniless. Coll. : ca. 1870–1900. Cf. *stumped*.

*case-ranging. An inspection of houses with a view to robbery : c. (— 1923). Manchon. See *casa*, 2.

cases, get down to. To ' get down to brass tacks ' ; talk seriously : lower classes' : C. 20. James Curtis, *The Gilt Kid*, 1936.

*case-vrow, C. 18–19 ; **case-fro,** late C. 17–18. See *casa*, 2. The *vrow* is Dutch for a woman, the *fro* indicates German influence thereon.

casein(e). ' The correct thing ' ; punning *the cheese*, q.v. Rare. † by 1900. Charles Kingsley in a letter of May, 1856. (The *-ine* form is incorrect.)

*caser. A crown-piece ; the sum of five shillings : c. (— 1874). In C. 20, the same, but low racing. Ex Yiddish.

*casey ; occ. **casscy.** Cheese. C. 19–20 c. **Cf.** *cassam, cash, caz*, qq.v. Ex L. *caseus*.

*cash ; cass. Abbr. *cassam, cassan*, cheese : c. : late C. 17–19 (B.E.) ; C. 18–19. See also caz.— 2. An Accountant Officer on duty : naval : C. 20. Bowen. (Only as *cash*.)

cash, equal to. Of undoubted and indubitable merit. Coll. : from ca. 1840 ; orig. (— 1835) U.S.

cash, in ; out. Having plenty of : no : money. (*In cash* occurs in Thackeray.) Coll. : from ca. 1840.

cash a dog. (Gen as vbl.n.) To cash a cheque against non-existent funds : bank-clerks' (esp. Anglo-Irish) : C. 20.

cash a prescription. To have a prescription made up. Coll. : from ca. 1880 ; ob.

cash in. To succeed, esp. financially : coll. : from ca. 1920. Ex *cash in*, to clear accounts, terminate a matter.—2. To die : coll. : C. 20. Ex : cash (or hand in, or pass in) one's checks. To die : orig. (— 1860), U.S., anglicised ca. 1875. *Checks* = counters in the game of poker. Cf. *peg out*.

cash up, v.i. and t. Settle a debt ; pay : from ca. 1830 ; ob. Barham ; Dickens, in *Martin Chuzzlewit* ; Sala, ' They'll never cash up a farthing piece.'

cashed-in. Dead ; killed : military : C. 20. F. & Gibbons. Ex *cash in*, 2, q.v.

Cashels. Great Southern and Western of Ireland railway stock : money-market, from ca. 1878 ; ob. The line had, at first, no station at Cashel.

cashier. To deprive of one's cash : late C. 16– early 17. Shakespeare—? elsewhere.

cask. A (small) brougham : ça. 1853–1900 ; Society. Less gen. than *pill-box*.

cask, bull the. See bull the cask.

Cass, the. The Casino, a low-class music-hall at Manchester (on the site now occupied by the Manchester Social Club) ; also known as *Mr. Burton's Night School*, because run by a Mr. Burton : mostly Mancunians' : ca. 1890–1910. *John o' London's Weekly*, Oct. 13, 1934.—2. (cass.) See cash.

*cassam, cassan, cassom, casson, casum. Cheese : mid-C. 16–20 c. The earliest and commonest form is *cassan* ; *cash*, an abbr., appears in C. 17 ; *casum* in C. 18. See casey, cash, and caz. Cf. the *cas* of Romany.

cast. Very drunk : Anglo-Irish (— 1935).

cast, at the last. At one's last chance or shift : c. 1450–1750 ; coll. > by 1600, S.E. Ex dicing.

cast, give a. To assist : waggoners' and estuary-sailors' coll. : mid-C. 19–20. H., 5th ed.

cast an optic. To look : sporting (— 1909) ; slightly ob. Ware.

cast beyond the moon. To make wild guesses : coll. soon > S.E. : from ca. 1540 ; ob. Heywood.

cast-iron horrors. See horrors, in the cast-iron.

Cast Iron Sixth, the. The 6th City of London Rifles : military : C. 20. F. & Gibbons. Ex endurance in training on Salisbury Plain.

cast(-)me(-)down. Cassidony, i.e. French lavender : sol. : ca. 1580–1800. Gerard, in his famous *Herbal* (1597), speaks of the 'simple people' who ' doe call it Castte me downe '.

cast-off. A discarded mistress : coll. : from ca. 1800.—2. In pl., landsmen's clothes : nautical : C. 19–20.—3. Also, any discarded clothes : coll. ; C. 19–20.

cast stones against the wind. To work in vain : C. 17–18 ; coll. soon > S.E.

cast up one's accounts. See accounts.

Castalian (of the Muses) and Castilian (of Castile) are occ. confused : C. 17–20.

caste is occ. misused for cast : mid-C. 19–20. Fowler.

*castell. To see, look : early C. 17 ; perhaps c. or coll., its history being problematic. Recorded in Rowlands, *Martin Mark-All*, 1610. ? ex *castle* as a vantage-point.

caster. See castor.—2. A cast-off or rejected person, animal, or thing : from ca. 1850 ; coll.— 3. In mid-C. 16–18 c., a cloak. Harman.

*Castieu's Hotel. The Melbourne gaol : Australian c. of ca. 1880–1910. Ex a man's name.

castle. Abbr. *castle in Spain* or the more gen. and English *castle in the air* : coll., C. 19–20.

*Castle, the. Holloway Prison : c. : late C. 19–20. James Curtis, *The Gilt Kid*, 1936.

Castle of St. Thomas. ' The Penitentiary in St. Thomas's parish, where the frail part of the Oxford belles are sent under surveillance ', Egan's Grose : Oxford University : ca. 1820–40.

castle-rag. A ' flag ', i.e. a fourpenny piece : rhyming s. (— 1859) ; † by 1914. H., 1st ed.

castor ; occ. caster. A hat, orig. of beaver's fur : in C. 17–early 18, S.E. ; ca. 1760–1810, coll. ; then s. Entick's *London*, 1640 ; Martin's Dict., 2nd ed., 1754 ; Moncrieff's *Tom and Jerry*, 1821 ; H., 1st–5th ed. (1859–74).

castor-oil artist or merchant. A surgeon ; a physician : military : from ca. 1905. F. & Gibbons ; B. & P. Cf.

Castor-Oil Dragoons, the. The Royal Army Medical Corps : military : from ca. 1905 ; ob. F. & Gibbons.

casual. A casual ward in a hospital ; an occasional workman, pauper, visitor, etc. : coll. ; resp. from ca. 1850 and from ca. 1820. Bee, 1823, notes it of a boarder in a lodging house.

casual, adj. Uncertain, undependable, happy-go-lucky, slightly careless and callous : coll., from ca. 1880 (S.O.D. records for 1883). In the 1930's, on the verge of S.E.—2. Confused with *causal* : late C. 16–20. Cf. *casuality* confused with *causality* : C. 17–20. O.E.D.

casuality. A casualty, a person wounded or killed. Sol. : from 1899.—2. See casual, adj., 2.

casualty. A casual labourer : Londoners' coll. : ca. 1850–1910. Mayhew, *London Labour*, II, ' The " casuals " or the " casualties " (always called amongst the men " cazzelties ")', E.D.D. Hence *casualty boy*, q.v.

casualty, adj. Casual : Londoners' coll. : mid-C. 19–20 ; ob. Mayhew, 1851, ' Red herrings, and other cas'alty fish '. Ex the dial. adj. *casualty*, for which see the E.D.D.

casualty boy. ' A boy who hires himself out to a costermonger ', E.D.D. : London coll. : ca. 1850–1910. Mayhew. Often *casalty boy*.

Cat. See Cat Street.

cat. A harlot : C. 16–19 ; in C. 19, ob. ; by 1850, †. Lyndesay, 1535, in his satire on wantons ; B.E. ; Dyche ; Grose. This sense of *cat* is due to Dutch influence.—2. Abbr. *cat o' nine tails* : apparently first in 1788, in Falconbridge's *African Slave Trade* : coll. ; by 1820, S.E.—3. In C. 20 c., punishment by the ' cat '.—4. Abbr. *tame cat*, q.v. —5. The female pudend : coll., C. 19–20 : otherwise *pussy*, cf. Fr. *le chat*.—6. Related is mid C. 19–20 (ob.) c. sense, a lady's muff (see muff). Brandon, 1839.—7. Also c. (— 1812), a quart pot, a pint pot being a *kitten*. It is implied by Vaux's *cat and kitten rig*.—8. A landlady in lodgings (rooms or boarding house) : from ca. 1820 ; ob.

Peake in his comedy, *Comfortable Lodgings*, 1827.—
9. See **Cheshire cat.**—10. Abbr. (— 1935), esp.
among actors, cf. *cat and mouse*, q.v.

cat, v. To vomit : late C. 8–20 : low coll. ; in
C. 20, mainly dial. Grose, 1st ed. Cf. *cat, shoot
the,* q.v.

cat, do a. See **do a cat.**

cat, flying. See **flying-cat.**

cat, free a. To steal a muff : c. (— 1864). H.,
3rd ed. See **cat,** n., 6.

cat, grin like a Cheshire. See **Cheshire cat.**

cat, not room enough to swing a. Cramped for
space ; very small : coll. >, in late C. 19, S.E. :
from ca. 1770. Smollett.

cat, old. 'A cross old woman ', Grose, 1st ed. :
coll. : mid-C. 18–20.

cat on hot bricks, like a. See **hot bricks.**

cat !, s'elp (or **s'help**) **the.** A variant of *bob, s'elp
me,* q.v. : low (— 1890) ; ob. F. & H. See also
swelp.

cat, shoot the. To vomit : C. 19–20 ; coll. *Lex.
Bal.,* 1811 ; Marryat in *The King's Own*, 1830, ' I'm
cursedly inclined to shoot the cat.' A C. 17–18
variant, *jerk the cat* ; a C. 17–20 ob. variant, *whip
the cat,* as in Taylor the Water Poet, 1630.

cat, sick as a. Vomiting ; very sick indeed :
coll. : mid-C. 19–20. Lyell.—2. Hence, extremely
annoyed : s. (— 1931) now verging on coll. Ibid.

cat, whip the. To indulge in a certain practical
joke : C. 18–19 ; coll. In C. 17–18, *draw* or *pull*
someone *through the water with a cat,* as in Jonson's
Bartholomew Fair, 1614, in B.E., and in Grose : for
an explanation of the origin of the phrases, see
Grose.—2. (Orig. of tailors), to work at private
houses : coll. ; from ca. 1785 ; ob. Grose, 2nd ed.—
3. To cry over spilt milk : Australian coll. (— 1916).
C. J. Dennis.

cat ?, who ate or **stole the.** A c.p. against
pilferers : C. 19–20, ob. ; coll. Perhaps ex an
actual incident.

cat ?, who shot the. A stock reproach to the
Volunteers : from ca. 1850. Extant in O.T.C.'s.

cat and dog life, lead a. (Of married couples) to be
constantly quarrelling : coll., from ca. 1560. B.E.
has *agree like Dog and Cat.*

cat and I'll kill your dog, you kill my. An exchange of (the lower) social amenities : C. 19–20 ;
coll. Cf. Scottish *ca' me, ca' thee.*

cat-and-kitten hunting or **sneaking.** The stealing of quart and pint pots (see **cat,** n., 7) : c.
(— 1859) ; ob. H., 1st ed.

cat and kitten rig. The ca. 1810–50 form
(Vaux) of the preceding.

cat and mouse. A house : rhyming s. (— 1857) ;
ob. ' Ducange Anglicus ', 1st ed.

Cat and Mouse Act. ' The Prisoners (Temporary
Discharge for Ill-health) Act of 1913 to enable
hunger-strikers to be released temporarily ' : 1913,
Punch, July 23. O.E.D. (Sup.).

Cat and Mutton lancers. Militia : East London :
1870 ; † by 1920. Ware. They often drilled on
Cat and Mutton Fields.

cat-burglar. A burglar that nimbly enters houses
from the roof : from ca. 1919 : coll. ; S.E. by 1933.
Cf. *garreteer* and *dancer.*

cat-faced. Ugly : low coll. (North of England) :
mid-C. 19–20. H., 3rd ed. Its original, *cat-face,* a
pejorative n., may be dial.

Cat Fleet, the. ' The First Battle Cruiser Squadron of the Grand Fleet ' : naval : ca. 1900–21.
Bowen. It included the *Lion* and the *Tiger.*

cat-harping fashion. Nautical, late C. 18–19 :
' Drinking cross ways, and not as usual over the
left thumb ', Grose, 1st ed. Ex *catharpin-fashion,*
q.v.

cat has kittened in one's mouth, to feel as if a. To
' have a mouth ' after being drunk : from ca. 1600 ;
coll. Field in his indelicate play, *Amends for
Ladies*, 1618. Cf. Fr. *avoir la gueule de bois.*

cat-heads. Nautical, C. 18–20 : the paps. Ex
the S.E. sense.

cat in hell without claws, no more chance than a.
A late C. 18–mid-19 c.p. applied to ' one who enters
into a dispute or quarrel with one greatly above his
match ', Grose, 3rd ed. Cf. *icicle's chance in Hades,
not an,* q.v.

cat in the pan, turn. To change sides, from self-
interest ; be a turncoat. Coll. : from — 1384 ;
ob. E.g. in Wyclif ; Bacon's *Essays* ; an anon.
song entitled *The Vicar of Bray* (ca. 1720) ; Scott in
Old Mortality. Whence *cat in (the) pan,* a turncoat
or traitor. Perhaps ex *cake in the pan,* i.e. a pancake : which is often turned.

cat jumps, see, occ. watch, how or **which way the.**
To observe the course of events : coll. ; from ca.
1820. Scott ; Lytton. Cf. *sit on the fence.*

cat-lap. Thin beverage, esp. tea : coll. : from
ca. 1780. Grose (1st ed.), Scott, Miss Braddon.

cat laugh, enough to—or it would—make a. (It
is) extremely funny, droll, ludicrous : coll. : 1851,
Planché ; 1898, Weyman. Apperson.

cat-market. Many persons all speaking at the
one time : coll. ; C. 19–20.

cat-match. A bowling match in which a dishonest expert is engaged with bad players : late
C. 17–18 c. B.E.

cat-meat pusher. A street vendor of cooked
horse-flesh : Cockney (— 1909). Ware. He sold
it from a barrow.

cat-nap. A short sleep had while sitting : coll. ;
from ca. 1850.

cat-o'-nine-tails. A nine-lashed scourge, until
1881 employed in the British army and navy ;
since, though decreasingly, for criminals. From
ca. 1670. From ca. 1700, coll. ; from ca. 1780,
S.E. In Head's *The English Rogue* ; Vanbrugh, in
The False Friend, ' You dread reformers of an im-
pious age, | You awful cat-a-nine tails to the stage ' ;
Smollett in *Roderick Random.*

cat on testy dodge, a. ' A ladylike beggar
worrying ladies at their houses for money—if only
a sixpence (tester) ', Ware : c. of ca. 1870–1914.

cat out of the bag, let the. See at **bag.**

cat-party. A party of women only : coll., C. 19–
20. Also *cats' party* : sporting (— 1888) ; slightly
ob. Cf. *bitch-* and *hen-party.*

cat-skin. An inferior make of silk hat : 1857,
Hughes ; ob. by 1900, † by 1920. (O.E.D.) Cf.
rabbit-skin.

cat speak (and a wise man dumb), enough or **able to
make a.** Astounding : coll. : late C. 16–20, ob.
D'Urfey, 1719, ' Old Liquor able to make a Cat
speak ' ; Dickens elaborates. The *man* addition
appears in 1661, in a form that shows D'Urfey to be
repeating a proverb : ' Old liquor able to make a cat
speak and a wise man dumb ' : a proverb implicit in
Shakespeare's *Tempest*, I, ii, ' Open your mouth ',
etc., and in one—perhaps an earlier—Shirburn
Ballad, ' Who is it but loves good liquor ? 'Twill
make a catte speake.' (Apperson.)

cat-stabber. An Army clasp-knife ; a bayonet :
military : C. 20. F. & Gibbons ; B. & P.

cat-sticks. Thin legs : late C. 18–mid-19 : coll. Grose, 1st ed. ? ex *trap-sticks*.

Cat Street. St. Catherine's Street : Oxford undergraduates' : late C. 19–20. Collinson. Orig. *Cat*.

cat up. A variant of *cat*, v. : late C. 19–20.

cat-walk. A ' brick-paved pathway, usually one brick (nine inches) wide, laid down across farm fields in Flanders ' : military : late 1914–18. F. & Gibbons.

cat with laughter. To laugh ' fit to burst ' : low (— 1923). Manchon. See *cat*, v.

cat-witted. Obstinate and spiteful : coll. : ca. 1660–1930. Contrast the dial. senses : scatter-brained, silly, conceited, whimsical.

[**Catachresis.** Most of those catachrestic usages —incorrectnesses, confusions, vaguenesses of sense— of the C. 16–mid-19 which appear in these pages are taken from the O.E.D. : this is not to say that I was ignorant of all or even most of them ; but since it was the O.E.D. which reminded me of the cata-chreses that I knew, I wish to ' render unto Caesar '. Nevertheless, I have added a certain number that are not to be found in the O.E.D., nor in Webster.— See also ' Solecism ', where I animadvert upon the interesting fact that an illiterate mistake is stig-matised as a solecism (or, in certain dictionaries, as a vulgarism), but a literate mistake is palliated as a catachresis.]

[**Catacombs, the.** This name for the great multi-cellular dug-out in Northern France is ineligible, despite a frequently held opinion.]

catalency. Incorrect for *catalempsy*, catalepsy : C. 16. O.E.D.

catamaran. ' An old scraggy woman ', Grose, 3rd ed. : from not later than 1791. Whence the soon prevailing nuance : a cross-grained person, esp. if a woman ; a vixenish old woman : coll. (— 1833). Marryat ; Thackeray, in *The Newcomes*, ' What an infernal tartar and catamaran ! ' ? a corruption of *cat o' mountain* (as in Fletcher's *The Custom of the Country*, 1616), which, in U.S., has, since ca. 1830, meant a shrew.

cataphract. A cataract : catachrestic : late C. 16–mid-17. O.E.D.

cataract. A black satin scarf worn by ' com-mercials ' for the surface and effect it offers to jewellery : ca. 1830–70. Ware.

catastrophe. The tail, the end. Late C. 16–early 19, jocular coll., as in Shakespeare, (Falstaff :) ' I'll tickle your catastrophe.'

catawamp(o)us ; occ. **catawamptious.** Avid ; fierce, eager ; violently destructive : orig. U.S. ; almost imm. anglicised by Dickens in *Martin Chuzzlewit*. The adv. (-*ly*) appeared notably in England in Lytton's *My Novel*, 1853. Perhaps, says W., suggested by *catamount*.

catawampus. Vermin and insects, esp. the stingers and biters. From ca. 1870 ; Mortimer Collins, 1880, ' . . . catawampuses, as the ladies call them '. Ex preceding.

catch. A person matrimonially desirable : coll. ; anticipated by Dryden's ' The Gentleman had a great Catch of her, as they say,' and Jane Austen's ' on the catch for a husband ', the term > gen. only ca. 1830–45. (S.O.D.)—2. In c., C. 17–19, a prize, a booty.

catch, v.i. To become pregnant : coll., mostly lower classes' : late C. 19–20.

catch, no. Unwelcome, profitless ; difficult : coll. : C. 20. Lyell. Prob. ex *catch*, n., 1.

catch (rarely **cut**) **a crab.** In rowing, to mull one's stroke, esp. by jamming the oar in the water as if a crab had caught it. Coll. : late C. 18–20 ; after G.W., S.E. Grose, Marryat, Hood.

catch a Tartar. Unexpectedly to meet one's superior ; be hoisted by one's own petard. Late C. 17–20 : coll. till ca. 1850, then S.E. Dryden, Smollett, Fanny Burney. For semantics, see Tartar.

catch bending. To catch (a person) at a disad-vantage : jocular coll. : C. 20. P. G. Wodehouse, *Psmith in the City*, 1910 ; Lyell. Esp. in a c.p., *don't let me catch you bending* (ob.). A person bend-ing is in a favourable position to be kicked.

catch-bet. A bet made to inveigle the unwary : low coll. ; from ca. 1870. H., 5th ed.

catch club, a member of the. A bailiff or his assistant : late C. 18–early 19 : jocular coll. Grose, 2nd ed.

*****catch cocks.** To obtain money on false pre-tences : military c., late C. 19–20 ; ob. Ware, who notes that the vbl.n. is *cock-catching*.

catch 'em (all) alive-o ! A c.p. of ca. 1850–80. Orig. a fisherman's phrase, but by 1853, if not a year or two earlier, it had a tremendous vogue. Its intent was to raise a smile, its meaning almost null. —2. (Gen. without the ' -o '.) A fly-paper : from ca. 1855 ; ob. Mayhew ; Dickens in *Little Dorrit*. —3. A small comb (cf. *louse-trap*) : ca 1860–1910. H., 3rd ed.—4. The female pudend : low : from ca. 1864 : ob.

catch-fake. The doubling of a rope badly coiled : nautical coll. : late C. 19–20. Bowen. I.e. a faked ' catch '.

catch-fart. A footman or a page : late C. 17–19. B.E., Grose.

catch it. To be scolded, reprimanded ; casti-gated : coll. ; from ca. 1830. Marryat, *Jacob Faithful*, 1835, ' We all thought Tom was about to catch it.'

catch me ! ; **catch me at it !** I'll do no such thing ! Coll. : from ca. 1770. Mrs. Cowley, Galt, Dickens (" Catch you at forgetting anything ! " exclaimed Carker ').

catch on. Coll. : to join on, attach oneself to : coll. : from ca. 1884.—2. To ' take ', be a success : from ca. 1886 : coll.—3. To understand, grasp the meaning or significance, apprehend : orig. (— 1884), U.S., anglicised ca. 1888 : coll.

catch, occ. **get, on the hop.** To surprise ; find un-prepared. From ca. 1861 : oll. *The Chickaleary Cove*, a popular song—the famous Vance its singer : ' For to get me on the hop, or on my ' tibby ' drop, | You must wake up very early in the morning.'

catch on the rebound. See **rebound.**

catch one bending. See **catch bending.**

catch one's death of cold. To get a severe chill : coll., from ca. 1870.

catch meself on, gen. in imperative. V.i., to pull oneself up or together ; recover one's common sense : lower classes' coll. : C. 20.

catch out. To detect in a mistake or a misdoing : 1815, Jane Austen : coll. >, by 1900, S.E. Ex cricket ; cf. *bowl out*. (O.E.D. Sup.)

catch-penny. A penny ' gaff ' (show or exhibi-tion) ; a broadsheet describing an imaginary mur-der. Coll. : ca. 1820–1910. Other senses are S.E.

[**catch-pole,** despite F. & H., is not ' eligible '. It occurs by the way, in Langland.]

catch the bird. To have a short sleep : nautical : late C. 19–20. Bowen.

catch the wind of the word. Quickly to apprehend (cf. *catch on*) : orig. Irish. C. 19–20 ; ob.

*catch the zig. To get ' done ' ; ' buy a pup ' : C. 20 racing c. John Morris : see *Slang*, p. 243.

catch up. To interrupt, ' pull up ', correct (a person) : from ca. 1840 ; coll. till ca. 1900, then S.E. Dickens, in *Barnaby Rudge*, ' You catch me up so very short.'

catched. Caught : S.E. >, by 1800, sol.

catchee. Pidgin English for *catch*, as *havee* for *have* : C. 18–20.

catcher. In ball-games, a catch ; esp. *knock up a catcher*, q.v. : coll. : C. 20.

catcher, knock up a. See also **knock up a catcher.**

catching harvest. A dangerous time for a robbery on account of congested roads : coll. : C. 18–mid-19. *A New Canting Dict.*, 1725.

catchup (ca. 1690), **catsup** (1730). Incorrect, via slovenly pronunciation, for *ketchup*. O.E.D. ; W.

catchy. Attractive, esp. if vulgarly so : 1831 : coll., as orig. were the senses : soon popular (e.g. of a tune), from ca. 1830, and tricky (as of examination questions), from ca. 1884. But from ca. 1890 all three meanings have been S.E. (S.O.D.)—2. Inclined to take an (esp. undue) advantage : (—)1859. H., 1st ed.—3. Spasmodic : coll. : U.S., 1872 ; England, 1883. O.E.D.—4. Merry : Scots coll. : 1804, Tarras, O.E.D.

catechi. Catechism(-lesson) : Public Schools' : late C. 19–20. (E. F. Benson, *David Blaize*, 1916.)

category. Inferior ; second- or third-rate : military coll. : late 1915–18. F. & Gibbons, ' This is a category sort of road.' Ex the 1915–18 military j. *category man*, a man pronounced unfit for front-line service or for very heavy service elsewhere.

caterpillar. An illicit or an illegal liver-by-his-wits : late C. 16–17 : orig. c., then s., then almost S.E.—2. Whence, a soldier : mid-C. 18–early 19. Grose, 2nd ed.—3. A ladies' school a-walking : Society : 1848 ; † by 1920. Ware. Cf. *crocodile*, 2, q.v.

caterwaul, v.. To make sexual love : late C. 16–20 (ob.) : coll. until ca. 1700, then s. The vbl.n. *caterwauling* is more gen. Nashe ; Congreve ; Smollett, concerning the servant-maids in *Humphry Clinker*, ' . . . junketting and caterwauling with the fellows of the country '.

catever, n. and adj. (A) queer (affair), (a) bad or inferior (thing). Low and Parlyaree : from ca. 1840. The spelling is various. Ex It. *cattivo*, bad.

catgut-scraper. A fiddler : late C. 17–20 ; ob. ; coll. Ned Ward, Wolcot, Mayhew.

Catharine Puritans. (Cambridge) members of St. Catharine's Hall : ca. 1860–1914. Punning Gr. καθαίρειν, to purify. Cf. *Doves*.

Catharine or **Catherine wheel, do a.** To do a lateral somersault, a ' cart-wheel ' : coll., ca. 1850–1900.

catharpin fashion. ' When People in Company Drink cross, and not going about from the Right to the Left ', B.E. : drinkers' : late C. 17–18. Ex Gr. κατὰ + πίνειν, to drink. The early form of *cat-harping-fashion*, q.v.

cathedral. A high hat : Winchester College, C. 19–20.

cathedral, adj. Old-fashioned ; antique. Coll. : late C. 17–early 19. B.E., Johnson, Grose.

Catherine Hayes. A drink made of claret, sugar, and nutmeg : ca. 1858–1890 ; Australian. Prob. ex the Irish singer so popular in Australia. Frank Fowler, 1859.

Catherine wheel. See **Catharine wheel.**

Catholic. Incorrectly, by Anglicans, pronounced *cartholic* ca. 1870–1910. John Gibbons (private letter, 1/5/35). *Catholic* for *Roman Catholic* is a catachresis noticed as early as 1676 by Elisha Coles, whose English Dict. has not received the attention it deserves.

catolla, catoller. A noisy fellow, either prating or foolish—or both. Early C. 19. Pierce Egan used it of a foolish betting man (1825).

cats. Atlantic Seconds : Stock Exchange, ca. 1875–85.

Cat's. (Cambridge) St. Catharine's Hall : from ca. 1870. (Oxford) St. Catherine's Society : from 1900—i.e. thirty-two years before the Non-Collegiate Delegacy attained *St. C. S.*—and often as *St. Cat's*. Hence, *Cat's man* : a member of either college.

cats, fight like Kilkenny. To fight even unto mutual destruction : coll. : C. 19–20.

cats and dogs, rain. To rain hard : coll. : Swift adumbrated this coll. in 1710 and employed it in 1738 (date of printing ; written ca. 1708) ; Shelley ; Barham. C. 19 humorists often added *and pitchforks and shovels*.

cat's face. A ' worker wanted ' notice in the window : tailors' : C. 20. E.g. *The Tailor and Cutter*, Nov. 29, 1928.

cat's foot, live under the. To be hen-pecked : coll. : late C. 17–19. Ray, 1678 ; Grose ; Spurgeon. (Apperson.)

cat's head. The end of a shoulder of mutton : Winchester College, from ca. 1830 ; ob. Cf. *dispar*, q.v.

cat's meat. The human lungs : low coll. : from ca. 1820. Egan's Grose. Ex the ' lights ' of animals, a favourite food of cats.—2. ' Small pieces of mutton and bacon . . . skewered on a stick and boiled ', Pettman defining *bobbetjes* : South African (— 1913).

cat's neck, who shall hang the bell about the. Who will take the risk ? C. 17–18 coll. : = *bell the cat*, q.v.

cats of nine tails of all prices, he has. A late C. 18–early 19 low c.p. applied to the hangman. Grose, 3rd ed. (at *cart*).

cat's party. See **cat-party.**

cat's paw. A dupe : late C. 18–20 ; coll. until ca. 1820, then S.E. *Cat's foot* was so used a century earlier.

cat's pyjamas, the. Anything very good, attractive, etc. : American (— 1920) anglicised by 1923 but † by 1933. Cf. *the bee's knees*.

cat's water. Gin : low : mid-C. 19–20. H., 1st ed. Cf. *bitches' wine* and esp. the semantic determinant, *old Tom*.

cat's whisker. A thin wire for establishing contact on a crystal (wireless) set : from ca. 1920 ; ob.

cat's whiskers, the. A variant of *the cat's pyjamas* (see above) : 1927, Dorothy Sayers in *Unnatural Death* ; virtually †.

catskin. See **cat-skin.**

Catskin Earls. The three senior earls in the House of Lords : Parliamentary ; from ca. 1860. The etymology is obscure : see F. & H.

catso. The male member : C. 17–early 18. Also, same period, a scamp, rogue, ' cullion '. The former sense, recorded in 1702, precedes the other by six years. Also an exclamation with later form *gadso*. Ex the It. *cazzo*, the *membrum virile*, the word has, in its different senses, several very English parallels.

catsoo'd. Drunk (1915–18); ex *catsoos*, a drink of beer at an estaminet (1914–18), the price—in the early days of the War—being *quatre sous*, approximately 2*d.* F. & Gibbons.

catsup. See **catchup**.

catting, vbl.n. 'Drawing a Fellow through a Pond with a Cat', B.E.: late C. 17–19; coll. Cf. *cat, (whip the)*, q.v.—2. A vomiting: C. 19–20, low: see **cat, (shoot the)**.—3. Running after harlots and near-harlots: coll.: late C. 17–early 19. See **cat, n.**

cattle, a pejorative fairly strong in C. 16–18, fairly mild (as in *kittle cattle* = women) in C. 19–20, applied to human beings: Gosson, 1579, ' Poets, and Pipers, and suche peevishe Cattel'; Shakespeare, in *As You Like It*, of boys and women; Evelyn, ' . . . concubines, and cattell of that sort'; G. R. Sims, in *The Dagonet Ballads*, ' Queer cattle is women to deal with.' Strictly, S.E.: but the contemptuous usage makes the term analogous to coll. It is the etymological kinship with *chattels* which prompted,—perhaps rather it determined,—the contempt. Note, too, that in the late C. 17–early 18, the word was wholly coll. in the sense recorded by B.E.: ' *Cattle*, Whores. *Sad Cattle*, Impudent Lewd Women', with which cf. Evelyn's phrase, preceded as it is by a reference to ' Nelly ', i.e. Nell Gwynn. In C. 18–early 19, *sad cattle* also meant gypsies, while in c. *black cattle* = lice; in C. 19 low coll., *small cattle* = vermin, lice (Baumann).

cattle-racket. A system of plunder: Australian coll.: ca. 1850–1900. Ex a wholesale plunder in cattle in New South Wales, app. in the 1840's. Morris.

catty. Spiteful and sly: gen. of women: from ca. 1885: coll. >, by 1910, S.E. *Cattish*, S.E. in the same sense, occurs a few years earlier. (S.O.D.) —2. Agile, smart; skilfully careful: Canadian (esp. lumbermen's) coll.: C. 20. John Beames.

caucus as a pejorative was, at first (say 1878–90), so close to being coll. as makes no difference. Its other senses, ex the U.S., have always been S.E. For this interesting and significant word see esp. the O.E.D., Thornton, Weekley, S.O.D.

caudge-pawed. Left-handed: coll. and dial.: mid-C. 17–20; ob. B.E., Grose. Cf. *cack-*, *car-* and *caw-handed*, also *lefty* and *maul(e)y*.

candle of hemp-seed, or hempen caudle. Hanging: jocular coll.: late C. 16–early 17. The latter in Shakespeare.

caul, be born with a. To be born lucky: coll.: C. 17–20, ob. Ben Jonson; Dickens.

cauli. Cauliflower: coll.: late C. 19–20. (*Time and Tide*, April 20, 1935.)

cauliflower. A clerical wig modish *temp.* Queen Anne; hence, v.i. and t., to powder a wig: both soon †.—2. Whence, ' any one who wears powder on his head ', Bee: ca. 1820–40.—3. The female pudend: C. 18–19. See Grose (1st ed.) for a witty, broad, and improbable origin.—4. The foaming top to (e.g. a tankard of) beer: from ca. 1870, ob. Ex Scots, where recorded as early as 1813: E.D.D. Contrast the Fr. *un bock sans faux-col*.—5. In pl., the 47th Regiment of Foot (after 1881, the North Lancashires): military: from ca. 1840. Ex its white facings. Known also as *the Lancashire Lads*. —6. Short for *cauliflower ear*: coll.: from ca. 1925. —7. A goods-engine drawing waggons laden with cauliflowers and other green-stuff that had come from the Channel Islands: **railwaymen's**: late C. 19–early 20.

caulk or caulking. A (short) sleep: nautical; from ca. 1820. Marryat. Perhaps ex:—2. A dram: nautical; from ca. 1800. Semantics: ' something to keep out the wet ' or ' the damp '.

caulk, v. To sleep, esp. if surreptitiously: nautical; from ca. 1835. Cf. n., 1.—2. V.t., to cease, ' shut up ': nautical, from ca. 1880. W. Clark Russell (O.E.D.). Ex the lit. sense.—3. Also nautical: to copulate with: from ca. 1840. Cf. the M.E. *cauk*, (of birds) to tread, ex L. *calcare*.

caulk my dead-lights ! Damnation: nautical (— 1887). Baumann. Cf. *damn my eyes !*

caulk up. To stamp, with one's spiked boots, on (a man): among Canadian lumbermen (playful little fellows): C. 20. John Beames.

caulker ; occ. misspelt **cawker.** Nautical: a dram: from ca. 1805; e.g. in Charles Kingsley. Cf. *caulk*, n., 2, and perhaps v., 1.—2. Anything incredible; esp. a lie: from ca. 1860. H., 3rd ed.; Clark Russell's *Jack's Courtship*. Perhaps influenced by *corker*. Cf. *crammer*: O.E.D.

causal. See **casual**, adj., 2.—**causality.** Idem.

cause. ' A particular local organization, enterprise, mission, or church ', O.E.D.: religious coll. (— 1893) >, ca. 1920, S.E. Ex *make common cause (with)*.

'cause. Because. In mid-C. 16–early 17, S.E.; ca. 1640–1780, coll.; thereafter, sol. (and dial.).

'cause why ? or ! Why; the reason why; the reason. In C. 14–16, S.E.; 17–18 coll.; 19–20 dial. and, elsewhere, increasingly sol. As for *'cause* alone, the pronunciation, as a sol., varies from *caws* through *coz* and *cuz*, to even *case*.

Caustic Barebones. Thos. Bridges (fl. 1759–75), the dramatist and parodist. Dawson.

caution. A person or a thing wonderful, unusual, or, esp., odd, eccentric: coll.: anglicised by Whyte-Melville in 1853 (*Digby Grand* ; again in *Good for Nothing*) ex U.S. (— 1835). I.e. one with whom caution should be employed.—2. Hence, at Oxford, from 1865, a ' cure ', a ' character '; and this has, in England, been the predominant usage, likewise coll.

cautions, the four. A mid-C. 18–early 19 c.p., explained thus by Grose, 1st ed.: ' I. Beware of a woman before.—II. Beware of a horse behind.— III. Beware of a cart sideways.—IV. Beware of a priest every way.'

cavalier. To play the cavalier, escort a lady: coll. >, by 1890, S.E.: ca. 1860–1910.

cavalry. Sol. for *calvary*, esp. in G.W. + among Tommies and ex-service men, in the sense of an open-air, life-size representation of the Crucifixion. (In Fr., *calvaire*.)—2. A very French moustache: military (— 1923). Manchon.

cavalry curate. A curate that, in a large parish, rides a horse in the discharge of his duties: from early 1890's: coll. >, by 1920, S.E.; slightly ob. (O.E.D. Sup.)

cavaulting, cavolting. Sexual intercourse: c. or low s.: C. 17–early 19. Whence *cavaulting-school*, a brothel: late C. 17–early 19 (B.E.). Ex Lingua Franca *cavolta*, riding and ' horsing ', q.v.; ex Low L. *caballus*, a horse. Cf. *cavorting*.

cave. (Political) a small group of politicians seceding, on some special bill or cause, from their party; the secession: 1866. (Cf. *Adullamites*.) Orig. *cave of Adullam*—see 1 *Samuel*, 22. 1–2.—2. Coll. abbr. *Cavalier*: ca. 1647–81. A. Brome, in *Songs*, 1661.

cave, v.i. See **cave in, 1**.

cave ! Schoolboys'. ? first at Eton College, for ' beware ! ' Direct ex the L. word. From ca. 1750 (?).

cave-dwellers. Brutal atavists : Society coll. : 1890 ; ob. Ware. Cf. *cave-man*, q.v.

cave in, v.i. To yield, esp. when further opposition is futile or impossible ; occ. *cave*. With *in*, coll. ; without, s. Anglicised ca. 1855 ex U.S. (− 1840) ex East Anglian dial., as is the v.t., to break down, smash, bash in : anglicised ca. 1885 ; but cf. the S.E. *cave* (C. 16–20), to hollow (out), and *cave in*, to subside concavely (late C. 18–20)—2. (Political) to form a ' cave ', a cabal : ca. 1880–1900.

cave-man. A ' he-man ', a rough and virile fellow : coll. : from ca. 1895. Hence *cave-man stuff*, rough treatment : C. 20. Cf. *sheik*, q.v.

cave of antiquity. ' Depôt of old authors ', Egan's Grose : Oxford University : ca. 1820–40. More prob., *Cave of Antiquity*, the Bodleian Library.

cave out. (Gen. ppl. adj., *caved out*.) To come to an end, be finished : coll. anglicised (− 1909) ex U.S. ' From the metal ceasing in a tunnel ', Ware.

caves is the Winchester College pronunciation of *calves* (of the legs). Wrench.

cavey. See **cavy.**

caviar(e). The obnoxious matter ' blacked out ' of foreign periodicals by the Russian Press Censor : from ca. 1888. *St. James's Gazette*, April 25, 1890, uses *caviar(e)* as a v.t. In Tsarist days, irreligious or socialistic matter ; *temp.* Soviet, powerfully religious or insidiously capitalistic opinions. The word, a good example of literary s., is ob.

cavish. See **cavy.**

cavolting. See **cavaulting.**

cavort. To prance (of horses) ; make a horse prance. Hence, to frisk, lit. and fig. Anglicised ca. 1900 ex (− 1834) U.S. ; coll.—rather low coll.—after ca. 1918. ' Perhaps cowboy perversion of *curvet* ', W.

cavy ; cavey. A Cavalier : coll. : ca. 1645–70 (O.E.D.). Whence adj., *cavish*, 1664.

caw-handed, late C. 17–20 (B.E.) ; **caw-pawed,** late C. 18–20 ; both ob. Awkward. In dial., *caw* is a fool, whence *caw-baby*, an awkward or timid boy : E.D.D. Cf. *caudge-pawed*, q.v.

cawfin. ' A badly found ship : marine : 1876, the date at which Samuel Plimsoll (d. 1898) finally got ' the Plimsoll line ' incorporated in law ; ob. A corruption, or rather a Cockney pronunciation, of *coffin*.

cawker. See **caulker.**

caxon, caxton and **Caxton,** (theatrical) a wig, C. 19–20, ob., is perhaps a corruption, after Caxton the printer's name, of † *caxon*, which = an old weather-beaten wig, says Grose (1st ed.), but ' a kind of wig ', says S.O.D. ; the latter gives it as S.E.—as prob. it was.

***caz,** in C. 19 c., is cheese. *As good as caz*, easy to do, a ' sure thing '. Vaux. Cf. (*the*) *cheese*.

caze. The female pudend : C. 19–20, ob.

cazzelty. See **casualty, n.**

***cedar.** In late C. 19–20 c., a pencil. Obviously ex the wood of that tree. Cf. East Anglican *cedar-pencil*, a lead pencil (E.D.D.).—2. A pair-oared boat, canvasless, in-rigged, easily upset : Eton, C. 19–20, ob.

cee. A small quantity of beer : C. 17–18, university s. > S.E. Cf. *cue*, q.v.

celebrate, v.i. To drink in honour of an event or on ; hence, to drink joyously : C. 20 ; coll. Ex S.E. *celebrate* (e.g. *an occasion*).

Celestial. A Chinese : from ca. 1860 : coll. ; by 1880, S.E.—if jocular, for otherwise the word is pure journalese, which has been described as ' not the language written by journalists but that spoken by politicians '.—2. A jocular coll. applied to a turned-up nose : from ca. 1865. It points to heaven. Cf. *star-gazer*, q.v.—3. See **Celestials,** 2.

celestial poultry. Angels : low coll. : from ca. 1870 ; virtually †.

Celestials. The 97th Regiment of Foot, which in 1881 became the West Kents : military : from ca. 1830. Ex its sky-blue facings.—2. (Rare in singular ; *celestials*.) Occupants of the gallery : 1884, *The Referee*, Oct. 5, ; ob. Ware. On *the gods*.

cell. Incorrect (C. 17) for *caul*, as *cellæform* (mid-C. 19–20) is for *celliform*. O.E.D.

cellar-flap. A dance performed within a very small compass : low coll. (− 1877) ; ob.

cellarous. Of, in, belonging or natural to a cellar. The jocular intention of Dickens's word—in *The Uncommercial Traveller*, 1860—makes it a coll., which, since it has not been seriously adopted, it remains.

cellars. Boots : London streets' (− 1909) ; ob. Ware. Opp. *garret*, the head.

cellier. An unmitigated lie : ca. 1681–1710 ; coll. Ex the impudently mendacious Mrs. Elizabeth Cellier of the Meal Tub Plot, 1680. In *The Pope's Harbinger*, 1682, '. . . a modern and most proper phrase to signifie any Egregious Lye '. See, e.g., the anon. pamphlet *The Tryal and Sentences of Elizabeth Cellier, for Writing . . . A Scandalous Libel Called Malice Defeated*, 1680.

'cello. Abbr. *violoncello* : from ca. 1880. Coll. >, by 1910, S.E.

cemetery (or **C.**), **the.** The Dogger Bank : fishermen's coll. : C. 19–early 20. Bowen. So many ' come to grief there every winter '.

censorium. An † incorrectness for the biological and psychological *sensorium*. O.E.D.

cent per cent. A usurer : coll. : C. 17–19. Cf. *sixty per cent*.

Centipedes, the. The 100th Foot Regiment : military : late C. 19–20. Ware. Ex the insect.

centipees. See **sank.**

centrals (or **C-**). Shares in the New York Central Railroad : Stock Exchange coll. (− 1895). A. J. Wilson, *Stock Exchange Glossary.*

centre of bliss. Coll. verging on S.E. : from ca. 1790 : *pudendum muliebre.* [Centre slang : see *Slang*, pp. 277–8.]

centrifugal (tending outward) and **centripetal** (tending toward the centre) are often—naturally enough !—confused by those who have no Latin : C. 18–20.

centuary. Century : a frequent spoken, occ. written sol. : C. 19–20.

centurion. One who scores 100 or over : cricketers' coll. : from ca. 1885 ; ob. *The Graphic*, July 31, 1886.

century. £100 : the turf : from ca. 1860.—2. 100 runs or more : from ca. 1880 : coll. >, by 1900, S.E. *The Graphic*, Aug. 11, 1883.

Century White. John White (d. 1645). Ex his *First Century of Scandalous Malignant Priests.* (Dawson.)

cephaleonomancy. Incorrect for *cephalonomancy*, the pretended art of divination by the boiling (occ. the broiling) of an ass's head : mid-C. 17–20. O.E.D.

'cept. Except : low, when not childish, coll. : C. 19–21. Baumann. (Also in dial.)

cert. Abbr. *certainty* : from mid-1880's (still mainly sporting) : s. >, by 1915, coll. Often *a dead cert. The Man of the World*, June 29, 1889, ' Pioneer is a cert. for the St. James's.'

Cert or Certif, the Higher (School) and the School. The Higher School Certificate ; the (lower) School Certificate : C. 20 : *Cert*, mostly Public Schools' ; *Certif* mostly other schools', and teachers'.

certain sure, for. Absolutely ; with certainty ; unhesitatingly : (rather illiterate) coll. : mid-C. 19–20. (Dorothy Sayers, *Have His Carcase*, 1932, ' We're all agreed, for certain sure, as deceased come to his death by cutting of his throat.')

certainty. (Gen. in pl.) A male infant : printers' : from ca. 1860. Cf. *uncertainty*.

certainty, a dead. A horse, etc., supposed to be certain to win ; a thing sure to happen. Coll. : 1859 +. Cf. the S.E. *moral certainty*.

cess. See **bad cess to.**—2. In South African coll. (from ca. 1860), ' an expression of disgust in common use, occasionally elaborated into " pooh-gaciss "', Pettman. Ex Cape Dutch *sis* or *sies* employed in the same way.

cession and **cessation** are occ. confused : C. 19–20. O.E.D.

c'est la guerre ! A military c.p. by way of excuse, apology : 1915–18. Anon., *C'est la Guerre : Fragments from a War Diary*, 1930. Ex the Fr. explanation (' It's the war, don't you know ! ') of any deficiency.

*chafe, v.t. To thrash : from ca. 1670 ; ob. Prob. orig. c. Coles, 1676 ; B.E. Cf. Fr. *chauffer* and (to) *warm*.

*chafe-litter. In mid-C. 16–early 17 c., a saucy fellow ; cf. *bawd physic*.

chafer, v. To copulate : low coll. : C. 19–20, ob. For etymology, cf. *chauvering*.

chaff. Banter, ridicule ; humbug : coll. Clearly in *The Fancy*, vol. I, 1821, but perhaps anticipated in 1648. For etymology, see **to chaff.**—2. (Christ's Hospital) a small article : from ca. 1860. Perhaps ex *chauffer*, haggling, influenced by *chattel*.

chaff, v. To banter, lightly rail at or rally, ' quiz '. S.O.D. dates at 1827, but cf. *chaffing-crib* and F. & H.'s extremely significant C. 17 example from the anon. ballad entitled *The Downfall of Charing Cross* : like the n., it > gen. only ca. 1830. Prob. ex *chafe*, to gall, fret, irritate.—2. Cf. the c. sense of ca. 1820–50 : ' to blow up [i.e. to boast] ; to talk aloud ', Egan's Grose, 1823.—3. (Christ's Hospital) v.t., to exchange, esp. small articles. From ca. 1860. W. H. Blanch, *Blue Coat Boys*, 1877.

chaff, adj. Pleasant ; glad : Christ's Hospital, from ca. 1865. Occ. *chaffy*.

chaff ! Interjection indicative of pleasure, joy. Christ's Hospital, from ca. 1865.

*chaff-cutter. A slanderer : c. of ca. 1840–90. Ex :—2. A knowing and plausibly talkative person : c. (– 1823) ; † by 1860. Egan's Grose. Cf. *chaff*, v., 2.

chaffer. A banterer ; a joker at the expense of others : coll. ; from ca. 1850. Mayhew, ' She was . . . the best chaffer on the road ; not one of them could stand up against her tongue.'—2. The mouth : Moncrieff, 1821 ; David Carey, in *Life in Paris*, 1822, ' For there you may damp your chaffer in fifty different ways.' ? etymology.—3. An Arctic whale, an Arctic grampus : nautical coll. : mid-

C. 19–20. Bowen. Ex Shetlands *chaffer*, the round-lipped whale.

chaffing-crib. A man's ' den ' ; the room where he receives his intimates. Moncrieff in *Tom and Jerry*, 1821. Low coll. ; † by 1900.

chaffy. Full of banter, ridicule, or badinage : mid-C. 19–20 : coll. >, by 1890, S.E. ; rare.—2. See *chaff*, adj.

chaft. ' Chafed ' : see **chafe.**

chai. Tea. In C. 17, among merchants and in middle-class society, *cha* was occ. used in England ; in C. 19, revived among soldiers as *chai*, it > s. Ex Chinese.

chain ?, who pulled your. Who asked you to interfere ? : a (low) c.p. : from ca. 1910 ; ob. Ex the noise resultant on pulling a w.c. flushing-chain.

chain-breaker. An under-vest or singlet : military : from ca. 1920. Formerly, those men taking part, as principals, in a strong-man act, wore only a vest.

*chain-gang. Jewellers ; watch-chain makers : c. ; from ca. 1860 ; ob.—2. ' A special set of stewards to help cope with a spate of passengers ' : nautical : C. 20. Bowen. Punning a convicts' chain-gang.

chain-lightning. Potato-spirit : lower London : 1885, *The Daily News*, Dec. 22 ; † by 1920. In U.S. as early as 1843 of any raw whiskey. Ex its effect : ' poisonous to a degree. Smuggled chiefly ', Ware.

Chain-Locker, the. The old Board of Trade office close to the Tower : C. 19.—2. The Registry-General of Shipping : C. 20. Bcth nautical. Bowen.

chain-smoke, v.i. To smoke (esp. cigarettes) incessantly : C. 20 : coll. >, by 1935, S.E. Ex S.E. *chain-smoker.*

chain up ! ' Shut up ! ' : low (– 1923). Manchon. Ex *chain up that dog* !

Chainy Tenth, the. The 10th Hussars : military : from the mid-1820's. F. & Gibbons. Ex the chain-pattern belt ' of the officers' uniform introduced in 1820 '.

chair, call a. To appoint a president ' at a tavern-party, when discussion ensues ', Bee : public-house : ca. 1820–60.

chair, put in the. To fail to pay (a person) : cab-drivers', ca. 1860–1900. *The Social Science Review,* vol. I, 1864.

chair, the. The electric chair (for criminals) : coll. : U.S., anglicised by 1931. C.O.D., 1934 Sup.

chair-bottomer. A cane-plaiter of chair-bottoms : proletarian coll. (– 1887) >, by 1920, S.E. (Baumann.)

chair days. Old age : Society coll. : 1898, Sir E. Arnold ; virtually †. Ware.

chair-marking. To write, not figure, the date in, or heavily to endorse, a cab-driver's licence, as a hint of the holder's undesirability : cab-owners', from ca. 1885. *The Pall Mall Gazette*, Sept. 15, 1890.

chair-warmer. A physically attractive woman ' who does nothing on the stage beyond helping to fill it ', Ware : theatrical : C. 20 ; ob.

chal. A man, fellow, chap (the feminine is *chai*, *chie*) : Romany ; in C. 19–20 used occ. in low coll. Its ultimate origin is unknown : see esp. Sampson at *čal.* Cf. *pal*, much more gen.

C(h)aldee, C(h)aldese. To trick, cheat, impose upon. Butler, ' He . . . Chows'd and Caldes'd you like a blockhead,' *Hudibras*, II. Ca. 1660–1720 ; coll. ? ex *Chaldee(s)* = an astrologer.

chalk. A point in one's favour : coll., from ca. 1850, ex the S.E. sense of a score chalked up in an ale-house. Edmund Yates, 1864.—2. A scratch, more gen. a scar : nautical, ca. 1830–1915. Marryat in *Poor Jack.*

chalk, v. To make (a newcomer) pay his footing : nautical, ca. 1840–1900.—2. In C. 18–19 c., to strike or slash, esp. a person's face. Cf. *chalker*, 2, q.v.—3. See **chalk off, chalk up.**

chalk, adj. Unknown ; hence, incompetent. Whence *chalk-jockeys*, jockeys unknown or incompetent or both. Racing : ca. 1870–90. See Addenda.

chalk, able to walk a. Sober : coll. (orig. nautical or military) : from ca. 1820. Scots, *line for chalk.* See also **walk the chalk.**

chalk, by a long. By much : from ca. 1840 ; coll. C. Brontë in *The Professor.* Slightly earlier is *by long chalks*, as in Barham, while *by many chalks* appears ca. 1880, as in ' the best thing out by many chalks ', Grenville Murray, 1883. Often with *beat*, and in C. 20 gen. in the negative. Ex ' the use of chalk in scoring points in games ', W.

chalk, give (someone) **a.** To beat, defeat, or swindle : low (— 1923). Manchon.

chalk against, n. and v. (To have) ' an unsettled misunderstanding or grudge ', Ware : lower classes': mid-C. 19–20 ; ob. Ex chalking a debt against a name.

chalk down. See **chalk out.**

Chalk Farm. An arm : rhyming s. (— 1857). ' Ducange Anglicus ', 1st ed. In 1914–18, the Tommy preferred *false alarm.*

chalk head. A person smart at figures : coll., from ca. 1850. *Punch*, 1856.—2. Hence, a waiter, rarely so called outside of London. *Punch*, 1861.

chalk is up, one's. One's credit is exhausted : public-house coll. (— 1887) ; ob. Ex *chalk up.*

chalk it up ! Just look at that ! : coll. (— 1923). Manchon (' Regarde-moi ça ! ').

chalk marquis. A sham marquis : lower classes' (— 1909) ; very ob. Ware, ' Never applied to any other title than this. [Prob. ex] some forgotten pun or play upon a name.' See **chalk,** adj.

*****chalk off,** v.t. To ' observe a person attentively so as to remember him ' : c. (— 1857) ; † by 1920. ' Ducange Anglicus ', 1st ed.—2. (Gen. in passive.) To rebuke : Glasgow (— 1934).

chalk out, occ. **down.** To mark out a course of action or conduct : from ca. 1570. Coll. in C. 16, thereafter S.E. (Contrast H. with F. & H. and with S.O.D.)

chalk up, occ. **chalk.** To consider in a person's favour : coll., from ca. 1890. Ex the S.E. sense, C. 16–20, to put to one's account, orig. by chalking the (usually, drinking) score on a wall. Cf. *challik it oop*, q.v.

chalk your pull ! Hold on ! ; steady ! : printers' (— 1887). Baumann.

chalker. A London milkman : ca. 1850–1900. Ex the addition of chalky water to milk. Cf. *cow with the iron tail.*—2. Gen. in pl. One who, at night, slashes the face of innocent citizens : a C. 18 Irish practice ; cf. *mohock.* Coll. whence *chalking*, ' the amusement [so] described ', Grose, 1st ed.

chalking him in. ' The steward's action of drawing a chalk line round any Western Ocean passenger who sits in the captain's chair, the penalty for which is a drink for every steward in the saloon ' : nautical coll. : late C. 19–20. Bowen.

chalks, by. An Australian coll. variant (ca. 1880–

1910) of **chalk, by a long.** Boldrewood, 1888, in the best of the bushranging novels. Ex Cumberland dial. E.D.D.

chalks, make. (Often as vbl.n., *making chalks.*) To be punished standing on two chalk lines and bending one's back : the Royal Naval School at Greenwich : ca. 1840–1900.

chalks, walk or **stump** one's. To move or run away ; make one's departure. From ca. 1840 ; perhaps orig. U.S., for Haliburton uses it in 1840 and De Vere includes it in his *Americanisms*, yet H., F. & H., and S.O.D. say nothing about U.S. ; cf. notably the evidence of the E.D.D. Bowen notes that *walk one's chalks* and *walk Spanish*, in late C. 19–20 nautical, = to desert. The origin is obscure : F. & H. notes a fanciful theory ; perhaps the phrase derives ex the walking of a chalked line.

chalks on, give. To be (much) superior to : late C. 19–20. Frank Richards, *Old Soldiers Never Die*, 1933, ' We all admired the Adjutant very much : he could give us all chalks on at swearing.'

Chalky. A frequent nickname of men surnamed White : naval and military : late C. 19–20. Cf. *Blanco*, q.v.

challik it oop ! Put it to my credit (esp. in a tavern) : theatrical c.p. (— 1909) introduced, presumably, by some dialectal (? Nottinghamshire) comedian ; ob. Ware.

cham or **chammy.** Pronounced *sham* : whence many puns. Abbr. *champagne.* *All the Year Round*, Feb. 18, 1871. Cf. *bubbly.*

cham, v. To drink champagne : from ca. 1875. †.

chamber-day. ' A day at the beginning of each half when " chambers " [the bed-rooms of scholars] were open all day for the re-arrangement of their occupants ' (E.D.D.) : mid-C. 19–20 : Winchester s. verging on j. N.b., one says *in* (not *in the*) *chambers.*

Chamber of Horrors. The Peeresses' Gallery in the House of Lords (contrast *cage*, 4) : Parliamentary, from ca. 1870. Ex the room so named at Madame Tussaud's. Cf. senses 3, 4.—2. A sausage ; gen. in pl. From ca. 1880. Cf. *bag of mystery.*— 3. ' Room at Lloyd's (Royal Exchange) where are " walled " notices of shipwrecks and casualties at sea ', Ware : City of London : late C. 19–20.—4. ' The corridor or repository in which Messrs. Christie (King Street, St. James's) locate the valueless pictures that are sent to them from all parts of the world as supposed genuine old masters ', Ware : Society (— 1909).—5. A family album : workmen's (— 1935).—6. See **House of Corruption** in Addenda.

[**chambering, chamberer.** Sexual indulgence, a loose fellow : despite F. & H., prob. always S.E.]

chambers. See **chamber-day.**

chameleon diet. A very meagre diet : hence, nothing to eat : late C. 17–18 ; coll. B.E.

chamming. Indulgence in champagne : from ca. 1875. Ob.

champ. A champion : coll. : from ca. 1915. Cf. :

champ up. To chew (up) ; eat up : (low) coll. (— 1887) ; ob. Baumann. Ex horses eating.

champagne shoulders. Sloping shoulders : Society : ca. 1860–80. Ware, ' From the likeness to the drooping shoulder of the champagne bottle as distinct from the squarish ditto of the sherry or port bottle '.

champagne weather. Bad weather : ironic Society coll. : ca. 1860–1910. Ware :

champagner. A courtesan : music-halls' : ca. 1880–1912. Ware. Ex the champagne formerly so frequently drunk by these perfect ladies.

champeen. An Australian variant (— 1915), e.g. in C. J. Dennis, of :

champion. Excellent ; arrant : coll., from the 1890's. Esp. predicatively, as ' That's champion ! ' Ex such phrases as *champion fighting-cock, champion pugilist.*—2. Also adv. : coll. : late C. 19–20.

champion slump of 1897, the. The motor-car : London, 1897–ca. 1910. Ware alludes to the unsuccessful *début* of the motor-car in 1896–7. Cf. *butter-coloured beauties.*

chance, v.t. To risk, take one's chances of or in : coll. ; from ca. 1850. Esp. *chance it,* used absolutely.

chance, main. By itself, *the main chance* occurs as early as 1597 in Shakespeare and notably in 1693, in Dryden's translation of *Persius* : ' Be careful still of the main chance, my son. *An eye to the main chance* appears first in Jonson's play, *The Case is Altered,* 1609, it is often preceded by *have* (a variant is *stand to the main chance,* 1579), and it may have originated in the game of hazard. Orig. = the most important issue or feature or possibility, it has, in C. 19–20, very rarely meant other than the chance of profit or advantage to oneself. Prob. always coll. (except in C. 20, when it is S.E.), though the O.E.D. hints a c. complexion.

chance, on the, adv., adj. (Acting) on the possibility *of* or *that.* Orig. (ca. 1780) coll. ; by 1830, at latest, S.E.

chance, stand a fair, good, etc. To be likely to do, (with *of*) to get. From ca. 1790 ; still of a coll. cast though virtually S.E. since ca. 1880.

chance, take a. To risk it, esp. if the chance is a poor one : C. 19–20 ; coll. in C. 19, S.E.—though not yet dignified—in C. 20. Cf. :

chance, take one's. At first, C. 14–19, S.E., to risk it ; from ca. 1800, to seize one's opportunity : coll. till ca. 1860, then S.E.

chance child. An illegitimate child : from ca. 1838 ; coll. till C. 20, then S.E. and somewhat archaic.

chance it, and. A C. 20 variant and derivative of the next : lower classes' coll.

chance the ducks, and. Come what may, as in ' I'll do it and chance the ducks.' A pleonastic c.p., from ca. 1870 ; ob. Recorded in H., 5th ed., and Northall's *Folk Phrases,* 1894. Cf. :

chance your arm ! Chance it !, try it on ! : coll., orig. tailors' : from ca. 1870 ; ob. Among soldiers, *chance one's arm* meant ' to take a risk in the hope of achieving something worth while ', from the late 1890's, the implication being the loss of one's stripes ; the phrase, however, prob. arose ex boxing. The variant, *chance one's mit,* belongs to C. 20. B. & P. ; O.E.D. (Sup.). Cf. preceding entry.—2. Hence, make an attempt : late C. 19–20 : tailors'.

chancellor of the exchequer. Jocularly coll. : C. 20 : the one who holds the purse-strings.

chancellor's egg. A day-old barrister : legal : late C. 19–20 ; ob. Ware.

chancer. A liar ; also, an incompetent workman, or one too confident of his ability : tailors' >, as to nuance 1, military by 1914 : from ca. 1870 : coll.

chancery, in. Fig. from ca. 1835 : coll. In parlous case, an awkward situation. Lit., pugilistic :

the head under an opponent's weaker arm to be punched with his stronger : from ca. 1815 and as in Moore's *Tom Crib's Memorial,* 1819.

chancet or **chanct ; chanst.** A sol. for *chance :* mostly Cockney, Australian (and American) : since when ?

chancy ; occ. **chancey.** (Seldom of persons) unsure, uncertain, untrustworthy : coll. : 1860. George Eliot. (In C. 16–18 Scottish, lucky. S.O.D.) *Chanciness,* coll., is rare.

*chandler-ken. A chandler's shop : c. (— 1812) ; † by 1890. Vaux.

chaney-eyed. One-eyed ; rarely and †, glassy-eyed. Low coll. : from ca. 1860 ; ob. *Chaney = chiney,* China, china, or Chinese, hence with small eyes or eyes like those of a China doll.

change, v.t. and i. To ' turn ', curdle (e.g. milk) : coll. and dial. : from ca. 1830.—2. V.i., to change one's clothes : coll. : C. 17–20.

change, give. To ' pay out ', punish : coll. : from ca. 1860. Gen. v.t., e.g. ' I gave him his change.'

change, give no. Absolute or (' he gave me no change ') v.t. : to give no satisfaction, esp. to reveal nothing. Coll., from ca. 1890.

change about or **over,** v.i. To change or be changed in position, circumstances, or post : coll. ; the former from ca. 1840 (Dickens, 1844), the latter from ca. 1860.

change about one, have all one's. To be clever, esp. to be quick-witted. Coll., from ca. 1880.

change artiste, quick. (Music-halls) one who changes costume for successive songs or scenes : from ca. 1870. Coll. in C. 19, S.E. in C. 20.

change bags. Knickerbockers for football, flannel trousers (? orig. grey) for cricket : Eton College, from ca. 1855 ; ob.

change foot. To play the turncoat : coll. : ca. 1600–1750.

change on, put the. To mislead, deceive. Dryden, 1677, ' By this light, she has put the change upon him ! ' ; Congreve, Scott. Coll., from ca. 1660 ; † by ca. 1900.

change one's note or **tune.** The former from ca. 1700, the latter from ca. 1570 : coll. To alter one's behaviour, professed opinion, speech, expression.

change out of, get no. To receive no satisfaction from ; fail to learn from. C. 20, coll. Cf. *give no change.*

change out of, take one's or **the.** To take the equivalent of a thing ; be revenged upon a person. Coll. : from ca. 1825. John Wilson, 1829 ; Whyte-Melville, 1854 ; Henry Kingsley, on several occasions. Often exclamatory, to the accompaniment of a blow, a neat retort, a crisply decisive act : *take your change out of that !*

change over. See **change about.**

changes, ring the. To change a better article for a worse (coll.), esp., 2, bad money for good (orig. c. >, ca. 1830, low s. > by 1869, gen. s. >, ca. 1900, coll.) : from ca. 1660, ca. 1780 resp. Smollett has ' ringing out the changes on the balance of power '. In C. 20 it also, 3, = to adopt different disguises in rapid succession and with baffling effect. Ex bell-ringing ; in sense 2, there is a pun on small change for larger coin (W.).

Channel-fever. Homesickness : nautical : mid-C. 19–20. Bowen. I.e. the English Channel.

Channel-groping. Cruising in home waters : naval : late C. 19–20. Ibid.

Channel-money. Subsistence-money paid to sailors waiting on a ship in dry dock : nautical coll. : late C. 19–20. Ibid.

chanst. See **chancet.**

*****chant.** Any distinguishing mark on personal effects. Vaux.—2. A person's name or address. Ibid.—3. A song sung in the street. Ibid. (at *chaunt*).—4. An advertisement in newspaper or hand-bill. All ca. 1810–90 ; c. >, except sense 4, low s. ca. 1850. For senses 1, 2, 4, the semantics are that these things proclaim a person's identity.

*****chant,** v. To talk ; sing songs in the street : c. and low, often as *chaunt* : from ca. 1840, ob. Mayhew, 'A running patterer . . . who also occasionally chaunts'.—2. To sell (a horse) by fraudulent statements : c. and low : from ca. 1810. *The English Magazine*, 1816. Prob. 'sing the praises of'.—3. Orig. c., then low, from ca. 1800 : to mark a person's name, initials, etc., on clothes, plate, etc. †. Vaux. I.e. to proclaim his identity. Cf. *chant*, n., 1, 2, 4.—4. To be advertised for : c. of ca. 1810–90. Vaux. Cf. n., 4.—5. V.i., to swear : sporting : 1886–ca. 1914. Ware.—6. V.t. In vagrants' c. of C. 20, thus in W. A. Gape, *Half a Million Tramps*, 1936, 'To "chant" this town,' i.e., to sing in it for alms.

*****chant, tip** (one) **a queer.** To give a false address to : c. of ca. 1810–90. Vaux. See **chant,** n., 2.

chanter, chaunter ; often **horse-cha(u)nter. A** horse-dealer that sells by fraudulent representation : from ca. 1817. Moncrieff, Dickens, Thackeray, Henley. Often *horse-chanter*.—2. In vagrants' c., a street patterer : ca. 1830–1900.

*****chanter(-)cull.** A contemporaneous c. variant of **chanter,** 2 : Ainsworth, 1834.

chant(e)y. See **shanty.**

chanting, chaunting, vbl.n. The dishonest sale of a horse by the concealment of its condition or temper and/or by *bishoping*, q.v. From ca. 1818. Often *horse-cha(u)nting*.—2. In c., street ballad-singing : ca. 1818–1900.

*****chanting ken.** A music-hall : late C. 19–20 c. *Ken* = a house or a place.

[**Chants.** Certain military chants and stock dialogues verge on c.pp. : borderline cases, like the indubitable chants, have been omitted as ineligible ; they may be consulted, *passim*, in B. & P., pp. 193–7, 220–1, 263–72.]

chap. A 'customer', a fellow. From ca. 1715 ; coll. In C. 20, rarely (unless prefaced by *old*) of an old or 'oldish' man. (Abbr. *chapman* ; ex the C. 16–early 18 sense, extant in dial., a buyer, a customer.) Grose, 'an odd chap' ; Byron ; Scott ; Thackeray ; Mrs. Henry Wood, 'You might give a chap a civil answer.' In post-War days, often used by and of girls among themselves. Cf. *customer*, *merchant*, qq.v., and the Scottish *callant*.—2. A male sweetheart : non-aristocratic coll. (— 1887). Baumann. Doubtless ex dial., where recorded before 1850.—3. A sailor : proletarian coll. (— 1887) ; ob. Ibid.

chap, v.t. To chaperon : from ca. 19 21. D. L. Murray, *The English Family Robinson*, 1933, ' Mrs. M. would chap. us if you're so fussy.'

Chapel ; only as **the Chapel.** Whitechapel : Cockneys' : mid-C. 19–20. Ware. Cf. *Ditch*, 1, and *Chapel*, adj.

chapel ; chapel of ease. A water-closet : from ca. 1860. H., 3rd ed. Cf. the S.E. meaning and the Fr. *cabinet d'aisance*.

chapel, v. (Of a don, gen. the Dean) to order (an undergraduate) to attend chapel twice daily for **a** specified period : university, passing to coll. and S.E. : from ca. 1845.

Chapel, adj. Of Whitechapel (London) : Cockneys' : mid-C. 19–20. Ware.

chapel, keep a. To attend chapel once : university, passing to coll. and j. : from ca. 1850.

chapel-folk. Nonconformists as opp. to Episcopalians (esp. Anglicans) : a snobbish coll. ; from ca. 1830.

chapel of ease. See **chapel,** n.

*****chapel of little ease.** A police station ; detention cell : c. (— 1871) ; ob. Cf. *chapel*, n.

chaperon. 'The cicisbeo, or gentleman usher, to a lady ', Grose, 3rd ed. : mid-C. 18–early 19 coll.

[**chaperonee, chaperonless, chaperonship,** are perhaps coll.—see the O.E.D.—but they much rather belong to semi-facetious journalese. They date from ca. 1884.]

*****chapped, chapt.** Thirsty : from ca. 1670. Ob. by 1930. Orig. c. : from ca. 1820, low. Head.

chapper. The mouth : low London (— 1909). Ware, 'From associations with chaps, chops, and cheeks ' ; cf., however, *chaffer*, 2.

chapper, v. To drink : low London (— 1909) ; ob. Ware. Ex the n.

chappie ; occ. **chappy.** Coll., from ca. 1820. At first = little fellow, but from ca. 1880 it = *chap*, esp. as a term of address with *old*, *my good* or *dear*, etc., or as = a man about town ; G. A. Sala, in *The Illustrated London News*, March 24, 1883, 'Lord Boodle, a rapid chappie always ready to bet on everything with everybody.' As a Society term it flourished in the '80's (Ware).

chappow. A raid : Anglo-Indian : from ca. 1860. Mayne Reid. Ex a Pushtoo word.

chappy. For the n., see **chappie.**—2. Talkative : a late C. 17–mid-18 coll. I.e. given to using his chaps, chops, jaws.

chaps me that ! (Galt's *chapse* is incorrect.) I claim that : Scottish children's coll. : mid-C. 19–20. Ex *chap*, to choose, bespeak. Cf. *bags I !*, q.v. O.E.D.

chapt. See **chapped.**

chapter, to the end of the. Always ; to the end ; until death : coll. : from ca. 1840. Occ. used in C. 20, in facetious endings to letters : cf. *to the last drop, till hell freezes, for ever—and after*.

char. Abbr. *charwoman* : from ca. 1875 : coll. Cf. *charlady* and S.E. *chore*.—2. In late C. 19–20 military : tea. In post-War days, vagrants' c. Ex *cha*, a S.E. form (C. 16–19).

char, chare, v. To come in to do the cleaning work in a house, shop, office, or institution. The S.O.D. records for 1732 ; in the C. 18, the meaning was simply, to do odd jobs. Coleridge, of all people, uses the word in 1810 in its mod. sense. Vbl.n., *charing* or *charring*, C. 19–20.

charwallah. A teetotaller : military (Regular Army) : C. 20. Frank Richards, *Old Soldiers Never Die*, 1933. Ex *char*, n., 2, and *wallah*. Cf. *bun wallah* and *wad-shifter*.

chara. A lower classes' abbr. (1927, F. E. Baily: O.E.D. Sup.) of *char-à-banc*. Also *charrie*, *-y* (1926 : ibid.). Cf. :

charabang (*ch-* pron. *tch*). Sol., from ca. 1835, for *char-à-banc* (since 1918 gen. spelt *charabanc*). Occ. *charrybong* (*ch-* pron. *sh*). The Fr. is *char à bancs*.

character. An eccentric or odd person : coll. : Goldsmith, 1773, 'A very impudent fellow this ! but he's a character, and I'll humour him ' ; Lamb, who was himself one. From ca. 1870, an odd person of much humour or wit : likewise, coll.

*character academy. ' A resort of servants without characters, which are there concocted ', F. & H., revised ed. (at *academy*) : c. : late C. 19–20.

*charactered. Branded on the hand ; ' lettered ', q.v. : C. 18–early 19, low if not indeed at first c. *A New Canting Dict.*, 1725 ; Grose, 2nd ed.

charades. ' The Christmas play performed at Bootham ' : Bootham School coll. : late C. 19–20. Anon., *Dict. of Bootham Slang*, 1925.

chare, char(r)ing. See char, v.

charge. A prisoner brought up for trial on a charge or accusation : from late 1850's. Sala.

charge, take. (Of a thing) to get out of control : coll. : 1890. (O.E.D. Sup.)

Charing Cross (pron. *Crorse*). A horse : rhyming s. (— 1857). ' Ducange Anglicus ', 1st ed.

*chariot. An omnibus : c. ; from ca. 1850 ; almost †. Whence *chariot-buzzing* (H., 1st ed.), pocket-picking in an omnibus ; cf. the neater Fr. argotic *faire l'omnicroche*.

charity-bob, the. ' The quick, jerky curtsey made by charity school-girls ', a curtsy rapidly vanishing as long ago as 1883 : coll. : ca. 1870–1915. Ware.

charity sloop. A 10-gun brig : naval coll. during Napoleonic wars. Bowen, ' Officially rated as sloops for the benefit of their commanders '.

charlady. Jocularly coll. for a charwoman : since the 1890's.

Charles James. Theatrical : late C. 19–20. As in ' Once I happened to mention to [a] manager . . . that my children would like to see the pantomime he was producing. "Right you are, old man," he said, " give me a ring any time and I'll see there's a Charles James for them." It took me some moments to realise that he meant a box, and I suppose that no one unacquainted with the peculiarities for [? of] rhyming slang would have realised it at all. Thus is Charles James Fox preserved in the memories of the people—an honour which so far as I am aware has never been conferred on any other politician ' : Edward Shanks in *John o' London's Weekly*, Dec. 8, 1934.

Charles O'Malley's Own. The 14th Hussars : an occ. military nickname of ca. 1842–80. F. & Gibbons. Ex Lever's novel (*Charles O'Malley*, 1841), ' in which the hero figures as an officer of the regiment '.

Charles William. The dummy man in life-boat exercises : Dartmouth R.N. College : C. 20. Bowen.

charley, charlie ; or with capitals. A night watchman : from ca. 1810. Vaux, 1812 ; Hood, 1845. † by 1900, except historically. Etymology unknown ; but prob. ex the very common Christian name.—2. A small, pointed beard : coll. : from ca. 1830. Hook, 1841. Ex *Charles I.*—3. With capital C, a fox : from ca. 1850 ; coll. Hughes in *Tom Brown's Schooldays*.—4. (Tailors') the nap on glossy cloth : from ca. 1865 (ob.) ; also 5, a round-shouldered figure or person : from ca. 1870 (ob.).—6. See charlies.—7. (Also old Charley.) An infantryman's ' pack ' : military : C. 20 ; ob. Hence, *little* (or *young*) *Charley*, his haversack. A hunchback used to be said to ' carry his little brother Charley on his back ' (F. & Gibbons).—8. The inevitable nickname of anyone surnamed Beresford : naval : C. 20. Ex *Charlie B.*, Admiral Lord Charles Beresford. (Bowen.) And of any

man surnamed Peace : military : C. 20. F. & Gibbons. Ex the notorious murderer.

Charley (or Charlie) Chaplin. An officers' moustache, about half an inch in extent : military : 1915. B. & P. Ex the moustache affected by the great comedian.—2. The village of Camblain Châtelain : military in G.W. Ibid.

Charley Chaplin's Army Corps. The Canadian Casualty Assembly Centre, at Shorncliffe, England : Canadian military in G.W. (B. & P.)

Charley Freer. Beer : sporting rhyming s. (— 1909) ; † by 1930. Ware.

*charley-ken. A watchman's (post or) box : c. : ca. 1810–50. Vaux. See charley, 1.

Charley Lancaster. A ' han'kercher ' = handkerchief. Rhyming s. (— 1857). ' Ducange Anglicus ', 1st ed.

charley-man. A variant (ca. 1820–40) of *charley*, 1. ' Jon Bee.'

Charley Noble. The galley funnel : naval : mid-C. 19–20 ; ob. Bowen. Ex a Commander Noble (ca. 1840), who insisted that the cowl of the galley funnel be kept bright. (F. & Gibbons.)

*charley-pitcher. A prowling sharper : c., from ca. 1855. Sala ; Besant & Rice. In C. 20, low ; ob. Etymology doubtful ; perhaps via *Charley [a] pitcher*.

Charley Pope. Soap : Cockney and military rhyming s. (— 1914). F. & Gibbons.

Charley Prescot. A waistcoat : rhyming s. (— 1857). ' Ducange Anglicus ', 1st ed.

Charley Wag, play the. To play truant : from ca. 1865. Charles Hindley, 1876. Henley, in 1887, ellipsed the phrase to *Charley-wag*, but he created no precedent.

charleys or charlies. (Always in pl.) The paps of a woman : from ca. 1840. ? etymology, unless on analogy of *fanny*, q.v. ; if, however, the term was orig. c., it may derive ex Romany *chara* (or *charro*), to touch, meddle with, as in Smart & Crofton. (Ware suggests origin in the opulent charms displayed by the mistresses of Charles II.) Hence occ. *Bobby and Charley*.—2. Thick twine-gloves : Winchester College, ca. 1850–80. Introduced by a Mr. *Charles* Griffith.

charlie. See charley.

charm. (Always pl.) A woman's breasts : C. 18–20. Until ca. 1840, S.E. ; then coll. and, very soon, s. as in ' flashes her charms ', displays . . . ? ex Fr. *appas*.—2. In singular, late C. 16–18 c. for a picklock. Greene ; Grose. Cf. S.E. *moral suasion*.

charming wife. A knife : rhyming s. (— 1914). F. & Gibbons. Contrast *trouble and strife*.

charms. See charm, 1.

charms, bunch of. A girl, esp. if attractive : coll. : C. 20.

charring. See char, v.—charry. See chara.

charter. To bespeak or hire, esp. a vehicle : from ca. 1865 : coll. Ex *to charter a ship*.

[Charterhouse s. is dealt with by A. H. Tod in his handbook, *Charterhouse*, 1900 ; all terms noted by him, and many others (owed to the kindness of Mr. David MacGibbon), are defined in the course of the present work. Cf. the entries at ' Eton ', ' Harrow ' ' Westminster ' and ' Winchester '.]

Charterhouse, sister of the. A great talker, esp. in reply to a husband : C. 16 coll. Tyndale, referring to the monks, says in 1528, ' Their silence shall be a satisfaction for her.' The foundation (1384) of this benevolent institution allows for women as well as men—Brothers and Sisters of Charterhouse.

charver. A sexual embrace : theatrical (orig. Parlyaree) : late C. 19–20. See **chauvering** and :

charver, v. To despoil ; to interfere with and spoil (one's business) : grafters' : late C. 19–20. Philip Allingham, *Cheapjack*, 1934. Ex the Romany for ' to copulate with (a woman) '. Hence :

charvered, ppl.adj. Exhausted, tired out : id. : id. Ibid. Cf. the low *fucked* in the same sense.

chase me, girls ! An Edwardian c.p. expressive of high male spirits. B. & P.

chase yourself ! Oh, go away ! : Australian s. (— 1915) now verging on coll. C. J. Dennis. Cf. *buzz off !* and *go and play trains !*

chaser. A drink taken immediately after another : coll. : C. 20. Esp. a ' tot of spirit taken after coffee ; small quantity of water taken after drinking neat spirits (also fig.) ', C.O.D., 1934 Sup.

chasing, vbl.n. The exceeding of a stated amount, or standard, of production : workmen's, from ca. 1880 ; s. tending to coll. Rae's *Socialism,* 1884.

chassé. To dismiss : Society, ca. 1845–1900. Thackeray, 1847, ' He was *chasséd* on the spot ' ; Yates, 1868. Ex Fr. *chasser,* to chase away, though perhaps imm. ex dancing j.

chaste though chased. A middle-class c.p. of ca. 1900–27. Too pedantic ever to have > very gen.

chat. As free-and-easy talk, always S.E., C. 16–20.—2. The female pudend : C. 19–20, ob. Ex the Fr. word. Cf. *cat* and *pussy.*—3. The truth ; ' the correct thing ', ' the ticket ' (? coll.) : from ca. 1815. Moore. — 4. The subject under discussion ; the point : coll. (ob.) : 1848, Lover (E.D.D.) ; Trollope, 1862, ' That's the chat as I take it.'—5. In mid-C. 19–20 Parlyaree, a thing, an object ; *anything.*—6. Impudence, in C. 20 as *back chat* : ca. 1870–1900 (*chat* is extant in dial.) : coll.— 7. G.W. +, a search for lice. Ex *chat(t),* a louse : see **chatt.**—8. A seal (to a letter) : c. of ca. 1810–60. Egan's Grose. Gen. in pl.—9. A house : c. (— 1879) ; ob. Ex *cheat,* q.v.—10. Also **chate, chatt,** often in pl. : the gallows : mid-C. 16–18 c.

chat, v. More frequent as v.i. than as v.t. ; more correct spelling, *chatt.* To search for lice : from ca. 1850 to G.W., low and perhaps c. ; in G.W. +, so gen. as to > a coll. for de-louse. Vbl.n., *chatting,* has since 1914 been much used and occ. responsible for obvious puns. (In Gavin Douglas's *Æneis, chat* may = to hang.)—2. To address tentatively ; to ' word ' : Australian (— 1916). C. J. Dennis.

*chat-hole. A hole made by convicts in a wall so that they can talk : c. : from ca. 1870.

chat up, v.i. Variant of *chat,* v. : military : G.W.

*chate. See **chat, chatt, cheat.**

Chateau Dif. The Stock Exchange : brokers' (— 1909) ; virtually †. Punning the *Château d'If* and *diff(s),* ' differences ' on settling days. (Ware.)

Chatham and Dover. Over ; as v., give over : London public-houses' rhyming s. (— 1909). Cf. :

Chatham rat. A seaman from the Medway depot : naval : late C. 19–20. Bowen. Rats abound there.

chati. A louse : New Zealanders' : C. 20. Ex *chat* ; prob. by Maori influence : see **koota.**

Chats. Shares in the London, Chatham and Dover Railway (now part of the Southern Railway). Stock Exchange, from ca. 1875 ; †.—2. The inevitable nickname of anyone surnamed Harris : lower classes' and naval : late C. 19–20. Bowen.— 3. (**chats.**) Articles of clothing : Glasgow (—1934). Ex *chat,* n., 5.

chatsby. Anything the name of which one has forgotten : theatrical (— 1935). Ex *chat,* n., 5, on *thingummy.*

*chatt, in C. 20 gen. *chat,* before G.W. rarely in singular. A louse : late C. 17–20. Orig. c., from ca. 1830 s., but very gen. only in G.W. +. B.E., Grose, H. Prob., as Grose suggests, ex *chattels* = live stock (q.v.) or *chattels* = movable property. Synonymy in F. & H. ; cf. *crabs, gentleman's companions, German ducks.*—2. In pl., dice : C. 19 low. —3, 4. See **chat,** n., 8, 10.

chatta. An umbrella : Anglo-Indian coll. : from ca. 1690. (Yule & Burnell.)

*chatte. An occ. variant of *chate,* the gallows : see **chat,** n., 10.

chatter-basket. A prattling child : esp. among nurses : orig. dial., coll. since ca. 1850. Much less gen. are the variants *chatter-bladder* (low), *chatter-bones* (mainly U.S.), *chatter-cart.* Cf. :

chatter-box, mod. **chatterbox.** Grose, 1st ed. : ' One whose tongue runs twelve score to the dozen '. Coll. till 1880, then S.E. Dickens, *The Old Curiosity Shop.* On the C. 16–17 *sauce-box.*

chatter-broth. Tea : the drink and the party : late C. 18–19. Grose, 1st ed. Cf. *scandal-broth* and the jocular S.E. *chatter-water,* which is very ob.

chatter-cart. See **chatter-basket.**

chatteration. Persistent or systematic chattering : from 1862 (O.E.D.). Perhaps rather a pedantic jocularity than a coll.

chatterer. A blow,—esp. if on the mouth,— that makes the recipient's teeth chatter : pugilistic : from ca. 1820 ; † by 1919. ' Peter Corcoran ', i.e. the poet Reynolds, 1827. Cf. :

*chatterers. The teeth : **c.** : C. 19–20 ; ob Egan's Grose. Cf. *grinders.*

*chattering. ' A blow given on the mouth ', Egan's Grose : c. of ca. 1820–60. Ex its effect.

chattering-box. A dissenting chapel : Oxfordshire s. (—1905), not dial. E.D.D. (Sup.).

chattering-broth. Tea : provincial (mostly Staffordshire) s., not dial. : from before 1897. E.D.D.

chattermag. Chatter (1895) ; a chatterbox (C. 20) ; to chatter (1909) : coll. Cf. *mag,* v. O.E.D. (Sup.).

*chattery. Cotton or linen goods or, occ., separate article : c. (— 1821) ; ob. Haggart.

chatting, vbl.n. To *chat,* v., q.v.

*chattry-feeder. A spoon : C. 19 c. Brandon. (Orig. and mainly at Millbank Prison.)

chatts. See **chatt.**

chatty. A pot—esp. if porous—for water : Anglo-Indian coll. : from ca. 1780.—2. A filthy man. Abbr. *chatty dosser* (see **dosser**). Ca. 1810–80 : low.—3. Among sailors, it survives as ' any seaman who is dirty or untidy, or careless in his appearance ' (Bowen).—4. (**Chatty.**) The inevitable nickname of anyone surnamed Mather : nautical and lower classes' : late C. 19–20. Bowen, ' From a celebrated character in naval fiction . . . whether the uncomplimentary meaning applies . . . or not '.

chatty. Lousy : low until G.W. : from ca. 1810. Vaux, 1812. A G.W. jest ran : ' He's a nice chatty little fellow.' Ex *chatt,* 1.

chatty but happy. (Of a ship) ' not very smart in appearance ' : naval c.p. : C. 20. F. & Gibbons. See **chatty,** adj.

chauki. See **chokey.—*chaunt.** See **chant.**

*chaunt the play. To expose and/or explain the ways and tricks of thieves : ob. c. ; from ca. 1845.

chaunted, properly chanted. Celebrated, hence famous. Lit.: in street ballads. Reynolds in his boxing verses, *The Fancy.* Reynolds (not to be confused with the prolific serial-writer) was the latest-comer of the great ' pugilistic ' trio of 1815–30 : Tom Moore, Pierce Egan, J. H. Reynolds.

chaunter. See chanter.

*chaunter cove. A newspaper reporter : c. from ca. 1840. Contrast *chaunting cove.*

*chaunter-cull. A writer of street ballads, carols, songs, last dying speeches, etc., for *ad hoc* consumption ; gen. to be found in a ' pub '. Not recorded before George Parker, 1781, but prob. existent from ca. 1720. C. ; ob. by 1890, † by 1900.

*chaunter upon the leer. C. and low, ca. 1830–70 : an advertiser. (By itself, *chaunter* is c. for a street singer, C. 18–19 : see chanter.)

*chaunting cove. A dishonest horse-dealer : c. of ca. 1820–90. Egan's Grose. See chanting.

chauvering. Sexual intercourse : Lingua Franca (?) and low : from ca. 1840. Whence the low *chauvering donna* or *moll,* a harlot. Cf. *charver,* q.v. Etymology obscure : but there is perhaps some connexion either with Fr. *chauffer,* to heat, with S.E. *chafe,* and with Northern dial. *chauve,* to become heated, to rub together or, more prob., with Romany *charvo* (or *charva,-er*),to touch, meddle with.

chav(v)y. A child : Parlyaree : from ca. 1860. Ex Romany *chavo* or *chavi.*

chaw. A yokel : from ca. 1850. Thomas Hughes. Abbr. *chaw-bacon,* q.v.—2. The process of chewing ; a mouthful (e.g. a quid of tobacco). From ca. 1740 : orig. S.E. ; from ca. 1860, either a low coll. or a sol. or—see E.D.D.—dial. for *chew.*—3. A trick, a hoax : University, ca. 1870–1900. Cf. a *bite,* q.v.—4. See ' Eton slang ', § 2.

chaw, v. To eat, or chew, noisily : C. 16–20. Until ca. 1850, S.E., then either low coll. or sol.—2. To bite : from ca. 1870. Kipling in *The Scots Observer,* 1890 (in a poem called *The Oont*), ' And when we saves his bloomin' life, he chaws our bloomin' arm.'—3. (University) to deceive, hoax, impose upon : ca. 1869–1914. Cf. *bite,* v.—4. To defeat, overcome : coll. (— 1887). Baumann.

chaw-bacon. A yokel : coll. ; from ca. 1810. *Lex. Bal.* ; Whyte-Melville in *General Bounce.*

chaw(-)over. To repeat one's words to satiety : low coll. (? ex Yorkshire dial.) ; from ca. 1820.

chaw the fat. A naval variant (late C. 19–20) of *chew the fat,* q.v. (Bowen.)

chaw(-)up. To destroy, smash, ' do for ' : from ca. 1840, mainly U.S. Dickens.

chawer. One who chews, esp. if roughly (— 1611) : orig. S.E. ; in C. 19–20, low coll. Cotgrave. Rare. The same applies to the C. 16–20 *chawing,* chewing, (fig.) rumination.

chaws. Sexual intercourse : low coll. : from ca. 1860 ; ob. Cf. *chauvering.*

chay, pron. *shay.* A sol. for *chaise,* as in *post-chay.* From ca. 1702. Mackenzie, 1771, ' The pleasure of keeping a chay of one's own ', O.E.D.

cheap, dirt or dog. The former from ca. 1835 (Dickens in *Oliver Twist,* 1838) ; the latter from ca. 1570 (Holinshed has it) and † by 1840. Coll. In C. 20, occ. *cheap as dirt* (Lyell).

cheap, feel. In ordinary sense, S.E., though not literary. In s., to feel ill after a bout of drinking : from ca. 1880 ; ob. Hence, *cheapness* : late C. 19–20.

cheap, on the. Cheaply ; economically. Coll. ; from the late 1850's. H., 1st ed.

cheap and nasty. Either lit. or = pleasing to the eye, inferior in fact. From ca. 1830 : coll. >, by 1890, S.E. *The Athenæum,* Oct. 29, 1864, '. . . or, in a local form, " cheap and nasty, like Short's in the Strand ", a proverb applied to the deceased founder of cheap dinners ' ; this gibe no longer holds good.

cheap and nasty bargain. An apprentice : nautical officers' : late C. 19–20. Bowen. Ex preceding.

cheap as dirt. See cheap, dirt.

cheap beer. ''Beer given by publicans at night-time to officers ' : policemen's (— 1909). Ware.

cheap-tripper. One who goes on cheap trips : coll. ; from ca. 1858. James Payn.

cheapness. See cheap, feel.

cheaps, the. A cheap edition, as of a 7s. 6d. novel re-issued at 3s. 6d. Publishers', booksellers', and bookbinders' : from ca. 1910 ; since ca. 1930, coll.

Cheapside, come at it, or home, by (way of). To buy a thing cheap : mid-C. 18–19 ; coll. Grose, 2nd ed. Variant : *get it by way of Cheapside.*

*cheat, occ. chate, chete, etc., is a mid-C. 16–19 c. word—gen. = thing, article—appearing in many combinations, e.g. *belly-cheat,* an apron, and *quack-ing-cheat,* a duck : in only a very few instances has this term penetrated English proper even to the extent of becoming s. Harman ; Grose. Etymology obscure. The unpreceded pl. means the gallows : cf. *chat,* n., last sense. (As a sham sleeve, it is S.E.)

cheat the worms. To recover from a serious illness : proletarian coll. (— 1887). Baumann.

cheatee. One who is cheated : coll. ; from ca. 1660, very rare in C. 18, revived in C. 19.

*cheating law. Card-sharping : late C. 16–early 17 c. Greene.

*cheats. Sham cuffs or wristbands : c. and low, late C. 17–early 19.—2. In Randle Holme's *Armoury,* 1688, a showy, fur-backed waistcoat. (See also note on *cheat.*)

check, get one's. To receive one's discharge, esp. from a medical board : military coll. : 1916–18. F. & Gibbons.—2. To be killed : military : late 1914–18. Ibid.

check, take. To be offended : coll. verging on S.E. : ca. 1660–1780. (O.E.D.) Ex dogs at fault.

check it up or check up. To enter a theatre with another person's discarded pass-out check : theatrical and theatre-goers' (— 1909) ; ob. Ware.

checker. An inspector : busmen's coll. : from ca. 1925. *The Daily Herald,* Aug. 5, 1936.

checks, hand in one's. See cash one's checks.

chee-chee. Of mixed European and Indian parentage. An adj. deriving from a Hindi exclamation = fie !—2. As a n., the minced English of half-breeds ; the half-breeds as a class. Both date from ca. 1780 : best classified as an Anglo-Indian coll. Yule & Burnell.

cheek. Insolence to an elder or superior : coll. : from ca. 1830 ; recorded in Marryat's *Poor Jack,* 1840, a locus exemplifying *give cheek = to cheek,* q.v. ; George Moore, *The Mummer's Wife,* 1884, ' If he gives me any of his cheek, I'll knock him down.' Cf. *lip.*—2. Audacity, effrontery, assurance : coll. : from ca. 1850. Mayhew, of doctors : ' They'd actually have the cheek to put a blister on a cork leg.' Cf. *face.*—3. A share : from ca. 1820 : low coll. Esp. in ' where's my cheek ? ' and the set phrase, *to one's own cheek,* all to oneself, as in ' Jon Bee ', 1823, and Lever's *Charles O'Malley,* 1841.—4. See cheeks.—5. A cheeky lout : London schools' (— 1887) ; † by 1920. Baumann.

cheek, v. To address saucily : from ca. 1840 : coll. Mayhew, Dickens. Occ., though † by 1920, *to cheek up*. Commonest form : *give cheek* ; v.t. with *to*.

cheek, have the. To be insolent or audacious enough (to do something) : coll. : mid-C. 19–20. Cf. *have the face* (or *front*).

cheek-ache, get or have the. To be made to blush ; to be ashamed of what one has done : artisans' and tailors' from ca. 1860 ; ob.

cheek it. To face it out : coll. : 1851, Mayhew (O.E.D.) ; 1887, Baumann (*cheek it out*). Ex *cheek*, v., q.v.

cheeker. One who speaks or addresses others impudently : 1840 (O.E.D.) : coll. Rare in C. 20. Ex *cheek*, v.

cheekiness. Impudence ; cool confidence ; audacity ; tendency to ' give cheek '. Coll., recorded in 1847 ; Aytoun & Martin ; Trollope in *The Three Clerks*. Ex *cheek*, n., l.

cheekish. Impudent ; saucy : coll., ca. 1850–1900. Mayhew.

cheeks. The posteriors : coll., from ca. 1750. Grose, by implication. Cf. *blind cheeks*. When, in 1928–30, dresses were the soul of wit, London clubmen heard, prob. ex the Stock Exchange, the rhyme, ' If dresses get any shorter,' said the flapper with a sob, | ' There'll be two more cheeks to powder, a lot more hair to bob ', sometimes known as *The Flapper's Lament*.—2. A jeering, insulting interjection : ca. 1860–80. H., 3rd ed.

cheeks and ears. A fanciful name for a head-dress not long in fashion : coll. : C. 17. It occurs in *The London Prodigal*, 1605.

cheeks near cunnyborough !, ask. (Cf. *cheeks*, 1.) Ask my arse ! Mid-C. 18–early 19 low London c.p. used by women only. See **cheeks ; cunnyborough** = **cunny** = **cunt.** Grose, 1st ed.

Cheeks the Marine. Mr. Nobody. A character created by Marryat, who conscientiously popularised it : *Peter Simple*, 1833. Fifty years later, Clark Russell, in his nautical glossary, defined the term as ' an imaginary being in a man-of-war '. By 1850 there had arisen the now ob. *tell that to Cheeks the Marine* = *tell that to the marines*, q.v. Prob. ex *cheeks*, 1, q.v.

cheeky. Saucy, impudent, insolent, ' cool '. ' Ducange Anglicus ', 1857 ; Henry Kingsley, 1859. Ex *cheek*, n., l, 2.

cheeky new fellow. See **new fellow.**

cheer, give (one) the. To bid a person welcome : proletarian coll. : from ca. 1870 ; ob. Baumann.

cheer o ! See **cheerio !**

cheerer. ' A glass of grog, or of punch ', Bee : public-house coll. : ca. 1820–80. Ex its effect. (The term occurs in Scots as early as 1790 : E.D.D.).

cheerio ! cheero ! A parting word of encouragement ; in drinking, a toast : coll. : resp. 1915 and ca. 1910. The former is rather more familiar, less aristocratic, esp. after G.W. See esp. B. & P. and O.E.D. (Sup.). Cf. *cheery-ho !*—2. Hence, adj. (from ca. 1919), mostly upper-class in use, as in Dorothy Sayers, *Clouds of Witness*, 1926, ' " He seemed particularly cheerio . . .", said the Hon. Freddy . . . The Hon. Freddy, appealed to, said he thought it meant more than just cheerful, more merry and bright, you know.' Ob.

cheers ! Often *three cheers !* A coll. expression of deep satisfaction or friendly approval : from ca. 1905.

cheery. Cheerful, lively : C. 17–20. Also, apt to cheer or enliven : C. 18–20, ob. On the border-line between coll. and S.E. ; Johnson considered it a ludicrous word—it is certainly unnecessary beside *cheerful*.

cheery-ho ! A post-G.W. variant of *cheerio !*

cheese. An adept ; a smart or a clever fellow : Public School and university : ca. 1860–1900. Ex *the cheese*, q.v.—2. See **cheese, the.**

cheese, v.t. Very rare except in *cheese it !*, be quiet ! : low from ca. 1855 ; previously c. (-- 1812), when also = run away ! Vaux. Ex *cease*.

cheese, believe or persuade or make believe that the moon is made of. To believe firmly, or to cause another to believe, something astounding or impossible or absurd ; hence, to be a fool, to befool another. Frith, ca. 1529 ; Wilkins the philosopher ; Ainsworth the lexicographer. Coll. ; in C. 18–20, S.E. Apperson.

cheese, hard. In comment or exclamation : bad luck ! From ca. 1870 ; coll. and dial.

cheese, howling. An overdressed dandy or ' blood ' : Cambridge University, ca. 1860–1895. Prob. ex the next ; cf. *cheese*, n., l.

cheese, the. The fashion ; the best ; ' the correct thing '. Recorded in *The London Guide* in 1818, apparently soon after the birth of this phrase, which seems to have > gen. only ca. 1840. Barham ; Reade, 1863, a character, concerning marriages, saying ' I've heard Nudity is not the cheese on public occasions.' Prob. ex the Urdu *chiz*, a thing (see Yule & Burnell ; F. & H.) ; but see **caz.** Cf. the derivative *the Stilton*.

cheese and crust ! A proletarian perversion and evasion (— 1909) of *Jesus Christ !* ; ob. Ware.

cheese-cutter. A prominently aquiline nose : from ca. 1870 ; ob. H., 5th ed.—2. The large, square peak of a cap : whence *cheese-cutter caps*. Ca. 1870–1910.—3. A peaked ' full-dress ' cap : *Conway* Training Ship : from ca. 1895 ; ob. Masefield, *The Conway*, 1933.—4. In pl., bandy legs : from ca. 1860 ; ob.

cheese it ! See **cheese**, v.—2. Occ. = *cave !*, q.v. : low : late C. 19–20. F. & Gibbons.

cheese-knife. A sword : military ; from ca. 1870. Cf. *toasting-fork*.

Cheese(-)mongers, the. The First Life Guards : from ca. 1788 ; ob. ' Come on, you damned Cheesemongers ! ' was heard at Waterloo. Ob. Also, from before 1890, called *the Cheeses*. The real ' etymology ' is obscure : perhaps many tradesmen > officers.

cheese-toaster. A sword : coll. : ca. 1770–1913 : military. Grose, 1st ed. ; Thackeray. Cf. in Shakespeare, *Henry V*, II, i, 8–11 (Oxford edition). In G.W. +, a bayonet. Cf. *cheese-knife* and *toasting-fork*. F. & H. gives the synonymy.

cheeser. An eructation : low coll. : C. 19–20, ob. —2. ' A strong smelling fart ', *Lex. Bal.*, 1811 ; ob.—3. A chestnut : Cockney's : late C. 19–20.

Cheeses and Kisses. Mrs, Missus : rhyming s. (— 1931).

Cheeses, the. See **Cheese-mongers.**—2. **cheeses, make.** (Schoolgirls') the making of one's dress and petticoat, after a rapid gyration of the body and a quick sinking to the ground or floor, spread into a cheese-like form. Hence, to curtsy profoundly. Coll. ; from ca. 1855. Thackeray, De Quincey, Besant & Rice. Ex Fr. *faire des fromages* : even Littré records it.

cheesing rows(, three). (Three) rousing cheers : C. 20. A deliberate Spoonerism.

cheesy. Showy, fine (opp. *dusty*) : coll. ; from mid-1850's. Surtees in *Ask Mamma*. Ex *the cheese*, q.v., at *cheese, the.*

cheesy-hammy-eggy-topside. A savoury popular with those who have sailed with Chinese cooks : (nautical) officers' : late C. 19–20. Cheese and ham with an egg on top.

[**chef.** A ship's cook : jocular naval coll. on the border-line of jocular S.E. : C. 20. F. & Gibbons.]

cheild (pron. *che-ild*). A derisively coll. C. 20 pronunciation, esp. with *my*, of *child* : in ridicule of the agonies of the transpontine drama. Infrequent before G.W., common in military fun, fairly gen. since.

chello. A variant of *jillo = jildi.*

Chelsea, get. To obtain the benefit of Chelsea military hospital : military, mid-C. 18–early 19. Grose, 3rd ed.

Chelsea College. See **Lombard Street.**

chemist, the. A medical officer : military : late 1914–18, and later. F. & Gibbons.

chemmy. The game of *chemin de fer* : coll. : from ca. 1920.—2. See **-y,** 2.

chemozzle. An occ. variant of *shemozzle*, q.v.

Chent. Incorrect for *Kent* : 1676, noted by Coles.

*Chepemans. Cheapside Market : C. 17 c. See **-mans.**

cheque, have seen the. To have exact knowledge : coll., from ca. 1870 ; ob.

cheque, little. See **little cheque.**

cheque, pass in one's. An Australian variant (— 1916), e.g. in C. J. Dennis, of *cash* (or *hand in*) *one's checks*, q.v.

Cher, the. The River Cherwell : Oxford undergraduates' : late C. 19–20. Collinson.

cheri or **Cheri.** A charming woman : Society : ca. 1840–60. Ware, 'From Madame Montigny, of the Gymnase, Paris. Her stage name remained Rose Cheri. She was a singularly pure woman, and an angelic actress. Word used by upper class men in society . . . to describe the nature of their mistresses.' (? rather *chérie*.)

*cherpin. A book : c. of ca. 1840–1900. Anon., *No. 747.* Etymology ?

cherrilet, cherrylet. Gen. in pl. A nipple : late C. 16–17. Sylvester, 'Those twins . . . Curled-purled cherrielets'. On the border-line between coll. and S.E.

*cherry. A young girl : c., latter half of C. 19. Cf. *cherry-pie* and *cherry-ripe*.

cherry-bounce. Cherry-brandy : coll. ; from ca. 1790 ; but in Robertson's *Phraseologia Generalis*, 1693, as *cherry-bouncer*. Cf. the S.E. sense, brandy and sugar.

Cherry-Breeches or **-Bums.** See **Cherubims.**

cherry-colour(ed). Either black or red : in a common card-cheating trick : low coll. : from ca. 1850. Cf. Grose's *cherry-coloured cat*, a black one.

cherry-merry. Merry ; convivial ; slightly drunk : coll. (— 1775). Perhaps the same as Middleton's *kerry merry*. ? *cheery* corrupted ; but cf. *chirping-merry*, q.v.—2. (Anglo-Indian) a present of money : coll. : from ca. 1850. H., 3rd ed. Cf. :

cherry-merry bamboo. A thrashing : Anglo-Indian, from ca. 1860 ; ob. H., 3rd ed. Lit., a present of bamboo : see **cherry-merry,** 2.

cherry nobs. (Very rare in singular.) Military policemen : military : C. 20. F. & Gibbons, 'From their red cap covers '. More gen. *red caps*.

Cherry-Pickers. See **Cherubims.**—2. (**cherry pickers.**) Inferior seamen : nautical : late C. 19–20. Bowen.

cherry-pie. A girl : from ca. 1870 ; ob. Cf. c. *cherry.*

cherry-pipe. A woman : low rhyming s. on c. *cherry-ripe*, a woman. From ca. 1880 ; ob.

cherry-ripe. A Bow Street runner : C. 18–early 19. Ex the scarlet waistcoat.—2. A footman dressed in red plush : from ca. 1860 ; ob.—3. A pipe : rhyming s. (— 1857). 'Ducange Anglicus', 1st ed.—4. In c., a woman : from ca. 1840. Cf. *cherry*.—5. Nonsense : rhyming s. (on *tripe*) : C. 20.

cherry-ripe ! A way of *calling ripe cherries !* Coll. : from ca. 1600. Herrick.

cherry-tree class. Two British battleships of a tonnage reduced by Washington, the U.S. capital : post-G.W. Bowen, 'Because they were cut down by Washington ', the cherry-tree hero of the truth.

cherub. See **cherubims,** 3.

Cherub Dicky. Richard Suett (d. 1805), a comedian. Dawson, 'Originally a choir-boy at Westminster Abbey'.

cherubim, singular, and **cherubims,** pl., are in C. 19–20 sol. or low coll. whenever they are not dial. Dickens has the former in *Dombey and Son,* 1848.

cherubims. Peevish children : late C. 18–early 19 ; coll. Facetiously allusive to 'To Thee cherubim and seraphim continually do cry' in the Te Deum. Grose, 1st ed.—2. (Military) the 11th Hussars : from ca. 1813. From their cherry-coloured trousers. *Cherry-Pickers*, because some of their men were captured when on outpost duty in a Spanish orchard. By low jocularity, *Cherry-Bums*. Also *Cherry-Breeches*. Cherubs, says the S.O.D., 'in early Christian art . . . were app. coloured red '.—3. Chorister, mod. choir, boys : from ca. 1850 ; ob. Also *cherubs*. Perhaps ex the Te Deum verse.

cherubims (or **-ins**), **in the.** Unsubstantial ; 'in the clouds' : C. 16–17 ; coll. ; rare. Udall.

Cheshire cat : often **cat.** An inhabitant of Cheshire : coll. nickname (— 1884). Ware (at *webfoots*). Ex :

Cheshire cat, grin like a. To laugh, or smile, broadly. Pejorative coll. : from ca. 1770. Wolcot, 'Lo, like a Cheshire cat our Court will grin ! '; Thackeray ; 'Lewis Carroll' in *Alice in Wonderland*. In C. 19 one often added *eating cheese, chewing gravel*, or *evacuating bones*. Origin still a mystery. I surmise but cannot prove *cheeser*, a cat very fond of cheese, *a cheeser* having > *a cheeser cat* > *a Cheshire cat* ; hence *grin like a Cheshire cat* would = to be as pleased as a 'cheeser' that has just eaten cheese. Or the development might be *cheeser : Cheshire-cheeser : Cheshire cat*.

Cheshire, the. 'The cheese ', 'the correct thing ', perfection : ca. 1870–1900. Ware.

chessy. Characteristic of good play at chess : coll. : 1883. O.E.D.

chest, chuck a. See **chuck a chest.** Cf. :

chest, chuck out one's. To pull oneself together ; stand firm : coll. : from ca. 1860 ; ob. The C. 20 sense (likewise coll.) is to make oneself appear manly, to show confidence. An occ. variant, *throw a chest.*

chest, get it off one's. 'To deliver a speech ; express one's feelings ', C. J. Dennis : (mainly) Australian s. (C. 20) >, by 1930, coll.

chest, over the. See **gun, over the.**

chest and bedding. A woman's breasts: nautical (— 1785); † by 1900. Grose, 1st ed. (at *kettle drums*).

chest-plaster. A young actor : theatrical : 1883–ca. 1890. A satirical description by the older actors : ' From the heart-shaped shirt-front worn with a very open dress-waistcoat, and starched almost into a cuirass . . . (*See* Shape and Shirt.) ' Ware.

chestnut. Abbr. *chestnut-coloured horse* : coll. : from ca. 1840.—2. A stale story or outworn jest. Coll., 1886 +, ex slightly earlier U.S. Perhaps ex ' a special oft-repeated story in which a chestnut-tree is particularly mentioned ', W. (cf. O.E.D. quotation for 1888) ; perhaps ex *roast chestnuts* (cf. *done brown*).—3. In pl., bullets : military of G.W., but not very gen. F. & Gibbons. Cf. Fr. *châtaignes*.

Chestnut Troop, the. 'A' Battery, Royal Horse Artillery : 1793 : military coll. >, in late C. 19, j. F. & Gibbons. Ex colour of the horses.

chestnuts. See **chestnut**, 2.

chesto !, chest-o ! ' Request to anyone to get off a chest lid, so that the chest may be opened ', Masefield. *Conway* Training Ship : from ca. 1880.

chesty. Weak in the chest ; of tuberculosis or pneumonia : coll. : C. 20. (O.E.D. Sup.)

*chete. See **cheat**.

Chev. A Chevrolet : motorists' coll. : from ca. 1925.

[**cheval de retour.** An old offender : occ. found in English books of ca. 1850–90 ; never used by the underworld, rarely by the police.]

Chevalier Atkins. A journalistic coll. variation, ca. 1895–1910, of *Tommy Atkins*. Ware.

chevisa(u)nce. Enterprise (esp. if chivalrous) ; prowess : catachrestic : 1579, Spenser. O.E.D.

chevoo. See **shevoo**.

Chevy Chase. A face : rhyming s. (— 1859) ; † by 1914, except as abbr., *chevy* or *chivvy*. H., 1st ed. ; Manchon.

chew. A quid of tobacco : low coll. ; from ca. 1840.

chew it over is an Australian variant (— 1916) of *chew the fat*.

chew the balls off. To reprimand severely : military : C. 20.

chew the cud. To be very thoughtful : coll., from ca. 1860.—2. To chew tobacco : from ca. 1845.

chew the fat or **rag** ; in C. 20, occ. **chew the grease** (Manchon). To grumble ; resuscitate an old grievance : military : from ca. 1880. Brunlees Patterson, *Life in the Ranks*, 1885. In G.W. there was a tendency to distinguish, thus : *chew the fat*, ' to sulk, be resentful ' ; *chew the rag*, ' to argue endlessly or without hope of a definite agreement ', B. & P. Moreover, in the C. 20 Navy, *chew the fat* additionally = ' to spin a yarn ' (Bowen).

chew the mop. A variant (from ca. 1920) of *chew the rag*, to argue : military.

chew up. (Gen. in passive.) To reprimand, to ' tell off ' : mostly military : C. 20. F. & Gibbons.

chewed rag or **string.** See **boiled rag**.

chewed up, be. To be very nervous and/or off colour : from ca. 1920. (G. Heyer, *Why Shoot a Butler ?*, 1933.)

chewing her oakum. (Of a wooden ship) beginning to leak, the caulking being bad : nautical : mid-C. 19–20 ; ob. Bowen.

*chewre. To steal : c. : C. 17–18.

chi-a(c)k, -hike, -ike. See **chiike**.

chic. Skill, dexterity, esp. in the arts ; finish, style ; elegance : coll. : from ca. 1855. Ex the Fr. Lever ; Yates, 1866, ' A certain piquancy and chic in her appearance '.—2. ' Style ' : artists' coll. : late C. 19–20.

chic, v. ' *To chic up a picture*, or *to do a thing from chic* = to work without models and out of one's own head ' : artists' s. (— 1891) verging on coll. F. & H. Ex preceding term.

chic, adj. Elegant, stylish : from late 1870's : coll. after ca. 1890. (Not so used in Fr.)

chice(-am-a-trice). Nothing ; no good : low and vagrants' : coll. : from ca. 1851. Egan's Grose has both forms and implies that the term was orig. Yiddish. Prob. ex Romany *chichi*, nothing, and the source of *shicer*, q.v.

chick. A child : whether endearment or neutral term. From M.E. onwards. Coll. almost S.E.— 2. Anglo-Indian coll. (— 1866) : abbr. *chickeen*, a Venetian coin (= 4 rupees). Esp. in " I'll buy you a chick.'

chickabiddy. A young girl : orig. (— 1860) costers'. Ex the nursery name for a chicken often employed as an endearment (— 1785) for a child. Grose, 1st ed. The *-biddy* may orig. have been *birdy* : W.

chickaleary cove. An artful fellow : costers' ; from ca. 1860. *The C. C.* was one of the famous Vance's songs ca. 1869. Prob. *chick* = a bird, *leary* = suspicious, alert, wide-awake : cf. *downy bird*, q.v.

chicken. C. 17–18 coll., ' a feeble, little creature, of mean spirit ', B.E. Whence the † *hen-hearted* and *chicken-hearted*, adjj., and *chicken-heart*, a coward, also coll.—2. A child (C. 18–20, coll.), *chick* being more usual.—3. In (— 1851) c., a pint pot : cf. *cat-and-kitten sneaking*, q.v.—4. A fowl of any age ; *the chicken*, fowls collectively : ⸝ coll. : C.19–20. O.E.D. (Sup.).

chicken, no. Elderly. From ca. 1700 : coll. Swift, ' . . . Your hints that Stella is no chicken ' ; Fielding ; Walpole ; Sala, ' I am no chicken.'

chicken, that's (gen. **your**). That's your concern : coll. (— 1931). Lyell. Now gen. *that's your pigeon*.

Chicken, the. M. A. Taylor, a noted barrister (d. 1834). Dawson, ' From his allusion to himself in his maiden speech (1785) as but " a chicken in the profession of the law " '.

chicken-butcher. A poulterer ; also, anyone shooting very young game. Coll. : late C. 18–20 ; ob. Grose, 2nd ed. In C. 20 Glasgow, *chicken-choker*.

chicken-feed. Small change : Canadian (and U.S.) : C. 20. (John Beames, *Gateway*, 1932.)

chicken-fixing. See **gilguy**.

chicken-food. Blancmange : naval : late C. 19–20. Bowen.

chicken got the axe, where the. I.e. ' in the neck ' ; severely, disastrously, fatally : a c.p. dating from ca. 1896 ; slightly ob. W. Cf. *where Maggie wore the beads*.

chicken-hammed. Bandy-legged : mid-C. 18–19 coll. Grose, 1st ed.

chicken nabob. A man returned from India with but a moderate fortune : late C. 18–early 19 coll. Grose, 2nd ed.

chicken-perch. A church : rhyming s. : late C. 19–20. B. & P.

chickens before they are hatched, count one's. Unduly to anticipate a successful issue. C. 16–20 ; coll. till C. 19, then S.E. Gosson, 1579 ; ' Hudibras' Butler, its populariser. Cf. **L.** *ante victoriam canere triumphum.*

chickery-pokery. See jiggery-pokery.

chicko, n. and adj. (A) very young (person, esp. a soldier): military: C. 20. **B. & P.** I.e. a mere chicken.

chicot. Verminous: military: 1916–18. **B. & P.**, 'From the French ill-success with *hitchy-koo*'.

Chidley Dyke. The line between Cheltenham and Southampton Docks: railwaymen's: C. 20; ob. Known to the passengers as *the Pig and Whistle Line.*

chie, occ. **chai.** See **chal.**

chief (the chief). The Chief Engineer, or, loosely, the First Mate: nautical coll.: mid-C. 19–20.—2. A Petty Officer, etc.: naval: C. 20. Bowen.—3. (chief.) A—gen. jocular—form of address: coll.; from ca. 1880. Partly ex sense 1. Esp. in *O.K.*, *chief* (post-G.W.): see **O.K.**

chief buffer, the. The Chief Boatswain's Mate: naval: late C. 19–20. Bowen.

chief housemaid, the. A 1st lieutenant, R.N.: naval: C. 20. Ibid. He is 'responsible for the cleanliness and good order of the ship'.

chief muck of the crib. 'A head director in small affairs', Bee: low: ca. 1820–80. Cf. *Lord Muck.*

***chife.** An occ. variant of *chive*: see **chive-fencer.** Grose, 1st ed. As is *chiff* (*Lex. Bal.*).

chigger. A variant of *gigger* or *jigger*, esp. as a private still. 'Jon Bee', 1823.

chiike, occ. **chy-ack** (or **chiack**) and **chi-hike**; rarely **chi-ak.** A street (orig. costers') salute; a hearty word of praise heartily spoken. From ca. 1855; low coll. H., 1st ed.; *The Chickaleary Cove,* where it is spelt *chy-ike.* Echoic. Etymology? Perhaps a corruption or perversion of *chuck,* v., 6 (n.b. esp. *chuck a jolly*).—2. Whence, in Australia, a jeering call, a piece of 'cheek': from ca. 1880.

chiike, **chy-ack,** v. To hail; praise noisily. Low coll.; from ca. 1855.—2. Among tailors: to chaff ruthlessly: from ca. 1865.—3. Whence, in Australia, to 'cheek', of which it is a corruption: from mid-1870's. Morris.—4. V.i., to make a 'row', a din: low coll.: from ca. 1880. O.E.D. (Sup.).

chiike with the chill off, give. To reprimand, scold, abuse. From ca. 1866; ob.

child, eat a. 'To partake of a treat given to the parish officers, in part of commutation for a bastard child', Grose, 1st ed. Mid-C. 18–mid-19 (coll.).

child, this. Oneself; I, me: coll.; orig. (− 1850) U.S., anglicised ca. 1890. At one time—before 1927, at any rate—there was a c.p.: *not for this child.* (Collinson)

childer. Children: in C. 19–20, low coll. when not dial.

Childers. A holding in 2¾% Consols redeemable in 1905: Stock Exchange from 1884, when Mr. Childers originated this stock in an 'attempt to reduce the interest on the whole of the Three per Cent. Debt' (A. J. Wilson, *Stock Exchange Glossary,* 1895); † by 1906, except historically.

children's shoes, make. To be fooled, mocked, depreciated: coll.: C. 17–19. Mrs. Centlivre.

child's play. Something very easy to do: coll. >, by 1880, S.E.; from ca. 1839, but dating from late M.E. in form *child's,* or *childer,* *game.*

chill, v.t. and i. To warm (a liquid). Coll.; from ca. 1820. Dickens, in *Boz,* 'A pint pot, the contents . . . chilling on the hob'. Abbr. *take the chill off,* also coll.

chill off, with the. A comment or exclamation indicative of dissent or depreciation or disbelief. Coll.; from ca. 1840. Cf. *over the left.*

chillum. (Anglo-Indian, from ca. 1780) a hookah, the smoking thereof, a 'fill' of tobacco therein: coll. rather than s. The orig. and proper meaning is that part of a hookah which contains the tobacco. Ex Hindi *chilam.*

Chilly Charley. Charles Clark (1806–80), topographer and *satirist.* Dawson.

Chiltern Hundreds, accept the. 'To vacate a favourable seat at the alehouse', Bee: public-house: ca. 1820–60. Punning S.E. sense.

chimbl(e)y, chimley. A chimney: (dial. and) sol.: C. 18–20.

***chime.** In c., to praise, esp. highly; puff; canoodle mercenarily: C. 19.

chime in, v.i. To join harmoniously in conversation, etc.: from ca. 1830; coll. soon S.E.

chime in with. To be in entire (subordinate) agreement with: from ca. 1820; coll. soon > S.E.

chimley. See **chimbley.—chimmy.** See the more gen. **shimmy.** (A. S. M. Hutchinson, 1908.)

chimney. One who smokes (esp. a pipe) a great deal: from ca. 1880; coll.

chimney-chops. A negro: coll.; late C. 18–mid-19 pejorative. Grose, 1st ed.

chimney-pot. The tall silk hat worn by men, also (long †) a riding-hat for women. Coll.; from ca. 1865. Abbr. *chimney-pot hat.* Cf. *bell-topper, stove-pipe.*

chimney-sweep(er). The aperient more gen. known as the black draught: ca. 1850–1900. H., 3rd ed. Cf. *custom-house officer.*—2. A clergyman: from ca. 1870; ob. Cf. *clergyman* = a chimney-sweep.

chimozzle. A variant (recorded in 1900) of *shemozzle.*

chimp. A C. 20 coll. abbr. of *chimpanzee*; orig. among the keepers at the Zoo.

chin. A talk: American s. (− 1914) anglicised ca. 1920. (O.E.D. Sup.) Ex:

chin, v. To talk, esp. if loquaciously or argumentatively: orig. (− 1880), U.S.; anglicised ca. 1890. From ca. 1920, also *chin-chin.* Vbl.n., *chinning,* a talk.—2. To hit (a person): low: from ca. 1910. Orig. on the chin, and esp. in Glasgow.

chin, up to the. Deeply involved; extremely busy. Coll.; from ca. 1860.

chin-chin! A salutation; in C. 20, a c.p. toast. This Anglo-Chinese term dates from late C. 18, but it > popular, outside of China, only in G.W., though it was general in the Navy in late C. 19 and, by 1909, common in 'club society' (Ware). Chinese *ts'ing-ts'ing,* please-please. (W.)—2. Hence also v., to greet: 1829, Yule & Burnell. Whence *chin-chin joss.*—3. See **chin,** v., 1.

chin-chin joss. Religious worship: pidgin-English (in Chinese ports): mid-C. 19–20. Ex preceding + *joss,* an idol. Yule & Burnell.

chin-chopper. A blow under the chin: boxing, from ca. 1870; ob.

chin-music. Conversation; oratory. Adopted ca. 1875 (Besant & Rice, 1876) ex U.S. where popularised by Mark Twain. Note, however, that Berkshire dial. had it as early as 1852 (E.D.D.).

chin-strap, come in on one's. 'To finish a march or a carrying party so fatigued that (fig.) only the *chin-strap* kept the body upright', B. & P.: military coll.: 1914.

chin-wag. Officious impertinence : ca. 1860–1900. H., 3rd ed.—2. Whence, talk, chatter : from ca. 1875. *Punch*, in 1879 : ' I'd just like to have a bit of chin-wag with you on the quiet.'

chin-wag, v.i. To talk : C. 20. Ex *chin-wag*, n., 2.

china ; chiner. (In C. 20, often *old china*.) A pal, a mate : abbr. *china plate*, rhyming s. (from ca. 1890) : C. 20, esp. in G.W.

China !, not for all the tea in. Certainly not ! ; on no account : Australian coll. : from the 1890's.

China-bird. (Gen. pl.) A naval man serving on the China Station : naval : C. 20. Bowen.

China orange. See **all Lombard Street.**

China Street. Bow Street (London) : c. : ca. 1810–50. Vaux. Ex proximity to Covent Garden and its oranges.

China Tenth, the. The 10th Hussars : military : 1810 ; slightly ob. In that year the Prince Regent was its colonel ; hence it was handled as carefully as valuable china. F. & Gibbons.

Chinaman. A left-hand bowler's leg-break : cricketers' : from ca. 1905. Ex the manner of Chinese script, right to left.

Chinaman's copy. An exact copy, including mistakes and emendations : typists' coll. (− 1935).

Chinaman's shout. ' Dutch treat ', q.v. : Australian : C. 20.

Chinas. Eastern Extension Australasian and China Telegraph shares : Stock Exchange, ca. 1885–1914.

chince. See **chinse.**

Chincha dung-boat. A sailing ship engaged in the guano trade from the Chincha islands : nautical coll. : C. 20. Bowen.

Chinee. A Chinese : coll. ; orig. and mainly U.S. ; anglicised ca. 1870. Cf. *chink*, 3.

chiner. See **china.**

Chinese compliment. A pretended deference to, and interest in, the opinion of another when actually one has fully made up one's mind : from ca. 1880 ; coll. soon S.E.

Chinese Rolls-Royce. A Ford car : Royal Army Service Corps's : G.W., and after ; ob. F. & Gibbons. Ex *Chinese* as a pejorative : cf. preceding entry.

chink. Money, esp. in coins. In pl., either coin (collective) or ready cash : only the latter sense (C. 16–20) has always been coll. After ca. 1830, *chinker* is very rarely used, *chink* taking its place. Shrewdly honest Tusser, ' To buie it the cheaper, have chinks in thy purse ' ; Jonson.—2. The female pudend : low coll., C. 18–20.—3. (Chink.) A Chinese : mainly Australian ; from ca. 1890. Cf. *Chinkie* and *John* (abbr. *John Chinaman*).—4. Prison : Devonshire s. : 1896, Eden Phillpotts in *Black and White*, June 27 (E.D.D.). Ex lit. S.E. sense of *chink*, a hole, on s. *clink*, prison.

chinkers. Money, esp. in coin. Coll. ; from ca. 1830. Sir Henry Taylor, 1834 ; Baumann in his *Slang Ditty* prefacing *Londonismen*, 1887. Derivatively developed from *chink(s)* and likewise echoic.—2. In C. 19–20 c., handcuffs joined by a chain.

Chinkie. A Chinese : Australian ; from ca. 1880 ; ob. A. J. Boyd, *Old Colonials*, 1882. Morris. By perversion of *Chinaman*. Cf. *Chink* (at *chink*, 3).

chinner. A grin : Winchester College : ca. 1885–1900. Wrench.

chinning, vbl.n. See **chin,** v.

chinny. Sugar : Regular Army's : late C. 19–20. F. & Gibbons. Ex Hindustani *chini*.

chinqua soldi. (Properly *cinqua s.*) Fivepence : theatrical and Parlyaree from ca. 1840. Ex It. via Lingua Franca.

chinse. A chance : a Winchester College deliberate corruption : C. 19–20. Wrench (*chince*).

chintz. A bed-bug : ca. 1880–1900. G. A. Sala, in *The Daily Telegraph*, Aug. 14, 1885. Ex the association of chintz with bedrooms.

chip. A child : late C. 17–early 19. B.E. ; Grose. Cf. *block, chip of the old*, q.v.—2. A sovereign : from ca. 1870. Miss Braddon in *Phantom Fortune*.—3. A slight fracture ; a piece chipped off : coll. ; from ca. 1870.—4. In C. 20 racing c., a shilling—the coin or its value.—5. With *not to care, a chip* = at all ; C. 16–20, ob. ; coll. > S.E. by 1600.—6. See **chips.**—7. A rupee : Regular Army's : late C. 19–20. Cf. sense 4, prob. a derivative.

chip, v. To ' cheek ', interrupt with (gen. deliberate) impertinence : Australia and New Zealand ; from ca. 1890. E.g. in C. J. Dennis. Perhaps ex the ' flying-off ' of wood-chips ; cf. *chip at*, q.v.—2. Hence, to chaff, in any way whatsoever : C. 20. (R. Keverne, *The Havering Plot*, 1928, ' Gurney chipped him in a friendly way.')

chip, brother. Orig. a ' brother ' carpenter, then anyone of the same trade or profession. Cf. *chips*, q.v. Often = *brother smut*. Coll. ; from ca. 1810. *Lex. Bal.*

chip at. To quarrel with ; to criticise adversely : coll. : from ca. 1800. Cf. *chip*, v., and the U.S. phrase, *with a chip on one's shoulder*. Cf. :

chip at, have a. To make fun of, to chaff : coll. (− 1923). Manchon.

chip in, v.i. To join in an undertaking ; contribute a share ; interpose smartly in a conversation, discussion, or speech : orig. (ca. 1870) U.S. ; anglicised ca. 1890. Perhaps ex *chips*, 5.—2. Hence, to interfere : C. 20. F. & Gibbons.

chip in broth, pottage, porridge. Resp. C. 17–early 19, late C. 17–18, late C. 18–20 (ob.) ; all coll. for a thing or matter of no importance. *The Church Times*, June 25, 1880, ' The Burials Bill . . . is thought . . . to resemble the proverbial chip in porridge, which does neither good nor harm ' (O.E.D.).

chip of the same or **old block.** See **block.**

chipper. Well, fit ; lively. Coll. ; orig. (1837) U.S., anglicised ca. 1880. Cf. Northern dial. *kipper*.

chipperow. See **chub-a-row !**

chipping. Vbl.n. (Ex *to chip*, q.v.) Impudence ; the giving of ' cheek ' : Australian : from ca. 1890.—2. The action of giving a tip : C. 20. Manchon. Prob. ex *chips*, 3.

Chippy. The inevitable nickname of a man surnamed Carpenter : mostly military : late C. 19–20. F. & Gibbons. Ex *chips*, 1.

chippy, adj. Unwell, esp. after liquor : cf. Fr. *gueule de bois* : from ca. 1870. Ex *cheap, feel*, q.v.—2. Apt to be impudent : coll. (− 1888). O.E.D. Cf. *chip in*, q.v.

chippy chap. A bluejacket of carpenter's rating : naval : late C. 19–20. F. & Gibbons. Cf. *Chippy*. Ex :

chips. A carpenter : esp. in Army and Navy ; from ca. 1770 ; in C. 20, coll. Grose, 1st ed. ; Clark Russell. Cf. the C. 17–19 proverb, *a carpenter is known by his chips* (Apperson).—2. Hence, in the Army of late C. 19–20, a Pioneer sergeant. F. & Gibbons.—3. Money : from ca. 1850. H., 1st ed.

Cf. sense 5.—4. (At Wellington College) a kind of grill, from its hardness : C. 19–20, ob.—5. Counters used in games of chance : orig. (— 1880) s., soon coll. (? ex U.S.).

chirography. Incorrect when = *chorography* : C. 17–20. O.E.D.

chiromancer. See **conjuror.**

chirp. To sing : coll. ; C. 19–20.—2. In c., to talk ; hence (— 1864), to inform to the police. H., 3rd ed.

chirper. A singer : C. 19–20, coll.—2. A glass of a tankard : from ca. 1845. Meredith in *Juggling Jerry*, 1862, ' Hand up the chirper ! ripe ale winks in it.'—3. The mouth : C. 19–20.—4. One who, gen. as member of a gang, haunts music-hall doors, tries to blackmail singers, and, if unsuccessful, enters the auditorium and hisses, hoots, or groans : music-halls', ca. 1887–1914.

chirpiness. Liveliness ; cheerfulness ; pleasing pertness : coll., from ca. 1865.

chirping-merry. ' Very pleasant over a Glass of good Liquor ', B.E. ; convivial : late C. 17–early 19 ; coll. Either the orig. of *cherry-merry*, q.v., or its explanation. (The Lancashire dial. form is *cheeping-merry*.) Grose, 1st ed., adds : ' Chirping glass ; a cheerful glass, that makes the company chirp like birds in spring.'

chirpy. Cheerful ; lively : coll., from ca. 1835. Justin M'Carthy ; Besant.

chirrup. To cheer or hiss at a music-hall according as a singer has paid or not : coll. : from ca. 1888 ; ob. Cf. *chirper*, 4, and *chirruper*.—2. Vbl.n., *chirruping* (*The Pall Mall Gazette*, March 9, 1888) suggests Fr. *chantage*.

chirruper. An additional glass of liquor : public-house coll. : ca. 1820–80. ' Jon Bee ', 1823.—2. A blackmailing hisser, occ. applauder, at a music-hall : coll. 1888. James Payn in an article, March 17, and *The Pall Mall Gazette*, March 6, 1888. See **chirrup,** v.

chirrupy. Cheery ; lively ; ' chirpy '. Coll. : from ca. 1870. Burnand, 1874 (O.E.D.) ; but in U.S. at least as early as 1861 (O.E.D. Sup.).

*chise ; occ. **chis.** A variant of *chiv(e)*, n. and v. : c. of ca. 1820–40. Bee. Cf. *chiser*.

chisel. To cheat : from ca. 1800. Prob. orig. dial., it > gen. only ca. 1840. Mayhew, who spells *chissel* ; Sala, who prefers *chizzle* ; also *chizzel* ; even *chuzzle*. Hence the old conundrum, ' Why is a carpenter like a swindler ?—Because he chisels a deal.' *Chiseller* and *chiselling* are natural but infrequent derivatives.

*chiser, chiver. Variants (ca. 1820–40) of *chiv(e)*, a knife : c. ' John Bee ', 1823. Cf. *chise*.

Chiswick. See ' Westminster School slang '.

chit. A letter or a note : used by Purchas in 1608, while its orig., *chitty* (still in use), is not recorded before 1673 : Anglo-Indian coll. ; since G.W., virtually S.E., esp. as = note, written authorisation, pass, an invoice.—2. Hence, an order or a signature for drinks in clubs, aboard ship, etc. : Society, ex India ; from ca. 1875 ; coll.—(3. As a very young or an undersized girl, always S.E., but as a pejorative for any girl or young woman it has a coll. flavour.)

chit-chat. Light and familiar conversation ; current gossip of little importance. C. 18–20 ; coll., by 1760 S.E. By alteration-reduplication.

chitterlings. Shirt frills : C. 16–19 : s. > coll., then—the frills going out of fashion—S.E. Lit., a pig's (smaller) entrails. Cf. *frill*.—2. Hence, the

human bowels : mid-C. 18–19. Grose, 1st ed., ' There is a rumpus among my chitterlins, i.e. I have the cholick.'

chitty. An assistant cutter or trimmer : tailors' : from ca. 1870 ; ob.

chitty-face. One who, esp. a child, is pinched of face, C. 17. In C. 18–19, baby-face. A pejorative. Extant in dial., mainly an adj. in *-d*. S.O.D. ranks it as S.E., but the authors' and the recorders' names connote coll. : Munday, ' Melancholy ' Burton, B.E., *A New Canting Dict.* (ca. 1725), Grose (1st ed.), H.

*chiv, chive. See **chive-fencer.**—2. The face : low Australian (— 1916). C. J. Dennis. Ex *chivvy* as at *Chevy Chase*.

*chiv, v. See **chive-fencer.**—2. Whence, to smash a glass in one's face : C. 20 c. Vbl.n., *chivving*. Charles E. Leach, *On Top of the Underworld*, 1933.

chivalry. Sexual intercourse : late C. 18–19 : low : ex Lingua Franca. Cf. *cavaulting, chauvering, horsing*, and :

chival(e)y. Human coition : C. 19 low. See preceding entry.

*chive-fencer. One who ' fences ' or protects murderers from arrest : c. (— 1909) Ex :—2. A street hawker of cutlery : costers' : from ca. 1850. See **fence(r)** ; *chive* (or *chiv*)—of Romany origin—is C. 17–20 c. for a knife, a file, a saw ; Romany and c. for to stab, to cut or saw (through), to ' knife ' : mid-C. 18–20 (Grose, 1st ed.).

*chiver. An occ. variant (— 1887) of *chive*, esp. as v. (see **chive-fencer**). Baumann.

chivey. A knife : nautical ex Romany : from ca. 1890. Cf. preceding entry.—2. (Also *chivy, chivvy*.) A shout, greeting, cheer, esp. if rough or chaffing ; a scolding. Coll. ; a corruption of *chevy* with sense deflected. From ca. 1810 (*Lex. Bal.*) and pronounced *chivvy*.—3. In c., the face, with further variant *chevy* : from ca. 1860 ; ob. Cf. sense 4 of :

chiv(e)y, chivvy, v. To run, go quickly, as in Moncrieff's *Tom and Jerry*, 1823, ' Now, Jerry, chivey ! . . . Mizzle ! . . . Tip your rags a gallop ! . . . Bolt ! ' Perhaps ex S.E. *Chevy Chase*.—2. To chase round (— 1830), as in H. Kingsley's *Austin Elliot*, ' The dog . . used to chivy the cats.'—3. Hence, to make fun of, ' guy ', worry : from ca. 1850. All coll.—4. In c., to scold : C. 19–20.

*chiving lay. The robbing of coaches by cutting the rear braces or slashing through the back of the carriage : mid-C. 18–early 19 c. Grose, 2nd ed.

chivvy. See **Chevy Chase.**—2. See senses 2 and 3 of **chiv(e)y, chivvy.**—3. As a term of address, ' old chap ' : lower classes' (— 1923. Manchon. Perhaps ex *chivvy*, a face : cf. *old top*.—4. The chin : military in Boer War. J. Milne, *The Epistles of Atkins*, 1902.

*chivy. Adj., relating to the use of the knife as a weapon : C. 19–20 (ob.) c. E.g. *chivy duel*, a duel with knives.

chizzel or **chizzle.** See **chisel.**—**Chloe.** See **drunk as Chloe.—choak ;** **choakee ;** **choaker.** See **choke ; choker ; chokey.**

choc. (Gen. in pl.) Abbr. *chocolate* : C. 20 ; since 1934, almost coll.

chock. To hit a person under the chin : Cockney coll. ; from ca. 1860. A semi-dial. variant of *chuck* (*under the chin*).

chocker, gen. **old chocker**. A man. Not, like *codger*, a pejorative. Cockney coll. ; from ca. 1860. Ex preceding.

chocks, pull the. See **pull the chocks.**

chocolate without sugar, give (a person). To reprove: military (— 1785) ; † by 1890. Grose, 1st ed.

choice !, you pays (yer or) your money and you takes (yer or) your. A C. 20 c.p. = you take whatever you choose. Ex the cry of showmen.

choice riot. A horrid noise : streets' : ca. 1890–1915. Ware.

choice spirit. The S.E. sense began with Shakespeare, but in C. 18 s., the term meant ' a thoughtless, laughing, singing, drunken fellow', Grose, 1st ed.

choke. Prison bread : low : from ca. 1880 ; ob.

choke, enough to make a black man. (Of medicine, food) extremely unpalatable : Cockney coll. (— 1887) ; ob. Baumann.

choke away, the churchyard's near ! (Cf. *churchyard cough*.) A late C. 17–early 19 c.p. jocular admonition to anyone coughing. Ray, 1678 ; Grose, 3rd ed.

choke, chicken : more are hatching. A similar C. 18–early 19, then dial., Job's comforting. Swift ; Grose, 3rd ed. (Apperson.)

choke-dog. Cheese : low coll. ; orig. and mainly dial. From ca. 1820 ; ob.

choke off. To get rid of a person ; put a stop to a course of action : coll. (— 1818) >, by 1890, S.E. (O.E.D.)

' choke-pear. A difficulty ; a severe reproof ; a ' settler ' (†) ; a gag (†) : from C. 16. Ex the instrument of torture (so named from an unpalatable kind of pear) so called. Coll. > S.E. by 1700 ; first two senses, archaic.

choke you ?, didn't that ; it's a wonder that didn't choke you ! C.p. comments on a bare-faced or notable lie : C. 19–20. Cf. the C. 17–18 semi-proverbial ' If a lie could have choked him, that would have done it ' (Ray).

choke your luff ! Be quiet : nautical : mid-C. 19–20 ; slightly ob. Bowen.

chokee. See **chokey.**

choker. A cravat ; orig. a large neckerchief worn round the neck. Often *white choker*, q.v. First record, 1848, Thackeray (*Book of Snobs*): ' The usual attire of a gentleman, viz., pumps, a gold waistcoat, a crush hat, a sham frill, and a white choker'.—2. A high all-round collar : from ca. 1868.—3. A garotter : from ca. 1800 ; coll. Cf. *windstopper*.—4. In c., a cell ; a prison : from ca. 1860 ; rare. See **chokey**.—Also, 5, a halter, the hangman's rope : C. 18–19.—6. A notable lie ; a very embarrassing question : low : late C. 19–20 ; slightly ob. Ware ; Manchon. Ex its supposed effect on the perpetrator.—7. A cigarette : military : 1915. F. & Gibbons. Prob. suggested by *gasper*.

chokered. Wearing a *choker*, q.v. *The London Review*, April 7, 1866 ; O.E.D. records it at 1865.

chokey, choky : rarely **cho(a)kee** or **chauki.** A lock-up ; a prison. In Anglo-Indian form C. 17, and adopted in England ca. 1850. Michael Scott has it in his *Cruise of the Midge*, 1836 ; Besant & Rice. Ex Hindustani *chauki*, lit. a four-sided place or building : Yule & Burnell.—2. Hence, imprisonment : from ca. 1880 ; rare.—3. G.W. +, a detention-cell, occ. a guard-room, ex the (— 1889) c. sense, a dark cell. Hindi *chauki*, a shed. Cf.

Queen's Chokey.—4. Derivatively, a prison diet of bread and water (1884).

choking (or **cold**) **pie** (or **pye**). ' A punishment inflicted on any person sleeping in company : it consists in wrapping up cotton in a case or tube of paper, setting it on fire, and directing the smoak up the nostrils of the sleeper,' Grose, 3rd ed.: coll. (— 1650) ; ob. by 1860 ; † by 1890. Howell's edition (1650) of Cotgrave's Dict.

choky. Having a gen. tendency or a momentary feeling of choking : from ca. 1855 ; T. Hughes, ' To feel rather choky ', 1857. Cf. the early and S.E. senses, which are, in C. 20, almost coll. : apt to choke the eater ; suffocating. O.E.D.

chol(l)ic(k), -e ; **cholicky.** Incorrect for *colic, colicky* : C. 17–20. O.E.D.

chonkey(s). A mincemeat, baked in a crust and sold in the streets : low coll. : mid-C. 19–20 ; ob. H., 1st ed. Etymology obscure : perhaps ex some noted pieman (Ware).

choom ; properly, but less gen., **chum.** A term of address much used by the Australian and New Zealand soldiers to an unknown English (not Welsh, Scottish or Irish) soldier : 1915–18. Ex *chum*, n., 1.

choops ! Be quiet, silent ! Anglo-Indian and military : C. 19–20. See **chubaree** for etymology and the gen. C. 20 form.

choose. To wish to have ; want : low coll. : from ca. 1760. In C. 20, almost S.E.

choosey. Fastidious ; given to picking and choosing : low coll. : C. 20. James Curtis, *The Gilt Kid*, 1936.

chootah. Small ; unimportant : Anglo-Indian : C. 19–20. Gen. *chota* or *choter*.

chop. In mid-C. 18–early 19 boxing s., a blow with the fist. Grose, 3rd ed.

chop, adj. In ' pidgin ', C. 19–20 : quick.

chop as in *first-*, *second-chop*, first- or second-rate or -class, rank or quality. Anglo-Indian and -Chinese coll., ex Hindi *chhap*, a brand. The attributive use is the more gen. and dates from late C. 18 : thus Thackeray, ' A sort of second-chop dandies '. Yule & Burnell, whence *no chop* (see **chop, no**).

chop, v. (The barter-exchange senses are S.E.)—2. To eat a chop : ca. 1840–1900. Mrs. Gore, 1841, ' I would rather have chopped at the " Blue Posts ".'—3. To eat (a human being), gen. in passive : West Africa, from ca. 1860 : ob. But, simply as ' to eat ', it is current, with corresponding n., ' food '. Either ex † *chop*, to devour, or suggested by *chopsticks*. W.—4. In c., to speak, as in *chop the whiners*, to say prayers : C. 18–19. Cf. *chop up*, q.v.—5. Esp., however, to do, or speak quickly : c. : C. 17–18.

chop, no. Inferior, insignificant, objectionable : coll. : from mid-1880's ; ob. (O.E.D. Sup.)

[**chop and change**, v. and n., is, despite F. & H., S.E. in all senses. See O.E.D.]

Chop-Back. (Gen. pl.) A Hastings fisherman : nautical : C. 18–20 ; ob. Bowen, ' From an old-time incident in a fight with Dutch traders '. Also *Hatchet-Back*, for the same grim hand-lopped reason : E.D.D. (Sussex nicknames.)

chop by chance. ' A rare Contingence, an extraordinary or uncommon Event ', B.E. : coll. : late C. 17–18 ; never very gen.

chop-chop ! Quickly ; immediately : pidgin ; from ca. 1860. James Payn. Prob. ex Cantonese dial.—2. Also as v., to make haste.

chop-church. In C. 16–early 17, S.E.; in late C. 17–18, coll.; in C. 19, archaic S.E.: an unscrupulous dealer or trafficker in benefices.

chop-logs. A C. 16–17 coll. perversion of *choplogic*.

*chop up. To hurry through, esp. in c. *chop up the whiners*, to gallop through prayers: late C. 17–19. B.E.

chopped hay. Knowledge imperfectly assimilated: coll. (– 1923). Manchon. Ex the stables.

chopper. 'A blow, struck on the face with the back of the hand', Moore in *Tom Crib's Memorial*, 1819. Pugilistic; ob. Occ. in coll. form, *chopping blow*.—2. A sausage-maker: tradesmen's: from ca. 1860.

chopper or **button on, have a.** To feel depressed: printers', from ca. 1850; ob. See also **button on, have a.**

chopping. (Of girls) vain and ardent; sexually on-coming: late C. 19–20; ob. Coll. Ex the S.E. sense. Cf. the idea in Fr. *avoir la cuisse gaie*.

chopping-block. In boxing, an unskilled man that yet can take tremendous punishment. From ca. 1830: coll.

chops. The mouth: C. 18 coll. Cf. S.E. senses.

chops, down in the. Depressed; melancholy; sad. Coll.: from ca. 1820; rare in C. 20, when the form (as occ. from ca. 1850) is *down in the mouth*, with sense of dejected.

chops, lick one's. To gloat: coll. in C. 17–18; S.E. thereafter, but hardly literary.

chops of the Channel, the. The Western entrance to the English Channel: nautical coll.: C. 19–20. Bowen.

chores, do. To 'char' (q.v.), do the cleaning work of a house: from ca. 1745: coll. when not dial. More gen. in U.S.

chortle. To chuckle gurglingly or explosively. Coined by 'Lewis Carroll' ex *chuckle + snort* (*Through the Looking Glass*, 1872) and soon popular, e.g. in Besant & Rice, 1876. For a while considered coll., but by 1895 definitely S.E. See my *Slang* at Portmanteau Words.—2. Hence, to sing: 1889, *The Referee*, Dec. 29, 'Chortle a chansonette or two'.—3. Hence, *chortle about* or *over*, to praise excessively: 1897, *The Daily Telegraph*, March 31 (Ware).

*chosen pals or **pells.** Highwaymen robbing in pairs, esp. in London: c.: mid-C. 18–early 19. Grose, 2nd ed. See **pal, n.**

Chosen Twelve, the. See **Apostles.**—**choter wallah.** See **barrow wallah.** Cf. **chootah,** q.v.

chounter. 'To talk pertly, and (sometimes) angrily', B.E.; late C. 17–18. ? ex *chant* influenced by *counter*; or is it not rather cognate with Devon dial. ppl. adj. *chounting* (the v. is unrecorded) = 'taunting, jeering, grumbling', E.D.D., which quotes it at 1746 ?

chouse. A swindle, hoax, humbug, imposition: from ca. 1700; ex *chouse* (= *chiaus*), a S.E. term of perhaps Turkish orig., the etymology remaining a partial mystery. From ca. 1850 at Eton and, as we see in R. G. K. Wrench, at Winchester, a shame, as in 'a beastly chouse', or an imposition, whence (– 1864) *chouser*, a 'sharp' lad. See O.E.D., Yule & Burnell, F. & H., and W.

chouse, v. To cheat; deceive; impose on: coll., from the 1650's; ob. Pepys, May 15, 1663, 'The Portugalls have choused us, it seems, in the Island of Bombay'; the anon. *Hints for Oxford,*

1823; Scottish Public-School s. at least as late as 1884. Cf. *diddle.* Vbl.n., *chousing.*

chouser. See **chouse, n.**

chout. An entertainment: East-End Cockney, ca. 1855–1910. H., 2nd ed. Etymology slightly problematic: ? a perversion of *shout*; or rather an adaptation of E. Anglican and Norfolk *chout*, a frolic or a merry-making (see E.D.D.).

chovey. A shop: costers': from ca. 1835; ob Brandon, 1839; H., 1st ed. Whence *man-chovey*, a shopman, and *Ann-chovey*, a shop-woman. ? etymology, unless a corruption of *casa* (perhaps on *chokey*).

chow. Food: from ca. 1870, mainly nautical ex 'pidgin'. Abbr. *chow-chow*, q.v.—2. Talk; 'cheek': theatrical, from ca. 1870; ob.—3. **(Chow.)** In Australia, a Chinese (– 1882). Morris. Prob. ex sense 1.

chow, v. To talk much; grumble: theatrical; from ca. 1870, C. n., 2, and:

chow ! An Anglo-Italian coll. (esp. in London) salutation: mid-C. 19–20. Ex It. *ciao* (coll. for *schiavo*), at your service.

chow, have plenty of. To be very talkative: theatrical; from ca. 1875.

chow-chow. Food of any kind (now *chow*); from ca. 1860; cf. S.E. senses. H., 3rd ed.—2. Also, chit-chat: from ca. 1870. H., 5th ed. Ex 'pidgin', where, lit., a mixture. See esp. Lady Falkland's *Chow-Chow*, 1857; ed. by Prof. H. G. Rawlinson, 1930.

chow-chow. To gossip, to chat: late C. 19–20. Manchon. Ex the n., sense 2.

chow-chow, adj. In Anglo-Indian coll., from ca. 1870:—Assorted, general, as in *chow-chow cargo* or *shop*; very good, very bad (as context shows), esp. when preceded by *No. 1.*

chow-chow chop. In Anglo-Chinese from ca. 1890: coll. rather than s. 'The last lighter containing the sundry small packages to fill up a ship', S.O.D.

chow-chow water. Eddies in the sea: Eastern nautical: late C. 19–20. Bowen, 'From the term used by Chinese pilots': cf. *chow-chow*, adj., q.v.

chow-up. A hot argument; a quarrel, a squabble: military: C. 20. F. & Gibbons. Ex *chow*, n., 2.

chowdar. A fool: from ca. 1860. Anglo-Chinese, says H., 5th ed.; but is it not an abbr. of the dial. *chowder-headed*, i.e. *jolter-headed* ?

Chrisake. Christ's sake: sol.: C. 19–20.

Christ-killer. A Jew: proletarian and military ca. 1850–1915. Mayhew; Ware.

christen. To call by the name of, give a name to: coll., from ca. 1640; in C. 20, almost S.E.—2. To change the markings on a watch: from ca. 1780 (G. Parker, 1781); orig. c.; not low s. until ca. 1850, as in H., 1st ed. (1859), and in Doran's *Saint and Sinner*, 1868. (Equivalent C. 19–20 c. is *church*.) Vbl.n., *christening*, late C. 18–20.—3. To add water to wines or spirits; any light liquor with a heavier: from ca. 1820. Scott, 1824, 'We'll christen him with the brewer (here he added a little small beer to his beverage).' Cf. *drown the miller.*—4. To souse from a chamber-pot: from ca. 1870. A school and college ceremony that is on the wane; but youth finds a chamber-pot symbolically ludicrous and emblematically important.—5. To celebrate (a meeting, a purchase, a removal, etc.): late C. 19–20. F. & H.

christened by a baker. (' He carries the bran in his face,' i.e. he is) freckled. Grose. Coll. : mid-C. 18–early 19.

christened with pump-water, he was. He has a red face. Coll. ; mid-C. 17–early 18. Ray.

christening, be out in one's. To be in error : proletarian coll. (— 1887). Baumann.

christening-wine. The ' champagne ' used in launching ceremonies : nautical : mid-C. 19–20 ; ob. Bowen.

Christer. An exclamation mark : authors' and typists' : C. 20. Ex exclamatory *Christ !*

Christian. A ' decent fellow ' ; a presentable person. Coll. In Shakespeare's *Two Gentlemen of Verona*, 1591, and until ca. 1840, it meant merely a human being, not an animal, the mod. sense beginning, as so many mod. senses have begun, with Dickens (see *Slang*).—2. Ca. 1805–40, the term = a tradesman willing to give credit. *Lex. Bal.*—3. The adj. (of a person, 1577 : humane ; of a thing or action, 1682 : civilised, respectable) follows the same course. (O.E.D.)

Christian compliments. ' A cough, kibed heels, and a snotty nose ', Grose, 3rd ed. : C. 18–19. Grose meant to write *Christmas*—see his reference at *compliments* and his MS. addition to the B.M. copy of the 1st ed. ; the 2nd ed. has ' *Christmass compliments.* A cough ', etc.

Christian pony. The chairman, or president, of a meeting : mid-C. 18–mid-19. Anglo-Irish. Grose, 2nd ed.

Christianable. As befits, fit for, a Christian : coll. : 1920. O.E.D. (Sup.).

Christians. Members of Christ's College, Cambridge : from ca. 1870.

Christians Arise. A Turkish big gun (or its shell) at the Dardanelles : military : 1915. F. & Gibbons. Ex :—2. (C. a.) The reveille bugle-call : military : from ca. 1910. Ibid.

Christmas, christmassing. Holly and mistletoe serving as Christmas decorations : from ca. 1820, 1840. Dickens, the former ; Mayhew, the latter. S.O.D. says it is nursery slang, F. & H.—coll. (The latter, I think.)—2. Something special to drink at Christmas time : Australian coll. : late C. 19–20.

Christmas, v. To ' provide with Christmas cheer ' : very rare : late C. 16–17. Adorn with decorations for Christmas : from ca. 1825. Celebrate Christmas : from ca. 1806. All three senses, coll. See ' The Philology of Christmas ', in *Words !* ; also O.E.D.

Christmas ! A mild, euphemistic expletive : late C. 19–20. Ware ; A. P. Herbert, *Holy Deadlock*, 1934. It is an evasion of *Christ !*

Christmas beef. See **beef, dressed like Christmas.**—**Christmas compliments.** See **Christian compliments.**

Christmas box. A Christmas present : low coll. (and dial.) : from ca. 1860.

Christmas Eve. To believe : rhyming s. : C. 20. P. P., *Rhyming Slang*, 1932. Less gen. than *Adam and Eve*.

Christmas-tree order, in. In heavy marching order : military : 1915 : ob. F. & Gibbons. Ex the soldier's appearance when he had *full pack up*, itself military coll. of C. 20. Sailors preferred *Christmas-tree*.

Christmassing. See **Christmas, n.**

Christmas(s)y. Pertaining to, looking like, Christmas : coll. : from ca. 1880. Baumann.

Christys. A coll. (in C. 20, S.E.) abbr. of

Christy('s) minstrels (— 1873) : Ruskin, in 1875, was app. the first to use the term in print. Ex one George Christy of New York.

chromo. Abbr. *chromolithograph, -ic* : coll. ; ' in use shortly after 1850 ', O.E.D.

chronic. Unpleasant ; objectionable ; unfair ; ' rotten '. (Rarely of persons : in same senses ; hence, formidable, excellent : C. 20. Manchon.) Late C. 19–20, ex the S.E. sense, acute (pain), inveterate (*c. complaint*). Ware, recording it for 1896, defines *chronic rot* as ' despairingly bad '. Whence :

chronic, something. Badly, severely, most objectionably : lower classes' : C. 20.

chronometer. A watch, however small : coll., either jocular or pretentious : C. 20.

chrony. A C. 17 variant of *crony*, 1.

chrysant. A chrysanthemum : coll. : from ca. 1890. (R. H. Mottram, *Bumphrey's*, 1934.) Also *chrysanth* (C. 20), as in *The Passing Show*, Jan. 20, 1934. Cf. *'mum*.

chub. An inexperienced person, esp. a callow youth : C. 17–18. B.E.—2. A blockhead : ca. 1600–1850 ; coll. Ex the short, thick river fish, whence also *chubby*, plump, S.E. (despite H.).

chub ! An abbr. (military : C. 20 : B. & P.) of :

chub-a-row or **chubarrow !** ; **chuprow !** ; occ. **chipperow !** ' Shut up ! ' : military, esp. the Regular Army's (resp. s., coll., s.) : mid-C. 19–20. F. & Gibbons. Ex Hindustani *chuprao*.

***chubbingly.** A late C. 17–early 18 c. variant of S.E. *chubby*. B.E., s.v. *bulchin*.

chubby or **dumpy.** A short, squat umbrella : coll. : 1925. Collinson.—2. **Chubby** is the nickname, since ca. 1920 among cricketers, of Maurice Tate.

chuck. A coll. endearment : C. 16–20, but ob. by 1800. ? ex *chick*.—2. Food of any kind, but esp. bread or meat (— 1850) : orig. c., but popularised in G.W. ? origin : cf. next 3 senses, esp. sense 5, and senses 7–9. Perhaps such food as one can chuck about without spoiling it.—3. Scraps of meat (cf. *block ornaments*) : from ca. 1860.—4. A particular sort of beefsteak : from ca. 1855 ; ob.—5. A measure for sprats : Billingsgate, from ca. 1840. Otherwise a *toss* ; cf. next.—6. A toss, jerk, or throw : coll. ; from ca. 1840.—7. Sea biscuit : nautical, from ca. 1840. (As for the next two senses) cf. 2–4.—8. (Military) mealy bread : from ca. 1855.—9. A schoolboy's treat : Westminster School : from ca. 1855. H., 2nd ed.—10. Abbr. *chuck-farthing*, a national sport : from ca. 1710 : coll.—11. See **chuck, get the.**

chuck, v. In c., to eat (— 1876). Hindley's *Cheap Jack*. App. later than and ex the n., 2nd sense.—2. As to toss, to throw with little arm-action, it has always been S.E., but as throw in any other sense, it is low coll. of C. 19–20.—3. (Pigeon fanciers') to despatch a pigeon : coll., then j. ; from ca. 1870.—4. To spend extravagantly (— 1876) : coll., as is the gen. late C. 19–20 form, *chuck-away*.—5. To abandon, dismiss, discharge (from gaol) ; (v.i.) give up (in C. 20, occ. = go back on an invitation that one has accepted) : often varied as *chuck up* : from ca. 1860. Whence *chuck it up !*, in C. 20 gen. *chuck it !* = drop it ! stop (talking, etc.) !—6. Also, in low coll., *chuck* often = do, perform (e.g. *chuck a jolly*, to begin bantering, chaffing, to support heartily, noisily) : the sense and the connotation of all such phrases will be obvious from the definition of the ' complementary ' nouns.—7. V.i., to be sexually desirous : late C. 18–mid-19. Grose, 3rd ed. Perhaps suggested by *chuck*, n., 1.

chuck, do a. See **do a chuck.**

chuck, get or **give the.** To be dismissed, to dismiss : from ca. 1880 ; low coll.—2. Hence, of a proposal for marriage or a courtship : from ca. 1920. E.g. in Dorothy Sayers, *Clouds of Witness*, 1926, ' I got the chuck from Barbara and didn't feel much like bothering about other people's heart-to-hearts.'

chuck, hard. A long or a difficult flight : pigeon fanciers' : from ca. 1875 ; in C. 20 j.—2. Ship's biscuit : nautical : late C. 19–20. C.O.D., 1934 Sup. See **chuck,** n., 7, and cf. *hard tack*.

*****chuck a chest.** To ' tell the tale ' : C. 20 vagrants' c. Prob. ex :—2. ' To throw forward the chest, as though prepared to meet the world ' : streets' : late C. 19–20. Ware.—3. Whence, ' to attempt to exercise undue authority ', ' throw one's weight about ' : military : C. 20. F. & Gibbons. Cf. *chuck out one's chest*, q.v. at *chest* . . .

chuck a curly. To malinger : military, from ca. 1870 ; ob. *Curly* = a writhing.

chuck a dummy. A faint on parade : military, from ca. 1890. Ex *chuck the dummy*, q.v.—2. Hence, ' to report sick without reasonable cause ' : military : C. 20. F. & Gibbons.—3. To lie down in the boxing ring : military (— 1935).

chuck a jolly. (Costermongers') from ca. 1850 : see **chuck,** v., 6.

chuck a shoulder. To give (a person) the cold shoulder : costers' (— 1909). Ware.

*****chuck a shoulder.** To attract someone's attention while a confederate robs him : c. : from ca. 1850. H., 2nd ed. See **stall.**

chuck [oneself] **about** or **into.** To move or act quickly, vigorously (— 1860) : coll. The *into* phrase also (— 1880) = fall into.

chuck-barge. ' Cask in which the biscuit of a mess is kept. Also equivalent to [fig.] bread-basket,' Ware : naval : late C. 19–20. Cf. *chuck*, n., 2.

*****chuck-bread.** Waste bread : late C. 19–20 vagrants' c. Ware.

chuck-farthing. A parish clerk : late C. 17– early 18. B.E. Ex a character in the *Satyr against Hypocrites*.

chuck her up ! In cricket, the fielding side's expression of delight : coll. : from ca. 1875.

chuck-hole. A coll. variant for the game of chuck-farthing : from ca. 1830 ; ob.

chuck in, v.i. To challenge : boxing ; from ca. 1820. Ex the old throwing a hat into the ring. Also, to compete. † by 1914.

chuck-in, have a. To try one's luck : ca. 1860– 1914 ; sporting.

chuck it ! See **chuck,** v., 5.

chuck off, to employ sarcasm ; **chuck off at,** to banter or chaff : Australian (— 1916). C. J. Dennis.

chuck one's hand in. To refuse to do, or stop doing, something : orig., military : C. 20. F. & Gibbons. Ex cards.

chuck one's weight about. To ' show off ' ; orig. military (— 1909). Ware.

chuck out. To eject forcibly (— 1880) ; to discard (thing or plan), from ca. 1910. Coll.—2. Hence, jocularly, to cause to leave : from ca. 1915.

chuck out hints. To hint (v.i.) : low coll. (— 1887). Baumann.

chuck out ink. To write articles : journalists' (— 1909) ; ob. Ware.

chuck over. To abandon (e.g. a sweetheart) : low coll. (— 1887). Baumann.—2. Hence, n. : late C. 19–20.

chuck seven. To die : low : late C. 19–20. (John G. Brandon, *West End*, 1933.) A dice-cube has no ' 7 '.

*****chuck the dummy.** To feign illness ; esp. to simulate epilepsy : c. (— 1890). Whence *chuck a dummy*, q.v.

chuck-up. A salute : military : from not later than 1915. F. & Gibbons, ' From the act of throwing up the hand to the forehead in saluting '.

chuck-up, give (a thing) **the.** To abandon it, to send it ' to the devil ' : low coll. (— 1923). Ex *chuck up* as at *chuck up the sponge*, 2.

chuck up the bunch of fives. To die : boxers' (— 1909). Ware.

chuck up the sponge. See **sponge.**—2. Hence *chuck up* (often corrupted, says H., 5th ed., to *jack up*), to abandon : coll. : from ca. 1860.

chuckaboo. A street endearment : mid C. 19–20. Ware. Cf. :

chuckaby. A C. 17 endearment : coll. So is *chucking*. O.E.D. Cf. *chuck*, n.

chuckaroo. A boy employed about a regiment : coll. among soldiers in India (— 1886). A corruption of Hindustani *chhokra*, a boy or youngster. Yule & Burnell.

chuckaway. See **Bryant & May's chuckaway.**

chucked. Slightly drunk : from ca. 1880. †. Cf. *screwed*.—2. Disappointed ; unlucky ; ' sold '. From ca. 1870 ; ob., except among artists, who, from late C. 19, apply it to a picture refused by the Academy. Cf. that delightful ca. 1879 ballad, *Chucked Again*.—3. Abbr. *chucked out*, forcibly ejected : see **chuck out.**—4. In c., amorous ; ' fast ' : from ca. 1800. Ex *chuck*, v., 7.

*****chucked** or **chucked up, be.** To be acquitted or released : c. ; from ca. 1860.

chucked all of a heap. Fascinated ; infatuated : London proletarian (— 1909). Ware.

chucked-in. Into the bargain ; for good measure. Coll. ; from ca. 1875. *Punch*, Oct. 11, 1884, 'Arry at a Political Picnic, reproduced in Baumann's *Londonismen*.

*****chucked up.** See **chucked, be.**

chucker. In cricket, either a bowler apt to throw the ball or a defaulting player. Both are coll. and both date from ca. 1880, the latter † and, post-1918, replaced by *quitter*.

chucker-out. A man, often ex-pugilist, retained to eject persons from meetings, taverns, brothels, etc. : low coll. (— 1880). *The Saturday Review*, March 31, 1883.

chucking-out. Forcible ejection (see preceding entry) : from ca. 1880. Occ. (1881 +) an adj., esp. in *chucking-out time*, closing time at a ' pub '.

chuckler. Anglo-Indian coll. : a native shoe maker. From ca. 1750. Ex Tamil.

chucks. A naval boatswain : nautical : late C. 19–20. Bowen.

chucks ! Cave ! Schoolboys' ; from ca. 1850. H., 3rd ed. Perhaps cf. *shucks !*

chucky. A coll. endearment (cf. *chuck*, n., 1) : from the 1720's ; ob. except in dial.—2. A chicken or a fowl : late C. 18–20 ; coll.

chuff. Impudent : low coll. (— 1923) ex dial. *chuff*, happy (— 1860). Manchon ; O.E.D.

chuff it ! Be off ! Take it away ! Coll. : ca. 1850 ; ob. H., 1st ed. Perhaps ex *chuff* as a term of reproach.

chugar(r)ow ! A corruption of *chubarrow !* or a contraction of *chuck* (or even *shut*) *your row !* : low : C. 20.

chul(l) or **chullo !** Hurry ! Military and Anglo-Indian, from ca. 1800. In C. 20, gen. *chello* or, in G.W., *jillo* or *jildi*. Hindi *chullo*, go along. Sala, in *The Illustrated London News* of June 19, 1886, says ' In Calcutta *chul* is a word that you may hear fifty times a day ' ; and n.b. Yule & Burnell.

chul(l), v. To succeed ; be satisfactory : of things or plans, as in ' It won't chul,' i.e. answer, do. From ca. 1860. Etymology obscure ; but perhaps suggested by *chull !*

chum ; in C. 18, occ. *chumm*. First recorded in 1684—Creech's dedication, ' To my chum, Mr. Hody of Wadham College '—this term seems at first to have been university s., which it remained until ca. 1800 ; a contemporaneous sense was ' a Chamber-fellow, or constant companion ', B.E. Almost immediately the term came to mean, also, an intimate friend and, in C. 18, a mate in crime : cf. *college chum*, q.v. Either s. or coll. in C. 17–18, it has in C. 19–20 been coll. Perhaps by abbreviation and collision of *chamber-fellow* or *-mate* : cf. the Fr. *chambrée* (a roomful of people, oneself included) and Grose's *camerade*. Cf. *mate, pal, sorry,* and the U.S. *buddy*. See Terms of Address, in *Words !*—2. On the *Conway* Training Ship, from ca. 1880 or a few years earlier, *chum* denoted anyone junior, *new chum* a newly joined cadet (Masefield, *The Conway*, 1933).—3. In Australia, a *chum* is an English immigrant : from ca. 1890. It represents *new chum*, a newcomer—esp. from England : this term dates from (—) 1839, while *old chum*, an experienced settler, antedates 1846 (C. P. Hodgson, *Reminiscences of Australia*) ; the latter has never, after ca. 1880 (see Morris), been much used. This use of *new* and *old* comes ex that, 4, in prisons for newcomers and old hands : c. (— 1812) ; † by 1900. Vaux.—5. See **choom**.

chum, v. To live together : from ca. 1730 (Wesley) ; coll., as is the rare C. 19 v.t., put as a chum (Dickens in *The Pickwick Papers*).

chum, long-eared ; long-faced chum ; long-haired chum. A mule ; a horse ; a girl : military : the third is the original (the 1890's) ; the others are of C. 20. B. & P. ; F. & Gibbons.

chumm. See **chum, n.**

chummage. The practice of rooming together ; more gen., money made, in several very different ways, from such practice : coll. : 1837, Dickens. Hence, *chummage-ticket*.—2. Among prisoners in gaols, garnish, footing : low s. verging on c. Orig. a London term (— 1777). Howard's *State of Prisons in England and Wales* ; Grose (1st ed.).—3. See **jury, chummage, and conter.**

chummery. Friendship ; friendliness ; rooms shared with a friend : coll., from ca. 1870 ; never very gen. ; ob., except in India, where it = ' a house where European employees of a firm . . . live together ' (Lyell). Besant & Rice.

chumming or **chumming-up.** Same as *chummage*, esp. as to garnish, footing : C. 19.—2. In C. 20, the forming of a friendship : coll.

chummy. A chimney-sweep's boy : from ca. 1835. Ob. by 1865, † by 1900. Dickens ; Thackeray ; Mayhew, in vol. II of *London Labour*, ' . . . Once a common name for the climbing boy, being a corruption of chimney '.—2. A coll. diminutive of *chum* = friend, ' pal '. Perhaps coined by Gilbert, 1864, in the *Bab Ballads*.—3. A low-

crowned, felt hat : ca. 1858–1900. H., 2nd ed. A friendly, comfortable piece of head-gear.—4. In Australia a post-1895 variant of *new-chum* (q.v.), an English newcomer : cf. *chum*, n., 3, q.v.

chummy, adj. Friendly, intimate ; sociable : coll. : from ca. 1880. Besant.—2. (Of a motor-car) affording comfort and space for three or four persons : coll. : 1922. Hence as n. (likewise O.E.D. Sup.).

chummy ships. Ships whose crews are ' friends ' : nautical coll. : late C. 19–20. Bowen. See **chummy,** adj.

chump. (S.E. or coll. > S.E. in sense of a blockhead.)—2. The head ; occ. the face : from ca. 1860. Esp. in *off one's chump*, very eccentric ; mad to almost any degree. H., 3rd ed. ; ' Master . . . have gone off his chump, that's all,' Besant & Rice, 1877.—3. A variant of *chum* = friend ; ca. 1880–1920. *Punch*, Oct. 11, 1884.

***chump, get** or **provide one's own.** To earn one's own living : c. : ca. 1860–1914. See esp. that prison classic, *Five Years' Penal Servitude*, anon., 1877, not to be confused with James Greenwood's *Seven Years' Penal Servitude*, 1884.

chump, or **chunk, of wood.** No good : rhyming s. (— 1859). Also, a ' chump ' or fool, ca. 1870–1900.

Chumps Elizas. Champs Elysées : ' *London*, Five Pounder Tourists' 1854, on ', Ware.

chumpy. Eccentric ; idiotic ; insane. Ca. 1870–1914. Ex *off one's chump*.

chunk. A thick solid piece or lump cut off anything (esp. wood or bread) : coll. and dial. : mid-C. 17–20. Ray's *Country Words*, 1691. App. ex *chuck* (O.E.D.)—2. ' Among printers, a journeyman who refuses to work for legal wages ', Grose, 2nd ed. : late C. 18–early 19. Cf. *flint* and *dung* among tailors.—3. A School Board officer : ca. 1870–1910.

chunk of wood. No good : rhyming s., contemporaneous variant of *chump of wood*, q.v.

chunky. Thick set. From ca. 1870 ; coll. Ex U.S. (1776). Thornton.

[**chupatty,** representing an object for which no English word exists, is ineligible ; but :]

chuprassy, in civilian use (— 1865) a messenger, in military usage, an Indian orderly (from ca. 1880), is Anglo-Indian coll., direct ex Hindi *chaprasi*, the wearer of a *chapras* or badge.

chuprow. See **chub-a-row.**

***church.** Illicitly to disguise a watch by changing its ' innards ' : c. : from ca. 1835 ; gen. as *church a yack*. Brandon, 1839. Cf. *christen*, q.v.

church, go to. To get married : coll. ; from late C. 16. Shakespeare, 1599, ' Counte Claudio, when meane you to goe to Church ? '

church, talk. To talk ' shop ' : coll. ; from ca. 1850 ; ob.

church-by-hand. ' An emergency or makeshift performance of Divine Service on board ship on Sunday, when the regular service cannot be held ' : naval : from ca. 1914. F. & Gibbons.

church-folk. Members of the Church of England as opp. to ' chapel folk ', Dissenters. From ca. 1870 ; coll. (Other senses, S.E.)

church parade. The walk-and-talk after church on Sunday mornings : coll. : from ca. 1870. Cf. *prayer-book parade*, q.v.

church-piece. A threepenny bit : Society (— 1909) ; ob. Ware.

church-service. A church-service book, i.e. one containing the Common Prayer, the lessons, the psalms in metrical version, etc. : **low coll.** (— 1859). Sala. (O.E.D.).

church-work. Work that proceeds very slowly : coll. ; from ca. 1600. Ex church-building.

churchify. To render ' churchy ' (q.v.) : 1843, Miall (O.E.D.) : coll. >, by 1900, S.E.

churchiness. The being ' churchy ', q.v. : from ca. 1880 : coll. >, by 1900, S.E.

churchwarden. A long-stemmed clay pipe : from ca. 1855 ; coll. Hood, 1857, ' Hang a churchwarden by my side for a sabre.' Churchwardens affected this ob. instrument. Cf. *alderman, yard of clay.*

churchy. ' Redolent ' of the Church ; obtrusive in religious observance. Coll. : from ca. 1860.

churchyard clock, as many faces as a. (Of a man) unreliable : naval : ca. 1860–1910. F. & Gibbons.

churchyard cough. A severe cough : coll. : late C. 17–20. B.E. Mainly jocular.

churchyard luck. The death of a child in a large, poor family : proletarian coll. (— 1909). Ware.

churl upon a gentleman, put a. To drink malt liquor immediately after wine : late C. 16–early 19. Coll. after ca. 1700. Esp. Apperson.

*chury. A knife : c. of ca. 1810–60. Vaux. Cf. *chivey,* n. ; prob., however, a misprint.

chuzzle. See **chisel.**—**chy-ack or -ike ; chyacke.** See **chiike.**

cicisbeo. A ribbon-knot attached to hilt of sword, neck of walking-stick, etc. : ca. 1770–1820 : Society. (S.O.D. gives as an unassimilated Italianism, but this usage of the word is slangy.) Ex the C. 18–20 sense, imported direct from Italy : a married woman's recognised gallant or ' servente '.

-cide, -icide. A suffix denoting -murder or -murderer. Often used in jocular coll. by the cultured, as in *time'cide,* a fribble or a pastime, and the happier *warricide,* a pacifist. This sort of thing easily > pedantic or otherwise objectionable, and should be *Fowlericided.*

cider-and. Cider with something else (esp. if liquid) : C. 18–20 ; ob. Coll. Fielding in *Joseph Andrews,* ' They had a pot of cider-and at the fire.' Cf. *hot with.*

cig. A cigar : ca. 1885–1900. Barrère & Leland.—2. From ca. 1890, a cigarette. P. G. Wodehouse, *Not George Washington,* 1907. Earliest record : 1895, W. Pett Ridge, *Minor Dialogues.*

cigaresque. Well furnished with cigars ; smoking or ' sporting ' a large or very expensive cigar. A jocular coll. (1839), in C. 20, almost S.E., after *picturesque* or *picaresque.*

Cilicia(n) and **Sicilia(n)** are still often confused, as they have been since ca. 1600.

cinch, v.t. (In Canada, as in the Northern States of America, the *c* is hard ; in England, as in the Southern States, it is soft ; in other parts of the British Empire, it varies.) ' Corner ', get a grip on, put pressure on : orig. (1875), U.S., anglicised ca. 1900, though never gen. But *it's a cinch /,* the screw is on !, it's as good as a certainty, has, during and since the G.W., been better received. F. & Gibbons. Ex *cinch,* a tight girth (Sp. *cincha*).

cinder. Any strong liquor mixed with water, tea, lemonade, etc. (— 1864) ; ob. H., 3rd ed., ' Take a soda with a cinder in it.'—2. A running track : abbr. *cinder-path* or *-track* : coll. : from ca. 1880. Occ. *cinders.*—3. A window : thieves' rhyming s. : C. 20. James Curtis, *The Gilt Kid,* 1936.

cinder, yours to a. See **yours to a cinder.**

cinder-garbler. A female servant : late C. 18–

early 19. Grose, 1st ed., adds : ' Custom House wit '. Cf. :

cinder-grabber. A female drudge : C. 19–20 ; ob. Ex preceding entry. Cf. *slavey.*

cinder-knotter. A stoker : naval (— 1909) ; ob. Ware.

cinder-sifter. A woman's ' hat with open-work brim, the edge of which was turned up perpendicularly ' : Society : ca. 1878–1912. Ware.

cinderella. Abbr. *Cinderella dance,* one ceasing at midnight : from ca. 1880 : coll. >, by 1900, S.E.

cinders. See **cinder,** 2.

cine. (Pronounced *sinny.*) In compounds, it = *cinema, cinematographic* : 1928 (O.E.D.) : coll. >, by 1935, S.E. owing to its frequency as a trade abbr.

cinema. Cinematograph, -graphic : coll. (1910) >, by 1920, S.E. (O.E.D. Sup.) Cf. preceding entry.

[Cinema slang : see ' Moving-Picture Slang '.]

cinerascent. Incorrect for *cinerescent* : C. 19–20. O.E.D. (Sup.).

cinquanter. An old ' hand ' or ' stager ' : ca. 1600–1800. Pedantic ; ex Fr. *cinquante,* 50.—2. A ' gamester and scurrilous companion by profession ': ca. 1600–60. (O.E.D.)

cinque and sice, set at. ' To expose to great risks, to be reckless about ' (O.E.D.) : ca. 1530–1720 : s. > coll. > S.E. Cf. *at sixes and sevens.*

circle train. A London underground train : London coll. : 1887, Baumann.—2. In C. 20, an Inner Circle train on the Metropolitan Line : coll.

circlers. Occupants of the dress-circle : theatrical (— 1909). Ware.

*circling boy. A ' rook ', a swindler, a gambler's or a thief's decoy : C. 17 c. Jonson. Cf. *run rings round,* q.v. at *rings round.*

circs. Circumstances : trivial coll. : from ca. 1880. Baumann. Prob. commercial.

circumbendibus. A roundabout way (lit.) : coll. : from 1681 (Dryden) ; ob. Ex *bend* + L. *circum,* around, + L. dative and ablative pl., *-ibus.*— Whence, 2, a long-winded story : coll. : from ca. 1780. Grose, 1st ed.

circumference. The waist of a large, fat person : coll. : C. 20. Cf. *girth.*

circumlocution office. A Government Office; any roundabout way of doing things. Coined by Dickens in *Little Dorrit,* 1857. Derisively coll. ; S.E. by 1900.

circumsession. Catachrestic for theological *circuminsession* : mid-C. 17–20. O.E.D.

circus. A noisy and confused institution, place, scene, assemblage or group of persons : coll. : American anglicised ca. 1895.—2. A raiding-party that moves from sector to sector : military : 1917. Also *travelling circus.* O.E.D. (Sup.).—3. An aeroplane squadron : military : 1917. B. & P. and, esp., F. & Gibbons. The most famous was Richthöfen's. —4. Artillery s., from 1914, as in R. Blaker, *Medal without Bar,* 1930 : ' Cartwright rode at the tail of the firing battery with " the circus "—G.S. wagons, mess-cart, water-cart and the odd bicycle-pushers.' —5. Any temporary group of persons that, bound together, are working at the same task, e.g. at an encyclopædia (for the masses rather than the classes) : coll. ; 1932.

Circus, Kaffir. See **Kaffir Circus.**

*circus cuss. A circus rider : c. : from ca. 1850. ? abbr. *customer.*

cirrhous, cirrhus. Incorrect for *cirrous, cirrus* : C. 18–20. O.E.D.

ciss ! See cess !—**Cissie, -y.** See **Sissie, -y.**

cit. Abbr. *citizen* : pejorative coll. ; from ca. 1640 ; ob. by 1830, and in C. 20, S.E. Rarely applied, in a city, to others than tradesmen ; in the country, to other than (gen. non-aristocratic) townsmen born and bred. ' The cits of London and the boors of Middlesex ', Johnson (S.O.D.). *Citess,* ca. 1680–1750, is rare.

***citizen.** A wedge for opening safes : c. : from ca. 1860. Whence, *citizen's friend,* a wedge smaller than a *citizen,* itself smaller than an *alderman* ; larger still, though only occ. used, is a *lord mayor.* The tools are used in the order of their size ; the terms are ob.

Citizens, the. The Leicester, or the Manchester, City ' soccer ' team : sporting : from the 1890's. (The former occurs in *The Observer,* Oct. 29, 1933.)

citt. A C. 17–early 18 variant (e.g. in B.E.) of *cit,* q.v.

City. (Always *the City.*) The district, or the business men therein, round the Exchange and the Bank of England : from ca. 1750 ; coll. till ca. 1800, then S.E. Abbr. *the City of London,* orig. the part within the old boundaries. Contrast *la Cité* in Paris.

City, something in the. In lit. vagueness, obviously S.E. ; but, pointedly coll. from ca. 1890, it denotes a shady financier, a nondescript and none too honest agent, and esp. a criminal or even a burglar. Ware.

***City College.** Newgate : c. (– 1791) ; † by 1890. Grose, 3rd ed. Cf. *college,* q.v.

City of the Saints, the. Grahamstown : South African coll. nickname of ca. 1865–90. Pettman.

City Road Africans. Harlots of that quarter : London streets' : ca. 1882–1910. Ware.

City sherry. Four-ale : East London : ca. 1880–90. Ware. Ex cclour (!).

city stage. The gallows : C. 18–early 19. (Once in front of Newgate, London, ' E.C.4 '.)

civet. C. 18–19, low coll. : *pudendum muliebre.*

civet-cat. A person habitually using civet perfume : C. 18 ; orig.—Pope, 1738—S.E., it soon > coll. and quickly ob.

civies, civvies. Civilian clothes : military : mid-C. 19–20. Barrère & Leland ; F. & Gibbons. (The officers' word is S.E. *mufti.*)

civil reception, a house of. A bawdy house : mid-C. 18–early 19. Grose, 1st ed.

***civil rig.** In vagrants' c., C. 19–20 (ob.), an attempt to obtain alms by extreme civility. *Rig,* a trick.

***civilian.** Any person, esp. a man, that is not a criminal : C. 19–20 (ob.) : c.

civility money. A tip claimed by bailiffs for doing their duty with civility : C. 18–early 19 ; orig. coll., it was S.E. by 1880. Motteux, 1708, ' four Ducats for Civility Money '.

civvies. See civies.

civvy, civy. (As in *civies,* the former *i* is, in either spelling, short), adj. Civilian, esp. with *life* or *clothes.* C. 20. Cf. the famous G.W. song, " When I Get my Civ(v)y Clothes on, Oh how Happy I Shall Be " : see B. & P.—2. Also, a civilian : coll. : orig. (1895), military. H. W. Nevinson, *Neighbours of Ours.*

civvy kip. A real bed as opp. a shake-down : military : 1915. F. & Gibbons. See *civvy,* 1.

-ck for **-ct** is frequent in sol., prob. from time almost immemorial : as in *effeck* and *respeck* (often spelt *respec').*

clack. As chatter, gossip, S.E. ; as tongue, coll.: late C. 16–20 ; ob. Greene, ' Haud your clacks, lads.' As ' a prattler or busybody ' (Dyche), coll.: C. 17–early 18.—2. A loud talk or chat, coll. : from ca. 1810 ; ob. James Payn, 1888, ' The old fellow would have had a clack with her.' Esp. in *cut your clack !,* ' shut up ! ' : late C. 19–20 (Manchon).—3. The v. is S.E. The word is echoic.

clack-box. The mouth : C. 19.—2. A persistent chatterer : C. 19–20, ob. Both have a dial. tinge. Ex the S.E. sense, the container of a pump's clack-valve. Cf. :

clack-loft : A pulpit : late C. 18–20 ; ob. Grose, 2nd ed. Cf. *hum-box.*

clacker. A person, esp. a soldier, delighting to spread rumours : mostly military : C. 20. F. & Gibbons. Ex *clack,* 3.

clagger. A duff made of flour and slush : nautical : late C. 19–20. Bowen. Ex dial. *clag,* to adhere.

***claim.** To steal : latter C. 19–20 c. ; ob. Cf. *convey, win, scrounge, souvenir.*—2. To arrest ; gen. in the passive : c. (– 1935). David Hume.

claim, jump a. To seize, or gain possession of, fraudulently. Lit., S.E. ex U.S. ; but fig. it is a coll. anglicised ca. 1880.

***claimed.** Under arrest. See *claim,* 2.

clam. One who says extremely little or is excessively secretive : coll. : C. 20. (The U.S. sense is, a close-fisted person.)

***clank.** In c., a pewter tankard : C. 19 ; late C. 17–18 (B.E.), a silver one. Hence, *rum clank,* a double tankard, as in B.E., who also records *clank-napper,* a stealer of silver tankards.

clanker. A notable lie, cf. *clinker* : ca. 1690–1840. B.E. ; Grose, 1st ed. Ex the noise of heavy metal : cf. *clank,* q.v., and *clanker,* silver plate, C. 17–18 c.

***clanker-napper.** A thief specialising in silver plate, esp. tankards : late C. 17–early 19 c. Cf. *clank-napper* (see **clank**).

clans, a or the gathering of the. Any considerable, or indeed inconsiderable, gathering-together of people, gen. of the same or similar character or pursuit or purpose. From ca. 1890 : coll., by 1933 S.E. Ex Scottish warfare of C. 16–18.

clap. Gonorrhœa : late C. 16–20 ; S.E. until ca. 1840, then low coll. Respectably : 'They sing, they dance, clean shoes, or cure a clap '—almost the sole instance in Johnson's formal works (this occurs in *London,* an admirable satirical poem, 1738) of a monosyllabic sentence. Ex Old Fr. *clapoir.*

clap, v. To infect with gonorrhœa : from ca. 1650. S.E. until ca. 1840, then low coll.—2. Catachrestically for *clip* (to embrace) and *clepe* (to call) : C. 15, C. 17 resp. O.E.D.—3. To take, seize : low (– 1857) ; ob. ' Ducange Anglicus ', 1st ed. Ex *clap one's hands on.*

clap, in a. Immediately ; occ., instantaneously. Coll. ; from ca. 1630 ; ob.

Clap-'em. See **Clapham.**

clap eyes on. To see, esp. unexpectedly or finally : coll. ; Dickens, 1838.

clap in, v.i. To come or go decisively ; enter vigorously ; put oneself forward : coll. : ca. 1600–1780. Marvell, 1672, ' Hearing of a vacancy with a Noble-man, he clap'd in, and easily obtained to be his Chaplain ' (O.E.D.).

clap of thunder. A glass of gin : coll. ; ca. 1810–40. Cf. *flash of lightning.*

clap on, v.i. To ' set to ' ; apply oneself energetically : coll. ; from ca. 1850. Surtees (O.E.D.).

clap on the shoulder, n. and v. (An) arrest for debt. C. 18 (? also C. 17) coll. Grose, 1st ed.

clap-shoulder. A bailiff or a watchman : rare coll. ; C. 17–early 19. Adj. in Taylor the Water Poet. The gen. form is *shoulder-clapper*.

Clapham (or Clap-'em), he went out by Had'em and came home by. ' He went out a-wenching, and got a clap,' Grose, 1st ed. : mid-C. 18–early 19 c.p. Punning *clap*, n.

clapper. The tongue (human) ; esp. that of a very talkative person : coll. : 1638, H. Shirley ; H., 1st ed. O.E.D.—2. In C. 20 c., ob. by 1932, a sandwich-man's boards.—3. A study ventilator : Shrewsbury School coll. : from ca. 1880. (Desmond Coke, *The Bending of a Twig*, 1906.) Ex the noise it makes as it is being closed.

clapper-claw. To thrash soundly and crudely : late C. 16–early 19. Coll. B.E., Grose. Lit., to scratch noisily.—2. Hence, to revile : late C. 17–20 ; ob. coll. almost S.E. (O.E.D.).

***clapper-dogeon** or, more correctly, -dudgeon. A beggar born, a whining beggar ; also as an insult. Mid-C. 16–19 : c. till ca. 1800, then low s. with an archaic tinge. Harman ; Jonson ; Ned Ward ; Sala. ? lit., one who assumes (' claps on ') grief, indignation, distress. Or, as O.E.D. suggests, *clapper + dudgeon*, the hilt of a dagger.

clapster. A frequent sufferer from *clap* (q.v.) ; a very loose man. C. 19–20 ; low coll.

clar. In piece-work, to earn as much as possible : factory-workers' : 1932. (*Slang*, p. 181).

Claras. Caledon an Railway stock : money market : from ca. 1880 ; ob.

Clare Market Cleavers. Butchers of that district : London coll. : ca. 1850–1900. ' The glory of Clare Market . . . was practically gone in '98,' Ware (whom see for an excellent account).

Clare Market duck. ' Baked bullock's heart stuffed with sage and onions—which gave a faint resemblance to the bird ', Ware : London : ca. 1850–1900. See the preceding.

Clarence. Like, though less than, *Cuthbert*, apt to be used as a jocular coll. : C. 20. See my *Name This Child*, 1936.

claret. Blood : from ca. 1600 (Dekker, e.g. in *The Honest Whore*, 1604). From ca. 1770, mostly in boxing ' circles ' (e.g. in Moore's *Tom Crib's Memorial*, 1819). Ex the colour. Cf. *badminton* and *bordeaux*. Hence :

claret, tap one's. To draw blood : from ca. 1770 ; pugilistic. Grose, 1st ed.

claret-christening. The first blood that flows in a boxing match : pugilistic (– 1923). Manchon. See claret.

claret-jug. The nose : pugilistic ; from ca. 1840 ; ob. Ex *claret*, q.v.

clargy. Clergy : sol. (– 1823). ' Jon Bee ' ; Baumann. Cf. *sarvice*.

clargyman. A rabbit : provincial, esp. Cheshire, s. (– 1898), not dial. E.D.D.

Clarian. A member of Clare, Cambridge University : from ca. 1850. Charles Whibley, witty Augustan, embalms it in *Cap and Gown* as ' stuke-struck Clarians '. Without the pun on *clarian*, the term would obviously not be unconventional.

Clarkenco. The Fourth Party in the House of Commons : political : late June–July, 1885. A telescoping of *Mr. Edward Clarke and Co.*, as it was also called (*The Referee*, July 19, 1885). Ware.

clashy. Anglo-Indian (coll. rather than s.) for a native sailor or tent-pitcher, loosely for a labourer, a ' low fellow ' : late C. 18–20. Ex Urdu.

class. Distinction ; sheer merit : athletics and, slightly, the turf : from ca. 1850 : coll. ' He's not class enough,' ' There's a good deal of class about him ' : he is not good enough ; pretty good. Cf. *classy*, q.v., and :

***class man.** A ' prisoner who has passed out of the first stage ', George Ingram, *Stir*, 1933 : c.

class, no. Without distinction or merit : lower classes' coll. : 1897, ' Soldiers ! Why, soldiers ain't no class.' Ware. Ex preceding.

class, take a. (Oxford) to take an honours degree : mid-C. 19–20 : coll. >, by 1880, S.E.

classic. Excellent, ' splendid ' : from ca. 1880 : coll. Ex burlesque S.E. sense : ' approved, recognised " standard " ', O.E.D.

classy. Stylish ; fashionable ; smart ; well-turned-out : from ca. 1890 : coll., lower middle class downwards. Cf. *class*, q.v.

[**clater** in Manchon is an error or, more prob., a misprint for *clatter*.]

clattery, adj. Clattering : coll. : from ca. 1880. O.E.D. (Also in Yorkshire dial. : E.D.D.)

***claw.** A stroke of the cat-o'-nine-tails : (– 1876) c. ; ob.

claw me and I'll claw thee. The C. 17–early 19 form of the C. 16 *claw me, claw ye* and the C. 20 *scratch my back and I'll scratch yours* : coll.

claw off. Severely to defeat or thrash : late C. 17–19, low coll., as is the sense, venereally to infect. B.E.—3. Also, to scold : same period and kind. Occ. *c. away*. Cf. earlier S.E. senses.

claw-back. See claw-poll.

claw-hammer (coat). The tail coat of full evening dress : coll. ; from 1869 in U.S. (Thornton) ; anglicised in 1879 (O.E.D.). (The *coat* is gen. omitted.) Ex a *claw*-hammer.

claw-poll, more gen. **claw-back.** A toady : coll., resp. C. 16–17, C. 16–19. Both S.E. after 1600.

[**claws, in one's.** In a person's power or possession : jocular of oneself, pejorative of another : late C. 16–20 : S.E. till C. 20, then virtually coll.]

***claws for breakfast.** Punishment with the cat-o'-nine-tails : (– 1873) c. ; ob. James Greenwood, *In Strange Company*. Cf. *claw*.

clay. Abbr. *clay-pipe* : coll. : from ca. 1860. Calverley in the *Ode to Tobacco*.

clay, moisten or **wet one's.** To drink : from ca. 1700 : coll. verging on S.E. In C. 19–20 also *soak*. Addison in *The Spectator*, ' To moisten their clay, and grow immortal by drinking '. Cf. S.E. *mortal clay*.

clay-brained. Very dull-witted : coll. >, by 1700, S.E. ; late C. 16–20, ob. Shakespeare.

clean, v.i. To change one's clothes : naval : late C. 19–20. Bowen, ' Even " clean into dirty clothes " is permissible.'

clean, in several senses as adj. and adv. is almost coll., as in *clean off his head*.—2. But as ' expert, clever ', it is wholly c. (– 1811) ; † by 1890. *Lex. Bal.*

clean, come. To tell, or confess, everything : U.S. ; anglicised ca. 1920. Dorothy Sayers, *The Five Red Herrings*, 1931, ' I'll come clean, as they say. I'd better do it at once, or they'll think I know more than I do.'

clean !, keep it. See **keep it clean !**

clean and polish—we're winning the war. A military c.p., by the ranks condemnatory of ' spit and polish ' (q.v.) : 1915–18. F. & Gibbons. Cf. :

clean as a button-stick. (Of a soldier) smart in appearance : military coll. : C. 20. F. & Gibbons. A button-stick was a device for polishing buttons.

clean as a pig-sty(, as). An Anglo-Irish ironic c.p. applied to a dirty house : late C. 19–20.

clean gone. Quite ' cracked ' ; mad : coll. : C. 20. Manchon.

clean leg up, give (one) **a.** To help him (esp. to obtain a job) : non-aristocratic coll. (— 1887) ; slightly ob. Baumann. Ex giving a person assistance over a fence.

clean one's front. See **front, clean one's.**

clean out. To deprive of money, gen. illicitly : orig. low, verging on c. : from ca. 1810. Vaux, 1812 ; Dickens, in *The Old Curiosity Shop,* ' He was plucked, pigeoned, and cleaned out completely.'—2. Ca. 1840–70, to thrash.

clean potato. The right, occ. the ' correct ', thing, esp. morally : coll. : from ca. 1870 ; ob.

clean ship. A whaling ship returning whale-less to port : whalers' coll. : late C. 19–20. Bowen.

clean-skins. (Rare in singular.) Unbranded cattle. Australia (— 1881) : coll. ; in C. 20, S.E. Morris.

clean straw. Clean sheets : Winchester College, ? C. 16–20 ; ob. ' Before 1540 the beds were bundles of straw on a stone floor,' F. & H. The same meaning is extant at Bootham School : see Anon., *Dict. of Bootham Slang,* 1925.

clean the board. To clear the board, etc., of all it contains ; make a clean sweep : coll. (— 1884). O.E.D.

clean up. To acquire (something) as profit or gain : coll. : C. 20 ; U.S., anglicised by 1910. O.E.D. (Sup.).

clean wheat, it's the. I.e. the best of its kind : coll., ca. 1865–1910. Cf. *A1.*

cleanie. One's best girl : military : from ca. 1919. Perhaps a blend of *clean + clinah.*

clear. (Exceedingly) drunk : c. and low : from late 1680's ; † by 1890. B.E. ; Vanbrugh, *The Relapse,* ' I suppose you are clear—you'd never play such a trick as this else.' Cf. *clear as mud.*

*clear, in the. With no evidence against one ; innocent, or app. so : c. : C. 20. (*The Passing Show,* May 26, 1934.)

clear, the coast is. The w.c. is at your disposal : euphemistic c.p. (— 1923). Manchon. Ex the fig. S.E. sense.

clear an examination paper. To answer all the questions : coll. (— 1893). On the analogy of *clear a dish,* eat all its contents. O.E.D.

clear as mud. Anything but clear ; confused : coll. : from ca. 1890.

clear crystal. White spirits, esp. gin ; loosely, brandy and rum. From ca. 1860 ; ob.

clear decks. To clear the table after a meal : nautical coll. : mid-C. 19–20. Bowen.

clear grit. (Canada) a member of the Canadian Liberal Party : ca. 1880–1900. *The Fortnightly Review,* May, 1884. Ex U.S. *clear grit,* the real thing.

clear off or out. To depart : from ca. 1830. The S.O.D. gives it as S.E., but in C. 19, at least, the term had a coll. taint, perhaps because it was used slightly earlier in U.S.—e.g. Neal, in *Brother Jonathan,* 1825, had ' Like many a hero before him, he cleared out.' Monetarily, *clear out* is gen. S.E., but as ' clean out ', q.v., or ' ruin ', it is coll. (— 1850), as in Thackeray's *Pendennis.*

clear-out, have a. To defecate : a low coll. (— 1923). Manchon.

clearing-out at custom-house, n. and adj. Easing (or eased) of an encumbrance : nautical : ca. 1820–60. Egan's Grose.

cleave, v.i. To be wanton (said of women only) : C. 18–early 19 ; low. The two opp. meanings of *cleave*—due to independent radicals—are present in this subtle term. *A New Canting Dict.,* 1725 ; Grose, 1st ed.

cleaved. See **cloven.**

cleaver. A butcher : coll. : C. 18–19. Ex the butcher's cleaver or chopper.—2. In late C. 18–early 19 low s., a forward woman ; a wanton. Grose, 2nd ed. See preceding entry.

cleavin(g). Boastful : Clare Market, London : ca. 1850–1900. Ex *Clare Market Cleavers,* q.v.

cleft. The female pudend : coll., C. 17–20. Ex the earlier S.E. (in C. 19–20, dial.) sense : the body's fork. In late C. 19–20 usage, as much euphemism as coll.—2. Adj. See **cloven.**

cleft stick, in a. In a very difficult position . from ca. 1700 ; coll. in C. 18 ; in C. 19–20, S.E.

*clem. To starve : c. 20 vagrants' c., ex dial.—2. In C. 20 circus s. (perhaps ex U.S.), a fight.

clencher. See **clincher.**—**clenchpoop.** See **clinchpoop.**

clergyman. A chimney-sweep : C. 19. Cf. *chimney-sweep.*

clergyman or **clerk, St. Nicholas's.** See at **Nicholas.**

[Clergyman's diction in the Church of England. The following passage, caustically true of many clerics, occurs in Ernest Raymond's *Mary Leith,* 1931 (Part I, ch. iii) : ' " All," when Mr Broadley was in high emotional state, showed a strange tendency to become " ull "—' " Brethren, shall we ull now rise and sing a hymn " ; the holy Apostles, on the crest of the wave of very strong feeling, changed most distinctly into " Thy holy Aparcels, O Lord " ; and at times—at really stirring times—" Lord " enriched and strengthened itself into something very like " Lorder ".' This passage is preceded by an equally pertinent one on cleric clichés.]

clericals. A clergyman's dress : coll. : from ca. 1860. Cf. *academicals.*

*clerk. To impose upon ; swindle : c. and low coll. : C. 18–early 19. *A New Canting Dict.,* 1725 ; Grose, 1st ed. Ex ignorance's suspicion of learning. —2. To act as a clerk : C. 19–20 ; coll. The vbl.n., *clerking,* occurs in C. 17, the ppl. adj. in mid-C. 16. Lamb, in 1834, ' I am very tired of clerking it.' (O.E.D.)

clerk of the works. ' He who takes the lead in minor affairs ', Bee : public-house : ca. 1820–50. Punning S.E. sense.

clerks, St. Nicholas's. See **Nicholas.**

clerk's blood. Red ink : coll. : C. 19–20, ob. Charles Lamb.

clever. " At first a colloquial and local word ", S.O.D. ; it still is coll. if = ' cunning ' or ' skilful ' and applied to an animal or if = ' well ', ' in good health or spirits ' (mid-C. 19–20). Esp. *not too clever,* indisposed in health ; the health sense is common in Australia and New Zealand.—2. Convenient, suitable : coll. : ca. 1750–1820.—3. ' Nice ' ; generally likable or pleasant : coll. : from ca. 1730 ; ob.— 4. (Of persons) well-disposed, amiable : coll. : ca. 1770–1830, extant in U.S. Goldsmith, ' Then come, put the jorum about, | And let us be merry and clever' (O.E.D.).—5. (Of planks, etc.) steady : Australian : from ca. 1910. Prob. ex sense 1.

clever boots. Gen. as a comment : a clever, occ. a sly, person. C. 20. Perhaps ex *clever shins*, q.v.

clever Dick. The same : schools' (— 1887) ; mostly London. Baumann. Cf. :

clever shins. A person sly to no, or little, purpose : schools', ca. 1870–1910. Baumann. Cf. *slyboots.*—2. Hence, more gen., a C. 20 coll. variant of *clever boots*. Manchon.

***cleyme ;** occ. **clyme** or **cleym.** An artificial sore : ca. 1670–1830 : c. Head ; B.E. furnishes an excellent account of this beggar's device. ? etymology, unless ex *cly*, to seize.

click. A blow, a punch : boxing ; from ca. 1770 ; ob. except in dial. Grose, 1st ed. ; Moore, in *Tom Crib's Memorial*, 'clicks in the gob'. (The wrestling term is j.)—2. A clique ; a 'push' (Australian sense) : Australian (— 1914). C. J. Dennis.—3. A successful meeting with an unknown member of the opposite sex : G.W. +. Much rarer than the corresponding nuance of the 4th sense of the v.—4.. Hence, a girl ; a sweetheart : Glasgow (— 1934)

click, v. To 'stand at a shop-door and invite customers in', Dyche, 1748. C. 18–early 19. Ex :—2. In c. and low, to seize : late C. 17–mid-19. B.E., Grose.—3. In printers' s., from slightly before 1860, 'A work is said to be "clicked" when each man works on his lines, and keeps an account thereof.' O.E.D. (Sup.).—4. In 1914 +, orig. military, 'to do a drill movement with a click' ; 'to click for a fatigue or a duty (i.e. to be put down for one)' ; (of a man) 'to click with a member of the opposite sex', i.e. get off with one, also absolutely as in 'He's clicked',—hence (a sense that Collinson misses), to be successful, to have a piece of very good luck (with variant 'he's clicked for something') and v.t. as in *click a Blighty*, to get a 'Blighty' wound (F. & Gibbons) ; (of a woman) to become pregnant, also to 'meet' a man, though the latter is gen. in form, *click with (a fellow)*. 'In all these senses', says Collinson in 1926, 'and the remark holds good, 'the word is still not uncommon'. Ex the click one hears when a small mechanical object falls into position, or when a key is turned. Cf., however, Scots *cleek in* (or *up*) *with*, to take up with (a person) : E.D.D.

click, one's ears go back with a. (Gen. *his ears went . . .*). An † 'near' c.p. indicative of pleasure manifested at good news : military : from not later than 1915. F. & Gibbons.

clicker. A shop-keeper's tout : late C. 17–19. Ned Ward in *The London Spy* : 'Women here were almost as Troublesome as the Long-Lane clickers.'—2. A foreman shoemaker apportioning leather to the workmen : orig. (C. 17) s., soon j.—3. In printing, from ca. 1770, a foreman distributing the copy : soon j.—4. In C. 18–early 19 c., one who shares out the booty or 'regulars', q.v.—5. A knockdown blow : boxing, from ca. 1815 ; ob.—6. One who, once or, esp., often, meets successfully with an unknown person of the opposite sex : G.W. + ; ex *to click*, 4.

clicket. Sexual intercourse : c. or low coll. ; late C. 17–18. Gen. as *be at clicket*. B.E., Grose. Ex the S.E. term, applied to foxes.

clickety click. (In the game of House) 66 : military : C. 20. F. & Gibbons. By rough-and-ready rhyming.

clicking, vbl.n. Success ; 'getting off' with a girl : from ca. 1915. See click, v., 4. Cf. P. G. Wodehouse's *The Clicking of Cuthbert*, 1922.

clickman toad. A watch : late C. 18–early 19. Perhaps orig. dial. Ex clicking sound. Whence— 2. A West-Countryman : s. (— 1788) and dial. ; † by 1890. Grose (2nd ed.), who tells an amusing anecdote.

clie. See cly, n.

client. A person, a fellow or chap : military : from ca. 1912. F. & Gibbons. Suggested by *customer*.—2. Hence, *client for Rouen*, a 'venereal' : military : 1915. B. & P.

***clift.** To steal : mid-C. 19–20 ; ob. H., 2nd ed. ? ex *have in a cleft stick*.

***cligh.** See cloy, v.

climacteric, climateric, climatic are occ. confused : C. 19–20. (O.E.D.)

***climb, on the,** adj. and adv. By 'cat'-burglary : c. : C. 20. James Curtis, *The Gilt Kid*, 1936.

climb down. To abandon a position, an assertion or boast : from mid-1880's : coll. >, by 1910, S.E.

climb the Mountain of Piety. To pawn goods : late C. 19–20 ; ob. Cf. Fr. *mont de piété*.

climb the rigging. To lose one's temper : naval : late C. 19–20. Bowen. Cf. *hit the roof* and *rear up*.

***climb the three trees with a ladder.** To ascend the gallows : c. : late C. 18–early 19. Grose, 2nd ed. Ex the three pieces of a gallows.

climb Zion. 'To rush up the fo'c'sle, chased by armed seniors', Masefield : *Conway* Training Ship, from ca. 1890.

clinah. See cliner.

***clinch.** A prison cell : mid-C. 19–20 c. (ob.) : H., 3rd ed. Hence *get*, or *kiss, the clinch* or *clink*, to be imprisoned.

clincher. A great lie : C. 19–20 ; ob. ; coll. Cf. *corker*.—2. A conclusive statement or argument : coll. ; 1804 (O.E.D.).

clinchpoop, occ. **clenchpoop.** A lout : coll. ; ca. 1570–1640.

cliner ; occ. **clinah.** A girl : Australian : C. 20. C. J. Dennis. Ex Yiddish : cf. *cobber*, 2, q.v.

***cling-rig.** See clink-rig.

clinger. A female dancing very close to her partner : from ca. 1890.

clink. A prison in Southwark, London : C. 16–17. In C. 18–20, any prison, esp. if small ; a lock-up ; a detention cell, this last nuance dating only from ca. 1880 and being mainly military (cf. *clinch*, q.v.) ; from 1919, occ. school s. for detention. Barclay, 1515 ; Marryat, 1835, 'We've a nice little clink at Wandsworth.' Echoic from the fetters (see **clinkers**).—2. Money (cf. *chink*) : Scottish coll. rather than dial. : from the 1720's. Ramsay, Burns, Hogg. Also, a coin : mostly military : from ca. 1870. Frank Richards, *Old-Soldier Sahib*, 1936.—3. Very inferior beer : from ca. 1860 ; ob. Sala. Cf. *bum-clink*.

clink, v. To put in prison : from ca. 1850. Also see clinch.

clink, kiss the. To be imprisoned. Low : late C. 16–early 19. A C. 19 c. variant, *get the clinch*.

***clink-rig ;** occ. corrupted to **cling-rig.** The stealing of (esp. silver) tankards from public-houses : c. ; ca. 1770–1880. Ex *clank*, q.v.

***clinker.** In c. of ca. 1690–1830, a crafty, designing fellow. B.E.—2. In c. C. 18–19, any kind of chain.—3. A hard, or smartly delivered blow : from ca. 1860 ; boxing. Thackeray. Ex S.E. *clink*, a quick, sharp blow.—4. A person or thing of excel-

lent quality : sporting s. (ca. 1860) >, ca. 1900, coll.
—5. A notable lie : mid-C. 19–20 ; ob.—6. Abbr.
(— 1923) of next. Manchon.—7. A prisoner :
military : 1914 or 1915 ; ob. F. & Gibbons. Ex
clink, n., 1.

clinker-knocker. A naval stoker : nautical, esp.
naval : late C. 19–20. Bowen.

***clinkers.** Fetters : c. and low ; late C. 17–early
19. B.E. Echoic ; cf. *clink*.—2. ' Deposits of
fæcal or seminal matter in the hair about the *anus*
or the female *pudendum* ', F. & H. ; low coll., from
ca. 1830. Cf. *clinkers in one's* . . . and the S.E.
sense, a hot cinder.

clinkers in one's bum, have. To be restless ;
uneasy. Low coll., from ca. 1840.

clinkerum. A prison ; a lock-up : C. 19. *Clink*
influenced by *clinkers*, 1.

clinking. First-rate ; remarkably good : from
ca. 1855 : coll. ; esp. in racing and games. *The
Sporting Times*, March 12, 1887, ' Prince Henry
must be a clinking good horse.'

clip, a smart blow, has a coll. ' look ', but it is
genuine S.E. The corresponding v., however, is
coll., late C. 19–20, and is always in forms *clip a
person one* or *clip a person on the* (gen.) *ear*.

clip, v. To move quickly ; run : coll., from ca.
1830. Michael Scott in *Tom Cringle's Log*, 1833.
Until ca. 1844, rarely of anything but ships.—2. See
preceding entry.

clipe. To tell tales : schools', ca. 1860–1900. Cf.
Chaucer's *clepe*, to speak of, and O.E. *clipian*, to call,
to name.

clipper. A splendid or very smart specimen of
humanity or horseflesh : orig. (— 1835), U.S.,
anglicised ca. 1845. Thackeray, 1848. Ex *clipper*,
any fast-moving ship or (from ca. 1830) the special
kind of vessel ; as horse, influenced by Dutch
klepper (W.).—2. See ' Rogues ' in Addenda.

clipping. (Of pace) very fast, ' rattling ' : coll. ;
1845, *Punch* (O.E.D. Sup.). Cf. *clipper*.—2. Hence,
excellent ; very smart ; dashingly showy : from
ca. 1855. H., 1st ed. ; Thackeray, *Philip*, ' What
clipping girls there were in that barouche.' Ex (*to*)
clip. Adv. in -*ly*.

clique, v.i. and t. To act as, or form, a clique :
coll. : from ca. 1880.

cliqu(e)y. Pertaining to or characterised by
cliques : from ca. 1875, though recorded in 1863
for U.S. (O.E.D. Sup.) : coll. for a decade, then
S.E.

clo. Clothes : low (mostly Cockney) coll. pronunciation, chiefly in the street cry, *clo ! old clo !* :
C. 19–20. Baumann.

***cloak.** A watch-case : C. 19 c. Ainsworth.

cloak, Plymouth. See **Plymouth cloak.**

cloak-father. ' A pretended author whose name
is put forth to conceal the real author ', O.E.D. :
coll. : ca. 1639–1700. Fuller. The O.E.D. cites as
S.E., but surely not ?

***cloak-twitcher.** A thief specialising in cloaks :
C. 18–early 19 : c. *A New Canting Dict.*, 1725 ;
Grose, 1st ed.

clobber ; occ. **clober.** Clothes : from ca. 1850 ;
at first, old clothes but from ca. 1870 also new ;
among soldiers in G.W., one's (full) equipment.
Chiefly Jewish, Cockney and C. 20 Australian.
Prob. ex Yiddish (*klbr*). (W. H. Davies, ' the
super-tramp ', considers it to be c.)

clobber, v. See **clobber up,** 2.

***clobber at a fence, do.** To sell stolen clothes :
c. ; from ca. 1855.

clobber out. An occ. C. 20 variant (Manchon) of
sense 2 of :

clobber up. To patch, ' transform ' (clothes).
Orig. a cobbling device. From ca. 1850.—2. To
dress smartly, v.t. and reflexive : from ca. 1860.
W. E. Henley. Also, occ. (gen. in passive), *clobber* :
not before ca. 1880.

clobberer. A transformer of old clothes : from
ca. 1855. Ca. 1880 it > j. *The Times*, Nov. 2,
1864. Cf. *clobber up*, 1.

clober. See **clobber,** n.

***clock.** A watch : C. 19–20 c. and low. (In
C. 16–18, S.E.) If of gold, *a red c.* ; if of silver, *a
white c.* : gen. abbr. to *a red, a white, 'un*.—2. A
face : from ca. 1870, ex U.S. Cf. *dial*.—3. A
dynamite bomb : London : 1880's. Ex a topicality of the dynamite scare at that time. Ware.—
4. A taxi-meter : taxi-drivers' : C. 20 ; by 1930,
coll.

clock, v.t. To time by a stop-watch : from ca.
1880 : sporting s. >, ca. 1910, coll. ; now verging on
S.E.

clock, know what's o'. See **o'clock.**

clock-calm. (Of the sea) dead-calm : nautical
coll. : late C. 19–20. Bowen. Ex a clock's shiny
face.

clock in (or **on**), **off** (or **out**). To sign the time
book on arrival or departure : from ca. 1905 ; coll.
>, by 1930, S.E. Factory and office phrases.

clock-setter. A busybody, a sea lawyer : nautical (— 1890) : *Century Dict.* Ex :—2. One who
tampers with the clock to shorten his hours :
nautical coll. : from ca. 1880.

clock stopped. No ' tick ', i.e. no credit. Tradesmen's c.p. : from ca. 1840 ; now rare, but not
ob.

clocking. Very fast time, esp. in athletics and
racing : 1888 ; coll. ; ob. (O.E.D.)—2. ' The
objectionable and mischievous practice . . . of
hitching the bell-rope or a separate cord round the
" flight " of the " clapper ", while the bell is " at
rest ", in order to pull the " clapper " against the
bell, with the frequent result of cracking the
latter ' : bell-ringers' s. (— 1901) >, by 1920, coll.
Rev. A. Earle Bulwer, *A Glossary of Bell-Ringing*,
1901.

clod. (Gen. pl.) A copper coin : non-aristocratic (— 1914). F. & Gibbons. Among Cockneys,
a penny (*The Evening News*, Jan. 20, 1936) ; also
among grafters (Allingham, *Cheapjack*, 1934).
Prob. ex both the colour and the weight.

clod, gen. v.i. To shell heavily : military : 1915.
F. & Gibbons, ' Suggested by the heaving up of the
earth as shells burst on impact '.

clod-crusher. A clumsy boot (gen. pl.) : coll. :
from ca. 1850. Cf. *beetle-crusher*.—2. Hence, a
large foot (gen. in pl.) : coll. ; from ca. 1860.—
3. Also, a heavy walker : coll. ; from ca. 1870.

clod-hopper. A clumsy boor : coll. : C. 18–20,
ex the C. 17–18 sense, ploughman. After ca. 1800,
S.E.—2. Gen. in the now more usual form :

***clodhopper.** A street dancer : c. (— 1933).
George Orwell, *Down and Out in Paris and London*.

clod-pate, clod-poll or **-pole.** A dolt : C. 17–20,
ob. ; coll. ; S.E. after ca. 1750. Like the preceding, in B.E., though the O.E.D. and S.O.D. say
nothing of their almost certainly coll. origin and
beginnings.

cloddy. Aristocratic in appearance : proletarian :
late C. 19–20. Ex well-formed or *cloddy* bull dogs
(' low to the ground, short in the back, and thickset ',

The Daily Telegraph, Nov. 13, 1895). Ex dial. *cloddy*, thick set, full-fleshed like a bull. Ware; E.D.D.)

clods and stickings. Skilly: paupers', from ca. 1840; ob.

cloister-roush. At Winchester College, ' a kind of general tournament ', Mansfield. Dating from early C. 19, † by 1890.

cloke. See **cloak**.

Clootie; Cloots. The devil: Scots coll. (and Northern dial.): from the 1780's. Burns has both; Barham (*Clootie*). Ex *cloot*, a division of a hoof; the devil has a cloven foot. (O.E.D.)

close in. Shut up: C. 14–17; coll. soon S.E.

close as God's curse to a whore's arse or **as shirt and shitten arse.** Very close indeed: mid-C. 18–early 19 c.p. or proverb. Grose, 1st ed.

close as wax. Miserly; stingy; secretive: from ca. 1770: coll. till mid-C. 19, then S.E. Cumberland, 1772; Charles Reade. (Apperson.) Cf. the S.E. *close-fisted* (C. 17–20, regarded by B.E. as coll.)

close call. A near thing; an incident almost fatal: coll.: U.S. (1880's) anglicised in late 1890's. (O.E.D. Sup.)

*close file. A secretive or uncommunicative person: c. or low, from ca. 1820; ob. *File* (cf. *blade*) = a man.

*close mouth. A disreputable establishment or resort: C. 20. Scottish c.

close one's dead-lights. To ' bung up ' one's eyes: nautical: ca. 1820–1910. Egan's Grose.

close thing. A narrow escape; an even contest. Coll. > S.E.: late C. 19–20. Cf. *close call.*

Closh. Collective for Dutch seamen: mid-C. 18–early 19. Grose, 1st ed. Ex Dutch *Klaas*, abbr. *Nicolaas*, a favourite Christian name in Holland.—2. Hence, a seaman from the Eastern counties of England: nautical: mid-C. 19–20. Bowen.

cloth. One's profession: C. 17–19; coll. > S.E. in C. 18. Esp. *the cloth*: the Church; clergymen: C. 18–20; coll. Swift, 1701; Dickens, 1836, of another profession, ' This 'ere song's personal to the cloth.'—2. Also, from ca. 1860 and coll., the office of a clergyman.

cloth, cut one's coat according to the. To act in sane accordance with the circumstances; esp., to live within one's means. Mid-C. 16–20. Coll. till C. 18, then S.E.

cloth in the wind, shake (occ. **have**) **a.** To be slightly drunk: nautical; from ca. 1830; ob.

cloth is all of another hue, the. That's a very different story: proverbial coll.: C. 15–17. Cf. *horse of another colour.*

cloth market. (Or with capitals.) Bed. Late C. 17–19: coll. (gen. with *the*). Ray, 1678; Swift. (Apperson.) Cf. *Bedfordshire.*

clothes-line, able to sleep (up)on a. Capable of sleeping in difficult place or position; hence, able to rough it, to look after oneself. Coll.; from ca. 1840.

clothes-pegs. Legs: rhyming s.: late C. 19–20. B. & P.

clothes-pin I am, that's the sort of. That's me! That's my nature. (Of men only; cf. *hair-pin.*) Coll.; from ca. 1865.

clothes sit on her like a saddle on a sow's back, her. A late C. 17–mid-18 c.p. applied to an ill-dressed woman. (B.E.)

clothing-crusher. A ' ship's policeman superintending the mustering of kits ': naval: C. 20. Bowen.

cloud. Tobacco smoke. Late C. 17–early 19 (cf. *blow a cloud*). B.E. gives it as tobacco, but his example shows that he means either tobacco being smoked or, more prob., tobacco smoke.

cloud, under a. As = out of favour, or in difficulties other than monetary, S.E.; as = in disgrace, coll. in C. 16–17, then S.E.

cloud-cleaner. Nautical of mid-C. 19–20 (ob.). ' An imaginary cloud jokingly assumed to be carried by Yankee ships ', Clark Russell.

cloud-compeller. A smoker, esp. of tobacco: from ca. 1860: jocular-pedantic >, ca. 1880, coll. (Like *cloud-assembler*, this is a Homeric epithet for Zeus.)

clouds, in the. Fantastic; fanciful; metaphysical. Also as adv. In C. 17, coll.; then S.E.

cloudy. In disgrace or disrepute; ' shady ': coll.: 1886, Stevenson (O.E.D.); ob. Cf. *murky.*

clout. A heavy blow: M.E. onwards. S.E. until ca. 1850, when it > low coll. and dial.; indeed it was far from literary after ca. 1770 (see Grose).—2. A handkerchief (unless of silk): the S.O.D. implies that this is S.E., but Jonson's *Gipsies*, B.E., John Hall's *Memoirs*, Fielding's *Jonathan Wild*, Grose (edd. of 1785–1811), Brandon, and H. tend to show that, from ca. 1600, it was low coll. verging on c.—3. A woman's ' sanitary ': low coll., C. 19–20, ob.

clout, v. To strike (a person) heavily: M.E. onwards; S.E. until ca. 1850, when it > low coll. and dial. Cf. sense 1 of the n.—2. Hence, to do eagerly, despatch vigorously: mostly military: C. 20. F. & Gibbons, ' That fellow clouted six eggs this morning for his breakfast.'—3. To seize; to steal: New Zealanders': C. 20. For semantics, cf. c. sense of *ding*, q.v.

clout, wash one's face in an ale. To get drunk: coll. (jocular): C. 16–17.

clout-shoe, clouted shoe. A yokel; a boor: ca. 1580–1750: coll. Cf. Spenser's *Colin Clout.*

*clouter. A pickpocket; one specialising in handkerchiefs: c. (– 1839); ob. Brandon.—2. Vbl.n., *clouting.*

clouting. A thrashing or a cuffing: see *clout*, v. —2. In C. 20 c., the carrying, by a woman shop-thief, of rolls of silk or cloth between her legs. Charles E. Leach. Cf.:

*clouting lay. The stealing of handkerchiefs from people's pockets: late C. 18–19 c. Grose, 2nd ed. Occ. abbr. to *clouting* (Vaux).

clouts. A woman's underclothes, from the waist down. Also, her complete wardrobe. Low coll.: C. 19–20; ob.

clove. A sol. form of *cloven*: C. 19–20. Baumann. Cf. *drove* for *driven.*

cloven, occ. cleaved or **cleft.** Ppl. adj., spuriously virgin: C. 18–early 19. *A New Canting Dict.*, 1725; Grose, 1st ed. Cf. *cleft*, n., q.v.

clover, in. (Gen. with *be* or *live*.) In great comfort; luxuriously; in pleasant and most welcome safety or security: C. 18–20: coll. >, in late C. 19, S.E. Ex cattle in clover.

clow. (Pronounced *clo.*) A box on the ear: Winchester College: C. 19. Perhaps on the auditory analogy of *bout—bow, lout—low*, as F. & H. suggests. Also, v.t.

*clows. (Gen. as pl.) A rogue: late C. 17–18 c. B.E., Grose. Perhaps cognate with :

*cloy, cloye. A thief; a robber: C. 18–early 19 c. Cf.:

*cloy, cligh, cly, to steal, is—like its derivatives—c., not s.: C. 17–early 19. Cf. C. 16–17 S.E. *cloyne*, cheat or grab.

*cloyer. A thief habitually claiming a share of profits from young sharpers : C. 17 c.—2. Also in c., the less specialised sense : a thief, a pickpocket : mid-C. 17–early 19. B.E.

club. The *membrum virile* : low : C. 19.—2. A very thick pigtail : coll. ; 1760–1920 ; S.E. after ca. 1800.—3. Short for *benefit club* : coll. ; from ca. 1880. *To be on the club* is to receive financial help from a benefit club.—4. (the Club.) Blackheath Rugby Football Club : sporting coll. : late C. 19–20. —5. An illicit drinking-den : Glasgow lower classes' : C. 20. MacArthur & Long, *No Mean City*, 1935.

club, v. (Of an officer) to get one's men into an inextricable position by confusing the order : from ca. 1805 : coll. > S.E. by 1890. Thackeray, Whyte-Melville.

club-fist. A man rough and brutal : late C. 16–17 ; coll. > S.E. by 1620.

club-land. The social district of which St. James's (London) is the centre : coll. ; from ca. 1870.

clubbability. The possession of qualities fitting a person to be a member of a club : coll. : from ca. 1875.

clubs are trump(s). Brute force rules, or is to rule, the day : coll. in C. 19–20 ; S.E. in late C. 16–18. Punning the card-suit.

clump. A heavy blow, gen. with the hand : mid-C. 19–20 : coll. (mostly Cockney) and dial.—2. Incorrect for a *clamp* : C. 19–20. (O.E.D.)

clump, v. To hit heavily : mid-C. 19–20 : coll. and dial. The ppl. adj. *clumping* = heavily walking.

clumper. A thick walking boot : coll., from ca. 1875. Ex *clump*, an additional half-sole.—2. A heavy hitter : C. 19–20 : coll. Ex *clump*, v.

clumperton. A countryman ; a yokel : C. 16–early 19 ; coll.

clumping. See clump, v.

clumsy cleat. A wedge of wood against which a harpooner, for steadiness, braced his left knee : whalers' coll. verging on j. Bowen.

clumsy Dick. An awkward and/or clumsy fellow : non-aristocratic coll. (— 1887) ; ob. Baumann.

*clush. Easy, simple ; 'cushy' : c. : from ca. 1840 ; ob. by 1880, † by 1900. Etymology ?

clutch, put in one's. To fall silent : motorists' (ca. 1920) > gen. by : 1928, Galsworthy, *Swan Song*. Ex motoring.

clutch-fist. A miser : C. 17–20 ; coll. till ca. 1800, then S.E. Adj., *clutch-fisted*, as in B.E.

clutching hand, the. Jocularly coll., C. 20 : greed. On the verge of S.E.—2. A quartermaster-sergeant : military : G.W. Prob. ex a lurid film so named. F. & Gibbons.—3. A D.H.6 aeroplane : Air Force : 1917–18. F. & Gibbons : a de Havilland used ' as an elementary training machine '.

clutter. A crowded confusion, a mess or litter : in C. 17–early 19, S.E. ; then coll. and dial. A variant of *clotter* (ex *clot*). Whence ?

clutter, v. To litter confusedly and abundantly : ca. 1670–1840, S.E. ; now coll. and U.S. (S.O.D.)

*cly. A pocket ; a purse ; money : c., ? and low : late C. 17–19. Indubitably c. is the late C. 17–early 19 sense, money. B.E., Dyche, Grose. So is *file a cly*, late C. 17–18, to pick a pocket. As mid-C. 16–18 v., to seize, take, to pocket, to steal : c., ? and low. See cloy, n. and v.

cly, fake a. See fake a cly.

*cly-faker. A pickpocket : c. (— 1812) ; ob. Vaux.—2. Hence the vbl.n., *cly-faking* (— 1851) ; ob.

*cly off. To carry off, away : C. 17 (? 18) c. Brome in his *Jovial Crew*.

*cly the gerke or jerk. To receive a whipping, a lashing : c. of ca. 1550–1850. See jerk.

*clye. A C. 16–17 variant of *cly*.—*clyme. See cleyme.

clyster-pipe. A doctor : C. 17.—2. An apothecary : C. 18–early 19. Both senses are low coll., the latter in Grose. Ex S.E. for a syringe.

c'm. Come (only in the imperative) : sol., esp. Cockney : C. 19–20. John G. Brandon, *The One-Minute Murder*, 1934, ' C'm on and git it over.'

*co. (Also coe.) A shortening of *cofe* or (q.v.) *cove*.—2. Co. or coy, so pronounced, is a sol. for *company* : late C. 19–20. Esp., . . . *and Co.*, and the rest of them : coll. : from ca. 1880.—3. *co*, where used jocularly, is either pedantic or coll., according to circumstances.—4. in co ; esp. *act in co*, to be leagued together : coll. (— 1823) ; ob. ' Jon Bee.'—5. A co-respondent : mostly Society (— 1923). Manchon.

co, and. And the rest ; et cetera : naval : from ca. 1912. Hamish Maclaren, *The Private Opinions of a British Blue-Jacket*, 1929, ' Sor some nise eye-lands and come after spisse knut mags [*spice, nut-megs*] and co—some times purls '.

co-ed. Co-educational : coll. : from ca. 1920. Prob. suggested by the American *co-ed*, a girl at a co-educational school or college.

co-op ; co-op store. A co-operative store : the longer form, early 1870's ; the shorter, early 1880's. Also a co-operative society : from early 1890's. O.E.D. (Sup.).—2. Hence, *on the co-op*, on the co-operative principle : from ca. 1910 : like the others, it is coll. Ibid.

coach. A private tutor : at first (1848, says S.O.D.) a university word, orig. Cambridge ; s., says Frank Smedley in *Frank Fairleigh*, 1850 ; but very soon coll. If not connected with a college, he was, until ca. 1880, known as a *rural coach*.—2. As a trainer of athletes (1885), a coll. now almost S.E. Whichever of *cab*, a ' crib ' (q.v.), and *coach* is the earlier, that one presumably suggested the other : since *cab* comes ex *cabbage*, q.v., the earlier is prob. *cab*.

coach, v. To travel, go, in a coach : coll. : C. 17–20 ; ob. Occ. with *it*.—2. To prepare (a pupil), teach him privately : from ca. 1848 ; s. soon coll., orig. university, as in Thackeray.—3. To train athletes : from ca. 1880 ; coll.—4. V.i., to read or study with a private tutor : from ca. 1849 ; s. > coll.

coach-fellow, occ. -companion. A companion, fellow worker, mate : jocularly coll. : ca. 1590–1800. Shakespeare, in the *Merry Wives*, ' You, and your Coach-fellow Nim '.

coach-wheel. A crown piece : late C. 17–20 ; ob. Grose. In late C. 17–19, *fore c.-w.*, half a crown ; *hind c.-w.*, a crown. B.E.

coach-whip. A Navy pennant : nautical : from ca. 1890. Cf. *duster*, q.v.

coachee, coachie, coachy. A coachman : late C. 18–20 ; ob. Coll. Thomas Moore, 1819, in *Tom Crib's Memorial*, in form *coachee*. See *-y*.—2. (Coachee.) See Billy Blue.

coaches won't run over him, the. He is in gaol: coll. (— 1813); † by 1900. Ray, 1813 (Apperson). Cf. *where the flies won't get at it* (see flies).

coaching. Private instruction (actively or passively): from ca. 1845. Coll.—2. (Rugby School) a flogging: C. 19; ob. by 1891.—3. The obtaining of high auction-prices by means of fictitious bidders: commercial (— 1866); ob. O.E.D.

coachy, adj. Resembling a coach-horse: coll. (— 1870). O.E.D.—2. Concerned with coaches or coach-driving: from ca. 1880; coll.

coachy, n. See coachee.

*coal, money: see cole.—2. A penny: grafters': C. 20. P. Allingham, *Cheapjack*, 1934.

coal and coke. Penniless: rhyming s. (on *broke*): C. 20.

coal-box. A chorus: music-hall, ca. 1850–1915. Mark Lemon in *Up and Down London Streets.*—2. A German shell that, of low velocity, bursts with a dense cloud of black smoke; esp. a 5·9: military: Oct. 1914. B. & P. Cf. *black Maria.*

coal-chisel. Incorrect for *cold chisel*: C. 18–20. (P. MacDonald, *R.I.P.*, 1933.)

coal-heaver. A penny, in the game of Crown and Anchor: military (and naval): C. 20. F. & Gibbons. Ex its colour.

Coal-Heavers, the. The Grenadier Guards: military: mid-C. 18–20. F. & Gibbons. Ex officers letting out soldiers to civilian employers. In C. 19–20, also *the Coalies.*

coal-hole, a. Work down in the coal-hole, often given as punishment to a working hand: *Conway* Training Ship: from ca. 1890.

coal-sack. Cul-de-sac: sol. (— 1909). Ware. —2. (Gen. pl.) A dark patch of cloud near the Milky Way: nautical: mid-C. 19–20. Bowen.

coal-scuttle (bonnet), n. and adj. A poke bonnet: from ca. 1830; ob., the fashion being outmoded by 1880—if not earlier. Dickens, in *Nicholas Nickleby,* '. . . Miss Snevellici . . . glancing from the depths of her coal-scuttle bonnet at Nicholas'.

coal up. To eat (heartily): stokers' (— 1909); slightly ob. Ware.

coal-whipper. A dock coal-heaver: nautical: C. 19. Bowen, 'Unloading . . by jumping off a staging in the days of primitive equipment'.

coaler. A coal-heaver: coll. (— 1887) verging on S.E. Baumann. Cf. *coaly.*

coaley, coalie. See coaly and Coal-Heavers. Coalies, the. See Coal-Heavers, the.

coaling or coally. (Of a part) effective, pleasant to the actor: from ca. 1850, ob. Also, fond of, partial to: ca. 1870–1910, e.g. Miss Braddon in *Dead Sea Fruit.* Theatrical.

coals, blow or stir the. To cause trouble between two parties: coll.; resp. C. 17–20, C. 16–18; ob. Both soon > S.E.

coals, call or fetch or haul over the. To call to task; reprimand; address severely: coll., resp. C. 19–20, late C. 16–18, late C. 18–20. Ex the treatment once meted out to heretics. See also haul, v., 2.

coals, carry no. To be unlikely to be imposed on, swindled, or tamely insulted: coll.: C. 16–19. B.E., whose definition is somewhat more racy. A C. 16–17 variant, as in Skelton, is *bear no coals.*

coals, let him that hath need blow the. 'Let him Labour that wants,' B.E.; also, stop no man from working. Coll. and proverbial: C. 17–18.

coals !, precious. See precious coals !

coals, take in one's (or one's winter). To catch a venereal disease: nautical, C. 19.

[coals of fire on the head of, heap : to return good for evil: has always, because of its Biblical connexion, been S.E.]

coals to Newcastle, carry. To do something ludicrously superfluous: late C. 16–20, being coll. till ca. 1830, then S.E. Heywood, Fuller, Scott. (Apperson.)

coaly, coaley, coalie. A coal-heaver or -porter: from ca. 1860. Mayhew.

Coast, the. The bank of the River Paraguay: coll., among Englishmen in S. America: C. 20. C. W. Thurlow Craig.

coast; coaster. To loaf, a loafer, about from station to station: Australian coll. (— 1890); ob. Morris.

coast is clear, the. See clear, the coast is.

coaster. See coast.—2. (Or C–.) A white man living on the Gold Coast: coll.; late C. 19–20.

*coat, v. To reprimand, esp. of a warder reprimanding a prisoner: C. 20 c.

coat, baste or coil or pay a person's. To beat him: C. 16–18: coll. Cf. *dust one's jacket.*

coat . . ., cut one's. See cloth.

coat, get the sun into a horse's. To allow a horse to rest from formal racing; hence, (of a trainer) to save oneself trouble: racing, from ca. 1880; †. *The Standard*, June 25 or 26, 1889: a forensic speech by Sir Charles Russell.

coat, turn one's. To desert one's cause or party: mid-C. 16–19: coll. >, by 1800, S.E.

coat, wear the King's. To serve as a soldier: from ca. 1750; coll. till C. 19, when S.E.; in C. 20, archaic. Cf. *wear the King's uniform.*

coat and badge. To cadge: military rhyming s.: C. 20. B. & P.

*coating, vbl.n. Giving a prisoner's history: c. (— 1935). David Hume. I.e. fitting him up nicely.

coax. One who coaxes, or is skilled in coaxing: coll.: from ca. 1860. Ouida (O.E.D.).

coax, v. To hide a dirty or torn part of one's stocking in one's shoes: mid-C. 18–early 19; coll. Grose, 2nd ed.—2. Hence, to deface or alter (a service-certificate): nautical: mid C. 19–20. Bowen.

cob. A chignon: coll.: ca. 1865–1914.—2. (Winchester College, ca. 1870–1930) a hard hit at cricket. Ex *cob*, v., 1.—3. In c., a punishment cell: from ca. 1860; ob. Perhaps cognate with :

cob, cobb, v. To strike, esp. on the buttocks with something flat (gen. a hand-saw, says Hotten): nautical (— 1769). Marryat in the *King's Own*: 'Gentlemen, gentlemen, if you must cobb Mrs. Skrimmage, for God's sake *let it be over all,*' i.e. with no clothes raised. Prob. echoic.—2. Hence, to humbug, deceive: coll., C. 19–20, ob., perhaps influenced by *cod.*—3. To detect, catch: schoolboys', C. 19. A variant of *cop*, v.: q.v.

cob o' coal. Unemployment relief: workmen's rhyming s. (on *dole*): from ca. 1925. *John o' London's Weekly*, June 9, 1934.

cob on, have a. To be annoyed: ships' stewards' (— 1935). Perhaps ex dial. *cob*, to strike, or the game of *cob-nuts.*

Cobb, by. By coach: Australian coll.: from 1870's; slightly ob. Morris. The Cobb who started a system of coaches long before 1860 was an American.

cobber. A great lie : C. 19–20, ob. Cf. *thumper*.
—2. A friend, comrade, companion : Australians' :
C. 20. A trustworthy correspondent (a writing
man) tells me that he heard it among racing-men of
the lower sort in the year 1900. Ex Yiddish *chaber*,
a comrade (cf. *cliner*). Dr Thomas Wood, *Cobbers*,
1934. See *Words !*, pp. 27–8.

cobbing, vbl.n. To *cob*, v., 1.

cobble. To detect ; catch : schoolboys' : C. 19.
Ex *to cob*, 3.

***cobble-colter.** A turkey, late C. 17–18 c., was
resuscitated by Disraeli in *Venetia*, his most
picaresque novel. *Cobble* = *gobble*.

cobbler. A drink of wine mixed with lemon-
juice, sugar, and ice, gen. taken through a straw :
coll. ; from ca. 1840 ; ex U.S. ? short for *sherry-
cobbler* ; cf. *cobbler's punch* ; perhaps, however,
' as patching up the constitution ', W.—2. The last
sheep to be shorn : Australian : from ca. 1890.
Ex *the cobbler's last*. Morris.—3. A ball : grafters' :
late C. 19–20. (P. Allingham, *Cheapjack*, 1934.)
Prob. ex *cobblers* (q.v.), abbr. *cobblers' stalls* (or
curls), low rhyming s.

***cobblers.** Testicles (human) : c. : C. 20.
James Curtis, *The Gilt Kid*, 1936.

Cobblers, the. The Northampton Association
Football Club : sporting : late C. 19–20. *The
News Chronicle*, Dec. 27, 1934, caption, ' Cobblers
Yield a Point.' Boots and shoes are made in pro-
fusion at Northampton.

**cobbler's door, knock at the ; give the cobbler's
knock.** In sliding or, less often, in skating, to rap
the ice in series of three taps with one foot while one
moves rapidly on the other. This rapping is occ.
called *the postman's knock*. Dickens in *Pickwick
Papers*. Coll. ; from ca. 1820.

cobbler's marbles. Sol. for *cholera morbus*, itself
catachrestic for malignant or Asiatic cholera : from
ca. 1860 ; ob.

cobbler's punch. See **punch, cobbler's.**

Cob's body, by). In oaths, a coll. corruption of
God's body : C. 18. (O.E.D.)

cobweb, in late C. 17–early 18, seems to have been
coll. for transparent or flimsy : B.E. cites *cobweb
cheat*, a swindler easily detected, and *cobweb
pretence*.

cobweb in the throat, have a. To feel thirsty :
coll. : from ca. 1830.—2. Hence, *cobweb throat*, a
dry throat after drinking liquor : late C. 19–20 ;
ob. A. H. Dawson's *Dict. of Slang*, 1913.

cocam. An occ. form of **cocum**, q.v.

cochineal dye. Blood : pugilistic ; ca. 1850–
1910. ' Cuthbert Bede ', 1853 : ' He would kindly
inquire of one gentleman, " What d' ye ask for a pint
of your cochineal dye ? " ' For semantics, cf.
bordeaux and *claret*.

cock. The penis : 1730, says S.O.D., but F. &
H.'s example from Beaumont & Fletcher's scabrous
play, *The Custom of the Country*, seems valid.
Always S.E. but since ca. 1830 a vulg. Prob. ex
cock, a tap.—2. A plucky fighter ; hence, a coll.
term of appreciation or address. Massinger, in
1639, has ' He has drawn blood of him yet : well
done, old cock.'—3. As chief or leader, despite the
coll. tang of *cock of the walk, the school*, etc., it has,
since 1800 in any case, been S.E., the term arising in
early C. 15.—4. A horse not intended to run or, if
running, to win : racing ; from ca. 1840 ; ob.—
5. In boxing, *a cock* = out, senseless, as in ' He
knocked him a regular cock ' or simply ' . . . a
cock ', where the term > an adv : ca. 1820–1920,

but ob. by 1900.—6. A fictitious narrative sold as a
broadsheet in the streets : low coll., recorded by
Mayhew in 1851 but prob. in use as early as 1840 ;
† by 1900. From ca. 1860 it derivatively meant any
incredible story, as in *The London Figaro*, Feb. 1,
1870, ' We are disposed to think that cocks must
have penetrated to Eastern Missouri.' Prob. ex
cock and bull story.—7. In c., abbr. *Cockney,
cockney*.—8. Among printers, a cock ensues when,
in gambling with quads, a player receives another
chance by causing one or more of the nine pieces to
fall, not flat as desired but, crosswise on another :
from ca. 1860, ob. by 1920.—9. Among tailors,
from ca. 1840, *a good cock* is a good, a *bad cock* a bad
workman.—[10. In ancient oaths, *cock* = God.—]
11. See **old cock.**—12. See **cocks.**

cock, v. To smoke (v.t.) : C. 19. Cf. *Broseley*.
—2. To copulate with, but gen. in the passive : low
coll., C. 19–20, ob. Whence vbl.n., *cocking*, and cf.
(*with*) *a cock in her eye* : sexually desirous.—3. To
see, examine ; speak of : gen. as *cock it* : tailors',
from ca. 1850 ; ob.—4. See **cock it over.**

cock. Adj. ex the n., 3 : chief ; foremost : coll. ;
from ca. 1660 ; ob. Etherege, in *The Man of Mode*,
' The very cock-fool of all those fools, Sir Fopling
Flutter '.

cock-a-bully. The gray (fish) : New Zealand
coll. (— 1896). Morris. A corruption of the
Maori name, *kokopu*.

cock-a-doodle. A ' donkey-drop ' (q.v.) : schoolboys' : ca. 1880–1910. Ex its ' high note '.

cock-a-doodle broth. Beaten eggs in brandy and
water : 1856 ; very ob. (Very strengthening.)

cock-a-doodle(-doo). Nursery and jocular for a
cock : C. 18–20. Echoic ex its crow (1573, O.E.D.)

cock-a-hoop (incorrectly-*whoop*). From ca. 1660 :
coll., in C. 20 S.E. : in C. 17–early 19, ' upon the high
Ropes, Rampant, Transported ' (B.E.), but only
predicative or complementary ; ca. 1830 it > an
ordinary adj. Ex the earlier *set* (*the*) *cock on* (*the*)
hoop or, as in Shakespeare, *set cock-a-hoop*, which
Ray explains by the practice of removing the cock
or spigot, laying it on the hoop, i.e. on the top, of a
barrel, and then drinking the barrel dry.

cock-a-loft. ' Affectedly lofty ', O.E.D. : coll. :
from ca. 1860 ; ob. Ex *cock-loft*.

cock a snook. See **cock snooks.**

cock-a-wax ; occ. **cock-o-wax.** A cobbler : ca.
1800–50. Lit., a fellow working with wax.—2.
Hence, anyone familiarly addressed : ca. 1860–
1900 : coll. H., 3rd ed. Ex *cock*, n., 2. Variant
lad o(f) wax.

cock-ale. A strong ale : ' pleasant drink, said to
be provocative ', remarks B.E. : coll. ; ca. 1680–
1830. Ned Ward ; Grose.

cock-alley. Also *c.-hall, -inn, -lane, -pit*, and
Cockshire. All low coll. : C. 18–20, the second and
the third being †, the fifth and sixth ob. *Pudendum
muliebre*.

cock-and-breeches. A sturdy boy, a small but
sturdy man : low coll. : from ca. 1830 ; ob.

cock-and-bull story. In this form from ca. 1700 ;
as *story* or *tale of a cock and a bull* from ca. 1608 :
coll., passing ca. 1850 to S.E. At first, a long rambling tale, then (C. 18–20) an idle, silly or incredible
story. John Day in *Law Tricks*, Sterne in *Tristram
Shandy*, Mrs. Henry Wood in *Henry Ludlow*. Cf.
the Fr. *coq-à-l'âne*.

***cock and hen.** A £10 note : thieves' and low
rhyming s. : from ca. 1870. *Slang*, p. 243.—2.
Hence, ten : C. 20. B. & P.—3. (Gen. **cockernen.**)

A pen : rhyming s., esp. grafters' : C. 20. Philip Allingham, *Cheapjack*, 1934.

cock-and-hen. (Gen. with *club*, occ. with *house*.) Adj. : admitting both sexes, for the once or constitutionally : coll. ; from ca. 1815. Moore in *Tom Crib's Memorial*.

cock and (by) pie !, by. A mild oath : coll. : mid-C. 16–mid-19. Thackeray. Perhaps *Cock*, God + *pie*, a Roman Catholic ordinal. (O.E.D.)

cock-and-pinch. The beaver hat affected by dandies of ca. 1820–30 ; † by 1900. Coll. (*Cocked* back and front and *pinched* up at the sides.)

cock-bawd. A man keeping a brothel : ca. 1680–1830 : low coll. B.E., Grose.

cock-billed. With yards crooked as a sign of mourning : nautical : late C. 19–20. Bowen. Cf. *a-cock bill*.

cock-brain. A silly light-headed person : late C. 16–18 ; coll. Adj., *cock-brained*.

cock-catching. See **catch cocks**.

cock-chafer or **-teaser.** A girl or a woman permitting—and assuming—most of the intimacies but not the greatest : low coll. (the latter term is far the commoner) : *c.-c.*, C. 19 ; *c.-t.*, C. 19–20.—2. Also low coll. is *c.-c.* = the *pudendum muliebre*, C. 19–20, while, 3, in c. of ca. 1860–90, it = the treadmill ; the latter (H., 2nd ed.) is unhyphenated.

cock-eye. A squinting-eye : recorded in 1825 ; *cock-eyed*, squinting : Byron, 1821. Both are coll. (O.E.D.).—Hence, 2, *cock-eye* and *cock-eyed*, from ca. 1895, = crooked ; inaccurate ; inferior. Lit., like a ' tilted ' eye.

cock-eyed. See **cock-eye**, 2.—2. Tipsy : from ca. 1930. Maurice Lincoln, *Oh ! Definitely*, 1933.

cock-eyed Bob. A thunderstorm off N.W. Australia : Western Australian (— 1894), hence pearlers' (— 1929). Morris ; Bowen. Applied also to a violent wind-storm off this coast, as in Ion L. Idriess, *Flynn of the Inland*, 1932.

cock-fighting, beat. To be very good or delightful ; to excel : coll., C. 19–20, though foreshadowed in Gauden's *Tears of the Church*, 1659.

cock-hall. See **cock-alley**.

cock-hoist. A cross-buttock : late C. 18–early 19 : coll. till C. 19, then j. Grose, 2nd ed.

cock-horse. Elated, cock-a-hoop, in full swing : ca. 1750–1870 ; coll. Ex (*ride*) *a cock-horse*, a child's improvised horse.

Cock Inn. The female pudend : low : C. 19–20 ; ob. Cf. *Cupid's Arms* and see **cock-alley**.

cock it ! There it is ! ; that's done it ! ; gone ! : lower classes' (— 1923). Manchon.

cock it over (a person). To ' boss ', to impose on : coll. (— 1923). Manchon. Ex *cock*, n., 3.

cock-lane. See **cock-alley**. Grose, 1st ed.

cock-linnet. A minute : rhyming s. (— 1909). Ware.—2. A dapper lad : East London (— 1909). Ibid.

cock-loft. The head : mid-C. 17–18 ; coll. Fuller, 1646 (Apperson). Lit., a garret ; cf. the proverbial *all his gear is in his cock-loft* and *garret* and *upper storey*.

cock-maggot in a sink-hole, like a. Very annoyed or peevish : proletarian coll. (— 1887) ; slightly ob. Baumann.

cock-o-wax. See **cock-a-wax**.

cock one's chest. The naval equivalent (—1909) of *chuck a chest*, q.v. Ware.

cock one's toes (up). To die : from ca. 1860 ; slightly ob. H., 3rd ed. Cf. the much more gen. *turn up one's toes*.

cock-pimp. A supposed, rarely an actual, husband to a bawd ; i.e. a harlot's bully : late C. 17–18 coll. B.E.

cock-pit, cockpit, the. A Dissenters' meeting-house : late C. 18–early 19. Grose, 1st ed. (at *pantile-house*).—2. The Treasury ; the Privy Council : a London coll. ; from ca. 1870. Ex an old Whitehall *cockpit*.—3. See **cock-alley**.

cock-quean. A man concerning himself unduly in women's affairs : either a sol. or a jocular perversion of *cotquean* : ca. 1830–80.

cock-robin. A soft, easy fellow : coll. : from ca. 1690 ; ob. B.E. ; Grose ; Montagu Williams, *Leaves of a Life*, 1890.

cock-robin shop. A small printery : printers', from late 1850's ; ob. H., 1st ed.

cock-shot. Anything set up as a target ; a shot thereat : coll. : resp. ca. 1840, 1880. O.E.D.

cock-shut. Twilight (also an adj.) : coll. > S.E. > dial. Recorded in 1598, 1594 : ' perhaps the time when poultry are shut up ', S.O.D.

cock-shy. Coll. ; in C. 20 verging on and by 1930 being virtually S.E. Cock-throwing and similar games : mid-C. 19–20. Mayhew.—2. A free ' shy ' at a target : from mid-1830's.—3. The missile : rare and ob. : from late 1830's.—4. The target (lit. or fig.) : 1836.—5. A showman's cock-shy ' booth ', etc. : from late 1870's. O.E.D.—6. *cock-shying* : see 1 and 2 : late 1870's. O.E.D.

cock-smitten. Enamoured of men : low coll., C. 19–20.

cock snooks or **a snook.** To put one's fingers derisively to nose : coll. ; late C. 19–20.

cock-sparrow. A barrow : rhyming s. : late C. 19–20. J. Phillips, *Dict. of Rhyming Slang*, 1931.

cock-stand. A priapism : a vulg. : C. 18–20.

cock-sucker. A toady : low coll. : C. 19–20. Mostly (? orig.) U.S.

cock-sure. Feeling quite certain (from ca. 1660) ; dogmatically sure of oneself (from ca. 1750). Coll. till ca. 1890, then S.E. Semantics obscure ; perhaps ex the action of a *cock* or water-tap ; perhaps a euphemism for *God-sure* (W.),—cf. *cock* for *God* in oaths.

cock-tail. A harlot : low coll. ; C. 19–20, ob.—2. A person of energy and promptness but not a ' thoroughbred ' : from ca. 1855 ; coll. Ex racing j.—Hence, 3, a coward : coll. ; from ca. 1860.—4. A whisked drink of spirits, occ. wine, with bitters, crushed ice, etc. : orig. (1809), U.S. ; anglicised ca. 1870 ; popularised in England during the G.W., when it > S.E. In senses 3 and 4, the usual spelling is *cocktail*, which, in C. 20, is the only spelling of sense 4.

cock-tail, -tailed, adj. Unsoldierly ; guilty of ' bad form ' : military, ca. 1880–1914. Either ex the n., 2nd and 3rd senses, or ex *turn cocktail*, i.e. to cock the tail, turn, and run.

cock-teaser. See **cock-chafer**. Often, as Manchon (1923) mentions, euphemistically abbr. to *C.-T.*

cock the eye. To wink ; leer ; look incredulous or knowing : from ca. 1750 : coll. until ca. 1800, then S.E. Smollett, in *Peregrine Pickle*, 1751, ' He . . . made wry faces, and, to use the vulgar phrase, cocked his eye at him.' (*Cock an eye* is merely, to glance.) Cf. *cock the nose*, (S.E. for) to turn it up in contempt.

cock-up. (Of a schoolmaster or monitor) to beat ; whence vbl.n. *cocking-up* : Charterhouse : C. 20.

cock-up. (Printers') a superior, i.e. a superior letter, as the o in N° ; from ca. 1860.

cock (up) one's toes. To die : c. and low ; from early C. 19. 'Fancy' Reynolds.

cock won't fight, that. That won't do ! That's a feeble story ! Tell that to the marines ! From the 1820's † : coll. Scott, *St. Roman's Well*, 1824 (E.D.D.). Ex the cock-pit.

cockalorum, occ. **cockylorum.** A very confident little man : coll. : 1715. Often as slightly contemptuous vocative. As adj., self-confident or -important : 1884 +. Ex *cock*, a leader (see **cock**, n., 2, 3), pseudo-L. *orum* ; cf. *cock-a-doodle-doo* (W.).

cockalorum (jig), hey or **high.** A coll. exclamation : from ca. 1860 ; ob. Prob. ex an old song-refrain.—As a schoolboys' game (leap-frog), S.E.

cockatoo. A small farmer : orig. in the wool districts and by the big squatters : from ca. 1863. (In C. 20, always **cocky**.) Australian : coll. Henry Kingsley in *Hillyars and Burtons*, 'The small farmers contemptuously called cockatoos '. Perhaps ex the crowding of cockatoos on new-sown corn.—2. Also as adj.—3. In C. 20 Australian c., a scout that gives warning of a policeman's approach.

cockatoo, v. To be a (small) farmer : coll. (— 1890). Boldrewood. Morris. Ex n., 1.

cockatoo fence. A fence made by a small farmer : Australian coll. (— 1884). Boldrewood in *Melbourne Memories*. Morris.

cockatooer. A ' cockatoo ' (sense 1): Tasmanian : ca. 1850–80. Morris.

cockatrice. A harlot ; a kept woman : late C. 16–18. Coll. Ben Jonson in *Cynthia's Revels* ; Marston in his most famous work, *The Malcontent* : ' No courtier but has his mistress, no captain but has his cockatrice ' ; Taylor, 1630 ; Killigrew.—2. A baby : coll. : C. 18–19. Resp. ex the fascination of the fabulous monster's eye, and the egg from which it was fabulously hatched.

***cockchafer.** See **cock-chafer**, 3.

cocked hat, knock into a. To damage very considerably (things, persons, and fig.) : coll. ; from ca. 1850. Orig. (1833 : Thornton), U.S. An officer's cocked hat could be doubled up and carried flat.

cocked-hat club. ' The principal clique amongst the members of the Society of Antiquaries.' At their meetings, a cocked hat lies before the president : ca. 1860–90. H., 3rd ed.

cocker. A foreman : tailors' : from ca. 1860.—2. A coll. Cockney term of address, dating from ca. 1870 ; ob. Clarence Rook, *The Hooligan Nights*, 1899. An extension (influenced by *cocky*, 3) of S.E. *cocker*, a supporter of cock-fighting.

Cocker, according to. See **at according to Cocker.**

cockernen. See **cock and hen**, n., 3.

cockie. See **cocky**, 1, 3.

cockies' joy. Treacle : Australian : late C. 19–20. See **cocky**, 5.

cockily. In a cocky manner : coll. ; from ca. 1860.

cockiness. Conceit ; undue self-assertion : coll. : from early 1860's.

cocking. Pert ; impudent : ca. 1670–1830 ; coll. *The Spectator*, 1711, ' The cocking young fellow '.

cocking a chest like a half-pay admiral. Putting on ' side ' : naval : late C. 19–20. Bowen.

cocking-up. See **cock-up.**

cockish. ' Wanton, uppish, forward ', B.E. : C. 16–20 : coll. > S.E. ca. 1800. As = lecherous

it is applied gen. to women and, except in dial., it > ob. ca. 1860.

cockles. (Always in pl.) *Labia minora* : C. 18–20 ; low coll. *Play at hot cockles*—see Northall's *English Folk-Rhymes*—is, in addition to its S.E. sense, *feminam digitis subagitare* : C. 18–20, low coll., ob.

cockles, cry. To be hanged : late C. 18–mid-19 : low. Grose, 2nd ed. Ex the gurgling of strangulation.

cockles of the heart, rejoice, warm, tickle the. To please mightily, cheer up : coll. ; from ca. 1669. Eachard, in his *Observations*, 1671, ' This contrivance of his did inwardly rejoice the cockles of his heart.' The S.O.D. mentions the proposed derivation ex the similarity of a heart to a cockle-shell and that ex *cardium*, the zoological name for a cockle ; F. & H. refers to Lower's once famous *Tractatus de Corde* (*A Treatise of the Heart*), 1669, where the term *cochlea* is used. The first is the likeliest.

cockloche. (Apparently =) a foolish coxcomb : C. 17. ? ex Fr. *coqueluche*.

cockney or **Cockney,** n. and adj. (One) born in the city of London : 1600 +. Coll. till ca. 1830 and nearly always pejorative. Orig. and until ca. 1870, ' born within the sound of Bow-bell ', B.E. Ex *cockney* = a milksop, earlier a cockered, i.e. pampered, child, a sense that developed from (?) *cock's eggs*, small eggs. The full history of this fascinating word has not yet been written, but see esp. O.E.D., Sir James Murray in *The Academy* of May 10, 1890 ; also W. and Grose, P. For an account of Cockney ' dialect ', see *Slang*, pp. 149–59. See also ' Cockney speech ' in Addenda.

Cockney-shire. London : C. 19–20, ob. ; coll.

Cockoolu. See **mounseer.**

cockpit mess. Eating one's meals in the cockpit with a marine sentry at hand—a punishment in the old training ship *Britannia* : naval : late C. 19–early 20. Bowen.

cockroach. A very small pearl-fishing boat : pearl-fishers' (— 1935). Because cockroach-infested.

cockroaches, get. See **box the Jesuit.**

cocks. (In trade, applied to) anything fictitious : ca. 1860–1910. Ex *cock*, n., 6.—2. Hence, esp., concoctions : pharmaceutists' (— 1909). Ware.—3. At Charterhouse (school), a gen. lavatory : from ca. 1860 ; ob. Ex the taps over the wash-bowls. See esp. A. H. Tod, *Charterhouse*, 1900.

cock's egg, give one a. To send on a fool's errand, esp. on April the First. Coll. : rare before C. 19, and ob. in C. 20. Cf. *pigeon's milk, strap oil*, and see *All Fools' Day* in *Words !*

cock's tooth and head-ache, I live at the sign of the. A late C. 18–early 19 c.p. answer to an impertinent inquiry where one lives. Grose, 3rd ed.

Cockshire. See **cock-alley.**

cocksy, coxy. Pert ; impudent ; bumptious : 1825 : (mostly schoolboys') coll. ; in C. 20 S.E. Ex *cocky* after *tricksy*. For second spelling, cf. *coxcomb* ex *cock's-comb*.

cocktail. See **cock-tail.**

cocky. An endearment : coll. : from ca. 1680 ; ob., except among Canadians and Cockneys. Ex (*old*) *cock*.—2. Adj., very pert ; saucily impudent ; over-confident : 1768 : coll. (cf. *cocking*). Hughes in *Tom Brown's School-Days*, ' It seems so cocky in me to be advising you.'—3. A low coll. form of address, ex *cock*, and presumably a chance-revival of *cocky* as an endearment : from ca. 1850.—4.

Brisk, active, as applied to the money market : Stock Exchange, ca. 1860–1910.—5. Abbr. *cockatoo*, q.v., a small farmer in Australia : from ca. 1880 (Sala speaks of it in 1887) and very gen., often non-pejorative, in C. 20.

cockylorum. See **cockalorum.**

cockyolly bird. Dear little bird : nursery and pet term (coll.) : from ca. 1830.

cocky's joy. See **cockies' joy.**

coco-nut (here, as in S.E., erroneously *cocoa-nut*) ; sol., *coker-nut*. The head : mainly boxing : from ca. 1830. Ainsworth. Cf. *boco*, q.v., and U.S. *coco(a)*.

cocoa for **coco** dates from an error in Johnson's Dict. ; moreover, as used for the earlier *cacao*, *cocoa* was orig. (C. 18) erroneous. W.—2. A schoolboys' perversion of *toko*, q.v. : late C. 19–early 20. Ware.

*****cocoa.** To say ; say so : c. rhyming s. : C. 20. James Curtis, *The Gilt Kid*, 1936, ' I should cocoa.'

coco(a)-nut, have no milk in the. To lack brains ; to be silly, even mad. From ca. 1850. See **coco-nut.**

coco(a)-nut, that accounts for the milk in the. A c.p. rejoinder on first hearing a thing explained : ca. 1860–1910. Ex ' a clever but not very moral story ', H., 5th ed. See **coco-nut.**

cocum(-am), cokum, kocum. Ability, shrewd-ness, cleverness ; that which is seemly, right, cor-rect ; luck, advantage : rather low (— 1851). Mayhew in *London Labour* ; *The Flippity Flop Young Man*, a ballad, ca. 1886.—2. A sliding scale of profit : publishers', ca. 1870–1914. Ex Yiddish c. *kochem*, wisdom. Cf. :

cocum, fight or **play.** To be cunning, wary, art-ful, esp. if illicitly : from late 1830's. Brandon, 1839 ; H., 1st ed. Likewise, *have cocum*, to have luck or an advantage ; be sure to succeed. Perhaps cognate with Ger. *gucken*, to peep or pry into ; but see preceding entry.

cod. The scrotum : from M.E. ; S.E., but in C. 19–20 a vulg. Ex O.E., M.E., S.E. and dial. sense, a pod.—2. In pl., a sol. for testicles : also from M.E.—3. In c., a purse ; whence *cod of money* = a large sum : late C. 17–early 19. B.E.—4. A fool : from ca. 1690 ; ob. Perhaps ex *cod's head*, also a fool : B.E. has both.—5. A friend, a ' pal ' : from — 1690, B.E. giving ' *an honest Cod*, a trusty Friend '. Abbr. *codlin(g)*, says F. & H. with reason. —6. (Often as *codd*) a pensioner of the Charterhouse : Charterhouse, ca. 1820–1905. Thackeray in *The Newcomes*. Perhaps ex *codger*.—7. A drunkard ; a drinking bout : tailors' (— 1909). Ware. Cf. n., 4, and *cod*, v., 2.

cod, v. To chaff ; hoax ; humbug ; play the fool : v.t. and i. : from ca. 1870. H., 5th ed. Ex *cod*, n., 4.—2. To go on a drinking or a womanis-ing spree : tailors' ; from ca. 1870 ; ob.—3. In C. 18 c., to cheat.

cod, on the. Drinking heavily : tailors' : late C. 19–20. Cf. *cod*, n., 7.

cod-banger. A gorgeously arrayed sailor : Bil-lingsgate (— 1909). Ware. Cod are banged on the head when wanted for market.

cod-hauler. A ship, or a man, from Newfound-land : nautical : mid-C. 19–20. Bowen. Ex the fisheries there.

cod-heids. Boots (or shoes) burst at the toes : Glasgow proletarian (— 1934).

cod-piece or collar ?, do they bite in the (with slight variations). ' A jocular attack on a patient angler

by watermen, &c.', Grose, 1st ed. : a mid-C. 18–early 19 c.p. *Cod(-)piece* : fore-flap of a man's breeches, C. 16–18.

Cod Preserves, the. The Atlantic Ocean : nautical : from ca. 1840 ; ob.

cod-whanger. A man engaged in fish-curing in Newfoundland : nautical : late C. 19–20. Bowen. Cf. *cod-hauler.*

coddam, coddem, coddom. A public-house and extremely elementary guessing-game played with a coin or a button : from ca. 1880 ; coll. I.e. *cod 'em.*

codder. One very fond of hoaxing or chaffing : from ca. 1860. Ex *cod*, v., 1.

codding, vbl.n. Chaff, humbug ; fooling ; non-sense : from ca. 1860.

coddle. One who is coddled or who coddles him-self : coll. ; (— 1830, when used by) Miss Mitford in *Our Village*. O.E.D.

coddom. See **coddam.**

coddy. ' A temporary foreman over a steve-dore's employees ' : nautical : late C. 19–20. Bowen. He ' cods ' 'em along.

coddy-moddy. A young gull : nautical : mid-C. 19–20. Bowen.

codge. A repair ; to repair : tailors' (— 1935). Much earlier in dial. ; perhaps a perversion of *botch.*

codger ; occ. **coger.** (Whimsically pejorative of) an old man : low coll. : 1756. Gen. with *old*, as in Colman's *Polly Honeycomb*, ' A clear coast, I find. The old codger's gone, and has locked me up with his daughter ' ; Smollett ; Barham.—2. During the approximate period 1830–1900, it occ. = a fellow, a chap. Dickens. ? ex *cadger.*

codling. A raw youth : ca. 1600–1750 ; coll. In late C. 18–early 19 (cf. C. 19–20 ob. *pippin*), a familiar term of address ; an endearment.

codocity. Gullibility : printers' : 1874 ; ob. Ware. Ex *cod*, n., 4, and v., 1.

Codrington's Manors ; Mostyn's Hunting Dis-trict ; Somerset Range. ' The three packs of hounds contiguous to Oxford ' : Oxford University : ca. 1820–40. Egan's Grose.

cods. See *cod*, n., 2.—2. (Cf. *ballocks*, q.v.) A curate : mid-C. 18–early 19 low. Grose, 1st ed. Often as *cods the curate*.—3. *The Bookseller*, Nov. 4, 1871 : ' The Cods and Hooks were the Whigs and Tories of Dutch William's land.'—4. With variant *cod's* ; a mid-C. 16–early 18 perversion or corruption of *God's*.

cods' eyes and bath-water. Tapioca pudding : Charterhouse : C. 20.

cod's-head. A fool : ca. 1560–1850. (Dunton in his ironically titled *Ladies' Dict.*, 1694.) In mid-C. 19–20 (ob.), as *cod's-head and shoulders*. Both forms are coll. Perhaps the source of *cod* = a fool.

cod's head and mackerel tail(, with). A sailing ship with the greatest beam well forward : nautical : mid-C. 19–20 ; ob. Bowen.

cod's opera. A smoking concert : tailors' : C. 20.

*****coe.** See **co**, 1.

coelebacy. Incorrect for *celibacy* : C. 17. O.E.D. Cf. *cœlo-* for *cœlo-.*

*****cofe.** An early variant of *cove*, q.v. (E.g. in B.E.) Likewise *coff* : C. 16.

coffee-and-b. Coffee and brandy : night-taverns' : 1880 ; ob. Ware.

coffee-colour. (Applied to persons) of mixed parentage : Anglo-Indian coll. (— 1886). Yule & Burnell. Cf. *annas of dark blood*, q.v.

coffee-house. The *pudendum muliebre*: low: late C. 18–19. Ex the popularity of coffee-houses in late C. 17–18.—2. A water-closet (variant *coffeeshop*): late C. 18–20, ob. Grose, 3rd ed.

coffee-house, -houser, -housing. To gossip during a fox-hunt, esp. while the huntsmen wait for hounds to draw a covert; one who does this; the act of doing this: sporting: from ca. 1875. Hawley Smart, in *Play or Pay*, ch. iv, 1878, speaking of horses: '. . . A hack, just good enough to do a bit of coffee-housing occasionally'. F. & H.; O.E.D. (Sup.).

coffee-mill. The mouth: ca. 1800–70. Moncrieff, ' Come, come, silence your coffee-mill.'—2. A marine engine: nautical: late C. 19–20. Bowen.

coffee-milling, vbl.n. ' Grinding ', working hard. Dickens, 1837. Aytoun & Martin's ' coffee-milling care and sorrow ' illustrates *c.-m.* as a v., to thumb one's nose at. Both ca. 1830–1900.

coffee-pot. One of the former small tank-engines of the Midland Railway: railwaymen's: late C. 19–20; ob.

coffee royal. ' The first mug of coffee in the morning under sail ': nautical: late C. 19–20. Bowen.

Coffee Ship, the. H.M.S. *Raleigh*: naval: early C. 19. Captain Tryon, who perished in the *Victoria*, established a canteen on board. (Bowen.)

coffee-shop. See **coffee-house**, 2.

coffee-whack. See **whack**, n., last sense.

***coffin, the.** A large box wherein, under a tarpaulin, an outcast may sleep: gen. price, fourpence. Post-War c. Orwell.

coffin-brig. An overweighted 10-gun brig: naval: early C. 19.—2. Hence, any unseaworthy vessel: mid-C. 19–early 20. Likewise, Bowen.

coffin-nail. A cigarette: from ca. 1885; in G.W. and after, occ. **nail.** Often in form of c.p., *another nail in one's coffin.* Cf. *gasper.*

coffins. The Funeral Furnishing Company's shares: ca. 1880–1915: Stock Exchange.

***cog.** Money; esp. a piece of money: C. 16–mid-18 c., mostly gamesters'.

cog, v. To cheat, wheedle; beg: C. 16–mid-19. Orig. either dicing s. or gen. coll.: cf. B.E.'s *cog a dinner*, ' to wheedle a Spark out of a dinner '. The S.O.D., like the O.E.D., considers wholly S.E. Perhaps ex *cog*, a wheel.—2. Hence, v.i., to cheat by copying from another: Scottish Public-Schools': mid-C. 19–early 20.—3. V.i., to agree well with another, as cog with cog: C. 19; coll. (Running like cogs.)—4. ' In school slang, to chastise by sundry bumpings or "coggings" on the posteriors for delinquencies at certain games,' E.D.D., 1898.

cog over. To crib from another's book: schoolboys', C. 19. Cf. *cog*, v., 2.

coger. See **codger.**—**cogey.** See **coguey.**

coggage ; coggidge. Paper ; writing paper ; a newspaper : Regular Army coll. : mid-C. 19–20. F. & Gibbons. Ex Hindustani *kaghaz.*

cogging, the cogging of dice, may orig. (— 1532) have been c. or low s. G. Harvey in *Four Letters.*

***cogman.** A beggar pretending to be a shipwrecked sailor : c. : C. 19. Bowen.

cognomen. A name : sol. ; from ca. 1850. A corruption of S.E. *senses.*

cogue (occ. **cog**) **the nose.** To take, hot, a good strong drink : nautical ; C. 19–20 ; ob. Ex *cogue*, to drink brandy, drink drams.

coguey. Drunk : ca. 1820–60. 'Jon Bee',

1823. Ex *cogue*, a dram. It is recorded in Staffordshire dial., as *cogy*, in 1816 : E.D.D.

coif. Incorrect when used for *quaich*, a cup. O.E.D.

coigne. Money : printers' (— 1909). Ware, A play upon coin and coigne or coin, or quoin, a wedge '.

coil up one's cables or ropes. To die : nautical : mid-C. 19–20. Bowen ; F. & Gibbons. Ex *slip one's cable.*

coin, post the. (Cf. *post the coal.*) To deposit money for a match : for a bet : sporting, ca. 1840–1900.

coin money. To make money both easily and quickly : from ca. 1860 : coll. Cf. :

coiny. Rich : coll. : from ca. 1890. Cf. preceding and *tinny.* (O.E.D Sup.)

***coke.** Cocaine : c. and low ; orig. U.S. (ca. 1910), anglicised ca. 1920. Esp. in Edgar Wallace's novels. Hence, *cokey*, a cocaine-addict : anglicised, as c., ca. 1920. E.g. in John G. Brandon, *The One-Minute Murder*, 1934.

coke, v. Catachrestic when applied to wood : C. 19–20. O.E.D.

coke, go and eat. Oh, run away ! Pejorative coll. : ca. 1870–1920. F. & H. cites as a variant, *go and sh*t cinders.*

Coke upon Littleton. A mixed drink of brandy and text (a red Spanish wine) : ca. 1740–1800. Ex the famous legal text-book. (O.E.D.)

***coker.** A lie : ca. 1670–1830 ; c. > low s. Coles, 1676 ; B.E. ; Grose (= *caulker*, q.v.). Cf. *caulker, corker* : undetermined cognates.—2. C.19–20 sol. for *coco*, esp. in *coker-nut.*

coker-nut. See **coco-nut.**—2. In pl., ' Well-developed feminine breasts ' : low London (— 1909). Ware.

cokes. A fool, a simpleton : ca. 1560–1700. B.E. indicates that the term was first used at Bartholomew Fair and in plays ; it is almost certainly (despite O.E.D.) either s. or coll., orig. at least. Perhaps ex *cockney.*

***cokey.** See **coke**, n.

cokum. An occ. variant of *cocum*, q.v.

col. A Parlyaree form of *cole*, or *coal*, money . see **cole.**

colcher ; occ. colsher. A heavy fall ; esp. *come a colcher* : dial. (— 1888) >, by 1893, coll. O.E.D. Ex dial. *colch, colsh*, a fall.

(Colchester,) weaver's beef (of). Sprats : coll., mainly Essex : mid-C. 17–mid-19. Fuller, 1662; J. G. Nall, 1866. (Apperson.)

Colchester clock. A large, coarse oyster : from ca. 1850 ; ob. A Londonism.

colco pari ? How much, what price ? : among British soldiers on the Salonika Front : 1915–18. Direct ex Bulgarian. (F. & Gibbons.)

cold. Ignorant : from ca. 1920. Will Scott, in *The Humorist*, Feb. 10, 1934 : ' You don't want to start cold.' Ex the disadvantage implied in *cold*, *have a person*, q.v.

cold, have a bad. To be in debt. A *very bad cold* indicates a rent-unpaid departure : ca. 1850–1920. Mostly a Londonism.—2. Gen., however, is the sense, to have gonorrhœa : C. 19–20.

cold, have or **have got** (a person). To have him at one's mercy or badly beaten : C. 20. Prob. ex U.S.

cold, leave. To fail to impress or convince or please : coll. : C. 20. ' My dear fellow, that leaves me cold.' Cf. the Fr. *cela me laisse froid* (F. & Gibbons).

cold, leave out in the. To neglect (a person); to ignore him : from ca. 1860 : coll. >, by 1890, S.E.

cold, the matter will keep. The matter may rest without harm or loss : coll. ; ca. 1660–1800. B.E.

. **cold at that, you will catch.** A c.p. or proverbial form of advice or warning to desist : coll. : mid-C. 18–early 19. Grose, 2nd ed.

cold blood. A house with an off-licence only : from ca. 1858 (ob.) : licensed victuallers' and public-houses'. H., 2nd ed.

cold-blooded. (Of a person) having a slow circulation : coll. (— 1893). O.E.D.

cold blow. See blow, n., 8. Specifically, *the Cold Blow* is Euston : taxi-drivers' : C. 20. (*The Evening News*, Jan. 20, 1936.)

cold burning. A private punishment by the pouring of water down a man's upraised arm so that it comes out at his breeches-knees : mid-C. 18–early 19 ; military (rank and file). Grose, 1st ed.

cold by lying in bed barefoot, he (or she) caught. A mid-C. 18–early 19 c.p. applied to a person fussy about his health. Grose, 2nd ed.

cold-canvass. ' Breaking in with just your visiting-card. Best thing to do is to use your intros. first, and leave the cold-canvass until you've found your feet,' Michael Harrison in *Spring in Tartarus*, 1935 : insurance s. verging on coll. : C. 20.

cold coffee. A hoax : Oxford University, ca. 1860–1910. H., 3rd ed. Because cold coffee is, except in very hot weather, a poor drink.—2. Bad luck : misfortune : from ca. 1860 ; ob. H., 3rd ed. Variant, *cold gruel.*—3. A snub or other unkindness in return for a proffered kindness : nautical, then gen. : from ca. 1870 ; ob. H., 5th ed.—4. Beer : artisans' : ca. 1874–1920. Ware.

cold comfort. Articles that, sent out on sale or return, or on approval, are returned : tradesmen's : from ca. 1870.

cold cook. An undertaker : from the 1720's. Grose, 1785 ; H., 1860. Whence :

cold cook's shop or **cookshop.** An undertaker's premises : from ca. 1830.

cold cream. Gin : from ca. 1860. *The Comic Almanack*, 1864. Cf. *cream of the valley.*

Cold Creams, the. The Coldstream Guards : military (— 1909). Ware.

cold enough . . . See brass monkey.

cold feet, get or **have (got).** To become, to be, discouraged, afraid : coll. : 1904 (O.E.D. Sup.). The U.S. *cold-footer* has not ' caught on ' in England.

cold four. Inferior beer (*four* ale): public-houses' (— 1909). Ware.

cold iron. A sword : coll., ca. 1690–1800. B.E., who adds : ' Derisory Periphrasis '.

cold meat. A corpse : from ca. 1780. Grose, 2nd ed. ; Moore, in 1819, ' Cold meat for the Crowner '.

cold-meat box. A coffin : from ca. 1820. ' The Pitcher ' in *The Sporting Times*, Aug. 3, 1889.

cold-meat cart. A hearse : ? earlier than ' Peter Corcoran ' Reynolds in *The Fancy*, 1820. Cf. :

cold meat of one, make. To kill : prob. from ca. 1820 (cf. preceding entry). Dickens, in *Pickwick*, causes a game-keeper to say to a bad shot, ' I'm damned if you won't make cold meat of some of us ! ' Cf. *cook one's goose.*

cold-meat ticket. An identity disc : military : G.W. (B. & P. ; F. & Gibbons.) Because it served to identify the corpse.

cold-meat train. Any train plying to a cemetery : from ca. 1860.—2. Also, however, the last train by

which officers can return to Aldershot in time for their morning duties : from ca. 1870. H., 5th ed.; R. M. Jephson in *The Girl He Left Behind Him*, 1876. Properly a goods train, it pulled one *ad hoc* carriage, called *the larky subaltern.*

cold north-wester. A bucket of sea-water poured over a new hand, by way of initiation : sailing ships' ; mid-C. 19–20 ; ob. Bowen.

cold pickles. A corpse : medical students' ; from ca. 1840.

cold pie (pye). See choking pie.

cold pig. The ' empties ', i.e. empty packing-cases, returned by rail to wholesale houses : commercial travellers', from ca. 1870 ; ob.—2. In c., a corpse (cf. *cold meat*) ; a person robbed of his clothes : from ca. 1850.

cold pig, v. From ca. 1830 : coll. Same meaning as :

cold pig, give. To awaken by sluicing with cold water or by pulling off the bed-clothes : s. passing to coll. Grose, 2nd ed. ; J. R. Planché ; Thackeray. From ca. 1750 in this form (now ob.) ; but from ca. 1600–1750, the form is *give a cold pie* : see choking pie.

cold shivers, the. A fit of trembling : coll. ; from ca. 1840.

cold shoulder of mutton. A mid-Victorian **s.** variant of the S.E. *cold shoulder* in its fig. sense.

cold storage. Cells ; prison : low and military : C. 20. B. & P.

cold tea. Brandy : a coll. of ca. 1690–1820. B.E. (Esp. among women.) Also see tea.

cold tongue. A senior's lecture or long reprimand : naval : ca. 1840–1900. Bowen.

cold-water army. The generality of teetotallers : coll. : from ca. 1870 ; ob. Cf. *water-waggon.*

cold without. Spirits mixed with cold water without sugar : coll. ; from ca. 1820. Barham ; Bulwer Lytton, 1853, ' I laugh at fame. Fame, sir ! not worth a glass of cold without.'

Coldstreamers. The Coldstream Guards : from ca. 1670 : coll. verging on S.E. (O.E.D. Sup.) Cf. *Nulli Secundus Club*, q.v.

*****cole**, much more frequent than *coal*, though the latter (money = coal = the fuel of life) is prob. correct, is money collectively ; there is no pl. From ca. 1670 ; it was c. until ca. 1730 ; in C. 20 rarely used except among Cockneys and soldiers, and at no time has it been applied to " futures " such as bills, promissory notes, bonds. Head, 1673 ; Grose. (For alternative etymologies, see coliander and cf. *cabbage*, n., 1, for *cole* = cabbage ; possibly ex foreigners' pronunciation of *gold* as *gōl.*)

*****cole, tip the.** Hand over money : c. then low : ca. 1660–1830. A C. 18–20 variant is *post the cole* (*coal*) or *the coin.*

[**cole-prophet**, though in Awdeley, is S.E. : see esp. Apperson.]

cole (gen. **coal) up !** They're paying out ! ; there's a pay-parade ! : military : late C. 19–20. B. & P. Ex *cole.*

colfabi(a)s. A water-closet at Trinity College, Dublin : from ca. 1820. Latinised Irish.

*****coliander** or **coriander (-seed** or **seeds).** Money : c. : from ca. 1690. B.E. Possibly the orig. form of *cole*, q.v.

Colinderies. The Colonial and Indian Exhibition held in London in 1886. A fairly gen. term. Current only in late 1886, 1887, and for a year or two later. Prob. suggested by the telegraphic address, *Colind.* Ware.

*coll. A C. 18 variant of *cull* : c. Harper, 1724, 'I Frisky Moll, with my rum coll.'—2. College ale : 1726, Amherst ; † by 1800. O.E.D.—3. College : schoolboys' : late C. 19–20. Collinson. Also as adj., e.g. in *coll-chap*.

collah carriage. A railway carriage filled with women : nigger minstrels' : ca. 1880–1900. Ware, 'Collah being Yiddish for young girls '.

collapse. To ' cave in ' ; suddenly lose courage : coll. : from ca. 1860.

*collar, n. See collar and cuff. Philip Allingham, *Cheapjack*, 1934.

collar, v. To appropriate ; steal : 1700. Leman Rede in *Sixteen-String Jack* ; Dickens in *Bleak House*.—2. To seize : from early C. 17 : coll. till ca. 1680, then S.E. though somewhat loose and undignified.

collar, against the. (Working) against difficulties —or the grain : from ca. 1850 : coll. till ca. 1890, then S.E.

collar, in ; out of. In : out of : employment. Coll. ; from ca. 1850. Ex the stable.

collar, put to the pin of the. Driven to extremities ; at the end of one's resources. A coll. phrase ex hard-pulling horses : ca. 1850–1910.

*collar and cuff. An effeminate : c., and—esp. among grafters—low : from ca. 1920. Philip Allingham, *Cheapjack*, 1934. Rhyming s. on *puff*, n., 2. Often abbr. to *collar*.

collar and elbow, n. The Cornwall and Devon style of wrestling : coll. : from ca. 1820.

collar-day. Execution day : late C. 18–early 19 ; low. Grose, 2nd ed. Ex the hangman's noose.

collar (or get) the big bird. To be hissed : theatrical : from ca. 1840 ; ob.

collar-work. Severe, laborious work : coll. from ca. 1870 ; in C. 20, S.E. Ex an uphill pull—all collar work—for horses.

collared. Unable to play one's normal game ; ' funky ' : C. 19–20, mostly gaming.

collared up. Kept hard at work, close to business : coll. ; from ca. 1850 ; ob.

collarology. The discussion, by tailors, of coat-collars : tailors' jocular coll. : 1928, *The Tailor and Cutter*, Nov. 29. Cf. *shouldology*, *sleeveology*.

colleckers, collekers. Terminal examinations with interviews : Oxford, from ca. 1895. Ex *collections*.

colle'ct. ' A gathering (in line) for an official purpose' : Bootham School : late C. 19–20. Anon., *Dict. of Bootham Slang*, 1925.

collect, v. To retrieve (objects) from a place : coll. : 1875. O.E.D. (Sup.).—2. Hence, to call for a person and then proceed with him : C. 20 coll. ' I'll collect you at Selfridge's and we'll tea at the Corner House.'—3. V.i. and v.t., to receive (something as) one's deserts : Australian (— 1916). C. J. Dennis.—4. To receive one's salary or wages : coll. : from ca. 1920.

collector. A highwayman ; occ., a footpad : late C. 18–early 19. Grose, 1st ed.

*college. A prison : this gen. sense arose ca. 1720, the orig. sense (C. 17) being Newgate, as indeed it remained until ca. 1800, when, too, from c. the term > low s. ' Velcome to the college, gen'l'mem,' says Sam Weller in Dickens.—2. (Often preceded by *New*) the Royal Exchange : late C. 17–18 : c. B.E.—3. (Gen. the college.) The workhouse : poor people's : late C. 19–20. Ware.

*College, King's. See King's College.

college, ladies'. A brothel : C. 18–early 19 ; low.

*college chum, collegian, collegiate. The first, C. 19 and not very gen. ; the second, C. 19–20, as in Dickens ; the third, the commonest, from ca. 1660 : the first and the third were c. before they > low s. : A prisoner (orig. of Newgate, *the City College*).—2. (Only *collegiate*.) A shopkeeper to a prison : c. : late C. 17–early 19. B.E. ; Grose.

*college-cove. A turnkey : c. (— 1823) ; † by 1890. Egan's Grose. See college, 1.

colleger. The square cap worn at universities : the mortar-board. University and Public School : from ca. 1880. Cf. the S.E. senses.

collegers. See colleckers.—collegian, *collegiate. See college chum.—collek(k)ers. See colleckers.

colli-mollie. See colly-molly.

collie shangle. A quarrel : Society : 1884. Popularised by Queen Victoria ex Scotch.

colligence. Incorrect for † *colligance* : C. 17. O.E.D.

Collins. A letter of thanks sent by departed guest to hostess : 1904 : coll. >, by 1930, S.E. Ex the *Collins* of Jane Austen's *Pride and Prejudice*. O.E.D. (Sup.) Cf. *bread-and-butter*.

collogue. To confabulate : from ca. 1810 (Vaux, 1812 ; Scott, 1811) : coll., perhaps whimsical. The earliest sense, to wheedle or flatter, v.i. and v.t., may possibly be coll.—it is hard to be dogmatic with C. 16–17 words—as Nashe's and Rochester's usage and B.E.'s recording seem to indicate. ? ex Gr. λόγος, a word, influenced by *colloque* (or *colloquy*) and *colleague*.

colloquials. Familiar conversation : Society : ca. 1890–1910. Ware.

colly-molly ; colli-mollie. Melancholy, of which it is a C. 17 jocular perversion. Nares. Cf. *solem(on)choly* .

colly-wobbles. A stomach-ache : coll. ; from ca. 1820. Egan's Grose, 1823 ; ' Cuthbert Bede '. Ex *colic*. Cf. the Australian *wobbles*, a cattle-disease from eating palm-leaves.

Colney Hatch. A match : rhyming s. : late C. 19–20. B. & P.

Colonel, the. Abbr. *Colonel Bogey* (golf) : coll. : C. 20.

Colonel Grogg. Walter Scott : ' so called by his youthful associates ' (Dawson). Ex his martial tastes.

Colonel Peerless's Light Infantry. N.Z. soldiers working at the base at Etaples : New Zealand military : latter half of G.W. Ex Colonel Peerless, the medical officer in charge.

Colonial goose. ' A boned leg of mutton stuffed with sage and onions ' : Australian (— 1898) ; ob. Morris. Ex predominance of mutton as bushman's diet.

Colonial oath !, my. An Australian variant (late C. 19–20) of *my oath !*, q.v. at *oath !, my*. Cf. Henry Lawson's story, ' His Colonial Oath ', in *While the Billy Boils*, 2nd series.

Colonies, the. Australia and New Zealand : Merchant Service coll. : C. 19–20 ; slightly ob. Bowen.

colory. See coloury.

colosh. Golosh : a. 19–20 sol. or incorrectness.

colour. A coloured handkerchief : sporting, chiefly boxing : from ca. 1840 ; ob. Adumbrated in Pierce Egan ; Mayhew.

colour-chest. A locker for signal-flags : naval coll. : C. 19. Bowen.

colour, off. Exhausted ; debilitated ; indisposed : from ca. 1860 ; coll.

colour of a person's money, see the. To see his money ; esp., to be paid. Coll. ; from ca. 1710. Dickens. (O.E.D.)

colour one's or **the meerschaum.** To > red-faced through drink : from ca. 1850 ; ob.

colour with, take. Ostensibly to ally oneself with : from ca. 1700 ; coll. > S.E. > †.

coloured on the card. With a jockey's colours inserted on a specific-race card : racing ; from ca. 1870 ; †.

coloury ; occ. **colory.** Coloured ; two-coloured : coll. ; from ca. 1850. C. Brontë. (O.E.D.)—2. Hence of such colour as shows good quality : commercial coll. : from ca. 1880. Ibid.

***colquarron.** The neck : late C. 17–early 19 c. B.E. Prob. Fr. *col*, neck + c. *quarron*, body.

colsher. See **colcher.**

colt. A barrister attending on a serjeant-at-law at his induction (1765) : legal, †. (S.O.D.)—2. A life-preserver, a ' neddy ' (q.v.) : a weapon affected by thieves and law-keepers : c. and low ; from ca. 1850.—3. a man (esp. an inn-keeper) that hires horses to highwaymen, thieves or burglars (B.E.) ; also, 4, a lad newly initiated into roguery : late C. 17–early 19.—5. One acting as a juryman for the first time : ca. 1860–90. H., 3rd ed.—6. A professional cricketer in his first season : coll. ; from ca. 1870. Ex *colt* in bowls.

colt, v. To make a newcomer pay his ' footing ' : late C. 18–20 ; coll. Ex *colt*, a very old term for an inexperienced or a newly-arrived person. Whence the † *coltage* : such a fine.

colt veal. Very red veal : coll. : late C. 17–early 19. B.E. ; Grose. Because ' young ', fresh.

colting. A thrashing : C. 19 coll. Ex *colt*, to beat with a colt, which is S.E.

colt's tooth, have a. To be fond of youthful pleasures ; to be wanton : late C. 14–19 : coll. till ca. 1790, then S.E. ; †. Chaucer ; Greene, 1588 ; Fletcher (the dramatist) ; Walpole ; Colman. Ex the lit. sense, one of a horse's first set of teeth. (Apperson.)

Columbine. A harlot : theatrical ; from ca. 1845 ; ob. Ex Harlequin's mistress.

Columbus. A failure : theatrical ; from ca. 1870 ; †.

column, dodge the. See **dodge the column.—column-dodger.** Ibid.

column of blobs (or **lumps**). Column of route : jocular military : from ca. 1899. B. & P.

columns. ' Rows of words, written vertically from a dictionary, as a punishment ' : Bootham School coll. : late C. 19–20. Anon., *Dict. of Bootham Slang*, 1925.

com. A commercial traveller : 1884, G. R. Sims in *The Referee*, Dec. 28 (Ware).—2. A comedian : theatrical (— 1887). *The Referee*, July 27, that year. (Ware).—3. (**com** or **comb,** more gen. **combies** (q.v. at *combie*) or **com(b)s.**) A woman's combination (C. 20, in -*s*) : C. 20. George Baker in *Ebenezer Walks with God*, 1931. Cf. *combie*, 2.—4. Commission in the agential or ambassadorial, not the pecuniary, sense : sporting : from ca. 1860 ; slightly ob. (Reginald Herbert, *When Diamonds Were Trumps*, 1908.)

comb and brush. ' Lush ', n. and v. : rhyming s. (— 1909) ; ob. Ware.

comb-brush. A lady's maid : ca. 1749–1820 ; coll. (? > S.E.). Fielding.

comb cut, have one's. To be humiliated ; hence, down on one's luck. Coll. soon > S.E. ; from ca. 1570. Middleton. Cf. Scott's ' All the Counts in Cumberland shall not cut my comb.' But *be comb-cut*, to be mortified or disgraced, has always been coll. (— 1860) ; ob. H., 2nd ed. Ex cock-fighting.

comb one's head. To scold : C. 18–19. A C. 19–20 variant, esp. as to rebuke, is *comb one's hair*.—2. With the addition of *with a joint* or *three-legged stool*, it means—as sometimes it does in the shorter form—to beat, thrash. Shakespeare, 1596, ' Her care should be, | To combe your noddle with a three-legg'd stoole.'

comb the cat. To run one's fingers through the cat-o'-nine tails in order to separate the tails : nautical and military ; ca. 1800–95.

combie. (Pron. *com-bēe*.) Abbr. *combination-room*, the fellows' common room : Cambridge University, from ca. 1860, ob.—2. A woman's combina-tion(s) : from ca. 1870 : Women's, nursery, and shop. Cf. *com*, 3.

combine. A combination of persons, esp. in commerce : orig. (ca. 1887) U.S., anglicised ca. 1910 : coll. till ca. 1930, when it > S.E.

combined chat. A bed-sitting room : theatrical (— 1935). Prob. ex *chat*, n., 5.

comboman. ' The name given in Central Australia to a white man who associates with native women ', *The Times Lit. Sup.*, May, 1934, in a review of Conrad Sayce's novel, *Comboman*, 1934 : coll. : from ca. 1925. I.e. a ' combination ' man.

combs. See **com,** 3.

come. The low n., noted by Manchon (1923) ; corresponding to, and ex, sense 1 of :

come. (Occ. **come off.**) ' To experience the sexual spasm ' (F. & H.) : low coll. : C. 19–20. Considered coarse, but it was orig. a euphemism and, in C. 20, how, if the fact is to be expressed non-euphemistic-ally, could one express it otherwise with such terse simplicity ?—2. To perform ; practise : coll., re-corded in 1812 (Vaux) but prob. from ca. 1800.—3. To play a dodge, a trick (v.t. with *over*) : 1785 ; coll. Greenwood, in *Tag, Rag, and Co*, 1883, ' We ain't two . . . as comes that dodge.'—4. To act the part of : O.E.D. records it at 1825 : coll. or s. : cf. *come the old soldier*, q.v.—5. To attain to, achieve : from ca. 1885 : dial. and coll.—6. To experience, suffer, as in *come a cropper* : this once coll. usage is now S.E. where the ' complement ' is S.E.—7. See **come it.**—8. Came : sol. : C. 19 (? earlier)–20. E.g. ' He come home yesterday.'—9. To become ; esp. in *come(s) of*, happen(s) to : non-cultured Canadian (and U.S.) coll. : late C. 19–20. E.g. in the novels by John Beames.

***come, to.** C. of ca. 1810–50, as in Vaux, 1812 : ' A thief observing any article in a shop, or other situation, which he believes may be easily purloined, will say to his accomplice, I think there is so and so *to come*.'

come about (one). To circumvent : C. 18 ; coll. Mentioned by Johnson.—2. To have sexual inter-course with : C. 19–20 (ob.) ; coll. : said of men by women.

come a colcher. See **colcher.—come a cropper.** See **come,** 6, and **cropper.**

come across. To be agreeable, compliant ; v.t. with *with*, to agree to ; give, yield ; lend : from ca. 1919. Ex U.S.—2. See also **across, come,** 2.

come again ! Repeat, please ! C. 20 : ? ex U.S.

come-all-over-queer, n. A *je ne sais quoi* of discomfort : low coll. : late C. 19–20.

come and have a pickle ! ' An invitation to a quick unceremonious meal ', Ware : Society : 1878–ca. 1910.

come and have one ! ; come and wash your neck ! Come and have a drink ! : resp., gen. coll. (from ca. 1880) and nautical s. (from ca. 1860). Ware. Cf. :

come and see your pa ! Come and have a drink ! C.p. : ca. 1870–1910.

come-at-able. Approachable ; accessible : 1687 (S.O.D.) ; coll. till ca. 1900, then S.E.

come back. To fall back, lose position : sporting ; from ca. 1880 ; ob.

come-back, make (occ. stage) a. To succeed after (long) retirement : (orig. sporting) coll. : from ca. 1920.

come-by-chance. A person or thing arriving by chance ; a bastard. Coll. : from ca. 1760.

*come clean. To give no trouble to the police when one is arrested ; to confess. C. 20 c.

come Cripplegate. To attempt to hoodwink officers : nautical : C. 19–20 ; ob. Bowen. Ex the tricks of crippled beggars.

come-day, go-day with (a person), **it's.** He's extravagant : military : ca. 1890–1915. Ware.

come dish about. A C. 18 drinking c.p. Ned Ward, 1709. (W. Matthews.)

come-down. A social or a financial fall or humiliation or *pis-aller* : from ca. 1840 ; coll. till C. 20, when S.E.

come down, v. To give, subscribe, or lend money (or an equivalent) : from ca. 1700, perhaps ex late C. 17 c. *come it*, to lend money. V.t. with *with*, from a few years later : coll. The v.i. in Steele's play, *The Funeral* ; Thackeray's *Pendennis*. The v.t. in Gay's *Beggar's Opera* : ' Did he tip handsomely ?—How much did he come down with ? '—2. See **down, be.**

come down (up)on (a person) **like a ton of bricks.** To scold, blame, reprimand severely : coll. ; from ca. 1850.

*come grass. To ' turn copper ', i.e. to become an informer, or to involve a confederate in trouble : c. : C. 20. David Hume. Ex *grass*, a policeman.

come home. (Of lost gear) to be restored to its proper place ; (of an anchor) to drag : nautical : late C. 19–20. Bowen.

come in if you're fat ! A C. 18 c.p. Swift, ca. 1708, ' Who's there ? . . . come in, if you be fat ' (Apperson). A thin person is prob. more expensive to entertain.

come in on one's chin-strap. See **chin-strap.**

come it. To cut a dash ; to move (lit. and fig.) fast : coll. (— 1840) ; ob., except in Glasgow, where it = to ' talk big '. Cf. *go it*. Thackeray, ' I think the chaps down the road will stare . . . when they hear how I've been coming it.'—2. To inform the police, disclose a plan, divulge a secret : c. (—1812). Vaux ; H., 1st ed.—3. To tell lies : low : ca. 1820–80. Bee, 1823.—4. To show fear : pugilistic, ca. 1860–1910. H., 3rd ed.—5. To succeed, manage : ex U.S., anglicised ca. 1895 ; coll., ob.—6. To lend money : c. : late C. 17–19. B.E.—7. A late C. 19–20 variant (low ; military) of *come the old soldier*. F. & Gibbons.—8. To ' try it on ' : Glasgow (—1934).

*come it as strong as a horse. (Of a criminal) to turn King's evidence : c. of ca. 1810–50. Vaux, who cites the synonymous *be coming all one knows*. Elaborations of *come it*, 2, q.v.

come it as strong as mustard. An intensive of *come it*, q.v., esp. in sense 3, or of *come it strong*, q.v. : low : ca. 1820–90. ' Jon Bee ', 1823.

come it over or **with.** To get the better of : s., > coll. by 1900 : from ca. 1840.

come it strong. To go to extremes ; exaggerate ; to lie : coll. ; from ca. 1820. ' Jon Bee ', 1823 ; Dickens in *Pickwick* ; Barham ; Thackeray. Cf. *make it hot* and see **come it as strong as mustard.**

come it with. See **come it over.**

come of. See **come,** v., 9.

come off, v.i. To pay : coll. : ca. 1580–1750. Variant of *come down*, q.v.—2. (Gen. of the man.) To experience the sexual orgasm : see **come,** v., 1.

come off it. See :

come off the grass ! Not so much ' side ' ! Don't exaggerate, or tell lies ! Ex U.S. ; anglicised ca. 1890. In C. 20, often abbr. to *come off it !* or even *come off !*

*come-on guy. He who gets hold of the ' mug ' for a gang of ' con men ' (confidence-tricksters) : c. : from ca. 1920. James Curtis, *The Gilt Kid*, 1936.

come on, my lucky lads ! ; come on, you don't want to live for ever ! These two c.pp., which were sometimes spoken together, were the C.S.M.'s or R.S.M.'s cries to his men the moment before the jump-off for an attack : military : in G.W. See, e.g., the description of the great attack in Hugh Kimber's very arresting novel, *Prelude to Calvary*, 1933.

come on, Steve ! A (mainly Cockney) c.p. adjuration that one should hurry : from ca. 1925. Ex the fame of Steve Donoghue as jockey.

come out. (Of girls) to make one's *début* in Society, gen. by being presented at Court : from ca. 1780 ; a coll. that, ca. 1840, > S.E.—2. Abbr. *come out on strike* : coll. at first ; since G.W., S.E. : from ca. 1890.

come out strong. To express oneself vigorously or very frankly : coll. ; from ca. 1850. Cf. S.E. *come out with*, to utter, and coll. *come it strong.*—2. To be generous : Public Schools' : from ca. 1890. P. G. Wodehouse, *The Pothunters*, 1902, ' " I'm a plutocrat." " Uncle came out fairly strong then ? " " Rather. To the tune of one sovereign, cash." '

come over. (Cf. *come it over*, q.v.) To cheat ; trick ; impose on : C. 17–20 : until ca. 1750, S.E., then coll. From ca.1860, gen. *get over* ; in C. 19–20, occ. *come it over.*—2. With *faint, ill, queer, sick*, etc., to become suddenly faint, etc. : coll. ; from ca. 1850.—3. In C. 20 New Zealand c., to admit an offence : cf. *come clean*, q.v.

come over at. To excite passion in (a person of the other sex) : U.S., partly anglicised by : 1928, A. E. W. Mason, *The Prisoner in the Opal*.

come over on a whelk-stall, (have). To be ' dressed to the nines ' : costers' (— 1909). Ware.

come round. To persuade ; make a deep impression on ; influence : coll. ; from ca. 1830. Thackeray, in *Vanity Fair*, ' The governess had come round everybody . . . had the upper hand of the whole house.'

come souse. To fall heavily : boxing : from ca. 1815. Tom Moore, 1819.

come the acid. See **acid.—come the bag.** An occ. variant of *come the old bag*, q.v.

come the artful. To try to deceive : coll. : from ca. 1840.

come the bat. See **bat,** n., 6.

come the don. See **come the nob.**

come the double. To take more than one's due or share : C. 20 : orig. military. F. & Gibbons

Esp. to try, unfairly, to obtain a second helping of food.

come the gypsy. To attempt to cheat or defraud : coll. ; from ca. 1840. Cf. the two *come the old* . . . entries.

come the heavy. To affect a much superior social position : from ca. 1860.

come the lardy-dardy. To dress oneself showily : from ca. 1860. Mostly London.

come the nob (occ. **the don**). To put on airs : from ca. 1855 ; ob. Mostly lower classes'.

come the old bag or **man** or **soldier.** (V.t. with *over*.) To bluff ; to shirk ; to domineer : late C. 19–20 : resp. low, gen., and military. Manchon (*bag*) ; F. & Gibbons (the other two). Ex :

come the old soldier. V.t., *over*. To wheedle ; impose on : coll. : from (? —)1825. Scott, in *St. Ronan's Well*, ' He has scarce the impudence . . . [Otherwise,] curse me but I should think he was coming the old soldier over me.' The idea is adumbrated in Shadwell's *Humours of the Army* : ' The Devil a farthing he owes me—but however, I'll put the old soldier upon him.'—2. See preceding entry.

come the Rothschild. To pretend to be rich : ca. 1880–1914 ; coll.

come the sergeant. To give peremptory orders : from ca. 1855 ; coll.

come the spoon. To make love, esp. if sentimental : from ca. 1865.

***come the Traviata.** In (harlots') c., to feign phthisis : C. 19 ; † by 1891. *La Traviata* is a Verdi opera, in which the heroine is a consumptive *prima donna*, based, of course, on *La Dame aux Camélias*.

come the ugly. To make threats ; from ca. 1870 ; coll.

come through a side door. To be born out of wedlock : coll. : from ca. 1860 ; ob. In a ca. 1880 broadside ballad, *The Blessed Orphan*.

come to grief. See **grief.**

come-to-Jesus collar. A full-dress collar : Canadian : C. 20. Because affected by revivalist preachers.

come to stay. (Adj. phrase.) With the quality of —possessing—permanency. Gen. as (*it*) *has come to stay*. Orig. (— 1888), U.S. ; anglicised ca. 1895. Coll. ; by 1933, S.E.

come to that ! In point of fact !, since you mention it ! : lower classes' coll. (— 1923). Manchon. ' Come to that, it was nothing special ! '

***come to the heath.** To give or pay money : c. of ca. 1810–40. Vaux suggests that there is a pun on *tipping* + *Tiptree Heath* (a place in Essex).

***come to the mark.** ' To abide strictly by any contract . . . ; to perform your part manfully . . . ; or to offer me what I consider a fair price . . .', Vaux : c. of ca. 1805–80. Whence the S.E. *come up to the mark*.

come to, or **up to, time.** In boxing, to answer the call of ' time ! ' ; hence, in sporting circles, to be ready, to be alert. Whyte-Melville, *M. or N.*, 1869.

come tricks. See **come,** 3.

come undone, unput, unstuck. To fall to pieces, lit. and fig. ; to experience disaster : coll. (orig. naval and military) : from late 1914.

***come up.** (Of favourites) to win : C. 20 : racing c.

come up !, before you. See **came up, before you.**

come up and see me some time ! A c.p. : from 1934. Ex a ' gag ' of Mae West's.

come up smiling. To smile though (esp. if heavily) ' punished ' : boxing ; from ca. 1860.—2. Hence, to face defeat without complaining or flinching : coll. ; from ca. 1870. John Strange Winter, in *That Imp*, 1887, ' And yet come up smiling at the end of it '.

come up to (the) scratch or **the chalk.** See **scratch.**

come Yorkshire over. See **Yorkshire.**

comedy-merchant. An actor : ca. 1870–1914. (*Merchant*, q.v., = chap, fellow, man.)

comether on, put one's or **the.** To coax, wheedle ; influence strongly : Anglo-Irish coll. (? dial.) : from ca. 1830. Ex *come hither*.

comf(a)ble. See **comforable.**

comflogisticate. To astound, or puzzle sorely : nautical (— 1923). Manchon. Cf. :

comfoozled. Overcome ; exhausted. Rare ; ? ca. 1830–1900. Perhaps coined by Dickens, when, in *The Pickwick Papers*, he makes Sam Weller say : ' He's in a horrid state o' love ; reg'larly comfoozled, and done over with it.' Like the preceding term, it is an artificial facetiousness.

comforable. Comfortable : sol. (— 1887). Baumann. Also *comfable* : C. 19–20.

comfort. (Gen. with *to do*, occ. with *that* . . .) A cause of satisfaction : C. 19–20 coll. ; earlier, S.E.

comfortable. Tolerable : coll. (— 1720) — 2. ' Placidly self-satisfied ' : coll. ; 1865. (S.O.D.)

comfortable importance or **impudence.** A wife : also a mistress virtually a wife : late C. 17–20 ; ob. B.E. Cf. Fr. *mon gouvernement*.

comfy. Comfortable : coll. (orig. Society) : from ca. 1830. Prob. influenced by *cosy*.

comic, n. A comic periodical : coll. ; S.O.D. records it for 1889.—2. A music-hall comedian : coll. : from ca. 1920.

comic cuts. See **cuts, comic.**

comic business. Flying : Air Force : 1915. F. & Gibbons.

comic-song faker. A writer of comic songs ; music-halls' : ca. 1880–1910. Ware.

comical, n. A napkin : ca. 1870–1910. (Mostly proletarian.)

comical, adj. Strange, queer, odd : 1793 (S.O.D.) ; coll.

comical farce. A glass : rhyming s. : late C. 19–20 ; ob. *The Evening Standard* Aug. 19, 1931.

comical, be struck. To be astonished : low coll. from ca. 1870 ; ob.

coming. (Gen. of women) forward ; wanton : C. 17–20 ; coll. till ca. 1850, then S.E. Fielding.— 2. Sexually capable : C. 18–19 ; low coll.—3. Pregnant : coll. ; C. 17–18.

coming ! Directly ! In a minute ! Coll. : from ca. 1700. Cf. *coming ?, so is Christmas*, said, C. 18–20, to a slow person.

***coming all one knows, be.** See **come it as strong as a horse.**

coming over . . . See **pin out.**

coming up in the next bucket. A variant of *up in Annie's room* (see **Annie's** . . .). Ex mining.

comma-hound. A proof-reader : publishers' and authors' : from ca. 1930.

commandeer. To gain illicit possession of, gen. by pure bluff : coll. : Boer War +. Cf. S.E. sense.

commandments, the ten. The finger-nails or ' claws ' of a person, esp. of a woman : from ca. 1540 ; ob.

Commem. Commemoration Day or Week : universities' : late C. 19–20. (Collinson.)

commend me to. Give me preferably, by choice : coll. ; from ca. 1710. (Orig. of persons ; post-1850, things.)

*commercial. In c., a thief or a tramp that travels considerably : ca. 1855–1914.—2. Abbr. *commercial traveller* : from ca. 1850 : coll. ; in C. 20 S.E.

commercial legs. Legs unfitted for drill : recruiting sergeants' : late C. 19–20 ; ob. Ware.

commish. Abbr. *commission*, a percentage on sales : from ca. 1895.

commissariat. The pantry : jocular coll. ; from ca. 1915. Popularised by the G.W.

*commission. A shirt : mid-C. 16–early 19 c. Harman. Ex It. *camicia*. See **camesa** and **mish.**

commissioner. A book-maker : from ca. 1860. Little used since ca. 1890.

commissioner of Newmarket Heath. A foot-pad : late C. 16–17. Nashe.

*commister. A rare variant (H., 1st ed.) of *camister* (q.v.), a clergyman.

committal, adj. Compromising ; involving, committing ; rashly revelatory : coll. : 1884, *Punch.* Ex *non-committal.* O.E.D.

commo. A communication trench : military : Nov., 1914. B. & P. For the shape, cf. *ammo*, q.v.

commodity. The *pudendum muliebre* : coll. ; late C. 16–19. Shakespeare, in *King John*, ' Tickling commodity ; commodity—the bias of the world.'—2. Occ., but only in c., a whore : late C. 16. Greene.

common. Common sense : lower classes' : C. 20. J. Curtis, *The Gilt Kid*, 1936, ' Use a bit of common '.

common bounce. ' One using a lad as a decoy to prefer a charge of unnatural intercourse ' : low, orig. perhaps c. : from ca. 1850 ; ob. in s.

Common Garden. A C. 17–19 facetious variant of *Covent Garden.*

common garden gout. Syphilis : late C. 17–18. B.E. Ex *Covent Garden* after *common-(or-)garden.*

common jack. A harlot : military ; C. 19–20, ob.

common-roomed, be. To be brought before the head of a college : University coll. (— 1886).

common sewer. A drink ; a taking or ' go ' of drink : from ca. 1860 ; ob. H., 2nd ed. Ex *sewer* = a drain.—2. A cheap prostitute : low : from ca. 1870 ; ob.

commoner. An ordinary harlot : late C. 16–early 19 ; coll. > S.E. by 1660.—A regular but mediocre boxer : pugilistic : ca. 1820–50. Bee.

commoner-grub. A dinner given, after cricket matches, by ' commoners ' to ' college ' : Winchester College : C. 19, † by 1890. (A ' commoner ' is not on the foundation.)

commoney. A clay marble : schoolboys', ca. 1830–1900. Dickens.

commons, house of. A privy : C. 18–early 19; coll. The S.E. form is *common house.*

commonsensical. Possessing, marked with, common sense : coll. ; from ca. 1870. ' The commonsensical mind ' occurs in *Fraser's Magazine*, Sept., 1880. After *nonsensical* ; the S.E. term being *common-sensible.*

communicator. A bell : jocularly coll. ; from ca. 1840. Esp. in *agitate the communicator.*

communiqué. A communiqué : sol. : C. 20. Very gen. in G.W.

communist. Ca. 1916 it > coll. for any lawless person ; since 1926 it has taken a very secondary

place to *bolshie*.—2. In the 1870's, a frequent sol. for a supporter of the Paris Commune (1870). O.E.D.

comp. A compositor : printers' : from ca. 1865. *Tit-Bits*, July 31, 1886, ' Applications for work from travelling comps are frequent.' Cf. *ass*, *donkey, galley-slave,* qq.v.

company, see. To live by harlotry ; esp., and properly, in a good way of business : low : from the 1740's ; ob. John Cleland, 1749 ; Grose, 1st ed.

company (with), keep, v.i. and v.t. To court ; to pay court to, or be courted by : low coll. (— 1861).

compete ; gen. **I'll compete.** I'm available ; I'll do it if you like : schoolgirls' : from ca. 1920 ; ob.

competition wallah. A competitioner, i.e. one who enters the Indian Civil Service by examination : the competition and the name began in 1856 : Anglo-Indian coll. The *wallah* is ex Urdu *wala* = Arabic *walad* = L. *-arius*, signifying a ' doer ', ' maker ', ' actor '.

compile. In cricket, to make abundantly, score freely to the extent of, as in ' England compiled 480 (runs).' S.O.D. records it for 1884.

complaining. ' The creaking of a ship at sea ' : nautical coll. verging on S.E. : C. 19–20. Bowen.

compleat. Apt to be used as a jocularly archaic coll. by the pedantically, the affectedly, or the ever-so-facetiously cultured, esp. in the book world : from ca. 1880. Ex Izaak Walton's *The Compleat Angler* ; e.g., in Oliver Onions's *The Compleat Bachelor*, 1901. *Complete*, obviously, has not the same antique connotation.

complement, -ary. See **compliment.**

complet ; gen. pronounced *complee.* Complete ; finished : soldiers' : 1915–18. Direct ex Fr. See **finni.**

complex. An obsession, esp. in *inferiority complex* (excessive modesty) : from 1910 but not at all gen. till ca. 1919 : orig. coll., but by 1936 verging on S.E. Ex Jung's—not Freud's—psychology, the term properly meaning ' a group of ideas associated with a particular subject ' (S.O.D.). See esp. Collinson, pp. 106–7.

compliment, -ary. In C. 19–20, sol. for *complement, -ary.* C. 19–20. The reverse is, in that period, rather rare.

compo. A monthly advance of wages : nautical coll. : from ca. 1850. Prob. ex *compo*, j. for a composition paid by a debtor (see O.E.D.).—2. Whence, in G.W. : pay : military coll.

comprador. In India, but † by 1900, a house-steward ; in China, a butler : coll. : from C. 16. The Portuguese *comprador*, a purchaser.

compree ? or ! (Do you) understand ? or ! : military coll. : G.W. I.e., Fr. *compris*, understood. F. & Gibbons.

compulsory. That irregular kind of football which is now called *run-about* : Charterhouse coll. : ca. 1850–90. A. H. Tod.

compy-shop. A truck-shop : workmen's coll. ca. 1850–1900. Ex *company-shop.*

coms. See **com,** 3.

comsah. A military variant (1916–19) of *oojah* (q.v.) on Fr. *comme ça,* like that, in that way. B. & P.

con. Abbr. *confidant,* 1825 ; *conundrum,* 1841 ; *conformist,* 1882 ; *Constitutional,* 1883 (Ware) ; *contract,* 1889 ; *construe,* n. (1905). All except the last are rare in C. 20. O.E.D.—2. A previous *conviction* : late C. 19–20 c. Charles E. Leach.—3. A *convict* : low (— 1909). Ware.—4. Abbr. *con camp,* q.v.

con, v. To rap with the knuckles : Winchester College, C. 19–20 ; ob. Ex the much older n., perhaps cognate with the Fr. *cogner*. Wykehamists, pre-1890, traditioned it ex Gr. κόνδυλος, a knuckle. —2. In C. 20 c., to subject to a confidence trick.— 3. In late C. 19–20 c., abbr. of *convict*.—4. To construe : Charterhouse : late C. 19–20.

con camp. A convalescent camp : military coll. : 1915. B. & P. Occ. abbr. to *con*.

*con-game, -man. A confidence trick, trickster : C. 20 (slightly earlier in U.S.) : c. >, by 1910, low.

Conan Doyle. Boil : rhyming s. : from ca. 1895. P. P., *Rhyming Slang*, 1932. Sir Arthur Conan Doyle achieved fame with the *Adventures of Sherlock Holmes*, 1892, a fame that was reinforced by *The Memoirs of Sherlock Holmes* late in 1893.

*concaves and convexes. A pack of cards devised for sharping : from ca. 1840 ; ob. Low and c.

concern. Any object or contrivance : somewhat pejorative ; from ca. 1830 ; coll., in 1930's verging on S.E.—2. The male or female genitals : from ca. 1840 ; s., whereas *thing* is perhaps more euphemistic than unconventional.

*concerned. Often used in c. periphrasis or c.p.: late C. 18–19. See e.g. *Alderman Lushington, Bolt-in-Tun, Mr. Palmer*.—2. (Occ. *with* or *in drink*.) Intoxicated : from ca. 1680 ; S.E. till ca. 1860, then coll. Ob.

concert. See consort.

concert grand. A grand piano suitable for concerts : coll. (— 1893) >, by 1920, S.E. (O.E.D.)

concertina. A collapsible wire-entanglement : military : 1916. B. & P.

concertize. ' To assist musically in concerts', Ware : musicians' coll. : 1885.

conchers. Cattle, either tame or quiet—or both : Australians' : from ca. 1870. † by 1912 and ob. by 1896.

conchie. See conchy.

conchologize. To study conchology ; collect shells : coll. : 1855, C. Kingsley. O.E.D.

conchy ; gen. *conchie* ; occ. *conshie* or *-y*. (Pron. *ko'nshee*.) Abbr. *conscientious objector*, i.e. to military service : 1917. See esp. George Baker's arresting, yet delicate, autobiography, *The Soul of a Skunk*, 1930.

concurrents. Incorrect for *concurrence* : ca. 1600–40. O.E.D.

concuss. (Gen. in passive.) To produce cerebral concussion in (a person) : C. 20. Prob. without reminiscence of, or allusion to, the S.E. sense, to injure by concussion : it is almost certainly a semi-jocular abbr. of *concussion*.

condemn. To curse, swear at : C. 20. Ex the euphemistic *condemn it !*, damn it !

condiddle. To purloin, steal : coll. ; ca. 1740–1860 ; extant in dial., where it arose. Scott in *St. Ronan's Well*, ' Twig the old connoisseur . . . condiddling the drawing.' Ex *diddle*, a, and to, cheat.

condition. See delicate condition.

condog. To concur : coll. : ca. 1590–1700 ; almost S.E. by 1660. *-dog* puns *-cur*.

Condolence. See Bay of Condolence.

condom is a variant of cundum.

conduit. The two Winchester senses (a water-tap, a lavatory)—see Wrench—are, now, almost certainly j. ; but orig. (? ca. 1850) they may have been s.

Condy. Condy's fluid : coll. : 1886 (O.E.D. Sup.).—2. Condy's crystals : coll. : C. 20.

coney and its compounds : see cony, etc.

confab. A talk together, or a discussion, esp. if familiar : coll. ; 1701 (S.O.D.). ' In close confab ', Wolcott, 1789. Ex *confabulation*. Also as v. : from ca. 1740 : not much used. Richardson.

*confect. Counterfeited : late C. 17–18 c. B.E., Grose. O.E.D. considers it S.E. ; perhaps it is c. only as *confeck* (Coles, 1676).

confectionary. Incorrect for *confectionery* : mid-C. 18–20. O.E.D.

confess. Confession, as in *go to confess* : Roman Catholic : from ca. 1890.

confess and be hanged ! A proverbial c.p. equivalent of You lie ! : late C. 16–17. Lit., be shrived and be hanged !

[confidence dodge, game, trick ; confidence man. Orig. (ca. 1880), these terms were perhaps coll.— witness F. & H.—but they very soon > S.E. Cf. *con man*, q.v.]

confirmable, confirmation, were, in C. 16, often confused with *conformable, conformation*. O.E.D.

confiscate. To seize as if with authority : from ca. 1820 ; coll. until C. 20, when, for all its looseness, the word is S.E.—2. Hence *confiscation*, ' legal robbery by or with the sanction of the ruling power ', O.E.D. : from ca. 1865 ; coll. till C. 20, when S.E.—3. And *confiscatory*, adj. to 2 : coll. : 1886 (O.E.D.).

confiscate the macaroon. An elaboration (ca. 1918–24) of *take the cake*. W.

conflab is a New Zealand (esp. military) corruption of *confab*, q.v. : C. 20.

conflabberate. To upset, worry, perturb (gen. as past ppl. passive). Ca. 1860–1920.

conflabberation. A confused wrangle ; an ' awful din '. Ca. 1860–1930. One of the half-wit jocularities so fashionable ca. 1840–1900, e.g. *absquatulate, spifflicate*, more popular in the U.S. than in the British Empire, which did but adopt them.

confloption. An unshapely or twisted thing, a distorted representation or grotesque figure : jocular (— 1887) ; ob. Baumann. Perhaps a perversion of *contraption*. Contrast the dial. senses : flurry, confusion (E.D.D.).

conflummox is an intensive of *flummox*, v. : from ca. 1860 ; virtually †.

confound it ! A coll. expletive : C. 19–20. Cf. sense 1 of :

confounded. Inopportune ; unpleasant, odious ; excessive. This coll., like *awful, beastly*, is a mere verbal harlot serving all men's haste, a counter of speech, a thought-substitute. From ca. 1760. Goldsmith, in *The Vicar of Wakefield*, ' What are tythes and tricks but an imposition, all confounded imposture.' From ca. 1850 its emotional connotation has been brutalised by association with *confound it !* = damn it !—2. Hence *confoundedly*, very : coll. : C. 18–20.

congee-house. See conjee-house.

congenital. Abbr. *congenital idiot* : C. 20 coll. (Not among ' the masses '.)

conger. An association of London bookseller-publishers that, ca. 1680–1800, printed and sold books as a close corporation, a none-too-generous ' combine ' : late C. 17–early 19 : coll. >, by 1750, S.E. >, by 1830, historical. See esp. B.E. Prob. (*pace* the O.E.D.) ex the *conger* or sea-eel, a lengthy, unpleasant creature.—2. Whence, to enter into such an association : coll. (— 1785) ; † by 1823. Grose, 1st ed. ; Egan's Grose.

congraggers. A variant of *congratters*, q.v. (D. L. Murray, *The English Family Robinson*, 1934).

congrats. An occ. variant of the next. Anthony Hope, *The Dolly Dialogues*, 1894, ' Dear old Dolly, —So you've brought it off. Hearty congrats.'

congratters. Congratulations, gen. as an exclamation : C. 20. Ex the preceding by Oxford -*er*. [**congrument** is one of those numerous ghost-words which are ' founded ' on a misprint—esp. on a misprint in a dictionary. O.E.D. (As they are hardly eligible here, I record extremely few of them.)]

conimbrum. Incorrect for *conundrum* : C. 17. O.E.D.

conish. Genteel ; fashionable : low (? also, or orig., c.) ; ca. 1800–40. Perhaps = ' tony ' and a corruption from *the ton*, q.v.

*****conish cove.** A gentleman : Scottish c. of ca. 1820–50. Egan's Grose.

conjee- or **congee-house.** A lock-up : military coll. (in India mostly) : from ca. 1830. Ex Tamil *kañji* ; *congee*—the water in which rice has been boiled—being a staple food of prisoners in India. Yule & Burnell.

conjobble. To arrange, settle ; discuss ; v.i., to chat together : 1694 ; ob. : coll. (O.E.D.)

conjoin. Occ. confused with *enjoin* : mid-C. 16–early 17. O.E.D.

conjugals. Conjugal rights : C. 20 cultured s. >, by 1930, coll.

conjurer, -or. A C. 17–18 sol. for all ' Astrologers, Physiognomists, Chiromancers, and the whole Tribe of Fortune-tellers ', B.E. Chiefly among the ignorant.—2. The evidence tends to show, however, that these terms were also employed in c. to = either a magistrate, a judge, or as for *cunning man*, q.v. See also **fortune-teller.**

conjurer (-or), no. One lacking brains and/or physical skill : coll. > S.E. ; from ca. 1660.

conk. The nose : low : 1812, Vaux ; H. Cockton, in *Valentine Vox*, 1840, ' Oh ! oh ! there's a conk ! there's a smeller !' Prob. ex *conch*, L. *concha* : cf. L. *testa* (a pot, a shell) = head.—2. ' A spy ; informer, or tell-tale ' : c. of ca. 1810–40. Vaux, who shrewdly relates it to sense 1 : cf. *nose*, an informer.—Hence 3, a policeman : low : ca. 1820–1910.—4. A blow on the nose : low : from ca. 1870 ; ob.—5. Hence, any blow on the body : from ca. 1920. See **konk** in Addenda.

conk, v. : gen. *conk out*. To fail, break down, esp. of an engine, a machine ; to die : aviation s. (1918) >, by 1921, gen. coll. Ex :

conked(, be). Dead, to die ; (of an engine) to stop, be stopped : aviation s. (1917) >, by 1920, gen. coll. Prob. ex *conquered(, be)*. For this and *conk*, see esp. B. & P. and O.E.D. (Sup.)

conker. A blow on the nose : from ca. 1820 ; ob. (But *conkers*, the game, is S.E.)

conk(e)y. Having a large nose : from ca. 1815. ' Waterloo ' Wellington was, post-1815, often called ' Old Conky ' from his large nose. Cf. *dook*, 3, q.v. —2. Hence, ' nosey ', inquisitive : from ca. 1840. Cf. *bowsprit, beak, nozzle* ; for synonymy, see F. & H.

Connaught Rangers, the. The 88th Foot Regiment in the British Army : military coll. (— 1864) >, by 1890, j. H., 3rd ed.

connect, v.i. To understand : C. 20. Ex telephones.

connect with. In boxing, from ca. 1920, **to hit.** *John o' London*, Feb. 4, 1933.

conner. Food : Regular Army's : late C. 19–20. B. & P. Ex Hindustani.

connotation, connote ; denotation, denote. Often confused : C. 19–20.

conny wobble. Eggs and brandy beaten up together : Anglo-Irish, C. 18–19.

conqueror. (As in *play the conqueror*.) A deciding game : games coll. : from ca. 1870. Cf. *decider*, q.v.

conscience. An association, gen. in a small company, for the sharing of profits : theatrical : ca. 1870–1900.

conscience, in (all). Equitably ; in fairness or in reason : coll. ; from ca. 1590. Swift. A mid-C. 16–17 variant is *of (all) conscience*. (O.E.D.)

conscience-keeper. ' A superior, who by his influence makes his dependents act as he pleases ', Grose, 2nd ed. : coll. : late C. 18–mid-19.

conscionary. Incorrect for *concionary* : C. 17. O.E.D.

consent. Incorrect for *concent*, a harmony in music : late C. 16–17. O.E.D.

conservatory roof. The transparent, streamlined roof fitted over the cockpit of a high-speed aeroplane : aviation : from 1934. *The Daily Telegraph*, Feb. 9, 1935.

consequence, of. As a result ; by inference : low coll., C. 19–20 ; earlier, S.E. (O.E.D.)

conservati've. A conservative. Jocular, ex Gilbert & Sullivan's opera *Iolanthe*, 1882, but popularised (as a coll.) only in C. 20.

conshie, -y. Less correct than *conchie, conchy*, q.v.

conshun's price. Fair terms or price : Anglo-Chinese ; from ca. 1850 ; ob. H., 3rd ed. Ex *conscience*.

considerable amount of concerted action. Conspiracy : Parliamentary : 1883. Mr. Herbert Gladstone, asked to withdraw ' malicious conspiracy ', substituted this phrase ; the younger Conservatives took it up for a few months. Ware.

considerable bend, go on the. To engage in a bout of dissipation : from ca. 1880 ; cf. *bender*, 3.

considering, adv. If one considers everything, takes everything into account : coll. ; from ca. 1740. Richardson, ' Pretty well, sir, considering ' (O.E.D.).

consimple. Consimile († adj.) : sol. : C. 16. (O.E.D.)

consign. To send, wish, as in *consign to the devil* : coll., from ca. 1900.

consolidate, v.i. To make sure of a job, to make good one's advances to a girl : military coll. : 1916. Ex military j., ' to take measures for holding a captured position to meet a counter attack ', F. & Gibbons.

consols. Abbr. *consolidated annuities* : (1770) in C. 18, Stock Exchange s. ; then gen. coll. ; finally (from ca. 1850) S.E. The consolidation of all Government securities into one fund took place in 1751.

consonant-choker. One who omits his *g*'s and slurs his *r*'s : ca. 1870–1910.

consort. ' Constantly confused in form and sense with *concert* ', W. : C. 17–20.

constable, outrun—occ. **overrun**—**the.** To go too fast or too far (lit. and fig.), as in an argument (Butler's *Hudibras*, I, 1663) : coll. ; † by 1850.— 2. Hence, mid-C. 18–20, to change the subject ; fall into debt (Smollett, in *Roderick Random* ; Dickens): coll. >, ca. 1880, S.E. ; very ob.

constant screamer. A concertina : non-aristocratic : ca. 1860–1915. Ware.

constician. A member of the orchestra : theatrical ; from ca. 1875 ; †.

constipated. Slow to part with money : from ca. 1925.

constituter. The 'Oxford *-er*' form of the next : Oxford undergraduates' : from late 1890's. Ware.

constitutional. A walk taken as exercise (for the good of one's constitution or health) : coll. : recorded by S.O.D. in 1829. Smedley, 1850, 'Taking my usual constitutional after Hall' ; 'Cuthbert Bede', 1853.

constitutionalize. To take a walk for health : coll. ; from ca. 1850. Like its origin, *constitutional* (q.v.), it is a university term, app. arising at Cambridge.

consumer. A butler : Anglo-Indian ; from ca. 1700. Semi-jocular on *consumah*.

contack. A contact : sol. : late C. 19–20. Likewise *impack* for *impact*.

contact. An acquaintance(ship) ; a connexion : both with a view to business or self-interest : coll., from ca. 1930, ex commercial j. (— 1925) ; prob. ex U.S., where the v. is frequent. Fast verging on S.E., at least the near-S.E. of trade.

[**contango** is so technical that it must rank as j ; s., however, in its slapdash formation. Ex *continue.* 1853.]

contempory. Contemporary : sol. (very frequent) : late C. 19–20.

contemptible and **contemptuous** are occ. confused : C. 19–20. Fowler.

Contemptibles, Old. The Regular Army and Reserves sent to France as an expeditionary force in 1914 : late 1915 : military coll. >, by 1918, S.E. Ex the Kaiser's alleged 'General French's contemptible little army'. F. & Gibbons ; O.E.D. (Sup.)

*****content.** Dead : C. 18–early 19 ; c. and low. *A New Canting Dict.*, 1725 ; Grose, 1st ed. I.e. content in death.

contentation and **contention** are occ. confused : C. 17. O.E.D.

conter. See **jury, chummage, and conter.**

context. To discover, or approximate, the sense of a badly written word from the context : printers' and typists' coll. (— 1909) >, by 1925, S.E. Ware.

continent, adj. and adv. On the sick list : Winchester College, C. 19–20. See also the entry at **Winchester College slang.**

continental, not worth a ; not care (or give) a. To be worth nothing ; care not at all. Orig. (— 1869) U.S. ; anglicised ca. 1895. In allusion to *continental money*, a worthless American currency note of ca. 1775–8. Thornton. Cf. *dam.*

continual, continuous. To confuse these is, in C. 20, to commit catachresis.

continuando, with a. For days on end ; for a long time. Often preceded by *drunk.* Coll. : ca. 1680–1750. B.E.

continuations. Trousers, for they continue the waistcoat : from ca. 1840. Whyte-Melville, 1853. (Cf. *dittoes, inexpressibles, unmentionables.*) Ex *continuations*, gaiters (as continuing knee-breeches : O.E.D.).

continute for **continuate** (adj.) ; **contoise** for **cointise** (heraldry). Errors noted by O.E.D.

contour-chasing, n. and adj. (Of an aeroplane) ' flying very low, and as it were following the slopes and rises of the ground ' : Air Force : 1915. F. & Gibbons.

contours. The curves of a woman's body : C. 20 : jocular coll. Ex *contour* as in the S.O.D.'s quotation from Scott : 'The whole contour of her form . . . resembled that of Minerva.'

contra. 'A novel "not passed" by Formmaster' : Bootham School : C. 20. Anon., *Dict. of Bootham Slang*, 1925. I.e., L. *contra*, against.

contra prep. 'Preparation at the end of term, when "contras" are allowed' : id. : id. Ibid.

contract. An undertaking ; esp. *it's a bit of a contract*, a rather difficult job : coll. : U.S. (ca. 1880) >, ca. 1890, anglicised. O.E.D. (Sup.)

contract, mess up the. To spoil, ruin, bungle anything whatsoever : military coll. : 1914. F. & Gibbons.

contraption. A contrivance, device ; small tool or article : dial. (1825 : E.D.D.) >, ca. 1830, U.S. coll. (Thornton) and, ca. 1850, English coll. Perhaps ex ' *contrivance* ' + ' *invention* '.

contra'ry. Adverse, inimical, cross-grained, unpleasantly capricious : from ca. 1850 : coll. Prob. influenced by the Scottish *contrair(y).*

contrection. Incorrect for *contrectation* : mid-C. 16–mid-17. O.E.D.

*****control fortune.** Not a euphemism but a c. term : to cheat at cards : C. 19–20 ; ob.

conundrum is s. in that sense, a pun, play on words, which arose at Oxford in 1644 or 1645 ; in C. 18 coll. ; ob. by 1800, † by 1830. Prob. ex a lost parody of a scholiast phrase. Tom Brown, Ned Ward. W. notes the similarity of *panjandrum.*— 2. A sausage : non-aristocratic (— 1923). Manchon. Suggested by *mystery.*

convalescence. A slack period : busmen's : from ca. 1930. *The Daily Herald*, Aug. 5, 1936. Opp. *belting*, 2.

convenience. A water - closet ; chamber - pot : C. 19–20 ; orig. euphemistic, after ca. 1918 a mildly humorous coll. (In C. 17–18 c., with variant *-cy*, a wife or a mistress.)

*****conveniency.** A mistress ; primarily, however, a wife : c. and low : late C. 17–early 19. B.E. Cf. :

*****convenient.** A mistress ; also, a harlot : c. and low : ca. 1670–1830. Etherege, 1676, ' Dorimant's convenient, Madam Loveit ' ; Shadwell ; B.E. ; Grose. Cf. *comfortable importance.*

convenient, adj. Handy, i.e. conveniently situated or placed : coll. : 1848. Thackeray.

conversation, a little. Cursing and/or swearing : C. 20 ; ob. Ware, 1909. Cf. *language*, q.v.

Conversation Cooke. Wm. Cooke (1766–1824), journalist and author of *Conversation*, a poem. Dawson.

Conversation Sharp. Richard Sharp (d. 1835), a critic and conversationalist. Ibid.

convey. To steal : mid-C. 15–20. Shakespeare : ' Convey, the wise it call.' Orig. euphemistic ; but in mid-C. 19–20 decidedly coll. in its facetiousness.

conveyance, a theft, C. 16–20 ; **conveyancer, a** thief, C. 18–19 ; **conveyancing,** thieving, swindling, from ca. 1750 ; **conveyer,** a thief, esp. if nimble (see Shakespeare's *Richard II*), late C. 16–20. In C. 19–20, all these are coll. and more or less jocular, though *conveyance* and *conveyer* were ob. by 1890, † by 1920.

convincing. Effective ; notable ; journalistic s. > j. : C. 20. In literary and art criticism, it was displaced, ca. 1929, by *significant.*

Convocation Castle. ' Where the . . . heads of colleges . . . meet to transact and investigate university affairs ', Egan's Grose : Oxford University : ca. 1820–40. Punning *Convocation*.

cony, coney. ' A silly Fellow ', a simpleton : from ca. 1590, archaic after 1820 ; coll. Greene, B.E., Grose. Cf. the C. 20 s. use of *rabbit*. (Variant, *Tom cony*.) Whence :

*cony-catch, to cheat, trick, deceive : c. and low : late C. 16–18. Greene ; Shakespeare, in *The Taming of the Shrew*, ' Take heed, signor Baptista, lest you be conny-catched in this business.' Ex :

*cony-catcher. A deceiver ; trickster ; sharper : c. and low ; ca. 1590–1840. John Day, Robert Greene, Walter Scott.

*cony-catching. Trickery ; cheating ; swindling : c. and low : late C. 16–early 19. Shakespeare, Middleton, Ned Ward ; the *locus classicus*, however, is Greene's series of pamphlets on cony-catching : and very good reading they are (see Dr. G. B. Harrison's reprints in the Bodley Head Quartos and my *Slang*, pp. 46–7). C1. *gull, warren*.—2. As adj., cheating, swindling : late C. 16–17. Greene.

*cony-dog. One who assists in cheating or swindling : c. : late C. 17–18._ B.E.

coo ! indicates astonishment or disbelief : mostly lower classes' coll. : from ca. 1890. Prob. ex *good gracious* (or *Lord*) *!* : cf. the frequent *coo lummy !*

cooee, cooey. (The *ee* sound long drawn out.) The Australian black's signal-cry, adopted by the colonists. Recorded in 1790—see esp. Morris—it has, since ca. 1840, been the gen. hailing or signalling cry. Coll. > S.E. As early as 1864, H. can say that it is ' now not unfrequently [*sic*] heard in the streets of London '. E. S. Rawson, *In Australian Wilds*, 1889, ' the startling effects of Jim's cooee '.— 2. The v.i. dates from 1827—or earlier.

cooee, within. Within hail ; hence, within easy reach. From ca. 1880 ; coll.

cook. To manipulate, tamper with ; falsify : coll. ; recorded in 1636 (S.O.D.). Smollett, 1751, ' Some falsified printed accounts, artfully cooked up, . . . to mislead and deceive '. H., 5th ed., ' Artists say that a picture will not *cook* when it is excellent and unconventional and beyond specious imitation.'—2. To kill, settle, ruin, badly worst : from ca. 1850. Mayhew. Cf. *cook one's goose* and *cooker*.—3. (Of persons) to swelter in the heat : coll. ; from ca. 1860.

cook-house official. A military variant of *latrine rumour*, q.v. : G.W. (B. & P.)

cook of the grot. A mess-orderly : naval officers' (— 1925). F. & Gibbons.

cook one's goose. To ruin ; defeat ; kill : from ca. 1850. ' Cuthbert Bede ', ' You're the boy to cook Fosbrooke's goose ' ; Trollope, 1861, ' Chaldicotes . . . is a cooked goose.' Cf. *do brown* and *settle one's hash*. (At this phrase, F. & H. gives an excellent synonymy of ' do for ' in its various senses.)

*cook-ruffi(a)n. A bad or bad-tempered cook : ca. 1690–1830 ; c., then low. B.E. Prob. ex the proverbial saying recorded by Ray in 1670, *cook-ruffian, able to scold the devil in* (or *out of*) *his feathers* (Apperson).

cooked. Exhausted, ruined, killed : late C. 19– 20. Manchon. Ex *cook one's goose*.

cooker. A decisive or a fatal act, a ' settler ' or ' finisher ' : low (— 1869,) ob. O.E.D. Cf. *cook*. v., 2, and *cook one's goose*.—2. See **Captain Cook**.—

3. A Gurkha knife : military : G.W. Ex the native name, *kukri*. F. & Gibbons.

cookie, cooky. A cook, but rarely of a man : coll. : from ca. 1770.—2. A harlot : Glasgow (— 1934).

cookie-shine. A tea-party : jocular coll. : ca. 1863–80. Reade. Ex *cookie*, a small cake. O.E.D.

Cookies, the. The 55th (or *Coke's*) Rifles : Regular Army in India : C. 20. F. & Gibbons.

cooking-day. ' Twenty-four hours devoted to Bacchus ' : naval (— 1909) ; ob. Ware. Ex special allowance of grog to the cook (Bowen).

cook's-galley yarn. A (wildly improbable) rumour : naval : C. 20. Bowen. Cf. *latrine rumour*, q.v.

Cook's guide ; C. tour, tourists. He who conducted, those who took part in a *tour* of the trenches by officers and N.C.O.s of an incoming battalion or by visitors : military jocular coll. : 1915–18. F. & Gibbons.

Cook's (or Cooks') Own, the. The Police Force : ca. 1855–90. Mayhew, ca. 1860 (see *Slang*, p. 93). On names of regiments and ex police predilection for cooks.

cook's warrant. A surgical operation, esp. if amputation : nautical (— 1887) ; ob. Baumann.

*cool. A cut-purse : late C. 16–early 17 c. Greene in 2nd *Cony-Catching*.

cool. (Esp. with *fish* or *hand*.) Impertinent, impudent, audacious, esp. if in a calm way : from ca. 1820 ; coll. till ca. 1880, then S.E. The same with the adv. *coolly*.—2. Stressing the amount in a large sum of money : from 1728 (S.O.D.) ; coll. Fielding, in *Tom Jones*, ' Mr. Watson . . . declared he had lost a cool hundred, and would play no longer.'—3. At Eton College, clear, effective, as in *cool kick* : mid-C. 19–20. Cf. :

cool, v. To kick hard and clear : Eton College : mid-C. 19–20.—2. In back s. (— 1857), look. ' Ducange Anglicus ' ; H., 1st ed. Thus *cool him !* is a costers' warning to ' look out ' for the policeman.

cool as a cucumber, adj. and adv. Cool(ly) and calm(ly) : from ca. 1700 ; coll. Gay, Scott, De Morgan. The C. 17 form was *cold as cucumbers*, as in Fletcher.

cool crape. A shroud : C. 18–early 19 : low. *A New Canting Dict.*, 1725. Ex *c.-c.*, ' a slight Chequer'd Stuff made in imitation of Scotch Plad [*sic*] ', B.E. Hence, *be put into one's cool crape*, C. 18, is to die.

cool lady. A female camp-follower that sells brandy : late C. 17–early 18. B.E. Ex :

cool Nant(e)s or Nantz. Brandy : ca. 1690–1830 ; coll. B.E., Grose. Ex the city of Nantes.

cool one's coppers. To quench the morning thirst after over-night drinking : from ca. 1860 ; coll. T. Hughes in *Tom Brown at Oxford*.

cool one's heels. To be kept standing ; esp. waiting : from ca. 1630 ; coll. > S.E. by 1700. A slightly earlier form was *hoofs*, applied lit. to soldiers.

cool tankard. (Like *cool crape—lady—Nantes*, it may be, but rarely is, spelt with a hyphen.) ' Wine and Water, with a Lemon, Sugar and Nutmeg ', B.E. Coll. : late C. 17–18 ; in C. 19–20 (ob.), S.E.

cooler. A woman : late C. 17–early 19 : low (? orig. c.). B.E., Grose. Ex the cooling of passion and bodily temperature ensuing after sexual intercourse.—2. Ale, stout, or porter taken after spirits (even with water) : from ca. 1820. Pierce Egan's *Tom and Jerry*. Cf. *damper*.—3. A heavy punch : boxers' (− 1823) ; † by 1900. 'Jon Bee.'—4. A prison : orig. (− 1884) U.S. ; anglicised, in c., ca. 1890 ; generalised, esp. as a detention cell, to s. in G.W.

coolie, cooly. ' A common fellow of the lowest class ' : from ca. 1800, orig. nautical.—2. Hence, a private soldier (− 1859) ; † by 1900. H., 1st ed.

Coolie Christmas. The Moharram as observed by the Indian immigrants : Natal coll. : C. 20. *The Graaf Reinet Advertiser*, May 2, 1902. Pettman.

coolieing, go. To hawk vegetables and/or fruit : South African coll. (− 1913). Pettman.

coolth. Coolness : S.E. >, ca. 1890, jocular coll. (O.E.D. Sup.)

cooly. See **coolie.**

coon. A man, esp. if sly and shrewd. Ex U.S., anglicised by *Punch* in 1860.—2. A negro : ex U.S. (− 1870), anglicised ca. 1890. Ex *racoon*. (Thornton.)

coon, a gone. A person in serious, or indeed in a hopeless, difficulty : orig. U.S. (− 1840), anglicised ca. 1860. H., 2nd ed. Origin doubtful : perhaps ex *racoon* after Scottish *gone corbie.* Calverley.

coon's age, a. A very long time, the racoon being notably long-lived : ex U.S. (− 1845), anglicised ca. 1870 but now ob. (Thornton.)

*****coop.** A prison : c. (− 1866) ; ob. James Greenwood in *Dick Temple.* Cf. :

cooped-up. In prison : low ; from ca. 1690. B.E. Cf. *coop*, q.v.

cooper. Stout half-and-half, i.e. stout with an equal portion of porter : coll. ; from ca. 1858. H., 2nd ed. Ex the coopers of breweries.—2. A buyer or seller of illicit spirits ; a ship engaged in such contraband : nautical coll. : from ca. 1880. Ex S.E. senses.—3. In C. 20 vagrants' c., a casual ward to be avoided. Ex sense 2 of :

coopered. Made presentable : coll. : 1829 (Scott). O.E.D. Prob. ex *horse-co(o)per.*—2. Illicitly tampered with ; forged ; spoiled ; betrayed, ruined : c. and low, esp. the turf : from ca. 1850. Mayhew. The other parts of the verb are rare. Cognate with *scuppered*, q.v. (In vagabondia, denoted by the sign ▽ : H., 2nd ed.)

coopering. The vbl.n. corresponding to *cooper*, 2 : the practice of such sales : nautical : mid-C. 19–20. Bowen.

Cooper's ducks with, be. To be all over with : London butchers' (− 1902) ; slightly ob. Apperson from *Notes and Queries.* Presumably of anecdotal origin.

cooppetty-coop. Money : naval : C. 20. F. & Gibbons note an anecdotal origin.

*****coor.** To whip : Scottish : c. of ca. 1810–80. Haggart's *Life*, 1821. Prob. ex S.E. *coir.*

coorse. A sol. form of *course* : C. 19 (? earlier)– 20. Baumann.

ccoshy. A sleep : military : G.W. Ex Fr. *coucher.* F. & Gibbons.

coot. A simpleton : orig. (1794), U.S. ; anglicised ca. 1850. Gen. as *silly coot* or *old coot.* Thornton. Ex the common coot's stupidity.—2. Hence, a person of no account : contemptuous Australian (− 1916). C. J. Dennis.—3. See *cootie*, whence it derives.

coota. An occ. form of *cootie.*

cooter. See **couter.**

cooter goosht. Bad food : Regular Army's : late C. 19–20. F. & Gibbons. Ex the Hindustani for ' dog's meat '.

cootie. A body-louse : nautical (C. 20) >, by

1915, at latest, military. Ex Malayan for a dog-tick. Moreover, *kutu* is common throughout Polynesia for any kind of louse : see, e.g. Tregear's *Mangareva Dict.* See *Words !*, revised ed.

cooty. Lousy : military (ex naval) : C. 20. Ex *cootie* or *coot*, 3.

cop. A policeman (− 1859) ; abbr. *copper.* H., 1st ed.—2. An arrest, as in *It's a (fair) cop* (spoken by the victim) : from ca. 1870 : low (? orig. c.). (In Cumberland dial. it = a prison. E.D.D.) Ex *cop*, v., 4.—3. A vocation or a job : Australian (− 1916). C. J. Dennis. Cf. :—4. Whence or cognately, an easy matter, gen. as *be no cop* : see **cop, be no.** In the Boer War, an English soldier wrote, ' We are going to a place called Spion Kop ; and I don't think it will be much of a " kop " for our chaps ',—it wasn't. (J. Milne, *The Epistles of Atkins*, 1902.)

cop, v. Catch, capture : from ca. 1700, S.O.D. recording at 1704.—2. Hence, to steal : low : mid-C. 19–20. E.D.D.—3. In mid-C. 19–20, it also = take, receive, be forced to endure, as in *cop it (hot)*, to be scolded, to get into trouble,—*cop the bullet*, get the sack,—*cop the needle*, become angry. The C. 20 *cop out* is a variant of *cop it hot.* In G.W., *cop it* = to die, while *cop a packet* = to be wounded, gen. severely.—4. As = arrest, imprison, perhaps as = steal, it was orig. (C. 19) c. ; in C. 20, low.—5. In racing c., C. 20, if a ' bookie ' wins on a race, he has ' copped ' ; and his clerk accordingly marks the book with a *C.* John Morris.—6. See **prop**, v., 2. The word derives 1—prob. ex L. *capere.* 2—via the Old Fr. *caper*, to seize. 3—whence the C. 17 S.E. *cap*, to arrest : *cap* to *cop* is a normal argotic change. Whence *copper*, q.v.

cop ! Beware ! Take care ! Anglo-Indian : mid-C. 19–20 ; ob. H., 3rd ed. ? ex *cop*, v., 3.

cop, be no (or **not much**). Of a task : to be difficult ; of an object : valueless. From ca. 1895. See **cop**, n., 4, and cf. *it's no catch*, which is earlier.

cop a dark 'un. See **dark 'un, cop a.**

cop a flower-pot. A Cockney synonym (by rhyming s. : C. 20) of *cop it hot* (see **cop**, v., 3). A news-vendor, in late Sept., 1935, said of Mussolini : ' He will cop a flower-pot if he goes on like this ' (*The New Statesman and Nation*, Sept. 28, 1935).

cop a mouse. To get a black eye : artisans' (− 1909). Ware.

cop it (hot). See **cop**, v., 3.

*****cop on the cross.** Cunningly to discover guilt : late C. 19–20 c.

cop out. See **cop**, v., 3.—2. Also, to die : military in Boer War and, occ., later. J. Milne, *Epistles of Atkins*, 1902.

cop the brewery, the curtain. See **brewery, cop the**, and **curtain, cop the.**—**cop the bullet, needle, sack.** See **cop**, v., 3.

*****copbusy.** To hand the booty over to a confederate or a girl : c. (− 1839) ; ob. Brandon.

cope. ' An exchange, bargain ; a successful deal ' : low : from ca. 1840 ; ob. Carew, *Autobiography of a Gipsy*, 1891. Prob. independent of the same word recorded, for C. 16–17, by the O.E.D.

(? *)copesmate. An accomplice : late C. 16– early 17 c. or low s. ; T. Wilson, 1570 ; Greene. Cf. the S.E.

coppa dah ! Catch this ! : military : C. 20. F. & Gibbons. Ex *cop there !*

copper. A policeman, i.e. one who ' cops ' or captures, arrests : orig. theatrical : from 1850's.— 2. A penny or a halfpenny : from ca. 1840. In pl., coll. for halfpennies and pennies mixed. ' Still used of the bronze which has superseded the copper coinage ', O.E.D., 1893.—3. In C. 20 c., an informer to the police. Cf. sense 1.

*copper, v. To inform against ; cause to be arrested : C. 20 c. Edgar Wallace, *Room 13*.

copper, catch. To come to harm : C. 16–17 ; s. > coll. Palsgrave. (O.E.D.)

*copper, come or turn. To inform the police : C. 20 c. Charles E. Leach ; David Hume. Cf. *copper, v.*

copper, worth one's weight in burnt. Of little worth : coll. (− 1887) ; slightly ob. Baumann. (In copper instead of in gold.)

copper-captain. A pretended captain : from ca. 1800 (? orig. U.S.) ; coll. > S.E.

copper-clawing. A fight between women : London streets' : from ca. 1820 ; ob. Ware suggests *cap-a-clawing.*

Copper-Face. Oliver Cromwell, whose sobriquet was *the copper-nosed saint.* Dawson. Cf. *Old Noll.*

*copper-house. A police-station : c. : C. 20. James Curtis, *The Gilt Kid*, 1936. Ex *copper*, a policeman.

*copper-man. A policeman : Australian c. ; ca. 1870–1910. Ex *copper*, n., 1.

copper-nose. The red, pimply, swollen nose of habitual drunkards : coll. ; from early C. 17 ; B.E. records the adj. *copper-nosed*, which until ca. 1660 was S.E.

copper-rattle. (Irish) stew : naval (− 1909) ; ob. Ware. Ex the noise made by the bones in the pot.

copper-show. A copper - mine : Australian (− 1916). C. J. Dennis.

copper-slosher. One apt to ' go for ' the police : 1882. Ware.

copper-stick. The *membrum virile* : low : C. 19–20 ; ob. Analogous is C. 19 *coral branch*.—2. From ca. 1880, a policeman's truncheon.

copper-tail. A member of the lower classes : Australian : late 1880's.

copper-tailed. See silver-tail.

copper-top. A red head ; often as nickname : mostly Australian (− 1916). C. J. Dennis.

coppers, clear one's. To clear one's throat : 1831, Trelawney (O.E.D.). Cf. :

coppers, cool one's. See cool one's coppers.

coppers, hot. See hot coppers.

coppers, hot. The hot, dry mouth and throat ensuing on excessive drinking : coll., from ca. 1840.

*copper's nark. A police spy or informer : c. ; from ca. 1860. Henley. *Nark* = spy.

copper's shanty. A police-station : low : ca. 1890–1915. Ware.

coppy, a tufted fowl ; adj., crested : dial. (−1880) >, by 1885, coll. Ex dial. *cop*, the top of anything. O.E.D.

copus. A drink of wine or beer imposed as a fine in hall : Cambridge University, C. 18–19. Johnson derives ex *episcopus* (cf. *bishop*, q.v.) ; H. ex *hippocras.*

copy(-)cat. A child given to copying others' work : elementary schools'.—2. Also a person annoyingly given to repeating or imitating others. Both, C. 20 coll.

copy of (one's) countenance. A pretence, hypocrisy ; sham, humbug : from ca. 1570 ; coll. passing in C. 17 to S.E. In *Westward Ho*, a play of 1607 : ' I shall love a puritan's face the worse, whilst I live, for that copy of thy countenance.'

copy of uneasiness. ' A copy of writ in any court ', Bee : ca. 1820–40.

copybook, blot one's. To spoil one's record : coll. : C. 20.

cor. God, as a low expletive : C. 19–20. Via *Gor*'.

coral-root. Incorrect for *coralwort* : mid-C. 19–20. O.E.D.

coram. A quorum : a late C. 16–17 sol. Nashe, Shakespeare.

Coras. The stocks and shares of the Caledonian Railway : Stock Exchange : from ca. 1885. On the analogy of *Doras*, q.v. A. J. Wilson, 1895 ; *The Daily Telegraph*, June 5, 1935.

corbiculum. Incorrect for *corbicula* : C. 19–20. O.E.D. Cf. *cordialgic* for *cardialgic*, ibid.

'cordin'. According ; accordingly : low coll. (− 1887). Baumann.

corditer. A sporting team from the *Excellent* : naval : C. 20. Bowen. Because ' hot stuff '.

Cordle, Lord and Lady. Two finely bedecked canaries sitting in a little carriage : London street-performers' coll. nickname (− 1887). Baumann.

corduroys. (A pair of) corduroy trousers : from ca. 1780 ; coll. ; in C. 20, S.E.

*core, v.i. To pick up small articles in shops : ca. 1810–60. Vbl.n., *cor(e)ing*. Perhaps ex Romany *čor*, to steal (Sampson).

corfee. A sol. pronunciation of *coffee* : centuries old, esp. among Cockneys. A *corfee-(h)ouse cut* is a cheesemongers' term (− 1909) for ' the back of bacon, without bones, and exceptionally used by coffee-house keepers ', Ware.

*coriander (seed). See coliander.

*coring mush. A boxer ; a fighter : c. : C. 20. James Curtis, *The Gilt Kid*, 1936. Ex Romany *koor*, to strike, to fight : the Romany *kooromengro* is., lit., a fight-man. For the second element, see mush, n., last sense.

Corinth. A brothel : C. 17–19 ; coll. >, by 1800, S.E. The ancient Greek city was noted for its elegance and modernity, also for its licentiousness.

Corinthian. A rake : late C. 16–18 ; coll. soon S.E., as is the adj.—2. A dandy, hence a fashionable man about town : ca. 1800–50 ; coll. > S.E., precisely as *swell*, which was in vogue by 1854, > S.E. One of the characters in Pierce Egan's *Life in London* is Corinthian Tom.

cork. Incorrect for *calk*, v. (late C. 18–20) and n., a sharp point on a horse-shoe : C. 19–20. O.E.D. (Sup.).—2. A bankrupt : ca. 1870–1900. H., 5th ed. Ex his lack of ' ballast '.—3. In Scottish coll., from ca. 1830, a small employer ; a foreman. (O.E.D.)—4. See corks.—5. A workman bringing a charge against his fellows : workshops' (− 1909). Ware derives ex *caucus.*

cork, draw a or the. In boxing, to draw blood : from ca. 1815 ; ob. Cf. *tap one's claret.*

cork and water. Any bottle of medicine : Bootham School : late C. 19–20. Anon., *Dict. of Bootham Slang*, 1925. Cf. :

cork-and-water club. Old scholars at Oxford University : id. : id. Ibid.

cork-brained. Foolish, light-headed : C. 17–20 ; coll. ; S.E. after ca. 1820. In B.E. as *corky-b.*

corked. (Of wine) tasting of cork : coll. (−1864) ; ob. ; H., 3rd ed.—2. Very drunk : C. 20. Lyell.

corker. Something that ends an argument or a course of action ; anything astounding, esp. a great lie. Recorded for 1837 ; app. orig. U.S. (O.E.D.) ;

s. >, by 1920, coll. Cf. *caulker, settler, whopper*, and esp. *put the lid on* (W.).

corker, play the. (Of persons) to be unusual, exaggerated, eccentric; in university and Public School, to make oneself objectionable. From ca. 1870. Anstey in *Vice Versa*.

corking. Unusually large, fine, good: from early 1890's: mostly U.S., s. >, by 1930, coll. App. ex *corker*, q.v., on the model of other percussive adjj. (*whacking, whopping*, etc.). O.E.D. (Sup.).—2. Hence, semi-adv., as in ' A corking great thing' (Manchon, 1923).

corks. A butler: from ca. 1860. H., 3rd ed. Cf. *chips*, a carpenter—2. Money: nautical and military; from ca. 1858. H., 2nd ed. Ex the floating property of corks.

corks! A lower classes' coll. interjection: not recorded before 1926, but heard by the writer in late 1921. Either a corruption, prob. euphemistic, of *cock's* as in *cock's* (God's) *body* (O.E.D. Sup.)., or an abbr., as I think, of *corkscrew!*, q.v.

corkscrew. A funnel on the early ships of the General Steam Navigation Company: nautical: late C. 19–early 20. Bowen. Ex the black and white bands painted spirally.

corkscrew! An evasion of *God's truth*: low London (— 1909). Ware. Cf. *cheese and crust*.

corkscrewing. The uneven walk due to intoxication: from ca. 1840; coll., as is

corkscrew, to move spirally (1837). Dickens: ' Mr. Bantam corkscrewed his way through the crowd' (S.O.D.).—2. *corkscrew out.* To draw out as with a corkscrew: coll.: 1852, Dickens (O.E.D.).

corkscrews. Abbr. *corkscrew curls*: coll.; from ca. 1880. Displaces *bottle-screws*.

corky. Frivolous; lively; restive: from ca. 1600: coll.; ob. Contrast the S.E. senses.

corky-brained. A coll. variant (C. 17–19) of *cork-brained*, q.v.

corn, a great harvest of a little. Much ado about nothing: coll.; C. 17–early 19.

corn, carry. See **carry corn.**

Corn, the. The Cornmarket, Oxford: Oxford undergraduates': late C. 19–20. Collinson.

corn in Egypt. Plenty, esp. of food: coll. (in C. 20, S.E.); from ca. 1830.

[**cornage.** For its catachresis in law, see the O.E.D.]

corned. Drunk (— 1785). Grose. Cf. *pickled* and *salted* for semantics. Not, as often supposed, an Americanism, as, however, *have corns in the head* (to be drunk) may possibly be. In dial., *corny*.

Corned Beef Island. A Corporation housing-estate: urban: from ca. 1925. ' Like bully-beef tins' (Allan M. Laing).

corned dog. Bully beef: military: C. 20. F. & Gibbons.

corned with oneself, be. (Very) well pleased with oneself: tailors': from ca. 1920. E.g. in *The Tailor and Cutter*, Nov. 29, 1928.

cornelian tub. A sweating-tub: late C. 18–early 19 coll. Grose, 3rd ed.

corner. A money-market monopoly with ulterior motives. From the 1850's. Coll. >, by 1900, S.E. (Thornton.)—2. **The corner:** Tattersall's subscription rooms: mid-C. 19–20, †; sporting. It is more than sixty years since ' Tatts ' was near Hyde Park Corner.—3. Also, Tattenham Corner on the Derby course at Epsom: sporting, from ca. 1870.—4. In c. (— 1891), a share; **the chance of a share in the** proceeds of a robbery.

corner, v. Drive into a fig. corner: ex U.S. (1824), anglicised ca. 1840: coll.—2. Monopolise a stock or a commodity: from the mid-1830's in U.S. (whence, too, the corresponding n.) and anglicised before 1860.

corner, be round the. To get ahead of one's fellows by unfair or dishonest methods: from ca. 1860.

corner-boy. A loafer: Anglo-Irish coll.: from ca. 1880; but recorded in U.S. in 1855 (Thornton). Prob. suggested by *corner cove*, q.v. Cf. *corner-man*.

corner, hot. See **hot corner.**

corner-cove. A street-corner lounger or loafer: coll.; from ca. 1850. Mayhew.

corner-creeper. An underhand and furtive person: coll.; ca. 1560–1720; S.E. after 1600.

corner-man. A loafer: coll., from ca. 1880 (recorded in 1885). Replacing *corner-cove*, q.v.—2. An end man, ' bones ' or ' tambourine ', in a negro-minstrel or an analogous show: from ca. 1860; ob. H., 3rd ed.

cornerer. A question difficult to answer: coll. (— 1887). Baumann. Ex *corner*, v., 1.

cornering. The practice of *corner*, v., 2; q.v.

corney. See **corny-faced.**

cornichon. A ' muff ' (e.g. at shooting): Society 1880–ca. 1886. Ex Fr. Ware.

Cornish duck. A pilchard: trade: from ca. 1865; ob. Cf. *Yarmouth capon*.

corns and bunions. Onions: rhyming s.: late C. 19–20. B. & P.

corns in the head, have. To be drunk: drinkers' (— 1745); † by 1860. Apperson.

cornstalk (or **C.**). A New South Welshman of European descent: coll.: from ca. 1825. Later (ca. 1880), and loosely, any Australian of the Eastern states. Peter Cunningham, 1827, ' From the way in which they shoot up '; rather, ex tendency to tall slimness. (Morris.)

cornuted. Cuckolded: late C. 17–18; coll. B.E. Ex a cuckold's horns. Cf.:

Cornwall without a boat, send (a man) **into.** To cuckold him: ca. 1565–1830. Painter, *Palace of Pleasure*, 1567; Halliwell. Punning † *corn(e)*, a horn, (in fortification) hornwork. Apperson. Cf. *cornuted*.

corny-faced. Red and pimply with drink: ca. 1690–1830. B.E. Cf. *corned*.

coroner. A heavy fall: from ca. 1870; ob. I.e. one likely to lead to an inquest.—2. **The Coroner** was the nickname applied, ca. 1870–1900, to Dr. E. M. Grace, ' W. G.'s ' brother.

corp. (Very rare as non-vocative.) Corporal: military coll.: C. 20. B. & P. Cf. *sarge*.—2. A corpse: nautical: late C. 19–20. Edwin Pugh, *A Street in Suburbia*, 1895; H. Maclaren, *The Private Opinions of a British Blue-Jacket*, 1929. Recorded in dial. as early as 1775: E.D.D.

corp out. To die: low (— 1923). Manchon. Prob. ex *corpse*, v., 2, after *conk out*, q.v.

corporal and four, mount a. To masturbate: low; late C. 18–20, ob. Grose, 1st ed.

Corporal Forbes or **the Corporal Forbes.** Cholera Morbus: Regular Army (esp. in India): from 1820's. Shipp's *Memoirs*, 1829. Yule & Burnell.

Corporal John. Marlborough, perhaps the greatest of British generals: orig. (ca. 1700), military; in mid-C. 18–20, only historical. Dawson.

corporation. A prominent belly: from ca. 1750; coll. C. Brontë, in *Shirley*, ' The dignity of an ample corporation '. Influenced by S.E. *corpulent*.

corporation's work, freeman of a. 'Neither strong nor handsome': c.p. of ca. 1780–1820. Grose, 1st ed. (Not very complimentary to corporate towns.)

corps commanders. (Singular very rare.) 'That species of lice with the Corps H.Q. colours, red and white', M. A. Mügge, *The War Diary of a Square Peg*, 1920 : military : 1915 ; ob.

corpse. A horse entered in a race for betting purposes only : the turf, from ca. 1870.

corpse, v. To blunder (whether unintentionally or not), and thus confuse other actors or spoil a scene ; the blunderer is said to be 'corpsed' : theatrical : from ca. 1855 ; ob. H., 1st ed.—2. To kill : low ; recorded in 1884. Henley & Stevenson in *Deacon Brodie*. Ex dial.

corpse lights. Corposants (St. Elmo's fire): nautical coll. : mid-C. 19–20. Bowen.

corpse-provider. A physician or a surgeon : from ca. 1840 ; ob.

corpse-reviver. Any powerful, refreshing drink : C. 20 ; ex a specific U.S. mixed drink.

corpse-ticket. A contemporaneous variant of *cold-meat ticket*, q.v. (F. & Gibbons.)

corpse-worship. A marked profusion of flowers at funerals : clubmen's : ca. 1880–1900. Ware says that 'this custom, set by the Queen at the mausoleum (Frogmore) immediately after the death of the Prince Consort [in 1861], grew rapidly . . . Finally, in the '90's, many death notices in the press were followed by the legend, "No flowers".'

corpus. Corpse : (dial. and) sol. : C. 19–20. (D. Sayers, *The Nine Tailors*, 1934.) Cf. *corp*, 2.

correct. The correct number or quantity ; esp. in (*up*) *to correct*, (up) to the correct or specified number, etc. : military coll. : 1916. B. & P.

correct, all present and. All correct : coll. : from ca. 1918. R. Knox, *Still Dead*, 1934, ' "Is that all present and correct ?" "Couldn't be better." ' Ex the military phrase (applied by a sergeant-major to a parade).

correct card, the. The right thing to have or do ; the 'ticket' : from ca. 1860, ex lit. racing sense. Often written *k'rect card*.

corro'boree, corro'bbery. A large social gathering or meeting (— 1892). Perhaps ex :—2. A drunken spree : nautical : late C. 19–20. Ware. Ex :— 3. A fuss, noise, disturbance (— 1874). Ex the lit. senses (Australian) ; properly a Botany Bay aboriginal word.

corroboree, v. To boil (v.i.) ; to dance. Australia : from ca. 1880 ; ob. For v. and n., see Edward Morris's neglected dictionary, *Austral English*, 1898.

corruption, occ. in pl. Natural sinfulness, 'the old Adam' : 1799 ; coll. until C. 20, when archaic S.E. (S.O.D.)

corruscate, corruscation. Incorrect for *coruscate, coruscation* : C. 17–20. O.E.D.

corsey. Reckless (betting or gambling) : sporting coll. : 1883 ; ob. Ware. Ex Fr. *corsé.*

Corsican, the. Something unusual : sporting ; ca. 1880–1913. Coined by F. C. Burnand (1836–1917), playwright and editor of *Punch.*

corybungus. The posterior : boxing ; ca. 1850–1900. Etymology ?

'cos. Because : coll. : C. 19–20. Baumann. Better spelt *'cause.*

*cosey. A late C. 19–20 variant of *carsey = casa, case* : qq.v.—2. Ware, however, notes that, in the London slums, it is (from before 1909) 'a small,

hilarious public-house, where singing, dancing, drinking, etc., goes on at all hours'. Prob. influenced by S.E. *cosy.*

*cosh. A life-preserver, 'neddy', i.e. a short, thin but loaded bludgeon, in C. 20 occ. of solid rubber ; also (rare before C. 20) a policeman's truncheon. From ca. 1870 : orig. c., then low. H., 5th ed ; Edgar Wallace *passim.* Prob. ex Romany.—2. With *the*, one who uses a **cosh** : C. 20 c.

*cosh, v. To strike with a cosh ; esp. thus to render unconscious : late C. 19–20 c. Ex the n.— 2. Hence merely, to hit : Cockneys' : C. 20.

*cosh-carrier. A harlot's bully : c. (— 1893). E.D.D. Ex *cosh*, n., 1. Hence, *cosh-carrying* : C. (— 1896) : O.E.D. (Sup.).

cosher, n., see **kosher.**—2. In late C. 19–20 c., one who uses a *cosh*, q.v.—3. A policeman : Berkshire s. (— 1905). E.D.D., Sup.—4. V.i., to talk familiarly and free-and-easily : coll. : from ca. 1830. Cf. Scottish *cosh*, on intimate terms, ex *cosh*, snug comfortable.

cosier. An inferior seaman : naval : C. 19. Bowen. Ex the † S.E. *cosier, -zier*, a cobbler.

cosma. Incorrect for *chasma*, a chasm : late C. 16–17. O.E.D.

coss. A blow, a punch : hatters' (— 1909). Perhaps ex *cosh* + *goss*, q.v. Ware.

cossack. A policeman : from late 1850's. H., 1st ed. ; *The Graphic*, Jan. 30, 1886, 'A policeman is also called a "cossack", a "Philistine", and a "frog".' All three terms are †.

cossid. A 'runner', i.e. a running messenger : Anglo-Indian coll. : late C. 17–20. Ex Arabic. (S.O.D.)

cossie. A swimming costume : Australian : from ca. 1919. Origin ?

cost. To be expensive : coll. : from ca. 1916. Norah Hoult, *Youth Can't Be Served*, 1933, 'Them things cost these times.' Abbr. *cost a lot of money.*

costard. The head : jocularly coll. (— 1530). Palsgrave (O.E.D.) ; Udall in *Ralph Roister Doister* ; Shakespeare ; B.E. ; Grose ; Scott. Ex *costard*, a large apple. Cf. :

coster. Abbr. (— 1851) *costermonger* (C. 16) orig. *costard-monger*, at first a seller of apples, then of any fruit, finally of fruit, fish, vegetables, etc., from a barrow. Cf. *costard*, q.v., and *barrow-man*, q.v.

costering. Costermongering : from ca. 1850 ; ob. Mayhew, 1851 (O.E.D.) ; H., 1st ed.

costermonger Joe. 'Common title for a favourite coster' : commercial London (— 1909). Ware.

costermongering. 'Altering orchestral or choral music, especially that of great composers' : musical : ca. 1850–1910. Ware. Ex Sir Michael Costa's adaptations of Handel.

costive. Niggardly : late C. 16–20 ; coll., in C. 20 S.E. and rare. Cf. *constipated.*

cot. Abbr. *cotquean*, a man meddling with women's work and affairs : coll. : late C. 17–18. B.E. Extant in dial.

cot, on the. 'A man of a bad character, trying to amend his ways—i.e. in a moral hospital, so to speak' : military : late C. 19–early 20. F. & Gibbons.

cotch. Except in dial., a sol. for *catch* : C. 19–20. In facetious usage, however, it is to be ranked as a coll.

cots. The shoe-strings of monitors : Christ's Hospital, ca. 1780–1890. Charles **Lamb.** Ex *cotton.*—2. God's, in ∞ll. oaths : C. 16–mid-18 (O.E.D.)

cotso. A variant of *catso*, q.v.

Cots(w)old lion. A sheep : mid-C. 15–mid-19. Ex the sheep-fame of the Cotswolds. Anon., ca. 1540 ; ' Proverbs ' Heywood ; Harington in his *Epigrams*. Cf. *Essex lion, Cambridgeshire nightingale*. (Apperson.)

cottage. Abbr. *cottage piano* : (— 1880) coll. > j. —2. A urinal : ca. 1900–12. Ware.—3. Hence, any lavatory : theatrical : from ca. 1910.

Cottagers, the. Fulham Football Club (' soccer ') : sporting : 1910, P. G. Wodehouse, *Psmith in the City*. They often play at Craven Cottage, London.

Cotterel's salad ; Sir James (Cotter's or) Cotterel's salad. Hemp : Anglo-Irish, C. 18–early 19. Grose, 1st ed. A baronet of that name was hanged for *rape*.

cotton, v.i. Prosper ; hence, agree together : coll. ; the former (†), from ca. 1560 ; the latter, from ca. 1600. In an old play (1605), ' John a Nokes and John a Style and I cannot cotton.' The primary sense (' prosper ') may arise ex ' a fig. sense of raising a nap on cloth ', W.—2. Hence, with *to*, ' get on ' well with (a person), take kindly to (an idea, a thing) : from ca. 1800 ; coll. Barham, ' It's amazing to think, | How one cottons to drink !'

Cotton, leave the world with one's ears stuffed full of. To be hanged : Newgate c. of ca. 1820–40. ' Jon Bee ', 1823. Ex the name of the Newgate chaplain, by a pun.

cotton-box. An American ship, bluff-bowed, for carrying cotton : nautical : C. 19. Bowen, ' The old clipper men used to speak of them as being built by the mile and sawn off in lengths when wanted.'

cotton in their ears, die with. A variant of Cotton, leave the world with one's ears stuffed full of.

cotton-lord, occ. -**king.** A wealthy manufacturer of, dealer in, cotton : 1823. Coll. >, by 1880, S.E. Cf. *cottonocracy, Cottonopolis*.

cotton on, v.i. ; v.t. with **to.** To form, or have, a liking or fancy (for a thing, plan, person) : coll. : C. 20. Ex *cotton*, 2. (O.E.D. Sup.)—2. To understand : from ca. 1910. C.O.D., 1934 Sup.

cotton-top. A loose woman preserving most of the appearances : ca. 1830–80. Ex stockings cotton-topped, silk to just above the ankles.

cotton up. To make friendly overtures ; v.t. with **to.** Both coll. ; from ca. 1850. See **cotton.**

cotton-wool, wrap in. To cosset, coddle : coll. ; from ca. 1870 ; now almost S.E.

cottonocracy. Cotton magnates as a class : coll. : 1845. (S.O.D.) Cf. :

Cottonopolis. Manchester : from ca. 1870 : coll. H., 5th ed. Cf. *cotton-lord* and *Albertopolis*.

cottons. Confederate bonds : from ca. 1870 ; Stock Exchange. Ex the staple of the Southern States, U.S.A.

Cotzooks ! A coll. corruption of *God's hooks* (nails on the Cross) : early C. 18. O.E.D.

couch a hog's head. Lit., to lay down one's head, i.e. to lie down and sleep : C. 16–17 c. ; in C. 18, low. Recorded in Harman, B.E., Scott (as an archaism). Occ. *cod's head.*

couch a porker. A variant of the preceding : c. : (?) C. 18.

cough-drop. A ' character ' ; a quick courter or ' love '-maker : low coll. : 1895, *The Referee*, ' " Honest John Burns " . . . objects to being called " a cough drop ".' Ware postulates ' 1860 on '.

cough-lozenge. A mishap ; something unpleasant ; esp. in *that's a cough-lozenge for* (somebody) : a virtual c.p. of 1850–60. Cf. preceding.

cough slum. See **slum, cough.**

cough up. To disclose : from C. 14, now ob. (not, as the S.O.D. says, †) ; S.E. in C. 14–17 ; coll. in C. 19–20.—2. To pay, v.i. and t. : from ca. 1895.— 3. (Likewise ex sense 1.) To produce, hand over : C. 20 ; perhaps orig. U.S.

coughing Clara. A heavy gun : military : late 1914. F. & Gibbons. Ex its report as heard from the Front.

couldn't speak a threepenny bit, I (etc.). I was unable to speak : London streets' (— 1909). Ware.

Coulson. A court jester : a coll. nickname (— 1553) soon > allusive S.E. Ex a famous fool so named. (O.E.D. : at *patch*.)

coulter-neb. The puffin : nautical : C. 19–20 ; ob. Bowen. Ex its sharp beak.

council and **counsel** are often misused one for the other : C. 18–20.

council-houses. Trousers : rhyming s. : from ca. 1925. Michael Harrison, *Weep for Lycidas*, 1934. Cf. *round the houses.*

council of ten. The toes of a man with in-turned feet : ca. 1858–90. H., 2nd ed.

councillor of the pipowder court. A pettifogging lawyer : coll. ; ca. 1750–1850. Ex *Court of Piepowders*, dealing summary justice at fairs ; Fr. *pieds poudreux.*

counsellor. A barrister : Irish c. (— 1889) and dial. (— 1862). Ex Scots (C. 19–20). E.D.D.

count. A man of fashion : ca. 1840–60 ; coll. Cf. *dandy, swell, toff.*

count, out for the. (Often preceded by *put*.) Ruined ; dead : from ca. 1880. Ex boxing.

count, take the. To die : from ca. 1890. Also ex boxing.

Count Eclipse. Dennis O'Kelly (d. 1787), owner of that now almost mythical racehorse Eclipse (b. 1764). Dawson.

count noses. To count the Ayes and *Noes* : Parliamentary : from ca. 1885 ; ob.

counter. An inferior officer of a counter or prison : C. 17. O.E.D.

counter-hopper. A Londoners' coll. variant (ca. 1850–1910 ; Mayhew, 1851) of the next. E.D.D.

counter-jumper. A shopman : coll. : 1831, an American example (O.E.D. Sup.) ; S. Warren, 1841 (O.E.D.) ; H., 2nd ed. ; G. A. Sala, 1864, ' He is as dextrous as a Regent Street counter-jumper in the questionable art of " shaving the ladies ".' Baumann, 1887, and Manchon, 1923, have *counter-skipper* : † by 1930.

counterfeit crank. A sham-sick man : mid-C. 16–18 : mostly c. Burton's *Anatomy.*

countermine. Incorrectly for *countermure* : ca. 1590–1740. O.E.D.

counterstrafe. To ' strafe ' (q.v.) in retaliation : artillerymen's and infantry officers' : 1916. B. & P.

counting-house. Countenance (n.) : non-aristocratic, non-cultured : ca. 1870–1910. Ware.

country, go to the ; in the country. See **go to the country.**

country, the. The outfield : from early 1880's : cricket s. >, by 1910, coll., now verging on S.E. Lillywhite's *Cricket Companion*, 1884 (O.E.D.). But *country stroke* appears as early as 1872. Also *country catching* (1888), c. *field(sman)* in 1890's. (W. J. Lewis.)

country, up the. See **up, adj.**

country-captain. A very dry curry, often with a spatch-cocked fowl; Anglo-Indian: coll.: from ca. 1790.—2. Also (— 1792, †), the captain of a *country-ship*, q.v.

country cousin. A dozen: rhyming s. (— 1909). Ware.—2. In pl., monthly courses: euphemistic (— 1923). Manchon. See **relations.**

country-crop, in Manchon, is an error for *county-crop*, q.v.

*****country Harry.** A waggoner: mid-C. 18–early 19 c. Grose, 2nd ed.

country-put. 'A silly Country-Fellow', B.E.: coll.; late C. 17–early 19. See **put, n.**

country-ship. A vessel owned in an Indian port: Anglo-Indian coll. (— 1775); *country-boat* occurs as early as 1619. (Yule & Burnell.)

country with (one), **be all up the.** To be ruin, or death, for: coll. (— 1887); virtually †. Baumann.

country work. Work slow to advance: coll. (— 1811); ob. *Lex. Bal.*

county, adj. Wrapped up in the affairs of county Society; apt to consider such society to be the cream of the social milk; very much upper-middle class. Coll.: from ca. 1880.

county-court. To sue a person in a county court: coll.: from ca. 1850.

county-crop. Abbr. *county-prison crop.* Hair cut close and as though with the help of a basin: a 'fashion' once visited on all prisoners: ca. 1858–1910. H., 2nd ed.—2. Hence, *county-cropped*: 1867, J. Greenwood (O.E.D.).

couped up. B.E.'s spelling of *cooped-up*, q.v.

coupla. Couple of: U.S., anglicised ca. 1905: (low) coll. D. Sayers, 1934, 'He'd had nothing to eat . . . for a coupla days.'

couple, a. A couple of drinks: coll.: late C. 19–20. Richard Keverne, *Menace*, 1935, 'Stopped at the "Swan" for a couple'.

couple-beggar. A hedge priest: coll.: C. 18–19. Swift, in *Proposal for Badges to the Beggars*; prob. the earliest record; Lever, in *Handy Andy.* Cf. *buckle-beggar.*

couple o(f) doorsteps. A sandwich: low: C. 20. F. & Gibbons. Ex *doorstep*, q.v.

couple of flats. Two bad actors: theatrical: ca. 1830–80. Ware. A pun on the two scene-screens.

coupled. Incorrect for *cupolaed*: C. 17. O.E.D.

coupling-house. A brothel: C. 18–19; low coll.

coupon. (Political) a party leader's recommendation to an electoral candidate: 1918. Collinson. The term soon passed from s. to j.; thence, ca. 1930, to S.E. *The coupon election* was that of 1918 (Great Britain).

courage, Dutch. See **Dutch courage.—*courber.** See **curber.**

course. A C. 17–20 incorrect spelling of *coarse.* E.g. in B.E.—2. Abbr. *of course*, as in *Course I did it* or *Course ! (What do you suppose ? !)*: late C. 19–20 coll. Baumann.

course with (a person), **take a.** To hamper him, follow him closely: coll.: mid-C. 17–early 19. B.E. Ex coursing.

court. To sue in a court of law: from ca. 1840: coll. Cf. *county-court.*

court card. 'A gay fluttering Fellow', B.E.; a dandy: coll.: ca. 1690–1800, then dial.

court cream ; court element ; court holy bread ; court holy water ; court water. Fair but insincere speeches, promises: C. 17–18 the first; the others

being C. 16–18. All are coll., as, orig., was the C. 17–18 *court promises.* (O.E.D.)

court martial. (Gen. hyphenated.) To try by court martial: from ca. 1855; coll.

court noll, courtnoll. A courtier: coll., pejorative; ca. 1560–1680. In C. 17, S.E.

court of assistants. Young men to whom young wives, married to old men, are apt to turn : a late C. 18–early 19 facetious coll. punning the S.E. sense. Grose, 2nd ed.

court of guard. Sol. for *corps de garde*: late C. 16–early 19. O.E.D.

court tricks. 'State-Policy', B.E.: coll.; mid-C. 17–18.

court water. See **court cream.**

*****cousin.** A trull: c.; — 1863. S.O.D.—2. In late C. 16 c., a (rustic) 'pigeon'. Greene.

cousin Betty. A half-witted woman: mid-C. 19–20; ob.; coll. Mrs. Gaskell, in *Sylvia's Lovers*, '. . . Gave short measure to a child or a cousin Betty '.—2. Also, a strumpet: C. 18–mid-19: c. and, latterly, low s. ' Jon Bee.'

cousin Jan or **Jacky.** A Cornishman: coll. and dial.: from ca. 1850.

cousin the weaver or, as in Swift and Fielding, **dirty cousin.** Prefaced by *my*, these two terms—the latter much the more gen.—were, in late C. 17–18, pejorative forms of address: coll.

cousin Tom. A half-witted man: in C. 18 if a beggar, in C. 19 of any such unfortunate, though not applied to a person of standing.

cousin trumps. One of the same occupation or, occ., character: mainly, like *brother smut*, as a familiar tu-quoque. Coll.; C. 19.

couta. A rare form of *couter.*—2. A barracouta (fish); Australian coll.: late C. 19–20.—3. Hence, a Southern Tasmanian (gen. the word is used in the pl.): Northern Tasmanians' nickname : C. 20. These fish being plentiful in Southern Tasmania.

couter, occ. **cooter.** A sovereign: perhaps orig. c., certainly always low and mainly vagrants' and Cockney: from ca. 1835. Brandon, 1839; Snowden's *Magistrate's Assistant*, 1846 (O.E.D.); H., 1st ed.; James Payn in *A Confidential Agent*, 1880. Ex Romany *kotor*, a guinea.

*****cove.** A man, a companion, chap, fellow; a rogue: from ca. 1560. In C. 16 often *cofe.* In C. 16–18, c.; still low. Harman, B.E., Grose; Dickens, in *Oliver Twist*, 'Do you see that old cove at the book-stall ?' Prob. cognate with Romany *cova, covo*, that man, and, as W. suggests, identical with Scottish *cofe*, a hawker (cf. *chap* ex *chapman*).—2. Hence, in Australia, the owner, the ' boss ', of a sheep-station: ca. 1870–1910. This sense owes something to :—3. *the cove* (or *Cove*), ' the master of a house or shop ', Vaux: c. of ca. 1800–70. Cf. next entry but one.

*****cove of (the) dossing-ken.** The landlord of a low lodging-house: C. 19 c. Cf. :

*****cove of the ken, the.** ' The master of the house ', Egan's Grose: c. of ca. 1820–70. Ex *cove*, 3.

Covent Garden. A farthing: rhyming s. on *farden* (— 1857). ' Ducange Anglicus.'

Covent Garden abbess. A procuress: C. 18–early 19. The Covent Garden district, in C. 18, teemed with brothels. See esp. Beresford Chancellor's *Annals of Covent Garden*; Fielding's *Covent Garden Tragedy*; and Grose, P. Cf. *Bankside ladies* and *Drury Lane vestal.*

Covent Garden ague. A venereal disease: late C. 17–early 19. Ray, 1678; Grose, 1st ed. Cf.

Drury Lane ague, and see **Covent Garden abbess** and **Covent Garden rails**.

Covent Garden lady. A variant (ca. 1800–30), noted in 1823 by Bee, of :

Covent Garden nun. A harlot : mid-C. 18–early 19. Grose, 1st ed. Cf. *nun* and *Drury Lane vestal*.

Covent Garden rails, break one's shins against. To catch a venereal disease : low : late C. 18–early 19. Grose, 2nd ed. Cf. *Covent Garden ague*.

Coventry, gone to ; or **he (she,** etc.) **has gone to Coventry.** He doesn't speak (to me, to us, etc.) nowadays : tailors' : late C. 19–20. Ex :

Coventry, send one to. To ignore socially : mid-C. 18–20 ; orig. military. Coll., > S.E. ca. 1830. Origin uncertain : perhaps ex Coventry Gaol, where many Royalists were imprisoned during the Civil War (see e.g. Clarendon's *History of the Rebellion*, VI, § 83). Lytton, in *Alice*, 'If any one dares to buy it, we'll send him to Coventry.' Cf. the County Antrim *go to Dingley couch*, the Ulster *send to Dinglety-cootch*, and see esp. the O.E.D. and Grose, P.

*cover. A pickpocket's assistant : c. : from ca. 1810. Vaux. Cf. *stall*, q.v. Ex :

*cover, v.t. and i. To act as a (thief's, esp. a pickpocket's) confederate : from ca. 1810 : c. and low. Vaux.—2. To possess a woman : low coll. : C. 17–20. Urquhart's *Rabelais*, 1653. Ex stallion and mare. Cf. *tup*.

*cover, at the. Adj. and adv., applied to a pickpocket cloaking the movements of the actual thief : c. : from ca. 1840. Charles E. Leach. See **cover**, n.

cover-arse gown. A sleeveless gown : Cambridge University, ca. 1760–1860.

*cover-down. A false tossing-coin : c. : C. 19 ; † by 1891. See **cap**, n., last sense.

cover-me-decently. A coat : ca. 1800–50. Moncrieff in *Tom and Jerry*.

cover-slut. Apron, pinafore : coll. ; C. 17–20, now archaic.

covered waggon. A fruit tart : *Conway* Training Ship (— 1891). Masefield.

*coverer. An occ. † variant (Egan's Grose, 1823) of *cover*, n.

covert-feme. Dryden's facetious manipulation of the legal *feme covert* : he uses *under covert-feme* of a man under his wife's protection. Cf. Dickens's jocular application of *coverture* in *Sketches by Boz*.

covess. A woman : late C. 18–mid-19. George Parker, Lytton. Ex *cove*, 1, q.v.

covetise (†) and **covetous** were, in C. 14–16, often written the one for the other. O.E.D.

covey. A man : low : from ca. 1820 ; ob. Pierce Egan, 1821 ; Dickens in *Oliver Twist*, 'Hullo, my covey ! what's the row ?' Diminutive of *cove*, q.v.

covey (of whores). 'A well fill'd Bawdy-house', B.E. : late C. 17–early 19 : coll.

covorly. Incorrect, for *cavally* (a fish) : mid-C. 19–20. O.E.D.

cow. A woman : in C. 18–20, low coll. Earlier, hardly opprobrious ; Howell, in 1659, speaks of that proverb which, originating *temp.* Henry IV, runs, ' He that bulls the cow must keep the calf.'—2. A harlot : C. 19–20 ; ob.—3. (Sporting) £1000 : from ca. 1860. Cf. *pony, monkey*.—4. Milk : Canadian : late C. 19–20. B. & P. Also, in C. 20, Australian : Ion L. Idriess, 1931.—5. (Always either *a cow* or, more strongly, *a fair cow*.) A (very) despicable person or an objectionable one ; a (most)

unworthy act ; an obnoxious thing : C. 20 Australian and hence N.Z. (C. J. Dennis.) Esp. (even of a man), *a fair cow*.—6. A member of the chorus : theatrical (— 1923). Manchon. Cf. sense 1.—7. A tramp's woman : tramps' c. (— 1935). Cf. sense 2.

cow, sleep like a. (Of a married man) ' i.e. with a **** at one's a-se ', Grose, 1st ed., who quotes the quatrain, ' All you that in your beds do lie, | Turn to your wives and occupy ; | And when that you have done your best, | Turn arse to arse, and take your rest ' ; for a variant here unquotable, see Grose, P. A mid-C. 18–mid-19 low coll.

cow and calf. To laugh : rhyming s. (— 1859) ; ob. H., 1st ed.

cow-baby. A faint-hearted person : coll. ; from ca. 1590. In C. 19–20, dial.

cow-bridges. ' The fore and aft gangways in the waists of old men-of-war, before the days of completely planked main decks ', Bowen : naval : C. 19.

cow climbed up a hill !, there was a. You're a liar ! : c.p. : C. 20. F. & Gibbons.

cow-cocky. A dairy-farmer : Australian : from ca. 1890. See **cocky**, n., 5.

cow come home, till the. C. 17–18 coll. See **cows come home.**

cow-cow, v.i. and t. To be in a rage ; to scold, reprimand severely : Anglo-Chinese ; mid-C. 19–20. H., 3rd ed.

cow-cumber, cowcumber. Cucumber : sol. in mid-C. 19–20 ; S.E. in C. 16–early 19. Dickens. (It is fairly gen. in dial.)

cow-(occ. bushel-, sluice-)c*nted. Low coll. pejorative applied to a woman deformed by childbearing or by harlotry : C. 19–20.

cow died of, the tune the old. See **tune the old cow . . .**

cow-feed. Salad ; raw vegetables : naval and military : C. 20. F. & Gibbons.

cow-grease or **-oil.** Butter : coll. : mid-C. 19–20. In C. 19, gen. *cow's-grease* ('Ducange Anglicus'). Cf. *cow-juice*, q.v.

cow-gun. A heavy naval gun : naval s. (from ca. 1900) >, by 1915, coll. O.E.D. (Sup.).

cow-handed. Awkward : late C. 18–19 coll. Grose, 1st ed.

cow-heart. Either jocular or pedantically sol. for coward : C. 19–20 (? earlier). Prob. suggested by :

cow-hearted. ' Fearful or Hen-hearted ', B.E. ; coll., verging on S.E. : mid-C. 17–20, ob. Cf. preceding.

cow-hitch. A clumsily tied knot : nautical (— 1867). Smyth. As in *cow-gun* and *cowhanded*, the idea is of unwieldiness.

cow-hocked. Thick-ankled ; large- or clumsy-footed. Coll. ; mid-C. 19–20.

cow-horn. A brass mortar on shipboard : naval : late C. 19–20 ; ob. Bowen. A perversion of *coe-horn*.

cow in a cage, as comely (or nimble) as a. Very ungainly or clumsy : coll. : 1399, Langland ; 1546, Heywood ; 1678, Ray ; 1732, Fuller. Apperson. Cf. *bull in a china shop*.

cow-juice. Milk : coll. ; late C. 18–20. Grose, 3rd ed. ; heard on the *Conway* Training Ship (— 1890), says Masefield. (Cf. *sky-juice*.) Esp. opp. *tinned cow*.

cow-lick. ' A peculiar lock of hair, greased, curled, brought forward from the ear, and plastered on the cheek. Once common amongst costermongers and tramps.' F. & H. ; H., 2nd ed., has it. Coll. >, by 1900, S.E. (First used in late C. 16,

prob. of a fashion different from that of the costers.)
Cf. *aggerawater*.

cow-oil. See **cow-grease.**

cow-pad. A third-term cadet employed in keeping the petty officers' quarters clean : Training Ship *Worcester* : late C. 19–20. Bowen.

cow-quake. A bull's roar : coll., mostly Irish and dial. : C. 19–20.

cow-shooter. A ' deerstalker ' hat, worn by seniors : Winchester College, C. 19.

cow-shot. A flat, scooping leg-stroke made by a batsman down on one knee and hitting against the flight of the ball : cricketers' s. (1904) >, by 1930, coll. Lewis. A more clumsy shot, made by a standing batsman, is termed an *agricultural* one : coll. : from ca. 1930.

cow-turd. A piece of cow-dung : late C. 15–20 : S.E. until C. 19, then a vulgarism. (O.E.D.)

cow-with-the-iron-tail. (Gen. without hyphens.) A pump, i.e. water mixed with milk : jocular coll. : from ca. 1790.

cowan A sneak, eavesdropper, Paul Pry ; an uninitiated person ; from ca. 1850. Ex freemasonry, certainly the last nuance and perhaps the others. Ex Scottish *cowan* or *kirwan*, a rough stone-mason ; or, less prob., Gr. κύων, a dog.

cowardise. Incorrect for *cowardous* : late C. 16. O.E.D.

coward's castle or **corner.** A pulpit, ' six feet above argument ' : coll. ; C. 19–20, ob.

cowle. Almost any document of a promissory or warranty nature, e.g. lease, safe-conduct : Anglo-Indian, from late C. 17.

cows-and-kisses. (But occ. unhyphenated.) The ' missus ' : wife or mistress (of house) ; any woman. Rhyming s. (— 1857). ' Ducange Anglicus '.

cow's baby, occ. **babe.** A calf : late C. 17–20 ; coll. B.E., Grose.—2. Hence, ca. 1820–60, ' any lubberly kind of fellow ', Bee, 1823.

*****cow's calf.** In racing c., C. 20 : ten shillings, in coin, currency note or value. Rhyming on *half* (a *sov.*).

cows come home, till the. An indefinite time ; for ever : mostly Canada, Australia, New Zealand : coll. : mid-C. 19–20. Ex U.S. (1824 : Thornton) ; orig. (1610), English, as *till the cow come home* (O.E.D.).

cow's courant. A ' gallop and sh–[t]e ', Grose, 2nd ed. : low coll. : late C. 18–early 19. *Courant* = *coranto*, a quick dance.

cow's grease (H., 1st ed.). See **cow-grease.**

cow's-spouse. A bull : late C. 18–mid-19. Grose, 3rd ed. Prob. *spouse* rather than *wife* by rhyming association : cf. *bubbly jock.*

cow's thumb, to a. Mid-C. 17–20, ob. ; coll. ' When a thing is done exactly, nicely [i.e. fastidiously], or to a Hair ', B.E. : is this ironical ?

cowsh. An Australian and New Zealand variant (— 1914) of *bullsh* (see **bull-shit**).

*****cowson.** A variant of ' son of a bitch ' ; applied also to things : c., and low : C. 20. James Curtis, *The Gilt Kid*, 1936. Prob. ex *cow*, 2.

cox. Abbr. *coxswain* : from ca. 1880 ; coll.—2. The same applies to the v. (t. or i.).

coxcomb. The head : jocular coll., punning *cock's comb* ; late C. 16–19. Shakespeare. Cf. S.E. senses. See esp. Weekley's *More Words Ancient and Modern.*

Coxey's army. A ' rag-time ' army : Canadian military in G.W. (B. & P.) Adopted from U.S.

coxy. See **cocksy.**

coxygeal. Incorrect for *coccygeal* : C. 19–20. O.E.D.

coy or **Coy.** See **co**, 2.

coyduck. To decoy, v.t., rarely v.i. : C. 19–20, coll. and dial. Prob. ex *coy-duck = decoy-duck*, and not, as Farmer ingeniously suggests, a blend of *conduct* and *decoy.*

coyote. The *pudendum muliebre* : C. 19. (Cf. *cat, pussy.*) Lit., the barking-wolf of the U.S.

coz. Abbr. *cousin* : used either lit. or to a friend : coll. ; late C. 16–early 19. Shakespeare.

cozier. See **cosier.**

cozza. Pork : cheapjacks' and costers' ; from ca. 1850. Charles Hindley, 1876. Origin ?

crab. A decoy at auctions : low, C. 19–20, ob.— 2. Abbr. *crab-louse,* a human-body louse, esp. and properly one of those unpleasant vermin which affect the pubic and anal hair : low coll., from ca. 1800. In B.E.'s day, *crab-louse* itself was coll.— 3. See **crabs.**—4. The action, or an instance, of finding fault : coll. : from ca. 1890. (O.E.D. Sup.) Ex *crab*, v.—5. A drawback : coll. : from ca. 1910. —6. A midshipman : naval : late C. 19–20. Bowen.—7. A type of aeroplane (Avro 504K) used for the training of novices : Royal Air Force : from ca. 1920. Because it is slow and esp. because of its well-splayed and much-braced undercarriage.

crab, v. To ' pull to pieces ', criticise adversely : low s. >, ca. 1840, gen. s. >, ca. 1870, coll ; from ca. 1810. (Vaux.) Occ. as v.i. : mid-C. 19–20. Cf. the S.E. senses, to oppose, irritate, and the C. 19–20 c. sense, to expose, inform on, insult, spoil. Vbl.n., *crabbing*.

crab, catch a. See **catch a crab.—crab, land.** See **land crab.**

*****crab, throw a.** A v.i. form (c. of ca. 1810–40) of *crab*, v. Vaux.

Crab and Winkle Line. The railway line between Tollesbury and Kelvesdon in Essex : railwaymen's : C. 20. Ex the crabs and periwinkles on the Essex coast.

crab-fat. Whale-oil for frost-bite : military : 1916. B. & P. As though against lice.

crab grenade. A flat, oblong German hand-grenade : military : 1915 ; ob. B. & P.

crab lanthorn. A peevish fellow : late C. 18– early 19 coll. Grose, 1st ed. Cf. *crab wallah.*

crab-louse. See **crab**, n., 2.

*****crab-shells.** Boots, shoes : from ca. 1780, perhaps orig. c., for in c. *crabs* = feet. Grose, 1st ed. ; Mayhew, ' With a little mending, they'll make a tidy pair of crab-shells again.' Cf. *trotter-* or *trotting-cases.*

*****Crab Street, in.** ' Affronted ; out of humour ', Vaux : c. (— 1812) ; † by 1890. A pun on *crabbed.* Cf. *Queer Street.*

crab wallah. An evil man : Regular Army's : late C. 19–20. B. & P. Cf. *crab lanthorn* and see **wallah.**

crabber. A fault-finder : coll. : C. 20. Ex *crab*, v. : q.v.

*****crabs.** In c., shoes : ca. 1810–50. Also feet : from ca. 1840. Abbr. *crab-shells.*—2. In gaming, esp. at hazard, a throw of two aces, ' deuce-ace ' (cf. *deuce, the*) : from ca. 1765 : Lord Carlisle, 1768 ; Barham. Whence :

crabs, come off or **turn out** or **up (a case of).** Of things : to be a failure, unfortunate. C. 19–20.

crabs, draw. See **draw crabs.**

*crabs, get. To receive no money: c. (— 1923). Manchon. Perhaps ex *crab*, n., 2: ? cf. Fr. low s., *recevoir peau de zébie*.

crabtree comb. A cudgel: jocular coll.: late C. 16–19.

crack. Abbr. *crack-brain*, a crazy or soft-headed person: coll.; C. 17–18. Dekker, Addison.—2. A harlot: ca. 1670–1820: orig. c., then low. D'Urfey, 1676 (O.E.D.); B.E.; Farquhar, ' You imagine I have got your whore, cousin, your crack '; Vanbrugh; Dyche, Grose. ? ex *crack*, the female genitals: low, C. 16–20.—3. A lie (the mod. form is *cracker*): ca. 1600–1820; coll. Goldsmith, ' That's a damned confounded crack.' Whence, prob., the coll. sense, a liar: C. 17.—4. In mid-C. 18–19 c., a burglar or a burglary: whence— both in Vaux—*cracksman*; and *the crack*, a (— 1812) variant of *(the) crack lay*.—5. Any person or thing— though very rarely the latter in C. 20—that approaches perfection: coll.; from ca. 1700 for persons, from ca. 1630 for things (cf. the adj.).—6. Hence esp. a racehorse of great excellence: from ca. 1850. E.g. in those very horsey publications, *Diogenes*, 1853, *Derby Day*, 1864, and *From Post to Finish* (1884), the third by Hawley Smart, the less popular Nat Gould of the '80's and '90's.—7. Cf. *the crack*, the fashion or vogue: ca. 1780–1840: fashionable world, as rendered by Pierce Egan, his cronies and his rivals. Grose, 2nd ed. Cf. *crack*, adj.—8. A crisp and resounding blow: coll.; S.O.D. records for 1838. Ex the crack of a whip or a shotgun.—9. Dry firewood: c., ' gypsy ', and low: from ca. 1840 (recorded in Mayhew in 1851). Ex the crackling sound it emits when burning.—10. ' A narrow passage [or alley] of houses ': London proletarian (— 1909). Ware.—11. See half a crack. Like *caroon*, *crack* is prob. a mere corruption or perversion of *crown*.—12. See ' Fops ' in Addenda. Ex sense 5.

crack, v. To boast, brag: C. 15–20, ob. S.E. till ca. 1700, then coll. and dial. Burton in his *Anatomy*: ' Your very tradesmen . . . will crack and brag.'—2. To fall into disrepute; into ruin: C. 17–19 coll. Dryden.—3. To collapse; break down (v.i.): sporting, from ca. 1870.—4. To break open, burgle: c. and low: from ca. 1720. Dickens in *Oliver Twist*, ' There's one part we can crack, safe and softly.' Esp. in *crack a crib*, to break into a house, likewise c. and low.—5. Wholly c.: to inform; v.t. with *on*: ca. 1850–1910.—6. To drink (cf. *crush*): late C. 16–20: coll. Gen. with *a quart* or *a bottle*. Shakespeare in the 2nd *Henry IV*, ' By the mass, you'll crack a quart together '; Fielding and Thackeray (*a bottle*).—7. V.i., a variant of *crack along*, q.v.: coll.: mid-C. 19–20. (O.E.D.)— 8. V.i., to fire (a rifle, shotgun, etc.); v.t., with *at*. Coll.; from ca. 1870.—9. In cricket, from ca. 1880, to hit (the ball) hard.—10. To smite (a person): Australian: late C. 19–20. E.g. ' He'll crack you one '; C. J. Dennis.

crack, adj. First-class; excellent: from ca. 1790; coll. Esp. of regiments, riflemen, and athletes. Thackeray, 1839, ' Such a crack-shot myself, that fellows were shy of insulting me.' Cf. *crack*, n., 5, 6.

crack, fetch a. See fetch a crack.

crack, in a. Instantaneously: coll.: from ca. 1720. Byron, 1819, ' They're on the stair just now, and in a crack will all be here.'

crack, must have been sleeping near a. See sleeping near a crack.

crack a boo. ' To divulge a secret; to betray emotion ', C. J. Dennis: low Australian (— 1916).

crack a bottle. See crack, v., 6.

crack a crib. See crack, v., 4.

crack a crust. To make a living; rub along. Superlatively, *crack a tidy crust*: coll., from ca. 1850. Mayhew, ' Crack an honest crust '; H., 1874, ' A very common expression among the lower orders '.

crack a Judy, a Judy's tea-cup. (Cf. the U.S. use of *Jane*, any girl.) To deprive a maid of her virginity. C. 19–20, low, ob.

*crack a ken or a swag. To commit a burglary: c.; the former, C. 18; the latter C. 19–20, ob.

*crack a whid. To talk: C. 19–20 (ob.) c. Vaux; Hindley's *Cheap Jack*. See whid.

crack along or on. V.i., to make great speed. V.t., *crack on or out*, to cause to move quickly, often with connotation of jerkily. Both coll., recorded in 1541. In C. 19, the adv. is often omitted. (S.O.D.)

crack-brain(ed), -headed, -skull, nn. and adjj. Indicative of craziness: all coll. quickly > S.E.; C. 16–19. Here *crack* = *cracked*.

*crack-fencer. A seller of nuts: low or c.; from ca. 1850; † by 1900. H., 1st ed.

crack-halter, -hemp, -rope, nn. and adjj. A gaolbird; a good-for-nothing ' born to be hanged '. All coll. passing rapidly to S.E.: the first and second, C. 16–17; the third, C. 15–early 19. Gascoigne and Dekker, *c.-halter*; Shakespeare, *c.-hemp*; Massinger and Scott, *c.-rope*.

crack hardy. To endure patiently, suppress pain or emotion; in low Australian, to keep a secret: C. 20. C. J. Dennis.

crack-haunter or hunter. The *membrum virile*: low, C. 19–20. Cf. *crack*, n., 2, 3.

crack-hemp. See crack-halter.

crack into (reputation, repute, fame, etc.). To render (famous, etc.) by eulogy: coll. (— 1892); ob.

crack-jaw. Difficult to pronounce: coll.: from ca. 1870. Miss Braddon.

*crack-lay, the. House-breaking: from ca. 1785; ob.; c. Grose, 2nd ed.

crack on, v.i. See crack along.—2. To pretend; esp. pretend to be ill or hurt: ? orig. military: from the 1880's, if not earlier. See the Kipling quotation at *blind*, v.

crack (or break) one's egg or duck. To begin to score: cricket; from ca. 1868.

crack-pot. A pretentiously useless, worthless person: coll.: from ca. 1860.

crack-rope. See crack-halter.

crack the bell. To fail; muddle things, make a mistake; ruin it: Cockneys' (— 1909); slightly ob. Ware.

crack the monica. To ring the bell (to summon a performer to reappear): music-halls': ca. 1860–90. Ware.

crack-up. To praise highly: coll.; from ca. 1840. James Payn, ' We find them cracking up the country they belong to.' Orig. (1835: Thornton), U.S.—2. V.i., to be exhausted; break down, whether physically or mentally: from ca. 1850; coll. Cf. *cracked*.

cracked. Ruined; bankrupt: from early C. 16; S.E. in C. 16–17, rare in C. 18, coll. in C. 19, ob. then † in C. 20. Mayhew, who has the more gen. *cracked up*.—2. Crazy: C. 17–20; S.E. until ca. 1830.—3. (With variant *cracked in the ring*) deflowered: C. 18–20, low, perhaps coll. rather than

s.—4. Penniless; ruined: low — 1860); **ob.** H., 2nd ed.

'**cracked in the right place**', as the girl said (occ. preceded by *yes ! but*). A C. 20 low c.p. in reply to an insinuation or an imputation of madness, eccentricity, or rashness. Heard in 1922 ; but older.

cracked-up. See sense 1 of **cracked.**

cracker. A lie ; a (very) tall story : C. 17–20, **ob.**: coll.—2. In C. 18, a pistol. Smollett.—3. A very fast pace, a large sum, a dandy, and analogically : from ca. 1870. *The Daily News*, Nov. 1, 1871, ' The shooting party, mounting their forest ponies, came up the straight a cracker.'—4. A heavy fall ; a smash : from ca. 1865 ; ob.—5. (The mod. sense, a thin, crisp biscuit, may derive ex the C. 17–18 c. and low *cracker*, a crust, as recorded by B.E. ; cf. the early C. 19 c. sense, ' a small loaf, served to prisoners in jails ', Vaux).—7. Leather, gen. sheepskin, trousers : South African coll. (— 1833). Pettman.—8. In mid-C. 17–early 19 c., the backside (as in Coles and B.E.).—9. In C. 20 c., and gen. in pl., prisoners that are insane or epileptic or suicidal or injured in head and spine.—10. (Gen. pl.) A cartridge : New Zealanders' : from ca.1910.

cracker-hash. Pounded biscuit with minced salt meat : nautical coll. : mid-C. 19–20. Bowen.

crackers. See **cracker,** 9 and 10.

crackers, adj. Crazy ; mad : lower classes' : C. 20. Ex :—2. *get the crackers,* to go mad : id. : late C. 19–20. F. & Gibbons.

crackey. See **crikey.**

crackiness. Extreme eccentricity ; craziness : coll. : from ca. 1860 ; ob.

cracking. Boasting. Burglary. See **crack, v.,** resp. 1, 3.

cracking, adj. Very fast ; exceedingly vigorous (— 1880) : slightly ob.

cracking, get. See **get cracking.**

cracking a (tidy) crust. See **crack a crust.**

*****cracking tools.** ' Implements of house-breaking', Egan's Grose : c. (— 1823) >, by 1860, low ; ob.

crackish. (Of women only) wanton : late C. 17–early 19 ; coll. B.E. Ex *crack,* n., 2.

crackle, crackling. The velvet bars on the hoods of ' the Hogs ', or students of St. John's, Cambridge : from ca. 1840. Cf. *Isthmus of Suez,* a covered bridge at the same college : ex L. *sus,* a pig.

*****crackmans, cragmans.** A hedge : C.17–early 19. c. Rowlands ; B.E. ; Grose. See **-mans.** Perhaps ex a hedge's *cracks* or gaps.

*****cracksman.** A house-breaker (see **crack, v.** 4) : from ca. 1810 ; orig. c. Vaux, Lytton, Barham, Dickens. The most famous of fictional cracksmen is Hornung's *Raffles.*—2. Hence, the *membrum virile* : from ca. 1850.

cracky. See **crikey.**

-cracy. -rule, -power, -government. Often, in C. 19–20, used in humorous or sarcastic coll. : as, e.g. in *beerocracy, cartocracy, dollarocracy, mobocracy.*

Cradock brick. A man of the Cradock district and town : South African nickname (— 1871). Pettman.

craft. A bicycle : youths' : ca. 1870–80. Ware. (Bicycles were still a novelty.)—2. **sweet craft,** a woman : nautical : C. 20. Manchon.

crag. See **scrag.**—*****cragmans.** See **crackmans.**

crag, long. A long purse : Aberdeen, either c. or low : late C. 18–mid-19. Shirrefs, 1790 (E.D.D.). Perhaps because a long purse (vaguely) resembles a long neck.

crail capon. ' A haddock dried unsplit ': nautical : mid-C. 19–20. Bowen.

cram. A lie, cf. the more frequent *crammer.* From ca. 1840. *Punch,* 1842, ' It soundeth somewhat like a cram.'—2. Hard, ' mechanical ' study (gen. for an examination), both the action and the acquisition : coll. ; from ca. 1850.—3. A ' crib ', an aid to study : university and school ; from ca. 1850. ' Cuthbert Bede ' in *Verdant Green.*—4. A coach or private tutor : from ca. 1855. Dutton Cook, in *Paul Foster's Daughter,* 1861, ' I shall go to a coach, a cram, a grindstone.'—5. (Of a crowd) a crush or jam : coll. : 1858, Dickens. (S.O.D.)

cram, v.i. and t. To tell lies ; to ply, hence to deceive, with lies. From ca. 1790 (recorded 1794, in *The Gentleman's Magazine*). Ex the idea of stuffing, over-feeding with lies.—2. To prepare oneself or another hastily, gen. for an examination (cf. the n., 2–4) : coll., from ca. 1800) : university and school. *Gradus and Cantabrigiam.*—3. To urge on a horse with spur and/or knee and/or hand or reins : sporting, from ca. 1830.—4. To coït with (a woman) : low : mid-C. 19–20. For semantics, see sense 1 : cf. *stuff* in its sexual sense.

cram-book. A book used for *cramming,* q.v. : coll. ; from ca. 1855. O.E.D.

cram-coach. A tutor that ' crams ' pupils for examinations : coll. ; from ca. 1880. (O.E.D.)

cram-paper. A list of prospective answers to be ' crammed ' for examination : coll. : from ca. 1875.

crammable. Capable of being mechanically learnt or soullessly prepared : coll. : from ca. 1865. O.E.D.

crammed, ppl. adj. (Of a person or a lesson) hastily prepared for an examination : coll. : from ca. 1835.

crammer. A liar : from ca. 1860. Cf. *cram,* n. and v.—2. A lie (cf. id.) : from ca. 1855. H. C. Pennell, *Puck on Pegasus,* ' I sucked in the obvious crammer as kindly as my mother's milk ' ; Trollope, 1880.—3. One who prepares students, pupils, for examination (cf. *coach, grinder*) : from ca. 1810 ; coll. Maria Edgeworth in *Patronage.*—4. A pupil or student ' cramming ' for an examination (like the preceding, ex *cram,* v., 2) : coll., rare ; from ca. 1812.

crammer's pup. (Gen. pl.) The pupil of a ' crammer ' (sense 3) : military (— 1923). Manchon.

cramming, vbl.n. The act of studying, less often of preparing another, for an examination : coll. ; from ca. 1820. ' Aspirants to honours in law . . . know the value of private cramming,' *Punch,* 1841 ; Herbert Spencer, 1869.—2. As adj., from ca. 1830. Southey.

cramp. Prayer ; to pray : Bootham School : late C. 19–20. Anon., *Dict. of Bootham Slang,* 1925. Ex the cramped position.

cramp, the. S.E. *cramp* : C. 19–20 ; coll.

cramp-dodge. Simulated writer's cramp : schoolboys' coll., mostly London (— 1887). Baumann.

cramp in the hand. Niggardliness ; ' costiveness ' : C. 19–20, ob. ; coll.

cramp one's style. See **style, cramp one's.**

*****cramp-rings.** Fetters : from ca. 1560 ; c. in C. 16–17, c. and low in C. 18. Harman, Dekker, Coles, Grose. Ex the S.E. sense, a gold or silver ring that, blessed on Good Friday by the sovereign, was considered a cure for falling sickness and esp. for cramp.

cramp-word. 'Crack-jaw' word; a word either very hard for the illiterate to pronounce or for most to understand: from ca. 1690: coll. B.E.: Dyche; Mrs. Cowley, 'Cramp words enough to puzzle and delight the old gentleman the remainder of his life'; Combe.—2. A sentence of death: C. 18–early 19 c. Dyche.

*cramped. Hanged; derivatively, killed: c. and low: C. 18–19. A development from † S.E. *cramp*, to compress a person's limbs as a punishment.

*cramping-cull. The hangman: c.: C. 18–early 19. *Cull* = man. Semantic.

cramps. See **Venetian cramps.—cranch.** See **craunch.**

crane. To hesitate at an obstacle, a danger: from ca. 1860: coll. >, by 1890, S.E. Ex hunting j.

craner. One who hesitates at a difficult jump: hunting coll.; from ca. 1860.

cranium. Jocular coll.; from ca. 1640: the head. In S.E. it is an anatomical term.

crank. Gin and water: late C. 18–early 19. Grose, 1st ed. Perhaps ex *crank*, pert, lively, exceedingly high-spirited, which may itself in C. 17–18, after being S.E. in C. 16, have been coll. (see B.E.), just as in C. 19 it > coll.—2. A person odd, eccentric, very 'faddy', mildly monomaniacal: orig. (— 1881), U.S., anglicised ca. 1890; in C. 20, coll. Prob. ex *cranky*, q.v.—3. In mid-C 16–18 c., a beggar feigning sickness or illness; also, the falling sickness. Harman. Ex Ger. *krank*, ill. Cf. *counterfeit crank*.

[**crank.** (Nautical) easily capsized: from late C. 17: despite F. & H., rather j. than unconventional.]

*crank-cuffin. A vagrant feigning sickness. C. 18 c. Ex *crank(e)*.

crank of, be a. See **cranky**, 2.—***cranke.** See **crank**, n., 3.

cranky. Crotchety; eccentric; slightly mad (rare): from ca. 1850; coll. >, by 1900, S.E. H., 1st ed. Cf. the S.E. and c. senses of *crank*, n. and adj.—2. Hence, *cranky on*, like *a crank of*, is C. 20 coll.: enthusiastic about, 'mad on'. Manchon.

cranny. The *pudendum muliebre*: low coll.; C. 19–20; ob. Whence *cranny-hunter*, its male opponent.—2. A half-caste: Anglo-Indian coll.: mid-C. 19–20. Ex *cranny* as applied, orig. and mainly in Bengal, to a clerk writing English, itself ex Hindustani *karani*. Yule & Burnell.

cransier. Incorrect for *creancer*: long †. O.E.D.

*crap or **crop.** Money: from ca. 1690. B.E. Orig. either c. or dial.; in C. 19 either s. or dial. Cf. *dust* for origin.—2. In c., C. 19, gallows: cf. *to crop*, to harvest. Vaux. Ex *crap*, v., 2.—3. (Printers') type that has got mixed; 'pie': from ca. 1850 (*crap* only).—4. A defecation: low coll.: mid-C. 19–20. Esp. *do a crap*. Ex:

crap, v. To defecate, evacuate: low coll: mid-C. 18–20. ? cf. *crop*, v.i., to take in the harvest.—2. In c., however, it = to hang: from ca. 1780. G. Parker. Cf. *crop*.

crape it. 'To wear crape in mourning': coll.: late C. 19–20. O.E.D.

crapping-casa, -case, -castle, or -ken. A w.-c.: low: C. 18–20 for all except *-castle*, which is C. 19–20; as *croppin-ken*, however, it occurs in Coles, 1676. Ob.—2. The third, in hospital, = a nightstool: C. 19.

crapple-mapple. Ale (?): Perthshire s.: from ca. 1880. Charles Spence, *Poems*, 1898 (E.D.D., Sup.).

crappo. A type of improvised French trench-mortar, somewhat like a toad: military: 1915–18. F. & Gibbons. Direct ex Fr. Army s. *crapaud*.

crash. Entertainment: C. 17 (? 18): S.E. or coll. Nares.—2. In C. 16, revelry: S.E.—3. (Theatrical) the machine that produces 'thunder'; this or any analogous noise: from ca. 1870; ob.

crash, v.i., occ. t., of an aeroplane: to come (bring) down, gen. violently, out of control: G.W. + (not heard, I believe, in 1914); at first coll., but almost imm. S.E. Its fig. use is coll. (— 1931). Lyell, 'He . . . slipped up on a piece of orange peel and crashed.'—2. Cf. the late C. 17–early 19 c. *crash*, to kill. B.E. Prob. ex North Country dial. *crash*, to smash.

crash-dive. 'The sudden submersion of a submarine on being surprised, or in imminent danger of being rammed': naval coll.: 1915. F. & Gibbons.

crash one's fences. To make mistakes: sporting, esp. hunting, coll.: late C. 19–20.

crasher. A person or thing exceptional in size, merit or, esp., beauty: coll.: from ca. 1908. A. E. W. Mason, *The Dean's Elbow*, 1930, 'Miss Lois . . . is considered . . . rather a crasher. . . . Not what I should call homey, but a crasher.'—2. A lie: Cheshire s. (— 1898). E.D.D.

crashing bore. A very tedious or tiresome person or, occ., thing: coll.: from ca. 1915. Anthony Berkeley, *Panic Party*, 1934, 'It's a crashing bore . . . to think of those dim cads knocking us for six like this, but . . . it's no use getting strenuous about it.' Ex aviation. Cf. *crushing*, q.v.

*crashing-cheats. The teeth: ca. 1560–1830. Until ca. 1750, c.; then low. Lit., crunching-things.—2. In mid-C. 16–early 17 c., fruit.

-crat, -ocrat. The same remark as at *-cracy*.

crate. A British aeroplane: Air Force: 1916. B. & P. By dysphemism.

crater, crat(h)ur. See **creature.**

crathe. Incorrect for *crach*, i.e. *cratch*: long † O.E.D.

craunch; occ. **cranch.** What can be craunched: coll.: from ca. 1870. A variant of *crunch* (v.). O.E.D.

craw. The human stomach: C. 16–20: pejorative coll. > S.E. (ob.). Whence *craw-thumper*, a Roman Catholic: from ca. 1780. Cf. *brisket-beater*. Grose, 1st ed.—2. Also, jocularly, a cravat falling broadly over the chest: coll.: ca. 1780–1830.

crawfish. To withdraw unreservedly from an untenable position: New Zealand soldiers' in G.W. The crayfish swims backwards.

crawl. A workman given to currying favour with foreman or employer: tailors'; mid-C. 19–20.

crawl, do a. See **do a crawl.**

crawl home on one's eye-brows. To return (esp., home) utterly exhausted: military coll. (1915) >, by 1919, gen. Lyell. Cf. *chin-strap*, q.v.

crawl with. To be alive, or filled, with: military coll. (1915) >, by 1920, gen. coll. F. & Gibbons; Lyell. On *be lousy with*.

crawler. A cab that leaves the rank to search for fares; this the driver does by coasting the pavement at a very slow pace: coll.; from ca. 1860. Rarely applied to taxis.—2. A contemptible sycophant: coll.; from ca. 1850. *The Evening News*, Sept. 21, 1885, 'The complainant call her father a liar, a bester [q.v.], and a crawler.'—3. A louse, a maggot, a nit: coll.: ca. 1790–1830 (O.E.D.). Cf. *creeper*, 4.

crawling on one's eye-brows. Exhausted, tired out: military: late 1914. F. & Gibbons.

crawling on you ?, what's. See **what's bit you ?**

crawly. Having, or like, the feeling of insects a-crawl on one's skin : coll. : 1860. Cf. S.E. *creepy.*

crawly-mawly. Weakly ; ailing : mid-C. 19–20 (ob.) coll. H., 3rd ed. Rhyming reduplication ex *crawl.* Adopted from Norfolk dial. of mid-C. 17–20.

cray. A crayfish : (low) Australian (– 1916). C. J. Dennis.

crayfish. A ' crawler ' ; a contemptible schemer : New Zealanders' : in G.W.

crayt(h)ur or **craychur.** See **creature.**

crazy. Very eager (*for* or *about*, or *to do*, something) : coll. : from the 1770's. (O. D. Sup.)

crazy-back ; crazy Jack. Bauman. 'vhom the O.E.D. has unfortunately overlooked) defines, resp., as *närrischer Fant*, a silly coxcomb, affected ' puppy ', and *verrücktes Weibsbild*, a crazy or a droll hussy : I know neither of these terms (London s. of ca. 1880–1910), but I suspect that, by a printer's error, the definitions have been transposed.

creak in his shoes, make one. To make him smart for it, give him a devilish bad time : London coll. (– 1887) ; ob. Baumann. (Creaking shoes are often painful.)

cream. ' Father-stuff ', as Whitman has it : low coll., C. 19–20. Hence, *cream-stick*, the *membrum virile* : C. 18–20, low coll.

cream (or green) cheese, make one believe the moon is made of. To humbug ; impose upon : coll. ; C. 19–20. Cf. *bamboozle.*

cream fancy (billy). A handkerchief, white or cream of ground but with any pattern. From ca. 1830 : mostly sporting. Brandon. Cf. *belcher.*

cream-ice jack. (Gen. pl. and *c.-i.-J.*) A street seller of ice-creams : London streets' (–1909). Ware, ' Probably from Giacomo and Giacopo ', common It. names, most such vendors being Italians.

cream jugs. Charkof-Krementschug Railway bonds : Stock Exchange, from ca. 1885 ; †.—2. The paps : low (– 1891).

cream of the valley. (Cf. *cold cream.*) Gin : coll. (– 1858) ; ob. Mayhew in *Paved with Gold.* Prob. suggested in opp. to *mountain dew, whiskey.* Occ. *cream of the wilderness* (1873 ; O.E.D.), ob.

cream-pot love. Love pretended to dairymaids for the sake of cream : late C. 17–early 19 coll. Ray, 1678 ; Grose, 1st ed. I.e. cupboard-love.

Creams. Abbr. *Cold Creams*, q.v. Ware.

cream-stick. See **cream.**

creamy. First-class, excellent : coll. ; from ca. 1880 ; slightly ob. Baumann.

*crease. To kill (a person) : c. : C. 20. James Curtis, *The Gilt Kid*, 1936. The word is proleptic.

creased. Fainted ; knocked unconscious : military : C. 20. F. & Gibbons. Perhaps on *curl up*, 2.

creases. Watercress : sol. when not a London street-cry, which latter is coll. : (? mid-)C. 19–20. Baumann, 1887.

create, v.i. To make a fuss, a ' row ' : from ca. 1910 (frequent among soldiers in G.W.). Ex *create a disturbance* or *fuss.*

creation !, that beats or **licks.** That's splendid, incomparable : ex U.S. (1834) ; anglicised ca. 1880 ; the *licks* form has never quite lost its American tang.

creature, often **crater, crat(h)ur,** all with the. In late C. 16–18, any liquor ; in C. 19–20, whiskey, esp. Irish whiskey, though Bee, I think wrongly, applies it specifically to gin. Coll. Shakespeare,

' I do now remember the poor creature, small beer.' Cf. S.E. *creature-comfort.*—2. See **brown creatures.**

credentials. The male genitals : jocular coll. ex commerce : from ca. 1895.

creek. ' Division between blocks of changing-room lockers ; division between beds ' : Bootham School : late C. 19–20. Anon., *Dict. of Bootham Slang*, 1925.

creek mat. A bedside mat : id. : id. Ibid.

creeme. To slip or palm something into another's hand(s) : coll. in late C. 17–18, dial in C. 19–20 (ob.) : ? orig. dial. B.E. ? ex the smoothness of cream.

creel. The stomach : Scottish : C. 19–20. E.D.D. Cf. *bread-basket.*

*creep, v.i. To escape : c. : from ca. 1930. James Curtis, *The Gilt Kid*, 1936.

*creep, at the, adj. and adv. Applied to robbing a place while people are there : C. 20 c. Charles E. Leach.

creep away and die ! Go away !, ' get out ! ': non-aristocratic c.p. (– 1923). Manchon.

creeper. A cringer ; a cringing lick-spittle : C. 17–20 ; coll. Cf. *crawl, crawler.*—2. A hack journalist ; ' penny-a-liner ' : from ca. 1820 ; † by 1890.—3. A paying pupil to a Ceylon tea-planter : Ceylon : from ca. 1890 ; ob. Yule & Burnell (at *griffin*).—4. A louse : low coll. : mid-C. 17–20. O.E.D. Cf. *crawler, 3.*—5. See **creepers.**

creepers. The feet : C. 19–20 (ob.) ; coll. Cf. *kickers, trampers.*

*creeping, vbl.n. Men and women robbing together : late C. 16–early 17 c. Greene.

creeping Jesus. A person given to sneaking and whining : ca. 1818 (O.E.D. Sup.) ; in C. 20, esp. Australian.

*creeping law. Robbery by petty thieves in suburbs : late C. 16–early 17 c. Greene. See **law.**

creeps, the. The odd thrill resulting from an un-defined dread : coll. : 1850, Dickens (E.D.D.) Occ. (now ob.) *cold creeps.* Cf. *cold shivers.* Edmund Yates, in *Broken to Harness*, '. . . In the old country mansions . . . where the servants . . . commence . . . to have shivers and creeps.' (The singular is rare.)

creepy. Given to creeping into the favour of superiors or elders : schoolboys' : late C. 19–20.

cremona. A krum(m)horn or cromorne : sol. : mid-C. 17–20. O.E.D.

creosotic, incorrect for *cresotic* ; **crepan** for *trepan.* O.E.D.

crest(s). The shield or arms of a college or a city : sol. : C. 19–20.

crevice. The *pudendum muliebre* : coll. ; C. 19–20. Cf. *cranny.*

[**crew,** when—in C. 16–20—used derogatively of a set or a gang, is almost, not—despite B.E. and Grose—quite coll. after ca. 1660 ; before 1600 it is almost c., as in Greene's Cony-Catching pamphlets.]

Cri, the. The Criterion (theatre, restaurant) at Piccadilly Circus : from ca. 1880.—2. Abbr. *crikey*, q.v.

crib, do a. See **do a crib.**

*crib. In C. 17–early 18 c., food ; provender. This sense is extant in dial : E.D.D. Brome.—2. Abbr. *cribbage* : coll. ; from ca. 1680. —3. (For origin, cf. sense 4.) An abode, shop, lodgings, public-house : from ca. 1810 ; orig. c., then low. Vaux ; Dickens, in *Oliver Twist*, ' The crib's barred up at night like a jail.'—4. A bed : from ca. 1820 ; c., then low. Maginn's *Vidocq* :

'You may have a crib to stow in.' Ex dia. sense (− 1790), a child's cot : E.D.D.—5. Hence, a 'berth', a situation, job : 1859, H., 1st ed.—6. A plagiarism : from ca. 1830 ; coll.—7. A literal translation illicitly used by students or pupils : coll. : from ca. 1825.

crib, v. To pilfer ; take furtively : from ca. 1740. Dyche's Dict., 5th ed., 1748 ; Foote, 1772, 'There are a brace of birds and a hare, that I cribbed this morning out of a basket of game.'—2. (For **crack a crib**, see **crack**, v., 4.—3. To plagiarise : coll. : 1778 (S.O.D.).—4. To use a 'crib', q.v. : from ca. 1790 ; coll.—5. To cheat in an examination : coll. ; from ca. 1840. *Punch*, 1841 (vol. I), 'Cribbing his answers from a tiny manual . . . which he hides under his blotting paper'.—6. To beat (a person) at fisticuffs : London streets' : ca. 1810–40. Tom Cribb defeated Belcher in 1807.—7. Hence, to thrash : low : from ca. 1840. Ware. —8. V.i., to grumble : military : late C. 19–20. F. & Gibbons. Prob. a back-formation ex *cribbiter*, q.v. In all senses, the vbl.n. *cribbing* is frequent.

crib, fight a. To pretend to fight : pugilistic (− 1791). Grose, 3rd ed. Ex the bear-garden.

crib-biter. A persistent grumbler : coll. ; from late 1850's ; ob. H., 2nd ed. Ex the S.E. sense of a horse that, suffering from a bad digestion, bites its crib, i.e. manger.

crib-cracker. A burglar : low (? orig. c.) : from ca. 1850. G. R. Sims, 1880.—2. Vbl.n., *crib-cracking*, in *Punch*, 1852.

Crib-Crust Monday. See **Pay-Off Wednesday**.

cribbage. The action of cribbing (v., 3, 4) ; what is cribbed : rare coll. ; from ca. 1830. Punning *cribbage*, the game.

cribbage-face(d), n. and adj. (A person) with a face pock-marked and therefore like a cribbage-board : from ca. 1780 ; ob. Grose, 1st ed. Cf. *rolled on Deal beach*.

cribbage-peg. (Gen. **pl.**) **A** leg : rhyming **s.** (− 1923). Manchon.

cribber. One who uses a crib (n., 6) : from ca. 1830 : coll.—2. A grumbler : military ; from ca. 1860. Prob. ex *crib-biter*, q.v.

Cribbeys or **Cribby Islands.** Blind alleys, hidden lanes, remote courts : late C. 18–early 19. Grose, 1st ed. Ex the Carribbee Islands, of which little—and that little unprepossessing—was known in C. 18, and gen. applied to the western quarter of the Covent Garden district.

***cribbing.** Food and drink : C. 17 c. Brome.—2. Also see **crib**, v., at end.

cricket, it's (that's, etc.) not. It's unfair : 1902 (S.O.D.), but adumbrated in 1867 (see Lewis) : coll., almost imm. > S.E.

Cricket Quarter. Summer Quarter (i.e. term) : Charterhouse coll. : mid-C. 19–20. A. H. Tod, *Charterhouse*, 1900.

cricket-ball. A hand-grenade of the shape and volume of a cricket-ball : military coll. : 1915–18. F. & Gibbons. It was used only in 1915 and it 'had to be lighted with a match' (Frank Richards).

cricketess. A cricketress : sol. : 1866. Lewis.

crik(e)y ; occ. **crick(e)y** or **crack(e)y**, the latter mostly American ; also **by crikey.** Orig. an oath (*Christ*), but by ca. 1835 merely an exclamation of surprise, admiration, etc. Barham, 'If a Frenchman, *Superbe !*—if an Englishman, Crikey !' Cf. the ob. *criminy*, in the same usages (Farquhar, 1700) and *jiminy*, q.v. These terms are either s. or coll., according to the philologists' point of view.

crim con. Abbr. *criminal conversation*, adultery. From ca. 1770, orig. legal ; then, by 1785, coll. ; then—from ca. 1850—S.E. Grose, 1st ed.

crimea. A (long or fierce-looking) beard : proletarian : 1856 ; very ob. Ware. Ex the hairiness of Crimean 'veterans'.—2. See **fusilier**.

crimes ! ; crimine or **criminy !** Variants (mid-C. 19–20 ; late C. 17–20) of *crikey* or *jiminy*. Farquhar, 1694, 'Oh ! crimine !' (E.D.D. ; W.).

crimp. To play foul : low s. or c. : ca. 1690–1750. B.E. Ex :

crimp, play. To play foul : low coll. : ca. 1660–1800. D'Urfey, Grose.

crimping-fellow. 'A sneaking Cur', B.E. : low coll. : late C. 17–18.

crimson dawn. See **red Biddy**.

crinckam, crincum. See **crinkum**.

crinkle-pouch. A sixpence : late C. 16–early 17 : coll.

crinkum, crincum ; occ. **crinkom**, C. 17, and **crinckam**, C. 18. A venereal disease : C. 17–18. O.E.D.

crinkum-crankum. The *pudendum muliebre* : ca. 1780–1870. Grose, 3rd ed. Ex the S.E. sense (cf. *crinkle-crankle*), a winding way. Cf. *crinkums*, q.v. —2. In pl. (*crinkum-crankums*), tortuous handwriting : coll. (− 1887) ; ob. Baumann.

crinkums. A venereal disease : C. 17–early 19. B.E. Cf. *crinkum* and *crinkum-crankum*.

crinoline. A woman : ca. 1855–95. Cf. *petticoat, skirt*.

Cripes ! Christ ! : low : late C. 19–20. Also *by cripes !* Cf. *crikey*, q.v.

cripple. A sixpence (− 1785) ; ob. in C. 20. Grose, 1st ed. Ex its aptness to be bent. Cf. *bender*.—2. A clumsy person ; a dull one : coll. ; mid-C. 19–20.—3. (Wellington College) a dolt : mid-C. 19–20.—4. A lobster minus a claw : nautical coll. : late C. 19–20. Bowen.

cripple !, go it, you. An ironic, often senseless, comment on strenuous effort, esp. in sports and games ; *wooden legs are cheap* was often, but since G.W. is seldom, added. Coll. ; C. 19–20. Thackeray, 1840.

cripple-stopper. A small gun for killing wounded birds : sporting coll. (− 1881). O.E.D.

Cripplegate. See **come Cripplegate**.

criq. Brandy : Canadian : C. 20. F. & Gibbons. Ex French-Canadian.

crisp. A bank or a currency note : from ca. 1850 ; cf. *soft*.

crisp, adj. New, interesting : from ca. 1920 ; slightly ob. Manchon.

crisp, talk. To say disagreeable things : coll. (− 1923). Manchon.

Crispin. A shoemaker : from ca. 1640 ; orig. coll., by 1700 S.E. ; rare in C. 20. Hence *St. Crispin's lance*, an awl, and *Crispin's holiday*, every Monday : both late C. 17–19 coll. Ex Crispin, the patron saint of shoemakers.

crit. A critic : C. 18 coll. (? coined by Fielding). O.E.D.

cro'-Jack eyed. Squinting : nautical : mid-C. 19–20. Bowen. Ex work aloft.

***croak,** in c., means both to die and to kill ; also (ob.) a 'last dying' speech : C. 19–20. Vaux (to die) ; Egan, 1823 (to hang) ; H., 1st ed., the n. sense : hardly before ca. 1850. Ex the death-rattle. Both senses appear also in dial.

***croaker.** In mid-C. 17–18, c. for a groat ; in C. 19, s. for a sixpence. B.E. Perhaps a pun—

suggested by *cripple*, 1—on *groat*.—2. A beggar : low : from ca. 1835. Brandon, 1839 ; H., 1st ed. Ex his complaints.—3. A dying person, a doctor, a corpse : the second being c. and low s., the first low coll., and the third (H., 2nd ed.) low s. : mid-C. 19–20. Hence, a beast killed to save it from dying : 1892 (O.E.D.)—5. A pronounced and persistent pessimist : from ca. 1630 ; coll. until ca. 1700, when it > S.E. Whence, prob., senses 2, 3.—6. (Gen. pl.) A potato : Anglo-Irish (— 1923). Manchon. Also *croker*. Possibly cognate with dial. *croke*, dross, core of fruit.

croaker's chovey. A chemist's shop : C. 19–20 low. Cf. *crocus-chovey*, q.v.

Croakumshire. Northumberland : mid-C. 18–19. Grose, 1st ed. Ex that county's defective *r*.

croakus. See **crocus**.

croby. ' Orig. a crust ; later, a piece of bread and butter ' ; † ' and superseded by " bar ", q.v.', says the anon. *Dict. of Bootham Slang*, 1925. Cf. *crug* and *cruggy*, qq.v.

croc. A file of school-boys or, much more gen., -girls walking in pairs : from ca. 1900 ; mostly school s. Abbr. *crocodile*, orig. university s. (— 1891), now coll.—2. Also, of course, the crocodile itself : coll. : rare before C. 20.

crock. A worthless animal ; a disabled person or (in C. 20 rarely) a ' duffer ' : from ca. 1879 ; coll. Either ex broken earthenware (1850) or the Scottish *crock*, an old ewe or (1879) a broken-down horse (S.O.D.).—2. Hence, a boy or a man that plays no outdoor games : Public Schools' coll. : from ca. 1890. P. G. Wodehouse, *St. Austin's*, 1903.—3. A bicycle : youths' : ca. 1870–80. Ware. Because a ' bone-shaker ' ?—4. A chamber-pot : Bootham School : C. 20. Anon., *Dict. of Bootham Slang*, 1925, adds ' crock rolling . . . A common practice in bedrooms.' Abbr. *crockery*.

crock up. To get disabled ; break down ; fall ill : from ca. 1890. Common in G.W. Ex preceding.

crocketts. A kind of makeshift cricket : Winchester College, C. 19–20. (R. G. K. Wrench.) Hence :

crocketts, get. (At cricket) fail to score : from ca. 1840 ; Winchester. See **Winchester College Slang, § 2.**

crocodile. A (gen. and orig. girls') school walking, two by two, in file (— 1870) : coll. In C. 20, S.E. The very rare v. occurs in 1889. (O.E.D.)— 2. A support of a plank serving as a seat : *Conway Training Ship* (— 1891). Masefield.

*****crocus.** See **crocus metallorum**.

*****crocus-chovey.** A doctor's consulting-room ; a surgery : mid-C. 19–20 c. H., 3rd ed. See **chovey**. Ex :—2. A chemist's shop : c. (— 1791). B. M. Carew, quoted by E.D.D.

crocus (metallorum) ; in C. 19–20 occ. *croakus*. A surgeon or a doctor (esp. a quack) : low (—1785) ; ob. Grose, 1st ed. ; Mayhew. Prob. ex *croak* after *hocus-pocus*, though the O.E.D. mentions a Dr. Helkiah *Crooke* and Coles has *crocus Martis*, a chemical preparation of iron, and *crocus veneris*, one of copper. Cf. *croaker*, by which also the old scientific term *crocus* was prob. suggested in this sense. At first, naval and military.—2. (Always **crocus**.) Among grafters, it bears the above-mentioned senses ; also, a herbalist, a miracle-worker. Philip Allingham, *Cheapjack*, 1934. For gen. information, see, in addition, Neil Bell, *Crocus*, a novel of the fairs, 1936.

*****crocus-pitcher.** An itinerant quack : mid-C. 19–20 c.

*****crocus-worker.** A seller of patent medicines : c., and Petticoat Lane traders' : late C. 19–20. ·

*****crocussing rig.** The practising of itinerant quackery : mid-C. 19–20 c. ; ob.

croker. See **croaker.—crokus.** See **crocus (metallorum)**.

*****crome.** The hook used by an ' angler ' (q.v.) : late C. 16 c. Greene, in *The Black Book's Messenger*.

crommel. Incorrect for *cromlech* : mid-C. 19–20. O.E.D.

crone. A clown : from ca. 1850 ; mostly Parlyaree. Prob. *clown* corrupted.

cronk. (Of a horse) made to appear ill in order to cheat its backers : from the 1880's : racing s. >, by 1890, gen. Ex Ger. *krank*, sick, ill. Morris.— 2. Hence, unsound ; dishonestly come by : from ca. 1890. *The (Melbourne) Herald*, 1893, July 4. Both senses are Australian. Cf. *crook*, adj.

crony. ' A Camerade or intimate friend ', B.E. : from 1650 ; university s. till ca. 1750, then gen. coll. Pepys, ' Jack Cole, my old schoolfellow . . . a great crony of mine ' (S.O.D.). Perhaps *crony* was Cambridge University's counterpart to the orig. Oxford *chum*. Its C. 17 variant *chrony* indicates the etymology : Gr. χρόνιος, contemporary, ex χρόνος, time. W. cites an instance for 1652.—Whence, 2, in c. or low s., an accomplice in a robbery : C. 18– early 19. *A New Canting Dict.*, 1725.—3. In C. 17–18, a tough old hen. B.E.—4. A Dumfries-shire c. term (C. 19–20) for a potato. The E.D.D. cites the derivative *crony-hill* ,a potato-field.

crook. A sixpence (— 1789) : low ; ob. by 1860, † by 1914. Ex *crook-back*, q.v.—2. A swindler, a thief ; a professional criminal : orig. (1886) U.S., anglicised ca. 1895 as a coll. ; by 1920, S.E. Perhaps ex *crook, on the* ; cf., as W. suggests, Fr. *escroc*.

crook, v.t. To steal : either c. or low s. (— 1923). Manchon. Ex *get on the crook* : see **crook, on the**.

crook, adj. Ill : Australian : C. 20. Prob. ex *cronk*, q.v., via *crooked*.—2. See

crook, go. To give way to anger ; to express annoyance : Australian : from ca. 1905. Prob. ex *crook*, adj.—2. Hence the c.p., *have you read the* (or, more gen., *that*) *little red book* ; if the man thus addressed looked interrogatively, one added *that little red book,* ' *Why Go Crook ?* ' Ca. 1910–20.

crook, on the. Dishonestly, illegally, illicitly ; leading a life of crime : in England before 1874 (? first used in U.S.) and, there, perhaps orig. c. H., 5th ed. Prob. suggested by (*on the*) *straight* : cf., however, *on the cross*.

crook-back. A sixpence (— 1785) ; † by 1900. Grose, 1st ed. Cf. *bender*, *cripple*, *crook*.—2. **Crook-Back.** Richard III of England (C. 15).

crook (occ. **cock**) **one's** or **the elbow** (occ. **little finger**). To drink (not of water) : ex U.S. (1830 : Thornton), anglicised ca. 1875 : coll. Besant & Rice, 1877.

crook one's elbow and wish it may never come straight. With the required pronominal adjustment, this phrase lent efficacy to an oath : late C. 18–early 19 low coll. Grose, 2nd ed.

crooked. Dishonestly acting (of persons), handled or obtained (things) : mostly Australian ; from before 1864. H., 3rd ed., ' A term used among dog-stealers and the " fancy " generally, to denote anything stolen ' ; ' Rolf Boldrewood ' speaks of ' a crooked horse '.

*crooked, adv. Illicitly, in a criminal manner ; furtively : c. : (?) mid-C. 19–20. James Curtis, *The Gilt Kid*, 1936, ' Sold crooked '.

crooked as a dog's hind leg. See **dog's hind leg.**—**Crooked Lane.** See **buy.**

crookshanks. A coll. nickname for a man with bandy legs : 1788, Grose, 2nd ed. Cf. the surname *Cruickshanks*.

crooky. To walk arm in arm ; v.t., to court (a girl) : coll. : mid-C. 19–20 ; ob. H., 2nd ed.

crool. Cruel : sol. : C. 19 (? earlier)–20. Also in *crool the pitch*.

Crop. ' A nick name for a Presbyterian ', Grose ; ' one with very short Hair ', B.E. Resp. mid-C. 18–early 19 and late C. 17–early 18 coll.—2. **crop,** money, see **crap,** n., 1.—3. **crop,** to hang, to defecate, is a variant of c. *crap*, v., 1 and 2. Cf. :

*crop, be knocked down for a. ' To be condemned to be hanged ', *Lex. Bal.* : c. of ca. 1810–50.

Crop the Conjuror. ' Jeering appellation of one with short hair ', Grose, 1st ed. : late C. 18- early 19 coll. Cf. *Crop*, 1.

cropoh. A Frenchman : nautical (— 1887) ; † by 1920. Baumann. Ex Fr. *crapaud*, a toad : cf. *frog*, q.v.

*croppen, croppin : see **crapping casa.**—2. The tail of beast or vehicle : C. 18–early 19 : c. *A New Canting Dict.*, 1725 ; Grose, 1st ed.

cropper ; esp. **come,** or **go, a cropper.** A heavy fall, fig. and lit. : from the late 1850's ; coll. H., 3rd ed. ; Trollope, 1880, ' He could not . . . ask what might happen if he were to come a cropper.' Ex hunting.

croppie. A variant of *croppy*, 2, q.v.—**croppin.** See **croppen.**—**croppin-ken.** See **crapping casa.**

croppled, to be. Fail in an examination, be sent down at a lesson : Winchester College : mid-C. 19–20. Ex (*to*) *crop* + *cripple*.

croppy or **Croppy.** An Irish rebel of 1798, when sympathy with the French revolutionaries was shown by close-cut hair : orig. coll., soon historical —therefore S.E.—2. Also, an ex-gaolbird : low (— 1857). ' Ducange Anglicus.'

crops, go and look at the. To visit the w.-c. : mid-C. 19–20 ; ob. Ex agriculture. Cf. *pluck a rose*.

*cross, gen. with **the.** Anything dishonest : from early C. 19 ; c. >, by 1870, low s. Opp. to *the square* as **crooked** is opp. to *straight*. Vaux ; Trollope in *The Claverings*.—2. Esp. a pre-arranged swindle : c. (— 1829).—3. Also, a thief : c. from ca. 1830. (The term occurs mostly in compounds and phrases ; these follow the v.)

cross, v. To bestride a horse : jocular coll. ; from ca. 1760 ; ob. (S.O.D.).—2. Hence, to have intercourse with a woman : from ca. 1790.—3. To play false, v.t. and (rarely), i. ; to cheat : low : C. 19–20. Egan's Grose.—4. In the passive, *be crossed*, mid-C. 19 university s. meant to be punished, e.g. by loss of freedom : ' Cuthbert Bede ' in *Verdant Green*, 1853 ; H., 3rd–5th edd. Ex the cross against one's name.

cross, adj. Out of humour, temporarily ill-tempered : coll. ; from ca. 1630.—2. Dishonest ; dishonestly obtained : c. : from ca. 1810. Vaux. Ex *cross*, n.

cross. Adv., unfavourably, adversely ; awry, amiss : from ca. 1600 ; S.E. till ca. 1840, then coll. (S.O.D.)

cross, come home by weeping. Finally to repent : C. 18–early 19 coll.

*cross, on the. Dishonest(ly), illegal(ly), fraudulent(ly) : from ca. 1810 ; orig. c. Vaux ; H., 1st ed. ; Henry Kingsley ; Ouida, 1868, in *Under Two Flags*, ' Rake was . . . " up to every dodge on the cross " .' See **cross,** n., 1.

cross, play a. Act dishonestly ; esp. in boxing, to lose dishonestly : ca. 1820–1920.

cross as the devil. A late C. 19–20 coll. variant, or perhaps rather intensive, of :

cross as two sticks, as. Very peevish or annoyed : coll. : from ca. 1830. Scott, 1831 ; Pinero, 1909. (Apperson.) Perhaps ex their rasping together, but prob. ex two sticks set athwart (W.).

Cross-Belts. The 8th Hussars : C. 18–early 20. ' The regiment wears the sword belt over the right shoulder in memory of the Battle of Saragossa [1700] where it took the belts of the Spanish cavalry,' F. & H.

*cross-bite, cross-biting. A deception, trick(ery), cheat(ing) : from ca. 1570 ; c. > s. > coll. > S.E. > †, the same applying to the slightly earlier v. Marlowe, G. Harvey, Prior, Scott, Ainsworth.—2. In late C. 16–18 c., ' one who combines with a sharper to draw in a friend ', Grose ; also v.

*cross-biter. A swindler, cheat, hoaxer : late C. 16–early 18 ; c. > s. > coll. > S.E.

*cross-biting law. ' Cosenage by whores ', Greene : late C. 16–17 c. Greene. See **law.**

*cross-boy. A crook, a dishonest fellow : Australian c. (— 1890). Ex *cross-chap*. (O.E.D. Sup.)

cross-built. (Of persons) awkwardly built or moving : coll. : ca. 1820–70. Bee.

cross-buttock. An unexpected repulse or rebuff : coll. (— 1864). H., 3rd ed. Ex a throw in wrestling.

*cross-chap, -cove, lad, -man, -squire. A thief. C. 19–20 c. ; *-squire* is †. Varied by *lad*, etc., *of the cross*. (See also the separate entries at **cross-cove** and **cross-man**.)

cross-country. Abbr. *cross-country runner* : athletics, C. 20 ; not gen.

*cross-cove. A swindler ; a confidence trickster : c. (— 1812) ; ob. Vaux.

*cross-cove and mollisher. A man and woman intimately associated in robbery : (— 1859) ; c. ; ob. H., 1st ed. See **cross,** n. ; **mollisher** : ex *moll*, q.v., ? after *demolisher*.

*cross-crib. A thieves' and/or swindlers' lodging-house or hotel : c. ; from ca. 1810. Vaux ; H., 1st ed. ; Baumann (misprinted *-crip*). Ex *crib*, n., 3.

*cross-drum. A thieves' tavern : c. : from ca. 1840. See **drum.**

cross-eye(s). A person with a squint : coll. : from ca. 1870.

*cross-fam or **-fan.** (Also n.) To rob from the person, with one hand ' masking ' the other : c. : from ca. 1810. Vaux. See **fam** and **fan.**

*cross-girl. A harlot that, specialising in sailors, gets all the money she can from the amorous and then bilks them by running away : c. (— 1861) ; ob. Mayhew.

cross I win, pile you lose. A C. 17 form of *heads I win, tails you lose.*

cross-in-the-air (or without hyphens). A rifle carried at the reverse : amateur soldiers' : ca. 1880–1914.

*cross-jarvey (-jarvis, Baumann) with a **cross-rattler.** ' A co-thief driving his hackney-coach ', Bee : c. : ca. 1820–90. See **cross,** adj., 2.

*cross-kid, occ. -quid. To cross-examine : c. (— 1879). Ex *kid*, to quiz.

*cross-kiddle. To cross-examine : c. (— 1879); ob. Horsley (cited by F. & H. at *reeler*).

*cross-lad. See cross-chap.

cross-legs. A tailor : low : ca. 1850–1910. Baumann.

*cross-life man. A professional criminal, esp. thief : c. (— 1878) ; ob.

*cross-man. A thief ; a swindler ; confidence man : c. (— 1823). Bee ; H., 3rd ed. See cross, n.

cross me (or my) throat ! Cross my heart ! ; i.e., honestly ! : a c.p. coll. interjection : C. 20.

*cross-mollisher. A female *cross-cove*, q.v. : c. (— 1812) ; ob. Vaux.

cross-patch. A peevish person : late C. 17–20 ; coll. B.E. Cf. the old nursery rhyme : ' Cross-patch, | Draw the latch, | Sit by the fire and spin.' Here, *patch* is a fool, a child (W.). In late C. 19–20, occ. *cross-piece* : Manchon.

*cross-squire. See cross-chap.

*cross-stiff. A letter : c. ; from ca. 1860 ; ob.

*cross, or go over, the Alps. To go to Dartmoor Prison : C. 20 c.

cross the damp-pot. To cross the Atlantic : tailors' ; from ca. 1860 ; ob.

cross the Ruby. To cross the Rubicon : ' Fast World, early 19 cent.' (Ware). Punning *ruby*, port wine.

crosser. An arranger of or participator in a dishonest act : sporting : from ca. 1870.

crossish. Rather bad-tempered or peevish : coll. : from ca. 1740 ; rare and ob. O.E.D.

crotcheteer. ' A patron of crotchets ' : Society : ca. 1880–1900. Ware.

Crouch-Back. Edmund, Earl of Lancaster (C. 13). Dawson.

Croucher, the. Jessop, the mighty hitter : cricketers' nickname : from ca. 1895.

crow. Gen. as a *regular crow*. A fluke ; unexpected luck : from ca. 1850. Ex billiards ; prob. the Fr. *raccroc*.—2. In c., with corresponding v., a confederate on watch ; if a female, often *canary*. From early 1820's. ' Jon Bee ', 1823.—3. A clergyman : late C. 18–20 ; ob. Ex black clothes.

crow, v. To bend (rails) for the two-foot or 4′ 8″ light-railway tracks : Public Works' (— 1935). —2. V.i., to act as a ' crow ' (n., 2) : c. : from ca. 1840. ' *No. 747* ', *The Autobiography of a Gipsy*, 1891 (E.D.D.).—3. Corresponding to crow, n., 2 ; v.i. : c. : late C. 19–20. W. A. Gape, *Half a Million Tramps*, 1936.

crow, a regular. A great success : lower classes' (— 1923). Manchon. Cf. *crow*, n., 1.

crow, no carrion will kill a. A coll., semi-proverbial saying applied to gross eaters, tough persons : C. 17–18.

crow a pudding, give or make the. See pudding, give the crow a.

crow-bait. A scraggy, esp. if old, horse : among Englishmen in South America : from ca. 1895. C. W. Thurlow Craig.

crow-eater. A lazy person (ex the eating habits of crows) : Australia, South Africa : from ca. 1875. —2. (Gen. in pl.) A South Australian : from the 1890's. Crows are very numerous in that State.

crow-fair. An assemblage of clergymen : late C. 18–19 ; coll. Grose, 1st ed. Ex their black clothes.

crow in a gutter, strut like a. To be over-proud : late C. 16–19 ; coll. Fulke ; Spurgeon. (Apperson).

crow to pluck (in C. 15, pull ; rarely pick) with anyone, have a. To have an unpleasant or embarrassing affair to settle : from C. 16 ; coll. till C. 18, when it > S.E. Shakespeare, ' Hudibras ' Butler, Scott. The phrase ' suggests animals struggling over prey ', W.

Crowbar Brigade, the. The Irish Constabulary : Anglo-Irish : 1848 ; ob. Ex ' crowbar used in throwing down cottages to complete eviction of tenants ', Ware. Whence :

crowbar landlord. One who resorts to such methods : Anglo-Irish : ca. 1850–90. Ware.

crowd. A company of people ; set, ' lot ' : Colonial (ex U.S.), from ca. 1870.—2. In G.W., a military unit : cf. *mob* and *push*.

crowd, may—might—will—would pass in a. Is just average : coll. : C. 20. An elaboration is *pass in a crowd with a push* (D. Sayers, *The Nine Tailors*, 1934). Cf. *there are worse in gaol*, q.v.

crowder. A full theatre or ' house ' : theatrical : from ca. 1870 ; ob.

crowdy-headed Jock. See Jock, 1.

crown ; always the crown. The sergeant-major : military coll. : C. 20. F. & Gibbons. Ex the badge of a crown on his sleeve.—2. The school tuck-shop : Charterhouse : C. 19–20. (A. H. Tod, *Charterhouse*, 1900.) Perhaps ex the old Crown Inn.—3. The school pavilion : Charterhouse : late C. 19–20. (Ibid.)

crown, v. To put a chamber-pot on a man's head : Australian universities', C. 20.—2. In c., to inspect a window with a view to burglary : C. 19–20 ; ob.—3. To hit (a person) on the *crown* : low : C. 20. George Ingram, *Stir*, 1933.

crown and feathers. The female genitals : low : C. 19–20.

crown-office. The head : late C. 18–early 19. Grose, 1st ed. Cf. :

crown-office, in the. Tipsy : late C. 17–18. B.E. Cf. preceding.

crownation. Coronation : sol., C. 17–20 ; rare after ca. 1920.

crowner. Coroner : in M.E. and early Mod.E. (e.g. in Shakespeare's *Hamlet*), it is S.E. ; then dial. and either coll. or sol., in C. 20 gen. the latter : esp. *crowner's quest*, a coroner's inquest (Manchon).—2. A fall on the crown of one's head : sporting : from ca. 1860. Whyte-Melville.

*crow's-foot. In c., the Government broad arrow : from ca. 1870 ; ob.

crow's-nest. ' Small bedroom for bachelors high up in country houses, and on a level with the tree-tops ', Ware : Society : mid-C. 19–20 ; ob. Ex nautical S.E.

cruel, cruelly, adj., adv. Hard, exceeding(ly) : resp. since M.E. and C. 16 : S.E. until C. 19, then coll. Pepys, July 31, 1662, ' Met Captain Brown . . . at which he was cruel angry '. The early history of the coll. *cruel(ly)* significantly parallels that of the adv. *bloody*.

cruel the pitch. To frustrate (a plan, etc.) ; to interfere greatly with one's schemes or welfare : C. 20. Ex cricket.

cruelty-van (or booby-hutch). A four-wheeled chaise : from ca. 1850 ; † by 1910.

crug. Food : from ca. 1820. Prob. ex *crug* (Christ's Hospital) bread : late C. 18–19 ; Lamb, ' a penny loaf—our crug '.—2. (Ibid.) a Christ's Hospital boy, esp. old boy : from ca. 1830.

cruganaler, cruggnailer. (Christ's Hospital) a biscuit given on St. Matthew's Day : C. 19–20.

Either ex *crug and ale* (see **crug**) or punning *hard as nails*.

cruggy. Hungry : C. 19–20 ; Christ's Hospital. Ex **crug**, q.v.

cruiser. A harlot : C. 19–20, ob. One that cruises the streets.—2. In c., a beggar : late C. 17–early 19. B.E. Ex habit of ' cruising about '.—3. A highwayman's spy : c. : C. 18–early 19.

crumb. A pretty woman : military ; from ca. 1830 ; † by 1914.—2. Plumpness : from ca. 1840. Dickens. Cf. *crummy.*—3. See **crums.**

crumb and crust man. A baker : coll. ; from ca. 1840.

crumbles. A set of mishaps causing one person to be blamed : nautical : late C. 19–20. Bowen.

crumbs. See **crums.**

crumbs, pick (in C. 16, **gather**) **up one's.** See **pick up one's crumbs.**

crummy. Plump ; esp. (cf. *bit of crumb*, q.v.) of a pretty woman that is full-figured, large-bosomed : from early C. 18, as is, 2, the c. sense, rich : both ex *crumby* (bread).—3. Lousy : from ca. 1840 ; perhaps orig. c., then Cockney (see H.), then low and military (certainly very common in G.W.) ; then, ex the Army, among tramps—see Jennings, *Tramping with Tramps*, 1932. Hence, the c. *crummy doss*, a lice-infested bed. ? ex a louse's vague resemblance to a small crumb.—4. Hence, dirty, untidy : nautical : mid-C. 19–20. Bowen.

crummy ! A C. 20 low variant of *criminy* (*crikey*) *!* Cf. *crums*, 2.

*****crump.** In late C. 17–early 19 c., one who helps litigants to false witnesses. B.E. Cf. *crimp* and *crimping fellow*, qq.v.—2. A hard hit or fall : Winchester College, from ca. 1850. S.E. *crump*, to hit briskly, the S.O.D. quoting ' We could slog to square-leg, or crump to the off,' 1892.—3. Hence, a ' coal-box ', i.e. a 5·9 German shell or shell-burst ; occ. of heavier guns : military : 1914 ; ob. B. & P. Hence :

crump, v.t. To shell with heavy guns : military : 1915 ; ob. Ibid.—2. The v. quoted at *crump*, n., 2, is considered by F. & H. and the E.D.D. to be s.

crumper. A hard hit or blow : from ca. 1850 : coll. Cf. *crump*, 1, q.v.—2. Whence, a great lie (cf. *thumper*) : from ca. 1880 : schoolboys'. Miss Braddon. (O.E.D.)

crumpet. The head : late C. 19–20 ; ob. Cf. *onion, turnip*, and F. & H., s.v., for synonymy. Esp. *barmy* (or *dotty*) *in the crumpet*, crazy, mad : Manchon.—2. A term of endearment : lower classes' : from late 1890's. (O.E.D. Sup.)

crumpet-face. A face covered with small-pox marks : mid-C. 19–20, ob. ; coll. H., 5th ed. Cf. *cribbage-face*, q.v.

*****crumpet, get a.** (Of a man) to copulate in a specific instance : c. : C. 20. James Curtis, *The Gilt Kid*, 1936.

crumpet-scramble. A tea-party : from ca. 1860 : coll. Derby Day, 1864, ' There *are* men who do not disdain muffin-worries and crumpet-scrambles.' Cf. *bun-fight.*

crumpler. A cravat : from ca. 1830 ; coll.—2. A heavy fall : circus and music-halls' and, in C. 20, hunting : from ca. 1850, as in ' Guy Livingstone ' Lawrence's *Hagarene*, 1874, and H. A. Vachell's *Moonhills*, 1934. Cf. *crusher*, 3, for semantics.

crums ; occ. **crumbs.** (Extremely rare in singular.) Lice : low (— 1923). Manchon. App. a back-formation ex *crummy*, 3.—2. As an exclama-

tion, it is synonymous with *crummy !* : mostly boys' : C. 20. Will Scott, in *The Humorist*, April 7, 1934, ' Crumbs, mater, shove a sock in it ! What tripe ! '

crunchiness ; crunchy. Fit(ness) for crunching or being crunched : coll. : from ca. 1890. O.E.D. (Sup.)

crupper. The human buttocks : jocularly coll., from late C. 16. Ex a horse's rump.

crush. A large social gathering, esp. if crowded : from ca. 1830 ; coll. Whyte-Melville, 1854 ; H. D. Traill, in *Tea Without Toast*, 1890, ' And we settled that to give a crush at nine | Would be greatly more effectual, and more intellectual, | Than at six o'clock to, greatly daring, dine.'—2. Hence (in the Army) a military unit : late C. 19–20. Cf. *crowd, mob, push.*—3. Hence, a set, a group : coll. : from ca. 1919. E.g. *Shakespeare—and That Crush*, by Richard Dark and Thomas Derrick, 1931.—4. An infatuation ; a strong liking or ' fancy ' for a person : U.S. (1914), anglicised in 1927. Esp. *have a crush on*. Ex *crushed on*, q.v.—5. Hence, the person for whom one has a ' crush ' : from ca. 1927. (O.E.D. Sup.)

crush, v.t., with *bottle, cup, pot, quart*. Drink : late C. 16–19 ; coll. Greene, 1592 (*a potte of ale*) ; Shakespeare (*a cup of wine*) ; Scott (*a quart*). Cf. *burst, crack.*—2. To decamp, run away : c. (? > low s.) : from ca. 1860. H., 3rd ed. Cf. *amputate* and esp. *crush down sides.*—3. See **crush the stir.**

*****crush down sides.** To run away, esp. to a place of safety ; also, to keep a rendezvous : Northern c. ; from ca. 1850. H., 3rd ed.

*****crush the stir.** To break out of prison : late C. 19–20 c. See **(to) crush**, 2, and **stir.**

crushed on. Infatuated with : Society : 1895 ; almost †. Suggested by *mashed*. Ware.

crusher. A policeman : from ca. 1840. Thackeray ; *Punch*, 1842 ; Sala. ? ex the size of his feet. (' He needs 'em big ; he has to stand about for hours,' a friend, 1933.) Cf. *flattie, flatty*, q.v.—2. Any thing or person overwhelming or very large or handsome : coll. : from ca. 1840. Thackeray of a woman, 1849. Cf. *whopper* and *crushing*, qq.v.—3. A heavy fall : sporting coll. (— 1887) ; ob. Baumann. Cf. *crumpler*, 2.—4. A ship's corporal : naval (— 1909). Ware. Ex sense 1.

crushing. First-rate ; excellent ; very attractive : coll. ; from ca. 1855 ; ob. H., 1st ed. Cf. *crusher*, 2, q.v., and *crashing bore.*

Crusoe. ' The great French ironworks at Creuzot ' : workers in iron (— 1909). Ware. Punning *Robinson Crusoe.*

crust ; occ. **upper crust.** The head : from ca. 1870. Cf. *crumpet*, q.v.—2. Impudence, ' cheek ' : from early 1920's. P. G. Wodehouse, 1924 (O.E.D. Sup.) ? ex face as hard as a crust.

crustily. Peevishly, snappishly : coll. : C. 18–20. Bailey's Dict.

crusty beau. Late C. 17–early 19 ; coll. : ' One that lies with a Cover over his Face all Night, and uses Washes, Paint, etc.', B.E. ; Grose.

crusty-gripes. A grumbler : low coll., mostly London (— 1887) ; slightly ob. Baumann. Cf. *belly-acher.*

*****crutch, under the.** See **arm, under the**, 2.

crutches are cheap ! (Cf. *wooden legs are cheap* and see **cripples.**) An ironic comment on strenuous physical effort, esp. in athletics : mid-C. 19–20 ; ob.

crutie or **-y**. (Gen. pl.) A recruit: naval (− 1923). Manchon. Cf. *rooky*.

cry. A crowd of people: pejorative coll. >, by 1660, S.E.: late C. 16–18. Shakespeare, in *Coriolanus*, 'You common cry of curs.' Ex hunting j. for a pack of hounds.—2. A fit of weeping: coll.: from ca. 1850.

cry, v.i. To weep: C. 16–20; coll. >, by 1700, S.E.; except in dignified contexts, where it still is indubitably coll. and where *weep* is requisite.

cry ! A libidinous good wish at nightfall; an exclamation indicative of 'surprise of a satiric character': London lower classes' (− 1909). Ware: 'Shape of Carai—probably introduced by English gypsies passing from Spain'. Cf. *caramba*. —2. An abbr. of *crikey*: low: mid-C. 19–20. Ware.

cry, or call, a go. To desist; give in. (With connotation: wisely and humorously.) Coll. (− 1880); the post-War *call it a day* is displacing it. Ex cribbage, where *cry a go* = *pass* in bridge.

cry and little wool, great (occ. **much**). A proverbial c.p. abbr. '*Great cry and little wool*', *as the Devil said when he sheared the hogs*. Much ado about nothing. From ca. 1570.

*****cry carrots and turnips**. To be whipped at the cart's tail: C. 18 c.

cry cupboard. To be hungry: coll.; from ca. 1660. Swift in *Polite Conversation*, ' *Footman.* Madam, dinner's upon the table. *Col[onel]*. Faith, I'm glad of it; my belly began to cry cupboard.' See also **cupboard, one's guts cry**.

cry off. To back out of an engagement or project: from ca. 1700; coll. > S.E. by 1800.

cry, the less you'll piss !, the more you. See **piss, the less** . . .

cry whore. To impute a fault, ascribe blame: coll.: ca. 1660–1800. Apperson.

cryptogamia. Incorrectly as a pl.: C. 19–20. O.E.D.

Crystal Palace, H.M.S. The Royal Naval Division depôt at the Crystal Palace: naval: G.W.— 2. **Crystal Palace Army, the**. The R.N.D.: id.: id. Likewise in F. & Gibbons.—3. **C- P-, the**. ' The huge iron mine superstructure at Loos, [captured] on Sept. 25, 1915 ': military: 1915–18. Ibid.

cu, cue. A cucumber: Covent Garden coll.: C. 20. (*The Daily Telegraph*, June 7, 1935.) Pl.: *cues*.

cub. An awkward, uncouth, uncultured or un-poised youth: from ca. 1600; prob. coll. at first; soon S.E.—2. In late C. 17–early 19 c., a tyro gamester. B.E.—3. At St. Thomas's Hospital, ca. 1690–1740, a surgeon's assistant; a coll. soon > official j. (O.E.D.)

cube. A cubicle: at certain Public Schools, e.g. Charterhouse: C. 20.

cubic. A Cubist painting: art coll.: from ca. 1921. See quotation at *Prime, the*.

Cubit, the ; punishment by the cubit. The treadmill: low (− 1823); † by 1890. Bee, ' *Cubit* being the inventor's name.' Cf. *Cubitopolis*.

Cubitopolis. The Warwick and Eccleston Square districts of London (S.W.1): ca. 1860–80. H., 3rd ed. Edmund Yates in *Land at Last*, 1866. So named by Lady Morley after *Cubitt* the large-scale building contractor. Also called *Mesopotamia*.

cuckold the parson. To ' sleep ' with one's wife before she is: coll. (− 1791); † by 1890. Grose, 3rd ed.

cuckoldshire, cuckold's-row. Cuckoldom: facetious coll.; C. 16–17. Likewise, in C. 16–18,

Cuckold's Haven or *Point*, a point on the Thames below Greenwich, was humorously used, with various verbs, to indicate cuckolding or being cuckolded. (O.E.D.)

cuckoo. A fool: from late C. 16: coll. Shakespeare in *2 Henry IV*, ' O' horseback, ye cuckoo.' In C. 19–20 gen. as *the*, or *you, silly cuckoo*.—2. A cuckold: late C. 16–18; coll. > S.E. Shakespeare. Prob. ex the Fr. *cocu*, a cuckold.—3. The penis: schoolboys, C. 19–20, ob. Perhaps a perversion of *cock*.—4. A person: 1924, Galsworthy; slightly ob. Prob. ex sense 1 Cf.—5. ' A torpedo-dropping aeroplane ': naval: from ca. 1914. Bowen.

cuckoo, v. See **cuckoo'd**.

cuckoo, adj. Mad, senseless, distraught: U.S., anglicised in early 1920's. Ex *cuckoo*, n., 1.

cuckoo, lousy as a. Extremely lousy (lit. sense): military coll.: 1915. B. & P. Cf. the Yorkshire saying, *as scabbed as a cuckoo*: E.D.D.

cuckoo'd, be or, gen., **get (all)**. To be or become very lousy: military: 1916. Ibid. Ex preceding.

cuckoos. Money: C. 17. ? c. Perhaps because the cuckoo sings and money talks.

cuckoo's nest. The *pudendum muliebre*: C. 19–20.

cucumber. A tailor: late C. 17–early 19. B.E., Grose. Cf.:

cucumber-time. The dull season: mid-July to mid-Sept. Tailors': late C. 17–20; ob. B.E.: ' Taylers Holiday, when they have leave to Play, and Cucumbers are in season.' Cf. the Ger. *die saure Gurken Zeit*, pickled-gherkin time, and the saying *tailors are vegetarians*, which arises from their living now on cucumber and now on ' cabbage ', q.v.

cud. A chew of tobacco: until ca. 1870, S.E., now dial. and coll., *quid* being much more usual.

cud, adj. Attractive, cosy; comfortable: Winchester College: 1st half C. 19. Wykehamistically deprived ex *kudos*.—2. Hence, pretty: ibid: mid-C. 19–20. (R. G. K. Wrench.)—3. At Christ's Hospital, mid-C. 19–20: severe. Baumann. Prob. ex *cuddy*, adj., q.v.

cuddie. A variant of *cuddy*, q.v. (Egan's Grose.)

cuddle-cook. A policeman: C. 20; mostly, lower classes'. Cf. *Cook's Own*, q.v.

cuddleable. Cuddlesome: coll.: from mid-1920's. O.E.D. (Sup.).

cuddling. Wrestling: esp. among devotees of wrestling and boxing: C. 19–20, ob.

cuddy. A nickname for a donkey: coll.: from ca. 1710. ? ex *Cuthbert*.—2. (**Cuddy**.) Admiral Collingwood of Napoleonic Wars fame: naval. Bowen.

cuddy, adj. (Of a lesson) difficult: Christ's Hospital, mid-C. 19–20, ob. Perhaps ex *cuddy*, a stupid chap: cf. preceding.—2. Hence *cuddy-biscuit*, a small hard biscuit.

cuddy-jig. The capers of a landsman endeavouring to keep his balance: nautical: mid-C. 19–20. Bowen. Ex *cuddy*, n., 1.

cuddy-leg. A large herring: (mostly Scots) nautical: late C. 19–20. Ibid.

cuds, cuds(h)o. In expletives, a corruption of *God's*: ca. 1590–1750: coll. (O.E.D.)

cue. A small quantity of bread; occ. of beer. As *cu* (q.v.) from *C̄*, so *cue* from Q (*q* = *quadrans* = a farthing). A university s. term that > S.E.: late C. 16–18. The S.O.D. quotes a 1605 text: ' Hast thou worn Gowns in the university . . . ate cues, drunk cees ? ' Cf. *cee*.—2. See **cu**.

*cue, v. To swindle on credit : c. : from ca. 1860. ? ex *Q. = query.*

cue-bite, v.i. To speak too soon on one's cues : theatrical (— 1935).

cuerpo, in. 'Without the cloak, so as to show the shape of the body,' S.O.D. Ex the Spanish for body, this phrase was presumably gallants' j. of C. 17: its unconventional use appears,C. 18, in the sense: without any clothing, naked, as in Smollett (coll.).

cuff ; often old cuff. A (foolish) old man : coll. ; ca. 1610–1820. ? ex *cuffin,* mid-C. 16–18 c. for a fellow, chap, itself prob. cognate with *cofe = cove.*— 2. Perhaps hence, a religious or a religious-seeming man : tailors' ; C. 19–20 ob.

cuff Anthony. See Anthony.—cuff or beat Jonas. See beat the booby.

cuff of, up the. In the good graces of : tailors' : late C. 19–20.

cuff(-)shooter. A beginner : theatrical ; from ca. 1870. Ex his display of linen.

cuff the logs. To be a riverman (river lumberman) : Canadian coll. : C. 20. John Beames.

*cuffen. A C. 16 variant of *cuffin,* q.v. at *cuff.*

cuffer. A lie ; an exaggerated story : military : from ca. 1870. Cf. *thumper.*—2. Hence, any story, a yarn : from mid-1880's. (O.E.D. Sup.)

cuffers, spin. To tell tall stories ; yarn. From ca. 1870. Ex *cuffer,* a fist.

*cuffin. See cuff, n., 1.—Cuffin-quire. See queer cuffin.—cuffing (C. 17). See cuff.

cui bono ? Properly, to whose advantage ? ; wrongly, to what purpose ? : mid-C. 19–20. W., 'attributed by Cicero to Lucius Cassius '.

cuirass. Same as *cure-arse,* q.v. : late C. 18. Grose, to the B.M. 1st ed. copy, has added the term with the note, ' Quasi *cure-a-se* ', but contrary to his gen. practice with these MS. addenda, he did not include it in the 2nd ed.

Culdee. Incorrect when applied to the Church of Iona : late C. 17–20. O.E.D.

*cule. Abbr. *reticule* : c. (— 1859) ; ob. H., 1st ed., implies it in *culling,* q.v.

*culing. See culling.

culiver. Incorrect for *caliver* : mid-C. 18–20. O.E.D.

*cull, cully. In C. 17 c., a constable. A deviation from :—2. In C. 17–18, c. for a fool, esp. a dupe ; in C. 19–20, though anticipated in C. 17 as *cully,* low s. for a man, companion, mate, partner : in C. 17–18, however, *cull* tended to mean any man, fool or otherwise, *cully* 'a fop, fool, or dupe to women' (Grose), as in Congreve's 'Man was by nature woman's cully made' (*The Old Bachelor,* 1693) : *cull* dates from ca. 1660, *cully* from ca. 1664. For etymology, see culls (cf. *ballocks,* a parson) ; but perhaps ex † S.E. *cullion* ; less prob. ex the Continental Gypsy radical for a man.—3. See rum cull.

*cull, bob and curst. Resp. ' a sweet-humour'd Man to a Whore, and who is very Complaisant . . . An ill'natur'd Fellow, a Churl to a Woman ', B.E. : c. : late C. 17–early 19. See cull, 2.

*culling, or culing. Stealing from carriage seats : c. or low ; from the mid-1830's. Brandon ; H., 1st ed. Ex *reticule.*

culls. Testicles : low coll., C. 16–17. Ben Jonson. Abbr. *cullions,* the same.

*cully. See cull. In late C. 19–20, often as a Cockney, also as a low, term of address to a man ; also, 2, a 'pal' : military : C. 20. B. & P.

cully-gorger. A theatre-manager (cf. *rum cull*);

a fellow actor : from ca. 1860 : theatrical ; † by 1930. H., 3rd ed. Ex *cully* (see cull, cully) + *gorger,* a 'swell'.

cully-shangy. Sexual intercourse : low ; C. 19. *Cully* ex *culls, shangy,* ex ?

culminate. To climb a coach-box : ca. 1780–1870 ; Cambridge University.

culp. 'A kick, or blow ; also a bit of any thing,' B.E. : late C. 17–early 19 low coll. (later dial.). Prob., as Grose (2nd ed.) suggests, influenced by *mea culpa.*

culty-gun. The *membrum virile* : low : C. 19. Ex L. *cultellus,* a knife.

culver-headed. Feebly foolish : coll. ex dial. : C. 19. H., 3rd ed. A culver is a dove, a pigeon, whence ' pigeon ', an easy gull for the ' rook '.

cum used facetiously for ' with ' or ' plus ' is coll. : from ca. 1860.

cum-annexis. One's belongings, esp. one's wife and children : West Indies, from ca. 1850 ; ob. Ex an official land-transfer locution affected at Demerara.

cum-div. Abbr. *cum dividend* : Stock Exchange s. > j. ; from ca. 1875. (Of a purchaser of stocks or shares getting the benefit of the dividend.)

cum grano. A coll. abbr. of *cum grano salis* (with a grain of salt) : from ca. 1850.

cummer, kimmer. A *female* intimate, acquaintance, or ' fellow ' or ' chap '. Orig. and still good Scots, these words have, in late C. 19–20, occ. been familiarly used by Sassenachs in these senses and thus > coll. H., 5th ed. Ex Fr. *commère.*

cummifo. ' Comme il faut ' : lower class coll. : 1889, *The Referee,* April 28. (Ware.)

cumsha(w). A present ; a bribe : Anglo-Chinese ' pidgin ' : from ca. 1835. Ex Chinese for ' grateful thanks '.—2. Unexpected or additional money : nautical : mid-C. 19–20. Bowen.

cund. To say or determine which way (a shoal of fish) is going : nautical coll. verging on j. : mid-C. 19–20. Smyth ; Bowen. Ex *cund* (gen. *cond*), to direct (a ship).

cundum. A ca. 1665–1820 form of a safety-sheath (cf. *French letter*), ex the name of its deviser, a colonel in the Guards. In 1667 those three aristocratic courtiers, wits and poets, Rochester, Roscommon and Dorset, issued *A Panegyric upon Cundum.* (Coll. rather than s.)—2. 'A false scabbard over a sword,' Grose, 2nd ed. : late C. 18–early 19 : military.—3. (Likewise ex sense 1.) ' The oil-skin case for holding the colours of a regiment,' ibid. : id. : id.

cunning. Quaintly interesting, pretty, attractive : orig. (— 1854) U.S. ; anglicised ca. 1880, but never very gen. (O.E.D.) Cf. *clever,* q.v.

cunning as a dead pig. Stupid : coll. : ca. 1705–50. Swift. (Apperson.)

*cunning man. 'A cheat, who pretends by his skill in astrology, to assist persons in recovering stolen goods,' Grose, 1788 : c. ; † by 1850.

cunning shaver. A sharp fellow, orig. illicitly : mid-C. 17–20, ob. ; coll. B.E. See shaver.

Cunningberry (or -bury). A variant (ca. 1820–50), recorded by ' Jon Bee ', of :

Cunningham ; often *Mr. Cunningham.* Ironical coll. for a simple fellow : mid-C. 18–early 19. Grose, resp. 2nd and 1st ed.

cunny. The *pudendum muliebre* : low coll. ; C. 17–20. Influenced by L. *cunnus,* it is actually an † form of *cony,* a rabbit. Cf. *pussy.*

cunny-haunted. Lecherous : C. 18–20, ob. ; low coll. Ex preceding term.

cunny-hunter. A whoremonger : C. 17–early 19 ; low. Punning *cunny = con(e)y.*

cunny-thumbed. Given to closing his fist, as a woman does, with the thumb turned inwards under the first three fingers : low coll. ; late C. 18–20. Grose, 1st ed. Ex *cunny*, q.v.—2. C. 19–20 schoolboys' : given to shooting a marble as a girl does. Other sex tests are these : an object thrown at a woman's shins or knees causes her to close her knees ; at her genitals, to open her legs, whereas a man closes his ; at her chest, to protect her breasts. A man walks from the hips ; a woman (unless an impenitent hiker or an athletic champion) usually from the knees. In threading a needle, a man holds the needle stationary and advances the thread towards the eyelet, whereas a woman directs the needle on to the stationary thread,—a difference that has originated a psychologico-physiological riddle. Apart from her voice, hair and breasts, a woman masquerading as a man is apt to forget that the proportionate breadth of the shoulders and esp. the hips, as well as the contour of the legs from hip to knee, are different in a man. In short, she would do well to wear long full trousers, for, in addition, her knees are much less bony, much more rounded, than a man's.

cunny-warren. A brothel : low (–. 1785) ; † by 1930. Grose, 1st ed.

cunt. (In back s., *tenuc*, the *e* being intruded for euphony.) The female pudend. In one form or another, it dates from M.E. ; ex a Teutonic radical corresponding to the L. *cunnus* (It. *cunno, conno*), itself related to *cuneus*, a wedge. Owing to its powerful sexuality, the term has, since C. 15, been avoided in written and in polite spoken English : though a language word, neither coll., dial., c., nor s., its associations make it perhaps the most notable of all vulgarisms (technical sense, *bien entendu*), and since ca. 1700 it has, except in the reprinting of old classics, been held to be obscene, i.e. a legal offence, to print it in full ; Rochester spelt it *en toutes lettres*, but Cotgrave, defining Fr. *con*, went no further than ' A woman's, &c.', and the dramatist Fletcher, who was no prude, went no further than ' They write *sunt* with a C, which is abominable ', in *The Spanish Curate*. Had the late Sir James Murray courageously included the word, and spelt it in full, in the great O.E.D., the situation would be different ; as it is, neither the Universal Dict. of English (1932) nor the S.O.D. (1933) had the courage to include it. (Yet the O.E.D. gave *prick* : why this further injustice to women ?)—2. (Cf. Romany *mindj* or *minsh*, the pudend ; a woman.) In C. 19–20 it also means woman as sex, intercourse with a woman, hence sexual intercourse. (It is somewhat less international than *fuck*, q.v.) See esp. Minsheu ; the Introduction to B. & P. ; Grose, P. ; *Lady Chatterley's Lover* ; A. W. Read, *Lexical Evidence*, 1935.

cunt !, silly. A low pejorative address or reference to a person : late C. 19–20. In 1914–18, the soldiers applied the term, with or without this or some other epithet, to material objects.

cunt-hat. A felt hat : low (– 1923). Manchon. There is a double pun : see **hat** and note ' felt '.

cunt-itch and **-stand.** Active physical desire in women : vulgarism : resp. C. 18–20, C. 19–20.

cunt-pensioner. A male-keep ; also, the man living on a woman's harlotry or concubinage : low coll. or perhaps rather a vulg. : C. 19–20 ; slightly ob. Often, in C. 20, euphemistically abbr. to *c.p.*

cunt-stand. See **cunt-itch**.

cunt-struck. Enamoured of women : C. 18–20 ; either a vulg. (more correctly, I think) or a low coll. Cf. *cock-smitten*, q.v.

cunting. Adj., expressive of disgust, reprobation, violence : late C. 19–20.

Cunts in Velvet. The Criminal Investigation Department : military (–1914).

cup such cover, such ; or **such a cup(,) such a cruse.** ' Implying similarity between two persons related in some way,' O.E.D. Coll. ; both ca. 1540–1700.

cup and can. Constant associates : ca. 1540–1830 ; coll. >, by 1600, S.E. Gen. *as merry as cup and can*, or *be cup and can*. Ex the cup's being filled and replenished from a can. (Apperson.)

cup-and-saucer player. A player in a comedy by T. W. Robertson (d. 1871), a pioneer of ' slick ' yet natural and workmanlike society-drama : theatrical, ca. 1866–90.

cup and wad. Tea and a bun in canteen or Y.M.C.A. or Church Army hut : military : G.W. (F. & Gibbons.)

cup even between two parties, carry one's. To favour neither of them : coll., C. 17–early 19. B.E.

cup man, cup-man. A toper : coll. > S.E. ; ca. 1830–1900.

cup of comfort or **of the creature.** Strong liquor : late C. 17–20 ; slightly ob. B.E. See also **creature**.

cup o(f) tea. A consolation : proletarian, gen. ironic : C. 20 ; slightly ob. Ware, ' Probably suggested by a cup of tea being " so very refreshing ".' —2. **one's cup of tea** = what truly suits one ; even one's ideal, one's mate : coll. : from ca. 1920. (Michael Harrison, *Weep for Lycidas*, 1934.) Cf. *ticket, be a person's* : q.v.

cup-shot. Tipsy : late C. 16–early 19 ; coll. >, by 1660, S.E. Fuller in *The Holy War*, ' Quickly they were stabbed with the sword that were cup-shot before.' Cf. *shot*, adj.

cup too low, a. Applied to one who, in company, is silent or pensive : late C. 17–18 ; coll. B.E. The phrase is extant in dial.

cup too much, have got or **had a.** To be drunk : mid-C. 17–19 ; coll. Ray, 1678 (Apperson). Cf. the preceding phrase.

cup-tosser. A juggler : C. 19 ; coll. Brewer suggests ex Fr. *joueur de gobelets.*—2. Whence, ' a person who professes to tell fortunes by examining the grounds in tea or coffee cups ', H., 3rd ed. : from ca. 1860 ; very ob.

Cupar justice. Hanging first and trying afterwards : C. 18–mid-19 : Scots coll. >, by 1810 or so, S.E. In 1706, A. Shields refers to ' Couper Justice and Jedburgh Law ' (see **Jeddart law**). Cf. *Halifax law, Lydford law*, and *lynching*.

cupboard, the. The sea : nautical : late C. 19–20. Bowen. Ex *Davy Jones's locker*.

cupboard, one's guts cry. One is hungry : low coll. : C. 18–mid-19. Grose, 2nd ed.

cupboard love. Interested affection : C. 18–20 : coll. ; S.E. after ca. 1820. ' A cupboard love is seldom true.' Hence *cupboard lover*, C. 19–20, rare.

cupboardy. ' Close and stuffy ' : Cockneys' coll. : late C. 19–20. Ware.

Cupid. A harlot's bully-lover : C. 19–20, ob. ; low.—2. With variant *blind Cupid*, ' a jeering name for an ugly blind man ', Grose, 1st ed. : mid-C. 18–early-19 coll.—3. See **Pam** (Palmerston).

Cupid's Arms or **Hotel.** See **hotel.**

Cupid's whiskers. Sweets with mottoes on them : coll. : late C. 19–20. Collinson.

Cupid, blind. See Cupid, 2.

Cupper. One of the inter-collegiate matches played for a cup : Oxford undergraduates' : C. 20. The Oxford-*er*.

cups, in one's. While drinking (rare in C. 20) ; intoxicated. From ca. 1580 : coll. (as in Nashe and Shadwell) until ca. 1720, then S.E.

*cur, turn. To turn informer or King's evidence : c. : mid-C. 19–20 ; ob. Baumann.

cur-fish. Small *dog*-fish : nautical : late C. 19–20. Bowen.

curate. Late C. 19–20 coll. : ' A small poker, or *tickler* (q.v.), used to save a better one ; also a handkerchief in actual use as against one worn for show. The better article is called a *rector*. Similarly when a tea-cake is split and buttered, the bottom half, which gets the more butter, is called the *rector*, and the other, the *curate*,' F. & H.

curate's delight. A tiered cake-stand : from ca. 1890. (Michael Harrison, *Weep for Lycidas*, 1934.)

*curb. A thief's hook : c. : late C. 16–18. Greene, Grose.

*curb. To steal, esp. with a hook ; gen. v.i. : late C. 16–early 18 c. Greene.—2. In C. 19 c., to strike.

*curber. A thief that uses a hook : late C. 16–18 c. Rowlands.

*curbing. An abbr. of the following term. Greene.

*curbing law. The practice of illegally hooking goods out of windows : late C. 16–18 c.

curbstone-broker. A guttersnipe : from ca. 1865 ; ob. In U.S., an illicit street-broker. (*Kerb*- is the more gen. spelling in C. 20.)

curbstone-sailor. A harlot : from ca. 1830. Cf. *cruiser*.

curby hocks. Clumsy feet : rather low : ca. 1850–1910. (See *hocks*.)

curdler. A blood-curdling story or play ; a writer thereof : coll (— 1887) ; ob. Baumann. Cf. *thriller*.

cure. An eccentric, an odd person (1856) ; hence, a very amusing one (— 1874). First printed in *Punch*, though ' he ' has ' no mission to repeat | The Slang he hears along the street '. Perhaps abbr. *curiosity* or, more prob., *curious fellow* ; popularised by an 1862 music-hall song. (O.E.D.)

cure-arse. A late C. 18–19 low coll. : ' a dyachilon plaster, applied to the parts galled by riding', Grose, 3rd ed. Cf. *cuirass*, q.v.

curio. Abbr. *curiosity* : from ca. 1850 (at first among travellers) ; coll. till ca. 1880, then S.E.

curiouser and curiouser. Ever more strange : coll. : late C. 19–20. Adopted ex Lewis Carroll.

curiosity. An odd person : ca. 1840–70 : coll. Displaced by *cure*, q.v.

curious, do. To act strangely : low coll. : mid-C. 19–20 ; ob.

Curjew. (H.M.S.) *Courageous* : nautical sol. (— 1788). Grose, 2nd ed.

*curl. See *curle*.—2. (Gen. pl.) A human tooth ' obtained by the body-snatchers ' : c. (— 1823) ; † by 1860. ' Jon Bee.'

curl, make (a person's) **hair.** To cause one to shudder, to frighten : coll. (— 1931). Lyell. (Contrast *curl one's hair*.) A low variant (late C. 19–20) is *make one's liver curl*.

curl, out of. Indisposed ; vaguely ill at ease : coll. : mid-C. 19–20. Ex the hair. Hence, *go out of*

curl, to collapse, as in Galsworthy, *The White Monkey*, 1924.

curl one's hair. To chastise ; scold, vituperate : C. 19–20 coll. ; ob.

curl paper. Toilet paper : either coll. or euphemistic : C. 19–20 ; ob.

curl up. To fall silent, ' shut up ' : from ca. 1860 ; ob.—2. (Sporting.) To collapse : coll. : from ca. 1890.

*curle. Clippings of money : late C. 17–18 c. B.E. Semantic.

curled darlings. Military officers : Society : 1856–ca. 60. Ware, who, noting that ' the Crimean War . . . once more brought soldiers into fashion ', refers to ' the waving of the long beard and sweeping moustache '.

*curls. See *curl*, 2.

curly. A cane : *Conway* Training Ship : from ca. 1885. Masefield.—2. (*Curly*.) The inevitable nickname of men with curly hair : coll. (— 1851). Mayhew.

curly-murly. A fantastic twist, esp. curl. : ca. 1720–1830. Also adj. : mid-C.19–20 : coll.

currant-cakey. Shaky : rhyming s. : C. 20. P. P., *Rhyming Slang*, 1932.

currants and plums. A threepenny piece : rhyming s. (— 1859) on *thrums*, q.v. H., 1st ed.

currency. N. and, occ., adj. of a person born in Australia, one of English birth being *sterling* : Australians' : from ca. 1825 ; † by 1914. P. Cunningham, 1827 ; Charles Reade in ' *It is Never Too Late to Mend* '. Morris.

curry-and-rice navy. The Royal Indian Marine : naval : late C. 19–20 ; ob. Bowen.

curry one's hide. To beat a person : coll. : C. 18–early 19. Ex S.E. *curry* in this sense.

curse, not to care or **be worth a.** I.e. extremely little : from M.E. onwards ; coll. S.O.D. supports *curse = cress* (A.-S. *cerse*) but notes that *damn* in this sense is very early. Prob. *cress* > *curse* under the influence of *damn* ; nevertheless, see **dam.** Langland has ' Wisdom and witt now is worth not a kerse.' Whereas *not worth a rush* or *a straw* have > S.E., *not worth a curse* has remained coll. because of its apparent meaning. Also *tinker's curse*.

curse flashes. To swear vigorously : Regular Army coll. : C. 20. Frank Richards, *Old Soldiers Never Die*, 1933. Perhaps on *curse like hell*.

curse of God. A cockade : coll. ; early C. 19. Cf. :

Curse of Jesus. The Clipper ship *Chersonese* : late C. 19–20. By ' Hobson-Jobson '. Bowen, ' Always very hard on her crew '.

curse of Scotland. The nine of diamonds : from 1710. Coll. > S.E. in C. 19. Orig. problematic. Grose, 1st ed. The various theories are as interesting as they are unconvincing : see H., 5th ed., and W.

cursetor, cursitor. A vagabond : from ca. 1560 : coll.—2. In mid-C. 18–early 19 c., ' broken pettyfogging attornies, or Newgate solicitors ', Grose, 1st ed. Ex L. *currere*, to run. Cf. the S.E.

[Cursing and swearing is, in its cause and its processes, akin to s. and coll. : see my *Slang* ; for the gen. subject of cursing and swearing, see Ernest Crawley's thoughtful and suggestive book, *Oath, Curse, and Blessing*, 1934, and Robert Graves's *Lars Porsena*, revised in 1935. Curses, oaths, asseverations and other exclamations that are s. or coll.— and perhaps a few that are neither s. nor coll.— appear in the present work.]

*curtail, curtal. A thief that cuts off pieces from unguarded cloth, etc., or from women's dresses; C. 18 c. Also, a thief wearing a short jacket; C. 16–17 c.

curtain, cop the. 'To gain so much applause that the curtain is raised for the performer to appear and bow': music-halls' (ca. 1880) >, by 1890, theatres'. Ware. Cf. curtain-taker.

curtain-lecture. A reproof, or lengthy advice, given in bed by a wife to her husband: from ca. 1630; orig. coll.; by 1730, S.E. The occ. curtain-sermon was † by 1900. (Apperson.)

curtain-raiser. A one-act play to 'play in the house': orig. (— 1886) theatrical s.; by 1900, coll.; by 1920, S.E. Ex Fr. lever de rideau.

curtain, take a. See take a curtain.

curtain-taker. 'An actor even more eager than his brethren to appear before the curtain after its fall': theatrical: 1882. Ware. Cf. curtain, cop the.

curtains. 'A [soldiers', esp. officers'] name given to one of the first modes of wearing the hair low on the military forehead (1870). The locks were divided in the centre, and the front hair was brought down in two loops, each rounding away towards the temple. The hair was glossed and flattened', Ware. Ca. 1870–85.

*curtal. A species of vagabond and thief: mid-C. 16–18 c. Ex his short coat. See curtail.

-cus, like -ibus and -orum, is a favourite suffix in mock-Latin words, which (e.g. circumbendibus) tend to have a (frequently jocular) coll. flavour. For this by-way, see esp. H. W. Fowler's stimulating, masterly, and remarkable Dict. of Modern English Usage, s.v. Spurious Latin.

cuse. Weekly order; (a book containing) the record of marks in each division. Winchester College: C. 19–20, ob. Ex classicus paper, the master's term.

cush. A cushion in: billiards coll.: C. 20. O.E.D. (Sup.). Cf. cushing.

cush, v.; cusher. C. 20 variants of cosh and cosher, qq.v.

cushing. A cushion: C. 16–20: S.E. till C. 18, then incorrect; C. 19–20 sol.

*cushion. To hide, conceal: c.: mid-C. 19–20, ob. H., 3rd ed. Ex S.E. sense, to suppress.

cushion, beside the. Beside the mark: coll.: late C. 16–early 19, verging on S.E. Ex billiards, a game played in England since C. 16. Cf. miss the cushion.

cushion, deserve a or the. To have done his duty and therefore deserving of rest (of a man to whom a child has been born): coll.: mid-C. 17–early 19. Ray, 1678.

cushion, miss the. To miss the mark; to fail; coll. (— 1529); app. † by 1700. Skelton; Clarke, 1639. (Apperson.)

cushion-cuffer, -duster, -smiter, and -thumper. A clergyman, esp. a violent preacher: coll.: the first, ca. 1680–1750; the second, ca. 1720–1820; the third, from ca. 1840 but ob.; the fourth, ca. 1640–1900. Thackeray, 1843. 'For what a number of such loud nothings . . . will many a cushion-thumper have to answer.'

cushionmong. Accouchement: Cockney sol. (— 1887); slightly ob. Baumann.

cushmawaunee! Never mind: among soldiers and sailors with Indian experience: mid-C. 19–20; ob. H., 3rd ed.

Cusby. La Cauchie, a town near Arras: military G.W. (F. & Gibbons.)

cushy. Easy, safe: of a job, task, or post. Not dangerous: of a wound (cf. Blighty, q.v.). S.O.D. records this military s. at 1915, but, to judge both from its possibly Hindustani origin (khush, pleasure) or its, to me, more prob. Romany one (kushto, good), and from report, it was used in the Indian Army some years before the G.W. (It is not impossibly a slurring of cushiony or an extension of dial. cushie, soft, flabby.)

cuss. As a coll. exclamation orig. (— 1872) U.S. and partly anglicised ca. 1900, it euphemises curse! —2. A person; gen., a man: coll.; both senses ex U.S. (— 1848), anglicised ca. 1880. Ex customer, perhaps influenced by curse.

cussèd. A low coll. form of cursèd, anglicised ca. 1882.

cussedness. Cantankerousness (persons); contrariness (things). Coll.: ex U.S. (from ca. 1850), anglicised ca. 1885. Baumann. The fourth general 'law' is, 'The cussedness of the universe tends to a maximum.'

*cussin. A man: c. (— 1887); virtually †. Baumann. Ex cuss, 2.

custom, it's an old (orig. Southern). In 1935 this, in the Southern form, > a c.p.; it is a line from a popular song. By the end of the year, and in fact by October, other words had begun to be substituted for Southern. In The Evening News of Jan. 4, 1936, we read of the man who, on being upbraided by his wife for kissing a girl in a square in London, W.2, explained that 'It's an old Bayswater custom'.

custom of the country. 'A bribe given to port officials to avoid delays': nautical coll.: mid-C. 19–20. Bowen.

customer. A man; chap, fellow: coll.; from late C. 16 but not common before 1800; gen. with queer or ugly. Cf. chap, merchant, artist, and Scottish callant, qq.v.

custom(-)house goods. 'The stock in trade of a prostitute, because fairly entered', Grose, 2nd ed.: mid-C. 18–early 19 low coll.

custom(-)house officer. A cathartic pill: mid-C. 19–20; ob. H., 2nd ed. Also customs.

Cut; always the C. The New Cut, a well-known plebeian street near Westminster: London coll. (— 1887). Baumann.

cut. A stage, a degree: coll. from ca. 1815; S.O.D. records in 1818; Dickens uses in 1835, (of a house) 'I really thought it was a cut above me.' — 2. A refusal to recognise, or to associate with, a person: from ca. 1790. The cut(-)direct (later dead cut) occurs ca. 1820.—3. A snub or an unpleasant surprise: coll.; ca. 1850–1910.—4. (Theatrical) an excision, a mutilation of the 'book' of a play: C. 18–20. Sheridan in the Critic, 'Hey . . . !— what a cut is here!'; The Saturday Review, April 21, 1883, 'Some judicious cuts.'—5. the cut: see cut, adj. C. 19.—6. See cuts.—7. A share: Australian and New Zealand coll.: late C. 19–20.

cut, v. To talk; speak; make (of words): in mid-C. 16–early 19, c.,—cut bene, e.g. is to speak gently; from ca. 1840 (? low) s. as in Thackeray's Pendennis, '[He] went on cutting jokes at the Admiral's expense.'—2. Ignore or avoid (a person); abandon (a thing, a habit): from ca. 1630; coll. Samuel Rowley, in The Noble Soldier, 'Why shud a Souldier, being the world's right arme |Be cut thus by the left, a Courtier?' Vbl.n., cutting. With this usage, cf. 3, the university (orig. s., then coll., now almost S.E.) cut lecture or hall or chapel, to absent oneself from these duties (— 1794).—4.

Move quickly; **run**: coll.; from ca. 1840. Earlier forms—all S.E.—are *cut away* (Cotton, 1678), *cut off*, and *cut over* (Lambarde's *Perambulation of Kent*; Nashe). Dickens, in *Little Dorrit*, 'The best thing I can do is to cut.' A C. 19 variant is *cut it*, q.v. After ca. 1860, the gen. form is the orig. nautical *cut and run* (lit., cut the cable and sail away); *cut one's lucky* (— 1840) being lower down the social scale, as also is (— 1823) *cut one's stick* (Egan's Grose): with the last, cf. *amputate one's mahogany*, the idea being that of cutting a staff for one's journey (W.); in gen., however, cf. U.S. *cut dirt* (1833): 'the horse hoofs make the dirt fly', Thornton.—5. (Theatrical) to excise: C. 18–20. See n., 4.—6. Excel (cf. *cut out*, q.v.): coll.; from ca. 1840. Whyte-Melville, in 1853, has *cut down*.

cut, adj. Tipsy: from ca. 1670. Head; B.E. Cf. *Punch*, 1859, 'He goes on the Loose, or the Cut, or the Spree.' Whence a *deep cut* or *cut in the back* (or *leg*), very drunk, late C. 17–early 19 (B.E.), and a *little cut over the head*, slightly drunk, late C. 18–mid-19 (Grose, 1st ed.): cf. *cut one's leg*, q.v.

cut ! See **cut it**, 2.

*****cut a bosh** or a **flash**. To cut a figure: mid-C. 18–early 19: c. See **bosh**.

cut a caper. To play a trick or prank; behave extravagantly or noisily: from late C. 16; coll. till ca. 1700, when it > S.E.

cut a dash or **shine** or **splash**. To make a display, a notable figure; be very successful, prominent: resp. early C. 18–20, C. 19–20 (orig. U.S.), C. 19–20: coll., the first being now S.E. Here, *cut* = make, do, perform. Cf. *cut a bosh*, q.v.

cut a dido. To 'cut a dash': naval: ca. 1835–60. Ex *cut up didoes*, with a pun on H.M. corvette *Dido*, very smart, of the 1830's. Bowen adds: 'The term was also applied to a sailing vessel tumbling about in a confused sea.'

cut a (e.g. fine, poor) **figure**. To make a . . . appearance: from ca. 1760; coll. until ca. 1890, then S.E. Lever in *Harry Lorrequer*, 'He certainly cut a droll figure.' The earlier, more dignified phrase is *make a figure*.

cut a finger. To break wind: low (— 1909). Ware. Cf. the Somersetshire *cut the leg*, to give off a foul smell (E.D.D.).

cut a shine or **splash**. See **cut a dash**.

cut a stick. To desert: naval: from ca. 1830. Bowen. Cf. *cut*, v., 4.

cut a tooth or **one's (eye-) teeth**. To become 'knowing', wide-awake: from ca. 1820: coll.; in C. 20, S.E. though hardly dignified. After ca. 1870, occ. *cut one's wisdom teeth*. See also **cut one's eye-teeth, have**.

cut above, a. See **cut**, n., 1.

cut and come again. Abundance, orig. of 'Meat that cries come Eat me,' B.E.: late C. 17–20; coll. Swift, Wm. Combe.—2. Whence, the female pudend: C. 19–20; low.

cut and run. Depart promptly; decamp hurriedly: coll (— 1861). Ex nautical j.

cut(-)away. A morning coat: from ca. 1845: coll.; in C. 20, S.E. (As adj., recorded in 1841, says the S.O.D., but anticipated in Jon Bee's description, 1823, of a dandy.)

*****cut bene whids**. To speak fair: c., as in B.E.: mid-C. 16–18. See **whids**. Variant with *benar*, q.v.

cut capers on a trencher. To dance within a very small compass: ca. 1850–1910; coll., mostly Cockney; cf. *cellar-flap*.

cut dead (— 1826) is a variant of *to cut*, v., 2, q.v.

cut fine. To reduce to a minimum, esp. in *cut it fine*, to leave a very small margin of money, space, or time: mid-C. 19–20: coll. >, by 1900, S.E.

cut for the simples. See **simples, be cut for the**.

cut in, v.i. To intrude; interpose briskly into a game or a conversation: from ca. 1820; coll. till ca. 1870, then S.E. Thackeray, '"Most injudicious", cut in the Major.'—2. Whence the n.: same period and promotion. Often written *cut-in*.

cut in the back or **leg**. See **cut**, adj.

cut into. (Winchester College) orig. to hit with a 'ground ash'; hence, to correct in a manner less formal than *tunding*, q.v.: C. 19–20, ob.

cut it. To run, move quickly: C. 19–20; coll See v., 4.—2. Interjection: cease! or be quiet! Also as *cut !*, *cut that !*, in C. 20 *cut it out !* From ca. 1850; coll. H., 1st ed.

cut it fat. To make a display; cut a dash; show off; from ca. 1830. Dickens, 1836, 'Gentlemen . . . "cutting it uncommon fat"'; Baumann, 1887. In the Dickens quotation, the sense of the whole phrase is perhaps rather, 'come it (too) strong'. *Cut it too*, or *uncommon, fat*, is indeed a separate phrase = overdo a thing; now ob.

cut it out ! See **cut it**, 2.

cut it short ! Make your story, or account, shorter ! Coll.: C. 19–20. Dickens.

cut mutton with. To partake of someone's hospitality: coll.; from ca. 1830.

cut no ice; gen. **that cuts no ice** ! That makes no difference, has no effect, is of no importance: orig. (1896), U.S.; anglicised ca. 1913. Thornton; O.E.D. (Sup.).

cut of one's jib. General appearance: orig. and still mainly nautical: from ca. 1820. Robert Buchanan, 1881, 'By the voice of you . . . and by the cut of your precious jib.'

cut of the simples. See **simples, be cut for the**.

cut off without a shilling. A late C. 19–20 jocular coll. variant of the S.E. phrase.

cut one's cable. An occ. variant (— 1931) of *cut the painter*, 2. Lyell.

*****cut one's cart**. To expose his tricks: (— 1851) c.; ob. Mayhew.

cut one's coat according . . . See **cloth**.—**cut one's comb**. See **comb cut**.—**cut one's lucky** or (perhaps orig. c., as Egan states) **stick**. See **cut**, v., 4, the latter ex the cutting of a staff before one begins a journey.

cut one's leg, have. To be drunk: late C. 17–mid-18. Ray, 1678 (Apperson). Cf. *cut*, adj.: q.v.

*****cut one's eye**. To become suspicious: c.: from ca. 1840. Cf. *cutty-eye*.

cut one's eye-teeth, have. To be alert or 'knowing': low (— 1864). H., 3rd ed. See also **cut a tooth**.

*****cut one's own grass**. To earn one's own living: c.; from ca. 1860; ob. Cf. *get one's own chump*, s.v. *chump*.

cut one's painter. See **cut the painter**.—**cut one's stick**. See **cut**, v., 4.

cut out. To find, put in the way of: late C. 17–19; coll. '*I'll cut you out business*, I'll find you Work enough,' B.E.—2. To supersede, outdo, deprive of an advantage: C. 18–20; coll. till ca. 1860, then S.E.; orig. nautical, but very early of sexual (or analogous) rivalry, as in R. Cumberland, *Wheel of Fortune*, 1779.—3. In Australia (— 1874), to detach (an animal) from the herd: orig. coll.; soon S.E.—4. To steal (esp. service stores): naval: late C. 19–20. Bowen. Ex senses 1, 2.

cut out of. To deprive of; destroy one's participation in, chances of getting: C. 17–20, ob.; coll., as in B.E.'s ' *Cut another out of any business*, to out-doe him far away, or excell, or circumvent.'—2. To cheat out of: C. 18–20; coll.

cut over the head. See cut, adj.

*cut queer whids. To speak offensively; use foul language: mid-C. 16–early 19 : c.

cut quick sticks. To depart hastily: C. 19–20; ob. Cf. *cut*, v., 4.

cut that ! See cut it.—cut the cackle. See cackle, cut the.

*cut the line or rope or string. To cut a long story short; to cease from keeping a person in suspense: c.: from ca. 1810, 1860, 1810, resp. Vaux.—2. (Only cut the line.) To cease work for the time being: printers' (– 1909). Ware. Referring to a *line of type*.

cut the, occ. one's, painter. To depart; decamp; depart in secret haste; to desert: orig., still mainly, nautical. From ca. 1840.—Hence, 2. To die: nautical: from ca. 1850. Bowen. Cf. *aloft*.
—3. Cut a person's painter, to send away, get rid of, render harmless: ca. 1660–1840. B.E.

*cut the rope or the string. See cut the line.

cut the rough (stuff). To cease doing or saying something obnoxious to another: Australian and New Zealand (lower classes', then military) coll.: C. 20. I.e. *cut out*, desist from.

cut throat. (More gen. with hyphen.) A butcher (lit.): C. 19–20, ob.—2. A dark lantern: coll.: ca. 1770–1840.—3. A game of bridge with three players only: coll. (– 1900).

cut under, v.t. To undersell, the gen. C. 20 form being *undercut*. From ca. 1870; coll. at first, S.E. since ca. 1895. L. Oliphant in *Altiora Peto* : ' Ned was all the time cutting under us by bringing out some new contrivance.'

cut up. To depreciate, slander; criticise very adversely : from ca. 1750; coll. till ca. 1800, then S.E. Goldsmith, 1759, ' The pack of critics . . . cutting up everything new.' Cf. the sense, to mortify, which is gen. in the passive, to be vexed, hurt, dejected : from ca. 1790; coll., in C. 20 almost S.E.—2. In the passive, to be in embarrassed circumstances : coll.; ca. 1800–70.—3. To turn up, become, show (up): coll.; ? late C. 18, certainly C. 19–20; ob.—4. To plunder, rob; to divide plunder : from ca. 1770; c. till ca. 1880, then (as in G. R. Sims's *How the Poor Live*) low.—5. To leave a fortune by will, v.i. (v.t. with *for*) : from ca. 1780. Gen. with *big, large, fat, rich* or *well*. Grose, 1st ed.; Disraeli, in *The Young Duke*, ' " You think him very rich ? " " Oh, he will cut up very large ", said the Baron.' This ' likens the defunct to a joint ' (of meat), W.—6. To behave: coll.; from ca. 1850. Hughes, in *Tom Brown's School Days*, ' A great deal depends on how a fellow cuts up, at first.' Cf.: *cut up nasty*, q.v.—7. To conduct (a contest) dishonestly : sporting : from ca. 1920. Prob. ex sense 4 (O.E.D. Sup.).

cut up didoes. See didoes, cut up.

cut up nasty, rough, rusty, savage, stiff, ugly, etc. To be quarrelsome, dangerous: coll.; the gen. phrase dates from ca. 1825. Dickens has *rough* in 1837, Thackeray *savage* in 1849, and *stiff* in 1856; *nasty* is the latest of those mentioned : hardly before 1900. Semantically similar to *cut*, v., 5, q.v.—2. In a race, cut up *rough, badly*, etc., signifies to behave badly, unfairly : from ca. 1880; orig. and gen. of horses.

cut up well. To look well when naked; be an attractive bed-fellow : in the language of (?) love : from ca. 1860; ob.—2. See also cut up, 5.

cutcha, kutcha. Makeshift; inferior; spurious; bad : Anglo-Indian and hence military; coll.; recorded in 1834, but in use in C. 18 (see French quotation in Yule & Burnell). Ex Hindi *kachcha*, raw, uncooked, hence rural, hence inferior, etc. Opp. *pukka*. (S.O.D.)

cutcher(r)y. A court-house; business office: coll.; Anglo-Indian, from early C. 17. Ex Hindi *kacheri*, a hall of audience. (S.O.D.).

[cute, says Manchon, is a n. = ' acuteness '. I doubt its existence. Perhaps confused with *cutie*, q.v.]

cute, 'cute, adj. ' Sharp, witty, ingenious, ready ', Dyche, 1748 : coll.: from ca. 1730. Foote has the adv. *cutely* in 1762, Goldsmith '*cuteness* (rare) in 1768.—2. Cf. the U.S. *cute*, used of things (– 1812), anglicised ca. 1850, esp. by schoolboys. Cf. the U.S. *cunning*.

cutey. See cutie.

Cuthbert. From 1917 (ob.), a government employee or officer shirking military service. Perhaps, says W., ' suggested by music-hall song on " Cuthbert, Clarence and Claude " '. Coined by ' Poy '. See my *Name This Child*.

cutie ; occ. cutey. A smart girl; loosely, any (young) girl : U.S. (– 1921) partly anglicised ca. 1930 owing to the ' talkies '. Ex *cute*, q.v. (O.E.D. Sup.)

[cutler's law. Pickpocketry : ? late C. 16–early 17 : ? c.—cutler's poetry. Wretched verse : ? coll. : ? C. 19.]

cuts. Scissors. small cuts : button-hole scissors. Tailors' : from ca. 1850.—2. Persons no longer friends : orig. schoolboys' (– 1871); rare, but coll., in C. 20. (O.E.D.) Ex *cut*, v., 2, or n., 2.—3. In expletives, a corruption of *God's* : C. 17–18.—4. A humorous seaman : late C. 19–20. Bowen. Ex S.E. *comic cuts*.—5. Shorts, esp. football shorts : Charterhouse : late C. 19–20. Prob. ex S.E. *cut short*.

cuts, comic. Admiralty intelligence reports; G.H.Q. communiqués : naval and military : 1915–18. Bowen.

cuts, have. To be excited : nautical : late C. 19–20. Bowen.

cutter, swear like a. I.e. violently : C. 19–20. Ex mid-C. 16–early 19 c. *cutter* = a robber, a bully.

cutter's mainsail. ' Corvus ', says Bowen without explanation : nautical : mid-C. 19–20. Perhaps the black guillemot : see E.D.D. at *cutty*, 2.

cuttee. See cutty, 2. Baumann, 1887. (A rare form.)

cuttie. See cutty, 2.

cutting. Underselling; keen competition : (– 1851); coll. > S.E.; in C. 20, *undercutting*. Cf. sense 2 of the adj.—2. Disowning or avoiding a person : see cut, v., 2.

cutting, adj. Blood-curdling (story, play, etc.): low coll., mostly London (– 1887). Baumann. Perhaps ex *cut to the heart* or *the quick*.—2. Cutting prices; underselling : coll.: 1851, Mayhew. (O.E.D.)

cutting-down. ' Cutting the clews of an unpopular shipmate's hammock and letting him down on deck ' : nautical coll.: mid-C. 19–20. Bowen.

*cutting-gloak. A rough apt to use the knife in a quarrel : c.: ca. 1810–50. Vaux, 1812 ; Egan's Grose, 1823.

cutting-out party. A predatory gang of cadets, esp. in the officers' pantry : *Conway* Training Ship (— 1891) ; ob. Masefield, *The Conway*, p. 113. Also, elsewhere, as Bowen shows.

cutting-shop. A manufactory of cheap, rough goods : ca. 1850–1900 ; coll. H., 3rd ed.

cuttle, a knife, in C. 16–18 low or coll. ; cf. the c. *cuttle-b(o)ung*, C. 16–18, a knife for cutting purses.

cutty. Abbr. *cutty pipe* : (— 1727) coll. : in C. 19–20, S.E. Cf. *nose-warmer*. *Cutty* is a mainly dial adj. = curtailed.—2. A coll., often humorous, semi-nickname for a testy, or esp. a naughty girl : from ca. 1820. Mostly in Scotland : see esp. the E.D.D. Often *cuttie*.—3. A black guillemot : (dial. and) nautical coll.: C. 19–20. Bowen.

*cutty-eye, v.i. To look, gaze, suspiciously : late C. 18–early 19 c. Grose, 2nd ed. V.t. with *at*.

*cutty-eyed. Looking suspiciously ; suspicious-looking : C. 19–20 (ob) c.

cutty-gun. A Scottish variant of *cutty*, 1 : mid-C. 19–20 ; ob. Bowen.

cutzooks ! An early C. 18 variant of *gadzooks !* O.E.D. Cf. *cuts*, 3.

cuz. A workman free of the ' chapel ' : printers' coll. > j. : from ca. 1720 ; ob. Bailey. Ex *coz*.

cycle. Abbr. *bicycle* or *tricycle* : from ca. 1880 : coll. till C. 20, then S.E. ; the same applies to the corresponding v.i.

cycling fringes. ' Especially prepared forehead-hair to be worn by such women bikers as had not abjured all feminine vanities ' : cyclists' coll. : 1897–ca. 1907. Ware.

cyclophobist. A hater of circulars : literary : 1882, *The Daily News*, Jan. 6. Ware.—2. Whence a hater of cyclists : 1897, *The Daily Telegraph*, Dec. 9. (Both are ob.)

*cymbal. A watch : mid-C. 19–20 c. ; ob. ' Ducange Anglicus.' Cf. *ticker*.

Cyprian. A prostitute : adumbrated long before, this term as used *temp.* Regency and George IV was fashionable s. ; now rare, archaic S.E. Ex *the Cyprian (goddess)*, Venus.

D

-d is frequently omitted in illiterate speech : prob. since centuries ago. E.g. *frien* (or *fren*) for *friend* ; and even in the past tense (preterite) of vv.

d or **dee.** A penny : coll. ; from ca. 1870 ; ob. except at Charterhouse : cf. *fa'd* and *ha'd*, qq.v. Ex the abbr. for penny, pence ; *d* = L. *denarius*, a rough equivalent of a penny. Hence, *be on the two d's*, to get the minimum pay : military : late C. 19–early 20. Manchon.—2. A detective : from ca. 1840. (In c., any police officer whatsoever.)—3. A damn, hence an oath ; esp. as *big d*. Coll. : popularised in Gilbert & Sullivan's *H.M.S. Pinafore*, 1877, ' What, never use a big, big D ? ', though Dickens, in 1861, has ' with a D '.—4. See **d-**.

'd. Had : coll. : 1741, Richardson, *I'd*, etc. (O.E.D.) Like the next it is pronounced *ud*.—2. Would : coll. : C. 17–20. Slightly earlier as *'ld* (or *ld*, † by 1800), which is rare in late C. 19–20, though it might well be preserved to distinguish it from *'d*, 1.

d.a. or **d.a.'s.** The menstrual flux : from ca. 1870. Abbr. *domestic affliction(s)*.

d. and d. Drunk and disorderly : police and, in C. 20, gen. ; from ca. 1870. Cf. *stropolous*.

d.b. Damned bad : theatrical coll. (— 1909) ; ob. Ware.

d.c.m. (or **D.C.M.**). A district court-martial : military coll. : C. 20. Punning the decoration.

D.I.O. See **damme ! I'm off**.

d.m.t. A jam roll : *Conway* Training Ship cadets' : ca. 1890–1914. Masefield. Ex ' damm tart '.

d.s.c. A decent suit of ' civvies ' : military : late 1918–19. F. & Gibbons. Punning *D.S.C.*, a military decoration.

D.T., The. *The Daily Telegraph* : orig. (—1873) journalistic, then gen. ; † by 1920, and ob. by 1905. —2. *d.t.*, from ca. 1858 ; *d.t.'s*, from ca. 1880 : low, post-War neutral, coll. abbr. of **delirium tremens** (' sometimes written and pronounced *del. trem* ', H., 5th ed. ; no longer so pronounced). G. R. Sims, 1880, and J. Payn, 1887, both use *d.t.*

d.t. centre. A minor club : literary : ca. 1880–1900. Ware.

d.v. Doubtful—very : theatrical (— 1909) ; ob. Ware.—2. **Divorce :** Society : ca. 1895–1915.

Another pun on the abbr. of *Deo volente* (if God so wishes). Ware.

da. A family and a child's abbr. of *dada* : coll. (— 1850).

da-erb. Bread : back s. (— 1859). H., 1st ed.

da da ! Good-bye ! : mainly nursery coll. : late C. 17–mid-18. Cf. *ta-ta*, q.v. O.E.D. Origin ?

*dab. An adept or expert ; ' dabster ', q.v. : late C. 17–20 : orig. c. ; by 1740, low ; by 1830, coll. Chesterfield, in letter of Aug. 17, 1733, ' Known dabs at finding out mysteries.' In C. 18, it has, in c., the sense, expert gamester (Dyche), while in C. 17–early 18 c. it means an ' expert exquisite in Roguery ', esp. in form *rum dab*, q.v. In C. 19–20, esp. among schoolboys. ? ex *dab*, to strike crisply, as the S.O.D. suggests, or ex L. *adeptus*, as H. proposes and I believe.—2. A bed : from ca. 1810 ; c. or low. Vaux ; Moncrieff in *Tom and Jerry*. ? origin and etymology. If any other example of back slang were recorded before 1850, I would postulate *bed > deb > dab* : prob., however, the term is a semantic development ex C. 18–20 S.E. *dab*, a flattish mass (e.g. of butter dabbed on something else). Certainly, however, *dab* is a variant for *deb* as back s. for a bed, in H., 1859.—3. Cf. the rare C. 18–early 19 coll. sense, a trifle.—4. In C. 19–20 c., the corpse of a drowned outcast woman : from ca. 1850. Ex *dab*, a small, flat fish. —5. A pimp ; esp. a bawd : c. : late C. 19–20. Manchon. Prob. ex sense 1.—6. A flat fish of any kind : London street coll. : C. 19–20. H., 1st ed. Cf. sense 4.—7. See **dabs**, 2.

dab, adj. Clever ; skilful or skilled ; expert ; very conversant. (Gen. with *at* or *in*.) C. 18–20, but never very common : in C. 19–20, coll. Ex *dab*, n., 1.—2. Bad : in back slang : from the 1850's. Diprose, *London Life*, 1877. Esp. *dab tros*, a bad sort : occ. used as an adj.

dab down. To hand over ; pay ; ' shell out ' : coll., C. 19–20. Cf. Yorkshire *dabs doon*, immediate payment (E.D.D.).

dab in, have a, v.i. To have a ' go ' : late C. 19–20. (J. Milne, *The Epistles of Atkins*, 1902.)

dab in the dook. A tip (lit., a pat on the hand): low and military : C. 20. B. & P.

*dab it up (with). To pair off (with a woman); arrange or agree to lie with her : c. >, by 1820, low ; from ca. 1810. Vaux.—2. 'To run a score at a public-house ', Egan's Grose : public-house coll. : ca. 1820–60.

dab !, quoth Dawkins when he hit his wife on the arse with a pound of butter. A mid-C. 18–mid-19 c.p. applied to impacts. Grose, 1st ed.

dab tros. A bad sort : back s. (— 1859). H., 1st ed. See dab, adj., 2. Cf. :

dabheno. A bad one, esp. a bad market : back s. (— 1859). H., 1st ed. Cf. dab, adj., 2.

dabs. A rare abbr. of dabster : coll., mostly London (— 1887); slightly ob. Baumann.—2. (Extremely rare in the singular.) Finger-prints : c. (— 1935). David Hume.

dabster. A ' dab ', q.v.; an expert : from ca. 1700 ; s. >, by 1850, coll. >, in late C. 19, mainly dial. Ex dab, n., 1, q.v.

*dace. Twopence. Late C. 17–19 ; c. and low. B.E. A corruption of deuce.

dacey. Of native Indian origin : Anglo-Indian coll. (— 1876). Ex Hindi des, country. (O.E.D.)

dacha-saltee. Tenpence ; a franc : from ca. 1850 ; Parlyaree and c. H., 1st ed. ; Reade, The Cloister and the Hearth. Ex It. dieci soldi via Lingua Franca. Cf. dacha-one, eleven(pence).

dad, dada, dadda. The first from before 1500, the others from before 1680 : coll. for father. Prob. ex child's pronunciation of father : cf., however, Sampson at dad. James I styled himself Charles I's ' Dear Old Dad '.—2. In Australia, at first coll. but soon official, dad is the name given, esp. in Anzac Day celebrations, to the fathers of those men who served with the Australian Force during the War. Cf. digger, 2.—3. In oaths and asseverations, God : coll. : 1678, Otway. In mid-C. 19–20, dial. and U.S. O.E.D.

dad-dad, mum-mum ; or daddy-mammy. A tyro's practice on a drum : military ; from ca. 1760. Grose.

daddle. The hand ; fist. From ca. 1780 : low. The S.O.D. says dial. : this it may orig. have been, but its use by and temp. Grose (1st ed.), George Parker, and Tom Moore indicates that it was common in London. ? etymology : cf. paddle. F. & H. gives synonymy. Cf. also flipper.

dad(d)ler. A farthing : low, esp. Cockney : C. 20. Perhaps a corruption of diddler.

daddy. Diminutive of dad, q.v. : father : coll. from ca. 1500.—2. A stage-manager : theatrical ; from ca. 1850. H., 1st ed.—3. The superintendent of a casual ward : from ca. 1860 : coll.—4. The man who, at a wedding, gives away the bride : ca. 1860–85. H., 2nd ed.—5. The person ' winning ' the prize at a mock raffle, faked lottery : from ca. 1860 ; c. then low. H., 3rd ed.

dadler. See daddler.

dado. (round the dining-room). A (knitted) abdominal belt : military, 1914 +. Ex the die-shaped part of a pedestal (W.).

*dads. An old man : c. : C. 18. Anon., Street-Robberies Consider'd, 1728. A perversion of dad. The -s indicates either familiarity or affection, or both : cf. ducks for duck (the endearment).

dad's will. Parental authority : Oxford University : ca. 1820–40. Egan's Grose.

daff ; daffy. Coll. abbr. of daffodil : mid-C. 19–20. Cf. mum, 2.

daffy (loosely daffey) ; **Daffy's Elixir.** Gin : from ca. 1820 ; ob. ' Corcoran ' Reynolds, 1821 ; Leman Rede, 1841. Ex a very popular medicine advertised as early as 1709, ca. 1860 called soothing syrup (applied also to gin) and in 1891 known as tincture of senna.—2. A large number of telegrams for delivery : Post Office telegraph-messengers' (— 1935).—3. See daff.

daffy, adj. Slightly mad ; soft in the head : dial. (— 1884) >, by ca. 1895, s. Ex Northern dial. daff, a simpleton. O.E.D. Sup.

daffy-down-dilly. A dandy : ca. 1830–80. Leman Rede in Sixteen-String Jack.

daft-man. To refuse (a person) perem ptorily or vigorously or to take no notice of him : tailors' : 1928, The Tailor and Cutter, Nov. 29. Lit., to render daft.

daftie. A daft person : coll. : from ca. 1870. (O.E.D.) Ex daft. (Slightly earlier in dial.)

dag. A ' hard case ' ; a wag ; a ' character ' : Australia, thence New Zealand : from ca. 1890. Prob. ex dagen, q.v.—2. See dags, 2.

dag at, be a. To be extremely good at : from the middle 1890's : Australians' ; hence, by 1920, New Zealanders'. Ex preceding.

dag up, v.i. To smarten oneself for guard or parade : military : C. 20. F. & Gibbons. Prob. ex dagging sheep.

*dagen, c. for an artful criminal or near-criminal, itself ex c. dagen or degen (q.v.), a sword.—2. See dags.

Daggarramereens. The Diego Ramirez Islands (E. of Cape Horn) : nautical : mid-C. 19–20. Bowen. By ' Hobson-Jobson '.

dagged. Tipsy : (— 1745) this term, perhaps orig., > solely, dial. ca. 1800. Ex dial. dag, to sprinkle. (O.E.D.)

dagger-ale. Inferior ale : late C. 16–17. Ex The Dagger, a low tavern fl. 1600 in Holborn. Cf. :

dagger-cheap. Very cheap : C. 17–18 ; coll. and archaic after ca. 1660. Bishop Andrewes, 1631, ' [The devil] may buy us even dagger-cheap, as we say.' Lancelot Andrewes, d. in 1626. See preceding.

daggle-tail. A slattern ; ' a nasty dirty Slut ' : from ca. 1560 ; coll. till ca. 1700, when it > S.E. ; ca. 1830 it > dial. and low coll. Cf. draggle-tail.

Dago. One of Latin race, but rarely of a Frenchman : ex U.S. (— 1858)—though anticipated in 1832 ; anglicised ca. 1900 : coll. In C. 17, Diego (James) was a nickname for a Spaniard. See Words ! and O.E.D. (Sup.).

dags. A feat, piece of work. ' I'll do you(r) dags ', i.e. ' something you can't ' ; (among schoolboys) ' do dags ', play foolhardy tricks. Coll. ; from ca. 1850. H., 1st ed. F. & H. proposes the A.S. daeg, the O.E.D. darg, one's task, as the origin ; ? a perversion of dare or darings (W.).

dags, on the. On furlough (as opp. a few days' leave) : naval : late C. 19–20. Bowen. Prob. ex the preceding.—2. Cigarettes : military : C. 20. F. & Gibbons. Perhaps ex dial. dag, the stem-end of a branch, the big end of a faggot (E.D.D.) : cf. fag ex fag-end.

daily. A daily maid-servant : from ca. 1920 : coll., now verging on S.E. (O.E.D. Sup.)—2. See Moving-Picture Slang, p. 6.

daily-bread. A wage-earner ; the working head of the house : from ca. 1860.

daily dozen, one's or the. Physical exercises, on rising in the morning : coll. : from ca. 1924.

daily eye-wash. An official Army communiqué : military : 1915 ; ob. It was heavily censored. See eye-wash.

Daily Levy, The. *The Daily Telegraph* : ca. 1860–1900. Ex Joseph Moses *Levy*, who, in 1856, took it over from its founder (1855), Colonel Sleigh, and made it London's first penny newspaper.

Daily Liar, The. *The Daily Mail* : jocular (not slanderous) : C. 20. Perhaps ex Cockney *Dily Mile*.

Daily Mail, n. Tail : rhyming s. : C. 20. B. & P.

dairs. Small unmarketable fish : nautical coll. : C. 19–20 ; ob. Bowen. Ex † dial *dairns*, the same.

Daily Wail (occ. **Whale**)**, The.** *The Daily Mail* : jocular : from ca. 1910.

dairy or **dairies.** The paps ; hence *sport*, later *air, the dairy*, expose the breast : low, from ca. 1780. Grose, 2nd ed. Cf. *charlies, charms, milky way,* and, in rhyming s., *cabman's rests,* and :

dairy arrangements. The female breasts : low (— 1923). Manchon. Ex preceding.

dairy on, get the. To see : notice (a person) : low s., perhaps orig. c. : from ca. 1910. Charles E. Leach, *On Top of the Underworld*, 1933. Origin ?

daisies. A pre-1879 abbr. of *daisy roots,* q.v. : boots.

daisies, turn up one's toes to the. To die : coll. (— 1842). Barham. Cf. *push up daisies* and *grin at the daisy-roots.* Hence :

daisies, under the. Dead : from ca. 1860 ; ob. In G.W. and after, gen. *pushing up daisies.*

daisy. N. (and, in England, a rare adj., 1757), an excellent or first-rate person or thing : the n. came ex U.S. (— 1876) and was adopted ca. 1890 ; Kipling used it in his poem, *Fuzzy Wuzzy.*

daisy, pick a. To defecate in the open air ; also, to retire to urinate. Mostly women's ; from ca. 1860 ; orig. a euphemism ; in C. 20, coll.

daisy-beaters. Feet ; the singular is very rare. C. 19. Cf. *creepers.*

daisy-cutter. A horse that hardly raises its feet from the ground : coll. : late C. 18–19. Grose, 1785.—2. Hence, any horse : C. 19–20 ; ob. Scott, Charles Reade.—3. In cricket, a ball that keeps very low after pitching, esp. on being bowled : coll. (1863) ; cf. *sneak(er).* F. & H. and Lewis.—4. A German shell that, on impact, burst instantaneously and scattered its fragments very close to the ground : New Zealanders' : in G.W. Cf. *grass-cutter,* q.v.

*daisy-kicker. A horse : c. and then low : from ca. 1770 ; ob. Cf. preceding.—2. The ostler of an inn, esp. a large inn : from ca. 1770 ; ob. Both are in G. Parker's *View of Society,* 1781 ; the second in Grose, 1st ed.

daisy-pusher. A fatal wound : military : 1916. B. & P. Ex :

daisy-pushing. Dead : military : 1915. F. & Gibbons. See also **daisies, under the.**

daisy recruits. (A pair of) boots : rhyming s. : ca. 1855–70. H., 1st ed. Cf. :

daisy roots. Boots : rhyming s. (— 1874). H., 5th ed. I have never heard the singular used. Often abbr. to *daisies.* Cf. the preceding term, which is less viable.—2. Hence, shoes : mostly grafters' : C. 20. Philip Allingham.

*daisyville, deuseaville. The country : c. and (?) low : resp. C. 19 and mid-C. 17–early 19. Coles, 1676.

[**dak, dawk.** (In India) any arrangement for, or method of, travelling by relay ; the letter-post.

Recorded in C. 14, the word, though unnecessary, has become Anglo-Indian ; j. rather than .coll. Hence, *dak bungalow,* a guest-house or a road-route (— 1853). See **dawk.**]

*dakma. To silence : c. ; rare in England and perhaps ex U.S. : C. 19.

Dally the Tall. Mrs. Grace **Dal**rymple Eliot (d. 1823), friend of George IV when Regent. Dawson.

dam. ' Damage ' (q.v.) : university : ca. 1900–15. Ware.

dam, not be worth or **care a.** (See **care a pin.**) Mid-C. 18–20 ; coll. Prob. ex a small Indian coin ; cf. *curse,* q.v. See esp. Yule & Burnell, W., and Grose, P. The *twopenny dam* is said to have been rendered fashionable by Wellington. Manchon.

dam of that was whisker, the. A c.p.—coll. and dial.—applied ca. 1675–1810 to a great lie. Ray, 1678 (Apperson). Is it possible that *whisker* may orig. have been *whisper* ? See also **whisker, the mother . . .**

damage. Expense ; cost : from ca. 1750 ; S.O.D. records it at 1755. Byron, ' Many thanks, but I must pay the damage.' Prob. ex *damage(s)* at law. In late C. 19–20, gen. as *what's the damage ?,* jocularly varying the much earlier *what's the shot ?* W.

damaged. Tipsy : from ca. 1865. Cf. *screwed.*

damager. A manager : theatrical : ca. 1880–1912. Ware. By sarcastic perversion.

damask. To warm (wine) : late C. 17–early 19. B.E. has ' *Damask the Claret,* Put a roasted Orange flasht smoking hot in it ' ? The ' warmth ' of damask, ' a rich silk fabric woven with elaborate designs and figures ' (S.O.D.).

*damber. A man belonging to a criminal gang : c. : mid-C. 17–18. Coles, 1676 ; B.E. Cf. *dimber* ; perhaps suggested by :

damme, or **dammy,** or **damme** (or **-y**)**-boy.** A profane swearer (gen. the single word) : coll. ; ca. 1610–1820. From mid-C. 17–early 18 (the hyphenated term), ' a roaring mad, blustering Fellow, a Scourer of the Streets ', B.E. ; this latter is possibly c. (Perhaps *damme !* is itself coll.)

dame. A house-master not teaching the Classics : Eton College : mid-C. 19–20.—2. A girl ; a sweetheart : Glasgow : from ca. 1932. Ex U.S., via the ' talkies ' ; nevertheless, the U.S. prob. derived this usage from Scots, where *dame,* a girl, appears as early as 1790 (Shirrefs, *Poems*) : E.D.D.

damfool ; occ., jocularly, **damphoole** or **-phule.** A damned fool : coll., n. and adj. : from, resp., ca. 1880 and ca. 1895. (O.E.D. Sup.) Whence :

damfoolishness. Damned foolishness : coll. : late C. 19–20.

damme !, I'm off. (Often *D.I.O.*) A men's c.p. of late C. 18–early 19, satiric of initials on cards of invitation, etc. Grose, 3rd ed.

dammit, as (e.g. **quick** or **soon**) **as.** Exceedingly (quick, soon) : coll. : C. 20. I.e. as saying *damn it !* Cf. :

dammit, (as) near as. Very nearly indeed : coll. : C. 20. (F. Grierson, *Mystery in Red,* 1931.)

damn'. Damned : coll. : late C. 18–20. Cf. *damn the . . .,* q.v., and see **damned.**

damn, not be worth or **care a.** The form and etymology preferred by the O.E.D. : see **dam.**

damn a horse if I do ! A strong refusal or rejection : coll. : ca. 1820–60. ' Jon Bee ', 1823, shrewdly postulates origin in *damn me for a horse if I do.*

damn all. Nothing: coll.: from ca. 1915. A bowdlerisation of *fuck all*. B. & P.

damn the (e.g. thing) **can** (or **could**) **one** (e.g. **find**). Not a (thing) can one (find): a coll. form of *not a damned thing can one (find)*: somewhat rare (— 1887). Baumann.

damn well. Certainly; assuredly: coll.: late C. 19–20. E.g. Winifred Holtby, 1934, ' " These things are not in our hands ", said the doctor . . . " Then they damn well ought to be ! " swore the merchant, appalled by the thought of all the money he had spent unavailingly.'

damnable. Confounded; objectionable: late C. 16–20; S.E. till ca. 1800, then coll. or a vulgarism.

damnably. In degraded usage, very, exceedingly: C. 19–20 coll. or vulgarism. Cf. preceding.

damnation, adj. and adv. From ca. 1750: damned; excessive(ly), very. Coll. (S.O.D.)

damned. An adj. expressive of reprobation or of mere emotional crudity or as an ever-weakening intensive (cf. *bloody*): late C. 16–20; S.E. till ca. 1800, then coll.—2. Adv., damnably; hence, very: mid-C. 18–20; S.E. till ca. 1850, then coll. In both senses, one tends to use *damned* before a vowel, *damn'* before a consonant.

damned, be. Used in intensive phrases: see **smart as be damned** and the like paragraph.

damned soul. A Customs House clearing clerk: from late 1780's. Grose, 2nd ed. Ex a belief that he has sworn never to make true declarations on oath.

damp. A drink: Dickens in *Pickwick*; not very gen. elsewhere. Gen. *give oneself a damp*, or *something damp.*—2. Also, rather rare v. reflexive (— 1862), whence prob.:

damp one's mug. To drink: low: from ca. 1860; slightly ob.

damp(-)pot. The sea; esp. the Atlantic: tailors': from ca. 1855.—2. A water-pot: tailors' coll.: late C. 19–20.

damp the sawdust. To drink with friends at the opening of a new tavern: licensed victuallers': from ca. 1860.

***damper.** In c., *damper*, after ca. 1860 gen. displaced by *lob*, is a till: C. 19. H., 2nd ed.—2. A spoil-sport, ' wet blanket ': coll.: from ca. 1815; in C. 20, rare.—3. A sweating employer, a ' last-ouncer ': tailors': from ca. 1860.—4. Ale or stout taken after spirits (and water): from ca. 1820, † by 1930.—5. A snack between meals: coll. and dial.: from ca. 1780; slightly ob. Grose, 1st ed.; Maria Edgeworth. See ' The Art of Lightening Work ' in *Words !*, p. 47, and cf. *snack, snap, tiffin*, and esp. *bever.*—6. A suet pudding preceding meat: schoolboys': C. 19–20, ob.—7. (Australia and New Zealand) a kind of bread, unleavened and baked in ashes: orig. (ca. 1825) coll. but by 1910 accepted as S.E. Peter Cunningham, 1827.—8. A lunch- or, more gen., dinner-bill: Society: 1886–ca. 1915. Ware notes the Fr. s. *douloureuse* and quotes Theodore Hook, ' Men laugh and talk until the feast is o'er ; | Then comes the reckoning, and they laugh no more ! '

damphool, -phule. See **damfool.**

damps. Denver & Rio Grande Railroad preference shares: Stock Exchange (— 1895). A. J. Wilson, *Stock Exchange Glossary*. A pun on the river mentioned.

Dams (or **d.**). Defensively armed merchant-ships and those connected with them: naval: 1915; ob. Bowen.

damsel. A hot iron used to warm a bed: contrast a *Scotch warming-pan*, q.v. The S.O.D. records it at 1727. Orig. it was undoubtedly either coll. or s., but by 1800 it had > S.E.; cf. the Fr. *moine.*—2. A girl, any girl: as employed in society and in the universities, post-G.W., the term has a facetious and coll. flavour.—3. A skate (fish): North Sea fishermen's: C. 19–20; ob. Bowen.

damson-pie. Abuse; a slanging match. Either coll. or dial.: Birmingham and ' the black country'; from ca. 1865. William Black, in *Strange Adventures of a House Boat*, 1888. The variant *damson-tart* occurs a year earlier (O.E.D.), but rather in the sense: profane language. Punning *damn !*

Dan. The inevitable nickname of anyone surnamed Coles: coll.: late C. 19–20. Bowen.

Dan Tucker. Butter: rhyming s. (— 1859), the rhyme being, as often, merely approximate. H., 1st ed.

***dance.** A staircase; a flight of steps: c. (— 1857); †. ' Ducange Anglicus.' Abbr. *dancers*, q.v.

dance, dance upon nothing (in a hempen cravat), **dance the Paddington frisk or the Tyburn jig.** To be hanged: low. The first, C. 19–20, the second C. 18–20, but both ob.; the third, late C. 17–19. *Paddington* refers to Tyburn. Hence, *the dance* (up)*on nothing*, like *the dance of death*, = hanging, C. 19–20. Hood, in *Miss Kilmansegg*, ' The felon . . . elopes | To a caper on sunny greens and slopes | Instead of the dance upon nothing.'—2. Among printers, from ca. 1850, type is said to dance when, the forme being lifted, letters fall out.— **3. dance Barnaby,** see **Barnaby.**

dance, lead (rarely **give**) **a person a.** To cause needless or excessive worry or exertion: from ca. 1520; coll. >, by 1900, S.E.

dance barefoot. Applied to a girl whose younger sister marries before her: coll.; ca. 1590–1800. (O.E.D.) Cf. the Yorkshire *dance in the half-peck*, ' to be left behind as a bachelor, on a brother's marriage ', E.D.D.

dance, fake a. See **fake a dance.**

***dance the stairs.** To break into a flat or an office; do quick a ' job ': C. 20c. Charles E. Leach.

dance to a person's whistle, pipe, etc. To follow his lead; unquestioningly obey. Coll. >, by 1700, S.E.; from ca. 1560.

danceable. Fit to dance with: coll.: 1860, Wilkie Collins (O.E.D.).—2. (Of a tune) suitable for a dance: coll.: from ca. 1890 (ibid.).

***dancer.** A ' cat' burglar: C. 19 c. Cf. *garreter* and *dancing-master.*

***dancers.** Stairs; a flight of steps: from ca. 1670; until ca. 1840, c.; then low s. or archaic c. Head; B.E.; Grose; Lytton. The term, occ. heard in G.W. and since, is ob. Because one ' dances ' down them.—2. (Also *Merry Dancers*) the Aurora Borealis: coll. > S.E., though in C. 20 mainly dial.: 1717. (S.O.D.)

dancing-dog. (Gen. pl.) A dancing man: from ca. 1880; ob. Ware, ' A satirical title applied . . . when dancing began to go out.' It again became popular ca. 1905 and ca. 1919.

dancing-master. A species of Mohock *temp.* Queen Anne: coll. See esp. *The Spectator*, No. 324 (1712). This dandy-rough made his victims caper by thrusting his sword between their legs.—2. The hangman: late C. 17–early 18; perhaps orig. c.—

3. In c., a 'cat' burglar : ca. 1860–1900. H., 3rd ed. Cf. *dancer*. Also called a *garreter* (H., 3rd ed.). —4. A boxer continually 'dancing about' : pugilistic (— 1923). Manchon.

dand. Abbr. *dandy*, a fop : ca. 1870–1900 : perhaps more dial. than s. Hardy. (O.E.D.)

dander. Anger ; a ruffled temper : coll. ; orig. (— 1832) U.S., though perhaps ex English dial. as H. implies ; (? re-)anglicised ca. 1860. Thackeray, in *Pendennis*, 'Don't talk to me . . . when my dander is up.' The S.O.D. proposes derivation either ex *dander* = dandruff or ex *dunder* = ferment ; the latter is preferable. But I suggest that the Romany *dander*, to bite,—*dando*, bitten,—may solve the problem. Whence *dandered*, angry, ruffled, anglicised ca. 1880 but never gen.

Dandies, the. The London Rifle Brigade : military : from ca. 1862. F. & Gibbons. Ex their smart appearance at the Hyde Park reviews.

dandification. The act or state of making look or looking like a dandy : coll., 1825 +. Ex :

dandify. To make resemble, give the style of, a dandy : coll. ; from ca. 1820. Whence the ppl. adj. *dandified*.

dandi. See **dandy**, 5.

dandiprat ; occ. **dandyprat(t).** A person physically, socially, or morally very insignificant : from ca. 1550 ; coll. till C. 19. The anon. play *Lingua*, 1580 ; Scott, 1821. Ex the C. 16–18 sense, a small coin worth 1½d.

dando. A heavy eater ; esp. one who cheats restaurants, cafés, hotels, etc. : from ca. 1840 ; † by 1920. Coll. Ex a 'seedy swell' so named and given to bilking. Thackeray ; Macaulay, 1850, in *Journal* : 'I was dando at a pastry cook's.'

dandy ; gen. **the d.** 'The ticket' ; precisely the thing needed, esp. if fashionable. S.O.D. records it at 1784 ; *dandy*, fop, occurring only four years earlier (? ex *dandiprat*), was perhaps s., or at the least coll., until ca. 1830.—2. Anglo-Irish, a small drink or 'go' of whiskey (— 1838) ; ob.—3. Anything first-rate ; also adj. : orig. (1794 : Thornton), U.S., anglicised ca. 1905.—4. In the West Indies, with variant *dandy fever*, the coll. name for *dengue fever* : 1828. (O.E.D.)—5. **dandy, dandi.** Anglo-Indian (coll. rather than s.) for a boatman on the Ganges ; from ca. 1680. And for : a small hammock-like conveyance carried by two men ; from ca. 1870.—6. In c., a bad gold coin (— 1883). Ex the modicum of pure gold.

dandy grey russet. A dirty brown : mid-C. 18–early 19 coll. Grose, 1st ed. Cf. dial. *dandy-go-russet*.

dandy horse. A velocipede : Society : ca. 1820–40. 'Jon Bee.'

*****dandy-master.** The head of a counterfeiting gang (— 1883) : c.

Dandy Ninth, the. The 9th (Service) Battalion of the Royal Scots : military : 1915. F. & Gibbons. 'Pride of the proud city are the . . . 9th Royal Scots, or Edinbro Highlanders, a territorial battalion, and the only kilted one in the regiment', R. J. T. Hills, *Something About a Soldier*, 1934.

dandyfunk. Pounded biscuit mixed with water, fat, and marmalade, then baked : nautical : late C. 19–20. Bowen. Prob. ironic.

dandypratt. See **dandipratt**.

dangle in the Sheriff's picture-frame. To be hanged : (c. or) low : late C. 18–early 19. Grose, 1st ed.

dang. A curse, a damn : late C. 19–20. Ex :

dang, v. To damn (e.g. *dang me !*) : euphemistic dial. (from ca. 1790) >, ca. 1840, coll. O.E.D.

dangle-parade. A 'short-arm' inspection : New Zealand soldiers' : G.W. Cf. *dingle-dangle*.

dangler ; dangling. An emotional friendship between two boys : schoolboys' : C. 20.

*****danglers.** A bunch of seals : c. (— 1859) : ? ex U.S.—2. Testicles : low : mid-C. 19–20.

dangling. See **dangler**.

*****danna.** Human ordure : C. 18–19 c. Hence *danna-drag*, the night-man's cart, C. 19 c. (Vaux), and *danna-ken*, the C. 18 c. form of the C. 19–20 *dunnekin*, which, orig. c., > s. and then, ca. 1900, low coll. and which, early in C. 19, pervaded dial.

Dansker. (Gen. pl.) A Dane : nautical coll. : C. 19–20. Bowen. I.e. Danish *Dansker*, the same. Cf. Shakespeare's use.

dant. A profligate woman ; a harlot : C. 16–17. Ex the Dutch, it is almost certainly c. or, at the least, low s. (Halliwell.)

dantiprat. A variant (C. 17) of *dandiprat*, q.v.

*****dap.** To pick up ; to steal, esp. luggage : C. 20 c. Perhaps ex S.E. *dab*, v., or *do up*.

daps. Slippers : Regular Army's : late C. 19–20. B. & P. Perhaps cognate with dial. *dap*, to move quickly and lightly (E.D.D.).

darbies. As handcuffs (from ca. 1660), prob. orig. s., certainly soon coll. ; but as fetters (from ca. 1670) always, though rare, s., ob. by 1860. Marryat, in *Japhet*, 'We may as well put on the darbies, continued he, producing a pair of handcuffs.' Ex a rigid form of usurer's bond called *Father Derby's*, or *Darby's*, *bands*.—2. Sausages : C. 19–20, ob. Ex ?

darbies and joans. Fetters coupling two persons : from ca. 1735, ex *Darby and Joan*.

darble. The devil : a coll. corruption, i.e. orig. a sol., of Fr. *diable*. From ca. 1850. H., 1st ed.

*****darby.** See **darbies**.—2. Ready money : from ca. 1675 ; orig. c., it > low ca. 1780 ; † by ca. 1850. B.E. ; Estcourt, in *Prunella*, a play (? 1712), 'Come, nimbly lay down darby ; come, pray sir : don't be tardy.' For etymology, cf. *darbies*.—3. A wholly c. sense is the mid-C. 19–20 one, a thief's 'haul'.

darby roll. A gait that results from the long wearing of shackles : from ca. 1820. 'Jon Bee', 1823. Orig. a c. or a police term, it > low gen. s., never very common and now ob. Cf. :

darby's dyke. The grave ; death : C. 19 low, prob. orig. c. : cf. :

darby's fair. The day on which a prisoner is removed from one prison to another for trial : C. 19 low. Cf. *darbies* and *darby roll*.

dard. The *membrum virile* : C. 17–18 ; low, perhaps c. Ex Fr. *dard*, a dart.

dare. A challenge ; act of defiance : from late C. 16 ; S.E. till late C. 19, when it > coll.

dark. Any person, place, thing not impregnated with Recordite principles : ecclesiastical : ca. 1855–80. H. Perhaps ex *darkest Africa*.

*****dark, get the.** To be confined in a punishment cell : c. : from ca. 1880.

dark, keep it. Say nothing about it ; gen. imperative. From ca. 1856 ; coll. 'Ducange Anglicus', 1857 ; Dickens, 1861 (O.E.D.). Prob. ex the long †, *keep a person dark*, i.e. confined in a dark room, as madmen formerly were ; cf. the treatment of Malvolio in *Twelfth Night*.

dark as a pocket. Extremely dark : merchant-servicemen's : late C. 19–20 ; ob. Ware.

dark (occ. black) **as Newgate knocker.** See **Newgate knocker, black as.**

dark as the inside of a cow. (Of a night) pitch-black : nautical : from ca. 1880. Cf. *dark as a pocket.*

*****dark cull(y).** A married man with a mistress that he visits only at night : C. 18–early 19 c. *A New Canting Dict.*, 1725 ; Grose, 1st ed.

dark horse. A horse whose form is unknown to the backers but which is supposed to have a good chance : the turf ; from ca. 1830. Disraeli, 'A dark horse . . . rushed past the grand stand in sweeping triumph,' 1831. Variant, from ca. 1840, *dark un.*—2. Hence, a candidate or competitor of whom little is known : from ca. 1860 ; in C. 20, coll.

dark house. The coll. form of *dark-room,* one in which madmen were kept : ca. 1600–1850.

dark it. (Esp. in imperative.) To say nothing, to ' cut it out ' : tailors' : 1928, *The Tailor and Cutter,* Nov. 29.

dark-lantern. ' The Servant or Agent that Receives the Bribe (at Court),' B.E. : ca. 1690–1770.

dark-lantern man, the. St. John of the Long Parliament. Ex his gloomy looks. (Dawson.)

dark 'un, cop a. To be put on over-time in the winter : dockers' : from ca. 1920. (*The Daily Herald,* late July or early Aug., 1936.)

darkened. Closed (eye) : pugilistic (— 1857) ; ob. ' Ducange Anglicus.'

Darkies. Generic for the Coal-Hole, the Cider Cellar, the Shades : ca. 1850–80. (These were places of midnight entertainment in or near the Strand.) Ware.—2. See **darky, 3.**

*****darkman.** A watchman : c. : C. 18. Anon., *Street-Robberies Consider'd,* 1728. Independent of *darkmans,* for lit. it is a man working in the dark, i.e. at night.

*****darkmans.** Night ; twilight : mid-C. 16–19 c. Harman, B.E., Scott. Occ. *darkman.* I.e. *dark + man(s),* q.v.

*****darkman's budge.** A nocturnal housebreaker's day-plus-night assistant : c. : late C. 17–18. B.E.

*****darkness, child of.** A bell-man : c. : late C. 17–early 18. B.E.

darks, the ; darky. The night ; occ. twilight : low ; mid-C. 18–20, ob. G. Parker, 1789 (*darkey*).

*****darky, darkey.** See **darks.**—2. A dark lantern : ca. 1810–1910 ; either low or c. Vaux.—3. A negro : coll. : orig. (1775 : Thornton), U.S. ; anglicised not later than 1840.—4. A white man with a dark skin : a generic nickname, from ca. 1880.—5. The inevitable nickname of men surnamed Smith : military : late C. 19–20. F. & Gibbons. Prob. at first a Gypsy nickname. Also, ironically, of men surnamed White (*The Observer,* Sept. 20, 1936).—6. A beggar that pretends to be blind : c. (— 1861). Mayhew.

darling in post-G.W. society use as a term of address for even a comparative stranger is rightly considered s., though by 1933 it had > j.

Darling shower. A dust-storm : Darling-River vicinity (Australia) : coll. (— 1898). Morris.

Darlo. Darlinghurst, Sydney : Sydneyites' : from ca. 1920. See **-o,** coll. and s. suffix.

darn, darnation, darned. A coll. form of *damn, damnation, damned.* ? orig. dial. ; in C. 19–20, mostly U.S. and euphemistic.

darning the water. ' Ships manœuvring backwards and forwards before a blockaded port ' : nautical : C. 19. Bowen. Ex darning socks.

dart. In boxing, a dart-like, i.e. straight-armed

blow : from ca. 1770 ; ob.—2. In Australia, idea, plan, scheme ; ambition (— 1887). Also, particular fancy, personal taste : from ca. 1894. Ex the idea of a ' darting ' or sudden thought. (Morris.) Cf. :

Dart, the Old. See **Old Dart, the.**

darter. Daughter. When not dial., this is sol. ; from C. 16 (? earlier).

Dartmoor crop. Short-cut hair : military : 1915 ; slightly ob. Ernest Raymond, *The Jesting Army,* 1930.

dash. A tavern waiter : ca. 1660–1830. B.E. Either ex his dashing about or ex his adding to drinks a dash of this or that.—2. For *cut a dash,* see **cut.**—3. A gift ; a tip : West Africa : from ca. 1780. Also v. : C. 19. Ex *dashee,* a native word : in fact, *dashee,* n. and v., is the earlier, C. 18 only, form of this ' Negrish ' term (O.E.D.).—4. An attempt, esp. in *have a dash at* : coll. (— 1931). Lyell. Cf. *have a cut* or *smack at.*

dash, v.i. To cut a dash ; coll. ; from ca. 1780.—2. (brewers and publicans) to adulterate : from ca. 1860. *The Times,* April 4, 1871, in leader on the Licensing Bill, ' [The publicans] too often . . . are driven to adulterate or dash the liquor.'

dash ! An expletive : coll. always, but euphemistic only when consciously used as an evasion for *damn !,* which orig. it represented : from ca. 1810. Ex the dash in *d—n.* The most frequent variants are *dash my wig(s) !,* ca. 1810–80, and *dash it all !,* from ca. 1870.

dash, do one's. ' To reach one's Waterloo,' C. J. Dennis : Australian (— 1916).

Dash !, s'elp me. A rather illiterate euphemistic coll. variant (— 1923) of *s'elp me God !* Manchon.

dash my buttons ! See **buttons.**—**dash my wig(s) !** See **dash !**

dash off ; dash out. To depart with a dash ; come out with a dash : coll. : late C. 18–20. Ex *dash,* v., 1. (O.E.D.)

dash on, have a. To bet heavily and/or wildly : the turf ; from ca. 1865, ob.

dashed, dashedly, adj., adv. Euphemistic coll. for *damned, damnably* : from ca. 1880. See **dash !** (O.E.D.)

dasher. One who cuts a dash ; esp. a showy harlot : from ca. 1790 ; coll. Dibdin, ' My Poll, once a dasher, now turned to a nurse.'—2. A brilliant or dashing attempt or motion : coll. (— 1884) ; ob. O.E.D.

dashing. A daring or brilliant action ; a showy liveliness in manner, dress, gen. behaviour : coll. : ca. 1800–95.

dashing, adj. Fond of ' cutting a dash ', making a show : from ca. 1800 ; coll. till C. 20, when S.E.

dashy. ' Dashing ', adj. ; coll. ; from ca. 1820 (perhaps after *flashy*) ; never very common and now ob.

data. Datum : incorrect as *phenomena* and *strata* are, in the singular, for *phenomenon* and *stratum* : rare before C. 20.

date. An appointment, esp. with a member of the opposite sex : coll. : from ca. 1905. Ex U.S. Cf. *date up,* q.v.—2. See **date !, you.**

date, v.i. To show its period, decade, year, etc., as in ' Fashion in dress dates so terribly '. Also, to be or become superseded, go out of fashion, quickly, as in ' Topicalities date so quickly.' Both senses are coll., somewhat cultured or, occ., snobbish, and arose ca. 1900 : ex the v.t. sense, likewise coll. (1896 : O.E.D. Sup.), to set definitely in a period, e.g. ' The War dates one so ! '—2. V.t., to caress *a posteriori*: low: C. 20. 'Etymology' legally unexplainable, but fairly obvious.

date, up to. Coll. as = (*brought*) up to the relevant standard of the time (— 1890); almost S.E.

date !, you. Well, you *are* a queer fish !: non-cultured (— 1923). Manchon. Origin ?

date up. (Gen. in passive.) To fill the time of (a person) with appointments: from ca. 1930; orig. U.S. Ex *date*, n.

datholite. Incorrect for *datolite* ('a borosilicate of calcium '): C. 19–20. O.E.D.

datoo. 'A westerly wind in the Straits of Gibraltar and Western Mediterranean ': nautical coll.: mid-C. 19–20. Bowen. ? ex Arabic.

daty. Soft-headed; sun-struck: military: C. 20. F. & Gibbons. By perversion ex the dial. *dateless* (knocked) unconscious, stupefied, foolish, crazy (E.D.D.).

daub. An artist: low coll.: mid-C. 19–20. H., 3rd ed. Ex *daub*, a bad painting.—2. A bribe: either c. or low s.: C. 18. *A New Canting Dict.*, 1725. Ex:

daub, dawb, v. (Vbl.n., **daubing.**) To bribe, gen. v.i.; low, perhaps orig. c.; ca. 1690–1850. B.E. Cf. *grease a person's palms*.

David, david; davy. An affidavit: the former, C. 19–20; the latter from ca. 1760. In O'Hara's play, *Midas*, 1764, 'I with my davy will back it, I'll swear.' A facetious variant is *Alfred David* or *Davy*, q.v. Also as oath in '*so help me Davy*, gen. rendered " swelp my *Davy* " ', H., 5th ed., the purer form occurring in H., 2nd ed. (1860).—2. **David Jones,** see **Davy.**

David (or **Davy**) !, **send it down**; often **send it down, David, send it down** ! A military c.p. apropos of a shower, esp. if likely to cause a parade to be postponed: C. 20. F. & Gibbons: B. & P. (Wales has a notoriously wet climate; David, the Welsh patron saint.) New Zealanders and Australians say *send her down, Hughie* !

David Jones; David Jones's locker. See **Davy Jones's locker.**

David's (later **Davy's**) **sow, (as) drunk as.** Beastly, or very, drunk: coll.; from ca. 1670. Shadwell, 1671. In Bailey's *Erasmus*, 1733, ' When he comes home . . . as drunk as David's sow, he does nothing but lie snoring all night long by my side.' Origin obscure, but presumably anecdotal. (Apperson.) Also *drunk as a sow*: see **sow.**

Davy, Davy Jones, Old Davy; David Jones. The spirit of the sea: nautical; from ca. 1750, Smollett being, in *Peregrine Pickle*, the first to mention it in print. *Davy Jones* is the orig. form, *David Jones* is recorded by Grose in 1785, *Old Davy* occurs in Dibdin in 1790, *Davy* arises ca. 1800. ? *Jonah* > *Jonas* > *Jones*, the *Davy* being added by Welsh sailors: such is W.'s ingenious and prob. etymology, perhaps suggested by *Davy Jones'(s) locker*, q.v.—2. See **David.**

Davy Debet or **Debt.** A bailiff: coll. verging on S.E.: ca. 1570–90. Gascoigne. Apperson, ' Debt personified '.

Davy Jones'(s), later **Davy's, locker.** The sea, esp. as an ocean grave: nautical. Apparently not recorded before Grose, 1785, and then as *David Jones's locker*.

Davy Jones's natural children. Pirates; smugglers: nautical, C. 19. (Mostly officers'.)

davy-man. That member of the crew of a ship captured by a privateer who was left aboard in order

to swear an *affidavit* as to her nationality: naval coll.: C. 19. Bowen.

Davy putting on the coppers for the parson(s). A nautical comment on an approaching storm: from ca. 1830; ob. This implies the sailors' belief in an arch-*devil* of the sea; cf.:

Davy's dust. Gunpowder: from ca. 1830; ? orig. nautical. Ex *Davy* = the devil.

Davy's locker. See **David Jones's locker.—Davy's sow.** See **David's sow.—dawb.** See **daub.**

dawg. A s. > coll. variation of *dog*, q.v.: late C. 19–20. Whence, perhaps orig. and certainly for the most part Australian, *put on dawg*, to put on ' side ', to behave arrogantly: C. 20. C. J. Dennis.

dawk, or **dak, travel.** To travel by relays, esp. in palanquins: Anglo-Indian (cf. *dak bungalow*, an inn, occ. a shelter-house, on a dak route); from ca. 1720; coll. >, by 1860, S.E. Ex Hindi.

daxie, daxy. A dachshund: coll.: 1899 (O.E.D. Sup.).

day ! Good day !: coll.: mid-C. 19–20. Cf. *afternoon* !, *morning* !, *evening* !, and *night* ! used in precisely the same voice- and manners-sparing way.

day, call it a. See **call it a day.—Day, the.** A variant of *der Tag*, q.v.

day, day ! Good day !; good-bye !: C. 17–18 coll.; somewhat childish.

Day and Martin. A negro: ca. 1840–1910. Ware, ' Because D. & M.'s blacking was *so* black.' Cf. *brown polish*, q.v.

day-bug. A day-boy: schoolboys': late C. 19–20. Ware. Cf. *night-flea*.

day-mates. The mates of the various decks: naval coll.: C. 19. Bowen.

daylight. A glass not full: university, ca. 1825–80. Ex the S.E. sense for the space between rim and liquor; the toast-tag, *No daylights* or *heel-taps* is still occ. heard.—2. For *burn daylight*, see **burn.**—3. A space between a rider and his saddle: from ca. 1870.—4. See **daylights.**

daylight in the swamp ! Time to get out of bed !: Canadian c.p.: C. 20.

daylight into one (coll.) or, both s., **the victualling department** or **the luncheon reservoir, let** or **knock.** To make a hole in, esp. to stab or shoot, hence to kill: in gen., from ca. 1840; but *let daylight into one* is low coll. recorded by the O.E.D. for 1793. In U.S., *make daylight shine through* (a person) occurs as early as 1774 (Thornton). Cf. *cook one's goose*, *settle one's hash*.

daylights. The eyes: from ca. 1750. Esp. in the pugilistic phrase, *darken one's daylights*. Fielding, ' D—n me, I will darken her daylights '; Grose, 1st ed.

day's pack(, the). Defaulters' punishment: military: C. 20. F. & Gibbons. Abbr. *pack-drill*.

dazzle with science. To out-box; fig., to defeat by sheer brains: coll.: C. 20.

dazzler. A showy person, esp. a woman; a brilliant act: from ca. 1835.—2. A dazzling blow (— 1883). O.E.D.—3. See **bobby dazzler.**

de- is often used in a s. or coll. sense or connotation, as in *de-bag*, q.v.

deacon. ' Boy who collects bread plates for replenishment ': Bootham School: late C. 19–20. Anon., *Dict. of Bootham Slang*, 1925. Cf. *angel*, 4, q.v.

deacon, v. This U.S. word, implying illicit or fraudulent treatment, or behaviour, has not ' caught on ' in the British Empire, except slightly in *deacon off*, to give (a person) the cue : late C. 19–20. Cf. *to doctor* (O.E.D.).

dead. Abbr. *dead certainty* : racing, from ca. 1870 ; ob.

dead, adj. (rarely) and adv. (often), has a coll. tinge that is hard to define : this unconventionality may spring from one's sense of surprise at finding so grave a word used to mean nothing more serious than incomplete, inferior, or than very, directly, straight, etc. See the ensuing phrases. It is, however, doubtful if *dead drunk* and analogous terms were ever, despite one's subjective impression, coll. : their antiquity is a hindrance to accurate assessment. The *dead* phrases may be spelt with or without a hyphen.—2. Dead easy : c. : from ca. 1920. James Curtis, *The Gilt Kid*, 1936.

dead, on the. Off liquor, teetotal : military : late C. 19–early 20. F. & Gibbons. Prob. *on the dead t.t.*

dead !, you'll be a long time. Enjoy yourself while you can and may ! : a late C. 19–20 c.p. Cf. the C. 18 proverbial *there will be sleeping enough in the grave* (Apperson).

dead against. Strongly opposed to : from ca. 1850. Coll. >, ca. 1890, S.E. but not literary.

dead alive, dead and alive. (Of persons) dull, mopish, cf. *deadly lively*, q.v. : C. 16–20 : S.E. till mid-C. 19, then increasingly coll.—2. Hence of things, esp. places : dull, with few amusements, little excitement (' a dead-and-alive hole ') : coll. ; from ca. 1850 ; now S.E.

dead amiss. Incapacitated, as applied to a horse : the turf : ca. 1860–1910. H., 3rd ed.

dead and done-for look, have a. To look most woe-begone, wretched : coll. (— 1887). Baumann.

dead ! and (s)he never called me ' mother ' ! A C. 20 c.p. satiric of melodrama, whence, in point of fact, the phrase is drawn. E.g. Christopher Bush, *The Case of the April Fools*, 1933.

dead as a door-nail, a herring, Julius Caesar, mutton, a tent-peg. Quite dead. All coll. orig.; all except the first still coll. The *door-nail* phrase occurs as early as 1350 and is found in *Piers Plowman*,—it was S.E. by 1600 ; the *herring*, C. 17–20, e.g. in Rhodes's *Bombastes Furioso*, 1790 ; the *mutton*, from (—)1770 ; the other two are C. 19–20, though *tent-peg* has since ca. 1910 been rare. Origins : *door-nail* is perhaps the striking plate of a door-knocker ; a *herring* dies very soon after capture ; *Julius Caesar* is deader than Queen Anne ; *mutton* is by definition the flesh of a dead sheep ; a *tent-peg*, like a *door-nail*, is constantly being hit on the head. Dial. has the synonyms : *dead as a hammer, maggot, nit, rag, smelt* (E.D.D.).

dead beat. A worthless idler, esp. if a sponger as well : orig. (— 1875) U.S., anglicised ca. 1900 and now verging on coll.—2. In Australian s. (— 1898), a man down on his luck or stony-broke. Morris.—3. Meat : rhyming s. (— 1914). B. & P.—4. Adj., completely exhausted : from ca. 1820 ; coll. Pierce Egan in *Tom and Jerry*, ' Logic was . . . so dead-beat, as to be compelled to cry for quarter.'

dead bird. A certainty : Australian : from ca. 1895 ; slightly ob. Morris, ' The metaphor is from pigeon-shooting, where the bird being let loose in front of a good shot is as good as dead.'

dead broke. Penniless ; occ., bankrupt or ruined : coll. : from ca. 1850.

***dead cargo.** Booty less valuable than had been expected : C. 18–20, ob. ; c. *A New Canting Dict.*, 1725 ; Grose, 1st ed.

dead cert, certainty. See cert and certainty.

dead cinch. An intensive of *cinch* (q.v.) in sense of ' dead cert '. Collinson.

dead earnest, in. In S.E., most earnest(ly) : as coll., undoubtedly, in very truth : from ca. 1870.

dead eyes for square ? Shall I pass at divisions (examinations) ? : *Conway* Training Ship : from ca. 1890 ; ob. Masefield.

dead-eyes under. (Of a ship) listing heavily : nautical : mid-C. 19–20. Bowen. Graphically proleptic.

dead finish, the. The extreme point or instance of courage, cruelty, excellence, endurance, etc. : Australian coll. (— 1881). O.E.D. (Sup.). Prob. ex *finish*, n., 1.

dead frost. A fiasco, complete failure : theatrical ; from ca. 1875. Rare in C. 20, when *a complete frost* is preferred and used over a much wider range.

dead give-away. A notable indication, or revelation, of guilt or defect : from ca. 1860.

dead gone. Utterly exhausted or collapsed : coll. ; from ca. 1870.

dead head. One who travels free, hence eats free, or, esp., goes free to a place of entertainment (cf. *paper*) : coll. : orig. U.S. (1849 : Thornton), anglicised ca. 1864. *The Daily Telegraph*, May 21, 1883, ' " Lucia di Lammermoor " is stale enough to warrant the most confirmed deadhead in declining to help make a house.' Whence v., and *dead-headism*. Orig. of ' passengers not paying fare, likened to dead head (of cattle), as opposed to live stock ', W.

dead heat. A race in which two (or more) competitors—animals or men—reach the goal simultaneously : from ca. 1840 (Tom Hood) ; coll. > S.E. by 1880.

dead horse. Work to be done but already paid for, work in redemption of a debt ; hence, distasteful work. Often as *work for a* or *the dead horse*, C. 17–20, or *draw* or *pull a* . . ., the former C. 19–20, the latter C. 17–18. Cartwright, 1651 ; B.E., who implies the use of *a dead horse* as also = a trifle. Coll. In Australia, *work off the dead horse*.—2. (West Indies) a shooting star : from ca. 1850. Ex a native Jamaican belief.

dead horse, flog a or the. To work to no, or very little, purpose ; make much ado about nothing ; cry after spilt milk. Coll. ; from ca. 1840.

[**dead letter** and **dead-lock,** the former in F. & H., the latter in H., have, prob., always been S.E.]

dead lights. The eyes : nautical ; from ca. 1860.

dead-lock. A lock hospital : Cockneys' : 1887 ; slightly ob. Ware.

Dead Louse. The *Daedalus* ship of war : late C. 18–mid-19 nautical. Grose, 2nd ed. Also *Dead Loss* (Ware at *Fiddler*).

dead low. (Of an atmosphere) absolutely still : nautical coll. : C. 19–20. Bowen.

***dead lurk.** Robbing a house during divine service : c. and low (— 1851) ; ob. Mayhew.

dead man. (Very rare in singular.) An empty bottle or pot at a drinking-bout or the like : late C. 17–20 ; orig. military. B.E. Cf. the later *dead marine*.—2. A loaf charged for but not delivered, or smuggled away by a baker's man to his master's prejudice : bakers', from ca. 1760. Grose, 2nd ed.—3. Hence the † sense, a baker (— 1860).

dead man, get a fart of a. Applied to anything extremely improbable : low coll. : ca. 1540–1720. Heywood, 1546 ; Robertson, 1681. (Apperson.)

*dead man's lurk. The extorting of money from a dead man's relatives : c. : from ca. 1850. See lurk.

dead marine. An empty bottle at or after a carouse : orig. nautical ; from ca. 1820.

dead meat. A corpse : from ca. 1860. Cf. *cold meat, croaker, pickles, stiff un*.

dead men. Empty bottles : see dead man, 1.— 2. Among tailors, misfits, hence a scarecrow, lit. and fig. : from ca. 1840.—3. Reefs and gasket-ends carelessly left hanging : nautical : mid-C. 19–20. Bowen.

dead men's shoes, waiting for. Expecting inheritances : C. 16–20 : coll. ; S.E. after ca. 1700. Phineas Fletcher, ' 'Tis tedious waiting dead men's shoes.'

dead nap. A thorough rogue : provincial low s., C. 19–20, ob. Cf. :

dead nip. An insignificant project turning out a failure : provincial s., C. 19–20, ob.

dead number. ' The last number in a row or street ; perhaps the *end* of the street ' : Cockneys' : late C. 19–20 ; ob. Ware.

dead oh ! ; deado. Adv., in the last stage of drunkenness : naval ; from ca. 1850.

dead on, dead nuts on. Clever at ; extremely fond of ; hence, at first ironically, very inimical towards. Coll. ; from, resp., ca. 1865 and 1870. Cf. the earlier *nuts on*, q.v.

dead one. See dead un.

dead-oner. A fatal casualty : military : 1915 ; ob. B. & P. Occ. corrupted to *deadomer*.

dead pay. Money drawn by ' widows' men ' (q.v.) : naval coll. : mid-C. 19–20. Bowen.

*dead set. A persistent and pointed effort, attempt ; esp. such an attack. From ca. 1720. C. >, in the 1770's, s. or coll. (low). *A New Canting Dict.*, 1725, ' *Dead Set*, a term used by Thief-catchers when they have a Certainty of seizing some of their Clients, in order to bring them to Justice.' *The Globe*, Nov. 2, 1889, ' Certain persons . . . are making a dead set against the field sports of Britain.'

dead soldier. A C. 20 military variant of *dead marine*, q.v. B. & P.

dead sow's eye. A button-hole badly made : tailors' : from ca. 1840 ; ob.

dead struck. (Of actors) breaking down very badly in a performance : theatrical ; from ca. 1860 ; ob.

*dead swag. In c., booty that cannot be sold : C. 19–20. Cf. *dead cargo*.

dead to rights. Adv., certainly, undoubtedly ; absolutely. ? orig. U.S. ; in England from ca. 1895, but never gen. and now ob. Cf. *to rights*, q.v.—2. In the (criminal) act : c. and low : late C. 19–20. James Spenser, *Limey Breaks In*, 1934, ' I had been caught " dead to rights ", as the crooks say.' Cf. *banged to rights*.

dead to the wide. See wide, to the.—2. dead to the world. See world, dead to the.

*dead un (or 'un). In C. 19–20 c., an uninhabited house.—2. A half-quartern loaf : from ca. 1870.—3. A horse that will be either scratched, ' doped ', or ' pulled ' (cf. *safe un*, q.v.) : the turf, from ca. 1870. H., 5th ed. ; Hawley Smart in *Social Sinners*, 1880.—4. A bankrupt company : commercial : late C. 19–20. Ware. Cf. *cadaver*.

dead with. See seen dead with.

dead yet, not. Very old : a theatrical c.p. (1883 ; ob.) applied to ' an antique fairy ' (Ware).

deader. A funeral : military : ca. 1865–1910.— 2. A corpse : from ca. 1880. Conan Doyle.—3. *Be a deader* also = to be (very recently) dead : late C. 19–20.

deadly. Excessive ; unpleasant ; very dull (gen. of places) : from mid-C. 17 ; coll. Cf. *awful, grim*. —2. Adv., excessively ; very : coll. ; from late C. 16. The S.O.D. records *deadly slow* at 1688, *deadly dull* at 1865.

deadly-lively, adj. and adv. Alternately—or combining the—dull (or depressing) and the lively ; with forced joviality, esp. to no purpose : coll. : 1823, ' Jon Bee '. Cf. *dead alive*.

deadly nevergreen(s). The gallows : late C. 18– early 19. Grose, 2nd ed.

deadomer. See dead-oner.

deady. Gin (— 1812) : Tom Moore, 1819. The S.O.D. says : ' Distiller's name ' ; F. & H. : ' From Deady, a well-known gin-spinner.' Ob., except in U.S. *dead-eye*.

deaf as the mainmast. Exceedingly deaf : nautical coll : C. 19–20. Bowen.

deaf one (or 'un). A cooked fig. : military : from ca. 1912. S. Rogerson, *Twelve Days*, 1933. Figs gen. cause a soft stool.

*deaf un, turn a. Not to listen : late C. 19–20 c. Charles E. Leach. (I.e., ear.)

deal. A lot (of . . .) : coll. ; from C. 16. ' Pregnantly for *a good* or *great deal*, etc.', O.E.D.— 2. Hence, adv., much : coll. : mid-C. 18–20.

deal, do a. To conclude a bargain : coll. ; late C. 19–20.

deal, wet the. To drink to the conclusion of a bargain(ing) : coll. ; from ca. 1860. Hindley, in *A Cheap Jack*, ' We will wet the deal '.

deal it out (to). To deal out punishment (*to a* person) : Australian coll. (— 1916). C. J. Dennis.

deal of glass about, there's a. A person or a thing is showy ; first-rate, ' the ticket '. ? ex large show-windows. From ca. 1880 ; ob.

deal of weather about, there's a. We're in for a storm : nautical coll. : mid-C. 19–20. Ware.

deal suit. A coffin, esp. if parish-provided : coll. : from ca. 1850. Cf. *eternity box* and the Fr. *paletot sans manches*.

dean. A small piece of wood tied round a small faggot : Winchester College ; from ca. 1850. Cf. *bishop*, n., 3.

*deaner, occ. denar, deener, or dener. A shilling : from ca. 1835 ; orig. tramps' c. ; in C. 20, racing and low. Common in Australia. Brandon ; H., 1st ed. ; *The Times*, Oct. 12, 1864. Prob. ex Fr. *denier* or Lingua Franca *dinarly*.—2. (Deaner.) Dean of a college : Oxford undergraduates' : 1899, *The Daily Telegraph*, Aug. 14.

dear ! ; o(h) dear ! Mild coll. exclamations (cf. *dear me !*, q.v.) : resp. C. 19–20, late C. 17–20. O.E.D. Perhaps *oh dear ! = oh, dear God* or *Lord* ; *dear* is an abbr. of *oh dear !*

Dear Joy. An Irishman : coll. : late C. 17–20 ; ob. B.E. ; Grose. Ex a favourite Irish exclamation. Cf. *dear knows !* : C. 19–20 : coll. : Northern Ireland and English provinces : abbr. *the dear Lord knows !* Cf. quotations in Thornton.

Dear Little Innocents ; Devil's Later Issue, the. The Durham Light Infantry : military in Boer War. J. Milne, *The Epistles of Atkins*, 1902.

dear me ! A mild exclamation : coll. : from ca. 1770. Perhaps ex It. *Dio mi (salvi) !*, God save me ! (W.) In dial. there are at least thirteen synonymns : E.D.D.

dear Mother, I am sending you ten shillings—but not *this* week. A lower classes' and military c.p. of C. 20. B. & P.

dearee. A C. 18 variant of *dearie*. (O.E.D.)

dearest member. The *membrum virile*. From ca. 1740 : orig. literary and euphemistic ; from ca. 1870, jocular and coll.

dearie, deary. A low coll. form of address used by women : late C. 18–20.

deary me ! Slightly more sorrowful or lugubrious than *dear me !* (q.v.) : coll. (? orig. dial.) : from ca. 1780. O.E.D.

death, done to. Too fashionable ; trite : coll. (— 1887) >, by 1910, S.E. Baumann.

death, dress to. To dress oneself in the extreme of fashion : coll. ; from ca. 1850. Cf. *dress to kill* and (q.v.) *killing*.

death, like. (Or, much later, *like grim death*.) Very firmly or resolutely : coll. ; from ca. 1780.

death, sure as. Absolutely certain : from ca. 1760 : S.E. >, ca. 1800, coll.

***death drop.** Butyl chloride, a very powerful drug : C. 20 c.

death hunter, later **death-hunter.** One who, to newspapers, supplies reports of deaths : from ca. 1730. Foote.—2. A seller of last dying speeches : from ca. 1850 ; coll. ; ob. by 1895, † by 1910. Mayhew.—3. Robber of an army's dead (— 1816) : ob. by 1860, † by 1890.—4. An undertaker : late C. 18–20. Grose, 1st ed.—5. Anyone else engaged in, living by, funerals : from ca. 1870 ; ob. H., 5th ed.—6. An insurance agent : mostly lower classes' (— 1934).

death on. (With *to be*.) Very fond of ; clever or capable at dealing with : orig. (— 1847) U.S. ; anglicised ca. 1875. (Cf. *dead (nuts) on, nuts on*.) In U.S. (1842 : Thornton), it also = fatal to—a sense anglicised ca. 1890.

Death or Glory Boys. The 17th Lancers : military coll. : late C. 18–20. F. & Gibbons, 'From their badge, a death's head with the words " Or Glory." ' Cf. *Bingham's Dandies* and *Horse Marines*, qq.v.

death's head upon a mop-stick. 'A poor, miserable, emaciated fellow,' Grose, 1st ed. : late C. 18–early 19.

deb. A *débutante* in society : coll. from ca. 1919 ; prob. ex U.S. See esp. Dorea Stanhope's series, ' The Débutante Market ' in *Time and Tide*, July, 1934 ; Michael Harrison, *Weep for Lycidas*, 1934, ' The usual dreary deb-parades they have in the country.'

deb, v. A G.W. term belonging to a certain English division, spreading to the other divisions of the same corps, and derived from the name of its commander, reputed to do this : (Of a general) to delay the zero hour of his attack until after the zero hours of the troops on his flanks and thus to ensure the safety of his flanks.

de-bag. An Oxford and (less) Cambridge term, from ca. 1890 : to remove the ' bags ' or trousers of (an objectionable fellow student).

debater. A debating society : Oxford undergraduates' : C. 20. The Oxford-*er*.

debblish. A penny : South Africa : from ca. 1870.

deboo. A début : sol. spelling : from ca. 1885.

debs. Debenture stock : Stock Exchange (— 1896).

debus, (loosely **debuss**), v.i. To get out of a bus or any motor transport : military s. (1915) >, by 1918,

coll. Opp. *embus(s)*. Hence, a *debussing point* was the place at which the men left the vehicles. F. & Gibbons.

decamp. To camp (v.i.) : catachrestic : late C. 17–mid-18. O.E.D.

decencies. ' Pads used by actors, as distinct from actresses, to ameliorate outline,' Ware : theatrical coll. : late C. 19–20.

decent, decentish. Passable ; fairly good or agreeable ; tolerable ; likable. Senses 1–3 arose ca. 1700 (the form in -*ish* ca. 1814) and, in C. 19–20, are S.E. The fourth sense is orig. and still Public-Schoolboyish (esp. in *decent fellows*).

decider. (Gen. **the d.**) The winning set from even, i.e., the 3rd or 5th : lawn tennis coll. : from ca. 1925. Occ. in other games, e.g. cards. Cf. *conqueror*, q.v. Ex racing, when a *decider* is a heat run off after a dead heat (O.E.D.).

decimate. Catachrestically as almost = annihilate : orig. and mostly journalistic : late C. 19–20. Esp. in *literally decimated*. Ex ' L. *decimare*, to put to death every tenth man of unit, as punishment for mutiny, etc.', W. The same applies to *decimation*.

deck. A pack of cards : late C. 16–20 ; until ca. 1720, S.E. (Shakespeare has it in the third *King Henry VI*) ; then dial. and, until ca. 1800, coll. ; very gen. in U.S. In C. 20 England, it is confined, more or less, to the underworld.—2. In Anglo-Indian coll., a look, a peep : C. 19–20. Variant *dekh*. Cf. *dekko*, q.v.—3. See **decker**, 3.—4. A landing ground : Royal Air Force : from ca. 1915. Orig. among R.N. aviators.

deck, go off the. To leave the ground : Air Force : 1915. F. & Gibbons. Perhaps at first of naval planes.

***deck, on the.** Penniless ; destitute : c. : from ca. 1925. James Curtis, *The Gilt Kid*, 1936. Prob. suggested by equivalent *on the floor*.

deckel is, in C. 20, gen. considered a misspelling of *deckle* in *d. edge* (uncut edge of a sheet of paper).

decker. A deck-hand : from ca. 1800 : coll. >, by 1850, S.E.—2. A deck-passenger, from ca. 1865. coll. (O.E.D.)—3. (**Decker**.) One who lives in ' the Deck ' or Seven Dials district of London (W.C.) costers' : late C. 19–20 ; ob. Ware.

deckie. Same as **decker**, 1 : coll. : from ca. 1910. O.E.D. (Sup.).

declare off, v.t. To cancel (an arrangement, a match, etc.) ; v.i., to withdraw, arbitrarily or unsportingly. Both coll. ; from the late 1740's. Fielding ; George Eliot, ' When it came to the point, Mr. Haynes declared off.' (O.E.D.)

decoct. Bankrupt : C. 16 ; either pedantic or affectedly facetious coll. Lit., thoroughly cooked, i.e. done to a turn. Cf. the C. 17 *decoctor*.

decolly. Décolleté(e) : sol. ; late C. 19–20. Cf. *neggledigee*.

Decomposition Row. Rotten Row, London : London Society s., ca. 1860–70. *The Literary Gazette*, April 12, 1862.

decoy-bird or **-duck.** A swindling-decoy : C. 17–20 ; low coll. ; S.E. after ca. 1790.

***decus.** A crown piece : late C. 17–19. Ex the L. motto, *decus et tutamen* on the rim. Shadwell ; Scott, ' Master Grahame . . . has got the *decuses* and the *smelts*.' B.E. cites as c., as it prob. was for some years.

dee. See **d.**—2. In c., a pocket-book : from ca. 1835 ; ob. Brandon ; H., 1st ed. Orig. Romany.

dee'd. Damned : C. 19–20. Barham (O.E.D.).

Dee-Donk. A Frenchman : Crimean War, when, by the way, the French soldiers called the English *I say's*, precisely as the Chinese mob once did (see Yule & Burnell). Cf. *Wee-Wee*, q.v.

'deed. Abbr. *indeed* : coll. : mid-C. 16–20. Since ca. 1870, mostly Scottish.

*decker. ' A thief kept in pay by a constable,' Haggart in his *Life*, 1821 : Scottish c. : †.

deener. See **deaner.**

deep. Sly ; artful : from ca. 1780. *Punch*, 1841, ' I can scarcely believe my eyes. Oh ! he's a deep one ' ; *a deep one* is defined by Grose (2nd ed.) as ' a thorough-paced rogue '. Ex the C. 16–20 S.E. sense, profoundly crafty.

deep end. See **end, go off the deep.**

deep grief. Two black eyes : ca. 1875–1900. Jocular on *full mourning*.

*deep-sea fisherman. A card-sharper on an ocean-liner : C. 20 c. Charles E. Leach.

deep-sinker. The largest-sized tumbler ; the drink served therein : Australian coll. : 1897, *The Argus*, Jan. 15. Ex deep-sinking in a mining shaft. Morris.

deer-stalker. A low-crowned hat, close-fitting and gen. of felt (— 1870) ; coll. soon > S.E.

deer-stalking, vbl.n. Running after women : jocular (— 1923). Manchon. By pun on *dear*.

deevie, -vy ; dev(e)y. Delightful, charming : 1900–ca. 1907, H. A. Vachell speaking of it in 1909 as †. A perversion of *divvy*, 4, q.v. O.E.D. (Sup.) records also the adv. in *-ily*.

deezer, the. The Deceased Wife's Sister Bill : political : 1907 ; ob. Collinson. A portmanteau word.

defamation. Deformation : sol., as is *deformation* for *defamation.* C. 19–20.

deferred stock. Inferior soup : ca. 1860–1900 ; in the City (see **City**). The body or solid part of soup is stock.

deffly. Deftly : in C. 18–20, sol. ; in C. 16–18, permissible. (O.E.D.)

deficient. A person mentally deficient ; also adj. C. 20 ; much less common than *mental* as adj.

definite. Dogmatic : late C. 19–20 ; coll. (Of persons only.—2. Definitive : catachrestic : C. 20.

definitely ! ; oh, definitely. Yes ! ; certainly : coll. : C. 20, esp. from ca. 1920 and non-proletarian. Notably (the clergyman in) Sutton Vane's arresting play, *Outward Bound*, 1924, and, satirically, A. A. Milne, *Two People*, 1931 (pp. 328–29), and Maurice Lincoln's novel, *Oh ! Definitely !*, 1933.

deformity. Difformity († S.E., want of uniformity or of conformity) : C. 16–19 : catachrestic. O.E.D.

*degen, occ. **degan ; dagen.** In late C. 17–early 19, c. for a sword. B.E.—2. A sense that, prob. after *knowing blade*, engendered that of an artful fellow : C. 19 low. Cf. *dag*, q.v. Etymology ?.

degommy. (Of officers) removed from command because of failure or incompetence : military : late 1914 ; ob. F. & Gibbons. Ex Fr. *dégommé*, lit. of gum removed from silk fabrics. Cf. *unstuck*, q.v.

degree, to a. To a serious, though undefined, extent : coll. : from ca. 1730.

*degrees, have taken one's. To have been imprisoned in an ' academy ' or gaol : c. : ca. 1820–50. ' Jon Bee.'

degrugger. A degree : Oxford undergraduates' : from ca. 1895. For the form, cf. *memugger* and *testugger.* (Ware.)

dekh. See **deck**, 2, and cf.:

dekho ; gen. **dekko,** n. (esp. **take a dekko**) and v. To see ; to, or a, glance. Vagrants' (— 1865), ex Romany *dik*, to look, to see (Sampson). In Army, esp. in G.W., common since ca. 1890, via Hindustani.

del. trem. See **D.T.**, 2.

delegate. A person seeking an advance : bank-clerks' (esp. Anglo-Irish) : from ca. 1923.

delerious. Incorrect for *delirious* : C. 18–20. O.E.D.

Delhi Spearmen, the. The 9th Lancers : military : from the Indian Mutiny ; ob. F. & Gibbons.

delible. Useless ; incompetent : Army officers' : 1916. F. & Gibbons. Cf. *degommy.*

*delicate. A false subscription-book used by a pseudo-collector of alms, etc. : mid-C. 19–20 ; c. and low. H., 3rd ed.—2. In c. alone (— 1845), a begging-letter.

delicate condition (late C. 19–20) or **state of health** (1850, Dickens), **in a.** Pregnant : euphemistic coll. (O.E.D. Sup.)

delighted ! Certainly ! ; with pleasure ! : C. 19–20 ; S.E. worn, in C. 20, to coll.

deliver the goods. See **goods, the.**

*dell. In mid-C. 16–early 19 c., a young girl ; but in C. 17–early 19 low s., a young wanton, a mistress (cf. *doxy*). Harman, Jonson, B.E., Grose, Ainsworth. Etymology ?.

delo diam. See **delo nammow.**

*delo nam o' the barrack. In late C. 19–20 c., the master of the house. *Barrack* = house, while *delo nam*, in back s., = old man.

delo nammow. An old woman : back s. (—1874). H., 5th ed. Earlier, *dillo namo*, q.v. There is also *delo diam*, an old maid (Ware).

delog. Gold : in back s. (— 1873). Hotten. Earlier *dlog*, q.v.

Delphi. The Adelphi Theatre : theatrical coll. : 1851. Mayhew ; Ware.

delude. See **elude.**

delve it. To work head down (as in digging) and sewing fast : tailors' : from ca. 1865.

dem. See **demn.**

demand the box. To call for a bottle : nautical : from ca. 1820 ; ob. Egan's Grose.

*demander (or **demaunder**) **for glimmer** (or **glymmar**). A pretended victim of fire : C. 16–18 c.

demi-. In facetious neologism and practice, often either coll. or near-coll., though rarely so used before C. 19.—2. As n., gen. pl., a convalescent ; a person half-fit : military (officers') : 1915. F. & Gibbons.

demi-beau. See **sub-beau.**

demi-doss. A penny bed : vagrants' and low ; ca. 1870–1914.

demi-rep. A woman whose general reputation or, esp., chastity is in doubt. First recorded in Fielding's *Tom Jones*, 1749, '. . . Vulgarly called a demi-rep ; that is . . ., a woman who intrigues with every man she likes, under the name and appearance of virtue . . . in short, whom everybody knows to be what nobody calls her.' By 1800, coll. ; by 1840 (except in the occ. variant *demi-rip*) S.E. ; by 1900, ob. Ex *reputation*.

dem. See **demn.**

demme !, a coll. variant of *damn !*, is recorded by O.E.D. for 1753.

demn ; dem. From late C. 17 in ' profane ' usage ; the latter the gen. form in C. 19–20. Orig. euphemisms ; but rather are they jocular coll. when facetious, esp. in derivatives *demd* (earlier *demn'd*) and *demnition* (as in *demnition bow-wows*, 'coined' by Dickens in *Nicholas Nickleby*). These three terms have all been popularly revived by the Baroness d'Orczy in her *Scarlet Pimpernel* romances.

demo. A (political) demonstration : political : from ca. 1930. James Curtis, *The Gilt Kid*, 1936.

demob. To demobilise : 1919. Gen. in passive.

demon, n. and adj. applied to 'a super-excellent adept'. Coll. ; from ca. 1882. *The demon bowler* = Spofforth, less fast but more skilful than Larwood ; *the demon jockey* = Fred Archer, who, fl. 1880's, holds several records still unapproached even by Steve Donoghue and Gordon Richards : See esp. the article by Sidney Galtrey ('Hotspur') in *The Daily Telegraph* of Oct. 7, 1933. Cf. *wizard* as adj.—2. A policeman : Australian c., from ca. 1875 ; ob.—3. Cf. the C. 20 Australian and New Zealand c. or low sense (rarely in singular) : a detective. Cf. :—4. An old hand at bushranging arrived from Tasmania (Van *Diemen's* Land) : Australian : ca. 1870–1900. Ware.

demonstrate. To make a fuss, 'go off the handle' ; exercise one's authority : 1916 +, esp. among ex-service men. Ex its (— 1830) technical sense, to make a military demonstration. Perhaps suggested by *create*, q.v.

demonstration. An instance of the preceding : military coll. : 1916. B. & P.

demure as a(n old) whore at a christening, as. Extremely demure : late C. 18–20 : coll. Grose, 2nd ed.

*demy. An illicit die (i.e. dicing) : C. 16–17 c. > s. Greene.—2. A urinal : Bootham School : C. 20. Anon., *Dict. of Bootham Slang*, 1925. Because it provides for only one of the two 'physical needs'.

demy-rep. See demi-rep.

den. A small lodging or, esp., room in which one —gen. a male—can be alone : from ca. 1770 : coll. >, by 1900, S.E. Cf. *snuggery.*—2. **the Den.** New Cross, London : C. 20.

dena ; denar, dener : see deaner.—**denarli :** see dinarl(e)y.

dennis. A small walking-stick : C. 19. App. unrecorded before 1823 (Bee).—2. (*Dennis.*) A pig : nautical : mid-C. 19–20. Gen. in address (*Dennis*). Hence, *hullo, Dennis !*, an insulting or derisive nautical c.p. of late C. 19–20 ; ob. Ware.

denotation, denote. See connotation, connote.

dental. Abbr. *dental student* : university coll. : from ca. 1905.

dented. See dinted.

dentity. An identity (person, not abstraction) : sol. (— 1887). Baumann.

deolali tap. See doolally tap. Also *deolalic tap.*

dep. A deputy, esp. a night porter at a cheap lodging-house : low (— 1870). Dickens, in *Edward Drood*, 'All man-servants at Travellers' Lodgings is named Deputy.'—2. In C. 20 c., a deputy-governor of a prison, esp. at Dartmoor.—3. At Christ's Hospital, C. 19–20, a deputy Grecian, i.e. a boy in the form imm. below the 'Grecians'.

depends, it (all). Perhaps ! Coll. ; late C. 19–20. —2. Also, when *depend* is used elliptically with the following clause and it = 'to depend on it', it is coll. (1700). S.O.D.

depose. See at dissolute.

depperty. A deputy : a mainly Cockney sol. (— 1887). Baumann.

deprave. Often confused with *deprive* : late C. 16–early 18. O.E.D.

depresh, the. The financial crisis that began in

U.S. in late 1929 and hit England in Jan., 1930 : orig. (1931), U.S. ; anglicised in 1933.

der Tag. 'Any much-desired date or goal' : Army officers' : 1915–18. B. & P. Satiric of the German phrase = 'the day when we Germans come into our own'.

derack ; deracks. A pack of cards ; in pl., the cards themselves ; military back s. : late C. 19–20. F. & Gibbons. Thus, *card* > *drac* > *derack*, and *s* is added.

derby. See darby.—2. **Derby dog.** The homeless dog that, at Epsom, is sure to appear on the course as soon as it has been cleared for the Derby : mid-C. 19–20 : coll. >, by 1890, S.E. (The race was founded in 1780 by the 12th Earl of Derby.)—3. **derbies.** See darby.—4: A Derby recruit : military coll. : 1916 ; ob. F. & Gibbons.

derby, v. To pawn : sporting : late C. 19–early 20. Ware derives from : the pawning of watches being excused on the grounds of their being lost or stolen at Epsom on Derby Day.

Derby crack, a. An outstanding race for the Derby : Cockney (— 1887). Baumann.

Derby Dilly. A section of the Tory party, so nicknamed in 1835. They followed Lord Stanley, afterwards Earl of Derby. (Dawson.)

Derby Kelly. Belly : rhyming s. (— 1900) B. & P. Gen. abbr. to *Derby Kell.*

dern, derned. See darn. Also durn, durned.

*derrey. An eye-glass : c. : from ca. 1860 ; ob.

derrey, take the. To quiz, ridicule : tailors', ca. 1850–1900.

derrick. The gallows ; hangman. As v., to hang. Orig. (1600) coll. ; by 1800, S.E. Ex *Derrick*, the name of the public hangman ca. 1598–1610. Cf. *Jack Ketch.*—2. Hence, a workhouse : tramps' c. (— 1935).—3. The *membrum virile* : low : C. 19–20.

derrick, v.i. 'To embark on a disreputable cruise or enterprise' : nautical : mid-C. 19–20. Bowen. Ex the n., sense 1.

derry. To dislike or have a 'down' on (a person) : Australian and New Zealand : from ca. 1905. Ex *derry on*, q.v.

Derry-Down Triangle. An Irish nickname for Castlereagh, the Irish member for Londonderry, who, during the troubles of 1796–98, caused Irish backs to be 'tickled at the halberts', Bee : ca. 1800–30.

derry on, have a. To have a 'down' on : Australian : from ca. 1895. Morris derives ex the comic-song refrain *hey derry down derry* ; but also operative is the dial. *deray*, uproar, disorder, itself ex Old Fr. *desroi, derroi*, confusion, destruction (E.D.D.) In C. 20, as e.g. in C. J. Dennis, *derry* is often used separately for : an aversion ; a feud.

dersay, I. I dare say ; perhaps : Cockney sol. (— 1887). Baumann.

derwenter. A released convict : ca. 1880–1900 : Tasmanian. Boldrewood. Ex the penal settlement on the banks of the River Derwent, Tasmania.

derzy. A tailor : Regular Army coll. : late C. 19–20. F. & Gibbons. Ex Hindustani *darzi*. Also, occ., *dhirzi.*

describe and **descry** were often confused ca. 1570–1780. O.E.D.

desert. A ladies' club : Society : 1892–ca. 1915. Ware, 'From the absence [? lack] of members.'

desert, swing it across the. To scheme one's way into hospital ; hence, to malinger : Egyptian

Expeditionary Force : 1915–18. F. & Gibbons. See **swing it.**

deserve a (or **the**) **cushion.** See **cushion, deserve a.**

desolate. Dissolute : sol. ; C. 18–20.

despatchers, dispatchers. False dice with two sets of numbers and no low pips : low ; perhaps orig. c. : from mid-1790's. *The Times*, Nov. 27, 1856. They soon ' despatch ' the unwary. Cf. *dispatches.*

desparado, Incorrect for *desperado* : C. 17. Cf.

desperancy, incorrect for *desperacy* : C. 17–early 19. O.E.D.

desperate, desperately, adj. and adv. Both from early C. 17 in loose sense of ' awful(ly) . Coll. ; the adv.—esp. as an intensive (= extremely, very) —remaining so, the adj. having, ca. 1750, > S.E.

desperately mashed. Very much in love : ca. 1882–1910. Cf. *mash*, q.v.

dessay. Dare say : daresay : sol. : C. 19–20. E.g. Milward Kennedy, *The Murder of Sleep*, 1932, ' I dessay he's forgotten Mr. Churt's 'ere.'

destiny. One's fiancé (rarely fiancée) : from ca. 1910 : middle-class coll.

dessicate. A frequent error for *desiccate* : late C. 16–20.

detail, but that's a ! or **a mere detail !** In the 1890's, the former was ' a current phrase ' humorously making light of something difficult or important ; the latter is the more gen. post-War form : a c.p. > coll. >, by 1930, S.E.

detachment. Incorrect for (legal) attachment : C. 18. As are *detainor, -our,* for (legal) *detainer* : C. 17–18. O.E.D.

deten. Detention : school coll. ; late C. 19–20.

detest, attest, protest and **testify** were, mid-C. 16–early 17, occ. confused. O.E.D.

detrimental. An ineligible suitor, also (and orig.) a younger brother to an heir to an estate : from ca. 1830.—2. Hence, a male flirt : from ca. 1850. All three nuances are Society slang, slightly ob. by 1920. 3. In C. 20, a male pervert : coll.

Detrimental Club. The Reform Club : Society ; late C. 19, rarely in C. 20.

deuce ; occ. **deuse,** C. 17–18 ; **dewce,** C. 17 ; **dewse,** C. 18 ; **duce,** C. 17–19 (O.E.D.). Bad luck, esp. in exclamations (e.g. *the deuce !*) : from ca. 1650. Hence, perdition, the devil, esp. in exclamations (e.g. *the deuce take it !*) : from ca. 1690. Cf. its use as an emphatic negative (e.g. *the deuce a bit*) : from ca. 1710. These three senses are very intimately linked ; they derive either from old Fr. *deus*, L. *deus*, or from *the deuce* (Ger. *das daus*) at cards : cf. *deuce-ace*, a throw of two and one, hence a wretched throw, hence bad luck.—2. Whence also the two at dice or at cards (mostly among gamesters) ; and 3, twopence (mostly among vagrants and Dublin newsboys) : both low and dating from ca. 1680. No. 3 is in B.E. as *duce*, q.v.

deuce, go to the. To degenerate ; to fall into ruin : coll. ; from ca. 1840.

***deuce-a-vil(l)e.** See **daisyville.**

deuce and ace. (A) face : rhyming s. : late C. 19–20. F. & Gibbons.

deuce and all, the. Much, in a violent or humorous sense : coll. (— 1762). Sterne. (O.E.D.)

deuce to pay, the. Unpleasant consequences or an awkward situation to be faced : from ca. 1830 ; in C. 20, coll. Thackeray, 1854, ' There has been such a row . . . and the deuce to pay, that I'm inclined to go back to Cumtartary.'

deuce (or **devil**) **with, to play the.** To harm

greatly ; send to rack and ruin : from ca. 1760 ; in C. 20, coll.

deuced. (Of things) plaguy, confounded ; (persons) devilish ; (both) excessive. Also as adv. From ca. 1774. Mme D'Arblay (O.E.D.) ; Michael Scott, in *The Midge*, 1836, ' Quacco . . . evidently in a deuced quandary.' Ex *deuce*, q.v.

deuced infernal. Unpleasant : Society : ca. 1858–70. H., 1st ed., Introduction (*jeuced* . . .).

deucedly. Plaguily ; extremely : coll. ; from ca. 1815. Thackeray. (O.E.D.)

***deuces.** In racing c., from ca. 1860 : odds of 2 to 1.

deuse. See **deuce.**

***deuseaville.** See **daisyville.** Hence *deuseaville-stampers*, country carriers : late C. 17–18 c. B.E.— ***deus(e)wins.** Twopence : 1676, Coles : c.

devast(itat)ion ; devastor. Incorrect for *devastation, devastator.* O.E.D.

devastating has from ca. 1924, been Society s., as in ' Quite too devastating, darling.' Cf. journalistic use. E. F. Benson, *Travail of Gold*, 1933, ' The banal epithets of priceless and devastating just fitted her.'

devey. See **deevie.**

devil. The errand boy in a printery—perhaps orig. the boy that took the printed sheets as they issued from the press : (— 1683) orig. printers' s., by 1800 printers' j. and gen. coll. ; by 1900, S.E. *Punch* in 1859 spoke of ' the author's paradise ' as ' a place where there are no printers' devils '.—2. In law, a junior counsel that, gen. without fee, does professional work, esp. the ' getting-up ' of cases, for another : from ca. 1850 ; in C. 20 considered as S.E.—3. Hence, a person doing hack work (often highly intelligent and specialised work) for another : from ca. 1880 ; coll. ; after ca. 1905, S.E. ' I'm a devil . . . I give plots and incidents to popular authors, sir, write poetry for them, drop in situations, jokes, work up their rough material,' G. R. Sims, 1889.—4. A (firework) cracker : from ca. 1740 ; coll. till ca. 1800, when it > S.E. Hence, perhaps, the C. 19–20 coll. sense, a piece of firewood, esp. kindling, soaked in resin.—5. A grilled chop or steak seasoned with mustard and occ. with cayenne : late C. 18–20 ; coll. soon S.E. Grose, 2nd ed., defines it as a broiled turkey-gizzard duly seasoned and adds, ' From being hot in the mouth '. Cf. *attorney.*—6. Gin seasoned with chillies : licensed victuallers and then public-house in gen. ; from ca. 1820. G. Smeaton, *Doings in London*, 1828.—7. (Fighting) spirit, great energy, a temper notable if aroused : coll. : from ca. 1820.—8. A sandstorm, esp. a sand spout : military (India and Egypt ; by 1890, South Africa) ; from ca. 1830. In C. 20, S.E. —9. Among sailors, any seam difficult to caulk : (? C. 18,) C. 19–20.—10. See **devil himself.**

devil, v. To act as ' devil ' to a lawyer : from ca. 1860.—2. To do hack work : from ca. 1880. In C. 20, both senses are S.E. See **devil, n.,** 2 and 3.

devil, a or **the,** followed by **of a**(n). An intensive of no very precise meaning : coll. ; from ca. 1750. Esp. in *a, the devil of a mess, row, man, woman.* Michael Scott, 1836, ' A devil of a good fight he made of it.'—2. Also, *the devil* (without *of*) is used intensively as a negative, as in ' The devil a thing was there in sight, not even a small white speck of a sail,' Michael Scott in *The Midge.*

devil, American. A piercing steam whistle employed as a summons : workmen's, ca. 1865–1910. *The Manchester Guardian*, Sept. 24, 1872.

devil, go to the. To fall into ruin : late C. 18–20 ; but the imprecation *go to the devil !* dates from C. 14.

devil, hold a light or **candle to the.** See **candle.**

devil !, how or **what** or **when** or **where** or **who the.** An exclamation indicative of annoyance, wonder, etc. : the second, from M.E. and ex Fr. *que diable !* ; the others C. 17–20 : coll. The first occurs in Pope, the second in Garrick, the fifth in Mrs. Cowley.

devil, little or **young.** A coll. term of address, playful or exasperated : C. 17–20.

devil, the. See **devil, a.—devil, young.** See **devil, little.**

devil, play the. To do great harm ; v.t., *with.* Coll. from ca. 1810 ; earlier, S.E. Egan, 1821, ' The passions . . . are far from evil, | But if not well confined they play the devil.'

devil a bit says Punch, the. A firm though jocular negative : ca. 1850–1910 ; coll. (Without *says Punch* : from ca. 1700.)

devil among the tailors, the. (Gen. preceded by *there's.*) A row, disturbance, afoot : late C. 18–20, ob. ; coll. Perhaps ex a tailors' riot at the performance of *The Tailors : a Tragedy for Warm Weather.* Cf. *cucumber time,* q.v.

devil (and all) to pay, the. Very unpleasant consequences to face : C. 15–20 ; coll. Swift in his *Journal to Stella,* ' Supposed', says the S.O.D., ' to refer to bargains made by wizards, etc., with Satan, and the inevitable payment in the end.'

devil and baker. A C. 20 coll. allusion to the proverbial *pull* or *haul devil, pull baker !,* said of a contest of varying fortunes, C. 17–20.

devil and ninepence go with (her, etc.) !, the. A semi-proverbial coll. : C. 18. T. Brown (— 1704), ' That's money and company.' (Apperson.) In C. 19–20 (ob.), with *sixpence* for *ninepence.*

devil and Tommy. See **Tommy, hell and.**

devil and you'll see his horns or **tail, talk of the.** Applied to a person that, being spoken of, unexpectedly appears : coll. proverbial, C. 17–20.

devil beats or **is beating his wife with a shoulder of mutton, the.** ' It rains whilst the sun shines,' Grose, 3rd ed. : semi-proverbial coll. : late C. 18–mid. 19.

devil by the tail, pull the. To go rapidly to ruin ; to take an undue risk ; to be at one's last shift. Coll. ; from ca. 1750.

devil-catcher or **-driver.** A parson : late C. 18–early 19. Grose, 1st ed. See also **devil-dodger.**

Devil Dick. Richard Porson, the scholar (d. 1808) : very combative. (Dawson.)

devil-dodger. A clergyman, esp. if a ranter : late C. 18–20. Lackington, 1791.—2. (Cf. *holy Joe.*) A very religious person : mid-C. 19–20. ' Ducange Anglicus.'—3. Also, a person that goes sometimes to church, sometimes to chapel (— 1860); ob. H., 2nd ed. Variants of sense 1 : *devil-catcher* (rare), *-driver* or *-pitcher,* and *-scolder,* all slightly ob. Cf. *snub-devil.*

devil doubt you, the. (Often with addition of *I don't* : which explains it.) A proletarian c.p. of late C. 19–early 20. Ware.

devil-drawer. A sorry painter : ca. 1690–1830 : coll. B.E. ; Grose.

devil go with you and ninepence or **sixpence.** See **devil and ninepence.**

devil himself, the. A streak of blue thread in the sails of naval ships : mid-C. 18–early 19 nautical. Grose, 1st ed.

devil is blind, when the. Never ; most improbably. Coll. : mid-C. 17–20 ; ob. Cf. *blue moon.*

devil-may-care. Reckless ; spiritedly free and easy, with connotation of real or assumed happiness. ? before Dickens in 1837 : coll. ; in C. 20, S.E.

devil may dance in his pocket, the. He is penniless : C. 15–early 19 coll. Because there is no coin with a cross on it : no coin whatsoever.

devil-on-the-coals. A small, very quickly baked damper : from ca. 1860 : Australian rural coll. : >, ca. 1900, S.E. The Rev. A. Polehampton, *Kangaroo Land,* 1862 (Morris).

devil-pitcher, -scolder. See **devil-dodger.**

devil take . . . ! Followed by *me, him,* etc. Variants of *take* are *fetch, fly away with, send, snatch.* Exclamations of impatience, anger. Coll. : C. 16–20 ; earlier in other forms.

devil to pay. See **devil (and all) to pay, the.**

devil to pay and no pitch hot, the. See **pay and . . .**

devil's (occ. **the old gentleman's**) **bed-post(s)** or **four-poster.** At cards, the four of clubs, held to be unlucky : coll. ; from ca. 1835. Captain Chamier, *The Arethusa,* 1837. Cf. :

devil's bedstead, the. The thirteenth card of the suit led : whist players' coll. (— 1887). Baumann.

devil's bones, teeth. C. 17–20, C. 19 : coll. : dice. Etherege, 1664, ' I do not understand dice . . . hang the devil's bones ! ' Cf. :

devil's books, the. Playing cards : C. 18–20, ob. ; coll. till ca. 1810, when it > S.E. Swift, 1729, ' Cards are the devil's own invention, for which reason, time out of mind, they are and have been called the devil's books.' Also, ca. 1640–1720, *the devil's prayer-book,* likewise coll. (Collinson.)

*****devil's claw(s).** The broad arrow on convicts uniforms : c. : from ca. 1850 ; ob.—2. ' A split hook to catch a link of chain cable ' : nautical coll verging on j. : mid-C. 19–20. Bowen.—3. A cable-stopper on a sailing ship : id. : id. Ibid.

devil's colours or **livery.** Black and yellow : coll. : mid-C. 19–20, ob.

devil's daughter. A shrew : coll. : mid-C. 18–20 ; from ca. 1820, mainly dial. Grose, 3rd ed., ' It is said of one who has a termagant for his wife, that he has married the Devil's daughter, and lives with the old folks.'

devil's daughter's portion. A mid-C. 18–early 19 c.p. applied—on account of their impositions on sailors and travellers—to Deal, Dover, and Harwich ; Helvoet and the Brill. Grose, 1st ed. (q.v.).

devil's delight, kick up the. To make a din, a disturbance : from ca. 1850 ; in C. 20, coll. Whyte-Melville in *General Bounce.*

devil's dinner-hour, the. Midnight : artisans' : late C. 19–20 ; ob. Ware, ' In reference to working late.'

devil's dozen. Thirteen : coll. ; ca. 1600–1850. From the number of witches supposed to attend a witches' sabbath. Cf. *baker's* (q.v.), *printers'* and *long dozen.*

devil's dust. Shoddy, which is made from old cloth shredded by the devil, a disintegrating machine : (— 1840, when Carlyle uses it) ; coll. recognised as S.E. by 1860. Popularised by a Mr. Ferrand in the House of Commons on March 4, 1842, when, to prove the worthlessness of shoddy, he tore a piece of devil's dust into shreds.—2. Gunpowder : military ; from ca. 1870 ; ob. Hawley Smart in *Hard Lines,* 1883.

devil's guts, the. A surveyor's chain : mid-C. 17–early 19 ; rural. Ray, 1678 ; Grose, 1st ed., ' So called by farmers, who do not like that their land should be measured by their landlords.'

devil's horns off, enough wind to blow the. A very strong wind : nautical : mid-C. 19–20. Baumann.

devil's in Ireland !, as sure as the. A coll. asseveration (– 1823) : ob. 'Jon Bee.'

Devil's Later Issue. See **Dear Little Innocents.**

devil's livery. See **devil's colours.**

devil's luck and my own (too), the. No luck at all : lower and middle classes' coll. : late C. 19–20. Ware. Cf. *devil's own luck*, q.v.

devil's own, adj. Devilish ; very difficult or troublesome or unregenerate, as e.g. in *devil's own dance* or *business*. Coll. : C. 19–20.

Devil's Own, the. (Abbr. *The Devil's Own Connaught Boys*.) The 88th Foot : military : from ca. 1810. The name is supposed to have been given by General Picton in the Peninsular War, when the 88th were devils in battle—and in billet.—2. (Only as *the Devil's Own*.) The Inns of Court Volunteers : bestowed by George III in 1803 (F. & Gibbons). Ex the personnel (see **devil**, n., 2). Mark Lemon, in his *Jest Book*, 1864, gives a fanciful etymology : '. . . lawyers always went through *thick* and *thin*.' Cf. *Devil's Royals*, q.v.

devil's own boy. A young blackguard ; a notable 'imp of the devil' : coll. ; C. 19–20, ob.

devil's own luck. Extremely bad, more gen. extremely good, fortune : C. 19–20 ; coll.

devil's own ship. A pirate : coll. ; C. 19.

devil's paternoster, say the. To grumble : C. 17–18 ; coll. Terence in English, 1614.

devil's picture-gallery, the. A pack of cards : coll. : late C. 19–20 ; ob. Collinson.

devil's playthings, the. Playing cards : C. 19–20, ob. ; coll. Cf. *devil's books*, q.v.

devil's prayer-book, the. See **devil's books.**

Devil's Royals, the. The 50th Foot, from 1881 the Royal West Kent Regiment : military : 1809, when at Vimiera, 'they charged a French column of five regiments with seven guns and routed it', F. & Gibbons.

devil's smiles. April weather ; alternations of sunshine and shower : C. 19–20, ob. ; coll.

devil's tattoo. An impatient or vacant drumming on, e.g. the table, with one's fingers, with one's feet on the floor. Coll. : after ca. 1895, S.E. Scott, Lytton, Thackeray.

devil's teeth. Dice : coll. (– 1860) ; ob. H., 2nd ed. Cf. *devil's bones*.

Devil's Wood. Delville Wood, 'the scene of terrific fighting in the Battle of the Somme' : military : (later) 1916. F. & Gibbons.

devilish, adv. Much, very : from early C. 17 : coll. ; in C. 19–20 almost S.E. Grose cleverly satirises its use. Orig. it had the force of the C. 20 *hellish* (adv.).

devils, blue. See **blue devils.**

deviltry. A coll. form of *devilry* : not gen. among the educated. From ca. 1850 in England, influenced by U.S. ; orig. and, except in facetious use, still mainly dial.

devor. A plum cake : Charterhouse, from ca. 1875. Ex the L.

devotional habits. Applied to a horse eager, or apt, to go on his knees : the stables (– 1860) ; ob. H., 2nd ed.

devy. See **deevie.**

dew. Whiskey ; **ooo.,** punch : Anglo-Irish : 1840, Lever (E.D.D.). Abbr. of *mountain-dew*, whiskey.

dew-beaters. Pedestrians out before the dew has

gone : coll. : mid-C. 17–19. Hackett's *Life of Williams*.—Whence, 2, the feet : c. : late C. 18–20, ob. Grose, 1st ed. ; Scott.—3. In C. 19 c. and (?) low : boots, shoes. Variants : *dew-dusters, -treaders* : mid-C. 19–20 (ob.) : Baumann.

dew-bit. A snack before breakfast : mid-C. 19–20 ; ob. ; coll. Cf. *dew-drink*, q.v.

dew-clap. Incorrect for *dewlap* : C. 16. O.E.D.

dew-drink. A drink before breakfast, as to farm labourers before they begin a non-union day's harvesting. Coll. : mid-C. 19–20. Like *dew-bit*, more gen. and early in dial. H., 3rd ed.

dew on, (have) got a. (To be) sweating : miners' : C. 20. *The Daily Herald*, Aug. 11, 1936.

dew o' Ben Nevis. Whiskey : taverns' : C. 20. Ex a specific whiskey. (Ware.)

dewce. See **deuce.**

dewitted, be. To be murdered by the mob, as were the brothers De Witt, Dutch statesmen, in 1672 : from ca. 1685 ; coll. till ca. 1720, then S.E. Cf. *lynch*.

***dews.** See **deuce**, 2. Esp. in *dews wins*, twopence.—**dewse.** See **deuce**, 1.

***dewse-a-vyle.** Cf. *deuseaville* and see **daisyville.**

***dewskitch.** A thrashing, esp. a sound one : (– 1851, ob.) vagrants' c., and low s.

dexter. (On the, belonging to the) right : facetiously coll. ex heraldry. From ca. 1870 ; in C. 20, rare in England, very gen. in U.S., esp. in sport (e.g. baseball). Atkin in *House Scraps* (a humorous ballad of the Stock Exchange), 1887 : 'His "dexter ogle" has a mouse ; | His conk's devoid of bark.'

dhirzi. See **derzy.**

dhobi, dhoby ; sometimes anglicised as **dobie, dobey, dobee.** A native washerman : Anglo-Indian coll. : C. 19–20. Ex Hindi *dhob*, washing. Among C. 20 Regular Army soldiers as among post-1840 Europeans resident in India, occ. loosely of any washerman or -woman. (Not to be confused with *dhoti*, the Hindu loin-cloth.)—2. Hence as v.i. and v.t., gen. in form **dobeying** (vbl.n.), clothes-washing : nautical : mid-C. 19–20. Bowen.

dhobi wallah. A variant, late C. 19–20, of sense 1 of the preceding.

dhoop. Incorrect for *doob* (an Indian grass) : C. 19–20. O.E.D.

diagram. (Facetious or) sol. for : diaphragm. C. 19–20.

dial. The face : low : from ca. 1830. Orig. *dial-plate* : *Lex. Bal.*, 1811. (Cf. *frontispiece*, esp. *clock*.) Variant, *dial-piece*.—2. In c., a thief or a convict hailing from Seven Dials, (now part of W.C.1), London : ca. 1840–90.

dial, turn the hands on the. To disfigure a person's face : ca. 1830–1910 ; low.

dial-piece, -plate. See **dial**, 1.—**alter one's dial-plate.** To disfigure his face : 1811.

dialectal (of dialect) and **dialectical** (of dialectics) are, C. 19–20, often confused.

[Dialogues verging on c.pp. : see note at Chants.]

Dials, the. The Seven Dials district, noted in C. 18–19 for being 'lousy' with low criminals : coll. : C. 19–20. Baumann. (Between Charing Cross and Oxford Street.)

diametarily. Incorrect for *diametrally*. O.E.D.

Diamond Coates. See **Romeo.**

diamond-cracking. Work in a coal mine : C. 19–20 ; cf. *black diamonds*.—2. In Australian c., from ca. 1870 : stone-breaking.

Diamond Dinks, Square Dinks, Triangle Dinks, the. The 2nd, 1st, 3rd Battalion of the New Zealand Rifle Brigade : N.Z. military in G.W. The 4th is the *Arse-Ups*, q.v. Ex the shapes of the shoulder-patches.

dibble. In C. 17, a moustache (?).—2. The *membrum virile* : low coll. ; C. 19–20. Ex the gardening instrument.—3. An affectionate form of *devil* : C. 19–20 ; affected by lovers.

dibble-dabble. An irregular splashing ; noisy violence ; rubbish : mid-C. 16–20 : coll. till C. 19, then dial. By reduplication of *dabble*. O.E.D.

dib(b)s. Money : from ca. 1810. H. & J. Smith, 1812 (O.E.D.). Prob. ex *dibstones*, a children's game played with sheep's knuckle-bones or with rounded pebbles.—2. A pool of water : nautical coll. : mid-C. 19–20. Bowen. Ex Scottish *dib*.—3. Fists ; esp. *use one's dibs* : C. 20. (George Ingram, *Stir*, 1933.) Cf. origin of sense 1.

*dice. The names of false dice are orig. c. and few > s. The terms, q.v. separately, are : *bristles, cinques, demies, deuces, direct contraries, fulhams, gord(e)s, graniers, langrets, sices,* and *trays* or *treys*. See also such terms as **bar(re)d, cater, flat, long, ventage.**

dice, box the. To carry a point by trickery : legal ; from ca. 1850.

dichrotal, dichrotism. Incorrect for *dicrotal, dicrotism* : from mid-1860's. O.E.D.

Dick. A man ; lad, fellow. As in *Tom, Dick and Harry* (see *Words !*, pp. 70–1) : late C. 16–20. Ex *Richard*. (Coll. rather than s.)

dick. A dictionary ; hence, fine words : from 1860 in U.S., and in Britain from ca. 1870. H., 5th ed. Cf. *Richard* (*Snary*).—2. An affidavit : recorded in 1861 (Dutton Cook, in *Paul Foster's Daughter*). See **dick, up to.**—3. A riding whip : from ca. 1860 ; H., 3rd ed. ? etymology.—4. The *membrum virile* : military, from ca. 1860. In 1915 +, though ob., *D.S.O.* facetiously = dick shot off. Perhaps suggested by either *derrick* or, less prob., *creamstick*.

*dick, v.t. and i. To look, peer ; watch : North County c. : from ca. 1850. H., 3rd ed. Ex Romany : cf. *dekko*.

Dick, clever. A smart, esp. a too smart fellow : lower classes' coll .(— 1923). Manchon.

*dick in the green. Inferior ; weak : c. : ca. 1805–1900. Vaux. Cf. *dickey*, adj.

Dick, in the days or **reign of Queen.** Never : coll.: from ca. 1660 ; ob. (Cf. *devil is blind, when the ; blue moon ; month of Sundays,*) Grose, 3rd ed., however, mentions that *that happened in the reign of Queen Dick* was applied to ' any absurd old story ' ; cf. *Dick's hatband,* q.v.

dick, money for. Money for nothing : military (— 1914). F. & Gibbons.

dick, swallow the. To use long words ; esp. to use them without knowledge of their meaning. Coll. ; from ca. 1870. See **dick, n., 1.**

dick, take one's. To take an oath : from ca. 1861. See **dick, n., 2.**

dick, up to. Artful, knowingly wide-awake ; also, up to the mark, excellent : from ca. 1870. J. Greenwood, *Under the Blue Blanket* : ' Aint that up to dick, my biffin ? ' As in the preceding term, *dick* abbr. *declaration* : cf. *davy* for *affidavit* (W.).

dick shot off. See **dick, 4.**

dicked in the nob. Silly ; insane : low : ca.

1820–60. Egan's Grose. Perhaps *ex queer ʊs Dick's hatband.*

dicken ! See **dickin !**

dickens (also **dickins**, C. 17–18 ; **dickings**, C. 19 ; **dickons**, C. 18–19, O.E.D.), **the,** rarely **a.** The devil, the deuce, esp. in exclamations : late C. 16–20 ; perhaps coll. Shakespeare, Urquhart, Gay, Foote, Sims ; C. Haddon Chambers, ' What the dickens could I do ? ' In origin a euphemistic evasion for *devil* ; either an attrition from *devilkin* (S.O.D.) or ex *Dicken* or *Dickon* (W.). Cf. *dickin !,* q.v.

dicker. A dictionary : C. 20. By the ' Oxford-*er* '. Cf. *dick,* 1.

Dick(e)y. The second mate : nautical : mid-C. 19–20. Bowen. See sense 6 of :

*dickey, dicky. A worn-out shirt : ca. 1780–1800 ; c. or low. G. Parker. H.'s extremely ingenious *tommy* (ex Gr. τόμη) perversely changed to *dicky* won't quite do.—2. Hence (— 1811) a sham, i.e. a detachable, shirt-front : low > respectable s. > coll., by 1900 > S.E. *Lex. Bal.*—3. A woman's under petticoat (— 1811) : coll. ; †—4. A donkey, if male : late C. 18–20 ; coll., ? orig. dial. John Mills, 1841. *Lex. Bal.,* ' Roll your dickey ; drive your ass.'—5. A small bird : mostly children's coll. ; from ca. 1850. Abbr. *dicky-bird.*—6. A ship's officer in commission, gen. as *second dickey,* second mate : nautical (— 1867).—7. A swell = London, ca. 1875–95. ? ex *up to dick.*—8. The *membrum virile* : schoolboys' : from ca. 1870. Ex *dick,* n., 4.—9. An affidavit : lower classes' : from ca. 1865. Ex *dick,* n., 2. (Manchon.)

dickey, dicky, adj. In bad health, feeling very ill ; inferior, sorry ; insecure ; queer : from ca. 1790 ; low at first. See **dickey with.**—2. Smart : London : ca. 1875–1910. ? ex *up to dick.* Cf. *dickey,* n., 7.

dickey-, gen. **dicky-bird.** A small bird : coll. : ca. 1845. Barham (O.E.D.).—2. A harlot : from ca. 1820. In the broadside ballad, *George Barnwell,* ca. 1830. Often as *naughty dick(e)y-bird.*—3. A louse : low : from ca. 1855 ; ob.—4. Gen. in pl., a professional singer : from ca. 1870 ; ob. Prob. influenced by dial. *dicky-bird,* a canary (E.D.D.).

dick(e)y-diaper. A linen-draper : ca. 1820–70. Bee. Lit., a fellow who sells diapers.

dick(e)y dido. A complete fool ; an idiot : mid-C. 19–20 (ob.) : lower classes'. Baumann.

Dick(e)y Dirt. A shirt : rhyming s. : late C. 19–20. F. & Gibbons.

dick(e)y domus. A small ' house ' or audience : theatrical : from ca. 1860 ; ob. Ex *dick(e)y,* adj., 1, and L. *domus,* a house or home.

Dick(e)y flurry. ' A run on shore, with all its accompaniments ' : nautical : late C. 19–20. Bowen. See **dickey, adj., 2.**

dick(e)y flutter. A bet : military : C. 20. F. & Gibbons. See **dickey, adj., 1.**

dick(e)y lagger. A bird-catcher : from ca. 1870 ; low. Ex *lag,* to seize.

dick(e)y leave. Absence without leave : military (— 1914). F. & Gibbons. Ex *dickey,* adj., 1.

dick(e)y run. A naval variant of *dick(e)y flurry,* q.v. : same period. Bowen.

Dick(e)y Sam. A native, occ. an inhabitant, of Liverpool : from ca. 1860 ; coll. ex Lancashire dial. H., 3rd ed., 1864 ; *The Athenæum,* Sept. 10, 1870, ' We cannot even guess why a Liverpool man is called a Dickey Sam.'

Dick(e)y Scrub. A variant of the nickname *Heigh-Ho,* q.v.

dick(e)y with, all. (Rare, except in dial., in the absolute use exemplified in Thackeray, 1837, 'Sam . . . said it was all dicky.') Queer; gone wrong, upset, ruined; 'all up with'. From ca. 1790. Grose, 3rd ed. Poole, in *Hamlet Travestied*, 1811 : ' O, Hamlet ! 'tis all dickey with us both.' Moore ; Barham. Origin ?

dickin, dicken ! ' A term signifying disgust or disbelief,' C. J. Dennis : Australian : C. 20. Sometimes *dickin on l*, stop that, it's too much to believe, it's disgusting. Ex *the dickens !*

dickings, dickins, dickons. See **dickens.**

Dick's hatband. A makeshift : proletarian and provincial : C. 19–20 ; ob. Ware. Ex :

Dick's hatband, as . . . as. Any such adj. as *queer* relates the second *as*. An intensive tag of chameleonic sense and problematic origin, mid-C. 18–early 19 ; surviving in dial., as in the Cheshire ' All my eye and Dick's hatband.' Grose, 2nd ed ; Southey. (Apperson.) In C. 19, occ. as *queer as Dick's hatband, that went nine times round and wouldn't meet.*

dicksee. See **dixie.**

dicky. See **dickey**, n. and adj., all senses.

dictionary, up to. Learned : coll. : C. 19.

did, does (or **do**) omitted : see ' Present infinitive '. —2. Occ., in sol. speech, *did* is inserted tautologically before *ought* : C. 19–20. E.g., Dorothy Sayers, *Have His Carcase*, 1932, ' I did ought to have spoke up at the time.'—3. (did.) Done : sol. : C. 19–20. Esp. in C. 20 jocular c.p., (*it*) *can't be did*, which is very ob.

diddeys. A C. 18 variant (Grose, 2nd ed.) of :

diddies. The paps : low ; from ca. 1780. Grose, 2nd ed. (as above). A corruption of *titties.*

diddle. Gin : from ca. 1720 ; in C. 19, low, but orig. c. Grose, 1st ed. ; Mayhew in *Paved with Gold*. Prob. ex *tipple*.—2. The sound of a fiddle : C. 19–20 (ob.), low coll. O.E.D.—3. A swindle : low ; from ca. 1840, ex the v. *Punch*, Sept. 5, 1885, ' It's all a diddle.' Ex v., 1.—4. Among schoolboys, the penis : from ca. 1870. ? an arbitrary variation on *piddle*.

diddle, v. To swindle ; ' do ' ; ' do for ', i.e. ruin or kill : from ca. 1803 (S.O.D. recording at 1806). Moore ; Scott, ' And Jack is diddled, said the baronet.' Ex Jeremy Diddler in Kenney's *Raising the Wind*, 1803.—2. To trifle time away (v.i.) : from ca. 1827, ob. ; coll.—3. To shake (v.t.) : coll., perhaps orig. dial. : late C. 18–20, ob. as coll. —4. Hence, to copulate with : low coll. or s. ; C. 19–20.—5. To toddle : rare (– 1923). Manchon.

***diddle-cove.** A publican : c. (– 1858). Ex *diddle*, gin.

diddle-daddle. Nonsense ; stuff and nonsense : coll. ; from ca. 1770.

diddler. A sly cheat, a mean swindler ; a very artful dodger ; occ., a constant borrower. Coll. ; from ca. 1800. Cf. *Jeremy Diddler* : prob. ex dial. *duddle*, to trick (W.).

diddling. Sly, petty cheating or meanly sharp practice ; chronic borrowing. Coll. ; from ca. 1810. Ex the v., 1.

diddlum, adj. Dishonest ; illicitly manipulated : low, esp. grafters' : C. 20. Philip Allingham, *Cheapjack*, 1934, ' " It's these ruddy diddlum machines wot's done it," he said.' I.e. *diddle 'em.*

diddlum buck. The game of crown and anchor : military : from ca. 1880. (F. & Gibbons.)

diddly-pout. The *pudendum muliebrs* : low ; from ca. 1860. ? rhyming s. on *spout.*

diddums ! Did you (or did he, etc.) then ! : nursery coll., in consoling a child : late C. 19–20. Manchon. And see esp. Norah March's excellent article entitled ' Away with all the " Diddums " Jargon ' in *The Evening Standard*, May 28, 1934. By perversion of *did you* (or *he*).

diddy. See **diddies.—diden.** See **did'n.**

***didek(e)i.** A gypsy : c. : C. 20. George Orwell, *Down and Out in Paris and London*, 1933. Ex Romany *didakeis*, half-bred gypsies (Smart & Crofton).

did'n ; diden. Didn't : sol. : C. 19 (? earlier)–20. *Time and Tide*, Nov. 24, 1934, ' Ran right into the back of 'er, diden 'e ? '

dido. Rum : military (mostly Regular Army) : C. 20. B. & P. Perhaps ex *didoes . . .*, q.v.

dido, cut a. A naval variant (C. 20) of the next. F. & Gibbons.

didoes, cut up (occ. **one's**). To play pranks : orig. (from ca. 1830) U.S. ; anglicised in the 1850's ; slightly ob. H., 1st ed. Etymology ?.

didyer. Did you : sol. : C. 19–20. Via *did yer.*

die. (Gen. pl.) A last dying speech ; a criminal trial on a capital charge : low : ca. 1850–70. H., 1st ed.—2. See **die of it.**

die by the hedge. (Or hyphenated.) Inferior meat : provincial coll. (? orig. dial.) ; C. 19–20, ob.

die dunghill. See **dunghill, die.**

Die(-)Hards, the. The 57th Regiment of Foot, now the Middlesex Regiment (British Army) : military, from 1811. Supposed to arise ex the colonel's words at bloody Albuera, ' Die hard, my men, die hard.' F. & H. ; F. & Gibbons.

die in a devil's or **a horse's nightcap ; one's shoes** (later **boots**) ; **like a dog ; on a fish-day.** To be hanged : coll. All four were current in late C. 17–18 ; the first and second survived in early C. 19. The second, with *boots* and owing to U.S. influence, has since ca. 1895 meant, to die in harness, at work.

die like a rat. To be poisoned to death : C. 17–18 ; coll. In C. 19–20, S.E. and of a blunted signification. Like the preceding set of phrases, it is in B.E.

die (of it), make a. To die : coll. : C. 17–20 ; ob. Cotgrave, 1611.

died of wounds. A military c.p. of the G.W. = *hanging on the barbed wire* and *up in Nellie's room.*

Diet of Worms, be or **have gone to the.** To be dead and buried : ca. 1710–1820. Addison, Grose. (Cf. *Rot-his-bone*.) When Luther attended the Diet at Worms in 1521, many thought that he would meet the fate of Huss.

Dieu et mon droit (pronounced *dright*), **Fuck you, Jack, I'm all right.** An occ. variant (–1914– 15) of *fuck you, Jack, I'm all right*, q.v.

diff. A difference, esp. in ' That's the diff ' : coll., orig. Stock Exchange : from ca. 1870. Ware, ' There is a great diff between a dona [a woman] and a mush. You *can* shut up a mush (umbrella) sometimes.'

different. Special, unusual, recherché : (1912, Canfield) >, by 1935, coll. O.E.D. (Sup.).

different, adv. Differently : from ca. 1840, sol. ; earlier S.E. Kingsley (in dialogue).

different ships, different long-splices. A coll. nautical variation, mid-C. 19–20, of the landsman's *different countries, different customs.* Bowen.

differential. A coll. (now almost S.E.) abbr. of *differential gear(ing)* : from ca. 1910.

diffs. Monetary difficulties : theatrical : from ca. 1870 ; ob. Ware. Contrast *diff*, q.v.

dig. In boxing, a straight left-hander delivered under the opponent's guard : from ca. 1815 ; used by Tom Moore in *Tom Crib's Memorial*, 1819. (As = any sharp poke, S.E.) Cf. such terms as *auctioneer, biff, corker, floorer, nobbler, topper.*—2. A(n intensive) period of study : school coll. (— 1887) ; slightly ob. Baumann, ' He had a dig at his Caesar *er hat seinen Cäsar geochst.*' Cf. *dig away.*—3. Dignity : ' elegant ' lower middle-class : from ca. 1890. Prob. ex *infra dig*, q.v. Ware.—4. Abbr. *digger*, 2, but not heard before 1915.

dig, v. To live, lodge : from ca. 1900. Ex *diggings*, q.v.

dig, on. On one's dignity : schoolboys' (— 1909). Ware. Cf. *infra dig.*

dig a day under the skin. To shave every second day : from ca. 1870 ; ob.

dig about, give (a person) **a.** To mock or chaff : lower classes' (— 1923). Manchon.

dig away, v.i. To study hard : school coll. (— 1887) ; slightly ob. Baumann. Cf. *dig out*, 2, q.v.

dig in the grave. A shave : military rhyming s. : C. 20. F. & Gibbons. As v. : gen. rhyming s. : from ca. 1880. *Everyman*, March 26, 1931.—2. The *spade* in Crown and Anchor : military rhyming s. : from ca. 1910. B. & P.

dig (oneself) in. To secure one's position : coll. : from 1915. Ex trench-warfare.

dig (a person) out. Esp. *dig me out*, call for me, ' tear me from lazy loafing in the house ' : Society : ca. 1860–1910. Ware. Cf. *diggings.*

Digby duck. (Gen. pl.) A dried herring : Nova Scotian and nautical : late C. 19–20. Bowen. Prob. on *Bombay duck*, q.v.

dig up. To look for, to obtain, both with connotation of effort and/or difficulty : U.S. (late C. 19) >, ca. 1910, anglicised. Ex mining.—2. To depart, make off : low : late C. 19–20. Manchon. —3. To tidy up (v.i.) : military : C. 20. F. & Gibbons.—4. To work hard : nautical : late C. 19–20. Bowen. Cf. *dig away*, q.v.

dig out after. To try hard to get (something) : lower classes' (— 1923). Manchon.

digger. The guard-room : military (— 1909) ; slightly ob. Ware, ' Short for " Damned guard-room." '—2. A common form of address—orig. on the gold fields—in Australia and New Zealand since ca. 1855, and esp. common in G.W. +. (Rarely applied to women, except jocularly.)—3. In 1915–17, a self-name of the Australian soldier and the New Zealand soldier. Prob. revived, ex sense 2, by those who ' shovelled Gallipoli into sandbags ', for this sense appears to have arisen *after* April 25, 1915 (Anzac Day). Beyond the two relevant Forces, however, only (late 1915 +) the Australian soldier was thus named. B. & P. (In post-War Australia and New Zealand, *Digger* is the official name for a man that served in the War. Cf. *dad*, 2.) Cf. *Aussie* and *dinkum*, n.—4. See the next two entries.

digger, up the. ' Up the line ' ; in the trenches : military : G.W. F. & Gibbons. Prob. *up the jigger* (where *jigger* = gadget or thingummy) influenced by *diggings.*

diggers. Spurs : late C. 18–20, ob. Grose, 1788. Cf. *persuaders.*—2. In cards, the spades suit : from ca. 1840. Cf. *diggums* and *big digger.*—3. The

finger-nails : low : **from ca. 1850 :** more gen. in U.S. than in the British Empire.

diggers' delight. A wide-brimmed hat made of felt : from ca. 1880 ; ob.

digging, n. Kneeling down to pray in dormitory at night : Shrewsbury School : from ca. 1880. Desmond Coke, *The Bending of a Twig*, 1906.

diggings. Quarters, lodgings, apartment : coll. ; orig. U.S. (1838), anglicised in late 1850's. (In S.E., *diggings*, gold-fields, and *digger*, a miner, date from the 1530's.) H., 1st ed. ; Clark Russell, 1884, ' You may see his diggings from your daughter's bedroom window, sir.'

diggums. A gardener : provincial coll. or s. : C. 19–20.—2. In cards (cf. *diggers*), the suit of spades : from ca. 1840.

diggy. ' Inclined to give sly digs ' : coll. : C. 20. O.E.D. (Sup.).

digital. A finger : facetiously and pedantically coll. ; from early Victorian days.

dignity men. (Extremely rare in singular.) ' The higher ranks and ratings of coloured seamen ' : nautical : late C. 19–20. Bowen. Ex the dignity of brief office.

digs. Abbr. *diggings*, q.v. : from ca. 1890. Ex Australian ; common in theatrical s. before becoming gen.—2. Prayers : Shrewsbury School : from ca. 1880. Desmond Coke, as at *digging*, q.v.

diject. Incorrect for *deject.* O.E.D.

dike, dyke. A w.-c. : (low) coll. : mid-C. 19–20. Ex S.E. sense, a pit. Hence, *do a dike*, to use the w.-c.

dikk ; dikk-dari. Worry ; worried : Anglo-Indian coll. : from ca. 1870. Ex Hindustani *dik(k)*, vexed, worried. Yule & Burnell.

dikkop, play. To try to deceive as does a plover (Dutch *dikkop*) when, as one approaches its nest, it simulates a broken wing : South African coll. : C. 20. Glanville, *The Diamond Seekers*, 1903. (Pettman.)

dilberries. Impure deposits about the anus or the pudend : low : C. 19–20. *Lex. Bal.* Cf. *clinkers.*

dilberry-bush. The hair about the pudend : low : mid-C. 19–20. Cf. :

dilberry-maker. The fundament : low (— 1811) ; ob. *Lex. Bal.*

dildo. An imagic substitute for the *membrum virile* ; a *penis succedaneus.* C. 17–20 ; orig. coll. ; in C. 19–20, S.E. ' Hudibras ' Butler's *Dildoïdes* ; Grose. Perhaps ex It. *diletto*, delight, hence this sexual substitute (cf. *dildo-glass*, a cylindrical glass), perhaps ex *dildo*, ' a tree or shrub of the genus *Cereus* ' (S.O.D.). See Grose, P.

dildo, v. To exchange sexual caresses with a woman : coll. ; ca. 1630–1820. Ex preceding.

dile. Sol. for *dial*, 1, q.v.

diligent like the devil's apothecary, double. Affectedly diligent : coll. : mid-C. 18–early 19. Grose, 2nd ed.

dilirious, dilirium. † errors for *delirious, delirium.* O.E.D.

dill. Incorrect *dilse*, the Scottish form of *dulse* : mid-C. 19–20. O.E.D.—2. Distilled water : pharmaceutical chemists' (— 1909). Ware.

dillo-namo. An old woman : back s. (— 1859). H., 1st ed. Later, *delo nammow*, q.v.

Dilly, the. The Piccadilly Saloon : ca. 1850–60. Later, *the Pic.*—2. Piccadilly (the London Street) : c. : C. 20. James Curtis, *The Gilt Kid*, 1936.

dilly. A coach : coll. ; ca. 1780–1850. ' The dillies ', Grose, 1st ed., remarks, ' first began to run in England about the year 1779,' but (see O.E.D.) in France by 1742. Ex *diligence.* ' The Derby dilly, carrying | Three Insides,' Frere, 1789.—2. From ca. 1850 : a night cart; ob. by 1910, † by 1930. H., 5th ed.—3. A duck : coll.; from ca. 1840, ex the call to a duck.—4. A coll. abbr. of *daffodilly* : 1878 (S.O.D.).

dilly, adj. **D**elightful : ca. 1905–25. O.E.D. (Sup.). Cf. *divvy,* 4, and *deevie.*—2. Foolish; half-witted : Australian (— 1916). C. J. Dennis. Perhaps ex *dippy* + *silly*; but more prob. ex Somersetshire *dilly,* queer, cranky (1873 : E.D.D.).

dilly-bag. A wallet; a civilian haversack : Australian coll.: from ca. 1885. In C. 20, often used by women for a small shopping-bag or for a general-utility purse-bag. In G.W., the Diggers occ. employed it as a facetious variation on *ditty-bag* for the small linen bag issued in hospitals for toilet and sentimental oddments. Ex *dilli,* a basket; *dilli* preceded *dilly-bag* by forty years. Morris.

dilly-dally. A doubling of *dally* : orig. (? Richardson in *Pamela*) coll.; S.E. by 1800. ' Prob. in coll. use as early as 1600,' O.E.D.—2. Also as coll. adj. (— 1909). Ware.

dim. Unimportant, undistinguished; colourless, insipid. (Persons only.) Oxford University : ca. 1927–34. Evelyn Waugh, *Decline and Fall,* 1928, ' Who's that dear, dim, drunk little man ? '; J. C. Masterman, *An Oxford Tragedy,* 1933, ' The dim little research fellow with clumsy manners and no conversation.' Suggested by *sub-fusc,* q.v.—2. Hence, dull, silly, stupid : Society : 1931; ob. A. A. Milne, *Two People,* 1931 (in sense : dull, boring). See the quotation at *crashing bore.* Cf. *opaque,* q.v.

dim-mort, in B.E., is, I believe, a misprint for *dimber mort,* q.v. at *dimber.*

dimback. A louse : military : C. 20. F. & Gibbons. Ex its dim-coloured back.

*****dimber.** Pretty, neat; lively : low, prob. orig. (— 1671), c.; † by 1840, except in dial. Whence the late C. 17–19 (perhaps always c.) *dimber-damber,* leader or captain of criminals or of tramps, as in Head, B.E., and Ainsworth's *Rookwood*; *dimber cove,* a handsome man, a gentleman (as in B.E.); and *dimber mort,* a pretty girl (presumably in B.E.: see **dim-mort**).—2. Moreover, *dimber-damber* has become a Cockney adj.: C. 19–20; ob.: ' smart, active, adroit ' (Ware).

dime museum. ' A common show—poor piece ' : theatrical : 1884–ca. 1900. Ware, ' From New York which has a passion for monstrosity displays, called Dime Museums—the dime being the eighth of a dollar.'

dimensions, take. To obtain information : police s.: from ca. 1880 ; ob. Ware.

*****dimmock.** Money : c. (— 1812) >, by 1860, low. Vaux ; H., 2nd ed. Hence, *flap the dimmock,* to display one's cash. Either ex *dime* = a tithe or ex *dime* = an American coin of 10 cents (minted ca. 1785).

[**din,** despite B.E., is not c.—nor otherwise eligible.]

din-din. Dinner; hence, any meal; food : nursery coll.: late C. 19–20. In a certain house I know, one woman invites her baby to ' din-din ', another calls ' din-din ! ' to her cats.

Dinah. A favourite girl or woman; a sweetheart : Cockney (— 1890). *Dona(h)* corrupted.

dinahs. Edinburgh and Glasgow Railway ordinary stock : Stock Exchange : from ca. 1870.

dinarlee (or -ly) ; dinali (or -y), etc. Money : from ca. 1845 ; low Cockney and (orig.) Parlyaree. Esp. in *nantee dinarlee,* [I have] no money. Mayhew in his *magnum opus.* Ex It. or Sp. (ultimately L. *denarii*) via Lingua Franca : the gen. view. Possibly, however, through the Gypsies ex the Arabic and Persian *dinar* (itself ultimately ex L. *denarius*), the name of various Eastern coins.

dincum. A rare variant of *dinkum.*

dine out. To go without a meal, esp. dinner : mid-C. 19–20 ; coll., ' among the very lower classes ', says H., 5th ed. Cf. *go out and count the railings, dining out,* and :

dine with Duke Humphrey. To go dinnerless (cf. *dine out*) : late C. 16–20 ; ob. Coll. till ca. 1820, then S.E. In *Pierce Pennilesse,* Nashe writes : ' I . . . retired me to Paules [*St. Paul's*], to seeke my dinner with Duke Humfrey ' ; Smollett ; *All the Year Round,* June 9, 1888. Prob. ex the Old St. Paul's Church part known as Duke Humphrey's Walk ; Humphrey, Duke of Gloucester, Henry IV's youngest son. See esp. the O.E.D. and F. & H. Cf. :

dine with St. Giles and the Earl of Murray. A Scottish coll. variant (C. 18–20 ; ob.) of the preceding. The Earl was buried in St. Giles' Church. W.

*****diner.** The C. 20 racing c. form of *deaner,* q.v.

dines !, by God's. A coll. oath of late C. 16–early 17. Perhaps ex *dignesse.* O.E.D.

ding, v.t., to strike, seems to have a coll. savour : actually, however, it is either S.E. (archaic in C. 19–20) or dial.—2. To *ding a person* is to abandon his acquaintance, or to quit him : ca. 1810–60, low. Vaux. Ex :—3. As to snatch, to steal, to hide, it is C. 18–19 c. (Capt. Alexander Smith, *A Thieves' Grammar,* 1719), whence *dinger,* a thief that, to avoid detection, throws away his booty. Grose, 2nd ed.—4. As = *dang,* a euphemism, mostly U.S.—5. Occ. confused with *din,* n.: mid-C. 18–20. O.E.D.

*****ding, knap the ; take ding.** To receive property just stolen : c. (— 1812) ; † by 1870. Vaux.

*****ding, upon the.** On the prowl : c. : C. 19. Bee.

*****ding-boy.** ' A Rogue, a Hector, a Bully, Sharper,' B.E.: late C. 17–18 c. Cf. *ding,* 3, q.v.

ding-dong. As adj. and adv., despite F. & H., it has always been S.E.—2. In (— 1859) rhyming s., a song : ob. by 1910, except as theatrical.

ding-fury. Anger : either dial. or provincial s.,— a discrimination sometimes impossible to make. C. 19–20 ; ob.

ding the tot ! Run away with the lot ! Rhyming s. : from ca. 1870 ; low.

*****ding (something) to (a pal).** To convey to a friend something just stolen : c. (— 1812) ; † by 1870. Vaux.

dingable. Worthless ; easily spared : c. (—1812) >, by 1840, low ; † by 1900. Vaux. Ex *ding,* 2.

dingbat. An officer's servant : Australian army : 1914. Apparently ex *dingo* + *batman.* B. & P.—2. ' A swab for drying decks ' : naval : from not later than 1915. F. & Gibbons. Perhaps ex the now mainly dial. *ding* to strike, dash down, move violently,—*bat* as in *brickbat.*

dingbats. Eccentric ; mad, gen. slightly : Australian military : ? before 1914. Perhaps a fanciful adaptation of the Fr. *dingot,* same meaning : cf. *dingo,* almost certainly ex Fr. *dingot,* itself (according to Dauzat) ex *dingue,* dengue fever. But, prob., imm. ex :—2. **the dingbats.** Delirium tremens : Australians' and New Zealanders' : C. 20 ; ob. —3. Hence, madness : id. : from ca. 1905 ; ob.

dinge. A picture, esp. a painting : Royal Military Academy : from ca. 1870 ; ob. Ex *dingy*.— 2. Black (colour) ; generic for Negroes : from ca. 1930. Michael Harrison, *Weep for Lycidas*, 1934. Ex *dinginess*. Cf. *dingy Christian*, q.v.

dinge. To render dingy : from ca. 1820 : coll. (ob.) and dial. Ex *dingy*. O.E.D.

*****dinger.** See **ding**, 3. (Grose, 1788.)

dingers. Cups and balls : jugglers', from ca. 1840. Ex the sound.

dinges or **dingus.** What-do-you-call-it ; what's-his-name : South African s. verging on coll. : late C. 19–20. Fossicker's 'Kloof Yarns' in *The Empire*, Aug. 27, 1898. Ex Dutch *ding*, a thing : cf., therefore, *thingummy*.

dingey. See **dingy Christian**.

dinghy. A small rowing-boat, esp. for pleasure : from ca. 1830 ; orig. Anglo-Indian coll. ; from ca. 1870, S.E. Ex Hindi *dengi*, a river-boat. (S.O.D.) —2. Dengue : low and military sol. : C. 20. B. & P.—3. (*Dinghy*.) The inevitable nickname of men surnamed Reed (Read, Reid) : naval and military : late C. 19–20. F. & Gibbons.

dingle. Hackneyed ; used up : Society, ca. 1780–1800. *The Microcosm* (No. 3), 1786. ? ex *dinged*, battered.

dingle-dangle. The *membrum virile* : low ; from ca. 1895. The term occurs in a somewhat Rabelaisian song. Ex *d.-d.*, a dangling appendage.

dingo. Slightly insane : British Army, 1915 + ; ob. Cf. *dingbats*, q.v.

dingy is, in C. 20, considered incorrect for *dinghy*, q.v.—2. Dengue : military s. verging on coll. : C. 20. F. & Gibbons.

dingy Christian. A mulatto ; anyone with some negro blood : mid-C. 18–mid-19. Grose, 1st ed.

dingus. See **dinges**.

dining out. (Of a seaman) undergoing punishment, esp. cells : naval : late C. 19–20. Bowen. See also **dine out.**

dining-room. The mouth : low : from ca. 1820 ; ob. ' Jon Bee ', 1823.

*****dining-room jump.** See **jump**, n.

dining-room chairs. The teeth : low : from ca. 1820. Bee. Ex *dining-room*.

dining-room post. Sham postmen's pilfering from houses : late C. 18–19 ; low or c. See esp. Grose, 2nd ed.

dinkum, occ. **dincum.** Work, toil : Australian : 1888, Boldrewood, 'An hour's hard dinkum ' ; ob. Ex Derbyshire and Lincolnshire dial. ; cognate with Gloucestershire *ding*, to work hard : i.e. *dincum, -kum*, is prob. a perversion of *dinging*, with which cf. *dink*, to throw, toss, a variant of S.E. *ding*, to strike. (E.D.D.)—2. See **Dinkums**.

dinkum, adj. (Often *fair dinkum*, occ. *square dinkum*.) Honest ; true, genuine ; thorough, complete : Australian : C. 20. C. J. Dennis. Perhaps ex *dinky*, adj., q.v. ; but actually *dinkum* prob. derives ex *fair dinkum*, for in Lincolnshire dial. we find *fair dinkum*, fair play, before 1898 ; the E.D.D. derives it ex Lincolnshire *dinkum*, an equitable share of work.

dinkum oil, the. The truth : Australian : from ca. 1910. C. J. Dennis. Ex *dinkum*, adj. ; cf. *the straight wire*, q.v.

Dinkums, the. (Rare in singular.) Those soldiers who had been on Gallipoli ; also, hence, the 1st Australian Division : Australian military : 1916 ; ob. B. & P. Ex *dinkum*, adj.

dinky. A mule : military : C. 20. F. & Gibbons. Prob. ironically ex :

dinky. Neat, spruce ; small and dainty : coll. (from ca. 1870) ex dial. *dinky*, itself ex Scottish *dink*, feat, trim, neat, as in Burns.

dinky-die. A variant (— 1914) of *dinkum*, adj. Jice Doone.

dinky doo. The number 22 in the game of House : military rhyming s. : C. 20. F. & Gibbons. —2. ' Thingummy ' : C. 20.

Dinner Bell, the. Edmund Burke (d. 1797). His long speeches interfered with M.P.s' dinners. Dawson.

dinner-set. The teeth : low : from ca. 1870. Cf. *dining-room chairs*.

Dinny Hayes, let loose ; Dinny Hayes-er. To punch ; a punch, esp. a mighty punch : Australian : C. 20. Ex a noted pugilist. John G. Brandon, *Th' Big City*, 1931, ' In New South [Wales] you just hauled off and spread the troublesome bloke on the floor with a Dinny Hayes-er.' Ibid., the other phrase.

dinoxide. Dioxide : incorrect form : mid-C. 19–20. On *binoxide*. O.E.D.

dinted, occ. **dented.** Damaged ; wounded, injured ; greatly diminished : of persons, reputations, or fortunes : facetious coll. ; from ca. 1910.

*****dip.** In c., with corresponding v. (1817), a pick-pocket, ' pick-pocketing ' (from ca. 1850). Cf. *****dive**, *diver*, qq.v.—2. Abbr. *dip-candle* : orig. coll., soon S.E. : from ca. 1815. Barham, ' None of your rascally dips.'—3. A pocket inkstand : Westminster School, C. 19–20, ob.—4. A tallow chandler : C. 18–early 19. Cf. sense 2.—5. A hit at, esp. a continuous hard hitting of, the bowling : cricketers' : C. 20. Neville Cardus, *Good Days*, 1934, ' After Macartney reached 200 in something like the time the average cricketer takes to score seventy, he waved his bat toward the pavilion, and signalled ; " What do you want, Charles ? " asked A. W. Carr : " a drink ? " " No . . . I want a heavier bat ; I'm going to have a ' dip '." One of the Nottingham bowlers, overhearing . . ., nearly fainted.' (Macartney—it was in 1921—went on to score 345 in 3 hours 55 minutes.)—6. Dripping (in cookery) : (low) coll. : mid-C. 19–20. (Neil Bell, *Andrew Otway*, 1931.)

dip, v. To pawn : mid-C. 17–20 ; coll. Ex the C. 17–20 S.E. sense, to mortgage, esp. lands, as in Dryden (' Never dip thyl ands '). *The Spectator* ; Thackeray ; B.E. has *dip one's terra firma*.—2. In the passive, to get into trouble ; be involved in debt : c. : from ca. 1670.—3. See n., 1.—4. To fail in an examination ; more gen. *be dipped* : naval : late C. 19–20. Ex ' the salute of dipping the ensign,' Bowen. Cf. :—5. To lose (e.g. a good-conduct badge), forgo (one's rank) : naval : late C. 19–20. Same origin. Bowen.

Dip, the. A cook's shop that, in C. 18–early 19, was situated ' under Furnival's Inn ' (Grose, 2nd ed.) and frequented by the lesser legal fry.

dip into. (Gen. with *pockets*.) To pick pockets : from ca. 1810.

dip one's beak. To drink : C. 19–20 ; low. (Cf. *moisten one's whistle*.) B.E. : ' He has dipt his Bill, he is almost drunk ' : low : late C. 17–early 19 ; extant in Cornish dial.

dip(t) stick. A gauger : C. 18–19.

diplomatial is a dictionary-error for *diplomatical*. O.E.D.

dipped, be. See **dip**, v., 2, 4.

dipped in wing. Worsted : C. 19–20, ob. ; coll. Perhaps ex *bee's-wing*, q.v.

dipped into one's (gen. **my**) **pockets, it** or **that has.** That has involved me in considerable expense : coll. (— 1887) ; slightly ob. Baumann. Perhaps ex **dip into,** q.v.

*****dipper.** A pick-pocket : mid-C. 19–20 ; orig. c., then low. Cf. *diver*.—2. An Anabaptist **or a** Baptist : the S.O.D., recording at 1617, considers it S.E., but—witness B.E. and Grose—it was prob. coll. until ca. 1820.

dipper (is) hoisted(**, the).** (There is) **a** strict rationing of water : nautical : C. 19–20. Bowen. ' From the old sailing ship custom of hoisting the dipper to the truck after the water has been served out to prevent men stealing more than their regulation pint.'

*****dipping.** Pick-pocketry : **c.** from ca. 1855. See **dip,** n., 1.

dipping-bloke. A pick-pocket : mid-C. 19–20 ; orig. c., then low. See **dip,** n., 1.

dippy. Extremely eccentric or foolish ; mad : from ca. 1910. Not impossibly ex Romany *divio*, mad, a madman (Sampson) ; cf., however, *dipso*, q.v.—2. Delirious : medical students' (— 1933). *Slang*, p. 191.

dips. A grocer : **s.** > coll. : C. 19–20 ; ob. Cf. 3.—2. The purser's boy : nautical : from ca. 1870. Ex :—3. The purser himself : from ca. 1830 ; nautical. Marryat. Ex *dip-candles*.—4. Doughboys : Australian coll. : mid-C. 19–20.

dipso, n. Abbr. *dipsomaniac*, a confirmed drunkard : C. 20 : cultured **s.** >, by 1930, coll.

diptheria. Frequent error for *diphtheria* : C. 19–20, as is *dipthong* for *diphthong*.

dire. Objectionable ; (very) unpleasant : from ca. 1920 (non-proletarian). Georgette Heyer, *Why Shoot a Butler ?*, 1933. Cf. *ghastly*, q.v.

direct O. A wireless operator employed directly by the shipowners : nautical : from ca. 1924. Bowen.

directly. Conjunction, as soon as, the moment after : 1795 : coll. R. H. Froude ; J. H. Newman ; Buckle. Abbr. *directly that* (or *when*). O.E.D.

dirk. The *membrum virile* : C. 18–20 ; orig. Scottish, then low jocular coll.

dirt. Brick-earth : late C. 17–20 ; coll.—2. Money : orig. (— 1890), U.S. ; anglicised ca. 1900. Cf. *dust*.—3. Shells : military : 1915. B. & P., ' Jerry put over a lot of dirt last night.' For semantics, cf. the soldiers' *clod* (v.) and *shit* (n.).—4. ' A mean speech or action,' C. J. Dennis : Australian (— 1916). Perhaps ex :

dirt (occ. mud), **cast, fling,** or **throw.** (V.t. with *at*.) To be vituperative, malicious : from ca. 1640 : coll. till ca. 1800, then S.E. Seldom (*throw*) ; Ned Ward (' Fling dirt enough, and some will stick ') ; ' John Strange Winter ' (*throw mud*).

dirt, do (a person). To play him a mean trick : C. 20 : mainly Australian. This is the chief use of *dirt*, 4, q.v. Cf. *dirty, do the.*

dirt, eat. To submit to spoken insult, degrading treatment : coll. (in C. 20, S.E.) ; from late 1850's. H., 3rd ed.

dirt ?, what's the. What's the scandal, hence the news ? : Society : from ca. 1932. (Evelyn Waugh, *A Handful of Dust*, 1934.)

dirt-baillie. An inspector of nuisances : Scottish (s., not dial.) : C. 19–20.

dirts, the. ' The dirty ', a mean trick : from ca. 1926. Anthony Weymouth, *Hard Liver*, 1936. On *bats* and *pots*.

dirty. A boy with a dirty mind : schoolboys' : late C. 19–20. Geoffrey Dennis, *Bloody Mary's*, 1934.

dirty, do the. To play a mean trick (*on* a person) ; coll., from ca. 1912 ; now verging on S.E. Here, *dirty* = *dirty trick*. (O.E.D. Sup.)

dirty a plate. See **foul a plate.**

dirty acres. An estate in land : mid-C. 17–20: coll. till ca. 1820, then S.E.—still facetious. B.E.

dirty beau. Coll. : ca. 1680–1810 : ' a slovenly Fellow, yet pretending to Beauishness ', B.E.

dirty dishes. Poor relations : coll. ; C. 19–20 ; ob. Somewhat low.

dirty-drunk. Exceedingly drunk : coll., mostly Anglo-Irish : C. 20. (Cf. *dirty drunken dribbler*, a person that spills his drinks : S.E. verging on coll.)

Dirty Half Hundred. The 50th Regiment of Foot (the 1st Battalion Royal West Kent) : from ca. 1810. Lever, in *Charles O'Malley*. Ex a Peninsular War incident : the soldiers, during a battle, wiped their brows with their black facings. Or rather, as in Napier's account of Vimiera : ' With faces begrimed with powder as black as their own lapels they came tumbling down on Laborde's division with a fearful war-cry.' Cf. *Blind Half Hundred*, q.v., and contrast *Dirty Shirts.*

dirty hougher. See **hougher, dirty.**

dirty left or **right.** A formidable left or right fist : Australian (— 1916). C. J. Dennis.

dirty puzzle. ' A sorry slattern or Slut,' B.E. : low coll. : ca. 1680–1830.

Dirty Shirt Club. The Parthenon (a publichouse) in Regent Street, London : ca. 1860–70. Ex its unwashed frequenters. H., 1864. Cf. :

dirty shirt march. The sauntering of male slumdom before, on the Sunday morning, it dresses for the midday meal : coll. ; from ca. 1870 ; ob.

Dirty Shirts. The 101st Regiment of Foot, now the 1st Battalion Munster Fusiliers : from 1857 : military. They fought gallantly in their shirtsleeves at Delhi in that year.—2. It seems that the 2nd Munster Fusiliers had won the same nickname early in the century.

dirty work at the cross-roads. Coïtion, or lesser amorous intimacies, with a woman : C. 20. Ex the (— 1900) sense, foul play, which often takes place at cross-roads. The pun is better unstressed.

dirzi, dirzy. See **derzy.**

dis. Disrespect : semi-jocular (— 1923). Manchon.—2. See sense 2 of :

dis ; sometimes **diss.** (Gen. v.t.) To distribute (type) : printers' (— 1889). Barrière & Leland.—2. Hence, occ., as n.

dis, ppl. adj. Disconnected : signallers' : from ca. 1910.—2. Hence, *go dis*, to go crazy : from ca. 1919. Lyell.

disab(b)illy. See **dishabbilly.**

disaster. A piastre : Australian and New Zealand soldiers' (Eastern front) : 1915–18. By rhyme and pun—the coin being of low value.

disception. Rare error (late C. 15–mid-16) for *disceptation*. O.E.D.

discomfit and **discomfort** were occ. confused in late C. 14–17. O.E.D.

discourse. To yaw-off on both sides : nautical : late C. 19–20. Bowen. I.e. *discourse*, with a pun on divagation in spoken discourse.

discret. A catachrestic spelling of that very technical adj. *discrete*. (In C. 16, *discreet* was occ. used thus, but that hardly confers archaism.)

discuss. To eat, drink: jocular coll.: 1815, Scott. *Discussion*, the consumption of food or drink does not follow until ca. 1860. (S.O.D.)

disgorge, v.i. and t. To pay up: coll.; C. 19–20. Ex the S.E. sense, to surrender something wrongfully appropriated.

disgruntled. Offended; chagrined; ill-humoured (temporarily): late C. 17–20. The S.O.D. records as S.E., but (witness B.E. and Grose) perhaps coll. in C. 17–18.

disguised. Drunk: s. or, perhaps rather, coll.: late C. 16–20; ob. In C. 18–20, the gen. form (almost S.E., by the way) is *disguised in liquor*. Massinger, in *The Virgin Martyr*, ' Disguised! How ? Drunk !' Goldsmith, of a handwriting in *She Stoops to Conquer*, ' A damned up and down hand, as if it was disguised in liquor.' Clark Russell, 1884, '. . . A third mate I knew, slightly disguised in liquor.' Ex the C. 16–20 *disguise*, to intoxicate with liquor. (Then, *disguise*, intoxication, is rare and rather S.E. than coll.)

disguised public-house. A workmen's political club: political: ca. 1886–1900. Ware.

disgusting. Unpleasant; silly: Society: from ca. 1920. Denis Mackail, *Greenery Street*, 1925, ' " You can have a Russian bath—if you know what that is." " Don't be disgusting," said Felicity—just to be on the safe side.' Cf. *filthy, foul*.

dish. An act of ' dishing ': 1891, Sir W. Harcourt (O.E.D.). Ex :

dish. To cheat; baffle completely; disappoint, ' let down '; ruin. From ca. 1798 : and see **dished up.** *The Monthly Magazine*, 1798; Moore; Moncrieff, 1821, ' I have been dished and doodled out of forty pounds to-day '; Disraeli, 1867, coined the famous *dishing the Whigs*. Ex meat being well cooked (*done*) and then served (*dished*): exactly analogous is *done brown*; cf. also *cook one's goose* and *settle one's hash* (W.).

dish, have a foot in the. To get a footing; have a share or interest in : coll. (— 1682). † by 1800. Bunyan. Ex a pig in his trough. (O.E.D.)

dish, have got a. To be drunk : coll.: ca. 1675–1750. Ray. (Apperson.)

dish-clout. A dirty and slatternly woman : late C. 18–20; coll. Grose, 1st ed.

dish-clout, make a napkin of one's. To marry one's cook ; hence, to make a misalliance : from ca. 1750 ; ob. ; a coll. of the proverbial kind. Grose, 3rd ed. Earlier (— 1678) as *make one's dish-clout one's table-cloth* (Ray) : Apperson.

dish-jerker. A steward: nautical: late C. 19–20. Bowen.

dish-water, dull as. A late C. 19–20 coll. variant of *ditch-water, dull as*. Collinson.

dish-wrestler. A dish-washer: low: from ca. 1925. James Curtis, *The Gilt Kid*, 1936.

dish out. To distribute (food) equally or decorations indiscriminately : military coll.: 1914. B. & P.

dis(h)ab(b)illy, n. Undress : which is pardonable. Adj., undressed : which is ludicrous. From ca. 1700 ; ob. Ex Fr. (*en*) *déshabillé*.

dished. (Of electrotypes) with letters having their centre or middle lower than their edge : printers' ; from ca. 1880.

dished up, be (whence *dish*, v.), is recorded by Grose, 2nd ed., for ' to be totally ruined '. In C. 20 displaced by *be dished* : see **dish.**—2. ' To be attended to in the sick bay ' (Bowen) : nautical : mid-C. 19–20.

disincommodate erroneously blends *discommodate* and *incommodate* : C. 17. O.E.D.

dislogistic. Incorrect for *dyslogistic* : C. 19–20. O.E.D.

dismal ditty. A psalm sung by a criminal just before his death at the gallows : ca. 1690–1820 : (perhaps orig. c., then) low, passing to low coll. B.E., Dyche, Grose.

dismal Jimmy. Mid-C. 19–20 coll., as in H. A. Vachell, *The Vicar's Walk*, 1933, ' Shown in his true colours, as a dog-in-the-manger, a spoil-sport, a wet blanket, a dismal Jimmy.'

dismals (, esp. in the). Low spirits : from ca. 1760 ; coll. till ca. 1840, then S.E. Ex M.E. *in the dismal*.—2. Mourning garments : ca. 1745–1830 : coll. (S.O.D.) L. *dies mali*, unpropitious days.

Dismember for Great Britain. ' The last political nickname given to Gladstone. About the time of the Home Rule Bill ' ; Society : 1886–early 87. Ware. (Gladstone supported Home Rule for Ireland.)

dispar, disper. A portion (cut in advance) of a leg or a shoulder of mutton (cf. *cat's head*) : Winchester College : from ca. 1830 ; ob. See esp. Mansfield's *School Life at Winchester College*, 1870, at p. 84. Prob. ex *to disperse* or perhaps *disparate* in the sense of unequal, or it may be a direct adoption of L. *dispar*.

dispatch. (*Despatch* is the inferior spelling.) V.t., to dispose quickly of food and/or drink : from ca. 1710 : coll. Addison. O.E.D.

dispatches ; des-. False dice : from ca. 1810 ; low, perhaps orig. c. Vaux. Cf. *des-, dispatchers*, q.v., and *doctors*.—2. In C. 18–early 19 legal : a mittimus. *A New Canting Dict.*, 1725 ; Grose, 1st ed.

disper. See **dispar.**

dispose. See **dissolute.**

disremember. To fail to remember : Anglo-Irish coll., C. 19–20 ; dial. and sol., mid-C. 19–20 ; fairly common in U.S., mid-C. 19–20.

dissecting job. Clothes requiring much alteration : tailors' : from ca. 1870.

diss. See **dis,** v.

dissolute and **desolate** are often confused by the ignorant : C. 16–20 sol. Less illiterate persons frequently stumble at *dissimulate* and *simulate*, while what we used to call the lower-middle class tends to err with *dispose* and *depose*.

distaff, have tow on one's. To have trouble in store, ex the sense of having work awaiting one, in hand : ca. 1400–1800. Coll. >, by 1600, S.E.

*distiller. One easily vexed and unable to conceal his annoyance : Australian c. : ca. 1840–90. Ex English c. *walking distiller*, the same : 1812, Vaux. See **carry the keg.**

distinctive is often misused for *distinct* and *distinguished* : late C. 19–20. Fowler.

distracted division. ' Husband and wife fighting ', Egan's Grose, 1823 ; † by 1860.

distress, flag of. See **flag of distress.**

districts (or **D-**). Shares in the District Railway : Stock Exchange coll. (— 1895) >, by 1920, j. (A. J. Wilson, *Stock Exchange Glossary*.)

district, on the. (Of a student) doing his midwifery course, which involves the care of the parturient poor in his hospital's district : London medical students' (— 1933). *Slang*, p. 191.

dit. See **dite.**

ditch. To throw away : nautical : from ca. 1870. (Bowen.) Ex *Ditch, the,* 2. Cf. *ditched,* q.v.

Ditch, the. Shoreditch : Cockney coll. : mid-C. 19–20. Ware. An inhabitant thereof : *Ditcher.* —2. **the d.**, the sea ; **the D.**, the Atlantic : coll. : from ca. 1860.—3. Calcutta : Anglo-Indian (— 1886) ; *Ditcher*, a Calcutta-ite. Ex the Mahratta Ditch. Yule & Burnell.

ditch-water, as dull as. Extremely dull : from ca. 1800 ; coll. till ca. 1880, then S.E.

ditch-water, clear as. Fig., far from clear : coll. : late C. 19–20. Manchon.

ditched. At a loss ; nonplussed : coll. : from ca. 1890.

*ditched, be. To get into trouble, be abandoned : Canadian and English c. (mainly vagrants') : C. 20. Orig. U.S. ; ex being thrown into a ditch from a moving train.

Ditcher. See Ditch, 1 and 3.

dit(e), not care a. A C. 20 coll. derivative of *not care a doit* (ineligible here). O.E.D. (Sup.).

dither. See all of a dither.—2. dithers, trepidation ; (an access of) nervous shiverings : from ca. 1860 : coll. (orig. dial.). H., 2nd ed. (Hence adj., *dithering*.) Perhaps ultimately ex *shiver*, via *didder.*

dither, v.i. To be very nervous on a given occasion ; to hesitate tremulously or bewilderedly : coll. when not dial. : from ca. 1880. Ex *dither*, n., 2.

ditto. The same : coll. when not used strictly in the way of business : late C. 17–20. Cf. *ditto(e)s.*

ditto(-)blues. A suit of clothes made of blue cloth : Winchester College : C. 19–20, ob.

ditto, brother smut. See brother smut.

dittoes, better **dittos.** A suit all of one colour and material : C. 19–20. Until ca. 1860, the gen. form is *suit of dittos*, which the S.O.D. records, as *suit of ditto*, as early as 1755. James Payn, 1882 : ' He was never seen in dittos even in September.' In C. 19, occ. applied to trousers only. Both senses, imm. they > gen., are coll. ; orig. tailors' s.

ditty. (Gen. in pl.) A fib ; a long circumstantial story or excuse. Coll. (mostly Australian and New Zealand) : late C. 19–20. Ex dial. : E.D.D.

ditty-bag. A small bag used by sailors for their smaller necessaries and sentimentalities : from ca. 1860. Orig., according to H., 3rd ed., and F. & H., coll. ; in C. 20, S.E. ? ex *dilli* : see dilly-bag.

div. A stock-and-share dividend : Stock Exchange : from ca. 1880.

dive. A place of low resort, esp. a drinking-den : coll. : orig. (ca. 1880) U.S., anglicised ca. 1905, though it was fairly well known considerably earlier (e.g. in *The Referee*, May 10, 1885). Ware. Many ' dives ' were, still are, in cellars or, at least, in basements.—2. A variant of *diver*, 2, q.v.

*dive, v.t. and i. To pick pockets : from ca. 1600 ; ob. In C. 17, c. ; then low s. Ben Jonson : ' In using your nimbles [i.e. fingers], in diving the pockets.'

dive for a meal (esp. *dinner*). To go down into a cellar for it : coll. : late C. 18–mid-19. Grose, 1st ed. Cf. *dive*, n., 1, q.v., and *diver*, 3.

dive in the dark. An act of coition : C. 19–20 ; low.

dive into one's sky. To put one's hand(s) in one's pocket(s) ; esp. to take out money. C. 19–20, ob. ; low.

dive the twine. Gen. *dived* . . ., applied to a school of fish that, ' surrounded by a purse-seine net drops down through the net and escapes before it can be . . . closed ' (Bowen) : Grand Banks fishermen's coll. : late C. 19–20.

*diver, rarely **dive.** (*Diver* only.) He who, assisting a ' curber ' (q.v.), sends in a boy to do the stealing : late C. 16–early 17 c. Greene, Dekker.— 2. A pickpocket : from ca. 1600 ; c. till ca. 1800, then low. Gay's *The Beggar's Opera* has a character named Jenny Diver. Baumann, 1887, ' Smashers and divers and noble contrivers.' Cf. *dip.*—3. One who lives in a cellar : low : late C. 18–mid-19. Grose, 1st ed. Cf. *dive*, n., 1.—4. See divers.—5. ' A liner's boatswain in charge of the wash deck party ' : nautical : late C. 19–20. Bowen *(the diver).*

divers. The fingers : C. 19–20 ; low. Cf. *pickers and stealers.* Cf. the U.S. c. term, *diving hooks*, appliances for picking pockets (late C. 18–19 : Thornton).

divers and diverse are often confused : C. 19–20. Orig. they were identical.

divest. Catachrestic for *vest* or *invest* : C. 17. O.E.D.

divi. See divvy, 2.

divide the house with one's wife. To turn her out of doors, ' give her the key of the street ' : mid-C. 18–19. Grose, 1st ed.

dividend(e). Incorrect for *dividend* : C. 16–17.— **divination** for **divinity** : C. 17. Both, O.E.D.

divine. Pleasant : ' nice ' : Society : from ca. 1920. Evelyn Waugh, *Decline and Fall*, 1928 ; *The Daily Mirror*, Nov. 1, 1933. Cf. *marvellous.*

divine punishment. Divine service : naval : 1869 (or a few years earlier) ; ob. Ware.

diviners († by 1921) ; **divvers.** Divinity Moderations : Oxford undergraduates' : from ca. 1898. (Oxford-*er*.) Ware.

diving-bell. A basement-, esp. a cellar-, tavern. Cf. *dive*, q.v. From ca. 1885. This term may, however, be rather older and hence constitute the germ whence sprang the U.S. *dive.*—2. ' A sailing-ship that was very wet and plunged badly ' : nautical : C. 19. Bowen. Ex S.E. nautical sense.

divolve. Incorrect for *devolve* : C. 15–20. O.E.D.

divot-digger. An inexperienced and/or clumsy golfer : Australian (— 1935).

divvers. See diviners.

divvies. See sense 2 of :

div(v)y. A division : military : from ca. 1880, esp. in G.W. As in ' the 29th Divvy ', which served on Gallipoli, 1915.—2. (Also *divi* : 1897, O.E.D.) A share ; a dividend (— 1890) : coll.—3. Also as v.i. and t., with variant *divvy up* : from ca. 1880.—4. As an adj., divine : from late 1890's ; † by 1921. Cf. *deevie*, q.v.

dixie, dixy. An iron pot, esp. as used in the Army, for boiling tea, rice, stew, vegetables, etc. Popularised by soldiers, who adopted it (–1879) ex Urdu.— 2. Also, the small, lidded can that, forming part of a soldier's equipment, is used for tea, stew, etc. Both senses were orig. s. or coll., but they soon > j., then S.E. and of gen. usage, which last they attained ca. 1917 or 1918. (In Frank Richards, *Old Soldiers Never Die*, the word is spelt *dicksee.*)—3. **Dixie** is the nickname, from ca. 1926, of W. R. Dean, who, for Everton in 1927–28, made a record in the English League (Association football) : 60 goals in 39 games.

Dizzy ; occ. **Dizzie.** The nickname given, ca. 1840, to Disraeli. Cf. *Pam.*—2. Whence *dizzy*, a clever man ; esp. in *quite a dizzy* : middle classes' : ca. 1870–1914. Ware.

dizzy. ' A man easily flustered ' : military : C. 20. F. & Gibbons.

dizzy, adj. Astounding : from ca. 1895. I.e., apt to render dizzy (O.E.D. Sup.). Cf. *dizzy limit.*

dizzy, get. See **get dizzy.**

dizzy age, (of) a. Elderly : near-Society : ca. 1860–1900. Ware, ' Makes the spectator dizzy to think of the victim's years.'

dizzy limit, the. The utmost : C. 20. Mostly Australian. C. J. Dennis. (It makes one dizzy.)

dlog. Gold : back s. (– 1859). H., 1st ed. More gen. *delog,* q.v.

d'n (care or know). Don't : low coll. (– 1887). Baumann. But *d'n know* is nearly always written *dunno* (likewise in Baumann) ; *d'n* being pronounced *dun,* with which cf. the *ud* of *'d* in its brevity and in its lightness of stress.

Do. Either of the Doherty brothers, the famous lawn-tennis players fl. 1897–1906.

do. A swindle, a fraud ; a trick : from ca. 1810 ; perhaps coll. Dickens, in *Boz,* ' I thought it was a do, to get me out of the house.' Ex *do,* v., 1.—2. Action, deed, performance, business, event ; (a) success. In C. 17–18, S.E., but from ca. 1820, coll., esp. in *make a do*—a success—*of it,* which dates back to Mayhew, 1851, or a little earlier.—3. A joke : middle classes' : ca. 1900–15. Ware.—4. An entertainment, a social function : C. 20. In *The New Statesman and Nation,* Sept. 23, 1933, we hear of ' a famous West Indies cricketer, who speaks perfect English ' (Constantine, no doubt) being puzzled by the phrase, *a slap-up do,* applied to a tea. The puzzlement was admittedly caused more by the *slap-up* than by the *do,* though the juxtaposition may also have been partly the cause. In this sense *do* obtained in dial. as early as 1820.—5. An attack ; an offensive : military : 1915 ; slightly ob. by 1930. B. & P.—6. In pl., a share : esp. *fair doo's* (or *do's*), q.v.

do. Does : sol. : throughout mod. English among the illiterate.—2. **do** or **does** omitted : see ' Present infinitive.'

do, v. To swindle, cheat : from ca. 1640. Kenney, in that amusing play, *Raising the Wind,* ' I wasn't born two hundred miles north of Lunnun, to be done by Mr. Diddler, I know.' Hence, to deceive, trick, without illegal connotations : C. 19–20. —2. In c., v.t. to utter base coin or ' queer ' (q.v.) : from ca. 1810. Vaux.—3. To give a bad time, punish : boxing ; ca. 1815–1900. Earlier, to defeat. Grose, 3rd ed., mentions that Humphreys, writing from the boxing ring, said : ' Sir, I have done the Jew ' (Mendoza). Cognate is 3, b,—to kill : low : 1823, Bee ; † by 1890. Cf. *do for,* 3.— 4. Visit, go over, as a tourist or as a pleasure-seeker : coll. ; from ca. 1850. Shirley Brooks, 1858, in the *Gordian Knot,* ' I did Egypt, as they say, about two years back.'—5. With *the amiable, polite, heavy, grand, genteel,* etc., *do* is coll., the exemplar being Dickens's *do the amiable* in *Boz.*— 6. See the senses implicit in *done, done-for, done-over, done-up,* qq.v.—7. To suffice (*that'll do me*), to answer its purpose : ? orig. (1846 : Thornton), U.S., anglicised ca. 1860.—8. Hence, to please, meet the requirements of (a person) : late C. 19–20. E.g. ' *You'll* do me ! '—9. Moreover, *do,* like *chuck, cop, get,* ' is a verb-of-all-work, and is used in every possible or impossible connection ' (F. & H.) : this shows very clearly in the following set of phrases in *do a . . . ,* where the status is s. or coll. according with the nature of the n.—10. To arrest : c. : C. 20. James Curtis, *The Gilt Kid,* 1936.

do a beer, a bitter, a drink, a drop, a wet. To take a drink of something stronger than milk or water, the domestic trio (coffee, cocoa, tea), or soft drinks. *Do* here = drink ; it dates from ca. 1850. All, orig. s., are, except *do a wet,* coll. in C. 20. Cf. *do a meal,* to eat a meal : same period and status.

do a bill. To utter a bill of exchange : commerce ; from ca. 1830. Barham, Thackeray.

do a bishop. To parade at short notice : military, C. 19. Perhaps ex a full-dress parade turned out, at short notice, for a chaplain-general.

do a bit. To eat something : coll. ; from ca. 1850.—2. (Of men) to possess, have, a woman : low coll. ; from ca. 1860.—3. The cricket sense is ineligible.

do a bit of stiff. To draw a bill : low commercial : from ca. 1850 ; ob.

do a bunk, a guy, a shift. To depart hastily or secretly : from ca. 1860. The second, orig. c. ; the commonest, the first.

do a bunk, a shift. To ease nature : low ; from ca. 1865.

*****do a bust.** See **bust, do a.**

do a cadge. To go begging : low coll. : from ca. 1820. See **cadge,** n. and v.

do a cat. To vomit : low : from ca. 1840. Cf. *cat, shoot the* (q.v.).

do a chuck. To effect an ejectment ; to depart. Low : from ca. 1850 ; ob.

do a crawl. To cringe : coll. : late C. 19–20.

*****do a crib.** To burgle : c. then, in C. 20, low : from ca. 1840.

do a doss. To go to sleep : low : from ca. 1850. Cf. *doss,* q.v.

do a drink (or drop). See **do a beer.**

do a duck. See **duck, do a.**

do a fluff. To forget one's part : theatrical : from ca. 1850.

do a Garbo, a Gaynor. See **Garbo** and **Gaynor.**

do a get. See **get, do a.**

do a grind, a mount, a ride, a tread. To have sexual intercourse (of men) : low : from ca. 1860.

do a grouse. To go a-seeking women : low : C. 19.—2. In C. 20, to grumble.

do a guy. (See **do a bunk, a guy . . .**)—2. Among workmen, to absent oneself, without permission, from work : from ca. 1865.—3. In c., to make an escape : from ca. 1860. In C. 20, low. Ex sense 1.—4. See **guy, do a,** 1.

*****do a job.** To commit a crime : C. 20 New Zealand c.

do a knee-trembler. See **do a perpendicular.**

do a meal. See **do a beer.**

do a mike or **a mouch.** To go on the prowl : from ca. 1860 ; low.—2. In C. 20, also to depart : low.

do a moan. To growl : naval (– 1909) ; ob. Ware.

do a mount. See **do a grind.**

do a nob. To make a collection : circus, showmen's : from ca. 1845.

do a perpendicular or **a knee-trembler.** To have sexual intercourse while standing : low : from ca. 1860 ; the former, ob.

do a pitch—a rush—a snatch. See **pitch**—**rush**—**snatch.**

*****do a push.** To depart ; esp. to run away : c. (– 1865) ; ob.—2. See **push, do a.**

do a ride. See **do a grind.**

do a rural. To ease oneself by the wayside : low : from ca. 1860 ; ob.

do a scrap. To have a fight : from ca. 1840.

do (one) **a shot.** To outwit ; to swindle : South African coll. (— 1890). Occ. *do* (one) *a shot in the eye.* Pettman.

do a shift. See **do a bunk** (both senses).

do a sip. To make water : back slang on *piss* : from ca. 1860 ; ob.

do a smile. See **smile, n.** (a drink).—**do a snatch.** See **snatch, do a.**

do a spread or **a tumble.** To lie down to a man : low coll. : from ca. 1840.

do a stagger. To walk : Oxford University : from ca. 1918. Cf. *stagger, v.*

do a star pitch. To sleep in the open (*à la belle étoile*) : low theatrical : from ca. 1850. Cf. *hedge square, q.v.*; and :

*do a starry. To sleep in the open : C. 20 c.

do a tread. See **do a grind.**

do a treat. See **treat, a.**

do an alley. To depart ; to hurry away : military : 1915 ; ob. F. & Gibbons. Ex Fr. *aller,* to go.

do as I do. An invitation to drink : ca. 1860–1910 : coll.

do brown. See **brown, do,** 2.

do down. To cheat or swindle : from the 1890's. Cf. *do, v.,* 1.—2. Hence, get the better of : coll. : from ca. 1908.

do for. To ruin, destroy ; wear out (person or thing) entirely : coll. ; from ca. 1750. Fielding (O.E.D.).—2. To attend to or on, as a landlady or a char for a lodger, a bachelor : orig. S.E. ; since ca. 1840, coll.—3. In c., to kill : from ca. 1850 ; in C. 20, low. Cf. *do, v.,* 3, *b.*—4. To convict : c. : from ca. 1850. H., 1st ed.

do gospel. To go to church : low coll. : from ca. 1860.

do it. To be in the habit of doing—or gen. ready to do—it, i.e. to have physical intercourse. As an evasion, euphemistic ; otherwise, coll.

do in. To kill : late C. 19–20. Cf. *do for,* 3.—2. Hence, to denounce to the police : low (— 1914). A. Neil Lyons (quoted by Manchon).—3. To defeat : Australian : C. 20. C. J. Dennis.—4. To spend (recklessly, utterly) : Australian (C. 20 : Dennis) ex English sporting (1886 : Ware).—5. To despatch, dispose of ; to spoil completely ; to cancel ; jocularly, to eat, to drink : from ca. 1920. In *The News Chronicle* of Aug. 30, 1935, there is this advertisement of Gaymer's cider : 'Guy Fawkes, my name is, | Famous for plottin', | And as it's Gaymer's | I'll do the lot in.'—6. To exhaust (a person) : coll. (— 1931). Lyell.

*do it away. To dispose of stolen goods : c. : from ca. 1810. Vaux. Cf. *fence,* **v.**

do it brown. See **brown, do,** 2.

do it fat (or **fine**). To act the fine gentleman : low (— 1923). Manchon.

do it now ! A commercial c.p. (— 1910 ; ob.). Collinson. Ex a business slogan.

do it up. See **do up,** 2.

do it up in good twig. (See **do up,** 2.) To live comfortably by one's wits : low : C. 19–20 ; ob.

do-little sword. A midshipman's dirk, indicative rather of authority than of violence : naval : mid-C. 19–20. Bowen.

do-more. A small raft, made of two logs : Canadian lumbermen's : later C. 19–20. Because a riverman can do more on two logs than on one log : John Beames

do on one's head, with the left hand, while asleep, etc. To do easily : coll. ; from ca. 1880. A

variant is, *do on the b.h.*, i.e. on the, or one's, bloody head.

do one's balls on. (Of a man) to fall utterly in love with : low coll. : late C. 19–20.

*do one's bit. In late C. 19–early 20 c., to serve a sentence. Ware.—2. In G.W., to serve in Army or Navy : ex the late C. 19–20 coll., do one's share, to help a general cause. In the Boer War, a soldier wrote of his fellows, 'They all do " their bit " well ' (J. Milne, *The Epistles of Atkins,* 1902).

do one's block. See **block, lose.**

do one's business. To kill : C. 18–20, low coll. (Fielding, Thackeray, Reade), as is the sense (from ca. 1850), to evacuate, defecate.—3. To have sexual intercourse with a woman (*one's* = her) : low ; from ca. 1860.

do one's dash. See **dash, do one's.—do one's luck.** See **luck.**

do one's money. To lose all one's money : mostly Australian and New Zealand : C. 20.

do one's nut. To lose one's head : lower classes' and military : C. 20. F. & Gibbons.

do one's stuff. To act as one intends ; perform one's social task : an Americanism anglicised along with *know one's stuff* (to be alert, competent) by 1931. E.g. David Esdaile in *The Daily Mirror,* Nov. 18, 1933 ; A. P. Garland, in *The Passing Show,* June 16, 1934, ' The spring sun shone brightly, and larks were doing their stuff overhead.'

do oneself well. See **do well.**

do over. Knock down ; persuade ; cheat, ruin : low coll. ; from ca. 1770. Parker, Dickens.—2. In C. 19 c., to search the pockets of ; c. *frisk.*—3. To seduce ; also, to copulate with : low ; mid-C. 19–20, ob. H., 5th ed.

do Paddy Doyle. See **Paddy Doyle.**

do proud. To flatter, act hospitably or generously towards : coll. ; from ca. 1830.

do reason or **right.** To honour a toast : coll. ; C. 19–20, ob.

do savage rabbits. See **savage rabbits.**

do svidanya ! Au revoir ! ; goodbye ! 1919 : military coll. (expedition in North Russia). F. & Gibbons. Ex Russian.

do the aqua. To put water in one's drink : public-houses' : mid-C. 19–20. Ware. L. *aqua,* water.

do the dirty. See **dirty, do the.**

do the downy. To lie in bed : from ca. 1840. ' Cuthbert Bede ', 1853, ' This'll never do, Gig. lamps ! Cutting chapel to do the downy.' C. *balmy, q.v.*

do the (e.g. **religious**) **dodge** (**over**). ' To pretend to be religious and so seek to obtain some favour ' (from a person) : coll. (— 1931). Lyell.

do the graceful. To behave gracefully or fittingly : non-aristocratic coll. : from ca. 1880. Ware.

do the handsome, occ. **the handsome thing.** To behave extremely well (in kindness, money, etc.) to a person : coll. ; from ca. 1840.

do the High. To walk up and down High Street after church on Sunday evening : Oxford University, ca. 1850–90. H., 5th ed.

do the polite. To exert oneself to be polite ; to be unusually polite : coll. : 1856 (O.E.D.).

*do the swag. To dispose of stolen property : c. : from ca. 1840. Cf. *fence* and *do it away.*

*do the trick. To gain one's object : from ca. 1810 : c. >, by 1830, s. >, by 1860, coll. Vaux.—2. Hence, (of a man) to perform effectually the act of kind ; (of a woman) to be devirginated : both low coll., from ca. 1840.

*do time. To serve a sentence in prison : from ca. 1870 ; c. till C. 20, when s. > coll. H., 5th ed. ; *The Cornhill Magazine*, June, 1884, ' He has repeatedly done time for drunks and disorderlies, and for assaults upon the police.'

do to death. To do frequently and *ad nauseam* : coll. ; C. 18–20.

do to rights. To effect or achieve satisfactorily ; to treat (a person) well : proletarian : mid-C. 19–20. Ware.

do up. To use up, finish ; disable, wear out, exhaust ; ruin financially : coll. : from ca. 1780 ; ob.—2. To accomplish one's object : coll. : C. 18–19.—3. In C. 19–20 (ob.) c., to quieten, gen. in *done up*, silenced.

do-ut-des. Selfish persons : Society : 1883–ca. 1905. Ware. A pun on L. *do ut des*, I give in order that you may give.

do well. To treat, entertain, well : from ca. 1895. Esp. *do oneself well* (in food and comfort). O.E.D. (Sup.).

do while asleep ; do with the left hand. See **do on one's head.**

do with . . ., (I) could. I would very much like to have : coll. (— 1887). Baumann. By meiosis.

do without, able to. To dislike (esp. a person) : late C. 19–20. Ex Yorkshire dial. ' Well, I could do without him, you know.'

do yer feel like that ? A satirical, proletarian c.p. addressed to any person engaged in unusual work or to a lazy one doing any work : late C. 19–20 ; ob. Ware.

do you hear the news ? See **news ?, do you hear the.**

do you know ? An almost expressionless coll. tag : 1883–ca. 1890. It > gen. in 1884 owing to its adoption by Beerbohm Tree in *The Private Secretary*. Ware.

do you sav(v)ey ? Do you know: middle classes' : ca. 1840–90. Ware. Cf. *do you know* and *don't you know.*

do you see any green in my eye ? D'you think I'm a fool ? What do you take me for ? A c.p. : from ca. 1850. Cf. the Fr. *je la connais*, sc. *cette histoire-là.*

do you to wain-rights. An intensification of *do to rights*, q.v. : East London c.p. of ca. 1874–1915. Ex murderer Wainwright. (Ware.)

*doash. In late C. 17–early 19 c., a cloak. B.E., Grose. Etymology ?.

doasta. Adulterated spirit, esp. if fiery, served in sailors' lodging-houses : nautical : late C. 19–20. Bowen. ? ex Hindustani.

dobbin. A sorry horse : coll. ; C. 19–20. Ex the S.E. sense, an ordinary draught horse. (Variant *dobin*).—2. Ribbon : c. and low : mid-C. 18–19. Hence *dobbin-rig*, the stealing of ribbon : late C. 18–20 (ob.) c. Grose, 3rd ed.

dobbs. Pork : military : late C. 19–20. F. & Gibbons. Origin ?

dobee, dobey, or **dobie.** See **dhobi.**

dobra. Good : military : 1919. In North Russia and Murmansk : ex Russian. F. & Gibbons.

doc. A coll. abbr. of *doctor*, in address and narrative : from ca. 1850 ; app., orig. U.S.—2. Hence, any sick-bay rating, esp. in address : naval : C. 20. Bowen.—3. See **doctor, 7.**

*doccy. See **doxy.**

dock. Orig. (1586–1610), as in Warner and

Jonson, prob. c. in its C. 19–20 S.E. sense, an enclosure for prisoners on trial in a law-court. (O.E.D.)—2. Hospital ; chiefly *in dock*. Late C. 18–20 : orig. nautical ; in C. 20, coll. Grose, 1st ed.—3. Among printers, the weekly work-bill or ' pole ' : from ca. 1860 ; ob.

*dock, v. To deflower (a woman) ; hence, to ' have ' a woman : from ca. 1560 ; ob. by 1800, † by 1840. Prob. orig. c. ; certainly always low. Harman, Middleton, B.E., Grose. (Gen. with *the dell*, q.v.) F. & H. proposes Romany *dukker*, to ravish ; but the S.E. *dock*, to curtail, with an implied reference to *tail* (q.v.), is obviously operative. —2. At Winchester College, C. 19–20, ob., to scratch or tear out or, as in R. G. K. Wrench, to rub out ; to knock down.—3. To take from (a person) part of his wages as a fine : dial. (ca. 1820) >, by 1890, coll. O.E.D. (Sup.).

dock, go into. To be treated for a venereal disease : late C. 18–20, ob ; nautical. Grose, 1st ed.

dock, in dry. Out of work : coll. : from ca. 1927. O.E.D. (Sup.).

dock-pheasant. A bloater : nautical : late C. 19–20. Bowen. Cf. *Billingsgate pheasant.*

dock - shankers. ' Dock - mates ' : nautical (— 1823) ; † by 1870. Egan's Grose, where, I surmise, the real meaning is, companions in a venereal hospital.

dock-walloping. Perambulating the docks to look at ships : nautical : late C. 19–20. Bowen.

dock to a daisy, (as like as) a. Very dissimilar : coll. (— 1639) ; † by 1800. Apperson.

docked smack smooth, be. To have had one's penis amputated : nautical : mid-C. 18–19. Grose, 1st ed.

docker. A dock labourer : from ca. 1880 ; coll. till ca. 1895, then S.E.—2. A brief from the prisoner in the dock to counsel : legal ; from ca. 1890.

docket, strike a. To cause a man to become bankrupt : legal and commercial j. > coll. > S.E. : ca. 1805–60.

dockets, play the game of. See **play the game of dockets.**

docking. ' A punishment inflicted by sailors on the prostitutes who have infected them with the venereal disease ; it consists in cutting off all their clothes, petticoat, shift and all, close to their stays, and then turning them out into the street ', Grose : low coll. ; ca. 1700–1850.

docking herself. (Of a ship) taking the mud and forcing a position for herself : nautical coll. : late C. 19–20. Bowen.

dockyard-crawl. The rate of work in the Royal dockyards : naval : late C. 19–20. Bowen. Cf. *Government stroke*, q.v.

dockyard-horse. An officer better at office-work than on active service : naval ; from ca. 1870.—2. (Gen. pl.) A man drawing stores for a (naval) ship : naval : late C. 19–20. Bowen.

dockyarder. A skulker, esp. about the docks : nautical ; from ca. 1860. The U.S. equivalent is *dock-walloper*. Cf. *strawyarder.*

Docs, the. The Duke of Cornwall's Light Infantry : military : C. 20. F. & Gibbons.

*doctor. A false die : Shadwell, 1688, constitutes the earliest record. Until ca. 1740, c. ; then low ; in C. 20 ob., very ob. Fielding, in *Tom Jones*, ' Here, said he, taking some dice out of his pockets, here are the little doctors which cure the distempers of the purse.' Ex a doctor's powers. Hence, late

C. 17–early 19 (as, e.g. in B.E.), *put the doctor(s) upon*, to cheat a person with loaded dice.—2. An adulterant, esp. of spirits (see Grose, 1st ed., 1785), but also of food, e.g. bread : among bakers (says Maton in *Tricks of Bakers Unmasked*), alum is called the doctor. O.E.D. records it at 1770.—3. Brown sherry : licensed victuallers', C. 19–20, ob. : because a doctored wine.—4. Earlier (– 1770), milk and water, with a dash of rum and a sprinkling of nutmeg : † by 1880.—5. The last throw of dice or ninepins : perhaps orig. c. : C. 18–19, mostly among gamesters.—6. The headmaster : Winchester College, from ca. 1830.—7. (Occ. doc.) A ship's cook : nautical, also up-country Australian : recorded by S.O.D. at 1860, but the evidence of H. shows that it must, among Englishmen, have been current some years earlier ; it existed in the U.S. as early as 1821 (Thornton). Ex food as health-ensurer.—8. A variant of *Cape doctor*, q.v. ; always *the doctor* (or *Doctor*) : 1856 (Pettman). But it is recorded for the West Indies as early as 1740 (O.E.D.).—9. A broker dealing specifically with overdue vessels : nautical and commercial s. (late 1890's) >, by 1920, coll. O.E.D. (Sup.).—10. See doctors.—11. Pill No. 9 in the Field Medical Chest : military : from 1914. Because so frequently prescribed.—12. Hence, 9 in the game of House : military : 1915. F. & Gibbons, as is sense 11.—13. A synonym of *punisher*, 3 (q.v.), as also is *gentleman*, 2.

doctor, v. Confer a doctorate upon, make a doctor ('philosophy', not medicine) : from ca. 1590 ; now very rare, yet not quite a ghost-word.—2. To treat; to make a doctor of, or as if of a doctor : from ca. 1730.—3. Hence, to practise as a physician (– 1865).—4. To adulterate ; tamper with ; falsify : from ca. 1770. Now coll.—5. Hence, to repair, patch up ; revise extensively, distort a literary work, a newspaper article : C. 19–20. (Thus far, S.O.D.)—6. To 'dope' (a horse) : sporting : from ca. 1860 ; little used after ca. 1910, *dope* being the fashionable word.—7. 'To undergo medical treatment' : coll. : from ca. 1880. All these senses are coll., though the fourth and the sixth had orig. a tinge of s.—8. 'To prepare the warriors, by certain "medicines" and incantations, for war,' Pettman : South African coll. : from ca. 1890. Ex *witch doctor*.

Doctor Brighton. Brighton : Society coll. (from ca. 1820) >, ca. 1895, gen. coll. Ware. I.e., Dr. Bright 'Un.

Doctor Cotton. Rotten : rhyming s. : C. 20. P. P., *Rhyming Slang*, 1932. Also *Dolly Cotton* and *John Cotton*.

Doctor Doddypoll. See doddypoll.

doctor draw-fart. An itinerant quack : C. 19–20, ob. : low coll.

Doctor Foster. 9 in the game of House : military : C. 20. Dr. Foster occurs in a nursery rhyme ; '9' is connected with pills ('number nine'), hence with medical officers. Cf. *doctor*, n., 12.

doctor (in one's cellars), keep the. Habitually to adulterate the liquor one sells : licensed victuallers', then public-house's : coll. ; from ca. 1860. H., 5th ed.

Doctor Inkpot. John Standish, a C. 16 Archdeacon of Colchester. Dawson. 'Writer of tracts.'

Doctor Jim. A soft felt hat, wide-brimmed : lower classes : 1896–ca. 1914. Ex Dr. Jameson's 'Africander felt' (Ware). Whence *Jimkwim*, *Jimmunt*.

Doctor Johnson. The *membrum virile* : literary :

ca 1790–1880. Perhaps because there was no one that Dr. Johnson was not prepared to stand up to.

doctor on one, put the. To cheat, orig. with false dice and, orig. perhaps, c. : late C. 17–20 ; ob. B.E.

doctor ordered, just what the. See just what.

doctored, ppl. adj. Adulterated ; patched-up (fig.) ; falsified : C. 18–20, coll. See doctor, v., 4.

*doctors. Counterfeit coin : c. (– 1923). Manchon. Prob. ex *doctor*, n., 1.

doctor's curse, gen. preceded by the. A dose of calomel (– 1821) : coll. ; ob. O.E.D.

doctor's shop. The number 9 (cf. *number nine*, q.v.) in the game of House : military : C. 20. F. & Gibbons. See doctor, n., 12.

doctor's stuff, occ. (C. 19–20) doctor-stuff. Medicine : coll. : from ca. 1770. 'He could not take Doctor's stuff, if he died for it.' (O.E.D.)

doctors upon, put the. See doctor, n., 1.

dod. A low coll. (†) and dial. interjection : from ca. 1670. Orig. a deformation of *God*. (S.O.D.)

dodder. 'Burnt tobacco taken from the bottom of a pipe and placed on the top of a fresh plug to give a stronger flavour,' F. & H. : mid-C. 19–20, Irish. Cf. S.E. *dottle*.

dodderer. A meddler ; a fool. (In S.E., a tottering, pottering old man.) C. 19–20, ob. ; mostly Cockney. Variant, *doddering old sheep's head*.

doddies. A selfish person : proletarian : ca. 1890–1915. Ware. A corruption of *do ut des* (man), q.v.

doddipool. See doddypoll.

doddle. Money very easily obtained : Glasgow (– 1934). Cf. *klondyke*.

doddy, or hoddy-doddy ('all head and no body'). A simpleton, an idiot : mostly Norfolk and orig. and mainly dial. : C. 19–20.

doddypoll. A M.E. and C. 15–18 nickname for a doll, a fool ; extant in dial. In late C. 16–mid-17, occ. *Doctor Doddypoll*. Apperson. Ex *dod*, to lop, poll, clip, and *poll*, the head. Cf. preceding.

dodge. A shrewd and artful expedient, an ingenious contrivance : from ca. 1830 ; coll. in C. 20. Dickens in *Pickwick* : '"It was all false, of course ?" "All, sir," replied Mr. Weller, "reg'lar do, sir ; artful dodge."' (Ex the corresponding v., which, like its derivative, *dodger*, is S.E., though the latter has a slightly coll. tinge.)

dodge, on the. Engaged in something dishonest : coll. : C. 20. O.E.D. (Sup.)

dodge Pompey. To steal grass : Australian : from ca. 1920. *Pompey* personifies the Law. Ex :—2. To avoid work on shipboard : naval (pre-G.W.) >, by 1918 at latest, gen. nautical. Bowen.

dodge the column. To shirk one's duty : military : 1899 (Boer War). See esp. B. & P.—2. Whence, (*column-*)*dodger* : military : 1914.

Dodger. Whysall (d. ca. 1930), the all-England cricketer.

dodger. See dodge.—2. A dram, a 'go' of liquor : from ca. 1850. H., 1st ed.—3. A shirker, malingerer : military : late C. 19–20. B. & P. —4. In C. 20 c., a half-sovereign ; ob. Ex its elusiveness.—5. A mess-deck sweeper : naval : late C. 19–20. Bowen. He thus avoids other duties.—6. A very frequent nickname of men surnamed Green : military : C. 20.—7. A good-conduct badge : military : C. 20. Ironic : cf. *canteen medal*, q.v. F. & Gibbons.—8. A sandwich : military (– 1914), because the meat therein dodges the consumer ? (Ibid.)—9. A clergyman, a priest : c. and low : mid-C. 19–20. Mayhew, *London Labour*, vol. IV, 1861. Abbr. *devil-dodger*, q.v.

dodgy. Artful : (low) coll. (— 1887) ; slightly ob. Baumann. See **dodge.**

dodipol. See **doddypoll.**

dodo. A stupid old man : Society : late C. 19–20 (ob.) ; coll. Ex the extinct bird. Cf. :—2. Scotland Yard : journalists' : 1885–ca. 1890. Ware.

*dodsey. A woman : c. : late C. 18–early 19. Grose, 2nd ed. Prob. a corruption of *doxy*.

doee. See **dooee.**

doer. One who cheats another : from ca. 1840 ; ob. O.E.D.—2. A ' character ' ; an eccentric or very humorous fellow : Australian ; from ca. 1905.

does, fair. See **fair doo's.**

does it ? A sarcastically intonated coll. retort : from ca. 1870 ; ob.

does your mother know you're out ? A c.p. of sarcastic or jocular implication : from 1838, says Benham in his *Book of Quotations*. *Punch*, 1841 ; *The Sun*, Dec. 28, 1864. F. & H., s.v., gives a very interesting list of such sapient phrases : all of which will be found in these pages.

does your mother want a rabbit ? A c.p. of the 1890's and pre-War C. 20 : non-aristocratic. B. & P. Ex the question of itinerant rabbit-vendors.

doesn't (or don't) give much away. Yield(s) few —or no—advantages ; very keen : coll. : from ca. 1880. Ware.

doey. See **dooey.**

[**dog,** when used of a person whether contemptuously or playfully, is considered by F. & H. to be coll., by the S.O.D. to be S.E. : the latter is, I think, in the right.]

dog. Abbr. *dog-watch* : nautical : from ca. 1890. —2. In the West Indies, a copper or a small silver coin, with variant *black dog* : (— 1797) nautical. (O.E.D.)—3. God : in coll. oaths : C. 16. O.E.D. —4. See **dog, put on.**—5. See **dogs.**—6. Soap : Bootham School : C. 20. Anon., *Dict. of Bootham Slang*, 1925.—7. A cigarette-end : c. : C. 20. M. Harrison, *Spring in Tartarus*, 1935.—8. A beggar-searcher for cigarette-ends : c. : C. 20. Michael Harrison, *Weep for Lycidas*, 1934.

dog. To post (a student) for examination on the last day : Oxford University (— 1726) ; † by 1800. Amherst. O.E.D.—2. V.i. To have sexual connexion on all fours, i.e. like a dog : C. 19–20 low.

dog, an easy thing to find a stick to beat a. ' It costs little to trouble those that cannot help themselves,' B.E. : mid-C. 17–18 coll.

dog, blush like a blue. See **blush.**—**dog, cash a.** See **cash a dog.**

dog,—fight bear, fight. To fight till one party is overcome : C. 16–20 coll. ; ob. Aphra Behn, Scott.

dog, he (she) worries the. A c.p. directed at a visitor whose approach repels even the house-dog : lower-middle classes' (— 1909) ; ob. Ware.

dog, put on ; occ. **carry dog.** To put on ' side ' : coll. : from ca. 1914. (O.E.D. Sup.) Cf. *doggy*, adj., 1.

dog, try it on the. See **try it on the dog.**

dog along. To fare tolerably, passably : Canadian coll. : C. 20. John Beames.

dog a swim. See **swim, give one's dog a.**

dog and bonnet. The lion-and-crown badge of the King's Own Scottish Borderers : military : C. 20. F. & Gibbons.

dog and cat, agree like. See **cat and dog.**

dog and maggot. Biscuits and cheese : Regular Army's : C. 20. B. & P.

dog at it, (an) old. Expert ; habituated : coll. ; C. 16–19. Nashe. The mod. form is *an old dog for a hard road*.

dog away one's time. To idle it away : Cockney (— 1887) ; slightly ob. Baumann.

dog-basket. ' The receptacle in which the remains of the cabin meals were taken—or smuggled—forward ' in sailing ships : nautical : C. 19. Bowen.

dog before its master, the. A heavy swell preceding a gale : nautical c.p. : late C. 19–20. Ibid.

dog-biscuit. An Army mattress : military : late C. 19–20 ; ob. F. & Gibbons. Ex colour and shape. Also *biscuit*.

dog bite my ear ! See **bite me !**

dog biting dog. Applied to one actor's adversely criticising another's performance : late C. 19–20 theatrical.

dog-bolt. A coll. term of contempt : mean wretch. C. 15–17, later use being archaic. (S.O.D.)

dog booby. An awkward lout ; a clodhopper : late C. 18–early 19 military. Grose, 1st ed.

*dog-buffer. A dog-stealer that kills all dogs not advertised for, sells the skins, and feeds the other dogs with the carcases : c. : late C. 18–19. Grose, 2nd ed.

dog-cheap. Exceedingly cheap : coll. (C. 16–20), F. & H. ; S.E., S.O.D. : prob. the latter.

dog-collar. A ' stand-up ' stiff collar, esp. a clergyman's reversed collar : from late 1860's ; slightly ob. Grenville Murray, ' The dog-collar was of spotless purity.' Whence :

dog-collar brigade, the. The Clergy : Glasgow : C. 20.

dog-drawn. Said (low coll.) of a woman from whom a man has, in the act, been forcibly removed : C. 19–20 ; ob.

*dog-end. A cigarette-end : vagrants' c. : from ca. 1920. James Curtis, *The Gilt Kid*, 1936.

*dog-fancier. A receiver of stolen dogs and restorer of the same to their owners—for a fee : c. (— 1861). Mayhew.

dog-fat. Butter : military : C. 20. B. & P.

dog-fight. An Air Force coll. (1915) >, by 1930, S.E., as defined, implicatively, by P. C. Wren, in *The Passing Show*, Aug. 18, 1934, ' But best sport of all was a dog-fight, an all-on-to-all scrap between a flight of British Bristol Scouts and a bigger flight of Fokkers, everybody shooting-up everybody, a wild and whirling mêlée from which every now and then someone went hurtling down to death in a blaze of smoke and fire.'

dog-gone, dog gone. Coll. euphemism for and ' fantastic perversion of *God-damned* ' (W.) : U.S. ; anglicised ca. 1860. H., 3rd ed.—2. Devoted : lower classes' (— 1909) ; ob. Ware.

dog-hole. A mean or a disgusting dwelling-place : coll. : from ca. 1570 ; ob.

dog in a blanket. A roly-poly pudding : coll. : mostly nautical : from ca. 1850. Sala.

dog in a doublet. ' A daring, resolute fellow ', Grose, 3rd ed. C. 16–early 19 coll. Ex German hunting-dogs, protected, in a boar-chase, with a leather doublet.

dog in a doublet, a (mere). ' A mean pitiful creature ', Northall : coll. (1577) ; now dial. Cf. :

dog in a doublet, proud as a. Exceedingly proud : coll. : late C. 16–17. Apperson.

dog in shoes, like a. Making a pattering sound: Anglo-Irish coll., C. 19–20.

[**dog in the manger, like a,** may orig. have been coll.: C. 16–20.]

dog is dead ?, whose. Variant, *what dog is a-hanging ?* What is the matter ? C. 17–20 coll.; ob. Massinger, 'Whose dog's dead now|That you observe these vigils ?' (O.E.D.)

Dog Lane. Friargate, York : Bootham School nickname : late C. 19–20. Anon., *Dict. of Bootham Slang,* 1925.

dog-Latin. Bad Latin ; sham Latin. Cf. *apothecaries'* or *bog* or *garden* or *kitchen Latin* : from ca. 1600 ; coll. >, by 1820, S.E.

dog laugh, enough to make a. Extremely funny : coll. : C. 17–early 19. Pepys ; Wolcot. (Apperson.) Cf. *cat laugh, enough to make a.*

dog-leech. A quack : C. 16–18 coll. (In S.E., a veterinary surgeon.)

dog-nap. A short sleep enjoyed sitting : coll. ; from ca. 1850. Cf. *cat-nap.* The variant *dog-sleep* is S.E.

dog-nose. See **dog's nose.**

***dog on anyone, walk the black.** A punishment inflicted on a prisoner by his fellows if he refuses to pay his footing : c. : late C. 18–mid-19. Grose.

dog on it ! An expletive affected, ca. 1860–90, by boys. Perhaps euphemistic for *God damn it !*

dog out in, not fit to turn a. (Of weather) abominable : coll. (— 1887). Baumann.

dog-shooter. A volunteer : C. 19 military then gen.—2. At the Royal Military Academy (— 1889), a cadet who, unable or unwilling to become an engineer, joins a class in another branch. Ob.

dog-stealer. A dog-dealer : jocular coll.(— 1854). Whyte-Melville.

dog that bit you, a hair of the. A drink taken to counteract drunkenness ; a drink the same as another's the night before : coll. (— 1546).

dog-throw. The lowest throw at dice (cf. *deuce*) : coll. (— 1830), verging on S.E. (O.E.D.)

dog to hold, give one the. To serve a person a mean trick : coll (— 1678) ; † by 1800. Ray, 1678. Cf. *holding the baby.* (Apperson.) Cf. :

dog-trick. A mean or 'dirty' action, trick : C. 16–19 coll. B.E.

dog-vane. A cockade : nautical : from ca. 1785 ; ob. Grose, 2nd ed.; songster Dibdin. Ex the S.E. sense.

dogged. Adv., very, excessively : mainly sporting (— 1819), prob. ex dial., where only is it extant. Perhaps the orig. of the U.S. *dog-gone.*

dogged as does it !, it's. Perseverance and pluck win in the end : a coll. c.p. dating from the mid-1860's.

dogger. A professional hunter of dingoes : Australian coll. : C. 20. The dingo is often described as a wild dog.—2. A dog : by 'the Oxford-*er* ' : from ca. 1910. (H. A. Vachell, *Martha Penny,* 1934.)

dogger, v. To cheat ; sell rubbish : Charterhouse ; from ca. 1860.

doggery. Manifest cheating : coll. : from ca. 1840 ; ob. Cf. S.E. *dog's trick.*

doggers. See **dog's lady.**

doggie, doggy. A pet name (coll.) for a dog : from ca. 1800.—2. In coal-mining, a middleman's underground manager (— 1845). Disraeli in *Sybil.* —3. (Esp. a cavalry) officer's servant : military : mid-C. 19–20 ; ob. Ware.—4. 'All round upright collar ' : London youths' (— 1909) ; ob. Ware.

Cf. *dog-collar.*—5. An officer assisting an admiral at his work ; 'a midshipman regularly attending a captain or flag officer ' : naval : from ca. 1910. Ex faithfulness to duty. O.E.D. (Sup.) ; Bowen.

doggo, lie. To make no move(ment) and say nothing ; to bide one's time : C. 19–20. Prob., 'like a cunning dog ' (W.). The *-o* suffix is common in s.

doggy, adj. Stylish ; smart, whether of appearance or of action : from ca. 1885. Ex a *sad dog, a bit of a dog.* Now, 'just a little too gay and dashing,' Denis Mackail, 1934.—2. N. : see **doggie.**— 3. (Of Latin) debased : coll. : 1898 (O.E.D. Sup.). Ex *dog Latin.*

dogs. (Always pl.) Sausages : low : from ca. 1860. Ex reputed origin. Cf. *bags of mystery.*— 2. Newfoundland Land Company's shares : ca. 1870–90 ; Stock Exchange.—3. **the dogs,** a greyhound race-meeting : coll. : 1929. (The Dog-Racing Bill is of 1928.) O.E.D. (Sup.).

dogs, go to the. To go to ruin ; to lead an extremely dissipated and foolish life. C. 16–20 ; coll. till ca. 1680, then S.E.

dogs, rain cats and. See **cats.**

dog's body. Pease pudding : nautical (— 1851). Clark Russell.—2. Any junior officer, R.N. ; esp. a midshipman ; hence, pejoratively, of any male : naval (>, by 1920, gen.) : late C. 19–20 ; F. & H. ; F. & Gibbons.

dog's bottom. A facetious term of address : from ca. 1930.

dog's breakfast. A mess : low Glasgow (— 1934).

dog's dinner, like a. Stylishly : low coll. : C. 20. James Curtis, *The Gilt Kid,* 1936, 'The geezer that was with her was dolled up like a dog's dinner with a white tie and all.'

dog's dram. A spit into his mouth and a smack on his back : mid-C. 18–early 19 low. Grose, 1st ed.

dog's face. A coll. term of abuse : coll. > S.E. ; from ca. 1670 ; ob.

dogs have not dined, the. A c.p. to one whose shirt hangs out at the back : mid-C. 18–early 19. Grose, 1st ed. (See *Slang,* p. 274.)

dog's hind leg, crooked as a. Very crooked (lit. only) : coll. : late C. 19–20. Apperson.

dog's lady or wife ; doggess ; puppy's mamma. 'Jocular ways of calling a woman a bitch,' Grose, 3rd ed. : coll. : late C. 18–mid-19.

dog's leg(s). The chevron(s), 'designating non-commissioned rank, worn on the arm, and not unlike in outline to the canine hindleg,' Ware : military : late C. 19–20.

dog's lug. A small bight in a sail's leech-rope : nautical : from ca. 1880. A characteristic variant on *dog's ear,* nautical j.

dog's match of it, make a. To do the act of kind by the wayside : low coll. : C. 19–20 ; cf. *to dog.*

dog's meat. 'Anything worthless ; as a bad book, a common tale, a villainous picture, etc.', F. & H. Coll. : from ca. 1820. Ex lit. sense.

dog's nose. Gin and beer mixed : low (— 1812) ; ob. Vaux. Occ. *dognose* ('Ducange Anglicus' ; Baumann).

dogs of war on (so-and-so) ! A gun-room or a ward-room c.p. = eject him (if possible) : naval : C. 20. Bowen.

dog's paste. Sausage—or mince-meat : low coll. : from ca. 1850. Cf. *dogs.*

dog's portion. A lick and a smell, i.e. almost nothing : late C. 18–20 (ob.) coll. In late C. 18–19 occ. applied to a distant admirer of women. Grose, 2nd ed. Cf. *dog's soup*.

dog's rig. Sexual intercourse, to exhaustion, followed by back-to-back indifference : mid-C. 18–19 : low. Grose, 2nd ed. Cf. *dog's match*.

dog's soup. Water : mid-C. 18–20 (ob.) coll. Grose, 1st ed. Cf. *fish-broth*.

Dog's Tail. The constellation of the Little Bear : nautical : from ca. 1860.

dog's vomit. Meat and biscuits cooked together as a moist hash : nautical : late C. 19–20. Bowen.

dog's wife. See **dog's lady**.

dogun or **D-.** A Roman Catholic : Canadian : late C. 19–20. Possibly ex that very Irish surname, *Duggan*.

doing. A thrashing ; a severe monetary loss : lower classes' coll. (– 1909). Ware. Ex dial. *doing*, a scolding : which in C. 20 is coll.

doing !, nothing. ' Certainly not ! ' in retort to a dubious or unattractive offer or an amorous invitation : from late 1890's. In 1927, a schoolgirl, writing on Queen Elizabeth, said, ' Philip of Spain asked her hand in marriage, but she replied : " Nothing doing ! " ' Ex *there's nothing doing*, no business being done.

Doin' It. Doingt, near Péronne : military : G.W. (F. & Gibbons.)

doings, in the. In the guard-room : military : from ca. 1914. F. & Gibbons. Ex :

doings, the. The thing (*any* thing) ; esp. what is at the moment needed or otherwise relevant : from ca. 1912. Perhaps ex the U.S. usage, the materials for a meal (1838) : Thornton. See esp. F. & Gibbons and B. & P. Cf. *gadget, ooja-ka-piv*.

dol. A dollar : lower classes' (– 1909). Ware.

doldrum. A dullard : a drowsy or a sluggish fellow (– 1812). O.E.D. Ex :

doldrums. Low spirits ; dullness : from ca. 1805 ; coll. till ca. 1890, then S.E. James Payn, 1883, ' Serious thoughts . . . which she stigmatised . . . as the doldrums.' Ex *dull* on *tantrum* : W.

dole. A trick, a stratagem : Winchester College : from ca. 1830. A development (though prob. straight from L. *dolus*) of the † S.E. sense, guile, fraud.

dole, go on the. To receive unemployment benefit : s. (ca. 1925) >, by 1930, coll.

dolefuls. Low spirits : coll. ; from ca. 1820. Miss Braddon. Cf. *dismals*.

dolifier. One who contrives a trick : Winchester College ; ex *dole*, q.v.

doll. A lady : Cockneys' (– 1864) ; † by 1900. Mayhew, ' If it's a lady and gentleman then we cries, " A toff and a doll ! " ' (O.E.D.) Because well dressed.

doll, Bartholomew. See **Bartholomew**.

*doll, mill. To beat hemp in prison : c. : mid-C. 18–early 19. Grose, 1st ed.

doll up, v.i. and reflexive. To dress oneself very smartly : mostly Australian : C. 20. Whence *dolled-up*, dressed ' to death '.

dollar. A five-shilling piece ; five shillings : C. 19–20 coll. ex U.S. ex C. 16–17 S.E. Hence *half-dollar* or *half a dollar*, half a crown.

dollar, holy. See **holy dollar**.—***dollar groin.** See **groin**.

dollars to buttons, it's. It is a sure bet : coll. : American >, before 1909, English. Ware.

dollars to doughnuts. Long odds : low coll. : from ca. 1920. James Curtis, *The Gilt Kid*, 1936.

dollop. A lot ; *the whole dollop*, the whole lot, esp. sum (– 1812) : coll ; †. Vaux.—2. A lump, esp. if ' formless ' or clumsy : low coll., or perhaps a vulgarism, ex dial. (– 1812). S.O.D. W. compares Norwegian *dolp*, a lump.

dolloping. The selling of goods at a ridiculously low price : cheapjacks' (– 1876). C. Hindley.

dollops of. ' Heaps ' of ; ' lots ' of : coll. (– 1923). Manchon.

dolly. A mistress : C. 17–early 19.—2. Also (– 1843), ' any one who has made a *faux pas* ', *Punch*, 1843. Cf. the C. 17 S.E. *doll-common*, a harlot ; in C. 17–early 18 coll., surviving as dial., *dolly* also bore this sense, plus that of a slattern.—3. A pet, i.e. a coll., name for a child's doll : from late C. 18.—4. A piece of cloth serving as a sponge : tailors', from ca. 1850.—5. A binding of rag on finger or toe : coll. and dial. (– 1888). O.E.D.—6. The *membrum virile* : low : C. 19–20, ob.—7. A ' donkey-drop ' (q.v.) : cricketers' (1906), as is 8, the sense (1926), a slow, easy catch. Lewis.—9. The inevitable nickname (*Dolly*) of all men surnamed *Gray* or *Grey* : C. 20. Ex the famous song, *Dolly Gray*.—10. See *Moving-Picture Slang*, § 4. (Also **Dolly**.) All ex *doll*, which in S.E. has a corresponding term for the first four.

*dolly. Perhaps only in *dolly pals*, dear friends or companions : c. : C. 19. Possibly a perversion of *dear* suggested by *dolly*, n., 1.—2. Adj., silly : foolish : from ca. 1850 ; ob. Dickens, ' You wouldn't make such a dolly speech,' where, however, the term may = babyish.

dolly-catch. The original (1895) of *dolly*, n., 8. E.D.D.

Dolly Cotton ; John Cotton. Rotten : rhyming s. : from ca. 1890. *Everyman*, March 26, 1931.

dolly-man, pitchy-man. A Jew : Anglo-Irish, esp. in the West : late C. 19–20. Prob., *dolly-man* derives ex *dolly-shop*, *pitchy-man* ex a huckster's *pitch*.

dolly-mop. A harlot : coll. (– 1833). Marryat. But in Cockney (– 1855, †), an ' amateur ' prostitute. Mayhew.—2. Also, a badly dressed maid-servant : ca. 1858–1905. H., 1860.

dolly-mopper. A womaniser, esp. if a soldier : military (– 1887) ; ob. Baumann. Ex preceding term, 1.

*dolly-shop. An illegal rag-and-bone shop or pawn-shop : from ca. 1840 : c. > low coll. Mayhew ; ' No. 747 ' (reference to 1845).—2. A fence's, i.e. a receiver's parlour : c. ; late C. 19–20.

dolly-worship. The Roman Catholic religion : Nonconformists' (– 1909). ' From the use of statues, etc.', Ware.

Dollymop. See **dolly-mop**, 1.

[**dolt-head ; doltish.** B.E. errs greatly in classifying these S.E. terms as c.]

–dom. Some of the C. 20 jocularities, e.g. Galsworthy's *devil-may-caredom*, verge on the coll. W.

dome. The head : coll. ; ' common ', says F. & H. in 1891. Its C. 20 use is gen. regarded as U.S. (Not in Thornton.)

dome-stick. A servant : sol., or, when deliberate, jocular coll., †. (– 1891.) Obviously suggested by the C. 17–18 spelling of *domestic*. Cf. *dram a-tick*.

doment. A variant of *do*, n., 3 : dial and (†) low coll. : from 1820's. O.E.D.

*domerar. See **dommerar**.

domestic afflictions. The menstrual period : coll. : from ca. 1850.

domin(i)e-do-little. An impotent old man : mid-C. 18–early 19 coll. Grose, 2nd ed.

Dominion, the. Canada : C. 20 ; coll. ? abbr. *dominion par excellence.*

domino. A knock-out blow : also as v. ; from ca. 1870. H., 5th ed. Cf. *domino with* (q.v.) Ex : —2. As an exclamation, it expresses completion— of a punishment in the Victorian Army and Navy (1864, H., 3rd ed.) ; among 'bus-conductors to signify 'full up' (— 1882) ; ob. All these senses are coll. ex the game of dominoes.—3. See **dominoes.**

domino-box. The mouth : from ca. 1820 ; orig. low, in C. 20 inelegant and ob. Bee, 1823. Contrast *box of dominoes* (see under).

domino-thumper. A pianist : from ca. 1880 ; ob. Barrière & Leland.

domino with, it is (or **it's**). It's the end of ; there is no hope for : C. 20. Ex dial. (1854) : ' " Domino," which the winner of a game of dominoes calls as he plays his last piece,' E.D.D.

dominoes. (Never singular.) The teeth, esp. if discoloured (contrast *ivories*) : from ca. 1820. Cf. *domino,* q.v.—2. The keys of a piano : from ca. 1880 ; ob. Hence :

dominoes, box of. A piano : from ca. 1880. See preceding.

dominoes, sluice one's. To drink : low (— 1823). Moncrieff in *Tom and Jerry,* Act II, scene 6. Cf. *dominoes,* 1, and *domino-box,* qq.v.

*dom(m)erar or **-er ; dummerer.** A beggar pretending to be deaf and *dumb* : mid- C. 16–18. Harman.—2. Also, ca. 1670–1750, a madman. Coles, 1676. Both are c.

Don. See **Ack.**

don. An adept, a 'swell' or 'toff' ; a pretentious person : coll. ; from ca. 1820. In C. 17–18 S.E. a distinguished person. Ex the Spanish dons as is 2, the English university coll. use, a fellow of a college : from ca. 1660 ; orig. pejorative. (O.E.D.) —3. (Gen. pl., and always **D.**) A Spaniard ; a Portuguese : nautical : C. 19–20. Bowen, 'A more polite term than *Dagoes* but not applied to other Latins.'

don, adj. Expert, clever ; excellent : from ca. 1860 ; ob. H., 2nd ed. Ex the preceding.

Don Caesar spouting. 'Haughty public elocution' : Society : ca. 1850–1900. Ware.

Don Peninsula. The world, the 'geographical' range, of the dons : Oxford University, ca. 1820–40. Egan's Grose.

don rags. A synonym of *collekkers,* q.v. : Oxford undergraduates' : C. 20.

dona, donah (mostly in sense 2), **donna, doner,** rarely **donnay.** A woman ; esp. the lady of the house : from the 1850's : Cockney and Parlyaree. H., 1st ed. Ex It. or Sp. via Lingua Franca.—2. Hence, in Australia, from ca. 1890 : a girl ; a sweetheart. 'Never introduce your dona(h) to a pal' has long been an Australian c.p.

dona Highland-flinger. A music-hall singer : rhyming s. (— 1909). Ware.

dona Jack. A harlot's bully : lower classes' (— 1909). Ware.

*donaker. A cattle-stealer : C. 17–early 18 ; c.

Donald. A glass of spirituous liquor, esp. whiskey : Scottish : 1869, Johnston, *Poems* (E.D.D.).

Doncaster-cut. A horse : coll (— 1529) ; † by 1600. Skelton. (Apperson.) Doncaster famous for horses.

donderkop. In address, blockhead : South African coll. (— 1897). Lit., dunderhead. Pettman.

done. See **do,** v.—2. Did : sol. : C. 19–20.

done brown. See **brown, done.**

*done, have one's drum. To have one's house searched by detectives : c. : C. 20. See **drum,** n., 2.

done, it isn't. It is bad form : coll. : from late 1870's. (O.E.D. Sup.). An upper-class counter, this. Hence, in C. 20, *the done* (correct) *thing.*

done-for. Exhausted ; cheated ; ruined ; in c., robbed, convicted to prison, or hanged : (—)1859 : see **do for.** The c. *done for a ramp* = convicted for stealing (H., 1st ed.).

done-over. Intoxicated : C. 19–20.—2. Possessed carnally (only of women) : C. 18–20 ; ob.—3. In c., same as *done* : see **do-over.**

done to death. See **death, done to.**

done to the wide ; done to the world. Utterly exhausted, defeated, or baffled ; ruined : from ca. 1908 : s. now verging on coll.

done-up. 'Used up, finished, or quieted' : coll. (— 1859). H., 1st ed.—2. 'Ruined by gaming, and extravagances,' Grose, 1st ed. (' *modern term* ', he adds) : ca. 1780–1860.

doner. See **dona.** And :

doner. One who is done for, ruined, fated to die : lower classes' : C. 20. Ernest Raymond, *The Jesting Army,* 1930.

dong. To strike ; to punch : New Zealanders' and Australians' : C. 20. Perhaps ex the *dong* emitted by a bell when struck ; perhaps a blend of *ding + dot.*

donk. A donkey : mostly Australian : C. 20.

donkey. A compositor (cf. *pig*) : printers' (— 1857). Variant *moke.*—2. A sailor's clothes-chest : nautical : from ca. 1860.—3. A blockhead, a fool : coll., from ca. 1840.—4. Even for an ass, *donkey* was orig.—ca. 1780—coll. and remained so for some fifty years.' Cf. *donkey dick,* q.v. Perhaps ex *Duncan* or *Dominic* : W.

donkey !, a penny (or **twopence or threepence**) **more and up goes the.** A (low) London c.p. expressing derision (— 1841) : coll. : ex a street acrobat's stock finish to a turn ; ob.

*donkey, ride the. To cheat with weights and measures : c. : C. 19. 'Ducange Anglicus.' Vbl.n., *donkey-riding.*

donkey, ride the black. See **ride . . .**

donkey, talk the hindleg off a. See **talk . . .**

donkey, whack one's own. To be occupied, or preoccupied, with one's own affairs : lower classes' coll. (— 1923). Manchon.

donkey ?, who stole the. Sometimes another person added, *the man in* or *with the white hat* : this latter represented also the occasion : ca. 1835–70. Ex an actual incident.

donkey dick. An ass : ca. 1780–1820. A variant of *donkey,* which is prob. ex *Duncan.* Grose, 1st ed. From early C. 19, *dick(y)* came to be used by itself.

donkey-drops. In cricket, from ca. 1887, slow round-arm bowling. A. G. Steel, 1888 ; the Hon. E. Lyttelton, in his *Cricket,* 1890. (Lewis.) Also *dolly* (see n., 7).

donkey-frigate. A 28-gun ship (between a frigate and a sloop) : naval : C. 19. Bowen.

donkey has of Sunday, have as much idea (of it) as a. To be wholly ignorant : Cockney (— 1887) ; ob. Baumann.

donkey in one's throat, have a. To have phlegm there : Cockney (— 1887) ; slightly ob. Baumann.

donkey's breakfast. (Orig. a man's) straw hat : Cockneys' : 1893 ; slightly ob. Ware.—2. A bundle of straw for a bed : nautical (— 1901). O.E.D. (Sup.).—3. Hence, a straw mattress : nautical : C. 20. Bowen.

donkey's ears. A shirt-collar with long points, already old-fashioned in 1891 : s. or coll. : ca. 1870–1900.—2. A variant, dating from just before G.W., of :

donkey's years. A long time : suggested by the sound of *donkey's ears*, when illiterately pronounced *donkey's yeers*, and the length of a donkey's ears : from ca. 1900.

donna and **donnay.** See **dona(h).**—**donneken.** See **dunnaken.** (Bee's spelling.)

donovan. (Gen. in pl.) A potato : Anglo-Irish : from ca. 1860. Cf. *murphy*. Ex the commonness of the surname.

don's or **dons' week.** The week before a general holiday ; esp. a week out of work before it : tailors' : from ca. 1860 ; ob.

Dons, the. The Wimbledon ' soccer' team : sporting : from ca. 1920.

don't. Do not : coll. : from ca. 1660.—2. As n., a reiteration of *don't*, a prohibition : from ca. 1890 : coll.—3. Also, done it : coll. : early C. 18. Swift. See *Slang*, p. 66.—4. And : does not : from ca. 1720, but sol. only since ca. 1840.

don't bother me now, (for) my hands are wet ! A military c.p. of the G.W. Ex the weary impatience of harassed mothers. (B. & P.)

don't bully the troops ! A military c.p. (C. 20) to an excessive or noisy talker. B. & P.

don't care a Pall Mall, (I). (I) don't care a damn : clubmen's : 1885–ca. 1890. Ware. Ex *The Pall Mall Gazette's* articles entitled ' The Maiden Tribute ' in July, 1885.—*Pall Mall*, a ' gal ' or girl.

don't dynamite ! Don't be angry ! : non-aristocratic c.p. of 1883–ca. 1900. Ware, ' Result of the Irish pranks in Great Britain with this explosive.'

don't fear ! See **don't (you) fear !**

don't know who's which from when's what, (I). (I, etc.) don't know anything about it : lower classes' c.p. : 1897–ca. 1905. Ware.

don't let me catch you bending ! See **catch bending.** (Collinson.)

don't look down, you'd soon find the hole if there was hair round it ! A drill-sergeant's c.p., on the fixing of bayonets : late C. 19–20. B. & P. Cf. *you're slower* . . .

don't lose your hair ! ' Keep your hair on ! ' : non-aristocratic : from ca. 1860 ; ob. Ware.

don't make a Judy Fitzsim(m)ons of yourself. See **Judy Fitzsim(m)ons.**

don't make me laugh (—I've cut my lip) ! A c.p. of C. 20. Collinson. The latter part is very ob.

don't mention that. A c.p. : ca. 1882–84, as the result of a libel case (Ware). Ex *don't mention it !*, q.v. at *mention*.

don't mind me ! Proceed : c.p., gen. ironic : C. 20. I.e. ' Go ahead—don't mind *me* ! '

don't-name-'ems. Trousers : jocular coll. ; from ca. 1850 ; † by 1930. Cf. *innominables*.

don't seem to. Be incapable of ; as in ' I don't seem to see it ' : coll. (— 1909). Ware.

don't sell me a dog ! Don't deceive me ! : Society : ca. 1860–80. Ware.

don't think !, I. I do think so ! : middle and lower classes' : from ca. 1880. Cf. *not half !*

don't turn that side to London ! A c.p. of con-

demnation : non-aristocratic (— 1909). Ware, ' From the supposition that everything of the best is required in the metropolis.'

don't (you) fear ! Take my word for it ! ; certainly not ! : coll. : mid-C. 19–20. Baumann. Cf. *never fear !* (q.v. at *fear, never*).

don't you forget it ! See **and don't you forget it !**

don't you know. As you well know ; please understand ! : coll. (— 1887) Baumann, ' Sehr gebräuchlicher Zusatz ' (a very frequent tag). In C. 20, almost meaningless except as a vague palliative. Cf. *do you know*, q.v., to which it may orig. have been an offset.

don't you wish you may get it ? A c.p. of ca. 1830–50 = I don't like your chance ! or I don't think ! Barham ; *Punch*, 1841, 1844.

doo-da or **dooda(h), all of a.** Excited : from late 1914. Ex the echoic refrain *doo-da, doo-da, doo-da day*, prob. on *all of a dither*.

doo flicker. ' Any mechanical tool, instrument, or gadget ' : Canadian military : 1915. B. & P. Cf. :

doo-hickey. ' An airman's term for any small, detachable fitting ' : 1915 ; slightly ob. F. & Gibbons. Of fanciful origin.

doocid. An affected, also a Cockney, variation of *deuced*. Manchon. As :

dood is of **dude.** Ibid.

doodle. A noodle : coll. ; from ca. 1620. Ford ; Grose ; Cobden, 1845, ' The Noodles and Doodles of the aristocracy.'—2. (Gen. of a child) the penis : mid-C. 18–20. Grose, 1st ed.

doodle, v. To make a fool of ; cheat : from ca. 1820. Moncrieff, ' I have been . . . doodled out of forty pounds to-day.' In C. 20, rare except in dial.

doodle-bug. A small, cheap car : motorists' (— 1935).

doodle-dasher. A man indulging in self-abuse : C. 19–20 low ; ob.

doodle-doo, gen. preceded by cock a. A child's or a childish name for a cock : C. 17–20 coll. Grose.

doodle-doo man. A cock-breeder or -fighter : C. 18–19 ; cockpit s.

doodle-sack. The *pudendum muliebre* : mid-C. 18–20 ; ob. Grose, 2nd ed. In S.E., a bagpipe : this origin, like so many in C. 18, is crudely anatomical.

dooee, occ. dooe ; doee. Two, as in *dooee salter*, two pence : Parlyaree : mid-C. 19–20. It. *due soldi*.

dooey, doey. Always *large do(o)ey*, a large cup of tea : orig., and mainly, carmen's : from ca. 1920. Ex the notice : *tea 1d., large do., 2d.*

doofer. Half a cigarette : workmen's (— 1935). Ex *do for now*, suffice for the present.

doog. Good : back s. (— 1859). H., 1st ed. Whence :

doogheno. A good one. *doogheno hit*, one good hit, i.e. a bargain, a profit. Back s. (— 1859). H., 1st ed.

dook. See **dukes.**—2. A sol. pronunciation of *duke* : C. 19 (? earlier)–20.—3. A huge nose : lower classes' : from ca. 1840 ; ob. Ware. Ex the Duke of Wellington's nose : cf. *conkey*, q.v.—4. An upper-form boy : Public Schools' ; late C. 19–20. See **nondescript.**

dook-reading. Palmistry : grafters' : late C. 19–20. Philip Allingham, *Cheapjack*, 1934.

dookie ; dukey. An unlicensed theatre ; ' penny gaff ' ; theatrical : from ca. 1860 ; ob. Perhaps ex a gaff-proprietor with a large nose : cf. *duker* and *dook*, 3. (Ware.)

dookin, dookering. Fortune-telling : gypsies', thence criminals' : from ca. 1835. Brandon ; H., 1st ed. Ex Romany *dukker*, to tell fortunes. Moreover, *dookering* among grafters means specific-ally ' [going] around from door to door telling for-tunes ' : Philip Allingham, *Cheapjack*, 1934.

dookin-cove. A fortune-teller : low : from ca. 1850. See **cove** and **dookin**.

dooks. (Extremely rare in singular.) The hands. More gen. *dukes*, q.v.

doolally (or **doolali**) **tap.** Off one's head ; mad : Regular Army. late C. 19–20. F. & Gibbons. Ex *Deolali*, a sanatorium in Bombay, and Hindu-stani *tap*, fever. Since ca. 1920, often abbr. to *doolally*. (See a so the Addenda.)

doolie. An ambulance : Anglo-Indian coll. : C. 18–20. Ex the S.E. sense, a litter or a rudi-mentary palanquin (C. 16 +). Yule & Burnell.

dooly, doolay. Milk : military : 1914 ; ob. Ex Fr. *du lait*. (F. & Gibbons ; B. & P.)

door, up to the. See **up to Dick.**

door and hinge. ' Neck and breast of mutton, a joint which bends readily amongst the cervical vertebrae,' Ware : Cockney's : mid-C. 19–20.

door-knob. A ' bob ' (shilling) : rhyming s. : late C. 19–20. B. & P.

door-knocker. A ring-shaped beard : prole-tarian : 1854–ca. 1915. Ware. (Also adj.)—2. A Nordenfelt machine-gun (used by the Boers) : military in Boer War. J. Milne, *The Epistles of Atkins*, 1902. Ex the noise.

door-mat. A heavy beard : 1856–ca. 1882. Cf. *crimea*, q.v.—2. Hence, says Ware, ' by 1882 . . . applied to the moustache only, probably because about this time the tendency to shave the beard and wear only a very heavy moustache became pre-valent '.

door-nail. See **dead as a door-nail.—door-plater.** See **brass-plater.—door-step.** See **doorstep.**

doorer. A doorsman or barker at an auction sale : London coll. : from the 1880's. *Answers*, Dec. 12, 1891 (E.D.D.).

dooring. Incorrect for *door-ring*. O.E.D.

[**doorsman.** One who, at shop or place of amuse-ment, invites the public to enter : from ca. 1855. By F. & H. considered as coll., by O.E.D. as S.E. Cf. *barker*.]

doorstep. A (gen. thick) slice of bread and butter : low (— 1885). Cf. *couple of doorsteps*, q.v.

doojie's joy. A poor specimen : *Conway* cadets' : from ca. 1885. John Masefield, *The Conway*, 1933. Origin ?

doo's. See **fair doo's.**

dooshman. An enemy : Regular Army : late C. 19–20. B. & P. Ex Hindustani.

dop. Alcoholic drink in gen. : South African coll. : C. 20. Ex *dop*, the native name for Cape brandy. O.E.D. (Sup.).

dope. A drug : 1889. Also, in C. 20, an anæsthetic : medical students'.—2. Drugging : from ca. 1900.—3. Adulterated liquor : Australian (— 1916).—4. Fraudulent information : 1901. Hence, 5, any information : from ca. 1910. All coll. ex U.S., where orig. of any thick lubricant or absorbent (S.O.D.) ; itself ex Dutch *doopen*, to dip : W.—Whence, 6, a fool, a bungler : military : 1915 (F. & Gibbons), though perhaps ex Cumberland dial. (1867 : E.D.D.), and, 7, ' news bulletin sent by wireless ' (Bowen) : nautical : from ca. 1925.—8. A heavy drinker : Australian : from ca. 1912. Ex sense 3.

dope, v. To take drugs : from ca. 1890 ; by 1920, coll. Ex n., 1.—2. To ' doctor ' or drug a person or a race-horse : from ca. 1900. Ware. Both senses were orig. U.S. The vbl.n. is frequent.

dope out. To discover, ascertain, comprehend : U.S. (1906, O. Henry) anglicised ca. 1917. Cf. *dope*, n., 5.—2. ' To work out ; get hold of ' : U.S. (1906), partly anglicised by 1934 owing to the ' talkies '. O.E.D. (Sup.) ; C. W. Thurlow Craig, *Paraguayan Interlude*, 1935.

dopey. A beggar's trull : low : mid-C. 18–early 19. Grose, 1st ed.—2. The podex : C. 18.—3. A drug-addict : c. and low : from ca. 1920. E.g. in John G. Brandon, *The One-Minute Murder*, 1934.

dopper. ' A heavy blanket overall once much favoured by North Sea fishermen ' (Bowen) : nautical coll. verging on j. Ex Norfolk dial. *dopper*, a thick woollen jersey.

dopy, adj. Dull, lethargic, half asleep (lit. and fig.) : C. 20 ; earlier in U.S. Ex *dope*, n., 1.—2. Stupefying : 1925, Edgar Wallace. (O.E.D. Sup.)

dor. Permission to sleep awhile : Westminster School : C. 17–early 19. Ex L. *dormire*, to sleep.—2. A dormitory : school s. (— 1920). O.E.D. (Sup.). Cf. *dorm*.

Dora. The Defence Of the Realm Act : 1914. Orig. s., soon coll. ; by 1920, S.E. and considered as officialdom's equivalent of Mrs. Grundy.

doras or **Doras.** The A shares of the South-Eastern Railway Deferred Ordinary Stock, the capitals being transposed : Stock Exchange : from ca. 1880 ; > † in 1915.

dorbie. An initiate : Scots Masonic : from ca. 1850. Hence *the dorbies' knock*, a masons' signal-rap. Ex *dorbie*, a stonemason, a builder.

dorcas. A sempstress, esp. in a charitable cause : coll. ; from ca. 1880. Ex the S.E. *Dorcas society, D. basket*, ex Dorcas in Acts, ix, 36.

dorm. A dormitory : schools' : late C. 19–20. Cf. *dor*, 2.

dormie. See **dormy.**

dormouse. Incorrect for *dormeuse* : C. 18. O.E.D.

dormy ; occ. **dormie.** A dormitory : at certain Public Schools, e.g. Rossall : late C. 19–20. Des-mond Coke, *The House Prefect*, 1908.

Dorothy, n. and, gen., adj. Rustic love-making : Society : late 1887–ca. 1890. Ex a musical comedy (1887–88) so named. (Ware.)

dorse. See **doss.**

dorse, v. To knock down on to the back : boxing : ca. 1810–80. Wilson, 1826. (O.E.D.)

dorse, send to. Knock out : boxing, ca. 1820–70. See **doss.**

do's, fair. See **fair doo's,** and **do,** n., 6.

***dose.** A burglary : C. 18–19 c. *A New Canting Dict.*, 1725 ; Grose, 1st ed.—2. A term of imprison-ment, esp. one of three months' ' hard ' : mid-C. 19–20 c. H., 2nd ed. Cf. *moon, stretch*. ? ex :—3. A defeat : boxing, C. 19–20, ob. Tom Moore, 1819.—4. As much liquor as one can hold—or somewhat more than is good for one : coll. ; from ca. 1850. Cf. *take a grown man's dose*, a great deal of liquor.—5. (? hence,) a venereal infection : low coll. ; from ca. 1860.(—6. A rare mistake for *doash*, q.v. : Grose's m.s. note to the B.M. 1st ed.)

dose, v. ; gen. **be dosed.** To infect venereally : low : from ca. 1870. Ex n., 5. Cf. :

dose, cop a. A phrase corresponding to *dose*, n., 2 and esp. 5 : low : from ca. 1870. Manchon.

dose of salts, like a. Very quickly ; esp. *go through* (something) *like* . . . : low, mostly Australian : C. 20.

dose of the balmy, have a. To sleep : coll. ; C. 19–20, ob. See **balmy.**

dosh. A 'bivvy' (1914) ; hence, a funk-hole (1915) : Canadian military. B. & P. Ex *doss,* q.v.

Dosinghem. See **Bandagehem.**

*doss (not before C. 19) ; (after ca. 1850, rarely) **dorse.** A, and to, sleep ; lodging, to lodge ; a bed. All implying extreme cheapness and/or roughness : late C. 18–20 ; vagrants', C. > ca. 1890, gen.s. G. Parker, 1789 ; Mayhew. Presumably imm. ex † *dorse, doss,* back ; ultimately ex L. *dorsum,* the back. (Cf. *dorse,* v.)—2. Hence, to ' hang the time out ', to loaf : telegraph-messengers' (1935).

doss, do a. See **do a doss.**

doss-house. A very cheap lodging-house : low : from ca. 1880. On *doss-ken.*

doss-down, n. ; **doss down,** v. A late C. 19–20 variant of the preceding. Lyell.

*doss-ken. The same : c. ; from ca. 1800. Cf. *dossing-ken,* q.v.

doss-man. The keeper of a cheap lodging-house : low : from ca. 1825.

doss-money. The price of a night's lodging : low : from ca. 1870.

doss out. To sleep in the open air : low (— 1923). Manchon.

doss-ticket. A ticket for a night's lodging : tramps' (— 1887). Baumann.

dosser. A frequenter of doss-houses : low : from ca. 1865. Whence (*h*)*appy dosser,* a homeless vagrant creeping in to sleep on chairs, or in passages or cellars : low (— 1880). Sims in *How the Poor Live.* Presumably ex *happy* but just possibly ex *haphazard.*—2. Hence, a tramp : tramps' c. : C. 20.—3. *The dosser* : the father of a family : from ca. 1885 ; ob. He who provides the *doss.*

*dossers' hotel. A casual ward : tramps' c. : C. 20. F. Jennings, *Tramping with Tramps,* 1932.

*dossing-ken or **-crib.** (Cf. *doss-house, doss-ken.*) A cheap lodging-house : c. : the former — 1838 ; the latter — 1851. See **doss.**

dossy. Elegant ; smart : from ca. 1885. ? ex *dosser,* the ornamental cloth used to cover the back of a(n imposing) seat ; or ex *D'Orsay,* for in Society, ca. 1830–45, one spoke of a man as ' a D'Orsay ' (a perfect gentleman)—ex the Comte D'Orsay (Ware).

do't. Do it : Society coll. of early C. 18. Scourged by Swift (see *Slang,* p. 66).

*dot. A ribbon. Hence, *dot-drag,* a watchribbon : C. 19 c. Haggart, 1821.

dot, v. To strike, gen. in form *dot* (a person) *one,* and esp. in sense ' give a black eye ' (Ware) : from the middle 1890's. W. Pett Ridge, 1895, *Minor Dialogues* ; C. J. Dennis has *dot* (one) *in the eye,* to punch (a person) in the eye.

dot, off one's. A variant (— 1923) of *dotty,* 2, Manchon. Prob. ex Yorkshire dial. : 1890. (E.D.D.).

dot, on the. (Constructed with *be.*) On the spot : Canadian : from ca. 1920. John Beames. Cf. *on the dotted line.*

dot, the year. A date long ago : coll. : late C. 19–20. Lit., ' the year 0 '. Esp. as in ' Ganpat ', *Out of Evil,* 1933, ' He's been in every frontier show [battle or skirmish] since the year dot.' Cf. ' I reckon *he* was born in the year dot, that 'orse was,' W. Pett Ridge, *Minor Dialogues,* 1895.

dot and carry, or go, one. A person with a wooden

or a shorter or a limping leg. The mid-C. 18–mid-19 form is *go* ; the C. 19–20, *carry.* Coll. Grose, 1st ed. ; Barham. Also as v.—2. An inferior writing or arithmetic master : late C. 18–early 19. Grose, 2nd ed. Ex an arithmetical process.

dots. Money : from ca. 1880. Collective-pl. synonyms are numerous.

dots on, put. To bore, to weary : orig. (1915 or 1916), military ; slightly ob. Prob. ex *dot one's* ' *i* ' ' *s.*

dotted line, sign on the. To sign ; jocular coll. : from ca. 1925. Ex the instructions on legal and official documents.

dotter. A penny-a-liner ; a reporter : from ca. 1870 ; ob.

dotties man. A greedy or selfish man : proletarian : ca. 1885–1915. Ware. See **doddies.**

dotty. Weak ; dizzy : sporting and gen. (— 1870) ; ob. Esp. *dotty in the pins,* unsteady on one's legs. Perhaps ex *dodder,* v.—2. Hence, idiotic ; (a little) mad : from ca. 1888.—3. As n., a low harlot's fancy man : c. (— 1891).

doubite. A street : ca. 1800–70 c. Matsell. More U.S. than Eng. Origin ?.

double. A trick : esp. in C. 18–19 *tip,* C. 19–20 *give the double,* to run away from one's creditors, then, from ca. 1850, to escape ; and in *put the double on,* to circumvent (— 1870).—2. An actor playing two parts ; also v. (from ca. 1800 and soon S.E.) : theatrical (— 1825).—3. Repetition of a word or sentence : printers'. from ca. 1870.—4. In c. a street-turning : from ca. 1870.—5. (Gen. *a double.*) Two score : fisheries' coll. : late C. 19–20. Bowen. Ex *double,* a basket containing from three to four dozen fish.

double, v. For the theatrical sense, see n, 2.—2. See **double up.**—3. To double one's effort or speed (v.i.) : coll. : from ca. 1885.

double-ace poker. See **kangaroo poker.—double, come the.** See **come the double.**

double act, do the. To get married, be married : low (— 1923). Manchon. Prob. ex *run in double harness.*

double-arsed. Large-bottomed : low coll. or a vulgarism : C. 19–20.

double back. To go back on an action, statement, opinion : coll. : mid-C. 19–20. Ex doubling back on one's tracks.

double-banked. ' Sleeping two in a cabin ' : nautical coll. : late C. 19–20. Bowen. Ex a rowing-boat double-banked.

double barrel. A field or opera glass : from ca. 1880 ; ob. Traill.

double-barrelled. Applied to a harlot natural and unnatural (see **fore-and-after**) : low : from ca. 1860.—2. Also to any person both normal and abnormal in sex : from ca. 1900.

double-bottomed. Insincere : coll. : C. 19–20 ; ob.

double-breasted feet, occ. **double-breasters.** Club feet : coll. : from ca. 1850 ; ob.

double-breasted water-butt smasher. A welldeveloped man ; an athlete : Cockneys' : ca. 1890–1914. Ware.

double Cape Horn. To be made a cuckold : nautical : late C. 18–mid-19. John Davis, *The Post Captain,* 1805. Ex horns attributed to cuckolds. (R. H. Case's ed. of the novel ; 1928.)

double-cross or **-double.** Winning, or trying to win, after promising to lose a race : sporting : from ca. 1870. The v. is *double, double-cross,* or *put the* *double on*, the last v.t. only : from ca. 1870.—2. Later, *double-cross*, etc., is much used by criminals for betrayal (n. and v.) in a criminal transaction : from ca. 1885 : see passim, Edgar Wallace's detective novels.

double-crosser. The agent of the preceding : rare before C. 20.

double-c**ted. Sexually large : low coll. **or** vulg. : from ca. 1800.

double dash ! Emphatic ' dash it ! ' : Cockney (— 1887) ; ob. Baumann.

double-decker. A ship having two above-water decks : from ca. 1870.—2. A tramcar or 'bus with seats on top as well as below : from ca. 1895. Both coll., the latter ex U.S.

double-diddied or **-dugged.** Large-breasted. N., *double dugs.* C. 19–20 : the n. is low coll. ; *double-diddied*, low s. ; *double-dugged*, low coll.

double-distilled. (Esp. of a lie) superlative **:** coll. : from ca. 1870 ; ob.

double-drummer. A particularly noisy kind of cicada : Australian children's : C. 20. Cf. *floury baker.*

double Dutch. See **Dutch, talk.** Cf. :

double Dutch coiled against the sun. Unintelligible ; nonsense : nautical : from ca. 1840.

*double-ender. A skeleton key with a ward at each end : c. : mid-C. 19–20 ; ob. ' No. 747.'

double event. Simultaneous syphilis and gonorrhœa (men), or defloration and conception : low : from ca. 1870.—2. A glass of whiskey and a glass of beer : public-houses' (esp. in Glasgow) : C. 20.

double figures, go into. To have 10 children at the least : lower classes' coll. (— 1923). Manchon.

double finn. A £10 note : low (? orig. c.) : from ca. 1870. See **finn** and :

*double finnip (etc.). The same : c. (— 1839). Brandon. See **finnif.**

double guts, n. ; **double-gutted,** adj. (Of a) person large-paunched : low coll. ; from ca. 1820.

double-headed. (Of a train) with two engines, one at the front and the other at the back : late C. 19–20 : railwaymen's coll., now verging on S.E.

double-header. A coin with two heads : low coll. : from ca. 1875.

double-hocked. Having extremely thick ankles : low : from ca. 1860.

double intenders. ' Knock-down blows—labial or fistful ', Ware : non-aristocratic (— 1909) ; virtually †.

double jug(g). The backside : late C. 17–19. Cotton ; Grose, 3rd ed.—2. In pl., the posteriors : C. 17–20, ob. ' Melancholy ' Burton.

double lines. Ship-casualty or casualties : nautical : from ca. 1870. H., 5th ed. Ex the manner of their entry at Lloyd's.

double-mouth(ed). (A person) large-mouthed, n. and adj. : coll. : C. 19–20.

*double, on the. (Of doors, gates) double-locked : c. : C. 20. George Ingram, *Stir*, 1933.

*double on, put the. See **double-cross.**

[Double passives, nearly always clumsy, and often cacophonous, are on the border-line between reprehensible catachresis and mere stylistic infelicity. See esp. Fowler.]

double-ribbed. Pregnant : low coll. : C. 19–20.

double scoop. ' Hair parted in centre, and worn low—gave way to the quiff ', Ware : military : ca. 1890–95.

double-shotted. (Of a brandy, or whiskey, and

soda) containing twice the usual proportion of alcohol : coll. : from ca. 1860.

double shuffle. A hornpipe step in which each foot is shuffled, rapidly and neatly, twice in succession : coll. ; from ca. 1830, esp. among costermongers. Dickens.—2. Hence a trick, a piece of faking : from ca. 1870.

double-shung. (Of men) excessively equipped sexually : C. 19–20 (ob.) : low. ' ? *double-slung.*

*double slangs. Double irons or fetters : **c.** (— 1812) ; ob. Vaux.

double-sucker. Abnormally developed *labia maiora* : low : from ca. 1870.

double thumper. An ' outsize ' in lies : from ca. 1850 : coll.

double-tide work. Extra duty : C. 19–20 : coll., orig. coastguardsmen's >, by 1880, gen. nautical. Bowen.

double-tongued squib. A double-barrelled gun : coll. G. W. Reynolds, 1864. Ob.

double up. To cause to collapse (v.i. sense is rare) : boxing (ca. 1814). Moore, ' Doubled him up, like a bag of old *duds.*'—2. To pair off, e.g., in a cabin (rare as v.i.) : coll. : 1837 (O.E.D.). H., 2nd ed. Occ. simply *double.*

Double X's, the. The 20th Foot Regiment, since 1881 the Lancashire Fusiliers : military : C. 19–20 ; ob. F. & Gibbons. Ex the figure XX.

doubler. A punch on side or belly : boxing : from ca. 1810. ' Peter Corcoran ', 1821, ' A doubler in the bread-basket.'

*doublet. A precious stone endorsed with glass : in C. 15–17, it was S.E. ; then it > c.—2. See **iron d.** and **stone d.,** a prison.

doubty. Doughty : incorrect form : C. 15–18. O.E.D.

douce. See **douse.**

doudon. A short, fat woman : non-aristocratic (— 1923). Manchon. Perhaps cognate with the Wiltshire *dowdy*, stunted in growth (E.D.D.).

Douglas with one eye and a stinking breath, Roby. The breech : nautical : mid-C. 18–19. Grose, 1st ed.

dough. Pudding : Public Schools', C. 19–20.—2. Money : U.S. (— 1851), then (from ca. 1880) Australia, then—ca. 1895—Britain. (Thornton.)

dough, one's cake is. See **cake is dough.**

dough-baked. Deficient in brains : coll. : from late C. 16 ; in late C. 19–20, dial. Wycherley, 1675, ' These dow-baked, senseless, indocile animals, women.' Cf. *half-baked.*

dough-cock. A half-wit aboard as seaman : nautical : late C. 19–20. Bowen.

dough-nut. (Gen. pl.) A Carley life-saving float : nautical : C. 20. Bowen. (Cheerful !)

Doughboy. An American infantryman : U.S. coll. (1867), anglicised ca. 1917. Thornton ; O.E.D. (Sup.), ' In allusion to the "large globular glass buttons of the infantry uniform " in the American civil war.'—2. (d-.) A punch in the face : low : from ca. 1919. G. Ingram, *Stir*, 1933, has it in its usual form : *give* (a person) *a doughboy.*

doughy. A baker : coll. (— 1823). Bee ; H., 3rd ed. Cf. *chips, dips.*—2. Hence, the nickname of any man surnamed Baker : naval and military : late C. 19–20. F. & Gibbons.

doughy, adj. (Of complexion) pale or pasty **:** coll. : from ca. 1860 ; ob. Ware. Cf. *underdone.*

doughy-nosed. (Of a seaman) in love : nautical : late C. 19–20. Bowen.

douse, dowse. To put, esp. down or (of a candle, lamp, etc.) out : low coll. : C. 18–20, chiefly in *douse the glim*, put out the light. Scott, Reade.—2. N., rare, except in *dowse on the chops*, a blow on the jaw : low : C. 17–19. Grose.

douser, a heavy blow ; **dousing (dowsing)**, a thrashing : resp. late C. 18–19 (Grose, 2nd ed.), C. 19. Both, low coll.

Dove. A member of St. Catharine's College, Cambridge : C. 19–20 ; ob. Suggested by *Puritan*, q.v. See Whibley in *Cambridge Wit*.

dove, soiled. A high-flying harlot : from ca. 1870 ; coll. Dove = purity.

dove-tart. A pigeon pie : coll. : from ca. 1850 ; ob. ' Cuthbert Bede '.

dove-cote. ' The quarters allotted to officers' wives on . . . the old Indian troopships ' : military : late C. 19–early 20. F. & Gibbons.

Dover, Jack of. A sole : late C. 14–17 : coll. ; then, in C. 18–early 19, dial. Chaucer. Dover is famed for its soles. (Apperson.)

Dover Castle boarder. A debtor compelled to sleep within the rules of the Queen's Bench Prison : debtors' : ca. 1850–81,—the prison was demolished in 1881. Ex the Dover Castle, the most prominent tavern in that district. Ware.

Dover waggoner !, put this reckoning up to the. (Gen. addressed to a landlord.) Score this up against me : a c.p. of ca. 1820–40. Bee, ' The waggoner's name being Owen, pronounced *owing*.'

Dovercourt beetle. A heavy mallet : nautical : mid-C. 19–20. Bowen. By a pun.

Dovers. Shares in the London and *Dover* Railway : Stock Exchange coll. (now only historical) : late C. 19–20. A. J. Wilson, *Stock Exchange Glossary*, 1895. *Dover A's* were gen. called *Doras*.

dowdying. A drastic practical joke practised in C. 18 by one Pearce, nicknamed *Dowdy* ex the burden, *dow de dow*, of one of his songs. Grose, 1st ed.

dowlas. A draper. Coll. ; from late C. 18. Ex the towelling so named ; popularised by Daniel Dowlas, a character in Colman's *The Heir at Law*.

dowling. A compulsory game of football : Public Schools (— 1871) ; ob. Ex the Gr. word for (a slave, or that for) to enslave. Desmond Coke, *The Bending of a Twig*, 1906, of the game as it is played at Shrewsbury School : ' Any number from three hundred down (or up) can play a dowling ; but it often happens that in reality some half-a-dozen punt the ball from end to end, while all the rest troop after it, like soldier-slaves round the great warriors of Ilium. And dowling is compulsory.' Cf. the quotation at *Skyte*.

*down. Alarm ; suspicion ; discovery : c. ; ca. 1810–1900. Vaux.—2. Hence *there is no down*, there is no risk ; all's safe.—3. A tendency to be severe towards : coll. (— 1893). S.O.D. Ex *down on*, be, 2. But cf. :—4. A prejudice against, hostility towards : Australian coll. : from ca. 1850. W. J. Dobie, *Recollections of Port Phillip*, 1856 (Morris). Ex sense 1.—5. See **Downs**.

down, v. To trick ; circumvent : C. 19–20 coll. —2. The sense, to bring, put, throw, or knock down, is—despite F. & H.—S.E., but *down a woman*, physically to prepare her for the act, is definitely low coll. if not s., from ca. 1850 : cf. *up*, v.

down, adv. (often with adj. force). Esp. with *to be* : depressed ; in low spirits : coll. : C. 17–20. Ben Jonson, ' Thou art so downe upon the least disaster.' (O.E.D.)—2. Wide-awake ; suspicious ;

aware : low (? orig. c.) : Vaux, 1812. Often with *to*, as in ' Down to every move,' Smedley, 1850. Cf. *up to*, aware of.—3. See :

down, adj. ' Engaged in fagging in the cricket field, etc. (Peculiar to College) ' : Winchester College coll. : from ca. 1860. Wrench.

down, preposition. See ' Westminster School slang '.

down, be or come. To be ' ploughed ' in a university examination : Australian coll. : 1886 ; ob.

down, up or. See **up or down**.

down a pit, be. To be greatly attracted by a role : theatrical : from ca. 1860 ; †.

down along. (Sailing) coastways down the English Channel : nautical coll. : mid-C. 19–20. Bowen.

down among the dead men. Dead drunk : ca. 1850–1900. ' Cuthbert Bede ', 1853.

*down as a hammer (see also **hammer, down as a**) or **as a tripper**. To be alert, wide-awake : c. : ca. 1810–40. Vaux. Elaborations on *down*, adv., 2.

*down buttock and sham file. See **buttock and tongue**.

*down(-)hills. Dice cogged to run low : late C. 17–early 19 : c. > low s. B.E. Cf. *up-hills*.

down on or upon, be. To be aware of, alertly equal to : from ca. 1790.—2. Hence, to pounce upon, treat harshly : s. (— 1860) >, by 1900, coll. H., 2nd ed.—3. See **down upon**.

down on (more gen. **upon**) **one, put a.** To inform on a person : from ca. 1840. Vaux.

down on the knuckle. See **knuckle, down on the**.

down pin, be. To be indisposed ; depressed : C. 19. Extant in dial. Ex skittles.

down south, esp. with **go** or **put.** (Of money) to go or be put in one's pocket, hence to be banked : from ca. 1890.

down the banks, get. To fail : Anglo-Irish coll. (— 1909). Ware, ' Probably the outcome of life amongst the bogs.'

down the Lane and/or into the Mo. (To take a stroll) in the Drury Lane district : Central London Cockneys' : ca. 1850–1910. *Mo* derives ex the long-disappeared Mogul Music Hall. (Ware.)

down the road. Vulgarly showy : coll. : (— 1859) ; ob. H., 1st ed. ; Sala, ' A racing and down-the-road look.' Ex Mile End Road, says Ware.

down the wind. See **weather, go up the**.

*down to, drop. To learn a person's designs or character : c. (— 1812) ; ob. Vaux. Cf. *drop to* and :

*down to, put (a person). To apprise one (of something) ; explain it to him : c. (— 1812) ; very ob. Vaux. See **down**, adv., 2.

down to dandy. Artful ; excellent : low : from ca. 1860 ; ob. Cf. *up to dick*.

down to it, get. See **get down to it**.

down to one, drop. To discover a person's character or designs : coll. : from ca. 1840.

down to something, put one. To explain ; prime ; let into the ' know ' : from ca. 1830.

down to the ground. Thoroughly ; extremely well : coll. : from ca. 1865. Miss Broughton, ' Suited me down to the ground,' 1867. (O.E.D.) In C. 16–17 S.E., *up and down*.

down upon (occ. **on**) **a person, be.** To scold, reprimand severely : coll. : from ca. 1810. Scott, ' We should be down upon the fellow . . . and let him get it well.'—2. See **down on, be** and **put a**.

down upon oneself, be or drop. To be melancholy : ca. 1810–60. Vaux.

downer. A sixpence : from ca. 1835. Brandon, 1839 ; Whyte-Melville. Ex Romany *tawno*, little one. Cf. *tanner.*—2. A knock-down blow : boxing ; from ca. 1815 ; ob. Moore, 1819.—3. A heavy fall : the turf (— 1923). Manchon.—4. A bed : tramps' c. (— 1935). Either ex *down* (cf. synonymous *feather*) or ex *get down to it*.

downish. Somewhat dejected : coll. : ca. 1670–1800.

*****downright, the.** Begging, esp. as a tramp : tramps' c. : C. 20. Whence :

*****downright, on the.** On the tramp, ' on the road ' : tramps' c. (— 1932). F. Jennings, *Tramping with Tramps.*—2. As in :

*****downrighter.** A destitute person that, quite openly, goes in for begging : c. : C. 20. W. H. Davies in a review by him in *The New Statesman*, March 18, 1933. Ex preceding.

Downs. Shares in the Belfast & County Down Railway : Stock Exchange (— 1895). A. J. Wilson, *Stock Exchange Glossary.*

*****Downs, the.** Tothill Fields Prison : c. : from ca. 1850 ; ob. Mayhew.

downstairs. Hell : C. 19 coll. Barham, ' Downstairs . . . old Nick.'

downy. An artful fellow : ca. 1820–80. Pierce Egan ; H., 5th ed. See the adj. Perhaps associated with *downy bird* (W.), but imm. ex *down on*, *be*, 1 : q.v.—2. A bed : from ca. 1850 ; ob. Trollope, ' I've a deal to do before I get to my downy.' Ex the down mattress.

downy, adj. Artful ; very knowing : from ca. 1820. Moncrieff, 1823, ' You're a downy von ' ; Dickens ; H. J. Byron, the dramatist. Ex *down*, n., 1. Cf. *downy*, n.—2. Fashionable : ca. 1855–90. ' *Ducange Anglicus*.'

downy, do the. See **do the downy.**

downy bird or **cove.** A clever rogue (— 1875, — 1821 resp.). In pl., gen. *the downies.* Egan ; Leman Rede, ' the downiest cove ' ; Greenwood. The *bird* form was suggested by a bird's down (cf. *downy-bit*), but the *downy* is ex *down*, n., sense 1.

downy bit. A half-fledged wench : low : from ca. 1830 ; ob.—2. An attractive young girl : low : from ca. 1880.

*****downy earwig.** A sympathetic person : c. (— 1932). F. Jennings, *Tramping with Tramps.*

downy flea-pasture. A bed : from ca. 1800. Cf. *bug-walk.*

dowry. A lot ; much : low ; from ca. 1850 ; ob. H., 1st ed. Prob. ex the S.E. word.

dowse. See **douse.**

dowser. A douceur : sol. : mid-C. 18–20 ; ob. Grose, 3rd ed.

*****doxe, doxey, doxie.** See **doxy.**

doxology-works. A church, a chapel : from ca. 1870 ; ob. Cf. *gospel-shop* and *preaching-shop*, qq.v.

*****doxy ;** also **doxey,** C. 17–19, and **doxie** or **doxey,** C. 17 ; occ. **doccy,** C. 16, and **doxe,** C. 16–17 (O.E.D.). In mid-C. 16–18 c., a beggar's trull, a female beggar. Harman, B.E., Grose. Prob. ex Dutch *docke*, a doll : cf., therefore, *dolly.* W.—2. Hence, in late C. 16–20 (ob.), a mistress, a prostitute. Chapman, Dunton, Grose.—3. Hence, in C. 19 low s., esp. in London and among patterers, a wife. Mayhew. (Dial. takes up two analogous ideas : a sweetheart (— 1818) ; app. later a slattern or (pejoratively) an old woman. E.D.D.) This *doxy* lends point to the quotation in :—4. **doxy,** opinion : coll. ; 1730. ' " Orthodoxy, my Lord," said

Bishop Warburton . . ., " is my doxy,—heterodoxy is another man's doxy." ' (S.O.D.)

Doyle, do Paddy. See **Paddy Doyle.**

Dozen, Old ; gen. **the** . . . The 12th Foot— from 1881 the Suffolk—Regiment : military : C. 19–20. F. & Gibbons.

dozen, talk (occ. **run**) **nineteen to the.** To talk very fast : from ça. 1850 ; coll. till C. 20, then S.E. Reade (*talk*), 1852 ; Sala (*run*), 1860. O.E.D. Cf. :

dozen, talk thirteen to the. To talk in the air, wildly, incoherently, without sense : coll. (— 1923). Manchon. Ex preceding.

dozenth. Twelfth : coll. ; from ca. 1710. (Hence, the rare *half-dozenth.*) Cobden, ' Let me repeat it—if for the dozenth time.' (O.E.D.)

dozing-crib. A bed : low (? c.) : mid-C. 19–early 20. Cf. *kip*, q.v.

Dr. Brighton ; Dr. Jim ; Dr. Johnson. See **Doctor Brighton** . . .

drab. Poison ; medicine : low (— 1851). Ex Romany, where *drabengro* (the suffix *-engro* = a man) is a doctor : see esp. Smart & Crofton and Sampson.—2. Despite F. & H., *drab*, a whore, a slattern, is S.E., as is the v.

drabbit ! Abbr. (*G*)*od rabbit !* An old, mainly dial., expletive. Cf. *drat it !*

drabby. An Indian transport-driver : Regular Army coll. : late C. 19–20 Ex Hindustani.—2. Hence loosely, any transport-driver : military : 1915. B. & P.

*****d'rac, drac.** (Gen. in pl.) A card : back s. in C. 20 c. Charles E. Leach, *On Top of the Underworld*, 1933. Also *derac(k).*

drach (pron. *dräk*). A drachma : among the English colony in Greece : late C. 19–20. T. B. Marle, *Candid Escort*, 1936, ' " Can you give me five drachs ? " he asked.'

draft on Aldgate pump. A spurious banknote ; fraudulent bill : c. late 1730–1850. Fielding, who notes it as ' a mercantile phrase ' ; Grose ; Bee. Also at *Aldgate.*

drag. A late C. 18–19 four-horse coach, with seats inside and on top. (In C. 20, a break.) Orig. s. or coll., as Moore's *Tom Crib*, Reynolds's *The Fancy*, and Lever's *Harry Lorrequer* (1819, 1820, 1839) clearly show ; it > S.E. ca. 1860. (In C. 17–18 S.E., also a cart or waggon, whence the robbery senses.)—2. In late C. 19–20 c., a van. Leach.—3. A chain : C. 19 c.—4. A street or a road (— 1851) : low, mostly Cockney. Mayhew.— 5. The robbing of vehicles : c., ca. 1780–1830. G. Parker, 1781. Now *van-drag*, q.v. Hence *done for a drag*, convicted for such robbery, and *go on the drag* (Grose, 1st ed.), to embark on, or to practise, such robbery : same period. But, from ca. 1850 (ob.), *go on* (or, more gen., *flash*) *the drag*, is to wear women's clothes for immoral purposes (*in drag*, thus dressed) : low if not c.—6. A trick or stratagem : C. 19–20, ob. ; low.—7. Three months' imprisonment : c. (— 1851). Henry Mayhew ; Charles E. Leach. Now rather *three moon.*—8. Its hunting senses are j.—9. An obstacle : coll. (— 1887). Baumann, ' That's where the drag is.'— 10. ' Petticoat or skirt used by actors when playing female parts. Derived from the drag of the dress, as distinct from the non-dragginess of the trouser ', Ware : theatrical (— 1887). Perhaps rather ex *go on the drag* (see *drag*, n., 5). Also as adj.—11. An arrest that the criminal considers is unjustified : c. (— 1935). David Hume. Perhaps ex sense 9.— 12. A harrow : Canadian coll. : late C. 19–20.

*drag, v. To rob vehicles : c. of ca. 1810–50. Vaux.—2. To arrest : c. : C. 20. Edgar Wallace, passim.—3. V.i. and t., to take a portion of the stakes in a gambling game as a reserve for future play : Australian and New Zealand : C. 20.

drag, in the. See 'dragged or dragged out'.

*drag, on the. See drag, n., 5.—2. 'On the off-chance of attracting the attention of a customer' : low or c. : from ca. 1840. 'No. 747.'—3. (Of Flying Squad cars) on patrol : c. : from ca. 1927.

drag, put on the. To go slowly, ease off. *Put the drag on a person*, to apply pressure, esp. to make him ease off or cease. Coll. : mid-C. 19–20.

*drag-cove. A carter : C. 19, mainly Cockney and orig. c. Vaux.

*drag-lay. The practice of robbing vehicles : late C. 18–early 19 c. Also *the drag*.

drag on, put the. See drag, put on the.

*drag-sneak. A practised robber of vehicles : c. ; late C. 18–19. Parker, Mayhew.

drag the pudding. To ' get the sack ' just before Christmas : tailors' : from ca. 1870 ; ob.

dragged. Late for duty : military : late C. 19–20 ; ob. F. & Gibbons. See sense 2 of :

dragged or **dragged out.** Physically exhausted : coll. ; from ca. 1860 ; ob.—2. (Only dragged.) Behindhand with one's work : tailors' : C. 20. Also *be in the drag*.

*dragged, be. To be returned to a convict prison to serve the rest of one's sentence : c. : C. 20. Edgar Wallace, *Mr. Reeder*, 1925.

dragged up. (Rare in other tenses.) Ppl. adj., educated, nurtured, brought up : from ca. 1690. Orig. Society s., B.E. remarking : ' As the Rakes call it ' ; in C. 19–20 coll.

*dragger. A vehicle thief : c. : late C. 18–20. George Parker ; Charles E. Leach. Ex *drag*, n., 5. —2. A fishing-boat using the otter trawl : Canadian nautical coll. : C. 20. Bowen.

*dragging. The practice of robbing vehicles : c. : C. 19. See drag, v.

*dragging lark. The practice of stealing from motor-cars : c. : from ca. 1910. James Curtis, *The Gilt Kid*, 1936.

dragging-time. ' The evening of a country fair day, when the young fellows begin pulling the wenches about', H., 3rd ed. : provincial coll. (— 1864).

draggle-tail. ' A nasty dirty Slut,' B.E. : coll. : late C. 17–mid-19. See (anatomical) tail and cf. *daggle-tail*, q.v.—2. Hence, a low prostitute : mid-C. 19–20 ; ob. H., 5th ed.

dragon. A sovereign : ca. 1825–90 ; low. Ex the device. Maginn.—2. A wanton : C. 17–19 coll. Fletcher. Cf. *St. George*.

dragon, blind. A chaperon : middle and upper classes' (— 1923) ; ob. Manchon.

dragon, water the. To urinate : low : C. 18–20 ; ob. Perhaps suggested by *dragon-water*, a popular C. 17 medicine.

dragon (up)on St. George. See riding Saint George.

dragoon it. To occupy two branches of one profession : coll. : mid-C. 18–19. Grose, 2nd ed. Ex Army : orig. a dragoon was a mounted infantryman armed with a carbine (cf., in Boer War and G.W., the Australian and New Zealand light horse).

dragsman. A coachman : coll. : from ca. 1810 ; in C. 20 S.E., ob. Egan.—2. A vehicle-thief : c., ca. 1810–1900. Vaux ; Mayhew. Less gen. than *drag-sneak*.

drain. A drink : coll. ; from ca. 1835. Dickens in *Boz*. Hence *do a drain* (cf. *wet*), to take a drink. Both, ob.—2. Gin : ca. 1800–80. *Lex. Bal.* Ex its urinative property.—3. The *pudendum muliebre* ; low : C. 19–20.

drain-pipe(s). Macaroni : (mostly London) school-children's (— 1887). Baumann.

drainings. A ship's cook : nautical : ca. 1830–1910. Cf. *slushy*. (Bowen.) Cf. :

drains. A ship's cook : nautical : late C. 19–20 ; ob.

*drake ; gen. in passive. To *duck* (a thief) in a pond : c. : ca. 1810–50. Vaux.

dram, dog's. See dog's dram.

dram-a-tick. A small glass of liquor served on credit : a late C. 18–early 19 punning coll. suggested by the C. 17–18 spelling of *dramatic*. Grose, 1st ed. Cf. *dome-stick*.

drammer. See drummer.

drank. (Past ppl.) drunk : from ca. 1830, sol. ; earlier, S.E.

drap. ' A nasty sluttish whore ', Egan's Grose : low : ca. 1820–50. A perversion of *drab*.

drapery miss. ' A girl of doubtful character, who dresses in a striking manner ' : non-aristocratic coll. : ca. 1870–1915. Ware. Ex the S.E. sense explained by Byron in a note to XI, 49, of *Don Juan*. Cf. *dress-lodger*, q.v.

drat ! A mild expletive ; occ. *drat you, him*, etc. ; *drat it !*, curse it ! Coll. : from ca. 1815 ; *dratted*, from ca. 1840. Dickens, ' Drat you, be quiet ! says the good old man ' ; Mrs. Henry Wood, ' That dratted girl.' Ex *(G)od rot !* : cf. *Gad* for *God* (W.).

draught. A privy : C. 17–18. Coll., F. & H. ; S.E., says the O.E.D. with reason.—2. A feeling of nervousness or vague fear : military (1918) >, by 1920, gen. ; ob. Lyell. On *wind up*.

draught on the pump at Aldgate, a. See draft and Aldgate.

draughty. Nervous ; (vaguely) afraid : military (1918) >, by 1920, gen. ; ob. Lyell. Ex *draught*, 2, q.v. : cf. *windy* in the same sense.

draw. A drawn game : from ca. 1870 ; orig. coll. ; in C. 20, S.E.—2. In cricket, a stroke made with the bat's surface inclined downwards : from ca. 1860.—3. An attraction, whether newspaper article or a game, a play or a preacher : from ca. 1880 ; coll.—4. A person, from ca. 1810, or a thing, a decade later, employed to *draw out* (q.v.) a person. —5. One so ' drawn ' : from ca. 1885. (O.E.D.)

draw, v.i. To attract public attention : coll. ; from ca. 1870. Hawley Smart, ' He usually kept " his show " running as long as it would draw ' ; by 1900, virtually S.E.—2. V.t. To elicit information from : coll., 1857, Reade (S.O.D.). More gen. *draw out*, q.v.—3. Flatter, tease, inveigle into vexation ; hence, make game of : coll. From ca. 1859. Thackeray, ' The wags . . . can always, as the phrase is, " draw " her father, by speaking of Prussia.'—4. In low coll., the sense in *dog-drawn*, q.v.—5. In c., to rob, pick the pockets of ; steal : C. 19–20. Vaux. Also *draw* (one) *of*, rob him of : ibid.

draw blanks. To fail ; be disappointed : coll., C. 19–20, ob. In S.E., *draw a blank*. Ex lotteries.

draw-boy. A superior article offered at a very low price : trade : mid-C. 19–20, ob. H., 3rd ed.

draw (a person's) cork. To cause his nose to bleed : pugilistic (— 1823) ; † by 1900. Egan's Grose.

draw crabs. 'To attract fire from the enemy artillery by exposing oneself on ground under observation' (B. & P.) : military : 1915. Ex *crabs*, body lice.

draw-fart, occ. preceded by **doctor**. An itinerant quack : low coll. : C. 19.

draw for. To borrow money from, as in ' She drew him for a dollar ' : coll. ; C. 19–20, ob.

draw it mild ! (Rare in other moods.) Expressive of derision ; incredulity ; supplication : coll. : 1837, Thackeray (O.E.D.) ; *Punch*, 1841 ; Barham ; Martin & Aytoun. ? ex public-houses ; cf. Barham's 'A pint of double X, and please to draw it mild,' W.

*****draw-latch.** A thief, esp. from houses : in C. 14–15, S.E. ; ca. 1560–1740, a member of an order of rogues (B.E.) ; in mid-C. 18–early 19, any house-robber (Grose, 1st ed.). The sense ' loiterer ' is S.E.

*****draw of.** See **draw**, v., 5.

draw off. V.i., to throw back the body in order to hit the harder : orig. (ca. 1860) pugilistic s. : in C. 20, gen. coll. H., 3rd ed. Cf. the nautical *haul off.*—2. V.t., with variant *draw one's fireworks*, to cool a man's ardour by lying with him : a low, woman's term : C. 19–20 ; ob. Cf. *cooler*.

draw out. To cause to talk, give an opinion ; elicit information : coll. ; from ca. 1775. Cf. *draw*, v., 2. Ex *drawing a badger* (W.).

draw plaster. To angle for a man's intentions : tailors' ; from ca. 1850 ; ob.

draw straws ; or **one's eyes draw straws.** To feel sleepy : coll. in late C. 17–early 19, then dial. Swift, in *Polite Conversation*, No. 3. (Esp.) Apperson ; but see also **straws, draw.**

draw teeth. To wrench the handles and knockers from street doors : ca. 1840–70. Orig. and chiefly medical students'. (Gen. as vbl.n. *drawing teeth.*)

draw the bow up to the ear ; draw (or **pull**) **the long bow.** See **bow.—draw the cork.** See **cork.** Cf. *tap the claret.*

*****draw the King's** or **Queen's picture.** To manufacture counterfeit coins : from ca. 1780 ; c. Grose, 2nd ed. (1788). After ca. 1860, perhaps s. In C. 20, ob.

draw the line at tick. (Of a woman) to be virtuous : serio-comics', esp. lady singers' (—1909); ob. Ware, ' A covered allusion to the textile fabric used for the covering of beds and mattresses.'

draw wool or **worsted,** v.t. and i. To irritate ; to foment a quarrel : tailors' : C. 19–20 ; ob.

drawed. Drew ; drawn : sol. in mid-C. 19–20. Baumann. The pronunciation *drore* for *draw*, as is *drawring*, is mainly Cockney, though it occurs in gen. illiteracy.

drawer, out of the top. See **top drawer, out of the.**

drawer-on. An appetiser (not of drink, which has *puller-on*) : coll., other senses being S.E. : C. 17–20, ob.

*****drawers.** (Only in pl.) Stockings, esp. if embroidered : c. : mid-16–18. Harman, Head, Grose. The origin ? Perhaps it is because one *draws* them on and off.

drawring ; dror(r)ing. A sol. (spoken rather than written) : C. 18–20. Also in *drawring-room.*

dread ! Drat !, as in ' Dread the fellow !' : Cockney (— 1887) ; ob. Baumann.

dreadful. A sensational story, article, print : coll. ; from ca. 1884 ; ob. Earlier and more gen., *penny dreadful*, q.v. Cf. *awful* and *shocker*.

dreadful, adj. Very bad, objectionable, etc., etc., etc. : coll. : from ca. 1860.

dreadful, as adv., was in C. 17–early 19 S.E. ; since, sol. (O.E.D.)

dreadfully. Very : coll. ; from ca. 1600. Cf. *awfully, bloody, terribly*.

dreadnought. A male pessary : low : from 1908. —2. A very high, stiff corset : low : from ca. 1909 ; ob.

dreadnoughts. (Like the preceding, ex the battleship.) Close-fitting (gen. thick) woollen or flannel female drawers : from 1908 ; low.

Dreado. H.M.S. *Dreadnought* : naval : early C. 20. Bowen.

dream, a. A very delightful or agreeably odd person : coll. : C. 20, chiefly among either the nation's youth and girlhood or romantic women. (As applied to things, even lovely dresses, it is S.E.) —2. See **wet dream.**

dredgerman. A sham dredger-man, actually a thief : (— 1857 ;) ob. See esp. Dickens's ' Down with the Tide,' in *Reprinted Pieces.* (Dickens's knowledge of unconventional English is very extensive, almost irreproachable.)

dredgy. A drowned sailor's ghost : nautical : late C. 19–20. Bowen. Because his corpse runs, or had run, the risk of being brought up by a dredge.

dreffle ; gen. **drefful.** Dreadful : (Cockney) sol. (— 1887). Baumann.

dress. At Winchester College, the players that come next in order after *six* or *fifteen* : because they attend matches ready to act as substitutes : from ca. 1850.

dress, more often **dress down.** To beat, thrash ; hence, scold severely : coll. ; from ca. 1660. Mrs. Centlivre, ' I'll dress her down, I warrant her.' I.e. to ' set to-rights ', W.

dress a hat. To practise a concerted robbery, from employers and by employees : low (— 1864) ; ob. See esp. H., 3rd–5th edd.

*****dress-fencer.** (A tramp or pedlar that is) a seller of lace : c. : C. 20. ' Stuart Wood ', *Shades of the Prison House*, 1932.

dress for the part. To be hypocritical : theatrical (ca. 1870) >, ca. 1880, Society coll. Ware.

dress-house. A brothel : from ca. 1820 ; ob. Implied in Bee. Cf. :

dress-lodger. A woman lodged, boarded, and (gen. well) dressed by another, whom she pays by prostitution : from ca. 1830 ; ob. Social-reform Kidd, 1836. Cf. *drapery miss*, q.v.

dress to death (later **to kill**) or **within an inch of one's life.** To dress ultra-smartly : coll. (— 1859). H., 1st ed.

dressed like Christmas beef. See **beef.** (Cf. *mutton dressed as lamb*.)—**dressed to** (or **up to**) **the knocker** (or **nines**). See **knocker** and **nines.— dressed up like a sore finger.** See **sore finger.**

dressing, gen. **dressing-down.** A thrashing ; a severe scolding or reprimand : coll. ; from late 1760's. Jane Austen, ' I will give him such a dressing.'

dressy. Fond of dress : 1768.—2. Very smartly dressed (—1834).—3. Of clothes, extremely fashionable : 1818. All three—the first appears in Goldsmith—were orig. coll., but a generation later they were S.E. (O.E.D.)

drift. To go, walk : mostly Public Schoolboys' and Society coll. (from ca. 1905) now verging on S.E. (Collinson.)

*drill. To entice by degrees: o.: late C. 17–mid-18. B.E. Ex the patience exercised in drill, or that in using a drill.

drill a hole in. To shoot a person with a rifle, also—in G.W.—with a machine-gun : from ca. 1830. The p.ppl. passive *drilled*, without complement, occurs in Marryat's *Peter Simple*. Both are coll.

drilling. 'Punishment by way of waiting, applied to needlewomen who make errors in their work,' Ware : workpeople's (— 1885) ; ob.

drily. A mildly erroneous spelling of *dryly* : C. 18–20.

drink, n. See big drink and cf. Thornton at *drink*.

drink, v. To supply with drink (water or stronger) : coll. : from ca. 1880. (O.E.D.)

[Drink, a drink, drinks ; invitations to drink—and the responses ; the chief alcoholic drinks ; tipsy : synonymies, in unconventional English, of all these may be found admirably set forth in F.& H. at *drinks* (esp.), *drunk, elbow-crooker, flesh and blood, gallon distemper, Gladstone, lush, pistol*, and *razors*. And see *passim* my *Words !* at ' Euphemism and Euphemisms ' and at pp. 128–30, 137, 176.]

drink hearty ! A coll. nautical toast of mid-C. 19–20.

drink like a fish. See fish, drink like a.

drink like a funnel. A C. 19 variant (Apperson) of the preceding.

drink till one gives up one's halfpenny ; only in past tense. (He) drank till he vomited : low : ca. 1675–1770. Ray. (Apperson.)

drink with the flies, n. and v. See Jimmy Woodser.—Drinking Parliament. See Drunken P——.

drinkitite. Thirst, but *on the drinkitite* is ' on the drink ' : East London (— 1909) ; ob. Ware. Cf. *bite-etite*.

drinks. Medicine : hospital nurses' (— 1933). *Slang*, p. 191.

drinks on, have the. To have (a person) at a disadvantage : lower classes' (— 1923). Manchon.

drip. Nonsense : from ca. 1920. For semantics, cf. *bilge* and S.E. *drivel*.—2. Hence, from ca. 1925, v.i., to talk nonsense.

dripper. A venereal gleet : late C. 17–early 19 : low coll. B.E.

dripping. A cook, esp. a bad one : from ca. 1860 ; ob. H., 3rd ed. Cf. *slushy*.

dripping tight. Completely drunk : lower classes' (— 1923). Manchon. I.e. ' soused ' ; an intensive of *tight*, 5.

*driss. An occ. form of *driz*, q.v.

drive. A blow ; a kick : coll. ; from ca. 1850. Henry Kingsley.—2. Energy : coll. ; from ca. 1905. By 1930, virtually S.E.

drive a quill. ' To work in an office ', C. J. Dennis : Australian coll. (— 1916). Ex the lit. S.E. sense (to write), recorded 120 years earlier.

drive to the last minute. To protract or defer as late as possible : coll. ; from ca. 1880.

drive French horses. To vomit : mid-C. 19–20 ; ob. Ex the *hue donc !* of French carters.

drive oneself to the wash. To drive in a basket-chaise : C. 19.

drive pigs to market. See pigs to market, drive one's.

driver. One who compels his employees to do more work for the same wages : s. (1851, Mayhew) >, by 1900, coll. (O.E.D.)—2. A captain notorious for crowding-on all possible sail : nautical coll. : mid-C. 19–20 ; ob. Bowen.

driver's pint. A gallon : late C. 19–20 (ob.): military.

*driz. Lace. Hence *driz fencer*, a seller of lace ; a receiver of stolen lace, hence of other material. C. : from ca. 1810. Vaux, Mayhew. Occ. *driss*.

*driz(-)kemesa. A lace shirt : c. of ca. 1830–70. Ainsworth, *Rookwood*, 1834, ' And sported my flashest toggery . . . My thimble of ridge, and my driz kemesa ', E.D.D.

drizzerable. Unpleasantly damp : C. 20. A. H. Dawson's *Dict. of Slang*, 1913. A blend of *drizzling + miserable*.

Drogheda Light Horse, the. The 18th Hussars : military : C. 19–20 ; ob. F. & Gibbons. Ex its first colonel, Lord Drogheda, who died in 1819.

drogy. A hydrographer in the Navy : naval : C. 20. Bowen.

dromack(k)y. A harlot : North of England s. ; ca. 1830–1900. Ex (a strolling actress that used to play the part of) Andromache.

drome. An aerodrome : 1914 : coll. >, by 1930, S.E. (O.E.D. Sup.)

*dromedary. A (bungling) thief ; hence, 2, a burglar : resp., late C. 17–18 c., C. 18 c. or low s. Also, in sense 1, *purple dromedary*, late C. 17–18 c. In C. 19–20 dial. (ob.), as in C. 16–17 S.E., a dull or stupid person. Ex the dromedary's ungainliness.

*drommerars, -ers. See dommerar.

droops, the. A sinking or droopy feeling ; lassitude : coll. : from ca. 1912. A London underground-railway advertisement of 1935 ran: ' Down those mid-morning " droops " with tea. You'll be better for a cup at 11 a.m.'

*drop, or rather the drop. Same as *drop-game*, q.v. Vaux, 1812.—2. A receiver of stolen goods : c. (— 1915). O.E.D. (Sup.).—3. A tip to a docker : nautical : C. 20. Bowen.—4. Hence, a tip : transport-workers' (— 1935) and underworld's (— 1936), the latter in J. Curtis, *The Gilt Kid*.

drop, v. To part with ; give : from ca. 1670 ; low.—2. Hence (1849), to lose, esp. money.—3. V.i., to understand : low (— 1909). Ware. Abbr. *drop to*, q.v.—4. To get rid of (a person) : New Zealand c. (— 1932).

drop, give one the. To give him the slip : coll. ; C. 18. Mrs. Centlivre. (O.E.D.)

drop, the new or, in C. 19, last. ' A contrivance for executing felons at Newgate, by means of a platform, which drops from under them,' Grose, 2nd ed. : ca. 1780–1900 ; coll.

drop a brick. See brick, drop a.

*drop a cog. To practise the *drop-game*, q.v.: late C. 17–early 19 c. B.E. See esp. Borrow's *Romano Lavo-Lil* (at *ring-dropping*).

drop a turd or one's wax. To defecate : low coll. : C. 18–20 ; C. 19–20 (ob.)

drop across. To scold severely : from ca. 1925. Lyell. Perhaps by confusion of S.E. *drop across*, to meet casually, and *drop on*, to scold or accuse.

drop anchor. To pull up a horse : the turf : from ca. 1860 ; ob.—2. Also, but gen. with *one's*, to sit down ; settle down : orig. nautical ; C. 19–20 coll.

*drop-cove. A specialist, C. 19–20 c., in the ' drop-game ', q.v. Vaux.

drop-dry. Water-tight : nautical coll. (— 1887) : in C. 20, S.E. Baumann.

*drop down to. See down to, drop.

*drop-game. The letting fall a coin, pocket-book, etc., in order to cheat the innocent person picking it up ; the piece so dropped is a *cog*. C. 19–

20 (ob.) c. The gen. mid-C. 19–20 term is *ring-dropping* or *fawney rig*.

drop in one's or **the eye, have a.** To be slightly tipsy : from ca. 1690 ; coll. B.E. ; Swift, 'You must own you had a drop in the eye, for . . . you were half-seas over.' Cf. dial. *drop in the head*.

drop—or **hang, slip,** or **walk**—**into.** To attack ; later, to criticise adversely. From ca. 1850 ; coll. The first, the most gen., prob. began in pugilism, where it means to thrash ; the second is rare and † ; the third is almost confined to physical aggression (including that of coïtion) and was orig. nautical ; the fourth is common.

drop it ! Stop ! Esp., stop talking or fooling. Coll. (— 1854). Whyte-Melville.

drop of gens, a. See **gens.**

drop off the hooks. To die : coll. (— 1857) ; ? orig. nautical. 'Ducange Anglicus.'

drop on. To call on, or 2, to scold or accuse, a person without warning ; 3, to thrash (cf. *drop into*) : the first, coll. ; the second, low ; the third, pugilistic. All from ca. 1850. ? cf. the U.S. *get the drop on* ; certainly cf. :

drop on, have the. 'To forestall, gain advantage over', orig. and esp. 'by covering with a revolver' : (U.S. and) Australian (— 1894). Morris : cf. *get the drop on* in Thornton.

drop on to or, loosely, **onto.** A variant—prob. the imm. origin of—*drop on.* 'Ducange Anglicus,' 1857.

drop one's bundle. See **bundle, drop one's.**

drop one's flag. To salute ; hence, fig. to lower one's colours, to submit : coll. (orig. nautical) ; from ca. 1840.

drop one's leaf. To die : coll. ; from ca. 1820. Egan's Grose. Ex the autumnal fall of leaves. Cf. *hop the twig*.

drop one's leg. (Of a woman) to curtsey : lower classes' (— 1923). Manchon. Prob. suggested by *make a leg*.

drop short. To die : coll. : from ca. 1820. ? ex *drop short in one's tracks*, or is this latter, as I suspect, much more recent ?

drop-shorts. Field artillery : military, mostly Australian and (naturally !) infantrymen's : 1915. Ex the shells occ. dropped short by one's own artillery.

drop the cue. To die : billiard-players' (— 1909). Ware. Cf. *drop off the hooks*.

***drop the main toby.** To leave the highroad ; turn off the main road : mostly vagrants' : mid-C. 19–20. H., 1st ed. See **toby.**

drop the scabs in. To work button-holes : tailors' : from ca. 1850 ; ob.

drop to. To come to understand a plot or plan, a man or his (bad) character : late C. 19–20 : s. >, by 1920, coll. Ex *drop down to* (q.v. at *down to, drop*). Cf. *tumble to*, q.v.

dropped on. Disappointed : tailors' : C. 19–20 ; ob.

***dropper.** A specialist in the *drop-game*, q.v. : late C. 17–19 c. B.E.—2. In late C. 17–18 c., also a distiller : B.E. at *rum dropper*.

dropping. A beating, thrashing, pugilistic or other : Royal Military Academy, ca. 1850–80.—2. Bribery : c. : C. 20. E.g. in Edgar Wallace, *Room 13*, 1924.

dropping member. The *membrum virile*, esp. if gonorrhœa'd : C. 19 low.

drops, fond of one's. Addicted to liquor : Cockney coll. (— 1887). Baumann. Ex *fond of a drop*, which is familiar S.E.

dropsy. A request to pay what is owed (esp. in money) : low (— 1935). Ex the effects of dropsy and perhaps with reference to *drop on*, q.v. Cf. :— 2. Salary : theatrical (— 1935).—3. Bribery : grafters' : C. 20. Philip Allingham, *Cheapjack*, 1934. Cf. *drop*, n., 3, 4, and v., 1.

drored. See **drawed.**—**dror(r)ing.** See **drawing.**

drouthy. Hesitant, wavering : Scottish (—1884). Ware.

drove. Driven : in late C. 18–20, a sol.

drown the miller. See **miller.**

drownd, to drown ; **drownded,** drowned : sol. ; C. 18–20. (Earlier, a S.E. variant.) Cf. *gownd*.

Drowning Flotilla. 'The Flanders Flotilla in the German submarine service, on account of its heavy casualties' : naval : 1917 ; ob. Bowen.

[**drub,** despite B.E. and Grose, has, I think, never been other than S.E., precisely as, despite F. & H., *to drug* and *a drug in the market* are S.E.]

drudge. A cabin-boy : nautical coll. : late C. 19–20. Bowen.

drug-store cowboy. (Gen. in pl.) A tyro cowboy, esp. one of those who carry a revolver dangling from a loose belt to somewhere near the knee : South American white men's derisive coll. : from ca. 1910 (C. W. Thurlow Craig, *Paraguayan Interlude*, 1935).

drugs. Pharmacology : medical coll. . late C. 19–20. *Slang*, p. 192.

***drum.** In c., a road, highway, street : from ca. 1840. Ex Romany *drom* (itself ex Gr. δρόμος), a road.—2. A building, house, lodging, or (in C. 20) a flat : c. and low (— 1859). H., 1st ed. ; Charles E. Leach.—3. Hence, a cell : c. : late C. 19–20. Ware.—4. (Ex *flash drum*,) a brothel : low : from ca. 1900.—5. Among tailors, a small workshop (hence, in C. 20, occ. a workman) : from ca. 1870.— 6. In Australia, from ca. 1860, a bundle of clothes carried on tramp : ob. by 1897, † by 1910. Hence, *hump one's drum*, to go on tramp : likewise †. Wm. Stamer, *Recollections of a Life of Adventure*, 1866 (Morris). Cf. *bluey* and *swag*, qq.v.—7. The ear : pugilistic : ca. 1860–1900. H., 3rd ed. Abbr. *drum of the ear*.

drum, v. To obtain, esp. custom(ers), by solicitation : from ca. 1840 ; coll. Cf. U.S. *drummer*, a 'commercial'.—2. In C. 20 c., *drum* (a place) is to ring or knock to ascertain if it is occupied. Charles E. Leach. Hence a *drummer* is a woman that does this, or that gets a job as a servant in a house some months before her man robs it ; *drumming*, robbery by these means.

drum and fife. Wife : military rhyming s. : late C. 19–20. *Everyman*, March 26, 1931.

drum, empty as an old. Extremely hungry : (mainly Cockney) coll. (— 1885) ; slightly ob. Baumann.

drum, follow the. See **follow . . .**

drum, tight as a. Extremely drunk : C. 20. An elaboration on *tight*. For *drunk as a drum*, see **wheelbarrow.**

***drum-up.** A drink of tea ; the making of tea : tramps' c. (— 1932). F. Jennings, *Tramping with Tramps*. Ex :

***drum up.** To make tea, esp. by the roadside : tramps' c. (— 1864) > also, by 1914, military s. 'No. 747' ; B. & P. Loosely, in C. 20, to cook a meal. Ex Romany *drom*, the highway.—2. Hence (?), to collect : military : from ca. 1915. F. & Gibbons.

drummerdairy. A dromedary : Cockney sol. (— 1887). Baumann.

drumbelo. A late C. 17–early 19 coll. variant of S.E. *drumble*, a dull, heavy fellow. B.E. ; Grose.

drummer. A horse with irregular fore-leg action : the turf : late C. 18–19. Grose, 1st ed. Ex the flourishes of a kettle-drummer.—2. A rabbit : late C. 19–20, ob.—3. In c., a thief that, before robbing, drugs his victim : from ca. 1855 ; ob. H., 1st ed.— 4. A trousers-maker : tailors' : from ca. 1860.— 5. See **drum**, v., 2.

drummer-up ; drumming-up. The agential and the vbl.n. of *drum up*, 1 ; esp. among labourers on public works, the man that makes tea for the gang ; the making of tea : C. 20.

***drumming.** See **drum**, v., 2.

Drummond. An infallible scheme, certain event : low : ca. 1810–50. Vaux. Ex the banking-house of Drummond & Co.

drummy. A sergeant-drummer : military : ca. 1870–1905. F. & Gibbons.

Drum's entertainment. See **Jack Drum's . . .**

drums, pair of. Trousers : tailors' : from ca. 1860.

drumstick. The *membrum virile* : C. 19–20 low ; ob.—2. In Madras Presidency, a pod of the horse-radish tree : coll. (— 1885).—3. See **drumsticks.**

drumstick-cases. Trousers : low : C. 19. Ex :

drumsticks. The legs : s. >, by 1840, coll. : Foote, 1770, ' What, d'ye think I would change with Bill Spindle for one of his drumsticks ? ' Orig. of a fowl's leg.

drunk. A debauch : coll. : from ca. 1860.—2. A tipsy person : coll. : from ca. 1880.—3. A charge of being drunk (and disorderly) : from 1883. (The various *drunk(en)* similes—Grose (3rd ed.), e.g., has *drunk as a wheelbarrow*—are recorded *passim* : see the key-nn. For a short synonymy, see F. & H. at *drunk*, and Apperson.)

drunk, on the, adj. Drinking continually for days : low coll. : from ca. 1870.

drunk to see a hole in a ladder, too. See **hole in a ladder.—drunk with a continuando.** See **continuando.**

drunkard, be quite the gay. To be somewhat tipsy : coll. : ca. 1870–1900.

drunkard, come the. To pretend tipsiness ; rarely, to be tipsy (†) : coll. ; from ca. 1860.

Drunken Barnaby. Richard Brathwait (d. 1673), that poet who, in 1638, published *Drunken Barnaby's Journal*.

drunken-chalks. Good conduct badges : military : ca. 1870–1910. Cf. *canteen medal*, q.v.

Drunken (or **Drinking**) **Parliament.** The Scottish Parliament that met (after the Restoration) on Jan. 1, 1661 : coll. nickname. (O.E.D.)

Druriolanus. Drury Lane Theatre : theatrical : ca. 1885–1910. On *Coriolanus* and with reference to Augustus Harris's nicknames *Augustus Druriolanus* and *the Emperor Augustus*.

Drury Lane ague. A venereal disease : mid-C. 18–early 19. Grose, 1st ed. Cf. *Covent Garden ague*, q.v., and cf. :

Drury Lane vestal. A harlot : mid-C. 18–early 19. Grose, 1st ed. In the C. 18, though little after ca. 1760, this district was residentially infamous. Cf. *Covent Garden nun* and *C.G. vestal*.

Drury-Laner, feel like a. To be indisposed : late C. 19–20. Perhaps, orig., ill from dissipation.

druv, v. Drove : (mostly Cockney) sol. : C. 19–20. Mayhew, 1861 ; Baumann. Cf. *drove*, q.v.

dry as . . . See the key-nn. ; Apperson has all— or most—of the phrases.

dry-bang, -baste, -beat, -rub. To beat severely : (*pace* O.E.D.) coll. ; C. 17–18.

***dry bath.** 'A search [of a prisoner] when stripped' : c. : C. 20. George Ingram in his prison-novel, *Stir*, 1933.

dry-blower. A gold-miner (s.), esp. one who dry-blows gold instead of sluicing it (coll.) : Australian : C. 20.

dry-bob. A cricketer, at Eton College : see **bob.** —2. A smart repartee : C. 17–18 coll.—3. Coïtion without (male) emission : mid-C. 18–19 low. Grose, 1st ed.

dry boots. A dry humorist : late C. 17–early 19 coll. B.E. ; Grose, 1st ed. Cf. *sly boots*.

dry ducking. A man's suspension by a rope to just above the water : nautical coll. : mid-C. 19–20. Bowen.

dry fist. A niggard : C. 17–18 coll. Adj., *dry-fisted*.

dry flogging. 'Corporal punishment with the clothes on' : nautical (esp. naval) coll. : mid-C. 19–20. Bowen. Cf. *dry ducking*.

dry guillotine, the. Severe imprisonment ; esp. imprisonment at Cayenne, most malarious : journalistic coll. : ca. 1860–80. Ware.

dry hash. A 'bad egg' ; ne'er-do-well ; loafer : Australia, ca. 1870–95.—2. 'A baked pudding made of corned beef, tinned salmon, or anything else that comes in handy' : mid-C. 19–20 : nautical coll. >, by 1930, S.E.

dry in. A c. or low s. variant (— 1923 ; slightly ob.) of *dry up*, v., 2. Manchon.

dry land ! You understand ! Rhyming s. (— 1859) ; ob. H., 1st ed.—2. For *dryland sailor*, see **turnpike sailor.**

dry lodging. Accommodation without board : lodging-house keepers', from ca. 1870. H., 5th ed. Cf. S.E. *dry*, without strong liquor ; but imm. ex Scots *dry lodgings* (Galt, 1823 : E.D.D.).

dry nurse. A junior that, esp. in the Army and Navy, instructs an ignorant superior in his duties : coll. : mid-C. 19–20 ; ob. H., 3rd ed. Ex the S.E. sense.

***dry room.** A prison : c. : C. 19–20, ob.

dry-rot. See **rot**, n.—**dry-rub.** See **dry-bang.**

dry scrub or **scrubber.** A marker's signalling of a 'magpie', the disk being rapidly moved up and down in front of the target : Regular Army (not officers') : from ca. 1920.

dry-shave. To deceive, befool, humbug (a person) : lower classes' (— 1923). Manchon. Prob. on *drub* reputed = *dry rub*.

dry smoke. A South African coll. as in Parker Gilmore, *Days and Nights in the Desert*, 1888, ' In his mouth was stuck a short pipe, out of which he was taking, in colonial parlance, *a dry smoke*—that is, it was alike destitute of fire or tobacco.' Pettman.

dry straight. To turn out all right (in the end) : coll. : from mid-1890's ; ob. O.E.D. (Sup.).

dry-up. A failure (cf. esp. *frost*) : theatrical : mid-C. 19–20 ; † by 1918.

dry up, v. Cease talking, notably in the imperative : s. >, by 1930, coll. : from ca. 1864. U.S. (— 1855). Rider Haggard, 1888, ' He . . . suddenly dried up as he noticed the ominous expression on the great man's brow.' Ex ' the figure of the "babbling" fountain ', W.—2. In c. of ca. 1850–1910, to decamp, take to one's heels. Baumann.

dry-walk, gen. **-walking.** A moneyless soldier's outing : military : ca. 1860–1914. (*Dry*, liquorless, is a U.S. import.)

d's, on the two. On twopence a day : military : ca. 1870–1910. Ex *d.*, pence.

d'see. Do you see ? Cockney coll. (— 1887). Baumann. Ex *d'ye see*.

duay. Mine ; my own. Hence, *come the duay*, to over-exercise one's authority. Military : 1915–18, but not very gen. F. & Gibbons derives it ex *Dieu et mon droit*.

*dub. A key, esp. a master or skeleton key : c. : late C. 17–mid-19. B.E. Ex the v.—2. A mediocre player : lawn tennis (— 1923) ; ob. Manchon. Perhaps cognate with Yorkshire *dubber-head*, a doll, but imm. ex :—3. (Also **dub-dub.**) A complete failure : military : G.W., and after. F. & Gibbons.—4. See **dubs.**

*dub, v. To open : mid-C. 16–18 ; (by confusion with *dup*), to close, gen. in form *dub up* (Vaux) : early C. 19 c. Prob. ex Walloon *adouber*, to strike, tap. W.

*dub, strike upon the. To rob (a house) : c. : late C. 17–early 19. B.E. See **dub,** n. 1.

*dub at a knapping jigger. A turnpike keeper : (? late C. 18) early C. 19 c. Vaux. *Jigger*, door or gate : and see **jigger.**

*dub-cove. A turnkey, gaoler, as is *dubsman*, occ. abbr. *dubs* : c. of (? late C. 18–)C. 19. Vaux ; the last in Henley.

*dub lay. The robbing of houses by picking the locks : late C. 18–early 19 c. Grose, 2nd ed. B.E. has ' *We'll strike it upon the dub*, . . . we will rob that place '.

dub o' the lick. ' A lick on the head ', Grose, 2nd ed. : late C. 18–mid-19 : low coll.

dub up. To ' fork out ' ; pay : s. (— 1823), now verging on coll. Bee. Developed from *dub*, v.—2. See **dub,** v.

dubash. An interpreter ; a commissionaire : Anglo-Indian ; from late C. 17. The former sense was † by 1902 ; the prevailing C. 20 one being, a European's native servant. Ex Hindi *dobashi*, a ' two-language man '. Yule & Burnell, 1903.

dubber. The mouth ; tongue : C. 18–19 c., as, in late C. 17–19, is the sense, 2, a picklock thief (B.E.).—3. In Anglo-Indian coll., more properly *dubba*, a leather bottle or skin bag : from late C. 17.

*dubbs. See **dubs,** 2.

dubby. Blunt ; dumpy : dial. (— 1825) >, by 1870, coll. O.E.D. (Sup.).

duberous (1818) ; **dubersome** (1837). In doubt ; dubious : (low) coll. and dial. O.E.D.

Dublin dissector. A cudgel : medical students', ca. 1840–1900. *Punch*, 1841.

Dublin packet, take the. To run round the corner : (— 1859) coll. ; ob. Punning *doubling*.

*Dublin packet, tip (a person) **the.** To elude openly ; give the slip quietly : c. (— 1812) >, ca. 1840, low, † by 1900. Vaux.

*dubs. A jailer : c. (— 1789) ; ob. Abbr. *dubs-man*.—2. (Also **dubbs.**) Money, esp. if of copper : c. (— 1823) ; † by 1870. ' Jon Bee.' Ex *dub*, a fraction of a rupee.

dubs, adj. Double : Winchester College ; from ca. 1830 ; ob.

Dubs, the. The Royal Dublin Fusiliers : military : late C. 19–20.

*dubsman. A turnkey. See **dub-cove.**

*ducat. See ducket.

ducats. Money, cash : theatrical (— 1853), ob. Earlier, gen. coll. : 1775. (S.O.D.) Prob. ex Shakespeare's Shylock. Cf. the use of *shekels*.

*duce, i.e. deuce, q.v., is twopence : c. : late C. 17–18. B.E. Moncrieff.

ducer, the. The second steward in a liner : nautical : C. 20. Bowen. Ex *duce = deuce*, two.

duchess. A woman of an imposing presence : from ca. 1690. B.E. Contrast *dutch*.—2. ' A woman enjoyed with her pattens on, or by a man in boots, is said to be made a duchess,' Grose, 1st ed. ; † by 1890.

duchess,—' hell ! ' said the. See ' **hell ! ' said the duchess.**

Duchess, ring up the ; I must ring up the Duchess. These two c.pp., applicable to resolution of a doubt or to settlement of a problem, arose in Jan., 1935, ex the play *Young England* : orig. and mainly London Society : ob.

duchess, the. The mother or the wife (*the old duchess*) of the person addressed : proletarian : resp. — 1909 and — 1923 ; ob. Ware ; Manchon. —2. A living lay-figure : silk trade : from ca. 1870 ; ob. Ware.

duchessy, adj. Like a duchess (— 1887) ; abounding in duchesses (— 1870) : coll. (O.E.D.)

duck. A decoy ; C. 19 coll. Abbr. *decoy-duck.*—2. A bundle of meat-scraps : low coll. (— 1864). H., 3rd ed. Cf. *faggots*.—3. A coll. endearment : from ca. 1590. Shakespeare. Hence, in admiration, as is the adj. *ducky*. Leman Rede, 1841, ' Oh, isn't he a duck of a fellow ? '—4. A soldier (gen. in pl.) of the Bombay Presidency : Anglo-Indian : from ca. 1800. Later, any official in the Bombay service. Ex *Bombay duck*, q.v.—5. A metal-cased watch : cheapjacks' : ca. 1850–1914. Hindley.—6. The face, as in *make a duck*, make a grimace : Winchester College : ca. 1860–1920. In cricket, however, *make a duck*, or *duck's egg*, is to score nothing, while *save* (— 1877) or *break* (— 1900) *one's duck*, is to score at least one run (Lewis) : *duck* occurs in 1868, *duck's egg* in 1863, and *duck-egg* in 1868 (O.E.D.).—7. Cf. the Anglo-Irish *duck* (*for dinner*), nothing to eat : late C. 19–20.—8. Abbr. *lame duck*, q.v. : from ca. 1780. Grose, 1st ed.

duck. To avoid ; to neglect to attend (e.g. a meeting) : coll. : C. 20. (E. Shanks, *The Enchanted Village*, 1933.)

*duck, do a. In c., to hide under the seat of a public conveyance so as to avoid paying (— 1889) ; but in gen. coll., to depart hurriedly (— 1900).

duck !, Lord love a. A mild proletarian expletive (— 1923). Manchon.

duck, make a. See **duck,** 6.

duck-disease ; duck's disease. ' Shortness of leg ', O.E.D. (Sup.) (the Army explained it differently) ; a nickname (*Duck's Disease*) for any very short man : (low) coll. : from ca. 1910.

duck egg. See **duck,** 6.

duck, fake the. See **fake the duck.**

duck-footed, adj. Walking with toes turned inwards : coll. : C. 19–20 ; ob. But *duck-legged*, with very short legs, is S.E.

duck-fucker. The man looking after the poultry on a warship : mid-C. 18–early 19 ; nautical. Grose, 1st ed.

duck in a thunderstorm. See **dying duck.**

duck of diamonds. A superlative of the admiring *duck*, 3 : coll. ; from ca. 1850 ; ob.

duck-pond. A canvas bathing-place for cadets : naval (— 1909) ; ob. Ware.

duck-shover, -shoving. A cabman who is guilty of breaking the rank and thus unfairly touting for custom; this extremely reprehensible practice; Melbourne: ca. 1869–1895. Morris. 2. (*d.-shoving.*) Hence (?), an evasion of duty: military: late C. 19–20. F. & Gibbons.

duckboard is military j., except when (ex its arrangement of colours) it = a Military Medal ribbon (1916 : B. & P.); but *duckboard-glide*, an after-dark movement along a trench, and *duckboard harrier*, a messenger, are military s. of 1917–18. It and he had to use the duckboard track. F. & Gibbons.

ducker. In diving, a header : sporting (— 1923). Manchon. Ex ducking one's head in water.—2. **the Ducker** is the swimming-pool at : Harrow School : late C. 19–20. J. Fischer Williams, *Harrow*, 1901. Ibid. I.e. *duck* + ' the Oxford-*er* '.

ducket. Any ticket ; esp. a raffle-card or a pawn-broker's duplicate : c. and low (— 1874); ob. H., 5th ed. A corruption of *docket*. Also *ducat*.

duckey. See **ducky.**

duckie. See **ducky.**

ducking, go. To go courting : low coll. : from ca. 1850; ob. Ex *duck*, 3.

ducking-money. Money exacted from a sailor the first time he went through the Strait of Gibraltar : naval coll. : C. 19. Bowen.

ducks. Aylesbury Dairy Company shares : Stock Exchange : from ca. 1880; ob. Aylesbury (Buckinghamshire) is ' especially noted for the rearing of ducks,' *Encyclopædia Britannica.*—2. A variation of *ducky*, 2, mostly in address : C. 20. James Curtis, *The Gilt Kid*, 1936.

ducks, fine weather for. See **fine weather** . . .

ducks and drakes with, later **of.** To squander money or potential money : from late C. 16 ; coll. till C. 19, then S.E. Chapman, ' Be like a gentleman . . . make ducks and drakes with shillings.'

duck's bill. ' A tongue cut in a piece of stout paper and pasted on at the bottom of the tympan sheet ', F. & H. : printers' ; from ca. 1860; ob. Ex shape.

duck's breakfast. A drink of water with nothing to eat : esp. New Zealanders' : C. 20. Cf. *Irishman's dinner*.

duck's disease. See **duck-disease.**

duck's egg. See **duck,** 6 ; *break one's duck's egg* occurs in 1867 (Lewis).

ducks in the pond. A term in the game of House : military : from ca. 1920. *The Evening News*, Nov. 21, 1935.

ducky ; duckie, adj. Expressive of admiration (see **duck,** 3) : coll. ; from ca. 1830.—2. N., an endearment, thus a variant of *duck*, 3 : from ca. 1815 ; coll. The former solely, the latter mainly, a woman's term.

dud. A delicate weakling (†); person without ability and/or spirit : orig. Scottish (— 1825), Jamieson speaking of ' a soft dud ' ; (?) used in U.S. in 1870 ; rare by 1896 ; resuscitated in G.W., from sense of an unexploding shell, hence of any very inferior or unsuitable object. In 1916 +, an adj. : e.g. ' a dud show ', a poor entertainment. These terms have prob. been influenced by the C. 17–20 dial. *dudman*, a scarecrow, but the word may derive ultimately ex Dutch *dood*, dead (W.).—2. See **duds.**

*****dud(d)-cheats.** Clothes and household effects : c. (— 1725); † by 1830. *A New Canting Dict.* Cf. *duds*, 1, 2, q.v.

*****dudder** or **whispering dudder, dudsman,** and **duffer** (q.v.). A pedlar of supposedly smuggled wares : late C. 18–early 19 ; the first two being c., the third also c. but only at first. Grose, 2nd ed. Ex *duds*, q.v.—2. One who passes off harmless powder as cocaine or morphia : Australian (esp. Sydney) c. (— 1931).

dude. A swell, fop : orig. (1883) U.S. and almost imm. anglicised ; coll. till ca. 1918, when it > S.E. The derivatives *dudine*, a female masher, and *dudette, dudinette*, a young girl aping the belles, did not catch on in England. Where the etymology is a mystery, but the occasion known to be the Æsthetic craze of ca. 1882–7, it is perhaps permissible to guess at *dud* (q.v.) influenced by *attitude*, the semantic transition being aided, maybe, by the dial. v.i. *dud*, to dress.—2. Light ; a light : either low s. or tramps' c. (— 1923). Manchon. Ex Romany.

duddering rake. ' A thundering Rake . . . one devilishly lewd ', *A New Canting Dict.*, 1725 : C. 18–early 19. See **dundering r.**

duddery. A clothier's booth : C. 17–early 19 low coll. Cf. the dial. senses.

duds. Clothes : mid-C. 16–17 c. (Harman, Head); in C. 18–20, low (Grose, Trollope). Ex C. 15 *dudde*, cloth, a cloak ; cf. *duddery*, q.v.—2. In C. 16–20 coll., occ. rags or old clothes.—3. The sense ' portable property ' is, orig. in mid-C. 17–18, English c., but in C. 19–20 it is mainly U.S. ' standard '.

*****duds, sweat.** To pawn clothes : C. 19–20 c.

*****dudsman.** A seller of so-called contraband clothes : c. ; (? late C. 18–)early C. 19. Cf. *dudder*, q.v.

due for the hammer or **the shillelagh.** An Anglo-Irish c.p. (C. 20) applied to a person about to be dismissed or to a team about to be beaten.

[**due to**, because of, is objected to by many purists, but the O.E.D. and W. support it ; moreover, the purists' preference, *owing to*, is, semantically, an exact equivalent.]

*****dues, the.** Money : orig. (— 1812) c. ; by 1860, coll. ; by 1890 ob. Vaux ; Ainsworth.

duey. Twopence : circus s. via Parlyaree : mid-C. 19–20. Baumann. Cf. *duce*.

duff. No good ; inferior : Glasgow : late C. 19–20. Cf.:

*****duff,** gen. preceded by **the.** The selling of actually or supposedly smuggled goods : late C. 18–early 19 c.—2. Food : nautical coll. : late C. 19–20. (A. E. W. Mason, *The Dean's Elbow*, 1930.) Ex the specific S.E. sense.

*****duff,** v. To sell inferior goods, esp. clothes, pretending they are stolen or smuggled : orig. (— 1781) c. ; by 1860, low.—2. Hence, to make old clothes appear new by manipulating the nap : coll. ; from ca. 1835.—3. To alter the brands of stolen horses or, esp., cattle (— 1869); hence, to steal cattle by changing the brands : Australian s. > coll. ; ob. Carton Booth in *Another England*, 1869 ; Boldrewood, *The Squatter's Dream*, 1890.—4. V.i. and t. To be a duffer (no good) ; to be a duffer at : ca. 1880–1915. Ware. Ex *duffer*, 4.

*****duff, man at the.** A seller of certain goods (see **duff,** n., 1. : C. 19 c. Cf. *duffer*, 1.

duff days. Thursday and Sunday, when that pudding appeared at the gun-room's dinner : naval coll. : C. 19. Bowen. Cf. :

duff night. Guest night on a warship : naval officers' : late C. 19–20. Bowen. Cf. preceding.

duff out of. To cheat or rob (a person) of : from ca. 1860 ; ob. Cf. *duff*, v., 1, 3.

***duffer.** A seller of pretended stolen or smuggled goods : mid-C. 18–19 ; orig. c. ; by 1860 low and slightly ob. Grose, 1st ed. ; Colquhoun, 1796, in *Police of the Metropolis*, ' A class of sharpers . . . duffers ' ; Dickens ; Thackeray.—2. A pedlar ; a hawker, esp. of women's clothes : low coll. : from late C. 18 ; ob.—3. A ' renovator ' of inferior goods, esp. clothes : low coll. ; from ca. 1850.—4. A worthless object, esp. counterfeit coin : low s. (— 1875) ; ob. Also, a person of no ability (— 1842), a dolt (from ca. 1870) : both coll.—5. A female smuggler : C. 19 nautical.—6. Ca. 1820–50, a professional cheater of pawnbrokers : low if not c.—7. In Australia, a cattle-stealer (or illicit brander) : s. > coll. ; from ca. 1870, though unrecorded before 1889. —8. An unproductive mine-claim : Australian coll. (— 1861). H. Finch-Hatton, *Advance Australia*, 1885. Cf. *shicer*, q.v. (O.E.D. ; S.O.D. ; Morris.)

duffer- or duffing-fare. A person driving in a cab to oblige the driver : London cabmen's : ca. 1900– 10. Ware.

duffer out. (Of a mine) to become unproductive : Australia (— 1885) ; coll. > j. by 1910.

duffing. The practice of selling worthless goods as valuable : low > coll. ; from ca. 1850. See **duff**, n. and v., and **duffer**, 1, 2.—2. In Australia, thieving of cattle (gen. preceded by *cattle-*) : s. (— 1881) > coll. by 1900.

duffing, ppl. adj. Inferior or counterfeit but offered as superior or genuine (— 1851) ; of a person selling such goods (— 1862).—2. Dull, stupid ; foolish : from ca. 1880 ; rare in C. 20.

duffing-fare. See **duffer-fare.**

duffy. A ghost or spirit : West Indies, chiefly among the negroes (— 1864). H., 3rd ed. ? ex *Davy Jones*.—2. A quartern of gin : London : ca. 1820–50. Bee. Ex *daffy*. But perhaps a misprint.

Duffo. A Devonport bluejacket or ship : naval : late C. 19–20. Bowen. By ' telescoping '.

dufter. An orderly room : military (Regular Army) : late C. 19–20. F. & Gibbons. Ex Hindustani *daftar*, an office.

dug-out. An over-age officer back in service : military : 1912 (O.E.D. Sup.). Because *dug-out* of his retirement. See esp. B. & P.—2. Hence, adj. : 1915. E.g. *dug-out king*, one who kept to his dugout (Australian : 1916), and *dug-out disease*, ' chronic fear of death and danger which kept those, whose rank permitted any choice, safe in their *dug-outs* ' (gen. : 1917).

dugs, of a woman's breasts or nipples, has, since ca. 1880, been a vulg., though it is permissible in S.E. if used as a strong pejorative.

***duke.** A handsome man, esp. if of showy appearance : gen. as *rum duke* (B.E.) : late C. 17– early 18 c. ; 2, hence (see **rum**), ' A queer unaccountable fellow ', Grose, 1st ed. : c. : late C. 18– early 19 ; often as *rum duke*.—3. Gin : ca. 1850– 80 ; a below-stairs term.—4. A horse : cabmen's ; ca. 1860–1910.—5. In c. also, a burglary, a robbery : from ca. 1840 ; ob. The first and second are derivable from the idea of aristocracy ; the third is etymologically problematic ; the fifth comes prob. ex Romany (cf. *dookin*).—6. See **dook**, 2 and 3, and **dukes.**

Duke. An occ. abbr. of **Duke of Kent.** P. P., *Rhyming Slang*, 1932.

Duke Humphrey. See **dine with Duke Humphrey.**

Duke of Fife. A knife : rhyming s. : late C. 19– 20. F. & Gibbons.

Duke of Kent. Rent : rhyming s. : 1932, P. P., *Rhyming Slang*.

duke of limbs. An ungainly fellow, esp. if tall : coll. : mid-C. 18–mid-19. Grose, 1st ed.

duke o(f) Seven Dials. ' Satirical peerage bestowed upon any male party dressed or behaving above or beyond his immediate surroundings ' : proletarian London : ca. 1875–1900. Ware. Seven Dials was a very poor quarter.

Duke of York. To talk : to walk : rhyming s. (— 1859 the latter, — 1873 the former).—2. A storm trysail : nautical : from ca. 1880.—3. A cork : rhyming s. : from ca. 1890. *The Evening Standard*, Aug. 19, 1931.

Duke of Yorks. Forks : rhyming s. (— 1874) ; ob. H., 5th ed.—2. Hence, fingers ; hence hands ; hence *dukes*, q.v.

duker. The proprietor of a large nose : streets' : ca. 1840–70. Ware. See **dook**, 3.—2. A lighter of a special type operating in the Mersey and Manchester Ship Canal : nautical : late C. 19–20. Bowen. Why ?

dukes, often, esp. in C. 20, pronounced *dooks*. Hands ; fists : low (— 1874). Ex preceding term. For such abridgements and similar ingenuity, see *Slang* at ' Oddities ' and *Words !* at ' Rhyming Slang '.

dukes, grease the. V.i., to practise bribery ; but the v.t. with *of* is much more gen. : low (— 1877). Horsley, *Jottings from Jail*.

dukes, put up the. To prepare for fisticuffs : orig. low s. ; in C. 20, low coll. From ca. 1880.

Duke's, the. The Argyll Rooms in Windmill Street : London : ca. 1860–1900. Ware. Ex *Duke of Argyll*.—2. The Duke of Wellington's, now the West Riding, Regiment : military : not before 1853 ; ob. F. & Gibbons.

dukess. A duchess : sol. : C. 19–20. Cf. *dook*, 2.

dukey. See **dookie.**

Dukie. (Gen. pl.) A boy of the *Duke* of York's Royal Military School : coll. : C. 20. O.E.D. (Sup.).

dukkering. See **dookin.**

dulay ; dupan. Milk ; bread, resp. : military : 1914 ; ob. B. & P. I.e. Fr. *du lait, du pain,* (some) milk, (some) bread.

dulcamara. A quack doctor : cultured coll. : ca. 1845–1910. Ex a character in *L'Elisir d'amore*, by Donizetti, who adopts the mediæval L. name for the herb gen. called bittersweet.

dulcerate, -ation. Incorrect for *dulcorate, -ation* : C. 16–17. O.E.D.

Duleep. Duleepsinhji : cricketers' : from 1925, when he first played for Cambridge. ' To cricketers he liked to be known as " Smith " ' (*Who's Who in World Cricket*, 1934).

dull in the eye. Tipsy : coll. : from ca. 1840 ; ob.

dull-pickle. A heavy, dull, stupid fellow : late C. 17–18 coll. B.E.

Dull Street, live in. I.e. in a dull quarter : coll. (— 1887) verging on S.E. Baumann. Cf. *Queer Street.*

dull-swift. A stupid fellow ; a sluggish messenger : coll. : mid-C. 18–early 19. Grose, 1st ed.

dullmajor. ' An interpreter in British prisoner of war camps in Germany ' : 1915–18. By ' Hobson-Jobson ' ex Ger. *Dolmetscher*. F. & Gibbons.

dully. A dull person : coll. : 1883 (O.E.D.). Cf. *stupid.*

*dum tam. A bunch of clothes carried on his back, but under his coat, by a beggar : North Scottish c. : C. 19. E.D.D., ' This seems to be a cant phrase denoting that although this is carried as beggars carry their children, it is mute.'

dumb. Stupid ; dull ; silent : S.E. ca. 1530–1650 ; (? revived) in U.S. as s.,—Thornton records it for 1843 ; anglicised, likewise as s., ca. 1920. See quotation **at marvellous.**

dumb arm. A maimed one : coll. : late C. 18–early 19. Grose, 1st ed.

dumb-cow. To brow-beat or cow : Anglo-Indian coll. (— 1886). Prob. ex Hindustani *dhamkana*, to chide or threaten, via the process of Hobson-Jobson. Yule & Burnell.

dumb-fogged, -foozled, ppl. adj. Confused, puzzled, confounded : coll. ; from ca. 1860 ; ob.

dumb glutton. The *pudendum muliebre* : mid-C. 18–19 low (Grose, 1st ed.) as is the synonymous *dumb squint*, C. 19. Hence *feed the dumb glutton*, mid-C. 18–19, or *the dummy*, C. 19–20 (ob.), to have sexual intercourse.

dumb insolence. Breaking wind on parade : military : 1916. F. & Gibbons. Ex military j. for ' silent insolence '.

dumb peal. A muffled peal : bell-ringers' coll. (— 1901). Rev. H. Earle Bulwer's *Glossary*.

dumb scraping. ' Scraping wet decks with blunt scrapers ' : nautical coll. : late C. 19–20. Bowen.

*dumb sparkler. A silent match : c. : mid-C. 19–20. ' No. 747.'

dumb-waiter. An elevator : rhyming s., mostly workmen's : from ca. 1920. *John o' London's Weekly*, July 9, 1934.

dumb watch. ' A venereal bubo in the groin ', Grose, 1st ed. : mid-C. 18–early 19 : low.

dumbfound. To perplex ; put to confusion ; silence : from ca. 1650 ; coll. until ca. 1800, then S.E.—2. Also, to beat soundly, thrash : ca. 1660–1820, as in B.E.'s ' I dumbfounded the sawcy Rascal.' After *confound*.

dumby. A variant, prob. the original, of *dummy*, 1. (Bee, 1823.)

dumfungled, adj. Dumbfounded : Cockney sol. (— 1887) ; ob. Baumann.

dummacker. A knowing person ; an astute one : ca. 1850–1910. H., 2nd ed. ? ironically ex dial. *dummock*, a blockhead.

*dummee. A variant (*Lex. Bal.* ; Egan's Grose) of *dummy*, 3, q.v.

*dummerer. See dommerar. — dummie. Bee's spelling of *dummy*, n., 3.

dummock. The posteriors : low : C. 19–20 ; ob. Perhaps ex Romany *dumo*, the back (Sampson), + *ock* as in *bittock*.

dummy. A deaf-mute : coll. ; from late C. 16. Ex *dumb*.—2. A person notably deficient in ability or brightness : coll. ; from ca. 1795.—3. In c., a pocket-book : from ca. 1810. Vaux. (Not in Grose, 1st, 3rd edd.)—4. A dumb-waiter : from ca. 1850.—5. An actor or actress that does not speak, a ' super ' : theatrical ; ca. 1870–1920.—6. A makeshift, substitute, or rudimentary bill : Parliamentary s. ; from ca. 1860.—7. In Australia, the grip-car of a Melbourne tram : coll. : ca. 1893–1905. Morris. Ex *Dummy*, the Northumberland dial. nickname for a colliery carriage : 1843 (E.D.D.).—8. A loaf of bread : c. (— 1909). Ware, ' Probably from the softness of the crumb ' ; cf. **sense 3.**

dummy, chuck a ; chuck the dummy. See the two relevant entries at **chuck.**

*dummy(-daddle) dodge. Pocket-picking under cover of a sham or ' dummy ' hand or ' daddle ' : c. of ca. 1850–1900.

*dummy-hunter. A pickpocket specialising in ' dummies ' or pocket books : c. : ca. 1810–1910. Vaux.

dummy run. A practice evolution : naval coll. : C. 20. Bowen.

dump. A small coin or sum of money : Australian coll. and s. resp. ; 1827, ca. 1840. Both ob. by 1895, † by 1910. Ex a small coin, worth 1*s*. 3*d*., called in as early as 1823 (Morris).—2. A button : c. (— 1859). App. only in *dump-fencer*, q.v. Ex sense 1.—3. In 1915 +, orig. military, a place : ex the j. sense, a place where war material, old or salvaged, is stored, for the most part in the open, hence a refuse heap, itself ex *dump*, v.—4. Hence, a hotel : tramps' c. (— 1923). Manchon.—5. Hence, a lodging-place or residence ; a cache of stolen goods : New Zealand c. (— 1932).

dump, v. To throw or set down heavily ; let fall heavily : ex U.S. (— 1830), anglicised ca. 1870 as a coll. that, ca. 1900, > S.E. Cf. the M.E. *domp*, to fall heavily,—whence *dump* perhaps on *thump*. W.—2. Hence, esp. in G.W. and after, to put, set, place, no matter how.—3. At Winchester College, to extinguish, as in ' dump the tolly ', i.e. the candle : mid-C. 19–20. (E.D.D.)

dump, not to care a. To care little or not at all : coll. ; from ca. 1800. Ex a metal counter.

dump-fencer. A button-seller : ca. 1855–1910 : low, perhaps c. H., 1st ed. For *fencer* = seller, cf. *driz-fencer*. See **dump**, n., 2.

Dumpies, the. The Nineteenth Hussars : from ca. 1860 ; ob. Ex the smallness of the men when the regiment was raised in 1859 : cf. the S.E. *Bantams* of the G.W.—2. Also, for similar reasons, a nickname of the 20th Hussars and the 21st Lancers : from ca. 1870 ; ob. F. & Gibbons.

dumplin(g). A short, thick-set man or woman : from ca. 1610 : until ca. 1800, coll. ; then S.E. ; now ob. Cf. *Norfolk dumpling*, an inhabitant of Norfolk, ex the prevalence of apple and, esp. plain, suet dumplings.

dumpling-depôt. The stomach : C. 19–20 ; ob. Cf., and after, *bread-basket*. J. J. Conington, *The Castleford Conundrum*, 1932, ' " This telegram produced some sensation ? " " . . . It did. F∂ir took 'em in the dumpling depot." '

dumplin(g) on, have a. To be with child : proletarian (— 1909) ; ob. *Ware*.

dumpling-shop. The human paps : lower classes' : C. 19–20 ; ob.—2. A variant (— 1923) of *dumpling-depôt*. Manchon.

dumps, the. A fit of melancholy ; depression : C. 16–20 ; S.E. until ca. 1660, then coll., esp. when preceded by *in*. *The Spectator*, No. 176 (1711), ' when I come home she is in the dumps.'—2. Money : from ca. 1835 ; ob. Barham speaks of suicide ' for want of the dumps '. Ex *dump*, n., 1.

dumpy. See **chubby.**

dun. A creditor importunately asking for what is his : from ca. 1628 ; orig. coll. ; in C. 19–20, S.E. Wycherley, ' insatiable . . . duns '. Possibly ex a stock name of the *John Doe, Tommy Atkins* type, as W.'s analogy from the Paston Letters seems to show.

dun, v. To persist in trying to get what is due to one : from ca. 1626 ; in C. 19–20, S.E. ; before, coll. Killigrew, ' We shall be revenged upon the rogue for dunning a gentleman in a tavern.' Prob., despite recorded dates, ex the n.

dun, adj. See **scruff,** n.

Dun Cow, the Old. The *River Clyde,* a steamer driven on the Gallipoli shore in April, 1915 : naval and military : 1915. Ex the wooden horse at the siege of Troy, ' whose site could be seen from her decks '. (Bowen.)

dun is the mouse, gen. **dun's the mouse.** A c.p. quibble made when *done* is mentioned, a mouse being *dun*-coloured ; when spoken urgently it connoted ' keep still ! ' Ca. 1580–1640. A later C. 17 form is *dun as a mouse,* which, implying no warning, prob. arises from the confusion of '*s* = *is* or *as* (or, though not here, *has*). (Apperson.)

dun territory. ' Circle of creditory to be had ', Egan's Grose : Oxford University : ca. 1820–40.

*****dunagan.** An early C. 19 variant (Egan's Grose) of *dunnaken,* q.v.

*****dunaker.** A stealer of cattle, esp. of cows : late C. 17–early 19 c. B.E. Variants, *dunnocker, donnaker.* Ex *dunnock,* q.v.

duncarring. Homosexuality : late C. 17–early 18. B.E. Prob. ex a person's name.

dunch. To *dine* at *lunch*-time : cultured middle class's : from ca. 1929 ; very ob. Somerset Maugham, *Cakes and Ale,* 1930, ' Verbs that you only know the meaning of if you live in the right set (like " dunch ") '.

Dundalks. Shares in the Dundalk Steam Company : Stock Exchange coll. (– 1895) soon > **j.** (A. J. Wilson's glossary.)

dundering rake. This (B.E., ca. 1690) is almost certainly the correct spelling of Grose's *duddering rake,* q.v. *Dunder* is a variant of the mainly Scottish *dunner,* to thunder.

[**dunderhead** and its variants have, despite H. and F. & H., always been S.E.]

dundrearies. A pair of whiskers that, cut sideways from the chin, are grown as long as possible : from Sothern's make-up in *Our American Cousin* (see the next entry) ; the fashion was antiquated by 1882, dead by 1892. This coll. term (1858) survives. Cf. *Piccadilly weepers.*

dundreary. A stammering, silly, long-whiskered dandy : coll. ; from 1858, the year of Tom Taylor's once famous comedy, *Our American Cousin,* in which Lord Dundreary appears ; hence, from ca. 1860, a foppish fool. The former †, the latter ob.

*****dunegan.** An early C. 19 variant of *dunnaken.* *Lex. Bal.*

dung. A workman at less than union wages : C. 19 ; in C. 20, merely historical.—2. Mid-C. 19–20, also a ' scab '.—3. Ca. 1760–1840, a journeyman tailor satisfied with regulation wages, Grose, 1st ed. With the last, contrast *flint,* q.v., and cf. *scab,* q.v.

dung-cart or **-fork.** A yokel ; a country bumpkin : coll. : C. 19–20 ; ob.

dung-drogher. A guano ship : nautical coll.: late C. 19–20. Bowen.

dungaree, adj. Low, coarse, vulgar : Anglo-Indian : from ca. 1830 ; ob. Ex the coarse blue cloth and the name of a disreputable Bombay suburb.

dungaree-settler. A poor settler in or of Australia : Australian coll.: ca. 1840–70. Anon., *Settlers and Convicts,* 1852 (Morris). Ex clothing himself, wife and family in clothes made of dungaree.

dunghill, die. To die contrite or cowardly ; esp. to repent at the gallows : coll. ; ca. 1755–1830. (O.E.D.)

dunna. See **dunno.**

dunnage. Clothes ; baggage : nautical : from ca. 1850. Mayhew. Cf. *duds.* Ex the S.E. sense, matting or brushwood used in packing cargo (W.).

dunnage-bag. A kit-bag : naval : late C. 19–20. F. & Gibbons.

*****dunnaken** or **-kin ; dunneken** or **-kin ; dunnyken** or **-kin ; dunagan, -egan.** A privy : late C. 19–20 ; c. >, by 1860, low coll. In C. 17–18, *dannaken* : orig. c., then low s. : see **danna.** Whence *do a d.,* to visit one : low : late C. 19–20. Manchon. (The form *dunnakew,* in B. M. Carew, 1791, is prob. a misprint.)

dunnaken-drag. A night-cart : ca. 1820–60. Egan's Grose. Cf. *danna-drag* at **danna.**

dunnaw. See **dunno.—dunneken** or **-kin.** See **dunnaken.**

dunner. An importunate creditor : from ca. 1690 ; coll. till C. 19, then S.E. ; in C. 20 somewhat archaic. B.E. *Dunning,* vbl.n., coming late is S.E.

*****dunnick-drag.** A variant pronunciation of *danna-drag* (q.v. at *danna*). Vaux.

dunno. Do not know : sol. : C. 19–20. Often *dunno !,* I don't know. Occ. *dunna* or *dunnaw.* See also **d'n.**

*****dunnock.** A cow : (? C. 17,) C. 18–early 19 c. Grose, 2nd ed. ? ex *dun,* adj.: *the dun cow* is famous and serves as a title to a satire by Robert Landor.

dunnyken or **-kin.** See **dunnaken.**

dunop. A pound (gen. sterling) : back s., from ca. 1865. *Dnuop > dunop,* for the sake of euphony. See *Words !,* article ' Rhyming Slang '.

duns. ' Tradesmen dealing with a ship or its crew ' : nautical : late C. 19–20. Bowen. They have the impudence to ask for their money.

duo. A duodenal ulcer : medical students' : from ca. 1920.

*****dup.** To open : mid-C. 16–18 c. ; now dial. Harman, Head. Elisha Coles, 1676, defines it as ' to enter [the house] '. Not *do up* but *do ope(n).*

dupan. See **dulay.**

durance. A prison : coll. ; ca. 1690–1750. B.E. (Unrecorded by O.E.D., this sense gives added point to *in durance vile.*)

duration, for the ; rarely **the duration.** For a very long time indeed : military : from 1915. Early in the G.W., one enlisted *for four years or the duration of the war.* B. & P.

Durham man. A knock-knee : late C. 18–early 19 coll. Grose, 3rd ed. : ' He grinds mustard with his knees : Durham is famous for its mustard.'

*****duria.** Fire : C. 19 c. ' Ducange Anglicus ', 1857. ? cf. Romany *dugilla,* lightning.

duritike. Incorrect for *diuretic* : C. 16. O.E.D.

durn, durned. Variants of *darn, darned* : low coll. : C. 19–20. Freeman Wills Crofts, *Mystery in the Channel,* 1931, ' It's durned strange they didn't tell you themselves, without your comin' to me abaht it.'

durra, dhurra. Indian millet : Anglo-Indian coll. : from late C. 18.

*****durrynacker.** A female lace-hawker, gen. practising palmistry ' on the side '. Vbl.n., *durrynacking.* Mayhew : mid-C. 19–20 c. ; ob. Ex Romany *dukker,* to tell fortunes : cf. *dookin,* q.v.

durzee. A variant of *derzy,* q.v.

dusodile. Incorrect for *dysodile* : C. 19–20. O.E.D.

dust. Money : coll. : from ca. 1600. Esp. in

down with one's or *the dust*, to pay, as in Fuller, 1665. 'The abbot down with his dust, and glad he escaped so, returned to Reading.' Prob. abbr. *gold-dust*.— 2. A disturbance, 'row', esp. in *kick up a dust*, cause a 'shindy' : from ca. 1750 ; s. until ca. 1890, then coll. (*Raise a dust* is S.E. and more lit.)

dust, v. To blind (fig.) ; befool, as in *dust the public* : Stock Exchange ; from ca. 1814 ; ob. Abbr. the S.E. *dust the eyes of*.—2. **dust** or **dust off** (or **out**), v. To depart hurriedly : in C. 17 S.E. ; in C. 19 U.S. s., whence C. 20 English s.

dust-bin. A grave : from ca. 1850 ; ob.

dust (a ship) down. To sweep her decks : nautical : late C. 19–20. Bowen.

Dust Hole, the. The Prince of Wales's Theatre in Tottenham Court Road : theatrical, from ca. 1840– 1900. (The theatre, which, ca. 1830–50, accumu- lated its sweepings under the pit while it was still the Queen's Theatre, moved in the late '80's.)— 2. Sidney Sussex College, Cambridge : ca. 1860–85. H., 3rd ed.

dust in the eyes, have. To be sleepy : cf. *draw straws* and *the dustman is coming.* Coll. : (? C. 18,) C. 19–20 ; ob. (*throw dust in the eyes*, like *bite the dust*, is S.E.)

dust it away, gen. in imperative. To drink about, esp. quickly : late C. 17–18 : coll. (*pace* the O.E.D.).

dust off. See **dust,** v., 2.

dust one's cassock, coat, doublet, or **jacket, with for him** (her) occ. added. To thrash ; † criticise severely. Coll. : the first and third, C. 18, Smol- lett ; the second, late C. 17–early 19, but anticipated in Tusser's 'What fault deserves a brushed cote' ; the fourth and sole extant, from late C. 17, as in Farquhar, Barham.

dust out. See **dust,** v., 2.

dust-up. A variant of *dust*, n., 2 : C. 19–20. Ware.

duster. A sweetheart (female) : tailors' : from ca. 1850 ; ob.—2. (Also **the red duster.**) A red ensign : nautical : from ca. 1895. Cf. *coach-whip.*

dustie. See **dusty.**

dusting. A thrashing ; (nautical) rough weather : both from late C. 18.

dustman. (Esp. *be a dustman.*) A dead man : late C. 18–early 19. Grose, 1st ed.—2. Sleep personified, esp. in *the dustman's coming*, used chiefly to children : coll. ; from ca. 1820 ; ob. Egan's Grose.—3. A gesticulatory preacher, apt to raise the dust : 1877, Blackmore (O.E.D.).—4. A naval stoker : naval : late C. 19–20. Bowen.

dustman's bell, the. Time for bed : nursery coll. : from ca. 1840. See preceding entry, sense 2. Ware.

dustman's hat. A slouch-hat of much the same shape as a dustman's : coll. : early C. 20. Collin- son.

dustoor(y). Commission as 'rake-off' ; dou- ceur ; bribe : Anglo-Indian, the shorter form, ca. 1680–1830 ; then, mainly, the longer. Largely displaced by *ba(c)kshee(sh).*

dusty ; dustie. A dustman : Cockney (– 1887). Baumann. Cf. *posty.*—2. 'A ship's steward's assistant—probably because this hard-worked official looks it' : naval (– 1909). Ware.—3. A nickname for any man named *Miller* : late C. 19–20. Because a miller is gen. dusty.—4. A C. 20 variant of *dustman*, 2. Manchon.

dusty, none or **not so.** Good (cf. *not so* or *too bad*) : from ca. 1854. Smedley, in *Harry Coverdale*, 'None so dusty that—eh ? for a commoner like me.' Ex

much earlier S.E. *dusty*, mean, worthless. Cf. *mouldy.*

dusty-bob. A scavenger : coll. : ca. 1850–1910.

dusty boy. A steward's assistant : naval : late C. 19–20. Bowen. Cf. *dusty*, 2 and 3.

dusty-nob or **poll.** A miller : coll. : C. 16–17 the latter ; C. 17–18 the former (rare). Cf. *dusty*, 3.

dusty pup. A 'dirty dog' : Australian coll. : from ca. 1920 ; ob.

[**Dutch.** Both n. and adj. were, in C. 17–early 18 (owing to trade rivalry and naval jealousy) very opprobrious or derisive ; the coll. sense endured throughout C. 18, some of the following phrases becoming S.E. in C. 19 ; but the few terms or phrases coined in C. 19 have remained s. or coll. See esp. 'Offensive Nationality' in *Words !* and Grose, P., s.v. *Dutch.*]

dutch ; esp. **my old dutch.** A wife : from ca. 1885 ; mostly Cockney and esp. costermongers'. Prob. coined by Albert Chevalier, who explained it by the resemblance of ' the wife's ' face to that of an *old Dutch clock* : cf. *dial*, q.v. (I used, with W., to consider it an abbr. of *duchess*, but Chevalier, I now feel tolerably certain, is right.)

Dutch, beat the. To do something remarkable : coll. (– 1775). Esp. in C. 19–20 *that beats the Dutch*, that beats everything, that's 'the limit', it's hardly credible.

dutch, do a. To desert ; run away ; abscond : military and Cockney : from ca. 1870 ; ob. Ware.

dutch, old. See **dutch.**

Dutch (or **double Dutch** or **Dutch fustian** or **High Dutch**), **talk.** To talk a foreign tongue, or gibberish. The third, used by Marlowe, may never have > coll. or gen. ; *High*, ca. 1780–1860 ; *Dutch* is C. 19–20 (ob.) ; *double Dutch* (H., 1st ed.), easily the com- monest since ca. 1860. All are coll. A humorous variant for linguistic dexterity is the ca. 1870–1900 *to talk double Dutch backwards on a Sunday.*

Dutch auction or **sale.** A mock auction or sale ; either at 'nominal' prices, esp. after the goods have been offered at a high price : coll. ; mentioned in 1872 as 'the old Dutch auction', hence presumably much earlier. H. has it in 1864.

Dutch bargain, i.e. one-sided : coll. ; from ca. 1650. With variant *wet bargain*, it also means a business transaction concluded with a drinking together.

Dutch brig, the. 'Cells on board ship or in the naval prisons' : naval : mid-C. 19–20. Bowen.

Dutch build. (Of a person having) a thick-set figure : coll. : mid-C. 19–20 ; ob. Baumann.

Dutch caper. A light privateering-ship, esp. if Dutch : naval : ca. 1650–1720. Bowen.

Dutch cheese. A bald-head(ed person) : low Cockney : 1882–ca. 1915. Ware, ' Dutch cheeses are generally made globular.'

Dutch clock ; old D.c. A wife : almost imm. abbr. to *dutch*, q.v. ; † by 1900.—2. A bed-pan : from ca. 1880 ; ob.

Dutch comfort. 'Thank God it is no worse,' Grose, 2nd ed. : coll. ; from ca. 1787. A C. 19 variant is *Dutch consolation* (H., 1st ed.).

Dutch concert or **medley.** Where everyone plays or sings a different tune : the former (Grose, 1st ed.) from ca. 1780, the latter C. 19–20 (ob.) and gen. of voices only. Coll.

Dutch consolation. See **Dutch comfort.**

[**Dutch courage,** courage induced by drink, has prob. been always S.E. So too, I think, **Dutch defence,** a sham one (Fielding).]

Dutch feast. 'Where the entertainer gets drunk before his guests', Grose, 1st ed. : coll. ; ca. 1780–1880. Cf. *Dutch treat*.

Dutch gleek. Drinks : ca. 1650–1870. Gayton, 1654.

Dutch have taken Holland, the. A C. 17–early 18 form of *Queen Anne's dead*.

Dutch medley. See **Dutch concert**.

Dutch nightingale. A frog : 1769, Pennant (O.E.D.) : jocular coll. >, by 1840, dial. ; ob. Cf. *fen nightingale*.

Dutch oven. The mouth : boxers' (— 1923). Manchon.

Dutch palate. A coarse palate, lit. and fig. : coll. : ca. 1675–1800.

Dutch party. See **Dutch treat**.

Dutch pegs. Legs : rhyming **s.** (— 1923). Manchon.

Dutch pink. Blood : 1853, 'Cuthbert Bede'. O.E.D. (Sup.). Ex the pigment so named.

Dutch pump. A punishment entailing vigorous pumping to save drenching or, occ., drowning : nautical coll : late C. 17–early 19. Bowen.

Dutch reckoning. A lump account, without particulars : ca. 1690–1800 : coll. > S.E. Cf. *altemal(l)*, likewise in B.E.—2. Among sailors (— 1867), 'a bad day's work, all in the wrong', Smyth.

Dutch red. A highly smoked Dutch herring : nautical coll. : late C. 19–20. Bowen.

Dutch row. 'A got-up unreal wrangle' : Cockney coll. (— 1909) ; ob. Ware remarks that, even in his day, it was rarely heard.

Dutch sale. See **Dutch auction**.

Dutch treat. An entertainment at which each pays his share : coll. ; from ca. 1875. Thornton records it for Iowa in 1903 ; in U.S.A. one finds also *Dutch lunch* and *D. supper*, while *D. party* is common to both England and U.S. in C. 20. Cf. *Dutch feast*.

Dutch uncle, talk to a person like a. I.e. severely. Coll. ; from ca. 1830. Ex the Dutch reputation for extremely rigorous discipline and the gen. idea resident in *patruæ verbera linguæ* and Horace's *ne sis patruus mihi*, the particular idea in Dutch *baas = boss =* master ; (ship's) captain.

Dutch widow. A harlot : coll. ; ca. 1600–1750. Middleton, 1608, 'That's an English drab, sir.'

Dutch wife. A bolster : from ca. 1880 ; ob. Ex the S.E. sense, an open frame used for resting the limbs in bed.

dutchess. See **duchess**.

Dutchie. A Dutchman ; occ. a German (see **Dutchman**) : allusive and nick-nominal : mid-C. 19–20 coll.

Dutchman. A German ; 'any North European seaman except a Finn' : nautical coll. : mid-C. 19–20. Bowen. (So too in U.S.) Ex earlier S.E.—2. A piece of quartz somewhat resembling an uncut diamond : South African diamond-diggers' (— 1913). Pettman. Perhaps ex the next entry. —3. The champagne of *Deutz & Gelderman* : middle-classes' : ca. 1870–1910. Ware.—4. (Gen. pl.) The 'mark' made by a drop of rain on still

water : children's (— 1923). Manchon. For semantics, cf. *dutch*, q.v.

Dutchman if I do !, I'm a. Certainly not ! Coll. ; from ca. 1850. Earlier (1837) is *I'm a Dutchman*, i.e. I'm somebody else : a coll. equivalent for disbelief ; Reade, 'If there is . . . gold on the ground . . ., I'm a Dutchman.'

Dutchman's anchor. Anything that, esp. if needed, has been left at home : nautical : from ca. 1860. Bowen, 'From the Dutch skipper who explained after the wreck that he had a very good anchor but had left it at home.'

Dutchman's breeches (occ. **breeks**). Two streaks of blue in a cloudy sky : nautical coll. (— 1867). Smyth. Sailors gen. use it in form, *enough to make a pair of breeches for a Dutchman*.

Dutchman's Cape. Imaginary land on the horizon : nautical coll. : mid-C. 19–20. Bowen.

Dutchman's drink. One that empties the pot : coll. ; from ca. 1860. Cf. :

Dutchman's headache, the. Drunkenness : coll. (— 1869) ; virtually † by 1920. (Apperson.)

Dutchmen. See **Dutchman**, 4.

Dutchy ; Dutchie. See **Dutchie**.

duty. 'Interest on pawnbrokers' pledges' : respectable lower classes' (— 1909). Ware, 'Evasive synonym'.

dwell. A pause : sporting coll. (— 1887) ; ob. Baumann.—2. A firmness in the market : Stock Exchange coll. (— 1923). Manchon.

dye. See **die**.

d'ye, d'you. Do ye, do you ? : coll. : C. 19–20. Cf. *d'see*, q.v.

d'ye want jam on both sides ? A military c.p. (1914 ; ob.) imputing unreasonableness. B. & P. More gen., *what do you want—jam on it ?*

dying duck in a thunderstorm, look like a. To have a ludicrously forlorn, hopeless, and helpless appearance : coll., orig. rural : from ca. 1850. (Ware.)

dying man's dinner. Something edible or potable snatched, opportunity favourable, when a ship is in peril and all hands at work : nautical : late C. 19–20 ; slightly ob. Bowen.

dyke. See **dike**.

dynamite. Tea : middle classes' : 1888–9. Ex Irish-American dynamiters' evasive term (*The Daily News*, Feb. 4, 1888). Ware. Cf. *dynamiter*.

dynamite, adj. (Of persons) violent, brutal, drastic, autocratic, powerful, expert—all or each to an alarming degree ; (of things) extremely dangerous or sudden. Coll., from ca. 1914. Cf. :

dynamiter. Any violent person : ca. 1882–90. Ware. See **dynamite**, n.

dynasty of Venus, the. 'Indiscriminate love and misguided affection', Egan's Grose : Oxford University : ca. 1820–40.

d'you feel like a spot ? See **how will you have it ?** (For *d'you*, see **d'ye**.)

dyspepsia. Delirium tremens : military hospitals' (— 1909) ; Ware.

dyspepsy. Dyspepsia : uncultured Canadian coll. : late C. 19–20. (John Beames, *Gateway*, 1932).

E

e, intrusive. In illiterate speech, *e* is frequently inserted before an *r* preceded by a consonant (esp. by a double consonant): prob. from time almost immemorial. E.g. *musheroom, umbrella.*—2. Sometimes an indication of exasperation, as in *Ker-rist* for *Christ* : see **kerwallop.**—3. Used for *-a-*, it is a mark of Cockney : C. 19–20. E.g. *fem(i)ly.* —4. In illiterate speech, it is also substituted for *i*, as in *ef* (if); for *o*, as in *ev* (of); and for *u*, as in *sepose* for *suppose*—see esp. the works of W. Pett Ridge. It is, in fact, the vowel to which illiteracy tends to reduce all vowel-sounds.—5. See the remark at *efink.*

'e-. See **h-** and **'ee.**

E.C. women. Wives of City men : snobbish Society : ca. 1881–1900. Ware. From the London postal district designated **East Central.**

'e dunno where 'e are ! A c.p. of the 1890's. *Quotations* Benham (cited by Collinson).

'e knows. A c.p. punning *Eno's* advertisements : from ca. 1905. Also *Eno's*, q.v.

E.P. or **e.p.** An experienced playgoer : theatrical : late C. 19–early 20. Ware.

each other as a nominative is sol. (— 1893) : 'occasionally heard', notes Henry Bradley, who cites 'We know what each other are doing.'—2. But *each other* for *one another*, never reprehensible in U.S., is—more's the pity, say the logical—losing that catachrestic stigma which resulted partly from the fact that its indiscriminate use occ. leads to ambiguity.

*eagle. The winning gamester : late C. 17–18 c. B.E. (Cf. the coll. > S.E. golf term.)—2. Chicken : R.N.C., Dartmouth : C. 20. Bowen.

eagle-hawking. The plucking of wool from dead sheep : Australian 'bush' (— 1898). Morris. Ex this habit of the Australian eagle-hawk.

Eagle-Takers. The 87th Foot, British Army : so named after Barossa, 1811, when they captured a French eagle. Moreover, its colours bear an eagle laurel-wreathed. See also **Aiglers, Faugh-a-Ballagh Boys** and **Old Fogs,** alternatives.

eagled. Punished by being spread-eagled : nautical : C. 19–20 ; ob. Bowen.

'Eaps, Eeps. Ypres : military : G.W. (B. & P.)

ear, on one's. In disgrace : U.S., anglicised by 1909. Ware.

ear, send away with a flea in one's (or the) **ear.** See **flea in one's ear, send away with a.**

ear-biter ; ear-biting. A persistent borrower ; borrowing : see **bite one's ear,** than which the two terms are slightly later.

ear-hole, on the. Cadging (esp. money) : military : C. 20. F. & Gibbons. Cf. *earwig*, v.

ear-swinger. An unemployed docker dunning his working mates for a loan : nautical : C. 20. Bowen.

Earl Beardie. Alex. Lindsay, 4th Earl of Crawford (d. 1454), a great fighter. Dawson.

Earl of Cork. The ace of diamonds : Anglo-Irish (— 1830) coll. Carleton, 'Called the Earl of Cork, because he's the poorest nobleman in Ireland '.

Earl of Mar's Grey Breeks. The 21st Foot, British Army : military : C. 18–19, but † by 1890. Ex the colour of the breeches and the orig. title, The Earl of Mar's Fuzileers.

Earl of Murray. See **dine with St. Giles.**

early. Keeping early hours ; rising early : coll. (— 1893) >, by 1920, S.E. (O.E.D.)

early, rise or **wake** or **get up very.** To be wide-awake, ready, astute : *rise*, C. 18 ; the other two C. 19–20, with *get up* the commoner in C. 20. Orig. coll. ; in C. 20, S.E. Swift.

early, small and. See **small and early.**

Early Bird, the. An express goods-train carrying provisions, through the night, to London : railway-men's : from ca. 1920. *The Daily Telegraph*, Aug. 15, 1936. Cf. *the Early Riser.*

early riser. An aperient : mid-C. 19–20 coll. Cf. *custom-house officer.*—2. 'A sharp, business-like person ' : coll. : U.S. >, ca. 1895, anglicised. Ware. Ex *early, rise*, q.v.

Early Riser, the. A fast freight train running to London : from ca. 1920. (It arrives early in the morning.) *The Daily Telegraph*, Aug. 15, 1936.

early-turner. A performer taking his ' turns ' early in the programme, hence before the more fashionable part of the audience has arrived : music-halls' coll. (— 1909). Ware.

early worm. One who searches the streets at dawn for cigar and cigarette stumps : coll. : from ca. 1870 ; ob. Ex S.E. sense. Baumann.

earn. To ' find ' or ' win ', i.e. to steal ; get by looting : naval and military : G.W. +. Cf. *make,* q.v. F. & Gibbons.

*earnest. A share of the booty : mid-C. 17–18 c. Head ; B.E. Cf. S.E. senses.

ears. ' Small advertisements appearing on each side of the title of the first page of a periodical ' (including newspapers) : copy-writers' s. (from ca. 1924) >, by 1930, coll. Alfred T. Chenhalls.

ears, tickle (a person's). To flatter : coll. (— 1931). Lyell.

ears are (or were) **worth, it's** (or it'd be) **as much as one's.** It is, would be, very risky for him : coll. : from ca. 1860.

ears back or **put back !, get your.** Get your hair cut : military c.p. : C. 20. F. & Gibbons.

'eart !, 'ave an. See **heart !, have a.**

earth. An early variant of *erth* (q.v.), three. H., 1st ed.

earth-bath, take an. To be buried. By itself, *earth-bath* = a grave. C. 19 low. *Lex. Bal.*

earth-stoppers. A horse's feet : coll. : ca. 1810–80. Moncrieff, 1823. Alluding to those who stop up foxes' earths.

earthed, be. (Of an aeroplane) to be brought down against its pilot's wish : Air Force coll. : 1915. F. & Gibbons. Ex a fox earthed.

earthern. Incorrect for *earthen* : C. 18–20 ; now rare. O.E.D.

earthly, no ; not an earthly. No chance whatsoever : coll. : resp. 1899 (Ware) ; 1907 (O.E.D. Sup.).—2. **no earthly** is also an abbr. of *no earthly good* : coll. : from ca. 1920. Galsworthy (cited by Collinson). Sc. *chance.*

earwig. A private and malicious prompter or flatterer : coll. > S.E. in C. 18 : late C. 1610–1880. Scott.—2. In C. 19 c. or low s., a clergyman. ' Ducange Anglicus ', 1857.

earwig, v. To prompt by covert assertions ; whisper insinuations to ; rebuke privately : C. 19–20 ; S.E. in the latter. Marryat, ' He earwigs the captain in fine style.' **Ex n., 1.** The vbl.n. *ear-wigging* is more frequently used than the v.

ease. To rob of, steal from : coll. : C. 17–20 ; in C. 17, jocular coll. ; in C. 18, c. ; in late C. 19–20, S.E. Jonson, 'Ease his pockets of a superfluous watch '.

ease oneself. To ejaculate seminally : coll. : C. 18–20. Somewhat euphemistic.

ease up ! Steady ! : coll. (— 1923). Manchon. Lit., slacken your pace !

east and south. The mouth : rhyming s. (— 1857). 'Ducange Anglicus.' After ca. 1895, *north and south.* Occ., ca. 1880–1900, *sunny south.*

east and west. Breast : rhyming s. (— 1923). Manchon.

East Country ship. A ship trading in the Baltic : nautical coll. : mid-C. 19–20. Bowen.

East of the Griffin. (In) East London : London coll. : 1885, *The Referee*, Oct. 11 ; very ob. Ware, ' Outcome of the city Griffin on his wonderful pedestal replacing Temple Bar '.

East (or e.) roll. A slow, gradual roll without jerks : nautical coll. : late C. 19–20. Bowen.

easterling. ' Erroneously used by early anti-quaries for *sterling* . . . the English silver penny of the Norman dynasty.' W.

Easterns. Shares in the Great Eastern Railway : Stock Exchange coll. (— 1895) >, by 1910, j. (A. J. Wilson's glossary.)

eastery. Private business : cheapjacks' (—1876) ; ob. Hindley in his classic ' editing ' of cheapjack life.

Eastralia. Eastern Australia : Australian coll. (— 1898) ; virtually †. Morris. On *Westralia.*

easy. A short rest, esp. as *take an easy* : coll. ; from ca. 1880.

easy, v.i. To dispose oneself suitably to the sexual embrace : low coll. ; from ca. 1900.

easy, adv. Without difficulty : in C. 19–20, coll. where not sol. ; earlier, S.E.—2. Comfortably ; at an easy pace, e.g. in *take it easy* ; without severity, as in *let one off easy.* Coll. (— 1779). Cf. the Irishism *be easy !*, don't hurry !

easy, honours. Honours divided : coll. (1884 : O.E.D.) >, by 1920, S.E. Ex cards.

easy, make. To gag ; to kill : mid-C. 18–early 19, low if not c. Grose, 1st ed. For the latter sense, *quiet* was occ. preferred.

easy a bit ! Don't hurry ! : coll. (— 1923). Manchon. Cf. *easy*, adv., 2.

easy as damn it or **kiss my a*se** or **my eye** or **pissing the bed, as.** Extremely easy : coll. : first, second, and third, C. 19–20 ; fourth, C. 18–20 (ob.). The polite variant and original of the second is *(as) easy as kiss my hand*, 1670, Cotton (Apperson). Cf. Shakespeare's 'easy as lying' and Ray's (1678) *easy as to lick a dish. Easy as an old shoe* and *as falling off* (*a chair, a log*, etc.) were orig. dial., not earlier than 1800.

easy does it ! Take your time : coll. ; from ca. 1840 ; ob.

*easy mort. Mid-C. 17–18 c. : ' a forward or coming wench ', B.E.

easy over the pimples or **stones !** Go slow ! Be careful ! Coll. : from ca. 1870. The former ex the barber's shop, the latter ex driving on bad roads.

[**Easy Street, in,** prosperous, is rather S.E. than coll.]

easy virtue. ' An impure, or prostitute ', Grose, 1st ed. : from ca. 1780 : s. >, by 1820, coll. >, by 1900, S.E. Cf. the S.E. *easy*, compliant.

eat coke ; eat crow. See **coke ; crow.**

eat. To enjoy enthusiastically : theatrical : from ca. 1932. John G. Brandon, *The One-Minute Murder*, 1934, ' The audience were, in theatrical parlance, literally eating this scene.'—2. To worry ; sorely puzzle : from ca. 1919. P. MacDonald, *R.I.P.*, 1933, ' But I don't *think* that's what's eating you.' See **what's biting you ?** and cf. dial *eat oneself,* to be very vexed (E.D.D.).

eat a child. See **child, eat a.**

*eat a fig. To break into a house : s. rhyming imperfectly on (*crack a*) *crib* : from ca. 1855 ; ob. c. H., 1st ed.

eat a sword, eat iron. To be stabbed : C. 16 : coll.

Eat-Apples, Eatables ; Eeetap(s). Etaples in France : military : G.W.

eat bull-beef. See **bull-beef, eat.**

eat like a beggar man and wag one's under jaw. ' A jocular reproach to a proud man ', Grose, 1st ed. : late C. 18–mid-19 : coll. c.p.

eat more fruit ! A c.p. of ca. 1927–34. Collinson. Ex the trade slogan.

eat one's boots, hat, head. Gen. as *I'll* or *I'd eat my . . ., hat* being the commonest and earliest (Dickens, 1836). A coll. declaration.

eat one's head off. To be idle ; cost more than its, or one's, keep. Orig. (— 1736) of horses ; then of servants (— 1874) ; finally (— 1920) of other employees. O.E.D. ; F. & H.

eat one's terms, occ. **dinners.** To go through the prescribed course of study for admission to the bar : a legal coll. (— 1834). Ex the eating of a few meals each term at an inns of court. (O.E.D.)

eat the wind out of a ship. To get nearer the wind than another ship is : nautical coll. : late C. 19–20. Bowen. Cf. *wipe* (a shooter's) *eye.*

eat up. To massacre (a man and his family) and confiscate his property (1838) ; hence, to vanquish in tribal battle (1859) : coll. Pettman. Prob. ex a Zulu metaphor. In late C. 19–20, gen. = to ruin, hence to be much too strong or too skilful for another.

eat vinegar with a fork. See **fork,** etc.—**Eatables.** See **Eat-Apples.**—**eaten a stake.** See **swallowed a stake.**

eatings. Board, meals, food : proletarian : C. 19. Ware.

eats. Food : C. 20 coll. Cf. *eat*, M.E., a meal, and C. 11–early 17, food, both S.E.

eau. Incorrect for *ea*, a canal : mid-C. 19–20. Confused with Fr. *eau*. O.E.D.

eautybeau. Beauty : music-hall transposition (— 1909) ; ob. Ware.

ebb-water. Lack of money : late C. 17–18. B.E. says it is c. ; perhaps it is, rather, low s. or low coll.

ebenezer. In fives, a stroke that so hits ' line ' as to rise perpendicularly : Winchester College. ? a Biblical reference or ex *Ebenezer*, coll. (1856) >, by 1890, S.E., a Nonconformist chapel (a term that —cf. *bethel*—is S.E. j. as used by Dissenters themselves). See also Addenda.

ebony. A negro : coll. : ca. 1860–1910. Abbr. *son of ebony* (1850).—2. (Gen. *Old Ebony.*) The publisher of *Blackwood's Magazine* ; the periodical itself. Ca. 1860–1900. Ex the colour of its cover.

ebony, bit or **piece of.** A variant (— 1923) of *ebony*, 1. Manchon.

ebony optic. A black eye ; *e.o. albonized*, the same—painted white : C. 19. ' Ducange Anglicus.'

eccer. (Pronounced *ekker*.) Exercise : Oxford undergraduates' : late C. 19–20. ' Oxford *-er*.' (Ware.)

ecclesiastical brick. A holystone : nautical, mostly officers' : late C. 19–20. Bowen. By elaboration.

-eck. Sol. for *-ect*, as in *rejeck* : C. 19–20. Cf. *ol'* for *old* (or as in *tol'*, told).

*eclipse. In gaming, a fraudulent man pulation of a die with the little finger : late C. 17–18, c.

ecliptical. Elliptical : a late C. 16–17 sol. Fuller. (O.E.D.).

eclogue. Dialogue(, conversation, discourse) : sol., C. 17. (O.E.D.) Cf. the C. 17 errors of *eclude* for *exclude*, *edention* for *edentation* (ibid.).

ecod. A mild oath (cf. *edad* and *edod*) : coll. : C. 18–19. ? ex *egad*, itself C. 17–20 (ob.).

ecstacy is an astonishingly frequent misspelling among those who should know better.

ed. Editor : only in compounds, as *city-ed* : C. 20 journalistic. Cf. :

ed (or **ed.**), **the.** The editor : journalists' and authors' coll. : C. 20. Neil Bell, *Winding Road*, 1934.

eddication. See **edication**.

edgabac. Cabbage : back s. (— 1859). H., 1st ed.

Edgarism. Atheism ; loosely, agnosticism : clubmen's : 1882. Ex *Edgar*, ' the villain-hero ' of Tennyson's prose play, *The Promise of May*. (Ware.)

*edge ! Run away !, be off ! : c. (— 1886) ; ob. Ware. A deviation from S.E. *edge* (*away*).

edge, outside. See **outside edge**.

edge, short top. A turned-up nose : tailors' : from ca. 1860.

edge, side. Whiskers : tailors' s. : from ca. 1860, as is :

edge, stitched off the : likewise tailors' : (of a glass) not full.

edge 'em. To commence drawing a crowd : market-traders' (e.g., Petticoat Lane) : C. 20.

edge of nothing, the thin. A coll. c.p. (— 1931) applied ' when people are very crowded and there is hardly room to sit ' (Lyell). Esp. *sit on the thin edge of nothing.*

edge off, or, v.t., out of. To slink away ; to desist gradually : coll. : from ca. 1860. Cf. the S.E. usages, whence it naturally develops.

edge on, have (got) an. To be impudent ; put on ' side ' : Public Schools' : C. 20. P. G. Wodehouse, 1903, ' Doesn't it strike you that for a kid like you you've got a good deal of edge on ? ' Contrast :

edge on, have the. To have a slight advantage over : Canadian coll. : C. 20. John Beames. Ex U.S.

edge up. (Gen. in imperative.) To move quickly : Glasgow (— 1934).

edgenaro. An orange : back s. (— 1859). H., 1st ed.

edgeways, not able to get a word in. To find oneself unable to take part in a conversation or discussion : coll. ; from ca. 1870 ; earlier and S.E., *edgewise*.

edication, edickation, eddication. Education : sol. : C. 19–20.

edify. Edifice : a C. 16 sol., for which there is the excuse that it occurs only in the pl. (O.E.D.)

edition, first, second, etc. One's first, second, or other child : journalists', authors', and publishers'

s. fast becoming a gen. bookish coll. : from ca. 1890. (There is prob. a further pun on *addition*.)

Edna. The inevitable nickname of men surnamed May : military (and naval) : C. 20. F. & Gibbons. Ex *Edna May*, the actress.

edod ! Rare coll. variant of *adod !* : late C. 17– early 18. O.E.D.

educated trimmer. An engineer officer : nautical, esp. executive officers' : late C. 19–20. Bowen. Opp. *bridge ornament*.

ee ; 'ee. Ye : coll. abbr. (— 1775) ; ob. Sheridan, ' Hark ee, lads ' (O.E.D.).

-ee. Often to humorous, occ. to coll. effect (imitative of legal terms) as in *kickee*, the person kicked : from ca. 1860. Somewhat pedantic.

eekcher. Cheek : central s. : from ca. 1880. Ware.

eel-skin(s). Very tight trousers : ca. 1820–60. Bulwer Lytton, 1827, ' a . . . gilt chain . . . stuck . . . in his eel-skin to make a show '.—2. A very tight dress : Society coll. : ca. 1881–90. Ware.

e'en. Even (= just, nothing else but) ' prefixed ' to vv. : mid-C. 16–19 coll. ; in C. 20, dial. Richardson, 1741. ' E'en send to him to come down.' (O.E.D.)

eenque ; eetswe. Queen ; sweet : transposed or central s. : from ca. 1870. Ware.

Eeps. See **'Eaps.—Eetap(s).** See **Eat-Apples**.

-eer is often jocular, occ. coll. as *profiteer* was at first (1915).

Eff, the ; the Effy. The Effingham Saloon, an East-End music-hall, fl. 1864.

effect, effection, effective. See **affect**.

effluvia is occ. used ignorantly as a singular (*effluvium*) : mid-C. 17–20. Cf. *data*.

effort. ' Something accomplished involving concentration or special activity ' : from ca. 1870 : S.E. >, by 1930, coll., esp. in *that's a pretty good effort* (C. 20). O.E.D. (Sup.) ; C.O.D. (1934 Sup.). —2. A ' thingummy ' ; an interjection : Bootham School (— 1925). Anon., *Dict. of Bootham Slang*, 1925.

Effy. See **Eff**.

efink. A knife : back s. (— 1859). H., 1st ed. *E-* is a common initial letter in back-s. words, for it ensures euphony.

*efter. A theatre thief : c. ; from ca. 1860 ; ob. H., 3rd ed. Perhaps *after* (the ' goods ') perverted.

egad ! A mild oath (' prob. for *ah God* ', W.) : C. 18–20 (ob.) ; coll. Slightly earlier *igad* ; occ. *egod* (C. 18). O.E.D.

egg. A person : coll., esp. in *good egg* and, as exclamation, *good egg !*, late C. 19–20, and *a bad egg*, a person (rarely a thing) that disappoints expectation : from early 1850's.—2. Abbr. *duck's egg* : cricketers' : 1876. Lewis. See **duck**, n., 6.—3. An aerial bomb : military : 1916.—4. A submarine mine : naval : 1916. Bowen.

egg, old. See **old egg**.

egg, sound. See **sound egg**.

egg-box. A box for table napkins : Bootham School : late C. 19–20. Anon., *Dict. of Bootham Slang*, 1925.

egg in that !, there's an. That's worth the trouble ! : semi-proverbial coll. (— 1923). Manchon.

Egg-Market, the. The Falkland Islands : whalers' : ca. 1830–1910. Ex swarming sea-fowl. Bowen.

Egg-Shells. H.M.S. *Achilles* : naval : C. 20. Bowen. By ' Hobson-Jobson.'

egg-trot. A coll. abbr. of *egg-wife's trot*, a gentle amble : ca. 1680–1900. Ex her pace when riding to market.

eggs, teach one's grandmother to roast, more gen. **suck.** To inform or lecture one's elders, superiors, or intellectual betters : coll. : from ca. 1700. Earlier forms are *teach one's dame* or *grandame* (*grannam*) *to spin* or *to grope ducks* (or *a goose*) or *to sup sour milk*. (Apperson.)

Eggs-a-Cook. Egyptians : Australian military : 1915–16. See :—2. Australian soldiers : a self-name, 1915–18. B. & P. Ex 'their being as " hard-boiled " as the eggs vended '—with this cry —' by the Egyptian hawkers '.—3. The 3rd Australian Division : Australian soldiers' : 1917 ; ob. Ex the colour-patch.

eggs (a penny, and four of them addle or rotten), come in with five. To interrupt fussily with worthless news or an idle story : coll. : ca. 1540–1880.

eggs are, be, or **is eggs, as sure as.** Undoubtedly ; certainly : coll. : the first two, late C. 17–18 (e.g. Otway) ; the third from (—)1772. The last perhaps, as A. de Morgan suggested, influenced by *X is X*, the logician's statement of identity. (Apperson.)

eggs are cooked !, the. Everything's done ! ; that's done it ! ; his number is up ! : New Zealanders' : from ca. 1910.

eggs for one's money, be glad to take. Gladly ' to compound the matter with Loss ', B.E. : semi-proverbial coll. : C. 17–18. Shakespeare, 1610 (Apperson).

egham, staines and windsor. A private coachman's three-cornered gala hat : coll. : ca. 1870–1900. Ex a once-famous business firm.

ego, often with capital. Myself ; yourself ; herself, himself : jocular coll. (— 1824) ; ob.—2. (ego !) See *quis* ?

egod ! See *egad* .

Egypt. Bread : military : C. 20 ; ob. F. & Gibbons. Perhaps ex *corn in Egypt.*

Egyptian charger. A donkey : mostly London : ca. 1820–50. Bee. Perhaps ex its frequent use by Gypsies.

Egyptian Hall. A ball : rhyming s. (— 1859). H., 1st ed.

eh ? What's that (you say) ? : coll. : C. 19–20. (O.E.D.'s earliest record is for 1837.)

eccespie. Pieces : transposed or central s. : from ca. 1860.—2. Hence, money : from ca. 1880. Ware.

Eiderdown. Ouderdon on the Western Front : military in G.W. (W. H. L. Watson, 1915.)

eight, one over the. One drink too many ; hence, slightly drunk : military (>, by 1925, gen.) : from not later than 1914. F. & Gibbons ; Lyell. Eight beers being considered permissible.

eight eyes, I will knock out two of your. A mid-C. 18–early 19 Billingsgate fishwives' c.p. The other six, as Grose, 2nd ed., enumerates them, are the two ' bubb*ies* ' (q.v.), the bell*y* (prob. implying the navel), 'two pope's eyes ' (? the anal and urinal orifices), and ' a *** eye ' (? what) : by the ' pope's eyes ' he perhaps means rump and anus, while by the asterisks he almost certainly understands the sexual aperture.

eighteenmo. Octodecimo : *book-world coll. ; 1858. Ex *18mo*, the abbr. form. (S.O.D.)

eighteenpence. Common sense : rhyming s. : C. 20. James Curtis, *The Gilt Kid*, 1936, 'He did not know Maisie had all that eighteenpence.' Also in P.P., *Rhyming Slang*, 1932.

*eighter. An 8-ounce loaf : c., mostly prisoners' : from ca. 1870.

Eiley Mavourneen. A non-paying debtor : commercial (— 1909) ; ob. Ware. Ex that song by F. W. Crouch, in which occur the words, ' It may be for years, and it may be for ever.'

either, either of + n. with a pl. v. : catachrestic : C. 19–20. Ruskin, 1874 (O.E.D.) ; Freeman Wills Crofts, *Mystery on Southampton Water*, 1934, ' This was not to say that during those wearing days either of them were idle.'—2. Catachrestic, too, is *either* (sing. n.) *or* (sing. n.) with a pl. v., as in Thirlwall, 1833, ' Religious rites by which either Thebes or Eleusis were afterwards distinguished ', O.E.D.— 3. Often *either* is used illogically, as twice in this short passage (from G. D. H. & M. Cole, *Superintendent Wilson's Holiday*, 1928) : ' He might have either been hidden in the vicinity or taken away, probably by car, to some distance. For traces either of burial or transport by road one would have to search by daylight.' To impute pedantry to a person indicating such lapses is to abdicate both logic and subtlety, or, at the least, both clarity and nuance.—4. See Addenda.

ek dum. See **ak dum**, 1. Thus in Richard Blaker, *Here Lies a Most Beautiful Lady*, 1935, of an Indian Army officer : ' " We'll go ek dum," said the Major.'

ekame. A ' make ', i.e. a swindle : back s. (— 1859). H., 1st ed.

ekker. An exercise (scholastic task) : Public Schools' and universities' (orig. Oxford) : from ca. 1890. ' The Oxford -*er*.'

ekom. A ' moke ', i.e. donkey : likewise back s. (— 1859). H., 1st ed.

elastic. Stretchable without permanent change of shape or size : coll. (in C. 20, almost S.E.) : from ca. 1780.

elbat. See **helbat**.

elbow, crook the. See **crook**. App. *lift the elbow* is not recorded before 1916 (O.E.D. Sup.).

elbow, knight of the. A gamester : coll. : ca. 1750–1840.

elbow, shake the. To play dice : coll. : from ca. 1690 ; ob. Vanbrugh, ' He's always shaking his heels with the ladies '—i.e. dancing—' and his elbows with the lords ' ; Scott in *Nigel*.

elbow ?, who is at your. A late C. 17–18 c.p. caution or warning to a liar. B.E. Cf. *watch your step !*

elbow-crooker. A hard drinker : coll. ; mid-C. 19–20 ; ob. Cf. *pot-walloper.*

elbow-grease. Hard manual labour : coll. (— 1639). Clarke's *Parœmiologia Anglo-Latina* ; Marvell ; B.E., 'A derisory Term for Sweat ' ; Grose ; George Eliot, ' Genuine elbow-polish, as Mrs. Poyser called it.' Cf. the Fr. *huile de bras* or *de poignet* (recently *de coude*), the primary sense being that of vigorous rubbing.

elbow in the hawse, (there's) an. A nautical coll. applied to a ship that, ' with two anchors down swings twice the wrong way, causing the cables to take half a turn round one another ', Bowen : mid-C. 19–20.

elbow-jigger or **-scraper.** A fiddler : coll. : from ca. 1820 ; ob. Egan's Grose.

elbow-shaker, -shaking. A gamester ; gaming, adj. and n. : coll. : the first from early C. 18, the second (—)1718 ; the third, C. 19–20, ob.

elbows, out at. (Of an estate) mortgaged : coll.; C. 18–early 19.

Elchi. See **Eltchi.**—**elch(er)wer.** See **helcherwer.**

elderly jam. An ageing woman : lower classes' : ca. 1880–1915. Ware.

eldest, the. The first lieutenant : naval s. verging on coll. : C. 19. Bowen. Contrast *the old man*, the captain.

electrify. Violently to startle : from ca. 1750 ; coll. till ca. 1850, when it > S.E. Burke ; Barham.

elegant. 'Nice' : coll. verging on s. : C. 18–early 19. Cf. *fair*, adj., 1 (q.v.).—2. Hence, first-rate, excellent : coll. ; from ca. 1840 ; ob. Prob. owing to influence of the U.S., where it was so used as early as 1765 (Thornton). As a jocular Irishism, it is spelt *iligant* : mid-C. 19–20. Cf. *nice*.

Elegant Extracts. The 85th Foot (British Army) on being remodelled in 1812 with officers chosen from other regiments : military ; ob. Ex Vicesimus Knox's and others' elegant-extract anthologies so popular ca. 1760–1820.—2. At Cambridge University, those students who, though 'plucked', were given their degrees : from ca. 1850 ; ob. H., 3rd ed. Cf. *gulf*.

elephant. A (large) corrugated-iron shelter : military : late 1916. *A baby elephant* is a small shelter. F. & Gibbons.—2. Hence, a (small) dug-out reinforced with corrugated iron : military : 1917. B. & P.

elephant, bang through the ; elephant, bang up to the. See **bang.**

elephant, cop the. To be tipsy : low (— 1923). Manchon. Ex *elephant's trunk*, q.v.

elephant, see the. To see the world ; gain worldly experience : coll. ; orig. (ca. 1840), U.S., anglicised ca. 1860. H., 2nd ed. ; Laurence Oliphant ; ob.—2. (Gen. *to have seen the elephant*.) To be seduced : from ca. 1875 ; ob. Cf. Fr. *avoir vu le loup*.

Elephant and Castle. Hell, as in 'How the Elephant and Castle !' : rhyming s. (*castle* being pronounced *caste'll*) : C. 20.

elephant dance. The double shuffle or 'cellar-flap', q.v. : ca. 1870–1910.

elephant trunk. An occ. variant of **elephant's trunk**, q.v. *The Evening Standard*, Aug. 19, 1931.

elephanter. Incorrect for *elephanta* : mid-C. 19–20. O.E.D.

elephants. See **elephant's trunk.**

elephant's ear. Sweet, 'a liliaceous plant bearing a single . . . leaf, resembling an ear' : Queenstown (South Africa) juvenile coll. (— 1913). Pettman.

elephant's trunk. Drunk : rhyming s. ; from ca. 1855. H., 1st ed. By 1873, often abbr. to *elephant's* or *elephants*. Cf. process in *china* (*plate*), q.v.

elevate. To render slightly drunk ; gen. in p. ppl. passive used as an adj. : from ca. 1700 ; in C. 18, S.E. ; then coll. Dickens, 'Except when he's elevated, Bob's the quietest creature breathing.'

elevation. Slight tipsiness : coll. ; from ca. 1820. Scott.—2. Opium (—1850) ; ob.—3. Whence, a 'pick-me-up' : coll. : mid-C. 19–20 ; now mostly dial. O.E.D.

elevator. A crinolette : Society : 1882–ca. 1900. Ware.

eleven-a-side. A tiny moustache affected by subalterns : Army officers' : 1915 ; ob. Collinson. I.e. eleven hairs on each side of the nose : ex cricket.

elevens !, by the. A jocular expletive : coll. :

(? coined by) Goldsmith, 1773 ; †. O.E.D. Prob. punning *heavens !*

elevenses. Morning tea : C. 20 coll. ex C. 19–20 dial. Dorothy Sayers, *Murder Must Advertise*, 1932, 'He goes out for his elevenses.' I.e. at eleven o'clock. Cf. dial. *elevener*.

*elf. Little : c. : late C. 17–mid-18. *Street Robberies Considered*. Ex *elf*, a dwarf.

eliminate. To kill (a person) : jocular coll. ; from ca. 1915.—2. Catachrestically for *isolate*, hence for 'deduce' : mid-C. 19–20. O.E.D. The same applies to *elimination*.

Ellenborough Lodge or **Park** or **Spike.** The King's Bench : ca. 1810–50. Ex Lord Chief-Justice Ellenborough (d. 1818), fl. 1802–18 in that office.

*Ellenborough's teeth. The *chevaux de frise* around the King's Bench Prison wall : c. ; ca. 1810–50. See preceding entry.

Ellersby. The London School Board : London : from ca. 1870 ; very ob. Cf. *Elsie* and :

Ellessea. The London Society of Compositors : printers' (— 1909). Ware.

Elliot-eye. 'An eye splice worked over an iron thimble' : naval coll. : late C. 19–20. Ex Admiral Elliot, its introducer into the Navy. Bowen.

ellum ; hellum. Sol. pronunciations of *elm*, *helm* : C. 19–20.

Elocution Walker. John Walker (1732–1807), lexicographer and teacher of elocution. Dawson.

elpa. See **helpa.**

elrig. A girl : back s. (— 1859). H., 1st ed.

else's, as in **somebody else's** : coll. ; from ca. 1660. Pepys.

Elsewicks. Shares in Armstrong, Mitchell & Co. : Stock Exchange coll. (— 1895). A. J. Wilson, *Stock Exchange Glossary*. Ex their 'scene of operations'.

Elsie. East London College : London University undergraduates' : C. 20 ; ob. since 1934, when renamed Queen Mary College.

El(t)chi(, Eltchee), the Great. Sir Stratford Canning, Lord Stratford de Redcliffe (d. 1880) : coll. : from ca. 1860 ; ob. Ex the name given him by the Turks. Ex Turkish *ilchi*, ambassador. W.

elude, delude, and illude are often used, sol., one for another : the same applies to their corresponding adjj. and nn. : C. 19–20.

elycampane, occ. **elecampane.** See **allacompain.** (Moncrieff, 1823.)

'em. Them : coll. from ca. 1880 ; earlier, S.E. though not, since ca. 1840, literary. Baumann.

emag. Game ; trick ; dodge : back s. (— 1873). Ware dates it 1870.

embroidery. Exaggerations ; fancy-work manipulations of or additions to the truth : coll. ; from ca. 1885. The corresponding v. is C. 17–20 S.E.

embus. The opp. to *debus*, q.v. : s. (1915) rapidly > coll. and j. Loosely, *embuss*.

Emden ?, didn't you sink the. An Australian Army c.p. (1915–18) contemptuous of arrogance or too good a 'press'. F. & Gibbons. The Australian cruiser *Sydney* destroyed the German cruiser *Emden* in 1914 at Cocos Islands.

emergency crew. A crew that, of men immune from the press gang, worked a ship for the real crew while danger threatened : nautical coll. : mid-C. 18–mid-19. Bowen.

eminent, -ency, and **imminent, -ency,** have, in C. 17–20, often been confused : hence sol.—The same applies, with some excuse, to *emigrant* and *immigrant*.

emit. Time : back s. : late C. 19–20.

Emma !, whoa. See whoa, Emma !

emma gee. A machine-gun(ner) : military : 1915. Ex signalese, *emma* being *m*. Cf. *pip emma, tock emma*, qq.v. B. & P. Cf. :

emma pip. (Gen. pl.) A military policeman : military : 1915.

emmanuensis. Incorrect for *amanuensis* : late C. 17–mid-18. O.E.D.

emmies. Shares in the Electrical and Musical company : Stock Exchange ; from ca. 1930. *The Daily Telegraph*, Nov. 18, 1933.

emperor, drunk as an. 'Ten times as drunk as a lord ', Grose, 3rd ed. : late C. 18–early 19. Cf. the allusive *bloody drunk* : see bloody.

Emperor's Chambermaids, the. The 14th Hussars : military : 1813, ex a chamber-pot captured at Vittoria. F. & Gibbons.

Empress pidgin. Discussion with Queen Victoria : naval : 1876–1901. Ware.

***empty.** Unpossessed of the riches reported : c. : C. 18. *A New Canting Dict.*, 1725.

empty, get the. To be dismissed : Cockneys' (— 1887). I.e. get the empty sack. (Baumann.)

empty bottle. A fellow-commoner : Cambridge (— 1794) ; † by 1870. Cf. *fellow-* and *gentleman-commoner*.

empyric(k). Incorrect for *empiric* : mid-C. 16–17. Cf. *enarrable* for *innarable* : late C. 15–early 16. O.E.D.

emshee. An occ. corruption of *imshee*, q.v.

Emsib. The Eastern Mediterranean Special Service Intelligence Bureau : military coll. : 1915–18. F. & Gibbons.

en is sol. for *-ing*, as in *shillen* : C. 19–20. ' How you getten on ? ', *Time and Tide*, Nov. 24, 1934.

enarrable. See empyric(k).

enclipse (C. 17) is perhaps a nonce-error for *eclipse*. O.E.D.

encumbrances. Children : coll. : from ca. 1830.

end. See business end.

end, at a loose. With nothing particular to do : coll. ; from ca. 1900. Orig., without occupation or employment.

end, fly off the deep. See fly off the handle.

end, go (in) off the deep. To get very excited or passionate : military (— 1918) > gen. by 1921, when *The Times Literary Supplement*, Dec. 22, has ' He never, to use the slang of the moment, " went in off the deep end " ' (O.E.D. Sup.) ; now verging on coll. F. & Gibbons. Ex leaping from a diving-board into the water at the deep end of a swimming-bath.—2. See quotation at *take a toss*.

end, no, adv. Immensely ; *no end of*, a great number or quantity of. The former is s., the latter coll. : the former dates from ca. 1850, the latter from ca. 1620. (O.E.D.)—2. Hence, *no end of a fellow*, a ' capital ' fellow, ' one of the best ' : coll. : C. 20. Lyell.

end of The Sentimental Journey. The female pudend : low coll. ; C. 19–20 ; ob. Sterne's witty novel ends with a significant '——'.

end-on. Straight ; standing on or showing its end : coll., C. 19 ; S.E., C. 20.—*Be end-on* : to have a priapism : low coll. : C. 19–20.

end up, get. To rise to one's feet : Australian (— 1916). C. J. Dennis.

end up, keep one's. To rub along ; maintain one's status, reputation, etc. From the late 1870's : coll. >, by 1910, S.E. Ex cricket.

endeca is incorrect for *hendeca* in *endecasyllable*, etc. O.E.D.

ender. A performer inferior to even an ' early-turner ', q.v. : music-halls' coll. (— 1909). Ware.

ends, at loose. Neglected (of persons), (of things) precarious : coll. ; from ca. 1860 ; ob. (Cf. *end, at a loose*, q.v.) Orig. nautical, of an unattached rope. W.

ends up, all. Easily : coll. : from ca. 1920. (O.E.D. Sup.) With a play on *anyhow*.

enemy, the. Time ; the clock, watch, etc. : coll. ; esp. as *how goes . . .?* or—ob. in C. 20— *what says . . .?* Dickens in *Nicholas Nickleby*, 1839. Hence *kill the enemy*, to pass time ; ob.

engaged ring. Engagement ring : coll., mostly London (— 1887). Baumann.

engine. A sewing-machine : tailors' : C. 20. E.g., *The Tailor and Cutter*, Nov. 29, 1928.

engineer and stoker. (Gen. pl.) A broker : rhyming s. : C. 20. J. Phillips, *A Dict. of Rhyming Slang*, 1931.

England's umbrella. Ireland : jocular coll. (— 1923). Manchon. For semantics, see Urinal of the Planets.

English. A key-translation, a crib : Winchester Colleges. verging on coll. : C. 19–20. Wrench. Ex *English*, to translate into English.

English burgundy. Porter : mid-C. 18–19. Grose, 1st ed. Cf. *British champagne*.

English cane. An oaken plant ; ? a cudgel : late C. 17–mid-18. B.E.

English manufacture. ' Ale, Beer, or Syder ', B.E. : late C. 17–18 : coll.

English pluck. Money : proletarian (— 1909) ; virtually †. Ware.

enif, adj. Fine : back s. (— 1859). H., 1st ed.

enin. Nine : back s. (— 1859). H., 1st ed. *Enin gen*, nine shillings ; *enin yanneps*, ninepence.

enjoy, followed by the infinitive (e.g. ' enjoy to do something '), is either low coll. or sol. (— 1864). The O.E.D., which points out that to use *enjoy* with an object denoting something not pleasant (as in *enjoy poor health*) is catachrestic : C. 19–20.

eno. One : back s. (— 1859). H., 1st ed.

enob. Bone : back s. : late C. 19–20. Ware.

enoptomancy. Incorrect for *enoptromancy* (divination by the mirror) : mid-C. 19–20. O.E.D.

Eno's. He knows : derisive : C. 20. Punning *Eno's Fruit Salt*. Also *'e knows*.

enough for anything after an adj. = either that adj. preceded by *very* or, gen., to satisfy anyone, in all conscience. Coll. : mid-C. 19–20. E.g. ' G.K.C. is witty enough for anything, don't you think ? '

enough to . . . See the key-nn. or -vv.

enquire (for *inquire*) is a hybrid form, but, though rightly frowned on by purists, it is not yet considered as indubitably catachrestic.

ensign-bearer. A drunken man ; a drunkard. Esp. one with a very red face : late C. 18–early 19. Grose, 2nd ed. (It serves as a flag.)

enthuse. To be enthusiastic ; speak enthusiastically : (mostly jocular or semi-jocular) coll. : orig. (— 1880), U.S. ; anglicised ca. 1900. Cf. the U.S. sense (1859 : Thornton), ' to kindle into enthusiasm '.

enthuzimuzzy. Enthusiasm : Society : ca. 1870–1900. Ware.

entrance-fee. Just enough money to order one drink at the canteen : military : from ca. 1910. B. & P.

envelope. To put (a note, a letter) into an envelope : coll. : 1857, De Morgan (O.E.D.). Rare and ob.

ephemeris is occ. used incorrectly for *ephemera* : C. 19–20. O.E.D.

epip. A pipe : back s. : from ca. 1865.

Epsom races. A pair of braces : rhyming s. (– 1857). 'Ducange Anglicus.'—2. Also, ca. 1850–1900, faces, now ' rhymed ' *airs and graces.*

Epsom salts. Coll., from ca. 1870, for *Epsom salt.*

equality (or **E-**) **Jack.** An officer treating those under him as equals : naval coll. : ca. 1810–70. Marryat, 1836.

equally as for **equally** or **as** (e.g. in ' *Stoke-hold* is equally as correct as *stoke-hole* ') is ' illiterate tautology ' : C. 19–20. Fowler.

*equipped, equipt. Rich ; well-dressed : c. : late C. 17–18. B.E. ; Grose, 1st ed.

-er is coll. when, in the game known among school-children as ' conquerors ', one speaks of e.g. a *niner*, nine chestnuts ' conquered '.—2. Illiterate for *-ow*, as in *medder*, q.v. Co-extensive with Mod. English.—3. See ' **Oxford -er, the** '.—4. Illiterate for *a*, as in *Isabeller*, and for *of*, as in ' A pint er beer '.—5. Coll. when agential as in *pea-souper* : mid-C. 19–20.

'Erb. A wag ; also in address to a person of name unknown to the speaker : Cockney and military : C. 20. F. & Gibbons. I.e. *Herbert.*

erf. (Gen. pl.) An egg : military coll. : late 1914–18. F. & Gibbons. I.e. Fr. *œuf.* Also *oof* (B. & P.).

Eries. Shares in the New York, Lake Erie, and Western Railroad : Stock Exchange coll. (– 1895) >, by 1910, j. (A. J. Wilson's glossary.)

erif. Fire : back s. (– 1859). H., 1st ed.

ʿeriff. A rogue ' just initiated, and beginning to practice ', Grose, 1st ed. : C. 18–early 19 c. Recorded first in *A New Canting Dict.*, 1725. Ex the sense, a canary (bird) two years old, for *canary* (*bird*) itself = a rogue.

erk. A lower-deck rating : nautical : late C. 19–20. Bowen. Perhaps ex dial. *irk*, to grow weary, or from officers' impatient ' They irk me, these —— ! ' See also **irk.** It is, in the aircraft engineering trade, the s. term for an aircraftsman : ? since 1916. *The Daily Herald*, Aug. 1, 1936. Prob. by telescoping.

errand, send a baby on an. To undertake a probable failure : coll. : mid-C. 19–20 ; ob.

error, and no. See **mistake, and no.**

ersatz girl. A temporary sweetheart ; a prostitute : prisoners-of-war s. : 1916. Ex Ger. *Ersatz*, a substitute.

erth. Three : back s. (– 1859). Hence, *erth-pu*, ' three up ', a street-game ; *erth sith noms*, three months' imprisonment ; *erth gens*, three shillings ; *erth yan(n)eps*, three pence. Also *earth.*

eruscation. An ignorant error for *coruscation* : C. 17. On the other hand, *erythism* is merely an incorrect spelling of *erethism*. O.E.D.

-ery is a frequent suffix in s. and coll., esp. in C. 20 and at schools and universities. Cf. *Hunnery*, q.v.

esclop. A policeman : back s. (– 1859). H., 1st ed. The *c* is never pronounced, the *e* gen. omitted : hence the well-known *slop.*

Eska, on Egyptian service, is the military nickname of men surnamed Moffatt : C. 20. Ex Arabic.

esma ! Listen : Eastern Expeditionary Force coll. : 1915–18. F. & Gibbons. Direct ex Arabic.

Espysay. The Society for the Prevention of Cruelty to Animals : coll. : from ca. 1880. Ware. Cf. *Ellersby.*

-esque is an often jocular, occ. coll. ending, as in *cigaresque*, q.v. The same applies to *-ess*, as, e.g., in *parsoness.*

esroch. A horse : back s. (– 1859) ; H., 1st ed. The *c* is added for naturalness. Occ. *esroph.*

-ess. See **-esque.**

esses emma. A sergeant-major : military signalese : 1914. F. & Gibbons.

Essex calf. A native of Essex : coll. : from ca. 1570 ; ob. G. Harvey, 1573 ; A. Behn ; Apperson. Cf. :

'Essex lion. A calf : from late 1620's (ob.): coll. ' Water Poet ' Taylor, 1630. Grose. (Apperson.) Essex being noted for its calves. Cf. *Cotswold lion*, *Rumford lion*, qq.v., and :

Essex stile. A ditch : coll. : C. 17–19. Camden, 1605 ; Grose, 1st ed. Ex the predominance of ditches over stiles in Essex. (Apperson.)

establish a funk. ' To create a panic—invented by a great bowler, at cricket, who enlivened this distinction with some cannon-ball bowling ' : Oxford University (– 1909) ; † by 1920. Ware. Cf. *bowl for timber.*

estacade. Incorrect for *estocade* : C. 18. O.E.D.

esuch. A house : back s. (– 1873) ; *c* for *o.* Cf. *esroch*, q.v.

esurient is catachrestic when, as from ca. 1820, used as = gastronomic. O.E.D.

-et for -ut. See **shet.**—2. For **-at**, as in **ketch** for *catch* : sol. : C. 19–20. See also *e*, 4.

et cetera ; etc. Catachrestically insulting when applied to persons : mid-C. 19–20. (Publishers sometimes put *etc.* at the end of an incomplete list of authors.)—2. For its slovenly use, see the astringent, invaluable Fowler.—3. A bookseller : c. : early C. 18. *Street Robberies Considered.* (Prob. ex booksellers' habit of short-titling books in their catalogues.)

eternal. Infernal ; damned : in C. 19–20, (dial. and) low coll. ; C. 17–18, S.E. Cf. U.S. *tarnal.*

eternity-box. A coffin : late C. 18–20 ; ob. Grose, 2nd ed.

[Eton slang. A. Clutton-Brock, *Eton*, 1900, writes thus : ' There are not many slang terms in common use at Eton. . . . At Winchester to " furk " (Latin *furca*, a fork) [1] means to expel. At Eton [it] is used only in connection with the wall game, and means to extract the ball out of the " bully " by a particular process. The player who performs this process is called the furker. Many . . . words peculiar to Eton are based on the " Lucus a non lucendo " principle ; . . . call over is termed " absence " because every one has to be present. . . .

2. The most common slang term at Eton . . . is " scug " ; this is primarily a term of abuse. It does not mean " cad ", like " lout " at Rugby, or " chaw " at Harrow. . . . It has various elusive meanings, ranging from a person of no account to one of dirty appearance, unpleasant habits, and undignified behaviour. . . . " Grub " at Eton is called " sock " [q.v.], and confectioners' shops are " sock shops ". To work hard is to " sap " (Lat. *sapio*, to be wise ?), and a " sap " is too often a term of abuse. To kick behind is to " fit ", and to kick on the shins is to " slick ". " Cheek " is [at Eton] " nerve ". When a boy is caned by his fag-master or any other boy in authority he is " worked off ".

---

[1] Both R. Townsend Warner and R. G. K. Wrench, however, derive—and correctly derive—the Winchester sense from an Old English word.

[For " pop ", see that term ; an excellent account of that institution occurs in this book by Clutton-Brock.]

3. The origin of . . . " wet-bobs " and " dry-bobs " is . . . unknown. That of the word " tug " is disputed. A tug is the oppidan word for a colleger, and is said to be derived from the Latin " gens togata ", the " gowned race ". A more probable explanation is that the word originally meant a certain waste part of the mutton on which the colleger was supposed to live. [Cf. Charles Lamb's " gag " and " gag-eater ", which once had the same meaning at Christ's Hospital.] Abbreviations are usually unfashionable at Eton [whereas at Charterhouse they are very general], and are considered the mark of a boy fresh from a private school. Thus, no one may say " ma " or " mi " for major or minor. An elder brother speaks of his younger brother as his " minor ", and a younger of his elder as his " major ". Cf. ' Harrow slang '.]

-ette, often jocular, is occ. coll., as in *munitionette*. Very rare before 1850.

euphemism and **euphuism** are sometimes used one for the other : mid-C. 19–20 : catachrestic.—2. For euphemism itself, see *Slang* and the essay in *Words !*

Euro. The *Europa* battle-ship : naval (— 1909) ; †. Ware.

Europe on the chest. Home-sickness : military : ca. 1880–1915. Ware.

Evans, Mrs. ' A name frequently given to a she cat, owing, it is said, to a witch of the name of Evans, who frequently assumed the appearance of a cat ', Grose, 1st ed. : coll. : mid-C. 18–mid-19.

evaporate. To run away : coll. : from ca. 1850. Dickens, ' The young man, looking round, instantly evaporated.' Ex S.E. sense, to disappear.

evatch. To have : back s. (— 1874). H., 5th ed. Instead of ' un-English ' *evah*.

***eve.** A hen-roost : C. 18–early 19 c. Extant, though ob., in dial. Prob. ex S.E. *eaves*.

evening wheezes. False news : lower classes' (— 1909) ; ob. Ex the lying rumours once more freely spread than nowadays. Ware.

evens, in. In even time (esp. of the 100 yards run in 10 seconds) : late C. 19–20 : athletics coll. >, by 1910, j.—2. **do evens,** to go at 20 miles per hour : cyclists' coll. : C. 20.

event, quite an. Something important, significant, or unusual : C. 20 coll.

ever in the **best, greatest, worst ever.** The best, etc., that has ever been : coll. : anglicised ca. 1930 ex U.S.

ever ?, did you. (Self-contained.) Have you ever seen, or heard, such a thing ? : coll. : mid-C. 19–20. O.E.D. (Sup.).

ever, seldom or. Seldom if(indeed) ever ; seldom or never : sol. ; C. 18–20.

ever a(n), e'er a(n). Any : in C. 19–20 (ob.), low coll. ; earlier, S.E.

ever is (or **was**), **as.** A coll. tag, orig. intensive, as in ' Bad riding as ever was ', 1708. Now approximately = ' mark you ' (parenthetic) and, mostly, rather illiterate. O.E.D. (Sup.).

ever so. Ever so much, as in *thanks ever so !* : mostly proletarian : from ca. 1895. Edwin Pugh, *Tony Drum*, 1898, ' " But I like you ever so," she faltered.'

ever since Adam was an oakum boy. Very old : naval coll. : C. 20. F. & Gibbons.

Ever Sworded, the. The 29th Foot, since 1881 the Worcestershire, Regiment : military : mid-C. 18–

20 ; ob. F. & Gibbons. Ex a custom resulting from a massacre in 1746.

ever the, adv. At all ; any : e.g. ' Ever the richer ', preceded by negative, = no richer. Coll. ; from ca. 1620. O.E.D.

Evergreens, the. The 13th Hussars : military . C. 19–20. Ex their motto *viret in œternum*. (F. & Gibbons.)

everlasting knock, take the. To die : sporting : 1889, *The Referee*, March 10.

everlasting shoes. The feet : coll. : from ca. 1870. H., 5th ed.

***everlasting staircase.** The treadmill : from ca. 1835 ; ob. Ca. 1850–90, occ. *Colonel Chesterton's everlasting staircase*, ex its improver. Brandon ; H., 1st ed.

Everton toffee. Coffee : rhyming s. (— 1857). ' Ducange Anglicus.'

every day and in every way, to which is often added **I shall get better and better.** A c.p. of ca. 1923–6. Ex Couéism.

every man Jack ; every mother's son. Absolutely everyone : coll. ; the former, from ca. 1840, e.g. in Dickens ; the latter, C. 14–20, e.g. in Shakespeare, Scott. (Apperson.)

every time. On every occasion ; without exception : coll., U.S. (1864) anglicised by 1880. O.E.D. (Sup.).—2. Hence, *every time !*, certainly ! ; I should just think so ! : coll. : C. 20.

every which way. In every manner or direction : jocular coll., orig. (1840) U.S. ; anglicised ca. 1910. Perhaps ex confusion caused by *every way* (*in*) *which*.

everybody or **everyone** followed by **they** (**them, their**). See **their**.

everything, in the predicate, = (something) very important, is coll. ; from ca. 1870. E.g. ' Bring the money ; that's *everything* !'

everything in the garden's lovely ! All goes well !: a C. 20 c.p., now ob. Ex :

everything is lovely. See **goose hangs high.**

everything is nice in your garden ! ' A gentle protest against self-laudation ' : 1896–ca. 1910. Ware supports with an anecdotal origin.

Eve's custom-house. The female pudend : late C. 18–19. Grose, 2nd ed., ' . . . Where Adam made his first entry.' Contrast *custom-house officer*.

***evesdropper.** A thief lurking about doors and watching his opportunity : c. (— 1725) ; † by 1800. *A New Canting Dict.*—2. A robber of hen-roosts : mid-C. 18–early 19 c. Grose, 1st ed. Ex *eaves*.

evethee. See **hevethee.**

evidence, v., as a mere synonym of *show*, is catachrestic : mid-C. 19–20. Fowler.

evif. Five : back s. (— 1859). H., 1st ed. Also *ewif*.

***evil.** In late C. 18–early 19 c., a halter. Grose, 2nd ed.—2. In C. 19 s., matrimony ; a wife. *Lex. Bal.*

evlenet. Twelve : back s. (— 1859). H., 1st ed. Naturally *evlewt*, looking un-English, was changed.

evolute. Incorrect for *involute* : C. 19–20. O.E.D.

***ewe,** or **white ewe,** gen. preceded by **the.** An important, because very beautiful, woman in a band of rogues, a criminal gang : c. : late C. 17–18. B.E. ; Grose, 1st ed.

ewe dressed lamb fashion, an old. An old woman dressed like a young girl : late C. 18–19 : coll. Grose, 1st ed. In C. 19–20 the usual form is *mutton dressed up to look like lamb* ; orig. and mainly Cockney.

ewe lamb. A uhlan : military : in G.W.

ewe-mutton. An elderly harlot or amateur prostitute : C. 19–20 ; ob.

ewif. A variant of *evif*, five ; *ewif* being more euphonious.

ex. Exhibition ; gen. **the Ex**, some specific exhibition, such as the Earl's Court Exhibition in 1899 : late C. 19–20. (Ernest Raymond, *A Family That Was*, 1929.)

Ex, His. His Excellency (the Governor-General) : Australian : C. 20.

exactly ! Certainly ! excellent ! Coll. : from ca. 1865. W. S. Gilbert, in *Bab Ballads*, 1869, ' " I'm boiled if I die, my friends ", quoth I, | And " exactly so ", quoth he ' (O.E.D.).

exagonal. Incorrect for *hexagonal* : C. 17. O.E.D.

exalt. To exult : catachrestic : C. 19–20.

exalted. (Other forms, very rare.) Ppl. passive, hanged : coll. : C. 19. Michael Scott, 1836.

exam. Examination : school s. >, in C. 20, gen. coll. ; from ca. the middle 1870's. James Payn, ' I read all about it for my exam.,' 1883.

examina. See ' Winchester College slang ', § 3.

exasperate or **hexasperate.** To over-aspirate one's *h*'s : from ca. 1850 ; ob. ' Cuthbert Bede ', 1853.

exceedings. ' Expenditure beyond income ' : Oxford University coll. (— 1909) ; ob. Ware.

Excellent's ulster. An oilskin : the (naval) Gunnery Schools', hence gen. naval : ca. 1840–90. Bowen.

Excellers, the. The 40th Foot, from 1881 the South Lancashires : C. 19–20 (ob.) military. Ex *XL'ers.*—2. Occ., the 12th Battalion, the London Regiment, formerly the 40th (XL) Middlesex Rifle Volunteers. F. & Gibbons.

except as a conjunction : see Fowler. To be avoided, except in archaic writing.

exceptionable and **exceptional** are, C. 19–20, frequently confused, as were, in late C. 14–17, **exception** and **acception**. O.E.D. See also Fowler.

excite !, don't. Keep cool ! : coll. (— 1934). C.O.D. (1934 Sup.). I.e. *don't excite yourself.*

exciting, adj. Excellent ; amusing, pleasant ; unexpected : coll. ; from ca. 1880.

excruciators. Very tight boots, esp. with pointed toes : coll. : from ca. 1865 ; ob.

excursioner, -ist. An excursion-agent : coll. ; from ca. 1890.

excuse ! Pardon me ! ; do not be offended : South African coll. (— 1906). Watkins, *From Farm to Forum*, at that date. Ex Dutch influence. (Pettman.)

execute. To cane : Public Schools' jocular coll. : late C. 19–20. Ian Hay, ' *Pip* ', 1907.

execution day. Washing day ; Monday : late C. 17–20 (ob.) : low coll. B.E. Ex hanging clothes on the line.

exes. Expenses : coll. (— 1864). H., 3rd ed.— 2. Those who were once something else : coll. ; from ca. 1820. Tom Moore, ' We x's have proved ourselves not to be wise.'—3. See **tommy and exes.**

*****exes** (or **exis**) **to fere.** Odds of 6 to 4 : racing c. : C. 20. For *exes*, see *exis* ; *fere* is *four* corrupted.

exhibition of oneself, make an. To show oneself in an unfavourable light : coll. ; from ca. 1880.

exis. Six ; esp. in *exis-evif gen*, 6 × 5 shillings, 30*s.*, and *exis-ewif yanneps*, 6 + 5 pence, 11*d.* Back s. (— 1859). H., 1st ed.—2. See **exes to fere.**

Exmas. Christmas : (low) coll. : late C. 19–20. (M. Harrison, *Spring in Tartarus*, 1935). Ex *Xmas.*

expect = to suppose or surmise and followed by a *that*, i.e. an immediately dependent noun-, clause has, since ca. 1870, been coll. when not dial. ; in C. 16–early 19, S.E.

expectible. Incorrect for *expectable* : C. 17–20. The O.E.D., which notes also the rare form of *expecting* for *expected*.

expecting, adj. With child : lower classes' coll. ; from ca. 1870. Baumann.

expended. Killed : nautical : mid-C. 18–early 19. Grose, 1st ed. Ex bookkeeping accounts.

expensive. Wealthy, sumptuous ; exceedingly or distinctively stylish : from ca. 1920 : s. >, by 1930, coll. Cf. *extensive*, q.v.

experience does it. A mid-C. 19–20 coll. rendering of *experientia docet*, (lit.) experiment teaches. Originated by Mrs. Micawber in *David Copperfield*.

explosion. The birth of a child : low : from ca. 1865 ; ob.

extensive. Showy ; given to, or actually, displaying wealth, fine clothes, conversational ability or effectiveness : (—)1859 ; ob. H., 1st ed. (Introduction).

extinguish. To reduce (an opponent) to silence : from ca. 1890, coll. ; earlier (1878), S.E.

extinguisher. A dog's muzzle (— 1890). *The Standard*, May 12, 1890.

extra. Dull, boring : from ca. 1929 ; ob. A. A. Milne, *Two People*, 1931.

extracted. Included in the list of *elegant extracts*, q.v. H., 3rd ed. Ob.

Extradition Court. The Second Justice-room at Bow Street : London legal and political : 1883, *The Daily News*, April 10. Ex the numerous extradition cases there tried.

extrumps or **ex(-)trumps.** Extempore ; without preparation (of a lesson) : Winchester College, from ca. 1860.

exudation. Percolation : catachrestic : late C. 18–20. O.E.D.

[**-ey** for *-y* or *-ie* is unnecessary, and often incorrect, in diminutives. See esp. Fowler.]

eye. A place where tradesmen (orig. and esp. tailors) hide stolen material : ' Called *hell*, or their *eye* : from the first, when taxed with their knavery, they equivocally swear, that if they have taken any, they wish they may find it in *hell* ; or alluding to the second protest, that what they have over and above is not more than they could put in their *eye*,' Grose, 1st ed. (at *cabbage*) : trade : mid-C.18–mid-19.—2. Incorrect for *nye* : C. 15–mid-18. O.E.D.

eye, all in the. All nonsense, humbug : ca. 1820–80. Cf. *Betty Martin*, q.v.

eye, be a sheet in the wind's. To be slightly drunk : nautical : 1883, Stevenson (O.E.D.). Gen. abbr. to *be a sheet in the wind.*

eye, glad. See glad eye.

eye, have a drop in the. See **drop in one's eye.**

eye, in the twinkling of an. See bedpost.

eye, lick the (or one's). To be happy, joyous : lower classes' (— 1923). Manchon.

eye !, mind your. Be careful ! From ca. 1850, low coll. ; earlier, S.E.

eye !, my or **all my.** See **Betty Martin** and cf. **eyes !, my.**

eye, pipe the ; or **put (the) finger in (the).** To weep : derisive coll. ; the former, C. 19–20 ; the latter, C. 16–early 19 (Grose, 3rd ed.).

eye, to have fallen down and trod(den) upon one's. To have a black eye : mid-C. 18–early 19. Grose, 2nd ed. (at *eight eyes*).

eye, wet an or **the.** To drink : from ca. 1830 ; ob.

eye-brows. See **eye-lashes.**

eye-glass weather. See **heye-glass weather.**

eye-glassy. Characteristic of the wearers of monocles : coll. : 1871, Meredith.—2. Hence, haughty, supercilious, haughtily contemptuous : coll. : 1907. O.E.D. (Sup.).

eye-hole. See **garter-hole.**

eye in a sling, have an ; with one's. (To be) crushed or defeated : proletarian coll. (— 1909). Ware.

eye-lashes or **-brows, hang (on) by the.** To be extremely persevering, tenacious, esp. in a difficulty : coll. ; from ca. 1850. The gen. ca. 1770–1850 form is *hang by the eye-lids*, applied to a dangerous position.

eye-limpet. An artificial eye : ca. 1875–1900.

eye of another shooter, wipe the. " To kill game that he has missed " (S.O.D.) : sporting : from ca. 1885.

eye-opener. The *membrum virile* : C. 19–20 low ; ob.

eye out of register. An inaccurate eye : printers' (— 1887). Baumann. Ex printers' j. *out of register.*

eye peeled or **skinned, keep one's (best).** To be wary : coll. : U.S. (1852 : Thornton), anglicised in late C. 19. Cf. *fly, wido, up to snuff.*

eye(-)sight, nearly lose one's. To obtain an unexpectedly and very intimate view of a member of the opposite sex : coll. ; from ca. 1860.

eye-teeth, draw (a person's). To make him less sure of himself : C. 20. Manchon. Cf. :

eye-teeth, have (cut) one's. To be experienced, prudent : coll. : C. 18–20. Apperson.

eye-wash. Something done, not for utility but for effect : coll. (— 1884) ; prob. orig. military. C. T. Buckland, in *Sketches of Social Life in India,* 1884, ' Most officers of any tact understand the meaning of eye-wash ' (O.E.D.). See esp. B. & P. Cf. *daily eye-wash,* q.v.

***eye-water.** Gin (— 1823) ; ob. C. >, by 1850, low. Egan's Grose ; H., 1st ed. ; Whyte-Melville ; *Judy* (an 1880's rival of *Punch*), Aug. 4, 1886, ' He imbibed stupendous quantities of jiggered gin, dog's nose, and Paddy's eye-water.'

eyeful, take an. ' To have a good look ' (**v.t.,** *at*) : coll. : C. 20. F. & Gibbons.

eyes, googoo. See **googoo eyes.**

eyes !, my. An exclamation indicative of surprise : ca. 1835–1910. Dickens, in *Oliver Twist,* ' My eyes, how green ! . . . Why a beak's a madg'strate.'

Eyes, the Old. The Grenadier Guards : military : C. 19–20 ; ob. F. & Gibbons.

Eyes and Limbs, the. ' The foot guards were formerly so called, by the marching regiments, from a favourite execration in use among them, which was, damning their eyes, limbs, and blue breeches,' Grose, 1st ed. : app. ca. 1720–60.

eyes are set, one's. One is drunk : coll. : C. 17. Shakespeare. O.E.D. (See also **eyes set.**)

eyes draw straws, one's. See both **draw straws** and **straws, draw.**

eyes out, cry one's. To weep long and bitterly : coll. ; from ca. 1705. Swift, ' I can't help it, if I would cry my Eyes out.'

eyes peeled or **skinned, keep one's.** See **eye peeled.**

eyes set (in one's or **the head), have** or **be with one's** or **the.** To be drunk : C. 17–18 coll. Shakespeare, ' O he's drunke . . . his eyes were set at eight i'th morning.'

Eyeties. Italians : military : G.W. (F. & Gibbons.) Ex the sol. pronunciation *Ey(e)talian.*

F

f for *th* is a mark of Cockney, as in *fanks* for *thanks, fing* for *thing* ; cf. *v* for *th,* as in *farver.*—2. But **f** or **ff** for *v* is a characteristic of Welsh English. See esp. Fluellen in *Henry V.*—3. See '**f** in Addenda.

F.A. or **sweet f.a.** See **Fanny Adams,** 2.

F.C.'s. False calves : theatrical coll. (— 1909). Ware, ' Paddings used by actors in heroic parts to improve the shape of the legs '.

f.h.o. ! ; **f.h.b.** Family hands off ! (sometimes explained as family hold off !) ; or, family hold back ! : middle-class domestic coll. c.p. indicating that a certain dish is not to be eaten by members of the family at a meal where guests are present : mid-C. 19–20.

f sharp. A flea : from ca. 1860 ; ob. H., 3rd ed. ; Lyell, ' " F " being the initial letter, and " sharp " because of the bite '. Cf. *b flat,* q.v.

face. A grimace : coll. : from ca. 1600 (S.O.D.). Shakespeare.—2. Great confidence, insolent boldness ; impudence : from ca. 1530 : coll. till C. 18, then S.E. Face is a principal character in Jonson's *The Alchemist.*—3. Credit, esp. in *push one's face,* to obtain credit by bluff or bluster : coll. : from ca. 1760. Goldsmith. Cf. U.S. *run*—or *travel on*—*one's face,* to go upon credit.—4. A contemptuous term of address : orig. and mainly Cockney : from ca. 1875. Cf. *face-ache* and *features.*

face, square. See **square face.**

face-ache. A C. 20 jocular term of address. Cf. *face,* n., 4. Prob. because the sight of the person addressed makes one's face ache with laughing. Cf. S.E. *face-ache,* neuralgia.

face but one's own, have no. To be penniless : prob. ex the gamesters' sense, to hold no court cards : late C. 18–early 19. Grose, 1st ed.

face-entry. Freedom of access to a theatre : theatrical (— 1874) ; ob. H., 5th ed. Cf. *face,* 3, q.v.

face-fungus. Moustaches ; esp. beard ; or both : jocular : C. 20. (D. Sayers, *The Nine Tailors,* 1934.)

face like a sea-boot. An expressionless face : nautical coll. : late C. 19–20. Bowen.

face-making. Sexual intercourse : mid-C. 18–early 19. Grose, 1st ed. Cf. *making feet for children's stockings.*

face the knocker. To go begging : tailors' : from ca. 1875.

face the music. To cope bravely with an unpleasant emergency : orig. (1850) U.S., anglicised ca. 1880. Coll.; post-War, S.E. Perhaps ex acting on the stage.

face-ticket, have a. To be so well known to the janitors that one is not asked to present one's ticket : British Museum Reading Room coll. (— 1909). Ware.

facer. A glass full to the brim : late C. 17–early 19 : c. >, by 1800, low coll. B.E., 'A Bumper without Lip-room'.—2. A blow in the face : pugilistic coll. : from ca. 1810 ; ob. *Lex. Bal.*— 3. Hence, a sudden check or obstacle : coll. ; from ca. 1825. Thackeray, 'In . . . life every man must meet with a blow or two, and every brave one would take his facer with good humour.'—4. Hence, a problem : coll. : mid-C. 19–20.—5. A dram : Anglo-Irish : mid-C. 19–20. H., 3rd ed.—6. A glass of whiskey punch : from ca. 1870 ; ob. H., 5th ed.

faces, make. To beget children : C. 18–early 19. —2. **(make faces at.)** To deceive, disappoint, or verbally attack a friend : c. ; ca. 1870–1920.

facey. A workman facing another as he works : tailors'. Hence, *facey on the bias*, one not directly in front, and *facey on the two thick*, a workman just behind one's *vis-à-vis*. From ca. 1870.

facias. See **fieri facias.**

facings, go or be put through one's. To be reprimanded or to show off : military s. > gen. coll. : from ca. 1865. In C. 20, S.E.

facings, silk. Beer-stains on the garments being made or altered : tailors' : from ca. 1870. Ex *watered silk*. Cf. *canteen-medal*.

fact. Factor : catachrestic : very rare before the crime-novel craze (from ca. 1922). E.g., A. Fielding, *Death of John Tait*, 1932, 'Altogether she was a strange fact in the case.'

*Factory, the. Old Scotland Yard : c. of ca. 1860–90. ' No. 747.'

facty. Full of facts : coll. but never very gen. : from ca. 1880. ' A " facty " [newspaper] article ', *The Pall Mall Gazette*, Nov. 2, 1883. O.E.D.

facy. Impudent, insolent : C. 17–20 ; coll. till C. 19, then dial. Ex *face*, n., 2.

fa'd, fa-d, fa-dee, far-dee. A farthing : Charterhouse : from ca. 1870. Cf. *ha'd*.

fad-cattle. Easily accessible women : C. 19. Cf. *cattle* ; *faddle*, to toy.

faddist, fadmonger. One devoted to a public or private fad : coll. ; from ca. 1880. Vbl.n., *fadmongering*.

faddle. To toy or trifle : coll. in C. 19 ; † by 1890, except in dial. Hence, n., a busybody ; also an affected and very effeminate male. The v. arose ca. 1680 (orig., to caress a child) ; the n. ca. 1800, though the sense, triflery, foolery, ' bosh ', hardly before 1850.

faddy. Full of fads : coll. : from ca. 1820. Mrs. Sherwood, 1824. Ex dial. (O.E.D.)

fade away ! Go away : smart s. (— 1913) ; ob. by 1920, † by 1930. A. H. Dawson's *Dict. of Slang*.

*fadge. A farthing : late C. 18–19 c. Grose, 3rd ed. ; Duncombe, *Sinks of London*, 1848.

fadge, v. To suit ; fit : late C. 16–19. Succeed : from ca. 1600. Both coll. The former in Nashe, Shakespeare, B.E., Horace Walpole ; the latter in Cotgrave, Borrow, Nares : ' Probably never better than a low word ; it is now confined to the streets.' Esp. in *it won't fadge*, it won't do or serve.—2. **fadge with**, to tolerate (a thing), agree or rub along with a person, is C. 17–early 18 and rather S.E. than coll.

fadger. A glazier's frame ; a ' frail ' : glaziers' ; from ca. 1860. H., 3rd ed. In C. 20, j. Ex *fadge*, v., 1.

fadoodle. A mere nothing, a useless trifle : lower classes' (— 1923). Manchon. Perhaps ex *faddle* on *flapdoodle*.

fag. Cf. **fag, stand a good** : possibly this phrase + *fag*, hard work, drudgery, weariness (1780 : O.E.D.), being a schoolboys' perversion of *fatigue* (W.), led to :—2. A boy doing menial work for one in a higher form : schoolboys' s. (— 1785) >, by 1850, gen. coll. Grose, 1st ed. ; Thackeray (of a young drudge in a painters' studio). Prob. ex *fag*, v., 1, but, despite the dates, perhaps ex *fag*, v., 2.— 3. Eatables : Christ's Hospital, from ca. 1800. Leigh Hunt, in his *Autobiography*, ' The learned derived the word from the Greek *phago*.'—4. See **fag, stand a good.**—5. A cigarette ; orig., an inferior cigarette (only from ca. 1915, any cigarette) : from ca. 1887. Abbr. *fag-end* and ? orig. military. ' Cuthbert Bede ', in 1853, speaks of ' the fag-ends of cigars ' (S.O.D.).

*fag, v. In c., to beat, thrash : late C. 17–19 ; after ca. 1830, low coll. B.E., Grose.—2. (? hence.) V.t., to have (a boy) as one's fag : schoolboys' : from ca. 1785 ; ob. Grose, 2nd ed.—3. V.i. (Ex n., 2.) To do menial jobs for a schoolfellow higher up in the school : from ca. 1805 : schoolboys' s. >, by 1860, gen. coll. In C. 20, both the n. and its derivative are, in this sense, gen. regarded as, therefore are, S.E.

fag, stand a good. Not to become easily tired : late C. 18–19 : coll. Grose, 3rd ed. Hence, *fag*, anything that causes weariness ; toil : coll. (— 1780). Hence, from ca. 1880, a wearisome thing ; a bore.

fag-end man. A collector—for a living—of cigarette-ends : lower classes' (— 1923). Manchon.

fag out. To serve as a fag ; esp. in cricket, to field : from ca. 1840 : coll., schoolboys', orig. and esp. at Winchester College. Lewis.

fagged out. Exhausted : coll. (— 1785). Grose. Perhaps ex dial. *fag*, to exhaust oneself in toil, and *fagged out*, frayed.

*fagger, figger or **figure.** A boy thief that, entering by a window, opens the door to his confederates or even hands the booty out to them : c. (— 1785) ; ob. Grose, 1st ed. ; whereas *figger* (Grose, 1st ed.) arose in late C. 18, *figure*, its derivative, is of C. 19– 20.

faggery, fagging. Serving as a *fag*, q.v., in a school : schoolboys' ; from ca. 1850, 1820, resp. De Quincey in his autobiographical sketches, 1853, ' Faggery was an abuse too venerable and sacred to be touched by profane hands.'

fagging. A beating, thrashing, thumping : low : not recorded before 1775, but prob. used as early as 1700. Ex c. *fag*, to beat.—2. See **faggery.**

fag(g)ot. A ' baggage ' ; a pejorative applied to a woman (— 1600), also—gen. preceded by *little*— to a child (— 1859) : low coll., the former in C. 20 being dial.—2. A rissole : low coll. ; from ca. 1850. Mayhew. Also, butcher's oddments or ' stickings ' (? hence the name) : low coll. (— 1859). H., 1st ed. —3. A man mustered as a soldier but not yet formally enlisted : late C. 17–19. B.E. Hence, a man hired to appear at a muster or on a muster-roll : C. 18–19. Grose, 1st ed. Both nuances are military ; the latter, also naval.

fag(g)ot, v. In C. 17–19, to bind, truss, i.e. as sticks in a faggot. Prob. coll. ; never, despite

B.E., was it ɔ.—2. C., however, is the sense, to garotte : late C. 19–20. Manchon.—3. In low s., v.t. and i., to copulate (with) ; to frequent harlots : C. 19. Ex *faggot*, n., 1.

fag(g)ot-briefs. A bundle or bundles of dummy briefs carried by the briefless : legal (— 1859). Sala, ' Pretend to pore over faggot briefs '. Ob.

fag(g)ot-master. A whoremonger : low ; from ca. 1825 ; ob. Cf. *faggot*, v., 3.

fag(g)ot-vote. ' A vote secured by the purchase of property under mortgage, or otherwise, so as to constitute a nominal qualification ', F. & H. : political coll. (1817, C.O.D.), ob. by 1920 ; S.E. by 1840. Gladstone, Nov. 25, 1879. Perhaps ex *faggot*, n., 3. Hence *fag(g)ot-voter*.

fag(g)oteer. Same sense, period, and status as *faggot-master*, q.v.

fag(g)otty. Incorrect for *faggoty* : mid-C. 19–20. O.E.D.

fail. To report a candidate as having failed in an examination : from ca. 1880 ; coll. till ca. 1920, then S.E.

fain I ! ; fains ! ; fain it ! ; faints ! A call for a truce ; a statement of opposition : schoolboys' : from ca. 1810. See also **faynights !** Prob. a corruption of *fen !*, ex *fend* ; or possibly ex *claim(s) I !* or *feign*. Cf. *bags (I)*, its opposite. The earliest forms are *fen !*, q.v., and *fin* or *fingy*, qq.v.

faints, the. A tendency to faint : coll. : from ca. 1890.

*fair ; always **the fair.** ' A set of subterraneous rooms in the Fleet Prison ', *Lex. Bal.* : c. : ca. 1810–50.

fair, adj. ' Nice ' : coll. verging on s. : C. 17. In C. 18, the word was *elegant*. See *Slang*, p. 28.— 2. Undoubted, complete, thorough : dial. (— 1872) >, by ca. 1885, s. (O.E.D. Sup.). See **fair cop** and (**at cow) fair cow.**

fair, adv.1 Fairly : coll. : C. 19–20.—2. Completely : dia . (1859 : E.D.D.) >, in the 1880's, coll.

fair, see. To ensure fair play by watching : coll. : Dickens, 1837. Ob. (O.E.D.)

*fair cop, it's a. It's a clear arrest : c. : late C. 19–20. Ware.

fair cow, a. See **cow,** 4.

fair dinkum. See **dinkum.**

fair doo's or **doos** or **does** or **do's.** A fair deal ; justice ; just proportion : military (ca. 1912) >, by 1920, gen. B. & P. Ex Yorkshire dial (1865 : E.D.D.).

fair-gang, the. Gypsies : coll. ; from ca. 1830 ; ob. by 1900, † by 1919. From their frequenting fairs in gangs or communities. Prob. a corruption of *faw-gang*, itself ex *Faa*, a Scottish-Gypsy surname (O.E.D.).

fair herd. A good attendance of strangers : Oxford University : 1883, *The Daily News*, June 13 ; ob. (Ware.)

fair itch. Utter imitation : low (— 1909) ; ob. Ware.

fair rations. Fair dealings ; honesty : sporting : from ca. 1875.

*fair roebuck. ' A Woman in the Bloom of her Beauty ', *A New Canting Dict.*, 1725 : c. : C. 18. Ex *fair roebuck*, a roebuck in its fifth year.

fair speech !, you have made a. A late C. 17–18 c.p. ' in derision of one that spends many words to little purpose ', B.E.

fair thing. A wise proceeding, a clear duty, justice ; enough, esp. in *a fair thing's a fair thing*. Coll. : C. 20. C. J. Dennis, 1916.

fair trade, -trader. Smuggling ; a smuggler : nautical (— 1887). Baumann ; Bowen.

fair-weather friend. One who writes only once a year and that in summer-time : Anglo-Irish : C. 20.

fair wind, give (something) **a.** To pass (e.g. the salt) : nautical : late C. 19–20. Bowen.

fairing. Cakes (or sweets) bought at a fair ; esp. gingerbread nuts : coll. when not dial. : from mid-C. 18. (O.E.D.)

fairish. Fairly large : coll. (— 1865).—2. As adv., in a pleasant manner ; to a fair degree : coll., 1836. (S.O.D.). Both perhaps orig. dial.

fairy. ' A debauched, hideous old woman, especially when drunk ' : proletarian (— 1909) ; ob. Ware.—2. A catamite : U.S., anglicised ca. 1924. Irwin ; M. Lincoln, 1933 ; O.E.D. (Sup.).— 3. A *fair*-headed girl : New Zealanders' nickname : C. 20.

fairy light. A Very light : military : 1916. By jocular perversion. F. & Gibbons.

fairy story or **tale.** A ' hard luck ' tale : low s. verging on tramps' c. : C. 20.

fairybabe. Incorrect for *fear-babe*, a bugaboo : C. 17. O.E.D.

[**faith** is, in C. 14–19, often used exclamatorily and expletively, by itself or in combination.]

faithful, one of the. A drunkard : C. 17 coll. *The Man in the Moon*, 1609.—2. A tailor giving long credit : late C. 18–19, either c. or low or c. > low. Grose, 1st ed. Hence, *his faith has made him unwhole*, too much credit has bankrupted him : Grose, 1st ed.

Faithful Durhams. The 68th Foot Regiment, from 1881 the Durham Light Infantry : military : traditionally from 1772 ; ob. F. & Gibbons.

faithfully. With obligating assurances : from late C. 16 ; coll. ' He promised faithfully to send the book the next day,' O.E.D.

faitor. See **fater.**

fake. An action, esp. if illegal ; a dodge ; a sham (person or thing) : from ca. 1825 : low. James Greenwood, 1883, ' Naming the house in [this] ridiculous way was merely a fake to draw attention to it.' For etymology, see the v., though it may abridge *fakement*.—2. Anything used in illicit deception or manufacture : 1866 (O.E.D.). Hence :—3. A mixture for making a horse safe (cf. *dope*) : ca. 1870–90. H., 5th ed. Cf. *dope*, n.—4. (Ex senses 1, 2.) A gadget ; a ' thingummy ' : Cockneys' : from ca. 1890. Clarence Rook, *The Hooligan Nights*, 1899.

*fake, v. To do anything, esp. if illegally or with merely apparent skill or ability ; to cheat, deceive, devise falsely ; tamper with ; forge ; ' dope ' (a horse) ; to steal. In c. and then, by ca. 1880, in low s., a verb of multiple usage : gen. only from ca. 1830 (cf. however, *fake away*), though doubtless used in c. as early as 1810, Vaux recording it in 1812. Vbl.n., *faking*. Perhaps ex L. *facere*, to do, influenced by *faire* as understood in Fr. c., but more prob. ex Ger. *fegen*, (lit.) to sweep, itself in extensive s. use (W.) : cf. *feague* (q.v.), which is either cognate or the orig. form.—2. To hit : Parlyaree : C. 20. Edward Seago, *Circus Company*, 1933.—3. V.i. To hurt, as in ' It fakes like hell ! ' : low s. or c. (— 1923). Manchon. Prob. ex :—4. V.t., to hurt : c. (— 1812). Vaux. Ex sense 1, possibly influenced by *ache*. Cf. *fake oneself*, q.v.—5. See **fake up.**

*fake a cly. To pick a pocket (see *cly*) : c. ; from ca. 1810 ; ob. Vaux.

fake a curtain. ' To agitate the act-drop after it has fallen, and so perhaps thereby induce a torpid audience to applaud a little, and justify the waiting actor to " take a curtain " ', Ware : theatrical : 1884.

fake a dance, step, trip. To improvise a step when, in dancing, one has forgotten the correct one : theatrical : from ca. 1860. Cf. :

fake a line. To improvise a speech : theatrical : from ca. 1860.

fake a picture. ' To obtain an effect by some adroit, unorthodox means ' : artistic coll. : from ca. 1860. Ware.

*fake a poke. To pick a pocket : c. : late C. 19–20. *The People*, Sept. 6, 1896. (Ware.)

*fake a screeve. To write a (begging) letter : c. ; from ca. 1810. Vaux.

*fake a screw. To make a false or a skeleton key : C. 19–20. Ibid.

fake a step or trip. See **fake a dance.**

*fake away ! Go it ! Splendid—don't stop ! C., perhaps only ' literary ' : ca. 1810–1900. Vaux. See **fake, v.**

fake one's pin. See **fake oneself.**

*fake one's slangs. To file through fetters : c. ; from ca. 1810 ; ob. See **slangs.** Vaux.

*fake oneself. To disfigure or wound oneself : C. 19 c. Cf. *S.I.W.* Cf. *fake one's pin*, to ' create ' a sore or wounded leg : likewise c. Ibid.

*fake out and out. To kill (a person) : c. : C. 19. Vaux, 1812.

fake-pie. A pie containing ' left-overs ' : straitened Society : 1880 ; ob. Ware.

*fake the broads. To ' stack ' the cards ; to work a three-card trick : c. ; from ca. 1840.

*fake the duck. To adulterate drink ; to swindle, cheat : c. ; from ca. 1830 ; †.

*fake the rubber. To stand treat : c. ; from ca. 1850 ; ob. H., 3rd ed.

*fake the sweetener. To kiss : c. : ca. 1840–1900. See **sweetener.**

fake up ; occ. simply **fake**, v.t. and reflexive. To paint one's face : theatrical ; from ca. 1870 ; ob.— 2. To adapt for the theatre : theatrical (— 1887). Baumann.—3. To falsify : mid-C. 19–20. Ibid.

faked ; occ. **faked-up.** Spurious ; counterfeit : low coll. ; from the 1850's. H., 1st ed. See **fake, v.**

*fakeman-charley. See sense 4 of :

*fakement. A counterfeit signature (— 1811), hence a forgery ; a begging letter, a petition (— 1839).—2. A dishonest practice (— 1838) ; hence, any trade, action, thing, contrivance (— 1857).—3. Small properties, accessories : theatrical ; from ca. 1875. The first senses, c. ; the second group, low ; the last, s. The term derives prob. ex *fake*, n., 1.—4. (Cf. sense 1.) Also *fakeman-charley.* A private mark of ownership : c. ; from ca. 1810 ; ob. Vaux ; H., 1st ed.

*fakement-chorley. Ware's variant of *fakeman-charley* : see last sense of *fakement.*

*fakement-dodge ; -dodger. The practice of writing begging letters ; the beggar or impostor employing this ' dodge ' : c. : mid-C. 19–20 ; ob. Mayhew.

faker. A maker, or a faker, of anything : low (— 1688). Randle Holme. Cf. the U.S. *faker*, ' a street-vendor of gimcracks, &c.', Thornton.—2. In c., a thief (— 1851) ; in C. 20, a pickpocket. Borrow, in *Lavengro*, ' We never calls them thieves here, but prigs and fakers.'—3. A jeweller : c. (— 1857). ' Ducange Anglicus.'—4. A circus per-

former, esp. rider : circus, from ca. 1875. Baumann *(fakir).*—5. A harlot's ' fancy man ' : low (— 1891) ; ob.

fakes and slumboes. Properties ; accessories : theatrical : from ca. 1880 ; †.

faking. Vbl.n., corresponding with all senses of *fake*, v., q.v. : low s. > coll. ; (—)1845.

fakir. See **faker,** 4.

fal. A girl : rhyming s. (1868) on *gal* ; ob. Ware.

falderals (or **-ols**). Silly ideas : coll. (— 1923). Manchon. Ex *falderal*, a trinket, a trifle ; imm. ex dial. sense : an idle fancy.

fall, v. To conceive a child : coll. : C. 19–20 ; ob.—2. In c., to be arrested (— 1883).—3. Hence, to go to prison ; e.g. *fall for three years* : c. : C. 20. ' Stuart Wood ', 1932.—4. (Prob. also ex sense 2.) To fail : c. and low s. : from ca. 1910. James Curtis, *The Gilt Kid*, 1936.

fall, have a bad or **good** or **lucky.** To have a piece of bad, or good luck ; make a (bad) strike : coll. (— 1887) ; ob. Baumann.

fall across. To meet (a person) unexpectedly : from ca. 1885 ; coll. till C. 20, then S.E.

fall down (on). To make a bad mistake or error (in or at) : s. >, ca. 1935, coll. : U.S. (ca. 1870) anglicised ca. 1910. Often with *on*. (O.E.D. Sup.)

fall-downs. Fragments of cookshop puddings ; collected, they are sold cheaply. Cockney : C. 19. Ware.

fall for. To be greatly attracted by (esp. a member of the other sex) : U.S. (ca. 1910), anglicised ca. 1920 ; by 1935, coll.

fall in. To be quite wrong : coll. ; from ca. 1900.

fall in the thick. ' To become dead drunk . . . Black beer is called thick, so is mud ' : low (—1909). Ware.

fall of the leaf, (at) the. (By) hanging : low or c. : ca. 1780–1840. George Parker.

fall through. To be unable to keep, or to go back on, an appointment : coll. : 1924, Galsworthy.

fallen away from a horse-load to a cart-load. Grown fat : a late C. 18–mid-19 c.p. Grose, 3rd ed.

false alarms. Arms (of body) : military rhyming s. : late C. 19–20.

false hereafter. A dress-improver or bustle : Society : ca. 1890–1900.

*fam ; occ. **famm** (B.E.) or **fem.** The hand : low, orig. c. : from ca. 1690 ; † by 1870. ? abbr. *famble*, q.v.—Hence, 2, a ring : c. of ca. 1770–1850.

*fam, v. To handle : C. 19–20 (ob). c. Vaux. Hence *fam a donna*, to caress a woman intimately ; *fam for the plant*, to feel for the valuables.

*fam-grasp. A hand-shaking : c. : late C. 18–19. Ex the v.t., late C. 17–19. The v. also = to agree, or to come to an agreement, with a person, a sense recorded by Coles in 1676. Lit., to grasp by the ' fam ' or hand.

*fam-lay. Shop-lifting, esp. of jewellery by one with viscous hands : c. : mid-C. 18–19. Grose, 2nd ed.

fam-snatcher. A glove : low : ca. 1820–60. Pierce Egan may have coined it.

*fam-squeeze. Strangulation : C. 19 c. Contrast *fam-grasp*, q.v.

*fam-struck. Baffled in a search ; handcuffed : C. 19 c.

fambly, famberly, fambly. Sol. for family : esp. Cockney : C. 19–20. Baumann *(famberly)*

*famble. The hand : mid-C. 16–20 c. Harman, B.E., Grose, Hindley. Prob. ex *famble*, to fumble

(O.E.D.).—2. Hence, a ring : C. 17–early 19 c. Shadwell.

*famble-cheat. A ring : mid-C. 17–18 c. Coles ; B.E. ; Dunton.—2. A glove : mid-C. 17–early 19 c. Coles.

*fambler. A glove : C. 17 c. Rowlands.—2. A seller of ' brum ' rings (rarely *famble*) : late C. 17–18 c.

*fambling-cheat. (Lit., a hand-thing ;) a ring : mid-C. 16–17 c. Harman ; Rowlands.

fambly. See fambely.

familiar way, in the. Pregnant : jocular coll. (— 1891), punning *in the family way*. Ob.

familiars. Lice : C. 19–early 20. Facetiously ex S.E. sense, a familiar spirit.

*family, the. The underworld of thieves : mid-C. 18–19 ; c. : Bamfylde-Moore Carew, 1749. Cf. *family-man*.

family, hands off ! See f.h.o. !

family head. ' An elaborate figure head of several figures ' : nautical : mid-C. 19–20. Bowen.

family hotel. A prison : coll. ; ca. 1840–1900. *Punch*, Jan. 31, 1857, ' In a ward with one's pals, | Not locked up in a cell, | To an old hand like me it's a family hotel.'

*family-man. A thief : c. (— 1788) ; ob. In pl., occ. *family people*. Ex *family*, q.v.—2. Also, a ' fence ' : mid-C. 19–20 c.

family of love. ' Lewd Women, Whores ', B.E. ; esp. a company thereof, Grose, 1st ed. : late C. 17–20 (ob.).

*family people. A c. (— 1812) variant of *family, the*, q.v. Vaux ; H., 1st ed.

family(-)plate. Silver money : jocular coll. ; from ca. 1850.

family(-)pound. A family grave : from ca. 1870.

*family-woman. A female thief : c. (— 1812). Vaux. On *family-man*.

famine. Lack of bread at meals : Bootham School : late C. 19–20. Anon., *Dict. of Bootham Slang*, 1925.

*famm. See fam, n.

famous. Excellent ; ' capital ' : coll. : from the 1790's. Southey, ' " But every body said," quoth he, " That 'twas a famous victory " ' (O.E.D.). Influenced by :

famously. Excellently : ' capitally ' : coll. ; from ca. 1600. Shakespeare, Lytton. (O.E.D.)

*fan. A waistcoat : c. ; ca. 1835–1900. Brandon ; Snowden, *Magazine Assistant*, 3rd ed. ? ex its spread.—2. An enthusiast, orig. of sport : ex U.S. (— 1889), anglicised ca. 1914 ; by 1930, coll. Abbr. *fanatic*.—3. Ca. 1680–1720, a fanatic : jocular coll. gen. spelt *fann* or *phan*. (O.E.D.)

fan, v. To beat, whip ; be-rate : low coll. : late C. 18–20. Now esp. *fan with a slipper*. Grose, 1st ed.—2. In c., to search a person, or his clothes : from ca. 1850. Mayhew. Cf. *frisk*, q.v.—3. Esp. to search illicitly (a man) for watch or wallet : c. : C. 20. Charles E. Leach.

fan-qui. See fanqui.—fan-tail. See fantail.

[Fanciful odds in betting. See **Burlington Arcade to a smock-shop, Lombard Street to a China orange, Pompey's pillar to a stick of sealing-wax, Waterloo Bridge to a deal plank**, etc.]

fancy. (Always the f.) The boxing world (from ca. 1810) ; boxers collectively (— 1820) : coll. ; by 1900, S.E. ; somewhat ob. Pierce Egan, ' The various gradations of the Fancy hither resort, to discuss matters incidental to pugilism.'—2. A ' best

girl ' : lower classes' (— 1923). Manchon. Abbr. *fancy piece*.

fancy, v. To have a (too) high opinion of oneself, of another, or of a thing : coll. : from ca. 1860.— 2. In the imperative, either as one word (*fancy !*) or two words (*fancy that !*) or preceding a phrase (e.g. ' Fancy you being in plus fours ! '), it expresses surprise : coll. : ? earlier than 1834, when (O.E.D.) Medwin has ' Fancy me boxed up in the narrow vehicle.'

fancy-(bloak or) bloke. A sporting man : coll. ; from ca. 1850 ; ob. by 1920. H., 1st ed. Ex *fancy*, n., q.v.—2. A *fancy-man*, q.v. : from ca. 1835. Brandon.—3. Hence, any woman's favourite male : from ca. 1880.

fancy frigate. A warship notable for smartness—but gen. ' very uncomfortable to live in ' : naval coll. : late C. 19–20 ; ob. Bowen.

fancy-girl. Same as *fancy-woman*, 2 : 1930, A. P. Herbert (O.E.D. Sup.).

Fancy Greens, the. The 36th Foot, from 1881 the Worcestershire, Regiment : military : C. 19–20 ; ob. F. & Gibbons, ' From the pea-green facings previously worn '.

fancy Joseph. A harlot's ' boy ' or bully (see fancy-man) : C. 19 low. Either with an allusion to Joseph and Potiphar's wife or an amplification of *joe*, a male sweetheart.

fancy-lay. Pugilism : low (— 1819) : ob. by 1890, † by 1918. Tom Moore. See lay.

fancy-man. (Cf. *fancy-bloke* and *f. Joseph*.) A harlot's protector and/or lover ; her husband : low (— 1821). Egan, ' Although " one of the fancy ", he was not a fancy man.' Ex :—2. A sweetheart : from ca. 1810 : low s. >, by 1860, coll. Vaux.— 3. A male keep : low (— 1811) ; ob. *Lex. Bal.* Cf. sense 2.—4. Rarely a pugilist ; often a follower of pugilism : but seldom used in the singular : from ca. 1845 ; ob. by 1900 ; † by 1920. In all senses, *fancy* is either a corruption of Fr. *fiancé* or, much more prob., ex *the fancy*, q.v. Notable synonyms of sense 1 : *mack*, *ponce*, and *prosser*, qq.v.

fancy piece. A harlot : low (— 1823). Egan's Grose. In C. 20, occ. of a man's favourite girl or woman, respectable or otherwise.

fancy religion. Any religion other than C. of E., R.C., and Presbyterian : naval and military : from the 1890's or earlier. Bowen.

fancy woman. A temporary mistress ; a kept woman : low coll. (— 1850). Cf. *fancy-man*, 3.— 2. In C. 19–20, a man's favourite female—often jocularly : low s. >, by 1860, coll. Vaux. Cf. *fancy-man*, 2.

fancy-work, take in. To make extra money by prostitution, ' do the naughty for one's clothes ' : low (— 1891). F. & H. The pun is best left unexplained ; cf. *fancy-man*, 1, 2.

fandangle. A fantastic or ludicrous ornament ; foolery ; nonsense : coll. : from ca. 1880. W. considers it an arbitrary deformation of *fandango*, ? after (*new-*)*fangle*(*d*).

fang-chovey. A dentist's ' parlour ' : low ; from ca. 1850. *Fang*, a tooth ; *chovey*, a shop. Also, *fang-faker*, a dentist : same comments.

*fann. See fan, n., 3.

fanning. A thrashing : late C. 18–19. See fan, v., 1.—2. In c., stealing : mid-C. 19–20. See fan, v., 2, and cf. *cross-fanning*, q.v.

fanny. The female *pudenda* ; the pudend : low : from ca. 1860 (perhaps much earlier). Variants, seldom used, are *fanny artful* and *fanny fair*.

Perhaps ex *Fanny*, the 'heroine' of John Cleland's *Memoirs of Fanny Hill*, 1749, the English classic of the brothel, as *La Fille Elisa*, 1877, or perhaps rather *La Maison Tellier*, 1881, is the French and *Bessie Cotter*, 1935, the American; the English novel, it may be added, is by far the most 'actionable'.—2. A can for liquor: naval: C. 20. F. & Gibbons; Bowen. Ex *Fanny Adams*, 1.—3. (**Fanny.**) The inevitable nickname of men surnamed Fields: military: C. 20. F. & Gibbons. Ex Fanny Fields, the music-hall actress.—4. (**Fanny.**) A member of the First Aid Nursing Yeomanry: military: 1914. B. & P.—5. (**Fanny.**) The cricketers' or footballers' nickname for Frederick Walden, capped for England at 'soccer' in 1914; retired from cricket in 1927. Ex *Fanny*; anyone small and neat (or dainty): late C. 19–20.—6. Talk; eloquence: c.: from ca. 1910. See **right fanny** and **fanny, put up the.**—7. Esp. a grafter's sales-talk: grafters': from ca. 1920. Allingham.

fanny, v.i. To 'tell the tale': market-traders' (e.g. Petticoat Lane): C. 20. Cf.:

***fanny, put up the.** 'To explain the working of a job to other criminals to induce them to come in' (David Hume): c.: from ca. 1930. Perhaps ex sense 6; perhaps ex sense 1,—for semantics, cf. *bullshit*.

Fanny Adams. Tinned mutton: naval (— 1889) >, ca. 1900, also military. Barrère & Leland; esp. B. & P. Ex Fanny Adams, a girl that, ca. 1812, was murdered and whose body, 'cut into pieces, 'was thrown into the river at Alton in Hampshire' (O.E.D. Sup.). Cf. *Harriet Lane*.—2. Hence, *F.A.*, nothing at all, often *sweet F.A.*: military: 1914. Euphemising *fuck all*, 'bugger all', (absolutely) nothing. B. & P.

***Fanny Blair.** The hair: rhyming s. (— 1859); †. H., 1st ed. A c. and U.S. variant of *Barnet fair*.

Fanny Nanny (or **n.**). Nonsense: nautical: late C. 19–20. Prob. a reduplication on the hypocoristic shape of the first syllable of *fantastic*: cf. *fantod*, q.v.

Fannys, the. (Members of) the First Aid Nursing Yeomanry Corps, founded in 1909: military coll. F. & Gibbons.

fanqui, fan-qui. A European: Anglo-Chinese: from ca. 1860; ob. H., 3rd ed. Lit., a foreign devil.

fant. See **phant.**

fantadlins. Pastry: ca. 1860–70: ? Cockney. H., 3rd ed.

fantail, fan-tail. A 'sou'-wester' of the kind affected, in C. 19, by coal-heavers and dustmen: from ca. 1850; ob. H., 1st ed; J. Greenwood in *Dick Temple*, 1877. Abbr. *fan-tail hat*, which must date from early C. 19.

fantail-boy. A dustman: low: ca. 1820–50. 'Jon Bee', 1823. Cf. preceding.

fantailer. A person with a tail-coat much too long for him: ca. 1820–50. 'Jon Bee.'

fantastically dressed. 'With more rags than ribbons', Grose, 3rd ed.: ironic coll.: late C. 18–early 19.

fanteague, on the. On the spree or 'loose': low: ca. 1875–1900.—2. Cf. *fanteague* or *fantigue*, dial. and coll. for a fuss, commotion, excitement, passion; a vagary; a joke, a 'lark': from ca. 1830. Dickens, 1837. Ex *fatigue* (see E.D.D. at *fantigued*), or perhaps ex *frantic* after *fatigue* (the rare variant *fantique* occurs—see O.E.D.—in 1825).

fantee or **fanti, go.** To run amok: orig. and mainly British West Africa (— 1917). Ex the S.E. sense, to go native, *Fantee* being the name of a Gold Coast tribe.

fanteeg, fantigue. See **fanteague, 2.**

fantod. A fad; a faddy naval officer: these senses are prob. S.E.—2. **the fantods,**—Galsworthy 1928, has the very rare singular,—restlessness, restless inquietude; esp. *give* (a person) *the fantods*, make him restless, uneasy, hence (in C. 20) nervy: U.S. (1885) anglicised ca. 1905. Imm. ex *fantad*, a fad, on Kentish *fantod*, restless; ultimately ex *fanteague* (q.v.) or *fantasy*. (O.E.D. Sup.)

fantosceny. A sol. form of *fantoccini*: C. 19–20. (O.E.D. Cf. dial. *fanty sheeny*.

far-away. In pawn: lower classes': 1884; ob. Ware, 'From a song'.—2. Hence (— 1909), to pawn: likewise ob. Ware, 'I far-awayed my tools this blessed day—I did !'

far(-)back. An inferior workman; hence, an ignorant fellow: tailors', from ca. 1870. Ex an apprentice's position at the back of the work-room.

far-dee. See **fa'd.**

far-keeper. An eye: Northumberland s. (— 1899), not dial. E.D.D. Ex *keek* = *peek* = peep, look.

far (enough) if . . .., I'll be. I'll certainly not (do so and so): Sheffield (low) coll.—not dial.: from ca. 1880. O.E.D.

far off. Preposition = far from. Coll.; from ca. 1860.

faradiddle. Bee's spelling (1823) of *taradiddle*, q.v.

farcidrama. Any light piece that fails: theatrical: 1885–ca. 90. Ex Ashley Sterry's name for H. J. Byron's posthumous half-finished comedy . . . *The Shuttlecock*, which was a 'frost'. Ware.

farden. A farthing: Cockney: from ca. 1840. (Also in dial.) Cf. *Covent Garden*.

***farcing, farsing.** The picking of locks: c.: late C. 16–early 17. Greene's 2nd *Conny-Catching*, 1592. ? *forcing*.

fare-croft. A cross-Channel Government packet-boat: nautical: ca. 1840–90. Bowen.

farfara. Incorrect for *fanfare*: C. 17. O.E.D.

***farger.** A false die: c.: late C. 16–early 17. Perhaps a perversion of *forger*.

Farinaceous City or **Village, the.** Adelaide: Australian coll. nickname: ca. 1870–1910. A. Trollope, 1873 (Morris). Wheat is the chief export of South Australia. Cf. *Holy City*, q.v.

farm. A cheap establishment for pauper children (— 1869); for illegitimate children (— 1874). Also v. (— 1838). Coll. soon > S.E. See esp. Dickens, *Oliver Twist*, ch. ii.—2. In c., a prison hospital. Hence, **fetch the farm,** to be ordered hospital diet and treatment. From ca. 1875.

farmer. A countryman; a clod-hopper: London coll. (— 1864); ob. by 1915, † by 1920. H., 3rd ed.—2. An alderman: low or c. (— 1848); prob. †.—3. See **farm, 1,** with its v.: coll. (—1869) > S.E. ca. 1900, though gen. as *baby-farmer*.—4. Gen. *be a farmer*, to be off duty: nautical: from early 1880's. (O.E.D. Sup.) Ex the purely imaginary joys of a farmer's life.—5. Hence, an inferior seaman: nautical: from ca. 1890. Bowen. —6. A hare: Kentish s. (— 1878). E.D.D. Ex its affection for the land.

Farmer White. J. C. White, the Somerset and England cricketer: cricketers': from 1931. He is also a farmer.

Farmer's Boy, the. An express goods-train carrying provisions to London : railwaymen's : from ca. 1920. *The Daily Telegraph*, Aug. 15, 1936. Cf. *the Feeder*.

*farsing. See **farcing**.

fart. An anal escape of wind, esp. if audible : C. 13–20 : S.E., but in C. 18–20, a vulgarism, as is the v. Chaucer, Jonson, Swift, Burns. In 1722, there appeared the 10th edition of the anon. author's pamphlet (I saw it listed in a bookseller's catalogue in 1933) *The Benefit of Farting Explain'd*, 'wrote' in Spanish [!] by Don Fart in Hando, Translated into English by Obadiah Fizle.—2. Hence, a symbol of contempt : C. 17–20. Crowne, 1685, 'A fart for your family ' (O.E.D.).—3. Hence, a contemptible person (cf. *silly cunt*) : low coll. ; from ca. 1860. —4. Also in *not care* or *give a fart for*, *not worth a fart* : the former, C. 17–20 (earlier *set not . . .*) ; the latter, C. 19–20.

fart, let a brewer's. (Occ. followed by *grains and all*.) To befoul oneself : low : late C. 18–mid-19. Grose, 2nd ed. Cf. the late C. 18–19 low coll., *not to trust one's arse with a fart*, to have diarrhœa (ibid.).

fart about. To dawdle ; to waste time ; play about : low coll., late C. 19–20. Ex dial.

fart-catcher. A footman or a valet (he walks behind) : mid-C. 18–19 : low. Grose, 1st ed.

fart-daniel. The *pudendum muliebre* : low : C. 19. Obscure : I surmise that *fart* = *farth*, alleged to = a litter of pigs, and that *daniel*—cf. *Antony pig*)—is the youngest pig (see E.D.D. at *daniel* and *farth*), hence that this strange term is orig. dial. (not in E.D.D.) ; it may, however, be merely a misprint for *fare-daniel*, dial. for a sucking pig that is the youngest of a litter.

fart-sucker. A parasite : low : C. 19–20 ; ob.

farthing, not to care a brass. Not to care at all : coll. >, by 1890, S.E. : from ca. 1800. Earlier, without *brass*. (James II, debasing the coinage, issued brass farthings, halfpence, and pence.)

farthing-faced chit. A small, mean-faced, insignificant person : Cockney (— 1909) ; ob. Ware.

farthing-taster. ' Lowest quantity of commonest ice-cream sold by London . . . itinerant . . . vendors ' : Cockneys' : ca. 1870–1914. Ware.

fartick, fartkin. Diminutives of *fart*, q.v. : C. 19 ; low coll.

*farting-crackers. Breeches : late C. 17–18 : **o.** B.E. Cf. *cracker*, q.v.

farting-trap. A jaunting car : Anglo-Irish : C. 19–20 ; ob.

fartleberries. Excrement on the anal hair : late C. 18–19 : low. Grose, 1st ed. Cf. *farting-crackers*.

fash one's beard. To get annoyed or exasperated : Scottish coll (? dial.) : 1789, Davidson (E.D.D.) ; Manchon. Cf. :

fashy, fashee. Angry : military : G.W. +. (Cf. Scottish *fash*.) Ex Fr. *fâché*. (F. & Gibbons.)

fast. A farce : New Zealanders', esp. soldiers' : 1915. A sol.

fast, v. To be short of money : ca. 1850–1900. ' Ducange Anglicus.' Cf. :

fast, adj. Short of money : coll. but orig. and mainly dial. : C. 19. Perhaps semantically = *bound fast*.—2. Dissipated ; 'going the pace ': coll. in C. 18, S.E. in C. 19–20.—3. Impudent : low coll. : ca. 1870–1900. *Don't you be so fast !* = mind your own business !—4. As in *I'm fast*, my watch is fast : coll. (— 1887) >, by 1900, familiar S.E. Baumann ; O.E.D.

fast and loose, play (orig. at). To be inconstant ; variable ; inconsistent : C. 16–20. Coll. till ca. 1700, then S.E. G. Harvey, Ned Ward, Dickens. Ex the game now—though even this is ob.—known as prick-the-garter, and played with a string or a strap.

*fast-fuck. A rapid or a standing coïtion : harlots' : C. 19–20.

*fast(e)ner. A warrant for arrest : late C. 17– early 19 c. B.E. ; Grose, 1st ed.

fastidious cove. A fashionable swindler : London : 1882–1915. Ware.

[**fastness**, a bog, is, by B.E. and Grose, 1st ed., treated as s. or coll. ; prob. S.E.]

*fat. In c., money : C. 19. More gen. in U.S. than in Britain.—2. ' The last landed, inned or stow'd of any sort of Merchandize whatever, so called by the several Gangs of Water-side Porters, &c.': late C. 17–early 19. B.E., Grose.—3. Hence, among printers, composition in which, e.g. in dictionaries and esp. in verse, there are many white spaces, these representing profit (— 1788). Grose, 2nd ed.—4. Hence (theatrical), a good part ; telling lines and situations : from ca. 1880. *The Referee*, April 15, 1888, ' I don't want to rob Miss Claremont of her fat, but her part must be cut down.' Cf. *grease*.—5. In journalism, a notable piece of exclusive news : from ca. 1890 (S.O.D.).—6. A lower-class nickname for a fat person (gen. a man) : late C. 19–20. Cf. *fatty*.

fat, adj. Rich : esp. with *cull* : late C. 17– early 19 c. ex C. 16 S.E.—2. Hence, in C. 19–20, abundant, profitable, very large, e.g. profits, income, takings. Also ironical, *a fat lot*, not much : from ca. 1860. H., 3rd ed.—3. Good : Australian (— 1890) : coll. the revival of a C. 17 S.E. usage.

fat, bit of. Something profitable : see **fat**, n., 3, 4 : C. 19–20.—2. Coïtion with a stout female : low : from ca. 1850 ; ob.

fat, cut it. See **cut it fat.**—**fat, cut up.** See **cut up.**

fat as a hen in the forehead or **as a hen's forehead.** Very thin : meagre : coll. ; the former, from ca. 1600, is in Cotgrave and Swift, but rare after 1820, when the latter, now ob., > gen. (Apperson.)

fat-arsed. Broad-bottomed : C. 19–20 coll. Cf. *barge-*, *broad-*, and *heavy-arsed*, the third in Richard Baxter's *Shove to Heavy Arsed Christians*, i.e. slow, dull ones.

fat burnt itself out of the fire, the. (And in other tenses.) The trouble blew over : lower classes' coll. (— 1909). Ware, ' Antithesis of " All the fat's in the fire ".'

fat-cake. ' A ridiculous name sometimes applied to *Eucalyptus leucoxylon* ': Australian s. or coll. (— 1898) ; ob. Morris cites Maiden's *Useful Native Plants*.

fat cock. A stout elderly man : jocular : from ca. 1850 ; ob. A ' double-sucker ', q.v.

*fat cull. See **fat**, adj., 1. In B.E. and Grose.

fat-face. A term of derision or abuse : coll. ; 1741, Richardson. (O.E.D.)

fat-fancier or **-monger.** A man that specialises in fat women : low : the former, C. 19–20 ; the latter, C. 19.

fat flab. A slice from the fat part of mutton-breast : Winchester College : from ca. 1860 ; ob.

fat or **full-guts.** A fat man or woman : low coll. : late C. 16–20, C. 19 resp. Shakespeare, ' Peace, ye fat guts, lie down ' (O.E.D.).

fat-head. A fool : from ca. 1840 : coll. (As a surname, C. 13.)

fat-headed, -pated, -skulled, -brained, -thoughted, -witted. Dull; slow; stupid. All coll.: resp. C. 18–20; C. 18–19; C. 18–19; C. 19; C. 19; C. 16–19, but soon S.E. Shakespeare has *fat*, slow-witted.

fat is in the fire, (all) the. It has failed; (C. 19–20 only) that's done it, it's all u.p.: coll.: the first sense from ca. 1600 (. . . *lies in the fire*, C. 16; *cast all the gruel in the fire*, Chaucer), as in Dekker; the second and third in Henry James, G. B. Shaw. Apperson.—Cf. *and then the band played!* and *good night!*

fat Jack of the bone-house. A very fat man: coll.; ca. 1850–1910.

fat lot, a. Always in actual or virtual negative, which = nothing; very little: coll.: 1899, Cutcliffe Hyne, 'Shows what a fat lot of influence . . . Congo has got' (O.E.D. Sup.); now verging on S.E.

fat one or un. A particularly rank breaking of wind; a 'roarer' (Swift): low: C. 19–20, ob.

fate. One's *fiancé* or *fiancée*: late C. 19–20; jocular coll.

***fater, fator, faytor.** In C. 17, a member of the Second Rank of the Canting Crew: in C. 18–early 19, a fortune-teller: both c. In C. 16–early 17 S.E., a cheat or impostor. Prob. ex Anglo-Fr. *faitour*. See Grose, P.

***father.** A 'fence' or receiver of stolen property: c.: mid-C. 19–20; ob. H., 1st ed. Prob. suggested by *uncle*, a pawnbroker. Cf. *father's brother*. —2. A master shipwright: nautical: C. 19. Bowen.—3. An admiral commanding a squadron: naval: C. 20. Ibid.

father !, go to. Go to hell !: c.p.: late C. 19–20; virtually †. Ex a music-hall song ('father' being dead). Prob. suggested by *go farther* and *ask father*.

father of a ——, the. A severe: esp. *father of a hiding* (or *licking*), a very severe thrashing: coll.: from ca. 1890. Cf. 'For three fardins I would take it from ye an' give ye the father an' mother of a good soun' blaichin'' in Seumas MacManus, *The Leadin' Road to Donegal*, 1895 (E.D.D., Sup.).

Father Derby's or **Darby's bands.** See **darbies.**

father-in-law. A step-father: mid-C. 16–20; S.E. until C. 19, then catachrestic and dial. (O.E.D.)

fatherhood. The having a certain, or the one, father: catachrestic: 1846. O.E.D.

fatherly. 'A talk from a master (not necessarily a reprimand)': Bootham School: C. 20. Anon., *Dict. of Bootham Slang*, 1925.

father's brother. A pawnbroker: jocular: from ca. 1850. Cf. *father*.

fati-gu'ed. A jocular pronunciation of *fatigued*; *fati-gu'e* is less gen. C. 20. Occ. *fattygew(ed)*. Perhaps orig. derisive of dial. pronunciation: see, e.g., the E.D.D.

fatness. Wealth: s. > coll.: C. 19; in C. 20, ob.—very ob.

fatted for the slaughter, being. A military c.p. of 1916–18 applied to men training hard during a so-called 'rest'. F. & Gibbons. Cf. *fattening* . . .

***fator.** See **fater.**

fatten-up. To write a telling part: theatrical: from ca. 1875. See *fat*, n., 4.

fattening for the slaughter. A 'rest', i.e. a period out of the line: jocular military: 1917; ob. B. & P.

fatty. A jocular epithet, endearment, or nickname for a fat person: coll.; C. 19–20.

fattygew(ed). See **fati-gued.**

fat(t)ymus, fat(t)yma. A fat man, woman resp.: facetious or endearing: ca. 1860–1900. Too artificial to last.

Faugh-a-Ballagh Boys. The 87th Foot, in late C. 19–20 the Royal Irish Fusiliers: military: from 1811. Ex *Fag an Bealac*, Clear the Way, the regimental march. Also *Aiglers* and *Old Fogs*. (F. & Gibbons.)

***faulk(e)ner.** (Cf. the spelling of *fast(e)ner*.) One that decoys others into dicing or card-playing; also a juggler: late C. 17–18 c. B.E. Perhaps ex *falconer*, via † *fawkener*.

fault, at. At a loss: orig. (1833), hunting s.; coll. by 1850, S.E. by 1870. (O.E.D.)—2. In fault: sol.: from ca. 1870.

faults. An incorrect pl., as in 'Where this happens, it is their own faults,' 1738. O.E.D.

***fauney.** See **fawney.**

favour. 'To deal gently with; to ease, save, spare': C. 16–20, S.E. till ca. 1790, then coll. and dial. (S.O.D.)—2. 'To resemble in face or features': orig. (early C. 17), S.E.; since ca. 1820, coll. and dial. (O.E.D.)

favourite vice. One's usual strong drink: club or man-to-man's: ca. 1880–1915. *The Daily News*, Oct. 6, 1885, 'When the bottles and the cigar-case are to the fore, even a bishop may enquire of you, with a jovial smile of born companionship, What is your favourite vice ?' (Ware). Replaced by *poison*.

***fawn(e)y, occ. forn(e)y, rarely faun(e)y.** A ring (hence *fawnied*, adj., ringed); ring-dropping (see **fawney-dropping**: the former low, the latter c.: late C. 18–19. Parker, 1781.—2. Also, though rare, a 'ring-dropper': late C. 18–early 19 c. Parker, 1781.—3. Ex sense 1 is U.S. *phoney*, illicit, sham, spurious, counterfeit: familiarised in England ca. 1930. Prob. *fawney* derives ex Irish *fáinne*, a ring.

***fawney, go on the.** To practise *fawney-dropping*, q.v.: late C. 18–19 c.

***fawney-bouncing.** Selling rings for a supposed wager: c.: mid-C. 19–20; ob. See esp. H., 1st ed. A *fawney-bouncer* is one who does this.

***fawney-dropper.** A ring-dropper: see next entry. C. 19 c. Cf. *money-dropper*.

***fawney-dropping** or **-rigging** (or **-rigging** : 'No. 747'). C.: C. 19, late C. 18–19 resp. Grose, 2nd ed., 'A fellow drops a ring, double gilt, which he picks up before the party meant to be cheated, and to whom he disposes of it for less than its supposed, and ten times more than its real, value.' See **fawney.**

***fawn(e)y-fam'd** or **-fammed; fawnied.** 'Having one or more rings on the finger', Vaux: c.: ca. 1810–60.

***fawn(e)y man.** A pedlar of bogus jewellery: tramps' c.: C. 20. Frank Jennings, 1932.

***fawney-rig.** See **fawney-dropping.—fawny.** See **fawney.**

fay appears in C. 14–19 coll. verging on S.E. expletives. † form of *faith*.—2. See quotation at *Noras*: ? meaning.

faynights. A late C. 19–20 variant of *fainits !*, q.v. at *fains !* Collinson.

***faytor.** See **fater.**

fazz. Grease: Post Office telegraph-messengers' (esp. in London); from before 1935.

***feager** (properly **feaguer**) **of loges.** A beggar with forged papers: C. 17 c. Rowlands. Cf.:

feague. To 'ginger up', esp. a horse (gen. by enlivening but ugly 'fundamental' means): late C. 18–early 19: low. Grose, 1st ed. Ex S.E. senses: beat; overcome, esp. by trickery: themselves ex Ger. *fegen*. Whence *fake*, q.v.: a form anticipated by C. 17 variant *feak*, to thrash.

*feaguer. See **feager**.

feak. The fundament: low: early C. 19. *Lex. Bal.* Perhaps ex *feague*.

feaker. See **faker**.

fear. To frighten: since ca. 1870, coll.; earlier, S.E. Also common in dial.: C. 19–20.

fear, for. Short for *for fear that* or *lest*: coll.: from ca. 1840.

fear !, never. No danger, or risk, of that !: coll. : ? earliest in Bulwer Lytton, 1838 (O.E.D.). Cf. *don't you fear !*, q.v.

fear !, no. Certainly not ! Coll.: from ca. 1880. Cf. *never fear*.

'feard. See **afeard**.

fearful, fearfully. Adj., adv.: a coll. intensive (cf. *awful, terrible*): from ca. 1880. Earlier in dial. D. Mackail, *Greenery Street*, 1925, 'I say, you're looking most fearfully fit.'

fearful frights. 'Kicks, in the most humiliating quarters ': lower classes': ca. 1890–1914. Ware.

fearnought. 'A drink to keep up the spirits. 1880 ', S.O.D.; ob.

fearsome. Timid: sol. when not dial.: from ca. 1860.

feastings even. Incorrect for *Fastens E(v)en*: Scottish and Northern. O.E.D.

feat. An exclusive piece of news: journalistic: adopted, in the early 1930's, from U.S.A. Abbr. (*special*) *feature*.

feather. The female pubic hair: either coll. or euphemistic: C. 18–19. Prior, Moore. Perhaps ex S.E. *feather*, (of a cock) to tread.—2. 'The wave made by a submarine's periscope': naval coll.: 1916. Bowen.—3. A bed: tramps' c.: C. 20. W. H. Davies in *The New Statesman*, March 18, 1918. Abbr. *feather and flip*, the same: rhyming s.: late C. 19–20. (Philip Allingham, *Cheapjack*, 1934.) On *kip*.

feather and flip. See **feather, 3**.

feather, high or **low in the.** With one's oar well or badly held while out of the water: sporting: from ca. 1870. Andrew Lang, *Ballad of the Boat Race*, 1878. Ex the S.E. *feather an oar*.

feather, in (full). Rich: coll.: from ca. 1860. H., 2nd ed.; Mrs. Henry Wood, 1871, 'Clanwaring, in feather as to cash . . ., was the gayest of the gay.'—2. In full dress: coll.: from ca. 1865. H., 5th ed.—3. Elated: coll.: from ca. 1870. Earlier *in high feather*: ca. 1815–70. Moore, 1819, 'The swells in high feather '.

feather, Jack with the. (Variant, *a plume of feathers*.) A trifling person: coll.: late C. 16–17.

feather, ride a. To be a jockey weighing less than 84 lb.: ca. 1810–1900; sporting coll.

feather, show the white. To show oneself a coward: orig. (− 1842) coll.; S.E. by ca. 1895. A cross-bred game-cock has a white feather in the tail.

feather-bed and pillows. A fat woman: low: ca. 1850–1910. Ex *feather*, q.v., and *pillow*, a large breast.

feather-bed lane. A rough road or lane: coll.: late C. 17–20; ob. B.E., Grose, 1st ed.

feather-bed soldier. A persistent, expert whoremonger: C. 19: coll. Cf. *carpet knight*.

feather-driver. A quill-driver, a clerk: coll.; late C. 16–17. Literary s.

feather in one's mouth, having (or **with**) **a.** 'Capable of showing temper, but holding it in': nautical: late C. 19–20; ob. Ex that foam at a ship's cut-water ' which shows there either has been, or will be, dirty weather' (Ware).

feather one's nest. To enrich oneself with perquisites, licit and/or illicit; to amass money: C. 16–20; coll. till ca. 1830, then S.E. Greene, Vanbrugh, G. Eliot.

feather to fly with, not a. 'Plucked': universities': late C. 19–20; ob. Ware.

*feathers. Money: wealth: c. or low: ca. 1855–1905. 'Ducange Anglicus.'—2. (**the feathers.**) Bed: from ca. 1880; very ob.

feature, n. and v., in newspapers and films, is s. (>, by 1925, cinematic coll.) if simply = either a part, or to present (prominently). U.S. (ca. 1897), anglicised ca. 1905. (O.E.D. Sup.)

features. A satirical term of address: ca. 1900–14. Ware. Cf. *face* and *face-ache*.

feaze. To harm; to trouble: Canadian: C. 20. Ex English dial.

Feb. February: coll.: C. 20. Ex the abbr. The only other months thus treated (so far !) are January, as *Jan*, and, rarely, August, as *Aug* (org).

*feck. To discover a safe method of robbery or cheating: C. 19 c. Duncombe, 1848. Ironically ex *feckless* or, more prob., a corruption of *feak* = **fake**, q.v.

fed to the back teeth. An intensive variant, dating from ca. 1910, of the next. Occ. *fed up . . .* or *fed to the wide*. (Manchon.)

fed-up. Bored: disgusted; (*with*) tired of: orig. military, possibly ex the Boers (witness Pettman): from ca. 1899. G. W. Steevens (d. 1900), 'We're all getting pretty well fed-up with this place by now.' Cf. Fr. *en avoir soupé*. W. In the G.W., a military c.p. ran, *fed-up, fucked up, and far from home.*

feed. A meal; an excellent meal: coll.: both from ca. 1805. Ex the stables. Bulwer Lytton, in *Paul Clifford*, 'He gave them plenty of feeds.'—2. Same as, and ex, *feeder*, 3: theatrical: from mid-1920's. J. B. Priestley uses it in 1929 (O.E.D. Sup.).

feed, v. To take food: M.E.–C. 20. Of animals, S.E.; of persons, coll. since ca. 1850.—2. In football, to back, v.i. and t.: from ca. 1880: coll. >, in C. 20, j. > S.E. Ex rounders.—3. In the theatre, to supply (the principal comedian) with cues: from ca. 1890.—4. In the universities, to 'cram': C. 18–19.—5. To bore or disgust: from ca. 1910. Cf. *fed-up*, its prob. origin.

feed, at. At meal; eating: coll.: from ca. 1880, *The National Observer*, 1890, vol. V, 'Statesmen at feed '. The C. 20 prefers *at one's feed*.

feed, be off one's. To have no appetite: from ca. 1830; s. > coll. ca. 1870. Michael Scott; Reade, 'No, doctor; I'm off my feed for once,' 1873. Variant with *oats*.

feed a part. (Theatrical.) To fill it out with small speeches or incidents (− 1892); ob. (O.E.D.)

feed the fishes. To be sea-sick: coll. (− 1884).—2. Hence, though rarely, to be drowned: from ca. 1890.

feed the press. To send 'copy' to the compositors slip by slip: journalistic (− 1891); ob.

Feeder, the. A G.W.R. express goods-train connecting 'several important services' carrying provisions to London : railwaymen's : from ca. 1919. *The Daily Telegraph*, Aug. 15, 1936. Cf. *the Bacca*, q.v.

*feeder. In c., a silver spoon ; any spoon : late C. 18–20 ; ob. Grose, 2nd ed. Hence *feeder-prigger*, a spoon-thief (' Jon Bee ').—2. In university s., a ' coach ' : mid-C. 18–early 19. Goldsmith : ' Mr. Thornhill came with . . . his chaplain and feeder,' 1766.—3. ' Actor or actress whose part simply feeds that of a more important comedian ' : theatrical coll. : 1800 ; ob. Ware.

feeding. Tiresome ; boring ; disgusting : from ca. 1910. Ex *feed*, v., 5 ; cf. *fed-up*, q.v.

*feeding-birk. A cookshop : c. : late C. 19–20. Ware, ' " Birk " being possibly a corruption of " barrack " '.

feeding-bottle. A woman's paps : low coll. C. 19–20 ; ob.

*feek. See **feke**.

feel. To take liberties with (one of the opposite sex) : low coll. : C. 18–20.—2. V.i., with infinitive, to feel, imagine, that one does : low coll. (— 1836) ; ob. (O.E.D.) Cf. *feel like*, q.v.

feel cheap. See **cheap, feel**.

feel like. To have an inclination for a thing or— esp. in form *feel like doing*—to do something : from ca. 1870, orig. (— 1855), U.S. : coll. A 1933–4 trade-slogan ran : ' *A.* I feel like a Guinness.— *B.* I jolly well wish you were ! '

feel like a boiled (or **chewed**) **rag**, or **like nothing on earth**. See resp., **boiled rag** and **nothing on earth**.

feel one's oats. See **oats, feel one's**.

feel one's own man. To feel (quite) oneself, i.e. fit or normal : coll. ; from ca. 1910. Cecil Litchfield in *Baffles*.

feel the collar. To perspire while walking : stable coll. (— 1909). Ware.

feel the draught. To be gravely inconvenienced ; esp., to be hard put to it financially : 1925 (O.E.D. Sup.).

feel the shrimps. See **can't you feel the shrimps ?**

feele. A girl ; a daughter ; loosely, a child (H., 1st ed.). In pl., occ. = mother and daughter. Low Cockney : from ca. 1840. Ex It. *figlia*, via Lingua Franca. In Parlyaree, often *feelier* (Seago, 1933). Cf. *dona(h)*, q.v.

feeler. A tentative question, comment, or device : from ca. 1830 ; coll. till ca. 1890, then S.E. *Tait's Magazine*, Sept., 1841, ' The *Times* is putting out feelers on the corn-law question.'—2. The hand : c. (— 1877) ; ob. Cf. *famble*.

feelier. See **feele**.

feet ?, how's your poor. A c.p. rampant in 1862, nearly † in 1890.

feet, officer of. An infantry officer : military : ca. 1750–1830. Grose, 1st ed. Cf. *foot-slogger*, q.v.

feet-casements. Boots ; shoes : low : from ca. 1840 ; ob. by 1920. Cf. *trotter-cases*.

feet for children's stockings, make. To beget children : low coll. : mid-C. 18–early 19. Grose, 1st ed.

feet uppermost, lie. To receive a man sexually : low coll. : C. 19–20 ; ob. Cf. *have a good look round*.

fegary, figary ; flagary. A whim ; a prank : coll. ; ca. 1600–1850. *Vagary* corrupted.

*fegs. A late C. 16–18, now dial., expletive : *faith* distorted ; cf. *fay*.

*feint. A pawnbroker : c. : ca. 1830–70. ? punning S.E. *feint* and c. *fence*.

*feke. Methylated spirits : c. (— 1932). See the next entry. Also *finish* (and *finish-drinker*).

*feke-drinker. A drinker of methylated spirits in either water or beer : c. : from ca. 1920. His life ' is a short one, and most of it he passes in prison in a terrible reaction ', T. B. G. Mackenzie in *The Fortnightly Review*, March, 1932. Presumably *feke* = *fake*, faked.

Felix. A man that stands another a drink : military : late C. 19–20 ; ob. F. & Gibbons.

fell. Fallen : sol. : C. 19–20, and prob. much earlier. Baumann.

fell a bit on. To act craftily or underhandedly : tailors' : from ca. 1850 ; ob. *Fell*, in tailors' j., = to stitch down (a wide edge) so that it lies smooth.

fell-and-didn't. A person lame-walking : tailors' : from ca. 1840.

fella(h) ; feller. A coll. pronunciation, the former somewhat affected and aristocratic, and form of *fellow* : resp. C. 20 and from ca. 1870. Esp. *young fella(h)*—or *feller—me lad*, jocular vocative : C. 20. (O.E.D. Sup.) Winifred Holtby, *Truth Is Not Sober*, 1934, ' Among the things a Fella does, correct grammar is not necessarily included ' (1931).—2. See :

feller in ' pidgin ', esp. in that of the South Seas and of Australia, is a tautological perennial—of no, or little, meaning and frequent use. Thus, in Ion L. Idriess, *Lasseter's Last Ride*, 1931, we find : ' " How much you want longa these feller spears ? " inquired Taylor ' ; a black gin defining a pair of well-worn corsets as ' that feller belly leggings ' ; and ' The [Australian] natives have no idea of counting. Any number above four they describe as " big feller mob ".'

fellow. As a male person it is S.E. of M.E.–C. 20 ; as ' chap ' it is coll. (— 1711). Note *my dear* or *good fellow* and *what a fellow !*—2. A sweetheart : coll. : late C. 19–20.—3. Jocularly, C. 19–20, of animals : coll.

fellow, a. One ; anybody ; even, myself : coll. : from ca. 1860. Hughes, 1861. (O.E.D.) In C. 20, esp. post-War, occ. used of themselves by would-be mannish girls.

fellow, old. A familiar, gen. affectionate, term of address : coll. : C. 19–20.—2. In some English schools it = a former member of the school (— 1844); ob. (O.E.D.)

fellow-commoner. An empty bottle : Cambridge (— 1785) ; ob. by 1900. Grose, 1st ed. The Oxford term was *gentleman commoner*. Contrast *empty bottle*, q.v.

fellow-feeling. A ceiling : rhyming s. : late C. 19–20. B. & P.

*felon. Felony : c. : C. 18. *A New Canting Dict.*, 1725 ; Grose. The term had existed in this sense in C. 14. See also **dose, 1**.

felonious. Thievish : (somewhat low) coll. : mid-C. 18–20.

feloosh. Money : coll. among soldiers with service where Arabic is spoken : C. 20. Direct ex Arabic.

felt. A hat made of felted wool : coll. until ca. 1600, then S.E. Dekker ; Moncrieff, 1823, ' Don't nibble the felt, Jerry.' (Caution : perhaps always S.E., even when, as occ. in C. 17, used of any hat whatsoever.)

*fem. See **fam, n.**

female, a woman, has long been pejorative : in C. 20 it has a coll. hue.

feme. In C. 16–early 17 a coll., jocular in this survival of Anglo-Fr. legal usage, for a woman. (S.O.D.)

*fen. A harlot; esp. a very low one: late C. 17–early 19.—Hence, 2, a procuress: C. 18–early 19. Both are c.; B.E., Grose, 1st ed. Prob. ex † *fen*, mud, filth.—3. A 'fence' (see n., 1): c.: late C. 17–18. B.E. (*not at fen*).

fen! An early (− 1815) variant of or alternative to *fains*, q.v.; esp. at marbles. Cf. also *fin*, and *fingy that* or *you*, Winchester College and Christ's Hospital resp. As a gen. term of protest or warning it has the † variant *fen live lumber!* (− 1877). Note F. & H. at *fains!*, *fen*, *fin*, and *finjy!*; and, here, see **fains!** Perhaps ex *fend*.

fen-nightingale. A frog; occ. a toad: coll.: from ca. 1860; ob. H., 3rd ed. Cf. *Cambridge-shire nightingale*, q.v.

*fence. A purchaser or receiver, and/or a storer of stolen goods: late C. 17–early 19 c.; then low; then, in C. 20, increasingly gen. B.E., Dyche, Grose, Dickens. Cf. *billy-fencer* and *father*. For etymology, see the v., 1.—2. A place where stolen goods are received or purchased, and/or stored: from ca. 1700. Always c. Cf. *dolly-shop*, *fencing-crib*.

*fence, v.i. To purchase or receive, and/or store, stolen goods: c.(− 1610). Rowlands, *Martin Mark-All*.—2. V.t. To spend (money): late C. 17–18: c. Coles, 1676; B.E. Both n. and v., 1, derive ex S.E. *fence = defence*, while *fence*, v., 2, is prob. a deliberate derivation from v., 1.—3. To sell: c. (− 1839). Brandon.

fence, over the. (Of a person) unashamed, scandalous; greedy; very unreasonable: New Zealanders' coll. variation (late C. 19–20) of S.E. *beyond the pale*. Perhaps ex local rules for cricket.

fence, sit (up)on the. (Rarely *ride*, occ. *be*.) To be neutral, waiting to see who wins: orig. political s., ex U.S. (− 1830), anglicised ca. 1870; in C. 20, coll.

fence-shop. A shop where stolen property is sold: low coll.: from ca. 1780; ob. G. Parker.

*fencer. A tramp; gen. with a defining term (as in *driz-fencer*), a(n itinerant) hawker: vagrants' c.: C. 19–20.—2. A receiver of stolen goods: c. > low: from ca. 1690; ob. B.E.—3. A horse that runs well near the barrier: the turf (− 1923). Manchon.

fences, crash one's. See **crash one's fences.** Cf. *rush one's fences*.

*fencing. The 'profession' of purchasing or storing stolen goods: orig. (ca. 1850), c.; in C. 20, low.

*fencing-crib, C. 19–20, **-ken,** late C. 17–early 19. A place where stolen property is purchased or hidden: c. The former, Ainsworth; the latter, B.E.

*fencing-cully. A broker or receiver of stolen goods: mid. C. 17–early 19. Coles; B.E.; Bailey; Grose, 2nd ed. See **fence,** n., 1.

*fend off. To take: New Zealand c. (− 1932). I.e. fend a thing off from another, i.e. for oneself.

Fenian, a. Threepence-worth of Irish whiskey and cold water: taverns': either from 1867, when the Fenians Allen, Larkin and O'Brien ('the Manchester Martyrs') were hanged for the murder of Police Sergeant Brett; or from 1882, when three Fenians were hanged—and therefore grew cold—for the murder of Cavendish and Burke in the Phœnix Park, Dublin. Also *three cold Irish*: which likewise was ob. by 1910, † by 1920. Ware.

feoffer, feoffo(u)r. Incorrectly for *feoffee*: C. 15–early 17. O.E.D.

fer. Far. A sol., only in pronunciation.—2. For: C. 18–20. Cf. *ter* for *to*.

ferdegew. A C. 16 (? later) sol.: farthingale. (O.E.D.)

fere. See **exes to fere.**

Ferguson, you can't lodge here(, Mr.). A London c.p., ca. 1845–50. (Ex the difficulties experienced, in 1845, by a drunk, not a drunken, Scotsman named Ferguson, in getting lodgings.) In denial or in derision.

Feringhee. A foreigner: Anglo-Indian: from ca. 1630. From ca. 1880, contemptuous. Ex the C. 10–20 Oriental, esp. the Persian and Arabic, hence also the Hindi adaptation of *Frank*, the *-ee* representing the ethnic suffix *-i*. (W.)

ferk!; **ferking.** See **furk!**, **furking.**—2. A variant of the Winchester *firk*, q.v. (R. G. K. Wrench.)

*ferm(e). A hole: C. 17–18: c. Dekker, Grose, 1st ed.—2. Occ. a cave, a prison. Ex Fr. *fermer*.

*fermedy or fermerly beggars. All beggars that lack sham sores: c.: late C. 17–18. B.E. Prob. ex Fr. *fermé*, closed, shut.

fernan bag. A small 'ditty bag' for tobacco and such trifles: nautical: C. 19. Bowen. Origin obscure; quite irrationally, I suspect a connexion with Pernambuco: cf. the † S.E. *Fernanbuck*, (of) Brazil.

Fernleaves. New Zealanders; esp. N.Z. soldiers: military coll.: 1915. F. & Gibbons. Ex the badge of the N.Z. soldiers.

*ferret. A dunning tradesman, esp. on 'young Unthrifts': c.: late C. 17–early 19 c. B.E.—2. Whence, a pawnbroker: c.: C. 18–early 19. *A New Canting Dict.*, 1725.—3. A barge-thief: late C. 19–20 c. F. & H.

*ferret, v.t. To cheat: c.: late C. 17–mid-19. B.E.; Grose, 1st ed. Ex the idea of sharpness. Cf. n., 1.

ferreting. (From the male angle) the act of kind: ex the method of hunting rats and rabbits with a ferret. C. 19–20; ob.

ferricadouzer. A knock-down blow: orig. pugilistic (− 1851); ob. Mayhew. Ex It. *fare cadere*, to fell, + *dosso*, back, prob. via Lingua Franca.

ferrup(s) appears in C. 17–19 exclamations; from ca. 1875, dial. ? echoic.

fess. To confess; own up: coll.: C. 19–20. More gen. in U.S. than in England.

fess, adj. Proud: schoolboys': C. 19–20; ob.

festive. 'Loud; fast; a kind of general utility word', F. & H.: ca. 1870–1910. Cf. :—2. (Of a new boy) 'who has not learnt his duty to his superiors and seniors', A. H. Tod: Charterhouse (− 1900). Hence *festivity*, cheekiness. Cf. *fess*, adj.

fetch. A success: coll.: C. 19.—2. A likeness—ex the S.E. sense, an apparition—as in 'the very fetch of him': coll.: from ca. 1830. (As = a trick or stratagem, S.E.)

fetch, v. (As = to attract greatly, S.E. though not dignified.)—2. To deal (a blow), make (a stroke or other movement): M.E.–C. 20: S.E. till C. 19, then coll.—3. To obtain a summons against (a person): coll.; from ca. 1840. Cf. *fetch law of*.—4. To go to (a certain prison), e.g. *fetch Pentonville*: c.: C. 20. 'Stuart Wood', *Shades of the Prison House*, 1932. Also, more gen., to attain to, get access to: coll.: from ca. 1875. See *farm*, 2; G. Ingram, *Stir*, 1933, 'A few tried to "fetch" the Asylum by feigning insanity.' Ex the sense in nautical j. : to arrive at.—5. (Of a pump) to empty the bilge : *Conway* cadets' coll. : from ca. 1860. John Masefield, *The Conway*, 1860. Prob. an abbr. of *fetch the water up*.

fetch a circumbendibus. Make a detour : C. 19–20 ; ob.

fetch . . . a crack. To strike (a person) : (? low) coll. : 1853, Dickens (E.D.D.).

fetch a howl. To weep noisily ; cry out : low coll. : C. 19–20. (*Fetch* = utter, however, is S.E. as in *fetch a groan* or a *sigh*.)

*****fetch a lagging.** To be imprisoned ; serve one's term : C. 19–20 c. ; ob. (By itself, *fetch*, to get, is S.E.)

fetch . . . a stinger. To strike (gen. a person) heavily : coll. : from ca. 1860.

fetch away. To part ; separate : coll. : from ca. 1850 ; ob. ' A fool and his money are soon fetched away,' F. & H.

fetch law of. To bring an action against : coll. (— 1832). Ob. (O.E.D.) Cf. *fetch*, v., 3.

fetch down. To bring down by blow or shot : coll. : from ca. 1700.—2. To force down (prices, value) : coll. ; from ca. 1840.

fetch the brewer. See **brewer.**—**fetch the farm.** See **farm.**

fetching. Attractive : from ca. 1880 : coll. until ca. 1925, then S.E. not yet literary.

fetid waistcoat. See **waistcoat, 2.**

fettle, in good or **proper.** Drunk : coll. : **ca.** 1875–1920.

few, a good. A fair number : coll. (and dial.) : from ca. 1860. (O.E.D.) Cf. :

few, (just) a. Adv., much, greatly ; decidedly, certainly : s. > coll. : from ca. 1760 ; ob. Dickens, in *Bleak House*, ' Mr. Smallwood bears the concise testimony, a few.' Cf. *rather !*, the U.S. *some*, and the Fr. *un peu*, which last may be the source.

few pence short in the shilling, a. A c.p. = ' silly ' ; half-witted ; (slightly) mad : C. 20.

ff for *v*. See ' **f for th** ', 2.

fi. Five : sol. : C. 19–20. Manchon. As in *fipence*.

fi-fa. Abbr. *fieri facias*, a legal writ : legal : C. 18–20. Cf. *fieri facias*, q.v.

fi-fi. See **fie-fie.**

fi-heath. A thief : back s. (— 1859). H., 1st ed. By euphonic manipulation.

fiasco. A fiancé ; occ., a fiancée : jocular coll. : from ca. 1920. Cf. *finance*.

fib. A trifling falsehood : early C. 17–20 ; a lie : C. 17–20. Coll. Perhaps ex † *fible-fable* (on *fable*) : W.—2. A liar : coll. (— 1861) ; an isolated pre-C. 19 instance occurs in C. 16 (O.E.D.). H. Kingsley, in *Ravenshoe*, ' " Oh ! you dreadful fib," said Flora.'—3. A blow : low coll. or s. : from ca. 1814 (O.E.D.), when boxing was at its palmiest. Ex *fib*, v., 3, 4.

fib. To tell a trivial lie : late C. 17–20. Dryden. Prob. ex *fib*, n., 1, q.v. Hence, 2, to tell a lie : in C. 18, chiefly among children (Johnson). Congreve, 1694, ' You fib, you baggage, you do understand, and you shall understand.'—3. To beat, thrash, strike : mid-C. 17–18 c. ; Head, Coles.—Hence, 4, in C. 19 pugilism, v.t. and i., to punch in rapid repetition. Southey, 1811 ; Thackeray (' My boy ; fib with your right '). Origin obscure : but cf. possibly *fake*, v., and certainly *fob*, v.

fibber. A liar, orig. small, soon great or small : coll. : from ca. 1720.

fibbery. The telling of lies : from ca. 1850 ; ob. ♪ coll. ' Ducange Anglicus.'

fibbing. The telling of lies : coll. ; from ca. 1740. Fielding.—2. In pugilism, C. 19, a rapid pummelling ; a sound beating. Tom Moore. See **fib,** v., 4.

*****fibbing-gloak.** A boxer : c. : early C. 19. Vaux. See **fib,** v., 4. *Gloak*, a man.

*****fibbing-match.** A prize-fight : c. : C. 19. Vaux. Ex *fib*, v., 4.

fice or **foyse.** ' A small windy escape backwards, more obvious to the nose than ears ', Grose, 2nd ed. : late C. 18–19 ; low coll. Earlier, S.E., esp. as *fist*.

fid. A quid of tobacco : late C. 18–20 (ob.) : nautical. Grose, 2nd ed. (Collinson's *fid*, a true derivative, is ineligible, being a mere personal ' neologism '. Ex *fid*, an oakum-plug for the vent of a gun.

fiddle. A sharper, occ. as *old fiddle* : C. 18–early 19. Ex *fiddle*, v., 2, q.v.—2. A watchman's or policeman's rattle : low : ca. 1820–50. Moncrieff. —3. A sixpence (cf. *fiddler*, 3) : from ca. 1850.—4. The female pudend : low : from ca. 1800. Cf. *strum*, v.—5. One-sixteenth of £1 : Stock Exchange : from ca. 1820 ; ob.—6. A writ to arrest : late C. 17–early 19 c. : B.E. ; Grose, 1st ed. Cf. *face the music*.—7. A whip : low : mid-C. 19–20 (ob.). ' Ducange Anglicus.'—8. ' A piece of rope and a long crooked nail ' for the picking of oakum : prison c. (— 1877).—9. An exasperating task or job : lower classes' coll. (— 1923). Manchon. Ex *fiddling job*.

fiddle, v. To play the fiddle : M.E.–C. 20 : S.E. till ca. 1820, then coll.—2. To cheat : C. 17–20 ; S.E. until ca. 1800, revived by the underworld ca. 1840. Mayhew.—3. Hence, to make a living from small jobs done on the street (cf. S.E. sense, to trifle) : mid-C. 19–20 ; ob. H., 1st ed.—4. To punch : pugilistic : ca. 1830–1900.—5. (In C. 19–20, gen. with adv. *about*) to play about intimately with, to caress familiarly, a woman, v.t. (*with* in C. 19–20) : C. 17–20 : coll. In this sense ' to play as on a fiddle ' is prob. cognate with ' *fiddle*, fidget with the hands ', which ' may belong . . . to Old Norse *fitla*, to touch with the fingers ', W.—6. To drug (liquor) : c. (— 1899). Clarence Rook, *The Hooligan Nights*. Perhaps ex sense 2.

fiddle, fit as a. Excellent ; in good health, condition, form : coll. ; from ca. 1610. Beaumont & Fletcher ; J. Payn. Cf. the dial. *as fine as a fiddle*.

fiddle, get at the. To cheat : low and/or commercial : late C. 19–20.

fiddle, hang up the. To desist, esp. from an enterprise : coll. ; from ca. 1870.

fiddle, have a face as long as a. To look dismal, extremely depressed : coll. ; C. 18–20.

fiddle, have one's face made of a. To be irresistibly attractive or charming : coll. ; from ca. 1660. Smollett, Scott.

fiddle, play first (ob.) or **second fiddle.** To occupy an important, esp. the most important, part or to have but a secondary place : coll. : from ca. 1770. Dickens, ' Tom had no idea of playing first fiddle in any social orchestra,' 1843.

fiddle, Scotch and **Welsh.** See those adjj.

fiddle, second. An unpleasant job : tailors' : ca. 1870–1915.

fiddle-back. ' A chasuble having a fiddle-shaped back ' : coll. : late C. 19–20. O.E.D. (Sup.).

fiddle-bow. The penis : cf. *fiddle*, n., 4. **Low** : from ca. 1830 ; ob.

fiddle-de-dee !, fiddle-faddle !, fiddlestick(s) !
Coll. interjections of resp. C. 18–20 (ob.), C. 17–early 19, C. 17–20 (ob.).

fiddle-face. A wizened-faced person : dial. and coll. : ca. 1850–1900. H., 1st ed. Prob. ex :—2. One with a long, unhappy face : coll. : late C. 18–20 ; ob. Hence adj. *fiddle-faced*. Cf. :

fiddle-headed. Plain ; ugly : nautical : from ca. 1840. Cf. *fiddle-face*, q.v.—2. Empty-headed : coll., first (O.E.D.) recorded in ' You fiddle-headed brute ! ' (to a horse), Whyte-Melville, 1854.

fiddle-strings, fret oneself to. See **fret** . . .

fiddle when one comes home, hang up one's. To be merry or witty abroad, but not at home : coll. : C. 19–20. Ex the C. 18–20 synonymous Derbicism *hang the fiddle at the door*.

fiddler. A sharper or a cheat : low : C. 19–20 ; ob. Ex *fiddle*, v., 2.—2. A prize-fighter, esp. one who jumps about a great deal : pugilistic : ca. 1830–1910. Ex *fiddle*, v., 4.—3. A sixpence : low (— 1853) ; † by 1920. H., 1st ed. Prob. ex *fiddler's money*, q.v. (Whence *fiddle*, sixpence.)—4. Also a farthing : ca. 1855–1900. H., 1859.—5. A capstan-house : nautical (— 1874) ; very ob. H., 5th ed. Because, on some ocean-going ships, it was the only place where passengers were allowed to smoke and because, while the sailors worked the capstan-bars, ' a man sometimes played on the fiddle to cheer them at their toil '.—6. (**Fiddler.**) The French racehorse, *Fille de l'Air* ; cf. *Potato* (or *-er*), the French horse, *Peut-Être* : both, sporting : first decade, C. 20. Ware.—7. A ' wangler ', a constant schemer or contriver : c. : C. 20. Anon., *Dartmoor from Within*, 1932. Perhaps ex *fiddle*, n., 8, influenced by v., 2.—8. A trumpeter : a bugler : military : late C. 19–20 ; ob. F. & Gibbons.

fiddler's bitch, drunk as a. Extremely tipsy : lower-class coll. : mid-C. 19–20. (A. Hyder, *Black Girl*, 1934.)

fiddler's fare. Meat, drink, and money : coll. : ca. 1780–1850. Grose. Cf. *fiddlers' pay*.

Fiddler's Green. The traditional heaven of sailors, esp. of those who die ashore : from ca. 1820 : nautical coll. Marryat, in *Snarley-Yow* :

' At Fiddler's Green, where seamen true,
　When here they've done their duty,
　The bowl of grog shall still renew,
　And pledge to love and beauty.'

Bowen defines it as ' a place of unlimited rum and tobacco '.

fiddler's money. All small change, esp. sixpences : coll. : mid-C. 18–early 19 ; since, dial. In C. 18, each couple paid 6*d*. ' for musick at country wakes and hops ', Grose, 1st ed. Cf. :

fiddler's pay. ' Thanks and wine ', B.E. : ca. 1660–1750 : coll. Cf. preceding entry. In C. 16–early 17, *fiddler's wages*, which gen. = thanks (without even the wine) : likewise coll.

***fiddlestick.** A spring saw : Scottish c. : ca. 1820–1910. Egan's Grose.—2. The male member : C. 19–20, ob. ; low. Cf. *fiddle-bow*.—3. A sword : late C. 16–17 jocular. Shakespeare.—4. Substituted for another word in jocular derision (hence coll.), as in ' " He won a patriot's crown," said Henry. " A patriot's fiddlestick," replied Bill.' C. 19–20. In this last sense, often (though not in C. 20) replaced by *fiddlestick's end*, q.v.

fiddlestick, not to care a. To care not a whit : coll. ; from ca. 1800.

fiddlestick's end(s). Nothing : late C. 18–early 19 : coll. Grose, 2nd ed. Cf. *fiddlestick*, 4.

fiddling. A livelihood from odd street-jobs ; esp. the selling of matches in the streets (M. Harrison, *Spring in Tartarus*, 1935) : low coll. (— 1851). Cf. *fiddle*, v., 3, q.v.—2. In low s. (— 1850), buying very cheaply and selling at a good price.—3. In c. esp. among gamesters, gambling : mid-C. 19–20 ; ob. ' Ducange Anglicus.'

fidfad, fid-fad. A ' fuss-pot ', an habitual fusser ; a fiddling trifle : coll. : from ca. 1750 ; ob. Goldsmith, 1754, ' The youngest . . . is . . . an absolute fid-fad.'

fidge. Fidgeting (habit, action) ; fidgetiness : C. 18–20.—2. A fuss : C. 19. Likewise coll. (when not dial.).—3. A fidgety person : coll. or dial. (— 1884). S.O.D. Also in phrase, *be in a fidge*, to be restless, fidgety. The term derives ex *fidge*, to fidget.

fidibus. A paper spill · cultured coll. (— 1829) ; ob. Ex C. 17 Ger. students' s. O.E.D., W.

***fidlam-** (or **fidlum-**)**ben**, late C. 18–19 (Grose, 1st ed.) ; **-cove**, C. 19. A general thief : c. Cf. *fiddle*, n., 1, and *St. Peter's son*.

fie-fie, occ. **fi-fi.** Of improper character (persons) : coll. ; from ca. 1810.—2. Hence, a woman of damaged repute : coll. ; from ca. 1860. ? begun by Thackeray, referring to Paul de Kock's novels.

fie-for-shame. The female genitals : school-girls' : from ca. 1820. Cf. *money*.

field. ' To support, take care of in swimming ' : Winchester College : mid-C. 19–20. Wrench. Perhaps ex fielding at cricket.

field, crop the. To win easily : horse-racing : from ca. 1870 ; ob. (Double pun.)

Field-Grey. A German soldier : coll. : 1914. Ex the colour of his uniform (*feldgrau*). See esp. W. F. Morris's exciting War novel, *Bretherton : Khaki or Field Grey ?*, 1929.

Field-Lane duck. A baked sheep's-head : late C. 18–19. Grose, 1st ed. Ex a low London thoroughfare leading from the bottom of Holborn to Clerkenwell and, for the greater part, demolished ca. 1870.

field of wheat. A street : rhyming s. : late C. 19–20 ; rare. (G. H. McKnight, *English Words*, 1923.)

field-running. The building of ' rickety houses rapidly over suburban fields ' : builders' : ca. 1860–1910. Ware. Cf. the ease with which tongue-in-cheek barbarians (financiers, they call themselves) evade, and the cynicism with which Governments allow them to evade, the strictures on ' ribbon-development ' in the 1930's.

fielder. One who backs the field, i.e. the rest, against the favourite : from ca. 1850. Also, a bookmaker : ca. 1865–90. The turf. Cf. :

fielding. The laying of odds against the favourite : horse-racing (— 1874) ; ob. H., 5th ed.

fields of temptation. ' The attractions held out to young men at the university ', Egan's Grose : Oxford University : ca. 1820–40.

fierce. Objectionable, unpleasant ; difficult, very inconvenient : from ca. 1920. From U.S., where it dates from ca. 1905. Richard Keverne, *Artifex Intervenes*, 1934, ' A rather fierce, night-clubbish woman '. Ex :—2. Exceptional in some way : U.S., anglicised ca. 1910. A. E. W. Mason, *The Dean's Elbow*, 1930, ' " Such a one ! " " A regular comic." " Fierce, I call him." '

fieri facias, to have been served with a writ of.
Have a countenance habitually red : late C. 16–20 ;
in C. 16–17, legal ; in 18–19, gen. ; in 20, † except
in legal s.—and even there it is decidedly ob. (Cf.
fi-fa, q.v.) Nashe, Dryden, Grose, H. Ex the
English pronunciation of the L. phrase (lit., cause to
be done !), with a pun on *fiery face*.

**fiery furnace has that (got) to do with you ?, what
the.** What the hell, etc. : euphemistic (— 1923) ;
ob. Manchon.

fiery lot. A fast man : coll. : ca. 1880–1900.
Cf. *hot stuff*.

fiery snorter. A red nose, *snorter* being a nose :
from ca. 1870 ; ob.

fif. Fifteen, in calling lawn-tennis scores :
(trivial) coll. : from ca. 1890.—2. Also of time :
coll. : C. 20. (E. F. Benson, *David of King's*, 1924,
' "Where and when ?" "Two fiff. Our ground".')

fifer. A waistcoat workman : tailors' : from ca.
1860.

fifteen-puzzle, a. Confusion ; incomprehensi-
bility : coll. : middle-class coll. : ca. 1880–90.
Ex a type of puzzle (movable cubes) very fashionable in 1879. Ware.

fifteen years of undetected crime. (Applied to)
the long service and good-conduct medal : naval
(ca. 1895) >, by 1910, also military. Bowen.

fifteener. A book printed in C. 16 : bibliographical coll. : 1830. In C. 20, S.E.

fifth, and so forth and so. And so on : c.p. :
C. 20 ; ob. Punning *fourth*.

fifth rib, dig or hit or poke one under the. To hit
hard ; dumbfound : coll. (— 1890). Ex C. 17–19
S.E. *smite under the fifth rib*, i.e. to the heart.

fifty-fifty, adv. Equally ; adj., equal : coll.,
orig. U.S. ; anglicised resp. ca. 1914, 1920. I.e., on
a basis of 50%. (O.E.D. Sup.)

fig, occ. **fig of Spain.** A contemptuous gesture
made by thrusting the thumb forth from between
the first two fingers : whence *not to care* or *give a fig
for a person* (see **curse, dam(n), straw**, etc.). In
C. 16–17 often as *fico*. Coll. Shakespeare, ' Fico
for thy friendship '.—2. The *pudendum muliebre* :
C. 19–20 (ob.) low. Semantically connected with
the gesture.—3. See **fig, in full.**—4. A coin (value
unknown) issued by a counterfeiter : c. (— 1798).
O.E.D. Also *fig-thing*.

fig, v. To ginger (a horse) : C. 19–20 ; stables'.
' Jon Bee ', 1823. Ex *feague*, q.v.—2. In c., mid-
C. 16–18, v.i., to steal. Cf. *feague* and *fake*.—3.
The same (late C. 19–20) as its original :

fig, give (a person) **the.** To defy with contemptuous gesture (see **fig, n.**) : from late C. 16 ; ob.

fig, in full. In full dress : s. >, ca. 1880, coll. :
from ca. 1840. Hughes, ' Where we go in full fig of
cap and gown ', 1861. Perhaps ex *feague* (v.) ; perhaps *fig-leaf* ; prob. abbr. *figure*.

*fig-boy. A pickpocket : c. of ca. 1550–1620.
O.E.D. Ex *fig*, v., 2.

fig-leaf. A small apron worn by women : from
ca. 1870 ; ob. H., 5th ed. Ex the fencing protective pad.

fig out, v.t. and reflexive. To dress in one's best :
coll. ; from ca. 1820 ; ob.

*fig-thing ; occ. **figthing.** See **fig, n.**, 4.

fig up. To restore, reanimate, enliven : coll.
(— 1819). T. Moore, ' In vain did they try to fig
up the old lad.' Ex *fig*, v., 1.

figaries. Roguery ; pranks : low coll., mostly
London (— 1887). Baumann. Ex the very gen.
dial. form of *vagaries*.

figaro. A barber : cultured : from ca. 1860 ;
ob. H., 3rd ed. Ex the popularity of the opera,
Le Nozze di Figaro.

*figdean. To kill : c. of ca. 1810–80. *Lex. Bal.*
? ex Fr. *figer*.

*figger, figure. See **fagger** and cf. *diver*.—2. A
Levantine trading-ship or trader, orig. from
Smyrna only : nautical : mid-C. 19–20. Bowen.
Ex the staple *fig*.

*figging-law or occ. **fagging-lay.** Pocket-picking : c. of C. 16–early 19, C. 18–early 19. Ex
fig, v., 2.

figgins. See **figs.**

figgy-dowdy and **-duff.** A boiled fruit-pudding :
nautical coll. : mid-C. 19–20, the former being used
orig. and mainly by West Country seamen. Smyth
(*-dowdy*) ; Bowen (both). Cf. Shropshire dial.
figgetty-dumpling, a boiled pudding made with figs.

fight. A party, as in *tea-fight* : coll. ; from ca.
1870. Cf. *worry*.

fight a bag of shit, not be able to. To be no good
at fisticuffs : low Australian coll. ; from ca. 1905.
More gen., *not to be able to fight one's way out of a
paper bag* : id. : C. 20.

fight or play cocum. See **cocum.**

fight in silver. To fight in silver spurs : cock-
fighting coll. (— 1823). Bee.

fight one's way out of a paper bag, unable to or can
(or could) not. See **fight a bag** . . .

fight space with a hairpin. To attempt the impossible : Oxford University coll. : 1882–ca. 1914.
Ware.

fight the old soldier. See **old soldier, fight the.**

fight (or **buck**) **the tiger.** To play against the
bank, orig. and esp. at faro : U.S. (*fight*, 1851 ;
buck, late C. 19), anglicised ca. 1900, but never
wholly acclimatised. Thornton.

Fighting Brigade, the. See **Old and Bold, the.**

fighting cove. A pugilist, esp. one travelling
with fairs : low ; mostly tramps' (— 1880).

fighting drunk. Quarrelsomely tipsy : coll. ;
from ca. 1890.

Fighting Fifteenth. The 15th Hussars : military
coll. : traditionally from 1760, ex their exploits at
Emsdorff. F. & Gibbons.

Fighting Fifth, the. The 5th Foot Regiment, in
late C. 19–20 the Northumberland Fusiliers : military coll. : from ca. 1810 ; ob. Also *The Old Bold
Fifth* and *Lord Wellington's Body Guard*, both from
ca. 1811 ; also *The Shiners*, from 1764. Cf. *Fighting Fours* and *Fighting Ninth*.

Fighting Fitzgerald. George Fitzgerald, a C. 18
swashbuckling dandy and duellist. Dawson.

Fighting Fortieth. The Prince of Wales's Volunteers, before 1881 the 40th Foot Regiment : military coll. : mid-C. 19–20. F. & Gibbons, ' Dating
from the Sikh Wars of 1843 and 1848 '.

Fighting Fours, the. The 44th Foot Regiment :
military coll. (— 1881). Ware.

Fighting Mac. General MacPherson of the
R.A.M.C. : English R.A.M.C.'s nickname for him
in G.W. (Philip Gosse, *Memoirs of a Camp-
Follower*, 1934.)

Fighting Ninth, the. The 9th Foot, from 1881 the
Norfolk Regiment : military coll. : C. 18–20 ; ob.
Also *The Holy Boys* : from ca. 1810.

Fighting Parson, the. See **Parson Bate.**

fightist. A fighter : jocular coll. : 1877, *The
Daily News*, Oct. 8 (O.E.D.) ; ob.

figs ; occ. **figgins.** A grocer : coll. : from ca.
1870. Ex his commodities.

fig's end. A c.p. replacing another word : cf. *fiddlestick's end* and *nothing.* Coll. ; C. 17–18. Shakespeare.—2. Also, same period, as exclamation.

figure. A price ; value ; amount to be paid : coll. ; from ca. 1840. In C. 20, S.E. Sala, 1883, 'The " figure " to be paid to Madame Adelina Patti for her forthcoming season '.—2. (Esp. in *no figure.*) The female breasts and buttocks : coll. ; from ca. 1870. The post-War term is *curves.*—3. A person untidy or, in appearance, grotesque (*quite a figure, such a figure*, etc.) : coll., 1774. (O.E.D.)—4. See **fagger.**

figure, v. In billiards (— 1891), to single out or ' spot '.—2. App. only as *figure on*, as in *The Gentleman's Magazine*, 1773, ' His antagonist . . . figured on him . . . at . . . whist, about £200,' i.e. totalled against him : non-proletarian ; † by 1900. O.E.D.

figure, cut a. See **cut a figure.**

*****figure-dancer.** One who alters the face value of banknotes, cheques, bills, etc. : late C. 18–19 : c. Grose, 2nd ed. Ex S.E. sense, a performer in a figure-dance.

figure-fancier. One who prefers his ' women ' to be large : low : ca. 1870–1910. Ex *figure*, n., 2.

figure-head. The face : nautical : from 1840 (in Marryat).

figure-maker. A wencher : low : from ca. 1875. Ex *figure*, n., 2.

figure of fun. An oddity : coll. : from ca. 1810 ; slightly ob. Cf. *figure*, n., 3.

figure on. See **figure, v.**, 2.

*****figure, occ. number, six.** ' A lock of hair brought down from the forehead, greased, twisted spirally, and plastered on the face ', F. & H. C. of ca. 1840–95. Mayhew, ' Hair . . . done in figure-six curls '. Cf. *aggravator*, q.v.

filbert. A very fashionable man about town : Society : ca. 1900–20. Popularised by the song about ' Gilbert | The filbert, | Colonel of the Nuts '. See **nut.**—2. The head, as in :

filbert, cracked in the. Slightly—or very—eccentric ; crazy : Cockney : from ca. 1880 ; ob. Baumann.

*****filch.** A hooked stick or staff wherewith to steal : c. : C. 17–18. Fletcher, 1622 (O.E.D.). Abbr. *filchman*, q.v. Grose gives variant *filel* : almost certainly a misprint for *filer*, q.v.—2. Something stolen : C. 17–20, increasingly rare.—3. A thief : more gen. *filcher* : from ca. 1770. Ex the v.—4. See **filch, on the.**

*****filch, v.** To steal ; pilfer ; rarely, rob : c. in mid-C. 16–early 18, then low s. : in late C. 19–20, low coll. Awdelay. Possibly ex *filchman* ; perhaps, however, cognate with *file*, q.v.—2. To beat, strike : c. : mid-C. 16–17. Cf. *fib*, v.

*****filch, on the.** On the watch for something to steal : c. (— 1877). Anon., *Five Years' Penal Servitude*, 1877. Cf. *bum, on the*, q.v.

*****filcher.** A thief, esp. an *angler*, q.v. In mid-C. 16–18, c. ; then low ; in C. 20, low coll. See **filch**, n., 2, and v., 1.

†**filching, vbl.n.** Theft, thieving, robbery : mid-C. 16–20 ; c. until C. 18, low until ca. 1850.

*****filching cove, mort.** A male, female thief : late C. 17–18 : c. B.E., Grose.

*****filchman.** A thief's hooked staff or stick : c. : mid-C. 16–17 ; cf. *filch*, n., 1. Awdelay, Head. The *man* is prob. *-man*, *-mans*, the c. suffix.

*****file ;** occ. **foyl-** or **file-cloy.** A pickpocket :

mid-C. 17–19 c. Head ; B.E. Cf. *bung-nipper* and *bulk*, q.v.—2. A man, a chap ; orig. a very cunning one : low (— 1812). Vaux ; Dickens. Often in combination, e.g. *old file*, an elder. Ob. The word may derive ex the tool ; perhaps, however, it is connected with Fr. *filou*, a pickpocket : cf. also Fr. *lime sourde* (O.E.D).

*****file, v.** To pick pockets ; to pick the pockets of ; occ., to cheat : c. : late C. 17–19 B.E. Cf. n., 1, and Fr. *filouter*.

*****file-cloy :** C. 17–18 ; in C. 18 **file-cly :** whence *file*, n., 1, q.v. Cf. :

*****file-lifter.** Also a pickpocket : c. of ca. 1670–1800. Cf. *file*, n., 1.

file on to. To grab ; take : Canadian (— 1932). John Beames. Perhaps ex military j.

*****filel.** The same as *filch*, n., 1 : q.v. as to form.

*****filer.** A pickpocket : c. of ca. 1670–1800. Rare. Ex *file*, v. (O.E.D.)

*****filing-lay.** Pickpocketry : C. 18–19 c. Fielding. Ex *file*, v.

*****fill, give** (a person) **a.** To put on the wrong scent ; to deceive : c. (— 1909). Ware.

fill a gentleman's eye. (Of a dog) to have thoroughly good points : sporting, esp. dog fanciers' : from ca. 1870. Ware.

fill one's pipe. To be able to retire from work : coll. : ca. 1810–1910. Egan, ' According to the vulgar phrase, to fill their pipe '.

fill the bill. To ' star ' : theatrical : ca. 1880–1910. Ex *bill*, a programme ; *fill* refers to the large letters ' featuring ' the star performer (W.).—2. Hence (? ex U.S.) to be effective, very competent, and, now †, to be a whopping lie : coll. ; from ca. 1885.

fillaloo. A din, an uproar : lower classes' (— 1923). Manchon. A perversion of *hullabaloo*. In dial. (— 1892) as *filliloo* or *fillyloo* : E.D.D.

*****filler.** A large coal, used in filling-out a sack with illicit intent : c. of late C. 16–early 17. Greene, *A Notable Discovery*, 1591.

*****fillet of veal.** A house of correction : c. (— 1857) ; † by 1900. ' Ducange Anglicus.'

fillibrush. To flatter ; praise insincerely, ironically : coll. : ca. 1860–90. H., 2nd ed. ? ex *filly*, q.v.

Fillin Jim. See **Phil and Jim.**

filling at the price. Satisfying : coll. ; from ca. 1840 ; ob. *London Figaro*, May 28, 1870, concerning baked potatoes. Perhaps ex Dickens's remark about crumpets in *Pickwick*, ch. xliv.

fillip, give nature a. See **give nature a fillip.**

fillup(pe)y. Satisfying : ca. 1840–80. Cf. *filling at the price.*

filly. A girl ; a wanton : from early C. 17. Etherege, ' Skittish fillies, but I never knew 'em boggle at a man before.'—2. In C. 19–20 c., a daughter. Ex Fr. *fille* ; cf. *feele*, q.v.—3. ' A lady who goes racing pace in round dances ' : ballrooms' (— 1909) ; virtually †. Ware.

filly and foal. ' A young couple of lovers sauntering apart from the world ' : proletarian (— 1909) ; ob. Ware.

filly-hunting. A search for amorous, obliging, or mercenary women : C. 19–20 low.

*****filtchman.** A C. 16 variant (a misspelling) of *filchman*, q.v.

filter. A synonym (— 1927 ; very ob.) of *trickle*, q.v. Collinson. Cf. *ooze.*

filth. A harlot : late C. 16–17 coll. > S.E. and dial. Shakespeare.

filthily. Very : **C.** 20. (G. Heyer, *Death in the Stocks*, 1935, ' He was filthily offensive.') Ex :

filthy. A C. 20 coll., pejorative and intensive adj., applied e.g. to an entertainment, holiday, present, etc., etc. Ian Hay, ' *Pip* ', 1907 ; Collinson. Cf. *foul.* It occurs in Devonshire dial. as early as 1733 (E.D.D.) in the sense : excessive. Cf. the Oxfordshire ' I be in a filthy temper ' (E.D.D., Sup. ; 1905).

filthy, the. Money : from ca. 1875. Abbr. :

filthy lucre. Money : jocular coll. (in C. 20, S.E.) from ca. 1870.

fimble-famble. A poor excuse or an unsatisfactory answer : coll. : C. 19. Ex the ideas implicit in S.E. *famble, fimble,* and *fumble.*

fin. An arm ; a hand : nautical > gen. : late C. 18–20. Grose, 1st ed (*one-finned,* having only one arm) ; Dickens ; Thackeray. *Tip the fin,* to shake hands : from ca. 1850 ; slightly ob.—2. Abbr. (occ. *finn*) of *finnup,* q.v.—3. Variant of *fen !,* q.v. Cf. *fains* and *fingy.*

final. The latest newspaper-edition on any given day : from ca. 1920 : coll., now verging on S.E. C.O.D. (1934 Sup.).

[*Final numbers.* In Royal Air Force coll., from ca. 1915, ' it is usual to allude to aircraft by the final numbers of their Service registry—thus " K 1833 " would be known in the Squadron as " 33 " to all and sundry. Nicknames and so on are rarely bestowed,' writes an R.A.F. officer.]

finals. (Orig. at Oxford.) The last of a series of examinations, esp. that for the B.A., B.D., B.E., or B.Sc. Coll. : from ca. 1894. Grant Allen. (S.O.D.)

finance. A fiancé, esp. if rich : jocular cultured ; also Society s. : from ca. 1905. ? ex U.S. Cf. *fiasco,* q.v.

financial. In funds : Australian : C. 20. Jice Doone, *to be a financial member,* to have paid one's due subscription.

find. A mess of three or four upper-form boys, breakfasting or teaing in one another's rooms in turn. Hence, *find-fag,* a younger boy attending to a ' find's ' wants. Harrow : late C. 19–20 ; ob.— 2. A person worth knowing, a thing worth having : C. 20 coll.—3. See **find, a sure.**

find, v. To suffer from, feel to an unpleasant extent (esp. the temperature) : coll. (ob.) and dial. in C. 19–20 ; formerly, S.E. (O.E.D.)—2. To steal : military, G.W. +. Cf. *earn, win* ; also *make.* Perhaps reminiscent of the C. 16–18 proverbial *find things before they are lost.* Cf. Ger. *finden* in military s. ; note, too, that Cæsar uses *invenire* thus in his *Gallic Wars.*

find, a sure. A person, occ. a thing, sure to be found : coll. : 1838, Thackeray. O.E.D.

find a pie. To find a person willing to make a small loan or to offer a drink : theatrical : C. 20. See **pie.**

find cold weather. To be ejected : public-houses ' (— 1909) ; ob. Ware. Cf. *give* (a person) *the key of the street.*

*find it. To back a winner : turf c. : C. 20. *Slang,* p. 245.

*finder. A thief, esp. in a meat-market : c., from ca. 1850. H., 1st ed.—2. A waiter : university, esp. Gonville & Caius College, Cambridge : C. 19.

*fine. A punishment, esp. imprisonment : Hence, v., to sentence : c. : C. 19–20 (ob.). *Lex. Bal.* A revival of C. 16–18 S.E.

fine, v. To confine : sol. : C. 19–20. *Lex. Bal.* (at *pear-making*).—2. See preceding entry.

fine, adj. Very large : coll., from ca. 1830. (Cf. *wee little.*) Often followed by *big, large,* etc. (O.E.D.)

fine, cut. See **cut it fine.** Also *run it fine* : from ca. 1890 : likewise coll. (O.E.D.)

fine and large, all very. A coll. c.p. comment expressing admiration or, more gen., incredulity or derision. Popularised by a music-hall song much in vogue 1886–8.

fine as a cow turd stuck with primroses. Very fine ; always satirical. Coll. (low) : late C. 18–early 19. Grose, 2nd ed. Perhaps suggested by :

fine (occ. **proud**) **as a lord's bastard.** Richly dressed or lodged : mid-C. 17–18 coll ; semi-proverbial. (Apperson.)

fine as fivepence or **fip(p)ence.** Very fine ; ' all dressed up ' : coll. : from ca. 1560. Wycherley, ' His mistress is as fine as fippence, in embroidered sattens.' Ex that coin's brightness. Cf. *neat as ninepence.* Dial. (see Apperson) has some picturesque variants ; coll. English, *grand* for *fine.*

fine day for the (young) ducks. An exceedingly wet day : C. 19–20, ob. The C. 20 prefers *great weather for ducks.* Coll.

fine days, one of these. Some day ; in the vague future : coll. : from ca. 1850. ? a development ex the C. 19 proverb, *one of these days is none of these days,* influenced by the Fr. *un de ces beaux jours.* In C. 19, occ. *mornings.*

fine(-)drawing. The sly accomplishment of one's (gen. illicit) purpose : tailors' : from ca. 1860 ; ob. Very delicate stitching being almost invisible.

fine ham-an'-haddie ! All nonsense : Glasgow (— 1934). Cf. *gammon and spinach.*

fine madam. A woman above her station : pejorative coll. : from ca. 1800.

fine twig, in. Finely, splendidly : low (— 1812). Vaux. (See *gammon the twelve*.)

fine weather for ducks. (Very) wet weather : coll. : 1840, Dickens (Apperson).

fine words butter no parsnips ! A sarcastic comment on fine-sounding statements or promises : coll. (C. 20, S.E.) ; from ca. 1750. C. 17 variants are *fair words,* or *those words,* and *mere praise,* etc.

finee ; occ. **finni** (q.v.) or **finny** or **finnee.** ' Done for ' ; no more (of supplies) : military : late 1914. Ex Fr. *fini.* Cf. *finish,* q.v. B. & P.

finee (etc.) **kapout** (or **kaput**). ' Napoo ' or ' finee ', qq.v., but much less gen. : military : 1916. Via Fr. Army s. ex Fr. *capot* (W.) or ex L. *caput,* the head. B. & P., ' In surrendering to the French, Germans would often say, " Kamarade, pas kapout," i.e. Don't shoot, don't kill me ! To which the answer was often, perhaps, " Fini kapout." Dauzat gives : "Capout : tué . . . véritable mot passe-partout, qui signifie tour à tour ' fini, abîmé, cassé, tué.' " '

[**fineering,** vbl.n. (The v. is very rare.) The ordering of specially made goods and the subsequent refusal to take them unless credit be allowed : C. 18. Goldsmith. Perhaps rather unassimilable than coll. Ex Dutch *fineeren,* to amass riches.]

finger. Abbr. *finger and thumb,* q.v. : 1868, says Ware.—2. ' An eccentric or amusing person,' C. J. Dennis : low Australian (— 1916). Why ?—3. A ' term of contempt for man or woman,' George Ingram : c. (— 1933). Cf. sense 2 and the dial. *finger of scorn,* a contemptible fellow (E.D.D.).—4.

Hence (?), an official: busmen's: from ca. 1930. *The Daily Herald*, Aug. 5, 1936.

finger. To caress a woman sexually: low coll.; from ca. 1800. Cf. *feel*.

finger, a bit for the. An extremely intimate caress, the recipient being a woman: C. 19 low.

*****finger and thumb.** A road: c. rhyming on Gypsy *drum*, q.v.: late C. 19–20.—2. Also (− 1859), rum: gen. rhyming s. H., 1st ed. ' Ducange Anglicus ', 1857, records it as *finger-thumb*, a form soon > rare.

finger-fuck. V.i. (of women only) to masturbate. Vbl.n. in *-ing*. C. 19–20 low coll.

finger in (the) eye, put. See eye, pipe the.

finger-post. A clergyman: late C. 18–20. Grose, 2nd ed. He points out the way to heaven, but does not necessarily follow it himself. ' Do as I say, not as I do.'

finger-smith. A midwife: C. 19–20; low. Vaux.—2. In c., a thief, a pickpocket (− 1823); ob. Egan's Grose.

finger-thumb. See finger and thumb, 2.

fingers are made of lime-twigs, (e.g.) **his.** He is a thief: coll.: late C. 16–mid-18. Harington, 1596; Bailey, 1736. Apperson.

fingy or finjy ! An exclamation of protest: Winchester College: from ca. 1840. Cf. and see fin, fen, and esp. fains.

fini. A rare variant of *finee*.—*finif, finip. See finnif and finith.

finish. The ' end ' of a person by death; social, professional, physical ruin: low coll.; from ca. 1820. Cf. *finish !*, q.v.—2. See Finish, the, 2.— 3. See feke.

finish. To kill; exhaust utterly, render helpless: from ca. 1600; S.E. until ca. 1830, then coll. Cf. *settle*.

finish ! I'm (or he's, etc.) done-for ! ; that's the end of it ! : orig. (1915) military. Possibly influenced by *finee*, q.v.; cf. *finish*, n.

Finish, the. A Covent Garden (opp. Russell St.) coffee-house (Carpenter's, says Bee) at which those making ' a night of it ' finished very early in the morning: late C. 18–early 19. Grose, 3rd ed.— 2. Hence (without *the* and uncapitalised), any such house of entertainment: C. 19. Thackeray.

*****finish-drinker.** See feke.

finished, be. To have finished (**v.t. or absolute**): loose coll.: C. 20.

finisher. Something constituting a person administering the final or decisive blow or touch: coll. (orig. pugilistic): from ca. 1815.

*****finith or finif.** Five; e.g. *finith to fere*, (odds of) 5 to 4: racing c.: C. 20. Of same origin as *finnif*, q.v.

finitive. In mid-C. 16–mid-17, misused for ' of the frontier ' and ' finical '. O.E.D.

finjy. See fingy.

fink. See I don't think !

*****finn.** See finnif.—**finned.** See fin, n., 1.—**finnee.** See finee.

finni. See finee. Dorothy Sayers, *The Five Red Herrings*, 1931, ' I says, finni ? meaning, is that O.K. ? complet ? 'ave yer done ? '

*****fin(n)if, -ip, -uf(f), -up ;** occ. derivatively **finny, finn, fin ;** in C. 20, occ. finnio (Chas. E. Leach). A £5 note, hence *double finnif* (etc.) = a £10 note, and *ready finnif* (etc.) = ready money. C.: from ca. 1835 ; in C. 20, often heard in low racing s. Brandon (1839) ; Snowden, *Magazine Assistant*, 1846 (O.E.D.). Ex Ger. *fünf*, five, via Yiddish.

finny. See finee.

fins, put out one's. To bestir oneself: C. 15 (? −C. 16); coll. Paston Letters. (O.E.D.)

*****finuf or finup.** See finnif.

fi'pence, fippence. Five pence: coll.: C. 17–20. Cf. U.S. *fip*.

*****fi(p)penny.** A clasp knife: Australian c.: ca. 1860–1910. Ex England, where recorded by Vaux in 1812. O.E.D.

*****fire.** Danger; *on fire*, dangerous: C. 19 c.

fire, v. To dismiss; expel: orig. (− 1885), U.S.; anglicised ca. 1905, though (says Ware) reaching England in 1896. Punning *discharge* (W.).

fire, catch on. To catch fire: either sol. or coll. (− 1886). O.E.D.

fire, like a house on. See house on fire, like a.

fire, pass through the. To be venereally infected: C. 19–20 (ob.); low.

fire, set the Thames on. (Gen. ironically or in sarcastic negative.) To be very able or clever. Coll. : late C. 18–20. In late C. 19–20, S.E. Foote, Jane Austen, Pinero (1915). See esp. Apperson and W.

fire a gun. To introduce a subject unskilfully, late C. 18–19 ; lead up to a subject : C. 19. Coll. ? ex military s. Grose, 2nd ed.

fire a shot. (Of the man *in coitu*) to have an emission: C. 19–20 low.

fire a slug. To drink a dram: late C. 18–20 (ob.); orig. military. Grose, 2nd ed.

fire-alarms. Arms: rhyming s. : C. 20. B. & P.

fire-and-light(s). A master-at-arms: naval coll. (and nickname): late C. 18–19. Bowen.

fire away. (Gen. an imperative.) To go ahead: coll. : from ca. 1770. FitzGerald.

fire-box. ' A man of unceasing passion ': ca. 1900–15. Ware classifies it as ' passionate pilgrims '.

fire-eater. A rapid worker: esp. among printers and tailors : ca. 1840–1920.—2. A bully ; duellist : ca. 1820–1900 : coll. > S.E.—3. In the 1860's, a ' swell ', esp. if inclined to boast.—4. In C. 20, during and after G.W., an excessively belligerent person, esp. if under no necessity to fight: coll. Cf. the S.E. and the U.S. usages, the orig. sense being that of a juggler that ' eats fire '. Hence adj., *fire-eating*.

fire-escape. A clergyman : from ca. 1850 ; ob. Cf. *devil-dodger*.

fire-fiend. An incendiary: coll. (− 1897). O.E.D.

fire-flaw. A sting-ray : nautical coll. : C. 19–20. Bowen. Corruption of *fire-flair*.

fire in the air. ' To shoot in the bush ', i.e. to ejaculate externally : low : C. 19–20.

fire out. Same as (*to*) *fire*, q.v. (In U.S., 1885; in England by 1896, says Ware.)

fire-plug. A (young) man venereally infected : low (1823) ; † by 1890. ' Jon Bee '. Suggested by *fire-ship*, q.v.

*****fire-prigger.** One who, pretending to help, robs at fires : c. or low : C. 18–early 19. See prigger and esp. Defoe's *Moll Flanders*.

fire(-)ship. A venereally diseased whore : low : ca. 1670–1850. Wycherley (O.E.D.); B.E.

fire-shovel when young, to have been fed with a. Have a large mouth : late C. 18–19 coll. Grose, 2nd ed.

fire-spaniel. A soldier apt to sit long by the barrack-room fire : military : from ca. 1870 ; ob. by 1910, † by 1918.

fire up, v.i. To light one's pipe : coll. : from ca. 1890. Ex a furnace.

fire(-)water. Very fiery spirits : ex U.S. (— 1826), anglicised ca. 1850 : coll. that, by ca. 1890, is S.E. ' Awful firewater we used to get,' T. Hughes in *Tom Brown at Oxford.*

fireworks. A brilliant display of skill or virtuosity : C. 19–20 coll. > S.E. ; often pejorative.— 2. Among tailors, ca. 1870–1915, a great disturbance or intense excitement.—3. Rockets, searchlights, star-shells, etc., over the front line : jocular military coll : 1915–18. F. & Gibbons.

fireworks on the brain, have. To be flustered : coll. : ca. 1870–1905. Cf. :

fireworks out of (a person), **knock.** To make him see stars : jocular (— 1923). Manchon, ' Lui faire voir trente-six chandelles.'

Firinghee. A variant of *Feringhee,* q.v.

firk. To beat : late C. 16–19, coll. > S.E. ? cognate with *feague* and *fig,* v.v—2. See **Winchester College slang,** § 5.

firkin of foul stuff. ' A very Homely '—i.e. plain—' coarse corpulent woman ', B.E. : low : late C. 17–mid-18.

firkytoodle (with frequent vbl.n., **firkytoodling**). To indulge in physically intimate endearments, esp. in those provocative caresses which constitute the normal preliminaries to sexual congress. Coll. : C. 17–19. Cf. *firk,* q.v.

firm. An association of two, three or four boys for the purchase and consumption of provisions : Shrewsbury School : late C. 19–20. Desmond Coke, *The Bending of a Twig,* 1906.

firm, a long. See **long firm.**

first. A first-class degree : (? mid-)C. 19–20. Likewise *second, third, fourth.*

first-chop. See **chop.**

first(-)class. Exceedingly good : coll. : 1870 (W. J. Lewis). ' From the universities [*first-class degree*] via the railways ', while ' *first-rate* is from the navy,' W.—2. As adv. : extremely well : 1895. (S.O.D.) Cf. *first-rate,* q.v.

first-classer. A person, thing, of the first class : coll. : 1925. (O.E.D. Sup.)

first-fleeter. One of the earliest settlers in Australia : Australian : ca. 1840–70. I.e., one who went there in the first fleet with Governor Phillips. O.E.D. (Sup.).

first flight, in the. Active, or first in, at the finish of a race or a chase : from ca. 1850 : coll. ? ex fox-hunting. Contrast the S.E. sense.

first-floor. The tenant or lodger occupying the first floor : coll. : from ca. 1860. O.E.D.

first-night wreckers. A theatrical coll. (1882–5) for a band of men intent on spoiling first-nights. Ware.

first-nighter. An habitué of first (orig. theatrical) performances : from ca. 1885 : journalistic s. >, ca. 1900, gen. coll., and, ca. 1910, S.E. Baumann.

first of May. The tongue : low (— 1857) ; † by 1920. ' Ducange Anglicus.'

first of the moon. ' Settling day, after pay ' : naval : C. 20. Bowen. I.e. of the month.

first on the top-sail and last in the beef-skid. (Of an A.B.) perfect : naval c.p. (— 1909) ; ob. Ware ; Bowen implies that it dates well back into C. 19.

first(-)rate, adv. Excellently ; in good health : coll. : from early 1840's. (The adj., C. 17–20, S.E.) See **first-class.**

first-rater. A person or thing that is first-rate : from ca. 1805 ; coll. till C. 20, then S.E.

first seven years. See **seven years.—First Tangerines, the.** See **Tangerines.**

[**fiscal.** The procurator fiscal : late C. 17–20 : S.E. verging on coll. Dorothy Sayers.]

fisgig. Fun (**gig**) made at the expense of another's face (**phiz**) : London jocular : ca. 1820–30. ' Jon Bee ', 1823.

fish. A seaman ; hence *scaly fish,* a rough, blunt sailor : late C. 18–early 19. Grose, 1st ed.—2. A man. Gen. derogatively. Always in such combinations as *cool fish, loose f., odd f.* (prob. influenced by *odd fellow*), *queer f.* (after *queer bird*), *scaly f.* († by 1920), *shy f.* Coll. : from ca. 1750, *queer* being the earliest, though *odd* and *scaly* are also of C. 18 ; *loose* (— 1831) ; *cool* (— 1861) ; *shy* (— 1891). O.E.D. ; F. & H. Orig., presumably, an angler's term (W.).—3. A piece, often collectively = pieces, cut out of a garment to ensure a better fit : tailors' ; from ca. 1870 ; ob.—4. The female pudend : low : from ca. 1850.—5. An instance or an act of fishing, esp. in *have a fish* : coll. ; (? —)1880. O.E.D.—6. A whale : whalers' coll. : C. 19–20. Bowen.—7. In oaths, as *God's fish !* (more gen. *Odds fish !*) : C. 18.

fish, bit of. A coïtion (see **fish,** n., 4) : low : from ca. 1850 ; ob.

fish, drink like a. To be constantly drinking (not innocuously) : coll. : from ca. 1640. In C. 20, S.E. Cf. C. 17–19, *drunk as a fish.* See esp. Apperson.

fish, pretty (in late C. 19–20, gen. **nice**) **kettle of.** A quandary ; muddle : coll. : C. 18–20. Richardson. Perhaps ex Scottish *kettle of fish,* a picnic.

fish ?, who cries stinking. Who would depreciate his own goods ? : C. 17–20 ; his own abilities ? : C. 18–20. Coll. B.E.

fish-bagger. A suburban tradesmen's derisive term of ca. 1880–1915 for ' those who live in good suburbs without spending a penny there beyond rent ', *The Graphic,* Sept. 27, 1884 (Ware).

fish-broth. Water, esp. if salt : jocular coll. : late C. 16–20 ; ob. Nashe, ' Belly-full of fishbroath '.

fish-eyes. Tapioca pudding : nautical : late C. 19–20. Bowen. Ex the appearance of that dish.

fish-face. A coll. term of abuse : ca. 1620–1750. Fletcher. (O.E.D.)

fish-fag. A vixenish or foul-mouthed woman : coll. : mid-C. 19–20. H., 5th ed. Ex S.E. sense, a Billingsgate fishwife.

fish-fosh. Kedgeree : Cockney (— 1887) ; slightly ob. Baumann. Reduplication on *fish.*

fish-gunners. The Royal Marine Artillery : naval : mid-C. 19–20 ; virtually †. Bowen. The implication being that all they hit was fish.

fish-hooks. (Singular very rare.) Fingers ; hence, hands ; low, and nautical : from ca. 1840.

fish-market. The lowest hole at bagatelle : gamblers' : C. 19–20. Cf. *simon.*—2. A brothel : ca. 1850–1910. Ex *fish,* n., 4.

fish nor flesh, be neither. (In C. 16, *flesh* occ. precedes *fish.*) To be hesitant, undecided, indeterminate : coll. ; C. 16–20. Shakespeare, ' She's neither fish nor flesh.' Variants : *neither fish, flesh, nor fowl* ; *neither fish, flesh, fowl, nor good red herring,* though, as in Dryden, the *fowl* is omitted at times.

fish of one and flesh or fowl of another, make. To exhibit partiality or make an invidious distinction : from ca. 1630 ; coll. till ca. 1850, then S.E.

fish on one's fingers, find. To devise and/or allege an excuse : late C. 16–early 17 : coll. Greene. (Apperson.)

fish to fry, have other. To have something else to do : coll. : mid-C. 17–20. Evelyn, 1660 ; Swift ; C. Brontë ; E. V. Lucas. (Apperson.)

fisher. A toady : C. 19.—2. In C. 20, an angler for benefit or compliment. Both senses are coll. Ex *fish*, v.—3. See :

Fisher. 'Treasury note signed by *Sir Warren Fisher*, replacing (Oct., 1919) the earlier *Bradbury*', W. At first s., it soon > coll. and, at its withdrawal from circulation on July 31, 1933, it was almost S.E. *The Daily Telegraph*, Aug. 1, 1933. Cf. *Bradbury*, q.v.

Fisheries, the. The Fisheries Exhibition held in 1883 : coll. : 1883 ; now only historical.

fisherman's. A C. 20 abbr. of the next. P. P., *Rhyming Slang*, 1932.

fisherman's daughter. Water : rhyming s. : late C. 19–20. E.g. in Julian Franklyn's *This Gutter Life*, 1934.

fisherman's walk, a. To which is gen. added *three steps and overboard*, which explains : nautical : C. 19–20 ; ob.

Fishermen, the. Grimsby Football Club : sporting : C. 20. Grimsby is a fishing port.

fishiness. See *fishy*, 1. Rare before C. 20, when coll.

fishing, go. To seek for an obliging or a mercenary woman : low : from ca. 1850 ; ob. Cf. *filly-hunting*, *fish* (n., 4), *grousing*.

fishing-fleet. 'The wives and families of naval officers spending the season at Malta' : naval : from ca. 1890. Bowen.

fishy. Morally or financially dubious ; equivocal, unsound : from ca. 1844 : s. >, by 1880, coll. *Punch*, 1859 : 'The affair is decidedly fishy.' Cf. *fish*, n., 2. Whence *fishiness*, the corresponding abstract n.—2. 'Seedy', indisposed : esp. in and ex *have a fishy*, i.e. a glazed, *eye*. Coll. ; from ca. 1860. (S.O.D.)

fishy about the gills. Having the appearance of recent drunkenness : Cockneys' (— 1909). Cf. *fishy*, 2, q.v. Ware, 'Drink produces a pull-down of the corners of the mouth, and a consequent squareness of the lower cheeks or gills, suggesting the gill-shields in fishes.'

*fisno. A warning, esp. in *give someone the fisno* : c. : from ca. 1840 ; † by 1920. 'No. 747.' Origin ?

fist. Handwriting : coll. > s. > coll. again ; from ca. 1470. In C. 15–17, prob. S.E. 'A good running fist', anon., *Mankind*, 1475. (W.)—2. A workman (tailor) : tailors' : from ca. 1860. Esp. *good* or *bad fist*.—3. Among printers, an index hand : from ca. 1880. Jacobi.

fist, v. To apprehend ; seize : coll. : late C. 16–20 ; ob. Shakespeare, 'An I but fist him once ! '—2. Whence the C. 19–20 low coll. sense, take hold of : ' Just you fist that scrubbing-brush, and set to work,' F. & H., 1891.

fist, give a person one's. To shake hands : coll. : late C. 19–20. Esp. in *give us your fist !*

fist, make a good, poor, etc., **at.** To do, or attempt to do, a thing, with a good, bad, etc., result : orig. (1834), U.S. ; anglicised ca. 1860. Coll.

fist, put up one's. To admit a charge : tailors' : from ca. 1860 ; ob.

fist-fucking. Masturbation : of males only (contrast *finger-fucking*) : low : C. 19–20.

fist it. (Of a woman) to grasp the *membrum virile* with sexual intent : low : C. 19–20.—2. To use one's hands, e.g. in eating with one's fingers : Australia and New Zealand (— 1846) : ob. by 1870 ; † by 1890. Morris.

fist-meat, eat. To receive a punch or slap in the mouth : coll. of ca. 1550–1700.

fistiana. Boxing and all that pertains thereto : jocular coll. ; from ca. 1840.

fistic. Related to boxing : (an increasingly low) coll. adj. : from ca. 1885.

fists(, esp. in one's). Grasp ; clutches : M.E. +; S.E. till C. 19, then coll.

*fit. Sufficient evidence to convict (a wrongdoer) : New Zealand c. (— 1932).—2. See **fit** (**in the arm**).

fit. Fought : (dial. and) low coll. : C. 18–20. (O.E.D.).—2. See **Eton slang**, § 2.

fit, adj. In excellent health : coll. : from ca. 1870. Ex sporting j.

fit as a fiddle : see **fiddle, fit as a.** For *awfully fit*, cf. *awfully*.

fit as a flea. Extremely fit or healthy : sporting coll. : mid-C. 19–20 ; ob. Reginald Herbert, *When Diamonds Were Trumps*, 1908.

fit as a pudding. Very fit or suitable : coll. : 1600, Dekker, ' 'Tis a very brave shoe, and as fit as a pudding' ; app. † by 1700. Apperson, who implies that it is prob. an abbr. of *fit as a pudding for a friar's mouth* (ca. 1575–1750) or, occ., *a dog's mouth* (1592, Lyly), itself a semi-proverbial coll.

fit end to end or **fit ends.** To have sexual intercourse : low : C. 19–20 ; ob.

fit (in the arm). A blow or a punch : London slums' : June, 1897–8. One Tom Jelly, arrested for striking a woman, declared that ' a fit had seized him in the arm' : this was too good for the populace to miss. Ware.

fit like a ball of wax (of clothes), i.e. close to the skin : coll. : from ca. 1840.

fit like a glove. To fit perfectly : coll. : from ca. 1770 ; coll. till ca. 1850, then S.E. (O.E.D.)

fit like a purser's shirt on a handspike. The nautical version of the next : mid-C. 19–20 : coll. Bowen.

fit like a sentry-box, i.e. very badly : military coll. : mid-C. 19–20 ; ob.

fit (a garment, hat, etc.) on a person is coll. : from ca. 1860.

fit to. (Of things) likely or 'enough' to (do something) : coll. ; from ca. 1770 ; ob.—2. Ready to, angry enough to (do something) : late C. 16–20. S.E. till ca. 1850, then coll. and dial. (S.O.D.)

fit to a T. Gen. v.t., to fit to a nicety : coll. : late C. 18–20. Ex the T-square used by architects.

fit to bust a double ration serve-out of navy-serge. Very fat : naval : C. 20.

fit to kill. Immoderately, excessively : coll. : U.S. (1856 : Thornton), anglicised ca. 1890.

fit(-)up. A stage easily fitted up ; hence, a small theatrical company : from ca. 1880 : theatrical s. >, by 1910, coll. Cf. **fit-up towns.**

fit up a show. To arrange an exhibition : artists' : from ca. 1870 ; ob.

fit-up towns ' do not possess a theatre, and . . . are therefore only visited by small companies carrying portable scenery, which can be fitted up in a hall or an assembly room', *The Referee*, July 22, 1883 : theatrical : from ca. 1880 ; ob. Ware.

Fitch's Grenadiers. The 83rd Foot Regiment, from 1881 the Royal Irish Rifles : military : 1793 ob. F. & Gibbons. Ex the (orig.) small stature of the men and its first colonel's surname.

fits, beat into. To ' beat hollow ' : coll. ; from ca. 1835. Hood, ' It beats all the others into fits ' (O.E.D.). In C. 20, often *beat to fits* (Manchon).

fits, give a person. To defeat humiliatingly : coll. ; from ca. 1870. Orig. U.S.

fits, forty. See **forty fits.**

fits, lick into. To ' beat hollow ' : coll. (—1887). Baumann. Ex *give a person fits.*

fits, scream oneself into. To scream excessively : coll. : from ca. 1840. (O.E.D.)

fits, throw (a person) **into.** To alarm or startle greatly : coll. : from ca. 1855.

***fitter.** A burglars' locksmith : c. ; from ca. 1860.

Fitz. A royal natural child : lower classes' : late C. 19–20. The prudent Ware thus wisely : ' Derivation obvious.'—2. A person of position or fortune going on the stage : theatrical : 1883. Ibid.

five. See **fives.**—2. **(the five.)** ' The five pounds weight allowed to apprentice jockeys' : turf : from ca. 1920 ; now verging on coll. O.E.D. (Sup.).—3. A five-eighth : Rugby football : from ca. 1910. Cf. *three,* a three-quarter.—4. Fifteen (in scoring) : lawn tennis players' : from ca. 1920. Cf. *fif.*

Five by Two. A Jew : rhyming s. : C. 20. P. P., *Rhyming Slang,* 1932. Cf. *four-by-two* and *buckle-my-shoe.*

Five-and-Threepennies, the. The 53rd Foot, from 1881 the Shropshire Light Infantry : military : C. 19–20 ; ob. Ex the 5 and 3, also ex the ensign's daily pay.

five-barred gate. A policeman : Cockneys' : 1886–ca. 1915. Ware, ' The force being chiefly recruited from the agricultural class '.

five-boater, -master, -rater. These are nautical coll. of obvious meaning, all three referring to ships : from ca. 1887. O.E.D.

five-eight (or **-eighth**). A mere lance-corporal : military : 1914–18. (That part of a corporal.)

five(-)fingers. The 5 of trumps in the card game of don or five cards : C. 17–19 : s. > j. Cotton in *The Compleat Gamester,* 1674 ; H., 3rd ed. Cf. *fives,* q.v.

five-master. See **five-boater.**

five o'clock, a. Afternoon tea at five o'clock : coll. : from ca. 1890. Cf. Fr. *des five o'clock à toute heure.*

five-oner ; five ones man. One who gets a 1st class certificate in each of his five examinations for lieutenant : naval : C. 20. Bowen.

five or seven. Intoxicated ; a drunkard : policemen's and Cockneys' : 1885–ca. 1914. Ex *five shillings or seven days,* ' the ordinary magisterial decision upon " drunks " unknown to the police ' (Ware).

five over five, adj. and adv. Applied to those who turn in their toes : from ca. 1820 ; ob. Egan's Grose.

five-pot piece. See **pot,** n., 5.

five-pounder. A cheap-excursionist : Jersey : 1883, *The Graphic,* March 31 ; ob. Ware.

Five P's. Wm. Oxberry (d. 1824), printer, publisher, player, poet, and publican. Dawson.

five-rater. See **five-boater.**

five-shares man. (Gen. pl.) A fisherman, whaler, etc., working for a share of the profits : nautical coll. : late C. 19–20. Bowen.

five shillings, the sign of. The tavern-sign of the crown. Hence *ten shillings, fifteen shillings,* the sign of the two, the three crowns. Mid-C. 18–early 19. Grose, 2nd ed.

five-star Frenchman. A Chargeurs Réunis steamer : nautical : C. 20. Bowen, ' From the painting of her funnel '.

fiver. Anything that counts five, but gen. a £5 note or occ. its equivalent : from ca. 1850. Whyte-Melville, ' Or, as he calls it, a fiver '.—2. In c., a fifth term of imprisonment (— 1872). O.E.D.

fivepence, fine or grand as. See **fine as fivepence.**

fivepence halfpenny. A military c.p. (G.W.) for something invisible or not there. F. & Gibbons. Ex the Government messing-allowance.

fives. A foot : C. 17.—2. From ca. 1820 : fingers, i.e. hands, fists. Bee.—3. Hence, a street fight : low, esp. Cockney : from ca. 1850.

fives, bunch of. A fist : from ca. 1822. Bee, 1823. Ex preceding entry, sense 2.

***fives going, keep one's.** Constantly to thieve, esp. to pickpocket : c. or low s. : ca. 1820–80. ' Jon Bee ', 1823.

fix. A dilemma : orig. (1833), U.S. ; anglicised ca. 1840 ; coll. till ca. 1890, then S.E.

***fix,** v. In c., to arrest : late C. 18–early 19.— 2. As a coll. verb-of-all-work, it is an importation —rare before 1840—ex the U.S. (1708 : Thornton) ; the n. *fixings* (in U.S., 1826) has been less warmly received.—3. To preserve (tissues) in, e.g., formalin : medical coll. (— 1933), now verging on j.

fix !, at the word. Be punctual, or sharp ! : military c.p. : C. 20. F. & Gibbons, ' Suggested by the Drill Book word of command, " Fix Bayonets ".'

fix it. To arrange matters : ex U.S. (— 1836) ; anglicised ca. 1850 : coll. Cf. :

fix up. To arrange, e.g. a rendezvous, esp. for another : ex. U.S., anglicised ca. 1855. In C. 20, occ. *be fixed up,* to have an appointment.—2. **fix** (a person) **up.** To provide him with lodgings or other quarters : coll. : from ca. 1888.

fixed bayonets. A brand of Bermuda rum : military : late C. 19–early 20. F. & Gibbons. Ex its sting and effects. But among prisoners of war in Germany in 1914–18 it was applied to a spirit made of potatoes and apt to render one ' fighting drunk '.

fixing. Strong drink : Australian (— 1889) ; ob. by 1912, † by 1924.

fixings. See **fix,** v., 2. Cf. *doings,* q.v.—2. As furniture : 1887, Baumann.

fixfax. See **paxwax.**

fiz, fizz. Champagne ; also, any sparkling wine : from ca. 1860. H., 3rd ed.—2. Occ., though very rarely in C. 20, lemonade mixed with ginger-beer : from ca. 1880.—3. A hissing sound : coll. ; 1842 (O.E.D.).—4. A fuss : from ca. 1730.—5. Animal spirits : from ca. 1850. These last two senses are coll.—and ob.—6. Ned Ward, in 1700, has *fiz* for *phiz.* Matthews.

fizz around. To ' buzz around ' ; move speedily and busily : from ca. 1930. ' Ganpat ', *Out of Evil,* 1933.

fiz(z)-gig. From such S.E. senses as a squib, a whirligig, a silly pastime, the word has come, in C. 20, to approximate, in its meaning, to *gadget.* Coll.—2. An informer to the police : c. of Sydney, N.S.W. : from ca. 1930.

fizzer. Any first-rate thing (e.g. a theatrical role) or, rarely, person : coll. (— 1866).—2. A very fast ball : cricketers' coll. (1904). O.E.D. (Sup.).; Lewis.—3. A charge-sheet : military : from ca. 1920.—4. A vendor of soft drinks : mostly Cockneys' : 1895, H. W. Nevinson. Ex :

fizzer-man. A camp-follower selling soft drinks : military : 1894 (O.E.D.). Collectively the ' fizzermen ' form the *fizzer-brigade*.

fizzing, adj. Excellent (— 1859). H., 1st ed. —2. Also as adv. : from ca. 1880 ; ob. C. *stunning*.

fizzle. A ludicrous failure : orig. U.S., anglicised ca. 1880 : coll. ; by 1900, S.E.

fizzle out. To tail off ; end lamely ; become a failure ; fail : orig. (ca. 1848), U.S. ; anglicised ca. 1870 ; coll. till ca. 1905, then S.E. Ex fireworks, esp. if damp.

flabagast, gen. **flabbergast.** To astound, physically or mentally ; utterly to confuse (a person) : coll. : from ca. 1772, when *The Annual Register* included it in ' On New Words '. Disraeli. Ex *flap* (or *flabby*) + *aghast* : W.—2. Hence the not very common and now ob. *flabbergastation* : 1845 (E.D.D.).

flabberdegaz. A ' gag ' or stop-gap words ; a piece of bad acting or instance of imperfect utterance : theatrical : ca. 1870–1915. Prob. ex :

flabbergast. See flabagast.

*****flag.** A groat or fourpenny piece : ca. 1560–1890 : c. Harman ; B.E. ; Mayhew, ' A tremendous black doll bought for a flag (fourpence) of a retired rag-merchant.'—2. An apron : low, or low coll. : from ca. 1845.—3. A sanitary pad or towel. Hence, *the flag* (or *danger-signal) is up* : she is ' indisposed ' : from ca. 1850.—4. Abbr. *flag unfurled*, q.v. : late C. 19–20 ; ob. Ware.—5. Words missed in composing : printers' (— 1909). Ex the appearance of the ' out ' words written at the side of the ' copy ' or of the proof. Ware.

flag, fly the. To post a notice that workmen are needed : tailors' : from ca. 1860. Cf. *cat's face up* and *flag-flying*, 2, q.v.

flag, show the. To put in an appearance, just to show that one is there : business and professional men's coll. : from ca. 1919.

flag-about. A strumpet : low, or low coll. : ca. 1820–70. Cf. *flagger*, q.v.

flag-flasher. One who, when off duty, sports the ' insignia of office '—cap, apron, uniform, badge, etc. : from ca. 1860. H., 5th ed. Ex *flag*, 2.

flag-flying. Adj. and vbl.n. corresponding to *flag*, n., 2 (cf. *flag-flasher*) and 3 (cf. *Captain is at home, the*).—2. A bill's being ' posted up when hands are required ' : tailors' (— 1889). Barrère & Leland. —3. Overbidding (occ., a tendency to overbid) at bridge : from ca. 1915 : s. >, by 1930, coll. O.E.D. (Sup.).

flag is up, the. See flag, 3.

flag of defiance. A drunken roisterer : nautical : mid-C. 18–early 19. Ex :

flag of defiance or bloody flag, hang out the. To have a red face owing to drink ; to be drunk : late C. 17–early 19 nautical. B.E. ; Grose, 1st ed., ' The flag of defiance or bloody flag is out,' etc.

flag of distress. ' The cockade of a half-pay officer ' : naval : late C. 18–mid-19. A MS. note by Grose to the B.M. 1st ed. copy : not, however, incorporated—as all such notes were orig. intended to be—in the 2nd ed. (1788).—2. An announcement-card for board, or board and lodgings : from ca. 1850 ; coll.—3. Hence, any outward sign of poverty : orig. nautical : mid-C. 19–20. H., 1st ed.—4. A flying shirt-tail : from ca. 1855 : low, esp. Cockney. Ibid.

flag unfurled. A man of the world : rhyming s. (— 1859) ; ob. H., 1st ed.

flag-wagging. Flag-signalling, esp. at drill : naval and military ; from ca. 1885.—2. Hence, in G.W., a signaller was called *flag-wagger*.

flagger. A harlot, esp. one walking the streets : low (— 1865) ; ob. Mostly London. Either ex pavement-*flags* or ex *flag-about*.

flagrant delight. A (mainly legal) jocular Englishing of *in flagrante delicto* : C. 20. Compton Mackenzie, *Water on the Brain*, 1933, ' To-night's the night for flagrant delight.'

flags. Clothes drying in the wind : low coll. : from ca. 1860. Cf. *snow*.—2. A flag lieutenant : naval nickname : late C. 19–20. Bowen.

Flags, the. The cotton market, Liverpool : Stock Exchange : from ca. 1890.

flam, humbug, a trick, a sham story, after being S.E. in C. 17–18, is in C. 19 coll., in C. 20 † except in dial. and Australian, the same applying dialectally to the rare adj. and the common v. Perhaps abbr. *flim-flam*, which, however, is recorded later : W. suggests that it derives ex Scottish *flamfew*, a trifle, gew-gaw.—2. The single beat of a drum : (— 1791 ; ob.) orig. military s. ; in C. 19 gen. s. > coll. ; in C. 20, S.E. but ob. Grose, 3rd ed.—3. In c., a ring : ca. 1850–70. H., 1864.

flamdoodle, flam-sauce. See flapdoodle.

flame. A sweetheart ; a kept mistress : after being S.E., this term, esp. as *an old flame*, a former sweetheart or lover, is in C. 19–20 increasingly coll. and jocular. The modern semi-jocular use is perhaps directly ex C. 17 Fr. ' *flamme* and *âme* riming in the Fr. classics almost as regularly as *herz* and *schmerz* in Ger. lyrics ', W.—2. In C. 19 low coll. or s., a venereal disease.

flamer. A person, incident, or thing very conspicuous, unusual, or vigorous ; e.g. as in Cockton's *Valentine Vox*, 1840, a ' stiff ' criticism : ca. 1808–1900.—2. In pl., a kind of safety-match giving a bright flame : from ca. 1885 ; ob. Baumann.— 3. An aeroplane coming down in flames : Air Force : from 1916. (P. C. Wren, in *The Passing Show*, Aug. 18, 1934.)

Flamers, the. The 54th Foot, in late C. 19–20 the Dorsetshire Regiment : military : 1781, when they took part in the burning of New London. F. & Gibbons.

flames. A red-haired person ; occ. as term of address or personal reference : coll. : ca. 1820–90. ' Jon Bee.' Cf. *carrots*, *ginger*.

flaming. Very or too noticeable or vigorous ; ' stunning ' : border-line coll. : from ca. 1800 ; ob. Ex the S.E. senses (C. 17 +), flagrant, startling.— 2. (Of tobacco) very strong : low (— 1887). Baumann.—3. Adj. and adv., ' bloody ' : euphemistic coll. ; from early 1890's. (O.E.D. Sup.). Cf. *ruddy*.

flaming onions. A German anti-aircraft projectile (some ten fire-balls on a chain) : military : G.W. (F. & Gibbons.) Ex the rows of onions sold by hawkers.

Flamingo. (Gen. pl.) An inhabitant of Flanders : from ca. 1910. Ernest Raymond, *Mary Leith*, 1931. By sound-suggestion ex Fr. *Flamand*, as if = ' flaming '.

flamp. To sell Army property illegally : Regular Army : late C. 19–20. Cf. *flog* in same sense.

flan. Red tape : naval : C. 20. Bowen. Ex *red flannel* on *red tape*.

Flanderkin. Late C. 17–18 coll. for ' a very large Fat Man or Horse ; also Natives of that Country ' (Flanders), B.E. Cf. the next three entries.

Flanders fortune. A small one : late C. 17–18 : coll. B.E.

Flanders piece. A picture that looks 'fair at a distance, but coarser near at Hand', B.E. : late C. 17–18 : coll.

Flanders reckoning. A spending of money in a place unconnected with that where one receives it : coll. : C. 17–18. Thos. Heywood. (Apperson.) Cf. *Flemish account*, q.v.

flanges. See **wingers, 2.**

flank. To hit a mark with a whip-lash (–1830). —2. To crack a whip (v.t.) : from ca. 1830. Both are coll. verging on S.E., the standard sense being, to flick ; ob.—3. To push or hustle ; to deliver (esp. a blow) : coll. ; from ca. 1860 ; ob. Cf. Fr. *flanquer un coup à quelqu'un*, whence, presumably, it derives.

flank, a plate of thin. A cut off a joint of meat : low coll. : from ca. 1860 ; ob.

flanker. A blow, kick ; retort : coll. : ca. 1860–1910. Whence *do a flanker*.—2. A shirker : military : late C. 19–20 ; ob. F. & Gibbons. Ex the 'advantages' of being on a flank.

flanker, do (a person) **a** ; absolutely, **work a flanker** (esp. in the Army). To deceive, trick, outwit, give the slip : lower classes' (– 1923). Manchon.

flankey. The posterior : low (perhaps orig. c.) : from ca. 1840. Duncombe.

flannel or **flannels.** Derisive coll., C. 20 : flannel drawers (women's). Variant : *red flannel(s)*.—2. (Only **flannel**.) See **hot flannel.**

⸢ **flannel** (often pron. flannin)-**jacket.** A navvy : contractors' : from ca. 1860 ; ob. Ware. From his flannel shirt or singlet. The *flannin* (or *-en*) form comes from dial.

flannel-mouth, n. and adj. (A) well-spoken (person, esp. if a man) : Canadian : C. 20. I.e. *soft-spoken.*

flannels, get one's. To obtain a place in a team (orig. cricket) : schools' ; esp. and initially Harrow : from ca. 1885. Coll. >, by 1910, S.E. Ex *flannels*, flannel garments.

flannen or **-in.** See **flannel-jacket.**

flap. A blow : coll. or dial. : C. 16–18. Ex the S.E. v.—2. A female of little repute, a jade : C. 17–20 ; coll., > dial. by 1800.—3. In c., sheet-lead used for roofing : mid-C. 19–20 (ob.). H., 5th ed. Ex the noise it makes when loose in the wind.—4. A garment or hat that has a pendent portion : ca. 1790–1920. (O.E.D.)—5. 'Any evolution on board or movement of warships' : naval : late C. 19–20. Bowen. Applied esp. to the bustle ensuing on an emergency order (F. & Gibbons).—6. An air-raid : Air Force : 1915. F. & Gibbons.

flap, v. To pay ; 'fork out'. Esp. in *flap the dimmock* (money). Low. From ca. 1840 ; ob.— 2. In c., rob, swindle : C. 19–20 ; ob.—3. V.i., fall or flop down : coll., from ca. 1660 (S.O.D.).—4. To talk (always with *about*) : from ca. 1925 ; slightly ob. Ex *flap one's mouth* (gen. *about*), the same : 1910, H. G. Wells (O.E.D. Sup.) ; ob.

flap, in a. Excited : naval : C. 20. Bowen. Ex *flap*, n., 5.

*flap a jay. To cheat or swindle a greenhorn : c. (– 1885). See flap, v., 2.

flap one's mouth. See **flap, v., 4.**

flap (in C. 16–17, occ. *slap*) **with a fox tail.** A rude or contemptuous dismissal ; a mild rebuke : coll. : C. 16–early 19. Palsgrave, 1530 ; Smollett ; Scott. (Apperson.)

flapdash. Very clean ; shining : lower classes' (– 1923). Manchon. Prob. by a confusion of words and ideas.

flapdoodle. Empty talk ; transparent nonsense : coll. ; from ca. 1830. (? orig. U.S.) Marryat, 1833, 'Flapdoodle . . . the stuff they feed fools on.' Also a v., as is very rare with the variants : *flap-sauce, flam-sauce, flamdoodle*.—2. The *membrum virile* : late C. 17–18 low coll. Cf. *doodle*. Like *flabbergast*, *flapdoodle* is arbitrarily formed.

flapdoodler. An empty, inept, talkative political charlatan : journalists' : ca. 1885–1910 ; then gen. but ob.

flapdragon, flap-dragon, flap dragon. Syphilis or gonorrhœa : late C. 17–early 19 : low. B.E. Ex the S.E. sense, a raisin snatched from burning brandy and eaten hot.—2. A Dutchman ; a German : pejorative coll. : C. 17.

*flapman. A convict promoted for good behaviour : prison c. (– 1893) ; ob.

flapper. The hand : low coll. (– 1833). Marryat ; *The London Miscellany*, May 19, 1866, 'There's my flapper on the strength of it.' Cf. *flipper*, q.v.—2. A slow or unskilful hunting man : sporting : from ca. 1850 ; ob. Whyte-Melville. (O.E.D.)—3. A dustman's or a coal-heaver's hat : coll. : ca. 1850–1900. Cf. *fantail*.—4. In the low coll. of sexual venery, the male member (cf. *flapdoodle*, 2) : C. 19.—5. There too, a very young harlot, a sense linking up with that in gen. s., a young girl (? ex that, mainly dial., sense of a fledgling partridge or wild duck) : both in F. & H., 1893, the latter being discussed in *The Evening News*, Aug. 20, 1892.—6. In society s. of early C. 20, 'a very immoral young girl in her early "teens "', Ware,—a sense surviving in the U.S. ; in England, however, the G.W. firmly established the meaning (already pretty gen. by 1905), *any young girl with her hair not yet put up* (or, in the late 1920's and the 30's, not yet cut short). Cf. Ger. *Backfisch* and *flap*, n., 2.—7. An Ayrton fan : military : 1916. Also, coll., *flapper fan*. B. & P.— 8. A variant of *flapping*, q.v., as n. and adj. : 1928 (O.E.D. Sup.).—9. Inevitable nickname of anyone surnamed Hughes : C. 20. Bowen.—10. See **flappers.**

flapper-bracket, -seat. A (mostly, motor-) bicycle seat at the back for the spatial transference of a youthful female : resp. s. (from ca. 1915) and coll. (from ca. 1918 ; ob.).

flapper fan. See **flapper, 7.**

flapper-shaker. The hand : low coll. ; from ca. 1850 ; ob. Ex *flapper*, 1.

flapper-shaking. Hand-shaking ; hence, a preliminary ceremony : from ca. 1850. 'Cuthbert Bede', 1853.

flapper vote, the. The 'franchise granted in 1928 to women of 21 years and over' : coll. : 1928. C.O.D. (1934 Sup.)

flappers. Extremely long pointed shoes, esp. those worn by 'nigger minstrels' : from ca. 1880 ; ob.—2. A sandwich-man's boards : tramps' c. : the 1920's. (The transition term between *clappers* and *wings*.) F. Jennings, *Tramping with Tramps*, 1932.

flapper's burr-(h)oles. Ears : workmen's (– 1935).

flapper's delight. A young subaltern : Army officers' : 1915–18. See **flapper, 6** (second nuance).

flapping ; occ. **flapper** (sense 7 of the n. above). Racing not subject to either Jockey Club or

National Hunt regulations : turf : 1910. (O.E.D.
Sup.) Ex lack of dignity.—2. Hence, from ca.
1915, as adj.

flapsauce, flap(-)sauce. See **flapdoodle**. (No connection with the † S.E. term.)

flare. Anything unusual, uncommon : nautical ;
from ca. 1850.—2. A quarrel, a row, a spree : coll. :
from ca. 1840. Cf. *flare-up*.

flare. In its C. 19–20 S.E. sense, to shine un-
steadily, *flare* seems to have, ca. 1660–1730, been c.,
then low s. and then, ca. 1760–1830, coll. : witness
B.E. and Grose, all edd. Prob. ex Dutch or Low
Ger. : cf. Ger. *flattern, fladdern,* and Dutch *vlederen* :
W.—2. To swagger : low coll. (— 1841) ; ob. Leman
Rede.—3. To whisk out (— 1850) ; hence (— 1851),
to steal lightly, deftly. Mayhew. Both : c.

*flare, all of a. Clumsily ; bunglingly : c. of ca.
1830–90. H. Brandon in *Poverty, Mendicity, and
Crime,* 1839.

flare-up, rarely **-out.** A quarrel, commotion, or
fight : coll. ; from ca. 1835. Hence, a spree or
orgy ; a jovial party : coll. (— 1847). Justin
M'Carthy, 1879, ' What she would have called a
flare-out '. Cf. the v.—2. Brandy : c.(— 1923).
Manchon. Ex the result of a light applied thereto.

flare up, v. To become extremely angry : coll.
(— 1849). ' Father Prout ' Mahony, '. . . Swore,
flared up, and curs'd ' ; Thackeray.

flaring, adv. Exceedingly ; vulgarly : coll. :
C. 19–20 ; ob. E.g. in *flaring drunk*.

flarty is obscure ; ? an outsider. It is grafters' s.
of C. 20. Philip Allingham, *Cheapjack,* 1934, ' " I'm
a flarty too," she told me in confidence. " I don't
really belong to the fair." ' Origin ?

*flash, n. and adj. (Underworld) cant ; relating
to the underworld or to its slang. Hence they often
connote trickery, crime, low immorality. Orig.—
1756, 1700 resp. (S.O.D.)—themselves c., they
rapidly > low s. > gen. s. > coll. > S.E. Ultimately ex *flash* = sudden flame ; intermediately ex
flash = ostentation ; imm.—of problematic birth.
Ca. 1810–30, the s. of the man about town, chiefly
the fast set and its hangers on (see esp. Jon Bee's
Dict. of the Turf, 1823) : s. > coll. > S.E. Cf. the
ca. 1760–1825 coll., verging on S.E., sense : fop,
coxcomb.—2. In c., late C. 17–mid-19, a peruke.
B.E.—3. A showy swindler ; a hectoring vulgarian
or *nouveau riche* : C. 17 coll. Shirley, ' The town is
full of these vain-glorious flashes.'—4. A boast or
great pretence uttered by spendthrift, quack, or
sciolist : C. 18. Dyche.—5. A portion or, as in
flash of lightning, q.v., a drink : late C. 18–19 :
low s. or low coll.—6. **the flash.** The banner or
other name-displaying cloth or card-device of a
bookmaker's stand : racing c. : C. 20. Abbr. *the
flash part.* Analogous is the grafters' sense : ' A
grafter's display. Anything to attract the crowd '
(Allingham) : C. 20.—7. Priority given, by news-
agencies, to sports' results : journalists' (— 1935).—
8. An electric torch : c. : from ca. 1910. James
Curtis, *The Gilt Kid,* 1936.

flash, v. To show ; esp. excessively, vulgarly,
or with unnecessary ' pomp ' or pretence : coll.
(— 1785). In C. 17, S.E.—2. V.t. with, e.g. *the
gentleman,* to show off as, pretend to be, e.g. a
gentleman : ca. 1795–1850.—3. V.i., with variant
flash it, to make a display, show off : ca. 1770–1830.
Cf. *flash it about* and *flash it away.* The term
derives ex *flash* in the sense, ' show as in a flash,
hence, brilliantly ' (see esp. W.), prob. influenced by
flash, n. and adj., qq.v.

*flash, adj. See **flash,** n., 1.—2. In c. of ca. 1810–
1900, knowing, expert ; cognisant of another's
meaning. *Lex. Bal.*—3. Orig. (— 1785) c., by
1870 low : showy, vulgar ; (in Australia, — 1893)
vain-glorious, swaggering. Perhaps ex C. 17–18
S.E. *flash,* show, ostentation.—4. Connected with
boxing and racing : ca. 1808–90.—5. In a set style :
ca. 1810–60) : c. > low. Also n. Rare except
in *out of flash,* q.v.—6. Occ. adv., as in *to dress flash,*
i.e. fashionably but showily and in bad taste.—7.
Imitation ; counterfeit : c. : form ca. 1880 ; ob.
Ware. (In the ensuing list of *flash* combinations,
only such are given as are not imm. and accurately
deducible from the mere collocation of n. and n.,
v. and n., and n. and adj.)

flash, adv. See **flash,** adj., 6.

*flash, out of. For showy effect or affectation : c.
(— 1812) >, by 1820, low s. ; † by 1900. Vaux ; Bee.

*flash, put. To put (a person) on his guard : c.
(— 1812) ; † by 1900. Vaux.

flash a bit. (Of women) to permit examination ;
behave indecently : low : from ca. 1840. Cf. *flash
it,* q.v.

*flash a fawn(e)y. To wear a ring : c. : from ca.
1815 ; ob.

*flash-case, -crib, -drum, -house, -ken, -panny.
A lodging-house or tavern frequented by thieves and
illegally favourable to them ; in sense 2 of that n.,
' fence ' : c. of resp. C. 19–20 ob. ; C. 19 ; C. 19–20
ob. ; C. 19–20 ; mid-C. 17–19 ; and C. 19, though
extremely rare in these senses. Vaux has the
second, fifth and sixth.—2. The meaning, a brothel,
is derivative, and, though orig. c., it gradually >
low : *flash-crib* is not used in this sense.

*flash-cha(u)nt. ' A song interlarded with flash ',
i.e. with cant : c. : ca. 1820–70. Egan's Grose.
Also *flash song* (Vaux), 1812.

*flash-cove, from ca. 1810 ; **-companion,** from ca.
1860. A thief ; sharper ; ' fence ' ; (only *flash-
cove*) landlord or a ' flash ken ' (Vaux).

*flash-covess. A landlady of a ' flash-ken ' : c. :
C. 19. Vaux.

*flash-crib and **flash-drum.** See **flash-case.**

*flash-dona. A variant of *flash girl,* q.v. : c. :
late C. 19–20. Ware.

*flash-gentry. The high-class thieves : from ca.
1820 ; ob. ; c. Conflation of n. and adj.

flash girl, moll, mollisher, piece, woman. A
showy harlot : low : from ca. 1820.

*flash-house. See **flash-case.**

flash in the pan. Coïtion *sans* emission : C. 18–
20 low coll. D'Urfey.

flash it. See **flash,** v., 3.

flash it or **flash one's meat.** (Gen. of men) to
expose the person : low : from ca. 1840.

flash it ! Let me see it ! Show it ! A low, esp.
a coster's reply to the offer of a bargain : from ca.
1820 ; ob.

flash it about or **cut a flash.** To make a display—
once, often, continuously ; to lead a riotous or even
a crapulous life : low : from ca. 1860. Cf. *cut a
dash.* Developed ex :

flash it away. To show off ; cut a figure : coll. :
ca. 1795–1860. O'Keeffe.

flash-jig. A favourite dance : costers' : ca.
1820–90. Perhaps ex *flash,* adj., 3.

*flash-ken. See **flash-case.** (B.E.)

flash kiddy. A dandy : low : ca. 1820–60. Cf.
kiddy, q.v.

flash-lingo. Underworld s. : low : late C. 18–19.
Grose, 1st ed. See **flash,** n., 1.

*flash-man. One who talks the s. of the underworld : c. : C. 19.—2. A chucker-out to a brothel : c. : C. 19. *Lex. Bal.* Imm. ex :—3. A harlot's bully or 'ponce' : late C. 18–20, ob. : low ; prob. orig. c. Grose, 2nd ed. (2nd nuance).—4. A patron of boxing : s. > coll. : ca. 1820–50. Moncrieff.

*flash mollisher. A woman thief or swindler : c. (— 1812) ; † by 1890. Vaux.—2. See flash girl.

flash-note. A counterfeit banknote : C. 19 low (? orig. c.).

flash o(f) light. A gaudily or vividly dressed woman : South London (— 1909) ; virtually †. Ware.

flash o(f) lightning. A dram of strong spirit, a glass of gin : from ca. 1780. Cf. (— 1862) U.S. usage.—2. Gold braid on an officer's cap : nautical : mid-C. 19–20 ; ob. H., 3rd ed.

flash one's gab. To talk, esp. much ; boast : low (— 1819). Tom Moore, 'His lordship, as usual, . . . is flashing his gab.'

flash one's meat. See flash it.

*flash one's sticks. To expose or draw (*not* to fire) one's pistols : ca. 1810–50 : c. Vaux.

flash one's ticker. To take out one's watch rather often : low : from ca. 1850.

flash-panny. See flash-case.

*flash patter. Cant (underworld slang) : c. : C. 19. E.g. in No. 747's autobiography, p. 410.

*flash song. See flash-cha(u)nt. Perhaps low s. rather than c.

flash(-)tail. A harlot picking up toffs at night : low (— 1868) ; ob.

flash the dibs. To spend one's money : low : from ca. 1840 ; ob.

*flash the drag. See drag, flash the.—flash the flag. See flag, 2.

*flash the hash. To vomit : late C. 18–19 : c. Grose, 2nd ed.

*flash the ivory or one's ivories. To grin or laugh : c. of late C. 18–19 and low s. of C. 19–20 resp. Grose, 1st ed. Contrast *tickle the ivories.*

flash the muzzle. To bring forth a pistol : low (— 1823) ; ob. by 1870, † by 1900.

*flash the screens. To pay : c. of ca. 1820–40. See pew, stump the.

flash the upright grin. (Of women) to expose one's sex : low : from ca. 1860 ; ob.

*flash the wedge. To 'fence' one's 'haul', 'swag ', or booty : c. : C. 19.

*flash to, be. To be aware of, to understand fully : c. : ca. 1810–60. Vaux.

flash toggery. Smart clothes : low (— 1834). Ainsworth in *Rookwood.*

flash vessel. A very smart-looking ship that is undisciplined : nautical : ca. 1860–1915.

*flash woman. A harlot mistress of a 'flash man' (3) : c. (— 1823) ; † by 1890. 'Jon Bee.'

flash yad. A day's enjoyment : ca. 1865–1910. *Yad* = *day* reversed.

*flashed-up. Dressed stylishly or in one's best : c., and low : C. 20. James Curtis, *The Gilt Kid*, 1936. Cf. *dolled-up.*

flasher. A would-be wit ; hence, an empty fop : ca. 1750–90 : coll. that perhaps > S.E. Mme D'Arblay, 1779, 'They are reckoned the flashers of the place, yet everybody laughs at them.'—2. A synonym of *quickee* (q.v.) : Glasgow (— 1934).—3. In Glasgow (— 1934), a 'dud ' bank-note.

flashery. Tawdry elegance ; showy or vulgar display or action : coll. : ca. 1820–80. Never much used.

flashily ; flashly. See flashy.

flashing it, go. To have sexual connexion : low : from ca. 1840 ; ob. Cf. *flash it* and *flash a bit.*

flashy. Showy, gaudy ; ostentatious : in late C. 18–20, coll. ; earlier, S.E. Hence advv. *flashly*, s., C. 19–20, but very rare in C. 20, and *flashily*, coll., C. 18–20. Miss Braddon, 1864, 'He chose no . . . flashily cut vestments.'

flashy blade or spark. A dandy : ca. 1815–30.—2. Hence, a cheap and noisy dandy or would-be dandy : ca. 1830–75. Both, coll. verging on S.E.

flat. A greenhorn ; a fool ; an easy 'gull' or dupe : from ca. 1760. Barham, ' . . . He gammons all the flats.' Cf. the C. 20 story of the girl that refused to live either with or in one. By contrast with *sharp.*—2. An abbr. of *flattie*, 4 : c. : C. 20. David Hume.—3. See flats.—4. (the flat.) The season of flat horse-racing : sporting coll. : from ca. 1910.

flat, do or have a bit of. To have sexual connexion : low : mid-C. 19–20.

*flat, pick up a. To find a client : harlots' c. : C. 19–20.

[flat !, that's. That is certain, undeniable ! Late C. 16–17. Shakespeare.—2. I'm determined (on that) ! C. 18–20. Addison. Perhaps both senses are best classified as literary with a strong coll. flavour.]

flat as a flounder or a pancake. Extremely flat, lit. and fig. : coll. The former : C. 17–19 ; the latter, C. 18–20, but with *cake* as early as 1542. Apperson. Ware notes the C. 18–20 variant (likewise coll.), *flat as a frying-pan.*

flat back. A bed bug : low : from ca. 1840 ; ob. by 1900, † by 1920.

flat broke. Penniless ; ruined : coll. : from ca. 1830.

*flat-catcher. An impostor, a professional swindler ; a decoy : orig. (— 1823), c. ; then low. Moncrieff, Mayhew, Whyte-Melville.

*flat-catching. Swindling : orig. (— 1821), c., then low. J. Greenwood, 1869, 'Flat-catching, as the turf slang has it '.

flat-cap. A citizen of London : coll. : late C. 16–early 18. Marston, 'Wealthy flat caps that pay for their pleasure the best of any men in Europe '. *Temp.* Henry VIII, round flat caps were fashionable ; citizens continued to wear them when they had become unfashionable.

flat chicken. Stewed tripe : proletarian (— 1909); slightly ob. Ware.

flat-cock. A woman : low (— 1785) ; † by 1890. Grose, 1st ed. Ex one of two possible anatomical reasons.

Flat Feet, the. The Foot Guards, British Army : from ca. 1860. H., 3rd ed.—2. Hence, various other line regiments ; also, militia men as opp. to regulars : military : from ca. 1870.

flat fish, gen. a regular. A dullard ; occ., an easy prey : from ca. 1850. Ex *flat*, stupid + *fish*, something hookable.

flat foot. A sailor not yet aged 21 : naval (— 1909). Ware. Ex :—2. Any sailor : naval, esp. marines' : from ca. 1895 ; ob. O.E.D. (Sup.).—3. A policeman : lower classes' (— 1935).

flat-iron. A public-house at a corner : low : from ca. 1860 ; ob. Ex its triangularity.

flat-iron jiff. A master man in a small way : tailors' : late C. 19–20. E.g. *The Tailor and Cutter*, Nov. 29. 1928.

*flat move. A plan that fails ; folly or mismanagement : ca. 1810–80 : c. >, by 1823, low **s.** Vaux ; ' Jon Bee '. I.e. a flat's action.

flat spin, go into a. See go into a flat spin.

flatch. A half : the rigid *flah* modified : back **s.** (– 1859).—2. A spurious *half*-crown : coiners' c. : from ca. 1870.—3. A *half*penny (– 1859). Senses 1 and 3 : H., 1st ed.

flatch yenork. A half-crown : back **s.** (– 1859). H., 1st ed.

flatiron gunboat. A gunboat of the 1870's–80's, ' with a short turtle back ' : naval coll. : that period. Bowen.

***flats.** Playing cards : c. (– 1812) ; ob. by '880, † by 1900. Vaux. Cf. *broads*, q.v.—2. False dice : ? c. : ca. 1700–1850. Cf. *Fulhams*.— 3. Counterfeit money : c. or low : ca. 1820–70.— 4. **sharps and flats** : jocular coll. for sharpers and their victims : C. 19–20. And, 5, for recourse to weapons : 1818, Scott (O.E.D.) ; † by 1900.—6. See **flats and chits.**—7. (Very rare in the singular.) Long, thin envelopes : among sorters on mail trains : C. 20. *The Daily Herald*, Aug. 5, 1936.

flats, mahogany. Bed bugs : low : from ca. 1850 ; ob. Cf. *flat back.*

***flats and chits.** Bugs and fleas, says Baumann, who classifies it as c. : but is this an error for *flats and chats*, bugs and lice ?

flats and sharps. Weapons : coll. : ca. 1780– 1850. Scott, in *Midlothian*, ' He was something hasty with his flats and sharps.'—2. See **flats**, 4.

flatt. (As, redundantly, in Grose.) See **flat.**

flattened out, ppl. adj. Penniless : tailors' : late C. 19–20.

***flatter-trap.** The mouth : c. or low : from ca. 1840 ; ob.

flattie, flatty. Among cheapjacks, one in a new ' pitch ' : ca. 1840–80.—2. A rustic ; an un-initiated person : low coll. : ca. 1855–80. H., 1st ed.—3. Hence (see, however, **flatty-gory**), a ' flat ', q.v. ; an easy dupe : ca. 1855–1915 : c. or low.—4. A uniformed policeman : c. and low : late C. 19–20. Because his feet go flat from so much ' promenading '. Cf. *flat foot*, 3.—5. A member of the audience : circus-workers' **s.** : C. 20. E. Seago, *Circus Company*, 1933. To showmen in gen., it means an outsider.—6. A small flat-bottomed sailing-boat : coll., esp. among boys : from ca. 1860.—7. One who goes out in a van in the summer but lives in a house in the winter : Gypsies' (– 1897). Abbr. *flattybouch*, same meaning. E.D.D.

***flatty-gory.** A ' flat ', a dupe or intended dupe : **c.** : ca. 1810–40. Vaux. Perhaps the origin of all senses of *flattie.*

***flatty-ken.** A thieves' lodging-house where the landlord is not ' fly ' to the tricks of the underworld : c. (– 1851) : ob. Mayhew. Ex *flattie*, 2, q.v., + *ken*, a place.

flavour, catch or get the. To be drunk : low coll. : from ca. 1860 ; ob.—2. To feel somewhat in-clined for sexual intercourse : low : from ca. 1870 : ? ob.

flawed. Drunk : late C. 17–19 : orig. c., then low. In C. 19, gen. = half drunk. B.E.—2. (Of women) no longer virgin though unmarried : coll. : C. 19–20.

flay or skin a flint. To be mean ; miserly : coll. > S.E. : mid-C. 17–19. Marryat, ' She would skin **a** flint if she could.' Cf. *flea-flint*, q.v.

flay (orig. and gen. **flea**) **the fox.** To vomit :

coll. : late C. 16–19. Cotgrave ; Urquhart ; H., 5th ed. The mod. term is *whip the cat.*

flaybottomist, late C. 18–19 ; **flaybottom**, C. 19–20 (ob.). A schoolmaster : jocular coll. Grose, 1st ed. (Cf. *bum-brusher* and *kid-walloper*.) Punning *phlebotomist.*

flea, fit as a. See **fit as a flea.**

flea and louse. A (bad) house : rhyming **s.** (– 1859). H., 1st ed.

flea-bag. A bed : low : ca. 1835–1915. Lever in *Harry Lorrequer*.—2. From ca. 1909, a(n officer's) sleeping-bag. Collinson.

flea-bite, in C. 16–17 occ. **-biting.** A trifling injury or inconvenience : coll. : late C. 16–18 ; in C. 19–20, S.E. The former in Taylor, 1630, and Grose ; the latter in Burton.

flea- or flay-flint. A miser : coll., > S.E. in C. 19 : C. 17–20 ; ob. D'Urfey, 1719, ' The flea-flints . . . strip me bare.' Ex *flay a flint*, q.v.

flea in one's or the ear, have a. To be scolded or annoyed ; to fail in an enterprise : coll. : C. 16–20. Heywood's *Proverbs*, 1546. (Anticipated in C. 15.) Cf. :

flea in one's (or the) ear, send away with a. To dismiss annoyingly or humiliatingly : coll. (– 1602). Middleton ; George Eliot ; Weyman, 1922. (Apperson.) Cf. dial. *flea in the ear*(*-hole*) and *flea in the lug*, resp. a box on the ears and a scolding or sharp reproof.

flea-pit. A flat (apartment) : from ca. 1919. (John G. Brandon, *The One-Minute Murder*, 1934.) On *flea-bag* with jocular allusion to S.E. *cubby-hole.*

flea the fox. See **flay the fox.**

fleas, jumpy as a bag of. Extremely nervous : ' windy ' : military coll. : from 1915. Frank Richards, *Old Soldiers Never Die*, 1933.

fleas, sit on a bag of. To sit uncomfortably ; be uncomfortable : coll. : from ca. 1830. If *of hen fleas*, then in extreme discomfort.

fleas for, catch (one's). To be very intimate with : of a man with a woman : low coll : C. 19–20 ; ob.

flea's leap, in a. Very quickly or promptly : coll. : from ca. 1840.

fleece. An act of thieving or swindling : C. 17 coll. The v. itself had a coll. flavour in C. 16–18. —2. The female pubic hair : (? C. 18 ;) C. 19–20 : low coll. Cf. *furbelow.*

fleece-hunter or **-monger.** A whoremonger : C. 19–20 (ob.) : low coll. Ex *fleece*, 2. Contrast *tuft-hunter.*

fleecer. A thief or swindler : C. 17–19 coll. Prynne. Cf. Yorkshire *fleecery.*

[**fleer**, in C. 17 often **flear**, to gain, etc., has, *pace* B.E. and F. & H., never been other than S.E.]

Fleet, Commander of the. See **Navy Office.**

fleet, go round or through the. ' To be flogged on board each vessel in the fleet ', S.O.D. : from ca. 1840 : nautical s., > j. : ca. 1880 ; ob.

Fleet, he may whet his knife on the threshold of the. He is not in debt : coll. : ca. 1650–1800. Fuller in his *Worthies* ; Grose in his *Provincial Glossary*. The reference is to the Fleet Prison (London), where debtors used to be imprisoned. (Apperson.)

***fleet note.** A counterfeit banknote : c. : ca. 1810–60. Is this the dial. adj. *fleet*, shallow ? Or *fleet*, the mainly dial. adj., skimmed ?

Fleet Street. Journalism : in C. 19 coll. and pejorative ; in C. 20 S.E. and neutral, the fourth estate being now a reputable body. Fleet Street became the centre of British journalism early in C. 18.

Fleet-Streeter. A journalist : C. 19–20 (ob.) : coll. In C. 19, ' a journalist of the baser sort ; a spunging *prophet* (q.v.) ; a sharking dramatic critic ; a *spicy* (q.v.) paragraphist ; and so on ', F. & H., 1893.

Fleet-Streetese. The English of the *Fleet-Streeter*, q.v. : coll. : in C. 20, neutral ; but in C. 19, to quote the same authority, ' a mixture of sesquipedalians and slang, of phrases worn threadbare and phrases sprung from the kennel ; of bad grammar and worse manners ; the like of which is impossible outside of *Fleet Street* (q.v.), but which in *Fleet Street* commands a price, and enables not a few to live.'

Flem. A Fleming : coll. (1909) by 1930 verging on S.E. (O.E.D. Sup.)

Flemish account. A bad account ; unsatisfactory remittance : coll. (by 1800 S.E.) : ca. 1660–1830 ; but extant, as s., among sailors as late as 1874 (H., 5th ed.). Its post-1820 use in S.E. is archaic. Cf. *Flanders reckoning*, q.v.—2. Hence, ' ship's books that will not balance ' : nautical : C. 19–20 ; ob. Bowen.

flesh !; flesh and fire ! As coll. exclamations : late C. 17–mid-18. Ex *God's flesh !* (Langland), where *flesh* has a spiritual or religious sense. O.E.D.

flesh and blood. Brandy and port equally mixed : from ca. 1825 ; ob.

flesh-bag. A shirt ; a chemise : low : from ca. 1810 ; ob. Vaux, 1812 ; *The London Magazine* (the like of which we need to-day), 1820 (vol. I), ' They are often without a flesh bag to their backs.'

flesh-broker. A match-maker : a bawd : late C. 17–early 19 : low. B.E., who has also, *spiritual flesh-broker*, a parson.

flesh-creeper. A ' shocker ' or ' blood ' or ' dreadful ' : 1887, Baumann ; † by 1930.

flesh, fish, nor good red herring, neither. See **flesh nor fish.**

flesh-fly (Cowper), **-maggot,** or **-monger ; flesh-market** or **-shambles ; flesh-mongering.** Rather (*pace* F. & H.) S.E. than coll., and all ob. or †.

flesh it. (Other forms are S.E.) To ' know ' a woman : C. 16–20 (ob.) : low coll. Cf. *fleshing*, q.v., and the S.E. *flesh one's sword*. (*Flesh*, generative organs, C. 16–20 literary : see Grose, P., at *flesh-broker*.)

flesh-tailor. A surgeon : C. 17 : jocular, but ? coll. or S.E. Ford, in *'Tis Pity She's a Whore*.

flesher. A shirt : military coll. : late C. 19–20 ; ob. F. & Gibbons. In the Army, it is worn next to the skin.

fleshing, go a. To go wenching : coll. : late C. 16–17. Florio, 1598.

fleshy, n. See **cat's head.**

fleshy part of the thigh. The buttock : jocular coll. : 1899–ca. 1912. Ex military new evasion. Ware, ' Came into use upon the news from S. Africa of Lord Methuen having been wounded in this region '.

flet. A halibut : nautical : C. 19–20. Bowen. Perhaps by perversion on perversion : which will, admittedly, explain anything, yet is undoubtedly operative now and then.

*fletch. A counterfeit coin : c. : ca. 1870–1910. Perversion of *flatch*, q.v.

flick, gen. **old flick.** Comical fellow : a low coll. salutation, jocular in tendency (— 1860) ; ob. H.,

2nd ed. ; *Punch*, July 28, 1883.—2. In C. 17 c., a thief. Rowlands, where wrongly printed *afflicke*. Abbr. late C. 16–early 17 *flicker*, a pilferer.—3. See **flicks.**

*flick, v. To cut : c. : from ca. 1670 ; ob. Coles ; B.E. ; Disraeli in *Venetia*. ? ex the flicking of a whip.—2. Gen. *flick along*. To cause (e.g. a motor-car) to move rapidly : from ca. 1915 : s. now verging on coll. Galsworthy, 1924.

*flicker. A drinking-glass. A *rum f.*, a large glass ; *queer f.*, an ordinary one. C. : mid- C. 17–early 18. Coles, 1676. Perhaps ex its flickering lights.

flicker. To drink : c. (? C. 18) C. 19. Ex *flicker*, n., q.v.—2. To grin ; laugh in a person's face : late C. 17–20 ; dial. after ca. 1830. B.E.

*flickers. A fainting : tramps' c. : from the early 1920's. F. Jennings, *Tramping with Tramps*, 1932. Ex U.S. c. *flicker*, in the same sense.—2. A variant, 1927–9, of *flicks*, q.v. Collinson.

flicking ; flickering. The former with *flick*, v., and *flicker*, v. ; the latter with *flicker*, vbl.n.

flicks, the. The films ; the moving pictures ; (*go to the flicks*) a cinema : 1927 (Collinson) ; ob. by 1935. Ex the flickering of the pictured screen ; imm. ex :—2. (**flick.**) A moving picture ; the performance at a cinema : 1926, Edgar Wallace (O.E.D. Sup.) ; † by 1936.

flier, flyer. At association football, a shot in the air : sporting : from ca. 1890.—2. See **flyer,** all senses.

flier, take a. To copulate without undressing or going to bed : low : from ca. 1780 ; ob. Grose, 1st ed.—2. To fall heavily : coll. (— 1931). Lyell. Ex the lit. S.E. sense, to take a flying leap.

flies !, no. Honestly ! ; without fooling ! : for sure ! : low (— 1923). Manchon. Perhaps abbr. *no flies in the ointment.*

flies about (a thing, a person), **there are no.** It, he, etc., is particularly good : Australian (— 1848) ; † by 1890. O.E.D. (Sup.). Whence :

flies on a person, there are no. (Occ. with *about* for *on*.) He is honest, genuine, not playing the fool : coll. (— 1864). H., 3rd ed.—But, 2, since ca. 1895, and owing to U.S. influence, it has meant : he is wide-awake ; esp. very able or capable.

flies won't get at it, where the. (Of drink) down one's throat : coll. : late C. 19–20. Cf. (at **coaches**) *the coaches won't run over him.*

flight, in the first. See **first flight.**

flight o(f) steps. Thick slices of bread and butter : coffee-houses' (— 1883). Ware. Cf. *doorstep*, q.v.

flight of turkeys. A Royal Marine landing-party : naval : C. 19. Bowen. Ex their red tunics.

flim. Abbr. *flimsy*, n., q.v.—2. Five pounds sterling : grafters' : C. 20. Philip Allingham. Ex sense 1 influenced by *finnif*, q.v.

flim-flam, n. and adj., is S.E. until C. 19, when it > coll. : since ca. 1850, it has been archaic. Cf. *flam*, of which it may possibly be a reduplication, even though the doubled form is app. the earlier.

*flimp ; rarely flymp. To hustle ; esp. thus to rob : c. (— 1839). Brandon. Hence *flimper* : a stealer from the person. ' Cf. west Flemish *flimpe*, knock, slap in the face,' O.E.D.—2. Hence, to swindle : low and military (— 1914). F. & Gibbons.—3. To have sexual intercourse with : from ca. 1850. Cf. the sexual vv. *bang* and *knock*, qq.v.

*flimp, put on the, gen. **v.i.** To rob on the highway ; to rob and garotte : c. : from ca. 1835 ; ob. Brandon.

*flimper. See flimp, 1.

*flimping. Stealing from the person: c. (—
1839).

flimsy. A banknote: from ca. 1810: low. *Lex.
Bal.* (*flymsey*). Occ. abbr. *flim* (— 1870). Also, in
pl., paper-money (— 1891). Ex the thin paper.—
2. Reporters' 'copy'; news: journalistic coll.:
from ca. 1859; in C. 20, S.E. Ex the thin copying-
paper.—3. Hence, a sheet of music, a street-song:
tramps' c. (— 1887). Baumann.—4. 'An officer's
report at the end of a commission or when leaving a
man-of-war': naval: from ca. 1890. Bowen.
Likewise ex sense 2.

flimsy, v. To write on *flimsy* (sense 2): journalists': from ca. 1885: coll. >, by 1910, S.E.

flinch-gut. Whale's blubber: whalers': mid-
C. 19–20. Bowen.—2. Hence the hold in which it
is stored: whalers': late C. 19–20. Ibid.

fling. A sowing of one's wild oats; a spree:
from ca. 1825: coll. soon S.E. Thackeray.
(With *have*.)

fling, v. To cheat or trick; v.t. with *out*: coll.:
mid-C. 18–20; almost †. Grose. Esp. *fling out of*,
e.g. money.

fling, in a. In a fit of temper: coll.: C. 19–20;
ob.

fling-dust, occ. -stink. A harlot that walks the
streets. C. 17–18 (? later): coll. Fletcher, 'An
English whore, a kind of fling-dust, one of your
London light-o'-loves', 1621 (O.E.D.).

fling (or flap) it in one's face. Of a harlot. to
expose the person: low coll.: C. 19–20.

fling out, v.i. To go out or away in noisy haste;
esp., in a temper: coll. > S.E.: C. 18–20.

flint. A worker at union, mod. trades-union,
rates: from ca. 1760. Opp. *dung*, q.v. Both
terms are in Foote's burlesque, *The Tailors*. Ob.
by 1890, † by 1910.

flint, old. A miser: coll. (— 1840). Dickens in
The Old Curiosity Shop. Ob.

flip. 'Hot small Beer (chiefly) and Brandy,
sweetened and spiced upon occasion', B.E., ca.
1690: orig. nautical; but S.E. by 1800. (Cf.
Sir Cloudesley, q.v.) Perhaps abbr. *Philip* (W.).—
2. A bribe or tip: low: C. 19–20.—3. (A shore)
flight or trip in an aircraft, esp. in an aeroplane:
aviators' (1914) >, by 1920, gen. (O.E.D. Sup.)
Ex the motion.—4. A mere nothing, a trifle: lower
classes' (— 1923). Manchon. Perhaps ex *flip*, a
flash or flicker of light.

*flip, v. To shoot, gen. v.t.: c. (— 1812); very
ob. Vaux.—2. To fly in an aircraft, esp. in an
aeroplane: aviators' (1915) >, by 1920, gen.—but
much less gen. than the corresponding n., whence, by
the way, it derives. F. & Gibbons.

flip-flap. A flighty woman: coll. > S.E.:
C. 18. Vanbrugh, 1702, 'The light airy flip-flap,
she kills him with her motions.'—2. A step-dance
(see cellar-flap); a somersault in which the performer lands on feet and hands alternately: the
former, from ca. 1860; the latter (showmen's),
late C. 17–early 19.—3. The arm: nautical
(— 1887). Cf. *flipper*. Baumann.—4. The *membrum virile*: from ca. 1650: cf. *dingle-dangle*.—
5. A (fireworks) cracker (— 1885); ob.—6. 'Broad
fringe of hair covering the young male forehead':
Cockneys': 1898–ca. 1914. Ware.

flipper. The hand: from ca. 1820: nautical,
soon gen. Egan's Grose; Barham. One flips it
about.—2. Esp. in *tip a person one's flipper*, shake
hands with. *Punch*, Oct. 11, 1884. Cf. *flapper*.

daddle, mauley.—3. That part of a 'scene' which,
painted and hinged on both sides, is used in trick
changes: theatrical coll.: from ca. 1870; ob.

flirt-gill, C. 16–17; gill-flirt, C. 18–early 19. A
wanton; a harlot. Orig. coll., soon S.E. Occ. *jill*;
abbr. *Gillian* = *Juliana*.

flirtina cop-all (sc. men). A wanton: low coll.:
from ca. 1860. ? after *concertina*.

*flit, do a. To run away with another's share:
c. (— 1933). Charles E. Leach.

flit, do a moonlight. To quit one's tenement,
flat, or house, or one's lodgings, by night and without paying the rent or (board and) lodging: (low)
coll.: mid-C. 19–20.

flivver. A cheap and/or small motor-car (1920)
or aeroplane (ca. 1925). O.E.D. (Sup.). Prob. ex
U.S. *flivver*, a failure,—itself perhaps a blend or
rather a confusion of *flopper* + *fizzler*.

float. The row of footlights; (also in pl.) the
footlights: theatrical: ca. 1860–1930. (In C. 20,
S.E.) Before gas, oil-pans with floating wicks were
used.—2. A till; the contents thereof: c. (— 1935).
David Hume.

float, v.i. To die, 'give up the ghost': Australian (— 1916). C. J. Dennis.—2. To make a
mistake: rare (— 1923). Manchon. Cf. *floater*, 5.

float one's hat. To get soaked; to lose one's hat
in the water: Canadian lumbermen's: C. 20.
John Beames.

float-up. A person's casual approach: New Zealanders': C. 20. Ex:

float up, v. To stroll up to a person or a group;
to arrive unexpectedly: New Zealand coll.: C. 20.

floater. (Cf. the American senses in Thornton.)
A suet dumpling: Cockney, mostly costers'
(— 1864). Often it floats in gravy. Cf. the U.S.
floating island. H., 3rd ed.—2. (Gen. pl.) An
Exchequer bill; any sound stock: Stock Exchange (— 1871). Because a recognised security.—
3. The penis: C. 19.—4. A mine adrift: naval coll.:
1916. Bowen.—5. A mistake, a faux pas; a
moment of embarrassment: university s. (ca. 1910)
>, by 1929 (Wodehouse), gen. to the upper and
middle classes. A. Lunn, *The Harrovians*, 1913);
Ronald Knox, 1934, *Still Dead*, 'It produced . . .
in the original and highly esoteric sense of that
term, a "floater".' Perhaps because it cannot be
recalled, though perhaps suggested by *faux pas*
slurred to *fōper*; cf., however, *float*, v., 2.—6. A
penny that does not spin: two-up players' coll.:
late C. 19–20.

*floating academy. The convict hulks: mid-
C. 18–mid-19 c. or low s. Grose, 1st ed. (at
academy). Cf. *Campbell's academy*, q.v., and *floating
hell*.

floating batteries. Broken bread dipped in tea:
military: ca. 1890–1914.

floating coach-and-four, the. The Isle of Man
paddle-ship *Ben-My-Chree*, after being re-boilered
and fitted with four funnels: nautical: C. 20.
Bowen.

floating coffin. A ship materially rotten:
nautical coll.: late C. 19–20. Bowen. Ex:—2. A
10-gun brig (also a *coffin-brig*): ca. 1800–80. Ibid.

floating-hell; occ., in sense 2 only, hell afloat.
The hulks: ca. 1810–50. *Lex. Bal.*, 1811. Ex the
repulsive conditions.—2. Hence, a ship commanded
by a brutal bully, hence by any rigid disciplinarian:
nautical coll.: from ca. 1850. Cf.:

floating L's. See L's, floating.

floating skeleton (or F.S.), the. 'The Russian

five-funnelled cruiser *Askold*' (Bowen): naval during the G.W.

flock of sheep. White waves (cf. ' horses ') of the sea : coll. : C. 19–20 ; ob.—2. A dominoes-hand set out on the table : from ca. 1870.

floey (or **Floey**), **drunk as.** Exceedingly drunk : proletarian (— 1909). Perhaps ex some very bibulous Flora. Ware.

*flog. To whip : from ca. 1670. Until ca. 1750, c. ; in C. 19–20, S.E. Coles, 1676. Prob. an echoic perversion of L. *flagellare.*—2. To beat, excel : ca. 1840–1910.—3. In late C. 19–20 military, to sell illicitly, esp. Army stores ; and, in post-G.W. c., to sell ' swag ' to others than receivers. F. & Gibbons ; B. & P. Ex *flog the clock* or *flog the glass.* (Cf. *flogging,* adj., q.v.)—4. Hence, to get the better of (a person), esp. in a bargain : military : 1915. F. & Gibbons.—5. Hence (?), to exchange or barter : c. : from ca. 1920. Anon., *Dartmoor from Within,* 1932.—6. See **flog it.**

flog a willing horse. To urge on a person already eager or very active : coll. : mid-C. 19–20.

flog it. To walk : military : from ca. 1912. F. & Gibbons. Ex the effort (*flog oneself along*).

flog the cat. To cry over spilt milk : nautical : mid-C. 19–20. Bowen.

flog the clock. To move its hands forward (— 1894) : coll. Prob. suggested by the nautical *flog the glass,* turn the watch-glass (— 1769) ; †. (O.E.D.)

flog the dead horse. See **dead horse.**

*flogged at the tumbler. Whipped at the cart's tail : c. : late C. 17–18. B.E.

flogger. A whip : late C. 18–19. George Parker, 1789.—2. ' A mop used in the painting room to whisk (charcoal) dust from a sketch ' : theatrical : ca. 1870–1920.

*flogging. ' A Naked Woman's whipping (with Rods) an Old (usually) and (sometimes) a Young Lecher ', B.E. : C. 17–18 c.—2. The frequent vbl.n. of *flog,* v., 3, q.v.

flogging, adj. Mean ; grasping : late C. 19–20 : coll. Ob. Cf. *flog,* 2.

*flogging-cove. An official dealing out the corporal punishment : c. : late C. 17–early 19. B.E.—2. A C. 18 variant of :

*flogging-cully. A man addicted to flagellation for sexual purposes : C. 18–early 19 : c. *A New Canting Dict.,* 1725 ; Grose, 1st ed. Cf. *flogging,* n., q.v.

Flogging Joey. Captain McCulloch, R.N., founder of the Coast Blockade : nautical : early C. 19. Bowen. He was a severe disciplinarian.

*flogging-stake. A whipping-post : late C. 17–19 c. until late C. 18, then low. B.E.

flogster. A person addicted to flogging as a punishment : coll. : C. 19–20 ; ob. A naval nickname for William IV when Duke of Clarence.

flooence is entirely unnecessary for *fluence,* q.v.

floor. That which nonplusses or discomfits one : ca. 1840–1920 ; coll. (O.E.D.)—2. A miscalculation : coll. : ca. 1845–1910. The former ex *floor,* v., 1 ; the latter, which has a corresponding but very rare v.i., is influenced by *flaw.*—3. As in *first-floor,* q.v.— 4. The ground outside a house : South African Midlands coll. (— 1913). Pettman. Cf. :—5. The ground ; e.g. *put on the floor,* to fail to hold (a catch) : cricket coll. : 1903 (O.E.D. Sup.).

floor, v. (Coll.) To vanquish, silence, or nonplus, esp. in an argument (— 1835). L. Oliphant, 1870, ' I floor all opposition.'—2. To drink ; ' get

outside of ' (— 1851) ; ob.—3. (Of an examiner) to plough : ca. 1840–1910.—4. (Also university) answer every question of ; reply brilliantly to (an examiner) : from ca. 1850 ; ob. Prob. ex sense 5. : —To do thoroughly ; complete, finish : 1836. (S.O.D.)—6. See **floored,** 2.—7. See ibid, 3.

floor, have or **hold the.** To be speaking ; esp. too much or to another's displeasure : coll. : froⅬ ca. 1850. Ex S.E., orig. political sense.

*floor, on the. Penniless : c. (— 1933). Charles E. Leach. Prob. ex boxing.

floor one's licks. To ' shine ' ; do unusually well : low : ca. 1840–1900.

floor the odds. (Gen. of a horse) to win despite heavy odds : the turf (— 1882). *The Daily Telegraph,* Nov. 16, 1882, ' The odds were . . . floored from an unexpected quarter.'

floored, ppl. adj. Senses as in *to floor,* q.v.—2. Dead drunk : from ca. 1810. Vaux.—3. Among painters : hung low at an exhibition, whether exhibit or exhibitor : from ca. 1860. H., 3rd ed. Opp. *skied,* q.v.

floorer. A knockdown blow (cf. *auctioneer*) : pugilistic (— 1819), > gen. ca. 1860.—2. Hence, unpleasant news, decisive argument or retort ; a notable check : from the 1830's.—3. In universities and schools : a question or a paper too difficult to answer : from ca. 1850.—4. In skittles, a ball that knocks down all the pins : from ca. 1840.—5. In c. : a thief that in assisting a man that he has tripped robs him : 1795 (O.E.D.).

floorer, first-, second-, third-. One who rooms on the first, second, third floor : lodging-houses' (— 1887). Baumann.

flooring. Vbl.n., in senses of *to floor,* q.v., but esp. among pugilists (— 1819). Tom Moore.

flop. The act or sound of a heavy or a clumsy fall ; a blow : late C. 17–20 coll. when not dial.— 2. Hair worn low down over the forehead by women: low London : 1881–ca. 1900. Ware.—3. A failure, e.g. of a book, a play, a project : from ca. 1890 : coll. >, by 1930, S.E. F. & H.—4. Hence, a ' soft ' person ; a spineless, toneless one : 1909, H. G. Wells (O.E.D. Sup.).

flop, v.t. In boxing : to knock down (— 1888) ; ob.—2. In gen. : v.i., to swing loosely and heavily : coll. ; C. 17–20.—3. V.i., move heavily, clumsily or with a bump : late C. 17–20 : coll.—4. V.t., throw with flopping suddenness : coll. ; from ca. 1820.— 5. To move, esp. wings, heavily up and down : coll. (— 1860). (S.O.D.)—6. (Of a book, play, plan) to fail : from ca. 1918 : s. now verging on coll. Cf. *flop,* n., 3.—7. To sleep : tramps' c. : C. 20. W. A. Gape, *Half a Million Tramps,* 1936. Ex S.E. *flop down.*

flop, adv. With a heavy or a clumsy fall. Often expletively. Coll. : from ca. 1725. J. Payn, ' She'll roll down, papa, and come flop.' (O.E.D.)

flop, do a. To sit or fall down : from ca. 1870.— 2. To lie down to a man : low : from ca. 1875. Contrast *flop a judy,* to cause a woman to lie ready for the sexual act : low : from ca. 1875.

flop about. To lie about, lazily and either lethargically or languorously : coll. : from ca. 1870.

flop in. To effect intromission : low : latter C. 19 (? C. 20).

flop on, e.g. **the gills.** A blow on the (e.g.) mouth : low coll. : from mid-C. 19.

flop out, v. Of a bather leaving the water with noisy awkwardness : coll. : from ca. 1870.—2. To knock down with a blow, cause to fall in a heap : coll. (— 1923). Manchon. Cf. *flop*, v., 1.

flop over, v.i. To turn heavily : coll. : from ca. 1860.

flop round. To loaf about : from ca. 1865 : coll.

flop-whop. Onomatopœic for a 'flopping' impact : coll. (— 1887). Baumann.

flopper. A weak or 'floppy' person : coll. (— 1923). Manchon. Cf. :

floppy. Apt to flop (see **flop**, v., intransitive senses) : coll. : 1858 (S.O.D.). Hence, n., *floppiness* and adv., *floppily*.—2. Hence, (very) drunk : low (— 1923). Manchon.

Floras. 'Preferred converted ordinary' shares in the Caledonian Railway : Stock Exchange (— 1895). A. J. Wilson, *Stock Exchange Glossary*. On *Coras*, q.v.

florence. A girl that has been tousled and ruffled : late C. 17–early 19 : coll. B.E. Cf. the ob. Northants *florence* (to go about untidily dressed), by which the Christian name, as a type, was prob. influenced.

Florrie Ford. A motor-car or -lorry : military : G.W. Ex *Ford* car + Miss *Florrie Forde*, the actress. (F. & Gibbons.)

flossification (— 1828) is incorrect for *florification*. O.E.D.

floster. A drink of sherry, soda-water, lemon, ice, and several other ingredients : from ca. 1860 ; ob. by 1900, † by 1924.

flouch or **floush**, **fall** or **go**. To collapse ; sag : coll. (— 1819) ; ob. Tom Moore, 'Georgy went floush, and his backers looked shy.' Ex dial. ; ultimately echoic. O.E.D.

flounce. 'The thick line of black paint put on the edge of the lower eyelid to enhance the effect of the eye itself' : theatrical (1854) soon > Society ; † by 1920. Ware.

*flounder. The corpse of a drowned man : c. : ca. 1870–1930. Barrère & Leland ; Manchon. Cf. *dab* in the same sense and status.

flounder, v. To sell and re-purchase a stock, esp. when at a loss on each occasion : Stock Exchange (— 1889). More gen. as *floundering*, vbl.n.

flounder and dab. A cab : rhyming s. (— 1857) ; ob. 'Ducange Anglicus.'

flourish. To have money, esp. much, in one's pocket : coll. Ex the semi-coll. sense, to be well off, itself ex the M.E.–C. 20 S.E. sense, to thrive.

flourish, take a. (Of the man) to have a hasty coïtion : mid C.18–19 low or low coll. Grose, 2nd ed.

flourish it. (Of either sex) to expose the person : low coll : mid-C. 19–20.

flourishing. Flourishingly. Often in reply to 'How are you (getting along) ?' Coll. : C. 19–20.

floury baker. A kind of locust : Australian children's : C. 20. Cf. *double-drummer*.

flous, gen. v.i. To deceive, cheat, shirk to the direct disadvantage of another : South African coll. (— 1913). Ex Dutch : cf. Ger. *Flause*, deceit, pretence. Pettman.

floush, fall or **go**. See **flouch**.

flower, flower of chivalry, flower-pot. The female pudend : low : C. 19–20. The second term puns the etymological meaning of its third vocable.

flower-fancier. A whoremaster : whoremonger : low : C. 19–20 ; ob.

flowers. Abbr. *monthly flowers*, the menstrual flux : C. 15–20 : until ca. 1840, S.E. ; then coll.

Ex Fr. *fleurs* = *flueurs* = L. *fluor* ex *fluere*, to flow (W.).

flowers !, say it with. A c.p. (from ca. 1925 ; ex U.S.) = send flowers ! ; also, say it nicely ! (Collinson.)

*flowery. Lodging ; entertainment : c. and Parlyaree : from ca. 1850 ; ob. H., 1st ed. Prob. ex It. via Lingua Franca.—2. Hence, a prison-cell : c. : C. 20.

flowery dell. A (prison-)cell : rhyming s. : C. 20. P. P., *Rhyming Slang*, 1932.

flowery language. A jocularly euphemistic coll. for obscenity and for blasphemy : from before 1893.

flowing hope. A forlorn hope : naval and military : ca. 1850–1914. Smyth. Orig. a sol.

'flu, flu ; occ. **flue**. Influenza : coll., gen. with *the* : from late 1830's. Southey, 1839, ' I've had a pretty fair share of the flue.' (O.E.D.)

flue. The Recorder, esp. of London : ca. 1750–1900. ? orig. c. Corruption of *flute*, 1.—2. As fluff, it is, despite F. & H., not 'unconventional '.— 3. See **flu**.—4. See **flue, in**, and the following entry.

flue, v. To put in pawn : low : from ca. 1860. Ex *in* or *up the flue*.

flue, be up one's. To be awkward for a person, as in ' That's up your flue ' : from ca. 1870 ; ob.

flue, in or **up the**. Pawned : from ca. 1820. Cf. *up the spout*, q.v. *Flue* is itself s. for the spout in a pawnbroker's shop.

flue or **spout, up the**. As in preceding entry.— 2. Collapsed, physically or mentally ; dead : low : ca. 1850–1910.

*flue-faker. A chimney-sweep : c. or low s. : ca. 1810–1900. Vaux.—2. A low sporting man : ca. 1855–1914. Because he bets on the great *sweeps* (H., 1859).

flue-scraper. A chimney-sweep : ca. 1830–1910. Suggested by *flue-faker*.

fluence (or **'fluence), the**. Delicate or subtle influence : Australians' and New Zealanders' : from ca. 1930. Ex the next, q.v. Neville Cardus, *Good Days*, 1934, ' Grimmett's fingers are always light and wondrously tactile ; when he passes the salt at dinner he imparts the "fluence".'

fluence on, put the. To persuade : mostly Australian and New Zealand : from ca. 1910. Abbr. *influence* and ex hypnotism, the orig. Australian sense, dating from ca. 1900 and ob. by 1924, being coll. : to hypnotise.—3. Cf. the Cockney sense of ca. 1850–85 : to 'attract, subdue, overcome by mental force ' (Ware).

flues, overheat one's. To get drunk : jocular (— 1923). Manchon. Lit., set the chimney on fire.

fluff, occ. **fluffings**. Short change given by clerks : railway : from ca. 1870. H., 5th ed. Cf. *menavelings*.—2. ' Lines ' imperfectly learned and delivered : theatrical : from ca. 1880. W. Archer, ' But even as seen through a cloud of fluff the burlesque is irresistibly amusing.'—Cf. **Major McFluffer**, q.v.—3. The female pubic hair : low : C. 19–20.—4. See **fluff, little bit of**.—5. A tip (gratuity) : transport-workers' : ca. 1890–1920. Prob. ex sense 1. Cf. *drop*, last sense.—6. Diffusely worded contribution to a newspaper : journalists' coll. : late C. 19–20. Cf. S.E. *woolly*.

fluff, v. To give short change : railways' : from ca. 1870. H., 5th ed.—2. Disconcert, nonplus, ' floor ' : from ca. 1860. Cf. *fluff in*, q.v.—3. To forget one's part : theatrical : from ca. 1880. George Moore, in the *Mummer's Wife*, 1885.—4. See **fluff it !**—5. (Of porters) when off duty, to hang about in the hope of tips : railwaymen's (— 1923). Manchon. Cf. sense 1.—6. (V.i.) To boast ; to tell lies : military : C. 20. F. & Gibbons. Perhaps ex sense 3.

fluff, do a. To forget one's part : theatrical : from ca. 1870.

fluff, little bit of. A girl : mostly Australian : C. 20. O.E.D. records it at 1903 ; C. J. Dennis, 1916. ? cf. *fluff,* n., 3.

fluff in. To deceive (a person) ' by smooth modes ' : lower classes ' (— 1909). Ware. Prob. ex *fluff,* v., 2.

fluff in the pan. A failure : from ca. 1860 : coll. : ex Scottish.

fluff it ! Go away ! Take it away ! (— 1859). Ob. H., 1st ed.

fluffer. A drunkard : from ca. 1880. Cf. *fluffiness.*—2. A player apt to forget his part : theatrical : from ca. 1880. See **fluff,** v.—3. A term of contempt : ' old ', says F. & H. in 1893. Untraced.

fluffing ; fluffings. The practice of, and the proceeds from, giving short change : railways ' : from ca. 1870. See **fluff,** n., 1, and v., 1.

fluffiness. Drunkenness : from ca. 1885. *Fun,* Aug. 4, 1886.—2. A tendency to forget words : theatrical : from ca. 1885.

fluffy. Of uncertain memory : theatrical : from ca. 1880. Ex *fluff,* n., 2. See also **Major McFluffer.** —2. Unsteady ; stupidly drunk : from ca. 1885.

fluke. A stroke of luck : coll. : from ca. 1860. Ex billiards. H., 2nd ed. ; Black, 1873, ' It is a happy fluke.'—2. An easy dupe, a ' flat ' : ca. 1800–30. Ex *fluke,* a flat fish.

fluke, v. To do a thing (well) by accident : coll. : from ca. 1880. Hence, vbl.n. and adj., *fluking.* Ex billiards.—2. To shirk : Eton (— 1864).

flukes, peak or **turn the.** To go to bed : nautical : mid-C. 19–20. Ex a whale's peaking the flukes, i.e. going under. O.E.D.

fluk(e)y ; gen. **flukie.** A whale : nautical coll. : from ca. 1920. (O.E.D. Sup.) Ex a whale's *flukes.*

fluk(e)y, adj. Chancy, uncertain ; achieved less by good management than by good luck : coll. : from ca. 1880. Hence, *flukiness,* abounding in flukes, and adv. *flukily.*

flumdiddle. A coll. variant (— 1923) of *flummery,* q.v. Manchon. I.e. *flummery* influenced by *diddle.*

flummergast, gen. as ppl. adj. To astound or confound : coll. (— 1849) ; ob. Variation of *flabbergast,* q.v.

flummery. Flattery ; polite nonsense : from ca. 1750 : coll. ; after ca. 1830, S.E. Ex the lit. sense, ' oatmeal and water boiled to a jelly ', not ' over-nourishing ', Grose, 1st ed. Cf. *balderdash.*

flummocks (rare), **flummox, flummux.** To perplex, abash, silence ; victimise, ' best ' ; disappoint, dodge, elude : 1837 : Dickens. Variant, † *conflummox.* Ex dial. Cf. *flabbergast.*—2. Hence, to confuse another player : theatrical : from ca. 1880.

flummocky. In bad taste : coll. (— 1891). *Blackwood's,* March 1891. Ex preceding.

flummox. A failure : 1857, ' Ducange Anglicus ' ; ob. Ex :

flummox, v. See **flummocks.**

flummox by the lip, to talk down ; vanquish in a slanging match : low : from ca. 1860 ; ob.

flummoxed. Silenced ; disappointed, outwitted ; spoilt ; ruined ; drunk ; sent to or sure of a month

in prison (c. only) : from the 1850's. H., 1st ed. ; *Punch,* Aug. 30, 1890, ' I'm fair flummoxed.' Ppl. adj. ex *flummox,* see **flummocks.** W hence :

*flummut. A month in prison : vagrants' c. (— 1851). Mayhew equates it to the beggars' sign. See **flummoxed.**

flummux, flummuxed. See **flummocks, flummoxed.**

flump. An abrupt or heavy fall, making a dull noise ; the noise : late C. 18–20 (ob.) coll. Cf. :

flump, v. To fall, or be set down, violently, thumpingly, or hurriedly : coll. : v.i., 1816 ; v.t., 1830 ; as adv., 1790. (S.O.D.) Thackeray, ' Chairs were flumped down on the floor.' ? a blend of *flop* and *thump* (W.).

flump, adv. With a ' flump ' : coll. : late C. 18–20. Grose's *Provincial Glossary.*

flunkey. A parasite, a toady : coll. : from ca. 1855 ; in C. 20, S.E. Ex sense, a man-servant esp. if in livery.—2. A ship's steward : nautical (— 1883) ; ob. W. Clark Russell.—3. A ward-room attendant : naval : from ca. 1880. Bowen.

flunkey out of collar. A footman out of work : 1857, ' Ducange Anglicus ' ; ob.

flurry one's milk. To be angry, perturbed, worried : low coll. : from ca. 1820 ; ob. Cf. Fr. *se faire du mauvais sang.*

flurryment. Confusion, bustle ; excitement, agitation : low coll. (— 1848). Pleonastic on *flurry,* ? after *flusterment.*

flush, v.t. To whip : coll. : mid-C. 19–20 ; ob. H., 3rd ed. Hence *flushed on the horse,* privately whipped in gaol : mid-C. 19–20, ob. : prob. c. Perhaps ex *flush,* to cleanse, or to make red.

*flush, adj., with *of.* Having plenty of money, esp. temporarily : C. 17–20. In C. 17, esp. as *flush in the pocket* or *fob,* c. ; in C. 18, low > gen. ; in C. 19–20, S.E. Dekker ; Trollope, ' Long before that time I shall be flush enough.' Cf. S.E. *flush of success* and *flush,* level, hence full.—2. Tipsy : C. 19–20 ; ob. Ex *flush,* level with, i.e. full to, the top.

flush, adv. Full ; directly : pugilistic, of a blow (— 1888). Ex C. 18 S.E.

flush a wild duck. To single out a woman for amorous attentions : low : C. 19–20 ; ob. Ex shooting ; *flush* = to cause to take wing.

flush hit. A clean hit ; a punch fair on the mark : pugilism : ca. 1810–1920 ; s. > j. by 1900.

flush on one, come. To meet a person suddenly, unexpectedly : coll. > S.E. : C. 17–20.

*flushed on the horse. See **flush,** v.

flusteration. A variant of *flustration.* Baumann.

flusticate. To confuse : C. 19–20 (ob.) : low coll. or sol. By *complicate* out of *fluster.*

flustrate. To confuse ; excite. (Gen. in past ppl. passive.) Sol. : C. 18–20 ; ob. *The Spectator,* (No. 493,) 1712, ' We were coming down Essex Street one night a little flustrated.' Ex *fluster.* Like next, occ. jocular.

flustration. Confusion, bustle ; excitement, flurry : sol., perhaps orig. nautical : from ca. 1740 ; ob. Smollett, ' Being I was in such a flustration ' ; Mortimer Collins. In C. 19–20, also *flusteration.*

flute. (Cf. *flue,* n.) A city recorder, esp. of London : ca. 1690–1820 : prob. c. B.E.—2. The male member : C. 18–19 : low. Variants *living flute, one-holed f., silent f.* Cf. the Romany *haboia* (English *hautboy*) in same sense. (Sampson.)—3. A pistol : ca. 1840–1910. Lover in *Handy Andy* (E.D.D., Sup.). Ex shape and ' tune '.

[flutist, flautist. See Fowler, who defends the former.]

flutter. A short visit or trip, esp. a joyous, informal one : coll. : 1857 (O.E.D.).—2. A venture, an attempt ; a spree ; a gamble : from ca. 1870. H., 5th ed. ; *The Saturday Review*, Feb. 1, 1890, ' Fond of a little flutter '.—3. The spinning of a coin : from ca. 1872.—4. See **flutter, have had a.** All senses refer to the flutter of excitement ; 3 also to the fluttering movement.

flutter. V.i., to gamble ; from ca. 1870. Cf. sense 3.—2. Also, to indulge in pleasure : from ca. 1880.—3. V.t., to spin (a coin), as in *flutter a brown* : from ca. 1870 ; ob. H., 5th ed.

flutter, be on the. To be on the spree ; sexually adept : low : ca. 1875. Cf. :

flutter, do or **have a.** To have a small gamble ; go on the spree ; (of either sex) to have sexual intercourse, for pleasure rather than passion : from ca. 1870 : s. >, by 1920, coll.

flutter !, give her a. Toss a or the coin ! C. 20.

flutter, have had a. To have had sexual experience ; to have lost one's virginity : low : from ca. 1875.

flutter a judy. To pursue a girl ; to possess one : low : from ca. 1850.

flutter a skirt. To be a (street-walking) harlot : low : from ca. 1850.

flutter for, have a. To try hard to do, get, etc. : coll. : (— 1873).

flutter (or **fret**) **one's kidneys.** To agitate ; greatly annoy : low : from ca. 1860. Cf. *flurry one's milk.*

flutter the ribbons. To drive (horses) : coll. : ca. 1860–1910.

flux. To cozen, cheat, outwit : late C. 18–early 19. Grose, 1st ed. Ex S.E. sense, to subject to a flux.

Fly. Admiral Martin, Commander-in-Chief of the Mediterranean Fleet : naval : early C. 20. Ex his fondness for tactical evolutions. Bowen.

fly. A printer's devil : late C. 17–mid-19 : printers'. Ex *fly* = a familiar spirit, a devil.— 2. A waggon : c. : late C. 18–early 19. All other vehicle senses are S.E. Grose, 2nd ed.—3. The act of spinning a coin : from ca. 1870 ; cf. *flutter*, n., 2. —4. A policeman : c. > low, (— 1857). Ob., except as a detective.—5. A customer : trade : ca. 1840–1910.—6. A trick, ' dodge ' : ca. 1860–1910. (O.E.D.)—7. **the fly** (or **Fly**). A locality infested by the tsetse insect : South African coll. : 1868, James Chapman, *Travels in South Africa*. (Pettman.)—8. A blow, punch : boxing (— 1887) ; ob. Baumann.

fly, v. To give way ; become damaged : pugilism (— 1865) ; ob.—2. To toss ; raise (e.g. a window) : c. (— 1857).—3. Send quickly, hastily : coll. : ca. 1845–1900. Darwin. O.E.D.—4. See **fly a kite** or **tile** ; **fly the mags.**—5. V.t., (of a horse) to outdistance easily : sporting (— 1887). Baumann.

fly, adj. Artful, knowing ; shrewdly aware : low (? orig. c.) : from ca. 1810. In Scots (*flee*), however, as early as 1724 (E.D.D.). Vaux. Variants *a-fly, flymy, fly to the game, fly to what's what*. Perhaps ex the difficulty of catching a fly, more prob. cognate with *fledge, fledged*, as Sewel, 1766, indicates (W.) ; though Bee's assertion that it is a corruption of *fla*, abbr. *flash*, is, considering the devices of c., not to be sneered at.—2. Dextrous : from ca. 1834 : low. Ainsworth.—3. (Of women) wanton : low :

from ca. 1880. Ex senses 1 and 2. Cf. U.S. *fly dame*, a harlot (— 1888).

fly, let. V.t., to hit out : coll. (— 1859). *Punch*, July 25, 1859, ' Lord Lyndhurst let fly and caught him . . . an extremely neat one on the conk.'

fly, make the fur or **feathers.** To attack successfully (*one's* for *the*) ; to quarrel noisily : coll. : orig. (1825), U.S. ; anglicised ca. 1860.

fly, not to rise to that. Not to ' bite ', i.e. not to believe : coll. : from ca. 1870 ; ob.

fly, off the. Laid up ; doing nothing ; retired, esp. from the giving or the pursuit of pleasure : low : from ca. 1850.

fly, on the. Off work ; walking the streets for fun ; on the spree : low : from ca. 1850.—2. In c., in motion : from ca. 1860. Cf. U.S. sense, in the air (1872 : Thornton).—3. Shrewdly, cunningly, secretly : low (— 1923). Manchon.

***fly, beg on the.** To beg from persons as they pass : c. (— 1861). Mayhew. Cf. *fly, on the*, 2.

***fly, take on the,** v.t. To beg from in the streets : c. : from ca. 1845 ; ob. Cf. *beg on the fly*, above.

fly a, the, kite. To raise money by means of accommodation bills : from ca. 1808. Whence *fly a bill*, to gain time by giving a bill (1860, O.E.D.).— 2. Merely to raise money (— 1880). In Anglo-Irish banks, it = to cash a cheque against non-existent funds : C. 20. Also *cash a dog, pay the bearer.*— 3. In c., to depart by the window (— 1860) : esp. from low lodging-houses. H., 2nd ed.—4. With *at*, to set one's cap at (— 1863). Henry Kingsley.— 5. (Gen. *fly the kite*.) To seek publicity : Society : from the 1890's ; ob. Ware.—6. To test public opinion by tentative measures : copy-writers' coll. : from ca. 1926. Cf. sense 2.

fly a tile. To knock off a man's hat : Stock Exchange : ca. 1820–1900.

fly-away. A tricycle : coll. (— 1887) ; ob. by 1905, † by 1920. Baumann.

fly-balance ; shotter ; sighter. A column of figures added correctly at the first attempt : bank-clerks' : C. 20 : resp. coll., now verging on j. ; s. ; s. Obviously *shotter* derives ex *at the first shot* ; *sighter* ex rifle-shooting.

fly-blow. A bastard : coll. (— 1875) ; ob. ? corruption of *by-blow*.

fly-blown. Tipsy : from ca. 1875 ; ob.—2. Penniless : Australian (— 1889).—3. Exhausted : low : from ca. 1880.—4. Devirginated ; also, suspected of venereal disease : low : from ca. 1885.

fly blue paper. To issue a summons : legal : from ca. 1890 ; slightly ob.

fly-boy. A variant of *fly*, n., 1. H., 5th ed.— 2. Gen. in pl., ' English " refugees " who crossed over to Ireland to evade conscription ' : Anglo-Irish pejorative, esp. at Dublin : G.W. F. & Gibbons. Sarcastic ex *fly*, adj., 1, with a pun on *fly*, to flee.

fly-by-night. A sedan chair on wheels : coll. ; *temp.*, the Regency.—2. A defaulting debtor ; his defaulting : coll. : 1823, ' Jon Bee '.—3. A harlot : from ca. 1860.—4. The female pudend : C. 19–20 low.—5. One who frequently moves about at night, e.g. a spreester : from ca. 1865.—6. A term of contempt for a woman : coll. : C. 18–early 19. Grose, 3rd ed. Ex witches broom-flying by night.

fly-cage. The female pudend : C. 19–20 low.

fly-catcher. The same : id.—2. An open-mouthed ignorant person : coll. : from ca. 1820.— 3. A fast aeroplane, officially a ' fleet-fighter ' : military (esp. airmen's) : 1915. F. & Gibbons.

*fly cop. A detective : U.S. >, by 1889, English c. Barrère & Leland ; Ware. Lit., ' a clever policeman '. Ex *fly*, adj., 1.

fly-disperser soup. Oxtail soup : from ca. 1860–1910.

fly-flapped. Whipped in the stocks or at the cart's tail : ca. 1785–1830. Grose, 2nd ed. Ex the C. 17–18 S.E. *fly-flap*, to beat.

fly-flapper. A heavy bludgeon : from ca. 1840 ; ob.

fly flat. A would-be expert : the turf : ca. 1885–1915. Barrère & Leland.

fly high or rather high. To get or to be drunk : low : from ca. 1860.—2. To keep good company and fine state ; venture for big stakes : coll. > S.E. : C. 19–20.

fly in a tar-box (in C. 19–20, glue-pot), like a. Nervously excited : coll. (— 1659) ; the former, ob. by 1800, † by 1900. Howell, 1659. (Apperson.)

fly laugh, 'twould make a. Very amusing : (? C. 17–) C. 18 coll. Apperson.

fly loo. See Kentucky loo.

fly low. To be modest and retiring : from ca. 1835 : coll., > S.E. by 1895.—2. In c., to hide from justice : ca. 1870–1920.

*fly man. An expert thief : c. : C. 20. E.g. in Edgar Wallace's *The Squeaker*, 1927.—2. A professional criminal : Glasgow c. : from ca. 1919. MacArthur & Long, *No Mean City*, 1935.

fly member. A very shrewd, sharp person : low (— 1909). Ware.

fly my kite. A light : rhyming s. (— 1857). ' Ducange Anglicus.'

fly off the handle. To lose one's temper : orig. (1825), U.S. ; anglicised ca. 1860. Also (— 1931), *fly off the deep end*, evidently influenced by *go (in) off the deep end* : Lyell.

fly on a wheel, break or crush a. To make much fuss about very little (— 1859) : coll. > S.E. by 1900.

fly on the wheel, the. One who considers himself very important : coll. > S.E. : late C. 16–20 ; ob. From Æsop's fable.

fly out. To grow angry ; to scold : C. 17–20 ; coll., > S.E. by 1700. Chapman, *The Spectator*, Thackeray.

*fly-paper, be on the. To be justiciable under the Prevention of Crimes Act : c. : from ca. 1912. James Curtis, *The Gilt Kid*, 1936. Ex :

*Fly Paper Act, the. The Prevention of Crimes Act (1909) : c. : 1910. Charles E. Leach. Cf. *Cat and Mouse Act*.

fly-pitch ; fly-pitcher. A cheapjack's ' pitch ' ; a cheapjack selling from a pitch : showmen's : C. 20. P. Allingham, in *The Evening News*, July 9, 1934.

fly-rink. A bald head : lower classes' : 1875 ; ob. Ware.

fly-slicer. A cavalryman : C. 19–20 (ob.) ; orig. late C. 18), a Life Guardsman (Grose, 1st ed.). Ex the brushing-away of flies with a sword.

fly-stuck (possibly S.E.) ; stuck (coll.). Bitten by the tsetse : South African : from ca. 1880 and esp. among hunters, as F. C. Selous, who uses both forms, makes clear in *A Hunter's Wanderings in Africa*, 1881. (Pettman.)

fly the blue pigeon. To steal lead from roofs : see blue pigeon : C. 18–19 c.

fly the flag. (Of harlots) to walk the streets : low : from ca. 1840.—2. To have the monthly flux : low : from ca. 1850.

fly the kite. See fly a kite.

*fly the mags. To gamble ; properly, by throwing up halfpence : c. (— 1812) >, by 1850, low. Vaux.

fly the pigeons. See pigeons, fly the.

fly to. See fly, adj., 1. Cf. *down to, up to, flash to*.

fly-trap. The mouth : from ca. 1790. Cf. *fly-catcher*, q.v.—2. The female pudend : C. 19 low. Cf. *fly-cage* and *-catcher*.—3. (Gen. pl.). A wire entanglement : military : 1915 ; ob. G. H. McKnight, *English Words*, 1923.

fly with, not a feather to. Penniless ; ruined : coll. : C. 19–20 ; slightly ob.

flyer. See flier.—2. (Gen. in pl.) A shoe : c. : late C. 17–18. B.E. In C. 19 low s., e.g. in Mayhew, *flyer* is an unwelted shoe.—3. In Winchester football, a half-volley : from ca. 1850.—4. A swift kangaroo : Australian coll. (— 1848) >, by 1890, S.E. O.E.D. (Sup.) ; Morris.—5. A breeder of homing pigeons : sporting coll. : mid-C. 19–20. Ware.—6. A speculation (in stocks and shares) : mostly Stock Exchange : U.S. (1848) >, by 1910, anglicised : coll. O.E.D. ; Manchon.—7. A smart, lively, very attractive person, esp. of a pretty girl : coll. : 1930, Temple Thurston (O.E.D. Sup.).—8. the Flyers. The Flying Squad : c. : from ca. 1920. E.g. in Edgar Wallace's *The Flying Squad*, 1928.—9. See flier, take a.

flying, look as if the devil had shit him or her. To be filthy or deformed : low coll. : C. 19–20 ; ob.

flying-arse-hole. An observer's badge : Air Force : 1915. B. & P. The badge consists of an O with the representation of a wing.

flying bedstead. The open stall (on wheels) of a dealer in old clocks and bric-à-brac : Cockneys' (— 1887). Baumann.—2. An Army bicycle or motor-cycle : military : G.W. (F. & Gibbons.)

Flying Bricklayers. The Royal Mounted Engineers : military : ca. 1880–1902.

*flying camp. A couple, or a gang, of beggars : c. : late C. 17–early 19. B.E. ; Grose, 1st ed., ' Beggars plying in a body at funerals '. Cf. S.E. sense.

*flying caper. An escape from prison : c. (— 1864) ; ob.

*flying-cat. An owl : c. : late C. 17–mid-18. B.E. Cf. Fr. *chat-huant* (O.E.D.).

flying county or country. A district where one can ride fast and safely : hunting : from ca. 1850 ; s. > j. by 1900. Whyte-Melville, ' Leicestershire, Northamptonshire, and other so-called " flying counties " '.

flying dustman. See stiff one.

Flying Dutchman. The London and Exeter express (G.W.R.) : coll. : ca. 1875–1915.—2. ' The Atlantic packet clipper *Dreadnought*. Also known as the *Wild Boat of the Atlantic* ' : nautical : late C. 19. Bowen.

*flying gigger or jigger. A turnpike gate : c. : mid-C. 18–19. Grose, 1st ed.

flying kite. A fancy sail, esp. if temporary : nautical coll. : mid-C. 19–20 ; ob. Bowen.—2. An aeroplane : Air Force coll. : 1914 ; ob. F. & Gibbons.

flying light. (Of a seaman that, when he joined his ship, was) possessed of nothing but the clothes on him : nautical coll. : mid-C. 19–20 ; ob. Bowen.

flying man. In Eton football : a skilful skirmisher (— 1864) ; ob.

flying matinée. A trench raid : military : 1916 ; ob. F. & Gibbons.

flying mess, in a. Hungry and having to mess wherever one can : military (— 1860) ; † by 1915. H., 2nd ed. Ex the difficulty of obtaining a good meal on a forced march.

flying onion. A kind of trench-mortar bomb : military : 1915. B. & P. Contrast *flaming onion.*

Flying P. Line, the. The Laeisz sailing-ships : nautical : mid-C. 19–20 ; ob. Bowen.

flying pasty. Excrement that, wrapped in paper, is thrown over a neighbour's wall : from ca. 1790 ; † by 1893. Grose, 3rd ed.

Flying Pig, the. A fast freight train bringing bacon to London : railwaymen's : from ca. 1920. *The Daily Telegraph,* Aug. 15, 1936. Cf. *the Farmer's Boy.*

flying pig. 'A large (9·45 inch) heavy trench-mortar shell' : military coll. : 1915–18. F. & Gibbons. Ex its appearance in the air.

*flying porter. An impostor that gets money by giving, to robbed persons, information that will (prob. not) lead to the arrest of the thieves : c. : late C. 18–19. Grose, 2nd ed.

flying stationer. A hawker of street-ballads, penny histories, etc. : late C. 18–19 : low. Grose, 3rd ed. Ex the fact that such a hawker keeps moving. Cf. the C. 19 *running patterer,* q.v.

flying trapeze. Cheese : rhyming s. : late C. 19–20. B. & P.

flymp. See flimp.—**flyms(e)y.** See flimsy, 1.

flymy. Knowing, artful, roguish ; sprightly ; low (— 1859). H., 1st ed. ; Henley. Ex *fly,* adj., 1, on *slimy.*

flyness. The abstract n. of *fly,* adj., 1 : late C. 19–20.

foal and filly dance. A 'dance to which only very young people . . . are invited' : Society (— 1909) ; ob. Ware. Cf. *filly and foal.*

foaled. Thrown from one's horse : hunting : C. 19–20 ; ob.—2. Manchon asserts that it = *fogged,* q.v. ; I doubt the validity of this.

*fob. A trick, cheat, swindle : orig. (1622), prob. S.E. ; but in late C. 17, c. ; in C. 18 low ; in C. 19, gen. s., almost coll. ; in C. 20, †. Ex M.E. *fob,* an impostor, ex Fr. *fo(u)rbe.*—2. A breeches or a watch pocket : in C. 17, c. or low ; C. 18, coll. ; C. 19, recognised ; C. 20, ob. The O.E.D. takes a rather different view of its status. 'Hudibras' Butler. Ex Ger. Variant, *fub.*

fob, v. To pocket : C. 19–20, ob. ; coll. Cf. *pocket,* v.—2. To cheat, rob ; procure dishonestly : C. 17–20 ; ob. Congreve ; Wolcot, 'To use a cant [i.e. fashionable s.] phrase, we've been finely fobb'd.' Cf. *fob,* n., 1.—3. To deceive ; trifle with : coll. > S.E. : late C. 16–20 ; ob. Shakespeare. In all senses, an early variant is *fub,* q.v.

*fob, gut a. To pick a pocket : low, ? c. : ca. 1815–90. Moore, 1819, 'Diddling your subjects, and gutting their fobs '.

fob of, fob out of. To cheat or deprive illicitly (a person) of (a thing) : coll. : from ca. 1840, 1850 resp. O.E.D. (Sup.). An extension of *fob,* v., 2.

fob off. To put off, or ignore, contemptuously, callously, unfairly, dishonestly ; deceive in any of these ways. (Variant *fub off.*) Coll. > S.E. : late C. 16–20 ; ob. Shakespeare, 'You must not think to fob off our disgrace with a tale.'

fob out of. See fob of.

fobus. A pejorative, gen. as term of address : C. 17–18. Wycherley, 'Ay, you old fobus '. Cf. *fogey,* q.v.—2. The *pudendum muliebre* : low (— 1893) ; ob.

fodder. Abbr. *bum-fodder,* q.v. : C. 19–20 low, verging on coll.

foei(-tock). An interjection of surprise, sorrow, sympathy : South African coll. : late C. 19–20. Ex Dutch *foei,* for shame !, and *tock,* why, to be sure ! Pettman.

fœtus, tap the. To procure abortion : medical (— 1893). By the way, *fœtus* should be *fetus,* as W. points out : mistaken pedantry (cf. *Welsh rarebit*).

*fog. Smoke ; occ. a smoke : c. : late C. 17–early 19. Grose, 1st ed. ? abbr. *fogus,* q.v.

fog, v. To smoke a pipe : either low s. or c. : C. 18–early 19.—2. Mystify, perplex ; occ. to obscure : coll. (orig. S.E.) : from ca. 1815. *The Daily Telegraph,* Sept. 29, 1883, ' We turns what we say into tangle talk so as to fog them.'—3. V.i., to set fog-signals along the line : railwaymen's : ca. 1885–1920. O.E.D.

fog-bound. Tipsy : C. 20. A. P. Herbert, *Holy Deadlock,* 1934, ' " Was I a bit tiddly last night ? " " Tiddly ? " " Tiddly. Skew-whiff. Fog-bound." '

fog-dog. The lower part of a rainbow : Newfoundland (esp. nautical) : mid-C. 19–20. Bowen. Cf. *stubb.*

fog in. To see (a place) by chance, to achieve (a purpose) by accident : Society (— 1909) ; virtually †. Ware.

fog(e)y ; occ. **fogay, foggi(e) ; fogram,** q.v. An invalid or, later, a garrison soldier or, derivatively, sailor : ? Scottish military : 1780. Grose, 1785, shows that, even then, *old* gen. preceded it. Ca. 1850, the sense > wholly that of an elderly person ; an old-fashioned, occ. an eccentric, person : a meaning it possessed as early as 1780. Thackeray, 1855, ' A grizzled, grim old fogy '. Grose derives ex Fr. *fougueux,* W. ex *foggy,* 2, q.v.—2. Hence, an old maid : low coll. (— 1887). Baumann (' eine alte Schachtel ').—3. Whence *fogyish,* old-fashioned, eccentric (1873),—*fogeydom,* the being a fogey, fogeys as a class (1859),—*fogeyism,* an example of fogeydom, a fogeyish trait (1859) : these three terms, somewhat coll. at first, had > S.E. by 1880.

fogged. Tipsy : from ca. 1840 ; ob. Cf. *foggy,* 1, its imm. origin.—2. Bewildered, puzzled, at a loss : coll. ; from ca. 1850.

fogger. A pettifogging lawyer : coll. (— 1600) > S.E. ; † by 1700. Ex *Fugger,* the merchant-financier family. S.O.D.

foggie. See fogey. This form is recorded for 1812.

foggiest (notion), have not the. To have no idea ; no suspicion. With *of* or *that.* Coll., now verging on S.E. : from ca. 1903. Variant, *faintest* : from ca. 1905 : by 1930, S.E.

fogging, vbl.n. Fumbling through one's part : theatrical : ca. 1885–1915.

foggy. Tipsy ; gen. slightly tipsy : from ca. 1820 ; ob. Cf. *hazy.*—2. Dull, thick-headed : from ca. 1770. Cf. *fogey,* q.v. Ex *foggy,* moss-grown, boggy, thick, murky, ex *fog,* rank grass.

*fogle. A (silk) handkerchief : c. : from ca. 1810 ; ob. *Lex. Bal.* ; Egan ; Dickens in *Oliver Twist.* ' Ger. *vogel,* bird, has been suggested, via " bird's eye wipe ",' W. ; perhaps rather ex It. *foglia,* a pocket ; cf. Fr. *fouille.*—2. Whence *fogle-hunter,* a thief specialising in silk handkerchiefs : from ca. 1820 ; ob. And *fogle-hunting,* occ. *f.-drawing* : from ca. 1820 ; ob. Bee.

fogo. See hogo.

fogram, fogrum. (Cf. *fogey*, q.v.) ' A fusty old man ', Grose 1st ed. : ca. 1775–1850.—2. Liquor ; esp. wine, beer, spirits of inferior quality : nautical (— 1867) ; ob. Smyth ; Bowen.—3. Adj., stupid, old-fashioned : app. earlier than *fogey* : witness e.g. Mme D'Arblay in 1772 and O'Keeffe, in *A Trip to Calais*, 1778, ' Father and mother are but a couple of fogrum old fools,' the *fogrum old* being significant. (O.E.D.)

fogramite. An old-fashioned or eccentric person ; coll. : ca. 1820–1900. Bee.

fogramity. An old-fashioned way or custom : Mme D'Arblay, 1796.—2. Hence, eccentricity.—3. A fogey, q.v. All coll. See preceding entry and *fogey*.

fogrum. See **fogram.**

fogue. To have a strong or objectionable odour : New Zealanders' (— 1935). Perhaps ex *fug*, *fuggy*.

*****fogus.** Tobacco : c. : mid-C. 17–19. Head, Ainsworth. Perhaps *fog*, a mist, + *us* as in *hocus-pocus.*

fogy. See **fogey.**—**fohm.** To form : see **fower** and **stan.**

foie-gras. Pâté de foie gras : coll. : 1818, T. Moore. (O.E.D. Sup.)

*****foil-(or foyl-)cloy.** A pickpocket ; thief ; rogue : c. : late C. 17–early 18. B.E. Cf. *file.*

*****foiler.** A thief : C. 17 (? –18) : c. Anon., *Nicker Nicked.*

*****foin.** A pickpocket : c. : late C. 16–early 17. Greene, 1591.

foin, v.t. and i. To have connexion with a woman : low : late C. 16–17. Ex S.E. sense.

*****foist, foyst, fyst.** A cheat, rogue, sharper, pickpocket : late C. 16–18 c. Greene ; Jonson : ' Prate again, as you like this, you whoreson foist you.'—2. A trick, imposture, swindle : C. 17 low or c.—3. A silent breaking of wind : low coll. : C. 16–early 19. Variants, *fice, fiste, fyce.*

*****foist, foyst, fyst,** v.t. and i. (very frequent as vbl.n.). To pick pockets ; trick, swindle : c. : late C. 16–18. Greene, Dekker, Middleton, Grose.—2. To break wind silently : low coll. : C. 16–early 18.—3. The dicing senses may have begun as c., the same applying to :

*****foister, foyster.** A pickpocket ; swindler : low, ? c. : mid-C. 16–17.

*****foisting.** See **foist,** v., 1.

fokesel, fokesill, foksl, fok'stl. Nautical incorrections of spelling for *fo'c'sle* : C. 19–20. Baumann ; Manchon.

foksl, fok'stl. See **fokesel.**

folks. Coll. if not indeed sol. for *folk*, people (indefinitely), individuals : late C. 18–20. See the quotation at *devil's daughter.* (Even *folk*, in this sense, is, in C. 20, coll., though certainly not sol.)—2. As = parents, family, relatives, it is S.E. though not literary. Cf. the U.S. sense : respectable people. (See esp. Fowler.)

follow. To accompany (a corpse) to the grave ; (also v.i.) to attend the funeral of (a person) : coll. : 1819 (O.E.D. Sup.).

follow-me-lads. Curls or ribbons hanging over the shoulder : coll. (— 1872) ; † by 1925. Contrast Fr. *suivez-moi jeune homme.*

follow the band or **the drum.** ' To belong to the Creed of the majority of a Battalion ' for Church parade : military : C. 20. F. & Gibbons. Contrast *fancy religion*, q.v.

follow your nose !, often with **and you are sure to go straight.** A c.p. (non-cultured) addressed to a person asking the way (— 1854). Other forms, e.g. *and you will be there directly* (C. 17), are earlier, and the phrase is clearly adumbrated in C. 14. (Apperson.)

follower. A female servant's sweetheart or suitor, esp. if he frequents the house : coll. : 1838, Dickens, ' Five servants kept. No man. No followers.'—2. A seaman serving always, if possible, under the one captain : naval coll. : C. 18. Bowen. —3. A young officer doing the same with a view to promotion : id. : id. Ibid.

fool, adj. Silly, foolish ; often a pejorative intensive : C. 13–20 : S.E. till C. 19, then (low) coll. and dial. Esp. in *a, the,* or *that fool thing.* (O.E.D.)

fool around (with). To dally riskily, with one of the opposite sex : v.t. and i. Coll. : from ca. 1880. In U.S., v.t., without *with.*

fool at the end of a stick, a ; a fool at one end and a maggot at the other : mid-C. 18–19 c.p. ' gibes on an angler ', Grose, 2nd ed.

fool-finder. A gen. petty bailiff : ca. 1785–1880. Grose, 3rd ed.

fool-monger. An adventurer, -uress ; swindler ; betting man : coll. : late C. 16–early 18.

fool-sticker. The male member. Occ. *fool-maker.* Low : C. 19–20.

fool-taker, -taking. A sharper, sharping : low coll. : late C. 16–mid-17. Greene, 1592.

fool-trap. A ' fool-monger ', q.v.—2. A stylish harlot.—3. The female pudend : low. All from ca. 1840.

fooleries, the. April-fooling : coll. : prob. from ca. 1880, on *Colinderies* and *Fisheries,* qq.v. Christopher Bush, *The Case of the April Fools,* 1933, ' April the First, and what people are accustomed to call " the fooleries ", sir, actually expire at midday.'

*****foolish,** adj. Of one who pays : harlots' c. : from ca. 1788 : ? ob. Grose, 2nd ed., ' Is he foolish or flash ? '

foolocracy. Government by, or consisting of, fools : jocular coll. : 1832. Sydney Smith.

foolometer. A means whereby to determine the public taste : jocular coll. : 1837, Sydney Smith (O.E.D.). In C. 20, S.E. Cf. S.E. *foolocracy.*

foolosopher, foolosophy. A silly pretender to, pretence of, philosophy : jocular coll. : from ca. 1550. Greene, ' That quaint and mysticall forme of Foolosophie ' (O.E.D.).

fool's father. The pantaloon or ' old un ' : theatrical : ca. 1870–1910.

fool's wedding. A party of women : coll. : from ca. 1875. Cf. *hen party.*

*****foont.** A sovereign : c. (— 1839). Brandon ; H., 1st ed. Ex either Fr. *vingt* or, prob., Ger. *Pfund.*

foot. Feet, as in ' Six foot two ' : coll. : C. 15–20.

foot ! ; or **foot !, foot !** Get out of it !, go away ! : coll. : C. 19–20 ; ob. Ware implies equivalence to Fr. *fous-moi le camp* and remarks that it is ' cast after the respectably dressed person who wanders into strange and doubtful bye-ways '.

foot, know the length of one's. To know a person well ; discover his weakness : coll. > S.E. : late C. 16–early 18. Later, *have* or *get* . . . : slightly ob. Apperson. Prob. orig. a shoemaker's metaphor (W.).

foot !, me or **my.** Rubbish ! ; not at all ! : low : late C. 19–20. C. J. Dennis ; Hugh Walpole, *Vanessa,* 1933, ' " But, Rose, you're wrong . . ."

" Wrong my foot ! you can't kid me." ' Occ. *pig's foot !*

foot a or the bill. To pay ; settle an account : coll. : from ca. 1844. Until ca. 1890, an Americanism.

foot-and-mouth disease. The tendency of golfers to talk at night of the day's exploits : jocular coll. : from 1923 or 1924 : cultured. (Ware, 1909, records that, in Lancashire, the phrase indicates ' swearing followed by kicking '.)

foot-bath. A too full glass : late C. 19–20 ; slightly ob. Ware.

foot in the grave, have one. To be seriously ill, near death ; very old : from ca. 1630 : coll. > S.E. ca. 1850.

foot in(to) it, put one's. To get into trouble ; cause trouble : coll. : from ca. 1790.

foot it. To walk : coll. : from ca. 1840. Cf. Fr. *faire du footing.*—2. To kick, ' hoof ' (q.v.), use one's feet : from ca. 1850 : sporting, esp. football.

foot land-raker. A footpad : C. 16–17 coll. (? jocular). Shakespeare.

foot-licker. A servant ; toady : coll. : C. 17–19. Shakespeare in *The Tempest.*

foot(-)lights, smell the. To come to like theatricals : theatrical coll. : from ca. 1870.

foot-pad. A pedestrian highwayman : orig. (C. 17), c. or low ; C. 18, coll. ; C. 19–20, S.E. Cf. *low pad* and see **pad.** For the vocabulary of footpaddery, see the relevant essay in *Words !*

foot-riding, vbl.n. Wheeling one's machine instead of riding it : cyclists' (— 1887) ; ob. T. Stevens, *Round the World on a Bicycle.*

foot-rot. Fourpenny ale : public-houses' : ca. 1895–1915. Ware. Cf. *rot-gut.*

*foot-scamp. A footpad : C. 18–early 19, low or c. Parker. See **scamp.**

foot-slogger. An infantryman : military coll. : from early 1890's. Cf. *foot-wabbler* and the Fr. equivalents, *pousse-cailloux, piou-piou.*—2. Hence, occ., a pedestrian : coll. : C. 20. The v., *foot-slog,* though likewise coll. (C. 20), is seldom used.—3. A policeman on his beat : Australian : from ca. 1920.

foot the bill. See **foot a bill.**

foot up. To ' total ' at the foot of a bill : coll. : ex U.S. (1840), anglicised ca. 1860. But as *foot* in S.E. for centuries before.

foot-wabbler, -wobbler. An infantryman : 1785, Grose ; ob. by 1860 : military. Cf. *mud-crusher* and *foot-slogger.* (Grose is notable on early military s.)

foot-walk (it). To travel on foot : Australian coll. (—1935).

football. A British 60-pound trench-mortar shell : military coll. : 1915–18. F. & Gibbons. (It was spherical.)

footer. Football : orig. university s. : from ca. 1880. See ' **Oxford -er, the** '.—2. Ca. 1885–1905, a player of Rugby football : universities'.—3. One who potters, ' messes ' about : s. when not dial. : from ca. 1750. It has a corresponding v. and vbl.n. : variant spelling *fouter (ing).* See Grose, P., at *forty.*

footing. Money paid, on beginning a new job, to one's fellow-workers : in C. 18, coll. ; but thereafter, S.E. Cf. *chummage.*

footle. Nonsense ; twaddle : from ca. 1893. Ex :

footle, v. To dawdle, potter, trifle about ; act or talk foolishly ; coll. : from ca. 1890 ; slightly ob.

By *futile* out of dial. *footer, fouter* (ex Fr. *foutre*), to trifle. F. Anstey in *Voces Populi.* (O.E.D.)

footler. One who ' footles ' : coll. : C. 20. Ex preceding.

footless stocking without a leg, a. Nothing : Anglo-Irish coll. (— 1909). Ware.

footlight favourite. A chorister that thrusts herself forward : theatrical coll. (— 1935).

footling. Insignificant ; trivial ; pettily fussy : coll. : from ca. 1893. Ex *footle,* v.

footman's inn. A wretched lodging ; a gaol : coll. : ca. 1600–1630.

*footman's maund. An artificial sore, made to resemble a horse's kick or bite : late C. 17–late 19 c. B.E. Cf. *fox's bite* and see **maund.**

Foot's horse, take or travel by (Mr.). To walk : coll. verging on S.E. : from ca. 1820 ; ob. Bee. Cf. *Shanks's mare.*

footy. Despicable ; worthless : coll. from ca. 1750 : in C. 20, ob. Grose, 1st ed. Ex Fr. *foutu.* See esp. Grose, P.

foozilow. To flatter, cajole : Anglo-Indian coll. (— 1886). Ex Hindustani. Yule & Burnell.

foozle. A miss : sporting s. > gen. coll. : 1890. Ex the v.—2. (Of a person) a bore ; an old ' fogey ' (q.v.) : coll. : 1860. Rhoda Broughton, ' Frumps and foozles in Eaton Square ' (, London, S.W.1). Prob. ex *fool + fizzle* : cf. next. (S.O.D. for dates.)

foozle, v. To miss ; make a bad attempt at ; bungle : sporting j. > gen. s. or coll. *The Field,* Feb. 25, 1888, ' Park foozled his second stroke.' Ex *footle + fizzle* ; or, more prob., dial. *footer* (to bungle) + *fizzle.* The vbl.n., *foozling,* bungling, is frequent in C. 20.

foozle about (with). To fool about (with) : coll. : C. 20. (G. D. H. and M. Cole, *Burglars in Bucks,* 1930.)

foozled, foozly. Blurred ; indistinct ; spoilt : coll. : from ca. 1890.

foozler. A bungler : from ca. 1895 : sporting j. > gen. s.

foozlified. Tipsy : nautical (— 1887) ; ob. Baumann. Cf. *foozle,* n., 2.

foozling. See **foozle,** v.

fop-doodle. A fop ; a fool ; an insignificant man : coll. : ca. 1640–1700.

fopper. A mistake : parvenus' sol. (— 1909). Ware. Corruption of *faux pas.* Cf. *fox paw.*

fop's alley, Fops' Alley. The gangway between stalls and pit, orig. and esp. in the Opera House : theatrical : ca. 1770–1830. Mme D'Arblay in *Cecilia,* 1782.

[**for-, fore-.** See Fowler.]

for certain sure. See **certain sure, for.**

for it, be. To be due for punishment ; hence, imm., in trouble : military s. (1915 : ? late 1914) >, by 1919, gen. coll. The *it* = punishment. F. & Gibbons.

for to. In order to : once S.E. ; but since ca. 1780, sol.

forage. To ' procure, seek, bring back ' [coll.] ; ' find places at other table than one's own, at meals ' [s.] : Bootham School (— 1925). Anon., *Dict. of Bootham Slang.*

forakers. A privy : Winchester College : C. 19–20. Either L. *forica > foricas > foricus >,* ca. 1860, *forakers* (W.) : or *four acres,* a field (H.). W.c.'s have had to endure much pedantic wit : cf. *Ajax.* R. G. K. Wrench gives it as *foricus* ; he adds ' Cf. Vulgars = Vulgus '.

foraminate. To have sexual connexion with (a woman): C. 19: low pedantic. Ex L. *foramen*, an orifice.

force. Catachrestic for *enforce*: rare before C. 20. *The Daily Telegraph*, Jan. 1, 1935, 'Hoad Does Not Force Follow On' (cricket in the West Indies).

Force, the. The Police: coll.: from ca. 1850. Cf. *the Profession*. Miss Braddon in *The Trail of the Serpent*, 1868. Abbr. *the Police Force*.

force-meat ball. Something inherently unpleasant endured under compulsion: C. 19. 'Jon Bee', 1823. ? ex the spiced, highly seasoned nature of *force-meat* and influenced by *forcement*.

force the voucher. See **voucher, force the.**

forced to be, be. To be necessarily: late C. 17–20: S.E. until mid-C. 19, then coll. (increasingly low). O.E.D.

force(d) put. Compulsion: 'Hobson's', i.e. no, 'choice': coll. > S.E.: ca. 1650–1820, then dial.

forceps. The hands: mainly and orig. medical: from ca. 1820; ob.

fore. A mostly proletarian and military coll. form of *before*: mid-C. 19–20.

fore-and-aft. To have sexual connexion: nautical: mid-C. 19–20; ob.

fore-and-aft rig. 'The single-breasted chief petty officer's uniform': naval: late C. 19–20. Bowen.

fore-and-after. A harlot that is 'double-barrelled', q.v.: from ca. 1850. ? ex, 2, the † nautical s. sense (— 1867), a cocked hat worn with the peak in front, Smyth: recorded in Southern Scots in 1839 (E.D.D.).

Fore and Afts, the. The Gloucestershire Regiment: military: late C. 19–20. App. 'coined by Kipling in his story "The Drums of the Fore and Aft"' (F. & Gibbons). See **Back Numbers.**

fore-bitter. 'A narrative song sung round the fore bitts in the dog watches, as opposed to a shanty, or working song': nautical coll.: mid-C. 19–20. Bowen.

[**fore-buttocks.** The female breasts: either cultured coll. or, prob., literary jocularity: ca. 1727; †. Coined by Pope at the height of his powers.]

fore-chains, (there's) a rat in your. A nautical c.p., 'the final insult to a sloppy ship' · late C. 19–20. Bowen, 'Its origin is obscure.'

fore-room. See **let . . .**

'fore you listed. A variant of *before you came up*, q.v.

forecastle, forecourt, forehatch, forewoman. The *pudendum muliebre*: all C. 19–20 and decidedly ob. terms in Venus-venery.

forecastle rat. A seaman that one suspects of being either the owners' or the officers' spy: nautical coll.: late C. 19–20. Bowen.

forecastle wireless. A rumour; rumours: nautical: from ca. 1925. Bowen.

forefoot. The hand: jocular coll.: late C. 16–20; ob. Shakespeare, Grose.

foregather. To come together in sexual intimacy: coll.: C. 18–early 19.

forego and **forgo** are often confused in writing: C. 19–20.

foreign line. Any line other than that on which the speaker is employed: railwaymen's coll. (— 1909). Ware.

foreign parts, gone to. Transported as a convict: ca. 1820–70. Bee.

foreigneering, vbl.n. and ppl.adj. Foreign (mat-

ters); like a foreigner: low coll.: from mid-1820's; slightly ob. I.e. *foreign* + pejorative suffix *-eer*. O.E.D.—2. Hence, *foreigneering cove*, a foreigner: c. or low (— 1909). Ware.

foreigners. Foreign stocks and shares: Stock Exchange coll. (1898: O.E.D. Sup.) >, by 1920, j.

foreman. The *membrum virile*: C. 17, ? later: coll., perhaps literary.—2. In Beaumont & Fletcher's *Philaster*, ed. of 1622, at v, iii, presumably s. and prob. = a goose. (O.E.D.)

foreman of the jury. One who monopolises the conversation: late C. 17–early 19. B.E. It is the foreman who delivers the jury's verdict.

forensic. Incorrect for *forinsec* (foreign): C. 18. O.E.D.

foreskin-hunter. A prostitute: low coll.: C. 19–20 (? ob.).

forest of debt. The payment of debts: Oxford University: ca. 1820–40. Egan's Grose.

***forestall.** In garotting, a look-out in front; the one behind is the *backstall*. C. of C. 19–20, ob. See **stall.**

forever gentleman. 'A man in whom good breeding is ingrained': Society: ca. 1870–1915. Ware. Contrast *temporary gentleman*.

***forger.** (Gen. pl.) A false die: gamblers' c.: late C. 16–early 17. Greene, *A Notable Discovery*, 1591.

forget. A lapse of memory ; an instance of such apse: coll.: from ca. 1820; ob. E.D.D.

forget about. To fail to remember the facts of or about; fail to take action about: coll.: from ca. 1895. O.E.D. (Sup.). Actually, this is a slipshod, unnecessary elaboration of *forget*.

forget it !, don't you. See **and don't you forget it !**

forget it !, (and) don't (you). An admonitory coll. c.p.: U.S. (— 1888) >, by 1900, anglicised. (O.E.D. Sup.)

forget oneself. (Of a child) to urinate or defecate unconventionally: euphemistic coll.: late C. 19–20. Cf. Fr. *s'oublier*.

forgot. Forgotten: once S.E. (Shakespeare, Pepys); since ca. 1850, except as an archaism, it is sol.

foricus. See **forakers.**

***fork.** A pickpocket: c.: late C. 17–early 19. Prob. ex *forks* in :—2. Also c.: app. from ca. 1810: a finger (Vaux); *the forks* (late C. 17–20) being the fore and middle fingers. Cf. *daddles, fives, grappling irons, pickers and stealers, ticklers*, qq.v.—3. A spendthrift: C. 18: ? c.—4. As crutch of the body, S.E. though hardly literary. But *the old fork* is coll. (late C. 19–20), esp. in *get on the old fork*, (of either sex) to coït.

fork, v. To pick pockets; esp. by inserting the fore and middle fingers: late C. 17–early 19: c. B.E. (as v.t.) In C. 19, variant: *put one's forks down*. Cf. C. 18–19 Edinburgh *fork for*, search for (E.D.D.).—2. V.t. and i., to dispose (a woman) for the sexual act: low: mid-C. 19–20 (? ob.).—3. Occ. abbr. *fork out*, q.v.—4. To protrude awkwardly: coll.: 1882 (? earlier). (O.E.D.)

fork, a bit on a. The female pudend; also, a sexual congress: low: C. 19–20. Hence, *get on the old fork*, to copulate: low coll.: late C. 19–20. Ex *fork*, n., last sense. Cf. *fork*, v., 2.

fork, eat (or **have eaten**) or, properly, **have been drinking** (Baumann)—**vinegar with a fork.** To be sharp-tongued or snappish: proverbial coll.: mid-C. 19–20; ob.

fork, pitch the. To tell a sad or doleful story: low coll.: from ca. 1860; ob.

fork and knife. Life: rhyming s.: late C. 19–20. (Alan Hyder, *Black Girl, White Lady*, 1934.)

fork in the beam ! A late C. 19–20 naval c.p., ' an order from the sub for all midshipmen to retire from the gunroom.' Ex a fork ' actually stuck into the beam in the old wooden ships '.

fork out ; rarely—except in U.S.—**over** or **up.** Hand over (valuables or money); pay, ' shell out ', q.v.: from ca. 1830 : s. > coll. by 1900 : Dickens, ' Fork out your balance in hand.' Ex *forks* = hands or fingers. Cf. *stump up* (W.).

forker. A dockyard thief or ' fence ' (q.v.): nautical : C. 19–20; extremely ob. Ex *fork*, v., 1. Cf. *forking*, q.v.—2. See :

forker, wear a. To be a cuckold : via *cornuted* : C. 17. Marston, 1606. (O.E.D.)

*forking. Thieving ; the practice of thieving : c.: C. 19. Ex *fork*, v., 1.—2. The undue hurrying of work : tailors' : from ca. 1850 ; ob.

forking the beam. The vbl.n. corresponding to *fork in the beam !*, q.v. (F. & Gibbons.)

*forkless. Clumsy ; unworkmanlike : c. (— 1821); ob. As if without *forks*, hands or fingers—prob. the latter.

forks. See *fork*, n., 2.—2. Only in pl., the hands : from ca. 1820. An extension of *fork*, a finger, or of *forks* as at *fork*, n., 2.

forlo(o)per. A teamster guide : South Africa : from ca. 1860 : coll.; in C. 20 S.E. The guide is gen. a boy who walks abreast the foremost pair of oxen. Dutch *voorlooper*, a ' fore-runner '. (O.E.D.)

forlorn hope. A gambler's last stake : coll.: late C. 17–19. B.E. Ex S.E. sense (orig. military). See O.E.D., and W.: *Romance of Words*.

form. Condition, fitness : orig. of horses (ca. 1760) and s.; by 1870, coll.; by 1900, S.E. Esp. *in* or *out of form*. Hawley Smart, in *Post to Finish*, ' When fillies, in racing parlance, lose their form at three years old, they are apt to never recover it.'— 2. Behaviour, esp. in *bad* or *good form* : coll. (1868) ex the turf, though anticipated by Chaucer and Shakespeare. In C. 20, by the class that uses this magic alternative and formula, it is considered S.E. —3. Habit ; occupation ; character : low coll. (— 1884); ob.—4. The height of one's attainment : Public Schools': C. 20. P. G. Wodehouse, 1902, ' He sneers at footer, and jeers at cricket. Croquet is his form, I should say.'—5. (Gen. with *in*) high spirits ; ' concert ' pitch : coll.: from ca. 1875. (O.E.D.)

form, a matter of. ' A merely formal affair ; a point of ordinary routine ': coll.: 1824, H. J. Stephen. O.E.D. (Sup.). Ex the legal *a matter of form*, ' a point of formal procedure ' (ibid.).

form ?, what's the. What's it like (at, e.g., a house-party) ? : Society : from the middle 1920's. Evelyn Waugh, *A Handful of Dust*, 1934, of a household, ' " What's the form ? " " Very quiet and enjoyable." '

-former, e.g. **fourth-former.** A pupil in the (e.g. 4th) form : Public Schools' coll.: C. 20.

*forney. A (finger-)ring. A variant of *fawney*, q.v.: C. 19–20 c.

fornicating-engine, -member, -tool. The male member : C. 19–20 ob.: low coll. Cf. :

fornicator. The male member. Whence *fornicator's hall*, the female pudend : C. 19 low. (? C. 20.)—2. In pl., the old-fashioned trousers with a flap in front : † by 1880, the trousers being antiquated even earlier.

forra(r)der, get no or **(not) any.** To make (no) headway : coll. (orig. illiterate, now mostly jocular): 1898, *The Daily Telegraph*, Dec. 15. Ware.

forsook. Forsaken : S.E. >, by 1880 at latest, sol. Baumann.

Fortescue ; forty-skewer. A fish having thorny spines on its fins (*pentaroge marmorata*): New South Wales : from late 1870's : coll. >, by 1910, S.E. *Fortescue*, recorded in 1882 in the Rev. J. E. Tenison-Woods's *Fish of New South Wales*, is a Hobson-Jobson adaptation of *forty-skewer*. Morris.

Forties, the. A well-known gang of thieves of the 1870's–early 80's : low (1887 —); † by 1910. Baumann. Ex *the Forty Thieves*.

fortin. (A) fortune : sol. (— 1887), esp. Cockney and provincial. Baumann.

Fortnum and Mason. A notable hamper : Society : mid-C. 19–20. Ware, ' From the perfection of the eatables sent out by this firm of grocers in Piccadilly,'—whence comes also the cleverest advertising-matter known to this century. (The firm was established in C. 18.)

fortune, a small. An extravagantly large sum paid for something, esp. for something small : coll.: from ca. 1890.

fortune-biter. A sharper, swindler : coll.: C. 18. D'Urfey.

*fortune-teller. A judge or, occ., a magistrate : c.: late C. 17–early 19. B.E., whose definition is so ambiguous that the term may, even there, bear the usual meaning : in which case that sense may orig. have been c. or, more prob., s. or low coll. Grose, 1st ed., seems, however, to be clear as to the ' judge ' interpretation, though he may merely be glossing B.E. Cf. *lambskin man, conjuror, cunning man*, which Egan considers as = a judge.

forty is, in C. 17–20 S.E. as well as coll., used frequently to designate a large though indefinite member, or quantity, or degree : Shakespeare, who has ' I could beat forty of them,' twice employs ' forty thousand ' in a highly hyperbolical manner common to the Elizabethan dramatists. *Forty pence*, a customary amount for a wager, C. 16–17, and the later *forty thieves* may be operative reasons for the continuance of this coll. or coll.-tending *forty*. (Onions.)—2. A sharper : Australian : from ca. 1925. (The O.E.D. Sup. records it at 1927.) Perhaps suggested by *the forty thieves*.

forty-faced. Arrant ; esp. shamelessly given to shameless deception : e.g. *forty-faced flirt* or *liar*.

forty fits, have. To be much perturbed or alarmed : coll.: late C. 19–20.

forty-foot, forty-guts. A fat, dumpy person (pejoratively) : the former stressing the shortness, the latter the fatness : low coll.: resp. from (—)1864, (—)1857. H., 3rd ed.; ' Ducange Anglicus '. Cf. *guts, tubby* or *tubs*.

forty-jawed. Excessively talkative : coll.: mid-C. 19–20. Cf. *jaw* and *forty-lunged*.

forty-legs. A centipede : late C. 17–20 : coll. (ob.) when not dial.

forty-lunged. Stentorian—or very apt to be. Coll.: from ca. 1850.

Forty-Niners. The earliest prospectors in California : U.S. coll., anglicised ca. 1900. They went there in 1849. Haskins, *Argonauts of California*, 1890.

forty to the dozen. Very quickly : with *talk*, more often *nineteen to the dozen* ; with *walk off*, the sense is to decamp very speedily. Coll.: from ca. 1860.

forty thieves (or **F.T.**), **the**. 'A famous class of contract-built 74-gun ships designed by Sir H. Peake, but ruined by Admiralty interference until they were the worst liners in the service': naval: C. 19. Bowen.—2. The 40th Pathans (Indian Army): military: late C. 19–20. F. & Gibbons. Ex numerals—and reputed habits.

forty-twa. A public urinal (Edinburgh): Scots coll.: ca. 1820–90. H., 3rd ed. Ex the number of persons seatable.

forty winks. A nap, short sleep: coll.: from middle 1820's. Egan, 1828 (O.E.D.); H., 3rd ed.; G. Eliot, 'Having "forty winks" on the sofa in the library', 1866.

Forum. A Warwickshire term (not. dial) explained in Lord Granville's speech at the Bright Celebration held in that city in June, 1883: 'I rise a stranger in this famous Town Hall known in Birmingham, I believe, by a still more classical name.' (Ware.)

forward station. 'A desirable coastguard station': nautical coll.: ca. 1850–1900. Bowen.

fosey-faced. See **fozy-faced.**

*foss ; phos(s). See **phos.**

fossick. (V.i., occ. with *about*; but **v.t.** only when used with *after, for, out, up*.) To search for anything: 1870; Australian s. > coll. ca. 1890. Ex the ideas, search for gold (1861), pick out gold (1852). Morris.—2. Whence vbl.n. *fossicking*, which is commoner than the other parts of the v.; also adj. (1859). Ex dial. *fossick*, a troublesome person: cf. *fuse.*

fossicker. A persistent searcher: from ca. 1890. Ex gold-mining senses. Australian.

fossicking. See **fossick, 2.**

fossilize. To look for fossils: coll.: 1845, Lyell. O.E.D.

fosterous. Phosphorus: sol. (– 1887); ob. Baumann.

Fostershire. Worcestershire: cricketers' jocular coll.: ca. 1907–13. Ex the famous sporting family. *Who's Who in World Cricket*, 1934.

fou, occ. **fow.** Drunk: in late C. 17–20, coll. Vanbrugh. Ex Scottish. In C. 20, *fou the noo* is often used, loosely but gen. jocularly, in same sense.

foul in C. 20 (mainly post-War) hyperbolical use is fairly to be described as s. > coll. of the *awful* and *terrible* kind. Cf. *filthy*, q.v. Desmond Coke, *Wilson's*, 1911, 'A foul row'; E. M. Delafield, *Gay Life*, 1933, 'He's terribly foul, isn't he?'

foul a plate (with). To sup or dine with a person: coll.: late C. 18–20; ob. except in Western Scotland in the form *dirty a plate.* Grose, 3rd ed.

foul as an Indiaman. (Of a ship) dirty: naval: C. 19. Bowen. Ex jealousy.

foul-weather breeder, the. The Gulf Stream: nautical coll.: mid-C. 19–20. Bowen.

Foul Weather Jack. Sir John Norris, an early C. 18 Admiral of the Fleet; Commodore Byron, a mid-C. 18 navigator. Dawson, 'From the bad weather that was supposed to attend them'.

*foulcher. A purse: c. (– 1877). Anon., *Five Years' Penal Servitude*, 1877. Is this cognate with or derived from Romany *folaso*, a glove?

founder in tears. A C. 15–16 sol. on the Eng. v. after Fr. *fondre.* (O.E.D.)

foundling temper. A very bad temper: London: from ca. 1880; ob. Ware, 'Proverbially

said of the domestic servants poured upon London by the metropolitan Foundling Hospital'.

foundry. A pork-butcher's shop; loosely, any shop: proletarian (– 1909); ob. Prob. ex 'the noisy vibrations of the sausage machine' (Ware).

fountain palace or **temple.** (Gen. pl.) 'Places of convenience, sunk below the roadways': London: the 1890's. Ware. Ex bright and cleanly appearance, the running water, etc.

four-and-nine(penny). A hat: ca. 1844–80. Thackeray; Viator, *Oxford Guide*, 1849. Occ. a *four-and-ninepenny goss.* Ex the price set by a well-known London hatter.

four-and-two. A sandwich: C. 20. (Neil Bell, *Andrew Otway*, 1931.) Cf. *four-by-two*, q.v.

four arf. A Cockney form of *four-half*, q.v. Ware.

four bag. A flogging: naval: mid-C. 19–early 20. Bowen; F. & Gibbons. The bluejacket received *four* dozen lashes; if also his discharge, then *four bag and a blanker*, the latter being his discharge ticket with one corner cut off.

*four-bones. The knees: c.: from ca. 1850; ob. *Punch*, Jan. 31, 1857.

four-by-three. Small; insignificant (rarely of persons): from ca. 1924. Dorothy Sayers, *Have His Carcase*, 1932, 'An adjectival four-by-three watering-place like Wilvercombe'.

four-by-two. An Army biscuit: military: from ca. 1912. F. & Gibbons. Ex *four-by-two*, a rifle pull-through (of that size in inches).—2. A Jew: Cockney soldiers' rhyming s.: 1914. B. & P.

four-eyes. A bespectacled person: uncultured coll.: from ca. 1870. H., 5th ed.

four-flusher. A braggart, a cheat: military coll.: from not later than 1918. F. & Gibbons. Ex U.S. senses, a pretender, a humbug, themselves ex poker j.

four-foot-one-and-a-half. A rifle: bluejackets': late C. 19–20. Ex length. Bowen.

four-half. Half-ale, half-porter, at fourpence a quart: 1884 (O.E.D.). Cf. *four thick*, q.v.

four-holed middlings. Ordinary walking shoes: Winchester College: C. 19; † by 1890.

four kings, the book (or history) of the. See **history of the four kings.** Cf. (*the*) *devil's picture-books.*

four-legged burglar-alarm. A watch-dog: jocular coll.: from ca. 1880.

four-legged fortune. A winning horse: Society: ca. 1880–1914. Ware.

four-legged frolic. Sexual connexion: low coll.: from ca. 1850. Perhaps ex the ob. C. 16–20 proverb, 'There goes more, *or* more belongs, to (a) marriage than four bare legs in a bed.'

four-letter man. A very objectionable fellow: rather low (– 1923); heard among Army officers as early as 1917. Manchon; B. & P. I.e., a *s-h-i-t.*—2. A *homo*(sexual): id.: from ca. 1930.

four-liner, n. and adj. (Something) very important: Society coll.: ca. 1890–1915. The origin appears in *The Daily News*'s words, 1890, cited by Ware, 'Four-lined whips [or messages] have been sent out on both sides of the House of Commons urging members to be in their places this evening.'

four-poster. A four-poster bedstead: coll.: 1836, Dickens.—2. Hence, a four-masted sailing-ship: nautical: mid-C. 19–20.

four seams and a bit of soap. A pair of trousers: tailors': from ca. 1870.

four, but more gen. **three, sheets in the wind.** Drunk : nautical, from ca. 1840.

four thick. 'Fourpence per quart beer—the commonest there is (in London), and generally the muddiest' : public-houses' : late C. 19–early 20. Ware. Cf. *four-half*.

four-wheeled kip. A taxi-cab : Dublin taxi-drivers' : from ca. 1910. A reference to fornication therein.

four-wheeler. A four-wheeled cab : coll. : from ca. 1846 ; coll. > S.E. ; ob. Cf. *four-poster.*—2. A steak : low coll. : from ca. 1880.

fourpenny bit. See **fourpenny one** and contrast *fourpenny pit*.

fourpenny cannon. Beef-steak pudding : London slums' (— 1909) ; ob. Ware. Ex shape or, more prob., hardness.

fourpenny (one). A cuff ; clip on the ear : rhyming s. on *hit* : C. 20. *The Evening News*, Feb. 29, 1936. (Presumably, orig. *fourpenny bit*.)

fourpenny pit. A fourpenny bit : rhyming s. : late C. 19–early 20. Ware.

fourteen, on his. On his demobilisation-furlough of fourteen days : military coll. : Dec., 1918–19. F. & Gibbons.

fourteen hundred ; or **f. h. new fives.** A warning cry = There's a stranger here ! Stock Exchange : from ca. 1885. Atkin, *House Scraps*, 1887. For a long time the Stock Exchange had never more than 1,399 members : the term has remained, though by 1930 it was ob. and though even as early as 1890 there were nearly 3,000 members.

*****fourteen penn'orth of it.** Fourteen years' transportation : c. : 1820–60. Bee.

fourth. A w.c. ; a latrine,—the vbl. phrases being *keep a fourth, go to the fourth* : *gone* [4] is the esoteric sign on an undergraduate's door. Cambridge s. (— 1860). H., 2nd ed. Not ex the Fourth Court at Trinity College, as ' explained ' by H., but perhaps (W.) ex a staircase-number. Cf. *rear(s).*—2. See **first.**

fourth estate, the. Journalists ; journalism as a profession : S.E., applied by Burke, > literary s. (— 1855) >, by 1910, outworn journalese : already in 1873 it was much in use among penny-a-liners (H., 5th ed.).

Fourth of July. A tie : rhyming s. : C. 20. B. & P.

fousty. Stinking : coll. when not dial. : from ca. 1810. ? ex *foist*, n., 3, influenced by *froust, frowst*.

fouter, v., and **foutering,** vbl.n. See **footer, 3,** for all remarks.

fouter or **footer, care not a.** To care not at all : coll. : late C. 16–20, ob.

foutie or **fouty.** See **footy.**

fow. See **fou.**

fower. (Pronounced *fo-er*.) Four : sol. : C. 19–20. Esp. in military commands. See **stan.**

fowl. A troublesome seaman : nautical : late C. 19–20. Also a *bird* or an *irk*. Perhaps there is a pun on *foul* and *queer bird*.

*****fox.** An artificial sore : c. (— 1862). Mayhew. Cf. *fox's bite*, q.v.—2. Shares in the Norfolk and Western Railroad : Stock Exchange (— 1895) ; now †. A. J. Wilson, *Stock Exchange Glossary*. Via ' Norfolks '.

fox, v. To intoxicate : C. 17–20 ; until ca. 1760, S.E. ; then coll. *The Sporting Times*, April 11, 1891, ' And so to bed well nigh seven in the morning, and myself as near foxed as of old '.—2. To cheat, rob : Eton (— 1859). H., 1st ed.—3. V.t. and v.i., to watch closely though slyly : London c. (— 1859) > low s. H., 1st ed. V.i., *fox about*. Cf. *fox's sleep*, q.v.—4. V.i., to sham : early C. 17–20 ; S.E. until C. 19, then coll. and dial. Ex a fox's habit of pretending to be asleep. (O.E.D.) This is prob. the sense posed by ' Ducange Anglicus ', 1857 : to be half asleep.—5. To criticise adversely a fellow-actor's acting : theatrical (— 1864). H., 3rd ed.—6. To mend a boot by ' capping ' it : from ca. 1790 (? j. >) s. > coll. > S.E. Grose, 3rd ed.

fox, catch a ; gen. **to have caught a fox** (B.E.). To be or become very drunk : C. 17–19 coll. A late C. 16–17 variant is *hunt the fox*. Cf.

fox-drunk. Crafty-drunk : late C. 16–17 : coll. Nashe.

Fox Hall. Vauxhall (gardens) : Society : mid-C. 18–mid-19. (Ware, at *chappie*.)

fox (or **fox's**) **paw, make a.** To commit a blunder, esp. in society or (of women) by carelessly allowing oneself to be seduced : late C. 18–19 low coll. Grose, 2nd ed. (*fox's paw*). A (prob. deliberate) perversion of Fr. *faux pas*. Cf. *fopper*, q.v.

fox to keep one's geese, set a. To entrust one's confidences and/or money to a sharper or an adventurer : coll. : from ca. 1630. ; ob.

foxed. Tipsy. See **fox, v.,** 1.

foxing. Vbl.n. *ex fox*, v., but not for sense 1, rarely for senses 2 and 6 ; mostly for sense 3.

fox's bite. An artificial sore : schoolboys' : from ca. 1850 ; ob. Cf. *fox*, n.

fox's paw. See **fox paw, make a.**

fox's sleep. A feigned sleep veiling extreme alertness : coll. : C. 17–20 : ob. In S.E., *fox-sleep*.

foxy. Strong-smelling : coll. verging on S.E. : C. 19–20.—2. The other *foxy* senses in F. & H. are all S.E.

*****foy.** A cheat, swindler : late C. 16–17. Perhaps c., certainly low.—2. A coll. expletive : late C. 16–early 18. I.e. *fay*, faith.

*****foyl-cloy.** See **foil-cloy.—foyse.** See **fice.— foyst, n.** and **v.** See **foist.—foyster.** See **foister.**

fozy-faced. Smug - looking : Glasgow coll. (— 1934). Ex dial. *fozy*, stupid, bloated.

f'r. For : coll. : C. 19–20. E.g. *f'r instance*, pronounced almost as if *frinstance*.

fragment. A dinner ordered by a master for a favoured boy, who could invite five school-fellows to share it : Winchester College : † by 1891. *Winchester Word-Book*. A *fragment* = three dishes or courses.—2. In Shakespeare, a pejorative term of address.

'fraid. Afraid : **a** coll., mainly childish, shortening : C. 19–20.

'fraidy cat. A frightened or a timorous person : coll., mostly children's : from ca. 1870.

frail. A woman : U.S., partially anglicised by Eric Linklater in 1931 (*Don Juan in America*). O.E.D. (Sup.).

frame. A picture : artists' : ca. 1890–1912. Ware. Ex *picture-frame.*—2. See **frame, v., 2 ;** variant more gen. : *frame-up.*

frame, v. To work up and present an unjustified case or serious complaint against : orig. and mainly U.S. ; acclimatised ca. 1924. See **Irwin.**—2. To effect a pre-arranged conspiracy, a faked result : U.S. (from ca. 1906), anglicised ca. 1924. Irwin ; O.E.D. (Sup.). Also n.

*****frammagem.** See **frummagem.**

franc-fileur. ' A man who gets away quickly and won't dance ' : Society : ca. 1890–1915. Punning Fr. sense. Ware.

France and Spain. Rain : rhyming **s.** : late C. 19–20. B. & P.

frangine. Brother : Canadian : C. 20. **F. &** Gibbons. Ex Fr.-Canadian.

frank. Obscene or tending to obscenity : book-world s. or j. : from ca. 1926. Whence *frank-ness.* Cf. Pope's usage : unchaste.

Frankenstein. A monster or a mechanism uncontrollable by its inventor or creator : a (journalistic) catachresis : from ca. 1840. Ex Mrs. Shelley's novel, *Frankenstein* (1818), wherein the titular character is the student-contriver, not the contrived monster. W.

frantic(ally). 'Awful(ly)', 'terrible' or 'terribly' : coll. : 1908 (O.E.D. Sup.). E.g. 'a frantic hurry' or 'muddle'. Ex :—2. Notable ; well-known ; confirmed : Public Schools' coll. : 1902, P. G. Wodehouse, 'Who's that frantic blood who owns all the land . . . ?'

frater. A beggar working with false papers, esp. **a** petition : mid-C. 16–20. Awdelay, Fletcher, Grose (1st ed.) ; David Hume, *Bullets Bite Deep*, 1932. Ex the begging friars.—2. 'A Wyke-hamists' relations are his *Pater, Mater, Frater* [brother] and *Soror* [sister] (*Nunky* and *Nevy* are now obsolete). Together they form his *Pitch-up*,' Wrench, 1901.

fraud. A thing either deceptive or spurious : coll. : late C. 18–20.—2. An impostor, humbug, hypocrite : coll. : 1850, Dickens (O.E.D.). Often jocularly.

Fray Bentos. Very well, esp. in reply to inquiries about one's health : jocular military : 1916 ; ob. B. & P. Ex the well-known brand of bully beef, with a pun on *très bien* (cf. *trez beans*, q.v.).

frazzle, to a. Very badly ; absolutely, utterly : orig. (1882), U.S. ; anglicised ca. 1905. Also *faded to a frazzle*, completely exhausted : ca. 1908–14. Ex Southern U.S. *frazzle*, a frayed-out end : cf. East Anglian *frazzle*, to fray out. Thornton ; E.D.D.

freak. An actor that loses caste by performing in some eccentric show : theatrical : late C. 19–early 20. Ware. Cf. *dime-museum.*

Freakeries, the. 'Barnum's freak and acrobat shows at Olympia' : London : 1898. Ware.

Fred Karno's army. The 'New Army' : military : late 1914–18. F. & Gibbons cite 'We are Fred Karno's Army, | A rag-time crowd are we ' ex a song given in B. & P. Ex 'the popular comedian, Fred Karno, noted for his troupe of whimsical oddities and caricaturists '. Cf. :

Fred Karno's navy. The Dover Patrol : naval during G.W. Bowen. Cf. *Harry Tate's navy.*

Freddy. A German, esp. a German soldier : rare military (esp. the Royal Warwickshire Rifles') : 1914–18. Ex *Friedrich* : cf. *Fritz*, q.v.

***free, v.** To steal (gen. a horse) : c. of ca. 1835–90. Brandon ; Snowden, 3rd ed., 1857. Cf. *convey*.—2. To make (a person) free ; to initiate : Public Schools' coll. : late C. 19–20. Ware.

free. Self-assured ; impudent : Oxford University (— 1864) ; † by 1921.

free and easy (often hyphenated). A social gathering (gen. at a public-house) where smoking, drinking and singing are allowed : (orig. low) coll. ; in C. 20, S.E. : from ca. 1796. The *Lex. Bal.* ; Macaulay, 1843 ; Cassell's *Saturday Journal*, Sept., 1891. A ribald club or society, fl. 1810–11, was known as the Free-and-Easy Johns.

free-and-flowing. A seaman's uniform with square collar : naval : mid-C. 19–20 ; ob. Bowen.

free(-)booker. A piratical publisher or an under-selling bookseller : journalists' : ca. 1880–1914. Punning *freebooter.*

Free-Born John. John Lilburne (d. 1657), famous for 'his defence of his rights as a free-born Englishman before the Star Chamber ' (Dawson).

free breakfast table, a. A political c.p. 'trotted out ' ca. 1906. Collinson. I.e. free of duties.

free fight. A general struggle or mellay : orig. U.S. (— 1855) coll., anglicised by 1873 ; in C. 20, S.E. H., 5th ed. Occ. *a free-for-all fight*, the *fight* sometimes being omitted.

free-fishery. The female pudend : low : C. 19–20 (? ob.).

free-fucking. A general sexual looseness ; unpaid coïtion ; fidelity to the other sex. Also adj. Low : rather a vulg. than a coll. : C. 19–20.

free gangway. 'General leave from a man-of-war ' : naval coll. : late C. 19–20. Bowen.

free gratis—for nothing ; f., g., and for nothing. Costing nothing : coll., orig. low : from ca. 1880.

[**free-handed, free-hearted, free of her favours**, given by F. & H., are S.E. ; *free of his patter*, full of talk, is low coll. only because of *patter*, the same remark, *mutatis mutandis*, applying to *free of his foolishness*, full of chaff.]

free(-)holder. A harlot's lover or 'fancy man ', q.v. : C. 19–20 (ob.) low.—2. 'He whose Wife goes with him to the Ale-house ', B.E. : late C. 17–early 19.

free-lance. A persistent adulteress : ca. 1888–1910. Ex the medieval mercenary earlier known as a *free companion* and renamed by Scott in *Ivanhoe.*

free of fumbler's hall or **Fumbler's Hall.** Impotent : (? late) C. 18–early 19 low. Grose, 2nd ed.

free of the bush. Extremely intimate (with a woman) : low : from ca. 1860.

free of the house. Intimate ; privileged : coll. in C. 19, S.E. in C. 20.

Free State coal. A South African coll. euphemism (dating from ca. 1880, and now slightly ob.) for dried cow-dung. R. Jameson, *A Trip to the Transvaal Gold-Fields*, 1886. Pettman.

free tank. Unlimited 'booze' : nautical, esp. naval ; also military : C. 20 ; ob. Bowen ; F. & Gibbons. Cf. *tanked.*

free trade or protection ? (Women's) knickers loose and open or closed and tight-fitting : low coll. : from ca. 1905.

free with both ends of the busk, make. To caress a woman with extreme familiarity : C. 18–20 (ob.). See **busk.**

freeman. The lover of a married woman : C. 19–20 (ob.) low.

freeman, v. ; make a freeman of. To spit on a (new boy's) penis : schools' (mostly Public) : ca. 1850–1920. Occ. *freemason.* Cf. *crown.*

freeman of a corporation's work. See **corporation's work.**

freeman of Bucks. A cuckold : C. 19 low. Punning *Buckinghamshire* and a *buck's* horns. Contrast *Bedfordshire.*

Freeman's !, it's Harry. There's nothing to pay : naval : from ca. 1870. F. & Gibbons ; Bowen. Ex :

Freeman's Quay, drink or **lush at.** To drink at another's expense : ca. 1810–80. Ex *free beer* distributed to porters and carmen at this wharf near London Bridge. *Lex. Bal.*, 1811 ; H., 1st–5th edd.

freemason, v. See **freeman, v.**

*****freeze,** v. To appropriate or steal : c. : C. 19. Cf. *freeze (on) to.*

freeze, do a. To feel extremely cold : coll. : late C. 19–20.

freeze on to. See **freeze to.**

freeze out. To compel to retire from business or society, by competition or social opposition : orig. (ca. 1867) U.S. ; anglicised ca. 1895 as a coll.

freeze the . . . See **monkey, cold enough . . .**

freeze to, in C. 20 gen. **freeze on to.** To take a powerful fancy to : late C. 19–20 ; ob.—2. Cling to, hold fast. Coll. : Australian (ex U.S., where common) : England slightly : in both countries from ca. 1880.

freezer. A very cold day (from ca. 1895, S.E.) ; a chilling look, comment, etc. : coll. : from ca. 1848. —2. An Eton jacket (without tail) : coll. or s. : from ca. 1880. ? abbr. *bum-freezer* or *-perisher.*— 3. A sheep bred for frozen export : New Zealand (— 1893) ; Australian, from ca. 1900. Coll. >, by 1920, S.E. (Morris.)

[French words : see the excellent account in Fowler.]

French, loose. See **loose French.**

French, speak. (Of a horse) to be an excellent steeplechaser : turf (— 1923). Manchon.

French article, cream, elixir, lace. Brandy : coll. : resp. — 1821, — 1788 (Grose, 2nd ed.), — 1860, — 1821. The second, gen. of brandy in tea or coffee—a French custom. See ' Offensive Nationality ', in *Words !* for coll., dial. and S.E. variations on the *French* theme, which was at its height ca. 1730–1820.

French crown, goods or **gout.** Syphilis : C. 17– 19 : coll. verging on S.E. *F. ache(s), fever, disease, measles, marbles, mole, pox,* are S.E. Cf. *French faggot-stick.*

French Devil, the. Jean Bart (d. 1702), an intrepid naval commander. Dawson.

French elixir. See **French article.**

French faggot-stick, a blow with a. A nose lost through syphilis : late C. 17–18 : low. B.E.

French fare. Elaborate politeness : C. 14–17 : coll. > S.E. In C. 14–early 16 often *frankish fare.*

French goods or **gout.** See **French crown.**

French kiss. A kiss applied heavily (' baiser très appuyé ') : coll. (— 1923). Manchon.

French lace. See **French article.**

French leave, take. To depart without intimation or as if in flight ; do anything without permission : from ca. 1770 : coll. in C. 18–mid-19, then S.E. Smollett, 1771. (Cf. Fr. *filer à l'anglaise.*) Ex the C. 18 Fr. custom of departing from a reception, dinner, ball, etc., etc., without bidding good-bye to host or hostess.

French (rarely **American, Italian** or **Spanish**) **letter.** A male sheath-pessary : low coll. : from ca. 1870. Cf. Fr. *capote anglaise.*

French pie. Irish stew : City of London restaurants' (— 1909). Ware.

French pig. A venereal bubo : C. 19–20 (ob.) low.

French pigeon. A pheasant mistakenly shot in the partridge season : sportsmen's (— 1893) ; ob.

French prints. Obscene pictures : coll. : from 1850. Thackeray. Ob.

Frencher. A Frenchman : pejorative coll. : ca. 1840–1900. C. Kingsley.

Frenchified. Venereally infected ; esp. with syphilis ; mid-C. 17–19 coll. B.E. Cf. *French gout.*

Frenchman. A (good, bad, indifferent) French scholar : coll. : from *temp.* Restoration.

Frenchman, the. Any foreigner : naval coll. (cf. later dial.) : ca. 1620–1720. Bowen.—2. Syphilis : C. 19 low. Cf. old technical *morbus gallicus.*—3. (A bottle of) brandy : Society : mid-C. 19–early 20. Ware, ' From this spirit being French '.

Frenchy. A Frenchman : coll. : recorded 1883, ? considerably earlier. Ex ob. S.E. adj. Miss Yonge, ' The squires had begun by calling him Frenchy ' (O.E.D.). In dial., any foreigner whatsoever.

fresh, adj. In one's first university term : university (? orig. Cambridge) ; from ca. 1800 ; ob. *Gradus ad Cantabrigiam,* 1803. Ex *freshman,* q.v.— 2. Forward, impudent : orig. (— 1848) U.S. (ex Ger. *frech*), anglicised ca. 1895. (W.)—3. Slightly drunk : coll. ; from ca. 1810. But in dial at least twenty years earlier : E.D.D. Marryat, ' I could get fresh as we call it,' 1829.—4. Fasting : opposed to eating and esp. drinking ; sober : M.E.–C. 20 : until C. 19, S.E. ; in C. 19 coll., in C. 20 Scottish only.

fresh as a daisy, a new-born thrush, an eel, flowers in May, paint, a rose. Very healthy, strong, active : coll., the second being low : resp. from ca. 1815, 1830, 1410, (1400–1600), 1440, 1850 ; the third and fifth soon > S.E. and indeed poetical, while the first is in C. 20 almost S.E. For the first, third, fifth and sixth (perhaps orig. ironic for the first or the third) see esp. Apperson.

fresh bit. (Of women, in amorous venery) a beginner ; a new mistress : low : from ca. 1840. Cf. *bit of fresh,* the sexual favour.

fresh hand at the bellows, (there's) a. A sailing-ship coll. c.p. of mid-C. 19–20 (now ob.), ' said . . . when the wind freshened, especially after a lull ' (Bowen).

fresh milk. A newcomer, newcomers, to the university : Cambridge University : ca. 1820–50. Egan's Grose. (Cf. *Freshwater Bay,* q.v.) Punning *freshman.*

fresh on the graft. New to the work or job : from ca. 1890. See **graft.**

fresh shot. Incorrect for *freshet* : C. 18. O.E.D.

fresh water. A. By way of punishment for working hands, a turn at pumping various tanks : Conway cadets' : from ca. 1880. John Masefield, *The Conway,* 1933. Cf. *coal-hole.*

fresh-whites. Pallor : lower classes' : mid-C. 19– early 20. Ware.

freshen one's way. To hurry : nautical (— 1893) s. > j. Ex *freshening wind.*

freshen the hawse. ' To serve out a tot after extra fatiguing duty ' : nautical : late C. 19–20. Bowen.

freshen up. To clean, smarten ; revive : coll. : from ca. 1850. An example of a S.E. term (*freshen*) being made coll. by the addition of pleonastic adv.

fresher. An undergraduate in his first term : university, orig. (— 1882) Oxford. Perhaps the earliest example of the Oxford *-er.* See *Slang,* pp. 208–9, and note that R. Ellis Roberts thinks that possibly it arose from a new man being described as *fresher than fresh.*

Freshers, the. ' That part of the Cam which lies between the Mill and Byron's Pool . . . Frequented by *freshmen,*' F. & H. : Cambridge University : from ca. 1880 ; ob. Cf. *fresher,* q.v.

freshman. A university undergraduate in his first year ; at Oxford, in his first term : late C. 16– 20 : orig., university s., but in C. 19–20 to be considered S.E. Nashe; Colman, 1767, 'As . . . melancholy as a freshman at college after a jobation'. Whence *fresher.*—2. Also an adj. : C. 19–20, ob.—3. The C. 17–20 *freshmanship* is, I think, ineligible.

freshman's Bible. The University Calendar : mostly Oxford and Cambridge : from ca. 1870 ; ob. Cf. *freshman's landmark*, q.v.

freshman's church. The Pitt, i.e. the Cambridge University, Press : Cambridge : from ca. 1870 ; ob. Ex its churchly architecture.

freshman's landmark. King's College chapel, Cambridge : Cambridge University : from ca. 1870. Ex its central situation and 'recognizability'.

freshwater bay, or **F.B.** The world of freshmen : Oxford University : ca. 1820–40. Egan's Grose. Cf. *fresh milk.*

freshwater mariner, seaman. A begging pseudo-sailor : ca. 1550–1840, 1690–1840, resp. as are Harman and B.E. Perhaps c., orig.

freshwater soldier. A recruit : late C. 16–18 : orig. coll. ; but in C. 17, S.E. Florio, 1598, defines as 'A goodly, great milke-soppe'. Cf. S.E. *freshwater seaman*, which may, just possibly, have at first been coll.

fret !, don't (you). You needn't worry : sarcastic coll c.p. : late C. 19–20. Cf. *I should worry !*

fret one's giblets, gizzard or **guts ; one's cream, kidneys.** To worry oneself with trifles : low coll. : in gen., from ca. 1850, the *gizzard* form antedating 1755 ; ob., except for *gizzard*. Cf. *flurry one's milk* and :

fret oneself to fiddle-strings. A coll. variant (— 1923) of, and prob. suggested by, the preceding. Manchon.

friar. A white or pale spot on a printed sheet : printers' : from ca. 1680. Contrast *monk*, q.v. In C. 19–20, both are j.

Friars. Blackfriars Station : London coll. (— 1909). Ware.

*frib. A stick : C. 18 c. *Discoveries of John Poulter*, 1754. ? etymology.

[**fribble,** a trifler, has, despite F. & H., never been eligible.]

Friday, black. See **black Friday.**

Friday face. A glum, depressed-looking face or person : coll. : from ca. 1590 ; ob. by 1889 ; by 1936 almost †. Greene ; Grose, 1st ed. (Adj., *Friday-faced*, from late C. 16 ; ob.) Variant, C. 18–20, *Friday look.* Ex Friday as a day of fasting. Apperson.

Friday while. Week-end leave : naval coll. : late C. 19–20. Bowen.

fridge. See **frige.** (This form occurs in W. Collin Brooks, *Frame-Up*, 1935.)

fried carpet. 'The exceedingly short ballet skirt . . . especially seen at the old "Gaiety"' : London theatrical : 1878–82. Ware.—2. 'An improved Cockneyism for "fish and 'taters"' : from ca. 1890 ; ob. *Tit-Bits*, Aug. 8, 1891 (E.D.D.). By jocular perversion.

friend, go and see a sick. To go womanising : low : from ca. 1860.

friend has come, my (little) ; I have friends to stay. The victim's announcement of the menstrual flux : C. 19–20 low : ob. Cf. *the captain is at home.*

friend in need. (Gen. pl.) A louse : low : C. 19–20 ; ob. ? ex C. 18 *gentleman's friend.*

friendly. Abbr. *friendly match*, one played for fun, not competition-points : from ca. 1894 : coll. for five years or so, then S.E.—2. An enemy shell

passing high overhead ; one of one's own shells falling short on one's own lines : military coll. : 1915. F. & Gibbons.

friendly lead. An entertainment organised to assist an unlucky, esp. an imprisoned man—or his wife and children : from ca. 1870 ; orig. c., by 1895 s., by 1910 coll., by 1920 S.E.

friendly pannikin. A drink shared with another from that utensil : Australian coll. : ca. 1860–1910.

friends to stay. See **friend has come.**

frig. An act of self-abuse : low coll. : C. 18–20. Ex the v.—2. See **frige.**

frig, v.t., i., refl. To masturbate : from ca. 1590 : low coll. Cotgrave ; Robertson of Struan. The imperative with *it* is late C. 19–20, occ. an exclamation : cf. *fuck it !* Ex L. *fricare*, to rub.—2. Hence, loosely, to copulate with : mid-C. 19–20.

frig about, v.i. To potter or mess about : low coll. : mid-C. 19–20. (It has been in use among *Conway* cadets since before 1891 : John Masefield, *The Conway*, 1933.) Cf. *bugger about.*

frig-pig. A fussy trifler : late C. 18–early 19. Grose, 2nd ed.

frigate. A woman : orig. (— 1690), nautical. Esp. *a well-rigged frigate*, 'a Woman well Drest and Gentile ' (i.e. Fr. *gentille*), as B.E. has it.

frigate on fire. A variant (ca. 1810–50) of *fire-ship*, q.v. Bee.

frigation. A frigatoon : naval : C. 19. Bowen. By perversion of the S.E. term, with a pun on *frig*, v.

frige ; occ. **frig.** Pronounced *fridge.* A refrigerator : cafés' and restaurants' : from ca. 1925. Heard in the Express Dairy in New Oxford Street, June 13, 1935, 'Who's got the key of the frige ?' Cf. the Fr. *frigo* for *viande frigorifiée.*

frigging. The practice, or an act, of self-abuse (cf. *frig*, n.) : low coll. : C. 17–20.—2. Trifling ; irritating waste of time : C. 18–20, ob. except with *about.*

frigging, adj. and adv. A low coll. intensive : *a frigging idiot* being an absolute fool ; *frigging bad*, exceedingly bad. From ca. 1820. Cf. *f**king*, adj., adv.

fright. Any thing or person of a ridiculous or grotesque appearance : coll. : from ca. 1750.

fright hair. 'A wig or portion of a wig which by a string can be made to stand on end and express fright ' : theatrical coll. (— 1909). Ware.

frightened of. Afraid of : coll. : from ca. 1830. In 1858 *The Saturday Review* could illuminatingly write, ' It is not usual for educated people to perpetrate such sentences as . . . " I was frightened of her." ' (O.E.D.)

frightful. An intensive adj. : coll. : from ca. 1740. (Cf. *awful, terrible.*) Dr. Johnson notes its constant use ' among women for anything unpleasing '.—2. A low coll. variant (C. 19–20) of :

frightfully. An intensive adv. : coll. : from ca. 1830. Ex preceding. Cf. *awfully* and P. G. Wodehouse, *Not George Washington*, 1907, ' Thanks . . . Oh, thanks. . . . Thanks awf'lly. . . . Thanks awf'lly. . . . Thanks awf'lly. . . . Oh, thanks awf'lly . . . (*with a brilliant burst of invention, amounting almost to genius*) Thanks *frightfully.*'

frightfulness. Anything, esp. behaviour, that is objectionable : jocular coll. : 1914 ; ob. Ex the lit. sense, which translated the German *Schrecklichkeit* (Aug. 27, 1914). W.

frigo. Frozen or chilled meat : American >, in early 1918, English military s., though never very gen. (F. & Gibbons.) An adoption of Fr. s., itself representing 'viande *frigorifiée*'.

frigster, frigstress. A male, female masturbator: coll.

frill. Affectation: late C. 19–20: coll. >, by 1920, S.E.—2. A girl; a woman: from ca. 1933. John G. Brandon, *The One-Minute Murder*, 1934, 'The hen, the frill—the skirt!'

frillery. Women's underclothing: low coll.: ca. 1888–1910. Cf. *frillies*.

frillery, explore one's. To caress a woman very intimately: low coll.: ca. 1888–1914.

frillies. Women's underclothing: coll.: ca. 1870–1910. Cf. *undies*, *scanties*, by the former of which it was gradually superseded: see *Words !*, p. 99.

frills. Swagger, conceit, 'side'. Hence *put on one's frills*, to swagger; also, low coll. or s., to grow very amorous. Also culture and accomplishments (music, dancing, foreign languages). Orig. (−1870), U.S.; anglicised ca. 1890. Kipling, 1890, 'It's the commissariat camel putting on his blooming frills' (recurring, in book form, in 1892).

frills, have been among a woman's. To have 'known' her: ca. 1860–1914.

fringe. Irrelevant matter: coll.: from ca. 1885; ob. (O.E.D.)

frint. A pawnbroker: low or c.: ca. 1810–50. *Real Life in London*, 1821. ? *friend* perverted.

frisco, frisko(e). A term of endearment: coll.: C. 17. Variant *friskin*.

frisk. As frolic and a lively dance-movement, it is S.E. as also is *frisker*, a dancer; but as sexual connexion it is low coll.: C. 19–20.—2. Only in *stand frisk*, to be searched: c. (−1812); † by 1900. Vaux. Ex

*frisk ; occ. friz (for senses 3, 4), v. To search (the person); examine carefully for police evidence: c. (−1781). Parker, Grose.—2. Hence to pick the pockets of, pick (a pocket, rob a till): c.: C. 19. Vaux.—3. To 'have' a woman: low: C. 19–20.—4. To hoax: ca. 1820–60. (O.E.D.)

*frisk, dance the Paddington. To be hanged: mid-C. 18–early 19: low or c. Grose, 1st ed.

frisk at the tables. 'A moderate touch at gaming': London coll.: from ca. 1880. Ware.

*frisker. A pilferer: c.: from ca. 1890. Ex *frisk*, v., 2.

frisko(e). See **frisco**.

frisky. Whiskey: from ca. 1890. Ex the popular saying (−1887), *whiskey makes you frisky*.

frisky, adj. Playfully amorous; fond of amorous encounters: coll.: from ca. 1890.—2. Bad-tempered: low London: from ca. 1880; ob. Ware.

Fritz. A German; gen. a German soldier: 1914 +, but, in 1917–18, less common than *Gerry*, *Jerry*, q.v. Also adj., which *Jerry* very rarely is, and, derivatively, a German shell, 'plane, etc.: 1915. A pet-name form of *Friedrich*, an extremely popular Ger. Christian name. See esp. *Words !*—2. An inevitable nickname of men with German surnames: C. 20.

frivol, frivel, frivole. To behave frivolously: coll., almost S.E.: from ca. 1865. W. Black, in *Yolande*, 1883, 'If you want to frivole . . . I shut my door on you.' Ex *frivolous*, ? on *fribble*.

frivoller ; frivolling. A trifler; trifling: coll.; resp. 1887 (Baumann), 1882 (O.E.D.).

*friz, frizz. See **frisk**, v., 1 and 2. Grose, 2nd ed. (*friz*).—2. (Only **friz.**) Frozen: sol. (−1887). Baumann.

frizzle. Champagne: ca. 1860–70. H., 2nd ed. ? a perversion of *fizz*.

*frizzler. A hawker: c.: from ca. 1840; † by 1920. 'No. 747.' Origin ?

*froe, occ. vroe. A woman, wife, mistress, whore: c.: late C. 17–19. B.E. Ex Dutch.

frog. A policeman: low s. verging on c.: from ca. 1855. 'Ducange Anglicus'; H., 2nd ed. More gen. in U.S. than in Britain. Ex his sudden leaping on delinquents.—2. (**Frog.**) A Frenchman (also *Froggy*): from ca. 1870. It has > the 'inevitable' nickname (also *Froggy*) of men with French surnames: lower classes'. (In Fr. s., orig. a Parisian.) Ex the toads on the Parisian shield and 'the quaggy state of the streets', F. & H.—3. In C. 17, however, it means a Dutchman: cf. *Froglander*.—4. A foot (cf. *creeper*): low: C. 19–20, ob. Ex the frog in a horse's hoof.—5. The bluejacket's 'frock, before the days of the jumper': naval coll.: C. 19. Bowen. Ex the tailors' frog.—6. Abbr. (−1935) of *frog and toad*: tramps' c.

frog-action. Bicycle polo, very popular in early C. 20 with the officers stationed at Whale Island (on the east side of Portsmouth harbour): naval. Bowen.

frog and toad. A (main) road: rhyming s. (−1859). H., 1st ed. Perhaps cf. :

*Frog and Toe. London: c. (−1857); † by 1900. 'Ducange Anglicus.' Perhaps cognate with preceding entry.

Frog-Eater. A Frenchman: low coll.: from ca. 1860; ob. Cf. *frog*, 2, and *Froggie*.

frog in the throat. A boat: rhyming s.: C. 20. B. & P.

frog it. To walk, to march: military: 1914 or early 1915. F. & Gibbons. Either ex *frog-march* or, by jocular perversion, ex *flog it*, q.v.

Froggie or Froggy. A Frenchman: from ca. 1870. *The Referee*, July 15, 1883. Also adj. All the *frog* terms for a Frenchman refer to the eating of *frogs*. Contrast *Froglander*.—2. See **frog**, 2.

Froglander. A Dutchman: late C. 17–19 (though after ca. 1820 only among sailors), and, in U.S., C. 19–20, though ob. B.E.

frog's march (gen. with **give the**) ; occ. **frog-march** or **-trot.** The carrying of a drunken man face downwards, e.g. to the police-station. Coll.: from ca. 1870. *The Evening Standard*, April 18, 1871 ; *The Daily News*, Oct. 4, 1884.—2. Also, from ca. 1884, a v.t.

frog's wine. Gin: ca. 1810–70. *Lex. Bal.* ? a reference to Holland: cf. *Froglander*.

from is pleonastic and therefore, strictly, a sol. before *hence*, *thence*, *whence*: C. 17–20.—2. For *since*, it is catachrestic, as in 'disabled from 1917': C. 19–20.

Froncey. French: low London: C. 19. I.e., Fr. *français*. Ware.

front. Bearing, deportment; style: coll. (−1923). Manchon. Cf. S.E. *front*, self-confidence, effrontery.

*front, v. To cover the operations of an associate pickpocket: c. (−1879); ob.—2. V.i. and t., to break in by the *front* door: c. (−1933). Charles E. Leach. Vbl.n., *fronting*.

front, clean one's. To clean one's *front* doorstep and proportionate share of the adjoining pavement: lower- and lower-middle-class coll.: late C. 19–20.

front attic, door, garden, parlour, room, window. The female pudend: low. None, I think, before

1800; Bee, 1823, has the fourth; F. & H. (1893) all six.

front-door mat. The female pubic hair: low: C. 19–20.

front(-)gut. The female pudend: low: C. 19–20; ob.

front name. A Christian name, esp. the first: when not culturedly facetious, it is low coll. (— 1895). Ex U.S. (— 1877).

*front office. Police headquarters: c.: C. 20; mostly and orig. U.S. (O.E.D. Sup.)

front parlour. See front attic.

front piece. A 'curtain-raiser': theatrical coll.: ca. 1885–1912. Ware.

front room. See front attic.

*front-stall. He who, in garotting or robbery with strangulation, keeps a look-out in front: c.: from ca. 1850; ob. See also back-stall and nastyman or ugly.

front window. See front attic.

front windows. The eyes; occ. the face: from ca. 1860.—2. Spectacles: C. 20; ob. A. H. Dawson, *Dict. of Slang*, 1913.

*fronting. See front, v., 2.

frontispiece. The face: pugilistic (— 1818); ob. Egan, Buckstone. Anticipated, however, with jocular (?) pedantry by the C. 17 and C. 18, e.g. by Hume. (O.E.D.)

froom or **frume.** Religious in the orthodox sense: Jewish coll.: late C. 19–20. Ex Ger. *fromm*.

frost. An utter failure or complete disappointment, whether thing, event, or person: theatrical s. > gen. coll.: from ca. 1885. *The Star*, Jan. 17, 1889, 'The pantomime was a dead frost.' W. ingeniously suggests that *frost* derives ex Wolsey's *killing frost* in Shakespeare's *Henry VIII*.—2. Lack of work: as in *have the frost*, to be unemployed: from ca. 1880; † by 1921.—3. A coolness between persons: late C. 19–20, ob. (O.E.D.)

frost bite me! See bite me!

frosty-face. 'One pitted with the small pox', Grose, 1st ed.: low or c.: ca. 1750–1890.

froudacious, froudacity, adj. and n. Inaccurate, -acy: Australia and, though much less, New Zealand: ca. 1888–93. Ex Froude the historian's statements concerning those two countries: on *audacious*. F. & H.

frought. See frout.

froust, frowst. A stink; stuffiness (in a room): coll.: from ca. 1870. Cf. *fug*, q.v. Ex *frousty*, q.v.—2. Hence, at Harrow School, additional sleep allowed on Sundays and whole holidays: from ca. 1875.—3. (Also ex sense 1.) A slacker in regard to sport: Sherborne School: C. 20. Desmond Coke, *Wilson's*, 1911.

froust, frowst, v. Rest lazily: coll. when not dial. (— 1884); ob. in coll.

frousty, frowsty. Unpleasant-smelling; fuggy: coll. when not dial.: 1865 (S.O.D.). Origin obscure.

frout. Angry; annoyed; vexed: Winchester College: C. 19–20. Ex the Hampshire dial. *frou(g)ht*, frightened, as R. G. K. Wrench suggests. (Winchester has a very large vocabulary, in which the boys have, for many years, been obliged to show their proficiency very soon after they first arrive.)

frow. See froe.—**frowst.** See froust.—**frowsty.** See frousty.

froze. Sol. for *frozen*: almost immemorial.

frozen limit, the. The utter limit of the obnoxious or the intolerable: coll.: from ca. 1915. Lyell. Cf. *dizzy limit* and see limit, the.

frozen mitt, give the. To cold-shoulder: U.S. anglicised in 1918. Collinson.

frozen on the stick. Paralysed with fear: aircraft engineers': from ca. 1931. *The Daily Herald*, Aug. 1, 1936. Prob. the joy-stick' of an aeroplane is implied.

fructicose. Incorrect for *fruticose*: C. 19–20. O.E.D.

fruit, old. See old fruit.

fruit of a gibbet. A hanged felon: coll.: C. 18. Gay. (Ware.)

fruitful vine. The female genitals: either low coll. (it appears in the *Lex. Bal.*) or 'dubious' euphemism, the double pun being indelicate: C. 19–20, ob.

fruition. Catachrestically (— 1885) for *fruit*. O.E.D.

fruity. Very rich or strong (e.g. language); very attractive or interesting or suggestive (e.g. story): coll.: 1900 (O.E.D. Sup.). Prob. suggested by *juicy*.

frume. See froom.

frumety-kettle. See furmity-kettle.

*frummagem; app. only as **frummagemmed**, choked, strangled, spoilt: c. of ca. 1670–1830. Head, Coles, Grose, Scott (in *Guy Mannering*). ? etymology.

[**frump,** n. and v., and **frumpish,** adj., are, despite F. & H., S.E. in all their senses.]

*frumper. A sturdy fellow: c. of ca. 1820–60. Kent, *Modern Flash Dict.*, 1825. Perhaps a survival of *frumper* = mocker, jester.

fry. To turn into plain English; gen. in passive: from ca. 1880; ob. James Payn, in *Grape from a Thorn*, 1881.

fry in one's own grease. To suffer the (natural) consequences of one's own folly; 'dree one's weird': coll.: C. 14–20. See esp. Apperson.

*fry the pewter. To melt pewter measures: c. of ca. 1850–1910. ? suggested by *fry the potato*.

fry your face, go and. A c.p. retort indicative of contempt, incredulity, or derision: ca. 1870–1905. Cf. the Suffolk *fry your feet!*, nonsense! E.D.D.

frying-pan. A collier brig from Whitby: nautical: C. 19. Ex the 'traditional wind vane, a large disc and a pointer' (Bowen).—2. (Gen. pl.) A hand: rhyming s. on sol. pronunciation *han*': C. 20, mostly military. F. & Gibbons.—3. See turnip. Mayhew, 1861; H., 5th ed., 1874; ob. On *warming-pan*.

frying-pan brand. 'A large brand used by cattle-stealers to cover the owner's brand', Morris: Australia (— 1857); ob.

frying-pan into the fire, jump from or out of the. To be thus worse off: from ca. 1520, with antecedents in Plato, Lucian, Tertullian: coll. until ca. 1890, then S.E. More, Harington, Garrick, Barham. See esp. Apperson.

fu-fu. Barley and treacle, 'a favourite dish in the early 19th century sailing ships': nautical: C. 19. ? origin: perhaps Bowen is wrong about the 'early', and the term derives from S.E. *fufu*, yam or plantain pounded into balls.—2. Hence, 'an amateur band raised in the ship's company': nautical: late C. 19–20. Bowen.—3. Hence, 'anybody inefficient at sea': nautical: C. 20. Ibid.

fuant. Excrement, esp. in pl. and of vermin (B.E.): C. 17–18 low coll. ? Fr. *puant* corrupted.

fub. See fob, n., 2, and fubbs.

fub, v. See **fob, v.**, of which it is a late C. 16–17 variant.—2. V.i., to potter about : cricketers' coll. (— 1906). Lewis. (Ultimately ex sense 1.)

fubbery, trickery, cheating, stealing, occurs in Marston. See **fob,** n. and v.

fub(b)s, n. ' A loving, fond Word used to pretty little Children and Women ' (B.E.), esp. if (small and) chubby : C. 17–18 : coll. Cf. the next two complete entries.

fubby. See :

fubs(e)y. Plump ; (of things) well filled : C. 17–20 (ob.) coll. ' Applied by Charles II to Duchess of Portsmouth ', W. ; Grose ; Marryat, in *Snarley-Yow*, 1837, ' Seated on the widow's little fubsy sofa '. Variant, *fubby.* Ex *fub(b)s,* q.v.

fubsiness. Fatness ; ' well-filledness ' : coll. : from ca. 1780. Ex preceding term.

fubsy. See **fubsey.**

fuck. An act of sexual connexion : from ca. 1800. (Ex the v., for which see etymology, etc.)—2. A person (rarely of the male) viewed in terms of coïtion, as in ' She's a good f.' : C. 19–20. These two senses are excellent examples of vulgarism, being actually S.E.—3. The seminal fluid, esp. if viewed as providing the requisite strength (*full of fuck,* potently amorous) : low coll. : C. 19–20.

fuck. v.t. and i. To have sexual connexion (with) : v.i. of either sex, v.t. only of the male : a vulg., C. 16–20. The earliest and latest dictionaries to record it are Florio (s.v. *fottere*) and Grose, the O.E.D., S.O.D., E.D.D. all ' banning ' it (cf. note at *cunt*) : the efforts of James Joyce and D. H. Lawrence have not restored it to its orig. dignified status. Either ex Gr. φυτεύω, L. *futuere,* Fr. *foutre,* the medial c. and the abridged form being due to a Teutonic radical and an A.S. tendency, or more prob., as A. W. Read (after Kluge) convincingly maintains, ex Ger. *ficken,* lit. to strike, hence to copulate with : cf., therefore, *bang* and *knock.* Transitive synonyms, many of them S.E. occur in Shakespeare (9), Fletcher (7), Urquhart (4), etc., etc. ; intransitive in Urquhart (12), D'Urfey and Burns (6), Shakespeare (5), etc., etc. See esp. B. & P. (the Introduction) ; Grose, P. ; and Allen Walker Read, ' An Obscenity Symbol ' (sec. II) in *American Speech,* Dec., 1934,—all at this term.—2. See **fuck off.**

fuck-beggar. An impotent or almost impotent man whom none but a beggar-woman will allow to ' kiss ' her : mid-C. 18–early 19 low coll. Grose, 1st ed., ' See buss beggar '.

fuck-finger, -fist. A female, a male, masturbator : low : C. 19–20, ob.

fuck-hole. The *pudendum muliebre* : C. 19–20 low. ? on *bung-hole.*

fuck (it) ! A low expletive : C. 19–20. Very gen. among those for whom delicacy and æsthetics mean little—or rather nothing. Manchon. Cf. *frig. it!,* q.v. at *frig,* v.

fuck off. To depart, make off : low : late C. 19–20. Cf. *bugger off, piss off,* qq.v.—2. Esp. in the imperative : id. : id.

fuck you, Jack, I'm all right ! A c.p. directed at callousness or indifference : nautical (late C. 19–20) ; hence military in G.W., and after. B. & P.

fuckable. (Of women) sexually desirable ; nubile : low coll. or a vulg. : C. 19–20. Cf. and contrast *fucksome.*

fucked and far from home. In the depths of misery, physical and mental : a military c.p. : 1915. (But believed to have existed as a low c.p.

from at least as early as 1910.) Ex the despair of a girl seduced and stranded.

fucker. A lover ; a harlot's ' fancy man ' : C. 19–20 low coll.—2. A pejorative or an admirative term of reference : from ca. 1850.—3, Hence, a man, chap, fellow : from ca. 1895 ; esp. in G.W., when the less Rabelaisian substituted *mucker.*

fucking, vbl.n. The sexual act regarded generically : C. 16–20 : vulg.

fucking, adj. (C. 19–20 low) ' a qualification of extreme contumely ', F. & H., 1893 ; but in C. 20, esp. in G.W., often a mere—though still a very low—intensive, occ. replaced by *mucking.*

fucking, adv. Very, exceedingly. Somewhat stronger and much more offensive than *bloody* (q.v.). From ca. 1840 ; perhaps much earlier—records being extremely sparse. Cf. *fucker,* 3.

fuckish. Wanton (of women) ; inclined, even physically ready, for amorous congress (men and women) ; C. 19–20 coll.

fucksome. (Of women) sexually desirable : a C. 19–20 vulg.

fuckster, fuckstress. A (notable) performer of, an addict to, the sexual act : a C. 19–20 vulg.—2. Hence, as a pejorative (' vieux cochon ', says Manchon) : late C. 19–20.

fud. The pubic hair : coll. when not Scottish or dial. : late C. 18–20, ob. as coll. Ex sense, a hare's or rabbit's scut.

fuddle. Drink ; a drink : c. or low : ca. 1680–1830. L'Estrange (O.E.D.) ; B.E. Ex the v.—2. Intoxication, drunken condition : coll. : from ca. 1760. O.E.D.—3. A drunken bout : low coll., or perhaps s. : from ca. 1810.—4. Derivatively : muddlement ; mental ' muzziness ' : from ca. 1825. (O.E.D.)

fuddle, the v., like **fuddler** and **fuddle-cap,** a drunkard, **fuddling,** vbl.n. and adj., and **fuddled,** ppl. adj., stupefied or muddled with drink, is, and prob. always has been, S.E. (far from literary), not c. nor s. nor even coll. : cf., however, F. & H.'s opinion with the O.E.D.'s.

fudge. A lie, nonsense ; exaggeration ; humbug or a humbug : 1790. Also (e.g. in Goldsmith, 1766), an exclamation, roughly equivalent to, though slightly politer than, *bosh !* Coll. : C. 18–20. Anecdotal orig. improbable ; perhaps ex Ger. *futsch,* no good, corrupted by Fr. *foutu* (W.), with the anecdote helping and *fudge,* v., reinforcing.—2. A forged stamp : schoolboys' : from ca. 1870.—3. A farthing : Dubliners', esp. newsboys' : late C. 19–20. Ex *fudge,* n. : cf. the Manx *not worth a fudge,* worthless or useless (E.D.D.).

fudge, v. To interpolate (as in Foote, 1776) ; do impressively very little (Marryat) ; fabricate (Shirley Brooks) ; contrive with imperfect materials, as e.g. writing a book of travel without travelling (Sala, 1859) ; forge (mostly schoolboys' : from ca. 1870). Coll. : all nuances slightly ob. and, in C. 20, almost S.E.—2. Botch, bungle, v.t. : coll. : from ca. 1700.—3. V.i., to talk nonsense, tell fibs : from ca. 1834.—4. Advance the hand unfairly in playing marbles : schoolboys' : from ca. 1875. In C. 20, almost S.E.—5. Copy, crib : also schoolboys' —and -girls' : from ca. 1870.—6. At Christ's Hospital (— 1877), v.i. and t., to prompt oneself in class ; to prompt another ; thence, to tell. Ex *fadge,* prob. influenced by *forge.*

fug. A stuffy atmosphere : from ca. 1888. ? ex *fog,* influenced by *fusty,* of which it is prob. a school-boys' or a dial. perversion (W.). In C. 20, coll.—

2. Hence (— 1923), one who likes a 'fug', a boy that doesn't play games: mostly schoolboys'. Manchon.

fug, v. To remain in a stuffy room: Shrewsbury School: from ca. 1888. Ex the preceding. Cf. *froust*, n., 2, and *froust*, v.

fug shop, the. The carpenter's shop at: Charterhouse (— 1900). A. H. Tod.

fugel, fugle, v.i. To cheat, trick: s. or dial.: C. 18–19. D'Urfey. (F. & H.'s definition is wide of the mark: perhaps the wish was father to the thought !)

fuggy. A hot roll: schoolboys': from ca. 1860. H., 3rd ed. ? etymology.

fuggy, adj. Stuffy: orig. (— 1888) schoolboys': from ca. 1910, coll. Perhaps a direct adoption of Scottish *fuggy*, *foggy*. F. & H.; O.E.D. (Sup.).— 2. Soft, effeminate: 'prep' schools': C. 20. Ex sense 1. (E. F. Benson, *David Blaize*, 1916.)

fugle. See **fugel.**

fugo. The rectum: C. 17–18: low coll. Cotgrave, D'Urfey.

fulham, fullam. A loaded die: practically never in singular. Mid-C. 16–early 19: low; in C. 17, perhaps c. Nashe, Shakespeare, Jonson, Butler, B.E., Grose, Scott. Fulham in South-West London was either a main manufactory or a notorious resort of sharpers. (A *high fulham* was marked 4, 5, or 6 ; a *low*, below 4.)

Fulham virgin. A loose woman: coll.: C. 19–20; ob. by 1905, † by 1927. Cf.—for same reason —*Bankside lady* and *Covent Garden nun*, qq.v.

fulk. 'To use an unfair motion of the hand in playing at taw' (marbles), Grose, 3rd ed.: schoolboys', mid-C. 18–early 19. Prob. ex dial., like so much other schoolboy s.; certainly it is extant in dial.

fulke. To have sexual intercourse (mainly v.i.): ca. 1820–1900: low pedantic. Ex the first and last words of Byron's *Don Juan*.

fulker. A pawnbroker: coll.: mid-C. 16–17. Gascoigne, 1566, 'The Fulker will not lend you a farthing upon it.' Ex Ger. (cf. *fogger*, q.v.).

full. Having eaten, occ. drunk, to repletion: low coll. since ca. 1830 ; earlier, S.E. (O.E.D.)— 2. Tipsy: coll.: from ca. 1850.—3. Having already sufficient money laid against a particular horse: bookmakers': from ca. 1880.—4. See **full up.**

full against. Very inimical to: gen. coll. from ca. 1870, ex earlier racing j. (see preceding entry, sense 3).

full as an egg. Very drunk indeed: Australian: from ca. 1925.

full as a goat. Extremely drunk: taverns': C. 18–19. Ware considers *goat* to be a corruption of *goitre*.

full as a tick. Replete (with food and/or drink): coll.: mid-C. 17–20; after ca. 1850, mainly dial.—2. Completely drunk: from ca. 1890: mainly Australian.

full as a tun(ne). Replete: coll.: ca. 1500–1660. Heywood the proverbist. (Apperson.)

full belly. One who ensures that his belly be full: C. 17 coll.

full blast, in. Very active ; highly successful: coll. (— 1859). Orig. North Country and ex the engine-room, esp. furnaces.

full bob. Suddenly ; in unexpected collision: C. 17–18 coll. Marvell, 'The page and you meet full bob.'

full-bottomed, -breeched, -pooped. Having a broad behind: coll.: **C.** 19–20, the first and third being orig. nautical.

full con. Flattery ; insincere compliment: military: from ca. 1908. F. & Gibbons. Cf. S.E. *confidence man.*

full dig, in. On full pay: ca. 1860–1910.

full due, for a. For ever: nautical: late C. 19–20. Bowen.

full feather, in. See **feather.**

full fig, in. See **fig.**—2. Adj. and adv., priapistic: low (— 1893) ; ob.

full-fledged. Ripe for the sexual act (of a girl): low coll.: C. 19–20.

full guts. A large-bellied person: C. 19–20, low coll. Adj., *full-gutted.*

full in the belly. Pregnant. Occ. abbr. to *full of it.* C. 19–20, low coll.

full house. A busy time: coll.: from ca. 1925. (Richard Blaker, *Night-Shift*, 1934, 'Sunday nights were, perhaps, the fullest house.') Ex *full house* notices at places of indoor entertainment.

full in the hocks or pasterns. Thick-ankled: coll., orig. stable s.: C. 19–20.

full in the waistcoat. Large-bellied: coll.: C. 19–20. Cf. *full guts.*

full march by [e.g.] **the crown-office, the Scotch Greys are in.** The lice are crawling down his (e.g.) head: a low c.p. of ca. 1810–30. *Lex. Bal.*

full jerry. To understand completely: New Zealanders': C. 20. See **jerry,** v.

full mouth. A chatterer: late C. 16–17 coll. Greene.

full of. Sick and tired of: Australian (— 1898) ; ob. by 1915, † by 1930. Morris. Cf. *full on* and *full up*, 2.—2. Covered with ; e.g. *full of mud*: South African coll. (— 1913). Pettman, 'It is an imitation of the Dutch idiom.'

full of beans. See **beans.**—**full of bread.** See **bread.**

full of 'em. Lousy ; full of fleas, nits: low coll.: C. 19–20.

full of emptiness. Empty: jocular coll.: late C. 18–20. Grose, 2nd ed.

full of f*ck and half starved. (Often preceded, occ. followed by *like a straw-yard bull*.) A friendly reply to 'How goes it ?' Low c.p., from ca. 1870 ; ob.

full of guts. Vigorous ; courageous ; (pictures, books, plays, etc.) excellently inspired: coll.: from ca. 1885. See **guts.**

full of it. See **full in the belly.**—2. Much impressed by any event or subject already mentioned: coll. (— 1887). Baumann.

full of oneself. Conceited ; somewhat ludicrously arrogant: C. 19–20 coll. Ex the C. 18–19 proverb, *He's so full of himself that he is quite empty.*

full on. More than ready ; eager: coll.: from ca. 1860.—2. Australian, from ca. 1890 : sated with, weary of, disgusted with ; ob. by 1914, † by 1920. Cf. *full up*, q.v.

full on for it or for one. Ready and extremely willing: gen. of an indelicate connotation: coll.: from ca. 1860.

full pack ; full pack up. See **Christmas-tree order.**—**full-pooped.** See **full-bottomed.**

full sail. Whiskers and beard: naval: C. 20. *The Evening News*, Feb. 25, 1936.

full suit of mourning, have or wear a. To have two black eyes: *half-mourning*, one black eye. Pugilistic: from ca. 1870 ; ob.

full swing, in. Very or fully active or engaged ;

highly successful : coll. (— 1861). *In the swing* is C. 18–20 ; *full swing* is C. 16–18. See **swing**.

full to the bung. Exceedingly drunk : low coll. : from ca. 1850. Cf. *bung-eyed*.

full up. Quite full ; full : coll. : C. 19–20. Whence perhaps :—2. (Constructed with *of*) sated ; weary ; disgusted : Australian and, later, New Zealand, from ca. 1890. Rolf Boldrewood in *The Miner's Right*. Variants *full* (if followed by *of*), *full on* (with object). Cf. *fed up* (with), q.v., the English counterpart.—3. Dead : taxi-drivers' (— 1935). Ex taxi-driving.

fullam. See **fulham**.

fuller's earth. Gin : ca. 1815–50. *Real Life in London*, 1821.—2. (**Fuller's Earth.**) New Zealand : theatrical and cinematic : from ca. 1912. Punning on the Fuller brothers, who, ca. 1910–30, owned a great number of N.Z. theatres and cinemas. (*The Daily Telegraph*, July 23, 1934.)

*fullied, be. To be committed for trial : c. : from ca. 1855. H., 2nd ed. Ex *fully committed*.

fullies. Women's drawers that are very full : feminine coll. : from 1933. See quotation at *neathie-set*.

fulness enough in the sleeve-top, there's not. A derisive reply to a threat ; it implies lack of muscle. Tailors' : ca. 1870–1920.

fumble, v.t., i., and absolute. To caress a woman sexually : coll. : C. 16–20 ; ob. Dunbar, Shebbeare, Goldsmith. (O.E.D.)

fumble-fisted. Clumsy : nautical coll. : from ca. 1860. Smyth.

fumbler. An impotent man, gen. old ; an unperforming or inadequate husband : mid-C. 17–19 coll. One of D'Urfey's titles is *The Old Fumbler*. Ex *fumble*, q.v.—2. The adj. *fumbling*, sexually impotent, C. 16–19, seems to have always been S.E.

fumbler's hall. ' The place where such [i.e. fumblers] are to be put for their non-performance ', B.E. : late C. 17–18 : coll.—2. The female pudend : late C. 18–19. For *free of fumbler's hall*, see **free of** . . . Cf. the dial. *fumbler's feast* mentioned by Southey in 1818.

fumitory. Incorrect for *fumatory* : C. 16–20. O.E.D.

fun. The breech or the behind : late C. 17–early 19. B.E. Prob. abbr. *fundament*.—2. A cheat, a trick : late C. 17–early 19. B.E. Both senses were orig. c. ? ex *funny* : certainly *funny business* is cognate, while U.S. *phoney business* is from another radical.—3. Difficult work ; exciting and/or dangerous events : military : from mid-1890's ; in G.W., from early Somme days (July, 1916), gen. bitterly ironical. (O.E.D. Sup.)

*fun, v.t. Cheat, trick, outwit ; with (*out*) *of*, deprive illicitly, dishonestly of : late C. 17–early 19 : orig. if not always c. Now dial., ob. B.E. ; Grose.

fun, do or, gen., **have a bit of.** To obtain or to grant, or enjoy together, the sexual favour : low coll. : from ca. 1850.

fun, have been making. To be tipsy : coll. : from ca. 1860 ; ob.

fun, like. Very quickly ; vigorously : coll. : from ca. 1815 : see **like**.—2. Also ironically as a decided negative : from ca. 1870.

fun at, poke. To joke (ob.), ridicule, make a butt (of). Also absolute without *at*. Coll. : from ca. 1835. Barham, ' Poking fun at us plain-dealing folks '.

fun (up)on, put the. To cheat, trick, outwit : late C. 17–early 19 : low. B.E. Ex *fun*, n., 2.

[**function** was, in 1915–18, employed by Army officers ' in almost any intransitive sense of *to make, do, act* ' : loose S.E. verging on coll. B. & P.]

functior, functure. A bracket candlestick made of iron and used for a night-light in college chambers : Winchester College (—1870). ? ex *fulctura*.

fundamental features. The posterior : cultured coll. : 1818, Moore : ob. *Blackwood's Magazine*, 1828, has it in the singular. Punning *fundament* : cf. *fun*, n., 1, and the jocular use of *fundamentally*.

funds. Finances ; supply of (esp. ready) money : coll. : 1728 (S.O.D.) : in C. 18 and C. 20, S.E. ; in C. 19, coll. Esp. *be in funds*, to have (temporarily) plenty of money. Thackeray.

funeral, it's his, my, your, etc. ; or negatively. It's his (not his, etc.) business, affair, concern, duty : orig., negative only and U.S. (1854), anglicised, mainly in the affirmative form, ca. 1880.

fungus. An old man (cf. S.E. *fossil* and † S.E. *funge*) : ? coll. : ca. 1820–90.

funk. Tobacco smoke ; tobacco ; a strong stink : resp. late and early C. 17–early 18 c. B.E. ; Ned Ward, 1703 (2nd nuance).—2. (A state of) fear, great nervousness, cowardice : orig. at Oxford, 1743, in *to be in a funk*. Often preceded by *cursed* (Grose), *mortal, awful, blue* (q.v.), or, in C. 19–20, *bloody*.—3. Among schoolboys, a coward : from ca. 1860. Anstey in *Vice Versa*, 1882. The second and third senses derive ex the first (itself prob. ex Flemish *fonck*), as appears from :

funk, v. ' To smoke ; figuratively, to smoke or stink through fear ', Grose, 1st ed. The *stink* sense occurs in 1708 ; that of smoking a pipe, five years earlier, and that of blowing smoke upon a person, four years earlier still. As to fear, the v.i. is recorded for 1737, the v.t., fear, be afraid of, not until a century later, and that of shirk, fight shy of, not until 1857, while the † sense, terrify, occurs in 1819 (e.g. in Mayhew, 1858).—3. With sense 1, connect ' to smoke out ', at least as early as 1720 : D'Urfey, Moncrieff ; with sense 2 (v.i.), cf. schoolboys' v.i. *funk*, unfairly to move the hand forward in playing marbles : from ca. 1810 ; ob. : cf. *fudge*, v., 4. (O.E.D. and S.O.D.) Perhaps n. and v. are ultimately derivable ex L. *fumus*, smoke, *fumigare*, to fumigate or smoke.

funk-hole. Any place of refuge, esp. a dug-out : military : 1900 (O.E.D. Sup.).—2. Hence, a safe job : id. : 1915. F. & Gibbons.

funk(-)stick. A person cowardly or very timorous : C. 20. A. E. W. Mason, *The Dean's Elbow*, 1930. Ex *funksticks*, q.v.

funk the cobbler. To smoke out a schoolmate (gen. with asafœtida) : from late C. 17 ; ob. by 1830, † by 1895. Ned Ward. See **funk**, v.

*funk 'um. A bag of lavender carried by a beggar more as pretence than as merchandise : c. : C. 20. (Michael Harrison, *Spring in Tartarus*, 1935.) Ex *funk*, v., 1 ; *'um = 'em*, them.—2. Hence, any perfume as merchandise : grafters' : from ca. 1910. Philip Allingham, *Cheapjack*, 1934.

funker. A pipe, cigar, fire : ca. 1800–70. Ex *funk*, n. and v.—2. A coward : from ca. 1860.—3. Among harlots, ' a girl that shirks her trade in bad weather ', F. & H. : from ca. 1865.—4. In the underworld, a low thief (— 1848) : c. ob. Duncombe.

funking-room. That room at the Royal College of Surgeons in which, on the last evening of their final examination during the adding of their marks, the students collect to hear the results : medical (— 1841) : ? †.

funkster. A coward : Winchester College : from ca. 1860. Cf. *funker*, 2.

funksticks. One who fears the fences (*sticks*) : hunting : 1889. (O.E.D.)—2. Hence, in South Africa, any coward : 1897, Baden Powell. (Pettman.)

funkum. See funk 'um.

funky. Afraid ; timid ; very nervous : coll. : from ca. 1837. Reade, ' The remaining Barkingtonians were less funky, and made some fair scores.' Cf. *windy*, (*have the*) *wind up*.

Funky Villas. Fonquevillers, near Hébuterne (in France) : military : G.W. (F. & Gibbons.)

funnel. The throat : coll. : C. 18–20, ob. Cf. *gutter lane*.

funniment. A joke, verbal or physical : from ca. 1845 (ob) : coll. Suggested by *merriment* and prob. coined by Albert Smith.—2. The female pudend : low : mid-C. 19–20, ob.

funnily, funniness, ex *funny*, adj., q.v., in the corresponding senses : C. 19–20.

funny. A narrow, clinker-built boat for sculls ; a racing-skiff : Cambridge and nautical s. > j. : from ca. 1799. Barham ; *The Field*, Jan. 28, 1882.

funny, adj. Strange, odd, queer : coll. : from early C. 19.—2. Hence, in late C. 19–20 coll. : dishonest.—3. Intoxicated : mid-C. 18–20 ; in late C. 19–20, only as a euphemism. Toldervy, 1756 (O.E.D.) ; *Slang*, p. 23.

funny, feel. To feel ill : from ca. 1895.—2. To be overtaken with drink or with emotion (e.g. of amorousness) : the former (†), from ca. 1800 ; the latter from ca. 1850.

funny bit. The *pudendum muliebre* : low : C. 19–20.

funny bone. The extremity—at the elbow—of the *humerus*, the ' funniness ' being caused by the ulnar nerve : coll. : from ca. 1840. Barham. Presumably by a pun on *humerus*, but greatly influenced by *funny feeling*, i.e. sensitiveness.

funny business. A shady transaction, dubious dealing ; monkeying about : s. >, ca. 1930, coll. : from ca. 1890. Ex a clown's *funny business*. Cf. the U.S. *phoney business* and *fun*, v., and n., 2.

funny for words, too. Extremely funny : coll. : late C. 19–20. Prob. suggested by *too funny for anything*, which was orig. (the late 1860's) U.S. (Thornton).

funny man. A circus clown : from ca. 1850. Mayhew, *London Labour*, III, 129.—2. A private joker : from ca. 1860. Both coll.

funny party. ' A warship's minstrel troupe or entertainers of any kind ' : naval coll. : late C. 19–20. Bowen.

funster. A maker of fun : coll. : 1887 : ob. Modelled on and suggested by *punster*. (O.E.D.)

fur. The (gen. female) pubic hair : low : C. 18–20.

fur, adj. and adv. Far : sol. : C. 19–20. Also *fer*.

fur and feather(s). Game : sportsmen : from ca. 1830 ; orig. s., then coll., then, in C. 20, j. or S.E.

fur fly, make the. See fly, make the fur.

fur out, have one's. To be very angry : Winchester College : from ca. 1870.

fur trade. Barristers : ca. 1830–80. ' Multiple ' journalist Reynolds, 1839.

furbelow. The female pubic hair : a C. 17–early 19 pun : cf. *fur*.

furch. Manchon's spelling of *furk !*, q.v.—**furfie, furfy.** See furphy.

[**furioso,** a blusterer, though cited by F. & H., is not unconventional but literary.]

furious joy. The *feu-de-joie* of military j. : military : late C. 19–20. F. & Gibbons. By ' Hobson-Jobson '.

furk ; also **ferk, firk.** To expel, drive away ; send on a message : Winchester College : from ca. 1850. Variants *furk down*, *f. up*. (Also see Eton slang, § 1.)

furk ! ; furking. Euphemistic variants (— 1923) of *fuck* (*it*) *!* and *fucking*. Manchon.

***furman.** An alderman : c. : late C. 17–early 19. B.E. Ex the fur-lined robes. Cf. *lambskin-man*, q.v.

furmity-faced. White-faced : coll. and dial. : C. 18–19. *Furmity*, also *fromenty* or *frum(m)ety*, is a dish of hulled wheat (L. *frumentum*) boiled in milk and variously flavoured.

furmity kettle, simper like a. To smile ; look merry : coll. : C. 18–early 19. In form *frumely-kettle*, however, it occurs in L'Estrange in 1668 ; and *simper like a pot that's ready to run over* is recorded by Apperson for 1631.

furnish. An embellishing or setting off : coll. : 1896 ; ob. (O.E.D.)

furnish, v.i. and t. To fill out ; regain strength and (good) appearance : coll. : from ca. 1860. Rarely of persons, gen. of horses. Henry Kingsley in *Ravenshoe*. Orig. stable s.

furniture picture. A picture sold to fill a gap on somebody's wall ; a picture painted solely as merchandise : artists' (— 1889) ; in C. 20, S.E. Barrère & Leland. Cf. *pot-boiler*, q.v.

furphy ; incorrectly **furphie, furfie** or -y. A false report, an absurd story : Australian military : from early 1915. Ex *Furphy*, the contractor supplying rubbish-carts to the camps at Melbourne. C. J. Dennis, 1916 ; B. & P. Hence :

furphy king. A man, esp. a soldier, making a habit of circulating rumours : Australian military : 1915–18. F. & Gibbons. Ex preceding.

furrow, or Cupid's or the one-ended furrow. The *pudendum muliebre* : low coll. : C. 19–20 (ob.). Whence *die* or *fail in the furrow*, do a ' dry-bob ', q.v., and *fall in the furrow*, to ' emit '.

furry tail. A non-unionist ; a ' rat '—whence the synonym. Esp. a workman accepting less than ' Society ', i.e. trade-union, wages : from ca. 1860 ; ob. Among printers, who, like tailors, have a large s. vocabulary. See *Slang* at ' Printers and Publishers ' and ' Trades '.

furry thing. (Gen. pl.) A rabbit : North Sea fishermen's euphemistic coll. : C. 19–20. For these fishermen, the mere mention of a rabbit brings ill luck. Bowen.

further first, I'll see you. I certainly won't ! Coll. (— 1851). In C. 20, the *first* is omitted. Mayhew, *London Labour and the London Poor*, I, 29.

Fury, the. The warship *Furious* : naval (— 1909) ; ob. Ware. Cf. *Dead Loss*.

fury, like. ' Like mad ', furiously, very hard or vigorously : coll. : from ca. 1840.

furze-bush. The female pubic hair, viewed as an entity. Occ. *furze*, which, however, stresses the hair as hair rather than as a mass. C. 19–20 low.

fusby. A woman : contemptuously pejorative : coll. : ca. 1719–1880. D'Urfey ; *Punch*, Nov. 29, 1845. (O.E.D.) ? ex *fubsy* influenced by *fussock* : qq.v.

fuschia. A very frequent error for *fuchsia*. Cf. *camelia* for *camellia*.

fuss. See **squeeze**, n., 6.

fuss-box. A post-1910, mostly upper-class variant of the next. O.E.D. (Sup.).

fuss pot, fuss-pot. A very fussy person : coll. (not the upper classes') : from ca. 1890.

fussock, fussocks ; a mere fussock. 'A Lazy Fat-Ars'd Wench ', B.E., who proceeds : ' *A Fat Fussocks*, a Flusom [? fulsome], Fat, Strapping Woman '. Grose (1st ed.) has ' an old fussock ; a frowzy old woman '. Coll. and dial. : late C. 17–19 ; † except as dial. Connected with (*to*) *fossick*, q.v., and :

fussock. To make much fuss, a noise : low, mostly Cockney (— 1923). Manchon. Imm. ex :

fussockin, fussickin. A fuss : Cockney (—1887). Baumann.—2. Hence, fussy : low, esp. Cockney (—1923). Manchon.

fussocks, a mere. See **fussock**.

fussy. (Of a garment) very, or too, elegant : from before 1923. Manchon. Ex S.E. *fussy about* (*clothes*).

fussy man, the. A school-attendance officer : urban : from ca. 1925.

fust. First : sol., esp. in Cockney : C. 19–20. Cf. *bust* for *burst* (W.).

fustian, n. and adj., bombast(ic), has never, I think, despite F. & H., been other than S.E.— 2. Wine ; but gen. with *white* = champagne, *red* = port, the latter occurring in Ainsworth, 1834. Low : late C. 18–19.

fustilarian. A low fellow, scoundrel : coll. : late C. 16–17. Shakespeare. ? *fusty* (see also next entry) + suffix *-arian* as a variation on the later-recorded :

fustilug(s), (Grose) **fusty luggs.** 'A Fulsom, Beastly, Nasty Woman ', B.E. Coll. : late C. 17–19. Junius. Common in C. 18–19 dial. as a big coarse person, a dirty slattern, a very untidy child. Cf. preceding entry. Lit., dirty ears or dirty thing.

fut, go. See **phut, go.**

[**futter,** coined by Sir Richard Burton, is, despite F. & H., S.E.—indeed literary—rather than unconventional. Ex Fr. *foutre*, it = to coït with.]

futures, gen. with **deal in** : to speculate for a rise or a fall, esp. in cotton : Stock Exchange coll. : from ca. 1880. In C. 20, S.E. Baumann.

fuzz. Abbr. *fuzz-ball*, q.v. : coll. : C. 17–early 18. In Holland's *Pliny*.

fuzz. To make drunk, esp. in p.ppl. passive, which = tipsy. Wood, 1685, ' The university troop dined with the Earl of Abingdon and came back well fuzzed.' Coll. : C. 17–18. Whence perhaps *to fuddle*, q.v. Its own etymology is uncertain : perhaps abbr. S.E. *fuzzle*, to intoxicate.— 2. To shuffle cards meticulously : change the pack : mid-C. 18–early 19. E. Moore in *The World*, 1753 ; Grose, 2nd ed. Prob. ex sense 1. (O.E.D.)

fuzz-ball. A puff-ball (the fungus *lycoperdon bovista*) : coll. : late C. 16–20. (S.O.D.) Of such long usage as to be, C. 19–20, virtually S.E.

*fuzz-chats. People camping on commons in the *furze* ; esp. Gypsies, showmen, cheapjacks : c. (— 1909). Ware.

fuzziness. A drunken condition ; hence incoherence, bewilderment ; a temporary dense stupidity : coll. : from ca. 1800 ; ob. The C. 20 prefers *muzziness*.—2. An intentional blurring : artists' and, later, photographers' s. (— 1866) : in C. 20 j.

fuzzy. Abbr. *Fuzzy-Wuzzy*, q.v. : military : late C. 19–20. Kipling. (O.E.D. Sup.)

fuzzy. Tipsy : coll. : from ca. 1770.—2. Hence, incoherent, temporarily ' dense ', bewildered : coll. : late C. 18–20 ; ob.—3. Rough, e.g. ' a fuzzy cloth ' ; big, vigorous, e.g. ' a fuzzy wench ' ; and esp. fluffy (1825) : of these three nuances, the first is coll., the second s., the third orig. coll. but soon S.E.—4. Prob. ex sense 1 is the nautical sense : rotten, unsound (of a ship) : from ca. 1860. Smyth.

Fuzzy-Wuzzy. A Soudanese tribesman, esp. as a dervish soldier : commemorated by Kipling in 1890 (reprinted in *Barrack-Room Ballads*, 1892). as ' a pore benighted 'eathen but a first-class fighting man '. Military : late C. 19–20, ob. Ex his ' 'ayrick 'ead of 'air '.

-fy is sometimes a jocularly coll. or, as in *argufy*, a sol. suffix : C. 19–20. But most such coinings have remained nonce-words.

fy out. To spy out : (low) Cockney (— 1887). Baumann. Ex *spy*.

*fye-buck (see also **buck**). A sixpence : in late C. 18, c. ; in C. 19, low ; † by 1885 ; already ob. in 1859. G. Parker's *View of Society*, 1781.

*fylch(e). See **filch.—fyst(e).** See **foist.**

G

G.G. George Grossmith : journalists' nickname. Dawson. Cf. *Society Clown*, q.v.

G.H. ! Queen Anne's dead ! : an abbr. of *George Horne*, q.v.

g.m. A.m. ; only of the 'small' hours, e.g. '2 g.m.', 'some time g.m.' : jocular (— 1923). Manchon. Perhaps ex ' *good morning* '.

G.P. ; the Street. Great Portland Street, London ; esp., the car-mart there : motor-trade s., now verging on coll. : from ca. 1928. R. Blaker, *Night-Shift*, 1934, ' Great Portland Street—" The Street " one and only and unmistakable ; " G.P."—the street of perdition.'

G.S. hairy. See **hairy**, n.

g.v. or G.V., the. The ' governor ' (q.v.) : somewhat jocular (— 1923). Manchon. Ex *gov.*

g.y. Abbr. *galley-yarn*, q.v.

ga-ga. See **gaga**.

gab. The mouth : low coll. : from ca. 1720, orig. Scottish. (*Gob*, q.v., is 'earlier.)—Hence, 2, talk ; idle chatter : coll. : from ca. 1790. Poole, 1811, ' Then hold your gab, and hear what I've to tell ' ; *Punch*, Sept. 10, 1887, ' Gladstone's gab about " masses and classes " is all tommy rot.' Ex *gob*, q.v., or rather ex :

gab, v. To talk fluently, very well ; too much : from ca. 1670 : (in C. 19–20, low) coll. Coles, 1676 ; Burns, ' gab like Boswell ' ; *Punch*, Sept. 10, 1887, ' Gals do like a chap as can gab.' Perhaps abbr. *gabble* and prob. distinct from S.E. *gab*, to tell lies, speak mockingly, though Coles's definition (' to prate or lie ') hardly supports such distinction.

gab, blow the. To inform, ' peach ' : low coll. : late C. 18–mid-19 ; ca. 1810, *blow the gaff* > more gen. (See **gaff.**) Grose, 1st ed.; Ainsworth in *Rookwood*.

gab, flash the, occ. **one's.** To show off in conversation : low (— 1819) ; ob. Moore.

gab, gift of the. 'A facility of speech, nimble-tongued eloquence ', Grose, 1st ed. : low coll. : from ca. 1780. Shelley in *Œdipus Tyrannus*. Earlier (? ca. 1640), *gift of the gob*, as in B.E. : the form prevalent until ca. 1780.

gab, stop your. Be quiet ! A C. 19–20 low coll. variant of Scottish *steek* (shut up) *your gob*.

gab-string. (Variant *gob-string*.) A bridle : C. 18–early 19 low. Grose, 1st ed.

gabber. A prater, ceaseless talker : coll. : from ca. 1790. (O.E.D.)

gabbey. See **gaby.**

gabble. A gossiper : coll. : C. 19.—2. A voluble talker : coll. : C. 19–20.—3. Rapid, continuous talk : from ca. 1600 : C. 17–18 S.E. > pejorative coll.

gabble, to. Talk rapidly, volubly, inconsequently : late C. 16–20 ; S.E. till ca. 1820, then a decidedly pejorative coll. The same applies to *gabbling*, vbl.n.

gabble-gabble. A contemptuous variation on *gabble*, n. and v., qq.v.

gabble-grinder. A gossiping or voluble talker : coll. : C. 19–20 ; ob.

gabbling. See **gabble,** v. **gabey.** See **gaby.**

gabster. An empty or an eloquent talker : coll. : C. 19–20 ; ob. Cf. *gab*, n. and v.

gaby, or **gabey** ; occ. **gabb(e)y.** A fool, dolt ; boor : coll. (— 1791). Grose, 3rd ed.; H. Kingsley, ' Don't stand laughing there like a great gaby.' ? ex *gape* (cf. *gape-seed*) influenced by *baby* ; it occurs in Lancashire dial. in 1740 (E.D.D.). *Gaby* is not to be connected with the Scottish adj. *gabby*, garrulous.

gad. An idle or trapesing slattern : low coll. (— 1859). H., 1st ed. Abbr. *gadabout*.—2. A shirt : tramps' c. (— 1923). Manchon. Ex Romany.

gad ! Coll. abbr. of coll. *by gad* (C. 17–20) : C. 19–20 ; ob. Cf. *egad, bedad ; gads me, gads my life*. Ex *God*.

gad, (up)on the. Impulsively ; suddenly : coll. : C. 17–18. Shakespeare. Here, *gad* = a spike : cf. *on the spur of the moment*.—2. Hence, on the move ; constantly making visits, gossip : coll. : from ca. 1815. Jane Austen.—3. On the spree : low : from ca. 1830.—4. Hence, from ca. 1850, (of women) on the town.

gad the hoof. To go without shoes ; hence to walk, roam about : low : from ca. 1845. Cf. *pad the hoof, hoof it*, qq.v.

gad up and down. To go a-gossiping : late C. 17–18 coll. B.E.

gad yang. 'A Chinese coasting junk ' : nautical : late C. 19–20. Bowen. Prob. *gad* because they gad about, and *yang* ex the Yangtse-kiang or as a typical Chinese name.

gadabout. A gossip moving from neighbour to neighbour ; a housewife too frequently talking to or visiting others ; a woman constantly out shopping, visiting, and otherwise enjoying herself : cf. the C. 18 proverb, ' gadding gossips shall dine on the pot-lid '. Coll. : from ca. 1837. Also adj. : coll., 1817 (O.E.D.). In C. 20, both n. and adj. are S.E.

gadget ; occ. **gadjet.** A small mechanical contrivance, a tool, a part of a mechanism : nautical coll. : from ca. 1855, though not in print before 1886 (O.E.D. Sup.). Prob. ex Fr. *gâchette*, a piece of mechanism (W.) ; cf. however, S.E. *gasket*.—2. Hence, an adjunct ; a knick-knack : coll. : from ca. 1914. The O.E.D. (Sup.) records it for 1915.—3. Hence, loosely, any small object : from ca. 1918. —4. *the gadget*, ' the trick ', the right thing to do : military : 1917. Manchon. Prob. ex sense 1.

gadsbud ! I.e. *God's bud !* (the infant Saviour) : coll. : late C. 17–18. Congreve. (Ware.)

gadso. The penis : late C. 17–mid-19 : low coll. Variant *catso*. Ex It. *cazzo*.—2. As an interjection : late C. 17–mid-19. Dickens, ' " Gadso ! " said the undertaker'. An interesting example of the (politely ob.) phallicism of many oaths and other expletives : cf. and see *balls, bugger, cunting, fuck, prick, twat*.

gadzooks. A mild expletive : either ex *gadso* or a corruption of *God's hooks* (? *hocks, houghs*, W.) : coll. : late C. 17–20 ; but since ca. 1870, only as deliberate jocularity or in ' period pieces '. There are many other *gad(s)* variations, but these need not be listed.

Gaelically utter. The Scottish accent ' when trying to produce English ' : Society coll. : ca. 1882–1910. Ware. Suggested by *too too*, q.v.

***gaff.** A fair : c. of ca. 1750–1845. *The Discoveries of John Poulter*, 1753. (Then grafters' s. : Philip Allingham, *Cheapjack*, 1934.) Also c., at least orig., are the senses :—2. A ring worn by the card-sharping dealer of the pack : early C. 19 : ex *gaff*, a hook.—And 3, a hoax, imposture ; stuff and nonsense (— 1877) : cf. Fr. *gaffe*, a social blunder.—4. An outcry ; cry, ' bellow ' : low : ca. 1820–50, C. M. Westmacott. (O.E.D.)—5. Any public place of entertainment : ca. 1810–50 : low (or c.).— Hence, 6, a low and cheap music-hall or theatre : low coll. : from ca. 1850. Mayhew. Also and often *penny-gaff*, 1856. Prob. ultimately ex sense 1. —7. Hence, talk, conversation : lower classes' (— 1923). Manchon.—8. Hence, the mouth : low (— 1923). Ibid. Cf. *gab*, 1.—9. In the G.W., it was occ. applied to ' any showy minor event [e.g. a trench raid] or affair ' : military. F. & Gibbons. Prob. ex sense 6. Cf. the corresponding sense of *show*.—10. A house that is being ' drummed ' (see **drum**, v., 2) : c. : C. 20. David Hume. Cf. :—11. The place or scene of the crime concerned : c. : C. 20. James Curtis, *The Gilt Kid*, 1936.—12. (Prob. ex senses 1–10.) An affair ; a criminal enterprise : c. : from ca. 1920. Ibid.

***gaff,** v.i. To toss for liquor : c. >, ca. 1820, low s. : ca. 1810–80. Vaux. Cf. *gaffing*.—Also, 2, to gamble : same period.—3. To play in a ' gaff ' (see n., 6) : from ca. 1860 ; ob.

gaff, blow the. To inform ; divulge a secret : low (perhaps orig. c.) : from ca. 1810. (Earlier *blow the gab*, see **gab.** See also **blow.**) Vaux ; Marryat.

gaff-topsail hat. A silk ' topper ' : nautical : late C. 19–20. Bowen.

gaffer. A husband : C. 18 coll. or dial.—2. An old man, esp. if a rustic (cf. *gammer*, q.v.), esp. as a term of address : coll. and dial. : late C. 16–20. Gay, Tennyson. Both these senses and the next six are ex *granfer* = grandfather.—3. Simply as term of address = ' my good fellow ' : coll. : late C. 16–20 ; slightly ob.—4. A master or employer : from ca. 1650 ; in C. 20, dial. Dyche, 1748, ' A familiar word mostly used in the country for master '.—5. Hence, a foreman : navvies' : from ca. 1840.—6. ' Mine host ' at an inn : low or c. (— 1887). Baumann.—7. Among athletes, a trainer (— 1888) ; ob.—8. The steward of a race-course : the turf : late C. 19–20.—9. A player at toss-penny : ca. 1828–80. ' Jon Bee.' Ex *gaff*, v., 1 or 2. (O.E.D.)—10. ' A market-master or fair-ground superintendent ' : grafters : from ca. 1880. Philip Allingham, *Cheapjack*, 1934. Cf. *gaff*, n., 1.

gaffer, v. To have sexual intercourse : C. 19. ? ex the v. implied in *chauvering* (sexual inter-course), q.v. : app. a corruption thereof.

gaffing. A way of tossing three coins in a hat to say who is to pay for drinks ; only he who calls correctly for all three is exempt from payment : low (? orig. c.) : ca. 1828–80. Pierce Egan.—2. Hence, toss-penny ; tossing of counters : low coll. (— 1859). H., 1st ed.

gag. Something placed in the mouth to silence or prevent the subject's cries : mid-C. 16–20. Perhaps always S.E., but ca. 1660–1800 it may have been c., then low ; witness B.E. (at *to gag*) and Grose.—2. Boiled fat beef ; more precisely, the fatty part of boiled beef : Christ's Hospital (— 1813) ; but see also section on Eton slang, § 3. Lamb. ? Etymology. Cf. *gag-eater*.—3. A joke ; invention ; hoax ; imposition ; humbug ; false rumour : from ca. 1805 : low s. >, ca. 1880, coll. : ob. Bee ; *The Daily News*, May 16, 1885. Ex sense 1.—4. Whence, interpolated words, esp. jokes or c.p. comments : theatrical (— 1847). *Pall Mall Gazette*, March 5, 1890, ' Mr. Augustus Harris pointed out that . . . actors and singers were continually introducing gag into their busi-ness.' In this quotation and often elsewhere, *gag* is collective, i.e. *gagging*, 3. Cf. *wheeze*. Ex pre-ceding sense, itself perhaps ex sense 1.—5. A criticism in Latin ; an analysis of some historical work : Winchester College : from ca. 1850. Mans-field. Ex *gathering*, an alternative name for this exercise.—6. A lie : c. : ca. 1860–1920. H., 3rd ed. ? ex theatrical *gag*.—7. An excuse ; a ' dodge ' : C. 20, mainly military. Often heard in the Army in 1914–18. Ex the ' lie ' and the theatrical sense.

gag, v. ' To put Iron-pinns into the Mouths of the Robbed, to hinder them Crying out ', B.E. ; in late C. 17–early 18, app. c. ; in C. 19–20, S.E. Ex the victim's gurgle (W.).—2. Hence, to hoax, v.t. and i. : low s. or coll. (? orig. c.) : from ca. 1777 ; † by 1880. Parker, Bee.—3. Take a rise out of (— 1864) : low coll. ; ob. H., 3rd ed.—4. To puff : low (— 1876). Hindley in his *Cheap Jack*.—5. Make up words ; speak ' gags ' (see n., 4), v.i. : theatrical, perhaps orig. low Cockney (see *London Labour*, III, 149) : ? first in 1852 in Dickens's *Bleak House*, ' The same vocalist gags in the regular business like a man inspired.'—6. As v.t., to fill up or enliven with a gag : 1861. (O.E.D.)—7. To lay information (v.t. with *on*) : c. (— 1891) O.E.D.— 8. V.t., to beg : tramps' c. : C. 20. W. A. Gape, *Half a Million Tramps*, 1936. Cf. *gag*, n., 7.

***gag, on the high**, adj. and adv. Telling secrets ; ' on the whisper ' : c. : ca. 1820–80. Kent, Dun-combe. Cf. *to gag*, last sense.

***gag, on the low.** In extreme destitution ; in lowest beggary ; with appalling bad luck ; in utter despair : c. : ca. 1820–80. Cf. preceding entry.

gag, strike the. To desist from joking or chaffing : low (? c.) : ca. 1830–70. Ainsworth in *Jack Shep-pard*. See *gag*, n., 3.

gag-eater. A Christ's Hospital term of re-proach : from ca. 1800 ; ex *gag*, n., 2, perhaps by way of *gag*, v., 1. (See also ' Eton slang ', § 3.)

gag-master. See *gagger*, 3.

gag-piece. (Theatrical) a play in which ' gags ' are, or can effectively be, freely used (— 1864). H., 3rd ed.

gaga ; incorrectly *ga-ga*. Evincing senile decay ; stupidly dull, fatuous ; ' soft ', ' dotty ' : 1921, Maurice Baring (O.E.D. Sup.). Adopted ex Fr. s., which may, seeing that it was orig. artists', derive ex *Gauguin* ; more prob., however, echoic of idiotic laughter. Esp. *go gaga*.—2. In *The Silver Spoon*, Galsworthy uses it (1926) for ' strait-laced '.

***gage.** A quart pot : c. : mid-C. 15–19. Promptorium Parvulorum (O.E.D.), Harman, B.E., Haggart. In C. 18, occ. a pint (pot) : Grose. In C. 19 c., occ. a drink. Ex the measure.—2. A pipe (for smoking) : mid-C. 17–early 19 c. Coles ; B.E., Grose, Ainsworth.—3. A chamber-pot : C. 18 coll. Variant spelling, *gauge*.—4. A small quantity of anything : low coll. (— 1864). H., 3rd ed. Ex senses 1, 2.—5. A greengage plum : lower classes' coll. (— 1923). Manchon.

***gager.** An early form of **gorger**. C. Hitchin, *The Regulator*, 1718.

***gagger.** In late C. 18–mid-19 c., one of those ' cheats who by sham pretences, and wonderful stories of their sufferings, impose on the credulity of well-meaning people ', Grose, 2nd ed. Ex *gag*, v., 2. Cf. *rum gagger*. Called *high* and *low gaggers* : also cf. *gag, on the high* or *low*.—2. Hence, a tramp, esp. one that begs : tramps' c. : mid-C. 19–20.— 3. An actor or music-hall ' artist ' ; from late 1840's, esp. one that often employs ' gags ' (*gag*, n., 4) : theatrical (— 1823). Egan's Grose ; *The Fortnightly Review*, April, 1887, ' Robson . . . was an inveterate gagger.' Variants : *gaggist* (rarely), *gag-master* (occ.), and *gagster* (fairly often).—4. The under-lip : Perthshire c. : C. 19–20 ; ob. (E.D.D.) Also *gegger*. Prob. ex † S.E. *gag*, v.i., to pro-ject.

***gagger**, v. To tell the pitiful tale : tramps' c. (— 1932). F. Jennings, *Tramping with Tramps*. Ex *gagger*, 2.

gaggery. A hoaxing kind of wit : ca. 1819–50 : coll. Cf. *gag*, v., 1. O.E.D.—2. The practice of employing ' gags ' (n., 4) : theatrical : from ca. 1860. Cf. :

***gagging.** The persuading a stranger that he is an old acquaintance and then ' borrowing ' money from him : ca. 1825–80 : c.—2. Loitering about for fares : cabmen's : ca. 1850–1910. Mayhew.— 3. The frequent employment of ' gags ' (n., 4) · theatrical (— 1883). Also as ppl. adj.—4. (Cf. senses 1, 2.) Begging (n.) : tramps' c. : C. 20. W. A. Gape : see *gag*, v., 8.

***gagging lark.** Unconcealed begging in the streets : c. : C. 20. James Curtis, *The Gilt Kid*, 1936. A tip silences the beggar's cries.

gaggist. See *gagger*, 3.

***gaggler's coach.** A hurdle : c. of ca. 1820–60. Duncombe. Ex *gaggler*, a goose. Or is this Kent's mistake, copied by Duncombe, for *gaoler's coach* (q.v.), also = a hurdle ?

gagster. See *gagger*, 3.

Gaiety girl. (Gen. pl.) One of the ' dashing singing and dancing comedians in variety pieces— from their first gaining attention at the Gaiety Theatre ' : theatrical coll. : from ca. 1890 ; ob Ware. Cf. :

Gaiety step. 'A quick, high dancing pas, made popular at the Gaiety Theatre': theatrical coll.: ca. 1888–92. Ware.

gail. A horse: either low or c.: early C. 19. ? connected with Romany *grei*.

‡gain-pain, the sword of a hired soldier, **is,** in English, a ghost word. S.O.D.]

gainst, 'gainst. Except in poetry, a late C. 16–20 coll.

gajo. An outsider: Parlyaree (— 1933). E. Seago. Ex Romany *gaujo*, a stranger.

gal. A girl: an upper-class coll.: from ca. 1840. Perhaps ex New England pronunciation (— 1796).— 2. A servant-girl: lower-class coll.: from ca. 1850. —3. A sweetheart: low coll.: from ca. 1860. Cf. *chap, fellow.*—4. A harlot: low coll. (— 1851); ob. Mayhew, 'Upon the most trivial offence . . . the gals are sure to be beaten . . . by their "chaps".'

gal-sneaker. 'A man devoted to seduction'; London lower classes': ca. 1870–1915. Ware.

galabieh, tighten one's. To tighten one's belt: Egyptian-service military coll.: from ca. 1920. The n. is direct ex Arabic.—2. Hence, from ca. 1925, to make the best of a bad job.

galaney. See **galeny.**

galanty (occ. **gallanty** or **gal(l)antee**) **show.** A shadow pantomime; occ. a magic-lantern show, but of silhouettes only: from ca. 1820. Ob. by 1900, † by 1930. This term, S.E. at origin and in C. 20, seems to have been coll. ca. 1850–90. ? ex It. *galanti.*

galany. See **galeny.**—**galavant.** See **gallivant.**

*galbe. 'Profile of a violent character, and even applied to any eccentricity of shape above the knees': c. (— 1909). Ware derives from Fr. *Galbe*, the Emperor Galba of 'pronounced profile and terrific nose': but is it not a sense-perversion of Standard Fr. *galbe* (from It. *garbo*), bodily contour ?

gale of wind dose. Very little whiskey in much water: nautical: late C. 19–20. Bowen. Opp. *second mate's nip.*

galen, Galen. An apothecary: coll.: ca. 1870–1910. By way of *Galen*, jocularly a physician. Ex the great physician of the 2nd century A.D.

galeny, galeeny, galan(e)y. A guinea-fowl: coll. or dial.: late C. 18–20. Ex L. *gallina. Temple Bar*, March, 1887.—2. In late C. 18–early 19, a fowl of any kind : c.

galimaufr(e)y, gallimaufr(e)y. As a medley, a jumble, and as 'a hodgepodge made up of the remnants and scraps of the larder' (Grose), it is S.E. But as a mistress, it is a late C. 16–17 coll. Shakespeare in *Merry Wives.*—2. In 'love'-making s., the female pudend : C. 19. Ex Fr.

galivant. See **gallivant.**

gall. Effrontery; impudence: late C. 19–20 low; more gen. in U.S., where app. it arose, than in England; cf., however, *gall is not yet broken,* q.v.

gall, on the. On the raw, i.e. on a tender spot (lit. or fig.): coll., ? > S.E.: C. 14–17. Chaucer, Skelton, Sanderson.

*gall is not yet broken, his. A mid-C. 18–early 19 c., esp. prison, saying of a man that appears dejected. Grose, 1st ed. Ironical on † *gall(s)*, courage.

[**gallant,** n., v., and adj., and **gallantry** in all senses given by F. & H., are S.E.]

Gallant Fittieth, the. The 50th Foot Regiment, British Army : military, coll. rather than s.: from 1808, ex its gallant share in Vimiera ; ob. Cf. *Gallants, the.*

gallantee (or **gallanty**) **show.** See **galanty show.**

Gallants, the. 'The 9th (Service) Battalion of the Royal West Surrey. A Great War nickname,' F. & Gibbons.

gallavant. See **gallivant.**

*gallersgood. Worthy of the gallows : c.: C. 18–early 19. Ware. I.e. *gallows-good.*

gallery. A commoner bedroom : Winchester College : C. 19. Ex a tradition of galleries in Commoners. Cf. *gallery-nymph.*—2. A showing of oneself in a ridiculous light : Shrewsbury School: late C. 19–20. Desmond Coke, *The Bending of a Twig*, 1906. Cf. *play to the gallery.*—3. A playing to the gallery : Public Schools' : C. 20. D. Coke, *The School across the Road*, 1910.

gallery, play the. To be, make an audience ; to applaud : coll. (— 1870); ob. Ex the theatre. *The Echo*, July 23, 1870, 'We were constantly called in to play the gallery to his witty remarks.' Cf.:

gallery, play to the. Orig. theatrical, then sporting, then gen.: to act so as to capture popular applause : from ca. 1870 : coll. Hence *gallery-hit, -play, -shot, -stroke,* etc., one designed to please the uncritical and those who like showy display.

gallery-nymph. A housemaid : Winchester College : C. 19. Ex *gallery*, 1, q.v.

galley. A synonym († by 1925) of Bootham School senses of *soap,* n. and v. (Anon., *Dict. of Bootham Slang*, 1925.)

[**galley, build a,** on which Grose expatiates, is ineligible.]

galley down-haul. An imaginary fitting, for the further confusion of a youngster for the first time at sea : nautical coll. : mid-C. 19–20. Bowen. Cf. *key of the starboard watch,* q.v.

galley down your back ! put a. Such-and-such a superior wishes to see you ! : printers' : from ca. 1870 ; ob. The galley—an oblong tray—would serve as a screen.

[**galley-foist** and **g.-halfpenny,** listed by F. & H., are S.E. : see the O.E.D.]

galley-growler or **stoker.** An idler ; malingerer : naval : from ca. 1850. Smyth. The galley is, of course, the cook-house : cf. *galley-yarn,* q.v.

galley-news; g.-packet (Smyth). See **galley-yarn. galley-slang.** 'A landsman's attempt at nautical jargon ' : nautical coll. : late C. 19–20. Bowen.

galley-slave. A compositor : printers' : late C. 17–19. Moxon. Ex the oblong tray whereon the type is made up for page or column.

galley-stoker. See **gally-growler.**

galley-wireless. News of destination, etc.: nautical : from ca. 1925. Bowen remarks that it ' reaches the men from the officers by way of the stewards '. Contrast and cf. :

galley-yarn. A lying or hoaxing story ; a swindle : nautical (— 1874). H., 5th ed. ; Henley & Stevenson in *Admiral Guinea*. Occ. abbr. to *g.y.* In this sense, ob. by 1910, † by 1930.—2. A rumour, esp. if *baseless* : late C. 19–20 nautical. As a lie, an empty rumour, *galley-packet* is a frequent synonym, dating from (—) 1867 : prob. the earliest form. *Galley-news* is of ca. 1880–1900. Cf. *cookhouse yarn, furphy, shave, sh*t-house rumour* or *yarn, transport tale.*

galleynipper. See **gallinipper.**

Gallicanism and **Gallicism** are, in C. 19–20, occ. confused. (O.E.D.)

gallied. 'Hurried, vexed, over-fatigued, perhaps like a galley-slave', Grose : C. 18–early 19 coll. More prob. ex dial. *gally,* to frighten.

galligaskins, S.E. in C. 16–17, is in C. 18–20 (ob.) a gen. jocular coll. for any loose breeches. Grose, 3rd ed. For the etymology of the S.E. word, see esp. W.

gallimaufr(e)y. See galimaufrey.

gal(l)inipper, occ. **gall(e)ynipper.** A large mosquito : West Indians' (— 1847). Ex U.S. usage (1801). Perhaps one that has a ' gallows ' nip or bite : see **gallows,** adj.

gallipot. An apothecary : late C. 18–20 (ob.) coll. Lit., a pot conveyed in a galley (vessel). Grose, 1st ed.; Michael Scott ; Thackeray in his *Book of Snobs.* Cf. *bolus.*

gallipot baronet. An ennobled physician : Society coll. : ca. 1850–1910. Ware. See **gallipot.**

gallivant, etc. ' A nest of whores ', Bee : London low : ca. 1820–40. ' Jon Bee ', 1823. ? a perversion of *galeny,* 2, q.v.

gal(l)ivant, occ. **gal(l)avant.** To gad about with or after, ' do the agreeable ' to, one of the other sex : coll. : 1823. Bee ; Dickens. Perhaps ex the n. (q.v.) ; perhaps a perversion of *gallant* (W.).—2. Hence, to gad about, ' trapes ' ; occ. fuss or bustle about : coll. : from ca. 1825. Miss Braddon, ' His only daughter gallivanting at a theaytre '. A humorous variation of *(to) gallant,* as in Galt's ' The witches . . . gallanting over field and flood ' (W.). The vbl.n. is common.

gallon distemper. Delirium tremens ; the less serious after-effects of drinking : C. 19–20 (ob.) coll. or s. Cf. *barrel-fever ; hot-coppers.*

galloot. See galoot.

galloper. A blood horse ; a hunter : ca. 1810–60 : low or c. *Lex. Bal.*—2. An aide-de-camp ; an orderly officer : military : from ca. 1870 ; in C. 20, j.

Galloper Smith. Lord Birkenhead (*the* Mr. Smith of the day) : ca. 1913–15. Collinson. Ex his quality as an Ulster leader.

galloping Lockhart. Gen. pl., ' the mobile Field Kitchens ' (F. & Gibbons) : military : 1914 ; ob.

gallore. See galore.

gallow-grass. Hemp : mid-C. 16–17 : s. > coll. I.e. ' halters in the rough ', F. & H. Cf. *neck-weed.*

gallows. (As = one who deserves hanging : S.E.)—2. Gen. in pl., a pair of braces : low coll. : 1730 ; then U.S. (1806) ; re-anglicised ca. 1830 ; in C. 19–20, mostly dial. Mayhew ; E.D.D.

gallows, adj. Enormous ; ' fine ' ; an intensive, cf. *bloody* : late C. 18–20, ob. except in dial. Parker, 1789, ' They pattered flash with gallows fun.' Whence :

gallows, adv. Very ; extremely : from ca. 1820 ; ob. except in dial. Byron, ' Then your Blowing will wax gallows haughty ! ' Also *gallus.*

gallows, a child's best guide to the. See **history of the four kings.**

gallows-apples of, make. To hang : low (? c.) : ca. 1825–80. Lytton. (O.E.D.)

gallows-bird. A corpse on, or from, the gallows : low coll. (— 1861) ; ob. Ex the S.E. sense, one that deserves to be hanged.

[**gallows-faced** or **-looking,** like g.**-clapper, -climber, -minded, -ripe,** etc., is S.E. ; the same applies to George Eliot's *gallowsness.*]

gallus. A frequent pronunciation and occ. spelling of *gallows,* adv. Cf. *allus.*

gally-pot. See gallipot baronet.

gally-swab. A cook's steward : *Conway* cadets' : from ca. 1880. John Masefield, *The Conway,* 1933.

*gallyslopes. Breeches : early C. 19 c. ? punning *galligaskins.*

galoot, occ. **galloot,** rarely **ge(e)loot.** A man, chap, fellow ; gen. a pejorative, implying stupidity or boorishness or moral toughness : orig. (1866), U.S., anglicised ca. 1880. Developed from the, 2, nautical s. sense (— 1835 ; † by 1900), a young or inexperienced marine. Marryat in *Jacob Faithful,* ' Four greater galloots were never picked up.' Ex :—3. A soldier : low or c. (— 1812) ; † by 1890. Vaux. ? ex Dutch *gelubt,* a eunuch. (S.O.D. ; W.)

galoot, on the gay. On the spree : low, mostly Cockney (— 1892). ' Ballads ' Milliken.

galoptious, galuptious ; goloptious ; or any with **-shus.** Delicious ; delightful ; splendid ; a gen. superlative : low : from ca. 1855 ; ob. *Judy,* Sept. 21, 1887, ' The galopshus sum of 20,000,000 dollars '. A fanciful adj. of the *catawampus, scrumptious* type, perhaps via Norwich dial. (H., 1864). See **goloptious.**

galore ; occ. † **gallore, gol(l)ore.** In abundance : from ca. 1670 : coll. till ca. 1890, then S.E.—though far from literary. In C. 19, also *in galore.* Prob ex Irish *go leor,* in sufficiency. Ned Ward, Grose, Reade.

galumph (incorrectly **gallumph**), like other humorous (esp. Lewis Carroll's) blends, looks coll but certainly isn't. Such blends, if adopted by the public, are, after the first few years, almost inevitably S.E. F. & H. records *galumph* as an Americanism : not a very shocking mistake, for the Americans adopted it warmly and used it frequently. (For blends, see *Slang* at the chapter on ' Oddities '.)

*gam. Pluck ; *gameness* : c. (— 1888).—2. With variant *gamb,* a leg, esp. if bow or otherwise ill-shapen ; nearly always in pl. : from ca. 1780 : c. G. Parker, 1781 ; Grose, 2nd ed. In low U.S. s., only of a girl's legs. It is also, as *gamb,* the heraldic term for a leg. Ex Northern Fr. *gambe* or else ex It. *gamba,* via Lingua Franca.—3. A hammock : training-ship *Britannia* : late C. 19. Bowen. Perhaps ex sense 2.—4. Abbr. *gamaroosh* : C. 20 ; mostly military.

*gam, flutter a. To dance : C. 19 c.—But *lift a gam =* to break wind : c. : mid-C. 19–20. Henley.

Gam-better. To humbug, deceive : political : ca. 1879–82. Ex Gambetta (1832–82), that Fr. statesman of Italo-Hebraic origin whose popularity began to wane in 1879. Ware.

*gam-case. A stocking : c. : late C. 18–mid-19. G. Parker, 1781. Ex *gam,* 2.

*gam it. To walk ; esp. to ' leg it ', run away : C. 19 c.

gamaliel. A pedant : a cultured coll. : C. 19–20 : † by 1921. Ex that Jewish doctor in the *Acts* who ' cared for none of these things '—things about which the multitude excited itself.

gamaroosh, -ruche, n. and, hence, v. (Of women.) (To practise) penilingism : late C. 19–20 low. Ex Fr. (? ex Arabic).

gambardier, or **gambolier** (or **-eer**). A member of the Royal Garrison Artillery : military, resp. coll. and s. : 1915. B. & P. ; Mark Severn, *The Gambardier,* 1930.

*gamb(e). See gam, 2.

gamble. Anything, esp. course or procedure, involving risk : coll. : from ca. 1820.—2. An act of gambling : coll. : from late 1870's. O.E.D.—3. Whence *on the gamble,* engaged on a course or spell of gambling : coll. : from ca. 1880.

gamble on that !, you can or **may.** Certainly ! Assuredly ! Coll. : from ca. 1870 in England ; ex U.S. (1866, Artemus Ward).

gambler. A mid-C. 18–early 19 class of sharper : low or c. Whence mod. S.E.

gamblous. Of, like to, gambling : Society coll. : coined by Joseph Chamberlain on April 29, 1885, in a speech made at a dinner given by the Eighty Club ; ob. Ware. Ex *gambling* + *hazardous*.

gambol. A railway ticket : railwaymen's : ca. 1880–1914.

gamboleer or **-ier.** See **gambardier.**

*****game.** (Collective for) harlots, esp. at a brothel : c. : late C. 17–early 19.—2. A simpleton, a dupe, a ' pigeon ' ; gen., however, a collective n. : c. : late C. 17–early 19. B.E., Grose.—3. The proceeds of a robbery : c. of ca. 1660–90.—4. A ' lark ' or source of amusement : coll. : Dickens, 1838 (S.O.D.).— 5. Preceded by *the*, game refers to some occupation and, except among thieves (where it is c.), is to be demarcated as coll. : among thieves it means thieving (1812, Vaux) ; among sailors, slave-trading (— 1860) ; among C. 17–early 18 lovers of sport, cock-fighting ; in amorous venery, coïtion (C. 17–20) ; among harlots, prostitution (C. 17–20).— 6. As plan, trick or dodge (esp. in pl.), the term— despite F. & H.—is gen. considered to be S.E. : nevertheless, I consider that *what is your (his, etc.) game* or *little game*, mid-C. 19–20 (' Ducange Anglicus ', 1857), is definitely coll.

*****game, v.** To jeer at ; pretend to expose ; make a game of : c. : late C. 17–18. B.E. (N.b. *make* († *a*) *game of* is S.E.)

game, adj. (Plucky : S.E.—Ready, willing : S.E.—Lame : S.E., says O.E.D. ; coll., says W. : from ca. 1785.) In c., (of men) knowing, wide-awake ; (of women) prone to venery, engaged in harlotry : C. 18–20. Cf. *game-pullet*, q.v.

[**game, cock of the**, a champion, like **game, die, to die resolute**, **game, play the**, to behave like a man and a gentleman, and (**the, his,** etc.) **game is up**, all is lost, are all metaphors from sport : and all, despite F. & H., are S.E., though *die game* may orig. have been coll.]

game !, it's a. It's absurd, or senseless ! : military coll. c.p. of 1916–18. ' Applied to the war and to the military machine ', B. & P.

*****game, on the.** Thieving : c. (— 1839) ; slightly ob. Brandon. Cf. *game-cove*, q.v.—2. Engaged in prostitution : harlots' c. : mid-C. 19–20. See **game, n., 5.**

game, stashed up the. See **stash up.**

game, the national indoor. Sexual intercourse : late C. 19–20 : coll.

Game Chicken, the. A coll. nickname for a famous boxer of ca. 1820 ; i.e. Hen Pearce, champion of England. See esp. Bernard Darwin, *John Gully and His Times*, 1935.

*****game cove.** An associate of thieves : C. 19 c. Ex *game*, n., 5.

game ever played, the first. Sexual congress : C. 19–20, coll. rather than euphemistic.

*****game publican.** A publican dealing in stolen goods or winking at his customers' offences : C. 19 : c. >, ca. 1830, low.

game pullet. ' A young whore, or forward girl in the way of becoming one ', Grose, 1st ed. : late C. 18–19 low (? orig. c.). Cf. *game woman.*

game ship. A ship whose captain and officers are susceptible to bribes for overlooking thefts from the cargo : nautical : ca. 1830–90.

*****game woman.** A harlot : C. 18–19 : c. >, ca. 1830, low. Cf. Etherege's ' the game mistress of the town '. See **game, n., 5.**

[**gameness, gam(e)y** (plucky ; malodorous), **gaminess** (malodorousness), and **gaming-house**, all listed by F. & H. as coll., have always been S.E.]

gamester. A harlot : C. 17 coll.—2. In the sense of wencher, C. 17, the term lies on the borderline of coll. and S.E.

gammer, as rustic title, C. 16–20 (ob.), is coll. > S.E. ; as term of address, = ' my good woman ', it is coll. Ex *grandmother*. Cf. *gaffer.*

gammocks. Pranks ; wild play : s. (— 1823) and (in late C. 19–20, nothing but) dial. ' Jon Bee.' Ex *game.*

gammon. Nonsense, humbug ; a ridiculous story ; deceitful talk ; deceit : low, prob. orig. c. (— 1805) ; in C. 20, low coll. Ex the late C. 18–19 c. sense, talk, chatter, gen. *gammon and patter*, q.v. (In C. 18–early 19, often spelt *gamon*.) Parker ; Hood, ' Behold yon servitor of God and Mammon . . . Blends Gospel texts with trading gammon.' Perhaps ex C. 17 sense, a beggar or seller of gammons of bacon. (Cf. Fr. *boniment(s)*.)—3. Wholly c. : one who engages the attention of a man to be robbed by a confederate : C. 19. Cf. *cover.*

gammon, v.i. To talk, esp. plausibly (— 1789).— 2. (V.i. and t.) To pretend : from ca. 1810.—3. Humbug or hoax ; tell deceitful or extravagant stories to ; deceive merrily or with lies or fibs ; flatter shamelessly : from ca. 1810. Likewise in Vaux. All senses orig. low ; from ca. 1850, low coll. Hume Nisbet, 1890, ' Oh, don't try to gammon me, you cunning young school-miss.' Cf. *bam, cod, flam, kid, pull one's leg, sell, soft-soap, take in.*— 4. V.i., act as ' cover ' to a thief : C. 19 (? C. 18) c. Ex n., 3. (S.O.D.)—5. To cheat (v.i.) at gaming : late C. 17–mid-18 : c. B.E. Prob. the origin of senses 1–3 and of n., 1. Its own etymology is obscure : but cf. *game*, v., 1.

gammon ! Interjection = nonsense ! bosh ! : from ca. 1825 ; low s. >, by 1860, low coll. Michael Scott, 1836, ' Gammon, tell that to the marines.' Ex n., 1, or ex *that's all gammon* (Vaux, 1812).

*****gammon, give** or **keep in.** To engage a person's attention—the former connotes by mere propinquity, the latter by conversation—while another robs him : C. 18–19 c. Capt. Alex. Smith, 1720 ; Haggart, 1821. Cf. *gammon*, n., 3.

*****gam(m)on and patter.** The language of the underworld, esp. of thieves : late C. 18–early 19 c. G. Parker, 1781.—2. The commonplace or familiar (hence almost jargonistic) talk of any trade or profession : late C. 18–20 ; ob. c. Grose, 2nd ed.— 3. A meeting ; a palaver : from ca. 1850 : c. See **gammon**, n., and **patter**, n.

gammon and spinach. Nonsense ; humbug ; deceit : low coll. : from ca. 1845 ; ob. Dickens, 1849, ' What a world of gammon and spinnage it is.' An elaboration of *gammon*, n., 1, after *gammon and patter.*

*****gammon lushy ; gammon queer.** To feign tipsiness, illness : c. : C. 19. Vaux. See **lushy.**

*****gammon the twelve.** To deceive the jury : c. (— 1812) ; ob. Vaux, who shows that *in fine twig*, cleverly or thoroughly, was often added. See **gammon**, v., 3.

gammoner. One who talks nonsense or humbug ; a specious or ulterior deceiver : from ca. 1830 slightly ob. Ex *gammon*, v., 1.—2. (Cf. *gammon*, n., 1.) One who covers the action of his thieving confederate : C. 19 c. Cf. *cover.*

gammoning. Vbl.n. and ppl. adj. corresponding

to *gammon*, **v.**, in all senses, though rarely in the last—*gammoning* which was † by 1900, while the other *gammoning*'s are extant though slightly ob.

*gammoning academy. A reformatory : c. : late C. 19–20. F. & H., revised ed. (at *academy*).

*gammy. The language of the underworld : C. 19 : c. ? ex *gammon and patter.*—2. A lame person (see **gammy**, adj., 4) : late C. 19–20.—3. A fool : Australian : ca. 1890–1910. Hume Nisbet in *The Bushranger's Sweetheart*, 1892.

*gammy, adj. False, spurious ; forged : c. (— 1839). Brandon. As in *gammy stuff*, spurious, i.e. worthless, medicine ; *gammy moniker*, a forged signature ; *gammy lour* (*low*(*r*)), counterfeit money. Perhaps ex *gammy*, n., 1.—2. Also c., but tramps' : mean ; hard (of householders) : mid-C. 18–20. Bampfylde Moore-Carew. Opp *bone.* Hence *gammy vil*(*l*)*e* or *vial*, a town in which unlicensed hawking is enthusiastically discouraged by the police.—3. Old ; ugly : theatrical : from ca. 1885 ; ob. ? ex next sense.—4. Halt and maimed : low coll. : from ca. 1870. *Gammy leg*, E.D.D., a lame leg ; *ganmy arm*, an arm injured permanently or temporarily ; *gammy-eyed*, blind, or sore-eyed. Either a corruption of *game* = lame or ex *gam*, n., 2. —5. Hence, 'disabled through injury or pain' : (low) coll. : from ca. 1890. O.E.D. (Sup.).

gamon. See **gammon**, n. and v.

gamp or **Gamp.** A monthly or sick nurse, esp. if disreputable ; a midwife : coll. (— 1864) ; ob.— Hence, 2, a fussy, gossiping busybody : coll. (— 1868). Brewer, quoting *The Daily Telegraph*, 'Mr. Gathorne Hardy is to look after the Gamps and Harrises of the Strand.' Ex Mrs. Sarah Gamp in Dickens's *Martin Chuzzlewit*, 1843 : as also in next two entries.—3. An umbrella, esp. a large one loosely tied : coll. : 1864. G. R. Sims.—4. *The Standard* : journalists' (— 1873) ; †. Cf. *Mrs. Harris* (another Dickens character : cf. sense 2), *The Herald*.

gamp, adj. ; **gampish.** Bulging, gen. of umbrellas : coll. (1881, 1864) ; ob.

Gamp, Mrs. A variant of *gamp*, n., **3** : coll. (— 1887). Baumann. Cf. *gamp*.

Gamp is my name and Gamp my natur' is itself a familiar quotation from Dickens, but if another (sur)name is substituted for that of Mrs. Gamp, it is a cultured c.p. of late C. 19–20. Collinson.

gampy. A low coll. variant (— 1887) of *gamp*, n., 3 ; ob. Baumann.

gamut, in the. A picture, a detail, etc., in tone with its accompaniments or environment : artists' : from ca. 1870 ; † by 1930.

*gan. The mouth ; occ. the throat : c. : mid-C. 16–early 19. Harman. ? ex Scottish *gane*. Cf. *gans*, q.v.

gan, v. Incorrect for *can* in † *to can thanks.* O.E.D.

gander. A married man : C. 17–20 coll. ; ob. Cf, *gander-month*.

Gander. A fop : London (mostly in Society) : ca. 1815–40. Ware, 'It is a perversion of Gandin, the Parisian description of fop.'

gander, v. Ramble ; waddle (like a goose) : coll. (— 1859). H. Kingsley.

gander, what's sauce for the goose is sauce for the. Let us be consistent ! Coll. (in C. 20, ? S.E.) : from ca. 1660. Head, Swift, Byron. Apperson quotes Varro's *idem Accio quod Titio jus esto.* Cf. the proverbs ' As is the goose so is the gander,' C. 18, and

'Goose, gander, and gosling are three sounds, but one thing,' C. 17.

gander-faced. Silly-faced : proletarian (mostly Cockney) coll. (— 1887) ; slightly ob. Baumann.

gander-month or **-moon.** The month after childbirth, when in C. 17–early 19 it was held excusable for the husband to err. Coll. ; † except in dial. Dekker, 1636 (O.E.D.).

gander-mooner. A husband during the ' gander-month ' : C. 17–19. Middleton, 1617.

gander-party. A party of men : opp. *hen-party* and cf. *stag-party.* Occ. *gander-gang.* Coll. : C. 19–20, ob. Orig. (— 1866), U.S. ; anglicised ca. 1880.

gander's wool. Feathers : coll. of the *cow-juice* type : C. 17–20 ; ob. Breton.

gang. A troop ; a company ; an underworld band of men : C. 17–20. Only from ca. 1850 has it ceased to be low coll. B.E., e.g., defines : ' An ill Knot or Crew of Thieves, Pickpockets or Miscreants'. Even in C. 20, when used contemptuously of a political party or section, or of a social, commercial, artistic, or journalistic—informal, yet effective— association or group, it has a coll. tinge, as in, e.g., Denis Mackail, *Greenery Street*, 1925, ' " Quite a party ? " " Yes ; quite a gang." '

ganger. An overseer or foreman of a working gang : coll. : from ca. 1849. It > S.E. ca. 1880. Mayhew ; *The Cornhill Magazine*, June, 1884.— 2. A member of the press gang : nautical coll. : C. 19. Bowen.

gangway ! Make way ! : *Conway* cadets' : from ca. 1860 : c.p. >, by 1900, j. Cf. :

gangway (or gangway, make way) for a naval officer ! A C. 20, esp. G.W., Army saying in reference to oneself or another desiring clear passage.

gannet. A greedy seaman : nautical : mid-C. 19–20. Bowen. Ex the bird.

*gans. The lips : c. : late C. 17–18. B.E. Cf. the differentiation of *mun, muns.* The E.D.D. notes the Scandinavian dial. *gan*, a fish-gill.

gantline. Incorrect for *girtline* : nautical : 1882 (O.E.D.). Or for *gauntlet* : nautical (— 1887). Baumann.

ganymede. (As a sodomist, late C. 16–19 literary.) A pot-boy ; *Hebe*'s ' opposite number ' : C. 17–20 (ob.) jocular and cultured coll. Ex *Ganymede*, cup-bearer to Zeus.

gaol-bird. One who has been often or long in gaol : from ca. 1680. Until ca. 1860, coll. Smollett, 1762, ' He is become a blackguard gaol-bird.'

gaoler's coach. A hurdle : ' traitors being usually conveyed from the gaol, to the place of execution, on a hurdle or sledge ', Grose, 3rd ed. : c. > low : late C. 17–early 19. Possibly the orig. of *gaggler's coach*, q.v. (In B.E. and Grose, 1st ed., as *goaler's coach* ; but *A New Canting Dict.*, 1725, has it correctly.)

gap. The female pudend : S.E. only if strictly medical and contextual : C. 18–20, low. Robertson of Struan, a '*φ*' poet who d. in 1746.—2. Mouth, esp. in *stop yer* (*your*) *gap !*, be quiet : low : late C. 19–20. *Slang*, p. 243.

gap, blow the. To inform, ' peach ' : a ca. 1820–90 variant of *blow the gaff.*

gap-stopper. A whoremonger : mid-C. 18–19 low. Grose, 1st ed.—2. The virile member : C. 19–20 low. Cf. :

gape. The female pudend ; gen. as *g. over the garter* : C. 19–20 low ; ob. Cf. *gaper*.

gape-seed, gapeseed. A cause of astonishment ;

a marvellous event, extraordinary or unusual sight, etc.: coll.: late C. 16–20, ob. Esp. with *seek* or *buy*, a vbl. phrase is frequent. (Florio, 1598, has the rare *gaping seed*.) Nashe; B.E.; Grose, 1st ed., 'I am come abroad for a little gapeseed'; C. 19–20 dial., *be fond of* or *gather* or *sow g.*, or *have a little g.* A folk-pun on *gape*.—2. One who stares with open mouth: from ca. 1880: coll.; ob.

gape-seed, be looking for. To be lazy and inattentive to one's work: C. 19 coll., C. 20 dial. (ob.).

gaper, or g. over the garter. The *pudendum muliebre*: C. 19–20 low; ob.—2. (*gaper*.) A very easy catch: cricketers': C. 20; slightly ob. P. G. Wodehouse, *A Prefect's Uncle*, 1903.

gaperies (or **G.**), **the.** Gay Paris: London: 1902–ca. 1912. Ware, 'The very last outcome of entertainments ending in "ies"'. Cf. *Colinderies, Freakeries*, etc. (*Gay Paree*.)

gapes, the. A bit of yawning; utter boredom: coll.: from ca. 1815. Jane Austen.

gapped, ppl. adj. Worsted; defeated: coll.: ca. 1750–1820. Ex S.E. sense, with the edges notched or cut about.

gaps with one bush, stop two. To accomplish two purposes at one time: C. 16–17; coll. till C. 17, then S.E. Cf. *kill two birds with one stone*.

gar in oaths (*begar !, by gar !, gar !*) is a corruption of *God* (cf. *gad*): late C. 16–20. (O.E.D.) Rather Anglo-French than purely English: cf., however, the U.S. pronunciation of *God* as *Gard*.

Gar and Starter, the. The Star and Garter Inn at Richmond: jocular Spoonerism (— 1874). H., 5th ed.

Garamity. See **Goramity.**

garbage. Clothes and personal effects: naval (— 1909); ob. Ware, 'Probably from the appearance of a box of clothes waiting the wash'—and perhaps suggested by *dunnage*.—2. 'The goodes gotten' in the 'lifting law' (criminal 'dodge'): c.: late C. 16–early 17. Greene, *Second Conny-Catching*, 1592.

Garbo, do a. See 'Moving-Picture Slang', § 10. Contrast *Gaynor*, q.v.

garboil is, mid-C. 16–mid-18, often used incorrectly for **garble.** O.E.D.

garden. The female pudend: C. 16–20. When a euphemism, S.E.; when used in jocular or amatory reference, *without* euphemistic intentions, it is cultured coll. (Occ., *garden of Eden*, indubitably a euphemism.)

Garden, the. Covent Garden Market: greengrocers', fruiterers', gardeners', orchardists': from ca. 1760: coll.—2. Covent Garden Theatre: theatrical coll. (— 1864). H., 3rd ed.—3. Hatton Garden: diamond-merchants' (— 1890): coll.—4. See **Academy, the.**

garden, v. See **gardening.**

garden or **garden-path, lead up the.** To blarney (a person), humbug, entice, mislead: from early 1920's. Ex gently suasive courtship.

***garden, put** (one) **in the.** To defraud (a confederate), esp. of (part of) his monetary share: c.: from ca. 1810; ob. Vaux (variants, . . . *bucket, hole, well*). Cf. *regulars*, q.v.

garden-gate. A magistrate: rhyming s. (— 1859). H., 1st ed.—2. The *pudendi labia minora muliebris*: low coll.—very rare as a euphemism: C. 19–20. Cf. *garden-hedge*.

Garden goddess. A harlot, not necessarily superior: C. 19. Cf. C. 18 *Covent Garden abbess*.

The Covent Garden district was harlot-ridden in C. 17–early 19. Cf.:

Garden-gout. Syphilis; gonorrhœa: C. 19 low. Cf. C. 18 *Covent Garden ague*.

garden-hedge. The female pubic hair: C. 19–20 low (ob.); rarely a euphemism.

Garden- or **garden-house.** A brothel: the *garden-* form is C. 17 coll. > literary; the *Garden-*, C. 18–early 19 low coll. See **garden**, 2, **Garden goddess**, and the various **Covent Garden** entries.

***garden-hop.** To betray (a confederate): c.: from ca. 1920. Edgar Wallace, *The Missing Million*. By rhyming s. on c. *shop*.

garden-Latin. Sham or extremely bad Latin: coll.: C. 19–20. Cf. *apothecaries'* and *kitchen Latin*; *bog* and *dog Latin*.

***garden-party.** Those prisoners who, suffering from phthisis, do their time in the open-air and sleep in special wards: c. (— 1932). T. B. G. Mackenzie in *The Fortnightly Review*, March, 1932.

garden-path. See **garden, lead up the.**

garden-rake. A tooth-comb: a low and jocular coll.: from ca. 1870.

garden steerage. Additional rest 'allowed to the bluejacket the morning after he has been busy on a night job': naval: late C. 19–20. Bowen.

garden-violet. See **violet.**

Garden whore. A harlot; a low harlot (cf. *Garden goddess*): C. 19 low.

gardener. The male member: cf. and ex *garden*: C. 19–20; ob.—2. An awkward coachman: coll. (— 1859); † by 1918. Ex the gardener's occ. relieving the coachman. Cabbies, wishing to annoy real coachmen, used to shout, 'Get on, gardener' (H., 1864). Cf. *tea-kettle coachman* or *groom*.

gardening. Patting the pitch, picking up loose bits of turf: cricketers' jocular coll. (— 1897). Lewis.

gards. 'Post guardship': nautical: C. 19. Bowen.

gardy-loo. Take care ! Look out ! A mid-C. 18–early 19 Scottish coll. Ex Fr. *gardez* [-*vous de*] *l'eau* or (via the supposed Fr. *gare de l'eau*) ex Fr. *gare l'eau*, i.e. the slops thrown into the street.—2. Hence, the act of so emptying the slops: same period and status.

gargle. A drink; drink: orig.—ca. 1859—medical for physic; gen. by 1889. Cf. *lotion*.

gargle, v.i. To drink; drink a lot, 'celebrate': orig.—? ca. 1880—medical; gen. by 1889. *The Morning Advertiser*, March 2, 1891, 'It's my birthday; let's gargle.'

gargle-factory. A public-house: from ca. 1870. Ex *gargle*, n., q.v.

garlic, smell. To smell something 'fishy', to have suspicions: Cockney (— 1887); slightly ob. Baumann.

Garman, or **German** likewise pron. *Jarman*, has been low coll. since ca. 1860.

garn ! 'Get away with you !' Low coll.: from ca. 1875. Ex *go on*. Runciman, *The Chequers*, 1888; *Ally Sloper*, March 19, 1892. Cf. *gorn*, q.v.

Garnet, Sir. See **Sir Garnet.**

garnish, in late C. 17–19 occ. *garnish money*. A fee exacted by gaolers and 'old hands' from a newcomer to prison: late C. 16–19: s. until ca. 1790; then coll. >, by 1830, S.E. Greene, B.E. (Abolished by George IV.)—2. Among workmen, mid-C. 18–19. an 'entrance fee'—wholly informal:

s. > coll. > S.E. Goldsmith. Occ. *maiden-garnish*. Not quite † in Northern—mainly Yorkshire—dial.—3. In C. 18–19 c., fetters, handcuffs. But, as the O.E.D. points out, this may well be a ghost-word due to a misapprehension by Johnson, copied by F. & H. Cf.:

*garnish, v. To fit with fetters; handcuff: **o.** (— 1755); † by 1900. Ex *garnish*, n., 1. But see **garnish**, n., last sense.

garrage. See **garridge.**—**garotte.** See **garrotte.**

garret. The head: from ca. 1785. Grose (2nd ed.), who also gives *upper storey*, q.v. Cf. also *cock-loft*.—2. Hence the mouth: low: C. 19. Ware.—3. The fob-pocket: c.: ca. 1810–70. Vaux, 1812: H., 1859.—4. 'A consultation of the members of a shop in relation to some trade or social difficulty': hatters': C. 19–20; ob. Ware. Cf. a printers' *chapel*.

garret, queer or **wrong in one's.** Crazy: s. when not dial. (— 1869). O.E.D. Ex *garret*, 1.

garret-election. A ludicrous, low popular ceremony practised at Wandsworth, London, when a new parliament opens, the ' voting '-qualification being open-air coïtion in or near Garret, a mean hamlet: C. 18–early 19. Coll.: or perhaps rather a legitimate folk-lore term. See Grose, 1785.

garret empty or **unfurnished, have one's** (occ. **the**). To have no brains; be a fool, somewhat crazy: from ca. 1790. Cf. Kentish (*be*) *not rightly garreted*.

garret-master. A cabinet-maker that, working on his own account, sells direct to the dealers: cabinet trade: from ca. 1850: in C. 20, S.E. and ob. Mayhew.

*garrete(e)r. A thief specialising in entering houses by garret-windows or sky-lights · c.: mid-C. 19–20 (ob.). Cf. *dancer, dancing-master*.—2. A literary hack: from ca. 1730: journalists' s., > gen. coll. ca. 1780, > S.E. ca. 1895: ob. Bentley, Macaulay. Ex S.E. sense, one who lives in a garret.

garridge ; garrage. A garage: sol.: from ca. 1910. (D. Sayers, *The Nine Tailors*, 1934.)

garrison-hack. A harlot: a soldier's drab: coll.: from ca. 1850; ob.—2. A woman that habitually flirts, somewhat indiscriminately, with garrison officers: from ca. 1875. *The Athenæum*, Feb. 8, 1890, ' The heroine is a garrison-hack, but the hero is an Australian.'

garrison sports. Washing out quarters: Regular Army jocular coll.: late C. 19–20; ob. F. & Gibbons.

*gar(r)otte. To cheat with the aid of cards concealed at the back of the neck: card-sharping c.: from ca. 1850.

*gar(r)otte, tip (one) the. To rob during or after throttling the victim: c.: from ca. 1850; † by 1900. The n. and the v., rob with or by throttling, with their natural derivatives, are S.E. ex the S.E. sense, execution by strangulation; see, however, **back-stall, front-stall,** and **ugly** or **nasty-man.** Ex Sp. *garrote*, a stick: cf. *garrot*, a surgical tourniquet.

*gar(r)otting. Vbl.n. corresponding with *gar(r)otte*, v., above.

garry, gharry. A (gen. light) carriage: Anglo-Indian coll.: from ca. 1800. Ex Hindi *gari*, a cart, a carriage. See Yule & Burnell.

garter, get over her or **the.** To take manual liberties with a woman: C. 19–20 (ob.) low coll.

garter, in the catching up of a. In a moment; quickly: coll.: from ca. 1690; ob. O.E.D.

garter-hole or **eye-hole.** Fillet-hole: bell-ringers' (— 1901), resp. s. and coll. (Rev. H. Earle Bulwer.)

garters. The irons; fetters: nautical (—1769); ob. Falconer. Pleasantly semantic.

garters, have one's guts for. See **guts for garters.**

garvy, garvie. (Gen. in pl.) A sprat: standard Scottish (from ca. 1740), whence, in pl., the 91st Foot Regiment (in late C. 19–20 the 2nd Connaught Rangers) in the British Army: military: 1823; ob. F. & Gibbons. Ex the lean appearance of the early recruits in the Fifeshire regiments. Cf. *Jack Sprat*.

gas. Empty talk; bombast; baseless boasting or threats: 1847, U.S.; anglicised ca. 1860. *Chambers's Journal*, June 29, 1867, ' I've piped off Sabbath gas in my time.'—2. A jet of gas: coll.: 1872 (S.O.D.).—3. See **gas, step on the.**

gas, v. To supply with gas; to light with gas: coll.: from ca. 1885: ob. by 1920; † by 1930. (O.E.D.)—2. Talk idly or for talking's sake; boast unduly or arrogantly (— 1874).—3. The sense, to deceive by such talk, is orig. and mainly U.S.

gas, give a person. To scold him; give a thrashing: ca. 1860–90. See (**give one) jessie,** by which it was perhaps suggested. (H., 2nd ed.)

gas, step on, occ. **tread on the.** To put on speed: U.S., anglicised ca. 1926. Ex motor-driving, *gas* being gasolene.

gas, turn off the. To cease, cause to cease, from overmuch talk or from boasting: from ca. 1880. Ex *gas*, n., 1. Cf.:

gas, turn on the. To begin talking hard or boasting: from ca. 1880.

gas and gaiters. Nonsense; mere verbiage, utter redundancy; exaggerated rubbish: from ca. 1928. An elaboration of *gas*, n., 1, after *gammon and spinach* (or *g. and patter*).

gas-bag. A person of too many words; a boaster: coll.: from ca. 1889. Ex *gas*, n., 1. Cf. *wind-bag* and *poison gas*, qq.v.—2. A balloon, airship: pejorative coll.: 1877; slightly ob. (O.E.D. Sup.)—3. ' The cloth bag in which the anti-gas respirator was carried ': facetious military: 1916; ob. B. & P.

gas-boat. ' A motor fishing vessel in the Grand Banks ': nautical: C. 20. Bowen. Here, *gas* = gasolene.

gas-pipe cavalry. Army cyclists: military (— 1923). Manchon.

gas-pipes. Very tight trousers: Cockneys': ca. 1890–1915. Ware.

gas out of one, take the. To take down a peg, the conceit out of one: from ca. 1885. See *gas*, n., 1.

gas round, to. Seek information slily: from ca. 1890: † by 1921. The gen. post-1918 phrase is *snoop* (a)*round*, q.v.

gascrome, gascromh. Incorrect for *caschrom*: C. 19–20. O.E.D.

gaseous. Apt to take offence on insufficient grounds: coll. (— 1864); † by 1920. H., 3rd ed. Ex the inflammability of gas.

gash. The mouth: orig. U.S. (1852) and rare in Britain except in jocular form, *an awful gash*: late C. 19–20.—2. The female pudend: C. 18–20: low coll.

gashion. Additional, free; often in pl. as n., ' extra of anything ' (cf. *buckshee*): naval: late C. 19–20. Bowen; F. & Gibbons. Prob. ex dial. *gaishen* (*gation*), an obstacle in one's way, perhaps via *additional*.

gashly. Ghastly : sol. when not dial. : C. 19–20. In C. 17–18, S.E., as in Sterne. Ex *gash*, ghastly, S.E. in late C. 16–18, then Scottish.

gashly, adv. Steadily ; esp. in *go gashly!* : military : C. 20. F. & Gibbons. Ex the Scottish and North Country *gashly*, shrewdly (E.D.D.).

gaskins. Wide hose or breeches : (in C. 18–19, jocular) coll. : C. 17–early 19. Johnson, ' An old ludicrous word '. ? abbr. *galligaskins*, q.v.

gasometer. A voluble talker ; a boaster : from ca. 1890 ; ob. Cf. *gas-bag*.

gasp. A dram of spirits : from ca. 1880. Ob. Ex its frequent effect.

gasp, v.i. To drink a dram of spirits : from ca. 1880 : †.

gasp my last if . . . !, may I. A non-aristocratic asseveration : coll. (— 1887) ; slightly ob. Baumann.

gasper. An inferior cigarette : from ca. 1912 : orig. military ; popularised during G.W. ; by 1930, coll. Ex its effect on one's ' wind ', i.e. staying powers.—2. Hence, any cigarette : from ca. 1925. Cf. *fag*.

gasping. Over-anxious : Glasgow (— 1934). Ex excited panting.

gaspipe, occ. **gas-pipe.** A steamer whose length, instead of five, is nine or ten times that of her beam : nautical : ca. 1880–1910.—2. An inferior or damaged roller : printers' : from ca. 1860 ; ob.—3. A rifle : esp. the Snider. *The Daily Telegraph*, July 9, 1883, ' The old Snider—the . . . gas-pipe of our Volunteers—continues to be used in many of the competitions.' Gen. ? ca. 1880–1910 ; specific, ca. 1875–95.

gaspipe-crawler. A tall thin man : gas-works' : ca. 1885–1914. Baumann. Cf. *lamp-post*.

gaspirator. A gas-mask : military : 1916 ; ob. F. & Gibbons. A telescoping of *gas-respirator*, itself abbr. *anti-gas box-respirator*.

gassed. Tipsy : orig. military : not, I think, before 1917. F. & Gibbons. Ex the stupefying effects of gas.

gassed at Mons. A military c.p., of 1916–18, in reply to an inquiry concerning a person's whereabouts. F. & Gibbons. The retreat from Mons took place in late Aug., 1914 ; poison-gas was not introduced till much later. Cf. *on the wire at Mons.*

gasser. A tremendous talker ; a boaster : from ca. 1888. Gen. with a modifying adj. Cf. *gas-bag* and *gasometer*, qq.v.

gassy. Full of empty talk or boasts ; given to these : 1863. (S.O.D.)—2. Very apt to take offence : ? coll. (— 1860). H., 2nd ed. Cf. *gaseous*.

gat, gats. A quantity ; number, group : schoolboys' : C. 19. See also the Shrewsbury sense of *penal*.—2. (*gat* only) a revolver : Canadian (— 1914), orig. U.S. (Ex *gatling gun*. See Irwin.) Since ca. 1924, thanks to gangster novels and films, the word has > fairly well known in Britain.

gate. The ' paying ' attendance at any outdoor sport or game : from ca. 1888. In C. 19, coll. ; C. 20, S.E. Ex :—2. (Occ. in pl.) money paid for admission thereto : coll. ? 1887, Baumann. Ex *gate-money*.—3. Preceded by *the* : Billingsgate, C. 18–20 fishmongers' ; Newgate (Prison) : C. 19 c. H., 3rd ed.—4. The mouth : New Zealanders' (from ca. 1910), esp. soldiers' in G.W.

gate, v. To confine wholly or partially to college-bounds : university (1831) : in C. 20, j. or S.E. Anon., *The Snobiad*, 1835 ; Bradley (' Cuthbert Bede '), 1853 ; Hughes, *Tom Brown at Oxford*, 1861.

*gate, on the. On remand : c. : late C. 19–20 ; ob. Cf. *fence, on the*. Perhaps imm. ex :—2. Forbidden to leave barracks : military : from ca. 1870. (F. & Gibbons.)—3. (Of a prisoner who is) in an observation-cell : c. (— 1933). G. Ingram, *Stir*, a novel of life in prison. The door is left open.—4. On the danger list at a hospital : lower classes' : from ca. 1925. Perhaps ex senses 1 and 3 by a confusion with the synonymous *be slated*.

gate-bill and **gate-money** are, despite F. & H., S.E. ; but **gate-race** (— 1864) or **-meeting** (— 1881), in the sense of a contest arranged less for the sport than for the money, is sporting s. > coll. H., 3rd ed.

gate-crasher, -crashing. One who attends, attendance at, a private party or entertainment without invitation : coll. : U.S., anglicised in late 1926. The v., *gate-crash*, which is rare, hardly—in England, at least—antedates 1930. Ex forcing one's way through a gate to attend an out-door sport.

gate-race. See **gate-bill.**

gate of horn, of life. The female pudend : the former, low ; the latter, gen. euphemistic and ineligible. C. 19–20.

gater. A plunge, headlong, into a ' pot ', q.v. : Winchester College : C. 19–20.

gates. The hour at which one must be in college ; the being forbidden to leave college, either at all or, as gen., after a certain hour : university : from ca. 1855. In C. 20, j. or S.E. Bradley, *Tales of College Life*, 1856 ; Lang, *XXXII Ballades*, 1881.

Gates, be at. To assemble in Seventh Chamber passage : Winchester College, ca. 1850–1910. Mansfield.

gates, break. To return to college after the latest permissible time : university : from ca. 1860. In C. 20, j. or S.E. Ex *gates*.

Gath, be mighty in. ' To be a Philistine of the first magnitude ', F. & H. Gath, a city in Philistia, is here, as in the next two entries, employed for Philistia (the land of the Philistines) itself. Coll. : mid-C. 19–20 ; ob. All three entries verge on S.E.

Gath, prevail against. To deal the Philistines a rousing blow : coll. : mid-C. 19–20 ; ob.

Gath !, tell it not in. Fancy *your* doing that ! Fancy your doing *that* ! Coll. : mid-C. 19–20.

gather the taxes. To seek employment at one shop after another : tailors' : ca. 1870–1920. Hence, *tax-gatherer*, a tailor seeking work.

gathering. See **gag**, n., 5.

gathers, out of. In distress (cf. *out at elbows*) : ? tailors' s. > gen. s. or coll. Ca. 1875–1915.

gations. An occ. spelling of *gashions* (see **gashion**).

'gator. An alligator : Australian coll. : late C. 19–20. (Earlier in U.S.A.)

*gatter. Beer. Frequently *shant of gatter*, a pot of beer : 1818. ? orig. c. : low s. >, ca. 1860, low coll. ; ob. Maginn in *Vidocq Versified* ; *Punch*, 1841 ; H., 1859. ? etymology : perhaps ex Lingua Franca ; perhaps ex Lingua Franca *agua* + *water*.

gaudeamus. A students' feast, a drinking-bout ; any merry-making : 1823, Scott (O.E.D.) : in C. 20, S.E. Ex first word (= let us rejoice) of a students' song in festive Latin.

[**gaudy**, an annual college dinner, hence any merry-making (†), has always, despite F. & H., been S.E.]

gaudy, adj., app. always in negative sentences. Good, esp. with *chance* or *lot* ; healthy : from ca.

1880; slightly ob. Hawley Smart in his best-known horse-racing novel, *From Post to Finish*, 1884; Galsworthy, *The Silver Spoon*, 1926, ' Only got one lung, and that's not very gaudy.' Ex notion of brilliance. Hence :

gaudy, adv. Very : lower classes' : C. 20. Galsworthy, *The White Monkey*, 1924, ' Ah ! It's a gaudy long wait.' Prob., like *ruddy*, a euphemism for *bloody*.

gaudy, as the devil said when he painted his bottom pink and tied up his tail with pea-green, Neat but not. A c.p. that, in C. 19, was addressed (by whom ?) to old ladies dressed in flaming colours.

gauge. See **gage.**

gauge of, get the. To ' size up '; discern a motive, penetrate a character : coll. : from ca. 1870 ; ob. Ex the S.E. *take the gauge of*.

gauge of it, that's about the. That is a tolerably accurate or equitable description : coll. : from ca. 1875.

gaum. See **maum.**

Gaw is merely a written variant of *Gor*.

gaw(-)gaw. A useless seaman : nautical : late C. 19–20. Bowen. Perhaps ex *gawpus*, q.v.

gawblim(e)y. See **gorblimy !** Cf. :

Gawd. A Cockney form of *God* : sol. Cf. *Cor*.

Gawd forbid. A variant of *God forbid*, q.v.

Gawd forgive (him) the prayers (he) said ! (He) did curse and swear ! : Cockney evasive c.p. : late C. 19–20 ; ob. Ware.

gawf. An inferior, red-skinned apple that can easily be made to look very attractive : costers' (— 1851). Mayhew. (They are now more highly considered.)

gawk, a simpleton, a fool, or an awkward person, is S.E. according to the O.E.D. and S.O.D. I cannot help thinking that at first, 1837, it was coll., though admittedly it was dial. as early as C. 17 (E.D.D.), and is S.E. in C. 20. Presumably ex *gawky*, n. (1724), and adj. (1724), always—it seems—S.E. The v. *gawk*, to gape or stare, to loiter about in a gaping manner, is orig. U.S. (1785) ; so far as it is used in Britain, it is coll., as also is *gawking*, vbl.n. and ppl.adj. ; *gawkiness*, however, is late (1873) and S.E.

gawm (or **G.**). See **gorm.**—**gawn.** See **gorn.**

gawney, goney. A fool : coll. when not dial. : from ca. 1770. (E.D.D.) ? by *sawney* out of *gawk*.

gawpus. An idle seaman : nautical coll. : from ca. 1870. Bowen. Ex dial. *gaupus* (*gawpus*), a simpleton.

gawsave. The National Anthem : low : C. 20. C. J. Dennis. Ex slovenly pronunciation of *God save (the King)*.

gay. (Of women) leading an immoral, or a harlot's, life : 1825, Westmacott (O.E.D.). In C. 20, coll. on verge of S.E.—2. Slightly intoxicated : C. 19–20 ; ob. Perhaps orig. a euphemism.—3. Impudent, impertinent, presumptuous : U.S. (— 1899), anglicised in 1915 by P. G. Wodehouse. O.E.D. (Sup.).

gay, all (so). ' All serene '; all correct, safe, excellent : C. 19

gay, feel. To feel amorous : C. 19–20. Orig. euphemistic ; in C. 20, jocular.

gay and frisky. Whiskey : rhyming s. : late C. 19–20. P. P., *Rhyming Slang*, 1932.

gay bit. A harlot : from ca. 1830 ; ob. Coll. See **bit.**

*gay cat. A tramp that hangs about for women : tramps' c. (— 1932). Ex U.S.

Gay Gordons, the. ' The Gordon Highlanders. In particular, the 2nd Battalion, the 92nd Highlanders ' : late C. 19–20 : rather sobriquet than nickname ; coll. verging on S.E. F. & Gibbons.

gay house. A brothel : C. 19–20 ; ob. Perhaps orig. euphemistic.

gay in the arse or groin or legs. (Of women) loose : coll. : C. 19–20 low. Cf. Fr. *avoir la cuisse gaie*.

gay it. (Of both sexes) to have sexual connexion : C. 19–20 ; ob. : coll.

gay life, lead a. To live immorally ; live by prostitution : coll. or s. : from ca. 1860.

gay old. An occ. variant of *high old*, q.v. : ca. 1885–1910.

gay tyke boy. A dog-fancier : ca. 1840–60 low. Duncombe.

gaying instrument, the. The male member : C. 19 ; low coll. *Lex. Bal.* Cf. :

gaying it, vbl.n. Sexual intercourse : C. 19–20 (ob.) ; low coll.

Gaynor, do a. See ' Moving-Picture Slang ', § 9. Like *Garbo* (q.v.), coll. rather than s.

[**gazebo,** despite F. & H., is ineligible ; nor, prob., is it dog-Latin.]

gazer. ' A pedlar who walks about a fair or market selling as he goes ' : grafters' : C. 20. Philip Allingham, *Cheapjack*, 1934.

gazob. A silly fool ; a (foolish) blunderer ; a ' softy ' : low (? orig. Australian) : late C. 19–20. Perhaps a corruption of *galoot*, q.v., or a blend of *galoot* + *blob* : cf. the U.S. *gazabo*, which, dating from ca. 1890, prob. derives ex S.E. *gazebo*, and may well represent the origin of *gazob*.

g'bye ! Good-bye ! : slovenly coll. : C. 20. (D. Mackail, *Greenery Street*, 1925.)

*geach. A thief : c. (— 1821) ; ob. by 1900, † by 1920. ? *thief* disguised. Cf. :

*geach, v.t. To steal : c. (— 1821) : † by 1920. Haggart, 1821. ? *thieve* perverted.

gear. The genitals, male and, more gen., female : late C. 16–19 : S.E. until C. 19, then coll. >, very soon, s.—2. As affair, business—even in *here's goodly gear*, here's a pretty kettle of fish—it is S.E.

gear !, that's the. That's right : military : 1915. B. & P. Lit., that's the correct instrument or equipment.

gear or gears, warm in one's. Settled down to work : C. 17–18 coll. Cf. :

gears, in his. Ready dressed : late C. 17–18 : coll. B.E., who notes also *out of his gears*, out of sorts, indisposed : perhaps, orig., s. Ex earlier *in his gears*, ready for work.

ged ! A coll. variant· of *gad !* = *God !* Late C. 17–19. Cf. vowel in *dem(me) !* W.

Geddesburg. Montreuil in 1916 : Army officers' jocular coll. On *Gettysburg* (U.S.A.) ex Sir Eric *Geddes*, who, in that year, established there his headquarters—he was Director General of Transportation, with 1,000 (or more) clerks. F. & Gibbons.

gee. A horse : s. (1887) >, ca. 1900, coll. Orig. a child's word. Abbr. *gee-gee*, q.v.—2. Grafters' s. of C. 20, perhaps ex *gee !*, q.v. : ' A grafters' accomplice or assistant who mingles with the crowd. Note : To give a grafter a gee is to buy something off him to encourage the crowd,' Philip Allingham, *Cheapjack*, 1934.—3. Bluff ; empty talk or ' fanny ' : c. : from ca. 1920. James Curtis, *The Gilt Kid*, 1936. Cf. *gee, put in the* (below).

gee. To fit, suit, be convenient or practical: only in negative phrases: late C. 17–20; ob. B.E.—2. (Of persons) to behave as is expected or desired; agree, get on well together: C. 18–20; ob. V.t. with *with*. Either ex next entry or a corruption of *go*.—3. To encourage, incite; delude: c. (— 1932). Anon., *Dartmoor from Within*, 1932. Perhaps ex *gee up* !

gee ! A command to a horse: gen. to turn to the right: coll.; 1628 (S.O.D.).—2. See **Jee** !

*gee, get at the. See **get at the gee.**

gee, give a. See **gee, n., 2.**

gee, on the. Annoyed, irritated: lower classes' (— 1923). Manchon. Perhaps ex *gee-up* !

*gee, put in the. To blarney; tell a plausible tale: c.: from ca. 1920. James Curtis, *The Gilt Kid*, 1936). Cf. *gee*, v., 3.

*gee, put on the. To 'swank'; act or talk pretentiously: c.: from ca. 1925. J. Curtis, *The Gilt Kid*, 1936.

gee-gee. A horse: s. (1869) >, ca. 1900, coll. Reduplication of *gee* ! Mostly among sportsmen and 'turfites'. *The Pall Mall Gazette*, April 14, 1889. (O.E.D.)—2. 'The nickname among journalists . . . of Mr. G(eorge) G(rossmith), better known, perhaps, as the Society Clown', F. & H., 1893.—3. A jocular perversion (— 1923) of *geeser*, 1.

gee-gee dodge. The selling of horseflesh for beef: trade (— 1884): ob. Greenwood, in *Veiled Mysteries*, 'The gee-gee dodge . . . was seldom . . . practised . . . it was impossible . . . to bargain for a regular supply.'

Gee-Gees, the. The Cavalry: infantrymen's: late C. 19–20; ob. Ware.

gee ho ! or **ho, gee ho** ! Equivalent to *gee* !: from ca. 1650: coll. Contrast *gee whoa* ! Also, same period, v.i. and t., say *gee-ho* (to).

gee up, occ. **hup** ! (To a horse) move forward ! Move faster: C. 18–20 coll.—2. To say 'gee up !': C. 19–20 coll. *Blackwood's Magazine*, Oct., 1824, 'Mr. Babb ge-hupped in vain.' The (*h*)*up* is not adv. but interjection.

gee whiskers ! See **jee whiskers** !—**gee whizz** ! See **Jee** !

gee whoa ! (To a horse) stop ! Rarer than *whoa* ! Coll.: C. 18–20.

*geekie. A police-station: Scottish c. (— 1893). ? ex *geek*, to peer about.

ge(e)loot, the form given by H., 3rd ed.: see *galoot*.

Geese, the. The Portuguese (soldiers in especial): military: 1917. B. & P.

geese, the old woman's picking her. Applied to a snowstorm: C. 19–20 proverbial coll., very gen. among school-children, who often add: *and selling the feathers a penny apiece.*

geese are swans, all his. He exaggerates in his praise, esp. of his own family or property: coll. (— 1529); in C. 20, rather S.E. Skelton; Burton; Newman in his *Apologia*, 'To use the common phrase . . .'

geese go bare-legged !, fie upon pride when. A proverbial c.p. retort to undue pride in the lowly: late C. 17–28. B.E.

geese on a common, like. Wandering, somewhat aggressively, at large: C. 19–20 coll.

geese when the gander is gone, he'll be a man among the. A C. 17–20 ob. coll. variation (ironical and = He'll be a man before his mother) of the C. 17–20 proverb *You're a man among the geese when the gander's away.* Apperson.

geeser (rare) or **geezer** ; occ. **geyser** (incorrectly); esp. **old geezer.** A person: in the 1890's, gen. of women; in C. 20, gen. of men (cf. *old buffer*). Low coll.: 1885 (O.E.D.). Albert Chevalier in his still-remembered *Knocked 'Em in the Old Kent Road*, 1890, ' Nice old geezer with a nasty cough '. Ex † *guiser*, a mummer, via dial.—2. Hence, occ., *my* (or *the*) *old geezer*, my ' old woman ' (wife): lower classes' (— 1923). Manchon.

*gegger. See **gagger, 4.**

gel (hard ɡ). A Cockney as well as an affected form of *girl* : C. 19–20. Prob. ex dial. Cf. *gal.*

gelatine (pronounced *jĕlăteen'*): the coll. spelling and pronunciation of *gelatin* (pronounced *gĕ'lătin*): C. 19–20.

geld ; occ. **gelt.** Money : South African s. verging on coll.: from ca. 1880. Ex Dutch *geld*, money, cash. Pettman. Cf. *gelt*, q.v.

gelding, a eunuch, is not, despite F. & H., unconventional, but *enter a man for the geldings' stakes*, to castrate him, is low coll., C. 19–20, ob., as is *he has entered for . . .*, to be a eunuch.

gell. An occ. variant of *gel*, q.v.

*gelt. ' Gilt ', i.e. money : late C. 17–early 19 c.: in C. 16–early 17, S.E.; in C. 19–20, grafters' s.; and see **geld.** B.E., ' *There is no Gelt to be got*, c., Trading is very Dead.' Prob. ex the Ger. for tribute, payment.

*gelter. Money : a C. 19 c. elaboration of *gelt*, q.v. Duncombe.

geluk ! I wish you luck !; ' also a birthday congratulation ': South African coll. (— 1913). Ex Dutch *geluk*, happiness, prosperity. Pettman, who notes also *gezondheid* (1875), occ. in form *santeit* (1896), I wish you good health !, ex Dutch *gezond-heid*, health.

*gem. A ring : late C. 17–early 18.—2. A gold ring : C. 18. *Rum gem*, a diamond ring : C. 18. All are c.—3. A ' jewel ' or ' treasure ' : (gen. playful) coll. : C. 19–20 ; ob. Because prized. O.E.D.

gem'man. See **gemman.**

gemini !, gem(m)iny !, jim(m)iny ! (In the earliest example, *gemony*.) An orig. not so low coll. oath or interjection, from ca. 1660, expressing surprise, often preceded by *oh* ! and occ. followed by *gig* (late C. 18–early 19) or *figs* (C. 19, chiefly Cockney). Dryden, 1672, ' O Gemini ! is it you, sir ? ' Ex *Gemini*, the Twins (Castor and Pollux), who figure in an old Roman oath), says the O.E.D.; ' Folk Etymology ' Palmer traces to a German and Dutch exclamation ex *O Jesu Domine !*: the former is preferable.

gemman or **gem'man.** A gentleman : sol.: mid-C. 16–20. Borrow in *Lavengro*.

gemonies (gen. with initial capital) is, in late C. 16–17, occ. misused to mean tortures. O.E.D.

gemony ! See **gemini** !

gen. A shilling : costers' (— 1851). Either abbr. *generalise*, q.v., or abbr. Fr. *argent*—see **gent.** Mayhew. For back slang, see *Slang* at ' Oddities '.

gen-net, ten shillings (back s.; H., 1859), is an occ. variant of *net gens.*

gender, to copulate, is, despite F. & H., ineligible. But *feminine gender*, the pudend, is (— 1835) schoolboys' ob. s., as in the rhyme, quoted—in part—by Marryat in *Jacob Faithful*: ' *Amo, amas*, | I loved a lass, | And she was tall and slender, | *Amas, amat*, | I laid her flat, | And tickled her feminine gender*,' F. & H.

general. A maid - of - all - work : coll.: 1884 (O.E.D.); Ware dates it at 1880. Abbr. *general* *servant.*—2. ' Chandler's shop—where everything may be obtained ' : urban low classes' (— 1909) ; slightly ob. Ware.—3. See **generalise**.

general, adj. Affable to all : late C. 16–17 : either S.E. or, more prob., coll. Shakespeare, ' Bid her be free and general as the sun.'

General Backacher. Major-General Sir William Forbes Gatacre (1843–1906) : military : ca. 1890–1906. He worked his men hard, but he was an able commander rather inconsiderately treated in the Boer War. (Ware.)

General One (or Vun) O'Clock ; Old Vun O'Clock. General von Kluck (1846–1934) : military : 1914 ; ob. (*The Observer*, Oct. 21, 1934).

generalise or **-ize**. A shilling : back—i.e. mainly costers'—s. : from ca. 1850. *The Saturday Review*, May 14, 1887, ' The difficulty of inverting the word shilling accounts for " generalize ".' (Cf. *gen*, q.v.) Ware records the form *general*.—2. Hence (— 1909) *Can you generalise ?*, can you lend me a shilling ? (Ware.) Virtually †.

generally always. Generally : late C. 19–20 : sol. when not Sussex dial. E.D.D., ' A superl[ative] form of *generally*.'

generating place. The female pudendum : C. 19–20 (ob.) low coll.

generating, or **generation, tool.** The male member : C. 19–20 (ob.) low coll. Solus *tool* is prob. the older term.

genetic and **generative** are sometimes confused, in educated sol., gen. the former for the latter : mid-C. 19–20. *The Expositor*, Dec. 1884 (O.E.D.).

Geneva print. Gin ; mostly in *read Geneva print*, to drink it : C. 17 coll. Massinger. (*Geneva > gin*.) Punning the kind of type used in Geneva bibles.

genitrave or **genitraf.** See **gennitraf**.

gen'lly. Generally : sol. (— 1887) ; prob. centuries old. Baumann.

gen'l'man. A gentleman : sol. and dial. : C. 19–20 ; prob. much older. Cf. *gem'man*.

gennet, gen-net. Ten shillings, separately or as a sum : back s. : from ca. 1860. See **generalise** and **gen**.

gen(n)itraf or **-trave.** A farthing : back s. : from ca. 1860. Ware. *Gnihtraf* euphonised.

genol. Long : back s. : from ca. 1860. *Gnol* euphonised.

gens ; occ. a drop of gens. *Gen*eral leave : naval : C. 20. Bowen.

gent. A loudly dressed vulgarian : from ca. 1560, though anticipated in C. 15 : in C. 16–18, S.E. : ca. 1800–40, coll. ; from ca. 1840, low coll., except when applied derisively to those who use the term. Glapthorne, Burns ; Thackeray, Disraeli. In 1846, magistrate Rawlinson : ' I hold a man who is called a gent to be the greatest blackguard there is.'—2. In c. (— 1859), money, esp. silver money : ex Fr. *argent* : cf. *gen*, q.v. H., 1st ed.—3. A sweetheart ; mistress ; *my gent*, my best girl. Low coll. : from ca. 1880 : ob. Prob. ex Fr. (*une femme*) *gentille*.—4. The adj., long †, was, pace F. & H., always S.E.

genteel, well-dressed, *apparently* a gentleman or a lady, has, from ca. 1880, been low coll.—except when depreciatory.

gentile. C. 19–20 (ob.) sol. for *gentle*, a maggot used by anglers as bait.

gentish. Like, characteristic of, a ' gent ' (q.v.) : ? S.E. or coll. : 1847 (O.E.D.) ; ob.

Gentle Annie. A certain Turkish gun at the

Dardanelles : military : 1915. F. & Gibbons. Also *Asiatic Annie*. Cf. *Beachy Bill*.

[**gentle craft, the,** whether shoemaking or angling, is, despite F. & H., S.E. of C. 16–20.]

*****gentleman.** A crowbar : c. : from ca. 1850 ; ob. See **alderman**.—2. See **punisher, 3.**

gentleman, do the. To go and urinate : lower classes' (— 1923). Manchon.

gentleman, put a churl (or beggar) upon a. See **churl.**

gentleman commoner. An empty bottle: Oxford University (— 1785) ; † by 1900. Grose, 1st ed. Cf. *fellow commoner*, q.v., *dead man, dead marine*. Such a student was, in general repute, deficient in intelligence.

gentleman in black, the (old). The devil : from ca. 1660 : s. >, in C. 19, coll. Dryden.

gentleman in black velvet, the (little). A mole. This was a Jacobite phrase after the death of William III, whose horse was said to have stumbled over a mole-hill. C. 18–19. Scott. (F. & H. erroneously give *brown* and the phrase, or toast, as Tory.)

gentleman in blue. A policeman : satirical coll. : mid-C. 19–20 ; ob. Ware.

gentleman in brown. A bed bug : coll. (— 1885) ; ob. G. A. Sala.

gentleman in red. A soldier : 1774 : either s. or jocular coll. ; ob.

Gentleman Jackson. John Jackson (1769–1845), champion boxer of England in 1795–1803. Dawson.—2. Peter Jackson, Australian aboriginal boxer : latter half of C. 19.

Gentleman Jones. Richard Jones (1779–1851), actor and dramatist. Dawson.

Gentleman Lewis. W. T. Lewis (1748–ca. 1811), actor. Ibid.

gentleman of fortune. A pirate : C. 19–20 (ob.) : coll., punning the S.E. sense : adventurer.

gentleman of four outs. See **gentleman of the three outs.**

gentleman of observation. A (spying) tout : the turf : C. 19.

gentleman of the back(door). A sodomist : *back door*, C. 18–20, ob. ; *back*, C. 19 : low coll. See also at **back.**

gentleman of the fist. A boxer : boxers' (—1819) ; ob. by 1900, † by 1910.

gentleman of the first head or **house ; gentleman of the five outs.** See **gentleman of the three outs.**

gentleman of the green-baize road. A cardsharper : gamblers' : C. 19–20, ob. Punning *gentleman of the road*, S.E. for a highwayman.

gentleman of the pad. A highwayman : 1718 : sometimes s., sometimes jocular coll. : † by 1870. See **pad** and **scamp.**

gentleman of the round. An invalided or a disabled soldier begging for his living : late C. 16–17 coll. Ben Jonson.

gentleman of the short staff. A constable : ca. 1830–80. Ainsworth.

gentleman of (the) three ins. (But *the* is rare and does not appear before ca. 1830.) ' In debt, in gaol, and in danger of remaining there for life ; or, in gaol, indicted, and in danger of being hanged in chains ', Grose, 1788 ; H., 1864, ' In debt, in danger, and in poverty '. A c.p. that > ob. ca. 1890, † ca. 1920. Prob. suggested by the contrasted :

gentleman of (rarely, and not before ca. 1830, **the) three outs.** ' Without money, without wit, and without mourners ', Grose, 1785,—it is the earlier

M

phrase. In 1788, he added, 'Some add another out, i.e. without credit.' Variants *four, five*; H., 1864, has *four* and refers to Ireland, where, he says, the retort to a vulgar fellow blustering of gentlemanliness was ' Yes, a gentleman of four outs—that is, without wit, without money, without credit, and without manners.' F. & H., 1893, cites ' Out of money, and out of clothes ; | Out at heels, and out at the toes ; | Out of credit, and in debt '. Ob. by 1893, but not yet †. Cf. the C. 16–17 *dunghill gentleman* and *gentleman of the first head* or *house*, which may themselves (see the O.E.D.) be coll. or even s.

gentleman of three ins and outs. See **gentleman of the three ins and outs.**

gentleman ranker. A broken gentleman serving in the ranks : military s. (− 1892) >, ca. 1900; gen. coll. >, ca. 1914, S.E. >, ca. 1919, somewhat ob. See Kipling's famous poem, *Gentleman Rankers*.

Gentleman Smith. William Smith, a C. 18 actor. Dawson. Cf. *Gentleman Lewis*.

gentleman who pays the rent, the. A pig : Anglo-Irish : mid-C. 19–20 ; ob. Ware.

gentleman's companion. A louse : coll. (− 1785) ; ob. by 1914, † by 1918. (In four years' active service, I never heard the term.) Grose, 1st ed. Cf. *bosom friend.*—2. Possibly, in late C. 17–18, it also = a flea. Ned Ward, 1709 (Matthews.)

gentleman's (or gent's) gent. A ' gentleman's gentleman ' or valet : C. 20. Both forms occur in that exciting and amusing novel, *Th' Big City*, by John G. Brandon, 1931.

gentleman's master. A highwayman : ca. 1780–1840. Grose, 1st ed. Ex gentlemen's obedience to his ' stand and deliver ! '

gentleman's, occ. lady's, piece. A tit-bit : (mostly children's) coll. : ca. 1880–1910. Bauman. (If used by adults to-day, it would hint at short rations.)

gentleman's pleasure-garden. The *genitalia muliebria* : low or jocular coll. : C. 19–20 ; ob.— Followed by *padlock*, it = a sanitary towel.

gentlemen's sons. The three regiments of Guards : coll. : ca. 1870–1914.

*gentry cofe, mid-C. 16–17 ; **gentry cove,** mid-C. 16–early 19. A gentleman : c. (Cf. C. 19 Devon *gentry man*.)—2. Whence *gentry cofe('s)* or *cove('s) ken*, a gentleman's house : likewise c. : † by 1850. B.E.

*gentry ken. A (? C. 18) C. 19 c. abbr. of *gentry cove's ken* (preceding entry).

*gentry mort. A lady : c. : mid-C. 16–early 19. This and the preceding two terms are in Harman.

gent's gent. See **gentleman's gent.**

genuine, n. and v. Praise : from ca. 1840, 1860 resp. : Winchester College. Wrench, ' Possibly from calling a thing " genuine." '

gēo-graphy. ' Burned biscuit boiled in water ' : nautical : late C. 19–20. Bowen.

geōcian (Č. 16), geocie (C. 16), geotick (C. 18), geoticall (C. 16). Incorrect for *goetian, goety, goetic, goetical*. O.E.D.

geode. Geoid : an educated sol. : C. 19–20. Bailey's *Festus*, 1839. (O.E.D.)

geom. (Pronounced *jŏm*.) Geometry: schools' : late C. 19–20.

Geordie, geordie. A pitman ; any Northumbrian : North Country coll. : from ca. 1760. Prob. ex the Christian name there so pronounced.—

2. A North Country collier (boat) : nautical : from ca. 1880.—3. The *George* Stephenson safety-lamp : miners' (− 1881).—4. A Scottish variant of the various senses of :

George, george. A noble (6*s.* 8*d.*, *temp.* Henry VIII) : abbr. *George-noble* : late C. 16–17.—2. A half-crown (piece) : ca. 1659–1820 : c. Shadwell. —3. A guinea : rare unless in form *yellow George* : c. (− 1785) ; † by 1870. Grose, 1st ed.—4. A penny : low : ca. 1820–70.—5. **brown george** : see **brown.**—6. **(George.)** George, Duke of Cambridge : military coll. : 1880–96. He was a very popular Commander-in-Chief. Ware.—7. As typical of any middle-class householder, esp. if married : coll. : C. 20.—8. An airman : military and naval : 1915. Cf. *Jack*, a bluejacket, and *Tommy*, a soldier.—9. Hence, in the Air Force, as a term of address to a stranger : 1915. F. & Gibbons. Cf. sense 7.

George !, by. (Occ. in late C. 19–20, simply *George !*) A mild oath : coll. abbr. *by St. George !* : 1731, Fielding (O.E.D.) ; earlier *by St. George, for George*, both in Ben Jonson, 1598 ; *before George*, 1678.

George !, let's join ; where's George ? These two c.p. phrases arose in 1935 ; they were burlesqued by the music-halls at least as early as Sept., 1935. Ex advertisements by Messrs. Lyons, who supplied the key and the answer : *at Lyonch* and *gone to Lyonch* (lunch at Lyons's). See **George, 7.**

George, riding (or the dragon upon) St. See **riding St. George.**

George Horne ! Queen Anne's dead ! Occ. *G.H.* Printers' : ca. 1880–1910. Ex a romancing compositor so named.

Georges man. A vessel fishing on the Georges Bank : Canadian fisheries' coll. : late C. 19–20. Bowen.

*Georgie (or -y) ; georgie. A quartern loaf : c. (− 1812) ; † by 1890. Vaux. Cf. *brown George*, q.v.

Georgie-Porgie or Georgy-Porgy. A coll. pet form of *George* ; any plump male child. (In 1883, R. L. Stevenson employed it as a v. = to fondle, but this use has not caught on.) From ca. 1870. Ex, as well as suggestive of, the nursery rhyme, ' Georgy-Porgy, pudding and (*or, loosely*, puddingy) pie, | Kissed the girls and made 'em cry.'

Georgium Sidus. The Surrey side of the Thames : London Society (− 1909) ; † by 1920. Ware.

geotick. See **geocian.**

geranium. A red nose : Cockneys' : from ca. 1882 ; ob. Ware.

Geraniums, the. The 13th Hussars : military : C. 20. F. & Gibbons, ' From the former green facings of their predecessors, the 13th Dragoons '.

gerd (e.g. *gerd-afternoon* in J. B. Priestley's *Far-away*, 1932). Good : an affected sol. characteristic of half-wits among the would-be superior : C. 20.

Gerines. The Royal Marines : mid-C. 19–20 ; ob. Bowen.

germ-peg. See **gim-peg.**

German, in late 1914–18, was generically an offensive term, sometimes coll., sometimes S.E. See *Words !* at ' Offensive Nationality '.—2. See **Garman.**—3. A German sausage : coll. (− 1883) ; ob. (O.E.D.)

German bands. Hands : late C. 19–20 rhyming s. B. & P.

German duck. ' Half a sheep's head boiled with onions ', Grose, 2nd ed. : late C. 18–19 († by 1893) coll. Because ' a favourite dish among the Ger-

man sugar-bakers in the East End of London',
H., 1864.—2. A bed bug: orig. and mainly Yorkshire: from ca. 1860; ob. H., 3rd ed.

German East. German East Africa: coll.:
C. 20. F. E. Brett Young, in *The Cage Bird*, 1933,
'When George and I were prisoners in German East
we had something in common with a vengeance, and
that was one shirt.' (Also in the same author's *Jim
Redlake*, 1930.)

German flutes. (No singular.) Boots: rhyming
s. (— 1857); † by 1914, when *daisy roots*, q.v., was
in full possession of the field. 'Ducange Anglicus.'

German gospel. Vain boasting; megalomania:
Nov., 1897–ca. 99. Ware, 'From a phrase addressed in this month by Prince Henry of Prussia
to his brother of Germany at a dinner: "The gospel
that emanates from your Majesty's sacred person",
etc.'

German Legion, the. The 109th Foot, now the
Leinster Regiment: military: from ca. 1860; ob.
F. & Gibbons. The battalion was, at that date,
'brought up to strength with men of the disbanded
German Legion . . . raised for the Crimean War'.

Germani. A German (soldier): soldiers' (East
African campaign): 1915–17. E.g. in F. E. Brett
Young, *Jim Redlake*, 1930. On the analogy of
certain Swahili words (e.g. *americani*).

gerrup! Get up!: slovenly coll. or, perhaps
rather, outright sol.: late C. 19–20. Cf. *siddown*,
q.v.

Gerry. A German; esp. a German soldier: late
1914 +, but not gen. till 1916, when it almost superseded *Fritz*, q.v. Usual spelling: *Jerry*. Ex
German. Occ. used as an adj.: 1915. B. & P.

***gerry.** Excrement: C. 16 c.; cf. *gerry gan*!
? ex L. *gero*, I carry; perhaps rather cf. Devonshire
gerred, bedaubed, dirty, itself connected with Fr.
bigarré, streaked (E.D.D.).

***gerry gan.** (See **gan** and **gerry**.) Lit., sh*t [in
your] mouth: a brutal C. 16–early 17 c. way of
saying 'shut up!'

[**gerrymander** and **gerrymandering**, orig. U.S.
(resp. 1812, 1813), were S.E., not unconventional,
when, ca. 1880, they gained a firm footing in Britain.]

Gers, the. The Germans, esp. soldiers: military:
1914–15. Cf. *Gerries* (whence *Jerries*).

gertcher. Get out of it, you!: low coll.: late
C. 19–20.

Gertie Lee. The number 33 in the game of
House: military rhyming s.: C. 20. F. & Gibbons.

Gertrude. See 'Moving-Picture Slang', § 4.
[**Gerund**, incorrect uses of :—See Fowler.]

gerund-grinder. A schoolmaster; esp. a pedantic
one: coll.: from ca. 1710; ob. Sterne, 'Tutors,
governors, gerund-grinders, and bear-leaders'.
Also, C. 19–20, *gerund-grinding*.

gesture. An action for the sake of show, good or
bad: when used trivially, it is coll.: from ca. 1925.
(As S.E.: 1916, says the O.E.D. Sup.)

get. A trick, swindle; a cheating contrivance:
posited by F. & H.; † by 1890.—2. A child, esp. **in**
one of his get, one of his offspring, of his begetting:
C. 14–20: S.E. till ca. 1750, then coll. (Grose,
2nd ed.); after ca. 1870, only of animals—unless
pejorative.—3. A variant (— 1923) of *get-up*, q.v.;
not very gen. Manchon.—4. A retrieving; the
return of a difficult ball: lawn tennis coll.: heard
in 1926; recorded by O.E.D. (Sup.) for March 22,
1927.

[**get.** If we consider *get* as a v. of all work, we
find that its rise and its increasing popularity are
mainly owing to U.S. influence (see W.'s *Adjectives
and Other Words*, my *Slang*, and Fowler's *Dict. of
Modern English Usage*). 'Its sense-development is
extraordinary, the intransitive senses springing
chiefly from reflexive, e.g. . . . *get (oneself) disliked*,' W. Except in the S.E. sense, to acquire,
obtain, receive, it is comparatively rare before 1870:
Grose gives no examples; in H., 1859, there is none,
while H., 1860, contains only *get-up*, n., and H.,
1874, the same. See also **got**.]

get, v. To become; feel, e.g. 'He gets ill every
winter,' 'He gets moody after drinking': late
C. 16–20; nominally S.E., but in C. 19–20 more
properly considered coll.—2. V.i., with intransitive
past ppl.: to complete an action: C. 18–20; S.E.
till ca. 1860, then coll. E.g. 'I'd be glad to get gone
from this town.' A rare construction. (O.E.D.)—
3. V.i., *get* as an auxiliary (from ca. 1650) is held by
the O.E.D. to be S.E., but there is a coll. taint in
such locutions as 'I got caught in the storm,'
1887 (S.O.D.).—4. V.t., have, take, eat (a meal):
coll. (— 1888), perhaps ex dial. (O.E.D.)—5. V.t.,
understand (rarely a thing), gen. as 'Do you get
me?': ex U.S.; anglicised ca. 1910.—6. To
corner (a person); get hold of, find and bring him,
there being an implication of subject's difficulty
and/or object's reluctance: coll.: 1879.—7. To
depart: mostly in the imperative. See **get!**—
8. In c., to steal: ca. 1820–60. Bee. Cf. *make*.—
9. To annoy or worry: coll., orig. (ca. 1880) U.S.,
anglicised ca. 1920. O.E.D. (Sup.).—10. To render,
succeed in rendering: coll., orig. (ca. 1890) U.S.,
anglicised ca. 1910. E.g. 'He gets me wild,' he
makes me angry. (O.E.D. Sup.)—11. To impress,
move, attract: coll.: from ca. 1915. E.g. 'That
play, Romance, got me properly.' (O.E.D. Sup.)
Prob. ex sense 9 influenced by sense 10.—12. **get
climbing, thinking,** etc., is simply a coll. form of
climb, etc., etc., or of *go climbing*, etc.: mid-C. 19–
20. It often expresses exasperation.—13. See **get
to** in the Addenda.

get! Abbr. *get out!*, go away! or clear out!
Orig. (1884) U.S., where usually *git!* Anglicised
ca. 1900, but found in Australia ca. 1890. Hume
Nisbet in *The Bushranger's Sweetheart*, 1892, 'None
of your damned impertinence. Get!' Cf.:

get, do a. To depart, retreat, hastily: Australian (— 1916). C. J. Dennis. Ex preceding.

[**get A**, in Felstedese (revised F. & H.), is not **s.**
but **j.**]

get a bit. To obtain money—or a woman: low:
late C. 19–20. Ware.

get a name. See **name, get a**.

get a pick on (a person). To pick on, ill-
temperedly mark out, quarrel with: Canadian:
C. 20. John Beames.

get about, v.t., with **her,** to effect intromission:
low coll. (amorous venery): from ca. 1880. Also,
absolutely, *get about it*.—2. V.i., (of news, gossip) to
spread, either (e.g.) 'The story got about,' often
with a *that* clause, or (e.g.) 'It got about that the
firm was bankrupt': coll.: from ca. 1848; since
ca. 1880, S.E.—3. V.i., to move about or round, **to**
travel, gen. with implication of frequency, though
this may be defined, as in 'He gets about a lot, *or* a
great deal': coll.: from late 1890's.

get above oneself. To be very, or too, satisfied,
or pleased with oneself: coll. (— 1923). Manchon.

get across; get it across. To succeed; esp. **to**
make oneself fully understood or suitably appreciated: resp. ca. 1915 and in 1913: coll. >, **by**

1933, familiar S.E. Ex U.S. *get it across the foot-lights.* (O.E.D. Sup.)

get all over. To handle and examine (a person)—'not necessarily for theft, but in all probability feloniously': low: mid-C. 19–20; slightly ob. Ware.

get along with you! Go away! Be quiet! Have done! Coll.: 1837, Dickens (O.E.D.).

get anything. To be infected, e.g. venereally; *get* replacing *catch.* Coll.: from ca. 1850. Merely a coll. absolute form of S.E. *get* = catch, C. 17–20.—2. (Wireless) hear; establish contact with a station: coll.: from ca. 1924.

get at. To assail; strike, as in ' Let me get at the foul-mouthed b—r ': from ca. 1890.—2. To banter, chaff, annoy, take (or try to take) a rise out of: from ca. 1890. *Ally Sloper's Half Holiday,* Jan. 3, 1891, ' " Your family don't seem to get on, missie . . ." " *On!* who're ye gettin' at ? " ' See also **get back at.**—3. To influence, bribe, corrupt a person or a group of persons; to 'nobble' (q.v.) a horse: orig. s. (1865), then, ca. 1880, coll. J. S. Mill (O.E.D.); *The Graphic,* March 17, 1883, ' Without any suspicion of being got at '.—4. To mean; intend to be understood: gen. as ' What are you getting at ? ' Coll.: from ca. 1905 : ? ex sense 2.

*****get at the gee.** To 'spoof' (v.i.): c. (— 1933). Charles E. Leach.

get away, get-away, getaway. An escape: 1890.—2. A means of escape; hence an exit: from ca. 1895; ex U.S., where in late C. 19–20 c. it means, a train or a locomotive.—3. An excuse, esp forethought: from ca. 1925. All orig. coll.; but in C. 20, senses 1 and 2 are S.E.

get away! As = go away, S.E., but as = don't talk nonsense, don't flatter, it is coll.: from ca. 1830. The form *get away with you!* is prob. to be considered S.E. Cf. *get along with you!*

get away closer! An 'invitation to yet more pronounced devotion': costers', hence gen. Cockneys' c.p.: late C. 19–20; slightly ob. Ware.

get away with it. To succeed beyond expectation and/or contrary to the full rights of the case: coll.: from 1918; ex U.S. (— 1912). F. & Gibbons; O.E.D. (Sup.).—2. Hence, 'just to scrape through a difficulty': coll. (— 1931). Lyell.

get back at. To chaff, banter; satirise, criticise; call to account: coll.: from ca. 1885. Cf. *get at,* q.v.

get back into your box! Be quiet! That's enough from *you!* Orig. (— 1893), U.S.; anglicised ca. 1900; slightly ob. Ex the stables.

get before oneself. To boast, threaten, be angry, unduly: low coll.: late C. 19–20; ob. Ware. Contrast *get behind oneself.*

get behind, v.t. An occ. variant of *get up behind,* q.v.—2. See :

get behind oneself. To forget an appointment, the date of an event, etc.: lower classes' coll.: mid-C. 19–20. Ware.

get busy. See **busy, get.**

get by, v.i. To escape notice, esp. when that notice is feared or inopportune. V.t., *get by with,* gen. followed by *it.* C. 20 : coll., ex U.S. Cf. *get past,* q.v.

get curly. To become troublesome: tailors': late C. 19–20. ? ex rucking.

get cracking. To begin work: Royal Air Force: from ca. 1925. I.e. cracking on speed.

get dizzy. To get angry: naval: from ca. 1920 Bowen.

get down on. To appropriate illicitly; to steal: New Zealanders': C. 20.

get down to brass tacks. See **brass tacks.**

get down to it. To begin to work seriously: C. 20 coll.: ? ex U.S.—2. To go to sleep: military coll.: from ca. 1910. (F. & Gibbons.)

get 'em. See **get them.**

get encored. To have a garment returned for alterations: tailors': from ca. 1875.

get even (with), v.i., t. To give tit for tat, have one's revenge (on): coll. (from ca. 1880); in C. 20, S.E. Ex S.E. *be even with,* on a par (or even terms) with.

get fits. To be impatient under defeat: lower classes' (— 1909).; ob. Ware.

get forrader. See **forrader.**

get going. The v.t., set going, start, prepare, is S.E., but the v.i., to begin doing something (work or play) vigorously or very well, ' get into one's stride ', is coll.: from ca. 1895. Esp. in ' Wait till I (he, etc.) get(s) going.'

get in, v.i.; **get into,** v.t. To effect intromission : low coll.: C. 18–20. *Get up.*—2. (v.i.) To strike victoriously; e.g. ' Get in with both fists': coll. (— 1897). Ex *get a blow in.* (Ware.)

get in bad. To make (a person) disliked; v.i., to cause oneself to become disliked: 1928 (O.E.D. Sup.). Ex U.S.

get in for it. To establish oneself firmly: lower classes' (— 1923). Manchon. Cf. :

get in with (a person). In S.E., to become familiar with: hence, as coll., to become a trusted and active associate with: from ca. 1910.

get in wrong; put in wrong with. To incur—cause another to incur—the dislike of (a person): U.S. coll., anglicised ca. 1932. C.O.D. (1934 Sup.).

get into. Put on clothes, boots, etc.: coll.: late C. 17–20. Lady Burghersh, 1813. (O.E.D.)—2. To become: coll. (— 1909). Used by Ware.—3. See **get in,** 1.—4. To become accustomed to; to learn : coll.: from ca. 1870.

get into a hank. To get angry: nautical: late C. 19–20. Bowen.

get into full swing; hot water. See **swing** and **hot water.**

get inside and pull the blinds down! A c.p. addressed to a poor horseman: Cockneys': mid-C. 19–20; ob. Ware.

get it. To be punished, physically or morally; to be reprimanded: coll.: from ca. 1870. Cf. *catch it.*—2. To be venereally infected : low coll.: from ca. 1875.

get it down fine. To have all details worked out: coll.: from ca. 1900. Ex the U.S. sense, to know all about a man's antecedents.

get it down one's or **the neck.** To swallow it: low coll. (— 1909). Ware.

get it every way. To profit, whatever happens: coll.: ex U.S.; anglicised ca. 1920.

get it hot. An elaboration, from ca. 1872, of *get it,* 1, q.v.

get it in the neck. To be defeated, thrashed (lit. or fig.), to receive a shock, to be grievously disappointed, severely reprimanded: from ca. 1916. Elaboration of *get it,* 1. Cf. *get it where . . .,* q.v.

get it off one's chest. See **chest, get it off one's.**

get it where the chicken got the axe. A lighter, more jocular form of *get it in the neck* : from ca. 1917.

get left. See **left, be** or **get.**—**get (or do you get me, Steve?** See **got me(, Steve)?**

get-off, n. An Air Force coll. dating from late 1914. See **porpoising.**

get off, v.t. Deliver oneself of, utter, esp. **a** witticism : orig. (1849), U.S. ; anglicised ca. 1875 : coll. ; slightly ob.—2. To let off ; excuse : esp. from punishment : mid C. 19–20.—3. To succeed in marrying one's daughters : coll. : from ca. 1860. (O.E.D.)—4. Hence, v.i., to get engaged or married : coll. : from ca. 1910. (Rarely of the man ; *then,* jocularly.)—5. Hence, to ' click ' with a member of the opposite sex : coll. : from ca. 1913.—6. V.i., to be let off a punishment, an irksome duty : escape : from ca. 1640 : in C. 17–early 19, S.E., then either coll. or near-coll.—7. **(get off it.)** To stop talking, befooling or chaffing a person, playing the fool, exaggerating, etc. : mostly in imperative : coll. (— 1923). Manchon.—8. To cease being obnoxious, presumptuous, or meddlesome : anglicised (ex U.S. coll.) ca. 1929 : verging on coll. Esp. *tell a person where he gets off.* Ex a conductor's or ticket-collector's or guard's telling a person where he gets off the tram, etc.

get off it ! See **get off,** 7.

get off my neck ! Stop trying to bluff or befool me ! : mostly military : 1915. F. & Gibbons. Cf. preceding.

get off with. To make friends with one of the opposite sex, esp. with a view to ' a good time ' : coll., orig. (1914 or early 1915) military >, by 1918, gen. F. & Gibbons.

get (money, ' a bit ') **on.** To back a horse : racing s. (from ca. 1869) >, ca. 1880, gen. coll.—2. To have connexion with (a woman) : low coll. : from ca. 1870. Ex the lit. sense, to mount.—3. V.i., to succeed, progress : coll. : from ca. 1780 : in C. 20, S.E. *The Pall Mall Gazette,* Dec. 29, 1871, ' That great Anglo-Saxon passion of rising in the world, or getting on '.—4. (? hence) to fare ; feel (in health) : coll. : from ca. 1880.—5. Hence, also v.i., agree—or disagree—with a person, with modifying adv. ; also, occ., absolutely, to agree well (with a person). Coll. : from ca. 1815. Never of things. ' We got on like a house on fire ' ; ' Oh, we get on, you know ! ' The S.E. form is *get along.*—6. To become elderly, or, esp., old : coll. : from ca. 1885. Abbr. *getting on in years.*—7. To depart : coll. : C. 20. Cf. the S.E. *get along.*

get on one's nerves. To affect morbidly, e.g. ' The clock gets on his nerves ' : coll. (from ca. 1870) >, by 1900, S.E. Cf. :

get (a person, a thing) **on the brain, or** (more gen. **have**) **on one's mind.** To be obsessed by, crazy about : coll. : from ca. 1870. Cf. *get on one's nerves,* q.v.

get on the home stretch. To be in sight of one's goal : coll. : late C. 19–20. Ex cribbage.

get on to. To suspect ; find out about : coll. : late C. 19–20. (James Spenser, 1934.)

get one on, v.t. and absolute. To land a punch (on) : pugilists' : from ca. 1880 ; ob.

get one's or another's back up. See **back up.**—
get one's books (or **cards**). See **books, get one's.**—
get one's goat. See **goat, get someone's.**

get one's own back. To have one's revenge (on), get even with : coll. : from ca. 1908. (O.E.D. Sup.) Ex the recovery of property.

get one's skates on. See **skates, put on one's.**

get one's tail up. Gen. in pl. and ' said of a crew which is getting out of hand and impudent to the officers ' : nautical : late C. 19–20. Bowen.

get-out. An evasion : coll. : C. 20. (James Spenser, *Limey Breaks In,* 1934.)

get out, v. To depart ; go away ; gen. in imperative : coll. : from ca. 1710 ; cf. *get,* q.v.—2. ' To back a horse against which one has previously laid ', F. & H. : racing (— 1884). Also *get round* (— 1893).—3. On the Stock Exchange (— 1887), to sell one's shares, esp. in a risky venture. (O.E.D.)—4. See **round the corner, get.**—5. V.i. (of things), to lengthen : coll., mostly Cockneys' : from ca. 1880. Edwin Pugh, *Harry the Cockney,* 1912, ' " Evenings are getting out, aren't they ? " '

get out ! Tell that to the marines ! Don't flatter ! Coll. : from ca. 1840. Dickens, ' Kit only replied by bashfully bidding his mother " get out ".' (O.E.D.)

get out (of bed) on the wrong side. To be irritable, testy : coll. : from ca. 1885. Ex the S.E. *to rise on the right side is accounted lucky,* C. 17–19. *The Globe,* May 15, 1890, ' If we may employ such a vulgar expression—got out of bed on the wrong side.'

get out of, e.g. **it, the scrape.** To escape the consequences of one's folly or mistake : be excused punishment or duty : coll. : from ca. 1880 ; in C. 20, S.E. Cf. *get off,* v.i.

get outside, or outside of. To eat or drink, gen. **a** considerable and specified amount : low coll. : from ca. 1890. S. Watson, in *Wops the Waif,* 1892.—2. (Of women only) to receive a man sexually : low coll. : from ca. 1870.

get over. To overcome (an obstacle, a prejudice) : coll. : from ca. 1700 ; since ca. 1895, S.E.—2. To recover from (illness, disappointment) : coll. : mid C. 18–20 ; since ca. 1900, S.E.—3. To dupe, circumvent, seduce : low coll. : from ca. 1860. Cf. *come over* and *get round.*—4. To astonish, impress : coll. : ca. 1890–1915. (J. Milne, *The Epistles of Atkins,* 1902.) Displaced by *get,* v., 11.

get past, v.i. ; **get past with** (gen. **it**). To escape detection ; hence to succeed against odds or justified (moral) expectation : coll. : from ca. 1915 : ? orig. military. Cf. *get by,* q.v.

get religion. To be converted ; become (very) religious : orig. (1826) U.S., anglicised ca. 1880 : in C. 19, s. ; low coll. in C. 20 ; now almost, though—thank God !—not quite S.E. Nevertheless, it is an expressive phrase that, for all its insensitive vulgarity, will prob. achieve linguistic sanctity.

get round. To circumvent, trick : coll. ; from ca. 1855, ex U.S. (1849).—2. To persuade, cajole ; hence, seduce (lit. or fig.), dupe : coll. : from ca. 1860. Cf. *get over,* 3.—3. To evade ; arrange, to one's own satisfaction, concerning : coll. : from ca. 1895.—4. In racing, same as *get out,* 2.

*get round the corner. See **round the corner, get.**

*get scrubbed. (Of the favourite or the second favourite) to lose the race : turf c. : C. 20.

get set. To warm to one's work ; become thoroughly used to or skilful at it : coll. : from ca. 1895. Ex the cricket sense : (of a batsman) to get one's eye in, itself s. in the 1880's, coll. in the 90's, and j. in C. 20.

get shut of. See **shut of.**

get straight, v.i. (the v.t. being S.E.). To free oneself of debt ; have a complication straightened out, one's home tidy, etc., etc. : coll. : from ca. 1875.

get that way. (Gen. *how do* or *did you get that way ?*) ' To get into the condition implied ' : coll., orig. (— 1922) U.S., anglicised by 1930. (O.E.D. Sup.)

get the ambulance ! (Gen. *git* . . .) A c.p. addressed to a drunk person : urban : 1897 ; ob. Ware.

get the bag or sack. See bag.—get the berry. See berry.—get the empty. See empty, get the.— get the go-by. See go-by.—get the jacket. See jacket, get the.—get the lead. See lead.—get the mitten. See mitten.

get the board. See board, get the.

*get the papers. To be indicted as an habitual criminal : c. (— 1935). David Hume. Mostly as a vbl.n.

get the poke. See poke, get the.—get the rasp or raspberry. See berry, get the, and raspberry.

get the sads. To become melancholy : lower classes' coll. (— 1909). Ware.

get the shilling ready ! Prepare to subscribe ! : a c.p. of 1897–8. With esp. reference to *The Daily Telegraph's* shilling fund for the London hospitals— part of the charity characterising the 60th year of Queen Victoria's reign. Ware.

get the shoot. To be dismissed : lower classes' (— 1909). Ware derives ex a flour-mill's shoots.

get the spike. To lose one's temper : low London : from ca. 1890 ; ob. Ware. Cf. *needle*, q.v.

get the staggers. See staggers, get the.—get the stick. See stick, get the.

get (th)em. To tremble with fear : G.W. + ; ob. : mainly soldiers'.—2. Also, but always in form *has*, or *have*, *got 'em*, to have the ' d.t.'s ' : from ca. 1900. See got 'em bad.

get there. To succeed in one's object or ambition ; *with both feet*, notably, completely. Coll. : orig. (— 1883), U.S. ; anglicised ca. 1893.—2. To become intoxicated : ca. 1890–1914.—3. (Of the man) to have sexual connexion : low coll. : from ca. 1860.

get through, v.i. To pass an examination ; succeed : coll. : from ca. 1850 ; in C. 20, S.E. ' Cuthbert Bede ', 1853, ' So you see, Giglamps, I'm safe to get through.'—2. V.t., to spend : late C. 19–20 ; coll. till ca. 1920, then S.E.—3. V.t., to complete ; do : coll. : late C. 17–20 : coll. ; then, in C. 19–20, S.E. ' He gets through an astounding amount of work—largely because he loves work.'

get together, v.i. To help each other, one another : coll. : from ca. 1920. Ex S.E. sense, to meet, assemble (late C. 17–20) : cf. the U.S. sense, to meet in amicable conference, to come to terms.

get-up. Dress ; general appearance, so far as it is prepared or artificial ; coll. : from ca. 1847. Whyte-Melville, George Eliot.—2. Hence, a masquerade dress ; a disguise : coll. : from ca. 1860. G. A. Sala. All these nuances are in C. 20 to be considered S.E.—3. ' Style of production or finish, esp. of a book, 1865 ', S.O.D. : publishers' coll. that, in C. 20, is S.E.

get up, v. To make, esp. as regards appearance or embellishment : always with adv. or adv. phrase : coll. : from ca. 1780 ; in C. 20, S.E. Leigh Hunt, ' The pocket books that now contain any literature are got up, as the phrase is, in the most unambitious style.'—2. V. reflexive, to dress : coll. : from ca. 1855 ; in C. 20, S.E. Albert Chevalier, 1892, in *The Little Nipper*, ' 'E'd get 'imself up dossy.' Hence to disguise oneself : coll. : from ca. 1860 : in C. 20, S.E. Also (though less gen.), from ca. 1860, v.i., as is the anon. *Eton School Days*, 1864, ' He felt confident in his power of getting up so that no one would recognise him.'— 3. V.i., to rise in the morning : from ca. 1580 : S.E.

till ca. 1880, then increasingly coll.—4. V.t., prepare (a case, role, subject, paper) ; arrange (e.g.) a concert : from ca. 1770, though anticipated in late C. 16–17 ; in C. 19, coll. ; but from ca. 1905, again S.E.—5. V.t., to have carnal knowledge of a woman : C. 19–20. (Rarely v.i. : C. 17–18 : prob. S.E.)

get up ! (To a horse) go ! get a move on ! Coll. : from ca. 1887 (O.E.D.). Occ. jocularly to persons : C. 20.

get up and look at you. (Of the ball) ' to rise very slowly after pitching ' : cricketers' jocular coll. (— 1888). Lewis.

get up behind. (V.t., with personal object) to endorse or back a man's bill or I.O.U. Vbl.n., *getting up behind*. Coll., mainly commercial : from ca. 1870.

get up early. See early.

*get up the mail. To provide money for a prisoner's defence : c. (— 1889). Cf. *mail* in S.E. *blackmail*.

get wet. See wet, get.

get (a person) wrong, gen. in form have got (him) wrong. To misunderstand ; have a wholly or mainly wrong opinion or impression of him. C. 20 ; ? ex U.S. Cf. *get in wrong*, q.v.

get your eye in a sling ! This proletarian c.p. of late C. 19–20 (ob.) constitutes a ' warning that you may receive a sudden and early black eye, calling for a bandage—the sling in question ', Ware.

get your hair cut ! A non-aristocratic c.p. of ca. 1885–1912. ' Quotations ' Benham ; B. & P. Ex a popular song.

getter, a sure. ' A procreant male with a great capacity for fertilisation ', F. & H. : Scottish coll. : C. 19–20.—2. See go-getter.

getting a big boy now. Of age : a c.p. ' applied satirically to strong lusty young fellows ' : late C. 19–20 ; slightly ob. Ex the ' leading phrase of the refrain of a song made popular by Herbert Campbell '. Ware. In C. 20, also *getting a big girl now*, applied to the other sex.

getting ox-tail soup. The maiming of cattle by cutting off their tails : Anglo-Irish : ca. 1867–83. Ware.

geyser. Incorrect for *geeser*, q.v. : late C. 19–20.

gezondheid ! See geluk !

gezumph. To swindle : grafters' : C. 20. Philip Allingham, *Cheapjack*, 1934. Ex Yiddish. Hence :

gezumpher. A swindler : id. : id. Ibid. See preceding.

gharry. See garry.

ghastly. A vaguely pejorative or a merely intensive adj. : coll. : from ca. 1860. Thackeray, ' A ghastly farce ' ; Denis Mackail, *The 'Majestic' Mystery*, 1924, ' " Ghastly," said Peter. " Filthy," answered James ' (of the weather). In C. 20, a frequent injunction is ' Don't be a ghastly idiot ! ,' as in F. Grierson, *Mystery in Red*, 1931. Cf. *awful, bloody, filthy, foul*.

ghastly. A pejorative or merely intensive adv. E.g. ' ghastly early in the morning '. Coll. : from ca. 1870. Cf. *shocking(ly)*.

ghaut serang. ' A crimp in the Indian ports ' : nautical coll. : late C. 19–20. Bowen.

gherkin. A jerkin, ' a leathern sleeveless coat issued in the winter ' : jocular military : 1915. B. & P.—2. A ' rooky ' (recruit) : Regular Army's : from ca. 1908. Ex his greenness.

ghost. One who, unknown to the public, does literary or artistic work for which another gets all the credit and most of the cash : from ca. 1884 : orig. journalistic or artistic s., then—ca. 1890— gen. coll., then—ca. 1910—S.E.—2. Meat : Regular Army's : late C. 19–20. B. & P. Ex Hindustani. —3. Salary ; but rare outside of *the ghost walks*, q.v.

ghost, v.i. To do unrecognised, and prob. ill-paid, work for another in art or literature : from ca. 1885 : ex, and of the same ' social ' ascent as *ghost*, n.,1.—2. To **s**hadow, spy upon : coll. : from ca. 1880 : ob. Rarely v.i. Ex S.E. sense, haunt as an apparition.

ghost, long. A very tall, thin person : coll. (— 1923). Manchon. Cf. *streak of misery.*

ghost of, not the. Not the slightest idea : 1934. E. M. Delafield, in *Time and Tide*, Sept. 21, 1935, ' " Who's that marvellous woman ? " " Darling, don't you know ? " " Darling, I haven't the ghost of." ' Cf. :

ghost of a chance, not the. No chance whatso-ever : coll. : 1857 (O.E.D.).

ghost of Joan. A nursing sister : military (not very gen.) : 1915 : ob. F. & Gibbons. Perhaps suggested by *St. John's* (*Ambulance*).

*****ghost story.** A ' bad luck ' story : tramps' c. (— 1932). F. Jennings, *Tramping with Tramps.* Ex U.S. : see Irwin.

ghost walks, the ; . . . does not walk. There is, is not, any money for salaries and wages : theat-rical : 1853, in *Household Words*, No. 183. Ex *Hamlet*, I, i.

[Ghost words :—Only a few are noted in these pages. The *locus classicus* is in the O.E.D. Sup. at ' List of Spurious Words '.]

ghosty. A ghost, esp. if small or friendly : coll. : from ca. 1900. Ex the jocular but S.E. adj.

ghoul. A newspaperman chronicling . even the pettiest public and private gossip or slander (cf. Oscar Wilde's witty differentiation) : journalists' : ca. 1880–1915. Ex Arabic *ghul*, a body-snatching demon.

giant. (Gen. pl.) A very large ' stick ' of asparagus : restaurants' coll. : from ca. 1880. Ware.

Gib. Gibraltar : military and civil service s. > gen. coll. : from ca. 1850. Once a convict settle-ment : whence the next entry. *The Pall Mall Gazette*, March 23, 1892, ' Stormy Weather at Gib '.

*****gib.** A gaol : c. (— 1877) ; ob. by 1914, † by 1921. See the preceding.—2. See **jib, cut of his.**—3. A forelock : nautical : late C. 19–20. Bowen. Prob. ex a whale's gib.

gib or jib, hang one's. To pout : nautical s. (ca. 1860) >, ca. 1890, gen. coll.

gib cat, melancholy as a. Exceedingly depressed, dispirited : coll. : C. 16–19. *Gib* = male (ex *Gilbert*) ; not, in itself, eligible. See Grose, P.

gib-face. A heavy jaw, an ugly face : coll. : mid-C. 19–20 ; ob. H., 2nd ed. Ex *gib*, the lower lip of a horse.

gibber. A stone suitable for throwing : Aus-tralian (Pron. *jibber*.) (— 1926). Direct ex Aborigine : Jice Doone.

gibberish, gib(b)rish, giberish, gibridge, gibrige, gibberidge. In C. 16–early 19, in the sense of under-world s.and Gypsy j., the word seems to have had a coll., even a s., taint. Prob. not ex *gibber*, than which it is earlier recorded, but from *Egyptian*, which, until recently, was gen. associated with *Gypsy*. (For modern gibberish, in technical sense, see *Slang*, p. 278.)

[**gibble-gabble,** senseless chatter, is not coll. nor **s.**, although it sounds like it and F. & H. class it **as** coll.]

gibby. A spoon : naval (— 1909). Ware ; Bowen. Origin ? Perhaps ex dial. *gibby* (*stick*), a hooked stick.

*****gibel.** To bring : c. (— 1837) : †. Disraeli in *Venetia*, his underworld novel.

giblet pie (or **G.P.**)**, the.** ' The American extreme clipper *Spindrift*, a particularly lofty ship said to be " all legs and wings " ' (Bowen) : nautical : late C. 19–early 20.

giblets. The intestines : coll. (— 1864). Brown-ing.—2. A fat man : low coll. : C. 19.

giblets, join. To marry : coll. verging on S.E. : 1681 as *j. g. together*, 1769 as *j. giblets*. (O.E.D.)—2. Whence, to copulate : late C. 18–20 low. In C. 19–20, also *do* or *have a bit of giblet-pie*.—3. To cohabit unmarried : late C. 18–early 19. Grose, 2nd ed. (for 2 and 3).

Gibson or **Sir John Gibson.** ' A two-legged stool, used to support the body of a coach whilst finishing ', Grose, 2nd ed. : coach-builders' : late C. 18–early 19.

giddy, in coll. speech, emphasises the word it pre-cedes : late C. 19–20. Manchon cites ' Up to the giddy hilt ' ; see also the next two entries.

giddy aunt !, my. A trivial, senseless exclama-tion : coll. : 1919, W. N. P. Barbellion (O.E.D. Sup.). An elaboration of *my aunt !* (see **aunt !, my**).

giddy goat, play the. To play the fool ; be ex-tremely happy-go-lucky ; live a fast life : coll. : from ca. 1890. *Ally Sloper*, March 19, 1892, has *giddy ox*. There is also the vbl.n., *giddy-goating*, 1891. (O.E.D.)

giddy kipper—whelk—whelp. A youth about town : London : ca. 1895–1914. Ware derives the first from *giddy skipper*, the second from the first, the third from the second.—2. (*g.k.* only.) ' A term of reproach at the Cheltenham Grammar School,' E.D.D., 1900.

[**gif(f)-gaf(f),**—cf. the odd proverbial saying, *giff-gaff was* or *is a good fellow*, C. 16–18, the C. 19–20 form (mainly dial.) being *giff-gaff*, i.e. fair exchange, *makes good friends*,—is good Scottish ; **giffle-gaffle**— cf. *gibble-gabble*—is dial. : both are ineligible, *pace* F. & H., who further err in including *gibus*, an opera hat.]

gift. Anything very easily obtained or won ; an easy task : coll. : from ca. 1830. Cf. *bunce*.—2. A stolen article sold very cheap : c. of ca. 1850–90. Mayhew, 1851 (E.D.D.).—3. See **gift-house.**

gift, not to have as a ; or in form **would not have as a.** Not to want at any price, even for nothing : coll. : 1857, Thomas Hughes in *Tom Brown's School Days.*

gift-house, occ. abbr. *gift.* A benefit club : printers' : from ca. 1870 ; ob.

gift of the gab. See **gab, gift of the.**

gifts as a brazen horse of farts, as full of. Miserly ; mean with money : low coll. : ca. 1787–1870. Grose, 2nd ed. Cf. *costive* and *to part.*

gig, in C. 17–18 often *gigg.* Of the ten Eng. senses listed by F. & H., those of a wanton (or a flighty girl),—a jest or piece of nonsense,—fun, a spree,—and a vehicle have always been S.E.—2. The nose : later C. 17–early 19 c., as is the sense, *pudenda muliebria.* Coles, 1676 ; B.E.—3. A door : prob. c. : late C. 18–early 19. Abbr. *gigger = jigger*, q.v. —4. (Esp. of a person.) An oddity : Eton, 1777 (S.O.D.) : † by 1870. Colman.—5. A farthing : mid-C. 19–20 ; ob. H., 1859. ? ex *grig.*—6. **The**

mouth : low (— 1871) : † by 1900. Perhaps cf. *gib-face* ; H. considers it to derive ex *grig*.

gig, v. To hamstring. 'To gigg a Smithfield **hank** ; to hamstring an overdrove ox ', Grose, 1785 : late C. 18–early 19 : either low or, less prob., c. Origin obscure, unless ex *gig*, to throw out, give rise to (see the O.E.D.'s v., 1).

gig-lamps. Spectacles : Oxford University, 1848 : by 1860, gen. s. Ex the lamps on a gig.— 2. One who wears spectacles : from ca. 1854. Popularised by ' Cuthbert Bede '.

gigg. See **gig,** n. and v.

gigger. A sewing-machine : tailors' : from ca. 1880.—2. Other senses : at *jigger*.

giggle, no. No fun ; no joke ; (very) unpleasant : low coll. : from ca. 1920. James Curtis, *The Gilt Kid*, 1936, ' It's no giggle being in the nick [in gaol], I can tell you.'

giggle-mug. ' An habitually smiling face ' : Cockneys' (— 1909). Ware.

giggles-nest ?, have you found a. Asked of one tittering, or laughing senselessly or excessively : low coll. c.p. : C. 19.

gigler, giggler, giglet, giglot, goglet. A wanton woman ; a giddy, romping girl (not in *gig(g)ler* form). The *-er* term may be c., C. 17–18 ; the other is S.E., the same applying to the adj. and to the adv. *giglet-wise*.

gigs !, by. A mild, rather foolish oath : ca. 1550–1700.

Gilbert, over the. See **over the Gilbert.**

[**gild,** v., has been somewhat misapprehended by F. & H. : *gild over* is to intoxicate slightly, and even that is S.E. : cf. S.O.D. and O.E.D.—2. Likewise, *gild the pill* has prob. been always S.E.]

gilden. Incorrect for *gilded* (adj.) : C. 16–20. O.E.D.

Gilderoy's kite, to be hanged (or **hung**) **higher than.** To be punished with excessive severity ; hence and gen., out of sight, gone : mid-C. 19–20 ; ob. Prob. of Scottish origin : see *Notes and Queries*, 7th Series, V, 357, and Thornton.

*****gile hather.** See **gyle hather.**

Giler, the. St. Giles, Oxford : Oxford undergraduates' : late C. 19–20. Collinson. ' Oxford *-er* ' + *the*, 2.

[**Giles's** (or **St. Giles's**) **bread,** as applied to the ' fat, ragged, and saucy ' (Grose, 2nd ed.), is perhaps to be considered rather coll. than S.E. : C. 18–early 19.]

gilguy. Anything whose name has slipped the memory : nautical : from ca. 1880 ; ob. R. Brown, *Spunyarn and Spindrift*, ' Sailors . . . if the exact name of anything they want happens to slip from their memory . . . call it a chicken-fixing, or a gadget, or a gill-guy ' (O.E.D. Sup.). Ex *gilguy*, ' often applied to inefficient guys ' (for bearing boom or derrick), Smyth. Cf. *jigger*, *gadget* (q.v.), *thingummy*, *what's-his-name*.

*****gilk** or **gilke.** A skeleton key : early C. 17 c. Rowlands. *?* *gilt* corrupted.

gill (or **jill**), a wench, and **gill flirt** have always, *pace* F. & H., been S.E. ; but **gill,** a fellow, a chap, is low s. or c. : Vaux, 1812 ; extremely ob. Gen. with another term, says Vaux, who aligns *gloak* and *gory*.

gill-guy. See **gilguy.**

gilliflower. One wearing ' a canary or belcher fogle round his twist [neck] ', Bee : low London : ca. 1820–50. If he wears many more colours he is a *tulip*.

gills. The flesh under the ears and jaws : since Francis Bacon's ' Redness about the cheeks and gills ' ; in C. 19–20, *pace* the O.E.D., the term has a very coll. hue, esp. in *rosy about the gills*, cheerful.— *blue, green, yellow*, or *queer about* . . ., dejected, indisposed,—and *white* . . ., frightened.—2. The corners of a stand-up collar : 1826 (S.O.D.) ; hence, 1859 (H., 1st ed.), a stand-up collar.

gills, a cant or **dig in the.** A punch in the face : pugilists' : C. 19–20 ; ob.

gills, grease the. To eat a very good meal : coll. : C. 19–20.

gilly. One of the audience : (circus) Parlyaree (— 1933). E. Seago. Perhaps (I greatly doubt it) derisive of the Scottish *gillie*.

gilpy. A youth : naval : C. 19. Bowen. Perhaps suggested by *hobbledehoy*, likewise ' less than a man and more than a boy ', but ex Scots *gilpy*, a lively young person.

*****gilt,** adj. Having golden or very fair hair : c. : from ca. 1920. James Curtis, *The Gilt Kid*, 1936.

gilt. Money : late C. 16–20 ; S.E. until ca. 1820, then s. (In C. 20 Australia, also wealth. C. J. Dennis.) Cf. *gelt*, q.v.—2. A skeleton key : c. : ca. 1670–1840 (Coles ; B.E.).—3. Whence, since ca. 1840, likewise in c., a crowbar. (' Pronounced *gilt* ', says ' Ducange Anglicus '.)—4. Also c., a thief, esp. a pick-lock : ca. 1620–1830.—5. ' A Slut or light Housewife ', B.E. : late C. 17–18.

*****gilt-dubber.** A C. 18–19 form of *gilt*. Grose, 1st ed. Also *rum dubber*, q.v.

gilt-edged. (Of ' paper ', i.e. shares, bills, etc.) exceptionally easy to negotiate : ex U.S. (ca. 1888) ; anglicised ca. 1895. Ex *gilt-edged* note-paper.— 2. Hence, first-class : coll. : from ca. 1898 in England.

gilt-horn. A complacent cuckold : C. 18. Because well-fee'd.

gilt off the gingerbread, take the. To destroy an illusion ; lessen a value : coll. (— 1830). Apperson.

gilt-tick. Gold : costermongers' : from ca. 1840 ; ob. *?* ex *gilded*.

Gilted Gabbart, the. Greenock : Port-Glaswegians' : late C. 19–20. Ex ' a gilt ship used as a vane on the Customs House Quay ' (Bowen).

*****gilter.** A (pick-lock) thief : c. : late C. 17–18 c. *Warning for Housekeepers*, 1676.

gim- or **germ-peg.** Incorrect for *gem-peg* : mid-C. 19–20. O.E.D.

gimbal (occ. **gimber**)**-jawed.** Very talkative, in gen. and in particular : coll. : C. 19. Ex the lit. U.S. sense, loose-jawed (— 1859).

gimcrack, showy simpleton or trifle, gew-gaw, and handy-man, is S.E. ; as ' a spruce Wench ', B.E., it is perhaps s. (late C. 17–early 19 low) ; the female pudend, low or low coll. : C. 19.—2. The adj., like the derivative *gimcrackery*, is also S.E., despite F. & H., who, further, wrongly make *gimlet-eye(d)* other than S.E.

gimlet. A half-glass of whiskey : (mostly Anglo-Irish) public-houses' (— 1935).

gimme. Give me : sol. : C. 19–20. Ex slurring.

gimmer. A woman, esp. an old one : pejorative, standard >, ca. 1850, coll. ; Scottish : from ca. 1770. Cf. *gammer*.

gin. A native woman (— 1830 ; anticipated in 1798) : Australian. Hence, 1830, the wife of an Aborigine. Orig. coll., but by 1860 standard Australian. Ex Aborigine. (Morris).—2. Hence, from ca. 1880, occ. facetious of any woman or wife ; also, an old woman (— 1893) ; ob.

gin and fog. Hoarseness caused by alcohol: theatrical: from ca. 1880. Ware.

gin and it. Gin and Italian vermouth: C. 20.

Gin and Gospel Gazette. *The Morning Advertiser*: journalists': later C. 19. Also known as *The Tap-Tub* and *The Beer-and-Bible Gazette*: the first and second terms by 1860; witness H., who further notes '*Tizer*.

gin-and-tatters. A dilapidated dram-drinker: coll. (— 1887). Baumann.

gin-bottle. A 'dirty, abandoned, . . . debased woman . . ., the victim of alcoholic abuse, within an ace of inevitable death': low urban (— 1909); slightly ob. Ware.

gin-bud. A gin-induced tumour or pimple on the face: low: ca. 1820–95. Bee; Baumann. Cf. *brandy-blossom*.

gin-crawl. A drinking-bout on gin: low coll. Ware quotes *The Bird o' Freedom* of March 7, 1883. Cf. *pub-crawl*.

gin-lane. The throat: low: from ca. 1830. Cf. *gin-trap*.—2. The habit of drunkenness, esp. on gin: from ca. 1835. Ainsworth, 'Gin Lane's the nearest road to the churchyard.'

Gin Palace (or **g.p.**); gen. **the.** Any naval ship *Agincourt*: naval: C. 19–20. Bowen. By 'Hobson-Jobson'.

gin-penny. Additional profit; 'bunce', q.v.: costermongers': from ca. 1850; † by 1920. Gen. spent on drink.

gin-spinner. A distiller: ca. 1780–1900. Grose, 1st ed. On *cotton-spinner*.

gin-trap. The mouth; the throat: low: ca. 1825–1910. Pierce Egan, 1827. (O.E.D.)

gin-twist. A drink made of gin and water, lemon and sugar: orig. (— 1823) coll.; ob. 'Jon Bee.' Cf. U.S. *gin-sling*.

gingambob, gingumbob; jiggumbob. A toy; bauble: late C. 17–20 (ob.): coll. B.E. has the second, Grose the first spelling, the third being C. 19–20.—2. (Gen. in pl.) The testicles: mid-C. 18–20; ob. Grose (1st ed.), who adds: 'See *thingambobs*.'

ginger. Spirit, pluck, energy: from ca. 1840: ? orig. U.S. R. L. Stevenson & Lloyd Osbourne in *The Wrecker*.—2. A cock with reddish plumage: from C. 18. Grose, 1st ed.—3. A reddish or a sandy colour: from ca. 1865, when used by Dickens.—4. A red- or sandy-haired person; 'carrots', q.v.: 1823, Bee. Whence the profligate c.p., *Black for beauty, ginger for pluck*.—5. A fast, showy horse; one that is, or appears to have been, 'figged', q.v.: from ca. 1825.—6. (**Ginger.**) The very frequent nickname of men surnamed Jones: naval and military: late C. 19–20. F. & Gibbons.

ginger, adj. Ginger-coloured; red- or sandy-haired (applied to persons and cocks): from ca. 1825: also dial.

ginger-beer. An engineer: nautical rhyming s. C. 20.

ginger group. 'Politicians actively impatient with their own party' (Allan M. Laing): political: 1934.

ginger-hackled. Red-haired (— 1785): ob. Ex the cockpit. Also *ginger-pated*: coll. (— 1785). Both forms are recorded by Grose, 1st ed.

ginger-pop. Ginger-beer: 1827 (S.O.D.): coll. —2. A policeman: 1887, 'Dagonet' Sims. Rhyming on *slop*, q.v.

ginger-up. To enliven: put mettle or spirit into: coll.: from ca. 1848: from ca. 1890, S.E. Disraeli,

1849. Ex 'figging' a horse (1823) or putting ginger in drinks (1825). O.E.D. Whence vbl.n. *gingering-up*.

ginger-whiskers. A man, esp. a soldier, dyeing his whiskers yellow: ca. 1820–60. Bee.

Ginger, you're barmy! An early C. 20, lower classes' c.p. B. & P.

gingerbread. Money: from ca. 1690; ob. Esp. in *have the gingerbread*, to be rich. B.E.—2. Showy but inferior goods: coll.: mid-C. 18–20; ob. Rare. Ex:

gingerbread, adj. Showily worthless: coll.: 1748. (The O.E.D. considers it S.E.) Nautically, *gingerbread hatches* or *quarters*, luxurious accommodation or living (mid-C. 19–20: coll.); *g. work*, carved and gilded decorations (coll. >, by 1800, S.E.: Smollett, 1757); *g. rigging*, wire-rigging (C. 19: coll).—2. **gilt off the gingerbread**, see **gilt**.

gingerbread-office. A privy: C. 17 coll. Ex *gingerbread* = luxury.

gingerbread-trap. The mouth: jocular coll.: 1865, Dickens: ob. (O.E.D.).

gingerly, adj. and adv., is considered by F. & H. to have orig. been coll.

gingery. Red- or sandy-haired; 'carroty': from ca. 1850: coll. until C. 20, when S.E. Miss Braddon, in *The Cloven Foot*, 'A false front of gingery curls '.—2. (Of horses) fiery: turf (— 1823). Bee.

gingham. An umbrella (rightly, one made of gingham).: coll.: 1861.

gingle- (or **jingle-)boy.** A coin: C. 17–18. Massinger & Dekker.—2. A gold coin: C. 19. Cf. *yellow boy* and *chinker*.

gingler or **jingler.** A coin: C. 19–20; ob. Ex the preceding.

gingumbob. See **gingambob**.

ginirally. Generally: sol. (— 1887). Baumann. Cf. *gen'lly*, q.v.

gink. A fellow: always pejorative: U.S. (ca. 1910), partly anglicised by P. G. Wodehouse in 1920 (O.E.D. Sup.) and (in New Zealand as a stupid fellow) thoroughly naturalised, owing to the talkies, by 1934. Possibly derived ex *gink*, a trick, whence Scots *ginkie*, a term of reproach applied to a woman: Godfrey Irwin, *American Tramp and Underworld Slang*, 1931; this seems more prob. than derivation ex *ginx's* (or *G-*) *baby*, an unwanted child, as in an extremely sentimental novel of the 1880's.

ginned-up. Tipsy: from ca. 1920. (D. Sayers, *Murder Must Advertise*, 1933.) Cf.:

ginnified. Stupefied with liquor, esp. and orig. with gin: coll.: late C. 19–20; ob.

ginnums. An old woman, esp. if fond of liquor, e.g. gin: low coll. (— 1893); ob.

*ginny. 'An Instrument to lift up a Grate, the better to Steal what is in the window', B.E.: c.: ca. 1670–1830. Head. ? ex dial. *ginny*, a (primitive) crane.

ginny. Affected by gin, applied esp. to the liver or the kidneys: coll.: 1888. (O.E.D.) Cf. *beery*.

gip. See **gyp**, all senses.—2. Abbr. *gipsy*: from ca. 1840: coll.

gip. To cheat (a person): U.S., anglicised by 1930. (O.E.D. Sup.). Ex *gip*, n., 2.

gip ! (To horses, S.E.) Indicative of surprise or contempt; also = go away ! C. 16–17 coll. I.e. *gee up*.

'gip', **quoth Gilbert when his mare farted** (Howell, 1659); '**Gip with an ill rubbing**', quoth **Badger when his mare kicked** (Ray, 1678). A c.p.

addressed to one who is 'pertish and forward';
† by 1800. Apperson.

Gip; gen. **Gippo, Gyp(p)o.** A gipsy: C. 20.—
2. Same as *Gippy*, 1: military: C. 20.—3. (Also
gypoo.) Grease; gravy; butter: military: from
ca. 1912. Ex dial. *gipper* or *jipper*, meat juice,
gravy. (O.E.D. Sup.)

gip (gyp, jip), give (a person). To thrash, punish,
manhandle, give a bad time: dial. (— 1898) >, by
1910 at latest, coll. Perhaps ex *gee-up !* (O.E.D.,
Sup.)

Gippoland. Egypt: military coll.: from ca.
1890. F. & Gibbons. See **Gip,** 2.

Gippy, Gyppy. An Egyptian (soldier): military:
late C. 19–20. Barrère & Leland.—2. A gipsy:
1913. (O.E.D. Sup.)

gipsy. A playful term of address to a woman,
esp. if she is dark: 1858, George Eliot, but prob. in
use some years earlier: coll. Ex sense, a hussy
(C. 18–19); ex C. 17–18 term of contempt.

girdle ?, ne'er an M by your. Have you no
manners ? Esp., haven't you the politeness to say
' *M*aster' ? Coll.: ca. 1550–1850. Udall in
Roister Doister; Swift; Scott. (Apperson.)

girdle, under one's. In subjection; under one's
control: ca. 1540–1880: coll. until C. 18, then
S.E.

**girdle behind you, if you are angry you may turn
the buckle of your.** 'To one Angry for a small
Matter, and whose Anger is as little valued ', B.E.:
late C. 16–early 18 coll.

girl. One's sweetheart or 'best girl': coll.:
from ca. 1790. E.g. 'Me and my girl '.—2. A
mistress: coll.: C. 19–20: abbr. (a) *kind girl*
(C. 18).—3. A harlot: coll.: from ca. 1770.
Abbr. *girl about*, or *of the town* (1711) and *girl of
ease* (1756). (O.E.D.) Cf. *tart* and see **girls.**—
4. Hence, a male harlot: c.: from ca. 1920.
James Curtis, *The Gilt Kid*, 1936.

girl, v.i. To consort with women; make love to
a woman: Oxford University coll.: from ca. 1919.
Dorothy Sayers, *Gaudy Night*, 1935, ' She remembered . . . an expression in use among the irreverent : "to catch a Senior girling ".' Ex *go
girling* (see **girling**).

girl, old. A woman of any age whatsoever: pet
or pejorative term, in reference or in address: from
ca. 1845.—2. A term of address to a mare: a pet
name : 1837, Dickens. O.E.D.

girl, one's best. The girl to whom one is engaged,
or wishful to be ; the fancy of the moment: coll.:
anglicised ca. 1890 ; orig. U.S. Cf. *girl*, 1, q.v.

girl and boy. A saveloy: rhyming s. (— 1859).
H., 1st ed. One of the comparatively few rhyming
s. terms that—unless here an indelicate innuendo is
meant—lack adequate reason or picturesqueness.

girl-catcher. See **girlometer.**

girl-getter. An affected, mincing, effeminate
male: low coll.: ca. 1870–1910. Does *getter*
here = *begetter* ? For such a man usually disdains
girls.

girl-shop. A brothel: low coll.: from ca. 1870:
ob. Cf. *girlery*, q.v.

girl-show. A ballet or a revue, esp. one that in
the 1890's was called a *leg-piece* and in C. 20 is
known as a *leg-show* : low coll.: from ca. 1880.

Girl Street. See **Hair Court.**

girl-trap. An habitual seducer: low coll.: from
ca. 1870 ; ob.

girlery. A brothel (cf. *girl-shop*) ; a musical-
comedy and revue theatre: the former from ca.

1870, the latter from ca. 1880 : coll. Ex Lamb's
girlery, girls collectively.

girlie. (Little) girl, mostly as an endearment:
coll.: late C. 19–20.

girling, go. To go looking for loose women, professional or amateur: low coll.: ca. 1860–1915.
Cf. *go on the loose* and *girl*, v.

girlometer, occ. **girl-catcher.** The male member:
low jocular coll.: from ca. 1870 ; ob. Perhaps on
foolometer, q.v.

girls, the. Harlots in the mass; lechery: coll.:
from ca. 1850. Cf. :

girls, to have been after the. To have syphilis or
gonorrhœa: low coll.: from ca. 1860.

girls are (hauling) on the tow-rope, the. A coll.
naval c.p. = ' homeward bound '. Late C. 19–20 ;
ob. F. & Gibbons: Bowen.

girnigo-gaby the cat's cousin. A reproach to a
weeping, a yelling child: C. 19 coll. H., 1864. I
surmise *girnigo-gaby* to be *crying-baby* corrupted ;
cat's cousin obviously refers to the shrill noise.
But cf. *Grinagog*, which prob. suggested it by
antiphrasis, and the dial. *girniga(w)*, ' the cavity of
the mouth ' (E.D.D.).

gis, g'is ! Give us (or give me) ! : sol.: mid-
C. 19–20.

git. Illiterate pronunciation of *get*: 1887, Baumann, but obviously very much older.

git ! See **get !** (Only occ. British.)—**giv.** See
stuff to give the troops. Also, in illiterate speech,
giv = gave, given.

give, v. For phrases (e.g. *give the go-by*, *the office*,
the tip) not listed here, see the resp. nn.—2. Gave ;
given: sol.: C. 18–20.

give (a person) **a double broad.** ' To hit with a
piece of marginal wood-furniture 8 picas wide ':
printers' (— 1933). *Slang*, p. 184.

give (a person) **a piece of one's mind.** Frankly to
impart one's ill opinion of him in gen. or in particular: coll.: 1865, Dickens.

give a pop. See **pop, give a.**

give a rolling. See **give him a rolling.**

give a shout. To call (another station): wireless
(orig. nautical wireless): from ca. 1925. Bowen.

give and take. A race in which a horse is
weighted according to its height: turf (— 1823):
ob. Bee.

give away, give-away. The betrayal, whether
deliberate or inadvertent, of a secret: from ca.
1880.

give away, v. To betray ; expose to punishment
or ridicule: from ca. 1878. In C. 20 mainly—but
not (?) orig.—U.S. Occ. *give dead away*.—2. V.
reflexive, to let slip a secret: (— 1883).—3. Incorrectly for *give way* : C. 17–20. ' ? = *give a way* ',
O.E.D.

give-away cue. An underhand betrayal of a
secret: low: from ca. 1885.

give (a ship) **beans** ; gen. **give her beans.** ' To
crack on sail in a strong wind ': nautical: late
C. 19–20 ; slightly ob. Bowen.

give (one) **best.** To acknowledge a person's
superiority ; admit defeat: orig. (— 1883), in
Australia, where also, as soon after in England,
it = to give up trying at anything. Keighley,
1883, ' I went to work and gave the schooling best ' ;
' Rolf Boldrewood '. Morris. Prob. ex :—2. In c.,
to leave (a person), avoid or abandon him (— 1877).
Horsley, *Jottings from Gaol.*

give gip or **gyp.** See **gip, give.—give her the gun.**
See **give the gun.**

give her the gun. To go to extremes : aircraft engineers' : from ca. 1932. *The Daily Herald*, Aug. 1, 1936.

give her the rush. ' To run out of one's ground to hit the ball ' : cricketers' coll. (— 1888) ; slightly ob.—as is the practice. (Lewis.)

give him a rolling for his all-over ! Give him a *Roland* for his *Oliver* ! : low Cockney (— 1909). Ware.

[**give in**, to yield, and **give out**, to fail, to cease, are, *pace* F. & H., S.E.]

give in . . . that. To admit, when close-pressed in argument, that . . . : coll. (— 1877). O.E.D.

give it a drink ! A c.p. hurled at a bad play or performance : theatrical and music-halls' (1897) >, by 1914, fairly gen. Ware. Cf. :

give it a rest ! Oh, stop talking ! C. 20 coll. ex U.S. *give us a rest !*

give it hot (with dative). To beat (soundly), scold (severely) : coll. : from ca. 1870.

give it mouth ! Speak up ! Low coll. : ca. 1865–1910. Orig. and mainly to actors. H., 5th ed., cites ' He's the cove to give it mouth ' as a ' low-folk ' encomium. Perhaps on *to give tongue*.

*****give it to** (a person) **for** (something). To rob or defraud one of : c. : ca. 1810–50. Vaux.—2. As to thrash or to scold, it may orig. have been coll., but it soon > S.E.—3. To pull a person's leg : low (—1812) ; † by 1890. Vaux.

give it to the Belgians ! See **Belgians.**

give it (up)on ?, what suit did you. How did you effect your purpose ? : low (— 1812) ; † by 1890. Vaux.

give jessie. See **jessie.**

give lip to. To speak insolently to : from ca. 1820 : nautical >, ca. 1860, gen. Haggart, 1821 ; Egan's Grose.

give (a ship) **muslin.** To make sail : nautical : late C. 19–20 ; ob. Bowen.

give nature a fillip. To indulge in wine and/or women : late C. 17–19 : coll. B.E.

give (a person) **one.** To give him a blow, a kiss, etc. : coll. : C. 19–20.

give (e.g. him) **one in the eye.** To thrash ; occ. to scold : from ca. 1880. Cf. *give it hot, something for oneself, what for, what's what.*

give one's head for naught (late C. 14–15) or **for the washing** (late C. 16–mid-19). ' To submit to be imposed on ', Halliwell. (Apperson.)

give out calendars. See **calendars, give out.**

*****give some stick.** To encourage punters to bet freely on (a certain horse, esp. the favourite) : racing c. (— 1933). Ex the use of the jockey's whip.

give (a ship) **something else to do.** Constantly to work the helm in order to check rolling or pitching : nautical : late C. 19–20. Bowen.

give (a person) **something for himself.** To thrash ; reprimand : coll. : late C. 19–20.

give (a person) **the air.** To dismiss : U.S., partly anglicised by 1934. C.O.D. (1934 Sup.).

give the bag, bullet, kick-out, pike, road, sack. To dismiss from one's employ : coll. : see the separate nn. *Bag* is the early form of *sack*, but see esp. **bag.** *Pike* and *road* are rare ; the former †, the latter ob. *Get* is commoner than *give the kick-out.*

give the ball air. ' To bowl the (slow) ball with a high trajectory ' : cricketers' coll. : 1919. Lewis cites E. R. Wilson, that nigh the most wonderful of all slow bowlers, as using the phrase in 1920.

give the belt. See **belt, give the.**

give the crock. To yield victory : lower classes' : from ca. 1880 ; very ob. Ware.

*****give the gooner.** See **gooner.**

give the gun to one's 'plane ; gen. **give her the gun.** To open the throttle : Royal Air Force : from ca. 1920.

give the miss in baulk. See **miss in baulk.**

give (a person) **the ram's challenge.** To nod to : tailors' (— 1928). ' Locus ' as in *give the ros(e)y.*

give (a person) **the road.** To avoid (him) : Canadian : from ca. 1910. John Beames.

give (a person) **the ros(e)y.** To blush at chaff : tailors' : 1928, *The Tailor and Cutter*, Nov. 29. From ca. 1890.

give way. (Of women) to permit the sexual embrace (— 1870). Perhaps orig. euphemistic and S.E., as often it still is ; but it also is a humorous coll.

give what for ; occ. **what's what.** (With dative.) To beat, thrash ; scold, reprimand : coll., the former C. 19–20, the latter C. 20 and gen. jocular.

give your arse a chance ! ; often preceded by *shut up* (or *stop talking*) *and.* A low, C. 20 c.p. : esp. in the Australian Forces, 1914–18.

give yourself a bit of an overhauling ! Go and have a wash and/or a clean-up : c.p. : from ca. 1912. Ex cleaning a motor-car.

given. Have given : sol., rather rare : C. 19–20. E. Raymond, *The Jesting Army*, 1930, ' But I given it. I can't do no more.'

given the deep six, be. To be heaved overboard ; to be buried at sea : nautical : late C. 19–20. Bowen. Prob. *six* refers to the length (in feet) of the coffin.

giver. A good boxer, esp. one with a hard punch : pugilistic : ca. 1820–1900. ' Peter Corcoran ' Reynolds in *The Fancy.*

gixie. An affected, mincing woman ; late C. 16– early 17.—2. A wanton wench : C.17. Both senses coll. on verge of respectability, the former being in Florio, the latter in Cotgrave, who remarks : ' A fained word '. Perhaps ex *gig* after *tricksy* (*trixy* in an old spelling).

gizz. A face : Scottish : C. 19. E.D.D. Perhaps influenced by *phiz.*

gizzard. The heart : low Australian (— 1916). C. J. Dennis. Cf. :

gizzard, fret one's. To worry oneself : low coll. (— 1755) ; ob. Johnson. Cf. *fret*, q.v., and *gizzard.*

gizzard, grumble in the. To be secretly annoyed : coll. (— 1765) : anticipated in C. 17 (? ex Yorkshire dial.). Whence *grumble-gizzard*, with which cf. *grumble-guts.*

gizzard, stick in one's. To continue to displease or render indignant : coll. : from ca. 1660. Pepys ; Swift, ' Don't let that stick in your gizzard ' ; in late C. 19–20, almost S.E. Ex the lit. sense, to prove indigestible.

glad, serve him (occ. **her, you,** etc.) **!** Serve him (etc.) right ! : from ca. 1910. Dorothy Sayers, *Clouds of Witness*, 1926, ' " Serve him glad," said Lord Peter viciously.' Ex North Country dial. (— 1891) : E.D.D.

glad eye, the. A come-hither look (gen. from female to male). Esp. in *give the g. e.* C. 20 : s. >, by 1930, coll. Ex † sense of *glad* (bright) : W.

glad rags, one's. One's best clothes : coll. : C. 20 ; U.S., anglicised ca. 1906 ; slightly ob (O.E.D. Sup.)

*gladd(h)er. (Often as vbl.n.) To employ a certain unascertained trick to relieve good citizens of their money : c. of ca. 1865 ; app. † by 1900. '*No. 747.*' Origin ?

gladiola. A sol. pl. of *gladiolus* : street flower-sellers' : late C. 19–20.

gladstone, a light travelling-bag, is S.E., but as an abbr. of the already jocular *Gladstone claret* (e.g. in Augustine Birrell's *Obiter Dicta*, 1885) it is coll. : 1864, H., 3rd ed. ; ob. Gladstone in 1860 reduced the import duty on French wines.

gladstonize. To say a lot and mean little : coll. : ca. 1885–1900.

*glanthorne. Money : c. : late C. 18–early 19. George Parker. ? *lanthorn* corrupted.

Glasgow Greys. The 70th Foot Regiment, from ca. 1881 the 2nd Battalion of the East Surreys : military : from soon after 1756 ; ob. At first, this regiment was recruited largely from Glasgow, and its facings were grey. F. & Gibbons.

Glasgow magistrate. A superior herring : inferentially from H., from ca. 1830. Ob. Cf. *Atlantic ranger, Billingsgate pheasant, Digby chicken, Dunbar wether, Gourock ham, Taunton turkey, Yarmouth capon.*

*glasiers. See glazier, 2.

glass, (to have) been looking through a. (To be) drunk : coll. : from ca. 1860 ; ob.

glass ?, who's to pay for the broken. Who is to pay for the damages ? Coll. : C. 19–20 : ob.

glass about, there's a deal of. A fine (though vulgar) display : low coll.—2. A c.p. retort to the boast of an achievement : low coll. Both ca. 1880–1914.

glass-eyes. A person wearing spectacles : coll. . ca. 1785–1900. Grose, 2nd ed. ; Baumann.

*glass house. A guard-room : esp. detention-barracks or cells for long-term prisoners : Regular Army : from ca. 1905. B. & P. Ex :—2. the Glass House. The military prison at North Camp, Aldershot : C. 20. So called ' presumably because it has a glass roof. It is known to, and dreaded for its severity by, every soldier . . ., just as the Naval Prisons at Chatham and Portsmouth are known and dreaded by every sailor in the Navy,' says ' Stuart Wood ', who ' served ' there in 1902, in *Shades of the Prison House*, 1932.

glass-house, live in a. To lay oneself open to criticism : coll. : from ca. 1845 ; now virtually S.E. Prob. suggested by the C. 17–20 proverb, *those who live in glass houses shouldn't throw stones.*

Glass-House Sailors. A synonym of *Crystal Palace Army* (see Crystal Palace). F. & Gibbons.

*glass-work. A method of cheating at cards by means of a tiny convex mirror attached to the palm of the dealer's hand : ca. 1820–80 : c.

glassy, the. Abbr. *the glassy eye*, ' a glance of cold disdain ', C. J. Dennis : Australian (— 1916). C. J. Dennis. Contrast :

glassy alley, the. The favourite or most admired : Australian (— 1916). C. J. Dennis. Ex game of marbles, a glassy alley being prized.

*glasyers. See glazier, 2.

*glaze. A window : c. of ca. 1690–1890. B.E., Grose (2nd ed.), Snowden.—2. Eye ; eyesight : c. (— 1788) ; † by 1900. Grose, 2nd ed. See glaze, mill a.

*glaze, v. (Of the dealer) to cheat, with a mirror, at cards : low or c. : ca. 1820–80. (See glass-work.) Pierce Egan.

*glaze, mill or star a or the. To break a window :

c. : ca. 1785–1890. Grose, 2nd ed. (at *star the glaze*).—2. Grose, 2nd ed. (1788), at *mill*, has ' I'll mill your glaze ; I'll beat out your eye,' † by 1900.

*glaze, on the, adj. and adv. (By) robbing jewellers' windows after smashing them : c. : from ca. 1719. Johnson's *Pirates and Highwaymen.*

*glaze, spank a or the. To break a window with the fist : c. (— 1839). Brandon.

*glazier. ' One that creeps in at Casements, or unrips Glass-windows to Filch and Steal ', B.E. : c. : mid-C. 17–early 19. Head, 1673.—2. Pl. only (in C. 16–17 often spelt *glasiers* or *glasyers*), the eyes : c. of ca. 1560–1830. Harman. Cf. :

glazier ?, is, rarely was, your father a. A c.p. addressed to one who stands in the light—esp. in front of a window, a fire, a candle, or a lamp. Grose (2nd ed.), who adds : ' If it is answered in the negative, the rejoinder is—I wish he was, that he might make a window through your body, to enable us to see the fire or light.' From ca. 1786.

*glaziers. See glazier, 2.

glean, v.t. and i. ; gleaning, vbl.n. To steal ; stealing : c. or low : ca. 1860–1910. Greenwood, *The Little Ragamuffin*, ca. 1880, ' Pinchin ', findin', gleanin', some coves call it.' (Baumann.)

gleaner. A thief of ' unconsidered trifles ' : low or c. : ca. 1860–1900. F. & H. Ex the preceding.

Glesca Kulies, the. The 71st Foot Regiment : military in the Peninsular War. F. & Gibbons. Lit., the Glasgow pickpockets or street-Arabs.

*glib ; in C. 18, occ. glibb. A ribbon : c. : mid-C. 18–early 19. ? ex its smoothness.—2. The tongue : mid-C. 19–20 ; ob. H., 3rd ed. Esp. in *slacken your glib !*, don't talk so much ! ? ex *glib(-tongued)*, which F. & H. wrongly include.

*glim, glym. A thief's dark lantern : late C. 17–early 19 c. B.E. Perhaps abbr. *glimmer* (of light). In C. 20, esp. ' an electric torch with the bulb covered over with paper except for a very small aperture ' (David Hume).—2. Hence, a candle : c. (— 1714) ; † by 1840, except in *douse the glim.*—3. A light of any kind : c. (— 1728).—4. A fire : c. (— 1785). Grose, 1st ed. Abbr. *glimmer, glymmar* or *-er.*—5. Whence, ca. 1840–90, the sham account of a fire sold by ' flying stationers ', q.v.—6. A match : either c. or low s. (— 1923). Manchon. Ex sense 3 rather than ex 2 or 4.—7. Low or c. is the sense, a venereal infection, ex that of fire : ca. 1850–1900.—8. See glims.—9. Eye-sight : c. of ca. 1820–60. Egan's Grose. Ex *glims*, 1.—10. A fiery drink (? gin) : ca. 1750–70. Toldervy, 1756. Cf. *rush-light.*

*glim, v. To burn, i.e. brand, in the hand : c. : late C. 17–early 19. B.E. Ex preceding.

*glim, douse the. To put out the light, gen. in imperative : orig., C. 18, c. ; ca. 1840, it > s., mainly nautical. Ex *glim*, n., 1–4. See douse.

*glim-fender. An andiron : c. of ca. 1670–1820. Coles ; B.E. A *rum g.-f.* was of silver : see rum. Ex *glim*, n.—2. A handcuff (but rare in singular) : c. : ca. 1820–70. ' Jon Bee.' Punning sense 1.

*glim-flash(e)y ; in C. 17, occ. glimflashly. Angry : c. : late C. 17–mid-19. Coles ; B.E. ; Lytton. ' No, Captain, don't be glimflashy ! '

*glim-glibber. A jargon ; applied esp. to under-world cant : low or perhaps c. (— 1844) : † by 1910. If *glibber* perverts *gibber(ish)*, then, lit., the term = a ' dark-lantern ' gibberish or lingo. O.E.D.

*glim-jack. A link-boy ; occ. a thief operating at night : c. : mid-C. 17–early 19. Coles, 1676.

*glim-lurk. A beggar's petition alleging loss by fire : c. of ca. 1845–80. Ex *glim*, n., 5. Mayhew. Cf. *lurker* and see **lurk.**

*glim-stick, glimstick. A candlestick : c. of ca. 1670–1830. Coles ; B.E. ; Grose. A *rum g.-s.* is of silver, a *queer g.-s.* is of brass, pewter, or iron. Cf. *glim*, n., 2. See **glim-fender** and **queer.**

*glimmer, glymmar or **-er.** Fire : c. of ca. 1560–1830. Harman ; B.E. ; Grose. C. *glim*, n., 4.—2. See **glimmers.**—3. A beggar ; c. of C. 20. Charles E. Leach, *On Top of the Underworld*, 1933.

glimmer, not a. Not (or none) at all : coll. : from ca. 1925. Only in answer to some such question as ' Have (had) you any idea how to do this, *or* that this would happen ? ' Abbr. *not the glimmer of an idea.*

*glimmerer. A beggar alleging loss by fire : ca. 1600–1830 : c. Dekker & Wilkins ; B.E. (O.E.D.) Cf. *glimmer* and :

*glimmering mort. A female ' glimmerer ', q.v. : ca. 1560–1660 c. Harman. See **mort.**

glimmers. The eyes (pl. only) : from ca. 1814 : low : ob. Ex *glimmer*, q.v.

glimmery. (Of an actor) having no clear conception of his part : theatrical : 1892 : ob. *The Athenæum*, April 9, 1892. (O.E.D.)

*glims, pl. only : eyes. From ca. 1790 : c. > low s. : ob. Grose, 3rd ed.—2. Whence, in pl. only, a pair of spectacles : orig. c., then low : from ca. 1860 : ob.

glims, puff the. ' To fill the hollow over the eyes of old horses by pricking the skin and blowing air into the loose tissues underneath, thus giving the full effect of youth ', F. & H. : shady horse-dealing and veterinary surgery : from ca. 1870.

glip. ' The track of oil left by a fast-swimming whale ' : whalers' and sailors' : mid-C. 19–20. Bowen. Perhaps cognate with Scottish and Northern *glid*, smooth (E.D.D.), possibly influenced by *slippery* ; cf. Northern *gliddy*, oily.

*glist(e)ner. A sovereign : c. >, ca. 1830, low : from ca. 1815. T. Moore ; Frank Jennings, 1932. Cf. *shiner* and *yellow boy.*

*glister. A glass or tumbler : c. (— 1889). ? ex the S.E. n. and v., *glister.*

*gloach ; gen., *gloak.* A man : c. (— 1795), Scottish according to Pierce Egan (1823) ; † by 1875. Potter's *Dict. of Cant.* ? cognate with *bloke.* Cf. *gill* and *gory.*

*gloak, v. To tell a piteous tale : tramps' c. (— 1932). Frank Jennings. Perhaps a corruption of *croak.*

gloar. To glower : sol. (— 1887). Baumann.

*globe. Pewter ; a pewter pot : c. : late C. 18–mid-19. Grose, 3rd ed. Ex the shape.

Globe-Rangers, the. The Royal Marines : nautical : ca. 1850–1914.

globe-trotter. A merely quantitative or spatial traveller : coll. (1883) : ob. Hence a long-distance or a frequent traveller : coll. : from ca. 1892. In C. 20, S.E. in both senses. *The Graphic*, August 7, 1886, ' Your mere idle gaping globe-trotter '.

globe-trotting is the vbl.n. to both senses of *globe-trotter*, q.v.

globes. The female breasts : coll. : from ca. 1860 : ob.

globos. Debenture shares in Bank of New Zealand Estates : Stock Exchange (— 1895). A. J. Wilson, *Stock Exchange Glossary.*

glope. To spit : ca. 1830–80 : Winchester College. Wrench. Cf. dial. *gloup*, to gulp.

gloque. A rare variant (Egan, 1842) of *gloak*, q.v.

glorified. Changed into something glorious (often sarcastically) : coll. : from ca. 1820. Lamb ; Thackeray, ' A glorified flunkey ' (O.E.D.).

glorification. A festive occasion, a ' spree ' : coll. : 1843. (S.O.D.)—2. A ' glorified ' variety or example of something usually inferior or unimpressive : coll. : from ca. 1885.

glorious. Divinely or ecstatically drunk : coll. : 1790, Burns (O.E.D.) ; Thackeray, ' I was taken up glorious, as the phrase is, . . . and put to bed.'

glorious sinner. A dinner : rhyming s. (— 1859). ? satirising gluttony. H., 1st ed.

gloriously. Ecstatically : always with *drunk* explicit or implicit. Coll. : 1784. Cowper. (O.E.D.)

glory ! is a low coll. exclamation of delight (— 1893). Quiller-Couch. Also *great glory !* and *how the glory !* Abbr. *glory be to God !*

glory, go to. To die : coll. : 1814. *Punch*, 1841. Ex *glory*, ' the splendour and bliss of heaven ', S.O.D.

glory, in one's. (At one's best : S.E.). Extremely gratified : coll. : 1895. (O.E.D.)—2. Esp. *leave one in his glory*, to depart, so that now he is (or sits) alone : 1887, Baumann.

*glory-hole. A small cell in which, at the court, prisoners are kept on the day of trial : c. : 1845 (O.E.D.).—2. A Salvation Army meeting-place : low : 1887 ; ob. Ware.—3. A dug-out : military : 1915. F. & Gibbons.—4. The fore peak : nautical : late C. 19–20 ; ob. Bowen.—5. Hence, the stewards' quarters : nautical : late C. 19–20. William McFee, *Sailors of Fortune*, 1930.

glory-hole steward. ' The steward who looks after the passenger stewards in their quarters ' : nautical : C. 20. Bowen.

Glory-oh, the. The warship *Glory* : naval (— 1909). Ware.

glove. A kind of drinking vessel : early C. 17. Dekker in *The Gull's Horn-Book.*

glove, fit like a. See **fit like a glove.**

gloves, go for the. To bet recklessly : the turf : from ca. 1870 ; ob. H., 5th ed. Ex women's tendency to bet in pairs of gloves on the ' heads I win, tails you lose ' principle.

gloves, win a pair of. To kiss a sleeping man : a kindly act meriting this reward : coll. : from ca. 1710 : ob. Gay, Grose.

glow, adj. Ashamed : tailors' : ca. 1870–1914. Ex *a glow of shame.*

glow, (all) of a. Coll. for *in a glow* : 1865, Dickens. O.E.D.

glow, got the. See **got the glow.**

glue. Thick soup : C. 19–20. It sticks to the ribs ! Cf. *deferred stock.*—2. Gonorrhœa : low : from ca. 1870.

glue did not hold, the. ' You were baulked . . . : you missed your aim,' Ray, 1813 : coll. : C. 19. (Apperson.)

glue-pot. A parson : mid-C. 18–20, ob. Grose, 1st ed. He joins couples together.—2. ' Part of the road so bad that the coach or buggy '—or motor-car—' sticks in it ', Morris : Australian coll. : recorded in 1892, but prob. dating from the 1870's or even '60's ; ob.—3. (Glue Pot, the.) London : showmen's : C. 20. P. Allingham, in *The Evening News*, July 9, 1934.

glue-pot has come unstuck, a or **the.** He gives off the odour of a genital exudation or of a seminal emission : a low c.p. : from ca. 1890.

[glum is—despite F. & H.—ineligible because S.E.; glump, glumpy, because dial.]

glum-pot. A gloomy or glum person : coll. : late C. 19–20.

glutman. A rush-time extra hand in the Customs : coll. verging on S.E. : ca. 1790–1850. See that interesting book, Colquhoun's *The Police of the Metropolis*, 1796.

glutton. A boxer that takes a lot of punishment before he is ' satisfied ' : pugilism : 1809. Cf. the S.E. *glutton for work.*—2. A horse that stays well : racing s. > gen. : from ca. 1850.

*glybe. A writing : c. (− 1785) ; † by 1890. Grose, 1st ed. A perversion of *gybe.*

*glym and its derivatives are defined at the preferable *glim*, etc.

*gnarl upon ; gnarling, adj. To spy or ' split ' on (a person) ; doing this, apt to do this : c. of ca. 1810–60. Vaux. Cf. :

*gnarler. A watch-dog : c. : C. 19. Egan's Grose. Lit., a snarler. Cf. *bleating cheat.*

*gnarling. See gnarl upon.

gnash. Incorrect for *nesh*, tender, physically soft : C. 18. O.E.D.

gnasp. To vex : coll. : C. 18–early 19. Bailey has it.

*gnawler. A late C. 19–20 c. variant of *gnarler*, q.v. Manchon.

*gnoff. See gonnof.

gnomon. The nose : jocular coll. : ca. 1580–1820. Stanyhurst, Cowper. (O.E.D.)

gnomonic. (?) Incorrect for *gnomic* : C. 18–20. O.E.D.

gnosh, v.t. To eat : military : C. 20. F. & Gibbons. Prob. a telescoping of *gnash one's teeth on.*

gnostic. A knowing person, ' a downy cove ' (q.v.) : ca. 1815–1900, but already ob. in 1859. Moore, in *Tom Crib*, ' Many of the words used by the Canting Beggars in Beaumont and Fletcher's masque are still to be heard among the gnostics of Dyot Street and Tothill Fields.'—2. Also as adj. (†).

gnostically. Artfully ; knowingly ; flashily : ca. 1820–95. Scott.

go. For the phrases not listed here, see the significant n. or adj. (F. & H.'s *go-between*, a pimp, is S.E.)

go. A three-halfpenny bowl of gin and water, esp.—and orig.—if sold at ' the Go Shop ', q.v. : ca. 1787–1820.—2. Whence (?) a draught, a drink : from ca. 1800. *Punch*, 1841, ' Waiter, a go of Brett's best alcohol.' Specifically, a quartern of brandy : same period. Thackeray in *The Hoggarty Diamond*, ' Two more chairs . . . and two more goes of gin ! ' Synonyms of the former are *bender, coffin-nail, drain, facer, gargle, lotion, nobbler, peg, reviver, slug, something, swig, tot, warmer, wet,* etc., etc.—2a. Hence, of food, as in ' We had a good go of cherries (of ices) ', Baumann, 1887.—3. The fashion, esp. in *all the go* (q.v.) and, late C. 19–20, *quite the go,—the go* having > † ca. 1840 ; the correct thing : from ca. 1787 (Grose's annotations to 1st ed. copy in the British Museum) : s. > coll. G. R. Sims, 1880, ' And all day long there's a big crowd stops | To look at the lady who's all the go.'—4. Hence, in the 1820's, a dandy, a notable swell. Egan, 1821, ' In the parks, Tom was the go among the goes.'—5. An affair, incident, occurrence : coll. or low coll. : 1796 (O.E.D.). Kenney, 1803, ' Capital go, isn't it ? ' (this stock phrase = a pleasant business) ; Dickens, ' A pretty go ! ' (stock ; = a startling or awkward business or situation, etc.) ; G. Eliot, ' A

rum go ' (stock, with variant *rummy* ; = a queer start, a strange affair).—6. Hence (− 1877), an occasion, a time ; e.g. ' I've twelve this go ' = I have [received] twelve [years] this time.—7. Hence, a bout, an attack, of sickness or illness : coll. : C. 20. (O.E.D. Sup.)—8. High spirits ; mettle, spirit ; energy, enterprise : coll. : 1825, Westmacott, in *The English Spy.*—9. A turn, an attempt : coll. : U.S. (1825), anglicised ca. 1835. Dickens, ' Wot do you think o' that for a go ? ' Gen. in *have a go at*, the object being anything from an abstruse subject to a woman.—10. A success, esp. in *make a go of it*, (C. 20) *make it a go* : orig. (− 1877), U.S. ; anglicised ca. 1895.—11. An agreement, a settled thing ; a certainty. Esp. in *it's a go*, occ. *is it a go ?* : mostly Australia and New Zealand (− 1914).—12. A chance ; esp. *give a person a fair go* : id. : from ca. 1910.—13. Working condition of the bells : bell-ringers' s. (− 1901) >, by 1930, coll. H. Earle Bulwer, *Glossary of Bell-Ringing.*

go, v. The sense, to be pregnant, as in Bacon, ' Women go commonly nine months,' is S.E.—2. Abbr. *go down*, v., 1, q.v. : from ca. 1740 ; coll. Fielding.—3. Gen. with *for*, as *to go for to* (do something), to be so foolish, brave, strict, etc., as to . . . , sol. or low coll. : from ca. 1750.—4. V.t., to wager. risk : 1768, Goldsmith : coll. Hence, to afford from ca. 1870. Also to stand treat : from ca. 1875—5. (Of things) to succeed : coll. : from ca. 1865 *London Opinion*, Jan. 13, 1866, ' His London-street railway scheme didn't go ' ; H. D. Traill, 1870.—6. Hence, to be accepted or acceptable ; to be valid or applicable : coll. ; orig. (ca. 1890) U.S., anglicised ca. 1910. E.g. ' That goes for (or with) me.' O.E.D. (Sup.)—7. (Of a politician or a constituency, with adj., as in ' Chelsea went red,' ' Mr. Maxton went conservative ') to become : coll. : from ca. 1889 ; ex U.S.—8. To ride to hounds : from ca. 1840 : sporting s. >, ca. 1895, j.—9. V.t., to eat : nautical : late C. 19–20. Bowen. Prob. ex sense 4, nuance 1.—10. Hence, to digest : mostly Canadian : late C. 19–20. (John Beames, *Getaway*, 1932, ' Your poor pa—he couldn't ever go pork an' onions.')—11. Abbr. *go for*, to attack : Australian : from ca. 1912.

go, a little bit on the. Slightly drunk : ca. 1820–80. Egan.

' go ', from the word. From the start : coll. : orig. (− 1838) U.S. ; anglicised ca. 1890.

go, great and little. See great go, little go.

go, high. See high go.

go, near. A narrow escape : coll. : from ca. 1825.

go, no. Either with *to be* or as an exclamation : 1825, Westmacott (O.E.D.) ; Dickens, ' I know something about this here family, and my opinion is, it's no go.' Occ. abbr. *n. g.* (ob.).

go, on the. On the verge of ruin or destruction : late C. 17–18 : coll.—2. In a (state of) decline : coll. : ca. 1725–1880. FitzGerald, 1842 (in a letter), ' As to poor old England, I never see a paper, but I think with you that she is on the go ' (O.E.D.).—3. Slightly drunk : 1821, Egan (O.E.D.) ; very ob.—4. On the move ; busy ; restlessly active : coll. : from ca. 1840.

go-ahead, adj. Progressive ; anxious to succeed —and usually succeeding : ex U.S. (like *going-ahead*, it occurs in 1840) ; anglicised ca. 1865. In C. 20, coll.

go ahead ! All right ! Proceed ! Ex **U.S.** (1835), anglicised ca. 1868. In C. 20, coll.

go all out on. To trust completely ; to make the most of (a person) : coll. : 1933, Compton Mackenzie. Ex athletics.

***go-along(er).** A fool ; an easy dupe : c. of resp. ca. 1845–1914 (Mayhew) and ca. 1810–90 (Vaux). Because he goes along when bid.—2. A thief : c. (— 1857). ' Ducange Anglicus ' ; H., 2nd ed. (This sense : only in the form *go-along*.)

go along, Bob ! ; come along, Bob ! These two c.pp., of ca. 1800–30, are of problematic and dubious meaning. ' Jon Bee '.

go-alonger. See *go along.

go and (do something). Where the *go and*-represents a mere pleonasm, the usage is coll. : from C. 15 or C. 16.—2. If = to be so silly, foolish, or unlucky as to do something, it is also coll. : from ca. 1875. Cf. *been and gone and* . . . (O.E.D.)

go and boil your head ! See at head.

go and eat coke ! A c.p. indicative of impatient contempt : London slums' (— 1909). Ware.

go and take a running jump at yourself ! (Rare in other moods.) Go to blazes ! : a c.p. (C. 20) expressive of scorn. E.g. in John G. Brandon, *The One-Minute Murder*, 1934. Cf. *go and play trains !* See play trains.

go as you please, adj. Unconfined by rules : athletics, ca. 1880. Hence, characterised by a general freedom of action : 1884 : coll.

go-ashore. ' An iron pot or cauldron, with three iron feet, and two ears, from which it was suspended by a wire handle over the fire,' Morris : New Zealand coll. (— 1849) >, by 1880, S.E. Ex Maori *kohua* by ' Hobson-Jobson '.

go-ashores. ' The seaman's best dress ', Smyth, 1867 : nautical coll. : from ca. 1850 : ob. (O.E.D.)

go at, have a. See go, n., 9.

go away. Abbr. *go-away dress* (a bride's) : Society coll : 1886. Ware.

go ba-ba (black sheep). See ba-ba.

go back of. See go back on.—2. See go behind.

go back on, v.t. To desert, turn against, or to fail, a person ; break a promise : ex U.S. (1868) ; anglicised ca. 1895. Variant *go back of* (not with persons) : 1888. O.E.D.

go bail !, I will or **I'll.** I'll be bound ! I'm sure ! Assuredly ! Coll. : from ca. 1880. Rider Haggard, in *Dawn*, ' He won't marry her now, I'll go bail ' (O.E.D.). Ob.

go behind, v.t. ' To disregard the writing for the sake of ascertaining the fact ', Thornton : orig. (1839 ; popularised in 1876), U.S. ; anglicised as a coll. ca. 1890. In C. 20, S.E. The variant *go back of* (late C. 19–20) is rare in Britain, frequent in U.S.

Go-Between, the. St. Alban's Church, Holborn : London : 1897–ca. 1912. Ware. Because ' High Church '.

go big ; go over big. (Of a play, a book) to be very successful : both U.S. and both anglicised in 1928. The latter was, in U.S., the earlier ; *go big* derives from it. (O.E.D. Sup.)

go blah. See blah, adj. Prob. ex :—2. To have one's mind go blank : from ca. 1907 : Parliamentary >, by 1930, gen. A. E. W. Mason, *The Dean's Elbow*, 1930, in reference to the year 1908 and to a prospective speaker in Parliament, ' If only his mind didn't go blank. Minds often did, even the best minds. Darkness descends on them, inextricable . . . These seizures . . . always chose ruinous moments. There was a slang phrase which described them—horribly graphic, too, like most

slang phrases. To go blah. Well, there it was ! He, Mark Thewless, would go blah this afternoon.' Perhaps *blah* represents a perversion of *blank*.

go-by. The act of passing without recognising (a person), dealing with or taking (a thing) ; an evasion or a deception. Esp. in *give* (e.g. him or it) *the go-by*, to ignore ; to abandon ; to refuse to recognise : from ca. 1655 : in C. 17–18, and indeed until ca. 1860, S.E. ; then coll. Stevenson, ' A French ship . . . gave us the go-by in the fog.' Also common in *get the go-by*, the corresponding passive.

go-by-the-ground. ' A little short person ', Grose, 2nd ed. : C. 18–19 coll. ; ob. except in dial. In late C. 16–17, *go-by-ground* (also, C. 17, adj.). Cf. Lincolnshire *go-by-the-wall*, a creeping, helpless person.

go close. Abbr. *go close to the winning-post* : sporting coll. (— 1909). Ware.

go crook. To speak angrily : Australian : from ca. 1910. See crook, adj.

go dis. See dis (disconnected) and cf. *gone dis*, q.v.

go-down. A drink : mid-C. 17–18 : s. >, by 1700, coll D'Urfey, Ned Ward Later, *go*, n., 2. The term survives in dial.

go down, v.i. ; go down with, v.t. To be accepted (by) ; be approved or allowed : C. 17–20 : in C. 17–18, S.E. ; then coll. Dekker ; Pepys ; Smollett, ' That won't go down with me.' Cf. *go*, v., 4, q.v.—2. V.i., to be rusticated : university : ca. 1860–1900. (In C. 20, simply to leave the university at the end of one's course.)—3. To become bankrupt : coll. (— 1892) : ob. Also *go under*, q.v.—4. To be sentenced, imprisoned : c. : C. 20. E.g. Edgar Wallace in *The Squeaker*, 1927.

go down one. To be vanquished : Cockneys' coll. (— 1909). Ware. Ex *going down one place* in school.

go due north. To go bankrupt : ca. 1810–80. I.e. to go to White-Cross Street Prison, once († before 1893) situated in the north of London.

go 'er on ! A Stock Exchange exclamatory c.p. made when a broker or a jobber wishes to continue buying or selling the same shares : C. 20. A commercial *attaboy !*

go fanti. To return to primitive life : scientific : from ca. 1880 ; ob. Ware.

go for. To attempt (to do) ; undertake : coll. : from ca. 1880 ; ob. ; orig. (— 1871), U.S.,—cf. that U.S. sense, to be in favour of, support, vote for, which is coll. found in coll. English ca. 1880–1910.—2. To attack, physically, lingually, or in writing (hence, esp. in the theatre, to criticise adversely) : ex U.S. (1838) ; anglicised ca. 1870. Baumann, 1887 ; *The Polytechnic Magazine*, Oct. 24, 1889, ' He went for the jam tarts unmercifully.'

go for the gloves. See gloves, go for the.

go for to [do, etc.]. ' Go and ' : sol. (— 1887). Baumann. Cf. *go to do*, q.v. See also go, v., 3.

go-getter. A very active enterprising person ; a pusher : coll. : U.S. (— 1922), anglicised by 1925. (O.E.D. Sup.) Ex *go and get what one wants*.

go home. To die : military : 1915. B. & P. Cf. *go out* and *go west*.

go hostile. See hostile.

go-in, gen. followed by *at*. A lit. or fig. attack : 1858.—2. A turn of work (— 1890). Both coll. O.E.D.

go in, v.i. To enter oneself ; set about it ; try : from ca. 1835 : from ca. 1890, S.E. Dickens, ' Go in and win ', advice offered to the weaker in a contest, esp. fisticuffs.—2. To die : military in the Boer War. J. Milne, *The Epistles of Atkins*, 1902. Ex dial. sense, ' to come to an end ', E.D.D.

go in at. To assail vigorously : coll. : from ca. 1810. In 1849, Dickens, ' Sometimes I go in at the butcher madly, and cut my knuckles open against his face.' Ob.

go in for. To seek ; attempt to obtain ; make one's object : coll. : from ca. 1860. Dickens, ' Go in for money—money's the article,' 1864.—2. Hence, apply oneself to, take up (e.g. as a hobby) ; to begin to do, to adopt as a profession, study as a subject : coll. : from ca. 1870.—3. To enter oneself as a candidate for : coll. : from ca. 1879 (O.E.D.).— 4. To venture on obtaining or on wearing : coll. : from ca. 1890.—5. To court (a woman : Society s. of ca. 1865–1900. Whyte-Melville in *M. or N.* Cf. *go in* and *go for*, 1.

go (in) off the deep end. See **end, go . . .**

go into. Attack vigorously ; punch fast and hard : boxing : 1811 : ob. by 1910, † by 1930. (O.E.D.)

go into a flat spin. (Gen. going . . .) To become muddled : aircraft engineers' : from ca. 1929. *The Daily Herald*, Aug. 1, 1936.

go it ; often **go it strong,** in C. 20 occ. **go it thick.** To act vigorously and/or daringly ; speak very strongly or frankly : coll. : C. 19–20. Bee. Dickens, ' I say, young Copperfield, you're going it.'—2. Hence, to live expensively and/or dissipatedly : coll. (— 1821). Egan, in *Tom and Jerry*, ' To go it, where's a place like London ? ' (the answer being, Any cosmopolitan capital).—3. To bombard heavily, make an artillery ' demonstration ' : military coll. : 1914. B. & P. Ex sense 1.

go it ! Keep at it ! Play, fight, etc., hard ! Coll. : from ca. 1820. Bee. ? ex *go it, ye cripples, (crutches are cheap)* : see **cripples.**

go it blind. To act without considering the consequences ; esp. to ' speed ', physically or morally, thus : from ca. 1840.

go it strong (or **thick**). See **go it.**

go native. See **native.** For the subject, see *The Fortnightly Review*, Dec., 1933.

go-off. (Time of) commencement : coll. : 1851 (O.E.D.). Esp. in the ob. *at one go-off* (1856) and in *at (the) first go-off,* at the very beginning : from ca. 1879.—2. In banking s., from ca. 1890, ' the amount of loans falling due (. . . going off the amount in the books) in a certain period ', O.E.D.

go off, v. To die : C. 17–20 (ob.) : coll. Shakespeare ; Dickens, ' She . . . was seized with a fit and went off.'—2. To be disposed of : goods by sale, women in marriage. Dickens, of the latter, in *Boz.* —3. To take place, occur ; occ. it almost = to succeed. Coll. : from ca. 1804. Maria Edgeworth ; Mrs. Gaskell, ' The wedding went off much as such affairs do.'—4. To deteriorate in freshness or (e.g. a horse) in form : coll. (— 1883).—5. (Contrast sense 3.) Not to take place : Society : ca. 1885–1915. Ware. (Esp. of an appointment or an engagement.)—6. ' To go on board ship' : naval coll. : C. 20. F. & Gibbons.

go off on. To blame, reprimand, abuse : nautical : C. 20. H. Maclaren, *The Private Opinions of a British Blue-Jacket*, 1929.

go off the deep end. See **end, go (in) off the.**

go off the handle. A C. 20 variant of *fly off the handle,* q.v.

go off the hooks. To die : from ca. 1830 ; ob. Cf. *go aloft* (see **aloft**).

go on. To talk volubly : coll. : from ca. 1860. With *at,* to rail at : coll. : 1873. (O.E.D.)

go on ! An exclamation of surprise, incredulity, or derision : coll. : from ca. 1875.

go . . . on . . . the first dots being any coll. or idiomatic or ' Saxon ' adj. (a literary adj. is very rare) ; the second dots being a pronoun or a n. representing a person ; the subject is gen. a person or else a thing endowed with personal qualities ; the object of *on* is shown at a consequent disadvantage —in fact, this construction is a coll. variation of the ethic dative. E.g., ' Just when I had saved enough money to retire, my bank went broke on me ' ; ' The servant went ill on him ', ; ' The egg went bad on the cook.' (From ca. 1895.)

*****go on,** orig. **upon, the dub.** To go housebreaking : late C. 17–early 19 c. See **dub.**

*****go on the sharpo.** To rob from buildings : tramps' c. (— 1932). F. Jennings.

*****go out, v.i.** To rob in the streets : c. (— 1823) ; ob. Bee, ' " I don't *go out*, now," said by a reformed rogue '. Cf. next entry.—2. To fall into disuse or into social disrepute : coll. : 1840 (O.E.D.). *Punch*, 1841, ' Pockets . . . to use the flippant idiom of the day, are going out.' Abbr. *go out of fashion* or *use.*—3. To die : military : 1915. B. & P. After *pass out* and *go west.*

*****go out foreign.** ' To emigrate under shady circumstances ' : c. (— 1909). Ware.

go out the back door. See **out the back door.**

*****go out together.** To go, habitually, thieving in company : c. of ca. 1810–90. Vaux. Cf. *go out,* 1 : q.v.

go out with the ebb. To die : nautical coll. : late C. 19–20. Bowen. Cf. military *go west.*

go over, to desert, is C. 17–20 S.E. ; but it is clerical s. when it = to join the Church of Rome (— 1861). Cf. *vert.*—2. To die : coll. : from ca. 1845. Abbr. *go over to join the majority.* Cf. *go off.* —3. In c., to search and rob a person (— 1889). Cf. *go through.*

go over big. See **go big.—go over the top.** See **top, go over the.—go phut.** See **phut, go.**

go round, v.i. To pay an informal visit : coll. : 1873, W. Black. (O.E.D.)

go round the buoy. To have ' a second helping of any food ' : nautical : late C. 19–20. Bowen.

Go-Shop, the. The Queen's Head tavern in Duke's Court, Bow Street (London, W.C.2) : late C. 18–early 19. ' Frequented by the under players ', Grose, 2nd ed. Ex *go,* n., 1, q.v.

go sick. To malinger : military coll. : 1915. Collinson. I.e. go on the sick-parade.

*****go the jump.** To enter a house by the window : c. : C. 19.

go the pace. See **pace, go the.**

go the whole hog. To act thorough-goingly : ex U.S. (1828) ; anglicised ca. 1850. See esp. Thornton and W. Cf. *whole-hogger*, q.v.

go through. To rob : ex U.S. (1867) ; anglicised ca. 1895.—2. To possess a woman : low coll. : from ca. 1870.

go through the Chapter House. (Of the ball) to pass through the stumps, in the days when there were only two : cricketers' : mid-C. 18–early 19. Lewis.

go through with. To complete (a difficult or distasteful task or duty) : mid-C. 16–20 : S.E. until ca. 1890, then of a coll. tendency.

go to do. To go and do ; to do : proletarian coll. : late C. 19–20. Cf. *go for to,* q.v. (E.g. Dorothy

Sayers, *Unnatural Death*, 1927, ' What a terrible thing, oh dear ! who would go to do a thing like that ? ')

go to father. See **father, go to.**

go to grass. To abscond ; disappear suddenly. Gen. in present perfect tense or as ppl. phrase, *gone to grass*. Ca. 1850–90.

go to grass ! ' A common answer to a troublesome or inquisitive person ', H., 1859 : ob. by 1880, † by 1900 in England : orig. (— 1848), U.S.

go to grass with one's teeth upwards. To be buried : from ca. 1810.—2. Hence, to die : coll. : from ca. 1820 : † by 1910. Cf. and see *landowner* and cf. the Devonshire *go round land.* ? an elaboration of the C. 17 *go to grass*, to succumb, be knocked down.

go to Halifax. See **Halifax ; to Bath,** see **Bath ; to Hanover,** see **Hanover ; to Putney,** see **Putney ; to Jericho,** see **Jericho.**

go to heaven in a string. To be hanged : coll. : ca. 1590–1800. Greene, 1592. (Apperson.)

go to hell and pump thunder ! A late C. 19 c.p. indicative of utter incredulity or derision. See **goose, go shoe a.**

go to Hell or Connaught ! Go away ! : coll. : from 1654. Ware. Ex a Parliamentary Act of that date.

go-to-meeting, adj. Best (of clothes) : coll. : ex U.S. (1825) ; anglicised ca. 1850, ' Cuthbert Bede ' having ' His black go-to-meeting bags '. Often preceded by *Sunday*.

go to one's chest. (Of things.) To annoy (a person) for a long time : low : 1914, A. Neil Lyons, in *Arthur's*, ' It goes to his chest ' (Manchon). Ex a cold going there.

go to pot. See **pot, go to.**

go to the bank. See **bank, go to the.**

*go to the country. To go to prison ; cf. *in the country*, in prison, esp. at Dartmoor : c. : C. 20. E.g. in E. Wallace, *The Brigand*, 1927.

go to the dogs. See **dogs.**

go uncling. To run after a married woman : Royal Air Force : from ca. 1920. Her children call him ' Uncle '.

go under. To become bankrupt ; disappear from Society : coll. (— 1879).—2. To succumb : coll. (— 1891) : since ca. 1918, S.E. ' He had " gone under " in the struggle, as the terribly expressive phrase runs,' H. C. Halliday, 1891.—3. To die : orig. (— 1849), U.S. ; anglicised ca. 1870, but never very gen.

go up. To be ruined, financially, socially, or politically : coll. (— 1864) : ob. More gen. in U.S. than in Britain.—2. See **gone up.**

go up for. To sit for (an examination) : coll. : from ca. 1885.

go up in the air. To ' explode ', lose one's temper violently : from ca. 1900.

go up one ! Good for you ! : a c.p. of late C. 19–20. Ex school-teacher's promotion of a successful pupil.

go (up)on the (e.g. **bush**). See the key-nn (e.g. **bush**).

go west. To die : popularised in the G.W., but adumbrated in late C. 16–18, as in Greene, *Cony-Catching*, Part II, 1592, ' So long the foists [thieves] put their villanie in practise, that West-ward they goe, and there solemnly make a rehearsall sermon at tiborne.' The basic idea is that of the setting sun ; pioneering in North America may have contributed. See esp. *Words !*

go while the going's good. See **going's good.**

go with. (Of things) to harmonise or suit : 1710 : S.E. until ca. 1880, then of a coll. hue.—2. To ' walk out with ' ; to affect in friendship or, gen., passion or love : low coll. : from ca. 1880.—3. To share the sexual congress with : low coll. : from ca. 1870.

*goad. A decoy at auctions or horse-sales : c. : C. 17–mid-18. Dekker ; B.E. Contrast :

*goads. False dice : c. : C. 18–early 19. Cf. *chapman*.

goal. In Winchester football of ca. 1840–1900, the referee.—2. (With derivative *goaler*, a gaoler.) A C. 19–20 sol. for *gaol* : in C. 17–18, a variant, S.E. but not literary : B.E., for instance, has *goaler's coach*. In late C. 19–20, much commoner in writing than in speech.

goaler. See preceding.

goalee ; gen. **goalie.** A goal-keeper : Association football coll. (ca. 1920) now verging on S.E. (O.E.D. Sup.)

goanna ; gohanna ; guana ; guano. An iguana : Australian coll. : resp. — 1891 ; 1896 (Henry Lawson), but ob. ; 1830 († by 1910) ; and 1802 (Barrington)—but † by 1900. Morris.

goat, a lecher, is not unconventional, but *goat*, to thrash, is low coll. of ca. 1860–1910. *Derby Day*, 1864.—2. A Maltese : nautical (esp. naval) : late C. 19–20. Bowen.

goat, get someone's. To annoy him : U.S. (ca. 1911), anglicised by 1916 : s. that, by 1937, is on the verge of coll. O.E.D. (Sup.). Perhaps ex Fr. *prendre la chèvre*, to take the milch-goat, often the poor man's sole source of milk.

goat, play the. To play the fool : 1879 : coll. In late C. 19–20, *giddy* is often added before *goat*. See also **giddy goat.**—By 1920, both forms were S.E. —2. To lead a dissipated life, esp. sexually : low : from ca. 1885.

goat, ride the. To be initiated into a secret society, esp. the Masons : low coll. : from ca. 1870. Ex the superstition that a goat, for candidates to ride, is kept by every Masonic lodge.

goat-house. A brothel : C. 19 coll. Ex *goat*, a lascivious man.

Goat Major, the. ' The lance-corporal who has charge of the Regimental Goat ' (Frank Richards) : Royal Welch Fusiliers' : C. 20.

goat-milker. A harlot : from ca. 1820. Cf. *goat-house*, brothel.—2. The female pudend ; low : from ca. 1840.

goatee. ' A tufted beard on the point of a shaven chin ' : from ca. 1855 : in C. 19, coll. ; in C. 20, S.E. Ex the tuft on a he-goat's chin.

goats and monkeys (at), look. To gaze lecherously (at) : coll. : 1749, Cleland ; † by 1890 at the latest.

goat's gig(g) or jig. Gen. or specific copulation : mid-C. 18–early 19 : low coll. Grose, 1st ed., ' making the beast with two backs '.

goat's wool. Something non-existent : proverbial coll. : late C. 16–20 : ob. Ex L. *lana caprina* (O.E.D.).

gob. A slimy lump or clot, esp. of spittle : mid-C. 16–20 ; S.E. till ca. 1830, then dial. and low coll. —2. The mouth : s. when not, as in the North, dial.: mid-C. 16–20. Cf. *gab*, n.—3. A portion : London schoolboys' (— 1887). Baumann. Also gen. s. (— 1859) : H., 1st ed.

gob, v. To swallow in large mouthfuls ; gulp : low : C. 18–20. Abbr. *gobble*.—2. To spit, esp. copiously : C. 19–20 low coll.

gob, have the gift of the. To be wide-mouthed : late C. 17–18.—2. To speak fluently, sing well : late C. 17–early 19. Cf. *gab, gift of the*, q.v.

gob-box. The mouth : low : ca. 1770–1910. Scott, in *Lammermoor*, ' Your characters . . . made too much use of the gob-box ; they *patter* too much.' An elaboration of *gob*, n., 2.

gob-full of claret. A bleeding at the mouth : boxing : ca. 1820–90. Bee.

***gob-stick.** A silver table-spoon : c. (— 1789) : † except in dial. Parker.—2. A wooden spoon : nautical : mid-C. 19–20. Bowen.

***gob-string.** A bridle : mid-C. 18–mid-19 : either c. or low. Grose, 1st ed. Cf. *gab-string*.

[**gobbet**, whether n. or v., is not, despite F. & H., unconventional.]

gobbie. See gobby.

gobble. A quick straight put at or into the hole : golf coll. (— 1878). O.E.D.—2. Mouth, esp. in *shut up your gobble !*, be quiet ! : low (— 1887). Baumann. Cf. *gobbler*, 3.—3. A C. 19 schoolboys' variant of *gobbler*, 2. E.D.D.

gobble-gut. A glutton : from ca. 1630 : S.E. until ca. 1790, then low coll.

gobble-prick. ' A rampant, lustful woman ', Grose, 1st ed. : low coll. : mid-C. 18–19.

gobble up. To seize ; appropriate ; use rapidly : coll. : ex U.S. (1861), where earlier *gobble* ; anglicised ca. 1890.

***gobbler.** In mid-C. 16–early 17 c., a duck. Harman.—2. A turkey cock : from ca. 1720 ; orig. low coll., but now S.E.—3. The mouth : low coll. : C. 19–20 ; ob.—4. A greedy eater : from ca. 1740 : S.E. in Johnson's day : but since ca. 1850, coll.

gobbling. Gorging : from ca. 1630 : S.E. until ca. 1840, then coll. Thackeray, in *Vanity Fair*, ' The delightful exercise of gobbling '.

gobby, or gobbie. A coastguardsman : nautical : from late 1880's ; ob. Ex *gob*, n., 1 ; see gobby loo. O.E.D. (Sup.) ; Bowen.—2. A quarter-deck man : naval : ca. 1830–90. Bowen, who adds : ' In the American [navy], any bluejacket '.

gobby fleet. Coastguard and post-guard ships : nautical : from ca. 1890 ; ob. Bowen.

gobby loo, according to Bowen, is the orig. form of *gobby*, 1.

goblin. A sovereign : low : from ca. 1880. Henley in Villon's *Straight Tip*, ' Your merry goblins soon stravag : | Boose and the blowens cop the lot.' Suggested by *sovrin*, the low coll. pronunciation of *sovereign*, as the fuller *Jimmy o' Goblin* (or *g*.) shows.

god. ' Often oddly disguised in oaths, e.g. *swop me bob*, for *so help me God !*,' W. As an oath, it occurs in many forms, but these are hardly eligible here.—2. A block pattern : tailors' : from ca. 1870 : s. > j.—3. A boy in the sixth form : Eton (— 1881) : ob. Pascoe's *Life in our Public Schools*.

God-amighty. The coll. and dial. form of *God-almighty*, lit. and fig. : C. 17–20.

God-awful. A stressing of *awful* in its coll. sense : (low) coll. : C. 20. Cf. *God's own*, q.v.

God bless you ! A c.p. addressed to one who sneezes : C. 18–20. Cf. the C. 18, proverbial ' He's a friend at a sneeze ; the most you can get out of him is a *God bless you*,' ' Proverbs ' Fuller, 1732.

God bless the Duke of Argyle ! A Scottish c.p. addressed to a person shrugging his shoulders, the insinuation being—lice. C. 19–20 ; ob. H., 3rd ed. Ex certain posts erected in Glasgow by his grace : thus common (Southern) report !

God-botherer. A parson : Royal Air Force's : from ca. 1920. Cf. *God-pesterer*, q.v.

God-forbid. (Gen. pl.) A child : rhyming s. on *kid* : late C. 19–20. Ware.

God have mercy (or, more gen., **Godamercy**), **horse !** ' An almost meaningless proverbial exclamation' that is also a coll. c.p. : coll. : ca. 1530–1730. Heywood's *Proverbs* ; 1611, in Tarlton's *Jests*, ' a by word thorow London.' (Apperson.)

God knows : I don't. An emphatic reply : coll. : C. 19–20. The C. 16–18 form is *God himself tell you, I cannot* : Florio, 1598. Cf. *Bramah knows !*

God knows—and He won't split. A C. 20 variant of the preceding.

God-mamma. Godmother : coll. verging on S.E. : 1828, Miss Mitford. O.E.D.

***God-man.** A clergyman : c. : from ca. 1920. Edgar Wallace, *Room 13*.

God pays ! A c.p. of soldiers and sailors, who assumed a right to public charity : C. 17–18. The C. 19–20 form is, *If I don't pay you, God Almighty will.* Ben Jonson, in *Epigrams*, ' To every cause he meets, this voice he brays, | His only answer is to all, God pays.'

God permit. A stage coach : late C. 18–early 19. Grose, 1st ed. Stage coaches were advertised to start ' If God permit ' or ' Deo volente '.

God-pesterer. A bishop : Royal Air Force's : from ca. 1920. Cf. *God-botherer*, q.v.

God-rest-ye. A frock coat : Glasgow (— 1934). Ex the exclamation.

God save. (Pl. **God saves.**) The national anthem : from ca. 1910. Cf. *the godders and langers* immortalised by ' Q ' (see *Slang*, p. 208).

Godamercy, horse ! See **God have mercy, horse.**

Godamercy me ! God have mercy on me ! : low (— 1887). Baumann.

Godblimey. See **gorblimey**, the much more gen. pronunciation.

goddess. A young woman : coll. of Englishmen in Malay : mid-C. 18–early 19. Ex Malay *gadis*, a virgin, by the process of Hobson-Jobson. Yule & Burnell.—2. The female ' galleryite ': see **gods.** Coll. : 1812 : very rare after 1890.

goddess Diana. A sixpence : rhyming s. on ' tanner ' : ca. 1855–1900. (Less gen. than *lord of the manor*.) H., 1st ed. ; *The Press*, Nov. 12, 1864.

godfather ; in C. 17, occ. **godfather-in-law.** A juryman : late C. 16–early 19 : coll. Shakespeare ; Jonson, ' I will leave you to your god-fathers in law ' ; Grose.—2. He who pays the bill or who guarantees the rest of the company ; esp. in ' Will you stand godfather ? and we will take care of the brat,' i.e. repay you at some other time : late C. 18–19 c.p. Grose, 2nd ed.

godfer. A troublesome child : lower classes' (— 1909) ; very ob. Ware. (*God-forsaken*.)

Godfrey. See **guess and by God, by.**

godhelpus. See **gordelpus.** Occ. **godhelpme** (Manchon).—2. **Godmanchester black pigs.** See **Huntingdon sturgeon.**

godown. A warehouse ; a store-room : Anglo-Chinese and Indian ex Malay *gadong* : from ca. 1550. Coll. >, in C. 19, S.E.—though there's not the slightest need of the word.

godpapa. Godfather : a childish or familiar coll. : from ca. 1825.

gods. In such oaths as *Gods me*, a corruption of *God save*.—2. Those occupying the gallery at a theatre : from ca. 1750 : s. that, ca. 1840, > coll. and is, in C. 20, considered as virtually S.E. Occ.

but not since ca. 1850, in the singular. *The Globe*, April 7, 1890, ' The gods, or a portion of them, hooted and hissed while the National Anthem was being performed.' F. & H.: ' Said to have been first used by Garrick because they were seated on high, and close to the sky-painted ceiling '. Cf. Fr. *poulailler* and *paradis*.—3. Among printers, the quadrats employed in ' jeffing ', q.v.: from ca. 1860. H., 2nd ed. Perhaps rhyming on abbr. *quads*.

God's (god's) occurs in numerous oaths : which do not concern us here. Cf. *gods*, 1.

gods, sight for the. A cause of wonderment ; coll. only when ironic : from ca. 1890. Hume Nisbet. Cf. the literary *enough to make the gods weep*.

God's mercy. Ham (or bacon) and eggs : country inns ' : ca. 1800–80. (Cf. *three-sixty-five*, q.v.) Ex a pious expression of thanks.

God's own. A great . . . ; esp. *God's own fuss*, a ' terrible ' fuss : expletive coll. (— 1923). Man-chon. Cf. :

God's quantity, any. Abundance : expletive coll. (— 1923). Ibid. Cf. preceding and *God-awful*, q.v.

Godspeed, in the. In the nick of time : coll. : ca. 1660–1820. L'Estrange. (O.E.D.)

goer. (Orig. of a horse.) An adept or expert ; one well grounded in a subject. Gen. with an adj., e.g. *a fast* (or *a hell of a*) *goer*. Coll. : from ca. 1850. G. A. Lawrence in *Guy Livingstone*. When applied to other than persons, it is S.E.

goes for my money, he. He's the man for me : coll. : ca. 1540–1660. Latimer, R. Harvey. (O.E.D.) Cf. *he's the man for my money*, which, however, can be varied according to persons and even animals or things—and is S.E.

goey. Lively ; progressive : 1907, P. G. Wode-house, *Not George Washington*. Ex *go*, n., 8.

goff. A Scottish variant of *golf* : in C. 20 jocular use, n. and v., it is coll.

goffer. (Gen. pl.) A mineral water : nautical, esp. naval : C. 20. Bowen. Because they are ' frills '.—2. Hence, ' a man selling mineral water or lemonade on board ship ' : naval : from ca. 1910. F. & Gibbons.

goffer, v. To ' bonnet ' a man : low London : from ca. 1890 ; ob. E.D.D.

goffer !, I'll draw you off a. A naval c.p. chal-lenge to an angry man : from ca. 1912. F. & Gib-bons. Ex *goffer*, n., 1.

gog. In oaths, a corrupt form of *God* : mostly C. 16–early 17 : coll.

gog, v. Gen. as vbl.n., *gogging*, ' the old sea punishment of scraping a man's tongue with hoop-iron for profanity ' (Bowen) : nautical : C. 19. Either ex or cognate with Lancashire *gog*, a gag for the mouth.

goggle, v. To stare ; roll the eyes : mid-C. 16–20 : S.E. till late C. 18, then somewhat coll. : in C. 20, rare except in dial. or in facetious coll.

goggler. A goggle-eyed person : coll. : from ca. 1800 ; ob.—2. An eye : from ca. 1820 : low. Ob.

goggles. A goggle-eyed person : coll. : >, by 1830, S.E. : C. 17–19. Beaumont & Fletcher, ' Do you stare, goggles ? '—2. The eyes, esp. if rolling or of a constrained stare : coll. : from ca. 1710. Byrom. Abbr. *goggle-eyes*.—3. Spectacles, esp. with round glasses : C. 18–20 : coll.—4. Hence, a nickname for anyone wearing glasses, esp. if they are large : C. 20.—5. The glasses protecting one from lachrymatory gas : military coll.: 1916. B. & P.

[**gogmagog**, like *God's penny*, is, despite F. & H., ineligible.]

gohanna. See goanna.

going. The condition of the ground for traffic, walking, hunting, etc. : orig. U.S. (1859) ; angli-cised ca. 1870 : coll. till ca. 1895, then S.E. *The Daily Telegraph*, Nov. 23, 1883, ' Going . . . wonderfully clean for the time of year '.—2. See a-going.

going (h)ome. A-dying : proletarian (— 1909) ; slightly ob. Ware.

going to buy anything ? An ' evasive request for a drink ' : urban : 1896 ; ob. Ware.

going to Calabar. A-dying : naval (— 1909) ; ob. Ware. Calabar is ' a white man's grave '.

going to keep a pianner-shop. Prosperous ; smartly dressed : Cockneys' (— 1909) ; ob. Ware.

going to see a dawg. I.e. a harlot or a kept woman : sporting : late C. 19–20. Ware. Cf. :

going to see a man. Going to get a drink : 1885, *The Referee*, Sept. 6. (Ware.)

going's quantity, (go) while the. The English ver-sion of the U.S. (*beat it*) *while the beating's good* and the Scots *go while the play is good* : coll. : in Eng-land from ca. 1912 ; slightly earlier in Australia. Lyell.

goings-on. Behaviour or proceedings, with a pejorative implication and gen. with a pejorative adj. : from ca. 1770 : coll. until C. 20, then un-dignified S.E. Douglas Jerrold, ' Pretty place it must be where they don't admit women. Nice goings-on, I daresay, Mr. Caudle.'

gol-mol. (A) noise or commotion : Anglo-Indian (— 1864). H., 3rd ed.

gold-backed one or **un.** A louse : mid-C. 19–20 ; ob. : low coll. H., 5th ed. Cf. *grey-backed*.

***gold braid.** (Collective n.) The principal warders : prisoners' c. : from ca. 1920. George Ingram, *Stir*, 1933.

gold brick. A fraud, a swindle ; a sham ; an app. chance of making a lot of money : U.S. (ca. 1888), partly anglicised by Wodehouse in 1915 ; James Spenser, *Limey Breaks In*, 1934. Ex the U.S. *gold-brick swindle*, a particular form of fraud. O.E.D. (Sup.).

gold-digger. A female attaching herself to a man for (her) self and pelf : U.S. (ca. 1925) ; anglicised by 1930. Ex the lit. S.E. sense.—2. Also *gold-digging*, the corresponding (not too) abstract n.

gold-drop. A gold coin : late C. 18–19. Mary Robinson, in *Walsingham*. (O.E.D.)

***gold-dropper.** A sharper that works the con-fidence trick by dropping money : see **fawney rig.** Ca. 1680–1830 : c. B.E., Dyche, Grose (1st ed.).

gold-dust. Tobacco, when supplies are short : nautical : late C. 19–20. Bowen.

gold-end man. A buyer of old gold and silver ; an itinerant jeweller : C. 17 coll. Jonson. ? a variation on *goldsmith's apprentice*.

gold-finder. An emptier of privies : coll. : C. 17–early 19. Cotgrave ; B.E. Cf. the C. 19 Warwick-shire *gold-digger*.—2. A thief ; a ' gold-dropper ', q.v. ; early C. 19.

gold hatband. An undergraduate aristocrat : university : ca. 1620–1780. Earle's *Microcosmog-raphy*. Superseded by *tuft*, q.v. ; see also **hat**, 1.

gold-mine. A profitable investment : from ca. 1850 : coll. till ca. 1885, then S.E. *The Saturday Review*, April 28, 1883, ' A gold mine to the . . . bookmakers '.

gold-washer. A 'sweater' of gold : C. 16 low or low coll.

*golden cream. Rum : c. (— 1889) ; ob. Clarkson & Richardson, *The Police*.

golden grease. A fee ; a bribe : coll. : late C. 18–19. Cf. *palm oil*.

*goldfinch. A rich man : C. 17–early 19 c. Dekker, B.E. Ex the colour of gold.—2. A guinea : C. 17–early 19 ; a sovereign : ca. 1820–1910. Both are either low or c. Same semantics. Cf. *canary*, 4, and *yellow boy*.

goldfinch's nest. The female pudend : low (— 1827) ; ob.

goldfish. A chorister that opens her mouth but does not sing : theatrical (— 1935).

goldsmith's window. A rich working that shows gold freely : from ca. 1890 : Australian coll. >, by 1920, S.E.

goldy- or goldie-locks ; goldilocks. A flaxen-haired girl or woman : mid-C. 16–20 : orig. S.E. ; in late C. 19–20, archaic except when coll. and applied to a child, often as a pet name.—2. **Goldy.** Oliver Goldsmith.

Goles !, by. A variant of *by golly !* : 1734, Fielding ; in C. 19, lower classes' ; in late C. 19–20, mostly dial. E.D.D.

Golgotha. ' Part of the Theatre at Oxford where the heads of houses sit ', Grose, 1st ed. : Amherst, 1726.—2. The Dons' gallery at St. Mary's, Cambridge : from ca. 1800. *Gradus ad Cantabrigiam*, 1803. Both † by 1890. The pun is on *head* (skull and important person) and *Golgotha*, ' the Place of Skulls ' (see New Testament).—3. Whence, a hat (— 1860) ; † by 1910. H., 2nd ed. All three senses are university s.

Goliah. Goliath : a C. 19–20 sol.

Goliath. ' A man of mark among the Philistines ' : literary : ca. 1880–1910.

goll. The hand : in late C. 16–early 19 coll., verging on S.E. ; in late C. 18–19 mainly dial. Dryden, ' Mighty golls, rough-grained, and red with starching '. Origin obscure.

gollop. To gulp ; swallow noisily and greedily : (low) coll. : C. 19–20. Ex *gulp*.

gollore. See galore.

gollumpus. A large, clumsy, loutish fellow : late C. 18–mid-19 coll. Grose, 1st ed. Prob. an arbitrary formation on *lump* (cf. modern *you great lump, you !*).

gollup. A variant of **gollop.** Egan's Grose.

golly. A tall person : schoolboys', not very gen. : C. 20. Prob. ex *Goliath*.

golly ! Abbr. *by golly*, an orig. Negroes' euphemistic corruption (1743) of *God* : anglicised in mid C. 19. Cf. *by goles !*

golopshus, goloptious. See galoptious. The best form is *goluptious*, for the term is a ' facetious perversion . . . of *voluptuous* ; cf. rustic *boldacious*,' W., *delicious* being the ' suggester '. The S.O.D. records it at 1856.

golore. See galore.

goloshes. India-rubber over-shoes : a coll. spelling of *galoshes* : late C. 18–20. *Galoshes* itself—witness Grose, 3rd ed.—had a coll. air at first. Ex Fr. *galoche* ; Grose's derivation ex *Goliah's shoes* is one of his portly jests.

'gom. A man : c. : C. 17. Beaumont & Fletcher.—2. The G.O.M. (Gladstone) : political : 1883–ca. 90. Ware.

gom ! Damn it : low : C. 19–20 ; ob. Baumann *God* corrupted.

gombeen-man. A usurer ; an extortionate middleman : Anglo-Irish : ca. 1862–1900 as coll., then ' Standard '. Ex Irish *gaimbin* = Medieval L. *cambium*. (W.'s *umpteen*, q.v., suggested by this word ?)

gomer. A large pewter dish. ? ex the † S.E. sense, a Hebrew measure.—2. Whence, a new hat. Both, Winchester College s. of ca. 1850–1915.

gommed ! Damned ! : low : C. 19–20. Baumann. Cf. *gormed, be*.

gommy. A dandy : C. 19. Ex Fr. *gommeux*.—2. A fool : coll. : ca. 1870–1910.—3. ' One who calls Mr. Gladstone a G.O.M., and thinks he has made a good joke ', *The Weekly Dispatch*, March 11, 1883 : † by 1900.

Gomorrah to you ! Good morning to you ! : a low c.p. of ca. 1900–14. Ware. Punning *good morrow* and (*to-)morrow*.

gomus. A fool : Anglo-Irish : ca. 1830–1920. Cf. Yorkshire *gomo* and the gen. dial. *gaum*.

gone, ruined, undone, is, despite F. & H., ineligible.—2. Went : sol. : C. 19–20.

gone coon. See coon, gone.

gone dis. Mentally deficient ; crazy, crazed : military : 1915. F. & Gibbons. Ex the signallers' *gone dis*, (of wires) having had a breakdown (*disconnected*) : 1914.

gone goose. A person left in the lurch, ship abandoned : nautical (— 1867). Smyth.

gone on. Infatuated with : low coll. : from ca. 1885. Baumann, 1887 ; *Illustrated Bits*, March 29, 1890, ' He must have been terribly gone on this woman.' S.E. has the absolute phrase *far gone*.

gone over a goodish piece of grass. (Of meat, esp. mutton) tough : lower classes' (— 1909) ; ob. Ware.

gone phut. See phut.

gone through the sieve. Bankrupt : commercial (— 1909) ; ob. Ware.

gone to Rome. (Of bells) become silent : Roman Catholic : from the 1880's. Ware.

gone to the pack. A New Zealand coll. variant (C. 20) of *gone to the dogs*.

gone up, one's number has. (He) has been killed : military : 1915. Ex turf j. (Manchon.)

gone west. Dead. See go west.

goner. One who is undone, ruined, or dead ; that which is (almost or quite) finished, extinguished, or destroyed : orig. (1847), U.S. ; anglicised ca. 1880. Nat Gould, 1891, ' Make a noise, or follow me, and you're a goner.'

goney. See gawney.

gong. A medal ; loosely, a decoration : Regular Army : late C. 19–20. F. & Gibbons. Ex Anglo-Indian *gong*, a ' metal disc, not musical, used in India for striking the hour ' (Yule & Burnell).—2. A bell : busmen's : from ca. 1925. *The Daily Herald*, Aug. 5, 1936.

[**gong** or **gong-house,** a privy (the former in Chaucer's *Parson's Tale*), and *gong-farmer* or *man* (the former in *Florio*, 1598), are, despite F. & H., all ineligible. All were † by 1800.]

gongster. A man on police speed-limit motor-patrol : motorists' : from April, 1935. On *gangster* and ex the warning *gong*.

goniv. An illicit diamond-buyer : South African diamond fields' : from ca. 1890 ; ob. Pettmann Also *gonoph* and therefore a variant of *gonnof*.—2. Whence (via Hebrew *genavah*, a theft, a thing stolen) *goniva(h)*, ' a diamond known to have been stolen or come by illicitly ', Pettman : South African c. : 1887, Matthews, *Incwadi Yami*.

gonna. (E.g., I'm) going to (do something): dial. and, esp. in U.S., low coll.: C. 19–20.

*gon(n)of, gonoph, gonov, gnof(f). (See also **gun.**) A thief; esp. a skilful pickpocket: c. from ca. 1835. Ex Hebrew *gannabh* via Jewish Dutch *gannef* (W.). Brandon, Mayhew, Dickens, Hindley, Clarkson and Richardson ('gunneffs or gonophs'). Cf. the C. 14–20 *gnof*, a bumpkin, a simpleton, as in Chaucer: this, however, is a different word.

*gon(n)of, etc., v. To steal; cheat; wheedle: c.: from ca. 1850; ob. Whence *gonophing*, etc., vbl.n.: Dickens in *The Detective Police*, reprinted 1857.

gonnows. God knows: sol.: C. 19–20. Ware.

goo. The mouth: low (— 1923) or perhaps orig. c. Manchon. I.e. *gob* perverted.—2. See **goo-wallahs.**

goo-goo eyes. Loving glances: Australian mostly: from ca. 1905. Neil Munro, 1906; C. J. Dennis. Prob. first in the baby-talk of lovers. Hence, occ., *goo-goo*, such a glance. (O.E.D. Sup.)

goo-wallahs, the. A sanitary squad: military: C. 20. F. & Gibbons. Ex low *goo*, an excremental 'button' (prob. abbr. *gooseberry*, with reference to sphericity), + *wallah*, q.v.

gooby. A simpleton, a dolt: from ca. 1890: coll. (1892, *Ally Sloper*, March 19). Prob. a corruption ex dial. *goff* or *goof*: cf. *goof*, *goofy*, and *goop*, *goopy*.

*good. Easily robbed (e.g. *upon the crack* or the *star*): c. of ca. 1810–1910. Vaux.—2. Solvent; esp. *good for*, able to pay: coll.: from ca. 1890. Ex the (— 1860) S.E. sense, 'safe to live or last so long, well able to accomplish so much', O.E.D. But Vaux, 1812, says that 'A man who declares himself *good for* any favour or thing, means, that he has sufficient influence, or possesses the certain means to obtain it,'—which puts back the S.E. sense some fifty years and perhaps indicates that this S.E. sense was orig. s. or coll.—3. The omission of *good* before *afternoon, day, morning*, etc., in greetings is a mostly Colonial coll. of late C. 19–20.

good, adv., when modifying a v. and = well: in C. 19–20, low coll.; earlier, S.E.

good ! Good night !: printers': from ca. 1870.

good !, be. A parting c.p. exhortatory to good behaviour: coll.: C. 20. (O.E.D. Sup.)

good, be any or **some** or, gen., **no.** To be to some extent useful; wholly useless: coll.: from ca. 1870.—2. When predicative with gerund following, coll. from ca. 1840. J. H. Newman, 1842, 'There is no good telling you all this,' O.E.D.—3. In *what good is it ?, are they ?*, etc., it is coll. from ca. 1865, Dasent using it in 1868. (O.E.D.)—4. (Of persons) *be no good*, to be worthless: coll.: from early 1890's (O.E.D.)

good, feel. To be jolly or 'in form': ex U.S. (1854: Thornton); anglicised ca. 1895: coll.

good, for. Completely; permanently: coll.: from ca. 1880. Abbr. *for good and all*.

good (or **good to me**), **it looks.** It looks very promising (to me): coll., orig. (ca. 1910) U.S., anglicised ca. 1918. O.E.D. (Sup.).

good a maid as her mother, a (occ. **as**). A C. 17 c.p. applied to a devirginated spinster. Howell's *Proverbs*, 1659.

good and all, for. Entirely; permanently; finally: from ca. 1515. In C. 16–early 19, S.E.; then coll. Horman in his *Vulgaria*, 1519; Wycherley, in *The Gentleman Dancing Master*, 'If

I went, I would go for good and all'; Dickens. See Apperson.

good as a play, gen. preceded by **as.** Very entertaining: proverbial coll.: from ca. 1630. Taylor the Water Poet; Arthur Machen, 1922.

good as . . ., as. It is extremely difficult to determine the status of the (*as*) *good as . . .* comparative phrases, many of which are either proverbs or proverbial sayings. G. L. Apperson lists the following: *as good as a Christmas play* (late C. 19–20 Cornwall)—*a play* (C. 17–20)—*ever drew sword* (late C. 16–17)—*ever flew in the air* (C. 17)—*ever struck* (C. 17)—*ever the ground went upon* with such variants as *ever stepped* (late C. 16–20)—*ever twanged* (mid-C. 16–17)—*ever water wet* (C .17–18)—*ever went endways* (C. 17 ?–18),—*George of Green* (C. 17–18)—*gold* (mid-C. 19–20)—*good for nothing* (C. 17)—*goose skins that never man had enough of* (Cheshire: C. 17–20),—*one shall see in* or *upon a summer's day* (late C. 16–19).—2. But Vaux's *good as bread* and *good as cheese* = thoroughly competent or able (in some specific relation): low: ca. 1810–50. Influenced by *the cheese*, q.v.

good as ever pissed. Extremely good: low coll.: from ca. 1710; ob. D'Urfey. Cf. the C. 17–18 proverbial saying, *good as ever went endways*.

good as ever twanged (often preceded by **as**). Of women only: very good: coll.: ca. 1570–1700. (Apperson.) Lit., as good as ever responded to a man's sexual aggress.

good as gold. Very good: coll.: 1843, Dickens. Gen. applied to children.

good as good(, as). Extremely good: coll.: from ca. 1880. Gen. applied to children: cf. (*as*) *good as gold*, q.v. Cf. Romance-languages emphasis by repetition of adjj. and advv.

good as they make 'em(, as). The best obtainable (things only): coll.: from ca. 1870.

good at it or **at the game.** An adept between the sheets: amatory coll.: C. 19–20.

good blood and so does black pudding, you come of. A proverbial c.p. reply to one boasting of good birth: C. 19.

good books ; bad books : be in one's. See **books.**

good boy. An occ. C. 19 variant of *good fellow*, q.v.

good bye-ee ! A c.p. form, ca. 1915–20, of *good-bye !* Collinson.

good cess ! Good luck ! Anglo-Irish (— 1845). F. & H.: 'Probably an abbreviation of "success "': but see **cess, bad,** its opposite.

good chap. A late C. 19–20 coll. variant of *good fellow*, q.v.

good enough, not. (Very) bad; esp., decidedly unfair: coll.: from ca. 1890.

good fellow, goodfellow. A roisterer, a boon companion: C. 16–20: S.E. until ca. 1660, then coll. Cf. Grose, 1st ed., '*Good Man*, a word of various imports, according to the place where it is spoken; in the city it means a rich man; at Hockley in the Hole, or St. Giles's, an expert boxer; at a bagnio in Covent Garden, a vigorous fornicator; at an alehouse or tavern, one who loves his pot or bottle; and sometimes, tho' but rarely, a virtuous man.'—2. In C. 17 c., a thief. Middleton in his most famous comedy.

good-for, n. An I O U: South African coll.: 1879. Rider Haggard in *Cetywayo*, 1882. (O.E.D.) —2. A Transvaal Government promissory note: ca. 1880–1900: South African coll. Pettman.

good for him (or **you**) ! Excellent work ! Splendid news ! Coll.: from ca. 1910.

good form. See **form.**

Good Friday. Alfred Bunn (d. 1860), theatrical manager. Dawson. Also *Poet Bunn*, for he was a versifier—of sorts.

good girl or **good one.** A harlot; a wanton wench : coll. : the former, C. 18–20, ob. ; the latter, C. 17–18. Cf. *good at it*, q.v.

good goods. Something worth having ; a success : sporting (— 1874) : ob. *The Sporting Times*, July 17, 1886, ' He was . . . rather good goods at a Sunday-school treat.' The superlative is *best goods* (— 1874). H., 5th ed.

good hunting ! Good luck ! : coll. : **from ca.** 1895. Orig. among sportsmen.

good in parts(, like the curate's egg). Now a potential proverbial saying, recently a ' battered ornament ' (H. W. Fowler), it was in the first decade of the century a cultured coll. Ex an illustrated joke in *Punch*. (Collinson.)

good ink(, that's). (That is) good, agreeable, pleasant : New Zealanders' : from ca. 1910. Cf. *good pup*.

good line. A smart or unusual remark : theatrical : from ca. 1920. (A. P. Herbert, *Holy Deadlock*, 1934.)

good look round for you won't see anything but the ceiling for a day or two !, have a. A military c.p. of 1915–18 ; applied to the ardour of soldiers-on-leave towards their wives. Cf. *feet uppermost*.

good looker. A pretty girl (woman) or handsome fellow : coll., orig. (ca. 1890) U.S., anglicised ca. 1920. O.E.D. Sup.) Also with hyphen.

good man, goodman. See Grose's definition at *good fellow*, above.—2. Gen. as one word :—A gaoler : C. 18–early 19 : low or coll.—3. The devil, always with *the* : C. 18–20 coll. ; ob. Cf. *the old gentleman*.—4. (Cf. sense 1.) *good man turd*. A contemptible fellow : C. 16–17 low coll. Florio.

good mark. See ' **mark, bad or good** '.

good morning ! have you used Pear's soap ? A c.p. of the 1920's. Collinson. Ex the famous old soap-firm's advertisement. Cf. *since when* . . .

good night, McGuinness ! ; good night, nurse ! C.pp. expressive of finality : resp. New Zealand, from ca. 1910 ; and gen., from 1914. Both are ob.

good night ! A c.p. retort expressive of incredulity, comical despair, delight : from ca. 1860 ; ob. In G.W., often *good night, nurse !* Cf. *carry me out, let me die, that's torn it*. An extremely suggestive adumbration occurs in Gabriel Harvey's *Four Letters*, 1592 (Bodley Head Quartos ed., p. 81) : ' Every pert, and crancke wit, in one odd veine, or other, [is] the onely man of the University, of the Citty, of the Realme, for a flourish or two : who but he, in the flush of his overweening conceit ? give him his peremptory white rod in his hand, and God-night all distinction of persons, and all difference of estates.'

good oil. Rare for *dinkum oil*, q.v.

good old . . . A (— 1891) familiar, i.e. coll., term of reference or address, gen. affectionate, occ. derisive. Albert Chevalier in *The Little Nipper*, 1892.

good one. See **good un.**

good people, the. Fairies : Anglo-Irish coll. >, ca. 1880, S.E. : from ca. 1800 ; ob. Scott ; C. Griffin ; R. L. Stevenson. Orig. and mainly euphemistic : cf. *Eumenides*: see *Words !* at ' Euphemism '. In C. 16–17 Scottish, *the good neighbours.*

good pup. Anything good, e.g. a successful sale, a good bargain, a comfortable dug-out : New Zealanders' : C. 20. Prob. at first a farmer's c.p. of commendation.

good sort, occ. g. old s. A generous, a sympathetic, or a readily helpful person : coll. (—1892) ; orig. only of men. Hume Nisbet, ' He seems a good sort.'

good strange ! A mild coll. oath : late C. 17–18. Perhaps *God's strings* (Ware).

good thing. As a *bon mot*, as something worth having, and as a successful speculation, it is hardly eligible, but as a presumed certainty it is racing s. (— 1884), whence, in C. 20, a gen. coll. applied to a business, an investment, etc.

good time. A carouse ; amusement and entertainment ; a sexually enjoyable occasion. Gen as *have a good time*. In C. 17, S.E.,—Pepys has it ; ob. till ca. 1840, when it appeared in the U.S. ; re-anglicised ca. 1870 as a coll. ; by 1930, virtually S.E. Trollope, 1863, ' Having . . . what our American friends call a good time of it ' ; H., 5th ed.

good to me, it looks. See **good, it looks.**

good tune played on an old fiddle, there's many a. An oldish woman may make an excellent bedfellow : late C. 19–20 : a c.p. >, by 1930, virtually a proverb.

good un. A person or thing of great merit : coll. : from ca. 1830.

good un (or one) !, that's a. What a fib (occ. good story) ! Coll. : C. 19–20.

good woman. ' A non descript, represented on a famous sign in St. Giles's, in the form of a common woman, but without a head ', Grose, 1785 ; hence, ' a not uncommon public-house sign ', H., 1864': the same authority adding that *the honest lawyer*, similarly represented, is another. The phrase is relevant because it was often employed allusively. † by 1920.

good-wool(l)ed. Plucky and energetic: s. when not, as prob. orig., dial. : from ca. 1845. Halliwell. Ex sheep with a good fleece.

good work ! Well done ! : C. 20 : coll. >, by 1930, S.E.

good young man. A hypocrite : proletarian c.p. of 1881–ca. 1914. Sponsored by Arthur Roberts in a song, says Ware, who notes that its opposite is *bad young man.*

gooder ; goodest. Deliberately used, it is coll. : late C. 19–20.—2. Unintentionally : C. 18–20 sol.

goodlish. Goodish : low coll. (— 1887). Baumann. Prob. a confusion of *goodly* + *goodish.*

goodman ; goodman turd. See **good man.**

goodness in mild expletives is coll. ; mostly mid-C. 19–20.

goods, bit (occ. **piece**) **of.** A woman, gen. as viewed in the light of her sexual attractiveness or potentialities : low coll. : from ca. 1860. Cf. *bit, piece*.—2. (**piece** only.) A person : coll. : from ca. 1870.—3. (**goods**.) A goods train : railwaymen's coll. (— 1887). Baumann.

goods, the. (Precisely) what is needed, esp. if of considerable worth or high merit. Gen. in *have the goods*, to be a very able person, and *deliver the goods*, to fulfil one's promise(s) : coll. : anglicised, ca. 1908, from U.S. (1870's). ? ex the U.S. sense (1852), the thing bargained for, the prize (see Thornton).—2. **the Goods.** The Gordon Highlanders : military : G.W. (F. & Gibbons). Magnificent soldiers.

Goodwin sands, set up shop on. To be ship-wrecked : ca. 1540–1750. In C. 16–17, often *Goodwins*. (Apperson.) Cf. *Tenterden steeple*, q.v.

goody. A matron,—but used only of, or to, a social inferior or, among the lower classes, equal : mainly rural : C. 16–20 ; ob. : in C. 16–18, wholly S.E. ; in C. 19, increasingly coll. ; in C. 20, archaic except in dial. Ex *goodwife*. Cf. *aunt(ie)*, *gammer*, *mother*. See esp. Florio, Johnson, and O.E.D. Whence the occ. coll. *goodyship* = the *ladyship* of jocular usage.—2. A religious hypocrite : coll. (— 1836) ; ob.—3. Gen. in pl., sweetmeats ; buns, cakes and pastry : from ca. 1760 ; occurring as *goody-goody* in 1745 (S.O.D.) : until ca. 1850, S.E. ; then coll.

goody, adj. Officiously or hypocritically or ignorant-tiresomely pious : 1830 : coll. till C. 20, then S.E. D. W. Thompson in *Daydreams of a Schoolmaster*, 1864.

goody !, my. My goodness ! : lower classes' (esp. women's) coll. (— 1887). Baumann.

goody, talk. To talk in a weakly or sentimentally good way : from ca. 1865. Coll.

goody-goody. Occ. a n. (ca. 1872) but gen. an adj. (1871). Both coll. in sense of a weakly or sentimentally good person.—2. See **goody,** n., last sense.

goody-la ! Good ! : military : 1916 ; ob. B. & P. Ex the Chinese Labour Corps's ' pidgin '.

goodyear !, what a or **the.** A (now) meaningless expletive : ca. 1550–1720. Cf. :

goodyear(s). Syphilis : C. 17 coll. Perhaps (!) ex *gougeer* ex *gouge*, a soldier's drab. But this may be deducing too much from the imprecative uses of *goodyear*, as in *a goodyear take ye !* and as in the preceding entry, in which the word = the deuce, the devil, a sense that may be operative in *Goodyer's pig*, q.v.

Goodyer's pig, like. Explained by the occ. accompanying tag, *never well but when in*—or *he is doing—mischief* : mid-C. 17–20. Mainly Cheshire. Who was Goodyer ? Cf. :

Goodyer's pigs did, they'll come again as. Never : proverbial coll. : ca. 1670–1750. Goodyer was prob. a notable farmer ; cf. preceding entry (likewise in Apperson). But *Goodyer* may be only a per-sonification of † Scottish *goodyer*, a grandfather.

goof. A person that is silly, ' soft ', or stupid ; hence adj. *goofy* : 1923, P. G. Wodehouse (O.E.D. Sup.), but certainly in use in 1922. Ex dial. *goof*, *goff*, a fool.—2. Hence, a man ever running after women : Royal Air Force : from ca. 1925. Also as v.t., to run after (a woman).

googlie, -y. See **bosie.**

googlie (-y) merchant. A bowler of ' googlies ' : cricketers' : 1924, H. C. Maclaren. (Lewis.)

googly, adj. Sentimental : C. 20. Charles Williams, *The Greater Trumps*, 1932, ' Henry and I would lean over the side of our honeymoon liner and hear your voice coming to us over the sea in the evening, and have . . . *heimweh*, and be all googly.' Perhaps ex *goo-goo eyes*.

gook. A tramp : low : 1914, A. Neil Lyons, *Arthur's* (cited by Manchon). Ex a dial. variant of *gowk*.

goolies. Testicles : low : late C. 19–20. Prob. ex dial. *gully*, a game of marbles.

*****gooner, give** (a person) **the.** To dismiss, reject, discard : c. : from ca. 1920. James Curtis, *The Gilt Kid*, 1936. Perhaps ex *give the go-by* + *goner*.

goop ; goopy. A fool, a fatuous person ; foolish,

fatuous : from ca. 1917. (O.E.D. Sup.) **Prob. a** corruption of *goof* ; cf. *looby, loopy*.

goori. A dog : New Zealanders' : late C. 19–20. A corruption of Maori *kuri*.

goose. (As a simpleton, S.E.) A tailors' smooth-ing iron, the handle being shaped like a goose's neck : 1605, Shakespeare : in C. 17–18 coll. ; in C. 19–20, S.E. Whence the C. 17–19 proverbial saying, ' A tailor, be he ever so poor, is always sure to have a goose at his fire.'—2. Abbr. *Winchester goose*, a venereal disease ; a harlot : low coll. (— 1778) ; † by 1870.—3. (Theatrical) a hissing : 1805 (S.O.D.), but not gen. before ca. 1850 : cf. *goose, get the.*—4. Abbr. *wayz(e)goose*, q.v. : printers' : from ca. 1860.—5. A scolding or a reprimand : coll. (— 1865) ; ob. by 1910, † by 1930. Prob. ex the theatrical sense.—6. A woman ; hence, the sexual favour : low : from ca. 1870.—7. See **goose, gone ;** also **Greenwich goose** and **guinea to a goose, a.**

goose, v. To condemn by hissing : hiss : theatrical and gen. : 1853 ; in 1854, Dickens, ' He was goosed last night.' Cf. *big bird, get the.*— Hence, 2, to ruin ; spoil utterly : coll. (— 1859). Cf. *cook one's goose.*—3. To befool, make a ' goose ' of (— 1899) ; ob. by 1920, † by 1925. Barrère & Leland.—4. To possess (a woman) : low : from ca. 1875.—5. V.i., to go wenching : low : from ca. 1870.—6. V.i., gen. as vbl.n., *goosing*, ' Thames watermen afloat looking for jobs ' : nautical : late C. 19–20. Bowen.

goose, be sound on the. To hold orthodox political opinions : orig. U.S. (1857) ; anglicised ca. 1890 : ob. Milliken in his *'Arry Ballads*, 1892.

goose, find fault with a fat. To grumble without cause : late C. 17–19 : coll. B.E.

goose, get the. To be hissed : theatrical : ca. 1860–1900. See **goose,** v., 1.

goose, (go !) shoe the. A derisive or incredulous retort : late C. 16–18. B.E. Cf. the late C. 19 equivalent, *go to hell and pump thunder !*

goose, guinea to a. See **guinea to a gooseberry.**

goose, hot and heavy like a tailor's. A late C. 17–mid-18 c.p. ' applied to a Passionate Coxcomb ', B.E. See **goose,** n., 1, and cf. *goose roasted . . .*

goose, not able or **unable to say ' boh ' to a.** Very bashful or timid : coll. : late C. 16–20.

Goose, Paddy's. See **Paddy's Goose.**

goose and duck. A copulation : rhyming s., from ca. 1870, on *fuck*.

goose-cap, goosecap. A dolt ; a silly person : late C. 16–early 19 : S.E. until C. 18, then coll., then, ca. 1800, dial. G. Harvey ; B.E. ; Grose.

[**goose-flesh** (rarely **-skin**), like **goose-riding** (by F. & H. unexplained) and **goose-step**, is, despite F. & H., ineligible.]

goose for, or **that laid, the golden eggs, kill the.** The proverbial forms : C. 15–20. The coll. form is *kill the goose with the golden eggs* : C. 19–20.

goose-gob (rare) ; **goose-gog.** A gooseberry : homely coll. : mid-C. 19–20.

goose-grease. A woman's vaginal emission : low : from ca. 1875.

goose hangs high, everything is lovely and the. All goes well : coll. C. 19–20 ; ob. Ex a plucked goose hanging out of a fox's reach.

goose is in the house, the. A tense-variable ex-pression for the hissing of a play, etc. : ca. 1800–50. Cf. *goose*, n., 3, the v., 1, and *goose, get the.*

goose-month. The period of a woman's confine-ment : coll. : late C. 18–mid-19. Ex *gander-month*, q.v.

goose-persuader. A tailor : C. 19–20 ; **ob.** Ex *goose*, n., 1.

goose roasted, a tailor's. ' A Red-hot smoothing Iron, to Close the Seams ', B.E. : late C. 17–18. See **goose**, n., 1.

goose-shearer. A beggar : C. 19–20 coll. : **ob.** Lit., cheater of fools.

goose-turd green. A light-yellow green : coll. : C. 17–18. Cotgrave.

goose without gravy. A severe blow that does not draw blood : nautical : ca. 1850–1914. Cf. *gooser*.

gooseberries. The human testicles : low : from ca. 1850 ; **ob.**

gooseberry. A fool : coll. (**ob.**) : ca. 1820–95. Ex *gooseberry fool*.—2. Hence (**?**), chaperon, or a save-appearances third person : 1837 (S.O.D.) : dial. until ca. 1860, then coll.—3. A (too) marvellous tale : journalistic s. (– 1870) >, ca. 1880, gen. coll. ; **ob.** by 1900, † by 1920. Occ. *giant* or *gigantic gooseberry*. See also **gooseberry season.**—4. See **gooseberry, play old ;** and for *old gooseberry*, see **gooseberry, like old,** and, more fully, **old gooseberry** itself.—5. A wire-entanglement device for blocking gaps ; an unused reel of barbed wire : military coll. : 1915 ; slightly **ob.** F. & Gibbons, ' From their prickly resemblance to the fruit.'

gooseberry, do or **play.** To act as propriety-third or chaperon : the former, 1877, in Hawley Smart's *Play or Pay*, and † by 1900 ; the latter, ca. 1837, and e.g. in G. R. Sims, 1880, and slightly ob. App. Devonshire dial. until ca. 1860. Cf. *gooseberry*, 2.

gooseberry, play old. (V.t. with *with*.) To play the deuce : coll. (– 1791) ; **ob.** Grose, 3rd ed. The v.t. form (with variant *play up*) also = to silence, or defeat, summarily : quell promptly : coll. : ca. 1810–80. Cf. preceding entry, q.v.—2. See **gooseberry, do.**

gooseberry, like old. Like the devil : coll. (– 1865). Ex next entry, *old gooseberry* being an † term for the devil. See ' The Devil and his Nicknames ' in *Words !*

gooseberry pudden (or **-in'**). Wife : rhyming s. on *old woman* : C. 20. J. Phillips's Dict., 1931.

gooseberry-eyed. Having ' dull grey eyes, like boiled gooseberries ', Grose, 3rd ed. : coll. : ca. 1789–1880.

gooseberry-grinder, gen. preceded by **Bogey the.** The behind : late C. 18–mid-19 low. Esp. in *ask Bogey the g.-g.* (Grose, 1st ed.) : see **ask** and **bogey.**

*gooseberry lay. The stealing of linen hanging on the line : C. 19 c. **?** from the notion, ' as easy as picking gooseberries '.

gooseberry-picker. A ' ghost ', q.v. : from ca. 1885 ; **ob.** by 1910, † by 1920.—2. A chaperon : ca. 1870–1900. H., 5th ed. ; *The Cornhill Magazine*, Dec., 1884. Ex children accompanying young people on gooseberry-picking parties.

gooseberry-pudden (rarely **-pudding**). A woman : low rhyming s. (– 1857) ; **ob.** ' Ducange Anglicus.'—2. Hence, a wife : **an** ' old woman ', q.v. : low : from ca. 1860.

gooseberry season. The silly season : journalists' : ca. 1870–1900. Occ. (see *The Illustrated London News*, July 18, 1885), *giant gooseberry season*, or *big g. s.* Cf. *gooseberry*, 3.

gooseberry wig. ' A large frizzled wig ', Grose, 3rd ed. : coll. : ca. 1788–1850. Perhaps, as Grose suggests, **ex a** vague resemblance to a gooseberry bush.

goosegog. See **goosgog.**

gooser. A knock-out blow ; **a** decisive coup : coll. : from ca. 1850 ; **ob.** **?** ex *cook one's goose* via *to goose*, q.v.—2. No score ; a ' goose-egg ', U.S. for *duck's egg*, q.v. : sporting : ca. 1885–1910.—3. The male member : low : from ca. 1871 ; **ob.**—4. A student at the Queen's College : Oxford undergraduates' : late C. 19–20. Ware. Cf. *Quagger*, q.v.

goose's gazette. A lying story ; a silly-season tale : coll. : ca. 1810–60. Cf. *gooseberry*, 3.

goose's neck. The male member : low : from ca. 1872. Ex *goose*, n., 1, 2, and 6. Cf. *gooser*, 3.

goosey, goosy, adj. With a goose-flesh feeling : coll. : mid-C. 19–20. Jefferies in *Amaryllis at the Fair.* (O.E.D.)

goos(e)y-gander. A gander : coll. : from ca. 1815. Baby language has both *goos(e)y-goos(e)y*, a goose, and *goosey-goosey gander*, a gander ; the latter occurs, e.g., in the well-known nursery rhyme recorded as early as 1842 by Halliwell in his *Nursery Rhymes.*—2. A fool : from ca. 1880.

Goosey Goderich. See **Prosperity Robinson.**

goosgog. A gooseberry : nursery and proletarian (– 1887) ex dial. Baumann. A variant of *goose-gog*, q.v., at *goose-gob.*

goosing. See **goose**, v., 6.

Gor. God : low coll., esp. Cockneys' : C. 19–20. Also *Gaw.* Esp. in *Gorblim(e)y.*

Gor' damn. Jam : rhyming s. : late C. 19–20. B. & P.

Goramity ; occ. **Garamity.** God almighty : West Indian negroes' coll. (– 1834). O.E.D. (Sup.).

Gorblimeries, the. Seven Dials, London : policemen's (– 1909) ; **ob.** Ware. Ex :

gorblim(e)y ; gawlim(e)y ! A corruption of *God blind me !* : orig. and mainly Cockneys' : 1870, says Ware for the latter form ; 1890, for the former.—2. Hence, ' an unwired, floppy, field-service cap worn by a certain type of subaltern in defiance of the Dress Regulations ' : military : 1915. F. & Gibbons.

gorblim(e)y, here come(s) the ——. A Cockney soldiers' derisive c.p. addressed to, or within the hearing of, another battalion or a section thereof : from late 1890's. B. & P.

gordelpus. A person frequenting casual wards : low (– 1909) ; **ob.** Ware. Ex *Gord (h)elp us !* See also **godhelpus.**

Gore. An occ. spelling (chiefly dial.) of *Gor.* E.D.D.

*goree. Money ; esp. gold money or gold : c. : late C. 17–mid-19. B.E. Ex Fort Goree on the Gold Coast. Cf. S.E. *guinea* and *old Mr. Gory*, q.v.

gorge. A heavy meal : from ca. 1820 : coll. until C. 20, when S.E. ' Jon Bee.' Ex the S.E. v. —2. Whence, a glutton : coll. (– 1923). Manchon.—3. A manager : theatrical : ca. 1873–1905. Ex *gorger*, 1.

gorgeous as a loose adj. expressing approbation is coll. : 1883 (S.O.D.).

gorgeous wrecks. Members of the Volunteer Defence Corps : 1915–18. F. & Gibbons. Ex *Georgius Rex*, from the *G.R.* of their brassards ; their advancing years. Occ., same period, *Government rejects* and *old gents.*

gorger. A theatrical manager : theatrical (– 1864). H., 3rd ed. Occ. *cully-gorger.*—2. An employer, a principal (– 1864). Prob. ex :—3. A gentleman, a well-dressed man : low : from ca. 1810 : † by 1910. *Lex. Bal.* Ex Romany *gaujer, gaujo, gorgio* (often in C. 20 tramps' c.), anyone not a gipsy, or, just possibly, ex *gorgeous* (H., 1859).—4. The sense, ' a man ', is very rare : c. : 1857, ' Ducange Anglicus '.—5. A voracious eater : from ca. 1790. App. coll., actually S.E., ex the S.E. v. Whence :

gorger, rotten. A lad that hangs about Covent Garden to eat discarded fruit : London : ca. 1870–1900. H., 5th ed.

gorgery. A ' gorge ' ; a (school-)feast : coll. : 1906, Desmond Coke, *The Bending of a Twig*. Cf. S.E. *gorger*, a glutton.

gorgie. One who is not a Gypsy : grafters' : late C. 19–20. Philip Allingham, *Cheapjack*, 1934. See **gorger**, 3.

[**gorgio.** See **gorger**, 3.]

Gorgonzola Hall. (Stock Exchange) ' formerly the New Hall : now [from ca. 1885] the corporation generally ', F. & H. Ex the colour of the marble. Ob.

gorm (or **G.**) ; **gawm.** God damn : low : mid-C. 19–20. Esp. in *gormed*, q.v.—2. Tobacco for chewing : tramps' c. (— 1932). F. Jennings, *Tramping with Tramps*.

gorm, v. To gormandize : from ca. 1890 ; virtually †. Ex U.S.A.

gorman. A *cormorant* : nautical coll. : C. 19–20. Bowen. Cf. Scots and Northern *gormaw*.

gormagon. (' Meaningless : pseudo-Chinese ', O.E.D. : but it may be a confused blend of *Gorgon*+*mason*.) A hypothetical monster of ca. 1750–1830 : coll. Grose, 1785, ' a monster with six eyes, three mouths, four arms, eight legs, five on one side and three on the other, three arses, two tarses [*penises*], and a **** [*pudendum muliebre*] upon its back ; a man on horseback, with a woman [*riding* ' side-saddle '] behind him.' Relevant is the *Gormagons*, properly *Gormogons*, an English secret society—a lay offshoot from the Masons—of ca. 1725–50 : evidently there was some ridiculous rite (cf. *goat, ride the*), for, in 1791, ' G. Gambado ' in his *Horsemanship*, speaks of ' the art of riding before a lady on a double horse, vulgarly termed *à la gormagon* '.

gormed, be. Be ' God-damned ' if . . . : low coll. oath : 1849, Dickens. *God* corrupted after dial. *gaumed*. Cf. *gommed*.

gormy-ruddles. The intestines : low : C. 19. Ex dial. *gormy-ruttles*, ' strangles ', i.e. horses' quinsies.

gorn. Gone : sol., mostly Cockney : C. 18–20. Occ. *gawn*.

gorra. Got a : Cockney : C. 19–20. *Slang*, p. 153. Cf. *norra*.

gorsoon. See **gossoon**.

gorspel, gorspil. Gospel : sol. pronunciation (Cockney and Australian) : C. 19–20.

***gory.** See **old Mr. Gory** and cf. *goree*, q.v.—2. A chap, a fellow : c. : ca. 1810–40. Vaux. Origin ? Cf. *cove, gill, gloak*, qq.v.

gos, gosse. Gossip, as term of address : coll. : ca. 1540–1660. Abbr. *gossip*. O.E.D.

Goschens. 2¾% Government Stock : ca. 1888–1905 : Stock Exchange coll. Created by Mr. Goschen in 1888. *Man of the World*, June 29, 1889, ' The nickname Goschens is going out of fashion.'

gosh is a corruption of *God* (cf. *Golly*) : 1757 ; though in 1553 it occurs thus in the anon. *Respublica* : ' Each man snatch for himself, by gosse ' (W.).

gosh. To spit : Winchester College : late C. 19–20. Wrench. Cf. *glope*.

gosoon, gosoun. See **gossoon**.

[**gospel** = ' Gospel truth ', (anything) absolutely true, n. and adj., is S.E. and in forms *all is*, or *is not, gospel*, and *take for gospel*, it dates from M.E.]

gospel, do. To go to church : low coll. : from ca. 1860 : ob.

gospel(or **gorspel, -il**)**-cove.** A clergyman : Australian (— 1916). C. J. Dennis.

gospel-gab. Insincere talk about religion : low coll. (— 1892). Hume Nisbet, ' With a little gospel-gab and howling penitence, [I] got the church people interested.'

gospel-grinder, -postillion, -shark or **-sharp,** are more gen. in U.S. than in England : coll. : from ca. 1855. Besant & Rice speak of ' a Connecticut gospel-grinder ', Mark Twain of a ' gospel-sharp ' in *Innocents at Home*. But in U.S. they merely = a parson ; in England they = a city missionary or a tract-distributor (H., 1st ed.) or a Sunday-School teacher (' Ducange Anglicus ', 1857).

gospel of gloom, the. Gloomy house-decoration and dresses : Society : ca. 1880–1900. Ware. Satirising the Æsthetes.

Gospel of St. Jeames, the. Snobbery : Society : 1847 ; ob. Ware. Ex Thackeray's *Jeames de la Pluche* in *The Yellowplush Papers*.

gospel of the tub, the. The mania for cold baths : Society coll. : ca. 1845–1910. Ware.

gospel-postillion or **-shark.** See **gospel-grinder**.

gospel-shop. A church or chapel ; gen. Methodist : coll. : from ca. 1780 : after 1860, chiefly nautical. (*Gospel-mill* is a U.S. variation.) J. Lackington, ' Mr. Wesley's gospel-shops ', 1791.

gospeller. An Evangelist preacher : pejorative coll. : from ca. 1880. Ex the † sense, one of the four evangelists, and the rare one, a missionary. Cf. *hot gospeller*, q.v.

goss. A hat ; at first a ' four-and-nine ' : coll. : 1848 (O.E.D.). Ex *gossamer hat*, a light felt fashionable in the late 1830's. Cf. :

gossamer. A hat (— 1859) ; esp. and orig. a very light one : ca. 1837–1900. Both Dickens and James Grant, in the late 1830's, mention ' ventilation ' gossamers ; Andrew Lang, in 1884, ' the gay gossamer of July '. Cf. *goss*, q.v.

gosse. See **gos** and **gosh**.—**gossip, up to one's.** See **up to the cackle**.

gossip pint-pot. A hard drinker : C. 16–early 17 coll. Hollyband. (O.E.D.)

gossoon ; earliest as **gosoun** ; occ., C. 19–20, **gosoon, gorsoon** (O.E.D.). A boy : Anglo-Irish : 1684 : S.E. until ca. 1850, then increasingly coll. Ex Fr. *garçon* via M.E. *garsoun*.—2. Hence, ' a silly awkward lout ; ' nautical (— 1867) ; ob. Smyth.

got with preceding **has** or **have** omitted : coll., esp. in U.S. : mid-C. 19–20. E.g. ' Got any money with you ? ' O.E.D. (Sup.)

got. For gen. remarks, see **get**, v.—2. A C. 20 variant of next, sense 2. John Brophy, *Water-front*, 1934, ' They got to do it, or else they'd never make money.'

got, has or **have.** I, you, we or they have or possess ; he has, etc. : coll., *got* being pleonastic (as also in next sense) : 1607, Shakespeare (S.O.D.).—2. Am, etc., bound (to . . .) : low coll. : 1868, J. Greenwood (see quotation at *hander*) ; the S.O.D quotes : ' The thing has got to be fought out,' 1889.

got ?, what has. What has happened to, become of ? Coll. : from ca. 1820 ; ob. a century later. Scoresby, in *Whale Fishery*, 1823, ' They all at once . . . enquired what had got Carr.' (O.E.D.)

got a clock(, he's). (He is) carrying a bag : a London c.p. of 1883–4. Ex dynamitards' activities.

got a collar on. Conceited ; vain ; arrogant : lower classes' (− 1909) ; ob. Ware.

got a face on (her, him). Ugly : proletarian (− 1909). Ware. Cf. *face-ache*.

got a skinful. See **skinful, have got one's.** Cf. :

got all (or more than) he can carry. Extremely drunk : coll. : C. 20.

got any hard ? A c.p. addressed in Southampton bars to a stranger and implying that he may have been to sea and that (faint hope !) he may have some hard tobacco to spare : from ca. 1920. (Something of a joke.)

got 'em bad, has or have. To be in earnest ; seriously affected (by illness, delirium tremens, love) : low coll. : from ca. 1870. Occ., in C. 20, *bad* is omitted. Cf. *get them.*

got 'em on (occ. **all on**), **have.** To be very fashionably dressed, often with the implication of over-dressing : low coll. : 1880 (*Punch*, Aug. 28) ; broadside ballads of the 80's. Ob. See also **got-up . . .** and **rigged-out.**—2. To have the advantage over (a person) : C. 20.

got line. (Of women.) Graceful and vigorous in dancing : theatrical : 1870 ; ob. Ware.

got me(, Steve)? ; get me(, Steve). Do you understand ? : U.S. c.p., anglicised by 1917. F. & Gibbons ; A. Christie, *Why Didn't They Ask Evans ?*, 1934, ' " I get you, Steve " . . . and . . . the queer phrase represented sympathy and understanding.'

got on, have. To have in evidence against : coll. : late C. 19–20. E.g., G. D. H. & M. Cole, *Superintendent Wilson's Holiday*, 1928, ' That's the gist of what we've got on [the arrested man], and it's my belief he'll find it a hard job to answer.'

got the glow. Blushing : London lower classes' (− 1909) ; ob. Ware.

got the morbs, adj. *Morbid*, melancholy : Society : ca. 1880–1910. Ware.

got the pants. Panting, breathless : low (−1909). Ware.

got the perpetual. Vigorous ; enterprising : lower classes' (− 1909) ; ob. Ware. Ex *perpetual motion.*

got the shutters up. Surly : lower classes' (− 1909). Ware.

got the woefuls. Sad ; wretched : non-aristocratic (− 1909). Ware.

got to ?, where has it, he, etc. What has become of it, him, etc. ? From ca. 1885 : s. in C. 19, then coll. Jerome K. Jerome in *Three Men in a Boat.*

got-up, n. An upstart : coll. : ca. 1880–1915. (O.E.D.) For form, cf. *had-up.*

got-up, dressed (ppl. adj.) : see **get up,** v., 1.— 2. Esp. well-dressed, in the low coll. variations : *got-up regardless* (abbr. *regardless of expense*),—*to kill,—to the knocker,—to the nines* : all from ca. 1880 : the first and the third are ob.

gotch-gutted. Pot-bellied : coll. when not, as gen., dial : late C. 18–19. Grose, 1st ed. Ex *gotch*, a pitcher or a (large) round jug. A late C. 17–mid-18 variant : *gotch-gutted.*

[**Goth** and **Gothic**, n. and adj., barbarian, uncouth, are, despite F. & H., S.E.]

Gotham. Newcastle : North Country s. (−1900) rather than dial. Ex dial. *gotham*, foolish, ignorant. E.D.D.

Gothicky. Gothic-like : coll. : 1893, Kate Wiggin in *Cathedral Courtship.* (O.E.D.)

gotta, gotter. Got to (do something) : sol. : late C. 19–20. (Ernest Raymond, *A Family That Was*, 1929.) Not exclusively U.S., as certain persons hold. Cf. *gerrup, siddown.*

Gott-strafers. See **strafe,** v., 1.

Gotter-dam-merung. A grotesque form of swearing : Society : 1862–3. Ware. Ex the performance of Wagner's *The Ring* in London in 1862.

goujeers, prob. a ' made ' word : see **goodyear.**

gourd. (Rare in singular.) A hollowed-out false die : low, or c., > j. : ca. 1540–1660. Ascham in *Toxophilus*, Shakespeare in *Merry Wives.* ? ex the fruit influenced by Old Fr. *gourd*, a swindle.

Gourock ham. A salted herring : mostly Scottish : ca. 1830–1900. Gourock was, before 1870, a well-known Clyde fishing village. Cf. *Glasgow magistrate*, q.v.

gout = venereal disease : e.g. in *Covent Garden*, or *Spanish, gout* : late C. 17–18.

gov. See **guv.**

government house. The house of the owner or manager of an estate : a Dominions' jocular coll. : from ca. 1880 ; ob. Ex *Government House.*

Government man. A convict : Australian coll. : ca. 1825–85. Applied esp. to assigned servants : see J. West, *History of Tasmania*, 1852, at ii, 127. (Morris.)

Government rejects. See **gorgeous wrecks.**

Government securities. Handcuffs ; fetters : from ca. 1850 ; ob.

Government signpost. The gallows : mid-C. 19. H., 1860.

Government stroke. A slow lazy stroke, hence a lazy manner of working : Australia : 1856. Trollope, 1873. Ex the anti-sweat motions of convicts : seen later in those of Government labourers, e.g. on the railway lines. Morris.

governor. A father : 1837 : s. >, ca. 1895, coll. Dickens in *Pickwick* ; *Answers*, April 20, 1889, ' To call your father " The Governor " is, of course, slang, and is as bad as referring to him as " The Boss " [!], " The Old Man ", or " The Relieving Officer ". ' (The last is never used as a term of address, *old man* practically never.) Occ. abbr. (*gov.* or) *guv*, q.v. Ex the third sense, whereas the second follows from the first.—2. A term of address to a strange man : s. > low coll. : from ca. 1855. H., 1860.—3. A superior ; an employer : coll. (occ. in address) : 1802 (S.O.D.), thus the earliest sense.

Governor-General, the. Macartney (b. 1886) : cricketers' nickname : from 1909, his first visit to England. Loosely ex his initials C.G. (*not* G.G.), aptly ex his masterly batting. *Who's Who in World Cricket*, 1934.

gov'nor. See **guvner.**

govy. A governess ; occ. as adj. : coll. : C. 20. An affectionate diminutive. (O.E.D. Sup.)

***gowk.** One ignorant of the various dodges : prison c. of C. 19. Ex Scottish for a fool.

gowk, hunt the. To go on (esp. an April) fool's errand : Scottish coll. : C. 18–20. See ' All Fools' Day ' in *Words !*

***gowler.** A dog, esp. one given to howling and growling : North-Country c. (− 1864). H., 3rd ed. Prob. *growler* perverted or ex dial. *gowl*, to howl.

gown, coll. for the undergraduates of Oxford or Cambridge, is, like *gownsman* (and even its abbr. *gown*), S.E.—2. Coarse brown paper : Winchester College : C. 19, but † by 1890. ? suggested by the rhyme and the coarseness of gown-material.

gownd. Gown : a C. 18–20 sol. Cf. *drownd(ed)* for *drown(ed)*. Common also in dial.

gowsers. Gownboys' shoes : Charterhouse : ca. 1830–75. A. H. Tod, *Charterhouse*, 1900. By telescoping.

goy ; goya. Resp., a Gentile man, woman : Jewish coll. : mid-C. 19–20. Ex Yiddish. Cf. *gorger*, esp. sense 3.

grab. A professional resurrectionist : medical s. (1823) > coll. : almost †. S. Warren's *Diary of a Late Physician*, 1830.—2. A policeman : 1849 : coll. : † by 1900. Albert Smith. (O.E.D.)—3. F. & H.'s other senses are S.E.

grab, v. To steal ; to arrest : 1812, Vaux, there- fore from a few years earlier : resp. low coll. and c. >, ca. 1870, s. >, ca. 1880, low coll. : so I believe, despite the O.E.D. Dickens in *Oliver Twist*, ' Do you want to be grabbed, stupid ? '

grab-all. A greedy or an avaricious person : coll. : from ca. 1870.—2. A bag wherein to carry odds and ends : coll. : from ca. 1890.

grab-bag. A lucky-bag : late C. 19–early 20. Ex U.S. Ware.

*****grab-coup.** The snatching, by a losing gambler, of all the available money and then fighting a way out : c. of ca. 1820–80. Bee. The variant *-game* arose, prob. in U.S., ca. 1850 ; *-racket* is certainly U.S. (— 1892), as in Stevenson & Osbourne's *The Wrecker*.

grab for altitude. See **altitude, grabbing for.**

*****grab-gains.** The snatching of a purse and then running away : c. of ca. 1840–1900. Cf. the C. 20 *smash-and-grab* (raid).

*****grab on,** v.i. To 'hold on', manage to live : low : from ca. 1850 ; ob. Mayhew.

*****grabber.** The hand, but gen. in pl. : from ca. 1810 (ob.) : c. >, by 1860, low. Cf. *pickers and stealers*.—2. A garotter : c. (— 1909). Ware.—3. Occ. a pickpocket : c. (— 1923). Manchon.

grabble, to seize, also to handle roughly or with rude intimacy, seems, in late C. 18–mid-19, to have been 'felt ' to be coll. : the O.E.D., however, con- siders it S.E. Cf. :

grabbling irons. A mid-C. 19 variant of *grappling irons* : fingers.

grabby. An infantryman : military (mostly in contempt by cavalrymen) and hence naval : ca. 1848–1912. (F. & Gibbons, 'From before the Crimean War '; I did not hear it in the G.W.) Whyte-Melville ; Bowen, 'Borrowed from the Hindustani'. Perhaps rather ex dial. *grabby*, greedy, inclined to cheat.

grace card. The six of hearts : Anglo-Irish : C. 18–20 ; ob. The proposed etymology—see F. & H., or H.—is too ' anecdotal ' for inclusion here.

grace o' God. ' The copy of a writ issued upon a bill of exchange ': commercial (— 1909). Ware.

*****Gracemans.** Gracechurch Street Market : C. 17–18 c. Rowlands, 1610. See *-mans.*

Graces, the Three. The brothers Grace : cricketers' coll. nickname (— 1887). Baumann. Punning mythology.

gracile. Gracefully slender : catachrestic : from ca. 1870. (Properly, lean, slender.) O.E.D.

gracing ; occ. **greycing.** A telescoping of *grey- hound racing* : sporting : 1927. O.E.D. (Sup.).

gracious, as H. shows in his Introduction, was, in mid-Victorian ecclesiastical s., made to = pleasant or ' nice ' or excellent.

gracious ! (C. 18–20), **gracious me !** (C. 19–20),

gracious alive ! (mid-C. 19–20), **good gracious !** (C. 18–20) are euphemisms > coll.

grade, make the. (Gen. in negative or interroga- tive.) To be able to do a thing ; to ' come up to scratch ': U.S. (— 1900), partly anglicised ca. 1930. Ex railway j.

graduate. An artful fellow : coll. : from ca. 1875 ; ob.—2. A spinster skilled in sexual practice : low coll. : from ca. 1885.—3. A horse that has proved itself good : the turf : from ca. 1870.—All ex the ob. S.E. sense, a proficient in an art or a craft.

graduate, to, v.i. Obtain a sound practical know- ledge of life, love, society, a livelihood, etc. : coll. : from ca. 1875 ; ob.

*****gradus.** In card-sharping, the making of a card to project beyond the rest : c. of ca. 1820–1910. Also known as *the step.* Cf. :

gradus ad Parnassum. (Lit., step to Parnassus ; properly, a dictionary of prosody.) A treadmill : literarys : ca. 1790–1870. Ex the ascent of Par- nassus and of the mill.

graft. Work, labour : coll. : from ca. 1870. Esp. in *hard graft*, (hard) work : in C. 20, mostly in the Army and in Australia and New Zealand. *Hard grafting* occurs in *The Graphic* of July 6, 1878. —2. Hence, any kind of work, esp. if illicit : low coll. (— 1874). H., 5th ed. Esp. in *what graft are you at ?*, what is your ' line ',—your ' lay ' ? Cf. the U.S. (orig. s.) sense, illicit profit or commission (mainly in politics), which, adopted into S.E. ca. 1900, prob. derives ex the Eng. term, as, ultimately, does its corresponding v.—3. Hence, the line one takes in a crime ; one's role therein : c. : C. 20. James Curtis, *The Gilt Kid*, 1936.

graft, v. To cuckold, ' plant horns ' on : low coll. : late C. 17–18. B.E.—2. To work ; esp. to work hard : coll., mostly Australia and New Zea- land : from ca. 1870. Earlier (ca. 1855–80), to go to work : English only (H., 1st ed.). Esp. in *where are you grafting ?* Prob. ex † *grave*, to dig, perhaps influenced by the gardening *graft* and even by *craft* (as in *arts and crafts*).—3. To be actively a criminal : c. : from ca. 1910. Edgar Wallace, *Room 13.*—4. To be or work as a grafter (see **grafter,** 4) : grafters' coll. : C. 20. Philip Allingham, *Cheapjack*, 1934.

grafter. ' One who toils hard or willingly ', C. J. Dennis : from late 1890's : mostly Australian. Ex *graft*, v., 2.—2. A swindler : coll., orig. (— 1900) U.S., partly anglicised ca. 1910. Cf. *graft*, n., 2.— 3. One who is actively a criminal : c. : from ca. 1912. Ex *graft*, v., 3.—4. ' One who works a line in a fair or market : as fortune-teller, quack doctor, mock-auctioneer, etc.': late C. 19–20. P. Alling- ham, *Cheapjack*, 1934. (Senses 3 and 4 follow naturally from sense 1.)

[Grafters' slang is the s. used by those who work a line at fair or market, e.g. as fortune-teller or quack doctor. Some of it is Parlyaree, some Romany, some Yiddish, some rhyming s. ; some of it, too, verges on c. The authority on the subject is Mr. Philip Allingham : see his fascinating *Cheapjack*, 1934.]

-gram, when used loosely, has a coll. hue, as in *pistolgram*, an instantaneous photograph.

gram-fed. ' Getting, or being given, the best of everything ': Anglo-Indian : 1880 (O.E.D.) : s. >, by 1910, coll. Ex *gram*, chick-pea.

grammophone ; even **gram(m)aphone.** Incorrect —the error is frequent—for *gramophone* : C. 20.

gramophone record. A canteen bloater : naval : late C. 19–20. Bowen. Because out of a tin.

gramp. To blow like a grampus : rare : from ca. 1925. Collinson. By back-formation.

grampus. A fat man ; esp. one who puffs freely : from ca. 1836 : coll. until ca. 1895, then S.E. Dickens.—2. A greedy, stupid person : Roxburghshire s. : C. 19–20 ; ob. E.D.D.

grampus, blow the. To drench a person : nautical : ca. 1810–1910.—2. To play about in the water : nautical s. > gen. coll. : ca. 1860–1915.

gran. A grandmother ; esp. in address : dial. and nursery coll. : late C. 19–20. Cf. *granny*.

***granam.** A late C. 16 form of *grannam*, 2.

grand. Abbr. *grand piano* : 1840 : coll. till C. 20, then S.E. *The Morning Advertiser*, March 28, 1891.

grand, adj. A gen. superlative of admiration : coll. : from ca. 1815. In late C. 19–early 20, mainly U.S., opp. *fierce*.—2. Adv., grandly : (low) coll. verging, in C. 20, on sol. : mid-C. 18–20. (O.E.D.)

grand, do the. To put on airs : coll. : from ca. 1885 ; ob. Baumann. Cf. *lardy-dah*.

[**Grand Old Man, the,** Gladstone, is on the borderline between coll. and S.E. In 1885, Joseph Chamberlain was named *the Grand Young Man* (Ware).]

grand slam. Complete or spectacular success : coll. : from ca. 1910. Ex the game of bridge.— 2. See **slam** (n.).

grand strut. The Broad Walk, Hyde Park : ca. 1820–80. Moncrieff, 1823, ' We'll . . . promenade it down the grand strut.'

Grand Trunks. Grand Trunk Railway (of Canada) shares : Stock Exchange coll. : ca. 1885–1900. Baumann.

grandad, grand-dad. A coll. childish and/or affectionate variation of *grandfather* : 1819, Byron. Cf. *granny, granty, grandma,* and :

grandada, grand-dada ; gran(d-)daddy. Grandfather : familiar coll. : resp. late C. 17–20 (ob.) and mid-C. 18–20.

grandma. An affectionate abbr. (C. 19–20) of *grandmamma* (1763), itself an affectionate form of *grandmother* : coll.

[**grandmaternal,** like **grandpaternal,** has been jocularised to the verge of coll.]

grandmother. (Gen. pl.) Any one of the big howitzers operated in France by the Royal Marine Artillery in G.W. : naval, hence military : 1915. Bowen. Also *granny* or, more gen., *Granny* (F. & Gibbons).

grandmother, all my eye and my. See **all my eye and my grandmother.**

grandmother, see one's. To have a nightmare : coll. : from ca. 1850 ; ob.

grandmother, shoot one's. To be mistaken or disappointed. Often as *you've shot your granny*. Coll. : from ca. 1860.

grandmother !, so's your. See **all my eye and my grandmother.**

grandmother !, this beats my. That *is* astonishing ! Coll. : from ca. 1880 : ob.

grandmother (or granny) how to (or to) suck eggs, teach one's. To give advice to one's senior ; esp. to instruct an expert in his own expertise : from ca. 1600. Cotgrave, Swift, Fielding. Occ., from ca. 1790, abbr. to *teach one's grandmother* or *granny*. Earlier forms are *teach one's (gran)dame to spin*, C. 16–17, *to grope ducks*, Cotgrave, 1611, or *a goose*, Howell, 1659, and *to sup sour milk*, Ray, 1670 ; ca. 1620–1750, *grannam* (or *-um*) was often substituted (see **grannam**) ; from ca. 1750, *granny*. A coll. phrase so gen. as almost to > S.E. (Apperson.)

grandmother (or little friend or auntie) with one, have one's. To be in one's menstrual period : low coll. : from ca. 1830. This process has attracted much cheap wit.

grandmother's review, my. *The British Review* : ca. 1820–60. Byron's nickname.

grandpa. Abbr. (C. 19–20) of *grandpapa*, itself coll. and affectionate—from 1753—for *grandfather*. (O.E.D.) Cf. *grandma*.

[**grangerise, grangerism, grangerite,** or **-izer,** are, despite F. & H., certainly S.E.]

***granna.** A loose variant of sense 2 of the next. Recorded (at date 1690) among the Sackville papers : see the Hon. V. Sackville-West, *Knole and the Sackvilles*, 1922. N.b., however, my comment at *gun*, n., 3.

grannam, occ. grannum. A coll. form of *grandam* = grandmother : late C. 16–early 19. Shakespeare ; Cibber in his *Rival Fools*, 1709, ' Go, fools ! teach your grannums : you are always full of your advice when there's no occasion for't.'— 2. Corn : c. : ca. 1560–1820. Harman, B.E., Grose. Ex L. (cf. *pannam*) influenced by *granary*.

grannam-gold. ' Old Hoarded Coin ', B.E. ; ' boarded money ', Grose (1st ed.) who prefers the preferable *grannam's* (or *-um's*) *gold* ; the S.E. form is *grandam-gold*. Coll. : late C. 17–18. I.e., supposed to have been inherited from the grandmaternal hoard.

Granny. See **grandmother.**—2. The inevitable nickname of men surnamed Hudson : military : late C. 19–20. F. & Gibbons.

granny ; occ. grannie, grannee (C. 17), **grany** (C. 18), **grannie,** Scottish : O.E.D. Grandmother : by that softening (or, via *grannam*) which is typical of affection. Coll. : 1663 (S.O.D.). ' An old Woman, also a Grandmother ', B.E.—2. ' Conceit of superior knowledge ' : low (— 1851) : ob. Mayhew. ? ex *teach one's grandmother to suck eggs*. —3. A badly tied knot apt to jam : nautical : ca. 1860. Abbr. *granny's knot*.

***granny,** v. To know, recognise ; swindle : c. (— 1851). Mayhew. Cf. *granny*, n., 2. Ex :— 2. To understand (v.t.) : c. : ca. 1845 in ' *No. 747* ', p. 409.—3. To disguise oneself : c. (— 1923). Manchon. Prob. ex sense 1.

granny ! A C. 20 variant of *so's your grandmother !* (see above). Manchon.

granny, shoot one's. See **grandmother . . .**— **granny, teach one's.** See **grandmother, teach . . .**

[**grant the favour** (v.i. ; v.t. with *to*), to ' take ' a man, is euphemistic not unconventional : this is a frequent error of F. & H.'s ; they, like 99.9% of people, fail to perceive that 90% of the world's obscene terms and locutions are the result of euphemism : neither the frank nor the mealy-mouthed realise that to call, e.g., the genitals by the one name and to eschew all others would soon lead to a lack of both obscene and euphemistic words and perhaps even minimise both euphemism and obscenity.]

granted ! A (genteel-low) coll. reply to an apology : from ca. 1905. Occ. *granted, I'm sure !*

granty. Grandmother : a coll. more familiar and less gen. than *granny*, of which it is an affectionate elaboration. From ca. 1850. More usual in Australia and New Zealand than in Great Britain. Cf. Scottish and Northern *grandy* (1747 : E.D.D.).

granum. An occ. C. 18 form of *grannam*. (O.E.D.)

grape-monger. A tippler of wine : C. 17 coll. Dekker.

grape-shot, adj. Tipsy : ca. 1875–1900. Whence the C. 20 *shot*.

grape-vine. Clothes line : rhyming s. : late C. 19–20. *John o' London's Weekly*, June 9, 1934.

graph. Ex *chromograph, hectograph*, etc., for a copy-producing apparatus : coll. : ca. 1880–1912. Whence :

graph, v. To take a number of copies of, by means of a ' graph ', q.v. : coll. : ca. 1880–1920. (O.E.D.)

-graph, -grapher, and **-graphy** are occ. employed in a word so jocular, e.g. *hurrygraph*, a hasty sketch, as to be almost coll.

graphyure. Incorrect for *graphiure* : mid-C. 19–20. O.E.D.

grapple. (Gen. in pl.) The hand : low (— 1877). See **grappler**, more common.

grapple-the-rails. Whiskey : Anglo-Irish c. > coll. (— 1785) ; ob. Grose, 1st ed. Because, after drinking it, one had to do this to remain upright.

grappler. (Gen. in pl.) The hand : from ca. 1850 : ? orig. nautical. Cf. *grapple* and :

grappling-irons. The fingers : nautical : from ca. 1855. H., 2nd ed. Cf. *grapple* and *grappler.—* 2. Handcuffs : ca. 1810–70. *Lex. Bal.* Presumably ex nautical S.E.

grass. Ground : 1625 (O.E.D.).—2. Abbr. *sparrow-grass* = asparagus : low coll. : from ca. 1830 ; earlier, S.E.—3. Green vegetables : Royal Military Academy and nautical : ca. 1860–1925.—4. A temporary hand on a newspaper : Australia (— 1889) ; ob. Whence the c.p. *a grass on news waits dead men's shoes.* ? ex the English printers' *grass* = casual employment (1888, O.E.D.) or ex *grass-hand*, q.v.—5. A policeman : racing s. : C. 20. Abbr. *grasshopper.—*6. Hence, an informer : c. (— 1933). Charles E. Leach.

grass, v. To bring to the ground : orig. (1814), pugilistic ; in C. 20, mostly of Rugby football and gen. considered S.E. Egan, Moore, Dickens.—2. Hence, to defeat, ca. 1880–1910, and to kill, ca. 1875–1914.—3. To discharge temporarily from one's employment : trade (— 1881) : ob. Ex a horse's going out to grass.—4. To do jobbing or casual work : printers' : from ca. 1894. O.E.D.—5. V.t., to inform on : c. : from ca. 1930. James Curtis, *The Gilt Kid*, 1936, ' Anyhow it was a dirty trick grassing his pals.' Ex *grass*, n., 6.

grass, be sent to. To be rusticated : Cambridge : ca. 1790–1880. Punning ' rustication '.

*grass, come. See **come grass.—*grass, cut one's own.** See cut one's own grass.

grass, give. Listed by F. & H. as coll., it is actually late C. 16–17 S.E. : a translation of L. *dare herbam.*

grass, go to. (Of limbs) to waste away : coll. : ca. 1840–1910.—2. For other senses, and for *go to grass !*, see go to grass.

grass, hunt. To be knocked down : s. or coll. : ca. 1870–1914.—2. At cricket, to field : ca. 1880–1910. A variation of *to hunt leather.*

grass, on the. (Of a horse that has) fallen : turf coll. (— 1923). Manchon.

grass, send one's calves out to. See calves.

grass, send to. To knock down : from ca. 1875 ; ob. Hindley. ? ex *hunt grass*.

grass, take Nebuchadnezzar out to. To ' take ' a man : low : from ca. 1870. *Take* = lead ; *Nebuchadnezzar* = the male member (why ?).

grass before breakfast. A duel : Anglo-Irish :

mid-C. 18–mid-19. Lover, in *Handy Andy.* (Ware.)

grass-comber. A countryman serving as a sailor : nautical : ca. 1860–1910. H., 3rd ed. ; Walter Besant, 1886, ' Luke was a grass comber and a land swab.' Earlier (ca. 1830–60), a farm-labourer passenger on a ship. On *beach-comber.*

grass-cutter. (Gen. pl.) A small bomb that, aeroplane-dropped,. bursts on impact and scatters shrapnel pellets at a low level, i.e. to kill persons rather than destroy inanimates : military : 1917. B. & P. Cf. *daisy-cutter*, 4, q.v.

grass grow under one's feet, let no. To lose no time or chance : C. 17–20 : coll. in C. 17, then S.E. A † variant is *on one's heel* (or *under one's heels*) : C. 16–early 19. Apperson.

grass-hand. A ' green ' or new hand : printers' : ca. 1875–1915. Cf. *grass*, n., sense, 4.

grass-widow. An unmarried mother ; a discarded mistress : C. 16–early 19 coll. More ; B.E. The former nuance is extant in dial.—2. A married woman temporarily away from her husband : coll. : from ca. 1858 ; orig. mainly Anglo-Indian. The second follows from the first sense, which prob. contains an allusion to a bed of straw or grass—cf. the etymology of *bastard* (W.).—3. Occ. as a v. : coll. : from ca. 1890.

grass-widower. A man separated temporarily from his wife : orig. (1862), U.S. ; anglicised ca. 1880. On *grass-widow*, 2.

grasser. A fall, esp. one caused by a punch : sporting (— 1887). Baumann.

grasses ! ' A cry directed at any one particularly polite ' : printers' (— 1909). Ware. Perhaps ex Fr. *gracieux* : cf. Scots *gracie*, well-behaved.

grasshopper. A policeman : rhyming s. (— 1893) on *copper*.—2. A waiter at a tea-garden : ca. 1870–1914. Ex his busyness on the sward. H., 5th ed.—3. A thief : c. (— 1893). *Pall Mall Gazette*, Jan. 2, 1893.

Grasshopper Falls. The great waterfall at *Gersoppa* on the Sheravati River : Anglo-Indian coll. (— 1886) by the process of Hobson-Jobson. Yule & Burnell.

grassing. ' Casual work away from the office ', F. & H. : printers' : from ca. 1889.

grassville. The country : early C. 19 : low. Punning *daisyville*, q.v.

grasswards, go. To fall : turf coll. (— 1923). Manchon. Cf. *grass, on the.*

*grassy. A c. variant (— 1935) of *grass*, n., 5. David Hume.

grateful and comforting. A c.p. of the 1920's. Collinson. Ex a famous advertisement by Epps's Cocoa.

gratters. Congratulations : university and Public School s. (— 1903) >, by 1933, gen. coll. (O.E.D. Sup.) Cf. *congrats.*

graunie. See **granny.—grave.** See **graves.**

grave-digger, like a. ' Up to the arse in business, and don't know which way to turn ', Grose, 2nd ed. : ca. 1790–1860.

grave-digger, the. Strong liquor : Anglo-Indian : late C. 19–20. Ware. Contrast *coffin-nail.—*2. Pl., the last two batsmen (in the batting-order) : cricketers' jocular coll. : 1887 ; ob. Lewis.—3. See **puff and dart.**

gravel. A rapidly diminishing supply of money in the market : Stock Exchange : 1884. (S.O.D.) Semantics : as the tide recedes, it leaves the gravel bare.

gravel, v. To confound, or puzzle greatly; 'floor', q.v.: mid-C. 16–20; coll. for a century, then S.E. Shakespeare, 'When you were gravelled for lack of matter'. Orig. nautical: cf. *stranded* (W.).

gravel-crusher. A soldier at defaulters' drill: military: ca. 1880–1900. Barrère & Leland.—2. Then, but soon ob. and now †, any infantryman: mostly cavalrymen's. Cf. *beetle-crusher.* Also *gravel-crushing*, n. and adj.—3. Strong and heavy farmers'-boots: Anglo-Irish: C. 20.

gravel-grinder. A drunkard: low: from ca. 1860: ob. H., 3rd ed. Ex:

gravel-rash. Abrasions resulting from a fall: coll.: from ca. 1855. 'Ducange Anglicus.' Perhaps jocular on *barber's rash.*—2. **have the g.-r.,** to be extremely drunk: from ca. 1860; ob. Ex the poor fellow's numerous falls.

gravelled. Very drunk: coll.: C. 20. Lyell. Cf. *gravel, v.*

gravelly. The adj. to *gravel*, n. (q.v.): 1887, Atkins, *House Scraps.* O.E.D.

graves. (Extremely rare in the singular.) Long, dirty finger-nails: lower classes' (— 1923). Manchon. Cf. *mourning.*

Gravesend bus. A hearse: (low) coll.: ca. 1880–1920. Cf. S.E. *journey's end.*

Gravesend sweetmeat. (Gen. in pl.) A shrimp: ca. 1860–1920. H., 3rd ed. Many being sold there.

Gravesend twins. Solid pieces of sewage: low (— 1874); ob. H., 5th ed. Our sewage system !

graveyard. The mouth: from ca. 1875; ob. Contrast *tombstone.*—2. 'A berth made over the counter of a coasting steamer': nautical: from ca. 1880. Bowen.—3. *the graveyard* (or *G.*): 'a portion of the Dutoitspan Diamond Mine . . . because so much money and labour was buried in it by the over-sanguine', Pettman: South African miners': late C. 19.—4. **(the g—.)** The Inscriptions Hall of the British Museum: late C. 19–20. *The Daily Telegraph*, April 17, 1935.

gravitation, for **gravidation,** is incorrect: C. 18. O.E.D.

gravy. The sexual discharge, male or female: low coll.: mid-C. 18–20; ob. Whence *give one's g.,* to 'spend'; *gravy-giver,* penis or pudend: *g.-maker,* pudend only: all, C. 19–20 (ob.) low, the first coll., the others s.

gravy !, by. A Scots exclamation: mid-C. 19–20; ob. Stevenson & Osbourne, *The Wrecker,* 1892. Prob. a corruption.

gravy-eye. A pejorative term of address: C. 19–20 low coll. Ex *gravy-eyed,* blear-eyed, a late C. 18 coll. > C. 19 S.E. The adj. is in Grose, 1st ed.—2. A turn at the wheel, 4–6 a.m.: nautical: ca. 1850–90.—3. The middle watch (12–4 a.m.): nautical: from ca. 1890. Likewise, Bowen.

***grawler.** A beggar: Scottish c.: ca. 1820–60. Egan's Grose. ? *crawler* perverted.

***gray.** A halfpenny (or, in C. 20, a penny) two-headed or two-tailed, esp. as used in 'two-up': c.: from ca. 1810. Vaux.—2. Abbr. *gray-back,* 1, q.v.: from ca. 1855; ob. H., 2nd ed.—3. Silver; hence, money: c. (— 1909). Ware. Ex the colour, *silvery-gray.*

gray as a badger, be; as grannam's (or -um's) cat. To have grey or white hairs from age: coll.: resp. C. 18–20 (ob.), C. 18–19.

gray-back, grayback; grey-. A louse: mid-C. 19–20, ob.: when not dial. it is coll.—and even then, chiefly U.S., though often used by British soldiers in G.W. Cf. *Scots Greys.*—2. (Mainly and orig. U.S.) a Confederate soldier: coll.: 1862, U.S.; 1864, England.—3. A big wave: nautical coll.: late C. 19–20. Bowen.—4. An Army shirt (grey in colour): military: C. 20. F. & Gibbons.

gray-backed un. The same as sense 1 of *gray-back.*

[**gray**(-) or **grey-beard,** whether old man or jug, jar, is, despite F. & H., S.E.]

gray-cloak. An alderman above the chair: C. 16–17 coll. Ex his grey-furred cloak.

gray goose. A big stone loose on the surface: Scots coll.: C. 19–20. Scott.

gray mare. A wife, esp. if dominant: C. 19–20 coll. Ex the proverb.

gray parson; gray-coat(ed) parson. A lay impropriator of tithes: coll.: the first, late C. 18–early 19 (Grose, 1st ed.); the second, C. 19; the third, ca. 1830 (Cobbett)—1910.

grayhound. 'A hammock with so little bedding as to be unfit for stowing in the nettings', Smyth: nautical (— 1867). Ex thinness.—2. Abbr. *Atlantic* or *ocean grayhound,* a fast ocean—esp. Atlantic—liner: from ca. 1887, the first being the S.S. *Alaska,* as W. reminds us; ob.: journalists'.—3. A member of Clare College: Cambridge: ca. 1830–80.

grays. A fit of yawning; listlessness: coll.: from ca. 1860: ob. Cf. *blues.*

graze, send to. To dismiss, turn out: ca. 1730–60. Swift, 1733, 'In your faction's phrase, send the clergy all . . .'

graze on the plain. To be dismissed: coll. (— 1869); ob. Cf. preceding.

grease. A bribe: coll. (— 1823). Bee. Hence *bribery.*—2. Flattery, fawning (cf. *butter*): coll. and dial.: from ca. 1870.—3. Profitable work: printers': from ca. 1850; ob. Ex *fat,* q.v.—4. A 'struggle, contention, or scramble of any kind, short of actual fighting': Westminster School (— 1909). Ware. Perhaps ex the resultant perspiration.—5. Butter: Australians' and New Zealanders' and *Conway* cadets': late C. 19–20. If inferior, *axle-grease.* Perhaps ex Yorkshire *grease,* strong, rancid butter (E.D.D.).

grease, v. To bribe: C. 16–20: coll. till C. 19, then S.E.—2. To cheat, deceive: C. 17 (? 18): coll., mostly low.—3. To flatter: C. 19–20: coll. Ex *grease one's boots,* q.v.—4. V.i., to run fast: Public Schools': C. 20. Desmond Coke, *The House Prefect,* 1908, 'Don't you see the old man greasing back ? He's got our bobby with him !' Cf. *grease off.*

grease, melt one's. To exhaust oneself or itself by violent action: coll.: from ca. 1830: ob. Southey. (O.E.D.)

grease a fat sow in the arse. To (try to) bribe, to give money to, a rich man: coll.: C. 18–mid-19. Heywood; Grose, 1st ed. Cf. the proverb, *every man basteth the fat hog* (sc. *and the lean one gets burnt*).

grease off. To make off; slip away furtively: low: 1899, Clarence Rook. Prob. suggested by *greased lightning.*

grease one's boots. To flatter; fawn upon: late C. 16–mid-19 coll. Florio; Ray, 1813. Cf. *grease,* v., 3. (Apperson.)

grease one's gills. To make a very good meal: C. 19–20 (ob.), low coll. Cf. *greasy chin,* q.v.

Grease-Pot or **Greasepot.** Grispot, a small village near Bois Grenier in the Armentières sector:

military in G.W. Philip Gosse, *Memoirs of a Camp-Follower*, 1934.

grease-spot. The figurative condition to which one is reduced by great heat: coll.: mainly Colonial: from ca. 1890. ? ex the U.S. (1836) sense, adopted in England ca. 1860 (H., 2nd ed., 'a minute remnant') as 'an infinitesimally small quantity' (Thornton), without reference to heat and gen. in negative sentences.

grease the fat pig or sow. A C. 17–20 variant (ob.) of *grease a fat sow* . . .

grease the ways. 'To make preparations in advance to secure influence to get an appointment or the like': naval coll.: from ca. 1880. Bowen. A variation of S.E. *grease the wheels*.

grease to. To make up to; to flatter: Public Schools': late C. 19–20. Desmond Coke, *The School across the Road*, 1910, 'You don't *really* mean you've chucked Warner's just because old Anson greased to you by making you a prefect.' Cf. *greaser*, 5, and *oil up to*, 2.

greased lightning, gen. preceded by *like*. This coll. 'emblem' of high speed is orig. (1833) and mainly U.S.; anglicised ca. 1850. It appears in cricket as early as 1871 (Lewis).

greaser. A Mexican: orig. (ca. 1849) and mainly U.S.; anglicised ca. 1875, though used by Marryat much earlier. Ex the greasy appearance.—2. A ship's engineer: naval: from ca. 1860. Ware.—3. An objectionable or disgusting fellow: lower classes' (— 1923). Manchon: 'Un sale type' is his definition.—4. An apology: Bootham School: from ca. 1880; † by 1925. See anon. *Dict. of Bootham Slang*, 1925. For semantics, cf. *butter* and *soft soap*. Cf. —5. A flatterer, sycophant: Sherborne Schoolboys': late C. 19–20. (Desmond Coke, *Wilson's*, 1911.) Occ. *greazer*. Cf. *grease to* and *greasing*, qq.v.—6. See **greasers**.

greaser, give (one). To rub the back of another's hand with one's knuckles: Winchester College: from ca. 1860 : ob.

greasers. Fried potatoes: Royal Military Academy: ca. 1870–1910. Cf. *boilers*.

greasing. Flattery; ingratiating manners; pretentiousness: Public Schools', esp. Shrewsbury School's: late C. 19–20. Desmond Coke, *The House Prefect*, 1908; his *The School across the Road*, 1910, 'Out in the studies, [the headmaster's] suggestion of the new name, Winton, was labelled variously as "a beastly greasing" and "a nasty oil".' Cf. *grease to* and *greaser*, 5.

greasy. Stormy (weather): nautical coll. (—1887). Baumann.—2. Pomaded: lower classes' coll. (— 1923). Manchon.

greasy chin. A dinner: ca. 1835–80. Ex the mid-C. 18–early 19 sense, 'a treat given to parish officers in part of commutation for a bastard', Grose, 1st ed. Cf. *eating a child*.

great ; great-great. An ancestor or a descendant in the 'great(-great)' degree: coll.: C. 20. O.E.D. (Sup.).

great, adj. Splendid; extremely pleasant; a gen. superlative: orig. (1809), U.S.; anglicised ca. 1895 : coll. Cf. *immense*, q.v.—2. In *run a great dog, filly,* etc., the sense is: the dog, etc., runs splendidly, a great race: sporting: from ca. 1897.

great big. A mere intensive of *big*: coll.: late C. 19–20. Cf. *fine*, q.v.

great Caesar ! An almost meaningless substitute for *great God !* : from ca. 1890. *Tit Bits*, March 19, 1892, 'Great Caesar ! There you go again !' Here

may be noted *great Jehoshaphat !*, in Besant & Rice's *Golden Butterfly* (1876), which contains also the (by 1914) † *great sun !* See also **great Scott !**

great dog or **filly.** See great, adj., 2.

great go, or **Great Go.** The final examination for the B.A. degree: Cambridge (hence, Oxford): from ca. 1820 : s. >, by 1860, coll. and, by 1870, ob.; by 1900, †. Cf. *little go* and *greater, greats*, qq.v., and see also go, n.

great-grandmother. See **Mother**.

great-great. See great, n.

great gun. A person, occ. a thing, of importance: coll.: from ca. 1815. Whyte-Melville, 'The great guns of the party'. Variant *big gun* (cf. *big noise*): from ca. 1865 ; ob.—2. A favourite or gen. successful 'wheeze' or practice: peddlers', mostly London: from ca. 1850. Mayhew, 'The street-seller's great gun, as he called it, was to . . .' Ex the S.E. sense : 'a fire-arm of the larger kind which requires to be mounted for firing', S.O.D.—3. See gun, great.

great guns ! An expletive: 1895; ob. Ex *blow great guns*, q.v.

great guns, blow. See blow.—great house. See big house.

great I am, the. Used jocularly of oneself, pejoratively of others, it connotes excessive self-importance : coll. : from ca. 1905. Ex *I Am*, the Self-Existent, God, as in Exodus iii. 14 (O.E.D.).

great intimate. This sense of *great*—such a phrase is app. independent of *great friend*—is † S.E., but we may quote Grose's (3rd ed.) low coll. equivalent of 'very intimate': *as great as shirt and shitten arse*. For other synonyms, see **thick**.

great joseph. 'A surtout. *Cant*,' says, in 1788, Grose, 2nd ed.; † by 1860. By *surtout* he prob. means overcoat, the gen. definition; and low s. is perhaps the more accurate classification. Ex Joseph's coat of many colours.

great life if you don't weaken, it's a. A G.W. c.p. carried on into civilian life, as, e.g. in G. D. H. & M. Cole, *Burglars in Bucks*, 1930.

great on. Knowing much about; very skilled in: coll.: from ca. 1875. Jefferies, 1878, 'He is very "great" on dogs' (S.O.D.). The S.E. form is *great at*, † *great in*: from late C. 18.—2. Very fond of: C. 20. Ultimately ex preceding, though perhaps imm. ex U.S., where the sense 'famous for' dates from 1844 (Thornton).

great Scott ! An exclamation of surprise ; also a very mild oath : orig. U.S. but soon anglicised, F. Anstey using it in *The Tinted Venus* in 1885 (O.E.D.). ? ex General Winfield Scott, a notoriously fussy candidate for the presidency. Cf. *dickens !, the*.

great shakes, no. See shakes.

***great smoke, the.** London : orig. (— 1874), c. : in C. 20, s. H., 5th ed.

great stuff. Excellent, whatever it may be ; also as n. : coll. : C. 20. E.g. *The Evening News*, Sept. 11, 1934, 'Great stuff, sweeps—that is, when you find one, see one, and speak to one !'

great sun ! See great Caesar !

great unwashed, the. The proletariat : at first (late C. 18), derisively jocular S.E. ; but since Scott popularised it, (non-proletarian) coll.—and rather snobbish.

great whipper-in. Death : coll. (? orig. hunting s.): from ca. 1860 ; slightly ob.

greater. The B.A. finals examination: Oxford (— 1893). Ex *greats*, q.v. An early example of the Oxford *-er*, q.v.; never very gen., and ob. by 1913, † by 1922.

Greater London, belong to. To be a well-known person : Society (— 1909) ; virtually †. Ware.

greats or **Greats.** That Oxford variation of *great go* (q.v.) which was first recorded and presumably popularised by ' Cuthbert Bede ' when, in *Verdant Green*, 1853, he wrote : ' The little gentleman was going in for his Degree, *alias* Great-go, *alias* Greats ' ; used again by T. Hughes in *Tom Brown at Oxford*. Until ca. 1895, s. ; since, coll. and applied (as abbr. *Classical Greats*) esp. to the examination for honours in Literæ Humaniores. Cf. *smalls* (and *little go*).

greazer. See **greaser, 5.**

Grecian. As roisterer, esp. ca. 1818–30, **it** is gen. considered S.E., though prob. it was orig. Society s. (Cf. *Corinthian*.) Ob. by 1840, † by 1860.—2. An Irishman, esp. a newly arrived Irish immigrant : (? low) coll. : from ca. 1850 ; ob. ; a variation of *Greek*, 3. Cf. next entry.—3. A senior boy : Christ's Hospital : from ca. 1820.

Grecian accent. An Irish brogue : coll. : ca. 1850–1930. See **Grecian, 2.**

Grecian bend. A stoop affected in walking by many women ca. 1869–90. *The Daily Telegraph*, Sept. 1, 1869, ' . . . What is called the " Grecian bend " '. The phrase was anticipated by *The Etonian* in 1821 (of a scholarly stoop) and is rarely used after ca. 1885. Cf. *Alexandra limp* and *Roman fall*.—2. H., 1874, defines it as " modern milliner slang for an exaggerated bustle " (dress-improver) : a derivative sense soon †.

*greed. Money : c. of ca. 1850–1900. ' Ducange Anglicus.'

greedy-gut or **-guts.** A glutton : (from ca. 1840, low) coll. : the former, mid-C. 16–early 18 ; the latter, C. 18–20. Florio ; Grose, 2nd ed. Cf. the old schoolboys' rhyme (ob. by 1900 ; ? † by 1920), ' Guy-hi, greedy-gut, | Eat all the pudding up,' the † singular being retained for the rhyme.

greedy scene. One in which a ' star ' has the stage to him- or herself : theatrical (— 1909). Ware.

Greek. A comparatively rare abbr. of *St. Giles Greek*, cant ; cf. the C. 17–20 *it is Greek to me*, half-way between S.E. and coll. Prob. orig. s., but soon merely allusive and therefore S.E. : C. 17–early 19. —2. As a card-sharper, a cheat, it is C. 16–19 S.E., as also is the C. 17 *merry Greek*, a roisterer.—3. An Irishman (' the low Irish ', H., 1859) : Anglo-Irish s. or coll., from ca. 1820 ; ob. ; Bee. Also in Australian s. before 1872.—4. A gambler ; a high-wayman : c. : early C. 19.—5. V., only as implied in *Greeking*, q.v.

*Greek fire. Bad whiskey : c. (— 1889) ; ob. Ex the S.E. sense. Cf. *rot-gut*.

[**Greek Kalends, at the.** Never. Despite F. & H., it has always been S.E. ; for coll. synonyms, see **blue moon, pigs fly, Queen Dick.**]

Greeking, vbl.n. and gerund. Cheating at cards : ca. 1816–40. *The Sporting Magazine*, 1817, ' A discovery of Greeking at Brighton, has made considerable noise . . . in the sporting world ' (O.E.D.). Displaced by S.E. *Greekery*.

green. Stage : theatrical (— 1935). Abbr. *greengage*, the same, prob. with allusion to the green cloth.

green, v. To make to appear simple ; to hoax : from ca. 1884 (Eton has the (— 1893) variant *green up*) ; slightly ob. T. C. Buckland in 1888, ' Green . . . as boys call it '. I.e. to treat as a green hand.

—2. To swindle, take in : (low) coll. or s. : 1884 (S.O.D.).

green, adj. Inexperienced, is—despite F. & H.—S.E.—2. (Gen. *be green*.) Cautious : railwaymen's : C. 20. Ware, ' Green through the railway world being the colour signal for caution '.

Green, send to Doctor or **Dr.** To put (a horse) to grass : late C. 18–19. Grose, 2nd ed. A punning coll.

*Green, sleep with Mrs. See **sleep with Mrs Green.**

green apron. A lay preacher : C. 18 : coll. In mid-C. 17–18, also an adj., as in Warren's *Unbelievers*, 1654, ' A green-apron preacher '. Ex the sign of office.

green as duckweed(, as). Extremely simple or foolish : low coll. (— 1887). Baumann.

green as I'm (or **you are,** etc.) **cabbage-looking, (I'm,** etc.) **not so.** (I'm, etc.) not such a fool as I (etc.) appear to be : lower- and lower-middle-class c.p. : late C. 19–20. (Ernest Raymond, *Mary Leith*, 1931.)

green-back. A frog : late C. 19–20 ; slightly ob. —2. A Todhunter text-book in mathematics : universities' : ca. 1870–1905. Ex colour of binding ; cf. *yellow-back*. Dr. Todhunter (d. 1884) published his famous text-books in 1858–69.

green-bag. A lawyer : late C. 17–early 19. B.E. Ex (the †) colour of brief-bag. Grose, 1st ed., is amusing on the subject. Cf. *black box*, q.v. ; and :

green bag ?, what's in the. ' What is the charge to be preferred against me ? ', Barrère & Leland : from ca. 1890 ; ob. Cf. preceding entry.

green bonnet, have or **wear a.** To go bankrupt : coll. : ca. 1800–1910. Ex the green cap formerly worn by bankrupts.

green cheese. See **cheese.**

green cloth. Abbr. *board of green cloth*, a billiard table : from ca. 1890 : coll.—2. Coll., too, is the sense, the green baize covering the table : from ca. 1870.

Green Dragoons. The 13th Hussars : military coll. : ca. 1860–1914. Ex their green facings when they were dragoons. F. & Gibbons.

green-envelope wallah. A soldier that sold green envelopes, which were not opened by one's own officers and were censored only at the Base : military coll. : 1915–18. F. & Gibbons.

green eye. A green marble : children's (— 1923). Manchon. ? ex (a) *greeny* (one).

[**green goods.** Counterfeit ' greenbacks ', the paper issue of the U.S. Treasury. Hence *green-goods man* or *operator*. Both orig. (— 1888) U.S. : heard occ. in the British Empire.]

green goose. A harlot : late C. 16–17 coll. Beaumont & Fletcher, ' His palace is full of green geese.' Cf. *idea in fresh bit*.

green gown, give a, either absolute or with dative. To tumble a woman on the grass : late C. 16–18 : coll. > S.E.—2. Hence, to have sexual sport, esp. (somewhat euphemistically) deflower a girl. C. 17–early 19 coll. ' Highwaymen ' Smith, 1719, ' Our gallant being disposed to give his lady a green gown '.

green-grocery. The female pudend : low : from ca. 1850 ; ob. ? ex *garden*.

green grove. The pubic hair (gen. female) : low : ca. 1850–1910.

green-hand(1)ed rake. See **Peter Collins.**

Green Horse, the. The 5th Dragoon Guards : military coll. : late C. 18–20 ; ob. F. & Gibbons. Ex their green facings.

Green Howards. The 19th Foot Regiment : military : mid-C. 18–20 : coll. until late C. 19, then the official name. F. & Gibbons. Ex the name of its 1738–48 colonel (the Hon. Charles Howard) and its green facings ; partly to distinguish it from the 3rd Foot, also at one time commanded by a Colonel Howard. Sometimes (not, I think, in C. 20) called *Howard's Garbage*.

green (in late C. 19–20, occ. **green stuff**) **in my eye ?, do you see any.** The most gen. form of *to see (any) green in a person's eye*, to consider him a greenhorn or a fool : 1840 : coll., mostly low. ' Quotations ' Benham ; Mayhew ; *Ally Sloper*, March 19, 1892 ' Ally Sloper, the cove with no green in his eye '. Ex *green* as indicative of inexperience or, esp., gullibility.

green jacket ; Green Jackets, the. (A member of) the Rifle Brigade : military coll. : from ca. 1820 ; ob. (O.E.D. Sup.) Ex the dark green of their superseded uniform.

*****green kingsman.** A pocket-handkerchief—gen. of silk—with a green ground : c. and pugilistic : ca. 1835–1910. Brandon. Cf. *belcher*.

Green Linnets. The 39th Foot, from ca. 1881 the 1st Battalion of the Dorsetshire Regiment : military coll. : mid-C. 19–20. Ex the colour of their facings. (F. & Gibbons.)

Green Marines. The old 45th Foot Regiment : military : C. 19.

green meadow. The female pudend : low : more coll. than euphemistic : from ca. 1850. Cf. *green grove* and see remarks at *grant the favour*.

green rag. The curtain : theatrical : from ca. 1840 ; † by 1900.

green-room, talk. To gossip about the theatre : 1839, Lever in *Harry Lorrequer* : coll. until ca. 1880, then S.E. (O.E.D.)

green sickness, despite F. & H., is ineligible. See **greens, 1.**

green stuff. See **green in my eye.**

Green Tigers, the. A C. 19 variant of *the Tigers*, q.v. (F. & Gibbons.)

green up. The gen. Etonian variation of *green*, v., 1.

greenacre. ' The falling of a set of goods out of the sling ' : dockers' : mid-C. 19–20. O.E.D. (Sup.). Perhaps ex Greenacre, a murderer (who buried the victim in sections in various parts of London) hanged at Newgate in 1837 : the rope broke.

greener. A new hand ; esp. one replacing a striker ; also a foreign workman newly arrived : ca. 1888–1910 (O.E.D. ; Manchon).

greenery-yallery. Characteristic of the Æsthetic movement in the art and literature of the 1880's. Coined in 1880 by W. S. Gilbert in *Patience*, which was first performed on April 23, 1881. Orig. s., it > coll. by 1890 and had, by 1910 > S.E. (as, e.g., it is in Hugh Walpole's *Vanessa*). This colour-scheme was a favourite with the Æsthetes.

greenfinch. ' One of the Pope's Irish guard ' : 1865, *The Daily Telegraph*, Nov. 1,—but prob. from a decade earlier. O.E.D.

greengage. See **green, n.** (In actors' rhyming s., from ca. 1880 : stage (n.). *The Evening Standard*, Aug. 19, 1931.)

greengages. Wages : rhyming s. : from ca. 1870. P. P., *Rhyming Slang*, 1932.

greenhead. A new hand, esp. if inexperienced : late C. 16–early 19 : coll. until ca. 1820 (see B.E. and Grose), then S.E.

greenhorn. A new hand ; also, a simpleton : from ca. 1680, but presumably several centuries older (see W.'s *Surnames* at *Greenhorn*). Coll. until C. 20, when S.E. In mid-C. 18–early 19, esp. ' an undebauched young fellow, just initiated into the society of bucks and bloods ', Grose, 1785 ; O.E.D. Ex a young horned animal. Cf. *greenhead*.

greenhouse. An omnibus : London bus-drivers' : ca. 1890–1914. Ex the large amount of glass in the windows.

greenie, greeny. The white-plumed honey-eater (*ptilotis penicillata*) : Australian schoolboys' coll. (— 1896). Morris.

greening for, have a. To be ' mad ' about (a person) : low (— 1923). Manchon. Ex *greens*, 4, or imm. ex dial. *greening*, a craving.

Greenland, come from. To be inexperienced : from 1838, Dickens ; ob. : a punning coll.

Greenlander. A new hand ; a simpleton : from ca. 1840 : ob. Ex preceding.—2. Occ. (— 1874), an Irishman ; ob. H., 5th ed.

[**greenly,** like **greenness,** is, despite F. & H., ineligible.]

greenman. A contractor speculating with money not his own : builders' : ca. 1875–1910.

*****greenmans.** The country : green fields : c. : C. 17–early 19. Cf. *daisyville* ; *-mans*.

greens. Chlorosis : coll. : C. 18–early 19. D'Urfey, ' The maiden . . . that's vexed with her greens '. Ex *green sickness*.—2. Inferior or worn-out rollers : printers' : from ca. 1870 : ob.—3. Green vegetables, e.g. and esp. cabbage and salads : coll. : 1725 (S.O.D.).—4. Sexual sport, esp. coïtion : low coll. : from ca. 1850. ? ex *garden*. Cf. the next six entries : all low s. that, except *fresh greens*, have > (low) coll. and all dating from ca. 1850.

greens, after one's, adj. (Of men) seeking coïtion : cf. *greens, on for one's* and see **greens,** last sense.

greens, fresh. A new harlot. Cf. *bit*, and see **greens,** last sense.

greens, get or **have** or **like one's ; give one's.** To obtain or enjoy the sexual favour ; to grant it. (Of either sex.) See **greens,** last sense, and :

greens, on for one's. (Gen. of women) eagerly amorous. Cf. *greens, after one's* ; see **greens,** last sense. Also, (of men) *go for one's greens*, to seek sexual intercourse.

greens, price of. The cost of a harlot's sexual embrace. See **greens,** last sense.

greens (or **taturs**) **!, s'elp me (my).** A low oath, orig. obscene—though this was rarely realised : mid-C. 19–20 ; ob. Mayhew, *London Labour*, iii, 144. See **greens,** last sense.

Greenwich, get. To become a ' Greenwich goose ', q.v. : nautical coll. : late C. 18–20.

Greenwich barber. A retailer of sand from at and near Greenwich in Kent : mid-C. 18–early 19. Ex ' their constant shaving the sand banks ', Grose, 1st ed.

Greenwich goose. A pensioner of Greenwich Hospital : naval and military : mid-C. 18–19. Grose, 1st ed. ; H., 3rd–5th edd.

greeny. The curtain : theatrical : ca. 1820–95. Egan.—2. A freshman : university coll. : ca. 1830–1900. Southey in *The Doctor*.—3. A simpleton : from ca. 1850 : mainly U.S.—4. See **greenie.**

greetin' fu'. Drunk : coll. : C. 19–20. The Scottish properly = crying-drunk, a sense here ineligible.

greeze. A crowd ; a gang : Westminster School : C. 19–20. Perhaps a perversion of *squeeze*.

grego. A rough greatcoat: mostly nautical: ca. 1820–80. Westmacott (O.E.D.); Marryat; Bowen, 'Borrowed from the Levant'.

gregorian, Gregorian. A kind of wig: late C. 16–20: a coll. that by 1690 was S.E.; now historical. Ex one Gregory, the Strand barber that 'invented' it, acc. to Blount, 1670.

Gregorian tree. The gallows: mid-C. 17–early 19: s. >, by 1750, coll. Ex 'a sequence of three hangmen of that name', *Gregory*, says F. & H.; prob. ex Gregory Brandon, a hangman, fl. *temp.* James I; successor, his son, Richard, gen. called 'Young Gregory'. In mid-C. 17, *Gregory* occ. = a hangman. (O.E.D.)

[**gregorine.** A louse, esp. in the head: C. 19: ex It.: thus F. & H. But the spelling is *gregarine*, ex L. *gregarius*, and the term is scientific for a parasitic protozoan.]

gregory. Abbr. *Gregory-powder*: 1897 (O.E.D.). Ex Dr. James Gregory (d. 1822).

Grenadiers. The Grenadier Guards: coll. from ca. 1835.

Greshamite. A fellow of the Royal Society: late C. 17–18: coll. soon > S.E. B.E. Cf. *Wiseacres' Hall*, q.v.

grey: see **gray** at all entries.—**greycing.** See gracing.

grey mare. One's or the fare: rhyming s.: C. 20. P. P., *Rhyming Slang*, 1932.

greyers. Grey flannel trousers and other-coloured coat: mostly undergraduates': from ca. 1925.

Greys, the. The Scots Greys: mid-C. 18–20: coll. till late C. 19, then familiar S.E. Orig. they were mounted on grey horses and in 1781 they began to be uniformed in grey. F. & Gibbons.

gribble. Socks, gloves, mufflers, chocolate, etc.: Northamptonshire soldiers' coll.: 1915–18. F. & Gibbons. Ex Mr. Gribble, a Northampton citizen, who maintained a fund for that purpose.

*****grick.** See grig, 1.

grid. A bicycle: 1924, D. H. Lawrence. O.E.D. (Sup.). Ex *grid*, a grid-iron.—2. Hence (?), the steam train that takes boys to and from school is known as *the grid* at: Hampton Grammar School: from ca. 1926.

griddle. To sing in the streets (whence vbl.n. *griddling*): low or c. (— 1851). Mayhew, 'Got a month for griddling in the main drag.' ? ex *grizzle* or perhaps ex Romany *ghiv*, to sing.

griddler. A street-singer, esp. without printed words or music: low or c.: from ca. 1855. Ex *griddle*. 'Seven Dials', says H., 1864, alluding to the former criminal centre of London (now part of W.C.1).

gridiron. A county court summons (— 1859): ob. Sala, 'He . . . takes out the abhorred grid-irons.' Ex, and orig., those of the Westminster Court, for its arms resemble a gridiron.—2. (the g-) 'The Honourable East India Company's striped ensign': nautical coll.: C. 19. Bowen.—3. The Grid(iron) is (— 1874) the Grafton Club, which had a notable grill.

gridiron, on the. (Either absolute, C. 19–20, or with defining circumstances, C. 16–18.) Harassed; in a bad way: coll.: late C. 16–20; ob.

gridiron and dough boys. The U.S. flag: nautical: ca. 1860–1910. H., 3rd ed.

gridiron grumbles at the frying-pan, the. 'The pot calls the kettle black': coll.: C. 19.

gridironing. The practice of taking a gridiron-shaped piece of land, knowing that nobody else would buy the intermediate strips, which one could acquire at leisure: Canterbury Province, New Zealand: ca. 1850–80: coll. Morris.

*****gridirons.** The bars on a prison-cell window: c.: from ca. 1870.

grief. Trouble: coll. (— 1891); ob. *The Sportsman*, Feb. 28, 1891, 'The flag had scarcely fallen than [*sic*] the grief commenced.' Ex *come to grief*.—2. See 'Moving-Picture Slang', § 6.

grief, bring to. To involve in great trouble; cause to fail: from ca. 1870: coll.

grief, come to. To get into serious trouble; fail: coll. (— 1857).—2. To fall from a horse or a carriage: coll. (— 1855), mainly sporting. Thackeray in *The Newcomes*, 'We drove on to the downs, and we were nearly coming to grief.'

griff. Abbr. *griffin*, 2, q.v.: 1829 (O.E.D.). Also of *griffin*, 3, 8.

griff, v. To deceive, take in (a person): Anglo-Indian, from ca. 1830; ob. Ex the n.

griffin. A greenhorn: from the 1850's. Ex next sense.—2. A new arrival from Europe: Anglo-Indian: 1793. Perhaps ex the unfortunate Admiral Griffin commanding in the Indian seas in 1746–8. See Yule & Burnell, who quote, for 1794, from Hugh Boyd, 'Griffin [capital letter], . . . the fashionable phrase here' (Madras).—3. A young subaltern: military: from ca. 1865.—4. An unbroken horse: Anglo-Chinese: from ca. 1875. Occ., esp. in senses 2 and 3, abbr. to *griff*, as, for the former in 1829, and for the latter in Besant & Rice's *By Celia's Arbour*, 1878.—5. A woman forbidding in appearance or manners: coll.: 1824: very ob. Cf. *gorgon* in S.E.—6. Hence, a chaperon; a caretaker: coll.: ca. 1830–1900.—7. An umbrella: fast male society, ca. 1859–70. H., 1860.—8. In c. (— 1888), a signal or warning: in G.W. +, s., esp. in *give* (ex *tip*) *the griffin*, v.i., or t. with dative, to give a warning, and in *the straight griffin*, the straight tip: in C. 20, (low) s. Occ. *griff*, as in Nat Gould's *Double Event*, 1891; rare in C. 20.—9. 'A grinning booby, who hath lost a tooth or two at top, and the same at bottom': app. ca. 1720–1850. 'Jon Bee.' —10. The derivatives *griffinage*, *griffinism*, are †: these refer mostly to senses 1–3.

griffins. The leavings from a contract feast: trade (— 1893); ob.

griffish, adj., of or like a newcomer to India, hence of any greenhorn: Anglo-Indian > gen.: 1836; ob. Ex *griff*, n. Yule & Burnell.

griffmetoll, griff-metoll. A sixpence: c.: ca. 1750–1800. ? ex *metal* + a device on the coin.

*****grig**; in early C. 19, occ. **grick** (Bee). A farthing: c. of ca. 1690–1860. B.E., Ainsworth. Cf. *gigg*.—2. In pl., cash: mid-C. 17–early 19.

grig, merry as a. Very active and lively: C. 18–20 (ob.) coll. Goldsmith, 'I grew as merry as a grig.' An extension of *a merry grig*, a jocose and lively person: C. 16–18 coll. > S.E. ca. 1820, when also it > archaic. Cotgrave, Wycherley, Grose. Ex the cricket or possibly the young eel.

grigs. See grig, 2.

grillatalpa. Incorrect for *gryllotalpa*: C. 18. O.E.D.

grim. Unpleasant: a C. 20 (rare before 1918) middle and upper class coll. intensive. Evelyn Waugh, *Decline and Fall*, 1928, 'Marriage is rather a grim thought'; Agatha Christie, *Why Didn't They Ask Evans?*, 1934, ' "I know," said Bobby.

"Absolutely grim."' Cf. *awful* and *ghastly*, and contrast *nice*.

*grim. To swindle: c.: late C. 16–early 17. Greene, 1591, 'The Cheater, when he has no cosin to grime with his stop dice.' ? cognate with Fr. *grimer*.

Grim, Mr. See old Mr. Grim.

griminess. Obscenity, eroticism in literature: literary coll.: 1895, *The Daily News*, Jan. 19; ob. Ware.

grin, on the (e.g. broad), adj. Grinning, e.g. broadly: coll.: from ca. 1800. In C. 18, *on the high grin*, as in Swift.

grin, stand the. To be ridiculed and laughed at: ca. 1820–50. Egan's Grose.

grin at the daisy-roots. To be dead and buried: Anglo-Indian (esp. Calcutta): from ca. 1880; ob. Ware. Cf. the (possibly derivative) military *push up daisies*, q.v.

grin in a glass case. 'To be shown as an anatomical preparation', F. & H.: coll.: mid-C. 18–mid-19. Grose, 1st ed. Ex the bodies and skeletons of criminals, formerly glass-cased at Surgeons' Hall.

grin like a Cheshire cat. See **cat, grin like a Cheshire**.

grinagog, the cat's uncle. A 'Cheshiring' simpleton; one who grins without reason: mid-C. 18–early 19. Grose, 1st ed. Punning *grin*. Cf. *girnigo gaby*, q.v.

grincomes, grincums. Syphilis: a C. 17 variant of *crinkums*, q.v. Jones, in *Adrasta*, 1635, 'In [a nobleman] the serpigo, in a knight the grincomes, in a gentleman the Neapolitan scabb, and in a serving man or artificer the plaine pox'.

grind. Hard work; routine: coll.: from ca. 1850. —2. Study, esp. for an examination: schools' (— 1856). T. Hughes.—3. A plodding student: schools': ca. 1870–1900, now only U.S. Cf. *grinder*, 2.—4. A walk, esp. a 'constitutional': university (— 1860).—5. A steeplechase: university (mainly Oxford): 1857, 'Cuthbert Bede'.—6. A training run; an athletic sports meeting: from ca. 1870: Oxford University. *Chambers's Journal*, April, 1872, 'The hero of a hundred grinds'.—7. The sexual act: late C. 16–20: low coll. Florio; D. H. Lawrence (*Love in a Haystack*). Esp. in *do a grind* (rarely of a woman), to coït: C. 19–20.—8. Grind, the. The ferry-boat at Chesterton: Cambridge University: late C. 19–early 20. Barrère & Leland.—9. A tutorial class of medical students: medical (— 1933). *Slang*, p. 192.

grind, v. To study (hard); read a text; prepare for examination: all with *with a 'coach'* understood and all v.i. (v.t. with *at*): school and university: from ca. 1835.—2. To work at a hard or a distasteful task, or at the daily routine: v.i., variants with *on* and *away*; v.t. with *at* or *through*: coll.: from ca. 1855.—3. V.t., to teach (a subject) in a plodding way, cf. *gerund-grinder*; to coach (a student): university: 1815 (S.O.D.): ob.—4. To ride in a steeplechase: 1857, G. A. Lawrence, in *Guy Livingstone* (O.E.D.); slightly ob.—5. V.i., to have sexual intercourse: low coll. (— 1811). *Lex. Bal.* Less gen. than *do a grind*.—6. To exhaust; be (like) hard work for: coll.: 1887; ob. Talbot Baines Reed (O.E.D.).

grind, do a. See **grind, n.**, 7, and **v.**, 5.

grind, on the. (Of either sex) being, at the time, incontinent; gaining a living as a prostitute: low: C. 19–20.

grind mustard with one's knees. To be knock-kneed: C. 18–early 19. See **Durham man**.

grind-off. See **grindo**.—grind the coffee-mill. See **coffee-mill**.

grind water for the captain's ducks. On a sailing-ship, to take the wheel at 6–8 a.m.: nautical: mid-C. 19–20; ob. Bowen.

*grind wind. To work the treadmill: c. of ca. 1880–1910.

grinder. A private tutor; a coach: university > gen.: 1813, Maria Edgeworth, 'Put him into the hands of a clever grinder or crammer.' Ob. by 1900, † by 1921.—2. A plodding student: schools': ca. 1870–1900.

grinder, take a. 'To apply the left thumb to the nose, and revolve the right hand round it, as if to work a . . . coffee-mill', F. & H. A Cockney retort to an attempt on his credulity or good faith. Cf. *take a sight* and *work the coffee-mill*. The term was ob. in 1900, † in 1919; already in *Pickwick* we hear that this 'very graceful piece of pantomime' is 'unhappily, almost obsolete'. A variation, presumably, upon 'cocking a snook'.

grinders. Teeth: coll.: C. 17–20. Ex S.E. sense (molars), as in Horace Walpole's 'A set of gnashing teeth, the grinders very entire'.

grindery. Shoemaking-material: shoemakers' (— 1887). Baumann.

grinding. Vbl.n. of *to grind*, q.v. at all senses.

grinding-house. A house of correction: C. 17–18 coll.—2. A brothel: C. 19–20 (ob.) low.

grinding-mill. A tutor's house where students are prepared for examination: university: ca. 1860–1900. Ex a coffee-mill.

grinding-tool. The male member: low: C. 19–20; ob.

grindo or grind-off. A miller: ca. 1862–1910. Ex a character in the play, *The Miller and his Men*.

grindstone. The female pudend: low: mid-C. 19–20. Ex *grind*, n., sense 7.—2. A private tutor; a coach: university: ca. 1850–1900. Ex *grind*, v., 3.

grindstone, hold or keep one's nose to the. To treat harshly: coll.: *hold* in C. 17–18; *keep* in C. 19–20. Variants in C. 19, *bring* or *put*. Ex C. 16–17 S.E. sense, to torture.—2. In C. 19–20, to study hard or toil unremittingly; to cause another to do so.

grindstone on his back, have the. To (go to) fetch the monthly nurse for one's wife's confinement: C. 18–19.

grinkcome, grinkum. See **grincomes**.

Grinning Dears, the. The Grenadiers: other infantry battalions' (— 1909); slightly ob. Ware.

grinning stitches. Careless sewing: milliners': from ca. 1870; ob. Because the stitches are wide apart.

grip. Abbr. *gripsack*, a traveller's handbag: orig. U.S., both are in C. 20 occ. used in the British Empire as coll.—2. ? hence, occupation, employment: Australian: C. 20. C. J. Dennis.—3. A place, e.g. a town: non-aristocratic: late C. 19–20.

grip, v.i. To seize sheep (for a shearer): Australian s. (1886) >, by 1910, coll. O.E.D.—2. To catch, seize, take; Public Schools' coll.: late C. 19–20.—3. Hence, to steal: Public Schools', esp. Charterhouse, s.: C. 20.

gripe or gripes. A miser; a usurer; occ. a banker: coll.: C. 17–18. Burton, 1621 (O.E.D.). —2. (gripe.) In late C. 16–17 c., a cheating gamester. Greene.

gripe-fist, -money, -penny. A miser or a usurer: coll., resp. C. 19, C. 17, C. 19. Cf. *gripe-all*, a grasping, mean person, C. 19 : ? S.E.

*****griper.** A collier bringing coal in barges to London : c. : late C. 16–early 17. Greene, 1591. Cf. *gripe*, 2, q.v.

gripes. Colic. When, in late C. 19–20, it is used of persons, it is coll.—either low or jocular (Earlier, S.E. ; as still of animals.)—2. See **gripe**.

gripes in a tangle. See **tip a daddle.**

gripper. He who catches sheep for the shearers : 1886 : ob. Ex *grip*, v., 1. (O.E.D.)—2. A miser : coll. (— 1887) ; ob. Baumann.

gripping. Mean ; miserly : Glasgow (— 1934). Cf. *gripe*.

grist. The *grist* metaphors are, despite F. & H., ineligible.—2. Sol. for *gist* : noted by Manchon in 1923.

gristle. The male member : low : from ca. 1850.

grit. Spirit ; stamina ; courage, esp. if enduring : orig. (1825, as *clear grit*), U.S. ; anglicised as a coll. ca. 1860. Thackeray. (*Clear grit* was, in U.S., not a mere synonym but an intensive.) Ex its hardness. Cf. U.S. *sand*.—2. A member of the Liberal or Radical Party : Canada : 1887 ; ca. 1884–7, a *Clear Grit*. The adj. *gritty* (U.S., 1847) has never caught on in England.

grizzle. One who frets : coll. : 1703, E. Ward (Matthews). Cf. :

grizzle, v. To fret ; complain whiningly or lachrymosely : coll. : 1842, ballad (O.E.D.). The low coll. form is *grizzle one's guts*.—2. To sing, esp. in the streets for a living : c. (— 1926). F. Jennings, *In London's Shadows*. Perhaps by pun ex *griddle*.

grizzle-guts, occ. **-pot.** A tearfully or whiningly ill-tempered or melancholy person : low coll. : from ca. 1875. Cf. *sulkington*.

grizzler. A grumbler ; a person given to fretting : dial. (— 1900) and coll. (C. 20). Ex *grizzle*, v., 1.—2. A street singer : c. : from before 1926. See **grizzle,** v., 2.

*****grizzling ; street grizzling.** Vbl.n. of *grizzle*, v., 2.

*****groaner.** A thief specialising in funerals and revivalist meetings : c. : ca. 1840–1900. Duncombe, *The Sinks of London*, 1848. Ex :

*****groaner and sigher.** A wretch 'hired by methodists and others to attend their meetings for the purposes of fraud', Potter, 1795. Cf. *groaner*.

groat, a cracked or **slit,** gen. in negative. Something worthless ; nothing : coll. : C. 17. Dekker, 'Peace, you cracked groats' ; Penn, 'The People . . . that would not trust an Archbishop about a Slit Groat' (O.E.D.).

groats. The chaplain's monthly stipend : nautical : ca. 1850–1914.

groats, save one's. To come off handsomely : university : mid-C. 18–early 19. Ex the nine groats deposited by every degree-candidate, who, with honours, recovers them. Grose, 1st ed.

groceries sundries. 'Wine and spirits sold furtively on credit to women' : grocers' (— 1909). Ware. Because so 'itemed'.

groceries, the. See **grocery,** 2.

Grocer's Express, the. A G.W.R. train running four times a week from London to Aberdeen with margarine, tea, coffee, cocoa : railwaymen's : C. 20.

*****grocery.** Small change in copper ; copper coins collectively : C. 18–early 19 : s. or, more prob., c. Bailey.—2. (With *the*, occ. in the pl.) sugar : ca.

1838–1910. Lytton, 1841, 'A pint of brandy . . . Hot water and lots of the grocery'. According to the E.D.D., however, *the groceries* is Anglo-Irish for a decanter of whisky and a bowl of sugar : Anglo-Irish : 1839, Lever.

grog. Rum diluted : 1770 .— 2. Spirits and water : from ca. 1790.—3. Strong drink in gen. : from ca. 1820. Orig. **s.,** all these senses were coll. by 1840, S.E. by 1870. ? ex *grogram*, whence *Old Grog*, the nickname of Admiral Vernon, who, in the summer of 1740, ordered the Navy's rum to be diluted and who wore a grogram cloak.—4. A party at which grog is drunk : coll. : 1888 : ob. (O.E.D.). —5. A 'groggy' (q.v.) horse : 1818, *The Sporting Magazine*, vol. ii (O.E.D.) : ob. by 1900, † by 1920.

grog, v. To drink grog : 1833 (S.O.D.) : s. >, ca. 1850, coll.

Grog, Old. See **Old Grog** and **grog, n.,** 3.

grog, seven-water. Extremely weak grog : nautical : from ca. 1830. Marryat.

grog-blossom. A pimple caused by strong drink : low (— 1791) : ob. Grose, 3rd ed. ; Thomas Hardy, 'A few grog-blossoms marked the neighbourhood of his nose.'

grog-fight. A drinking party : military (— 1864): ob. H., 3rd ed.

grog on board, have. To be drunk : C. 19–20 (ob.) nautical. Egan's Grose.

grog-shop. The mouth : pugilistic : from ca. 1840 ; ob. Thackeray.

grog-tub. A brandy bottle : nautical : ca. 1860–1914.

grogged, be. To be tipsy : ca. 1840–1900 : coll. Cf. Grose, 1796, 'A grogged horse ; a foundered horse'. Ex *grog*, v. : q.v.

groggified. A late C. 18–19 variant (Grose, 2nd ed.), latterly nautical, of the first sense of :

groggy. Tipsy : 1770 : ob. Grose, 1st ed. Ex *grog*, n., 1, 2.—2. Whence, (of horses) tender-footed : stables s. > j. : 1828. Youatt, 1831, in *The Horse* : ob.—3. Whence, unsteady on one's feet : pugilistic and gen. : from ca. 1830. Thackeray. (For these three senses, O.E.D.)—4. In poor health : C. 20. Cf. Australian *crook*.

*****grogham.** A horse, esp. if old : c. in late C. 18–19, then low ; ob. Grose, 1st ed. Origin ? Cf. *prad*.

*****groin.** A (race-course) betting ring : c. : C. 20. Esp. among pickpockets and race-course thieves, who frequently refer to the betting rings as *the bob* (shilling) *groin* and *the dollar* (five-shilling) *groin*. David Hume. Perhaps suggested, anatomically, by *joint*, 5.

*****groiny.** A ring ; a diamond—or other precious stone—when in a ring : c., and grafters' s. : C. 20. Margery Allingham, *Look to the Lady*, 1931. A diminutive of the preceding.

gromal. An apprentice : nautical coll. : mid-C. 18–19. Bowen. A corruption of dial. *gom(m)eral(l)*, *-el(l)*, *-il(l)*, a simpleton (E.D.D.).

grooly. Sinister : from ca. 1920 ; now almost coll. Ronald Knox, *Still Dead*, 1934, 'Dashed cowardly of me, but . . . It's just the tiniest bit grooly, isn't it ?' A blend of *gruesome* + *grisly*.

groom. A croupier : gamblers' c. > s. : late C. 19–20. Baumann.

groovy. Of settled habits or rutty mind : coll. : only from ca. 1880, although *grooviness*, likewise coll., is recorded by the O.E.D. as early as 1867.

[**grope**, to feel a woman, and **grotto**, the pudend, are, despite F. & H., S.E.]

*groper. A blind man : **c. :** mid-C. 17–mid-19. Coles, 1676.—2. (Gen. in pl.) a pocket : c. or low : late C. 18–early 19. G. Parker.—3. A midwife : low (? orig. c.) : C. 18–mid-19. E. Ward ; Grose, 1st ed.—4. The blindfolded person in blind-man's-buff : ca. 1810–1914. (O.E.D.)—5. **(Groper.)** A West Australian : Australian (— 1926). Jice Doone. I.e. a ' sand-groper '.

groperess. A blind woman : low : ca. 1820–60. ' Jon Bee '. Ex *groper*, 1.

Groperland ; occ., sol., **Gropherland.** Western Australia : from ca. 1925. See **groper**, 5.

groping for Jesus. Public prayer : lower classes' : 1882. Ware. Ex Salvationists' cry, *grope for Jesus—grope for Jesus !*

gropus. ' The coat-pocket—from the manner of groping for its lesser contents ', says ' Jon Bee ', 1823 : ca. 1820–50.

grot. A mess(-room) : naval : C. 20. Bowen. I.e. a grotto.

grottae. An incorrect pl. of *grotto* : **C. 17.** O.E.D.

grouce. See **grouse**, n. and v.

ground, be put on the. To be made an insurance inspector : insurance s. : C. 20. (Michael Harrison, *Spring in Tartarus*, 1935. He spends much time visiting prospective clients.

ground, go down to the. To defecate : C. 17 coll. Middleton in his *Family of Love*, ' Do you go well **to** ground ? ' Cf. C. 19 medical j., *get to the ground*.

ground, suit down to the. To be thoroughly acceptable or becoming : coll. : from ca. 1875. Miss Braddon, ' Some sea coast city . . . would suit me down to the ground.' But *down to the ground* is occ. used with other vv. Cf. the M.E. *all to ground* (W.).

ground floor. (Always **the g. f.**) The inside of a bus, i.e. the lower deck : busmen's : from ca. 1931. *The Daily Herald*, Aug. 5, 1936.

ground floor, let in on the. (Of the promoters) to allow to share in a financial or commercial speculation on equal terms : orig. U.S. ; anglicised ca. 1900 : mainly Stock Exchange and commerce. From the opp. angle, *get*, or *be let, in on the g.-f.*

ground-parrot. A small farmer : Australian (— 1898) ; ob. Suggested by *cockatoo*, n., 1, and ex the *ground-parrot* or *psittacus pulchellus*. Morris.

ground-squirrel. A hog, a pig : nautical : ca. 1790–1860. Grose, 3rd ed.

ground stunt. An aeroplane attack at a low altitude : Air Force coll. : 1915 ; ob. F. & Gibbons.

ground-sweat. A grave : c. or low : late C. 17–mid-19. B.E. Esp. in *have*, or *take, a ground-sweat*, to be buried. Cf. dial. *take a g.-s. about anything*, to worry oneself greatly, and the C. 19 dial. proverb, ' a ground-sweat cures all disorders.' (E.D.D. ; Apperson.)

ground wallah. Any R.A.F. member working only on the ground : Air Force coll. : 1915. F. & Gibbons.

ground (or floor) with one, mop (or wipe) up the. To thrash soundly ; fig., to prove oneself vastly superior to : coll. : from ca. 1880. Henley & Stevenson, 1887, ' I'll mop the floor up with him any day.'

grounder. A low-keeping ball : cricketers' coll. : 1849 ; ob. Lewis. Cf. *sneak(er)*.—2. In angling, a catching the ground : 1847, Albert Smith (O.E.D.) : s. > j. or coll.—3. A knock-down blow : from late 1880's : s. ; in C. 20, coll

grouse. A grumble : orig. (ca. 1890) soldiers' s. ; since G.W., gen. coll. Ex :

grouse ; occ., but not after 1914, **grouce, v.** To grumble : dial., from ca. 1850 (see W.), >, by ca. 1880, soldiers' s. that, ca. 1919, > gen. coll. Kipling, 1892, ' If you're cast for fatigue by a sergeant unkind, |— Don't grouse like a woman, nor crack on, nor blind.' ? cognate with Old Fr. *groucier* ; and ? cf. U.S. *grout*, to grumble (1836 : Thornton).—2. To coīt with a woman : dial. and s. : mid-C. 19–20. Ex dial. *grouse*, to pry, search.

grouse, do a. To look for, or successfully follow, a woman : low : from ca. 1850 ; ob. Either ex the ' running down ' of the bird or ex *grouse*, to shoot grouse.

grouser. A grumbler : 1885, J. Brunlees Patterson, *Life in the Ranks* (O.E.D. Sup.) : soldiers' >, by 1920, gen. coll. Ex *grouse*, v., 1, q.v.—2. One who runs, sexually, after women : low : from ca. 1855 ; ob. by 1914, † by 1920.—3. A rowing man, a ' wet bob ' : sporting : ca. 1880–1910.

grousing. A sexual search for women ; the habit thereof. Cf. *go grousing = do a grouse*. Both, low : from ca. 1850 ; ob.—2. Vbl.n. of *grouse*, v., 1, q.v.

grout(e). To work or study hard : Marlborough and Cheltenham Colleges : from ca. 1870. Ex the S.E. sense, dig with the snout.

grouter, on a or the. Out of one's turn, interferingly ; unfairly : Australian military (1916) ; by 1919, gen. low s. Esp. *come in on a grouter*, e.g. to obtain an issue to which one is not entitled. Ultimately, perhaps, of the same origin as the preceding term ; imm. ex the j. of the game of two-up, where it is applied to one who enters the game only when it seems likely that the spinner will ' spin out ' or fail to ' head them '. Prob. a corruption of *go-outer*.

grouty. Peevish ; sulky : coll. : orig. (1836), U.S. ; anglicised ca. 1870 ; ob. Ultimately ex Eng. dial. *grouty*, thundery.

Grove of the Evangelist. St. John's Wood : ca. 1870–1910. Cf. *Apostle's Grove*.

*grow, v.i. To be allowed to let one's hair and beard grow : prison c. : ca. 1870–1915. Also to *grow one's feathers*.

grow !, I've seen 'em. A discontented military c.p. (of the G.W.) at the app. unduly rapid promotion of a junior. F. & Gibbons.

growed. Grew ; grown : sol. (and dial.) : C. 19–20.

growl you may—but go you must ! A nautical c.p. uttered ' when the watch below have to turn out of their bunks to shorten sail in bad weather ' : late C. 19–20. Bowen. The moderation of the language indicates the gravity of the need.

growler. A four-wheeled cab : coll. : 1865 (S.O.D.). ? ex its own tendency to creak—or its driver's to grumble.—2. Hence, *work the growler*, to go in a cab from ' pub ' to ' pub ' : low coll. : late C. 19–20 ; ob. Manchon.

growler-shover. A cabman : low : late C. 19–early 20. Ware. Ex preceding.

growlery. One's private sitting-room : jocular coll. : ex Dickens's coinage in *Bleak House*, 1852–3. Cf. *den*, *snuggery*. (O.E.D.)

growly. Subject, temperamentally or incidentally, to moroseness or ill temper expressed in growls : coll. : from ca. 1920.

grown. The corpse of an adult : undertakers' : from ca. 1870 ; ob.—2. An adult : coll. (— 1923). Manchon. Abbr. *grown-up*, q.v.

grown-man's dose. A very large drink ; much liquor : coll. : from ca. 1860.

grown(-)up. An adult : coll. : from ca. 1810. (In C. 20, S.E.) Dickens, in *Our Mutual Friend*, 'I always did like grown ups.'

groyze. To spit : *Conway* cadets' (— 1891) ; ob. John Masefield, *The Conway*, 1933. Perhaps cf. dial. *growze* (etc.), to have a chill before a cold.

grub. Food ; provisions of food : 1659. Until ca. 1830, low. Ca. 1750–1830, gen. in *grub and bub*, or *bub and grub*, food and drink (see **bub**) : of the latter, Parker in 1789 says : ' A mighty low expression '. Maginn ; Thackeray, 1857, 'He used to . . . have his grub too on board.'—2. Whence, a meal, a feed : from ca. 1855 ; ob. Hughes.—3. (For etymology, cf. sense 5.) A short, thick-set person (rarely a woman) : coll. : C. 15–17.—Cf. 4. A dirty and slovenly, gen. elderly, person : coll. : from ca. 1890.—5. A low-keeping ball ; a ' grounder '—and, like it, only of a bowled ball : cricketers' : ca. 1820–1910. Ex the lowly ' insect ' so named.

grub, v.i. To eat : from ca. 1720 : low until ca. 1840. *A New Canting Dict.*, 1725 ; Dickens in *Pickwick*. Ex n., 1, q.v.—2. Whence, v.t., provide with food : from ca. 1810. Vaux.—3. Whence, to beg food : low : ca. 1840–1900.—4. To cut off a cock's feathers under the wings : cock-fighters' : from ca. 1700. Kersey's ' Phillips '. (O.E.D.)

grub, like. Greatly : enthusiastically. ' I am on like grub,' Baumann, 1887. Low ; ob.

grub, ride. To be sullen ; ill-tempered : coll. (— 1785) ; ob. by 1860, † by 1890. Grose, 1st ed. ? ex dial., which has *the grubs bite* (a person) *hard* in the same sense.

grub along. To get along, fig., as best one can : low (— 1888).

grub-crib. See **grub-shop.**

grub-hamper. A ' consignment of sweet edibles from home ' : Public Schools' : late C. 19–20. Ware.

*grub-hunting, vbl.n. Begging for food : tramps' : from ca. 1845.

grub it. A variant of *grub*, v., 1 : C. 19–20 ; very ob.

grub-shite. To befoul ; hence, make very dirty : low : ca. 1780–1860. Grose, 1st ed. Lit., **to** befoul as a grub befouls.

grub-shop, -crib, -trap. The first and second, an eating-house : low : from ca. 1840. Also, a workhouse : from ca. 1850.—2. The first and third, the mouth : low : from ca. 1860.

grub-spoiler. A ship's cook : nautical : late C. 19–20. Bowen.

grub-stake. One's share of the rations : military coll. : 1914. F. & Gibbons. Ex the S.E. mining sense.

grub-stake, v.t. To give (an author) money to keep him going while he writes a book : publishers', hence also authors', coll. : from ca. 1920. Cf. the n.

*grub-stealer. A beggar stealing food from another : tramps' c. (— 1887). Baumann.

Grub Street, as the ill-fed corpus of literary hacks, is S.E., but *Grub Street news*, ' lying intelligence ' (Grose, 1st ed.) or ' news, false, forg'd ' (B.E.) is, in late C. 17–18, coll. Ex that C. 17 hack-, i.e. ' grub-', inhabited street near Moorfields which has, since 1830, been known as Fore Street. See Grose, P., and Beresford Chancellor's *Annals of Fleet Street*.

grub-trap. See **grub-shop.** Baumann.

grubber. An eater : low : from ca. 1860. Ex *grub*, v., 1.—2. A workhouse : tramps' c. (— 1900). E.D.D. ; J. Stamper, *Less than the Dust*.—3. A casual ward : tramps' c. (— 1932). ' Stuart Wood.'—4. An occ. variant of *bone-grubber*, esp. in sense 1.

*grubber-dock. A workhouse infirmary : tramps' c. (— 1931). J. Stamper, Ibid., 1931 (see **grubber,** 2).

grubbery. An eating-house : from ca. 1820. Bee.—2. A dining-room : from ca. 1830.—3. Food : ca. 1830–1905. Trelawney. (O.E.D.) Ex *grub*, v., 1.—4. The mouth : from ca. 1870. All low, except the jocular third.

grubbing, vbl.n. (see **grub**, v.). Eating : from ca. 1815. Moore, ' What with snoozing, high grubbing, and guzzling like Cloe '.—2. Food : from ca. 1865 : ob.

*grubbing-crib or **-ken.** An eating-house : low if not indeed c. : from ca. 1830 ; ob.—2. (*-crib* only) a workhouse : tramps' : from ca. 1850. Mayhew. Cf. *mungarly casa.*

*grubbing-crib faker. The proprietor, occ. the manager, of a low eating-house : low : from ca. 1850 : ob. Ex preceding term.

*grubby. A c. diminutive of *grub*, food : ca. 1820–60. Cf. *bubby.*

*grubby-ken. A low eating-house : ca. 1820–50 : c. Ex preceding.

gruel. Punishment ; a beating : coll. : from ca. 1795. Scott in *Guy Mannering*, '. . . Great indignation against some individual. "He shall have his gruel," said one.' Gen. in phrases. *Give one his*, or *get one's*, *gruel*, to punish, be punished ; in boxing, knock out or be knocked out ; in c., to kill, be killed. Also, *gruelled*, floored ; *gruelling.* a beating ; heavy punishment : also adj. (Occ. *take one's gruel*, to endure a beating like a man, as in *Sporting Life*, Dec. 15, 1888.) Cf. *settle one's hash* and *cook one's goose* and consider *serve one out*, pugilistic ex nautical *serve out grog.*

gruel, v. To punish ; exhaust : coll. : 1850, Kingsley (O.E.D.). Ex the n.

gruel-stick. A rifle : military : C. 20. F. & Gibbons. Cf. *cheese-toaster*, a bayonet.

grueller. A ' settler ' ; a knock-down blow ; a poser : coll. : 1856, Kingsley. (O.E.D.). Ex *gruel*, v.

gruelling, vbl.n. and ppl. adj. : see **gruel,** n. (1882 : O.E.D.)

gruffle. To speak gruffly in a muffled way : dial. (— 1825) >, by 1900, coll. Echoic. O.E.D. (Sup.)

Grumach Gillespie. Archibald Campbell (1598–1661), Marquis of Argyle. Lit., squint-eyed. Dawson.

grumble-guts. An inveterate ' grouser ' : C. 19–20 coll., now mainly dial., which also has *grumble-belly* or *-dirt*. Variant, *grumble-gizzard*, C. 19–20 ; ob. Cf. :

grumble in the gizzard, C. 18–20 (ob.) ; **of the** gizzard, C. 17. To murmur or repine : coll. B.E. ; Grose, 1st ed.

grumbler. Fourpence-worth of grog : Londoners' : ca. 1820–50. Bee.

grumbles, be all on the. To be cross or discontented : low coll. : from ca. 1865. The O.E.D. records *the grumbles*, jocular coll. for ill humour, at 1861.

grumbletonian. A (constant) grumbler : coll. : from ca. 1710 ; ob. Orig.—ca. 1690–1730—the nickname of the Count(r)y Party, in the oppositiou (Macaulay's *History*, ch. XIX).—' Coined on *Muggletonian* ', W.

grumbly. Like a grumble : 1858, Carlyle.—2. Inclined to grumble : ibid. Both coll. (O.E.D.)

grummet. The female pudend : low : nautical : from ca. 1860 ; ob. Ex *grummet-hole*, itself ex *grummet*, a little ring serving merely to tie gaskets (Manwayring, *Seaman's Dict.*, 1644—cited by W.).

grumpish, grumpy. Surly ; peevish : coll. ; in C. 20, S.E. : resp. 1797, 1778 (O.E.D.). Sala, ' Calling you a " cross, grumpy, old thing ", when you mildly suggest . . .'

grundy. A short fat person, rarely of a woman : rare coll. : C. 16. Foxe in *Acts and Monuments*, 1570. *Mrs. Grundy* : see at **Mrs.**

*****grunt.** Anon., *Street Robberies Consider'd*, 1728. defines it as a hog : if this is correct, the term is c. ; but prob. it is an error for sense 1 of :

*****grunter.** (In M.E., any grunting animal. Hence :—) A pig : c. in mid-C. 16–18 ; coll. (mainly jocular) in C. 19–20. Brome ; Tennyson.—2. In C. 17 c., also a sucking pig. B.E. Ex *grunting cheat*.—3. A shilling : late C. 18–early 19 : low, ? orig. c. Grose, 1st ed. On *hog*. But from ca. 1840, sixpence : ob. *Household Words*, June 20, 1885, ' The sixpence . . . is variously known as a " pig ", a " sow's baby ", a " grunter ", and " half a hog ".'—4. A policeman : low (— 1820) : ob. *The London Magazine*, vol. i, 1820.—5. A constant grumbler : tailors' : from ca. 1870.—6. ' Any type of wireless spark transmitter other than quenched gap, or high frequency ' : naval : from ca. 1922. Bowen.—7. A motor-car : lower classes' (— 1923) : ob. Manchon.

grunter's gig. A smoked pig's ' face ' or chap : late C. 18–mid-19. Grose, 1st ed.

*****grunting cheat.** A pig : c. : ca. 1560–1730. Fletcher in *The Beggar's Bush*. Cf. :

*****grunting peck.** Pork ; bacon : c. : ca. 1670–1850. Coles ; B.E. ; Bailey ; Grose. See **peck** and cf. *bleating cheat*.—2. Tea : low (— 1923). So, at least, says Manchon. His *grunting-peg* is erroneous.

Grunts, Bridge of. See **Isthmus of Suez.**

gruts. Tea : low coll. : from ca. 1810 : ob. *Lex. Bal.* Perhaps cognate with dial. *grout*, small beer.

guacho. A sol. spelling of *gaucho*, one of a South American half-breed race of mounted herdsmen : from ca. 1830. *Gaucho* is Sp. (O.E.D. ; W.)

guana, guano. See **goanna.**

guard. A conductor on an omnibus : busmen's : from ca. 1927. *The Daily Herald*, Aug. 5, 1936. Ex railway j.

guard. To see that horses or hounds from one stable are separated in a race : sporting s. > coll. > j. : 1893 (O.E.D.).

guard-fish. Erroneous spelling of *garfish* : Australian : 1847, Leichhardt. Morris.

guard-mounter. An article kept solely for guard-duty : military : from ca. 1925. The best-dressed man is excused guard.

guard the ace. To form ' a destroyer screen round big warships at sea ' : naval : 1914. Bowen. Ex bridge.

guardee. A soldier of the household Guards : from ca. 1905.—2. Hence, *guardee* (or *guardsman's*) *wriggle*, also *tickling his ear*, an exaggerated salute affected by the Guards : military : from ca. 1910. B. & P.

guardian angel. An observation-balloon man's parachute : Air Force : 1915. F. & Gibbons.

Guards of the Line, the. The 29th Foot, in late C. 19–20 the Worcestershire, Regiment : military nickname : from before 1877. F. & Gibbons.

guardsman's wriggle. See **guardee**, 2.

guardy, -ie. An affectionate abbr. of *guardian* : coll. : from ca. 1890.

gubb. A young sea-gull : nautical : C. 19–20. Bowen. Origin ?

gubber. A beach-comber on the look-out for odds and ends : nautical : mid-C. 19–20. Bowen.

gubbins as fish-offal is S.E., but as the name given to the primitive inhabitants of a Dartmoor district near Brent Tor, it is coll. : from ca. 1660 ; ob. by 1850, † by 1900.—2. Hence (?), a fool : military and schools' : late C. 19–20. F. & Gibbons.—3. Rubbish, trash : coll. : late C. 19–20. Ex S.E. sense. Ibid.

gubbrow. To bully, dumbfound, perturb : Anglo-Indian coll. (— 1886). Ex Hindustani. Yule & Burnell.

gud. An expletive perversion of *God* : ca. 1675–1750. Otway. (O.E.D.)

[**gudgeon**, a bait, an easy dupe, is, like the v.i. and v.t., S.E., though *gudgeon*, to be gullible, admittedly has a coll. tang.]

guer(r)illa, properly employed in **guer(r)illa (warfare)**, is a catachresis when, as in C. 19–20, it is used for **guer(r)illero**, a guerilla fighter. W.

guess !, I. I'm pretty sure : coll. : orig. (1798) U.S., anglicised ca. 1885 but still recognised as from abroad. (Baumann.) Ex the M.E.–early Mod. Eng. *guess*, (rather) think, suppose, estimate. Cf. Thornton.

guess and by God (or, euphemistically, **Godfrey**), by. (Of steering) at hazard : naval (—1909). O.E.D. (Sup.).

guessing, keep (a person). To keep one uncertain or in the dark : coll., orig. (— 1905) U.S., anglicised by 1910. O.E.D. (Sup.).

guff. Humbug ; empty talk ; foolish bluff ; nonsense : from ca. 1888 (? orig. U.S.). Prob. ex *guff*, a puff, a whiff. Cf. *gup*, q.v.—2. Whence, impudence : Dartmouth College, where *guff rules* = ' privileges of the Senior Cadets ' : from ca. 1890. Hence, *guffy*, impudent. Bowen.

guffin. A person both clumsy and stupid : from ca. 1860 : s. when not dial. (after 1920, the latter only). Miss Braddon. (O.E.D.)

guffoon. The Anglo-Irish form of the preceding. Ex It., says Ware.

guffy. A soldier : nautical : from ca. 1880 ; ob. Clark Russell. ? ex *guffin*.

guffy, adj. See **guff**, n., 2.

guggle. The windpipe : late C. 17–20 ; ob. except in dial. (O.E.D.). Ex the v.—2. A gurgling sound : coll. : from ca. 1820.

guggle, v. To gurgle (of which it is the coll. form) : C. 17–20. Johnson.

gugusse. ' An effeminate youth who frequents the private company of priests ' : Roman Catholics' : from the early 1880's ; ob. Ware, noting its Fr. origin, adds : ' In Paris (1880) the word was taken from the name of one of the novels specially directed about this time at the French priesthood.' I.e. *Gugusse*, a s. form of *Auguste*.

guide-post. A clergyman : late C. 18–early 20. Inferentially from Grose (all edd.) at *parson* (a signpost). For a parallel vice-versality, cf. *chimney-sweep* and *clergyman*.

guiders. Reins : coll. : from ca. 1830 ; ob.—2. Sinews : low coll. when not dial. : from ca. 1820. Cf. *leaders.*

guillotine, v.t. To place (a delinquent) with his head jammed under the shutter in the hammock netting and then aim missiles at the exposed portion of his anatomy : *Conway* cadets' (— 1891). John Masefield, *The Conway*, 1933.

guilt. Sense of guilt : a catachresis : ? only in Tillotson, 1690. (O.E.D.)

guinea, yellow as a. Very yellow : C. 19–20 : coll. >, by 1900, S.E. ; ob. Collinson.

guinea-dropper. A sharper, esp. one who drops counterfeit guineas : C. 18. Gay in *Trivia*. Cf. *gold-finder* and *ring-dropper.*

Guinea-gold. Sincere ; utterly dependable : coll. verging on S.E. : C. 18–early 19. Semantics : *sterling.* Moreover, Guinea gold, from which the guinea was coined in C. 18, was ' of a magnificent yellow ' (Ware).

guinea-hen. A courtesan ; a harlot : C. 17–early 18 : s. >, by 1700, coll. Shakespeare. With a punning allusion to her fee.

guinea-pig. A gen. term of reproach : coll. : ca. 1745–1830. Smollett, ' A good seaman he is . . . none of your guinea-pigs.' Cf. sense 6, q.v.—2. One whose fee is a guinea, esp. a ' vet ', a medical man, a special juryman : coll. : ca. 1820–70.—3. From ca. 1870, a public-company director, one who merely attends board meetings.—4. Ca. 1870–90, an engineer officer doing civil duty at the War Office. H., 1874.—5. Also, ca. 1875–1915, a clergyman acting as a deputy. *The Saturday Review*, Aug. 25, 1883.—6. A midshipman in the East Indian service : nautical : ca. 1745–1930. (Yule & Burnell.)

guinea-pigging. Acting as a company-director for the sake of the fee : 1890.—2. As a clerical deputy : 1887. Both coll. (O.E.D.)

guinea to a gooseberry, (it's) a. (It is) long odds : sporting : ca. 1880–1910. Hawley Smart, 1884, ' Why, it's a guinea to a gooseberry on Sam ! ' A ca. 1865–90 variant : *a guinea to a goose* (Baumann). Cf. the City *Lombard Street to a China orange.*

guinea-trade. Professional services of the deputy, stop-gap, or the nominal kind : 1808 (S.O.D.) ; ob. Perhaps rather jocular coll. than s. Punning *Guinea trade.*

Guinness is good for you ! A c.p. of 1930–. Dorothy Sayers in her *Strong Poison*, 1930 ; *Slang*, p. 173. Ex the great brewery's slogan.

Guise's Geese. The 6th Foot, from ca. 1881 the Royal Warwickshire Regiment : military : C. 19–20. Ex Guise, its colonel ca. 1735–63 ; but imm. ex *Guise's Greens*, its late C. 18–20 variant,—*Guise* being pronounced *Geeze*. F. & Gibbons. Also called *The Saucy Sixth*, C. 19–20.

guiver. Flattery ; artfulness : theatrical : from ca. 1890.—2. Whence, in Australia, C. 20, it is gen. s., with additional sense of fooling, nonsense, esp. if plausible ; make-believe. C. J. Dennis. This odd word is an extension of *guiver*, adj.—3. ' The . . . sweep of hair worn down on the forehead, lower and lower as the 1890's proceeded ' : among Cockney boy-' swells ' : from ca. 1890 ; virtually †. Ware. Perhaps ex *guiver lad* or ex *guiver*, adj.

guiver, v.i. To humbug ; fool about ; show off : sporting (— 1891) ; ob. Ex preceding.—2. Hence, to make-believe : Australian : C. 20.

guiver, adj. Smart ; fashionable : low (— 1866).

Vance in *The Chickaleary Cove*. ? ex the Northern dial. *givour*, gluttonous ; cf. :

guiver lad. A low-class dandy ; an artful fellow : ca. 1870–1900. Mainly Cockney. Cf. *guyvo* and *artful member*, qq.v.

gulf. (The group or position of) those who barely get their degree, ' degrees allowed ' : Cambridge University : 1827 (O.E.D.) ; Bristed, *Five Years in an English University*. † by 1920.—2. One who, trying for honours, obtains only a pass : Oxford University : from ca. 1830 : † by 1921. See **gulfed** in :

gulf, v. To place in the ' gulf ', sense 1 (occ. sense 2) : university : from ca. 1831, Cambridge ; 1853, Oxford (O.E.D.). † by 1920. According to H., 1860, *gulfed* denoted a man ' unable to enter for the classical examination from having failed in the mathematical . . . The term is now obsolete.'

gulf, shoot the. To achieve a very difficult task ; ironically, to achieve the impossible : coll. : ca. 1640–1760. Howell ; Defoe, ' That famous old wives' saying '. Perhaps, as Defoe asserts, ex Drake's ' shooting the gulf ' of Magellan. O.E.D.

gulf it. To be content with, or obtain, a place in the ' gulf ' : Cambridge University, 1827. Anon., *Seven Years at Cambridge*, 1827 (O.E.D.). Ob. by 1890, † by 1920. Ex *gulf*, n., 1 ; rarely sense 2.

gull, as a simpleton, fool, or dupe,—as a trick, fraud, or false report, is S.E., but as a trickster or swindler, late C. 17–19, it is s. S.E. also is the v. in its various senses, though it may possibly have been orig. coll. in that of dupe. Almost certainly S.E. are *gullage* and *gullery*,—*gullable*, *gullible*, and *gullish*,—and *guller* ; perhaps, too, *gull-catcher*.

gull-finch. A simpleton ; a fool : C. 17 coll. ' Water Poet ' Taylor.

***gull-groper.** One who (gen. professionally) lends money to gamblers : c. : C. 17–early 19. Dekker, ' The gul-groper is commonly an old monymonger.' Ex the S.E. *grope a gull*, to ' pluck a pigeon '.

gull in night-clothes. A rook (the bird) : naval : late C. 19–20. F. & Gibbons. Ex the darkness of night.

gull-sharper. ' One who preys upon Johnny Raws ', Smyth : nautical : ca. 1850–1915.

gullet. The throat : always loose Eng., it was coll. in late C. 17–mid-18 : B.E., ' a Derisory Term for the Throat, from Gula '. In C. 20, almost coll.

gullfinch. See gull-finch.

gully, the throat, is low coll. : C. 19–20 (ob.). Ex C. 16–17 S.E. sense (gullet).—2. As a large knife, it is, despite F. & H., ineligible, for it is dial.—3. The female pudend : low (? s. or coll.) : from ca. 1850 ; ob.—4. **the gully.** The fielding-position between point and slips : cricketers' coll. (— 1920) >, by 1934, j. Lewis.—5. In c. of C. 19–20 (now virtually †), a person given to telling lies. Vaux, 1812.

gully, v. Dupe ; swindle : low : ca. 1830–1910. Ainsworth, ' I rode about and speephified, and everybody gullied.'

gully-fluff. ' Beggar's velvet ' ; orig. the fluff that forms in pockets : low coll. : from ca. 1820 ; ob. Cf. S.E. *flue.*

gully-groper. A long cattle-whip : Australian : ca. 1870–1900. Cf. *gully-raker*, 3.

gully-gut. A glutton : mid-C. 16–19 coll. In C. 16–17, often *gulli(e)-gut.*

gully-hole. The gullet, the throat ; the female pudend. C. 19–20 (ob.) ; low.

gully-raker. A wencher : low : C. 19–20.—2. The male member : low : C. 19–20, ob.—3. In Australia, a long whip, esp. for cattle : from ca. 1880. A. C. Grant, *Bush Life in Queensland*, 1881. Ex the ca. 1845–80 sense, 4, a cattle thief : H., 1864.

gully-raking. Cattle thieving : Australian : from ca. 1845 ; ob.

gully-shooting, vbl.n. Pointing oars upwards when rowing : *Conway* cadets' (– 1891). John Masefield, *The Conway*, 1933.

gulpin. A simpleton ; a person (ignorantly) credulous : coll. (– 1860). H., 2nd ed. Besant, 1886, ' Go then, for a brace of gulpins ! ' Because he will gulp down anything ; imm. ex the next sense.—2. A marine : nautical : from ca. 1800 ; ob. Cf. *tell that to the marines.*

gulpy. Easily duped : coll. : C. 19–20 ; ob. Cf. *gulpin*, 1.—2. (Of the voice) broken by gulps of emotion : coll. : from ca. 1860. By the O.E.D. considered S.E.

gulsh, hold one's. To keep quiet, refrain from talking : from ca. 1840 : more dial. than (provincial) coll. Ex Northamptonshire *gulsh*, silly talk ; ribaldry.

gum. Chatter : coll. : ca. 1750–1860. Smollett. —2. Abusive talk : coll. or s. : ca. 1780–1840. Grose, 1st ed., ' Come, let us have no more of your gum.' Ex the *gums* of the mouth.—3. Abbr. *chewing-gum* : orig. U.S. ; anglicised ca. 1905 as a coll., now verging on S.E.

gum !, by. A mild oath : low coll., and dial. : from ca. 1825. Pierce Egan in *The Life of an Actor. God* corrupted ; or, as Ware suggests, a telescoping and slovening of *God almighty*. In C. 20, esp. in Australia and New Zealand, often *gum !*

Gum, old mother. Pejoratively, an old woman : low coll. : from ca. 1850 ; ob.

gum-smasher or **-tickler.** A dentist : from ca. 1860 ; ob. Cf. *snag-catcher.*

gum-sucker. A native of Tasmania, inaccurately says F. & H. ; properly, a person Victorian-born,— loosely, a native of other States, inclusive of—and esp.—Tasmania. Coll. : from ca. 1820 ; slightly ob. Ex the habit, among boys, of eating gum from eucalyptus or acacia trees, as in P. Cunningham's *Two Years in New South Wales.* Morris.—Hence 2, a fool : also Australian, but not very gen. : ca. 1880–1900.

gum-sucking. A low variant (– 1923) of *French kiss.* Manchon.

gum-tickler. A drink ; esp., a dram : ca. 1814–1915. Dickens, ' I prefer to take it in the form of a gum-tickler,' 1864.—2. See **gum-smasher.**

gum-tree, be up a. To be in a predicament ; be cornered : Australian : from ca. 1895. Cf. the much earlier U.S. sense, be on one's last legs, whence prob. the Australian. ? ex an opossum being shot at. Cf. :

gum-tree, have seen one's last. To be done for : Australian (– 1893) : s. > coll. ; ob. F. & H. But Baumann, 1887, classifies the phrase as nautical : prob. both lexicographers are correct.

gum-tree !, strike me up a. Variant, *up a blue gum(-tree)*. An Australian coll. expletive : from ca. 1905. The gum-tree has very hard wood and is difficult to climb.

gumbler. See **querier.**

gummagy. Given to scolding or snarling : low coll. : C. 19–20 (ob.). Ex *gum*, 2, q.v.

gummed. (Of a ball) close to the cushion : billiards : from ca. 1870.

gummey. Grose's 1st ed. spelling of *gummy*, adj.

gummie, gummy. A toothless person : low coll. : from ca. 1840. Gen. as *old gummy*. Ex the extent of gum displayed.—2. A dullard ; a fool : C. 19–20 ; ob. Ex *gummy*, adj.—3. (More U.S. than British.) Medicine ; properly, a medicament. Also *gummy-stuff*. C. (– 1859) ; ob.—4. A ' swell ' : sporting : ca. 1875–1910. Ware. Ex Fr. *gommeux*, a young man of fashion ; ' imported by English racing bookmakers '.—5. A gum-digger : New Zealand and Australian coll. : C. 20. (O.E.D. Sup.)—6. A shark : Australian : from ca. 1925. Ex the lavish display of teeth.

gummy, adj. Thick, fat : applied mostly to a drunkard, human ankles, and equine legs : coll., though by O.E.D. considered as S.E. : ca. 1735–1890. Grose, 1st ed.

gummy ! A late C. 19–20 low variant of *by gum !* Manchon.

gummy, feel. To perspire : university : ca. 1880–1914.

gummy composer. An old and insipid composer : musical coll. (– 1909). Ware. Ex *gummy*, n., 1.

[**gump,** a dolt, given by F. & H., is dial. and U.S. coll.]

gumption. Common sense ; shrewdness ; practical intelligence : coll. : 1719 (S.O.D.). Grose, in his *Provincial Glossary*, ' Gawm, to understand . . . Hence, possibly, gawmtion, or gumption, understanding.' Orig. Scottish. A C. 18–mid-19 variant is *rum gumption*, latterly one word, where *rum* = first-class.

gumptious. Shrewd ; coll. : from ca. 1880 ; ob. —2. Vain of one's ability : low coll. : ca. 1850–95. Lytton in *My Novel.*

gums !, bless her, his, its, your, etc. A facetious form of *bless your soul !* From ca. 1860 ; ob.

gun. A flagon of ale : s. and—in C. 20 wholly— dial. : 1645 (S.O.D.). Cf. the Anglo-Irish sense (a toddy glass) and *gun, in the.*—2. A tobacco pipe : jocular coll. : from ca. 1705 ; ob.—3. A lie : c : ca. 1680–1770. Perhaps ex the loud voice characterising a liar or a lie. But there may be some error : the Knole Park vocabulary (see note at *granna*) defines it as ' lip ' : but I suspect that vocabulary of being very careless and inaccurate : *grannam* is well attested (not *granna*) ; so is *gentry mort*, not *gentry more* (as in the ' Knole ') ; so too *heave a bough*, not (as at Knole) *heave a book*,—*half bord*, not (as there) *half-berd*,—*lurries*, not (as there) *lucries* ; *margery*, not (as there) *magery.*—4. A thief ; a pickpocket : c. (1845 in ' *No 747* ' ; ' Ducange Anglicus ', 1857) >, ca. 1880, low s. Cf. *gunner* and *gun-smith.* Abbr. *gon(n)oph, gon(n)ov* or *-of(f).*—5. Hence, a ' rascal ', ' beggar ', as a vaguely pejorative term of reference : from ca. 1890 ; ob : more Australian than English. ' Rolf Boldrewood.'—6. A revolver : orig. (– 1889) and mainly U.S. ; anglicised ca. 1900 and, with the influx of U.S. gangster novels and films, > gen. ca. 1925 ; heard occ. in the Army in 1914–18.—7. In c. of ca. 1810–50, a look, inspection, observation. Vaux, ' There is a strong *gun* at us, . . . we are strictly observed.' Cf. the v.—8. Gonorrhœa : low : late C. 19–20.

*gun, v. To look at, examine : c. of ca. 1810–95. Vaux ; Baumann. Perhaps ex sighting an object before shooting at it. (Extant in Sussex dial.)

gun, give her the. See **give her the gun.**

gun, give the. See **give the gun.**

gun, great. A joyous scamp : from before 1923 Manchon.—2. See **great gun.**

gun, in the. Tipsy: late C. 17–early 19. B.E. Ex *gun*, 1. This phrase may have suggested *sun, in the* (q.v.).

gun, over the ; chest, over the. Settlement, esp. judicial and domestic : from before 1900. John Masefield's history of the *Conway*, 1933.

gun, son of a. See **son** and cf. *son of a bitch*.

gun, sure as a. Adv., with complete accuracy or certainty ; adj., wholly certain, inevitable : coll. : from ca. 1680 ; ob. Jonson, ' He has spoke as true as a gun, believe it ' (*as a gun* becoming inseparable from *sure* only in late C. 17) ; B.E. ; ' Father Prout ' ; Manville Fenn.

gun-bus. ' A gun-carrying aeroplane ' ; esp. ' the first Vickers' " pusher " machine ' : Air Force : 1915 ; ob. F. & Gibbons.

gun-case. A judge's tippet : coll. : from ca. 1895. (O.E.D.)

gun-fire. Early-morning tea (or a cup of tea) : military : from ca. 1912. F. & Gibbons ; B. & P. Prob. ex the morning gun of a garrison town, but perhaps by analogy, ex *gunpowder*, a coarse or common (though orig. a fine green) tea. Sidney Rogerson, *Twelve Days*, 1933, remarks, ' Very brown, very sticky, but very stimulating.'

gun-man. A lawless fellow likely to carry a rifle or, esp., a revolver : coll., orig. (ca. 1902) U.S., anglicised ca. 1925 ; now verging on S.E. (O.E.D. Sup.)

gun-runner. One engaged in illegally conveying firearms (and ammunition) into a country : coll. : 1899, *The Athenæum*, Oct. 21. (O.E.D.)

gun-smith. A thief : low (– 1869) ; ob. An elaboration of *gun*, 4.

Gunboat. An ' inevitable ' nickname of men surnamed Smith : naval and military : late C. 19–20. F. & Gibbons. Ex the well-known early C. 20 boxer, ' Gunboat ' Smith.

gundiguts. ' A fat, pursy fellow ', Grose, 1st ed. : low coll. : late C. 17–mid-19 ; ob. Ex Scottish *gundie*, greedy. Cf. *greedy-gut(s)*.

gungoo. Genuine ; complete, entire : naval : C. 20. F. & Gibbons. ? a perversion of *damn' good*.

gun(n)eah, guniah, guniar. See **gunyah.**—

***gunnef.** See **gonnof.**

***gunner.** A thief : low or c. (– 1889) : ob. Extension of *gun*, 4.—2. One who lies in order to do harm : 1709, Steele : † by 1760. Cf. *gunster*, q.v.—3. ' A Merchant Service warrant officer in the East ' : nautical : late C. 19–20. Bowen.

Gunners, the. The *Arsenal* Football Club : sporting : late C. 19–20.

gunner's daughter, hug (C. 19) or **kiss** (– 1785) or **marry** (1821) **the.** To be flogged : nautical : † by 1900. Grose, 1st ed. ; Byron ; Marryat. A *gunner's daughter* is a cannon : a nautical jocularity and prob. eligible here as s. > coll.

gunner's tailor. The rating who made the cartridge-bags : naval (– 1867) ; † by 1900. Smyth.

gunnery Jack. A gunnery lieutenant : naval : late C. 19–20. Ware. Cf. **guns.**

***gunning,** vbl.n. Thieving—' profession ' or an instance : c. (–1868) > low. Ex *gun*, n., 4, q.v.

gunnya(h). See **gunyah.**

***gunpowder.** An old woman : c. : late C. 17–early 19. B.E. ; Grose, 1st ed. Either ex dry, yellow skin compared with the powder, or because, in the underworld, likely to be peevish, apt to ' go up in the air '.—2. Some fiery drink : ca. 1755–80. Toldervy. Cf. *wild-fire* and *slug*. (O.E.D.)

guns. A gunnery-lieutenant : naval : from ca. 1910. F. & Gibbons ; Bowen. Cf. **gunnery Jack.**

guns, gas and gaiters. A naval c.p. (C. 20) ' applied to the gunnery officers, who were the first to introduce the polished gaiters for work in the mud at Whale Island ', Bowen.

gunster. ' A Cracker, or bouncing Fellow ', a harmless liar (contrast *gunner*, 2) : ca. 1700–60. Steele in *The Tatler*, No. 88. (S.O.D.)

gunyah ; occ. guniah, guniar, gun(n)eah, gunnya(h), gunyer, gunyio. ' A black-fellow's hut, roughly constructed of boughs and bark ' : this sense, late C. 18–20, is S.E. But when applied to a white man's hut or, derivatively, house, it is coll. : late C. 19–20. Ex Aborigine. Morris. Cf. *hump(e)y*, q.v.

gup. Gossip, scandal : coll. : Anglo-Indian, with stress on its idleness : *gup-gup* is recorded for 1809 ; *gup* doubtless soon followed. Familiarised in Britain in 1868 by Florence Marryat's *Gup*, a rather catty account of society in South India. Ex Hindi *gap*, tattle. See Yule & Burnell.—2. From ca. 1920, however, the sense of the term has, in England, been much influenced by *gush* and *tosh*, *tush* ; and even by 1883 (O.E.D. Sup.) it represented, also, silly talk.

gup ! Go up *!* ; (to a horse) get up *!* A C. 16–17 coll. corruption of *go up*. G. Harvey. Followed by *drab, quean*, or *whore*, it is a c.p. form of address.

gurge. A whirlpool : nautical coll. : C. 19–20. Bowen. Ex dial. *gurgise*, † S.E. *gurges* (direct ex L.), the same.

gurk, v.i. To belch : coll. (– 1923). Manchon. Echoic ; or ex *gurgle*, itself echoic.—2. Hence, occ. as n.

gurrawaun. A coachman : Anglo - Indian (– 1864) ; ob. A native corruption of *coachman*.

gurrell. A fob : Westminster slums (? c.) : ca. 1850–80. H., 1860.

gush. A smell, a whiff (e.g. of tobacco) : coll. : 1838, Dickens : ob. (O.E.D.)—2. Talk too effusive and objectionably sentimental : coll. : from ca. 1865. *The Church Times*, Sept. 17, 1886, ' Not mere gush or oratorical flip-flap '.—3. Ca. 1870–80, ' the newspaper work necessary for a continuance of the " largest circulation " ' : the C. 20 has other names for this ' slush '.—4. Hence, in late C. 19–20, a newspaper article designed to this end. Manchon.

gush, v. To talk (gen. v.i.) too effusively and sentimentally ; often, also insincerely : coll. : from early 1860's ; Webster records it in 1864. Miss Broughton, Miss Braddon. Ex the burbling spring and the garrulous brook.

gusher. An over-effusive and (gen. insincerely) sentimental talker : coll. : 1864, Edmund Yates in *Broken to Harness*.

gushing, adj. (The n., also coll., is rare.) Excessively sentimental and effusive, either inanely or insincerely : coll. : 1864, *Fraser's Magazine*, p. 627, ' What, in the slang of translated Cockneys, is called the Gushing School '.—2. Coll. adv. in *-ly* : 1865. (O.E.D.)

gushy. (Adj.) The same as preceding adj. : coll. (– 1889). O.E.D.

gusset. The female sex : coll. : late C. 17–19. Cf. *placket*.

gusset, brother or **knight** or **squire of the.** A pimp : low coll. : resp. late C. 17–19, C. 19–20, C. 19.

gusset of the arse. The inner side of the buttocks late C. 18–19 low coll. Burns.

gusseteer. A wencher : C. 19 coll., somewhat derisory. Ex *gusset*, q.v. Cf. :

gusseting. Wenching : C. 19 coll., low or jocular. Punning S.E. sense.

gussie. An affected and/or effeminate man : Australian : from ca. 1905. Ex *Gus*, the Christian name. Cf. *Nancy*, which, however, connotes sexual perversion.

gust. A guest : jocular : from ca. 1905 ; ob. (See *Slang*, p. 17.) Cf. *finance*, q.v.

gut. The belly : low coll. and dial. in C. 19–20 ; until ca. 1800, S.E.—2. Gluttony : low coll. in C. 19–20 : ob.

gut. V.i., to cram the guts : low coll. : 1616 (O.E.D.). This accounts for F. & H.'s ' to eat hard, fast, and badly ' (schools'), now ob.—2. As to remove or destroy the contents or inside of (v.t.), it is, despite F. & H., good Eng., but *gut a house*, to rob it, is C. 17–19 c.,—*gut an oyster*, to eat it, low s. of late C. 17–20 (ob.),—*gut a quart pot*, empty it, is C. 18–20 low s.,—*gut a job* (Moore in *Tom Crib's Memorial*), to render it valueless, is C. 19 low s.

gut-entrance. The female pudend : low : from ca. 1840. Cf. *front-gut*.

gut-foundered. Extremely hungry : coll. : mid-C. 17–mid-19. In dial. it = ' diseased from the effects of hunger ' (E.D.D.).

gut-f**ker, **-monger,** **-sticker.** A sodomite : low : C. 19–20 ; ob.

gut-head. A person stupid from over-eating : coll. : C. 17. (O.E.D.)

gut-pudding. A sausage : late C. 17–18 : ? coll. or S.E.

gut-puller. A poulterer : low : from ca. 1850. Ob.

gut-scraper. A fiddler : jocular coll. : C. 18–20. D'Urfey. Also *catgut-scraper*. A C. 17 variant is *gut-vexer*.

gut-stick. The male member : low : C. 19–20 ; ob. Cf. *cream-stick*. Hence *have a bit*, or *a taste, of the g.-s.*, (of women) to coït.

gut-sticker. See **gut-f**ker.**—**gut-vexer.** See **gut-scraper.**

guts. The stomach and intestines : mid-C. 16–20. Until ca. 1830, S.E. ; then coll. ; then, in C. 20, low coll.—2. A (very) fat person ; rarely of a woman : low coll. from ca. 1660 (earlier, S.E.) ; ob., unless preceded by an adj. ; extant in dial. Cf. Shakespeare's ' Peace, ye fat-guts.'—3. Abbr. *greedy-guts* : low : late C. 19–20.—4. Spirit, real quality, energy : artists' s. and gen. coll. : from ca. 1890.—5. Whence, courage : coll. : from ca. 1892. F. & H. Cf. the exactly similar ascent of *pluck*, q.v.—6. The essentials, the important part, the inner and real meaning : coll. : from ca. 1908. ' Let's get at the guts of it ' or ' of the matter ' : a very gen. locution. Ex the S.E. (1663) sense, ' the inside, contents of anything ', S.O.D. Cf. *have guts in one's brain*.

guts, fret one's. To worry oneself greatly : low (? s. or coll.) : from ca. 1840.

guts, ward-room officers have stomachs, and flag-officers palates,—midshipmen have. A naval c.p. : mid-C. 19–20 ; ob. Bowen. (Cf. *horses sweat, men perspire, and women feel the heat*.)

guts, with or **without,** adj. Strong or weak, gen. of things, esp. books, pictures, etc. Low coll. > coll. (ob.) : from ca. 1890.

guts and garbage. A (very) fat man : mid-C. 18–mid-19 : low. Grose, 1st ed.

guts are ready to eat my little ones, my great ; my

guts begin to think my throat's cut ; my guts curse my teeth; my guts chime twelve. I'm very hungry : coll. (the first, low) : resp. late C. 18–mid-19 ; late C. 18–20 ; late C. 18–19 ; mid-C. 19–20 ; ob. The first three are (? first) recorded by Grose, 1785, 1785, 1788, resp., the fourth by F. & H. Not ' cast-iron ', but adaptable to other than the first person singular.

guts but no bowels, have plenty of. To be unfeeling ; even hard, merciless : coll. : late C. 18–20 ; ob. Grose, 3rd ed. Cf. dial. *have neither gut nor gall in one*, to be heartless and lazy.

*guts, come one's. To confess ; to ' peach ' : c. : from ca. 1930. James Curtis, *The Gilt Kid*, 1936.

guts for garters ; gen. **I'll have your,** though other persons and tenses occur. A race-course (and other low) c.p. : from before 1932. *Slang*, p. 242.—2. It also means, to defeat utterly, to damage severely.

gut's horn, the. A dinner bugle-call : military : C. 20 ; ob. F. & Gibbons.

guts in one, have (no). To be spirited, energetic, a ' good fellow '—or the opposite, which is much the more gen. : coll. : from ca. 1890. Cf. *guts*, 4.

guts in one's brain(s), have. To have a solid understanding ; be genuinely intelligent : coll. : ca. 1660–1890. Butler, 1663 ; Swift, ' The fellow's well enough if he had any guts in his brain.' (Apperson.) Cf. *more guts than brains*, below.

guts into it, put one's. Do your best, esp. physically ; perhaps orig. aquatic, Row the best you can. Coll. : from ca. 1880.

guts than brains, more. Adj., silly ; brainless : late C. 18–20. Grose, 1st ed. Also *have more . . .* Cf. the G.W. soldiers' *more ball(ock)s than brains*, *more brawny than brainy*. Cf. *guts in one's brain(s)*, above.

guts to a bear, not fit to carry. Worthless ; very uncouth : coll. : ca. 1650–1880. Howell, Wolcot, Scott. See Apperson.

gutser ; occ. **gutzer.** A heavy fall : from ca. 1905. Fig. from ca. 1914. Both low. In G.W. applied esp. to a fall from an aeroplane and to a sharp rebuff or disappointment. Construction : *come a gutser*. F. & Gibbons.

gutsiness. Energy ; spirit : from ca. 1890. Courage : C. 20. Both, s. > coll. but also ob. Ex :

gutsy. Energetic ; spirited : coll. : from ca. 1890.—2. In C. 20, occ. = courage.

gutted. Penniless ; temporarily without cash : low : ca. 1820–1910.

gutter. The female pudend : low : C. 19–20 (ob.). Cf. Sanskrit *cushi*.—2. Esp. *in the gutter*, (of an advertisement) occupying an inside position, next to the fold (*gutter*) in the paper : copy-writers' coll. : from ca. 1920. The term *gutter* is common among printers and publishers.

gutter, v. To fall stomach-flat in the water : Winchester College : from ca. 1860. Cf. Fr. *piquer un plat-ventre*.

gutter, lap the. To be extremely drunk : low : from ca. 1850. Perhaps suggested by *gatter*, q.v. : but cf. *gutter-alley*.

gutter-alley, -lane. The throat : C. 17–19 the latter, C. 19 the former. Jocular coll. (See also at **gutter-lane.**)—2. A urinal : from ca. 1850 ; ob. by 1900, † by 1915.

gutter-blood. A ragged rascal : Scottish coll. (— 1818) ; ob. Scott, *Midlothian*.—2. A vulgarian, a *parvenu* : mainly Scots coll. : from ca. 1855 ; ob.

gutter-chaunter. A street singer : low, mainly Cockney : ca. 1840–1900.

gutter-crawling. Route marching through streets : military : C. 20. F. & Gibbons. Cf. *gutter-merchant*.

gutter-hotel. The open air : tramps' c. : from ca. 1870 ; ob. Cf. *hedge-square* and *daisyville*, qq.v.

gutter-kid. A street arab : Cockney coll. (— 1887). Baumann.

gutter-lane. See gutter-alley. 'Throat' synonyms are : *beer street*, *Holloway*, *gin-* and *red lane*, *peck alley*. Ex L. *guttur*, the throat, fig. gluttony : indeed Bailey, 1721, spells it *Guttur Lane*. (Cf. next entry.)

gutter lane (or ' capitalled '), **all goeth** (C. 17)—or **goes** (C. 18–20)—**down.** He spends all his money on his stomach. A proverbial coll. : C. 17–20 ; ob. Prob. suggested by Gutter Lane, London, with pun on L. *guttur*. Cf. preceding entry.

[**gutter-literature**, like *g.-journalism* and *g.-press*, is S.E. : but see **awful, blood and thunder, shocker.**]

[**gutter-master**, a C. 17 term of reproach, is on the verge of eligibility.]

gutter-merchant. An itinerant vendor : coll. (— 1923). Manchon. He walks in, or almost in, the gutter.

***gutter-prowler.** A street thief : c. : ca. 1840–1910.

gutter-slush, -snipe. A street arab : resp. s., and coll., from ca. 1880 (in C. 20, S.E.). 1885–1910, and coll., from ca. 1880 (in C. 20, S.E.). With the latter, which follows from the S.E. sense, a gatherer of refuse from the gutter, cf. Fr. *saute-ruisseau*, an errand-boy (W.).

guttie, -y. A glutton : coll. : C. 19.—2. A very fat person : low coll. : C. 19–20 ; ob. Ex the Scottish adj.—3. A gutta-percha ball : golfers' s. : 1890 (O.E.D.).

[**guttle**, to eat (or drink) greedily ; *guttler*, a gormandiser ; *guttling*, given to coarse eating and/or over-drinking,—all, despite F. & H., are S.E.]

guttle-shop. A tuck-shop : Rugby School : from ca. 1860.

gutty. See guttie.—**gutzer.** See gutzer.

guv or **gov.** Abbr. *governor*, q.v. : low : from ca. 1880.

guvner, -or, = **governor**, q.v. Occ. *gov'nor*.

guy, an ill-dressed or ugly person, is gen. considered S.E. : but was it not orig. (1823, Bee) coll. ? —2. A dark lantern : low, or c. (— 1811) >, ca. 1860, low : ob. by 1900, † by 1935. *Lex. Bal.* Esp. in *stow the guy*, conceal the lantern. Ex Guy Fawkes's plot.—3. A Christian as opposed to a Jewish crimp : ca. 1830–80 : low or c.—4. A jaunt or expedition : Cockney (— 1889). *The Sporting Times*, Aug. 3, 1889, ' A cheerful guy to Waterloo was the game.' Cf. *do a guy*.—5. Whence, a decamping (— 1898) : low.—6. A man, fellow, chap : orig. (— 1896), U.S. ; anglicised ca. 1910.— 7. Whence, in Australia and, by 1920, in New Zealand, ' a foolish fellow ', C. J. Dennis : from ca. 1910.—8. An American soldier : military : 1918. B. & P. Ex the frequency with which Americans use *guy* in sense 6.—9. The manager, the chief : circus s. verging on coll. (— 1923). Manchon. Ex sense 6.

guy, v. To hiss : theatrical : from ca. 1870 ; ob. ' If orig. U.S., may be . . . from Dutch *de guig aansteken*, to make fun ', W.—2. Whence, to quiz, make an object of ridicule : coll. : from ca. 1880. Cf. U.S. sense (e.g. in Thornton). Also **as v.i.**, to

poke fun : Cockneys' : C. 20. Edwin Pugh, *The Cockney at Home*, 1914.—3. To run away ; escape : c. or low (— 1874). H., 5th ed. Cf. :

***guy, do a.** To give a false name : c. (— 1887) : † by 1910. *Fun*, March 23, 1887.—2. To run away ; escape : c. (— 1889, Clarkson & Richardson) >, ca. 1892, low. In C. 20, gen. s., often and wrongly deemed U.S. Cf. *guy*, v., 3. Referable to Guy Fawkes.

guy, great. A post-G.W. derivative of *guy*, n., 6. For sense, see the quotation at *sound egg*.

guy on, clap a. Put a stop to ; cease (v.t.) : nautical : 1814 : ob. by 1910, † by 1930. Ex *guy-rope*. O.E.D.

guy to, give the. To run away from ; give (someone) the slip (— 1899). Ex *guy*, n., 4, 5.

guying, n. Hissing : theatrical (— 1885). Jerome K. Jerome.—2. Ridicule : coll. : from ca. 1890.

Guy's. Guy's Hospital : coll. (— 1887). Baumann. Cf. *Bart's*.

guyver. See guiver.

guyvo. A smart fellow ; a dandy : naval : C. 20. F. & Gibbons. Ex *guiver*, adj., q.v.

Guz. See Guzzle.

[**guzzle**, n. and v. ; *guzzler* ; *guzzling*, n. and v. : all are S.E. Prob. the sound is responsible for the frequent imputation of coll., esp. for *guzzle*, liquor.]

Guzzle. Devonport : naval : late C. 19–20. Bowen. Ex *guzzle*, liquor. In C. 20, often abbr. to *Guz* : F. & Gibbons.

guzzle-guts. A glutton or a heavy drinker : low (— 1788) ; ob. Grose, 2nd ed.

Guzzle-Pawnee. The inevitable military nickname (— 1935), on Egyptian or Indian service, of men surnamed Drinkwater. A pun on Hindustani *pawnee*, water.

gwennie (-y), or **G.** A high-angle, anti-aircraft gun on board ship (cf. *archie*) : naval : C. 20. F. & Gibbons ; Bowen. Ex *Gwendolen*, an aristocratic name.

g.y., all a. All on one side or askew ; crooked : North Country coll. (? and dial.). From ca. 1860. Cf. *all* (q.v.) *of a hugh*.

***gybe.** A written paper : c. of ca. 1560–1660. Harman.—2. A pass, esp. if counterfeit : ca. 1560–1830 : c. Awdelay, Dekker, B.E., Scott. (Often spelt *jybe*.) Perhaps ex Ger. *Schreiben*, a writing.

***gybe**, v. To whip ; castigate, esp. in past ppl. passive : late C. 17–18 c. B.E. Ex the S.E. sense.

gybing (i.e. gibing), occ. **gybery** or **gibery**, n. Mockery ; jeering. In late C. 17–18 (witness B.E. and Grose) it seems to have been coll.

gybs. Prayers : Charterhouse : late C. 19–20. Why ?

***gyger.** See jigger.

Gyle. The ' Shortened familiar, and secretive title for Argyle Rooms, Windmill Street ' : London fast life : ca. 1850–78. Ware.

Gyles. See hopping Giles.

gym. Abbr. *gymnasium* : orig. and mainly schools' (— 1887). Baumann.

gymmy. See -y, 2.

gymnasium. The female pudend : low jocular s. : from ca. 1860.

gyne(i)ocracy, gynæ(or -œ-)ocracy. Catachrestic for *gynæcocracy* or *gynocracy* : C. 17–20. O.E.D.

gynie. Gynæcology : medical students' (—1933). *Slang*, p. 190.

gyp. A college servant : Cambridge University : from ca. 1750. In C. 19–20, also Durham University. Cf. the Oxford *scout* and the Dublin *skip*. Etymologies proposed : Gr. γύψ, a vulture (symbolic of rapacity), by Cantabs, popularly ; *Gipsy Joe*, by *The Saturday Review* ; *gypsy*, by the S.O.D. ; and, I think the most convincing, the C. 17 *gippo* (Fr. *jupeau*), a garment, hence a varlet—cf. the transferred sense of *buttons*—by W.—2. Abbr. *gypsophila* : coll. : C. 20. O.E.D. (Sup.).

gyp. To cheat (v.t.), swindle : Canadian : C. 20. From U.S. ; ex S.E. *Gypsy*. (John Beames.)

gyp ! See **gip.**

gyp, give (a person). See **gip, give.**

gyp-room. 'A room where the gyps keep table furniture, etc.' : from ca. 1870 : Cambridge coll. >, by 1900, S.E. (O.E.D.).

gype, adj. Looking like a boxer or a boxer's clothes, etc. : tailors' : late C. 19–20. Origin ?.

gypoo, Gyp(p)o. See **Gipo.**

gypper. A Gypsy : late C. 19–20.

Gyppy. See **Gippy.** But note that *Gyppies* (not *Gi-*) = Egyptian cigarettes : coll. : C. 20. E.g. in F. Brett Young, *Jim Redlake*, 1930.

gyro. A gyroscope : coll. : from mid-1890's.— 2. A gyro-compass : coll. : 1914 (O.E.D. Sup.).

Gypsies of Science. The British Association : literary coll. : ca. 1845–1900.

gyte. A child : pejorative low : from ca. 1820 : Scots. Ex *goat*.—2. A first-year pupil at the Edinburgh High School : Scots : from ca. 1880. Ex Scots *gyte*, a foolish fellow.

gyvel. The female pudend : Scots low coll. : C. 18–20 (ob.). Burns.

H

h' is an unsatisfactory variant ('invented' by Swift, ca. 1708) of *ha*, q.v. (*Slang*, p. 66.)

h-. 'As criterion of educated speech from 19 cent. only. "The *h* and other points of etiquette" (Thackeray, 1848)', W. The intrusive *h-*, however, has always been a sol.

h.i.c. Hole-in-corner paper : Bootham School (— 1925). Anon., *Dict. of Bootham Slang*.

h.o.p., on the. A jocular elaboration of *on the hop*, 1 (s.v. *hop*), q.v. ; ob. s.

h.s. 'Hot stuff', esp. in the sexual sense : from ca. 1930. Compton Mackenzie, *Water on the Brain*, 1933, 'She's h.s. all right.'

ha' d, ha-d, ha-dee. A halfpenny : Charterhouse : from ca. 1870. Obviously *ha'* = half ; *d* is the sign for pence. Also, rarely, *hadee*.

ha or ha'. Have : a worn-down form : in C. 19–20, low coll. when not dial. Occ. it > '*a*' or *a*.

hab. A Negro (and dial.) pronunciation of *have* : C. 18–20.

hab or nab, hab-nab, habs-nabs ; hob-nob, adv. At random, by hook or by crook, hit or miss : coll. : from ca. 1540 : the *a* forms ob. by 1760, † (except in dial.) by 1800 ; the *o*, ob. by 1840, † (except in dial.) by 1860. 'Hob-nob is his word ; give't or take't,' Shakespeare, whereas Udall revealingly spells *habbe* or *nhabbe*. Cf. *hab or nab* (= *ne habe*), have or have not. Variant : *at*, or *by*, *hab or nab*. See also **hob and,** or **or, nob.**

haberdasher. A publican : jocular coll. : C. 19. Moncrieff. Because he sells *tape*, q.v.

haberdasher of (nouns and) pronouns. A schoolmaster : late C. 17–19 ; now archaic. The longer and orig. form, not after C. 18. B.E.

habit-shirt. A profligates' s. term of ca. 1820–50. As the exact meaning is obscure, Bee is quoted in full : 'A sham plea put in (on) to save appearances. Worn by the *ladies* ; but gentlemen should "look well to't", as Hamlet says, or it will be all *Dickey*.' See **dickey,** n., and cf. *belly-plea*.

habitual, n. A confirmed drunkard, criminal, *drug-taker*, etc. : coll. : 1884. (S.O.D.) Contrast *chronic*, q.v.

haby. A *haber*dashery department (in a store) : trade : C. 20. (E. R. Punshon, *Information Received*, 1933.)

hack, for a sorry horse or a sorrier writer, is S.E., as also for a gash caused by a kick ; as a harlot or a bawd, however, it is s. : from ca. 1730 ; almost †.

Ex *hackster* or *hackney* (*woman* or *wench* or *whore*), which are rather S.E. than coll.—2. See **garrison hack.**—3. As used in Public Schools for a kick, blow, punch, it verges on s. : C. 20. E. F. Benson, *David Blaize*, 1916, has 'A juicy hack'. Also as v. : C. 20 ; e.g. in A. Waugh, *The Loom of Youth*, 1917.

hack and manger, at. (Gen. with *live*.) In clover : coll. : ca. 1660–1890. Ex *hack*, the rack that holds fodder for cattle. (Extant in dial.)

hack of a dress, make a. To wear it daily : coll. (— 1887) ; ob. Baumann.

hackery. A bullock-cart : late C. 17–20 Anglo-Indian. (Before 1880, at least) rarely used among natives : W., however, suggests ex Hindi *chhakra*, a two-wheeled cart.

hackle. Pluck, spirit. Whence *to show hackle*, to be willing to fight : coll. (— 1860). H., 2nd ed. Ex *hackle*, a long shining feather on a cock's neck. Cf. *hackles up*.

hackle as a variant of *heckle* in political sense is coll. (— 1923). Manchon.

hackle, cock of a different. An opponent of a different, gen. better, character : coll. (— 1865). See **hackle** and cf. :

hackles. Whiskers : jocular coll. : from ca. 1880 ; ob. Cf. :

hackles up, with the. Very angry ; at fighting-point : coll. when, from ca. 1880, applied to men. Ex cock-fighting.

hackslaver. To splutter, hesitate in speech, stammer : low coll. (— 1864) ; ob. H., 3rd ed. Ex † S.E. *hack*, same meaning.

hackum, occ. *-am* or *-em*. A bravo, a blustering bully : coll. : from ca. 1650 ; ob. by 1820, † (in England) by 1860. Variant : *Captain Hackum*, in B.E. and Grose, the former designating it—wrongly, I think—as c. Obviously a variation of S.E. *hacker* ex *hack*, to gash. (But *hackster*, its variant, is S.E.)

hacky. Of, or like, a hack (horse) : coll. : 1870. —2. (Of a cough) hacking : coll. : from ca. 1899. O.E.D.

had, deceived, tricked, 'done' : see **have.**—2. **had,** wholly redundant in component tenses,— where it is either past tense or past ppl. (gen. the latter),—is frequent in C. 15–16 and not rare since. Sol. Bishop Bekynton, 1442, 'He might never have had escaped' (O.E.D.).

Had 'em, Haddums. Rare except in *to have been*

at Haddums, late C. 17–18 (B.E.), or in the mid-C. 18–early 19 c.p. (Grose, 1st ed.) *to have been at Had'em and come home by Clapham*, punning *Hadham* and *clap*: properly, to have caught *clap* or gonorrhœa; loosely, syphilis. (These topographical and coll. puns were much commoner before ca. 1830 than after.)

had enough(, have). (To be) tipsy: coll.: C. 19–20. I.e. more than enough.

had on! 'Sucks!', a term of triumph or defiance at certain schools: from the 1880's. See esp. Ernest Raymond, *Once in England*, 1932, at p. 12.

had one and (or but) the wheel came off(, we). A lower-class and military c.p. directed at an unintelligible speaker or speech: C. 20. B. & P.

had-up. An examination (of a person) by the police: ca. 1820–70. 'Jon Bee.' Ex S.E. *had up*, brought before a magistrate.—2. A person 'had-up': legal coll.: late C. 19–20. (R. Hichens, *The Paradine Case*, 1932.)

haddick. A haddock: sol. (— 1887). Baumann.

*haddock. A purse: (low or) c.: from ca. 1810; ob. Vaux; Ainsworth.—2. Money: fishmongers' (— 1874). H., 5th ed.—3. 'Haddock is the English version of the Latin *ad hoc*. (Cf. Rt. Hon. J. H. Thomas),' editorial footnote to editorial entitled 'Haddock Intervention' in *The Week-End Review*, Oct. 7, 1933: cultured s.: late 1933–4.

haddock to paddock, bring. To lose everything: C. 16 coll. and proverbial.

haddocks. Great North of Scotland Railway ordinary stock: Stock Exchange: from ca. 1885.

Haddums. See Had 'em.

hadee. See ha'd. (Rare.)

Hades. Hell: orig. euphemistic S.E.; in C. 20, esp. in *go to Hades!*, jocular coll.—2. See **hell, as much** . . .

hadland. One who has lost the land he once owned: coll.: ca. 1590–1660. Cf. *lackland*.

hæma-, hemastatic(s). Incorrect for *hœmo-* or *hemostatic(s)*: mid-C. 19–20. O.E.D.

hæmatoid. A cultured euphemism for unconventional *bloody*: ca. 1920–6. Manchon.

haeremai!; occ. **horomai!** († by 1898). A 'Maori term of welcome, lit. come hither . . . It has been '—from ca. 1880—'colloquially adopted': New Zealand. Morris.

hag, an old or ugly woman, is S.E., as is the † *hagged*, haggard.—2. At Charterhouse (school), any female; at Winchester College, a matron, as also at Charterhouse: both ca. 1850.

*haggard. A proposed dupe that keeps aloof: c. of ca. 1592. Greene. Ex the S.E. sense: a wild, unreclaimed bird that does not return to the wrist.

haggis debate. A debate referring to Scotland: Parliamentary (— 1909). Ware. Cf.:

Haggisland. Scotland: jocular coll.: C. 19–20; ob. (Until C. 18, haggis—as is very little known—was a popular English dish.)

haggle, despite F. & H., is S.E., as is *haggler*, except as, in London vegetable-markets, a middleman (ca. 1840–1900): Mayhew.

hagrerwa(i)ters is a variant of *aggerawater*, q.v. (Ware.)

hagship, your. A contemptuous term of address, occ. of reference, applied only to women: C. 19–20 (ob.) low coll. Ex S.E. sense, personality of a hag.

hail and rain. A train: rhyming s. (— 1923). Manchon.

[**hail fellow well met, be,** to be on very easy or

over-familiar terms, is prob. to be considered S.E. (From ca. 1580. Occ. *hail-fellow*.)]

hail up. To 'put up, as at an inn': Australian coll.: ca. 1880–1910. Ware. Does this represent a perversion of *hale oneself up*?

hailed for the last time, be. To die: nautical, coll. rather than s. (— 1891); ob. Clark Russell in *An Ocean Tragedy*.

Haines! 'Intimation of sudden retreat. Heard in Liverpool, whence it arrived from New York', says Ware in 1909. But it did not spread to the rest of England, and even in Liverpool it has long been †.

hain't, haint. Have not; am not: a sol. contraction (— 1887). Baumann. See also *ain't*.

hair. The female sex; women viewed sexually: low: ex *hair*, the female pubic hair. This, like the following, is C. 19–20: *after hair*, looking for a woman, ob.; *bit of hair*, the sexual favour; *plenty of hair*, an abundance of girls; *hair-monger*, a womaniser; *hair to sell*, a woman prepared—at a price—to grant the favour.

hair phrases. The following, despite F. & H., are S.E., though it is arguable that the third and fourth have at first been coll.: **against the hair, of a** (or † **one) hair, to a hair; split hairs** (earlier **cut the hair).** S.E. also are put up one's hair, (of women) to become grown-up, and **not to turn a hair,** orig. of horses.

hair, comb one's. See **comb.**

hair, lose one's. To lose one's temper: **s.** (— 1931) verging on coll. Lyell. Opp. *hair on, keep one's.*

hair, not worth a. Worthless: coll.: C. 19–20 (ob.).

hair about the heels. Underbred: coll. when, from ca. 1880, applied to persons. Orig. of horses. Cf. *hairy about the fetlocks.*

hair-brush (grenade). A handled grenade used in 1914–15: military coll. F. & Gibbons. Ex its shape.

Hair Court. Sexual connexion, esp. in *take a turn in Hair Court*, occ. amplified *take . . . Court, Girl Street*: C. 19–20 (ob.) low.

hair curl, make one's. See **curl, make one's hair.**

hair cut, get one's. To visit a woman: low: late C. 19–20. Cf. *see a man about a dog*, s.v. *dog*.—2. For **hair cut !, get your,** see get . . .

hair-divider or -**splitter.** The male member: low coll.: from ca. 1850, 1810 (*Lex. Bal.*) resp.; ob. Cf. *beard-splitter.*

hair grows through his hood, his. 'He is on the road to ruin': coll.: mid-C. 15–early 18. Skelton, Deloney, Motteux. Apperson.

hair-lip. Incorrect for *hare-lip*: C. 18. O.E.D.

hair of, within a. Almost: coll. (— 1933). Lyell, 'He was *within a hair of* being dismissed.'

hair of the dog that bit you, a. See at **dog.**

hair on, hold or, more gen., keep one's. To keep one's temper: from late 1860's ('Quotations' Benham). Gen. in imperative. Variant, *wool*. 'App. playful advice not to *tear one's hair*', W.

hair-raiser. An exciting adventure-story: coll.: from ca. 1910.

hair-restorer. A made-up story; humbug: mostly lower classes': 1914, A. Neil Lyons in *Arthur's*, cited by Manchon; slightly ob. Ex the (mainly reputed) virtues of hair-restorers.

hair-splitter. See **hair-divider.**

hair stand on end, make one's. To astound; frighten: orig. (C. 17) coll., soon S.E.

hair than wit, having more. Often preceded by *bush natural.* (Rather) stupid, silly : C. 16–19 coll. > proverbial. Apperson.

hairs, get or **have by the short.** So to hold (lit. and fig.) that escape is painful or difficult : (low) coll., esp. among soldiers : from mid-1890's. Ex the hair on one's nape or that around the genitals. P. G. Wodehouse, *The Head of Kay's*, 1905, 'We have got them where the hair's short. Yea. Even on toast'; Galsworthy, *The Silver Spoon*, 1926, 'If [she] is not taken by the short hairs, she'll put it across everybody.'

hairy. A draught-horse ; any rough-coated horse : military : 1899, Conan Doyle (O.E.D. Sup.). Hence, *G.S. hairy*, a Government horse : military : 1915 (see B. & P.).—2. A slum girl : low Glasgow : C. 20. MacArthur & Long, *No Mean City*, 1935. Ex *hairy, the*, q.v. in Addenda.

hairy, adj. Difficult : Oxford University : ca. 1850–1900. Clough.—2. Splendid, famous : from ca. 1890 : ob. Kipling, 'The Widow of Windsor with a hairy gold crown on her head.'—3. (Of women only) desirable : low : from ca. 1860.—4. Ill-bred ; bad-mannered : 1906 (O.E.D. Sup.). Ex *hairy about* (or *at*) *the fetlocks* or *heel*, q.v.—5. Angry ; (angry and) excited : Anglo-Irish : 1914, James Joyce (O.E.D. Sup.). Collinson (*get hairy*).

hairy, feel. To feel amorous : low : from ca. 1860. Cf. *hairy*, 3.

hairy about (or **at** or **in**) **the fetlocks** (or **heel**). See *hairy*, adj., 4. From late 1890's. Ex the stables. O.E.D. (Sup.).

hairy bit. An amorous and attractive wench : low : from ca. 1860.

hairy-heeled. Same as *hairy*, adj., 4, and of same origin : 1930, A. E. W. Mason (O.E.D. Sup.).

hairy Jock. See **Jock, hairy.**

hairy oracle or **ring.** The female pudend. Whence *work the hairy oracle*, to go wenching. Low : from ca. 1870.

Hairyfordshire. The female pudend : low : from ca. 1865. Whence *go to Hairy ordshire*, to coit. Obviously punning *Herefordshire*.

hake's teeth. 'A series of deep soundings in the Bristol Channel' : nautical : late C. 19–20. Bowen. A hake's teeth being well-defined.

hakim. 'A medical man.—*Anglo-Indian* ', H., 1864 : C. 17–20.—2. (Yule & Burnell) 'the authority' ; a governor. Anglo-Indian coll. : late C. 17–20. Both ex Hindi ; the former ex *hakim*, wise, the latter ex *hakim*, a master.

halbert. Whereas *get the halbert*, to be promoted sergeant, and *be brought to the halberts*, i.e. flogged, are † j. or S.E., *carry the halbert in one's face*, (of officers) to show that one rose from the ranks, is C. 18 military s. > coll. : cf. the G.W. *temporary gentleman* and the S.E. C. 18 *old halbert*.

half, when used as elliptical n. with the orig. n. omitted, is gen. to be considered coll. : e.g. = a half-year at school, a half-back at football, a half-pint or gill of liquor. Rare before 1820 and not common before 1865.—2. See **one,** 6.—3. See **half seven.**

half, v. Go halves : coll. : 1889 (O.E.D.).

half !, not. See **not half !**

half a bar. Ten shillings : Cockneys' : C. 20. (*The Evening News*, Jan. 20, 1936.)

*half a bean or **counter.** Half a guinea (Vaux) or sovereign : C. 19 c., C. 19–20 c. > low. See **bean** and **counter** ; cf. *half a quid*.

half-a-brewer. Tipsy : low : mid-C. 19–20 ; ob. Ware.

half a bull or **tusheroon.** Half-a-crown : C. 19 ; C. 19–20 low. H., 1859. See **bull** and **tusheroon.**

half a crack or **jiffy** or **tick.** 'Half a mo ' : low coll., s., low s., resp. : C. 19, C. 19–20 (ob.), C. 19–20. —2. Half a crown : C. 20. (R. Knox, *The Body in the Silo*, 1933.) Only *half a crack.*

half a dollar. Half-a-crown : from ca. 1900, due to U.S. influence.—2. A collar : rhyming s. : late C. 19–20. B. & P.

half a farthing I'd (do, have done it), for. It wouldn't take (have taken) much to make me . . . : coll. (— 1887) ; ob. Baumann.

half-a-foot o' port. A glass of that wine at Short's in the Strand : London : mid-C. 19–20. Ware. Because served in a long champagne-beaker.

*half a hog. Sixpence : late C. 17–19 : c. then low. B.E., Grose. Cf. *grunter* and *hog.*

half a mo. A cigarette : Cockneys' and soldiers' : from ca. 1910. B. & P.

half a one. £500 : Stock Exchange coll. (— 1895) >, by 1920, j. (A. J. Wilson.) See **one,** 6.

*half a quid. Half-a-guinea (Vaux, 1812) ; by 1830, half-a-sovereign : c. >, by 1850, low.

half a stretch. Six months in prison : c. (—1859). H., 1st ed. See **stretch.**

half a ton of bones done up in horsehair. 'A thin ill-conditioned young horse ' : sporting (— 1909) ; ob. Ware.

half-a-yennork. Half-a-crown : low : from ca. 1855. See **yennork.**

half an eye, see with. To be alert of mind ; often with the implication that the deduction is easy to make. Coll. : from ca. 1530 : in C. 19–20, S.E. The nautical *have half an eye*, ex the same sense, is perhaps to be considered as coll.

half an ounce. Half a crown : C. 18–early 19. Silver, in C. 18, being assessed at five shillings an ounce. *A New Canting Dict.*, 1725.

half an Oxford. Half-a-crown : from ca. 1870. P. P., *Rhyming Slang*, 1932. On *Oxford scholar* = dollar.

half and half, gen. hyphenated. A drink of ale and beer, or ale and porter, in equal quantities : from ca. 1710 (ob.) : s. >, ca. 1800, coll. ; in C. 20, S.E. Ned Ward, *A Vade Mecum for Maltworms*, 1715 ; 'Peter Corcoran' Reynolds, 'Over my gentle half-and-half '.

half and half, adj. Half-drunk : from ca. 1715 (slightly ob.) : in C. 18, s. ; in C. 19 coll. ; in C. 20, S.E.

half-and-half coves, occ. **boys, men,** etc. Cheap would-be dandies : low : ca. 1820–60. Moncrieff.

half-and-halfer. A person, an object, that is neither the one thing nor the other : coll. : late C. 19.

half-baked. Irresolute : ca. 1800–60 : coll. Ex the C. 17 S.E. sense, not thorough-going.—2. (? hence) half-witted ; silly : perhaps orig. (1842) U.S. and anglicised ca. 1860, though recorded in dial. in 1855 : coll. H., 1860 ; Besant, 1886, 'Not quite right in her head—half-baked, to use the popular and feeling expression '; *Notes and Queries*, 1864, records the Cornish proverb, 'He is only half-baked ; put in with the bread and taken out with the cakes,'—so perhaps *not* American in origin. In C. 20, it implies lack of intelligence (but not downright silliness) plus a lack of culture.

*half board or **borde.** Sixpence : mid C. 17–early 19 c. Coles. See **borde.**

half-bull white. See **white, n.**

half-cock, go off at. (Variant *half-cocked*.) 'To ejaculate before completing erection', F. & H.: low : from ca. 1850. Ex a gun.

half-cocked. Slightly intoxicated : Australian : 1888, Fergus Hume (O.E.D.) ; ob. Ex dial., where recorded over fifty years earlier.

half-cracked. Somewhat unintelligent or mad : low coll. (— 1887). W. P. Frith, 'What is vulgarly called half-cracked ', 1887.

half-crown ball. Generic for : 'a respectable, commonplace hop': middle-classes' coll. : ca. 1880–1914. Ware.

half-crown battalion. Any Second Sixth Battalion : military : 1915. F. & Gibbons, 'From the notation [2/6] entered in official documents '.

half-crown word. A rare or, esp. a difficult word : low coll. : from ca. 1860 ; ob. Cf. *jaw-breaker* and *sleeve-board*, qq.v.

half-crowner. A publication priced at 2*s.* 6*d.* : booksellers' coll. : from ca. 1880 ; ob. Baumann, 1887.

half-cut. Half-drunk : lower classes' : from ca. 1860 : ob. See **cut.**

*half flash and half polish. Having a smattering of cant and an imperfect knowledge of the world : c. of ca. 1810–50. Vaux ; Egan's Grose. Cf. *foolish*, q.v.

*half-fly flat. A criminal's rough-worker : **c.** : from ca. 1830.

half-go. 'Three pennyworth of spirits, for mixing with . . . water': public-houses' : ca. 1890–1914. Ware.

half-gone. Half-drunk : coll. : late C. 19–20. F. & Gibbons.

half-hour gentleman. A man whose breeding is superficial : society coll. : ca. 1870–1914. Ware. Cf. *temporary gentleman*, q.v.

*half-inch. To steal : c. and low s. (— 1914). Charles E. Leach. Rhyming s. on *pinch.*—2. To draw near to (an object) : New Zealanders' : from not later than 1915. Perhaps ex *inch by inch.*

*half jack. Half a sovereign : c., or low : mid-C. 19–20 ; ob.

half-joe. Eight dollars : see **joe,** 4.

half-laugh and purser's grin. A sneer or an unpleasant innuendo : nautical, esp. naval : ca. 1880–1915. Clark Russell ; Bowen.

half-man. A landsman or a youth rated as an A.B., but not with his pay : nautical coll. : ca. 1860–1910. Bowen. Cf. :

half-marrow. An incompetent sailor ; a seaman that, having served his time, is not yet rated as A.B. : (mainly Northern and Scots) nautical : ca. 1850–1930. Cf. mining *h.-m.*, a partner.

half-moon. A wig : coll. : C. 18–19.—2. The female pudend : C. 17 low.

half-mourning. A black eye : rather low (— 1864) ; ob. Cf. *full mourning*, two black eyes.

half-nab or **-nap.** At a venture ; hit or miss : a C. 18-early 19 low corruption or perversion of *hab-nab*, q.v.

half-nelson. Partly drunk : low (— 1923). Manchon. Ex the wrestling-hold.

half-nicker. Ten shillings ; a 10*s.* note, half a sovereign : New Zealanders' : C. 20. Ex dial. *half-a-nicker* (1895 : E.D.D.).

half-off or **-on.** (Often without hyphens.) Half-drunk : low : from ca. 1870. See **on.**

half-past kissing time and time to kiss again(, it's). A low c.p. reply to a female asking a man the time : mostly London : ca. 1870–1910. Ex a popular

ballad. Cf. *an hour past hanging time* in Swift's *Polite Conversation* and see also **kissing-time.**

half-past nines. Very large feminine foot-wear : Cockneys' (— 1909). Ware. Nines being a large size for women.

half-pie. Insincere ; little respected ; (rather) contemptible : New Zealanders' : C. 20. See **pie.**

half-rats. Partially intoxicated : low : 1897 ; ob. Ware, who notes the equally low variant, *half up the pole*, dating from a decade or so earlier.

half-rem. See ' Winchester College slang ', § 6.

half-rinsed. Slightly drunk : New Zealanders' : from ca. 1912.

half-rocked. Half-witted ; silly : dial. >, ca. 1860, coll. Ex a West Country saying that fools have been cradle-rocked bottom upwards. A West Country synonym (wrongly, I think, included by F. & H.) is *half-saved* : see Mortimer Collins's *Frances*, ch. xlii. Cf. *rocked in a stone kitchen.*

half round the bend. Not mad, but often doing very silly things : naval : late C. 19–20. Bowen.

*half-scrag. (Collective n.) Half-castes : c. : from ca. 1860. The reference in ' *No 747* ' at p. 16 is to ca. 1865.

half-screwed. Half-drunk : from ca. 1835. Lever, ' He was, in Kilrush phrase, half-screwed . . . more than half tipsy.' See **screwed.**

half sea. Mid-Channel : nautical coll. : from ca. 1860. Bowen.

half-seas over. Half or almost drunk : late C. 17–20 : nautical > gen. : C. 19–20, coll. B.E., Smollett, Thackeray. Either *half sea's over* or a corruption, as Gifford maintained, of *op-zee zober*, ' over-sea beer ', a heady drink imported from Holland ; but, in C. 16, the phrase = halfway across the sea, which rather rebuts Gifford. Cf. the nautical *slewed*, *sprung*, *three sheets in the wind*, and *water-logged.*

half seven (eight, nine, etc.), at. At half-past seven (etc.) : military (other ranks') : from ca. 1920. E.g. ' We move off at half eight, sir.'

half-slewed. Half-drunk : nautical > gen. **slewed** ; *half-slewed* may, however, have been prompted by *half-screwed*, q.v.

half-snags. Half-shares : low coll. : C. 19–20 (ob.). Ex *half-snack(s)*. See esp. Walford's *Antiquarian*, 1887, p. 252.

half-termer. A half-term holiday : Public Schools' : C. 20.

half-timer. A scholar working half the day and going to school the other half : primary schools' coll. (from 1870) >, by 1900, S.E.—2. A kipper : nautical : C. 20. Bowen. Because so small on a dish.

*half tusheroon. Half-a-crown : c. (— 1857). ' Ducange Anglicus.'

half-un. A half-glass of spirits and water : low coll. : from ca. 1865 ; ob.

half up the pole. See **half-rats.**

halfpenny good silver, think one's. To think extremely well of one's abilities : coll. : ca. 1570–1700. Gascoigne.

halfpenny howling swell. A pretender to fashion : ca. 1870–80. Ware.

halfpennyworth of tar, lose the ship for a. To lose or spoil by foolish economy : a C. 19–20 coll. perversion of C. 17–18 *sheep*, often—in dial.—pronounced *ship.*

halfperth, halfporth, halfp'worth. See **ha'p'orth.**

Halifax !, go to. Go to blazes ! : coll. : 1669 (O.E.D.) ; in C. 19–20, mostly U.S. and re-anglicised

ca. 1870, esp. in dial. (See Apperson.) Euphemising *hell* but ultimately ex the C. 16–20 *Hell, Hull, and Halifax*, q.v. Cf. *Bath, Jericho, Putney*, qq.v.; see also **Hull**.

hall. (Gen. pl.) A music-hall : coll. (— 1887). Baumann.

hall, v. Dine in hall : Oxford University coll. rather than s. : from ca. 1860. Ex j. *hall*, dinner in hall (1859 : S.O.D.).

Hall, the. Leadenhall Market : fishmongers' s. > coll. : mid-C. 19–20. H., 3rd ed. Cf. (*The*) *Garden, the Lane*.

Hall by the Sea, the. The Examination Hall of the Royal Colleges of Physicians and Surgeons : medical : ca. 1880–1915. Situated on the London Embankment, i.e. near the Thames !

hall of delight. A music-hall : Australian : ca. 1890–1910. Hume Nisbet. (I myself did not hear it ; never, I believe, very gen.)

hallabaloo. An early form of *hullabaloo*.

hallan(d)-, or **hallen-, shaker.** A vagabond ; esp. a sturdy beggar : Scots coll. : C. 16–20 ; ob. *Hallan*, a partition wall in a cottage.

hallelujah gal(l)op. A hymn in a quick, lively measure, 'invented by General Booth to attract the multitude' : Salvationists' coll. : from the 1890's. Ware. Cf. :

hallelujah hell-sniffle of a(n). A truly 'awful' (something or other) : Canadian (— 1932). John Beames.

hallelujah-lass. A female member—esp. if young —of the Salvation Army : coll. : from ca. 1899.

halligator ; properly **alligator.** A herring : eating- and coffee-houses' : mid-C. 19–20. Ware.

hallion, hallyon ; hellion ; hullion. 'A rogue ; a clod ; a gentleman's servant out of livery ; also a shrew', F. & H. : Scots coll. and Northern dial. : late C. 18–19. Scott, 1817, 'This is a decentish hallion'; Crockett, 1895, 'I can manage the hullions fine.' ? ex Fr. *haillon*, a rag, a tatter.

hallo, baby ! how's nurse ? A military c.p. addressed to a girl pushing a 'pram' : from ca. 1908. B. & P.

hal(l)mote, when defined—as, ca. 1650–1800, it often is by writers on Church (e.g. Fuller) and Law (e.g. Blount and Jacob)—'a holy or an ecclesiastical court', is a decided catachresis. (O.E.D.)

*halls. See **work the halls**.

halloo-baloo ; halloo-bo-loo ; hallybaloo. Early forms of *hullabaloo*. (O.E.D.)

halo racket, work the. To grumble, be discontented : low : from ca. 1860. Ex the Heaven-placed saint dissatisfied with his halo. See **racket**.

halperthe, halp(w)orth(e). Early forms of *ha'p'orth*, q.v.

halter-sack. A gallows-bird ; also as a gen. pejorative : late C. 16–mid-17 : coll. Beaumont & Fletcher, in *A King and No King*, 'Away, you haltersack, you.'

halvers ! An exclamatory claim to something found : coll. and dial. (— 1816) : ob. except in dial. Scott.

halves. Half-Wellington boots : Winchester College, ca. 1840–85. (Pron. *hāves*.)

halves, cry or **go.** To claim, or to take, a half share or chance : coll. : from ca. 1850. Mayhew, 'He'll then again ask if anybody will go him halves.'

ham and eggs. Legs : rhyming s. : from ca. 1870. P. P., *Rhyming Slang*, 1932.

*ham-cases, hams. Trousers : c. : ca. 1770–1860, **ca.** 1720–1830 resp., though *ham-cases* may be the

earlier : those things which encase the hams. Cf. Romany *hamyas*, knee-breeches.

ham diet, be for. To be 'crimed' : Scottish military : G.W. F. & Gibbons.

ham-match. A stand-up lunch : low (— 1890) ; ob. : mostly London.

ham pilot. A clumsy pilot and/or one rough on his machine : Royal Air Force : 1932. From U.S.A.

hamble. To hamstring : a C. 17–18 cultured sol. (S.O.D.) Properly, to maim, mutilate.

Hamburg. A 'bazaar', i.e. false, rumour : Anglo-Indian : late C. 19–20 ; very ob. Ware. Semantics : *made in Germany*.

*hamlet. A high constable : c. : ca. 1690–1830 ; it survived in U.S. till ca. 1900. B.E. Cf. Yorkshire *play Hamlet*, or *hamlet, with*, to play the devil with, to scold.—**2.** (**Hamlet.**) An omelette : theatrical : 1885. Ware, 'Started on Ash Wednesday [of that year] by the actors of the Princess's Theatre, where Mr. Wilson Barrett was then playing *Hamlet*. These gay souls dined and supped at the Swiss Hotel, Compton Street, and necessarily therefore found themselves before omelettes.'

hammer. A vigorous puncher, esp. with the stronger arm : pugilistic : from ca. 1830 ; ob. Also *hammerer*, as in Moore's *Tom Crib*, 1819, and *hammerman*, as in Bee's *Dict*.—**2.** Hence, a boxer ; a stalwart bodyguard : late C. 19–20. E.g., John G. Brandon, *Th' Big City*, 1931.—**3.** An impudent lie : from ca. 1840 ; ob. Cf. *whopper*.

hammer, v. To punish ; beat : pugilistic **s.** (— 1887) and then gen. coll. Baumann.—**2.** To declare (a member) a defaulter : Stock Exchange (— 1885). Ex the hammer-taps preceding the head porter's formal proclamation. Frequently as a ppl. adj., *hammered* : see esp. A. J. Wilson, *Stock Exchange Glossary*, 1895, for the procedure. In the printing and allied trades a youth is said to be *hammered out* when he completes his apprenticeship and leaves the shop, at which point all those who are working in the shop seize a hammer and bang on a bench : this is a coll. verging on j., and belongs to late C. 19–20.—**3.** To depress (a market, stocks, prices) : Stock Exchange : 1865 (S.O.D.) Vbl.n., *hammering*.

hammer, at or **under the.** For sale : auctioneers' : from ca. 1855, but adumbrated 140 years earlier : *at* being †. In C. 20, *under the hammer* has > coll. and, before 1920, S.E. Cf. L. *sub hasta*. (W.)

*hammer, down as a. Wide-awake, 'fly' : c. : ca. 1810–1905. Vaux ; Moore. See also **down as a hammer.**—**2.** (Variant, *down like a hammer*) very prompt to act ; peremptory, merciless : coll. : from ca. 1860. The *as a* form is †.

hammer, swing the. To malinger : military : C. 20. F. & Gibbons. Cf. *swing the lead*.

hammer, that's the. That's all right ; that's excellent : (low) coll. : from ca. 1860 ; ob. Cf. :

hammer, up to the. First-rate ; excellent : from early 1880's : s. >, ca. 1900, coll. ; ob. Lit., up to the standard. (O.E.D.)

hammer and tongs. Occ., as in Marryat's *Snarley-Yow*, an expletive (†) ; gen. an adv. = violently, and preceded by *at it*, as in G. Parker's 'His master and mistress were at it hammer and tongs.' Coll. : from ca. 1780 ; *with h. and t.*, ca. 1708–80. Ex a vigorous smith's blows on the iron taken with the tongs from the fire.

hammer-headed. Stupid ; oafish : coll., perhaps : the O.E.D. considers it S.E. Mid-C. 16–20 ; ob.

Nashe. Ex the hardness of a hammer.—2. Hammer-shaped : mid-C. 16–20 ; S.E. till C. 19, then coll. Dickens.

hammer into. To succeed, finally, in teaching (a person something) or convincing (a person of something) : coll. : mid-C. 17–20 : S.E. until ca. 1830, then coll.—2. To fight and defeat : coll. (— 1931). Lyell, ' One of the boys lost his temper and fairly hammered into him.' Cf. *pitch into.*

hammer-man. See hammer, n., 1.

hammer on, v.i. To reiterate again and again : coll. (— 1888) : ob.

hammer out. To discuss (v.t.) until settled, gen. with connotation of difficulty, occ. with that of obtuseness : late C. 16–20 ; coll. till ca. 1720, then S.E. D'Urfey.

hammered, ppl. adj. See hammer, v., 2.—

hammered out. See hammer, v., 2.

hammerer. See hammer, n., 1.

hammering. Heavy punishment ; a defeat : pugilistic s. > gen. coll. : from ca. 1830.—2. Overcharging for time-work, e.g. corrections (which are, from author's and publisher's stand-point, always over-charged) : printers' : from ca. 1860 ; ob.— 3. See hammer, v., 3.—4. The transmission of wireless messages : nautical : from ca. 1924. Bowen.

hammering-trade. Boxing : boxers' (— 1819) ; ob. by 1900, † by 1920. Moore, ' The other . . . made, express, by Nature for the hammering trade.'

*****hammerish.** Same as, and ex, *down as a hammer* : ca. 1810–50. Vaux.

Hammers. The West *Ham* ' soccer ' team : sporting : C. 20. (*The Sunday Referee*, Oct. 15, 1933.)

hammers to one, be. ' To know what one means ', F. & H. : (low) coll. : ca. 1860–1910.

Hammersmith, have been at or gone to. To be soundly drubbed : boxing coll. : from ca. 1820 ; ob. Egan's Grose. Punning the London suburb, part of which is ' tough ', and *hammer*, n., 1.

hammock, the moon's stepping out of her. The moon is rising : nautical coll. (— 1887) ; ob. Baumann.

hammock-man. A seaman attending to the midshipmen : naval : late C. 19. Bowen. Cf. *midshipmen's devil,* q.v.

hampered. Entangled : ca. 1630–90, S.E. ; late C. 17–18 coll. ; then S.E. again. Ex *hamper,* a fetter, as in Browne's *Britannia's Pastorals,* ' Shackles, shacklockes, hampers, gives and chaines '

Hampshire hog. A native of Hampshire : C. 17–20 : coll. Drayton in *Polyolbion.* Ex the county's famous breed of hogs.

Hampstead donkey. A louse : low : ca. 1865–1900.

Hampstead Heath. The teeth : rhyming s. : from ca. 1880. *The Referee,* Nov. 7, 1887. Cf. *Hounslow Heath,* q.v. It is, in C. 20, often abbr. to *Hampsteads* : witness *The Daily Express,* Jan. 25, 1932.

Hampstead Heath sailor. A landlubber : ca. 1875–1905. Cf. *freshwater sailor.*

Hampsteads. Teeth : a late C. 19–20 abbr. of *Hampstead Heath,* q.v. (*The Daily Express,* Jan. 25, 1932.)

Hampton Wick, often abbr. to **Hampton.** The penis : rhyming s. : late C. 19–20. B. & P. On *prick.*

*****hams.** See ham-cases.

hanced. Tipsy : C. 17 coll. Taylor the Water Poet. Cf. *elevated.*

hand. Orig. (C. 17), nautical for a sailor, a sense it has retained ; but as early as 1792 it had > gen. coll. for one skilful *at* anything ; in C. 20, it verges on S.E.—2. Of a person in reference to character (e.g. *a loose hand*) : coll. : 1798 ; ob. O.E.D.—3. A skilful touch with horses : coachmen's and sporting : from ca. 1855, j. > s. or coll. ; ob. Whyte-Melville.—4. See hands, all.

hand !, bear a. Make haste ! : coll. : late C. 18–20 ; ob. Grose, 3rd ed.

hand, bring down, or **off, by.** To masturbate (v.t.) : low coll. : from ca. 1800 ; *down* is †. (Of men.)

hand, bring up by. Manually to induce a priapism : low : from ca. 1850.

hand, cool or **fine** or **good** or **neat** or **old** or **rare.** An expert : coll. : resp. 1845,—1880,—1748,— 1892,—1861, (? —) 1797. In *cool,* and occ. for the others, the stress is on character, not skill : this gen. coll. tendency dates from ca. 1798 (S.O.D.).— 2. See hand, old, below.

hand, get or **give a.** To be applauded or to applaud : theatrical : from ca. 1870. Ex the S.E. *give one's hand,* as in Shakespeare.

hand, get or **have the upper.** To gain or have an advantage (v.t. with *of*) : coll. (— 1886) ; in C. 20, S.E. : ? always S.E. Stevenson, in *Kidnapped.*

hand, green. An inexperienced person, esp. workmen : C. 18–20 : orig. coll. ; but since ca. 1860, S.E. See green, adj.

hand, heavy on ; hot at hand. Hard to manage : coll. : ca. 1860–1912. Cf. :

hand, light in. Easy to manage : coll. : ca. 1860–1910.

*****hand, long.** See long hand.

*****hand, old.** An ex-convict : Australian : ca. 1860–1905. T. McCombie, *Australian Sketches,* 1861 ; 1865, J. O. Tucker, ' Reformed convicts, or, in the language of their proverbial cant, " old hands ".' Morris.

hand, stand one's. To pay for a round of drinks : Australian : ca. 1890–1915. Hume Nisbet in *The Bushranger's Sweetheart,* 1892.

hand, such a thing fell into his. He has improved another's notion, invention, etc. : coll. : ca. 1660–1800. B.E.

hand and pocket shop, the first three words being often hyphenated. An eating-house where cash is paid for what one orders : coll. : ca. 1785–1840. Grose, 2nd ed.

hand-cart cavalry. Stokes trench-mortar brigades : military : 1916–18. F. & Gibbons. The mortar was transported in a hand-cart.

hand-grenade. An Army water-bottle : military : 1915. F. & Gibbons. Ex its shape.

hand in, get one's, v.i. To practise so as to become proficient : coll. : from ca. 1875. Ex much earlier cognate S.E. phrases.

hand in one's checks or **chips.** See cash one's checks. Mostly U.S.

hand is (or was) out, his or **her.** He is or was ' ready to take all and everything at all times ' : non-aristocratic c.p. (— 1909) ; ob. Ware.

hand it to. To admit the superiority of : coll., orig. (— 1916) U.S., anglicised ca. 1930. (O.E.D. Sup.)

hand-me-downs. Second-hand clothes : low coll (— 1874). H., 5th ed.—2. In C. 20, also = ' ready-mades ' : cf. *reach-me-downs.* A C. 19 variant, in the former sense, is *hand-em-downs.*—3. Whence *hand-me-down shop,* a shop where such clothes may be bought ; also (— 1909), an illegal pawnbroker's : low coll. Ware.

*hand like a fist. A handful of trumps ; an unbeatable hand : gamblers' (at cards) : from ca. 1870.

hand like a foot. A large, rough hand ; vulgar, clumsy handwriting : coll. : from ca. 1705 ; ob. Swift.

hand of it, make a. To turn something to account ; profit by it : coll. : C. 17–early 19. Ex C. 16 S.E. *make a hand*, v.i.

hand on, get a. To suspect ; be distrustful of : tailors' : from ca. 1870 ; ob.

hand (or heart) on, e.g. **his halfpenny, have his.** 'To have an eye on the main chance, or on any particular object ', Apperson : C. 16–20 : coll. till C. 19, then dial.

hand on it, get one's. To caress a woman genitally : low coll. : from ca. 1850.

hand-out. A meal handed out to the indigent : U.S., anglicised ca. 1920. (M. Harrison, *Spring in Tartarus*, 1935.)

hand over fist. Hand over hand ; very quickly : coll. : from ca. 1880.

hand over head. Hurriedly ; without method or reason ; thoughtlessly : coll. : from ca. 1440 : ob. except in dial. Latimer.

hand-running. Straight on ; in due succession : coll. when not, as gen., dial. : from ca. 1825 ; † except in dial. (O.E.D.)

hand-saw. Same as *chiv(e)-fencer*, q.v. : Cockney (— 1859). H., 1st ed. Prob. the correct term (which is ob.) should be *hand-saw fencer* : H. is here ambiguous.

hand to fist. Cheek by jowl ; intimate(ly) : mid-C. 17–19 coll. Grose. Ex the † S.E. *hand to hand*.

hand up. To betray ; sneak on : Winchester College : ca. 1860–1910.

handbasket portion. A woman whose husband receives numerous presents from her parents and/or relatives : late C. 18–mid-19 : coll. Grose, 2nd ed.

handbinders, manacles, may (see F. & H.) possibly be C. 17–early 18 coll.

handed, be. See ' Westminster School slang '.

hander. A second or assistant in a prize fight : sporting (— 1860) ; † by 1921.—2. A cane-stroke on the hand : schoolboys' (— 1868) ; ob. J. Greenwood, ' You've been playing the wag, and you've got to take your hànders.'

handfist, -ing. Incorrect for *handfast, -ing* : C. 18–20. O.E.D.

*handful, a. Five : racing c. : C. 20. Cf. *fives*(, *a bunch of*). Hence, *win with a couple of handfuls*, by ten lengths, i.e. easily (*Slang*, p. 243).

[**handicap,** n. and v., has, whether lit. or fig., always, *pace* F. & H., been S.E.]

handie-dandie, handy-dandy. Sexual connexion : (mainly Scots) coll. : C. 16–18. Ex the child's game.

handies. ' A fondling of hands between lovers ', C. J. Dennis : Australian : C. 20. Esp. in *play at handies*, to fondle thus.

handkercher, hankercher. Handkerchief : sol. and dial. : C. 19–20. (O.E.D.) Cf. *hankie*.

handky is a rare variant of *hankie* (-*y*), q.v.

handle. A nose : low : ca. 1810–1920, but ob. by 1900. *Lex. Bal. Modern Society*, Aug. 27, 1887, ' A[n] . . . intriguing . . . old lady, with an immense handle to her face '. Ex the C. 18 jocular *handle of the face*, as in Motteux.—2. A title : nearly always in form *handle to one's name* : coll. :

1833, Marryat ; Thackeray, 1855. In C. 20, occ. loosely used to include *Dr.* and even *Mr.*

handle, v. As = to use, e.g. *handle one's fists*, it is S.E., but as = to palm (cards) it is cardsharpers' c. : from ca. 1860.

handle, fly off the. See **fly off the handle.**

handle the ribbons. To drive a coach or a carriage : coll. (— 1827) : ob. Moncrieff ; Milliken, ' He 'andled the ribbings to rights,' 1892 in his lively '*Arry Ballads*.

handle to one's name. See **handle, n., 2.**

hands, all. ' All the members of a party, esp. when collectively engaged in work ', O.E.D. : coll. : from ca. 1700. Farquhar, Dickens. Ex *all hands*, the complete (ship's) crew.

hands off ! Keep off or away ! Coll. : from ca. 1560.

hand's turn. A stroke of work : coll. (— 1881) ex dial. (1828). O.E.D.

hands up ! Oh, stop talking ! : (low) coll. (— 1888). Ex police command to surrender.

handsaw. A street seller of knives and razors : low : ca. 1835–1900. Ex the lit. S.E. sense. Cf. *chive-fencer*, q.v.

[**han(d)sel,** n. and v., should not have been included by F. & H.]

handsome as an adj. is, despite F. & H., ineligible. As an adv., esp. in *handsome is that handsome does* (' a proverb frequently cited by ugly women ', Grose), it was, in C. 15–mid-18, S.E. ; then coll. ; then, after ca. 1850, low coll. As n. : see **handsome thing.**

handsome-bodied in the face. Ugly : derisively coll. (— 1678) : † by 1893, ob. by 1860.

handsome reward, ca. 1785–1830, meant, as a jocular coll., a horse whipping. Grose, 3rd ed. Ex the ambiguous language of ' lost ' advertisements.

handsome (thing), do the. To behave extremely well ; esp. to be very generous : coll. (— 1887). Manville Fenn, in *This Man's Wife.*

handsomely over the bricks ! Go cautiously ; Be careful : an ob. (— 1893), mainly nautical coll. elaboration of the nautical *handsomely !*, carefully !, not so fast ! F. & H. ; Bowen.

handspike hash. The enforcing of discipline : sailing-ships' : late C. 19–20. Bowen. Cf. *belaying-pin soup.*

handsprings, chuck. To turn somersaults : low coll. : from ca. 1860.

handstaff. The male member : from ca. 1850 : coll. (mainly rural). Ex the handling of a flail.

handy, play at. An English form of *play at handies* (see *handies*) : C. 20. Manchon.

[**handy blows.** Fisticuffs : late C. 16–mid-19. The O.E.D. considers it S.E. ; F. & H., coll., as do B.E. and the editor of *A New Canting Dict.* Prob. coll. ca. 1660–1740.—**handy man,** occ. **handy-man,** a man of all work, is certainly S.E., for *handy*, dextrous, like *handy*, convenient or near, is S.E. ; and *handy man*, a sailor—dating from Kipling's early work—is a special application thereof. But **handy for,** conveniently situated for, is coll. : late C. 19–20.]

handy billy (or **B.**). ' A small tackle used for a variety of purposes ' : naval coll. : late C. 19–20. F. & Gibbons.

handy-dandy. See **handie-dandie.—handy for.** See **handy blows,** at end.

handy Jack. A lower classes' coll. and pejorative form of *Jack of all trades* : but C. 19–20. Ware.

hang. The general drift or tendency, gen. in *get*

the hang of: coll. (— 1847): perhaps orig. U.S., where recorded—see Thornton—in 1845 as *acquire the hang of*. Darley; *The Daily Chronicle*, April 4, 1890, 'He gets what some call the hang of the place.'—2. (Always in a negative sentence.) A (little) bit: pejorative coll. (— 1861); ob. H. Kingsley, 'She can't ride a hang.'

hang, v. In expletive locutions, as *hang him! (and) be hanged!*, (*go and*) *hang yourself!*, *hang it!*, and *hang!*, it indicates disgust, annoyance, or disappointment, and sometimes *hang* (*it*)! = *damn* (*it*)! Coll.: late C. 16–20, though anticipated in C. 14, as in Chaucer's ' Jelousie be hanged be [*by*] a cable! ' Shakespeare, 'He a good wit ? Hang him, baboon ! '; Grant Allen, 'Hang it all . . .'—a common form of the exclamation. Cf. the † proverbial *hang yourself for a pastime* (— 1678). See esp. the O.E.D.

hang aback. A coll. nautical variant of *hang back* (to show reluctance), in the specific sense, to shirk duty : C. 19–20. Bowen.

hang about or **around.** To haunt, v.t., loaf, v.i. : coll. : orig. U.S. ; anglicised ca. 1895.

hang an arse. To hold (oneself) back ; hesitate : late C. 16–20, ob. : S.E. in C. 17, then coll., then in C. 19–20 low coll. Marston, Smollett, Tomlinson in his valuable *Slang Pastoral*. Cf. S.E. *hang a leg* or † *the groin*.

hang-bluff. Snuff: rhyming s. (— 1857); †. 'Ducange Anglicus.' Displaced, ca. 1870, by *Harry Bluff*.

hang-by. A hanger-on, a parasite : coll. : late C. 16–17 ; then dial. Jonson.

hang-dog. A pitiful rascal : C. 18 coll. Fielding. (The adj. is S.E., as, indeed, the O.E.D. considers the n.) Lit., fit only to hang a dog.

hang-gallows look. A villainous appearance : coll. on verge of S.E. : late C. 18–19. Grose, 1st ed. (The n. *hang-gallows*, a gallows-bird, is wholly S.E.)

hang in. To set to work ; do one's best : low coll. : C. 19–20, ob.

hang-in-chains. 'A vile desperate fellow', Grose, 1st ed. : coll. : ca. 1780–1830.

hang in the bellropes. To postpone marriage after being ' banned ' in church : coll. : from ca. 1750 ; ob. by 1900, † by 1930, except in dial. Apperson.

hang it ! See **hang. v.**

hang it on. See **hang on**, eligible sense, and cf. :

hang it on with (a woman). To make her one's mistress : low (— 1812) ; † by 1900. Vaux.

hang it out. To delay a matter : (? low) coll. : Australian (— 1890) ; slightly ob. ' Rolf Boldrewood.' Ex *hang about*, q.v. Cf. *hang on* and *hang out*, v., 2.

hang it up. See **hang up, v.—hang of, get the.** See **hang, n.,** 1.

hang off, v.t. To fight shy of : printers' : from ca. 1860. A slight deviation from C. 17–20 S.E. senses, to hesitate, hang back, raise objections.

hang-on. 'A hanger-on, a mean dependant' (O.E.D.) : coll., I think, though given as S.E. by the O.E.D. : late C. 16–early 17.

hang on, v. To sponge on ; pursue a person or a design, is, despite F. & H., ineligible. But (gen. as *hang it on*) in sense, to delay a matter, it is low : from ca. 1810. Vaux. Cf. *hang it out*, q.v.

hang on by one's eyelashes (in C. 20 **eyebrows**). To persist obstinately or most courageously : from ca. 1860 : coll.—2. Also, in C. 20, to be near to ruin, death, or defeat, *eyebrows* being much pre-

ferred in this sense. A variant of both senses is *hang on by the skin of one's teeth*, likewise coll.

hang on by the splashboard. To catch a 'bus, tram, etc., as it moves ; hence, barely to succeed : from ca. 1880 : coll.

hang one's bat out to dry. To place one's bat in an impotent position : cricketers': 1895, C. B. Fry. (Lewis.)

hang one's hat up. To become engaged to a girl ; *hanging one's hat up*, thus engaged : non-aristocratic : late C. 19.

hang one's latchpan. To look and/or be dejected ; to pout : low coll. when not dial. : C. 19–20, ob. Ex *latchpan*, a pan to catch the drippings from a roast.

hang-out. A residence or lodging : low s. > coll. : from ca. 1820 ; ob. by 1910, virtually † by 1934. ' Ducange Anglicus ' has *hangs-out*. Ex :

hang-out, v. To reside, live, lodge ; be temporarily at (e.g. a dug-out in the trenches) : orig. low or prob. c. (— 1811) ; by 1835 gen. s. ; in C. 20, coll. *Lex. Bal.*, 'The traps [*police*] scavey where we hang out '; Dickens. Ex the ancient custom of hanging out signs. Cf. (— 1871) U.S. *hang out a shingle*, to carry on a business.—2. Hence (of inanimates), to be, to exist, be located : coll. : from ca. 1910. Lyell, 'I hear you've got a job in Foster's factory. Where does it actually hang out ?'—3. To last, to endure : Australian (— 1916). C. J. Dennis. Cf. (perhaps ex) *hang it out*, q.v.

hang out the flag of distress. See **flag of distress.** —2. To live in furnished lodgings : urban (— 1923). Manchon.—3. To be an ordinary street-harlot : low (— 1923). Ibid.

hang out the washing. To set sail : nautical : mid-C. 19–20. Bowen.

hang-over. A ' morning after the night before ' feeling : from ca. 1910.

hang saving ! ' Blow the expense ! ' : coll. c.p. : C. 18. Swift, *Polite Conversation*, II. Nowadays, *hang the expense !* : C. 19–20.

hang-slang about, gen. v.i. To ' slang ', vituperate : low : ca. 1860–1910. An elaboration of *slang*, v.—2. To ' hang about ' with illicit intention : c. or low (— 1923). Manchon.

hang-up. A gallows-bird : coll. : ca. 1560–1660. (*Hang-rope* and *-string* are S.E.)

hang up, v. (Gen. as *hang it up.*) To give credit, lit. chalk it up : prob. orig. (— 1725) c. ; by 1785, low ; ob. by 1890, † by 1921.—2. V.t., to rob, with assault, on the street ; to garotte : c. : ca. 1870–1915. Cf. S.E. *hold up*.—3. V.t., to postpone, leave unsettled : coll. : G. Rose, 1803 (O.E.D., which considers the phrase S.E., as it certainly is in C. 20). *The Cornhill Magazine*, June, 1887.—4. V.i., to be in dire straits, physical or monetary ; e.g. *a man hanging* is one ' to whom any change must be for the better ', F. & H. : low coll. : ca. 1860–1910.—5. V.t., to tie up a horse : Australian (— 1860) ; coll. W. Kelly, *Life in Victoria*, 1860. Ex securing horses to posts.

hang up one's hat. To die : (? low) s. > coll. : ca. 1850–1914.—2. To make oneself very much at home : coll. : from ca. 1855. Occ. with an implication of ' honest ' courting and often of a married man living in the wife's house, as in Trollope's *The Warden*.

hang up the hatchet. See **bury the hatchet.**

hang up the ladle. To marry : society : mid-C. 18–early 19. Ware.

hanged. Confounded, gen. as in ' Oh that be

hanged !' Coll.: from the middle 1880's. (O.E.D.). Ex dial. where recorded in 1864 : E.D.D. Cf. *hang*, **v.** (*I'll be hanged if* is familiar S.E.)

[**hanger-on**, considered by Grose as coll., is S.E.] **hangers.** Gloves ; esp. gloves held in the hand : ca. 1875–1910.—2. (Gen. in *pot-hooks and hangers* and very rare in the singular.) Strokes with a double curve, as *l* : **a** nursery coll : from ca. 1705. Swift.

hanging. Fit to be hanged : coll. : C. 19–20, ob. See **hang up, v.,** 4.

Hanging Committee. The Royal Academy committee that chooses pictures : painters' coll. (— 1887). Baumann. A pun.

Hanging Jervis. John Jervis, Admiral Lord St. Vincent (*temp.* Nelson) : naval. He was ungentle in his enforcement of discipline. (Bowen.)

hanging Johnny. The male member ; esp. if impotent or diseased : low : C. 19–20 (? ob.).

Hanging Judge, the. This nickname on the verge of being mere sobriquet has been given to various judges apt to give the capital sentence ; e.g. Toler (early C. 19), Hawkins (late C. 19), Avory (1920's and early 30's).

(hanging) on the barbed wire. A military c.p. reply to an inquiry as to a man's whereabouts : 1916–18. F. & Gibbons ; B. & P. Ex men left dead on the wire after an attack. Cf. *up in Annie's room*.

hangman. A pejorative term ; a jocular endearment : mid-C. 16–20, but rare after 1650. By the O.E.D. considered S.E. ; the latter use is, I believe, coll.

hangman's day. Monday (in U.S., *hanging day*, Friday) : low coll. : ca. 1830–1900.

hangman's wages. Thirteen-pence-halfpenny : 1678, Butler : ob. by 1820, † by 1880 : coll. Dekker, 1602, **has** 'Why should I eat hempeseed at the hangman's thirteen-pence-half-penny ordinary ? ', and *thirteen-pence half-penny wages* occurs in 1659. The C. 17 execution fee was **a** Scottish mark, fixed by James I at 13½*d*.

hangs-out. See *hang-out*, n.

hank. A spell of rest or comparative (physical) ease : coll. : from ca. 1810 ; ob. Vaux ; Egan's Grose ; *Sporting Life*, Dec. 7, 1888, concerning a boxing-match, 'The company . . . called out, " No hank ! " '

hank, v. To tease, bait, worry ; persecute : coll. : from ca. 1820 ; ob.

hank, in (a). In trouble ; in difficulty : coll. : C. 17–19.

hank, Smithfield. An ox infuriated by ill-treatment : ca. 1780–1830. Grose, 1st ed.

hank (up)on one, have a. To have a profitable, e.g. a blackmailing, hold on a person : coll. : ca. 1600–1840 (extant in dial. and in U.S.). In Vaux it takes the form, *have* (a person) *at a good hank*. Ex *hank*, a coil of rope.

hanker, v.i. To long. V.t. with *after*. From ca. 1640 ; it seems to have, ca. 1680–1825, been considered coll.,—witness B.E., and Grose (edd. of 1785–1823). The same applies to the vbl.n. *hankering*.

hankercher ; hank(e)ycher (Baumann). See **handkercher.** Cf. :

hankie, hanky ; rarely **handky.** A handkerchief : nursery coll. : late C. 19–20. C. J. Dennis.

hankin, n. Passing off bad work for good : commercial : from ca. 1870 ; ob.

*hankins. Breeches : c. : C. 18. Anon., *Street-Robberies Consider'd*, 1728.

hanktelo. ' A silly Fellow, a meer Cods-head ', B.E. : late C. 16–early 19 : coll. verging on S.E. In Nashe as *hangtelow* ; Grose, 1st ed.

hanky. See **hankie.**—2. Abbr. *hanky-panky* : 1924, Galsworthy (O.E.D. Sup.).

hanky-panky. Legerdemain ; hence, almost imm., trickery, double or underhand work : 1841, *Punch*. Also adj., as in *hanky-panky business*, conjuring or ' dirty work ', and *hanky-panky tricks* or *work*, double-dealing. An arbitrary word—cf. *hoky-poky*—perhaps ex (*have a*) *hank* (*on one*), q.v. above ; or perhaps, as W. suggests, ex ' *hokey-pokey* by association with *sleight of hand* '. Cf. *jiggery-pokery*, q.v.

hanky-panky bloke. A conjuror : theatrical : ca. 1860–1920. Ex preceding.

hanky-spanky. Dashing (of persons) ; esp., well-cut, stylish (of clothes) : ? low : from ca. 1880 Prob. ex *spanking*, q.v., by *hanky-panky*, q.v.

hanky worker. One who gets out of strait jackets : showmen's (— 1934). P. Allingham, *The Evening News*, July 9, 1934. Cf. *hanky-panky bloke*.

Hannah, that's the man as married (occ. **that's what's the matter with the man . . .**). Excellent ! Good for you ! Most certainly ! Orig. to designate a good or happy beginning. A rather low c.p., mostly Shropshire, then London : ca. 1860–1905. H., 1864.

Hanover !, go to. Go to hell : Jacobites' : ca. 1725–80. Ware. Cf. *Halifax, Jericho, Bath*, etc. E.D.D. notes also the dial. *what the Hanover !* and, concerning the Suffolk *go to Hanover and hoe turnips !*, remarks : ' Said to date from the time of the [first two] Georges, who were so unpopular in the east [of England] '.

Hanover (or to Hanover) jack. An imitation sovereign : low (? orig. c.) : ca. 1880–1914. Ware, who cites a police report of 1888, offers an unconvincing derivation.

Hans. A Dutchman ; a German (in C. 20, the only sense) : coll. : from ca. 1570. Abbr. *Johannes*, John. Cf. *Fritz*, q.v.

Hans Corvel's ring. The female pudend : C. 18–19 low coll. Prior. Ex a tale by Poggio.

Hans-en(or in)-Kelder. An unborn child : low : perhaps orig. c. : often as a toast to the expected infant : ca. 1630–1830. Brome, Dryden, Grose. Ex Dutch, lit. Jack in (the) cellar.

Hans the Grenadier. See **Carl the care-taker.** Cf. *Hans Wurst*, ' the popular German nickname for a German infantryman ' (F. & Gibbons).

Hansard. The reports of Parliamentary proceedings and speeches : coll. : 1876, Leslie Stephen (O.E.D.). Published by Messrs. Hansard since 1774.

hansel. See **handsel.**

hanseller, han'-seller. A low coll. form of S.E. *hand-seller*, a cheapjack : ca. 1850–1910. Hindley, in *Adventures of a Cheap Jack*.

hansom. A chop : costermongers' : ca. 1870–1925. ? punning the notions ' goes quickly ' and ' good to look at ', or ex the normal shapes.

ha'n't, han't. Have not : sol. : C. 18–20. Cf. *aint* and (for *am not*) *aren't*.

Hants. Hampshire. Such abbrr., when written, are S.E. ; but if spoken as genuine equivalents of the original names they are coll. This notice is to serve as generic for all the British counties that are so abbr. in coll. speech: e.g. *Bucks, Lancs, Wilts,* but not, e.g. *Som.* nor *Cambs.* Rare before ca. 1890.

hap-harlot. A rug, a coarse coverlet : coll. : ca. 1550–1760, then dial. (in C. 20, †). Lit., a cover-knave. Cf. *wrap-rascal,* q.v.

hap worth a cop(p)eras. See **ha'porth o' coppers.**

ha'penny. A coll. form (C. 16–20) of *halfpenny.* (O.E.D.)

ha'penny harder, a. (Of the money-market) slightly better in tendency : Stock Exchange coll. : C. 20. Ex the lit. sense as applied to a specific ' security '.

ha'p'orth. A coll. contraction of *halfpennyworth* : 1728, Swift (O.E.D.). Earlier contractions, also to be rated as coll., are—see the O.E.D. at *halfpenny-worth*—*halpworthe,* ca. 1490,—*halporthe,* 1533,—*halfperth,* 1692,—*halfp'worth,* 1719. Swift also has *halfporth,* but this is rare. A late (? before 1873, Browning) contraction is *ha'p'worth.*

ha'porth o' coppers. Habeas corpus : legal : from ca. 1840 ; ob. Ex the C. 18 sol. pronunciation *hap worth a coperas* quoted by Grose (3rd ed.).

ha'porth of liveliness. Music : costers' : from ca. 1845 ; ob. Mayhew.—2. A dawdler, a slow-coach : low (— 1893) ; ob.

happen. Adv. (orig. a subjunctive : cf. *maybe*), perhaps, perchance : at first (— 1790) and still mainly Northern dial., but from ca. 1845 it has been increasingly used as a coll., esp. in the non-committal *happen it does, happen it (he,* etc.) *will.*

happen in, v.i. To pay a casual visit : coll. : ex U.S. (— 1855) ; anglicised ca. 1895.

Happy. The inevitable nickname of anyone surnamed Day : late C. 19–20 : mostly naval and military. Bowen. Ex *O, happy day !*

happy, adj. Slightly (and, properly used, cheerfully) drunk : coll. : 1770 (O.E.D.). Marryat.

Happy and Chatty, the. H.M. Cruiser *Immortalité* : naval : when, in 1895–8, she was on the China Station under Sir Edward Chichester. Bowen. Partly rhyming, partly allusive to her condition.

happy days. Strong ale and beer mixed : public-houses' (esp. at Glasgow) ; from ca. 1920.

[**happy despatch,** better **dispatch,** death, cited by F. & H., is rather euphemistic than coll. An extremely ' approximate ' rendering of the Japanese *hara-kiri.* See **hari-kari,** itself a solecism.]

happy dosser. See **dosser.**

happy Eliza. A female Salvationist : 1887–ca. 1910. Ex a broadside ballad that points to ' Happy Eliza ' and ' Converted Jane ' as ' hot 'uns in our time '.

happy family. A number of different animals living quietly in one cage : coll. : ca. 1850–1915. Mayhew.

[**happy-go-lucky,** despite F. & H., is S.E. So, too, is *happy land,* Heaven.]

happy hunting-ground. ' A favourable place for work or play ', F. & H. : coll. (— 1892) >, ca. 1900, S.E.—2. The *pudendum muliebre* : low : from ca. 1870.

happy landings ! (Esp. over a drink) good luck ! : Air Force members' : 1915–18. (*The Evening News,* July 25, 1934.) It is extant among aircraft engineers : witness *The Daily Herald,* Aug. 1, 1936.

happy returns. Vomiting : Australia : low : ca. 1880–1930.

Happy Valley. A Somme valley famous in the Battle of the Somme (July–Nov., 1916) : ironic military nickname in late 1916–18. B. & P.

ha'p'worth. See **ha'p'orth.**

haramzeda. A scoundrel ; very gen. as term of abuse : Anglo-Indian (— 1864). Ex Arabo-Persian for son of the unlawful. Yule & Burnell.

harbegeon. A sol. spelling and pronunciation of *habergeon* : C. 15–20. (Even the correct form, however, has been merely historical since C. 16.) O.E.D.

[**harbour (of hope),** the female pudend, is salaciously euphemistic S.E.]

***hard.** Hard labour : c. (— 1890) : in C. 20, low. —2. Third class, on e.g. a train. ' Do you go hard or soft ? ', i.e. third or first : late C. 19–20. Abbr. *hard seat* or *hard arse.*—3. Preceded by *the,* whiskey : from ca. 1850 ; ob.—4. See **hard up, have a.**—5. Plug tobacco : from mid-1890's : coll. >, by 1930, S.E. Bowen ; O.E.D. (Sup.).

hard, adj. (Of beer or cider) stale or sour : late C. 16–20 : S.E. till ca. 1680 ; then coll. till mid-C. 19, then s. when not dial. ' Hard drink, that is very Stale, or beginning to Sower ', B.E.—2. Intoxicating, spirituous : coll. : orig. (ca. 1874) U.S., anglicised in mid-1880's. (O.E.D.)—3. See **tired.**

hard, die. To die fighting bravely : coll. : C. 19–20 ; ob. Cf. *the Die-Hards,* q.v., and the S.E. sense, to die impenitent.

hard, in the. In hard cash ; cash down : coll. (— 1830) ; ob.

hard-a-Gilbert. Hard-a-port : naval officers' : late C. 19–early 20. Bowen, ' Gilbert being an old-time wine merchant whose port was supplied to ward-rooms '.

hard-a-weather. Weather-proof ; physically tough : nautical coll. : 1848. Clark Russell, ' They were hard-a-weather fellows.'—2. Hence, a sailor : nautical coll. (— 1923), not very gen. Manchon.

hard-arsed. Very niggardly, monetarily costive : low : from ca. 1850.

hard as a bone ; as nails. Very hard : unyielding ; physically or morally tough : coll. : resp. ca. 1860–1930 and from 1838 (Dickens in *Oliver Twist*).

hard at it. Very busy, esp. on some particular work : coll. : from ca. 1870.

hard-bake. A sweetmeat of boiled brown sugar (or treacle) and blanched almonds : schoolboys' (— 1825) : in C. 20, gen. considered S.E. Hone, ' Hardbake, brandy-balls, and bull's-eyes '.

hard-baked. Constipated : low coll. (— 1823); ob. by 1893. ' Jon Bee.'—2. Stern, unflinching : coll. : ? orig. U.S. (— 1847).

hard bargain. A lazy fellow ; an incorrigible : coll. : from ca. 1850.—2. A defaulting debtor : trade : from ca. 1860 ; ob.—3. Occ. as synonymous with *hard case,* 4.

hard bit or **mouthful.** An unpleasant experience : coll. : ca. 1860–1910.—2. (Variant, *bit of hard*) the male member in priapism ; hence (for women) the *coitus.*

[**hard-bitten** is S.E., not—as in F. & H.—coll. ; and **hard-boiled,** despite popular opinion, is also S.E.—though a quite unnecessary Americanism and despite its having, in the U.S., been orig. coll.]

hard case. An incorrigible : orig. (1842), U.S. ; anglicised ca. 1860.—2. In Australia and New Zealand, a person morally tough but not necessarily incorrigible ; also a witty or amusing dare-devil,— one who loves fun and adventure ; a girl ready for sexual escapades : all coll. from ca. 1880.—3. A defaulting debtor : trade : from ca. 1865. Cf.

hard bargain, q.v.—4. A brutal officer : nautical : from ca. 1865. Cf. *hard horse*, q.v.

hard cheddar. See hard cheese.—hard cheek. See hard lines.

hard cheese. Bad luck ; orig., esp. at billiards : Royal Military Academy (— 1893) ; in C. 20, gen. in sense and in distribution. A humorous variant is *hard cheddar* (e.g. Neil Bell, *Andrew Otway*, 1931).

hard-cut. Dropped cigar-ends : low (? c.) : ca. 1890–1920. Cf. *hard-up*, n., 1.

hard doer. A wag ; an irrepressible, devil-may-care, dryly amusing person ; a ' sport ' : Australian : s. >, by 1930, coll. : C. 20. Cf. *hard case*, q.v., and the U.S. *hard doings*, hard work, rough fare. Occ., from ca. 1910, abbr. *doer*.

hard-drinking. Vbl.n., drinking to excess : C. 17–20 : coll. till ca. 1750, then S.E.

hard for soft, give. (Of men) to have sexual intercourse : low coll. : from ca. 1860.

hard ?, got any. See got any hard ?

hard hit, be. To have had a heavy loss, esp. of money : coll. : 1854.—2. To be very much in love : coll. (— 1888). Miss Braddon, in *Gerard*. Occ. *hit hard*.

hard(-)hitter. A bowler hat : Australian : C. 20. Jice Doone.

hard horse. A brutal or tyrannical officer : nautical (— 1893) ; virtually †. F. & H. ; Bowen.

hard in a clinch—and no knife to cut the seizing. In a very difficult position—and no app. way out : a nautical c.p. : late C. 19–20. Bowen. Here, *seizing* is cordage.

hard lines. Hardship : orig. nautical (— 1855) ; ob. ? ex ropes unmanageable from wet or frost ; *lines*, however, was in C. 17 *lot*. Difficulty ; an unfortunate occurrence, severe action : coll. : from ca. 1858. W. Black, ' I think it's deuced hard lines to lock a fellow up.' In South Africa, also *hard cheek* (Pettman) : late C. 19–20.

hard-lying money. ' The extra allowance granted to officers and men for service in destroyers and torpedo boats . . . compensation for wear and tear of uniform and clothing, etc. Extended in the War to crews of motor launches and other auxiliary small craft. (Abolished in 1923.) ' : naval coll. : C. 20 ; ob. F. & Gibbons.

hard-mouthed, wilful, is S.E., but as = coarse-spoken it is coll. of ca. 1860–1910. Ex the stables.

hard neck. Extreme impudence : tailors' : from ca. 1870 ; ob.—2. Hence, a very impudent or brazen person ; occ. as adj. : C. 20, esp. in Glasgow.

hard nut. Abbr. *hard nut to crack* : a dangerous foe ; a ' hard case ' (senses 1 and 2) : coll. (? orig. s.) : from ca. 1875.

hard-on, adj. With the *membrum virile* in erection : low : from ca. 1860.—2. Also as a n. : from ca. 1890 (? ex U.S.). Cf. *horn*.

hard on the setting sun. A journalistic coll. phrase indicative of scorn for the Red Indian : in 1897, *The People* (on June 13) refers to it as ' a characteristic bye-word ' ; virtually and happily †. Ware.

hard-puncher. ' The fur cap of the London rough ', F. & H. : low : ca. 1870–1905. H., 5th ed. Ex a vigorous boxer's nickname. Cf. *bendigo* and *hard hitter*, qq.v.

hard-pushed. In difficulties, esp. monetary : coll. (— 1871). Cf. *hard-up*, adj., and :

hard put to it. In a—gen. monetary—difficulty : coll. : cf. *hard-run*. Late C. 19–20.

hard row to hoe. A difficult task : coll. : orig.

(1839), U.S. ; anglicised ca. 1860. Gen. as *he*, e.g., *has a hard* . . .

hard-run. Very short of money ; ' hard up ' : coll. : late C. 19–20.

hard Simpson. Ice : milk-sellers' : ca. 1860–80. Ware. See Simpson.

hard-skin. ' A rough, wild-living man ' : coll., esp. military : 1915. B. & P. After *rough-neck* (?).

hard stuff. Intoxicating liquor : Australia, whence New Zealand : from ca. 1890. Prob. ex U.S., where *hard* = intoxicating (1879).—2. Whiskey (gen. *the hard stuff*) : Glasgow (— 1934).

hard tack, whether ship's biscuits or coarse fare, is S.E. in C. 20 ; perhaps orig.—1841—nautical s. Lever in *Charles O'Malley*.—2. As = insufficient food, it is coll., mostly Cockneys' : ca. 1810–1910.

hard(-)tail. (Gen. pl.) A mule : military : C. 20. F. & Gibbons. Cf. *long-eared chum*, q.v.

hard thing. A C. 20 New Zealand variant of *hard case*, 2. Only of men.

hard-up. A gleaner and seller of cigar-ends : low (— 1851) ; ob. by 1920, † by 1930. Mayhew. See also topper-hunter and hard-cut.—2. Hence, a very poor person : low coll. (— 1857) ; ob. ' Ducange Anglicus.'—3. Hence, one who is temporarily penniless : from ca. 1860.—4. A cigarette-end : low : 1923, Manchon,—but prob. dating from ca. 1870. Ex sense 1.—5. Hence, a cigarette made from fag-ends : c. and low : from ca. 1924. (Michael Harrison, *Weep for Lycidas*, 1934.) Also known as *kerbside Virginia* and *pavement twist*.

hard-up, adj. In want, gen. of money : s. >, ca. 1880, coll. : 1821 (S.O.D.). Hence *hard up for*, sorely needing. Haggart, Hook ; *The London Figaro*, Jan. 25, 1871, ' For years, England has been a refuge for hard-up German princelings.' Ex nautical j. (steering). Cf. *hard-pushed—put to it—run*, qq.v. ; *dead-broke* ; *stony*.—2. Intoxicated : low coll. : ca. 1870–1900.—3. Out of countenance ; exhausted, esp. in swimming : Winchester College : from ca. 1850 ; ob.

hard up, have a. To have a priapism : low : late C. 19–20.

hard-up merchant. A C. 20 variant of *hard-up*, n., 1. Desmond Morse-Boycott, *We Do See Life*, 1931.

hard-upness, -uppishness, -uppedness. Poverty, habitual or incidental : coll. : resp. 1876, 1870, ca. 1905.

hard word on, put the. To ask (a person) for something, esp. a loan : Australian (— 1914). Jice Doone. Cf. *put the nips in* and *sting*.

hardening squad. ' Men being trained before returning to France after convalescence ' : military coll. : 1915. B. & P.

hardiness. Hardness : ' often an error of copyists and editors ', O.E.D., esp. in C. 16–17.

hardly with superfluous negative, as in ' I couldn't hardly tell what he meant ' : sol. : C. 19–20 ; earlier, S.E. (O.E.D.)

hardware. ' Ammunition in general, and shells in particular. Jocular ', Ware : military and naval : from ca. 1880. Very gen. in G.W.

*hardware bloke. A native of Birmingham ; a ' Brum ', q.v. : c. of ca. 1870–1915.

*hardware-swag. Hardware carried by them for sale : tramps' c. (— 1887). Baumann.

hardy annual. A constantly recurring bill : Parliamentary : from ca. 1880.—2. A stock subject : journalistic : from ca. 1885. *The Pall Mall Gazette*, Aug. 16, 1892, ' The readers of the *Daily*

Telegraph are once more filling [its] columns . . . with " Is Marriage a Failure ? " The hardy annual is called " English Wives " this time.'

hare, v.i. To run very fast : Shrewsbury School coll. : late C. 19–20. Desmond Coke, *The House Prefect*, 1908. By 1920, fairly gen. S.E.

[**hare**, to harass, scare, is, despite F. & H., ineligible.]

hare, swallow a. To get exceedingly drunk : coll. : late C. 17–mid-19. B.E. ; Grose, 1st ed., proposes *hair*, ' which requires washing down ', but the phrase was perhaps suggested by the old proverbial *to have devoured a hare*, to look amiable.

hare and hunt with the hounds, hold or **run with the.** To play a double game : C. 15–20 : orig. coll. ; then, in C. 16, proverbial ; then, in C. 18–20, S.E.

[**hare-brained**, like **hair-brained**, is, despite F. & H., to be considered S.E.]

hare in a hen's nest, seek a. To try to do something (almost) impossible : late C. 16–17 coll. *Hare* synonyms, all (I think) S.E. rather than coll. and all certainly proverbial, are *catch*, or *hunt for, a hare with a tabor*, C. 14–20,—*take hares with foxes*, C. 16–17,—and *set the tortoise to catch the hare*, C. 18–20, ob. (O.E.D. and Apperson.)

hare of, make a. To render ridiculous ; expose the ignorance of : coll., mostly and orig. Anglo-Irish : from ca. 1830. Carleton ; Lever, ' It was Mister Curran made a hare of your Honor that day.'

hare-sleep. Feigned sleep : C. 17–18 : coll. > S.E.

hare's foot, kiss the. To be (too) late : coll. : C. 17–18. Cf. :

hare's foot to lick, get the. To obtain very little —or nothing. Coll. : C. 19–20 ; ob. Scott, ' The poor clergyman [got] nothing whatever, or, as we say, the hare's foot to lick.'

hari-kari. A corrupt, almost sol. form of *hara-kiri* : from ca. 1860. Ex low coll. Japanese for belly-cut, long and often Englished as *happy dispatch*. Still more corrupt is *hurry-curry*. (The practice is mentioned as early as in Cock's *Diary*, 1616.)

haricot beans. Bullets : military, not very gen. : 1915–18. (G. H. McKnight, *English Words*, 1923.)

haricot veins. Varicose veins : sol. : late C. 19–20. (Ware.)

hark-ye-ing. ' Whispering on one side to borrow money ', Grose, 1st ed. : mid-C. 18–early 19. The late C. 17–early 18 preferred *harking*, as in B.E.

harker. A man on listening-patrol : military coll. : 1914–18. F. & Gibbons. Ex Scottish *harker*, a listener.

harlequin. A sovereign : theatrical : ca. 1860–1905. Ex its glitter.—2. The wooden core of a (gen. red) india-rubber ball : Winchester College : ca. 1870–1900.

harlequin Jack. ' A man who shows off equally in manner and in dress ' : lower classes' : late C. 19–20 ; ob. Ware.

[**harlotry**, a harlot, and, as adj., disreputable : despite F. & H., ineligible.]

*harman. A late C. 17–19 abbr. (as in B.E. ; Lytton, *The Disowned*) of :

*harman-beck. A constable : c. of ca. 1560–1880. Harman ; B.E. ; Scott ; Borrow. Prob. ex *next* + *beck* (= *beak*), q.v. ; but perhaps ex *hard man*, a severe one ; or even ex postulated *har-man*, he who cries *ha(r)*, stop !,—cf. † *harr*, to snarl.

*harmans. The stocks : c. : ca. 1560–1820,

though ob. by 1785. Harman, B.E., Grose. If the *-mans* is the c. suffix (q.v.) found in *darkmans*, *lightmans*, etc., then the *har-* is prob. *hard*, for the notion, hardness = the gallows, is characteristic of c.

haro. To yell : coll. : C. 19. Ware. Ex *cry haro*.

harness, the routine of one's work, as in *in harness*, at work, and *die in harness*, i.e. at one's post or still working, is held by the O.E.D. to be S.E. But I think that at first (say 1840–80) it was coll. ; in C. 20 it is certainly S.E. ? suggested by Shakespeare's ' At least we'll die with harness on our back,' *Macbeth*, V, v (W.).—2. An infantryman's equipment : jocular military coll. : 1914–18. B. & P.

harp. The tail of a coin, esp. as a call in toss-halfpenny : Anglo-Irish (— 1785) ; ob. by 1860. Grose, 1st ed. The tail of a coin bore Hibernia with a harp. Cf. *music* and *woman*, qq.v.

harp, playing the. See **playing the harp.**

[**harp on**, to repeat or return to sickeningly, **is**, *pace* B.E., Grose, and F. & H., ineligible here.]

harpeian, harpyan. Erroneous forms and pronunciation of *harpyian*, of or like a harpy : C. 17–19. O.E.D.

harper. A brass coin, value one penny, current in Ireland in late C. 16–early 17 : coll. Ben Jonson. (S.E. : *harp-shilling*.) Ex the harp thereon represented.

harpers !, have among or **at you (my blind).** A c.p. ' used in throwing or shooting at random among a crowd ', Grose : ca. 1540–1830. Considered proverbial as early as 1542 (Heywood).

harquebus of crock. A sol. for *harquebus à croc* : late C. 16–17 (O.E.D.).

harras, harrass. In C. 19–20, incorrect for *harass*. Influenced by *embarrass*.

harridan. A woman half whore, half bawd : c. late C. 17–18. B.E.—2. ' A hagged old woman ', a disagreeable old woman : orig. (— 1725) coll. ; S.E. by 1895. *A New Canting Dict.*, 1725.

Harriet Lane. ' Australian canned meat—because it had the appearance of chopped-up meat ; and Harriet Lane was chopped up by one Wainwright ' : lower classes' : ca. 1875–1900. Ware. Cf. *Fanny Adams*, q.v.

Harrington. A brass farthing : ca. 1615–40 coll. Jonson, 1616, ' I will not bate a *Harrington* o' the sum.' Ex Lord Harrington, who, in 1613, obtained the patent of coining them. Just as *Bradbury* will doubtless come to be considered S.E., so, because of its historical associations, has *Harrington* been listed by the O.E.D. as S.E.

[**Harrow slang.**—J. Fischer Williams, *Harrow*, 1901, writes thus pertinently :—' As to language, the inhabitants of Harrow speak, generally, the English tongue. But . . . they cut short certain words of their last syllable or syllables and substitute the letters " er ". [See ' the *Oxford* -er '.] Thus Duck Puddle becomes " Ducker ", football " footer ", and Speech-Room " speecher ", blue coat " bluer ". . . . Some years ago the number of these changes was strictly limited, but latterly the custom has been spreading. Harrow has often been made responsible for a variation of this final " er " into either " agger " [q.v.] or " ugger " . . . but these seem to have arisen at a famous Oxford college . . ., and Harrow is guiltless of this invention. Perhaps the only other word of the Harrow language worth noticing is " Bill " for " names-calling " or " call-over " [roll-call is the usual S.E. term]. Some have suggested that this is a corruption of " Bell ", the School bell being rung to call the boys together, but probably " Bill " is the truer word, and is used in the older English sense of list.' Orig. coll., *bill* is in C. 20 to be considered as j.— Cf. ' Eton slang '.]

Harry. A rustic : late C. 18–early 19 c., then dial. (ob.). Grose, 2nd ed.—2. The ' literary ' shape of *'Arry*, q.v. : 1874 : coll. > S.E.

Harry !, by the Lord. Perhaps jocular ex app. later *old Harry*, the devil : late C. 17–20 ; ob. Congreve, Byron, Besant. (O.E.D.)

Harry, old. For this and *play old Harry*, see **old Harry.**

Harry,—Tom, Dick, and. As generic for the mob, any and everybody, it was orig. coll., but in C. 20 it is S.E. See ' Representative Names ' in *Words !*

Harry Bluff. Snuff : rhyming s. (— 1874) ; ob. (Cf. *hang-bluff*, q.v.) H., 5th ed.

Harry Common. A womaniser : jocular coll. : late C. 17–18. Cf. Shakespeare's *Doll Common.*

Harry Freeman's. See **Freeman's** ; cf. :

Harry Frees (or **f.**). Fruit and vegetables given by the public : Grand Fleet bluejackets' : C. 20. Bowen. Ex the preceding.

Harry gave Doll, what. Sexual connexion : low coll. : C. 18–19.

Harry Lauders. Stage hangings : theatrical rhyming s. (on *borders*) : from ca. 1905. *The Evening Standard*, Aug. 19, 1931.

Harry Randall (loosely **Randle**). A handle ; also, a candle : rhyming s. : C. 20. B. & P. Ex a comedian, famous ca. 1900. Cf. *Jack Randall.*

Harry-Soph. One who, having kept the necessary terms, ranks, by courtesy, as a bachelor : Cambridge University (— 1720, as in Stukeley's *Memoirs*) ; > † before 1893 but after 1873. Earlier (— 1661), *Henry Sophister*. ? ex *Henry VIII*—see Fuller's *Worthies*, p. 151—and *Sophista*, in the form *sophista Henricanus*. A University joke refers to Gr. ἐπίσοφος, very wise. (O.E.D.)

Harry Tate. A plate : rhyming s. : from ca. 1910. B. & P.—2. ' The R.E.8, a slow 'plane used solely for observation ' : Air Force : 1915 : ob. Ibid.—3. State : rhyming s. : from ca. 1920. P.P., *Rhyming Slang*, 1932.

Harry Tate's Cavalry. The Yeomanry : military : from ca. 1910 ; very ob. F. & Gibbons. Cf. :

Harry Tate's Navy. The Royal Naval Volunteer Reserve : naval : ca. 1905–14.—2. The Motor Boat Reserve : naval : 1915–18. Bowen. Ex the great comedian. Cf. *Fred Karno's Army.*

Harry Twitcher. Henry Brougham, orator (1778–1868). Ex a facial tic. Dawson.

Hartfordshire (B.E.'s spelling). See **Hertfordshire.**

ha(r)th-pace ; hearth-pace. A C. 17 error for *half-pace*, a platform, a stair-landing. (O.E.D.)

hartichoke, -chough. In C. 19–20, C. 17–18 resp., low coll. > sol. for *artichoke.*

*hartmans. The pillory : c. : ? C. 18–early 19. Baumann. A variant of *harmans*, q.v.

harum-scarum. Four horses driven ' tandem ' : sporting : ca. 1862–1900. Cf. *suicide.*

harum-scarum. Adv., 1674 ; adj., 1751 ; n., 1784 (O.E.D.). Coll. Wild(ly) ; reckless(ly) ; giddy, giddily. Anon., *Round about Our Coal Fire*, 1740, ' Tom run harum scarum to draw a jug of ale.' Perhaps, as W. suggests, *hare'em*, *scare'em* ex † *hare*,

to harass : cf. Smollett's *hare'um scare'um* and Mme D'Arblay's *harem-scarem*. Cf. Westcott's famous novel, *David Harum*, 1899. (*Harum-scarumness*, though coll., is comparatively rare.)

harumfrodite. A Cockney sol. for *hermaphrodite* : late C. 19–20. Kipling, ' 'Ee's a kind of a giddy harumfrodite—soldier and sailor too ' (W.).

harvest for, of, or **about a little corn, make a long.** To be tedious about a trifle : coll. proverbial : C. 16–20 ; since ca. 1820, mainly dial.—indeed, in C. 20, otherwise †. Greene ; Richardson in *Clarissa.*

Harvey. An occ. abbr. of the next. (P. P., 1932.)

Harvey Nichol. A pickle : C. 20. P. P., *Rhyming Slang*, 1932. Ex those well-known West End linen-drapers and furnishers who have, since 1905, been one of the combine known as Debenhams, Ltd. Pl. : *Harvey Nichols*, the orig. form.

Harwich !, they're all up at (old). They're in a nice mix-up or mess ! : semi-proverbial c.p. (— 1923). Manchon. Why ? Perhaps by folk-etymology. Ex dial. *harriage*, disorder, confusion (E.D.D.).

has, I. I have : sol. (— 1887 ; prob. centuries old). Baumann.

has(-)been. Any antiquated thing or, more gen., person : coll. from ca. 1825 ; orig. Scots (C. 17–19) as in Burns. In C. 20, S.E. Rare as adj. Cf. *never(-)was.*

hash. As a medley, S.E. ; as a fig. mess, coll., esp. in *make a hash of*, to fail badly with or at : C. 19–20.—2. One who ' makes a hash ' of his words : coll. when not Scots : mid-C. 17–20, ob. Burns.—3. Work in school : Charterhouse (—1900). A. H. Tod. Cf. *hash*, v., 2.—4. Hence, a class or form : ibid. : C. 20.

hash, v. To spoil : coll. but not very gen. : C. 19–20.—2. Study hard : Cheltenham School : ca. 1860–1915. Also at Charterhouse : witness A. H. Tod, 1900. Cf. *hasher*, q.v.

*hash, flash the. To vomit : mid-C. 18–mid-19 c. Grose, 2nd ed.

hash pro. A scholarship pupil : Charterhouse : C. 20. See **hash, n.,** 3.

hash, settle one's. To subdue, silence, defeat ; kill : 1825, but recorded in 1807 in U.S., where perhaps learnt by the English in the war of 1812 : s. >, in C. 20, coll. Browning, in *Youth and Art*, " You've to settle yet Gibson's hash.' Cf. *cook one's goose.*

hash-up. A ' mess ', a bungling ; fiasco : coll. : from ca. 1905. Ex :

hash up, v. To spoil, ruin (a chance, an entertainment, etc.) : coll. : C. 20. E.g. James Spenser, *Limey Breaks In*, 1934–2. To re-serve ; mangle and re-present : côll. (in C. 20, S.E.) : from ca. 1740.

hasher. A football sweater : Charterhouse : from ca. 1880. A. H. Tod, *Charterhouse*, 1900. Cf. *hash*, n., 3.

hask. A fish-basket : nautical (esp. fishermen's) coll. : mid-C. 19–20. Bowen. Prob. ex dial. *hask*, hard ; but perhaps cognate with *husk* (n.).

Haslar hag. A nurse at the Haslar Hospital : nautical : from ca. 1880 ; †.

Hastings sort, be none of the. To be too slow ; slothful : esp. of one who loses a good chance by being dilatory : mid-C. 16–mid-19 : proverbial coll. Grose, 3rd ed., explains by ' the Hastings pea, which is the first in season ' ; but is not the phrase merely a pun ? The personal is recorded before the vegetable sense; the capital *H* is folk-etymology. Cf. *Hotspurs*, q.v.

hasty, precipitate, 'very Hot on a sudden' (B.E.),—which dates from early C. 16,—seems to have, ca. 1680–1810, been coll.: witness B.E. and Grose.

hasty g. A hasty generalisation: Cambridge University: ca. 1880–1900.

hasty pudding. A muddy road: coll.: ca. 1790–1870. Grose, 3rd ed., 'The way through Wandsworth is quite a hasty pudding.'—2. A bastard: low: from ca. 1870.

hat. A gentleman commoner; a 'tuft', q.v. Cambridge University (— 1830); ob. by 1900, † by 1920. In the *Gradus ad Cantabrigiam*, 1803, he is a *hat commoner*; in Earle's *Microcosmography*, 1628, a *gold hatband*.—2. An occ. abbr. of *old hat*, the female pudend: ca. 1760–1830. See **old hat.**—3. Hence, an old-hand harlot: Scots: ca. 1820–1910. Ex preceding sense.—4. In such asseverations as *by this hat* (Shakespeare), *my hat to a half-penny* (ibid.), and *I'll bet a hat* (? C. 18–early 19). O.E.D.—5. See **bad hat.**—6. A condition or state, thus *be in a deuce of a hat* = to be in a 'nice mess'; *get into a hat*, to get into a difficulty: low: late C. 19–20; ob.

hat !, all round my. A derisive and mainly Cockney c.p. retort; also, all over, completely: ca. 1880–1925. Milliken. Perhaps ex the broadside ballad, 'All round my hat I wears a green willow.'—2. Hence, *feel all round one's hat*, to feel indisposed: lower classes', esp. Cockneys': C. 20. Manchon.

hat, bad. See **bad hat.**—**hat, black.** See **black hat.**

hat, eat one's. Gen. as **I'll eat my hat, if** . . . A strong asseveration: coll.; seemingly originated or, at the least, recorded first by Dickens in *Pickwick*, who also sponsors the much rarer *eat one's head*; there is, however, another form, . . . *old Rowley's* (Charles II's) *hat.*

hat, get a. To do the 'hat-trick', q.v.: cricketers': ca. 1890–1914.

hat, get (occ. **be**) **in(to) a** or **the.** See **hat, 6.**

hat, hang up one's. See at **hang.**—**hat !, I'll have your.** See **hat !, shoot that.**—**hat, keep under one's.** See **keep under one's hat.**

hat !, my. A mild, coll. exclamation: C. 20. Cf. *my aunt !*

hat, need a new. To have become conceited coll.: C. 20. Cf. *head, get a big.*

hat, old. See **old hat.**

hat, pass (or **send**) **round the.** To make a collection: from ca. 1857: coll. till C. 20, when, by the G.W. at latest, it > S.E., as *go round with the hat* seems to have always been.

hat !, shoot that; occ. **I'll•have your hat !** A derisive c.p. retort: ca. 1860–72: mainly London. Cf. *hat !, all round my*, q.v.

hat, talk through one's. To talk nonsense: coll., orig. (— 1888) U.S., where at first it meant to bluster; anglicised ca. 1900.

hat !, what a shocking bad. A Cockney c.p. remark on an objectionable person: ca. 1890–1910. Anstey, 1892, 'Regular bounder ! Shocking bad hat !' As a 'bounder', a 'bad lot', *bad hat* survives: see at **bad** and cf. *old hat*, q.v.

hat ?, where did you get that. A c.p. of ca. 1885–1914. Cf. *hatter ?, who's your*, q.v. Ex a popular song. ('Quotations' Benham.)

hat covers (e.g. his) **family, (his).** He is alone in the world: coll.: from ca. 1850.

hat off, with his. Charged with a 'crime': military: from ca. 1920. A soldier removes his hat when he is being tried for an offence.

hat-peg. The head: low: ca. 1875–1915. Cf. *block.*

hat(-)trick. Three wickets with successive balls: cricket: 1882. Orig. s.; in C. 20, j. > S.E. *The Sportsman*, Nov. 28, 1888, 'Mr. Absolom has performed the hat trick twice.' In the good old days, this feat entitled its professional performer to a collection or to a new hat from his club.

hat up, hang one's. See **hang one's hat up.**

hat-work. Hack-work; inferior writing: journalists' (— 1888); † by 1921. Rider Haggard in *Mr. Meeson's Will.* Perhaps work that could be done with one's hat almost as well as with one's head.

hatband, (as) queer (occ. **odd, tight,** etc.) **as Dick's** or occ. **Nick's.** Very queer, etc.: late C. 18–20, ob. Prob. ex some local half-wit. Grose, 3rd ed. (at *Dick*).

hatch, be hatching. To be confined in childbed: low: from ca. 1860; ob.

hatch, match, and dispatch column; or **hatches, matches, despatches;** or **the hatched, matched, dispatched column.** Births, marriages, and deaths announcements: journalistic: ca. 1885–1914. Occ., also †, *cradle, altar, and tomb column.*

Hatch-Thoke. A Founder's Commemoration day: Winchester College: C. 19–20. Wrench, 'Said to be from the old custom of staying in bed [see **thoke**] till breakfast, which was provided at Hatch '.

hatches, tight under. Henpecked: lower classes' (— 1923). Manchon. Imm. ex:

hatches, under (the). In (gen. serious) trouble of any kind: coll.: mid-C. 16–20; ob. by 1890, † by 1925.—2. Dead: nautical: late C. 18–early 20. Dibdin in *Tom Bowling.* In C. 17, often (*be*)*stow under hatches*, to silence (as in Marston), distress; *bestowed under hatches* = the shorter phrase, C. 17–early 18; *be under (the) hatches* dates from early C. 17 and occurs in Locke. Ex the lit. nautical sense, below deck.

hatchet. A very plain or an ugly woman: tailors': ca. 1870–1920. Ex *hatchet-faced.*

hatchet, bury (and dig up) the. See at **bury.**

hatchet, sling or **throw the.** To exaggerate greatly; tell yarns; lie: low: the former —1789 and ob., the latter —1821.—2. (Gen. with *sling*.) To sulk; skulk; sham: nautical: from ca. 1850. Whence the vbl.nn. *hatchet-slinging* and *-throwing*; the former in G. Parker, 1789. 'App. a variant on *draw the longbow.*' W.—3. (**sling** . . .) To make off; escape: c. (— 1923). Manchon. By prob. deliberate confusion with *sling one's hook*, q.v. cf. *hook, sling one's*, 1.

Hatchet-Back. See **Chop-Back.**

hatchet-face(d), applied in S.E. to a long, thin face, was, ca. 1680–1750, coll. and = very plain or even ugly: B.E., 'Hatchet-fac'd. Hard-favor'd, Homely'—whence, by the way, the U.S. as distinct from the mod. Eng. sense of *homely.*

hatchway. The mouth: nautical > low gen.: from ca. 1820; ob. Egan's Grose.—2. The female pudend: nautical > low gen.: from ca. 1865. Cf. *fore-hatch*, q.v.

hate. A bombardment: 1915: military. In 1916–18, the usual German night or morning bombardment. 'An allusion'—furthered, I believe, by Frank Reynolds's famous cartoon in *Punch*, in Feb.,

1915—'to the *Hymn of Hate*, perpetrated (Aug., 1914) by one Lissauer', W.—2. Since the G.W., but ob. by 1934, a scolding or esp. a (gen. morning) grumble.

hate. To dislike : Society coll. : from ca. 1919. Denis Mackail, *Greenery Street*, 1925, 'I should hate it, of course, but I shouldn't mind it.'

hate, stir up a little. 'To shell the enemy when he seemed quiet', F. & Gibbons : 1915–18. Ex *hate*, n.

hatfler. A 'flat' (person) : centre s. : from ca. 1860 ; ob.

hatful. Much, esp. money and in horse-racing : coll. (— 1859). Miss Braddon, 'He had won what his companions called a hatful of money on the steeple-chase.'

hath-pace. See **ha(r)th-pace.**

hatless brigade, the. Those men who do not wear hats : C. 20 : coll. >, by 1930, familiar S.E. (Collinson.)

hatter. A miner that works alone : Australia, 1864 : s. >, by 1890, coll. R. L. A. Davies, 1884, 'Oh, a regular rum old stick ; he mostly works [as] a "hatter"'.—2. Hence, a criminal, esp. a thief, working on his own : Australian c. (— 1893) ; ob. By 1890, the term has the connotation, 'A man who has lived by himself until his brain has been turned', Marriott Watson, in *Broken Billy* : this sense was prob. prompted by the next entry, sense 1. Prob. ex (*his*) *hat covers his family*, q.v. See esp. Morris.

hatter, (as) mad as a. Very mad ; extremely eccentric : coll. : orig. (1836, Haliburton) U.S., where *mad* meant angry, as generically it still does ; anglicised in 1849 by Thackeray in *Pendennis* ; well established in England by 1863, when appeared F. A. Marshall's farce, *Mad as a Hatter* ; it was 'Lewis Carroll' who, in 1866, definitely fixed the English sense. 'The *hatter* may orig. have been *adder*, or Ger. *otter* . . . both adder and otter. *Attercop*, spider . . . has some support in *mad as a bed-bug*[, another U.S. phrase],' W.

hatter ?, who's your. A London (chiefly Cockney) c.p. of ca. 1875–85. Cf. *hat ?, where did you get that*, q.v.

hatting. Vbl.n. and ppl.adj. corresponding to *hatter*, 1 : Australian (— 1890) coll. : ob. Morris.

hatty, an elephant : Anglo-Indian coll. See **hutty.**

haul. To worry, pester : coll. : ca. 1670–1750. Gay.—2. (Gen. with *up*) to bring up for reprimand : coll. (— 1865). Ex the more gen. *haul over the coals*, coll., 1795. Cf. *coals, call over the*, q.v., and *haulable*, q.v.

haul ashore. To retire from the sea : nautical : late C. 19–20. Bowen. Cf. *swallow the anchor*.

haul-devil. A clergyman : low : ca. 1865–1910. Cf. *devil-dodger*.

haul off and take a binge. See **binge, have a.**

haul one's wind. To get clear : nautical coll. (— 1823). Egan's Grose. Ex lit. sense.

haul over the coals. See **haul, 2.**

haulable, adj. Applied to a girl whose company renders an undergraduate liable to a fine : university (Oxford and Cambridge) : ca. 1870–1914. Ex *haul*, v., 2.

hauling sharp. On half rations : nautical : late C. 19–20. Bowen.

häuser. A meat pie : Bootham School : late C. 19–20. Origin ? (Anon, *Dict. of Bootham Slang*, 1925.)

havage, havidge. 'An assemblage or family of dishonest or doubtful characters', Bee : low : ca. 1820–50. Ex dial. *havage*, lineage, family stock, + (*William*) *Habberfield*, a criminal whose family was such.

have. (Gen. in pl.) One who has, esp. money and/or property ; gen. contrasted with *have-not*, a needy person : coll. : 1836 (S.O.D.).—2. A trick or imposture ; a swindle : from ca. 1880. Cf. *a catch* or *a have.* Ex :

have, v. To cheat (— 1805) : perhaps orig. c. G. Harrington, in *The New London Spy*, 'Had, a cant word . . . instead of . . . cheated'.—2. Hence, to trick, deceive (1821) : low. Egan.—3. Hence, to humbug, fool (— 1893 ; prob. as early as 1825), low > gen.—4. To possess carnally : a vulgarism of C. 16–20. In C. 20, gen. of women by men, but previously said 'indifferently of, and by, both sexes', F. & H.—5. (Gen. *have it.*) To receive, or to have received, punishment, a thrashing, a reprimand : coll. : late C. 16–20. Shakespeare.—6. To have caught (someone) in discussion, argument, or put into a fix : coll. : 1820 (O.E.D.).—7. To represent as doing or saying something : coll. The O.E.D. states that it is U.S. and cites a passage, written in 1928 ; but surely it has been used in England since at least as early as 1921 ?—8. Redundant use was frequent in C. 15–16—and has not, among the uneducated, been uncommon since—in the compound tense : sol. The most gen. C. 19–20 form is *if I (you, he,* etc.*) had have*, or *had've, done it, gone, seen it*, etc., etc. Cf. *of*, have, used in same way.

have ?, is that a catch or a. A low c.p. acknowledgment that the speaker has been 'had' or fooled. Should the other essay a definition, the victim turns the tables with *then you catch*—or, as the case may be, *have—your nose up my a***.* Ca. 1885–1900.

have a banana ! A c.p. of ca. 1905–15, esp. among the lower classes. B. & P.

have a cab. To be drunk : London : late C. 19–early 20. Ware.

have a cob on. See **cob on, have a.**

have a down. See **down, n.**

have a go. To hit the bowling, esp. if rashly : cricketers' coll. : 1894, Norman Gale. (Lewis.)

have a good look round. See **good look . . .**

have a heart ! See **heart !, have a.**

have a heat. See **heat, have a.**

have any, not. See **any.—have a binge.** See **binge, have a.**

have by the short hairs. See **hairs, get . . .**

have for breakfast ; occ. **before breakfast** (as a rare appetiser). A humorous way of implying that a thing is easy to do, (gen.) a man easy to beat. E.g. 'Why ! I have one like him every day before breakfast' or 'I could have *or* do with six like him for breakfast.' For task or feat, the *before breakfast*, often with *do* or *have*, is preferred. C. 20 coll. : mostly Australia and New Zealand.

have had it. To have been seduced : C. 19–20 low coll.—2. In C. 20, however, usually (of a girl) to have had sexual experience,—there having arisen a (mostly subconscious) opinion that no woman but a half-wit, or in sheer ignorance, is ever, in the strict sense, seduced against her will.

have got = have : see **got, have.—have it.** See **have, v., 5.**

have it, let one. To strike hard ; punish (lit. or fig.) severely : coll. : ? orig. U.S., where it is recorded as early as 1848 ; anglicised in the 1880's. Cf. :

*have it off. To engage successfully in a criminal undertaking, esp. by oneself : c. : from ca. 1925. James Curtis, *The Gilt Kid*, 1936. Prob. ex Yorkshire dial. *have off*, as in ' He has a good deal off,' he knows a lot about it or is well acquainted with the matter (E.D.D., Sup.).

have (or take) it out of one. To punish ; exact a compensation from : coll. : from ca. 1870. ? ex preceding phrase. Cf. *have*, v., 5.

have it out with one, (v.i., have it out). To reprove freely ; come to a necessary understanding, or settle a dispute, with a person : coll. : from ca. 1860 (Ware). *The Daily News*, April 2, 1883; John Strange Winter, ' Instead of . . . having it out, he . . . fumed the six days away.' ? ex the S.E. *have out*, to çause a person to fight a duel with one.

have-not. (Gen. in pl.) See have, n., 1. 1836.

have-on. A variant (— 1931) of *have*, n., 2, gen. as ' a mild joke to deceive a person ' (Lyell).

have on. To engage the interest or the sympathy of, esp. with a view to deceit (seldom criminally): dial. (— 1867) > (low) coll. ca. 1870 ; slightly ob. O.E.D. (Sup.) ; F. & H. Cf. *string on*, q.v., and the S.E. *lead on* and (see *have on toast*) the † S.E. *have in a string*.

have on the raws. To touch to the quick ; tease : low coll. : from ca. 1860 ; ob. Lit., raw flesh, raw places.

have on toast. To deceive utterly, hence to defeat heavily in argument : from ca. 1870 : (orig. low) s. > coll.—2. In C. 20, to have at one's beck and call or ' just where one wants him '. Cf. the C. 16–18 S.E. *have in a string*, i.e. at command (see Apperson, *have*).

have one's brains on ice. ' To be very cool-headed and collected ' : coll. (— 1931). Lyell.

have the edge on. See edge on.—have one's guts for garters. See guts for garters.

*have the goods on. To have abundant evidence for the conviction of (a person) : N.Z. c. (— 1932).

have (a person) to rights. (Gen. in passive.) To defeat : lower classes' coll. : from ca. 1880. Ware.

have towards, occ. with or at. To pledge in drinking : the first and third, C. 17–18 and S.E. ; the second, C. 19 and coll. Michael Scott, ' " Have with you, boy—have with you," shouted half-a-dozen other voices.'

[have up, to bring before the authorities, esp. in the law-courts : not coll., as claimed by F. & H., but S.E.—as early as Caxton.]

have you a licence ? A c.p. addressed to one clearing his throat noisily : mid-C. 18–early 19. Grose, 1st ed. Punning *hawking* and ' the Act of hawkers and pedlars '.

Havelock's saints. Teetotallers : military : mid-C. 19–20 ; virtually †. Dating from a fact—and the time—of the Indian Mutiny. (Ware.)

haven-screamer. A sea-gull : nautical : late C. 19–20. Bowen.

Havercake Lads. The 33rd Foot Regiment, since ca. 1881 the 1st Battalion of the West Riding Regiment : military : late C. 18–20 ; ob. F. & Gibbons. Its recruiting sergeants, in leading a party had an oatcake on their swords. (Also the self-given name of the inhabitants of part of Lancashire : from before 1855.)

haves. Half-boots : Winchester College. See halves, the better spelling.

hav(e)y-cav(e)y. (Of persons only) uncertain, doubtful, shilly-shally : also an adv. Late C. 18–

early 19 : coll. ex dial. Grose, 2nd ed. A Northern and Midland anglicisation of L. *habe, cave*, have (and) beware !

havidge. See havage.

*havil. A sheep : c. (— 1788) : † by 1860 in England. Grose, 2nd ed. Origin ?

havildar's guard. The cooking of the fry of fresh-water fish spitted in a row on a skewer : coll., in and around Bombay (— 1886). Ex *havildar*, a Sepoy non-commissioned officer. Yule & Burnell.

havoc(k). In late C. 17–mid-18, esp. in *make sad havoc*, this term app. had a strong coll. taint.

havy-cavy. See havey-cavey.

haw-haw, adj. Affected in speech (rarely of women) ; rather obviously and consciously English upper-class : (mostly Colonial) coll. : mid-C. 19–20, esp. in and since G.W. Cf. *bit of haw-haw*, q.v.

hawbuck. An ignorant and vulgar rustic : 1805 (S.O.D.) : coll. till C. 20, then S.E. and ob. Ex *haw*, either the fruit of the hawthorn or a hedge + *buck*, a dandy (W.).

hawcubite. A noisy, violent street roisterer, one of a band infesting London ca. 1700–1 ; hence a street bully or ruffian. Coll. > S.E. Except historically, used very rarely after ca. 1720. F. & H. : ' After the Restoration there was a succession of these disturbers of the peace : first came the Muns, then followed the Tityre Tus, the Hectors, the Scourers, the Nickers, the Hawcubites, and after them the Mohawks.' ? ex *hawk* ; cf. :

*hawk. A sharper, esp. at cards ; a ' rook ' : orig. (C. 16), c. ; from ca. 1750, low ; ob. B.E.—2. A bailiff ; a constable : C. 16–early 19 : s. > coll. Jonson, Ainsworth.

*hawk, v. To act as a decoy (cf. *button*, n.) at a fair : c. (— 1851) ; ob.—2. The v., to spit with difficulty and noise, is, despite F. & H., ineligible.—3. V.i., to pull : Canadian : C. 20. John Beames.

hawk !, ware. A warning, esp. when bailiff or constable is near : low coll. : C. 16–mid-19. Skelton has the phrase as a title ; Grose, 1st ed.

hawk and buzzard, between. Perplexed and undecided : proverbial coll. (— 1639) : ob. by 1780, † by 1820, except in dial. L'Estrange, ' A fantastical levity that holds us off and on, betwixt hawk and buzzard, as we say, to keep us from bringing the matter in question to a final issue.' Apperson.

hawk and pigeon. Villain and victim : Society coll. : late C. 19–early 20. Ware.

hawk from a handsaw (when the wind is southerly) know a. (Gen. in negative.) To be discerning ; occ. lit., have good eyesight, hence to be a person of sense : proverbial coll. : C. 17–20. Shakespeare and Barbellion, the longer form ; Mrs. Centlivre, the shorter in the negative. (Apperson.)

hawk one's brawn. See brawn, hawk one's.

hawk one's meat. (Of a woman) to peddle, i.e. display, one's charms, esp. of breast : low : late C. 19–20. Cf. *dairy*, *sport one's*, q.v.

hawk one's mutton. To be a prostitute : mostly Cockney : mid-C. 19–20. Contrast *hawk one's meat*.

hawker, vbl.n. hawking. Peddler, peddling : C. 16–20 ; app. coll., ca. 1680–1820, when it was applied specifically to news-vendors.—2. A severe cough : lower-class coll. : from ca. 1870. (Neil Bell, *Crocus*, 1936.) Ex *hawking*, or clearing one's throat.

*hawker's gag. Boot-laces carried as an excuse for begging : tramps' c. (— 1932). Frank Jennings, *Tramping with Tramps*.

hawse or **hawses, cross** or **come across** or **fall athwart one's.** To obstruct or check; fall out with: nautical: ca. 1840–1910. A *hawse* being 'the space between the head of a vessel at anchor and the anchors, or a little beyond the anchors', O.E.D. Cf.:

hawse,—I'll cut your cable if you foul my. A nautical threat: ca. 1850–1925. Smyth. Cf. preceding entry.

hawse-holes, creep (or **come**) **in** (or **through**) **the.** To rise from the forecastle: nautical, esp. the Navy (− 1830); ob. Marryat, 'A lad who creeps in at the hawse-holes . . . was not likely to be favourably received in the midshipmen's mess.' Hence, *hawse-pipe officer*, one so risen: naval: mid-C. 19–20 (Bowen). Cf. *halberd*, q.v.

hawser, esp. in C. 17–18, is occ. used in error for *hawse* (see **hawse, cross . . .**).

hay! or **hey!,** as interpellation or in address, evokes—not among the cultured—the c.p. reply, *no, thanks!* or *not to-day!* or, rarely, *straw!* Late C. 19–20.

hay, hit the. See **hit the hay.**

hay, make. (Transitively with *of*.) To cause confusion; defeat heavily whether manually or verbally; upset; 'kick up a row': university (− 1817); the v.i. was ob. by 1920. H. Kingsley, the v.i.; v.t. in Maria Edgeworth and *The Pall Mall Gazette*, June 9, 1886, 'Sussex made hay of the Gloucestershire bowling.'

*****hay-bag.** A woman: c. (− 1851): in C. 20, mainly U.S. Mayhew. 'Something to lie upon', F. & H.; also perhaps from the appearance of old drabs.

hay-band. An inferior cigar: low (−1864); † by 1915. H., 3rd ed.

hay, lass, let's be hammered for life on Sunday! A lower classes' c.p. of late C. 19–early 20. Ware. Prob., at first, metal-workers'.

hay-seed. A countryman; esp. if very rustic: orig. (− 1889), U.S.; anglicised as a coll., ca. 1905 in Britain, but in Australia and New Zealand ca. 1895. Ex hay-seeds clinging to outer garments. Also *hayseed*.

hay while the sun shines, make. Profitably to employ one's time: proverbial coll. (− 1546) >, ca. 1800, a S.E. metaphor. Anticipated by Barclay in 1509.

haying. Haymaking: coll. (− 1887). Baumann. Ex dial.

haymaker. A jolly sort of fellow: tailors': C. 20. Ex *make hay while the sun shines.*—2. A swinging blow: boxers': from ca. 1920. (O.E.D. Sup.) Cf. *cow-shot* and *agricultural*, qq.v.

haymaking. Practical joking: University and Army: from ca. 1880; extremely ob. Ware. Perhaps ex *making hay while the sun shines.*

haymaking drill. Bayonet exercise: military: late C. 19–20; ob. F. & Gibbons. Ex prodding sacks filled with straw.

Haymarket hector. A whore's bully: C. 17–19: coll. Marvell. Cf.:

Haymarket ware. An ordinary prostitute: C. 19–20, but ob. by 1910, † by 1920. Cf. preceding entry and cf. *barrack hack.*

hayseed. See **hay-seed.**

haystack, sails like a. Sails ugly or clumsy to look at: nautical coll.: late C. 19–20.

haystack, unable to hit a; I, he, etc., **couldn't hit a haystack.** A coll. c.p. applied to a bad aimer, esp. a bad shot: mid-C. 19–20. Contrast the *haystack* phrase at *hit*, v.

haze. To harass or punish with overwork or paltry orders; constantly find fault with: nautical coll. > j. > gen. S.E.: Dana, 1840. Ex dial. *haze*, to ill-treat, frighten: W.

haze about. To loaf; roam aimlessly about: coll.: ob.: 1841, *Tait's Magazine*, VIII, '. . . Hazing about—a capital word that, and one worthy of instant adoption—among the usual sights of London' (O.E.D.).

hazel-geld, -gild. To beat with a hazel stick · (? jocular) coll.: late C. 17–early 19; the former, perhaps an error, is in B.E.; the latter in Grose, 1st ed. (For *oil of hazel*, see **oil.**)

hazy. Stupid or confused with drink: 1824, T. Hook: coll.; in C. 20, almost S.E. and slightly ob. Barham, 'Staggering about just as if he were hazy'.

Hazy Brook. Hazebrouck on the Western Front: military coll.: 1914–18. F. & Gibbons.

he; hee. A cake. A *young he*, a small cake. Charterhouse (school): from ca. 1860; ob. Cf. *she*, q.v.—2. It, where personification does not hold good: coll.: C. 19–20. Baumann cites 'Shut him up well,' close the door well.—3. Often as a sol. for *him*: contemporaneous with the language.

He-Cat. (Any) H.M.S. *Hecate*: naval: C. 19–20. Bowen.

he-male. A very manly fellow indeed, all confidence and coition: middle classes': ca. 1881–1910. On *she-male*, q.v. (Ware.) Whence:

he-man. A virile fellow; a 'cave-man'; one who 'treats 'em rough': from ca. 1906: s. >, ca. 1930, coll. (Collinson.) Whence *he-man stuff.* Cf. B.E.'s *great he-rogue*, 'a sturdy swinging Rogue'.

he-man stuff. 'Cave-man' methods: from ca. 1908. ? orig. U.S.

he never does anything wrong! An ironic c.p. applied to one who never does anything right: music-halls' (1883), then gen.; † by 1920. Ware.

he worships his creator. A Society c.p. (− 1909) directed at a *self-made* man with a high opinion of himself. Ob. Punning *Creator*, God. (Ware.)

head, the obverse of coin or medal, and **head,** a *coiffure*, are, though cited by F. & H., clearly S.E.— 2. A man-of-war's privy: nautical, but perhaps rather j. than s. or coll.: ca. 1870–1910. The gen. C. 20 form—† by 1930—is *heads.* Cf. *rear(s)*.— 3. See **heads.**—4. A postage stamp: mid-C. 19–20: dial. >, by 1860, coll. Ex the sovereign's head thereon. (O.E.D. Sup.).

head, v.t. To toss (a coin); *head browns*, to toss pennies: Australian: late C. 19–20. C. J. Dennis. Lit., to make a coin turn up heads.

[**head** phrases and compounds that, listed by F. & H., are S.E.:—*fly at one's head, give one his head, hit the right nail on the head, on head* (as in *do on head*, act rashly, and *run on head*, incite, act incitingly), *over head and ears, take one in the head,* come into one's mind, *without head or tail* or *cannot make head or tail of it, have at one's head,* to cuckold, and *head-fruit*, the result of being cuckolded.]

*****head, (can) do on one's.** To do easily and joyfully: c.: from ca. 1880.—2. Hence, in C. 20 gen. s., to do easily.

head, eat one's. See **hat, eat one's.**

head, fat or **soft in the.** Stupid: coll.: C. 19–20.

head, get or **have a big; or a swelling in the.** To become or be conceited: ? orig. (− 1888) U.S.; established in Britain, however, by 1893. Cf. *hat, need a new,* q.v.

head, have a. To have a headache from drinking : coll. : from ca. 1870. In C. 20 often *have a* (*shocking*) *head on one* (Lyell). Cf. *have a mouth* and Fr. *gueule de bois.*

head, have maggots in the. To be eccentric ; crotchety : low coll. : from ca. 1860. Cf. *bee in one's bonnet.*

head, have no. To be crack-brained, irresponsible : (? low) coll. : from ca. 1870. Contrast *have a head on.*—2. (Of drinks) to be flat : this is S.E.

head, hurt in the. To cuckold : C. 18 coll.

head, knock on the. To destroy, kill ; put an end to : low coll. : from ca. 1870. *The Weekly Dispatch*, May 21, 1871, of a disorderly house.

head, off one's. Out of one's mind ; crazy : coll. : from ca. 1845. Hood ; Mark Pattison. (O.E.D.)

head, out of one's own. Imagined, invented, thought of by oneself : rather coll. than S.E. : 1719, Defoe. ' Were not all these answers given out of his own head ? ', Jowett.

head-and-gun money. ' The . . . bounty of £5 a head on the crew of an enemy armed ship captured or sunk ' : naval coll. : 1915–18 ; ob. Bowen. Prob. after S.E. *blood-money.*

head (or **neck**) **and heels, bundle out.** To eject forcibly : low coll. : from ca. 1860. In S.E., *neck and crop.*

head-beetler. A foreman or ganger : (? orig. Anglo-Irish) workmen's (— 1864) ; ob.—2. Hence, almost imm., a bully : workmen's : ob. by 1910, † by 1915. *Chambers's Journal*, Sept. 18, 1886, ' The " beetle " was a machine for producing figured fabrics by the pressure of a roller, and head-beetler probably means the chief director of this class of work.'

***head bloke.** See **head screw.**

***head bully,** or **cully, of the pass** (or **the passage**) **bank.** ' The Top Tilter of that Gang, throughout the whole Army [*of criminals and vagabonds*], who Demands and receives Contribution from all the Pass Banks in the Camp ', B.E., who has *bully*, Grose (1st ed.) preferring *cully.* C. of ca. 1670–1820. See **pass(age) bank** and **top.**

head cook and bottle-washer. One in authority (cf. *head-beetler*) ; a foreman ; a boss : low coll. (— 1876). Hindley.—2. A general servant : pejorative (— 1887). Baumann.—3. In C. 20, often applied to a person temporarily doing a general servant's work.

***head cully of the pass,** or **the passage, bank.** See **head bully . . .**

head (or **beard**) **for the washing, give one's.** To yield tamely : C. 17 (? — 18) coll. Butler, in *Hudibras*, ' For my part it shall ne'er be said, | I for the washing gave my head.' A late C. 16–early 17 variant : *. . . polling.* Cf. Fr. *laver la tête à quelqu'un.*

head full of bees. See **bees, his head is full of.**

***head-guard.** A hat ; esp. a billy-cock : o. (— 1889) ; †.

head in a bag, get or **put the.** See **bag.**

head in chancery, get one's or **the.** See **chancery.**

head is full of proclamations, one's. Or **have a head full . . .** To be ' much taken up to little purpose ', B.E. : coll. : ca. 1560–1770. Fenton's *Bandello* ; Cotgrave ; Berthelson's *English-Danish Dict.*, 1754. Apperson.

head like a sieve, have a. To be very forgetful : coll. : from ca. 1880.

head-mark, know by. To recognise (a cuckold) by his horns : low : mid-C. 18–20, ob. Punning the S.E. sense.

head-marked, adj. Cuckolded, cuckold : low : mid-C. 18–20 ; ob.

head off, argue or **talk one's.** To be excessively argumentative or talkative : coll. : from ca. 1885. Milliken. (In fact, *one's head off* is an adv. = excessively. We can speak of a person's *yawning his head off.*) Cf. :

head off, beat one's. To defeat utterly : coll. : from ca. 1850. Thackeray, ' He pretends to teach me billiards, and I'll give him fifteen in twenty and beat his head off.' Cf. :

head off, eat one's or **its.** To cost, in keep, more than one's or it's worth : C. 18–20 : coll. Orig., of horses ; gen. from ca. 1860. Anon., *The Country Farmer's Catechism*, 1703, ' My mare has eaten her head off at the Ax in Aldermanbury.'

head on, have a. To be alert or knowing : low coll. (— 1893) ; ob. Cf. the S.E. *have a head on one* or *on one's shoulders.*

head on, put a (**new**). To damage a man's face : ? orig. U.S. (— 1870), anglicised by 1890.—2. Hence, to defeat, gen. heavily ; get much the better of : ? orig. (— 1880) U.S. ; anglicised by 1890. Also *put a new face on.*—3. To make malt liquors froth : public-house s. > gen. coll. : from ca. 1860 (*Head*, froth on top, is itself S.E.)

head on one, have a. See **head, have a.**

head or tail. See **heads or tails.**

head over heels, for earlier and logical **heels over head**, was orig. coll.—a popular corruption : from ca. 1770. Thackeray. (O.E.D.)

head over turkey. An Australian (— 1916) variant of preceding. C. J. Dennis.

head-piece, brain(s), late C. 16–20, was S.E. until C. 20, when increasingly coll.

head-rails. The teeth : nautical (— 1785) >, ca. 1840, gen. ; extremely ob. Grose, 1st ed. ; ' Cuthbert Bede ', in *Verdant Green* ; Baumann, who cf.'s the Homeric ἕρκος ὀδόντων, the hedge or fence of the teeth ; Bowen.

head-robber. A plagiarist : journalistic : ca. 1880–1914.—2. A butler : low (— 1893) ; ob.

***head screw,** occ. **h. bloke.** A chief warder : prison c. (— 1893).

head-serag, in C. 20 **-serang.** An overseer, master ; one in authority or a ' big-wig ' : Bengali English coll. and nautical s. (— 1864) >, ca. 1900, gen. s. Ex Persian *sarhang*, an overseer, a commander.

head-worker. A schemer, a shirker, a malingerer : military coll. : G.W. F. & Gibbons.

headache, as much use as a ; no more use than a headache. Useless : C. 20. E.g. D. Sayers, *Unnatural Death*, 1927.

header. A blow on the head : boxing : 1818 ; ob. (O.E.D.)—2. A notability : tailors' : ca. 1860–1920. Cf. *big-wig.* Perhaps ex † S.E. sense, a leader.—3. See :

header, take a. To plunge, or fall, headlong into the water : coll. : implied in 1849.—2. To leap, app. dangerously : theatrical : from ca. 1860.—3. To go direct for one's object : coll. (— 1863).

heading-'em, vbl.n. The tossing of coins for bets : low : from ca. 1880.

headless, hop. To be beheaded : grimly jocular S.E. > coll. : C. 14–17. (O.E.D.)

headquarters, often ' capitalled '. Newmarket : turf s. (— 1888) >, in C. 20, j. Because the most important racing and training centre.

heads, the. Those in authority, the singular being *one of the heads* : coll. : from ca. 1895 : more

gen. Colonial than English : very common in the
A.I.F.

heads and tails, lie. To sleep heads to head-rail
and foot-rail alternately : low coll. : from ca. 1860 ;
ob.

heads I win, tails you lose. A mock bet ; also = I
cannot fail ! Occ. used as an adj. Coll., orig. low
(— 1846). Anticipated by Shadwell, 1672, in
Epsom Wells : ' Worse than *Cross I win, Pile you
lose.*' Apperson.

heads or tails ; head or tail. A phrase used in
tossing coins to gain a decision : coll. : late C. 17–
20. Otway. (O.E.D.)

heady, intoxicating, was by B.E. considered coll.,
as it may well have been in his day.—2. Very
ingenious (things) or shrewd (ideas, plans, actions) :
C. 20 : coll. : mostly Australia and New Zealand.—
3. Biliously headachy : mostly aviators' coll. :
1934 (Nov.), *The Air Review.*

heady whop. A person with an extraordinarily
large head : Cockney : ca. 1880–1900. Merely
whopping head corrupted.

heaf. A variant of *heef,* q.v.

heake. Incorrect for *heck* (lower half of a door) :
C. 17. O.E.D.

health, for one's. (Always in negative or interrogative.) For nothing, the implication that one *is*
there, doing this, etc., for money, i.e. for profit :
coll. : orig. (1904), U.S., Thornton citing ' I'm not
in politics for my health '—nor, presumably, for the
body politic's : anglicised ca. 1912.

Healtheries, the. The Health Exhibition, London, 1884: coll.; ob. by 1900, † by 1915. Prompted
by *the Fisheries,* q.v., of 1883. Cf. also *Colinderies,
Inventories.*

healthy. Large ; excellent : coll. : from ca.
1920. E.g. ' a healthy cheque '.

heap. A large number, a great deal : coll. :
mid-C. 17–20. Keats. Often, mid-C. 16–20, in pl.,
as in Hughes, ' She will be meeting heaps of men.'

heap, adv. Much : orig. (1834), U.S. ; anglicised ca. 1850. Also, from ca. 1880, *heaps.*

heap, in the. (Of a horse) that is losing : Glasgow racing (— 1934). It is in the ruck.

heap, strike (from ca. 1895, often **knock**) **all of a.**
To cause to collapse : coll. (— 1818). Scott,
' Strike, to use the vulgar phrase, all of a heap.'
In C. 18, the form was *strike all on a heap,* recorded
for 1711, but Richardson adumbrated the mod. form
with ' He seem'd quite struck of a heap,' 1741.
(O.E.D.)

*****heap o(f) coke.** A fellow, man, comrade :
thieves' rhyming s. (— 1909) on *bloke.* Ware. In
theatrical s., it refers to ' the guv'nor ' (father ;
managing director) : from ca. 1890. *The Evening
Standard,* Aug. 19, 1931.

heap o(f) saucepan lids. Money : rhyming s. on
dibs : from ca. 1880. Ware.

heaped, ppl.adj. Joined in the sexual act :
C. 16–20 : low coll. Tourneur, ' O, 'twill be
glorious to kill 'em . . . when they're heaped.'—
2. Hard put to it, ' stumped ' : racing : ca. 1880–
1915. Hawley Smart in *From Post to Finish.*

heaps. See **heap,** n. and adv.

*****heapy.** Short for *heap o' coke,* q.v. Ware, 1909.

hear. To attend church ; v.t., sit under the
preaching of : coll. : ca. 1780–1910. Cowper, 1783,
in a letter, ' There are, however, many who have left
the Church, and hear among the Dissenters.'
(O.E.D.)

hear a bird sing. To learn privately : coll. : late

C. 16–17. Shakespeare. In C. 19–20, *a little bird
told me* (so).

hear of it. To be blamed, reprimanded for it :
coll. : late C. 16–20. Shakespeare. Occ. in C. 19–
20, *about.*

hear say or **tell, to.** Hear it said, related (that
. . .) : in C. 20, ' considered vulgar ' (W., 1920), i.e.
low coll. Orig. S.E. with ellipsis of *people, persons,
someone,* etc., before the second v.

hearing. A scolding, a reprimand : coll. when
not, as gen., dial. : from ca. 1810 ; ob. Scott in
Old Mortality. Ex *hear of it,* q.v.

*****hearing cheat.** (Gen. in pl.) An ear : c. : mid-
C. 16–early 19. Harman, Grose.

heart appears in various ejaculations, e.g. (*Lord* or
God or *Lord God*) *bless my heart* : coll. : C. 19–20 ;
heart alive !, C. 19–20 coll. The earliest, *for God's
heart* appears in Chaucer. (O.E.D.)

heart !, have a. Show mercy ! ; steady ! : coll. :
late C. 19–20 ; slightly ob. Often jocular, esp. **as**
'ave an 'eart ! Ex *have the heart* (*to do* something).

heart, next the, adj. or adv. Fasting(ly) : mid-
C. 16–17, coll. ; in C. 18–19, dial. Nashe. Here,
heart = the stomach : cf. S.E. *heartburn* and Fr.
mal au cœur.

heart alive ! See **heart.**

heart and dart. A fart : rhyming s. : from ca.
1860 ; ob.

heart and part. Erroneous, C. 16–20, for S.E.
art and part.

heart on one's halfpenny, have one's. See **hand
on . . .**

heart in one's boots, one's. (In sentences with *is*
or *sinks* ; in phrases, preceded by *with.*) Afraid,
extremely dejected : coll. : C. 19–20 ; anticipated
by Garrick's ' soul and spirit . . . in her shoes ',
a form still heard. The C. 15–early (? all) 18 form
is *in one's hose,* as in Skelton, Breton, Motteux.
(Apperson.)

heart out, slave one's. To worry oneself **to**
death : coll. (— 1887) ; ob. Baumann.

heart to grass, take. A C. 16–17 coll. form of
heart of grass, a corruption of *heart of grace,* esp.
when preceded by *take.*

heart up, enough to have one's. Enough to make
one spew : low coll. (— 1887). Baumann.

hearth-pace. See **harth-pace.**

heartbreaker. A love-lock ; a pendent curl :
coll. : 1663, Butler, who applies it to Samson : ob.
by 1860, † by 1900.

heartburn. A bad cigar : ca. 1870–1925 :
mainly Cockney.

hearthstone. Butter : eating-houses' ; late
C. 19–20. Ware. Prompted by *doorstep,* q.v.

heartie. See **hearty, my.**

*****heart's ease.** (Occ. as one word without
apostrophe.) A twenty-shilling piece : c. : late
C. 17–early 19. B.E.—2. Gin : c. : ca. 1690–1830.
B.E.; Grose.

hearts of oak. Penniless : late C. 19–20 :
(ironic) rhyming s. on *broke.* E.g. in *The Passing
Show,* July 7, 1934.

hearty, n. and adj. Strong drink ; drunk : low :
ca. 1850–1915.—2. (Gen. *a hearty.*) A person
enjoying boisterous health and few brains, esp. if a
devotee of outdoor games and sport : from ca.
1920 : coll., orig. undergraduates', >, by 1935,
S.E. Partly in opp. to *arty.* (See also **guts
than brains, more,** and, in Michael Harrison's *Weep
for Lycidas,* 1934, a devastating description and
indictment.)—3. Hence, adj., sporting ; occupied

in sport or in strenuous exercise : mostly, as orig., university coll. Not, it would seem, before 1924 or 1925. E.g. ' I've just had a very hearty week-end.'

hearty (incorrectly **heartie**), my. A Northern dial. (1803 : E.D.D.) and hence a nautical form of address : from ca. 1835 ; ob. Marryat. Whence, the ' only just ' S.E. sense, a sailor.

*****hearty-choke (and, or with, caper-sauce) for breakfast, have a.** To be hanged : orig. (— 1785), c. ; in late C. 19, low ; in C. 20, †, except in the doubly-punning *a (h)artichoke and a (h)oyster*, a hanging-breakfast. Grose, 1st ed. ; Danvers, in *The Grantham Mystery,* ' Compelled to have a hearty-choke for breakfast some fine morning '. Punning *artichoke.* Cf. *vegetable breakfast,* q.v.

[**heat**, a preliminary bout or trial, has, despite F. & H., always been S.E.]

heat !, have a. Warm yourself (by the fire) ! : Anglo-Irish c.p. invitation : late C. 19–20.

heat, on, sexually excited, is low coll. when applied, C. 19–20, to women.

heathen philosopher. One whose breech is visible through his trousers : late C. 17–18. B.E. Ex dress-despising philosophers.

heathenish. Abominable, offensive, ' beastly ' : coll. : from ca. 1855. (O.E.D.) Ex S.E. sense of ' barbarous ', as in Shakespeare.

Heathens. The Black*heath* Rugby Football Club: 1891 : a journalistic jocularity >, ca. 1905, sporting s. *The Pall Mall Gazette,* Nov. 16, 1891, ' The Oxonians . . . got two goals, while the Heathens were unable to score.' (O.E.D.)

*****heave.** An attempt to cajole, deceive, or swindle, esp. in *a dead heave,* a flagrant attempt to do so : C. 19, and prob. earlier : c. Bee.

*****heave.** To rob, v.t. : c. : ca. 1560–1830 : extant, according to F. & H., in 1893 in Shropshire dial., but unrecorded by E.D.D. Esp. in *heave a bough* (for *heave a book,* see comment at *gun,* n., 3), rob a booth, mid-C. 16–18, and *heave a case,* rob a house, C. 18–early 19 : occ., by confusion of these two senses (as in Head), *heave a booth* = to rob a house. Harman ; Coles's and Dyche's dictionaries. Ex the S.E. sense, to lift : cf. *lift,* v.—2. To throw, toss, hurl : late C. 16–20 : S.E. until ca. 1830, then nautical j. and gen. coll. (O.E.D.) and dial.

heave ahead or **on,** v.i. To hurry, press forward : nautical coll. : C. 19. Marryat. Ex the advancing of a ship by heaving on a cable attached to some fixed object in front of her (Smyth).—2. Hence, gen. in imperative, get on with one's job or story : nautical coll. : mid-C. 19–20. Bowen.

heave around. To proceed vigorously : *Conway* cadets' (— 1891). John Masefield, *The Conway,* 1933. Cf. :

heave in sight. When not nautical j., this is gen. coll. (from ca. 1830).

[**heaven, heavens,** occur in mild ejaculations, which are, in C. 20, almost coll.]

heaven, feel one's way to. To caress a woman with progressive intimacy : low coll. : C. 19–20, ob. By itself, *heaven,* thus used, is a euphemism.

heaven and hell. A shell : military rhyming s. : from 1914.

Heaven, Hell, and Purgatory. Three taverns situated near Westminster Hall : C. 17. Jonson in *The Alchemist.*

heaven-tormentor. (Gen. pl.) A sail above the sky-sail : late C. 19–20 ; ob. Bowen.

heavens, adv. Very : **a** coll. (ob.) and dial. intensive : from ca. 1875. Esp. of rain and with *hard,* as in D. C. Murray's *The Weaker Vessel,* ' It was raining heavens hard.'—2. Exclamation : see **heaven.**

*****heaver.** A thief ; esp. one who steals tradesmen's shop-books (Grose, 2nd ed.) : c. : late C. 18–early 19. Ex *heave,* v., 1.—2. A breast ; the bosom : c. · mid-C. 17–early 19. Coles.

heaves, the. Spasms : proletarian (— 1909). Ware, ' Graphic description'.

Heavies, the. ' The regiments of Household Cavalry, 4th and 5th Dragoon Guards, and 1st and 2nd Dragoons ', F. & H. : military coll. (— 1841). Lever. Ex their heavy equipment.—(In next two senses, small *h.*)—2. Bugs, esp. bed-bugs : low : ca. 1850–1910.—3. In late C. 19–20, esp. in G.W., the heavy artillery : military. Cf. sense 1.

heavy, come or **do the ;** occ. **do it heavy.** To put on airs ; affect superiority : s. or low coll. : from ca. 1880.—2. In C. 20, esp. since the G.W., abbr. *do the heavy father,* to be severely parental. Ex *heavy father* (1898), *heavy uncle* (ca. 1899), repressive or pompous father, pompously dignified uncle theatrical s. >, by 1925, gen. coll. (O.E.D. Sup Cf. *heavy stuff,* q.v.

heavy, the. Porter and stout : abbr. *heavy wet,* q.v. : 1823 ; ob. (O.E.D.)

heavy-arse. A sluggard : low coll. : late C. 19–20. Cf. :

heavy-arsed. Inert, lethargic, apathetic : C. 17–18 coll. One of Richard Baxter's titles was, *Shove to Heavy-Arsed Christians.*

heavy brown. Porter : low : ca. 1820–50. Bee, who is, however, ambiguous, thus : ' *Heavy*—heavy wet, or brown—porter.' Cf. *heavy wet,* q.v.

heavy cavalry or **dragoons** or **horsemen** or **(the) heavy troop.** Bugs ; esp. bed-bugs : ca. 1850–1910. The commonest are the first two ; *h.d.* is recorded by H., in 1864, as of Oxford University. Cf. *heavies,* 2, and contrast *infantry, light.*

heavy father. See **heavy, come the,** 2.

heavy grog. Hard work : workmen's : ca. 1860–1914. Ex the drink.

heavy grubber. A hearty eater ; a glutton : low coll. : from ca. 1858 ; ob. Dickens in *Great Expectations.*

heavy hand. Deep trouble : lower classes' coll. (— 1909). Ware.

heavy horseman. (Gen. pl.) A ship-looter working in the daytime, esp. on the Thames : nautical : C. 19. Bowen. Contrast *heavy cavalry.*

*****heavy lurker.** A ' teller of the piteous tale ' in a large way : c. : C. 20. ' Stuart Wood ', 1932.

heavy merchant. He who represents the villain : theatrical (— 1909). Ware.

*****heavy plodder.** A stockbroker : c. : ca. 1845–90. Duncombe.

heavy stuff. Unsympathetic and over-paternal advice or moralising : coll. : C. 20. Ex *heavy, come the,* q.v. ; ult. ex the theatrical sense, serious, esp. sombre or tragic (1826).—2. In G.W. military coll. verging on S.E., it signified (as it still does) heavy shelling or, properly, big shells. F. & Gibbons.

heavy, or **howling, swell.** A man, occ. a woman, in the height of fashion : ca. 1830–1910 : perhaps rather coll. than s. Anstey, 1892, ' We look such heavy swells, you see, we're all aristo-crats.' Punning *heavy,* having great momentum, and undoubtedly prompted by *heavy swell,* a sea running high.

heavy uncle. See heavy, come the, 2. Cf. *heavy father* (ibid.).

heavy wet ; occ. abbr. to heavy. Malt liquor ; esp. porter and stout : 1821, Egan : ob. Lytton, 'I had been lushing heavy wet,' 1830.—2. An extremely ' severe ' drinking-bout : ca. 1850–1925.

heavyside (or **H.**). Incorrect for *Heaviside* (*layer*) : 1913. O.E.D. (Sup.).

hebdomadal. A weekly magazine or review : 1835 (S.O.D.) : orig. jocular S.E. ; in late C. 19–20, journalistic ; ob.

Hebe or **hebe,** a waitress or a barmaid, is (now trite) S.E., but as pubic hair and the genitals, a sense omitted by the O.E.D. though given by Bailey, it is perhaps coll.

Hebrew. Unintelligible speech, jargon : coll. : 1705, Vanbrugh, ' Mighty obscure . . . All Hebrew.' Cf. *Greek*, a century older and S.E.

heck !, by ; what the heck ! Orig. (— 1892), Lancashire exclamations of surprise or indignation : by 1905, at latest, they had > gen. coll. Prob. ex dial. (*h*)*eck !,* indicating surprise or conveying a warning ; *heck* is perhaps a euphemism for *hell* : cf. the Lancashire *ecky,* a mild oath, and *go to ecky,* ' go to hell ! ', of mid-C. 19–20, and possibly the Scottish and Irish *hech* (or *hegh*), as in *hech, sirs !,* though this expletive *hech* is more prob. an elemental like *ha* or *ho.* (E.D.D.)

hectastyle. Incorrect for *hexastyle* : C. 18. O.E.D.

hectic. Exciting, esp. with tendency to dissipation or to excessive activity (as in *a hectic time*) ; (of a book) sensational in theme, luridly indelicate in language, or both : C. 20 coll., esp. since G.W.

hectic show, a. Dangerous flying : Air Force : 1915 †. F. & Gibbons. Ex preceding + *show.*— 2. A bitter infantry-battle : infantry officers' : 1916 †. B. & P.

Hector, hector, as a bully, a swashbuckler, is rather S.E. than coll., though († 1670) John Hacket's ' One Hector, a phrase at that time '— ca. 1640—' for a daring ruffian ' tends to show that at this period it was, by some at least, held to be coll. *The Hectors* were a swashbuckling band : see hawcubite.—2. The v. is S.E., as is *hectoring,* adj. and n.

Hector's cloak, wear. To be rightly rewarded for treachery : coll. : C. 17–early 18. Ex Hector Armstrong who, the betrayer of Thomas Percy, Earl of Northumberland in 1569, died a beggar. But *take Hector's cloak,* C. 17–early 18 (then dial, now †), is ' to deceive a friend who confides in one's fidelity ', Apperson.

hedge, a covering bet, and **hedge,** to bet ' opposite ' for safety, are, despite F. & H., ineligible, as are the figurative senses.

hedge, as adj., is a (mainly †) pejorative prefixed to nn. to connote ' connected with, born under, plying a trade under a hedge, esp. one by the roadside ; hence low, paltry, rascally, ignorant '. That many of these terms had a coll. taint appears from B.E. and Grose ; yet it is more correct to regard as S.E. all *hedge* compounds except the few that follow.

hedge, (as) common as the. Applied to whore or strumpet : coll. : late C. 17–18. B.E. Cf. the S.E. *hedge-whore,* ' a low beggarly prostitute ' (Grose). Cf. *highway.*

hedge, hang in the. (Esp. of a law-suit) to be undecided : coll. : late C. 17–18. B.E.

hedge, take a sheet off a. To steal openly : coll. : C. 17 (? 18 also).

hedge-bird. 'A Scoundrel or sorry Fellow ', B.E. : C. 17–mid-18 coll. (? S.E. till ca. 1680).

hedge-bit. A hedge-whore ; a (gen. dirty) harlot favouring the open air : C. 19–20 low ; ob.

***hedge-creeper.** A robber of hedges : mid-C. 16– early 19 : coll. till ca. 1690, then low s. or c.

hedge-docked. Seduced in the open air : low : C. 19.

hedge-hopping, n. Flying very low : Air Force : 1915 +. F. & Gibbons.

hedge or by stile, by. By hook or by crook : late C. 17–18 : coll. B.E.

hedge-popper. ' A trumpery shooter ', F. & H. ; *hedge-popping,* the shooting of small birds in and about hedges. Both sporting s. > coll. : from ca. 1860 ; ob.

***hedge-square** (occ. **street**), **doss** or **snooze in.** T) sleep in the open air, esp. in the country : vagrants' c. (— 1876) ; ob. J. Greenwood, in *Under the Blue Blanket.* Cf. *starry, do a.*

hedgehog. A many-oared boat : nautical : C. 19. Bowen. Ex that animal's appearance.

hee. See he, 1.

hee-haw. A donkey : nursery coll. : mid-C. 19–20.

heebie (or **-y**)**-jeebies, the.** A fit of depression or irritation : U.S. (1927) >, by 1928, anglicised. Ex a dance that, so named, resembled the *Blues* (O.E.D. Sup.) ; perhaps a reduplicated perversion of S.E. *creepy* or *the creeps* : cf. the Scottish adv., *heepie-creep,* 'in a creeping, sneaking manner' (1873 : E.D.D.).

heef dry or **wet.** To fight, make a campaign, on dry land or on sea : military (— 1923). Manchon. Ex dial. *heaf,* to settle down, to reside or live.

heel. down (or **out at**) **heel**(**s**) is S.E., not—*pace* F. & H.—coll. The same applies to *heel-tap,* liquor left in the bottom of a glass, but *heel-taps,* a London dustmen's † dance, is perhaps coll.

heel, hairy at the. See hairy about . . .

heel-tap !, take off your. A toast-master's injunction to drain one's glass : coll. : mid-C. 18– mid-19. Grose, 2nd ed.

heel up, v.i. To follow behind a person : Glasgow (— 1934).

heeler. A plunge, feet first, into water : Winchester College : from ca. 1860.—2. A lurch to the side : coll. : from ca. 1890. O.E.D. (Sup.).—3. Hence, a boat inclined to lurch thus : coll. : 1926 (O.E.D. Sup.).—4. A fast sailing-ship : nautical coll. : late C. 19–20. Bowen. Prob. ex dial. *heeler,* a quick runner.

heels. The following phrases, cited as coll. by F. & H., are S.E. :—*get* or *have the heels of, go heels over head, lay by the heels, take to one's heels, tread upon* (or *be at, upon*) *the heels of.*

heels, bless the world with one's. To be hanged : coll. : ca. 1560–1650. Painter in his *Palace of Pleasure.*

heels, cool or **kick one's.** See cool one's heels.

heels, his. The knave of trumps : cribbage s. > j. : late C. 18–20. Grose, 1796. Cf. *nob,* q.v.

heels, kick up one's. See heels, turn up one's.

heels, lift one's. (Of a woman) to lie down for coïtion : low coll. : C. 18–20.

heels, turn—occ. **tip, topple ; kick, lay**—**up one's.** To die : coll. The first, much the most gen., C. 16– 20, e.g. Nashe, in *Pierce Penniless* ; *topple,* late C. 16–19, in Nashe's *Lenten Stuff* ; none of the other three ' antedated ' C. 17 or ' postdated ' C. 19.

hefty. Big and strong : coll. : orig. (— 1871), U.S. : anglicised ca. 1905 (Thornton defines it as

C

'heavy, bulky', which prob. derives ex Eng. dial., but in Eng. coll. usage the connotation of strength is essential, unless the reference is to a thing—and then the tendency is to join it to another adj. as in 'a hefty great book').—2. Hence, adv.: exceedingly: coll.: late C. 19–20. (O.E.D. Sup.)

heifer. A woman, gen. a girl: low coll.: C. 19–20; ob.—2. A charwoman: Charterhouse: † by 1900, as A. H. Tod notes in his *Charterhouse.*

heifer-paddock. A school for older girls: Australian: ca. 1880–1900. Mrs. Campbell Praed, *Australian Life*, 1885, 'I shall look over a heifer-paddock in Sydney, and take my pick.'

***heigh-ho.** Stolen yarn: Norwich c.: ca. 1855–1910. Ex the form of apprising the 'fence' (q.v.) of stolen yarn. H., 2nd ed.—2. **Heigh-Ho.** Henry Norris (1665–1725), comedian. Ex one of his songs. Dawson.

height has occ., C. 16–19, been used erroneously for *hight*, to adorn. O.E.D.

heights of connubial bliss, scale the. If jocular, it is coll.: otherwise, obviously, it is a weak S.E. euphemism. C. 19–20, ob.

heightth. Height: in late C. 18–early 19, it was coll.; since ca. 1860, it has been low coll. >, in C. 20, sol. This represents a comparatively rare spelling, a frequent pronunciation—until Johnson's day, in fact, a variant S.E. pronunciation.

Heine, Heinie; occ. **Hiney.** The Canadian (and later the U.S.) soldiers' name for 'Fritz' or 'Jerry', qq.v.: 1914–18 (and after). Ex *Heinrich*, an extremely common Ger. Christian name. F. & Gibbons.

(h)elbat. A table: back s. (— 1859). 'The aspirate is a matter of taste,' H.

helch(er)wer; helsh-. A welsher: centre s.: from ca. 1860; ob.

helio, n. and v. Heliograph: by coll. abbr.: from ca. 1890. Kipling, in *Many Inventions*; *The Daily News*, Sept. 4, 1897, 'Messages had to be helio'd under a hot fire at short range' (O.E.D.).—2. Heliotrope: coll.: from ca. 1920. O.E.D. (Sup.).

he'll. He will (cf. *she'll*, she will): coll. contraction: C. 18–20.

[**Hell.** ' A dark corner near Third Pot, famed for its growth of violets ', Wrench : Winchester College : C. 19–20: prob. rather j. than eligible. Ex the Hampshire *hell*, a dark place in the woods.]

hell is frequent in imprecations, esp. in *hell !, go to hell !, hell's bells !* (Colonial), and the quaint † *go to hell and pump thunder !*—2. As a place of confinement, the 'den' in prisoner's base, a workman's receptacle for refuse or stolen remnants (see **eye**), and as a gambling house—all listed by F. & H.—it is S.E., though the third sense may, orig., have well been coll. or even c.—witness Anon.'s *Defence of Cony-Catching*, 1592 (pp. 57–8).—3. As the female pudend, C. 18–20, it is low coll.: see **hell, put the devil into.**—4. Fun; esp. in *just for the hell of it*: coll.: C. 20. E.g. in James Spenser, *Limey Breaks In*, 1934.

hell, all to; occ. **gone to hell.** Utterly ruined: coll.: C. 19–20.

hell and high water, between. In a great difficulty: nautical coll.: C. 20. (W. McFee, *The Beachcomber*, 1935). A deviation from S.E. *between the devil and the deep sea.*

hell, as much chance (or hope) as a snowflake in; or **as an icicle in Hades.** Almost no chance at all: Australian coll.: from ca. 1910. Lyell.

hell, give. To trounce, punish severely; vituperate: coll.: from ca. 1830.

hell, gone to. See **hell, all to.**

hell !, I'll go (hopping) to. A coll. expletive connoting surprise or indignation: C. 20. (Manchon.)

hell, kick up or **play.** To cause a (tremendous) disturbance or great trouble: coll.: from ca. 1840. See **hell and tommy.**

hell, lead apes in. See **apes.**

hell, like. With extreme vigour; desperately: coll.: from ca. 1850. Thackeray, 'I tried every place . . . and played like hell.'—2. Very badly: C. 20 coll.—3. Not at all ! Certainly not ! E.g. 'Did you go ?—Like hell (I did) ! ' C. 20 s. > coll.

Hell, Little. 'A small dark covered passage, leading from London-wall to Bell-alley', Grose, 2nd ed.: mid-C. 18–early 19.

hell, put the devil into. To have sexual connexion: C. 18–20 'literary' coll.: ex Boccaccio.

hell, raise. To make a tremendous noise or disturbance: C. 19 coll. > C. 20 S.E. Variant, *hell's delight.*

hell, silver. A gambling house where only silver stakes are allowed. This, like *dancing hell*, was orig. (ca. 1840) coll. but soon > S.E.

hell, to. Intensely. Always with *hope* or *wish*: low coll. (— 1891). Nat Gould, in *Double Event*, 'I hope to h— the horse will break his neck and his rider's too.'

hell and spots. A C. 20 variant (s. >, by 1934, coll.) of the next. Richard Blaker, *Night-Shift*, 1934, 'Another sort of woman could have knocked hell and spots off of you.'

hell and tommy, esp. in *play h. and t.* and, in C. 20, *like h. and t.* A picturesque intensive (s. > coll.): slightly ob. App. first printed, 1832–4, in *The Caesars*, by De Quincey, 'Lord Bacon played Hell and Tommy when casually raised to the supreme seat in the council.' Genesis obscure; *and tommy* is a tag added to *(play) hell*, precisely as *and Betty Martin* is tagged to *(all) my eye.* Ware, who does support *Hal and Tommy* (Henry VIII and Thomas Cromwell playing havoc with Church property), proposes *hell and torment* (by corruption or perversion),—than which I have not heard, nor can I think, of a likelier origin. In Northumberland dial. (1894 : E.D.D., Sup.), *play hell and tommy with =* ' to set utterly at variance '.

hell-bending, vbl.n. Preaching; esp., fervid preaching: Canadian: from ca. 1910. John Beames.

hell-born babe, hell-cat, -hag, -hound, -kite. A man or a woman of a devilish character: C. 16–20, ob. Perhaps orig. coll., but certainly soon S.E.

hell-box or **-hole.** A coll. variation of *hell*, a receptacle for (esp. stolen) remnants. Cf. *cabbage*, q.v.—2. (Only *hell-box*.) A galley-stove: nautical: late C. 19–20. Bowen, 'Most frequently in the Canadian and American ships '.

hell breaks loose, gen. **hell is broke loose,** describes extreme disorder; *hell broke loose* as a n. = anarchy, noisy topsy-turvydom: coll. soon > S.E.: late C. 16–20. Byron, in *Vision of Judgement*, 'And realised the phrase of " Hell broke loose " '.

hell-broth. Bad liquor: (low) coll.: from ca. 1850; ob. Ex S.E. sense.

hell-cart. A hackney carriage: coll.: ca. 1630–1700. Perhaps orig. *hell-cart coach.*

hell-driver. A coachman: late C. 17–mid-18 coll. B.E.

hell-fire, adv. Extremely, 'damned', damnably,

'devilish': coll. (— 1760); **ob.** C. Johnston, in *Chrysal*, 'The weather in summer is *hell-fire* hot, in winter *hell-fire* cold' (O.E.D.). Cf. and (?) ex *hell-fired*, q.v.

Hell-Fire Dick. 'The driver of the Cambridge Telegraph' (coach) and 'a favourite companion of the University fashionables': Cambridge University nickname (— 1811). *Lex. Bal.* He died in 1822 (Egan's Grose); Bee says his name was Owen.

Hell-Fire Jack. A violent or reckless officer, not necessarily unpopular: sailing-ships' nickname: mid-C. 19–20. Bowen.

hell-fired, adv. Extremely, 'damned': coll.: 1756; ob. Toldervy, in *The Two Orphans*, 'He is a h–ll-fir'd good creature' (O.E.D.). Ex S.E. sense.

hell for leather, often hyphenated. Desperately and vigorously (or swiftly): coll.: from ca. 1875 (W.). Kipling, 1892, 'When we rode hell-for-leather, | Both squadrons together, | Not caring much whether we lived or we died'. Perhaps out of *all of a lather* by *leather*, skin as affected by riding (W.).

hell, Hull and Halifax,—Good Lord deliver us,—from. A proverbial coll. = save us from evil: C. 16–20. (The most usual form is *from Hull, hell, and Halifax, Good Lord deliver us !*) Ex the celebrated Gibbet-Law of Halifax: this consisted in execution of prisoners and *subsequent* inquiry into their demerits; as early as 1586, *to have had Halifax law* had been extended to the procedure of inquiry made after condemnation. (Apperson, at *Halifax*.) See **Halifax !, go to.**

hell-matter. Old, battered type: printers': from ca. 1865; ? orig. U.S.: ob.

hell mend (him) ! Curse (him) !: coll.: late C. 19–20.

hell of a (e.g. mess). Very much of a ——. A coll. intensive: 1778 (S.O.D.). Cf. *devil of a* ——.

Hell (late C. 19); **Hell Passage** (C. 20). St. Helen's Passage, Oxford: undergraduates'. Collinson.

'hell !' said the duchess (when she caught her teats in the mangle). The fuller form is the original; it dates from ca. 1895 and was frequently heard in the G.W., though rarely in the ranks. In post-War days, the shorter form is much the more heard, gen. without the slightest reference to the original: cf. Michael Arlen's novel, *Hell ! said the Duchess*, 1934. So well established is the phrase that *The Times Literary Supplement*, Jan. 11, 1936, could wittily head a review of Daniel George's *A Peck of Troubles*, with the words, 'Said the Duchess'.

hell-scrapers. Shrapnel: a Boer name: 1899–1901. J. Milne, *The Epistles of Atkins*, 1902.

hell-ship. A ship with brutal officers: nautical coll.: late C. 19–20. Bowen, 'Borrowed from the Americans'.

hellish, adv. 'Sometimes a mere coarse intensive', O.E.D.: coll.: from ca. 1750.

hellite. A professional gambler: coll. (— 1838) >, ca. 1870, S.E.: ob. by 1900, † by 1920. 'Ducange Anglicus.'

hell's bells ! Hell ! : coll.: late C. 19–20; orig. Colonial. In 1932, at Sydney, Lieut. Joe Maxwell brought out his typically Australian War-book, *Hell's Bells and Mam'selles*. By rhyme: cf. *here's cheers !* Also in construction (C. 20) as in 'Regular **hell's bells** of a fuss', H. C. Bailey, *Mr. Fortune Wonders*, 1932.

hell's delight. See **hell, raise.**

hell's like ! 'Like hell !': a coll. intensive: C. 20. (John Brophy, *Waterfront*, 1934.)

hellum. See **ellum.**

helluva or **heluva.** Hell of a: coll. slurring, as in A. A. Milne, *Two People*, 1931, 'Making a heluva bad job of it'. Not merely, nor even orig., U.S.

[**help,** a servant, is U.S. but, despite F. & H., ineligible.]

help, v. With *can, could*, often erroneously with *not* omitted: coll.: from ca. 1860. Whateley, 'In colloquial language it is common to hear persons say, "I won't do so-and-so more than I can help," meaning, more than I can not help,' as when J. H. Newman, in his *Apologia*, wrote, 'Your name shall occur again as little as I can help, in the course of these pages.' (O.E.D.). See esp. Fowler.

help ! A derisory exclamation on hearing a tall story: rare before C. 20. (*So help me God* > coll. only in its corrupted forms, e.g. *s'elp me Bob*: see **s'elp.**)

helpa. An apple: back s. (— 1859). H., 1st ed. The *h* is optional: cf. *helbat.*

helping foot !, he deserves a. He needs kicking: ironic c.p. (— 1923). Manchon.

helpless. (Very) drunk: coll.: from ca. 1860. Cf. *gravelled* and *paralytic.*

helsh(er)wer. See **helch(er)wer.**

helter-skelter. A privateer: naval: C. 19. Bowen. Ex his methods: see next entry.

[**helter-skelter,** adv., is by B.E. and Grose regarded as coll.: in their time, ca. 1690–1800, it prob. was. Etymology unsolved: I trepidate *helter*, to put a halter on (cf. dial. *heltering*, the breaking-in of colts), to hang, + *kelter*, order,— hence, in defiance of order (the *s* being euphonic); *helter-kelter* is, by the way, found in the Essex and Kentish diall.]

heluva. See **helluva.—hemastatic.** See **hæmastatic.**

hemelytrum. Incorrect for *hemi-elytrum*: 1826 (O.E.D.).

hemispheres. The female breasts: 'literary' coll. when not a mere euphemi sm: C. 19–20.

hemp, hempy, hemp-seed or **-string,** like **stretch-hemp,** a candidate for the gallows, rarely a halter, are rather S.E. than coll. (although *hempy*, it seems prob., was orig. coll.). The same holds for *hempen candle, circle, collar, cravat, croak, garter, habeas, necktie,* the hangman's noose, a halter; for *hempen fortune,* bad luck, i.e. death by the gallows; and for Randolph's *hempen squincy*, hanging. The following six entries, however, were, at least orig., coll.:—

hemp, young. 'An appellation for a graceless boy', Grose, 1785: coll.: late C. 18–early 19.

hemp in the wind, wag. To be hanged: coll.: ca. 1530–1620. Sir Thomas Moore. (Never, I think, very gen.)

hemp is growing for the villain, the. A c.p. applied to a rogue: C. 19. Bee. Earlier, *hemp is grown for you* (Ware).

hempen bridle. A ship's rope or rigging: coll.: C. 18.

hempen fever, die of a. To be hanged: mid-C. 18–mid-19: (? s. >) low coll. Grose, 1st ed.; Ainsworth, 'Three of her [*four*] husbands died of hempen fevers.' Cf. Nashe's *hempen circle*, Skelton's *hempen snare* (Onions), Hoccleve's *hempen lane*, and Dekker's *hempen tragedies*.

hempen widow. A woman widowed by the

gallows: late C. 17–mid-19: (? **s.** >) low coll.; perhaps orig. c. B.E., Grose, Ainsworth.

hen. A woman: from ca. 1620: jocular s. > coll.—2. A mistress: same period; ob.: low. Brome.—3. Drink-money: Cockney (— 1892); ob. Milliken.

hen-frigate. A ship 'bossed' by the captain's wife: nautical (— 1785); ob. Grose, 1st ed. Cf. *hen-house*, q.v.; but prob. an abbr. of B.E.'s *hen-pecked frigate*.

hen-fruit. Eggs, collectively: Canadian: C. 20. (Cf. *cackle-berry*, q.v.) John Beames.

[**hen-hearted**, timorous, has, despite Grose and F. & H., always been S.E.]

hen-house. A house in which the woman rules; also called a *she-house* (cf. *hen-frigate*, above): coll. (— 1785): ob. by 1870, † by 1900. Grose, 1st ed.— 2. A building in which live soldiers' wives: military: C. 20. Manchon.

hen-party. An assemblage of women: coll. (orig. low): from ca. 1885. Occ. *-convention* or *-tea*. Cf. *bitch-*, *cat-*, *tabby-party*.

hen-peck. (Of a wife) to rule, domineer over the husband: coll.: 1688 (S.O.D.). Byron. Ex:

hen-pecked. Ruled, domineered over by a wife: coll.: 1680, 'Hudibras' Butler; (S.O.D.); B.E. gives *hen-pecked frigate* (see **hen-frigate**) and *hen-pecked husband*; *The Spectator*, No. 479, 'Socrates . . . the undoubted head of the sect of the hen-pecked'. Perhaps suggested by the C. 16–18 proverb, *It is a sad house where the hen crows louder than the cock.*

hen-toed. With one's feet turned in as one walks: coll.: C. 19–20; ob.

Henri Clark. To flatter: theatrical; esp. at Drury Lane: 1883–ca. 90. Ware, 'From the flattering stage-mode of a singer of this name'.

Henry Sophister. See **harry soph.**

hens. 'Gillygate end of old 3rd and 4th XI's playing pitch', *Dict. of Bootham Slang*, 1925.

*****hens and chickens.** Pewter measures; esp. quarts and pints: c. (— 1851); ob. Mayhew.

hep! 'Left!' in military commands, as being so much easier to pronounce explosively: C. 20.

her. She: low coll. or sol.: C. 17–20; recorded in 1698 (O.E.D.), but only predicatively, i.e. coll. Sol. only when nominatively. There are extremely few records for pre-1840. E.g. ' Her and me was born here; us be great frien's.' Cf. *him*, *me*, *us*, qq.v.

Her Majesty's carriage. A prison van: ca. 1880–1901; then *His M. c.*, ob. Baumann.

Her or **His Majesty's naval police.** See **naval police.**

Her Majesty's tobacco pipe. The furnace in which forfeited tobacco from the Customs is burnt: ca. 1850–80. *The Echo*, Jan. 27, 1871. This wasteful custom was changed ca. 1880 and the forfeited tobacco went to workhouses (? always).

herbaceous border. A naval sloop of the *Flower* class: naval officers': 1915–18. Bowen.

herbs!, good or **sweet** ('erbs! or). Excellent!; excellently!: a c.p. (— 1923), mostly of postmen. Manchon.

here. Redundant between *this* and its n. (cf. *that there*, e.g. *thing*): mid-C. 18–20 sol. Foote, in *The Orators*, 'I should be glad to know how my client can be tried in this here manner' (O.E.D.) Ex *this*, e.g., *thing here*, where *here* is added for emphasis: cf. Fr. *ce(tte)* . . . *-ci* or *-là*.—2. Redundant after *belong*, as in 'I'm a stranger, I don't belong here': coll.: from ca. 1890. (O.E.D.)—3. Cf. *here*, as

n. = this place, as in ' Between here and London': coll.: C. 19–20. O.E.D. (Sup.).

here, I'm not. I feel disinclined for work or conversation: tailors': ca. 1860–1915.

here-and-thereian. A 'rolling stone': coll.: ca. 1700–1860. Cibber, Grose (2nd ed.).

here goes! Now for it!; there's not much chance, but I'll *try*: coll.: 1829, J. H. Newman, in a letter. (O.E.D.)

here we (or **you**) **are!** This is what's needed: coll.: both from ca. 1845.

here we are again! A C. 20 c.p.; orig. (from ca. 1880) a form of greeting. Possibly originated by Harry Paine (? Payne), that clown who, at Drury Lane in the 1870's and -80's, began the Boxing Night harlequinade with a somersault and a cheerful ' here we are again!'

here (or **yere**) **they come smoking their pipes!** A c.p. by Billingsgate fish-buyers when, at auctions, the bids were rapid and high: 1870's. Ware, 'It probably meant independence and determination.'

Herefordshire weed. An oak: (when not Herefordshire dial.) coll. (— 1860). E.D.D.

here's cheers! A coll. (— 1931) variant of the next. Lyell, who cites also *here's God bless us* (C. 20).

here's fun!; here's jolly good luck! Two C. 20 coll. variants of the preceding. Lyell.

here's hoping! A mostly G.W. variant of:

here's how! A late C. 19–20 coll. toast. ? used before Kipling, 1896, in *Seven Seas.*

here's looking to you. See **here's to you.**

here's luck! I don't believe you!: tailors': from ca. 1860.

here's more hair on your navel!; here's mud in your eye! C. 20 toasts, the former mostly Australian.

here's to it! A most indelicately anatomical toast: C. 19–20: coll. See **it.**

here's to you! A toast: in some form or other, from late C. 16. At first coll. (with ellipsis of *a toast*); by 1700, S.E. Late C. 19–20 coll. variants are *here's looking to you* and *here's looking towards you.* (Lyell.)

heresy-shop. A Nonconformist church: Roman Catholic priests': C. 19–20. Cf. *schism-shop*, q.v.

hermetic(al), erroneously for *hermitic(al)*: C. 18–20; a cultured sol. O.E.D.

hermit, or **bald-headed h.** The male member: low: C. 19–20, ob.—2. In Gypsy s., a highwayman: C. 19. Longfellow.

hern. Hers: (dial. and) sol.: C. 15–20. Baumann. Cf. *hisn*, q.v.

herohotic. (Of novels) sexually outspoken: literary: 1897–ca. 1900. Ware. Punning *erotic* and *hot* (amorous) *hero*.

herring, dead as a (shotten). Quite dead: coll.: late C. 16–20, ob. Herrings very quickly die on being removed from the water.

herring,—neither fish, flesh, fowl, nor good red. See **fish.**

herring, neither (or **no**, or **never a**, or, gen., **the devil a**) **barrel the better.** All (gen. bad) alike: proverbial coll.: mid-C. 16–20. Bale, in his play, *King John*, ca. 1540; Jonson, Fielding, FitzGerald (Apperson.)

herring (or, 1869, **a whale**), **throw a sprat to catch a.** To forgo a small in the hope of a great advantage: proverbial coll. (— 1826). Grant Allen, in *Tents of Shem*, ' He's casting a sprat to catch a whale.'

herring-gutted. Tall and very thin: coll.: C. 18–mid-19. Arbuthnot.

herring-hog. A porpoise: nautical coll.: mid-C. 19–20. Bowen. Ex dial.

Herring Joker. A Nova Scotian, man or ship: nautical: late C. 19–20. Ibid. Here, *joker* = chap, fellow.

Herring-Pond, be sent across the, or **cross the H.-P. at the King's expense.** To be transported (– 1785): coll.; perhaps orig. c.: † by 1870. Grose, 1st ed. By itself, *herring pond,* the sea, or *H.-P.,* the North Atlantic Ocean (1616), is jocular S.E. rather than coll. (In Cornish, *herring-pool.*)

herrings in a barrel, like. Very crowded; packed very close: coll. (– 1891): ob., the post-G.W. preference being for *like sardines (in a tin).*

her's is a frequent written illiteracy, i.e. sol., for *hers.* Cf. *it's* for *its, their's* for *theirs.*

Hertfordshire kindness. An acknowledgment—or a return in kind—of favours received; also and esp. a drinking twice to the same man: coll.: ca. 1660–1830. B.E., Swift, Grose. Ex a Hertford-shire custom, says Fuller in his *Worthies.*

Herts Guards, the. The Hertfordshire Terri-torials of the Bedfordshire Regiment: military: late 1915–18. F. & Gibbons. From October, 1914, to August, 1915, they served with the 4th Guards Brigade.

he's, hes. His: sol. and dial.: C. 19 (or earlier)–20.

he's saving them all for Lisa (or Liza)! A now ob. c.p. applied, from before 1909, by the lower classes to 'a good young man who will not use oaths or strike blows', Ware. Ex the youth who wouldn't give a beggar a penny because he was saving them all for his girl.

Hesiod Cooke. Thomas Cooke (1703–56), trans-lator of Hesiod. (Dawson.)

hess-u-hen! 'A way of asking for a copy of *The Sun* newspaper', Ware, 1909: lower middle classes': † by 1920. I.e. *s u n.*

hev. Have: sol., esp. Cockneys': C. 19–20.

hevethee. A thief: centre s.: from ca. 1860; ob.

hexarch. Incorrect for *exarch*: C. 17–20 (O.E.D.). Contrast *exagonal* for *hexagonal.*

hexasperate. See exasperate.—**hey!** See **hay!**

hey-gammer-cook, play at. To coït: C. 18–early 19. C. Johnson.

heye-glass weather, it's. It's foggy: a pro-letarian c.p. aimed at the wearer of a monocle or eye-glass: 1860; very ob. Ware.

Hibs, the. The *Hibernian* Football Club: sporting: C. 20.—2. The Hibernians, an Irish political group: Anglo-Irish: 1914; ob.

hic is a slovenly spelling (e.g. in *Street-Robberies Consider'd,* 1728) of **hick.**

***hiccius-doccius, hictius-doctius, hixius-doxius, etc.,** the variants being unrecorded after ca. 1790. A juggler; a trickster, a shifty fellow: c.: ca. 1678–1810. Butler, Wycherley. Either an arti-ficial word of spurious L. (cf. *hocus-pocus*), or a corruption of *hicce est doctus.* The term was orig. (1676, Shadwell) and frequently used in jugglers' patter.

hiccius-doccius or **-doxius,** etc. Slovenly: ca. 1730–1800. North, in the *Examen,* 'The author with his hiccius-doxius delivery'.—2. Drunk: ca. 1780–1820. Grose, 1st ed. Perhaps ex *hick,* to hiccup.

[**Hiccobites, a** C. 18 drinking club, is **s.** by forma-tion: *hiccup-ites.*]

***hick.** An (easy) prey to sharpers: c.: ca. 1685–1750. B.E.—2. Whence, a—gen. simple—country-man: **s.** > coll.: ca. 1680–1830: now mostly U.S.: see esp. Irwin. Ex the familiar by-form of *Richard,* as *Bob* is of *Robert.*

hick(a)boo. An air-raid; a warning that an air-raid is imminent: Air Force men's: 1916. F. & Gibbons; Manchon, 'Déformation d'un mot hindou signifiant aigle'.

Hickenbothom, Mr. 'A ludicrous name for an unknown person, similar to that of Mr. Thingam-bob', Grose: coll. (– 1791); † by 1890. Grose's etymology, *Ickenbaum* (an oak-tree), is nonsense; the word is perhaps a pun on *hick,* q.v., and *bottom,* the posteriors.

hickery-pickery. Hiera picra (a purgative drug) · low coll., or sol.: C. 19–20.

hickey. (Not quite) drunk: late C. 18–19: low (? orig. c.); more U.S. than Eng. Grose, 1st ed. Ex *hiccius-doccius,* adj., or else ex dial. *hick,* to hiccup.

hickitserpu. A sticker-up (esp. of skittles): centre s.: from ca. 1860; ob.

hicra-picra. Hiera picra: sol., or low coll. (– 1857). O.E.D. See **hickery-pickery.**

hictius-doctius. A late C. 17 variant of *hiccius-doccius.*

hide. The human skin: O.E.–mod. Eng.: S.E. >, ca. 1710, low coll. C. Coffey, in *The Devil to Pay,* 1731, 'Come, and spin, you drab, or I'll tan your hide for you.'—2. Impudence; excessive self-assurance: Australian: C. 20. Jice Doone.

hide, v. To flog, thrash: low coll., prob. ex dial. (1825); ob. Ex *tan one's hide,* q.v.

hide and seek, he plays at. 'A saying of one who is in fear of being arrested . . . and therefore does not choose to appear in public', Grose, 1785; ob. by 1860, † by 1890. (*Hide and seek,* as a game, has, in dial., at least thirteen variants.)

***hide up.** (Of police or other authorities) to defend or shield (a wrongdoer): c.: from ca. 1920. E.g. in Edgar Wallace, *The Flying Squad.*

[**hidebound,** despite Grose and F. & H., has always been S.E.]

hideously. Very: mostly Society: from ca. 1920. Denis Mackail, *Greenery Street,* 1925, 'It was so hideously awkward.' Cf. *fearfully.*

hidgeot, hidgit. An idiot: ˌ sol.: C. 19–20. Ware.

hiding. A thrashing; occ., from ca. 1890, a heavy defeat. Low coll.: 1809 (S.O.D.). 'Cuth bert Bede', 1853, 'May the Gown give the Town a jolly good hiding.'

higgledy-piggledy, adv. and adj. In a confused jumble: coll.: late C. 16–20: from ca. 1895, S.E. Florio; Miss Broughton, in *Nancy,* 'We are all higgledy-piggledy—at sixes and sevens.' Johnson, 'corrupted from *higgle* . . . any confused mass', and therefore connected with *higgler,* a hawker,—*higgler* being S.E., not coll.; but more prob. a 'reduplicated jingle on *pig,* with reference to huddling together', W.

high. Intoxicated: 1627, May in his *Lucan* (O.E.D.): from ca. 1880, mostly U.S.—2. As (of game) tainted, it is S.E., but as (of a prostitute) venereally infected, it is low coll.—3. Obscene: low coll.; like preceding sense, from ca. 1860 and ob.

High, the. The High Street, Oxford: undergraduates' **s.**: late C. 19–20. Collinson. Cf. *the Broad, the Corn, the Turl.*

high and dry, adj. = stranded, is, despite Egan and F. & H., ineligible, but *the High and Dry*, the High Church party, is Church s.: 1854, Conybeare, in *Church Parties.* Also adj. (— 1857.) *The Graphic*, April 10, 1886, ' In the Church have we not the three schools of High and Dry, Low and Slow, and Broad and Shallow ? ' See the other two terms.

high and mighty. Arrogant ; imperious : coll. (— 1825). J. W. Croker ; Nat Gould, ' None of your high and mighty games with me.'

high-bellied ; high in the belly. Advanced in pregnancy : low coll. : from ca. 1850. Also *high-waisted.*

High Church Trumpet, the. Dr. Sacheverell (1674–1724), churchman and politician. (Dawson.)

high collar and short shirts. A music-halls' (1882), hence urban c.p. directed at cheap ' swells ' ; † by 1900. Ware.

high-day. Catachrestic for *hey-day* : C. 17– early 18. Tom Brown, 1687. O.E.D.

high eating. Eating skylarks in a garret : jocular coll. : late C. 18–early 19. Grose, 2nd ed. Cf. *high living*, q.v.

high enough, you can't get. A jeering comment on failure : low coll. : from ca. 1850 ; ob. ' Probably obscene in origin ', F. & H.

high feather, in. See **feather, in full.**

high-flier. See **high-flyer.**

***high-fly, be on the.** To practise the begging-letter ' game ' or ' lay ' (C. 16 *law*) : c. (— 1839) ; ob. Brandon in *Poverty, Mendicity and Crime*, 1839. Collectively, *the high-fly* is those who carry on this trade.—2. To tramp as a beggar : from ca. 1850 ; ob.

high-flyer, -flier. As a very ambitious or pretentious person, S.E. ; **s.** as a bold adventurer, a fashionable prostitute, an impudent and dissolute woman : from ca. 1690, only the second nuance being extant. Perhaps s. is sense, 3, a fast mail-coach : Scott, 1818, in *Midlothian* ; † by 1870.—Also old **s.** are :—4. One who frequents the gallery of a theatre : C. 18. D'Urfey, 1719.—5. And, a gross exaggeration : ca. 1770–80. G. J. Pratt, in *The Pupil of Pleasure.* O.E.D.—6. In c., a genteel beggar (— 1851), as in Mayhew's *magnum opus* ; a begging-letter writer, from ca. 1839.—7. Ex the c. senses comes that of a broken-down gentleman, as in *The Standard*, June 20, 1887 ; ob. by 1915, † by 1920.—8. ' A swing fixed in rows in a frame much in vogue at fairs ', F. & H. : circus (— 1859).—9. A slave-ship : nautical : late C. 19–20 ; ob. Ware.

***high-flying** (over-ambitious, -pretentious, or -extravagant, is S.E., as is the corresponding n. ; but) in c. signifies begging, esp. by letter : from ca. 1839 ; ob.

***high game, high-game.** A mansion : c. (—1889) ; ob.

high(-)gig, in. Lively : ca. 1815–70 : coll. Moore, ' Rather sprightly—the Bear in high-gig '. See **gig.**

high(-)go. A frolic ; a drinking-bout : low coll. : from ca. 1820 ; ob. Cf. *go*, n., 2 and 6.

high-hat. To treat (a person) superciliously : an American coll. partly anglicised by 1930.

high, home, and easy. Very slow, under-hand lob bowling : cricketers' : ca. 1825–1900. Lewis.

high hook. That angler of a party who *hooks* the heaviest fish : anglers' coll. : from early 1890's. O.E.D. (Sup.) Prob. ex :—2. Same as *high line*, 2.

high horse, be on or **get on** or **ride the.** See **horse, ride the high.**—**high in the belly.** See **high-bellied.**

high in the instep, be. To be (over-)proud : coll. : from ca. 1540 ; in C. 19–20, mostly dial. Fuller, in his *Church History.*

***high jinks.** A gambler who, at dice, drinks to intoxicate his, gen. ' pigeon ', adversary : c. : ca. 1770–1820. (In S.E., a dicing game for drinks.)— 2. A frolic ; a very lively, and often noisy, party or gathering or behaviour : coll. (— 1861). Hughes, in *Tom Brown at Oxford*, ' All sorts of high jinks go on on the grass plot.' Ex the S.E. sense.

high jinks, be at one's. To be stiffly arrogant in manner ; ' ride the high horse ' : low coll. : from ca. 1865 ; ob.

high jump(s), be for the. See **jump(s), be for the high.**

high-kicker. A dancer specialising in the high kick ; whence, almost imm., a wild ' spreester ' : coll. : from ca. 1870.—2. In C. 20, gen. ' a girl who is over fond of " a good time ", somewhat fast ' (Lyell) : coll.

high-kilted. Indecorous ; obscene : Scots coll. (in C. 20, standard) : C. 19–20. The same holds of *Highland bail*, the right of might, as in Scott's *Antiquary.*

***high law.** Highway robbery : c. : ca. 1590– 1660. Greene, *Cony-Catching* pamphlets, No. 1.

***high-lawyer.** A highwayman : c. : late C. 16– mid-17. Greene, 1591 ; John Day in *The Blind Beggar*, ' He wo'd be your prigger, . . . your high-lawyer.' Lit., one who practises the high (i.e. the highway) ' law ' or ' lay ' or ' game '.

high line. A good catch : Grand Banks fishermen's coll. : from ca. 1890. Bowen.—2. Hence, ' the most successful fishing boat or clipper of the season ' : from ca. 1895 : id. Ibid. Also, occ., *high hook.*

***high-liver.** A thief lodging in an attic : C. 19 c. Ex the gen. s. or jocular coll. sense, one who lodges in garret or loft, with its vbl.n., *high living* (— 1788), as in Grose, 2nd ed. Cf. *high eating*, q.v.

high-lows. Laced boots reaching up over the ankles : orig. (1801), trade s. >, ca. 1860, gen. coll. ; and, by 1895, S.E. ' In contrast with " top " boots and " low " shoes ', S.O.D.

***high(-)men** or **runners.** Dice so loaded that they fall ' high ' : orig. (1592), c. ; by C. 18, low s. ; in C. 19–20, gen. considered S.E. The *runners* form, 1670. (Extremely rare in singular.)

High-Mettled Mary. Bolingbroke, statesman (1678–1751). Dawson.

high-nosed. Arrogant ; supercilious, ' superior ' : (low) coll : from ca. 1860 ; ob.

high old. Excellent ; very merry, jolly, or joyous : coll. : from ca. 1880 : *high old time* occurs in *The Illustrated London News*, Feb. 10, and *The Referee*, March 11, 1883 ; *high old liar*, in J. Newman's *Scamping Tricks*, 1891 ; *high old drunk*, a mighty drinking-bout, before 1893. Orig. (— 1869) U.S. All the *high old* phrases except *h.o. time* are ob. An extension of † *high time* in this sense. Ware ; F. & H. ; O.E.D. (Sup.).

***high(-)pad** or **-toby** or, occ., **-toby-splicer** or **-splice toby.** The highway, esp. as a place for robbery : c. : resp. mid-C. 16–early 19, C. 18– mid-19, first half C. 19, latter half C. 19. See **pad** and **toby** and cf. *drum*, q.v., and :

***high pad** or **high tobyman** or **high-toby gloak.** A highwayman, esp. if well armed and well mounted : c. : resp. C. 17–early 19, C. 19, C. 19 (Vaux).

high part, the. The gallery : Dublin theatrical (— 1909). Ware. Cf. *the gods.*

high-pooped. Heavily buttocked : nautical **s.** > low coll. : from ca. 1830 ; ob.

high port, at the. See **at the high port.**

high-priori. A burlesque coll. perversion of *a priori* : from ca. 1740. ? ' coined ' by Pope (' We nobly take the high Priori Road ').

high-rented. Hot : low coll. : from ca. 1850 ; ob.—2. Very well known to the police : c. : from ca. 1860 ; ob. Cf. *hot,* q.v.

high ropes, be on the. To be excited : late C. 17–early 19 ; (very) angry : C. 18–mid-19 ; standing on one's dignity : C. 19–20, ob. All coll. Resp. B.E., Grose (2nd ed.), Mrs. Henry Wood (in *Trevlyn Hold*). ? ex circus tight-rope walking and trapeze-work.

high(-)runners. See **high men.**

high-seasoned or **highly spiced.** Indelicate ; obscene : coll. verging on S.E. : C. 19–20.

high shelf, the. The ground : lower classes' (— 1909). Ware.

high-, or **clouted-, shoe(s).** A rustic : mid-C. 17–early 19 : coll. > S.E. The occ. form, *high-shoon,* is often used as an adj.

high-sniffing. Supercilious ; pretentious, ' superior ' : (low) coll. : from ca. 1860 ; ob. Cf. *high-nosed,* q.v.

high spots, hit the. To go to excess (of dissipation or merry-making) ; to attain a very high level : U.S. (— 1910), anglicised ca. 1927. Likewise *high spot* (gen. pl.), ' the outstanding parts or features of something ' : anglicised ca. 1925. O.E.D. (Sup.).

high-stepper. A very fashionably dressed or mannered person : from ca. 1860 : coll. until C. 20, when S.E. Adj., *high-stepping* : same period, same comment. Ex a high-stepping horse.—2. Pepper : rhyming s. : C. 20. F. & Gibbons.

high-stomached. Very courageous : prob. S.E. rather than coll.—2. Disdainful, haughty : coll. rather than S.E. Both from C. 16 ; ob. and, since ca. 1850, archaic.

high(-)strikes. Hysterics : if unintentional, a sol. (— 1838) ; if deliberate, jocular coll. : from ca. 1850 ; ob.

high-tailing. Running away without looking behind ; bolting : Canadian coll. : C. 20. F. & Gibbons. Ex the flight of scared horses.

high tea. An ample tea with meat : coll. (1856) ; from ca. 1895, S.E. *Sporting Life,* Dec. 15, 1888. Perhaps *high* is here merely intensive (W.).

*high(-)tide or **water.** Temporary richness or plentifulness of cash : resp. late C. 17–20, C. 19–20 : ob. B.E. ; Bee. (Contrast *low water.*) Orig., prob. c. ; by 1830, coll.

*high-toby. Highway robbery, but only by mounted men : ca. 1810–70. Vaux, Ainsworth.

*high-toby gloak. See **high pad.**

high-up. High ; fig., of high rank or position : dial. >, in late 1890's, coll. O.E.D. (Sup.).

high-waisted. See **high-bellied.**

high water. See **high tide.**

high-water mark, up to (the). In excellent condition ; also, a gen. approbatory locution : coll. : from ca. 1860 ; ob.

high wood, live in. To hide, esp. to lie low and keep quiet : low : from ca. 1840 ; ob. by 1900, † by 1920. Ex High Wood, i.e. that H.W. which was the nearest to London. Cf. *hide and seek,* q.v.

highball. A drink of whiskey served in a tall glass : 1899 ; by 1930, coll. Orig. and mostly American. O.E.D. (Sup.).

highbrow. A person affecting intellectual superiority : coll., orig. (1911), U.S. ; anglicised ca. 1917. Cf. *lowbrow,* q.v.—2. Hence, as adj., anglicised at about the same time. (Mencken.)

higher Malthusianism. Sodomy : cultured s. : ca. 1860–1900, Ex Thomas Malthus, the political economist's (d. 1834) *Essay on Population,* 1798.

highfalute. To rant ; use fine words : mainly and orig. U.S. : anglicised ca. 1875 as s., but never very gen. Cf. :

highfalutin(g). Rant or bombast : orig. (—1850), U.S. ; anglicised ca. 1865 : coll. till C. 20, when S.E. *The Pall Mall Gazette,* May 3, 1886, ' A glib master of frothy fustian, of flatulent high-falutin', and of oratorical bombast '.

highfalutin(g) ; gen. without **g.** Bombastic, absurdly pompous, whether in conversation or in behaviour : orig. (1848), U.S. s. ; anglicised, as coll., ca. 1862 ; ' now common in Liverpool and the East End of London ', H., 1864 ; in C. 20, S.E.—a very useful word. Friswell, in *Modern Men of Letters,* 1870, ' High-falutin' nonsense '. (In C. 19, hyphenated very often, in C. 20 rarely.) Ex Dutch *verlooten,* says H. ; more prob. an elaboration of *high-flown,* perhaps influenced by *floating* (W.).

Highgate, sworn (in) at. Sharp, clever : coll. (from ca. 1840, mainly dial.) : mid-C. 18–19. Colman, 1769, ' I have been sworn at Highgate, Mrs. Lettice, and never take the maid instead of the mistress ' ; Hone's *Every Day Book* (ii, 79–87) ; Apperson. Ex a C. 18 custom prevalent at Highgate public-houses—see Grose, P.

Highland fling. A speech, or series of speeches, delivered in Scotland : political : 1880–ca. 1915. Ware. Applied orig. to Gladstone's famous Midlothian speeches.

highly spiced. See **high-seasoned.**

highty-tighty ; hoity-toity. A wanton, **or,** as B.E. phrases it, ' a Ramp, or Rude Girl ' : resp. late C. 17–18, C. 18–early 19 : orig. low, then gen., coll. But *hoity-toity* is rare as a n. ; usually it goes with *wench,* as in Grose.

highty-tighty ; hoity-toity, adj. Peremptory, quarrelsome : C. 19–20.—2. Uppish : late C. 19–20 ; this, the prevailing C. 20 sense, comes ex dial. The *-i-* form is coll., the *-oi-* orig. coll., in C. 20 S.E. ' The earliest record, *upon the hoyty-toyty* (1668), suggests the *high ropes* [q.v.] and *tight rope,* or simply a jingle upon *high,*' W. See esp. W. : *More Words Ancient and Modern.*

highway, (as) common as the. See **hedge, (as) common as the.**

higly-pigly. A ca. 1660–1800 variant of *higgledy-piggledy,* q.v.

higry-pigry. See **hickery-pickery.** (Graves, in *The Spiritual Quixote.*)

hike. A blow, a knock : schools' : ca. 1860–90. (Solely on the evidence of a MS. note in the British Museum copy of the 1864 Hotten).—2. A long walk, esp. for exercise and (?) pleasure : dial. and U.S. >, Eng. coll. ca. 1926. Ex the v.

hike, v., orig. (1809) dial., = to tramp (from 1927, for pleasure and/or exercise) ; **hike off,** orig. (— 1788) c., = to run away. Grose, 2nd ed. Becoming, except in dial., disused in England, *hike* went to U.S., whence it returned, to gen. coll. usage in England, ca. 1926. (Like *hick,* q.v., it has been very gen. considered an Americanism.)—2. To pull, or drag, esp. with a great effort : coll., ex dial. : 1867 (S.O.D.).

hike about. Wander about : coll. ex dial. : C. 19–20. Perhaps influenced by U.S. college use (see Thornton).

hike off. See hike, v.—2. Also, to carry off ; to arrest : both (low) coll. : mid-C. 19–20 ; the latter, ob.

hiked up, be. ' To be shanghaied, or shipped unwillingly ' : nautical : late C. 19–20. Bowen. Cf. *hike*, v., 2.

hiker ; hiking. One who ' hikes ' (*hike*, v., 1); n. and adj. (connected with, characteristic of) the going for long walks. Both coll. : 1927. See hike, v., 1.

[**hilding** is not, as given by F. & H., coll., but S.E.]

hill, over the. See over the hill.

hill-topper. A ' sex-novel ' : journalists' : ca. 1894–1900.

hillman. The foreman of the dustmen : Cockney (— 1887) ; very ob. Baumann.

hillo ! Hello !, hullo ! : non-aristocratic variant (coll. and dial.) : C. 19–20. Baumann ; E.D.D.

hills or **Hills, the.** The Gogmagog Hills, a common morning's ride : Cambridge University (— 1803).—2. St. Catherine's Hill : Winchester College : C. 16–20 (Wrench). Without *the*.

hilltop literature. Solid advice : journalistic coll. of ca. 1898–1914. Ware, ' Derived from danger-board warnings to cyclists on the summits of steep hills '.

hilly. Difficult, as in *hilly reading* and *hilly going* (hard to do) : coll. : from ca. 1870 ; ob. Cf. *steep*, q.v.

hilt(s), loose in the. Unsteady ; conjugally unfaithful : coll. : mid-C. 17–early 18.

him. He : predicatively, coll. ; nominatively, sol. : resp. late C. 16–20, C. 18–20. Cf. *her*, q.v.

him !, I've got. Now I know or have guessed (it) ! : coll. (— 1887). Baumann.

himses or **H-.** A fellow workman or -men : tailors' : C. 20. *The Tailor and Cutter*, Nov. 29, 1928, ' A bit of a case Himses '. Cf. *umses*, q.v.

hinchinarfer. A woman of gruff voice and shrieking-sisterhood tendencies : proletarian : ca. 1880–1915. Ware cryptically observes : ' Obscure erotic '.

hind. Person, fellow, chap : coll. : C. 16. E.g. in Douglas's *Æneid*. (O.E.D.)

hind boot. The breech : low : C. 19–20, ob. Cf. *hinder end*.

hind coach-wheel. A five-shilling piece : late C. 17–early 20 ; †. Cf. *fore c.-w.*, q.v.

hind leg, kick out a. To make a rustic bow : coll. : mid-C. 18–20, ob. Grose, 3rd ed.

hind leg off a horse (dog, donkey, etc.), talk the. See talk the . . .

hind-paw. (Gen. pl.) A foot ; loosely and rarely, a leg : jocular proletarian (— 1923). Manchon.

hind-shifters. The feet or heels : coll. : ca. 1820–70. Lamb, in *Elia*, ' They would show as fair a pair of hind-shifters as [anyone] in the colony.'

[**hinder blast**, C. 16 for crepitation, is only very doubtfully eligible.]

hinder end, parts, world. The breech : (low) coll. : C. 19–20 ; ob. Cf. :

hinder entrance. The fundament : low coll. : C. 19–20 ; ob. Cf. :

hinders. Hind-quarters : coll. : from ca. 1890 ; slightly ob. (O.E.D. Sup.) Ex dial. : 1857 (E.D.D.).

Hindoo punishment. The ' muscle-grind ' in gymnastics : circus (— 1875) : † by 1920. Frost, in *Circus Life*.

Hindoos. (Singular very rare.) ' Such Europeans as came from India to the Cape either to recruit their health or to take up their residence ', Pettman : South African coll. : ca. 1825–70. Cf. *Cape doctor*, q.v.

Hiney. See Heine.

hing aff. Get off ! : Glasgow (— 1934). Lit., ' hang off ! ' Cf. :

hing-on, a. A walking arm-in-arm : Glasgow coll. (— 1934).

hinge and pluck. The heart, liver and lungs of a killed pig : butchers' (— 1887). Baumann.

hinges, off the, adv., adj. Confused(ly) ; slightly indisposed : coll. : C. 17–20 ; † by 1820, except in dial. Cotgrave, Motteux.

hinterland. The breech : (low) coll. : cf. *hinder end*, etc. ' Old ', says F. & H. in 1893, but not, I feel sure, older than 1880, the S.E. sense being recorded only at 1890. F. & H. may well be thinking of *hinderlands*, rare for *hinderlings*, the posteriors. Perhaps cf. Romany *hinder*, to defecate.

hip (1762), **hip(p)s** (1710). Morbid depression : 1710 : coll. ; ob. by 1870 ; † by 1910. (See hyp.) Usually ' spelt with *y* in the [n.] but with *i* in the v., etc.', S.O.D. Ex *hypochondria*.

hip, v. To depress the spirits of : coll. : from ca. 1840. Prob. ex *hipped*, q.v.

[**hip, catch** or **get** or, gen., **have on the.** To have or get at a disadvantage, is S.E., while *hipe*, n. and v., is wrestling j.]

hip-hop, adv. Hoppingly : coll. : ca. 1670–1920. Villiers, in *The Rehearsal* ; Congreve. Reduplication of *hop*. (The O.E.D., perhaps rightly, considers it S.E.—at least after ca. 1700.)

*hip-inside. An inner coat-pocket, *hip-outside* being an outer : c. (— 1839) ; ob. Brandon.

hip, Michael, your head's on fire ! A low c.p. addressed to a red-haired man : mid-C. 18–mid-19. Grose, 1st ed.

hipe. A rifle ; gen. in *slope hipe* : military : late C. 19–20. *Rifle* being less easy to pronounce, *ripe* none too easy, and *slope* perhaps effecting the form. (See esp. B. & P.)

hipped. Melancholy, bored, depressed ; slightly indisposed : coll. : 1710 (S.O.D.) ; ob. Ex, *hypochondria* ; cf. *hyppo*, *hyps*, nn., and *hippish*, q.v.

hippen. The green curtain : theatrical, but perhaps only in Northumberland ; certainly never very gen. : ca. 1870–1905. ? ex Scots coll. *hippen* (i.e. hipping cloth), a baby's napkin.

hippish. Low-spirited : coll. : 1706 (S.O.D.). Gay, ' By cares depress'd, in pensive hippish mood '. Cf. *hipped*, q.v., and *hip*, *hyp(pos)*, nn.

Hippo, the. The London Hippodrome : Londoners' : late C. 19–20.

hippo. An occ. variant, recorded for 1725, of *hypo*, *hyppo*, q.v. (Never *hipo*.)—2. Hippopotamus : coll. : 1872 (O.E.D.). Selous.—3. Ipecacuanha : Anglo-Irish (— 1900). E.D.D.

hippy. Morbidly depressed : coll. : from ca. 1890. Cf. *hipped*, *hippish*, qq.v.

hips, down in the. Dispirited ; indisposed : coll. : 1729, Swift ; ob. by 1890, † by 1910. Ex a phrase applied to horses injured in the haunch-bone.

hips,—free of her lips, free of her. Proverbial coll. : C. 19–20 ; somewhat ob. *Hips* here = buttocks, hence sex.

hips, long in the. Broad-buttocked : coll. : C. 19–20 ; ob. Cf. *hips to sell.*

hips, walk with the. ' To make play with the posteriors in walking ', F. & H. : C. 19–20 coll. ; ob. A lower rather than a middle or upper class allurement to lewdery.

hips to sell(, with). Broad-buttocked : low coll. : C. 19–20 ; ob.

Hipsy hoy. A boy : rhyming s. : C. 20. B. & P.

hircarra(h). See **hurkaru.**

hiren, a harlot, is, despite F. & H., ineligible. As a sword, a fighting hector or bully, it is, so far as I know, unrecorded save by F. & H. : at present, it is suspect.

his. ' The use of *his* with familiar words, as " he knew *his* Homer from beginning to end ", is purified slang ' (Greenough & Kittredge, 1902) : coll. : mid-C. 19–20.—2. The enemy's : military coll. : 1914–18. B. & P. Opp. *ours.*

his legs . . . See **legs grew.—his nabs, nibs.** See **nabs, nibs.**

hishee-hashee. See **soap and bullion.**

hisn, his'n ; occ. **hissen.** *His,* when used predicatively or, gen., absolutely : sol. when not, as mostly, dial. : C. 15–20. Prob. *his* influenced by *mine* opp. *my* (S.O.D.).

hiss, the. The warning of a master's approach : Winchester College : C. 19–20.

hisself. Himself (in the accusative and without—as in *his true self*—any stress on *self*) : sol. : C. 19–20. Baumann.

hissen. See **hisn.**

hist, n. and v. (Pronounced *hïghst.*) Hoist : sol. : C. 19–20. Baumann.

historical. (Of a costume or hat) seen more than three times : Society : 1882, *The Daily News,* Dec. 26 ; † by 1915. Ware.

[**historical** or **wrought** or **illustrated shirt.** Not coll. but † S.E. : late C. 16–19. ' A shirt or shift worked or woven with pictures or texts ', F. & H.]

history of the four kings, study the. To play at cards : coll. : mid-C. 18–mid-19. Cf. the mid-C. 18–early 19 coll. *a child's best guide to the gallows,* a pack of cards, as also is the n. part of the defined locution. Grose, 1st ed. (both).

hit, a success, like **make a hit,** to score an outstanding success, was orig., I think, coll., *pace* the O.E.D. : from ca. 1815. But *hit* (*it*), to guess a secret, attain an object, is, *pace* F. & H., certainly S.E., as, prob., was *hit in the teeth,* to reproach (v.t., *with*).

hit, to go to and then travel along or work or play at or rest in, as in *hit the road* or *trail, the high spots, the haystack,* was orig. and still U.S. : these usages can hardly be said to be fully anglicised ; but they prob. will be—very soon too !

***hit,** ppl.adj. Convicted : c. : orig. and mostly at the Old Bailey : from ca. 1860.

hit, hard, ppl.adj. See **hard hit.—hit a haystack.** See **haystack** and **hit, v.**

hit it off. To agree well with a person : coll. on verge of S.E. (in C. 20, indubitably S.E.) : from ca. 1780. ' Trollope, in *Barchester Towers.*—2. To describe accurately : the (from ca. 1735) coll. form of S.E. *hit* : in C. 20, S.E., which, acc. to the O.E.D., it always has been. Trollope, in *The Duke's Children.*

hit it up ; orig. **hit things up.** ' To behave strenuously ; riotously ', C. J. Dennis : Australian : C. 20.

hit on the tail, v.t. To coït with : C. 16–17 coll. Skelton.

hit or miss. A kiss : rhyming s. : late C. 19–20. George Orwell, *Down and Out in Paris and London,* 1933.

hit the hay. To go to bed : U.S. (orig. tramps') anglicised in 1929 by Conan Doyle. (O.E.D. Sup.)

hit the high spots. See **high spots.—hit the road.** See **hit,** v. An interesting parallel is the Norfolk dial. *hit the road,* to walk fast, as in P. H. Emerson, *On English Lagoons,* 1893 (E.D.D.).

hit the roof. To flare up, be or become extremely angry : coll. : C. 20. Cf. and see **housetop, be at the,** the idea being that of S.E. *fly into a rage.*

hit things up. See **hit it up.**

hit (a person) up for (something). To ask (a person) for : Colonial and South-American-English s. : C. 20. C. W. Thurlow Craig, *Paraguayan Interlude,* 1935, ' I . . . hit him up for a job, and here I am.'

hit where one lives. To mean much to, make a great impression on, a person : 1907, P. G. Wodehouse, *Not George Washington,* ' This is just the sort of thing to get right at them. It'll hit them where they live.'

hit with. (More gen. *struck with,* q.v.) Prepossessed by : coll. : ca. 1885–1915.

hitch. Temporary assistance ; unimportant help through a difficulty : coll. : from ca. 1890 ; ob.

hitch, v. To marry ; gen. in *hitched,* ppl. adj., married : orig. (1857) U.S., app. first as *hitch horses* : anglicised ca. 1890. In C. 20, the prevailing form is *hitched up,* which is very gen. in the Southern-Hemisphere Dominions. Ex *hitch* (*up*), to harness.

hitchy-koo. Verminous, lousy : military : 1914 ; ob. B. & P. Ex a music-hall refrain's resemblance to *itching, itchy.*

Hittite, hittite. A prize-fighter : a pugilistic pun : ca. 1820–1910. More gen., however, as Bee (1823) phrases it : ' *Hittites*—boxers and ring-goers assembled '.

hive. The female pudend : low : from ca. 1850 ; ob. Ex *honey,* q.v.

hive it. To effect coïtion : low : from ca. 1860 ; ob. Ex preceding.

Hivite. A student of St. Bees, Cumberland : schools' and universities' (— 1860). H., 2nd ed.

hixi(o)us-doxi(o)us. See **hiccius-doccius.**

ho, out of all. Beyond all bounds : coll. : late C. 14–20. Chaucer, Swift. (After ca. 1870, † except in dial. Ex *ho !*) A late C. 16–19 variant is *out of all* (*w*)*hooping,* which appears in Shakespeare's *As You Like It,* and, as *past all w.,* in Kingsley's *Westward Ho !* (Apperson.)

hoaky or **hokey, by (the).** An expletive : mainly nautical, but perhaps orig. Scots : from ca. 1820 ; ob. Barham, Lover, Manchon. ? ex *holy poker.*

hoax, v. and n., and its derivatives *hoaxer* and *hoaxing,* were orig. (1788) coll., which they remained until ca. 1830. First recorded in Grose, 2nd ed. Orig. university wit, says Grose. Prob. ex *hocus* (*-pocus*) ; cf., possibly, Romany (*hoax* or) *hokano,* to cheat, and *hookapen,* a hoax, a falsehood.

hob. A dolt ; a rustic clown : C. 14–early 19 : until ca. 1680, S.E. ; then coll. when not dial. Ex *Robert.*

hob, be on the. To be a teetotaller : military : late C. 19–20. F. & Gibbons, ' The tea-kettle on the hob '.

hob and nob, hob or nob, hob nob. Orig. mere variants, but the only C. 19–20 forms, of *hab or nab* (etc.), q.v.—The only specific ' individual ' senses are, 1, as v. : to drink together. 1763, coll.,—in

C. 20, S.E. ; be on very friendly terms (v.t., *with*), 1828 ; coll. till C. 20, when S.E.—2. As n. : a toast (very rarely as *h.n.*, occ.—in C. 18–19—as *hob a nob*), 1756, always coll. ; adv. or adj., on terms of close friendship or good-fellowship, 1851, coll. till C. 20, then S.E.—See also hob-nob, below. (Dates : S.O.D.) The *hab, nab* form was influenced by *Hob*, a familiar by-form of *Robert* (W.).

Hob Collingwood. The supposedly unlucky four of hearts : C. 18–19 Northern coll.

hob-job. An unskilled or clumsy job ; an odd job : s. and dial. : from ca. 1855.

hob-jobber. A man or boy alert for small jobs on the street : (low) coll. : mostly London : from ca. 1850 ; ob.—Also vbl.n., *hob-jobbing*.

hob-nob. A c.p. gracing a ' mutual ' drinking : ca. 1760–1830 : coll. > S.E.—2. A drinking together or to each other's health : 1825 : coll. till C. 20, then S.E. (See hob and nob, above.)—3. A familiar, intimate conversation : coll. (— 1876) ; in C. 20, S.E.

hobbadehoy, hobbe(r)dehoy. See hobbledehoy.

hobber-nob(ber). A corrupted form of *hob or nob* (see hob and nob) : from ca. 1800 ; ob.

Hobbes's voyage. Coll. : late C. 17–18. Vanbrugh, in *The Provoked Wife*, ' So, now, I am in for Hobbes's voyage ; a great leap in the dark.' Some topical origin.

hobbinol, a—gen. uncouth—countryman, is S.E. Cf. *hob*, q.v.

hobble, as amorous v. (see F. & H.), is ob. S.E. ; but as an awkward or puzzling situation it is (from ca. 1775) coll. and dial. ; and as to arrest, to commit for trial, it is c. (— 1789) and ob.—2. To *hobble a plant* is to *spring* it (see plant, a cache) : c. : ca 1810–50. Vaux.

hobble, in a. In trouble ; hampered ; perplexed : coll. : late C. 18–20 ; ob.—2. In c., committed for trial : late C. 18–20 ; ob.

*hobbled (upon the legs). On the hulks ; in prison ; transported as a convict : c. : late C. 18–mid-19. Parker, Vaux.—2. Whence (?), *hobbled*, committed for trial : c. : late C. 18–20 ; ob.

hobbledeg(or j)ee. A jog-trot : coll. (— 1788) : ob. by 1880, † by 1900. Grose, 2nd ed. I.e. *hobble* + a fanciful ending.

hobbledehoy ; also hobba(r)d(e or y)hoy, hobbe(r)-dehoy. A boy not yet quite a man : coll. : 1540, as *hobbledehoye* in Palsgrave. In C. 18, gen. in rhyme, ' hobbledehoy, neither man nor boy '. Prob. *hob* (see above) + some now indeterminable ending—perhaps Fr. *de haie, de haye*, of the hedge (see hedge)—with *-le-* (rare before 1700) or *-a(r)-, -e(r)-*, acting as a euphonic.

hobbledehoyish ; hobbledehoyhood. Awkwardly youthful ; the age when a boy is such : the former (— 1812), coll. ; the latter (1836) hardly gen. enough to be coll.

hobbler. An unlicensed pilot ; a landsman acting as tow-Jack : orig. (1800), nautical s. ; by 1900, j. As a boatman, Isle of Man dial.

hobby. (A horse in common use : S.E.—) A translation : university. Whence *to ride hobbies, to use* ' cribs '. Ca. 1870–1910.

Hobby, Sir Posthumous('s). A man fastidious or whimsical in his clothes : coll. : ca. 1690–1830. B.E. ; Grose, 2nd ed. Punning *hobby*, an avocation.

hobby-horse. A wanton, a prostitute : late C. 16–17 : coll. (Other senses, S.E.) Ex the S.E. sense, a horse in common use : cf. *hobby*.

hobby-horse, v. To romp ; play the fool, esp. in horse-play : coll. : ca. 1630–1890.

hobby-horsical. Connected with, devoted to a hobby ; whimsical : jocular coll. : 1761, Sterne.—2. In late C. 18–early 19, and perhaps orig., ' a man who is a great keeper or rider of hobby horses ', i.e. hacks. Grose, 1st ed.

hobnail. A countryman ; a boor : coll. : from ca. 1645 ; in C. 19–20, S.E. ; ob. Beaumont & Fletcher, in *Women Pleased*, ' The hob-nail thy husband's as fitly out o' th' way now.'

hobnailed. Boorish : coll. till C. 19, then S.E. : C. 17–20 ; ob. Ex preceding. Occ. *hobnail* (earlier, by the way, as adj. than as n.).

hobo, pl. **hoboes.** A tramp ; esp., in C. 20, one who works. Orig. (— 1891, Flynt), U.S. ; anglicised ca. 1905. The v. has not ' caught on ' in England.—2. Hence, a useless fellow : military : from ca. 1910.—3. In New Zealand and Australia, in post-G.W. days, it is often applied to a rough-and-ready fellow. The etymology remains a puzzle : see esp. Irwin, who quotes a tramp's C. 20 distinction : ' Bums loafs and sits. Tramps loafs and walks. But a hobo moves and works, and he's clean.'

hobson-jobson. ' A native festal excitement ; a *tamāsha* . . . ; but especially the Moharram ceremonies ', Yule & Burnell : Anglo-Indian, prob. orig. (ca. 1850) military ; the form *hossy-gossy* occurs as early as 1673. Ex the Mahommedan wailing-cry, *Yā Hasan ! Yā Hosain.* (In S.E., a certain linguistic process.)

Hobson's. See sense 2 of :

Hobson's choice. That or none : coll. : 1649, Somers Tracts, ' I had Hobson's choice, either be a Hobson or nothing ' ; B.E. ; Steele, in *The Spectator*, No. 509 ; Cibber, in *The Non-Juror*, ' Can any woman think herself happy that's obliged to marry only with a Hobson's choice ? ' The etymology ex Thomas Jobson, that Cambridge livery-stable keeper (d. 1630) who let out his horses only in strict rotation, is seriously damaged by Richard Cock's ' We are put to Hodgson's choise to take such privilegese as they will geve us, or else goe without,' 1617—one of W.'s happiest discoveries.—2. A voice : theatrical rhyming s. : late C. 19–20 ; now gen. abbr. to *Hobson's*.

hock, in. Laid by the heels ; swindled : low : late C. 19–20, ob.—2. In prison : c. : late C. 19–20. Prob. ex Dutch s. *hok*, debt, as the C.O.D. (1934 Sup.) notes, and perhaps influenced by *hock*, a rod, a chain, with a hook at the end. Cf. the U.S. sense, in pawn, which, in C. 20, is occ. heard in England, as is *hock*, to pawn.

hock, old. Stale beer : late C. 18–19 : (low) coll. Ex *hock*, the white German wine—orig. *Hochheimer*, that made at Hochheim, on the Main.

*hock-dockies ; in C. 19, occ. hock(e)y-dockies. Shoes : c. (— 1789) ; † by 1893, perhaps by 1880. Rhyming reduplication on *hocks*, q.v.

hockelty ; hocly. The *hock* or penultimate card, esp. in faro : from mid-1860's. O.E.D. (Sup.).

hockey. Drunk, orig. with stale beer : ca. 1788–1880. Grose, 2nd ed. Ex *hock, old*, q.v. Cf. *hickey*.

hockey club, the. A, the, venereal hospital : New Zealand soldiers' : in G.W. Ex a hockey-club-shaped instrument used in the treatment of disease.

*hock(e)y-dockies. See hock-dockies.

hocking. A variant of *houghing*, q.v.

hocks. The feet : low coll. (— 1785) ; in C. 19–

20, gen. the feet and ankles; **ob.** Grose, 1st ed. Ex a quadruped's hocks.

hocky. See **hockey.—hocly.** See **hockelty.— hocum.** See **hokum.**

hocus. A juggler, a conjuror; an impostor: ca. 1650–1720. Abbr. *hocus-pocus*, q.v. In Witts' *Recreations*, ca. 1654, as *hocas.*—2. Jugglery; deception: from ca. 1650; in C. 19–20, S.E.; † except in sense of criminal deception, shady trickery.—3. Drugged liquor: orig. (— 1823), s.; by 1890, S.E. Also *hocus-pocus*. Bee.

hocus, v. To 'hoax' (q.v.): 1675: coll. till C. 19, then S.E. Whence *hocusser* and *hocussing*, C. 19–20 nn.—2. To drug, esp. with liquor (— 1836, Dickens, in *Pickwick*, ch. xiii): ex slightly earlier, now ob., sense, to stupefy with liquor (and then rob): 1831 (S.O.D.): coll. until ca. 1880, then S.E.: cf. *snuff*, q.v. To *hocus* horses as early as 1823 (Bee). All senses ex the n.

hocus, adj. Intoxicated (— 1725): ob. by 1830, † by 1860. Ex the v. *A New Canting Dict.*, 1725; Grose.

hocus-pocus; in C. 17, often **hocas-pocas.** The name of, or for, a juggler: Jonson, in *The Staple of News*, 1624; in 1634, a title runs, 'Hocus Pocus Junior, *The Anatomie of Leger de main*'; in 1656, defined by Blount.—2. Hence, a trickster: from ca. 1720.—3. A juggler's trick; hence, imm., deception, trickery: 1647.—4. As a juggler's formula: 1632.—5. A juggler's or impostor's stock in trade: from ca. 1650. Also *hocus-trade*, C. 17.— 6. Drugged liquor (— 1823); † by 1893, *hocus* being then gen.—All these senses were orig. s., prob. low s., but soon > coll.; by 1850, only the third, fourth, and fifth were much used; in C. 20, only the third and fifth, both of which have, since ca. 1810, been S.E. Either ex an actual juggler's name (slightly latinised, no doubt), or ex *hoc est corpus (filii)*, mentioned (by Tillotson) as a juggler's phrase, the latter theory being bolstered by the Scandinavian *hokuspokusfiliokus* (W.). N.B., the C. 17 sense, a bag used by jugglers, was too rare to be coll.—6. See 'Occupational Names' in the Addenda.

hocus-pocus, v. To cheat, trick: from ca. 1770. —2. V.i., to juggle, practise trickery: 1687, L'Estrange. Both orig. coll., but in late C. 19–20, S.E. (Dates, O.E.D.) Ex the n.

hocus-pocus, adj. Juggling, cheating, fraudulent: 1668 (S.O.D.): coll. until C. 19, then S.E. Wycherley; Macklin, in *Love à la Mode*, 'The law is a sort of hocus-pocus science that smiles in yer face while it picks yer pocket.'—The adv. is rare: *hocus-pocusly*.

hocus-pocus, play. To play the juggler (fig.): coll.: ca. 1659–1740. Bentley.

hocus-trade. See **hocus-pocus,** n., 5.

hocus-trick. A juggling trick, hence a swindle: coll.: ca. 1675–1700. Ex *hocus*, n.

hod or **Hod;** occ. **Brother Hod.** A bricklayer's labourer: coll. (— 1791); ob. Grose. Ex the hod used for carrying bricks and mortar; abbr. *hodman.* —2. A bookmaker's money-bag: turf c.: C. 20. *Slang*, p. 243.

hod of mortar. A pot of porter: rhyming s. (— 1859); ob. H., 1st ed.

hoddie-doddie; better **-y.** A squat person: coll.: ca. 1530–1850. In C. 17–18, gen. in form of jeering rhyme or c.p., *Hoddy-doddy, All arse and no body*; the rhyme was, in a contemporary song, applied to the Rump Parliament.—2. A fool; a cuckold: ca.

1595–1800; cf. *hoddy-peak* (the reference being to a snail's horns). Cognato with *hodmandod*, q.v., in being prob. a rhyming perversion of *dodman*, a snail. —3. A lighthouse's revolving light: nautical: late C. 19–20; ob. Bowen. Ex West Country dial.

hoddy-doddy, adj. Dumpy: coll.: from ca. 1820; † except in dial. Ex n.

hoddy-peak; in C. 16, often **peke.** A fool, a dolt: C. 16–early 17.—2. A cuckold: ca. 1585–1640. Both senses orig. coll., but by 1590, at latest, S.E. The *hoddy*, as in *hoddy-doddy*, may at first have been = a snail; cf. *hodmandod*. (*Hoddy-poll*, C. 16, same meanings, may orig. have been coll.)

[**Hodge,** a typical English rustic, is not, as in F. & H., coll., but S.E., and the same holds of *hodge-podge*, a M.E. corruption of *hotch-potch*.]

hodman. Oxford University s. > coll.: 1677, S.O.D., which defines thus, 'A term of contempt applied by [those] undergraduates of Christ Church . . . who were King's Scholars of Westminster School, to those who were not, and hence to other undergraduates'. After ca. 1790, merely historical. (Cf. *squill*). Ex the S.E. sense, a bricklayer's labourer: cf. *hod*, q.v.

hodmandod. A shell-snail: coll.: 1626 (S.O.D.); ob. except in dial. Ex *dodman*, a snail: cf. *hoddy-doddy*, q.v.—2. A deformed person: coll.: ca. 1660–1900.—3. A Hottentot: low coll., almost sol.: 1686; † by 1850. Captain Cowley in *Harris's Voyages*.

hodmandod, adj. Short and clumsy: from ca. 1820; ob.: coll. when not dial. Ex preceding; prob. suggested by *hoddy-doddy*, q.v.

***hog.** (Pl. **hog.**) A shilling: orig. (ca. 1670), c.; in C. 19–20, low s. Coles.—2. In C. 18–early 19, occ. a sixpence: also c., whence the U.S. sense. Prob. ex the figure of a hog on a small silver coin.— 3. A student of St. John's College, Cambridge: Cambridge (— 1690); † before 1889. Also *Johnian hog*. A. de la Pryme, in *Diary*, 1690.—4. See **Hampshire hog,** the *Hampshire* being almost never omitted.—5. **the Hog.** Richard III of England. (Dawson.)—6. See **road hog.**

hog, v. To appropriate, esp. appropriate and eat or drink, greedily: orig. (1887), U.S.; anglicised ca. 1912; > coll. ca. 1930.—2. To coït, v.i. and t.: low: C. 19–20, ob.—3. **hog it,** to sleep soundly, esp. snoringly: coll. (— 1923). Manchon.—4. To be, behave like, a road-hog: coll.: 1925. O.E.D. (Sup.). Also *hog it.*

hog, go the whole. See **go the whole hog.—hog, Johnian.** See **hog,** n., 3.

hog-grubber. 'A narrow-soul'd sneaking Fellow', B.E.: coll.: late C. 17–early 19. Hence adj., *hog-grubbing*: C. 18–early 19.—2. 'A Thames waterman, licensed by the Trinity House': London watermen's: ca. 1840–80. Mayhew, cited by E.D.D.

hog in a squall or **storm, like a.** Beside oneself; out of one's senses: nautical coll. (— 1887); slightly ob. Baumann.

hog in armour. A lout in fine clothes: coll.: ca. 1650–1930. Hence 'Thackeray's "Count Hogginarmo"' (S.O.D.). In C. 20, S.E.—2. Larwood & Hotten, in *Signboards*, 1867, 'a favourite epithet applied to rifle volunteers [from ca. 1850] by costermongers, fishmongers and such-like'.—3. An ironclad: naval: ca. 1860–90. Bowen.

hog it. See **hog,** v., 3 and 4.

hog-rubber. A(n ignorant) rustic: pejorative coll.: C. 17. Jonson, Burton. (O.E.D.

hog-shearing ; shearing of hogs, vbl.n. Much ado about nothing : coll. : C. 17–18. Ex the full text of the *much cry and little wool* proverb.

hog-wash. Bad liquor, esp. 'rot-gut', q.v.; 1712, Arbuthnot (O.E.D.) : coll. >, 1800, S.E.— Hence, 2, worthless, cheap journalism : journalistic : from ca. 1880. Cf. *slush*, q.v.

hog-yoke. Nautical, C. 19, thus in Bowen : 'The old-fashioned wooden quadrant in American ships and Grand Bankers, so-called from its likeness to the wooden yoke put over hogs to prevent them breaking through fences '.

hoga, that wcn't. That won't do ! Anglo-Indian (— 1864) ; ob. H., 3rd ed.

Hogan(-Mogan) ; Hogen(-Mogen). A Dutchman : a coll. affected by satirists, ca. 1670–1700. Ex *hoogmogendheien*, the Dutch for high and mighty lords, as applied to the Dutch States-General. See that fine scholar, G. Aitken's *Satires of Andrew Marvell* (1892), p. 128.—2. Hence, any 'high and mighty' person : coll. : ca. 1640–1750.—3. Also as corresponding adj., with additional sense, potent (of drink) : ca. 1650–1730. Cf. :

hogan-mogan rug. A strong drink, esp. ale : coll. : ca. 1650–1720. Dryden, in *The Wild Gallant*, 'I was drunk ; damnably drunk with ale ; great hogan-mogan bloody ale.' Cf. the preceding entry.

hogmagundy. Sexual intercourse : orig. Scots : ca. 1820–90, (not very gen.) Southern coll. ? ex *hogmanay*.

hogmanay. A wanton : Scots C. 19–20 (ob.) coll. Ex the Scots national festival of Hogmanay, New Year's Eve.

hogo, a flavour, a taint, may orig.—ca. 1650— have been coll., but it very soon > S.E. Ex Fr. *haut goût*. Also *fogo*, which is a C. 19 corruption.

Hogs Norton, have been born at. To be ill-mannered, uncouth : proverbial coll. : mid-C. 16– mid-19. Often in orig. form, which adds : *where the pigs play on the organs*. The reference is to ' the village of Hock-Norton, Leicestershire, where the organist once upon a time was named Piggs ! ', so it is said (Apperson, q.v.).

hogs (or pigs) to a fair or fine market, bring one's. To profit ; do well : coll. : C. 17–20, ob.—2. Also, ironically : C. 18–20.

hogs (or pigs) to market, drive one's. To snore : C. 18–20 : coll. Swift, 'He snored so loud that we thought he was driving his hogs to market'; Grose, 1st ed., has the abbr. form *drive one's hogs*. Ex the notable grunting of driven pigs.

hog's wash of the fo'c'stle head. The deck-hands on a merchant ship : nautical : C. 20.

*****hogshead, couch a.** To lie down and sleep : c. of ca. 1560–1840. Ex *hog's head*, a person, 1515 (S.O.D.).

hoi polloi. Candidates for pass degrees : university : ca. 1860–1915. Ex the Gr. for ' the many '. Cf. S.E. sense.

hoick. A jerk as one's stroke begins or ends : rowing coll. (— 1898). O.E.D. (Sup.). Ex :

hoick, v. To raise, hoist, esp. with a jerk : coll. : late C. 19–20. Prob. ex *hike*, v., 2.—2. Hence, to force (an aeroplane) to mount steeply : coll. : 1916. (O.E.D. Sup.)—3. Hence, v.i., to climb steeply, jerk oneself up (and *out of*) : coll. : from ca. 1925 (O.E.D. Sup.)—4. To spit (mostly as v.i.) : Bootham School (— 1925). Anon., *Dict. of Bootham Slang*.

*****hoise.** A C. 19 variant of :

*****hoist.** A confederate helping a thief to reach an open window : late C. 18–mid-19 c. Grose, 2nd ed. —2. Hence, a shop-lifter : C. 19, c. > low.—Cf. 3, **hoist, the.** Shop-lifting : c. (— 1812). Vaux.

*****hoist,** v. To rob by means of *the hoist*, q.v. ; to shop-lift : c. : ca. 1810–60.—2. Implied in *hoisting*, 2. —3. V.i., to drink : (low) coll. : from ca. 1860 ; ob.

hoist, give a, v.t. To do a bad turn : tailors' : from ca. 1870 ; ob.

*****hoist, go upon the.** To enter a building by an open window : c. : ca. 1787–1860. Grose, 2nd ed. Cf. *heave*, v., 1, q.v.

hoist, on the. On ' the drunk ' : (low) coll. : from ca. 1860 ; † by 1930.

hoist him in ! A mid-C. 19–20 nautical c.p. verging on j., for it constitutes an order ' to wel come the captain or senior officer over the side, a relic of the old way of embarking in bad weather with a whip on the yard arm '.

hoist in. A drink of liquor : ca. 1865–1920. Ex *hoist*, v., 3.

hoist in, do or have a. To have sexual intercourse : low : from ca. 1850. (Rarely of women.)

*****hoist-lay.** Shop-lifting : c. : ca. 1810–60.—2. ' Shaking a man head downwards, so that the money rolls out of his pockets ', F. & H. : ca. 1830–1900 : c. Also *hoisting*, 2., q.v.

hoist one's pennants. To grumble ; be severely critical : nautical : late C. 19–20. A display of all pennants means ' I don't understand your signal '.

*****hoister.** A shop-lifter ; a pickpocket : c. : resp. C. 19–20 and C. 19. The latter is in J. H. Jesse's *London*, vol. i, 1847. Ex *hoist*, v., 1.—2. A sot : (low) coll. : from ca. 1860 ; ob. Ex *hoist*, v., 3.

*****hoisting ; hoist-lay.** Shop-lifting : late C. 18– 19 c.—2. See **hoist-lay,** 2 : c. : late C. 18–early 19. Grose, 2nd ed.—3. (**hoisting.**) Grose's military ceremony is folk-lore, not coll.—4. (**hoisting**) drinking : low coll. : from ca. 1860 ; ob. Ex *hoist*, v., 3.

hoik. An occ. variant of *hoick*, esp. the v.

[† **hoit, hoyt,** to romp, be riotously inclined, is, despite F. & H., ineligible.]

hoity-toity. See **highty-tighty.**

hok is incorrect for *hough*, q.v.

hokey. Prison : low : late C. 19–20. Perhaps ex *chokey* on *hokey-pokey.*

hokey !, by (the). See **hoaky.** Occ. varied to *by the hokeys* and, in late C. 19, to *by the hokey-pokey.*

hok(e)y-pok(e)y. A cheat, a swindle : low coll. : from ca. 1845.—2. Nonsense : low coll. : from ca. 1875.—3. A, indeed any, cheap ice-cream sold in the streets : low coll. : from ca. 1884. A C. 19 street-cry ran ' hokey-pokey, pokey ho ' ; a C. 19– 20, ' hokey-pokey, a penny a lump '. All these senses are ex *hocus-pocus* ; the third is not—as some wit proposed—ex It. *o che poco !*, oh, how little. (The form *hokery-pokery* is Northern dial.)

hokey-pokey, adj. Swindling ; illegal, illicit : low coll. (— 1887). Baumann. Ex n., 1.

hokum ; occ. **hocum.** Anything designed to make a melodramatic or a sentimental appeal ; bunkum : U.S. (ca. 1920), anglicised by 1926. Prob. ex *hocus(-pocus)* on *bunkum*. O.E.D. (Sup.).

hol. See **hols.**

Holborn, the. The Holborn Restaurant in London : coll. (— 1887), verging on S.E. Baumann, ' feines Restaurant in Holborn '.

Holborn Hill, ride backwards up (Grose, 1st ed.). To go to be hanged : mid-C. 18–early 19 s. : perhaps orig. c., but certainly soon low coll. Congreve has *go up Holborn Hill* ; *ride up Holborn* occurs at least as early as 1659 (see Nares), while Jonson, in *Bartholomew Fair*, alludes to *the heavy hill . . . of Holborn*. Such was the route to Tyburn, where criminals were hanged, the criminals riding backwards. The last execution at Tyburn, so therefore the last procession thither, was in 1784, the executions thereafter taking place near Newgate.

hold. (To bet, wager : S.E.—) V.i. To conceive a child : coll. : C. 18–20. Ex the C. 17–20 S.E. sense of animal conception. Variant *hold it.*— 2. In billiards, to hole, v.t. : s. > j. : 1869. ' A corruption of *hole*, by association of *holed* and *hold* ', S.O.D.—3. (V.t.) To hold one's own against, be (clearly) a match for : sporting s. (−1883) >, in C. 20, gen. coll. (O.E.D.)—4. To be in funds : low coll. (? orig. s.) : at first, Cockney : from ca. 1870. In C. 20, mostly Australian. Esp. in *do you hold ?*, C. 19, and, C. 20 Australia, *are you holding ?*

hold a candle to, and hold a candle to the devil. See **candle**.

hold a good wind. (Of a ship) to have ' good weatherly qualities ' : nautical coll. : mid-C. 19–20 ; slightly ob. Bowen.

hold down (e.g. a job). To overcome the difficulties of ; hence to do satisfactorily, with the connotation of keeping abreast of the ' snags ' and problems of a difficult job : coll., orig. (ca. 1890) U.S., anglicised ca. 1910. Perhaps ex :

hold down (a claim). To reside long enough on a claim to establish ownership under the homestead law : mining s. : U.S. (1888) and Australia (ca. 1890).

hold hard ! ; hold on ! Wait a moment ! ; stop ! Coll. : the former (orig. in S.E., of pulling at a horse's reins) from ca. 1760 ; the latter from ca. 1860 and orig., and long mostly, nautical. Colman, 1761, ' Hold hard ! hold hard ! you are all on a wrong scent ' ; Edmund Yates, 1864, in *Broken to Harness*, ' I told Meaburn to hold on.' (Although *hold on* often occurs in moods other than the imperative, *hold hard* very rarely does.)

hold in hand. To amuse ; vividly to interest ; have a marked ascendancy over : coll. : from ca. 1860 ; ob. Ex the † S.E. sense, keep in expectation.

hold it ! Stay in precisely that position ! : painters' s. (from ca. 1895) > coll. ca. 1910 in the theatrical, and ca. 1925 in the cinematographic world.

hold my hand and call me Charlie ! A c.p. dating from ca. 1930 ; slightly ob. (Mostly derisive.)

hold on ! See **hold hard !**

hold on by the eyebrows, or eyelashes, or eyelids. See **eyelashes**.

hold on like grim death ; hold on to. To be courageously or obstinately persistent about ; apply oneself diligently to : the former, coll. ; the latter, coll. in C. 19, S.E. in C. 20. Both from ca. 1850 ; the former was perhaps orig. U.S.

hold on the slack. To do nothing : nautical coll. : mid-C. 19–20. Bowen. I.e. the slack of the rope.

*hold-out. A mechanical device, esp. in poker, for ' holding out ', i.e. concealing, desirable cards until they are useful : gamblers' c. : ca. 1860–1900, though app. not recorded before 1893. Maskelyne, in *Sharps and Flats*, 1894. (O.E.D.)

hold out on. To keep something (esp. money or important information) back from (a person) : orig. U.S. ; anglicised ca. 1924.

hold the market. ' To buy stock and hold it to so large an extent that the price cannot decline ',

F. & H. : Stock Exchange s. (ca. 1880) >, ca. 1890, gen. coll.

hold the stage. To have the eye of an audience : theatrical : from ca. 1875.—2. To attract most of the attention ; do all the talking : coll. : from ca. 1895.

hold tight ! See **tight !, hold**.

hold-up. (A highwayman ; a bushranger : orig. (ca. 1888), U.S. ; never properly anglicised, and never gen.)—2. A highway robbery ; any robbery in which a person is held up at firearm-point : orig. U.S. ; anglicised ca. 1905 as a coll. ; by ca. 1933, S.E.

hold-up, v. Rob on the highway, hence waylay and rob, hence to cheat : orig. (1887), U.S. ; anglicised as a coll. ca. 1895 ; in C. 20, S.E. Cf. Australian *stick up*.—2. In c., to arrest : ca. 1880–1915.

hold up your dagger hand. A C. 17 drinking c.p.

(hold up your head :) there's money bid for you. (Don't be so modest ! for) people think well of you : C. 17–mid-19 : a semi-proverbial c.p. Swift, the longer form ; Marryat, the shorter, preceded by ' as the saying is '. Apperson.

hold with. To approve of ; agree with : coll. : from ca. 1895. Ex S.E. sense, to side with : cf., in S.E., the † *hold on*, the ob. *hold of* or *for* (S.O.D.)

hold your jaw ! Be quiet : (low) coll. : from ca. 1750. Foote. Occ. in other moods than the imperative. Cf. *hold hard !*

holding, ppl. adj. In funds : Australian : C. 20 : s. > coll. See **hold**, 4. Esp. *how are you holding ?*, how much money have you ? : also New Zealand.

holding back. ' Trying to avoid being cured of wound or sickness ' : military coll. : 1915. B. & P. Merely an extension of the S.E. sense.

[holding the baby(, left). Jocular S.E. rather than s. or.coll. : late C. 19–20. E.g. of a person left with stocks and shares that cannot be sold. Ex men holding the baby outside a shop while the wives take an unconscionable time inside.]

holding up the corner. A coll. phrase satirical of a leaning idler : C. 20. Ware.

hole. The *pudendum muliebre* : low coll. : C. 16 (? earlier)–20. See also **better 'ole**.—2. Hence, like *c**t*, it has come to signify coïtion or women viewed as sexual potentialities or actualities, as in ' He likes a, *or* his, bit of hole ' or ' Hole means everything to that blighter.'—3. The anus : low coll. in C. 19–20, but in C. 14–18 a vulgarism (as in Chaucer's ribald *Miller's Tale*). Abbr. *arse-hole.*— 4. As a prison-cell, a dungeon, it is, despite F. & H., perfectly good Eng., and as, in C. 17–18, a printery specialising in unlicensed books, it is rather printers' j. than coll. or printers' s.—The following two senses were S.E. previous to ca. 1870, then, *pace* the O.E.D., they > coll. : 5, a small, dingy abode or lodging (1616) ; 6, a monetary or social difficulty, a mass, a scrape : 1760, Smollett. (Dates, S.O.D.)— 7. A place : mostly military and Society : from ca. 1915. Perhaps ex *better hole*, q.v.—8. (Gen. in pl.) A shilling : tramps' c. (− 1935). Also grafters' s. (− 1934). Philip Allingham, *Cheapjack*.—9. A tunnel : railwaymen's coll. : mid-C. 19–20. (*The Passing Show*, April 7, 1934.)

hole. (Gen. v.t.) ' To effect intromission ', F. & H. : low : C. 19–20. Ex n., 1. The v.i. is gen. expressed by *to hole it*.

hole, better ; gen. **better 'ole**. A better, esp. a safer place ; esp. *if you know of a better 'ole, go to it*, which > in 1915 (the year of Captain Bruce Bairns-

father's cartoon), a c.p. not yet † ; Bairnsfather)'
play of the same title (staged in 1916) reinforced the
cartoon.—2. Hence, one's wife's, or, occ., one's
sweetheart's pudend : mostly military : 1916–19.

hole, bit of. See **hole, n.**, 1 and 2.

hole, put a bit of wood in the. See **wood in
it !**

***hole, put in the.** Contemporary with the
synonymous *garden, put in the.*

hole !, suck his. A low ' dovetail ', or c.p. retort,
on receiving ' Yes ' to the question, ' Do you know
So-and-so ? ' : from ca. 1870 ; ob.

hole-and-corner, underhand or secret, is S.E., as is
h.-and-c. work, ' shadiness ' ; but *h. and c.* work,
sexual connexion, is mid-C. 19–20 low coll.

hole in a ladder, unable (or **too drunk**) **to see a.**
Excessively drunk : coll. : from ca. 1860.

hole in (anything), make a. To use up largely,
esp. money or drink : coll. : from ca. 1660. In
C. 20, S.E.—2. To interrupt, break ; upset, spoil :
coll. : from ca. 1850. Only in such locutions as :
make a hole in one's manners, to be impolite (ob.) ;
. . . *in one's reputation,* (of a man) to seduce a girl,
(of a girl) to allow herself to be seduced ; . . . *in
the silence,* to make a noise, esp. an excessive (and
occ. continuous or continual) noise : orig., these
were prob. to be considered jocular S.E., but they
promptly > coll.

hole in one's coat(, pick a). (To find) a cause
for censure, a moral flaw : coll. : late C. 16–19.
Shakespeare, ' If I find a hole in his coat, I will tell
him my mind ' ; Burns on Grose, ' If there's a hole
in a' your coats, I rede you tent it.'

hole in one's pocket, burn a. See **burn.** . . .

hole in the water, make a. To commit suicide by
drowning : (jocular > low) coll. : from ca. 1850.
Dickens, 1853 (O.S.D.) ; E. Phillpotts, *Yellow Sands,*
1926. Cf. *hole in anything, make a,* 2.

hole it. See **hole, v.**

hole of content or **of holes.** The female pudend :
C. 16–19 : orig. euphemistic, but in C. 18–19 low
coll. Also *queen of holes.*

hole to hide it in, give or **lend a.** To grant the
sexual favour : low coll. : C. 19–20.

holed, ppl.adj. (Of the woman, with *well-,
large-,* etc.) having a pudend of a specified kind :
C. 19–20 : low coll.—2. (Of a man) in, or at, sexual
congress : C. 19–20 low coll.

holely. Incorrect for *holey* (adj.) : C. **16.**
O.E.D.

holer. A man promiscuously and actively
amorous : low coll. : C. 16–20, ob. Also *hole-
monger.*—2. A whore ; a light woman : C. 18–
mid-19 : coll. This word, not nearly so gen. **as**
F. & H. implies, is a reminiscence of the C. 13–15
use, gen. as *holour,* applied only to men.

holey dollar. See **holy dollar.**

holiday. (Gen. pl.) A spot carelessly left untarred or unpainted : nautical coll. (— 1785).
Grose, 1st ed. ; Bowen.—2. Hence, a gap ' left
between slung hammocks or clothing hung up to
dry ' : nautical : late C. 19–20. Bowen.

holiday, blind man's. See **blind man's holiday.**

holiday, gone for a, adj. Imperfect, incomplete,
flawed : coll. : from ca. 1860 ; ob. Cf. *holiday,* n.,
in nautical coll. (— 1785) and Cornish dial., resp. a
spot left untarred or unpainted and a part left
undusted, unswept, uncleaned.

holiday, speak. To use choice English : coll. :
late C. 16–17. Shakespeare.

holiday, take a. To be dismissed, esp. from a job :

slow) coll. : C. 19–20 ; ob. Cf. *get the bag* or *sack*
(s.v. *bag*).

holiday at Peckham, have a. To go without
dinner : coll : C. 19. Ex :

holiday at Peckham or **with him, it is all.** It is all
over with it or him : coll. : ca. 1790–1910. Punning on *peck,* food, and *peckish,* hungry.

[**holiday bowler,** a bad bowler (at bowls), is cited
by B.E. and Grose as coll., but *holiday,* suited only
for a holiday, frivolous, hence inferior, is S.E., as in
the C. 17–18 proverbial *she's a(n) holiday dame.*]

holiday cutter, a. A minor punishment, the
delinquent pulling in the cutter instead of going
ashore : *Conway* cadets' : from ca. 1890. John
Masefield, *The Conway,* 1933. Analogous is the
Conway's holiday messenger, the delinquent attending
on lower deck instead of going ashore : Masefield.

holing, n. Whoring ; womanising : low coll. :
C. 19–20 ; ob. See **hole, v.**

holla-baloo. A variant, recorded by Baumann,
of *hullabaloo.*

Hollanders. Pointed wax moustaches : South
London : 1875–85. Ware. Ex W. Holland, a
popular theatre-lessee owning ' the finest pair of
black-waxed sheeny moustaches ever beheld '.

holler, v. To shout ; cry for mercy : a low coll.
form of *hollo, holloa, hollow* : app. orig. (— 1699),
U.S., anglicised ca. 1870. (O.E.D. Sup.)

Holler Cuss. The Fr. race-horse *Holocauste* competing in the Derby of : 1899 : sporting. Ware.

hollis. A small pebble : Winchester College :
ca. 1870–1920. ? ex a boy's name. (Wrench.)

hollop. Orlop : a nautical sol. : C. 18–20.
Smollett, in *Peregrine Pickle.*

hollow. Cooked poultry : gourmets' (— 1823).
Egan's Grose. Because disembowelled.

hollow, adj. Complete, thorough ; very easy :
coll. : 1750 (S.O.D.) Esp. with *thing* and *victory*
(or *defeat*), the former (synonymous with the latter)
being a set phrase in C. 18–early 19, as *hollow win* is
in C. 20. Ex :

hollow, adv. Completely, thoroughly, very
easily : 1668 (S.O.D.) Esp. with *beat,* as in Townley, 1759, ' Crab was beat hollow.' Skinner, in his
fascinating *Etymologicon,* pertinently suggested
that *hollow = wholly* corrupted. The mainly U.S.
form, *all hollow,* occurs in Foote's *The Orators,* 1762.

hollow meat. ' Rabbit or hare . . . unpopular
when served out to a ship's company ' : nautical
coll. : late C. 19–20. Bowen. Prob. suggested by
dial. *h.m.,* poultry as opp. to butcher's meat
(E.D.D.).

Holloway. The female pudend : low punning :
from ca. 1860 ; ob.

Holloway Castle. Holloway Prison : London
lower classes' (— 1893). Ware, who mentions that
it is occ. called, evasively, *North Castle* : it is
situated in North London.

Holloway, Middlesex. The lower bowel : low,
doubly punning : ca. 1865–1910.

Holly. A philippic : Society : ca. 1880–90. Ex
John *Holl*ingshead, who, as lessee of the Gaiety
Theatre, ' for many years issued scathing proclamations signed with his name, printed in the house
bills ' (Ware).

hols. (Rarely *hol,* a single day's holiday.)
Holidays : orig. and mainly schools' : C. 20. The
O.E.D. (Sup.) dates at 1906, but the term was in use
at least five years earlier. See also Addenda.

holt. A hold, a grip : low coll. : from ca. 1880,
ex U.S. (1825), ex Eng. dial. of C. 14–20. O.E.D. ;

Thornton.—2. Hence, **a** speciality : Canadian (— 1932). John Beames.

holus-bolus. The head ; occ. the neck : nautical : ca. 1870–1905.

holus-bolus, adv. All together ; completely ; at a gulp ; in confusion ; helter-skelter : orig. (— 1847), dial. ; coll. from ca. 1860, perhaps thanks to T. Hughes (as dial.) in *Tom Brown's Schooldays* ; Wilkie Collins, in *The Moonstone*, 'He put [the silver] back, holus-bolus, in her pocket.' The O.E.D. suggests by facetious latinisation of *(the) whole bolus* or as through Gr. ὅλος βῶλος.

Holy Aunt. A High Anglican c.p. term for the Roman Catholic Church : late C. 19–20. On the Roman Catholics' ' Holy *Mother* Church '.

Holy Boys. The 9th Foot, from ca. 1881 the Norfolk, Regiment : from ca. 1810 (ob.) : military. F. & Gibbons. In the Peninsular War, they bartered Bibles for drink and gained a reputation for sacking monasteries. Frank Richards, in *Old-Soldier Sahib*, 1936, explains it thus : ' [The Norfolk Regiment] once sold the Bibles given them by a pious old lady, before going overseas, to buy beer.'

Holy City, the. Adelaide : Australian coll. : from ca. 1870. R. & F. Hill, in *What We Saw in Australia*, 1875. Ex its many churches. Morris. Cf. *Farinaceous City*, q.v.

Holy Cod. Good Friday : atheists' : 1890 ; ob. Adopted from Fr. free-thinkers' *la Sainte Morue*.

holy dollar. A dollar out of which a *dump* (q.v.) has been punched : Australia : ca. 1820–80. Elsewhere, ca. 1850–1910, also as *holey d.* Referred to in *The Hobart Town Gazette*, Aug. 10, 1822, though not so named. Punning *holey*. (Morris.)

holy father. ' A butcher's boy of St. Patrick's Market, Dublin, or other Irish blackguards [pl., *sic*], among whom the exclamation, or oath, *by the holy father*, (meaning the pope) is common ', Grose, 1785 : Anglo-Irish : (prob.) ca. 1750–1850. Cf. *holy lamb*, q.v.

holy fowl. A pious (esp. outwardly pious) woman : ecclesiastical : late C. 19–20.

holy friar. A liar : rhyming s. : late C. 19–20. Manchon.

Holy Ghost, the. The winning post : turf rhyming s. : C. 20. (P. P., *Rhyming Slang*, 1932.)

Holy Ghost shop. A church : low (— 1909). Ware.—2. The Theatre Royal : low (— 1909) ; † by 1930. Ibid.

holy ground. See **holy land**.—**holy iron.** See **holy poker.**

holy Joe. One who is good at Scripture : *Conway* cadets' : from ca. 1865. John Masefield, *The Conway*, 1933.—2. Hence (?), a pious person : coll. : late C. 19–20. Barrère & Leland. Imm. ex :— 3. A parson, a chaplain : nautical (— 1874). H., 5th ed. ; Baumann.—4. Hence, ' the shallow, circular-crowned hat worn by clergymen ' (*Slang*, p. 198) : ecclesiastical : C. 20.

holy (jumping mother of) Moses ! See **Moses** and cf. the former of :

holy kicker ! ; holy smoke. Exclamations expressive of amazement : late C. 19–20.

holy lamb. A thorough-paced villain : Anglo-Irish : ca. 1760–1870. Grose, 1st ed. Orig., prob. blasphemous. Cf. *holy father*, q.v.

holy land or **ground** (occ. with capitals). St. Giles's, London, or rather (Seven Dials) the underworld part thereof : perhaps orig. c. : the former — 1821, the latter —1819 ; both prob. from ca. 1810. Ob. by 1890, † by 1920. A pre-1819 chant runs :

' For we are the boys of the holy ground, And we'll dance upon nothing '—i.e. be hanged—' and turn us round.' An early explanation has it that the name is ' in compliment to the superior purity of its Irish population ' (*The Fancy*, vol. i : 1821), while *The Licensed Victuallers' Gazette* of April 3, 1891, refers to ' the Irishmen of the Holy Land '. Cf. *Palestine*, q.v.—2. Any neighbourhood affected by Jews : (low) coll. : from ca. 1875. Cf. *New Jerusalem*, q.v., and the next entry.—3. (Only **holy ground.**) A portion of the *Conway's* main deck consecrated by the Bishop of Liverpool for church-services : *Conway* cadets' : from ca. 1885. John Masefield, *The Conway*, 1933.

holy of holies. The Grand Hotel at Brighton : from ca. 1890. Because a favourite with Jews. Cf. preceding entry.—2. A private room ; a ' den ' or ' sanctum ' : coll. (— 1875) ; in C. 20, S.E., as indeed it was in C. 19 except when jocular or derisive. Nat Gould, in *The Double Event*, ' Fletcher did not venture into that holy of holies.'—3. The female pudend : low : C. 19–20. Punning *holey*.

holy poker or **iron.** A university bedel (rarely as *h. iron*) : ca. 1850–1910.—2. As an oath (in C. 20, mild) : the former (— 1840) has variant *h. pokers*, without *the* ; the latter (— 1886), ob. by 1910, was † by 1920. (Cf. the next entry.) Ex the mace carried by an esquire bedel.—3. The penis : low : from ca. 1860 ; ob. Punning *hole*, n., 1 ; cf. *poke*, v.

holy show ! ; h. lance ! A mild oath : ca. 1850–1910 : the latter, not gen. Cf. *holy poker*, 2, q.v.

holy smoke ! See **holy kicker.**

holy terror. A very formidable person ; a person of tiresome manner or exasperating habits : coll. : from ca. 1890.

holy than righteous, more. (Of a garment) torn or holey ; (of a person) wearing ragged or torn clothes : (orig. low) coll. : from ca. 1885. Baumann.

holy water, as the devil loves. Not at all : coll. : mid-C. 16–20. (Holy water having, in theology, the virtue of routing the devil.)

holy-water sprinkler. A spiked club : coll. : C. 19 (and prob. centuries earlier). The S.E. is *h.-w.* †*springle* or *sprinkle*, though, in this sense, even those forms must orig. have been coll., as the sense, a fox's brush (C. 18 and prob. C. 17), was orig. sporting s.

holy workman, he is a. An ecclesiastical c.p. of C. 16 applied to ' him that will not be saved by Christ's merits, but by the works of his own imagination ' (Tyndale, 1528). Cf. *a merely moral man.*

hom forty. A frequent variant of *hommes-forty*, q.v. (B. & P.)

Home. Great Britain and Ireland ; esp., and gen., England : Colonial, prob. first in U.S. (by 1912 very ob., says Thornton) in C. 18. In C. 20, mostly Australian and New Zealand. Esp. as *at h., go h.* A coll. usage bordering on—indeed, by the O.E.D. considered as—S.E.—2. (**the Home.**) The preventive-detention part of Camp Hill Prison : from ca. 1925.—3. (**home** ; gen. **the home.**) A convict prison : c. (— 1932). ' Stuart Wood ', *Shades of the Prison House*.—4. (**home.**) A dug-out in the front trench : New Zealand soldiers' : 1915–18.

home, bring oneself. See **home, get,** 3.

home, carry or **send.** To bury, to kill : coll. : C. 18–20, ob. Ex late C. 16–20 coll. > S.E. *send to one's last home.* Cf. *home, go,* q.v.

home, get. To ' land ' a blow effectively : boxing s. > gen. coll. : C. 19–20. Ex S.E. *pay or* *touch home.*—2. To reach the winning-post : turf and athletics : late C. 19–20, s. > coll.—3. Specifically games and the turf, orig., is the sense, to recover a loss, come out quits : from ca. 1809 : in C. 20, S.E. Also *bring oneself home*, from ca. 1760, as in Miss Burney ; likewise S.E. in C. 20.—4. To induce the sexual spasm in a woman ; also, to get her with child : low coll. : C. 19–20.

home, go. To die : C. 19–20 coll. Esp. in *gone home*, dead. Note, however, that *go to one's last home* is a S.E. euphemism. Cf. *home, carry* or *send*, q.v.—2. (Of clothes) to begin wearing out ; to wear out : lower classes' (— 1923). Manchon.

home, make oneself at. To make oneself very comfortable in another's abode or lodging : coll. (— 1892) >, by 1925 or so, S.E.

home, see (a person). To reprimand ; to 'tell off ' : C. 20. Ernest Raymond, *The Jesting Army*, 1930.

home about, nothing to write (or cable). See **nothing to . . .**

home and fried. ' Safe and correct ' (F. & Gibbons) : military : late C. 19–20. Possibly rhyming s. on *home and dried*.

home-bird. A hen-pecked husband ; a milksop : coll. : from ca. 1870.

home-folk(s). One's relatives and/or friends, neighbours : coll., orig. (ca. 1880) U.S., anglicised ca. 1900. O.E.D. (Sup.).

Home for Lost Dogs. A medical (now ob.) nickname, from ca. 1875, for a large and well-known London medical school, whither flock those who, even if there they obtain their degree, would never have been brilliant physicians or surgeons.

home on the pig's back ! Very successful ! ; thoroughly (and easily) : a c.p., mostly among New Zealanders and Australians : from ca. 1910. Cf. (?) *save one's bacon.*

Home Rule or **h. r.** Irish whiskey : ca. 1880–1914. Cf. :

home-rulers. ' Roast potatoes, as baked in the streets ' : London : 1882–ca. 1914. Ware. Because so many potatoes came from Ireland.

home-stretch. See **get on the home-stretch.**

home sweet home. The female pudend ; orig., no doubt, the conjugal one : low : from ca. 1870 ; ob.

[**home to, come.** To touch deeply, esp. in one's conscience ; impress lastingly : from ca. 1620 : S.E. till ca. 1850, then tending more and more to coll.]

homee. Rare for **omee.**

Homeless Fleet, the. ' The pre-War Home Fleet . . . always being pushed about from port to port ' : naval : early C. 19. Bowen.

homer. In error for *omer*, a Hebrew measure of $5\frac{1}{10}$ pints : C. 18–19. (A *homer*, properly, is a Hebrew measure of about 80 gallons.) O.E.D.

homesters. A team playing on their own ground : sporting s. (1891) >, ca. 1900, coll. >, ca. 1920, S.E.

homeward-bound stitches are designed to last only till one is paid off : nautical : from ca. 1870. Bowen. Cf. :

homeward-bounder. A vessel bound for home : coll. (— 1867). Admiral Smyth.

homey, adj., and **hominess.** See **homy.**—2. **homey** is a theatrical variant (C. 20) of *omee*, q.v. This form is prevalent also among grafters : Philip Allingham, *Cheapjack*, 1934.

hommes-forty. A French railway van or truck for the transport of troops : Western Front Army,

1914–18. F. & Gibbons. Ex the marking, ' 40 hommes, 8 chevaux ' (40 men or 8 horses). Cf. *ommes and chevoos*, q.v.

homo. A man : the orig., and a C. 19 alternative (never gen.), of *omee*, q.v. Lingua Franca. This, as opp. adoption pedantic or jocular of L. *homo*, is adumbrated—perhaps even illustrated by this (ca. 1843) from Southey's *Common-Place Book*, ' One of these homo's had 800 head of game in his larder ' (O.E.D.) ; also in Moncrieff, 1843. Cf. the U.S. *hombre* (ex Sp.). Occ. in jocular opp. to *woman* : men's : C. 20.—2. A homosexual : from ca. 1925. (Compton Mackenzie, *Water on the Brain*, 1933.)

homo genius. A genius : 1887, Baumann ; virtually †. Punning *homogeneous* and *genius homo*.

homolo-, in Webster, is incorrect for *homalo-* : from ca. 1860. O.E.D.

*****homon(e)y.** A woman ; a wife ; C. 18 c. *The Discoveries of John Poulter*, 1754, ' My homoney is in quod.' Cf. *homo*, with which it is cognate.

homy, occ. **homey.** Home-like ; resembling or suggesting home ; unobtrusively comfortable : coll.: from ca. 1855. Kingsley, ' I like to . . . feel " homey " wherever I be.' Whence *hominess*, *homelikeness*, quiet comfort : coll. : 1885. (O.E.D.)—2. Affable ; friendly : coll. : C. 20. See quotation at *crasher*.

Hon., the, requires the Christian name (or initial) before the surname, its omission being a sol. Fowler.

hondey. An omnibus : Manchester : ca. 1860–1900. Abbr. *hondeybush* (i.e. *omnibus* corrupted).

hone. The female pudend : either euphemistic or low coll. : C. 18–19. D'Urfey, ' So I mav no more pogue the hone of a woman.'

honest, chaste, was always S.E., despite F. & H., whose second sense, a coll. one, immoral but within the law, arose ca. 1850 and disappeared with the C. 19. As an adv. (= *honestly*) it is coll. only when, exclamatory, it means ' It's true,—on my word it is.'

honest, the. The truth : non-aristocratic, non-cultured coll. : late C. 19–20. Francis E. Brett Young, *White Ladies*, 1935, ' Why, I'm proud to drive anyone there, miss, and that's the honest.' Abbr. *the honest truth*.

honest a man as (any in the cards) when all the kings are out, as. A knave : C. 17–mid-19 coll., the longer form being gen. till C. 19.

honest as the skin between the brows or horns(, as). As honest as may be : coll. : resp. mid-C. 16–17, C. 17. Still, Jonson, Shakespeare ; Jonson. Cf. the coll. > S.E. similes *as honest a man as ever broke bread*, late C. 16–20 (ob.) ; *as ever trod on shoe-leather*, late C. 16–19 ; *as the sun ever shone on*, late C. 18–20 ; and *as honest a woman as ever burnt malt* : late C. 16–17. (Apperson.)

honest broker. A matrimonial agent : lower middle classes' : from ca. 1880 ; ob. Ware.

honest fellow. See **jemmy,** n., 2. Cf. the C. 20 *stout fellow.*

honest Indian or, gen., **Injun !** Honour bright ! Coll. : orig. (— 1884), U.S. ; anglicised ca. 1895, mostly owing to Mark Twain's books ; ob.

Honest Jack. Felton, the murderer of the Duke of Buckingham (1628) ; John Lawless, Irish agitator (d. 1837). Dawson.

Honest John. Earl Spencer (1782–1845), statesman. Ibid.—2. John Burns : late C. 19–20.

honest man and a good bowler, an. A person that combines two qualities rarely found together,—for, says Quarles in 1635, ' He hardly can Be a good bowler and an honest man,' the special combination soon being made generic and then proverbial. Coll. : late C. 16–early 18. Shakespeare, in *Love's Labour's Lost*, V, ii ; Ray. (Apperson.)

honest-to-God or **-goodness**, adj. and adv. Real(ly), genuine(ly), thorough(ly) : coll., orig. (— 1916) U.S., anglicised by Galsworthy in 1921. O.E.D. (Sup.).

Honest Tom. Thomas Warton (1728–90), the poet and critic. He was somewhat uncouth.

honest woman (variant of), **make an**, v.t. To marry a mistress : low coll. (and dial.) : from ca. 1560. Wycherley, in *Love in a Wood*, ' *Dap.* Why she was my wench. *Gripe.* I'll make her honest then.'—2. From ca. 1890, often jocular and meaning simply to marry (and thus give a higher official status to), and, as such, ordinary coll. Collinson.

honey, an endearment,—the same applies to compounds, e.g. *honeycomb*,—is S.E., as the *semen virile* it is C. 19–20 low s., and, in form *poor honey*, a harmless, foolish, good-natured fellow, it is C. 18– early 19 coll. when not dial.—2. Abbr. *pot o' honey*, money : rhyming s. (— 1923). Manchon.

honey-blob. (Gen. in pl.) A large and ripe yellow gooseberry : Scots coll. Horace Walpole, in a letter of 1744.

honey-bucket. A latrine-receptacle for excreta : Canadian military : from 1914. B. & P.

honey-fall. A piece of good fortune : ca. 1820– 50. It is, however, extant in dial. : E.D.D. Bee. Perhaps by fusion—or a confusion—of *honeymoon* and *windfall*.

honey for a halfpenny, sell. To think very poorly of : coll. : late C. 16–17.

honey moon. (In C. 19–20, one word.) The first month after marriage : coll. (at first low) : mid-C. 16–18.—2. In C. 19–20, the holiday spent together by a newly married couple before they settle down in their home : at first, perhaps coll., but very soon S.E. Ex *sweetness* = tenderness. Cf. the proverbial *it is but honeymoon with them* : C. 16–17.

honey or all turd with them, it is all. They are either sworn friends or bitter enemies : coll. c.p. or perhaps proverb : mid-C. 18–mid-19. Grose, 3rd ed.

honey-pot. The female pudend : C. 18–19 low s. > coll. or euphemism > coll. D'Urfey. Cf. *honey*.

Hong-Kong !, go to. Go away ! : coll. : late C. 19–20. Hong-Kong is prob. a euphemism for Hell ; cf. *go to Bath, Halifax, Jericho, Jerusalem.*

honky-donks. A marine's feet : naval : late C. 19–20. F. & Gibbons. Ex East Anglian *honka-donka*, thick, heavy boots. Cf. *hock-dockies.*

honour !; honour bright ! Upon my honour !, or as an emphatic or anxious query. Coll., orig. Anglo-Irish and somewhat low : resp. ca. 1840–80 (as in Selby's *Antony and Cleopatra Married*, 1843) and from ca. 1819 (e.g. Moore's *Tom Crib* and W. Black's *Beautiful Wretch*).

honour mods. Honour moderations : Oxford University coll. : C. 20. (O.E.D. Sup.)

honours (are) easy or **even !** We (etc.) are level : coll. : C. 20. Ex bridge.

hoo-ha. An argument, a ' row ' ; an artillery demonstration : military : from ca. 1905. B. & P. Echoic.

hooa. See **hoor.**

hooch, hootch. Alcoholic liquor, esp. spirits : U.S. (ca. 1902), partly anglicised in G.W. Ex

Alaska *hoochino*, a very strong drink, made by Alaskan natives. F. & Gibbons ; Irwin ; O.E.D. (Sup.).

hood, by my. An asseveration : mid-C. 14–early 17 ; coll. Shakespeare. Origin unknown. (O.E.D.)

hood, put a bone in one's. To cuckold : mid-C. 16–17 coll. The anon. play, *The Nice Wanton*, 1560, ' I could tell you who putteth a bone in your hood.'

hood, two faces under one. Double-dealing, n. : coll. : C. 15–18. B.E. In early C. 19, often *hat* for *hood :* Jon Bee.

hood for this fool, a. A proverbial c.p. of ca. 1550–1620.

hoodlum. (A boy rough : U.S. only : from ca. 1872. Hence :) Any, esp. if dangerous, rough : orig. (ca. 1876) and still mainly U.S. ; anglicised ca. 1895. Prob. by printer's error for *noodlum*, ex *Muldoon*, the name of the leader of a San Franciscan gang of street arabs ; another suggestion is that it comes from the gang-cry, *huddle 'em !* : unlikely. Bartlett ; Thornton. Cf. *hooligan, larrikin* and *tough*, qq.v.—2. Also *hoodlumism*, coll., never very gen.

hoodman. A blind man (cf. *groper*, q.v.) : C. 18– early 19 : ? orig. c.

hoodman, adj. Blind : C. 18–early 19.—2. Intoxicated : C. 19 low. Prob. ex :

hoodman blind. Blind drunk : C. 19 low. ? ex *hoodman*, adj., 1.

hoodoo. Such an adverse charm as the evil eye ; any person or thing causing bad luck (cf. *Jonah*, q.v.) : orig. (— 1885), 1881 resp., U.S. ; anglicised, as a coll., ca. 1910, but common in Australia several years earlier. Prob. *voodoo* corrupted ; *voodoo* being a Dahomey native word. (The v. has not been welcomed in Great Britain—nor in its Dominions.)—2. Hence, adj. : unlucky : anglicised ca. 1920.—3. A useless hand shanghaied by a crimp as an A.B. : nautical : from ca. 1910. Bowen.

hooer. See **hoor.**

hoof. A human foot : low coll. : late C. 16–20. 1836, in M. Scott's *Cruise of the ' Midge '* ; Sydney Watson, 1892, ' Teddy, look out, yer've got yer hoof on my trotters.' Cf. *trotters*, q.v.

hoof, v.t. To kick : low coll. : from ca. 1860. Cf. *toe*, q.v., and *hoof out*.—2. V.i. ; also *hoof it*. To dance : from mid-1920's. (O.E.D. Sup.)

hoof, bang or **beat** or **pad the.** To walk, tramp, run away : low coll. : resp. C. 17, mid-C. 17–mid-19 (in C. 17, *beat it on the hoof*), and —1838 and ob. ; the first in Cotton, the second in Grose and, the older form, in B.E., the third in Dickens. Also, occ., *be upon the hoof*, ca. 1710–78. Cf. *hoof it*, q.v., and Shakespeare's ' Rogues, hence, avaunt . . . Trudge, plod, away ith' hoof ' (*Merry Wives*).

hoof, under the. Down-trodden : coll. : from ca. 1840. (In C. 20, S.E.)

hoof-and-mouth disease. Boasting, esp. at night to one's wife, of one's exploits at golf : jocular coll. : from ca. 1923. Also *foot and mouth disease*, q.v.

hoof in, recognise or **see one's.** To discern personal interference or influence in a matter : coll. : 1860, Thackeray. Ex *the devil's hoof*.

hoof it. To go on foot ; tramp : low coll. : late C. 17–20. B.E. ; Cumberland, in *The Fashionable Lover*, has *hoof* without *it*—prob. for the metre, though the usage occurs from ca. 1640. Cf. *hoofing*, q.v.—2. See **hoof**, v., 2.

hoof out. To eject ; dismiss, discharge : low coll. : from ca. 1850. Ex *hoof*, v.

hoof-padder. A pedestrian : low : C. 19. Cf. *hoof*, n., and *pad*, v.

hoofing, vbl.n. Walking ; tramping : (low) coll. mid-C. 17–20. From ca. 1850, gen. *hoofing-it*. Brome. (O.E.D.)

hoofy. Splay- or large-footed : low coll. : C. 19–20, ob.

Hooghly mud. Butter : nautical : late C. 19–20. Bowen, ' Originating in the ships on the Indian trade '.

hooha. See **hoo-ha.**

*****hook.** (Gen. pl.) A finger : c. : from ca. 1820 ; ob. Maginn, in *Vidocq Versified*.—2. A thief, esp. a pickpocket : c. : from ca. 1560. *Jack Juggler*, an anon. C. 16 play, ' So yonder cometh that unhappy hook ' ; Edgar Wallace, *passim*.—3. An advantage, ' catch ', imposture : low coll. (? s.) : from ca. 1860 ; ob. Cf. *hook, on the*, 2, below.— 4. Hence (?) and ex sense 2 : that member of a confidence-trick gang whose job it is to introduce the prospective victim : c. (— 1935). David Hume.—5. See **hooks.**—6. A shirker : military : C. 20. F. & Gibbons. Perhaps ex *Hooky Walker*.

*****hook,** v. To rob, steal, esp. to steal small articles from a (gen. shop-)window by cutting a small hole in it and ' fishing ' with a piece of string that has a hook attached : mid-C. 16–18 c. in specific sense ; C. 17–20, low coll. in gen. sense.—2. Overreach, trick, gen. in past ppl. passive : low (? orig. c.) : late C. 17–18.—3. To obtain, esp. in marriage : coll. : from ca. 1800 : gen. of a woman, as in John Strange Winter's *Army Society*, ' I wonder if Mrs. Traff has contrived to hook him for her sweet Laura.' Ex *hook a fish*.—4. See **hook it.**—5. ' To move with a sudden twist or jerk ' : M.E.–Mod.E. ; till C. 19, S.E. ; then coll. rapidly > s. and dial. (S.O.D.)

hook ! An exclamation implying doubt : Oxford University : ca. 1860–1910. ? ex ' ? ' or ex *hook*, v., 3, or ex *hookey Walker*, q.v.—2. Run away ! : 1908, A. S. M. Hutchinson, *Once Aboard the Lugger*, ' " Hook ! " said Bob. David asked : " What's hook ? " " Run away." ' Ex *hook it*.

hook, on one's own. On one's own account, at one's own risk and/or responsibility : coll. : orig. (1812), U.S., anglicised ca. 1845. Thackeray in *Pendennis*. Origin not yet properly determined.

hook, on the. At an advantage : coll. : late C. 17–18. Congreve, ' Consider I have you on the hook.'—2. On the ' thieve ' : c. : C. 19–20 ; ob. Ex *hook*, v., 1, or n., 2.

hook, sling or **take one's.** To run away ; depart, secretly or hastily, or both : low : from ca. 1860. H. (*sling*) ; Baumann, 1887 (both forms) ; Kipling, 1892, ' Before you sling your 'ook, at the 'ousetops take a look.' In C. 20, rarely *take*. Cf. *hook it*, q.v. —2. Nautical, and only in the *take* form, is the sense, to weigh anchor : from ca. 1890 ; ob.

hook and eye, adv. Arm in arm : tailors' : from ca. 1860. Ex the S.E. term, a metallic fastening, as for a dress.

*****hook and snivey ; hook-em** (or **'em** or **hookem)- snivey,** a corruption dating from ca. 1800 ; (after ca. 1820, the corrupted) **hookum snivey.** (In C. 20, *snivey* often > *snivv(e)y*.) Abbr. *hook and snivey, with nix the buffer*, an underworld trick for feeding a dog (*buffer*) and an additional man for nothing (*nix*) ; see **hook,** n., 2, and **snivey.** C. : ca. 1775– 1850. G. Parker's illuminating *View of Society* ; Grose, 2nd ed.—2. Hence (of course omitting *with nix the buffer*), an impostor specialising in this

trick : ca. 1790–1860. (Cf. *hook-um-snivey*, **v.**)— 3. Cognately, and gen., like the next sense, in form *hook-um* (or *hookum*) *snivey*, ' a crook of thick iron wire in a wooden handle, used to undo the wooden bolts of doors from without ', F. & H. : likewise c. : ca. 1800–1905.—4. A sarcastic or derisory affirmation accompanied with hand to nose, or as an irrelevant answer (= no one) to, e.g. ' Who did that ? ' : low, orig. and mostly Cockney : ca. 1850– 1915. H.—5. Hence, adj. in senses 1 and 2 : late C. 19–20 : mostly dial.

hook (at the end), with a. (Often tagged with *of it*.) A phrase implying ' Don't you believe it ! ' : low, ob. : the shorter form, (—)1823 ; the longer, (—)1864, and resp. Bee and Traill. Accompanied by a crooking of the forefinger. Cf. *over the left* for the practice, *Hooky Walker* for the phrase.

*****hook 'em snivey.** A variant of *hook and snivey*.

hook it. To decamp ; depart hastily : (low) coll. : from ca. 1850. Mayhew, Dickens, H. Kingsley. As *hook*, v.i., however, it dates from much earlier and comes ex *hook*, v., last sense. Whence *hook, sling one's*, q.v.

hook-me-dinghy. Anything whose right name has temporarily slipped one's memory : naval : from ca. 1890. Bowen. Cf. *wifflow gadget* and the prob. derivative *ooja-ka-piv*.

hook off. To remove (illicitly) : low (— 1887). Baumann. Cf. *hook*, v., 1 and 5.

hook on to. To attach oneself to ; follow up : (orig. low) coll. : from ca. 1890. Milliken, 1892, ' It's nuts to 'ook on to a swell.'

[**hook or by crook, by.** Despite F. & H., this is S.E.]

hook-pointed (Scots **-pintled**). Imperfectly erected : low amorous coll. : C. 19.

*****hook-pole lay.** To plunder a man after pulling him from his horse by means of a long, hooked pole : c. : C. 18. Smith's *Highwaymen*, 1720.

hook-um-snivey. To cheat, esp. by feigned sickness : low : ca. 1855–80. The *and* of *hook and snivey*, q.v., corrupted to *um*. H., 1859.

hook up with. To get into a quarrel with ; to fight (a person) : Canadian (— 1932). John Beames.

hooked, ppl.adj. Duped, tricked : see **hook, v.** esp. in sense 2.

hooked up. Dead : low (— 1923). Manchon. Ex *hooks, drop . . .*, q.v.—2. Provided with sweetheart or a temporary girl : low : C. 20. Alan Hyder, *Black Girl, White Lady*, 1934.

Hookee Walker (*Lex. Bal.* spelling). See **Hooky Walker.**

*****hookem snivey.** See **hook and snivey.**

*****hooker.** A thief, esp. an ' angler ' (q.v.) : c. : ca. 1560–1870. (One of the third rank of canters.) Harman.—2. A sharper : C. 17–18 c. B.E.—3. A pickpocket, esp. a watch-stealer : c. (— 1888) ; ob. *Tit Bits*, Nov. 17, 1888. Cf. the C. 19–20 U.S. c. sense, a harlot, and C. 20 sense, a drink of strong liquor.—4. A ship : depreciative or affectionate nautical s. (1823) >, ca. 1880, coll. Perhaps ex Dutch *hoeker*, huckster : W. Often *old hooker* (— 1865).

hookerman. A ship : nautical coll. (— 1894). Ex preceding, last sense. (O.E.D.)

hookey, play. To play truant : from ca. 1890. (Orig. American.)

Hookey (Walker). See **Hooky (Walker).**

*****hooks.** The hands : c. : from ca. 1825. Ex *hook*, a finger. Also *hooks and feelers*, as in the anon. *Five Years' Penal Servitude*, 1877 ; a thief, referring to hard work in prison, says that, when a man is released, ' in a week or two [he] can bring his hooks and feelers into full trim again '. Cf. *c**t-hooks*.—2. Spurs : military : late C. 19–20. F. & Gibbons.

hooks, catch. To get into trouble : military : C. 20. F. & Gibbons. Ex fishing.

hooks, drop or **go** or **pop off the.** To die : low : resp. — 1859, — 1872, and 1837. Perhaps ex a felon's corpse dropping, from sheer decay, off the hooks from which it has been suspended.—2. (Gen. with *go*) to get married, usually of women : coll. (— 1876) ; ob.

hooks, off the, adj. Ill-tempered, peevish : mid-C. 17–mid-19. Pepys, 1662 ; B.E.—2. Out of sorts or order : C. 17 (? also early C. 18).—3. Slightly mad : late C. 18–mid-19. Scott, 1825, ' Everybody that has meddled in this . . . business is a little off the hooks . . . in plain words, a little crazy.' Cf. S.E. *unhinged*.—4. Dead : low : from ca. 1860. This sense from *drop* (etc.) *off the hooks* ; all senses except the last, which is s., are coll.

hooks, off the, adv. To excess : coll. : C. 17. D'Urfey.—2. Immediately ; summarily : coll. : from ca. 1860. Trollope, in *Castle Richmond*, ' Baronets with twelve thousand a year cannot be married off the hooks.' (O.E.D.)

*hooks and feelers. See **hooks.**

*hookum-snivey. See **hook and snivey** and **hookum snivey.**

hookum. A regulation ; *the h.*, ' the correct thing ' : military coll. : late C. 19–20 ; ob. F. & Gibbons. Ex Hindustani *hukam*.

Hooky. The inevitable nickname of any man surnamed Walker : late C. 19–20 : mostly naval and military. Bowen. Ex *Hooky Walker*, q.v.— 2. (**Hooky.**) Sir Montague Browning after the loss of his hand : naval : C. 20. Bowen.

hooky, adj. Rural Canadian coll. (mid-C. 19–20), as in John Beames, *An Army without Banners*, 1930, ' " Hooky ", as country folk call a cow given to using her horns '.

hooky !, by. See sense 1 of the next entry.—

hooky, play. See **hookey, play.**

Hooky Walker ! A phrase signifying that something either is not true or will not occur : (low) coll., from ca. 1810. *Lex. Bal.* Also *Hook(e)y !*, as in Bee, and *by hooky !*, as in Manchon.—2. Be off ! : (low) coll. : from ca. 1830. Since ca. 1840, gen. abbr. to *Walker !*, as in Dickens's *Christmas Carol*, 1843, ' " Buy it," said Scrooge. " Walker ! " said the boy.' Acc. to Bee, ex John Walker, a prevaricating hook-nosed spy.

hoolerfer. A fool : centre s. : from ca. 1860 ; ob. Cf. *hugmer*.

Hooley. A magnificent fur-collared and -lined overcoat : London : 1897–ca. 1912. At first, favourable ; after Millionaire Hooley's bankruptcy in 1898, pejorative. Ware. Cf. :

Hooley, v. ' To pile success on success ' : City of London coll. : 1894–8. (On Dec. 10, 1897, Horatio Bottomley spoke thus significantly, ' But, you know, when you apply, if I may use the phrase, " Hooleying " finance to any good industry, there must be a certain finality about it.'

hooligan. A lively rough, not necessarily nor usually criminal : from ca. 1895 : s. till ca. 1910, then coll. Ex a ' joie-de-vivre ' Irish family (the Houlihans) resident, in the middle 90's, in the Borough (London) : W. Ware derives it from ' Hooley

Gang, a name given by the police in Islington to a gang of young roughs led by one Hooley '. W.'s is preferable. Cf. *hoodlum, larrikin,* and *tough,* qq.v. (The derivatives, e.g. *hooliganism,* do not belong to unconventional speech.)

hoop. The female pudend : low : C. 19–20 ; ob.

hoop, v. To beat, thrash : late C. 18–mid 19. Grose, 1785.

hoop, go through the. To pass the Insolvent Debtors' court : C. 19. Ex circus tricks.—2. Hence, to have a bad time of it : coll. : C. 20.—3. To be up for punishment : military : from ca. 1910. F. & Gibbons.

hoop, put through the. To give a bad time, to punish : coll. : C. 20. Opp. senses 2 and 3 of the preceding.—2. Hence, to reprimand ; question closely : coll. : from ca. 1912.

hoop it. See **hoop, go through the,** 1.—2. To run away : c. (— 1839) ; † by 1900. Brandon. Perhaps a perversion of *hop it.*

hoop one's barrel. To beat, thrash : low (— 1785). Grose, 1st ed. Cf. *hoop,* v.

hoop-stick. The arm : low : ca. 1860–1910.

hooped up, get. See **hoop, go through the.**

hooper's, or **hoopers, hide.** Coïtion : C. 18–mid-19 low, but never very gen. D'Urfey, 1719, in the notorious *Pills.* Ex the S.E. sense, hide-and-seek.

hooping, out of all ; in C. 19, occ. past all hoop-ing. See **ho.**

hoops-a-daisy ! A variant, or possibly the origin, of *upsadaisy !*, up ! : coll. : C. 19–20.—2. Occ. a joyful exclamation, as in D. Sayers, *The Nine Tailors*, 1934, ' Hoops-a-daisy ! . . . I've got it,' Wimsey speaking as he uses a fishing-line.

hoor, hooer, hooa or **hua.** A sol. pronunciation of *whore* : C. 19–20.

hooray ! This coll. form of *hurrah, hurray* is half-way between dignity and impudence : C. 18– 20.—2. Good-bye ! : New Zealanders' : C. 20.

hooroo ! ; **hooroosh !** C. 20 variants of the preceding, sense 1. Coll.

hoosh. A thick soup with plenty of body : 1905, R. F. Scott, *The Voyage of the ' Discovery '* (O.E.D. Sup.). Just possibly ex dial. *hoosh !*, used in driving or scaring away pigs or poultry : such soup is a staple dish of explorers ; its frequent appearance may well have induced a vigorous *hoosh !*, go away : but cf. :

hoosh out, v.t. To force (water) out : from before 1923. Manchon. Ex Irish dial. *hoosh*, to heave, to raise.

hooshgoo. A cook : Canadian : C. 20. Just possibly ex *hoosh.*

hoot. Money ; payment, wage ; compensation : New Zealand and soon Australia (— 1896). Ex Maori *utu* (money), often pronounced with clipped terminal. Morris.

hoot, care a. Care infinitesimally ; always in negative or interrogative—i.e. potentially or implicatively negative—phrases or sentences : coll. : from ca. 1905. Possibly ex S.E. *hoot,* a cry of disapprobation, a shout expressive of obloquy ; prob. an adoption of U.S. *hoot,* an abbr. of, and used in the same sense as, U.S. *hooter,* an atom, the least bit (1839), Thornton.

hootch. See **hooch.**

hooter. A wooden trumpet designed to make a horrible noise : C. 20 coll. >, by 1930, S.E.

hooting pudding. A plum-pudding containing so few plums that they can be heard hooting to one another across the vast : provincial : from ca. 1860 ; ob.

hoots in hell, not to care two. A military variant (— 1914) of *hoot, care a,* q.v. F. & Gibbons.

hop. A ball, if informal ; a dance : coll. : from ca. 1730. Jane Austen, ' At a little hop at the park, he danced from eight o'clock till four.'—2. (*hop* or *Hop.*) A policeman : low Australian (— 1935). Perhaps suggested by synonymous *cop.*

Hop- in **Hop-Monday** and **-tide** is an error for **Hock-** : C. 16. (*Hob-* for *Hock-* may, as the O.E.D. points out, be only a scribal error.)

hop, on the. (Esp. *catch on the hop.*) Unawares : (orig. low) coll. (— 1868). In that famous ballad, *The Chickaleary Cove.*—2. In the nick of time : coll. : ca. 1872–1905.—3. At a disadvantage : coll. : from ca. 1880 ; ob. Perhaps ex *on the hip* (W.).—4. (Adj.) On the go ; unresting : coll. : from ca. 1890. Milliken.—5. Hence, adj., enjoying oneself, having a riotous time : coll. (— 1923). Manchon.

hop-and-go-kick. A lame person : tailors' : from ca. 1860 ; ob.

hop and hang all summer on the white spruce. A Canadian lumbermen's c.p. : from ca. 1890. John Beames.

hop-harlot. See **hap-harlot,** of which it is an occ. variant.

hop in. To arrive : coll. : from **ca.** 1820 ; virtually †. Cf. *pop in.*

hop it. To depart quickly : coll., orig. Cockney : from ca. 1912. Cf. *hop the twig,* 1. In the form *'op it !,* it is (when not illiterate) a jocular c.p. : see esp. the leading article in *John o' London's Weekly,* March 23, 1935.

hop-merchant. A dancing-master : low coll. : late C. 17–19. B.E. Occ. *hoppy.* Cf. *caper-merchant.*—2. A fiddler : C. 19–20.

hop-o'-my-thumb. A dwarf : coll. : C. 16–20 ; slightly ob. (Palsgrave has *upon,* the usual C. 16 form.) Smollett, ' You pitiful hop-o'-my-thumb coxcomb '. In C. 20, gen. considered S.E. Cf. *Jack Sprat,* q.v.

hop off. To die : 1797, Mary Robinson, ' Must look in upon the rich old jade, before she hops off ' (O.E.D.); ob. Cf. Craven dial. *hop* and *hop the twig,* 2, q.v.

Hop Out. Hopoutre, a suburb of Poperinghe : Western Front military in G.W. F. & Gibbons.

hop-out. A definite challenge to fight : mostly Australian : from ca. 1908. Ex :

hop out, v. To challenge (a person) to fight : lower classes' and military : C. 20. Ibid.

hop-over. An attack : military coll. : 1916. Ibid. Ex *hop the bags,* q.v.—2. Also as v.i. : likewise mostly facetious. B. & P.

hop (or **jump**) **over the broom(stick).** See **broom-stick.**

hop-picker. A harlot : low (? orig. c.) : from ca. 1880. Also *hopping wife.*

*hop-pickers. The queens of all four suits : gambling, c. : from ca. 1885.

hop-pole. A tall, slight person : (low) coll. : 1850, Smedley.

hop the bags. To attack ; ' go over the top ' : military : from 1916. B. & P. Ex sandbags forming the parapet of the trench.

*hop the twig. To depart, esp. if suddenly : orig. (— 1785), c. : from ca. 1860, low ; slightly ob. Grose, 1st ed. ; *All the Year Round,* June 9, 1888,

' *To hop the twig* . . . and the like are more flippant than humorous.' Ex bird-life.—Whence 2, to die : low : 1797, Mary Robinson, in *Walsingham* (cf. *hop off,* above). *Punch,* in its 1st volume, ' Clare pines in secret—hops the twig and goes to glory in white muslin.' Cf. and see **croak, go west, kick the bucket, lose the number of one's mess, slip one's cable, snuff it.**

hop the twigs. See **twigs.**

hop the wag. To play truant or ' Charley Wag ' (q.v.) : low : from ca. 1850 ; ob. Mayhew, ' They often persuaded me to hop the wag.'

hop-thumb. A C. 16–17 variant of *hop-o'-my-thumb,* q.v.

hop whore, pipe thief(, hangman lead the dance) ! A proverbial c.p. of ca. 1530–1660. ' Proverbs ' Heywood ; Davies of Hereford. (Apperson.)

hope (or **I hope**) **it keeps fine for you** ! A military c.p., often ironic, of the G.W. Ernest Raymond, *The Jesting Army,* 1930.

hope (or **I hope**) **your rabbit dies** ! A jocular imprecation : C. 20. E.g. in Dorothy Sayers, *Have His Carcase,* 1932.

hope (**you've got**) **!, what a ;** some hope ! A discouraging c.p. reply to one confident of obtaining some privilege : C. 20, esp. in G.W. Cf. *hopes !, some,* q.v.

hopeful ; much more frequently **young hopeful.** A boy, youth, young man : ironic coll. : from ca. 1855, *cp.* 1720, resp. ' Cuthbert Bede ', in *Tales of College Life,* has the former. Occ. of a girl.

hopes !, some or what. A c.p. expressive of extreme scepticism : C. 20, esp. among the Tommies in the G.W. Cf. *hope you've got !, what a,* above.

Hopkins ; Mr. Hopkins. A lame person : jocular coll. (— 1785) ; ob. Grose, 1st ed. Cf. *hoppy* and :

Hopkins !, don't hurry. In mid-C. 19–20 U.S., ironic to slow persons ; but in C. 17–18 England it implied, Don't be too hasty, and took the form *as well come* (or *hasty*) *as Hopkin(s), that came to jail over night, and was hanged the next morning.* Cf. preceding term.

hopper. The mouth : low : mid-C. 19–20 ; ob.— 2. In error, C. 19, for *hooper,* the wild swan. (O.E.D.)—3. A grasshopper : Australian coll. : late C. 19–20.—4. A sewage-boat or -ship : low, mostly London : C. 20. (M. Harrison, *Spring in Tartarus,* 1935.)

hopper, go a. To go quickly : sporting : **ca.** 1870–1915.

hopper-arsed. Large-bottomed : coll. : late C. 17–early 19. B.E. ; D'Urfey, ' Hopper-arsed Nancy ' ; Grose, ' from . . . resemblance to a small basket, called a hopper '.—2. Sometimes, however, it appears to = shrunken-arsed : B.E.'s definition is susceptible of this meaning ; not so Grose's.

*hopper-docker. A shoe : c. : ca. 1810–50. Vaux. Perhaps a corruption of *hock-dockies,* q.v.

hopping Giles. A cripple : s. (— 1785) >, ca. 1850, coll. ; ob. Ex *St. Giles,* the patron of cripples. Grose, 1st ed. ; *Household Words,* June 27, 1885. Cf. :

hopping Jesus. A lame person : low : from ca. 1860 ; ob. Cf. *creeping Jesus.*

hopping to hell. See **may I go hopping to hell** !

hopping wife. See **hop-picker.** In Anon., *Indoor Paupers,* 1888.

hoppo. A customs-house officer : Anglo-Chinese coll. : from ca. 1710. Ex Chinese *hoo-poo,* the Board of Revenue ; abbr. *hoppo-man.* Yule & Burnell.

hoppy. A lame person : coll. : C. 19–20 ; ob.— 2. A dancing-master : mid-C. 19–20.—3. A fiddler : low coll. (— 1892) ; ob. S. Watson, in *Wops the Waif*.

*hops in, (to have) got one's. (To be) tipsy : c. (— 1933). Charles E. Leach, *On Top of the Underworld*.

hopthalmia. Ophthalmia : medical students' (— 1887). Baumann.

horizontal. A courtesan : fast life : 1886 ; ob. Ware. Ex Fr. *horizontale*. Cf. the next entry, sense 2.—2. A bad crash : Air Force : 1915. F. & Gibbons. Cf. *gutser*.

horizontal refreshment. Food taken standing, esp. a snack at a bar : jocular coll. : from ca. 1890 ; ob.—2. Coïtion : low pedantic coll. : from ca. 1870. Cf. :

horizontalise. To have sexual intercourse : low pedantic : from ca. 1845 ; ob.

horn. The nose, esp. if noisy : C. 19–20 ; ob. low coll. Also *horn(e)y*.—2. As a drink, almost wholly U.S. since C. 18. See Thornton.—3. Gen. in pl., indicative of one's having been cuckolded : despite F. & H., this sense and the v. *horn*, to cuckold, are definitely S.E. : likewise S.E. are most of the *horn(s)* = cuckoldom terms listed by F. & H. ; all that are relevant follow hereinafter.—4. The physical sign of sexual excitement in the male ; in C. 19 often used loosely of women. Low coll. : mid-C. 18–20. Always preceded by the. Cf. *horn, have the*, q.v.—5. The male member : coll. : C. 18 ; being the origin of the preceding sense.

horn, at the sign of the. In cuckoldom : late C. 17–early 19 coll.

horn, come out of the little end of the. To get the worst of a bargain, be reduced in circumstances ; after great efforts, to fail : coll. : the first two senses, C. 17–early 18 ; the third, from ca. 1840 and mostly U.S. Moreover, in the C. 17–18 usages, the form is almost always *be squeezed through a horn*.

horn, cure the. To have sexual intercourse : C. 19–20, low coll.

horn, get or **have the.** To have a priapism : late C. 18–20 : low coll.

horn, in a. A phrase that advises disbelief or refusal : (ex Eng. dial.) mostly U.S., where recorded as early as 1840 ; it never > very gen. in Britain and was † by 1910.

horn, wind one's or **the.** To publish one's having been cuckolded : C. 17–18. Cf. the C. 17–18 proverb, *he had better put his horns in his pocket than wind them*.—2. To break wind : C. 18–mid-19 low.— 3. To blow once so hard : from ca. 1850. In C. 20, gen. *blow one's horn*.

horn and hide, all. (Of cattle.) Nothing but skin and bone : Australia (— 1890). In C. 20, S.E.

horn and the hoof !, by the. C. 17 : ' A Butcher . . . sweares by the horne and the hoofe (a poor othe . . .) ', Day, 1640. (O.E.D.)

horn-colic. A temporary priapism : mid-C. 18– mid 19 low. Grose, 1st ed. (*horn cholick*). Cf. *Irish toothache*, q.v.

[**horn-fair**, as described in Grose, belongs to folklore, not here.]

horn-fisted. With hard, callous hands : nautical coll. : mid-C. 19–20. Bowen.

horn-grower or **-merchant.** A married man : coll. : C. 18.

horn in. To interfere ; v.t. with *on* : U.S., anglicised ca. 1930. Dorothy Sayers, *Have His*

Carcase, 1932, ' Glaisher might not like this horning in on his province.' Ex cattle.

horn-mad. As stark-mad, even at being cuckolded, it is—like *horn-work*—S.E., but as extremely lecherous it is a C. 19–20 (ob.) low coll.

horn-pipe or **hornpipe.** A cry of condemnation by the audience : theatrical : 1885, *The Daily News*, May 6 ; very ob. (Ware.)

horn-pipe, dance the. To be a cuckold : C. 17–18 jocular coll.

horn-pipes in fetters. A jigging dance : Cockney (— 1851) ; † by 1900. Mayhew.

horn-rimmers. Horn-rimmed spectacles : coll. : from ca. 1927. (O.E.D. Sup.) By process of ' the Oxford *-er* '.

*horn-thumb. A pickpocket : ca. 1565–1620. Jonson, ' A child of the horn-thumb, a babe of booty . . . a cut-purse '.

Horncastle, the member for. A cuckold : C. 18– early 19 jocular coll.

horned range(s). A fife-rail ; a shot-rack : nautical coll., the latter naval (and † by 1890) : C. 19–20. Bowen.

Horner, Miss. The female pudend : C. 19–20 (ob.) : low.

hornet. A cantankerous person : (low) coll. : from ca. 1840 ; ob. Ex the S.E. sense, a virulent and persistent enemy. Cf. the ironical Gloucestershire saying, *he is as mild as a hornet*.

horney and **hornie.** See **horny.**

hornification ; hornify. A priapism ; to procure one : late C. 18–20 ; ob. : low coll.

horning, vbl.n. and ppl.adj. of *horn*, 4, q.v.

Hornington, old. The male member : C. 19 low. Cf. *horny*, n.

hornpipe. See **horn-pipe.**—**horns.** See **horn,** n., 3.

horns, draw or **pluck** or **pull** or **shrink in one's.** To retract, withdraw, cool down : coll. : from C. 14, mid-C. 17 (ob.), late C. 16, and C. 15 († by C. 17), resp. All were orig. coll., but they quickly > S.E. ; then, excepting the last, they seem to have been coll. ca. 1760–1890, from which date they have certainly been S.E. Cf. *retire into one's shell*, also ex a snail.

horns-to-sell. A loose wife : coll. : C. 18–mid-19. —2. A cuckold : coll. : same period.

Hornsey, knight of. A cuckold : mid-C. 17– early 19 punning coll. The anon. play, *Lady Alimony*. Cf. *Horncastle, member for.*

hornswoggle. Nonsense, humbug : ca. 1860– 1905. Ex U.S. *hornswoggle*, to cheat, deceive (1852). ' Believed to be of *American* origin ', H., 1864 ; Thornton.

horny, horney, hornie. Scots coll. for the devil : late C. 18–20. Gen. *auld Hornie*.—2. A constable : c. of ca. 1810–70. Vaux. Extant in Anglo-Irish s. : witness E.D.D.—3. The nose : low : ca. 1820–1910. Bee. Ex *horn*, 1.

horny, adj. With rising *membrum* ; disposed for carnal woman : C. 19–20 low coll. Esp. in *feel horny*.

horny, old. (Or with capitals.) The male member : C. 19–20 low coll.—2. See **horny,** n., 1.

horomai ! See **haeremai !**

horrible. Excessive ; immoderate : mid-C. 15– 20 : S.E. till ca. 1830, then coll. Lady Mary Wortley Montagu, 1718, ' This letter is of a horrible length '. (O.E.D.) The same applies to the adv. Cf. :

horrid. Offensive; detested; very bad or objectionable : coll. : from ca. 1665. Esp. as a feminine term of strong aversion. (S.O.D.)

horrid, adv. Horridly; very objectionably : 1615 : coll. till ca. 1830, then low coll., and finally, in C. 20, sol.

horrid horn. A fool, a half-wit : Anglo-Irish of the streets : ca. 1850–1900. Ex Erse *omadhaun*, a brainless fellow. H., 1859.

horridly. An intensive before adjj. denoting qualities objected to : coll. : late C. 18–20.

horrors. (Gen. with *the*.) The first stage of *delirium tremens* : low coll. : from ca. 1859. H., 1860.—2. Low spirits, a fit of horror : coll. : from ca. 1765 ; ob. Goldsmith ; Miss Ferrier ; F. W. Robinson, in *Mr. Stewart's Intentions*, 1864, 'Sermons always gave me the horrors.'—3. (Without *the*.) Sausages : see **chamber of horrors.**—4. In c., handcuffs : from ca. 1860 ; ob.—5. (Rare in singular.) Oro cigarettes : military : 1916–18. Occ. '*orrors*.

Horrors, Chamber of. See **Chamber of Horrors.**

horrors, have the blue. To have *delirium tremens* : coll. (— 1887) ; slightly ob. Baumann. Ex *horrors*. Cf. :

horrors, in the cast-iron (or **stone-wall**). Suffering from delirium tremens : Anglo-Irish : C. 20.

horse. A lottery ticket hired out by the day : ca. 1725–80. Fielding.—2. A day-rule : ca. 1820–50 : legal. (O.E.D.)—3. Work charged for before completion : workmen's : 1760. Abbr. the orig. form, **horse-flesh,** q.v.—4. A £5 note : low : from ca. 1860.—5. (With capitals.) Horsemonger Lane Gaol : c. of ca. 1850–90. Mayhew. Also *the Old Horse*.—6. An arrogant or supercilious officer : nautical (— 1867) ; ob. Smyth.—7. Hence, a strict disciplinarian : naval : mid-C. 19–20 ; ob. Ibid.—8. See **salt horse.**

horse, v. To possess a woman : coll. : C. 17–20, ob. Ex a stallion covering a mare.—2. To flog : C. 19 coll. Cf. *horsed, be* (q.v.).—3. To outdo another, esp. at piece-work : workmen's : ca. 1860–1910. *All the Year Round*, July 13, 1867.—4. See **horse it** and cf. *dead horse* and *horse*, n., 3.

horse, all. (Of a jockey) very small : coll. : 1860, O. W. Holmes. Not typically U.S.)

horse, as good as a shoulder of mutton for or **to a sick.** Utterly useless or worthless : coll. : mid-C. 16–mid-18. Jonson.

horse, as holy as a. Extremely holy : C. 16 coll., somewhat proverbial. Palsgrave.

horse, as strong as a. (Of a person only) very strong : coll. : from ca. 1700. Ned Ward ; Douglas Jerrold, in *Mrs. Caudle*, 'You're not as strong as a horse.' (Apperson.)

horse, eat like a. To have a very large appetite : coll. : C. 18–20.

horse, flog (occ. **mount on) a dead.** 'To engage in fruitless effort' : coll. (in C. 20, S.E.) : from ca. 1840. Ex :

horse, flog (also **work, or work for) the dead.** See **dead horse** and **horse**, n., 3.

horse, old and **one-.** See resp. **old horse** and **one-horse.**

horse, put the cart before the. See **cart.** . . .

horse, put the saddle on the right. To apportion (esp. blame) accurately : coll. : C. 17–18. B.E. Cf. the C. 17–mid-18 proverbial *the fault of the horse is put on the saddle.*

horse, ride (occ. **mount) the high.** To put on airs, stand on one's dignity ; (haughtily) take offence :

coll. : from ca. 1715. Addison has *great*, while in C. 19–20 one occ. finds *be on* or *get on*. Prob. ex a *high hobby-horse* in the nursery.

horse, salt. See **salt horse.**

horse, sick as a. Very sick without vomiting : late C. 17–19 : coll.

horse, talk. To talk big or boastingly : coll. : 1891, Kipling. Ex *talk horse*, i.e. of the turf. (O.E.D.)

horse, the gray mare is the better. See **gray mare.**

horse and cart. Heart : rhyming s. (— 1909). Ware.

horse and foot. With all one's strength : coll. : ca. 1600–1760. (Extant in dial.) Horace Walpole.

horse and harness, come for. That is, for one's own ends : coll. : C. 15–16. Caxton. (O.E.D.)

horse and man. (Often preceded by *undone*.) Completely : C. 17 coll. ? ex jousting.

horse !, and thou shalt have grass,—live. Well, let's wait and see ! Later on, we'll see ! In C. 18–early 19, coll., as in Swift's *Polite Conversation* ; then dial., mainly Lancashire. (Apperson.)

horse away. To spend in a lottery (cf. *horse*, n., 1).

horse-box. The mess-room of the sergeant-major(s) of Marines : naval : late C. 19–20. Bowen.—2. See :

horse-boxes. (Rare in singular.) 'The senior military officers' cabins in the old naval troopers' : naval : ca. 1850–1910. Bowen.

horse-breaker. A woman hired to ride in the park : ca. 1860–70 : Society.—2. Hence, a courtesan given to riding, esp. in the park : Society (— 1864) ; ob. by 1900, † by 1915. *Public Opinion*, Sept. 30, 1865, 'These *demi-monde* people, anonymas, horse-breakers, hetairæ . . . are by degrees pushing their way into society.'

horse-buss. A resounding kiss ; a bite : coll. (— 1785) ; † by 1890. Grose, 1st ed. A development from *horse-kiss*, q.v.

horse-capper (or **-coper**), **-courser** (or **-coser**), or **-chaunter.** A dealer in worthless or tampered horses. The last, C. 19–20 (ob.) has always been low coll. ; *h.-capper* is a corruption of *h.-coper*, which, despite its taint of unsavouriness, was always S.E. ; both *-courser*, low coll. after ca. 1750, and *-coser* were orig. S.E., the latter being somewhat dial.

horse-collar. A halter : an occ. variation, mainly C. 18, of *horse('s)-nightcap*, q.v.—2. The female pudend : low : C. 19–20 ; ob.—3. A very long wide collar : tailors' : from ca. 1860.

horse-coser or **-courser.** See **horse-capper.**

horse-duffing. See **duff,** v., and **duffing** (esp. *cattle-duffing*).

horse-faker. A horse-dealer : low (— 1887). Baumann. Cf. *horse-capper.*

horse-flesh. See **horse,** n., 3 ; **horse it ;** and **dead horse.** (*Horse-flesh* is orig.—C. 17—printers' s.)

horse foaled on an acorn, a or **the.** The gallows : ca. 1670–1850 : low proverbial > literary s. Smollett, Grose ; Lytton, Ainsworth.—2. 'The triangles or crossed halberds under which soldiers were flogged ', F. & H. : ca. 1790–1870 : military.

horse-godmother. 'A large masculine woman', Grose, 1st ed. : (rather low) coll. : ca. 1570–1890 ; now—and perhaps orig.—dial. Wolcot, 'In woman angel sweetness let me see, | No galloping horse-godmother for me ' ; Thackeray.

horse is soon carried, a short. ' A little Business is soon Dispatched,' B.E. : coll. : ca. 1670–1770.

horse is troubled with corns, that. That horse is foundered : jocular coll. : mid-C. 17–mid-18.

horse it. To charge, in one's week's tally, for work not yet completed, the unprofitable remainder being *dead horse*, q.v. : workmen's (— 1857).—2. See also **horse**, n., 3, and cf. *horse*, v., 2.—3. To work hard : coll. : C. 20.

horse-kiss. A rough kiss : coll. : ca. 1670–1760. Cf. *horse-buss*, q.v. Extant in dial. as ' a pretended kiss which is really a bite,' E.D.D.

horse ladder, send for a. To send on a fool's errand : rural (esp. Wiltshire) coll. : mid-C. 18–early 19. The victim was told that it was needed *to get up the horses* (*to finish a hay-mow* : Grose, 3rd ed.).

horse-latitudes. That space in the Atlantic which, lying north of the trade winds, is noted for baffling winds : nautical : from ca. 1775 ; ob. ' Perhaps adapted from Sp. *golfo de las yeguas*, " the gulph of mares, so the Spaniards call the great ocean, betwixt Spain and the Canary Islands " (Stevens), supposed to be from contrast with the *golfo de las damas* (of ladies), from Canaries to West Indies, usually smooth and with favourable winds,' W.

horse-laugh. A guffaw : coll. >, ca. 1890, S.E. : from ca. 1710. Pope. ? punning *hoarse*.

horse-leech. An insatiable person ; a whore : coll. : mid-C. 16–mid-17. Jonson. Prob. ex :— 2. A quack : late C. 16–17. Hall, in *Satires*, 1597, ' No horse-leech but will look for larger fee.' Ex lit. S.E. sense.—3. Whence too : an extortioner ; a miser : coll. : from ca. 1545 ; ob. (This sense should not, perhaps, be distinguished from the first. The O.E.D. considers it S.E.)

horse-load to a cart-load, fall away from a. To put on weight suddenly : ironic coll. : mid-C. 17–early 19. B.E. ; Swift.

horse-marine. An awkward person : ca. 1830–60. H., 1860. Perhaps ex the heraldic and † *horse-marine*, a sea-horse. W. Cf.

horse-marines, the. ' A mythical corps, very commonly cited in jokes and quizzes on the innocent ', F. & H. : coll. : from ca. 1820 : ob., except in form *the marines*. Scott, ' Come, none of your quizzing . . . Do you think we belong to the horse-marines ? ' Imm. ex :—2. The 17th Lancers: military : C. 19–20 ; ob. F. & Gibbons. In 1796, on a passage to the West Indies, they did duty as marines.

horse-marines !, tell that to the. Don't be silly !, or Do you think I'm a fool ? ! Coll. : ca. 1830–1910. (See **marines**.) Occ. amplified with *the sailors won't believe it* or *when they're riding at anchor*. Perhaps suggested by † *horse-marine*, sea-horse (in heraldry) : W.

horse-milliner. As a dandified trooper, hardly eligible.—2. A saddle- and harness-maker : coll. : ca. 1815–80. Ex the S.E. sense.

horse-nails. Money, esp. cash : low (— 1859). Cf. *brads*. H., 1st ed. Cf. *haddock*.

horse-nails, feed on. ' So to play as not so much to advance your own score as to keep down your opponent's,' F. & H. : cribbage : ca. 1860–1914.

horse-nails, knock into. To defeat heavily : low coll. : from ca. 1870 ; ob. Cf. *knock into a cocked hat*.

horse- or horse's-nightcap. A halter ; esp. in *die in a horse('s)-nightcap*, to be hanged : low coll.,

ex low s. (? ex c.) : late C. 16–19. Cf. *anodyne necklace, choker, hempen cravat, Tyburn tippet*.

horse of another colour, (that's) a. (That is) quite another matter : coll. (in C. 20, S.E.) : orig. (1790's) U.S., anglicised ca. 1840 by Barham. Undoubtedly suggested by Shakespeare's ' My purpose is indeed a horse of that colour ' (*Twelfth Night*, II, iii, 181). O.E.D. and Sup.

Horse of Troy, the. The collier *River Clyde* : naval and military : 1915. F. & Gibbons. She lay off ' V Beach ', near Cape Helles, throughout the fighting on Gallipoli.

horse-pox. An intensive of *pox*, esp. in adjuration or asseveration : mid-C. 17–18 low coll. E.g. ' Ay, with a horse-pox '.

horse-Protestant. A churchman : tailors' : from ca. 1860 ; ob.

horse-sense. Common sense, esp. if unrefined and somewhat earthy : orig. (1833), U.S. ; anglicised ca 1895 as a coll.

horse-shoe. The female pudend : C. 18–20 (ob.) low. Cf. *horse-collar*.—2. (Gen. *Horseshoe*.) H. L. Collins, the Australian test captain in 1926 : cricketers' : from 1926. Ex his luck in winning the toss. (*Who's Who in World Cricket*, 1934.)

horse sick, enough . . . See **sick, enough to make a horse**.

horse-sovereign. ' A twenty-shilling piece with Pistrucci's effigies of St. George and the Dragon ', F. & H. : coll. (mostly low) : ca. 1870–1900. *London Figaro*, Jan. 26, 1871.

horse to market, run before one's. To count unhatched chickens : coll. : late C. 16–17. Shakespeare. (O.E.D.)

horse with (or Bayard of) ten toes, ride (up)on a. To walk : coll. : C. 17–early 19. Cf. *marrowbone* (punning *Marylebone*) *stage*[*-coach*] and *Shanks's mare*, qq.v.

horsed, be. To be flogged ; to take on one's back a person to be flogged : coll. : ca. 1675–1895. ' Hudibras ' Butler ; Smollett ; *Notes and Queries*, Jan. 1, 1881. Ex the wooden horse used as a flogging stool.

horses and mares, play at. To coït : schoolboys' : from ca. 1850 ; ob.

horse's head is swollen so big that he cannot come out of the stable, his. He owes much money to the ostler : a C. 17 c.p.

horse's leg. A bassoon : military bandsmen's (— 1909). Ware, ' From its shape '.

horse's meal. Food without drink (esp. without strong liquor) : ca. 1780–1850 : s. >, by 1820, coll. Grose, 1st ed. Cf. *dog's supper* and dial. *horse-feast*.

horse's necklace. A contemporaneous variant of *horse* (or *horse's*)*-nightcap*, q.v.

horse's nightcap. See **horse-nightcap**, than which it is more gen.

horses together, they cannot set (occ. **hitch** or **stable**) **their.** They cannot agree : mid-C. 17–18 coll., as in Swift and Garrick ; C. 19–20 dial.

horstile. See **hostile**.

horsy-face. An unpopular officer, esp. if he had a long face : naval : mid-C. 19–20 ; slightly ob. Bowen.

hortus. A perfect example of C. 18 pedantic s. : the female privy parts. Bailey. L. for ' garden ', q.v.

hose, in my other. Expressive of refusal or disbelief : late C. 16–17 coll. Florio. The early C. 20 equivalent is *not in these trousers*. Cf. *I don't think !, in a horn*, and *over the left*, qq.v.

hosed and shot. (Gen. preceded by *come in* and in past tense.) Born to a good estate : ca. 1670–1750. Cf. *born with a silver spoon in one's mouth*, q.v.

hospital game. Football, esp. Rugby : non-aristocratic coll. : 1897 ; ob. Ware, 'From the harvest of broken bones it produces '.

hospitality, partake of Her or **His Majesty's. To** be in gaol : jocular coll. : 1894 (O.E.D. Sup.).

hoss, as a familiar term of address, is U.S. (1844), but *old hoss*, occ. *old horse* (q.v.), has to some extent been anglicised.—2. Moreover, *hoss* is, in England, a sol. (— 1887) for *horse*. Baumann.

host, mine, a tavern-keeper, is by F. & H. considered coll., but this is extremely doubtful : in C. 20, it is a journalistic cliché. Likewise *to reckon without one's host,* to count one's chickens before they are hatched, was orig. (C. 15), in this its fig. sense, coll., to judge by Caxton's 'It ys sayd in comyn that . . .' (see O.E.D.) ; but it very soon > S.E.

[**hosteler** is mentioned here because Grose wrongly held it to be coll. and gave it the punning etymology of *oat-stealer*.]

hostile ; often pronounced *horstile.* Angry, annoyed ; esp. *go hostile,* to get angry : Australian and New Zealand military : in G.W.—and after.

hostilities (only). Those who joined the Navy for ' the duration of hostilities only ' : naval : 1914–18. Bowen. Cf. *duration,* q.v.

hot. A mellay at football ; a crowd : Winchester College (— 1878). The second sense is ob.

hot, v.i. To crowd, or form a mob : Winchester College (— 1878) ; ob. Also *hot down* and *hot up* : R. G. K. Wrench.—2. To heat : coll. from mid-C. 19 ; earlier—from late M.E.—it was S.E. ; but in C. 20, except when playfully or jocularly among the cultured, it is low coll.—indeed almost a sol.—3. To reprimand severely : coll. : 1920 (O.E.D. Sup.). Ex *give it hot,* in the same sense.

hot, adj. Of F. & H.'s six senses, two—lustful (or passionate) and violent (sharp, severe)—have always been S.E., as, of course, has *hot-blooded,* amorous, lecherous.—2. Alive ; vehement : coll. : from ca. 1860.—3. Very reckless, boisterous ; careless of decorum ; (of a literary work) licentious : coll. : from ca. 1885. J. Runciman, in *The Chequers,* 1888.—4. In c., well known to the police : from ca. 1830 ; ob. (F. & H.'s appended senses, dangerous and uncomfortable, are S.E.)—5. Venereally diseased : low : C. 19–20 (? ob.).—6. (Of a horse, in C. 20 also of persons) much betted-on. Esp. in *hot favourite.* Orig. (1894) racing, from ca. 1905, gen. sporting s.—7. Exceedingly skilful : C. 20. Cf. *hot on* and *hot stuff,* qq.v. Collinson.—8. In C. 20 insurance s., applied to a very likely insurer, a promising ' prospect ', q.v. Ex *hot* in children's games.—9. Excessive, extreme : from ca. 1910. C. J. Dennis. Cf. *hot, make it,* q.v.—10. (Of a Treasury bill) newly issued : coll. : 1928. O.E.D. (Sup.). Cf. :—11. Novel, new : Bootham School (— 1925) ; by 1933, gen. *Dict. of Bootham Slang.*

hot, catch or **get it ; give it hot.** To be severely thrashed, defeated, or reprimanded ; to thrash, defeat, reprimand severely : coll. : from ca. 1680 for *give,* ca. 1859 *catch,* and 1872 *get.*

hot, cop it. See *cop,* v., 2.

hot, make it. To ask too much ; exaggerate grossly ; in short, to behave as if one were ignorant of the limits and limitations imposed by the commonest decency : C. 20 s. >, by 1930, coll. Esp. in

don't make it too hot ! Prob. ex S.E. *make it hot,* i.e. uncomfortable, *for.*

hot, not so. Bad ; unattractive ; inefficient ; ineffective : from ca. 1930. Ex U.S.

hot a stomach as to burn the clothes off his back, have so. To pawn one's clothes for drink : mid-C. 18–early 19 : coll. Grose, 2nd ed.

hot air. Boastful or exaggerated talk ; talk for the sake of effect : from ca. 1910. Ex U.S., where used by George Ade in 1899.—2. Hence, *hot-air merchant,* rare in England, and *hot-air artist,* a person indulging in this sort of thing : anglicised ca. 1913. (O.E.D. Sup.).—3. For *hot-air round,* see *round,* n., 2.

hot and hot, adj.-adv. and n. (Dishes) served, in succession, so soon as cooked : 1771, Smollett, the adj.-adv. ; 1842, Tennyson, the n. : coll. till ca. 1880, then S.E. Occ. in fig. usage. (O.E.D.)

hot and strong, give it (to) a person. ' To punish . . . severely, either physically or verbally ' : coll. : late C. 19–20. (Lyell.)

hot-arsed. Extremely lascivious (only of women) : low coll. : C. 19–20. Cf. S.E. † *hot-backed.*

hot as similes to be considered for this dictionary are these :—(Perhaps, but most probably not) *hot as* (a) *toast,* C. 15–18, and *warm as* (a) *toast,* C. 19–20, *hot as coals,* ca. 1550–1620, and *hot as fire ; hot as blazes,* C. 19–20, however, is downright s., while *hot as hell* is merely coll. ; *hot as buggery* is low s. > low coll. ; (of a person only) *hot as if* (e.g.) *he had a bellyful of wasps and salamanders,* ca. 1700–50.

hot at. See *hot on.*—**hot beef.** See *hot meat.*

*****hot beef, give.** To cry ' stop thief ' : underworld rhyming s. (— 1877) ; ob. Horsley. Cf. *beef,* n.

hot blanketeer. ' A woman who pawns her blankets while they are warm from being slept in—she redeeming them before night-time ' : proletarian : late C. 19–20 ; ob. Ware.

hot bricks, like a cat on, adj. and adv. Restive(ly) ; uncomfortable (or -ly) : coll. : from ca. 1880. J. S. Winter, ' Lady Mainwaring looked . . . like a cat on hot bricks.'

hot cakes, like. See *cakes, like hot.*

hot coppers. (Occ. singular.) The parched throat to be expected after a drinking-bout : low : 1830, Pierce Egan ; ob. Thackeray, ' " Nothing like that beer ", he remarked, " when the coppers are hot." ' Cf. *cool one's copper,* also *mouth.*

hot corner. ' A position in which one is threatened or bullied ' : non-aristocratic coll. : ' 1854 on ', says Ware.

hot cross bun. Son : theatrical rhyming s. : late C. 19–20. *The Evening Standard,* Aug. 19, 1931.

hot down. See *hot,* v., 1.

hot flannel ; warm flannel ; flannel. A drink of gin and beer, heated after the addition of sugar, nutmeg, etc : coll. : resp. 1789 (Parker), 1823 (Bee), and 1858 (Mayhew). Cf. *hot-stopping,* q.v.

[**hot-foot,** in hot haste, like † *hot-house,* a brothel, is S.E.—despite F. & H.]

hot gospeller. A fanatical preacher, or a preaching fanatic : coll. (— 1893). Since G.W., gen. thought to have come from the U.S.—an opinion prob. wrong.

hot lot. A late C. 19–20 variant of *hot member,* q.v. Manchon.

hot meat ; occ. **hot mutton** or **beef.** A fast woman, a prostitute ; the female pudend · low : C. 19. Cf. *bit,* q.v.

hot member ; hot un. A debauchee, an either

sex rake : C. 19–20 (ob. the former).—2. A person contemptuous of the conventions : C. 19–20. (Both senses are low coll.)—3. A dangerous and/or quarrelsome person : low s. > coll. : from ca. 1880, *h. m.* being very ob. Ware. (The earlier term— *h. m.*—may have been suggested by *hot shot*, q.v.) Cf. *hot stuff*, q.v.

hot milk. The *semen virile* : low : C. 19–20 (? ob.).

hot on. Extremely severe towards or in respect of : C. 20 s. > coll.—2. Unusually good or skilful at : from ca. 1895 : coll. Variant, *hot at.* Cf. *hot stuff* (*at* or *on*).

hot place, the. Hell : orig. (ca. 1840) euphemistic ; but from ca. 1890, coll. *Blackwood's Magazine*, March, 1891.

hot pot, a heated drink of ale and brandy, has, despite Grose and F. & H., been prob. always S.E. Cf. *hot flannel* and *huckle-my-buff*, qq.v.

hot potato. A waiter : (approximately) rhyming s. : 1880 : orig. and mainly music-halls'. Ware.

hot potato, drop like a. To abandon with—often callous or unseemly—alacrity : (orig. low) coll. >, ca. 1920, S.E. : from before 1893. F. & H.

hot press. 'A particularly vigorous comb by the Press Gang' : nautical : late C. 18–mid-19. Bowen (The Press Gang was disenrolled in 1835.)

hot pudding for supper, have a. (Of women only) to coït : low : C. 19–20. Ex *pudding*, the male member.

*hot seat. A variation of the confidence trick : c. : from ca. 1919. Charles E. Leach, *On Top of the Underworld*, 1933. Cf. *rosary.*

hot shot (indeed), a ; hot shot in a mustard pot (when both one's heels stand right up), a. Always preceded by the v. *to be*, which is gen. in the present tense, and indicative of contemptuous irony : ca. 1650–1750. Ex *hot-shot*, one who shoots eagerly with a firearm.

hot socks. 'Gaily coloured hose', C. J. Dennis : Australian (– 1916).

hot stomach. See **hot a stomach . . .**

hot-stopping. Hot spirits and water : 1861, Whyte-Melville, 'No man can drink hot-stopping the last thing at night, and get up in the morning without remembering that he has done so ' (O.E.D.) ; ob. Cf. *hot flannel* and *hot tiger*, qq.v.

hot stuff. A person very excellent, skilful or energetic (*at*, e.g., a game) : coll. : from the early 1890's.—2. A person out of the ordinary in degree, —dangerous,—(mostly of women) sexually hot or lax : coll. : C. 20. Collinson.—3. A thing that is remarkable, behaviour that is either remarkable or censurable, a striking action : coll. : C. 20. In G.W. military s. : heavy shelling.—4. Hence as adj. or as an admiring exclamation : coll. : from ca. 1910. For all four senses, see esp. Collinson and the O.E.D. (Sup.).

hot-stuff. v. To requisition : military : 1914. Ex the n. Whence :

hot-stuffer. A thief : an illicit scrounger : military : 1915. B. & P.

hot tiger. Hot-spiced ale and sherry : Oxford University (– 1860) ; ob. by 1919, † by 1930. Cf. *hot flannel, hot pot,* and *hot-stopping*, qq.v.

hot time (of it), give (a person) a. To make him thoroughly uncomfortable ; to reprimand severely : coll. : late C. 19–20. Manchon. See also **hot catch it.**

hot un. See **hot member** and **hot stuff.**

hot up. See **hot, v., 1.**

hot water. (Constructed, sense 1 with *cost* (*one*), sense 2 with *be in*.) Trouble ; great discomfort : coll. : ca. 1535–1750.—2. Hence, a scrape : coll. : from ca. 1760. Gayton, 1659, 'This same search hath not cost me hot water (as they say)',—cited by Apperson ; Lord Malmesbury, 1765, 'We are kept, to use the modern phrase, in hot water ',—cited by O.E.D. ; *Punch's Almanack*, Nov. 29, 1846, 'The *Times* newspaper first printed by steam, 1814, and has kept the country in hot water ever since.' (Until ca. 1890, *The Times*, until ca. 1900 *Punch*, had much less of a reputation for respectability than they now enjoy (?).)

hot-water play. A farce : theatrical coll., adopted in 1885 from U.S. ; ob. Ware, 'The actors [? characters] in the play always being in difficulties until the fall of the curtain '.

hot with. Spirits with hot water and sugar : coll. : 1837 (S.O.D.) ; Thackeray, 1862, fig. (O.E.D.) Cf. *cider and* and *cold without*, and contrast Fr. *café avec.*

[**hotch-potch,** despite F. & H., has always been S.E.]

hotel ; occ. **Cupid's hotel** or **Cupid's Arms.** The female pudendum : low : C. 19–20, ob. Cf. *Cock Inn.* (This kind of coll. humour is moribund, thank heaven !)

hotel-barbering, n. Bilking ; lodging at hotels and departing without paying the bill : low (– 1892) ; † by 1930. *The Daily Chronicle*, March 28, 1892.

hotel-beat. 'A frequenter of hotels with no means of payment' : adopted, before 1909, from U.S. (Ware.)

Hotel Lockhart. A lower classes' c.p. 'satirical attack upon doubtful grandeur' : ca. 1890–1914. Ware.

hotel warming-pan. A chambermaid : C. 19–20 ob. In C. 18, *Scotch warming-pan*. A C. 19–20 variant : *warming-pan.*

Hotspurs, you are none of the. A c.p. retort to, or comment on, a noisy braggart, with the implication that he is a coward : ca. 1720–1870. Cf. *Hastings sort*, q.v.

Hottentot. 'A stranger come from the West [sc. of London]', G. R. Sims : East End of London (– 1880) ; † by 1919. Esp. in the playful street-cry, *Hottentots !*—2. A fool : low coll. : C. 19. Ex the Hottentots' reputation for stupidity.

hottie. An Edinburgh High School term for ' one who has something pinned to his back of which he knows nothing ', E.D.D. : mid-C. 19–20.

hough ; occ., erroneously, **hok.** To kick ; act roughly towards : Hampton Grammar School (– 1935). Ex :—2. To hack, in Rugby football : ibid. : from ca. 1920.

hougher, dirty. A term of contempt : Hampton Grammar School (– 1935). Ex sense 1 of *hough.*

houghing. Rough or ' dirty ' play : ibid. : from ca. 1925. Ex *hough*, q.v.

hound. An undergraduate not on the foundation : King's College, Cambridge : late C. 18–early 19. *The Anecdotes of Bowyer.*—2. Applied pejoratively to a man, it is S.E., whence *dirty dog*, whence *dusty pup*, q.v. But when = person, as in *drink-hound*, a drunkard (Evelyn Waugh, *Vile Bodies*, 1930) and *gloom-hound*, a gloomy person (John G. Brandon, *The One-Minute Murder*, 1934), it is s., verging on coll., of the upper and upper-middle classes, and it dates from ca. 1919. Cf. the use of *wallah.*—3. Orderly officer : Army officers' : from ca. 1925. Suggested by *orderly dog,* q.v.

Hounslow Heath. The teeth : rhyming s. (— 1857). ' Ducange Anglicus.' Also *Hampstead Heath,* which displaced it ca. 1890.

houri of Fleet Street. A harlot : orig. (ca. 1880) journalistic, > gen. ca. 1890, † ca. 1910.

house, the audience in a theatre, is always S.E. (Abbr. *playhouse.*)—2. An ' exclusive set at parties and dances—a group whose members sit together and dance together ' : middle classes' (— 1909); virtually †. Ware. (Post-War Society would speak of a ' gang '.)—3. A gambling form of lotto : military s. (from late 1890's) >, by 1915, coll. Its other name, *box and numbers,* partly explains the semantics. See also **little Jimmy** in the Addenda. Frank Richards, *Old-Soldier Sahib,* 1936, gives, at pp. 69–72, an excellent account of the game.—4, 5. See senses 4, 5 of :

House, always preceded by **the.** The Stock Exchange : coll. : from ca. 1810.—2. The House of Commons : from ca. 1820 : coll. till C. 20, then S.E. ' Jon Bee ', 1823.—3. Christ Church, Oxford : from ca. 1868 : s. till ca. 1890, then coll. till ca. 1930, then S.E.; cf. *Peterhouse,* q.v. Dorothy Sayers, *Clouds of Witness,* 1926, ' " Used to know him at the House." . . . " Whose house ? " . . . " Oh, Christ Church, Oxford." '—4. The workhouse : proletarian coll. (— 1861). Mayhew.—5. The public-house : coll., mostly Cockney (— 1887). Baumann.

house, be atop of (occ. **on**) **the.** A C. 17 variant of *housetop, be at the,* q.v.

House, father of the. The oldest-elected member of the House of Commons : from ca. 1850 : Parliamentary s. >, ca. 1890, coll.

house-bit ; occ. **-keeper** or **-piece.** A paramour servant : low : from ca. 1850 ; ob.

house broke up. A military c.p. indicative of complete despair : from ca. 1870 ; ob. Ware.

house-dove. A stay-at-home : 1579 (S.O.D.) : coll. till ca. 1600, then S.E. ; † by 1800.

house-farmer or **-knacker.** Resp. London coll. and s. for ' landlord ', gen. pl., as in Baumann, who, in 1887, scathingly describes them as ' Londoner Blutsauger, die den Armen schlechte, wohlfeile Wohnungen vermieten.'

house of call. ' The usual lodging Place of Journey-men Tailors ', B.E. : late C. 17–18 tailors' s. > coll. in early C. 18 and S.E. by 1790. (Also of other occupations.)

house of civil reception. A brothel : C. 18–early 19 coll. Grose.

House of Commons ; house of office. A water-closet : the former, always s.; the latter, orig. coll. but S.E. by 1690. Resp. mid-C. 19–20, ob ; C. 17–19. Chapman, in *May-Day,* 1611, ' No room save you turn out my wife's coal-house, and her other house of office attached to it ' ; Smollett

house of parliament. A ' convention of workmen in their shop ' : tailors' (— 1909). Ware. Cf. a printer's ' chapel '.

house on fire, like a. Very quickly or energetically : coll. : from ca. 1805. W. Irving, 1809, ' like five hundred houses on fire ' ; 1837, Dickens. (O.E.D.)

house on one's head, pull (in C. 19 occ. **bring**) **an old.** To involve oneself in trouble : coll. : C. 17–mid-19. Topsell. (O.E.D.)

house out of the windows, throw (in C. 16–17 occ **cast,** in C. 17 often **fling**) **the.** To make a great noise or disturbance in a house : mid-C. 16–mid-19 coll., then dial. Dickens, in *Boz,* quotes it in form ' regularly turned out o' windows ', i.e. in an uproar. (Apperson.)

house-roof, up in the. See **housetop, be at the.**

house-tailor. An upholsterer : coll. : late C. 17–18. B.E.

house-wallah. One who, esp. a Gypsy who, lives in a house in contradistinction to a tent : Gypsies' coll. (— 1900), esp. in Hampshire. E.D.D.

house that Jack built, the. A prison : low : from ca. 1860 ; ob. Baumann.—2. ' The first permanent building in the Whale Island Gunnery School ' : naval : late C. 19–20 ; slightly ob. Bowen.

house (or **tenement** or **apartments**) **to let.** A widow : resp. mid-C. 18–20 (ob.), C. 18–19, C. 19–20 (ob.). Grose, 2nd ed.

house under the hill. The female pudend : low : C. 19–20 ; ob.

housebreaker. A breaker-up of houses : industrial : from ca. 1895. Ware.

household brigade, join the. (Of men) to marry : coll. (— 1881) ; ob. *Home Tidings,* April, 1881. Punning the name of the English regiment.

Houseman. A member of the college of Christ Church, Oxford : from ca. 1868 : orig. s. ; by 1890, coll. : by 1905, familiar S.E. *The Oxford Spectator,* late 1868, ' While [it] is called Christ Church by strangers, by others it is called the House, and they themselves Housemen.' Ob. (O.E.D.)

houser. A house-match : Public Schools' : from late 1890's. P. G. Wodehouse, *Tales of St. Austin's,* 1903.

houses, (as) safe as. Perfectly safe : coll. : 1859 (O.E.D.). E. Yates, 1864, ' I have the means of doing that, as safe as houses.' Perhaps, as H. suggests, the phrase arose ' when the railway bubbles began to burst and speculation again favoured houses '.

housetop (or **top of the house** or, C. 16–early 17, **house-roof), be at** (or **up in**) **the.** To be, become, very angry (cf. *hit the roof*) : coll. : *up in,* ca. 1540–1660 ; *at,* ca. 1630–1800, then dial. Anon., *Scoggin's Jests,* 1626. (Apperson.) Cf. *up in the boughs* (see at **boughs**).

housewife. The *pudendum muliebre* : C. 19–20 (ob.) low. (The other senses listed by F. & H. are S.E.)

housey, adj. Belonging to the Hospital : Christ's Hospital : C. 19–20.

housey-housey ! The c.p. cry with which players of ' House ' are summoned : coll., mostly military : C. 20.

housle. To hustle, of which, presumably, it is a corruption : Winchester College : from ca. 1850 ; ob. by 1920.

hove-down. Bed-ridden, confined to bed : nautical (— 1887). Baumann.

hoveller. A beach-thief, a lawless boatman : nautical (in C. 20, S.E.) : from before 1769, when recorded by Falconer. Ex his living in a hovel. Cf. *beach-comber,* q.v.

how. A howitzer : military coll. : late 1914. B. & P.

how !, and. The U.S. variant, partly anglicised by 1933, of the English *rather !* Now verging on coll. By ellipsis, thus : ' " Fred Perry is a great player." —" And how [very great a player he is] ! " ' ; ' " That's pleasant."—" And *how* [pleasant] ! " '

how, as. (= *how* = conjunction *that.*) E.g. ' I

do not know as how I can '; frequently *seeing as how*. Sol.: mid-C. 17–20; earlier, S.E. Cf. *as* = conjunction *that*.—2. Interrogatively, *as how ?* = in what way ?: coll.: C. 20. Ronald Knox, *Still Dead*, 1934, ' " I think he's too stupid . . ." " As how ?" " Oo, I mean about why he ran away . . ." ' A blend, or perhaps a confusion, of *as for instance* and *how*.—3. Also, tautologically, as in *The Morning Post*, July 8, 1785, ' *Bet Cox* swears . . . that, *though as how* she was with the Prince, one night when he was drunk, yet that did not compensate her for the wear and tear with his attendants,' quoted in *Beside the Seaside*, 1934.

how !, here's. See **here's.**

how and about. Concerning; all about: coll.: ca. 1750–1830. Richardson, in *Grandison*, ' Emily wrote you all how-and-about it.' (O.E.D., which—wrongly, I feel—gives it as S.E.)

how are you off for soap ? A city c.p. of ca. 1830–45. Marryat. in *Peter Simple*, ' Well, Reefer, how are you off for soap ? '

how came, or come, you so ? (Often hyphenated and occ. preceded by *Lord !*) Intoxicated : 1816 (O.E.D. Sup.): low s. >, by 1840, coll.; ob. by 1880, † by 1900.

how do or **how-do.** A shortening of *how do you do ?* : Society (— 1887). Baumann.

how do we go ? What chance is there (' of obtaining something unspecified yet known to the person questioned ') ? : military c.p.: 1915 ; slightly ob. B. & P. Prob. an abbr. of *how do we go about (getting) it ?*

how-do-you-do, how-d'ye-do. A fuss, a noisy difficulty, a ' mess' : low coll.: from ca. 1835. In C. 20, gen. preceded by (*a*) *pretty*.

how do you like your eggs cooked or **done ?** An Australian c.p. (from ca. 1908), gen. as an unkind comment on misfortune : very soon, however, there was evolved the c.p. reply, *scrambled, like your brains, yer* (or *you*) *bastard !*

how-d'ye-do. A shoe : from ca. 1890. P. P. *Rhyming Slang*, 1932.

how goes ? How goes it ? : C. 20. Dorothy Sayers, *Have His Carcase*, 1932.

how-howish. See **howish.**

how is that for high ? ; how the blazes ! See resp. **high** and **blazes.**

how'll you have it ? See **how will . . .**

how many more ? How many more minutes (till . . .) ? : Bootham School coll. (— 1925). Anon., *Dict. of Bootham Slang*.

how much ? What do you say, mean ? A coll. request for an explanation : from ca. 1850 ; not quite extinct, though ob. so early as 1914. F. Smedley, 1852, ' " Then my answer must . . . depend on the . . ." " On the how much ? " inquired Frere, considerably mystified.'

how we apples swim ! A c.p. applied to a parvenu, a pretender, a person ' out of the water': mid-C. 17–19. Hogarth, in *Works*, vol. iii, ' He assumes a consequential air . . . and strutting among the historical artists cries, how we apples swim.' In C. 19 often tagged with *quoth the horseturd.* Cf. *humble-bee* . . ., q.v.

how will (gen. **how'll**) **you have it ?** Either a specific or, hence, a vague general invitation to take a drink. Lyell gives, as the commonest coll. invitations to drink, the following, all of which are of late C. 19–20, except the last two—rarely heard before ca. 1910 :—*what'll you have ?, what's yours ?, how'll you have it ?, what is it ?, name yours !, let's*

have one !, *what about a small spot ?* and *d'you feel like a small spot ?* Cf. *what's your poison ?* (see **poison**) or *name your poison !*

Howard's Garbage. See **Green Howards.** Contrast :

Howard's Greens, the. The 24th Foot Regiment, in late C. 19–20 the South Wales Borderers : military : from ca. 1720 ; ob. Ex its facings and the name of its colonel, 1717–37. Contrast *Green Howards*.

howdy, -ie. A midwife : low Scots coll. (and Northern dial.) : C. 18–20, ob. ? ex *holdie* ex *hold*, friendly. Ramsay, Scott, Galt. (O.E.D. ; E.D.D.) —2. (Only **howdy**) how do you do ? : C. 19–20 dial. and slightly ob. low coll.

howdydo ? How do you do ? : C. 19–20 : coll. ; now archaic. (Denis Mackail, *Summer Leaves*, 1934.)

however. (Interrogative and conjunctive as in ' However did you manage it ? ') How, in any manner or circumstances ? : coll. : 1871. S.O.D.— 2. After *but*. See **but . . . however.**—3. Placed at the end of a sentence, *however* is coll. : mid-C. 19–20. E.D.D.

howish. Vaguely feeling somewhat indisposed : mid-C. 18–early 19.—2. ' All overish ' (q.v.) : late C. 18–mid-19. Both coll. In late C. 17–early 19, also *I know not howish* and *I don't know howish*, while *how-howish* occ. occurs ca. 1720–80. Dryden, 1694, ' I am—I know not howish.' (O.E.D.)

howl. Something very amusing : C. 20. (D. Sayers, *Murder Must Advertise*, 1933.) Ex *howlingly funny*, or ex *howler*.

howl, fetch a. See **fetch a howl.**

howler. A glaring (and amusing) blunder : from before 1890 ; recorded first in 1872 (S.O.D.) of a bitterly cold day ; then 2, at least as early as 1875 (though this sense is ob.), of a—lit. or fig.—heavy fall, a serious accident, esp. in *come*, or *go, a howler*, as in Stephens & Yardley's *Little Jack Sheppard*, 1886, ' Our hansom came a howler ' ; also, a tremendous lie : C. 20 (Lyell). Lit., something that howls or cries for notice, or perhaps, as W. proposes, by way of contracting *howling blunder*.—3. A fashionably dressed man : London : 1896–ca. 1914. Ware. Ex *howling swell*, q.v. in :

howling, adj. A general intensive : 1860, H., 2nd ed. (see *bags*) ; 1865, Sala, ' howling swells ', a *howling swell*, orig. low, being, ca. 1865–1910, a very fashionably but over-dressed man. Applied also to e.g. a lie, a cad, trousers (e.g. *howling bags*, i.e. extravagantly cut or patterned : † by 1905 : see **bags.**) S.E. itself has *howling* as an intensive, as e.g. in the Biblical *h. wilderness.*

howling comique. A ' very bad comic singer indeed ' : music-halls' (— 1909) ; ob. Ware. Cf. *howler*, 1, and *howling*.

howlingly. A gen. intensive adv. : late C. 19–20 : s. till ca. 1910, then coll. : now on the verge of S.E.

how's battle. A coll. greeting of 1934–6, among the cultured. A result of the Crisis : *battle of life*.

how's the way ? How are you ? ; good-day to you ! : New Zealand coll. : C. 20.

how's things ? How goes it ? : coll. : C. 20. Lyell. (See quotation at *old socks*.)

how's your (often **yer**) **belly** (**off**) **for spots ?** A lower classes' c.p. (= how are you ?) of ca. 1900–25.

how's your father ? A military c.p. of 1915–17, ' turned to all sorts of ribald, ridiculous and heroic uses ' (B. & P.). Ex a music-hall song.

how's your poor (often **pore**) **feet ?** A mainly London c.p. : ca. 1862–70 ; revived ca. 1889, but ob. again by 1895, † by 1910. G. A. Sala, in *Breakfast in Bed*. According to Ware, (presumably as *how are your poor feet ?*, an occ. variant) ' from a question addressed by Lord Palmerston to the then Prince of Wales upon the return of the latter from India ' : but that visit ' postdates ' 1862, when (see *All the Year Round*, 1863, x, 180) it was indubitably current.

hows'ever, howsomdever are C. 19–20 sol. forms of :

howsomever. Nevertheless ; however. M.E.– C. 20 : until ca. 1750, S.E. ; then (dial. and) coll. ; from ca. 1830, low coll. ; in C. 20, low coll. > sol. Dorothy Sayers, *Have His Carcase*, 1932, ' Howsomever, it looks like a plain suicide.'

*hoxter. An inside pocket : c. : ca. 1810–80. Vaux, 1812 ; Egan's Grose, 1823 ; Ainsworth. ? ex *huck*, a hip, a haunch.—2. Additional drill : Royal Military Academy : ca. 1885–1914. Ex *extra* via *hextra*.—3. Money : see **huxter.**

hoy. A coll. exclamation of address at a distance (see also **whoy-oi**), hence a summons to attention (esp. in *give a person a hoy*) ; also = *steady !* : late C. 19–20. Used very much earlier in dial. : E.D.D. A mean between archaic *ho !* and *hullo !*

*hoys, hoise. See **hoist.** (A C. 19 variant. Egan's Grose.)—**hua.** See **hoor.**

hub. As an, or the most, important city (gen. *hub of the universe*), it is S.E., but as a husband, it is a low coll. abbr. of *hubby*, q.v. : from ca. 1810 ; ob. Combe, 1812 ; Hood, ca. 1845. (O.E.D.)

hubbie. An incorrect form of *hubby*, q.v.

[**hubble-bubble**, n., a hookah, confused speech, and adj., confused, are S.E.]

hubble-de-shuff. Quickly and irregularly : military s. > coll.—2. Hence, confusedly : coll. Both senses, C. 18. ' Old military term ', says Grose. ? ex Northern dial. *hobbleshow*, (a) tumult, rabble, confusion.

hubbub may possibly, in C. 17–18, have been coll. ; in C. 19–20, definitely S.E. Perhaps ex an Irish cry or interjection : W.

hubby. A husband : coll. : E. Ravenscroft, in *London Cuckolds*, 1688 (O.E.D.) ; 1798, Morton, in the epilogue to his comedy, *Secrets Worth Knowing*, ' The wife poor thing, at first so blithe and chubby, | Scarce knows again her lover in her hubby.' Cr. *hub*, q.v., and :

hubbykins. A still more hypocoristic form of *husband* as a vocative : coll. : late C. 19–20. Dorothy Sayers, *Clouds of Witness*, 1926, ' She called him hubbykins.'

hubris. ' Accomplished, distinguished insolence ' (Ware) : academic s. >, by 1890, coll. : from early 1880's : ob. Direct ex Gr. On Oct. 28, 1884, *The Daily News* wrote thus : ' Boys of good family, who have always been toadied, and never been checked, who are full of health and high spirits, develop what Academic slang knows as *hubris*, a kind of high-flown insolence.'

huck. To bargain : C. 15–17 : coll. prob. in C. 16 only, otherwise S.E. ; in C. 18–20 (ob.), dial. Holinshead, 1577, ' If anie man hucked hard with him about the price of a gelding[, he said] : " So God helpe me . . . he did cost me so much," or else, " By Jesus, I stole him." '

huckle-my-buff or **butt.** ' Beer, egg, and brandy, made hot ', Grose, 1785, at which date Grose spells it *butt* ; in the 2nd and 3rd edd., however, it is *buff*,

as again in the *Lex. Bal.* and in Egan's ed. ; Ainsworth, in *Rookwood*, returns to *butt*. Since the term is extant, though ob., in Sussex dial. as *h.-my-buff*, *butt* is prob. a misprint : see too **huggle-my-buff.**

huckster, n., despite F. & H., has always been S.E., but *in huckster's hands*, late C. 16–early 19, prob. was coll. orig., at least in sense : in a bad way.

hucksum, the hip, may be C. 19 coll. ex Southern dial. (see E.D.D. at *hock*), but *huck-* or *huckle-bone*, the same, is certainly S.E.

huddle. To have sexual connexion : low coll. : C. 18–20, very ob. Ex C. 17 S.E., C. 18–20 dial., where it = to hug or embrace. E.D.D.

*hue. To lash ; punish (esp. severely) with the lash : late C. 17–18 c. B.E. ? ex the resulting *hue* of the victim's flesh, or, more prob., ex S.E. *hue*, to assail or drive with shouts.

Hue and Cry, the. *The Police Gazette* : mostly journalistic (— 1923). Manchon. Ex the *wanted*'s.

*huey. A town or a village : tramps' c. of ca. 1840–80. Mayhew. Origin ?

huff, as a Winchester College abbr. of *huff-cap* (q.v.) is s. from before 1870 and now †. Mansfield, 1870 ; Adams, 1878.—2. In c. (— 1832), now †, to rob by throwing one's arms over the victim's shoulders and then taking (esp. money) from the pockets (O.E.D.).—3. As a low coll. for a (mean) trick, an (artful) dodge, ca. 1860–1910, it is prob. ex the removal of a piece at draughts, wherein *huff*, v. and n., is j. (F. & H.'s other senses of the n., as both of the v., are ineligible because S.E.)

huff, stand the. ' To be answerable for the reckoning in a public-house ', Grose, 2nd ed. : coll. — 1788) ; ob. by 1860, † by 1893. Prob. jocularly on *huff*, a slight blast.

huff and ding. ' To Bounce and swagger ', B.E. : low coll. : C. 17–early 18. See **ding.**

huff-cap as † a swaggering bully,—likewise the corresponding adj.,—was always S.E., but as strong ale it was orig. (1577) coll., soon S.E., by 1700 † (except at Winchester College, where in C. 19 it survived as *huff*, q.v. ' From inducing people to set their caps in a bold and huffing style ', Nares.

huff-snuff, a bully, a person apt to take offence, was prob. coll. orig., but if so it very quickly > S.E. († by 1800). Lit., blow snuff, i.e. show resentment.

huffa ! An exclamation : C. 16–early 17. Ex C. 15 interjectional *huff*.

huffed. Killed ; esp. by a fall from an aeroplane : military, esp. Air Force : 1915. F. & Gibbons ; Manchon. Ex the game of draughts.

huffer, a threatening swaggerer, may possibly have been orig. (C. 17) coll.

huffle. To ' bagpipe ', which, says Grose, 1785 (neither term appears in later edd.), is ' a piece of bestiality [? *penilingism*] too filthy for explanation '. Low : C. 18–early 19.

[**huffy,** like **huffed, huffily, huffiness,** is, despite F. & H., good S.E.]

hufty-tufty ; huftie-tuftie, adj. Swaggering . coll. : late C. 16–early 17. Nashe.

*hug. The act or (as in *put on the hug*) the practice of garrotting : c. (— 1864) ; ob. by 1890, † by 1910. *The Home Magazine*, March 16, 1864.

[**hug,** used fig. (to cherish, cling to), has, despite F. & H., always been S.E.]

hug, close. (Gen. *the c. h.*) Coïtion : coll. : C. 18–early 19. D'Urfey, ' They've a new drug | Which is called the close hug.'

hug, give the. To close (with) and grapple the body (of) : pugilistic : C. 19–20, ob.

hug brown Bess. See **brown Bess.**

hug-centre. ' Head-quarters of public love-making ' : coll. : U.S. (— 1882), anglicised ca. 1885 ; ob. by 1915, † by 1930. Ware.

hug-me-tight. A jersey, a jumper, a pull-over : Glasgow (— 1934). Cf. *huggers*, q.v.

hug it as the devil hugs a witch. To hold a thing as if one fears to lose it : coll. : mid-C. 18–early 19. Grose, 2nd ed.

hug the ground. To fall ; be hit off one's legs : pugilistic : C. 19.

hug the gunner's daughter. See **gunner's daughter.**

[**hugger-mugger**, whether n., v., adj., or adv., has, *d* pite F. & H., always been S.E.]

hugger-mugger, in. Secretly : C. 16–20 ; S.E. till ca. 1830, then (in C. 20, low) coll. The C. 16 form is *in hucker-mucker.* ' Perhaps partly sug-gested by M.E. *huke*, . . . cloak ', W.

huggers. Stockings : Glasgow lower classes' (— 1934). They cling.

*****hugging, n.** Garrotting : c. of ca. 1850–90. Ex *hug*, q.v.

huggle-my-buff. A ca. 1750–80 form of *huckle-my-buff*, q.v. Toldervy, 1756.

Hugh Prowler. See **Prowler, Hugh.—Hughie !, send her down.** See **David.—Hughli, -y.** See **Hooghly.**

hugmatee. Some kind of ale : either c. or fashionable s. of ca. 1698–1710. In *Letters to Phalaris*, Bentley names it along with *humpty-dumpty* and *three-threads*, qq.v. ; ' facetious ' Tom Brown, ca. 1704. Perhaps, as Murray (always ingenious on drinks,—cf. his *bingo*) brilliantly sug-gested, ex *hug me t'ye.*

hugmer ; ugmer. A fool : centre s. on *mug* from ca. 1860 ; ob.

hugsome. Sexually attractive (rarely of men) ; esp., sexually cuddlesome : coll. : late C. 19–20.

[**hulk**, to hang about, is not coll. but dial.]

hulkey. See **hulky.**

hulking, adj. Bulky, unwieldy ; ungainly, clumsy : coll. : late C. 17–20. Ex S.E. *hulk*, an unwieldy mass (as in J. Beresford, 1806), a heavy ungainly person (as in Ned Ward, 1698). Cf. :

hulky, adj. (Occ. as n.) Unwieldly ; ungainly, clumsy : coll. (— 1785). Grose, 1st ed.

hull. Whole, as in ' the hull of us ' (all of us) : sol. (— 1887). Baumann.

hull between wind and water, to. Possess a woman : C. 19–20 (†) : nautical s. > low coll. Cf. *between wind and water*, q.v.

hull-cheese ' is composed of . . . mault and water . . . and is cousin germane to the mightiest ale ', Taylor the Water Poet, 1622 : C. 17 c. > s. By 1670 it was proverbial in the form, *you have eaten some hull-cheese*, you are drunk, and as such, latterly only in dial., it remained in C. 19.

Hull, hell, and Halifax. See **Halifax,** also **hell.**

hullabaloo. A tumultuous noise or confusion ; an uproar : from ca. 1760 : coll. till ca. 1840, then S.E. Prob. ex Northern or Scottish dial. Smollett, 1762, spells *hollo-ballo* ; another frequent early form is *halloobal(l)oo.* Evidently a rhyming reduplica-tion on *halloo.*

hullo, features ! See **features.** (Ware classifies this † ' friendly salute ' as proletarian.)

hulver-head. ' A silly foolish Fellow ', B.E. Whence *hulver-headed*, adj. Coll. in late C. 17–18, then dial. Lit., *hulver* = holly.

hum. Very strong ale : ca. 1615–!720 : coll.

1616, Jonson ; Fletcher. Perhaps orig. c. Cf. *stingo*, q.v.—2. A hoax, a trick, a cheat : 1751 (S.O.D.) ; ob. by 1900 ; † by 1920. From ca. 1850, the word was somewhat low. *The World*, No. 164 (1756) ; Lamb, 1806, ' I daresay all this is hum ', where its derivation ex *humbug* appears very clearly. —3. A lie : ca. 1820–1900. Bee, ' *Hum*—a whispered lie.'—4. A person at church : c. : C. 18–early 19. *A New Canting Dict.*, 1725. **?** ex *amen* mumbled into a resemblance to *hum !*—5. A stink : low : from ca. 1890. (Cf. *hum*, v., 4.) Collinson. Perhaps ex Northern dial. *humming*, anything gnawed and then left by rats (see E.D.D.). —6. The ship *Hermes* : naval (— 1909). Ware. Cf. *Dead Loss.*

hum, v. To be all astir, very lively : coll. : 1726 (S.O.D.). In form is (are), *was* (were), etc., *humming.*—2. Cheat, bamboozle, humbug : 1751 (S.O.D.) : ob. by 1860, † by 1880 : orig., prob. s., but by 1760 it was coll. Goldsmith, in his *Life of Nash*, ' Here Nash, if I may be permitted the use of a polite and fashionable phrase, was humm'd.' Ex *humbug*, q.v.—3. Hence, to cadge : military : late C. 19–20. F. & Gibbons.—4. As = to mumble, esp. in *hum and ha(w)*, it has always been S.E.—5. To stink : low : from ca. 1895. Prob. ex the corresponding n. (*hum*, sense 5) ; Ware, how-ever, implies that the v. is the earlier and that it dates from considerably before 1895, and states that ' this is an application from the humming of fermentation in an active manure heap.'

hum, make things. (Cf. *hum*, v., 1.) To acceler-ate, lit. and fig. ; keep busy and moving : coll. : orig. (— 1887), U.S., but anglicised by 1895. Ex the *hum* of activity (W.).

*****hum-box.** A pulpit : c. : ca. 1720–1895. *A New Canting Dict.*, 1725 ; Mayhew, in *Paved with Gold.* The idea : the box noted for humming and hawing. Cf. *cackle tub*, q.v.

*****hum-box patterer.** A parson, esp. when preach-ing : c. : C. 19. G. W. M. Reynolds.

*****hum-cap.** ' Old, mellow, and very strong Beer ', B.E. : late C. 17–18 c. Ex *hum*, n., 1.

human. A human being : mid-C. 16–20 ; S.E. till ca. 1830, then U.S. (see Thornton), as it still is, but in C. 20 it is in England either affected S.E. or jocular coll. according to the context.

Humber keel. See **billy-boy.**

humble. A homily : a C. 16 (? also C. 17) sol. Lever, in *Sermons*, 1550. (O.E.D.)

humble-bee in a cow-turd thinks himself a king, a. A proverbial c.p. of ca. 1650–1800. See also **how we apples swim !** (Apperson.)

humble-cum-dumble, your. Your humble ser-vant : jocular (— 1823) ; † by 1900. Bee.

humble-pie, eat. To apologise ; be very sub-missive, even to humiliation : from ca. 1830 : dial. till ca. 1850 ; coll. till ca. 1895, then S.E. Thack-eray, 1855 ; Manville Fenn, ' Our savings are gone and we must eat humble pie for the future.' By a pun ex *umble pie*, i.e. one made from a deer's *umbles* ; cf. dial. *to eat rue-pie* (W.).

humbug. A † hoax, † befooling trick ; an im-posture, fraud, sham : coll. : ca. 1740 ; perhaps not (see O.E.D.) till ca. 1754, when F. Killigrew issued *The Universal Jester*, a collection of ' conceits . . drolleries . . . bon-mots, and humbugs ', tracked down (see ed. 1860) by H., who also discovered that ' Orator Henley [d. 1756] was known to the mob as Orator Humbug '. The term, however, occurs for certain in 1751—in *The Student*, ii, 41, a notable

locus.—2. An impostor, a cheat, a 'fraud': coll.:
1804 (S.O.D.). Dickens in *Pickwick*, 'You're a
humbug, sir . . . I will speak plainer . . . An
impostor, sir.' Prob. this sense dates back to ca.
1762, for in 1763 we find a mention of the quasi-
Masonic society, *the Humbugs*.—3. Deception,
pretence, affectation: coll.: 1825 (S.O.D.). Cf.
humbug!, q.v. Etymology obscure; perhaps ex
hum (and haw) + bug(bear). Cf., however, Nashe's
'without humdrum be it spoken', in *Saffron
Walden*.

humbug, v. Impose upon, hoax, delude: coll.:
1751, Smollett, 'The most afflicted of the two taking
his departure with an exclamation of "Humbugged,
egad!"'—2. V.i., to practise or be a humbug: coll.:
1753 (S.O.D.). Whence *humbug about*, q.v.—3.
Change or transfer by fraud or trickery (v.t.): 1821
(S.O.D.): low coll.; ob.—4. V.t and, more often,
i., to cajole: esp. in *h. of*, cajole or cheat out of
something (ca. 1760–1870), and *h. into*, cajole or
hoax into doing something (from ca. 1810). These
four nuances are all coll. As used in the following
quotation, *humbug* is ob.: H. Kingsley, in *Ravenshoe*, 'She was always ready to help him, provided,
as she told him, "he didn't humbug".' Cf. preceding entry for etymology.

humbug, adj., corresponding to senses 1 and 2 of
the n.: coll.: 1812 (O.E.D.).

humbug! Stuff and nonsense! Coll.: from ca.
1825. Ex the n., 3.

humbug about. To play the fool: C. 19–20:
coll. Ex the v., 2.

humbug-and-derricks. (Gen. pl.) A cargo
steamer: sailing-ships': mid-C. 19–20; ob.
Bowen.

humbug into and † **humbug of.** See **humbug, v.,**
last sense.

humbug(g)able. Gullible: coll.: 1825, Southey.
Rare in C. 20. But the seldom-used *humbug(g)-
ability* is recorded as early as 1798.

humbugger. A cheat: low coll.: ca. 1751–1890.—
2. A hoaxer: coll.: from ca. 1752; ob.—3. One who
constantly fools about, an habitual deceiver: coll.:
from ca. 1760. Henry Brooke, in *Poems*, at that
'On Humbugging': 'To you . . . the humbuggers
of hearts', 1778.

humbuggery. Imposture; deception; pretence:
from ca. 1830; ob. More gen. in U.S. than in
Britain, where the word is apt to recall *buggery*.

humbugging, n. Deception, hoaxing (C. 18–20,
ob.); pretence, foolery (C. 19–20). Coll. A.
Murphy, 1752, 'The never enough to be admired
Art of Humbugging came into Vogue'; Henry
Brooke, 1778, see **humbugger, 3.** (O.E.D.)

humbugging, adj. Swindling (ob.), hoaxing:
from ca. 1800: coll.—2. Deceitful, pretentious:
coll.: from ca. 1830. Thackeray, 1840, 'Do you
not laugh . . . at the humbugging anniversary of a
humbug?'—3. Apt to cajole or to play the fool:
(rather low) coll.: from ca. 1860.

humbuggism. An occ. coll. variant, now ob., of
humbugging, n., q.v.: from ca. 1840. Tom Moore,
1842, 'By dint of sheer humbuggism'.

humdrum. A wife, occ. a husband: C. 17–early
19 coll. (Other senses of the n., like all senses of the
adj., are S.E.) By 'reduplication on *hum*, with
reminiscence of *drum*', W.

humdudgeon; humdurgeon. An imaginary illness: coll. (— 1785). Grose, 1st ed., spells it *humdurgeon*, the O.E.D. *humdudgeon*, thus linking the
word with *dudgeon*, ill humour. Grose, 'He has got

the hum durgeon, the thickest part of his thigh is
nearest his a*se; i.e. nothing ails him except low
spirits.' The saying was † by 1890.

humdurgeoned, adj. Annoyed: late C. 18–mid-
19 coll. Lytton. Ex preceding.

humging. A whip-top: Restoration period.
Lit., 'goes with a hum'.

humgruffin. A hobgoblin; a repulsive person.
Also, a derisive term of address: 1842, Barham:
coll.; ob. Prob. *hobgoblin* corrupted by association with *griffin*. (O.E.D.)

humgumptious. Knowingly deceitful or artful:
low: ca. 1820–70. Ex † dial. *humgumption*, self-
importance, nonsense, itself presumably ex *humbug + gumption*. (Bee, at *hum*.)

humla. An attack: Regular Army: C. 20.
B. & P. Ex Hindustani.

humm. A C. 17–18 variant of *hum* (esp. n., 1).

hummer. (Cf. *rapper, whopper*.) A notable lie
(B.E., Grose): late C. 17–early 19,—being a special
application of the sense, 'a person or thing marked
by extreme energy, activity, etc. . . . 1681'
(S.O.D.); of persons, it has since ca. 1880 been
mainly U.S. Ex *hum*, v., 1.—2. An impostor, a
pretender: s. > coll.: ca. 1760–1820. Henry
Brooke, 'Our hummers in state, physic, learning,
and law', 1778. A variant of *humbug*, n., 3, which
it may have preceded.

hummie. A callous growth, induced by continual friction, on the back of the neck: dockers'
s. (— 1887) > coll.; ob. ? ex *hump* or *hummock*.
(O.E.D.)

humming. Extremely intense, active, busy, (of
blows) hard, or (ob.) large: from ca. 1650: s. >,
ca. 1790, coll. Fielding, 'Landlord . . . You seem
to drive a humming trade here.' Ex *hum*, v., 1.—
2. (Of liquor) very strong: coll.: 1675 (S.O.D.);
ob. B.E., '*Humming Liquor*, Double Ale, Stout,
Pharaoh [q.v.]'; *humming tipple*, Ned Ward, 1714.
Cf. *hum*, n., 1, *stingo*, and *humming October*. Perhaps ex the hissing of frothy liquor, perhaps ex
subsequent humming in the head (O.E.D.).

humming, adv. Exceedingly: coll.: C. 18.
Farquhar. Ex adj., prob. sense 1.

humming bird. (Gen. pl.) A shell that, in its
flight, makes a humming sound: military: in G.W.

humming October. Very strong ale from the new
season's hops: coll.: from ca. 1710; ob. by 1890,
† by 1910. Often just *October*, lit. ale brewed in
October.

hummum(s). A brothel: the form *hummum* is
prob. coll., while *hummums* is either s. or, more
prob., coll.: late C. 17–18. B.E.; Grose. (See
O.E.D. and esp. Beresford Chancellor's informative
Covent Garden). Ex Arabic *hammam*, a hot bath,
some Turkish bath establishments (*hummums* in
S.E.) being or becoming little better than brothels.

hump; sense 1 always preceded by the. Temporary ill humour; a sulky fit: from ca. 1725, but
not gen. before ca. 1860. Esp. in *get*, or *have, the
hump*: Jerome K. Jerome, in *Idle Thoughts*, 1886,
'He has got the blooming hump.' Also *have the
hump on* or *up* (recorded by H., 1860): ca. 1862–
1900. Perhaps ex *hip* on *dump(s)*: W.—2. 'A
long walk with a swag on one's back': Australia:
ca. 1890–1914. Boldrewood. See **hump, v.,** last
sense.—3. (**the Hump.**) Portland: nautical: late
C. 19–20. Bowen. Ex the Bill's shape and the
feeling induced.

hump, v.i. To have sexual intercourse: ca.
1760–1800, Grose in 1785 remarking: 'Once a

fashionable word'. It was transported to the U.S., where it survives in c. (Irwin).—2. To spoil, botch : low (mostly Cockney) : ca. 1850–1900. Mayhew.— 3. To shoulder and carry : Australia : from ca. 1850, perhaps orig. gold-diggers' s., as W. Howitt's *Two Years in Victoria*, vol. i, 1853, tends to show. As early as 1857, one spoke of *humping it*, but gen. the phrase is *hump one's swag* (Howitt), *one's drum* (— 1886) as in Lawson's *When the World was Wide*, 1896, and in C. 20 (*one's*) *bluey*, this last being re-corded in 1890. See **bluey** and cf. *hump*, n., 2. Morris. Ex the *hump* of a bent back. Cf. the familiar-S.E. *hump oneself* (to depart).—4. See **hump oneself.**

hump, get or **have the.** See **hump**, n., 1.

hump on or **up, have the.** See **hump**, n., 1.

hump oneself. To hurry : Shrewsbury School : from ca. 1880. Desmond Coke, *The Bending of a Twig*, 1906.

hump it. See **hump**, v., 3. In G.W., esp. 'to march with full kit' (F. & Gibbons).—2. To die : lower classes' (— 1923). Manchon. Ex *hump*, v., 3.

hump(e)y. As an Australian native hut, it is coll. (1846 as *umpee*, 1873 as *humpy*) >, ca. 1880 ,j. ; but as a settler's small and primitive house, it is s. (1881) >, ca. 1910, coll. A. C. Grant, R. M. Praed, 'Rolf Boldrewood', Gilbert Parker. Ex Aboriginal *oompi* ; 'the initial *h* is a Cockney addition', Morris. Cf. *gunyah*, q.v.

Humphrey, dine with Duke. See **dine.**

*humpty-dumpty. A rank or disastrous failure ; a fiasco : c. : from ca. 1920. James Curtis, *The Gilt Kid*, 1936. Ex ' Humpty Dumpty had a great fall ' in the nursery rhyme.

humpty-dumpty. Ale boiled with brandy : coll. : late C. 17–20, ob. B.E. ; Disraeli, in *Venetia*.— 2. A short, dumpy, round-shouldered, gen. clumsy person : coll. (— 1785) : in C. 20, usually considered S.E. Grose. Prob. by reduplication on *hump* by reminiscence of *dump*. with intrusive *t* (O.E.D.) ; or perhaps a reduplication on a corrupt or diminutive form of *Humphrey* (W.).—3. Also adj. Both n. and adj. are occ. abbr. to *humpty*. *A Dict. of Slang and Colloquial English* (the abridged F. & H.), 1905 : ' As adj. and adv., short and thick, all of a heap, all together.'

humpy, n. See **humpey.**—2. Adj. : depressed ; dispirited : 1907, P. G. Wodehouse, *Not George Washington*. See **hump**, n., 1.

humstrum, despite Grose and F. & H., is S.E., except when, as in C. 18, it is applied jocularly to a violin : then, it is coll.

Hun. Jocular, or pejorative for a very objection-able person : coll. : from 1914 to ca. 1920 strongly ; virtually † by 1929. For pre-coll. history, see W.— 2. Hence, a flying cadet : Air Force : late 1915 ; ob. F. & Gibbons. He was destructive of the instructional 'planes.

Hun-hunting. A search for enemy 'planes : Air Force coll. : G.W. (F. & Gibbons).

Hun-pinching, n. ' Raiding an enemy trench in order to secure prisoners for the benefit of the Intelligence Department' : military : 1917–18. Ibid.

Hun-pox. Chicken-pox : military : 1915. B. & P. Suggested by S.E. *German measles*.

hunch. A suspicion ; an intuition or premoni-tion : orig. and still mainly U.S. (not long pre-G.W.); anglicised by 1916, thanks to the Canadian soldiers. (—The v.i. and t., to jostle, is ineligible.)

Hundred and Worst, the. The 101st Regiment : a G.W. military nickname ex an unsuccess at Tanga. F. Brett Young, *Jim Redlake*, 1930.

hunder-hand. A ' sudden blow given with advantage' : street boys' : 1880. Ware. I.e. *underhand blow.*

hung for **hanged** (by the neck) is, in C. 19–20, increasingly considered a sol.

hung, be. To have one's picture accepted and hung at an exhibition, esp. that of the Royal Academy : artists' coll. : mid-C. 19–20. Ware.

hung beef. ' A dried bull's pizzle ', esp. as an instrument of castigation : low (— 1811) ; very ob. *Lex. Bal.*

hung up, be. To be held up, hence at a standstill, (ob.) in a fix : coll. : 1879, says Ware, who implies that it came from America and that it is a Society phrase—which, it may be added, had > gen. by 1910 if not a decade earlier.

hungarian. A hungry person : C. 17 : ? orig. c. or merely and prob. jocular coll. ; certainly pun-ning *Hungarian*.—2. Hence, a beggar, a thief, a freebooter : C. 17, perhaps orig. c. (Occ. adj. in both senses.)

hunger, erroneously for *hungri*, i.e. *hungry* : C. 14–25, e.g. in *The Digby Mystery*, ca. 1485. (O.E.D.)

hungered, a or **an.** Improperly for *a-hungered*, *anhungered* : C. 14–20. O.E.D.

hunger drops out of one's nose. One is extremely hungry : proverbial coll. : C. 16–17. Skelton ; Cotgrave ; Howell in his *Letters*. Apperson.

hungry as a hunter, as. Very and healthily hungry : coll. : from ca. 1800 or slightly earlier. Lamb, in a letter of 1800, ' I came home . . . as hungry as a hunter' ; Marryat ; Mrs. Henry Wood. Other *hungry as* phrases, all coll., are *hungry as a church mouse* (C. 17–20, dial. from ca. 1800), *as a hawk* (from ca. 1640, e.g. in R. L. Stevenson), *as a June crow* (C. 19–20, ob., pro-verbial), *as a kite* (C. 16–20, in C. 19–20 dial. : cf. *as a hawk*), *as a wolf* (from ca. 1540, e.g. in Lytton, cf. the C. 19 Leeds *hungry as a dog*), and *as the grave* (C. 19–20, ob., mainly dial.). Apperson.

Hungry Hundred, the. ' The first batch of [R.N.R.] lieutenants admitted . . . on the Emer-gency List in the 'nineties ' : naval ; † by 1914. Bowen.

hungry Liz,—' A 6-inch howitzer now (Oct. 1918) collecting war-loan subscriptions in Bethnal Green [London] is called.' W.

hungry quartz. Unpromising quartz : Aus-tralian mining s. >, ca. 1900, coll. : from ca. 1880. Ex the S.E. application to poor land and fishless rivers.

Hungry Six, the. ' The first Flying Squadron [of warships] sent round the world under Admiral G. Phipps Hornby in the 'seventies. They were on " bare navy " ' (Bowen) : naval : ca. 1875–90.

hunk. A steward in the 3rd class : nautical : C. 20. Bowen. Perhaps ex Scots *hunk*, a slut, or, more prob., ex :

hunk, v. To clean : (naval and) military : late C. 19–20. F. & Gibbons. Origin ? Also, among telegraph-messenger boys, *hunk up*, to polish (one's buttons).

hunkers, on one's. In a squatting position : Scottish coll. : late C. 18–20. R. L. Stevenson. (O.E.D.)

[**hunks.** A miser. C. 17–20. Despite Grose and F. & H., ineligible.]

Hunland. The country behind *any* enemy lines occupied, wholly or in part, by German soldiers: Air Force coll.: 1915. F. & Gibbons.

Hunnery, the. The Department of German: Liverpool University students': 1915–18. Collinson.

Hunnish. Jocular, or seriously pejorative for objectionable, unsporting: from 1914; ob. by 1921, † by 1929. Ex *Hun*, q.v.—The adv. (in -*ly*) was seldom used.

hunsup. A corrupt, indeed a dial. and low coll., form of S.E. *hunt's-up*. O.E.D.

***hunt.** To decoy a ' pigeon ' (q.v.) to the gaming tables: c.: late C. 17–19. Mostly as vbl.n. (B.E.). —2. See hunted, be.

hunt, in or **out of the.** Having a (good) chance or none; in or not in 'the swim': coll.: late C. 19–20.

hunt-about, n. A prying gossip: coll.: from ca. 1850; ob.—2. A harlot ever walking about: low coll.: from ca. 1860; ob.

hunt-counter. A beggar: late C. 16–17 coll. Shakespeare.

hunt grass. To be knocked down: pugilists': C. 19. Cf. *grass*.—2. Occ., though mostly U.S., to be very puzzled (— 1869); ob. by 1900, † by 1910.

hunt leather or **the leather.** To field: cricket s. (— 1892) >, ca. 1900, coll. Now mostly journalistic j.—and something out-moded.

***hunt the dummy.** To steal pocket-books: c. (— 1811); ob. *Lex. Bal.* A Catnach chorus: ' Speak to the tattler, bag the swag, | And finely hunt the dummy.' See **dummy.**

[**hunt the squirrel, v.; hunting the squirrel, n.** This post-boys' and stage-coachmen's amusement— see Grose—belongs not here but to folk-lore.]

hunted, be. ' A man whose turn comes for him to drink, before he has emptied his former glass, is said to be hunted,' Grose, 1st ed.: drinkers': ca. 1770– 1840. Cf. *chaser*, q.v.

hunters, pitch the, v., with vbl.n. **pitching the hunters.** Low coll. (mostly costermongers' and cheap jacks'): ca. 1845–1914. Mayhew, 1851, ' Pitching the hunters is the three sticks a penny, with the snuff-boxes stuck upon sticks; if you throw [? *knock down*] your stick, and they fall out of the hole, you are entitled to what you knock off.'

hunter's moon, the. An October moon, the moon next after the harvest moon: rural coll. >, in C. 20, S.E.: C. 18–20, ob. Kingsley, 1855.

***hunting.** The vbl.n. corresponding to *hunt*, v., q.v.—2. hunting, good. See good h.

hunting flotilla. An anti-submarine flotilla in the Grand Fleet: naval coll.: 1916; ob. Bowen.

Huntingdon sturgeon. A native or an inhabitant of Huntingdon: 1667–ca. 1900, though ob. by 1830. Ex a young, flood-drowned donkey thought, in May, 1667, to be a sturgeon by the people of Huntingdon, a black pig by those of Godmanchester, the latter being called *Godmanchester black pigs*, the former *Huntingdon sturgeons.* Braybrooke's Pepys (the *Diary*), cited by Apperson.

Huntley and Palmer, take the. A variant (ca. 1894–1928) of *take the biscuit, take the cake.* W. Pett Ridge, in his clever *Minor Dialogues*, 1895; McKnight, *English Words*, 1923. Huntley & Palmer being the notable makers of biscuits.

Hunt's dog, (which) will neither go to church nor stay at home,—like. A mid-C. 17–20 ob., mainly rural and latterly dial., proverbial c.p. applied to any very unreasonably discontented person. Grose, who explains it by a certain labourer's

mastiff. (Ascribed to, or claimed by, various counties: see Apperson.)

hup, v.i. and **t.** To cry *hup* (to a horse) in order to urge on or to turn to the right: coll.: from ca. 1820. Scott in *St. Ronan's Well.* (O.E.D.)

hupper sukkles. Upper circles: Society: ca. 1845–70. Ware, ' Introduced by Thackeray in the *De la Pluche* [Yellowplush] *Papers.*' These Papers appeared in *Fraser's Magazine* in 1838–40; in book-form, in 1841.

hurdy-gurdy. As = a barrel-organ, this term was orig. (ca. 1845) coll., for properly it means, or rather meant, a lute-like instrument. Echoic.

hurkaru. A messenger: Anglo-Indian coll.: from ca. 1800; earlier as *hircar(r)a(h), hurca*(or *u)-ca*(or *u)rra(h).* Ex Hindustani *harkara*, messenger, emissary, spy. Yule & Burnell.

hurly-burly, strife, a commotion, an uproar: mid-C. 16–20. Until ca. 1850, S.E.; since, increasingly though still but slightly coll. Also adj. and † adv. Ex S.E. *hurling and burling.*

hurrah-boat. An excursion steamer: naval (— 1909). O.E.D. (Sup.); Bowen.

hurrah boy. (Gen. pl.) A college student: 1928 (O.E.D. Sup.); ob.

hurrah clothes. One's best clothes: mostly naval: from ca. 1905. (O.E.D. Sup.)

hurrah cruise. ' A naval cruise to attract popular attention ': naval; from ca. 1920. Bowen. ? ex:

hurrah party. ' Naval men going ashore for a spree ': naval: C. 20. Ibid. Cf. *banzai party*, q.v.

hurra(h)'s nest. The utmost confusion: nautical from ca. 1845, but orig. (1829 or earlier) U.S.; prob. anglicised mainly by the popularity of R. H. Dana's *Two Years Before the Mast*, 1840. Rare in C. 20; † by 1910 (i.e. in Britain).

hurricane. A very crowded—properly a fashionable—assembly at a private house: ca. 1745–1815: fashionable s. > coll. Mrs. Delany, Mrs. Barbauld. (Occ. as v., spend in or at a ' hurricane '.) O.E.D. Cf. *bun-worry, tea-fight*, qq.v.

hurricane-jumper. A rating that joined the Navy as a youth without going to a training-ship: naval: late C. 19. Bowen. (See also **northorigger.)**—2. (**the H. J.**) H.M. Cruiser *Calliope*, after escaping from the Samoan hurricane (1889): id.: id. Ibid. See esp. R. L. Stevenson, *A Footnote to History.*

hurridun. A late C. 17–early 18 variant of *harridan*, q.v. B.E.

hurroosh. A coll. form of C. 19–20 S.E. *hurroo*, a cry of triumph or joyous excitement. Kipling, 1891, in *Plain Tales*, ' There was a wild hurroosh at the Club.' (O.E.D.)—2. Also v.i. and v.t.: from ca. 1890.

hurry. ' A quick passage on the violin, or a roll on the drum, leading to a climax in the representation ', F. & H.: from ca. 1835: musical s. > j. (not in O.E.D.). Dickens, in *Boz*, ' The wrongful heir comes in to two bars of quick music (technically called a hurry).'

hurry, be in no. To have, or take, plenty of time: coll. (— 1858). Buckle. (O.E.D.)

hurry, not . . . in a. Not very soon: coll.: from ca. 1835. (O.E.D.)

hurry-curry. As a curricle or swift car—cited by F. & H.—it is a S.E. nonce-word.—2. See **hari-kari** (corrupt for *hara-kiri*). From ca. 1860.

hurry-durry, hurrydurry. Rough, boisterous, impatiently wilful: mainly nautical coll.: ca. 1670–

1720. Wycherley, in *The Plain Dealer*, ' 'Tis a hurrydurry blade.' Reduplication on *hurry*.—2. As a comparatively rare n., C. 18, it is a coll. variant of Scottish *hurry-burry*.—3. A late C. 17 exclamation of impatience or indignation : coll. Otway, Mrs. Behn. (O.E.D.)

hurry-scurry. A (hurried, disorderly) rush or a crowded rushing-on or -about : coll. : 1754 (S.O.D.). Ex the adj.

hurry-scurry, v. 'To run or rush in confused and undignified haste' (S.O.D.) : coll. : from ca. 1770. Prob. ex the n.

hurry-scurry, adj. Characterised by hurried disorder : coll. : 1732 (S.O.D.). A reduplication on *hurry* suggested by *scurry*.

hurry-scurry, adv. Pell-mell ; in hasty and marked disorder : coll. : 1750 (S.O.D.). Ex the adj.

hurry up. (Gen. in imperative.) To hurry : coll. : late C. 19–20 ; Ware, however, dates it from 1850, makes it Anglo-Indian, and goes so far as to say that it ' originated in the river steamer navigation of U.S.A.' at, presumably, a date earlier than 1850. N.b., both v.i. and v.t.

hurry-whore. A harlot ever walking : C. 17 (– 1630) coll. Taylor the Water Poet, ' Hyreling hackney carryknaves and hurry-whores '. Prob. with reference also to what is coarsely known as ' a short time ' (q.v.).

hurt, v.i. To suffer injury, esp. to feel pain : C. 14–20 : S.E. till ca. 1880, then coll. E.g. ' Does your foot still hurt ? ' (O.E.D.)

husband's boat. The Saturday London-to-Margate boat in the summer season : (lowish) coll. : ca. 1865–1914. A Vance ballad, ca. 1867, was entitled *The Husband's Boat*.

husband's supper, warm the. To sit, with lifted skirts, before a fire : low : from ca. 1860 ; ob.

husband's tea. Weak tea : low coll. : from ca. 1850 ; ob. Cf. *water bewitched*.

husbin. Husband : sol. (– 1887). Baumann.

***hush.** To kill, esp. to murder : c. of C. 18–19. *A New Canting Dict.*, 1725 ; Grose, 1st ed., ' hush the cull '. Cf. *silence*.

hush-boat. See **hush-ship.**—**hush-crib.** See **hush-shop.**

Hush-Hush Army, the. General Dunsterville's force in the Caucasus and at Baku in 1918–19 : military of that period. F. & Gibbons. Ex the secrecy observed in its formation and departure. Cf. :

Hush-Hush Crowd, the. The Tank Corps in its early days (June–Dec., 1916) : military : late 1916–17. F. & Gibbons. Cf. :

Hush-Hush Operation. A projected, never-executed attack on that part of the Belgian coast which was occupied by the Germans : military coll. : 1916–17. Ibid.

hush-(hush-)ship. (Often *hush-boat*.) A seemingly peaceable vessel that, carrying several guns, lures German submarines to its eager arms : 1915–18, and after : orig. coll., but by 1918 S.E. Bowen. Cf. *Q-boat*, q.v.

hush-hush show. ' A very secret affair ' (Lyell) : coll. : orig. (1917), military >, by 1919, gen. On preceding phrases ; see **show.**

hush-money. Money paid to ensure silence ; blackmail : C. 18 coll. (the O.E.D. records at 1709) ; C. 19–20 S.E. Grose, 1st ed.

hush-shop, occ. -**crib.** An unlicensed tavern : low coll. (*h.-crib* may well be c.) : from ca. 1843 ;

ob. *The Globe*, Sept. 18, 1872, ' At Barrow-in-Furness the new Licensing Act has had the effect of calling numerous hush-shops into existence ' ; first recorded in Bamford's *Life of a Radical*, 1844 (O.E.D.).

hush up, v.i. To be, more gen. become, quiet, silent, or still : coll. : C. 18–20, ob. Cf. the v.t. sense, which is S.E. (O.E.D.)

husky. Gooseberry fool with the *husks* retained : Winchester College : ca. 1840–80. Mansfield. Cf. *non-husky*.—2. An Eskimo or his language ; esp. an Eskimo dog : 1864 (S.O.D.) : coll. till C. 20, then S.E. : mostly Canadian. *Eskimo* corrupted.

husky, adj. Well-built and sturdy and rough : coll. : ex U.S. (– 1889), anglicised ca. 1918, though Canadianised by 1900. Perhaps because so many such men have husky voices ; perhaps influenced by *husky*, an Eskimo dog (strong and hardy).

***husky-lour, huskylour.** A guinea : c. : late C. 17–18. B.E. Ex *lour* (q.v.), money, + *husky*, dry. (Dry money = hard cash = a specific coin.)

hussy, huzzy. When, in C. 19–20, used jocularly as = woman, lass, esp. as a term of address, verges on coll. ; otherwise wholly S.E.—2. See **huzzy,** below. Ex *housewife*.

hustings (occ. **hoistings**), **you are all for the.** A mid-C. 17–18 proverbial c.p., app. = you're all due for trouble. ? ex *Hustings*, long the supreme law court of London. (The political sense of *hustings* did not arise before C. 18.)

hustle, n. ' Push ' ; energetic activity : ex. U.S. (ca. 1890) ; anglicised, as a coll., ca. 1905. Now almost S.E. Cf. and contrast sense 2 of :

hustle, v.i. and t. To have sexual connexion (with) : low : ca. 1830–1910.—2. As = to hurry, bustle, greatly bestir oneself, it is gen. considered as a coll. ex the U.S., but it is S.E. of more than a century's standing.—3. See **hustling,** 2.

***hustler.** A pickpocket that relies on jostling and hustling his victims : ca. 1825–1910 : c.—2. One who works energetically and impatiently : ex U.S. (1886), where, however, there is frequently a connotation of (often slight) unscrupulousness : anglicised ca. 1905, coll. till ca. 1925, then S.E. Ex *hustle*, v. 2.—3. An employee whose duty is to hurry people on to ' Tube ' (q.v.) trains in London : 1920 : s. > j. > coll. (W.)

hustling. Impatiently energetic work : genesis as for *hustle*, v., 2.—2. ' Forcible robbery, by two or more thieves seizing their victim round the body, or at the collar ', Bee : c. : from ca. 1820 ; ob.

hutch. A place of residence, sojourn, or occ. employment : low coll. : ca. 1860–1915. Ex S.E. sense, a hut, cabin, small house. Cf. *diggings*, q.v.—2. Hence, *the hutch*, the guard-room : military : C. 20. F. & Gibbons.—3. A study : Public Schools' : late C. 19–20. Desmond Coke, *The House Prefect*, 1908.

hutty. An elephant : Anglo-Indian coll. : post-1886 but pre-1892 ; *hatty*, however, was used prob. as early as C. 18. Kipling, in *The Road to Mandalay*. Ex Hindustani *hattee*, properly *hathi*, an elephant.

huxter ; occ. **hoxter.** Money : low, being ' much in use among costermongers and low sharpers ', H., 1874, therefore prob. c. at first and mainly : ca. 1860–1910. Also in pl. ? ex *hoxter*, 1, q.v.

huzzy, -ie ; also **hussy.** A housewife's companion, i.e. a pocket-case for needles, thread, etc.

A reduction of *housewife* : C. 18–early 19. Richardson, Scott. (O.E.D.)—2. See also **hussy.**

hy-yaw ! An exclamation of astonishment : Anglo-Chinese coll. (— 1864). H., 3rd. ed.

Hyde Park railings. A breast of mutton : West London street s. : late C. 19–20 ; ob. Ware. Ex appearance of the bone-system.

hyacine, as used by Spenser for *hyacinth* (the gem), is a corrupt form.

hybern-, for *hibern-,* is, e.g. in *hybernate,* an incorrect form : C. 17–19. (Like the following *hydr-*group, with the exception of *hydro,* this is merely a written error.) (O.E.D.)

hydræleum, -lon, -olean, hydroleon, etc., are erroneous for *hydrelæon* or *-um.* (O.E.D.)

hydraform is erroneous for *hydriform* : from ca. 1820. (O.E.D.)

hydrargysm. Erroneous for *hydrargyrism,* an obscure medical term. (O.E.D.)

hydrazoa. In error for *hydrozoa* : from ca. 1840. (O.E.D.)

hydro. Abbr. *hydropathic* (*establishment*) : orig. (1882), coll. ; in C. 20, S.E. (O.E.D.)

hydrogogy. An erroneous form of *hydragogy* : ca. 1570–1700. Later *hydrogogue.* (O.E.D.)

hydroptic(al). A C. 17 error (after *epilepsy, epileptic*) for *hydropic(al).* (O.E.D.)

hydropyretic is erroneous for *hidropyretic* : from ca. 1850. (O.E.D.)

hydrotic(al). A C. 17–20 error for *hidrotic(al).* By confusion with *hydro-* derivatives. (O.E.D.)

hyemnal is in error for *hiemal* : ca. 1670–1800. ? after *autumnal.* (O.E.D.)

hyking, n. ' Calling out at or after any one ' : proletarian (— 1909) ; ob. Ware. A perversion or a corruption of *chyack,* esp. in the form *chy-ike.*

hyloist, occ. **hu-.** A C. 19–20 mistake for *hylist,* one who affirms that matter is God. Thomas Love Peacock. (O.E.D.)

hymastatics. Incorrect for *hæmostatics* : C. 18–20. O.E.D.

[**hymeneal sweets, coïtion,** and **hypogastric cranny,** the female pudend, both listed by F. & H., are ineligible, being mere pedantic euphemisms.]

hymenial is erroneous for *hymeneal* : C. 17–20. (O.E.D.)

hymns and prayers. (Esp. unmarried) men and women : late C. 19–20 ob. jocular coll. Suggested by *hims and hers.*

hyp (1736), gen. **the hyp.** Also in pl., (*the*) *hyps* (1705). Low spirits : coll. ; ca. 1705–1895. (See **hip, n.** and **v.,** and **hypo, hyppo.**) Ex *hypo-*

chondria. Lamb, in *The Pawnbroker's Daughter,* ' The drops so like to tears did drip, | They gave my infant nerves the hyp.'

hyp, Michael. See **hip, Michael.**

hyp'd. An † variant of *hypped,* q.v.

hyper. Abbr. *hypercritic* and *hyper-Calvinist* : coll. : resp. late C. 17–early 18 (as in Prior) and mid-C. 19–20, ob., as in Spurgeon. (O.E.D.)

hypernese. ' Ziph ', q.v. ; schoolboyish gibberish (e.g. *pegennapy,* penny) : Winchester College : ca. 1830–60. *The Press,* Nov. 12, 1864. [Hyphens. See ' Hyphenation ' in Addenda.]

hypnotic. Catachrestic (late C. 19–20) for *narcotic* or *soporific,* n. and adj. (F. W. Crofts, *Sudden Death,* 1935, ' The [sleeping-]draughts were merely a quite ordinary mild hypnotic.')

hypo. Abbr. *hyposulphite* (now technically known as *thiosulphate*) *of soda* : from ca. 1860 : coll., though not perhaps till *thiosulphate* arose in 1873.— Also adj. (Both : O.E.D.)—2. See :

hypo ; occ. **hyppo.** (Very) low spirits : coll. : 1711 ; † by 1880. Abbr. *hypochondria.* (Cf. *hip, hypocon,* and *hyp,* qq.v.) In 1711 Mandeville brought out his *Treatise of the Hypochondriack and Hysterick Passion, vulgarly called the Hypo in Men and Vapours in Women.* In the same year, Joseph Collett, merchant, wrote from Rio de Janeiro, ' I have a better Stomach than usuall and have perfectly forgot what the Hyppo means ', Oct. 15th in his *Private Letter Books,* edited by H. H. Dodwell in 1933.

hypochondria, in its physiological sense, is C. 18 catachrestic when used as a singular. (O.E.D.)

hypocochoana, like **hypopecouana,** is a corrupt form of *ipecacuanha* : late C. 17–18. (O.E.D.)

hypocon, occ. **hyppocon.** Abbr. *hypochondria* : coll. : 1704 to ca. 1710. ' Facetious ' Brown. This is earlier than *hip(p), hip(p)s, hyp, hyps,* qq.v.

hypothenuse. Hypotenuse : an erroneous spelling that, in late C. 16–mid 19, was S.E. ; from then till C. 20, catachrestic ; and in C. 20, coll. So too the adj. *hypothenusal.* Ex late L. *hypotenusa.* (O.E.D.)

hypped (1710) and **hyppish** (1732). See **hipped, hippish.**

hyps, gen. *the hyps* (1705). See *hyp* and cf. *hypo,* q.v. (For a tabulation of the earliest records of the various forms of the various *hip, hyp,* words, see Grose, P., s.v. *hyp.*)

hypt. An † variant of *hyp'd = hypped* : see however, *hipped.*

I

I after a v.t. or a preposition is, in C. 19–20, resp. sol. and, gen. illiterate—i.e. low, coll.

i = *in* occurs in such † mild or trivial oaths as *icod, i'faith, ifecks* or *i'fegs, igad* or *i'gad.*—2. Long **i** for *ai, ay* (e.g. *daily, day > dily, dye*) is a mark of Cockney. Cf. ' *ah* for *ou* ', q.v. Short *i* for *ĕ* is another mark of Cockney speech and, like the preceding, almost (one surmises) immemorial ; e.g. *git* and *stiddy* (steady).

I am. See **great I am.**

I believe yer or **you, my boy !** Of this c.p., not wholly disused even yet, *The Referee,* on Oct. 18, 1885, wrote : ' 'Tis forty years since Buckstone's

drama, *The Green Bushes,* was first played at the Adelphi, and since Paul Bedford's [that most popular actor's] " I believe yer, my boy ! " found its way on to tongues of the multitude.' Cf. *Bedford go,* q.v., and :

I believe you—but thousands wouldn't ! A c.p. indicative of friendship victorious over incredulity : C. 20. Perhaps ex preceding (q.v.).

I.D.B. An illicit diamond-buyer : South African coll. : 1884. Ex *I.D.B.,* illicit diamond-buying. Pettman.

I desire. A fire : rhyming s. (— 1859) ; ob. Cf. *I suppose.*

I don't think ! See **think, I don't**. Occ. *fink*.

I hope it keeps fine for you ! See **hope it keeps fine** . . .

I refer you to Smith ! An allusive imputation of a lie or a boast : 1897–ca. 99. Ware, 'From a character named Smith with an affliction of lying in *The Prodigal Father* (Strand Theatre, 1897).'

I say ! A coll. exclamation, indicative of surprise : late C. 19–20. Ware implies that orig. it was proletarian.

I says. I say : sol. : C. 19–20. In illiterate speech, it is often repeated needlessly, as in D. Sayers, *The Nine Tailors*, 1934, 'And I says, " No ", I says '.

I subscribe ! Yes (on being offered a drink) : coll. : ca. 1870–1910.

I suppose. The nose : rhyming s. (— 1859). 'Ducange Anglicus.' Cf. *I desire*.

I.T.A. 'Irish toothache ', sense 2 (q.v.) : proletarian (— 1909). Ware.

I won't—slightly. I certainly shall : military c.p. : from ca. 1930.

-ible is often wrongly used for *-able* : e.g. *incontestible*. (Rarely distinguishable in speech.)

Ibsênity. A characteristic, or the chief characteristics, of Ibsen (d. 1908), esp. of his plays : ca. 1905–14 : jocular coll., coined by *Punch* on *obscenity*. (W.)

ice, cut no. See **cut no ice**.

ice-cream ship, the. The Cunard-liner *Antonia* : nautical : 1922 ; ob. Bowen.

ice-Jack. An ice-cream seller : coll. (— 1923). Manchon.

icicle's chance in Hades or **hell, not an.** Not the least chance : coll. : from ca. 1910.

-icide, in nn. and adjj., denotes killer of, killing ; the person, etc., represented by the n. forming the main part of the word : sometimes (rarely before C. 20) so extravagant or jocular as to be coll.

ickitserpu. See **hickitserpu**.

ickle. Little : nursery coll. : since when ? See esp. Norah March's article in *The Evening Standard*, May 28, 1934.

ictus. A lawyer : C. 19 legal. A telescoped corruption of L. *iuris consultus*.

idæa is an † erroneous form of *idea* : C. 16–early 18. O.E.D.

idder. See **kidder !**

iddy (or **itty**) **umpty.** A signaller : military : late C. 19–20. F. & Gibbons. Ex a phrase used in India for teaching Morse to native troops.—2. Hence, a R.E. lineman repairing telephone and telegraph wires : military : G.W. Ibid.—3. **the Iddy** (or **Itty**) **Umpties.** The 17th Division : military : from ca. 1910. Ibid. Ex their dot-and-dash sign.

idea !, the. What an idea ! ; well, I never ! : coll. : C. 20. Manchon.

idea ?, what's the big. What folly have you in mind ? : coll. ; orig. U.S., anglicised ca. 1930. O.E.D. (Sup.)

idea-box or **-pot.** The head : resp. C. 19, late C. 18–20 (ob.). Grose, 1st ed. Cf. *knowledge-box*, q.v.

ideagraph, etc., is erroneous for *ideograph*, etc. : from ca. 1835. So too *idealogical*, etc., for *ideological*, etc. : from ca. 1797. (O.E.D.)—And, C. 19–20, *idealogue* for *ideologue*. (O.E.D.)

idee. (An) idea : C. 15–20 : S.E. till C. 18, then low coll.

identical, the. The very same person, thing, or

statement : coll. (— 1891). N. Gould, in *The Double Event*, ' " I'm the identical," said Jack.'

identified with, be ; identify oneself with. Catachrestic when simply = to be associated, associate oneself, with : C. 20. Ex U.S.

identity. A person, esp. of some—gen. **rather** quaint—importance. Chiefly in phrase, *an old identity* : coll. : orig. (1862) New Zealand ; then (— 1879) Australia. Ex a topical song by R. Thatcher. Morris.—2. In C. 20 Australian, mostly ' a person long associated with a locality ', Jice Doone.

idiot-fringe. Factory-girls' hair combed down, fringe-wise, over the forehead : London jocular : ca. 1885–1900. Baumann.

idle fellowship. (Gen. pl.) A sinecure fellowship : Oxford and Cambridge Universities' coll. (— 1884) ; ob. Ware.

idles, the. Idleness, whether healthily deliberate or morbidly lazy : C. 17–20 : coll. Gen. preceded by *sick of*, i.e. with. Apperson.

idolathite or **-yte.** Erroneous forms of *idolothyte* : C. 16–18. (O.E.D.)

idonk. An idea : military : 1915. F. & Gibbons. Perhaps influenced by Fr. *dis donc !*

-ie. See **-y**, an extremely common coll. suffix.

ietqui. Quiet : sporting (— 1909). Ware. By transposition.

if is often omitted in coll. speech, as in ' And yet, come to the rights of it, he'd no business there at all ' (Baumann) : C. 19 (? earlier)–20.

if as how. If ; as in ' If as how anyone had come up ' (Baumann) : sol. (— 1887).

if my aunt had been a man she'd have been my uncle. A C. 18–mid-19 proverbial c.p. in derision of one who has laboriously explained the obvious. Apperson.

if only I had some eggs I'd make (or **cook**) **eggs-and-bacon—if I had the bacon !**, with slight variations. A military c.p. of the G.W.

if-shot or **-stroke.** An unsound stroke : cricketers' coll. : 1897, Ranjitsinhji. (Lewis.)

if you call yourself a soldier, I'm a bloody Army Corps ! A military c.p. implying superior soldierliness in the speaker : 1915 ; slightly ob. B. & P.

ifs and ands. Conditions and stipulations ; circumlocution ; hesitation : coll. : C. 16–20, but since ca. 1820, mainly dial. and rurally proverbial. More, 1513 ; Davenport, 1624 ; Richardson, 1748 ; Sir Robert Horne, in *The Times*, May 30, 1924 (Apperson.)

-ify, for *-efy :* incorrect in *rarify* and *stupify*.

iggerance, igorance. Ignorance : a frequent sol. pronunciation among the illiterate : C. 19–20.

iggri, -ry. Hurry up ! : coll. of soldiers with service in Egypt : late C. 19–20. Ex Arabic.

Iggry Corner, at Bullecourt, a spot dangerous because of shell-fire in 1917. F. & Gibbons.

ignoramus. An ignorant person : C. 17–20. In C. 17, coll. ; then S.E. Ex *Ignoramus*, a nickname for the title-role lawyer in Ruggle's lawyer-satirising play, 1615,—this latter being ex a Grand Jury's endorsement to a bill of indictment.

Ignoramus Jury. The Grand Jury that, in 1681, rejected a bill of indictment against the Earl of Shaftesbury : late C. 17 : coll. : then historical, therefore sanctuaried among the museum-pieces of reconditely allusive S.E. (O.E.D.)

igorance. See **iggerance**.

I'll. I shall, or I will : coll. : C. 18. O.E.D. Cf. *Ile* (at *ile*, 1).

*Ikey. A Jew, esp. a Jewish receiver of stolen goods : c. (— 1864) in C. 19, low in C. 20. H., 3rd ed. also *Ikey Mo*. Ex *Isaac*.—2. In C. 20, occ. a pawnbroker of any nationality.—3. The 'inevitable' nickname of men with Jewish surnames or features : late C. 19–20.

ikey, adj. Smart or smartly dressed ; alert, wide-awake, artful : low : from ca. 1870 ; ob. Ex the preceding, sense 1.—2. Hence, conceited : low (— 1889) ; slightly ob. Barrère & Leland.

*Ikey Mo. Same senses, period, and genesis as *Ikey*, n. Ex *Isaac Moses*.

ile. (Ile.) I shall, I will : coll. : C. 16–17. O.E.D.—2. (ile.) A low coll. and dial. pronunciation of *oil* : C. 19–20 (in late C. 19–20, mostly U.S.). —3. (Gen. *ile*, not *Ile* or *Isle*.) Dance (n. and v.) : rhyming s. (—1909). Ware. Abbr. *Isle of France*.

iligant. See illigant.

ilk, of that. As = of that class, set, or family, it is a mid-C. 19–20 sol. ; the phrase properly 'implies coincidence of name with estate, e.g. [*Lundie of that ilk* =] *Lundie of Lundie*', W.

'ill. A vowelled form of '*ll* : (dial. and) lower-class coll. : C. 19–20.

I'll. A coll. abbr. of *I shall, I will* : C. 17–20 (O.E.D.). Cf. *I'il* and *Ile* (at *ile*, 1).

ill, be. To vomit : C. 19–20 ; euphemism >, ca. 1910, coll.

ill-convenient and its n. in -ence. (The being) inconvenient, ill-suiting : C. 18–20 ; S.E. till ca. 1820 ; coll. ca. 1820–70 ; then low coll. (O.E.D.)

*ill fortune. Ninepence (as a single coin) : c. : late C. 17–early 19. B.E. ; Grose. 2nd ed. Because not a shilling. Cf. *picture of ill luck*, its synonym.

I'll give you Jim Smith ! I.e. a thrashing : (mostly London) streets' c.p. : 1887–ca. 90. Ware. Ex a pugilist prominent in 1887.

I'll go hopping to hell ! ; often preceded by *well* ! : a C. 20 c.p. indicative of astonishment or admiration.

I'll have a basinful of that ! A (mostly lower-classes' and lower-middle classes') c.p. directed at a long word or a new one : 1934–5. A synonym, from ca. 1910, is *I'll have two of those l*, as in Michael Harrison, *Spring in Tartarus*, 1935.

ill to, do. (Gen. in negative.) To coït with (a woman) : Scots coll. : C. 19–20 ; ob.

*illegitimate. A counterfeit sovereign, *young illegitimate* being a 'snide' half-sovereign : c. of ca. 1820–70. Bee (1823). By a pun.—2. A low-grade costermonger : from ca. 1840 ; ob. by 1915, † by 1920.

illegitimate, adj. 'Applied to steeple-chasing or hurdle-racing, as distinguished from work on the flat ', F. & H. : racing (— 1888) : in C. 19, s. : in C. 20, coll. or j.

illigant ; more correctly iligant. Elegant : Anglo-Irish : C. 18–20 ; † except as an archaic jocularity or as a typical example of the Irish pronunciation of English. See also elegant.

illination. Erroneous for *illinition* : C. 17–20.— So illipsis for *ellipsis* : C. 18–20. O.E.D.

[illiteracies are in this dictionary termed solecisms (' sol.'). For a classification, see Fowler.]

illude and *elude* are often, in C. 16–20, confused. So are illusion and *allusion*.

[illuminated, having an interlinear translation, is given by the O.E.D. as college s. : true ; American.]

illure, illurement are erroneous forms of *allure*,

allurement : late C. 16–17. Due to the influence of words having prefix in *il-*. (O.E.D.)

illustrated clothes. See historical shirt.

illustricity, illustriousness, is very faulty in its form : C. 17–18. (O.E.D.)

I'm. A coll. abbr. *I am* : mid-C. 17–20. Cowley, 1647, ' No : I'm undone ' (O.E.D.).

I'm afloat. A boat, or a coat : rhyming s. (— 1859 the former ; — 1874 the latter). H., resp. 1st and 5th ed.

I'm so frisky. Whiskey : C. 20 rhyming s.

image, esp. in *you little image*. A term of affectionate reproach : coll. : from ca. 1870 ; ob.

I'm in the boat—push off ! A variant, less gen., of *fuck, you, Jack, I'm all right*. B. & P.

imbibation. Erroneous for *imbibition* : from ca. 1820 ; ob. O.E.D.

immanent, imminent, eminent, have, since ca. 1600, often—mostly the second for the first or for the third—been interconfused. So too the corresponding nn. and advv. All catachreses. O.E.D.

Immelmann. To have or to get one's own back : aircraft engineers' : from ca. 1917. *The Daily Herald*, Aug. 1, 1936. Ex the name of a well-known aviator—one of the three greatest German G.W. ' aces.' He died in action on June 18, 1916 : see Franz Immelmann, *Immelmann*, published in English in 1935. Max Immelmann was known as *der Adler von Lille*, the eagle of Lille.

immense. A general superlative ; splendid : from ca. 1760. G. A. Stevens, 1771, ' Dear Bragg, Hazard, Loo, and Quadrille, | Delightful, extatic ! immense ! ' Cf. *great*, q.v.

immense, adv. Immensely ; very : 1754, Murphy, ' An immense fine Woman '. (O.E.D.)

immensely. As a mere intensive : coll. : C. 19–20. Cf. *immense*, adj., q.v.

immensikoff. A fur-lined overcoat : ca. 1868–1905. Ex a song, *The Shoreditch Toff*, sung ca. 1868 by Arthur Lloyd, who described himself as Immensikoff and wore a coat heavily lined with fur (F. & H.).

immergent is, ca. 1650–1820, occ. used—erroneously, of course—for *emergent*=urgent. O.E.D.

immigrant ; imminent. See eminent, immanent

immortal. Excessive ; inhuman : coll. : ca. 1540–1650. (O.E.D.)

immortally. Infinitely ; superhumanly : coll. : from ca. 1540.

Immortals. The 76th Foot Regiment, British Army : military ; from ca. 1804 ; ob. F. & Gibbons. In the Mahratta War, 1803–4, most of the men were wounded, very few killed, and so men kept reappearing. Known also as *the Pigs* and *the Old Seven-and-Sixpennies*, qq.v.

imp. As a mischievous child, S.E.—2. One who prepares cases for a (law) ' devil ', q.v. : legal : from ca. 1855 ; ob.

impack. See contack.

impale. To possess a woman : low : C. 19–20. ob.

impall. An † erroneous form of *impale*. O.E.D.

impartial was, in late C. 16–18, occ. used in error for *partial*. (O.E.D.)

impayable, adj. Beyond anything ; ' the limit ', ' priceless ' : coll. : 1818 (S.O.D.) ; ob. Direct ex Fr. ; cf. Fr. *c'est impayable !*

imperance, -ence ; also † impurence. Impudence, impertinence : sol. : 1766, Colman, ' I wonder at your impurence, Mr. Brush, to use me in this manner.'—2. Hence, an impudent person : from ca. 1835. Dickens, in *Pickwick*, ch. xiv, ' " Let me alone, imperence," said the young lady.' Corruption of *impudence*, not a contraction of *impertinence*. Cf. :

imperent. Impudent ; impertinent : sol. James Grant, 1838 (O.E.D.). Cf. preceding entry.

imperial, as a tuft of hair on lower lip, has, despite F. & H., always been S.E., but as adj., (of a fall) on one's head, it is sporting s. : 1861. Suggested by *imperial crown*. Cf. *crowner*.

imperial pop. Ginger beer : Cockneys' : in 1854. The *imperial* was in honour of Napoleon III, who in that year passed in state through London. Ware.

imperiality, as ' an imperial right or privilege ', is a C. 19–20 ghost-sense fathered by Webster and ' based on a misprinted quotation from Tooke '. The right word would be *imperialty*. (S.O.D.)

Imperials, the. British soldiers : Colonial military coll. : 1915–18. F. & Gibbons.

impertinacy, impertinat. Erroneous for *impertinency, impertinent* : C. 15–17. (O.E.D.)

implement. ' Tool, a Property or Fool, easily engag'd in any (tho' difficult or Dangerous) Enterprize ', B.E. : coll. : late C. 17–18.

implement, to. Fulfil (a promise). Ca. 1927–33 this term was so abused that it might, for that period, be fairly considered as cultured, even pedantic, s.

implicit for **explicit** (C. 18), a sol. ; for ' absolute ', ' unmitigated ', (C. 17), a catachresis. (O.E.D.)

impo. See **impot.**

importance. A wife : from ca. 1640 ; in C. 19–20, low coll. ; ob. Rochester. Less gen. than *comfortable importance*, q.v.

importune as = to import, portend, is catachrestic. Spenser, imitated by Marston. (O.E.D.)

importunity of friends. Book-world c.p. or coll., ca. 1660–1780 : ' the stale Excuse for coming out in Print, when Friends know nothing of the matter ', B.E. (Still a frequent make-believe.)

impose. ' To punish (a person) by an imposition ' : † university and ob. school s. : from ca. 1885. (O.E.D.)

imposh. A Public Schools' variant of *impot* : C. 20. E. F. Benson, *David Blaize*, 1916.

imposs or **impos.** Impossible : coll. : from early 1920's. (O.E.D. Sup.)

impost. That weight which, in a handicap race, a horse has to carry : racing : 1883 (S.O.D.).

*impost-taker. A usurer that, attending the gaming tables, lends money at exorbitant interest : ca. 1690–1830 : c. B.E., Grose. Cf. *sixty per cent.*, q.v.

impot ; in Australia and New Zealand, occ. *impo.* A schoolboys' contraction of *imposition* (a punishment-exercise) : from ca. 1890 : in C. 20, coll.

imprac. Impracticable : coll. (— 1923). Manchon.

impregnate is, in C. 17–18, occ. used erroneously for *impregnable*. (O.E.D.)

impressa, an erroneous form of *impresa* : late C. 16–17.—2. Of *impress* (a distinctive mark) : C. 17.—Likewise, *impress* is in C. 19 an occ. error for *imprest*, to lend, advance money. And vice versa. (O.E.D.)

imprimatur and **imprimature** are, in C. 19–20, occ. confused, the one for the other. O.E.D.

improve, on the. Improving : coll., mostly Australian : from ca. 1925.

improve the occasion, to turn to spiritual profit, seems, ca. 1855–90—nor is it yet †—to have been ' much in use among Chadbands and Stigginses ', H., 5th ed. H. calls it s., but it is perhaps rather a Nonconformist c.p. Lawrence, in *Guy Livingstone*, 1857 (O.E.D.).

Imps or **imps.** Imperial Tobacco Company shares : Stock Exchange : from ca. 1919.

impudent stealing. ' Cutting out the backs of coaches, and robbing the seats ', Grose, 2nd ed. : ca. 1788–1830. (Not a mere description (hence S.E.), but a definition).

impure. A harlot : fashionable s. until ca. 1830, then coll. : 1784. Ob. by 1890 ; † by 1930 ; being S.E. in C. 20.

imshee ; imshi ; imshy ! Go away ! : G.W. + ; orig. military. Ex Arabic. (Also, intensively, *imshee yaller !*)

imshee (etc.) **artillery.** Trench-mortar batteries, esp. the 3-inch Stokes : Australian military : 1915 ; ob. Because, after firing, they hurried away.

[**in,** n., a person in (esp. a political) office : despite F. & H., this is S.E.]

in, preposition : all phrases not found here—and only a few are listed here—must be sought at the dominant n. or pronoun.—2. If suppressed, as before *these days* (at this time or age), it produces a coll. : C. 19–20.—3. ' Within the sphere of (a particular class or order of things) ' : coll. : 1866, Ruskin, ' The newest and sweetest thing in pinnacles ' (O.E.D. Sup.).

in, adv. In office : C. 17–20 : political coll. >, in C. 19, S.E. Shakespeare.—2. In season : from ca. 1850, though anticipated in C. 17 : coll. till C. 20, then S.E. Mayhew, 1851, ' During July cherries are in as well as raspberries '.—3. Fashionable : coll. : from ca. 1860.—4. See **in it** and **in with.**—5. At the wickets : from ca. 1770 : cricket coll. >, ca. 1860, S.E.—6. In c., in prison (— 1862). ' It is the etiquette among prisoners never to ask a man what he is in for,' Anon., *Five Years' Penal Servitude.* Cf. *inside*, q.v.—7. To the good ; with a profit (of e.g. £1000) : from ca. 1890 : s. >, ca. 1905, coll.

in is often used erroneously for *un-*, as in *inguilty.* Instances : too numerous to mention, nor need they be listed, here. Note, however, that many once S.E. words in *in-* have been displaced by those in *un-* with the gradual weakening of the Latin tradition. See esp. Fowler.

-in' for *-ing*, when not a coll. affectation by the upper and upper-middle classes (huntin', shootin' and fishin', you know), is a low coll. bordering on, and in C. 20 considered as in fact being, sol. It is contemporaneous with the whole of Mod. E.

in, and a bit. With a little extra ; with a tip in addition : coll. (— 1923). Manchon.

in, well. See **well in.**

in-and-in, play at. To have sexual connexion : low coll. : C. 17–early 19. Glapthorne, Cotton, D'Urfey. Cf. *in-and-out, play at.*

in-and-out (also, and gen., in pl.), inside working, intimate or secret details, is S.E., but the adj., when = variable, uneven (as applied to a horse's ' form '), is sporting s. (— 1885) >, in C. 20, coll. >, ca. 1930, S.E.—2. An *in-and-out* is a pauper frequently returning, for short periods, to the workhouse or casual ward : low : from ca. 1880. Ware. —3. **the In and Out.** The Naval and Military Club in Piccadilly : naval and military officers' : from not later than 1914. F. & Gibbons, ' From the words "In" and "Out", painted on the pillars of the approach to the courtyard in front.'—4. Stout (the drink): rhyming s.: late C. 19–20. B. & P.

in-and-out, play at. to coït: C. 17–20 low coll. Cf. *in-and-in*, q.v.

in-and-out shop. 'A shop through which one can walk in and out along a passage, where the goods are hung up for inspection' (O.E.D. Sup.): coll., orig. and mainly Londoners': C. 20.

in Annie's room. See **Annie's room.**

in course. Of course: sol.: C. 19–20. (Graham Shepard, *Tea-Tray in the Sky*, 1934.)

[**in dock, out nettle** is proverbial and therefore ineligible. For this phrase, see esp. Apperson.]

in everybody's mess and nobody's watch. A cadger chary of work: a naval c.p. of ca. 1880–1910. Bowen.

in for, gen. with *it.* Due to receive punishment, incur trouble: C. 17–20. Coll. till late C. 18, then S.E.—though not dignified. Cf. the modern *for it*, q.v.

in for (a person), **get it.** To remember to one's disadvantage: (rather low) coll.: from ca. 1860. *Derby Day*, 1864 (p. 121).

in for it. (Of a woman), pregnant: lower classes' (— 1923). Manchon.

*****in for patter,** adj. and adv. Waiting for trial: c. (— 1859); ob. Also *in for pound* (1887, Baumann.)

in for the plate. Venereally infected: low: ca. 1810–70. *Lex. Bal.*

in her Sunday best. With all canvas set: sailing-ships' coll.: mid-C. 19–20; ob. Bowen.

in it, be. See **in with.**—2. Sharing in the benefits of robbery or swindle: c. (— 1812). Vaux.—3. See **like the man** . . .

in it, for all there's. Esp. with *play one's hand.* To one's or its utmost capacity: (somewhat low) coll.: from ca. 1880.

in it, little or **nothing** or **not much.** (Gen. preceded by *there's.*) Much of a muchness; virtually no difference: racing s. (ca. 1905) >, by ca. 1912, gen. coll. (O.E.D. Sup.)

in-laws. One's parents-in-law: 1894 (O.E.D.): s. >, ca. 1905, coll. Attributed to Queen Victoria by *Blackwood's Magazine*, Jan. 24, 1894.

in on. Participating in, admitted to a share of, some thing or some affair of unusual interest or importance: coll.: from ca. 1919. 'Am I to be in on this?'

in Paris. Eloped: Society: mid-C. 19–early 20. Ware. Because elopers so often went there.

*****in smoke.** In hiding: New Zealand c. (— 1932). Thereby shrouded.

in the drag. Behindhand: tailors' (— 1909). Ware.

in the tub. 'In the bad books of seniors'; (of a ship) having incurred the Admiral's displeasure: naval: late C. 19–20. Bowen.

in the wind. Drunk: nautical (— 1823); ob. Egan's Grose; Bowen. See **three sheets in the wind.**

*****in town.** 'Flush of money', Vaux: c. of ca. 1810–60.

in with (or **in it with**), **be.** To be on guard against or 'even with' (a person): low coll.: ca. 1860–1905.—2. To be on intimate or profitable terms with: late C. 17–20: coll. till C. 19, then S.E. Surtees, in *Hillingdon Hall*, 'He was in with the players too, and had the *entrée* of most of the minor theatres.'—3. Hence, to be in partnership with: (orig. low) coll.; in C. 20, S.E.: from ca. 1810; Vaux.—4. Hence, in the swim: coll.: from ca. 1860.—5. To be compared with, count beside: coll. (— 1889).

inamoretta. In mistake for, or a corruption of, *inamorata*, prob. by confusion with *amoretto*: C. 18. Mrs. Manley. (O.E.D.)

inceasible is erroneous for *incessable*, ceaseless, incessant. (O.E.D.).

incert (†) is an erroneous form of *insert.* O.E.D.

[**inch,** to move slowly or by very small degrees, is S.E.]

Inch and Pinch. Gallipoli Peninsula: New Zealand soldiers': 1915; ob. Ex '*Peninsula*' reversed. Cf. *Pinch an Inch.*

inch before (or **beyond**) **one's nose, not to** (**be able to**) **see.** To find oneself in the dark: C. 17–20 coll. Apperson cites two examples of the now rare affirmative.

inch in, v.i., to encroach, seems to have been coll. in C. 17–18. B.E., Grose. So too the vbl. n., *inching-in.*

incident. An illegitimate child: Society: adopted, before 1909, from U.S.; ob. Ware.

incipience, -nt, are occ., C. 15–17, used erroneously for *insipience, -nt.* So too *incypyent.* O.E.D.

incision is, in C. 17, occ. used erroneously for *insition*, engrafting. (S.O.D.)

incog. A coll. abbr. of *incognito*, n., adj., and adv.: resp. from ca. 1690, 1705, 1709. B.E., Gray, Disraeli.—2. Intoxicated: ca. 1820–1900: low. Bee. Ex *cog*(*ue*), a dram, by way of *disguised*, q.v.

incognita. A disguised harlot: fashionable s. > coll.: C. 18. Cf. *anonyma*, q.v.

incon(**e**)**y.** '? Rare, fine, delicate, pretty, nice': fashionable s. of the c.p. kind: ca. 1585–1640. Shakespeare, 1588. ? etymology. — Also adv. (O.E.D.)

inconstancy is occ., ca. 1580–1630, used in error for *incontinency.* O.E.D.

incumbrances. Children: (? low) coll.: C. 19–20. Gen. *encumbrances.*

indaba. A(n important) meeting or conference: from ca. 1907: South African coll. >, ca. 1920, s. Ex *indaba*, 'a native council meeting for the discussion of business important to the tribe', Pettman.

indeed and indeed! Really and truly: coll.: from ca. 1670. Wycherley, 'Indeed and indeed, father, I shall not have him' (O.E.D.).

indentures, make. To stagger with drink: C. 17–18 coll. Rowlands; Franklin, *Drinker's Dict.*, 1745. (The legal documents had their tops or edges indented, mainly for identification.) Apperson.

indescribables. Trousers: coll. (jocular): 1794. Dickens. Of this orig. euphemistic, but by 1850 jocular and semi-satirical group, the two commonest synonyms are *inexpressibles* and *unmentionables*, qq.v.; others are *indispensables*, *ineffables*, *inexplicables*, *innominables*, *unutterables* and *unwhisperables*, qq.v. The earliest is *inexpressibles* (1790), the latest *unutterables.* By 1900, all except *indescribables*, *indispensables*, *inexpressibles*, and *unmentionables* were †; the second > † ca. 1920. Not belonging to this class, yet cognate, is *sit-upons* (— 1860).

index. The nose: sporting: 1817; ob. Cf. *gnomon*, q.v.—2. The face: (low) coll., or s. > coll.: from ca. 1818; ob. Egan. Cf. *dial.*

[India, the female pudend, is literary rather than coll. Donne.]

India husband. That actual owner of an East Indiaman who chartered her to the Company: nautical coll.: mid-C. 18–mid-19. Bowen. By deviation from S.E. *ship's husband.*

India-rubber man. See **bungy man.** Bowen. Ex his elasticity.

India wipe. A silk handkerchief: ca. 1790–1840: low. Grose, 3rd ed. See **wipe,** n.

Indian. A Maori (1769); an Australian Aboriginal (1770): catachrestic (Australian, New Zealand): ob. by 1840, † by 1890. Morris.

Indian Warner. Thomas Warner, a C. 17 governor of Dominica. He had Indian blood. (Dawson.)

indicated, ppl. adj. (Always with v. *to be.*) Necessary (occ.); (gen.) desirable, advisable: coll.: from ca. 1915. E.g., 'a drink was indicated'. Ex S.E. sense, to suggest, to point to.

indict and **indite** are occ. confounded. So *indite* for *invite* and *inscribe.* (O.E.D.)

Indies, black. See **black.**

[Indirect question:—See Fowler.]

indijaggers. Indigestion: Oxford undergraduates': from ca. 1908. Used, e.g., by Lord Peter Wimsey in Dorothy Sayers, *Strong Poison,* 1930. See **-aggers** and cf. *Maggers' Memugger.*

indispensables. Trousers: coll.: 1841 (O.E.D.); by 1900, † by 1920. Cf. *indescribables,* q.v.

individual, when merely = person, dates from ca. 1740: until ca. 1870, S.E.; then coll. when contemptuous, low coll. > sol. when unintentional. See esp. Fowler.

indorse ; more gen. *endorse.* To cudgel. Esp. *indorse with a cudgel.* Coll. (– 1785); † by 1880. With a pun on † *dorse,* the back. Grose, 1st ed. —2. V.t. and i., to practise sodomy (on): low: from ca. 1780. Whence:

indorser. A sodomite: low (– 1785); ob. by 1870, † by 1900. Grose, 1st ed.

Indy. India: C. 16–20: until C. 18, S.E.; then coll. till late C. 19, when it > sol.

ineffable, the female pudend, is a literary synonym, but as one not to be named, an anonymous journalist (1859), or a tremendous swell (1861, †), it is coll., while *ineffables,* trousers, is a coll.: 1823 (O.E.D.); ob. by 1880, † by 1900. Leigh Hunt, 'The eatables were given up for the ineffables'.

inescaturation is erroneous for *inexsaturation:* C. 17. O.E.D.

['Inevitable' or inseparable nicknames. See **Nicknames.**]

inexpleable, -ly. Erroneous for † *inexpleble, -ly* (insatiable, -bly): C. 16–18. O.E.D.

inexplicables. Trousers: coll.: Dickens, 1836, in *Boz :* † by 1890. Cf. *ineffables, inexpressibles.*

inexpressibles. Trousers: coll.: from ca. 1790. Grose, 3rd ed. Wolcot; Dickens, 'Symmetrical inexpressibles, and scented pocket-handkerchief'. Cf. *indescribables,* q.v.

infædation is an † erroneous form of *infeudation.* O.E.D.

infant. Walter Hancock's steam-carriage, 1832: coll.: 1832–ca. 1840.

infantry. Children: from 1613: in C. 17–18, S.E., in C. 19–20 (ob.), jocular coll. Jonson describes a teacher as 'terror to the infantry'.

infantry, light. See **light infantry.**

Infants, the. The Infantry: cavalrymen's: late C. 19–20; ob. Cf. *Gee-Gees,* q.v.

[infare, cited by F. & H., is ineligible.]

inferior. Any non-prefect member of the school: Winchester College: from ca. 1840; ob. Mansfield.

Inferior Portion, the. The younger Tories: political: 1885–ca. 90. Ex a Gladstone-written phrase, which 'took at once, and was satirically used' (Ware).

inferiority complex. See **complex.**

infernal. Execrable, detestable, excessive: coll.: 1764 (S.O.D.).—2. In C. 17–early 19, sometimes an adv.: 1646, Lady Mary Verney, 'Besides coaches which are most infe[r]nell dear.'

infernally. An intensive adv.: C. 19–20. Ex the idea of *hellish(ly),* q.v.

inferred. 'The common journalistic *faux pas* of using "inferred" in the sense of "implied"': catachrestic: rare before C. 20. Peter Quennell in *The New Statesman,* Dec. 30, 1933.

[Infinitive for infinitive preceded by *do* or *does* is coll. (late C. 19–20), only in dialogue. E.g., A. A. Milne, *Two People,* 1931, ' "Anybody know its name ?" . . . "Sizilietta." ']

infirmary, my or the answer's in the. I.e. in the *affirmative,* which it puns: coll.: C. 20; very ob. Prob. ex some boxer's fate.—2. Hence, my answer is unfavourable, or a piece of bad news: from ca. 1910 and imm. much more gen. than sense 1.

inflicted and **afflicted** are frequently confused by the illiterate.

influ. An occ. variant (– 1923; ob.) of *flu,* q.v. Manchon.

influence. See **'fluence.**

influence in the right quarter, have. A virtual c.p., naively ironic, applied to a man that has got a menial or otherwise distastful job: New Zealanders': in G.W.

info. Information: Australian, mostly low and esp. among racing touts: from ca. 1930.

infra dig. Unbecoming (act); undignified: coll.: 1824 (S.O.D.). Scott. Abbr. *infra dignitatem.*—Hence, 2. Scornful, proud: Winchester College: from ca. 1860. Also *sport infra-dig duck,* to look scornful: ibid. Wrench.

-ing added to a n., e.g. *admiralling,* indicates the active state of being that which the n. (e.g. *admiral*) denotes. Often preceded by *a-,* as in 'Hudibras' Butler's *a-colonelling.* Certain final consonants of the original n. are doubled. Coll.—2. For *-in(n), -en(n), -on(n),* it is sol.: C. 18–20. See quotation at **handle the ribbons.**

ingan. See **ingun.**

Ingee. India: sol. (– 1887). Baumann. (Cf. *Injun.*) Whence *injee-rubber* (ibid.).

ingenious, ingenuous : often confounded since ca. 1600. So, too, the nn. and advv.

ingle, a catamite, and v., to sodomise, to caress, are, despite F. & H., ineligible, as is *ingler,* a sodomist; but we may note *ingle* used (from ca. 1840) catachrestically for an open fireplace; *ingle-nook,* the female pudend, is a mere literary synonym.

*ingler. A dishonest horse-dealer: ca. 1820–1910. *The Modern Flash Dict.,* 1825.

ingot(t)ed. Rich: coll. (in C. 20, S.E.): ca. 1860–1905. E. Yates. Cf. *inlaid.*

ingun, occ. **ingan.** An onion: Cockney (– 1823); ob. 'Jon Bee.'

inhabitable is, from ca. 1520, often confused with *habitable* and *inhabited.* (French influence.) O.E.D.

inhalent is wrong for *inhalant,* C. 19–20. Ibid.

Iniskillen men. The militia: late C. 17–18

pejorative. Ex a famous regiment 'fam'd . . . in the late Irish Wars', B.E.

[Initials for names : objectionably for surnames, as in 'My regards to Mrs. S.' addressed to her husband ; unobjectionably when affectionately for Christian names. Both usages are coll. : mid-C. 19–20. I have even heard *P* for *pater* as a term of address ; cf. the *P.A.* hereinunder.]

injun !, honest. Honestly ! An orig. (1876) U.S. coll., anglicised ca. 1905 : mostly among boys. Ex (*Red*) *Indian*, very rarely used in this phrase. Cf. the U.S. *get up one's injun*, = British *irish* and *paddy* (temper), qq.v.

-ink for **-ing** is a very gen. sol. : since when ? E.g., John Brophy, *Waterfront*, 1934, 'Girls lose their character, drivink out on dark roads with young good for nothinks.' Also esp. *anythink* and *somethink*.

ink, sling. To be an author : coll. : ex U.S., anglicised ca. 1890.—2. To be a clerk : coll. : C. 20.

ink-bottle. A clerk : artisans' (— 1909) ; slightly ob. Ware.

[**ink-horn** or **-pot**, pedantic, has, despite F. & H. always been S.E.]

ink in one's pen, have no. To be penniless, occ. witless : C. 16–17 coll.

Ink-Line, The. Fleet Street : London taxi-drivers' : from ca. 1905. (*The Evening News*, Jan. 20, 1936.) Cf. *the Cold Blow, the Pill-Box, Spion Kop*, qq.v.

ink-slinger. An author, a journalist : coll. : orig. (1887), U.S. ; anglicised ca. 1890. Milliken. —2. Occ., in late C. 19–20, a clerk ; esp. in the Navy, who use it for a purser's clerk. Ware.

ink-slinging. Authorship, journalism : coll. : from ca. 1890. Milliken.—2. In C. 20, occ. 'clerking'. Cf. :

ink-spiller. A clerk : Cockney (— 1887). Baumann. Cf. *ink-slinger*, 2.

[**inkle-weaver**, even in *great* or *thick as inkle-weavers*, is ineligible.]

[**inkosi.** See **enkosi**.]

inky, n. See 'Moving-Picture Slang', p. 3.

inky, adj., often as a one-word reply evasive of a direct answer ; 'can't talk about it now !' Tailors' : from ca. 1860 ; ob. Cf. S.E. *dirty*.—2. Tipsy : orig. (ca. 1915) military ; ob. F. & Gibbons ; Manchon. Perhaps suggested by *blotto*, q.v.

*inky smudge. A judge : underworld rhyming s. : late C. 19–20. James Curtis, *The Gilt Kid*, 1936.

inlaid ; well-inlaid. Rich ; temporarily in funds : late C. 17–early 19. B.E. ; Grose. Cf. *ingotted*, q.v., and Yorkshire *inlaid for*, provided with.

innards. The stomach ; guts : C. 19–20 ; orig. euphemistic, then, ca. 1870, coll. ; in C. 20 regarded as low coll. Corruption of S.E. *inwards*.

innards, fill one's. To eat : low coll. : from ca. 1860.

inner being (— 1923) or **inner man** (from ca. 1855), **the.** The stomach ; one's appetite : jocular coll. Esp. in *satisfy the inner man.* Ex *the i. m.*, the mind, the soul. Cf. *inside lining* and *M. le Ministre de l'Intérieur.*

[**innings**, a spell, a turn, is S.E. ex cricket ; but note :]

innings, have (a) good. To be lucky, esp. in money matters : coll. : from ca. 1860.—2. To live a long time : coll. (— 1870). In C. 20, both senses are S.E.

innings, have a long. To live a long time ; *have had a long innings*, to die at a ripe old age : coll. : from ca. 1860 ; in C. 20, S.E. Cf. *not out (96)*, 96 and still alive.—2. Also as for preceding entry, sense 1.

innocent, n. and adj., half-wit(ted), is S.E. (latterly dial.).—2. An undeserved term of imprisonment : c. (— 1896). Ware.

innocent as a devil of two years old (as). A mocking assent to a declaration of innocence : coll. : ca. 1660–1770. Ray, Swift. (Apperson.) The equivalent *new-born babe* (or *child unborn*) simile is S.E.

innocent of. Free from, devoid of : coll. : 1706 Addison (O.E.D.).

innocents, massacre or slaughter of the. 'Devoting to extinction a number of useful measures which there was not time to pass', *The Times*, July 20, 1859 : Parliamentary : the former from — 1859, the latter from — 1870.

innominables. Trousers : coll. : ca. 1835–90. Southey. Cf. *indescribables*, q.v.

inns a court is a coll. form of *inns of court* : C. 17–early 19. O.E.D.

inquiration. An inquiry : London jocular : ca. 1885–1900. Baumann. Prob. ex Essex dial.

insane, when applied to things, is coll. : from ca. 1845.

insanitary suspector. A sanitary inspector : jocular (— 1935).

inscipient, erroneous for *incipient*.—**inscision, -tion**, for *incision*.—**inscyde**, †, for *incide*. (All O.E.D.)

insecty. Abounding in, or of the nature of, insects : coll. : 1859, Alex. Smith (O.E.D.).

inside, n. A passenger riding inside a vehicle : coll. : 1798 (S.O.D.) ; ob. Scott. Cf. *outside*.—2. The entrails : coll. and dial. : from ca. 1740. Also in pl. : from ca. 1760.

inside, adj. Secret, intimate, trustworthy (information) : from ca. 1880 : coll. till C. 20, when S.E.

*inside, adv. Inside a prison : c. (— 1888). Ware.

inside and outside ! A toast of ca. 1805–50 : low coll. *Lex. Bal.* Abbr. *the inside of a c**t and the outside of a gaol.*

inside lining. Food and drink, a meal. Esp. in *get an inside lining.* Low coll. (— 1851) ; slightly ob. Mayhew. Cf. *inner lining.*

inside of. Within (of time) : mid-C. 19–20 : coll., mostly Colonial ex U.S. ' Rolf Boldrewood '. 1888, ' He knocked the seven senses out of him inside of three rounds.'

inside of a(n). ' The middle or main portion of a period of time, exclusive of the beginning and end,' O.E.D. : coll. : from ca. 1890 ; ob. Hardy, in *Tess*, ' Home for the inside of a fortnight.' Ex preceding term.

inside of everything, know the. To be especially well informed : from ca. 1880 : coll. till C. 20, then S.E.

inside out of, take the. To empty (a glass) ; gut (a book) : coll. (— 1843) ; ob. Moncrieff, ' Haven't you taken the inside out of that quart of gatter yet ? ' (See **gatter**.)

inside running. An advantage : late C. 19–20 : orig. a sporting coll. ; in C. 20, S.E. 'The inside track of a curved race-course being shorter than the outside,' W. Cf. *inside track*, q.v.

inside squatter. A settler in a civilised district ;

Australian coll. : **ca.** 1870–1900. **Cf.** *outside squatter*, q.v.

inside the mark. Moderate : coll. : adopted from U.S. before 1909 ; slightly ob. Ware.

inside the probable. Probable ; within probability : coll. (-- 1909) ; perhaps orig. American, certainly ob. Ware. Cf. the preceding.

inside track, be on (or **have**) **the.** To be safe or at a point of vantage ; (with *of*) to understand thoroughly : sporting s. >, by 1890, coll. : from ca. 1865 ; ob. See **inside running.**

inside walker. A screw-steamer : nautical : late C. 19–20. Bowen, 'Borrowed from " Pidgin " English.'

inside worry, do an. To copulate : low coll. : from ca. 1840.

insides. See **inside,** n., 2.

insignia is erroneous when used as a singular (with pl. *-as*) : from ca. 1770. O.E.D.

insinuator. A slow, twisting ball : cricketers' jocular coll. : 1845 ; ob. Lewis.

insition. An † erroneous form of *incision* : C. 17–18. O.E.D. (As = engraftment it is S.E.)

-insky. A comic suffix added to almost any word ; often abbr. to *-sky*, as in *buttinsky*, one who butts in. C. 20. Prob. ex U.S.—2. Also in imitation of Russian, as is *offsky.*

insolute. Erroneous for *insolite* : late C. 15–18.—
insomnious catachrestically as = troubled with dreams. Mainly a lexicographical aberration introduced by Blount. (O.E.D.)

inspector of pavements. A person in the pillory : ca. 1820–40. Egan.—2. A man out of work : from ca. 1840 ; ob. by 1914, † by 1920 ; also as :

inspector of public buildings. A man out of work : from ca. 1870 ; † by 1920.

inspire. To impart—unavowedly—a tendential, esp. an official tone to an article : journalists' (— 1884) : orig. coll.; in C. 20, gen. S.E. *The Daily Telegraph*, Feb. 14, 1889, ' All the inspired papers keep laying stress upon this fact.'

inspired. Tipsy : coll. : C. 19–20 ; ob.—2. See **inspire.**

institution. A widely recognised and established practice or object ; an idea, an invention : coll. (1839) : ex U.S. (1788). In C. 20, almost S.E. O.E.D.

[**instrument** as female pudend is, despite F. & H., ineligible.]

instrumentation. ' Erroneously used for : Performance of instrumental music ; playing on instruments (with reference to style) 1856,' O.E.D.

insurance-anchor. A spare bower : merchant-servicemen's jocular coll. : late C. 19–20. Bowen.

i'n't, i'nt. An † coll. abbr. of *is not* via *isn't* : ca. 1740–1850. (O.E.D.)

in't. Abbr. († except in poetry, where archaic) of *in it* : except in poetry, coll. : C. 17–19. (O.E.D.)

*int. A sharper : C. 17 c. Brathwayte, ' His nipps, ints, bungs and prinados.' ? ex *interest* or ex L. *intus.*

intellects. Intellectual power(s) ; ' wits ' : late C. 17–20 : S.E. until ca. 1860, then—when not an archaic survival—coll. ; from ca. 1890, low coll. (O.E.D.)

intended. A prospective and affianced husband or wife : coll. : 1767 (S.O.D.) Gen. as *my, your,* etc. *intended.*

intense. Serious : soulful : coll. : **ca.** 1878–

1920. **Du Maurier,** 1889, ' Fair Æsthetic to Smith who has just been introduced, " Are you intense ? " ' —2. Hence, excited ; excitable : Society coll. : from ca. 1920. Evelyn Waugh, *Vile Bodies,* 1930, ' " Darling, I *am* so glad about our getting married." " So am I. But don't let's get intense about it." '

intentions. One's hitherto unavowed intention in regard to a proposal of marriage : coll. : 1796, Jane Austen (S.O.D.). Only of the man, esp. if bashful or ' dishonourable '.

Inter. The University of London Intermediate Examination : from ca. 1870 : coll. in C. 20 ; orig. s. Cf. *matric,* which, likewise, was orig. an abbr.—2. Hence, adj., as in *Inter arts* : late C. 19–20.—3. Esp. *the Third Inter,* the Third International : Socialist coll. : post-G.W. (James Cleugh, *Orgy by Numbers,* 1934.)

inter-'varsity. See **'varsity.**

interduce. To introduce : sol. (— 1887). Baumann.

interesting condition, be in an. To be with child : coll. : from ca. 1745. Smollett, ' I cannot leave her in such an interesting condition ' ; Dickens, in *Nicholas Nickleby.*

interloper. An unlicensed trader, interfering smuggler ; hanger-on ; busybody : C. 16–20 ; ob. Coll. till ca. 1750, then S.E. Minsheu ; B.E.

internatter. An international player : Oxford undergraduates' : from the middle 1890's. Charles Turley, *Godfrey Marten, Undergraduate,* 1904, ' He is an " internatter ", you see, and I don't think he ever forgets it.' By ' the Oxford *-er* '.

internecine, though etymologically incorrect as defined by Johnson, has so engrafted itself on the language that it cannot be condemned even as catachrestic : though I see that the O.E.D. classifies *internecion,* ' mutually deadly destruction ', as improper.

[Interpolation is a minor characteristic of unconventional speech ; prob. it does not antedate the C. 20, for it was rare before the G.W. E.g. *not bloody likely, abso-bloody-lutely, cheer-(most-)frightfully-ho !* This last occurs, e.g., in Dorothy Sayers, *The Unpleasantness at the Bellona Club,* 1928.

intersturb, erroneous for † *interturb.*—**intersusception,** for *intro-* or *intus-susception.* O.E.D.

into, in to. ' The two words should be written separately when their sense is separate,' Fowler, who cites, as erroneous, ' Lord Rosebery took her into dinner.' This catachresis has > distressingly gen.

into (a person) **for** (a sum of money), **be.** To owe a person so-much, to have let him down for a stated amount : Canadian coll. : late C. 19–20. John Beames, *Gateway,* 1932, ' I wouldn't give that fellow Dow much rope . . . He's into me for ninety dollars, and I can't get a cent out of him.'

into (a man), **be.** To fight : coll. (— 1864). H., 2nd ed. Cf. *pitch into, slip into,* qq.v.

into (a woman), **be** or **get.** ' To possess a woman carnally,' F. & H. : low coll. : C. 19–20. Cf. *be* or *get up*—see **up.**

into next week. Violently ; fatally ; into insensibility : coll. : mid-C. 19–20. Gen. **with** *knock* ; occ. with *hit, skid,* etc. See the **entry at knock into a cocked hat.**

intricate. A sol. (— 1923) for *intimate.* Manchon.

intro. An introduction (to a person) : **coll.** : 1899, Clarence Rook ; Michael Harrison, see the quotation at *cold-canvass.*

introduce (the) shoemaker to (the) tailor. To kick on the posterior : lower classes' (— 1909) ; ob. Ware.

inuendo. An erroneous spelling of *innuendo* : C. 18–20. O.E.D.

[**invade.** To grope, or to coït with, a woman : C. 17–19. A literary euphemism, as are F. & H.'s *be improperly intimate*, or *have improper intercourse, with*, and *interrural trench*.]

invalidish, invalidy. Valetudinarian ; rather ill : coll. : resp. 1855 (in C. 20, S.E.), 1894. S.O.D.

inveigle. To wheedle (one) out of something) : coll. : from ca. 1845 ; ob. E. E. Napier, 1849, ' He managed to " inveigle " me out of sixpence.' O.E.D.

Inventions ; Inventories. The Inventions Exhibition, London, 1885 : coll. : 1885 ; ob. by 1900, † by 1920. Ware. Cf. *Colinderies, Fisheries, Healtheries*, qq.v.

invest, v.i. (v.t. with *in*) To spend money (on), lay out money (for) : coll. : from ca. 1860.

inveterate. Obstinately prejudiced ; malignant, virulent ; embittered : C. 16–20. S.E. till ca. 1860, then coll. ; in C. 20, low coll. Dickens, 1861, ' I felt inveterate against him ' (O.E.D.).

inviduous. A sol. pronunciation of *invidious* : C. 19–20.

Invincibles. Invincible Brotherhood : Fenian coll. : 1883–ca. 1900. Ware.—2. Preston North End Football Club in 1888–89, when they ' won the League Championship without losing a match and . . . the F.A. Cup without having a goal scored against them ' (*Athletic News Football Annual* : 1935–36) : sporting coll. : 1888–90.

invitant. Erroneous for an invited person : C. 17–19. Galt. (O.E.D.)

invite. An invitation : late C. 16–20. S.E. until ca. 1830, then coll. ; in C. 20 low coll. if not indeed sol. Dickens, ' The invites had been excellently arranged.'

[**inward**, an intimate, C. 17, is ineligible.—2. In pl., see **innards**.]

-ious as a pejorative suffix tends to be s. or coll. E.g., *robustious*.

ipecac. A coll. abbr. of *ipecacuanha* : late C. 18–20 : S.E. until ca. 1890, then coll.

Ips. Ypres : military coll. : 1914–18. B. & P. Also *Eeps*.

ipsal dixal. An unsupported statement : Cockney (— 1860) ; ob. by 1895, † by 1910. H., 2nd ed. Ex *ipse dixit*.

ipsolateral is incorrect for *ipsilateral* : 1913. O.E.D. (Sup.).

Irish, n. Irish whiskey : from ca. 1880 ; ob. : coll. verging on S.E. Crackanthorpe.—2. Anger : orig. dial. >, ca. 1870, s. See also **Irish up** and cf. *paddy*, a synonym. Presumably ex Irish impetuosity.

Irish, adj. A derogative : from ca. 1690. In addition to the ensuing phrases, there are many in dial. (see esp. Grose, P.). Probably ex Irish uncouthness and lack of general education before C. 19.

Irish, weep. To shed insincere tears : C. 19–20. Coll. verging on S.E.

Irish, you're. You're talking gibberish : low coll. : C. 19–20.

Irish apricot. A potato : late C. 18–19. Grose, 1st ed. C. 19 variants, *Irish apple* or *lemon*. ' It is a common joke against the Irish vessels, to say that they are loaded with fruit and timber ; that is, potatoes and broomsticks,' Grose.

Irish Arms, the ; occ. **Irish arms.** Thick legs : mid-C. 18–mid-19. ' It is said of the Irish women ', remarks Grose, 1st ed., ' that they have a dispensation from the Pope to wear the thick end of their legs downwards '. Also *Irish legs*.

Irish assurance. ' A bold forward behaviour ', Grose, 1st ed. : mid-C. 18–mid-19. Cf. *dipped in the Shannon*, q.v.

Irish battleship or **man-of-war.** A barge : naval : mid-C. 19–20 ; ob. Bowen.

Irish beauty. A woman with two black eyes : mid-C. 18–early 19. Grose, 3rd ed. With allusion to pretty, black-eyed colleens.

Irish draperies. (Exceedingly rare in singular.) Cobwebs : (English) lower classes' (— 1909). Ware.

Irish evidence. False evidence ; a perjured witness : mid-C. 18–mid-19. Grose, 1st ed.

Irish fortune. *Pudendum muliebre* and pattens : C. 19. Cf. *Whitechapel fortune*, q.v.

Irish horse. Salt meat ; corned beef : nautical (— 1887) ; ob. Baumann.

Irish hurricane. ' A flat calm with drizzling rain ' : nautical : mid-C. 19–20. Bowen.

Irish legs, see **Irish arms**.—**Irish lemon**, see **Irish apricot**.—**Irish man-of-war.** See **Irish battleship**.

Irish pennants. Fag-ends of rope, etc. : nautical : C. 19–20 ; ob. Bowen.

Irish promotion. See **Irish rise**.

Irish rifle. A small comb : from ca. 1840 ; † by 1920.

Irish rise. A reduction in pay or position : coll. : ca. 1850–1910. Also *Irish promotion*.

Irish root. The penis : low : ca. 1830–1914. Cf. *Irish toothache*.

Irish theatre. A guard-room : military (— 1864) : ob. by 1900, † by 1914. H., 3rd ed. Cf. *mill*.

Irish toothache. A priapism : low : C. 19–20 ; ob. In late C. 19–20, gen. simply *toothache*. Cf. *Irish root*, q.v.—2. Pregnancy : lower classes' (— 1909). Ware. Also *I.T.A.*

*****Irish toyle.** A thief in the semblance of a pedlar : mid-C. 16–18 c.—2. A member of the twelfth order of rogues : C. 17 c. Both in B.E.

Irish up, get one's. To become angry : low : from ca. 1880. See **Irish**, n.

Irish wedding. The emptying of a cesspool : low : ca. 1820–50. Bee. Cf. :

Irish wedding, to have danced at an. To have two black eyes : coll. : from ca. 1840 ; ob.

Irish welcome. An invitation to come at any time : coll. verging on allusive S.E. : late C. 19–20. Benham.

Irish whist(, where the jack takes the ace). Coïtion : low : from ca. 1850 ; ob.

Irishman, the Wild. The Irish mail train between London and Holyhead on the L. & N.W. Railway : coll. : from ca. 1860. *The Times*, Mar. 27, 1862, ' The Irish express train (better known as the Wild Irishman) between London and Holyhead . . .' (O.E.D.)

Irishman's dinner. A fast : C. 19–20 jocular coll. ; ob.

Irishman's harvest. The orange season : London costermongers' : ca. 1840–1910. Cf. *Irish apricot* and *Irish lemon*, qq.v.

Irishman's hurricane. A dead calm : nautical : C. 19–20, ob. Cf. *Irish hurricane*.

Irishman's promotion or **rise.** A reduction in wages : coll. (— 1889). Barrère & Leland. Also *Irish rise*.

Irishman's reef. 'The head of a sail tied **up**': nautical s. (— 1880) > j.

Irishman's rest. 'Going up a friend's ladder with a hod of bricks': lower classes' (— 1909). Ware.

Irishman's rise. See Irishman's promotion.

irk. A troublesome seaman: nautical: late C. 19–20. Bowen. Abbr. *irksome.* Also *bird* and *fowl.* Cf. *erk,* which is prob. a derivative.—2. An air mechanic: Air Force: 1915. B. & P. By concertina-ing.

iron. Money: ca. 1780–1840. Grose, 1st ed. —2. A portable firearm, esp. a pistol or a revolver: from ca. 1835.—3. See **irons.**—4. A male harlot: c.: from ca. 1920. James Curtis, *The Gilt Kid,* 1936. A corruption of *nigh enough,* q.v.

iron, v.i. and t. To speak ironically to: sol. when not deliberate: ca. 1820–95. Bee's *Dict. of the Turf.*

iron, bad. A failure; a mishap; bad luck: workmen's: from ca. 1860; ob. Cf. *bad bread.*

iron, shooting and thieving. See shooting and thieving resp.

iron-bound. A hard-baked pie: low: ca. 1870–1915.

iron-bound, adj. Laced with metal. E.g. *iron-bound hat,* a silver-laced hat. Coll.: ca. 1780–1930. Grose, 1st ed.

iron cow. The village pump: C. 19 coll. Cf. *cow-juice,* q.v.

[**Iron Division, the.** The 13th Division: military of G.W.: rather sobriquet than nickname.]

iron doublet. A prison: C. 18–early 19. A variation of *stone doublet.*

iron foundries. Heavy shelling: military: 1915–18. B. & P. Cf. *coal-box.*

iron hand, the. The Closure of 1876: political coll. of Victoria, Australia. Morris. Ex *the iron hand in the velvet glove.*

iron hoop. Soup: (military and Cockney) rhyming s.: late C. 19–20. B. & P.

iron horse. A locomotive: from ca. 1860, ex U.S. (1846). In C. 19 coll.; in C. 20, outworn S.E.—2. A bicycle; occ. a tricycle: cyclists': ca. 1875–1900.

iron horse, v. Toss: Cockneys': from ca. 1880. P. P., *Rhyming Slang,* 1932. Most Cockneys pronounce *toss* to rhyme with *horse.*

iron rations. Tinned meat: nautical and military coll.: from ca. 1860. In C. 20, S.E.—2. Whence, shell-fire, esp. if severe: military: 1915; ob. B. & P. Cf. *iron foundries.*

iron toothpick. A sword: military: ca. 1870–1910. Contrast *toothpick,* q.v.

iron with one's eyebrow(s), polish the King's. To look out of grated, esp. prison, windows: ca. 1780–1840. Grose, 1st ed.

ironbark, adj. Unyielding; hard: Australian (— 1888); ob. 'Rolf Boldrewood', in *Robbery under Arms,* 'I always thought he was ironbark outside and in.' Cf. :

ironclad, adj. Severe, hard; unyielding: ca. 1884–1910. Mostly U.S., ex the vessel.

ironing. Irony: sol. when not a jocular perversion: from ca. 1740. Rare in C. 20. (O.E.D.)

ironmonger's shop by the side of a common, keep an. (To which is often added: *where the sheriff sets one up.*) To be hanged in chains: ca. 1780–1830. Grose, 1st ed. Cf. *iron with . . .,* q.v.

[**irons.** Fetters. Despite F. & H., this is ineligible.]

irons, fresh or new off the. Fresh from school or college; inexperienced; brand-new: coll.: from ca. 1680; ob. O.E.D.

irons in the fire (or **on the anvil**), **have many or other.** To have many interests; to employ various means to one end: C. 16–20: coll.; in C. 20, S.E. The *on the anvil* form, recorded in 1612, was ob. by 1850, † by 1900. For *many, other* or *more* is occ. found. (Apperson.) Ex a smithy.

Ironside(s). 'Common as an Eng. nickname, from Edmund II onward,' W.—2. Cromwell: 1644–47.—Hence, 3, his men: 1648 +; Perhaps ex *Ironside's men.* In all senses, coll. (Extant as surname.)

irrascible. Erroneous for *irascible.* Rare in C. 20.—**irrelentlessly,** for *relentlessly*: C. 17–18.—**irremediless,** for *remediless*: C. 17–early 18.—**irrevalent,** a frequent perversion of *irrelevant*: C. 18–20. O.E.D.

irreverend, -ly. In late C. 16–mid-19, often confused with *irreverent, -ly.* Ibid.

irrigate (one's canal). V.i. and t., to take a drink; pour drink down: jocular coll.: C. 18–20; ob. Ex the L. sense, to moisten.

irruption and **eruption** are often confused: C. 17–20. (O.E.D.)

Isabella. An umbrella: rhyming s.: from ca. 1855. H., 1st ed.

I'se. I am; occ., I shall: dial. and sol.: C. 18–20.

-ise, -ize in vv. With few exceptions, the latter is preferable. See esp. Fowler. (My own practice is reprehensibly inconsistent.)

-ish. A suffix that, when added to adjj., is either coll. or of a coll. tendency: C. 18–20. Grose, P., at *moreish*; Collinson.—2. When attached to cardinal numbers, esp. when indicative of the time (as in *fourish,* at about four o'clock), it is decidedly coll.—and C. 20. (Cf. *all-overish,* q.v.). 'Now, in coll. use, possible with nearly all monosyllabic adjj., and some others,' S.O.D.—3. Added to proper names, it is coll.: from ca. 1840. Tennyson, 1845, 'I feel . . . Martineauish about it' (O.E.D.).

island, drink out of the. To drink until—and after—one sees the rising bottom of a wine bottle: drinking s.: late C. 18–early 19. Grose, 2nd ed.

Island of Bermuda. See **Bermudas.**

Isle of Bishop. 'Orthodox', i.e. good, mead: Oxford University: ca. 1820–40. Egan's Grose.

Isle. See **ile,** 3.

Isle of Bull-Dogs. The area within the proctors' authority: Oxford University: ca. 1820–40. Egan's Grose.

isle of fling. A coat: East End of London: ca. 1875–1910. ? origin. Perhaps rhyming on *lining.*

Isle of Flip. Eggs and sherry: Oxford University: ca. 1820–40. Egan's Grose.

Isle of France. A dance: rhyming s. (— 1859); ob. H., 1st ed. Cf. *ile,* 3 (q.v.).

Isle of Matriculation. Entrance into the University: Oxford University: ca. 1820–40. Egan's Grose.

ism. A doctrine or a theory: 1680 (O.E.D.): coll. Ex such words as *Jesuitism, Puritanism.* Cf. *ology,* q.v.

isn't. A coll. form of *is not*: from C. 16.

isofagus, †. Erroneous for *œsophagus.* O.E.D.

issue, join. Erroneous when = to come to an agreement, to agree: from ca. 1775. O.E.D.

issue, the (whole). The complete set, number, amount; 'the lot': military: from 1915. Ex an *issue* or distribution of, e.g., cigarettes. B. & P.

issues, pool one's. To work in profitable unison : coll. : from ca. 1860 ; ob.

is't. Abbr. *is it* : coll. when neither dial. nor poetic : before C. 19, normal S.E.

-ist. A n. suffix ; often jocular, occ. coll., in C. 19–20. Shelley.—2. (Without hyphen) a holder of an *ism*, q.v. : from ca. 1810 : coll. till ca. 1880, then S.E. (O.E.D.)

Isthmus of Suez. The bridge at St. John's College, Cambridge, also called the *Bridge of Grunts* : Cambridge University : ca. 1850–1910. Punning its synonym *Bridge of Sighs* and *sues*, swine, with reference to *hog*, n., sense 3, q.v.

it. As an indefinite object of a v., as in *walk it, cab it* : orig. S.E. ; but from ca. 1880, coll. (So too in curses.)—2. A chamber-pot : C. 19–20 ; ob.—3. The female, occ. the male, sexual organ : C. 19–20 ; orig. and still mainly euphemistic.—4. ' Coll. use of *it* for the consummate is [orig.] U.S.', W. : from ca. 1910 in England. E.g. ' He thinks he's it ' or ' just it '.—5. In quotation from books or news- papers, etc., *it* used with *says* or *tells* dates from C. 12 : S.E. till C. 19, then coll.—6. Sexual appeal : from ca. 1920. Now jocular coll. Ex the novels of ' Victoria Cross ' and Elinor M. Glyn.—7. In *gin and it*, it = Italian vermouth : coll. : from ca. 1910.—8. For stylistic infelicities, see Fowler.

it, be for. See **for it, be.**

it, of. As in ' We had a nice time of it ' : coll., gen. ironic (— 1887). Baumann.

it can't be did ! See **did, 3.—it isn't done.** See **done, it isn't.**

it snowed ! A c.p. indicative of misery or disaster : lower classes' ; adopted, before 1909, from U.S.A. (Ware.)

Italian quarrel. ' Death, poison, treachery, re- morselessness ' : Society (— 1909) ; virtually †. Ware.

itch. To feel a sexual urge : C. 17–20 low coll. Cf. *itch in the belly.*

itch and scratch. A match (ignition) : rhyming s. : late C. 19–20. B. & P.

itch-buttocks, play at. To have sexual inter- course : late C. 16–19 ; coll. Florio.

itch in the belly, have an. To be sexually excited : ca. 1660–1900 : coll. Cotton, D'Urfey.

itcher. The female pudend : C. 19–20 low ; ob. Ex *itch*, v. Also *itching Jenny.*

itchiness. In C. 20, coll. ; in C. 19, S.E. See **itchy.**

itching Jenny. See **itcher.**

itching palm. See **palm.**

Itchland. Wales : late C. 17–early 18. B.E.— 2. Scotland : C. 18–mid-19. *A New Canting Dict.*, 1725. Cf. *Scratchland*, q.v.

Itchlander. A Scotsman : C. 18–mid 19. Ex preceding term.

itchy. Affected with or like an itch : C. 16–20 : S.E. until ca. 1840, then coll.

*item. A hint or a warning : c. : C. 19. Bee, ' It was I that gave the item that the traps were a coming.'

-itis. A suffix indicating—or facetiously im- puting—a disease : often a jocular coll. in late C. 19–20. E.g. *jazzitis* (1919). W.

it's. A written sol. for possessive *its* : C. 18–20. —2. (Occ. *its.*) Coll. for *it is* : C. 17–20.—3. It, as in ' It's being so cold that day ' · coll. (— 1887). Baumann.

it's a great life (if you don't weaken) ! A G.W. variant of *this is the life*, q.v.

it's a way they have in the Army ! A military (mostly officers') c.p. of 1916–18. B. & P.

itty umpty. See **iddy umpty.**

Ivan. A Russian private soldier : military coll. : 1914 ; † by 1920. B. & P. Cf. *Tommy.*

I've. I have : coll. : from ca. 1740. Richard- son, ' A queer sort of name ! I've heard of it somewhere ' (O.E.D.).

I've seen 'em grow ! ; I've sh** 'em ! Military c.pp. of the G.W., resp. indicative of contempt at rapid promotion and of scorn for soldiers of another unit. B & P.

ivories. The teeth : from ca. 1780, ob. Egan ; Thackeray, ' Chatter your old ivories at me ;' *Punch*, 1882, ' Sluicing his ivories ' (cf. *ivories, rinse . . . the*).—2. Dice ; billiard-balls : from ca. 1830. (Very rare in singular.)—3. See **tickle the ivories.**

ivories, box of. A set of (good) teeth in one's mouth : low (— 1860). H., 2nd ed. Also *cage of ivories* : H., 2nd ed.

ivories, flash the. To show one's teeth : low : C. 18–20 ; ob. See *flash the ivory.*—2. Occ., to smile.

ivories, punch the. To vamp on the piano : jocular coll. (— 1923). Manchon. Contrast *tickle the ivories.*

ivories, rinse or sluice or wash one's or the. To drink : C. 19–20 ; ob. Moncrieff. See **ivories,** sense 1.

ivories, tickle the. To play the piano : mid- C. 19–20 coll. Cf. *ivory-thumper*, q.v.

ivory. See **ivories,** various senses. Rare in singular, except when collective.—2. A pass-ticket on a railway ; to a theatre, etc. : ca. 1855–1910.

ivory, black. (African) negroes as merchandise : 1873 (S.O.D.) ; slightly ob.

*ivory, flash the. See **flash the ivory.**

ivory, touch. To play at dice : (—) 1864 ; ob. Sala. (O.E.D.)

ivory box. The mouth : pugilists' : ca. 1880– 1910.

ivory carpenter. A dentist : low jocular coll. : ca. 1885–1915.

[**ivory gate,** the female pudend, is a literary euphemism.]

ivory-hammerer or **-thumper,** occ. *-spanker.* A pianist : from ca. 1860 ; ob. Cf. *ivories, tickle the.*

ivory pearl. Girl : rhyming s. : C. 20. *John o' London's Weekly*, June 9, 1934. More gen. is **ocean pearl.**

ivy bush, like an owl in an. Having a large wig or very bushy hair : anticipated in 1606 (Day) but properly of ca. 1705–1840. Swift, Grose. (Apper- son.)

ivy-leaf. See **pipe in . . .**

-ize as a v. suffix is often coll. in tendency in late C. 18–20.—So also *-izer* as a n. suffix.

J

j or **J.** See **jay.** Also *J.A.Y.* (Ware.)—2. (J'.) Do you : low coll. : mid-C. 19–20. Garnett Radcliffe, in *The Passing Show*, Jan. 27, 1934, ' Stick 'em up ! J'hear me, you big stiff ? ' By slurring.

J.S. or **N.** or **D.** Judicial Separation or Nullity of Marriage or Divorce : legal coll. (— 1896). Ware.

J.T. A euphemism (— 1923) for *John Thomas*, 2. Manchon.

jab. A poke, prod, or stab : coll. and dial. (Scottish form of *job*) : from ca. 1820.—2. In boxing s. (in C. 20, gen. coll.), an abrupt blow with the fist : from ca. 1850.

jab, v.i. and t. To poke, prod, stab, thrust : coll. and dial. : from ca. 1830. Both n. and v. may have owed their widespread coll. usage in part to U.S. influence : witness F. & H.'s error.—2. Hence, to strike smartly (e.g. *jab him one !*) : late C. 19–20. C. J. Dennis.

jabber. Chatter ; incoherent, inarticulate, or unintelligible speech : in C. 18, coll. ; then S.E. Ned Ward, in *Hudibras Redivivus*, ' And stopp'd their bold presumptuous labour, By unintelligible jabber.'

jabber, v. To chatter ; speak fast and indistinctly, talk gibberish : from ca. 1500 : coll. till C. 19, then S.E. Pope, in *The Dunciad*, ' Twas chatt'ring, grinning, mouthing, jabb'ring all.' Imitative : cf. *gab(ble)* and *gibber.*

jabberer. One who jabbers (see the v.) : from ca. 1675 : coll. till C. 19, then S.E. with a coll. tinge. ' Hudibras ' Butler.

jabbering. Vbl.n. of *jabber, to*, q.v. : C. 16–20 : coll. till C. 19, then S.E.—2. The same applies to the adv. in *-ly*.

jabber(k)nowl. See **jobbernowl.**

[**jabberment**, chatter, nonsense, gibberish, from ca. 1640, is a rare literary form.]

Jab(b)er(s) or **Jabez** or, rarely, **Japers, by** (Anglo-Irish **be**). A low oath : first recorded in 1821 and as *by jappers*. Presumably a corruption of *Jesus* via the Anglo-Irish *Jasus*. Cf. *begorra*, q.v.

jabberwock. A weird monster : coined by Lewis Carroll in *Through the Looking Glass*, 1871. In C. 19, s. ; in C. 20 verging on coll. and, by 1920, recognised by W. as S.E. *The Globe*, Aug. 25, 1917, ' This super-Jabberwock.'

jabez. See **jabbers.**—2. Whence (?), v., to play a dirty trick ; 1923, Manchon.

jacco. A C. 17 (? also C. 18) corrupt form of *jackal*. (O.E.D.)

jack. (The capital is fairly gen. where a person is designated ; otherwise the initial letter is in lower case.) The c. senses are a farthing (late C. 17–early 18) ; a seal (C. 17–18, a corruption of *jark*, q.v.) ; an abbr. (not later than 1845) of *Jack in a box*, 6 ; and a policeman (ca. 1865),—this last > gen. Australian s. ca. 1910. Ware.—2. Almost c. is the (— 1851) gaming sense, a counter resembling a sovereign.—3. The least bit : coll. : ca. 1500–1650. (In negative and interrogative sentences.)—4. A variety of polyanthus : coll. (— 1879).—5. A single carnation (sold as a choice carnation) : horticultural s. (— 1878). (O.E.D.)—6. A variety of tea-rose : coll. : abbr. *Jacqueminot* : 1883.—7. A jack-boot : coll. : C. 19–20 ; ob.—8. A Jacobin pigeon : coll. : ca. 1740–1830.—9. A coll. abbr. of *jackal* : from ca. 1890. (O.E.D.)—10. Orig. s. or

coll. but long recognised as S.E. are the senses : the small bowl aimed at in the game of bowls (C. 17–20), as in Shakespeare's *Cymbeline* ; a pitcher, gen. one of leather and often as *black jack* (late C. 16–20) ; a boot-jack (late C. 17–20) ; an ape (from ca. 1500 ; long ob.) ; a peasant (C. 16–20 ; ob. by 1800) ; a male, as in *jack-hare, -rabbit*, etc. (C. 16–20) ; a male sweetheart (C. 15–20 ; now archaic),—cf. *Jill* ; a term of contempt (from C. 14, but rare after C. 18). —11. Orig. (ca. 1660) S.E., but in C. 19–20 coll., is the sense a knave in a suit of cards.—12. Scots C. 19 coll. : a jakes.—13. Nautical : the Union Jack : from ca. 1650. Kipling.—14. A sailor : coll. : from ca. 1700. Dibdin. Earlier as *sailor Jack, Jack the sailor*.—15. A Jacobite : coll. : ca. 1695–1750. Swift.—16. A post-chaise : low : ca. 1810–50. Vaux.—17. In amorous venery and low s., both the penis and an erection thereof : C. 19–20, ob.—18. See **Jack in the water.**—19. (Jack.) A low coll. term of address to any man one doesn't know : C. 19–20. Prob. orig. nautical.—20. A native soldier : Anglo-Indian coll. : 1853 (Yule & Burnell) ; † by 1886. Abbr. *Jack-Sepoy*.—21. Horse-flesh salted and so washed as to lose its horsy flavour : 1904 (O.E.D. Sup.)—22. The inevitable nickname of any man surnamed Sheppard (etc.) : naval and military : late C. 19–20. Bowen. Ex the C. 18 prison-breaker.—23. H., 2nd ed., has ' a low prostitute ', but this definition of 1860 is not repeated in 1864 : I suspect it to be an error caused by confusion with ' a male sweetheart ' (see sense 10).

*jack, v. In c., to run away quickly : from ca. 1840 ; ob.—2. In low s., to copulate : C. 19–20, ob. —3. See **jack it.**—4. App., to lock, as in *gig(g)ers jacked* in Anon., *The Catterpillers of the Nation Anatomized*, 1659 : c. : C. 17.—5. See **jack up.**

Jack, Cousin. See **Cousin Jack.—Jack, every man.** See **every man Jack.** Occ. *every Jack man*, †.

jack, lay (occ. **be**) **on the.** V.i. and t., to thrash or to scold soundly : coll. of ca. 1550–1640. In *Jacob and Esau*, a play, ' If I wrought one stroke to-day, lay me on the jack ' ; North, 1579, ' Lay it on the jacks of them.'

jack, on one's. Alone ; without assistance : low : C. 20. James Curtis, *The Gilt Kid*, 1936. Ex *on one's Jack Jones*, q.v. at **Jack Jones.**

jack, play the. To play the rogue : C. 17.—2. To play the fool : C. 19. Both coll.—3. V.t. with *with*, as in Shakespeare's *The Tempest*, ' Your fairy . . . has done little better than play the jack with us.'

Jack, poor. (A) dried hake : 1667 (O.E.D.) : coll. till ca. 1705, then S.E. Also *dry* or *dried Jack.*

Jack-a (occ. **-o'**)**-dandy** ; occ. **Jack Dandy.** A little fop, a petty dandy, an insignificant little fellow : coll. : ca. 1630–1920. Brome, Cumberland, Ainsworth.—2. Brandy : rhyming s. (— 1857) : gen. as *Jack Dandy.* ' Ducange Anglicus ' has the shorter form.

Jack-a-green. See **Jack in the green.**

Jack-a-Lent, occ. **Jack o' Lent.** A dwarf, a puppet : late C. 16–18 : coll. till ca. 1660, then S.E. Shakespeare.—2. A simpleton, a nobody : C. 17–19 : coll. till C. 18, then S.E. Both ex the puppet thrown-at during Lent.

Jack Adams. A fool : late C. 17–19 : coll. till ca. 1850, then nautical s. for a foolish and stubborn person.

Jack Adams'(s) parish. Clerkenwell: C. 18–early 19. Prob. ex an actual idiot.

Jack Barrel. A minnow: nautical: late C. 19–20. Bowen.

Jack Blunt. A blunt fellow: 1898 (O.E.D.): coll. till ca. 1910, then S.E.

Jack Boot. John Stuart (1713–92), 3rd Earl of *Bute.* Dawson.

Jack boot(s). The ' boots ' (q.v.) at an inn: ca. 1800–50 : coll. till ca. 1820, then S.E.—2. **Jack Boots.** Henry Compton (1632–1713), Bishop of London. (Dawson.)

jack-boy. A postillion: low: ca. 1810–50. Vaux. See **jack,** n., 16.

Jack and Jill. A (small) hill: rhyming s. : C. 20. *John o' London's Weekly,* June 9, 1934.

Jack and Jill. A till ; a bill : from ca. 1890. P. P., *Rhyming Slang,* 1932.

Jack ashore. A lower classes' coll. (— 1909) for a ' larky ', rather tipsy sailor. Ware.

Jack at a pinch. A person employed in an emergency ; esp. a stop-gap clergyman : coll. : from ca. 1620 ; very ob., except in dial. B.E.

Jack at warts. A conceited little fellow : C. 19 coll. Ex dial. *Jack at the wat,* the small bag of a pig's intestines.

Jack Brag(ger). A boaster : C. 16–20 coll. ; almost †.

Jack Dandy. See **Jack-a-Dandy.**

Jack Drum's entertainment. Ill-treatment, esp. an ignominious dismissal : coll. : ca. 1570–1660. Gosson ; Nashe, ' I would give him Jacke Drummes entertainment, and send him packing '; John Taylor, 1649. Occ. *Tom Drum's entertainment,* as in Holinshed. Apperson.

Jack Dusty ; Jack in the dust. A ship's-steward's assistant : resp. nautical, mid-C. 19–20, and naval, id. Bowen. Cf. *dusty boy,* q.v.

Jack Frost. A coll. personification of frost : from ca· 1825 ; ob.

Jack-hold-my-staff. A too humble servant : coll. : C. 17. Mrs. Behn. (O.E.D.)

Jack (or **Johnny**) **Horner.** A corner : rhyming s. : C. 20. B. & P.—2. See **Johnny Horner.**

Jack in a (or **the**) **box,** gen. hyphenated. A child's toy : recorded in 1702, but prob. much earlier : coll. soon > S.E.—2. A sharper, a cheat : c. : ca. 1570–1830. Dekker. Prob. ex the fifth sense.—3. A street pedlar : late C. 17–18 : coll. Ned Ward.—4. See **Jack in the cellar.**—5. The consecrated host : pejorative coll. : ca. 1545–1700. —6. A small but powerful screw, used by burglars : c. of ca. 1840–1910. ' *No. 747* ', in a ' locus ' valid for 1845, likewise valid for the abbr., *Jack* (pp. 423, 439 resp.); Albert Smith, 1848. Prob. ex the nautical s. > coll. sense (— 1801), 7, a large wooden male screw.—8. The male member : C. 19–20 ob. Ex sense 1.—9. A game in which one throws at an object placed on the top of a stick set in a hole, beyond which the object, if hit, must fall clear to become the thrower's property : C. 19–20 ob. (low) coll.—10. A coll., mainly Australian name of the plant *stylidium graminifolium* : from ca. 1850. Ex the sensitive stigma-column.

Jack in (C. 17–18 an) **office.** An imperious petty official : from ca. 1660 : coll. till C. 19, then S.E. Cf. *Jack in the pulpit,* q.v.

Jack in the basket. A mark (orig. a basket) ' on top of a pole to serve as a beacon ' : nautical coll. : mid-C. 19–20 ; ob. Bowen.

Jack in the cellar or low cellar (occ. **the box**). A child in the womb : ca. 1750–1900. Smollett. Cf. *Hans en* (occ. *in*) *kelder,* q.v.

Jack in the dust. See **Jack Dusty.**

Jack in the green. A chimney-sweep enclosed in a framework of boughs in a First of May procession : from ca. 1800 ; ob. by 1890 : coll. >, ca. 1850, S.E.

Jack in the orchard, get. To achieve sexual intromission : C. 19–20 low.

Jack in the pulpit. A pretender ; an upstart : coll. : C. 19.

Jack in the water ; occ. **Jack.** A handy man at boat-house or landing-stage : (low) coll. ; from ca. 1835. Dickens in *Boz.*

jack it. To die : low (— 1909). Ware.

Jack Johnson. A heavy Ger. shell, esp. a 5·9 : 1914–18 : military. Ex the large and famous negro boxer (fl. 1907–12) via the black smoke issuing voluminously from the shell burst : moreover, Johnson's American nickname, as the O.E.D. (Sup.) reminds us, was *the Big Smoke.* Occ. abbr. to *Johnson,* q.v.

Jack Jones. Alone : (imperfect) rhyming s., esp. military : C. 20. F. & Gibbons.

Jack Ketch, occ. **J. Kitch.** A hangman, an executioner ; c. >, ca. 1750, s. > coll. in C. 19 : ca. 1705–1880. Earlier allusions are to the actual person ; e.g. Anon., 1676, ' There stands Jack Kitch, that son of a Bitch.' Ex the famous executioner of ca. 1670–86. Cf. *Derrick* and *Gregory Brandon,* qq.v.

Jack Ketch's kitchen. That room in Newgate in which the hangman boiled the quarters of those dismembered for high treason : C. 18 : perhaps orig. c. Ex preceding.

Jack Ketch's pippin. A candidate for the gallows : C. 18 low. Also called a *gallow's apple.*

Jack Muck. A merchant seaman : naval : ca. 1870–1914. Bowen.

Jack Nasty. A sneak ; a sloven : (low) coll. : from ca. 1855 ; ob. T. Hughes. Cf. :

Jack Nasty-Face. A common sailor : nautical : late C. 18–early 19.—2. A cook's assistant : C. 19–20 nautical.—3. A dirty fellow : mid-C. 19–20 coll. (now ob.), prob. orig. nautical.—4. Any ugly man : naval : C. 20. Bowen.—5. Female pudend : low : ca. 1820–70. ' Jon Bee.'

Jack northwester. The north-west wind : nautical coll. : from ca. 1740 ; ob.

Jack-o'-Dandy. See **Jack-a-dandy.**

Jack of all trades. One who (thinks he) can do everything : C. 17–20 : coll. till C. 18, then S.E. and gen. contemptuous. Minshull, Dryden.

Jack of legs. An unusually tall man : coll. : ca. 1770–1890. Grose, 1st ed.—2. A large clasp-knife ; late C. 18–19. (A corruption of *jocteleg.*) Also as *jackyleg,* q.v.

Jack of or on both sides. A neutral ; a runner with both hare and hounds : coll. : ca. 1550–1880 : extant in dial. Nashe, Defoe, Spurgeon. (Apperson.)

Jack of Tilbury. Sir John Arundell (1495–1561), Vice-Admiral of the West. Dawson.

Jack out of doors. A vagrant : C. 17 : coll. quickly > S.E.

Jack out of office. A discharged official : derisive coll. : ca. 1540–1790. Shakespeare, ' But long I will not be Jack-out-of-office.' Contrast *Jack in office,* q.v.

Jack pudding (or **Pudding**). A merry Andrew ;

a clowning assistant to a mountebank : coll. : 1648 (S.O.D.); ob. by 1830, † by 1900. Cf. Fr. *Jean Potage.*

Jack rag, every. A C. 19 (mainly dial.) variant of *every man Jack*, q.v.

Jack Randall. A candle : rhyming s. (— 1859). Ex the famous boxer. (H., 1st ed., erroneously spells as *Randle*.) Cf. *Harry Randall.*

Jack Robinson. The penis : low : C. 19–20, ob. Cf. *John Thomas.*

Jack Robinson, before one can say. Instantly : late C. 18–20 coll. Fanny Burney, Dickens, Hardy. According to Grose, 1st ed., 'from a very volatile gentleman . . . who would call on his neighbours, and be gone before his name could be announced ' : which seems improbable. (Apperson.)

Jack (S)(s)auce. An impudent fellow : coll. : ca. 1560–1750. (Cf. *sauce-box*.) G. Harvey, ' A Jack-Sauce, or unmannerly puppy.' See **sauce.**

Jack-Sepoy. A native soldier : Anglo-Indian coll. : ca. 1840–70. Yule & Burnell.

Jack Shalloo. A braggart : naval : ca. 1850–1900. Bowen. Perhaps ex dial.-*shallock*, a dirty, lazy fellow. But see **Jack Shilloo** for more prob. origin.—2. Whence ' a happy-go-lucky careless officer, and hence a slack ship is called a Jack Shalloo ship ' (Bowen) : naval : C. 20.

Jack Shay ; jackshea. A tin quart-pot : Australia (— 1881) ; ob. ? prompted by *char*, n., 2, q.v. ; more prob. punning, or rhyming on, *tay*, † S.E. and present Irish pronunciation of tea ; possibly at first *Jack Shea* (rhyming with *tay*). (Morris.)

Jack Shilloo. A boaster : naval : late C. 19–20 ; ob. F. & Gibbons. A *Jack*-personification of Anglo-Irish *shilloo*, a loud shouting, as in Lover, 1840 (E.D.D.). Also *Jack Shalloo*, q.v.

Jack Snip. An inferior tailor : C. 19–20 ; ob.

Jack Sprat. An undersized man or boy : mid-C. 16–20 ; ob., except in dial. Pejorative *Jack* with pejorative *sprat*. Whence presumably *Jack Sprat could (or would) eat no fat, his wife could (or would) eat no lean.*

Jack stickler. A busybody : coll. : ca. 1570–1690.

Jack Straw. A nonentity : coll. : ca. 1590–1910. Nashe, ' These worthless whippets and Jacke-Strawes.' Ex the C. 14 rebel (cf. *Guy Fawkes*).

Jack Straw's castle. The female pudend : C. 19 low.

Jack tar (Tar). A sailor : 1781, George Parker : coll. : often abbr. *jack*, occ. *tar*.—2. A hornpipe : ca. 1820–90.

***jack the interim.** To be remanded : c. of ca. 1860–1914.

***Jack the Jew.** A Jewish thief or ' fence ' of the lowest order : c. of ca. 1820–60. ' Jon Bee.'

Jack the Painter. Very strong tea, drunk in the bush : Australia : from ca. 1850 ; ob. G. C. Mundy, *Our Antipodes*, 1855. Ex the mark it leaves around one's mouth. Morris.

***Jack the slipper.** A treadmill : c. : from ca. 1860 ; ob.

jack up. To give way, collapse, become bankrupt, become utterly exhausted.—2. V.t., to ruin ; exhaust utterly ; destroy. Both from ca. 1870 and both coll. (perhaps orig. dial. : see E.D.D.). Perhaps ex *jacked*, q.v. below.—3. To abandon, ' chuck up ' : late C. 19–20 ; slightly ob. Ex dial. Edwin Pugh, *Tony Drum*, 1898 ; Ian Hay, *Pip*,

1907, ' If I find the life utterly unbearable . . . I shall jack it up.' Perhaps cognate with S.E. *jerk.*

Jack Weight. A fat man : coll. : late C. 18–mid-19. Grose, 1st ed.

jack whore. ' A large masculine overgrown wench,' Grose, 1st ed. : ca. 1760–1860. (Extant in Hampshire dial. for ' a strong Amazonian sailors' trull ', E.D.D.)—2. A wencher : low : mid-C. 19–20 ; ob. Manchon.

jackanapes—' old colloquial ', says F. & H.—was prob. such only in the C. 16–17 sense, a tame ape or monkey ; otherwise S.E.—2. (J.) Wm. de la Pole, 1st Duke of Suffolk. (Dawson.)

jackanapes, (as) full of tricks as a. Exceedingly mischievous : C. 17–18. B.E. Cf. the C. 17–18 proverb, *there is more ado with one Jack-an-apes than (with) all the bears.*

jackaroo, jackeroo. A young Englishman learning sheep- and/or cattle-farming : Australia (— 1880) : s. >, by 1900, coll. Either ex *Johnny Raw* after *kangaroo* or ex the Brisbane Aborigines' name (orig. for a garrulous bird) for a white man. Morris. Cf. *colonial experience*, q.v., and :

jackaroo, v. To lead the life of a *jackaroo*, q.v. : Australia (ca. 1887) ; ob. : s. > coll. Morris.

jackass. A stupid, ignorant fellow : coll. > S.E. : from ca. 1830 ; ob. Barham.

jackass frigate. A small frigate that sails slowly : nautical s. > coll. : ca. 1830–70. Marryat, in *Peter Simple.*

jacked. (Of a horse) spavined, lamed : late C. 18–19 coll. In late C. 19–20, *jacked up*. (See **jack up,** above.) Perhaps ex *to jerk.*

jackee-ja or **Jacky-ja(r).** ' A canoe on the Greenland coast ' : nautical : C. 20. Bowen. Perhaps by ' Hobson-Jobson ' ex an Eskimo word.

jackeen, Jackeen. (Often *Dublin jackeen*.) A self-assertive but worthless fellow ; esp. a Dublin rough : Anglo-Irish : from ca. 1840 ; ob. : coll. Ex *Jack* + pejorative *-een*, as in *squireen.*

***jacken-closer.** A seal : ca. 1820–60 : o. Corruption of *jackrum.*

jacker (or **J.**) A boy in a training-ship : naval : late C. 19–20 ; ob. Bowen.

jackeroo. See **jackaroo.**

Jackery. (Gen. in pl.) A favoured stationhand : Australia : ca. 1885–1910.

jacket, the cooked skin of an unpeeled potato, S.E.—2. ' A soldier who wears a jacket (chiefly cavalry or horse artillery) ' : military (— 1909) ; extremely ob. Ware. Cf. *jacket, get the.*

***jacket, v.** To swindle ; betray ; deprive of one's birthright or situation : c. of ca. 1810–50. Vaux.—2. To thrash : coll. : from ca. 1875. Ex the vbl.n., itself ex *fall upon*, or *dust* or *lace, the jacket of.*—3. To put in a strait jacket ; threaten to lock (a person) up as a madman : lower classes ' (— 1909). Ware.

jacket, dust (a person's). See **dust,** v.

jacket, get the. To receive an appointment to the Royal Horse Artillery : military coll. : C. 20. F. & Gibbons. ' In allusion to the R.H.A. uniform jacket, in contradistinction to the tunic of the Royal Artillery.'

jacket, give a red-laced. To flog : military : ca. 1800–50.

jacket, line one's. To fill one's stomach : C. 17–early 19 : coll.

jacket, send in one's. To resign · jockeys' : ca. 1870–1905. Hawley Smart.

jacket job. A good job (e.g., a barman's) in the steward's department : nautical : C. 20. Bowen. 'From the distinctive uniform.'

jacket-reverser. A turn-coat : jocular coll. : C. 19.

jacketing. A thrashing ; severe reprimand : coll. (— 1851). Mayhew, 'I don't work on Sundays. If I did, I'd get a jacketing.' Cf. *jacket*, v., 2.

***jacketing concern.** The vbl.n. of *jacket*, v., 1, q.v. : c. : c.a. 1810–50. Vaux.

jackety. Of or like a jacket : coll. : from ca. 1850. Surtees. (O.E.D.)

jack(e)y. Gin : orig. (1799) either c. or low. *Lex. Bal.* ; W. S. Gilbert, in *H.M.S.* '*Pinafore*', 'I've snuff, and tobacky, | And excellent jacky.' Cf. *old Tom* for the semantics.—2. (**Jacky.**) Admiral of the Fleet Lord Fisher : naval : late C. 19–20. Bowen.

jackman. See **jarkman,** for which it is merely erroneous.

Jacko. A Turk, esp. a Turkish soldier : military (Gallipoli and Palestine forces) : 1915–18. F. & Gibbons.

***jackrum.** A marriage-licence : c. of ca. 1800–50. Cf. *jukrum*, q.v.

jacks, the. Military police : Australian and New Zealand military, 1914–18. (Very rare in singular.) See **jack,** n., c. senses.—2. Hence, in New Zealand c. (—1932), the police.

jacks, be upon their. To have an advantage : coll. : C. 17–18. Ex bowls.

Jack's alive. A sharp run round : coll. (—1894) ; ob. Ex the mainly Scottish game.—2. The number 5, esp. in the game of House : military rhyming s. : C. 20. B. & P.

Jack's delight. A sea-port harlot : sea-port s. > coll. : from ca. 1840 ; ob.

jackshea. See **Jack Shay.**

Jackson, jammed like. See **jammed like Jackson.**

Jackson's hens, fly up with. To become bankrupt : from ca. 1570 : coll. till C. 19 then dial.—2. Hence, *make one fly with Jackson's hens*, to ruin a person : C. 17–18.

Jackson's pig, it's gone over Borough Hill after It is lost : rural coll. verging on dial. (esp. Northants) : mid-C. 19–20 ; ob. Apperson.

jacksy-pardy (occ. **-pardo**). The posteriors : low : from ca. 1850 ; ob.

***jacky.** See **jackey.**

Jacky. See **jackey.**

Jacky (or **Johnny**) **hangman.** A Jack hanger, i.e. *lanius collaris* : Natal coll. (mostly juvenile) : from ca. 1890. Ex 'the bird's habit of hanging his captures on thorns until they are to his taste', Pettman.

Jacky Winter. The brown flycatcher, a small bird common about Sydney : coll., New South Wales : from ca. 1890. 'It sings all through the winter, when nearly every other species is silent,' Morris.

jackyleg(s). A large pocket-knife : Scots coll. : late C. 19–20, ob. Ex *jocteleg.*

Jacky's yacht. The battleship *Renown* : naval : ca. 1892–94. Bowen. The flagship of Admiral Fisher : see **jackey,** 2.

***jacob.** A ladder : C. 18–20 c. >, by 1900, low. *Memoirs of John Hall*, 1708. Perhaps, as Grose suggests, ex Jacob's dream.—2. A thief using a ladder : c. of ca. 1710–80.—3. A familiar name for a jay : C. 18–mid-19. Cf. *poll.*—4. Hence, a soft

fellow ; a fool : ca. 1810–60. *Lex. Bal.*—5. The male member : C. 19 low. Cf. *dick.*

Jacobite, jacobite. A sham shirt ; a shirt collar : late C. 17–mid-19. B.E.

Jacob's ladder. A rent in which only the woof threads remain, e.g. 'a longitudinal flaw in the leg of a ballet-girl's tights,' H. : theatrical > gen. s. (— 1859) ; ob. Sala.—2. The female pudend : C. 19 low. Cf. *jacob*, last sense.

[**jade,** contemptuous for a woman, is, despite F. & H., ineligible.]

jag, (a bout of) intoxication, **on a jag,** on a drunken spree, and **have a jag on,** gen. supposed to be U.S., were orig.—C. 17–20, ob.—Eng. dial., whence U.S. and Eng. s. usage in late C. 19–20. Lit. sense, a load. (But *jagged*, tipsy, is a solely U.S. term.)

jag, v.t. To hunt, pursue : South African coll. : 1850, Gordon Cummings, *A Hunter's Life in South Africa.* Ex Dutch *jagen*, to hunt, chase. Pettman.—2. Hence, to arrest : military : C. 20. B. & P.

jag up. To punish : military : from ca. 1912. F. & Gibbons. Prob. ex the preceding, sense 1.

***jagger.** A gentleman : c. of ca. 1835–1910 : more U.S. than Eng. ? ex Ger. *jäger*, a sportsman (Brandon.)—2. As hawker, it is ineligible.

Jaggers. Undergraduates at Jesus College : Oxford undergraduates' (— 1899). Ware.—2. Hence, Jesus College itself : Oxford undergraduates' : C. 20. Collinson. By the process of 'the Oxford *-er* '.—3. **the Jaggers.** The 5th Battalion of the 60th Rifles, in late C. 19–20 the King's Royal Rifle Corps : military coll. : C. 19–20. When raised in 1798, they were composed mainly of German Jäger (riflemen, marksmen). F. & Gibbons.—4. A messenger-boy : late 1890's and early C. 20. Ex 'the name of one who went from London to Chicago at a moment's notice in the 'nineties' (A. H. Dawson, *Dict. of Slang*, 1913.)

***jague.** A ditch : c. of mid C. 17–mid-19. Head & Kirkman ; Grose. ? cognate with *jakes.*

jail-bird. A prisoner ; a thorough scoundrel : C. 17–20 : coll. till C. 19, then S.E. Davies of Hereford. Cf. *queer* (or *quire-*) *bird*, q.v.

jail-khan(n)a. A gaol (jail) : Bengal Presidency coll. (— 1886). A hybrid ex *khan(n)a*, a house, a room. Yule & Burnell.

jailer ; loosely **jailor.** A policeman : Glasgow (— 1934). Not ex the current S.E. sense, but coined anew from *jail.*

jake (or **J.**) A Jebacca boat : Canadian (and U.S.) nautical : mid-C. 19–20 ; slightly ob. Jebacca is at Cape Ann, Mass. (Bowen.)—2. (jake only.) Methylated spirits : c., mostly tramps' : from ca. 1920. W. A. Gape, *Half a Million Tramps*, 1936.

jake, adj. Honest, upright ; equitable, correct ; 'O.K.', excellent : Colonial and U.S. : C. 20. (I cannot adduce an early example, but *jake* was certainly used, in these senses, at least as early as 1910.) Prob. ex *jannock*, q.v. Often elaborated to *jake-a-loo*, occ. to *jake-a-bon* or *tray jake*, i.e. *très* (very) *jake.*

jake, adv. Well, profitably ; honestly, genuinely : Colonial : from ca. 1905. Ex preceding.

jake with the lever up. Excellent ; extremely satisfactory or pleasant : Canadian : from ca. 1920. See **jake,** adj.

***jake-drinker.** A variant—recorded by the same authority—of *feke-drinker.* C. 20 : c.

jakes. A privy : from ca. 1530 ; slightly ob. : S.E. till ca. 1750, then coll. Shakespeare, in *Lear*, ' I will tread this unbolted villain into mortar, and daub the walls of a jakes with him ' ; Sir John Harington's *Metamorphosis of Ajax*, ed. by Jack Lindsay, 1928. Prob. an abbr. of *Jack's place*.

[**jakes-farmer, -man.** An emptier of cesspools : late C. 16–17. Ineligible.]

jalouse as = regard with jealousy, begrudge jealously, is late C. 19–20 catachrestic. O.E.D.

jam, a crush, a crowd, is ineligible, as is **jam,** excellence, good luck, though **jam on it,** luxury, is (late C. 19–20) coll.—2. A difficulty, awkward ' mess ' : coll. : from ca. 1920. Ex sense, crowd, crush. Esp. in *get into a jam*.—3. As clear profit, an advantage, or a certainty of winning, it is late C. 19–20 s. (orig. racing) > coll.—4. Hence, a joy, a great pleasure : preparatory schools' : C. 20. E. F. Benson, *David Blaize*, 1916, ' It had been " jam " to see the Head stamp on that yellow-covered book.'—5. A sweetheart ; a mistress : low : from ca. 1870. (Also *bit of jam*, esp. as an attractive girl.) Hence, *lawful jam*, a wife : late C. 19–20, ob.—6. The female pudend : C. 19–20, ob. Whence *have a bit of jam*, to coït.—7. The pool at the game of nap : gaming s. : from ca. 1850. —8. A gymnastics shoe : Bootham School : late C. 19–20 ; † by 1925, says the anon. *Dict. of Bootham Slang* issued in that year. I.e. *gym* with the vowel from the second syllable.—9. See **jam-jar** below.

*jam, v. To hang : c. : mid-C. 18–early 19. Grose, 2nd ed. ? = *jamb*.—2. To spread with jam : coll. : from ca. 1850.

jam, adj. Smart ; neat : **low** : ca. 1880–1905. Ex *jam* = excellence.

jam, bit of. A very pretty girl : lower classes' : from ca. 1890 ; ob. See **bit of** . . . and cf. *jam-tart*, 1.

jam, money for. See **money for jam.**

jam, not all. Despite its apparently coll. tinge the phrase is S.E. But *real jam* is coll., † *jam and fritters* is s. : ex *jam*, n., 3.

jam-jar. A tram-car : rhyming **s.** : C. 20. B. & P.

jam-jar ; occ. abbr. to **jam.** A motor-car : rhyming s. : from ca. 1925. Philip Allingham, *Cheapjack*, 1934.

Jam-Jug(, the). The Russian cruiser *Zhemtchug* : naval : ca. 1915–20. Bowen. By ' Hobson-Jobson.'

jam on both sides. See **d'ye want jam.**

jam on it. Something pleasant : naval (−1900) > military. See **jam,** n., 3, and cf. *jammy*, q.v.

jam-pot. A high collar : Australian : ca. 1880–1900.—2. The female pudend : low : C. 19–20.

jam-tart. A mart : rhyming s. : mid-C. 19–20. B. & P.—2. Whence, a sweetheart ; a wife ; a mistress ; a harlot : low : from ca. 1860.—3. The market, esp. if favourable : buyers and sellers thereat : Stock Exchange : ca. 1880–1914.

jam-tin. A hand-grenade improvised from a jam-tin : military coll. : 1915, then rare. B. & P.

jam-up, adj. and adv. (In) the pink of perfection : low coll. : ca. 1850–90. Also *real jam* : from ca. 1880. Cf. *jammy*, q.v.

Jamaica discipline. ' The regulated distribution of booty among the crew of a pirate ' : nautical coll. : C. 19–20 ; ob. Bowen.

jamberoo. A ' good time ' ; esp. a drinking-bout : Australian (− 1935). A perversion of :

jamboree. A frolic, a spree : **s.** >, in C. 20, coll. : orig. (− 1872) U.S. ; anglicised, esp. in Australia, ca. 1890. Origin unknown.

*james. A crowbar : c. : C. 19–20 ob. Cf. *jemmy*, q.v. Vaux.—2. A sovereign (money) : c. : from ca. 1855 ; ob. Mayhew, in *Paved with Gold*.— 3. A sheep's head : low : from ca. 1825 ; ob. Cf. *bloody jemmy*, q.v.

James and Mary. A famous sand-bank in the Hoogly River below Calcutta : Anglo-Indian coll. : C. 18–20. Ex the wreck, there, of the *Royal James and Mary* in 1694. Yule & Burnell.

Jamie Moore, have been talking to. To be tipsy : Scots coll. : C. 19–20 ob.

jammed, be. To be hanged (see **jam,** v.), hence to meet any violent death : ca. 1800–50. *Lex. Bal.*

jammed like Jackson. A C. 19–20 naval c.p. verging on the proverbial, ' and when something goes seriously wrong, or leads to a disaster ', F. & Gibbons. Ex John Jackson who, in 1787, refused to listen to his pilot and ' nearly wrecked his ship in consequence '.

Jammy. (Gen. pl.) A native of Sunderland : nautical : late C. 19–20. Bowen. Possibly a corruption of *Sammy*, q.v.

jammy. Exceedingly lucky or profitable : from ca. 1870 : (low) coll. Hence, in C. 20, excellent, ' topping '. Ex *jam*, good luck. Cf. *am on it* and *jam-up*, qq.v.

jammy bit of jam. An intensive of *jam*, n., 5 : 1883, says Ware.

jams. Abbr. *jimjams*, q.v. Always *the jams*.

Jan. See **Feb.**

*jan. A purse : C. 17 c. Rowlands, in *Martin Murk-All* ; Jonson.

Janc, the. The Junior Army and Navy Club : naval and military officers' : C. 20. F. & Gibbons.

janders. Jaundice : sol. (− 1887) and dial. Baumann.

*jane. A sovereign : c. of ca. 1860–1910. *The Times*, April 14, 1864. Prob. suggested by the † S.E. sense, a small silver coin of *Genoa*.—2. A woman ; a girl. Australian (− 1916). C. J. Dennis. ? ex U.S. Cf. *judy*, 1. By 1933 it was used thus in Glasgow, with the additional sense : a sweetheart. Also in England, in the Australian sense : 1933, D. Sayers, *Murder Must Advertise*.

[**jane-of-apes,** a pert girl, cited by F. & H., is a literary though jocular nonce-word, while *jango*, liquor, is dial. Moreover, *janizary*, one of the rabble, as in B.E. and Grose is a mere S.E. transference of sense.]

Jane Shore. Tinned meat : naval : C. 20. Bowen. Suggested by *Harriet Lane* and *Fanny Adams*, for they too were decapitated.—2. A whore : rhyming s. : C. 20. More gen. *Rory o' More*. B. & P.

[**Janeite,** an admirer of Jane Austen's works, is rather literary j. than coll. : C. 20.]

jankers. Defaulters : their punishment ; punishment cells ; defaulters' bugle-call : military (1915) ; orig. (ca. 1910) naval. F. & Gibbons ; Bowen. Echoic : prob. ex *janglers* or *jangles*.— 2. Whence, *jankers king*, a provost-sergeant, and *jankers man*, a defaulter : military : 1915. F. & Gibbons.

jannock, jonnick, jonnock, jonnuk. Honest, loyal, equitable ; proper, customary ; conclusive : dial. >, ca. 1840, provincial coll. >, in 1914, fairly gen. coll. (Its use in Lancashire has been wittily satirised by C. E. Montague in *A Hind Let Loose*,

1911.) Whence the C. 19 *die jannock*, to die game or with bravado. In Australia, where it dates from ca. 1890, it is rather s. than coll. and is gen. pronounced *jonnuk*.—2. Also adv.

janty. A ship dressed with flags : nautical, esp. naval : C. 19. Bowen. Ex *jaunty*, elegant.

January chickens, have. To have children in old age : proverbial coll. : C. 19.

Jap. A Japanese : late C. 19–20 coll.—2. Also adj. : dated by Ware as early as 1860 and classified, as to *Jap crock*, as a Society term. (Cf. *Chink*, Chinese.)

Japan. Bread : military : 1915 ; ob. F. & Gibbons. Ex Fr. *du pain*, (some) bread. Also *dupan*.

japan. To ordain (a priest) : from ca. 1755 ; ob.: mainly university. Ex the clerical black coat. (The sense, to make shiny and black, is S.E.)

Japanese knife-trick. Eating with one's knife : low : ca. 1885–1910.

[**jape**, n. and v. Jest. V.t., copulate with. Despite F. & H., ineligible.]

jap(p)ers, be or by. See jab(b)ers.

jar. (A source of) annoyance : Public Schools' coll. : 1902, P. G. Wodehouse, *The Pothunters*. That which jars on one.

jar, on or **upon a** or **the.** Ajar : from ca. 1670 : S.E. till ca. 1850, then coll.

jarbee. An able seaman : naval (— 1909) ; ob. Ware ; Bowen. A perversion of *A.B.*

[**jargoon**, considered by Charles E. Leach (*On Top of the Underworld*, 1933) to be c., is actually S.E.]

jargoozle. To mislead, lit. and fig. : C. 19–20 ob.: coll. Prob. by *bamboozle* ex † S.E. *jargogle*, to confuse.

*[**jark** ; often **jarke.** A seal : c. : mid-C. 16–19. Harman. Often corrupted to *jack*. ? cf. Romany *jarika*, an apron.—2. Whence, a safe-conduct pass : C. 19–20, ob.—3. A watch : low (? orig. c.) : C. 19–20, ob. More gen. *yack*.

jark it. To run away : low : ca. 1820–60. Bee. ? ex *jerk* : cf. C. 20 *put a jerk into it*.—2. In C. 17–18 c., it occurs in *blot the scrip and jark it*, where *jark* = to seal.

***jarkman.** A writer of begging letters ; an habitual carrier, or a fabricator, of false papers : c. : mid-C. 16–mid-19. Harman, B.E., Ainsworth.

jaro, give (a person). To scold, vituperate : New Zealand : C. 20. (O.E.D. Sup.) Prob. ex Maori *iaua !*, hold ! or stay ! ; but cf. *jyro* (Addenda).

jarrehoe. A man servant : Wellington College : C. 19–early 20. ? origin.

jarring or **railroading.** A reprimand : Public Works' (— 1935). Ex *give a person a jar* (jolt) or else ex *jar on one's nerves*.

jarrock is a much-copied error for † *jarecork*, a red or purple dye-stuff. O.E.D.

jarvel. A jacket. "Old", says F. & H.: I find no other record.

Jarvey, the Fighting. Bill Wood : pugilistic : ca. 1810–30. 'Jon Bee.' Ex :

jarvis or **jervis** ; **jarv(e)y, jarvie.** A hackney coachman : s. >, ca. 1870, coll. : the *-is* forms in late C. 18–early 19 : the *-(e)y, -ie* forms from 1819, ob. by 1898, † by 1910 except as = the driver of an Irish car. Grose, 3rd ed. ; Serjeant Ballantine in his *Experiences*.—2. Hence, a hackney coach : ca. 1819–70. Moncrieff.—3. Occ. as v.i., to drive a carriage : 1826 : † (O.E.D.). Ex the proper name, 'perhaps in allusion to *St. Gervase*, whose attribute is a whip or scourge ' ; W.

jas(e)y or **jaz(e)y.** A (worsted) wig : ? orig. c. : by 1840 coll. : by 1870, S.E. : 1789, George Parker. Ex *Jersey* (*flax*).

jasey (or **jazey**), **cove with a.** A judge : ? orig. c. : C. 19.

***Jason's fleece.** A citizen swindled out of his money : late C. 17–early 19 : either c. or low s. B.E.

jass is a C. 17–18 error for *eyas* (hawk). O.E.D.

jasy. See jasey.

***jaum.** To discern ; discover : c. of ca. 1815–1900. Haggart ; Egan's Grose, where it is spelt *jaun*. Origin ? Possibly cognate with dial *jaum* (= *jam*), to corner in an argument (E.D.D.).

jaundy. A master-at-arms : naval (— 1909). Ware, 'Supposed to be from "gendarme ". The more gen. form is *jaunty*, recorded by the O.E.D. (Sup.) for 1904. Also *jonty*. Whence :

jaunty's boat's crew. 'The men remaining in one of the old naval hulks after the ships had drawn their companies ' : ? ca. 1800–40—a dating that affects *jaundy*.

java or **Java.** Tea ; coffee : Canadian : C. 20. B. & P. Cf. S.E. *Mocha*.

javel. A dock-loafer, gen. also a thief : nautical : C. 18. So Bowen. An extension of † S.E. *javel*, a low fellow, a rogue.

jaw. (Continual) talk ; impudence : coll. >, in C. 20, undignified S.E. : mid-C. 18–20. Smollett, ' "None of your jaw, you swab," . . replied my uncle.'—2. A talk, speech, lecture : low coll : from ca. 1800.

jaw, v. To chatter ; speak, esp. if impudently or violently ; (v.t.) abuse grossly : (low) coll. : mid-C. 18–20. Smollett, 'They jawed together . . . a good spell ' ; Thackeray.—2. To address abusively, scold or address severely : low coll. : from ca. 1810. Marryat.

jaw, hold or **stow one's.** To fall or be silent : coll. >, ca. 1890, undignified S.E. : from ca. 1850. Foote (*hold*). In C. 19–20, often *stop*, as in H. Kingsley's *Geoffry Hamlyn*.

jaw-bone. Credit ('tick') : Canadian (ca. 1860) >, ca. 1880, military. (O.E.D. Sup.)—2. Hence, *call one's jaw-bone*, to live on credit : from ca. 1890. F. & H.

jaw-breaker. A word difficult of pronunciation : coll. : 1839, Lever, 'high Dutch jawbreakers '. Baumann, 1887, has the rare variant, *break-jaw*. Cf. the U.S. form, *jaw-cracker*.—2. A hard punch on the jaw : pugilistic coll. of ca. 1860–1900.

jaw-breaking, adj. Difficult to pronounce : coll. : from ca. 1840. Thackeray.—2. The adv. in *-ly* is recorded for 1824. (O.E.D.)

jaw like a sheep's head, all. Nothing but talk : coll. : from ca. 1870. Hindley.

jaw-me-dead. A very talkative fellow : late C. 18–mid-19. Grose, 1st ed. Baumann (1887) has *jaw-me-down*, which he classifies as nautical : so, too, Bowen.

jaw-smith. A (demagogic) orator : coll. : ca. 1860–1900 : more U.S. than English.

jaw- (or **jawing-**) **tackle.** The organs of speech : nautical : from ca. 1830, 1858 resp. ; ob. Trelawney, 1831 ; C. Reade, 'Ah ! Eve, my girl, your jawing tackle is too well hung.' Baumann, 1887, records the variant *jawing-gear*.

jaw-twister. A (— 1874) ob. coll. elaboration of *jaw-breaker*, q.v. H., 5th ed.

jaw-work ! 'A cry used in fairs by the sellers of nuts,' Grose, 1st ed. : coll. or c.p. : mid-C. 18–mid-19.

jawaub. See **juwaub.**

jawbation. (Also *jobation*, q.v.) A general confabulation : coll. and dial. : C. 19–20. Ex :—2. A scolding : coll. : C. 18–20. Cf. :

jawing. A talk : (low) coll. : late C. 18–20.—2. A scolding : low coll. : C. 19–20.

jawing-gear. See **jaw-tackle.**

jawing-match. Wordy warfare : (low) coll. : from ca. 1815 ; ob. Moore.

jawing-tackle on board, have one's. ' To be saucy or impudent ', Egan's Grose : ca. 1820–1920.

jawkins. A club bore : clubmen's coll. : ca. 1846–50. Ex Thackeray's *Book of Snobs.*

jay. A wanton : late C. 16–early 17 coll. > S.E. Shakespeare.—2. An amateur ; an inferior actor : theatrical : ca. 1870–1905.—3. A simpleton (occ. as *j*) : coll. (— 1889) ; ob. (Ware dates it at 1880.) *Punch*, Feb. 22, 1890, ' She must be a fair j as a mater.' The *j* prob. abbr. *juggins.* Its U.S. origin shows clearly in C. 20 nuance, a fool, and in the New Zealand c. sense (— 1932), an easly victim.

jay, flap a ; play or scalp one for a. To befool or swindle (a simpleton) : low coll. (— 1887) ; ob. Baumann. More U.S. than Eng.

jay-walker. (Hence, *jay-walking*.) One who crosses a street to the peril of the traffic : 1925 : s. (ex U.S.) >, ca. 1934, coll. Ex U.S. *jay*, a provincial ' loon '. See esp. Logan Pearsall Smith in *The New Statesman*, June 15, 1935.

jaz(e)y. See **jasey.**

jeames. A flunkey ; a footman : 1846 : coll. in C. 19, S.E. in C. 20. Thackeray instituted the term in the *Diary of C. Jeames de la Pluche, Esq.*—2. **(Jeames.)** *The Morning Post* : journalists' : ca. 1859–1885. H. 2nd ed. Ex *James* affectedly pronounced.

Jebbel. The inevitable military nickname, on Egyptian service, of men surnamed Hill : from ca. 1920. Ex the Arabic for a hill.

Jedburgh, Jeddart, or Jedwood justice. Hanging first and trying afterwards : C. 18–20 : Scots coll. > historical S.E. A. Shields, 1706, ' Couper Justice and Jedburgh Law.' Ex a piece of summary justice done at this Scots border town. Cf. *Cupar justice, Halifax law, Lydford law.*

jee. A variant of grafters' **gee** (q.v.). George Orwell, *Down and Out*, 1933.

Jee ! or **Gee !** An orig. euphemistic, now mostly U.S. coll. corruption of *Jesus !* : mid-C. 19–20. Whence, **jee whizz !,** indicative of surprise : late C. 19–20, as in C. J. Dennis.

jee whiskers ! A New Zealand facetious variant (— 1935) of *jee whizz* (see preceding).

jeer. See **jere.**

Jeese or **Jeez !** Jesus ! : low : C. 20 : ex U.S.

jeff. A rope : circus s. > ,by 1900, j. : from ca. 1850. Dickens in *Hard Times.*—2. A man, chap, fellow : tailors' : late C. 19–20. Gen. in combination : e.g. *flat-iron jeff*, q.v.

jeff, v. ' To throw or gamble with quadrats as with dice,' Jacobi : printers' (— 1888). Ex U.S. (1837).

jeffy. See **jiffy.**

***jegger.** See **jigger,** n., 1.—**Jehoshaphat.** See **jumping Jehoshaphat.** (A sonorous name for the mild purpose.)

[**jehu,** a furious driver, hence a coachman, is merely jocular S.E.]

jeldi (or **-y**). See **jildi.**

jellico, occ. **jeelyco.** Angelica sylvestris : coll. (— 1853) >, ca. 1880, S.E. (O.E.D.)

jelly. A buxom and pretty girl : low : ca. 1840–1910. Perhaps ex Scots *jelly* = excellent.—2. The *semen virile* : low coll. : C. 17–20 ; ob. Fletcher, in *The Beggar's Bush.* Cf. :

jelly-bag. The scrotum.—2. The female pudend. Both low coll. : C. 17–20, ob.

jelly-belly. A fat person : low coll. : C. 19–20. Cf. *forty-guts.*

jelly-dog. A harrier (dog) : sporting (— 1897). With harriers, one hunts hares, which are gen. eaten with jelly. O.E.D.

jelly-dogging. Vbl.n., hunting with harriers : sporting s. : 1889, R. S. S. Baden-Powell. (O.E.D.)

***jem.** A gold ring. (A *rum gem* = a diamond ring.) Mid-C. 18–mid 19 c. Grose, 1st ed.

Jem (occ. **Jim**) **Mace.** A face : rhyming s. : late C. 19–20. B. & P. Ex the noted pugilist.

jemeny ! An occ. spelling (— 1923) of *jeminy !,* q.v. Manchon.

jemima. A chamber-pot : low : C. 19–20 ; ob. —2. A servant girl : Londoner's jocular coll. (— 1887) ; ob. Baumann. Cf. *Biddy*, q.v.

jemimas. Elastic-sided boots : coll. : C. 20.

jeminy !, often preceded, occ. followed, by *o(h).* A variant of ob. *gemini*, q.v.

jemmily. Neatly : coll. : ca. 1830–90. Ex *jemmy,* adj., 1.

jemminess. Neatness, spruceness : low coll. : ca. 1755–1890. See **jemmy,** adj.

jemmy (in C. 19, occ. *jimmy*). A short crowbar used by housebreakers : ? orig. (— 1811) c. : by 1870, coll. ; by 1910, S.E. *Lex. Bal.* ; Dickens, in *Oliver Twist.* Earlier *jenny*, q.v. ; ca. 1810–30, occ. called a *jemmy rook* (*Lex. Bal.*) ; in U.S., *jimmy.* Cf. *james*, q.v.—2. A dandy : coll. : ca. 1752–1800, thereafter gen. *jemmy jessamy* († by 1900), though the two terms were orig. distinct. *The Adventurer*, No. 100, 1753, ' The scale . . . consists of eight degrees ; Greenhorn, Jemmy, Jessamy, Smart, Honest Fellow, Joyous Spirit, Buck, and Blood.' See also **jemmy jessamy,** adj., separate entry.—3. Hence, a light cane, orig. and esp. one carried by a ' jemmy ' or dandy : ca. 1753–1800.— 4. Hence, also, a finicky fellow : naval : ca. 1760– 1800. Bowen, ' Adopted by the mutineers of 1797 for all officers.'—5. A sheep's head cooked : coll. : from ca. 1820 ; ob. Cf. *bloody jemmy.*—6. A shooting-coat ; a greatcoat : coll. : ca. 1830–1910. Dickens, ' Your friend in the green jemmy.'—7. A term of contempt, esp. as *all jemmy* (more gen. *all jimmy*), all rot ! : ca. 1860–1910.

jemmy, adj. Dandified, smart, neat : coll. : ca. 1750–1860 ; extant in dial. A. G. Stevens, ' Dressed as jemmy . . . as e'er a commoner in all England.' Ex † *gim*, smart, spruce.—2. Hence, sharp, clever : ca. 1760–80.—3. A pejorative : low : ca. 1860–1910. Ex *jemmy*, n., last sense.

Jemmy Donnelly. A jocular coll. name given to three kinds of large timber tree : Queensland : from ca. 1880 ; ob. Morris.

Jemmy Ducks. (Occ. *Billy D.*) The ship's poulterer : nautical : ca. 1860–1905.

Jemmy Grant. See **Jimmy,** n., 2, and **Jimmy Grant,** 2.

jemmy jessamy, gen. with capitals. Adj., dandified, effeminate : ca. 1785–1860. Variant, *Jemmy Jessamine*, not before 1823. See **jemmy,** n., 2.

jemmy-john. A low coll. corruption (— 1864) of *demijohn.* T. B. Aldrich.

Jemmy o' Goblin. A sovereign : (orig. theatrical) rhyming s. (— 1895). More frequently

Jimmy o' Goblin, occ. abbr. (— 1909) to *Jimmy* (recorded by Ware).

jemmy rook. See **jemmy, n., 1.**

Jemmy Squaretoes. The devil : nautical : C. 19–20. Bowen. Cf. *Old Squaretoes*, q.v.

Jemmy Twitcher. John Montagu, 4th Earl of Sandwich (d. 1792). Ex Gay's *The Beggar's Opera*, in which a highwayman, so named, betrayed his friends.

jenkers. An occ. form of *jankers*, q.v.

Jenkins' hen, die like. I.e., unmarried : Scots coll. : C. 18–19.

Jenny. Sir Robert Peel (1788–1850). Dawson.

jenny. A small housebreaking crowbar : late C. 17–early 19 c. B.E. Cf. *jemmy*, n., 1., *bess*, *betty*, and the Ger. *Peterchen, Klaus, Dietrich* (W.).—2. A she-ass : C. 19–20 : coll. >, by 1890, S.E. Abbr. *jenny ass.*—3. 'A losing hazard into the middle pocket off a ball an inch or two from the side cushion,' F. & H. : 1856 (S.O.D.) : billiards s. > j. >, in C. 20, S.E.—4. A hot-water bottle : coll. : from ca. 1880 ; ob.

*jenny. To comprehend : c. (— 1909). Ware. Perhaps a perversion of *granny*, v., or *jerry*, v.

Jenny Hills. (Very rare in singular.) Pills : rhyming s. : late C. 19–20.

Jenny Lea or **Lee.** Tea : rhyming s. : late C. 19–20. Also *Rosy Lee* and *you and me.*—2. A flea : id. (— 1923). Manchon. P.P., *Rhyming Slang*, 1932, differentiates thus : *Jenny Lea*, tea ; *Jenny Lees*, fleas.

jenny linda or **-er, Jenny Linda** or **-er.** A window : rhyming s. (— 1857). 'Ducange Anglicus.' On *winder*, the low coll. pronunciation, ex Jenny Lind, the famous mid-C. 19 singer.

Jenny Willocks. A very effeminate male ; a hermaphrodite : Glasgow (— 1934).

Jenny Wren. A wren : coll. : mid-C. 17–20. An excellent example of the people's poetry (' twopence coloured ').

jere or jeer. (The latter is rare and erroneous.) A turd : c. : C. 17–18 (?–19).—2. Hence (?), one's posterior : low ; esp. showmen's : C. 19–20. Neil Bell, *Crocus*, 1936.

Jeremiah. A fire : rhyming s., esp. urban labourers' : C. 20. *John o' London's Weekly*, June 9, 1934. Cf. *Anna Maria*.

Jeremiah, v. To complain : lower classes' coll. (— 1909) ; slightly ob. Ware. Cf. :

Jeremiah-mongering. ' Deplorable and needless lamentation' : Society : 1885–86. 'Invented to describe the behaviour of those who after the fall of Khartoum '—the country is going to the dogs, sir ! —' went around maintaining that England had indeed come to a finality ' (Ware).

jeremy diddler (or with capitals). A shark or sharper ; a shabby and dishonest borrower : coll. : 1803, Kenney names thus a man in *Raising the Wind* ; ob. Personification of *diddler*, q.v.

Jericho. A place of banishment, retirement, concealment, or desirable distance, esp. in *go to Jericho*, which in the imperative = go to the devil ! : s. > coll. : from ca. 1635. Ex 2nd Samuel x. 4–5. Cf. *Halifax*, q.v.—2. A water-closet : ca. 1840–1915 : low.—3. A rough quarter of Oxford : Oxford University : ca. 1840–80. ' Cuthbert Bede ', 1853, ' The purlieus of Jericho would send forth champions to the fight.'

Jericho, have been to. To be tipsy : C. 18–early 19 : drinkers'. Apperson.

Jericho Jane. A long-range Turkish gun firing

into Jericho from the Shunet Nimrin hills in 1918 : among Australian soldiers in that region. F. & Gibbons. Contrast *Asiatic Annie*.

Jericho to June, from. A long way : coll. : ca. 1835–1915. Barham.

jerk, a witty sally, a retort ; a lash with a whip : both S.E. despite F. & H.—2. A musculo-tendinous reflex (action) : medical students' (— 1933). *Slang*, p. 192. E.g. a ' knee-jerk '.

jerk, v. To write, as in *jerk a poem* : (low) coll. : ca. 1860–1905.—2. To accost eagerly : coll. or s. : ca. 1740–1810. 3. To rob (a person of) : c. : from ca. 1880. Baumann.

*jerk, cly the. To be whipped at the post : C. 17–18 c.

Jerk, Dr. A flogging schoolmaster : coll. : ca. 1740–1830. Foote.

jerk, in a. Instantly : coll. : ca. 1760–1820. G. A. Stevens, ' Put wine into wounds, | You'll be cured in a jerk.' Extant in dial.

*jerk a gybe. To forge a licence : mid-C. 17–18 c. Head & Kirkman.

jerk a part. See **sling a part.**

jerk a wheeze. To tell a ' wheeze ' with brilliant effect : theatrical : 1860, says Ware, but he, I believe, antedated it by a decade—perhaps even by two decades.

jerk chin-music. To talk : ca. 1870–1910 : coll., mostly U.S.

jerk in(to) it, put a. To act smartly or vigorously ; hurry : from ca. 1912. Ex physical training and prob. suggested by *jump to it*. (B. & P.)

jerk-nod. See **yerknod.**

jerk off, v.i. and **v. reflexive.** To masturbate : low coll. : C. 18–20. An ob. low s. variant is *jerk one's jelly* or *juice*.

jerk the cat. See **cat, jerk the.**

jerk the tinkler. To ring the bell : jocular : ca. 1830–1925. Dickens, in *Oliver Twist*.

jerker. A tippler : low : ca. 1830–1900. ? ex *jerk one's elbow.*—2. A steward : nautical : from ca. 1850 ; ob.—3. A harlot : urban (mostly London) : from ca. 1860 ; ob. Ex *jerk*, v., 2.—4. A chamber-pot : low : from ca. 1870 ; ob.

jerks. Delirium tremens : coll. : from ca. 1820. —2. Physical training : from ca. 1905 : perhaps orig. naval or military. Abbr. *physical jerks.*

jeroboam, wine-measure, -bottle, or -goblet, is S.E.—2. A chamber-pot : ca. 1820–80. Whence *jerry*, 3.

jerran. Anxious ; (greatly) concerned : Australia : ca. 1820–1900. Peter Cunningham, ' Rolf Boldrewood.' Ex *jirrand*, Botany Bay Aborigine for afraid. (Morris.)

jerrawicke. Australian-made beer : Australian coll. : ca. 1850–60. Morris. ? ex Aborigine.

Jerry ; occ. **Gerry.** N. and adj., German ; esp. (of) a German soldier : 1914 + ; ob. From mid-1916, more gen. than *Fritz(y)*. Often half-affectionately, as in ' Poor old Jerry's copping it hot from our heavies.' B. & P.

*jerry. A fog, a mist : c. of ca. 1810–80. Vaux. —2. Also c. (— 1887), a watch : ob. (Baumann.) The gen. C. 20 term is *kettle.*—3. A chamber-pot : low : from ca. 1825. Ex *jeroboam.*—Hence, 3, *a*, a cup, as in *the cricket* or *sports jerry* : Charterhouse : late C. 1920—4. A (hard, round) hat : ca. 1840–70. Abbr. *Tom and Jerry hat*, q.v.—5. A celebration of completed indentures : printers' : from ca. 1870 ; ob.—6. A low beer-house : from ca. 1850 : coll. >, ca. 1880, S.E. Abbr. *jerry-*

shop.—**7.** A jerry-builder: 1890 (S.O.D.): >, ca. 1920, coll.—**8.** A recognition, discovery, ' tumble ': low : from ca. 1880. Ex the v.—**9.** A variant of *gerry*, q.v.

jerry, v.i. and t. To recognise ; discern, discover, detect ; understand : low : from ca. 1870. Prob. ex *jerrycummumble*, q.v. Cf. *rumble*, itself prob. suggested by *tumble*, the latter prob. ex *jerrycummumble*.—**2.** To jibe (at) ; chaff maliciously : low : ca. 1850–90. Ex *jeer*.

jerry, adj. Unsubstantial ; constructed unsubstantially : from ca. 1880 : coll. till C. 20, then S.E. Cf. next two entries. ? etymology : perhaps ex *Jerry*, familiar and/or contemptuous for *Jeremiah*. More prob. a corruption of *jury* (as in *jury-mast, -leg*, etc.), as W. suggests.

jerry-builder. ' A rascally speculating builder,' F. & H. : recorded in 1881 (S.O.D.) but arising in Liverpool ca. 1830 (F. & H.). The vbl.n. *jerry-building* occurs in a Liverpool paper of 1861 (W.).

jerry-built. Unsubstantial(ly built) : 1883 : coll. till C. 20, then S.E. *The Daily Telegraph*, March 23, 1883 ; J. Newman in *Scamping Tricks*, 1891. ? ex or = *jury-built* (W.) : see **jerry**, adj.

*****jerry-getting, -nicking, -stealing.** The stealing of watches : c. (— 1888) ; ob.

jerry-go-nimble. Diarrhœa : coll. : C. 19. Earlier, *thorough-go-nimble*.—**2.** An antic or ' jack pudding ' (q.v.) : C. 19 coll. > S.E. Henley & Stevenson.

Jerry Lynch. A pickled pig's-head : low : mid-C. 19–20 ; ob.

*****jerry-nicking.** See **jerry-getting**.

Jerry over ! ; Jerry up. Resp. a night and a day warning that a German 'plane was overhead : military coll. : 1917–18. (F. & Gibbons.)

jerry-shop. A (low) beer-house : from ca. 1830 : s. > coll >, ca. 1860, S.E. Often abbr. *jerry*, as in Mayhew, ' A beer-shop or, as he called it, a jerry.'

jerry sneak. A henpecked husband : 1763, Foote instituted the character in *The Mayor of Garratt* : coll. : † by 1860.—**2.** In c., a watch thief : C. 19–20 ; ob.

*****jerry-stealing.** See **jerry-getting**.—**Jerry up !** See **Jerry over !**

jerry wag. A spreester, esp. if half drunk : ca. 1820–70. ' Jon Bee.'

jerry-wag shop. A coffee shop or stall : ca. 1820–70. Ibid.

jerry(cum)mumble. To shake, tousle, tumble : C. 18–early 19. Cibber the shorter, Grose (1st ed.) the longer form. Perhaps on *stumble*. Whence, perhaps, *tumble*, to understand (v.t. with *to*), *jerry*, the same, and *rumble*, the same : qq.v.

jerrymander. See **gerrymander**, for which it is erroneous.

Jersey, Mr. Mrs. Langtry : a turf nickname. Ex her sobriquet, *the Jersey lily*. (Dawson.)

Jersey hop. ' An unceremonious assembly of persons with a common taste for valsing ; from Jersey, U.S.A. ' : ca. 1883–1900. Ware.

Jerusalem ! Indicative of surprise. Mid-C. 19–20. Perhaps the origin of *Jee !* (q.v.). Cf. *Jerusalem, go to*.

Jerusalem, be going to. To be drunk : drinkers : C. 18–early 19. Cf. *Jericho, to have been to*, q.v. Both terms occur in Franklin's *Drinker's Dict.*, 1745. (Apperson.)

Jerusalem !, go to. Go to blazes ! C. 19–20. Cf. *Jericho !, go to*.

Jerusalem cuckoo. A mule : military (in

Palestine) : 1917–18. B. & P., ' From its melodious note.' In Warwickshire dial., an ass (E.D.D.).

Jerusalem (or Jews') letters. Tattooing : nautical (— 1923). Manchon.

Jerusalem parrot. A flea : low (— 1923). Manchon.

Jerusalem pony. An ass : from ca. 1820 ; ob.: s. >, ca. 1850, coll. Bee. Ex Christ's entry into Jerusalem on an ass. Cf. *Egyptian charger*.—**2.** Hence, a needy clergyman doing *locum tenens* work : clerical : from ca. 1850 ; ob. Cf. *guinea pig*.

Jerusalem the Golden. Brighton : from ca. 1870. Ex the numerous rich Jews there.

jervis. See **jarvis**.

jes', jes. Just (adv.) : sol. (— 1887). Baumann.

jess (falconry) is wrongly defined in many notable dictionaries. See O.E.D. or S.O.D.

jessamine. A C. 19 variant of :

jessamy. As n., a fashionable man next above a ' jemmy ' (see n., 2) : ca. 1750–1830.—**2.** As adj., dandified, effeminate : ca. 1680–1850. Head, G. A. Stevens. (For both, see also *jemmy jessamy*. Like *jessamine*, of which it is a corruption, it is ex the flower (*jasmine*)).

Jessie. An effeminate man : Glasgow (— 1934). Cf. *Nancy* and *Pansy*.

jessie or **jessy, give** (a person). To thrash : non-aristocratic (— 1860) ; slightly ob. H., 2nd ed. Origin ? Perhaps—via *Jess*—it is a corruption of *give a person gas*, q.v.

Jesso. The inevitable nickname of anyone surnamed Read : naval and, hence, military : late C. 19–20. Bowen. Why ?

jest. Just : dial. and lower classes' coll. : C. 19–20.—**2.** A sol. (— 1923) for *gist*. Manchon.

jester. A ' joker ' (q.v.), chap, fellow : coll. : ca. 1860–1905. See also **artist, merchant**. A very interesting s. and coll. synonymy exists for a fellow.

jesuit. A sodomite : coll. : ca. 1630–1820. Whence *jesuits' fraternity*, the world of sodomy, as in Rochester, ' The Jesuits' fraternity | Shall leave the use of buggery.' Cf. *box the Jesuit* and the opprobrious sense attaching to *Jesuit* even in S.E. The Society of Jesus is here made the scapegoat for all monastic orders,—against whom, as against sailors, the charge of masturbation is often laid.—**2.** A graduate or an undergraduate of Jesus College, Oxford : Oxford University : ca. 1760–1890. Smollett, in *Humphrey Clinker*.

Jesuit, box the. See **box the Jesuit**.

Jesus appears in blasphemous oaths ; often disguised, as in *jab(b)ers, by*, q.v.

Jesus'-eyes. Forget-me-nots : Roman Catholic coll. (— 1909). Ware.

Jesus wept ! A low c. p. expressive of commiseration or disgust or annoyance : C. 20.

*****jet.** A lawyer : c. : C. 18–early 19. *A New Canting Dict.* Cf. *autem jet*, a parson (see **autem**).

[**jet**, to strut, like **jetter**, a pompous man, is S.E., despite F. & H.]

jet one's juice. (Of men) to experience the sexual spasm : low : C. 19–20 ; ob. Cf. *come*, q.v.

jeuced infernal. See **deuced infernal**.

Jeune Siècle. ' Conversion of *fin de siècle*, and describing people . . . of the same social behaviour. Of course from Paris ' : Society coll. : first decade of C. 20. Ware.

Jew, a hard bargainer, despite F. & H. is S.E., but the v.i. and t., *jew*, to drive a very hard bargain, to overreach or cheat, is coll. : 1845 (S.O.D.).—**2.** A ship's tailor : nautical : late C. 19–20. O.E.D. (Sup.). Cf. *jewing*, q.v.

Jew(-)bail. Insufficient or worthless bail : mid-C. 18–mid-19 : coll. Grose, 1st ed. ; Bee.

Jew-balance. A hammer-headed shark : nautical : late C. 19–20. Bowen.

Jew boy. A (young) Jewish male : mid-C. 19–20 : coll. >, ca. 1920, S.E. Mayhew, 1861.

Jew fencer. A Jewish street buyer or salesman, esp. of stolen goods : low : from ca. 1850. See fencer (not *fence*).

Jew food. Ham : Charterhouse : C. 20. Ironic.

*Jew-Jack. See **Jack the Jew.**

Jewburg. A C. 20 South African punning variant of *Joburg*, q.v.

Jewel of Asia. 'A certain heavy Turkish gun at the Dardanelles' : military : 1915 ; ob. F. & Gibbons. Cf. *Asiatic Annie.*

jewing, vbl.n. Tailoring ; sewing : nautical : late C. 19–20. Bowen. Cf. *Jew*, 2. Hence, *jewing-bag*, the bag in which a sailor keeps his sewing-gear : id. : id. Ibid.

Jew's compliment. See **Judische compliment.**

Jew's eye, worth a. Extremely valuable : late C. 16–20 ; ob. Perhaps ex eyes put out by medieval torturers to enforce payment. G. Harvey, 'Let it everlastingly be recorded for a soverain Rule, as deare as a Jewes eye' ; Grose.

Jew's(-)harp. A hair-comb with tissue paper applied to one side : on blowing against the other, one can produce queer music : C. 19–20 : s. >, ca. 1890, coll. Punning the S.E. musical instrument so named.

Jew's letters. See **Jerusalem letters.**

Jews on a pay-day, (as) thick as two. (To be) intimate : Cockney (— 1887). Baumann.

Jew's poker. One who lights Jews' fires on Saturdays (the Jewish Sunday) : from ca. 1870. *Lloyd's Weekly*, May 17, 1891.

Jezebel, an objectionable or shrewish woman, is, despite F. & H., ineligible.—2. The male member : C. 19–20 low. Perhaps ex *2nd Kings* ix. 33 : 'And he said, throw her down. So they threw her down.'

jib. The underlip (as in *hang one's jib*, to look dejected) ; also, the face (as in nautical *cut of one's jib* (q.v.), one's personal looks or look) : coll. and dial. : from ca. 1820.—2. A first-year undergraduate : Dublin university : from ca. 1840 ; ob. Lever.—3. A horse given to jibbing : 1843 (S.O.D.) : coll. >, ca. 1895, S.E. Mayhew.—4. See **jibb.**—5. A 'flat-folding, "chimney-pot" hat, closed by springs set in centre of vertical ribs' : Society : 1848–80. Ware. Ex Fr. *gibus* (from the inventor's name).

jib, v. As to shirk or funk, prob. to be considered S.E.—2. To depart (esp. hastily or slyly) : low coll. : from ca. 1850.

jib draw !, long may your big. 'Good luck !', esp. to a man leaving the service : naval (— 1909). Ware. Of erotic origin.

jib of jibs. An impossible sail : nautical coll. : ca. 1850–1910. Ex nautical j. for the outermost jib (a triangular stay-sail). Cf. *sky-scraper.*

*jibb. The tongue ; hence language, speech : C. 19–early 20 tramps' c. Ex Romany *chib, jib*.

jibber the kibber. To deceive seamen and thus wreck ships ' by fixing a candle and lantern round the neck of a horse, one of whose fore feet is tied up ; this at night has the appearance of a ship's light,' Grose, 2nd ed. : late C. 18–early 19. The phrase is mysterious : *jibber*—by itself, however, unrecorded

before 1824—gen. = to talk confusedly, here prob. = to confuse. But what is *kibber* ? unless it be a rhyme-tag ?

jickajog. A pushing ; a commotion : low : C. 17–mid-19. Jonson. Euphonic reduplication on *jog*. Cf. *jig(ga)-jog(gy)*.

jiff (1790, ob.) ; gen. **jiffy** (1785) ; occ. **jeffy** (— 1791). A moment : coll. Rare except when preceded by *in a*. Grose, 3rd ed. ; H. & J. Smith ; Thackeray ; Milliken (*jiff*). ? etymology, perhaps suggested by *jiffle*, to fidget. (O.E.D. ; E.D.D.)

jiffess. An employer's wife : tailors' : from ca. 1860 ; ob.

jiffy. See **jiff.**—2. **jiffy-quick** is a variant of *in a jiffy* : coll. : 1927 (O.E.D. Sup.).

jig. Abbr. *jigger*, c. senses, q.v.—2. Applied to a person, a domestic animal, etc. : jocular coll. : C. 18–19. Bentham, 'This Lord and Lady Traction are the queerest jigs you ever saw ' (O.E.D.).—3. A swindler : Winchester College : ca. 1840–70.—3a—Hence, a clever fellow : ibid. : from ca. 1860.—4. A swindle, a low joke, an object of sport : ibid. : from ca. 1870. (The other F. & H. senses are S.E., as are those given by F. & H. for the v.)

jig, on the. Fidgety : coll. : from ca. 1880. Jefferies, in *Wood Magic*. O.E.D.

jig, the feather-bed or **the buttock-** or **Moll Peatley's.** Copulation : low coll. : C. 17–20 ; ob.

jig-a-jig ; in C. 19 often jig-jig. N. and v. for sexual intercourse : low : v. from ca. 1840, n. from ca. 1900. F. & H. says U.S., but this is very doubtful : almost certainly Eng., perhaps orig. dial. In the 1840's there was a street-ballad entitled *Jig Jig to the Hirings*, wherein *jig-jig* occurs as a v. (B. & P.) Popularised in and by the G.W., when used by French touts in form *jig-a-jig très bon*. Echoic. Cf. *jig-jog* and *jiggle*.

jig by jowl. Cheek by jowl : late C. 17–18 coll. D'Urfey.

jig is up, the. The game is up : late C. 18–20 : S.E. till ca. 1850, then coll. ; in C. 20, s. and dial. Contrast *on with the dance.*

jig-jog, jigga-jog(gy). A jolting movement : coll. verging on S.E. C. 17–20. Marston.

jig(g)amaree. A trick ; a fanciful contrivance : recorded in England from ca. 1845 ; ob. : coll., esp. in U.S. (where recorded in 1824). Ex various diall. Halliwell. Fanciful on *jig*.

jiggalorum. A fanciful, gen. worthless, trifle : coll. C. 17–18. Cf. *cockalorum*.

jig(g)ambob, occ. **jiggembob.** See **jiggumbob.**

Jigger. An 'inevitable' nickname of men surnamed Lees : mostly naval and military : late C. 19–20. F. & Gibbons.

*jigger. Its c. senses are :—A door : mid-C. 16–19. Harman, Coles, Mayhew. Also as *jig, gigger, gyger, jegger*.—2. A door-keeper : C. 18–20, ob. Parker. Also *jigger-dubber*.—3. A key, a lock : ca. 1815–70. Bee.—4. A whipping-post : C. 18–early 19. John Hall.—5. A private or secret still : ca. 1820–1910. Bee.—6. Its s. senses.—7. A fiddlestick : C. 18–19.—8. A bridge or rest : billiards : 1847 (S.O.D.).—9. The curtain : theatrical : from ca. 1850 ; ob.—10. A prison cell : 1896, Max Pemberton (O.E.D.). Ex next.—11. A guardroom : military (— 1882).—12. G.W. military : the front line, esp. as a trench, a sense merging (the semi-coll., semi-S.E.) *jigger*, gadget + *jigger*, an alternative of *digger*, a trench.—Low s. are :—13. The penis ; 14, the female pudend : C. 19–20.

jigger, v.t. and i. To shake or jerk often and

rapidly : coll. : 1867 (S.O.D.). Ex *jig*, **v.** of motion.—2. To circumvent, damage, ruin : from ca. 1860. Ex *jiggered !*, q.v. Cf. *jiggered up*.—3. To imprison, shut up : 1887, Hall Caine (O.E.D.); ob. Gen. with *up*.

jigger, not worth a. Worthless : (low) coll.: 1861, *Punch*, 'The churches here ain't worth a jigger—nor, not half-a-jigger.'

*jigger-dubber. A door-keeper, turnkey : c.: ca. 1770–1880. Parker, Bee. See **jigger**, esp. 1, 2, 3.

jigger it ! Curse it ! A C. 20 variant of *jiggered*, q.v.

jigger-stuff. Illicitly distilled spirits : ca. 1840–1900 : low (? orig. c.).

jigger-worker. A vendor of illicitly distilled spirits : ca. 1840–1905.—2. A drinker of whiskey, esp. if illicitly distilled : low (— 1896) ; ob.

jiggered, ppl. adj. Made from a secret still : from ca. 1880. *Judy*, Aug. 4, 1886, 'Jiggered gin.' Suggested by *jigger-stuff*, q.v., and *jigger-gin*.

jiggered !, be. As in *I'm* or *I'll be, jiggered !*, *you be jiggered !* Marryat, 1837 (S.O.D.). Possibly a deliberate fusing and perversion of *Jesus* and *buggered* ; cf. however, *sniggered*.

jiggered up. Exhausted : nautical (— 1867). Smyth. Cf. *jigger*, v., 2, but prob. ex *jiggered !*, *be*.

jiggery-pokery ; occ. **jackery-pokery.** Humbug ; underhand work : ? orig. (ca. 1880) tailors' s. ; coll. by 1900. Ex Scottish *joukery-paukery* ex *jouk*, a trick. Cf. *hanky-panky*, hocus-pocus, W.

jigget, occ. jiggit, v.i. To jig, fidget, hop about, shake up and down : coll. : 1687. Mrs. Behn, Miss Mitford, Kipling (O.E.D.). Diminutive of *jig*.

jiggety, jiggity. Having a hopping or jerky movement : coll. : from ca. 1880.

jiggle, v.i. and t. To have sexual intercourse with : low : from ca. 1845. Ex the S.E. sense. Hence *jiggling-bone*, the male member. Cf. *jig-a-jig*, q.v.

*jiggot o' mutton. A leg of mutton : c. (—1909). Ware. Fr. *gigot*.

jig(g)umbob. Also *jig(g)ambob*, *-embob*, *-ombob* ; *gig(g)umbob*, etc. ; *gingam*(or *um*)*bob*. Something odd or very fanciful ; something unspecified : coll. : C. 17–20 ; ob. Beaumont & Fletcher, 'What Giggombob have we here ?' Rare of a person. Ex *jig*, n. : cf. *kickumbob* and *thingumbob*, q.v.

jil-crow-a-berry. 'The Anglicised pronunciation and spelling of the aboriginal name for the indigenous *Rat-tail Grass*' : Australian coll. (—1898). Morris.

jildi, jildy ; jildo ; occ. **jeldi**(-y) ; very often **jillo.** Adj. and adv., lively ; look sharp ! : Regular Army's : late C. 19–20. Ex Hindustani. (Also, as adv., *on the jildi* : B. & P.) Cf. Romany *jido*, *jidilo*, lively.—2. V. See Addenda.

*jilt. A crowbar : c. (— 1859) ; ob. H., 1st ed. In pl., housebreaking tools in general.

*jilt, to. Enter a building slyly or on false pretences, and then steal : c. : from ca. 1860 ; ob.

jilt-flirt is erroneous for *gill-flirt*.

*jilter. A thief acting as in **jilt, to**, q.v. : c. : from ca. 1860. Also called a *note-blanker*. (Such thieves work in pairs.)

Jim, Dr. Dr. Leander Starr Jameson (of Jameson's Raid) : from the late 1880's.

Jim Brown. Town : rhyming s. (—1893).

Jim Crow. See **Billy Barlow.**

jim-jam. A knick-knack : coll. (— 1592) ; † by

1700. A reduplication on the first syllable of *gimcrack*.—2. Delirium tremens : in pl. only (*the j.-j.*) : 1885. Often called *the jams* (ob.). Perhaps influenced by *whim-whams*.—3. Also pl. only : peculiarities : coll. (— 1899). O.E.D.—4. (Pl., *the j.-j.*) The fidgets ; nervousness ; the 'creeps' ; low spirits : coll. : C. 20. E.g. A. S. M. Hutchinson, 1908 ; Galsworthy, 1926. Ex sense 2. Cf. dial. *antrims*, whims, perhaps ex *tantrums*. Also *the jimmies* : coll. : from ca. 1920. O.E.D. (Sup.).

Jim Mace. See **Jem Mace.**

jimbugg. A sheep : Australia : from ca. 1850 ; ob. More gen. is *jumbuck* (— 1845) : orig. the natives' pidgin English : the word meaning, in Aborigine, a white mist, the only thing with which a flock of sheep could be compared. Morris.

jiminy. Se **gemini.**

jimkwim ; jimmant. Corruptions of *Doctor* (or *Dr.*) *Jim*, q.v. Ware.

Jimmie's. See **Jimmy's.**—**jimmies, the.** See **jim-jam, 4.**

jimmy. A mainly U.S. variant of *jemmy*, n., 1, q.v.—2. (**Jimmy.**) A new chum or immigrant : Australian (— 1859) ; † by 1897. Also (— 1867) *Jimmy* (or *Jemmy*) *Grant*, presumably after *immigrant*, though see **Jimmy Grant**, 2. Morris. (Only *Jimmy* :—) In South Africa (esp. Natal) by 1878, notes Pettman.—3. A contrivance ; anything faked ; a concealed helper : showmen's : from ca. 1850.—4. Abbr. *Jimmy o' Goblin*, q.v. at *Jemmy o' Goblin*. Both forms occur in Neil Bell's *Andrew Otway*, 1931.—5. 'The nickname used as an alternative to Shiner for all naval Greens' (Bowen) : late C. 19–20. Also, in C. 20, for military Greens.

jimmy, adj. See **jemmy, adj.**

jimmy, all. All nonsense : Cambridge University : ca. 1860–1910. See also **jemmy, n., 7.**

Jimmy Bung(s). A cooper : naval (— 1909). Ware (*Bung*) ; Bowen (*Bungs*). Prob. ex *bung-hole*. Also *Bungs*, q.v.

Jimmy Ducks. The rating in charge of the ship's poultry : naval : ca. 1800–50. Bowen. Cf. *duck-fucker*.—2. Hence, a galley boy, a butcher's assistant : nautical : mid-C. 19–20. Ibid.

jimmy (or J,) **fixing.** 'A mechanical contraption of any description' : merchant service : late C. 19–20. Bowen. Cf. *hook-me-dingly*, q.v.

Jimmy Grant. See **jimmy, n., 2.**—2. An emigrant : rhyming s. : from late 1850's. Also *Jemmy Grant.*

Jimmy Low. A eucalyptus timber-tree : Australia (— 1889). After some New South Wales 'character'. Morris. Cf. *Jemmy Donnelly*, q.v.

Jimmy-o, like. 'Like billy-o,' which prob. suggested it : military (— 1923). Manchon.

Jimmy o' Goblin. See **Jemmy o' Goblin.**

Jimmy Riddle. To urinate : rhyming s. (on *piddle*) : late C. 19–20. B. & P.

Jimmy Round. (Gen. pl.) A Frenchman : naval : late C. 18–early 19. Ware derives it from the Fr. *je me rends*, I surrender. Cf. *kamerad*, q.v.

Jimmy Skinner. A dinner : rhyming s. (—1896').

Jimmy the Bunting. A signalman : naval : late C. 19–20. Bowen. With a pun on *Baby Bunting* and *bunting*, flags in the mass.

Jimmy the One. The First Lieutenant : naval : C. 20. Bowen. Cf. *one-pipper*.

Jimmy Woodser. A drink by oneself : Australian : C. 20. Also a *drink with the flies*, which is C. 20 coll.

Jimmy's. St. James's Restaurant in Piccadilly: ca. 1870–1910. (The site of the present Piccadilly Restaurant.)

jingbang, occ. **jimbang**. (Sometimes hyphenated. Always preceded by *the whole*.) A lot, or group, complete: mainly Scots coll. (— 1891). Stevenson, 'The only seaman of the whole jingbang.'

jingle. A two-wheeled carriage. Despite F. & H., ineligible.—2. (Cf. *jink*, 1.) Money: New Zealanders' (— 1935). Cf. *chink, chinkers*.

*****jingle-box.** A leathern drinking vessel tipped with silver and hung with bells, in C. 17 use among topers: C 17–18. B.E., who says 'formerly'; Grose.

jingle-boy. See **gingle-boy.**

jingle-brains. A wild harum-scarum fellow: C. 17–18; coll. Extant in dial.

*****jingler.** A horse-dealer frequenting country fairs: late C. 17–18 c. B.E.

jingo !, by the living. A C. 19–20 (ob.) elaboration of:

jings !; more gen. *by jingo;* in late C. 18–20 Scotland, always (*by*) *jing*(*s*). A mild oath: coll.: from ca. 1694 as an exclamation, but in 1670, and prob. much earlier, it was a piece of conjurer's gibberish. (S.O.D.)—As a noisy patriot, it is S.E. The word comes prob. ex Basque *J*(*a*)*inko*, God, via the Basque harpooners on British whalers. W.

jiniper-, in C. 18–19 **juniper, lecture.** A scolding: late C. 17–mid-19: coll. B.E.'s *jiniper-l.* is obviously a misprint, but it may have reproduced a Cockney pronunciation.

jink. Coin, money: late C. 19–20. Perhaps on *chink*, q.v.: but cf. *jingle*, 2.—2. In pl., see **high jinks.** (F. & H.'s *jink* and *jinker*, copulate, copulator, are ineligible because dial.)

jink one's tin. To pay, 'shell out'; rattle one's money: low: from ca. 1850; ob.

jinker. A light sulky, with room for only one person; esp. one used in speed-trotting trials: Australian coll. (from ca. 1910), now verging on S.E. Ex *jinker*, a vehicular contrivance for the transport of tree trunks.

jinket. To be very merry; dance about: coll., the former 1742, ob., the latter 1823, ob. Ex *jink*. (O.E.D.)

jinks. See **high jinks.**—2. **Jinks the Barber.** A secret informant: middle classes': mid-C. 19–20; ob. Ware, 'The general barber being such a gossiper. Jinks is a familiar name '—coll., from ca. 1820—'for an easy-going man'.

*****jinny.** A Geneva watch: c.: late C. 19–20; ob. Ex *Geneva*.

Jinny Spinner (or **j.-s.**). A cockroach: nautical: late C. 19–20. Bowen.

*****jip;** esp. **stick of jip.** Indian ink: c.: mid-C. 19–20. '*No. 747.*' Cf. *jipping*, q.v.

jip, give one. See **gip, give.**

jipper, jippo. Gravy: nautical: from ca. 1850. Occ. it = juice, syrup, or even dripping (E.D.D.). In the C. 20 British Army, *jippo*, and among the Australians occ. = stew. A correspondent remembers it being, ca. 1905 at school, used of the slimy outside of pudding. Perhaps ultimately ex † *jippo*, a tunic, ? hence a scullion. Just possibly, a *Gippo* being a man of brown colour, ex sense 2; but I shouldn't be surprised if it were proved to be a corruption of *sipper*.—2. *Jippo*, an incorrect form of *Gyppo*, an Egyptian.

*****jipping**, vbl.n. Staining (part of a horse) with Indian ink to conceal a blemish: c.: mid-C. 19–20. '*No. 747* ': cf. *jip*.

jippo. See **jipper.**

jirrand. See **jerran.**

jist, adv. Just: sol. (— 1887). Baumann. Likewise *jes*.

jitters, the. A feeling, a bout, of (extreme) nervousness or of irritation, annoyance: from ca. 1930. (*The Passing Show*, July 15, 1933.) Cf. *jim-jams*. Perhaps a perversion of S.E. *twitter*, a trembling.

Jix. Sir William Joynson-Hicks, the Home Secretary of 1926–30. Nickname (journalistic > gen.) by fusion of *Joynson* + *Hicks*. His death in 1932 stopped the late 1928 + 1932 usage of his name as a synonym for interfering prudery. See esp. P. R. Stephensen, *Policeman of the Lord*, 1928, and his *The Well of Sleevelessness*, 1929. Cf.:

Jixi, occ. **-y.** A two-seat 'taxi' licensed in 1926: coll.: 1926–27. Sir Wm. Joynson-Hicks was then Home Secretary: cf. *Jix*, q.v. On *taxi* (O.E.D. Sup.).

jo. See **joe, n.**—2. An exclamation, a warning: Australia: from ca. 1853; ob. Also *joe, joey*. Ex Charles Joseph La Trobe, the Victorian Governor at that time. W. Howitt, *Two Years in Victoria*, 1855. (Morris.) Also a v. (— 1861), with variant *joey*. T. McCombie, *Australian Sketches*, 1861.—3. A banjo: mostly Canadian: C. 20. (John Beames.)

jo-jo. A man with much hair on his face: Melbourne (Australia): low: ca. 1880–1905. Ex a Russian 'dog-man', ostensibly so named, exhibited in Melbourne ca. 1880. Morris.

joan, Joan. A fetter, esp. in *Darby and Joan*, fetters coupling two prisoners. C. 18–19. Suggested by *darbies*, handcuffs or fetters.

Joan, homely. A coarse, ordinary woman: C. 17–18 coll. B.E. In dial., *Joan Blunt*.

Joanna; occ. **Johanna** or **-ner.** A piano: rhyming s. (— 1923) on *pianner*. Manchon.

Job. A henpecked husband: lower and lower-middle classes' coll.: 'coined' by Douglas Jerrold, in *Mrs. Caudle's Curtain Lectures*, 1846; ob. (Ware.) Ex the Biblical character.

job as transaction—situation—piece of work—occurrence—a jab—is S.E., despite F. & H.—2. A guinea: c. of ca. 1670–1830. Coles. Whence *half a job*, half a guinea. Occ. *jobe*.—3. A robbery: C. 18–20, c. >, ca. 1850, low. Defoe, in *Moll Flanders*, 'It was always reckoned a safe job when we heard of a new shop.' O.E.D.—4. A clock: c. (— 1923). Manchon. Why ?—5. A recruit: military: from ca. 1910. Perhaps abbr. a *bad job*.

job, v. To coït with: coll.: C. 16–20. Anon. play of *Thersites*, 1537; Burns. All other senses listed by F. & H.—e.g. to prod—are S.E.; except, 2, *job* = *jobe*, q.v.—3. To smite: coll.: C. 20. C. J. Dennis. Ex *job*, to prod; cf. *jab*, v., 2, q.v.

job, be on the. 'To mean honestly; to be genuine; to "run straight"; to work quickly and steadily; to achieve complete success; to be bent on,' F. & H. Coll.: from ca. 1880.

job, do a. To conduct a funeral: undertakers' coll. (— 1864). H., 3rd ed.—2. See *****do a job.**

job, have got the. To have a commission to bet on a horse: racing: from ca. 1875.

job for her, do a woman's. To accomplish the sexual act with her—and to her pleasure. Low coll.: from ca. 1850.

job for him, do a man's. To ruin; knock out; kill : low coll. : from ca. 1860.

job for oneself, do a. To defecate : late C. 19–20 : (? orig. low) coll.

Jobanjeremiah. A maunderer : lower classes' (– 1909) ; ob. Ware, ' Combination of the two doleful patriarchs.'

jobation. A (tedious) reproof or rebuke : coll. : from ca. 1865 ; ob. Ex *jobe*, v. The alternative form *jawbation* has been influenced by *jaw*, n. and v. Colman, 1767, in *The Oxon in Town*, ' As dull and melancholy as a fresh-man . . . after a jobation.'

jobbed, that job's. It's finished : coll. : 1840, Marryat, ' That job's jobbed, as the saying is ' (O.E.D.) ; ob.

[**jobber** is ineligible because it is S.E. So too is *jobbery*.]

jobbernowl, -nol(l), -nole. A fool's head ; a fool : coll. : late C. 16–20 ; ob. ? ex *job(b)ard*, a simpleton. The *-nol(l)* forms not before ca. 1670, and rare after 1750.—2. Adj., stupid : coll. : from ca. 1825 ; ob.

***jobberknot, -nut.** (Or hyphenated.) A tall, clumsy fellow : C. 19 c.

jobbing. Sexual intercourse : mainly Scots coll. : C. 17–20.

***jobe.** See job, n., 2.

jobe, occ. **job.** To rebuke lengthily and tediously : coll. : ca. 1670–1830. ' Cambridge term ', Grose, 2nd ed. (following Ray). Ex ' the lengthy reproofs of Job's friends,' S.O.D.

[**Job's comfort—comforter—news—post** are all S.E. Cf., however :]

Job's dock, be laid up in. To be treated in hospital for a venereal disease : coll. : C. 18–early 19. Grose, 2nd ed. Cf. *Job's ward*, q.v.

Job's tears. The seeds of *Coix lachryma*, ' which are used for necklace-making by the native tribes on Cape York peninsula, are there called *Job's tears*, Morris. *Australia* (– 1897). But also of the natives of Papua, where they are worn only by widows as a sign of mourning : cf. Job when ' separated ' from his family.

Job's turkey, as poor as. Exceedingly poor : coll. of ca. 1820–1910 : mainly and perhaps orig. U.S.

Job's ward. The ward for venereal patients in St. Bartholomew's Hospital : mid-C. 18–mid-19 : prob. orig. medical. Grose, 2nd ed.

Job's wife. A wanton and scolding woman : coll. : C. 19.

Jo'burg, Joburg. Johannesburg : Ware says, ' *Military*, 1900 on,' but it is more prob. miners' coll. originated a decade earlier. (The town was founded in September, 1886.)

joby. A vendor of sweets and refreshments : Eton College : late C. 19–20. *The Saturday Review*, July 14, 1934.

jock. ' Private parts of a man or woman,' Potter, *Dict. of Cant and Flash*, 1790 : low. (Of a woman, very rare after ca. 1880.) See **jock, v.** N.b., *jock-strap* is athletes' and footballers' S.E.— 2. Abbr. *jockey* : coll. : from ca. 1825 ; ob.

Jock. A North Country seaman, esp. a collier : coll. : mid-C. 18–19. Also *crowdy-headed Jock*. ' Jock being a common name, and crowdy the chief food, of the lower order of the people of Northumberland,' Grose, 2nd ed.—2. A Scot ; in G.W. a Scottish soldier. Coll. : from ca. 1870. In C. 16–19 dial., *Jocky*.—3. Hence, the ' inevitable ' nick-

name of men with a Scottish surname or accent : late C. 19–20.

***jock, v.** To coït with a woman : late C. 17–19 : c. till C. 19, when low. B.E. Cf. *jockum-cloy* ; also *jockum*, which it prob. abbr. ; hence *jock*, n., 1.

Jock, hairy. (Gen. pl.) A variant of *Jock*, 2, second nuance—but not in his hearing ! B. & P.

Jock Blunt, look like. To be out of countenance through disappointment : C. 18–early 19. Ramsay. Contrast *Jack* (occ. *John*) *Blunt*, q.v., and its dial. counterpart *Joan Blunt*.

***jockam.** See jockum.

jockey, n., is, in all senses listed by F. & H., S.E. ; but see **jockeys.**—2. **the Jockey.** Charles Howard (1746–1815), the 11th Duke of Norfolk, at one time Lord-Lieutenant of the West *Riding*. (Dawson.)— 3. (**jockey.**) The piece of bread added to a ' toke ' (small loaf) to make up the correct weight : prison c. : C. 20. (James Spenser, *Limey Breaks In*, 1934.) —4. A ' bus-driver : busmen's : from ca. 1920. *The Daily Herald*, Aug. 5, 1936.

jockey, v., in sense to cheat, is, again despite F. & H., ineligible.—2. At Winchester College, from ca. 1820, to appropriate, engage, supplant : all ob.

jockey not ! ; **jockey up !** Winchester College ob. cries of (*a*) exemption, (*b*) participation. (Cf. *bags I* and *finge*, qq.v.) Mid-C. 19–20. Wrench.

***jockey-stick.** The thin piece of wood with which the ' jockey ' (see n., 3) is attached to the ' toke ' : prison c. : C. 20. James Spenser, *Limey Breaks In*, 1934.

jockey (or bag) the over. So to run as to get all the bowling to oneself : cricketers' : from ca. 1860. In C. 20, *bag* is much the commoner.

jockeying. ' Vehicular racing ' : London streets' : C. 19. Ware.

jockeys. Top-boots : trade : from ca. 1850 ; ob. Mayhew.

[**jocko,** a chimpanzee, is familiar S.E. verging on coll.]

[**jocktelear,** a small almanac, *jocteleg* (or *jackleg*), a large pocket-knife, and *Jocky*, a Scot, are, despite F. & H., all ineligible because dial.]

***jockum** ; occ. **jockam.** The penis : c. : mid-C. 16–early 19. Harman.

***jockum-cloy.** To coït with (a woman) : C. 17– early 19 c. B.E. Ex *jockum* + *cloy*, qq.v. Cf. *jock*, v.—2. Also n.

***jockum-gage.** A chamber-pot : c. : C. 17–19. B.E. Ex *jockum*.

***jockum-gagger.** A man living on his wife's harlotry : ? C. 18–early 19 : c.

joe. Abbr. *Joe Miller*, q.v. : 1834 (O.E.D.).—2. (Also *joey*.) A fourpenny piece : ca. 1840–1910. Ex *Joseph* Hume, politician and financial expert (1777– 1855). E. Hawkins, *Silver Coins of England*.—3. A marine : nautical : ca. 1850–1900. Abbr. *Joseph*. —4. A Portuguese and Brazilian gold coin : 1772 (S.O.D.) : coll. >, ca. 1880, S.E. Ex *Johannes*, recorded in 1762 in U.S., where *jo* occurs in 1765. Derivatively a nautical name for the sum of sixteen dollars : ca. 1790–1850 : John Davis, *The Post Captain*, 1805 (ed. R. H. Case, 1928).—5. (More gen. *jo*) a companion, a sweetheart : S.E.—6. As exclamation, see jo !—7. See **joes.**—8. **Joe** or **Joey.** A police-trooper : Australian miners' derogatory in the 1850's. Prob. of same origin as *jo*, 2.—9. A penny : New Zealanders' (– 1935). Cf. sense 2.

joe, v.i. To poke fun ; to take liberties with text or audience : theatrical : ca. 1865–1900. H.

Kingsley. Ex Australia, where (— 1861) it means —gen. as v.t.—to ridicule ; insult grossly ; now ob. See jo, 2. Also joey.

*Joe (occ. Jo) Ronce. A harlot's bully : rhyming s. (on *ponce*) : C. 20. Hence, **the Jo(e) Roncing stakes**, ' poncing '. Both are in James Curtis, *The Gilt Kid*, 1936.

Joe, Artful. Joseph Chamberlain (1836–1914) : nickname (— 1887) ; † by 1930. Baumann.

Joe, not for. See Joseph, not for.

Joe Blake. A cake : rhyming s. : late C. 19–20. B. & P.—2. A snake : Australian rhyming s. : C. 20.—3. Beefsteak : rhyming s. (— 1933).

*Joe Blake the Bart(h)lemy, v. To visit a prostitute : c. and low (— 1859) ; ob. H., 1st ed.

Joe Hook. Crook : rhyming s. : C. 20. P. P., *Rhyming Slang*, 1932. Other ' rhyming ' *Joe's* are *Joe Blake, Joe Rook, Joe Skinner*, all noted by the same glossarist.

Joe Manton. A fowling-piece made by Joseph Manton (d. 1837), a well-known London gunsmith : coll. : 1816 (S.O.D.) ; ob. by 1890, † by 1910. Also *Manton*. See Joe Miller, 2.

Joe Miller. A jest-book : coll. : 1789, George Parker ; ob. Ex comedian Joseph Miller (1684–1738), whose name was ' identified ' with a book pub. in 1739 but not compiled by him.—2. Hence, a jest, esp. if a stale one : coll. : 1816. Scott, ' A fool and his money are soon parted, nephew ; there is a Joe Miller for your Joe Manton ' (S.O.D.). Cf. *chestnut*.

Joe Miller of it, I don't see the. I don't see the joke ; or the fun of doing it : coll. : ca. 1830–95.

Joe Rook. A book : C. 20. P. P., *Rhyming Slang*, 1932.

Joe Savage. A cabbage : rhyming s. (— 1859).

Joe Skinner. Dinner : late C. 19–20. Cf. *Lilley & Skinner* and contrast *Joe Hook*, q.v.

joes, the. Melancholy thoughts : (low) Australian (— 1916). C. J. Dennis. Why ? Cf. *jim-jams*, q.v.

joey. A fourpenny piece : from ca. 1855 ; †. ' Ducange Anglicus ', 1857 ; H., 1859, ' The term originated with the London cabmen.' See joe, n., 2. —2. A marine : nautical : from ca. 1830 ; ob. F. & Gibbons. Cf. *joe*, n., 3 ; but prob. ex *jolly*, n., 2.—3. A clown : theatrical : from ca. 1830. Ex Joe Grimaldi, who to the early C. 19 was what Grock is to C. 20.—4. A very young kangaroo : Australian coll. : 1839. Hence, a hewer of wood and drawer of water (1845), punning *kangaroo* as typical of an Australian ; from ca. 1870, any other young animal ; hence, from ca. 1880, a little child, a baby. Ex Aborigine *joé*. Morris.—5. See jo, 2. —6. A newly entered prisoner in a convict prison : o. : ca. 1865 is the date of the reference in ' *No 747*.' —7. See joe, 8.

joey, v. See jo, 2, and joe, v.—2. To ' mug ' or attract the public's attention, while the ' mugger ' is up-stage : theatrical : mid-C. 19–early 20. Ware. Ex *joey*, n., 3.

joey ! See jo, 2.

[jog, v.i. and t., to colt (with), is a literary euphemism, while—again despite F. & H.—*jog-trot* has always been S.E.]

jog the loo. To pump briskly : nautical coll. : C. 19–20. Bowen. Obviously *loo* is water (Fr. *l'eau*).

jogger. To play and sing : theatrical or, rather, Parlyaree (— 1893) ; ob. Ex It. *giocar*, to play. See Parlyaree and cf. :

joggering omee (or omey). A musician, esp. if itinerant : Parlyaree (— 1893) ; ob. See jogger.

*jogue. A shilling : c. of ca. 1810–60. Vaux. ? the origin of *bob*.

*jogul. To ' play up ', or simply to play, at any game, esp. cards : gaming c. (— 1859). Ex Sp. *jugar*. H., 1st ed.

Johanna, -ner. See Joanna.

John. A first-year cadet : Sandhurst : from ca. 1870. Ex *Johnny Raw*.—2. A chap, a fellow (C. 19–20) ; occ. a male sweetheart : C. 20. Ex *Johnnie*, 1.—3. Abbr. *Sir John*, a priest : rare and rather S.E. than coll. ; *Sir John* being certainly S.E.—4. A policeman : C. 20 : mostly Australian (— 1916). *The Westminster Gazette*, Sept. 18, 1901 O.E.D. Sup.). C. J. Dennis. Perhaps suggested by *John Peel* (of the song) and *peeler* ; but prob. abbr. *Johnnie*, 5.—5. A Chinaman : U.S. (ca. 1870), anglicised ca. 1890.—6. Dried fish : nautical : late C. 19–20. Bowen.—7. A coll. term of address, C. 19–20, as in Desmond Coke, *The Bending of a Twig*, 1906 : ' All men-servants are Johns at Shrewsbury ' ; for its Westminster usage, see **Westminster School slang**. Cf. sense 2.

[John-a-Nokes (like John-a-Stiles), despite F. & H., is S.E., as are *John-a-dreams,—among the maids, John Cheese* or *Trot* (a rustic, a dolt), *John Chinaman*. See *Words !* at ' Representative Names ' for a group of such names.]

John-and-Joan. A homosexual pervert : C. 18–mid 19 coll.

John Audley ; occ. Orderly ! Abridge the performance ! : theatrical : from ca. 1810. Ex the actor-manager John Richardson (d. 1837), who used to ask ' Is John Audley here ? ' whenever another ' house ' was waiting, though tradition (H., 1864) has it that John Audley or Orderly taught him the wheeze.—2. Also occ. as a v. Also, to depart : circus s. : C. 20 (E. Seago, *Circus Company*, 1933).

[John Barleycorn is S.E.]

John Barleycorn, or Sir J. B., is nobody with him. He's no drinker : proverbial c.p. : C. 17–18.

John Barleycorn's, or Sir John Barleycorn's, the strongest knight. Malt liquor is strong stuff : proverbial c.p. : C. 17–18. Ray.

John Blunt. See Jack Blunt.

John Collins. A drink made of soda water, gin, sugar, lemon and ice : Australia : from ca. 1860. *The Australasian*, Feb. 24, 1865, ' That most angelic of drinks for a hot climate . . .'

John Company ; occ. Johnny Company. The Honourable East India Company : coll. : from ca. 1785 ; now only historical. Ex Dutch *Jan Kompanie*, by which the Eastern natives speak of the Dutch East India Company and government.

John Cotton. See Dolly Cotton.

John Crap(p)o. See Johnny Crapose.

John Des paper. See ' Winchester College slang ', § 7.

John Drawlatch. A sneaking person : coll. > S.E. : C. 16–17. Heywood's *Proverbs*, 1546.

*John Davis. Money : c. (— 1926). F. Jennings, *In London's Shadows*.

John Finality. The 1st Earl of Russell (1792–1878), who ' always spoke of the Reform Bill of 1831 as a " finality " ' (Dawson).

John Ford's altar (a master's desk), John Ford's bath (horse-trough), John Ford's hat (= ?), John Ford's leg (roly-poly pudding) : Bootham School (— 1925). Anon., *Dict. of Bootham Slang*.

John Fortnight. The tallyman : London work-men's : late C. 19–20 ; ob. Ware, 'From his calling every other week.'

John Gray's bird, like. Fond of company, even if it be rather above one : coll. : C. 16. Gascoigne. (Apperson.)

John Hop. A policeman : New Zealanders' : C. 20 ; ob. Rhyming on *Cop.*

John Long (in C. 18–19, occ. **Tom Long**) **the carrier, stay for** or **send by.** To wait, or postpone for, a long time : coll. : C. 16–19. Cotgrave.

John Orderly. See **John Audley.**

John Roberts. A, or enough, drink to keep a man drunk from Saturday to Sunday night : Anglo-Welsh (— 1886). Ex the author of the Sunday Closing Act.

John Roper's window. See **Roper's window.**

John Thomas. A flunkey : low coll. : ca. 1860–1910.—2. The male member : low : from ca. 1840. Cf. *dick.*

John (occ. **Joan**) **Thomson's man.** A uxorious husband : Scots coll. : C. 16–19. Dunbar.

John Tuck. A Chinese mandarin : nautical : late C. 19–20. Bowen. Cf. *John*, 5.

Johnian. A student of St. John's College, Cam-bridge : Cambridge University coll. >, in C. 19, S.E. : mid-C. 17–20. But *Johnian hog* (— 1785, Grose, at *hog*) and *J. Pig* (from ca. 1800) are s.

Johnnie, Johnny. A fellow, a chap ; a sweet-heart : coll. : from ca. 1670 ; ob. Ramsay, Kipling.—2. A (fashionable) young man about town : from ca. 1880.—3. A tiger : sportsmen's : 1815 (O.E.D.).—4. A penguin : nautical (— 1898). —5. A policeman : low : from ca. 1850. Occ. (ca. 1860–80) *Johnny Darby*, perhaps influenced by *darbies* and Fr. *gendarmes.* Mayhew, Besant & Rice.—6. A half-glass of whiskey : Anglo-Irish : from ca. 1860 ; ob. (Earlier (— 1827), Dumbarton-shire dial.)—7. A Greek : nautical : late C. 19–20. Bowen. Perhaps ex prevalence of the name *Johannides.*—8. A Turk ; rarely a German : mili-tary : G.W. (F. & Gibbons ; B. & P.)—9. The nickname of men surnamed Walker : naval and military : late C. 19–20. Ex the celebrated whiskey. (F. & Gibbons.)

Johnnie Rutter. Butter : rhyming s. : from ca. 1880. P. P., *Rhyming Slang*, 1932. Contrast *Johnnie Horner.*

Johnnies and Sallies. Kinds of 'Kaffirs', the former being specifically shares in the Johannesburg Consolidated Investment Company (*The Con-tinental Daily Mail*, Aug. 29, 1933). Stock Ex-change : C. 20. E.g. *The Evening Standard*, Feb. 5, 1935.

Johnny Armstrong. Manual work, hand-power : jocular nautical : from ca. 1920. (O.E.D. Sup.) Cf. *elbow-grease.*

Johnny Bates'(s) Farm. See **Bates' Farm.**

Johnny Bono. An Englishman : East End of London : from ca. 1850 ; ob.

Johnny Bum. A male donkey : jocular : late C. 18–mid-19. Grose, 1st ed. Ex a euphemism for *jack ass, ass* being pronounced *arse.* Grose.

Johnny cake. A cake cooked in a frying pan or baked in the ashes : Australia (— 1861) : coll. Adoption of a U.S. term, which (orig.—1775—*journey-cake*) denotes a thin cake made of Indian meal and toasted before a fire. (Morris ; Thornton.)

John(ny) Crapose. Frenchman : low : C. 19–early 20. The singular is *Crapo* or *Crappo*—but not very frequent. Ware ; Bowen. Ex Fr. *crapaud*, a

toad (not a frog).—2. (Gen. *John Crappo.*) Hence, a British seaman wearing a moustache : nautical : ca. 1815–50. Bowen.

Johnny Darby. See **Johnny**, 5.—2. In pl., hand-cuffs : ca. 1860–1915.

*Johnny Gallacher (or **Gallagher**). A uniformed policeman : tramps' c. (— 1935). Cf. the synony-mous *John.*

Johnny hangman. See **Jacky hangman.** (Wood-ward, *The Birds of Natal*, 1899.)

Johnny Haultaut. A man-of-warsman : mer-chant service : ca. 1870–1910. Clark Russell. Perhaps ex *haul tight.*

Johnny Horner. Round the corner ; i.e. to, at, a 'pub' : rhyming s. (— 1909). Ware.—2. See **Jack Horner.**

Johnny Newcome. A new-born child : coll. : from ca. 1830 ; ob.—2. An inexperienced youth ; a landsman : nautical : from ca. 1850 ; ob.

Johnny Raw. A novice ; a recruit : coll. : 1813 ; ob. *The Sydney Bulletin*, Feb. 26, 1887, 'He was a new-chum—a regular Johnny-Raw.'—2. A morning drink : provincial : from ca. 1870 ; ob.

Johnny Scaparey, do a. To abscond : circus-employees' : mid-C. 19–20. It. *scappare*, to escape.

Johnny Squarehead. A German (soldier) : mili-tary : in G.W.

Johnny Turk. The orig. form of *Johnnie (-y)*, 8. B. & P.

Johnny Won't Hit To-Day. J. W. H. T. Douglas, the English all-rounder, slow-scoring batsman : Australians' : 1920's.

Johnny Walker, still going strong like. A c.p.: from ca. 1925 ; slightly ob. Collinson. Ex the famous advertisement of a famous whiskey.

Johnson. Abbr. *Jack Johnson*, q.v. : 1916, *The Wipers Times*, Feb. 12, 'The Johnsons. A Shout. A Scream. A Roar,' a very apt description of their advent and explosion. B. & P. (2nd ed.).

join up, v.i. To enlist : coll. : from 1914.

joined, be. To be married. Coll. : C. 19–20. Cf. *join giblets* (see giblets).

*joint. In c. (— 1885) partnership ; a concerted robbery (— 1887, Baumann) : ob.—2. 'An outside bookmaker's paraphernalia of list-frame, umbrella, etc., some of which are joined together in movable pieces,' O.E.D. : the turf from ca. 1896.—3. A wife : low : C. 20 ; ob. Ware. Because *joined.*—4. Any place or building : low : ex U.S. (— 1883), whence adopted ca. 1905 in Australia (very com-mon in the A.I.F.), ca. 1910 in England. Whence the next entry.—5. Hence, a brothel : New Zea-land c. (— 1932).—6. (Cf. senses 2, 4, 5.) In grafters' s. of C. 20 : a tent ; a stall ; any stand from which, or object with which, a grafter pro-vides amusement. Philip Allingham, *Cheapjack*, 1934.—7. A fellow, chap : from ca. 1895, but not very gen. ; mostly Cockneys'. Edwin Pugh, *The Cockney at Home*, 1914, 'I'm a joint as likes plenty of room' ; Ernest Raymond, *Mary Leith*, 1931. Perhaps cf. sense 3.

joint, jump the. To assume command : low Australian (— 1916). C. J. Dennis.

*joint, work the. To swindle with a jockeyed lottery table : c. (— 1895). Ex *joint*, 1.

jokee. The 'victim' of a joke : coll. : from ca. 1870.

joker. A man, chap, fellow : from ca. 1810. (Pepys's 'At noon . . . to the Trinity-house, where a very good dinner among the old jokers' is misleading.) Cf. *artist, merchant, shaver*, and see Herring Joker.

*joker, little. See little-joker.

jolah. A haversack : Regular Army's : late C. 19–20. Ex Hindustani. (B. & P., 3rd ed.)

Jollies, the. See jolly, n., 2, quotation from Bowen : ? C. 17–early 19.

jollification. Jollity ; a merry-making : coll. : 1798 (S.O.D.). Scott. Whence :

jollify. To behave merrily ; become, occ. make, slightly drunk : coll. : from ca. 1820.

jollily. Excellently, splendidly ; delightfully : from ca. 1560 : S.E. till ca. 1850, then coll. ; slightly ob. (Cf. *jolly*, adj., 1 and 2.) M. C. Jackson, 1878. (O.E.D.)

jollocks ; jollux. A parson : low : late C. 18–19. Possibly a euphemising (suggested by *jolly*, adj.) of *ballocks*, q.v. (cf. *cods*, a curate) ; prob. ex dial. *jollock*, jolly, hearty (O.E.D.).—2. (*jollux*.) A fat person : ca. 1795–1815. O.E.D.

jolly. The head : late C. 18–mid-19. Also *jolly nob*. Grose, 1st ed.—2. A Royal Marine : nautical : from ca. 1829. Also (— 1867) a *Royal* (or *royal*) *jolly*. (Cf. *tame jolly*, q.v., a militiaman.) Marryat ; Kipling ; Bowen, ' Taken from the old nickname of the City Trained Bands.'—3. the confederate of a thief or a swindler ; esp. a sham purchaser : c. (— 1856) ; ob. Mayhew, Greenwood.—4. A pretence ; an excuse : c. : from ca. 1850 ; ob. J. W. Horsley.—5. Praise, a recommendation ; chaff, abuse : low (orig. Cockney) coll. : from ca. 1855. H., 1859 ; Vance, in *The Chickaleary Cove*.—6. Hence, a cheer : from ca. 1870 ; slightly ob. Esp. in *give* (e.g. *him*) *a jolly*, chiefly in imperative.—7. Abbr. *jollification* : coll. : 1920. O.E.D. (Sup.).

jolly, v.t. and i. To joke ; rally, chaff ; vituperate : from ca. 1860.—2. To cheer : from ca. 1890.—3. V.i., to make a sham bid (at an auction) : 1869 (O.E.D.) : c. > low ; ob.—4. To treat (a person) pleasantly so that he stay in, or become of, a good humour : orig. (1893), U.S. ; anglicised ca. 1910. Esp. with *up* or *along*. (S.O.D.)

jolly, adj. Excellent ; fine ; indicative of general approbation (in mid-C. 19–20, often ironical) : C. 14–20 ; S.E. till C. 19, then coll. *The Daily Telegraph*, 1869, ' He is annoyed when young ladies use slang phrases, such as awfully jolly.'—2. Extremely pleasant, agreeable, suitable, charming : mid-C. 16–20 : S.E. till ca. 1860, then coll.—3. Slightly drunk : from ca. 1650 ; euphemistic S.E. till C. 19, then coll.—4. ' Healthy and well developed ; well conditioned ; plump ' : coll. and dial. : from ca. 1660. (S.O.D.) Whence.—5. Fat ; too fat : the turf : from ca. 1885.

jolly, adv. with adv. or adj. (In mid-C. 19–20, often ironical.) Very ; exceedingly : mid-C. 16–20 : S.E. till C. 19, then coll. Dickens in *Oliver Twist*, ' " He is so jolly green," said Charley.'

jolly, chuck a. See chuck a jolly.

jolly along. A variant (— 1923) of *jolly*, v., 4. Manchon.

jolly boys. ' A group of small drinking vessels connected by a tube, or by openings one from another,' F. & H. : coll. : from ca. 1890 ; slightly ob.

jolly dog. A boon companion, merry fellow : coll (— 1785) >, ca. 1870, S.E. : slightly ob. Grose. Cf. S.E. *jolly fellow*.

jolly for. To support a friend with kindly chaff or praise : ca. 1850–1925 : mostly Cockney. Cf. jolly, n., sense 6.

jolly jumper. A light sail set above a ' skyscraper ' (q.v.) : nautical (— 1883) ; ob. Clark Russell.

jolly nob. See jolly, n., 1.

Jolly Polly. Gallipoli : military : 1915 ; ob. B. & P. By ' Hobson-Jobson '.

jolly Roger. A pirate's flag : nautical coll. > S.E. : from ca. 1880. Stevenson, in *Treasure Island*, ' There was the jolly Roger—the black flag of piracy—flying from her peak.'

jolly-up. A ' beano ' ; a drinking-bout : lower-middle class : from ca. 1905 ; ob. Alec Waugh, *The Balliols*, 1934.

jolly utter. Unspeakable : London cultured : 1881–ca. 1890. *Punch*, 1881 ; W. S. Gilbert's *Patience*, 1881 ; *The Referee*, Feb. 18, 1883. (Ware.) Cf. *utterly utter*.

jolt. To coït with (a woman) : low : C. 19–20.

jolt, pass a. ' To deliver a short sharp blow ' : Australian (— 1916). C. J. Dennis.

[jolt-, jolter-head, a dolt, and its adj. are, despite F. & H., ineligible.]

jomer. A fancy girl ; a sweetheart : c. (— 1839) >, ca. 1850, theatrical and Parlyaree ; † as theatrical. Perhaps a corruption of It. *donna* (cf. *dona*(*h*), q.v.), it is always—in contradistinction to *blower, blowen*—a complimentary term, says Brandon.

[Jonah, a bringer of ill luck, is—despite F. & H.— S.E.]

Jones, Mrs. See Mrs. Jones.

jonnick, jonnock, jonnuk. See jannock.—jonty. See jaundy.

joo. Did you ? : slovenly coll. : C. 20. Denis Mackail, *The ' Majestic ' Mystery*, 1924, ' When joo get down, Langley ? '

jor (' r ' rasped). A sol. pronunciation of *jaw* : since when ? In illiterate speech, any vowel + *w* tends to be pronounced *awer, ewer*, etc., with the ' e ' clipped short.

jorb. Sol. pronunciation of *job* : mostly Cockney and Australian : C. 19–20. C. J. Dennis.

jordan ; in C. 17–18, often jordain ; in C. 16–17, occ. jurdain(e), jurdan or jurden. A chamber-pot : C. 14–20 ; ob. : S.E. till ca. 1840, then dial. and low coll. (In C. 19, occ. a slop-pail.) ' Prob. an application of the baptismal name *Jordan*, very common in M.E.', W.—2. A blow with a staff : c. : late C. 17–mid-19. B.E.—3. The Atlantic : journalists' : ca. 1870–1910.

Jordan, over ; this side of Jordan. Resp., dead ; alive : coll. (— 1889). Barrère & Leland ; Manchon. Ex its use in ' pietistic language to symbolise death ' (O.E.D. Sup.).

jorram, of a boat-song other than Gaelic, is catachrestic : late C. 18–20. (O.E.D.)

[jorum, a drinking bowl, despite F. & H., is S.E. But the derivative sense, a large number or quantity, is dial. and, thence, in late C. 19–20, s. verging on coll.]

José. A canteen attendant : naval : C. 20. Bowen, ' A relic of the days when the Maltese did a lot of this business.'

Joseph. A marine : nautical : C. 19–20 ; ob.— 2. As coat, or woman-proof man, it is S.E.

Joseph !, not for. A scornful refusal : 1844, C. Selby, *London by Night* : ob. by 1900, † by 1920. Also (— 1867) *not for joe !*, which is extant : Galsworthy, *Swan Song*, 1928, ' Not if he knew it—not for Joe ! ' Cf. *Archibald, certainly not !*

Joseph and Jesse ! A political c.p. of 1886.

Satiric of Joseph Chamberlain and Jesse Collings, imm. after the latter assumed office. ' As Mr. Chaplin rather neatly put it . . ., " the voice is the voice of Jesse, the hand is the hand of Joseph," ' *The Daily News*, Feb. 26. (Ware.)

Joseph's coat. A many-coloured coat ; a dress of honour : coll. : from ca. 1890. Kipling, ' A Joseph's jury-coat to keep his honour warm.'

Josephus rex, you are. You're joking : a late C. 18–early 19 c.p. *Jo-king, rex* being L. for king. Grose, 1st ed.

josh. A fool ; a sleepy fellow : coll. : mid-C. 19–20 ; ob. ? ex *joskin*, q.v.

josh, v.t. and i. To banter ; indulge in banter : U.S. (1880's), anglicised by 1935, thanks to the ' talkies '. O.E.D. and Sup. Perhaps ex Northern dial. and Scottish *joss*, to jostle, push against : possibly influenced by ' Josh Billings ', that humorist whose writings were, ca. 1866–95, a household name in the U.S.A.

josh about or **around,** v.i. To move clumsily or carelessly : C. 20. E.g. in John G. Brandon, *Th' Big City*, 1931. Prob. ex S.E. *jostle* influenced by *josh,* n. : q.v.

josher. An occ. variant of *josser,* 6.

joskin. A country bumpkin : low : from ca. 1810 ; ob. *Lex. Bal.* Prob. ex dial. *joss,* to bump, after *bumpkin* itself. (O.E.D.)—2. Hence, ' a green hand under sail ' : nautical : from ca. 1830 ; ob. Bowen.—3. Hence, a recruit : military : C. 20.

joss. An idol : Anglo-Chinese ' pidgin ' : C. 18–20. Ex Portuguese *Deos,* God. Whence *josshouse,* an idol temple : mid-C. 18–20. Yule & Burnell. Cf. *chin-chin joss,* q.v.—2. Luck : nautical : late C. 19–20. Bowen. Ex sense 1.

josser. A simpleton (– 1886) ; ob. except among tailors (see, e.g. *The Tailor and Cutter,* Nov. 29, 1928). Prob. ex *joskin.*—2. An old roué (– 1892) ; †.—3. (Gen. with *old*.) A fellow : from ca. 1890. Perhaps ex *joskin,* q.v.—4. A parson : Australia : ca. 1885–1910.—5. A ' swell ' : Hong-Kong (– 1909). Ware. Prob. ex *joss,* q.v., as sense 4 is —even more prob.—6. An outsider : Parlyaree : (? late C. 19–) C. 20. Edward Seago, *Circus Company,* 1933. Prob. ex sense 1 influenced by *joskin,* 2. Also *josher.*

jossop. Syrup, juice, sauce, gravy : schoolboys' : from ca. 1860 ; ob. (Manchon.) Perhaps a corrupt blend of *juice + syrup.*

*****jostle.** To cheat : c. : late C. 18–20. (Cf. *hustle,* v., and *hustler.*) Whence :

*****jostler.** A swindler : Glasgow c. : C. 20—and prob. from well back in C. 19.

jottle (v.i.) ; **do a jottle ; go jottling.** To copulate : low : C. 19–20 ; ob.

journalese. Inferior journalistic writing : 1882 (S.O.D.) : coll. till ca. 1930, then S.E. According to a certain journalist, most journalese is written— or spoken—by politicians.

*****journey.** A term in prison : c. (– 1932). ' Stuart Wood ', *Shades of the Prison House.*

journey, this. On this time or occasion : coll. : 1884 ; slightly ob.

journeyman gentleman tailor. A silk hat ; a frock coat : tailors' : C. 20.

journeyman parson. A curate : London : ca. 1820–1900. Bee. Because apt to be moved about far more than is a full-blown clergyman.

journeyman soul-saver. A scripture-reader : ca. 1860–1900.

Jove ! ; **by Jove.** A coll. exclamation, assevera-

tion : from ca. 1570. Shakespeare, ' By Jove, I always took three threes for nine ' ; Miss Ferrier. (O.E.D.)

jow. (Gen. in imperative.) To go away ; be off : Anglo-Indian : from ca. 1860 ; slightly ob. H., 1864. Ex Hindustani ; cf. Romany *jaw* (and Sampson's *ja*).

[**jowl** (a jaw, a cheek) ; **cheek by jowl.** Despite F. & H., both are S.E.]

joy-bag. A (sand-)bag in which a man carries souvenirs to take home on leave : military : 1915– 18. F. & Gibbons.

joy-ride. A ride at high speed, esp. in a motorcar : orig. (1909), U.S. ; anglicised ca. 1912 as a coll.—2. Hence, v.i. and *joy-rider, -riding.*

joy-spot. Any well-known place of enjoyment : Western Front officers' coll. : 1915–18. F. & Gibbons.

joy-stick. The control-lever of an aeroplane : 1915 : s. > by 1925, coll. ; now verging on S.E. Ex its vibration or else ex the joy one experiences in handling it.—2. The penis : low : late C. 19–20.

joy-waggon. A practice aeroplane at a flyingschool ; Air Force : 1915 ; ob. F. & Gibbons.

joy-wheeler. A girl given to pleasure, esp. ' joyrides ' : 1934, H. A. Vachell, *Martha Penny.*

joyful, O be. See **o be joyful.**—2. Cf. *sing ' O be joyful' on the other side of one's mouth,* q.v. at ' *o be joyful' on . . .*

joyous spirit. See **jemmy,** n., 2. (Transient s.)

jube. A coll. abbr. of *jujube* (the lozenge) : from ca. 1840.

jubilee. A very pleasant time : Winchester College : C. 19–20 ; ob.—2. A postage stamp commemorating the Silver Jubilee of King George V, May 6, 1935 : coll.

jubilee track. A two-foot gauge track used mostly by petrol-locomotives and waggons : Public Works' : 1935. Cf. :

jubilee waggon. A two-foot gauge skip : id. : id.

jubileeve it ? Do you believe it ? (or,!) : a c.p. dating from the Silver Jubilee (May 6, 1935) to the death (January 20, 1936) of H.M. King George the Fifth. Ex an advertisement by Shell. In 1887 (Queen Victoria's first Jubilee), moreover, there was a popular song in which the singer, speaking of the contemporary jollifications, declared that they were, ' would jubilieve it, quite driving me mad '.

Judaic superbac(e)y. A ' Jew in all the glory of his best clothes ' : Covent Garden Theatre and vicinity : 1887–ca. 1899. Ware.

[**judas,** a traitor, **judas-coloured, judas-hole** : all, despite F. & H., are S.E.]

jude. A harlot : low (– 1886). Henley. Also *judy,* q.v.

*****judge.** An expert, sagacious thief or swindler : c. : ca. 1810–50. Vaux.

judge and jury. A mock trial, the fines being paid in beer : tailors' : from ca. 1870.

judgmatic. Judicious ; judicial. So *judgmatical.* Adv. *judgmatically.* All coll. and slightly ob. : resp. 1835, 1826, 1814. O.E.D. dates. But *judgmatical* (even 1826 = J. Fenimore Cooper) was orig. U.S., Thornton recording it at 1774. On *dogmatic.*

judicial and **judicious** are often confused : C. 18– 20. (Neatly exemplified by R. Keverne in *The Man in the Red Hat,* 1930.)

Judische (or **Jew's**) **compliment.** A large penis but no money : low : from ca. 1850 ; ob. Cf. *Yorkshire compliment,* q.v.

judy. A girl, esp. one of loose morals : from ca. 1810 : prob. orig. c. ; always more or less low ; common among C. 19 sailors. Also, later, *jude*. Vaux, 1812 ; Runciman, *The Chequers*. Ex *Punch and Judy*, or, like *jane*, direct ex the Christian name. —2. A simpleton, a fool : orig. (1824), U.S. ; anglicised ca. 1850. Esp. in *make a judy of oneself*, play the fool, act the giddy goat.—3. In C. 20, gen. = a woman of ridiculous appearance, but also, in low s., any woman.

Judy Fitzsimmons of yourself !, don't make a. Don't be a fool! : Anglo-Irish (— 1932). Of topical origin, ex *make a judy of oneself*, to play the fool : anglicised ca. 1850 ex U.S. : see **judy**, 2.

judy-slayer. A 'lady-killer' : London **Jews'** (— 1909). Ware. Cf. *judy*, 1.

[**juff.** The cheek ; in pl., the posteriors. F. & H., adding 'old'. In neither O.E.D. nor E.D.D. nor, as far as I know, elsewhere. Perhaps—cf spurious *joves*—by error on Fr. *joues*, cheeks.]

*****jug.** A prison : C. 19 c., C. 20 low. Also *stone jug*, q.v. Ainsworth, 1834, the first English user, the term occurring in U.S. in 1815 (O.E.D. Sup.) ; Dickens, Thackeray. Ex Fr. *joug*, a yoke, via ob. Scots *joug(s)*, a pillory.—2. As a mistress and as a term of contempt, it is, despite F. & H., indubitably S.E.—3. Abbr. *juggins*, q.v.—4. A bank : c. : from ca. 1860. *Cornhill Magazine*, 1862 ; Charles E. Leach, 1933.

*****jug,** v. To imprison ; lock up : orig. (ca. 1840) c. ; by ca. 1860, low. See the n., and cf. Scots *joug*, to confine in the jougs.—2. To deceive, humorously or, more gen., illicitly : low : from ca. 1870 ; ob.

jug-bitten. Tipsy : coll. : ca. 1620–1750. Taylor the Water Poet.

jug-loops. Hair worn with tiny curls on the temples : low Cockney : ca. 1885–1905. Baumann.

*****jugelo(w).** A dog : c. of ca. 1810–50. Vaux. Ex Romany *juggal*, pl. *juggalor*.

jugful, not by a. Not by a long way : coll. : ex U.S. (1834), anglicised ca. 1850 ; ob. by 1910, † by 1930.

jugged, arrested, imprisoned : see **jug**, v., 1.

juggins ; occ. **jug.** A fool : s. >, in C. 20, (low) coll. : 1882 (S.O.D.). *Punch*, July 17, 1886, ' Yah ! Wot a old juggins he is ! ' Prob. suggested by *muggins*, q.v.

juggins-hunting. 'Looking for a man who will pay for liquor' (Ware) : taverns' (— 1909). Ex preceding. Contrast :

juggins's boy. 'The sharp and impudent son of a stupid and easily ridiculed father' : low London : 1882. Ware.

*****juggler's box.** The branding-iron : c. : late C. 18–early 19. Grose, 2nd ed.

*****juggling law.** In late C. 16–early 17 c., it is a branch of criminal activity practised among the devotees of certain games. Greene, *A Disputation*, 1592, ' *The Juggling Law*, wherein I will set out the disorders at Nyneholes and Ryfling [i.e. dicing], how they are only for the benefite of the Cutpurses.'

juggo. In the punishment-cell ; hence, out of action, ill : military : from ca. 1910. F. & Gibbons. Ex *jugged* : see **jug**, v., 1.

juice. Emoluments, profits of office or profession : coll. : ca. 1520–1640. Latimer, Sir E. Hoby. (O.E.D.)—2. Money : ca. 1695–1730. Ned Ward in *The London Spy*, 1698 (see *Slang*, p. 69).—3. Juiciness of colour : C. 19–20 artists. S.O.D. Cf. *juicy*, fifth sense, q.v.—4. Abbr. *sky-juice*, q.v.

Also, gravy : a solely Charterhouse sense : C. 20.—5. Petrol : 1909. Hence, from ca. 1918, *step on the juice*, to accelerate. O.E.D. (Sup.).—6. Electricity ; electrical current : electricians' s. (1903) >, ca. 1920, gen. s. O.E.D. (Sup.).

juice, v.i. To rain : low (— 1932). *Slang*, p. 244. Ex *juice*, n., 4.—2. To weep ; v.t., to reprimand : Bootham School (— 1925). Cf. *juice-meeting*.

juice, bright-work. See **bright-work juice.**—**juice, bug.** Hair-oil.—**juice, cow.** See **cow-juice.**—**juice, fresh.** Fresh water. All four terms are Conway cadets' s. : from ca. 1890. John Masefield, *The Conway*, 1933.

juice for jelly, give. (Of a woman) to experience the sexual spasm : low : C. 19–20. (Otherwise, *juice* in this sense is rare.) Cf. *jelly*, q.v.

juice-meeting. A reprimand ; any address to the school : Bootham School (— 1925). Anon., *Dict. of Bootham Slang*. Cf. *juice*, v., 2.

juicer. See 'Moving-Picture Slang', § 5.

juicily. Excellently ; 'splendidly' : 1916, E. F. Benson.

juicy. As (of women) amorous, it is S.E.—2. Piquant, bawdy : low coll. (— 1880). Greenwood. —3. (Of weather) wet, very rainy, drenching : coll. : 1837 (S.O.D.).—4. Rich in money, etc. : coll. : from ca. 1620. Contrast *dry*, q.v.—5. In artists' s. : 'characterised by rich liquid colouring, 1820 ', S.O.D.—6. Excellent : 1916 : E. F. Benson (O.E.D. Sup.). Cf. *juicily*.—7. Drunk : Glasgow (— 1934).—8. (Of stocks and shares) attractive in price : Stock Exchange : from ca. 1920. E.g. *Time and Tide*, Sept. 8, 1934, ' But still, with this juicy price in prospect, the shrewd professionals are hesitant.'

*****jukrum.** A licence : late C. 17–early 19 c. B.E. Cf. *jackrum*.

Julius Caesar. The male member : low : from ca. 1840 ; ob.

Julius Caesar, dead as. Certainly, or long, dead : coll. : C. 19–20 ; ob.

Julius Caesar was a pup, not since. In, or for, a devilish long time : from ca. 1890.

Julyflower is a coll. perversion of *gillyflower* : mostly C. 19, though dating from C. 16. (O.E.D.)

jumbaree. Jewellery : theatrical : ca. 1870–1905. ? ex *jamboree*.

jumble. A jumble-sale, or articles therefor : coll. : from ca. 1930. O.E.D. (Sup.).—2. (Also *jumbling*.) An unintentional confusion in the ringing of the bells ; i.e., technically, a ' breakdown ' : bell-ringers' coll. (— 1901). H. Earle Bulwer's *Glossary*.

jumble, v.i. and t. To have sexual intercourse (with) : late C. 16–18 : S.E. >, ca. 1650, coll. Stanyhurst, Barnfield, Randolph, D'Urfey.—2. To take for a drive : coll. : C. 19–20 ; ob. For origin, cf. :

jumble-gut lane. A rough road : low coll. : late C. 17–early 19. B.E.

jumbler. A performer of the sexual act : coll. : C. 17–18. Ex *jumble*, v., 1.

jumbling. See **jumble**, n., 2.

jumbo. A clumsy, heavy fellow : from ca. 1820 : coll. >, ca. 1900, S.E. ' Jon Bee.'—2. In C. 20, gen. of a very fat boy or man : coll. > S.E.—3. An elephant : coll. : from ca. 1882. ' Chiefly in allusion to a famous elephant at [the London] Zoo (d. 1885),' W. ; it was sold to Barnum in Feb., 1882 (O.E.D.).—4. Whence *Jumbo*, the Elephant and

Castle Tavern in South London: public-house frequenters': from 1882. Ware.—5. 'The big fore-staysail': grand Banks fishermen's: from ca. 1883. Bowen.—6. A big goods-train engine: railwaymen's: first decade, C. 20.

jumboism. 'The hesitative policy of the Liberal Whigs': Conservatives' nickname therefor: 1882, at the time of 'the Jumbo craze' (see **jumbo, 3**). Ware. Cf. *bad as your breath* . . ., q.v.

Jumbo's trunk. Tipsy: rhyming s. on *drunk*: esp. ca. 1880–85. Manchon. On *elephant's trunk*, q.v.

jumback. See **jimbugg.—jumm**, in F. & H., is ineligible.

***jump**; occ. **dining-room jump.** 'Robbery effected by ascending a ladder placed by a sham lamp-lighter, against the house intended to be robbed . . . Because, should the lamp-lighter be put to flight, the thief . . . has no means of escape but that of jumping down,' Grose, 2nd ed.: c. from ca. 1787; † by 1890.—2. A window (on the ground floor): c.: C. 19–20. Vaux.—3. Pl., see **jumps.**—4. The n. corresponding to *jump*, v., 5: same period. Esp. *have a jump.*—5. A fright: coll.: late C. 19–20. Desmond Coke, *The House Prefect*, 1908, 'Good heavens, Manders! . . . You did give me a jump.'

***jump**, v. To seize and rob (a person): c.: ca. 1780–1890. Also to rob (a building) by way of *jump*, n., 1: c.: C. 19.—2. To seize and arrest: Australian: ca. 1870–1900. 'Rolf Boldrewood.'—3. To possess oneself of a mining right, in the owner's absence. Gen. with *a* or *the claim*. From ca. 1854, when in *The Melbourne Argus*; *jumping of claims*, however, occurs in U.S. in 1851 (Thornton): coll. >, ca. 1870, S.E. Marryat, in *Mountains and Molehills*, 'If a man jumped my claim, . . . I appealed to the crowd.'—4. Hence, in South Africa, to appropriate (goods) wrongfully: 1871, *The Queenstown Free Press*, Aug. 18, 'Five thousand bricks were jumped the other night from . . .'s brickyard at Klipdrift.' Pettman.—5. To copulate, v.i. and t.: C. 17–20 coll.; ob.—6. To try a medicine: medical: from ca. 1860; ob.—7. See **jump a ship.**—8. (Also *jump with.*) To agree, tally: a S.E. sense, despite F. & H.

jump, at the first. At the very beginning (of proceedings): coll.: ca. 1570–1700.

jump or jumps, be for the (high). To be about, or obliged, to face a difficulty or a very unpleasant task: military (ca. 1912), esp. as to be on the crime-sheet, hence due for trial. F. & Gibbons. Ex steeplechasing. Also, in G.W., *be up for the long jump* (Ibid.).

jump, from the. From the beginning: coll. (in C. 20, tending to S.E.): app. orig. U.S. (1848) and anglicised ca. 1870.

***jump, go the.** To rob as in *jump*, n., 1: c.: C. 19. Baumann.

jump, not by a long. Not by a long way: non-aristocratic coll. (— 1887); ob. Baumann.

jump, on the. On the move; active; restless: coll.: 1900, *The Daily News* (of May 4), 'Keeping the foe on the jump' (O.E.D.).

jump, see how the cat will. To watch the course of events before committing oneself: coll.: from ca. 1820. Scott, Bulwer-Lytton.

jump a bill, to dishonour an acceptance, like *jump one's bail*, to abscond, is orig. and mainly U.S., partly anglicised ca. 1890.

jump a ship. To desert: nautical: C. 20. Bowen.

jump at. To accept eagerly: coll. >, ca. 1905, S.E.: 1769 (S.O.D.). J. Payn, 1882, 'He might well have jumped at such an offer.'—2. To guess: coll.: from ca. 1890.

jump-down. 'The last place . . . in course of erection on the outskirts of . . . civilised life,' Staveley Hill, in *From Home to Home*, 1885: Colonial: ca. 1880–1910.

jump down a person's throat. A variant (—1887) of *jump upon*, q.v. Baumann.

jump on. See **jump upon.**

jump one's horse over a or the bar. To sell horse, bridle and all, to the landlord of a public-house: Colonial: ca. 1880–1905. *The Daily Telegraph*, March 20, 1886.

jump out of one's skin. To be greatly startled: coll.: C. 19–20.

jump to it. To bestir oneself: military, esp. N.C.O.s': from ca. 1912. B. & P. Cf. *put a jerk in it* (see **jerk** . . .).

jump up. To get the best of (a person); or the reverse: tailors': from ca. 1850.

jump up behind. To endorse the bill of a friend: commercial: from ca. 1870. Cf. *endorse.*

jump (up)on. To criticise severely: coll.: 1868 (S.O.D.). M. E. Braddon, 'In vulgar phraseology, to be "jumped upon".'

jumpable. 'Open for another to take': Australian coll.: 1884, Boldrewood. Ex *jump*, v., 3.

jumped-up. Conceited, arrogant: (orig. low) coll.: from ca. 1870. H., 5th ed., 1874. Ex dial. —2. Upset, nervous: low coll.: ca. 1880–1910. Cf. S.E. *jumpy.*

***jumper.** A thief entering houses by the windows: c.: from ca. 1787; ob. Grose, 2nd ed. See **jump**, n., 1.—2. A tenpenny piece: Scottish c. of ca. 1820–50. Haggart.—3. The illegal appropriator of another's mining-claim: from ca. 1855: coll. >, ca. 1880, S.E.—4. 'Now the technical term for the seaman's upper garment, but originally [ca. 1850–75] a slang term for a duck jacket slipped on to protect clothing during a dirty job on deck,' Bowen.—5. The inevitable nickname of a man surnamed Collins or Cross: naval and military: late C. 19–20. F. & Gibbons. The latter ex *jump across*, the former of anecdotal origin.—6. A (gen., travelling) ticket-inspector: orig. (1900), railwaymen's. O.E.D. (Sup.).—7. A light buggy: Canadian coll.: C. 20. John Beames. Ex its motion.

jumping cat, the cult of the. The practice of waiting before committing oneself: coll. (— 1896); † by 1920.

jumping-jack. A sea-gull: nautical (— 1896): coll. rather than s.

jumping Jehoshaphat or Jupiter or Moses(, by the). Mild oaths: mid-C. 19–20 coll.; ob. *Jehoshaphat* is occ. employed alone, often in the sol. form *Jehosophat.*

jumping-off place. A point of departure: coll.: orig. (1826), U.S.; anglicised ca. 1870. In C. 20, S.E.

jumping-powder. A stimulant: s. >, ca. 1890, coll.: ca. 1825–1914. Blaine, 1840, in *Encyclopædia of Rural Sports*, 'Fortified . . . by a certain quantum of jumping powder.'

jumps. Delirium tremens (— 1879).—2. The fidgets: coll. (— 1881). (Both with *the*.)—3. As a garment, it is (despite F. & H.) S.E.

jumps, be for the high. See **jump, be for the high.**

jumpy as a bag of fleas. See **fleas, jumpy as** . . .

June too-too. June 22, 1897, the sixtieth anniversary of the Queen's reign : non-aristocratic c.p. : 1897 only. Punning ' 22 ' and satirising the ' too-too ' of the Æsthetes. Ware.

Jungle, the. The West African share market : Stock Exchange : C. 20. Abbr. *jungle-market*, which the O.E.D. records for 1901.—2. The Salvation Army Hostel in Blackfriars Bridge Road : c. : from ca. 1920. Michael Harrison, *Weep for Lycidas*, 1934 ; W. A. Gape, 1936.

jungles. Shares in West African businesses : Stock Exchange coll. (1904) >, by 1930, j. O.E.D. (Sup.). Ex preceding. sense 1.

jungli. Uncouth : unrefined : Anglo-Indian coll. (— 1927). O.E.D. (Sup.). I.e. *jungly*, *-gli* imitating a Hindi suffix.

junior. Smaller ; lower ; the less good. (So *tight junior*, the smallest, lowest.) Winchester College : C. 19–20 ; ob. The opp. is *senior*. Wrench.

juniper. Gin : from ca. 1820 ; ob. by 1910, † by 1920. Bee, 1823 ; J. E. Ritchie, in *The Night Side of London*. Gin = *de genièvre* = juniper, though *gin* is actually abbr. of *geneva*.

juniper-lecture. See **jiniper-lecture.**

junk, as old or inferior cable, fig. salt beef, is S.E. Whence, however, sense of (*a*) miscellaneous, second-hand stuff, hence (*b*) rubbish : orig. (1842), U.S. ; anglicised as coll., resp. ca. 1880 and ca. 1900 ; both nuances now verge on S.E.—2. Whence liquor ; dregs : Australian (and U.S.) nautical : C. 20. Bowen.

junket. A mixture ; mix-up, confusion : coll. (— 1923). Manchon. Ex the dish.

junket, v. To exult (*over*) : Winchester College : from ca. 1850 ; ob. Ex the S.E. v.

junket ! Indicative of self-congratulation : Winchester College : C. 19–20 ; ob. Wrench.

[**junt** (a trick), wrongly defined, is also wrongly included by F. & H. : it is S.E.]

Jupiter. Used in mild oaths of C. 17–20 : literary until C. 19, then coll. if used with a smile.—2. (Also *Jupiter Tonans*. Cf. *the Thunderer*.) *The Times* newspaper : Fleet Street : ca. 1850–1900.

Jupiter Carlyle. The Rev. Alex. Carlyle (1722–1805), who impressed his many notable friends and acquaintances as having a Jovian head. Dawson.

Jupiter Junior. *The Daily Telegraph* : Fleet Street : ca. 1870–1900. Ex **Jupiter**, 2.

Jupiter Placens. Lord Brougham (d. 1868.) In contrast to *Jupiter Tonans*, 1. Dawson.

Jupiter Scapin. ' A tricky minister ' : political and Society's coll. : late C. 19–early 20. Ware. Ex the Parisians' nickname, ca. 1810, for Napoleon I.

Jupiter Tonans. Lord Chancellor Erskine (1750–1823).—2. See **Jupiter**, 2. Dawson.

*jurk. A rare C. 19 variant of *jark*, **q.v.** ' Ducange Anglicus ', 1857.

jury. An assertion ; a profession of faith, etc. ⁊ costermongers' : from ca. 1850 ; ob.

jury, chummage, and couter. Knife, fork, and spoon : Regular Army's : late C. 19–20. B. & P. Ex Hindustani.

jury—hang half and save half. The jury may be *a Kentish, a London,* or *a Middlesex jury* : a proverbial c.p. : resp. C. 18–19 ; late C. 18–mid-19 ; C. 17–19. The implication, as Middleton in 1608 suggested of the third, ' Thou . . . wilt make haste to give up thy verdict, because thou wilt not lose thy dinner.' (Apperson.)

just. Certainly ; indeed ; ' rather ! ' : 1855 : coll. till ca. 1920, then S.E. Milliken, 1892, ' Wouldn't I just ! '—2. Quite, very, truly, as in ' It's just splendid ! ' : coll. : from ca. 1905. [just exactly. ' Bad tautology ', Fowler. Mid-C. 19–20.]

just nicely. Tipsy : euphemistic : from ca. 1930. (G. Heyer, *Death in the Stocks*, 1935.) Abbr. S.E. *just nicely drunk.*

just quietly was, in the G.W., a tag-c.p. among New Zealanders. It had virtually no meaning.

just what the doctor ordered. A c.p. of approval applied to anything particularly applicable or suitable or to anything very good or very pleasant : C. 20.

justass. A mid-C. 18–early 19 coll. pun on *justice* (a person). Grose, 1st ed.

justice, do. To pledge (a person) ; drink to : late C. 17–18. B.E.

Justice Child, do. To inform to the police or to a magistrate : c. of ca. 1690–1750. B.E. The reference is prob. to Sir Francis Childe, the elder (1642–1713) ; *A New Canting Dict.*, 1725, makes *child* a vocative,—which seems less likely and certainly less pointed.

justices' justice. Justice (esp. if severe) of the kind administered by petty magistrates : from ca. 1830 : coll. till ca. 1890, then S.E. [justum in F. & H. is a nonce-word.]

jutland, Jutland. The posteriors : low punning coll. : C. 18–mid-19.

juvenile. (Gen. pl.) A book for children : booksellers' and publishers' : from ca. 1898. S. >, ca. 1920, coll. ; now almost S.E.

juventate, erroneous for *juventute* : from ca. 1770. (O.E.D.)

juwaub, a refusal, a dismissal ; as v., to refuse, reject. Anglo-Indian : from ca. 1830. H., 1864. Ex Hindustani **jawaub, an answer.** (Also, and better, **jawaub.**)

jybe. See **gybe.**

K

k. See **ka' me, ka' thee.**—2. For such obscure words gen. spelt with a *c* as are looked-for in vain under *k*, see *c* : e.g. *kushy* is a possible form of *cushy*, but it will be found only at *cushy*.—3. Sol. for *qu* : mostly Cockney : C. 19–20. E.g. (*h*)*arlekinade*.—4. See **ink**.—5. For *ct*, *k* is an illiteracy ; e.g., *ack* for *act* : immemorial.

K.A.B.G.N.A.L.S. These letters, which, in back s., form *back slang* (the needless *c* being omitted), are ' uttered rapidly to indicate that this mode of conversation will be agreeable to speaker ' (Ware) : mostly Cockneys' (— 1909). Also *kabac genals.*

K.B.H. See **K.H.B.**

K.D.G.'s, the. The King's Dragoon Guards : military coll. : from ca. 1881. F. & Gibbons.

K.G.5. H.M.S. *King George V* : naval coll. : 1912. Ibid.

K.H.B. A ' King's hard bargain ', more gen.

'King's bad bargain'; an undesirable sailor or, occ., soldier: coll.: 1925, 'Taffrail' (O.E.D. Sup.).

k-legged. Knock-kneed; shaky on one's legs: printers': from ca. 1860. In dial., *k* or *kay* denotes 'left', as in *k-pawed*, Cheshire and Lancashire for left-handed.

k-nut. See **knut.**

k.o.; occ. **kayoe.** V. and occ. n. Knock-out. Also *give one the K.o.* Orig. and mostly pugilists': C. 20, ex U.S.

K.S. Kuala Solor: Federated Malay States coll.: C. 20. (Somerset Maugham, *The Casuarina Tree*, 1926.)

ka' me, ka' thee. One good turn deserves another: proverbial coll. (— 1546) >, ca. 1700, S.E. Other forms *k, kay, kawe, kob*; Ray, C. 17, has *claw*, which, being also the earliest form, may provide the origin. Cf. the late C. 19–20, *scratch my back and I'll scratch yours.*

kabac genals. See **K.A.B.G.N.A.L.S.**

kadi. See **cady.**

kaffir. A prostitute's bully; hence, a low fellow: low: ca. 1860–1910.

Kaffir circus. The market where, on the Stock Exchange, transactions in South African land, mining, and other stocks are effected: South African and London financial: from the early 1890's. A. J. Wilson, 1895; Pettman. Ex *Kaffirs*, q.v.

Kaffir piano. The marimba, a musical instrument: South African coll.: 1891. Pettman.

Kaffirs. South African Mining Shares: Stock Exchange s. >, by 1920, coll.; now almost S.E.: 1889, *The Rialto*, March 23, 'Even Kaffirs raised their sickly heads.'

Kaffir's (occ. **Caffre's**) **lightener.** A full meal: South African: from ca. 1860; ob.

kai-kai. Food; feasting: New Zealand: mid-C. 19–20. Reduplication of Maori *kai* (food), itself used by the New Zealand soldiers in the G.W. F. & Gibbons. Cf. *kapai.*

kail through the reek, give one his. To reprimand, or punish, severely: Scots coll.: C. 19–20. Scott. Ex the unpalatableness of smoke-tasting soup.

kaio. A 'popular corruption in the South Island of New Zealand of *Ngaio*,' the Maori name for *myoporum lœtum*, a tree whose wood is used for gun-stocks: from ca. 1870. Morris.

kakker-boosah. Prematurely voided excrement: low (— 1823); † by 1890. Bee. See **cack.**

kalsomine is erroneous for *calcimine*: from ca. 1860. O.E.D.

kamerad! Stop; that's enough; don't make it too hot!: military: 1915; ob. Ex the Ger. soldiers' cry (lit., 'comrade!') on surrendering. B. & P.—2. Also (1916), v., to surrender; cry 'enough!'; ob. Ibid. (3rd ed.).

kan du! A military variant of *can do*, 2. As if ex Hindustani.

kanga. Abbr. *kangaroo*: Australian coll.: from ca. 1890.

kangaroo. A native—not an Aborigine—of Australia: 1827 (S.O.D.): coll. >, ca. 1860, S.E. Cf. *wallaby*; a post-War Australian Rugby-team called itself *the Wallabies*.—2. 'A tall thin man, especially ill-shaped and round-shouldered': nautical coll.: late C. 19–20; ob. Ware.—3. **the Kangaroo**, Lt.-Col. Sir George Cooke (1768–1834): early C. 19 military. Ex *James Cook*, discoverer of New South Wales, kangaroo-land par excellence.—

4. The nickname of a type of aeroplane: Air Force: 1915; ob. F. & Gibbons.

kangaroo-droop or, more gen., **-hop.** A feminine affectation, hands being brought, palm downward, to the breast: cf. *Grecian bend, Roman fall.* Coll., Australian: ca. 1875–1900. Morris.

*kangaroo (or **Anzac**) **poker**; also **double-ace poker.** A gambling game played by confidence-tricksters: c., and police s.: from ca. 1916. Charles E. Leach, *On Top of the Underworld*, 1933. Prob. introduced by Australian soldiers in 1915, when hundreds of them were evacuated, wounded, from Gallipoli to England.

kangaroos. West Australian mining shares; dealers in these: Stock Exchange: 1896 (Morris).

kanits. A stink: back s. (— 1874). Whence *kanitseno*, a stinking one. Ob.

kant [see **cant.—Kanuck**] see **Canack.—kanurd.** A loose form of *ken(n)urd*, q.v.

kapai. Good; agreeable; (mostly North Island) New Zealand: mid-C. 19–20. *The New Zealand Herald*, Feb. 14, 1896. Borrowed direct from Maori, where *kapai* = this is good. Morris.

kap(o)ut. Finished, dead; no more: military: 1915. B. & P. (Only predicatively.) Ex Ger. *kaputt.* Cf. Low Ger. *kaputt* (or *kapuut*) *gaan*, to die; Devonshire dial. has rare *go capooch*, to die, recorded by the E.D.D. Sup. for 1881.

karibat. Food: Anglo-Indian (— 1864). H., 3rd ed. Ex Hindustani for curry and rice, the staple dish of both Europeans and natives in India.

Karno. See **Fred Karno** . . .

*kate. A master or skeleton key: c. of late C. 17–mid-19. B.E. Cf. *bess, betty, jenny*; also *jimmy*: see esp. **betty.**—2. Hence, a picklock: C. 18–mid-19. Grose, 1st ed.—3. (Also *katy, Katy.*) A wanton: (mainly Scots) coll.: C. 16–early 19.

Kate Karney. The Army: military rhyming s.: late C. 19–20. F. & Gibbons.

Kate Mullet, as knowing as. Stupid: C. 19–20; ob. Quiller-Couch, in *Troy Town*, '. . . They say she was hanged for a fool.'

*kath (or **K.**). An indefinitely long term of imprisonment: New Zealand c. (— 1914).—2. Hence, 'the duration' (q.v.): New Zealand military: 1915–18. O. J. T. Alpen, *Cheerful Yesterdays*, ca. 1930.

Kathleen Mavourneen system. The hire-purchase system: Anglo-Irish (— 1932). Ex the refrain of the song: 'It may be for years and it may be for ever.'

katterzem. A parasite: Scottish (— 1909). Ware. Ex Fr. *quatorzième*, fourteenth: he being willing to go, at a moment's notice, to prevent the number of guests being thirteen.

kayoe. See **k.o.—kaze**, despite F. & H., is S.E.

kebrock. A cap: Canadian military: G.W. Ex Fr.-Canadian. F. & Gibbons.

keck. See **kek.**

keck-handed. Left-handed: schools' and dial.: C. 19–early 20. Cf. *k-legged*, q.v.

keddlums. A cooks' and children's perversion (— 1923) of *kettle.* Manchon.

kedge. To cadge: Cockney (— 1887). Baumann.

kedger. A fisherman; a mean fellow: nautical (— 1867). Admiral Smyth. Prob. *cadger* influenced by *kedger*, a kedge-anchor. Imm. ex:—2. A beggar specialising in fees for trivial services: c. (— 1823); † by 1890. Bee adds *kedgers' coffee-*

house and *hotel*, a resort resp. daily and nightly of 'every kind of beggars'.

kedgeree-pot. A round pipkin : Anglo-Indian coll. : C. 19–20. Yule & Burnell.

kee-gee. 'Go, vigour' : East London : ca. 1860–1915. Ware. Prob. ex *qui-vive*, for cf. *key-vee.*

keek-cloy. See **kicks.**

*****keekers.** The eyes : Scots c. : C. 19–20. Ex *keek*, to look. Cf. *peepers.*

keel. The posteriors : Scots coll. : C. 19–20 ; ob.—*keel over* (F. & H.) : ineligible.

*****keel-bully.** A lighterman carrying coals to and from the ships : late C. 17–18 : c. >, ca. 1770, s. >, ca. 1800, coll. >, ca. 1860, S.E. See B.E., Grose. Mostly derisive.

[**keel-haul, -ing,** even fig., are S.E.]

keelie. A (gen., street) rough : from ca. 1850 : Scots s. >, ca. 1870, coll. Ex *the Keelie Gang*, an Edinburgh band of young blackguards, ca. 1820 (O.E.D.). Cf. *hoodlum* and *hooligan*, qq.v. ; see also **larrikin.**

keen as mustard. Very keen : coll. : C. 20. Lyell. Ex the next, orig. with a pun on *Keen's mustard.*

keen (on). Fond (of) ; eager (for) ; greatly interested (in) : coll. (— 1897) : by 1930, almost S.E. Mary Kingsley, '. . . If they don't feel keen on a man surviving ' (O.E.D.). ' Keen on a girl.'

[**keep.** As board and lodging. (despite F. & H.) always S.E. ; as a kept woman (rarely man) it may orig. have been coll. : long S.E.]

keep, v. To live ; reside ; lodge : C. 14–20 : S.E. till ca. 1770, then coll. and mainly Cambridge and U.S. Shakespeare ; Grose.—(2. Other senses in F. & H. are S.E.)

keep a cow,—as long as I can buy milk I shall not. Why have the expense of a wife when one can visit a whore ? Proverbial c.p. : C. 17–20 ; ob. Bunyan.

keep a pig. To have a lodger : Oxford University : mid-C. 19–early 20. Esp. of a freshman quartered on a senior undergraduate.

keep a stiff upper lip is coll. (orig.—ca. 1815— (U.S.) >, in C. 20, S.E. Not to show fear or sorrow.

keep [a person] back and belly. To clothe and feed : coll. : C. 18–20 ; ob.

keep ' cave ! ' To watch, and give warning : Eton College : C. 19–20.

keep chapel. See **chapel.**

keep company. As = go into society, S.E.—2. (V.t., *with*.) To be or act as a sweetheart ; coll. : from ca. 1830. Dickens in *Sketches by Boz*, ' Mr. Wilkins kept company with Jemima Evans.'

keep down the census. To abort ; masturbate : low : mid-C. 19–20 ; ob.

keep hold of the land. ' To hug the shore ' : nautical coll. : late C. 19–20 ; slightly ob. Bowen.

keep in with. To maintain, esp. friendly, relations with : late C. 16–20 : S.E. till ca. 1875, then coll. W. Black, in *Yolande*, 1883.

keep it clean ! Don't be indelicate, smutty ! : c.p. : from the late 1920's. Cf. S.E. *clean fun.*

keep it dark. See **dark.**

keep it up. To prolong a debauch : from ca. 1780 : coll. Grose, 2nd ed. Ex the S.E. sense, to continue doing something.

keep off the grass ! Be cautious ! : a coll. c.p. orig. proletarian : late C. 19–20. Ware. Ex notices in parks.

keep nit. To keep watch ; to be on the ' qui-

vive ' : Australian : C. 20. John G. Brandon, *Th' Big City*, 1931, uses it of keeping watch for gamblers or for a gang. Possibly *nit* is an abbr. of dial. *nitch*, a notch : if so, *keep nit* = keep tally = keep tab. But much more prob. a corruption of *keep nix* (q.v. at *nix !*).

keep one's (or the) boiler clear. (Esp. in the imperative.) To ' watch your stomach—in reference to health ' (Ware) : engineers' : mid-C. 19–20. As a C. 20 wit has said, in approximately these words : ' What a lot of trouble people would spare themselves if only they would keep their bowels open and their mouths closed.'

keep one's eyes skinned. To maintain a sharp look-out : coll. : U.S. (1846), anglicised ca. 1860. Occ. *peeled* for *skinned.*

keep one's hair on. See **hair on.** (Esp. in the imperative.)—**keep one's pecker up.** See **pecker up.**

keep oneself to oneself. Coll. form of *keep to oneself*, i.e. avoid the society of others : from ca. 1890.

*****keep open house.** To sleep in the open air : tramps' c. : from ca. 1850 ; ob. See also **hedge-square, star-pitch,** and **starry.**

*****keep sheep by moonlight.** (V.i.) To hang in chains : C. 18–early 19 c.

keep sloom. To remain quiet ; say nothing : tailors' : from ca. 1860.

keep the doctor. To sell adulterated drinks : low coll. : C. 19–20 ; ob.

keep the door. To be a brothel-keeper : low coll. : C. 18–mid-19.

keep the pot boiling. See **boiling.**

keep (something) under one's hat. (Esp. in the imperative.) To say nothing about : from ca. 1925. *The Humorist*, April 7, 1934 ; T. F. Tweed, *Blind Mouths*, 1934.

keep up, old queen ! A c.p. (— 1909) of farewell ' addressed by common women to a sister being escorted into a prison van ' ; slightly ob. Ware.

keep up to the collar, v.t. Keep hard at work : coll. (— 1861) ; ob. T. Hughes, ' Hardy kept him pretty well up to collar.'—2. Hence, v.i., to work hard, to be flustered, worried : coll. (— 1923). Manchon.

keep your hair on ! A c.p. of ca. 1867–1913 offered on any mishap. ' Quotations ' Benham ; B. & P. See **hair on, keep one's.**

keep your nose clean ! Avoid drink ! : military c.p. (— 1909). Ware.

keep your thanks to feed your chickens ! I don't need, desire, any thanks : semi-proverbial c.p. (— 1681) ; very ob. W. Robertson, *Phraseologia Generalis.*

keep yourself good all through ! Be entirely good ! : a Society c.p. : 1882–ca. 1890. Ware.

keeper of overdrafts, the. The manager : bank-clerks' : C. 20. Jocular on the titles of museum-officials.

*****keeping-cully.** ' One who keeps a mistress, as he supposes, for his own use, but really for that of the public,' Grose, 1st ed. : c. : ca. 1660–1840.

keeps, for. For good ; permanently ; in cricket, defensively : coll. >, by 1920, S.E. : from 1880 in Australia (app. earliest in cricket sense), ca. 1890 in England. I.e. to keep for good. Cf. :

keeps !, no. A school-children's c.p. (— 1923) in playing games : ' We won't keep things this game,' or ' We're not playing for keeps.' Manchon Cf. preceding.

*****keffel.** A horse : c. late C. 17–mid-19. B.E.

(It survives in dial., where first recorded in 1825. Ex Welsh *ceffyl*, E.D.D.)

keg. The stomach : from ca. 1885 (orig. dial.); rare in C. 20.

keg, little bit o(f). Human copulation : low (— 1909). Ware. Lit., a small piece of common meat.

keg-meg. Tripe; derivatively *keg-meg shop*: low (— 1857). ' Ducange Anglicus '. A variant of dial. *cag-mag*, inferior meat, refuse. Cf. *cag-mag* above. 2. Hence (?), an intimate talk : (low) coll. : 1883, J. Payn in *Thicker than Water*.

kegged, be. To be jeered at : nautical : mid-C. 19–20 ; ob. Bowen. Ex *cag(g)*, q.v.

keifer. ' Generic for *mutton* (q.v.),' F. & H. : see **monosyllable, the.**

kek or **keck.** An especially heavy mail : Post Office telegraph-messengers' (esp. in London): from ca. 1920. Perhaps ex dial. *keck*, a jolt, a blow.

kelder. Belly ; womb : low coll. : mid-C. 17–early 19. Brome.

Kelly from the Isle of Man. A C. 20 (now ob.) c.p. ex a popular song. Collinson.

Kelly's eye. One, esp. a solitary one : mostly in house (the gambling game): military : C. 20 Anecdotal ex a one-eyed Kelly. Also *Kelly's wonk*.

*kelp. See **calp.**

*kelp, v.t. To lift one's hat to (a person): c. of ca. 1800–50. Vaux.

[**Kelso boots,** heavy feet-shackles : C. 18–early 19. *Kelso convoy*, the act of accompanying a friend a short distance : C. 19–20 ob. Scots : ? coll. or dial. The same query applies to *kelty*, a bumper glass, also listed by F. & H. : I consider all three to be dial.—except perhaps the third. E.D.D.]

kelter ; occ. **kilter.** As order, condition, it is dial. and S.E.—2. As money, it is c. of ca. 1780–1820. George Parker, 1789. Also dial : ? before it was c.—the earliest dial. record being 1808. E.D.D. ; O.E.D.

kemesa. See **camesa.**

[**Kemp's morris,** listed by Grose, is ineligible.]

Kemp's shoes to throw after you !, would (that) I had. I wish I could bring you good luck : a C. 17–early 19 c.p. Ex a lost topical reference. Grose, 1st ed.

*ken. A house (in compounds, house or place): c. : ca. 1560–1860 ; thereafter somewhat literary,—except in compounds. Harman, B.E., Lytton, Henley & Stevenson. The O.E.D. essays no etymology, W. proposes abbr. *kennel*, I suggest a corruption of Romany *tan*, a place, or a corruption of the original whence *tan* itself springs. (H., 3rd and later edd., refers us to ' *khan*, Gipsy and Oriental.' The word does not exist in Romany in this form ; but there is the Hindustani *khan(n)a*, a house, a room, which appears, in various forms, in the various Gypsy dialects.) For *bob-* or *bowman-ken*, see **bob-ken** ; for *boozing-ken*, see **boozing.**

*ken, bite or **crack a.** To rob a house : c. : resp. late C. 17–18 (B.E.), late C. 19–20 ob.

*ken, burn the. See **burn the ken.**

*ken-crack lay. Housebreaking : c. : C. 19–20, ob. See **ken** and **lay.**

*ken-cracker, -miller. A housebreaker : c. : resp. late C. 18–20 (ob.), late C. 17–early 19. B.E. ; Grose, 1st ed. (both).

kenird. Drink : back s. (— 1887). Baumann. Cf. *kennurd* for the euphonic *e*.

kennedy. A poker : low London : ca. 1820–

1900. Bee, 1823. **Ex** one Kennedy killed in ' tough ' St. Giles's by a poker. Hence, *give one kennedy*, hit one with a poker, as in Henley's *Villon's Good Night*. ' Frequently shortened to *neddy*,' H., 1859.

[**kennel,** female pudend ; **kennel-raker,** scavenger. S.E., despite F. & H.]

*kenner. A C. 19 (?–20) variant of *ken*. Manchon. Influenced by *khanna*, q.v.

kennetseeno. Stinking : manipulated back s. or central s. (— 1859). H., 1st ed.

*kennick. ' A mixture of flash-patter [i.e. cant] and padding-ken [or low lodging-house] talk,' says ' *No 747* ' at p. 17 in a reference valid for the year 1865. Fanciful ex *ken*, q.v.

kenning by kenning, vbl.n. ' Increasing a seaman's wages by the work he does, a term principally used by the old whalers '; nautical coll. : from ca. 1860 ; ob. Bowen. A natural development ex Scottish and Northern dial. *kenning*, a little.

ken(n)urd. Tipsy : back s. (— 1859) on *drunk*. H., 1st ed. (Since *knurd* is ugly.) Mayhew has it in 1851 in form *kanurd* (E.D.D.).

Kensingtons, the. The 13th London Regiment : military : from ca. 1915 (?). (See esp. ' *The Kensingtons* ', by Sergeants O. F. Bailey & H. M. Hollier, 1936.) Ex their headquarters' being in Kensington.

kent. A coloured cotton handkerchief : low : from ca. 1810 ; ob. Vaux. Also :

Kent clout or **rag.** See preceding entry. H., 1859.

Kent-Street ejectment or **distress.** The removal, by the landlord, of the street door when rent is in arrears : (low) coll. : ca. 1780–1830. Grose, 1st ed. Ex a Southwark practice.

[**Kentish fire,** a salvo of applause : S.E., despite F. & H. and Manchon.]

Kentish knocker. A Kentish smuggler : C. 19 : local coll. > S.E. Ex *Kentish Knock*, the sandbank facing the Thames-mouth. (O.E.D.)

Kentish long-tail. A native of Kent : coll. nickname : C. 13–20 ; since ca. 1750, dial. The legend behind the name is in Layamon's *Brut*, vv. 19555–86. Apperson.

Kentucky loo ; fly loo. Betting on certain antics of flies : students' : mid-C. 19–20 ; virtually †. Ware.

kenurd. See **kennurd.**

kep. An occ. variant of *kip*, n., 3.

kep, v. Kept : sol. (— 1887). Baumann.

Keppel's snob, put up at the. To be a snob : naval : ca. 1870–1910. Ware. I.e. at *The Keppel's Head*, an inn named after Admiral Keppel (d. 1786): pun on *nob*, head.

[**ker-,** intensive s. or coll. prefix, indicative and imitative of effort, as in *ker-wallop*, is U.S (1852) : it has never > gen. in the British Empire. Cf. the *k* in *knut* : see **kn-.**]

kerb-walker. A singer on the pavement-edge : Glasgow (— 1934).

*kerbside Virginia. See **hard-up,** n., 5.

kerbstone broker. A stockbroker operating outside the Stock Exchange : orig. (1860), U.S.; anglicised ca. 1890 as coll. ; by 1920, S.E.

kerbstone jockey. A soldier in the Transport (*A.S.C.*) : New Zealand soldiers' ; in G.W. A safe job, comparatively ; esp. as the horses were heavily harnessed.

kerel. A chap, a fellow : South African coll. : late C. 19–20. Also (simply *kerel*), a term of address = ' old chap '. Ex Dutch; **cf.** † S.E. *carl* (cognate with *churl*). Pettman.

kernel of the nuts. See k-nut and filbert.

Kerry security. ' Bond, pledge, oath—and keep the money,' Grose, 1785. Coll. : late C. 18–mid-19.

Kerry witness. One who will swear to anything : coll. : from ca. 1825 ; ob.

kerseynette. Erroneous form of *cassinette* : 1846 onwards. O.E.D.

kersplosh ! Splash ! : Australian (— 1916.) C. J. Dennis. See **ker-**.

kerte(r)ver-cartzo. A venereal disease, esp. syphilis : low London : ca. 1850–90. (Cf. *catever* and *catso* (*gadso*), qq.v.) H., 1859. Ex Lingua Franca.

kervorten. A quartern : a Cockneyism : mid-C. 19–20 ; ob. ' *No. 747* ' (= reference of 1845) ; H., 5th ed. By perversion.

ketch. To catch ; also as n. : Cockney (— 1887). Baumann. Cf. *kedge*. Whence *ketched*, caught.

Ketch ; Jack Ketch. See **Jack Ketch**.

Ketir Mug. The inevitable nickname, on Egyptian service (— 1935), of men surnamed *Braines* or *Brayne* (etc.). Ex the Arabic for ' big ' + *mug*, face.

kettle. The female pudend : low coll. : C. 18–20 ; ob. D'Urfey.—2. An ironclad or other iron-built vessel : nautical : ca. 1870–1914.—3. In c., a watch. A *red kettle* is a gold watch ; a *white*, a silver one. Mid-C. 19–20.

kettle, cook the. To make the water in the kettle to boil : South African coll. : from the late 1890's. Hicks, *The Cape as I Found It*, 1900. (Pettman.) Cf. the English *run the bath*.

kettle and coffee-mill. Boiler and engine : from ca. 1870 ; ob. Bowen remarks that it was applied by sailing-ship men to wind-jammers ruined by the intrusion of ' these monstrosities '.

kettle black, pot calling the. See **black a*se** and cf. the proverbial *the kiln calls the oven burnt house* (C. 17–19). Apperson.

kettle of fish, a pretty. See **fish**.

kettledrum. An afternoon tea-party on a big scale : coll. : from ca. 1860 ; ob. Mrs. Henry Wood, ' Bidding the great world to a kettle-drum.' Cf. *drum*.—2. **kettledrums**, or **Cupid's kettledrums**, a woman's breasts : low : ca. 1770–1850. Grose, 1st ed.

kew. A week : back s. (— 1859). H., 1st ed. Pl. either *kews* or *skew*.

key, a translation, is S.E.—2. The penis : C. 18–20, ob. : sometimes euphemistic, but gen. low coll. ' Lets a man in and the maid out ', F. & H. (Cf. *lock*, last sense, q.v.) Whence *keyhole*, the female pudend, for which F. & H.'s *keystone of love* is a mere literary euphemism.

key, v.t. So to word (an advertisement) that one can check its selling-appeal : publicity men's and publishers' : from ca. 1920 : s. > j. >, by 1934, S.E.

key, his wife keeps the. He is addicted to drinking on the sly : proletarian (— 1887). Baumann.

key of the street, have the. To be shut out for the night ; to have no home : from ca. 1835 : coll. till C. 20, then S.E. Dickens in *Pickwick*.

key under the door (occ. **threshold**), **leave the.** To go bankrupt : C. 17–19 : coll. Swift ; Ray, 1670, *lay the key* . . ., a variant. (Apperson.)

key-vee(, on the). Alert : lower classes' : 1862. Ware. Ex *qui-vive*. Cf. *kee-gee*.

keyhole. See **key**, n., 2.

keyhole (occ. **keyholed**), **be all.** To be tipsy :

low : from ca. 1860 ; ob. Perhaps because a drunk man has difficulty in finding the keyhole.

***keyhole-whisperer** or **-whistler.** A night's lodger in barn (see **skipper**, whence *skipper-bird*) or outhouse : tramps' c., resp. 1845 (' *No. 747* ') and 1851 (Mayhew) ; ob.

keystone under the hearth(, keystone under the horse's belly). A C. 19 smugglers' c.p. > proverbial, the reference being to the hiding of contraband spirits below the fireplace or in the stable. Wise, *The New Forest*, 1863. (Apperson.)

khabbar, khubber. See **kubber**.

khaki. A Boer War volunteer : military : 1900 ; †.—2. Pease-pudding : low : C. 20 ; ob. Ware. Ex colour.

Khaki Election, the. The General Election in Britain at the time of the Boer War : political coll. ; ob. Collinson.

khalishee. (Gen. pl.) A native Indian sailor : nautical coll. : mid-C. 19–20 ; ob. Bowen. ? a corruption of *Khalsa(h)*, the Sikhs collectively.

khanna. A house, compartment : often used very incongruously in Anglo-Indian coll. : late C. 18–20. Yule & Burnell. (See also **ken**.)

kia ora ! Good health to you ! ; good luck ! : New Zealand (and occ. Australian) : from ca. 1870. Ex Maori *keora ta-u* and *k. tatu*. See esp. Morris.

kibber. See **jibber the kibber**.

kibe is catachrestic when = to kick, to gall : C. 19–20. O.E.D.—2. *kibe ?*, to whose benefit ? : Universities' (— 1909) ; ob. Ware. Ex *cui bono*.

kibosh. (The *i* gen. long.) Nonsense ; anything valueless : low : 1860 (H., 2nd ed.): ob. *Punch*, Jan. 3, 1885, ' ' Appy New Year, if you care for the kibosh, old chappie.' Occ. *kiboshery*. By *bosh*, nonsense, out of *kibosh*, *put the* : qq.v.—2. Fashion ; the correct thing : low : from ca. 1888 ; ob. E.g. ' That's the proper kibosh.'—3. See **kibosh on, put the**.

kibosh, v. To spoil, ruin ; check ; bewilder ; knock out (lit. and fig.) : from ca. 1880 (E.D.D.). Milliken in his *'Arry Ballads*.

kibosh, put (a person) **on the.** To calumniate : low : late C. 19–20. Manchon. Ex *kibosh*, n., 1. Contrast :

kibosh on, put the. Same senses as in **kibosh**, the v. : 1836, Dickens, in *Boz*, ' ' Hooroar,'' ejaculates a pot-boy . . ., '' put the kye-bosh on her, Mary ! '' ' ; ' Put the kibosh on the Kaiser ' was a G.W. soldiers' c.p. Perhaps ex Yiddish, which has *kyebosh* or *kibosh*, eighteen pence (cf. *kye*, q.v.): a sense that has got into East End of London s.

kiboshery. See **kibosh**, n., 1.—**kibs(e)y.** See **kyps(e)y.**

kick. The fashion ; vogue : from late C. 17 ; very ob. Preceded by *the*. (If preceded by *a*, a singularity is indicated.) Hence, *high kick*, ' the top of the Fashion ', B.E. ; *all the kick*, ' the present mode ', Grose.—2. A sixpence : from ca. 1700 ; slightly ob., except in *two and a kick*, half-a-crown. Only in compound sums, e.g. ' fourteen bob and a kick ', Moncrieff.—3. The hollow in the butt of a bottle : trade : from ca. 1860. (Occ. *kick-up*.) Mayhew. ? cognate with *kink*, W. pertinently asks.—4. A pocket : c. : from ca. 1850. Mayhew. Prob. ex *kicks*.—5. A moment (cf. *jiffy*) : low coll. : from ca. 1855 ; ob. Esp. *in a kick* H., 1st ed.—6. (Cf. *the boot*) dismissal from a job : 1844 (S.O.D.). Preceded by *the* and esp. in *get the kick*. Cf. *kick out, get the*, q.v.—7. A complaint, a ' grouse ' ; a refusal : coll : mid-C. 19–20 ; orig.

(1839), U.S. E.g. ' He has a kick coming.' Ex the C. 14–20 S.E. v., to resist, be recalcitrant, wrongly included by F. & H., as is that of ' to recoil '.— 8. A chance ; an attempt, ' go ', as in ' Let's have one more kick ' (Baumann) : coll. (— 1887) ; ob.

kick, v. To die : ? c. (— 1725) > s.—2. To escape : C. 18 c. Also *kick away* (*A New Canting Dict.*, 1725). In C. 19–20, but ob., is *kick it* : low.— 3. V.t., ask for (money) ; borrow from (a person) : low : from ca. 1790 ; ob. Mayhew, ' Kick him for some coppers.' Cf. *break shins* and *kick for the boot*, qq.v.—4. V.t., demand money, work, a rest, etc., from (a person) : esp. tailors' : 1829 (O.E.D.). (See also the n., seventh sense.)

kick, get the. See **kick out, get the.**

kick, have the. To be lucky : athletic ex football : ca. 1880–1915.

kick a (person's) **lung out.** To castigate severely : low (— 1909). Ware. Prob. ex U.S.

kick at waist. To fit badly at the waist : tailors' : ca. 1870–1920.

*kick away. See **kick, v., 2.**

kick coming, a. A (gen. a serious) objection ; obstacle.—2. An effort. Both late C. 19–20 coll. Cf. *kick,* n., 7, 8.

kick down the ladder, as in Thackeray's *Snobs,* viii, is ineligible.

kick for the boot. To ask for money : tailors' : from ca. 1850. Cf. *kick,* v., 3, and :

kick for trade. To ask for work : tailors' : from ca. 1855 ; ob. Cf. preceding.

kick, or **odd kick, in one's gallop.** A whim ; strange fancy : mid-C. 18–19 coll.

kick in the guts. A dram of spirits : low : ca. 1770–1860. Grose.

kick in the pants. See **thump on the back.**

kick it. See **kick, v., 1 and 2.**

kick-off. A start : City s. (— 1887) >, ca. 1900, gen. coll. Esp. *for a kick-off.* Baumann. Also v. Ex football.

kick on one's side, have the. To have the luck : sporting coll. (— 1887) ; slightly ob. Baumann.

kick one's heels. See **cool one's heels.**—2. See **kick up one's heels.**

kick out, v.i. To die : 1898 (O.E.D.). Prob. ex U.S. Cf. *kick the bucket.*—2. Hence, to run away ; make off : C. 20. Manchon.—3. Hence, to get out of bed : from ca. 1910.

kick out, get or **give the (dirty).** To be dismissed ; to dismiss (from employment) : C. 19–20 : with *dirty,* s. : without, coll. till ca. 1920, then S.E. Also *get* or *give the kick* : coll. : late C. 19–20 (Lyell).

kick over the traces. To ' go the pace ' ; to be recalcitrant : from ca. 1860 : the former sense verging on S.E., the latter S.E. since ca. 1905. Ex a fractious horse.

kick-shoe. A dancer ; a buffoon : coll. : ' old ', says F. & H.—but how old ?

kick the bucket. See **bucket, kick the.**

kick the cat. (Gen. **he kicked the cat.**) To show ' signs of domestic dissatisfaction ' : lower classes' coll. (— 1909). Ware.

*kick the clouds or **the wind.** To be hanged : resp. c. (— 1811), ob., often amplified with *before the hotel door* (*Lex. Bal.*), and s. or coll. : late C. 16–early 19 (Florio).

kick the eye out of a mosquito, can or **be able to.** This coll. Australian expression (— 1888 ; ob.) indicates superlative capacity. ' Rolf Boldrewood.'

kick the stuffing out of. To maltreat ; to get the better of : orig. U.S. ; anglicised as low, ca. 1900.

*kick the wind. See **kick the clouds.** Manchon, erroneously (I believe), gives it as *kick up the wind.*

kick-up. A disturbance ; quarrel : late C. 18–20 : coll. (in C. 20, S.E.). Grose, 3rd ed. ; Wolcot, ' There'd be a pretty kick-up—what a squall ' ; Dickens.—2. A dance : late C. 18–early 19. Grose, 3rd ed.—3. As a v., it is, in itself, S.E., even when = to die and even in *kick up a breeze, dust, shindy,* etc. : see-**breeze, dust, shindy.**

kick up at. To reprimand : at certain Public Schools, esp. Marlborough : late C. 19–20. Charles Turley, *Godfrey Marten, Schoolboy,* 1902 (pupil *loquitur*), ' Pollock . . . has been kicking up badly at me in the last week. He says my prose is " the immature result . . ." '

kick up one's dust in the park. To stroll there : Society (— 1909) ; ob. Ware. Ex Fr. *faire sa poussière . . .*

kick up one's heels. To die : C. 16–19 : orig. coll. but soon S.E. Cf. *kick,* v., 1, *kick out,* and *bucket, kick the.*

[**kick up the wind.** See **kick the wind.**]

kicker. A dancing-master : coll. : ca. 1830–70. (Cf. *hop-merchant.*) Selby, 1838.—2. A horse : nautical (— 1887). Baumann.—3. An auxiliary motor fitted into a sailing ship. : Canadian (and U.S.) nautical coll. : from ca. 1890 ; ob. Bowen. Ex its action on the ship.

kickeraboo or **-poo.** Dead : West Indies ' pidgin ' : late C. 18–19. Grose, 1st ed. Prob. ex *kick over the bucket* rather than ex *kick the bucket.*

kickers. The feet : low : C. 19–20 ; ob.—2. A fit of nervousness, or of nerves : from ca. 1930. R. H. Mottram, *Bumphrey's,* 1934 (concerning aviation), ' I won't go if it gives you the kickers.' Cf. *jitters,* which it may ' folk-etymologise '.

kicking-in. A fag's duty at football : Winchester College : ca. 1820–70.

kicking-strap. An elastic strap inside a garment : tailors' : from ca. 1860. Ex the strap adjusted on a horse to prevent his kicking.

*kicks. Breeches : late C. 17–early 19 ; trousers : C. 19–20, ob. The former, c. ; the latter, low. B.E. ; Moore, ' That bedizen'd old Georgy's bang-up togs and kicks.' Cf. *kickseys, kicksies,* q.v.— 2. See **pair o(f) kicks.**

kicks than halfpence or **ha'pence, more.** Esp. with *get,* more trouble than profit or money ; hence, more unkindness than kindness : coll. (in C. 20, S.E.) : 1824, Scott, ' Monkey's allowance . . . more kicks than halfpence.' Cf. *monkey's allowance,* q.v.

kicksees, kickseys, kicksies. Breeches : C. 18– mid-19.—2. Trousers : mid-C. 19–20, ob. (As breeches, perhaps orig. c.) Cf. *kicks,* q.v.—3. Shoes : low (— 1823) : † by 1895. Bee.

[**kickshaw(s),** a trifle, etc., **kicksy-wicksy,** and **kicksy-winsy** are, despite F. & H., ineligible.]

kicksie. See **kicksy.**

kicksies. See **kickseys.**—**kicksies-builder.** A tailor : c. or low (— 1887) ; ob. Baumann. Ex : —2. A trousers-maker : c. or low (— 1857). ' Ducange Anglicus.'

*kicksters. A pair of breeches : c. (— 1839) ; † by 1900. Brandon.

kicksy ; occ. **kicksie.** Disagreeable ; apt to give trouble : ca. 1850–90. ' Ducange Anglicus ' ; H., 1st ed. I.e., apt to kick.

kicky, adj. Kicking (ball) · cricketers' coll. : 1888, A. G. Steel. (Lewis.)

*kid. (The 1599 Middleton-Massinger quotation given by both F. & H. and the O.E.D. may belong to sense 1; perhaps to sense 3.) A child, esp. if young: late C. 17–20: orig. c. or low; ordinary s. in C. 19–20. J. Payn, 'He thinks how his Missis and the kids would enjoy the spectacle.' Ex the young of a goat.—2. A thief, esp. a young and expert one: c. (— 1812); ob. by 1880, † by 1896. Vaux; Bee; Egan's Grose.—3. A man, esp. if young: low (— 1823); ob., except in U.S. and, in England, except when applied to a (clever) boxer, e.g. Kid Berg; this boxing nuance is allied to the preceding sense. 'Jon Bee'; Bulwer Lytton.— 4. A policeman: c. of ca. 1875–1905. Thor Fredur. —5. Chaff, leg-pulling, 'gammon and devilry', Hindley; H., 5th ed.: low (— 1874) >, ca. 1900, ordinary s. Esp. in *no kid* (! or ?). Ex *kid*, v., 2, q.v.—6. See **kids**.—7. (Gen. *kiddy*.) A flat dish wherein sailors measure their ration: nautical (— 1887) Baumann.—8. Cheese: Winchester College: late C. 19–20. Wrench. Cf. origin of sense 1.

kid, v. To lie in; v.t., get with child: low coll., low s., resp.: C. 19–20; ob.—2. To cheat; hoax; wheedle, flatter: from ca. 1810, orig. c. *Lex. Bal.* —3. Hence (mostly v.t.), to chaff, quiz: low (— 1859) >, ca. 1900, ordinary s. H., 1st ed. Cf. *kid on*, q.v. Senses 2 and 3 ex the idea: to treat as a child.—4. Hence, v.i. (often with *that . . .*), to pretend, to give the impression . . . : from late 1870's. Esp. *stop kidding !*, let's talk seriously: late C. 19–20.

kid, hard. See hard kid.

*kid, nap the. To become pregnant: c. (—1811); ob. *Lex. Bal.*

kid, no. See kid, n., 5.—kid, with. See kidded.

kid-catcher. An official who seeks non-attend-ants-at-school: London School Board's: late C. 19–early 20. Ware.

*kid-ken. See kidden.

*kid-lay and -rig. The robbing of apprentices or errand-boys of the parcels entrusted to them: c.: resp. late C. 17–early 19 and C. 19 (ob. by 1859). B.E.; Vaux and H., 1st ed.—2. (Only kid-lay.) One of the gang practising this 'lay': c.: C. 18. *A New Canting Dict.*, 1725.

kid-leather. Generic for young harlots: low: C. 19–20.

kid on. To lead on, persuade, by 'gammon' or by deceit: c. (1839, Brandon) > low (1851, Mayhew) >, ca. 1900, ordinary s. Cf. *kid*, v., 2. Contrast:

kid oneself; occ. kid oneself on. To be conceited; to delude oneself: low > ordinary s.: from ca. 1860. See kid, v., 2, and kid on.

*kid-rig. See kid-lay and cf. *kinchen-lay*, q.v.

kid-stakes. Pretence; foolery; flattery: Australian: C. 20. C. J. Dennis. Prob. orig. horse-racing, ex *kid*, n., 5.

kid-stretcher. A man fond of young harlots (see kid-leather): low: C. 19–20; ob.

kid up. To dress oneself properly or in style: military (— 1923). Manchon. Contrast :—2. kid oneself up, to delude oneself: lower classes' coll. (— 1923). Ibid. Ex *kid oneself*.

kid-walloper. A schoolmaster: coll.: late C. 19–20. Recorded in Yorkshire dial. in 1889 (E.D.D.).

kidded; occ. with kid. Pregnant: low: C. 19–20; ob. See kid, v., 1.

*kidden, slurring of less usual *kid-ken*; occ. *kiddy-ken*. A lodging house frequented by thieves,

esp. by young thieves: c. (— 1839); ob. by 1890; † by 1920. Brandon in *Poverty, Mendicity and Crime.*

kidder. As dealer, huckster, S.E. > dial.—2. A glib, persuasive speaker; an expert in chaff: low (— 1859) >, ca. 1900, ordinary s.—3. Hence, one given to pretending: low (— 1880) >, by 1900, gen.—4. A person employed by a (usually hawker-) tradesman to "buy" and therefore to stimulate genuine sales: tramps' c. (— 1932). F. Jennings, *Tramping with Tramps.*—5. (Also *Kidder.*) A Kidderminster carpet: Cockney (— 1887). Baumann.

kidder? Where?: Regular Army's: late C. 19–20. B. & P. Ex Hindustani. Opp. *idder !*, here !: id.: id. Ibid.

kiddey, kiddie. See kiddy.

kiddier. A pork-butcher: low: from ca. 1860; ob. H., 2nd ed. ? pejorative on *kid*, a young goat.

kiddily. Fashionably, smartly, showily: low: from ca. 1820; † by 1914. Bee.

kidding. Vbl.n. of *kid*, v., 2 and 3, and of *kidder*, 4. Cf. *kid*, n., 5.

kiddish. Childish: 1897, *The Daily News*, Dec. 13: s. >, ca. 1920, coll. (O.E.D.)

kid(d)l(e)ywink. A raffle: low (— 1884); ob.— 2. A small village shop: from ca. 1855; ob. H., 1st ed. (Cf. West Country dial. sense, an ale-house.)—Whence, 3, the late C. 19–20 nautical sense, 'a seaman's beershop in the Western English ports': from ca. 1870.—4. A woman of unsteady habits: from ca. 1860; ob. H., 2nd ed.

kiddo. A term of address to a girl or, mostly by the father, to a daughter of any age whatsoever: from the late 1880's. (Christina Stead, *Seven Poor Men of Sydney*, 1934.) Cf. *boyo.*

kiddy. A man, youth, boy: low (— 1860); ob. by 1910, † by 1920.—2. A little child: 1888, Rolf Boldrewood, 'They'd heard all kinds of rough talk ever since they was little kiddies': s. >, ca. 1910, coll. Occ. *kidlet*. Ex *kid*, n., 1.—3. A flash, but minor, thief: 1780, Tomlinson in his *Slang Pastoral*: ob. by 1875, † by 1914. Whence *rolling kiddy*, a dandy thief (1840, Lytton).—4. (Only with difficulty separated from preceding sense.) A dandy, esp. one who dresses like a flash thief (see preceding sense): low: ca. 1820–1910. Byron, 'A kiddy . . . a real swell.'—5. A harlot's bully: c. (or perhaps low): ca. 1830–1910.—6. 'A hat of a form fashionable among "kiddies"': ca. 1860–1900: c. or low. (O.E.D.)—7. A stage-coach driver, says F. & H., citing Dickens in *Boz*: actually Dickens uses it as the adj., q.v.—8. See kid, n., 7.

kiddy, v.t. To hoax, humbug: low (1851) >, ca. 1880, ordinary s.; ob. Mayhew.

kiddy, adj. Fashionable, smart, showy, flash: low: ca. 1805–1900. Also, arrogant: nautical (— 1887); ob. Baumann. Moncrieff, 'That kiddy artist . . . the dandy habit-maker'; Dickens, 'In the celebrated "kiddy" or stage-coach way.'

*kiddy-ken. See kidden.

*kiddy-nipper. 'Taylors out of work, who cut off the waistcoat pockets of their brethren . . . thereby grabbling their bit', or money, says Grose, 1st ed.: c.: late C. 18–mid-19.

kiddyish. Stylish; somewhat showy: low: ca. 1815–60. 'Think of the kiddyish spree we had,' *Jack Randall's Diary*, 1820. Ex *kiddy*, adj.—2. Gay; frolicsome: low (— 1860); ob. H., 2nd ed.

kidknapper. A C. 17–18 form of *kidnapper*, q.v.

kidlet. See **kiddy**, n., 2, and **kid**, n., 1. Cf. :

***kidling.** A young thief, esp. if his father is in the same profession : c. of ca. 1820–60. 'Jon Bee', 1823.—2. A baby ; a little child : 1899 (O.E.D.) : s. verging on coll.

kidment. Humbug ; 'gammon', 'blarney': c. (— 1839) >, by 1860, low ; ob. Brandon.—2. Hence, a false story, a begging letter, etc. : c. : from ca. 1845.—3. Professional patter : cheapjacks' s. : from ca. 1850.—4. A pocket handkerchief, esp. 'one fastened to the pocket, and partially hung out to entrap thieves' : c. of ca. 1835–1910. Brandon ; H., 1st ed.—5. Hence, from ca. 1860, any inducement to crime : c. ; ob.

kidna, kitna. How much : Anglo-Indian (— 1864) ; ob. : coll. H., 3rd ed.

***kidnap.** To steal children : orig. (late C. 17), c. >, ca. 1750, s. >, ca. 1800, coll. >, ca. 1840, S.E. Ex *kid*, n., 1, + *nap* = *nab*, to steal. Recorded four years later than :

***kidnapper** ; occ. † **kidknapper**. A child-stealer, orig. one who sold the children he stole to the plantations in North America : 1678 (S.O.D.). In late C. 18 used also 'for all recruiting crimps', Grose. For rise in status, see back-formational **kidnap**.

kidney. As kind, class, disposition, S.E. (mid-C. 16–20) although ca. 1740–1890 it had a coll. tinge.—2. F. & H.'s second sense (a waiter) arises from a misunderstanding.—3. A fractional part of a shilling : Stock Exchange : from ca. 1890. Ex *Cadney*, the first broker known to deal under $\frac{1}{12}$.

kidney-hit. A punch in the short ribs : boxing : from ca. 1860.

kidney-pie. Insincere praise : New Zealanders' : from ca. 1912. Cf. *kid*, n., 5.

kids. Kid gloves : coll. : from ca. 1885. Baumann, 1887 ; in *Illustrated Bits*, July 13, 1889, a shop-dialogue runs : 'Certainly, miss . . . Some undressed kids.'—'Young man ! I only require gloves.'—2. The study of children's diseases ; 'the children's department in a hospital' : medical students' (— 1933). *Slang*, p. 192.

***kid's-eye.** A fivepenny piece : Scottish c. of ca. 1815–50. Haggart.

***kidsman.** One who teaches boys how to steal, esp. one who also boards and lodges them : c. of ca. 1835–1900. Brandon ; Baumann.

kie show. A wild-man or wild-beast show : grafters' : C. 20. Philip Allingham, *Cheapjack*, 1934. Origin ?

Kiel whale. 'A nauseous fish-meal, served . . . as a staple dish' : among British prisoners of war in Germany : 1915–18. F. & Gibbons.

kiff, all. All right ; all correct : military : 1915 ; ob. Gen. as an (emphatic) affirmative and prob. suggested by Fr. s. *kif-kif*, equal, similar, the same (esp. in *c'est kif-kif*, it makes no odds). B. & P., 3rd ed.

kift. A 'booze' (?) : Ayrshire s. : 1892, Hew Ainslie, *A Pilgrimage to the Land of Burns*, 'To . . . invite them all to that ancient hostelry for a "kift owre a chappin "' (E.D.D., Sup.).

kikimoreyism. 'Swank', 'side', pose : 1923, Manchon. Origin ? (I surmise an error.)

***kilkenny.** A frieze coat : late C. 17–early 19 : c. > low ca. 1760. B.E.—2. A penny : from ca. 1870. P.P., *Rhyming Slang*, 1932.

kill. A ruined garment : tailors' : from ca. 1860.

kill, v. See 'Moving-Picture Slang', § 3.—2. 'To hurt badly, put *hors de combat*,' Wrench :

Winchester College : C. 19–20. Prob. ex the Anglo-Irish use : cf. *kilt*, q.v.

kill, dressed (or got-up) **to.** See **dressed**.

kill-calf or **-cow**. A butcher ; a murderous ruffian ; a terrible person : coll. : ca. 1580–1750 : coll. quickly > S.E. ; extant in dial.—2. Also as adj., murderous. (Nares.)

kill-devil. Rum, esp. if new : mid-C. 17–20, ob. : coll. (orig. West Indian). Thus also in C. 18 America : see, e.g. W. E. Woodward, *Washington*, 1928.—2. A gun : C. 18. Ned Ward, 1703.

kill-priest. Port wine : provincial : late C. 18–20, ob. Grose, 1st ed. Cf. preceding.

kill that baby ! Turn out the spot-light : film-industry c.p. : from ca. 1930. A *baby* because it is only a small light.

kill-the-beggar. Inferior whiskey : Anglo-Irish : from ca. 1850. Cf. *kill-devil* and *-priest*.

kill the canary. To evade, or malinger at, work : bricklayers' (— 1909). Ware.

kill-time. A pastime ; a stop-gap : mid-C. 18–20 : coll. >, ca. 1890, S.E.—2. Also adj.

kill who ? Ca. 1870–1915, a proletarian c.p., 'satirical protest against a threat' (Ware).

killed off. Removed from (or lying under) the table because intoxicated : ca. 1805–1900. Bee, 1823, 'Borrowed from a phrase used of our brave defenders by Mr. Windham, minister-at-war' (William Windham, 1750–1810) ; Baumann.

killers. Eyes (never in singular) : Society s. of ca. 1775–1800. C. Whibley, in *Cap and Gown*, quotes one Mansell (1780) : 'Their eyes (in fine language . . . killers).'

killick. A petty officer's arm-badge : blue-jackets' : late C. 19–20. F. & Gibbons. It is shaped like an anchor or killick.

killing. Extremely funny : coll. : from ca. 1890. Prob. ex *killingly funny*.—2. The senses fascinating or irresistible (C. 17–20), exhausting (from mid-C. 19), despite F. & H., have always been S.E.

[**Kilmarnock-cowl** and **K. whittle**, listed by F. & H., are dial.]

kilo. Abbr. *kilogramme* : coll. : 1870, *The Daily News*, Dec. 2. (O.E.D.)—2. Abbr. *kilometer* : coll. : C. 20, esp. in G.W., by the soldiers, who rarely used it in sense 1.

kilt, ppl. adj. Killed (gen. as a gross exaggeration and merely = severely hurt, beaten, defeated): Anglo-Irish and jocular : C. 19–20. Marryat.

kilter, esp. in U.S. : see **kelter**.

kiltie (-y), or **K.** A Highland soldier : coll. : from late 1840's, orig. Scottish. E.D.D. ; J. Milne, *Epistles of Atkins*, 1902 ; B. & P. Ex their kilts. Cf. *Jock*.

kim kam (occ. hyphenated), adv. and adj. (In) the wrong way ; out of order : coll. : late C. 16–early 19, then dial. In Cotgrave and Shakespeare, *clean kam* ; North, 1740, *chim-cham*. (Apperson.) Prob. *clean* (wholly) *cam* (awry, crooked).

***kimbaw.** To cheat, trick ; esp. beat severely and then rob : c. of ca. 1690–1830. B.E., Ainsworth. Ex *a kimbo* (*akimbo*) : cf. (*to*) *cross*, q.v

***kin.** A thief ; *the kin*, thieves collectively : c. : C. 18. *A New Canting Dict.*, 1725.

***kinchen, kinchin.** A child ; a young boy (or girl), a young man : c. : from ca. 1600, though forty years earlier in combination. In C. 19–20, convicts' c. Ex Ger. *Kindchen*, a little child (S.O.D.). Cf. next three entries.

***kinchen-** (or **kinchin**) **co** (C. 16–18) or **cove** (C. 17–19). A boy brought up to stealing : c. : from ca.

1560. (Before C. 19, rare in *cove* form.) Harman, B.E., Lytton. See **co** and **cove**.—2. (Only as *k. cove*. Head, Grose.) A small man (cf. *kinchen*, q.v.) : c. of ca. 1660–1830.—3. A man who robs or kidnaps children : c. : C. 19.—4. See **kinchen-mort, 1**.

***kinchen** (or **-in**) **-lay**. The practice of robbing children : c. of ca. 1835–80. Dickens in *Oliver Twist*. Cf. *kid-lay* or *-rig*, q.v.

***kinchen-mort** or **-cove**. One of 'Beggars' children carried at their mother's backs,' Grose (2nd ed.), who, to distinguish from the second sense, adds *in slates*, i.e. in sheets : c. : ca. 1560–1830. Cf. *kinchen co(ve)*, q.v.—2. Also a young girl trained to thieve : mid-C. 18–early 19 c. Grose.

kincob. 'Uniform, fine clothes, rich embroidered dresses,' H., 3rd ed. : Anglo-Indian coll. : from ca. 1840 ; ob. Loosely ex proper sense, gold brocade (1712). Persian-Hindustani origin. See esp. Yule & Burnell.

kin'd. A satirical pronunciation (*kinned*) of *kind* : Society : late 1884, only. Ex Barrett's production of *Hamlet*, in which, in Oct., 1884, 'he made this reading, "A little more than kin and less than kin'd".' (Ware.)

kind. Adv., kindly : C. 17–20 : S.E. till ca. 1820, then coll. ; since ca. 1880, sol. Dickens, 1849.

kind-heart. A dentist : jocular coll. : ca. 1610–40. Jonson.

kind of. Adv., in a way, somewhat ; as it were : coll. : orig. (— 1800), U.S. ; anglicised ca. 1850, Dickens using it in *David Copperfield*. (Cf. *sort of*.) Often—this is a sol.—spelt *kinda, kinder*.

kind of (with pl. n. and v.), **these**. C. 16–20 ; S.E. till late C. 18, then coll., as Holcroft, 1799, 'These kind of barracks . . . are . . . more expensive' (O.E.D.).

kind of a sort of a. A coll. (gen. jocular) variation of *kind of a* and *sort of a*, themselves both coll. forms of *kind of, sort of* (e.g. *thing*).

kinda, kinder. See **kind of**.—2. Hence, *kinderway, in a* : somehow or other ; mediocrely. Manchon.

kindly, adv. Easily, readily, spontaneously, congenially : C. 15–20 ; S.E. till ca. 1880, then coll. —and dial.

[**kindness**, the sexual favour, is euphemistic S.E.]

King. King William's Town (on Buffalo River) : South African coll. : 1880. Pettman.—2. The steward in charge of this or that on a modern liner : nautical : C. 20. Bowen. Thus, *the linen king, the crockery king, the silver king*.—2. See **King Death**.

King-at-Arms. Incorrect for *King-of-Arms*, in heraldry : mid-C. 16–20. O.E.D.

King Coll. Colley Cibber (1671–1757), the actor-dramatist. Dawson.

King Death or **k. d.** Breath : C. 20. P. P., *Rhyming Slang*, 1932. Occ. abbr. to *King*.

King Dick. Admiral Sir Frederick *Richards* when he was First Sea Lord in the [eighteen-] nineties,' Bowen.—2. A brick : rhyming s. : late C. 19–20.

King Jog. Mr. Lambton when Lord Durham : ca. 1820–35. *The Creevey Papers*. Because he said that 'one can jog along on £40,000 a year.'

King John's men, one of. Occ. amplified with *eight score to the hundred*. A little under-sized man : late C. 18–19 : from ca. 1850, mainly nautical. Grose, 1st ed.

King Lear. An ear : from ca. 1870. P. P., *Rhyming Slang*, 1932. Contrast *King Death*.

king pin(, the). The leader ; most important

person : Australian (— 1916). C. J. Dennis. Perhaps ex ninepins.

kingdom come. The after-life : late C. 18–20 : s. >, ca. 1920, coll. Grose, 1st ed. ; Wolcot, 'The Parson frank'd their souls to kingdom-come.' Hence, *go, send, to k.c.*, to die, kill. Ex *thy kingdom come* in the Lord's Prayer (O.E.D.).

King's (or **Queen's**) **bad bargain**. See **bad bargain**.

King's-Bencher. A notable galley orator : nautical : mid-C. 19–early 20. Bowen. Cf. *bush lawyer*, q.v.

King's birthday, the. Pay day : military : from ca. 1908. F. & Gibbons.

king's books ; books or **history of the four kings**. A pack of cards : ca. 1650–1850 : coll. >, ca. 1800, S.E. Urquhart, Foote. Cf. *devil's books*, q.v.

***King's College.** The King's Bench Prison : c. late C. 18–mid-19. Grose, 3rd ed.

[**king's** or **queen's cushion** or **chair**. Ineligible because S.E.]

King's English, clip the. To be drunk : drinking s. (— 1745) >, ca. 1800, coll. ; † by 1890.

King's hard bargain. A late C. 19–20 variant of *King's bad bargain*. Bowen. Cf. *K.H.B.*

***King's** (or **Queen's**) **Head Inn**. Newgate Prison : c. of ca. 1690–1830. B.E. Also called *the Chequer Inn in Newgate Street*.—2. Any prison : c. : ca. 1790–1850.

king's horse, (you, he, etc.) shall have the. Ac.p. directed at a liar : ca. 1670–1840.

King's keys, the. Crowbars and hammers used to force locks and doors : legal : ca. 1810–60. Scott in *The Black Dwarf*.

King's man or **K.-m**. See **kingsman**.

King's Men, the. The 78th, from 1881 the Seaforth Highlanders : military coll. : C. 19–20 ; ob. F. & Gibbons. Ex a Gaelic motto : *Cuidich'r Rhi*, Help the King. Also *the Kingsmen*.

King's parade, the. The quarterdeck : naval : C. 19. Bowen. Ex the display made by the officers.

***King's** (or **Queen's**) **Pictures**. Money ; esp. coins : C. 17–20, ob. : c. >, ca. 1780, s. >, ca. 1850, coll. Brome, B.E., Grose. Also, in C. 19–20, *King's* (or *Queen's*) *portrait*.

King's plate. Fetters : low (— 1811) ; ob. by 1880, † by 1910. *Lex. Bal*.

King's whiskey. Customed whiskey (the illicit stuff being plain *whiskey*) : Anglo-Irish coll. : mid-C. 19–20.

Kingsley's Stand. The 20th Foot, in late C. 19–20 the Lancashire Fusiliers : military : late C. 18–20 ; ob. Their commander of 1754–69 was Wm. Kingsley ; despite heavy losses at Minden, the regiment volunteered for guard-duty the next day. F. & Gibbons.

kingsman. A handkerchief green-based, yellow-patterned : costermongers' (— 1851) ; ob. Mayhew ; 'The favourite coloured neckerchief of the costermongers,' F. & H. A very emphatic one is a *kingsman of the rortiest* († by 1910) : Ware.—2. (Gen. with capital *K*.) A member of King's College, Cambridge : Cambridge University (— 1852) : coll. >, ca. 1900, S.E.

Kingsmen, the. See **King's Men, the**.

Kingswood lion. An ass : ca. 1820–90 : coll. or s. Egan's Grose. Cf. *Jerusalem pony*, q.v.

***kinichin.** A rare C. 19 variant of *kinchen*. 'Ducange Anglicus.'

kink. A whim ; a mental twist : S.E. (The adj. *kinky* is U.S. coll.) But—2, as large number (of persons), it is Bootham School s., † by 1925.

kinkling. (Gen. pl.) A periwinkle : nautical : mid-C. 19–20. Bowen. By corruption. Also in Dorset dial. (— 1851) : E.D.D.

kins. A suffix, coll. in tendency, seen both in the euphemising of oaths (e.g. *bodikins*) and in diminutives (e.g. *babykins*). O.E.D. (Sup.).

kinyans. Spirituous liquor(s) : naval : ca. 1860–1910. Bowen. Origin ?

*****kip.** A brothel : 1766, Goldsmith, ' Tattering a kip '—wrecking a brothel—' as the phrase was, when we had a mind for a frolic ' : low (? orig. c.) : † by 1880, except in Dublin, where it has > s. Ex Danish *kippe*, a hut, a mean alehouse ; ? cf. Romany *kipsi*, a basket,—*kitchema*, an inn.—2. A bed ; a hammock : low (— 1879, perhaps orig. c.) and nautical. Cf. *doss*, *letty*, *lib(b)*, and *lig*, qq.v.— 3. A lodging or a lodging-house, a doss-house : low (— 1883). *Answers*, Jan. 31, 1891.—4. Sleep : unrecorded before C. 20 ; perhaps it arose in G.W., when it was much used by British soldiers.[—5. Grose's sense has always been S.E.]—6. ' A small chip used for tossing pennies in the occult game of two-up ', C. J. Dennis : late C. 19–20 : s. >, by 1920, coll. >, by 1930, j. Perhaps a corruption or a perversion of *chip*.

*****kip,** v. To play truant : low (? c.) : ca. 1815–60. Haggart.—2. To lodge ; sleep : c. : from ca. 1880. Barrère & Leland. Cf. *doss*, v., and :

kip down. To go to bed ; dispose oneself for, go to, sleep : a C. 20, mainly military, variant of *kip*, v., 2. B. & P.

*****kip-house, -shop.** A tramps' lodging-house : tramps' c. : resp. from ca. 1885 ; and (— 1932) : T. B. S. Mackenzie.—2. (*kip-shop* only.) A brothel : military : 1914 ; ob. B. & P. Cf. *knocking-shop*.

Kiplingism, gen. pl. (One of) the errors and/or solecisms in Dr. T. *Kipling's* ed. (1793) of the Codex Bezæ : Cambridge University coll. rather than s. : ca. 1794–1840. O.E.D. (Sup.).

kipper ; esp. **giddy kipper.** A person, esp. if young ; a child : C. 20. O.E.D. (Sup.). Cf. *queer fish*.—2. See next.—3. A tailoress help : tailors' (— 1933).

[**kipper** and **kips(e)y** in F. & H. are ineligible, but **kipper**, a stoker (from being roasted), is naval (— 1909) ; ob. Ware.]

kipsey. A house ; the home : low Australian (— 1916). C. J. Dennis. ? ex *kipsey*, a wicker-basket, influenced by *kip*, n., 3.

kirb. A brick : back s. (— 1859). H., 1st ed.

*****kirk,** v.i. To break into a house while its occupiers are at church : c. (— 1933). Charles E. Leach. See also **kirkling**.

kirk and a mill of, make a. To make the best of : C. 18.—2. To use as one wishes : C. 19–20. Galt. Both senses are Scots coll. (O.E.D.)

kirker is Scots > gen. coll. in *Auld Kirker* and *Free Kirker* : from ca. 1880. (The secession was in 1843.)

Kirke's (wrongly **Kirk's**) **Lambs.** The 2nd Foot, British Army : military : 1682 ; but in C. 19–20 merely historical. Ex its first colonel, Percy Kirke (d. 1691), and ex the Paschal Lamb on its colours.

*****kirkling ; cracking a kirk,** vbl.nn. Breaking into a dwelling while its occupants are at *kirk* or church : c. ; from ca. 1850. Cf. U.S. *****kirk-buzzer**.

kisky. Drunk ; stupid with drink : from ca. 1860 ; ob. Perhaps ex fuddled speech or ex Romany *kushto*, good (cf. *feel pretty good*) or else, as Baumann suggests, on *frisky* and *whiskey*.

kismisses. ' The raisins issued as rations in Indian waters ' : nautical : late C. 19–20. Bowen. ? ex Hindustani.

kiss. As the sexual favour, S.E.—2. ' A drop of wax by the side of the seal ' of a letter : coll. (mostly rural) : from ca. 1825 ; ob. Thackeray, Dickens.—3. (Gen. pl.) A full-stop : shorthand-typists' (— 1935).

[**kiss**, v. ; **kissing**, n. Whether sexual or of light touching in billiards : S.E.]

kiss-curl. A small curl lying on cheek or temple : coll. (in C. 20, S.E.) : from 1854, says Ware. *Punch*, 1856, ' those pastry-cook's girl's ornaments called kiss-curls '.

kiss-me-quick. A small bonnet, once fashionably worn on the back of the head : 1852 (O.E.D.) : coll. >, ca. 1890, S.E.—2. A ' kiss-curl ', q.v. : from ca. 1890 ; ob. : coll >, in C. 20, S.E.

kiss me, sergeant ! A military c.p. to a sergeant when unusually officious or to the orderly sergeant ordering ' Lights out ! ' : 1914–18. B. & P.

kiss my ——. See **a*se**. (Also as adj.) Cf. the old proverbs, *He that doth kiss and do no more, may kiss behind and not before* and *Kiss one where one sat on Saturday* (or *Sunday*). Apperson.

kiss my hand, as easy as. See **easy as damn it**.

kiss the Clink, the Counter. To be confined in the Clink (see **clink**, n.) or in the Counter prison : mid-C. 16–18 coll. J. Wall, Rowlands.

kiss the babe. To take a drink : bon viveurs' (— 1913) ; ob. A. H. Dawson's *Dict. of Slang*.

kiss the hare's foot. See **hare's foot**. (The following phrases defined by F. & H. are S.E. : *kiss the claws* (perhaps orig. coll.) or *hands*, to salute ; *kiss the dust*, to die or be defeated ; *kiss the post*, to be shut out.)

kiss the maid. To lose one's head in an early form of the guillotine : late C. 17–mid-18. B.E.

kiss the master. To hit the jack : bowls : ca. 1570–1660. Gosson.

kisser. The mouth : pugilists' (— 1860) >, ca. 1900, gen. low s. Cf. *kissing-trap*.—2. In pl., the lips : likewise pugilistic (— 1896) ; ob.

kisses. Shares in the Hotchkiss Ordnance Company : Stock Exchange : ca. 1890–1910.

kissing-crust. ' The soft-baked surface between two loaves ; also the under-crust in a pudding or pie,' F. & H. : coll. : 1708, W. King's *Art of Cookery* ; Barham, ' A mouldy piece of kissing-crust as from a warden pie.'

[**kissing-strings.** Bonnet-strings tied under the chin, ends loose : † S.E.]

kissing-time(, it's) ; or **half-past kissing-time(, it's time to kiss again).** A c.p. (— 1923) to children (continually) asking one what time it is. Manchon. —2. See **half-past . . .**

kissing-trap. The mouth : low and boxers' : from ca. 1850 ; ob. On *potato-trap*, q.v.

[**kist(-fu)-o'** whistles or **whustles,** an organ, is Scots dial.]

kistmutgar. See **kitmegar**.

kit. A dancing-master, a fiddler : ca. 1720–1830. Ex *kit*, a small fiddle formerly much used by dancing-masters. *A New Canting Dict.*—2. A set, collection of things or (rarely in C. 20) persons, esp. in *the whole kit* : coll. : 1785, Grose ; Shelley, in *Œdipus Tyrannus*, ' I'll sell you in a lump the whole kit of them ' (O.E.D.). Cf. the U.S. *whole kit and boodle*. Prob. ex the military sense.—3. **(the whole kit.)** In low C. 19–20 : *membrum virile* and *testes*.

Kitch, or k. A recruit in Lord Kitchener's New Army : military : late 1914–16. F. & Gibbons.

kitchen. The stomach (cf. *victualling office*, q.v.) : low coll. : from ca. 1850.—2. The female pudend : low : from ca. 1860.

***kitchen co, kitchen mort.** Awdelay's variants (1561) of *kinchen co(e)* and *kinchen mort*, qq.v.

[kitchen-Latin, -medicine or -physic, -stuff, despite F. & H., are S.E.]

***kitchener.** A thief haunting a 'thieves' kitchen ', q.v. : c. : from ca. 1840.

Kitchener wants you ! A military c.p. to a man selected for filthy, arduous or perilous work : 1915–16. B. & P. Ex a famous enlistment-poster.

Kitchener's mob. A late 1914–15 military coll. for ' the men who joined up in response to Lord Kitchener's Appeal, in Aug., 1914 ', F. & Gibbons. Cf. *Kitch*, q.v.

kitchenite. ' A loafing compositor frequenting the kitchen of the Compositors' Society house,' F. & H. : printers' : from ca. 1870.

kitching. Kitchen : sol. (— 1887). Baumann. (N.B., -*ing* is common, in illiterate speech, for -*en*, -*in*.)

kite, as a shark or sharper, or in gen. detestation, is S.E.—2. An accommodation bill ; a bill of exchange, esp. if worthless : commercial : 1805 (S.O.D.). Hence *fly a kite*, to ' raise the wind ' by such bills.—3. Hence, a cheque : esp. a blank or a worthless cheque : c. : C. 20. Edgar Wallace, in *The Gunner*, 1928 ; Charles E. Leach, in *On Top of the Underworld*, 1933 ; David Hume, *The Gaol Gates Are Open*, 1935. See also **kite lark**.—(4. As a recruiting sergeant, it is F. & H.'s error.)—5. Any type of aircraft : Royal Air Force : from ca. 1919.

kite, v. To move like a kite through the air ; also fig. : coll. : 1863, Le Fanu, ' He has been " kiting " all over the town ' (O.E.D.)—2. V.i, same as *fly a kite* : see **kite**, n., 2 : from ca. 1860 : commercial.—3. As v.t., to convert into an accommodation bill, it is not very gen. : from ca. 1900 : commercial.

kite, blow out the. To have a full stomach : Cockneys' (— 1909). ; ob. Ware.

kite, fly a. See **kite**, n., 2 : 1805 ; app. orig. Anglo-Irish.—2. As to put out a feeler, it is later and S.E.—3. See **kite-flying**, 2.

***kite, pull a.** To make a face, a grimace : c. (— 1887). Baumann.

kite-flyer. One who raises money or maintains credit by the issuing of bills of exchange and/or accommodation : commercial : from ca. 1830. See **kite**, n., 2.—2. Hence, a passer of worthless cheques : c. (— 1935). David Hume.

kite-flying. The vbl.n. corresponding to the preceding senses 1 and 2 : resp. from ca. 1820 and in C. 20.—2. Whoremongering : low : ca. 1820–60. ' Jon Bee '.

***kite-lark.** (With *lark*, cf. the c. senses of *law* and *lay*.) ' Stealing letters in transit, removing any cheques they may contain, and, after suitable manipulation, cashing them at the banks ' : c. : C. 20. A gang that operates this ' racket ' is known as a *kite mob*. Charles E. Leach, *On Top of the Underworld*, 1933. See **kite**, n., 3.

***kite-man.** A crook specialising in cheques and bills of exchange : from ca. 1920. (See **kite**, n., 2, 3.) E.g. Edgar Wallace in *The Double*, 1928.

***kite-mob.** See **kite lark**.

***kites.** The practice of forging cheques, and/or issuing cheques against a merely nominal bank-

balance : c. : C. 20. James Curtis, *The Gilt Kid*, 1936. Ex *kite*, n., 3.

kitmegur. An under-butler, a footman : Anglo-Indian (Bengal) coll. : from ca. 1750. More correctly *kitmutgar* or *khedmutgar*, *khid-* ; *kistmutgar* is an † sol. Yule & Burnell.

kitna. See **kidna**.

***kitten.** A pint or half-pint pewter pot : c. : from ca. 1850 ; ob. See **cat and kitten**.

kitten, to. To be brought to bed of a child : low coll. : C. 19–20.

Kitties, the. The Scots Guards : military : from ca. 1840 ; ob.—2. (Also **kittys**.) Effects, furniture, stock : s. or coll. : late C. 18–mid-19. Grose, 3rd ed.

[kittie (or kittock) and kittle-breeks, in F. & H., are ineligible.]

kittle cargo. A clergyman : nautical s. (— 1923) verging on coll. Manchon. Ex necessity to mind one's language.

kittle-pitchering. ' A jocular method of hobbling or bothering a troublesome teller of long stories ' (Grose, 1st ed.) by constant inquiries about minor points : ca. 1780–1850.

kitty. The prison at Durham ; hence, esp. in the North of England, any prison : 1825 : s. and dial. Hone. ? ex *kid-cote*.—2. In card games, the pool : 1892, *The Daily Chronicle*, March 5 : coll. >, in C. 20, S.E.—3. A pet-name form of *kitten* : C. 18–20 : coll. till C. 19, then S.E.—4. for *kittys*, pl. only, see **kitties**.—5. (**Kitty**.) The inevitable naval, hence military, nickname of any man surnamed Wells : late C. 19–20. Bowen. Ex some naval celebrity or ' character '.

kivey. A man, fellow, chap : from ca. 1850 ; ob.: low. Bradley, in *Verdant Green*. This diminutive of *cove* (see also **covey**) was possibly influenced by L. *civis*, a citizen.

Kiwi, kiwi. ' A man on ground duty and not qualified for flying service ' : Air Force : 1917 ; ob. F. & Gibbons, ' From the name of the flightless bird of New Zealand.'

kiwi (or Kiwi) king. ' Any officer fussy about polish ' : military : 1916–18. B. & P. Ex ' A well-known dressing for leather.'

klaar. Ready (1852) ; clear (— 1912) : South African coll. Ex Dutch *klaar*, which is used in both these senses. Pettman.

klep. A thief : from ca. 1880. A somewhat low abbr. of *kleptomaniac*.

klep, v. To steal : from ca. 1885 ; ob. Ex. the preceding.

klip. A diamond : South African diamond fields' s. >, by 1920, coll. : from the middle 1880's. Matthews, *Incwadi Yami*, 1887. Ex Cape Dutch *klip*, a rock, a pebble. Pettman. Cf. :

klip, v. To put a stone behind (a wheel) to prevent a vehicle from running backwards : South African coll. : 1878, Roche, *On Trek in the Transvaal*. For origin, cf. the n. Pettman.

klobber. See **clobber**.

klondyke. Money easily obtained : Glasgow (— 1934). Cf. *bonanza* for semantics.

klondyke, adj. Mad : lower classes' : 1897–ca. 1914. Ware. Ex Klondyke gold-fever.

kloop. A coll. imitation of a cork being drawn : from ca. 1870.

Klosh. See **Closh**. (Bowen.)

kn-. Common to the Teutonic languages, but, in S.E., silent since C. 17. In C. 20 ' there has been a s. tendency to reintroduce the *k*- sound in *knut*,

Knightsbridge ', W. Cf. *ker*, q.v., and the jocular pronunciation (connotative also of emphasis) of *twenty* as *ter-twenty*.

knab, knap, and compounds. See **nab, nap,** etc. But see also **knap.**

[**knack.** A trick, a trinket, etc., is S.E., while F. & H.'s definition as penis is almost certainly an error ; *knack-shop* also is S.E.]

knacker. An old and worn-out horse : coll. ex dial. : from ca. 1858. H., 1st ed. ; W. Bradwood. —2. As a horse-slaughterer, it is S.E.

***knacker** ; gen. in passive. To kill ; ruin : c. or perhaps merely low s. (— 1887). Baumann. Ex sense 2 of the preceding.—2. (Rare except as *knackered*, ppl. adj.) To rob (a person) of something : Conway cadets' (— 1891). J. Masefield, *The Conway*, 1933.

knackers. The testicles, occ. of animals : low : C. 19–20. Prob. ex dial *knacker*, a castanet or other ' striker '.—2. The shares of Harrison, Barber & Co., Ltd. (horse-slaughterers) : Stock Exchange : ca. 1890–1910. A. J. Wilson, *Stock Exchange Glossary*.

knap. A cheating trick at dice : ca. 1650–1720 : ? orig. c. > j. > S.E. ' Hudibras ' Butler. (O.E.D.)—2. ' A manual retort rehearsed and arranged,' F. & H. : theatre : ca. 1850–1900.

knap, to strike crisply, is S.E.—2. Its other senses, receive, endure, steal, all derive from that of ' to take ' : c. or low : from ca. 1810. Vaux ; H., 1864, ' Oh, my ! won't he just knap it if he can ! ', i.e. take anything if there's a chance. (Cf. the Whitby *knap*, a person not strictly honest.) In combination :—*knap a clout*, to steal a handkerchief ; *knap the swag*, to grab the booty ; *knap seven penn'orth*, to be sentenced to seven years : all being c.

knap, give or **take the.** To give or to get a sham blow : ca. 1850–1900.

***knap a jacob from a danna-**(or **-dannaken-, dunnigen-)drag.** To steal a ladder from a night-cart : c. : ca. 1810–90. Vaux ; Egan's Grose.

knap a hot un. To receive a hard punch : boxing : from ca. 1820 ; ob.

Knap is concerned, Mr. ; Mr. Knap's been there. She is pregnant : low : ca. 1810–1910. Vaux, 1812 ; Egan's Grose, 1823.

***knap the glim.** To catch a ' clap ', q.v. : c. : from ca. 1810 ; ob. Vaux.

***knap the rust.** To become (very) angry : c. : from ca. 1810 ; † by 1910.

knap the stoop. To be made ' inspector of the pavement ', q.v. : c. : ca. 1820–70.

knapped, be. To be pregnant : low : ca. 1820–90. Egan's Grose.

knapper. The head : low : from ca. 1840. Because the ' receiver general ', q.v.—2. (Rare in singular.) The knee : from ca. 1760 : since ca. 1820, dial. : ob. T. Brydges. (O.E.D.)

***knapper's poll.** A sheep's head : late C. 18–early 19 c. Grose, 2nd ed.

***knapping-jigger.** A turnpike or toll gate : c. of ca. 1830–95. Ainsworth.

***knapping-jigger, dub at the.** To pay at the turnpike : c. (— 1859) ; † by 1900. H., 1st ed.

Knap's been there, Mr. See **Knap is concerned.**

knapsack descent. A soldier or soldiers in every generation of a family : non-aristocratic coll. : late C. 19–20. Ware.

knark. A ca. 1850–1900 variant of *nark*, q.v. Mayhew ; Baumann.

knat. A hard task ; a tyrant ; a person not

easily fooled : tailors' : from ca. 1860 ; ob. ? the perversion—or the survival of an † form—of *gnat*.

knave. A dunce : Christ's Hospital : from ca. 1820 ; ob.

knave in grain. A late C. 18–mid-19 jocular coll. for a corn-factor, a miller. Grose, 2nd ed.

knave's grease. A flogging : C. 17 jocular coll. Withals's Dict.

knealing is C. 18–20 erroneous for *ncaling*, an old form of *annealing*. Cf. † *kneck*, possibly erroneous for *kink* ; † *knede* for *need* ; *knevel* for *kevel*. O.E.D.

knee, break one's. To be deflowered ; made pregnant : coll. : C. 19–20 ; ob.

[**knee, give** or **offer a,** is S.E., as also is F. & H.'s *knee-trick*.]

knee-drill. Kneeling, to order, for prayers : Salvation Army j. (1882) >, ca. 1895, jocular coll., gen. used loosely as = praying. Ware.

knee-high to a(n) . . . Very small or young, esp. in *knee-high to a mosquito* or *a duck* : orig. (1824), U.S. ; anglicised ca. 1890. Thornton.

knee-trembler. A standing sexual embrace : low coll. : from ca. 1850.

knees, sit on one's. To kneel down : coll. : C. 19–20.

kneller. See **knuller.**

knick-knack, trinket, is S.E. ; female pudend, low, C. 19–20.

knickers. Men's knickers ; women's drawers : a coll. abbr. of *knickerbockers* : 1881 (S.O.D.).

***knickers and stockings.** A term of penal servitude : c. (— 1932). ' Stuart Wood ', *Shades of the Prison House*.

knicks. Women's drawers : C. 20. Abbr. *knickers*, q.v.

knife. A sword : M.E.–mod. E. : literary till C. 19, when it > military coll. (—2. As = to stab, it is, despite F. & H., ineligible ; as = to strike at secretly, it is American.)—3. A shrew : lowest London : C. 19. Ware, ' Suggestive of being " into you " in a moment.'—4. To ' blue-pencil ' (a manuscript) : theatrical : ca. 1880–1915. Ware. Punning *cut*.

' **knife** ', before one can or could say. Very quickly, swiftly, or suddenly : coll. : 1880, Mrs. Parr, *Adam and Eve* ; ' Rolf Boldrewood ' ; Kipling. O.E.D. Cf. *Jack Robinson* . . ., q.v.

knife and fork, lay down one's. To die : low coll. : from ca. 1860. (S.E., however, is *play a good knife and fork*.)

knife and fork tea. High tea : lower-middle class's coll. : 1874 ; slightly ob. Ware.

knife-board. A seat running lengthways on the roof of an omnibus : 1852 (S.O.D.) : coll. >, ca. 1890, S.E. Leech's cartoon in *Punch*, May 15, 1852 (O.E.D.).

knife it. To decamp ; esp. as imperative, stop !, go away !, run ! : low (— 1812) ; ob. Vaux ; H., 1st ed. Cf. *cut it out !*

knifer. A sponging shark : low : from ca. 1890 ; ob. F. & H.—2. A rough apt to stab with a knife : low (— 1905). O.E.D. (Sup.)

knifey. (Of a person, esp. a customer) that cuts things painfully fine when dealing in the money-market : stockbrokers' (— 1935).

kniff-knaff. Some kind of jest : ca. 1680–1700. E. Hooker. (O.E.D.)

knifish. Spiteful : tailors' : from ca. 1860 ; ob.

knight and barrow pig. ' More hog than gentleman. A saying of any low pretender to precedency,' Grose. 1st ed. : c.p. of ca. 1780–1840.

knight of the . . . ' Forming various jocular (formerly often slang) phrases denoting one who is a member of a certain trade or profession, has a certain occupation or character, etc.', O.E.D. Most are ironical (cf. *carpet-knight*, q.v.) and orig. were, prob., derisive, of the many sets or classes of knights and/or of the various orders of knighthood. Some are c., some s., some coll., some S.E., even literary, and long demoded. A few arose in C. 16, many in C. 17–18 ; the numerous C. 19 additions are s. or coll. ; the practice is, fortunately, †. The principal phrases—drawn from F. & H. and O.E.D. —are these :—**blade**, a bully : late C. 17–18 : c. > s. —**brush**, an artist (— 1885) : coll. ; also, a house-painter : jocular coll. : from ca. 1890 ; ob.— **cleaver**, a butcher : jocular coll. : from ca. 1870 ; ob.—**collar**, one who has been hanged : ca. 1550– 1660.—**cue**, a billiard-marker : jocular coll. : 1887 (O.E.D.) ; ob.—**elbow**, a sharping gambler : late C. 17–mid-18.—**field**, a tramp : C. 16–early 17.— **forked order** or (without the) **Hornsey** : jocular : resp. ca. 1660–1750, ca. 1630–1700. (Contrast *order of the fork*, below.)—**grammar**, a schoolmaster : perhaps merely literary : ca. 1690–1740.—**green cloth**, a gambler : orig. (— 1881), U.S. ; anglicised ca. 1885 ; ob.—**Hornsey.** See **forked order.**—**industry (the** being occ. omitted) : from ca. 1650 : prob. literary. Fr. *chevalier d'industrie.*—**jemmy**, a burglar : Society : late C. 19–early 20. Ware.— **knife**, a cutpurse : C. 17. Jonson.—**lapstone**, a cobbler : jocular coll. : C. 19–20 ; ob.—**napkin**, a waiter : from ca. 1850 : jocular ; ob.—**needle**, **shears, thimble**, a tailor : resp. 1778, Foote ; from ca. 1780, Grose (1st ed.) ; late C. 18–20, Grose, 1st ed. All orig. jocular s. or coll. but by 1860, almost S.E.—**order of the fork**, one who digs with a fork : jocular coll. : from ca. 1620. J. Taylor the Water Poet. Contrast *forked order*, above.—**pen**, a clerk or (cf. *quill*) an author : from ca. 1860 ; ob. : resp. jocular coll. and near-literary.—**pencil**, a bookmaker : jocular : from ca. 1880 ; ob. or †.— **pestle**, an apothecary : C. 17–20 ; ob. : jocular coll. —**petticoat**, a brothel's bully : low coll. : ca. 1880– 1910.—**piss-pot**, a physician or an apothecary : from ca. 1860 ; ob.—**pit**, a fancier of cock-fighting : from ca. 1870 ; ob. : jocular coll. or perhaps journalistic.—**post**, a notorious and/or a professional perjurer : from ca. 1580 ; ob. : c. till ca. 1750, then s. ; since ca. 1840, S.E. Also, *the K. of the P.*, Titus Oates of the Popish Plot : C. 17. (The most widely used of all.) Nashe, Ford, Mrs. Centlivre, W. T. Moncrieff. ? ex (*fit for*) the *whipping-post.* F. & H.'s other sense is suspect : see **whipping-post** and **knighted in Bridewell.**—**quill**, an author : late C. 17–20 ; ob. : coll. soon > S.E.— **rainbow**, a footman : ca. 1780–1880. Grose, 1st ed. —**road**, a highwayman, esp. a notable one : from ca. 1660 : c. till ca. 1750, then s. ; from ca. 1840, S.E. and literary. In C. 19, occ. a footpad, and in C. 20 a tramp. In late C. 19–20, occ. a ' commercial ', O.E.D. (Sup.).—**rumpad**, the same : c. : ca. 1815–40. Moore.—**shears.** See **needle.**— **spigot**, tapster or publican : from ca. 1820 ; ob. : jocular coll. Scott.—**sun**, an adventurer : literary : from ca. 1720 ; † by 1910. Punning the *Knights of the Golden Sun*, an order of chivalry.—**thimble.** See **needle.**—**trencher.** A good trencher-man : from ca. 1780 : jocular. Grose, 2nd ed.—**vapour**, a smoker : C. 17 ; perhaps a nonce-word (Taylor the Water Poet).—**wheel**, a cyclist : prob. S.E. : from ca. 1880 ; ob.—**whip**, a coachman : from ca. 1810 ;

ob. : jocular s. > coll. Bee.—**whipping-post**, a disreputable person, esp. a sharper : ca. 1815–60. Scott.—**yard**, a shop-assistant : ca. 1885–1910.

knighted in Bridewell or **bridewell, be.** To be whipped in prison : late C. 16–17. Cf. *knight of the post* and *the whipping-post*, qq.v.

Knight's. Shares in the Witswatersrand Mining Company : Stock Exchange (— 1895). A. J. Wilson, *Stock Exchange Glossary.*

knights, be the guest of the cross-legged. To go dinnerless : C. 18–early 19. Ex the effigies in the Round Church (in the Temple, London), a rendezvous of hungry men looking for jobs from the lawyers and their clients. Cf. *dine with Duke Humphrey.*

knit it ! Stop ! ; ' shut up ! ' : Glasgow (— 1934).

knitting-needle. A sword : military : ca. 1850– 1910. Cf. *tooth-pick*, q.v.

knob. The head : from ca. 1720. Hence, *one on the knob*, a blow on the head (Grose). Gen. *nob.*— 2. Abbr. *knobstick*, q.v. : 1838 (S.O.D.).—3. A ' nob ' or ' big wig ' : see **nob** in that sense. Cf. : —4. An officer : naval : ? mid-C. 17–mid-19. Bowen, ' Apparently introduced into the British service with the amalgamation with the Scottish Navy.'

knob, v. To hit : 1818 : from ca. 1815. Prob. ex *hit on the knob.*

knob of suck. A piece of sweetmeat : provincial : C. 19–20 ; ob.

knob on to. To pay court to ; fall in love with : Cockney (— 1887) ; slightly ob. Baumann.

knobs, make no. Not to hesitate or be scrupulous : coll. : ca. 1670–1770.

knobs on !, (the) same to you with. The same to you—only more (so) : from ca. 1910. B. & P. Ex :

knobs on, with, adj. Embellished ; generous.— 2. Adv., with embellishments ; with interest, forcibly. Both, C. 20. Ex *knob* = excrescence = ornament.

knobstick ; occ. **nobstick.** A non-unionist ; a workman that takes less than the agreed price or one who works while his fellows are on strike : workmen's : from ca. 1825 ; ob. : s. >, ca. 1870, coll. >, ca. 1900, S.E.—2. A master paying less than union wages : workmen's : from ca. 1850 : s. >, ca. 1880, coll. >, ca. 1905, S.E. Mayhew.

knock. A copulation : low coll. : C. 16–17. See the v.—2. The penis : C. 18–20. More gen. *knocker.*—3. A lame horse : horse-dealers' : from ca. 1860. *The London Review*, June 18, 1864, ' The knock . . . is a great favourite for horse-coping purposes, as he is often a fine-looking animal.'—4. An innings : cricketers' coll. : from ca. 1919. E.g. *The Daily Express*, May 13, 1935, ' Nourse's perfect knock.'

knock, v.t. and **i.** (Of a man) to have sexual intercourse (with) : low coll. : late C. 16–20. Florio, ' *Cunnata*, a woman nocked.' See **nock**, n., for possible etymology, and cf. the mainly U.S. *knocked-up*, pregnant.—2. To rouse or summon one by knocking at his door, v.t. : coll. : C. 18–19. Abbr. C. 19–20 S.E. *knock up.*—3. To astound, alarm, confuse ; to ' floor ' : coll. : from ca. 1715 ; ob. except in *that knocks me !*, that confounds or is too much for me.—4. To impress greatly, to ' fetch ', to surprise : 1883, *The Referee*, May 6, ' " It's never too Late to Mend " . . . is knocking 'em at the Pavilion'. Cf. Chevalier's song title, 1892, *Knocked*

'Em in the Old Kent Road.—5. See **knock about.**—
6. V.i., to welsh : racing c. (— 1932). Prob. ex
sense 3.

knock, get the. To drink too much, become
drunk : from ca. 1860 ; ob.—2. To be dismissed
from employment : from ca. 1860 ; ob. Cf. *get the
sack.*

knock, take the. To lose to the bookmakers
more than one can pay : the turf (— 1890).
Hence, from ca. 1895, to suffer a financial loss.—
2. To be drunk : C. 20. Manchon.

knock about, v.i. To wander much, roam, gen.
aimlessly : coll. : from ca. 1850. Mayhew, ' I've
been knocking about on the streets.' In C. 20,
however, one can say, e.g. ' He's knocked about the
world for many years,' where *knock = knock about,*
v.i. From ca. 1880, also *knock (a)round.*—2. To
pass round, esp. in *knock about the bub* (drink) :
low (— 1781) ; ob. G. Parker.

knock-about, adj. Noisy and violent (e.g.
comedians) : theatre : 1891.—2. The n., a ' knock-
about ' performer or performance, is recorded four
years earlier.—3. Abbr. of next.

knock-about man or **hand.** A handy man :
Australian coll. : from ca. 1875. W. Harcus, 1876,
' Knockabout hands, 17s. to 20s. per week.' Also
(— 1889) *knock(-)about.* Cf. *rouseabout,* q.v.
(Morris.)

knock about spare. (Gen. as p. ppl.) To have
nothing particular to do : military coll. : G.W.
(B. & P.)

knock acock. To ' floor ' ; astound : coll. :
C. 19. See **cocked hat.**

knock all of a heap. See **heap.**

knock along. An Australian variation (com-
mented-on in the Tichborne case, 1874) of *knock-
about,* v.i. ; very ob. Ware.

knock at the cobbler's door. See **cobbler's
knock.**

knock-back. A refusal ; a grave disappointment : coll., esp. Australian : C. 20.

knock bandy. To astound, ' flabbergast ' :
tailors' : from ca. 1860.

knock (or let) daylight into. See **daylight.**

knock-down. Strong liquor : late C. 17–19.
B.E. In mid-C. 18–20, but ob., *knock-me-down,*
Grose, 1st ed.—2. An introduction : Australian :
C. 20. Cf. v., last sense. C. J. Dennis. Ex U.S.

knock down, v. To call upon, nominate, urgently
invite : coll. ; slightly ob. : 1759, Goldsmith,
' . . . Had knocked down Mr. Spriggins for a song '
(O.E.D.). But *knock down for a song,* to sell very
cheaply, is S.E.—2. To reduce considerably in
amount or degree : coll. : from ca. 1865. E.g.
to knock down prices, colours.—3. To spend in
drink or other riotous living : Australia : 1869,
Marcus Clarke, ' Knocked down thirteen notes, and
went to bed as light as a fly.' Morris.—4. To introduce (one person to another) : C. 20 Australian
ex (— 1896) U.S.

knock 'em down. To gain applause : proletarian
(— 1887). Baumann.

knock-'em-down business. Auctioneering : low
coll. : from ca. 1860.

knock-'em-downs ; k.-me-d. A coco-nut shy :
coll. : from ca. 1825. Bee. Loosely, skittles :
from ca 1860.

knock for six. To overcome drastically, foil
utterly, inconvenience gravely : from ca. 1899.
' It knocked me for six ' is a Tommy's description
of a knee-wound in the Boer War : J. Milne, *The*

Epistles of Atkins, 1902. J. C. Masterman, *An
Oxford Tragedy,* 1933 ; A. Berkeley, 1934 (see
quotation at *crashing bore*). Ex cricket.

knock-in. The game of loo ; a hand at cards :
from ca. 1860 : low s. > coll.—2. The same as
knock-out, n., 1.

knock in, v.i. To return to college after the gate
is closed : university : 1825, C. M. Westmacott.—
2. To join in (cf. *chip in*) a game of cards : clubmen's and gamblers' : from ca. 1860.—3. To make
money : costermongers' (— 1909). Ware. I.e., into the pocket.

knock in the cradle. A fool ; but gen. as *to have
got a knock . . .,* be a fool. Coll. : ca. 1670–1850.
Resp. B.E., Ray.

knock into a cocked hat. See **cocked hat.**—
knock into fits. See **fits.**—**knock into** (gen. **the
middle of) next week.** See **week.**—**knock spots off**
or **out of.** See **spots.** These four = to defeat
utterly, be much better than : C. 19–20. The first
and second are coll., the others s.

knock it back (invariable). To eat ; occ. to
drink : mostly military : from ca. 1912. B. & P.

knock it down. To applaud by hammering or
stamping : low : from ca. 1860 ; ob.

knock it out of one. To exhaust ; punish
severely : coll. >, ca. 1910, S.E. *Punch,* 1841,
' The uphill struggles . . . soon knock it all out
of him.'

knock-me-down. See **knock-down,** n., 1.—2. As
adj., violent, overpowering, overbearing : coll. :
1760, Foote, 'No knock-me-down doings in my
house.' (O.E.D.)

knock-me-downs. See **knock-'em-downs.**

knock-off. Time to leave off work : C. 20 coll.
Abbr. *knock-off time.*

knock off. Two of F. & H.'s senses—v.t., to
deduct, and v.i., to cease (esp. work)—are S.E.—
2. To die : C. 18–20 ; very ob. Tom Brown in a
letter of 1704.—3. To complete or despatch easily
or hastily : coll. : from ca. 1815. Peacock ; *The
Pall Mall Gazette,* Nov. 29, 1891, ' A specimen of the
" consumptive manner " as knocked off by Mr.
Lang.'—4. Hence, to steal : nautical (C. 20) >
military in 1915. Bowen. Cf. S.E. sense, to
deduct.—5. To do, commit, esp. in *knock off a job,*
to commit a crime : c. (— 1932). Anon., *Dartmoor
from Within.* Ex sense 3.—6. To arrest (a person) :
c. (— 1933). Charles E. Leach, *On Top of the
Underworld.*

knock off corners. To be successful : music-
halls' : ca. 1880–1914. Ware cites *Entr'Acte,*
April 16, 1885 : ' Just as Arthur Williams had commenced to " knock corners off " at the music hall,
he is once more summoned to the Gaiety. More
study ! '

***knock-off, on the ;** adj. and adv. A-thieving
in any way : c. : from ca. 1925. James Curtis,
The Gilt Kid, 1936.

[**knock on the head,** to frustrate or kill, is S.E.]

knock-out ; occ. (— 1860) **knock-in.** One who,
at auctions, combines with others (hence, also, the
combination) to buy at nominal prices : from ca.
1850 : coll. >, in C. 20, S.E. Ex :—2. **knock-out,**
an illegal auction : from ca. 1820 : coll. >, ca. 1890,
S.E. ' Jon Bee.' (These auction senses are also used
as adjj.)—3. Applied in admiration, or by way of
outraged propriety, to a person, esp. one who does
outrageous things ; also to an astounding or outrageous thing. Chiefly as *a regular knock-out.*
From ca. 1894. Perhaps ex boxing, a *knock-out*

being a champion, but more prob. ex *knocker*, 3, q.v.—4. As a knock-out blow, it is S.E.

knock out, v. Corresponding to the n., senses 1 and 2 : from ca. 1870 : coll. >, ca. 1905, S.E.—2. To make (very) quickly or roughly : coll. : from ca. 1855. Dickens, Hardy. (O.E.D.)—3. Hence, **to earn** : Colonial : from ca. 1895. Ex *knock up*, fifth sense, q.v.—4. To render bankrupt : from ca. 1890. —5. To leave a college by knocking at the gate after it has been shut : university : from ca. 1860. Cf. *knock in*, v., 1.—6. ' To bet so persistently against a horse that from a short price he retires to an outside place,' F. & H. ; to force out of the racing quotations : from ca. 1870 : mostly the turf. (—7. To defeat : S.E.)—8. To fail (a candidate) in an examination : late C. 19–20. Ex boxing.

knock out drops. A liquid drug—gen. butyl-chloride—' put in liquor to facilitate robbing ' : U.S. (1876), anglicised ca. 1904 : low. (O.E.D. Sup.) H. C. Bailey, *Mr. Fortune Wonders*, 1933, ' "Chloral hydrate " . . . "That stuff ! Knock-out drops. The common thieves' dope for putting a man to sleep ".'—2. In Australia, ' drugged or impure liquor ' : from ca. 1910. C. J. Dennis.

knock out an apple. To beget a child : 1818, Keats in a letter of Jan. 5 ; † by 1890. (Thanks to Allen Walker Read.)

knock out of time, v.t. To punch so hard that one's opponent cannot rise at ' Time ' : boxers' : from ca. 1880 : s. >, ca. 1890, coll. >, ca. 1910, S.E.

knock-outs. Dice : gamblers' s. : from ca. 1850.

knock over, v.i. To give way ; to die : from ca. 1890 : s. >, ca. 1905, coll. ; ob.

knock round. See **knock about**, v., 1.

knock saucepans or **smoke out of.** To attack violently ; gen., however, to defeat utterly : Australia : ca. 1885–1905. ' Rolf Boldrewood ', both uses in *Robbery under Arms*.

knock-softly. A fool ; a simpleton ; a too easy-going person : coll. : 1864 ; ob.

knock spots off. See the group at *knock into a cocked hat.*

knock the bottom (or **filling** or **inside** or **lining** or **stuffing** or **wadding**) **out of.** To confound, defeat utterly ; render useless, valueless, or invalid : coll. : resp. 1875, ca. 1880, ca. 1890, ca. 1890, 1889, ca. 1895. The O.E.D. compares *it won't hold water.* Cf. :

knock the end in (gen. v.i.) or **off** (gen. v.t.). To ' spoil the whole show ' : military : 1915. F. & Gibbons. Ex preceding.

knock-toe. A ' Deal lugger-rigged galley-punt, in which there was little room for the feet ' : nautical : C. 19. Bowen.

[**knock under**, abbr. *k.u.* (*the*) *board*, despite F. & H., is S.E.]

knock up. To exhaust, become exhausted, is S.E., as are to rouse by knocking at the door, to put together hastily.—2. To gain, in class, a place (v.i. and v.t., e.g. ' He knocked Jones up ') : Christ's Hospital : from ca. 1830. Cf. *ox up*, q.v.— 3. Make (so many runs) by hitting : cricket coll. : 1860 (Lewis). Ex :—4. To earn : coll. : from ca. 1885. Cf. *knock out*, v., 3.—5. See **knocked up**, its only part.—6. To arrange (e.g. a dance) : (low) coll. (— 1887). Baumann.

knock up a catcher ; gen. **to have knocked up** . . . To be put on an easy job : dockers' : from ca. 1921. (*The Daily Herald*, late July or early Aug., 1936.) Ex cricket.

knock-upable. Easily fatigued : coll. : from ca. 1870. George Eliot. (Ware.)

knockabout, n. and adj. See **knock-about.**

knocked, wounded ; **knocked cold**, killed : New Zealanders' and Australians' : in G.W., and diminishingly afterwards.

knocked off one's pins. Flabbergasted : coll. (— 1880). Trollope.

knocked out. Unable to meet engagements : commercial coll. : from ca. 1860.

knocked up. Exhausted : see **knock up**, 1.—2. Pregnant : low : C. 19–20 ; mainly U.S. Ex *knock*, v., 1.

knocked up a catcher(, to have). (To be) de-tected, found out : mostly military (— 1914). F. & Gibbons. See **catcher.**—2. See **knock up a catcher.**

Knocker. An ' inevitable ' nickname of men surnamed Walker or White : naval and military : late C. 19–20. Ibid.

knocker. A (notable or frequent) performer of the sexual act : C. 17–20 ; ob. : low coll. Barry, in *Ram Alley.*—2. The penis : from ca. 1650 ; ob. : low (? coll.).—3. One of striking appearance : C. 17–19. Whence *knock-out*, n., 3.—4. A (kind of) pendant to a wig : ca. 1818–38. (O.E.D.)—5. A person given to discouraging or fault-finding : coll., orig. (ca. 1910) U.S., partly anglicised ca. 1927. O.E.D. (Sup.).—6. A person taken by the police : tramps' c. (— 1932). Frank Jennings, *Tramping with Tramps.*—7. A person that contracts debts without the intention to repay them : Glasgow (— 1934).

knocker, on the ; **knocker-worker.** Resp. adj. (or adv.) and n. applied to one who sells things by going from door to door : low s., esp. grafters' : C. 20. Philip Allingham, *Cheapjack*, 1934. He is constantly using the door-knocker.

knocker, up to the. (Very) healthy, fit, or fashionable ; adv., exceedingly well : 1844, Selby, in *London by Night.*

knocker-face or **-head.** An ugly-face (or its owner) : low : from ca. 1870 ; ob.

*****knocker-off.** A thief specialising in motor-cars : c. : from ca. 1920. Ex *knock off*, v., 4. E.g. in Edgar Wallace, *The Door with Seven Locks*, 1926.

knocker on the front door, have a. To have achieved respectability : lower and lower-middle classes' coll. (— 1909). Ware.

knocker-worker. See **knocker, on the.**

knockers. Small curls worn flat on the temples : coll. : ca. 1890–1915.

knocking. Sexual intercourse : low coll. : late C. 16–20, ob. except in combination.

knocking-house or, more gen., **-shop.** A brothel : low : mid-C. 19–20. H., 2nd ed., has the latter.

knocking-jacket. A nightgown, nightdress : low coll. : ca. 1700–1850. D'Urfey.

*****knocking-joint.** A brothel : C. 20 : c. >, by 1915, low s. Ex *knock*, v., 1.—2. The stand of a bookmaker that intends, if unlucky, to welsh : racing c. (— 1932).

knocking-shop. See **knocking-house.**

[**knot**, a set or group of persons, has always been S.E. : in C. 17–18, however, it was, like *crew*, used often of the underworld.—As v., to coït, **it is** S.E.]

knot, tie with St. Mary's. To hamstring : coll. : C. 19.

knot it. To abscond : low : from ca. 1860 ; ob

knot with the tongue that cannot be undone or untied with the teeth, knit or tie a. To get married : coll. : late C. 16–mid-19 ; then dial. Lyly, Swift, Scott. (Apperson.)

[**know,** to possess carnally, has always, despite F. & H., been S.E.]

know, be all. To be a bookworm : proletarian coll. (— 1887). Baumann.

know, don't you. See don't you know.

know, in the. Possessing special and/or intimate knowledge : coll. : 1883, *The Referee*, April 29, 'As everybody immediately interested knows all about them, perhaps Refreaders would like to be in the know likewise.'

know, we or **you** or **do you (?).** A mildly exclamatory or semi-interrogatory (virtual) parenthesis : coll. : from ca. 1710. Addison, 1712 ; Jane Austen, 'Do you know, I saw the prettiest hat you can imagine.' (O.E.D.)

know a great A from a bull's foot, (2) **a thing or two,** (3) **a trick or two,** (4) **a trick worth two of that,** (5) **how many blue beans make five,** (6) **how many days go to the week,** (7) **how many go to a dozen,** (7a) **one's book,** (8) **one's life,** (9) **one's way about,** (10) **something,** (11) **the ropes,** (12) **the time of day,** (13) **what's o'clock,** (14) **what's what,** (15) **which way the wind blows.** To be well-informed, experienced, wide-awake, equal to an emergency. Nos. 5 and 14 are s., the others coll. ; nos. 7, 9 and 15 are almost S.E.—No. 1, C. 18–20, ob. ; no. 2, late C. 18–20 (Holcroft) ; no. 3, C. 18–20, ob. ; no. 4, late C. 16–19 (Shakespeare) ; no. 5, C. 19–20, see blue beans ; no. 6, C. 17–18 ; no. 7, from ca. 1850 ; no. 7a, from ca. 1880 ; no. 8, from ca. 1890, ob. ; no. 9, from ca. 1860 ; no. 10, from ca. 1870, ob. ; no. 11, from ca. 1850, orig. nautical ; no. 12, from ca. 1890 ; cf. no. 13, from ca. 1520 (Dickens) ; no. 14, *what is what* from ca. 1400, *what's what* from ca. 1600 (e.g. in Jonson and Wycherley) : see esp. Apperson ; no. 15, from ca. 1540 ; ob. by 1890 ; †. Cf. *know one point more than the devil*, q.v.

know B from a battledore, not to. See B and cf. *know a great A from a bull's foot*.

know it !, not if I. Not if I can help it : coll. : 1874, Hardy. (O.E.D.)

Know-it of **Know-all Park.** A know-all : coll. : from ca. 1910. (Compton Mackenzie, *Water on the Brain*, 1933.)

*****know life,** in the C. 19 underworld, meant, to know the shady tricks and the criminal acts, but not necessarily to be a criminal oneself. Vaux.

know much about it, not. Not to know how to deal with ; esp. of a batsman towards a bowler : coll. : C. 20.

know of, not that I. So far as I know : coll. : from ca. 1880.

know of, not that you. A defiant expression addressed to someone in reference to something he proposes or is about to do : coll. : ca. 1740–1820. Richardson, 'As Mr. B. offer'd to take his Hand, he put 'em both behind him.—Not that you know of, Sir !' (O.E.D.)

know one point, occ. **an ace, more than the devil.** To be (very) cunning : coll. : C. 17–18. Prob. ex Spanish. Cf. the Cornish *know tin*—tin occurring in many forms. Both are much stronger than *know a thing or two*, etc.

know one's way about, the ropes, the time of day, what's o'clock (etc.). See know a great A.

know one's stuff. See do one's stuff.

knowed. Knew ; known : sol. : C. 18–20. (Often as deliberate jocularity.)

knowing, shrewd, artful, is, despite F. & H., ineligible, for it has always been S.E.—2. Stylish ; knowing 'what's what' in fashion, dress, manners : coll. : ca. 1795–1860. Jane Austen ; T. Hughes, 'Tom thought his cap a very knowing affair.'

knowing bloke. A sponger on recruits : military (— 1887) ; ob. Brunlees Patterson in *Life in the Ranks*. (But *knowing one* is S.E.) For *knowing codger* (— 1859) see knowing, 1, + *codger*.

knowledge-box. The head : (— 1785) coll. >, ca. 1890, S.E. Grose, 1st ed. But *knowledge-casket* (— 1901) has not taken on. (In U.S. c., *knowledge-box* is a school. Irwin.)

knowledgeable. Having or showing knowledge or mental ability : from ca. 1830 : dial. >, ca. 1860, coll. Hence *knowledgeably* (— 1865) and *knowledgeableness* (— 1886). O.E.D.

known, n. A well-known person : coll. : 1835 (O.E.D.). Never very gen.

knows, all one. (To) the best of one's ability ; (to) the utmost : coll. : from ca. 1870. Other forms are possible : *all one knew, all they know* or *knew*.

[**knub,** to rub against, tickle, listed by F. & H., is dial.]

*****knuck.** A thief, esp. a pickpocket : c. of ca. 1810–60. Vaux ; Ainsworth, in *Rookwood*. Ex *knuckle*, n., 1.

*****knuckle.** A pickpocket, esp. an expert : c. of ca. 1780–1840. Parker.—2. Abbr. *knuckle-duster*, q.v. ; never very common : coll. : from ca. 1870.

*****knuckle,** v. To pick pockets, esp. if expertly : c. of ca. 1785–1870. Parker ; Grose, 3rd ed.—2. To pummel, punch, fight with one's fists : c. : from ca. 1860 ; ob. [—3. To acknowledge defeat, give in : S.E., whether as *knuckle* or as *knuckle down* or *under* ; so too is *knuckle down* (*to*), to apply oneself earnestly (to).]

*****knuckle, down on the.** (Almost) penniless : either c. or low : from ca. 1840 ; ob. '*No. 747*' (reference to year 1845).

*****knuckle, go on the.** To practise pickpocketry : c. of ca. 1810–70.

knuckle, lie on the. See lie on the knuckle.

knuckle, near the. Slightly indecent : coll. (1895, W. Pett Ridge) >, by 1930, S.E. Cf. the c.p., *the nearer the bone the sweeter the meat*.

*****knuckle-bone, down on the.** Penniless : c. : from ca. 1880. Baumann.

*****knuckle-confounders** or **-dabs.** Handcuffs : c. of ca. 1780–1850. Grose, 1st ed.

knuckle-duster. A knuckle-guard that, made of metal, both protects the hand and gives brutal force to the blow : orig. (— 1858), U.S. and c. ; anglicised, ca. 1865, as coll. ; by 1900, S.E. *The Times*, Feb. 15, 1858.—2. Hence, a large and either heavy or over-gaudy ring : low : from ca. 1870. H., 5th ed.

knuckled. Handsome · tailors' : from ca. 1860 ; slightly ob.

*****knuckler.** A pickpocket : c. : ca. 1810–90. Vaux. Ex *knuckle*, v., 1. Cf. :

*****knuckling-cove.** The same : id. : id. Ibid. Ex *knuckle*, v., 1.

knuller ; occ. **kneller.** A chimney-sweep given to soliciting custom by knocking or ringing at doors : low : ca. 1850–1900. ? ex *knell*.—2. A clergyman : low : ca. 1860–1910. Ex sense 1 via *clergyman*, q.v.

knut, k-nut. (The *k-* pronounced.) A very stylish (young) man about town; a dandy: from ca. 1905. Prob. *nut* orig. = head and *knut* has perhaps been influenced by *knob*, q.v. See also **filbert** and **kn-**.

Knuts, the. Important persons crossing to France during the G.W.: Dover Patrol nickname. Ex preceding.

knutty. The adj. of *knut*: 1915; ob.

ko-tow, kotow! (Properly **k'o-tou, k'o-tou!**) Thank you!: Anglo-Chinese coll.: C. 17–20.

kocks nownes! A coll. perversion of *God's wounds*: C. 16–mid-17. O.E.D.

kokum. Sham kindness: Australian c. (— 1896); ob. Also *cocum*, q.v. Perhaps this strange word is cognate with Sampson's χοχανο, lying, counterfeit: cf. χοχανι, a sham horoscope (Welsh Gypsy).

kollah. A loose spelling of *calloh*, q.v. (Ware.)

konk. See **conk**, n. and v.

*****konoblin rig.** The stealing of large pieces of coal from coal-sheds: c. (— 1811); † by 1900. *Lex. Bal.* This may be the original of *nobble*: but what is its own etymology?

komate. A dead or a wounded soldier: a sick horse: New Zealand soldiers': 1915–18. Ex Maori *ka maté*, dead.

kooferred, be. To be killed: naval (African Squadron): ca. 1860–1910. Bowen, 'Borrowed from the Swahili.'

kool. To look: back s. (— 1859). H., 1st ed.

koota, kooti, kuti. New Zealand forms (late C. 19–20) of *cootie*, q.v.

kootee. A house: Anglo-Indian (— 1864). H., 3rd ed. (Not in Yule & Burnell.) But is not 'house' a misprint for 'louse'?

kop. Illiterate for *cop*.

kop-jee. The head: lower classes': 1899–1901. Ware. (Boer War influence.) Cf.:

kopje walloper. A diamond-buyer visiting the Kimberley fields: from ca. 1886; ob. Ex *kopje*, a small hill. Pettman.

Kosbs, the. The King's Own Scottish Borderers: an occ. military nickname: C. 20. F. & Gibbons.

kosal kasa. One shilling and six pence: Yiddish trading coll.: C. 19–20. Ex Hebrew words for '1' and '6'. Ware.

*****kosh, occ. kosher.** A short iron bar used as a weapon: c. (— 1874). H., 5th ed. Prob. ex Romany *kosh(t)*, a stick. Occ. spelt *cosh(er)*.—2. Hence, in G.W. military, a trench-club. B. & P.— 3. In late C. 19–20, to hit (a person) with a kosh, as 'He'll cosh him one.'

kosher; occ. cosher. See **kosh**.—2. Adj., fair; square: East End of London: from ca. 1860. Ex Hebrew *kasher*, lawful, esp. as applied to meat.

*****kotey.** An illiterate form of *quota*, q.v.

[**kotoo, kotow, kowtow,** despite F. & H., is S.E.]

Koylis, the. The King's Own Yorkshire Light Infantry: military: C. 20. F. & Gibbons.

*****kradying-ken.** A low lodging-house: c.: 1845.

'*No. 747*', p. 419. A corruption of (the only app. later) *pratling-ken*.

Krakenhohe. A local, late 1918–early 1919 military c.p. 'cuss-word'. F. & Gibbons, 'A German town, found hard to pronounce by our men, who passed it in their advance after the Armistice.'

k'rect. Correct: sol. (— 1887). Baumann. For *k'rect card*, see **correct card**.

krop. Pork: back s. (— 1874). H., 5th ed.

Kruger-spoof. Lying: 1896–97. Ware. Ex promises made by President Kruger in 1896—but not kept.

Kruger's tickler or **tiddler.** A little feather brush used, in the celebrations after Ladysmith and Mafeking, to tickle fellow-celebrants' faces: coll.: Boer War. Collinson.

Kruschen feeling, that. Verve and energy: a c.p.: from ca. 1925; slightly ob. Collinson. Ex an advertisement of Kruschen Salts.

kuanthropy. An inferior, indeed an incorrect, form of *kynanthropy*: from ca. 1860. O.E.D.

kubber, properly **khubber,** occ. **khabbar** (or **-er**). News: Anglo-Indian (— 1864). H., 3rd ed. Hindustani *khabar*, news—esp. of game.

kudize. To esteem, honour; praise, extol: students' (— 1887); virtually †. Baumann. Ex:

kudos. Glory, fame: university s. (from ca. 1830) >, ca. 1890, gen. coll. Gr. κῦδος. As rare † v., *kudos* occurs in 1799, *kudize* in 1873: both, pedantically ineligible.

kutcha. See **cutcha.**—**kuti.** See **koota.**

kwy. Death: fast life: ca. 1800–40. Ware. Ex *quietus*.

kyacting. Playing the fool, or jocularity, during hours of work: naval (— 1909). Ware. This may be a confusion of *chy-ack* (or *-ike)ing* and *skylarking*.

kybosh. See **kibosh** and cf. *kyebosk*.

kye. Eighteen pence: costermongers': from ca. 1860. Abbr. Yiddish *kye*, 18, + *bosh*, pence. Cf. *kibosh*, q.v.—2. Hence (?), a bluejacket mean with his money: naval: late C. 19–20. Bowen. ? cf. U.S. s. *kike*, a Jew.

kye-bosh. See **kibosh on.**—**kyebosh.** See **kibosh**.

kyebosk. A low Cockney variant of *kibosh*. Baumann, 1887.

kynchen. See **kinchen.**

'k'you! (Pronounced as the letter q.) Thank you!: slovenly coll. (verging on sol.) abbr.: from the 1890's.

kypher, v.i. and t. To dress (her): lower classes' (— 1909). Ware. Ex Fr. *coiffer*.

[**kypsey,** occ. **kipsey,** a wicker basket, is S.E. > dial.]

kyrie eleison, give or **sing a.** To scold (v.t. with *to*): ecclesiastical (1528, Tyndale) >, ca. 1600, gen. coll. (as in Taylor the Water Poet): † by 1780. Ex the Gr. for 'Lord, have mercy'. O.E.D.

kỹsh. A cushion; a small, flat, square squab used for sitting on and for carrying books: Marlborough College: late C. 19–20. By corruption of '*cush*ion '.

L

l is occ. omitted in illiterate speech, esp. in *all*; thus *all right* > *a*' (pron. *aw*) *right* or *orright*. C. 19–20.

L.L. (Slightly) fraudulent: financial: 1870. Ware. I.e. *limited liability*.—2. The best whiskey: Dublin taverns': late C. 19–early 20. Ware. Ex *Lord Lieutenant*.

L's, the three. Lead, latitude, look-out: nautical coll.: from ca. 1860. Smyth; Clark Russell. Dr. Halley added a fourth, *longitude*.

L.S.D. Money: coll.: from ca. 1835: in C. 20, S.E. Hood, ' But, p'raps, of all the felonies de se, . . . Two-thirds have been through want of £ *s. d.*' (O.E.D.)

la ! An exclamation: C. 16–20: polite till ca. 1850, then low coll. and dial. Cf. *la, la !*, q.v.—2. (Often pronounced *law*): in C. 17–20, a low coll. euphemism for *Lord !*, this sense merging with the preceding. Cf. *lor*', *lawks*, qq.v.

la-di-da, or occ., as in Baumann, **la-de-da ;** also **lardy-dardy**, q.v. Very stylish ; affectedly smart of costume, voice, manners : from ca. 1860 : coll. ' Its great vogue was due to a music-hall song of 1880—*He wears a penny flower in his coat, La-di-da !* ', W., who suggests imitation of affected *haw-haw* (q.v.) speech.—2. Also, from 1883 (O.E.D.), a n.: derisive coll. for a ' swell '. Cf. † U.S. *la-la*, a ' swell '. And :—3. ' Elegant leisure, and liberal expenditure ': (mostly London) streets' (— 1909); ob. Ware.—4. Occ. as v.: 1867, S. Coyne, ' I like to la-di-da with the ladies ' (O.E.D. Sup.).

la, la !, or **la-la !** A coll. imitation of a French exclamation : C. 18–20.—2. Also, C. 16–20 (ob.), an expression of derision : polite >, ca. 1850, somewhat trivial and coll. Cf. *la !*, q.v.

lab. Laboratory: school and university s. >, by 1910, coll.: late C. 19–20. J. C. Masterman, *An Oxford Tragedy*, 1933, ' " I must go too. I want to go up to my Lab," said Mottram.'

labbering. ' The struggling of a hooked fish ': nautical coll.: late C. 19–20. Bowen. Ex dial *labber*, ' to dabble or splash in water ' (E.D.D.).

Labby. Henry Labouchere (1831–1912), the witty journalist (editor of *Truth*) and politician.

[**labour**, to beat ; prob. *labourer*, a mid-wife ; *labour-lea*, to copulate, are all ineligible, the third being an † Standard Scottish euphemism.]

Labour, the ; gen. **on the Labour**, on unemployment-relief : working classes' coll. : from ca. 1921. (Michael Harrison, *Spring in Tartarus*, 1935.)

lac, lack, lakh, esp. in pl. A large number or quantity : Anglo-Indian : from ca. 1885. Kipling. Ex Hindustani *lak(h)*, a hundred thousand.—2. Earlier, in (— 1864) Anglo-Indian coll. that, ca. 1910, > standard, it meant 100,000 rupees.

lace. Strong liquor, esp. spirits, added to tea or coffee: coll. >, ca. 1750, S.E. : C. 18–20, ob. *The Spectator*, No. 488 (i.e. in 1712).—2. By inference, sugar : C. 18. Ex :

lace, to intermix with spirits : S.E. (from ca. 1675). (With sugar, ca. 1690–1720, is prob. s. or coll.) Ex *lace* as an adornment, an accessory. W. —2. Also S.E. is *lace*, to flog, to thrash, again despite F. & H.—3. To wear tight stays (v.i.) from ca. 1870 ; coll. >, ca. 1895, S.E. : ob.

lace into. A C. 20 coll. variant of *lace*, to thrash. Lyell.

lace-ups. Laced-up boots : coll. (— 1887). Baumann.

laced, ppl.adj. Intermixed with spirits : S.E.— 2. Sugared : ca. 1690–1750 : s. or coll. B.E.

laced mutton. A woman, esp. a wanton : ca. 1575–1860. Whetstone, 1578 ; Shakespeare, in *Two Gentlemen*, ' She, a lac'd mutton, gave me, a lost mutton, nothing for my labour ' ; B.E. ; *Lex. Bal.* Cf. *mutton* and *mutton dressed as lamb*, the latter at *lamb*.

Lacedemonians, the. The 46th Foot Regiment, since ca. 1881 the 2nd Battalion of the Duke of Cornwall's Light Infantry : military : late C. 18–20 ; ob. F. & Gibbons. Ex its colonel's speech, made in 1777, under fire, about the Lacedemonian discipline. Also *Murray's Bucks* and *the Surprisers*.

lacing, spirits added to tea or coffee, is S.E. But as a flogging, it is C. 17–20 coll. (B.E., Grose.)

[**lack-Latin**, an ignorant person, like **lack-land**, a propertyless one, is S.E.]

Lack(e)ry. The Regular Army nickname for any man surnamed Wood : late C. 19–20. F. & Gibbons. Ex :—2. *lack(e)ry*. A stick, piece of wood : Regular Army : mid-C. 19–20. Ex Hindustani *lakri*.

lactory is erroneous for *lactary* : mid-C. 17–20. (O.E.D.)

lad. A dashing fellow : coll. : late C. 19–20 ; anticipated in Udall's *Roister Doister*, ca. 1553, ' I trowe they shall finde and feele that I am a lad.' Cf. *lad of the village*.

lad o' wax. A cobbler : coll. : from ca. 1790 ; ob. by 1890, † by 1920. Baumann notes the variant, *cock-a-wax*, q.v.—2. A boy ; a poor sort of man (contrast *man of wax*, a ' proper ' man) : C. 19 coll.

*lad of, occ. **on, the cross.** See **cross, n.**

lad of the village, gen. in pl. A dashing fellow or cheerful companion, esp. if a member of a set : late C. 19–20 coll. Perhaps an extension of *lad*, q.v. (or vice versa), or, more prob., ex :—2. (Gen. in pl.) One of a set of thieves and pickpockets congregating at a given spot : c. of ca. 1820–80. ' Jon Bee.'

ladder. The female pudend : C. 19–20 low. Semantics fairly obvious.

ladder, climb or **go up** or **mount the.** To be hanged : semi-proverbial coll. : ca. 1560–1870. In C. 17–19, *to bed* or *to rest* is gen. added. Harman, *climb three trees with a ladder*. Cf. (and see) the following few of many synonyms : *catch* or *nab the stifles, cut a caper upon nothing, dance the Paddington frisk, preach at Tyburn cross, trine, wear hemp* or *a Tyburn tippet*.

ladder, groom of the. A hangman : either S.E. or jocular coll. : ca. 1640–1700.

ladder, unable to see a hole through a. See **hole in a ladder.**

laddie, laddy. A coll. endearing form, mainly Scots, of *lad* : mid-C. 16–20.

laddle. A lady : chimney-sweeps' (esp. on May 1): mid-C. 19–early 20. On that date, the sweepers' wives, collecting money for the men, carried brass ladles. (H., 1860). ' Ducange Anglicus,' 1857, classifies it as c.

ladidah. See **la-di-da.**

ladies. Cards : gambling (hence almost c.): 1890, *The Standard*, March 15.

ladies' cage. The Ladies' Gallery : parliamentary (— 1870). See also **cage, n.**

[**ladies' fever**, syphilis, like **ladies' delight**, (etc.), the penis, is euphemistic S.E.]

ladies' finger or **wish**. A tapering glass of spirits, esp. if gin : (low) coll. : ca. 1850–1910.—2. In Australia, but gen. as *lady's finger*, a very short, thin banana : from ca. 1890 : coll. on the verge of standard, which latter it > ca. 1920.

ladies' grog. Grog that is hot, sweet, strong, plentiful : from ca. 1840 ; ob.

Ladies' Mile, the. Rotten Row, in London's Hyde Park : Society > gen. : from ca. 1870 ; ob. *The Daily News*, May 10, 1871. Punning the names of horse-races.

ladies' tailoring. Sexual intercourse : low : from ca. 1815 ; ob. Cf. *stitch*.

ladle. To enunciate solemnly and pretentiously : theatrical coll : from ca. 1870 ; ob.

[**ladron** and **lad's leavings** in F. & H. are ineligible.]

lads, one of the. A variant of *lad of the village*: coll : C. 20. Lyell.

lady. A hunch-backed woman : ca. 1690–1870. B.E. Cf. *lord* (q.v.), by which suggested.—2. A **wife** (esp. *my old lady* : cf. *old woman*) : low coll. : from ca. 1860 ; earlier, S.E. Cf. *lady, your good*, q.v.—3. Madam, as term of address : M.E.–C. 20 : polite till ca. 1860, then increasingly coll. and low. (See W.'s comment.)—4. The reverse of a coin : low : C. 19–20, ob. Ex *tail*, via sex.—5. A quart or a pint pitcher upside down : low : C. 19–20, ob.—6. He who attends to the gunner's small stores : nautical (− 1711) ; † by 1920. Whence, in the same period, the † *lady's hole*, the place where such stores are kept. Both terms were coll. by 1750, S.E. by 1800 at latest.—7. With sense 2, cf. : mother, gen. *the old lady* : (jocular) coll. (− 1887). Baumann.

lady, old. The female pudend : low : C. 19–20, ob.—2. A coll. term of address to animals, esp. mares and bitches : from ca. 1840. O.E.D.

lady, perfect. A prostitute : low when not jocular : from ca. 1880. Ex the claims of such women—or ex male irony.

lady, your good. Your wife : C. 18–20 : S.E. till ca. 1860, then low coll. Cf. *your* or *the missus* and Fr. *votre dame*. (Rare in other ' persons '.)

lady-bird, ladybird. As endearment, S.E.—2. A whore : C. 16–20 ; ob. Brome, Moncrieff. Cf. *bird*, q.v.

[**lady-chair**, given by F. & H., is S.E. ; cf. *king's cushion*, q.v.]

Lady Dacre's wine. Gin : ca. 1810–50. *Lex. Bal.*

[**lady-feast**, an abundance of sexual love,—**lady-flower** or **star**, the female pudend,—and **lady-ware**, the male genitals (also trinkets), are all S.E. euphemisms : despite F. & H.]

lady-fender. A woman given to nursing the fire : servants' : C. 19–20, ob.

***lady green**, or with capitals. A clergyman, esp. a prison chaplain : c. : from ca. 1880 ; ob. ? ex inexperienced mannerism.

lady, or Lady, Jane. The female pudend : low : from ca. 1850 ; ob.—2. ' A stout, handsome, cheery woman ' : Society : 1882–ca. 1915. Ware.

lady-killer. A male flirt : from ca. 1810 : coll. >, ca. 1890, S.E. Whence **lady-killing**, n. and adj., which arose, the adj. in 1825, the n. in 1837 (O.E.D.): same change of status. Cf. *masher*.

Lady Lavery. (Gen. in pl.) An Irish Free State legal-tender note : Anglo-Irish, esp. among bank-clerks : from ca. 1925. Obviously ex that notability.

lady marm. An affected, pretentious woman : lower classes' coll. (− 1923) Manchon. Variant : *stuck-up marm*.

lady of easy virtue. See **easy virtue.**—**lady of pleasure**. S.E. euphemism.—† **lady of the lake**, a mistress : S.E.

lady of the gunroom. A C. 19 variant (coll. verging on S.E.) of *lady*, 6. Bowen.

lady (or Virgin) of the Limp. A coll. variant (military) of the S.E. *the Hanging Madonna* or, esp., *the Leaning Virgin*, the displaced Basilique de Notre-Dame de Brébières, at Albert : 1914–18. B. & P.

lady of the manor. An occ., late C. 19–20 variant of *lord of the manor*, sixpence. B. & P.

lady-sitter. A lady who allows herself to be appraised—and painted : painters' (− 1887) ; ob. Baumann.

ladyfied. Having the appearance (*l'air mais pas la chanson*) of a fine lady : coll. : from ca. 1880.

lady's finger. See **ladies' finger.**

lady's hole. See **lady**, 6.

lady's ladder. Rattlins set (too) close : nautical : from ca. 1850.

[**lady's low toupée** (in D'Urfey, *toppie*). Ineligible : S.E. euphemism.]

lady's pocket-handkerchief. ' Any light fancy sail or flying kite ' : nautical pejorative : C. 19–20 ; very ob. Bowen.

ladyship, her. Our ship : nautical coll. rather than s. (− 1887) ; slightly ob. Baumann.

***lag**. (Also *lage*, q.v.). Water : c. : ca. 1560–1870. Harman.—2. Also, wine : c. : late C. 16–19.—3. Hence (also *lage*), a ' wash ' of clothes : c. : ca. 1560–1860. Harman. Esp. in *lag of duds*, in C. 17–18 often corrupted to *lag-a-duds*.—4. A transported convict : c. (− 1811) ; † by 1895. *Lex. Bal.* Prob. ex *lag*, v., 4. (It may well date back to 1740 or so.) Hence, any convict : from ca. 1830 : also c. Prob. via *returned lag* (1828, Bee).—5. A sentence of transportation : c. (− 1821) ; † by 1895. Hence (also *lagging*) a term of penal servitude : c. : from ca. 1850.—6. A ticket-of-leave man : c. : from ca. 1855. ' Ducange Anglicus.' Usually *old lag* (− 1856), which also = a one-time convict.—7. A fag : Westminster School (− 1881).—8. As the last, hindermost, person : S.E.

***lag**, v. To urinate : c. : ca. 1560–1850.—2. To wash (gen. with *off*) : c. : ca. 1560–1700. Harman.—3. Also v.t., to water (spirits) : c. of ca. 1810–60. Vaux.—4. To transport as a convict : c. : from ca. 1810 ; † by 1900. Vaux ; Dickens. Ex † *lag*, to carry away.—5. To send to penal servitude : c. : from ca. 1850. Edgar Wallace, passim.—6. Midway between these two senses : to arrest : from ca. 1823 : c. >, by 1900, low and military. De Quincey ; Nat Gould. (O.E.D.)—7. V.i., to serve as a convict : c. : C. 20. Ex sense 5.—8. To inform on (a person) to the police, to ' shop ' : c. : from ca. 1870.—9. As to carry off or steal, and as to be last or very slow, it is S.E.

***lag, old**. See **lag**, n., 6.—**lag-a-duds**. See **lag**, n., 3.

***lag-fever**. Illness feigned to avoid transportation : ca. 1810–90. *Lex. Bal.*

***lag-ship**. A convict transport : c. of ca. 1810–80. Vaux.

***lage**. See **lag**, n., 1, 3. Esp. *lage of duds*. Ex Old Fr. *l'aige* or *l'aigue*, the water : ? cf. *newt* for (a)*n ewt*.—2. V., see **lag**, v., 1–3.

***lagger**. A sailor : low (? orig. c.) > nautical :

from ca. 1810 ; ob. Vaux. Perhaps ex *lag*, to loiter.—2. A convict during or after imprisonment : c. : 1819 (O.E.D.) ; ob.—3. An informer to the police : from ca. 1870 : c. Ex *lag*, v., 8.—4. A bargeman that, lying on his back, pushes the barge along with his feet on the roof of a subterranean canal : nautical : from ca. 1880. Bowen. An extension of sense 1, possibly influenced by sense 2.

*lagging. The vbl.n. corresponding to *lag*, v., 4–7, qq.v. Esp. as a penal term of three years : c. (— 1932). Anon., *Dartmoor from Within*. Cf. the next three entries.

*lagging, be. A variant of *lag*, v., 7 : c. : C. 20. E.g. in Edgar Wallace, *The Brigand*, 1927.

*lagging and a lifer. Transportation for life : c. of ca. 1835–90. Dickens. See lifer.

*lagging-dues will be concerned. He will be transported : c. : ca. 1810–60. Vaux.

lagging-gage. A chamber-pot : low if not indeed c. : C. 18–19. Ex *lag*, v., 1.

*lagging-matter. A crime potential of transportation : c. of ca. 1810–60. Vaux.—2. Hence, a crime likely to result in penal servitude : c. : from ca. 1860.

laid. A pollack : nautical : mid-C. 19–20. Bowen. Possibly ex dial. *laidly*, ugly : it is not a handsome fish, for its lower jaw protrudes.

laid. Lay (past tense) ; lain (past ppl.) : sol. : C. 18–20.

laid on the shelf ; laid (up) in lavender. Pawned : resp. C. 19–20, late C. 16–20 (slightly ob.).—2. (The latter phrase only) : ill ; out of the way : turf : from ca. 1870.

laid on with a trowel. See trowel ; cf. *lie with a latchet*, q.v.

Laird of Lag, the. Sir Robert Grierson (d. 1733), very severe towards the Covenanters. Dawson.

lairy. 'Slow, slack ; also cunning' : *Conway* cadets' (— 1891). John Masefield, *The Conway*, 1933. A corruption of *leary, leery*.

laisser (or -ez-)-faire, adj. Apt to let things slide : coll. (— 1931). Lyell.

lake-wake is an error for *lyke-wake* (O.E.D.) : C. 15–20. Cf. *late-wake*.

laker-lady. An actor's whore : theatrical : C. 18–early 19. ? ex *lady of the lake* or ex *lake* (now dial.), to play amorously.

lakes, abbr. ; Lakes of Killarney. Mad : rhyming s. (on *barmy*), esp. among grafters : C. 20. Philip Allingham, *Cheapjack*, 1934.

lakin !, by (our). A (low) coll. form of *by our Lady* : C. 15–mid-17. O.E.D.

lakh(s). See lac.

laldie, give (something). To enjoy it greatly : Glasgow (— 1934). Ex dial. *give laldie*, to punish.

lall-shraub. Claret : Anglo-Indian coll. : from ca. 1780. Ex Hindustani *lal-sharab*, red wine. Yule & Burnell, ' the universal name . . . in India '.

*lally. Linen ; shirt : c. (— 1789) ; † by 1890. Parker. Gen. *lully*, q.v.

lam. A hard nit : cricketers' coll. (— 1902). E.D.D. Ex :

lam, v. ; lamb ; old spelling lamm(e). To beat, thrash : 1596, though implied in 1595 in *belam* : S.E. >, in C. 18, coll. ; in late C. 19–20, low coll. Dekker, ' Oh, if they had staid I would have so lamb'd them with flouts ' ; Grose ; Anstey (d. 1934). Cognate with Old Norse *lemja*, lit., to lame ; fig., to flog, thrash. Cf. *lamback, lambaste, lambeak*,

lamb-pie.—2. To hit hard : cricketers' coll. : 1855. Lewis.

lam (it) into one ; lam out, v.i. To hit out ; give a thrashing : mainly schoolboys' : from ca. 1875.

lama. Erroneous for *llama*, the animal : mid-C. 17–20. Contrast *llama*, q.v. (O.E.D.)

lamb, as an easy-going person, a simpleton,—as (esp. as *Nottingham lamb*) a cruel or a bludgeon man (cf. *mint-sauce*, q.v.),—and as a term of endearment : despite F. & H., it is S.E.—2. See pet lamb. —3. See Kirke's Lambs.—4. An elderly woman dressed like a young one : C. 19–20, coll. mostly Cockney, and gen. as *mutton dressed as lamb, mutton dressed lamb-fashion*.

lamb, v. See lam.—lamb, skin the. See skin the lamb.

lamb and salad, give, v.t. To thrash : mid-C. 19–20 ; ob. Elaboration on *lam*, q.v. Cf. lamb-pie.

lamb-down. To make a man get rid of his money to one : 1873, Marcus Clarke : low Australian ; ob. Morris.—2. To spend in drink : Australian : 1873, J. Brunton Stephens ; ob. Ex *lam*, q.v.

lamb-fashion. See lamb, n., 4.

lamb-pie. A thrashing : low coll. : C. 17–mid-19. Cf. lamb and salad.

[lamback, 1589, to beat, thrash, and as n. ; lambacker, 1592, a bully ; lambeak, 1555 as v., 1591 as n. ; lambskin, to beat, a heavy blow (1573) : these began as S.E. and did not survive long enough to > coll.]

lambaste. To beat, thrash : 1637 : S.E. >, in C. 18, coll. ; in C. 19–20, (dial. and) increasingly low coll. Davenant, ' Stand off awhile, and see how Ile lambaste him.' Ex *lam*, q.v., on *bumbaste*, q.v.

lambasting. A thrashing : 1694, Motteux, ' A tight lambasting ' : S.E. >, ca. 1750, coll. ; from ca. 1860, low coll. and dial.

Lambeth, n. and v. Wash : South London (— 1909) ; very ob. Ware, ' From the popular cleansing place in S. London being the Lambeth baths.'

lambie. See lamby.

lambing. See lamming.

lambing-down. Vbl.n. of *lamb-down*, q.v.

Lambs, the. The Royal West Surrey Regiment : military : late C. 18–20. Ex *Kirke's Lambs*, q.v., and the orig. Regiment's badge of a lamb. F. & Gibbons.—2. See Sweet Lambs, the.—3. Lambs. Light Armoured Motor Batteries : military : 1915 ; ob. F. & Gibbons.

*lambskin (occ. lamb-skin) man. A judge : c. of ca. 1690–1830. B.E. Ex judge's gown, lined and bordered with ermine (Grose). Cf. *furman*, q.v.— 2. See lamback.

[lamb's wool, a hot drink of spiced ale, is, despite F. & H., definitely S.E.]

lamby. (Gen. pl.) A mizzen-top man : naval (— 1891). Ware ; John Masefield, *The Conway*, 1933.

lame as a tree. See tree, lame as a.

lame as St. Giles, Cripplegate(, as). Very lame indeed—' applied to badly-told untruth ' : coll. : C. 17–19. Ware. Ex the frequenting of that church by cripples, St. Giles being their patron.

[lame dog over a stile, help a, despite F. & H., is S.E.]

lame duck, a defaulter, see duck.—2. A scapegrace : Australian coll. (— 1895) ; ob.

lame-hand. An inferior driver : coaching : ca. 1800–70.

lame post, come by the. To be late (esp. of news) :

from ca. 1650 : coll. >, ca. 1700, proverbial S.E. Fuller, 1732, records, 'The lame post brings the truest news.'

lamentable, despicable, wretchedly bad : late C. 17–20 : jocular S.E. verging on, indeed occ. descending to, the coll. Cf. *deplorable.* (O.E.D.)

lamm(e). See lam.

[**Lammas, at lat(t)er,** never, is, despite F. & H., ineligible.]

Lammermoor lion. A sheep : C. 18–mid-19 mainly Scots jocular coll. Cf. *Cotswold lion* ; contrast *Essex* or *Rumford lion,* qq.v.

Lammie Todd ! I would—if I got the chance ! From ca. 1860 ; ob. : tailors'. Prob. ex a well-known tailor's name.

lammikin, a variant of *lambskin* (see **lamback**).

lamming. A beating, thrashing : 1611, Beaumont & Fletcher, 'One whose dull body will require a lamming' : S.E. till C. 18, then coll. ; from ca. 1850, low coll.

lammy, a chiefly nautical term, is, despite F. & H., ineligible.—2. A term of address : dustmen's (– 1823) ; † by 1900. Bee suggests derivation ex Fr. *l'ami,* as in ' Ohé ! l'ami.'

lamp. An eye : late C. 16–20 : S.E. till C. 19, then s., gen. in pl. *Lex. Bal.* In C. 19 c., a *queer lamp* is a blind, squinting, sore or weak eye. Cf. Fr. c. *lamper* and U.S. *lamp* (partly anglicised as c. by 1920), to gaze at.—2. (Extremely rare in singular.) Spectacles : late C. 19–20 : low, mostly Cockney. Milliken. Abbr. *gig-lamps,* q.v.

lamp-lighter, (off) like a. (Off) 'like a streak' coll. : from ca. 1840 ; ob. E.D.D., which notes the variant *like lamp-lighters.*

[**lamp, smell of the,** is impeccable S.E., while **lamp of life,** the male, **lamp of love,** the female pudend, and **lance,** the penis, are S.E. euphemisms.]

lamp-post. A tall, very thin person : (low) coll. : from ca. 1870. Cf. *hop-pole* and *reach me down a star.*

lamp-post, between you and me and the. In confidence : urban coll. (– 1887) ; slightly ob. Baumann. Cf. *bed-post,* q.v.

lamps. See **lamp,** both senses.

Lancashire Lads, the. The 47th Foot, in late C. 19–20 the Loyal (North Lancashire) Regiment : military : 1782 ; ob. F. & Gibbons details an anecdotal explanation.—2. The Lancashire Fusiliers : military coll. : late C. 19–20. Ibid.

Lancashire lass ; gen. pl. A tumbler : rhyming s. (on *glass*) : from ca. 1880. P. P., *Rhyming Slang,* 1932.

lance-jack. A lance-corporal : military coll. : late C. 19–20. F. & Gibbons.

*****lance-knight, lanceman, lanceman-prigger.** A highwayman : c. of ca. 1590–1640. The first in Nashe, the other two in Greene. See **prigger.** Perhaps *lanceman* was suggested by Fr. *se lancer.*

*****lancepresado, lanspresado, lansprisado.** One who comes into company with but two pence in his pocket : c. of ca. 1690–1800. B.E.—2. Other senses, S.E. Ex *lancepesade, lanceprisado,* a lance-corporal in an army of mercenaries.

lance- (or rear-rank) private. A private 'on approbation', on trial ; inferior : jocular military coll. : from ca. 1906. B. & P.

lancer. A shot missing the target : Regular Army : C. 20. F. & Gibbons. Perhaps because of the splinters it causes to fly from the framework.

Lancs (pronounced *lanks*), **the.** The (–) Lanca-

shire Regiment : military coll. : C. 20. E.g., F Brett Young, *Jim Redlake,* 1930.

land, to arrive, cause to arrive, set down, is S.E.—2. To cause a horse to win (v.t.) ; (v.i.) to win : sporting coll. : 1853, Whyte-Melville.—3. To establish, set one 'on his feet', make safe : 1868, Yates (O.E.D.) ; Hindley, 'I bought a big covered cart and a good strong horse. And I was landed.'—4. (V.t.) to deliver, get home with : boxers' (– 1887). Baumann ; 1888, J. Runciman, 'Their object is to land one cunning blow.' Earlier *lend,* playful for *give* (W.).

land !, my. A mild Canadian (and U.S.) oath : mid- C. 19–20. (John Beames.) Ex English dial. ; *land = Lord.*

[**land-car(r)ack or frigate,** a mistress : despite F. & H., † S.E.]

land crab. A military policeman : military (not very gen.) : G.W. (F. & Gibbons.)—2. A type of aeroplane : Air Force : 1915 ; now only historical. (Ibid.)—3. The super-express engine of the L.M.S. railwaymen's : from ca. 1930. Ex the abundance of outside machinery.

land-face. See **ship one's land-face.**

land or **lands in Appleby ?, who has any.** A c.p directed at one who is slow to empty his glass : late C. 17–early 19. B.E. Perhaps orig. ex of cider.

land lies, see how the. To ask how stands one's account or bill, esp. at a tavern : coll. : late C. 17–early 19. B.E., Grose.—2. Gen. sense is S.E.

land-loper or **-lubber.** A vagabond, a pilfering tramp : C. 17–early 19 coll. ; after ca. 1860, low. B.E., Grose. The earlier form, *land-leaper,* was S.E.—2. As a nautical term, S.E.

*****land navy, the.** Pretended sailors : vagabonds' c. (– 1909). Ware.

land of incumbents. Good clerical livings : Oxford University : ca. 1820–70. Egan's Grose, 1823. See also **land of promises** and **land of sheepishness.**

[**land of nod,** sleep, is S.E., despite F. & H.]

land of promises. A freshman's ambitions : Oxford University s. > coll. : ca. 1820–60. Egan's Grose, 1823. Cf. *land of incumbents* and following entry.

land of sheepishness. The being a schoolboy : Oxford University : ca. 1820–50. Egan's Grose. Cf. *preceding entry* and *land of incumbents,* qq.v.

*****land-pirate, -rat.** A highwayman, footpad, or vagabond thief : C. 17–early 19. : the former, c. ; the latter, S.E. : resp. Dekker, Grose ; Shakespeare.

land-raker. A vagabond, esp. if a thief : late C. 16–mid-18 : coll. Shakespeare. Cf. *land-pirate, -rat,* q.v.

land-security. A C. 19 variant of *leg-bail,* q.v.

land-shark. As land-grabber and as one preying on sailors : S.E.—2. A usurer : C. 19–20 (ob.) coll., mostly low when not U.S.—3. A custom-house officer : coll. : 1815 ; Scott, in *Guy Mannering* ; ob.—4. A lawyer : nautical (– 1860): coll. H., 2nd ed.

*****land squatters.** (Very rare in singular.) Those tramps who, in their begging, do not specialise in either themes or localities : tramps' c. (– 1932). Frank Jennings, *Tramping with Tramps.*

land-swab. A landsman ; an incompetent seaman : nautical : from ca. 1840. See also **swab.**

landabrides. Erroneous for † S.E. *lindabrides,* a mistress. O.E.D.

landed estate. The grave : coll. : C. 19–20, ob. Cf. *Darby's dyke* and *landowner.*—2. Dirt under one's nails : low coll. : from ca. 1870 ; ob.

lander. A blow or punch that reaches its mark : pugilistic (— 1923). Manchon.

landies. Gaiters : Winchester College : ca. 1840–80. Ex *Landy & Currell*, the firm that supplied them.

landlady, bury the. To decamp without paying : low : C. 19–20, ob. Cf. *burn the ken* and *moonshine* ; contrast *bury a moll*.

landowner, become a. To die : late C. 19–20, esp. among soldiers in G.W. Prob. a development ex *landed estate*, q.v.

Land's End or **land's end, at (the).** At last ; sooner or later : proverbial coll. : ca. 1540–1600. 'Proverbs' Heywood. Ex the geographical feature, perhaps ; prob., however, in reference to *land-end*, 'a piece of ground at the end of a "land" in a ploughed field', O.E.D.

Land's End to John o' Groats, from. All the way ; thoroughly : proverbial coll. : from ca. 1820 ; ob. Scott, Peacock.

land's sake !; for the land's sake ! A non-aristocratic exclamation : late C. 19–20. E.g. Galsworthy, *The White Monkey*, 1924. I.e. *Lord's sake*. Cf. **land !, my**, q.v.

lane, a nautical 'highway', is S.E.—2. The throat : from ca. 1550. Udall. Gen. preceded by *the*. Esp. *the narrow lane* (Udall, 1542 : † by 1800) or *the red lane* (1785, Grose) and *Red Lion Lane* (1865 ; now † : O.E.D.). Cf. *gutter lane*, q.v.—3. See **Lane, the.**

Lane, another murder down the. Another (melo)drama at Drury Lane Theatre : theatrical : from ca. 1880 ; ob.

Lane, Harriet. Preserved, gen. tinned, meat : nautical and military : ca. 1870–1910. Ex a girl, so named, found chopped into small pieces.

Lane, the. Abbr. of :—*Drury Lane Theatre* : theatrical (— 1880). G. R. Sims. Cf. *Lane, another murder down the*, and *Garden, the*.—2. *Mincing Lane* : (mostly Colonial) brokers' : from ca. 1870.—3. *Mark Lane* : corn-factors' : from ca. 1860.—4. *Chancery Lane* : legal : from ca. 1850.—5. *Petticoat Lane* : c. : from ca. 1870.—6. *Horsemonger Lane Gaol* : c. of ca. 1850–90. Mayhew. (This gaol was demolished before 1896.)

langers and godders. (The singing of) *Auld Lang Syne* and *God Save the King* : Oxford University, but not .very gen. : C. 20. See **'-er', the Oxford.**

langolee. The male member : low : mid-C. 19–20; ob. ? a perversion of Welsh Gypsy *trangluni*, tools (Sampson).

*langret. A die so loaded that it shows 3 or 4 more often than any other number : mid-C. 16–18 : c. > s. > coll > j. >, by 1700, S.E. and archaic. Greene. Ex *lang* = long.

Langtries. Fine eyes : Society : ca. 1880–1900. Lily Langtry, 'the Jersey Lily', shone as one of the most beautiful women of her time (1852–1929) ; went on the stage in 1881 and had a tremendous success ; married Sir Hugo de Bathe in 1899. Just as in the Orient, to the natives every gentleman is *Mr. Mackenzie* (occ. *MacGregor*), so, at Aden and Suez, every pretty woman is (or was until 1924, at the least) *Mrs. Langtry.* (I.e. in address.)

language. Bad language ; swearing, obscenity : 1886 (S.O.D) : low coll. Besant. Often in the imperative = 'Mind your bad language !'

language of flowers, the. 'Ten shillings—or seven days ; the favourite sentence of Mr. Flowers, a very popular and amiable magistrate at' : Bow Street

Police Court : 1860–83. Ware. Contrast *say it with flowers*.

[**lank**, as adj., has always been S.E., while F. & H.'s **lank sleeve** is merely a special nuance of the S.E. sense.]

lank comes a bank, after a. A proverbial c.p. in reference to pregnant women : ca. 1650–1820.

Lanky and York, the. The Lancashire and Yorkshire line : railwaymen's : late C. 19–20.

lanspresado, -prisado. See **lancepresado.**

[**lant, lantern-jawed**, and **-jaws**, are, despite F. & H., definitely S.E.]

lantern (late C. 18–19) or **lanthorn** (late C. 17–19), **dark.** A servant or an agent receiving a bribe at court : ca. 1690–1820. B.E.

lantern, Ballarat. A candle set in the neck of a bottle whose bottom has been knocked off : coll., Victoria (Australia) : ca. 1870–1910. Wood & Lapham, *Waiting for the Mail*, 1875. Morris. Ballarat is a noted mining town. Cf. *soldiers' pomatum.*

lap. Any potable : from ca. 1565 ; ob. In C. 16–19 c., butter-milk, whey (Harman) ; in late C. 17–19 c., also pottage (Head). In C. 18–20, also tea (G. Parker) and, from 1618, less gen. strong drink : low except, as often in mid-C. 19–20, when jocular. Among C. 19–20 (ob.) ballet-girls, it gen. denotes gin. Ex the v.—2. In athletic terminology, it is S.E.

lap, v. As = to drink, it is S.E., though undignified when used of persons ; in C. 19–20, jocular or trivial.—2. As an athletic term, it is (again despite F. & H.) S.E.

lap, go on the. To drink (strong liquor) : low s. > low coll. : from ca. 1885 ; ob. *Punch*, Sept. 25, 1886, ' Grinds 'ard, never goes on the lap, | Reads Shakespeare instead o' the *Pink 'Un*.'

lap-clap. A copulation; a conceiving : low coll. : C. 17–mid-18. Hence, *get a lap-clap*, to become pregnant.

lap-feeder. A silver table-spoon : low : C. 19–20 ; ob.

lap-priest, in F. & H., is a S.E. nonce-word.—**lap the gutter.** See **gutter.**

lapel, ship the white. To be promoted from the ranks ; esp. to become an officer of marines : naval coll. : mid-C. 18–early 19. (In 1812, marine officers began to wear, not white lapels but epaulettes.)

lapful. A husband, a lover ; an unborn child : resp. low s., low coll. : C. 19–20, ob.

lapland or **Lapland.** The female pudenda : low : from ca. 1840.—2. The society of women : low coll. : from ca. 1850. Punning *lap* and *Lapland.*

*lapper. Drink, esp. if liquor : c. ; C. 19–20, ob. —2. But *rare lapper* = a hard drinker.

.*lappy cull. A drunk man : c. : C. 18. C. Hitchin, *The Regulator*, 1718. Cf. *lushing man.*

lapsy lingo. A lapsus linguæ : lower classes' sol. (— 1909). Ware.

larboard peeper, one's. One's left eye : nautical (— 1887) ; ob. Baumann.

larbolians, -ins (both in Smyth); **larbowlines** (Bowen). Men in the *larboard*, or port, watch : nautical (— 1867) ; ob.

lardy ; lardy-dardy ; lardy-dah. Adj., affected, 'swell', though *lardy* (abbr. *lardy-dardy*) very rarely = affected. Somewhat low : resp. 1890 and ob., 1861 (Miss Braddon). ca. 1870 and a mere variant of *la-di-da* (q.v.). See also **lardy-dardy** below.

lardy-dah ; also **la-di-da** (q.v.) A fop, a ' swell ' : from ca. 1880 ; somewhat low.

lardy-dah (or **la-di-da**), **come** or **do the**. To dress for the public ; to show off in dress and manner : low : from ca. 1883. See **la-di-da**, of which *lardy-dah* is a corruption.

lardy-dardy, v.i. To act the ' swell ' ; be affected ; show off : 1887, G. R. Sims, ' Other men were lardy-dardying about . . . enjoying themselves ' (O.E.D.). Cf. *la-di-da*, 4.

lareover (or **lare-over**) ; **lay-over, layer-over**. A word used instead of one that must, in decency, be avoided : late C. 17–early 20 : the first, coll. and dial. ; the others, S.E. (B.E.) Cf :

lareovers for meddlers. ' An answer frequently given to children, or young people, as a rebuke for their impertinent curiosity,' Grose : c.p. : C. 18–early 19 ; then dial., gen. as *layers for meddlers*.

large, adj. gen. used as adv. Excessively : (low) coll. : from ca. 1850. Thus, *dress large*, i.e. showily ; *go large*, i.e. noisily ; *play large*, i.e. for high stakes ; *talk large*, i.e. boastfully. Cf. *fine and large*, q.v.

large house. A workhouse : low coll. : from ca. 1850. Cf. *big house*.

large order. Something big or exaggerated or very difficult : coll., by 1930 verging on S.E. : 1890, *The Pall Mall Gazette*, Feb. 17. Ex commerce. Cf. *tall order*.

larikin. An occ. variant of *larrikin*, q.v.

lark. A game ; piece of merriment or mischief ; trick : 1811, *Lex. Bal.* : s. >, ca. 1870, coll. Dickens, in *Pickwick*, ' " Here's a lark ! " shouted half a dozen hackney coachmen.' For etymology, see the v.—2. A boat : from ca. 1785 : c. > s. >, ca. 1850, nautical s., > ca. 1870, nautical j. ; ob. Grose, 2nd ed. Prob. *ark* (q.v.) perverted.—3. Abbr. **mud-lark*, q.v.—4. A line of business : grafters' : late C. 19–20. P. Allingham, *Cheapjack*, 1934. Cf. *lay*, 2 and *law*, 2.

lark, v. See the amorous and the sporting sense of *larking*.—2. To play (esp. the fool) ; be mischievously merry ; go on the ' spree ' : 1813, Colonel Hawker ; Barham, ' Don't lark with the watch, or annoy the police.'—3. To ride in a frolicsome way or across country : 1835, ' Nimrod ' (O.E.D.) : sporting s. >, ca. 1870, coll.—4. V.t., tease playfully : 1848, Thackeray (O.E.D.) : s. >, ca. 1880, coll.—5. V.t., to ride (a horse) across country : from ca. 1860 : sporting s. >, ca. 1880, coll. ; ob.—6. To jump (a fence) needlessly : 1834, Ainsworth ; ob. (O.E.D.) Ex the n., which is ex the Northern dial. *lake*, sport. Whence *skylark*, q.v.

lark, go on or **have** or **take a**. To be mischievously merry : go on the spree : from ca. 1815 : s. >, ca. 1870, coll. Cf. :

lark, knock up a. Same as preceding : 1812, Vaux ; † by 1890 : prob. c. > low s.

larker. A person given to (mischievous) fun : from ca. 1825 : s. >, ca. 1870, coll.

larkiness. The abstract n. of *larky*, q.v. : coll. : C. 20. (O.E.D. Sup.)

larking, n. Cunnilingism : low : C. 18–19 (? 20). Grose, 1st ed. ; absent in latter edd.—2. Fun ; a mischievous frolic : from ca. 1812 : s. >, ca. 1870, coll. Beddoes, ' Professors of genteel larking.'—3. Sporting senses of *lark*, v. (q.v.)

larking, adj. Given to ' larks ' (see **lark**, n., 1) ; sportive : 1828, J. H. Newman : s. >, ca. 1870, coll. (O.E.D.)

larkish. Fond of, or of the nature of, a ' lark ' (q.v.) : from ca. 1880. Whence *larkishness*.

larks with, come half. To impose on the credulity of (a person) : low (— 1923). Manchon. See **lark**, n., 1.

larksome. Fond of a ' lark ', apt to indulge in ' larks ' : coll. : from ca. 1870.

larky. Ready or inclined to play ' larks ' (see **lark**, n.) : 1841 (O.E.D. Sup.) : s. >, ca. 1870, coll. H. Mayo, ' When the Devil is larky, he solicits the witches to dance round him ' (O.E.D.).—2. Hence, occ. as adj. : C. 20. O.E.D. (Sup.).

larky subaltern's train. See **cold-meat train**.— Larrence. See **lazy Laurence**.

*larries. A C. 18 variant of *lurries* (see at **lurry**). *The Scoundrel's Dict.*, 1754.

larrikin ; occ. **larikin**. A (gen. young) street rowdy : orig. and mainly Australian : 1870 or a few years earlier : s. >, ca. 1890, coll. >, ca. 1910, S.E. *The Melbourne Herald*, April 4, 1870, ' Three larikins . . . had behaved in a very disorderly manner in Little Latrobe-street.' Cf. *hoodlum*, *hooligan*, *tough*, qq.v. Also as adj. : 1870, Marcus Clarke. See esp. Morris. Etymologies proposed : *leary kinchen* (see separate words), fantastic ; a pronunciation of *larking*, ineptly fantastic ; *Larry*, a common Irish pet-form of *Lawrence*, + *kin*, O.E.D. ; perhaps orig. Cornish, where *larrikin = a* ' larker ' (q.v.), suggested by W., not to the exclusion of the preceding, which seems the most likely.

lar(r)ikiness. A female larrikin : 1871 : same remarks as for preceding, q.v.

larrikinism. The habits and tricks of larrikins : 1870 : remarks as for *larrikin*, q.v. *The Australian*, Sept. 10, 1870, ' A slight attempt at " larrikinism " was manifested.'

larrup ; occ. **larrop** and † **lirrop**. To beat, thrash : coll. and dial. : from ca. 1820. Fonblanque, 1829, ' Is this a land of liberty, where a man can't larrop his own nigger ? ' (O.E.D.) ? ex *lee-rope*, as an early glossarist proposed, or, as W. proposes, suggested by *lather*, *leather*, and *wallop*, qq.v.

larruping. Vbl.n. of preceding : a thrashing. Coll. and dial. : from ca. 1825. Peake.

Larry, (as) happy as. Very happy : Australian coll. : late C. 19–20.

Larry Dugan's eye-water. Blacking : mostly Anglo-Irish : ca. 1770–1820. Ex a very well-known Dublin shoe-black. Grose.

lars ; larse. Last : sol. (esp. Cockneys') and dial. : C. 19–20. (R. Blaker, *Night-Shift*, 1934.)

lascar. A tent-pitcher ; (in full, *gun-lascar*) an inferior artilleryman : Anglo-Indian coll. : from late C. 18 ; both ob. (As a sailor, S.E.)

lash. Violence : Australian (— 1916). C. J. Dennis. Perhaps ex *lash out at*.

lash, v. To envy. Gen. as *lash !*, used as a taunt : the Blue Coat school (— 1877) ; ob. Blanch.

lash-up. A break-down ; a failure, a fiasco or ' mess-up ' : naval (late C. 19–20) >, by 1915, military. F. & Gibbons.—2. Hence, a turmoil : nautical (— 1935).

lashin(g)s. (Gen. of drink, occ. of food, rarely of anything else.) Plenty : coll., orig. Anglo-Irish : 1829, Scott, ' Whiskey in lashings ' ; 1841, Lever, ' Lashings of drink,' these quotations illustrating the gen. forms ; the former is ob. Perhaps ex, or for, *lavishings* (W.) ; prob. ex † S.E. *lash* (*out*, to squander. Cf. *whips*, q.v., and :

lashin(g)s and lavin(g)s. Plenty and to spare : Anglo-Irish coll. : from ca. 1840.

la'ship. A coll. form of ladyship : C. 18–early 19. O.E.D.

[**lask** in F. & H. is † S.E. for a looseness of the bowels.]

lass in a red petticoat. A wife well-endowed : proverbial coll., esp. in *the lass in the red petticoat shall pay for,* or *piece up, all* : ca. 1660–1800. J. Wilson, *The Cheats,* 1664. (Apperson.)

lassitudinarian. A person of infirm health : Society : 1894–1914. Ware. Punning *Latitudinarian* and *valetudinarian.*

last. A person's most recent joke, witticism, etc. : coll. : 1843 (S.O.D.). E.g. ' X's last is a scream.'

last, the. ' The end of one's dealings with something ' : coll. : 1854 (S.O.D.). Dickens, ' If it ever was to reach your father's ears I should never hear the last of it ' (O.E.D.).

last bit o(f) family-plate, the. The final silver coin : artisans' (— 1909). Ware.

last compliment. Burial : coll. : from ca. 1780 ; ob.—2. As the sexual favour, it—with the synonymous *last favour*—is S.E., as also is F. & H.'s *last feather.*

last drink, take one's. To die by drowning : Canadian lumbermen's coll. : late C. 19–20. John Beames.

last hope. An iron ration : military : 1915–18. F. & Gibbons. (Used only in emergency.)

last shake o(f) the bag. Youngest child : proletarian : C. 19–20 ; ob. Ware.

last ship, a. A nautical coll. (C. 19–20), thus in Bowen, ' Anything that is the epitome of excellence, for the sailor always has good things to say, and odious comparisons to make, of his last ship, no matter what she was like.

laster. The flow of the tide : nautical : C. 19. Bowen. ? the ebb-flow, ' the last of it '.

lasting, adj. (Of a horse) having staying power : sporting : from ca. 1810.

lat or **lat-house.** A latrine : C. 20 military. B. & P. Occ. *the lats.*

*****latch.** To let in : c. of ca. 1720–1850. *A New Canting Dict.*

latch-drawer (in F. & H.) is S.E.

latch-key. A crowbar : Irish Constabulary's : 1881–82. Ware. Because so often used by them in evictions.

latch-opener. The ' price ' of a drink (cf. *entrance-fee*) : military : C. 20. B. & P.

latch-pan. The under lip. Hence, *hang one's latch-pan,* to pout, be sulky : coll. and dial. : C. 19–20. Ex lit. sense.

late. Keeping late hours : coll. : from ca. 1630. ' Having to do with persons or things that arrive late ' : coll. : 1862, ' the " late " mark '. But *late fee,* earlier *late-letter fee,* has passed from coll., via Post Office j., to S.E. (S.O.D.)

late play. A holiday beginning at noon : Westminster School : C. 19–20 coll.

[**late unpleasantness, the.** In U.S., before 1916, the U.S. Civil War. In British Empire, the Great War. Perhaps orig. coll., but prob. always S.E.]

late-wake, like **lake-wake,** is erroneous for *lyke-wake* : C. 18–20.

-later, -latry ; -olater, -olatry. One who worships ; (excessive) adoration, worship. In mid-C. 19–20, this suffix is occ., as in *babyolatry,* so jocular as to verge on coll., even in nonce-words.

latest, the. The latest news : coll. : C. 19–20. Baumann, ' What's the latest ? '

lath-and-plaster. A master : rhyming s. (— 1857). ' Ducange Anglicus.'

lather. The sexual secretion : low : C. 19–20 ; ob. Hence *lather-maker,* the female pudend.

lather, v. To beat, thrash : from ca. 1795 : coll. >, ca. 1890, S.E. Cf. *lace, lather, larrup, strap,* qq.v.

[**lathy,** thin, despite F. & H., is S.E.

Latin for ' goose '. A dram : ca. 1820–50. ' Jon Bee.' Ex *brandy is* . . .

Latiner. A Latin scholar ; one who speaks Latin : coll. : 1691 (S.O.D.).

latitat. An attorney : coll., though perhaps orig. legal s. : 1565, Cooper's *Thesaurus.* Foote, in *The Maid of Bath,* ' I will send for Luke Latitat and Codicil, and make a handsome bequest to the hospital.' † by 1860 in England, the term derives ex an old form of writ. (For legal s., see my *Slang,* published in 1933.)

latrine rumour. False news : a wild story ; a baseless prediction : military : 1915. Ex the fact that latrines were recognised gossiping places. Cf. *cookhouse rumour, ration-dump r.* or *yarn,* and *transport r.* or *tale.* See esp. B. & P. and Stephen Southwold's essay on rumours in *A Martial Medley,* 1931.

-latry, -olatry. See -later.—**lats, the.** See **lat.**

latter end. The posteriors : mid-C. 19–20 : jocular coll. >, ca. 1910, S.E. According to Baumann, a careful observer, it was at first a boxing term.

lattice. See **red lattice.—latty.** See **letty.**

laugh and joke. A smoke : rhyming s. : C. 20. *John o' London's Weekly,* June 9, 1934.

laugh on the other, or wrong, side of one's face or **mouth** is, despite F. & H., indubitably S.E.

laughing, be. To be ' comfortable, safe, fortunate ' : military coll. : 1915 ; ob. (Hence, more gen., to be winning : Glasgow.) B. & P., ' He's got a job at Brigade Headquarters, so he's laughing '. Ex one's laugh at such good luck.

laughs. A make-up : theatrical (— 1935). I.e., putting on one's laughs.

lauk ! See **lawk !**

launch. A lying-in : coll. : from ca. 1786 ; ob. by 1880, † by 1910. Grose, 2nd ed. Prob. ex nautical v., but perhaps cognate with † dial. *launch,* to groan.

launch, v. (Gen. in passive.) To reverse a boy's bed while he is asleep : Public Schools : ca. 1810–90. G. J. Berkeley, *My Life,* 1865.

launderer, be a. To commit a Stock Exchange ' washing ' (itself j., not s.) : Stock Exchange : from ca. 1930. ' A City Man's Diary ' in *The Evening Standard,* Jan. 26, 1934.

laundress, despite F. & H., is in all senses S.E.

Laurence. See **lusk.**—2. **have Laurence on one's back, have a touch of old Laurence,** to be lazy : coll. : C. 19–20 ; ob. except in dial. See **lazy Larrence.**

laurestinus is an error for *laurustinus,* an evergreen flowering shrub : late C. 17–20.—So *laure-, lauristine,* erroneous for *laurustine,* the same. (O.E.D.)

lav. Lavatory : C. 20. (Dorothy Sayers, *Murder Must Advertise,* 1932.)

lavender, all. Always negative : ' It ain't all lavender,' its not all fun or all pleasant : lower classes' coll. (—1923). Manchon.

lavender, lay (up) or **put in.** (The *put* form not before C. 19.) To pawn : from ca. 1590 ; slightly

ob. Greene, in his *Upstart Courtier*. Like the next sense, **ex** the preservative virtues of lavender.—2. ' To put out of the way of doing harm, as a person by imprisoning him or the like ' : from ca. 1820 ; ob. Scott, in *Nigel*. (O.E.D.)—3. See **laid on the shelf**, 2.—4. As = put carefully aside for prospective use, it is S.E.

lavender-cove. A pawnbroker : low : from ca. 1850 ; slightly ob. Ex preceding.

lavish. Bacon fat ; the fat on 'shackles ' (q.v.) : mostly military : C. 20. Semantics : ' rich '.

law, the old sporting term, is S.E.—2. A phase of crime, esp. of theft ; a trick or ' lay ' (q.v.) : c. : ca. 1550–1650. Esp. in Greene's ' coney-catchers '. See also **lurk, packet, rig, slum.**

law ! or **Law !** Lord ! : late C. 16–20 ; in C. 19–20 low coll., perhaps orig. euphemistic. Prob. arising from cumulative force of *la !* (q.v.), *lo !*, and *Lor'* (q.v.). W. See also **lawk(s), laws,** and **lors.**

law in the Mat(t)o. A ·44 Colt revolver : among Englishmen in Brazil : C. 20. C. W. Thurlow Craig, *A Rebel for a Horse*, 1934.

law-lord. A judge having, by courtesy, the style of ' Lord ' : Scots coll. : from ca. 1770.

lawed, it is, was, etc. It is settled by law : coll. and dial. : C. 19–20 ; ob.

lawful blanket or **jam.** A wife : low : the former from ca. 1810 ; the latter from ca. 1850 ; ob. *Lex. Bal.* Henley, 1887, ' Gay grass-widows and lawful jam.' Cf. *Dutch*, contrast *jam tart.*

lawful picture. A coin ; in pl., gen. money : coll. : C. 17–18.

lawful time. Playtime : Winchester College : C. 19–20 ; ob.

lawk !, lawks. Lord ! : coll. (rather low) : from ca 1765 ; earliest as *lauk*, latest as *lawks*. Dickens in *Pickwick*, ' Lawk, Mr. Weller . . . how you do frighten me.' Occ. (C. 19–20, ob.) *lawk-a-daisy* (*me*) i.e. *lackadaisy* = lackaday !, and (C. 19–20) *lawk-a-mussy*, the latter a corruption of *Lord have mercy !* Either ex *lack* as in *good lack !* or ex *Lord* influenced by *lack* and *la !* or *law !*, qq.v. See also **lor' !**

lawless as a town-bull. Quite lawless ; very unruly : proverbial coll. : ca. 1670–1800.

lawn. A handkerchief, esp. if of white cambric : low coll. : from ca. 1810 ; ob. Vaux.

lawner. Refreshment served on the lawn to a hunt : middle and upper classes' : from ca. 1925. (Evelyn Waugh, *A Handful of Dust*, 1934.) ' The Oxford-*er*.'

Lawrence. See **Laurence** and **lazy Larrence.**

laws ! ; **laws-a-me !** ; **lawsy !** A low coll. form (cf. *law, lawks, lors,* qq.v.) of *Lord !* : from ca. 1875.

lawt. Tall : back s. (— 1859). H., 1st ed.

lawyer. An argumentative or discontented man, esp. one given to airing his grievances : military coll. : late C. 19–20. F. & Gibbons. In Australia, such a man is called *bush lawyer* : coll. : C. 20.

*lawyer, high (occ. **highway**). A highwayman : c. : ca. 1590–1640. Greene. Ex *law*, 2, q.v. Cf. *martin, oak, scripper, stooping,* qq.v.

lawyer must be a great liar, a good. A frequent c.p. in conversations turning on the law : ca. 1670–1780. Ned Ward, 1703. (Apperson.)

lawyering, n. and adj. (Concerning, of) a lawyer's profession : coll. : from ca. 1860.

lawyers go to heaven, as. (Gen. preceded by *fairly and softly* or *by degrees*, etc.). Very slowly :

from Restoration days : proverbial coll ; in C. 19–20, mainly dial. (Apperson.)

lay, a wager, is S.E.—2. An occupation, esp. if criminal ; a ' line ' ; a trick : from ca. 1705 : c. >, ca. 1840, low. *A New Canting Dict.* Hence *avoirdupois-lay*, q.v. ; *fancy-lay*, pugilism, C. 19 low ; *kinchen-lay*, q.v. ; etc., etc. Prob. ex *law*, 2, q.v.—3. Hence, a hazard, chance : 1707, Farquhar : c. >, ca. 1800, low : † by 1850. See **lay, stand a queer.**—4. A quantity : c. : ca. 1815–50. Haggart. Perhaps ex fusion of senses 1 and 2.—5. Hence, some ; a piece : Northern c. : from ca. 1850 ; ob. H., 1st ed.—6. ? hence, a share in the capture : whale-fishers' (— 1887). Baumann.—7. (Also from sense 5.) Goods : c. : ca. 1820–50. Haggart.—8. (Butter)milk : c. : C. 17. Middleton & Dekker in *The Roaring Girl*. Ex Fr. *lait*.—9 Borrowed money : Regular Army's : from ca. 1925. Prob. ex sense 4 of :

lay, v. As to wager, as to search or lie in wait for (also *lay by, lay for*) : S.E., despite F. & H.—2. To lie (down) : M.E.–C. 20 : sol. in C. 18–20, except when nautical Cf. *laid*, q.v.—3. See **lay into.**—4. V.i. and v.t., to borrow (money) : Regular Army's : from ca. 1920.

lay, a good. Anything advantageous ; esp., an economical way of cutting : tailors' : C. 19–20 >, ca. 1890, coll.

*lay, on the. At (illicit) work : C. 18–20 c.—2. On the alert, e.g. for something to steal : C. 19–20 c. See **lay, n., 2.**

*lay, stand a queer. To run a great risk : c. : from ca. 1720 ; † by 1850. *A New Canting Dict.*, 1725. See **lay, n., 3.**

lay a duck's egg. In cricket, to score nothing : sporting : from ca. 1870 ; ob. See **duck's egg** and **blob.**

lay a straw. To stop (v.i.) ; mark a stopping-place : coll. : C. 16–mid-17. Barclay, Bullein, Barnaby Rich. (Apperson.)

lay a or **in water.** To defer judgement ; esp. too long : coll. : C. 15–early 17 ; *in* not before C. 16. (The *a* is, of course, the preposition as in *a-board*.) Lyly, ' I see all his expeditions for warres are laid in water ; for now when he should execute, he begins to consult.' (Apperson.)

*lay-about. A professional loafer : c. (— 1932) Scott Pearson, *To the Streets and Back*. I.e. ' lie-about '.

lay about (one), fight vigorously, etc. : S.E.—2. To idle : sol. for *lie about* : mid-C. 19–20.

lay at. To (attempt to) strike : C. 15–20 : S.E. till C 19, then dial. and coll.

lay by the heels. To put in stocks (†) or in prison : C. 18–20 : coll. >, ca. 1860, S.E.

lay-down. A rest ; a sleep : sol. : C. 19–20. Ex *lay*, v., 2, q.v.

*lay down, gen. **lay them down.** To play cards : c. : mid-C. 19–20 ; ob.—2. See **lay**, v., 2.

lay down one's, or **the, knife and fork.** To die : low coll. (— 1859) ; ob. H., 1st ed. Cf. *hop the twig, lose the number of one's mess, peg out,* qq.v.

lay down the law. To dogmatise : coll. : 1885 (O.E.D.). Ex lit. sense, declare what the law is.

lay, or **lay himself, down to his work.** (Of a horse, etc.) to do his best : sporting : from ca. 1885 ; slightly ob. *Illustrated Sporting and Dramatic News*, May 20, 1893. (O.E.D.)

lay in, v.i. To attack with vigour : coll. : from ca. 1888.—2. V.i., to eat vigorously : from ca. 1800 : S.E. >, ca. 1880, low coll.

lay, occ. **cast, in one's dish.** To object to something in a person; accuse of : coll. : mid-C. 16–mid-19. T. Wilson in *Rhetorique*, Harington in *Epigrams*, Butler in *Hudibras*, Scott in *Old Mortality* (Apperson).

lay into. To thrash : 1838, Douglas Jerrold : s. >, ca. 1870, coll. Cf. *pitch into*.

lay into its collar. (Of a horse) to pull hard : Canadian coll. : late C. 19–20. (John Beames.)

lay it on. To exaggerate, etc. : S.E.—2. **lay it on thick**, the same : coll. : mid-C. 19–20. See **thick**.

lay me in the gutter. Butter : rhyming s. (— 1923). Manchon.

[**lay off**, v.i., to give over, is dial. and U.S.]

lay off to (a person). To try to impress (him) : lower classes' coll. (— 1923). Manchon. Perhaps ex nautical j.

lay or lie on the face. To be exceedingly dissipated : lower classes' (— 1909) ; slightly ob. Ware.

lay on to be. To pretend to be : lower classes, esp. Cockneys' : 1914, A. Neil Lyons, ' I don't lay on to be a saint ' (Manchon).

lay one's shirt. To stake one's all : sporting s. > coll. : mid-C. 19–20. If the stake is lost, one *does* (or *has done*) *one's shirt* : late C. 19–20 sporting.

[**lay oneself open, lay oneself out** or **forth** (to exert oneself in earnest), and **lay oneself out for** (to be ready to participate in anything), all in F. & H., are S.E.]

lay out, to intend, propose, is S.E., but to overcome or disable, esp. with a punch, also to kill, is s. : orig. (1829), U.S. ; anglicised ca. 1860. Ex the *laying-out* of a corpse.

lay over, in F. & H., is (there unavowed) U.S.— **lay-over.** See **lareover**.

***lay the razor.** A term, ca. 1865, in racing c. (or perhaps s.), as in ' *No. 747* ' ; of obscure meaning : Possibly, to judge precisely when to spur one's horse to win the race.

lay-up. A drink, a ' go ' (q.v.) : low (— 1891) ; ob. Newman, in *Scamping Tricks*, ' A strong lay-up of something neat.'—2. A period in prison : c. : C. 20. George Orwell, *Down and Out*, 1933.

lay up in lavender. See **lavender**.

laycock. See **Miss Laycock**.

layer. A bookmaker ; a betting-man : mid-C. 19–20 : sporting s. >, ca. 1880, coll. >, in C. 20, S.E.—2. A lazy fellow : lower classes' coll. (—1923). Manchon. I.e. one given to lying in bed.

layer-over. See **lareover.**—**laystall, leystall. lay-stow** : S.E., despite F. & H.

laze. A lazy rest : coll. : from ca. 1860. Ex the S.E. v.

laze-off. A rest from work : coll. : 1924, Galsworthy, *The White Monkey*.

lazy as Ludlam's, or **(David) Laurence's, dog.** (Sussex dial. has *Lumley's*.) Extremely lazy : proverbial coll. from ca. 1660 : ob. by 1870, † except in dial. by 1900. According to the proverb, this admirable creature leant against a wall to bark. Cf. :

lazy as Joe the marine who laid down his musket to sneeze. Exceedingly lazy : C. 19 semi-proverbial coll. Prob. ex :

lazy as the tinker who laid down his budget to fart. The acme of laziness : late C. 18–early 19 low, semi-proverbial coll. Grose, 3rd ed. Cf. two preceding entries.

lazy-bones. A loafer or a very lazy person : coll. : from ca. 1590. Harvey, ' Was . . . vivacitie a

lasie-bones ? ' Cf. *lazy-boots.*—2. Lazy-tongs or, as it is occ. called, lazy-back : coll. (— 1785) ; ob. (Despite F. & H., *lazy-tongs* itself is S.E.)

lazy-boots. ' A lazy-bones ' (q.v.) : coll. : from ca. 1830 ; ob. Mrs. Gaskell. Cf. *sly boots* and *clever boots*.

lazy Eliza. A big, long-distance shell passing high overhead with a slow rumble : military : 1915 : ob. F. & Gibbons. (Most shells with personal names are feminine.)

lazy Larrence, Laurence, Lawrence. The incarnation of laziness : from ca. 1780 or perhaps even from ca. 1650 : coll. (ob.) and dial. Perhaps in reference to the gen. heat of St. Lawrence's Day, Aug. 10, or to the legend of the martyred St. Lawrence being too lazy to move in the flames. (Apperson ; E.D.D. ; Prideaux's *Readings in History*, 1655.) See also **Laurence**, 2.

lazy-legs. A ' lazy-bones ' (q.v.) : coll. : 1838, Dickens (O.E.D.) ; ob.

lazy man's load. An excessive load carried to save a second journey : coll. (— 1791) : in C. 20, almost S.E., slightly ob. Grose, 3rd ed.

lazy-roany. Lazzaroni, or Neapolitan beggars : nautical (— 1887). Baumann.

'ld. (Pronounced *ud*.) Would : coll. : late C. 16–20. Shakespeare. In C. 19–20, gen. *'d*.

'le. Will or shall, as in *sheele* (C. 16–17) and *shele* (C. 17). O.E.D. Cf. *'ll*, q.v.

[**lea-rigs**, given by F. & H., is ineligible as dial.]

Lea toff. ' One who displays his distinction, in a hired boat, rowing up and down the River Lea ' : Cockneys' (— 1909) ; ob. Ware.

lead in its theatrical senses is S.E.—2. Abbr. *friendly lead*, an entertainment designed to assist some unfortunate : from ca. 1850 : c. >, ca. 1880, s.

lead, dull as. (Of a person) extremely dull : coll. (— 1923). Manchon.

lead, get the. To be shot : late C. 19–early 20.

lead, sling the. A Glasgow variant (C. 20) of :

lead, swing the. To loaf ; malinger, evade duty : C. 20, orig. and mainly military, by folk-etymology corruption ex *leg, swing the* (q.v.), known to be nautical, the issue being confused by the sailors' technical phrase for taking the soundings, *heave* (never *swing*) *the lead.* Actually, this duty, assumed by soldiers to be easy and to admit of loafing, is both arduous and skilful, for its performer is ' bang under the [chief] officer's eye—and usually the captain's and pilot's as well, and in a tight spot of navigation at that,' Mr. H. G. Dixey in a private letter (March 14, 1934) to the author. Whence *lead-swinger*, q.v.—2. Hence, loosely, to ' tell the tale ' (q.v.) ; to boast : from ca. 1919.

lead apes in hell. See **apes in hell.**

lead me to it ! That's easy ! ; with pleasure ! : a coll. c.p. of C. 20. Dorothy Sayers, *The Nine Tailors*, 1934, ' " Can you ride a motor-bike ? " " Lead me to it, guv'nor ! " '

lead-off. The first or most important article in a newspaper : journalists' coll. (— 1887). Baumann.

lead off, v. To lose one's temper, be angry : military : from ca. 1910. F. & Gibbons. Perhaps ex boxing.

lead towel. A pistol : low : mid-C. 18–early 19. ' Jon Bee.'

lead-swinger. A loafer, schemer, malingerer : C. 20 military. B. & P. Ex *lead, swing the.* Cf. *leg-swinger*, q.v.

lead up the garden. See **garden, lead up the.**

leaden favour or **pill.** A bullet : American, anglicised before 1909. Ware.

Leadenhall Market sportsman. ' A landowner who sells his game to Leadenhall market poulterers' : sporting : ca. 1870–1915. Ware.

leader. ' A remark or question intended to lead conversation (cf. *feeler*). 1882 ' : coll. ; slightly ob. (S.O.D.)—2. **the leader,** the commanding officer ; *the grand leader,* the senior general or other officer commanding a garrison : semi-jocular military (officers') : from ca. 1933. Ex newspaper accounts of Herr Hitler (*der Führer*).

leading article. The nose : coll. (— 1886) ; ob.— 2. The female pudend : low : mid-C. 19–20 ; ob.— 3. ' The best bargain in the shop—one that should lead to other purchases ' : tradesmen's : from ca. 1870 ; ob. Ware.

leading heavy. (Gen. pl.) The role of a serious middle-aged woman : theatrical : from the late 1880's ; prob. from U.S.A. Ware.

leading question, unfair question, **a** poser : catachrestic : late C. 19–20. Fowler.

leading-strings. ' The yoke-lines on a ship's rudder ' : nautical : late C. 19–20. Bowen.

leaf. Furlough : naval (late C. 19–20) >, by 1914, military. F. & Gibbons. Ex the frequent Welsh pronunciation of *leave.*

leaf, drop one's. To die : low (? orig. c.) : C. 19–20 ; ob. Manchon. Ex :

*****leaf, go off with the.** To be hanged : Anglo-Irish c. > low : from ca. 1870 ; ob. Grose, 2nd ed. Either ex the autumnal fall of leaves or ex a hanging-device shaped like the leaf of a table. Cf. :

*****leafless tree.** The gallows : c. of ca. 1825–70. Lytton in *Paul Clifford.*

leaguer is occ., ca. 1670–1830, used in error for † *leaguer* (i.e. *ledger* in † sense). O.E.D.

leak. The female pudend : low : C. 18–20 ; ob. Gay.—2. A urination : a vulgarism or a low coll. : mid-C. 19–20. Esp. in *do* or *have a leak.* Cf. the v. —3. See **leek,** 3.

leak, v. To make water : a vulgarism : from ca. 1590 ; ob. Shakespeare.

leak, spring a. To urinate : low : ca. 1860–1910. Ex nautical j.

leaky, unable to keep a secret, despite F. & H. is S.E. ; but *leaky,* in the particular sense, talkative when drunk, is a proletarian coll. dating from ca. 1880 (Ware).—2. Tearful, apt to weep : lower classes' (— 1923). Manchon.

lean, adj. and n. Unprofitable (work) : printers' (— 1871). From C. 17 in a different sense, but this (e.g. in Moxon) is j. Contrast *fat,* q.v.—2. Un-remunerative : (dial. and) coll. (— 1875).

lean and fat. A hat : rhyming s. (— 1857). ' Ducange Anglicus.'

lean and lurch. A church : rhyming s. (— 1857). ' Ducange Anglicus.'

lean as a (1) **rake,** (2) **shotten herring.** Extremely thin : resp. late C. 16–20, S.E. >, ca. 1700, coll., but in C. 19–20 mainly dial. ; and proverbial coll. from ca. 1650 (after ca. 1830, mainly dial.).

lean-away. A drunkard : Australia : ca. 1890–1910.

lean off it or **that !** Cease leaning on it ! : coll. : 1829, Marryat, ' Lean off that gun ' ; ob.

lean on your chin-straps ! A military c.p. used when marching up a steep hill : military : 1915 ; ob. F. & Gibbons.

leap, to copulate, like *leaping-house,* is S.E.—2.

leap ! All safe ! : c. : C. 18. *A New Canting Dict.,* 1725.

leap, do a. To copulate : low coll. : C. 19–20.

leap (occ. **go**) **a whiting, let.** To let an opportunity slip : proverbial coll. : ca. 1540–1780. Heywood, Breton. (Apperson.)

leap at a crust. ? to be very hungry ; or, snatch at any chance whatsoever : semi-proverbial coll. : ca. 1630–1750. Draxe ; Swift. (Apperson.)

leap at a daisy. To be hanged : coll. : ca. 1550–1620. Anon., *Respublica* ; Greene ; *Pasquil's Jests,* 1604, ' He sayd : Have at yon dasie that growes yonder ; and so leaped off the gallows.' (Apperson.)

leap at Tyburn or **in the dark, take a.** To be hanged : low (? orig. c.) : C. 17–early 19. D'Urfey, ' All you that must take a leap in the dark . . .'

*****leap-frog.** A crab : c. (— 1857). ' Ducange Anglicus.'

leap-frogging. ' Penetration by successive " waves ", each " wave " or " leap " remaining in the trench or other objective that it [has] captured. Introduced by the British in 1917 ' : military coll. >, by late 1918, j. B. & P.

leap in the dark or **up a ladder.** A copulation : C. 18–20 low ; ob. Cf. *leap, do a,* and *leap at Tyburn,* q.v. (In S.E., *leap in the dark* is often applied to death or to any other great risk.)

leap over nine hedges, ready to. Exceedingly ready : coll. : ca. 1660–1800. Ray.

leap over the hedge before one comes to the stile. To be in a violent hurry : proverbial coll. : ca. 1540–1800. Heywood, Gascoigne, Ray, Motteux.

leap (or **jump**) **the besom, broom(-stick), sword.** (U.S., **book.**) To marry informally : C. 18–19 coll. See the nn. separately. The *sword* form, military.

leap the stile first, let the best dog. Let the best or most suitable person take precedence or the lead : coll. : C. 18–early 19.

leapt, to have. (Of frost) to thaw suddenly : coll., mainly rural : 1869, H. Stephens, ' When frost suddenly gives way . . . about sunrise, it is said to have " leapt " ' (O.E.D.).

learn. To teach : from M.E. ; S.E. till ca. 1760, then coll. ; from ca. 1810, low coll. ; since ca. 1890, sol. Chiefly in *I'll learn you !* (often jocularly allusive). Cf. Fr. *apprendre,* to learn, also to teach.

learned men. C. 19 nautical coll., thus : ' In the old coasters, certified officers shipped for foreign voyages to satisfy the regulations.' Bowen.

learning-shover. A school-teacher : Cockneys' : 1869 ; ob. Ware.

learning the follows. The ringing of ' call changes ' : bell-ringers' (— 1901). H. Earle Bulwer's glossary of bell-ringing.

*****leary, leery.** Artful ; wide-awake ; (suspiciously) alert ; c. >, ca. 1830, low : from ca. 1790. Grose, 3rd ed. Prob. ex dial. *lear,* learning, cleverness (cf. S.E. *lore*). Cf. *peery,* q.v.—2. ' Flash ' ; showy of dress and manners : low : ca. 1850–75. H., 1st ed. Cf. *chickaleary.*—3. (Of personal appearance) somewhat wild : from ca. 1850.—4. In Australia (— 1916), low, vulgar. C. J. Dennis.

leary bloke. A showy dresser, gen. of lower classes : low (— 1859) ; † by 1880. H., 1st ed. Cf. *leary,* 2, and *chickaleary cove.*

leary-cum-Fitz. A vulgarian actor : theatrical : ca. 1890–1914.

least in sight, play. To hide ; make oneself scarce ; keep out of the way : low : ca. 1780–1870. Grose, 1st ed.

leastaways. A C. 19–20 variant of:

leastways ; leastwise. At least : C. 16–20 : S.E. till C. 19, then coll. ; in C. 20, low coll. In C. 19–20, also dial.

leather. Skin : C. 14–20 : S.E. till ca. 1700, then coll. till ca. 1780, when it > s. Hence, *lose leather*, C. 18–20 (ob.), to be *saddle-galled*.—2. Hence, the female pudend : C. 16–20 low coll. Whence, *labour* or *stretch leather*, to coït, C. 16–19 and C. 18–20, and *nothing like leather*, nothing like a good ****, C. 19–20.—3. As a football or a cricket ball, it is S.E., as are *hunt leather* and *leather-hunting*.

leather. To beat, thrash : from ca. 1620 : coll. >, ca. 1820, S.E. Prob. at first with a strap. Cf. *lather, tan, dust*, qq.v.

***leather, the.** A kick with booted foot : c. : C. 20. J. Curtis, *The Gilt Kid*, 1936.

leather-bumper. (Gen. pl.) A cavalryman : infantrymen's : late C. 19–20. F. & Gibbons.

leather-flapper. A keen horseman : sporting : from ca. 1865 ; virtually †. '*No. 747*.'

Leather Hats, the. The 8th Foot, in late C. 19–20 the King's Regiment (Liverpool) : military : C. 19–20. F. & Gibbons.

leather-head(ed), n. and adj., (a) blockhead : late C. 17–20 ; ob. Davenant ; B.E.

leather-jacket. (As fish, S.E.—) 2. Applied to various Australian trees : Australian coll. (— 1898) verging on S.E. Ex their tough skin. Morris.—3. A rough-and-ready pancake : Australian coll. : 1846, G. H. Haydon, *Five Years in Australia Felix*, '. . . Dough fried in a pan ' (Morris). Tough eating !—4. A small insect destructive of grass : coll. : C. 20. *The Daily Telegraph, passim* in April, 1935, in reports on the cricket-ground at Lord's. Ex its appearance.

leather-lane. The female pudend : C. 18–20 low ; ob.—2. As an adj., paltry, it is c. of ca. 1810–60. Vaux ; Egan's Grose. Always as *Leather Lane concern*.

leather-neck. A soldier ; more gen., a Royal Marine : nautical and esp. naval : mid-C. 19–20 ; ob. Bowen. Cf. *mud-crusher*.

leather-stretcher. The male member : C. 18–20, ob. : low. Ex *leather*, n., 2. Hence, *go leather-stretching*, to have sexual intercourse.

leathering. A thrashing : from ca. 1790 : coll. Ex *leather*, v.

leathern convenience, -cy. A stage-coach ; a carriage : Quakers' j. >, ca. 1790, jocular coll. ; † by 1860. B.E. ; C. K. Sharpe, 1801, ' I left Oxford with Stapleton in his mama's leathern conveniency.'

[**leathernly,** clumsily, sordidly, despite F. & H. is † S.E.]

leathers. A person wearing leggings or leather breeches, e.g. a postboy : coll. : ca. 1835–1910. Dickens ; Thackeray, in *Pendennis*. Cf. *boots, buttons*, q.v.—2. The ears : low : from ca. 1860.

leave. A (favourable) position for a stroke : billiards : from ca. 1850.

leave, take French. See French leave.

leave . . . be. To let be ; cease, or abstain, from interfering with : coll. : from ca. 1825.

leave an R in pawn. To desert : naval : C. 19. Bowen, ' The man's name in the ship's books being marked " R " for " run ".'

leave cold. See cold.

leave go (of), hold (of), (loose of), v.i. To let go : coll. : from ca. 1810.

leave in the air. See air.—**leave in the lurch.** See lurch.

leave in the briers or **seeds.** To bring to, or leave in, (grave) trouble : semi-proverbial coll. 1533, Udall (*briers*) ; ca. 1590, Harvey (*seeds*). Rare since ca. 1820. Apperson.

leave it all to the cook !, I'll. I won't take that bet : sporting c.p. of ca. 1820–40. Egan's Grose. (A cook is a good judge of meat, a betting-man of horseflesh.)

leave the minority. To die : Society : 1879 ; ob. Ware. On *join the majority*.

leave the sea and go into steam. To transfer to a steam-driven ship : sailing-men's c.p. : ca. 1860–1900. Bowen.

leave-yer-(h)omer. ' A handsome, dashing man . . . Derived, very satirically, from " That's the man I'm goin' to leave me 'ome for " ' (Ware) : lower class women's : late C. 19–20.

leaving-shop. An unlicensed pawn-broker's shop : low coll. (— 1857) ; ob. *The Morning Chronicle*, Dec. 21, 1857 ; J. Greenwood.—2. Hence, allusively, the female pudend : low : from ca. 1860 ; ob.

leccers. (Pron. *lekkers.*) Lectures : Oxford undergraduates' : from late 1890's. Ware. (Ox-ford-*er*.)

[**lecher, the v.,** is, despite F. & H., just as much S.E. as the n.]

led-captain. A toady, sponge, pimp : from ca. 1670 : coll. >, ca. 1800, S.E. ; † by 1880. Wycherley, in *Love in a Wood*, ' Every wit has his culley, as every squire his led captain.' Prob. ex *a led horse*. (But † *led friend*, a parasite, was always S.E.)

ledding. Sol. for *leaden* : Cockney and Australian : C. 19–20. C. J. Dennis.

leddy, the. A ship's figurehead, no matter what it represents : nautical : mid-C. 19–20. Bowen. Ex the old Scots and dial. *leddy*, a lady.

ledger. (Gen. in pl.) A ledger-clerk : bank-clerks' coll. : late C. 19–20. Cf. *voucher*.

Leeds. Lincolnshire and Yorkshire ordinary shares : Stock Exchange : ca. 1885–1915.

leek. A chimney-sweep not brought up to the trade : coll. : ca. 1850–1910 : low. Mayhew. Ex his *greenness*.—2. A Welshman : very late C. 17–early 19 c. *Street Robberies Considered*, ca. 1728. Cf. :

Leek, the. A fast goods-train running to Llanelly (in Wales) : railwaymen's : from ca. 1910. *The Daily Telegraph*, Aug. 15, 1936. See leek, 2. Cf. *the Bacca*, q.v.

Leekshire. Wales : low : C. 18–19. Ex the racial emblem.

***leer.** A newspaper : c. of ca. 1785–1870 G Parker, in *Life's Painter*, 1789. *?* ex Ger. *lehren*, to read ; much more prob. ex *the lure*, q.v.

***leer, roll the.** See roll the leer.

leerily. The adv. of *leary* : 1859. See leary. Farrar, in *Julian Home*, 1859 (O.E.D.).

***leery.** See leary.

leetle. Little : late C. 17–20 : on borderland between S.E. and (gen. jocular) coll. Cf. *lickell*, q.v.

leeward, go to. To put oneself at a disadvantage : nautical coll. : mid-C. 19–20. Cf. :

leeward of (occ. **on**), **get to.** ' To fall foul of a man ' : nautical coll. : late C. 19–20. Bowen. Ex nautical j.

lef. See lep.

left, adj. Revolutionary ; socialist(ic) ; communistic : coll. (? before 1918) ; in 1930's verging on S.E. ' In Kiel, where the revolution started, matters appear to be going "left" with a vengeance,' *The Daily Chronicle*, Dec. 2, 1918 (W.).

left, be or **get.** To fail; be outdistanced metaphorically; be placed in a difficult position: coll.: orig. (ca. 1980), U.S.; anglicised ca. 1895. Abbr. *be* or *get left in the lurch* (Ware).

left, over the; over the left shoulder. In the wrong way. But gen. a c.p. used to negate one's own or another's statement, the thumb being sometimes pointed over that shoulder: from ca. 1610; slightly ob. In C. 19–20, when the phrase is somewhat low, *shoulder* is gen. omitted. Cotgrave; H. D. Traill, 1870, ' Don't go ? . . . It's go and go over the left . . . it's go with a hook at the end.'

left-forepart. A wife: mid-C. 19–20; ob. ? ex-*left rib.* Cf. *Dutch,* q.v.

left-hand man of the line, the. ' The sentry on the last post westward of the British line in Flanders': jocular military coll.: 1914–18. F. & Gibbons.

[**left-handed, left-handed wife, left-hander, are** S.E.]

left her purse on her piano. A c.p. constituting a ' satirical hit at self-sufficiency ': non-aristocratic: late C. 19–early 20. Ware.

left in the basket. See **basketed.**

left shoulder, over the. See **left, over the.**—**left-off,** gen. in pl. Left-off clothes: coll.: from ca. 1890.

*****lefter, over the.** See **over the lefter.**

Lefty. A proletarian ' inevitable nickname' (late C. 19–20), as in Francis D. Grierson, *Murder at Lancaster Gate,* 1934, ' Lefty Harris, they called him, on account of his being left-handed.'

leg. A swindling gambler at race-courses: 1815 (O.E.D.); ob. Abbr. *blackleg* (q.v. in turf sense). Dickens in *Pickwick,* ' He *was* a horse-chaunter: he's a leg now.'—2. A point: card-players': from ca. 1860. H., 3rd ed.—3. A bow, as in *make a leg*: S.E.—4. See **legs.**—5. A footman: fast society: ca. 1860–1910. Ware, ' From the display of the lower limbs.'

leg, v. To trip up: from ca. 1880: also dial. *The Saturday Review,* April 22, 1882, ' They legged the copper, and he fell to the ground.'—2. Gen. as *leg it,* to run away: S.E.

[Of F. & H.'s *leg* phrases, many—despite the ' look ' of some—are S.E.:—**make** or **scrape a leg** (to bow), **in high leg, leg up** (assistance), **lift a leg** (make water), **shake a free** or **loose leg, not a leg to stand on,** † **fight at the leg, put one's best leg foremost,** (put) **the boot on the other leg, leg of mutton** (adj.), **be** or **get on one's legs** (but see **legs, get on one's hind**), **get** or **set on one's legs, fall on one's legs, feel one's legs, have the legs of one, on one's last legs, stand on one's own legs, stretch one's legs.]

leg, as right as my. As right as may be; decidedly: from ca. 1660; ob.: low coll.—2. Occ. as adj., perfectly right, ' a bit of all right ': C. 18–20; ob.

leg, break a. To give birth to a bastard: low coll.: from ca. 1670; ob. R. Head, in *Proteus Redivivus.* The proverbial form gen. added *above the knee*; gen., too, as *to have broken her leg.* See also **broken-legged.**

leg, cut one's. To get drunk: C. 18–early 19 coll.

leg, drop the. To decamp: lower classes' (— 1923). Manchon.—2. To make a leg, to bow or curtsey: rural coll. (— 1923) and dial. Ibid.

leg (or **arm** or **throat**), **have a bone in one's.** To be incapacitated: coll., as a playful refusal: from

ca. 1540. Udall, 1542, ' Allegeing that he had a bone in his throte and could not speake '; Torriano, 1666, ' The English say, He hath a bone in his arm and cannot work '; Swift, ca. 1706 (pub. 1738), ' I can't go, for I have a bone in my leg.' In C. 19–20 dial., to *have a bone in the arm* or *leg* is to have a shooting pain there.

leg, lift one's. To coït: low: C. 18–20; ob. Anon., in *Duncan Davidson,* a song. (But, gen. of a horse, *lift a leg,* to walk, is S.E.)

leg, make a. (Of a woman) to display one's leg(s): lower classes' coll. (— 1923). Manchon.

leg, make one's. To feather one's nest: id. Ibid. Contrast the preceding.

leg, pull one's. To befool; impose on: coll. (— 1888); now on verge of S.E. Ex *tripping-up.*

leg, show a. To rise from bed: orig. naval coll. (in C. 20 verging on S.E.): from ca. 1830. In C. 20, gen. in the imperative. Cf. military *rise and shine !,* q.v.

leg, swing the. To loaf; malinger: nautical: from ca. 1860. (Corrupted by the Army to *swing the lead*: see at **lead**). Ex a dog running on three legs, sometimes to rest the fourth, sometimes to elicit sympathy (Mr H. G. Dixey, in a letter to the author). Cf. *leg-swinger, -swinging, swinging a leg.*

leg-and-leg, adv. and adj. (Of a game) when each player has won a ' leg ' or point; level: cards coll.: from ca. 1860. In Anglo-Irish, *horse-and-horse.*

leg-bags. Trousers: from ca. 1855; ob.—2. Stockings: ca. 1870–1910.

leg-bail (and land-security), give or **take** To escape from custody; to decamp: from ca. 1760: semi-proverbial coll. >, ca. 1700, S.E.; slightly ob. Ray, Grose.

leg-business. Sexual intercourse: low coll.: C. 19–20; ob.—2. Ballet-dancing: from ca. 1870. Cf. *leg-shop* and *leggy.*

leg-drama, -piece, -show. A play or a ballet distinguished for the amount of leg shown by the female participants: resp. from ca. 1870, 1880, 1890.

leg-grinder. A revolution round the horizontal bar as one hangs by one's legs: gymnastic coll. (— 1887). Baumann. Cf. *muscle-grinder,* the same exercise as one hangs by one's arms.

leg in, get a. To win another's confidence, esp. to gain proof of confidence and/or esteem: coll.: from ca. 1890. Nat Gould.

leg in, own a. To have an interest, a share in (horses): sporting: from ca. 1865; ob. ' *No. 747.*'

leg-lifter. A male fornicator: C. 18–20 (ob.) low. So *leg-lifting,* fornication.

leg-maniac. An ' eccentric, rapid dancer ': theatrical coll.: ca. 1880–1915. Ware.

leg of mutton. A sheep's trotter: low: from ca. 1850. (Adj.: S.E.)

leg of the law. A lawyer: C. 19–20; ob.: low. Varying *limb of the law.*

leg off or **shot off, have a.** (Of an animal) to have a leg broken, e.g. by a shot: South African coll.: 1906, Watkins, *From Farm to Forum.* Ex Cape Dutch idiom. Pettman.

leg on or **over, lay** or **lift a.** To coït with a woman: low coll.: C. 18–20. D'Urfey, Bruns. Cf. *leg, lift one's,* and *leg-lifter.*

leg-piece. See **leg-drama.**

leg-shaker. A dancer: (low) coll.: C. 19–20; ob.

leg-shop. A theatre specialising in the display of the female form: from ca. 1872; ob. Cf. *leg-business, -drama, -show.*

leg shot off. See **leg off.**

leg show. See **leg-drama. Very** common in 1914–18, *leg-show* is applied less to the programme as a whole than to the underclad personnel in action or to a leggy 'number'. B. & P.

leg-swinger. A loafer; malingerer: nautical: from ca. 1860. (Corrupted by the Army to *lead-swinger*, q.v.) Ex *leg, swing the*, q.v. Cf. :

leg-swinging or swinging the leg. Loafing; pretended illness or injury: nautical: from ca. 1860. See **lead, swing the.**

legal, the. Abbr. *the legal fare*: lower classes' coll. (− 1923). Manchon.

[**legem pone** and **legerdemain**, despite F. & H., are both S.E.]

legend. Catachrestic for *legion*: late C. 16–20. Shakespeare, Mrs. Behn. (O.E.D.)

*****leger.** A giver of short weight in coals.—2. **legering** (*law*), this practice. Ca. 1590–1650: c. Greene. Ex Fr. *léger*, light.

*****legged.** In irons: c. > low: **ca.** 1830–70. Brandon.

*****legger.** One pretending to sell smuggled, but actually selling shop-worn, goods: ca. 1785–1830: c. Grose, 2nd ed.—2. A reprimand by a master: Charterhouse: C. 20. Ex *lecture* by 'the Oxford-er'.

leggings. Stockings: (somewhat low) jocular coll.: from ca. 1870; ob.

leggism. The art or the character of a 'leg' (q.v., sense 1): from ca. 1820; ob.

leggo ! 'Leg it !'; run !: low: late C. 19–20.—2. Let go !: sol.: mid-C. 19–20. (D. Sayers, *Murder Must Advertise*, 1933.)

leggy. As long-legged, S.E.—2. Notable for the display of leg: from ca. 1865. Cf. *leg-business*, *-shop*, qq.v. *The Daily Telegraph*, Jan. 10, 1866, 'Leggy burlesques' (O.E.D.).

leggy-peggy. A (little) leg: nursery (− 1887). Baumann.

legit, the. A C. 20 theatrical abbr. of *legitimate drama*. See **legitimate, the.**

legitimacy. The reason for much early emigration to Australia: Australia: ca. 1820–60. Ex the legal necessity of the voyage. Peter Cunningham. Cf. *legitimates.*

legitimate. A sovereign (coin): Londoners': ca. 1820–50. Bee. Prob. ex *legitimate sovereign* (king).

legitimate, adj. Applied to flat racing as opp. to steeplechasing: racing (− 1888).

legitimate, the. Legitimate drama, i.e. good (mainly Shakespearean) drama, as opp. to burlesque: theatrical (− 1887).

legitimates. Convict emigrants: Australian: ca. 1820–60. See **legitimacy.** Morris.

[**leglin-girth, cast a.** To conceive a child. Ineligible: Scots dial.]

legs. A tall, thin person, esp. if a man: coll.: C. 19–20. Cf. *lamp-post.*

legs, be or get on one's hind. To be speaking, rise to speak, esp. if formally: jocular coll. (− 1897). Without *hind*, it is S.E.—2. To fall into a rage (occ. with *rear* instead of *get*): C. 20. Ex a horse rearing.

legs, give—or show—(a clean pair of). To run away; decamp: coll. (− 1883).

legs, have. To be (considered) fast (e.g. of ship, train, runner): coll.: from ca. 1870.

legs, make indentures with one's. To be tipsy: C. 18–early 19. Ray.

legs, merry. See **merry legs.**

legs and arms. Weak beer: tailors': from ca. 1860. Because without body.

legs eleven. The number 11 in the game of house: military: C. 20.—2. Hence, eleven o'clock: military: from 1914.—3. A very tall thin man: military: from ca. 1915. F. & Gibbons

legs grew in the night, therefore could not see to grow straight,—his. A jeering c.p. addressed to a crooked-legged man. Grose, 3rd ed. Cf. *buy one's boots . . .*

legs in a bed, more belongs or goes to marriage than four bare. A c.p., > proverbial when applied to a portionless couple: from ca. 1540; ob. Heywood, 1546; Swift; Scott; Apperson. Cf. the C. 17–18 proverb, *there belongs more than whistling to going to plough.*

legs on one's neck or to ground, lay one's To decamp; run away: coll.: C. 17–early 19, C. 17–20, the latter extant only in dial.

Legshire. The Isle of Man: C. 19–20; **ob.** Ex the heraldic bearings.

leisure hours. Flowers: rhyming s. (− 1909). Ware.

lemma. An error for *lemna*, a genus of aquatic plants: mid-C. 18–20. O.E.D.

lemme. (Pronounced *lemmy*.) Let me: sol.: C. 19–20.

lemon. An unattractive female, esp. if a girl: U.S., anglicised by 1932. C.O.D., 1934. Ex :— 2. Something undesirable: from ca. 1921. Esp. in *the answer is a lemon* (see below); but also as in *The Daily Express*, Dec. 13, 1927, 'Middlesbrough seem to have picked a lemon, for the draw gives them South Shields as opponents' (O.E.D. Sup.).

lemon, squeeze the. To make water: C. 19–20: low. Ob.

lemon, the answer is a. A derisive-reply c.p. (orig., ca. 1910, U.S.): in England from ca. 1920; ob. Ex the bitterness of a lemon as an eaten fruit.

lemon-rob. Lemon- or lime-juice as an antiscorbutic: nautical (− 1867); slightly ob. Smyth. Subjectively pejorative.

lemoncholy. Melancholy: London (− 1909); ob. Ware. By jocular transposition and slight distortion of *melan.* Cf. :

lemonjolly. A jocular distortion of *melancholy*: ca. 1860–1910. Occ. *lemon colly, lemon* punning *melan.* Cf. *colly molly*, q.v.

lend. A loan: coll. from ca. 1825 ex C. 16–20 dial. 'For the lend of the ass you might give me the mill,' old ballad.

lend, v. Give, as in 'Lend me a lick of the ice-cream !': proletarian coll. (− 1887). Baumann.

lend us your breath to kill Jumbo ! A proletarian c.p. of 1882–ca. 1910. Ware, 'Protest against the odour of bad breath.' (See **jumbo, 3,** and **jumbo-ism.**)

lend us your pound ! Pull your weight (on the rope): a jocular nautical c.p.: late C. 19–20. Bowen.

lenety. See **lenity.**

length. 42 lines: 1736 (O.E.D.): theatrical s. >, ca. 1880, theatrical coll. Fielding; G. Parker; Dickens, 'I've a part of twelve lengths.'—2. Six months' imprisonment: c.: from ca. 1850. H., 1st ed. Cf. *dose, moon, stretch*, qq.v.

length of a . . ., go the. To lend as much as a (guinea, etc.): coll. (− 1887). Baumann.

length of one's foot, get the. See **foot, get the length of one's.**

lenity. Incorrect for *lenitive.* : C. 16–19. Also *lenety.* O.E.D.

[**lenten-faced, lenten fare,** in F. & H., are S.E.]

Lents. The Lent Term boat-races : Cambridge University : 1893 (S.O.D.) : coll. till C. 20, then S.E.

lep ; occ. **lef.** Left, esp. in words of command : military : C. 19–20. (Andrew Buchanan, *He Died Again*, 1933.) In the same way, *right > ri*, as in *ri turn !, ri wheel !*

leracam. Mackerel : back s. (— 1859). H., 1st ed. Occ. *luracham.*

[**leri(com)poop, leripup, liripipe, liripoop, luripup ;** also two r's. S.E.]

lernilite is erroneous for *lennilite* : from ca. 1867. O.E.D.

lerry-come-twang. A fool : Restoration period. Ex a popular refrain-tag of the time.

Lesbian. A woman sexually devoted to women : coll (— 1896) >, ca. 1930, S.E. Ex the Sapphic legend. (In neither O.E.D. nor S.O.D.)

-less in mid-C. 19–20 usage often borders on the coll.

'less or less. Unless : Canadian (and U.S.) coll. ; mid-C. 19–20. Ex English dial. usage. Cf. *'cept.*

lesson. See **simple arithmetic.**

-let. A diminutive that, in C. 18–20, occ. has a coll. force.

let, to. (Of a canvas) sparsely filled : painters' (— 1909) ; ob. Ware.—2. See **apartments to let.**

let alone. (Prepositional phrase.) Much less ; not to mention : coll. : 1816, Jane Austen ; Barham, 'I have not had . . . [a] brown to buy a bit of bread with—let alone a tart.' Occ. *letting alone* (1843 ; ob.). O.E.D.—2. **let me, him,** etc., **alone** († **for doing,) to do something**) coll. : C. 17–20. Shakespeare, ' Let me alone for swearing ' ; Dryden, ' Let me alone to accuse him afterwards.' O.E.D.

let daylight into. To stab, shoot ; kill : coll. : C. 19–20. See also at **daylight.**

let-down. A disappointment ; deception : coll. (— 1894).—2. The v. : S.E.

let down (a person's) **blind.** To indicate that he is dead : coll. (— 1923). Manchon.

let down easily or **gently.** To be lenient to : coll. : 1834, M. Scott, ' By way of letting him down gently, I said nothing.'—2. Occ. = *let down*, to disappoint : late C. 19–20 : coll.

let drive, aim a blow, is S.E.—**let fly** : see **fly.**

let 'em all come ! A c.p. expressive of cheeky defiance : 1896 : lower classes' >, by ca. 1912, gen. Ware relates its origin to the manner in which the British received the German Emperor's message of congratulation to Kruger, on the repulse of the Jameson Raid, the U.S.A.'s communication concerning the English boundary dispute with Venezuela, and the shortly ensuing tricoloured agitation in the French press. Cf. *let her rip !*

let 'em trundle ! ' Clear out ! ', go away : app. ca. 1695–1730. Congreve, *The Way of the World*, 1700 (cited by G. H. McKnight).

let go. To achieve sexual emission : low coll. : C. 19–20.—2. Not to mention ; all the more reason, e.g. ' Let go he wasn't there ' : lower classes' coll. — 1923). Manchon. On *let alone . . .*

let go the painter. See **painter.**

let her fizzle. ' To keep on all possible sail in a strong wind ' : Canadian (and U.S.) nautical : from ca. 1870 ; ob. Cf. :

let her rip ! Let it (etc.) go freely ! ; damn the consequences ! : coll. : mid-C. 19–20. Perhaps orig. U.S. (as Ware and Thornton think).

let her roll ! Let's have it ! ; ' on with the dance ! ' : Canadian lumbermen's : C. 20. John Beames. Ex logging.

let-in. An illegal victimisation ; **a robbery ;** a gross deception : coll. (— 1923). Manchon. Ex :

let in, v. To victimise ; deceive, cheat : coll. : from ca. 1830. Thackeray, ' He had been let in terribly . . . by Lord Levant's insolvency.' Ex ice giving way.—2. V.i., to deal, gen. followed by *with* : university (mostly Oxford) : from ca. 1860 ; ob. T. Hughes, *Tom Brown at Oxford.* Cf. :

let (another or oneself) **in for.** To involve in : coll. : late C. 19–20 ; by 1935, S.E. Always with— occ. jocular—implication of unpleasantness.

let into. To attack ; abuse ; beat : from ca. 1850 ; ob. Mayhew, ' Those that let into the police, [got] eighteen months.' Cf. S.E. *let out at.*

let it run. To write as fully as the facts allow : journalistic coll. : late C. 19–20.

let loose. See **let oneself loose.**

let-loose match. A bull-baiting : sporting : ca. 1820–40. Egan's Grose.

let me chat yer (or **you**) **!** Let me tell you ! : a New Zealand soldiers' c.p. in the G.W.

let me die ! A synonym of *carry me out !*, q.v. : ca. 1860–1914.

let off steam. See **steam.**

let on. To admit ; betray : dial. (— 1725) >, ca. 1830, coll. Haliburton, 1835 ; Boucicault, ' Don't let on to mortal that we're married.'—2. Hence, mostly in Australia and New Zealand and from ca. 1880, occ. to pretend, make believe, give to understand : coll. : orig. dial. >, by 1828, Southern U.S. (Thornton).

let oneself loose. To speak **or** act without restraint : coll. : C. 19–20.

let out. As speak strongly, strike out, it is, despite F. & H., clearly S.E.—2. To disclose a secret, information, v.i. : from ca. 1870 : coll., mostly U.S. (The v.t. is S.E.)—3. A gen. v.i. of action, but esp., v.t., to give a horse his head ; v.i., to ride at greater speed : coll. : from ca. 1885. ' Rolf Boldrewood.' —4. See **lets out her fore-rooms.**—5. To exonerate, vindicate, clear from all suspicion of guilt : coll. : C. 20. Adopted, ca. 1918, from U.S.A., where employed before 1909 (Ware). ' This new piece of evidence certainly lets him out.' See almost any post-War detective novel.

let out a reef. To unbutton after a meal : from ca. 1850 : nautical >, ca. 1880, gen. coll.

let rip. See **rip,** but cf. *let her rip.*—**let slide.** See **slide.**—**let the cat out of the bag.** See **cat.**

let-up. A pause, a cessation : orig. (1837) and still mainly U.S. ; partially adopted ca. 1880 : coll. till C. 20, when S.E. (Thornton.)—2. Hence, ' a sudden disappearance of artificial causes of depression,' F. & H. : Stock Exchange : from 1880's. In C. 20, S.E.

let up, v.i., to become less (esp. less severe), to cease, is orig. (ca. 1857) and still mainly U.S. : rare in England before C. 20. Coll. Cf. :

let up on. To cease to have—esp. anything pejorative—to do with : coll. : orig. (1857) and still mainly U.S. (Thornton.)

letch-water. The sexual secretion : low coll. : late C. 18–20 ; ob. See S.E. *letch.*

let's ! Let us (sc. do something expressed or implied) ! Coll. : late C. 19–20. Often *yes, let's !*

lets, no. Without hindrance or modification: schoolboys': from ca. 1850. Cf. *fain I* and *fen.*

let's have one ! See **how will you have it ?**

let's hear from you ! Hurry up !; look lively: military c.p.: G.W. (F. & Gibbons.) Ex the vocal numbering of a rank of soldiers.

lets out her fore-rooms,—she lies backwards and. She is a harlot, esp. one not professed: proverbial coll.: ca. 1630–1850. Motteux.

let's play silly buggers ! Let's pretend we're mad !; (playfully) Let's do something silly !: a lower classes' (from early C. 20) >, by late 1914, military c.p.; ob. B. & P. Cf. *run away and play trains !*

lettary. A lodging; lodgings: grafters': late C. 19–20. Philip Allingham, *Cheapjack*, 1934. A variant of **letty**, q.v.

letter. Abbr. (— 1896) of *French letter*, q.v.—2. Hell; only in *what the* (*bloody*) *letter !*, what the (bloody) hell !: euphemistic (— 1923). Manchon. Ex *'ell* = l[*etter*].

letter, go and post a. To coït: low: mid-C. 19–20; ob. Cf. *see a man about a dog.*—2. Occ., to visit the w.c.: C. 20.

letter-fencer. A postman: low London (—1909). Ware.

letter in the post office, there is a. See **flag**, n., 3; it is synonymous with the phrase there: late C. 19–20; ob.

letter-man. (Gen. pl.) A steward doing his first trip with a company: nautical: late C. 19–20. Bowen. Because presumed to have had a letter of introduction to the seniors.—2. **letter man.** One who has been in prison an indicated number of years: prison c. (— 1933). Charles E. Leach. Each year an alphabetical letter is assigned by the prison authorities to indicate the current year of a sentence.

*letter Q. An underworld dodge known also as the *billiard slum* or *mace*, q.v. Hence, *go on the* (*letter*) *Q*, to practise this dodge: c.: ca. 1810–60. Vaux, ' Alluding to an instrument used in playing billiards '.

*letter-racket. Begging by letter: vagrants' c.: from ca. 1810. Vaux.

*lettered. Branded; burnt in the hand: C. 18–early 19 c. Cf. *charactered.*

letting alone. See **let alone**, 1.

letty. A bed; a lodging. Also v.i., to lodge. Parlyaree (— 1859); in C. 20, mainly theatrical. Ex It. *letto*, a bed, via Lingua Franca. H., 1st ed.; J. Frost, *Circus Life*, 1875; Ware; E. Seago, *Circus Company*, 1933. Also occ. *latty*. (See section on Parlyaree, in my *Slang*.)

[**levant**, v.; **levant me !**; **levanter :**—despite F. & H., these are S.E.]

level, on the. Adj. and adv., honest(ly), fair(ly): coll., orig. (— 1900) U.S., anglicised by 1905. Perhaps ex U.S. (*act* or *work*) *on a broad level*, be trustworthy. Cf. *square*, *straight*, and contrast *crook*, *cross.*

level best. One's best or utmost: coll.: orig. (1851), U.S.; anglicised ca. 1870. E. Hale, 1873, ' I said, " I'll do my level best, Doctor." '

level-coil, play. To coït: c.: C. 17–early 18: low. Ex S.E. † *level-coil*, a rough, noisy game.

level pegging. (Of competitors) keeping level; also n. This s. (from before 1900) has, by 1920, > coll. Collinson.

leven. ' In back s., is sometimes allowed to stand for *eleven*, for . . . it is a number which seldom occurs. An article is either 10*d.* or 1*s.*', H., 1859.

Levi Nathan. The U.S. *Leviathan*: nautical: early C. 20. By ' Hobson-Jobson ' and ' from the favour she won with wealthy Hebrews '. (Bowen.)

leviathan. A heavy backer of horses: sporting journalists' (— 1887); virtually †. Baumann. Ex S.E. sense.

[**levite**, whether clergyman or dress, is † S.E.: despite F. & H.]

levitor is catachrestic for *levator*: C. 17–20. O.E.D.

levy. A shilling: low: from ca. 1860. H., in 3rd ed., says Liverpool. Ex U.S. *levy* (1832), an abbr. of *eleven* or perhaps even *elevenpenny bit*: see esp. Bartlett, 1848, and Thornton. (—As v., in C. 17 occ. erroneously for *level*. O.E.D.)

[**lewd infusion** is euphemistic S.E.]

Lewis. A coll. military abbr. (1915 +) of *Lewis gun*, ' a kind of magazine-fed, gas-operated, and air-cooled machine-gun ', S.O.D. Ex its American inventor, Colonel Isaac Newton Lewis. (See esp. B. & P., pp. 214, 328.)

Lewis Cornaro; gen. **a.** A water-drinker: London: ca. 1820–40. Bee. (Topical.)

leystall. See **laystall.**

liable to. Used in error for *incident to*: 1631–1746. (S.O.D.)

liar myself, I'm a bit or something of a. A c.p. reply to a liar: orig. (— 1896), U.S.; adopted in British Empire ca. 1900 as a coll.; since G.W., S.E.

*lib. Sleep: c. of ca. 1670–1800. R. Head.—2. A bank-note: c.: C. 19.—3. (*Lib*; gen. pl.) A Liberal: 1885, *Punch* (Baumann).—4. (Always *the Lib.*) The Library: Charterhouse (— 1900). A. H. Tod, ' A collection of Library books is " Lib. Coll." '

*lib, v. To sleep, lie down; also to coït: c. of ca. 1560–1870. Harman, B.E., Grose. Also *lyp* (C. 16–17).—2. As castrate, S.E.

*lib-beg, libbege; lyb beg(e), lybbeg(e); lib-(b)edge. A bed: c. of ca. 1560–1860. Harman, Rowlands, Head, B.E., Grose.

*lib-ken, libken; lipken, lypken; lib- or lybkin. A house; a lodging: c. of ca. 1560–1880. Harman, Jonson, B.E., Grose, Scott, Mayhew. Ex *lib + ken*, qq.v. Cf.:

*libben. A private house: c. of ca. 1670–1860. Coles. Ex preceding.

[**liberty hall**, or with capitals. Not coll., but allusive S.E.]

library. A theatre-ticket agency: theatrical: C. 20. Denis Mackail, *Romance to the Rescue*, 1921, ' In the Christmas holidays people will go to any show that the libraries tell 'em to go to.'

licence ?, have you a. See **have you a licence ?**

licet. Allowed, permissible: Winchester: C. 19–20. Wrench. Ex L. *licet*, it is permissible.

lick, a blow, is S.E. and dial. But see **licks.**—2. A hasty wash; a dab of paint: coll.: from ca. 1650. Cf. *lick and a promise* and *licked.*—3. A drinking bout: low (— 1886); ob. *The Daily Telegraph*, March 3, 1886.—4. A turn of speed or work, esp. if great or vigorous: (dial. and) U.S. and Australian coll.: 1837 (S.O.D.). See **licks, big.**

lick, v. To beat, thrash: perhaps orig. c. or low (it's in Harman) >, ca. 1700, gen. s.: from ca. 1535. (See also **lick into fits.**)—2. To defeat, surpass: s. >, in C. 20, coll.: from ca. 1800. De Quincey.—3. To astound, puzzle: from ca. 1855. ' Ducange Anglicus.' See **licks me, it.**—4. V.i., to ride at full speed : Australian (— 1889) ; ob., except of a motor-car (Lyell). See lick, at full. ' Rolf Boldrewood '. —5. See licked.—6. F. & H.'s other senses, ineligible.

lick, (at) a great or, more gen., full. At a great or at full speed : coll. : U.S. (? orig.) and Australian : from ca. 1888. ' Rolf Boldrewood '.

lick and a promise, a. A piece of slovenly work, esp. a hasty, inadequate wash of hands and/or face : coll. : from ca. 1870.

lick and a smell, a. Almost nothing, esp. as to food ; a ' dog's portion ', q.v. : coll. : mid-C. 18–20. Grose.

[lick-box, -dish, -fingers, -pan, -pot, -sauce, -trencher ; lick-penny ; lick-spigot (a tapster); lick-spittle (and v.) :—despite F. & H., all S.E.]

lick into fits. To defeat thoroughly : from ca. 1875. Ex lick, v., 1.

[lick into shape, like lick the trencher (to toady) : S.E. despite F. & H.]

lick of the tar-brush, a, the. A, the, seaman : nautical : late C. 19–20. Bowen. Ex the utility of tar on shipboard.

lick one's (more gen., the) eye. To be well pleased : low coll. : mid-C. 19–20 ; ob.

lick out of. To drive (something) out of (a person) by thrashing : from ca. 1880 ; ob. O.E.D.

lick-spigot ; 1.-twat. Resp. fellatrix, fellator. Low : resp. C. 18–20, ob. ; C. 17–20.

lick-up. Trade s. of mid-C. 19–20 as in quotation at smother.

lick you, I'll. This threat in C. 18–early 19 evoked the following ' dovetail ', i.e. c.p. reply : If you lick me all over, you won't miss my a***. Grose.

licked, lickt, ppl.adj. Applied to ' Pictures new Varnished, Houses new Whitened, or Women's faces with a Wash ', B.E. : coll. : late C. 17–20.

lickell. Little : C. 18–mid-19 coll. Ex little on mickle. Cf. leetle, q.v.

licker. Anything excessive, in size, degree, quality : C. 18–20 ; ob. Cf. the adj. licking, also spanker, thumper, whopper, qq.v., and lick, v., 3, its imm. origin.

lickidation. Liquidation : sol. (— 1887). Baumann.

licking. A thrashing : from ca. 1755 : s. >, ca. 1800, coll. Toldervy. (O.E.D.)—2. A defeat : from ca. 1800 : s. >, in C. 20, S.E.

licking, adj. First-rate, splendid, excellent : from ca. 1680 ; ob. by 1900 ; by 1936, all but †. Cotton, Eden Phillpotts. (O.E.D.) Cf. licker, q.v.

licks, with my, your, his, etc. A thrashing : late C. 18–20 : coll. (†) and dial. Burns. Ex lick, n., 1.

licks, big. Hard work ; also adv., by hard work, ' great guns ' : Australian, from ca. 1888 (e.g. in ' Rolf Boldrewood '), but ob.; orig. (— 1861), U.S. Cf. lick, (at) a great.

licks, give (something) big. To enjoy greatly : Glasgow : C. 20. Exactly equivalent, semantically, to laldie, give, q.v. : cf. punish.

licks me, it. It's beyond my comprehension : coll. : from ca. 1855. Anon., Derby Day, 1864. Ex lick, v., 2 ; cf. it beats me. (The past tense occurs : e.g. in ' It licked me how the bottom itself did not tumble clean away from the ship,' The Durham County Advertizer, Nov. 10, 1871.)

lid. A hat, a cap, or (in Glasgow, at least) even a bonnet : from ca. 1905.—2. A steel helmet : soldiers' : from 1915. B. & P. Cf. battle bowler and tin hat.

lid, dip one's. To raise (lit., lower) one's hat : Australian (— 1916). C. J. Dennis. See lid, 1.

lid,—like pot, like (pot-) ; or with such for like. (Also a lid worthy of such, or the, kettle.) A proverbial coll. expressive of suitability, similarity, adequacy : C. 16–18. Palsgrave, Urquhart, Fuller. (Apperson.)

lid on (it), that's put the. (Cf. lie with a lid on, q.v.) That's done it ; nothing more's to be said ; that's finished it ; ' good night ! ' : late C. 19–20 c.p.

lie, n. See white lie and whole cloth ; also trowel and loud one.

lie, v. To be in pawn : C. 17 : coll. Anon., The Man in the Moon, 1609.—2. To lay : late M.E.–C. 20 : erroneous, and—as such—coll. ; rare in C. 19–20. Fielding.

[lie-abed, n., and lie down, be brought to bed : despite F. & H., clearly S.E.]

lie as fast as a dog can lick a dish ; as fast as a dog (or horse) will trot. To tell lies ' like anything ' ; semi-proverbial coll. : resp. C. 16–17 ; C. 16–20, but in C. 19–20 mainly dial. Apperson.

lie at the Pool of Bethesda. (Of theological candidates) to await employment : theological students' (— 1909). Ware. Ex Ger.

lie back and let, etc. See lets out her fore-rooms.

lie by one, not to let anybody. To be a liar : C. 17–18 coll. Ray.

lie by the wall. To be dead : C. 15–20 : coll. till C. 18, then dial. (Apperson.)

lie doggo. See doggo.

lie down. To take a reprimand, a lie, a beating, etc., abjectly. Only in take lying down. 1888, The Saturday Review, Aug. 4. (O.E.D.)

lie fiat. See lie low ; † by 1910.

lie in. To remain in one's room when one is supposedly out on leave : Royal Military Academy : ca. 1870–1914. Ex the S.E. sense.

lie in state. To lie between two women : low : C. 19–20 (? ob.).

lie laid on with a trowel. An outrageous and obvious lie : coll. (— 1931). Lyell. Ex S.E. lay it on with a trowel.

lie like a flat-fish. To tell lies adroitly : nautical : late C. 19–20. Bowen. By pun on lie.

lie like truth. To tell a lie with seemly verisimilitude : coll. (— 1876). C. Hindley, ' [Cheapjacks] are always supposed, and by common consent allowed, to lie like truth.'

lie low. (Also † lie flat.) To hide one's person or one's intentions ; occ., but † by 1910, to keep to one's bed : coll. : from ca. 1845. F. Anstey, ' So you've very prudently been lying low.'

lie nailed to the counter. See counter.

lie off. ' To make a waiting-race ', F. & H. : the turf (— 1896).

lie on the face. See lay on the face.

lie on the knuckle. (Of a ship) to be ' drawn alongside the entrance to a dock, generally waiting for a tug ' : nautical coll. : late C. 19–20. Bowen.

lie out of one's ground. To ' lie off ' (q.v.) too long and so, unintentionally, lose the race : the turf (— 1896).

lie with a latchet. A thorough-going lie : coll. : C. 17–20, but since 1820, only dial. Ray, Fuller. (Apperson.). Also known as a † lie made of whole cloth, or (in dial.) out of the whole stuff, and one laid on with a trowel.

lie with a lid on, gen. preceded by that's a. Coll., but mostly dial. : 1880, Spurgeon. (Apperson.)

lied, v. Lay : sol. : C. 18–20. Baumann.

life, bet your. See bet your life.—life, it's a great. See it's a great life.—*life, know. See know life.—life, lag for. See lifer, 1 ; also lag.

life, nothing in my young. Gen. preceded by *he* (or *she*) *is*. He means nothing to me : from ca. 1930. Orig. among the youthful and of one sex for the other. E.g. in Achmed Abdullah's story in *Nash's Magazine*, Feb., 1935.

life, not on your. Certainly not ! : coll. : from middle 1890's.

life, this is the. See this is the life !—life !, we ain't got much money but we do see. See we ain't . . .

life and everlasting, for. (Esp. of sales) final ; without appeal : lower and lower-middle classes' coll. : mid-C. 19–early 20. Ware.

life of him, me, etc., for the ; for my, etc., life (ob.). Gen. preceded by *cannot*. To save one's (exaggerated) life : coll. : 1809, Malkin, ' Not knowing how for the life of him to part with those flattering hopes ' (O.E.D.).

life-preserver. A loaded bludgeon or stick, properly one used in self-defence. F. & H. gives as U.S. c. : rather is it S.E. (1837 : S.O.D.).—2. The penis : low : from ca. 1840 ; ob.

life there's soap, while there's. A jocular c.p. variation on the old proverb : C. 20.

lifeboat party, the. A nucleus battalion left out of an engagement : jocular military : 1916–18. F. & Gibbons.

*lifer. One sentenced, for life, to transportation (1830 ; † by 1890) or (from ca. 1860) to penal servitude : c. R. Dawson, *The Present State of Australia*, 1831 ; Dickens. Also, *lag for life* (ob.).—2. Penal servitude (orig. transportation) for life : 1832 : c. Besant, ' Twenty-five years . . . as good as a lifer.' Cf. *lagging and a lifer*, q.v. (O.E.D.)

*lift. A thief, esp. from shops : c. : late C. 16–early 19. Greene, ' A receiver for lifts, and a dishonourable supporter of cut-purses '. Cf. *lifter* and *shop-lift*, *-lifter*.—2. A theft ; plunder : c. : late C. 16–mid-19. Also *lifting*.—3. A kick : coll. : orig. footballers' : late C. 19–20.—4. Hence, a punch : lower classes' coll. (— 1923). Manchon.—5. As assistance, it is S.E.—6. Conceit, ' side ' ; presumption : Shrewsbury School : from ca. 1885. (Desmond Coke, *The Bending of a Twig*, 1906.) Whence the adj., *lifty*, recorded by the same author. Cf. *roll*, q.v.

*lift, v. To steal, v.i. and t. : c. (1526) >, ca. 1750, gen. s. Skelton, Greene. From ca. 1850, gen. applied to stealing cattle and horses.—2. Hence, to transfer matter from one periodical to another : journalists' and printers' (— 1891).—3. ' To bring (a constellation) above the horizon in sailing, etc.' : coll. : 1891. Kipling. (O.E.D.)—4. The sporting senses are S.E.—5. See lifted, be.—6. To arrest : low Glasgow (— 1934).

lift, a good hand at a dead. A person reliable in emergency: coll.>, by C.19, S.E. C. 17–mid-19. Grose.

lift-leg. Strong ale ; ' stingo ', q.v. : C. 18–mid-19 : low. Cf. :

lift-leg, play at. To have sexual intercourse: C. 18–mid-19 low. Also *lift one's leg*.

lift or raise one's elbow, hand, little finger. To drink, esp. to excess : late C. 18–20 ; > , ca. 1860, coll. The *hand* phrase admits the addition of † *to one's head* (Grose, 2nd ed.). Cf. :

lift (up) the hand(s) ; occ. the arm. To do a little physical work : from ca. 1890. ' Rolf Boldrewood ' (O.E.D.). See also the preceding entry.

lifted, be. ' To be promoted unexpectedly or undeservedly ' : naval coll. : C. 19. Bowen.

*lifter. A thief, esp. from shops : c. : ca. 1590–1830 ; from ca. 1750, gen. s. Shakespeare, ' Is he so young a man and so old a lifter ? ' Ex *lift*, v., 1.—2. (Gen. in pl.) A crutch : S.E. or coll. in C. 16–mid-17, then low or c. until ca. 1870, when it fell into disuse. Coles and B.E. classify it as c.—3. A heavy blow : from the late 1880's. (O.E.D.)—4. A horse given to kicking : stables' coll. (— 1909). Ware.

*lifting. Thieving ; theft ; late C. 16–20 ; ob., except for the stealing of live stock : c. >, ca. 1750, gen s. Greene. Also in late C. 16–mid-17, *lifting law* (Greene, *passim*).

lifty. See lift, n., 6.

*lig. A bed : c. of ca. 1720–1840. *A New Canting Dict.*, 1725. Perhaps *lib* (q.v.) influenced by dial. *lig*, to lie (down). Cf. U.S. c. *lig-robber* in Irwin.—2. A weighted fish-hook : nautical coll. : late C. 19–20. Ex East Anglian *lig*, a load.

[lig-by, ligby, a bedfellow, a concubine, despite F. & H. is S.E.]

light. Credit : low or rather workmen's : from ca. 1820. Bee, 1823, says that it is orig. printers' s. and gives ' strike a light, to open an account, of the minor sort, gen. applied to ale-house scores.'—2. Hence *get a light*, obtain credit ; *have one's light put out*, exhaust one's credit. H., 1st ed.—3. As a notable or conspicuous person, even when the application is jocular, the term is S.E.

light, wanton, is—by itself or in combination—S.E., despite F. & H.—2. In or of silver : c. (— 1923). Manchon. Prob. on *white*, q.v.

[light, bring to, may orig. have been s. or even c. Vaux, 1812, ' A thief, urging his associates to a division of any booty they have lately made, will desire them to *bring the swag to light*.']

light, make a. See make a light.

light, not worth a. Worthless ; useless : low coll. : late C. 19–20. Philip Allingham, *Cheapjack*, 1934.

light, put out one's. To kill : C. 17–20 : S.E. till ca. 1820, then (increasingly low) coll. ; in C. 20, indeed, it is s. *The Graphic*, Sept. 27, 1884, ' So now, the malefactor does not murder, he " pops a man off ", or " puts his light out ".'

light !, strike a. A late C. 19–20 coll. exclamation. Prob. ex the imperative of the lit. S.E. phrase.—2. In the indicative, *strike a light* is, to commence work : sheet-metal workers' : C. 20. *The Daily Herald*, Aug. 11, 1936. Ex a job of welding.—3. See light, n., 1.

light and dark. A park : late C. 19–20. P. P., *Rhyming Slang*, 1932.

light as . . . The similes verge on but do not > coll. (E.g. *light as a feather, a fly, a kiss, the Queen's groat*, though the last—C. 17—may after all be coll.) Apperson.

light-blue. Gin : ca. 1820–40. ' Peter Corcoran ' Reynolds ; Randall's *Scrapbook* ; Egan's Grose. Cf. *light-wet*, q.v.

light bob. A light-infantry soldier : 1785, Grose : military s. >, ca. 1880, S.E. Whyte-Melville, ' A light-bob on each side, with his arms sloped '.

Light Bobs, the. The 13th Foot Regiment, from ca. 1881 the 1st Battalion of the Somerset Light Infantry : military : C. 19–20 ; ob. F. & Gibbons.

light-comedy merchant. A comedian pure and simple : theatrical : 1887, *The Referee*, March 13. (Ware.)

light fantastic, the. The foot as the means of dancing; dancing : coll. : from ca. 1840. Stirling Coyne, 'Then you're fond of sporting on the light fantastic.' Ex Milton's 'Come and trip it as you go | On the light fantastic toe' (*L'Allegro*).

*light-feeder. A silver spoon : c. from ca. 1850 ; ob.

[**light-fingered**, despite B.E., Grose, F. & H., has always been S.E.]

light food. Tobacco for chewing instead of a meal to eat : lower classes' (— 1909). Ware.

light frigate. A woman of loose morals : ca. 1690–1760. B.E. Cf. :

light horse. A courtesan ; a harlot : ca. 1620–1700 : Society s. > coll.—2. See 'Rogues' in Addenda.

*light horseman. A thief operating as one of a gang on the Thames : C. 19–20 ; ob. Colquhoun ; *The Daily News*, Jan. 9, 1899. (O.E.D.)

light-house, lighthouse. A red-nosed person, gen. male : ca. 1810–90. *Lex. Bal.*—2. A pepper-castor : naval (— 1909). Ware ; Bowen.—3. A tramp acquainted with the police or with their methods : tramps' c. (— 1932). Frank Jennings, *Tramping with Tramps*.

light infantry. Fleas : C. 19–20 ; ob. Cf. *light troops*, contrast *heavy dragoons*.

light-o ! A request for more light, shouted to anyone standing in the light : *Conway* cadets' coll. (— 1891). John Masefield, *The Conway*, 1933.

light out. To leave hastily and, gen., secretly : orig. (1878), U.S. ; anglicised ca. 1900 ; by 1930, coll. Cf. *skin out* and *vamoose*.

light stags. Shoes : Canadian (esp. lumbermen's) : from ca. 1905. John Beames.

*light the lumper. To be transported : c. of ca. 1795–1830. Perversion of *lump the lighter*.

light-timbered. (Of persons) limber ; slender-limbed ; weak : coll. : late C. 17–mid-19. B.E. Cf. the S.E. *light(ly) built*.

light (or candle) to the devil, bear or hold a. See **candle to . . .**

light troops. Lice : ca. 1810–90. *Lex. Bal.* Cf. *light infantry* and *heavy dragoons*.

light up, v.i. To light one's pipe, cigar, cigarette : coll. : from ca. 1860. T. Hughes. (O.E.D.)—2. V.i., to light the lamps ; put on the lights : coll. : late C. 19–20.—3. To give (a person) a dose of cocaine : c. : from ca. 1920. E.g. in E. Wallace, *The Flying Squad*, 1928.

[**light-weight,** n. and adj., are, despite F. & H., simply S.E.]

light-wet. Gin : ca. 1820–60. Randall's *Scrapbook*, 1822. Cf. *light blue, blue ruin, satin,* and *lightning*.

*lighter. See **lump the lighter** and **light the lumper.**—2. An animal's *lights* : low Cockney and tramps' c. (— 1932). Scott Pearson, *To the Streets and Back*.

*lightmans. Daylight, dawn, day : c. of ca. 1565–1860. Harman, B.E., Grose. Opp. to *darkmans*, q.v. Ex *light* ; see **-mans.**

lightning. Gin : low (perhaps orig. c.) : from ca. 1780 ; ob. G. Parker. (Cf. *blue ruin*.) Hence, *flash o' lightning*, a glass of gin (— 1811) ; *Lex. Bal.*

lightning, like greased. Very swiftly : orig. (1833, *as g. l.*), U.S. ; anglicised ca. 1845 as a coll. Hood, 1842, 'I will come, as the Americans say, like greased lightning.' Thornton.

lightning-conductors. 'Naval full-dress trousers,

with the broad gold stripe down the seam' : naval : C. 20. Bowen. Ex the brightness of the stripes.

lightning curtain-taker. A performer rushing in front of the curtain on the least approbation : theatrical coll. >, by 1920, S.E. : 1884. Ware.

lights. The eyes : from ca. 970 : S.E. till ca. 1810, then boxing s. *The Sporting Magazine*, 1815, 'He mill'd the stout Caleb and darken'd his lights' (O.E.D.) ; 1820, 'Peter Corcoran' Reynolds. Also *daylights* and *top-lights*.—2. A fool : low : ca. 1858–1910. H., 2nd ed. Ex an animal's *lights*, influenced by *light-headed*.

lights up ! A play-goers' c.p. indicative of condemnation : ca. 1900–15. Ware.

lignum. *Polygonum*, a wiry plant : Australian coll. (— 1880). By contraction.

Ligoniers, the. The 7th Dragoon Guards : military coll. : mid-C. 18–20 ; ob. F. & Gibbons. Ex Earl *Ligonier*, their colonel in George II's reign.

like, n. Always preceded by *the* and (esp. from ca. 1860) gen. in the pl. and followed by *of* (rarely † *to*) : such a person or thing, in C. 19–20 often pejorative : coll. : from ca. 1630, the first record being a letter by Rutherford in 1637, 'In a broken reed the like of me' ; *likes* occurring in 1787 ('the likes of me') ; Cobbett, 'the like of this' ; Du Maurier, in *Trilby*. (O.E.D.)

like, v. Misused as in *like*, adj., 3 (*had liked to . . .*), q.v.

like, adj. Inaccurately constructed with the dative, etc., instead of with the elliptical possessive : C. 14–20 : catachrestic verging, in C. 18–20, on coll. Historian Freeman, 'His domestic arrangements . . . are rather like a steamer' (O.E.D.).—2. Likely, with *to* and the infinitive : i.e. 'that may be reasonably expected to . . .' : C. 14–20 : S.E., indeed literary, to ca. 1790, then increasingly coll. A. E. Housman, 1896, 'Such leagues apart the world's ends are, | We're like to meet no more.' O.E.D.—3. Apparently about to : sometimes confusedly as in *had like to* = *was like* (i.e. *likely*) *to*, or, worse still, *had liked to* = *had been like* (i.e. *likely*) *to*. From ca. 1550 : S.E. (except in the † and ob. confused constructions) until ca. 1820, then coll. and dial. Mrs. Carlyle, in letter of 1853, 'I am like to cry whenever I think of her.' O.E.D.

like, adv., at the end of a phrase or a sentence. Somewhat, not altogether ; as it were, in a way ; in short, expressive of vagueness or after-thoughted modification : (dial. and) low coll. : 1801, 'Of a sudden like' ; Scott, Lytton, De Quincey, E. Peacock. O.E.D.

like, conjunction. Like as : the v. being often omitted in the *like* clause. Late C. 15–20 : S.E. till ca. 1880, then increasingly coll., in C. 20, low coll. ; from ca. 1930, gen. considered a sol. J. K. Jerome, 1886, 'Did [Robinson Crusoe] wear trousers ? . . . Or did he go about like he does in the pantomime ?' Prob., in the main, ex the semi-prepositional force of *like* combined with the suppression of *as* in *like as*. O.E.D. (See esp. Fowler.)—2. Also in such phrases as that in H. C. Bailey, *Mr. Fortune Wonders*, 1932, 'I came down [at] half-past seven. like usual' : sol. : late C. 19–20.

like, anything—nothing—something, in comparison (e.g. Payn, 'Not that Pye is an archangel, nor anything like it'), are S.E. ; but the elliptical *something like*, something like what is obligatory, intended, or desired, is late C. 18–20 coll. The O.E.D. quotes ' "This looks something like, Sir," said she.' 1798. Often by itself.

like, feel. See feel like.—like, most or very. See like as not.

like ?, what. (Absolutely or as in ' what like is he ? ') Of what character, nature, quality ? : dial. (— 1820) >, coll. 1860, (low) coll.

like a . . ., like anything, etc., where speed, energy, or intensity is indicated, have a coll. tendency that often > coll. or, if the second member is coll. or s., even s. Many of the following phrases, which are s. unless otherwise designated, are found at the resp. n., pronoun, adj., or adv. :—*like a basket of chips* (Moore, 1819), † ; *l. a bird* (from the 1860's : ' Quotations ' Benham), coll. ; *l. a dog in a fair* (Barham), † ; *l. a house on fire* (1857, see house on fire), s. > coll. ; *l. a shot* (1850, Smedley), coll. ; *l. a streak* (— 1890), coll. ; *l. a thousand*, or *a ton*, or *a cart-load, of bricks* (from ca. 1840), cf. *l. bricks* ; *l. a tom-tit on a horse-turd* (gen. in another sense : see horse-turd) ; *l. anything* (from ca. 1680 ; *as anything*, 1542), coll. ; *l. be(-)damned* (C. 20),—cf. *smart as be damned*, i.e. ' damned smart ' ; *l. beans* (ca. 1820–1900) ; *l. billy-(h)o* (late C. 19–20) ; *l. blazes* (— 1845 ; Disraeli, De Quincey), cf. *l. a house on fire* ; *l.* † *boots* or *old boots* (1868, Miss Braddon ; prob. earlier), cf. *l. the very devil* ; *l. bricks* (1835, Dickens), † by 1914 ; *l. buggery* (see buggery); *l. fun* (1819, Moore), s. > coll. ; *l. hell* (see hell); *l. hot* † *cake* or *cakes* (— 1888), orig. U.S. ; *l. mad* (from ca. 1660), coll., as in Pepys's ' A mad coachman that drove like mad ' ; *l. old boots* (mid-C. 19–20) ; *l. one o'clock* (from before 1847 : orig. ' of a horse's movement ' (very rapid), says Halliwell), contrast *l. one o'clock half-struck*, separate entry ; *l. shit to a shovel* (late C. 19–20, low, ob.) ; *l. smoke* (C. 19–20) ; *l. thunder* (from ca. 1830, ob. ; M. Scott) ; *l. the very devil* (from ca. 1830 ; M. Scott) ; *l. wink(e)y* (— 1896) and *l. winking* (Barham).

like a birch-broom in a fit. See birch-broom.— l. a bird. See bird.—l. a book. See book.—l. a dose. See dose of salts.—l. a whale. See whale.— l. Christmas beef. See beef.—l. greased lightning. See lightning.

like a halfpenny, or a penny, book,—you talk like. A c.p. remark to a fluent or an affected or pedantic speaker : low coll. : ca. 1880–1910.

like as. As : sol. : mid-C. 19–20. J. Storer Clouston, 1932.

like as not(, as) ; like enough ; most (ob.) or very like. Probably : coll. and dial. : resp.—1897 (but *as like as*, without *not*, occurs in 1563, Foxe ; 1611, Shakespeare, ' Most like I did ' ; 1610, Shakespeare, ' Will money buy 'em ? . . . Very like.' O.E.D.

like for to (do something). Likely to : lower classes' coll. (— 1923). Manchon.

like it but it doesn't like me, I. Applied to food, drink, work, etc. : a semi-jocular coll. c.p. : late C. 19–20.

like it or lump it. To like or, disliking, put up with it : from ca. 1860 : coll. See lump, v., 3.

like it you may do the other thing !, if you don't. Equivalent, and allusive to, the preceding : coll. (— 1864). H., 3rd ed.

like . . ., like . . . These proverbial ' consequences ', e.g. *like mother, like daughter*, look—or some of them look—rather coll., but they are the very flesh and bone of S.E. (Apperson for examples.)

like mother makes it. See mother makes it, like.

like nothing on earth. See nothing on earth.

like one o'clock half-struck. Hesitatingly : 1876,

Hindley : low ; ob. Contrast *like one o'clock*, s.v *like a* . . .

like something the cat has brought in, or, in Australia, like something the cat brings in of a wet night. A c.p. applied to a person looking utterly disreputable or very bedraggled : from ca. 1920. Also *look what the cat's brought in !*

like that !, I. A derisive or indignant ' Certainly not,' ' I certainly don't think so ' : coll. : late C. 19–20. Cf. *not half*, q.v.

like the man who fell out of the balloon : he wasn't in it. He stood no chance : c.p. : C. 20. (*The Humorist*, July 28, 1934.)

like to meet her in the dark(, he'd, I'd, etc.). Plain : lower classes' : from ca. 1884 ; slightly ob. Ware.

likely, had. A catachrestic variation of † *was likely*, came near (to be or do . . .) : C. 17–18. Cf. *like*, v., and *like*, adj., 3 : qq.v.

likely !, not. Certainly not ! : coll. : 1923, Manchon ; but in use before the G.W. and prob. from late C. 19.

*likeness, take a. To take a criminal's measurements and record physical characteristics, almost solely of the face : c. of ca. 1810–1910. *Lex. Bal.* Ex *likeness*, a portrait.

likes, the. See like, n.—likes of, the. See like, n.

[likewise as conjunction is considered by Fowler to be an illiteracy ; rather is it an infelicity.]

l'il. Little : a drunken or an endearing contraction : C. 19–20 coll.

*lil(l). A pocket-book : c. : from ca. 1810. Vaux. Prob. ex Romany *lil*, paper, a book. See esp. Sampson. Cf. Borrow's *Romano Lavo-Lil*, i.e. *Romany Word-Book* or *Glossary*.—2. Hence, any book : from ca. 1840 : tramps' c.—3. A five-pound note : c. (— 1896) ; ob.

lill for loll (or law). Tit for tat : C. 15–17 : coll. Perhaps jinglingly ex A.-S. *lael*, a bruise. (O.E.D.)

Lilley and Skinner. Dinner : London rhyming s. : from ca. 1910. Ex the well-known boot- and shoe-makers and retailers ; the firm was established in 1835.

[Lilliputian, n., like lily-liver(ed),—despite F. & H.,—is S.E.]

lily benjamin. A white greatcoat : C. 19 low. See benjamin ; cf. *lily shallow*.

lily of St. Clements. See St. Clements.

lily shallow. A white driving-hat : Society, esp. the ' whips' ' : ca. 1810–30. *Lex. Bal.*

*lily-white. A chimney-sweep : c. of ca. 1690– 1830. B.E.—2. A Negro : C. 18–early 19 : low.

Lily-Whites, the. The 17th Foot (now the Leicestershire), also the 59th Foot (now the East Lancashire) Regiment : military : resp. C. 19 and C. 19–20. Ex their white facings. (F. & Gibbons.)

lily-white groat. A shilling : low : ca. 1890– 1914. See white.

limb. A very mischievous child : 1625, Jonson, ' A limb o' the school, . . . a little limb of nine year old ' : coll. ; slightly ob.—2. Hence, depreciatively, of older persons : coll. : C. 18–20 ; ob. except in combination, e.g. *limb of Satan* (Estcourt, 1706).

*limb, v. To tear to pieces ; to thrash : c. or low (— 1857) ; ob. ' Ducange Anglicus.'—2. To cheat : c. (— 1878) ; ob. Hatton, *Cruel London*.—3. To bring to the stocks : low : C. 19. Baumann.

limb !, blow of my last. A coll. asseveration : nautical (— 1887) ; ob. Baumann.

limb of the bar. A barrister : 1815 : coll. >, ca. 1860, S.E. Ex :

limb of the law. A lawyer ; a lawyer's clerk : 1730 : coll. >, ca. 1800, S.E.

limber up. To answer one's name : naval : from ca. 1916. Bowen. (Indicative of military influence.)

limbered, ppl. adj. Arrested ; in detention or prison : C. 20 military. Ex *limber,* to imprison,— cf. *in lumber, lumbered, Lombard Street,* qq.v.,— influenced perhaps by *limbo,* q.v., and certainly by S.E. *limber,* the detachable front of a gun-carriage.

limbo. A prison ; any place of confinement : from ca. 1590 ; † by 1910 : coll. till C. 18, then s. ; in C. 19–20, c. Grose ; Moncrieff ; Anon., *Five Years' Penal Servitude,* 1877, ' It was a heartless, cruel robbery . . . Before that occurred he had never been in limbo.' Ex the theological sense, esp. the phrase *in limbo patrum.*—2. Pawn ; a pawnshop : ca. 1690–1820. Congreve.—3. The female pudend : C. 19 low.—4. Bread : military : late C. 19–20. F. & Gibbons. Perhaps because often it is, on active service, ' as hard as *hell* '.

limbs, duke or duchess of. A gawk : from ca. 1780 ; ob. : low. Grose, 1st ed.

Limburger, that's the. That's ' the cheese ', i.e. excellent, correct, splendid : late C. 19–early 20. See **cheese.**

limby. A man that has lost a leg : New Zealanders' : in G.W. Cf. *wingy,* q.v.

lime-basket or **-kiln, as dry as a.** Exceedingly dry : coll. : from ca. 1835 ; the former, † by 1915. Dickens, Hume Nisbet.

lime-juice. Lime-light : theatrical : ca. 1875–1915. Ware. (Thus does sound generate sense !) —2. A ' new chum ' : Australia (— 1886) ; ob. by 1896, † by 1910. Ex the lime-juice served on outgoing ships. Cf. :

lime-juicer. The same as *lime-juice,* 2 : ibid. : ca. 1858–1900. Cornwallis, *The New World,* 1859. O.E.D. (— In U.S. : see **limey.**)

lime twig, -twig, limetwig. As a snare, S.E.—2. A thief : late C. 16–early 17 : c. : Greene, third *Cony-Catching,* 1592.

Limehouse. ' To use coarse, abusive language in a speech ' (Lyell) : coll. (— 1931). Ex the S.E. sense, ' to make fiery (political) speeches such as Mr. Lloyd George made at Limehouse in 1909 ' (O.E.D. Sup.).

Limericks. Shares in the Waterford & Limerick Railway : Stock Exchange coll. (— 1895) >, by 1910, j. A. J. Wilson, *Stock Exchange Glossary.*

limey, Limey. An Englishman : C. 20 U.S. >, in 1933, partly anglicised, thanks to Spenser's *Limey,* a notable book on the U.S. underworld. Ex *lime-juicer,* the U.S. (— 1881 but †) term for a British ship or sailor, lime-juice being served on British ships as an anti-scorbutic. Cf. *lime-juice,* q.v.

limit, the. Esp. in *that's the limit.* A person, act, or thing that is the extreme (or beyond) of what one can bear, gen. in jocular use : coll., orig. (ca. 1903), U.S. ; anglicised ca. 1908. (O.E.D. Sup.) Cf. *dizzy limit,* and *frozen limit,* qq.v.

limit, the sky is one's. One is ambitious ; one rises in the world : 1933, *The Daily Mirror,* Oct. 26.

*limiting law. In c. of late C. 16–early 17, as explained by Greene in *A Disputation,* 1592, ' The *lymitting Lawe,* discoursing the orders of such [professional criminals] as followe Iudges, in their circuites, and goe about from Fayre to Fayre.'

[**limlifter,** in F. & H., is a mere variant of S.E. † *limb-lifter.*]

limmick. Salt : Regular Army : late C. 19–20. F. & Gibbons. A perversion of Hindustani *namak.*

limping Jesus. A lame person : low : C. 19–20 ; ob. Cf. *dot and carry one.*

Lincoln and Bennett. A superior men's-hat : Society coll. : ca. 1840–1910. Ware. Ex the maker's name. (The firm was established ca. 1800 ; it is now styled Lincoln, Bennett & Co., Ltd.)

Lincolnshire Yellow-Belly (or y— b—). A native of Lincolnshire : C. 18–20. Ex the yellow-bellied frogs of the Lincolnshire fens.

lindabrides. See **landabrides.**

line, a vocation, a profession, a ' lay ', is, despite F. & H., excellent S.E.—2. A hoax : low coll. : ca. 1850–1910. Esp. in *get* (e.g. *him*) *in a line,* get some sport out of him. Cf. *get into a line,* s.v. *line, cut the.*—3. **the line,** the line of bookmakers on a race-course : racing-men's s. verging on c. : C. 20.— 4. A large amount of stock ; a large number of shares : stockbrokers' coll. (— 1935). (Cf. the technical sense in insurance : see O.E.D. Sup.).— 5. A customer that has purchased heavily is known to drapers, hosiers, and their like as *a good line* : C. 20. Ex *a good line* of drapery-stock : a sense that is S.E.—6. A printed form : Public Works' (— 1935). See also **pay-off line** and **sub-line.**

[**line,** v., to copulate with, and to fill (e.g. *line one's jacket, pockets, stomach*), is S.E., again despite F. & H.]

*line (or string), cut the. To end suspense : c. : ca. 1810–60. Vaux. Cf. 2nd nuance of **line, get into a.**

line, draw the. ' To lay down a definite limit of action beyond which one refuses to go,' S.O.D. : from ca. 1885 : coll. >, ca. 1933, S.E. Baumann.

line, fake a. See **fake a line.**

*line, get into, or **on, a ;** keep **in a** (tow)-**line.** To end suspense ; to engage in conversation a person to be robbed by one's confederate(s), also *get in a string,*—cf. *line,* n., 2 ; to keep in suspense, also *keep in tow* or *in a string.* C. of ca. 1810–60. Vaux.

line, good. See **good line.**

line, have in. To have the measure of (a person) : military : C. 20. Frank Richards, 1933, ' Even the young soldiers . . . had him in line.' Cf. *have* (a person) *taped.*

[**line, on the.** Hung on the line at the Royal Academy : S.E., well established.]

line, the devil's regiment of the. Felons ; convicts : coll. : ca. 1870–1914.

line-age ; also **linage.** Payment by the line : journalists' : from ca. 1888 : s. till C. 20, then j. Punning *lineage.*

line-o'-battler. A battle-ship : naval coll. (— 1887) ; slightly ob. Baumann.

line of the old author, a. A dram of brandy : late C. 17–early 19. B.E.

line on, get a. To get information about, or a clue to (either identity or meaning) : coll., orig. (1903) U.S., anglicised not later than 1925. O.E.D. (Sup.). Ex markmanship.

line up ; line up to. To approach (v.i. and v.t.) ; to accost : Australian (— 1916). C. J. Dennis.

lined, be. (Gen. of women) to be married : lower classes' (— 1909). Ware. Ex *lines,* 1.

[**linen, cool in one's,** to die, is, despite F. & H., S.E.]

linen, the. The stage curtain : theatrical : ca. 1880–1910. Cf. *the rag.*

linen, wrap up in clean. To couch smutty or sordid matter in decent language : coll. : C. 18–19. We still say *nicely wrapped up.*

*****linen-armourer.** A tailor : late C. 17–mid-19 : c. >, ca. 1800, jocular S.E. (B.E.)

Linen Cook. Robt. Cook (mid-C. 17–early 18), eccentric vegetarian of Ipswich and Bristol. (Dawson.)

linen-draper. Paper : rhyming s. (— 1857). ' Ducange Anglicus.'—2. Esp. a newspaper.

Linenopolis. Belfast : coll. (— 1886) >, ca. 1910, S.E. ; ob. Cf. *Cottonopolis.*

liner. As abbr. *penny-a-liner,* S.E.—2. A picture hung on the line : artistic s. (— 1887) >, in C. 20, coll. W. P. Frith in his *Autobiography.*—3. A battle-ship : naval (— 1887) ; very ob. Baumann. Cf. *line-o'-battler.*

lines. A marriage certificate : from ca. 1825 : dial. and coll. >, ca. 1900, S.E. Anon., *Fast Life : An Autobiography,* ' Those good-natured ladies who never had their lines.'—2. Reins : from ca. 1850 : dial. and (mostly U.S.) coll.

lines, hard. Bad luck : coll., prob. orig. nautical : 1824, Scott, ' The old seaman paused . . . " It is hard lines for me," he said, " to leave your honour in tribulation ".' (O.E.D.) Perhaps punning *tack* (orig.,rope, line),as W. Ingeniously suggests.

lines like a butter-box. A nautical c.p. (late C. 19–20) applied to ' a clumsy, full-bodied ship' (Bowen). Cf. *sardine-tin.*

liney, liny. Wrinkled : coll. (— 1887). Baumann. E.g. ' a liney face '.

-ling. A diminutive S.E. suffix, gen. contemptuous ; in nonce-usages, verging, in C. 19–20, on coll.

ling-grappling, vbl.n. Caressing a woman sexually : low : C. 19–20 : app. ob.

[**lingo** and **Lingua Franca,** despite F. & H., are S.E. ; so are F. & H.'s **lining, get within the lining** of one's smock, and linsey-woolsey. Note, however, that H., 1859, says that ' Slang is termed lingo among the lower orders ' : this is a coll., ob. in C. 20.

linguistic is catachrestic when made to = of, or concerned with, language or languages : mid-C. 19–20. S.O.D.

*****link.** To steal from a person's pocket : c. : ca. 1820–60. Haggart.

link and froom. These related terms in Yiddish and hence in low London s. date, as to the latter at any rate, from the 1880's. Ware. See **froom,** of which *link* is the opp.

linkister. A linguist ; esp. an interpreter : nautical (— 1867). Smyth. (Also dial.)

linkman. A ' general man-servant about kitchen or yard ' : West London coll. (— 1909). An extension of S.E. sense.

[**links.** Sausages : not s. but dial. Because linked together.]

linnen. See linen.

lino. A coll. abbr., from ca. 1880, of *linoleum* (1863).—2. In C. 20, among printers and journalists, a coll. abbr. of *linotype* (1888), itself contracting *line of type.*

Linseed Lancers. The Royal Army Medical Corps : C. 20 military, esp. in G.W. ; not, however, derisive after July, 1916. F. & Gibbons ; P. Gosse, *Camp-Follower,* 1934.

lint-scraper. A surgeon, esp. if young : coll. : 1763, Foote ; Thackeray. Ex the lit. S.E. sense.

liny. See liney.

lion. A person or a thing of (esp. fashionable) interest ; hence, *see the lions,* to go sight-seeing : both, S.E.—2. A great man's spy : C. 18 : coll., perhaps > S.E.—3. An inhabitant of, or a visitor to, Oxford : Oxford University : from ca. 1780 ; in C. 20, ob. Grose, 1st ed.—4. A citizen : London smart s. : ca. 1780–1800. O.E.D.—5. A hare : ca. 1825–35 : coll. verging on S.E. Westmacott, Lytton, Ex certain restrictions on game.

lion, as valiant as an Essex. Timid : C. 18–early 19. Cf. :

lion, Cotswold or **Lammermoor ; lion, Essex** or **Romford.** Resp., a sheep ; a calf. *Cotswold lion* or *lion of Cotswold,* mid-C. 15–mid-19. Anon., *Thersites ;* Ray ; Grose. See also **Essex l., Lammermoor l., Romford l.**

lion, tip the. To squeeze a person's nose and flatten it to his face : late C. 18–mid-19. Grose, 1st ed.

Lion Chang, or **long L.C.** Li Hung Chang, an eminent Chinese who passed through London in 1896, to which year and place the nickname is, virtually, confined. Ware, ' His entourage also obtained, in several instances, droll names. Lo Feng Luh became Loafing Loo, Viscount Li became Lud Lulliety, and S'eng became Seng-Song.'

lion comique. A leading comic singer : music-halls' coll. : ca. 1880–1905. Ware.

[**lion-drunk, lion-hunter, lioness** (but the C. 16 sense, a harlot, may be s., while that of a lady visitor to Oxford—1808—is certainly s.), **lionize,** are all, in all senses and despite F. & H., good S.E. ; so are **lion's provider, lion's share** and **put one's head into the lion's mouth.**]

Lions, the. The 4th King's Own, now the King's Own Royal Regiment : military : C. 18–20 ; ob. Ex the lion badge. F. & Gibbons. (Badges, facings, and mottoes are responsible for many nicknames of regiments.)—2. Millwall Football Club : sporting : C. 20. Their ground is *the Den* : cf. Daniel in the lion's den. Cf. :

lion's den. The headmaster's study : various schools' : late C. 19–20.

lions in the Army, they tame. A Regular Army c.p. : late C. 19–20. (Frank Richards, *Old Soldiers Never Die,* 1933.) In reference to military discipline.

lip. Impudence ; abuse : low : from ca. 1820 (perhaps orig. c.). Haggart, ' giving him plenty of lip '.—2. A house : c. : ca. 1820–50. Egan's Grose. Ex *lib-ken,* q.v.

lip, v. To sing : c. (1789, G. Parker) >, ca. 1860, low s. ; ob. Esp. in *lip a chant,* sing a song.—2. To speak, utter : coll. : from ca. 1880 ; rare after 1918. *Punch,* Jan. 10, 1885, ' I had great power, millions lipped my name.'

[**lip, all betwixt cup and :** S.E.—**make a lip :** S.E., as also are **lip-clap, lip-labour** or **-work,** and **lip-salve** or **-wash,** all in F. & H.]

lip, button one's. (*button one's mouth* is † S.E.) Gen. in imperative. C. 19–20 : s. verging on coll. ; once (— 1868) common among schoolboys.

lip, carry or **keep a stiff upper.** See keep.

lip, give it. ' To talk vociferously ', C. J. Dennis · Australian (— 1916).

lip-lap. A child born in the East Indies ; esp. if Eurasian : East Indian coll. : mid-C. 18–20. Perhaps ex Javanese *lap-lap,* a dish-clout. Yule & Burnell. Cf. *chee-chee,* q.v.

lip-thatch or **-wing.** A moustache : jocular coll. verging on S.E. : resp. 1892 (Kipling), 1825 (Westmacott) : ob. O.E.D.

lipey; occ. lippy. A low London term of address: ca. 1870–1915.

*lipken. See libken.

lippy. Impertinent: from ca. 1890. Ex *lip*, .*t.*, 1. (O.E.D. Sup.)—2. See lipey.

lips hang in your light, your. (Occ. his, her, etc.) A proverbial c.p. = you're a (born) fool. C. 16–17. Skelton (*eye* for *light*); Davies of Hereford; ' Phraseologia ' Robertson. (Apperson.)

liq. See what will you liq ?

liqueur of four ale. A glass of bitter: City (— 1909); ob. Also *City sherry*. Ware.

liquid fire. Bad whiskey: (low) coll.: C. 19–20; ob.

liquor. A drink: from ca. 1860; mostly U.S. Also *liquor-up*.—2. The water used in adulterating beer: publicans' (— 1909). Ware. (Obviously, a euphemism.)

liquor, v.t. To supply, or to ply, with liquor: mid-C. 16–20: S.E. till C. 18, then coll. till ca. 1850, then s. Also, late C. 19–20, *liquor up*. Surtees.— 2. V.i., to drink alcoholic liquor: orig. (1836), U.S.; anglicised ca. 1840. Marryat. Also, from 1845, *liquor up*.—3. To thrash, esp. in *liquor someone's hide*: ca. 1680–1800. D'Urfey. Punning *lick*. [liquor, in. S.E., despite its associations—and F. & H.]

liquor ?, what's your. What will you drink ?: coll. (— 1887); slightly ob. Baumann. Cf. *what's your poison ?*

liquor one's boots. To cuckold: C. 18: T. Brown.—2. To drink before a journey (cf. S.E. *stirrup-cup*): among Roman Catholics, to administer extreme unction: ca. 1780–1890. Grose.

liquor up. See liquor, v., 1 and 2; and the n.

liquored, drunk, 1667, now gen. liquored up (not before C. 19); liquorer, a hard drinker (— 1885; ob.); liquoring, vbl.n., hard drinking, C. 19–20, now gen. liquoring-up. All ex the v., 1 and 2. Cf.:

Liquorpond Street, to have come from. To be drunk: ca. 1825–1910. Buckstone, in *23, John Street, Adelphi*, ' I don't know where you are, sir; but you seem to have just come from Liquorpond Street.'

liquors. Water: Bootham School (— 1925). Anon., *Dict. of Bootham Slang*.

Lisa. See Liza.

*lispers. The teeth: c. of ca. 1785–1860. G. Parker. Cf. *listeners*.

list. See add.—2. Short for *list of geldings in training*: the turf: 1890. Hence, *put on the list*, to castrate. S.O.D.

listen to oneself. To think: Anglo-Irish coll.: C. 19–20. Ware.

listener. An ear: low and boxers': from ca. 1820; ob. (Gen. in pl.) Bee.

listman. A ready-money bookmaker: from ca. 1885; ob.: the turf. Ex the list of prices exhibited by his side.

[lists of love, like litter, little (paltry), little ease, and Little Englander, despite F. & H., are S.E., while Little Guid, the devil, is dial.]

lit (slightly), gen. well lit (quite), tipsy: from ca. 1920. Cf. *light-house*, q.v. Also *lit up*, slightly drunk (Lyell).

literally = in its strongest admissible sense: catachrestic: late C. 19–20. Even more catachrestic when, as in C. 20, it is used as a mere intensive,—in fact, it is then a slovenly coll.

literature. Any printed matter whatsoever, as in ' the literature of patent-medicines ': coll.: 1895 (S.O.D.).

litery. Literary: sol.: C. 19–20. (Manchon.)

lithia. Short for *lithia water*: coll.: 1893 (S.O.D.)

*little alderman. A sectional ' jemmy ': c. (— 1889). Cf. *alderman*.

Little Barbary. Wapping: s. > coll.: late C. 17–early 19. B.E., Grose.

little beg. Little beggar, as a ' friendly term applied by upper form to lower form boys': Public Schools': late C. 19–20. Ware.

*little ben. A waistcoat: c.: C. 19–20; ob. Ex *benjamin*, q.v.

little bird told me, a. A semi-proverbial c.p. (C. 19–20) in reply to the (not necessarily expressed) question, ' Who told you ? '

little bit of . . . See all right, fluff and keg and sugar.

little breeches. A familiar term of address to a boy: ca. 1770–1850. Grose, 1st ed.

little Charley. See charley, 6.

little Chats (or little chats). Arbitration ordinary stock in the London, Chatham & Dover Railway: Stock Exchange (— 1895); † by 1920. A. J. Wilson, *Stock Exchange Glossary*. Cf. *Chats*, q.v.

little cheque, a. A c.p. *à propos* of the repayment of a loan: ca. 1893–95. Ex *Two Roses*, a popular comedy, in which this phrase is often spoken by Digby Grant played by a famous actor. (A. E. W. Mason, *The Dean's Elbow*, 1930.)

little clergyman. A young chimney-sweep: ca. 1787–1860. Grose, 2nd ed. See clergyman; contrast *chimney-sweep*.

little Davy. The penis: low: C. 19–20; ob.

little deers. Young women, esp. if associated—or declaring themselves associated—with the stage: Anglo-American Society (— 1909); † by 1920. Ware. Punning *dear* to form the feminine of *stag* in its Society sense.

little devil. See devil.

little end of the horn, the. A difficulty; distress: hence, *come out at the little end of the horn* = to come to grief, be worsted. Coll.: C. 17–20; after 1800, mostly dial. and U.S. (See esp. Apperson and Thornton.)

Little England. Barbados: West Indies': C. 19–20, ob. Cf. *Bim*.

Little England beyond Wales. Pembrokeshire: late C. 16–20; coll. till C. 19, then S.E. See esp. E. Laws's *History of Little England beyond Wales*, 1888. (Apperson.) But *Little London*, Penrith, is prob. dial., as is *Little London beyond Wales*, Beaumaris.

Little Fighting Fours, the. The 44th Foot Regiment, since ca. 1881 the Essex Regiment, rather the 2nd Battalion of the 2nd Essex: military: C. 19–20; ob. Ex low stature and high courage. F. & Gibbons; R. J. T. Hills. Cf. S.E. *Bantams*.

little finger. The male member: female euphemistic: C. 20.

little finger, cock one's. To drink often—and much. Coll.: C. 19–20.

little go. The first examination to be passed for one's B.A. degree: university coll.: 1820: Oxford († by 1864) and Cambridge. Thackeray. Cf. *smalls*.—2. Hence, one's first imprisonment: c. (— 1909). Ware, ' First invented by a fallen university man.'

little-go-vale. ' Orderly step to the first examination,' F. & H. : Oxford University : ca. 1820–40. Egan's Grose.

Little Grenadiers, the. The Royal Marines : military : 1761 ; ob. F. & Gibbons. Ex their grenadier caps and their stature less than that of the average grenadier in C. 18.

little grey home in the west. A vest : rhyming s. in G.W., and after. B. & P., ' From the popular song of that name.'

little house. A privy : from ca. 1720 : S.E. till ca. 1850, then dial. and, in New Zealand, coll. Ex *petty house*, q.v.

*****little joker.** The hidden pea in the thimble-rigging game : c. : from ca. 1870. ? ex the card-game sense of *joker*.

Little Lons. Little Lonsdale Street, Melbourne : Australian (– 1916). C. J. Dennis.

little man. A footman : Eton College : ca. 1850–1915.

little man in the boat. The navel : trivial : late C. 19–20. (Also in a very indelicate metaphorical c.p.)

little Mary. The stomach : coll. : 1903. Ex Barrie's *Little Mary.* (O.E.D. Sup.)

little man in the boat. See boat.

little more Charley behind. ' More lumbar width—speaking of feminine dress or costume ' : theatrical (– 1909) ; ob. Ware.

little-pigger. A supporter of a modified Colonial Preference : political coll. : ca. 1905–10. Collinson. Opp. *whole-hogger* in its political sense.

little red book, the. See crook, go.

little side. A game between houses only : Rugby school : from ca. 1870 : coll. > j.

little sister. The female pudend : low : C. 19–20 ; ob.

*****little smack.** A half-sovereign : c. (– 1926). Frank Jennings, *In London's Shadows.*

*****little snakesman.** A young thief that, entering by a window, opens the door to the gang : c. of ca. 1780–1890. G. Parker.

little spot. See spot.

little steps. Children : coll. (– 1923). Manchon. Either ex their gait or ex the staircase effect of a normal family.

Little Sussex. The Duke of Sussex, son of George III : 1st half of C. 19. *The Creevey Papers.* He was the shortest of the King's sons.

Little Willie. See Willie.

Little Witham, be born at ; go to school at ; belong to, etc. To be stupid : coll. (more or less proverbial) : late C. 16–mid-19 ; extant only in dial. Punning *wit* ; Nashe, e.g., has *small Witam . . . little Brainford.* (Apperson.)

littler, littlest. Smaller, -est ; younger, -est. C. 19–20 : unintentional, they are sol. or dial. ; deliberate, they (though rarely *littler*) are jocular coll., as in *the littlest ones* (the youngest children), *The Observer,* 1932, Christmas number.

live, energetic, forceful, is S.E. (though mostly in U.S.).—2. Jocular s. verging on coll., esp. as *a real live* —— ; e.g. ' A real live glass milk jug ', 1887 (S.O.D.), ' A real live philosopher ', 1890 (ibid.).

live bach(e). To live as a bachelor : Society coll. (– 1909). Ware.

live eels. Fields : rhyming s. (– 1857). ' Ducange Anglicus.'

live horse. Work additional to that included in the (gen., week's) bill : workmen's : C. 19–20 ; ob. Opp. to, and suggested by, *dead horse*, q.v.

live even in a gravel pit, he would. A semi-

proverbial, mainly rural, c.p. applied, ca. 1660–1750, to a cautious, niggardly person. Ray, Fuller. (Apperson.)

live lumber. Soldiers or passengers on board ship : nautical : ca. 1780–1910. Grose, 1st ed. ; Baumann.

live message. (Gen. pl.) A message in course of transmission : telegraphers' coll. (1870) >, by 1910 j. Ware.

live-on. A fine girl or woman : low : late C. 19–20 ; ob. Ware. Cf. *leave-yer-homer*.

live one. A shell that will explode : military coll. verging on j. : G.W. (B. & P.)

live sausage. See sausage.

live stock. Fleas ; lice ; in short, body vermin : from ca. 1780. Grose, 1st ed.—2. In C. 19, also cattle. Bowen.

live with, can or be able to. To be able to play (a person) on level terms : sporting : from ca. 1928.

live wire. An indefatigable but not necessarily reliable news-gatherer : journalistic coll. : C. 20. Ex the familiar S.E. sense.

liveliness, a certain. A bombardment ; officiousness : military : 1915–18. B. & P. Ex a meiosis sponsored by Mr. Winston Churchill.

lively. A lively person : coll. : 1889, Clark Russell, in *Marooned.* O.E.D.

lively-hearty. A sailor : nautical coll. (– 1923). Manchon.

liven. To make, or to become, lively : coll. : 1884 (S.O.D.). In C. 20, gen. *liven up*.

livener. A ' pick-me-up ', q.v. ; a morning dram : s. (– 1887) >, by 1910, coll. Baumann.

liver curl. See curl, make one's liver.

liver, have a. To be irritable, bad-tempered : coll. : from ca. 1890.

liver and grapes. ' Fried liver and bacon for the wardroom breakfast ' : naval : C. 20. Bowen. Why *grapes* ?—unless it = *grapeshot*.

liver-faced. Pale- or white-faced ; cowardly : low (– 1857). ' Ducange Anglicus.'

liverish. ' Livery ' (q.v.) ; having the symptoms attributed to a liver out of order : coll. : 1896. *The Daily News,* July 9, 1896, an advertisement. O.E.D.

Liverpool Blues. The 79th Foot, British Army : military : ca. 1778–84.

Liverpool button. ' A kind of toggle used by sailors when they lose a button ', F. & H. : nautical s. > j. : from ca. 1850 ; ob.

Liverpool house. The midship deckhouse : sailing-ship coll. : C. 19. Bowen.

Liverpool tailor. A tramping tailor (status of workman) : tailors' : ca. 1870–1910.

Liverpool weather. ' In the Merchant Service, a special brand of dirty weather ' : coll. : late C. 19–20. Bowen.

[**Liverpudlian** and **living fountain,** despite F. & H., are S.E.]

livery. ' Liverish ' : coll. : from ca. 1895. Cf. *liverish*, q.v.—2. Hence, in C. 20, irritable, bad-tempered, morose, gloomily silent. Cf. *liver, have a*.

livery, be one of the. To be a cuckold : ca. 1680–90. Betterton. (O.E.D.)

Liveyer(e), Livyere. A permanent inhabitant of the Labrador coast : Canadian coll. (– 1901). Ex *live here.* O.E.D. (Sup.)

living with mother now. A females' c.p. addressed to proposals of marriage or mistress-ship : 1881–ca. 1914. Ware notes that orig. it was ' the refrain of a doubtful song '.

Liz. See **Lizzie**, 1.

Liza, he's saving them all for. See **he's saving . . .**

Liza !, outside. Be off ! A low c.p. of ca. 1880–1905.

Lizzie. A (cheap) motor-car, orig. and mainly a 'Ford': 1921. By personification. Also *tin Lizzie*. Occ., from ca. 1924, *Liz*.—2. A big gun, or its shell: naval: 1915; ob. F. & Gibbons, 'Suggested by the firing of the big fifteen-inch guns of H.M.S. *Queen Elizabeth*'.—3. (Also lizzie.) Cheap *Lisbon* red wine: c. and low: from ca. 1920. James Curtis, *The Gilt Kid*, 1936.

'll. A contraction of *will* or *shall*: from ca. 1575: in C. 16–mid-18, S.E. after *I, she, thou, we, ye, you*; later, coll., as always after any other word. Occ., before C. 19, written *'le, as in I'le, Ile*. (O.E.D.)

llama. Erroneous for *lama*: C. 19–20. Contrast *lama*, q.v. (Correctly, *lama* is the Tibetan dignitary, *llama* the South American animal.)

lliana. Erroneous for *liana*: from ca. 1860. O.E.D.

'lo ! Short for *hollo(a), hullo*: late C. 19–20: coll., mostly Colonial.

load, a ; loads. A great quantity or number: coll.: both being of C. 17–20. Shakespeare; Clough, ' Loads of talk with Emerson all morning ' (O.E.D.).—2. A venereal infection: Australia: late C. 19–20: low. Hence *get a load*.

load, v.i. To buy heavily ; *unload*, v.i. and t., sell heavily ⊦ Stock Exchange : 1885 : coll. till C. 20, then S.E.—2. V.t., to conceal a horse's broken wind by putting well-greased shot into its throat: c.: from ca. 1860. ' *No. 747*.'

[load, have (taken) a—get one's. To have as much drink as one can carry: in late C. 16–17, S.E.; thereafter dial. and U.S. s. Moreover, *lay on a* or *give one his load*, to thrash, is C. 16–17 S.E.]

load of hay. A day: rhyming s. (— 1859). H., 1st ed.

load of loose. The debris thrown up by, or the burst of, a big shell: military : 1915 ; ob. B. & P. I.e. a load of loose stuff.

[loaded, tipsy, is, despite F. & H., U.S.: hence, ineligible.]

loaded-up, be. Have in hand large quantities of a thing—e.g. stocks—as security. Stock Exchange : from ca. 1886 : coll. till C. 20, then S.E.

loads of. See **load, a.**

loaf. A dawdle ; a lounge : s. >, in C. 20, coll. : orig. (ca. 1855), U.S. ; anglicised ca. 1870. Ex the v., which, however, probably comes ex *loafer*, q.v.— 2. See **loaf of bread**.

loaf, v. To lounge, idle, take things very easily : coll. ; in C. 20, S.E. Orig. (ca. 1838), U.S. ; anglicised ca. 1850, though Dickens uses it in 1844. H. Kingsley, ' This one loafed rather energetically.' Cf. **loaf away**.

loaf, be in a bad. To be in trouble, in a difficulty : ca. 1780–1850. Grose.

loaf away. Pass (time) in idling : from ca. 1850 (orig. U.S.): coll. till C. 20, then S.E. Cf. *loaf*, v., q.v.

loaf o(f) bread. Dead; the head (gen. *loaf*): rhyming s.: late C. 19–20. B. & P.

loafer. An idler : coll. ; in C. 20, S.E. : orig. (1835), U.S. ; anglicised ca. 1850, though Dickens uses it earlier in his *American Notes*. Prob. ex Low German (*land)läufer*, a landloper. See esp. O.E.D., Thornton, W.—2. Hence, a cadger : rare coll. : C. 20. Manchon.

Loaferies, the. The Whitechapel Workhouse : East London : 1898–ca. 1905. Ware, ' From the tenderness shown towards the inmates ' and on such names as *Colinderies* and *Freakeries*.

[loaferess, loafering and **loaferish** have not reached England ; ob. in U.S.]

loafing, vbl.n. Aimless lounging ; deliberate idling : orig. (1838), U.S. ; anglicised ca. 1850 as a coll. >, in C. 20, S.E. Cf. :

loafing, adj. Lounging ; deliberately idle : orig. (ca. 1838), U.S. ; anglicised ca. 1850 as a coll. >, by 1905, S.E. T. Hughes, ' A . . . poaching, loafing fellow '.

loamick. See **lomick**.

loap. See **lope**. A C. 18 variant.

*****loaver**. Money : c. (— 1851) >, ca. 1880, low s. Mayhew. Prob. a corruption of *lowre* (= *lour*, q.v.) by Romany *luva* (pronounced *loover*),—cf. Sampson at *lovo*. Lingua Franca, says H. in 1864.

[loaves and fishes, benefits, profit, is, despite F. & H., ineligible.]

*****lob** ; in C. 18, often **lobb**. A snuff-box ; any box ; a till : c. : resp. 1718 († by 1800) ; ca. 1750–1810 ; from ca. 1810 (slightly ob.), as in valuable Vaux.—2. **lob, the** : see **lob, go on the**.—3. The head : boxing : ca. 1850–1910. H., 1st ed.—4. A partial priapism : low coll. : C. 18–19.—F. & H.'s other senses are S.E. or S.E. > dial.—6. A yorker : Winchester College cricketers' : ca. 1850–90. Wrench.

lob, v. To droop ; sprawl : late C. 16–20 ; ob. : S.E. >, ca. 1800, s. Egan.—2. The cricket term, whether v. or n., is S.E.—3. To arrive : Australian (— 1916). C. J. Dennis. (Also military, esp. in *lob back*, to return to one's battalion . 1915–18. B. & P.)

*****lob, dip** or **frisk** or **pinch** or **sneak a.** To rob a till : from ca. 1810 : c. : all slightly ob. See also **lob-crawler** and **-sneaking**.

*****lob, go on the.** To go into a shop to get change for gold and then secrete some of the change : c. : ca. 1750–1820. C. Johnson ; Grose, 2nd ed.

*****lob, make a good.** To steal much money from a till : c. of ca. 1810–60. Vaux.

*****lob-sneak, -crawler** ; **lob-sneaking.** A till-robber ; till-robbing : c. : from ca. 1865 ; slightly ob. See **lob**, n.

*****lobb.** See **lob**, n., 1.

lobcock, a blockhead, is S.E.—2. A large, relaxed *membrum virile* : mid-C. 18–19 low coll. Grose, 1st ed. Ex *lob*, v., 1.—3. See ' Occupational Names ' in Addenda.

*****lobkin.** A house ; a lodging : c. : late C. 18–early 19. Grose, 2nd ed. A survival and perversion of *lib-ken*, q.v.

loblolly is S.E., but **loblolly-boy**, a doctor's assistant, is naval s. (1748, Smollett) >, ca. 1860, S.E., and merchant-service s., in C. 19, for a steward, also for a spiritless boy at sea (from ca. 1850 ; ob.), while *loblolly-doctor*, a ship's doctor or surgeon, is nautical s. of C. 18. Both ex *loblolly*, gruel.

lobs. An under-gamekeeper : ca. 1860–1920.— 2. Abbr. *lobster*, q.v.—3. Talk : tramps' c. of ca. 1840–1910. A perversion of Romany *lavav*, pl. of *lav*, a word.

lobs ! Look out ! : schoolboys' : ca. 1850–1910. Baumann.—2. Truce, truce ! : id. : C. 20. Manchon.

[Lob's pound, despite F. & H., is ineligible—even in the sexual sense.]

lobscouse, a meat-and-vegetable hash, **is** nautical j. and dial., but **lobscouser,** a sailor, is nautical **s.** (— 1884) >, in C. 20, S.E. and ob. Cf. *scouse.*

lobster. One of Hazelrigg's regiment of Roundhead cuirassiers : 1643–77. Ex the complete suits of armour, encasing them as a lobster's shell the lobster. Clarendon.—2. A British soldier : 1687, T. Brown, is app. the earliest indisputable record ; ob. by 1901, † by 1915. B.E., Grose, W. W. Jacobs. Also *boiled lobster,* q.v. Ex the red coat. (O.E.D.)—3. As a bowler of lobs in cricket, jocular S.E., the normal word being *lob-bowler.*—4. ' Often carelessly used in Australia for the crayfish ' : mid-C. 19–20. Morris. (Cf. *locust.*)

lobster, v. To cry ; cry out : Winchester College : ca. 1850–1910. Prob. ex the Hampshire dial. *louster,* to make an unpleasant noise.

lobster, boil one's. (Of a clergyman) to turn soldier : military : ca. 1785–1840. Grose, 2nd ed. Because clerical black is exchanged for red and because an unboiled lobster is bluish-black, a boiled one is red. Cf. :

lobster, boiled. Same as *lobster,* n., 2 : ca. 1875–1905. In contradistinction to, and suggested by :

lobster, raw or unboiled. A policeman : 1829–ca. 1910 : s. >, ca. 1870, coll. Ex the blue uniform equated with the colour of a raw lobster : see **lobster, boil one's.**

lobster-box. A military transport : nautical : 1833, M. Scott, ' Lobster-box as Jack loves to designate a transport ' ; † by 1915, as is the sense, a barrack : mainly military (— 1860), H., 2nd ed. Ex *lobster,* n., 2.

lobster-cart, upset one's. To knock a person down : coll. : orig. (1824) and mainly U.S. ; † in England. Cf. *apple-cart,* q.v.

lobster-kettle of my cunt, I will not make a. ' A reply frequently made by the nymphs of the Point at Portsmouth, when requested by a soldier to grant him a favour ', Grose, 2nd ed. : ca. 1785–1860. Ex *lobster,* n., 2.

lobster-pot. The female pudend : C. 19–20 low ; ob.—2. An indian troop-ship of the *Serapis* class : naval : late C. 19–early 20. Bowen. Cf. *sardine-tin.*

lobster-smack. A military transport (cf. *lobster-box,* q.v.) : 1829, Marryat (O.E.D.) : jocular coll. >, ca. 1880, S.E. Ex *lobster,* n., 2.

lobster soldier. A Marine : naval : late C. 19–20.

lobtail. To sport or play : nautical : ca. 1850–1910. Ex a whale smacking the water with his flukes.

loc man. (Gen. pl.) A pilot : nautical : ca. 1850–1910. Bowen. Perhaps abbr. *local man.*

local. A public-house in one's own district : coll. : C. 20. E.g. *The Evening News,* Sept. 11, 1934.

[**locale** is erroneous for *local,* a place, locality : C. 19–20. Thus O.E.D. ; Fowler, however, recommends *locale.*]

*****lock.** A place for storing stolen goods : c. : late C. 17–early 19. B.E.—2. Hence, a receiver of such goods : c. of ca. 1690–1870. B.E. (This sense is also expressed by *lock-all-fast,* q.v.)—3. A line of business or behaviour : ca. 1780–1830 : low ; perhaps orig. c. G. Parker.—4. A chance, gen. **in** *stand a queer lock,* have a poor one : c. of ca. 1720–1860. *A New Canting Dict.,* 1725. Hence, prob., the next sense.—5. As in Grose (1st ed.), *to stand a queer lock,* bear an indifferent character ; †.—

6. The female pudend : mid-C. 18–20 : low. Also *lock of all locks* (G. A. Stevens, 1772). The male counterpart is *key,* q.v.

*****lock-all-fast.** A late C. 17–18 variant of *lock,* 2 B.E.

[**lock-hospital** and **lock-up house,** despite F. & H., are S.E.]

*****lock-up chovey.** A covered cart : c. >, ca. 1860, low : ca. 1810–1910. Vaux.

lock-ups. Detention in study : Harrow School : from ca. 1830 ; ob.

lockees. Lockhouse : Westminster School : C. 19–20.

*****locker.** A thieves' middleman : C. 18 c. C. Hitchin, 1718. Ex *lock,* 2.—2. A bar-room : nautical coll. · from ca. 1850 ; ob.—3. The female pudend : C. 19–20 low, mainly nautical.—4. A purse : lower classes' coll. (— 1923). Manchon.

locker, Davy Jones's. See **Davy Jones.**—**locker, shot in the.** See **shot.**—**lockeram-** or **lockram-jawed** is S.E.

lockers, be laid in the. To die : nautical (1813, Scott) >, ca. 1890, S.E. Cf. *lose the number of one's mess,* q.v.

locksmith's daughter. A key : ca. 1780–1890. Grose, 1st ed. Cf. *blacksmith's daughter.*

loco. A coll. abbr. of *locomotive,* an engine : 1896 (S.O.D.).

locomotive. A hot drink of burgundy, curaçoa, egg-yolks, honey, and cloves : coll. : ca. 1885–1910.

locomotive tailor. A tramping workman tailor : tailors' : from ca. 1870.

locomotives. The legs : from 1841 ; ob. by 1900, † by 1920. W. T. Moncrieff, in *The Scamps of London.*

locum. Abbr. *locum tenens* : medical, clerical : from ca. 1900. *The Scotsman,* March 11, 1901, ' Acting . . . as " locum " . . . during the severe illness of the minister ' (O.E.D.).—2. Hence, a locum-tenency : medical : C. 20. R. Austin Freeman, 1926, ' I am doing a locum. Only just qualified, you know.'

*****locus.** See **locust,** v.

locus away. To remove under the influence of drink : low (? orig. c.) : 1898 (prob. earlier). Ex *locus(t),* v., and see **locust,** n.

*****locust.** Laudanum : c. : from ca. 1850 ; ob. Mayhew. Also *locus(s),* esp. when used in the wider sense, a drug (' generally . . . snuff and beer ', H., 1st ed.). The term occurs in combination (*locus-ale*) as early as 1693. Perhaps ex Sp. *locos,* pl. of *loco,* lunatic. (O.E.D.)—2. In Australia, ' popularly but . . . erroneously applied to insects belonging to two distinct orders ', cicadas and grasshoppers : 1846. Morris.—3. A very extravagant person : Society (— 1909) ; ob. Ware. A resuscitation of the C. 16–17 S.E. sense.

*****locus(t),** v. To drug a person and then rob him : c. (— 1859). H., 1st ed., where spelt *locuss.*—2. Earlier (*locus,* 1831), to stupefy with drink. Cf. *locus away* and **locust,** n., 1.

loddy. A perverted abbr. of *laudanum* : ca. 1810–70. L. M. Hawkins. (O.E.D.) Cf. dial. *lodlum* and *lodomy* (E.D.D.).

lodge. The school sanatorium : Bootham School (— 1925). Anon., *Dict. of Bootham Slang.*

lodger. A person of no account : low : from ca. 1840 ; ob. Ex ' It's only a lodger ! ' Cf. *hog,* q.v.—2. A convict awaiting his discharge : prison-authorities' (— 1889).

*lodging-slum. The stealing of valuables from high-class lodgings hired for the purpose : c. of ca. 1810–70. Vaux. See slum.

log. The lowest boy in form or house : Public Schools' : ca. 1860–1910.—2. Abbr. *logarithm*, coll. : C. 19–20 : universities'.—3. See logs, 2.

log-juice. Cheap port-wine : 1853, Cuthbert Bede ; slightly ob. (O.E.D.)

log-roller. A political or a literary ally, gen. not too scrupulous : orig. (ca. 1820), U.S. ; anglicised ca. 1865 : coll. till C. 20, then S.E. See :

log-rolling. 'Co-operation in the pursuit of money, business, or praise ', F. & H. : orig. (1823), U.S. ; anglicised ca. 1865 : coll. till ca. 1895, then S.E. Ex mutual assistance in the actual rolling of logs. See esp. O.E.D. and Thornton.—2. Also adj.

log up, v.i. To make a log-support for a windlass : Australia (– 1890) : coll. Morris, who quotes ' Rolf Boldrewood ', 1890, *The Miner's Right*.

*loge. A watch : c. : late C. 17–early 19. B.E. Ex Fr. *horloge*.

-loger, -logy. See -ologer, -ology.

*loges. A pass or warrant : c. : early C. 17. Hence, *feager of loges*, a professional beggar with false passes. Rowlands.

logged. (Of a ship) on her beam-ends : nautical coll. : late C. 19–20. Bowen. Perhaps ex dial. *log*, v.t., to rock.—2. Utterly drunk : from ca. 1920. (R. Knox, *Still Dead*, 1934.) Ex *water-logged*.

[loggerhead, n. and adj., loggerheaded, be at or come to loggerheads ; S.E.]

loggo, logs, esp. in ' Any loggo ? ' : a London street-cry : mid-C. 19–20. See -o.

logie. Sham jewellery : theatrical : from ca. 1860 ; in C. 20, S.E. and ob. Ex David *Logie* the inventor. H., 1st ed. ; Sala, ' The plastering of girdles with zinc "logies".'—2. Sewage : Winchester College : from ca. 1870 ; ob.

*logier. A pocket-book : c. of ca. 1820–50. Bee. Ex Dutch or Yiddish.

logio.—Erroneous for *loggia*. (O.E.D.)—logograph, C. 19–20, for *logogriph*. (S.O.D.)

logs. A lock-up ; a minor prison : Australian coll. (– 1888). ' Rolf Boldrewood ', 1888, ' Let's put him in the Logs.' Morris, ' In the early days '—see G. Barrington, in his *History of New South Wales* —' a log-hut, and often keeping its name when made a more secure place '. Ob. however, by 1910, † by 1930. Cf. the † U.S. *log-box*.—2. (Rare in singular.) ' *Logs*. Fines inflicted at sea . . . officially logged by the captain ' : nautical coll. : late C. 19–20. Bowen.—3. (the Logs.) ' The timber pond in Portsmouth Harbour ' : naval : late C. 19–20 ; ob. Ibid.

-logy. See -ologer.

loke. A locum tenens : medical : from ca. 1905. Ware. Ex *locum*, q.v.

lol ; occ. loll. A students' social evening or spree : Stellenbosch students' : ca. 1885–1900. Pettman, who derives it ex Dutch ' *lollen*, to sit by the fire, to chat '.

loll, a favourite child, is ineligible ; as abbr. *lollipop* it is s. but rare (see lolly). S.E., too, are *loll*, v., and its derivatives *loller*, *lollpoop* (occ. *loll*).—2. See lol.

loll-shraub, -shrob. Claret : Anglo-Indian coll. : from ca. 1815. Ex Hindustani for ' red wine '.

loll-tongue, play a game at. To be salivated for syphilis : ca. 1785–1850. Grose, 2nd ed. ? ex panting from the effects of the treatment.

lollipop, lollypop. A sweetmeat : coll. : from ca.

1787. Grose, 2nd ed. ; C. Selby, ' Our hearts we cheer, with lollypops.' ? ex Northern dial. *lolly*, the tongue.—2. The *membrum virile* : C. 19–20 (ob.) ; low. Also *ladies' lollipop*.—3. Fig., over-sweet writing : from ca. 1850 ; ob. : coll.—4. As an adj., from ca. 1835 : coll. Cf. :

lollipop dress. A ' stripy dress, generally red and white, suggestive of sticks of confectionery ' : theatrical coll. : 1884. Ware.

lollop. A lounger, loafer : coll. : from ca. 1840. Ex the v.—2. The action or an act of lolloping : coll. : 1834 (S.O.D.). Ex the v.

lollop. To lounge about : coll. : 1745, C. H. Williams, ' Next in lollop'd Sandwich, with negligent grace.' Ex *loll*, v.—2. To bob up and down : coll. : from ca. 1850. Mayhew, ' Its head lolloping over the end of the cart ' (O.E.D.).—3. To proceed clumsily by bounds : coll. : 1878, Lady Brassey, ' We lolloped about in the trough of a heavy sea.' But for date cf. *lolloping*, adj., 2.

lolloping. Vbl.n. of *lollop*, v., in all senses : coll. —2. Adj., lounging, slovenly, idle : coll. : 1745.—3. Moving by clumsy bounds : coll. : 1844, Stephens in *Advice of a Gentleman*, ' [Long-pasterned horses] have usually a lumbering lolloping action, neither fast nor pleasant.'

lollopy. Lazy : coll. : from ca. 1855. Cf. *lolloping*, adj.

[lollpoop. ' A lazy, idle Drone ' : a C. 17–18 coll. verging on S.E.]

lolly. A sweetmeat : 1862 (O.E.D.) : dial. and, in Australia and New Zealand, coll. Ex *lollipop*, q.v.—2. The head : boxers' : ca. 1855–1910 ; ob. H., 1st ed. Cf. *crumpet*.—3. A shop : grafters' C. 20. Philip Allingham, *Cheapjack*, 1934. Perhaps because it seems a sweet thing to have. Hence, *lolly-worker*, ' a swindler who starts a shop and immediately sells the alleged goodwill ' (Allingham).

*lolly, v.t. To give (a fellow crook) away to the police : c. (– 1933). Charles E Leach, *On Top of the Underworld*. Prob. abbr. *lolly-shop* by a grim pun on *shop*, to betray to the police.

lolly-banger. A ship's cook : nautical : ca. 1872–1914. Perhaps ex *lolly* influenced by *loblolly*, q.v.

lollypop. See lollipop.—lolpoop. See lollpoop.

*lolly-worker. See lolly, n., 3.

Lombard fever. The ' idles ' : coll. : 1678, Ray ; † by 1870. A perversion of the S.E. † *fever-lurden* (cf. S.E. † *lurden*).

*Lombard Street, in. In prison : c. of ca. 1810–60. Vaux. See lumber, n. and v. (esp.), lumbered, limbo, and limbered.

Lombard Street to a Brummagem sixpence, a China orange (the commonest form), an egg-shell, ninepence. (Gen. preceded by *all*.) In C. 20, the second occ. > *all China to an orange*. A c.p. indicative of very heavy, indeed the longest possible odds ; a virtual certainty : coll. : resp. 1826, G. Daniels, ob. : 1849, Lytton ; 1752, Murphy, † ; 1819, Moore, ob. Ex the wealth of this London street. (See esp. Apperson.) Also *Chelsea College to a sentry-box* (1819) and *Pompey's pillar to a stick of sealing-wax* (1819), likewise in Tom Moore).

Lombards. Shares in the Lombard-Venetian Railway : Stock Exchange coll. (– 1887). Baumann.

lomick ; loamick. The hand : Shetland and Orkney islanders' s., not dial. : from ca. 1880. E.D.D. Ex Orkney dial. *lomos*, the hands.

London, agree like the clocks of. To disagree at, and on, all points : proverbial coll. : late C. 16–early 18. Nashe, Ray. The elder Disraeli ascribes it, tentatively, to some Italian clock-maker.

London Blizzard. Leighton Buzzard : railway-men's : from ca. 1920. *The Daily Herald*, Aug. 5, 1936. By rhyming equivalence.

London, put or **show** or **turn the best side to.** To make the best display one can : coll. : 1873, *Cassell's Magazine*, Jan. ; Baumann ; Ware, ' Making the best of everything '. Cf. *Humphrey's toppers.*

London flitting. See **moonlight flitting.**

London fog. A dog : rhyming s. : late C. 19–20. B. & P.

London ivy ; L. particular. A thick London fog (cf. *pea-souper*) : coll. : both 1852, in Dickens's *Bleak House* ; the former was ob. by 1920.—2. (Only **London ivy.**) Dust : Cockneys' (— 1909). Ware.

London jury. See **jury—hang half.**

London ordinary. Brighton beach : ca. 1864–1915. H., 3rd ed. Trippers feed there.

London Smash 'Em and Do for 'Em Railway. The London, Chatham & Dover Railway : late C. 19–20 ; now only historical.

London smoke. A yellowish grey : Society coll. : ca. 1860–90. Ware, ' Became once a favourite colour because it hid dirt.'

London Thieving Corps, the. The London Transport Corps (now the Army Service Corps) : Crimean War military. F. & Gibbons.

London waggon. ' In the days of the Press Gang [abolished in 1835], the tender which carried the victims from the Tower of London to the receiving ship at the Nore ' : nautical : ca. 1770–1840. Bowen

Londons. Shares in the London & North-Western Railway : Stock Exchange coll. (— 1895) >, by 1910, j. A. J. Wilson's glossary.

Londony. Characteristic of London : coll. : 1920, Denis Mackail, *What Next ?*, ' More Londony than any native '.

Londrix. London : ca. 1860–80. H., 3rd ed. Prob. ex Fr. *Londres.*

lone duck or **dove.** A woman no longer ' kept ' ; a harlot ' working ' in houses of accommodation : low : from ca. 1860 ; ob.

lone star. A second lieutenant : military officers' : 1915 ; ob. F. & Gibbons. Because he has only one star, whereas a first lieutenant has two. Contrast :

lonely star. A woman advertising that she wishes to write to lonely soldiers : military : 1916–18. F. & Gibbons.

[**long.** The foll. terms in F. & H. have always been S.E. :—*long and* (*the*) *short of it, long-headed, long robe, long-tailed, long-tongue*(*d*), and *long-winded.*]

long. A ' bull ' : Stock Exchange (— 1888) ; ob. —2. A rifle : Fenian : from ca. 1885. Cf. *short*, a revolver.—3. See **John Long.**—4. See **long, the.**

long, adj. Tall : M.E.–C. 20 : S.E. till ca. 1870, then coll., mostly jocular.—2. (Of numbers, or of numbered things) large. Chiefly in *l. trump, l. suit* (both in cards), *l. family, odds, price* : 1746 coll. (O.E.D.)—3. (Of liquor) diluted : lower classes' coll. (— 1923). Manchon. Ex *long drink*, a big one.

long, adv. Along ; e.g. ' Come long, Bill ! ' : coll., mostly lower classes' (— 1923). Manchon.

long lie. Additional time in bed on certain days :

Shrewsbury School coll. : from ca. 1880. Desmond Coke, *The Bending of a Twig*, 1906. Cf. the Public School sense of *froust* (*frowst*) and *thoke*, qq.v.

long !, so. Good-bye : coll. : 1834. (S.O.D. and O.E.D.) In the Colonies, often pronounced *soo'-long*. ? ex *for so long as you're away good luck !*

long, that. Thus or so long : low coll. : late C. 19–20. See **that,** adv.

long, the. The summer vacation : university coll. : 1852, Bristed ; Reade, 1863.

Long Acre. A baker : rhyming s. (— 1857). ' Ducange Anglicus.'

long and slender like a cat's elbow. A C. 18–mid-19 ironic proverbial c.p. T. Fuller, *Gnomologia*, 1732.

long attachment. One tall, one short (other-sex) person walking together : coll. : from ca. 1860 ; ob. In jocular S.E., *the long and* (*the*) *short of it.*

long balls ; gen. l. bowls. Long-range firing : naval : C. 19. Bowen. Ex *long bowls*, whether in sense of ninepins or in the Scottish one of a game played by throwing heavy bullets is not certain.

long beer, drink. A large measure of liquor : coll. : 1859, Trollope. (O.E.D.)

long Bertha. A variant of *big Bertha*. See **Bertha.** (F. & Gibbons.)

***long bill.** A long imprisonment : c. : from ca. 1860. Cf. *lifer*, q.v. A short term is *a short bill.*

long-bow, draw or **pull the.** To tell unlikely stories : coll. ; in C. 20, S.E. : resp., from ca. 1668, C. 19–20. L'Estrange ; Thackeray, ' What is it makes him pull the long-bow in that wonderful manner ? '

long-bow man. A liar : coll. : ca. 1678–1830. Ray, Motteux. (O.E.D.)

long bowls. See **long balls.**

long chalk. See **chalk, not by a long.**

long clay. A long clay pipe : coll. : from ca. 1860. Cf. *churchwarden*, q.v.

long-cork. Claret : 1829, Marryat : † by 1900. Ex the long corks.

long-crown. A clever fellow, esp. in the proverb, ' That caps long-crown, and he capped the devil ' : coll. and dial. (— 1847) ; † except in dial.

long dispar(s). The loin : Winchester College. See **dispar.**

long drink. See **long beer.**

long-eared bastard or **chum.** See **chum, long-eared.** The former term, affectionate or neutral, the latter contemptuous. Cf. *long-faced one.*

long Eliza. A blue and white vase ornamented with tall china-women : sailors' and traders' : from ca. 1880. See esp. *The Pall Mall Gazette*, Dec. 4, 1884. Ex Ger. *lange Lischen*, tall Lizzies.

long enough, I, you, etc., **may** (do something). It's pretty hopeless : coll. : C. 16–20. In C. 19–20 gen. followed by *before* + v. Palsgrave, Browning. O.E.D.

long eye. The female pudend : ' pigeon ' : from ca. 1850.

long face. A solemn or a downhearted expression : coll. : from ca. 1785.

long-faced chum. A variant of the next. See **chum, long-eared.**

long-faced one. A horse : military (— 1896). Cf. *long-eared bastard*, q.v.

long feathers. Straw ; bedding stuffed with straw : military (— 1879) ; † by 1915.

long fifteens. Some class of lawyers : C. 17. L. Barry, in *Ram Alley*. O.E.D.

long firm. A swindling group of phantom capitalists : 1868 : commercial coll. *Orchestra,* Jan. 2, 1869. Presumably ex *long* (!) credit expected, or ex ' choosing its victims at a distance ', W.

long fork. A stick used as a toasting fork : Winchester College : ca. 1830–70.

long gallery. The act or the practice of trundling the dice the whole length of the board : ca. 1790–1850. Grose, 3rd ed.

long ghost. A tall, awkward person : ca. 1860–1910. H., 3rd ed. Cf. *lamp-post.*

long glass. A very long, horn-shaped glass filled with beer on special occasions : Eton College s. > j. : ca. 1820–70. Brinsley-Richards, *Seven Years at Eton,* 1883.

long-haired chum. A female friend or sweetheart : from ca. 1870 : tailors' >, in C. 20, soldiers' and sailors'. See also at **long-eared chum.**

*****long hand, the.** Pickpocketry : c. (— 1923). Manchon. Therein, a long, thin hand is useful.

Long Harry. Henry Wilkinson (1610–75), ' an Oxford Professor of Divinity and member of the Westminster Assembly ' (ca. 1650). Dawson.

long-head. A ' shrewd-head ' or very shrewd or cunning person : lower classes' coll. (— 1923). Manchon. Ex dial.

long hogs. A sheep's first growth of wool : coll. : ca. 1840–1900.

long home, one's. The grave : C. 14–20 : S.E. >, ca. 1820, coll. Dickens.

long hope. Long expectations in studying for a degree : Oxford University : ca. 1820–40. Egan's Grose.

long-horn. A biplane of the ' pusher ' type : Air Force coll. : from ca. 1917 ; ob. F. & Gibbons.

long hundred. Six-score fresh herrings : Billingsgate coll. : from ca. 1870. Ex *long hundred,* 120. H., 5th ed.

long in the mouth. Tough : low coll. : from ca. 1850 ; ob.

long in the tooth. Elderly : from ca. 1910 : (low) coll. >, by 1930, S.E.

jump, be up for the long. See **jump, be for the.**

long jump, the. The transference of an air squadron to active service overseas : Air Force : 1916. ; ob. F. & Gibbons.

long lady. A farthing candle : late C. 18–early 19 coll.

long lane. The throat : C. 19–20 ; ob. See **lane, 2.**

long lane, for the. Of something borrowed without intention of repayment or restoration : coll. : C. 18–mid-19. ? ex the proverb *it's a long lane that has no turning.*

long leg. ' A big difference in the draught forward and aft in a sailing ship ' : nautical coll. : mid-C. 19–20 ; ob. Bowen. Ex nautical j. *long-legged,* (of a ship) drawing much water.

long legs ; long un. A tall person : C. 18–20 coll. Cf. *lamp-post.*

long Meg. A very tall woman : late C. 17–early 19. B.E. Ex an actual woman, known as Long Meg of Westminster.

long nose, make a. To put a derisive thumb to the nose : 1868 (O.E.D.).

long oats. ' A broom or fork-handle used to belabour a horse ', F. & H. : military : ca. 1870–1914. Cf. *Thorley's food for cattle.*

*****long one** or **'un.** A hare : poachers' : from ca. 1810. *Lex. Bal.* Contrast *long tail,* 4.—2. A

pheasant : poachers' (— 1909). Ware. Prob. suggested by *long tail,* 4.

long paper. Paper for impositions : Winchester College : from ca. 1860.

long pig. Human flesh as food : 1852, Mundy, in *Our Antipodes* : nautical >, ca. 1895, S.E. Prob. ex Fijian phrase.

long pull. An over-measure of liquor, given (customarily or occasionally) to improve trade : publicans' coll. (— 1909). Ware.

Long Shanks. Edward I (d. 1307) : coll. > S.E. —2. (In lower case.) A tall man : coll. : late C. 17–20. B.E., Grose.

long shilling. A drive ' from the Royal Exchange to the east corner of Catherine-street, in the Strand ', Grose : London hackney-coachmen's : ca. 1740–80.

long ship. A ship ' in which it is a long time between drinks ' : nautical : C. 20. Bowen.

long-shore butcher. A coastguardsman : nautical : ca. 1820–1905.

long shot. A bet laid at large odds : turf s. (— 1869) >, in C. 20, gen. coll. *Leisure Hour,* May, 1869.

long sight, not by a. Not by a long way : coll. : late C. 19–20.

*****long-sleeved top.** A silk hat : c. (— 1889) ; ob.

long-sleeved 'un. A long glass (of liquor) : Australian : from ca. 1890 ; ob. Ex :

long-sleever. The same ; also the glass itself : Australian (— 1888). Morris.

long stomach. A greedy eater : ca. 1780–1870 : coll. Grose, 2nd ed.

long suit, one's. One's forte or speciality : C. 20 : coll., now verging on S.E. Ex card-games.

long tail, as applied to one of the riff-raff, is S.E. —2. A native of Kent : from ca. 1620 : coll. till ca. 1750, then dial. Also *Kentish long-tail,* q.v.—3. A Chinaman : nautical : from ca. 1865 ; ob.—4. A pheasant : sporting coll. : 1854, Smedley.—5. A greyhound : coursers' and dog-fanciers' (— 1864) ; ob. H., 3rd ed.—6. One or another : c. : ca. 1730–70. Johnson.

long-tailed bear, (that's) a. You lie ! : non-aristocratic evasive c.p. : late C. 19–early 20. Ware, ' Bears have *no* tails.'

long-tailed beggar. A cat : low (mostly nautical) coll. : from ca. 1830 ; ob. Marryat, in *Peter Simple* ; H., 5th ed.—2. In c. (— 1923 : Manchon), the same as :

*****long-tailed finnip** or **'un.** A bank-note of high denomination : c. : from ca. 1835. Brandon ; Snowden's *Magazine Assistant.* Cf. *flimsy,* q.v.

long tea. Tea poured from a high-held pot ; urine : schoolboys' : ca. 1850–1910.

long togs. A landsman's clothes ; esp. full-dress clothes : nautical : from ca. 1830. Also adj. as in Marryat's ' them long-tog, swallow-tailed coats '.

long Tom. A large, long-range gun : nautical (also † *long Tom Tuck* : Bowen) and military coll. : from ca. 1865. Cf. *long-winded whistler,* q.v. Also, a nickname for specific cannon.—2. Hence, a penis : low : from ca. 1898. (Whence an obscene riddle current during the Boer War.)

long-tongued as Granny. Very apt to blab : coll. : ca. 1720–1830. Ex Granny, an idiot (d. 1719) that could lick her own eye.

long tot. A lengthy set of figures for addition, esp. in examinations : from ca. 1885 : coll. Ex *tot* (q.v.), itself abbr. *total.*

Long Town. London : Anglo-Irish (— 1823) · † by 1900. ' Jon Bee.'

long trail, the. ' In the China clippers, the homeward route round Australia ': mid-C. 19–20 ; virtually †. Bowen.

long 'un. See **long legs** and **long one.**

long vac. The summer holiday : at schools, some universities (cf. *long, the*), the law-courts : coll. : late C. 19–20.

long-winded paymaster. A person that takes long credit : late C. 17–early 19. B.E., Grose.

long-winded whistler. A chase-gun : nautical : ca. 1865–90. Smyth. Cf. *long Tom.*

long word, a. A word indicative of a long time : coll. : from ca. 1860. ' Since I've been in London, and that's saying a long word ', *The Cornhill Magazine*, Dec., 1861 ; ' " Never " is a long word,' *The Standard*, July 28, 1883. O.E.D.

longa in ' pidgin ' represents ' at ', ' for ', ' of ', ' to '. See quotation at the ' pidgin ' usage of **feller.** Ex *belonging to.*

longanimity. Catachrestic for *longinquity* : C. 17–20. O.E.D.

Longbelly. ' A Natal [coll.] corruption of the name of the native chief, Langelibelee, who gave so much trouble in 1873 ', Pettman. Virtually † by 1920.

longs, the. The latrines at Brasenose : Oxford University : from ca. 1870 ; † by 1930. Built from funds donated by Lady Long. Still so called at Trinity College, Oxford : but because of their length.

Long's. Short's winery almost opposite Somerset House : the Strand, London : mid-C. 19–20 ; ob. Ware.

***longs and shorts ;** also **longs and broads.** ' Cards so manufactured that all above the eight are a trifle longer than those below it,' F. & H. : cardsharpers' c. : from ca. 1860. H., 3rd ed.—2. Orig. (— 1823), *longs and broads* = cards. Egan's Grose.

longshore lawyer. An unscrupulous lawyer : coll. (— 1823) ; ob. Bee.

longshore owner. (Gen. pl.) A shipowner that sent ill-found ships to sea : nautical coll. : ca. 1850–1910. Bowen. Cf. S.E. *arm-chair tactician* or *strategist.*

Lonsdale's ninepins. Those nine boroughs for which Lord Lonsdale used to provide the members : Parliamentary : late C. 18–early 19.

[**loo** (the game), n. and v., despite F. & H., is S.E., as are the following *loo-* words :—**look (for) babies or cupids in the eyes** ; **look pricks** ; **loon** (while **play the loon** is Scots) ; **loose** (= wanton, dissipated and its compounds ; **on the loose** ; **shake a loose leg.**]

'Loo, the. Woolloomooloo, a rough district of Sydney : Australian coll. : C. 20. C. J. Dennis.

loo ! Milk ! : milkmen's cry (— 1823) ; ob. ' Jon Bee.' Ex Fr. *lait.*

looard. A nautical spelling of *leeward* : coll. (— 1887). Baumann.

looby. A fool ; an idle, dull fellow : C. 14–20 : S.E. till ca. 1820, then coll. and dial. Disraeli, ' Her looby of a son and his eighty thousand a year '. Cf. *loopy*, q.v.—2. In C. 20, occ. as adj. in sense of *loopy*, q.v. (B. & P.)

loocha, -cher. ' A blackguard libertine, a lewd loafer ' : Anglo-Indian coll. : from ca. 1820. Ex Hindustani *luchcha.* Whence *Loocha Point*, Louisa Point, Matheran, India. Yule & Burnell.

loo'd, or looed, be. To be very short of money : nautical (— 1923). Manchon. I.e. to be to leeward. Imm. ex :—*loo'd.* ' beaten, defeated ',

Barrère & Leland : coll. : from middle 1880's ; ob. Ex the game of loo. (E.D.D.)

loof-faker. A chimney-sweep : 1859, H., 1st ed. ; ob. Doubtless *loof* is an approximate back-s. perversion of *flue* : *flue* > *floo* > *oolf* > *loof.*

look. To look surprised ; stare : C. 17–20 : S.E. till ca. 1850, then coll.

look a gift-horse in the mouth. To criticise a gift or a favour : C. 16–20 : coll. till C. 18, then S.E. ' Hudibras ' Butler.

look alive. To be alert ; bestir oneself : coll. : C. 19–20. Also, in late C. 19–20 lower classes' coll., *look slimy* (ob.). Cf. *look sharp* and *look slippery*, qq.v.

look as if butter would not melt in one's mouth. See **mouth.**

look as if one had eaten live birds. To be unwontedly lively : from ca. 1867 : ob. *The Quarterly Review*, cxxv, p. 231 (Apperson).

look at, cannot. To have no chance against : coll. : 1895 (O.E.D.). Ex cricket, where it appears as early as 1862 : Lewis.

look at, have a. ' To look at for the purpose of examining ' : coll. : 1885. S.O.D.

look at him (it, me, you, etc.**), to.** Judging from his (my, etc.) appearance : coll. : 1846, Bentley's *Miscellany* (vol. xx), ' No one would think me more than five- or six-and-thirty, to look at me.' O.E.D.

look at the maker's name. To drain a glass : coll. : from ca. 1860 ; ob. Also *bite one's name in the pot.*

***look at the place.** (Of thieves) to examine a house, etc., beforehand, to see if there is anything unusual about it : C. 19–20 : c. Vaux.

look behind one, not or **never to.** Advance or prosper without interruption : coll. : 1852, Serjeant Bellasis. (O.E.D.) The gen. C. 20 form is *never to look back* (1893, O.E.D.). Perhaps ex racer leading easily (W.).

look big. See **big.—l. blue.** See **blue.—l. botty.** See **botty.**

look Cro'-Jack-eyed. To squint : nautical : mid-C. 19–20. Bowen.

look down one's nose. To look glum : coll. : C. 19–20 ; ob.

look down one's nose at. To despise : coll. : from ca. 1840.

look'ee. A low coll. form of *look you !* (C. 18–20) = mind this !

look for a needle in a bottle of hay or **in a haystack.** To look for something virtually impossible to find : proverbial coll. : resp. late C. 16–19, C. 19–20. Greene, Hood.

look goats and monkeys at. See **goats and monkeys.**

look here ! Mind this ! ; mind what I say ! : coll. : C. 17–20. Shakespeare. Also *look you !* : late C. 16–20. Shakespeare, ' Look you how he writes.' (O.E.D.)

look-in. A chance of success : sporting : 1870, *Bell's Life*, Feb. 12.—2. See **look-up, n.**

look in, v.i. ' To use a wireless receiver adapted for television ' : coll. : Aug. 1928. O.E.D. (Sup.).

look into the whites. To be about to fight : lower classes' : from ca. 1885 ; ob. Ware. Sc. *of each other's eyes.*

look like a billy-goat in stays. To look very silly : nautical : late C. 19–20. Bowen.

look like a tooth-drawer. To be thin and meagre : coll. : C. 17. Beaumont & Fletcher, in *Philaster* ; Ray (as a semi-proverbial phrase). Apperson.

look like nothing on earth. See **nothing on earth.**

look lively. To be drunk : low coll. : from ca. 1850.

look nine ways for Sunday(s). To squint : nautical : from ca. 1850 ; ob. Ex the C. 16–18 coll. *look nine ways* confused with the dial. *look both* (later *all*) *ways for Sunday*.

look old. To be severe or cautious : streets' coll. (— 1909). Ware.

look on, v.i. Applied to a horse meant not to do its best : the turf : from ca. 1870.—2. To read (a book, etc.) at the same time (*with* another person) : coll. : late C. 19–20.

look on the wall and it will not bite you. A derisive c.p. addressed to a person ' bitten with mustard ', Ray : ca. 1670–1760.

look one way and row another. To do the opposite of what one seems to intend to do : coll. : ca. 1580–1880. Melbancke, 1583 ; D'Urfey ; Spurgeon, 1869. (Apperson.)

look out, that is X's. That is X's concern or sole business : coll. : 1844 (S.O.D.).

look-out house. The watch kept ' by ordained masters on defunct incumbents ', Egan's Grose : Oxford University : ca. 1820–40.

look-see ; occ. **looksee.** A look-round, an inspection : from early 1880's. (O.E.D. Sup.) Almost certainly ex pidgin, hence nautical, *look-see,* to look and see.—2. Hence, a periscope or a telescope : 1915–18 : resp. military and naval. F. & Gibbons. —3. (Ex 1 and 2.) Looks, appearance : 1926 (O.E.D. Sup.).

look-see, v. See preceding, 1.

look sharp. To exercise great care or vigilance : S.E.—2. To be quick ; to hasten : coll. : from ca. 1815. Cobbett, ' They shall look sharp if they act before I am ready for them ' ; Dickens ; Manville Fenn. O.E.D. Cf. the next two entries.

look slimy. See **look alive.**

look slippery. To be quick : see **slippery.** (Ware, 1909, considers it essentially naval.)—**look slippy.** See **slippy.**

look-stick. A telescope : naval : late C. 19–20. Bowen. Cf. *look-see,* 2.

look through a glass. To become tipsy : low coll. : from ca. 1840 ; ob.

look through a hempen window. To be hanged : coll. : ca. 1625–1700.

look to, or watch, one's water (for him). To follow a person's movements, watch him very closely : coll. (semi-proverbial) : from ca. 1540 : in C. 19–20, dial. only. Heywood, 1546 ; Manley, *The New Atlantis.* (Apperson.)

look towards one. To drink his health : low coll. : 1848, Thackeray ; ob. See also **looks towards.**

look-up ; occ. **look-in.** A short visit : coll. (— 1923). Manchon. Ex sense 2 of :

look up, v.i. To improve : s. >, in C. 20, coll. (in C. 19, mainly commercial) : 1822, *The Examiner,* ' Foreign Securities are generally looking up.' O.E.D.—2. V.t., to visit, gen. informally : coll. : from ca. 1835. Dickens, in *Pickwick,* ' He used to go back for a week, just to look up his old friends.'

look you ! See **look here !**—**looker.** See **good-looker.**

looking as if he hadn't got his right change. Mad- or wild-looking : Cockneys' (— 1909). Ware.

looking as if one could not help it. Looking like a simpleton or a faint-heart : coll. : late C. 18–20 ; ob. Grose.

looking-glass. A chamber-pot : ca. 1620–1830,

then dial. (n.b. the E.D.D. entry). Beaumont & Fletcher ; B.E. ; Grose. Prob. ex the attention paid to it by physicians.

looking like a bit of chewed string. An elaboration of *chewed string,* q.v.

looking lively. Slightly intoxicated : coll. : late C. 19–20. Lyell.

looking seven ways for Sunday. Squinting : London lower and lower-middle classes' : late C. 19–20. Ware. Cf. **look nine ways,** q.v.

lookit ——— ! Look at ———! : Canadian (and U.S.) : from ca. 1880. Beames.

looks towards you !, I. Your good health ! : lower classes' coll. : mid-C. 19–20. See **look towards.**—2. Hence, **I** congratulate you ! : lower classes' ironic c.p. (— 1923). Manchon.

looksee. See **look-see. looney.** See **loony.**

Loonies. ' Bootham Park Asylum ; that end of the playing pitches ' : Bootham School (— 1925). Anon., *Dict. of Bootham Slang.* Ex *loony,* 2.

*****loonslate, loonslatt.** Thirteen pence halfpenny : c. : late C. 17–18. B.E. Cf. *hangman's wages,* q.v.

loony ; often **looney ;** occ. **luny.** Crazy : (lower classes') coll. : 1872.—2. Hence, a fool ; a lunatic : id. : 1869. (E.D.D.) Ex *lunatic* influenced by *loon.* Cf. *dippy, dotty, potty,* and :

loony, be taken. To go crazy, mad : (proletarian) coll. : late C. 19–20. A. Neil Lyons, *Arthur's,* 1914, ' Took looney, or what is it ? ' (Manchon.)

loony-bin. A lunatic asylum : Cockneys' : from ca. 1890. Ex *loony,* 2.

loop-liner. A short pint, sold at about three-quarters of the price of a full pint : Anglo-Irish, esp. Dubliners' : from ca. 1920 ; ob. A play on *porter,* the short pint being invariably of this beverage : the Loop Line, running through the centre of the city of Dublin, is an accommodation line linking two systems ; similarly a *loop-liner* is an accommodation *porter* that lacks the dignity of a full pint.

loopy. Slightly mad : s. (or coll.) : late C. 19–20. ? ex *looby,* q.v., influenced by ironic allusion to Scots *loopy,* crafty. Occ. *looby.*

loos-wallah. A rascal ; a thief : Regular Army : late C. 19–20. F. & Gibbons. In Hindustani, ' thief-fellow '.

loose. To lose : sol. : C. 19–20. Often used by persons that should know better.

loose, adj. See remarks at **loo.**—2. (Of time) not strictly observed : coll. : 1892, Sir H. Maxwell, ' Breakfast is not on the table till a loose ten.' Ob. O.E.D.—3. Absent without leave : New Zealand soldiers' : 1915–18.

loose, have a screw. See **screw.**—**loose, play fast and.** See **fast and loose.**

loose, run. (Of a horse) to race unbacked : the turf : 1884, Hawley Smart.

loose, turned. (Of a horse) handicapped at a very low rate : the turf : from ca. 1880 ; ob. Cf. preceding entry.

loose a fiver. (To have) ' to pay extravagantly for any pleasure or purchase ' : proletarian (— 1909). Ware.

loose-box. A carriage kept for a kept woman's use : C. 19. Cf. *mot-cart.*

loose end. A late C. 19–20 variant of *loose fish,* 2. Manchon.

loose end, at a († *after* or *on* a). Not regularly employed ; not knowing what to do : from ca. 1850 (*at a* . . . recorded first in 1860) : coll. ex dial. (O.E.D.) Ex freedom from tether (W.). Cf. :

loose end, leave (a matter) **at a.** To leave unsettled : coll. : from ca. 1864.

loose ends, at. Neglected : coll. : from ca. 1870 ; ob. Cf. preceding entry.

loose fish. A harlot : coll. : 1809, Malkin ; † by 1895. (O.E.D.)—2. A person of irregular, esp. of dissipated habits : coll. : 1827, Egan, ' Known among the loose-fish who frequent races by the name of thimble-rig.'—3. An independent member : Parliament : 1864 ; ob.

loose French. (Gen. *loosing F.*) To use violent language in English : urban (mostly Cockney) : ca. 1890–1915. Ware.

loose hold. To let go : coll. : from ca. 1695. Dryden. Cf. *leave go*, q.v.

loose-hung. (Of persons) unsteady : low coll. : from ca. 1820 ; ob.

loose-wallah. An occ. variant of *loos-wallah*, q.v. (B. & P.)

loosen (a person's) **hide.** To thrash : 1902, *The Daily Chronicle*, April 11 (O.E.D.).

loot. Pillage ; plunder : 1788 : military coll >, ca. 1870, S.E. Ex Hindustani *lut*, but prob. influenced by *lootie*, a native irregular of India, hence a bandit. See esp. Yule & Burnell.—2. A lieutenant : late C. 19–20 naval and military. Bowen ; B. & P. Ex mispronunciation as *lootenant*. Cf. *luff*.

loot, v. To plunder ; carry off as booty : from ca. 1840 : military coll. >, ca. 1870, S.E. The same ascent characterises *looter* and. *looting*.

lop. A penny : Anglo-Irish (— 1935). Perhaps ex dial. *lop*, a flea : cf. the fig. use of *flea-bite*.

[**lop**, to lounge, idle, is, like *lop about*, S.E., despite F. & H. ; the same applies to *loplolly*, a mere variant of *loblolly*, q.v.]

lope. To run ; run away : from ca. 1570 : S.E. till ca. 1690, then s. and dial. B.E. ; Grose, ' He loped down the dancers.'—2. To steal : c. (— 1874). H., 5th ed.

loper. Abbr. *landloper*, q.v.

lor', Lor' ! A slovenly form of *Lord* : low coll. : 1835 (S.O.D.). Cf. *law*, q.v.

lor (or **Lor')-a-mussy !** Lord have mercy ! (= surprise) : low coll. : 1865 (prob. much earlier). Dickens. Cf. *Lord-a-mercy !*, q.v. (O.E.D.)

lord. A hunchback : late C. 17–20 ; ob. B.E. ; Lamb, ' A deformed person is a lord.' A hunchback used often to be addressed as *my lord*. Perhaps ex Gr. λορδός, bent backward, a technical and medical term. Cf. *lady*, q.v.—2. An occ. abbr. of *lord of the manor*, q.v.

Lord ! In C. 14–16, dignified ; in C. 17–20, trivial when not profane. Shakespeare, ' O Lord, I must laugh ' (S.O.D.).

lord, drink like a. To drink hard : proverbial coll. : C. 17–18. Whence :

lord, drunk as a. Very drunk : from ca. 1670 : coll. till C. 19, then S.E. Cf. *emperor*, q.v.

lord !, my. See **lord, 1.**

lord, swear like a. To swear copiously and/or vigorously : coll. > S.E. : C. 16–17.

Lord-a-mercy (on us) ! ' The Lord have mercy (on us) ! ' as an exclamation of surprise : low coll. when not sol. : C. 19–20. Eleanor Smith, 1808, ' Lord-a-mercy upon those that had a hand in such a business.' O.E.D.

Lord Adam Gordon's Lifeguards. The 3rd Hussars : military coll. : late C. 18–20 ; ob. F. &

Gibbons. They served as escorts to Lord Adam Gordon, in 1782–98, commanding the Forces in Scotland.

Lord Baldwin. See **Queen Anne.**

Lord Blarney. Lord Carnarvon : Anglo-Irish : 1885 ; very ob. Ware. On his appointment as Lord Lieutenant of Ireland in 1885, he made many flattering speeches (see, e.g. comment in *The Daily News*, Nov. 14, 1885).

Lord Harry. See **oid Harry.**

[**Lord bless me !** An oath so trivial as to verge on the coll. : from ca. 1780. Horace Walpole.]

Lord Crop. Lord George Gordon of the Gordon Riots : d. in 1793. Dawson.

Lord George, the. The Lloyd George old age pension : working-class sol. : from ca. 1917. (M. Harrison, 1935.)

Lord have mercy (up)on me. The ' iliac passion ', a ' colic ' of the small guts : late C. 16–17 medical coll. used, according to *Junius' Nomenclator*, by ' the homelier sort of Phisicians '. (O.E.D.)

Lord John Russell. A bustle or dress-improver : rhyming s. (— 1859) ; † by 1900.

Lord knows how or **what** or **who, the.** Some person or thing of unspecified but considerable potentialities ; phrases indicative of irritation, wonderment, admiration, or, as gen., the completeness of one's own ignorance. Coll. : late C. 17–20. *The Gentleman's Journal*, March, 1691–2, ' Here's novels, and new-born adventures . . . and the Lord knows what not.' In C. 20, usually—but, I believe, wrongly—held to be S.E.

Lord love a duck ! See **duck !, Lord love a.** Cf. :

Lord love us ! A jocular, also a low coll., form of *Lord love me !* (itself trivial) : late C. 19–20.

Lord Lovel. A shovel : rhyming s. (— 1857). ' Ducange Anglicus.'

Lord lumme or **lummy !** See **lumme !**

Lord Mansfield's teeth. The spikes along the top of the wall of the King's Bench Prison : ca. 1790–1830. Ex Sir Charles Mansfield (1733–1821), Lord Chief Justice.

***lord mayor.** A large crowbar : c. (— 1889). D. C. Murray. Opp. *alderman*.

lord mayor, v. To swear : rhyming s. : late C. 19–20. B. & P.

lord mayor's coal. A (piece of) slate : coll. : ca. 1840–80. Barham.

Lord Mayor's fool, like my or **the.** Fond of everything good : proverbial coll. : from ca. 1670. Ray ; H. Kingsley in *Geoffrey Hamlyn* : † by 1910. Often as *the Lord Mayor's fool, who likes everything that is good*. Swift has *like my Lord Mayor's fool, full of business and nothing to do*. (Apperson.)

Lord Minimus. Jeffrey Hudson, a famous Court dwarf of mid-C. 17. Dawson.

Lord Muck. See **Muck, Lord.**

lord of the foresheet. A sailing-ship's cook : jocular nautical : late C. 19–20. Bowen.

lord of the manor. A ' tanner ' (q.v.), i.e. sixpence : rhyming s. (— 1839). Brandon ; H., 1st ed. This is the earliest record of a rhyming s. term ; its inclusion in Brandon, moreover, significantly implies that ' Ducange Anglicus ', 1857, was right in classifying all such terms as c.

Lord Piccadilly. Another nickname of *Old Q*, q.v.

Lord Wellington's Bodyguard. The 5th Foot Regiment, in late C. 19–20 the Northumberland Fusiliers : military : 1811, when they ' furnished the guard at Wellington's headquarters ' ; ob. F. & Gibbons.

lords, the. The first cricket eleven : Winchester College : from ca. 1860 ; ob.

Lord's Own, the. H.M.S. *Vengeance* : naval : C. 20. Bowen, ' " Vengeance is Mine, saith the Lord ".'

lordsake. For the Lord's sake : Scots coll. : from ca. 1860. O.E.D.

lordy ! or **Lordy !** Lord ! : (dial. and) low coll. : mid-C. 19–20. Cf. *law !, lawks !, lor*'. Abbr. :

Lordy me ! A (dial. and) low coll. corruption of *Lord (have* or) *help me* : C. 19–20. Ware.

lorification is erroneous for *lorication* : C. 18–20. O.E.D.

lorry-hopping. Lorry-jumping : military : 1915 ; ob. F. & Gibbons.

lors ! Lord ! : low coll. : 1860, George Eliot. (O.E.D.) Cf. *laws !*

lose. The act, or an instance, of losing (a horse-race) : racing : 1884. O.E.D.

lose, v.t. To be much superior to ; overcome, defeat easily : coll. : C. 20.

lose one's hair. See **hair.**

lose one's legs. To become tipsy : from ca. 1770 ; ob.

lose one's number. To be ' crimed ' : military : C. 20. B. & P.

lose one's rag. See **rag, lose one's.**

lose out, v.i. To lose ; be swindled or merely fooled : coll. : Australia : late C. 19–20. Perhaps ex the † S.E. *lose out*, recorded by O.E.D. at 1869.

lose the number of one's mess. See **mess.**

loser, as a billiards term, is S.E.—despite F. & H. —2. A handicap, obstacle, disappointment : low : from ca. 1920. James Curtis, *The Gilt Kid*, 1936, ' It was a bit of a loser, feeling bored before the trial had started.'

lost a cart-load (or cartful) and found a waggon-load. See **cart-load.**

lost it, he's. He is in a bad temper : Charterhouse : C. 20. I.e. lost his temper.

lost the key of the 'angar door. An Air Force c.p. : from ca. 1930. Flying Officer B. J. Hurren, *Stand Easy*, 1934. Ex a topicality explained in that book.

lot. A group of associated persons, or of things of the same kind : from ca. 1570 : S.E. until ca. 1875, then (except for merchandise and live stock) coll. W. Benham, 1879, ' Their crew seem to have been a lazy lot.' O.E.D.—2. A person, gen. pejoratively as in *a bad lot*, or ironically as in *a nice lot* : from ca. 1846 : coll. >, in C. 20, S.E. Thackeray, in *Vanity Fair*, (à propos of Miss Sharp) ' A bad lot, I tell you, a bad lot '. Ex the auction-room (W.).— 3. See **lot, red.**—4. See **lot, the, 2.**

lot, a ; lots. A considerable quantity or number ; adv., a good deal. Coll. : *lots* from ca. 1810, *a lot* from ca. 1835. Also with adj. as in *a good lot* (Keble, 1835), *a great lot*. Either followed by *of* or absolutely. O.E.D.

lot, hot. See **hot lot.**

*lot, red ; white lot. Resp. a gold and a silver watch : c. (-- 1933). Charles E. Leach. See *red and *white.

lot, the ; the whole lot. The whole of a stated quantity or number : coll. : 1867, Mrs. Henry Wood, ' He's crunching the lot ' (a quart of gooseberries). O.E.D.—2. See ' Moving-Picture Slang ', § 11.

*lot, white. See **lot, red.**

[loteby (or ludby) and Lothario, despite F. & H., are both S.E.]

Lothbury, go by way of. To be loth : coll. : ca. 1560–1660. Tusser. For punning topicalities, cf. *Clapham, Needham, Peckham*, qq.v.

lotherwite. Corrupt for *lairwite* (a fine for fornication or adultery) : C. 16–17. (O.E.D.)

lotion. A drink—rarely of aught but liquor, and esp. of gin : 1876, Hindley. Cf. † *lotium*, a low coll. form of *lotion*.

lotman. A pirate : nautical coll. : ? late C. 18–mid-19. Smyth ; Bowen. ' Alleged ', says O.E.D. : but why should Admiral Smyth fabricate the word ? Ex *lot*, a share (in the booty).

lots. See **lot, a.**

Lot's wife. Salt : nautical : late C. 19–20. Bowen. Cf. and see :

Lot's wife's backbone, (as) salt as. Extremely salt : lower classes' (— 1909). Ware. Ex the Biblical story.

Lottie is an inevitable nickname (C. 20) of men surnamed Collins. F. & Gibbons. Ex the celebrated actress, Lottie Collins. Cf. *Jumper*, q.v.

Lotties and Totties. Harlots : orig. (— 1885) and mainly theatrical. Ware. Ex the frequency of those diminutives in that class.

lotus, n. and esp. v. (To) hocus : low rhyming s. : 1885. Ware. Influenced by *locust*.

loud. (Of dress or manners) showy : 1847, Albert Smith, ' Very loud patterns ' : coll. till C. 20, then S.E. (As strong-smelling : S.E. ; ob. except in U.S.)

loud one, a. A big lie : coll. : ca. 1670–1850. Ray ; Scott, in *Ivanhoe*, ' " That's a lie, and a loud one," said the Friar.'—2. A noisy breaking of wind : low : mid-C. 19–20.—3. A misfortune : military : G.W. Prob. ex the bursts of heavy shells. (F. & Gibbons.)

loudly. Showily, of dress or manners : 1849, Thackeray : coll. till C. 20, then S.E. (O.E.D.)

Louis. A harlot's bully : low (-- 1935). Adopted from U.S. Cf. Fr. *Alphonse*.

lounce. A drink : nautical : from ca. 1850 ; ob. Ex *allowance*.—2. See **lownce.**

lounge. A chief meal ; a treat : Eton and Cambridge : 1844, Disraeli ; *The Press*, Nov. 12, 1864, ' I don't care for dinner . . . Breakfast is my lounge.'—2. As a loitering-place, it is, despite Grose, S.E.—3. A lounge suit : C. 20 : tailors' coll., now verging on S.E. See, e.g., *The Tailor and Cutter*, Nov. 29, 1928.

lounge-lizard. A sleek adventurer frequenting lounges in the expectation of women, their money and caresses : U.S. s. (1923), anglicised by 1925 ; by 1935, coll. (Krapp's prophecy as to its lack of viability has been proved false.)

*lour, loure, lowr(e). (See also **loaver.**) Money ; in C. 19, gen. of coin : c. : from ca. 1565. Harman, Head, Grose, Brandon, Richardson (author of *The Police*, 1889). Ex C. 14–16 S.E. *lower*, a reward, recompense, itself ex Old Fr. *louier*, a reward ; cf. Romany *loor*, to plunder, and *looripen*, plunder, booty.

*lour, gammy. Counterfeit coin : c. (— 1839). Brandon.

[louse, care not a ; not worth a louse. S.E., despite F. & H.]

louse, mean as a. Stingy ; miserly : non-aristocratic coll. (— 1887). Baumann.

louse, prick a. To be a tailor : coll. : C. 17–mid-19. Hence *louse-pricking*, vbl.n., tailoring, also as adj. : C. 18–mid-19, e.g. in Toldervy (O.E.D.)

louse a grey head of his own, he will never. A c.p. of C. 18–early 19 : He will never live to be old. Grose.

louse-bag. ' A black bag worn to the hair or wig ', Grose, 1st ed. : coll. : ca. 1780–1830.

louse for the sake of its skin or hide, skin a. To be extremely thrifty : coll. : late C. 16–18. In C. 19–20, *flea* is substituted for *louse*. (Apperson.)

louse-house. A lock-up ; a prison : late C. 18–early 19. Grose, 1st ed.

louse-ladder. ' A stitch fallen in a stocking ', Grose, 1st ed. : ca. 1780–1840. Extant in dial.

Louse-Land ; Louseland. Scotland : late C. 17–early 19. B.E. Cf. *Itchland.*

louse miss its footing on one's coat it will break its neck, if a. To have a very threadbare coat, clothes : proverbial coll. : mid-C. 14–mid-18. Langland, Palsgrave, ' Gnomologia ' Fuller. (Apperson.)

louse-trap. A fine comb : low : late C. 17–20. In B.E., a *Scotch l.-t.*—2. A woollen body-belt or sheep-skin coat : military 1914–18. B. & P.

louse-walk. A back-hair parting : low : ca. 1820–80.

Lousy. The village of La Houssoye near Albert : Western Front military in G.W.

lousy. Contemptible ; mean ; filthy : late C. 14–20 : S.E. till C. 20, when, esp. after G.W., coll. and used as a mere pejorative.—2. (Of paint) full of skin from too long keeping : painters' : from ca. 1860 ; ob.

lousy with. Full of : 1915 : orig. military, as in ' lousy with guns ' ; esp. in ' lousy with money '. Ex the prevalence of lice.

Lousy Wood. Leuze Wood, the scene of fierce fighting on the Somme in 1916 : military : late 1916–18. F. & Gibbons. By ' Hobson-Jobson '. Cf. *Lousy.*

lout, ' a heavy idle Fellow ' (B.E.) : S.E.—2. Anyone of the poorer classes : Rugby school : from ca. 1855 ; ob. T. Hughes in *Tom Brown's School-days.*

***louter.** A professional thief and thug : c. (— 1923). Manchon. Perhaps ex preceding.

lovanenty ! ; occ. **lov(e)anendie !** A C. 19–20 Scots coll. exclamation of surprise.

love, no score, is S.E.—2. An endearing term for a person or a thing ; a ' duck ' : coll. : 1814, Jane Austen, ' The garden is quite a love.' O.E.D. [Of the **love-** compounds listed by F. & H., the following are S.E. :—love-apple, l.-brat or -child, **l.-dart** or dart of love, **l.-flesh,** **l.-juice,** **l.-ladder,** **l.-liquor,** **l.-lock,** love's channel or fountain or harbour or paradise or pavilion, love's picklock, some of which, obviously, are very ' literary '.]

love a duck ! See **duck !,** Lord love a. Occ. *luvvaduck* (Will Scott, *The Humorist*, April 7, 1934).

love and leave you, I must ; gen. **I must love you,** etc. This post-G.W. c.p. on parting from a person prob. comes ex dial. : see Dr. Bridge, *Cheshire Proverbs*, 1917.

love-curls. Hair that, cut short, is worn low over the forehead : Society coll. : ca. 1880–1914. Ware.

love-lane. The female pudend : C. 19–20 ; ob. : low coll. verging on S.E. euphemism. Hence, *a turn or an ejectment in l.-lane,* an act of copulation.

love-letter. (Gen. in pl.) A bill of exchange : bank-clerks' (— 1935). Ironic.

love of Mike !, for the. For goodness' sake ! : (low) coll. : mid-C. 19–20 : Anglo-Irish > gen.

love-pot. A drunkard : C. 19 coll. Cf. *toss-pot* and *lushington.*

love us !, Lord. See **Lord love us !**—love your heart !, or you or it, Lord. A low coll. exclamation (cf. *Lord love us !*, q.v.) : resp. 1833 (T. Hook), † by 1910 ; 1841, Lytton ; 1843, Dickens. O.E.D.

loveage. Tap-lashes ; ' alls ' (q.v.) ; ' ullage ' (q.v.) : coll. (— 1860) ; ob. H., 2nd ed.

lovely. A very pretty girl : from ca. 1930. Ex —2. (Gen. pl.) A débutante ; a young married woman in Society : from ca. 1926 ; ob.

lovely, adj. Attractive, delightful ; excellent : coll. : C. 17–20. Markham, 1614 ; Walton, ' This trout looks lovely.' Cf. :

loverly. A late C .19–20 sol., also an ironically jocular s. form of *lovely* (q.v.), due partly to mis-pronunciation, partly to S.E. *loverly*, like or in the manner of a lover.

lover's knot, tie the true. To coït : C. 19–20 ; ob. ? low coll. or euphemistic S.E.

lovey ; in C. 18, occ. **lovy.** A term of endear-ment ; from ca. 1730 : S.E. till ca. 1820, then increasingly low coll. Fielding, 1731 ; Foote, ' I go, lovy.' Cf. :

lovey-dovey. An endearment, whether in ad-dress or in reference : (low) coll. : 1819 (O.E.D.). A reduplication on *lovey*, q.v.

low or **Low,** adj. Low Church : coll. : 1854, S. Wilberforce : 1881, Trollope, ' Among [these Low Church prelates] there was none more low, more pious, more sincere.' O.E.D.

low, lie. To bide one's time ; keep quiet : from ca. 1881 : s. >, coll. Orig., presumably U.S., for the popularity of Joe Chandler Harris's *Uncle Remus* (1880) put the phrase into gen. circu-lation. Low coll., or rather sol., is *lay low* in this sense.

low and slow. An epithet-c.p. applied to the Low Church : from ca. 1855 ; ob. Cf. *high and dry,* q.v.

low-brow, n and adj.. One who is not, occ. one who does not claim to be, intellectual : orig. (1913), U.S. ; anglicised (both n. and adj.) ca. 1923, as s. ; by 1932, coll. ; now almost S.E. (O.E.D. Sup. ; Mencken's *The American Language.*) Opp. to *high-brow,* q.v.

low comedy. A low comedian : theatrical : 1884, Jerome K. Jerome. (O.E.D.) Prob. an abbr. of *low-comedy merchant*, a low comedian : recorded by Ware for 1883.

low countries ; Low Countries. (Preceded by *the*.) The female pudend : low : C. 18–mid-19.

low-down, vulgar, is S.E.—2. As n., a mean trick : C. 20 s. verging on coll. ; ex U.S.—3. Information : U.S., anglicised ca. 1930, esp. by bank-clerks. (K. G. R. Browne, in *The Humorist*, July 28, 1934, ' He will lurk for days in the most unlikely places . . . to get the low-down on the home-life and marital customs of the pink-chested buzzard or the mottled wattle-rat.')

***low Fulhams.** See **low men.** (From ca. 1670 ; † by 1850.)

***low in the lay.** Almost, or quite, penniless : c. : 1830, Lytton ; ob.

[**low-lived** (cf. *low down,* 1) is, despite F. & H., good S.E.]

low man. A Junior as contrasted with a Senior Optime or Wrangler : Cambridge University : from ca. 1850.

***low men.** False dice so loaded as to show low numbers : late C. 16–19 : prob. orig. c., but by 1700 prob. S.E. Nashe, Florio. Also *low Fulhams,* q.v., and *low-runners* (C. 17–18), the latter being almost certainly c.

*low pad. A footpad : c. of mid-C. 17–mid-19. Head, Grose, Ainsworth. Contrast *high pad*, q.v., and see also **pad**, n. and v.

low-runners. See **low men.**

low tide or **water, be at, in.** To be in difficulties, rarely other than monetary : coll. : resp. late C. 17–early 19, late C. 18–20 (in C. 20, S.E.). B.E. ; Dickens, ' I'm at low-water mark, only one bob and a magpie.' Nautical in origin : stranded by ebbing tide (W.).

*low toby and **low-toby man.** See **toby.**

lowance. A coll. form of *allowance* : esp. nautical : mid-C. 19–20. (Manchon.)

lowdah. ' A native pilot in Eastern waters ' : nautical coll. verging on j. : late C. 19–20. Bowen. ? ex Hindustani.

lower. To drink (a glassful, etc.) ; low coll. : C. 19–20.

lower regions. Hell : from ca. 1870 : coll. >, ca. 1915, S.E.

*lowing(-)cheat or **(-)chete.** A cow : c. : ca. 1560–1750. Harman. See **cheat.**

*lowing-lay or **-rig.** The stealing of cattle, esp. cows : c. of ca.1810–60. *Lex. Bal.* See **lay** and **rig.**

lowlands, the. The female pudend : low : late C. 18–mid-19.

lownce or **lounce.** A ration of food : naval coll. : late C. 19–20. Manchon. I.e. (*al*)*lowance.*—2. See **lounce.**

*lowr, lowre. See **lour.**—**£. S. D.** See at **L.**—**lubber,** n. and adj., even in nautical sense, S.E. as is *lubberland* (the paradise of indolence).

Loyals, the. The 81st Foot, in late C. 19–20 the Loyal (North Lancashire), Regiment : military coll.: from the mid-1790's. F. & Gibbons. Ex the regimental motto.

lozenge. (Gen. pl.) A revolver or pistol cartridge, more gen., bullet : military : 1915 ; ob. F. & Gibbons. Contrast *cough-drop*, q.v.

lubber's(-)hole ; until ca. 1830, occ. **lubber-hole.** An opening in the maintop, preferred by tyros and timids to the shrouds : from ca. 1770 ; ob. by 1910 : nautical s. >, ca. 1840, coll. >, ca. 1880, S.E. Captain Cook ; Wolcot ; D. Jerrold, ' Go up through the futtock-shrouds like a man—don't creep through lubber's-hole.' (O.E.D.)—2. Hence, any cowardly evasion of duty : nautical (— 1860) ; ob. H., 2nd ed.

lubra. A woman : low pejorative coll. : late C. 19–20 rural Australian. Ex the ' standard ' sense, a black woman, recorded first in 1834. Much less gen. than *gin*, q.v. (Morris.)

lubricate. V.i., to drink (— 1896) ; v.t., ply with drink, C. 20. *The Daily Express,* ' His late employers . . . had dismissed him for . . . " lubricating the police ".' (O.E.D.)

lubricated, well. Drunk ; very drunk : C. 20. Cf. *oiled, well oiled.*

luck ; good luck. A treading in (esp. human) dung ; a beraying : C. 18–early 19. Grose. See **luck, shitten.**

luck, do one's. (Gen. in present perfect tense.) To lose one's good fortune : Australian : C. 20. C. J. Dennis.

luck, down on (occ. **in**) **one's.** Unlucky ; impoverished : from ca. 1848 : s. till ca. 1920, then coll. Thackeray, ' When Mrs. C. was particularly down on her luck, she gave concerts and lessons in music.'

luck, fisherman's. The being wet, hungry, and ' fishless ' : coll. : from ca. 1855.

luck, greasy. A full cargo of oil : whalers' : from ca. 1830.

luck, shitten. Good luck : ca. 1670–1830. Ex the proverb, ' shitten luck is good luck.' Ray, Grose. Cf. the belief that a bird's droppings falling on a person confer good luck on him.

luck !, worse. More's the pity ! : coll. : 1861, Miss Yonge. O.E.D.

luck to (e.g. **him, it**) **!, bad** or **good.** A c.p., pejorative or approbatory (occ. ironically or jocularly congratulatory) : coll. : C. 19–20.

*lucky. Plunder : c. : from ca. 1850 ; mostly U.S. ; ob.

lucky, adj. (Of persons) handy : C. 18 coll. (The O.E.D. considers as S.E.)

lucky, cut (occ. **make**) **one's.** To decamp : low London : from ca. 1830 ; slightly ob. M. C. Dowling, 1834, ' You'd better cut your lucky.'

lucky !, strike me. A mild asseveration (' agreed ! ' ; ' sure ! ') : coll. (— 1887). Baumann.

lucky, touch. To experience good luck : coll. : late C. 19–20. Collinson.

lucky bag. The female pudend : mid-C. 19–20 ; ob. : low. Punning the S.E. term.

*lucky bone. The small bone of a sheep's head, this being considered a charm : c (— 1883). Sala in *The Illustrated London News*, Nov. 10, 1883.

lucky old sergeant-major, the. The ace (shaped like a crown) in the game of house : military : C. 20. F. & Gibbons. Ex the sergeant-major's badge : a crown.

lucky piece. An illegitimate son (occ. daughter) by a well-to-do father, generous enough to set up the mother in comfort : lower classes' (esp. rural) : late C. 19–20. Lit., a lucky coin.

[**lucries.** See note at **gun,** n., 3.]

lud ! A trivial ejaculation : coll. : ca. 1720–1850. Ex *Lord !*—2. In address to a judge (*my Lud* or even *m'Lud*) : a form so minced as to be coll. or, at the least, near-coll. ? recorded in law before 1898, Besant, ' " My Lud," said Mr. Caterham, " my case is completed " ' (O.E.D.). In the House of Lords, the clerks used *my Lud* as early as 1830 (ibid.).

Ludgate, take. To go bankrupt : coll., mostly commercial : 1585, Higgins ; † by 1700. Ludgate Prison was mainly for bankrupts and debtors. O.E.D.

Ludgate bird. A person imprisoned for debt ; a bankrupt : C. 17. John Clarke, 1639.

*Lud's bulwark. Ludgate Prison : c. : ca. 1690–1830. B.E. Cf. *Ludgate, take.*

luff. Speech, talk : low : ca. 1820–60. Egan, 1821, ' Hold your luff.'—2. A lieutenant : naval : from ca. 1835 ; ob. E. Howard, 1836. Ex the gen. pronunciation (*le'f-tenant*). Cf. the now more gen. *loot*, 2, q.v. (Rare except as *first l., second l.*)

luff, spring one's. To display agility in climbing : jocular nautical coll. (ex the S.E. sense). The term (slightly ob.) app. arose in the 1860's.

lug. An ear : standard in Scots ; in late C. 16–20 English, s.—mainly jocular. Lyly, ' Your clumsy lugs ' ; Moncrieff, ' He napp'd it under the lugs, too.'—2. See **lugs.**—3. A pawn-shop : see **lug, in.**

lug, v. To pull violently, carry with effort, there being the implication of ponderousness in the object : without that implication, S.E. ; with it, coll. of mid-C. 17–20. Culpepper, Horace Walpole, Help. O.E.D.—2. V.i., to drink steadily, is † S.E., despite H. and F. & H.

lug, in. In pawn : low (? orig. c.) : from ca. 1840. H., 2nd ed. Ex :

lug-chovey. A pawnbroker's shop : c. : from ca. 1830.

[lug in, lug out, like lug-loaf, blow in one's lug, and lay one's lugs, are, despite F. & H., ineligible : resp. S.E., S.E., S.E. ; standard Scots, the same.]

lugger and the girl is mine !, once aboard the. A male, either joyous or derisively jocular, C. 20 c.p. ; slightly ob. ? ex a popular song : cf. A. S. M. Hutchinson's novel, *Once Aboard the Lugger—the History of George and Mary*, 1908.

lugow. To fasten, place, put : Anglo-Indian coll. : from 1830's. Ex Hindustani *lagana*. Yule & Burnell.

lugs. Affected manners, 'airs', 'swank'. Hence, *put on (the) lugs*, put on style, be conceited. Both low coll. from ca. 1890.

lugs !, if worth his. (Sc. *he would . . .*) If worth his while ! Scots coll. : C. 14–20. Ex lug, n., 1.

luke. Nothing : c. of ca. 1820–70. D. Haggart, 1821. Problematically ex dial. *luke*, a leaf (hence a trifle) or, more prob., Northern dial. *luke*, a look (? not worth a look) ; H., 1864, describes it as North Country cant ; also, note the earliest record.

[lull, ale, despite F. & H., is S.E. despite its semantic ingenuity.]

lullaby. The male member : low : mid-C. 19–20. (? ob.)

lullaby-cheat. A baby : c. of ca. 1670–1840. Head, Ainsworth. See cheat.

lully ; occ. lally (q.v.). Wet or drying linen : c. of ca. 1780–1870. Grose.—2. Hence, a shirt : low : from ca. 1860. Ware.

lully-prigger, -prigging. A stealer, stealing, of linen, esp. hanging on the fence or line : c. of ca. 1780–1880. G. Parker.

lumb. Too much : c. of ca. 1720–1800. *A New Canting Dict.*, 1725. ? a perversion of *lump*.

lumber. A room : c. of ca. 1780–1830. G. Parker. Ex the Lombard Room (for the storing of valuables).—2. A prison, only in *lumber, be in*, q.v.

lumber, v. To pawn : somewhat low (? orig. c.) : from ca. 1810 ; ob. Vaux. Ex S.E. *put to lumber*, hence ultimately ex *Lombard*. (Pepys in 1668 uses *Lumber Street* for *Lombard Street*.)—2. To arrest, imprison : c. of ca. 1810–90 ; rare except, and extant only in, the passive (see **lumbered**). Vaux.

lumber, be in. To be in detention ; in prison : C. 19–20 c. ; ob. Vaux. Cf. *lumbered, Lombard Street, limbered* and *limbo*, qq.v.

lumber, live. See live lumber.

lumber-house. A house for the storage of stolen property : c. (— 1811). *Lex. Bal.* ; *Ally Sloper's Half-Holiday*, May 4, 1889. Ex S.E. *l.-house*, a pawnbroker's.

lumbered, ppl.adj. Pawned : from ca. 1810 ; ob. : low (? orig. c.).—2. Arrested ; in prison : c. (— 1812). Vaux. Cf. *limbered*, q.v.

lumberer. A tramp, a vagrant : ca. 1760–1820 : perhaps orig. c. ; certainly low.—2. A swindling tipster : low : from ca. 1887. Barrère & Leland.—3. Hence (?), a lying adventurer : Society : ca. 1890–1914. Ware.—4. A confidence man : c. (— 1933). Charles E. Leach.—5. A pawnbroker :

C. 19–20, ob. : S.E. till ca. 1880, then (mostly U.S.) c.

lumme !, lummy ! Esp. as *Lord l. !* A low coll. exclamation : C. 19–20. Ex *love me*.

[lummo(c) king, heavy, awkward, clumsy, is dial.]

lummy. See lumme !—2. First-rate : low : 1838, Dickens in *Oliver Twist* ; Milliken, 1892, ' 'Ardly know which is lummiest '. Prob. ex dial. : cf. the N. Yorkshire *lummy lick*, a delicious mouthful (E.D.D.).

lump, anything exceptional (gen. as to size) : S.E., as is the sense, a party, an association.—2. (Also in pl.) A great quantity ; adv. (*a lump*), a lot, greatly : s. (in C. 20, perhaps rather coll.) and dial. : *a lump* from ca. 1710, *lumps* from ca. 1520. Skelton ; Leigh Hunt ; Farmer, ' I like that a lump.'— 3. (Gen. *the lump*.) The workhouse : vagrants' c. : from ca. 1870. H., 5th ed. Also *Lump Hotel*. Cf. *pan* and *spinniken*, qq.v.

lump, v. To thrash ; ca. 1780–1840 ; then dial. Grose, 1st ed.—2. To punch, strike : low : ca. 1780–1830. Grose. Like preceding sense, ex the S.E. meaning, to thresh.—3. To dislike, be displeased at : coll. : orig. (1833), U.S. ; anglicised ca. 1860. Dickens, 1864, ' If you don't like it, it's open to you to lump it.' (—4. As to take in a lump, drink at a draught, put in a lump sum, e.g. as a bet, it is S.E.)—5. To carry : Australian : C. 20 Prob. influenced by *hump* in the same sense.

Lump Hotel. See lump, n., 3.

lump and bump. A fool ; a simpleton : rhyming s. (on *chump*) : late C. 19–20. Philip Allingham, *Cheapjack*, 1934.

lump of bread. A C. 20 variant of *lump of lead*. Manchon.

lump of coke. A man, chap, fellow : s. rhyming on *bloke* (— 1859). H., 1st ed. In C. 20, gen. *heap of coke*.

lump of ice. Advice : rhyming s. (— 1909). Ware.

lump o(f) jaw on(, have a). (To be) talkative : low (—1909). Ware.

lump of lead. The head : rhyming s. (— 1857). ' Ducange Anglicus.' Cf. *pound of lead*.

lump of school. A, rarely to, fool : rhyming s. (— 1909). Ware.

lump o(f) stone. A county jail : c. (— 1909). Ware. Cf. *stone-doublet* and *-jug*.

lump the lighter. To be transported : c. of ca. 1780–1875. Grose, 1st ed. ; H., 5th ed. Perhaps *lump* here = strike, hit (as in *hit the track*), i.e. unpleasantly or forcibly meet with.

lumper, a riverside labourer : S.E., as is the scientific sense (opp. to *splitter*).—2. A riverside thief : ca. 1780–1840 : c. G. Parker.—3. A contractor for loading and unloading ships : from ca. 1780, ob. : s. >, ca. 1870, coll. Grose, 1785 ; Mayhew. (Cf. O.E.D. dating.)—4. Such a fraudulent seller of clothes-materials as makes the flimsy seem the better cause, e.g. the old new, the flimsy solid : c. : ca. 1850–1910. Mayhew. Cf. the somewhat different *duffer*.—5. A militiaman : 1869, Blackmore ; ob. by 1920, † by 1935.—6. A potato : from ca. 1840 : Anglo-Irish coll. >, in C. 20, S.E.

Lumpers, the. The Lifeguards : military : C. 19–20. F. & Gibbons. Ex their stature : lumping fellows !

lumping. Great ; heavy ; bulky ; awkward, ungainly : coll. and dial. : 1678, ' lumping bargains ' ; 1887, ' a lumping yokel '. Stigmatised by Johnson as ' low '.

lumping pennyworth. A (great) bargain : coll. : ca. 1700–1860 ; then dial. Arbuthnot. Hence :

lumping pennyworth, get or **have got a.** To marry a fat woman : coll. verging on c.p. : C. 18– early 19. Grose.

[**lumpish**, despite F. & H., is S.E.]

lumps. See lump, n., 2.—**lumps out of, knock.** To command much applause : theatrical : ca. 1884–1910. Coun, *Nutts about the Stage*, 1885.

lumpshi(o)us. Delicious : low coll. (orig., prob. s.) : 1844, Buckstone ; ob. ? by *scrumptious* out of *lovely*. Cf. *luptious*, q.v.

lumpy, pregnant, is low coll. verging on S.E. ; (of ground) rough, S.E.—2. Tipsy : from ca. 1810 ; ob. by 1910, † by 1930. *Punch*, 1845.—3. Costly : booksellers' : ca. 1890–1915.

lumpy roar. A grandee, or a ' swell of the first water ' : low London : 1855–ca. 1860. Ware says that it may represent *l'Empereur* Napoleon III, ' who became popular in 1855 by his visit to England . . . and [by] his encouragement of English trade '.

lun. A harlequin : late C. 18–early 19 : theatrical. Grose, 1st ed. By ' collision '.—2. A clown : C. 19, mainly U.S. and theatrical. ? a contraction of *harlequin* or, more prob., ex Shakespearean *lunes*, mad freaks, as in *Winter's Tale*, II, ii, 30. (Onions.)

*****lunan.** A girl : vagrants' c. : from ca. 1835. Brandon. Ex Romany *loobni* (cf. Sampson at *lubni*), a harlot.

lunar, take a. To glance, look, keenly ; properly, upwards : late C. 19–20. Galsworthy, *The Silver Spoon*, 1926, ' " Taking a lunar " at flying grouse.' Ex *take a lunar observation*.

lunch. Luncheon : 1829 (S.O.D.) : coll. till ca. 1919, then S.E. Abbr. *luncheon*. For *lunch(eon)* and its synonymy, see ' The Art of Lightening Work ' in *Words !*—2. A paper sold at lunch-time, esp. one giving the cricket scores : newsvendors' coll. : 1921.—3. Any meal other than breakfast ; a large dinner, a heavy supper : Canadian coll. (– 1932). John Beames.

lunch. (The v.i., always S.E.—) To provide lunch for : coll. : 1892 (S.O.D.).

luncheon reservoir. The stomach : low jocular : from ca. 1860 ; ob. Cf. *bread-basket* and *victualling office*. Cf. :

lung-box. The mouth : low : from ca. 1850. Cf. *potato-trap*.

lunger. A person diseased or wounded in the lungs : coll. : 1893. Kipling. (O.E.D.)

[**lungis**, a lazy fellow, a loafer, is † S.E., despite F. & H.]

lungs. ' A large and strong-voiced man ', Johnson : coll. : ca. 1680–1740.—2. An underworkman in the ' chymical art ', Johnson : ca. 1610–1750 : coll. >, ca. 1700, S.E. Jonson, ' That is his fire-drake, his lungs, his zephyrus, he that puffs his coals.'

Lunnon. London : (dial. and) low coll. : C. 18– 20.

luny. See loony.

luptious. Lovely ; delicious : late C. 19–20 ; ob. Ex *voluptuous* + *delicious*. Cf. *lumpshious* and *scrumptious*. (This type of ' made ' words was common in the Victorian period ; the vogue has waned.)

luracham. See ler-ac-am.

[**lurch**, a trick, a cheat, is S.E., as is the v. So too

are *give one a lurch* and *leave in the lurch*, though the latter may possibly be s. in B.E.'s sense, ' Pawn'd for the Reckoning.' All despite F. & H.]

lurcher, a rogue, is S.E., but *lurcher* or *lurcher of the law*, ' a bum bailiff, or his setter ' (Grose, 1st ed.) is s. of ca. 1780–1840. Ex dial. *lurch*, to slink about.

[**lurdan, -en**, a rogue, a loafer ; **lurdenry**, roguery : S.E. and dial., despite F. & H.]

*****lure.** ' An idle pamphlet ', B.E. : c. of ca. 1690– 1780, when it > *leer*, q.v.—2. When used for a trap, a snare, it is catachrestic : mid-C. 15–20 (O.E.D.).

*****lurk** ' is mostly applied to the several modes of plundering by representations of sham distress ', Mayhew : c. : from ca. 1850 ; ob. Prob. ex the v. Cf. *law, lay, racket, rig, slum* ; also *bereavement lurk, dead lurk, lurker*.—2. In Australian low s. verging on c., it = ' a plan of action ; a regular occupation ', C. J. Dennis : late C. 19–20.—3. In app. temporary c. of ca. 1840–60, it = an eye or eyesight. ' *No. 747* ', with valid reference to the year 1845.—4. An occasional customer : grafters' : late C. 19–20. Philip Allingham, *Cheapjack*, 1934. Cf. v., 3.

*****lurk,** v. To beg with ' faked ' letters : c. : from ca. 1850 ; ob. Mayhew. Perhaps a corruption of dial. *lurch*, to slink about : cf. *lurcher*.—2. **be lurked**. ' To be ordered to do some unpleasant job without a chance of avoiding it ' : nautical : mid-C. 19–20. Bowen. Cf. (? ex) the † S.E. *lurk*, to shirk work. —3. V.i., to sell, on the move, to an occasional customer : grafters' : C. 20. Allingham. Ex n., 4 (q.v.).

*****lurk, go on** or **upon a.** To get money by a ' lurk ', q.v. : c. : from ca. 1850 ; ob. Mayhew.

*****lurker.** A none too honest Jack of all trades : c. : from ca. 1860 ; ob.—2. A begging impostor equipped with sham documents, false letters, faked seals and crests and signatures, etc. : c. : from ca. 1850 ; ob., except as a professional teller of the piteous tale. See esp. Mayhew's *London Labour*, I, 233, and ' Stuart Wood ', *Shades of the Prison House*, pp. 78–9. Also *lurksman*.

*****lurking**, n. and adj. Fraudulent begging ; being a ' lurker ' (sense 2) : c. : both from ca. 1850 and both in Mayhew's *London Labour*, vol. I.

*****lurksman.** See lurker, 2.

*****lurries.** The more gen. form of :

*****lurry.** (Gen. in pl.) Money : c. of ca. 1670– 1830. R. Head in *The Canting Academy* ; Grose. In the pl., the sense is rather ' all manner of cloaths ', Coles, 1676, or ' Money, Watches, Rings, or other Moveables ', B.E. Prob. a corruption of *lour(e), lowre*, influenced perhaps by dial. *lurry*, to pull, drag (E.D.D.).—2. As *gabble*, it is S.E. > dial.— 3. As a variant of *lorry* (Collinson), it is rather Northern dial. (– 1927) than a coll.

luscious. Very pleasant ; very fine : Bootham School (– 1925). Synonymous is *mellow* : the two are frequently conjoined. Anon., *Dict. of Bootham Slang*, 1925.

lush. Drink, i.e. strong drink : from ca. 1790 ; ob. ? orig. c. ; certainly low. Potter ; Vaux ; Lytton, ' " Bring the lush and the pipes, old bloke ! " cried Ned . . . ; " we are never at a loss for company " '.—2. A drink : low (– 1892) ; ob. Hume Nisbet.—3. A drinking-bout : from ca. 1840 ; ob. : low. Colonel Hawker's *Diary* (O.E.D.) ; *The Licensed Victuallers' Gazette*, Jan. 16, 1891.—4. A drunkard : low : from ca. 1890 ; ob. Abbr. *lushington*, q.v. These four senses are either ex S.E. *lush*, adj. (cf. *lush*, adj., below), as the O.E.D. proposes, or ex *Lushington*, a well-known

London brewer, as F. & H. claims, or ex *the City of Lushington* (see **lushington**), or, as W. suggests, ex Shelta *lush*, to eat and drink.—5. A dainty : Eton College : C. 19. Either ex *lush*, as above, or ex *lush*, S.E. adj.

lush, v. To drink, v.i. : from ca. 1810 ; ob. : low. *Lex. Bal.* Also *lush it* : from ca. 1830 ; ob. Cf. *boose, bub, liquor, soak, wet.*—2. To drink, v.t. : low : perhaps from ca. 1810 (see *Lex. Bal.*) ; certainly from 1830, when used by Lytton in *Paul Clifford*, ' I had been lushing heavy wet ' ; Dickens, 1838, ' Some of the richest sort you ever lushed.'— 3. To treat, ply with drink : low : from ca. 1820 ; ob. Haggart, ' We had lushed the coachman so neatly, that Barney was obliged to drive ' (O.E.D.). Ex the *n.*, first three senses. For an excellent synonymy of all three senses, see F. & H. at *lush*, v.

lush, adj. Tipsy : low : from ca. 1811 ; ob. Vaux. Also *lush(e)y*, from ca. 1810. *Lex. Bal.*, ' The rolling kiddeys . . . got bloody lushy.' Either ex S.E. adj. *lush* or ex s. *lush*, *n.*, q.v. above. (The *lush*, *n.*, v. and adj., are now extant mainly in dial. and in U.S. c.)—2. Erroneously used of colour : mid-C. 18-20. (O.E.D.)

lush at Freeman's Quay. To drink at another's expense. See **Freeman's Quay** and **Harry Freeman's.**

*****lush cove.** A drunkard : c. (— 1839). Brandon's definition (in ' Ducange Anglicus '), ' public house ', is an error—prob. for ' a frequenter of the public house '.

*****lush-crib.** A low public-house ; a gin-shop : c. : from ca. 1810 ; ob. Vaux. Cf. *lush-ken.* Ex *lush*, *n.*, 1. Cf. *boozer, drum, panny, pub, Tom and Jerry shop.*

*****lush-house.** The same : c. or low (— 1896) ; ob. F. & H., in *lush-crib* synonymy.

lush it. See **lush**, v., 1.

*****lush-ken.** A low public-house or alehouse ; a gin-shop : c. : from ca. 1790 ; ob. Potter, Vaux. Ex *lush*, *n.*, 1. Cf. *lush-crib* and *lushing-ken.*

lush-out. A drinking-bout : low (— 1823) ; † by 1920. ' Jon Bee.'

*****lush-panny.** Same (— 1896) as **lush-ken** : c. or low ; ob. Cf. *lushery* ; see **panny.**

[**lushborough, lushburg,** a brass coin, is † S.E., despite F. & H.]

lushery. A low public-house : low (— 1896). F. & H. in *lush-crib* synonymy.

lushey. See **lush**, adj., 1.

lushing. The vbl.n. of *lush*, v., all senses. Cf. :

lushing, adj. Given to drink : low : mid-C. 19-20 ; ob. Mayhew, 1861, speaks of a harlot nick-named Lushing Loo.

*****lushing-ken.** A low public-house, a drinking bar : c. : from ca. 1880. L. Wingfield, 1883, ' Unable . . . to steer clear of lushing-kens ' (O.E.D.).

*****lushing-man.** A drunkard : c. of ca. 1850–1910, mostly U.S. Ex *lush*, v.

lushing-muzzle. A punch on the mouth : boxing and nautical : ca. 1820–1900. Egan's Grose. See **lushing** and **muzzle.**

lushington or **Lushington.** A drunkard : rather low : from ca. 1840 ; ob. *The Comic Almanack,* 1840 ; Mayhew ; ' Rolf Boldrewood ', 1890, ' The

best eddicated chaps are the worst lushingtons when they give way at all.' (Cf. *Admiral of the red, boozer, gin-crawler, pot-walloper, soak(er), wetster.*) Either ex *lush*, n., 1, and punning the surname *Lushington,* or ex *Lushington the brewer,* or else ex *the City of Lushington,* a convivial society that, flourishing ca. 1750–1895, had a ' Lord Mayor ' and four ' aldermen ' (O.E.D.) : cf. the next three phrases.

Lushington, deal with. To take too much drink : ca. 1820–90. Bee. Cf. :

Lushington is concerned, Alderman. Applied to one who is drunk : low : ca. 1810–1900. Vaux, where also *he has been voting for the Alderman.* Cf. :

Lushington is his master. He is apt to drink too much : ca. 1825–90. (The C. 20 phrase is *the booze has got him down.*) See **lushington.**

lushy. See **lush**, adj., 1.

lushy cove, a drunkard : c. (ob.) : from ca. 1810. Vaux ; Mayhew. Also *lush cove.*

[**lusk,** despite F. & H., is † S.E. for an idler, as are F. & H.'s *lust-proud, lusty Lawrence* (wencher), and *lute* (a literary euphemism).]

luvvaduck ! See **love a duck !**

lux. An excellent or splendid thing : Christ's Hospital : from ca. 1840 ; ob. Prob. ex *luxuriant,* says Blanch, the Hospital's annalist. Cf. :

luxer. A handsome fellow : Winchester College : ca. 1850–1915. Either ex *luxury,* as Adams suggests, or ex L. *lux,* a light.

luxuriant is often misused for **luxurious :** from mid-C. 17. (O.E.D.)—2. In C. 17–mid-19, *luxurious* for *luxuriant* is S.E. ; ca. 1850–1910, rare ; after ca. 1910, a catachresis.

-ly omitted in advv. is a constant characteristic of sol. speech : ' immemorial '.

lyb-beg, lybbege. See **lib-beg.**

lycæum is erroneous for *lyceum* : late C. 16–19. O.E.D.

Lyceum, the. See **Academy, the.**

Lydford law. To hang first and try afterwards ; hence, any arbitrary procedure in judgement : late C. 14–20 (ob. by 1870, except in dial.) : coll. >, by 1700, S.E. Langland, T. Fuller, ' Molière ' Ozell, Kingsley. (Apperson.) Ex Lydford, ' now a small village on the confines of Dartmoor . . . formerly the chief town of the stannaries ', O.E.D. Cf. *Halifax law,* q.v., and *Jedburgh justice,* q.v.

[**lyer-by, lyerby, lig-by,** is S.E., despite F. & H.]

lying down, take it. See **lie down.**

lylo ! Come here ! : Anglo-Chinese (— 1864). H., 3rd ed.

*****lymitting law.** See **limiting law.**

Lymps, the. The Olympic theatre : theatrical (— 1864) ; † by 1920. H., 3rd ed.

*****lyp.** To lie down : c. of ca. 1560–1700. (Cf. *lib,* the gen. form.) Whence :

*****lyp-ken, lypken.** See **lib-ken** and cf. *libben* and *lobkin.*

lyre-bird, be a (bit of a). To be (a little) apt to tell lies : Australia : C. 20 ; ob. Punning *liar* and (native to Australia) *lyre-bird.*

lyribliring, warbling, singing, is prob. S.E. (long †). I have not discovered on what F. & H.'s ' Old Cant ' is based. Cf. the jocular synonym, *lyribbising* (recorded by A. H. Dawson in 1913), app. a blend of *lyric + improvising.*

M

'm. Am: coll.: from ca. 1640. Cowley, 1647, 'No: I'm undone' (O.E.D.).—2. Abbr. *ma'am* (q.v.): low coll.: C. 18–20. Pronounced as brief and indistinct *um* or *em*.

m'. My: slovenly coll., as in *m'dear* (vocative): C. 19–20.

m. and v. (A) tinned-meat-and-vegetable ration: military (officers') coll: 1915–18. F. & Gibbons. Also *Maconochie*, q.v.

m.b. coat and/or **waistcoat.** A long coat and/or a cassock waistcoat worn by some clergymen: clerical: from ca. 1840, but not recorded till 1853, in Dean Conybeare; ob. Ex 'mark of the beast' in reference to Popery.

m.d. or M.D. A physician; a person holding the degree of Doctor of Medicine: coll. when spoken, i.e. pronounced *em dee*: mid-C. 18–20. (O.E.D.)—2. Money down: political coll. (in reference to electioneering bribery): 1857. Ware.

m.p. A policeman: from ca. 1860. H., 3rd ed. ? ex 'mounted policeman'.

m.t. An empty truck, van, or gen., carriage: railway: from ca. 1860. H., 3rd ed. By pun on *empty*. Cf. *Moll Thompson's mark*, q.v.—2. An empty bottle: from ca. 1858; ob. More usual in U.S. than in the British Empire. Cf. *dead marine*, q.v.

M (occ. **by** but gen.) **under the girdle, carry** or **have an.** To be courteous of address: coll.: ca. 1550–1820; extant in dial. as *keep* 'Master' *out of sight*, to be lacking in respect. Udall, 'Ne'er an M by your girdle?'; Haughton, in a late C. 16 play, 'Hark ye . . . methinks you might do well to have an M under your girdle'; Swift. Ex 'master' and 'mistress'. (Apperson.)

ma. Abbr. *mamma*: from ca. 1820 (? orig. dial.): coll. >, ca. 1890, low coll. Cf. *pa.*—2. (**ma.**) See **me,** 2.—3. At certain Public Schools, *ma* and *mi* indicate (Smith) *major* and (Smith) *minor*: mid-C. 19–20. These terms are rather coll. than s. (See also 'Eton slang', *sub finem*.)

Ma State, the. New South Wales: Australian coll. nickname: late C. 19–20. N.S.W. was the first Australian State to be founded.

ma'alish. See **maleesh.**

ma'am. A coll. contraction of *madam*: 1668, Dryden. Very gen. in C. 18–mid-19 in Society, and still etiquette in addressing a queen or a royal princess; since ca. 1850, chiefly parenthetical or terminal. 'Also written as vulgar *marm, mem, mim, mum, -m*', S.O.D.

ma'amselle. A coll. abbr. of *mademoiselle*: late C. 18–20. Fr. *ma'm'selle*.

mab. A slattern, a loose-moral'd woman, is S.E. —2. A cabriolet: ca. 1820–95. Moncrieff; Baumann. A personifying perversion of *cab-*.

mab, gen. **mab up.** To dress carelessly: late C. 17–early 19: coll. verging on S.E. Ray (*mab*), B.E. (*mab up*). Gen. in ppl. form *mabbed up*. Ex *mab*, n., 1.

mac, occ. **mack.** Abbr. *mackerel*, a pimp: 1887, Henley: low s.—2. (Only as **mac.**) A coll. abbr. of *macadam*: 1851, Mayhew; slightly ob. (O.E.D.) —3. A rare spelling of *mack*, 2.—4. An abbr. (1932) of *tarmac* (lit. and fig. senses): Royal Air Force's.

macaroni, occ. **maccaroni,** a dandy (1760–75), is S.E., as is the adj.—2. A merry fop, esp. if an Italian: coll.: C. 18. Addison, 1711, *The Spectator*, No. 47.—3. An Italian: somewhat low:

C. 19–20. **Ex** the national dish, as is the preceding sense.—4. A pony: rhyming s. (– 1857). 'Ducange Anglicus.'

Macaroni Parson, the. Dr. Dodd, Shakespearian scholar and forger (executed in 1777).—2. John Horne Tooke, parson, philologist, and politician 1736–1812). Dawson.

macaroni-stake. A race ridden by a gentleman rider: ca. 1820–30. Bee. Prob. ex *macaroni*, 1, q.v.

[**macaroon**, given by F. & H., is S.E.]

maccacco. See **murkarker.—maccaroni.** See **macaroni.**

*mace. 'A rogue assuming the character of a gentleman, or opulent tradesman, who under that appearance defrauds workmen, by borrowing a watch, or other piece of goods, till one [that] he bespeaks is done' (i.e. swindled), 1785, Grose: c. of ca. 1780–1850. Parker, 1781.—2. Any dressy swindler of tradesmen: from ca. 1850; ob. H., 1st ed.—3. Swindling; fraudulent robbery: c.: from ca. 1800.—4. A sham loan-office: c. (–1879); ob. Presumably ex *mace*, a club, a metal-headed staff.

*mace, v.t., occ. v.i. To swindle, defraud, whether gen. or in sense of *mace*, n., 1.: from ca. 1790, when recorded by Potter (O.E.D.); 1821, Egan, in *Life in London*: c. Ex *mace*, n., 1 —2. To welsh: c. (– 1874). H., 5th ed.

*mace, give it him (a tradesman) **on** or **upon the.** To obtain goods on credit and never pay for them: c. (– 1812); ob. Vaux; H., 1st ed. Cf. *mace, strike the.*

*mace, man at the. An operator of a sham loan-office: c. (– 1879); ob.

*mace, on (the). On credit: c. (– 1893). P. H. Emerson, in *Signor Lippo*.—2. (Only on the **mace.**) On the 'mace' racket: c.: C. 19–20. Vaux, 1812; W. T. Moncrieff, 1830, 'He's been working on the mace.' Cf. *macer, macing*, qq.v.

*mace, strike the. The v.i. form of *mace*, v., q.v.; esp. as a variant of *mace, give it on the*, q.v.: c.: from ca. 1810. Vaux.

*mace-cove, -gloak, -man (and **macer,** q.v.). A swindler: c.: resp. from ca. 1810 (e.g. in *Lex. Bal.*); 1812, Vaux, †; from ca. 1780, and often spelt *maceman*.—2. The third is also, from ca. 1870, a welsher, and, ca. 1880–1900, a 'swell mobsman', q.v. Ex *mace*, n., q.v.

*mace the rattler. To travel in a train without paying: c.: from ca. 1880.

*macer. A swindler, whether gen. (from ca. 1819) or, ca. 1820–50, as an exponent of *mace*, n., 1: c. Ex *mace*, v.—2. A welsher: c. (– 1874). H., 5th ed.

*MacGorrey's Hotel. Chelmsford Gaol: c.: C. 19. Ware. Ex a governor so named.

machine, a carriage, bicycle, etc., is S.E., as is † *machiner*, a coach-horse.—2. The male, the female pudend: low coll.: C. 19–20; ob. Prob. ex Fr. *machine*, the male member. (Cf. *thing* and Fr. *machin*.)—3. A 'French letter': low coll.: ca. 1790–1860. Grose, 3rd ed.

*macing. See **mace,** v.—2. 'Severe, but regulated thrashing by fists': non-aristocratic: mid C. 19–early 20. Ex *Jem Mace*, a notable English pugilist.

*macing-cove. A variant of *mace-cove*. Mayhew, 1861.

mack. See **mac,** 1.—2. A coll. abbr. of *mac(k)intosh*: late C. 19–20.—3. A Celtic Irishman: derisive coll.: ca. 1615–1700. (O.E.D.)

Mack, the. The sail training-ship *Macquarie*: nautical: early C. 20. Bowen.

mack !, by (the) ; occ. simply **mack !** A trivial, coll. asseveration : ca. 1560–1670. Anon., *Misogonus* ; Cotton. Ex *by the Mass* prob. influenced by *by Mary*. O.E.D.

Mack Sennett. See ' Moving-Picture Slang ', § 8. Coll., not s.

macked steamer. Nautical, thus : ' In the middle 19th century, . . . a shoddily built . . . steamer ' (Bowen) : nautical. I.e., a ' made ' steamer in Northern dial.

Mackay, the real. The real thing, ' the goods ' : coll. : from ca. 1929. R. C. Woodthorpe, *The Shadow on the Downs*, 1935. Margery Allingham, *Death of a Ghost*, 1934, spells it *McKie*. An adaptation of the U.S. *McCoy*, genuine, excellent ; ' from the pugilist, " Kid " McCoy, who was for some time at the head of his class ' (Irwin).

MacGregor or MacKenzie, Mr. See **Langtries.**

mackerel, a pimp, is S.E., despite F. & H.'s inclusion and despite B.E.'s classification as c.— 2. Adj., smeared ; blurred : printers' : from ca. 1730 ; ob. A corruption of *mackled*, ex S.E. *mackle.*

mackerel-back. ' A very tall, lank Person ', B.E. : late C. 17–18. Hence *mackerel-back(ed)*, long-backed : late C. 18–early 19. Grose.

macnoon. A loose, mainly Australian variant of *maghnoon*. E.g. in Ion L. Idriess, *Lasseter's Last Ride*, 1931.

Maconochie (incorrectly **-achie**). A tinned stew of meat and vegetables : military coll. : from 1915. B. & P. Abbr. *ration of Maconochie's stew* ; prob., as the O.E.D. (Sup.) implies, even *Maconochie ration* was orig. coll. Ex the makers' name. Cf. *m. and v.*, q.v.—2. A telephone-box ; stomach : military : 1916. B. & P., 3rd ed. Ex the shape, and the receptacle

Maconochie Cross ; M. Medal. Military Cross ; Military Medal : military : 1915 : ob. F. & Gibbons.

Macrooms. Shares in the Cork & Macroom Railway : Stock Exchange coll. (– 1895) >, by 1910, j. Wilson's *Stock Exchange Glossary.*

mad, adj. (Construction : *mad at*, with a person ; *mad about*, about a thing or person.) Angry, vexed : C. 14–20 : S.E. till C. 19, then coll. and mostly U.S. Nat Gould, 1891, ' My eye ! won't he be just mad.'— 2. (Of a compass-needle) with its polarity disturbed : nautical coll. : late C. 19–20. Bowen. Suggested by *erratic.*

mad, like. See the entry at **like a . . .**

mad !,—you are of so many minds, you'll never be. A semi-proverbial c.p. of ca. 1670–1750. Ray, Swift. (Apperson.)

mad as a buck. Very angry ; crazy : late C. 16–17 : proverbial coll. Shakespeare, ' It would make a man mad as a buck to be so bought and sold.' Cf. dial. *mad as a tup* (ram).

mad as a hatter. Exceedingly angry (an ob. sense) ; crazy : coll. : 1837, Haliburton ; 1849, Thackeray ; cf. Lewis Carroll's ' (the) Mad Hatter '. F. & H. suggests *hatter* = *atter* = adder ; but prob. *hatter* is a dealer in hats and there is prob. some topical reference. Cf. *mad as a weaver.*

mad as a March hare. (In late C. 14–15, e.g. in Chaucer, *March* is omitted.) Eccentric ; mad : proverbial coll. : from ca. 1500. Skelton, ' Thou mad March hare.' Ex sexual excitement. Cf. :

mad as a weaver. Very angry ; crazy : proverbial coll. : C. 17.

mad as May-butter. Exceedingly eccentric;

mad ; excited : C. 17 : proverbial coll. Fletcher, 1626. Ex difficulty of making butter in May.

mad as mud. Exceedingly angry : from ca. 1925. Richard Keverne, *The Havering Plot*, 1928, ' Joan will be as mad as mud with me for telling. Cf. *mad*, 1.

*mad dog.** Strong ale : c. : ca. 1580–1620 Harrison's *England.*

mad major, the. ' Any very eccentric or excessively daring officer, especially if . . . of that rank ' (B. & P.) : military coll. : 1914–18. Ex a legend about a foolhardy and bloodthirsty officer.

mad Mick and banjo. A pick (rhyming s.) and shovel : Australian, esp. military : C. 20.

[**mad minute**, rapid fire, is journalese and ineligible.]

mad money. A girl's return fare, carried lest her soldier friend got ' mad ', i.e. too amorous for her : New Zealand soldiers' : 1916–18. Mostly a legend, and concerning ọnly English girls.

mad on, have a. To be in an ugly mood : Canadian coll. : from ca. 1870. I.e. a mad fit. Ex *mad*, a fit of anger : same period and status. John Beames.

*mad Tom.** A rogue that counterfeits madness : C. 17–18 c. Also *Tom of Bedlam.*

mad up, get one's. To become very angry : from ca. 1880 ; mostly U.S. ex (– 1847) Eng. dial. O.E.D.

mad woman. An empty coach : coaching : ca. 1800–70.

madam, as a kept mistress, as a bold girl or artful woman, and as an ironical address, is, despite F. & H., certainly S.E.—2. A pocket handkerchief : c. (– 1879) ; ob. Perhaps because a mark of at least outward respectability.—4. Nonsense ; line of talk : c. : from ca. 1930. James Curtis, *The Gilt Kid*, 1936. Perhaps suggested by the synonymous *fanny.*

madam-sahib. See **mem-sahib.**

*Madam Van.** (In Grose, 1st ed., erroneously *M. Ran.*) A whore : late C. 17–early 19 c. B.E.

[**madcap**, despite F. & H., is S.E., as is the † *madpash*.]

madding is gen. misunderstood as = maddening (actually it there = raving) in *far from the madding crowd*, itself a casual alteration of *far from the madding crowd's ignoble strife.* (Gray's *Elegy*.) W.

maddy. A large mussel : nautical coll. : C. 19–20. Bowen. Ex ob. (? †) Scots *moddy*, the same.

*made,** stolen, see **make**, v., 1.—2. Lucky : tramps' c. (– 1933). *The Week-End Review*, Nov. 18, 1933—anon. article entitled ' Down and Out '.

made beer. College swipes bottled with rice, nutmeg, etc., to recondition it : Winchester College coll. : ca. 1840–90. Mansfield.

made in Germany. Bad, valueless : late C. 19–20 : coll. >, by 1915, S.E. (Ware.)

made to walk up Ladder Lane and down Hemp Street. Hanged at the yard-arm : nautical : C. 19. Bowen. By ' allusive topography ' : cf. *gutter lane.*

made up strong. Heavily yet effectively painted and powdered : (low) coll. : C. 20.

madge, occ. **madge howlet.** The female pudenda : low : from ca. 1780 ; ob. Grose.—2. A woman : Scots coll. : C. 19. Jamieson.

*madge-cove or -cull.** A sodomite : resp. ca. 1820 –60 (Bee) and c. of ca. 1780–1850 (Grose, 1st ed.).

madza. Half. Hence *madza caroon*, half a crown ; *madza saltee*, a halfpenny ; *madza poona*, half a sovereign ; also *madza-beargered*, half drunk,

and *madza round the bull*, half a pound of steak.
Parlyaree : from ca. 1850. Ex It. *mezzo*, a half,
via Lingua Franca, and gen. pronounced *medzer*.

mafeesh ! Finished ; done with ; dead : Eastern
Front military in G.W. C. J. Dennis, 1916 ; B. & P.
Ex Arabic.

maffick, to rejoice wildly as a crowd, orig. s.,
rapidly > coll. and, by 1902, S.E. Ex the rejoicing at the relief of *Mafeking* (South Africa) on
May 17, 1900. Revived in Nov., 1918, it is now
moribund. (W. ; O.E.D.)

mafish is an occ. variant of *mafeesh*.

mag. Talk ; chatter : coll. : 1778, Mme
D'Arblay, ' If you have any mag in you, we'll draw
it out ' ; slightly ob. Ex *magpie*.—2. A chatterer :
coll. : from ca. 1890.—3. A magazine : coll. :
C. 19–20. Wolcot, ' Hawkesbury . . . who wrote
in mags for hire.'—4. A halfpenny : c. : 1781, G.
Parker. Ex *make*, a halfpenny, influenced by *meg*,
a guinea. Cf. *magpie*, 2. ' Ducange Anglicus '
defines it as a penny (1857).—5. A magpie : C. 19–
20 coll. verging on S.E.—6. A ' magpie ' : shooting : 1895 (O.E.D.). See **magpie**, 4.—7. A mag-
neto : motorists' coll. : 1919.—8. A face : low :
1899, Clarence Rook. Perhaps ex :

mag, v.i. To talk (noisily), chatter ; to scold :
coll. : 1810 (O.E.D.). Ex the n., 1.—2. To steal :
Scots c. : from ca. 1815 ; ob. Scott.

*****mag, on the**. On the look-out for victims : c. of
ca. 1845–60. ' *No. 747.*' Perhaps, via *mag*, n., 5,
a perversion of *on the make*.

*****mag-flyer ; mag-flying**. A player of, a game of,
pitch and toss : c. : resp. 1882, 1883. Ex *mag*, n.,
4, q.v.

*****mag-stake**. Money obtained by the confidence
trick : c. : from ca. 1838 ; ob. See **magsman**.

Maga. *Blackwood's Magazine* : literary s. >,
ca. 1860, coll. >, ca. 1890, S.E. : 1825, in *Blackwood's* itself. Abbr. *magazine* : cf. *mag*, n., 3.

magazan is erroneous for *mazagan* (a kind of
broad bean) : late C. 18–20. O.E.D.

[**Magazine** or **Review** when omitted from titles of
periodicals gives them a coll. tinge, as in *The
English* : C. 18–20.]

Magdalen marm. An unsatisfactory servant :
Southwark coll. : ca. 1840–90. Ware, ' A servant
from the Magdalen, a refuge for fallen women in the
Blackfriars Road, which existed there until about
the middle of the [19th] century. The women who
went out as servants had been too often pampered
there.'

[**magdalene, Magdalene**, a reformed whore, is S.E.]

[**magery**. See note at gun, n., 3.]

magg. A variant of *mag*, n., 4.

magged. Irritable, irritated ; (of a rope) frayed :
nautical : late C. 19–20. Bowen. Cf. Bedfordshire *magged*, exhausted, itself prob. ex the very old
dial. *maggle*, to tease, to exhaust, itself perhaps
cognate with L. *mactare* (to afflict or punish), as
Joseph Wright seems to imply.

Maggers. See **Memugger**.

maggie, a girl, is Scots.—2. As = *magpie*, 6, it is
shooting s. : C. 20.—3. A magnetic detector:
wireless operators' : from ca. 1925. Bowen. Cf.
mag, n., 7.—4. (**Maggie**.) H.M.S. *Magnificent* ; the
White Star liner *Majestic* : resp. naval (C. 20) and
nautical (late C. 19–20). Bowen.

Maggie Ann. Margarine : from ca. 1910 : military >, by 1919, gen. B. & P. Cf. *marge*.

Maggie Rab or **Rob(b)**. A bad halfpenny or wife :
Scots coll. : C. 19–20.

Maggie wore the beads, where. ' In the neck ',
i.e. disagreeably, disastrously : a c.p. of ca. 1905–25.
W. (at *neck*). Cf. *where the chicken got the axe*.

magging. Talk(ing) ; chatter : 1814, Pegge.
Ex *mag*, v., 1.

[**maggot**, a whim, a whimsical fellow, like *maggot-
pated* (or *-headed*) and *maggoty*, has always been S.E.,
despite F. & H.]

maggot, acting the. See **acting the maggot**.

maggot, mute as a. Excessively silent : lower
classes' coll. (— 1923). Manchon.

maggot at the other, a fool at one end and a. A
c.p. directed at an angler : late C. 19–20. Ibid.

maggot-boiler. A tallow-chandler : from ca.
1786 ; ob. Grose, 2nd ed.

maggoty. Very drunk : Anglo-Irish, esp. public-
house s. : C. 20. Cf. *mouldy*, adj., 3.

maghnoon. A fool, dolt, idiot : Eastern Front
military : 1915. B. & P. Direct ex Arabic.

Magic Carpet, the. A fast goods-train ' not from
Arabia, but Kidderminster, bringing fine weaves to
London's floors ' : railwaymen's : from ca. 1920.
The Daily Telegraph, Aug. 15, 1936. Cf. *the
Biscuit* and *the Bacca* (q.v.).

[**magistrand**, despite F. & H., is S.E.]

magistrate. A herring : Scots : C. 19–20, ob.
Cf. *Glasgow magistrate*.

magnet. The female pudend : low coll. : C. 18–
20 ; ob.

Magnificat, correct. To find fault unreasonably
and presumptuously : mid-C. 16–mid-18 : coll. till
C. 17, then S.E. Palsgrave, Nashe, L'Estrange. Ex
the idea of changing the Church service. (Apperson.)

Magnificat at matins, like or **sing**. (To do things)
out of order : late C. 16–17 : coll. soor. > S.E.
Bishop Andrewes, 1588 ; Urquhart, 1653.

magnificent, high and mighty, is S.E.—2. In pl.
' a state of dignified resentment ' : 1836. Marryat,
' Jack walked his first watch in the magnificents.'
Ob. by 1910, † by 1930.

Magnificent Hayes. Rear-Admiral John Hayes,
who (d. 1838) splendidly handled the *Magnificent* in
the Basque Roads in 1812. Dawson.

magnify. To signify : from ca. 1710 ; after ca.
1870, dial. Steele, ' This magnified but little with
my Father ' (O.E.D.).

magniloquent, pompous, is a catachresis. Kingsley, 1850. O.E.D.

magnolious. Large, splendid, magnificent : from
ca. 1870 ; almost †. Ex the splendour of the
magnolia.

[**magnum** is S.E., as is *magnum bonum* : both
despite F. & H.]

magpie. An Anglican bishop : C. 18–20 coll.
Ex the black and white vestments.—2. His vestments : coll. : from ca. 1880.—3. Whence, the
' blue naval uniform with white trousers for semi-
tropical service ' : naval : C. 20. Bowen.—4. A
halfpenny : c. : 1838, Dickens (O.E.D.). An
elaboration of *mag* in same sense.—5. A pie :
low : C. 19–20, ob.—6. ' A shot striking a target,
divided into four sections, in the outermost but
one ', F. & H. : 1884, *The Times*, July 23 : military
coll. >, by 1900, j. Ex the black and white disk
(cf. a magpie's colour) with which such a shot is
signalled from the butts.

Magpies, the. Newcastle United Football Club :
sporting : C. 20. Ex their magpie-coloured jerseys.

magpies' nest. The female pudend : low coll. :
C. 18–20 ; ob.

mags. A gratuity expected by servants : Scots coll. : from ca. 1830 ; ob.

*magsman ; occ. **megsman.** A street swindler ; a confidence trickster : 1838, *The Town*, Jan. 27 ; Mayhew ; G. R. Sims. Ob. Ex *mag*, n., talk.—2. In ' *No. 747* ', the reference being to 1845—the sense was † by 1900, he is a fashionably dressed swindler travelling in, or awaiting trains.

mahcheen. A merchant : Anglo-Chinese (— 1864). H., 3rd ed. Ex Chinese pronunciation.

mahogany. A dining-table : coll. : 1840, Dickens, ' You three gentlemen with your legs under the mahogany in my humble parlour.' Also *mahogany tree*, q.v.—2. A drink of two parts gin to one part treacle : from ca. 1790 : s. ex Cornish dial. ; long † except in dial. Boswell. Ex the colour.—3. A strong mixture of brandy and water : from ca. 1815 ; ob.—4. Salt beef : nautical ; from ca. 1840 ; ob. Ex its hardness.

mahogany, amputate one's. To run away : from ca. 1850 ; very ob. Cf. *cut one's sticks*.

mahogany, have one's feet under another man's. To live on another : coll. : from ca. 1845 ; ob. Cf. *mahogany tree*, q.v. Ex :—2. To dine with another person : 1840, Dickens (see **mahogany,** 1).

mahogany-flat. A bug : ca. 1860-1905. Cf. *heavy cavalry* and *Norfolk Howard*.

mahogany tree. A dining-table : 1847, Thackeray : coll. ; † by 1920. Cf. *mahogany,* 1.

Mahometan gruel. Coffee : ca. 1787–1900 ; coll. Grose, 2nd ed. Because orig. coffee was drunk mostly by the Turks.

maid, kiss the. To be executed by the ' maiden ', q.v. : C. 17–18 coll. B.E.

maid,—neither wife, widow, nor. See **maiden-wife-widow.**

Maid Marian in the usual sense is (despite F. & H.) S.E.—2. A big woman : Leicester Square, London : ca. 1882–90. Ware. Ex a giantess so named.

maidan (pronounced *mydahn*). A plain, an open space ; parade-ground : Regular Army's, resp. coll. and s. : late C. 19–20. B. & P. Ex Hindustani.

maiden. A decapitating machine : late C. 16–19 : coll. (mostly Scots) >, ca. 1800, S.E.—2. The cricketing term is S.E.

[**maiden-gear,** like **maidenhead,** is S.E., despite F. & H.]

Maiden Town. Edinburgh : Scots coll. : C. 18–mid-19. Ex ' a tradition that the maiden daughter of a Pictish king sought protection there during a time of civil war ', F. & H.

maiden-wife-widow. The widow of a man ' that could never enjoy her maidenhead ', Randle Holmes, 1688 : coll. : ca. 1680–1800.—2. A whore : coll. : ca. 1670–1850. Ray, Fuller. Gen. *neither maid, wife, nor widow*.

maiden's prayer, the. A (sausage-shaped) observation-balloon : military : 1915–18. (Anatomical.) Also *the virgin's dream*.

maids adorning. The morning : rhyming s. (— 1859). H., 1st ed.

Maidstone jailor. A tailor : rhyming s. (—1857) ; ob. ' Ducange Anglicus.'

maik. A frequent variant, in Scotland and Dublin (esp. among the Dublin newsboys) of *make*, n., 1.

mail. To post (a letter) : orig. (1828), U.S. : anglicised ca. 1860 as coll. ; in C. 20, S.E., but not at all gen. H., 3rd ed. ; S.O.D.

*mail, get up the. To find the money for a prisoner's defence : c. : from ca. 1840 ; ob. Ex *mail*, payment : cf. *blackmail*.

mail up ! A coll. c.p. ' shout of joy and expectation when letters and parcels [have] arrived from home ' : military : C. 20. B. & P.

mailed fist. Needless threats ; boasting : 1897–ca. 99. Satiric of the Kaiser's farewell speech to his brother Henry, when sent forth by him ' to conquer China with a fleet of two sail—all of which ended in leasing a coaling-station by China to Germany '. Ware.

mails. Mexican railway shares : Stock Exchange : from ca. 1890. (F. & H.)

main, as dicing and cock-fighting term, is S.E., as is *main chance*.—2. The main line : railwaymen's coll. (— 1887). Baumann.

main, turn on the. To weep : 1837, Dickens (O.E.D.) ; ' Cuthbert Bede ', in *Verdant Green,* ' You've no idea how she turned on the main and did the briny.' Cf. *turn on the water-tap(s)*.

main avenue. The vagina : low : C. 19–20 ; ob.

main-brace, splice the. To give out grog ; hence, to drink : nautical : 1805 (O.E.D.). Perhaps ex the strengthening influence of good liquor (W.). Hence, *(with) main-brace well spliced,* thoroughly drunk.

main-sheet. Strong drink ; esp. brandy : Jamaica : from ca. 1880.

*main toby. A main road : c. of ca. 1800–90. See **toby.**

mainga. Water : South African coll. : C. 20. F. & Gibbons. The perversion of a Zulu word, *amanzi* or *manzi*, in which the *a* is pronounced *ah*.

mains, the. A brothel : used by the Army in Germany : from late 1918 ; very ob. B. & P.

major, the. The sergeant-major : military and marines' coll. : C. 20. Bowen. Also (*major*), as term of address.—2. For *major* and *minor* as used at Eton, see ' Eton Slang,' § 3. See, further, **ma,** 3.

Major Grocer. Incorrect for *Major Groce*, an Australian fruit : C. 19–20. Morris. *Groce* is, presumably, itself incorrect for *Grose* : see quotation in Morris at *Major Buller*, and Grose, P., p. 383.

Major McFluffer ; Fluffy. A ' sudden lapse of memory, and use of words to call the attention of the inattentive prompter ' : theatrical (— 1887).—2. **fluffy** is also an adj. See **fluff,** v.i. Ware gives an anecdotal origin.

major in. To take (e.g. Latin) as a major subject : from ca. 1925 : coll. >, by 1933, S.E. Ex *major subject(s)* or perhaps direct ex U.S. *major,* a major subject.

major sa(u)ltee. A corruption of *madza sa(u)ltee,* q.v. at *madza*.

[**majority, go over to,** or **join, the (great).** To die : S.E. despite F. & H.]

mak gauw ! Be quick : South African coll. : late C. 19–20. Ex Dutch *maken,* to make, to do ; *gauw,* quick. Pettman, who confines it to Dutch-speaking districts.

*make. A halfpenny : c., from ca. 1545 ; since ca. 1860, only dial. and Scottish and Dubliners'. Harman.—2. A successful theft or swindle : c. (— 1748) ; † by 1910. Dyche, 5th ed. ; H., 5th ed. (Cf. O.E.D. dating.)—3. See **make, on the.**

make, v. To steal : late C. 17–20 : c. >, in C. 20, low (very common, e.g., among soldiers in G.W.). B.E. Cf. the exact synonym in Fr. c. : *faire*.—2. Hence, to appropriate : Winchester College : late C. 18–20 (Wrench). Ex dial. The sense of unlawful acquisition was very common in 1914–18, as in ' We've made three shovels last night ; that brings us up to correct.' B. & P., 3rd ed., p. 331.—3. The sense, ' to earn ' is S.E.—4. With ellipsis of infinitive : coll. : not recorded before, but prob. at least ten years earlier than, 1888, *The Times*, Aug. 11, ' The enemy will not play the game according to the rules, and there are none to make him ' (O.E.D.).—5. To catch (a train, boat, etc.) : from ca. 1885 : in 1930's, verging on coll. Ex the C. 17–20 S.E. sense, orig. nautical, ' arrive at '.

[The following make terms (listed by F. & H.) are S.E. :—**make a House, make away with, make horns** (reproach with being a cuckold), **make it up, makepeace, makeshift** (a thief), **make up** (theatrical n. and v., to invent, an invention), **makeweight**.]

*make, on the. Intent on booty or profit : orig. (— 1887), c. >, by 1900, s. >, by 1930, coll. Baumann. Adapted from U.S.

*make a break. To run away from the police : New Zealand c. (— 1932).

make a light. To see, look ; to find : Australian ' pidgin ' (— 1859). Henry Kingsley. (Morris.)

make a mess of. See **mess of.**

make a row over the stones. (Of a ship) ' to pound heavily in the sea ' : nautical : late C. 19–20 ; ob. Bowen.

make a straight arm. To offer a bribe : nautical : late C. 19–20. Bowen.

make a wry mouth. To be hanged : semi-proverbial coll. : C. 17. Cotgrave.

make all right. To promise to pay for vote : electioneering coll. : mid-C. 19–early 20. Ware.

make and mend. The naval half-holiday on Thursday, nominally for attending to one's clothes : naval : C. 20. Bowen.

make buttons. See **buttons, make.**

[**make dainty ; make nice.** To scruple : S.E. verging on coll.]

make dead men chew tobacco. See **tobacco, make . . .**

make down. To re-make so as to fit a smaller wearer : coll. : from ca. 1890. O.E.D.

make 'em, as — as they. A coll. variant of *as — as they make them*, exceedingly, as — as possible. Prob. mid-C. 19–20. Lyell.

make ends meet. To coït : low jocular : C. 19–20 ; ob.

make free with the land. To hug the shore : nautical coll. : C. 20. Bowen.

make good. To succeed : orig. (1911), U.S. ; anglicised ca. 1913 as a coll.

make hay. To cause confusion, disorder, trouble : coll. (— 1863) ; ob. H. Kingsley.

make horns. A † coll. variant of *make faces* (see **faces**).

make indentures. See **indentures.**

make-it. A corruption of (bakers') *make-weight* : sol. (— 1909), mostly London. Ware.

make it warm for. To punish, thrash : coll. : from ca. 1880. Ware. Cf. *warm one's jacket.*

make leg. To become prosperous : London lower classes' (— 1909). Ware.

make mouths. To grin ; jeer : coll. : C. 19–20.

make one's coffin. To charge (a person) too highly for an article : tailors' (— 1909). Ware.

make one's money. To make money ' on the side ', e.g. by giving short change, purloining cigarette-cases : waiters' : late C. 19–20. Cf. *makesures*, q.v.

make one's numbers. To make oneself known : naval : C. 20. Bowen. Ex ships hoisting signals to convey their identity.

make one's pile. To amass a fortune : orig. (1861), U.S. ; anglicised ca. 1875 : coll.

make out. In *how do you make it out that . . .*, or *how do you make that out*, in what way do you come to believe that ? Coll. : 1887, Lewis Carroll. O.E.D.—2. In sense ' get on (badly, well) ', it is S.E. of mainly U.S. usage, despite its coll. ring.

make settlement in tail. See **tail, make settlement in.**

make them, as good, bad, etc., **as they.** As good, bad, etc., as may be : from ca. 1870 : coll. >, by 1920, S.E. George Moore, in *Esther Waters*, ' You are as strong as they make 'em ' ; Grant Allen, ' As clever as they make them '.

make tracks. To depart hurriedly : orig. (1833), U.S. ; anglicised ca. 1860. Thornton.

make up, v.i. ; **make up to,** v.t. To make love (to a person) : coll. : from ca. 1820. E.D.D.

make up one's leg. To make money : costermongers' (— 1909). Cf. *make leg*, q.v. Ware.

make up one's mouth. To obtain one's living : low coll. : from ca. 1880 ; ob. Cf. † S.E. sense, to finish a meal with something very delicious.

make yes of it. To agree ; to accept : lower classes' coll. (— 1923). Manchon.

makee-learn. A new-hand, a beginner : naval : C. 20. Bowen. Ex Pidgin.—2. Hence, in the Army, a young officer : C. 20. F. & Gibbons.

makesures. Petty pilferings : potmen's : C. 19–20 ; ob. Cf. *make one's money*, q.v.

-making ; as, and esp., in **shy-making** and **sick-making.** An adjectival ' suffix ' fathered, perhaps in derision of the German love of compounds, by Evelyn Waugh : the fashion (not yet quite extinct) raged in 1930–3. See esp. Evelyn Waugh's *Vile Bodies*, 1930. Rather s. than coll. and restricted almost wholly to the educated and/or the cultured, esp. in Society and near-Society ; never very gen. outside of London.

makings, material : S.E. But as = (small) profits, earnings : coll. : 1837, H. Martineau (O.E.D.).

maknoon. Mad ; silly : coll. among troops in Egypt : late C. 19–20. F. & Gibbons. An Arabic word.

[**malady of France,** like **malinger** and **malingerer,** is, despite F. & H., S.E.]

Malay. Mohammedan : Western Province (South Africa) coll. : from ca. 1840. James Backhouse, *A Visit to the Mauritius and South Africa*, 1844. Ex the importation of Malacca slaves (whose religion was Mohammedanism) by the Dutch. Pettman. Cf. *Coolie Christmas* and *Hindoos*, qq.v.

maleesh or **malish,** or, properly, **ma'alish** (pronounced *marleesh*). Never mind ; ' san fairy ann ! ' : Eastern Front military in G.W. ; in Egypt since late C. 19. F. & Gibbons. Direct ex Arabic.

malkin. The female pudend : low Scots : from ca. 1540 ; ob. Cf. *pussy*, q.v.

malkin-trash. A person dismally dressed : coll. late C. 17–early 19. B.E.

mall. Credit (' tick ') : metal trades' (— 1909). Ware. Possibly ex *mall* (or *maul*), a heavy hammer.

mallet. Erroneous for *mallard* (the bird). O.E.D.

malleting bout. A bout with fisticuffs : low : ca. 1820–50. Bee. On *hammering*.

malley. A gardener : Anglo-Indian (— 1864) H., 3rd ed.

[**malmsey-nose,** despite Grose, is S.E., as is *maltworm*.]

Mals. ' Members of an amalgamated society ' :

political coll.: 1897, Sidney & Beatrice Webb, *Industrial Democracy* (E.D.D. Sup.).

malt. To drink malt liquor: low coll.: 1813, Colonel Hawker (O.E.D.); 1835, Marryat, ' Well, for my part I malt.'

malt, shovel of. A pot of porter: London public-houses': ca. 1820–60. Bee.

malt above the meal, water, wheat,—have the. To be tipsy: Scots coll.: resp. C. 19–20; from ca. 1670; from ca. 1540, ob. Heywood, 1546 (*wheat*); Ray (. . . *water*); Scott (. . . *meal*). (Apperson.)

malt-horse, or M— H—. A native of Bedford: C. 17–21. ' Because of the high quality of malt produced from [Bedfordshire] barley,' Hackwood; cf. Drayton's *Polyolbion*, XXIII (1622). Apperson.

malt-pie. Liquor: jocular coll.: C. 17. Heywood the dramatist. (O.E.D.)

*__**maltooling.**__ The picking of pockets in omnibuses: c. (— 1861); ob. Mayhew. Properly by a woman (*mal* = *moll*); and cf. *tool*, to drive.

maltoot, maltout. A sailor, esp. in address or as a nickname: 1785, Grose; † by 1880. (After that, *matlo(w)*, q.v.) Ex Fr. *matelot*, a sailor.

malty. Tipsy: from ca. 1820; ob. ' Jon Bee.' Cf. *malt*, v., q.v.

malum. To understand (gen. v.t.): Regular Army's: late C. 19–20. F. & Gibbons. Direct ex Hindustani.

mam. Mother: childish coll.: C. 16–20; ob. Cf. *mammy*, *dad*, qq.v.—2. Also a variant abbr. of *madam*: coll.: C. 17–20. Cf. *marm*.

mammæform is erroneous for *mammiform*: C. 18–20. O.E.D.

[**mammet**, despite F. & H., is indisputably S.E.]

mammy. Mother: except perhaps when used by children, coll.: from ca. 1520. Skelton, ' Your mammy and your dady | Brought forth a godely babi ! ' (O.E.D.)

mamsell. Mademoiselle: coll.: from ca. 1840. Thackeray.—2. A French girl: coll.: late C. 19–20, esp. in G.W. among the soldiers. Cf. *ma'amselle*.

man. A husband, a lover: C. 14–20: S.E. till ca. 1850; then coll. and dial. Esp. in *my* or *her man*. —2. In its university sense, it is S.E.—3. The ' head ' of a coin in tossing: coll.: 1828, Bee. Contrast *woman*.—4. In *the late* or *the present man*: the former, the present holder of a post, an office: coll.: 1871, Beaconsfield. O.E.D.—5. As used in c., see **-mans**.—6. A C. 20 coll.: ' an exclamatory form of address in common use all over South Africa, employed often enough quite irrespective of either the age or the sex of the person addressed ', Pettman. Cf.:—7. In English Public Schools (C. 20) as in P. G. Wodehouse, *Mike*, 1909, ' Awfully sorry, you know, man.' Coll.

man, v. To coït with a woman: low coll.: C. 19–20; ob.

[**man** terms that, listed by F. & H., are actually S.E.:—**man about town** and **man of the world, man of Kent** and **Kentish man, a man or a mouse, man in black, man-root, mannish wood,** and **man's meat**.]

man, dead. A supernumerary: coll.: ca. 1650–1800. Pepys.

man, get behind a. To endorse a bill: C. 19–20, ob.: mostly commercial.

man, go out and see a. To have a drink: C. 19–20. Ex the excuse.

man,—if my aunt had been an uncle, she'd have been a. A derisive c.p. (in C. 19–20 occ. varied by the scabrous . . . *she'd have had a pair of b***s under her a****) applied to a ridiculous surmise:

mid-C. 17–20. Ray. Cf. *if pigs had wings, what lovely birds they'd make.*

man, nine tailors make a. See **ninth.**

man, old. A chief, a captain, an employer: coll.: 1847, Howitt.—2. A father: coll.: from ca. 1850. —3. A husband: coll.: from ca. 1855. Cf. *old woman.*—4. A term of address: (?) mid-C. 19–20: coll. verging, in C. 20, on S.E.

Man, the Sick. Turkey: journalistic: from ca. 1870; ob.

man-a-hanging. A person in difficulties: coll.: C. 18–19. H., 5th ed.

man alive ! A term of address, esp. in surprise or reproof: coll.: ca. 1829, J. B. Buckstone. In C. 20, occ. as one word. Cf. Thornton.

man among the geese when the gander is gone, he'll be a. He'll be important if nobody of importance is there; also a gen. c.p. derisive of a man's ability: C. 18. Apperson.

man and wife. A knife: rhyming s. (— 1914) F. & Gibbons. Contrast *trouble and strife.*

man before his mother, he'll be a. See **mother.**— **man, feel one's own.** See **feel.**

man-box. A coffin: ca. 1820–70. ' Peter Corcoran ' Reynolds in *The Fancy.*

man-chovey. See **chovey.**

man-eater. A horse prone to biting (people): coll.: 1879, Mrs. A. E. James (O.E.D.).—2. ' A particularly tough officer ': (mostly Atlantic) sailing-ships': late C. 19–20; virtually †. Bowen.

man for my money, the. The right person: coll.: 1842, Lever (O.E.D.).

man Friday. A factotum: C. 19–20, ob.: coll. verging on S.E.

man in blue. See **blue.** (Contrast S.E. *man in black*, a parson.)

man in the boat, the little. The clitoris: low: mid-C. 19–20.

man in the moon, as a dolt, is S.E.—2. ' A mythical personage who finds money, for electioneering, and for such electors as vote straight,' F. & H.: jocular coll., ob.: 1866, *John Bull,* Sept. 1 (O.E.D.).

man in the street. The average person: 1831, Greville (O.E.D.): Newmarket s. >, ca. 1840, coll. >, ca. 1890, S.E. Cf. U.S. *man in the car* and see ' Representative Names ' in *Words !*

man-killer. ' Porter, stout, cooper—the black beers ' (Ware): teetotallers' (— 1909).—2. ' A hard-working sailing ship in which accidents were frequent ': nautical coll.: ca. 1850–1910. Bowen. —3. The cumbersome, very heavy tank-engine of the L.M.S.: railwaymen's coll.: first decade, C. 20.

man o' war. Any among the bottom boats at ' Bumpers ' (q.v.): Shrewsbury School: late C. 19–20. Desmond Coke, *The Bending of a Twig,* 1906.

man of cash. A gambler in luck: London sporting: ca. 1820–60. Bee.

man of many morns. A procrastinator: Scots coll.: C. 18–20; ob.

man (or Man) of Sedan, the. A political nickname for Napoleon III: coll.: Sept. 2, 1870–1873 (year of his death). Ware.

man of straw. See **straw.**—**man of wax.** See **lad o(f) wax.**

man shall have his mare again, the. All will end well: a proverbial c.p.: late C. 16–mid-19. Shakespeare, Addison, Creevey. (Apperson.)

man that's carrying the brick. A man at all religious: Regular Army's: from ca. 1905.

Frank Richards, *Old Soldiers Never Die*, 1933. Perhaps by rhyme : *hod > God, hod man > God man.*

man Thomas. The penis : low : C. 19–20. Cf. *John Thomas*, q.v.

man-trap. A widow : coll. (mostly low) : 1773, Goldsmith. Cf. the macaronic pun *vir-gin* (late C. 19–20).—2. The female pudend : low : from ca. 1775. Grose, 1st ed. Ex preceding sense.—3. A lump of excrement : low : C. 19–20 ; ob.

manablins, manav(i)lins. See **menavelings.**

manage. To succeed against odds ; contrive to make the inadequate serve : coll. : 1899 (O.E.D.), *The Speaker*, July 29, ' He managed almost without a hitch.'

management (or M—), the. The officers, esp. the senior ones of a unit : Territorial Army's : from ca. 1925.

managing director, the. The commanding officer : Regular Army officers' : from ca. 1933. Prob. ex *leader*, 2 (q.v.).

manany. ' A sailor who is always putting off a job of work ' : nautical : C. 20. Bowen. Ex Sp. *mañana*, to-morrow.

mana(r)vel. To pilfer small stores : nautical : from ca. 1865. Smyth. Perhaps ex, or at the least prompted by :

manav(i)lins. See **menavelings.**

*Manchester, manchester. The tongue : c. : 1812, Vaux ; ob. by 1900. ? via *yarn* ; perhaps rather a pun on *mang*, q.v.

Manchester-bred. Explained by the gen. affixed tag, *long in the arms and short in the head* : a c.p. (— 1869) > proverbial. W. Carew Hazlitt.

Manchester school of nutrition. ' High-feeding, emphatically introduced by certain medical men of that city ' : Society : ca. 1860–70. Ware.

Manchester silk. Cotton : commercial : from ca. 1850.

Manchester sovereign. A shilling : low : from ca. 1860 ; ob.

manchet. See **brewer's basket.—mand.** See **maund.**

mandarin (or M.). A politician ; a Government official, esp. if pompous : coll. : 1916. F. & Gibbons. Ex S.E. *mandarin*, a very important or a great man.

*mander. A remand : c. (— 1877) ; ob. Greenwood. Ex *remand.*—2. A remanded prisoner : c. (— 1887). Baumann.

mandevil(l)e. A C. 19 dictionary corruption of † *mantevil.* (O.E.D.)

mandozy. A telling hit : low : ca. 1800–70. Ex Daniel *Mendoza*, the Jewish boxer, who (1764–1836) did not, however, possess a powerful punch and who published a book on boxing in 1789 and took an inn in Whitechapel ca. 1800 ; perhaps with a pun on *man dozy.*—2. Hence, an endearment among London's East-End Jews : from ca. 1820.

*mang. To talk ; boast (mainly Scottish) c. of ca. 1810–90. Vaux. ? a corruption of *mag*, to talk, influenced by Romany *mong*, beg, request.

*mangaree, mangarlee or -ly. See **mungaree, mungarly, munjari.**

*mange. A variant (— 1909) of *mungaree*, q.v. Ex It., ' through the organ-grinders' lodging-houses ' (Ware).

mangle. The female pudend : low : from ca. 1860 ; ob.—2. A machine-gun : Air Force : 1915–18. F. & Gibbons. Proleptic.

manhandle. To handle roughly ; maltreat : from ca. 1864 : s. >, ca. 1910, coll. H., 3rd ed.

? *handle as a man would* or, as W. suggests, ex Devon dial. *manangle*, to mangle.

manhole. The female pudend : low : from ca. 1870. Ex S.E. sense.

-mania, in C. 19–20, occ. so fanciful as to verge on coll.

maniorable. A mistaken form of *manurable* : C. 17–18. O.E.D.

manner a . . . ?, what. What kind of : sol. : C. 17–early 19. Corrupted *of.*

manners, after you is. A c.p. indicative of the speaker's — gen. jocularly assumed — inferiority : ca. 1650–1850. Brome.

manners of, all. Incorrect for *all manner of.* Manchon, 1923.

manny. A derivative of *mandozy*, 2 (q.v.) : Jewish East London : from ca. 1880. Baumann ; Ware defines it as ' a term of endearment or admiration prefixed to Jewish name, as " Manny Lyons ".' Contrast dial. senses.

manœuvre. See **apostle.**

*manor. A police-district : c. : from ca. 1920. E.g. in Edgar Wallace's " thriller ", *The Gunner*, 1928.

Manton. See **Joe Manton.**

*-mans. (Always preceded by *the.*) A c. suffix of ca. 1560–1890, though † in most words by 1840. It means either ' state of being ' or ' thing ' according as an abstraction or an object is indicated ; though it may simply be a disguise-appendage, a deliberately misleading amplification, as a glance at the *-mans* words shows. Perhaps ex L. *mens* via the Fr. advl. ending *-ment*, or simply a perverted and extended use of *man*, a human being. Cf., however, the Welsh Gypsy suffix *-imen* (? a variant of the much commoner Romany and Welsh Gypsy *ben*), found in words adopted direct ex English, as *aidlimen*, idle,—*gladimen*, glad,—*madimen*, mad, and its radical form *-men*, which Sampson derives ex the Gr .' middle passive participle-μενος ' and notes as orig. attached to loan-vv., as in *zilvimen*, jealous (§ 201) ; certainly relevant is the Welsh Gypsy *-moni*, app. derived ex Bengali *·man*, with which cf. Sanskrit *manaḥ*, mind, mood (Sampson, § 205). See such words as **crackmans, darkmans, gracemans, harmans, lightmans, ruffmans, togemans.**

Mantalini. A male milliner : middle-class coll. : ca. 1840–60. Ex ' the milliner's husband in Dickens's *Nicholas Nickleby* ' (Ware).

manual compliment or subscription. A blow ; a ' sign-manual ', q.v. : C. 19–20, ob. : coll. ? prompted by Fielding's ' manual remonstrances '.

manuary. A consecrated glove : a C. 19 lexicographical error. O.E.D.

manufacture. Liquor prepared from English products : ca. 1720–1850 : coll. *A New Canting Dict.*, 1725.

manúka. Incorrect pronunciation of *mánuka* (pron. *máh-nooka*) : New Zealand : mid-C. 19–20. Morris.

many a. Many of . . . : sol. : C. 15–16. Mandeville, Berners. O.E.D.

many a one. Many a person : C. 16–20 : in C. 20, gen. considered coll.

map. A dirty proof : printers' : from ca. 1860. Ex the markings.—2. A young whiting : nautical : ? mid-C. 19–20. Bowen. Origin ?—3. Face, head, skull : military and lower classes' : C. 20. B. & P. Cf. *dial.* and the Scottish sense : a portrait.

map, not on the. Barely credible : impossible :

military coll.: 1916. F. & Gibbons. **Cf.** *off the map*, insignificant, obsolete (coll.: from ca. 1915), and *on the map*, important, prominent (coll.: from ca. 1915). O.E.D. (Sup.).

maple. 'In New Zealand, a common settlers' corruption for any tree called *Mapau* ': C. 19–20. Morris.

Maps. J. Nicholson, a C. 18 bookseller at Cambridge. Dawson.

mapsticks !, cry. I cry you mercy !: low coll.: ca. 1705–50. Swift. (O.E.D.) Prob. *mapsticks* is a low perversion of both *mopsticks* and *mercy*.

mar. An illiterate pronunciation (and spelling) of *ma*, q.v.: mid-C. 19–20. Manchon.

Marble Arch. The female pudend: low: from ca. 1850. Punning some such phrase as (*at*) *the entrance to Hyde Park*.

marbles. Furniture ; movables : somewhat low : 1864, H., 3rd ed. ; 1867, Trollope ; ob. Ex Fr. *meubles*, furniture. Hence, *money and marbles*, cash and effects.—2. As syphilis (gen. *French m.*), S.E. —3. Testicles : low : C. 19–20. Cf. *pills*.—4. Shares in the Marbella Iron Ore Company : Stock Exchange (— 1895). A. J. Wilson, *Stock Exchange Glossary*.

march. See **dirty-shirt march.—March hare.** See **hare.—march in the rear of a whereas.** See **whereas.**

march-past. 'Roast meat and vegetables in the lower-deck dinner ': naval : C. 20. Bowen.

marchioness, a slatternly general maid, is allusive S.E. verging on coll., just as *mare*, a woman, is allusive S.E., as in *grey mare* proverb.

Marconi mast. 'The tall racing yacht's mast in which the top-mast is socketed instead of being fiddled. First seen in "Istria", whose owner was facetiously said to have fitted it to wireless for more whiskey when supplies ran out ': nautical : from ca. 1925. Bowen.

Marcus Superbus ; Marcus Superfluous. A grandee : theatrical : 1896–ca. 99. The former, ex 'the name given to himself by Mr. Wilson Barrett in his play, *The Sign of the Cross* (1896) '; the latter, coined by Miss Louie Freear, a burlesque actress, a few months later. Ware.

mare, Shanks's. See **Shanks.** (Cf. the Fr. s. *par le train 11*.)

mare (to) go, money makes the. Money can do most things : proverbial coll. : late C. 16–20 ; ob. Florio, Breton, N. Bailey, Kingsley. Perhaps punning *mayor*.

mare or lose the halter, win the. To play double or quits : coll. : C. 17–18. In Northants dial., *saddle* for *halter*.

mare to market, go before one's or the. To do ridiculous things : ca. 1670–1830 : coll.

mare with three (occ. two) **legs, (two- or) three-legged mare.** The gallows : coll. : ca. 1565–1850. Ainsworth, in *Rookwood*.

mare's dead ?, whose. What's the matter ? : rural coll. : late C. 16–mid-18. Deloney, Shakespeare, Swift. (Apperson.)

[**mare's nest** and **mare's tail**, in F. & H., are unexceptionably S.E.]

margarine mess. (Gen. pl.) A motor-car : Nov., 1897–8, mostly in London. Ex *butter beauty*, q.v. (Ware.)

marge. Margarine : from ca. 1905. (*margarine* itself, 1873 : O.E.D.)

Margery. An effeminate : low London : ca. 1850–1900. Ware. Cf. *Nancy*.

***margery-prater.** A hen : c. of ca. 1570–1820. Cf. *cackling-cheat*, q.v.

Maria. See **black Maria.**

marigold ; occ. **marygold.** A gold coin, esp. a sovereign : ca. 1660–1700. Cowley. Ex the colour.—2. One million pounds sterling : City men's : from ca. 1855. H., 1st ed.

***marinated.** Transported as a convict : c. : ca. 1670–1830. Head, Grose. Ex 'the salt pickling fish undergo in Cornwall ', H., 1st ed.

marine. An ignorant and/or clumsy seaman : nautical : 1840, Dana ; ob.—2. An empty bottle : from ca. 1800 ; ob. John Davis, *The Post Captain*, 1805 (ed. R. H. Case, 1928) ; Trelawney. Also *dead marine*. Cf. *marine officer*, Grose, 1785, the term being † by 1840, and *marine recruit* (— 1860 ; †), in H., 2nd ed. See esp. Mark Lemon's *Jest Book* (1864), p. 161, for anecdotal etymology.

***mariner, freshwater.** See **freshwater.**

marines, tell that (tale) to the. *I* don't believe it, whoever else does ! : c.p. : 1830, Moncrieff. Earlier (— 1823) *that will do for the marines* (but the *sailors won't believe it*), as in Byron. Orig. nautical : cf. the opinion held by sailors of marines implicit in *marine*, both senses.

mark. A fancy or preference : 1760, Foote, ' Did I not tell you that old Moll was your mark ? ': coll. ; in late C. 19–20, low coll.—2. A person : c. : from ca. 1850. Cf. ' *mark, bad* or *good* ', q.v.—3. A victim, esp. a prospective victim : c. (— 1885).—4. A newcomer, esp. if she is ingenuous, among prostitutes : prostitutes' c. (— 1923). Manchon. Cf. senses 2, 3.—5. (Prob. ex sense 3.) A good giver : tramps' c. (— 1935).—6. Abbr. *mark of the beast*, q.v.—7. **the mark**, the pit of the stomach : boxing : 1747, J. Godfrey, *The Science of Defence* (O.E.D.). Also (— 1823 ; †) *Broughton's mark*, ex the famous C. 18 boxer.—8. See ' **mark, bad** or **good** '.

***mark,** v. To watch ; pick out a victim : c. : from ca. 1860 ; perhaps, however, implied in Brandon, 1839, ' *Marking*—watching, observing '.

mark, bad or **good.** A man who does not, or does, pay his employees regularly and in full : Australian : from ca. 1840 ; ob. R. Howitt, 1845. A *good mark* was the earlier. Morris. Cf. *mark*, n., 2, q.v.

mark, easy or **soft.** A person easily fooled or persuaded : U.S. (late C. 19), anglicised by 1933. O.E.D. (Sup.) ; C.O.D. (1934 Sup.). Cf. *mark*, n., 3.

mark, off one's. Having run away : Glasgow (— 1934). Ex foot-racing.

mark, toe the. See **toe.**

Mark Lane, walk penniless in. To have been cheated and to be very conscious of the fact : proverbial coll. : late C. 16–early 17. Greene. (Apperson.)

[**mark of mouth.** Despite F. & H., this is clearly S.E.]

mark of the beast. The female pudend : low : from ca. 1715. D'Urfey. Also *mark*.—2. 'The white patches on the collar of a midshipman's uniform ': naval : late C. 19–20. Bowen.

mark-off or **tick-off** or **tick-down.** The process of checking the entries in one set of bank account-books with those in another set : bank-clerks' : C. 20 : s. verging on coll.

mark on . . ., a. A person with a very pronounced fondness for (something) : dial. and s. : from ca. 1880 ; ob. Miss Braddon, 'Vernon was . . . a mark on strawberries and cream.'

mark one. A nursing sister, esp. one belonging to Queen Mary's Nursing Service : naval : G.W. F. & Gibbons.

mark time on. To keep (a person) under observation, have a ' down ' on him ; to retain, stick to (a thing) : military, resp. coll. and s. : 1915 ; ob. F. & Gibbons. Ex Army j.

mark up. To know or learn all about (a person) : tailors' : from ca. 1870.—2. To give credit for : coll. : 1899, *Tit-Bits*, July 22, ' I shaved a gentleman who asked me to mark it up ' (O.E.D.).

marker, a Cambridge word, is S.E., despite F. & H.—2. But as a receiver of stolen goods it is late C. 16–early 17 c. Greene.—3. Something worthy to be compared : 1895, H. P. Robinson, ' It ain't a marker to what's ahead ' (O.E.D.) ; ob.

market. The betting-ring : racing : from ca. 1880.

market, go to. To attempt something : coll. : 1890, ' Rolf Boldrewood ' (O.E.D.) ; ob.

*market, in the. Having plenty of money : c. (— 1935). David Hume. Opp. *on the floor.*

market-dame, a harlot, is C. 18 coll. verging on S.E.

market-fever. See **pencil-fever.**

market-horse. A horse kept on the lists simply for the betting : turf : from ca. 1873. H., 5th ed. Cf. *market* and *marketeer.*

market-place. The front teeth : provincial s. verging on dial. : from ca. 1850 ; ob.

marketeer. A betting-man specialising in the study of horses that are favourites : racing s. verging on c. : from ca. 1870 ; ob. H., 5th ed.

*marking. A watcher ; a watching : c. : from ca. 1830 ; mostly U.S., though see **mark,** v.

marking M., n. and adj. Rapid(ity) of action : Anglo-Irish (— 1909). Ware. *M.,* the Virgin Mary.

marley-stopper. A splay-footed person : streets' (— 1887) ; ob. Ex *marble* and the stopping of a marble with one's feet.

marm. See **ma'am.**—2. Marmalade : low coll. : late C. 19–20. Cf. *marge.*

marm-puss. A wife : tailors' : from ca. 1870 ; ob.—2. (Also **marm-poosey.**) A showily dressed landlady : public-house frequenters' : 1863 ; slightly ob. Ware.

marmaid. A mermaid : nautical : mid-C. 19–20. Baumann.

marmalade, (the) true. An † variant of *jam, real,* q.v.

Marmalade Country, the. Scotland : music-halls' coll. : ca. 1905–14. Ware. Ex the marmalade that is a staple industry of Scotland.

marmite. A pot-shaped bomb (or, loosely, shell) : military officers' : 1917–18. Adopted from Fr. s.

[**marmoset, maroon,** and **marplot,** in F. & H., are all S.E.]

marouski, marowsky. See **marrowskying.**

Marquis of Granby. A bald-headed person : C. 19–20, ob. Ex one.

marquis of marrowbones. See **marrowbones, marquis of.**

marriage, there belongs more to. See **legs in a bed.**

marriage face. A sad face : middle classes' (— 1909) ; ob. Ware, ' Because generally a bride cries a good deal, and so temporarily spoils her looks '.

[**marriage lines.** See **lines,** of which it is the S.E. original.]

marriage music. The crying of children : late C. 17–mid-19. B.E.

*married. Chained or handcuffed together : c. : mid-C. 18–20, ob. Grose, 1st ed.

[**married man's cotillon** is euphemistic S.E. ; S.E. also, though given in F. & H., are *marrow, marrow-bones and cleavers, martext, martin-drunk, martinet.*]

married on the carpet and the banns up the chimney. Living together as though man and wife : coll. (somewhat low) : C. 19–20 ; ob.

married the widow, have. To have ' made a mess of things ' : C. 19. Ex Fr., with pun on the guillotine—' the widow '. Ware.

married to brown Bess. (Having) enlisted : military : late C. 18–19. Ex *hug brown Bess.* (Ware.)

Marrow Men. T. Boston the elder (1677–1732) and his followers, opponents of an Act of Assembly in 1720 ; they based their opinions on *The Marrow of Modern Divinity* (ca. 1647). Dawson.

marrowbone(-and-cleaver), like **marrow-pudding,** is low for the penis, as obviously is *a bellyful of marrow-pudding,* pregnancy : C. 19–20, ob.

marrowbone (occ. **Marylebone**) **stage** or **coach, go in** or **ride by the.** To walk : ca. 1835–1910. Prob. suggested by *Marybone = Marylebone.* Cf. *Bayard of ten toes* and *Shanks's mare,* q.v.

marrowbones, the knees, is jocular S.E., but as pugilists, C. 17, e.g. in Fletcher, 1625, and as fists (regarded as weapons), ca. 1810–1910, it is s.

marrowbones, marquis or **marquess of.** A lackey : late C. 16–17. Nashe.

[**marrowskying.** The transposition of the initials of words (as in *poke a smipe,* smoke a pipe), with variant adj. and n. *marrowsky* or *mowrowsky* : ca. 1860–1900. H., 2nd ed. In 1848 described by Albert Smith as *Gower Street* dialect (cf. *medical Greek*), it was affected by students of London University and constitutes *spoonerism* before the letter. Perhaps ex the name of a Polish count, as the O.E.D. suggests. See esp. *Slang* at ' Oddities '.]

marry. See **marrying.**

marry ! An exclamation : C. 14–mid-19. Orig. an oath, it soon > harmless. Ex (*the Virgin*) *Mary.* Often, in C. 16–19, with asseverative tags or with *gip, up,* etc. Cf. :

marry ! come up, my dirty cousin. A c.p. addressed to one affecting excessive delicacy : from ca. 1670 ; in C. 19–20, dial. (Apperson.)

marry the mixen for the sake of the muck. To marry an undesirable person for the sake of the money : proverbial coll. : from ca. 1730 ; since ca. 1850, dial. A *mixen* is a dung-heap ; *muck,* q.v., is a pun. (Apperson.)

marry up. To bind or busy in marriage : coll. : from ca. 1820. J. Flint, 1822, ' I believe that the girls there are all married up.' O.E.D.

marrying, vbl.n. ; **marry,** v.t. Stockbrokers' s. (— 1935), thus :—' When a broker receives simultaneous orders to buy and sell the same security, he can marry the deal. I.e. he puts one bargain against the other.' (A correspondent.)

marshal is catachrestic when used for *martial.*

Marshall or **marshall.** A £5 Bank of England note : ca. 1860–80. Ex a Bank of England official. Cf. *Abraham Newland, Bradbury, Fisher,* qq.v.

Marshland, arrested by the bailiff of. Stricken with ague : coll. : from ca. 1660 ; in C. 19–20, dial. ' Proverbial ' Fuller, Grose (*Provincial Glossary*), Smiles. (Apperson.)

*marter in Greene's *Second Cony-Catching*, 1592, is either a perversion of, or a misprint for, *marker*, 2 (q.v.).

martialist. An officer in the army: Society: 1885, *The Daily News*, Dec. 31; † by 1915. Ware.

*martin. An honest victim of rogues: c.: late C. 16–mid 17. Greene. ? ex the bird.—2. A boot: tramps' c. (— 1893); ob. P. H. Emerson. ? origin.—3. See St Martin.—4. See Betty Martin.

martingale. The doubling of stakes at every loss: 1815 (O.E.D.): s. >, by 1850, j. Whence:

martingale, v.i. To double the bet at every loss: s. (— 1823) >, by 1850, j. Bee.

Martin's hammer knocking at the wicket. Twins: C. 18–mid-19 coll. In C. 19–20, dial. and gen. in form, *she has had Martin's hammer knocking at her wicket*, she has twins. Halliwell. Ex the Fr. *Martin* (or, as in Lafontaine, *Martin-bâton*), a man armed with a staff.

marvellous as used in Society since ca. 1920 is s. for 'pleasant', 'nice'; a mere counter of a word! See, e.g., 'Slang Words' in *The Daily Mirror* of Nov. 1, 1933, and Ibid., Oct. 26, 1933 (*too, too marvellous*); M. Lincoln, *Oh! Definitely*, 1933, 'If you forbade that girl to say "marvellous", then stopped her from saying " definitely ", she couldn't speak at all.'

marwooded, ppl.adj. Hanged: lower classes': ca. 1875–83, executioner Marwood dying at the latter date. Ware.

Mary or **mary.** An aboriginal woman; occ. of a Kanaka: Queensland: from ca. 1880; ob. Morris. Cf. *Benjamin*, q.v.

Mary! or **mary!** (In 'jeffing' with quads) no score!: printers': from ca. 1870; ob. Ex *marry!*, q.v. For the very interesting printers' s., see *Slang*.

Mary Ann. A female destroyer of recalcitrant labour-sweaters: ca. 1865–90: mostly Sheffield. H., 5th ed.—2. A dress-stand: dress-makers': from ca. 1870.—3. A sodomite: from ca. 1890; ob. (Cf. *Cissie, Jessie, Margery, Nancy*, and *Pansy*.) *Reynolds's Newspaper*, June 2, 1895. Hence, 4, an effeminate actor: theatrical: late C. 19–20.—5. An exclamation: 'san fairy ann', whence it derives: 1916–18. F. & Gibbons.

Mary Jane or **mary jane.** The female pudend: low: from ca. 1840; ob.

marygold. See **marigold.**—**Marylebone stage.** See **marrowbone stage.**

mas; **Mas John** or **mas john**; also **mess-John.** By itself, *mas* is a low coll. abbr. of *master*: ca. 1570–1730, as in Whetstone and Mrs. Centlivre. *Mas John*, however, is jocular or contemptuous coll., ca. 1660–1840, for a Presbyterian minister as opp. to a Roman or an Anglican clergyman (in C. 19, S.E.), as in Jeremy Taylor, Burke, and Scott. O.E.D.

mascot. A person or thing that brings, or is believed to bring, good luck: 1881: s. >, ca. 1905, coll. >, ca. 1930, S.E. Ex E. Audran's opera, *La Mascotte*, played in London on Dec. 29, 1880, the word deriving ex Provençal *masco*, a sorcerer. O.E.D.

mash. A sweetheart: 1882; † by 1915, except in Australia (C. J. Dennis, 1916). Also *masher*, q.v. —2. A dandy: from ca. 1883; †. Cf. *masher*. Ex *mash*, v.—3. Only in *make* (Society) or *do* (rather vulgar) *a mash*, to make a 'conquest': 1883–ca. 1912. Ware. Ex *mash*, v.—4. Mashed potatoes: lower classes' coll. verging on sol. Even *mashed*, in this sense, is coll. Both: C. 20. Manchon (the latter). Cf. *mash*, n., 2.

mash, v.t., occ. v.i. To court or ogle or (attempt to) fascinate a girl or a woman; not often used of a woman 'bewitching' a man: 1882, Leland, ' These black-eyed beauties '—Gypsies—' by mashing men for many generations . . .'; ob. Prob. ex the S.E. sense, to crush, pound, smash utterly, but perhaps, as Leland suggests, ex Romany *mash* (*masher-ava*), to allure, entice. Orig. (ca. 1860), U.S. Also *mash it* and:

mash, make a. See **mash,** n., 3.

mash, on the. Constantly courting or ogling women: 1888; † by 1920.

mash that! Hold your tongue!: low London (— 1909). Ware. Prob. ex S.E. sense of *mash*, v.

mash-tub. A brewer: coll.: from ca. 1850; ob. Hence, ca. 1870–1900, *The Morning Mash-Tub*: *The Morning Advertiser*, because of its brewery interests: Fleet Street.

mashed, n. See **mash,** n., 4.

mashed, adj. Flirtatious; 'smitten'; amorous: 1883; † by 1920. Ex *mash*, v., but perhaps suggested by *spoony on*, 'mash being regarded as spoon-diet', W. Also *mashy* (Baumann, 1887).

mashed on. In love with: from ca. 1883; † by 1920. See esp. *The Pall Mall Gazette*, Oct. 11, 1883, quoted by O.E.D. Ex *mash*, v.

masher. A 'lady-killer': 1882, but not very gen. till 1883; ob. Ex *mash*, v., q.v.—2. A dandy, a fop: 1883; ob. The two senses merge, for the term was almost always applied to a flirtatious dandy, as T. A. Gartham in *The Pall Mall Gazette*, l.c., makes clear.—3. A lover: Glasgow: C. 20.

masher, adj. Smart; dandified: 1884 († by 1915), *The Globe*, Feb. 7, 'What are . . . masher canes to students immersed in Mill or Emerson . . . ?'

masher blue. A weak blue, with tiny white dots: ca. 1884–90. Affected by 'mashers' for their waistcoats. *The Girl's Own Paper*, Nov., 1884. O.E.D.

masherdom. The world of the 'masher', q.v.: coll.: 1883; † by 1920. Also *mashery*.

mashers' corners. ' The O.P. and P.S. entrances to the stalls of the old Gaiety Theatre ': Society: late 1882–ca. 85. Ware. Ex *masher*, n., 1.

mashery. † by 1920. 'Masherdom': 1887, Baumann.

mashing. Dandified flirtation by men; as adj., given to or characterised by such flirtation: 1883; ob. Ex *mash*, v.—2. 'A little screw of paper containing tea and sugar mixed ': lower classes': late C. 19–20. W. A. Gape, *Half a Million Tramps*, 1936.

Mashona piano. A late C. 19–20 South African coll. (cf. *Kaffir piano*) for ' a somewhat crude, but ingenious musical instrument made by the Makalakas, consisting of a wooden frame, with iron tongues of different lengths fastened upon it in a row, each emitting when struck a different musical note ', Pettman.

mashy. See **mashed,** adj.

maskee! Never mind!; it doesn't matter: Anglo-Chinese (— 1864). H., 3rd ed. Origin problematical: cf., however, *ma'alish*, ex the Arabic, and Skeat's ingenious derivation ex Portuguese *mas que*.

*maskin. Coal: c.: C. 18–mid-19. ? origin.

maskins!, **by the.** A corruption of *by the mass!*: C. 17–20; in C. 19–20, dial.

masnel is a wholly incorrect form of † *masuel*, a battle-mace. O.E.D.

*mason. A person, esp. a horse-dealer giving worthless notes in payment for horses : c. of ca. 1750–1800. *The Discoveries of John Poulter*, 1753. Ex superstitions regarding masonry.—2. Also, v.i.

*masoner. The same as *mason*, n.,q.v. Poulter.

masonics. Secrets : Society coll. : mid-C. 19–early 20. Ware, 'From the secret rites of Freemasonry. Not that there are either secrets or rites in Freemasonry—at all events in England—where combined secrets are neither wanted nor expected.'

*masoning. The giving of worthless notes for horses purchased : c. of ca. 1750–1800. See mason.

masonry. Secret signs and passwords : coll. : 1841, Lytton ; ob. Ex S.E. sense.

*mason's maund. A sham sore that, above the elbow, counterfeits a broken arm : c. : late C. 17–early 19. B.E. Cf. *maund*, q.v.

[mass. Frequently employed in oaths in late M.E. and early Mod. E.]

massa ; occ. mas'r. Master : in Negroes' English : recorded 1774, Foote (O.E.D.) ; doubtless in use very much earlier. Mostly in U.S., but not to be considered U.S.

massacre of the innocents. See innocents.

massacree. 'Unlettered pronunciation for massacre ', Bee, 1823. (Also in dial.)

*masse-stapler. A rogue disguised as a woman : c. : C. 18–early 19. ? origin.

Massey-Harris. Cheese : Canadian : C. 20. B. & P. Ex the Massey-Harris self-binder + the costiveness of cheese.

massy. A corrupt, sol. form of *mercy*, chiefly in exclamations, e.g. *massy sakes* and *Lord-a-massy* : mid-C. 19–20 ; ob. O.E.D.

[master-can, a chamber-pot, is ineligible because it is Scots dial.]

master of (a person), get the. To become, or act the, master over : proletarian coll. (— 1887). Baumann.

master of impediment. 'Troublesome preparation for the schools ', Egan's Grose : Oxford University : ca. 1820–40.

*master of the black art. A beggar : c. : late C. 16–17.

master of the mint. A gardener : jocular coll. : mid-C. 18–19. Grose, 2nd ed. Cf. :

master of the rolls. A baker : mid-C. 17–20, ob. ; jocular coll. Peacham, Grose. Cf. *burn-crust*, *dough-puncher*, *doughy*, *fourteen-to-the-dozen*.

master of the wardrobe. One who pawns his clothes to buy liquor : ca. 1780–1830. Grose, 2nd ed. Cf. two preceding entries.

master-vein, be hit on the. To take a man ; to conceive : late C. 16–17. Greene, ' My faire daughter was hit on the master vaine and gotten with child,' O.E.D. Cf. *masterpiece*.

masterful for *masterly*, though once S.E., is now a catachresis. Fowler.

masterpiece. The female pudend : low : C. 18–20. ; ob. Cf. *master-vein*, q.v.

masterpiece (o)f night work. A very pretty harlot : low (— 1909). Ware.

mastodonton is incorrect for *mastodon* : C. 19–20. O.E.D.

mat. (A) matter, esp. in *what's the mat ?* : schoolboys' : late C. 19–20.—2. A matinée : theatrical coll. : 1914, Gertrude Atherton (O.E.D. Sup.).—3. See mats.

mat, on the. Up for trial (from late 1890's) ; hence, in trouble (ca. 1915) : military >, by 1920, gen. coll. F. & Gibbons ; Lyell. Ex the small

square mat on which the accused soldier stood in a barracks orderly-room.

match !, a. Agreed ! ; done ! : coll. >, by 1650, S.E. : late C. 16–early 18. Shakespeare, ' A match, 'tis done ' ; Farquhar. O.E.D.

match and pocket the stake(s), lose the. (Of women only) to coït : C. 19–20 : low.

match ! quoth Hatch (or Jack or John) when he got his wife by the breech or when he kissed his dame,—a. A c.p. of ca. 1670–1750. Ray, ' Proverbial ' Fuller. (Apperson.)

matches. Shares in Bryant & May, Ltd., the English manufacturers of matches : Stock Exchange : from ca. 1890.

mate. A companion, partner ; comrade ; friend : late C. 14–20 : S.E. except in Greene's *Third Cony-Catching* (1592), where it verges on c., and except when—from ca. 1450—it is used as a vocative, this being (in C. 19–20, somewhat low) coll. : orig. nautical. Stanyhurst, Miss Braddon. O.E.D. Cf. *matey*, q.v.

Mate, the. Astley the race-horse owner and famous sportsman of ca. 1860–95, and brother of Hugo Astley, well-known in the entertainment-world of ca. 1870–1900. Reginald Herbert, *When Diamonds Were Trumps*, 1908.

mater. Mother ; one's mother : from ca. 1860 : chiefly schoolboys' and undergraduates'. Hemyng in *Eton School Days*, 1864. Simply the L. word adopted in English. Cf. *pater*, q.v.

materials. Whiskey-punch : Anglo-Irish evasive coll. : late C. 19–20. Ware.

maternal. A mother : 1867, Routledge's *Every Boy's Annual*, Dec. ; ob. O.E.D. Either short for *maternal parent* or the adj. used as a n.

maternity jacket. A double-breasted tunic worn in the : Air Force : G.W. F. & Gibbons.

mat(e)y. A mate, companion, comrade : from ca. 1830 : eligible only as a term of address (for it is then coll.), as in H. Kingsley's *Geoffry Hamlyn*, ' " Matey," says I, (you see I was familiar, he seemed such a jolly sort of bird), " matey, what station are you on ? " ' Slightly ob. Cf. *mate*, q.v.

mat(e)y. Characteristic of a ' mate ' (as imm. above) ; friendly, ' chummy ' : coll. (now verging on S.E.) : from ca. 1910. Ex the preceding.

maths. A coll. abbr. (? orig. among schoolboys) of *mathematics* : from ca. 1875. At Dulwich College, it is *math* (Collinson).

mathy. See -y, 2.

Matilda. See waltz Matilda. Among New Zealanders (— 1932), gen. carry Matilda.

*matin-bell. A thieves' meeting-place : c. : C. 19–20 ; ob.

matinée dog. Mostly in *try it on the matinée dog* : theatrical : ca. 1885–1915. Ware. Satiric both of vivisection and of frequenters of *matinées*, at which the dramatic performance is gen. inferior to the acting done in the evening. Whence *try it on the dog*.

matineer. A frequenter of matinées : theatrical coll. : from either 1884 or 1885, the two years during which there was a rabies for matinées. Punning *mutineers*. (Ware.)

matlo(w). A sailor : from ca. 1880 : mainly nautical and, in C. 20, military, and often as a nickname. Ex Fr. *matelot*, a sailor : cf. *maltout*, q.v. Philip MacDonald, *Patrol*, 1927.

matric. A coll. abbr. of *matriculation* : 1885, *Punch*, March 16. (O.E.D.)

matrimonial. Coïtion in the usual position ; occ. *m. polka*. Low : from ca. 1850 ; ob.

matrimonial peacemaker. The penis: mid-C. 18–20. Grose, 2nd ed. It is doubtful whether this is not sometimes a mere S.E. euphemism.

matrimony. A mixture of two drinks or edibles: s. and dial.: 1813. O.E.D.

mats. (Virtually non-existent in singular.) Trench 'duckboards': military: G.W. (F. & Gibbons.)

matter, as near as no. Very near(ly) indeed: coll.: from ca. 1890.

matter with ?, what is the. What troubles or ails or is amiss with . . . ?: coll.: 1715, Defoe, 'I beseech what is the matter with you.' O.E.D.—2. In late C. 19–20, it also = What objection is there to . . . ?: jocular coll.

mattress-jig. Sexual intercourse: low coll. when not S.E. euphemism: C. 18–19.

maty. See matey.

maukes, maux, mawkes. See mawkes.—maukin. See malkin.

mauldy. Left-handed: Australian (— 1926). Jice Doone. Possibly cognate with Aberdeenshire *mauly*, abbr. *maulifuff*, a woman without energy, a girl apt to make a fuss (E.D.D.); but prob. a corruption of *mauley*, q.v., for this latter form also occurs in Australia in the sense of *mauldy*.

mauled. Exceedingly drunk: late C. 17–mid-19. B.E., Grose.

mauler. (Gen. pl.) A fist: late C. 19–20. Manchon. Prob. suggested by:

mauley; occ. **mawley** or **morley.** A fist, the hand: low: 1781, G. Parker; Moncrieff; Miss Braddon. Hence *slang* or *sling a person one's mauley*, to give a person one's hand, shake hands with; *tip a mauley*, give a hand; *fam the mauley*, shake hands.—2. Hence, a finger; virtually always in pl.: c.: 1845 in '*No. 747*'; ob.—3. Handwriting, 'a fist'; a signature: low: from ca. 1850; ob. Mayhew. The term derives ex *maul*, v.; or is perhaps 'a transposition of Gaelic *lamh*, hand, used in tinkers' s. or Shelta', W., 'in form *malya*'; the Romany s. is *mylier*.—4. See mauldy.

maum, in phrase *maum and gaum* and gen. as *mauming and gauming.* To 'paw' (a person): low coll.: ca. 1735–1860 (O.E.D.). Perhaps cognate with dial. *malm*, to besmear.

*****maund.** Begging; (with prefixed word) some specified begging imposture: C. 17–early 19 c. Rowlands, B.E., Grose (*mason's maund*, q.v.). Cf. *maunder.*

*****maund,** v.t. and v.i. To beg: c.: ca. 1565–1800. Harman, Beaumont & Fletcher, B.E. Prob. ex Fr. *mendier* or *quémander* influenced by Romany *mang*. O.E.D.—2. To ask: c.: ca. 1565–1700. Harman.

*****maund, mason's.** See mason's maund.

*****maund abram.** To beg as a madman: C. 17–18 c. Rowlands. See abram.

*****maund it.** To go a-begging: c.: C. 17–18. Ex *maund*, v., q.v.

*****maunder.** A beggar: c.: C. 17–mid-19. Rowlands, Lytton. Ex *maund*, v.

*****maunder,** v. To beg: c.: ca. 1610–1770. Middleton & Dekker; Dyche. Ex *maund*, v., of which it is a mere extension, perhaps suggested by Fr.

*****maunder on the fly.** To beg of people in the streets: c.: ca. 1850–90. H., 1st ed.

*****maunderer.** A professional beggar: c.: ca. 1610–1840. Middleton & Dekker; Ainsworth, in *Rookwood.* Ex *maunder*, v. Cf.:

*****maundering,** ppl. adj. Begging; given to begging: c.: ca. 1610–1700.

maund(e)ring-broth. A scolding: late C. 17–early 19. B.E. Ex *maunder*, to grumble.

*****maunding.** The, or an, act of begging: c.: 1610, Rowlands; † by 1850. O.E.D.—2. Adj., begging; given to or characteristic of begging: c.: ca. 1600–1720. W. Cartwright, 'Some counterfeiting trick of such maunding people', O.E.D.

*****maunding cove.** A beggar: c.: C. 17–18. Anon., *Sack for my Money*, ca. 1603.

[**maw,** belly, is S.E., as is **mawworm**, while **mawther** (or **mauther**) is dial.; but **maw**, mouth, may perhaps, as applied to human beings (its S.E. sense, in this connexion, is jaws or mouth of a voracious mammal or fish), be considered c.—as 'Ducange Anglicus', 1857, considers it.]

maw !, hold your. Stop talking: coll.: C. 18–19.

maw-wallop. A filthy dish of food: low coll.: late C. 18–mid-19. Grose, 2nd ed.

maw-wormy. Captious; pessimistic: coll.—theatrical, and non-aristocratic: 1885, *Entr'Acte*, June 6. Ware. (Stomach-worms cause peevishness.)

mawkes. A whore: coll.: C. 17–18. Lodge; *Street Robberies Considered.*—2. A slattern, esp. if dirty or vulgar: coll. verging on S.E.. late C. 17–20; dial. after ca. 1820. Grose, 2nd ed.

mawkish. Slatternly: ca. 1720–70. *A New Canting Dict.*, 1725.

mawley. See mauley.—mawpus. See mopus.

max. Gin; properly, very good gin: low: ca. 1810–1900. *Lex. Bal.*; Byron, 'Oh ! for a glass of max'; Mayhew, Baumann. Abbr. *maxima, -e, -us*, or -*um*. Cf. :

maxie. A great error, big mistake: Scottish: 1868, G. MacDonald, *Robert Falconer*, 'Horror of horrors ! a maxie'; ob. E.D.D.

May. The college Easter Term examination, says Bristed, 1852; more safely defined as the college May examination: Cambridge coll. > j. > S.E. Occ. *Mays*.

May-bees don't fly all the year long. A c.p. reply to one beginning a statement with *it may be*: mid-C. 18–20; ob. Grose, 2nd ed. In Swift, *May-bees don't fly now.* Also *this month.* The Scots form is *maybes* (or *May-bees*) *are no aye honey-bees.*

May-game of one, make a. To befool a person: coll. > S.E.: late C. 16–early 19. B.E., who defines *May games* as 'Frolicks, Plaies, Tricks, Pastimes, &c.'.

May-gathering. Sheep-stealing: c.: C. 19. Cf. *bleat-marching* and *fleecy-clamming.*

may God blind me. 'The original invocation'—† by 1909—'of the gutterling': whence *Gorblimey* (q.v.), etc. Ware.

May hill, to have climbed or **got over** (or **up**). To have survived the late spring, gen. considered a tricky month: proverbial coll.: from ca. 1660; ob. Perhaps in allusion to an actual May Hill. Apperson.

May-term. The Easter, i.e. the summer, term at Cambridge: coll. (— 1905) verging on S.E. (O.E.D.)

mayn't. May not: coll.: C. 19–20.

Maypole. Countess Schulenburg, a mistress of George I. Dawson. Ex her thinness.

Mays. See May.—2. The Cambridge May (now held in early June) boat races: s. (— 1879) > j. >, by 1900, S.E. (O.E.D.)

mazard. See **mazzard**.

mazarine. A common-councilman of London : coll. : from ca. 1760 ; ob. *The Annual Register*, 1761. Ex the gown of mazarine blue.—2. A platform under the stage : theatrical : from ca. 1860 ; ob. H., 3rd ed. ? ex It. *mezzanino*.

mazer. See **mazzard**.

mazuma. Money ; esp. cash : Canadian (— 1914). B. & P. Adopted from U.S. Ex Yiddish.

mazzard ; also **mazard** and **mazer.** The head : jocular coll. verging on S.E. : *mazer*, ca. 1580–1660 ; *maz(z)ard*, C. 17–20, ob.—2. The face (not *mazer*) : ca. 1760–1890 : jocular coll. verging on S.E. Horace Walpole, ' His . . . Christian's mazard was a constant joke ' (O.E.D.). Sense 2 ex sense 1, which, as to *mazzard*, derives ex *mazer*, a drinking-bowl.—3. (Again, not *mazer*) the head of a coin : Anglo-Irish : C. 19–20 ; ob. Maria Edgeworth. (O.E.D.)

mazzard. To knock on the head : C. 17–18 coll. verging on S.E. (Not very gen.)

McKie. See **Mackay, the real**.

me. (As nominative, i.e.) I : C. 16–20 : loose S.E. till C. 18, then, as subject, dial. and sol., as in Dickens's ' Me and Mrs. Boffin stood the poor girl's friend ' ; predicatively, coll.—somewhat low coll. verging on sol., as in Swift's ' Impossible ! it can't be me.'—2. My : mid-C. 13–20 : S.E. till C. 16, then dial. and, when not dial., sol. (Cf. dial. and slurred, almost sol. *mă*, my.)—3. Myself : when deliberate, it is a literary affectation ; when unintentional, it is coll. verging on sol. Baumann, ' I turned me round.' (Not to be confused with the ethical dative, ' I'll buy me a paper,' itself ob.)

me, and. Especially in view of the fact that I am . . . : low coll. : from ca. 1810. Maria Edgeworth, 1812, ' Which would be hard on us and me a widow '. O.E.D.

me and you. A menu : from ca. 1910. P. P., *Rhyming Slang*, 1932.

me I. ' Used expletively in passages of a narrative character ', O.E.D. : C. 17–early 19, low coll. verging on sol., in such phrases as *then says me I* (e.g. in Vanbrugh's *Æsop*) and *what did me I but* . . . (Not to be confused with, though perhaps generated in part by, the ethical dative.) O.E.D.

[**meacock,** n. and adj., **meal(y)-mouthed, measure,** n. and v., **meat and drink,** are all, despite F. & H., S.E.—and always have been !]

[**Meads.** College cricket-ground : Winchester, perhaps rather j. than coll. : C. 19–20. Wrench, ' The Itchen valley consists entirely of *water-meads*.']

meal-mouth. ' A sly sheepish Dun ', B.E. : coll. or s. : late C. 17–18.

meal-sack, gen. -**tub**. A stock of sermons : clerical : from ca. 1860 ; ob.

mealer. One pledged to drink intoxicants only at meals (— 1890). Barrère & Leland.—2. One who, lodging at one place, eats elsewhere : coll. : orig. (1883), U.S. ; anglicised ca. 1887.

mean, disobliging, petty, (of a horse) vicious, is U.S.—2. The phrase *to feel mean*, to feel ashamed or guilty, is recorded by Marryat in 1839 as U.S., but it > anglicised ca. 1860 as s. ; by C. 20, coll.

mean, v. ' To intend with determined purpose ', O.E.D. : coll. : from ca. 1840. E.g. ' Well, anyway, I *mean* to do it ! ' Esp. in *mean business*.

mean a thing. (Always in negative or interroga-

tive sentences.) To mean, to signify, anything ; be of importance : coll. : from ca. 1927. ' He doesn't mean a thing in my young life.'

mean to do without 'em !(, I). I.e. without women : a c.p. popularised on the music-halls by Arthur Roberts in 1882 ; † by 1910. Ware.

mean to say, I. A coll. tautological form, dating from the early 1890's, of *I mean*, itself verging on coll. when, as frequently, it connotes apologetic modification or mental woolliness. (The phrase occurs in Yorkshire and Cheshire dial. before 1900 : E.D.D.)

meaning-like. In earnest : low coll. (— 1887). Baumann. (For *meaningly*.)

measle, v.i. To become pitted with measle-spots : coll. : from ca. 1880.

measles. Syphilis : medical students' ironic (— 1933). *Slang*, p. 192.

measly. Contemptible ; of little value : 1864, Miss Braddon, ' To think that the government . . . should have the audacity to offer a measly hundred pounds or so for the discovery of a great crime ! ' —2. Miserable-looking, ' seedy ' : ca. 1860–1900. H., 3rd ed.

measure is catachrestic when, as in C. 17–18, used, e.g. by Burney, to render L. *modus* as translation of Gr. τρόπος, ἁρμονία. S.O.D.

measure, be (a person's). To be just the person needed : low s. (— 1857) >, by 1880, non-aristocratic coll. ' Ducange Anglicus ' ; Baumann, ' He's our measure *das ist unser Mann*.'

measure, get (late C. 18–mid-19) or **take** (late C. 17–early 19) **one's.** To coït with ; to marry : coll., the former sense being low. Lacy, in *Sir Hercules Buffoon*, ' Gin I'd let him alane, he had taken measure o' th' inside of me as well as o' th' out.'

measure out. To knock down ; to kill : low coll. (— 1891) verging on s.

measured, be. To be exactly suited, e.g. with a part written to one's fancy or ability : theatrical : 1859, Blanchard Jerrold.

measured for a suit of mourning, be. To receive a black eye : boxing : 1819, Moore in *Tom Crib's Memorial* ; ob. by 1900, † by 1930.

meat. Something profitable or pleasant : coll. : from ca. 1885. *The Westminster Gazette*, Dec. 28, 1897, ' There is a good deal of meat for the actors ' (O.E.D.).—2. Generic for the human body (rarely the male) as an instrument of sexual pleasure ; hence, for the female pudend and/or the male : low coll. : late C. 16–20 ; slightly ob. Gosson ; Killigrew, ' Your bed is big enough for two, and my meat will not cost you much.' Cf. *mutton*, q.v., and the ensuing entries and *meaty*, 2 and 3.—3. ' The thickest part of the blade of a bat ' : cricketers' coll. : 1925, D. J. Knight (Lewis).—4. Tissues for microscopical examination : medical students' (— 1933). *Slang*, p. 192.

meat, a bit of. Coïtion : low (s. rather than coll.) : C. 18–20.—2. A harlot : low : late C. 19–20. Manchon. See **meat, 2**.

meat, cold. See **cold meat**.

meat, feed (a person). To supply with very rich and nutritious food : 1920, P. G. Wodehouse. O.E.D. (Sup.). Here, *meat* is opp. *milk*, the food of infancy.

meat, flash. To expose the person : late C. 18–20 : low.

meat, fond of. Frequently amorous : low : C. 19–20.

meat, fresh. A harlot new at her trade : low : C. 19–20.

meat, price of. The cost of a sexual embrace : low : C. 19–20.

meat, hot. See hot meat.

meat, raw. A harlot (less gen., any woman) naked in the sexual act : low : C. 19–20. Contrast *meat, fresh*.

meat, the nearer the bone the sweeter the. A mid-C. 19–20 low c.p. applied by men to a thin woman viewed as a bed-mate. Ex the old proverb, *the nearer the bone the sweeter the flesh* (mid-C. 16–20) : Apperson.

meat and drink. An amorous carouse : low : C. 19–20 ; ob.

meat-axe, savage as a. Extremely angry : U.S. coll., anglicised ca. 1905. (Thornton.)

meat-flasher, -flashing. An exposer, the exposure, of the person in public : low : C. 19–20. Ex *meat, flash*, q.v.

meat-fosh. A (warm) meat-hash : Cockneys' (— 1887). Baumann. ? Fr. *farci*.

meat-hook. A curl on the temple (as worn by the London coster) : Cockneys' (— 1887) ; slightly ob. Baumann.

meat-house. A brothel : low : C. 19–20 ; ob. Cf. :

meat-market. A rendezvous of harlots ; the female breasts ; the female pudend ; low : C. 19–20.

meat-merchant. A bawd : low : C. 19–20 ; ob. Contrast :

meat-monger. A man given to wenching : low : C. 18–19.

meat of, make (cold). To kill : orig. (1848), U.S. ; anglicised ca. 1870.

*meat-safe. A pugilistic variant (— 1920, but already ob.) of *bread-basket*, q.v. W.—2. That oblong box-pew (gauze-fronted and curtain-sided) in which, at divine service, the condemned murderer sits in the prison chapel : c. (— 1932). ' Stuart Wood ', *Shades of the Prison House*.

meat-skewer. A bayonet : jocular military coll. : from ca. 1910. F. & Gibbons.

meat-ticket. A variant of *cold-meat ticket*. Ibid.

meater. A cowardly dog (lit., one that will bite only meat), hence a cowardly man : low (mostly Cockneys') : late C. 19–20. Ware.

meaty, plump, is S.E.—2. Sexually enjoyable : low coll. : from ca. 1820.—3. Obscene : book-world coll. : C. 20.

mebbe. Perhaps : (dial. and) proletarian coll. : C. 19–20. Lit., *maybe*.

mebu. A ' pill-box ' : Army officers' : late 1917–18. F. & Gibbons. Ex the Ger. technical name, ' maschinengewehr-eisenbeton-unterstand '.

Mecænas, Mecenas. Incorrect forms of *Mœcenas* : mid-C. 16–20. Spenser. O.E.D.

[**mechanic,** given by F. & H., has always been S.E.]

mechanical cow. See shorthorn.

med, medic, medical, medico. A doctor, whether physician or surgeon or both combined ; a student of medicine. Thus, *med*, orig. (1851) U.S., was anglicised ca. 1860 and in C. 20 is ob. ; *medic*, as doctor, is C. 17–18 S.E., C. 19 rare coll., and as medical student is s., orig. (1823) U.S. and very rare in Great Britain, where it is ob. in C. 20 ; *medical* is coll. in both senses, and, though recorded first (1823) in Hawthorne, it may be orig., as it is mainly, English (Halley, 1834 ; Masson, 1864) ; *medico*, student, is C. 19–20, but the more gen. sense of

doctor arises in late C. 17, is S.E. till ca. 1850, and is thereafter coll. See esp. O.E.D. and F. & H.

med lab. Medical laboratory : medical students' coll. (— 1933). *Slang*, p. 190.

medal, a putty ; occ., though † by 1930, **a paper** medal with a wooden string. Recognition of merit, ' by way of humorous encouragement ' : military coll. : C. 20. Collinson.

medal (or medals) to-day, you're wearing your ; or medal showing ! Your fly is undone ; you have a fly-button showing : mid-C. 19–20 : jocular c.p. verging on euphemistic S.E.

medder. Meadow : sol. : C. 19–20. Baumann.

meddlers, lare-overs for. See lare-overs.

meddling duchess. An ' ageing, pompous woman who fusses about and achieves nothing ' : lower classes' : ca. 1880–1915. Ware. See the corresponding sense of *duchess*.

Medes and Persians. Jumping on a boy when he is in bed : Winchester College : ca. 1840–1910.

medic and medical. See med.

medical Greek. ' Marrowskying ', q.v. : coll. verging on S.E. : from ca. 1800 ; ob. H., 2nd ed. Also known as *Gower Street dialect*.

medicine. Liquor : from ca. 1850 ; ob. Mayhew. Cf. *poison*, q.v.—2. Sexual intercourse : from ca. 1855 ; ob. Hence *take one's medicine* = to drink ; to copulate.

medicine, take († a). To take a purgative : coll. : 1830, Southey. (O.E.D.)

medicine and duty. The number 9 in the game of House : military : 1915. B. & P. For semantics, cf. *number nine*, 2.

medico. See med.

Medics, the. The Army Medical Corps : military coll. (not very gen.) : 1914–18. F. & Gibbons.

Mediterranean Greys, the. The 50th Foot Regiment : military : 1793 and for a few years after. Ex ' the elderly look of all ranks ' stationed at Gibraltar in that year. (F. & Gibbons.)

medium. ' A person engaged by a squatter, part of whose " run " is offered by Government at a land lottery ' or ballot. ' The medium takes lot-tickets . . ., attends the drawing, and, if his ticket is drawn before his principal's land is gone, selects it, and hands it over on payment of the attendance fee,' F. & H. : Australian coll. : from ca. 1880 : coll. >, ca. 1900, S.E. ; ob.—2. In *the happy medium* it is catachrestic (— 1887), *the happy mean* being the correct phrase. Baumann.

medlar. The female pudend : low : C. 17–mid 19.

medza, medzer. See madza. Cf. :

medzies ; metzes. Money : Parlyaree and theatrical : (? late C. 19-) C. 20. E. Seago, *Circus Company*, 1933. Ex It. *mezzo* : cf. *madza*, q.v. Hence, *nanty metzes*, ' broke ', penniless.

meech, meecher, meeching. See miker, etc., and mooch, etc.

meer-swine. A porpoise : nautical coll. : mid-C. 19–20 ; ob. Bowen. By Ger. influence ex *seahog* ; but imm. ex Scots.

meerschaum. The nose : boxing (— 1891) ; ob. *Sporting Life*, March 25, 1891.

meet. An assignation : Australian coll. (—1916). C. J. Dennis.

[**meetinger** is S.E., as are these others in F. & H. : **meg(, roaring), megrim, (to) mell, melt** (sexual verb), **member** (penis), **merchant(, play the), mercury, mercury-woman, mercurial, meridian, merkin, mermaid, merry** (wanton), **merry-andrew,** merry-begot, merry dog, merry Greek, merry-man, merry pin(, in a), merry thought, mess-mate, messel (properly *mesel*, misunderstood by F. & H.), and mettlesome. Whereas meg, a wench, and **Meg's** diversions are dial.]

*meg ; occ. megg. A guinea : c. : ca. 1685–1820. Shadwell. Cf. *mag* (coin).—2. In late C. 19–20 dial. and till ca. 1860 in c., a *meg* is a half-penny ; in the U.S. C. 19–20 underworld, *me(i)g* is a five-cents piece. ? etymology.—3. See **Meg of Westminster.**

*meg. To swindle : c. (— 1887). Baumann.

Meg of Westminster, as long as. Very tall (esp. if of a woman) : coll. : late C. 16–18. *The Life and Pranks of Long Meg of Westminster*, 1582 ; Grose. In C. 18, *long Meg* was a nickname for any very tall woman. Ex a 'legendary' character.

*megg. See meg, n.

*megging, n. and adj. Swindling : c. (— 1887). Baumann.

megs. First Preference Stock in the Mexican Railway : Stock Exchange : from ca. 1890.

*megsman. See magsman.

mcisensang. A missionary : Anglo-Chinese (— 1864). Ex Chinese pronunciation of the English word. (H., 3rd ed.)

*mejoge. A shilling : c. of ca. 1750–80 and perhaps much later. John Poulter. ? ex *meg*, q.v. Cf. *midgic*, q.v.

melanotype is erroneous for *melanotype* (from ca. 1865), as *melanogogue* is for *melanagogue* (mid-C. 17–18). O.E.D.

melancholy, as . . ., as. Apperson (to whom praise be !) cites the following four coll. similes : *as melancholy as a* (gen. *gib*) *cat*, ca. 1590–1840, e.g. Lyly, Shakespeare, D'Urfey, Lamb ; *as m. as a collier's horse*, ca. 1650–1750 ; *as m. as a sick monkey*, from ca. 1830 (ob.), as in Marryat's *Midshipman Easy* ; and *as m. as a sick parrot*, ca. 1680–1840, as in Mrs. Behn.

*mell. The nose : c. of ca. 1720–1850. ? ex the † S.E. sense, a mace or club.

mell, dead as a. Quite dead : Scots coll. : late C. 18–20 ; ob. Cf. preceding.

mellish. A sovereign : mostly Londoners' low s. : ca. 1820–50. Bee. Perhaps ex Fr. *miel*, honey.

mellow. Almost drunk : C. 17–20 : coll. till C. 19, then S.E. Cotgrave, Garrick.—2. See luscious.

melon. A new cadet : Royal Military Academy : from ca. 1870 ; ob. Ex his greenness, as is 2, the Australian and New Zealand sense (late C. 19–20), a simpleton, a fool.—3. Abbr. *paddy-melon*, a small kangaroo : Australian coll. : from ca. 1845.

melon-cutting. A sharing of spoils or profits : Stock Exchange : 1908. O.E.D. (Sup.). Cf. *melon*, 1.

*melt. To spend (money) : c. from ca. 1690 ; ob. B.E. Also *melt away* (C. 18).—2. Hence, to cash (a cheque or a bank-note) : 1868, Reade and Boucicault in *Foul Play* (O.E.D.) : low s. verging on c.—3. Hence, to discount (a bill) : financial (— 1909). Ware.—4. V.i., to be spent on drink : ca. 1760–1800. Foote.—5. To defeat : boxers' (— 1823) ; † by 1900. See melting.

melt in the mouth, look as if butter would not. See butter.—melted, 'twill not cut butter when it's hot or. See butter.

melted butter. The *semen virile* : low : C. 18–20.

melter. He who administers a sound beating : boxing : ca. 1820–1900. Bee. Cf. :

melting. A sound beating : pugilistic : ca. 1820–1900. Ex *malleting*, says 'Jon Bee' ; much more prob. ex Scots *melt*, to knock down, orig. by a stroke in the side, where lies the *melt* or spleen (Jamieson).

melting moments. The coïtion of a fat man and woman : low : ca. 1810–90. *Lex. Bal.*—2. Hence, ardent passion : non-aristocratic coll. (— 1887). Baumann.

melting-pot. The female pudend : low : C. 19. Cf. *melted butter*, q.v.

melton. Dry bread : tailors' : from ca. 1860 ; ob. Prob. ex *Melton* (*cloth*), a strong smooth cloth with close-cut nap.

Melton hot day. A melting hot day : sporting and clubs' : June 3, 1885, and for a week or two later. The Derby, run on that day, was won by Melton. Ware.

mem. A low coll. form of *ma'am*, q.v. : 1700, Congreve (O.E.D.).—2. A memorandum : of which word, as of *memento* (Baumann, 1887), it was orig. a mere written abbr. : coll., 1818, Moore (O.E.D.) Cf. *memo*, q.v.

mem, the. The mistress of the house : coll. (India and the F.M.S.) : late C. 19–20. E.g., Somerset Maugham, *The Casuarina Tree*, 1926. Abbr.

mem-sahib, the. One's wife : Anglo-Indian (orig. Bengal Presidency) coll. : late C. 19–20. Adoption of the Indian alteration (itself dating from ca. 1857) of *ma'am, madam*. S.O.D. ; Yule & Burnell. Cf. (the now ob.) *madam-sahib*, the form used at Bombay, and *burra be(e)bee*, q.v.

member. A person : C. 16–20 : S.E. till mid-C. 19, then s. and dial. Gen. as *hot m.* (q.v.), *warm m.*, etc. Ex *member of the community*.

'member. To remember : childish coll. : C. 18–20.

member for Cockshire, the. The penis : from ca. 1840 ; ob. Punning *male* (or *privy*) *member* and *cock*.

member-mug. A chamber-pot : low coll. : late C. 17–19. Ex *member*, the male member.—2. An out-of-doors boy : Westminster School : ca. 1850–1910.

memo. Orig. (1889) a mere written abbr. of *memorandum*, it was by 1895 a gen. accepted coll. ; by 1930 it may well have > S.E. Cf. *mem*, 2.

memory-powder, you want a little. Your memory is bad : c.p. of ca. 1885–1910. Baumann.

Memugger, Maggers'. The Martyrs' Memorial : Oxford undergraduates' : from late 1890's. Ware. (' Oxford -er.')

men. See man for all senses and phrases.

menagerie. The orchestra : theatrical (—1859) ; ob. H., 1st ed. Ex the noise.

menavelings ; maniv(i)lins, the usual form. Odd money in the daily accounts : railway clerks' : from ca. 1863. H., 3rd ed.—2. Hence, in low s. of late C. 19–20 : odds and ends, extras, broken victuals. Cf. *manablins*.

mend. To bandage : lower classes' coll. : mid-C. 19–20 ; ob. Ware.—2. To produce (e.g. a story) better than (somebody else) : coll. : from ca. 1870 ; earlier, S.E.

mend as sour ale mends in summer. To become worse : from ca. 1540 : coll. till C. 19, then dial. ' Proverbs ' Heywood, Wither, Swift. (Apperson.)

mend or correct the Magnificat. See **Magnificat.**

mending, vbl.n. Something to be repaired ; nautical for repairing (as in *mending wool*) : coll. : from ca. 1860. (O.E.D.)

Mendinghem. See **Bandagehem.—menjar(l)y.**
A rare variant of *mungar(l)y.*

mensh !, don't. Don't mention it ! : a lower-middle-class c.p. : C. 20.

mental. A person mentally deranged, mad : coll. : 1913 (O.E.D. Sup.). Ex *mental case* or *m. defective.* (The adj. is S.E.)

mention it !, don't. A phrase in deprecation of apology or thanks : coll. : 1854, Wilkie Collins (O.E.D.). Prob. an abbr. of *don't mention it, for it's a trifle.*

mentisental. Sentimental : East London (— 1909) ; ob. Ware. By transposition : cf. *lemoncholy.*

mephisto. A foreman : tailors' : from ca. 1870 ; ob. Abbr. *Mephistopheles.*

mephites is incorrect for *mephitis* : C. 18–20. O.E.D.

Merc or **Merce.** A Mercedes motor-car : Society : from ca. 1920. (M. Lincoln, *Oh ! Definitely,* 1933.)

mercer's book, the. Proverbial coll., ca. 1590–1602, for debt, esp. the debts of a gallant. Nashe, 'Divers young Gentlemen shall creepe further into the Mercers Booke in a Moneth, then they can get out in a yere ' ; Jonson. O.E.D.

merchant. A fellow, 'chap' : S.E. in mid-C. 16–early 17, lapsed till ca. 1880, then revived as a coll. (esp. among actors) verging on s. Cf. *customer* and *client.* (*play the merchant* : S.E.)

merchant of capers. A variant of *caper-merchant,* q.v.

merchant of eel-skins. No merchant at all : semi-proverbial coll. : ca. 1540–1670. Ascham, in *Toxophilus* ; A. Brewer, 1655. (Apperson.)

merchantable. See **scruff,** n.

mercy, cry (one). To cry mercy ; beg a person's pardon : coll. when *I* is omitted : late C. 16–18. Shakespeare, ' Oh, cry you mercy, sir, I have mistook.'

mere country put, a. A virtually c.p. elaboration of *put,* n., 1 (q.v.) : ca. 1690–1750.

Merica or **-ka.** Rare spellings of *Merrika,* q.v.

meridian. A drink taken at noon : app. ca. 1815–1910 : Scots coll. verging on ' standard '. E.D.D.

Merino(e)s, pure. (Members of) the ' very first families ' : Australian, esp. New South Wales : from ca. 1825 ; ob. Peter Cunningham, 1827. ' The pure merino is the most valuable sheep,' Morris.

merits. Ca. 1820–50 as in ' Jon Bee ', 1823 : ' High flash '—i.e. fashionable s.—' for the extreme of a thing, used negatively in general ; as, " Sir, you do not enter into the merits of—the wine, the joke ", &c.'

Merrika (or -er) ; Merrican, -kan, -kin. America ; American : sol. (— 1887). Baumann.

Merry Andrew. Andrew Boorde, an early C. 16 traveller and author. (Dawson.)

merry-arse(d) Christian. A whore : low coll. : ca. 1810–70. *Lex. Bal.*

merry as . . . Of the following similes listed by Apperson, all or nearly all must orig. have been coll. :—*merry as a cricket* (mid-C. 16–20) ; *m. as a Greek* (mid-C. 16–18) ; *m. as a grig* (from ca. 1560 ; in C. 20, dial.) ; *m. or happy as a king* (mid-C.16–mid-19) ; *m. as a* [*mag*]*pie* (late C. 14–early 17) ; *m. as beggars* (ca. 1650–1750) ; (*who so*) *m. as he that hath nought to lose* (?) (ca. 1660–1780) ; *m. as mice in malt* (ca. 1630–1880) ; *m. as the maids* (ca. 1630–

90) ; *m. as three chips* (ca. 1540–90) ; *m. as tinkers* (ca. 1650–1700).

merry bit. A willing wench : C. 19–20 low ; ob. Cf. *merry-legs.*

merry bout. A copulation : ca. 1780–1830. *The Newgate Calendar,* 1780. O.E.D.

merry Cain. See **Cain, raise.**

merry dancers. The Northern Lights : from ca. 1715 : coll. and dial. Also (*the*) *dancers.*

Merry Dun of Dover. A legendary ship—drawn from Scandinavian mythology—' so large that, passing through the Straits of Dover, her flying jib-boom knocked down Calais steeple ; while the fly of her ensign swept a flock of sheep off Dover Cliff. She was so lofty that a boy who went to her mast-head found himself a grey old man when he reached the deck again,' F. & H. : nautical : ca. 1840–1900. H., 3rd ed.

merry-go-down. Strong ale : ca. 1470–1620 (Golding, Nashe) ; then dial. Not c., though described as such by F. & H. : see esp. Apperson.

merry-go-sorry. Hysteria : coll. verging on S.E. : late C. 16–early 17. Breton.

merry-go-up. Snuff : ca. 1820–50. Egan, 1821, ' Short but pungent like a pinch of snuff.'

merry-legs. A harlot : low coll. : C. 19–20 ; ob.

merry-maker. The male member : low : mid-C. 19–20 ; ob.

merry men of May. Currents caused by the ebb-tides : nautical : C. 19–20 ; ob.

mervousness. Fear of Russia : political (— 1887) ; † by 1915. Ex *Merv,* a Russian city, + *nervousness.* Baumann.

meself. Myself : S.E. in C. 9–16 ; coll. in C. 17–mid-18 ; then low coll. till ca. 1830 ; then sol. except in dial. (*Myself* > gen. in C. 14.)

mesne tenant is catachrestic for one who holds property from a mesne lord : from ca. 1850. S.O.D.

Mesop. See **Mespot.**

Mesopolonica. A destination on the Eastern Front, it not being certain whether Mesopotamia or Salonica was intended : Army officers' : 1916–18. F. & Gibbons.

Mesopotamia. Belgravia, also known as *Asia Minor, the New Jerusalem* : ca. 1860–4 : fashionable. E. Yates, in *Broken to Harness.* Cf. *Cubitopolis,* q.v.—2. A walk at Oxford : Oxford University (— 1886) ; ob.

Mesopotamia ring, the true. Pleasing, high-sounding, and incomprehensible : coll. : ca. 1880–1910. Ex *the* or *that blessed word Mesopotamia,* itself almost eligible on the same count, with the same meaning, and arising ex a plausible ascription of spiritual comfort.

Mespot. Mesopotamia : 1915 : orig. and still largely military : at first, officers'. F. & Gibbons. Also, occ. *Mess-Pot, Mesop* and *Mess-Up.*

mess. A difficulty, notable failure, muddle : 1834, Marryat (O.E.D.) : coll. till ca. 1890, then S.E. Hence, *make a mess of,* to bungle ; *clear up the mess,* to put things straight ; *get into a mess,* to involve oneself in difficulties. J. W. Palmer, ' What a mess they made of it ! '—2. Its use at Winchester College (see Mansfield) is hardly eligible ; the same holds of *middle mess.*

mess. To interfere unduly ; gen. as vbl.n. *messing,* applied to police interference : low coll. : from ca. 1870 ; ob. Also *mess about,* extant.

mess ! A proletarian exclamation (— 1923). Manchon. Euphemistic for *shit !*

mess, be scratched out of one's. A variant (Baumann, 1887 ; now ob.) of :

mess, lose the number of one's. To be killed : naval (— 1887). Baumann. Manchon's *be stretched of one's mess* I believe to be an error for the preceding. F. & Gibbons cites *be put out of one's mess* : military : G.W. In the Boer War, a military variant was *lose one's number*, as in J. Milne, *The Epistles of Atkins*, 1902.

mess about. See **mess** (the *v.*).—2. To take (sexual) liberties : low coll. : from ca. 1873. V.t. form, *mess about* or *m. a. with*.—3. V.i. and t., to play fast and loose ; swindle, put off : low coll. : from ca. 1890.

mess clout. The duster supplied weekly to each mess : *Conway* cadets' coll. (— 1891). J. Masefield, *The Conway*, 1933.

mess-John. See **mas John**.

mess of, make a. See **mess**, n. 1.—2. To defeat utterly, overcome easily or signally : from ca. 1910.

Mess-Pot. See **Mespot**.

mess-traps. Cooking utensils : nautical, esp. naval, coll. (—1887) ; ob. Baumann. Here *traps* = odds-and-ends, ' things '.

mess treat. A ' tip given by an old boy to his former mess to provide a special feed (usually at tea) ' : *Conway* cadets' coll. (— 1891). John Masefield, *The Conway*, 1933.

mess-up. An elaboration, or perhaps merely a slovenly derivative, of *mess*, n., 1. : coll. : from ca. 1916, when I remember hearing it at Pozières.—2. **Mess-Up.** See **Mespot**.

messer. A bungler, muddler : coll. (slightly low) : from ca. 1905.

messman's horror. A hungry man : naval : C. 20. Bowen. The messman thus loses his ' perks '.

Messolini. Mussolini : from Sept., 1935. In Australia he is *Muss*, while in the U.S. he is often called *Muscle-inski*.

Met, the. The Metropolitan music-hall : London (— 1896) ; † except historically.—2. The Metropolitan Railway : London coll. : late C. 19–20.—3. In pl. (*Mets*), stocks and shares therein : from ca. 1886 : Stock Exchange s. >, by 1910, coll. Baumann.

metal. Money : coll. : C. 19–20, ob. (Cf. S.E. usage for precious metal, gold.) Ex *precious metal*.—2. See **mettle**.—3. Sweetmeats : Anglo-Indian (— 1864) ; nearly †. H., 3rd ed.

metal rule. An oath ; an obscenity. Also as v., in *you be metal-ruled !*, you be damned ! Printers' : from ca. 1860 ; ob. Ex the dash (—) in print.

metal (or, as gen., **mettle**) **to the back.** Constantly courageous and/or energetic : coll. : ca. 1590–1760. Shakespeare ; Coffey, 1733, ' The girl is mettle to the back.' Apperson.

metallician. A bookmaker : racing : ca. 1870–90. H., 5th ed. Ex bookmakers' use of metallic pencils and even books. Cf. :

metallics. Money : turf (— 1923). Manchon. An elaboration of *metal*, 1.

metals. Rails : railwaymen's coll. (— 1887). Baumann.

Meteors. The Meteorological Service at the Front : military : 1916–18. F. & Gibbons.

meter. See **-ometer**.—2. A term of abuse in the Army : late C. 19–20. Ex Hindustani : lit., a scavenger.

metho. Methylated spirits, esp. as drunk by ' down-and-outers ' : Australian (— 1935).

Methusalem. Esp. in *old as Methusalem*. Methuselah : mid-C. 17–20 : always corrupt ; in mid-C. 19–20, low coll. Cowley. Influenced by *Jerusalem*. (O.E.D.)

Methuselier or **-ilier.** A member of the Australian Remount Unit : Australian coll. : 1916. F. & Gibbons. Ex *Methuselah* on *fusilier* : most of the men were over military age.—2. A member of the Volunteer Training Corps (special constables, etc.) : mostly Anglo-Irish : from 1915 ; ob.

metro, the. The underground-train system of Paris ; hence occ. that of London : C. 20. Fr. (*le*) *métro* (abbr. *Métropolitain*), itself often loosely used.

mets or **Mets.** See **Met, the, 3.**

mettle. The *semen virile* : low coll. : C. 17–20 ; ob. Field, 1612, (*mettle of generation*). The gen. late C. 19–20 term, esp. in the Colonies, is *spunk*. Ex S.E. *mettle*, (of animals) natural ardour and vigour).—2. Hence, *fetch mettle*, to masturbate : C. 18–19. Grose, 1st ed.—3. **mettle to the back.** See **metal to . . .**

metzes. See **medzies.**

mew-mew ! Tell that to the marines : tailors' : from ca. 1860 ; ob.

mi. See **ma, 3.**

mia-mia (pron. *mi-mi*) ; occ. **miam, mimi** or **mi-mi.** An aboriginal hut : Australian coll. (— 1845) >, ca. 1870, ' standard ' ; in 1871 and later, applied to any hut : coll. >, by 1880, ' standard '. Ex Aboriginal. Morris. Cf. *gunyah* and *hump(e)y*, qq.v.

mice-feet o', make. To destroy utterly : Scots coll. : C. 18–19.

mices, like **mouses**, is sol. except when jocular : C. 18–20.

[**mich** (**-er, -ery, -ing**), now dial., **michael** (a man), **middle, middle-gate** or **-kingdom, midget, miff,** v. and adj., **mightily, milch-cow, mild, milk** (to plunder or drain), **milk and water, milk-livered, milksop, mill** (bring grist to the ; also **put through the mill**), **mill-round, mine of pleasure, mingle-mangle, minckins, minikin, mint of money, minx, miraculous cairn, mishmash, miss, mix,** v., **mizmaze** (also dial.), are S.E. ; while, again despite F. & H., **midge** and **miff-maff** are dial.]

Michael, your head's on fire. (Often preceded by *hip !*) A c.p. addressed to a red-headed man : mid-C. 18–mid-19. Grose, 2nd ed.

Michaelmas rent in Midsummer noon, spend (one's). To spend money that should be laid by for a definite purpose : proverbial coll. : ca. 1600–1860. Camden. (Apperson.)

miching Malicho, or mallecho in Shakespeare's *Hamlet* is prob. s. : meaning and etymology are alike uncertain, though *miching* prob. = skulking, perhaps = a dirty trick (O.E.D.). Note, too, Romany *malleco*, false (Smart & Crofton), and Welsh Gypsy *maleko !*, look out for yourself ! (Sampson). Moreover, Ware states that in April, 1895, he ' heard a man in the gallery of the Palace of Varieties (London), after several scornful phrases, say derisively, " Oh—ah—minchin maleego ".' I believe that the phrase may = our modern ' dirty dog ! ', for the Romany *malleco* is prob. cognate with Turkish Gypsy *maklo*, spotted. (L. *maculatus*.)

mick ; mickey or **micky ; occ. mike.** (Or with capital initial.) An Irishman : orig. (— 1869), U.S. : anglicised ca. 1890 : more gen. in Canada, Australia, and New Zealand than in Britain. Ex *Michael*.—2. Hence, an Irish seaman (nautical : late

C. 19–20) or soldier (military : same period). Cf. *Jock*. Both *Jock* and *Mick* are now vocatives of a wide range.

mick, do a. See **mike, do a.**

mickle and **muckle** are mere variants, therefore *many a mickle makes a muckle* is erroneous. Fowler.

Micks, the. The Irish Guards : military : C. 20. F. & Gibbons. Ex *mick*, 2.

micky. See **mick.**—2. A young bull running wild : Australia : from ca. 1880. Grant, 1888, ' There were two or three mickies and wild heifers '. Prob. ex ' the association of bulls with Irishmen ', Barrère & Leland. (Morris.)—3. A New Zealand corruption (— 1898) of Maori *mingi*, orig. *mingi-mingi*, a shrub or small tree (*cyathodes acerosa*). Morris.—4. (Also **Mikey.**) Sick, esp. after liquor : low : late C. 19–20. Ex *Bob, Harry and Dick*, the same : rhyming s. : 1868. Ware.

microcoustic is incorrect for *micracoustic* : mid-C. 19–20. O.E.D.

micturition is catachrestic when made to = an act of urination (for properly it = a morbid desire to urinate) : 1799, O.E.D.

mid. A midshipman : coll. : 1798, Mrs. Ann Bennett (O.E.D.). Also *middy*, q.v.—2. Jewish pronunciation of *with* : since time almost immemorial. Cf. ' Jon Bee ', 1823, ' The Cockneys come it *vid*,'—but not in C. 20.

mid-Vic. (The adj. is exceedingly rare.) A mid-Victorian : cultured s. : from ca. 1932 ; already very ob.

mid vire. A midday ' wire ' or telegram, ' giving last prices in the coming-on races ' : sporting men's, orig. (— 1909) and mainly in Paris ; ob. Ware.

midden. A filthy slattern : Scots coll. : C. 19–20.—2. **eating midden,** a glutton : Scots coll. : C. 19–20.

midder. Midwifery : medical students' (—1933). *Slang*, p. 192. (Influence of ' the Oxford -*er* '.)

middies. Midland Railway ordinary stock : Stock Exchange : from ca. 1885.

middle. A social, literary or scientific article for the press : 1862 : coll. till C. 20, then S.E. Abbr. *middle article*. Hence *middle(-)man*, a writer of such articles ; ob.—2. A finger : c. : C. 18–mid-19. —3. A middle-weight : boxing coll. : 1902, P. G. Wodehouse, *The Pothunters*.

middle, v. To cheat, befool : ca. 1869–1905. E. Farmer, *Scrap-Book*. (O.E.D.)

middle-cut, an old Winchester College word, is virtually S.E.

middle finger or leg. The male member : low : C. 19–20.

middle hills. See **morning hills.**

middle piece. The chest : boxing : ca. 1817–1900. Cf. :

middle storey. The stomach : ca. 1670–1800 : jocular coll. Crowne.

middle stump. Penis : cricketers' : C. 20.

middle-watcher. The slight meal snatched by officers of the middle watch (about 2.30 a.m.) : nautical coll. (— 1867). Smyth.

Middlesex clown (gen. in pl.). A native or an inhabitant of Middlesex : jocular coll. : mid-C. 17–early 19. Fuller ; Grose, in the *Provincial Glossary*. (Apperson.)

Middlesex jury. See **London jury.**

Middlesex mongrel. A C. 18 variant of *Middlesex clown.* (Lord Hailes, 1770.)

middling. Moderately large : late C. 16–20 : S.E. till ca. 1850, then coll. (somewhat low) except in *middling size, stature, degree*. Blackmore, ' A middling keg of hollands, and an anker of old rum '. O.E.D.

middling, adv. Moderately, tolerably : C. 18–20 : S.E. till ca. 1830.—2. Fairly well (success, health) : coll. : 1810, W. B. Rhodes, ' We are but middling—that is, but so so.' O.E.D.

middlingish, adv. Somewhat ; moderately : (low) coll. and dial. : 1820. O.E.D.

middy. A midshipman : coll. : 1833, Marryat. Ex *mid*, q.v.

midge-net. A lady's veil : (low) coll. : ca. 1858–1910. H., 2nd ed.

*****midgic.** A shilling : New Zealand c. (— 1932). Prob. ex *mejoge*, q.v.

Midlands, the. The female pudend : low jocular : from ca. 1830 ; ob.

midnight's arse-hole, as white as. Black as pitch : low coll. : ca. 1550–1640. Anon., *Jacob and Esau*, ca. 1557 (in Dodsley's *Old Plays*).

Mids or **mids.** Shares in the Midland Railway : Stock Exchange : C. 20. Cf. *middies*, q.v.

midshipman's half-pay. Nothing : nautical : from ca. 1850.

midshipman's nuts. Broken biscuit, esp. and properly if hard (as dessert) : nautical coll. : from middle 1840's ; ob.

midshipman's roll. A hammock badly rolled : naval coll. : mid C. 19–20. Bowen.

midshipman's watch and chain. A sheep's heart and pluck : ca. 1780–1850 : orig. nautical. Grose, 1st ed.

midshipmen's devil. ' The steward who looked after the midshipman's mess in the Blackwallers ' : naval : latter half of C. 19. Bowen.

midshipmen's parade. The lee side of the quarter-deck, the weather side being reserved for seniors : naval : ca. 1820–60. Bowen.

midshipmite. A midshipman : when not nautical, it gen. connotes smallness (*mite*) : 1833, Marryat : coll. A perversion.

midsummer, be but a mile to. To be somewhat mad : coll. : ca. 1460–1570. *The English Chronicle* (O.E.D.) Cf. :

Midsummer noon. Madness. Gen. as *'tis Midsummer noon with you*, you are mad : late C. 16–mid-19. Cf. Shakespeare's *midsummer madness, midsummer noon*, popularly associated with lunacy, and the old proverb, *when the moon's in the full, then wit's in the wane.* (Apperson.)

miff. A petty quarrel ; a tantrum, a fit of anger : coll. and dial. (since ca. 1850, mainly dial.) : 1623, C. Butler, ' . . . Lest some of the bees take a miff.' Cf. *miffy* and *mifty*, qq.v.

miffiness. A tendency to take offence : coll. and dial. : 1845, Ford's *Handbook of Spain*. O.E.D.

miffy. The devil : (low) coll. : C. 19. ? ex *miff*. Also in dial. ; the E.D.D. derives it ex Old Fr. *maufé*, devil.

miffy, adj. Easily offended : coll. and dial. : C. 18–20. Cibber, Blackmore. Whence *miffiness*, q.v. Also :

mifty. Apt to take offence : late C. 17–18. B.E. Like preceding, ex *miff*, q.v.

might, subjunctive, ' is often used *colloq.* (*a*) with pres. inf. to convey a counsel or suggestion of action, or a complaint that some action is neglected ; (*b*) with perf. inf. to express a complaint that some not difficult duty or kindness has been omitted ' : the former, Meredith, 1864 ; the latter, Manville Fenn, 1894. O.E.D.

mighty. Very considerable in amount, size, degree: late C. 16–20: S.E. till ca. 1840, then familiar S.E. rapidly > coll. Borrow, 'mighty damage'. O.E.D.

mighty, adv. Very greatly: C. 13–20: S.E. till ca. 1750, then coll. Johnson, 'Not to be used but in very low language'. (In C. 19–20, often ironical.)

mighty ! ; **mighty me !** Coll. interjections: Scots: from ca. 1865. (Also in dial.)

mighty, high and. See **high and mighty.**

mike or **Mike.** An Irishman, esp. if a labourer: coll.: from ca. 1873. Cf. *mick*, q.v., and, like that term, ex *Michael*.—2. A wasting of time; idling, esp. in *do*, or occ. *have, a mike*, to idle away one's time: low: 1825, Egan. Prob. ex S.E. *mich(e)*, to skulk. O.E.D. Cf. *mike, v.*—3. A microphone: from ca. 1927.—4. A microscope: medical students' (— 1933). *Slang*, p. 190.

mike, v. To 'hang about', either expectantly or idly: low: 1859, H., 1st ed. Where tramps are concerned, the gen. word is *mooch, mouch*. Ex S.E. *mich(e)*. Cf. *miker*.—2. A variant (C. 20: F. & Gibbons) of sense 2 of:

mike, do a. See **mike, n.,** 2.—To decamp; to evade duty: military and low (— 1914). F. & Gibbons. Also *do a mick*.

Mike and George. A decoration of the Order of St. *Michael* and St. *George*: military: 1915; ob. F. & Gibbons.

mike (at), take a. To have a look (at): low: C. 20. E.g. in John G. Brandon, *West End*, 1933.

miker. A loafer; a 'scrounger' (q.v.): low: from ca. 1880. Ex *mike, v.* Cf. *miking*, q.v.

mikerscope. Microscope: sol. (— 1887). Baumann.

Mikey. See **Micky,** 4.

miking, n. and adj. Idling; skulking; 'scrounging': low: from ca. 1880. Ex *mike, v.*

***milch-kine.** (The singular, *milch-cow*, is very rare.) Applied by gaolers to their prisoners, who, when they 'bleed' freely, will 'have some Favour, or be at large', B.E.: c.: late C. 17–early 19.

mild, draw it. See **draw it mild.**—**mild-bloater.** See **bloater.**

mildewed. Pitted with smallpox: euphemistic (— 1923) for *poxed*. Manchon.—2. A synonym of *measly* and *mouldy*, qq.v.: from ca. 1920; ob. Ibid.

mile. (With a plural numeral) miles: late C. 13–20: S.E. till C. 19: ca. 1800–50, coll.: since ca. 1850, dial. and low coll. Dickens, 1850, 'I'd go ten thousand mile.' O.E.D.

mile of an oak, within a. Near enough; somewhere (derisively): late C. 16–18: coll.; sometimes a c.p. Porter, 1599, 'Where be your tools ? . . . Within a mile of an oak, sir'; Aphra Behn; D'Urfey, 'Your worship can tell within a mile of an oak where he is'; Swift. (Apperson.)

***miler.** Also *myla*. A donkey: vagabond c.: from ca. 1850. Ex Romany *meila*, occ. *moila*, prob. ex dial. *moil, moyle*, a mule, and perhaps ultimately ex L. *mulus*. Cf. Romany *Meilesto-gav*, lit. donkey's town, i.e. Doncaster. (Smart & Crofton.)—2. A man or a horse specially trained or qualified for a mile race: sporting: from ca. 1886. Baumann.—3. *-miler.* A journey, esp. a walk, of a stated number of miles: coll.: 1856, Dickens, 'I went out this morning for a 12-miler' (O.E.D. Sup.).

Miles's boy. See **Ralph.** ('Jon Bee', 1823.)

milestone. A yokel, a country booby: low

(? orig. c.): from ca. 1810; ob. by 1890, † by 1910. Vaux, 1812. Cf. *milestone-monger.*

milestone, let run a. To cause a die to run some distance: gaming: 1680, Cotton; † by 1800.

***milestone-inspector.** A professional tramp: tramps' c. (— 1932). Frank Jennings, *Tramping with Tramps.* Ex:

milestone-monger. A tramp: coll.: from ca. 1860; ob. Cf. *milestone*, q.v.

milikers. Militia: low London: 1870; ob. Ware. By slovenly slurring.

military. Porter (the drink): taverns': ca. 1885–1900. Ware. Ex its strength.

milk. Sexual 'spendings': low coll.: from ca. 1660; ob. John Aubrey. Cf. *milk, v.,* 1.—2. A milksop: proletarian (— 1887). Baumann.

milk, v. To cause sexual ejaculation: low coll. bordering on S.E.: C. 17–20; ob. Jonson, in *The Alchemist*; D'Urfey.—2. To bet against one's own horse knowing that it cannot win; to keep (a horse) a favourite at short odds when he has no chance or may even be scratched: sporting: ca. 1860–95.—3. To obtain possession, or sight, of by trickery or artifice: from ca. 1860: coll. till ca. 1910, then S.E. E.g. *milk a telegram*, to see it before the addressee does. Prescott, *Electrical Inventions*, 1860, '. . . a wire could be milked without being cut or put out of circuit.'—4. V.i., to withdraw part of one's winnings before a session is finished: gamblers': from not later than 1923. O.E.D. (Sup.). Ex the S.E. sense in 'That cow milks well.'

milk, Bristol. See **Bristol milk.**

milk, cry over spilt. See **spilt milk.**

milk, give down one's. To pay: coll. almost S.E.: ca. 1590–1800. Marlowe, L'Estrange.

milk and water ! 'Both ends of the busk !': a late C. 18–early 19 toast. Grose, 3rd ed.

milk boiled over, (e.g.) his. (E.g.) he was careless: proverbial coll.: ca. 1730–1800. 'Proverbial' Fuller. (Occ. in other persons but rarely in other tenses.)

milk-bottle. A baby: lower classes' (— 1909). Ware.

milk-fever. See **pencil-fever.**

milk-hole. 'The hole formed by the *roush* (q.v.) under a *pot* (q.v.)': Winchester College (— 1896); ob. F. & H.

milk, hot. See **hot milk.**

milk in the coco-nut, no. Silly; mentally deranged: low: from ca. 1850; ob. Cf. the U.S. *account for the milk in the coconut*, to solve a puzzle (1853, says Thornton).

milk-jug or -pan ; also **milking-pail.** The female pudend: low: C. 18–20; ob. Ex *milk, n.,* 1.

milk off one's liver, wash the. To rid oneself of cowardice: coll.: C. 17–mid-18. Cotgrave.

milk over the fence. To steal milk from neighbours' cows: from ca. 1870. Gen. as vbl.n. phrase, *milking over . . .* *The Milk Journal*, Sept., 1871.

milk-shop or **-walk.** The female breasts: low: C. 19–20; ob. Cf. *milky way*, q.v.

milk the pigeon. To attempt an impossibility: coll.: mid-C. 18–20; ob. Grose, 1st ed. The corresponding S.E. phrases are *milk the bull* or *the ram.*

milk-woman. A wet-nurse: Scots coll.: C. 19–20. Hence, *green m.-w.*, one recently delivered.—2. A female masturbator: low: C. 19–20; ob.

***milken.** A variant of *mill-ken*, q.v. ('Ducange Anglicus.')

milker. An interceptor of telegrams : from ca. 1865 : coll. Ex *milk*, v., 3.—2. The female pudend (cf. *milk-jug*) : low : C. 19–20.—3. A masturbator : low : C. 19–20 ; ob.

milker's calf. A mother's child, esp. if a boy : Australian rural (— 1888) ; ob. 'Rolf Boldrewood'. Ex standard sense, a calf still with the cow.

milking. Vbl.n. of *milk*, v., 2, q.v. *The Times*, Jan. 2, 1862.

milking-pail. See milk-jug.

milking-pail, carry or work the. Racings : ca. 1860–95. For meaning, see milk, v., 2.

milkman. (Cf. *milker*, 2. ; *milk-woman*, 2.) A masturbator : low : C. 19–20 ; ob.

milks ; Milwaukees ; Pauls. Shares in the Chicago, Milwaukee and St. Paul Railroad : Stock Exchange (— 1895) : resp. s., coll > (by 1910) j., and s. > (by 1900) coll. Wilson's *Stock Exchange Glossary*.

milky. A milkman : non-aristocratic coll. (— 1887). Baumann. Cf. *postie*.

*milky, adj. White : C. 19–20 (ob.) c. Only in *milky duds*, white clothes (see duds) and *m. ones*, white linen rags. Brandon (*m. ones*) ; H., 1st ed. (*m. ones*).—2. Cowardly ; *turn milky*, to become afraid : c. : C. 20. James Curtis, *The Gilt Kid*, 1936. Ex fear-caused pallor.

milky way. The female bosom : from ca. 1620 : poetical S.E. till ca. 1800, after which it rapidly > low s. : ob. Cf. *milk* (*-shop* or) *-walk*.

mill. A chisel : c. : ca. 1605–1830. Dekker, Grose.—2. Hence (?), a housebreaking thief : C. 17 : c. Dekker. ? abbr. *mill-ken* (q.v.), recorded much later.—3. The female pudend : C. 18–20 ; ob. : ? low coll. (or perhaps s.) or euphemistic S.E. D'Urfey.—4. A fight, esp. with the fists : from ca. 1819 : s. >, ca. 1860, coll. >, ca. 1890, S.E. (T.) Moore, in *Tom Crib's Memorial* ; 1825, Westmacott ; T. Hughes, 'A good hearty mill'. ? ex *windmill* or ex the v.—5. See mill, go through the, 2. —6. The treadmill : c. : 1842, Barham ; † by 1910. —7. A prison : c. : 1838, Dickens ; Mayhew, 'A month at the mill '.

*mill, v. To rob (a building) : c. of ca. 1565–1840. Until C. 17, only in *mill a ken* (see ken). Harman.—2. To steal (v.t. and i.) : c. : C. 17–early 19. Middleton & Dekker ; Jonson, 1621, ' Can they cant or mill ? '—3. To beat, thrash, punch, pummel : C. 18–20 (ob.) : orig. c. ; by C. 19, low s. (Cf. *mill . . . glaze*, q.v.). Hence v.i., to box, fight (occ. *mill away*) : C. 19–20, ob. ; as in Thackeray. Also v.t., to fight with (a person) : at Public Schools, esp. Harrow : from ca. 1860 (?). Arnold Lunn, 1913.—4. To kill : c. : from late C. 17, † by 1920. B.E., Dyche, Grose. (N.b., senses 3 and 4 derive ex sense 1, which connotes ' break in(to) ' or ' through ', 'knock out ').—5. To send to the treadmill, hence to prison : c. : ca. 1838–1910. Dickens, in *Oliver Twist*. Cf. *lag*, v., q.v.—6. See mill . . . glaze.—7. (Ex sense 3.) Esp. *mill the bowling*, to wear it down : cricketers' : 1833, Nyren, ; ob. (Lewis.)

mill, go or pass through the. To have (severe) experience : S.E.—2. Hence, to go through the bankruptcy court : coll. or s. : from ca. 1840 ; ob. —3. To go to prison : c. (— 1889). *The Daily News*, July 4, 1889.

mill, safe as a thief in a. Not safe or honest at all : coll. : ca. 1660–1780. With allusion to ' a Miller, who is a Thief by his Trade ', B.E.

*mill a quod. To break out of gaol : c. (—1753) ; † by 1890. Poulter.

mill-clapper. The tongue, esp. of women : late C. 17–20, ob. : coll. B.E.

*mill doll or M.D. A prison : ca. 1780–1830 : c. Messink, Bee.—2. According to Vaux, 1812, it is ' an obsolete name for Bridewell house of correction, in Bridge-street, Blackfriars, London '.

*mill doll, v. To beat hemp in prison : c. : ca. 1750–1840. Fielding. Also *mill dolly*, recorded in 1714 in Smith's *Lives of the Highwaymen*. (O.E.D.)

*mill . . . glaze. While *m. a* or *the glaze* is to break open a, the window (late C. 17–mid-18, B.E.), *m. one's g.* is to knock out his eye (C. 18–early 19, Grose) : both are c.

*mill-ken. A housebreaker : c. : ca. 1669–1870. *The Nicker Nicked* ; Fielding. (O.E.D.) See mill, v., 1, and mill, n., 2. Cf. :

*mill-lay. Burglary : c. : ca. 1780–1870. Grose, 2nd ed. Ex *mill*, n., 2.

[mill-pond. The Atlantic, esp. the part traversed by ships going from England to Canada and the U.S. : jocular S.E. bordering on coll. : 1885, Grant Allen. O.E.D.]

*mill-tag, -tog, -tug, -twig. A shirt : c. : resp. from ca. 1850 (Mayhew), 1835 (Brandon), 1745 (B. C. Carew), and 1820 (Haggart, Egan : Scots c.) : all these are ob. Perhaps ex *mill*, n., 6. Cf. *camesa* and *mish*, qq.v.

mill-wash. Canvas for lining of waistcoats and coats : tailors' : from ca. 1860 ; ob.

miller. A murderer : late C. 17–early 19 : c. B.E. Ex *mill*, v., 4.—2. A boxer : 1812, *The Sporting Magazine* (O.E.D.) ; 1823, Bee ; ob. by 1890, † by 1920. Ex *mill*, v., 3.—3. A vicious horse : 1825, Westmacott : sporting : † by 1890. Ex senses 1 and 2.—4. A ' Joe Miller ', q.v. H., 3rd ed., 1864.—5. A white hat : coaching : ca. 1830–80. Ex the whiteness of flour.

miller (also †miller's thumb), drown the. To add too much water, esp. to flour or to spirits : coll. : from ca. 1815 ; in C. 20, rare except in dial. Also *put out the miller's thumb*, 1767, and *put out the miller's eye*, 1678, Ray, and 1834, Esther Copley (O.E.D.).—2. (Only *drown the miller*.) To go bankrupt : Scots coll. : ca. 1800–80. A. Scott, 1805.

miller, give (one) the. To pelt with flour, etc., in thin paper bags, which naturally burst immediately on contact : coll. (— 1864) ; ob. H., 3rd ed. ; Hindley.

miller's daughter. Water (n.) : rhyming s. : late C. 19–20. B. & P.

miller's eye. (See miller, drown the, 1.) A lump of flour in a loaf : coll. : from ca. 1830 ; ob.

miller's mare, like a. Clumsily : C. 17 : coll., semi-proverbial. Beaumont & Fletcher ; Killigrew. A miller being no trainer of good horses. (Apperson.)

miller's waistcoat (that takes a thief by the neck every day), as stout as a. A C. 18–early 19 c.p., which glosses the proverb *many a miller many a thief* and that of miller, tailor and weaver in a bag. (Apperson.)

milliner's shop. The female pudend : low : from ca. 1840 ; ob.

milling. A beating, a thrashing : 1810, Combe, ' One blood gives t'other a milling ' ; ob.—2. A fight ; fighting : 1815, *The Sporting Magazine* (O.E.D.) ; Moore ; ob.—3. Robbery ; theft : c. : ca. 1565–1840. Harman. (For the origin of these three senses, see mill, v., resp. 3, 3, 2 or 1).—4. (Of horses) kicking : sporting (—1897) ; † (O.E.D.). Cf. *miller*, 3.

milling, adj. Fighting, pugilistic : from ca. 1810; ob As in :

milling-cove. A pugilist : low : ca. 1810–1905. Vaux, Ainsworth. And in :

milling-match. A prize-fight ; boxing-match : sporting : 1819, Moore ; † by 1920.

million to a bit of dirt, (it's) a. (It's) a sure bet : sporting : from ca. 1860 ; ob. Ware.

Mills spud. A Mills grenade : jocular military : 1916 ; ob. F. & Gibbons. Ex its shape, not unlike that of a large and knobbly potato.

millstone, look or see through a. To be very perceptive or well-informed or shrewd of judgement : from ca. 1530 : coll. till C. 18, then S.E. Occ. *see into* (C. 16–17) ; occ. . . . *a brick wall* (C. 19–20). Often *see as far into a millstone as another* (Palsgrave, 1540). Apperson.

millstone (occ. **milestone** or **brick wall**), **run one's head against a.** To resist stupidly ; attempt the impossible : from ca. 1835 : coll. verging on S.E. In C. 20, only *brick wall*.

millstones, one's eyes drop ; weep m. Applied to one unlikely to weep : late C. 16–17 : coll. 1594, Shakespeare, 'Your eyes drop millstones when fools' eyes drop tears.'

milt. The semen. Hence *milt-market* or *-shop*, the female pudend ; *double one's milt*, to ejaculate twice without withdrawal. Low : C. 19.

milton. An oyster ; coll. : 1841, Thackeray, Aytoun & Martin, 'These mute inglorious miltons are divine', which offers a clue to the semantics : cf. the S.E. phrase, *close as an oyster*.

*milvad. A blow : Scots c. : 1821, Haggart ; † by 1900. Hence *milvader*, to strike. Origin ?

*milvadering, n. Boxing : Scots c. : 1821, Haggart ; † by 1910. Ex preceding. Perhaps cf. the dial. *mulvather*, to confuse or bamboozle.

Milwaukees. See **milks.**

mim. A low coll. variant, C. 19–20, of *ma'am*, q.v. Cf. *mem, mum*.

mim ! Excuse me laughing ! ; you make me laugh ! : telegraphists' : C. 20. Ex code.

mimpins. Some kind of pretty sweetmeat : schoolboys' : 1820 ; long †. Leigh Hunt. O.E.D.

mince. An abbr. of *mince-pie* (see **mince-pies**) : late C. 19–20, esp. in boxing ; ob.

mince, v.t. and i. To dissect : medical students' : from ca. 1840.

mince-pies. Eyes : rhyming s. (— 1857). 'Ducange Anglicus.' Later, occ. † *mutton-pies*.

minchin malacho (or **maleego**). See **miching malicho.**

*mind. To be at hand to help (a crook) : c. : C. 20. E.g. in Edgar Wallace's *Room 13*. Cf. *minder*, 2.

mind ! Note what I say ! : coll. : 1806, J. Beresford, 'So I bar Latin, mind !' O.E.D.

mind, if you don't. If you're not careful (to avoid . . .) : coll. : from ca. 1835. M. P. R. James, 1839, 'They'll see you, if you don't mind.' O.E.D.

mind, I'm a good. I have a good mind (to do . . .), i.e. I think of (doing . . .) : sol. : C. 19–20. Surtees, 1852. Ex confusion with *I've a* . . . (O.E.D.)

mind !, never. Don't let that trouble you ! ; mind your own business ! : coll. : ca. 1814, anon. in *Gonzanga*, 'Never mind, father, don't be obstreperous about it.' O.E.D.

mind one's book. (Of a schoolboy) to be diligent in one's studies : coll. : from ca. 1710 ; ob. Addison, 'Bidding him be a good child and mind his book '. O.E.D.

mind the grease ! Let me pass, please ! : lower classes', presumably rhyming s. (— 1909). Ware.

mind the step ! See **step !, mind the.**

mind to, have a. To be disposed (to do something). With the infinitive suppressed, it is coll. : from ca. 1850. Mrs. Stowe, 'I don't need to hire . . . my hands out, unless I've a mind to.' Prob. ex such sentences as 'enquire what thou hast a mind to ', 1671. O.E.D.

mind your eye ! Be careful ! : coll. : 1737, Bracken (O.E.D.). Cf. :

mind your helm ! Take care : nautical : C. 19–20. Cf. preceding.

mind your P's and Q's. See **P's and Q's.**

Minden Boys. The 20th Foot Regiment, since ca. 1881 the Lancashire Fusiliers : military : latter C. 18–20 ; ob. Ex their bravery at the battle of Minden, 1759. (F. & Gibbons.)

minder. A child left to be taken care of : 1865, Dickens : coll. till ca. 1890, then S.E. (O.E.D.).— 2. A pickpocket's assistant ; one who 'minds' as in **mind*, q.v. : c. : C. 20. Edgar Wallace, resp. *The Flying Squad* and *Room 13*.

mindjer ; mindyer. Mind you : the former is even more illiterate than the latter : C. 19–20. Baumann.

mine arse. See **bandbox.**

Mine-Bumpers, the. The Third Battle Squadron : naval : 1915–18. Bowen.

mine in a Portuguee pig-knot. 'Confused, not knowing where to begin a yarn ' : nautical : late C. 19–20. Bowen. The key is in *yarn*.

mine-jobber. A swindler : City coll. : from ca. 1880. Ware. Ex the frequent flotation of worthless companies.

mine uncle('s). See **uncle.**

mine's. Mine **is** : coll. : C. 19–20. E.g. 'Mine's a gin.'

minge. Female society : military : 1915–18. F. & Gibbons. After *binge*, n. (q.v.), ex Suffolk *minge* (the female pudend), itself ex the E. Anglian v. *minge* (E.D.D.).—2. In c., the female pudend : late C. 19–20. James Curtis, *The Gilt Kid*, 1936. Ex Romany, as is the Suffolk dial. word.

mingle. An official meeting of officers and nurses in hospital : Army officers' coll. : 1915–18. F. & Gibbons.

mingy. Miserly, mean ; hence (from not later than 1915) disappointingly small : coll. Thinned ex *mangy* (W.) and prob. influenced by *stingy*. App. first 'lexicographed ' by W., 1920, but (as 'mean ') definitely remembered by the author at least as early as 1910.

minikin, tickle (the). To play the lute or viol : coll. : ca. 1600–40, mostly by the dramatists with a sexual innuendo (*minikin*, an endearment for a female). Marston (?), 'When I was a young man and could tickle the minikin . . . I had the best stroke, the sweetest touch, but now . . . I am fallen from the fiddle, and betook me to [the pipe].' O.E.D.

ministering angel. A sister of Queen Mary's Nursing Service : naval : 1914–18. F. & Gibbons. Cf. *mark one*, q.v.

minnie. A German trench-mortar : from 1915 : military.—2. Hence, the projectile it propels : from not later than March, 1916. Ex Ger. *minenwerfer*, lit. a mine-thrower. See B. & P.

Minnie P. play. A play in which a little-maid variety-actress has the chief part : theatrical coll. : 1885–ca. 1900. Ware, ' From Miss Minnie Palmer's creations, chiefly in *My Sweetheart* '.

Minnie's husband. See **Carl the caretaker.** Ex *minnie*, q.v.

minnywoffer. A variant, perhaps rather the orig., of *minnie*, both senses ; rare after 1916.

minor. A water-closet, says F. & H., referring to Grose, 1785 : the term is in no edition of Grose : F. prob. telescoped *mine uncle's* (Grose, 1st ed.) and *minor clergy* (Grose, 2nd ed.).—2. A younger brother : schools' (orig. and esp. Eton) : 1863, Hemyng, *Eton School Days*, ' " Let my minor pass, you fellows ! " exclaimed Horsham.' See also ' **major and minor** '.

minor clergy. Young chimney-sweeps : ca. 1787–1900. Grose, 2nd ed.

mint. While *mint of money* is prob. to be considered S.E., *mint* (money), which dates from C. 8, is S.E. till ca. 1550, coll. till ca. 1850, then low s. Harman, Jonson, Grose. In C. 19–20, gen. *mint-sauce*, q.v.—2. Gold : mid-C. 17–18 c. Coles ; B.E. ; Grose.

mint, adj. Absolutely as new ; clean and with leaves uncut : esp. in *a mint copy* : booksellers' s. (– 1927) >, ca. 1932, j.

mint-hog. An Irish shilling : Anglo-Irish : low : C. 19–20 ; ob.

mint-sauce. Money : from ca. 1825 ; ob. : low. Egan ; J. Greenwood, 1867, ' The requisite mint sauce (as that horribly slangy and vulgar B.P. terms money).' The corresponding U.S. term (now ob.) : *mint-drops* (1837, J. Quincy Adams ; prob. earlier). Thornton. See **mint,** n., 1.

minus. (Predicatively) without ; short of : coll. : 1813. (Baumann, however, dates it from mid-C. 18.) As in ' *minus* one horse ', 1840, or ' He was considerably minus at the last Newmarket meeting ' (1813). Rarely † *minus of*. O.E.D.—2. As an adj., lacking, non-existent : from ca. 1850 : coll. Bristed, 1852, ' His mathematics are decidedly *minus*.' O.E.D.

miracle. A corrupt form of *merel*, a game : C. 17–18. (O.E.D.)

miraculous. (Very) drunk : Scottish (– 1920). Perhaps abbr. *in miraculous high spirits*. E.D.D.

mis. A variant of *miss*, q.v. Manchon.

mischief, ruin or a mischievous person, is S.E., but *the mischief*, the devil, is coll. : 1583, Hollyband, ' What the mischief is this . . . ? ' ; Beaumont & Fletcher, ca. 1616, ' In the name of mischief . . .' O.E.D. (But *with a mischief* is S.E.).

mischief, go to the. To go to the bad : coll. : 1818, Susan Ferrier, ' Boys may go to the mischief, and be good for something—if girls go, they're good for nothing I know of.'

mischief, load of. A wife : C. 18–early 19 : coll. bordering on S.E. Grose, ' A man loaded with mischief, . . . with his wife on his back '. Revived by Ashley Dukes in 1924–5.

mischief, play the. (V.t., with.) To play havoc : coll. : 1867, Trollope, ' That butcher . . . was playing the mischief with him.' O.E.D.

mischievious. Mischievous : a frequent sol. : (?) C. 17–20. Ex C. 15–17 stressing of 2nd syllable.

misegun. Mazagan (a kind of bean) : low coll. or a sol. : C. 19–20. Scott. O.E.D.

miserable as a bandicoot. An Australian coll. synonym (C. 20) of :

miserable as a rat in a tar-barrel. Thoroughly depressed : nautical coll. : late C. 19–20. Bowen.

miserables, the. A splitting headache after ' the night before ' : proletarian coll. (– 1887) ; ob. Baumann.

misery. Gin : low : ca. 1820–1910.—2. (In cards) misère : coll. : from ca. 1830.—3. (**Misery.**) H.M. Cruiser *Mersey* : naval : C. 20. Bowen, ' A brute of a ship to handle '.

misery, streak of. See **streak of misery.**

misery-bowl. ' Relief-basin—at sea ' : tourists' (– 1909) ; slightly ob. Ware.

Misery Junction. ' The angle forming the southwest corner of the York and Waterloo Roads . . . From the daily meeting here of music hall " pros " who are out of engagements, and who are in this neighbourhood for the purpose of calling on their agents, half a dozen of whom live within hail ' (Ware) : theatrical : ca. 1880–1914.

misfit. A clumsy man : tailors' : from ca. 1850.

misfortune, have or **meet with a.** To give birth to an illegitimate child : coll. and dial. : C. 19–20. Mrs. Carlyle, Marryat. Hence, *misfortune*, a bastard : from ca. 1860. Carlyle. O.E.D.

***mish.** A shirt ; a chemise : c. : from ca. 1670 ; † by 1870. Head ; Grose. Abbr. *commission* (q.v.), the anglicised form of *camesa*, q.v.—2. Mission : Public Schools' : C. 20. (Arnold Lunn, *The Harrovians*, 1913.)

***mish-topper.** A coat ; a petticoat : ca. 1670–1850 : c. Coles, 1676 ; B.E. ; Grose. Lit., that which ' tops ' or goes over a ' mish ' (q.v.).

misle. See **mizzle.**

Misleading Paper, the. *The Times* : a nickname : 1876–ca. 1890. Ware, ' Given . . . when it began to lose its distinctive feature as the " leading paper " in Liberal policy '.

misli. See **mizzle.**

miss ; more correctly **mis.** A miscarriage : women's (– 1923). Manchon.

miss, give (e.g. **it**) **a.** To avoid doing something or seeing some person or thing ; cease doing something : coll. : from ca. 1912. Ex billiards, *give a miss in balk* (' avoid hitting the object ball ', S.O.D.), itself often used in the same way. P. G. Wodehouse, 1907, ' And James . . . is giving this the miss in baulk ! '

miss a tip. To have a fall : circus-men's : mid-C. 19–20. Seago. See also **tip,** n.

Miss Adams is an occ. variant of *sweet Fanny Adams* (see **Fanny Adams**).

Miss Brown. The female pudend : low : late C. 18–19. Grose, 3rd ed. Cf. *brown madam*, q.v., and *Miss Laycock*, q.v.

miss is as good as a mile, a. A narrow escape serves as well as an easy one ; ' a failure by however little is still a failure ' ; proverbial coll. : from ca. 1820. Scott. Earlier, *an inch in a miss is as good as an ell*.

Miss Laycock. The female pudend : low : late C. 18–19. Grose, 2nd ed. Cf. *Miss Brown*.

Miss Molly. See **molly.**

Miss Nancy. An effeminate man : coll. from ca. 1880. Baumann. Ex dial. (– 1824). Also *Nancy*. Hence, *Miss-Nancyism*, effeminacy : from ca. 1885. Cf. *cissy* or *sissy*.

miss of, feel the. To feel the lack or the loss of : from ca. 1855 : S.E. till ca. 1880, then (low) coll. George Eliot, 1860 ; Baumann, 1887 ; ' Rita ', 1901, ' 'Tis now you'll feel the miss o' your mother.' O.E.D.

miss of, find or **have** (a). (The *miss* often preceded by *great, heavy, little, no*.) To feel regret at, or the disadvantage of, the loss or absence of some person or thing : C. 13–20 : S.E. till C. 19, then coll. (from ca. 1880, low) and dial. Anna Seward. O.E.D.

miss of, there is no (great). There is no (great) regret or disadvantage in the loss, privation, or absence of some person or thing : C. 14–20 : S.E. till ca. 1820 ; then dial. and coll. (increasingly low), the latter being ob. O.E.D.

miss one's guess. To be mistaken : Canadian coll. : C. 20. (John Beames.) Ex U.S.

miss one's tip. See **tip.**—**Miss Right.** See **Right.** [See **Right, Mr.**—] **miss the bus.** See **bus.** Also **boat.**—**miss the cushion.** See **cushion.**

missafic. Incorrect for † *missific* : C. 17. O.E.D.—**misshit** or **miss-hit.** Incorrect for *mishit* : late C. 19–20. O.E.D. (Sup.).

missioning. Mission-work : coll. (— 1887), now almost S.E. Baumann.

missis ; gen. missus. (Occ. written as *Mrs.*, and always occurring as either *the missus* or, less gen., *my, your, his*, etc., *missus*.) A wife : orig. (— 1839), dial. >, ca. 1847, low coll. Thackeray, 1848, ' Bowing to the superior knowledge of his little Missis '.—2. (Among servants) a mistress of the house : low coll. : 1837, Dickens. In this sense, often without *the, my*, etc. (O.E.D.for dates.)

missle. See **mizzle.**

[Misspelling :—A few of the commonest examples involving confusion or implying a wrong origin are given *passim* in these pages : I owe most of these to the O.E.D., esp. in the matter of learned or technical words—see, notably, the latter end of *H*.]

missuses. The pl. of *missis* (q.v.), *missus*. Baumann.

missy. (In address.) Miss : coll. : C. 19–20. More gen. in U.S. than in England.

mist, Scotch. See **Scotch mist.**

mistake, and no. Undoubtedly ; for certain : coll. : 1818, Lady Morgan, ' He is the real thing, and no mistake ' ; Thackeray. (O.E.D.) Also *and no error* (— 1887), as in Baumann.

mister. In address with the name omitted : mid-C. 18–20 : S.E. (= *sir*) until ca. 1820 ; then coll. ; by 1860, low coll. *Punch*, Jan. 22, 1901, ' Please, mister, when are we going to get through ? ' O.E.D.

mistook. Mistaken : S.E. until ca. 1850, then coll. ; in C. 20, a sol.

mistress roper, or with capitals. A marine : ca. 1840–95. Because he is clumsy with ropes : ? punning *miss the ropes* (a *miss-the-roper*).

mit. See **mitt.**

Mitcham whisper. A shout ; almost a shout : 1880, Spurgeon, *Ploughman's Pictures* : coll. Cf. *Irish whisper*, a very audible whisper. At Leigh (in Lancashire), a *Leigh whisper* is an unearthly yell. Apperson.

mitching. vbl.n. Playing truant : Canadian coll. : mid-C. 19–20. Ex Eng. dial. : see E.D.D.

mite ; occ. in C. 19–20, **mitey.** A cheesemonger : 1765, Foote, ' Miss Cicely Mite, the only daughter of old Mite the cheesemonger ' ; ob.—2. A particle, a tiny bit : C. 17–20 : S.E. till ca. 1840, then coll. (increasingly low).—3. A whit or a jot : late C. 14–20 : S.E. till mid-C. 19, then coll. C. D. Warner, 1886, ' Not a mite of good ' (O.E.D.).

mitey. See **mite,** 1.

*mitney. A policeman : c. (— 1923). Manchon.

Origin ? Perhaps ex *mittimus*, 2 or 3, or ex an unrecorded *mitteny* (adj. to *mittens*, fists).

mitre. A hat : universities' (— 1896) ; ob.

mitt ; in C. 20, occ. **mit.** A glove : from ca. 1811 ; ob. Vaux. Ex first sense of *mitten*.—2. (Gen. **the mitt.**) Hand-work, work by hand : tailors' : C. 20. Ex *mitten*, 1.

mitt, the frozen. The cold shoulder : C. 20. F. & Gibbons. See **mitten, get the.**

mitten. A hand ; a fist : low (mostly pugilistic) : from ca. 1810 ; ob. Vaux.—2. A boxing glove : ? orig. (— 1859), U.S. ; anglicised ca. 1880. H., 1st ed. ; J. Greenwood.—3. See **mittens.**

mitten, get or **give the.** (In U.S., occ. simply *mitten* for *give the mitten to*.) To be jilted or to jilt : *get the m*., orig. (1838), U.S., but anglicised ca. 1870, also meaning to be dismissed ; *give the m*., orig. (1848), U.S., and anglicised ca. 1870, with further sense, to dismiss. Both slightly ob. Prob. ex *mittimus* (q.v.) with allusion to *mitten*.

*mittens. (Very rare in singular.) Handcuffs : c. (— 1933). Charles E. Leach, *On Top of the Underworld*.

mittens, easy as, adj. Free in speech and/or manner ; free and easy : low (s. bordering on coll.) : from ca. 1890 ; ob. Mostly London. Milliken.

mittens, handle without. To handle roughly : coll. soon > S.E. : from ca. 1675 ; ob. Ray, Johnson. In late C. 19–20, gen. *handle without gloves* or *with the gloves off*.

mittimus. A dismissal from one's post, as in *get one's m*., which also means to receive one's ' quietus ', q.v. Coll. : from late C. 16. Nashe, ' Out of two noblemen's houses he had his mittimus of ye may be gone.' (O.E.D.)—2. As a magistrate, it is jocular S.E. rather than coll. (C. 17–18). The L. *mittimus*, we send.—3. The v., ' commit to jail by a warrant ' (O.E.D.) is jocular S.E.

mivvy. A woman ; a lunatic : low (— 1923). Manchon. Perhaps a perversion of *miffy*, n., or possibly the adj.

mix. A mess, a muddle ; a state of confusion : coll. : from ca. 1880. Cf. *mix-up*.

mix 'em. See **mixum.**

mix (C. 19) or **join** (late C. 18–19) **giblets.** To marry : low. ' Jon Bee.'

mix it. To fight vigorously : Australian (— 1916) >, by 1918, gen. and, by 1936, coll. C. J. Dennis. Cf. U.S. *mix-in*, a fight.

mix it up. See **mix up,** v.

mix-metal. A silversmith : late C. 18–mid-19 : coll. Grose, 1st ed.

mix them. To mix one's bowling : cricketers' coll. : from mid-1890's. Lewis.

mix-up. Confusion ; a mess, a muddle : coll. : from ca. 1895. Cf. *mix*.—2. A fight, esp. a general scrimmage : C. 20. Cf. *mix it*, q.v.

mix up, v. Mainly as *mix it up*, ' to agree secretly how the parties shall make up a tale, or colour a transaction in order to cheat or deceive another party ', Bee : ca. 1820–95.

mixed. Confused, bewildered : coll. : from ca. 1870. *Punch*, Sept. 4, 1880, ' Rather mixed after twenty-one hours' continuous sitting '.—2. Slightly drunk : low coll. : from ca. 1871 ; ob. *Leeds Mercury*, Aug. 29, 1872.

mixer ; good mixer. A sociable person ; one who gets on well with others : U.S. (resp. early C. 20 and late C. 19), anglicised ca. 1924 : coll. >, by 1933, S.E. Somerset Maugham, 1925, *good mixer*. (The opp. is *bad mixer*.) O.E.D. (Sup.).

mixum ; occ. **mix 'em**. An apothecary : coll. : ca. 1630–1720. Glapthorne, ' Mr. Mixum, your apothecary '.

*mizzard. The mouth : c. : from ca. 1890 ; ob. P. H. Emerson. Corruption of *mazzard*, q.v.

*mizzle or **mis(s)le** ; occ. † *misli*. To decamp ; depart slyly : orig. (ca. 1780), c. >, ca. 1820, low s. G. Parker, ' He preferred mizzling off to France.' Ex Shelta *misli*.

mizzle, do a. (As n., *mizzle* does not otherwise occur.) To decamp : low : from ca. 1850. Ex preceding ; cf. the next two entries.

mizzled. Tipsy : low (— 1923). Manchon's definition in Fr. s. is illuminating : *parti pour la gloire.*

*mizzler. A fugitive ; one who departs slyly : orig. (— 1834), c. >, ca. 1840, low s. Ainsworth. Hence, *rum mizzler*, one clever at getting away.

mo. A moment, esp. in *half a mo* : low coll. : late C. 19–20. Ware. Ex *moment*.—2. See **down the Lane.**—3. (Also **Mo.**) Medical officer : Army officers' in G.W. (E. Raymond, *The Jesting Army*, 1930. I.e. *M.O.* telescoped.)

mcab. A hat ; esp. the turban-shaped hat in feminine vogue, 1858–9 : university (mainly Cambridge) : ca. 1858–80. H., 3rd ed. Ex ' Moab is my washpot,' Psalms lx. 8 : the approximate shape. —2. A lavatory at : Winchester College : from ca. 1860 ; †. Mansfield.

Moabite. A bailiff : late C. 17–19. B.E. Cf. *Philistine*, q.v.

moach. See **mooch.**—**moak.** See **moke.**

moan. A complaint or grievance : naval : from not later than 1914. Bowen.

moan, v. To complain, grumble ; to do so habitually : naval : from not later than 1915. F. & Gibbons. Ex dial. Cf. the military *grouse.*

moan, do a. See **do a moan.**

mob. The rabble, the disorderly part of the population (1688). The populace, the crowd (1691). S. till ca. 1750 ; coll. ca. 1750–1820 ; then S.E. Burke, 1790, ' A mob (excuse the term, it is still in use here) which pulled down all our prisons ' ; T. Hale, 1691, ' the beliefs of the mob ', in the second sense. (O.E.D.) Cf. the C. 18–mid-19 proverb, ' The mob has many heads but no brains.' Abbr. *mobile*, q.v., itself a shortening of *mobile vulgus*, the fickle or excitable crowd.—2. A gang of criminals, esp. of thieves : orig. (1845 in ' *No. 747* ') c. > low by 1851 (Mayhew) ; as early as 1843 as *swell mob*, q.v. Prob. ex :—3. (Gen. in pl.) A companion in crime : c. (— 1839) ; † by 1890. Brandon ; H., 1st ed.—4. In Australia, a gang of roughs : late C. 19–20 : s. > coll. Ex :—5. A group or crowd of persons, esp. if possessing common interests : coll. >, in C. 20, S.E. : Australia, from ca. 1880. ' Rolf Boldrewood ' speaks, in 1884, of ' the " Dunmore mob ".' (N.B., mob as (part of) a herd, a flock, is ' standard ' Australian now recognised as S.E.) Morris.—6. In late C. 19–20, esp. in G.W., a military unit, esp. a battalion or a battery. (Not disrespectful.) S. rapidly > coll. (B. & P. ; F. & Gibbons.)—7. A harlot (cf. *mab*) : c. : 1665, Head ; 1697, N. Lee ; Grose. † by 1830. O.E.D.—8. A ' rag ' (concerted mischief) : Charterhouse : late C. 19–20.

mob, v. To crowd ; hustle ; attack in a disorderly mob : from early C. 18 : coll. till ca. 1800, then S.E. Ex *mob*, n., 1 and 2. (O.E.D.) Whence *mobbing*, q.v.—2. To ' rag ' : Charterhouse : late C. 19–20. Cf. *mob*, n., 8, and *mob up* and *mobbish*.

mob-handed. In a ' mob ' ; in a group : grafters' : C. 20. Philip Allingham, *Cheapjack*, 1934.

mob-up. To hustle (a person) : Charterhouse : ca. 1870–1910. A. H. Tod, *Charterhouse*, 1900. Cf. *mob*, v.

mob store. A mobilisation store : military coll. : 1915. F. & Gibbons.

mobbing, vbl.n. corresponding to *mob*, v., 1 : 1734, North (O.E.D.) : coll. > ca. 1800, S.E. H. Walpole, ' The night will be full of mobbing, bonfires, and lights '. (Perhaps the same holds of the adj. *mobbish*, late C. 17–20, ob.)

mobbish. Inclined for a ' rag ' : Charterhouse : C. 20. Ex *mob*, n., 8.

mobile. The rabble, the rough part of the population : 1676, Shadwell, ' Do you hear that noise ? the remaining rogues have raised the mobile.' (O.E.D.).—2. Whence, the populace : from ca. 1680. Shadwell, ' The mobile shall worship thee.' Both senses, orig. coll., were S.E. by 1700 ; ob. by 1830, † by 1850 except historically. Cf. *mob*, n., 1 and 2.

mobile, do a. To route-march in or into the desert : Egyptian-Front military : 1915–18. F. & Gibbons. Ex the *mobile column* of military j.

mobility. The low classes : 1690, B.E. and Dryden : s. till ca. 1750, coll. ca. 1750–1810, then S.E. ; ob. by 1840, † (except historically) by 1915. In *the Maccaroni and Theatrical Magazine*, Jan., 1773, appeared this notice :—' Pantheon's : the *Nobility's*, Oxford Road ; the *Mobility's*, Spawfields' (see Chancellor, *Pleasure Haunts of London*). Ex *mob*, n., 1, on *nobility*.

mobocracy. The rabble as a ruling body : 1754, Murphy (O.E.D.) : coll. till ca. 1810, then S.E. Ex *mob*, 1, and, though much less, 2. (Derivatives : S.E.)

*mobsman. A pickpocket : from ca. 1850 ; ob. Mayhew.—2. But orig. (ca. 1845), a member of the ' swell mob ' (q.v.), properly *swell mobsman* ; hence, any well-dressed swindler (— 1859). H., 1st ed.

moche. See **mooch.**

mocho. Mocha coffee : low (— 1887) ; ob. Baumann.

mock-duck or **-goose.** A piece of pork that, stripped of crackling, is baked with a stuffing of sage and onions : coll. : from ca. 1875. O.E.D.

*mock-litany man. A sing-song beggar : Anglo-Irish c. (— 1909). Ware.

mockered. Full of holes ; (of a face) pitted : low : from ca. 1850. Ex Romany *mockodo*, *mookeedo*, dirty, filthy (*moker*, to foul).

mocteroof, v.t. and i. To doctor damaged fruit or vegetables : Covent Garden : from ca. 1860 ; ob. E.g. chestnuts are shaken in a bag with beeswax (F. & H.). ? etymology. Perhaps a corruption of *new-proof.*

Model, the. Pentonville Prison : low : from ca. 1855 ; ob. Ex *model prison.*

model of, the (very). Some person or thing that very closely resembles another : orig. (— 1849) and still dial., > (of) coll. ca. 1890. Crockett. (E.D.D.)

[**Modern Babylon**, London, is S.E., as are **modest** (small), **mollycoddle** (v.) and **moddly-coddly**, **mollycoddish**, **mome**, **Mondayish**, **mondongo**, **money-bags** or **-grubber**, **monkey** (an endearment ; also the v.), **monkey-tricks**, **monkeyings**, **mons Veneris**, **montem**, **month**, **month's mind**, **moon** (a wig), **cry for the moon**, **level at the moon**, **moon-calf**, **moon-eyes**, **moonflaw**, **moonlight** (v.), **moon's minion**,

moonshine (unreality, a month, poached eggs and sauce), **moonshine** (adj.), **moonshiny, moony** (silly), **mop** (an endearment, a grimace, a fool), **mope** (n. and v.), **moped, moppet, mopsy, morning-star, morsel** and **dearest morsel, moss-rose, mossy cell** or **face** or **vale, mother** as hysteria and as term of address, **mother's son, mount** (to wear), **mount-falcon, mount of Venus, mounts of lilies, mouse** (an endearment ; to bite), **mousle, mouth** (v.) and **give mouth, mouth-glue, mouthing ; mundungus ; mollie, mop** (a statute fair), **mort** (large quantity or number), are dial :—all despite F. & H.]

modest quencher. A small drink : from ca. 1860 ; ob. : coll. H., 3rd ed.—2. Hence, in C. 20, ' an expensive drink or simply a drink of any kind ' (Lyell).

modestines. An incorrect form of *modestness* : ca. 1540–1640. O.E.D.

modicum. An edible thirst-relish : 1609, Dekker ; soon †. O.E.D.—2. The female pudend : low : ca. 1660–1840. Cotton. (Cf. † S.E. jocular sense, a woman : cf. *bit*, *piece*, qq.v.)

mods or **Mods.** The first public examination for B.A. degrees : Oxford University : coll. : 1858, J. C. Thomson, ' Between the ' ' little-go ' ' and ' ' mods ' ' he learns nothing new ' (O.E.D.). Ex *Moderations*.

modsman. A candidate for ' mods ' : Oxford coll. (— 1887). Baumann.

moey ; occ. **mooë(y).** The mouth : low : from ca. 1850 ; ob. H., 1st ed. (at *mooe*). Ex Romany *mooi*, mouth, face.—2. The female pudend : low : from ca. 1855 ; ob. H., 1st ed. (*mooe*).

moffling chete. See **muffling cheat.**

mofussil. Rather provincial ; countrified : from ca. 1840 : coll. >, ca. 1890, S.E. Ex the n., which (*the Mofussil*) is standard Anglo-Indian for the country districts or anywhere out of a capital city. Ex Hindustani. See esp. Yule & Burnell. Hence :

mofussilite. An inhabitant of a rural district : Anglo-Indian coll. : from ca. 1845. Ex preceding term.

mog. A cat : mainly schoolboys' : C. 20. Collinson. Perhaps ex dial. *moggy*, applied to various animals.—2. Hence, a cat's-skin tippet or other fur : racing s. or c. (— 1932). *Slang*, p. 247.

moggy. An untidily dressed woman : low : from ca. 1880 ; ob. (Also dial.) Ex dial. *moggy*, a calf, a cow (E.D.D.) : cf. the preceding.—2. A cat : Cockneys' (and dial.) : late C. 19–20.

mogue, v.t. and i ; n. To mislead ; joke, gammon : low and tailors' : 1870, Bell's *Life*, June 19. Whence *no mogue*, honestly, and *moguing*, n., gammon. ? cognate with *mug*, a fool.

moguey. A coll. corruption of Maori *moki* (or *mokihi*), a raft : mid-C. 19–20. Morris.

mohack. See **mohock.**

mohair. A civilian ; a tradesman : military : 1785, Grose ; ob. by 1870, † by 1890. Ex the mohair buttons worn by civilians ; soldiers have metal buttons.

Mohammed Ali. A regimental institute : coll. among regular soldiers in India : from ca. 1920. Such institutes are often supplied by a merchant so, or analogously, named.

mohawk, for *amuck* (a frenzied Malay), is catachrestic : C. 18–early 19. O.E.D.—2. See **mohock.**

mohican. A very heavy man that rides a long way in an omnibus for sixpence : ca. 1845–60. *Tait's Magazine*, 1848, 2nd Series, vol. XV.

mohock ; occ. **mohack** or **mohawk.** (Or with capitals.) An aristocratic ruffian night-infesting London, ca. 1710–15. From 1711 : coll. > S.E. ; ob. by 1760, except historically. Ex *Mohawk*, a member of a Red Indian tribe. Swift, ' A race of rakes, called the Mohocks, that play the devil about this town every night '.

moiety, a part, a share, is loose S.E.—2. A wife : coll. > S.E. : from ca. 1735 ; ob. Punning *better half*.

moira. A drink of any kind ; esp. beer : mostly New Zealanders' : in G.W. Ex Arabic.

moiré, n., for *moire*, is catachrestic : from ca. 1850. O.E.D.

moist one's clay. To drink : from ca. 1830. In C. 20, gen. *moisten* . . .

moist round the edges. Very slightly tipsy : rare : C. 20.

moisten, v.i. To drink : from ca. 1840 ; ob. Also *moisten one's chaffer* (— 1864) or *clay* (q.v.).

moke. An ass : s. and dial. : 1848, J. L. Tupper (O.E.D.) ; Thackeray. ? ex *moggy*, q.v., or perhaps Romany *moila*, an ass (cf. *miler*, q.v.), or rather ex Welsh Gypsy *moχio* or *-a*, a donkey : Sampson supports the third origin and notes that *moχio* existed at least 50 years before the first recorded instance of *moke* ; moreover, Brandon, in 1839, records *moak* as a c. word of Gypsy origin and, at that time, mainly Gypsy use. Cf. *mokus*.—2. A fool : orig. (1871), U.S. ; anglicised ca. 1890 ; ob.—3. A very inferior horse : Australia : 1888, ' Rolf Boldrewood ', ' I am regular shook on this old moke.' Cf. sense 1.—4. A variety artist that plays on several instruments : theatrical (— 1890). *Century Dict.*

Moke Train, the. The Army Service Corps : military : late C. 19–20. F. & Gibbons. Ex ' Military Train ', its title in 1857–70. Also, occ., *Muck Train*.

moko. A pheasant mistakenly shot before the shooting season : sportsmen's : from ca. 1860. H., 2nd ed. ? ex *moke*.—2. A variant (— 1923) of *mocho*. Manchon.

mokus. An occ. s. (ob.) and dial. variant of *moke*, 1, 3, qq.v. : mid-C. 19–20. Prob. ex *moke* + *-us*, a ' characteristic Romany termination of masculine loan-words ', Sampson.

molasses in winter, slow as. Exceedingly slow : coll. : late C. 19–20. Collinson. In winter, molasses is very stiff.

mole. The penis. Whence *mole-catcher*, the female pudend. Low : C. 19–20, ob.

molionet is an incorrect form of *molinet* : mid-C. 17–mid-18. O.E.D.

*****moll.** A harlot : C. 17–20 : c. >, ca. 1890, low. Middleton, ' None of these common molls neither, but discontented and unfortunate gentlewomen ' (O.E.D.). Ex the familiar form of *Mary*.—2. An unmarried female companion of a criminal or a tramp : c. : from ca. 1820. ' Jon Bee.' Cf the U.S. *gun moll*, a woman that carries a revolver for her ' man '.—3. A girl : from ca. 1835 : c. >, ca. 1860, low. Brandon. In U.S. c., *moll* is ' any woman, regardless of character or condition ', I. : so too, in C. 20, among English grafters (Allingham). —4. Hence, from ca. 1890, a sweetheart : low.

Moll(-)Blood. The gallows : Scots coll. : ca. 1810–50. Scott.

*****moll-buzzer.** A pickpocket specialising in women : c. : from ca. 1855. Perhaps orig. U.S. Whence *moll-buzzing*, this practice.

Moll Cutpurse. Mary Frith (d. 1649), notable pickpocket and the heroine of Dekker & Middleton's *The Roaring Girl*, 1611. (Dawson.)

moll-hunter. A man 'always lurking after women': low: late C. 19–20. Ware. See **moll**, 1 and 3.

moll Peatley's, or—prob. erroneously—**Pratley's, gig.** Copulation: C. 18–early 19: low. Budgell, in *The Spectator*, 'An impudent young dog bid the fiddlers play a dance called Moll Patley.' Ex *moll*, 1, perhaps allusively to some whore surnamed *Patley* or *Peatley*.

*****moll-sack.** A lady's hand-bag; occ. a small market basket: c.: from ca. 1838. Brandon; H., 1st ed.

moll-shop. A brothel: low: 1923, Manchon; but in use before G.W. Also *molly-shop*.

Moll Thompson's mark. 'M.T.' = empty. 'Empty packages are said to be so marked,' F. & H.: ca. 1780–1890. Grose, 1st ed.; H.

*****moll-tooler.** A female pickpocket: c.: from ca. 1858; ob. H., 1st ed.

*****moll-wire.** A pickpocket specialising in robbing women: c.: from ca. 1865; ob.

*****molled;** gen. **molled up.** Sleeping with a woman not one's wife: c.: 1851, Mayhew.—2. Accompanied by, esp. arm in arm with, a woman: low: from ca. 1860. Both senses ex *moll*, but resp. ex sense 1 (or 2) and sense 3.

*****mollesher;** more gen. **mollisher.** A—gen. a low —woman; a thief's mistress: c.: from ca. 1810; ob. Vaux (*-ish-*), Mayhew (*-esh-*). Ex *moll*, 1.

moll's three misfortunes, a. In the B.M. copy of the 1st ed., Grose has written: 'Broke the [chamber-]pot, bes—t the bed and cut her a–se.' But this low c.p. of ca. 1785–1820 was included in no ed. whatsoever.

molly. An effeminate man; a milksop: coll. >, in C. 20, S.E.: 1879, L. B. Walford (O.E.D.), though possibly existing a century earlier: the entry in Grose (1st ed.) is ambiguous. Ex *Miss Molly*, q.v.—2. A sodomite: coll.: 1709, E. Ward; ob. Cf. *pansy*. But ca. 1895–1914, a merely effeminate fellow was often called a *Gussie*; in C. 20, esp. after the G.W., a sodomite is a *nancy*, a *Nancy-boy*, or a *cissy* (*sissy*), this last also applying to a milksop.—3. A wench; a harlot: coll.: 1719, D'Urfey, 'Town follies and Cullies, And Molleys and Dollys, for ever adieu' Ob. (As a country lass, it is dial.) All ultimately ex *Mary*: cf. *moll*, q.v.

Molly, Miss. A milksop, an effeminate fellow: from ca. 1750; ob.: coll. >, ca. 1890, S.E. Grose. Cf. *molly*, all senses, and *Miss Nancy*, qq.v. (But *Miss Mollyism*, C. 19–20 (ob.), is S.E.)

molly-head. A simpleton: from ca. 1900; ob. ? orig. U.S. Ex *molly*, 1.

Molly Maguires. An Irish secret society that, ca. 1843, aimed to intimidate bailiffs and their like: app. not recorded before 1867 (W. S. Trench): coll. quickly > S.E. Ex their usually dressing in *women's* clothes and ex Connor Maguire, a noted C. 17 conspirator, says Dawson.

molly-mop. An effeminate man: coll.: 1829, Marryat; ob. Ex *molly*, 1. (O.E.D.)

[**molly-puff.** A gamblers' decoy: ca. 1625–70: ? c. Shirley, 'Thou molly-puffer, were it not justice to kicke thy guts out ?' (Perhaps ex *molly*, 3 + *puff*, to advertise.) But F. & H.'s definition is prob. wrong, for Shirley's term is, likely enough, a mere variant of *mullipuff* (q.v. in O.E.D.), a fuzzball, used as a term of contempt.]

molly-shop. See **moll-shop.** (Manchon.)

mollygrubs. See **mulligrubs.—mollyhawk.** Incorrect (from ca. 1880) for *mollymawk* = *mallemuck*. O.E.D.

molly's (or **Molly's**) **hole.** The female pudend: low: C. 19–20; ob. Ex *molly*, 3.

molo. Tipsy: military: C. 20. F. & Gibbons. Perhaps ex Romany: cf. *motto*, q.v.

molo(c)ker. A renovated hat: trade (– 1892); ob. Ex *molo(c)ker*, v., to renovate an old hat by ironing and greasing: trade (– 1863). Sala. ? ex the inventor's name.

molrower. A wencher, esp. a whoremonger. low: from ca. 1860; very ob. Ex:

molrowing, vbl.n. Whoring: low: from ca. 1860; ob. Ex:—2. Caterwauling: low: from ca. 1858; ob. H., 2nd ed.; Milliken, 'Beats 'Andel's molrowings a buster'. Perhaps a fusion of *miauling* and *caterwauling*.

mompyus. See **munpius.**

monacholite, like **monalechite,** a 'blundered form', is almost catachrestic for *monothelite*: C. 15. O.E.D.

monaker, monarch, etc. A sovereign (coin): from ca. 1855; ob.: low. Orig. (– 1851), a guinea. Mayhew.—2. The ten-oared boat: Eton College: ca. 1890–1915.—3. A name or title: orig. tramps' c., it >, in all extant forms, gen. though somewhat low s. ca. 1900. The forms are these :—*monaker*, from ca. 1860 (though Baumann implies from mid-C. 18), not very gen. ; *monarch* (– 1879), ob., *Macmillan's Magazine*, 1879, vol. XL ; *monarcher* (cf. *monarcher, big*, q.v.), app. first in P. H. Emerson, 1893 ; *monekeer*, 1851 (Mayhew), † ; *moneker*, from ca. 1852, while *monneker* arises ca. 1855 ; *monica*, from ca. 1890 ; *monnaker* (cf. *monaker*), from ca. 1865 ; *mon(n)ick* (– 1895), as in *The Times*, Nov. 11, 1895, † by 1914 ; *mon(n)icker*, a frequent form, from ca. 1880 ; and *mon(n)iker*, the most gen. form of all (– 1874), H., 5th ed. The etymology is mysterious : I. proposes *Ste Monica*, *Monica* deriving from L. *monitor*, an adviser, ex *monere*, to advise, to warn ; Ware asserts that it derives 'from Italian lingo for name, Monaco being the Italian for monk' ; I suggest *monarch*, a king, hence that which rules and determines, hence that which, by designating, partly rules a man's life ; W., however, thinks that it may be a Shelta word, and gives the meaning as 'sign' ; but recent opinion 'favours' *monogram*, which, I freely admit, is supported by :—4. A signature (– 1859). H., 1st ed. This sense, however, causes me to wonder if the term be not a blend of *monogram + signature* ; and this sense may possibly be earlier than sense 3.

monaker (etc.), **tip** (a person) **one's.** To tell one's name : low : from ca. 1860. (Manchon.)

monarch(er). See preceding.—2. **monarcher, big.** An important person : tramps' c. (– 1893) ; ob.

Monas or **monas.** Isle of Man Railway shares : from ca. 1890 : Stock Exchange.

Monday, adj. An intensive : from ca. 1890 ; very ob. : low. Kipling, 1892, in *Snarleyow*, 'You may lay your Monday head | 'Twas juicier for the niggers when the case began to spread.' ? by misunderstanding or by corruption ex *multy*, q.v.

Monday, black. See **black M.—M., bloody.** See **bloody M.—Monday, St.** See **St M.**

Monday mice. The numerous black eyes seen that morning after the week-end drinking : London streets' : late C. 19–20 ; slightly ob. Ware.

Monday pop. One of the celebrated **popular**

concerts at St. James's Hall, London : coll. : 1862, Geo. Eliot in letter of Nov. 26. (Ware.)

moneke(e)r ; monekeur (very rare). See **monaker, monarch,** 3.

money. Money's worth ; a way of investing money : coll. : 1851, Mayhew, 'In February and March . . . green fruit's not my money' ; ob.—2. A (gen. very young) girl's private parts : low : from ca. 1780 ; ob. Grose, 1st ed.

money, a pot—or **pots**—**of.** A large amount of money ; a fortune : coll. : from ca. 1870. Mrs. H. Wood 1871, *pots* ; Trollope, *a pot.* (O.E.D.)

money, eggs for. An excuse, a trick. Esp. in *take eggs,* to suffer a trick, accept an excuse. Coll. : C. 17. Shakespeare, *The Winter's Tale.*

money, hard. Coin, as *soft money* is notes : coll. : from ca. 1848.

money, it's like eating. This is a costly business : semi-proverbial coll. c.p. (— 1887). Baumann.

money, not (a person's). Not to one's taste or choice : coll. : late C. 19–20. Esp. as in Manchon, 'You ain't everybody's money.' Prob. suggested by (*the*) *man for my money,* q.v.

money, so and so for my. So and so is what I like, desire, would choose : coll. : C. 17–20. W. Haughton, 1616, *English-Men for my Money*—a title. O.E.D.

money, Spanish. Fair words and compliments : late C. 17–18. B.E.

money, the man for (e.g.) **my.** See **man for my money.**

money-bag lord. An ennobled banker : Society coll. : 1885–ca. 1914. Ware. Cf. *gallipot baronet.*

money-box, -maker, and (†) **-spinner.** The female pudend : low : C. 19–20 ; ob.

money-bug. A millionaire : anglicised in 1898 from U.S.A. ; ob. Ware.

money burns in (e.g.) **his pocket**(, e.g. **his**). He cannot keep money ; is impatient to spend it : from ca. 1530 : coll. till ca. 1860, then S.E. More, Cornwallis (1601), Farquhar, T. Hughes. (Apperson.)

*money-dropper. A swindler who, dropping counterfeit money, gets good change from some 'flat' : c. : 1748, Smollett ; Grose, 2nd ed. † by 1905. Cf. *ring-dropper.*

money for jam(, **it's**). (It is) sure money or, more gen., money easily obtained or earned : coll. : C. 20. Manchon. Cf. *jam,* n., 3.—2. Hence, (it's) too easy ! : from ca. 1910. B. & P.

money for old rope. (Always predicative.) Something for nothing or almost nothing : (low) coll. : C. 20. James Curtis, *The Gilt Kid,* 1936.

money makes the mare to go. See **mare to go.**

money talks. Money is very powerful : semi-proverbial c.p. bordering on S.E. : 1586, Pettie, 'The tongue hath no force when gold speaketh' ; 1666, Torriano, 'Man prates, but gold speaks' ; 1915, P. G. Wodehouse, 'The whole story took on a different complexion for Joan. Money talks' ; A. Palmer, 1925, in *The Sphere,* '"Money talks . . . So why not listen to it ?"' Cf. the late C. 16–18 *what will not money do ?* (Apperson.)

mongar(l)ey. See **mungar(l)y.**

mongey. Food : military : 1914. B. & P. Ex Fr. (*du*) *manger.*

*mongrel. A sponger ; a hanger-on among cheats : c. : ca. 1720–1890. *A New Canting Dict.,* 1725.

*monic or **monick.** A mainly c. variant of **monaker** : late C. 19–20.

monica, monick, monicker, moniker. See **monaker, monarch,** 3.

monied, monies. Incorrect for *moneyed, moneys* : from before mid-C. 19.

moniker. See **monaker.**

monish. Money : mostly Yiddish (— 1887). Baumann. Ex *money* or rather *moneys.*

monk. A term of contempt : low : from ca. 1860. H., 3rd ed.—2. A dark or an over-inked spot in a printed sheet : printers' : 1683, Moxon (O.E.D.) : s. >, ca. 1830, j. Perhaps ex the Westminster Abbey associations of Caxton's press. Cf. *friar,* q.v.—3. Abbr. *monkey,* the animal : mid-C. 19–20 : (low) coll.—4. A sickly parrot : from the 1890's. Ware. Ex head indrawn and dejected.

Monk Lewis. M. G. Lewis, author of *The Monk,* a famous work (1795).

*monkery ; occ. **monkry.** The country : tramps' c. : 1790, Potter (O.E.D.) ; Egan ; Mayhew ; P. H. Emerson.—2. (Preceded by *the*) tramps or other vagrants collectively : tramps' c. : 1851, Mayhew.—3. The practice of going on tramp : tramps' c. : from ca. 1850. Mayhew, 'He had followed the " monkry " from a child' (O.E.D.).—4. Hence, *on the monkery,* on tramp (Mayhew, 1851). All senses are either ex *monkery,* a monastic, hence a quiet life (H., 1st ed.) or, less prob., ex the idea of itinerant monks ; all, too, are ob. Cf. *deuseaville,* q.v.—5. (Ex senses 1 and 4.) A district : grafters' s. : from ca. 1880. Philip Allingham, *Cheapjack,* 1934.

*monkery, on the. See **monkery,** 4.

monkey. See **Modern Babylon.**—2. £500 (in U.S. $500) : 1856, *The Druid* ; Whyte Melville. (The O.E.D. cites an 1832 text in which, prob. erroneously, it = £50.) Among stockbrokers, however, *monkey* (in C. 20) = £50,000 of stock, i.e. 500 shares of £100. Cf. *pony.*—3. 'A vessel', i.e. a container, ' in which a mess receives its full amount of grog', F. & H. : nautical (— 1867) : s. >, ca. 1890, j. Smyth. Prob. ex *suck the monkey* (see below).—4. A hunting flask (for drinking) : hunting s. or coll. : ca. 1850–80. Surtees (O.E.D.).—5. See **monkey up.**—6. A sheep : rural Australian : from ca. 1880 ; ob. A. C. Grant, *Bush Life,* 1881.—7. The instrument that propels a rocket : military (— 1860) : s. >, ca. 1895, j. H., 2nd ed.—8. A hod : bricklayers' (— 1885) : s. >, ca. 1905, j.—9. A small bustle or dress-improver (— 1889) ; † by 1896 : coll. *Notes & Queries,* June 22, 1889.—10. A padlock : c. (— 1812). Vaux ; Leach, 1933.—11. A mortgage (see **monkey on a house**) ; a writ on a ship : nautical : late C. 19–20. Bowen. 12. A clerk, esp. if unimportant : mechanics' (— 1909). Ware. Cf. Fr. s. *le singe,* ' boss '.

monkey, cold enough to freeze the balls off a brass. Exceedingly cold : low coll. (mainly Australian) : late C. 19–20.

monkey, suck the. To drink liquor, esp. rum, from a cask with a straw through a gimlet hole (cf. *admiral, tap the,* q.v.) : nautical : 1785 ; ob. Grose, 1st ed. Cf. *monkey,* 3 ; perhaps it is a telescoping of the idea expressed in sense 3.—2. To drink liquor from a bottle ; hence, to tipple : gen. s. : 1797 ; ob.—3. To drink rum out of coco-nuts, from which the milk has been drawn off : nautical : 1833, Marryat ; ob.

monkey,—' they're off ', said the. A c.p., applicable esp. to a race : lower classes' : C. 20.

monkey and the nut, a or **the.** 'The Cunard houseflag with its lion and globe : nautical : C. 20 Bowen.

monkey-board. The conductor's or the footman's place on an old-style omnibus or on a carriage: coll.: 1842, Mrs. Trollope (O.E.D.); J. Greenwood. † by 1895.

monkey-boat. A small boat used in docks: 1858 (O.E.D.).—2. A long, narrow canal boat: 1864, H., 3rd ed. Both senses are nautical s. >, ca. 1905, j.

Monkey Brand is 'often applied derisively to an ugly face' (Collinson): from ca. 1910. Ex that well-known Lever Brothers' advertisement in which a monkey gazes at itself in a frying-pan.

monkey-cage. A grated room from which a convict sees his relatives and friends: low: from ca. 1870. Cf. Fr. *parloir des singes.*

monkey-coat, jacket. A close-fitting, short jacket, 'with no more tail than a monkey': nautical: 1830: s. >, ca. 1890, j. N. Dana, 1830; R. H. Dana, 1840,—both *monkey-jacket*, app. orig. U.S.

monkey-hangers. Port Glasgow men: Greenock seamen's: late C. 19–20. Topical: Bowen gives the anecdote.

monkey is up. See **monkey up.—monkey-jacket.** See **monkey-coat.**

monkey island. 'The uppermost tier of a big ship's bridge': nautical: late C. 19–20. Bowen.

monkey-monk. (Applied to persons.) An intensive of *monk* or a pejorative of *monkey*: 1934, Richard Blaker, *Night-Shift.*

monkey-motions. Physical drill: military: ca. 1890–1914. (Ware.) Also naval: late C. 19–20; ob. (Bowen.)

monkey off one's back, take the. (Gen. in imperative.) To calm oneself: low (— 1887). Baumann. See **monkey up.**

monkey on a gridiron, sit like a. To be a bad, or very ungraceful, horseman: coll. (— 1923). Manchon.

monkey on a, gen. one's or the, house; monkey on or up the chimney. A mortgage on a house: mainly legal: 1875; ca. 1885. Ob. Cf. *monkey with a long tail,* q.v. 'Prob. suggested', says the O.E.D., 'by the initial *m* of *mortgage.*'

monkey on or up a stick. A thin man with jerky movements: coll.: ca. 1880–1920. Ex the now seldom seen toy so named (1863).

monkey on a wheel. A bicyclist: from ca. 1880; ob.

monkey on horseback without tying his tail ?, who put that. A low c.p. applied to a bad horseman: late C. 18–early 19. Grose, 2nd ed.

monkey on one's back, have a. A ca. 1880–1910 variant of *monkey up,* q.v.

monkey-poop. 'The half deck of a flush decked ship': nautical coll. verging on j.: late C. 19–20. Bowen.

monkey-pump. The straw in *monkey, suck the,* 1, q.v.: nautical (— 1867); ob. Smyth.

monkey-shines, monkey-like antics or tricks, is U.S. (1847) and has never been properly anglicised, though it was occ. heard, ca. 1875–1905, in Britain.

monkey-tail, hold on by somebody's. To take someone's word for a story: nautical (— 1887). Baumann. Punning *tale*; cf. *monkey about,* (S.E. for :) to play the fool.

monkey up, get one's. To make, but gen. to become, angry: s. (— 1859) and dial. H., 1st ed. Also, in predominant sense, *one's monkey is up* (1863, O.E.D.) or † *have a* or *the monkey on one's back* (— 1864). Anon., 1877. *Five Years' Penal Servi-*

tude, 'My monkey was up, and I felt savage '; 'Rolf Boldrewood', 1888, 'The mare, like some women when they get their monkey up, was clean out of her senses.' ' Perhaps alludes to animal side brought uppermost by anger ', W. Cf. *back up,* q.v.

monkey up, put one's. To anger a person : from ca. 1865. Cf. preceding entry.

monkey up the chimney. See **monkey on a house** and :

monkey with a long tail. A mortgage : legal (— 1886); ob. Cf. *monkey on a house, monkey up the chimney,* qq.v.

monkey with a tin tool(, like a). A low coll. phrase denoting self-satisfaction or impudence : from ca. 1863 ; ob. H., 3rd ed.

monkey's allowance. More rough treatment than money : 1785, Grose ; Marryat, 1833, 'When you get on board you'll find monkey's allowance': s. >, ca. 1840, coll. ; ob.

monkey's grease, (as) useless as. Useless : C. 18 : coll. 'Proverbial' Fuller. (Monkeys are thin.)

monkey's island. An occ. variant of *monkey island,* q.v. (F. & Gibbons.)

monkey's money. Payment in kind, esp. labour, goods, or, most of all, fair words : ca. 1650–1800 : coll. Urquhart, 1653, 'Paid for in court fashion with monkey's money '. Cf. *money, Spanish,* q.v.

monkey's orphan. '19th century naval name for the disappearing ship's fiddler ', Bowen.

monkey's parade. A (length of) road frequented by lads and lasses, esp. with a view to striking an acquaintance ('clicking '): (low) urban, esp. London : C. 20. Also **monkey-parade** (Addenda).

monkey('s)-tail. A short hand-spike : nautical s. >, ca. 1860, j. : 1833, Marryat.—2. A nail : rhyming s.: late C. 19–20. *John o' London's Weekly,* June 9, 1934.

monkry is an occ. early variant of *monkery* (q.v.). Mayhew.

monk's rhubarb. Catachrestic when used of garden rhubarb : from ca. 1730. O.E.D.

Monmouth Street finery. Tawdry clothes, furniture, etc. ; pretence, pretentiousness : ca. 1850–80 : low coll. Mayhew. Monmouth (ca. 1890 > Dudley) Street was long a well-known market for second-hand clothes.

monnaker, monneker, monnicker, monniker. See **monaker, monarch.**

mono. A monotype machine or process : printers' s. (— 1910) >, ca. 1925, coll. Cf. *lino,* q.v.

monocular eyeglass. The breech : low : ca. 1860–1910.

monodelph(, etc.) for **monadelph(, etc.)** is incorrect : from ca. 1828. As is *monograph* (e.g. in Albert Smith, 1849) for *monogram.* O.E.D.

monos. The 'King's scholar who at 4 p.m. announces, in Latin, the finish of the day's work ': Westminster School (— 1909). Ware. The Gr. word for ' alone '.

monosyllable. The female pudend : either polite s. or a vulgarism ; ob. by 1880, † (except among the cultured) by 1915. Anticipated in Lucas's *The Gamesters,* 1714, thus, 'Perhaps a bawdy monosyllable ',—i.e. *c**t,*—' such as boys write upon walls ', but app. [1] first ' dictionaried ' in 1788, Grose, 2nd ed. (which, by the way, has been shamefully neglected by lexicographers), as ' a woman's commodity ' (see **commodity**). Omitted by O.E.D., as is *c**t* (q.v.), the word both connoted and denoted by *the monosyllable,* of which ' Jon Bee ' remarks, in 1823, ' of all the thousand monosyllables in our language, this *one* only is designated by the definite article; therefore do some men call it "the article", "my article", and "her article" as the case may be'. For a fuller treatment, see my edition of Grose. (¹ Bee says, 'Described by Nat Bailey as *pudenda mulieris*': I find it in neither the 1st ed., 1721, nor the supplementary volume, 1731.)

mons. A crowd; to crowd (v.i.): Winchester College: ca. 1860–1920. ? L. *mons*, a mountain, or an abbr. of *monster* or *monstrous*.—2. (Gen. **Mons.**) A catachrestic abbr. of *monsieur*: C. 18–20; ob. ('Regarded in Fr. as intentional impertinence', W.)

Mons, gassed at. See **gassed**.—**Mons, on the wire at.** A variant of the preceding. F. & Gibbons. (There was no 'wire' at Mons.)

Mons Meg. The female pudend: low: C. 19. ? ex the C. 15 gun in Edinburgh Castle.

[Monsham. See 'Westminster School slang'.]

monstrous, adj. An intensive (very great, iniquitous, etc.): coll.: ca. 1710–1840. Swift, 'We have a monstrous deal of snow'; F. Burney, 'this monstrous fatigue'; Cobbett, 'Here is a monstrous deal of vanity and egotism'. O.E.D.

monstrous, adv. A general intensive (cf. *awfully*, *bloody*, q.v.): coll.: ca. 1590–1850. Shakespeare, 'monstrous desperate'; Congreve; Mrs. Trollope, 'monstrous good friends'. (O.E.D.)

monteigh. Incorrect for *monteith* (C. 17–18), as *monticole* (C. 19–20) is for *monticule*. O.E.D.

month, a bad attack of the end of the. Shortness of money: jocular coll.: from ca. 1870. I.e. waiting for the month's salary to be paid.

month of Sundays. A long time: coll.: from ca. 1830. Marryat, 1832 (O.E.D.).

monthlies, the. Menstruation: 1872 (O.E.D.): a vulgarism >, ca. 1895, low coll. Cf. *flowers*.

month's end, an attack of the. See **week's end**.

***montra.** A watch: c.: ca. 1810–50. Vaux. Ex Fr. *montre*.

moo-cow. A cow: childish coll.: 1812, Combe, 'The moo-cow low'd, and Grizzle neighed'; Thackeray. Cf. *bow-wow*, *cock-a-doodle-doo*.

Moo-Cow Farm. Mouquet Farm: military; esp. among the Australians, who, in the Battle of the Somme, fought fiercely there (near Thiepval): latter 1916; ob. F. & Gibbons.

mooch. An idling, 'scrounging', skulking, hanging about, looking for odd jobs. Hence, *on the mooch*, adj. and adv., engaged in one of these 'activities'; in Wiltshire dial., shuffling(ly). H., 1st ed., 1859; *The London Herald*, March 23, 1867. Also *mouch*. (Cf. *mike*, q.v.) Ex the v.—2. See sense 5 of:

mooch, v. (Also *mouch*; cf. *mike*, q.v.) To idle, sneak, hang about (often with *about*); slouch (with *along*): low: 1851, Mayhew. Also dial. Prob. ex *mike*, v., influenced by Fr. *mucher*, to hide, skulk.—2. 'To sponge, slink away and allow others to pay for your entertainment', Barrère & Leland: ca. 1855–1910. 'Ducange Anglicus.'—3. V.t., to steal, pilfer: 1861, Mayhew (to steal things one finds lying about): ob.: prob. c. > low s. and dial. O.E.D.—4. To be a tramp: tramps' c.: late C. 19–20. Gen. as vbl.n.: *mooching*. Cf. :— 5. 'To walk round and round the decks in company': *Conway* cadets' (— 1891). Also *come* (or *go*) *for a mooch*. John Masefield, *The Conway*, 1933.

mooch, do a. See **do a mike**.

moocher; moucher. A lazy loiterer or hanger-about; a loitering thief (gen. a pilferer); a tramp: a (professional) beggar: low: from ca. 1855. 'Ducange Anglicus'; Mayhew. Also *mutcher*. Cf. dial. senses: see E.D.D. Ex the preceding.—2. A synonym of **bug-hunter**: c. (— 1861); ob. Mayhew.—3. A customer owing money to the bank: Anglo-Irish bank-clerks': C. 20. Cf. *delegate*, q.v.

Moocheries or **Muckeries, the.** 'The Inventories' (Inventions Exhibition), held at South Kensington, London, in: 1885. Ex *mooch*, v.; *Muckeries* being a jocular perversion.

moochi. An Indian shoemaker: Regular Army coll.: late C. 19–20. B. & P. Ex Hindustani.— 2. Hence, any shoemaker: Regular Army s.: C. 20. Ibid.

mooching, mouching. Vbl.n., see **mooch**, v.—2. Adj., from ca. 1860. Also dial.

Moochy. See **Mouchey**, 2.

moody. 'Gentle persuasion, blarney, flattery': grafters': C. 20. Philip Allingham, *Cheapjack*, 1934. Origin ?

moody, v. To flatter; to wheedle: id.: id. Ibid. Ex the n.

mooë, mooey. See **moey**.

mooer. A cow: coll.: ca. 1820–1910. Ex *moo*, v. Cf. *moo-cow*, *mower*, qq.v.

mooi. Fine; handsome: South African Midlands coll.: from ca. 1880. Ex the Dutch *mooi* (handsome, pretty, fine), which, among the Cape Dutch, 'has to do duty for almost every shade of appreciation', Pettman.

***moon.** A month's imprisonment: c.: 1830, Moncrieff, 'They've lumbered him for a few moons, that's all.' Hence, *long moon*, a calendar month. Cf. *drag*.

moon, v. (Gen. with *about*, *along*, or *around*.) To idle, lounge, or wander as in a dream: coll.: 1848, Albert Smith (O.E.D.); Charlotte Yonge, '. . . When you were mooning over your verses'.— 2. Occ. v.t. with *away*, as in Besant & Rice, 1877, 'I might have mooned away the afternoon in the Park.'

moon, a blue. See **blue moon**.

moon, find an elephant in the. To find a mare's nest: ca. 1670–1830. Butler, *The Elephant in the Moon*. Ex the C. 17 Sir Paul Neal, who thought that a mouse in his telescope, as he looked through it, was an elephant in the moon.

moon, shoot (occ. **bolt** or **shove**) **the.** To depart, with one's valuables and, if possible, furniture by night without paying the rent: coll.: 1823, Egan's Grose, *shove* († by 1870), c.; *bolt*, † by 1905, occurring in 1825, and *shoot* in 1837. O.E.D.

***moon-curser.** A link-boy, esp. one that lights his clients into a pack of rogues: c.: 1673, Head; † by 1840. (In dial., a ship-wrecker.)

moon-eyed hen. A squinting wench: ca. 1780–1890. Grose, 1st ed. (*m.-e.* itself is S.E.)

moon-faced. Japanese-faced: non-aristocratic (— 1887); ob. Baumann.

moon, God bless her !,—it is a fine. A proverbial c.p. greeting the new moon: from ca. 1670; ob. Aubrey. (Apperson.)

moon is made of green cheese, make believe the. See **cheese**.

moon knows about Sunday, know no more about it than the. To know nothing about it: coll. (— 1887); slightly ob. Baumann.

***moon-man; moon's man.** A Gypsy: C. 17–early 19: c. (after 1800, perhaps low s.): Dekker, B.E., Grose.—2. A robber by night: late C. 16–17:

coll. Shakespeare (*moon's man*); 1632, Sherwood, who defines as a brigand (O.E.D.)

moon-raker. A Wiltshire man: from ca. 1765: coll., slightly ob. Grose, 2nd ed., says that some Wiltshire rustics, seeing the moon in a pond, tried to rake it out: Wiltshire people prefer a more complimentary legend. *The Moon-Rakers* are the 62nd Foot, in late C. 19–20 the Wiltshire Regiment (military: late C. 18–20; ob.).—2. Hence, ca. 1830–1900, a smuggler: dial. (mostly) and coll.—3. A blockhead: from ca. 1840, ob.: coll. >, ca. 1900, S.E. Ex sense 1.—4. A sail above the sky-sail, also an imaginary sail above the ' sky-scraper ', q.v.: nautical, resp. (— 1867) j. and (— 1896) s.

moon-raking, vbl.n. and ppl.adj.: from ca. 1865; ob. Coll. >, ca. 1895, S.E. See **moon-raker.**

moon-shooter. See **moon, shoot the.** From ca. 1890.

mooner. A dreamy idler, lounger, wanderer: coll.: 1848, Albert Smith. In C. 20, S.E.

mooney. A variant spelling of *moony,* q.v. Baumann, 1887.

moonish. An occ. variant (— 1923) of *moony,* 3. Manchon.

moonlight. Smuggled spirits: from ca. 1809; > ob. ca. 1890. Scott. (O.E.D.) Ex the night-work of smugglers: cf. *moonshine,* q.v. (As v., S.E.)

moonlight flit, flitting. A removal of household goods by night without paying the rent: resp. dial. (— 1824) >, ca. 1865, s.; s. (— 1721) >, ca. 1880, coll. O.E.D.; F. & H., where the occ. late C. 19–early 20 variant, *London flitting,* is recorded.

moonlight wanderer. One who does a ' moonlight flit ' or ' London flitting ': ca. 1820–70. ' Jon Bee.' See preceding entry.

moonlighter. A harlot: from ca. 1850; ob. (—The Anglo-Irish sense is S.E. as is *moonlighting,* n. and adj.)

moonraker. See **moon-raker.—moon's man.** See **moon-man.**

moonshee. A native teacher of, an amanuensis in, languages. This sense (1776) is prob. to be rated as ' standard '; but as = a learned person (—1864), *moonshee* is coll. (H., 3rd ed.), as is ' Indian interpreter ': military: late C. 19–20 (B. & P.). A so *moonshi, munshi, munshee.* (O.E.D.; Yule & Burnell.)

moonshine. Smuggled spirits: 1785, Grose: coll. >, ca. 1890, S.E. Often with a specific sense: white brandy, in Kent, Sussex: gin, Yorkshire. Cf. U.S. c. *shine.*—2. In C. 20, it occ. = ' adulterated alcoholic liquor ' (Lyell) and is, in this sense, to be considered coll.

moonshine, gilded. Bogus bills of exchange: ca. 1820–1910, but ob. as early as 1880. Bee. Ex the metaphorical S.E. sense of *moonshine*: unreality.

moonshine in the mustard pot (for it). Nothing: coll.: ca. 1630–1700. Gen. preceded by *one shall have.* Cf. S.E. *moon*(*shine*) *in* (*the*) *water.* (Apperson.)

moony. A noodle: coll.: from ca. 1850. Ex: —2. Adj., silly, which is S.E.—3. But *moony,* drunk, (gen.) slightly drunk, is s.: 1854 (O.E.D.); very ob.—4. Romantic: Glasgow coll. (— 1934).

Moor, the. (The prison on) Dartmoor: c.: C. 20. Edgar Wallace, passim (e.g. *The Squeaker*).

moored in Sot's Bay (or s. b.). ' Drunk and incapable ': nautical: late C. 19–20. Bowen. Cf. *gutter lane.*

Moorgate rattler. A ' swell ' of that London district: Cockneys': 1899–1910. Ware.

Moorish, Mohammedan: C. 16–20: S.E. till ca.

1830, then coll., increasingly low; ob. Southern India and Ceylon (S.O.D.). Cf. Anglo-Indian use of *Moor* in Yule & Burnell.

moosh is a variant (— 1914) of *mush,* 4 (B. & P.); also of *mush,* 2.

mootch. See **mooch.**

mop. See **Modern Babylon,** list at.—2. A drinking-bout. Hence *on the mop,* on the ' drunk ' or the drink. Low: from ca. 1860, ob., as is :—3. A drunkard, same period. Cf. *lushington,* q.v.: see also **lush.**—4. Hair: lower classes' coll. (— 1935). Ex *mop of hair.*

mop, v. To empty a glass or pot: ca. 1670–1810. Cotton. Cf. *mop up,* 1.—2. To collect, obtain, appropriate: coll.: from ca. 1850; † by 1905. Cf. *mop up,* 2.—3. (Gen. in passive.) To defeat heavily: 1910, P. G. Wodehouse, *Psmith in the City,* ' This is pretty rocky . . . We shall get mopped.' Cf. *mop up,* v., 7.—4. To hurry: Post Office telegraph-messengers' (— 1935). Cf. *mopping up the miles.*

mop, chew the. See **chew the mop.**

mop down. To empty a glass, etc.: a C. 20 variant of *mop up,* v., 1. Gen. in form *mop it down,* to drink freely. See song in B. & P. at p. 40.

mop-eyed. See **mope-eyed.**

mop out. (Cf. *wipe out,* q.v.) To floor, kill; ruin (— 1892); † by 1910: low. Gen. in passive. Milliken, 1892, in his *'Arry Ballads.* Cf. *mop up,* v., 5.

mop-squeezer. A housemaid: low: 1771 (O.E.D.); Grose, 2nd ed. Ob. Cf. *slavey,* q.v.

mop-stick. A ninny, a simpleton: low (— 1887); slightly ob. Baumann. Also *mopstick.*

mop (or wipe) the † earth, floor, † ground with one. (Occ. with *up* after *mop.*) To knock a person down (— 1887).—2. Hence, in C. 20, to overcome easily. Cf. *mop up,* 7.

mop-up. A severe trouncing, in single fight or, gen., in battle: C. 20; ob. Conan Doyle, 1900, ' Better six battalions safely down the hill than a mop up in the morning.' O.E.D. The military *mopping-up,* not used before July, 1916 (if memory serves me aright,—though F. & Gibbons may be correct in dating it at Feb., 1917), is applied to the work done by the parties sent on after, or by the men left behind from, the attacking troops to clear the captured lines of a lurking foe and of obstructions. Also as adj., as in *mopping-up party* or, occ., *wave*: early 1917. By the end of the G.W., it had > j.

mop up, v. To empty (e.g. a glass): from ca. 1810. *Lex. Bal.* Cf. *mop,* v., 1, and *mop down,* qq.v.—2. Also, to eat: rare before ca. 1890.—3. To collect, obtain, appropriate: from ca. 1855. Mayhew.—4. V.i., to stop talking, gen. in imperative (— 1887); ob.: low. Walford, *The Antiquarian,* April, 1887.—5. To kill, slaughter: mainly military and naval (— 1887). Baumann; Rider Haggard. Cf. the n., q.v. Cf. *wipe out,* q.v.—6. V.i. (absolute) and v.t., to capture or subject isolated machine-gun, bombing, and other posts after the main body of an attack has moved on: military: G.W. +. See B. & P. at *mopping-up* and cf. *mopper-up.*—7. Hence, or ex sense 5, to defeat utterly: s. (from ca. 1918) >, by 1930, coll. Lyell. —8. See **mopping up the miles.**

mope-eyed (occ. **mop-eyed**) **by living so (or too) long a maid, you are.** A proverbial coll. or a c.p. of ca. 1645–1720. Herrick, Ray, B.E. (Lit., *mope-eyed* = purblind.) O.E.D.; Apperson.

moper. A deserter : military (— 1887) ; virtually †. Baumann.

mopes, the. Low spirits, esp. if shown : from ca. 1825 : coll. till C. 20, then S.E. Hone, ' I have got the mopes ' ; Thackeray. O.E.D.

moph. A variant (Bee, 1823) of *muff*, a fool.

mophy. (Of a youth) delicate and well-groomed : seamen's : late C. 19–20. Bowen. Prob. ex :

mophrodite, Fielding, 1742 ; **morphrodite,** Vanbrugh, 1706. Hermaphrodite : sol. : C. 18–20. O.E.D.

mopper-up. A member of a mopping-up party (see **mop up,** v., 6) : military : G.W. +. *The Times,* Nov. 27, 1917, ' Ten men detailed as moppers-up ' (W.). Cf. :

Mopper-Up, the. A fast goods-train travelling to London with food-supplies : railwaymen's : from ca. 1920. *The Daily Telegraph,* Aug. 15, 1936. Cf. *mop up,* v., 3.

mopping-up, n. See **mop-up,** n.—See **mop up,** v., 6.—Adj. to latter of these.

mopping up the miles, vbl.n. Speeding : motorists' coll. (— 1935). Ex *mop up,* v., 2.

*****moppy.** Drunk : c. : from ca. 1820 ; † by 1915. Egan's Grose.

mops, in the. A perversion, ca. 1830–1910, of *in the mopes.* See **mopes.**

mops and brooms. Half-tipsy : coll. : 1814, *The Sporting Magazine ;* Hardy (O.E.D.) ; ob. With *be.* Ex the drinking customary at *mops* (statute hiring-fairs), the girls carrying a mop or a broom to indicate the kind of work they desired. Hence :

mops and brooms, feel all. To be full of bitterness and sorrow : low (— 1887). Baumann.

mops(e)y. A (gen. short) homely or, esp., dowdy woman : late C. 17–20 : coll. till ca. 1830, then S.E. ; † by 1910. B.E., Grose. Ex *mopsy,* an endearment.

mopus. A moping, or a dull, stupid, person : coll. : ca. 1690–1820 ; then extant only in dial. B.E., Johnson. Ex S.E. *mope,* n. and v.—2. A small coin : ca. 1690–1860 : c. >, ca. 1750, s. B.E. ; Tait's *Edinburgh Review,* 1841.—3. In pl. (often *mopusses*), money : ca. 1765–1905 : low. Anon., *The Stratford Jubilee,* 1769, ' If she has the mopus's, I'll have her, as snug as a bug in a rug ' ; 1892, M. Williams (O.E.D.). ? ex Sir Giles *Mompesson,* an early C. 17 monopolist.

morai. Incorrect for *marae* or *marai* (human-sacrificial altar) : from ca. 1780. O.E.D.

moral. Likeness ; counterpart. Rare except in *the very moral of* : low coll. : 1757, Smollett ; G. Parker, Smedley, ' Rolf Boldrewood '. Slightly ob. Perhaps ex the † S.E. sense, a symbolical figure, but prob. by a sol. for *model.*—2. A ' moral certainty ', which it shortens : orig. and still mainly racing : 1861, Whyte-Melville ; 1869, J. Greenwood, ' Everything that is highly promising becomes, in the slang of the advertising tipster, a moral.' (O.E.D.)

moral Cremorne, the. The Fisheries Exhibition of : 1883 : Society. Ware, ' So named because there had been no illumination fêtes since the closing of immoral Cremorne Gardens '.

moral-shocker. A novel dealing with sex : ca. 1890–1914 : Fleet Street. Loose for *morals-shocker.* Cf. *hill-topper,* q.v.

Moral Surface, the. Sir Robert Peel (d. 1850). Bestowed by his enemies in allusion to hypocritical Joseph Surface in Sheridan's *School for Scandal.*

Moray coach. A cart : from ca. 1805 ; ob. : Scots jocular coll.

morbs, get the. See **get the morbs.**

more unnecessarily preceding comparative of adjj. and advv. : in early Mod. English, permissible ; since ca. 1720, only in poetry and when unintentional, hence sol. Cf. *most.*—2. The more, as in ' more fool you ! ' : coll. (— 1834). Ainsworth ; Baumann.—3. No more, as in ' more she ain't ' : sol. (— 1887). Baumann.—4. Moreover : coll. : from ca. 1930. E.g. in *The Daily Telegraph,* Oct. 19, 1935 (boxing notes).

more like, preposition. Nearer : coll. : C. 20. W. Headlam, 1902, ' . . . 4 . . . I gladly adopted more like 12.' O.E.D.—2. Abbr. *more like it,* better, more acceptable or reasonable or sensible : coll. : C. 20.

more sauce than pig, ca. 1670–1750, like **more squeak than wool,** C. 18, indicates greater show than substance. Proverbial coll. : resp. B.E., Swift ; North. Cf. the C. 19–20 dial. *more poke (bag) than pudding.* Apperson.

more so, adv. An intensive, *so* representing the omitted part : coll. till C. 20, then S.E. : 1876, Besant & Rice, ' The English servant was dressed like his master, but " more-so " ' (O.E.D.). Often *only more so* (Milliken, 1892).

more than the cat and his skin, you can't have. A semi-proverbial, non-aristocratic c.p. (— 1887) ; ob. A variant of *having one's cake and eating it.* Baumann.

more war ! A Cockney c.p. directed at a street quarrel, esp. among women : 1898. In reference to the Spanish-American War. (Ware.)

more wind in your jib ! The c.p. of sailors in a ship with foul wind on meeting another with a fair wind : mid-C. 19–20. Bowen. (Thus will the wishers' ship gain a fair wind.)

moreish (occ. **more-ish**) ; **morish.** That makes one desire more : coll. : from ca. 1706, though not in print till 1738. Swift, ' *Lady S.* How do you like this tea, Colonel ? *Col.* Well enough, Madam ; but methinks 'tis a little more-ish.'

morepork (kind of a fellow). A ' dull dog ' ; a fool : Australian coll. : from ca. 1840 ; very ob. R. Howitt, 1845 ; ' Rolf Boldrewood ', 1890. Ex the bird named more properly *mopoke.* Morris.

morgan rattler. ' A cane or stick with a knob of lead at one or both ends, and short enough to be carried up the sleeve ' : low s. (— 1902) ex dial. (— 1866) ; † by 1910. E.D.D. Prob. ex a man's name. Cf. *cosh* and *neddy* in analogous senses.

Morgan's orchard. In cribbage, 4 : cribbage-players' (— 1935). Why ?

morgray, morgree. Erroneous for *morgay* (C. 19–20) and *mogra* (C. 19–20). O.E.D.

Morgue, the. At Messrs. Bickers' book-shop in Leicester Square (it is now in Charles Street, Haymarket) in the 1890's, ' a side-window . . . packed with " remainders ", the *memento mori* of the publisher's reader and the town traveller alike ', Arthur Waugh in *The Spectator,* Jan. 25, 1935 : London book-world s. of the period.

*****mork.** A policeman : c. (— 1889) ; ob. Clarkson & Richardson. Prob. a corruption of Romany *mo(o)s(h)kero,* a constable.

morley. See **mauley.** (Borrow's spelling, W.)

morning. An early drink : 1718, Ramsay (O.E.D.) ; 1854, R. W. Van der Kiste : mostly Scots : coll. till ca. 1860, then S.E. Also, from ca. 1890, *morning-rouser.*—2. **(morning !)** Good morning !: coll.: from ca. 1870. 'Henry Seton Merriman', 1895, ' " Morning—morning ! " he cried. "Good morning ", replied Luke ' (O.E.D.). Contrast :

morning ! or **morning to you !**, or **the top of the morning to you !** (Cheerily) good morning ! : from ca. 1870 : orig. and still mainly Anglo-Irish : coll.

morning after the night before, the. A coll. c.p. applied to the effects, or to a person showing the effects, of a drinking-bout : C. 20, esp. Australian.

morning-drop. The gallows : ca. 1810–90 : ? orig. c. *Lex. Bal.* ; Baumann.

morning hills. † Winchester College term. Mansfield, 1866, ' On holidays and Remedies we were turned out for a couple of hours on to St. Catherine's Hill . . . once before breakfast (Morning Hills), and again in the afternoon (Middle Hills).'

morning-rouser. See **morning,** 1. Cf. *eye-opener*, q.v.

*****morning sneak.** One who robs houses or shops while—before the household is up or the staff arrived—the servant or the shopman is cleaning steps, windows, etc. : c. (− 1812) : ob. by 1890, † by 1920. Vaux.—2. In C. 18 c., *the morning sneak* is ' to walk about the Streets in a Morning betimes, and 'sping [*sic*] any Body to go out of Doors, then immediately the Thief goes in,' as *The Regulator*, 1718, has it.

morning's morning. A variant (ca. 1895–1914) of *morning*, 1.

morocco, in. Naked : Gypsy s. : C. 19–20 ; ob. Longfellow. O.E.D. Cf. *leather,* n.

morocco man. An agent of a fraudulent lottery assurance : ca. 1795–1830 : s. > coll. Colquhoun, *Police of the Metropolis,* 3rd ed., 1796. O.E.D.

moron. A half-wit : orig. (ca. 1922), U.S. ; anglicised in 1929 as a coll. Norah James in *Sleeveless Errand,* Feb., 1929. (See O.E.D. (Sup.) and Mencken, *The American Language.*) Ex the technical sense, ' one of the highest type of feeble-minded ' (U.S. : 1910), itself ex Gr. μωρός, foolishly stupid.

morone. Incorrect for *maroon* : from ca. 1830. O.E.D.

Morpheus, in the arms of. Asleep : coll. : C. 19–20. Morpheus is properly the god of dreams.

morphodite. See **mophrodite.**

morrice, morris. To be hanged : c. of ca. 1720–70. *A New Canting Dict.*—2. (Often with *off.* Grose, 1st ed.) To decamp ; depart : from ca. 1760 ; ob. Cowper, 1765 ; Grose ; Dickens ; Grenville Murray, ' The fellows . . . flirt with them, and morris off to town in spring for better amusement.'—3. To move rapidly : sporting : ca. 1825–60. O.E.D.

morrice (or **morris), do a.** A variant (? from ca. 1770 ; ob.) of *morrice,* 2.

Morse (or **Moss) caught his mare, as.** Asleep. See **napping, catch.**

*****mort ;** occ. **morte** (early). A woman ; c. : ca. 1560–1890. Awdelay ; B.E., ' a Wife, Woman, or Wench ' ; Disraeli.—2. A harlot ; a near-harlot : from ca. 1565 : c., † by 1910. Harman.—3. A yeoman's daughter : c. : late C. 17–18. B.E., Grose. Also *mot,* late C. 18–19 only : ' Arabian ' Burton. All senses prob. cognate with or ex Dutch *mot* as in *mot-huys,* a brothel (Hexham) ; note, however, that Dr. John Sampson, in *The Times Literary Supplement* of June 21, 1928, derived *mort* ex *amourette.* (See **Modern Babylon** list.)

*****mort, autem-, dimber-, kinchen .** See autem, dimber, kinchen.

*****mort, strolling** or **walking.** A female tramp : c. : late C. 16–19. Chettle (*walking*).

mortal. Very great ; ' awful ' : coll. : from ca. 1715 ; ob. Countess Cowper, 1716, ' [They] take mortal pains to make the Princess think well of the Tories ' ; Dickens.—2. ' As an emphatic expletive (with *any, every,* or a negative) ' : coll. : 1609, Jonson, ' By no mortal means (!) ' ; ' every mortal thing ', 1843. Cf. ' no *earthly* chance '.—3. Tediously long : 1820, Scott, ' Three mortal hours ' ; Stevenson, ' They performed a piece . . . in five mortal acts.'—4. Short for *mortal drunk* (cf. at *mortally*) : from ca. 1808 : Scots and Northern coll. and dial. ; ob. Jamieson's Dict. ; Stevenson & Osbourne. (For all four senses, O.E.D.)

mortal, adv. Excessively ; ' deadly ' : C. 15–20 ; ob. : S.E. till ca. 1750 ; then, as in Warburton, coll. till ca. 1820, after which it is low coll. (as in Thackeray's ' mortal angry ') and dial. O.E.D. Cf. :

mortally. Extremely ; ' awfully ' : coll. : mid-C. 18–20. E.g. *mortally drunk.* Cf. preceding.

mortar. Abbr. of *mortar-board,* q.v. : low coll. : from ca. 1870. (The C. 17 *mortar* = *mortier* and is S.E. ; F. & H., at *mortar-board,* errs notably.)—2. The female pudend : low : C. 19–20 ; ob.

mortar, bricks and. Houses ; house property : coll. : from ca. 1905.

mortar, have one's finger in (the). To dabble in building : coll. : ca. 1630–1750. Berkeley MSS., 1639 ; Gerbier, *Discourse of Building,* 1662 ; Swift. See Apperson.

mortar-board. A trencher-cap, worn at universities and some Public Schools : coll. : 1853, ' Cuthbert Bede ', ' " I don't mind this 'ere mortar-board ".'

mortar-pounder. A ship's doctor : nautical : late C. 19–20. Bowen.

mortarie. Erroneous for *mortuary* (C. 16–17) ; as *mortne, mortné,* for *morné* (C. 18–20). O.E.D.

mortgage-deed. A pawn-ticket : from ca. 1860 ; ob. H., 3rd ed. Cf. *tombstone,* q.v.

mortial. Mortal : sol. : C. 19–20. Mayhew, 1861.

moschkener. See moskeneer.

Moses ! ; by the holy (jumping mother of) Moses ! ; by the piper that played before Moses ! ; holy Moses ! ; walking Moses ! A (low) coll. asseveration : resp. from ca. 1858, ob. ; 1876, Hindley (in full), ob. ; 1890, Hume Nisbet, † ; 1855, Strang ; from before 1923, when in Manchon.

Moses, prickly. The mimosa : Australian bushmen's (− 1887). Morris.

Moses, stand. Ca. 1790–1920 : ' A man is said to stand Moses when he has another man's bastard child fathered upon him, and he is obliged by the parish to maintain it,' Grose, 3rd ed. Contrast dial. *say Moses,* to make an offer of marriage (E.D.D.). —2. Hence, absolutely (of a man only). To adopt a child : lower classes ' ; mid-C. 19–20. (Neil Bell, *Crocus,* 1936.)

mosey ; occ. **mosey off.** To decamp ; depart quickly : orig. (1836), U.S. ; anglicised ca. 1890 ; ob. (The other U.S. sense, to hasten, be ' lively ', bustle about, has not been anglicised.) See esp. Thornton. ? etymology.

mosey along. To jog along : orig. (− 1877), U.S. ; anglicised ca. 1890 ; slightly ob. Kipling, 1891, ' I'll mosey along somewhow ' (O.E.D.).

*mosh. To leave a restaurant without paying: c.: from ca. 1860; ob. A deliberate corruption of *mooch*, v., 2, q.v., though imm. ex the next entry.—2. V.t., to pawn: c. (— 1923). Manchon. A rare corruption of *mosk*, q.v.

*mosh, the. The practice of ' moshing ' (see preceding entry): c. (— 1857); ob. ' Ducange Anglicus.'

mosk. To ' moskeneer ' (q.v.), which it shortens: C. 20: perhaps orig. c.

moskeneer ; occ. **moskeener, moshkeneer, moschkener, moskuiner.** To pawn (v.t. or i.) for more than the article is worth : ? orig. (— 1874), c. > low. H., 5th ed.; Henley, 1887, ' Fiddle, or fence, or mace, or mack ; Or moskeneer, or flash the drag '. Ex modern Hebrew *mishken*, to pawn, by Yiddish corruption (O.E.D.).—2. Hence, he who does this (— 1893), as in P. H. Emerson. Cf. *mosker.*

moskeneering. The profession of pawning at unfair prices : see preceding and **mosking.**

mosker. A professional pawner at prices unfair to the pawnbrokers : low (? orig. c.): 1883 : *The Daily Telegraph*, July 9, in a long article.—2. In C. 20 c., esp. a professional pledger of ' fired ' sapphires, paste diamonds, and the like who sells his pawn-tickets at a profit.

mosking. Ex *mosk*, q.v., a C. 20 variant of *moskeneering*, q.v.: low (? orig. c.): 1902, *The Standard*, June 5 (O.E.D.), ' The practice of obtaining a living by professional pawning—known as " mosking ",' which word has almost superseded *moskeneering.*

mosky. A dolphin : nautical : late C. 19–20. Bowen. Whence ?

Moslemin, in the singular (e.g. in Hope's *Anastasius*), is catachrestic ; so are *Moslemah* (e.g. in Scott) and *Moslemins* (e.g. Milman) as pl. of *Moslem*. C. 19–20. O.E.D.

mosque. A church ; a chapel : either c. or low : ca. 1780–1830. G. Parker.

*moss. Lead : c.: from ca. 1787 ; ob. Grose, 2nd ed., ' Because both are found on the tops of buildings '. Cf. *blue pigeon*, q.v.—2. Money : ? orig. (— 1859), U.S., though adumbrated in early C. 17 ; ob. Prob. ex *a rolling stone gathers no moss.*

Moss caught his mare, as. See **Morse . . .**

moss-dog. A stingy fellow ; a miser : low and military (— 1914). F. & Gibbons. Ex *moss*, 2.

mossel. Morsel : sol. : C. 19–20.

Mossie ; mossie. The Cape sparrow : South African coll. : from ca. 1870. Layard & Sharp, *The Birds of South Africa*, 1875–84. Ex Dutch *musch*, a sparrow. Pettman.

mossker. An occ. variant of *mosker*, q.v.

mossoo. Monsieur ; a Frenchman : low coll. (almost sol.) : 1870 ; slightly ob. Cf. *mounseer.*

mossy. Dull ; stupid : s. or jocular coll. : ca. 1595–1605. ' Mossy idiots ', 1597. O.E.D. For etymology, cf. U.S. *mossback* and :

mossy-back. An old-fashioned person : orig. U.S. ; anglicised as coll. ca. 1890 ; ob.

mossyface ; old mossyface. The ace of spades : low : from ca. 1860 ; ob.—2. In late C. 18–mid-19, however : the female pudend. Grose, 2nd ed.—3. **Mossy Face** was the G.W. ' Air Force name for the Bois d'Havrincourt on the Western Front ' (F. & Gibbons).

most, pleonastic before superlative of adjj. and advv. : C. 15–20 : S.E. till ca. 1720, then permissible in poetry ; otherwise sol. O.E.D. Cf. *more.*

most of you !, all there but the. A low c.p. applied to copulation : from ca. 1850 ; ? ob.

*mot, mott. A girl : c.: 1785, Grose ; ob. by 1880, † by 1915, except in Ireland, where it has, since late C. 19 (if not earlier), been used in low s., not necessarily pejoratively. But *mot of the ken* (Mayhew) = matron of the establishment. A thinned form of **mort*.—2. A harlot : c. : from ca. 1790 ; ob. Grose, Vaux, Maginn, Henley. A variant of *mort*, q.v.

mot, v.i. To go wenching : c.: C. 19–20 ; ob. Ex *mot*, n., 2.

mot-cart. A brougham : ca. 1820–70 : low (prob. orig. c.).—2. A mattress : low : (— 1890). Barrère & Leland. Ex *mot*, 2.

*mot-case. A brothel : c.: mid-C. 19–20 ; ob. (Manchon.) Ex *mot*, n., 2.

mote, v.i., with vbl.n. *moting*. To drive or ride in a motor-car : coll. : 1890–ca. 1907. A prospectus of June, 1890 (*moting*) ; *The Westminster Gazette*, Jan. 18, 1898, ' Leaving London about midday we shall mote to Ascot.' O.E.D.

moth. A harlot : from ca. 1870 ; very ob. : low. Either ex the attraction of night-lights or ex † S.E. sense, ' vermin '.

Mother. A Western Front nickname for various big howitzers (9·2's). F. & Gibbons. A 12-inch was gen. called *grandmother* ; a 15-inch, *great-grandmother* (B. & P.).

mother. See list at **Modern Babylon.**—2. A female bawd : low coll. : late C. 17–20, but in C. 18 gen., and in C. 19–20 only, applied to the keeper of a brothel. B.E., Grose. Also, in reference, *the mother*. Also **mother abbess** (C. 18–mid-19; see abbess), **m. damnable**, q.v., **m. midnight**, q.v., **mother of the maids**, q.v.—3. Abbr. (— 1909) *mother and daughter*. Ware.

mother ?, did you tell your mother. See **mother know . . .**

mother, he'll be a man before his. A derisive c.p. either in retort or, more gen., in comment : from C.17 ; ob. Not in polite circles.

mother and daughter. Water : rhyming s. (— 1864). H., 3rd ed.

Mother Bunch. A short, stout woman : lower classes' coll. (— 1923). Manchon.

Mother Carey's chickens. Snow : nautical (— 1864). H., 3rd ed.—2. Applied to faring alike and paying the same : ca. 1820–50. ' Jon Bee.'—3. Applied to a small gun : naval : C. 20. Bowen.

mother damnable. A female brothel-manager : C. 19–20 ; ob. See **mother.**

Mother Hubbard. The poet Spenser : late C. 16. Ex his *Mother Hubbard's Tale.* Dawson.

mother-in-law. A step-mother : C. 16–20 : S.E. till ca. 1860 ; then catachrestic.—2. A mixture of ' old and bitter ' (sc. ales), hence the etymology : 1884, *The Daily Telegraph*, July 3 ; ob. Mostly public-house.

mother-in-law's bit. A small piece : coll. : from ca. 1780. Grose, who thereby designates a step-mother ; cf. preceding entry, sense 1.

mother know you're out ?, does your. A derisive c.p. addressed to a person showing extreme simplicity or youthful presumption : 1838, in Bentley's *Miscellany*, ' " How's your mother ? Does she know that you are out ? " ' (O.E.D.) Baumann, 1887, has *what will your mother say ?* and *did you tell your mother ?*—2. Also in more gen. circumstances (— 1895). Both uses, slightly ob. by 1915 ; now moribund.

mother makes it, like. Very well cooked; extremely tasty : lower classes' coll. : late C. 19–20. Collinson. Prob. with allusion to many married men's stock complaint, ' Umph ! not like (my) mother makes it.'

mother midnight. A female bawd : low : late C. 17–18. B.E.—2. A midwife : low : late C. 17–20 ; ob. The latter sense (B.E., Grose) always predominated.

mother of all saints or souls,—of masons,—of St. Patrick. The female pudend : low : resp. G. A. Stevens, 1785 ; Grose, 3rd ed. (say 1791), likewise ob. ; ca. 1810–70, ' Jon Bee ' ; *Lex. Bal.*, 1811. Anglo-Irish and ob. All are low.

mother of the maids. A female brothel-keeper : low coll. : ca. 1787–1830. Grose, 2nd ed. Ex— and in derision of—the ca. 1570–1800 title of the head of the maids of honour in a Royal household.

Mother of the Modern Drama. A certain English actress that, in 1884, ' took up high matronly ground in a lecture . . . at Birmingham ' : theatrical : 1884–ca. 1910. Ware. She spoke of retiring at the age of forty : she had already passed that age.

mother sold her mangle ?, has your. An urban (mostly London) c.p. of no special application : somewhat low : ca. 1870–1900.

mother or grandmother to suck eggs, teach one's. See **eggs**.

mother's blessing, or M. B. Proletarian (— 1861 ; ob.), as in Mayhew, ' My husband's bedridden, and can't do nothink but give the babies a dose of " Mother's Blessing " (that's laudanum, sir, or some sich stuff) to sleep 'em when they's squally.'

mother's meeting. ' The captain's address to a ship's company ' : naval (bluejackets') : from ca. 1912. F. & Gibbons.

mother's milk. Gin : from ca. 1820 ; ob. : low. Moncrieff.—2. Hence, spirits of any kind : from ca. 1860 ; very ob. Dion Boucicault.

mother's (or mothers') ruin. Gin : late C. 19–20. Perhaps it is rhyming s.

mother's white-haired boy. A mother's darling : coll., gen. derisive : from ca. 1895.

motor. A *fast* man about town : London Society : 1896–ca. 99. Ware.—2. A tutor for examinations : Oxford University : 1897–ca. 1900. Ibid. Simply a pun on *coach*.

***mott.** See **mot**.—**motte**, the *mons veneris*, is very doubtfully eligible.

motter. ' Name given to the motor carriage on its very first official appearance in London on Lord Mayor's Day, 1896 ' : Cockneys' : 1896–8 (or 9). Ware.

motting, vbl.n. Wenching ; whoring : C. 19–20 low ; ob. Ex *mot*, v., q.v.

mottled. Dull, boring ; disgusting : from ca. 1929 ; very ob. A. A. Milne, *Two People*, 1931 (see quotation at *throw up*).

***motto.** Drunk : tramps' c. (— 1923). Manchon. Ex Romany.

mottob, n. Bottom : back s. (— 1859). H., 1st ed.

moty. A motor-car ; also adj., as in *moty car* : sol. and dial. : C. 20.

mouch, moucher, mouching. See resp. **mooch, moocher, mooching**.

mouchey, Mouchey. A Jew : low : from ca. 1860 ; ob. H., 3rd ed. Ex or cognate with *Moses* : cf. Ger. *Mauschel* (Baumann). Cf. *Yid*, q.v.—2. (**Mouchy** or **mouchy**.) The inevitable

nickname of men surnamed Reeves : mostly military : C. 20. F. & Gibbons.

mought, v. Might : once (C. 16–17) S.E ; now only dial. and sol. (O.E.D. ; Manchon.)

moulder. ' A lumbering boxer, one who fights as if he were moulding clay,' Bee. 1823 : pugilists' : ca. 1820–1900.

mouldies. Old clothes ; *moult the mouldies*, get rid of, change, one's old clothes : Cockney : 1895, James Greenwood, *Inside a 'Bus*. I.e. clothes going mouldy. Cf. *mouldy*, adj., 2.

mouldy. A purser's steward : nautical : from ca. 1875 ; very ob. Ex *mouldy provisions*.—2. A torpedo : naval : 1915. F. & Gibbons ; Brown. Prob. ex Scottish and Northern dial. *moudie*, a mole, ex *mould*, earth. Hence, *squirt a mouldy*, to fire a torpedo : F. & Gibbons.

mouldy, adj. Grey-headed : from ca. 1860 ; ob. H., 3rd ed. Cf. *mouldy-pate*, q.v.—2. Worthless : coll. : from ca. 1890, as in ' a mouldy offer '. Anticipated in 1876 by Stevenson, ' I have had to fight against pretty mouldy health ' (O.E.D.). Ex the S.E. senses, decaying, decayed, lit. and fig. Cf. *dusty*.—3. Very drunk : Anglo-Irish (esp. public-houses') : C. 20. Cf. *maggoty*.

mouldy-grub. (Gen. in pl.) A travelling showman ; an open-air mountebank : low : from ca. 1860 ; ob. H., 3rd ed. Hence, vbl.n., *mouldy-grubbing*, the work of such persons. In S.E., the term is † for *mulligrubs*.

mouldy one or 'un. A copper coin : low : from ca. 1850 ; ob. Ex colour.

mouldy-pate. A lackey with powdered head : ca. 1860–1900. H., 3rd ed.

mounch-present (as in Awdelay). See **munch-present**.

mounseer or Mounseer. A Frenchman : mid-C. 17–20 : S.E. till C. 19, then (low) coll. when not jocular S.E. ; ob. W. S. Gilbert, e.g. in *Ruddigore*. Cf. *mossoo*, q.v. Baumann, 1887, has the nautical *Mounseer Cockoolu*, which was † by 1930.

mount. A bridge : c. : C. 18–19. But only in **Mount, the**, q.v.—2. A saddle-horse : coll. : 1856, Whyte-Melville, ' A dangerous and uncontrollable mount '.—3. A copulation : low coll. : from ca. 1856 ; ob. Cf. *ride*.—4. Hence (?), a wife or a mistress : from ca. 1856 : low.—5. Any machine ; *on a mount*, driving a derrick, etc., etc. : Public Works' (— 1935). Ex S.E. *mount*, the mounting of a machine.

mount, v. To get upon in order to copulate with : late C. 16–20 : S.E. till C. 19, then (of animals) coll. or (of persons) low coll.—2. To supply, ' set up ' : ca. 1770–1890. D. Graham, 1775, ' The old woman . . . mounted [Tom] like a gentleman,' O.E.D.—3. (Occ. v.i.) to prepare for representation on the stage : theatrical (— 1874) coll. > S.E. in C. 20. H., 5th ed.—4. In c., v.i., to swear falsely, commit perjury, for money : from ca. 1780 ; ob. G. Parker ; *The Daily Chronicle*, March 6, 1902 (O.E.D.). Vbl.n., *mounting*.—5. (Likewise in c.) *mount for = bonnet for*, q.v. Vaux, 1812 ; † by 1900.—6. To read the record of the previous convictions of (a criminal) : c. (— 1933). Charles E. Leach. Cf. sense 3.

***Mount, the.** London Bridge : c. (— 1718) ; † by 1900. C. Hitchin, *The Regulator*. In approaching it, one mounts a rise.

Mount Misery. ' Monkey Island, from its coldness in bad weather ', Bowen : nautical : late C. 19–20.

Mount Pleasant. The *mons veneris* : low : from ca. 1880 ; ob. Ex the London district and the pubic eminence. Cf. *Shooter's Hill.*

mount the ass. To go bankrupt : coll. : late C. 18–mid-19. Ex the old Fr. custom of mounting a bankrupt on an ass, face to tail, and leading him through the streets.

mount the cart. To be hanged : lower classes' coll. : C. 18–early 19. Ware. The victims proceeded in a cart to the place of execution.

mountain-dew. Scotch whiskey : 1816, Scott : coll. >, ca. 1860, S.E. Bee, 1823, defines it, however, as contraband whiskey.

mountain of piety, climb the. To pawn some of one's effects : jocular coll. (— 1891) ; ob. By itself, *mount(ain) of piety* is S.E., C. 17–20, ob.

mountain-pecker. A sheep's head : low (— 1859) ; † by 1910. H., 1st ed. Cf. *jemmy,* 5, q.v.

mounted pitcher. ' A grafter who talks and demonstrates from the top of his stall high above the crowd ' : grafters' coll., verging on j. : late C. 19–20. Philip Allingham, *Cheapjack,* 1934. Hence, *work mounted,* to do this : id. : id. Ibid.

*mounter. A swearer of false evidence, a giver of false bail : c. : from ca. 1780 ; ob. Implicit in G. Parker, 1781 ; Vaux. Ex *mount,* v., 4.

Mounties, the. The Canadian *Mounted* Police Force : from ca. 1890 : Canadian s. >, ca. 1930, coll. Occ. in singular, a member of that force. See esp. the cinema.—2. Hence, the Camel Corps in Egypt : coll. (— 1931). O.E.D. (Sup.).

Mournful Maria. ' The Dunkirk syren, employed to give warning of enemy air attacks and long-range shelling ' : military : 1916–18. F. & Gibbons.

Mournful Monday. The day (Oct. 30, 1899) of the British defeat by the Boers at Nicholson's Nek : journalistic coll. > S.E. : late 1899–ca. 1905. O.E.D.

mourning. The adj. (bruised) is S.E.—2. As n., two black eyes. Hence, *half-mourning,* one black eye. Gen., however, *in mourning,* bruised, black, either (of eyes) *to be in mourning* or (of persons) *have one's eyes in mourning* : mostly pugilistic : 1814 (O.E.D.), *The Sporting Magazine* ; 1820, ' Peter Corcoran ' Reynolds. See also **Blackwall.**—3. Both vbl. forms are likewise, from ca. 1880, applied to dirty finger-nails.

mourning, (full) suit of. Two black eyes (— 1864). H., 3rd ed.

mourning-band. A dirty, esp. a black, edge to a finger-nail : from ca. 1880.

mourning-coach horse. ' A tall, solemn woman, dressed in black and many inky feathers ' : London middle classes' : ca. 1850–90. Ware.

mourning shirt. As an unlaundered shirt, it is jocular S.E. (C. 17–19).—2. A flannel shirt, since it requires comparatively infrequent laundering (— 1908). O.E.D.

mouse. A raised bruise : pugilistic : 1854, ' Cuthbert Bede ' ; ob. Ex the bluish colour.— 2. Hence, a black eye (cf. *mourning,* q.v.) : from ca. 1860. H., 3rd ed. ; 1895, *The Westminster Gazette,* ' A black eye in true cockney slang is known as a mouse.'—3. F. & H. says that it also = the face, the mouth : prob. this is fleeting s. of the 1890's, but I find no other record of these two senses.— 4. The penis : low : C. 19–20 ; ob.—5. A woman, esp. a harlot, arrested for brawling or assault : London police's : ca. 1780–1800. R. King, 1781

(O.E.D.).—6. A barrister ; occ. a solicitor (cf. the c. sense of *mouthpiece*) : ca. 1888–1910 : low (? orig. c.). Nat Gould.

mouse ! Be quiet, or talk low ! ; softly ! : low : C. 19. Mostly U.S.

mouse, (as) drunk as a. Very drunk : C. 14–20 ; ob. : proverbial coll. Orig. *(as) drunk as a drowned mouse.*

mouse-buttock. See **mouse-piece.**

mouse-digger. Winchester College, ca. 1840–1910. Mansfield, 1866, ' Plying the mouse digger (a kind of diminutive pick-axe) in search of mice '.

mouse-foot !, by (the). A mild coll. oath : ca. 1560–1640. A. Dent, 1601, ' I know a man that will never sweare but by Cocke, or Pie, or Mouse Foot. I hope you will not say these be oaths.'

mouse-hunt. A wencher : coll. : late C. 16–mid-17. Shakespeare. ? also *mouse-hunter.*

mouse in a cheese, speak like a. I.e. faintly ; indistinctly : proverbial coll. : late C. 16–20 ; ob.

mouse in a churn, warm as a. Very snug : proverbial coll. : ca. 1670–1720. Ray.

mouse-piece or **-buttock.** (In beef or mutton) that part immediately above the knee-joint : coll. and dial. : C. 19–20 ; ob. In S.E., *mouse.*

mouse tied with a thread, as sure as a. Very far from sure : proverbial coll. : ca. 1540–1600. ' Proverbs ' Heywood. (Apperson.)

mouse-trap. The mouth : low : C. 19–20 ; ob.— 2. The female pudend : low : from ca. 1850 ; ob.— 3. A sovereign : low : from ca. 1855. Ex ' a fancied resemblance of the crown and shield to a set trap ', F. & H.

mouse-trap, the parson's. Marriage : late C. 17–19. B.E. ; Grose, 1st ed.

mouser. The female pudend, the ' cat ' (q.v.) : low : C. 19–20 ; ob.—2. A battalion man, because, like a cat, he remains in quarters, to watch the mice : militia : C. 19. C. James, in his *Military Dict.,* 1802 (O.E.D.)—3. A detective (— 1863 ; ob.) : low (? orig. c.). O.E.D.

mouses. See **mices.**

mousgeron, a C. 18 error for *mousseron,* a white mushroom. O.E.D.

mouth. See list at **Modern Babylon.**—2. A noisy, prating, ignorant fellow : late C. 17–mid-19 ; anticipated in Shakespeare. Dyche. Cf. *mouth almighty,* q.v.—3. A dupe (Cotton, 1680) ; hence, a fool (1753, Poulter) : c. >, as in H., 3rd ed., low s. ; ob.—4. Spoken impudence (cf. *cheek* and esp. *lip,* q.v.) : C. 19–20 ; ob. Not very gen.—5. The dry or furry mouth caused by a debauch : low coll. : from ca. 1870. ' He has a mouth this morning.' Cf. *hot coppers.*

[**mouth, down in the,** dejected, is S.E. (C. 17–20) : since ca. 1890, almost coll.]

mouth, occ. face, laugh on the wrong side of one's, is S.E., but **sing on the . . .** is coll. : from ca. 1760.

mouth, shoot one's. See **shoot off one's mouth** and **shoot one's mouth off.**

mouth !, shut your. Stop talking ! : low coll. (— 1895). Cf. Fr. *ferme !*

mouth almighty. A noisy, talkative person : low : ca. 1860–1910. H., 3rd ed.

mouth and will die a lip, you are a. A low, abusive c.p. of ca. 1860–80. H., 3rd ed. Ex *mouth,* n., 2 (esp.) and 1.

mouth-bet. A verbal bet : the turf : from ca. 1860 ; ob.

mouth half cocked. A person gaping and staring

ignorantly at everything he sees : **coll.** : late C. 17–early 19. B.E., Grose (1st ed.).

mouth like the bottom of a bird-cage or (Manchon) **parrot-cage, have a ;** or **one's mouth feels like the bottom,** etc. To have a ' mouth ' after drinking : from ca. 1920.

mouth-organ. A Stokes-mortar bomb : military : 1916 ; ob. F. & Gibbons, ' From the sound made by the air passing through the holes round the base of the shell as it starts '.

mouth-pie. A feminine scolding or wrangle : Cockneys' (— 1909). Ware.

mouth thankless. The female pudend : low Scots : mid-C. 16–early 17. Kennedy, A. Scott.

mouth that cannot bite or **says no words about it.** The female pudend : C. 18–mid-19 : low coll. ; occ. euphemistic S.E. D'Urfey (latter form).

mouth wide, open one's. To ask a high price : coll. : from ca. 1890. C. Roberts, 1891, ' To use a vulgarism, he did not open his mouth so wide as the other ' (O.E.D.). In C. 20, often of things other than money and occ. *open one's mouth too wide.*

mouther. A blow on the mouth : boxing : 1814 (O.E.D.) ; slightly ob.

mouthful. A long word, esp. a name, that ' fills ' the mouth : coll. : 1884. O.E.D. Cf. :

mouthful, say a. To say something important or arresting : U.S. (ca. 1920), anglicised in 1929. (O.E.D. Sup.)

mouthful of moonshine, give one a. To feed on fair words : late C. 18–mid-19 : coll. Ray, ed. of 1813. (Apperson.)

*mouthpiece. A defending counsel ; a solicitor : c. (— 1857). ' Ducange Anglicus ' ; H., 1st ed. ; J. Greenwood ; Charles E. Leach, 1933.

movables. See **moveables.**

move, a (gen. clever or sly) action or movement, is S.E., but *flash to* (e.g. *every move*), 1812, was perhaps orig. c. († by 1900), *fly to* . . . (see **fly**) is low s. ; *up to* (— 1859), perhaps orig. coll., is S.E. in C. 20.

move, *v.i.* To depart, make a start ; move away or off : mid-C. 15–20 : S.E. till ca. 1750, then coll. Toldervy, Haliburton. O.E.D.

move off. To die : coll. : from ca. 1760 ; ob. Foote, ' Whether from the fall or the fright, the Major mov'd off in a month ' (O.E.D.). Cf. *go off.*

move on, get a, *v.i.* To hurry ; make progress : coll. : orig. U.S. ; anglicised ca. 1907. (Lyell.)

move the previous question. To speak evasively : Society (— 1909) ; ob. Ware. Ex Parliamentary j.

move to. To bow to (a person) : app. ca. 1900–20. A. H. Dawson, *A Dict. of Slang,* 1913.

mov(e)ables is S.E. except ca. 1690–1830 in the sense of swords, jewellery, watches, small objects of value, which is c. B.E., Grose.

movie, rarely **movy.** Of the cinema : from ca. 1914 : coll. Esp. in *a movie star.* Ex :—2. A moving picture : coll., orig. (1906 or 1907) U.S., anglicised ca. 1913. Much less gen. than the derivative :

movies. Moving pictures : the cinema : U.S. (— 1913), anglicised as a coll. ca. 1917. W., ' Current [1920] use of *movies* (U.S.) is curiously like that of Tudor *motions* for a puppet-play.'—2. ' The 80-foot motor launches built in the U.S. . . . during the [G.W.] ' : naval : 1917 ; ob. Bowen.—3. A warship's searchlights : id. : id. Ibid.

Moving-Picture Slang. Most of the terms in the following short article, ' It is Said in Filmland :

' Slanguage " the " Movies " Have Made ', reprinted—with many thanks to the proprietors and the editor—from *Tit-Bits,* March 31, 1934, date, in England, from ca. 1930 :—

The visitor to a foreign country expects to hear the natives speaking a tongue which is unlike his own, but it comes as a surprise to a visitor to a modern studio to find the technicians and artists speaking one of the strangest languages ever evolved.

2.[1] Every trade and profession has its own jargon, but the film world has a colourful compilation of expressions unlike those in other walks of life.

3. " Niggers " are not men of colour, but blackboards used to " kill " unwanted reflections from the powerful lights. The latter, however, are not called lights but " inkies " (short for incandescent), or " sun arcs " (searchlights), or " baby spots " (powerful lamps giving a very narrow beam), or " broads " (lights which give flat, over-all lighting). " Spiders " are the switches into which connections are plugged. When it is bristling with cables on all sides it is not unlike a giant spider. The " organ " is not a musical instrument but a control panel which enables the technicians to start up the cameras and sound-recording apparatus, switch on red warning lamps outside the doors, and cut out all telephones.

4. " Gertrude " is not a young lady, but a giant steel crane, with a camera at its head, which enables shots to be taken of players going up staircases or along balconies. " Dollies ", too, have nothing to do with femininity ; they are the low trucks, with pneumatic-tyred wheels, on which cameras follow stars as they hurry through hotel foyers or along the decks of liners.

5. Here are some more studio terms. " Juicers " are electricians ; " lens hogs " are stars who are over-anxious to hold the dead centre of the picture. A " wild " scene has nothing to do with Hollywood parties, it is the terse description for scenes, usually of cars, aeroplanes or trains, which have appropriate fake sounds added in the laboratory after they have been photographically recorded.

6. When a film is completed it is " in the can ". Every time a scene is successfully " shot " [2] it is called " a take " ; the whole of the day's " takes " are then assembled and shown to the producer in a private projection room, but are then known as " the rushes " or " the dailies ". Exposed film is " stuff " ; unexposed film is " raw stock " If too much film has been shot on a scene, the surplus is known as " grief ". The chemicals in which film is developed are known as " soup ".

7. But not all studio terms are coined ; as in other walks of life, many of the expressions used owe nothing to slang and everything to tradition.

8. For instance, a broadly funny situation is known as " a Mack Sennett " ; a film cheaply and hurriedly made is known as " A Poverty Row Picture ", in commemoration of the days when Gower Street, Hollywood (nicknamed Poverty Row), was the home of small independent companies turning out pictures quickly and cheaply.

9. " To do a Gaynor " means to smile upwards through eyes swimming with tears, a tribute to Janet Gaynor's ability to switch on the " sunshine through the tears ".

[1] The paragraph-numbers are not in the original. (Editor.)
[2] This is S.E. (Editor.)

10. " To do a Garbo ", on the other hand, means to be proud, aloof, and unbending.

11. But perhaps the most picturesque phrase of all is " the lot ", which is always used to describe the company's land surrounding the studio. It has been in use since the days when, before studios were thought of, all " interior " scenes were made in the open air (sunlight being the only satisfactory illuminant thirty years ago), and for which purpose hard-pressed pioneers rented vacant building lots.

mow. To copulate with : Scots and Northern dial. or coll. : C. 16–early 19. The word, occ. as a n., survived in low s. till late C. 19. Scots, either dial. or coll., is *mowdiwark* or *-wort*, the penis.

*****mow-heater.** A drover : c. : mid-C. 17–mid-19. Coles, 1676. Ex the drovers' habit of sleeping on hay mows (Grose, 2nd ed.).

*****mower.** A cow : c. : ca. 1670–1830. Coles, 1676. Perversion of *mooer*, q.v.

Mowree. A New Zealand seaman : nautical : late C. 19–20. Bowen. Ex *Maori*.

[**mowrowsky.** See **marrowskying.** Ware's form and spelling.]

mozzy. Judy ; cf. *Swatchell, Punch.* Show-men's : from ca. 1850. ? via Lingua Franca ex It. *moglie*, wife.

Mr. See **mister.—Mr. and Mrs. Wood.** See **Wood** in front.—**Mr. Burton's Night School.** See **Cass, the.—Mr. Ferguson, Knap, Mackenzie, Nash, Palmer, Pullen, Right, Smith.** See each name.

Mr. Whip. See **Billy Blue.**

Mrs. An occ. written form of *missis* (*missus*), q.v. (—See **Modern Babylon** list.)

Mrs Chant. Aunt : C. 20. P. P., *Rhyming Slang,* 1932. Cf. :

Mrs Ducket(t). A bucket : C. 20. (P. P., 1932.)

Mrs. Gamp, Mrs. Harris. (Gen. together.) *The Standard, The Morning Herald,* esp. when they were owned by a Mr. Baldwin : ca. 1845–60 : journalists'. Ex Mrs. Gamp and her imaginary friend Mrs. Harris in Dickens's *Martin Chuzzlewit* and the way those inter-appealing newspapers had of pretending to be independent.

Mrs Green. See **sleep with Mrs Green.**

Mrs. Jones. A water-closet : low : from ca. 1860 ; ob. H., 2nd ed. Gen. as *visit* or *go to see Mrs. Jones.* Cf. *my aunt's* and *Sir Harry.*

Mrs. Kell(e)y !, you must know. A c.p. ' with no particular meaning ', gen. addressed to ' a long-winded talker ' : London : 1898–1905. Ex a ' phrase used for two years at all times and places by Dan Leno '. Ware.

Mrs. Langtry. See **Langtries.**

*****Mrs. Lukey Props.** A female brothel-keeper : tramps' c. (– 1896) ; ob.

Mrs. Partington. A personification of impotent and senile prejudice ' : 1831 ; ob. : coll. >, ca. 1890, S.E. Sydney Smith.—2. Also, ' a kind of Malaprop ', F. & H. : coll., in C. 20 verging on S.E. but very ob. Besant & Rice, 1872, ' As Mrs. Partington would say, they might all three have been twins.'

Mrs. Suds. A washerwoman, a laundress : 1757, Foote ; ob. : coll.

M's and W's, make. To be drunk, esp. walk un-steadily : printers' : from ca. 1860.

mss or **MSS** (earlier **MSS**ᵗ), as a singular, is cata-chrestic. Written only.

mubblefubbles. Low spirits : ca. 1585–1670. Lyly, Gayton, O.E.D. ? echoic ; cf. *mulligrubs.*

much ?, how. See **how much.**

much !, not. Not likely or certainly not ! : coll. : from ca. 1885.

[**much matter of a wooden platter.** Much fuss about a trifle : ca. 1630–1750. A proverb verging on coll. Apperson.]

much of a . . ., with a negative. A great . . . ; a . . . of a noteworthy quality or to any great degree. Coll. : from ca. 1840. Dickens, ' He don't lose much of a dinner.' In C. 20, gen. of persons, e.g. ' not much of a scholar ', O.E.D.

much of a muchness. Of much the same size, degree, value or importance ; very much alike ; coll. : 1728, Vanbrugh (O.E.D.) ; 1860, *Punch* ; 1876, G. Eliot, ' Gentle or simple, they're much of a muchness.'

much wit as three folks—two fools and a madman. Always preceded by *as* ; gen. also with *have.* (To be) tolerably clever or cunning ; also (to be) a fool. A derisive c.p. bordering on the proverbial. Mostly Cheshire. Ray, Lytton. (Apperson.)

[**muchly** is jocular S.E.—S.E. also are **muck** (money), **muck-worm** (a miser), **muckender** or **-inder, muckerer** or **mokerer** (a miser), **muddle,** n. and v., **muddle away, muddle-head, muff-** or **muffin-cap, muggy** (of weather), **mughouse, mule** (obstinate person), **mull,** a cow (also dial.), **mum** (see **mum,** 2), **mum-budget, mumble-crust, mumbo-jumbo, mumchance, mumming-show,** (beat to a) **mummy, mumpish, mumps, mumpsimus, mun-dungus** or **-go,** n. (tobacco : verging on coll.) and adj. (stinking : ditto), **mushroom** (upstart), **muss** (an endearment), (dead as) **mutton, mutton-head,** (return to one's) **muttons, muzzle** (the mouth ; to kiss) ; **muzzard** like **muddle,** to coït with (a woman), and **mugger,** a hawker, a Gypsy, is dial. :—All are wrongly listed by F. & H.]

mucidine is an error for *mucedin(e)* : from ca. 1870. O.E.D.

muck. In *run a muck* = *run amuck, muck* is catachrestic : 1687 (S.O.D.) ; rare in C. 20.—2. A very untidy, an uncleanly condition : (low) coll. : 1766, Goldsmith, ' She observed, that " by the living jingo, she was all of a muck of sweat ".' Gen. *be in a,* or *all of a, muck.*—3. Filth, dirt, esp. if an oozing mass : C. 14–20 : S.E. till ca. 1840, then coll., increasingly low. Dickens, Calverley. Like sense 2, O.E.D.—4. Anything (soil, gravel, clay) excavated : Public Works' coll. : late C. 19–20.—5. Anything vile or disgusting : coll. : 1888, *The Sportsman,* Nov. 28, ' Drinking sech like muck.'—6. A coarse brute : low coll. : from ca. 1885. Baumann. Anticipated in ' Muck' : that's my opinion of him ', 1884, Henley & Stevenson.—7. Hence, an infantryman ; the infantry : cavalry-men's (– 1909) ; virtually †,—as are the cavalry. Ware.—8. A heavy fall, lit. or fig. : from ca. 1892 ; ob. Abbr. *mucker,* q.v. : see also **mucker, go a.**—9. A failure : Public Schools. coll. : late C. 19–20. D. Coke, *The Bending of a Twig,* 1906, ' Make a muck of it.' Cf. sense 5 of :

muck. To make dirty : from ca. 1830 : S.E. till ca. 1895, then coll. (increasingly low).—2. F. & H.'s ' to spend ' is almost certainly an error for, and caused by the quotation in :—3. To excel ; beat : low : from ca. 1850 ; ob. Mayhew, ' He'd muck a thousand ! '—4. Hence, to ruin (a person) : low : from ca. 1890. Milliken, ' I'm mucked, that's a moral '.—5. To fail in or at : 1899, Kipling, ' I shall muck it. I know I shall ' (O.E.D.). Cf. *muck up,* 2.—6. See :

[muck !, mucker, mucking, have from ca. 1915 represented *fuck !*, etc. Except when used jocularly, these are mere printers' words ; and even when jocular, they derive from these letter-equivalences of the actual vulgarisms and are deliberate. Frequent in War books of 1929–30, and since. A century hence, some curious errors will arise in respect of *muck = fuck*, etc.]

muck, chief. (Of a person) a trump : low (— 1887) ; ob. Baumann. Cf. :

Muck, Lord. A person unjustifiably, or in the speaker's opinion unjustifiably, important or esteemed : (low) coll. : from the 1890's. Prob. suggested by the preceding term.

muck about. To fondle or caress very intimately : low, mostly costers' : from ca. 1880. Stronger than *mess about*, q.v.—2. V.i., wander aimlessly ; potter about : s. >, ca. 1915, coll. : 1896, Kipling, ' Our Colonel . . . mucks about in 'orspital ' (O.E.D.).

muck and halfpenny afters. A bad, pretentious dinner : lower-middle classes' (— 1909) ; virtually †. Ware.

muck and truck. Miscellaneous articles : commerce (— 1898) ; ob. O.E.D.

muck-cheap. ' Dirt-cheap ' : coll. : from ca. 1870 ; ob. Cf. *muck*, n., 3. Cf. the Fr. *salement bon marché* (Manchon).

muck-fork. A finger ; occ. a hand : low : from ca. 1850.

muck-heap. A filthy sloven : coll. : ca. 1860–1910. Cf. *muck-suckle*, q.v.

muck in, v.i. To share rations, sleeping quarters and certain duties ; an informal method and group, this social unit of the Army was arranged by the men themselves and respected by N.C.O.'s ; it protected and furthered its own interests. Military (rare outside of English units) : 1915+. See esp. though passim, Frederick Manning's *Her Privates We*, 1930 ; and B. & P. at *mucking-in* (3rd ed., p. 141).—2. Hence, v.t., *muck in with*. F. & Gibbons.

muck of, make a. A coll. variant of *muck up*, 2 : from late C. 19.

muck out. To clean out (of money) ; ruin : low : from ca. 1855. H., 1st ed.

muck-snipe. A ruined person, esp. gambler : low : ca. 1850–1910. Mayhew.

muck-spout. A foul-mouthed talker : low : from ca. 1870 ; ob.

muck-suckle. A filthy woman : low coll. : ca. 1860–1900. Cf. *muck-heap*, q.v.

***muck toper feeker.** An umbrella-maker : Scots c. : ca. 1820–80. Egan's Grose. Prob. the form should be *mush-topper feaker* : see mush and mush-faker.

muck-train. A commissariat train : military : ca. 1885–1914.—2. See **Moke Train.**

muck up. To litter : late C. 19–20 : (low) coll. Mrs. Caffyn, ' Mucking up my rooms ' (O.E.D.).— 2. To spoil, ruin, e.g. a person but esp. a plan : from ca. 1885. Cf. *muck*, v., 4. Baumann.—3. Hence, as n., a complete failure ; confusion or muddle.

muck-up in a dixie. A stew : military : from ca. 1910.

muckcook. To laugh behind one's back (v.i.) : low : ca. 1880–1905. Origin ?

mucked out, ppl.adj. Penniless : low : from ca. 1820 ; ob. Egan's Grose ; H., 1st ed.

mucker. (See the **muck !, mucker, mucking** entry.—) 2. A heavy fall : from ca. 1850. Esp.

in *come* or (ob.) *go a mucker* ; often fig., come to grief. Kingsley, 1852, ' Receiving a *mucker* ' (lit., of a horse) ; J. Payn, 1876, ' A regular mucker ' (fig.). Because frequently caused by road-filth or muck. O.E.D.—3. A quartermaster : military : ca. 1885–1910.

mucker, v. To have a heavy fall ; hence fig., come to grief : from ca. 1860 ; ob. Kingsley.— 2. V.t., to ruin (one's chances) : 1869, ' W. Bradwood ' (O.E.D.). Ob.

Muckeries, the. See **Moocheries, the.**

muckhill at one's door, have a good. To be rich : proverbial coll. : ca. 1670–1720. Ray. Here, as in next, *muckhill* = dung-heap. (Mostly rural.)

'muckhill on my trencher', quoth the bride,— ' you make a '. A c.p. of ca. 1670–1750 and = You carve me a great heap. Ray, Fuller. (Apperson.)

muckibus. Tipsy : low : ca. 1755–1850. Horace Walpole, 1756. Ex *muck*, n.

muckin ; occ. **mucking** or **mukkin.** Butter : Regular Army's : late C. 19–20. F. & Gibbons. Ex Hindustani *makkhn*.

mucking. See the **muck !** . . . entry.—2. An act of ' messing about ' : coll. : 1904, Kipling, ' His photographic muckings ' (O.E.D.). ? no singular. Ob. ; see **mucking-about.**—3. Rubbish, a ' mess ' : coll. : 1898, Kipling, ' She's only burning muckings ' (O.E.D.).—4. See **muckin.**

mucking, adj. Dirty ; disgusting : low coll. (— 1887). Baumann.—2. See **muck !**

mucking-about. A ' messing about ' : s. > coll. : from ca. 1905.—2. An intimate fondling : low (mostly costers') : from ca. 1880. See **muck about.**

mucking-togs ; muckintogs. A mackintosh : low perversion : 1842, Barham ; ob.

mucking-in, vbl.n. and ppl.adj. See **muck in.**

Muckle Flugga Hussars, the. ' The ships on the Northern Patrol of the 10th Cruiser Squadron ' : naval : 1915–18. Bowen. Ex Muckle Flugga, the most northerly of the Orkneys.

mucko. Orderly man : military : C. 20. B. & P. He did the dirty work.

mud. A fool, ' a dull, heavy-headed fellow ', Dyche : low (? orig. c.) : ca. 1710–1850. Whence *one's name is mud* (Bee, 1823) : > coll. : extant.— 2. A non-society (i.e. non-trades union) man : printers' : from ca. 1786 : ob. by 1900, † by 1920. Grose, 2nd ed. Cf. *dung* among tailors.—3. A ' mud-student ', q.v. : C. 20. O.E.D. (Sup.).

mud, clear as, (very) obscure, is S.E., whence **sure as mud,** absolutely certain, is school **s.** : 1899, Eden Phillpotts (O.E.D.) ; slightly ob.

mud, mad as. See **mad as mud.**

mud, one's name is. One has been heavily defeated ; one is in disgrace : from ca. 1820. ' " And his name is mud ! " ejaculated upon the conclusion of a silly oration, or of a leader in the *Courier* ', 1823, ' Jon Bee '. See also **mud** : the sense has changed, for in C. 20 mire, not a dull fool, is understood to be the origin.

mud-crawling. ' Country route marching in wet weather ' : military : C. 20. F. & Gibbons. Cf. :

mud-crusher. An infantryman (not often applied to an officer) : military : from ca. 1872. H., 5th ed. ; Sir G. Chesney, 1893, ' " You are too good be a mud-crusher, Tommy ", said the Major . . . patronisingly ' (O.E.D.). Cf. *beetle-crusher*, *swaddy*, *toe-footer*, *worm-crusher*, and the Fr. *pousse-cailloux*, pebble-pusher. See esp. *Words !*

mud-fog association. A scientific association in gen., or some particular one : coined by Dickens,

1838, in *Bentley's Magazine*; referred to by C. Dickens, Jr., in *Household Words*, May 1, 1886. Ca. 1860–75, it was rarely used for other than the British Association for the Promotion of Science, esp. at the universities : H., 2nd to 5th edd. Coll. : † by 1896.

mud-gunner. (Gen. pl.) A machine-gunner : military, mostly Australian : 1915 ; virtually †. Rare and possibly ex a mis-hearing of *mug-gunner*, q.v.

mud-head or **mudhead.** A stupid person : coll. : 1838, Haliburton ; D. C. Murray, 1883, ' That old m.-h.'. The adj., *mud-headed*, 1793, is S.E. but likewise ob. O.E.D.

mud-hen. A female speculator : Stock Exchange : U.S., anglicised by 1896.

mud-hole. ' A salt-water lagoon in which whales are captured ', F. & H. : whalers' (— 1893) : coll. >, ca. 1910, j. Ex the churning-up of the water.

mud-honey. Mud ; esp. street slush : low : ca. 1870–1914.

mud-hook. An anchor : nautical (— 1884). ' H. Collingwood ' O.E.D.—2. Hence, the anchor in the game of crown and anchor : nautical and military : C. 20. F. & Gibbons.

Mud Island. Southend : East London's nickname : ca. 1900–14. Ware. Ex its muddy estuary.

mud-lark or **mudlark.** A waterside thief that, niding under a ship at low tide, receives small stolen packets from the crew : c. (— 1796). By 1820, a sea-shore scavenger, who often waded out up to his, or her, waist. The first in Colquhoun's *Police of the Metropolis*, the second (also *mud-larker*, or *mudlarker*) in Egan's Grose and in Mayhew ; the first, ob. by 1890, the second > s. by 1850, coll. by 1900. Suggested by *skylark*.—3. A man that scavenges in gutters, esp. for metal, e.g. horse-nails : c. or low : ca. 1820–50. Bee.—4. Hence an official cleaner of common sewers : coll. (— 1859) ; ob. H., 1st ed. ; Ogilvie.—5. A street arab : coll. : 1865, *The Saturday Review*, July 4. O.E.D.—6. A member of the Royal Engineers : military coll. (— 1878). O.E.D.—7. Any person that, belonging to bank, counting-house, etc., has often, in the course of his work, to be out in the open air : City (London) : from ca. 1860 ; ob. H., 3rd ed.—8. A hog : ca. 1780–1830. Grose (1st ed.), who does not, as stated by F. & H., father, 9, the sense, ' a duck ' ; this definition occurs first in the *Lex. Bal.*, 1811 : ca. 1810–30.—10. A race-horse that revels in muddy ' going ' : Australian sporting coll. : C. 20.—11. (**Mud-Lark** ; gen. pl.) A native of, a person long resident in, Victoria (Australia) : Australian : C. 20.

mud-larker. See **mud-lark**, 1, second part, q.v. : 1840, Marryat. Ob.

mud-major. An infantry major : military (— 1896) ; † by 1915. Because, on parade, he was on foot. Cf. *mud-crusher* and *mud-picker*, qq.v.

mud-pads. The feet : lower classes' (— 1923). Manchon. Contrast *mud-pipes*.

mud-picker. A military policeman in garrison : military : ca. 1895–1910.—2. A soldier in the Engineers : military (— 1923). Manchon.

mud-pilot. ' The pilot who takes a ship from Gravesend to the entrance of her dock ' : nautical : late C. 19–20. Bowen.

mud-pipes. Gum-boots : lower classes' (— 1923). Manchon.

mud-player. A batsman fond of a wet wicket : cricket : ca. 1890–1914.

mud-plunger. An infantryman : (mainly) military : from ca. 1890 ; ob. Cf. *mud-crusher*, q.v., and see ' Soldiers' Slang of Three Nations ' in *Words!*

mud-plunging. A tramping through mud in search of alms : tramps' c. : from ca. 1880. *The Daily Telegraph*, Feb. 8, 1883.

mud-pusher. A crossing-sweeper : urban lower classes' : from ca. 1870. Ware.

Mud-Salad Market. Covent Garden : low London : from the late 1870's ; ob. *Punch*, Aug. 14, 1880, ' Mud-Salad Market belongs to his Grace the Duke of Mudford [!]. It was once a tranquil Convent Garden.'

mud-show. An outdoor show, esp. an agricultural one : Society (— 1909) ; ob. Ware.

mud-slinger ; -slinging. A slanderer ; slander : coll. (orig. low) : from ca. 1890.

mud-student. A student of farming : from ca. 1855. (O.E.D.)—2. Esp. at the Agricultural College, Cirencester (— 1864 ; ob.) H., 3rd ed.

muddie. A childish attempt at, or corruption of, *mother*. Manchon, 1923. Prob. via *mummy*.

mudding-face. A fool ; a soft fellow : low : ca. 1870–1915. Presumably ex *mud*, a fool, and prob. by a pun on *pudding-face*.

muddle. Slight tipsiness : coll. (— 1923). Manchon. Prob. by *muddled* out of *muzzy*.

muddle on. Though half-drunk, to continue drinking : coll. : late C. 17–18. B.E.

muddler. A clumsy horse : turf coll. : from ca. 1886 ; ob.

mudge. A hat : c. (— 1888). *The Sportsman*, Dec. 22, 1888. ? etymology : is it perchance a sense- and form-perversion of *mush*, an umbrella ?

mudger. A milksop : low : 1830, Lytton, ' Girl-faced mudgers' ; ob. by 1880, † by 1910. ? ex dial. *mudge*, to move, budge, hence one moving very quietly.

mudlark. See **mud-lark**.—**mudlarker.** See **mud-larker**.

muff. The female pudend, outwardly : late C. 17–20 ; ob. : orig. c. ; by 1920, low. B.E., who quotes the toast, *to the well-wearing of your muff, mort*.—2. ' A foolish silly person ', Vaux, 1812 : orig. c. >, by 1880, gen. s. ; ob. Ca. 1850–75 it occ. connoted weakness of mind : H., first five edd. H., 2nd ed., ' *muff* has been defined to be " a soft thing that holds a lady's hand without squeezing it " .' Perhaps (cf. sense 1) ex (the *softness* of a) *muff*, the covering for female hands ; Vaux less prob. suggests that it is a perversion of *mouth*, 3.— 3. Whence, orig. in athletic sport, a clumsy and/or a stupid person : 1837, Dickens, ' " Now butter-fingers "—" Muff " . . . and so forth ' (O.E.D.). s. >, ca. 1880, coll.—4. A failure : 1871, *Punch*, Feb. 25, of a book ; ob. Esp. (1896), anything badly bungled. Coll. Ex the v.—5. See **muff, not to say**.—6. A buff, i.e. a muffling-pad attached to a clapper : bell-ringers' (— 1901). H. Earle Bulwer, *A Glossary of Bell-Ringing*, 1901. Abbr. *muffler*.

muff. To bungle, physically or otherwise, esp. at games : 1846, ' Muffed their batting ' (Lewis) ; 1857, G. A. Lawrence, ' I don't see why you should have muffed that shot.'—2. V.i., to fail in an examination : 1884, Julian Sturgis : orig. Eton College s. >, ca. 1890, gen. coll. ; ob.

muff, not to say ; say neither muff nor mum. To say not a word : mid-C. 15–20 : coll. till C. 18, then dial. Stapylton. Ex *muff*, an echoic word 'representing an inarticulate sound', O.E.D.

muffed, ppl. adj. Bungled; clumsily spoilt, missed : from ca. 1860 : s. > coll.

muffin. A fool : low : 1830, W. T. Moncrieff; † by 1910. Ex *muff*, n., 2, prob. by a pun on the light *flat* cake.—2. Whence, at games a constant misser of a shot or a ball : coll. (— 1895); ob. Mostly U.S. Funk & Wagnalls.—3. A man that chaperons or acts as companion to women : from before 1923. Manchon. Prob. ex senses 1 and 2.— 4. One's 'girl', by arrangement, for the social life of a season : Canadian : 1856, Miss Bird : ob. (O.E.D.)—5. A cap of the 'pill-box' type : late .. 19–early 20. F. & Gibbons (at *quiff*).

muffin, cold. Mediocre; (almost) worthless : Cockney : ca. 1890–1910. Milliken.

muffin-baker. A Quaker : rhyming s. (— 1859). H., 1st ed.

muffin-countenance or **-face.** A hairless one, says F. & H. ; an expressionless one, says the O.E.D. with reason : resp. 1823, ob., and 1777 (I. Jackman). Whence :

muffin-faced. Having an expressionless face : C. 19–20, ob. Bee, however, in 1823, implies that it indicates a face with protruding muscles : † by 1890.

muffin-fight ; muffin-worry. A tea-party : coll.: resp. ca. 1885–1910 and 1860, H., 2nd ed. (also in Ouida, 1877). O.E.D. Cf. *bun-worry, tea-fight*.

muffin-puncher. A muffin-baker : Cockneys' (— 1909). Ware.

muffin-walloper. (Gen. pl.) A scandal-loving woman delighting to meet others at a tea-table : London middle classes' : ca. 1880–1914. Ware.

muffing, ppl.adj., bungling, from ca. 1840. John Mills. O.E.D.—N., clumsiness, clumsy failure : from ca. 1860. Both s. > coll. ca. 1890.

muffish. Foolish, silly ; esp. clumsy : coll. : 1858, Farrar (O.E.D.). See muff, n., 2, 3.

muffishness. The quality of being a *muff*, 2, 3, q.v. : coll. : 1858, Farrar (O.E.D.).

muffism. Foolishness ; an action typical of a *muff*, 2, 3, q.v. : coll. : 1854, Lady Lytton : coll. ob. by 1900, almost † by 1930. (O.E.D.)

muffle, a boxing-glove, is prob. S.E. (ca. 1810–40). So, perhaps, is :

muffler, in the same sense : mid-C. 18–20 ; ob.— 2. A stunning blow : boxing : ca. 1820–1905.—3. A crape mask : 1838, Glascock : c. ; ob. Ex the much earlier S.E.

*muffling-cheat. A napkin ; a towel : c. of ca. 1560–1840. Harman ; Grose, 1st ed.

mufti. Plain clothes worn by one who, at work, wears a uniform : 1816 : s. >, ca. 1880, coll. >, ca. 1910, S.E. 'Quiz'; Marryat, 1833, 'In a suit of mufti', the post-1850 form being *in mufti*. O.E.D. Perhaps jestingly ex *mufti*, a Moham-medan priest, via the theatre, which, in early C. 19, represented officers off duty wearing 'flowered dressing-gown and tasselled smoking cap', W.—2. A chaplain on a man-of-war : naval : ca. 1830–50. Marryat, in his *King's Own*.

mug. The face : 1708, *The British Apollo*, 'My Lawyer has . . . a Temple-Mug' (O.E.D.). Prob. ex mugs 'made to represent a grotesque human face '.—2. Hence, the mouth : 1820, J. H. Reynolds, 'Open thy mug, my dear' (O.E.D.). Ob. by 1900, † by 1920.—3. A cooling drink : coll. (1633, S.O.D.) >, ca. 1850, S.E. ; ob.—4. A fool ; an easy dupe ; a 'duffer' : 1857, 'Ducange Anglicus'; Mayhew.

I.e. something into which one can pour any-thing.—5. An examination : from ca. 1852 ; ob. : university and school.—6. Hence, one who studies hard : school : from ca. 1880.—7. See mugs.—8. A mist, a fog : s. and dial. ; the former (as in Ash's Dict., 1775), ca. 1770–80 ; the latter, extant, with further senses, a drizzle, gloomy damp weather.

mug, v. To grimace : theatrical >, ca. 1880, gen. : 1855, Dickens, 'The low comedian had "mugged" at him . . . fifty nights for a wager' (O.E.D.). Slightly ob. Cf. *mug up*. Prob. ex *mug*, to pout : see sense 7, this paragraph.—2. To strike, esp. punch, in the face : boxing : 1818 (O.E.D.) ; ob. Ex mug, n., 1.—Hence, 3, (— 1859), to fight (v.t.), chastise, thrash : H., 1st ed.—4. To bribe with liquor : s. (†) and dial. : 1830 (O.E.D.). Also, in s. and dial., v.i. and v. reflexive, to get drunk : from ca. 1840.—5. Hence, to swindle, to rob (esp. by the garrotte) : low : from ca. 1860 ; ob. Mayhew.—6. V.i., to study hard : 1848 : mostly school and university. (V.t. with *at*.) Perhaps ex the theatrical sense. Occ. *mug away* or *on*. (O.E.D.)—7. Also v.t., to study hard (at) : from ca. 1880. More gen. *mug up*.—Hence, 8, to take pains with (e.g. a room) : Winchester College : from ca. 1870 ; ob. 'He has mugged his study and made it quite cud' (i.e. comfortable), F. & H.—9. (Gen. with *together*), v.i., to crowd in a confined space (— 1878). E.D.D.—10. See mug oneself, 2. —11. To pout ; to sulk : s. (ob.) and dial. : from ca. 1730. Collins the poet. Perhaps ex dial. *mug*, v.i., to drizzle, rain slightly. O.E.D. Cf. sense 1.— 12. To kiss (gen. v.t.) : low Australian (— 1916). C. J. Dennis. Ex *mug*, n., 1.

mug away or **on.** See mug, v., 6 : resp. 1893, 1878. (Prob. years earlier.) O.E.D.

mug-faker. See mugger, theatrical sense.—2. A camera : grafters' : from ca. 1920. Philip Alling-ham, *Cheapjack*, 1934.

mug-gunner. A machine-gunner : Australian military : 1915. Ex initials and the dangerous (*mug's*) job.

*mug-hunter. A robber of drunken men, esp. at night : c. (— 1887) >, ca. 1900, low.

mug in together. A lower classes' post-G.W. corruption of *muck in*, 1.

*mug John. A policeman : Australian c. (— 1935). Ex *mug*, n., 4, + *John*, 4.

*mug-lumberer. A fashionably dressed swindler : c. (— 1923). Manchon. Ex *mug*, n., 4, + *lum-berer*, 2.

mug oneself. See mug, v., 4.—2. To make one-self cosy : low : from ca. 1880 ; ob.

mug-trap. A duper or swindler of fools : 1892, Milliken : low. Cf. *mug-hunter*, q.v.

mug up. V.i., and, more gen., v.t., to study hard : mostly school, university and Army : from ca. 1860 ; ob.—2. V.t. and v.i., to paint one's face : theatrical : 1859, H. ; 1892, Milliken, 'You're mugged up to rights.'—3. To eat : mostly in the Grand Banks schooners : late C. 19–20. Bowen.

mugger. One who studies hard : mostly schools' (— 1883). James Payn.—2. (Also **mug-faker** : 1887, Baumann.) A comedian specialising in grimaces : theatrical : 1892 (also prob. earlier), *The National Observer*, Feb. 27, 'None had ever a more expressive ˜gnomy than this prince of muggers.'— 3. (Also **muggar, muggur.**) A crocodile : Anglo-Indian : 1844 : coll. or, more prob., S.E. See O.E.D. and Yule & Burnell. Ex Hindustani.

*muggill. A beadle : c. of ca. 1600–20. Rowlands, in *Martin Mark-All.* ? etymology.

mugging. Vbl.n. to *mug*, v., 1, 2, 3, 5, 6, qq.v.

muggins. A simpleton, 'juggins' (q.v.), fool : U.S. (ca. 1870), anglicised ca. 1880. Ex *mug*, n., 4, suggested by the surname *Muggins*.—2. A borough-magnate or a local leader : ca. 1890–1910.—3. See :

muggins, talk. To say silly things : 1881, *Punch*, Sept. 10. O.E.D.

[**muggle.** Recorded for 1607 in Middleton and for 1617 in T. Young, this word is perhaps s. 'Origin and meaning obscure', says the O.E.D., but the O.E.D.'s quotations lead me to hypothesise 'sweetheart' in Middleton and 'girl' in T. Young, with etymology in It. *moglia*, a woman.]

*muggled. An adj. applied to cheap goods offered for sale as contraband : c. : from ca. 1850 ; ob. Mayhew. A perversion of *smuggled*.

muggles. Restlessness : ca. 1740–1800. Robertson of Struan, in *Poems*, 1750.

muggur. See **mugger**, 3.

muggy. Drunk : low : from ca. 1858 ; ob. H., 1st ed. Ex dial. *muggy*, damp.

mugs, cut. To grimace : theatrical : from ca. 1820 ; ob. Egan's Grose. Cf. *mug*, n., 1.

mug's corner. The fielding position at mid-on ; that at short leg : cricketers' : ca. 1890–1910. (*The Observer*, March 10, 1935.)

mugster. One who studies hard (i.e. 'mugs') : schools' (— 1888) ; ob.

mugwump. A great man ; an important one : from ca. 1830, and orig. and mainly U.S. : perhaps orig. coll., but certainly soon S.E. Ex the Red Indian for a chief.—2. The v. and the derivatives are certainly S.E.

mukkin. See **muckin**.

mule. A sexually impotent man : low coll. : from ca. 1870. A mule being unable to generate.— 2. A day hand in the composing room : printers' : from ca. 1860 ; ob.

mule, shoe one's. To embezzle : coll. : ca. 1650–1720. Nares.

mulga, a lie ; mulga wire, an unfounded report, usually incorrect ; **it came over the mulga**, a c.p. applied to a tale of doubtful authenticity : Australian : C. 20. Cf. the S.E. *bush telegraph*.

mull. A muddle, a mismanagement, a failure : 1821, Egan, 'Somebody must make a mull' : s. >, ca. 1860, coll. Esp. in *make a mull of*. Prob. ex *muddle* on analogy of *mell, meddle*, W., or perhaps ex dial. *mull*, to pulverise, cause to crumble (O.E.D.).— 2. Hence, or perhaps ex the v., from ca. 1865, a simpleton ; a clumsy fellow. Chiefly *old mull, regular mull*.—3. A Civil Service officer of the Madras Presidency : Anglo-Indian : from ca. 1835. Abbr. *mulligatawny*. Yule & Burnell. Cf. *Duck* and *Qui-Hi*, qq.v.

mull, v. To spoil, muddle : orig. and mainly athletics : coll. : 1862, *Sporting Life*, June 14, 'Pooley here " mulled " a catch' (O.E.D.). Ex the n., 1.

muller, v.t. To cut down a tall hat into a low-crowned one (occ. called a *muller*) : trade : 1864–ca. 85. *The Builder*, Nov., 1864. The hat was also called a *Muller-cut-down*. Ex *Müller*, a murderer that attempted to disguise himself in this way.

mulligatawny. See **mull**, n., 3. Ca. 1810–20. 'Quiz', 1816. ? ex the high seasoning of this East Indian soup and the peppery temper of many officials.

mulligrubs ; in C. 19–20, occ. **mollygrubs**.

Colic : from ca. 1615 : S.E. till C. 19, then coll. Fletcher, in *Monsieur Thomas* ; 'Cuthbert Bede', 1853. O.E.D. Ex :—2. (Esp. in *be in one's mulligrubs.*) Depressed spirits (cf. *mubble-fubbles*) : C. 17–20 (anticipated in 1599 by Nashe's *mulligrums*, which persists in dial.) : S.E. till C. 19, then coll. Scott (of a drink), 'Right . . . as ever washed mulligrubs out of a moody brain'. Both senses, esp. the latter, are ob. A fantastic formation, perhaps on *mouldy grubs*.

Mullingar heifer. (A development from the *Lexicon Balatronicum's Munster heifer*, q.v.) A thick-ankled girl : Anglo-Irish : from ca. 1860 ; ob. H., 3rd ed.

Mullingars. Shares in the Midland Great Western Railway of Ireland : Stock Exchange coll. (—1895). A. J. Wilson, *Stock Exchange Glossary*. Mullingar is a market, assize and county town 50 miles N.W. of Dublin (Bartholomew's *Gazetteer*).

mullock. Rubbish ; a worthless thing : Australian coll. : from ca. 1890. Ex the mining-j. senses, rock without gold, refuse of gold-workings, ex Eng. dial. Whence the next two entries.

mullock, poke. (V.t. with *at*.) To tease ; to deride : Australian : C. 20. C. J. Dennis. Ex preceding. Cf. *poke borak* (see **borak**).

mullock over. To shear incompletely or very carelessly : Australian shearers' : from ca. 1890. *The Age*, Sept. 23, 1893. Morris. Ex *mullock*, q.v.

multa, multie, multi, multy (q.v.). Very : Parlyaree : mid-C. 19–20. E.g. in :

multee kertever (or **-iver**) or **multicattivo.** Very bad : theatrical (— 1887) ex (— 1859) Parlyaree ; very ob. in the former. H., 1st ed. Ex It. *molto cattivo*, very bad, via Lingua Franca. Cf. :

multy. An expletive and/or intensive adj. : low and Parlyaree : mid-C. 19–20. Henley, 1887, 'How do you melt the multy swag ?' E. Seago, *Circus Company*, 1933, shows that, in C. 20, it occ. means 'bad' : prob. ex *multee kertever*, q.v. Ex It. *molto*, much, very.—2. Adv. See **multa**.

mum. Silence, esp. if connoting a refusal to speak : coll. : 1562, J. Heywood ; Butler ; *The Pall Mall Gazette*, Jan. 7, 1890, 'If the policy of " mum " continues' (O.E.D.). Ob. Ex *mum*, a representation of an inarticulate sound : cf. *muff, not to say.*—2. As a silent person, as adj. and v., and as an interjection, it is S.E.—3. See **mums**.—4. Mother, gen. as term of address : orig. (— 1823), dial. ; > coll. ca. 1880. Also, in C. 20, **mums**. Abbr. *mummy*, q.v.—5. A low coll. variant of *ma'am*, q.v. : C. 19–20. Cf. *mem*.

mum as a quasi-adv. (strictly silent), esp. in *to stand mum*, is coll. : C. 16–19. Archaic except in dial. R. Bridges, 1894, 'Don't stand there mum', O.E.D.

mum-glass. The Monument erected in memory of the Great Fire of London (1666), on Fish Street Hill, London, E.C. : late C. 17–20 ; ob. B.E., Dyche & Pardon, Grose. Ex S.E. sense, a glass used for drinking *mum*, a kind of beer brewed orig. in Brunswick (O.E.D.) : the shape.

*mum your dubber ! Silence ! : from ca. 1780 ; ob. : c. G. Parker. See **dubber**.

mumble-crust. A coll. nickname for a toothless person : ca. 1550–1620.

mumble-matins. A coll. nickname for a priest : ca. 1560–1630.

mumble-news. A tale-bearer : 1588, Shakespeare, 'Some mumble-news, some trencher-knight, some Dick ' : coll. >, in C. 19, S.E. ; ob. by 1860, † by 1900.

mumble-peg. The female pudend : low : C. 19. ? ex the game.

mumble-sparrow. ' A cruel sport practised at wakes and fairs ', a handicapped man (gen. with arms tied behind his back) attempting to bite off the head of a handicapped cock sparrow. Coll. > S.E. : ca. 1780–1820. Grose.

mumble-te-peg, mumbledepeg, mumblety-peg. Erroneous forms of *mumble(-the)-peg.* Mid-C. 17–19. O.E.D.

mumbo-jumbo. Meaningless jargon : coll. : from ca. 1880. Ex the S.E. sense : an object of senseless veneration, itself ex a West African word.

mumchance that or **who was hanged for saying nothing, look** or **sit like.** A c.p. applied to a silent, glum-looking person : late C. 17–mid-19. B.E., Grose. Cheshire substitutes *mumphazard* and *stand.* Apperson.

mummer. An actor : contemptuous s. : 1840, Carlyle. Ex the S.E. sense, an actor in a dumb show or in a mumming. Whence *mummerdom*, rather S.E. than unconventional.—2. The mouth : low, esp. boxing : ca. 1780–1870. Grose, 1st ed. Ex *mun(s)* and *mums*, qq.v.

mummery-cove. An actor : low : ca. 1830–80. Cf. *cackling-cove*, q.v.

mummies, Mummies. Egyptian securities : Stock Exchange : 1903, *The Westminster Gazette*, Feb. 17 (O.E.D.). Mummification being an Egyptian process and mummies a source of interest.

mumming-booth. ' A wandering marquee in which short plays are produced ' : theatrical coll. : late C. 19–20 ; ob. Ware.

mummy. Mother, esp. as term of address : orig. (— 1790), dial. ; > coll. ca. 1880 and ' in recent years fashionable in England ', O.E.D., 1908. Ex *mother* or *mammy*, q.v.

mump. To deceive, overreach, cheat : ca. 1650–1740 : s. >, ca. 1710, coll. ; very gen. until ca. 1705. Fuller, Wycherley, North. Ex Dutch *mompen*, to cheat. (2) To disappoint : coll. : ca. 1700–40. Kersey. Both senses constructed with (*out*) *of*.—3. V.i., to beg, be a parasite : from ca. 1670 ; ob. : orig. c. >, ca. 1750, low s. Head, Macaulay. —4. V.t., to obtain by begging : from ca. 1680 ; ob. F. Spence.—5. (V.t.) To call at (a house) on a begging round : from ca. 1865 : c. >, ca. 1890, low s. ; ob. (For these five senses) O.E.D.—6. To talk seriously : low (— 1857) ; ob. ' Ducange Anglicus.'

mumper. A beggar : from ca. 1670 ; ob. : c. >, by 1720, low s. Until ca. 1720, a genteel, then any beggar (witness Head, 1673, and Grose, 1785). Extant also as dial.—2. Hence, a sponger : ca. 1720–1830. Macaulay, 1849, ' A Lincoln's Inn mumper was a proverb.'—3. A half-bred Gypsy : ca. 1870–1900 : c. Hindley.

mumper's (or -ers') hall. A beggar's ale-house : late C. 17–mid-19 : c. until ca. 1720, then low s. B.E. (a pertinent description) ; Grose, 1st ed. [Mumpers' talk is tramps' c. Thus ' No. 747 ', *The Autobiography of a Gipsy*, speaks of ' that strange mixture of thieves' Latin and mumpers' talk which has so often done duty for genuine Romnimus ' (Romany).]

mumping, vbl.n. and ppl.adj. Begging : resp. from ca. 1690 (c. > low s.) and from ca. 1825 (low s., ob.) : n. in Motteux, adj. in Lytton. Cf. the

dial. *Mumping Day*, Boxing Day : C. 19–20 ; ob. (Prob. S.E. is C. 15 *mumpin(g)s*, alms.)

mumple-mumper. An occ. C. 19 variant of *mummer*, 1, q.v.

mumps, the. Very low spirits : non-aristocratic coll. (— 1887). Baumann. Cf. *dumps*.

***mumpus.** A perversion of *mumping*, q.v. Baumann.

mums. The lips : late C. 18–19. More gen. *muns*, q.v. Cf. also *mun*.—2. See *mum*, n., 4.

mum's the word ! Silence : coll. : C. 18–20. T. Brown. Earlier, *mum for that !* (S.E.).

mumsie or **-y.** Mother : domestic and nursery coll. : late C. 19–20. (Evelyn Waugh, *A Handful of Dust*, 1934.) Cf. *mummy*, q.v.

mun ; often **munn,** (early) **munne.** The mouth : C. 14–20 ; s. († by ca. 1880) and dial. E.D.D. Ex Norwegian dial. *munn*, the mouth. Cf. *muns*, q.v. Also *muns* (q.v.) and *mund*.—2. One of a band of London street ruffians ca. 1670 : coll. Shadwell, 1691 (O.E.D.). Cf. *scourer*, *mohock*. ? etymology if not ex *mun*, the mouth : perhaps they were very loud-mouthed fellows.

munch, v.i. To eat heavily ; ' stuff ' : proletarian coll. (— 1923). Manchon. Cf. *Munching House*, 2.

munch-present. A servant that tastes of his master's presents to a friend : app. c. : ca. 1560–90. Awdelay.—2. A glutton : C. 16(?–17) : coll.—3. A taker of bribes : late C. 16–17 : coll.

Munching House. Mansion House (London) : City (— 1885) ; slightly ob. Ware. ' From the lusty feeding going on there '.—2. Hence (*m.-h.*), a cheap restaurant : lower classes' : C. 20. Manchon.

mund, munds. A C. 19 variant of *mun*, 1, and *muns*, qq.v.

mundane. A person of fashion : Society coll. : ca. 1890–1910. Ware. Ex Fr. *mondain(e)*.

mundicative. Incorrect for *mundificative*, a cleansing medicine : late C. 16–20. O.E.D.

munduc. ' The seaman left to take charge of the boat on the pearl fishery, while the others are diving ' : pearl-fishers' : late C. 19–20. Bowen. Prob. ex the Malayan *munduk*, a mole : a sense that accords well with nautical humour.

[†**mundungus,** both n. and derivative adj., are S.E. verging on coll.]

***mung.** To beg, gen. v.i. : tramps' c. : from ca. 1810 ; ob. *Lex. Bal.*, Mayhew, P. H. Emerson. Ex Romany *mong*, request, beg (*mongamengro*, a beggar). Cf. *mang* and *mump*, qq.v.

***mungaree** or **munjari** ; **mungarly.** Food ; scraps of bread ; a meal : Parlyaree and tramps' c. : from ca. 1855. Mayhew, Hindley, Emerson. Ex It. *mangiare* (cf. Fr. *manger*), to eat, hence food, via Lingua Franca. For the form, cf. *dinarly*, q.v. Also *mange*, q.v.—2. Begging, ' working as a tramp ' : tramps' c. (gen. as *mongaree* or *-gery*) : C. 20.

***mungarly-casa** or **-cass(e)y.** A baker's shop : Parlyaree and tramps' c. : from ca. 1858. H., 1st ed. *The Times*, Oct. 18, 1864. Ex preceding + It. *casa*, a house.

munging, vbl.n. Begging : Northern s. (ob.) and dial. (— 1859). H., 1st ed. Ex dial. *munge*, to grumble in low, indistinct tones (E.D.D.).

mungo. An important person. a ' swell ' : 1770, Colman, in *The Oxford Magazine* : soon †, presumably s. ? ex *Mungo*, a common name for a Negro (1768). O.E.D.

*munge, n. Dark, darkness : c. : C. 18. C. Hitchin, *The Regulator*, 1718. Origin ?

mungy. Food : naval and military : from ca. 1860. Bowen. Either ex Fr. *manger*, to eat, or a re-shaping of *mungaree*, q.v. Hence, *mungy-wallah*, a man working in the cook-house : military : late C. 19–20.

munitionette. A female worker on munitions : coll. : 1915, *The Daily Sketch*, Nov. 19. O.E.D. (Sup.). Ex :

munitions. The production of munitions; munition-work : coll. : from late 1915. The Ministry of Munitions was created in mid-1915. (O.E.D. Sup.)

munjari or -y. See mungaree. The *-y* form occurs in Philip Allingham's *Cheapjack*, 1934.

*munns. See muns.

munpins or, better, mompyns. The teeth : C. 15–mid-16 : coll. Lydgate. Lit., mouth-pins (see mun, 1). Also *mone pynnes* (as in Lydgate) and *munpynnys* (as in Skelton). The O.E.D. considers it S.E.

*muns ; in C. 17–early 18, occ. munns ; in C. 19, occ. munds. The face : from ca. 1660 : c. >, ca. 1720, low s. Head, Grose. See mun, 1.—2. Occ. the lips (cf. *mums*, q.v.), the mouth (— 1823), the jaws : C. 18–20, ob. Foote, 1760, ' Why, you jade, . . . I must have a smack at your muns ' ; Bee.

munshi. See moonshee.

Munster heifer. A thick-legged and/or thick-ankled woman : Anglo-Irish : ca. 1810–60. *Lex. Bal.* Cf. *Mullingar heifer*, q.v.

Munster plums. (Singular app. unrecorded.) Potatoes : Anglo-Irish >, ca. 1850, gen : from ca. 1780 ; ob. Grose, 1st ed. Cf. *Irish apricots* and *murphies*.

mur. Rum : back s. (— 1859) ; very gen. in G.W. among soldiers. H., 1st ed.

murder, cry blue. To make an excessive outcry : 1887, ' John Strange Winter '. O.E.D.

murder, look like God's revenge against. To look angrily : coll. : C. 18–mid-19. Grose.

murder-house. A military hospital : military (other ranks') : from ca. 1920.

murder is out, the. The mystery is solved : C. 18–20 : S.E. >, ca. 1830, coll. Ex the proverbial *murder will out* (late C. 13–20), Apperson.

murderin' Irish ! ; orig. murder an' Irish ! A lower classes' exclamation indicative of a climax : mid-C. 19–early 20. Ware.

Murdering Thieves, the. The Army Service Corps : military : C. 20 ; very ob. F. & Gibbons. For origin, cf. *Moke Train*, q.v.

*murerk. The mistress of the house : tramps' c. : from ca. 1855. H., 1st ed. ? *burerk* perverted.

murg. A telegram : Post Office telegraph-messengers' (— 1935). Ex :

murginger. A telegraph-boy : id. : from ca. 1920. A perversion of *messenger*.

murine is a C. 17 error for *marine*, v., = marinate. O.E.D., ' or misprint '.

murkarker or murkauker. A monkey : ca. 1850–80 : low coll. seldom heard outside London. H., 1st ed. Ex *Jacko Macauco* or *Maccacco*, a famous fighting monkey of ca. 1840–5 at the Westminster Pit. (In S.E., *macaco* is any monkey of the genus *macacus*.) Also *maccacco*.

murky. Containing secrets, ' shady ' ; sinister, discreditable : esp. in (e.g. *his*) *murky past* : from ca. 1920 : jocular coll. Ex the late C. 18–20 senses, very dark (of colour) and dirty, grimy. Richard

Keverne, *The Man in The Red Hat*, 1930, ' I felt pretty sure she was terribly worried . . . But, by Gad ! I'd no idea things were quite as murky as they are.' The sense is anticipated in P. G. Wodehouse, *Love among the Chickens*, 1906, ' I was . . . thinking about my wretched novel. I had just framed a more than usually murky scene.'

murph, but gen. murphy. A potato : from resp. ca. 1870, ca. 1810. *Lex. Bal.*, Thackeray. Ex the very common Irish surname : cf. *donovan*, q.v.—2. Morpheus, i.e. sleep : sol. : 1748, Smollett, in *Roderick Random* : H., 2nd ed. (Only *Murphy*.)

Murphy's countenance or face. A pig's head : from resp. ca. 1810 († by 1890) and ca. 1860. Vaux in *Dict.* and *Memoirs* (1812, 1819). Cf. *murphy*, 1.

[murrain is frequent in C. 16–early 18 cursings. Lit., a plague.]

Murray's Bucks. See Lacedæmonians.—Murrumbidgee whaler. See whaler.

murse. Incorrect for *murre*, C. 17–20. O.E.D.

murtherer. (Gen. pl.) A cannon for use against, rather the men than the material of a ship : naval coll. : C. 18–early 19. Bowen.

muscle bo'sun. A physical-training officer : naval : C. 20. Bowen. A synonym of *india-rubber man.*

muscle-grinder. See leg-grinder.

*muscle in. To intrude, by violence, on another's ' racket ' : American c. anglicised ca. 1928 and, by 1935, > gen. s. = to poach, fig., on another's preserves. (C.O.D., 1934 Sup.) Abbr. *muscle one's way in.*

Museum headache. Extreme ennui ; impatient boredom : London writers', authors', journalists' : 1857–ca. 1914. Ware, whose quotation from *The Daily News* of Dec. 11, 1882, shows that the phrase referred to the waiting for books in the British Museum Reading Room.

museuming. The visiting of museums : coll. : 1838, ' A day or two museuming '. O.E.D.

Mush. The inevitable military nickname, on Egyptian service, for men surnamed Knott or Nott : from ca. 1920. Ex the Arabic for *not.*

mush, *mush-top(p)er, mushroom. An umbrella : resp. low (— 1851], Mayhew, but recorded in a compound in 1821 ; from ca. 1820, † by 1880, c., as in Haggart; low, 1856, very ob., Mayhew. Ex the shape.—2. (Only mush : pronounced *moosh*.) The mouth : boxing, then low : mid-C. 19–20 ; prob. U.S., orig. Matsell, Walford.—2, *a.* In C. 20 New Zealand, the face. Ex the softness of mush and the mouth.—3. (Only mush, in senses 3–6.) A cab-proprietor in a small way ; (also *little mush*) a cab-driver owning his own vehicle : from ca. 1890 ; ob. by 1910, † by 1930. Abbr. *musher*, q.v.—4. The guard-room : cells : military : late C. 19–20. F. & Gibbons. Origin ? Perhaps ex dial. *mush*, to crush.—5. Other senses of *mushroom* : see mushroom.—6. Porridge : nautical coll. : C. 19–20 ; slightly ob. Bowen. A particularisation of the S.E. sense.—7. A man : c. : late C. 19–20. James Curtis, *The Gilt Kid*, 1936. Only in combination : see, e.g., coring mush and rye mush. Ex Romany *moosh*, a man.

mush, gush, and lush. ' Mean interested criticism—critiques paid for either in money or feastings ' : authors' and journalists' : ca. 1884–1905. Ware.

mush-faker, *mush-top(p)er-faker, mushroom-faker. A mender of umbrellas : resp. low (— 1851),

Mayhew; c. of ca. 1820–50, Haggart; o. or low (– 1839), ob. by 1860, Brandon, Mayhew. Ex *mush*, 1, and *faker*, q.v. Cf. :

mush-faking, occ. **mushfaking**. Umbrella-mending : low : from ca. .1857. P. H. Emerson.

mush-rat. Musk-rat : Canadian sol. (and English dial.) : late C. 19–20. (John Beames.)

mush-top(p)er. See **mush**, 1.—**mush-top(p)er-faker**. See **mush-faker**.

musha. An interjection connoting strong feeling : from ca. 1830 : Anglo-Irish coll. >, by 1870, S.E. Lover. Ex Irish *maiseadh*, if it be so. S.O.D.

*mushed(-)up. Well-dressed : c. (– 1933). Charles E. Leach, *On Top of the Underworld*. Perhaps ex *molled up* influenced by *mushy*, qq.v.

musher. Same sense as **mush**, 3, q.v. : 1887, *The Globe*, April 22 (O.E.D.) ; ob. by 1900, † by 1920. Seldom used outside of the cab-trade.

musheroom. A mushroom : sol. (and dial.) : C. 19–20. E.g., in F. Brett Young, *Jim Redlake*, 1930.

mushiness. See **mushy**.

mushing, vbl.n. ' Cab-owning on a small scale ' : cab-men : ca. 1887–1915. Cf. *mush*, 3, and *musher*. *The Globe*, April 22, 1887 (O.E.D.).

mushroom. See **mush**, 1.—2. A circular hat with a low crown, esp. a lady's with brim down-curving : coll. : from ca. 1864 ; ob. H., 3rd ed.—3. The female pudend : low : C. 19.—4. ' The great clock to be seen in most taverns ' : tavern-frequenters' (– 1909). Ware. Ex shape.

mushroom-faker. See **mush-faker**.

mushy. Insipid ; gushingly sentimental : from early 1870's : coll. >, by 1910, S.E. George Eliot, 1876, ' She's not mushy, but her heart is tender ' (O.E.D.). Whence *mushiness* (– 1890).

music. A C. 18 abbr. of *music's paid, the*, q.v. Grose, 1st ed.—2. The reverse or ' tail ' of a coin, but only in ' calling the toss ' : Anglo-Irish : ca. 1780–1930. Grose, 1st ed. Ex the harp on the reverse of an Irish farthing or halfpenny.

music, face the. See **face the music**.

music, it makes ill. Applied to unwelcome news : coll. : late C. 17–mid-18. B.E.

music as a wheelbarrow, you make as good. A semi-proverbial c.p. to one who plays badly or is unpleasantly noisy : C. 18. ' Proverbs ' Fuller.

music-box. A piano : jocular coll. : 1849, Thackeray : C. Reade, in *Hard Cash*.

music-duffing, vbl.n. Reconditioning old musical instruments : low (– 1923). Manchon. After *cattle-duffing*.

music-hall howl. The singing heard in music-halls : musicians' coll. (– 1909). Ware, ' The result of endeavouring rather to make the words of a song heard than to create musical effect '.

musical. (Of horses) with defective respiration : C. 20. Cf. *roarer*, q.v. O.E.D.

Musical Box, the. ' A widely celebrated Whippet Tank in the action at Villers Bretonneux, Aug. 8, 1918 ' : military ; now only historical. F. & Gibbons.

*music's paid, the. (See also **music**, 1.) ' The Watch-word among High-way-men, to let the Company they were to Rob, alone, in return to some Courtesy ', B.E. : c. : late C. 17–early 19. Grose.

muskin, gen. preceded by *unaccountable*. A chap, fellow, man, esp. if odd : ca. 1750–60. Johnson, ' Those who . . . call a man a cabbage, . . . an odd fish, an unaccountable muskin '. O.E.D. **?** a perversion of the C. 16 endearing *muskin*.

muslin. Sails, collectively ; esp. the lighter sails : nautical : from ca. 1820 ; ob. *Blackwood's Magazine*, 1822, ' She shewed as little muslin as required ' (O.E.D.).—2. The fair sex : from ca. 1883 ; ob. by 1910, † by 1920. Hawley Smart, 1884. (Cf. *skirt*, q.v.) Gen as :

muslin, a bit of. A woman, a girl : 1823, Moncrieff, ' A bit of muslin on the sly ' ; C. Griffin ; Thackeray. Ob. by 1910, † by 1918. Cf. :

muslin, a piece of. The same : ca. 1840–1900. W. T. Moncrieff, 1843. Much less gen. than preceding term ; prob. influenced by *piece*, a girl.

Muss. See **Messolini**.—**mussy**. See **muzzy**, 1.

must. ' As a past or historical present tense, *must* is sometimes used satirically or indignantly with reference to some foolish or annoying action or some untoward event.' Late C. 14–20 : S.E. till ca. 1850, then coll. ' Just when I was busiest, I must go and break my leg ! ' O.E.D.

musta or **muster**. The make or pattern of anything ; a sample : Anglo-Chinese and -Indian : C. 16–20 ; in 1563 as *mostra*, which is the Portuguese origin. Coll. Yule & Burnell. H., 3rd ed., ' Very gen. used in commercial transactions all over the world '.

mustard (at), be. To be excellent (at anything) ; (of a woman) *be mustard*, to be sexually ' hot stuff ' ; from late 1920's. Lyell. Ex *hot stuff + keen as mustard*.

mustard-plaster on his chest !, put a. A c.p. applied to ' a doleful and dismal pallid young man ' : lower-classes' : ca. 1880–1914. Ware. Ex a comic song written in connexion with Colman's mustard by E. Laman Blanchard (1820–89).

mustard-pot. The female pudend : C. 19–20 : low.—2. A ' carriage with a light yellow body ' : lower classes' : late C. 19–20 ; ob. Ware.

muster. As used by *Conway* cadets, ' to line up outside galley or store-room for more food ' (Masefield), it is rather j. than eligible.—2. See **musta**.

muster one's bag. To be ill : nautical, esp. naval. : late C. 19–20. Bowen. Ex taking one's kit-bag to the sick-bay.

mustn't. Must not : coll. : 1741, Richardson, ' I mustn't love my Uncle.' O.E.D., but prob. in spoken use from ca. 1705.

mustn't-mention-'ems. Trousers : ca. 1850–1910. Cf. *unmentionables*, q.v.

*mutcher. See **moocher**. Extremely rare form in C. 20.

mute. An undertaker's assistant acting as a mourner silent supposedly from grief : from ca. 1760 : coll. till ca. 1840, then S.E. Grose.

mute as a fish. Silent : C. 15–20 ; ob. : coll. >, by 1600, S.E. Burgh & Lydgate. Galsworthy, 1915, has *dumb as fishes*. Apperson. In late C. 18–20, often *mute as fishes*, and dial. offers at least six variants.

mutiny. The rum-ration : naval : late C. 19–20. Bowen. Because, without it, the men would mutiny.

mutt. A ' stupid ', a fool, a gawk : U.S. (1910), anglicised in France in 1918. Ex *mutton-head*, q.v., (O.E.D. Sup.)

Mutt and Jeff. The British War Medal and Victory Medal : military : 1918. B. & P. Ex the famous pair of comic figures. Cf. *Pip, Squeak and Wilfred*.

mutton. A loose woman ; prostitutes collectively : 1518, Skelton ; Shakespeare ; D'Urfey. Ob. by 1820, † by 1900. Rare in C. 19 except as *laced mutton*, q.v.—2. Sexual pleasure ; the female pudend ; the sexual act : from ca. 1670 ; ob. E.g. in *fond of his mutton*, fond of the act. Almost solely from the man's stand-point. Rochester ; H.—3. A sheep : late C. 16–20 : in C. 19–20, jocular but (except as used at Bootham School) still S.E.—4. See **muttons**.

mutton, bow-wow. See bow-wow.

mutton, cut one's. To dine : low s. bordering on coll. : from ca. 1850 ; ob. Ex the S.E. *eat* or *take a bit of*, or *one's, mutton with*, to dine with (C. 18–20, ob.).

mutton, give (a person) **the cold shoulder of.** A non-aristocratic punning elaboration (— 1887 ; ob.) of *give the cold shoulder*. Baumann.

mutton, in her. Having carnal knowledge of a woman : low : C. 19–20, ob. *Lex. Bal.* Ex *mutton*, 2, q.v.

mutton ?, who stole the. A c.p. of ca. 1830–50 addressed jeeringly to a policeman. Brewer. Ex the Force's failure to detect the culprit in a theft of mutton.

Mutton-Bird. (Gen. pl.) A resident in North Tasmania : Southern Tasmanians' : C. 20. Opp. *couta*, 2 (q.v.). Mutton-birds abound in Northern Tasmania.

mutton-chopper. A mutton-chop (sc. whisker) : ca. 1890–1900 : mostly Cockney. Milliken. N.B. *mutton-chop*, in this sense, is S.E.

mutton-chops. A sheep's head : low (— 1864) ; ob. H., 3rd ed.

mutton-cove. A ' mutton-monger ', q.v. : low : from ca. 1830 ; ob.—2. **(M.C.)** The Coventry-Street end of Windmill Street, once a resort of harlots : ca. 1840–70 : low London. Ex *mutton*, 1.

mutton dressed as lamb or (ob.) **lamb-fashion.** An old woman dressed like a young one : low : mostly Cockney : from ca. 1860. Cf. the older form, *an old ewe dressed lamb-fashion*, q.v. at old ewe.

mutton-eyed. ' Sheep's-eyed ', q.v. : from ca. 1850 ; ob. Mainly jocular.

mutton-fed. Big, fat, and red-faced : coll. (— 1923). Manchon, ' A mutton-fed policeman '.

mutton-fist or **-hand.** A large coarse hand, esp. if red : resp. 1664, Cotton, ' Lifting his Mutton-fists to th' skies ' ; from ca. 1820 and not very gen.—2. A printer's index-hand : printers' (— 1888). Jacobi. (O.E.D.)

mutton-head. A dull or stupid person : coll. : 1804 (O.E.D. Sup.). Ex the well-known stupidity of sheep. Ex :

mutton-headed. Dull ; stupid : s. (1788) and dial. Grose. Ex the well-known stupidity of sheep.

mutton in long coats. Women : low : late C. 17–19. B.E. ; Baumann. Cf. :

mutton in a silk stocking, leg of. A woman's leg or calf : low : late C. 17–20. B.E. ; Baumann.

mutton-monger. A wencher : from ca. 1530 ; ob. by 1830, † by 1850. More, 1532 (O.E.D.) ; Florio ; Chapman, ' As if you were the only noted mutton-monger in all the city ' ; Coles ; Grose. Ex *mutton*, 1. Cf. *muttoner*, q.v. F. & H. provides a long synonymy.—2. A sheep-stealer : ca. 1660–1750. Cotton, B.E.—3. A considerable eater of mutton : mid-C. 17. W. M., 1649, ' A horrible Mutton-monger, a Gorbelly-Glutton ', O.E.D.

mutton of, make. To kill (a person) : low coll. : late C. 19–20. Manchon (*refroidir*).

mutton-pies. The eyes : rhyming s. : ca. 1880–1910. *The Referee*, Nov. 7, 1887, ' Bright as angels

from the skies | Were her dark-blue mutton-pies.' Cf. the very much more gen. *mince-pies*, q.v.

mutton-quad. An em quad : printers' (— 1871). Ex *m* for *mutton*. O.E.D. Cf. *mutton-thumper*.

mutton rabble. A ' sheep-chase ' : Bootham School (— 1925). Anon., *Dict. of Bootham Slang*. Cf. *rabble*, q.v.

mutton-shunter. A constable : policemen's : 1883–ca. 1915. Ware. Policemen keep harlots moving.

mutton-thumper. A bungling workman ; a young apprentice bookbinder : late C. 18–20 : bookbinders'. MS. note in the British Museum copy of Grose, 2nd ed. ; F. & H. Ex the sheepskin used in binding.

mutton-tugger. (Prob.) a ' mutton-monger ', q.v. : presumably s. : ca. 1600. ' The nurseries of wickedness, the nests of mutton tuggers, the dens of formall droanes ' (O.E.D.).

mutton-walk (or with capitals). The saloon at Drury Lane theatre : ca. 1820–80 : London fast life. Egan, 1821, *Real Life.*—2. (? hence) any resort of harlots, esp. Piccadilly : from ca. 1870.

muttoner. A ' mutton-monger ', q.v. : C. 17–early 19. Halliwell. Ex *mutton*, 1.—2. A blow on the knuckles from a cricket-ball : Winchester College : ca. 1850–90. Cf. *mutton-fist*, q.v.

muttongosht. Mutton : domestic Anglo-Indian coll. (—1886). Lit., mutton-flesh. Yule & Burnell. For its hybridity, cf. *jail-khana*.

muttonous. Slow ; monotonous : low : ca. 1880–1910. Ex *monotonous* on *gluttonous*.

muttons. The tax on live stock : 1881, *The Daily News*, Feb. 1. O.E.D.—The Turkish loans of 1865 and 1873, these being in part secured on the sheep-tax : first recorded, 1887 (Baumann). Both are Stock Exchange and ob.

muvver. See -uvver.

muzz ; occ. **muz** (†). One who studies hard, reads much and studiously. *The Trifler*, No. 5, 1788, ' The almost indelible stigma of a Muz ' ; 1899, W. K. R. Bedford. Ob. (O.E.D.) Ex :

muzz, v.i. To study diligently ; to ' mug ', q.v. (V.t. with *over*.) S. J. Pratt, 1775, ' For ever muzzing over a musty book '. Since ca. 1890, mainly at Westminster School : cf. the Eton *sap*, q.v. ? ex *muse*, (be)*mused*.—2. V.t. To fuddle ; make ' muzzy ' (q.v.) : 1787, ' Fred. Philon ', ' Apt to get muzzed too soon '. Cf. *muzzle*, v., 4.—3. V.i. to loiter or ' hang about ' : ca. 1778–1810. Mme D'Arblay, 1779, ' You would not dare keep me muzzling here.' ? cognate with *muse*, v. All three senses, O.E.D. ; for the first, cf. remarks at ' Westminster School slang '.

muzzed. Fuddled ; stupidly tipsy : 1787, see quotation at *muzz*, v., 2.

muzzel ; occ. **muzzle.** A charm ; *work the muzzle* (or *-el*), to sell charms : grafters' : C. 20. Philip Allingham in *Cheapjack*, 1934, postulates a Yiddish origin.

muzzing, vbl.n. To *muzz*, v., all senses.—2. Ppl.adj., studying hard ; given to intent study : 1793, J. Beresford : ob. O.E.D.

muzzle. A beard, esp. if long, straggly, and/or dirty : ca. 1690–1830. B.E. ; Grose, 1st ed. Ex S.E. *muzzle*, the mouth.—2. See **muzzel**.

muzzle, v. To strike on the mouth : low, esp. pugilistic : from ca. 1850 ; ob. Mayhew, 1851, ' Just out of " stir " [q.v.] for muzzling a peeler.'— 2. Hence, to fight ; to thrash : low (— 1859) ; ob. H., 1st ed.—3. Hence, to throttle, garotte : **c.** ;

from ca. 1860 ; ob. H., 3rd ed.—4. To drink to excess : s. from ca. 1850 ex (— 1828) dial. ; ob. as s. Also, v.t. to fuddle : s. (from ca. 1850 ; ob.) ex dial. (— 1796). O.E.D.—5. To take, ' bag ', get : orig. (1890, ' Rolf Boldrewood '), Australian > gen. ca. 1895 ; ob. Barrère & Leland, 2nd ed. Prob. ex S.E. *muzzle*, put a muzzle on. O.E.D.

(muzzled) bull-dog. A main-deck gun : naval : ca. 1865–1905. Admiral Smyth, 1867.—2. ' The great gun which stands housed in the officers' ward-room cabin ', ibid. : ca. 1865–80.

muzzler. A blow on the mouth : from ca. 1810 : boxing. *Lex. Bal.*—2. A dram ; a (quick) drink : low : from ca. 1850 ; ob. H., 5th ed. Ex *muzzle*, the mouth.—3. A strong head wind : from the middle 1870's : nautical coll. >, by 1910, S.E. Bowen ; O.E.D. Cf. *nose-ender*, 2.

muzzling, vbl.n. Hitting on the mouth : boxing : 1819 ; ob. O.E.D. Cf. *muzzler*, 1.

muzzy. (Of places) dull, gloomy ; (of weather) overcast : coll. and dial. : 1727, Mrs. Delany, who spells it *mussy* ; 1821, Coleridge, ' This whole long-lagging, muzzy, mizly morning '. Prob. ex dial. *mosey*, hazy, muggy.—2. Stupid, hazy of mind, spiritless : coll. : 1728, Mrs. Delany ; Keats, 1817, ' I don't feel inclined to write any more at present for I feel rather muzzy ' ; Thackeray. Cf. *muzz*, v., 2. Perhaps ex dial. *mosey*, stupefied with liquor, or ex *bemused*.—3. Stupefied, more gen. stupid, with liquor : coll. and dial. : 1775, Thomas Campbell ; Thackeray ; J. Payn. Ex preceding senses.—4. Blurred, indistinct : coll. : from ca. 1830. Washington Irving, 1832. Ex senses 1, 2, and esp. 3. O.E.D.

my ! ; oh my ! A (low) coll. exclamation : 1707, J. Stevens, ' Such . . . Sayings are a Discredit . . . : As for Instance . . . my Whither d'ye go ' ; 1849, Mrs. Carlyle, ' Oh, my ! if she didn't show feeling enough.' O.E.D. Abbr. *my God !*—2. *o(h) my* is an abbr. of *o(h), my Gawd*, a sword : late C. 19–20. B. & P.

my for me occurs in street oaths and asseverations, e.g. in *s'elp my bob* for *s'elp me, bob* for *so help me, God* : low (— 1864). H., 3rd ed.

my arse . . . See arse in (or on) a band-box.

my aunt ! A coll. interjection : late C. 19–20. Cf. *giddy aunt, my*.

my aunt (Jones). A water-closet : low euphemistic : from ca. 1850 ; ob. H., 1st ed. (*my aunt*). The longer form (H., 5th ed.), ca. 1870–1905, gen. dispenses with *my*. Cf. *Mrs. Jones*.

my bloater. See bloater.

my boy !, I believe you. See I believe you, my boy.—my colonial oath ! See colonial oath !, my.

my eye ! Occ. my eyes ! († by 1860). A coll. exclamation of surprise, wonderment, or admiration : slightly ob. Moore, 1819, ' My eyes ! how prettily Tom writes ' ; M. E. Braddon, 1876, ' My eye, ain't I hungry ! '—2. my eye, all. See all my eye.—3. my eye and Betty Martin. See Betty Martin.

my giddy aunt ! See giddy aunt.—my gracious ! See gracious.—my hat ! See hat !—my land ! See land !, my.—my lord. See lord.—my nabs. See nabs.—my oath ! See oath !, my.

my oath, Miss Weston ! On my word of honour ! : naval : C. 20. F. & Gibbons. Ex the respect felt for Miss Agnes Weston, the naval philanthropist.

my pippin. See pippin.—my stars (and garters) ! See stars !—my tulip. See tulip.—my uncle. See uncle.—my watch. See watch, his.—my wig. See wigs.—my word ! See word !

*myla. See miler, 1.

mylier. An occ. C. 19–20 form of *mauley*, q.v. at end of entry.

*myll. See mill, n. and v.—mynt. See mint.

[myrmidon, a constable's attendant or assistant, is S.E.—despite B.E.'s designation as c., Grose's inclusion as s., and F. & H.'s listing.]

myrtle, my. A low London term of address : late C. 18–early 19. Bee. Cf. *jessamy* and *tulip*.

mystery. A sausage : somewhat low : from ca. 1885 ; ob. More gen. is *bag of mystery*, as in Henley, 1887, and much more gen. is *mystery bag*, as in *The Sportsman*, Feb. 2, 1889.

mystery ship. A Decoy Ship or Q Boat : 1916, Alfred Noyes (O.E.D. Sup.) : coll. >, almost imm., S.E. Bowen ; B. & P.

N

-n' for *-nd* : sol. : since when ? E.g. *han'*, hand. —2. Occ. for *-nt*, as in *don'*, don't, *won'*, won't, and ' Can' [can't] you come ter-morrer ? ' : sol., esp. Cockney : also immemorial.

'n. Than : a coll. abbr. pronounced either as a final *n* or as very short *en* ; e.g. *more'n* = *morn* or *mor-en*. C. 18–20. Also dial. Cf. *'an*, q.v.—2. In : on : coll. : C. 19–20. More gen. in dial. and in U S. than as a coll. ; the person that uses *'n* for *in*, gen. uses it also for *on*. (See *passim* the books by C. W. Thurlow Craig.)

'n'. And : another coll. and dial. abbr., similarly pronounced : late C. 17–20. (Cf. *yn*, q.v.) In familiar speech, esp. ' more'n more ' and ' bread'n butter '.—2. (By itself, *n'* ; in composition, *'n* or *n.*) Not : mostly dial., but occ. sol. or low coll. : mid-C. 18–20. E.g. ' I didn' care ', ' doesn' '

n.a.d. Shamming : military hospitals' (— 1909) ob. Ware. Ex the initials of *no appreciable disease*. Cf. *n.y.d.* (q.v.) and *p.u.o.*, which latter

was a G.W. confession as to the *unknown* origin of that *pyrexia* which was trench-fever.

n.b.g. or, as in the other ' initial '-words, more gen. with capitals. No bloody good : coll. : C. 20. Contrast *n.g.*

n.c. 'Nuff ced, i.e. enough said : from ca. 1870. (Ware states American origin.) Cf. *o.k.*, q.v.

n.c.d. (N.C.D.). See no can do.

n.d. (Of a woman) trying to look young : Society : late C. 19–early 20. Ware. Ex librarians' *n.d.*, no date.

n.e. or N.E. See north easter.

n.f. A smart or cunning tradesman : printers' : from ca. 1865 ; ob. Abbr. *no flies.*—2. Among artisans (— 1909), it means *no fool*. Ware.

n.g. No go ; no good : orig. (1840), U.S., anglicised ca. 1890 ; ob. Thornton.

N.H. A bug : from ca. 1875 ; ob. Abbr. *Norfolk Howard*, q.v.

n.n. A necessary nuisance, esp. a husband : Society (— 1909) ; † by 1919. Ware.

n. (or **N.**) **wash.** See **notergal wash.**

n.y.d. Drunk : military hospitals' (— 1909) ; ob. Ware. I.e. *not yet diagnosed.* Cf. *n.a.d.,* q.v. —2. **Not** yet dead : jocular : from ca. 1915. Same origin. (B. & P.)

na poo. See **napoo.**—**Naafi.** See **Nafy.**

*nab ; occ. **nabb** or **nab(b)e.** The head : c. of ca. 1560–1750. Harman (as *nabe*) ; Head. Cf. *nob* and *napper,* qq.v.—2. The head of a stick : c. : early C. 17. Dekker (O.E.D.). 3. A hat ; a cap : c. of ca. 1670–1830. Shadwell, Fielding, Grose. Cf. *nab, a penthouse,* q.v. Abbr. *nab-cheat* or *-chete,* q.v.—4. A fop : c. : ca. 1690–1750. B.E. (Matsell's recording is of an archaism.)—5. One who ' nabs ', esp. a police officer : 1813 : c. >, ca. 1860, low s. ; ob. O.E.D.—6. See **nabs.**

*nab ; occ. **nab(b)e** or **nabb.** To catch ; to arrest : from ca. 1685 : c. >, ca. 1860, low s. F. Spence, Shadwell. Cf. *nap* and *nobble,* qq.v.—2. It soon > a gen. c. v. of action : see **nab the rust, the stifles,** etc.—3. Linking senses 1 and 4 with the n., sense 3, is B.E.'s ' *I'll Nab ye,* i.e. I'll have your Hat or Cap.'—4. To seize ; to steal : low s. : from ca. 1814. *The Sporting Magazine,* 1814, ' All was lost, save what was nabb'd to pay the cost ' (O.E.D.).— 5. To cog (a die) : C. 18 c. or low s. ; in its orig. form, *nap* (B.E.), it was certainly c.—6. V.i., to snatch at something : C. 19–20 ; ob. : low.—7. (Cf. senses 1, 4.) To detect (an incident) : Shrewsbury School : late C. 19–20. E.g. in Desmond Coke, *The House Prefect,* 1908.

[**nab,** to bite gently, is dial., as are **nail** (disposition), **off at the nail,** (possibly) **nale, Narrowdale noon, nary, nash-gab** (impertinence), **nation** as adj. ; whereas the following are S.E. :—**nabob, nag** (a whore), **nail** or **right nail on the head(, hit the), nail to the counter, nakedness** (the private parts), **nameless(, the ;** or **name-it-not :** both euphemistic), **Nantz, nap** (a short sleep), **nappy, n.** (strong ale) and adj. (heady ; drunk), **nasty** (see the entry), **nation** as n., **natural** as idiot and natural wig, **nature** (the generative organs) and **nature's garb, naughtiness** (immorality), **naughty** (loose-moralled ; obscene), **naughty dream** (a sexual one), †**naughty man** (a whoremonger), **naughty pack** (a wanton ; as = an endearment, dial.), **navigator** (a navvy), **nay** (to deny), **nay-word** (a proverb).]

nab, a penthouse. A large hat : c. or low s. of ca. 1750–1820.

nab-all ; also **nabal(l).** A fool : early C. 17 s. > coll. Rowlands.—2. As a churl or a miser, C. 17– 20 (ob.), it is S.E.

*nab-cheat or **-chete.** A hat or cap : c. of ca. 1530–1830. Copland, B.E. See **cheat.**

*nab-girder. A bridle : c. of ca. 1670–1870, though ob. as early as 1820. Coles, B.E., Grose. Also *nob-girder.* Ex *nab = nob,* the head, + *girdle* perverted.

nab it (on the dial). To receive a blow (on the face) : low : from ca. 1820. But *nab it,* like *nap it,* also = to receive (gen., unexpected) punishment : low and dial : C. 19–20.

nab the bib. To weep : from ca. 1830 : low. Earlier (— 1812), *nap the bib,* which, recorded by Vaux and used by Egan, was prob. c. ; and later (1860 +), with variant *nap one's bib,* which also meant, to carry one's point, by weeping, then by any similar means (H., 3rd ed.).

*nab the regulars. To divide a booty : c. : from ca. 1840.

nab (or, in C. 19–20, **nap**) **the rust.** To take offence

(cf. *rusty,* q.v.) : from ca. 1850 : low· and dial. ob. Ex :—2. The turf sense, (of a horse) to become restless (— 1785). Grose, 1st ed.—3. To receive unexpected punishment : C. 19–20 (ob.) : c. > low s. Prob. influenced by *nab the teize,* q.v.

*nab the snow. To steal linen, esp. from hedges : c. : from ca. 1780. Grose, 2nd ed.

*nab the stifles. To be hanged : c. : C. 19–20 ; ob. See **stifles.**

*nab or **nap the stoop.** To stand in the pillory : late C. 18–early 19 c. Grose, 1st ed.

*nab or **nap the teize.** To be whipped, privately. in prison : late C. 18–mid-19 c. Grose, 1st ed ? ex *tease,* for in C. 19, it is often spelt *teaze.*

nabb ; occ. **nabbe.** See **nab,** n. and v.

nabber. A bailiff ; a constable : low : from ca. 1810 ; ob.—2. A thief, esp. a pilferer : low and (— 1808) Scots dial. Ex *nab,* v., 1. Cf. :

*nabbing-cheat. The gallows : c. (— 1719) ; † by 1850. ' Captain ' Alexander Smith.

*nabbing-cull. A bailiff ; a constable : c. : ca. 1775–1840. Tomlinson. Cf. *nabman.*

nabby. A Scottish form of *nobby,* adj., q.v.— ***nabe.** See **nab,** n. and v.

*nabman. A constable : c. of ca. 1815–40. Ex *nab,* v., 1.

nabob. Gen. pl., ' senior passengers in the East Indiamen ' : nautical : late C. 18–early 19. Bowen. —2. A capitalist : ca. 1858–90. H., 2nd ed. Ex the S.E. sense.

nabrood. (Pronounced *nay-brood.*) Neighbourhood : sol. (— 1887). Baumann.

*nabs ; in C. 19, occ. **knabs.** (Mainly North Country) c. >, ca. 1830, low s. : from ca. 1790 ; ob. Potter. *His nabs,* he ; (rare) *your nabs,* you ; but *my nabs,* either I, myself, or my friend (cf. C. 16 *my nobs,* my darling). O.E.D. Cf. *watch,* q.v. Perhaps a corruption of *neb,* a nose, a face : for semantics, see *nibs,* which is a variant.

*nabs, queer. See **queer nabs.**

*nabs on. A hall-mark : c. (— 1889) ; ob. Ex *nab* = head.

*nace. See **nase.**

nack = **knack,** a trick, is S.E.—2. A horse : c. (— 1889). Ex *nag,* q.v.

nackers. Properly *knackers :* low and dial. C. 19–20. The testicles.

nacky is a mere variant (ob.) of S.E. *knacky,* ingenious.

naf. The female pudend : ? back s. on *fan,* abbr. *fanny,* q.v. : from ca. 1845. If not obscure dial. of independent origin—ex or cognate with *naf(f),* the navel (— 1866), or with *naf(f),* the hub of a wheel (— 1796), E.D.D.—then this is perhaps the earliest of back-s. terms. Halliwell.

Nafy or **Naffy ;** properly **Naafi ;** loosely **Narfy** (though pronounced thus by Indian Army officers). The canteen : naval and military : from ca. 1930. Ex the ' Navy, Army, and Air Force Institute '.

nag. A riding horse (esp. if small) or pony : C. 15–20 : coll. except in Scotland and the North of England, where dial. Anon., *The Destruction of Troy,* ca. 1400 : ' He neyt [= neighed] as a nagge, at his nose thrilles [= nostrils] ' ; Coryat ; Johnson, ' A horse in familiar language ' ; Henley.—2. The penis : low : ca. 1670–1750. Cotton. Ex preceding sense (semantics : ' to ride '). Cf. *nags,* q.v. —3. As a whore or other opprobrium, it is S.E.

nag. To scold or persistently to find fault (**v.t** with *at*) : orig. (— 1828), dial. >, ca. 1840, coll. >, ca. 1890, S.E. Orig. sense, **to gnaw.**

nag, tether one's. To coït : low Scots : C. 19–20. Contrast :

nag (or **dragon**), **water one's** or **the.** To make water : low : mid-C. 19–20 ; ob.

***nag-drag.** A three-months imprisonment : c. : from ca. 1850 ; ob. See **drag.**

nag-tail, the little. High cockalorum : children's coll. (– 1923). Manchon. Via nursery-rhyme *ride a-cock horse* . . .

naggie. See **naggy.** The female pudend : low : C. 19–20 ; ob. Cf. *nag*, n., 2.

naggle. To toss the head stiffly and affectedly : coll. († by 1910) and dial. : from ca. 1840. Halliwell. Cf. S.E. *naggle*, to haggle, quarrel.

naggy or **naggie.** A pony ; a very small riding horse : coll. and dial. from ca. 1780. Blackmore, ' Then the naggie put his foot down.' O.E.D.

nags. The testes : low : C. 19–20 ; ob. Cf. *nag*, n., 2 : ? on (*k*)*nackers*.

nail. ' A person of an over-reaching, imposing disposition '—i.e. a ' shrewdy ', a crook—' is called a nail, a dead nail, a nailing rascal,' Vaux, 1812 : low : ca. 1810–1915. Ex the v., senses 2 and 4.— 2. ' The central sconce at the east and west ends of the school were so called,' Adams's *Wykehamica* : from ca. 1840 : Winchester College. Whence *stand up under the nail*, to stand there throughout school time for having told a lie ; later he received a ' bibler ' or was ' bibled ', Mansfield.—3. (Gen. pl.) A cigarette : military : from ca. 1910. F. & Gibbons. Abbr. *coffin-nail*.

nail, v. To catch or get hold of or secure : 1760, Foote, ' Some bidders are shy . . . ; but I nail them.'—2. Hence, to rob or steal : low : from ca. 1810. Vaux.—3. To catch or surprise (a person) in a fix, a difficulty : 1766, Goldsmith, ' When they came to talk of places in town, . . . I nailed them ' (O.E.D.).—4. Hence, in late C. 19–20 c. > low s. : to arrest (a person).—5. To strike smartly, to beat : Scots s. : from ca. 1805 ; ob.—6. Hence, to succeed in hitting : Dowden, 1886 (O.E.D.), but prob. very much earlier. In Scots at least as early as 1785 (E.D.D.).—7. To overreach ; to cheat : low : ca. 1810–30. Vaux.—8. To back-bite : printers' : from ca. 1870. Also *brass-nail* ; cf. *nail-box*, q.v.—9. ' To impress for any kind of fagging. Also, to detect ' : Winchester College (– 1889). Ex sense 1.

nail, naked as my. See **naked.**—**nail, dead as** . . . See **door-nail.**

nail, off the. Tipsy : Scots coll. : from ca. 1820. Galt, 1822, ' I was what you would call a thought off the nail.' Cf. Scots *off at the nail*, mad.

nail, on the. At once : late C. 16–20 : coll. >, ca. 1870, S.E. Nashe (*upon*, as is gen. till C. 18) ; Gay. Ex hand-nail and a drinking custom : see **supernaculum** and cf. Fr. *payer rubis sur l'ongle* (W.).—2. Under discussion : coll. : ca. 1885–1910. W. T. Stead, 1886. (O.E.D.)

nail-bearer. (Gen. in pl.) A finger : C. 18– mid-19 : ? S.E. or coll.

nail-box. A favourite spot for back-biting : printers' : from ca. 1870. Cf. *brass-nail*.

nail in one's coffin. A drink of liquor : coll. : from ca. 1820. Egan's Grose. Gen. as *here's another nail in your*, occ. *my*, rarely *his*, *coffin*.—2. See **coffin-nail**.

nail in one's coffin, drive or, occ., **put a.** To do anything likely to shorten one's life : C. 19–20 : coll. till C. 20, then S.E. In 1789, Wolcot anticipated, thus : ' Care to our coffin adds a nail, no

doubt ' (O.E.D.).—2. **To hasten or advance a** project, a piece of work : S.E.

nail-rod or **nailrod.** Orig. (ca. 1885), a stick of ' Two Seas ' tobacco : † by 1915. Ex the shape. (Morris.)—2. Hence (– 1896), any coarse, esp. if dark, stick of tobacco ; ob. by 1915, † by 1925. Both senses, New Zealand and then Australian. *The New Zealand Herald*, Nov. 8, 1886 (O.E.D.) ; 1896, H. Lawson.

nailed-up drama. Drama dependent upon elaborate scenery : theatrical : ca. 1881–1914. Ware. First used in reference to just such a drama, *The World*.

nailer. An exceptionally good or marvellous event, thing or person (esp. a hand *at* . . .) ; a gen. term of excellence : 1818, Macneill (O.E.D.) ; ca. 1890, Marshall in ' *Pomes* ' *from the Pink 'Un*, ' At guzzling the whole lot were nailers '. Cf. the ob. U.S. *nail-driver*, a fast horse.'—2. An extortioner, a usurer, ca. 1888–1925. Ex *nail*, v., 2.—3. See **nailor**.—4. ' An obvious, gross lie ' : late C. 19–20. Lyell. Ex dial.—5. (**the nailer**.) See **boy with the boots**.—6. See **nailers** (Addenda).

nailing, vbl. n. See **nail**, v., all senses.—2. Adj. : excellent : 1883, *Pall Mall Gazette*, March 29 (O.E.D.).—3. Adv. : very, exceedingly : 1884, Mrs. E. Kennard (O.E.D.) ; 1894, George Moore, ' A nailing good horse once '. Ex *nail*, v., 1, influenced by *nailer*, 1.

***nailor ;** more correctly **nailer.** (Constructed with *on*.) A prejudice (against) : c. (– 1887) >, by 1900, low. Baumann.

nailrod. See **nail-rod**.

nails often occurs in late C. 14–early 17 oaths and asseverations. E.g. (*by*) *God's nails*.—2. See **nail**, n., 3.

nails, eat one's. To do something foolish or unpleasant : coll. : C. 18–19. Swift.

nails, hard as. In good condition : from ca. 1860 : coll. till ca. 1905, then S.E.—2. Unyielding, harsh, pitiless : coll. (– 1889) >, ca. 1920, S.E.

nails, right as. Perfectly fit : coll. : from ca. 1890. Ex preceding, sense 1.

nails on one's toes, before one had. Before one was born ; long ago : coll. : C. 17. Shakespeare, in *Troilus and Cressida*, ' Whose wit was mouldy ere your grandsires had nails on their toes '. Cf. *before you come up*, q.v.

nair. Rain : back s. : from ca. 1870 ; ob., as, except among costers, is all back s. : see *Slang* at ' Oddities '. Cf. *nire*, q.v.

naked, n. Raw spirit : somewhat low : from ca. 1860 ; ob. Ex the adj.

naked similes were prob. all coll. in origin, but their very force soon made them S.E. and proverbial. The chief non-dial. ones are :—**naked as a cuckoo**, C. 17–20, latterly dial. and in Dekker as **naked as the cuckoo in Christmas** ; **naked as a needle**, mid-C. 14–20 (ob.), in P. J. Bailey, 1858, **nude as a needle** ; **naked as a shorn sheep**, C. 17–18 (Gayton, 1654) ; **naked as a stone**, C. 14–15 ; **naked as a worm**, C. 15–16 ; **naked as one's** (gen. my) **nail**, ca. 1530–1700 (Heywood, 1533,—Massinger,—' Phraseologia ' Robertson) ; **naked as truth**, C. 17 (suggested by the late C. 16–20 S.E. *the naked truth*), ' Lest it strip him as naked as truth ', in the Somers Tracts. For all : Apperson.

nale, an ale-house, is Scots (prob.) coll. : C. 18– early 19. Extant in Gloucestershire.

nale or **nael, neel.** Lean : back s. (– 1859). H., 1st ed. (Often adj., rarely v.)

nam. A man : back **s.** (— 1859). Ibid. Hence, *nam esclop*, a policeman.

nam ; (not before C. 16) **n'am.** Am not : C. 9–16 : S.E. till ca. 1500, then coll. Gascoigne, 1576, ' I n'am a man, as some do think I am.' O.E.D.

namase. See **nammous.**

namby-pamby. Affected ; effeminate : from ca. 1745 : coll. till ca. 1780, then S.E. Ex. Carey's, Pope's, and Swift's nickname (1726 +) for *Ambrose* Philips, poetaster (d. 1749).

name, get a. To get a (very) bad name : coll. : C. 20. E.g. Denis Mackail, 1925, ' If they weren't jolly careful, their beloved house would be getting what is known as " a name ".'

name !, give it a ; name yours ! Invitations to drink : coll. : late C. 19–20. Lyell. See **how will you have it.**

name, lose one's. ' To be noted for punishment ' (F. & Gibbons) : military : C. 20. I.e. to have one's name taken.

name, to one's. Belonging to one : coll. : 1876, Whyte-Melville (O.E.D.).

name in vain, take one's. To mention by name : coll. : C. 18–20. Swift. Ex the Biblical *take the name of the Lord in vain.*

name into it, put one's. To advance a matter greatly : tailors' : from ca. 1860 ; ob. Ex putting the tailors' name on a garment.

name is mud, his. See **mud.**

name of, by the. Having the name (of) : from ca. 1670 : S.E. till ca. 1830, then coll. and U.S. Thackeray, 1841, ' A grocer . . . by the name of Greenacre ', O.E.D.

name of . . .(, in the). Some of these asseverations are C. 19–20 coll. ; e.g. *name of goodness*, which is also dial. E.D.D.

name (or number) on, have one's. (Of a bullet) that hit a soldier : military coll. in G.W. F. & Gibbons. Cf. *addressed to*, q.v.

name to go to bed with, a nice. An ugly name : dial. >, by 1887, coll. Baumann. Cf. the Fr. **s.** *un nom à coucher dehors* (Manchon).

name yours ! See **name !, give it a.**

nameless creek, the. ' A lucky place whose whereabouts is for that reason untold ', F. & H. : anglers' j. > coll. : from ca. 1860 ; ob.

*nammous or **namous ;** occ. **nammus** or **nommus ;** rarely **namus** and **†namase.** To depart, esp. furtively and/or quickly : c., esp. among coster-mongers : from ca. 1855. J. E. Ritchie, *The Night Side of London Life*, 1857 ; *The London Miscellany*, March 3, 1866. Slightly ob. Prob. a corruption of *vamos, vamoose*, perhaps shaped by *nim* and Ger. *nehmen*. H. postulates back s. on *someone* (' simpli-fied ' presumably, as *summon*) : wrongly, I believe.

nam(m)ow. A woman ; esp. *delo n.*, an old woman : back s. (— 1859). H., 1st ed.

*nammus, namous. See **nammous.**

Namurs, the. The Royal Irish Regiment, earlier (C. 19) the 18th Foot : military : from ca. 1810. Also, from ca. 1850, *Paddy's Blackguards.*

namus. See **nammous.**

nan. A serving-maid : C. 18 : coll. (somewhat low). *A New Canting Dict.*, 1725. Ex *Nan*, a by-form of *Anne*.

nan ! What did you say ? : mid-C. 18–20 : coll. (e.g. in Foote) till ca. 1810, then dial., where ob. by 1920. Ex *anan, anon*. O.E.D., E.D.D.

nan-boy. An effeminate man : late C. 17–20 ; ob. : coll. Cf. *nan* the n.—2. A catamite : C. 19–20 : coll. Sense 1, ? influenced by *Nancy*.

Nana ; Nana-ish. Outrageous ; indecent : club-men's coll. : late 1880–ca. 85. Ware. Ex Zola's *Nana*, that novel which, dealing with a ' swell ' courtesan, owes its best scene to Otway.

nana. A banana : nursery coll. : late C. 19–20. Cf. *nanny*, 4.

Nance. A variant (C. 20) of the next. Norah Hoult, *Youth Can't Be Served*, 1933.

Nancy, Miss Nancy, Nancy boy. A catamite : (low) coll. : C. 19–20. Also as adj. : rare before C. 20. E.g. Hugh Walpole, *Vanessa*, 1933, ' But he isn't one of those, you know. Not a bit nancy.'—2. Also, an effeminate man : C. 19–20 ; ob. except in dial. Cf. *molly*, q.v.—3. (Only as **nancy, Nancy.**) The breech, esp. in *ask my Nancy* : low (perhaps orig. c.) : ca. 1810–1910. Vaux. See **arse !, ask my.**

Nancy Dawson. Grog : naval : C. 19–20 ; very ob. Bowen, ' Men were summoned to draw it by that popular old air.'

Nancy Lee. An occ. C. 20 variant of *Rosy Lee*, tea. Much less gen. than :—2. A flea : rhyming s. : from ca. 1860. *Everyman*, March 26, 1931.

nanna. An occ. variant of sense 3 of :

nanny. A whore : late C. 17–19 : coll. Ex *Nanny*, the female name. Mostly in combination : see, e.g., **nanny-house.**—2. A she-goat : from ca. 1890 as a coll., but in dial. before 1870 (E.D.D.) Abbr. *nanny-goat.*—3. (A) nurse : 1864 (O.E.D. Sup.) : children's coll. that, by 1933, was on the verge of S.E.—4. A banana : (mostly London) street boys' (— 1909). Ware. Cf. *nana.*

nanny-goat. A she-goat : coll. : 1788, T. Day (O.E.D.). Cf. *nanny*, 1, and *billy-goat.*—2. An anecdote : 1860, Haliburton ; ob. Semi-rhym-ing s.

nanny-goat, play the. To play silly tricks ; be-have like a fool : coll. : from ca. 1905. Ex slightly earlier dial : see E.D.D. Cf. *goat, play the.*

Nanny-Goats, the. The Royal Welch Fusiliers, orig. the 23rd Foot Regiment : military : mid-C. 19–20. Also, *the Royal Goats.* Ex the goat as mascot. (F. & Gibbons.)

nanny(-)hen, as nice as a. Very affected ; delicate ; prim : C. 16–17 : coll. The *nanny-hen* is merely *nun's hen* (see **nice as a nun's hen**) and may, in fact, have rarely been used : see Apperson at *nice.*

nanny-house or **shop.** A brothel : low coll. : resp. late C. 17–19 (B.E. ; Grose) ; C. 19–20, slightly ob. (and not recorded before 1825 : O.E.D.) F. & H. give an imposing synonymy : e.g. *academy, case, flash drum, knocking-shop, molly-shop, number 9, pushing-school, trugging-ken, vrow-case, whore-shop.*

*nantee ; nanti (rare), **nanty.** No ; not, or nor, any. Also absolutely : I have none ; ' shut up ' (abbr. *nantee palaver*, q.v.) ; stop ! (e.g. ' Nanty that whistling ! ') : from ca. 1850 : Parlyaree and c. > also, by 1900, gen. theatrical. Mayhew. Among grafters : beware ! (Allingham, *Cheapjack*, 1934.) Ex It. *niente*, nothing, via Lingua Franca as is most Parlyaree.—2. Hence adj. : of no account : Par-lyaree (— 1909). Ware.

nantee medzies or **nanty metzes.** See **medzies.**

nantee narking. Great fun : low taverns' : ca. 1800–50. Egan's *Life in London.* Lit., ' no crab-bing '.

nantee palaver ! Hold your tongue ! : from ca. 1850. Lit., no talk. Cf. :

nantee panarly ! Be careful ! : from ca. 1850. See **nantee.**

nantee worster. No worse; a person no worse: low London : late C. 19–20. Ware.

nanti, nanty. See nantee.

Nap. Napoleon : a nickname of ca. 1810–30. Cf. *Boney*, q.v.

*__nap.__ An infection of syphilis or gonorrhœa : c. : late C. 17–18. B.E.—2. An instance of : ' By Cheating with the Dice to secure one Chance ', B.E. : c. : late C. 17–18. Rare : the v. is much commoner.—3. An arrest : throughout C. 18 : c. or low s. *Street Robberies Considered*, ca. 1728.—4. Presumably, a sheep, the term occurring only in *napper of naps*, a sheep-stealer : late C. 17–18 : c. B.E., Grose. These four senses derive ex the c. v., q.v.—5. A hat : c. of C. 18. Ex *nab*, n., 3.—6. Strong ale or beer : Scots coll. : late C. 18–19. Tarras, 1804 ; Jamieson. Ex *nappy*.—7. A Napoleon, i.e. a twenty-franc piece : coll. : 1820, Moore (O.E.D.) ; † by 1920. By abbr.—8. A pretended blow : theatrical : from ca. 1850. Mayhew. Esp. in *give* and *take the nap*. ? ex *knap*. O.E.D.—9. A very pointed moustache : London : 1855–ca. 70. Ware. Re-introduced by Napoleon III, who visited London in 1855.

*__nap__, v. See the n., 1, and 2. : same period and status. The infection is gen. conveyed by *nap it* (B.E., Grose). The etymology, like the relation to *nab*, is vague ; cf. the cognate S.E. *knap*.—2. To seize, catch ; arrest : c. : from ca. 1670 ; ob. Head, ' If the Cully naps us, And the Lurries from us take ' ; D'Urfey (O.E.D.). In John Poulter, 1753, the sense weakens : ' Nap my kelp (hold my hat).'—3. Hence, to steal : c. : from ca. 1690 ; ob. B.E., Vaux. E.g. *nap the wiper*, steal the handkerchief.—4. To receive severe punishment (prob. ex. sense 1) : gen. as *nap it* : low : from ca. 1815 ; ob., except in dial.—5. To cog (a die) : late C. 17–18 c. cognate with sense 2 : both prob. ex *knap*.—6. Hence, v.i. and t., to cheat : c. of ca. 1670–1760. Coles.—7. A low variant of S.E. *knap* : late C. 17–20.—8. The horse-racing v. is j., not s.

nap, go. To risk everything : ca. 1884, Glover, *Racing Life* : coll. (? orig. racing s.) >, ca. 1920, virtually S.E. Ex the card game.

*__nap a winder.__ To be hanged : c. : C. 19. Lit., catch something that winds one.

nap and double. Trouble (n.) : rhyming s. : C. 20. Margery Allingham, *Mystery Mile*, 1930.

*__nap it.__ See nap, v., 1 and 4. E.g. *nap it at the nask* (see **nask**), to be lashed at Bridewell : late C. 17–18 c. B.E.

nap-nix. An amateur playing minor parts for experience : theatrical : from ca. 1860 ; ob. H., 3rd ed. Ex *nap*, to take or receive, + *nix*, nothing.

*__nap on.__ To cheat, try a cheating trick on : ca. 1670–1760 : c. Head.—2. Also, however, it means to strike or to strike at : C. 17–early 18. (See, e.g. the O.E.D.'s quotation from Head & Kirkman, where the sense is ambiguous.) Here, *nap* (cf. Greene's ' worse than nabbing on the neckes to Connies ') is prob. S.E. *knap* corrupted.

nap on, go. To bet, everything one has, on : from the 1880's : racing coll. >, by 1900, S.E. (O.E.D.)

nap or nothing. All or nothing : clubmen's : 1868–ca. 1900. Ware.

*__nap the bib, the regulars, the rust, the teaze or teize.__ See **nab the bib**, etc.

nap the rent. See **pew, stump the** : with which it is contemporaneous as well as synonymous.

nap toco for yam. To get the worst of it, esp. in fisticuffs : low : ca. 1820–70. ' Jon Bee.' ? ex Gr. τόκος, interest. See **toco**.

napkin, be buried in a. To be asleep ; half-witted : C. 19–20, ob. : coll.

napkin, knight of the. A waiter : C. 19–20, ob. : coll. bordering on S.E.

napkin, take sheet and. To sleep and eat (with someone) : coll. : C. 17–18. Mewe. O.E.D.

napkin-snatching. The stealing of handkerchiefs : ca. 1820–60 : low or c. Egan's Grose.

napkin under one's chin, stick a. To eat a meal : from ca. 1750 ; ob. : coll. Foote. (Like *napkin, take . . .*, above, this phrase verges on S.E.)

napoo ; rarely **napooh.** Finished (esp., empty), gone ; non-existent ; dead ; ' nothing doing ! ' ; ' it's no use arguing any longer ', ' (it's) no good ' : orig. and mainly military : 1915 ; ob. Ex Fr. *il n'y en a plus*, there is none left, in reply to inquiries for drink.—2. Hence, also from 1915, v., to finish ; occ. to kill.—3. As an adj., the term does not exist except in *The Pall Mall Gazette*, Feb. 15, 1917, cited by W. For senses 1 and 2, see esp. B. & P. and cf. *san fairy ann*, q.v.

napoo finee. An occ. elaboration of *napoo*, 1, and *finee*, qq.v. : military : 1916–18. F. & Gibbons.

*__napp.__ See nap, n. and v.

*__napper.__ A cheat ; a thief : c. of ca. 1670–1840. Coles ; B.E. Esp. in *napper of naps* (see nap, n., 4).—2. A false witness : low or c. : C. 18.—3. See **rain-napper.**—4. The head : s. and dial. : from ca. 1780. Grose, 1st ed. Esp. in *go off one's napper*, go mad. ? etymology, unless ex *nab*, the head (cf. *nap*, 5.)—5. Hence, the mouth : low : late C. 19–20. A. Neil Lyons, *Clara*, 1912, ' You keep your napper shut ' (Manchon).—6. A hat : c. of ca. 1800–70. See nap, n., 5. H., 3rd ed.

*__napping.__ Cheating : from ca. 1670 ; ob : c. until C. 19, then low s.—2. See nap, v.

napping, as Moss (in late C. 18–mid-19, often **Morse**, as in Grose) **caught his mare.** Asleep ; by surprise : a coll. proverbial c.p. of ca. 1569–1870 ; in C. 19, dial. ' The allusions to this saying and song in C. 16–17 are very numerous,' Apperson. App. one Moss caught his mare by feeding her through a hurdle (Apperson, quotation of 1597).

napping, catch or **take.** To take by surprise or in the act : 1562, Pilkington (O.E.D.) ; Grose, in the elaborated form (see preceding entry) : coll. till C. 19, then S.E. Lit., to catch asleep.

nappy. Beer : early C. 18. Ned Ward (cited by W. Matthews in *Notes and Queries*, June 15, 1935).—2. A napkin : nursery coll. : C. 20 (and prob. from mid-C. 19). Collinson.

nappy, adj. (Of a horse) that has ' these here little lumps along the neck and withers about as big as a nut ' (' No. 747 ') : horse-copers' : mid-C. 19–20.

naptha. See **'p for ph .'**

nare. Never. Only if spelt thus is it low coll. and dial (C. 18–20), for obviously it represents and is pronounced in the same way as *ne'er*.

Narfy. See **Nafy.**

narikin. A new-rich : 1923, Manchon ; ob. Ex Japanese.

*__nark.__ A police spy ; a common informer : c. (— 1864). ' No. 747 ' ; H., 2nd ed. ; Arthur Morrison, in *Mean Streets*. Often *copper's nark*, i.e. ' nose ' (q.v.). Ex Romany *nak*, the nose. Cf. *nark*, v.—2. Hence, in C. 20 low s. a spoil-sport ; a spiteful or nagging person. C. J. Dennis. Influenced by *nark*, v., 4.—3. Hence, rancour ; a spite (*against* a person) : low (— 1923). Manchon.

—4. 'A man eager to curry favour by running about and doing odd jobs for a superior' : military : from ca. 1908. F. & Gibbons.—5. A person on inquiry from head office : London clerks', managers', etc. : from before 1935.—6. See grafters' sense of **bogey**, n.

*nark, v. To watch ; occ., look after : c. (— 1859). H., 1st ed. Ex the n. Cf. *tout*, v.—2. Hence, to see : low (— 1886). ' Pomes ' Marshall. —3. V.i., to act the informer : 1896, A. Morrison, in *Child Jago*, ' It was the sole commandment that ran there : " Thou shalt not nark " ' (O.E.D.). Cf. *nose*, *stag*, qq.v.—4. To annoy, exasperate : C. 20 low s. ex dial. (— 1888) slightly influenced by the c. senses. (E.D.D.)—5. In Australia, it also = to foil : C. 20. C. J. Dennis.—6. See :

nark it ! ' Shut up ! ' ; be quiet ! : military and low : from ca. 1912. F. & Gibbons. Prob. ex *nark*, v., 5.

nark yer !, I'll. An Australian c.p. (from ca. 1915) combining the senses of *nark*, v., 4 and 5.

Narky. H.M.S. *Narcissus* : naval : C. 20. F. & Gibbons.

narp. A shirt : Scots, either c. or, less prob., low s. (— 1839). Brandon. Origin ?

narrative. A dog's tail : middle class jocular : ca. 1900–14. Ware. Punning *tail—tale—narrative*.

narrish. Thrifty : coll. (— 1889) ; ob. London society, Oct., 1889. Ex S.E. *narrowish*.

narrow. Never (a) ; not (a), not (one) : coll. and dial : 1750, Fielding, ' I warrants me there is narrow a one of all those warrant officers but looks upon himself to be as good as arrow a squire of £500 a year.' Ex *ne'er a*.—2. While it is S.E. as = mean, parsimonious, close(ly investigating or made), (very) small, it is low coll. or s. as = stupid, foolish, ignorant : from ca. 1850 ; ob.—3. The bowling sense, ' When the Bias of the Bowl holds too much ', B.E., is either j. or coll. of late C. 17–20 ; ob.—4. For *narrow squeak*, see **squeak**.

narrow, 'tis all. ' Said by the Butchers one to another when their Meat proves not so good as expected ', B.E. : late C. 17–18 c.p.

narrow lane, the. See **lane**, 2.

narrow-striper. A Royal Marine Light Infantryman : naval : late C. 19–20. Bowen.

nary a. Never a . . . : dial. and sol. : C. 19–20. Perhaps ex *ne'er a*. Cf. *narrow*, q.v.

nasal. The nose : boxing : 1888, *Sporting Life*, Nov. 21, ' Planted a couple of well-delivered stingers on Harris's nasal '. Virtually † by 1920.

*nase. Also *nace*, *naze*, *nazie*, *nazy*. Drunken; (of liquor) intoxicating : c. : from ca. 1530 ; fl. till ca. 1690 as *nace*, *naze* ; then only as *nazie*, *nazy*, or *nazzy* : see **nazy**. Copland (*nace*), Harman (*nase*), B.E. (*nazie*), Grose (*nazie*). ? ex *nose*, Fr. *nez*. See also **nazy**.

*nash. To go away from, to quit, person(s) or place : c. of ca. 1810–50. Vaux, ' Speaking of a person who is gone, they say he is nash'd.' Ex Romany *nash*, *nasher*, to run.

*Nash is concerned, Mr. C. of ca. 1810–50 : Vaux, see quotation, preceding entry.

nasie (Coles, 1676). See **nazy**.

*nask or naskin. A prison : c. of ca. 1670–1830. Coles, 1676 (*naskin*) ; Higden, 1686, Juvenal (*10th Satire*), *naskin* ; ca. 1690, B.E., *nask* and *naskin* ; Grose, id. ? ex † Scots dial. *nask*, a withe + c. *ken*, a place, *nask* being an abbr. Whence, *the Old Nask*, the City (London) bridewell ; *the New Nask*, the Clerkenwell bridewell ; and *Tuttle* (in Grose, *Tothi-*

fields) Nask, that in Tothill Fields : all in B.E. and all c.

Nasties ; gen. the N—. Nazis : 1934 ; ob. By ' Hobson-Jobson '. Cf. *Nazi-scrammer*.

nasty, ill-tempered, disagreeable, dangerous, unpleasant in its results, is S.E. verging on coll. (the O.E.D. gives it, rightly no doubt, as S.E., and the E.D.D. as coll.), except when used by children to mean ' naughty ' (coll. : late C. 19–20) : *nasty far* (— 1902) is also S.E. ; but *nasty one*, a fig. blow, a set-back, as in ' Ouida ', 1880, is coll., and so is *nasty knock*, 1886, at least orig., for in C. 20 it is rather S.E. than unconventional ; *nasty one in the eye*, a set-back, an affront, is, however, definitely coll. (— 1902).

nasty, cheap and. Outwardly pleasing, actually worthless : coll. (— 1864) until ca. 1905, then S.E. In London, ca. 1860–80, the phrase often ran ' . . . like Short's in the Strand ', with reference to a cheap restaurant that now has a much better reputation.

nasty face. See **Jack Nasty-Face**.

*nasty man. He who, in a garrotting gang, does the critical work ; or he who, for a cracksman on a desperate job, acts as a garrotter : c. : from ca. 1840 ; ob. The reference (p. 419) in ' No. 747's ' *Autobiography* is valid for 1845 ; Trevelyan in *The Competition Wallah*.

Natal fever. A heat-induced indisposition for exercise : South African coll. : 1909, *The East London Dispatch*, June 7. Pettman.

Natal rum. ' A vile spirit distilled from sugar refuse and nothing behind " Cape smoke " [q.v.] in its effects ', Pettman : 1885, W. Greswell, *Our South African Empire*.

natchrel, -ril. Natural : sol. and dial. : C. 18–20. C. J. Dennis.

nater. An international player : sporting (— 1923) ; ob. Manchon. Also **internatter**, q.v.

Nathaniel, (down) below. Even lower than hell : ca. 1860–1915. Nathaniel being Satan, says Ware : but *Nathaniel* may be rhyming s. on *hell*.

nation as n. is S.E., as an adv. = very (— 1785) it is coll. († by 1870) and dial. ; as adj. (very great or large) it is C. 19–20 dial. As all three, common in late C. 18–20 U.S. The adj. derives ex the n. (Sterne, 1762, ' The French have such a nation of hedges ') and occurs in U.S. as early as 1765 (*nation profit*), while the adv., in U.S., 1788 (*nation fine*), derives either ex the U.S. adj. or the n. The word itself is a euphemistic abbr. of *damnation* (adv.). Thornton and O.E.D.

native ; gen. collectively **the natives,** ' silly people, generally ; the untravelled population of any town, wrapped up in incipient [? *innate* or *insipid*] simplicity are *natives* ', Bee : London coll. : from ca. 1820 ; ob. Cf. :

native cavalry. ' The unbroke horses of countrymen, when they resort to races, fairs, fights, &c.', Bee : London : ca. 1820–60. Cf. preceding entry.

natomy ; nattermy. See **atomy**, of which it is a mainly dial. variant.

nat'ral. Natural : low coll. (— 1887). Baumann.

Nats, the. The National Party : in South Africa : from ca. 1926. (W. Saint-Mandé, *Halcyon Days in South Africa*, 1934.)

nattermy is the form given by Ware. See **natomy.**

natty. A ' natty ' person : coll. : 1820, Moore ; ob. O.E.D. Ex :

natty, adj. Orig., and in c., app. clever, smart with the hands : see **natty lad**.—2. Smartly neat, spruce : from ca. 1785 (implied in the adv., q.v.) : s. till ca. 1860, then coll. ; in C. 20, S.E. Surr, 1806, ' A natty spark of eighteen '.—3. Of things, very neat, dainty : s. till ca. 1860 ; coll. ca. 1860–1910 ; then S.E. 1801, Wolcot, ' Thy natty bob '.—4. Hence, of persons, daintily skilful : from ca. 1820 : s. >, ca. 1860, coll. ; in C. 20, S.E. Prob. ex *natty lad*, q.v. For etymology, cf. the † S.E. *netty*, *nettie* (e.g. in Tusser, ' Pretty . . . fine and . . . nettie '), but prob. a corruption of *neat* (W.) or perhaps ex Fr. *net*. N.B., the other parts, *nattily*, *nattiness*, mid-C. 19–20, were, prob., orig. coll., but they soon > S.E. (O.E.D.)

natty, adv. Nattily, i.e. smartly, daintily, neatly, hence skilfully : from ca. 1785 : s. >, ca. 1860, (low) coll. G. Parker, 1789, ' A kind of fellow who dresses smart, or what they term natty '. Ex the adj.

***natty lad**. A young thief, esp. if a pickpocket : c. of ca. 1780–1870. Grose, 1st ed. See **natty**, adj., 1, and the etymology.

natural. A mistress, a harlot : ca. 1685–1830 : perhaps orig. c. ; never better than low s. Shadwell, ' My natural, my convenient, my pure '.—2. A child : coll. : late C. 18–early 19. Grose, 1st ed. By abbr. ex *natural child, daughter, son*. (—3. F. & H.'s definition as ' bastard ' is an error accounted for by a misreading of the entry in Grose, edd. 1–5.)—4. Ace and 10 at vingt-et-un : from ca. 1900. Manchon. Perhaps because such a hand naturally makes 21.—5. See next two entries.

natural, for (or **in**) **all one's** (gen. **my**). For or in all one's life ; ever : C. 20 : s. >, by 1930, coll. As in the next entry, sc. *life* after *natural* ; as also there, perhaps an allusion is understood to *for the term of his natural life*.

natural !, not on your. Certainly not ! : C. 20. See preceding entry.

naturally ! Of course : coll. : late C. 19–20. (Strangely, not in O.E.D.)

naughty. Flash ; loudly smart : low : ca. 1860–1910. Vance, 1864, speaks of trousers as ' werry naughty '. Prob. *naughty*, immoral, influenced by *natty*, adj., 3.

naughty, do the. To play the whore ; to coït (of women only) : from ca. 1850 : low coll. Also, ca. 1860–1910, occ. *go naughty* : ordinary coll.

naughty, the. The female pudend : mid C. 19–20.

naughty house, if used by the prim, is S.E. ; if by the lewd, a coll. : C. 19–20.

nautical triumvisetta. ' A singing and dancing nautical scene by three persons, of whom two are generally women ' : music-halls' (— 1909) ; very ob. Ware. Perhaps a blend of *triumvirate + set*, with an Italianate suffix (*a*).

nav. Abbr. *navigator*, q.v.

Nav. House, the. The Royal Naval College at Portsmouth : naval : C. 20. Bowen.

naval police, Her or **His Majesty's**. Sharks : nautical : mid-C. 19–20 ; ob. Ware. They are sharp deterrents of desertion at sea.

[**navee**. Jocular S.E., not coll., spelling : fathered and popularised by Gilbert : late C. 19–20.]

navel, gall one's. To grow wanton : C. 18 coll. ; cf. the C. 17–18 :

navel, proud below the. Amorous : coll. bordering on S.E., as in Davenant's *Albovine*, 1629, ' Whenever I see her I grow proud below the navel.'

navel-tied. Inseparable : C. 18–early 19 coll.

Gen. *they have tied their navels together*, as in Ray's *Proverbs*, ed. of 1767.

navels, wriggle. To copulate : C. 19 : low coll. Cf. *giblets*, q.v.

naverage. A catachrestic form of *naufrage* : C. 17(?–18). O.E.D.

navigator. A ' tatur ', i.e. potato : rhyming s. (— 1859). H., 1st ed. Occ. *nav* (— 1902).

navigator Scot. A hot ' tatur ' ; gen. a hot baked potato : rhyming s. (— 1859). H., 1st ed.

Navvies. See sense 3 of :

navvy. A labourer working on excavation, earth-works, or similar heavy tasks : 1832, De Quincey : coll. >, by 1865 (witness H., 3rd ed.), S.E. Ex *navigator*, S.E. (ca. 1770–1870), same sense.—2. The navigating officer : nautical : late C. 19–20. Bowen.—3. Gen. pl., ' General Steam Navigation's ships ' : nautical : late C. 19–20. Ibid.

navy !, thank God we've got a. A military c.p. muttered when things are going wrong : C. 20 ; esp. in G.W. F. & Gibbons, ' Said to have originated in a soldier's sarcastic comment when . . . watching a party of the old Volunteers marching by one Saturday night '. I suspect, however, that it is a very old c.p. ; Evan John in his arresting *Charles I* (published in 1933) suggests that it was originated by Sir John Norris, temp. Charles I.

Navy Office, the. The Fleet Prison : low : ca. 1810–40. Lex. Bal. Whence, *Commander of the Fleet*, the warden there. Ib. Ex the old name for the Admiralty building (see Pepys's *Diary*, July 9, 1660 : O.E.D.)

Nawpost, Mr. A foolish fellow : late C. 17–18 : c. p. coll. B.E. ; Grose, 1785. Presumably, one foolish enough, if hungry, to gnaw a post.

' Nay, stay ! ' quoth Stringer when his neck was in the halter. A c.p. applied to one speaking too late : ca. 1670–1750. Ray, Fuller. (Apperson.) Ex a topical instance, perhaps of an innocent man.

Nazarene foretop. ' The foretop of a wig made in imitation of Christ's head of hair, as represented by the painters and sculptors ', Grose, 2nd ed. : ca. 1785–1820 : on the border-line between S.E. and coll.

naze. See **nase**.

Nazi-scrammer. An actor or actress that, because of Jewish blood, has left Germany to perform, permanently, in another country : theatrical : 1935, *The Daily Express*, Sept. 20. See **scram**.

nazie. See **nazy**.

nazold. A silly person ; a vain fool : 1607, Walkington : coll. till ca. 1840, then only as dial. Cf. S.E. *nazzard*, which app. = dial. *azzard* and, significantly, *azzald*, which may be cognate with *ass*.

***nazy** ; occ. **nazzy**. Drunken : from early 1670's : c. (ex *nase*, q.v.) until ca. 1780, then low ; from ca. 1830, dial. (ob. in C. 20). Coles, 1676 (*nasie*) ; B.E. (as *nazie*) ; *A New Canting Dict.*, 1725, *nazy-cove* and *-mort*, a male and a female drunkard ; Grose (*nazie*, 1785 ; *nazy*, 1788) ; Robinson's *Whitby Glossary*, 1855 (*nazzy*). Cf. :

***nazy-nab**. A drunken coxcomb : c. : C.18. *A New Canting Dict.*, 1725. Ex preceding.

ne'. Never : a clipped, slovenly coll. of the upper classes and of drunks : since when ? John Dickson Carr, *The Eight of Swords*, 1934, ' His daughter and my son—hurrumph, ne' mind.'

***ne-dash**. See **nedash**.

neagues ; neakes. See **'Sneaks !**

[**near**, parsimonious, or on the left side, is S.E., as are **neat** (undiluted), **neb**, **necessary** (a privy : now dial.), **neck of** (**on or in the** : close upon), **neck of anything**(, **break the**), **neck-question, neck-verse, ne'er-do-well,** n. and adj., **negotiate** (contrive, manage to do or pass), **Negro, neighbourly, nephew, nervous cane, nest** (a centre, a place), **nes(t) cock or nestle-cock, nestling, nether end or eye, nettle, nettle-bed, nettled, nettler, newcome** (n.), **newgate** (to imprison) ; whereas **Ned Stokes** is dial. :—all despite F. & H.]

near-. Approximating to, incomplete(ly) ; ostensible ; a substitute for, hence artificial (things) ; superficial : coll. : from ca. 1925 in England ; ex (— 1919) U.S. : see esp. Mencken. In such phrases as *near-silk,* artificial silk ; *near-thinker,* almost or ostensibly a thinker. By 1937, knocking at the S.E. gates. Cf. the late C. 16– early 17 S.E. usage, exemplified in *near-wretched,* Ben Jonson, and *near-isle,* Lisle, 1625 (O.E.D.).

near and far. The bar : public-house rhyming s. (— 1909). Ware.

near—in C. 17 occ. **like—as fourpence to a groat, as.** For practical purposes the same : mid-C. 16– 20 : coll. till C. 19, then dial. (Apperson.)

near the knuckle. See **knuckle, near the.**

neardy. A master, a foreman, a parent ; a ' boss ' : Northern coll. : from ca. 1860 ; ob.

nearer the bone. See **meat, the nearer the bone.**

neat. (Ironically) rare ; fine : ca. 1825–1915 ; ob. by 1890. T. Creevey, 1827, ' So much for my new find ! Is he not a neat one ? ' (O.E.D.

neat as a band-box, a new pin, ninepence, wax. As neat as possible ; very neat indeed : coll. : resp. C. 19–20, C. 19–20, C. 17–20 (see at *ninepence*), ca. 1840–1910.

neat but not gaudy. Sprucely neat : orig. serious (ca. 1630–1800) and presumably S.E. ; then —even in Lamb's ' A little . . . flowery border . . ., neat not gaudy ', 1806—it takes an ironical turn (cf. *neat,* above), which finds itself recognised as a c.p. when, in 1838, Ruskin, in *The Architectural Magazine* for Nov., writes, ' That admiration of the " neat but not gaudy ", which is commonly reported to have influenced the devil when he painted his tail pea green.' (Apperson.) In 1887, *Lippincott's Magazine* for July has, ' The whole thing " Neat, but not gaudy, as the monkey said " on the memorable occasion " when he painted his tail sky-blue ",' which presents a diversion from the orig. sense and likewise constitutes a c.p. But by 1902, F. & H. can give as a ' common ', i.e. gen., c.p. : *neat, but not gaudy : as the devil said when he painted his bottom red and tied up his tail with sky-blue ribbon.* After 1930 one has often heard *neat but not gaudy* or this plus *as the monkey said* ; the longer forms only occ.

neaters. Undiluted rum ; rum before it is made into grog : naval officers' : C. 20. Bowen. (By process of ' the Oxford *-er* '.

neathie-set. A woman's term for a set of feminine underclothes : from 1933. In *Books of To-Day,* Nov., 1934, C.G.T., in a poem entitled *Too Much of Too Little,* writes, concerning advertisements : ' I'm weary of their " woollies ", | Their " step-ins " and their " pullies ", | Their " tighties " and their " fullies ", | Their darling " neathie-sets ".' (Cf. the quotations at *briefs* and *undies.*) Ex *underneath.*

neb. A face, esp. a woman's : (low) coll. : C. 17–18. Extant in dial. Ex *neb,* a bird's bill.

Nebuchadnezzar. The penis, esp. in *take N. out to grass,* (of a man) to have sexual intercourse : low : ca. 1860–1915. Ex its liking for ' greens ', q.v.—2.

A vegetarian : ca. 1870–1910. Ex the Biblical Nebuchadnezzar's eating of grass.

Nec Ultra. The west side of Temple Bar, London ; fashionable London : Society : C. 19. D. Jerrold (the first), cited by Ware. Punning the L. phrase.

necessary. A bedfellow, esp. a woman : coll. : C. 18–early 19.—2. With *the* : *ad hoc* money, funds : coll. : 1897, *The Daily News,* Sept. 6 (O.E.D.). Cf. *needful,* q.v.

neck ; occ. **brass-neck** (Manchon). Impudence ; very great assurance : C. 20. Ex Northern dial. : see E.D.D. Cf. *cheek* and *lip.*

neck, v. To hang : coll. : C. 18–mid-19. Cf. S.E. senses, strike on the neck, behead ; imm., however, prob. ex the *neck* hanging phrases.—2. To swallow, drink : coll. : from ca. 1820 ; ob. ca. 1900–20, but then (witness O.E.D. Sup.) revived. Cf. the C. 16 coll. usage : Barclay, 1514, ' She couthe well . . . necke a mesure . . . : she made ten shylynge [i.e. little] of one barell of ale,' which, *pace* the O.E.D., is clear enough.—3. See **necking.**

neck, in the. With unpleasant results ; severely : U.S. (ca. 1890), anglicised by H. G. Wells in 1908 : s. >, by 1935, coll. Esp. with *get it.* Cf. *where Maggie wore the beads* and *where the chicken got the axe.* W. ; O.E.D. (Sup.).

neck, lose or win by a. To lose or win by very little : from ca. 1850 : coll. till C. 20, then S.E. For origin, cf. **neck and neck.**

neck, put it down one's. See **neck, wash one's.** Cf. the U.S. *shot in the neck,* drunk.

neck, talk through (the back of) one's. To talk extravagantly, catachrestically : 1904 (O.E.D. Sup.).—2. Hence, to talk nonsense : from ca. 1920. Both senses had, by 1930, > coll.

neck, wash one's or **the.** To drink : low : ca. 1820–1900. ' Jon Bee ' ; Baumann. In C. 20, *put it down one's neck* (Manchon).

neck and crop. Violently ; all of a heap ; entirely : 1816, Hone : coll. >, ca. 1890, S.E. Hardy, 1872 ; Hall Caine in *The Manxman,* 1894. (Apperson.)

neck and heels. Impetuously ; whole-heartedly : coll. (— 1887). Baumann.

neck and neck. Almost equal ; close : from ca. 1835 : coll. till C. 20, then S.E. Ex horses running almost level in a race. W. S. Landor to Browning, Feb. 11, 1860, ' You and your incomparable wife are running neck and neck, as sportsmen say ' : H. C. Minchin's *Walter Savage Landor,* 1934.

neck as long as my arm, I'll first see thy. I'll see you hanged first ; you be hanged ! A mid-C. 17– mid-18 c.p. Ray, 1678. (Apperson.)

neck-basting. Liquor-drinking : low (— 1887) ; slightly ob. Baumann.

[**neck-beef,** coarseness ; S.E. ; *as coarse as neck-beef* : S.E. bordering on coll. : ca. 1770–1920. Cf. Sedley's ' She is very pretty, and as cheap as neck-beef,' 1687 (O.E.D.).]

neck-cloth. A halter : low coll. : ca. 1815–70. Cf. *necktie,* q.v.

neck it, unable to. Lacking moral courage : low coll. : from ca. 1840 ; slightly ob. Ex *neck,* v., 2. Cf. the S.E. *swallow* = to tolerate.

neck-oil. Liquor ; esp. beer : low coll. : from ca. 1830. H., 2nd ed. ; Ware. Cf. *neck,* v., 2.

neck or nothing. Desperate(ly) : from ca. 1675 : coll. till ca. 1850, then S.E. Ray ; Cibber ; Swift, ' Neck or nothing ; come down or I'll fetch you down '; Byron. (Apperson.) Either a hanging or a steeplechasing phrase.

neck-squeezer. A halter : low coll. : ca. 1810–70. Cf. *neck-cloth, necklace.*

***neck-stamper.** A pot-boy at a tavern : c. : ca. 1670–1820. Coles ; Grose, 1st ed.

neck-weed. A halter (cf. *gallows-grass,* q.v.) : ca. 1560–1830 : coll. >, ca. 1600, S.E.

neckerchief on the way to Redriffe, the Devil's. The halter ; the gallows : low coll. : ca. 1810–60. *Notes and Queries,* 1886.

necking, vbl.n. and ppl.adj. Love-making. Orig. and mainly U.S. ; partly adopted in England ca. 1928, esp. in *necking* (cf. *petting*) *parties.* Lit., hugging each other around the neck, and ultimately ex Scots.

necklace. A halter : C. 17–mid-19 : coll. soon > S.E. Cf. *neck-cloth,* and :

necktie, a halter ; *wear a hempen necktie,* to be hanged : C. 18–early 19 coll. Cf. the U.S. *necktie sociable* (— 1878), *n. party* (— 1893), a lynching : Thornton. In English c., a *necktie-party* is a hanging : 1932, 'Stuart Wood', *Shades of the Prison House.*

necky. Impudent, cheeky : *Conway* cadets' (— 1900). John Masefield, *The Conway,* 1933. Ex *neck,* n.

Ned. The inevitable nickname, from the 1890's, of Australian men surnamed Kelly. Ex the notorious bushranger, Ned Kelly.

***ned.** A guinea : c. of ca. 1750–1890 ; then in U.S. as a 10-dollar piece. *Discoveries of John Poulter* ; G. Parker : H., 5th ed.—2. Abbr. *neddy,* 1, q.v. : from ca. 1830.

Ned Fool. A noisy fool or idiot : coll. : late C. 16–early 17. Nashe.

Ned Skinner. Dinner : rhyming s. (— 1909.) Ware.

***nedash.** Of no use ; nothing : c. of ca. 1810–50. Vaux ; Egan's Grose (*ne-dash*). Ex Romany *nastis, nastissa, nestis,* I, you, he, etc., cannot ; ? ultimately L. *nequeo.*

neddy. An ass : C. 17–20 : coll. Wolcot, 1790. Ex *Edward.* Occ. abbr. *ned* ; also called *Jack* or *Tom.* (The very few pre-1790 examples are not indisputable.)—2. Hence, a fool : coll. and dial. : from ca. 1820. 'Jon Bee' ; Thackeray, 'Long-eared neddies, giving themselves leonine airs '.—3. A guinea : c. : ca. 1760–1850. See **ned,** 1.—4. A life-preserver : c. : 1845 in ' *No. 747* ' (p. 423) ; 1857, ' Ducange Anglicus ' ; 1859, H. ; 1864, *The Cornhill Magazine.* Also *billy, cosh,* qq.v. According to Brewer, ex one *Kennedy,* whose head was smashed in with a poker ; prob., however, semantically ex sense 2 above.—5. A large quantity ; plenty : Anglo-Irish : from ca. 1860 : ob. H., 3rd ed.

neddyvaul (or **N.**). The chief, leader, conqueror : street boys' (mostly London) : late C. 19–early 20. Ware. A corruption of *Ned* (the head) *of all.*

necee peeress. ' An E.C. [East London] or city [rather, City] bride of little or no family, and an immense fortune, both of which are wedded to some poor lord or baronet ' : Society (— 1909) ; ob. Ware. Lit., an *E.C.* peeress.

needful, the. *Ad hoc* money : coll. : 1771, Foote, ' Then I will set about getting the needful ' ; *The Comic Almanack,* 1836, ' Needy men the needful need ' ; Dickens ; *The Free Lance,* Oct. 6, 1900. Cf. *necessary,* q.v.

Needham. Poverty : **allusive S.E. of ca.**

1570–1890. Prob. coll. in *on the high-road,* or *in the high-way,* to *Needham.* Fuller, Ray, Spurgeon Needham (in C. 16, occ. *Needam* ; in C. 17, occ. *Needom* or *Needome*) : a small town near Ipswich (O.E.D. ; Apperson.) Cf. :

Needingworth, it comes from. It is worthless or inferior : coll. : C. 17. John Clarke, 1639. Cf. preceding : another topical allusion on the border-line between S.E. and coll.

***needle.** A sharper ; a thief : c. of ca. 1780–1850. Potter, 1790. Abbr. *needle-point,* q.v. : ex the notion of extreme sharpness.—2. The penis : both low coll. and, in C. 18, S.E. (E.g. in Nabbes, Dorset, Rochester).—3. With *the* : irritation ; nervousness : 1887, *Punch,* July 30, ' It give 'im the needle . . . being left in the lurch this way ' ; 1900, G. Swift, the nervousness sense, which is mainly athletic, esp. rowing. O.E.D. Prob., as W. suggests, influenced by *nettle* (e.g. † *get the nettle,* become angry), but imm. ex *cop* or *get the needle* (see **needle, cop the**).—4. Hence (without *the*), ill feeling : 1899, Clarence Rook, *The Hooligan Nights,* ' It was a fight with the gloves. But there was a bit of needle in it. It was all over Alice.'

needle, v. To irritate, annoy : 1881, G. R. Sims. Also *get* or *give the needle,* below. Ex *cop* or *get the needle* (see next entry).—2. V.i., to haggle over a bargain and if possible gain an advantage : c. of ca. 1810–50. Vaux. Ex the n., 1, q.v. : but cf. n., 3.

needle, cop, get, or **take the ; needle, give the.** To become annoyed ; to annoy : resp. (—1874), 1898, 1897 ; 1887. H., 5th ed. ; cf. *needle,* n., 3, and v., 1. Ware classifies it as, orig., tailors' s. : ' Irritated, as when the needle runs into a finger '.

needle and pin. Gin : rhyming s. : late C. 19–20. B. & P.

needle and thread. Bread : rhyming s. (—1859) ; ob. H., 1st ed.

needle-book or **-case.** The female pudend : low : C. 19–20 ; ob. Cf. *needle-woman.*

needle-dodger. A dressmaker : from ca. 1860 ; ob. ? on *devil-dodger.*

needle-fight. ' A boxing match in which the combatants have a personal feeling or grudge against each other ' : sporting coll. (— 1931). Lyell. Ex the S.E. sense, one ' that arouses much interest and excitement ' (O.E.D. Sup.), prob. influenced by *needle,* n., 4. Cf. *needle-match.*

needle-jerker. A tailor : from ca. 1805 ; ob. O.E.D. Cf. *needle-dodger.*

needle-match. A dispute : Glasgow (— 1934). Ex the *needle-match* (a very important one) of sporting j., on *needle-fight,* q.v.

***needle-point.** A sharper : c. of ca. 1690–1890. B.E., Grose, Vaux, Baumann. (Occ., C. 19, *needle-pointer.*) Because so sharp. Cf. *needle,* n., 1, and v., 2.

needle-woman. A harlot : coll. : 1849, Carlyle : ob. Cf. *needle-book.*

***needy.** A nightly lodger ; a beggar ; a tramp : c. verging on low s. : from ca. 1859. H., 1st ed. ; P. H. Emerson. Ex :

***needy mizzler.** A very shabby person ; a tramp that departs without paying for his lodging : tramps' c. : from ca. 1810 ; ob. Vaux ; H., 2nd ed. See **mizzler.**

***needy-mizzling.** C. : from ca. 1820. *Temple Bar,* 1868, ' He'll go without a shirt, perhaps, and beg one from house to house.' Ex preceding.

neel. See **nale,** second entry.

ne'er a face but his own. Penniless : low : late C. 17–18. B.E. Obviously alluding to the heads and faces on coins. Occ. *nare* . . . ; often *never* . . .

ne'er-be-lickit. Nothing whatever : Scots coll. : from ca. 1870. *The Encyclopædic Dict.*, 1885, ' Nothing which could be licked by a dog or cat '.

neergs. Greens (vegetables) : back s. (— 1859). H., 1st ed.

neetewif, neetexis, neetrith, neetrouf. See **nete-wif, netexis, netrith, netrouf.**

[Negatives used catachrestically :—See Fowler.]

neggledigee ; niggledigee or **gée.** Negligee, ' a woman's undressed gown ' (Grose) : low coll. when not a sol. : mid-C. 18–early 19. Shebbeare ; Grose, 2nd ed. (N.B., *négligé* comes later.)

Negro, wash a. To attempt the impossible : coll. : C. 17. Middleton & Dekker ; Barrow, in *Sermons*, ca. 1677, ' Therefore was he put . . . to wash Negros . . . to reform a most perverse and stubborn generation.' O.E.D.

negro's-head, gen. in pl. **(negroes' heads).** A brown loaf : nautical : late C. 18–early 19. Grose, 2nd ed. Ex the colour ; also ex the hardness of the Negro's Head nut. Cf. *brown George.*

negro-nosed. Flat-nosed : late C. 17–20 ; ob. Coll. (e.g. in B.E.) till C. 19, then S.E.

Neill's Blue Caps. See **Blue Caps.**

neither. Either : sol. : C. 15–20. (Gen. erroneously after a negative). E.g. in *The Humorist*, Dec. 23, 1933, ' You ain't picked the best one to come out with, neither ! '

neither . . . or. Neither . . . nor : catachresis : immemorial. A certain writer of detective ' thrillers ' perpetrated this in 1932, ' Looking neither to the right or the left '.

neither sugar nor salt, be. Not to be delicate ; esp. not to fear rain : proverbial coll. : C. 18–20 : ob. Swift. Ex sugar melting in rain. (Apperson.)

Nelson's blood. Dark rum : naval : (? mid-) C. 19–20. Bowen.

nenanecking. A variant of *shenanecking,* i.e. *shenanigan* : nautical : late C. 19–20. Bowen.

Nellie, -y. A giant petrel : nautical coll. (— 1875). Pettman, *Africanderisms,* 1913.—2. Any H.M.S. *Nelson* : naval : C. 19–20. Bowen.

nenti. A late C. 19–20 form of *nantee,* q.v. P. H. Emerson, 1893.

Neptune's Bodyguard. The Royal Marines : military : ca. 1850–1910. Also the *Admiral's Regiment, the Globe-Rangers* or *-Trotters, the Jollies,* and the *Little Grenadiers.*

Neptune's sheep. A nautical variant of *white horses* (waves white-crested) : late C. 19–20. Bowen.

nerve. A dashing dandy : Society coll. : ca. 1750–60. *The Adventurer,* No. 98, 1753, ' Buck, Blood, and Nerve.'—2. Impudence ; supreme ' cheek ' : (orig. low) coll. : 1899, *The Critic,* Jan. 21. Ex the S.E. sense, courage, assurance, esp. Disraeli's ' You have nerve enough, you know, for anything,' 1826 (O.E.D.). Cf. *nervy.*

nerver. A ' pick-me-up ' drink of strong liquor ; a tonic : Cockney (— 1887) ; ob. Baumann.

nerves, get on one's. See **get . . .**

nerving is an illicit tampering with a horse to make it more spirited and saleable : horse-copers' : mid-C. 19–20. ' *No. 747.*' Cf. *nerve,* 2.

nervy. Very impudent ; impudently confident : 1897 : middle 1890's ; slightly ob. Ex S.E. *nervy,* boldly brave.—2. ' Jumpy ', having bad nerves ; excitable or hysterical : coll. : 1906. S.O.D.

nescio, sport a. To pretend not to understand anything, esp. in an old university custom : university : ca. 1810–50 (perhaps 150 years earlier : cf. next). *Lex. Bal.*

nescio, stay with. To circumvent with pretended ignorance : Cambridge University : C. 17–18. J. Hacket's *Life of Archbishop Williams.*

-ness. ' Much used in mod. jocular formations, e.g. *Why this thusness ?* ', W., 1920.—2. A suffix frequently substituted by the illiterate, esp. Cockneys, for other abstract suffixes : almost immemorial. Edwin Pugh, in *The Cockney at Home,* 1914, has *romanticness* and *sarcasticness* ; the *-ness* is gen. added to the adj.

nest ; gen. **nest in the bush.** The female pudend : low coll. when not euphemistic S.E. : C. 18–20 ; ob. G. A. Stevens (longer form), Burns (the shorter).

nest, v. To defecate : C. 17–early 18 : ? coll. or dial. (Scots) or S.E. (F. & H.)

nest-egg. A sum of money laid by : late C. 17–20 : coll. till C. 19, then S.E. Orig. (as in B.E.), gen. as *leave a nest-egg.* Ruskin.

nestling, keep a. To be restless and/or uneasy : late C. 17–18 coll. B.E. Ex the restlessness and anxiety of a mother bird for her chicks.

nestor. An undersized boy : Winchester College : from ca. 1860 ; ob. Ex wizened, shrunken Nestor, who in allusive S.E. = an old man.

***nests.** (App. never in singular.) Varieties : c. (—, 1851) ; ob. Mayhew. ? perversion of *sets.*

net. Ten : back s. (— 1859). H., 1st ed. Cf. *netgen,* q.v.—2. A let : lawn-tennis coll. : C. 20. O.E.D. (Sup.). Cf. *tennis* for *lawn tennis.*

net, all is fish that comes to. All serves the purpose : proverbial coll. : mid-C. 17–20. In late C. 19–20, rarely without *my, his,* etc., before *net.*

netenin. Nineteen : back s. (— 1859). H., 1st ed. Cf. :

netewif. Fifteen : back s. (— 1859). Ibid. Also *neetewif.*

netexis. Sixteen : back s. (— 1859). Ib. Cf. preceding two entries.

netgen. A half-sovereign ; the sum of ten shillings : back s. (— 1859). H., 1st ed. Composed of *net,* 10 + *gen,* a shilling (q.v.)

Netherlands, the. The male or the female privities : low : C. 18–20 ; ob.

netnevis. Seventeen : back s. (— 1859). H., 1st ed. Cf. :

nettheg, often written **net-theg.** Eighteen : back s. (— 1859). Ibid. Cf. :

netrouf. Fourteen : back s. (— 1859). Ib. Also *neetrouf.* Cf. preceding two entries.

nettle, to have pissed on a. To be peevish, ill-tempered ; very uneasy : mid-C. 16–18 coll., then dial. Heywood ; Greene, in *The Upstart Courtier* ; B.E.

nettle in, dock out. A phrase implicative or indicative of fickleness of purpose ; or of senseless changing of order : proverbial coll. : mid-C. 14–18. B.E.

nettle stuff. ' The special rope yarn used for making hammock clews ' : nautical coll. : mid (?) C. 19–20. Bowen.

neuf. An incorrect form of *neaf, nieve,* the fist : early C. 17. O.E.D.

Neurope, n. and adj. New Europe : philately ; 1919, *The Daily Chronicle,* Nov. 13. W.

nevele ; loosely **nevel.** Eleven : back (— 1859). H., 1st ed. ; Manchon.

never, on the. On credit; by wangling: military (1915) >, by 1919, gen. B. & P. From ca. 1925, often *on the never-never*. Prob. abbr. *on the never-pay system*.

never (or **ne'er** or **nare**) **a face but his own.** See **ne'er a face** . . .

never fear. Beer: rhyming s. (— 1859). H., 1st ed.—2. See **fear !, never**.

Never-mass, at. Never: coll.: mid-C. 16–17. Anon., *Thersites*, ca. 1550 ; 1631, R. H., 'As our Country Phrase is, when Hens make Holy-water, at new-Never-masse'. O.E.D.

never-mention-'ems. Trousers: coll.: 1856; ob. Cf. *unmentionables*, q.v. (O.E.D.)

never-mind ! See **mind !, never.**

never never ; or with capitals. Abbr. *never never country* or *land*, the very sparsely populated country of Western Queensland and Central Australia: Australian coll.: 1900, H. Lawson, 'I rode back that way five years later, from the Never Never' (O.E.D.). Because, having been there, one swears *never, never* to return; the derivation ex an Aboriginal word for unoccupied land is prob. invalid.—2. Also with *country* or *land* : the future life, esp. heaven: Australian coll.: from ca. 1888 ; ob. 'Rolf Boldrewood'.

never-never, on the. See **never, on the.**

never-never policy, the. 'The late Mr. Cook's . . . much-parodied . . . slogan, *Not a penny off the pay. not a minute on the day*. (The General Strike, May, 1926)' : political coll. ; now only historical. Collinson.

never no more. Never more, never again : c.p.: late C. 19–20. (Somerset Maugham, *The Casuarina Tree*, 1926.)

never out, the. The female pudend : low: C. 19–20 ; ob.

never-squedge. 'A poor pulseless, passionate youth—a duffer': low London (— 1909). Ware. Perhaps *never-squeeze* (a girl).

never-too-late-to-mend shop. A repairing tailor's: tailors': from ca. 1860 ; ob.

never trust me ! A c.p. oath = never trust me if this doesn't happen : (mostly low) coll. and mostly London : late C. 16–20 ; ob.

Never-Wag Man of War. The Fleet Prison: low : ca. 1820–50. Egan.

never-waser. (Rarely of things.) One who never was a success : orig. (ca. 1890) circus s. >, ca. 1905, gen. *The Sportsman*, April 1, 1891. Cf. *has been*, q.v. (In U.S., often *never-was* : O.E.D. Sup.)

neves(s) ; more gen. **nevis.** Seven : back s. (— 1859). H., 1st ed. Whence :

*nevis-stretch. Seven years' hard labour : c.: from ca. 1860. Ex preceding.

nev(v)y ; nev(v)ey. Nephew : occ. low coll. but gen. dial. : C. 19–20. Also see **frater.**

New. New College, Oxford : Oxford University coll. : mid-C. 19–20. (A. Fielding, *Death of John Tait*, 1932.)

new. A fresh arrival : *Britannia* training-ship (— 1909). Ware. (Cf. *new fellow*, q.v.) Whence *new, new !*, the cry of a senior cadet wanting something done by a youngster : Bowen.

new !, tell us something. A coll. c.p. retort on stale news : late C. 19–20. Lyell.

New Billingsgate. 'Gorgonzola Hall', q.v. : Stock Exchange (— 1887) ; ob.

new brat. The Bootham School form of the next. Anon., *Dict. of Bootham Slang*, 1925.

new bug. A new boy : orig. (ca. 1860), Marlborough School ; in C. 20, fairly gen.

new chum ; new-chum. A new arrival, esp. if from Great Britain or Ireland : Australian coll. (in C. 20, S.E.), often slightly contemptuous. T. L. Mitchell, 1839, 'He was what they termed a "new chum", or one newly arrived'; R. M. Praed, 1885 ; Mrs. H. E. Russell, 1892. Whence the rare *new chumhood* (1883, W. Jardine Smith). Morris. See also **chum.**

new collar and cuff. To refurbish an old sermon : clerical : from ca. 1870 ; ob.

*New College. The Royal Exchange : c. : late C. 17–early 19. B.E. (as *College*, perhaps carelessly) ; Grose. See also **college.**—2. Whence *New College students*, 'golden scholars, silver batchelors, and leaden masters', Grose, 1st ed. : which, as James Howell's *Proverbs*, 1659, makes clear, is a c.p. flung at the gradual dulling of their intelligence. C. 17–early 19.

new drop. 'The scaffold used at Newgate for hanging criminals ; which, dropping down, leaves them suspended', Grose, 1788 : ca. 1785–1850 : perhaps orig. c. : certainly never better than low s.

new fellow. A naval cadet in his second term, a 'first-termer' being a *cheeky new fellow* : *Britannia* training-ship : late C. 19–early 20. Bowen. Cf. *new*, q.v.

new Gravel Lane bullock, fifty ribs a side. A red herring : nautical : late C. 19–20. Bowen. Cf. *Billingsgate pheasant.*

new growth. A (gen. cancerous) tumour : medical coll. (— 1933). *Slang*, p. 192.

new guinea, a or **the.** The first possession of an income : Oxford University : ca. 1820–40. Egan's Grose, 1823 (where 'cant' obviously = slang).

new hat. A guinea : cheapjacks' : ca. 1870–1915. C. Hindley, 1876.

new head, give a. To supply a new title and a few lines of introduction to old matter, to deceive the reader into thinking the whole article or 'item' new : journalistic coll. : late C. 19–20.

new iniquity. Australian immigrants : New Zealand (mostly Otago) : coll. : ca. 1862–80. Opp. *old identity*, q.v. at identity. Morris.

New Jerusalem. Warwick and Eccleston Squares district : ca. 1865–1900. Cf. *Cubitopolis.*

*new knock, the. A C. 20 c. variant of *new drop*, q.v. Edgar Wallace in *The Squeaker*, 1927.

New Light ; occ. **new light.** A Methodist : coll. : from ca. 1785 ; ob. Grose, 2nd ed.—2. One who attends the gaols in order to engineer escapes : c. : ca. 1820–50. Egan's Grose.

new lining to his hat. A bluejacket's pay, 'still received on the cap instead of in the hand' : naval : late C. 19–20. Bowen.

new Navy. Comforts and improvements introduced into the Navy : naval coll. (old bluejackets') : from ca. 1920 ; ob. Bowen.

new pair of boots, that's a. That's quite another matter : middle-class coll. : 1883, *Entr'Acte*, March 17 ; ob. Ware.

new pin, bright or **clean** or **neat** or **nice** or **smart as a.** Extremely bright, etc. ; very smart ; first-class : coll. : from ca. 1880. R. L. Stevenson, 1882 (*clean* . . .) ; Elworthy, 1886 (*neat*) ; P. H. Emerson, 1893 (*smart* . . .). Obviously, however, *as a new pin* often merely = wholly ; it dates back at least as far as Scott, 1829, 'Clear as a new pin of every penny of debt'. Apperson.

new plates. See **plates.**

new settlements. A final reckoning: Oxford University: ca. 1820–40. Egan's Grose.

New South. New South Wales: Australian coll.: late C. 19–20. See the quotation at *Dinny Hayes.*

Newcastle, carry or **send coals to.** See **coals.**

Newcastle hospitality. Roasting a friend to death; more gen., killing a person with kindness: North Country coll.: mid-C. 19–20. (Rather coll. than dial.) Apperson.

Newcastle programme. 'Extreme promises, difficult of execution': political coll.: 1894–ca. 1900. Ware. Ex 'a speech of extreme Radical promise made by Mr. John Morley at Newcastle'.

Newgate, specifically, from C. 13, the prison (demolished in 1902) for the City of London, was by 1590, 'a common name for all prisons' (Nashe). (Cf. *Newman's,* q.v.) Whence the following; of which it is exceedingly difficult, if not impossible, to determine the exact status:—

Newgate, as black as. Frowning; soiled (dress): low coll.: ca. 1820–80. Bee. Cf. *Newgate knocker, black* or *dark as.*

Newgate, may soon be afloat at Tyburn,—he that is at a low ebb at. A c.p. of ca. 1660–1810: condemnation at Newgate might well end in a hanging (one's heels afloat) at Tyburn; also fig. Fuller in his *Worthies,* Grose in his *Provincial Glossary.* Apperson.

Newgate bird or **nightingale.** A gaol-bird; a thief, a sharper: *bird,* C. 17–19 coll., e.g. in Dekker (see also **bird**); *nightingale,* C. 16 coll., e.g. in Copland.

Newgate collar (rare: gen. **Tyburn collar**), **frill, fringe.** 'A collar-like beard worn under the chin', F. & H.: resp. ca. 1820–90 (c. or low s.); ca. 1860–1900 (c. or low s.); ca. 1860–1920 (id.). H., 2nd ed., *frill* and *fringe.* Cf. *Newgate knocker* and *Newgate ring.*

Newgate frisk or **hornpipe.** A hanging: c. or low s.: resp. ca. 1830–90; ca. 1825–80. Esp. preceded by *dance a.* Maginn has 'toeing a Newgate hornpipe'.

Newgate knocker. 'A lock of hair like the figure 6, twisted from the temple back towards the ear', F. & H.: low coll.: from ca. 1840; ob. Mayhew. The fashion was at its height ca. 1840–55. Cf. *aggerawators,* q.v., and *Newgate ring.*—2. (Cf. *Newgate, as black as.*) *As black,* or *dark, as Newgate knocker,* extremely black or (esp. of a night) dark: coll.: from ca. 1880; ob. Apperson.

Newgate ring. Moustache and beard worn as one, without whiskers: s. or low coll.: ca. 1820–90. Cf. *Newgate collar* and *Newgate knocker.*

Newgate saint. A condemned criminal: ca. 1810–80: c. or s. or low coll.

Newgate seize me (if I do, there now)! Among criminals, an asseveration of the most binding nature: c. of ca. 1810–60. 'Jon Bee', 1823.

Newgate solicitor. A pettifogging attorney: c. or s. or low coll.: ca. 1785–1840. Grose, 2nd ed.

Newgate steps, born on. Of criminal, esp. thievish, extraction: late C. 18–mid-19: c. or low s. or low coll. Bee, 1823, 'Before 1780, these steps . . . were much frequented by rogues and w—s connected with the inmates of that place.'

Newington Butts. Guts: C. 20. P. P., *Rhyming Slang,* 1932. Often abbr. to *Newingtons.*

Newland. See **Abraham Newland.**

*Newman's. In C. 17, *Numans*; in C. 18, **no** record; ca. 1805–50, *Newmans.* Newgate: c.

The *New* of *Newgate* + *mans,* q.v., a place. But while *Numans* stands by itself, *Newman's* is rare except in the following combinations :—

*Newman's Hotel. Newgate: c. of ca. 1805–50. *Lex. Bal.* Ex preceding.

*Newman's lift. The gallows: c. of ca. 1805–50. Ibid. Contrast:

*Newman's Tea-Gardens. Newgate: c. of ca. 1805–50. Ib. Cf. *Newman's Hotel.*

[**newmarket,** as a method of tossing coins, is prob. to be considered as S.E.]

Newmarket Heath, a fine morning to catch herrings on. A c.p. = the C. 20 *a fine day for ducks.* C. 17–mid-18. John Clarke, 1639. (Apperson.)

Newmarket Heath commissioner. A highwayman: coll.: ca. 1800–50. Ex notorious locality.

new scum. A new boy; collectively, new boys: Shrewsbury School: from ca. 1870. Desmond Coke, *The Bending of a Twig,* 1906. Cf. *new bug,* q.v.

news?, do you hear the. A nautical c.p. (amounting indeed to a formula) 'used in turning out the relief watch': mid-C. 19–20. Bowen.

news!, tell me. Often preceded by *that's ancient history.* A c.p. retort to an old story or a stale jest: C. 18–20; ob. Swift. Cf. *Queen Anne's dead.*

Newtown pippin. A cigar: low: ca. 1880–1910. Ex its fragrance.—2. A dangerous type of riflegrenade: military, esp. Australian: 1915.

New York nipper; gen. pl. A kipper: C. 20. P. P., *Rhyming Slang,* 1932.

newy. 'The "cad" paid to look after the canvas tent in "Commoner" field', F. & H.: Winchester College: ca. 1860–1915. See **cad,** school sense.

next, as — as the. As (any adj.) as possible: coll.: late C. 19–20.

next of skin. See **skin, next of.**

Next Parish to America. Arran Island: Anglo-Irish coll. (— 1887). Ware, 'Most western land of Ireland'.

next way, round about, is at the far door. You're going a long way round: a C. 17 proverbial c.p. John Clarke, 1639. (N.b., *next* = nearest = shortest.)

N.F. ; N.G. ; N.H. See at beginning of **N.**

Niagara Falls. Stalls (of a theatre): theatrical rhyming s.: C. 20. *The Evening Standard,* Aug. 19, 1931.

[**nias** in F. & H. is S.E., as are **nice** (simple; squeamish or precise), **niche, nick** (a dent; the critical instant), **nick,** v. (four senses), **knock a nick in the post, nick with nay, nick-nack, nickname, nickumpoop** and **nincompoop, niddicock, niddipol, nidget** or **nigit, niece, nig** (to trifle, e.g. as an artist), **night-bird, night-cap** (drink; halter), **-gear, -hawk** (etc.), **-house, -hunter, -jury, -magistrate, -man** and **-farmer, -rail** or **-vale, -shade, -sneaker, -walker** (except perhaps as a bellman, C. 17), **nilly-willy, nimble, nimrod** (sportsman), **nine-eyed, ningle, ninny(-hammer,** a fool), **nip** (a pinch; a sip, a drink; a taunt), **nip,** v. (in corresponding senses), **nip-cheese** (a miser: also dial.), **nip in the bud, nipperkin, nipping, nit** (a louse's egg); dial. are **niffnaffy** and **nipshot(, play).**]

*nib. A gentleman: from ca. 1810; ob.: c. until ca. 1880, then low. Vaux. (Also from ca. 1840, *nib-cove*). Whence *half-nib(s),* one who apes gentlemen. ? ex the C. 17 Cambridge, esp. King's College, **nib** (either s. or j.), a freshman. More prob., as W. points out, a thinned form of *nob,* q.v.: cf *nab* and (*his*) *nabs* ; see **nibs**.—2. A fool : printers' : from ca. 1860 ; ob.

*nib, v. To catch ; arrest : from ca. 1770 : c. until ca. 1850, then low s. ; ob. Ex *nab*, q.v.—2. To nibble : C. 17–20 : S.E. until C. 19, then low coll. (†) and dial. Ex *nibble*.

*nib-cove. See **nib**, n., 1.

*nibbing cull. A (petty) thief ; occ. a fraudulent dealer : c. : ca. 1770–1820.

*nibble. To catch : C. 17–20 ; ob. : c. >, ca. 1860, low s. Middleton, ' The rogue has spied me now : he nibbled me finely once.'—2. To steal, pilfer : c. : C. 19–20 ; ob. Vaux.—3. To copulate : low : C. 19–20 ; ob.—4. To consider, eagerly but carefully, e.g. a bargain, an offer. V.t. with *at*. Coll. : C. 19–20.

nibble, get a. To obtain an easy job : tailors' : from ca. 1850 ; ob.

*nibbler. A (petty) thief ; occ. a cheating dealer : c. : C. 19–20 ; ob. Vaux.

nibby. A late C. 19–20 low variant (Manchon) of and derivative ex :

*niblike. (See also **nibsome**.) Gentlemanly : from ca. 1830 ; ob. : c. until ca. 1860, then low s. Ainsworth, ' All my togs were so niblike and splash.'

*nibs. (See also **nabs**.) Self : *my nibs*, myself ; *your nibs*, you or, as term of address, ' friend ' ; *his nibs*, the person mentioned ; also (— 1860), the master or a shabby genteel (cf. *nib*, n., 1, q.v.), or, among tailors (— 1928), a well-dressed workman. From ca. 1820 : c. >, ca. 1840, low s. >, ca. 1890, gen. s. Haggart, 1821 ; Mayhew ; Chevalier, 1893, in his song, *Our Little Nipper*. Ex *nabs*. There is prob. some connexion with *nib*, n., 1 : cf. *his lordship*, jocularly applied to anyone, with which cf. *his royal nibs*, him, in A. Adams's *Log of a Cowboy*, 1903 (O.E.D.). Note also the analogous *nose-watch*, q.v.—2. Delicacies : proletarian (— 1923). Manchon. Ex *nibble*.

nibso. A ca. 1880–1915 variant of the preceding, 1 : low.

*nibsome. Gentlemanly ; (of houses) richly furnished, etc. : from ca. 1835 ; ob. : c. >, ca. 1860, low s. G. W. M. Reynolds, 1839, ' Betray his pals in a nibsome game '.

nice. (See entry at **nias**.)—2. Agreeable ; delightful : coll. : 1769, Miss Carter, ' I intended to dine with Mrs. Borgrave, and in the evening to take a nice walk ' ; Jane Austen ; Mary Kingsley. O.E.D. (Often with an *ad hoc* modification.) Cf. *nice and*, q.v.

nice, not too. A Society coll. : from ca. 1870. Ware, ' First degree of condemnation—equals bad '.

nice and. Nicely, in sense of ' very ' : coll. : 1846, D. Jerrold, ' You'll be nice and ill in the morning.' It is the phrase only which has coll. force : *nice*, by itself, however ironical, is S.E. : witness Jerrold's ' A nice job I've had to nibble him.' O.E.D. ; Fowler.

nice as a ha'porth of silver spoons. Ridiculously dainty or fastidious : proverbial coll. : C. 16. ' Proverbs ' Heywood, 1546 ; ənon., *Jack Jugeler*. Cf. :

nice as a nanne, nanny, or nun's hen. Very affected or fastidious : proverbial coll. : C. 15– early 18. Wilson in his *Rhetoric*, 1560 ; Ray. (Apperson.)

nice as nip. Precisely what's needed ; exactly : Northern and Midlands coll. : from ca. 1850. See

e.g. F. E. Taylor's *Lancashire Sayings*, 1901. (Apperson.)

nice as nasty, Objectionable : lower classes' (— 1909). Ware. A euphemism.

nice joint. A ' charming, if over-pronounced, young person ' : urban, mostly Cockneys' (— 1909) : ob. Ware.

nice place to live out of, it's a. A c.p. (— 1909) indicating unpleasantness ; ob. Ware.

nice thin job. The ' mean evasion of a promise ' : lower classes' coll. : 1895–ca. 1914. Ware.

nice to know, not. (Only of persons) objectionable : coll., mostly jocular : C. 20 (D. Sayers, *Murder Must Advertise*, 1933.)

niche-cock. The female pudend : low coll. : C. 18–20 ; ob. (By itself, *niche* is S.E.)

(nichels or) nichils in a bag or in nine holes, nooks, or pokes. Nothing whatsoever : late C. 16–20 : coll. till C. 19, then dial. R. Scot, 1584 (*in a bag*, † by 1700) ; Fuller ; Bailey, ' Nichils are . . . debts . . . worth nothing.' Ex L. *nihil*. Apperson.

nichevo. No more ; dead : North Russia Expeditionary Force coll. : end of G.W. F. & Gibbons. Direct ex Russian.

Nicholas, Saint. The devil jocular coll. verging on S.E. : late C. 16–early 19. Whence (*Old*) *Nick*. Nares. Ex the patron saint of scholars and ? thieves.

Nicholas, clergyman or clerk or knight of St. Or as *St Nicholas's clergyman*, etc. A highwayman (? ever in the singular) : ca. 1570–1820 (*knight* not before late C. 17) : coll. >, by 1660, S.E. Foxe, Shakespeare, John Wilson, Scott (*clerk*) ; R Harvey, 1598 (*clergyman*). Ex preceding entry, perhaps by a pun on † S.E. *St Nicholas*('*s*) *clerks*, poor scholars.

Nicholas Kemp. A proverbial coll., only in the phrase quoted by Quiller-Couch in *Troy Town* : ' Like Nicholas Kemp, he'd occasion for all.' From ca. 1880 ; ob.

Nicholls. A complete riding habit : Society coll. : from ca. 1860. Ware, ' From the splendid habits made by Nicholls, of Regent Street ', London.

nick. (See entry at **nias**.)—2. The female pudend : low coll. : C. 18–20 ; ob. Robertson of Struan, who, like G. A. Stevens, tended to obscenity. —3. Abbr. *Old Nick* (q.v.), the devil : coll. : 1785 (E.D.D.)—4. Only in *nick and froth*, q.v.—5. (**the nick.**) The proper, the fashionable, thing or behaviour : ca. 1788–1800. Lord R. Seymour in *Murray's Magazine*, vol. 1. O.E.D.—6. (**the nick.**) Good physical condition or health : almost always *in the nick* : late C. 19–20. C. J. Dennis.—7. See **nick, on the**.—8. (**the nick.**) A prison (' Stuart Wood ', 1932) ; a police-station (Charles E. Leach, 1933) : c. (from 1919). Prob. ex sense 3 of the v., but imm. ex military s. (from ca. 1910), the guard-room, detention-cells (F. & Gibbons).—9. See **nicks**.

nick. To cheat, defraud (*of*) : coll. : late C. 16– 20 ; very ob. Taylor the Water Poet. (O.E.D.)— 2. To catch, esp. unawares : from ca. 1620. Fletcher & Massinger. In C. 20, occ. to get hold of, as in Galsworthy, *The White Monkey*, 1924, ' Wait here, darling ; I'll nick a rickshaw.'—3. Hence, in C. 19–20, to arrest : low s. or perhaps c. *The Spirit of the Public Journals*, 1806, ' He . . . stands a chance of getting nicked, because he was found in bad company,' O.E.D.—4. To steal ; purloin : 1826 (E.D.D.) ; 1869, *Temple Bar*, ' I bolted in and nicked a nice silver tea-pot ' : c. >, by 1880, low s.—5. To in-dent a beer-can : C. 17–18 : either coll. or, more prob., S.E. So too the vbl.n.—6. To copulate with : low coll. : C. 18–20 ; ob.—7. V.i., to drink heartily : Scots s. : late C. 18–19. Jamieson.

Nick, old. See **Old Nick.**

*nick, on the. Stealing ; going to steal : c. (— 1887). Baumann. Ex *nick,* v., 4.

nick, out of all, adv. Past counting : excessively ; coll. : late C. 16–17. Shakespeare, in *Two Gentlemen,* ' He lov'd her out of all nick.'

*nick, out on the, adj. and adv. Out thieving : c. : from ca. 1870. H., 5th ed.

nick and froth. A false measure (of beer) ; cheating customers with false measures : coll. : C. 17–mid-18. Rowlands, B.E. Anticipated, however, in Skelton's *Elynour Rummynge,* ' Our pots were full quarted, | We were not thus thwarted | With froth-canne and nick-pot.' The *nick* was a dent in the bottom of the beer-can, the *froth* implied an excessive amount.—2. Hence, a publican : ca. 1660–1800 : coll. Ned Ward has *nick and froth victualler* (1703).

nick me ! An imprecation of ca. 1760–80 : coll. Foote. (O.E.D.) Ex v., sense 2.

nick-nack ; also **knick-knack.** (See entry at **nias.**)—2. The female pudend : low : C. 18–20 ; ob.—3. In pl. only, the human testicles : low : C. 18–20. Cf. *knackers.*

nick-ninny. ' An empty Fellow, a meer Cod's head ', B.E. : late C. 17–early 19.

nick-pot. A tapster ; an inn-keeper : C. 17–18 : s. or coll. Rowlands.—2. A fraudulent measure or beer-pot : C. 17–18 : s. or coll. See **nick and froth, 1.**

nick the pin. To drink not too much, i.e. fairly : coll. : ca. 1690–1730. B.E. ; Kersey, ' To the Pin plac'd about the middle of a Wooden Bowl or Cup ' (O.E.D.).

*nicker. One who, at cards, is a cheat : ca. 1660–1730 : s. or low coll., though perhaps orig. c.—2. One of a band of disorderly young men delighting in the breaking of windows by throwing copper coins at them : ca. 1715–20 : coll. Gay, in *Trivia,* ' His scatter'd Pence the flying Nicker flings.' Ex *nick,* to hit the mark.—3. A pound sterling : criminals' c. (— 1932) : ' Stuart Wood '). Also in racing c., where it further signifies a sovereign or a £1 currency note : C. 20. Also in New Zealand lower-class s. (pre-G.W.) and then in military s. Common, too, among grafters : Philip Allingham, 1934. Whence *half-nicker,* q.v. In c., the pl. is *nicker* : witness James Curtis, *The Gilt Kid,* 1936.

nickerers. New shoes : Scots c. or, more prob., s. ; certainly it soon > s. C. 19. Jamieson. Ex the creaking sound : see **nick,** n. and v., in E.D.D.

nickery. A nickname : low coll. : ca. 1820–30. Bee. By corruption.

nickey ; nickin. See **nikin** and **Old Nick.**

[Nicknames. Those of persons (e.g. *Dizzy*) and of regiments (e.g. *the Docs*) will be found *passim* in the course of these pages.

' Inevitable ' nicknames are of two classes : general ; particular. The general denote nationality (*Fritz, Frog, Ikey, Jock, Mick, Taffy*) or a physical trait (*Bluey, Bunty, Snowy, Tich, Tiny*).

The particular, which are the ' inevitable nicknames ' *par excellence,* attach themselves to certain surnames ; like the general, they are rarely bestowed on women. The following [1] are the most frequently heard :—*Betsy* Gay ; *Blanco* White (cf. *Chalky*) ;

---

[1] For details, see each nickname at its alphabetical place.

Bodger Lees (cf. *Jigger*) ; *Bogey* Harris ; *Brigham* Young ; *Buck* Taylor ; *Busky* Smith (cf. *Dusty* and *Shoey*) ; *Chalky* White ; *Charley* Peace ; *Chats* Harris ; *Chatty* Mather ; *Chippy* Carpenter ; *Dan* Coles ; *Darky* Smith ; *Dinghy* Read ; *Dodger* Green (cf. *Shiner*) ; *Dolly* Gray ; *Doughy* Baker (cf. *Snowy*) ; *Dusty* Miller and, occ., Jordan, Rhodes, Smith ; *Edna* May ; *Fanny* Fields ; *Flapper* Hughes ; *Ginger* Jones ; *Granny* Henderson ; *Gunboat* Smith ; *Happy* Day ; *Hooky* Walker ; *Jack* Sheppard (-erd, -herd) ; *Jesso* Read ; *Jigger* Lees ; *Jimmy* Green (cf. *Dodger*) ; *Johnny* Walker (cf. *Hooky*) ; *Jumper* Collins or Cross ; *Kitty* Wells ; *Knocker* Walker or White ; *Lackery* Wood ; *Lottie* Collins ; *Mouchy* Reeves ; *Nobby* Clark(e) and, occ. Ewart, Hewart, Hewett, Hewitt ; *Nocky* Knight;, *Nutty* Cox ; *Pedlar* Palmer ; *Piggy* May ; *Pills* Holloway ; *Pincher* Martin ; *Pony* Moore ; *Rattler* Morgan ; *Shiner* Black, Bright, Bryant, Green, White, Wright ; *Shoey* Smith ; *Shorty* Wright ; *Slinger* Woods ; *Smoky* Holmes ; *Smudger* Smith ; *Snip* Parsons, Taylor ; *Snowy* Baker ; *Spiky* Sullivan ; *Spokey* Wheeler, Wheelwright ; *Spud* Murphy ; *Taffy* Jones, Owen and, as above, any Welshman ; *Timber* Wood (cf. *Lackery*) ; *Tod* Hunter, Sloan ; *Tom* King ; *Topper* (occ. corrupted to *Tupper*) Brown ; *Tottie* Bell ; *Tug* Wilson ; *Wheeler* Johnson ; *Wiggy* Bennett. (A small Army group consists of Arabic words : see **Eska, Jebbel, Ketir Mug,** and **Mush.**)

These ' inevitable ' names app. arose first in the Navy (see esp. *Pincher* ; cf. *Nobby* and *Tug*) and soon—by 1890 or so—reached the Army ; the G.W. effectually distributed them among the lower classes, a few (e.g. *Dolly* and *Tug*) among the upper classes. They derive from the commonness of some phrase, as in ' *Happy* Day ' and ' *Hooky* Walker ' ; from an historical or a vocational association, as in ' *Pedlar* Palmer ', ' *Dusty* Miller ', and ' *Shoey* Smith ' ; from a merely semantic suggestion, as in ' *Lackery* (or *Timber*) Wood ' and ' *Shiner* White ' ; rarely from a neat phrasal connexion as in ' *Jumper* Cross ' (*jump across*) ; occ. from a well-known trade article or advertisement, as in ' *Blanco* White ' and ' *Johnny* Walker ' ; from a famous personage, as in ' *Pincher* Martin ', ' *Nobby* Ewart ', ' *Spiky* Sullivan '—the largest of the ascertained-origin groups ; and from some anecdotal cause or incidental (or local) notoriety, as in ' *Pills*[1] Holloway ', ' *Rattler* Morgan ', ' *Wiggy* Bennett ', whose origins are, at this date, either unascertainable or ascertainable only with great difficulty.

F. & H. ; Bowen ; B. & P. ; and personal research. For an article on the subject, see *A Covey of Partridge,* 1937.]

nicks. See **nix.**—2. Stolen goods : Londoners' (— 1890). E.D.D. Ex *nick,* v., 4.

*nickum. A sharper ; a cheating tradesman or inn-keeper : c. : late C. 17–mid-18. B.E. Ex *nick 'em,* cheat them. (In Scots dial., a wag ; a tricky person. E.D.D.)

nicky. See **nikin** and **Old Nick.**—2. A ' saved end of a cigarette, nipped out '—*nicked* with one's nails—' for smoking later ' (F. & Gibbons) and gen. worn behind the ear : military : 1914–18.

Nicodemus. A fanatic : Restoration period. Ex Biblical history and Church dissension.

nidderling. A catachrestic form of *niddering,* itself based on an erroneous late C. 16 reading of

---

[1] See, however, at the term itself.

nithing, a base coward. From **ca.** 1660. See O.E.D. at *niddering*.

nidget. Idiot: sol. and dial.: C. 18–20. Ex *an idiot*.

niet dobra ! No good ! : a c.p., at the latter end of the G.W., among members of the North Russian Expeditionary Force. F. & Gibbons, ' Usually with an intermediate English expletive, e.g. " Niet blanky dobra " ' : cf. *no bloody good*. Cf. *nichevo*, q.v.

niff, v.i. To smell unpleasantly : Dulwich College : from late 1890's. Collinson. Back-formation ex *niffy*, adj. Also as n.: see Addenda.

niffle. To smoke : *Conway* cadets' : late C. 19–20. John Masefield, *The Conway*, 1933. Rather by a blend of *niff* and *sniffle* than ex the latter only.

niffy. ' A strong, nasty smell ' : military : C. 20. F. & Gibbons. Ex :

niffy, adj. Smelly : Sussex dial. >, ca. 1890, low s. Ex dial. n. and v., *niff*, smell ; stink.—2. See **nifty**.

Niffy Jane. H.M.S. *Iphigenia* : naval : C. 20. Bowen. By ' Hobson-Jobson '.

nifty. Smart, fashionable ; fine, splendid ; (somewhat blatantly) skilful : orig. (1868), U.S. ; anglicised ca. 1890. Bret Harte's ' Nifty ! Short for magnificat ' is a joke, but the term may be a perverted telescoping of *magnificent*. (Occ., in C. 20, in sol. form *niffy*, q.v., the error being partly caused by the popularity of *niffy*, 1, q.v.)

*****nig.** A clipping of money ; such clippings collectively. Gen., however, in pl. : clippings. Late C. 17–early 19 c. B.E. ; Grose, 1st ed. Prob. *nick* perverted.—2. A Negro : (low) coll. : orig. (1864), U.S. ; anglicised ca. 1870. Abbr. *nigger*, q.v.—3. Gin : back s. (— 1859). H., 1st ed.—4. A trick or ' dodge ' : Blue Coat Schoolboys' (— 1887). Baumann.

*****nig**, v. To clip money : late C. 17–early 19 c. Implied in B.E.'s *nigging*.—2. To catch ; arrest : mid-C. 18 c. ? *nick*, v., 3, influenced by *nab*, v., 1.—3. To have sexual intercourse : low : C. 18. Abbr. *niggle*, to copulate.

Niger. C. J. Fox. Ex his dark complexion. Dawson. Also *the Young Cub*.

niggar (†) ; gen. **nigger.** A Negro : coll., often pejorative : 1786, Burns ; 1811, Byron, ' The rest of the world—niggers and what not '. Ex. † S.E. *neger* (L. *niger*).—Hence, 2, a member of some other dark-skinned race : somewhat catachrestically coll. : from ca. 1855. O.E.D. (See also Fowler.)—3. See ' Moving-Picture Slang ', § 3.

nigger-driver ; -driving. One who works others excessively hard ; this practice : coll. : from ca. 1860. Ex the cruelty of some overseers of slaves.

nigger-spit. The lumps in cane sugar : low : from ca. 1870 ; ob.

nigger stock. ' Kaffirs ', q.v. : Stock Exchange (— 1923). Manchon.

niggers ! An oath : low coll. : C. 17. Whence *niggers-noggers* ! Cf. *jiggers* !, ex *Jesus*. Often, ca. 1640–80, abbr. to *nigs* !, preceded by (*God's*)s or *cuds*. Glapthorne. O.E.D.

niggers in a snow-storm. Curry and rice ; stewed prunes and rice : naval : late C. 19–20. Bowen.

*****nigging.** Vbl.n., the clipping of money : c. : late C. 17–early 19. B.E., Grose.

*****niggle** ; in C. 16–early 17, often **nygle** ; in C. 17–18, often **nigle.** Occ. the n. of :—*niggle*, etc., v.i. and v.t., to have sexual connexion with a woman :

ca. 1565–1820 : c. >, ca. 1720, low s. (Extant in U.S. c. : Irwin.) Harman ; Rowlands, who says that ca. 1610, *wap* was more gen. ; in 1612, however, Dekker has ' And wapping Dell that niggles well, and takes loure for her hire ' ; B.E. ; Grose. Whence *niggler*, 1.

niggledigee or **niggledigée.** See **neggledigee.**

*****niggler.** A lascivious or very amorous person : c. : C. 17–18. Marston. Also *nigler*.—2. (Also **nigler.**) A clipper of money : c. : late C. 17–18. B.E., Grose. Ex *nig*, v., 1.

*****niggling.** Keeping company with a woman, sexual intercourse : c. : C. 17–early 19. Dekker, Brome, B.E., Grose. Ex *niggle*, v., q.v. Cf. *niggler*, 1.

nigh, adj. Near ; close (e.g. ' a nigh fit ') : low coll. : C. 19–20. Baumann.

*****nigh enough** (or **enuff**). A passive homosexual ; esp. a male harlot : c. : from ca. 1920. James Curtis, *The Gilt Kid*, 1936. Cf. *collar and cuff*, q.v.

night. See the entry at **nias** as well as the here-ensuing *night* entries.

night ! Good night ! : coll. : late (? mid-)C. 19–20. Cf. *day !*, *evening !*, and *morning !*

night !, good. That's done it ! Coll. : late C. 19–20 ; ob. Cf. *that's torn it !*

night and day. A play : rhyming s. (— 1859). H., 1st ed.

night-cap. (See entry at **nias.**)—2. A nocturnal bully : coll. : ca. 1620–30. Webster in *The Duchess of Malfi*. O.E.D. (—3. A wife : this is F. & H.'s error for † S.E. *night-cape.*)—4. See **horse's night-cap.**

night-flea. A boarder : Essex schools' (— 1909). Ware. Contrast *day-bug.*

night-fossicker ; n.-fossicking. A nocturnal thief of gold quartz or dust ; such thieving : Australian coll. : from ca. 1860. Also just *fossicker, fossicking*. See **fossick.**

night hawk. (Gen. pl.) A night-watchman steward : nautical : late C. 19–20. Bowen.

night of it, make a. To spend the night in gambling and/or drinking and/or whoring : coll. : from ca. 1870.

night ops. See **ops, night.**

night-physic or **-work.** Copulation : late C. 16–early 18 : jocular coll. when not euphemistic S.E. Massinger, ' Which . . . ministers night-physic to you ? '

night-snap. A nocturnal thief : C. 17 : low s. Fletcher.

night to run away with another man's wife, a fine. A fine night : a proverbial c.p. of late C. 16–18. Florio, Rowley, Swift (*a delicate night*). Apperson.

night-walker. A bellman ; a watchman : either c. or low s. : late C. 17–mid-18. B.E. All other senses (e.g. a harlot), despite B.E., are S.E.

night with you and a file of the morn's morning !, all. ' A slang form of saying "good-night !" ' : Aberdeenshire : 1882 ; ob. E.D.D.

nightie, nighty. A night-dress : coll. : from early 1890's.—2. Hence, occ., a surplice : from ca. 1897 : jocular coll. Abbr. *night-dress* or *n.-gown* + familiar *ie, y*. O.E.D.

nightingale. See **Arcadian, Cambridgeshire, Dutch, Newgate,** and **Spithead nightingale.**—2. A soldier that, being punished, ' sings out ' : military : ca. 1770–1830. Grose, 2nd ed.—3. A harlot : low : from ca. 1840. Because most active at night.

nighty. See nightie.—nigle ; nigler ; nigling. See niggle, niggler, niggling.

nigmenog. See nimenog.—nigs. See nig, n., 1. Also abbr. *niggers !*, q.v.

nihil-ad-rem. Vague (of things) ; unconscious : Winchester College : ca. 1860–1910. E.g. ' He sported nihil-ad-rem duck.' L., lit. ' nothing to the purpose '.

nikin ; occ. nickin ; also nikey, i.e. nick(e)y ; also nis(e)y, nizey or nizzie. A soft simpleton : coll. : late C. 17–18. B.E., Grose. The -*k*- forms are prob. ex *Nick*, the -*s*- and -*z*-, ex Fr. *niais*, foolish. —2. (Only nickin, nikin, ni(c)k(e)y.) Abbr. *Isaac* : C. 17–19.

nil, n. and adj. Half profits, etc. ; half : low : from ca. 1859 ; ob. H., 1st ed. ; Baumann.

Nile, down the. In Nile Street, Hoxton : low London : C. 20. Charles E. Leach.

*nim ; occ. nym. A thief : c. of ca. 1620–40. Taylor the Water Poet. Ex :

nim ; occ. nym. (Whence Shakespeare's Nym.) To steal, pilfer (v.i. and v.t.) : C. 17–20 : low s. till mid-C. 17, then c. : from ca. 1850, still c. but archaic. John Day, 1606, in his *Isle of Gulls* ; ' Hudibras ' Butler ; Gay, in *The Beggars' Opera* ; G. P. R. James, *The Gipsy*. Ex A.-S. *niman*, to take.

nimak ; occ. nimma(c)k. Salt : Regular Army's : late C. 19–20. Ex Hindustani. Cf. *muckin*.

nimble as similes are coll. :—(as) nimble as a cat (up)on a hot backstone, late C. 17–early 19 (backstone, occ. bakestone in C. 19), the gen. C. 19–20 form being (up)on hot bricks ; (as) nimble as a bee in a tar-barrel, C. 19–20, ob., a cognate phrase being to bumble like a bee in a tar-tub ; . . . as a cow in a cage, C. 19–20 (ob.) jocular ; . . . as a new-gelt dog, C. 19–20 (ob.), mainly rural ; . . . as an eel (wriggling in the mud ; in a sandbag), C. 17–20, being in C. 19–20 mainly dial. ; . . . as ninepence, from ca. 1880, also dial., prob. ex the proverb, a nimble ninepence is better than a slow shilling (C. 19–20 ; latterly dial.), with which cf. the late C. 19–20 Gloucestershire a nimble penny is worth a slow sixpence. Apperson.

nimble-hipped. (Gen. of women.) Active in the amorous congress : C. 19–20 ; ob. Coll. verging on S.E.

*nimbles. The fingers : early C. 17. Jonson, 1621, ' Using your nimbles | In diving the pockets ', O.E.D. The S.E. adj. *nimble-fingered* is recorded the same year.

nimenog ; occ. nigmenog. ' A very silly Fellow ', B.E. ; a fool : late C. 17–18 : coll. Grose, 2nd ed. Presumably cognate with *nigit* and the dial. *nidyard*, S.E. *niddicock*.

*nimgimmer ; nim-gimmer. A surgeon, doctor, apothecary, ' or any one that cures a Clap or the Pox ', B.E. : c. : late C. 17–early 19. Grose, 1st ed. Ex *nim* + ?

nimma(c)k. See nimak.

nimmer. A thief : ex *nim*, v., q.v. for period and changing status.

nimming. Theft ; thieving : see nim, v., for period and status.

nimrod. The penis : low : C. 19–20 ; ob. Because ' a mighty hunter '. Cf. :

nimshod. A cat : low : from ca. 1870 ; ob. ? a corruption of *Nimrod*, or is it a mere coincidence that the vocable may = *nim*, to take, + *shosho* or *shoshi*, Romany for a rabbit. Not ex dial.

nin. Drink · children's coll. : C. 16–17. Cot-

grave (' Before they can speak '). O.E.D. By corruption.

nincum-noodle. A *noodle* with *no income* : jocular London : ca. 1820–40. Bee. Baumann has *nincum*, a noodle.

nine-bob-square. Out of shape : C. 19–20 : coll. († by 1902) and dial. In dial., cf. *nine-bauble-square* and *nine-bobble-square*. ? lit. ' nine-cornered-square '.

nine corns. A small pipeful, a half-fill, of tobacco : mid-C. 19–20 : coll. († by 1902) and dial. (ob. ; mostly Lincolnshire). See esp. E.D.D.

nine lives and (or but) women ten cats' lives, cats have. A mid-C. 18–mid-19 c.p. Grose.

nine mile nuts. ' Anything to eat or drink very sustaining. From the nutritive qualities of chestnuts—especially in Japan ' : Japanese pidgin English (— 1909) ; slightly ob. Ware.

nine shillings. Nonchalance ; cool audacity : late C. 18–20 ; ob. Grose, 3rd. ed. A perversion.

*nine-tail bruiser or mouser. The cat-o'-nine tails : prison c. : ca. 1860–1910.

nine-two is the coll. form of S.E. *nine-point-two* (gun) : military : 1914 ; ob. B. & P.

nine ways or nine ways at thrice or nine ways for Sunday(s), look. To squint : coll. : resp C. 16–20 (ob.), as in Udall ; C. 17, as in G. Daniel (O.E.D.) ; and C. 19–20.

nine winks. A short nap : ca. 1820–50. Bee. Cf. *forty winks*.

nine words at once, talk. To speak fast or thickly : C. 17 : coll. Cotgrave.

ninepence, bring one's noble to. See noble to ninepence.

ninepence, grand or neat or nice or right as. Extremely neat, nice, right : coll. : C. 17–20 for *neat* (e.g. Howell, 1659), C. 19–20 for the three others : *grand*, Dickens ; *right*, Smedley, 1850 ; *nice*, T. Ashe, 1884, but implied in H., 2nd ed. See also neat as a bandbox.

ninepence, nimble as. See nimble as.

ninepence, right as. A coll. variant (from ca. 1885) of *nimble as ninepence*, q.v. Baumann suggests an influence by *ninepins*.

ninepence, the devil and. See devil and . . .

ninepence for fourpence. A political c.p. of 1908–9. Collinson. Ex the national health insurance scheme.

ninepence to nothing, as like as. Almost certainly : coll. : C. 17. Ray.

ninepence to nothing, bring (one's). To waste or lose property : C. 18–20 : coll. till ca. 1850, then dial. In C. 16–17, *bring a shilling to ninepence*. Apperson.

ninepins. The body as life's container ; life in gen. : low : 1879, G. R. Sims, in the *Dagonet Ballads*, ' It's a cold . . . as has tumbled my ninepins over.' Ob.

niner. A convict serving nine years : coll. : 1897, Waring. O.E.D.—2. (Gen. pl.) A senior naval cadet : in the training-ship *Britannia* : late C. 19–early 20. Bowen. ? ex *ninth term*.

nines (rarely nine, †), to or up to the. To perfection ; admirably : coll. : late C. 18–20. (Ca. 1870–80, *up to the nines* also = up to all the dodges : H., 5th ed.) Burns, 1887, *to the nine*, as also Reade in *Hard Cash* ; T. Hardy, 1876, *up to the nines*, a form that appears to be recorded first in 1859, H., 1st ed., in the phrase *dressed up to the nines*. ? ex *nine* as a mystic number connoting perfection (W.). Also *got-up to the nines*.

nineteen bits of a bilberry, he'll make. A pejorative c.p. of ca. 1660–1700. Ray.

nineteen to the dozen. See **dozen**.

nineteenth hole, the. The bar-room of a golf club-house : golfers' : from not later than 1927. (O.E.D. Sup.) A golf-course has 18 holes.

ninety dog ; always in form : **90 dog.** A pug-dog : streets' (— 1909). Ware, 'Referring to aspect of tail '.

ninety-eight out of, have. To get one's own back on (a person) : tailors' : late C. 19–20. E.g. in *The Tailor and Cutter*, Nov. 29, 1928.

ninety-nines, dressed up to the. An elaboration of *dressed* (*up*) *to the nines* : coll. (— 1887) ; ob. Baumann.

ninety-seven (gen. **97**) **champion frost.** A lower-classes' c.p. applied in 1897–9 to motor-cars, which, in 1896–7, were something of a 'frost' or failure. Ware.

ning-nang. A worthless thoroughbred : veterinary : from ca. 1890. Ex horse-dealers' s. (—1864). H., 3rd ed. In Northern dial., *ning-nang* is applied also to a worthless person.

ninnified. Foolish : coll. : C. 20. James Spenser, *Limey Breaks In*, 1934. Ex S.E. *ninny* + *-fied*, made.

***ninny.** 'A canting whining Begger ', B.E. : c. of late C. 17–mid-18. Ex S.E. sense, or perhaps imm., as prob. the S.E. is, from *an innocent*, as the O.E.D. suggests.

ninny-broth. Coffee : late C. 17–18. Ned Ward in *The London Spy*.

ninth, occ. in C. 18 **tenth, part of a man.** A tailor : C. 18–20 ; ob. : coll. Foote, 1763, 'A journey-man-tailor . . . this whey-faced ninny, who is but the ninth part of a man.' Ex the proverbial *nine tailors make a man* (late C. 16–20) : in C. 17 also *two* (Dekker & Webster) or *three* (Apperson).

niog ot takram. Going to market : back s. (— 1859). H., 1st ed.

***nip.** A thief, esp. a cut-purse or a pickpocket : c. of late C. 16–18. Greene. **?** ex the v.—2. A cheat : c. : late C. 17–early 19, when it was the prevailing c. sense, a cut-purse gen. being a *bung-nipper*, q.v. B.E. ; Grose, 1st ed.—3. S. of ca. 1820–50 : 'Passengers who are taken up on stage-coaches by the collusion of the guard and coachman, without the knowledge of the proprietors, are called nips,' De Quincey, 1823 (O.E.D.).—4. See **nips.**

***nip, v.** ; also **nipp(e), nyp.** To steal, esp. to pick pockets or to cut purses : c. : ca. 1570–1830. (V.i. and v.t.) Harman (the stock phrase, *nip a b*(*o*)*ung,* to cut a purse), Greene, Cleveland ; B.E., 'to Pinch or Sharp anything '. Ex the S.E. sense, to pinch (cf. s. *pinch*, q.v.), and ex :—2. To catch, snatch, seize neatly, take up smartly (also with *away out, up*) : from ca. 1560 : chiefly dial (earliest record) and s. H. Scott (dial.), F. Godwin, C. B. Berry. O.E.D.—3. To 'pinch ', i.e. arrest : c. : from ca. 1560. R. Edwards, ca. 1566, 'I go into the city some knaves to nip '; Mayhew. O.E.D.—4. (Prob. ex preceding sense.) To move, to go, almost always quickly or promptly : orig. (— 1825), dial. > s. ca. 1880. Often with *out* (*The Daily Telegraph*, Jan. 2, 1883, 'I nipped out of bed ') or *up* ; *nip in* = to slip in, *nip along* = to depart hurriedly or rapidly, or to move with speed. E.D.D.—5. To coït with (a woman) : low (— 1923). Manchon.—6. V.t., to cadge from : military : C. 20. F. & Gibbons. Prob. ex sense 2. Cf. *sting*, q.v.—7. To detect : Shrewsbury School coll. : from ca. 1880.

E.g. in D. Coke, *The Bending of a Twig*, 1906. Cf. sense 2.

nip, as white as. As white as snow : proletarian (— 1887). ; slightly ob. Baumann. Ex dial. (— 1861) and the herb cat-mint, ' covered with a fine white down ' (E.D.D.).

nip along—in—out—up, etc. See fourth sense of **nip, v.**

nip and tuck, adv. and adj., occ. as virtual n. (a neck-and-neck race). Neck and neck ; almost level or equal(ly) : coll. : orig. U.S. ; anglicised ca. 1890. In U.S., *rip and tuck*, 1833 ; *nip and tack*, 1836 ; *nip and chuck*, 1846 ; *nip and tuck*, 1857 : an illuminating example of semantic phonetics or, rather, phonetic semantics. Thornton.

nip-cheese, a miser, is S.E., as are *nip-cake, -crust, -farthing* ; the last, like *nip-cheese*, is also dial. ; solely dial. are *nip-corn, -currant, -fig, -prune, -raisin, -screed, -skin, -skitter* (E.D.D.). But *nip-cheese*, a ship's purser, is nautical s. : 1785, Grose ; Marryat ; 1867, Smyth ; Bowen. Ob. by 1907. Ex some pursers' ' pinching ' part of the cheese and other food.

nip-louse. A tailor : low : from ca. 1850 ; ob. Cf. *nip-shred*, q.v.

nip-lug. A teacher : Scots s. or coll. : C. 19–20 ; ob.

nip-lug, at. At loggerheads : Scots coll. : C. 19–20 ; ob.

Nip or **Nyp Shop, the.** The Peacock tavern in Gray's Inn Lane : London : ca. 1785–1810. ' Because Burton Ale is there sold in Nyps ', Grose. MS. note of 1786 in B.M. copy of *The Vulgar Tongue* (1st ed.)—a note incorporated in the 2nd ed. (1788).

nip-shred. A tailor : mid-C. 17–mid-18 : s. > coll. K. W., 1661, 'Though her nimble nipshred never medles with the garments ' (O.E.D.). Cf. *nip-louse*, q.v.

nipp, nippe. See **nip, v.**, 1–3.

nipped !, before you. Before you went to school (see **nip**, v., 4) : a military c.p. (1915–18) addressed to a younger man or newer soldier and implying that the elder man was already performing some military work or duty years before. F. & Gibbons.

nippence, no pence, | half a groat wanting two-pence. Nothing, a groat being fourpence : a C. 17 rhyming c.p. Ray, Fuller. (Apperson.) Cf. *if we had eggs*, q.v.

***nipper.** A thief, esp. a cut-purse or a pickpocket : c. : ca. 1580–1830. Fleetwood, 1585, ' A judiciall Nypper ' (O.E.D.), i.e. a very skilful one, this being a stock phrase (see Grose at *nypper*) ; John Day ; Grose. Ex *nip*, v., 1.—2. ' A boy who assists a costermonger, carter, or workman ', O.E.D. : low coll. (and dial.) : from ca. 1850 ; ob. Mayhew, 1851. Prob. because he ' nips ' about, therefore presumably dial. orig. (see **nip**, v., fourth sense).—3. Whence, a boy, a lad (in C. 20, esp. if under say 12) : from ca. 1859. H., 1st ed. ; *The Daily News*, April 8, 1872 (O.E.D.) ; 1888, *The Referee*, Nov. 11, ' Other nippers—the little shrimps of boys . . .'; Chevalier in *The Idler*, June, 1892, ' I've got a little nipper, when 'e talks | I'll lay yer forty shiners to a quid | You'll take 'im for the father, me the kid,' which rather bears out the O.E.D.'s quotation from Williams's *Round London*, 1893, ' The mind of the East End " nipper " is equal to most emergencies.' —4. Whence (?), a boy or ' cad ' : Marlborough School : from ca. 1875 ; ob.—5. See **nippers.**—6. A frosty day : coll. (— 1887) ; ob. Baumann.—7.

A cabin-boy: sailing-ships': from ca. 1865; slightly ob. Bowen.

*nipper, v. To catch; to arrest: c. (>, ca. 1830, low s.): ca. 1820–50. 'Jon Bee'; Egan (1824, in vol. IV of *Boxiana*). Ex *nip*, v., 3, q.v.

*nippers. Handcuffs or, occ. shackles: c. of ca. 1820–1920. Haggart; Egan's Grose; Matsell. Ex *nip*, v., 3.—2. 'A burglar's instrument used from outside on a key', F. & H.: c.: from ca. 1840. Also *American tweezers.*—3. Eye-glasses, esp. pince-nez (whence the name): from ca. 1875 and prob. ex U.S. (Lowell, 1876).—4. A policeman: c. (— 1887) >, by 1930, low. Baumann. Occ. *nipper* (Manchon).—5. **(the nippers.)** The lowest form: many Public Schools': C. 20. Ian Hay, *The Lighter Side of School Life*, 1914.

nippiness. See **nippy**, adj., 2.

*nipping, n. and adj. See **nip**, v., 1: same period and status. Esp. in Greene.

nipping Christian. A cut-purse: low s. of ca. 1800–60. F. & H.

nipping-jig. (A) hanging: early C. 19: ? c. > low s. F. & H.

nippitate; -ato, atum, -aty (occ. **-ati**). Strong, prime liquor, esp. ale: ca. 1575–1700. The O.E.D. considers both the n. and the derivative adj. as S.E., prob. rightly; F. & H. thinks it may have been c. Laneham, Stubbes, Nashe, Oliffe, Urquhart. Etymology obscure: but cf. *nip*, v., 2.

*nipps. See **nips**.

nippy. The penis: children's: from ca. 1850; ob. ? ex *pee.*—2. A waitress in Lyons's restaurants and tea-shops: from 1924: j. >, by 1930, coll., indeed by 1935 almost s. Dorothy Sayers, *Un-natural Death*, 1927, '"Nippy" found dead on Wandsworth Common.' 'The word is a registered trade mark of the company,' O.E.D. (Sup.). Ex *nippy*, lively.—3. Hence, any waitress, esp. in a cheap establishment: from ca. 1930.

nippy, adj. As = mean, stingy, or curt, snappish, it is familiar S.E.—2. Lively, nimble, active, sharp or prompt: 1853, Surtees; Burleigh, 1898, 'He . . . liked to see them keen and "nippy" at every soldierly task.' O.E.D. Hence, in C. 20, *nippiness.*—3. Well-dressed; smartly fashionable: lower classes' (— 1923). Manchon. Just possibly influenced by Fr. *nippé*, 'togged up' (Kastner & Marks).

*nips; nipps, nyps. Shears for clipping money: c.: late C. 17–mid-19. B.E.; Grose, 1st ed.

nips in(to), put the. To ask a loan (from a person): Australian and New Zealand: from ca. 1908. Cf. *sting*, q.v., and *put the hard word on.*

nipsitate. A C. 17 variant of *nippitate*, q.v. Davenport, 1639. O.E.D.

nire. Rain: Cockney back s. (on *rine*): before 1859. H., 1st ed. Cf. *nair*.

nisey or nisy. See **nikin** and **nizey**.

nit. (See list at **nias.**)—2. 'Wine that is brisk, and pour'd quick into a Glass', B.E.: coll.: late C. 17–mid-18. ? ex † *nitty*, full of air bubbles.—3. As a wanton, it is Scots: rather dial. than coll.—4. A military policeman: military: 1915; ob. F. & Gibbons. Cf. the fig. sense of *lousy*.

nit, dead as a. Quite dead: coll. and dial.: late C. 18–20; ob. except in dial. Wolcot, 1789; Hardy, 1874, '[The Sheep] will all die as dead as nits.' O.E.D.

nit, keep. See **keep nit**.

nit-squeeger, i.e. **nit-squeezer**. A hair-dresser: low: 1788, Grose, 2nd ed.; ob.

'nitiated; 'nitiation. Initiated; initiation: lower classes' (and Canadian lumbermen's): from ca. 1920. John Beames.

nitraph. A farthing (pronounced *farthin*'): back s. (— 1859). H., 1st ed.

nits will be, gen. become, lice. A proverbial c.p., > in C. 18 a proverb, applied to 'small matters that become important', B.E.: mid-C. 17–18. Isaac D'Israeli ascribes it to Oliver Cromwell.

nitsky. A C. 20 variant of *nix*, nothing. Alan Hyder, *Black Girl, White Lady*, 1934.

nitty. A disturbance, racket, squabble: nautical: 1830, Marryat, 'I never seed . . . such a nitty kicked up 'tween decks, in my life' (O.E.D.). Ob. Prob. ex dial. *nitter* or *nitty-natter*, to be constantly grumbling.

*nix; nicks. Nothing; occ., in mid-C. 19–20 but ob., nobody. Orig. c. >, ca. 1815, low s. >, ca. 1860, gen. s. G. Parker, 1789, 'How they have brought a German word into cant I know not, but nicks means *nothing* in the cant language': prob. ex coll. Ger. *nix* (= *nichts*) via coll. Dutch, as the O.E.D. implies. Also *nix my doll*, q.v. Cf. *nix-nie.*—2. **(nix.)** A master (or mistress): Bootham School (— 1925). Anon., *Dict. of Bootham Slang.* Perhaps because he 'nicks' delinquents.

nix! A warning, esp. among schoolboys and workmen, of somebody's approach. Esp. in *keep nix*, to keep watch. Ob. H., 2nd ed., 1860; Routledge's *Every Boy's Annual*, 1869. Also (recorded in 1883) *nix*(, e.g. *lads*,) *buttons !* Prob. ex Romany *nisser*, to avoid, influenced by *nix my dolly*, q.v.

nix, deberr! No, my friend: London: ca. 1810–30. 'Jon Bee', 1823, 'Borrowed of the Russians who lay in the Medway, 1810 '.

nix goot. No good: among prisoners of war: 1914–18. B. & P. I.e., Ger. *nichts gut.*

*nix my doll. Nothing: c. of ca. 1810–30. Vaux. A mystifying elaboration of *nix*, q.v., when the latter began to > well known.

*nix my dolly. Never mind!; prob. a mere variant of *nix my doll*, nothing (to worry about): 1834, Ainsworth, 'Nix my dolly, pals, fake away,' in a popular song that popularised the phrase which soon >, as it may orig. have been, merely 'literary' c.; certainly † by 1890 and ob. by 1860.

nix-nie. Nothing at all: South African (—1913). Elaboration of *nix*, q.v. Pettman.

nix(e)y! No!: circus-workers' (— 1887). Baumann. Ex *nix* and *nix !*

niz-priz. A writ of *nisi prius*: legal: mid-C. 19–20. H., 3rd ed.

nizey, nizi, nizy, nizzie, nizzy. (Also **nisey, nisy.**) A dunce, simpleton, fool: coll.: mid-C. 17–early 19. (The rare *nizi*, only C. 17; *nisy* only C. 18.) Either ex Fr. *niais*, foolish, or ex † S.E. *nice*, foolish. Coles, 1676; Ned Ward; Johnson, 'a low word '.—2. A coxcomb: late C. 17–early 18: coll., I think, though B.E. says c. See also **nikin**.

no. Any: sol. (— 1887). Baumann, 'I didn't want no tellin'.'—2. For stylistic improprieties, see Fowler.—3. See **there's no ——**.

[In F. & H., the following **no-** terms should have been omitted as S.E.:—(the) **noble art** = pugilism, **nod** = a fool, **nod, v., nodcock or nodcoke, noddipol** (or **noddypoll**), **noddy** (a fool; a buggy), **noddy** the adj., **Knave Noddy** (the knave of trumps), **noddy-headed** (witless), **noddy-pate or -peak(e)**, **nodgecock**, **nog or (k)noggin** (a measure; a mug), **nohow** the adj., **noise, n. and v., make a noise at one, noli-**

me-tangere, a repellent person, no-man's-land, nonplussed or -ust, nonsense (a trick), nonesuch (something unequalled), nonjuror, noodle the v., noodledom, nookery, noose = to marry, nose, v. (except in c. sense), nostrum, notch the v., notional, notionate ; whereas nobby, a fool, and nog = noggin, are dial.]

no. 1. See number one.

no battle. Not worth while, no good : printers' : from ca. 1870 ; ob. Because not worth fighting for or because there's no fight to see.

no bon. See bon.

no-beyond jammer. A 'perfectly beautiful woman' : low (— 1909) ; virtually †. Ware. Lit.: as ' jam ', incomparable.

no can do. Cannot do ; impossible : pidgin and ' passe-partout ' English : mid-C. 19–20. Whence N.C.D., the naval refusal of an invitation : late C. 19–20. Bowen.

no catch(, it's, etc.). (It's) very hard work, very disappointing, unpleasant, dangerous : coll. : late C. 19–20. See catch, n., and cf. the equivalent no cop at cop.

[no catchy no havy. If I'm not caught, I can't have a beating or come to any harm : mid-C. 18–19 Negro saying quoted by Grose, 2nd ed. But unless such terms and phrases are taken up by the British, they are ineligible.]

no chicken. See chicken.—no class. See class.

no compree ! I don't understand : military c.p. : 1914–19. Cf. compree, q.v.—2. Hence, No thanks !: id. : 1915–19. F. & Gibbons.

no cop. See cop, no.

no earthly. See earthly, not an.—no end. See end.—no error, and. See mistake, and no.—no fear. See fear.

no flies ; also (see H., 5th ed.) no(-)fly. Artful, designing : printers' : from ca. 1870. Also n. f., q.v. In C. 20, there are no flies on (so and so), he's no fool, he's a good, sound fellow : which appears to come from the U.S.A. (Thornton).—2. ' An emphatic addition made to an assertion . . . It really means " no error " or " no mistake " . . . as " A jolly fine girl, and no flies ! " ' H., 5th ed. (1874).

No Flint. Charles, Earl Grey, a British general in America in C. 18. He preferred cold steel to bullets. Dawson.

no flowers—by request ! A jocular c.p. : C. 20. See corpse-worship.

no fool. See fool.

no go(, it is, etc.). No use ! ; it's impracticable or impossible : 1830, Moncrieff ; 1852, Notes and Queries, Jan. 17, ' My publisher coolly answered that it was no go ' ; 1896, Farjeon, ' But it was no go '.

no goody-la ! The opp. of goody-la !, q.v.

no grease ! An engineers' c.p. : (— 1909) imputing lack of polish or manners. Ware.

no-how, no-howish. See nohow, nohowish.

no kid. No mistake ; lit., without deception : from ca. 1890. P. H. Emerson.

no mistake, and. See mistake, and no.

no more wit than a coot(, have). (To be) stupid : C. 16 coll. Apperson.

no moss ! No animosity ! : tailors' : from ca. 1870 ; ob.

no name, no pull. If I don't mention names, there can—or should—be no offence, no libel action : tailors' : from ca. 1870 ; ob. Cf. :

no names, no pack-drill. The soldier's equivalent of the preceding : C. 20 c.p. (Drill with a heavy pack up is a very common military punishment.) B. & P.

no number nines. See what ! no number . . .

no odds ! It doesn't matter ; never mind : coll. : 1855, Dickens.

no. one or 1 ; no. two or 2. See number one ; number two.

no possible probable shadow of doubt, no possible doubt whatever is a c.p., either independent, or in retort on, or confirmation of, of that there is no possible doubt. Late C. 19–20, among the cultured. Ex Gilbert & Sullivan. (Collinson.)

no rats ! A proletarian c.p. (— 1909 ; ob.): ' He (or she) is Scotch.' Ware, ' A Scot is always associated with bagpipes, and . . . no rat can bear . . . that musical instrument.'

no repairs. See repairs.

no return ticket ! A London lower-classes' c.p. (— 1909) : He, or she, is mad ! Abbr. he's going to Hanwell [lunatic asylum] and has no return ticket. Ware.

no Robin Hood. No bloody good : rhyming s., esp. military : from ca. 1910. B. & P.

no sir ! ; no sir-ree. (Accent on the last syllable.) This emphatic negative, recorded in U.S. in 1847, has in post-War England > a c.p. (Thornton.)

no such. Catachrestic for none such : late C. 19 (? earlier)–20. Freeman Wills Crofts, The Cask, 1920, ' You can't have seen a letter from me, because no such exists.'

no two ways about it. (There's) no alternative ; no room for a difference of opinion : coll. : C. 20. Ex U.S.

Noah's ark. An overcoat, long and closely buttoned : coll. : from ca. 1858 ; ob. by 1905, † by 1920.—2. A lark (whether bird or, more gen., fun) : rhyming s. : 1887, The Referee, Nov. 7.—3. Dark : rhyming s. : C. 20, esp. among urban labourers. John o' London's Weekly, June 9, 1934. (—4. The nautical sense is S.E.)

Noah's doves. ' Reinforcements at sea when Armistice was signed ' : Australian military : late 1918 ; now only historical. F. & Gibbons. Cf. rainbow, q.v., and olive-branch.

Noakes. See John o' Nokes and, for secondary sense, Nokes.

nob. (In C. 18, also nobb.) The head : from ca. 1690 : c. >, ca. 1750, low s. >, ca. 1810, gen. s. B.E. ; K. O'Hara, 1733, ' Do pop up your nob again, | And egad I'll crack your crown ' ; Barham. Cf. (? ex) nab, the head, q.v.—2. A blow on the head : from ca. 1810 ; very ob. : orig. sporting.— 3. In cribbage, ' the knave of the same suit as the turn-up card, counting one to the holder ', O.E.D. : 1821, Lamb. See also nob, one for his.—4. A person of rank, position, or wealth : 1809 (O.E.D.) ; Lex. Bal., 1811 ; Westmacott, 1825, ' Nob or big wig ' ; Dickens, Thackeray ; Anstey. (In the C. 19 Navy, a lieutenant : Bowen.) Earlier in Scots dial. as nab or knab(b) : 1742, R. Forbes (E.E.D.). These Scottish forms militate against abbr. nobility ; this sense prob. derives ex sense 1 : cf. the heads, important persons.—5. Hence, a fellow of a college : Oxford University : ca. 1820–60. Westmacott, 1825.—6. Abbr. knob-stick, q.v. : workmen's coll. : from ca. 1865 ; ob. J. K. Hunter, Life Studies, 1870 (O.E.D.).—7. A sovereign (coin) : ca. 1840–90. Ex the head.—8. The game of prick- (or cheat-)the-garter : c. of ca. 1750– 1800. John Poulter, 1753, ' We got about three pounds·from a butterman at the Belt or Nobb.'—

9. The **nose** : Scottish and North Country s. : 1796 (E.D.D.). Cf. sense 1.

nob, v. To punch on the head, v.t. and v.i. : boxing : 1812, both in *The Sporting Magazine* ; ob. 1823, Moncrieff, ' I've nobb'd him on the canister.'—2. To collect (money) ; make a collection from (persons) : showmen's : both 1851, Mayhew, e.g. ' We also " nobb ", or gather the money ', and ' We went to " nob " them.' O.E.D. Perhaps ex cribbage or ex *nob* = a sovereign.—3. See **nob it.**

nob, come the. To give oneself airs : from ca. 1820 ; ob. Ex *nob,* n., 4.

nob, do a. A variant (— 1875) of *nob,* v., 2. T. Frost, *Circus Life* ; Manchon. See also **do a nob.**

nob, one for his. A point in cribbage for holding the knave of trumps : 1870, Ware & Hardy in *The Modern Hoyle* (O.E.D.).—2. Hence, a punch on the head : boxing : from ca. 1870.

*****nob, pitch the.** See **prick-the-garter.** From ca. 1820 ; † by 1890 ; prob. c.

nob-a-nob, adj. Friendly, intimate : 1834, Ainsworth ; † by 1890. Corrupted *hot-nob.*

nob-cheat or **-chete.** See **nab-cheat.—nob-girder.** See **nab-girder.**

*****nob in the fur trade.** A judge : c. : ca. 1838, G. W. M. Reynolds, ' Let nobs in the fur trade hold their jaw ' ; † by 1880. Ex the fur on the robe.

*****nob it.** To prosper without much work ; to succeed by shrewdness : c. of ca. 1810–40. Vaux. Also *to fight nob-work,* gen. as vbl.n.

*****nob-pitcher.** C. of ca. 1810–90. Vaux, 1812, ' A general term for those sharpers who attend at fairs, races, etc., to take in the flats at prick-in-the-garter, cups and balls, and other similar artifices.'

nob-stick. See **knob-stick.**

nob-thatch. Hair (of the head) : 1866, Yates, ' You've got a paucity of nob-thatch, and what 'air you 'ave is gray.' Ob. Ex *nob,* n., 1. Cf. :

nob-thatcher. A wig-maker : from ca. 1790 ; ob. Grose, 3rd ed.—2. A (gen. female) straw-bonnet maker : 1823, Moncrieff : ca. 1820–1900. Cf. *noddle-thatcher.*

nob the glazes. To collect money from persons at first-floor windows, performers standing upon each other's or even one another's shoulders : showmen's and circus s. (— 1875). T. Frost, *Circus Life.* See **nob,** v., 2, and **glaze.**

nob-work. Mental occupation : low : from ca. 1820. (Cf. *head-work.*) Ex :

*****nob-work, fight.** See **nob it.—nobb.** See **nob,** n., 1 and v., 2.

nobba, occ. **nobber.** Nine, gen. as adj. : Parlyaree via Lingua Franca : from ca. 1850. E.g. *nobba saltee,* ninepence. Ex Sp. *nova* or It. *nove.* Cf. the interchangeable *b* and *v* of *sabe, savv(e)y.* ' Slang introduced by the " organ-grinders " from Italy ', H., 1864 : from ca. 1850.

nobber. See preceding entry.—2. A blow on the head : boxing : 1818 ; ob. Moore, 1819, ' That flashy spark . . . received a nobber.' Ex *nob,* v., 1.—3. A boxer skilful at head-punches : boxing : from ca. 1820 ; ob. *The Sporting Magazine,* 1821, ' Randall . . . a nobber of first-rate excellence '. (Both senses, O.E.D.)—4. A collector of money, esp. for showmen or minstrels, or, in C. 20, for a beggar : 1890, *The Echo,* Oct. 30, ' Only a nobber can know the extraordinary meanness of the British public ' ; P. H. Emerson. Ex *nob,* v., 2.

nobbily. Smartly, esp. if rather showily : from ca. 1858. H., 1st ed. Ex *nobby,* adj.

nobbing. The giving or the getting of blows on the head : boxing (— 1825). Ob. The corresponding adj. is recorded at 1816 (O.E.D.).—2. Going round with the hat (— 1859) : showmen's : H., 1st ed. In the pl., money collected : 1851, Mayhew, ' Fifteen shillings of nobbings '. Ex *nob,* v., 2. Cf. *nobbing-slum,* q.v.

*****nobbing-cheat.** See **nubbing cheat.**

nobbing-slum. The bag (or the hat) for collecting money : showmen's : from ca. 1890. Cf. *nobbing,* 2, and *nob,* v., 2, qq.v.

nobbish. A variant of *nobby,* adj., q.v. From ca. 1860 ; ob. H., 2nd ed.

nobble. To strike on the head ; to stun : low : from ca. 1880 ; ob. Ex *nob,* n., 1.—2. To tamper with a horse, e.g. by laming it, to prevent it from winning : the turf : 1847. Lever, 1859, ' A shadowy vision of creditors " done ", horses " nobbled " ', O.E.D. ' App. a modern frequentative of *nab,* v., q.v. (W.)—3. Hence, to obtain a person's help or interest by underhand methods : 1865. O.E.D.—4. To appropriate dishonestly, even to steal : 1854, Thackeray, ' After nobbling her money for the beauty of the family '. O.E.D. Cf. *knoblin rig,* q.v., for form.—5. To swindle out of : 1854, Thackeray, ' I don't know out of how much the reverend party has nobbled his poor old sister at Brighton.'—6. To seize, catch, get hold of : low (? orig. c.) : 1877, Greenwood, ' There's a fiver . . ., and nine good quid. Have it. Nobble him, lads, and share it betwixt you '; Somerset Maugham, *Cakes and Ale,* 1930, ' She nobbled Jasper Gibbons. In a little while he was eating out of her soft hand.'—7. Hence, to kidnap : c. : C. 20. (Evelyn Waugh, *Decline and Fall,* 1928.)

nobble-tree. The head : provincial : ca. 1870–1910. Ex *nob,* the head.

nobbled, ppl.adj. See *nobble,* v.

nobbler. A blow on the head : boxing : from ca. 1880. (—2. A short stick for killing fish : prob. j., therefore ineligible.)—3. Hence, any finishing blow or stroke : from ca. 1885.—4. An assistant of thimble-riggers and card-sharpers, i.e. a decoy ; also, a pickpocket working in the vicinity of these riggers and sharpers : c. : from ca. 1835. Brandon ; H., 1st ed. ; C. Hindley.—5. One who disables horses a little before a race : the turf : 1854, Whyte-Melville. See **nobble,** v., 2.—6. A pettifogging lawyer : North Country : from ca. 1860 ; ob. H., 3rd ed.—7. A drink, esp. of spirits : Australian coll. : 1852, G.E.P., ' To drain a farewell " nobbler " to his Sally ' ; 1859, Fowler, *Southern Lights and Shadows,* ' The measure is called a nobbler, or a break-down ' : coll. >, ca. 1905, S.E. Because it gets hold of one. Whence *nobblerise.*—8. A prospective customer : Petticoat Lane : C. 20.

nobblerise. To drink frequent ' nobblers ' : Australian coll. : 1864, J. Rogers. Morris.

nobbling, vbl.n. See **nobble,** all senses.—2. Adj., in good health : coll. : ca. 1820–40. *The Spirit of the Public Journals,* 1825 (O.E.D.). Cognate with *nobby,* adj.

nobby, n. Always *the nobby.* The smart thing : 1869, E. Farmer ; ob. (O.E.D.) Ex *nobby,* adj.—2. Inevitable nickname (**Nobby**) for any man surnamed *Clark(e)* : late C. 19–20. Also, ' the naval nickname which, originally given to Admiral Charles Ewart on account of his dapperness, has spread to all Ewarts and Hewetts ' (Bowen) : C. 20. *Nobby* also a loose variant of **Knobby** (Addenda).

Clarks are *Nobby* because clerks used, in the City, to wear top hats, i.e. *nobby* hats.—3. The ship *Niobe* : naval (— 1909). Ware.

nobby, adj. Very smart, elegant, or fashionable. Of persons : from ca. 1808. A broadside ballad of ca. 1810, ' A werry nobby dog's meat man '. (Cf. *nifty*, q.v.) Of places or things : 1844, C. Selby, ' My togs being in keeping with this nobby place ' ; 1852, ' The nobbiest way of keeping it quiet '. Ex Scots *knabbie* or *knabby* (1788, Picken, ' Mony a knabbie laird ', O.E.D.) ; see also **nob,** n., 4.

noble. A mainly girlish, chiefly school-girlish, coll. of approbation for persons or things, esp. in *that's (very) noble of you* : C. 20. Ex aristocratic connotation.

noble blood to market and see what it will bring, send your. A C. 18 c.p. addressed to one boasting about or trading on his high birth. Apperson.

noble to ninepence, bring a or **one's.** To dissipate money idly or wantonly : semi-proverbial coll. : from ca. 1565 ; ob. by 1820, except in dial. Ful-well, 1568, ' For why Tom Tosspot, since he went hence, | Hath increased a noble just unto nine pence ' ; Bailey's *Colloquies of Erasmus* ; 1914, R. L. Gales in *Vanished Country Folk*, ' As a child I remember " Their noble has come to a ninepence " as the commonest of sayings.' Apperson.

Nobody's Own. The 13th, also the 20th, Hussars : military : mid C. 19–20. F. & Gibbons, ' As not being allotted in their title to any Royal personage or other person of distinction, as with other cavalry regiments outside the Household Brigade ' ; R. J. T. Hills, *Something About a Soldier*, 1934.

nobs. An endearment applied to a woman : coll. : ca. 1520–80. Skelton. ? origin.

Nobs' House, the upper. The House of Lords : low : ca. 1820–50. Bee. Cf. :

Nobs' Houses, the. The Houses of Parliament : low : ca. 1820–50. Bee. Cf. :

Nobs' (occ. **Nob's) Nob, the.** King George IV : ca. 1820–40. Bee. (He was a famous dandy.) Like the preceding, ex *nob*, n., 4.

nobsey. A mistress : coll. : mid-C. 16. Harpsfield. Ex *nobs*, q.v. O.E.D.

nock. (As the posteriors, esp. the breech, it is S.E. : but see **nockandro.—**) 2. The female pudend : low : late C. 16–18. Florio, Cotton. Lit., *a notch*. Cf. :

nock, v. To ' occupy ' a woman, gen. v.t. : low coll. : late C. 16–18. Florio ; Ash in his Dict. In C. 19–20, *knock*, which was prob. suggested by this.

nockandro. The posteriors, esp. the breech : coll. : C. 17. Cotgrave, Urquhart, Gayton. Prob. *nock*, a notch, + Gr. ἀνδρός, of a man. Cf. *nock*, n., 1, q.v.

nocky. ' A silly, dull Fellow ', B.E. : late C. 17–early 19 ; *nocky* extant in dial. Also, as in Grose (1st ed.), *nocky boy.* The etymology is obscure : but perhaps via *knock in the cradle*, q.v.—2. **Nocky** is an ' inevitable ' nickname of men surnamed Knight : military : C. 20. F. & Gibbons. Of unascertained origin, prob. anecdotal.

nocturne. A harlot : Society s. bordering on euphemistic S.E. : ca. 1875–1915. Prob. ex ob. S.E. *nocturnal* (late C. 17–20) : a night-walker, a harlot.

nod, land of. (Occ. with capitals ; always preceded by *the*.) Sleep : C. 18–20 : coll. till C. 19, then S.E. Swift, ' I'm going to the land of Nod ' ; Grose ; Scott, 1818, in *The Heart of Midlothian*. Punning the Biblical place-name.

nod, on the. On credit : coll. : from ca. 1880. *The Rag*, Sept. 30, 1882, ' A pay-on-the-nod, | An always-in-quod young man '. Contrast the C. 18 proverb, *a nod of an honest man is enough*.

nod is as good as a wink to a blind horse, a. A semi-proverbial c.p. applied to a covert yet comprehensible hint, though often stupidity in the receiver is implied. C. 19–20. Dorothy Wordsworth, *Journal*, 1802. (Apperson.)

noddle. The head : coll. (orig., perhaps jocular S.E.) : 1664, Butler, ' My Head's not made of brass | As Friar Bacon's noddle was ' ; L'Estrange ; Thackeray. Ex the S.E. sense of C. 15–mid-17 *noddle* (cognate with *noll*) : the back of the head.—2. The head as the seat of intelligence—or the lack of it. Coll. ; often playful, often derisive : 1579, Tomson ; 1611, W. Baker, ' The wit enskonsed in thy noddell ' ; Dickens. O.E.D.

noddle-case. A wig : coll. : ca. 1700–80. Facetious Tom Brown. Cf. :

noddle-thatcher. A wig-maker : coll. : ca. 1715–1800. Cf. *nob-thatcher*, q.v.

noddleken. See **nuddikin.**

noddy-headed. (See the entry following **no.)—** 2. Drunk : coll. : ca. 1850–1910.

noffgur. A fashionable harlot : low : ca. 1885–1910. Barrère & Leland quote from an anon. song : ' Wrong 'uns at the Wateries, | Noffgurs at the Troc, | Coryphées by Keltner, | Tartlets anywhere.' Etymology obscure : ? *naughty girl* telescoped.

noggin. The head : s. or coll. : ca. 1800–60. Ex S.E. sense.

[**noggy.** Drunk : dial. and perhaps provincial s. : C. 19–20. E.D.D.]

nohow ; occ. **no-how.** The adj. (= indistinct) is S.E., as is the adv. (by no means, in no manner). Preceded by *all*, it = out of sorts, and is coll. : from ca. 1850. Dickens.—2. In solecistic speech, often with a superfluous negative, e.g. in Reade's ' That don't dovetail nohow ' (O.E.D.).

nohowish. Unwell : nautical (— 1887). Bauman. Ex *nohow*, 1.

noise, a big. See **big noise.**

noise like a(n) . . ., make a. To pretend to be a (thing) ; (momentarily) to suppose oneself to be an (animal ; occ. a person) : a c.p. locution : from ca. 1920. Dorothy Sayers, *Unnatural Death*, 1927, ' And now we'll just make a noise like a hoop and roll away.'

*noisy-dog racket. The stealing of brass knockers from doors : c. of ca. 1810–60. *Lex. Bal.* ? ex the accompanying barks of a provoked dog or simply ex the noise the operation was apt to make.

nokes ; Nokes. ' A Ninny or Fool ', B.E. : coll. : ca. 1690–1890.—2. See **John-a-Nokes.**

Nokkum. (Gen. pl.) A Scottish Gypsy tinker : their own word : mid-C. 19–20. The reference in ' *No. 747* ' (p. 49) is valid for 1865.

nol. Long : back s. (— 1859). H., 1st ed.—2. **Nol.** See **Old Noll.**

[**noli me tangere** (or hyphenated). Syphilis. Scots coll. : C. 17–early 19. Perhaps, however, merely a specific instance, for all other senses are S.E. Lit. (in L.), touch me not !]

noll ; occ. **nol, nole, nolle,** these three being † by 1750. The head : C. 9–20 : S.E. till C. 18, then coll. till ca. 1820, then (except as jocular archaism) dial.—2. A person, esp. as a simpleton, gen. with *dull* or *drunken* : late C. 14–mid-17. : S.E. verging on, indeed sometimes actually, coll.—3. **Noll, Old.** See **Old Noll.—**4. **Noll.** Oliver Goldsmith. (Dawson.)

nominate. See **poison.**—**nomm(o)us.** See **nammous.**

non-car(e)ish. Insouciant: coll. (— 1923). Manchon.

non-col. A group of pupils exempted, or the rule by which they are exempted, from the practice of writing '*columns*' (q.v.): Bootham School (— 1925). Anon., *Dict. of Bootham Slang.*

Non-Coll, adj. and n. Non-Collegiate: Oxford and Cambridge Universities' coll.: from ca. 1875. *Durham University Journal,* Dec. 13, 1879, 'The Cambridge "non-colls"'. O.E.D.

non-com. A non-commissioned officer: coll. (orig. military): from ca. 1862. H., 3rd ed. (1864); J. S. Winter, 1885, 'Well-tipped quartermasters and their favourite tools among the non-coms.' Cf. the Fr. s., *sous-off* = *sous-officier* (W.).

non-con., Non-Con., Non-con. A Nonconformist: coll.: from ca. 1680; ob. Flatman; Grose, 1st ed.

non est. Absent: coll.: 1870, Brewer. Lit., he is not (sc. found, L. *inventus*). Abbr.:

non est inventus, adj. Absent: coll.: 1827, De Quincey, *Murder as One of the Fine Arts*; ob. by 1890, † by 1915. Ex legal 'S.E.'

non-husky. See **husky.**

non-licet, adj. Illegal; esp. unbefitting a Wykehamist: Winchester College: from ca. 1890. 'Don't sport non-licet notions,' Wrench, *The Winchester Word-Book,* 1891. Ex the legal S.E.

non me. A lie: lower classes', mostly Cockneys': 1820–ca. 30. Ex Queen Caroline's trial, whereat the Italian witnesses said *non mi ricordo* (I don't remember) to every important question. Ware.

non-plus, catch (a person) **on the.** To catch at unawares: coll. (— 1887).; ob. Baumann.

non-stop. A big shell passing far overhead: military: 1915; ob. F. & Gibbons. Ex a non-stop train.

nonce. Understanding, as in 'There's no nonce about him': sol. (— 1887); ob. Baumann. A perversion of *nuance* or a confusion of *nous* and *sense,* or of *nonsense* and *sense.*

nondescript. A boy in the middle school: certain Public Schools': late C. 19–20. In the same schools, *squeaker* (see sense 3) and *dook* (last sense): Ian Hay, *David and Destiny,* 1934.

nonesuch, nonsuch. The female pudend: low: C. 18–20; ob.—2. In allusive S.E. bordering on semi-proverbial coll. (gen. ironic): late C. 16–17. Wither, 'A spotless Church, or perfect Disciplines | Go seek at None-such.' Ex Nonsuch, near Epsom in Surrey. O.E.D. Cf.:

Nonesuch, he's a Mr. He's very conceited: c.p. of ca. 1885–1910. Baumann.

[**nonny-nonny.** A meaningless refrain useful esp. for palliating obscenity: C. 16–18; extant only as an archaism. Perhaps coll. rather than S.E. F. & H. give it as = a simpleton: but is this so? I find no support.]

nonplush. Nonplus; occ. nonplussed: sol. when not dial., nor as ca. 1820–40, jocular. Bee.

nonsensational. Sensationally nonsensical: critics': 1897, *The People,* Feb. 28; † by 1909. Ware. On *non-sensational* and telescoping *nonsensically sensational.*

nonsense. 'Melting butter in a wig', Grose, 3rd ed.: late C. 18–early 19.—2. Money: c. or, more prob., low s.: from ca. 1820. Egan, 1821, 'Shell out the nonsense: half a quid Will speak more truth than all your palavers.' By antiphrasis.—3. A

small division of the Third Form: Eton College: mid-C. 19–20: s. > j.

nonsuch. See **nonesuch.**

noodle, a simpleton (from ca. 1750): perhaps orig. coll.; otherwise, always S.E.—2. 'A man belonging to the Northumberland Yeomanry or Volunteers': Northumberland s.: 1891; ob. E.D.D.

Noodles, the House of. The House of Lords: ca. 1820–60. Bee. Cf. *Nobs'* . . ., q.v.

*****nook.** A penny: c., esp. vagrants': C. 20. Manchon; James Curtis, *The Gilt Kid,* 1936. Origin?

noom. The moon: back s. (— 1859). H., 1st ed.

noomony. Pneumonia: Canadian sol. verging on (lower-class) coll.: C. 20. John Beames, *Gateway,* 1932, 'You'll get the noomony one of these days, goin' on the way like you do.'

noose, nooze. To hang: from ca. 1670; ob.: ? orig. c.; certainly low s. till C. 19, then coll. Head, Grose. (—2. V.t., to marry, late C. 17–20, is jocular S.E.)

nope. A blow, esp. on the head, from ca. 1720: s. († by 1870) and Northern dial. *A New Canting Dict.,* 1725; Grose. Cognate with C. 15 *nolp,* of equally obscure origin: cf. *culp,* q.v.—2. This U.S. pronunciation of *no,* the semi-exclamatory adv., has, esp. since 1918 and as a low coll., gained ground in the British Empire. ('Ganpat', *Out of Evil,* 1933.) —3. A slovenly, occ. jocular, 'collision' of *no hope!*: low coll.: C. 20, but rare before the G.W.

Noper Force, the. The North Persian Force, operating in the latter half of 1918: military. B. & P. Prob. with a pun on *nope,* 3.

nor. Than: dial. (from C. 15) and, in C. 19–20, low coll. Thackeray, 1840, 'You're no better nor a common tramper,' O.E.D. (*—nor* = *north* is S.E.)

nor an 'un. Not a single one: sol., not very gen.: mid(?) C. 19–20. Richard Blaker, 1930.

Nor' Loch trout. A joint or leg of mutton: Scots s.: ca. 1770–1810. Jamieson, 'This was the only species of *fish* which the North Loch, on which the shambles were situated, could supply.'

nor'-wester. A glass of potent liquor: nautical coll.: 1840, Marryat; ob. O.E.D.

Noras. Great Northern Railway deferred ordinary stock: Stock Exchange: from ca. 1885; ob. Atkin, 1887, 'For we have our Saras and Claras, | Our Noras and Doras for fays.'

Noravee yawl. A Norway yawl: nautical coll.: C. 19–20. Bowen.

Norfolk boy, the. Porson's nickname at Eton—and after. Dawson.

Norfolk capon. A red herring (cf. *Glasgow magistrate,* q.v.): coll.: from ca. 1780; ob. Grose, 1st ed. Smith, *The Individual,* 1836, 'A Norfolk capon is jolly grub.' Cf. also *Yarmouth capon,* q.v.

Norfolk dumpling. An inhabitant, esp. a native, of Norfolk: coll.: C. 17–20. Day, in *The Blind Beggar,* 1600; Ray, 'This referres not to the stature of their bodies; but to the fare they commonly feed on and much delight in'; Grose, 1st ed. True, Mr. Ray; nevertheless, this dish does tend to make children and even adults round and fat. Apperson. Cf. *Norfolk turkey,* q.v.

Norfolk Howard. A bed-bug: coll.: from ca. 1863; ob. H., 3rd ed. Ex one Joshua Bug, who in June, 1862, changed his name to Norfolk Howard.

Norfolk Howards. The Norfolk Regiment (in C. 19, the 9th Foot): military: from ca. 1870. Ex the preceding, in the jocose way of soldiers.

[**Norfolk nog.** A kind of strong ale : ca. 1720–60 : coll. rapidly > (? always was) S.E. Vanbrugh, 1726, ' Here's Norfolk nog to be had at the next door.']

Norfolk turkey. An inhabitant, esp. a native, of Norfolk : coll. : C. 19–20 ; ob. Anon., *Ora and Juliet*, 1811, ' The boorish manners of those Norfolk turkeys ' (O.E.D.). Cf. *Norfolk Dumpling*, q.v., see **Norwicher**, and note the C. 16–20 (ob.) proverb *Essex stiles* (ditches), *Kentish miles, Norfolk wiles, many men beguiles*, with variants ; glance also at *Yorkshire* and at *north*, sense 1.

*__*nork.__ A variant (virtually †) of *nark*, n., **1.** Baumann.

norp, gen. v.i. To insert phrases apt to ' fetch ' the gallery, i.e. to ' gag to *or* for the gods ' : theatrical : from ca. 1870 ; ob. Perhaps ex Yorkshire dial. (at least as early as 1869 : E.D.D.) *norp* or *naup*, to hit the mark, to succeed, ex the much earlier *norp, naup*, to strike, e.g. with a stick, gen. on the head.

Norperforce. The North Persian Force operating at the end of the G.W. : military coll. : late 1918–19. F. & Gibbons. Also **Noper Force,** q.v.

norra. Not a : Cockney : C. 19–20. Julian Franklyn, *This Gutter Life*, 1934, ' Yus, norra bad uncle Ned '. Cf. *gorra*.

Norsker. A Norwegian : nautical coll. : mid-C. 19–20. Bowen. Ex Scandinavian *Norsk* (Norse).

north. A frequent C. 20 abbr. of *north and south*, q.v. (B. & P.)

north, adj. Intelligent ; mentally and socially alert ; cunning : from late C. 17 ; ob. Rare except in *too far north*, too clever or knowing, as in Smollett, 1748, and Mrs. A. M. Bennett, 1797 (O.E.D.) ; Ashton, in his *Social Life in the Reign of Queen Anne*, quotes however this illuminating passage : ' I ask'd what Countrey-man my Landlord was ? answer was made, Full North ; and Faith 'twas very Evident, for he had put the *Yorkshire* most damnably upon us.' Cf. the C. 19–20 dial. *to have been as far North as anyone*, to be no more of a fool than the next man (E.D.D.).—**2.** Strong, gen. of drink : nautical : from ca. 1860. Hence, *due north*, neat, without water, and *too far north*, drunk ; contrast this phrase in sense 1. *The Glasgow Herald*, Nov. 9, 1864. Cf. *another point(, steward) l*, q.v.

north and south. The mouth : rhyming s. : from ca. 1880.

North Castle. See **Holloway Castle.**

North Country compliment. An unwanted gift of no value to either the donor or the recipient : coll. : from ca. 1870 ; ob. H., 5th ed.

north-easter. A bluejacket that, on pay day, finds he is not entitled to receive any : naval : late C. 19–20. Bowen. Ex the bitterness of a North-East wind. Occ., in C. 20, abbr. to *N.E.*: F. & Gibbons. The adj. is *North-East* (or *n.-e.*), as in *The Saturday Review*, Oct. 20, 1934.

north eye. A squint : showmen's s. and Southern dial. : from ca. 1850. P. H. Emerson, 1893. Cf. the other dial. phrases in E.D.D. (F. & H. too soon discouraged.)

North Sea Rabbits. Herrings as food : New Zealand soldiers' : 1916–18. Ex the abundance of herrings in N.Z. camps in England and of rabbits in N.Z.

Northallerton. (Rare in singular.) A spur : coll. : ca. 1790–1880. Grose, 3rd ed, ' That place, like Rippon, being famous for making them '.

northen-spell. A corrupt form of *knur(r) and spell* (a game) : C. 19–20. O.E.D.

Northern Glance, the. The Aurora Borealis : nautical coll. : mid-C. 19–20. Bowen. Presumably suggested by S.E. *Northern Lights.*

Northo. H.M.S. *Northumberland* : naval : C. 20. Bowen.

northo-rigger. Gen. pl., ' In the late Victorian and Edwardian Navy, ratings who had entered as youths instead of through the harbour training ships. Now seldom heard ', Bowen, 1927. Also *hurricane-jumper.*

Northumberland's arms, Lord. A black eye : mid-C. 17–20 : s. >, ca. 1680, dial. († except in Northumberland). Grose, 2nd ed. Either from the dark-colour fusils [i.e. light muskets] carried by the Percys' retainers or from the black and red predominant in the spectacles-resembling badge [1] of this powerful family (E.D.D.). [1. Note as relevant the heraldic sense of *fusil*.]

Norway neck-cloth. ' The pillory, usually made of Norway fir ', Grose, 1st ed. : ca. 1784–1830.

Norwegian house-flag. One of ' the windmill pumps that used to be compulsory in Norwegian sailing ships' : nautical : ca. 1850–1910. Bowen. I.e. as inevitable as a house-flag.

Norwicher. One who drinks too much from a shared jug, glass, etc., i.e. an unfair drinker : ca. 1860–1900. H., 3rd ed. ; *The Athenæum*, Aug. 15, 1896 (? relevant). (Not in E.D.D.) Origin obscure ; but see *Norfolk wiles* in the ' Cf.' part of *Norfolk turkey*. These territorial amenities are common enough (cf. *Yorkshire*).

*__*nose.__ An informer (1789, Parker : ' *Nose.* Snitch '), esp.—from ca. 1810—a paid spy (Vaux, 1812) : c. Often, from ca. 1870, *a policeman's nose* : contrast sense 3. Also *noser*, q.v.—**2.** Hence, a detective policeman, as in Greenwood's *Dick Temple*, 1877 : c. of ca. 1875–1910.—**3.** One who supplies information to criminals : c. : C. 20. Edgar Wallace, *The Clue of the New Pin*, 1923. Ex sense 1.

nose, v. (See entry imm. after **no.**—**2.** To bluster, to bully : this is a ' ghost ' sense fathered by Johnson and copied by (e.g.) Ash and Grose. See O.E.D.)—**3.** V.i., to inform to police ; to turn king's evidence : c. : from ca. 1810 ; ob. *Lex. Bal.*, ' His pal nosed, and he was twisted for a crack,' i.e. hanged for burglary. Cf. *nose upon*, q.v.—**4.** Hence, v.t., to spy on, keep under police observation ; to watch (a building) : c. : C. 20. Edgar Wallace *passim* : e.g. *Room 13.*

[**nose** phrases. Such as are not recorded hereinafter—and they are fairly numerous—are S.E. : see esp. F. & H. at IV, 67–9, and the O.E.D., at *nose*, 215–17.]

nose, at one's (very). Very close : from ca. 1520 : coll. and dial.

nose, † **candles** or **dewdrops in the.** Mucus depending from the nose : low : late C. 18–20.

nose !, follow your. A C. 17–20 c.p. ' said in a jeer to those that know not the way, and are bid to Smell it out ', B.E. ; Swift ; Grose. In C. 19–20, often *follow your nose, and you* (or *for it*) *can't go wrong.*

nose, good. A smell-feast : low coll. : late C. 17–20 ; ob. B.E.

nose, make a bridge of someone's. To pass him by in drinking : late C. 17–20 ; ob. Swift ; Grose, 1st ed.—**2.** Hence, to supersede : same period ; ob. Ray.

*nose, on the. Watching : o. (— 1839) >, ca. 1900, low s. ; ob. Brandon.

nose, parson's. See parson's nose. Cf. :

nose, recorder's. The rump of a fowl : coll. : ca. 1820–90. Westmacott, 1825. O.E.D.

nose, wipe (a person's). See at wipe.

nose and chin. A ' win ' (q.v.), i.e. a penny : low (orig. c.) rhyming s. of ca. 1855–1905. H., 1st ed.— 2. Gin : rhyming (— 1909). Ware. Cf. needle and pin.

nose-bag. Such a visitor as carries his own food : waiters ' : 1860, H., 2nd ed.—2. An hospitable hotel or boarding-house : middle classes' : late C. 19–20 ; ob. Ware. Cf. sense 1.—3. A bag holding food for human beings : 1925, P. G. Wodehouse (O.E.D. Sup.).—4. A veil : low : ca. 1865–1915.—5. Hence, a gas-mask : jocular military : 1915–18.—6. A hand-bag : from ca. 1885 ; ob. The Cornhill Magazine, April, 1887, ' So I yesterday packed up my nosebag, and away I posted down to Aldgate.' All these senses ex the S.E. one.

nose-bag, put on the. To eat either hurriedly or at work—or both. (Low) coll. : from ca. 1870. H., 5th ed. Ex the stables. Cf. nose in the manger, q.v.

nose-bag, straight from the. (Of news) reliable, authoritative : racing (— 1914) >, by 1915, military. F. & Gibbons. Cf. straight from the horse's mouth.

nose-bag in one's face, have the. To have been ' a private man, or rode private ', Grose, 2nd ed. : military : ca. 1780–1830. Ex S.E. nose-bag.

nose-bagger. A variant, from ca. 1865, of nose-bag, 1. Ware.

nose cheese first, see the. To refuse contemptuously : low : C. 19–20 ; ob.

nose-cough. A heavy breathing through the mouth on account of a stoppage in the nose : non-aristocratic (—1887). Baumann.

nose-dive. A snatch, a swoop, an attempt, as in ' 'E makes a nose-dive at me eats, but I donged 'im ' : Australian : from ca. 1919. Ex the nose-dive made by an aeroplane.

nose em. See nose my.

nose-ender. A straight blow on the nose : boxing : 1854, ' Cuthbert Bede '. Cf. noser.—2. A strong head-wind : nautical coll. : mid-C. 19–20. Bowen. Cf. muzzler, 3.

*nose-gent ; nosegent. A nun : c. : ca. 1565– 1830. Harman ; Grose, 1st ed. ? etymology.

nose in, shove one's. To interfere, interpose rudely : low coll. (— 1887). Baumann.

nose in the manger, have or put one's. To eat, esp. to eat heartily : coll. : from ca. 1860 ; ob. T. Hughes, 1861, Tom Brown at Oxford. Ex the stables.

nose is a lady's liking, a long. A low c.p. of C. 19– 20. Length of the male nose being held to denote a corresponding length elsewhere, as the size of a woman's mouth is supposed to answer to that of another part. F. & H., as for most of the ' anatomicals ' not marked ' Grose ' in this volume.

nose is always brown, his. A low c.p. applied, in C. 20, to a sycophant. Cf. arse-crawler.

nose itches !, my. A C. 18–20 c.p. invitation to kiss, the dovetail being either, as in Swift, ' I knew I should drink wine, or kiss a fool,' or, in C. 18–20, ' I knew I would shake hands with a fool,' or, in C. 19–20, ' I knew I was going to sneeze or to be cursed, or kissed, by a fool.'

nose my (' Ducange Anglicus ', 1857) is itself ex noser-my-knacker, q.v. : mid-C. 19–20 ; ob. Also nose em, nose 'm.

nose of. To cheat, swindle (a person) of (something) : ca. 1650–90. O.E.D. gives as S.E., but the O.E.D.'s quotations (Brome ; Brian, Piss-Prophet) indicate coll. Cf. :

nose of, wipe one's. To deprive or defraud (one) of (something) : late C. 16–mid-18. Again the O.E.D. gives as S.E. ; again I suggest coll. Bernard, 1598, ' " . . . Who wipes our noses of all that we should have ' ; Cibber, 1721, ' Thou wipest this foolish Knight's Nose of his Mistress at last ' (O.E.D.), which, by the way, recalls ' He'll wipe your son Peter's nose of Mistress Lelia ' in anon.'s Wily Beguiled, ca. 1606. Cf. nose-wiper, q.v.

nose of wax ; or waxen-nose († by C. 18). Anything, esp. any person, very pliable, exceedingly obliging or complaisant or easy-going : coll. verging on S.E. : ca. 1530–1830. Scott, 1815, ' I let . . . the constable . . . manage the business his ain gate, as if I had been a nose o' wax.' Apperson.

*nose on. To give information to the police about (a person) : c. : C. 20 (and prob. earlier). Edgar Wallace passim. Ex nose upon, q.v., or perhaps ex nose, v., 3.

nose-paint. Alcoholic drink : South Lancashire jocular s. (— 1905), not dial. E.D.D. (Sup.).

nose-rag. A pocket-handkerchief : from ca. 1835 : low. Haliburton. Cf. nose-wiper.

nose swell, make one's. To make a person jealous or envious : coll. : from ca. 1740 ; ob. State Trials, 1743, ' He heard Lord Altham say, . . . my wife has got a son, which will make my brother's nose swell,' O.E.D. Cf. the S.E. put one's nose out of joint, of which it is prob. a jocular elaboration, and the C. 18 (? S.E.) variant, make one's nose warp (Ray).

nose to light candles at, a. A (drunkard's) red nose : coll. : late C. 16–20 ; ob. Nashe. ' Their noses shall bee able to light a candle.'

nose up my arse !, your. An expression of the utmost contempt : mid-C. 19–20. Cf. the milder ask † mine or my arse !, q.v.

nose upon, v.t. To tell something of a person so that he be injured and, if possible, one's self profited : low coll. : from ca. 1810 ; ob. Vaux. Whence perhaps nose on, q.v.

nose-warmer. A short pipe : from ca. 1880.

*nose-watch. I ; me : c. of ca. 1570–1630. Cf. nibs (esp. my nibs), which affords a very significant analogy. Harman, ' Cut to my nose watch . . . say to me what thou wilt.' See watch.

nose well down(, with). In a great hurry : military coll. : C. 20. F. & Gibbons. Ex marching with head down.

nose-wipe. A pocket-handkerchief : low : from ca. 1820. Cf. nose-wiper, q.v.

nose-wipe, v.t. To cheat, deceive : coll. : ca. 1620–1750. Burton. (O.E.D.) Again, reluctantly, I differ from the O.E.D. as to status : cf. nose of, wipe the.

nose-wiper. A pocket-handkerchief : from ca. 1894. Lord C. E. Paget, 1895, ' Charged with my relay of nose-wipers, I was close to his Majesty on the steps of the throne,' O.E.D. Ex nose-wipe, n., q.v.

nosebag. See nose-bag.—nosegent. See nosegent.—nosender. See nose-ender.

nosegay. A blow on the nose : boxing : ca. 1820–50. Egan's Grose.—2. A warrant officer : naval (— 1923). Manchon.

Nosegay Nan. Mrs. Abington (1737–1815), the actress. Her name as a flower-girl. Dawson.

nosegay to him as long as he lives, it will be a. A mid-C. 17–early 18 semi-proverbial c.p. applied to one who has a very big and/or long nose. Ray, 1678. (Apperson.)

noser. ' A bloody or contused nose ', H., 1859 ; pugilistic ; very ob. Ex :—2. A blow on the nose : mostly boxing : from ca. 1850. Mayhew.—3. A strong head-wind : nautical coll. : from ca. 1850.—4. A paid spy : c. of ca. 1860–1910. *The Cornhill Magazine*, vol. II, 1862, ' There are a few men and women among thieves called nosers . . . They are in the secret pay of the police.' Ex *nose*, v.—5. One who inspects—esp. by smelling—fruit or flowers but does not buy : Covent Garden (—1909). Ware.—6. The nose-dive of an aeroplane : Air Force : 1914. B. & P. Ex sense 2.

noser-my-knacker. Tobacco (pronounced *tobakker*) : rhyming s. (— 1859). H., 1st ed.

nos(e)y. Inquisitive : from ca. 1906. Esp. *Nosey Parker*, a prying person (from not later than 1910) : hence *nosey-parkering*, inquisitive(ness).

nosper. A person : back s., low London (—1909). Ware.—2. Hence (—1909), a stranger. Ibid.

nosrap. A parson : back s. (— 1859). H., 1st ed.

nossall or -oll. A horse given to kicking and/or other vicious behaviour : London farriers' : late C. 19–20. Perhaps cf. dial. *nozzle*, to strike violently, to do things vigorously.

nosy. See nos(e)y.

not, either repeated or with another negative where only the one is understood : from C. 15 : S.E. till ca. 1665, then a vulg. when not dial.—2. With dependent clause omitted, as in E. P. Oppenheim, 1907, ' " She is coming back . . . ? " " The chambermaid thought not, sir " ' : coll. : prob. from as early as the 1890's. O.E.D. (Sup.). [not phrases. See the key n., adj., or adv. Cf., however, next few entries].

not all there. See there, all.—**not a sixpence to scratch with.** See scratch with.

not-class. Not first-rate : coll. (— 1887). Baumann.

not fucking likely. See abso-bloody-lutely.—**not likely !** See likely, not.—**not much !** See much !, not.

not half, adv. Much, very ; as in ' not half screwed, the gent was ! ' : (mostly Cockney) ironic coll. : C. 20.—2. As exclamation, esp. of emphatic assent ; as in ' " Did you like it ? "—" Not half ! " ' : id. : from ca. 1905. For both senses, see B. & P. and Lyell.

not if I am in orders for it ! A military c.p. of refusal : from ca. 1930. I.e. I wouldn't do it even if I were, in Daily Orders, instructed to do so.

not Jack out of doors nor yet gentleman. One not quite a gentleman ; one of ambiguous status : C. 17 semi-proverbial coll. John Clarke, 1639. (Apperson.)

not meant. (Of a horse) not intended to win : the turf : ca. 1860–1910. H., 3rd ed.

not out. See innings, have a long.

not so as (or that) **you'd notice.** See notice, not . . .

not so old nor yet so cold. A late C. 17–mid-18 semi-proverbial c.p. of doubtful and perhaps dubious meaning. Swift, *Polite Conversation*. (Apperson.)

not worth a . . . These similes all have a coll.—

several, indeed, a s.—ring. Some will be found at the key n., but for convenience I summarise Apperson's masterly forty, and add one :—**not worth a bands' end,** mid-C. 19–20 dial. ; **bean,** late C. 13–20, but in C. 19–20 only = penniless ; **button,** C. 14–20, ob ; **cherry,** late C. 14–15 ; **chip,** C. 17 ; **cobbler's curse,** late C. 19–20 dial. (cf. *tinker's curse*) ; **cress,** C. 14–15 ; ? hence, **curse,** C. 19–20 ; **dodkin, do(i)tkin,** or **doit,** from ca. 1660, ob. ; **fart,** C. 19–20, low ; **farthing,** C. 17–20 ; **fig,** C. 16–20 ; **flea,** C. 15–17 ; **fly,** late C. 13–20, ob. ; **gnat,** late C. 14–16 ; **gooseberry** (Shakespeare) ; **groat,** C. 16–early 19 ; **haddock,** C. 16 ; **hair,** early C. 17 ; **haw,** late C. 13–16 ; **hen,** late C. 14–mid-16 ; **herring** (cf. *haddock*), C. 13 ; **leek** or **two leeks,** C. 14–mid-17 ; **louse,** late C. 14–20, latterly dial. ; **needle,** C. 13–15 ; **nut,** late C. 13–mid-14 ; **pea** or **pease,** late C. 14–early 17 ; **pear,** C. 14–16 ; **pin,** from ca. 1530, ob. ; **point** or **blue point,** ca. 1540–1690 ; **potato** (Byron, ? nonce-use) ; **rush,** occ. **bulrush** or **two rushes** (cf. *leek*), mid-C. 14–20, ob. ; **sloe** (cf. *haw*), C. 13–14 ; **straw,** late C. 13–20 ; **tinker's curse,** mid-C. 19–20, orig. dial. ; **rotten apple,** mid-C. 15–early 16 ; **egg,** C. 15–19 ; **ivy leaf,** late C. 14–mid-15 ; **onion,** C. 16 ; **shoebuckles,** C. 17 ; **three halfpence,** mid-C. 17–early 18. (Apperson's *not worth hiring, who talks of tiring* is irrelevant ; and in late C. 19–20, *farthing* is gen. *brass farthing*.)

not worthy to. Most of these are to be found at the key vv. ; most of them deal with the tying of another person's shoe-laces or the cleaning of another's foot-wear, even as early as ca. 1410. See Apperson at **not worthy** : I go into no further detail here, for the phrases unrecorded herein are hardly unconventional.

notch. The female pudend : low coll. : late C. 18–20 ; ob. Grose, 1st ed. Cf. *nock*, q.v.

note. ' Intellectual signature, political war-cry ': Society coll. : from ca. 1860 ; ob. Ware quotes *The Daily News*, Nov. 18, 1884, ' Culture is the " note " of Boston'.

note, change one's. To tell a (very) different story : late C. 17–20 : coll. till ca. 1850, then S.E. Ex modulated singing.

*****note-blanker.** See jilter.

note-shaver. A usurious bill-discounter : commercial coll. (— 1902). Orig. U.S.

noter. A note-book : Harrow School : late C. 19–20. Oxford *-er*.

notergal wash ; occ abbr. to **n.** (or **N.**) **wash.** Grubbiness : lower classes' : 1857–ca. 80. Either ex *no wash at all* or ex *Nightingale wash*, Florence Nightingale having stated that a person could, if necessary, keep himself clean with a pint of water per day. Ware.

'nother. Another : slovenly, when not nursery, coll. : since when ? (Denis Mackail, *Summer Leaves*, 1934.)

nothing. See dance, neck, and say.—2. Ironically spoken it = something very considerable : coll., mostly Australian : late C. 19–20. C. J. Dennis.—3. Not at all ; certainly not : coll., orig. (— 1888) U.S., anglicised not later than 1910. E.g. ' Are you ill ? ' ' Ill, nothing ! ' (O.E.D. Sup.) Cf. *my foot !*

nothing, no. Nothing whatever : coll. : from the 1830's. *Harper's Magazine*, March, 1884, ' There is no store, no post-office, no sidewalked street,—no nothing.' Cf. the (— 1854) Northants dial. *a new nothing to hang on one's sleeve*, nothing at all. O.E.D. and Sup.

nothing below the waist. No fool : tailors' c.p. (— 1928). See the quotation at *rub about*.

nothing but. Nothing else ; *anything else but*, anything but, anything except. Both of C. 20 ; the former being coll., the latter catachrestic. E.g. John G. Brandon, *The One-Minute Murder*, 1934, ' As far as that poor devil's concerned . . . it's accident and nothing but,' i.e. nothing but an accident.

nothing but up and ride ? A semi-proverbial c.p. = Why, is it all over ? ; is that the end ? Ca. 1650–1750. Howell, 1659 ; Ray ; Fuller, 1732. Apperson.

nothing doing ! See **doing !, nothing.**

nothing in my young life. See **life, nothing** . . .

nothing like leather. A c.p. applied to anything that smacks—esp. if one-sided or tendentially—of the doer's or the speaker's trade (orig. that of a currier) : late C. 17–20. L'Estrange, 1692 ; Mrs. Gaskell, 1855. In C. 20, esp. from ca. 1929 and prompted by the competition of Uskide and its similars, the phrase has > a leather-sellers' and shoemakers' slogan, which has in its turn re-popularised the c.p. The anecdotal ' etymology ' is that a cobbler once extolled leather for its value in fortifications. Apperson ; W.

nothing on earth, feel (or look) like. To look or feel wretched or ill : coll. (— 1927) >, by 1933, S.E. (Collinson.)

nothing to do with the case ! That's a lie ! : a polite c.p. dating from W. S. Gilbert's *The Mikado*, March 14, 1885 ; ob., though we still, occ., hear the original, *The flowers that bloom in the spring, tra-la, have nothing to do with the case*, words sung with alluring vivacity by George Grossmith. Ware.

nothing to write home about. Unremarkable ; unusual ; mediocre : coll. : late C. 19–20. During the G.W., Australian soldiers preferred *nothing to table home about*.

nothing to make a song about. See **song about.**

nothink. See **-ink.**

notice, not so as (occ. **so that**) **you'd.** Not so much—or to such an extent—as to be noticeable : from ca. 1929. In addition to its being a c.p., the phrase is coll. by its very structure.

*****notice to quit.** Danger of dying, esp. from ill-health : from ca. 1820 : c. until ca. 1850, then coll. ; ob. Egan's Grose. Esp. *have notice to quit*, ' to have a fatal illness and to know that it is fatal ' (Lyell).

notion. A term or a custom peculiar to : Winchester College (— 1891). Wrench.

nottamizer. A dissecting surgeon : ca. 1825–60. Smeaton, 1828. Ex *atomy*.

Nottingham Hussars, the. The 45th Foot Regiment : military : ca. 1830–80. F. & Gibbons. They came from Nottinghamshire.

Nottingham lamb. See **lamb.**

nottub. A button : back s. : late C. 19–20. Ware.

nought. Anything : sol. : C. 18–20. Baumann, ' I don't see nought of him.'

nouns ! A C. 16–18 oath = (*God's*) *wounds* ; coll. Earliest as *Cock's* or *Od's nouns*, *nouns* by itself being unrecorded in print before 1608. O.E.D.

nourishment, sit up and take. To become alert or healthy after apathy or illness : from ca. 1890 : coll. till ca. 1920, then jocular S.E. Ex the sick-room + S.E. *take notice*, (esp. of babies) ' to show signs of intelligent observation ', Dickens, 1846 (O.E.D.).

nous. Intelligence ; esp. common sense : coll. :

1706, Baynard, ' A Demo-brain'd Doctor of more Note than Nous ', O.E.D. ; 1729, Pope, who, as still sometimes happens, writes it in Gr. characters (νοῦς) ; Barham ; Reade. ' Curiously common in dial.', W. Ex the Gr. philosophic sense of mind or intellect, as in Cudworth, 1678.—2. App., ca. 1820–40, it = uppishness. Bee ; therefore London fashionable s.—3. Ex sense 1, the rare *nous*, to understand : from ca. 1858 ; ob. H., 1st ed.

nous-box. The head : 1811, *Lex. Bal.* : s. >, ca. 1880, coll. ; ob. Ex preceding.

nouse. Wolcot's and H.'s spelling—which has no justification—of *nous*, q.v.

nova. Nine, gen. in sums of money : from ca. 1890, but much less gen. than *nobba*, q.v. : Parlyaree. P. H. Emerson, 1893. Ex It. *nova*.

Nova Scotian pump. ' A bucket with a line attached to draw water from overside, referring to the hard work in Nova Scotian ships ' : nautical : late C. 19–20. Bowen. Cf the next three entries.

Nova Scotian soda. Sand and canvas supplied, instead of soda, for cleaning paint-work : nautical : late C. 19–20. Bowen. Cf. *Nova Scotian towing.*

Nova Scotian sun(-light). The moon(-light) : nautical : late C. 19–20. Bowen. A moonlight night being, in a hard-worked Nova Scotian ship, considered as opportune for some job, by the men deemed unnecessary.

Nova Scotian towing. ' Towing a boat with the dories out forward, to save expense of a tug ' : Grand Banks fishermen's : late C. 19–20. Bowen. Cf. the preceding three entries.

novelty, the, the female pudend, C. 18–20 (ob.). may be euphemistic S.E.

novi. (Pl., **novis.**) A new boy : several English Public Schools' : late C. 19–20. Ex L. *novi* (*homines*), the newcomers, the new-rich.

now. Really, truly, indeed : coll. : mid-C. 19–20. E.g. R. Keverne, *Menace*, 1935, ' " I damned near went to my own funeral." " Did you now ? " said Mr. Harris with zest.'

now or never. Clever : rhyming s. (— 1909). Ware.

now then, only another nineteen shillings and eleven pence three farthings to make up the pound before I begin the service. A military c.p., from ca. 1908, by ' anyone desirous of raising a loan or of starting a " bank ",' B. & P.

now then, shoot those arms out ! You wouldn't knock the skin off a rice-pudding ! A drill-sergeants', esp. a physical-training instructors', c.p. : from ca. 1910. B. & P.

now we shall be sha'n't. A jocular perversion of *now we sha'n't be long* : a non-aristocratic c.p. : Dec., 1896–ca. 1900. Ware.

now we sha'n't be long. See **sha'n't be long.**

now we're busy ! A c.p. implying action : 1868 : ob. Ware, ' Also an evasive intimation that the person spoken of is no better for his liquor, and is about to be destructive ' : a c.p. dating from the 1880's ; † by 1920.

nowhere, be. To be badly beaten, hopelessly out-distanced : 1755. From ca. 1820, often figurative. In gen. use from ca. 1850 ; in C. 20, coll. (O.E.D.) J. Greenwood, 1869, ' The brave Panther when he has once crossed the threshold of that splendid damsel . . . is, vulgarly speaking, nowhere.' Contrast the U.S. sense, utterly at a loss, completely ignorant.

nowheres. See **somewheres.**

nozzle. The nose: mainly pugilistic: **1755**, Johnson (E.D.D.); Grose, 1st ed.; Meredith, in *Harry Richmond*, ' Uncork his claret . . . ; straight at the nozzle.' Ex S.E. sense, a small spout, etc., the word itself being a diminutive of *nose*.

nozzle, v.t. To shrink (gen. clothes): tailors': from ca. 1870; ob. Prob. ex steaming-process.— 2. Hence, to pawn: also tailors': from ca. 1875.

nozzler. A blow, esp. a punch, on the nose: mostly pugilistic: 1828 (O.E.D.).

n^{th}, esp. **to the nth (or n^{th} plus one or 1).** To the utmost: loosely, exceedingly: 1852, Smedley, ' Minerva was . . . starched to the nth,' O.E.D.: coll. till. ca. 1910, then S.E.: largely, university and scholastic. Less gen. (except in S.E., i.e. lit. usage), *n^{th} power, n^{th} degree.*

[**nu-** terms listed wrongly by F. & H. are these :— S.E., **numps** (a dolt), **numskull(ed), nuncle, nup(son),** nurse (wet-nurse; the billiards v.), **nut** (the pope's eye), **nut-hook, nut to crack, nuts** (small round coals). Dial.: **nut,** a harum-scarum ass.]

***nub.** The neck: c.: ca. 1670–1830. Coles, 1676; B.E.; Grose, 1st ed. Extant, though very ob., in East Anglian dial. as the nape of the neck (E.D.D.). Perhaps cognate with dial. sense, knob; but cf. the app. earlier v., to hang.—2. (? hence,) the gallows: c.: late C. 17–early 19. B.E.—3. Copulation: c.: C. 18–early 19. *A New Canting Dict.*, 1725. ? ex dial. sense, a protuberance: cf., however, the C. 18–20 dial. v. (see e.g. Grose's *Provincial Glossary*), to jog or shake.—4. A husband: c. > low s.: late C. 18–19. H., 2nd ed. Either ex preceding sense or ex *an hub*.

***nub,** v.t. To hang (a person) by the neck: c. of ca. 1670–1840. Head; Fielding. ? origin, the earliest dates of n. and v. being somewhat hazy.

***nubbing,** vbl.n. Hanging: c.: ca. 1670–1840. Coles; implied in Head's *nubbing-cheat*. B.E., Grose.—2. Sexual intercourse: mid-C. 18–early 19: c. Grose. Ex *nub,* n., 3.

***nubbing-cheat**: occ., in C. 19, **-chit.** The gallows: c.: ca. 1670–1840, then only as an archaism. Head, B.E., Grose, Maher, ca. 1812 (*nubbing-chit*), Ainsworth. Cf. *nubbling-chit.* See **cheat, chete.** F. & H. gives a brave synonymy: e.g. *Beilby's ball-room, crap, hanging-cheat, (the) queer-'em, (the) stifler, Tyburn cross, wooden-legged mare,* qq.v.

***nubbing-cove.** The hangman: c.: mid C. 17– early 19. Coles, 1676; B.E.; Grose. See **nubbing, 1.**

***nubbing-ken.** The sessions-house: c. of mid C. 17–early 19. Coles; B.E.; Grose.

***nubbling-chit.** A corrupt, rare variant of *nubbing-chit* (see **nubbing-cheat**): C. 19 only. Martin & Aytoun in their picaresque *Bon Gaultier Ballads,* 1841.

nubbly. Smutty: late C. 19–20; ob. Galsworthy, *The Silver Spoon,* 1926, ' He spent some time in making a list of what George Forsyte would have called the " nubbly bits ".' An extension of sense ex S.E. *nubbly,* knobby.

nucloid. A reserve ship with only a *nucleus* crew: naval officers': ca. 1890–1910. Bowen.

nuddikin. The head: low: C. 19–20; ob. H., 2nd ed. Also *noddleken.* Cf. dial. *noddle-box.*

nudil is a C. 17–18 error for *nodule.* O.E.D.

nuff. Enough, esp. in *to have had one's nuff,* to have had enough, i.e. more than enough, drink; to be drunk: military: ca. 1880–1910.

nuff ced or **said.** See **n.c.**

***nug.** An endearment, gen. with *my (dear):* **c.:** late C. 17–early 19. B.E. Ex:

***nug,** v. To fondle; to coït with, though occ. v.i. F. & H. The word is very rare in print, but it is implied in *nugging-dress* and *-house,* qq.v. C. of late C. 17–mid-19. ? a corruption of *nudge*: cf. dial. *nug,* to nudge, jog with the elbow, knock or strike (E.D.D.).

nugget. A thick-set young beast (esp. heifer or calf): Australian, mostly rural: from ca. 1850: coll. >, ca. 1890, S.E. Mundy's *Antipodes,* 1852 (O.E.D.). Often *a good nugget* (Morris).—2. Hence, a short, thick-set person: Australian coll.: from ca. 1890. Often as a nickname. This usage is paralleled in late C. 19–20 Eng. dial. Ex shape. Cf. *nuggety,* q.v.—3. Any boot-polish: Australian coll.: from ca. 1910. Ex the specific brand of boot-polish.

nugget, v. (Gen. v.t.) To appropriate (usually one's neighbour's) unbranded calves: Australian s. >, ca. 1900, gen. Australian s. Mrs. C. Praed, 1885 (O.E.D.); R. M. Praed, 1887. Ex *nugget,* n., 1. (Whence vbl.n., *nuggeting*: 1887.)

nuggets. Money, esp. cash: coll.: from ca. 1890; ob. Milliken, 1892.

nuggety. Thick-set, esp. if short: Australian: from ca. 1885: coll. >, ca. 1905, S.E. *The Daily News,* April 9, 1887. Ex *nugget,* n., 1.

***nugging,** vbl.n. Sexual intercourse: late C. 17– mid-19 c. Mainly in next four.

***nugging-cove.** A fornicator: C. 18–mid-19 c. Ex *nug,* v., q.v.

***nugging-dress.** An odd or exotic dress; esp. a loose dress affected by, and characteristic of, harlots: late C. 17–mid-19: c. B.E.; Grose, 1st ed. Cf.:

***nugging-house.** A brothel: c.: mid-C. 18– mid-19. Grose, 1st ed. Ex *nug,* v.

***nugging-ken.** The same: c.: mid-C. 18–early 19. Ex *nug,* v.

***null.** To strike, beat, thrash: c. of ca. 1780– 1870. Grose, 1st ed. Ex S.E. *annul.*

***null-groper.** One who sweeps the streets in search of nails, old iron, etc.: c. of ca. 1820–60. Egan's Grose. Prob. *nail-groper* perverted.

Nulli Secundus Club. The Coldstream Guards: military: ca. 1880–1914.

***nulling-cove.** A boxer: ca. 1810–1910: **c.** >, ca. 1850, pugilistic s. Vaux. Ex *null,* q.v.

***Numans.** Newgate: C. 17 c. Rowlands. I.e. *New + mans* (q.v.) Later *Newmans, Newman's,* q.v.

[**Number.** For wrong use of, in pronouns, see e.g. **their, them, they.**]

number. A bed-room in hotel or large boardinghouse: coll.: C. 20. O.E.D. (Sup.). Ex the fact that it has one.

***Number Nine** or **9.** The Fleet Prison: c. of ca. 1820–50. Bee. It was situated at No. 9, Fleet Market.—2. Occ. abbr. of:

number nine (or **9**) **king.** A medical officer: military: 1915; ob. Ex *number nine,* the standard purgative pill, given to all and sundry. See B. & P. at *sick,* p. 161. Cf. *the doctor* (q.v.) in the game of house.

number nip. The female pudend: low: C. 19– 20; ob.

number of one's mess, lose the. See **lose the number.—number on.** See **name on.**

number one. One's self or one's own interests, esp. in *look after,* or *take care of, number one.* C. 18– 20: S.E. until C. 19, then coll. T. Pitt, in *Diary,* 1704–5 (O.E.D.); Dickens; *Judy,* July 29, 1871,

'If a man doesn't take care of No. 1, he will soon
have 0 to take care of.' Cf. *one*, 1.—2. Urination ;
occ., a chamber-pot : children's : late C. 19–20.
Manchon, 'I want to do number one.' Cf. *number two*, 1.—3. The cat-o'-nine-tails ; punishment
therewith : prison j. and prison c. (— 1889) ; ob.
Cf. *number two*, 2.—4. The first lieutenant : naval
(— 1909). Ware.—5. See **number ones**.—6. A
close crop of the hair, according to Service regulation : military coll. : 1915. F. & Gibbons.—7. For
the Fenian sense, see **A/1**, 2.—8. (Cf. sense 3.) ' No.
1 diet, with close confinement,' George Ingram,
(*Stir*), 1933 : prisoners' c. : from ca. 1920.

number one (or **1**) **chow-chow**. (Of a meal)
exceptionally good ; (of an object), utterly worthless : Anglo-Indian coll. (— 1882). Yule & Burnell.
See **chow-chow**.

number one (or **1**)**, London,**—**be at**. To have the
menstrual discharge : low : mid-C. 19–20 ; ob.
Cf. *number one*, 2.

number ones. A seaman's best uniform :
naval : late C. 19–20. Bowen.

number six. See **Newgate knocker**.—**number
sixes**. See **sixes**.

number two. Defecation : nursery : late C. 19–
20. Cf. *number one*, 2.—2. The birch : prison j.
and prison c. : from ca. 1885 ; ob. Cf. *number
one*, 3.

number up, have one's. To be in trouble ; dead :
military : C. 20.—2. *one's number is up*, however, =
he won't live (being destined for death) or, less often,
he is sure to be detected : the former a gen. coll. ;
the latter, military s. : C. 20. B. & P., p. 338.

number was dry !, before your. A military c.p. of
1915–18. (F. & Gibbons.) See **nipped !, before you**.
I.e. before the ink first used to write down his regimental number had dried.

numbers, by. In an orderly, indeed somewhat too
' regimental ', manner : military coll. : late C. 19–
20. Ex drilling by numbers, esp. instructions to
recruits.

numbers, consult the book of. To call for a
division, put the matter to the vote : Parliamentary :
ca. 1780–1850. Grose, 1st ed. Cf. (*the*) *book of
words*. Ex the Biblical Book of Numbers, which
contains a census of the Israelites (W.).

numbers the waves, he. (Other persons, rare.)
He wastes his time or engages in an impossible task :
late C. 18–mid-19 semi-proverbial c.p. Ray, 1813.
(Apperson.)

[Numerals are coll. **in** *a twelve*, *a fifteen* (etc.), a
motor-car of 12, 15 h.p. : motorists' and motor-
trade's : from ca. 1910. (Richard Blaker's novel of
a garage, *Night-Shift*, 1934.)]

***numms, nums**. A dickey ; a clean collar on a
dirty shirt : late C. 17–early 19 c. B.E., Deane
Swift on Dean Swift, 1755 (O.E.D.) ; Grose, 1st ed.
? etymology.

nun. A courtesan ; a harlot : from ca. 1770, ob. :
S.E. >, ca. 1810, coll. or s. Foote, Egan. (Perhaps much earlier : see **nunnery**.) Cf. *abbess*.

nunky (occ. **nunkey**) ; **nunks**. Coll. forms of †
S.E. *nuncle*, an uncle : resp. late C. 18–20 ; from
ca. 1840 (ob.). Charlotte Smith, 1798, ' Old nunky
looks upon you as still belonging to him ' (O.E.D.) ;
The Comic Almanack, 1841, ' Come, nunks, one
game at Blindman's-buff.'—2. A Jew more or less
a money-lender : lower classes' (— 1923). Manchon. Cf. *uncle*, q.v.

nunnery. A brothel : late C. 16–20 ; ob. : S.E.
till ca. 1780, then s. Nashe ; Fletcher, in *The Mad

Lover, 1617 (O.E.D.) ; Grose, 1st ed. ; Egan. Cf.
nun, q.v.

***nunquam**. A very dilatory messenger : c. : ca.
1560–1620. Awdelay. Ex L. *numquam*, never.
Cf. S.E. *numquid*, an inquisitive person.

nuntee (or **-y**). An occ. variant of *nantee*.

nunyare. Edibles ; a meal : Parlyaree : from
ca. 1855. A corruption of *mungaree*, q.v. Ex It.
mangiare, to eat. Mayhew, *London Labour*, iii,
201.

nuppence. No money : from ca. 1885 ; ob. Ex
no pence after *tuppence*.

Nuremberg egg. A watch, egg-shaped : C. 16–
early 18 : coll. Invented there.

nurse. An old man's maid-*cum*-mistress : low
coll. : C. 19–20 ; ob.—2. A capable first lieutenant
' nursing ' a figure-head captain : naval coll. : ca.
1800–40. Smyth.

nurse, v. To cheat (gen. *out of*) : either c. or s. :
from ca. 1780 ; ob. Grose, 1st ed.—2. (Of trustees)
to eat up property : from ca. 1858. H., 1st ed.
Cf. *nurse, be at*, q.v.—3. To cheat a rival company's omnibus of passengers by keeping close to
it ; gen. by having one bus before, one behind :
1858 : omnibus drivers' and ticket-collectors'.—4.
To hinder a horse in a race by hemming it in with
slower ones : the turf : from ca. 1892. P. H.
Emerson, 1893.

nurse, be at. To be in the hands of (esp. dishonest) trustees : ca. 1780–1840. Grose. (Cf.
nurse, v., 2, q.v.) Gen. of the estate.

Nurse Nokes. James Nokes, a C. 17 actor. Ex a
famous role. Dawson.

nursed in cotton, be. To be brought up very, or
too, tenderly : late C. 18–mid-19 coll. Ray, 1813.
(Apperson.)

nursery. A race for two-year-olds : the turf :
from ca. 1882. Coll. till C. 20, then S.E.—2. **the
nursery**, the female pudend : low : C. 19–20 ; ob.

nursery business. The playing of successive
cannons : billiards : from ca. 1890. (As a series of
cannons made by keeping the balls close together,
nursery is S.E.)

nursery noodle. A very fastidious critic :
literary : ca. 1900–14. Ware.

nurse's vail. A nurse's petticoats wet with
urine : low : C. 19–20 ; ob. by 1890 ; virtually † by
1920. Punning *vail*, a gratuity.

nursey, nursie. A coll., mainly children's, form
of *nurse*, n. : from ca. 1810. (O.E.D.).

nut. The head : 1858, Mayhew, ' Jack got a
cracker '—a ' heavy punch—' on his nut.'—2.
Hence, brains, intelligence : 1888, J. Runciman ;
ob.—3. A person : coll. : 1887, Manville Fenn, ' He
is a close old nut,' (O.E.D. : slightly ob. Esp. *an old
nut* ; cf. *a silly chump* (W.).—4. A ' tough ' youth :
Australian s. or coll. : 1882, A. J. Boyd, ' He is a
bully, a low, coarse, blasphemous blackguard—
what is termed a regular Colonial nut ' ; ob.
O.E.D. Cf. the Staffordshire dial. sense, a hard-
headed fellow, and the Yorkshire one : a troublesome, disobedient boy (E.D.D.).—5. Whence, a
dare-devil : Australian : from ca. 1895. (Morris).
Esp. *the nut*.—6. A dandy, esp. if in a cheap way :
from late 1903 ; ob., except as *knut*, *k-nut*. Cf.
filbert, q.v. Prob. ex *nutty*, 3, q.v.—7. A drink,
esp. of liquor : low : from ca. 1898 ; ob.—8. A
present ; an action designed to please : c. or low s. :
ca. 1810–50. Vaux. Cf. *nut*, v., 1.—9. **the Nut**.
The Keppel's Head inn at Portsmouth : naval
(— 1891). Ex *nut*, n., 1.—10. See **nuts**.

nut, v. To curry favour with ; to court, to ogle : ca. 1810–90 : ? orig. c. Vaux. Cf. *nut, n.*, 8, and *nuts*, 1.—2. To punch on the head, gen. v.t. : boxing : from ca. 1870 ; ob. Ex *nut, n.*, 1.

nut, crack a. To drink a (gen. silver-mounted) coco-nut shell full of claret : Scots coll. : ca. 1820–80. Scott ; *Notes and Queries*, 1889 (7 S., viii, 437).

nut, do one's. See **do one's nut.**

nut, off one's. Crazy : 1873, Miss Braddon (O.E.D.). Ex *nut, n.*, 1.—2. In liquor, drunk : low : 1860, H., 2nd ed. ; ob. by 1910, † by 1930.

nut, sweet as a. See **sweet as a nut.**

nut, work one's. To think hard ; to scheme : orig. (— 1902), dial. ; >, ca. 1905, s., esp. in Australia. Also *work one's head* : cf. *head-worker*. Cf. *nut out*, q.v.

nut at, be a. To be extremely good at (e.g. a game) : from ca. 1900. Whence *nut*, a dandy.

nut-crack. Nut-crackers (the instrument) : from ca. 1570 : S.E. till C. 19, then low coll. (S.O.D.)

Nut-Crack Night. Hallowe'en : coll. (C. 18–19) and dial. (C. 18–20 ; ob.). Brand, 1777. Because nuts were, in C. 18, flung into the fire. O.E.D.

nut-cracker. The head ; hence a sharp blow thereon : boxing : from ca. 1870 ; ob. Ex *nut, n.*, 1.—In the pl. :—2. A pillory : coll. : late C. 17–early 19. B.E. ; Grose, 1st ed. ? ex the shape.—3. The fists : boxing : from ca. 1870 ; ob. Ex *nut-cracker*, q.v.—4. A curved nose and protuberant chin : C. 19–20 (ob.) : coll. Ex S.E. *nut-cracker* as adj. describing ' the appearance of nose and chin . . . produced by the want of teeth ' (O.E.D.).—5. The teeth : coll. : C. 19–20.—6. The 3rd Foot Regiment : military : ' from the Peninsular War, and, according to tradition, with special reference to the Buffs at Albuera [1811] ', F. & Gibbons. *Chambers's Journal*, Dec. 23, 1871.

nut-cut. Roguish, mischievous : ca. 1860–1914. H., 3rd ed. (' Anglo-Indian '). Cf. *nut, n.*, 6.

nut 'em. Mostly as *nutted 'em !*, an exclamatory c.p. when the pennies turn up two heads in ' two-up ' : Australian and New Zealand : C. 20. Ex *nut*, the head.

nut out. To consider ; work out : military from ca. 1908. F. & Gibbons, ' I've got to nut it out.' Prob. ex *nut, n.*, 2, and *nut, work one's*, qq.v.

nut-rock, adj. and n. (A) bald (person) : lower classes' (— 1935). A ' nut ' bare as a rock.

nut-worker. A schemer ; a shirker ; a malingerer : military : from ca. 1906. F. & Gibbons. Ex *nut, work one's.*

nutting, vbl.n. Ogling ; paying of court ; currying of favour : ca. 1810–90. See **nut, v.**, 1.

nutmegs. The human testicles : low coll. : C. 17–20 ; ob. Grose, 1st ed. Cf. *nuts, n.*, 2, and *apples.*

nuts. A delightful thing, practice, experience : from ca. 1589 (Apperson) : S.E. until ca. 1780, then coll. until ca. 1850, then s. ; ob. Fletcher, Cotton, Lamb, Milliken. (O.E.D.) Almost an adj., as in Grose, 1st ed., ' It was nuts for them ; i.e. it was very agreeable to them.' (A particularly good example occurs in Head & Kirkman, 1674, ' It was honey and nuts to him to tell the guests,' Apperson.) Prob. ex C. 16 *nuts to*, an enticement to, ' recorded in

a letter from Sir Edward Stafford to Burghley (1587) ', W. Cf. *nut, v.*, 2, q.v.—2. The (gen. human) testicles : low coll. : late C. 18–20. Perhaps suggested by the † S.E. sense, the *glans penis*.—3. Barcelona Tramway shares : Stock Exchange : from ca. 1900. Ex *Barcelona nut.*

nuts, adj. Crazy : orig. (ca. 1905), U.S. ; anglicised, thanks mainly to ' the talkies ', in 1929. Ex *off one's nut*, 1 (see above).

nuts, for. (Always with a negative, actual or implied.) At all : coll. : 1895, W. Pett Ridge in *Minor Dialogues ;* 1899, *The Times*, Oct. 25, ' They can't shoot for nuts ; go ahead ' (O.E.D.)

nuts on or **upon, be.** To set high value upon ; be devoted to ; fond of or delighted with (person or thing) : 1785, Grose : *on* not before ca. 1840 ; *upon* rare after ca. 1870. *Punch*, 1882 (LXXII, 177), ' I am nuts upon Criminal Cases, Perlice News, you know, and all that.'—2. Hence, to be very clever or skilful at : from ca. 1880.—3. Hence, to detest : 1890, *Punch*, Feb. 22. Ex cleverness or skill directed *against* some person or thing. Cf. :

nuts on or **upon, be dead.** The same as the preceding in all three senses : from ca. 1890, though 1894 is the earliest O.E.D. record. Orig. an intensive, it >, by 1910, merely the more gen. form of *be nuts on.* Anticipated in 1873 by William Black's ' My aunt is awful nuts on Marcus Aurelius.'

nutted, ppl.adj. Deceived or tricked by a friend : low : from ca. 1860 ; ob. H., 2nd ed. Ex *nut, v.*, 2, possibly influenced by sense 1, and *nuts*, 1.—2. See **nut 'em.**

nutty. Amorous ; with (*up*)*on*, fond of, in love with, enthusiastic about : 1821, Egan, ' He was so nutty upon the charms of his fair one.' Slightly ob. Ex *nuts on, to be*, q.v.—2. Not quite right in the head : *The Pall Mall Gazette*, May 27, 1901 (O.E.D.). Semantically ex sense 1 : cf. S.E. *be mad about a girl*. (In Glasgow, since ca. 1920, it has had the nuance, ' romantic ', as Alastair Baxter, the begetter of *A Survey of the Occult*, 1936, tells me.)—3. Spruce ; smartly dressed or turned out : 1823, Byron (of a girl), ' So prim, so gay, so nutty, and so knowing ' ; ob. Perhaps ex *nuts*, 1, q.v. ; cf. *nut, n.*, 6.—4. Whence, agreeable : ca. 1890–1920. Milliken, 1893, ' Life goes on nutty and nice.'—5. Spicy ; piquant : 1894, Sala in *London up to Date*, ' The case, he incidentally adds, promises to be a nutty one ' ; slightly ob. Ex the nuts in a cake via the idea of fullness of detail.—6. Dandyish : 1913 (S.O.D.). Ex *nut, n.*, 6.—7. (**Nutty.**) The inevitable nickname of men surnamed Cox : naval and military : late C. 19–20. F. & Gibbons. Prob. ex sense 3 or sense 4, but perhaps ex *nuts, n.*, 2, by indelicate association.

*nux. The object in view ; the ' lay ' or ' game ' : c., orig. and mainly North Country : from ca. 1860 ; ob. H., 3rd ed. ? ex L. *nux*, a nut, hence a nut to crack.

*nygle. See **niggle.**—**nym.** See **nim.**

[**nymph of darkness** or **the pavement.** A harlot : euphemistic S.E. But *nymph of the pave*, recorded by H. in 1859, is s. († by 1890).]

nyp. See **nip.**—**Nyp Shop.** See **Nip Shop, the.**—**nypper.** See **nipper.**

O

[Under **o**, F. & H. lists the following ineligibles.
S.E. :—**oaf** (a lout), **oafdom, oafish ; oar,** oarsman ;
ocean greyhound ; October (ale) ; **odd** (strange),
odd man out, oddity, odds ; odour (repute) ; **off,** in
cricket ; **off-chance ; ogle,** to examine, consider,
and corresponding **ogler ; oil (of man)** and **oil,** to
flatter ; **old shoe ; old song ; old trot ; old woman**
(a man of womanly habits) ; **olive branches,**
children ; **Oliver, give a Roland for an ; omnibus,**
a man of all work ; **open house ; oppidan ;**
opiniator ; optic, an opera- or spy-glass ; **optime ;**
organ-pipes (in dress-making) ; **orifice** (the female
pudend) ; **ornament** (the same) ; **out,** in cricket and
in politics ; **stand out ; out and out,** adv. and adj. ;
out-Herod ; out of countenance, cry, (at) elbows,
(of) frame, hand, heart, (at) heel, (of) pocket,
temper, out of the way (uncommon ; see, however,
c. sense) ; **outer** (in rifle-shooting) ; **outrider,** a
highwayman ; **outsider,** an ignorant or a person
unattached or (virtually) unknown ; **overdo ; overs,**
amount in excess ; **overscutched** or **overswitched** or
overwhipped housewife, a whore ; **owl,** a person
much about at night ; **owl,** to sit up at night ; **owl-**
light, dusk. Dial. :—**outing** (an apprentice's coming of journeyman age).]

o or **O.** Overseer : printers' (— 1909). Ware.

o', preposition ; in C. 16–17, occ. **o.** Of : late
C. 16–20 : S.E. until C. 19, then coll. and dial.
Shakespeare ; Browning, 1864, ' Just a spirt | O' the
proper fiery acid ' (O.E.D.), though here it is prob.
to be considered poetic licence. Esp. in *o'clock,*
John o' Groats, Jack o' lantern. ' Formerly in many
others, as *Inns o' Court, man o' war, Isle o' Wight,*
but in these *of* is now usually written, even when *o'*
is familiarly pronounced . . . It is usual in the
representation of dialectal or vulgar speech,'
O.E.D.—2. On, as in *o' nights* : M.E. onwards :
S.E. till ca. 1810, then coll. and dial. W. A.
Wallace, 1890, ' He went to church twice o' Sundays.' O.E.D.

-o was orig. incorrect in such words from Sp. and
It. as *ambuscado, bastinado, salvo* (of artillery). W.
—2. A frequent adj.-ending among Britishers and
Americans in Paraguay and the Argentine, owing to
the influence of Sp. ; e.g. *tremendo,* tremendous.
See C. W. Thurlow Craig, *passim.* —3. As a suffix-
tag (e.g. in *all alive-o*), it is a C. 19–20 coll. derivative ex the metre-tag common in songs. Often
jocular or affectionate, as in *on his owny-o.* See,
e.g., **all alive-o, billy-o, loggo.**

O.A. (Gen. pl.) An old Alleynian : Dulwich
College coll. : late C. 19–20. Collinson.

O.B., the. The Old Bailey : policemen's s., and
c. : mid-C. 19–20. Ware.—2. Oscar Browning, the
Cambridge historian and famous, eccentric don
(1837–1923) : Cambridge University : from ca.
1880 ; ob.

o (or **oh**) **be easy,** sing. ' To appear contented
when one has cause to complain, and dare not ',
Grose, 3rd ed. Coll. : ca. 1785–1830.

o (or, more gen, **oh**) **be joyful.** A bottle of rum :
nautical : ca. 1850–1910. H., 3rd ed.—2. Earlier
(— 1823), of brandy or any other good liquor ; † by
1860. Egan's Grose.

' **o** (or **oh**) **be joyful ' on the other side of his mouth,**
make one sing. (Gen. **I'll make you . . . your**
mouth.) A c.p. threat : mid-C. 18–early 19.
Grose, 2nd ed.

o-be-joyful works. A public-house : late C. 19–
early 20.

o begga me, ex the alternative **o Bergami !**
You're a liar ! : London lower classes' : ca. 1820–
30. Ex Bergami, a lying Italian witness at Queen
Caroline's trial. Ware. Cf. *non me.*

O.C. Grease. The master cook : military : from
ca. 1915. Cf. :

O.C. Swills. The Controller of Salvage ; any
Salvage Corps officer : military : G.W. (F. & Gibbons.)

O.D. An ordinary seaman : nautical : **C.** 20
Bowen. (Cf. *ord.*) Whence :

O.D.'s delight. German sausage : nautical :
C. 20. Ibid.

o.d.v. or **O.D.V.** Brandy : jocular (— 1887) :
virtually †. I.e. *eau-de-vie.* Baumann.

o.k. ; gen. **O.K.** All right ; correct ; safe ; suitable ; what is required ; comfortable, comfortably
placed : orig. U.S. s. ; >, ca. 1880, Eng. s. and ca.
1895, Eng. coll. (For its use by ' the great Vance ',
see Addenda.) Thornton records it at 1828 and
gives an anticipation (likewise by Andrew Jackson)
at 1790 : but on these two instances the O.E.D.
throws icy water and gives 1840 as the date. It
either = *oll* (or *orl*) *korrekt* (or *k'rect*) or is a Western
U.S. error for *order recorded* (Thornton inclines to
the latter origin) ; or again—the fashionable (but
not the O.E.D. Sup.'s) view of the 1930's—it may
represent the Choctaw (*h*)*oke*, it is so, for Jackson
presumably knew the Choctaw word and it was his
opponents who, wishing to capitalise his well-known
illiteracy, imputed (so it is held) the *orl k'rect* origin
to the phrase's first user. *The Graphic,* March 17,
1883, ' It was voted O.K., or all correct ' ; 1889,
Answers (No. 56), ' John Jenkins . . . was O.K.
with Matilda Ann at Williams Street ' ; the label
on bottles of Mason's ' O.K.' Sauce—cf. *oke,* q.v.
(Such fanciful etymologies as *aux Cayes* and *och aye !*
can be summarily dismissed ; *o.k.* is an evergreen
of the correspondence column.)

o.k. ; O.K., v.i. and, more gen., v.t. To pass as
correct : orig. (— 1885), U.S. ; anglicised as a coll.
ca. 1900. E.g. *to o.k. an account, a document.*

O.K., baby ! An American c.p. partly anglicised
in 1932. See, e.g., letter in *The Daily Mirror,* Nov. 7,
1933.

O.K. by me !, it's. I agree, or approve : an
Americanism anglicised by 1933.

O my. See **my !,** 2.

o.p. ; O.P. Opposite the prompter. (Cf. *p.s.,*
prompt side.) Theatrical s. (— 1823) >, ca. 1870,
coll. >, ca. 1900, j. Both in Egan's Grose, 1823.—
2. Earlier (ca. 1809–20, though recorded later), **old**
price(s), in reference to ' the demonstrations at
Covent Garden Theatre, London, in 1809, against
the proposed new tariff of prices ', O.E.D. Byron
alludes to it in a letter of June 12, 1815, to Moore.—
3. (Of spirits) over-proof : j. when lit. ; when fig.,
it is coll., as—to borrow from the O.E.D.—in
Walch, *Head over Heels,* 1874, ' " Pshaw ", cried
Sandy (Clan MacTavish) in his beautiful O.P.
Scotch ',—which, you'll admit, is neat, as well as
being adumbratory of the 1933–4 *mot,* ' What
matter if your English be bad so long as your
Scotch is good ! '—4. The booksellers' use of the
term for ' out of print ' dates from ca. 1870 : j.
rather than coll. (H., 5th ed.) Cf. *out of print,* q.v.

o.p.h. ; O.P.H. Off, as in ' Dammit ! I'm off.'
Jocular : late C. 19–20. (Obviously, *off* is perverted to *oph* ; but the pronunciation, gen. slow,
is *O—P—H*.—2. Old Parliamentary Hand : political : 1886 ; ob. First applied, by *The Times*, to
Gladstone. (Ware.)

O.P.T. Other people's tobacco, a favourite
' brand ' ; esp. *smoke O.P.T.* : jocular coll. : C. 20.
Also *O.P.*

*o per se o ; or with capital *o*'s. A crier : early
C. 17 c. Dekker.

O. Pip or **O. pip.** An observation-post : military
coll. : G.W.—and after. F. & Gibbons. Ex
signalese.

o.s. or **O.S.** Very large ; ' *outsize* ' : from ca.
1930. Ex drapers' j. George Joseph, in *Everyman*, Jan. 5, 1934, of an imagined performance of
La Bohème : ' An O.S. Mimi loved by a C.3
Rudolph '.

o.t. (or **O.T.**), **it's.** It's (very) hot : non-aristocratic : from ca. 1880. Ware.

o.v. or **O.V.** The oven, or that open space below
the stage in which the Pepper's-ghost illusion is
worked : showmen's and low actors' : late C. 19–
early 20. Ware.

[**O.V.O.** A low phrase listed by Ware with the
remark, ' Quite inexplicable. No solution ever obtained from the initiates.' Perhaps it's just as well.]

o yes ! A jocular perversion of *oyez !* : from
before 1887 ; slightly ob. Baumann.

oaf. A wiseacre : coll. : late C. 17–mid-18.
B.E. Ex S.E. sense.

*oak. He who, in highway robbery, keeps watch
on behalf of the highwayman : c. : late C. 16–early
17. Greene, 1591. He affords security.—2. A
man of good substance and credit : late C. 17–mid-
19 : c. >, ca. 1750, s. B.E. ; Grose, 1st ed. Ex
the solidity of oak. Cf. † U.S. *oak*, strong.—3. An
oaken, hence an outer door, esp. in *sport oak*, in
C. 19–20 gen. *sport one's oak*, to shut one's outer
door as a sign that one is engaged : 1785, Grose :
university s. >, ca. 1820, coll.—4. A joke :
rhyming s. : late C. 19–20. Ware.—5. An occ.
spelling of *oke*, q.v.

oak, close as. Very retentive of secrets ; secretive : semi-proverbial coll. : C. 17–18. Shakespeare ; Colman, 1763, ' I am close as oak, an
absolute free-mason for secrecy.' Apperson.

oaken towel. A cudgel, orig. and mainly of oak ;
hence *rub one down with an oaken towel*, to cudgel,
to beat him : low (? orig. c.) : C. 18–mid-19.
Grose. In U.S. c., *an oak towel* is a policeman's
club : see Irwin.

oaks, felling of. Sea-sickness : C. 17 coll.
Jocular, as Withals (1608) shows in his *Dict.* ? ex
vomiting upon the oak of a ship.

oakum, pick. To be in a poor-house : lower
classes' coll. (— 1887). Ex the same phrase in S.E.
(to be in prison). Baumann.

oar in every man's boat, occ. † barge, have an. To
be concerned in everyone's affairs : mid-C. 16–20,
ob. : coll. >, ca. 1650, S.E. Udall, Florio, Howell.
Cf. :

oar in, put or **shove an** or **one's.** To interfere :
resp. coll. from ca. 1730, as in Moncrieff, 1843 ;
s. from ca. 1870, as in Mrs. Henry Wood (1874).
Coffey, 1731, ' I say, meddle with your own affairs ;
I will govern my own house, without your putting
in an oar.' Ex preceding ; there is, however, the
transitional *put an* (or *one's*) *oar in every man's boat*,
as in Brathwait, 1630. Apperson.

oars. A waterman : C. 17–19 : either coll. or
S.E. As = oarsman, certainly S.E.

oars, first. A favourite, esp. in *be first oars with* :
coll. : 1774, C. Dibdin's song, *The Jolly Young
Waterman*, ' He was always first oars when the fine
city ladies | In a party to Ranelagh went, or Vaux-
hall ' : whence the origin. O.E.D.

oars, lie or **rest (up)on one's.** To take things
easily : resp. 1726, Shelvocke, and † by 1920 ; 1836,
Lady Granville : both coll. till ca. 1850, then S.E.
O.E.D. Ex leaning on the handles of one's oars.

oat. An atom or particle, but esp. in *have not an
oat*, to be penniless : from ca. 1870 (ob.) : low.
H., 5th ed. Perhaps suggested by *groat*, but more
prob., as H. suggests, *iota* corrupted.

oat-stealer. An ostler : C. 19–20 ; ob. Jocular
coll. H., 3rd ed. Ex *ostler*, q.v.

oath, Highgate. See **Highgate, sworn at.**

oath !, my. A mild expletive : mostly Australian and New Zealand : late C. 19–20. Ex the more
trivial senses of S.E. *oath*. See also **colonial oath.**

oath, take an. To drink (liquor) : low : C. 19 ;
mostly U.S.

oatmeal. (Gen. in pl.) A profligate roisterer
(one of a set) : coll. : ca. 1620–40. Ford, in *The
Sun's Darling*, 1624 ; see also Nares. Semantics
obscure.

oatmeal, all the world is (gen. not). Everything
is delightful : proverbial coll. : ca. 1540–1700.
Udall, Swetnam. (Cf. *beer and skittles*.) ? ex oatmeal as food.

oatmeal, give (a person) his. To punish ; rebuke severely : mid-C. 18–early 19. Boswell.
(A. W. Read, in *Agricultural History*, July, 1934.)

oatmeal party. Scotsmen : naval coll. : late C.
19–20. F. & Gibbons. Ex the staple Scottish food.

oats, earn a gallon of. (Of horses) to fall on the
back and roll from side to side : provincial coll. :
C. 19. Halliwell.

oats, feed of. A whip ; a whipping : mostly
rural : C. 19–20 ; ob.

oats, feel one's. To get bumptious or very high-
spirited : orig. (ca. 1840), U.S. >, ca. 1905, anglicised as a coll. ; now verging on S.E. Ex a horse
feeding on oats.

oats, have one's. To sow one's wild oats (see
oats, wild) ; to ' enjoy ' a woman : low (— 1923).
Manchon.

oats, off one's. Indisposed : coll. (— 1923).
Manchon. Ex a horse off his oats, i.e. eating too
little. Cf. *off one's chump*, q.v.

oats, wild. A dissolute young man : coll. : ca.
1560–1620. Gen. a nickname. Becon (d. 1570),
' Certain light brains and wild oats '. Prob. ex,
though recorded some twelve years earlier than,
sow one's wild oats, to commit youthful follies, while
to have sown . . . indicates reform : coll. ; in late
C. 19–20, S.E. : 1576, Newton, ' That wilfull . . .
age, which . . . (as wee saye) hath not sowed all
theyr wyeld Oates ' (F. & H., checked by O.E.D.).
Ex the folly of sowing wild oats instead of good
grain ; cf. Fr. *folle avoine* (W.).

Oats and Barley. Charley : rhyming s. (— 1859).
H., 1st ed.

oats and chaff. A footpath : rhyming s.
(— 1857) ; ob. ' Ducange Anglicus.'

ob. Abbr. *obit* : Winchester College : C. 19–20.
See **obit** itself.

ob and sol. Scholastic, hence any subtle disputation : late C. 16–17 : coll. 1588, ' Very skilfull in
the learning of ob and sol '. Also *obs and sols*, as in

Burton, 1621; occ. *sols and obs.* Abbr. *objection and solution* in C. 16 books of theology. The derivative *ob-and-soller*, a subtle disputant, is either a nonce or a very rare usage. O.E.D.

Obadiah. A Quaker: C. 18–mid-19: coll. Ex the common Quaker name.

obbo. An observation balloon: military: 1915–18. F. & Gibbons.—2. Observation-work: policemen's: from ca. 1919. Charles E. Leach, *On Top of the Underworld,* 1933.

obbraid, obbrayd. A corrupt form of *upbraid*: C. 16. O.E.D.

Obeum, the. The name of a latrine at Cambridge: Cambridge University: from ca. 1890; ob. Ex Oscar Browning, popularly reputed to be its propagandist. On *odeum,* a hall for the playing of music. Cf. *O.B., the,* q.v.

obfuscated; obfusticated. Drunk: coll.: from ca. 1855; ob. The former is in 'Ducange Anglicus', 1857; the latter (Dec. 30, 1872) is a sol. Also *obfuscation*: H. Kingsley, 1861, 'In a general state of obfuscation'. Ex S.E. sense, to stupefy. Contrast *sub-fusc,* q.v.

obit. An obituary notice: journalistic: 1874, W. Black in *The Athenæum,* Sept. 12, 'It was the custom of his journal to keep obits in readiness.' Prob. ex *obituary,* not a revival of mid-C. 15–17 S.E. *obit,* the same.

objec(k). Sol. for *object*: C. 19–20. Cf. *subjec(k)*.

object. A laughing-stock; 'gape-seed': coll.: from ca. 1820. Cf. '*little object* (of children) = a half-playful half-angry endearment,' F. & H. Ex S.E. *object of pity, mirth, derision,* etc.

obligate. To make indebted, to bind, a person by a kindness or a favour: late C. 17–20: S.E. till ca. 1860; then—except in U.S. (where coll.)—slightly sol., or at least catachrestic; ob.

oblige. To favour a company (*with,* e.g., a song): coll.: 1735, Pope. O.E.D.

Obo. Prince Obolensky, the speedy Oxford and England Rugby wing three-quarter: sporting: from Dec., 1935, when he achieved fame in the match, England *v.* the All Blacks.

obof. An old buffer over forty: jocular military: 1916–18. F. & Gibbons. Ex conscripted middle-aged men.

obnoxious. Injurious: mid-C. 17–20: catachrestic. By confusion with *noxious.* O.E.D.

obolize is erroneous for *obelize*: C. 19–20. O.E.D.

obs. Obligations: (lower) middle classes' (− 1923); almost † by 1933. Manchon. By abbr.

***observationist.** One (gen. a pedlar, hawker, etc.) who spies out likely booty for thieves: c. (− 1889); ob. Barrère & Leland.

observe. To preserve; retain: catachrestic: C. 15–16. O.E.D.

obsquatulate. An occ. form of *absquatulate,* q.v.: H., 1859.

obstacle. An obelisk: sol. (− 1823). 'Jon Bee.'

obstain(e). Catachrestic forms of *abstain*; † by C. 18. O.E.D.

obstreperlous, -olous, -ulous; obstropalous, -olous, -ulous; also abstrepolous, -ulous, Obstreperous: from ca. 1725: sol. when not deliberately jocular; Halliwell, however, in 1847, characterises it as 'genuine London dialect'. Resp. first recorded: ca. 1780, ca. 1760, 1727; 1773 (Goldsmith), ca. 1770, 1748 (Smollett); ab-

forms only in C. 18. Commonest: *obstropolous, -ulous.* (O.E.D.)

obstroculous. An occ. Australian variant of the preceding. E.g. in Ion L. Idriess, *Flynn of the Inland,* 1932.

obvious. (Of women) stout: Society: 1897–ca. 1914. Ware. Ex the signs of pregnancy.

obviously severe. 'Hopelessly rude of speech': Society: ca. 1890–1914. Ware.

Ocac. See **Okak.**—**Ocakery.** See **Okakery.**

occabot. Tobacco: back s. (− 1859). H., 1st ed. (*tib fo occabot,* bit of tobacco).

occasion. A notable celebration, a special ceremony, an event of note: coll.: from ca. 1860. Dickens; in C. 20, esp. *a great occasion.* Ex *special occasion.*

occasion, improve the. To offer a prayer; give a homily or moral address: coll. (mostly clerical): from ca. 1860. G. Macdonald, 1865, in *Alec Forbes.* The more gen. sense, to profit by a chance, is S.E.

occifer. An officer: late C. 19–20. Ware. Also *ossifer.*

occupant. A harlot: late C. 16–early 17: a vulg. Marston, 1599. Ex *occupy,* q.v.—2. A brothel: C. 17: a vulg. Cf. *nanny-house.* Ex preceding sense.

occupy. (V.t. and v.i.) to cohabit (with); lie with: C. 16–early 19: S.E. in C. 16, then a vulg., as in Florio, Rowley, Hexham, Rochester, D'Urfey, Grose. 'In consequence of its vulgar use in this sense, this verb was little used in literature in the 17th and 18th century; cf. [Shakespeare, 2nd *Henry* IV, at II, iv, 159] 'as odious as the word *occupy*', Onions. Cf. L. *occupare amplexu* and see **fuck.**

occupying-house. A brothel: late C. 16–17: a vulg. Florio.

ocean pearl. A girl: rhyming s.: late C. 19–20. B. & P. Also *ivory pearl,* q.v.

Ocean Villas. Auchonvillers, a town near Arras: military: G.W. (F. & Gibbons.)

ocean wanderers. Any fish (gen. herrings) issued as rations: military: from 1914. B. & P.

ocean wave. A shave: rhyming s.: C. 20. *John o' London's Weekly,* June 9, 1934.

oceans. A (very) large quantity or number: from ca. 1840: coll. almost S.E.

***ochive;** also **oschive.** A knife: c.: C. 18–20; ob. *A New Canting Dict.,* 1725, defines *oschive* as a bone-handled knife, as if ex L. *os,* a bone + *chive,* a knife, but *oschive* may be an etymologising theory and perversion of *ochive.* Ex Romany *o chif,* the knife. More gen., *chive*; occ. *chif(f)*: see **chive,** n. See also **oschive.**

ochorboc. Beer: Italian organ-grinders' (− 1909). Ware. It. *bocca* (mouth), thus: *occa + b* + intrusive *oc.*

***ochre.** Money: c. >, ca. 1870, low s.: 1854, Dickens, 'Pay your ochre at the doors'; ob. Also, gold, money. Ex the colour of gold. Cf. with caution, *gilt.*

o'clock, know what's. To be alert; shrewd: low coll.: from ca. 1835. Dickens, Thackeray. Ex the S.E. sense, to know the real state of things.

[**o'clock, lie at.** This miners' term, despite its promising appearance, is j.]

o'clock, like one. See **like** . . .

-ocracy. See **-cracy.**

October; october. Blood: boxing: from ca. 1850; ob. 'Cuthbert Bede', 'Now we'll tap your best October.' Ex *October* (*ale* or *cider*). Cf. *claret,* q.v.

octodrant. Erroneous for *octant :* late C. 17–20. O.E.D.

octopi. Octopuses : C. 19–20 : a cultured sol. ex the mistakenly assumed L. origin. (The scientific pl. is *octopodes.*)

od, 'od ; occ. **odd.** Also with capitals. God, in oaths and asseverations : coll., though orig. euphemistic S.E. : C. 17–early 19. Whence *od rabbit it !,* 1749, Fielding,; *od rat it !* (also in *Tom Jones*), whence *drat (it) !,* q.v. ; *od rot it !,* from ca. 1810 ; *od save's !* (lit., God save us), C. 19–20, mainly and in C. 20 only dial. See esp. O.E.D. and E.D.D. Cf. *ods,* q.v.

odd, of age, *years* being omitted, as in Hood's ' His death . . . At forty-odd befell,' 1845, app. the earliest record. Here, *odd* denotes a small surplus (in years) over and above a ' round number '. O.E.D.

odd-come-short. In pl., odds and ends : rural coll. : 1836, T. Hook ; slightly ob.—2. Some day : coll. : from ca. 1875 ; ob. Usually *one of these odd-come-shorts* (as in Harris's *Uncle Remus*); but except in U.S., much less gen. than :

odd-come-shortly. The same : coll. : C. 18–20 ; ob. Swift, ' Miss, when will you be married ? . . . One of these odd-come-shortly's, Colonel ' ; Grose, 2nd ed. ; Scott.

odd fish. See **fish.**

odd job man. One ' who professes to do anything and only does his employer': trades' (— 1909). Ware.

oddish. Tipsy: low coll. : from ca. 1850 ; **ob.** Cf. *queer,* adj., 2, q.v.

odds ! See **ods.**

odds, above (Australian) or **over** (English) **the.** Outside the pale ; exorbitant : C. 20 : s. >, by 1930, coll. C. J. Dennis. Ex horse-racing.

odds, it is or **makes no.** It makes no difference (in good or ill) : C. 17–20 : S.E. till C. 19, then coll. T. A. Guthrie, ' But there, it's no odds ' (O.E.D.).

odds, shout the. To talk too much, too loudly, or boastingly : lower classes' : from ca. 1910. F. & Gibbons. Ex the race-course.

odds ?, what's the. What difference does it make ? : coll. : mid-C. 19–20. (Dickens's ' What is the odds . . . ? ' is S.E. ;) Trollope, 1880 ; Besant. (O.E.D.)

odds ?, where's the. A low coll. form (— 1887) of the preceding. Baumann.

odds, within the. Possible or possibly ; esp. just or barely possible : sporting coll. (— 1887) >, by 1890, gen coll. Baumann.

odds and sods. " ' Details " attached to Battalion Headquarters for miscellaneous offices : batmen, sanitary men, professional footballers and boxers on nominal duties, etc.' : military : 1915 ; ob. B. & P.—2. Hence, hangers-on ; miscellaneous persons : from 1919.

odds of, be no. As in ' It's no odds o' mine ' (Greenwood), no concern of mine : (low) coll. : mid-C. 19–20. Baumann.

odling (vbl.n.), cheating : either S.E. or a rare catachresis : late C. 16–mid-17.

odno. Lit., nod. Rare except in *ride on the odno,* to travel by rail without paying : back s. : 1889, *The Sporting Times* ; ob.

ods, od's ; odds. (Also **ads, uds.**) God's, gen. in combination, in late C. 16–early 19 coll. oaths and asseverations ; extant as a jocular archaism. The second member is frequently perverted, as in *bud* ex *blood, nouns* or *oons* ex *wounds, zooks* ex *hooks.* Cf. :

ods bods. A C. 18 reduction of and corruption of : **ods bodkins,** a jocular exclamation, is a late C. 19–20 perversion of *ods bodikins,* lit. God's little body, a C. 17–19 oath. See **ods.**

of, v. Have : sol. : C. 19–20. (Never for the infinitive.) Frequent among the illiterate and not unknown in the Dominions and in U.S., among the literate though not, of course, the cultured. E.g. ' I would of done it.' Even more sol. when unnecessary, as in ' If I had of done it ': here, however, *(ha)ve* is more gen. : see **have.** Ex the slurred pronunciation of '*ve = have,* as in ' I would've done it.'

of, preposition. Intrusive or tautological, as in the next entry and as is frequent, in low coll. (i.e. in sol.), esp. after a present participle : C. 19–20. Greenwood, ca. 1880, ' They're takin' of her to the pit-hole ' (Baumann) ; D. Sayers, 1933, ' Bill Jones says he rekollects of me standing in the Dispatch.'—2. Its omission is C. 19–20 coll. in, e.g., ' What colour was her dress ? '—3. On : late C. 14–20 : S.E. until mid-C. 18, then coll. ; in C. 20, increasingly low coll. ; prob. soon to be a sol Sheridan, 1777, ' Oh, plague of his nerves ! ' (O.E.D.)—4. (Always *of a* or *of an.*) At some time during, in the course of : S.E. until C. 19, then coll., as in *of an evening.*—5. For sins against grammar, see Fowler.—6. Like : sol. : mid-C. 19–20. D. Sayers, *Murder Must Advertise,* 1933, ' A charm or a trinket or something of that.' I.e. *of that sort.*

of ?, what are you doing. What are you doing ? (dial. and) low coll. : C. 19–20. Abbr. or slovenly corruption of † *what are you in the doing of* (W.). Cf. *of,* preposition, 1, q.v.

of a skew. Askew : sol. : C. 19–20. Baumann.

of it. See **it,** of.

off, v. To depart, go away : low coll. : 1895, *The Westminster Gazette,* Sept. 21, ' He took down his hat, and off'd,' O.E.D. In C. 20, gen. *off it.* Ex dial. : 1889 (E.D.D.).—2. To die : military : 1914–18. B. & P.—3. **off with,** to remove or take off instantly : from ca. 1890 : sol. when not jocular (coll.) *The Daily News,* Feb. 23, 1892, ' They offed with his head,' O.E.D.—4. To refuse, reject : 1908, A. S. M. Hutchinson, *Once Aboard the Lugger,* ' I haven't offed that yet—haven't refused it, I mean ' ; ob.

off, adj. Out of date ; no longer fashionable : coll. : 1892, *Illustrated Bits,* Oct. 22, ' Theosophy is off—decidedly off.' Perhaps ex restaurant j. (' Chops are off ').—2. Hence, stale ; in bad condition, e.g. of a cricket pitch : low coll. : from ca. 1895. ' Smells a little bit off, don't it ? ', F. & H. Abbr. *off colour.*—3. Hence, out of form : coll. : from ca. 1896.—4. Hence, in ill health : coll. : from late 1890's.

off, preposition. Having lost interest in ; averse to : coll. : C. 20. Desmond Coke in *The House Prefect,* 1908, ' You can see Bob's off you ' ; Manchon, 1923, ' He's dead off jam ' ; Collinson, 1927, ' I'm rather off dogs at present.' Ex *off, cannot be,* q.v.

off ! Abbr. *switch off,* q.v.

off, a bit. (Slightly) crazy : C. 20. Collinson. Abbr. *a bit off his head.*

off, be. To depart ; run away : coll. (— 1887). Baumann ; 1892, *Ally Sloper,* Feb. 27.

off, cannot (or **could not**) **be.** As in Greenwood, ca. 1880, ' I couldn't be off likin' it,' I could not help —or refrain from—liking it : (low) coll. : mid-C. 19–20. Baumann.

*off, have the bags. To have independent means —and live on them : c. (— 1887). Baumann.

[**off and on**, as adj. = vacillating, is, despite H., S.E.]

off bat. Point, in cricket : Winchester College : coll. or j. : mid-C. 19–20.

off chump. Having no appetite : stables' (– 1909). Ware. Perhaps *off champing*. Cf. *oats*, *off one's*.

*****off duty.** Not engaged in stealing : c. (– 1887). Baumann.

off-go. A start, a beginning : Scots coll. : 1886, R. L. Stevenson. O.E.D.

off it. See *off*, v.—2. A variant of *off one's chump* or *nut* or *rŏcker*, etc. See those nn.

off of. Off ; from sol. : mid-C. 19–20. ' That takes the beauty off of it ' ; ' He took it off of me.' Baumann.

off one's chest ; off one's chump, coconut, nut, onion, pannican, rocker, top traverse. See the nn.— **off one's feed** or **oats.** See *feed* and *oats*, *off one's*.

off the hinge. Out of work : low : from ca. 1850 ; ob. Ex :

off the hinges. Out of order ; upset ; disheartened : coll. till C. 18, then dial., where it gen. = in bad health, spirits, or temper. Cotgrave. (Apperson.) Ex a door unhinged.

off the hooks. Crazed, mad (gen. temporarily) ; coll. : C. 17–mid-19. Beaumont & Fletcher ; Scott.—2. Crestfallen (this sense was ob. by 1750, † by 1800) ; ill-humoured : coll. (ob.) : from ca. 1630 ; in C. 19–20, mainly dial. Davenport, 1639. (—3. In dial., also shabby, worn out, ailing.)—4. Out of work : coll. : C. 18. North, *Lives of the Norths*, 1740. (This interpretation is not perfectly certain.) For all : Apperson.

off the horn. (Of steak) very hard : low : from ca. 1870 ; ob. H., 5th ed.

off the rails. See **rails.**—**off with.** See *off*, v., 3.

offer up. To lift ; to help to raise : London labourers', esp. in the building trade : late C. 19–20. (By ellipsis.) Holway Bailey in *The Observer*, March 31, 1935.

offhandish. A coll. form (– 1887) of *off hand*, brusque, inconsiderate, casual. Baumann.

office. One's *office* is one's ' ordinary Haunt, or Plying-[? playing-]place, be it Tavern, Ale-house, Gaming-house or Bowling-green ', B.E. : late C. 17–18.—2. A signal, a (private) hint ; a word of advice ; (in sporting s.) valuable information : C. 19–20 : ? orig. c. Esp. in *give the office* (1803) and *take the office* (1812, likewise in Vaux), the latter slightly ob. (O.E.D.)—3. An aeroplane cockpit : Air Force : from 1915. F. & Gibbons. Ex its speaking-tube and writing-pad.—4. An orderly-room : military jocular coll. : C. 20. B. & P.

office, v. To give information (about something) ; warn, intimate to : low (? orig. c.) : 1812, Vaux ; Moore, 1819, ' To office . . . To the Bulls of the Alley the fate of the Bear '.

office, cast of (e.g. your). ' A Touch of your Employment ' : coll. : late C. 17–18. B.E. prob. means a helping hand from one in a (good) position.

office, cook's. The galley : nautical : from ca. 1850 ; ob.

office, give one the. See **office**, n., 2.

office-sneak. A stealer of umbrellas, overcoats, etc., from offices : coll. : from ca. 1860.

officer bloke. A batmen's coll. for the officer they serve : military : C. 20. B. & P.

officers' mess. ' Any female working in officers' quarters, or any female companion of officers ' : military : from ca. 1910. B. & P.

officer's mount. A harlot : military (the ranks') : late C. 19–20. Punning Army j. for a horse.

officers of the 52nds. Young men rigidly going to church on the 52 Sundays in a year : city of Cork (– 1909). Ware. As if of the 52nd regiment.

offish. Distant ; reserved : coll. : from ca. 1830. L. Oliphant, 1883. Cf. *stand-offish*.—2. (Pronounced *off-fi'sh* and not, as in sense 1, *o'ff-ish*.) Official ; authentic : military : 1916–18.

offishness. Aloofness ; reserve : coll. : from ca. 1880. Ex *offish* and, like it, of persons only.

offitorie, offytorie. Corrupt C. 16 forms of *offertory*. O.E.D.

offsider. An assistant : Australians' and New Zealanders' : C. 20. Orig., 2, a cook's offsider : late C. 19–20. Both are coll.—3. Hence, a ' pal ' ; Australian : from ca. 1919.

-offsky. A comic suffix imitative of Russian : C. 20. Cf. *-insky*.

ofter. A frequenter or habitué : sporting : ca. 1884–1910. Ware. Ex *oft*, often.

og. See **ogg.**

og-rattin. Au gratin : London restaurants' (– 1909). Ware.

ogg or **og.** A shilling : New Zealanders' : C. 20. A corruption of *hog* (a shilling), q.v.

ogging of tekram. Going to market : back s. (– 1859). H., 1st ed.

ogle. See **ogles.**—2. ' An ocular invitation or consent, side glance, or amorous look ', F. & H. : coll. : C. 18–20. Cibber, 1704, ' Nay, nay, none of your parting ogles.' Ex :

*****ogle,** v.i. and t. (See the first o entry.—) To look invitingly or amorously (at) : from ca. 1680 : c. until ca. 1710, coll. till ca. 1790, then S.E. Implied in B.E.'s *ogling*, ' casting a sheep's Eye at Handsom Women ' ; and in the Shadwell quotation at *ogling* ; D'Urfey. Ex Low Ger. *oegeln*, same meaning.—2. To look ; to look at : c. and S.E. : from ca. 1820 ; ob. Haggart, 1821, ' Seeing a cove ogling the yelpers '. Ex S.E. sense, to examine.

*****ogled,** with determining word, e.g. *queer-ogled*, squinting : late C. 18–20 ; ob. : c. >, ca. 1840, low s.

*****oglen, rum.** ' Bright, piercing eyes ', Bee : c. : ca. 1820–50. Cf. etymology of *ogle*, v., 1.

ogler. A punch in the eye : boxing s. (– 1887) ; ob. Baumann.

*****oglers.** Eyes : c. : from ca. 1820 ; ob. Haggart. A variation on :

*****ogles.** (Extremely rare in singular.) Eyes : mid-C. 17–20 : c. until ca. 1805, then boxing s. until ca. 1860, finally low gen. s. ; ob. Coles, 1676 ; B.E. ; Dyche ; Grose ; ' Cuthbert Bede ' ; Thackeray. Ex the v. Hence, *queer ogles* (see also **ogled**), cross eyes ; *rum ogles*, bright or arresting eyes.

ogling. (The ppl. adj. is S.E.—) Vbl. n., the throwing of amorous or insinuating glances : from ca. 1680 : c. until ca. 1710, then coll., then, by 1790, S.E. Shadwell, 1682, ' They say their Wives learn ogling in the Pit,' a marginal gloss reading : ' A foolish Word among the Canters for glancing ' (O.E.D.).

oh. See **o be . . . ;** also **after you, dummy, Jupiter, Moses, my, swallow.**

oh, go to spue. The popular shape of *Ogotaspuotas*, on a flag in a meeting at Hyde Park in favour of the Cretans : London : 1897. Ware.

oh, la-la ! A military c.p. indicative of joviality : 1915 : very ob. B. & P., ' Borrowed from the French and in use chiefly among officers '.

oh, my leg ! A low c.p. addressed, ca. 1810–50, to one recently liberated from gaol. ' Jon Bee.' A gibe at the gait caused by fetters.

oh, to be shot at dawn ! A jesting c.p. for anyone (including oneself) in trouble : military : 1917–18. B. & P. Ex death for desertion.

oh well ! it's a way they have in the Army. See **it's a way.**

oh yeah ! Oh, no ! ; You think you know all about it, but, in my opinion, you don't : adopted ca. 1930, via the ' talkies ', from U.S., where *yes* often > *yeah. The Daily Mirror*, June 28, 1934, ' item ' headed ' Oh Yeah ! '

oick. A variant of *hoick*, v., 4.

oickman. A labourer, shopkeeper, etc. ; hence, an objectionable fellow : Bootham School (— 1925).

oil. An oil-painting : coll. : from ca. 1890. By 1920, almost S.E. (Gen. in pl.)—2. See **oils,** 2.— 3. **the oil,** esp. *the dinkum* (occ. *good*) *oil* : the truth. Orig. and mainly Australian. C. 20. Ex prospecting for oil-springs.—4. Hence, in New Zealand c. (— 1932), it = information.—5. In addition to its popularity in proverbs and proverbial sayings (there are 89 in Apperson), *oil* is of frequent occurrence in various humorous and/or ironic phrases that began as coll. and may have > S.E. ; indeed, since it is arguable that all except **oil of giblets** were always S.E., it is better to list them all together :—**oil of angels,** a gift, a bribe, late C. 16–17, as in Greene (and see below) ; **oil of barley** or **malt,** beer, mid-C. 17–early 19, as in B.E. ; **oil of Baston** (a topographical pun ; *basting*), a beating, C. 17, Withals,— with which cf. **oil of gladness** (Grose, 2nd ed.), **hickory** (gen. as **h. oil**), **holly** (C. 17), **rope** (C. 18, Mrs. Centlivre), **stirrup** (late C. 18–mid-19, Grose, 2nd ed. : also as **stirrup-oil**), **strappem** (C. 19), and **whip** (mid-C. 17–mid-18, Fuller), and also the C. 18–20 dial. (ob.) **birch, hazel** (also in form **h. oil,** coll. and dial.), **oak, strap,** the form **strap-oil** occurring as C. 19–20 jocular coll. ; **oil of giblets** or **horn,** the female spendings (this, certainly, is low s. !), C. 19–20 ; **oil of palms** (Egan's Grose), or **palm-oil,** a bribe, C. 19–20, ob.—cf. *oil of angels* ; **oil of tongue,** flattery, with which cf. the late C. 14– mid-15 S.E. **hold up oil,** to consent flatteringly (Apperson), and the rare **oil of fool,** flattery, as in Wolcot (O.E.D.).—6. Pretentiousness ; presumption ; ' side ' : Public Schools' : C. 20. (D. Coke, *The School across the Road,* 1910.) Cf. *greasing,* q.v.

oil, v. To cheat : Charterhouse : late C. 19–20. Hence *oiler,* 3.—2. See Addenda.

oil, good or **dinkum.** See **oil,** n. 3.

oil, strike. To have good luck, be successful : orig. U.S. ; anglicised ca. 1875 ; by 1920, coll. Ex the S.E. sense, to discover oil-springs.

oil-butt. A black whale : whalers' : late C. 19– 20. Bowen. Ex the abundance of oil which its carcase yields.

oil-can. A shell from a German trench-mortar : military : late 1914–18. F. & Gibbons. Ex its shape.

oil-painting, be no. To be plain-looking ; ugly : coll. : late C. 19–20. Cf. *picture* and *pretty as paint,* qq.v.

oil-rag. A cigarette : rhyming s. (on *fag*) : C. 20. P. P., *Rhyming Slang,* 1932.

oil of . . . See **oil,** n. 5.

*oil of angels. Money : beggars' and tramps' c. (— 1926). F. Jennings, *In London's Shadows.* Cf., 2, the phrase at **oil,** n. 5.

oil-rag. A gunner : artillerymen's : C. 20. Ex his frequent use thereof.

oil the knocker. To fee the porter : from ca. 1850 ; ob.

oil the wig. To become tipsy, while *oil one's wig* is to make a person tipsy : provincial s. or coll. : late C. 18–19. Cf. *oiled.*

oil up to. To attempt to bribe (a person) : 1934, *The Passing Show,* 1934. Cf. *oil,* v. Prob. ex : —2. To toady to : Harrow School : late C. 19–20. Arnold Lunn, *The Harrovians,* 1913. Cf. *oil,* v., 2, in Addenda.

oiled. Slightly tipsy : 1916, E. V. Lucas (S.O.D.). Gen. *well-oiled.* Cf. *oil of barley* (beer) and :

oiler. A person (gen. male) addicted to drink : 1916. Prob. ex preceding.—2. An oilskin coat : coll., orig. (middle 1880's) U.S., anglicised, esp. in the Navy, by 1900. Cf. *oilies.*—3. A cheat : Charterhouse : late C. 19–20. Ex *oil,* v. Cf. *bumfer.*

oilies. The same as *oiler,* 2, than which, in English use, it is slightly earlier : coll. : late C. 19–20. Bowen. Also in dial.

oiliometer. Incorrect for *oilometer* : 1876. O.E.D.

oilous. A C. 19–20 dictionary error of *oileous,* C. 17 S.E. for ' oily '. O.E.D.

oils. See **oil,** 1.—2. (Very rare in the singular.) An oilskin coat : coll. : 1891, J. Dale, *Round the World.* O.E.D. Cf. *oiler,* 2, and *oilies.*

oily. An oilskin coat : 1926, Richard Keverne. Cf. *oiler,* 2 ; *oilies* ; *oils,* 2.

oily wad. A seaman not specialising in anything : naval : from ca. 1914. Bowen. Ex the time such men ' have to spend cleaning brass-work with oily wads '.—2. Any one of nos. 1–36 of ' the first British oil-burning torpedo-boats ' : naval : from ca. 1916. Ibid.

oiner. A cad : university : ca. 1870–1915. Etymology obscure : ? Gr. οἰνίζω, smell of wine.

ointment. Money : coll. : C. 15–17. Ex the C. 13 fabliau, De la Vieille qui Oint la Palme au Chevalier. F. & H.—2. The *semen virile* : low : C. 18–20, ob.—3. Butter : medical students' : from ca. 1859. H., 2nd ed.

Okak ; properly **Ocac.** The Officer Commanding Administrative Centre : Army officers' : 1915–18. F. & Gibbons.

Okakery ; Ocakery. The Records Depot : id. : id. Ibid. Ex preceding.

oke ! ' O.K.', adj., q.v. ; yes ! : C. 20 U.S. >, ca. 1930, anglicised, thanks (?) mainly to ' the talkies ' (q.v.). Richard Church, in *The Spectator,* Feb. 15, 1935, ' A child replied " oke " to something I said. After a shudder of dismay, I reflected that this telescoped version of " O.K.", now used to mean " Right you are ", or " I agree ", or any other form of assent, will ultimately appear in the text-books as a legitimate word, with an example quoted from a poet who is at present mute and inglorious.' Prob. ex *o.k.,* q.v. But cf. the Choctaw (*h*)*oke,* it is so (Thornton) : which may well—in Britain at least—have > operative because of the interesting label on bottles of Mason's ' O.K.' Sauce.

ol' ; occ. spelt **ole.** A slovenly form of *old.* Co-extensive with mod. English. In Westbourne Grove, London, W., stands ' Ole Bill's ', an eating-house.

old. Money : low : 1900, G. R. Sims, *In London's Heart,* ' Perhaps it's somebody you owe a bit of the old to, Jack.' ? abbr. *old stuff.*—2. Much : coll. : early C. 19, but rare. See the Scott quotation in *old*, adj., 2.

old, adj. Crafty, clever, knowing : from ca. 1720 ; ob. Defoe, ' The Germans were too old for us there ' (O.E.D.). Esp. in such phrases as *old bird, dog, file, hand, soldier, stager*, qq.v.—2. A gen. intensive = great, abundant, excessive, ' splendid ' : coll. : mid-C. 15–20. Anon., ca. 1440, ' Gode olde fyghting was there ' (O.E.D.) ; Tarlton, 1590, ' There was old ringing of bells ' ; Cotton, 1664, ' Old drinking and old singing ' ; Grose ; Scott, 1814, ' So there was old to do about ransoming the bridegroom ' (O.E.D.). From ca. 1860, only with *gay, good, grand, high,* and similar adjj., as in *The Referee*, March 11, 1883, ' All the children . . . had a high old time,' and with *any* as in ' any old time ' or ' any old how ' (Manchon).—3. Ugly : c. : late C. 18–early 19. Grose, 3rd ed. Perhaps ex *old Harry, Nick, One, Roger*, etc., the devil.—4. (Mostly in terms of address.) Indicative of affection, cordiality, or good humour : coll. : 1588, Shakespeare, ' Old Lad, I am thine owne ' (O.E.D.) ; B.E. ; Grose ; Hume Nisbet, 1892, ' Now for business, old boy.' Also *old bean, chap, fellow, man, thing, top,* etc.—5. Hence, of places familiar to one : coll. : late C. 19–20. Often *good old*, q.v.—6. A gen. pejorative : C. 16–20 : S.E. or coll. or s. as the second member is S.E. or coll. or s. ; the practice itself is wholly (orig., almost wholly) unconventional. E.g. *old block, fizgig, fogy, stick in the mud*. See the second member of such phrases when they are not listed below.—7. In combination with (e.g.) *Harry, Nick, One, Scratch*, qq.v., the devil : coll. : from Restoration days, the earliest record in the O.E.D. being *Old Nick* in L'Estrange, 1668 ; *old,* however, was, in S.E., applied to Satan as early as C. 11. Ex the S.E. sense in this connexion : primeval. See also *old Bendy*.

old, any. See old, adj., 2.

old, good. An approving phrase that gives a coll. and familiar variation to *good*. C. 19–20. Perhaps ex *old,* adj., 2, and 4, qq.v.—2. In the G.W. Army, a c.p. ' gag ' ran : ' Some say good old X : we say fuck old X *or* him ' ; extant ; prob. pre-War.

old Adam. The penis : low coll. : C. 19–20. Ex S.E. sense, natural sin.—(*as*) *old as Adam*, very old indeed, is S.E., not coll.

Old Agamemnons. ' The 69th Foot, now [1902] the 2nd Batt. of the Welsh Regiment ', F. & H. : military : late C. 18–20 ; ob. Ex the days when they were marines on the *Agamemnon*. See also *Ups and Downs*.

old and bitter. A mother-in-law : proletarian (—1935).

Old and Bold, the. The 14th Foot Regiment, which, ca. 1881, changed into the Prince of Wales's Own (West Yorkshire Regiment) : military : C. 19–20 : ob. Also known as *Calvert's Entire, the Powos, the Fighting Brigade*.

old as Charing Cross or **as Paul's** (i.e. St. Paul's) or **as Paul's steeple.** Ancient ; very old indeed : coll. : ca. 1650–1820. Howell, 1659 (*Paul's steeple*) ; Ray, 1678 (*Charing Cross*) ; Other topographical similes are † *old as Aldgate* and, in dial., † *Cale Hill,* † *Eggerton,* † *Glastonbury tor,* † *Pandon Gate* ; cf. S.E. *old as the hills*.

old as my tougue and a little older than my teeth, as. A c.p. reply to an inquiry as to one's age : coll. (slightly ob.) and dial : C. 18–20. Swift, *Polite Conversation*, Dial. I. (Apperson.)

old as the itch, as. Extremely old : (low) coll. : C. 18. Fuller.

old bach. A confirmed bachelor : coll. : from early 1870's. (O.E.D. Sup.)

old bag. An ' old sweat ' ; pejoratively, an old soldier : lower classes' coll. (— 1923) ; ob. Manchon.

Old Bags. John Scott (1751–1838), 1st Earl of Eldon ; at one time Lord Chancellor. Dawson.

Old Bailey underwriter. A forger on a small scale : ca. 1825–50. Moncrieff, *Van Diemen's Land*, 1830. ? orig. c. ; certainly low.

old bean. A term of address : from ca. 1917 ; slightly ob. by 1933. Collinson. See old, adj., 4.

old beeswing. A s. vocative (ob. by 1910, † by 1920). See beeswing, and old cock.

old (or, as with all names for the devil, **Old**) **Bendy** or **bendy.** The devil : C. 19–20 dial. rather than coll. Dial. also are : old a'ill thing, old bogey, botheration, boy (q.v.), carle, chap (q.v.), child, cloots or Cloots, dad, fellow (q.v.), gentleman (q.v.), hangie, Harry (q.v.), hooky, hornie, lad (q.v.), Mahoun, man (q.v.), Nick (q.v.), or Nicker or Nickie or Nickie Ben, one (q.v.), Sam, Sanners or Sanny or Saunders, Scrat(t), Scratch (q.v. : also coll.), Scratchem, Smith, smoke, sooty, soss or Soss, and thief. For the coll. and s. terms, see under ; cf. also *old*, adj., last sense. My essay ' The Devil and his Nicknames ' in *Words* !

old Bill. A veteran ; any old soldier, esp. if with heavy, drooping whiskers : military coll., mostly officers' : 1915 ; very ob. F. & Gibbons. Ex Captain Bairnsfather's Old Bill.

old Billy. The devil, but rarely except in *like old Billy*, like the devil, i.e. hard, furiously, etc. Astley, 1894 (O.E.D.). Cf. the *like* similes.

old Billy-o. An occ. variant (— 1923) of the preceding. Manchon.

*old bird. An experienced thief : c. : 1877.—2. An experienced, knowing person : coll. : from ca. 1887. Cf. *old dog, old hand, old soldier, old stager* qq.v.

old blazes. The devil : low : 1849 ; ob. See old, adj., last sense.

old block. See chip of the old block.—**old bloke.** See bloke.

Old Bold, the. The 29th Foot Regiment (in late C. 19–20, the 1st Battalion of the Worcestershire Regiment) : mid-C. 19–20 ; ob. Also *the Ever-Sworded 29th*. Cf. :

Old Bold Fifth, the. The 5th Foot (in late C. 19–20, the Northumberland Fusiliers) : military : mid-C. 19–20. Also *the Fighting Fifth* (†), *Lord Wellington's Bodyguard, the Shiners*.

old boots. The devil. Only in . . . *as old boots* and esp. *like old boots*, a gen. intensive adv. Smedley, 1850, ' was out of sight like old boots ' ; Milliken, ' I jest blew away like old boots.' See old, adj., last sense.—2. See old shoes.

old boy. A coll. vocative : C. 17–20. Shakespeare. Cf. *old chap*. See old, adj., 4.—2. See entry at old Bendy : coll. and dial : C. 19 (? earlier)–20.—3. Any old or oldish man, or one in authority, esp. one's father, a headmaster, the managing director, etc. : coll. : C. 19–20. Cf. *old man*, q.v. This (like the preceding sense) always, except in the vocative, goes with *the*.—4. A strong ale : brewers' coll. : ca. 1740–80. O.E.D.

Old Braggs, the. The 28th Foot (in late C. 19–20, the 1st Battalion of the Gloucestershire Regiment) : military : from ca. 1750. Ex the name of its colonel (1734–59) with a good-humoured pun on *brag*. Also *the Slashers* (C. 19–20 ; ob.). F. & Gibbons.

Old Brickdusts, the. The 53rd Foot, from ca. 1881 the King's Shropshire Light Infantry : military : C. 19–20. Ex the brickdusty hue of their facings. (F. & Gibbons.)

old buck. A coll. term of address : C. 20. P. G. Wodehouse, *Love among the Chickens*, 1906 ; Collinson. Cf. *old horse*.

Old Bucks. The 16th Foot (in late C. 19–20, the Bedfordshire Regiment) : military : from 1809. F. & Gibbons. Also known as *the Feather-Beds* and *the Peace-Makers*.

old buffer. See **buffer** in relation to **old**, adj., 6.

Old Buffs, the. The 3rd Foot (in late C. 19–20, the East Kent Regiment, gen. called *the Buffs*) : military : C. 19–20. See **Buffs.** Also *Nut-Crackers* and *Resurrectionists*.

old buster. Old chap, gen. as vocative : 1905, H. A. Vachell in *The Hill*, ' You funny old buster ! ' ; ob. by 1920, † by 1930. Ex *buster*, 5.

Old Cars. Old Carthusians : from ca. 1880 : ' justly considered a vulgarism ', A. H. Tod, *Charterhouse*, 1900.

Old Canaries, the. The 3rd Dragoon Guards : military : late C. 19–20. F. & Gibbons. Ex their yellow facings.

old chap. A coll. vocative (— 1823). Egan's Grose ; Anstey. See **chap** and **old**, adj., 4.

old Charley. See **charley**, 6.

Old Chich. Sir Edward Chichester, very popular in the 1880's and 1890's : naval. Bowen.

old China. A variant, mostly as a vocative, of *China* (or c), a mate or companion, q.v.

old chum. See **chum.** (Ca. 1840–1900 ; increasingly rare. C. P. Hodgson, *Reminiscences*, 1846.)

old cock. See **cock** (= man, fellow) in relation to **old**, adj., 4. Used both in address (Mark Lemon, 1867, ' Mr. Clendon did not call Mr. Barnard old cock, old fellow, or old beeswing ') and in reference = an (old) man (Marriott-Watson, 1895, ' He was a comfortable old cock . . . and pretty well to do ').

old cockalorum (or **-elorum**). A very familiar variation (— 1887) of the preceding, slightly ob. Baumann.

old codger. See **codger** (Colman, 1760), and **old**, adj., 6.

old crawler, esp. preceded by **regular.** A pejorative, whether in reference or in the vocative : late C. 19–20 : (mainly Australian) coll. or s. ' Rolf Boldrewood ', 1888. Prob. ex *pub-crawler* or *crawler*, a contemptible person, a toady.

old cuff. See **cuff**, 1, and **cuffin** in relation to **old**, adj., 4. (B.E.)

Old Daph. Sir Wm. Davenant, dramatist (1606–68). Dawson.

Old Dart, the. Great Britain, esp. England : Australian : C. 20. Ex *dart*, 2, q.v.

old Davy. The devil : coll., mainly lower classes' (— 1923). Manchon.

old ding. The female pudend : low : C. 19–20 ; ob. Egan's Grose. ? ex *ding*, to strike.

old dog. See **old dog at it.**—2. Abbr. *gay old dog* : coll. : C. 19–20.—3. (Of a person) ' a lingering antique ', F. & H. : coll. : 1846, Dickens ; ob. Ex sense 1.—4. A half-burnt plug of tobacco remaining in a pipe : low : from ca. 1850 ; ob.

old dog at common prayer. (Of a clergyman) ' A Poor Hackney that cou'd Read, but not Preach well ', B.E. : late C. 17–mid-18. Cf. :

old dog at it, be. To be expert at something : coll. : ca. 1590–1880. Nashe, ' Olde dogge at that drunken, staggering kind of verse ' ; Butler ; B.E. ; Grose, 1st ed. Cf. the S.E. proverbial *old dog for a hard road*.

*old donah. A mother : tramps' c. (— 1893) >, by 1914, also Cockney s. P. H. Emerson. See **donah** ; cf. *old gel* or *woman*.

*Old Doss. Bridewell (London) : c. of ca. 1810–95. *Lex. Bal.* ; Baumann. See **doss.**

Old Dozen, the. The 12th Foot (in late C. 19–20, the Suffolk Regiment) : military : C. 19–20.

Old Dreadnought. Admiral the Hon. Edward Boscawen (1711–61) : naval : C. 18. Bowen.

old driver. The devil : low : C. 19–20 ; ob. Cf. *skipper*, q.v.

old dutch or **Dutch**, gen. preceded by **my**, occ. by **your** or **his.** One's wife : from the middle 1880's. When Albert Chevalier introduced the term into one of his songs (cf. the later, more famous poem, *My Old Dutch*), he explained that it referred to an old Dutch clock, the wife's face being likened to the clock-face. Prob. influenced by *duchess* (cf. my etymological error, at *old dutch*, in the 1st ed. of *Slang*).

Old Ebony. *Blackwood's Magazine* : journalistic and literary : from ca. 1860 ; ob. Ex the sober black lettering, etc., on the front cover. Cf. *Maga.*

old egg. A very familiar term of address (rarely to women) : coll. : late 1918 ; ob. (O.E.D. Sup.)

old ewe dressed lamb-fashion, an. An old woman dressing like a young one : coll. : 1777, *The Gentleman's Magazine*, ' Here antique maids of sixty three | Drest out lamb-fashion you might see ' ; Grose, 1785, as above. † by 1900. See **mutton dressed as lamb**, the mod. form.

Old Eyes, the. The Grenadier Guards : military : C. 19–20. Also *the Bermuda Exiles*, † ; *the Coal-heavers* ; *the Housemaids' Pets* ; *the Sand-Bags*, ob.

old fellow. A coll. vocative : 1825, C. M. Westmacott (O.E.D.). See **fellow.**

Old Fighting Tenth, the. The Lincolnshire Regiment : military coll. : late C. 19–20. F. & Gibbons. Orig. the 10th Foot Regiment.

old file. A miser : see **file.**—2. An old, or rather an experienced, man : low : from ca. 1850 ; ob. Ex sense 1 ; cf. *old*, adj., 6.

Old Five and Threepennies, the. The 53rd Foot : military : C. 19–20 ; ob. Ex the number ' 53 ' and the C. 19 daily pay of an ensign. Also *the Brick-dusts*.

old fizgig. See **fizgig.** Leman Rede & R. B. Peake, 1836. Ob.

old floorer. Death : low : from ca. 1840 ; ob. Cf. S.E. *the leveller.*

Old Fogs, the. The 87th Foot (in late C. 19–20, the Royal Irish Fusiliers) : military : ex the battle-cry, *fag an bealach* (clear the way) influenced by :

old fogy. See **fogy.**—**old fork, the.** See **fork, the old.**

old four-by-two. The quartermaster : military : from ca. 1912. B. & P. Ex *four-by-two*, a rifle *pull-through*.

old fruit. A jocular term of address : ca. 1912–25. Cf. *pippin*, q.v., and *old bean*.

old gal. See **old girl.**

Old Gang, the. Uncompromising Tories : political coll. nickname : from ca. 1870. Ware.

old geezer. See **geezer.**

old gel. A Cockney variant of *old donah*, q.v. · C. 20. B. & P.

old gentleman. The devil : **s.** > coll. ; also dial. C. 18–20. T. Brown, 1700 (O.E.D.) ; Barham.—2. A card slightly larger and thicker than the others : cardsharpers' c. : 1828, G. Smeeton, *Doings in London.* Ex sense 1 (the very devil for the sharped).—3. Time personified : C. 18. Ned Ward (1703) : cited by W. Matthews.

old gentleman's bed-posts. A variant (— 1874) of *devil's bed-posts,* q.v. (H., 5th ed.)

Old Gents, the. A synonym of *Gorgeous Wrecks* : coll. : 1915 ; ob. F. & Gibbons.

old geyser. I.e. *old geezer* : see **geezer.**

old girl or **gal.** A wife ; a mother : resp. low (— 1887) > respectable coll. and, from ca. 1895, low s. that has remained such. Baumann (*my old girl,* my wife) ; *The Idler,* June, 1892 (*the old gal,* wife). Cf. *old woman,* q.v.

old gooseberry. The devil : low : from ca. 1790. Grose, 3rd ed. ; 1861, H. Kingsley in *Ravenshoe* ; ob. App. orig. only in the next entry.—2. Hence (?), wife : low London (— 1909). Ware.

old gooseberry, play (up). To play the devil : coll. : from ca. 1790 ; ob. Grose, 3rd ed. ; Dickens ; H. Kingsley, 1865, ' Lay on like old gooseberry.'

old gown. Smuggled tea : low : from ca. 1860 ; ob. H., 2nd ed.

Old Grog. Admiral Edward Vernon (1684–1757). Ex his grogram coat. Dawson. (See also **grog.**)

old hand. An experienced person ; an expert : coll. : 1785, Grose. See **old,** adj., 1. Cf. *old bird, dog, file, soldier, stager,* qq.v.—2. An ex-convict : c. (mostly Australian) : 1861, T. McCombie, *Australian Sketches.* Morris.—3. *The Old Hand* : a coll. nickname for Gladstone from 1886 until his death. Baumann.

old Harry. The devil : coll. : from ca. 1740 ; ob. Grose, 1st ed. Cf. *the Lord Harry* (q.v.), 1687, Congreve.—2. In B.E. : ' A Composition used by Vintners, when they bedevil their Wines ', which explains the semantics. (For this B.E., see *Slang.*)

old Harry, play. To play the devil : coll. : 1837, Marryat, ' They've played old Harry with the rigging.' Cf. *old gooseberry, play.* Ex preceding entry. H.'s etymology (*old hairy*) is very ingenious : but, I fear, nothing more.

old Harvey. The large boat (launch) of a man-of-war : nautical : from ca. 1850 ; ob.

Old Hard-Heart. Admiral Sir A. K. Wilson, V.C. (1842–1921) : naval : late C. 19–20. Bowen. Also *Tug.*

old hat. The female pudend : low : 1754, Fielding ; Grose, ' Because frequently felt '. Ob.—2. A rank-and-file supporter of Sir James M'Culloch : Victoria (Australia) : ca. 1885–90. The anecdotal origin is less than usually suspect. Morris.

Old Honesty. Charles Lamb the essayist (1775–1834). Dawson.

old horney (horny) or **Hornington.** The penis : low : C. 18–20 ; ob. Cf. the indelicate sense of *horn* and *Miss Horner,* the female pudend.

old horse ; also **salt horse.** Salt junk : nautical : from ca. 1858. H., 2nd ed.—2. (Also and esp. *old hoss.*) A coll. vocative : orig. U.S., ' but now in common use here among friends ', H., 5th ed. (1874 ; but H. died in 1873.)

Old Horse, the. See **horse,** n., 5.

old house on or **over one's head, bring an.** To get into trouble : from ca. 1575 (ob.) : coll. till C. 19, then proverbial S.E. Gascoigne ; Sedley. (Apperson.)

old huddle and twang. App. a coll. intensive of *old huddle,* a miserly old person : ca. 1575–1640. Both are in Lyly, 1579. Cf. *old file,* q.v.

old identity. See **identity.**

old image. A very staid person : coll. : 1888, ' Rolf Boldrewood ', ' You're a regular old image, Jim, says she ' ; slightly ob. ? ex *graven image.*

Old Imperturbable. Philip Mead, Hampshire and England batsman : cricketers' coll. nickname. *The Observer,* June 14, 1936. (In August, 1936, he exceeded W. G. Grace's aggregate of runs in first-class cricket : his calmness has been held responsible for this audacity.) From ca. 1930.

Old Inniskillings, the. The 6th (Inniskilling) Dragoons : military coll. : C. 19–20 ; ob. Also *the Skillingers,* by a rhyming or an abbr. perversion of *Inniskilling.*

old iron. Shore clothes ; *work up* (i.e. refurbish) *old iron,* to go ashore : nautical : C. 19–20, ob. Ex the re-painting of rusted iron. Cf. *clobber.*

old iron. ' Small pilferings of any sort of material entrusted to workmen on a job ' : South Lancashire s. (— 1905) rather than dial. E.D.D. (Sup.).

old iron and brass. A pass : military rhyming s. : C. 20. B. & P.

old Jamaica. The sun : nautical rhyming s. : late C. 19–20. Bowen. Abbr. *old Jamaica rum.*

old jacker. A senior boy retained to show the youngsters the ropes : training-ships' : late C. 19–20 ; ob. Bowen.

Old Jocks, the. The Scots Greys : military : late C. 19–20. F. & Gibbons.

old lad. A coll. vocative : late C. 16–20. See **old,** adj., 4.

old lady. A term of address to a woman come down in the world : low (— 1823) ; † by 1900. Bee.—2. A card broader than the rest : cardsharpers' c. : 1828, G. Smeeton. See **old gentleman.**—3. The female pudend : low : C. 19–20. Cf. *old man,* n., 1.—4. One's wife or mother : coll. : from ca. 1870. (O.E.D. Sup.) Mostly U.S.

Old Lady of Threadneedle Street, the. The Bank of England : coll. : 1797, Gilray ; *Punch,* 1859, ' The girl for my money. The old lady of Threadneedle Street '. Ex its position in London, its age, and its preciseness.

old lag. See **lag,** n.—**old licht** or **light.** See **light,** n.

old ling. The same as *old hat,* 1 : low : mid-C. 18–mid-19. Grose, P.

Old Loyals, the. The 23rd Battalion of the London Regiment (Territorial) : military : late C. 19–20. F. & Gibbons. Ex its motto.

old man. The penis : low : C. 19–20. Cf. *old lady,* 3, and *old woman,* 4.—2. The captain of a merchant or a passenger ship : from ca. 1820 : orig. U.S. ; anglicised ca. 1860 (witness H., 3rd ed.). W. Clark Russell, *Sailors' Language,* 1883.—3. Whence, the officer in charge of a battalion : military : C. 20.—4. A husband : low (also jocular) coll. : 1768, Sterne ; 1848, Thackeray ; 1856, Whyte-Melville. O.E.D.—5. A father : low coll. : orig. (— 1852), U.S. ; anglicised ca. 1855. Cf. *old woman.* (Thornton.)—6. A coll. vocative : 1885, *Punch,* Aug. 24 (O.E.D.). Cf. *old boy, chap, fellow.*—7. A full-grown male kangaroo : Australian coll. : 1827, Peter Cunningham, *Two Years in New South Wales* ; J. Brunton Stephens. ' The aboriginal corruption is *wool-man,*' Morris.—8. A master, a ' boss ' : late C. 19–20 : **s.** >, ca. 1920, coll. : ? orig. U.S.—9. Hence, the governor of a prison :

c. (— 1932). Anon., *Dartmoor from Within.*—10. ' The ridge between two sleepers in a feather bed ', F. & H. : low (— 1902).—11. A blanket for wrapping up a baby or young child : nurses' : late C. 19–20.—12. A headmaster : schoolboys' : C. 20.

old-man, adj. Large ; larger than usual : Australian coll. : 1845, R. Howitt ; slightly ob. Ex the kangaroo : see preceding entry, sense 7. Morris. Cf. *piccaninny*, adj.

old man's milk. Whiskey : low coll. : from ca. 1860 ; ob. (Different in dial.)

Old Mob. The nickname of ' a noted Hawker ' (B.E.) : ca. 1690–1700.

Old Morality. W. H. Smith, the leader of the House of Commons in 1886–91. Dawson.

old mother Hubbard, that's. That's incredible : non-aristocratic c.p. of ca. 1880–1910. Ware. Ex the nursery-rhyme.

old moustache. An ' elderly vigorous man with grey moustache ' : lower classes' : ca. 1880–1914. Ware.

*****old Mr. Goree** or **Gory.** A gold coin : mid- C. 17–early 19 : c. >, ca. 1750, s. Coles, 1676 ; B.E. ; Grose. Perhaps ex the bright colour ; ? cognate with Romany *gorishi*, a shilling, ex Turkish *ghrush* ; most prob., however, ex the place (*Goree*).

old Mr. Grim. Death : coll. : C. 18–mid-19. Cf. *old floorer*.

old mud-hook. A frequent variant of *mud-hook*, 2 (q.v.). B. & P.

old nag. A cigarette : mostly military rhyming s. (on *fag*, q.v.) : C. 20. B. & P.

old Nick. The devil : coll. : 1668, L'Estrange. (The date of F. & H.'s earlier record is suspect.) Suspect also is ' Hudibras ' Butler's etymology : ' Nick Machiavel had no such trick, | Though he gave's name to our Old Nick.' Often abbr. to *Nick*, q.v. Certainly ex *Nicholas*, perhaps influenced by Ger. *Nickel*, a goblin (W.). Cf. *old Harry* ; see **old**, adj., last sense.—2. See **boy with the boots.**

Old Nol(l). Oliver Cromwell : a coll. nickname : from ca. 1650 ; ob. B.E., Grose. *Nol*(l), abbr. *Oliver*, puns *noll*, the head, and *noll*, a simpleton.

Old Nosey. The Duke of Wellington : coll. : 1851, Mayhew, but prob. in spoken use thirty years earlier (cf. *conky*, q.v.) ; ob. by 1890, † by 1910. Like many other persons of character, Wellington had a very big nose.

old one, often spelt **old 'un.** The devil : C. 11–20 : S.E. until C. 18, then coll. ; ob. Grose. See **old**, adj., last sense.—2. A quizzical familiar term of address : coll. (— 1811) ; slightly ob. *Lex. Bal.*—3. Hence, one's father : coll. : 1836, Dickens. (Like preceding senses, with *the*.)—4. Hence, the pantaloon (who was gen. the fool's father) : theatrical : from ca. 1850 ; ob.—5. A horse more than three years old : from ca. 1860 : racing coll. > S.E. —6. The headmaster : Public Schools' : late C. 19–20. (P. G. Wodehouse, *Tales of St. Austin's*, 1903.)

Old One-Eye. H.M.S. *Cyclops* : naval : C. 20. Bowen. Ex the legend of the Cyclops.

Old One O'Clock. See **General One O'Clock.**

old oyster. A low vocative : from ca. 1890 ; ob. Milliken, 1892, ' Life don't want lifting, old oyster,' which puns the Shakespearian tag.

old palaver. See **palaver**, n., 1.

old paste-horn. (Gen. a nickname for) a large-nosed man : mostly shoemakers' : from ca. 1856 ; ob. See **paste-horn** and cf. *conky*, q.v.

old peg(g). ' Poor Yorkshire cheese, made of skimmed milk ', Grose, 1st ed. : late C. 18–mid-19

coll., C. 18–19 dial. (E.D.D.). ? because hard and dry.

Old Peveril. Sir Walter Scott (d. 1832). Ex his *Peveril of the Peak*, 1823. Dawson.

old pharaoh. A variation of *pharaoh*, q.v. : late C. 17–early 19. G. Meriton.

old pip. An upper-classes' coll. term of address : from ca. 1930. E.g. in John G. Brandon, *West End !*, 1933. Cf. *old fruit.*

old plug. See **plug**, n., 1.

old Poger. (The devil.) Prob. a ghost word fathered by the *Lex. Bal.*, 1811, and copied by Egan and F. & H. : error caused by mingling the successive *old peg* and *old Roger* in Grose, first three edd. Perhaps, however, *poger* is a misprint for *poguer* = poker ; see :

old poker ; Old Poker. The devil : coll. : 1784, Walpole, ' As if old Poker was coming to take them away '. Perhaps ' he who pokes ', but more prob. *poker* = hobgoblin, demon : if the latter, then S.E. until C. 19, then coll., after ca. 1830, mainly U.S. ; except in U.S., † by 1880. Cf. *poker, by the holy*, which it may have suggested.

old pot. An old man : late C. 19–20 : see **old**, adj., 4 and 6, and **pot**.—2. **the old pot**, one's father : low : late C. 19–20 ; ob. P. H. Emerson.

old pot and pan. ' Old man ' = husband, father ; occ. ' old woman ' = wife, woman : mid-C. 19–20 rhyming s. († by 1915 for a woman).—2. Hence, any Commanding Officer : military : C. 20. B. & P.

old put. See **put**, 2.

Old Q. Wm. Douglas, 4th Duke of Queensberry (1724–1810), sportsman and rake. Dawson.

old raspberry. A red-nosed ' character ' : lower classes' (— 1923). Manchon. Ex the colour.

old rip. See **rip.**

old Robin. An experienced person : coll. : ca. 1780–1830. J. Potter, 1784 (O.E.D.). Cf. *old bird, hand, soldier, stager*, qq.v. See **old**, adj., 1.

old Roger. The devil : coll. : ca. 1720–1840. *A New Canting Dict.*, 1725. Cf. *old Harry, old Nick.*—2. The pirates' flag : 1723 ; by 1785, replaced by *jolly Roger.*

Old Rowley. Charles II : Restoration period. Ex the saying " A Roland for an Oliver ", in contradistinction to Cromwell. Dawson.

*****Old Ruffin.** An early C. 19 form of *Ruffin*, the devil : c. Ainsworth.

old salt. An experienced sailor : nautical coll. : C. 19–20. See **old**, adj., 1.

Old Saucy Seventh. The 7th (Queen's Own) Hussars : military : C. 19–20 ; ob. Also † *Lily-White Seventh, Old Straw-Boots* (ob.), *Old Straws* (ob.) and † *Young Eyes.*

old scratch or **O— S—.** The devil : low coll. : 1740 (O.E.D.) ; Smollett ; Trollope. In late C. 19–20, mostly dial. See also **Scratch.**

Old Seven and Sixpennies, the. The 76th Foot (from ca. 1881, the 2nd Battalion, West Riding Regiment) : C. 19–20 ; ob. Ex the number ' 76 ' and the (former) amount of a lieutenant's pay. Also *the Immortals* and the *Pigs.*

old shaver. See **shaver.** Cf. the more gen. *young shaver.*

old shell. An old (sailing-ship) sailor : nautical : mid-C. 19–20 ; ob. Ex S.E. *shellback.*

old shoes. Rum : low : late C. 19–20 ; ob. Ware. Why ?

·**old shoes** (occ. **boots**), **ride in** (or, more gen., **wear**) **another man's.** To marry, or to keep, another man's mistress : coll. : C. 19–20 ; ob.

old shoes ! up again ! ' No rest for the wicked ! ' : semi-proverbial coll. (— 1887) ; ob. Baumann.

old shopkeeper. See shopkeeper.

old shovel-penny. ' The paymaster, who is generally an ancient ' (Ware) : military (— 1909) ; ob.

Old Slop. *The Times* : London : ca. 1840–50, when that newspaper, having no will of its own, was trying to attract attention. Ex Fr. *salope*, a slut. Ware.

old socks. A term of address : Canadian : C. 20. Garnett Radcliffe, in *The Passing Show*, Jan. 27, 1934, ' Hey, Morrison, old socks. How's things ? '

old soldier. An experienced, esp. if crafty, man : coll. : 1722, Defoe, ' The Captain [was] an old soldier at such work ' (O.E.D.). See old, adj., 1. Cf. *come the old soldier*, q.v. Contrast :—2. A simple fellow, gen. in the proverbial *an old soldier, an old innocent* : mid-C. 19–20 ; very ob. R. L. Stevenson in *St. Ives*, 1894. Apperson.—3. An old quid of tobacco ; a cigar-end : low : late C. 19–20.

old-soldier, v. To ' come the old soldier over ' (a person) : coll. : 1892. O.E.D. Cf. :

old soldier, fight the. To shirk duty ; sham sick : nautical : early C. 19. John Davis, *The Post Captain*, 1805 (ed. R. H. Case, 1928). I.e. like an ' old soldier ' (q.v.).

old soldier—old shit(e). A military c.p. : C. 20.

old spit and polish (or **shine**). See spit and polish, 2.

old split-foot. The devil : low jocular : ? orig. U.S. (Lowell, 1848) ; very ob.

old sport. A coll. term of address : 1905 (O.E.D. Sup.) Ex *sport*, a good fellow.

old square-toes. A coll. nickname for a pedantic, old-fashioned man : from ca. 1860 ; ob. *The Sun*, Dec. 28, 1864.—2. But *square-toes* appears as early as 1785 (Grose, 1st ed.) for ' one's father ' or ' father ' ; † by 1860.

old stager. A very experienced person : coll. : 1711, Shaftesbury, whence we see that the term was orig. applied to travellers by stage-coach (O.E.D.) ; the gen. sense was well established by 1788 : witness Grose, 2nd ed. Cf. *old hand*.

old stander. A naval seaman transferring from ship to ship as his captain is transferred : naval coll. : C. 18–mid-19, Bowen virtually implies. Cf. *old stager*.

Old Steadfast. Woodfull, the Australian test cricketer of 1926–34 and captain in 1930–4 : cricketers' nickname : from 1930. Also, as in *The Daily Telegraph*, April 23, 1934, *the Rock* or *the Unbowlable*.

Old Steams. Shares in the City of Dublin Steam Company : Stock Exchange (— 1895). A. J. Wilson, *Stock Exchange Glossary*.

old stick. A pejorative applied to a person (cf. *stick*, q.v.) : coll. : C. 19–20 ; ob. See old, adj., 6. Cf. next entry.—2. A complimentary vocative : ca. 1800–70. Halliwell. Cf. *old*, adj., 4.

old stick in the mud. (In vocative and reference) a very staid person : coll. : from ca. 1820. Moncrieff, 1823, *Tom and Jerry*.

Old Strawboots or **Straws.** See Old Saucy Seventh and Strawboots. Ex having, at Warburg (1760), substituted straw-bands for outworn boots. Very ob. if not †.

old strike-a-light. One's father : ca. 1850–60. F. & H., at *governor*. Ex his exclamation on being asked for loans.

old stripes. See stripes.

Old Stubborns. The 45th Foot (from ca. 1881, the Sherwood Foresters) : military : C. 19–20.

Old Subtlety. William Fiennes (1582–1662), the 1st Viscount Saye and Sele (Dawson).

old sweat. An old soldier, esp. of the Regular Army : military : from ca. 1890. F. & Gibbons. Ex his strenuous efforts. Cf. *old soldier*, q.v.

Old Tay Bridge. A middle-aged lady bank-clerk : bank-clerks' nickname : late C. 19–20. The old bridge across the Forth of Tay at Dundee was blown down in 1879.

old thing (**Old** or **Ould Thing, the**). The language of the Irish tinkers : those tinkers' (— 1891). O.E.D. at *Shelta*.—2. A familiar term of address : coll. : 1913, Galsworthy, ' My dear old thing ' (O.E.D. Sup.).—3. Beef and ' damper ' : Australian coll. : ca. 1845–80. Ibid. Prob. ex ' —, the same old thing ! '

old thirds. Three men working on the one job or together : tailors' (— 1935). Cf. *partners*.

Old Tick. The same as *Old Q.* (Dawson.)

old-timer. One given to praising old times : coll. : 1860, *Music and Drama* ; ob. Mostly U.S.— 2. One long established in place or position : from ca. 1810 : coll. until ca. 1905, then S.E. except when used as term of address.

old toast. The devil : low : C. 19–20 ; ob. Occ. *old toaster*, likewise ob. (Cf. the U.S. *old smoker*.) Prob. ex :—2. ' A brisk old fellow ', Grose, 1st ed. : c. or low s. : ca. 1690–1830. B.E.

old Tom. Gin ; esp. very good strong gin ; low : from ca. 1820 ; ob. ' Jon Bee ', 1823 ; H., 5th ed. (q.v. for etymology) ; A. S. M. Hutchinson, making great play with it in *Once Aboard the Lugger*, 1908. Brewer's etymology ex one Thomas Chamberlain, a brewer of gin, may be correct.

Old Tony. Anthony Cooper (1621–83), the 1st Earl of Shaftesbury. (Dawson.)

old top. A s. vocative : from ca. 1920 ; slightly ob. by 1930. P. G. Wodehouse, 1923 (O.E.D. Sup.). Cf. *old bean*.

old tots. See tots, old.

Old Toughs, the. The 103rd Foot (in late C. 19–20, the Royal Dublin Fusiliers) : military : from ca. 1750. F. & Gibbons. Ex long and arduous Indian service. Also *the Bombay Toughs.*

old trout. A C. 19–20 survival, now slightly ob., of *trout*, q.v., ' That awful old trout ', applied in 1934 by a ' bright young thing ' to a dowdy authoress.

old truepenny. See truepenny.—**old turnip.** See turnip, 2.—**old 'un.** See old one.—**old Vun O'Clock.** See General One O'Clock.

old whale. An old sailing-ship seaman : nautical : from ca. 1860 ; ob. Bowen.

old whip. See whip, old.

old whiskers. A ' cheeky boys' salute to a working-man whose whiskers are a little wild and iron-grey ' : mid-C. 19–20. Ware.

Old White Hat. John Willis, clipper-ship owner : nautical : mid-C. 19–very early 20. Bowen. Ex the white top-hat he was so fond of wearing.

old wigsby. A ' crotchety, narrow-minded, elderly man ' : middle classes' coll. : C. 19–20 ; ob. Ware. Cf. Fr. *perruque*.

old wives' Paternoster, the. ' The devil's paternoster ', i.e. a grumbling and complaining : coll. : ca. 1575–1620. H. G. Wright, 1580, ' He plucking his hatte about his eares, mumbling the olde wives' Paternoster, departed.' Apperson.

old woman. A wife : low (except when jocular) coll. : 1823, ' Jon Bee '. Cf. *old man*, 4.—2. A mother : low coll. : orig. (1834), U.S. ; anglicised ca. 1850. Thornton. Cf. *old girl*, q.v.—3. A prisoner that, unfit for hard work, is put to knitting stockings : prison c. : from ca. 1860.—4. The female pudend : low : C. 19–20. Cf. *old man*, 1.

old woman's poke. A shuffling of cards by the juxtaposed insertion of the two halves of the pack : card-players' coll. (— 1887). Baumann.

oldest. Eldest : C. 14–20 : S.E. until ca. 1830, then dial. and low coll.

olds. Old persons ; old members of a set, class, etc. : coll. : 1883, Besant, ' Young clever people . . . are more difficult to catch than the olds,' O.E.D.

oldster. The nautical sense (a midshipman of four years' service) is j.—2. An elderly or an experienced person : coll. : 1848, Dickens in *Dombey and Son* (O.E.D.).

ole. See ol'.

olivander. An error for † S.E. *olivaster* (cf. Fr. *olivâtre*) : from ca. 1850. O.E.D.

olive-branch. A contemporary synonym of *rainbow*, q.v. (F. & Gibbons.)

olive oil ! Au revoir ! : 1884, orig. music-halls'; ob. Ware.

***Oliver** ; occ. **oliver.** The moon : c. : ca. 1780–1900 ; nearly † by 1860 (H., 2nd ed.). G. Parker. Esp. in *Oliver is up* or *O. whiddles*, the moon shines, and *O. is in town*, the nights are moonlight. Ainsworth, in *Rookwood* (1834), has ' Oliver puts his black night-cap on,' hides behind clouds. Perhaps *Oliver* was ' coined ' in derision of Oliver Cromwell : cf. *Oliver's skull*.—2. Among tramps conversant with Romany, *Olivers* (rare in singular) are stockings : from before 1887. Baumann.—3. A fist : abbr. (— 1909) of rhyming s. *Oliver Twist*. Ware.

Oliver ?, do you. Do you understand ? : C. 20 : abbr. rhyming s., *Oliver Cromwell* on *tumble* (pronounced *tumbell*), to understand. W.

Oliver Twist. See **Oliver**, 3. (Mid-C. 19–20 ; ob.)

Oliver's skull. A chamber-pot : low : ca. 1690–1870 ; ob. by 1820. B.E.

oll. All : (dial. and) low coll. : C. 19–20. (*The Observer*, June 2, 1935, in a cricket report.)

ollapod. A (gen. country) apothecary : coll. : ca. 1802–95. H., 3rd ed. ; Baumann. Ex George Colman's *The Poor Gentleman*, 1802. (Sp. *olla podrida* ; lit., putrid pot.)

'oller, boys, 'oller ! A collar : rhyming s. : late C. 19–20. B. & P.

***olli compolli.** ' The by-name of one of the principal Rogues of the Canting Crew ', B.E. : c. : late C. 17–mid-19. What was his role, unless he were, perchance, the Jack-of-all-trades ? And what the etymology of this rhymed fabrication unless on *olio* ?

-ology. Often, from ca. 1810, in jocularities verging on the coll. *John Bull*, April 28, 1917, ' Don't pin your faith too much to ologies and isms ' (W.). Here, as in *-ometer* (q.v.), the *-o-* has been adopted from the preceding element, the radicals being Gr. λόγος, a word, and Gr. μέτρον, a measure.

omacle. An incorrect form of *onycle*, onyx : C. 14–16. O.E.D.

omalo. Incorrect for *homalo-* in scientific combinations : from ca. 1865. O.E.D.

***omee** ; **omer** ; **omey** ; **homee, homey.** A man ; esp. a master, e.g. a landlord : c. and Parlyaree (>, in late C. 19, also gen. theatrical) : from ca. 1840. ' *No. 747* ', p. 409, is valid for 1845 ; H.,

1st ed. Ex It. *uomo* via Lingua Franca. See quotation at *parker*.

-ometer. Jocular formations were popularised by Sydney Smith's *foolometer* : e.g. *girlometer*, q.v.

omms and chevoos. A French van or truck on troop-trains in France : military : G.W. (F. & Gibbons.) Ex the marking, ' Hommes 37–40. Chevaux en long 8.'

omnes. A mixture of ' odds and ends of various wines ' : wine-merchants' (— 1909). Ware. Ex *alls*, L. *omnes* meaning all.

omni-. All-. Often, from ca. 1860, so fantastic as to border on coll.

omni gatherum ; or as one word. A variant of *omnium gatherum*, q.v.

omnibus. The female pudend : low : from ca. 1840.—2. A harlot : low : ca. 1850–1910.

omnium. Combined non-Government stocks of which the constituents may be handled separately : Stock Exchange coll. : from ca. 1894. L. *omnium*, of all things. O.E.D.

omnium(-)gatherum ; also o. **getherum,** C. 17 ; o. **githerum,** C. 16. A mixed assemblage of things or persons : coll. : 1530 (O.E.D.). Mock L. ending added to *gather*.—2. Hence a medley dance popular in mid-C. 17 : coll.—3. Omnium (in S.E. sense) : coll. : ca. 1770–95. O.E.D.

omnium gatherum, adv. Confusedly, promiscuously : mid-C. 17 : coll. Ex preceding.

omo- is incorrect (C. 17–20) for *homo* ; **omoio-** (C. 19–20) for *homoio-, homœo-*. O.E.D.

on, adj. Concupiscent : low coll. : C. 18–20 ; ob. Halliwell.—2. Whence, ready and willing : coll. : from ca. 1870. E.g. *are you on ?*, are you agreed, prepared, willing ?—3. Whence, fond of : 1890, L. C. O'Doyle, ' Woddell was not much on beer ' (O.E.D.) : coll. >, ca. 1930, almost S.E.—4. No : back s. (— 1859). H., 1st ed. E.g. *on doog*, no good.—5. Tipsy : low, esp public-house : C. 19–20. O.E.D. records at 1802 ; H., 2nd ed. Gen. *a bit on*. Perhaps ex *on the booze*.—6. Present ; nearby ; likely to appear : Winchester Coll. : from ca. 1830 ; ob. ? ex *on view*.—7. Possible ; feasible : billiard and snooker players' coll. : from ca. 1930. Horace Lindrum, in *Lyons' Sports Sheet*, Dec. 23, 1935, ' The majority of amateur [snooker] players . . . wildly attempt shots that are not " on ".' Lit., on the table : cf. *on the cards*, possible or almost probable.

on, adv. or adv.-adj. Having money at stake, a wager on (something) : from ca. 1810 : racing coll. until ca. 1885, then S.E. *The Sporting Magazine*, 1812 (O.E.D.) ; *The Standard*, Oct. 23, 1873, ' Everyone . . . had something on.' Since ca. 1870, gen. *have a bit on*, as in George Moore's *Esther Waters* : this phrase is coll.—2. Hence, standing or bound to win : racing (— 1874) > gen. coll. ' You're on a quid if Kaiser wins,' H., 5th ed.

on, preposition. Of : C. 13–20 : S.E. until ca. 1750, then coll. till ca. 1790, then low coll. (in C. 20, indeed, virtually sol.) and dial. Esp. in *on't* = of it. Partly ex *o'* being = both *of* and *on*.—2. Superfluous in this sense : sol. : mid-C. 19–20. ' Who's that you're meaning on ? ', where *meaning on* should correctly be simply *meaning*, though the *on* arises actually from the implied sense, ' whom are you getting at ? ' (Baumann.)—3. See **on**, adv., 2.—4. With : coll. : C. 19–20. See **onto**, 2, and in that quotation substitute *on* for *onto*.—5. To be paid for by : coll. : C. 20. Esp. in ' The lunch is on *me*.'

(O.E.D. Sup.)—6. To the detriment, or the ruin, or the circumventing, of : C. 20, ' I hope he won't go bankrupt on us.' Sometimes, to one's loss, as in ' Our old cat died on us.'

on phrases :—See the key words.

on, hot. See hot on.

once. Energy, vigour ; impudence : low : 1886, *The Referee*, Oct. 24, ' I like Shine—I cannot help admiring the large amount he possesses of what is vulgarly called " once " ' ; virtually †. Ware, ' The substantivising of " on "'—most emphatic.'

once, in. First time ; at the first attempt : low coll. : late C. 19–20. G. R. Sims, 1900, ' You've guessed it in once, father.' Cf. S.E. *in one*.

once a week. ' Cheek ' (n. and v.) : rhyming s. (— 1914). F. & Gibbons.

once-a-week man ; or Sunday promenader. A man in debt : London : ca. 1825–40. Egan, *Real Life in London*. Sunday was the one day on which he could not be arrested for debt. (Ware.)

once before we fill and once before we light. A drinking c.p. recorded by Ned Ward in 1709.

once-over. A quick, penetrating glance : coll. adopted, in 1919, ex U.S. (British soldiers had heard it in France often enough in 1918.)

oncer. A person in the habit of attending church only once on a Sunday : coll. : from ca. 1890. (O.E.D. Sup.) Opp. *twicer.*—2. A £1 note : c. (— 1933). Charles E. Leach.

onces. Wages : artisans' (— 1909) ; ob. Ware. Ex *once a week*.

oncet. See onct.

oncoming. (Of women.) Sexually responsive : coll. : late C. 19–20.

onc't, onct ; oncet, onest. Pronounced *wunst*. Once : sol. : C. 19–20. Baumann.

one. Oneself ; one's own interest : coll. : 1567, R. Edwards, ' I can help one : is not that a good point of philosophy ' (O.E.D.) ; † by 1830. In C. 19–20, *number one*, q.v.—2. A grudge ; a score ; a blow, kiss, etc. : 1830, Galt, ' I owed him one ' (O.E.D.) : s. >, ca. 1890, coll.—3. A lie : late C. 19–20 : s. >, ca. 1920, coll. Esp. ' That's a big one ! '—4. Erroneous form of *own*, adj. : C. 17. O.E.D.—5. Erroneous for *wone*, abundance, resources : C. 15. O.E.D.—6. ' " One " in Stock Exchange parlance, when applied to stock, means one thousand nominal ; a " half " or " half-a-one " is, therefore, five hundred pounds. " Five " = five thousand pounds nominal,' A. J. Wilson, *Stock Exchange Glossary*, 1895. These terms are coll. verging on j.—7. See :

one, a. A very odd or amusing person : from ca. 1905. ' He's a one ! ' Cf. *one for*, q.v.

one, on a. Under open arrest : military (other ranks') : from ca. 1925. The *one* is the *charge-sheet* on which his name appears.

one a-piece, see. To see double : coll. : 1842, *Punch* (ii, 21) ; ob.

one-acter. A (short) play in one act : theatrical coll. : from ca. 1910. Ex *one-act play* by ' the Oxford -*er* '.

one and a peppermint-drop. A one-eyed person : low London (— 1909) ; slightly ob. Ware.

One and All, the. The Duke of Cornwall's Light Infantry : military : late C. 19–20. F. & Gibbons. Ex the county motto.

one-and-thirty. Drunk : semi-proverbial coll. : mid-C. 17–18. Ray. Ex the scoring of full points at the old English game of one-and-thirty.

one and t'other. Brother : rhyming s. : late C. 19–20. B. & P.—2. Mother : C. 20. P.P. *Rhyming Slang*, 1932.

one another for each other. See each other, 2.

one-armed landlord. A pump : Somersetshire s. (— 1903) rather than dial. E.D.D. Ex the cheapness of water compared with beer.

one better, go. To do better, to ' score ' : from ca. 1890 : s. >, ca. 1910, coll. *The Spectator*, May 7, 1892 (O.E.D.). Ex play at cards.

one-bite. (Gen. pl.) A small, sour apple—thrown away after being tested with one bite : costers' : from ca. 1870. Ware.

one consecutive night. A c.p. denoting ' enough ' : Society and theatrical : 1890, *The Daily News*, Aug. 15 ; † by 1915. Ware.

one-drink house. A public-house where only one drink is served within (say) an hour : coll. of London lower classes : ca. 1860–1905. Ware.

one-er, †onener, oner, wunner. A person, a thing, of great parts, remarkable (e.g. a notable lie), most attractive, dashing ; an expert : 1840, Dickens, ' Miss Sally's such a one-er for that, she is ' ; 1857, Hughes, *wunner* ; 1861, Dutton Cook, *onener* (pron. *wun-ner*) ; 1862, Thackeray, *oner*. In C. 20, rarely other than *oner*. Perhaps *oner* is ex *one*, something unique, influenced—as W. suggests—by dial. *wunner*, a wonder. (Cf. *one, a*, q.v.)—2. Esp. a knock-out blow : 1861, Dutton Cook, as above.—3. Something consisting of, indicated by, characteristic of or by, ' 1 ' : coll. : 1889 (of cricket). Esp. of one church-going a day. (For all three) O.E.D.—4. Esp. a shilling : low : late C. 19–20 ; ob. Cf. (and prob. ex) *one of them*, 2.

One-Eyed City, the. Birkenhead : C. 20. (John Brophy, *Waterfront*, 1934.) Mostly among ' Liverpudlians '.

one for, a. ' A devotee, admirer, or champion of (anything) ' : coll. : from ca. 1930. O.E.D. (Sup.) Prob. ex *a one* (q.v. at *one, a*).

one for his nob. See nob, one for his.

one-gun salute, get a. To be court-martialled : naval coll. : C. 20. F. & Gibbons. The ship on which the Court is to be held fires one gun at 8 a.m.

one hand for yourself and one for the ship ! Be careful : a nautical c.p. (C. 19–20) addressed to a youngster going aloft. Bowen.

one-horse. Insignificant ; very small : coll. : orig. (1854), U.S. ; anglicised—mostly in the Colonies—ca. 1885. Goldwin Smith, 1886, ' Canada has been saddled with one-horse universities.' (Thornton.)

one hundred and twenty (gen. written ' 120 ') in the water-bag. An Australian rural c.p. (C. 20) applied to a very hot day. Sc. *degrees*.

one in, adj. ' Hearing another's good fortune and wishing the same to oneself ', F. & H. : tailors' : from ca. 1870. Contrast *one out*, q.v.

one in ten. A parson : coll. : late C. 17–19. B.E. Ex *tithe*.

one in the eye. A misfortune, a set-back, a snub, an insult : late C. 19–20. G. R. Sims, 1900, ' It was . . . " one in the eye " for her aunt ' (O.E.D.).

one-legged donkey. ' The single-legged stool which the old coastguard was allowed for purposes of rest, designed to capsize the moment he drowsed off ' : nautical : C. 19. Bowen.

one lordship is worth all his manners. A C. 17 c.p. punning *manors*.

one nick or nitch. A male child, *two nick* (*nitch*) being a baby girl : printers' : from ca. 1860. Ex an anatomical characteristic.

one o'clock, like. See **like one o'clock.**

one of + pl. n. + **who** (**which,** or **that**) **is** (**was,** etc.). Incorrect for *one of . . . are* (*were,* etc.). ' He is one of those men who is always right,' properly ' are always right '. An error arising in faulty thinking : cf. *these kind of* . . ., q.v.

one of my cousins. A harlot : coll. : late C. 17–early 19. B.E., Grose. Ex a lie frequently told by the amorous-vagrant male.

one of the best. See **best, one of the.**

one of the boys. A variant of *one of the lads,* q.v. at *lads.* See also **b'hoy.**

one of them or **us.** A harlot : coll. : resp. C. 19–20 (extant only with stressed *them*) ; mid-C. 18–mid-19, as in Grose, 1st ed. Cf. *one of my cousins.*—2. (Only **one of them.**) A shilling : urban lower classes' (— 1909). Ware.

one of those. A catamite ; any homosexual : euphemistic : C. 20. See the quotation at **Nancy,** 1.

one of those, I (really) **must have.** A non-aristocratic c.p. of ca. 1880–3. Ware. Ex a comic song.

one on (him, you, etc.) !, **that's.** That is a point against you ! : coll. : late C. 19–20.

one out, adj. I'm lucky ! : tailors' : from ca. 1870. Contrast *one in,* q.v. Cf. :

one out of it ! I'm keeping out of this ! : tailors' : from ca. 1870.

one over the eight. See **eight, one over the.**

one-pip(per). A second lieutenant : military : 1915. F. & Gibbons. The New Zealanders preferred *one-star artist.* See next entry but one.

one squint, etc. See **squint is better . . .**

one star, one stunt. An Army c.p. (1914 +), now ob., meaning that second lieutenants in the infantry frequently got killed in their first battle. They wore one star. See **stunt.**

one two, preceded by **a, his, the,** etc. Two blows in rapid succession : boxing coll. : from ca. 1820. Egan, ' Belcher . . . distinguished for his one two '.

one under the arm. An additional job : tailors' : from ca. 1870 ; ob. Ex things carried comfortably under the arm.

one up, be or **have gone.** To have obtained the next step in promotion : military coll. : C. 20. F. & Gibbons. Cf. :

one up on, be. To have scored an advantage over (a person) : coll. : C. 20.

one or a marble (up)on another's taw, I'll be ! I'll get even with him some time ! : low : ca. 1810–50. Vaux.

one with t'other, the. Sexual intercourse : low : C. 17–18. Anon. song, *Maiden's Delight,* 1661, in Farmer's *Merry Songs and Ballads,* 1897.

one word from you and (s)he does as (s)he likes, with other pronominal variations. He ignores your commands : c.p. : C. 20. Sarcastically ex *one word from me* (etc.) *is enough* or *he* (etc.) *obeys.*

onee. One : low theatrical : from ca. 1850 ; ob. Influenced by Parlyaree.

oneirocracy. A catachrestic form of † *oneirocrisy* : C. 17. O.E.D.

onener, oner. See **one-er.**

one's eye. A hiding-place for ' cabbage ' (q.v.) : tailors' : from ca. 1850 ; ob.

one's name on it. See **name on it.—onest.** See **onct.**

ongcus or **-cuss** ; **onkiss** ; mostly **oncus** or, esp., s. **onkus.** (Of food) good ; (of a place) passable : New Zealanders' : from ca. 1914, chiefly among the

soldiers.—2. (Ex the second nuance.) Inferior or bad ; unjust : Australians' : from ca. 1914. It is, however, possible that sense 2 is the earlier and that the origin is the U.S. *ornery.*

*****onicker.** A harlot : c. : from ca. 1880 ; ob. Walford's *Antiquarian,* 1887. Cf. **one nick,** q.v.

*****onion.** A seal, gen. in pl. *bunch of onions* : c. : 1811, *Lex. Bal.* ; ob. Esp. if worn on a ribbon or a watch-chain ; occ. applied to other objects there worn. Ex the shape.—2. The head, esp. in *off his onion,* crazy : from ca. 1890 : low >, by 1920, gen. Ex the shape.—3. ' Part of a knot speed ' : nautical : C. 20. Bowen ; F. & Gibbons, ' We got sixteen and an onion out of her.' Jocular on *fraction.* 4. Abbr. *flaming onion,* q.v.

onion, feel much of an. To feel very bored : lower classes' (— 1923). Manchon.

onion, it may serve with an. An ironical C. 17 c.p. Howell. (Apperson.)

onion, off one's. See **onion,** 2.

*****onion-hunter.** A thief of seals worn on ribbons, etc. : c. : 1811. See **onion,** 1.

onish. (Pron. *onnish.*) Rather late : e.g. ' It's getting onish.' C. 20 : coll.

onk. (Gen. pl.) A franc : military : late 1914 ; ob. F. & Gibbons. By perversion.

onker. A sailing-ship on the Baltic timber trade : Thamesside : late C. 19–20. Origin ?

onkiss or **onkus.** See **ongcus.**

only is frequently misplaced, as in ' We only heard it yesterday ' for ' We heard it only yesterday ' : this catachresis is coeval with the language. (Baumann.)—2. Except : sol. (— 1887). Baumann, ' They never came, only on Tuesdays.'

on't. On it : C. 15–20 : S.E. until C. 19, then coll.

'on't. Won't : sol. : C. 19–20. Baumann.

onto, corresponding to **into,** is S.E. ; where = *on to,* it is catachrestic : mid-C. 19–20. See esp. the O.E.D. and Thornton's acrid comment.—2. On, in sense of ' with ' : sol., or low coll. : from ca. 1870 or perhaps a decade or two earlier. Baumann cites ' He had a strange habit of somerseting onto him ' (cf. S.E., ' He had a strange way with him ').

on'y. Only : sol. : C. 19–20. Like **'on't,** it is very illiterate. Baumann.

oodles. A large quantity, esp. of money : orig. U.S. ; anglicised ca. 1890. *The Overland Monthly,* 1869 (iii, 131), ' A Texan never has a great quantity of anything, but he has " scads " of it or oodles or dead oodles or scadoodles or " swads ".' Prob. ex (*the whole*) *boodle* (O. W. Holmes), with which cf. *caboodle,* q.v.

oof, ooftish. Money : low : resp. from ca. 1885 ; from ca. 1870 (and ob.). *The Sporting Times,* Dec. 26, 1891, ' Ooftish was, some twenty years ago, the East End [Yiddish] synonym for money, and was derived from [Ger.] *auf tische* [properly *auf dem tische*], " on the table ", because one refused to play cards for money unless the cash were on the table '. Cf. *plank down,* q.v.—2. (Gen. pl.) An egg : military or Western Front in G.W. (F. & Gibbons.) Ex Fr. *œuf.* Only *oof* in this sense.

oof-bird. A source, gen. a supplier, of money : 1888. Ex preceding *on the golden goose.* Whence *the feathered oof-bird,* (a supplier, a source of) money in plenty.

oof-bird walk, make the. To circulate money : low : from ca. 1888 ; ob.

oofless. Poor ; temporarily without cash : from ca. 1889. See **oof.** Contrast : *oofy.*

oofs. See **erfs.**—**ooftish.** See **oof.**

oofy. Rich; (always) with plenty of cash: low: from ca. 1889. See **oof.**

ooja(-ka-piv or **ka-(or -cum-)pivvy,** the latter being the original corruption), is prob. a corruption of the nautical *hook-me-dinghy* or else ex Hindustani (as Manchon says); military, C. 20, it means a 'gadget'—anything with a name that one cannot at the moment recall. Further corruptions were *ooja-cum-spiff* and, later still, *oojiboo*, with which cf. the Canadian *hooza-ma-kloo*. B. & P.—2. Hence, *the old oojah*, the Colonel: military: from ca. 1905. Manchon.

oolfoo. A fool: low: late C. 19–20. Ware. By transposition and addition. Also *oolerfer*: centre s.: from ca. 1860.

Oom Paul. Paul Kruger (1825–1904) when President of the South African Republic. Lit., Uncle Paul.

ooman. Woman: sol. and dial.: C. 19 (prob. earlier)–20. Baumann. Cf. *'on't*.

oons ; occ. **oun(e)s.** A coll. variation, late C. 16–20 (very ob.), of *zounds*. O.E.D.

oopizootics, the. 'An undiagnosed complaint', C. J. Dennis: Australian (— 1916). Jocularly artificial word.

Ooty. Ootacamund: Anglo-Indian: late C. 19–20. (Philip Gosse, *Memoirs of a Camp-Follower*, 1934.)

ooze. To depart: from ca. 1920. D. Mackail, 1930, ' I've got some work this afternoon. Shall we ooze ? ' Cf. *filter* and *trickle*.

oozle. See **ouzle.**

op, n. Optime: coll.: Cambridge University: 1828, *The Sporting Magazine*. O.E.D.—2. Opera: Society: from ca. 1870; virtually †. Ware.—3. See **ops.**—4. Operator; *esp. wireless op*: nautical: from ca. 1922.

'op it. See **hop it.**

opaque. Dull; stupid: London: ca. 1820–40. Bee. (Adumbrates *dim*, q.v.)

open. An open golf-championship, as *the British open*: sports coll.: from ca. 1920.

open-air. An open-air meeting: Salvation Army's coll.: 1884. Ware.

open arse. A medlar: C. 11–20: S.E. till ca. 1660, then low coll. till ca. 1820, then dial. Grose, 1st ed. (at *medlar*), cites a C. 18–early 19 c.p.: (*it is*) *never ripe till it is rotten as a t—d, and then* (*it is*) *not worth a f—t.*—2. Hence, a harlot: C. 17–mid-18. Davies, *The Scourge of Folly*: ca. 1618, puns thus on *meddler, medlar* : ' Kate still exclaimes against great medlers . . . I muse her stomacke now so much shoulde faile | To loath a medler, being an open-tail ' (O.E.D.). See also **open up.**

open c or **C.** The female pudend: low: C. 19–20; ob. (? orig. printers'.)

open house, keep. See **keep open house.**

open lower-deckers. To use bad language: naval: late C. 18–mid-19. Bowen, ' The heaviest guns were mounted on the lower decks.'

open one's mouth too wide. To bid for more than one can pay for: from ca. 1880: Stock Exchange s. >, ca. 1920, gen. coll.

open the ball. See **ball, open the.**

open to. To tell, or admit, to (a person): London lower classes': 1895, *The People*, Jan. 6, ' I knew then that Selby had got a bit more [money] than he opened to me '; slightly ob. Ware.

open up, v.i. (Of a woman, sexually) to spread: low coll. bordering on S.E.: mid-C. 19–20. Ex

S.E. sense, to become open to view. Cf. the rare C. 17 *open-tail*, a harlot, a light woman, and *open arse*, q.v.

opener. Any case, bag, package, etc., opened by customs officials: customs' s. (ca. 1908) >, by 1930, coll. O.E.D. Sup. Either by ' the Oxford *-er* ' or ex the frequent order, *open her !*

oper, no. No chance, esp. of surviving a battle: military: 1915; ob. F. & Gibbons; B. & P. I.e. *no hope*.

opera buffer. An actor in opera bouffe: theatrical: 1888; ob. Punning *opera-bouffer*.

opera house. A workhouse: C. 19. Ex L. *opera*, work. F. & H. (? elsewhere.)—2. A guard-room; detention-quarters or -cells: military: from the 1890's. F. & Gibbons.

operation. A patch, esp. in trousers-seat: tailors' (—1909). Ware.

operator. A pickpocket: coll. bordering on S.E.: C. 18. Ex the † S.E. sense, one who lives by fraudulent operations.

ophido- iš, in combination, erroneous for *ophio-*. C. 17–19. O.E.D.

opiniated. Opinionated: sol.: late C. 19–20. (Dorothy Sayers, *Unnatural Death*, 1927.)

opinionatre, opiniona(s)try. Incorrect forms of *opiniatre, opinia(s)try* (ca. 1660–1700), as *opinitive* is (late C. 16–17) of *opinative*. Other erroneous *op*-words are **oplitic, oplophorous,** by *hop-*; **opportunity** for *importunity* (late C. 16–17); †**oppurtenance** for *appurtenance*, †**opreption** for *obreption*; **opstropolous** (see **obstreperlous**); †**optain(e)** for *obtain*. O.E.D.

-opolis. See **-polis.**

ops, night. Night-operations (in manœuvres): military coll.: from 1915. Also in medical s.

opsh. Something optional; esp. a ball where fancy dress is optional: 1933, F. Morton Howard in *The Humorist* of Dec. 16, ' There was a fancy-dress dance . . . of the sort known locally as an " opsh ".'

opt. The best scholar: schools' (— 1887). Abbr. L. *optimus*. Baumann.

optic. (Gen. in pl.) An eye: C. 17–20: S.E. till ca. 1880, then jocular coll. *Licensed Victuallers' Gazette*, April 10, 1891, ' A deep cut under the dexter optic '.

[or and nor. See Fowler.]

***oracle.** A watch: C. 18 c. or low s. Swift, ' Pray, my lord, what's o'clock by your oracle ? ' Prob. S.E. *oracle* influenced by L. *hora* (cf. Romany *ora*, hour, watch).—2. The female pudend: low: C. 18–20. Gen. *hairy oracle*.

oracle, work the. To raise money: from ca. 1820. ' Jon Bee ', 1823 ; J. Newman, *Scamping Tricks*, 1891. Hence, 2, to contrive a robbery: c. (— 1887). Baumann. Ex S.E. sense, to obtain one's end by (gen. underhand) means.—3. **work the double, dumb,** or **hairy oracle,** (gen. of the man) to copulate: low: C. 19 (? earlier)–20; ob.

orange. The female pudend: Restoration period.

orange, sucked. A very silly fellow: lower classes' coll. (— 1923). Manchon.

orange dry, squeeze or **suck the.** To exhaust, drain, deplete: late C. 17–20 (*squeeze* > † ca. 1860): S.E. until ca. 1880, then coll.

Orange Lilies, the. The 35th Foot (from ca. 1881, the 1st Battalion Royal Sussex): military: from ca. 1760; ob. Ex ' the facings till 1832 and the plumes awarded for gallantry at Quebec in 1759 ', F. & H.

Orange Peel. Sir Robert Peel (1788–1850) when Chief Secretary for Ireland. Dawson, 'Because of his strong anti-Catholic opinions' and punning *orange-peel.*

orate. To hold forth, 'speechify': C. 17–20: S.E. till ca. 1830, then lapsed until ca. 1865, when, under the influence of U.S. (where still serious), it was revived as a jocular term that, ca. 1910, > coll. Cf.:

oration, v.i. To make a speech: coll.: from ca. 1630; slightly ob. J. Done, 1633, 'They . . . had marvailous promptitude . . . for orationing'; Meredith. Ex the n. O.E.D.

Orator Henley. John Henley (1692–1756), pamphleteer and lecturer.

[**orator to a mountebank,** a quack doctor's decoy, is perhaps late C. 17–mid-18 coll. but prob. S.E.—a mere special application of the S.E. sense. B.E.]

orbit, catachrestic for **orb**: C. 18–20. The O.E.D. incriminates Defoe, Scott, Jowett.

orch. Orc (a fierce cetacean; hence, a devouring monster): C. 17 erroneous form. O.E.D.

orchard. The female pudend: low: C. 19–20; ob. See **Jack in . . .**

orchestra; in full **orchestra stalls.** Testicles: rhyming s.: late C. 19–20. On *balls.*—2. (Always **o. stalls.**) Prison cells: police jocularity: from ca. 1920.

orchid. A titled member of the: Stock Exchange: from ca. 1880. Because decorative.

orchids and turnips. People important and insignificant: jocular coll. (— 1923). Manchon. Cf. the Fr. s. phrase, *les grosses et les petites légumes.*

ord. An ordinary seaman: naval (not officers'): C. 20. Bowen. More gen. *O.D.*

order, a large. An excessive demand or requirement: 1884, *The Pall Mall Gazette*, July 24, 1884, '. . . An agreeable piece of slang, a very large order' (O.E.D.). Also, from ca. 1910, *a big order.* Obviously ex the placing of an unusually large order for goods.

order, a strong. A very good horse: the turf (— 1923). Manchon.

order of the . . ., the. E.g. . . . *of the bath,* a bath; . . . *of the boot,* a kick, a violent dismissal; . . . *of the push,* a dismissal. All are coll. and essentially middle-class; from ca. 1880. (See e.g. **push, order of the.**) Perhaps suggested by such *knight* mock-titles as *knight of the pigskin,* a jockey.

order of the day, the. The most usual thing to do, think, etc., at a given period: coll.: from ca. 1790. Arthur Young, 1792 (O.E.D.).

***order-racket.** The obtaining of goods from a shopkeeper by false money or false pretence: ca. 1810–70. Vaux. See **racket.**

orderly buff. An Orderly Sergeant: military: C. 20. F. & Gibbons.

orderly dog. An Orderly Corporal: id.: id. Ibid.

ordinary. A wife: low coll.: C. 19–20; ob. Cf. *old dutch.*—2. A bicycle: 1923, Manchon. Ex *an ordinary bicycle* opp. a motor-cycle.

ordinary, adj. Ordinary-looking, plain: from ca. 174C: S.E. till ca. 1880, then coll. and (esp. in Cambridgeshire) dial. *Knowledge,* Aug. 10, 1885. O.E.D.

ordinary, out of the. Unusual: coll.: late C. 19–20. (Cf. the etymologically equivalent *extra-ordinary.*)

-ore for **-oor,** as in **pore** for **poor,** is a distinctive mark of illiterate speech.—2. So is **-ore** for **-orn,** as in **tore** for **torn, wore** for **worn.**

orf. Off: sol.: C. 19–20. Independently, or as in *orfis,* q.v. Also for equivalent *ough* as in *corf.* This incorrect sound is typical of Cockney. See also **-rf.**

orfis, orfice. Office: sol.: mostly Cockney and Australian: C. 19–20. C. J. Dennis.

organ. A pipe: ca. 1780–1850. Grose, 1st ed. Hence, *cock one's organ,* smoke a pipe. Presumably ex the resemblance to an organ-pipe.—2. A clothes' trunk: Scottish servants': C. 19–20; ob.—3. A workman lending money to his fellows at very high interest: printers': from ca. 1860. Hence, *play the organ,* to apply for such a loan, and, among soldiers, *want the organ,* to be trying to borrow money (F. & Gibbons).—4. See 'Moving-Picture Slang', § 3.

organ, carry the. To shoulder the pack at defaulters' or at marching-order drill: military: ca. 1870–1910.

organ, want the. See **organ, 3.**

organ-pipe. The wind-pipe, the throat; hence the voice: low s. > coll.: from ca. 1850; slightly ob. Ex the shape and purpose of both.

oricle. Oracle: sol.: mostly Cockney and Australian: mid-C. 19–20. C. J. Dennis.

orinoko, pron. *orinoker.* A poker: rhyming s. (— 1857); ob. 'Ducange Anglicus.'

orl. A 'phonetic' spelling that is unnecessary.

orlop, demons of the. Midshipmen and junior officers: naval jocular coll. (— 1887); virtually †. Baumann.

ormenack. Sol., mostly Cockney, for *almanack*: C. 19–20.—2. Hence, in C. 20, a year: 1914, A. Neil Lyons, ''Arf a ormenack dead wasted' (Manchon).

ornary, ornery. Ordinary: illiterate coll. (and dial.): C. 19–20. Baumann. Contrast the American sense: unpleasant, intractable, bad-tempered, etc.,—for which see Thornton's admirable *American Glossary,* 1912.

Oronoko. Tobacco: 1703, Ned Ward. Rare. (W. Matthews.)

ornithorhynchus. A creditor: Australian: ca. 1895–1915. I.e. a duck-billed platypus: F. & H. explain as 'a beast with a bill'.

orphan collar. A collar unsuitable to the shirt with which it is worn: jocular (— 1902). Orig. U.S.

orright. All right: sol.: C. 19–20. Also **aw right.** See '**l** omitted '.

'orrors. See **horrors, 5.**

Orosmades. 'A nickname given to the poet Thos. Gray (1716–71) when at Cambridge' (Dawson).

Orstrylia, -lian. The Cockney pronunciation of *Australia, -lian*: C. 19–20.

orter. Ought to: sol. spelling, low coll. pronunciation: C. 19–20. H., 3rd ed., at *party.*

orthopnic is a C. 17 error for *orthopnoic.* O.E.D.

O's, the. Clapton Orient Football Club: sporting: C. 20. Cf. *the Bees.*

os ace. An illiterate pl. of *o ace* for *o-yes,* i.e. *oyez*: C. 17. O.E.D.

oscar. Money, esp. coin: Australian rhyming s. (C. 20) on *cash.* Ex Oscar Asche, the Australian actor (1871–1936).

***oschive.** See **ochive.**

Oserlander. Gen. pl., 'small river craft on the Rhine and Meuse': nautical coll.: late C. 19–20.

Bowen (? cf. the Ger. place-names, *Osche* and *Oscheleben*.)

osocome. An error for † *nosocome*, a hospital. O.E.D.

ossifer. See **occifer.**

ossy. Horsey (adj.): 1881, Earl Grenville (O.E.D. Sup. at *bean*).

ostiarius. A prefect doing, in rotation, special duty, e.g. keeping order : Winchester College coll. or j. : C. 19–20. Revived by Dr. Moberly ca. 1866. L. *ostiarius*, a door-keeper.—' The official title for the Second Master,' Mansfield, 1866 ; ob.

ostler. An oat-stealer : late C. 18–mid-19. I suspect that this is rather a Grose (1st ed.) pun than, except jocularly, an actual usage. Cf. *oat-stealer*.

ostracy. An error for *ostracism*, as in North, 1579 : ca. 1570–1700. O.E.D.

otake. A C. 15 error for *out-take*, preposition. Ibid.

otamy. An † corruption of *atomy*.

ote. C. 16 corrupt form of *hote* (ex *hight*, to bid, sell, name), Spenser. O.E.D.—2. Also of *wot* ex *wit*, to know. Ibid.

*****other, the.** Homosexuality as a criminal offence : c. : from ca. 1925. James Curtis, *The Gilt Kid*, 1936. As opp. to prostitution.

other half, the. ' The return drink in the ward-room, all naval drinks being traditionally a half-measure ' : naval coll. : C. 20. Bowen.

other side, the. Mail travelling in the opposite direction : railwaymen's, esp. on mail trains : from ca. 1920. *The Daily Herald*, Aug. 5, 1936.

other thing !, if he doesn't like it he may do the. I.e. ' lump it ', or go to hell : coll (— 1887). Baumann.

other thing, the. The contrary, reverse, opposite : coll. : from ca. 1923. Ex the preceding.

otherguess. Different : from ca. 1630 : S.E. until ca. 1820, then coll. and dial. Cf. † S.E. *othergates*.

otherwise for *other* is catachrestic : rare before C. 20. Fowler.

otomy ; occ. **ottomy.** A C. 18–19 form of the dial. and (low) coll. *atomy*, q.v. Swift, Grose, Ainsworth. Whence *ottomise*, q.v.

otter. A sailor : C. 18–20 ; very ob. *Street Robberies Consider'd*.—2. N. and adj. ; also *otto*. Eight : occ. eightpence : Parlyaree and costers' s. : from ca. 1850. Ex It. *otto*, via Lingua Franca. P. H. Emerson, 1893, ' I'll take otto soldi.' See **soldi.**

otter-down. An erroneous form of *eider-down* : ca. 1750–1800. E.g. in Johnson. O.E.D.

otto. See **otter, 2.**

ottomise. To anatomise : mid-C. 18–mid-19 : low coll. Grose, 1st ed. Ex *otomy*, q.v.

ottomy. See **otomy.**

Ouds, the. The **O**xford **U**niversity **D**ramatic **S**ociety : Oxford University s. (from ca. 1890) >, by 1920, coll.

ought. Nought (a cipher) : sol. and dial. : from ca. 1840. Dickens, 1844, ' " Three score and ten ", said Chuffey, " ought and carry seven ".' Prob. ex *a nought > an ought*. Hence, *oughts and crosses*, a children's game : 1861, Sala. O.E.D.—2. A C. 18 mis-spelling of *ort*. O.E.D.

ought. Been obliged. Esp. in **ought to** (present infinitive), **didn't ; ought to** (perfect infin.), **hadn't.** Should not—ought not to—do ; should not—ought not to—have done : C. 19–20 : low coll. >, ca. 1880, sol. Particularly illiterate is this example from Baumann : ' Didn't 'e ought to stay ? ', i.e.

' Ought he not to have stayed ? ' Also in affirmative (see examples at O.E.D., *ought*, 236, IV, 7, c). A survival of *ought*, past ppl. of *owe*.

oughta, -er. Ought to : sol. : C. 19–20. Baumann.

ould. Old : low coll. (and dial.) : C. 19–20. Baumann.

*****ounce.** A crown (coin) : c. of ca. 1720–1830. *A New Canting Dict.*, 1725. Silver being formerly estimated at five shillings an ounce.

'ounds. A coll. form of *wounds* (e.g. God's wounds) : C. 18. Cf. *zounds*.

our —. A familiar way of referring to that thing or, more gen., person : C. 19–20. Dorothy Sayers, *Murder Must Advertise*, 1933, ' I've an idea our Mr. Willis was a bit smitten in that direction at one time.'

our 'Arbour. See **'Arbour.—Our Billy.** See **Billy, Our.**

our noble selves ! A C. 20 upper-middle class toast.

ourick. A Gentile (gen. pl.) : pejorative Jewish coll. : late C. 19–20. Ex Yiddish.

ourn. Ours : mid-C. 17–20 : dial. and low coll. Partly ex † S.E. *our(e)n*, our ; partly ex *our* on *mine*. Cf. *hern, hisn, yourn.*

ours. British, or Allied : military coll. : 1914–18. B. & P. Opp. *his*.

our's. Ours : sol. : C. 19–20. Cf. *her's*.

ourous for *orous* is catachrestic, as in *humourous* for *humorous*. Cf. Galsworthy, *The Silver Spoon*, 1926, ' The rumourous town still hummed.'

Ouse whale. Fish served at school meals : Bootham School (— 1925). Anon., *Dict. of Bootham Slang.*

ouster-le-mer. A law-dictionaries error for *oulter-le-mer.* O.E.D.

out, n. (Mostly in pl.) One out of employment or (esp. political) office : 1764 : coll. till ca. 1790, then S.E. Goldsmith, Chatterton. Ex the adj.-adv.—2. A dram-glass : public-house and low : ca. 1835–70. Dickens, in *Sketches by Boz*. These glasses are made *two-out* (half-quartern), *three-out* (a third), *four-out* (a quarter).—3. An outing or excursion ; a holiday : from ca. 1760 : dial. and, from ca. 1840, coll. ; very ob. as the latter. (O.E.D.)—4. An outside passenger on a coach, etc. : 1844 ; ob. : s. >, ca. 1850, j. J. Hewlett, 1844, ' Room for two outs and an in ' (O.E.D.).—5. (Also in pl.) A loss : lower classes' coll. (— 1909). Ware.

out, v. To disable ; knock out : 1896, *The Daily News*, June 15 (O.E.D.) : boxing s. >, by 1930, coll. Ex *to knock out*.—2. Hence, in c. (>, ca. 1915, low s.), to kill : 1899, *The Daily News*, Sept. 11 (O.E.D.), but prob. dating from 1897 or 1898 : see **out**, adj., sense 10.—3. See **out it** and **out with.**

out, adj. (See the first **o** entry.—) 2. Unfashionable : coll. or, as the O.E.D. classes it, S.E. : 1660, Pepys in *Diary*, Oct. 7, ' Long cloakes being now quite out ' ; ob. ? ex *go out of fashion*.—3. (Of a girl, a young woman) at work, in domestic service : coll. >, ca. 1890, S.E. : 1814, Jane Austen.—4. Tipsy : C. 18–mid-19. ? ex *out*, astray. F. & H.—5. Having been (esp. recently) presented at Court : Society coll. >, ca. 1890, S.E. : 1866, Mrs. Gaskell (O.E.D.) ; 1877, *Belgravia*, Aug., p. 189. Ex *to come out at Court*.—6. Wrong, inaccurate : coll. or, as the O.E.D. holds, S.E. : mid-C. 17–20. Ex *out in one's count, guess, estimate*. —7. Having a tendency to lose : s. verging on coll. : from ca. 1850 ; ob.   Ex *out of luck.*—8. Not on sale : from ca. 1830 : market-men's coll. > j. Ex *out of stock.*—9. In c. : (recently) released from gaol : from ca. 1880.   Ex *out of gaol.*—10. Dead : c. : 1898, Binstead, *The Pink 'Un and the Pelican.* Ex *to knock out.*   Cf. *out*, v., 2.—11. See next entry, 3.—12. See **out with.**

out, adv.   The orig. form of all the adj. senses : see preceding entry.—2. See **all out.**—3. In existence ; one could find : coll. >, ca. 1905, S.E. : from ca. 1856.   G. A. Lawrence, 1859, ' Fanny was the worst casuist out ' (O.E.D.).   ? ex *out before the world* or *out on view.*

out ?, does your mother know you're. See **mother** . . .   The c.p. reply is, *Yes, she gave me a farthing to buy a monkey with ! are you for sale ?* (Manchon).

out, play at in and.   See **in and** in **and in and out.**

out after, be.   A mainly lower classes' coll. variant (— 1923) of familiar S.E. *be out for,* to be exceedingly keen to obtain.   Manchon.

[**out and out,** adv. and adj. : S.E., despite F. & H. and others.]

*out-and-outer.   A very determined, unscrupulous fellow : c. of ca. 1810–70.   Vaux.   Ex *out and out,* adv.—2. Hence, a person or thing perfect or thorough of its kind : from ca. 1814 ; ob.—3. Hence, a ' whacking great ' lie : from ca. 1830 ; ob.—4. A thorough-going supporter : coll. : 1833 ; slightly ob.—5. ' An out-and-out possessor of some quality ' : coll. : 1852, Thackeray.—6. A thorough scoundrel : from ca. 1870.   Ex sense 1.—7. A thorough bounder, an ' impossible ' person : from ca. 1905.   O.E.D.

out at elbows or **heels.** See **elbows** and **heels.**

out at leg.   (Of cattle) feeding in hired pastures : rural coll. : C. 19–20 ; ob.

out for an airing.   (Of a horse) not meant to win : the turf : 1888, *The Sporting Times,* June 29. Opp. *on the job* (see **job**).

out it.   To go out, esp. on an outing : coll. : 1878, Stevenson, ' Pleasure-boats outing it for the afternoon '.   Ex ob. S.E. *out,* v.i.   O.E.D.

out of (occ. **Christ's,** but gen.) **God's blessing** (occ. **heaven's benediction,** Shakespeare in *Lear*) **into the warm sun.**   From better to worse : proverbial coll. : mid-C. 16–mid-19.   Palsgrave, 1540, ' To leappe out of the halle into the kytchyn, or out of Christ's blessynge in to a warme sonne ' ; Howell ; 1712, Motteux, who misunderstands it to mean ' out of the frying-pan into the fire '.   Skeat derives it ex the congregation hastening, immediately after the benediction, from the church into the sun.   Occ. *out of a* or *the warm sun into God's blessing,* from worse to better (Lyly).   Apperson.

out of collar.   (Of servants) out of place : 1859, H. ; † by 1910.

out of commission.   Requiring work : clerks' coll. (— 1909).   Ware.

*out of flash.   See **flash, out of.**—**out of mess.** See **mess, out of.**

out of it, the hunt, the running.   Debarred ; having no share, no chance ; wholly ignorant : from ca. 1880 : coll. till C. 20, then S.E.   Ex sport.

out of print.   Dead : booksellers' : from ca. 1820 ; very ob.   Egan's Grose.   Cf. *o p.*

[**out of school.**   See ' Westminster School slang '.]

out of sorts.   See **sorts, out of.**

out of the cupboard, come.   To go out to work on one's first job : lower classes' (— 1909).   Ware.

*out of the way (for so and so).   In hiding because

wanted by the police (for such and such a crime) : c. : from ca. 1810 ; ob.   Vaux.

*out of town.   ' Out of cash ; locked up for debt ', Bee : c. of ca. 1810–50.   Opp. *in town,* q.v.

*out of twig.   Reduced by poverty to the wearing of very shabby clothes : c. of ca. 1810–60.   Vaux. who notes *put out of twig,* to alter a stolen article beyond recognition, and *put oneself out of twig,* to disguise oneself effectually.

(out) on one's own.   Peerless ; a very good sort (of fellow) : coll. : C. 20.

out or down there.   Turn out or be cut (or knocked) down : boatswains' c.p. to lazy seamen : C. 19.   Bowen.

out the back door, go.   To go down to the beach at Gallipoli, esp. on fatigues : New Zealand soldiers' : in 1915.

out there.   On the Western Front : military coll. : late 1914–18.   F. & Gibbons.   Also *over there.*

out with.   To bring out, to show : coll. : 1802, R. & M. Edgeworth (O.E.D.) ; e.g. *out with a knife.*—2. Hence, to utter, esp. unexpectedly, courageously, etc. : coll. : 1870, Spurgeon, ' He outs with his lie ' (O.E.D.).—3. Gen. *be out with,* to be no longer friendly towards : (mostly nursery) coll. : from before 1885.   Ware.

outcry.   An auction : C. 17–19 ; † S.E. in England by ca. 1800, but surviving in India as a coll. until late C. 19.   H., 3rd ed. ; Yule & Burnell. (Also mid-C. 18–19 dial. : E.D.D.)

outer.   A betting-place, in the open, overlooking a race-course : low Australian : from ca. 1920. Cf. ;

outer, on the.   Penniless : Australian : from ca. 1920.   Jice Doone.   I.e. on the outer edge of prosperity ; ex running on the outside track.

outer edge, the.   See **outside edge.**

outface it with a card of ten.   See **card of ten.**

outfit.   A travelling party ; a party in charge of herds, etc. : coll. : orig. (1870) and mainly U.S.—2. Whence, Canadian and Australian military coll. : a battalion, a battery, an aeroplane squadron, etc. : G.W. +.   (Also U.S.)

outfit, the whole.   The whole thing or collection of things : coll. : from ca. 1910.

outing.   A pleasure-trip, an excursion : orig. (— 1821), dial. >, ca. 1860, coll. >, ca. 1905, S.E. *The Sun,* Dec. 28, 1864, blames H. for omitting this term.—2. The vbl.n. of *out,* v., 2 : q.v.

*outing dues.   Execution (for murder) : c. : late C. 19–20 ; ob.   G. R. Sims.   Ex *out,* v., 2.

[**outparter.**   A spurious or ghost word. See O.E.D. at *outparter* and *outputter.*]

outrun the constable.   See **constable.**

outs.   See **out,** n., 1 and 5.—2. Out-patient department of a hospital : medical (— 1933).   *Slang,* p. 192.

outs, be (at).   To quarrel ; to be no longer friends : coll. : C. 19–20 ; ob.

outs, drink the three.   To drink copiously : a coll. c.p. : C. 17.   Two specific meanings : S. Ward, 1622, ' Wit out of the head, Money out of the purse, Ale out of the pot ' ; T. Scott, 1624, ' To drink by the dozen, by the yard, and by the bushell '.   O.E.D.

outs, gentleman of (the) three.   See **gentleman of** . . .   (Baumann, 1887, has *four outs* : without wit, money, credit, or good manners.)

outs of, make no.   To fail to understand ; misunderstand : (somewhat low) coll. : C. 19–20 ; ob. Possibly influenced by, or a corruption of, *make orts of,* to undervalue ; cf. S.E. *make* (a person) *out,* to understand him.

outside. An outside passenger : 1804 (O.E.D.) : coll. till ca. 1890, then S.E.—2. The utmost : coll. : from ca. 1690. B.E. Esp. in *at the outside.*

outside, preposition. More thán, beyond : (low) coll. : from before 1887. Baumann cites novelist Greenwood, ' Tuppence outside their value '.

outside, at the. At the (ut)most : from ca. 1850. Esp. of number or price : e.g. ' In a few weeks, at the outside, we may expect to see . . .', *The Literary Gazette*, Jan., 1852. (O.E.D.) Ex *outside*, n., 2.

outside !, come. Fight it out ! : coll. : late C. 19–20. Ex lit. sense.

outside, get. See **outside of, get.**

outside edge, the. ' The limit ' : C. 20. Lyell. App. first recorded by Ian Hay in ' *Pip* ', 1907. Orig. a skating variant of *the limit.* Also *the outer edge* (Collinson).

outside, Eliza or **Liza !** Get out of this ! : a low c.p. : from ca. 1850 ; ob. Ware defines it as ' drunk again, Eliza ' and says that it is ' applied to intoxicated, reeling women '.

outside of. Except ; beyond (the number of, the body of) : coll. : orig. (— 1889), U.S. ; anglicised ca. 1905. E.g. ' Outside of the habitués, nobody was there.'

outside (of), get. To eat or drink (something) : from ca. 1890. Also *be outside of* : same period : ob. Cf. the U.S. sense, to understand.—2. (Of a woman) to coït with : low : from ca. 1870.

outside of a horse. On horseback : coll., mostly Australian : 1889, ' Rolf Boldrewood '.

outside the ropes. Ignorant (of a particular matter) ; being merely a spectator : 1861, Lever, ' Until I came to understand . . . I was always " outside the ropes ",' O.E.D.

outside walkee. A paddle-steamer : nautical : late C. 19–20. Bowen. Ex pidgin : cf. *inside walkee*, the reference being to the position of the motive power.

outsider. (See the first o entry.—) 2. One who fails to gain admission to the ring : the turf : coll. : from ca. 1860. Ex *outsider*, a non-favourite horse, a sense that, despite the O.E.D., may have been coll. at its inception (1857).—3. A person unfit to mix with good society : coll. : from ca. 1870.—4. A homeless person : Glasgow (— 1934). Pregnantly ex the lit. sense.

*outsiders. Nippers with semi-tubular jaws used in housebreaking : c. and j. : 1875 (O.E.D.).

outsize. A person (gen. female) rather larger than the majority : from ca. 1890. Ex drapery j. The O.E.D. records it for 1894 as *rather an out size* and as S.E. ; yet I believe that spelt as one word (C. 20) it is to be considered coll. Certainly such a phrase as *an outsize in thunderstorms, punches*, ' *hates* ', *efforts*, etc., is jocular coll. of C. 20.

outward-bounder. A ship outward-bound : nautical coll. : 1884, Clark Russell. O.E.D.

ouzle, pronounced and gen. spelt **oozle.** To obtain illicitly or schemingly : New Zealand soldiers' : 1915 ; ob. Perhaps ex *ooja + wangle.*

Oval, the. The Kennington Oval Cricket Ground : coll. (— 1887) >, by 1900, S.E. Baumann.

ovate. To greet with popular applause, with an ovation : journalistic coll. : 1864, Sala ; *The Saturday Review*, May 3, 1890, ' Mr. Stanley . . . was " ovated " at Dover.' O.E.D.

ovator. One who participates in a popular welcome (to another) : journalistic coll. : 1870, *The*

Evening Standard, Oct. 22. O.E.D. Like preceding, ex S.E. *ovation.*

oven. The female pudend : low : C. 18–20, ob. D'Urfey. Perhaps with reference to the C. 16–19 (extant in dial.) proverb, *he* (or *she*) *that has been in the oven* [as a hiding-place] *knows where to look for son, daughter*, etc.—2. A large mouth : ca. 1780–1910. Grose, 1st ed. Ex S.E. *oven-mouth*, a wide mouth.

oven, in the same. In the same plight : low coll. : C. 19–20 ; ob.

oven-door. A bass-fiddle : South Lancashire jocular (— 1905). E.D.D. (Sup.).

over, be all. To make a great fuss of, esp. with caresses : C. 20. (Of a monkey) ' He'll be all over you as soon as he gets to know you,' which indicates the semantics : *The Humorist*, July 28, 1934. (Lyell.)—2. Hence, to be infatuated with : from ca. 1925.

over, do. To possess a woman : low coll. : C. 18–20 ; ob.

over, get. To get the better of : coll. : 1870, Hazlewood & Williams.

over, put it. See **put it over.**

over-and-over. An acrobatic revolution of oneself in the air, a complete turn (or more) : acrobats' coll. (— 1887). Baumann.

over at the knees. Weak in the knees : C. 19–20 ; stable coll. ; in C. 20, S.E.

over-boyed. (Of a ship) officered by youths : naval coll. : ? mid-C. 18–mid-19. Bowen.

over-day tarts. The darkened and damaged appearance about the gills and fins of a herring more than 24 hours caught : fish trade (— 1889). Ex the blood there extravasated and its resemblance to an overflowing jam tart.

over-eye. To watch (carefully) : non-aristocratic coll. : C. 19–20 ; ob. Ware. Ex *oversee.*

over shoes, over boots. Completely : coll. : late C. 16–early 19. Shakespeare, Breton, Welsted (1726), Scott. Cf. the S.E. *over head and ears.* (Apperson.)

over the air. By wireless : (mostly nautical) coll. : from ca. 1925. Bowen.

*over the Alps. In Dartmoor prison ; loosely, in any prison : c. : from ca. 1920. Edgar Wallace *passim.*

over the bags. See **bags, mount the.—over the bender.** See **bender.—over the broom(stick).** See **broom(stick).—over the chest.** See **chest.—over the coals, call over the.** See **coals.**

over the door, put. To turn (someone) out into the street : coll. : C. 18–mid-19. Cf. *give the key of the street*, q.v.

over the Gilbert. (Of naval routine) gone wrong : naval : C. 20. Bowen. Why *Gilbert* ?

over the gun. See **gun, over the.**

over the hill. Past mid-Atlantic ; occ. (of a ship) over the horizon : nautical : late C. 19–20. Bowen.

over the left (shoulder). See **left.**

*over the lefter. (Of a partridge or a pheasant) shot before the season begins : poachers' c. (— 1909) Ware.

over the lid ; over the plonk. Variants (1917–18) of *top, over the*, q.v.

over the side. Absent without leave : naval : C. 20. F. & Gibbons. I.e. of the ship.

over the stile. (Sent) for trial : rhyming s. (— 1859). H., 1st ed.

over the top. See **top, over the.**

over the top, go. To be married, to marry : jocular : from 1919. Ex military sense.

*over the water. In King's Bench Prison : London c. : ca. 1820–50. 'Jon Bee.' The reference is to the 'other' side of the Thames.

over there. See **out there.**

overbroke. Too much, too heavily ; esp. **bet overbroke,** applied to a bookmaker : the turf : C. 20.

overdraw the badger. See **badger.** (? ex † S.E. *overdraw one's banker.*)

overflow and plunder. A method of fleecing the audience by sending them from dearer to yet dearer seats : theatrical : ca. 1880–1900. Barrère & Leland.

overheat one's flues. To get drunk : low, mostly Cockney (— 1887). Baumann.

overlander. A tramp (see **sundowner**) : Australian : from ca. 1890 ; ob. Morris.

overrun the constable. See **constable, outrun** or **overrun.**

overseen. Somewhat drunk : late C. 15–20 : S.E. till C. 17, then coll. till ca. 1820, then dial. L'Estrange. Cf. *overshot, overtaken,* qq.v.

overseer. A man in a pillory : mid-C. 18–early 19. Grose, 1st ed. Ex the C. 16–17 S.E. sense, one who looks down at anything, hence a spectator.

overshot. (Very) drunk : C. 17–20 ; ob. Marston, 1605 (O.E.D.) ; Lyell. Cf. :

oversparred. Top-heavy ; unsteady ; drunk : nautical : 1890, Clark Russell ; ob.

overtaken. Drunk : late C. 16–20 : S.E. till C. 18, then coll. till ca. 1850, then dial. Hacket, 1693, 'I never spake with the man that saw him overtaken' ; Congreve ; Halliwell ; Mrs. S. C. Hall. Ex *overtaken in* or *with drink.*

overtoys box. A cupboard-like box for books : Winchester College : from ca. 1880.

-ow. For Anglo-Indian vv. in *-ow*, see **puckerow** (which note can be supplemented by reference to Yule & Burnell at *bunow* and *lugow*). C. 19–20.

owl. A harlot : C. 19–20 (ob.) : coll. verging on S.E.—2. A member of Sidney Sussex College, Cambridge : Cambridge University : ca. 1810–90.

owl, v.i. To smuggle : coll. : ca. 1735–1820. Ex *owler, owling,* qq.v.—2. To sit up **at** night : from the 1890's ; ob.

[**owl, catch the.** This country trick, mentioned by Grose, 1st ed., belongs to folklore.]

owl (or **by owls**), **live too close to the,** or **near a, wood to be frightened by an.** To be not easily frightened : C. 18–early 19 as proverbial coll., then dial. Swift, however, has 'Do you think I was born in a wood to be afraid of an owl ?'

owl, take the. To become angry : coll.: late C. 18–mid-19. F. & H.

owl in an ivy-bush, like an. See **ivy-bush.**

owl-light, walk by. To fear arrest : coll. : ca. 1650–1700. Howell. (Apperson.)

owler. A person, a vessel, engaged in smuggling sheep or wool from England to France : late C. 17–early 19 : orig. c. or s., though the O.E.D. considers it to have always been S.E. (B.E., Grose.) Ex ob. S.E. v., *owl.* Cf. :

owling. Such export : late C. 17–early 19. See preceding entry for status.

owls to Athens, bring. To bring 'coals to Newcastle' : proverbial coll. : late C. 16–18. Melbancke's *Philotinus,* 1583 ; Hacket's *Williams,* 1693. Apperson.

own, on its or **one's.** On its or one's own account, responsibility, resources, merits : from ca. 1895 :

coll.—2. Hence, by oneself ; alone ; independently : C. 20 coll.—3. **on** (or **out on**) **one's own.** See **out on one's own.**

own back, get one's. See **get one's own back.**— **own man, feel one's.** See **feel one's own man.**

own up. To confess ; admit (v.t. with *to*) : coll. : 1880, Trollope, 'If you own up in a genial sort of way, the House will forgive anything.'

owned, be. To make many converts : clerical : ca. 1853–75. Conybeare. Cf. *seal.*

owner. The captain of a ship : naval : C. 20. Bowen. Hence, *owneress,* his wife : O.E.D. (Sup.). —2. A visitor from on shore, come to look over the ship : id. : id. F. & Gibbons.

owner's man. A captain or officer protecting the owner's interest by cheese-paring ; an officer related to the owners : nautical coll. : late C. 19–20. Bowen.

ownest. An † wrong form of *honest,* O.E.D.— 2. (E.g. *my*) *ownest own,* (my) dearest one : Society (— 1887) >, by 1910 at latest. rather cheap. Baumann.

owny-o, on one's. 'On one's own' (q.v.); lonely : C. 20. Jocular *-o* and endeary *-y.*

owt. (Dial. form of *ought,* n., q.v.—) Two : back s. (— 1859). H., 1st ed.

owtherquedance. A mistaken form of *outrecuidance* : C. 18–20. O.E.D.

ox has (hath) trod on his foot, the black. He knows what poverty, misfortune, ill-health, old age, etc., is : proverbial : from ca. 1530 : coll. till ca. 1750, then S.E. ; ob. Tusser, Ray, Leigh Hunt.

ox-hide, oxhide, has since 1858 been catachrestically explained as a measure of land : by confusion with *hide* (skin and measure). O.E.D.

ox-house to bed, go through the. To be cuckolded : late C. 17–early 19 : semi-proverbial coll. B.E., Grose. Obviously because he has horns.

ox-pop. A butcher : low : ca. 1810–80.

oxer. An ox-fence : fox-hunting : 1859, G. A. Lawrence, 'A rattling fall over an "oxer"'; Whyte-Melville ; Kennard, *The Girl in the Brown Habit,* 1886.

oxford ; Oxford. A crown piece : low : ca. 1885–1914. Hence *half-oxford,* a half-crown piece : ob. Binstead, *The Pink 'Un and the Pelican,* 1898. It is an abbr. of *Oxford scholar,* q.v. below. —2. As in 'Are you Oxford or Cambridge ?', i.e. 'Are you at (or, were you at) Oxford or Cambridge University ?' : coll. : C. 19–20. Baumann.

Oxford,—send verdingales (farthingales) **to Broadgates at** or **in.** A c.p. of ca. 1560–1670 (later in dial.) in reference to farthingales so big that their wearers could not enter an ordinary door except sideways. Heywood (1562), Fuller, Grose's *Provincial Glossary.* Apperson.

Oxford bleat. From ca. 1925 (coll.), as in Denis Brown in *The Spectator,* Jan. 5, 1934, where he speaks of an exaggerated form of the Oxford or Public School accent : 'Surely it is permissible to suggest what [outsiders] rudely call the Oxford Bleat by writing down the directions given me the other day as "past a whaite house, between the water-tah and the pah station".'

Oxford bags. See **bags.**

Oxford Blues, the. The Royal Horse Guards : late C. 17–20 : military. Ex the colour of their facings, introduced in 1690.

Oxford clink. The C. 18–mid-19 sense, a play on words, a mere jingle, is prob. S.E.—2. A free pass : theatrical : ca. 1890–1915.

Oxford '-er'. At Oxford, it began late in 1875 and came from Rugby School (O.E.D. Sup.). By this process, the original word is changed and gen. abridged; then -er is added. Thus, *memorial* > *memugger*, the *Radcliffe* Camera > *the Radder* (for *the* is prefixed where the original has *the*). Occ. the word is pluralised, where the original ends in *s*: as in *Adders*, Addison's Walk, *Jaggers*, Jesus College. This -er has got itself into gen. upper-middle class s. See esp. *Slang*, revised ed. (1935), pp. 208–9.

[**Oxford glove.** App. a very loose-fitting glove: C. 17: coll. Nares, quoting Dekker. *Oxford Glove* may, however, have been j. of now obscure meaning.]

Oxford scholar. Five shillings (piece or sum): New Zealanders' rhyming s. on *dollar*: C. 20. Also from ca. 1870, in the S.W. of England; now ob. Cf. *shirt collar* (*Everyman*, March 26, 1931.)

***oxo.** Nothing: c.: from ca. 1930. James Curtis, *The Gilt Kid*, 1936. Suggested by the popularity of *Oxo*, the beef-extract; prob. by rhyming s. on the letter *o* regarded as the cypher 0.

oyl. See oil (of barley, hazel, etc., etc.).

oyez. Confused by Skene (late C. 16–early 17) with *outas* (L. *huesium*). O.E.D.

oyster. A gob of phlegm: low coll.: late C. 18–20. Grose, 1st ed.—2. The female pudend: low: C. 19–20; ob. (Cf. *the oyster*, the semen.)—3.

Profit, advantage: jocular: ca. 1895–1915. Ex a prophet's (*profit !*) and an oyster's beard.—4. (Gen. in pl.) One of the holes in a cooked duck's back: domestic: late C. 19–20.

oyster, a choking or **stopping.** A reply that silences: coll.: ca. 1525–1600. Skelton (*stopping*); Udall (the same); J. Heywood, 1546 (*choking*).

oyster, as like as an apple to an. Very different: coll.: ca. 1530–1680. More, 1532, 'Hys similitude . . . is no more lyke then an apple to an oyster'; L'Estrange, 1667. In 1732, Thomas Fuller has the form, *as like as an apple to a lobster*. Apperson.

oyster, old. See old oyster.

oyster-faced. Needing a shave: low (mostly London): ca. 1895–1915. See oyster, 3.

oyster part. A part in which one speaks but a sentence: theatrical coll. (— 1923). Manchon.

oysterics. 'Panic in reference to oysters creating typhoid fever': middle classes': ca. 1900–8. Ware. Ex *oysters* + *hysterics*.

oysters, drink to one's. To fare accordingly (esp., badly): coll.: mid-C. 15–early 16. J. Paston, 1472, 'If I had not delt ryght corteysly . . . I had drownk to myn oystyrs.' O.E.D.

ozimus, ozymus. A mid-C. 16–mid-18 error for *osmund*, iron imported from Sweden. E.g. in Edward VI's *Journal* and Hume's *History*. O.E.D.

P

p for b. A characteristic of Welsh pronunciation of English. E.g. *pridge* for *bridge*. See esp. Fluellen's speeches in *Henry V*.

p for ph is a C. 18–20 sol. E.g. in *naptha* for *naphtha*; *diptheria* for *diphtheria*.

-p is sol. for -pt, as in 'He kep me waitin'' or 'I slep rotten': C. 19–20; and prob. from much earlier.

P.A. (Only in the vocative.) Father: C. 20. E.g. Beatrice Kean Seymour, *Daughter to Philip*, 1933. The *pa* in *pater*.

p and q; **P. and Q.** Of prime quality: C. 17–20: coll. in C. 17, dial. thereafter. Rowlands (*Pee and kew*, as it is sometimes written). Origin obscure.

p.b. or **P.B., the.** The public: theatrical (— 1909); † by 1930. Ware. Also *the pub* (ibid.).

P.B.I. The infantry: infantrymen's coll.: from 1916. B. & P. I.e. poor bloody infantry.

p.c. (or **P.C.**). Poor classes: Society: from ca. 1880; ob. Ware.

p.d. or **P.D.** An adulterating element in pepper: trade: from ca. 1870. I.e. 'pepper-dust'.

p.d.q.; **P.D.Q.** Pretty damn(ed) quick: late C. 19–20. *The Free Lance*, Oct. 6, 1900, 'I'd be on my uppers if I didn't get something to do P.D.Q.' Cf. *p.o.q.*

P.G. H.M.S. *Prince George*: naval coll.: G.W. (F. & Gibbons.) Likewise **the P.R.** is H.M.S. *Princess Royal* (ibid.).—2. A pro-German: among prisoners of war, in Germany: 1915–18.—3. A paying guest: jocular coll.: from ca. 1910.—4. P. G. Wodehouse, the great humorous novelist: coll.: from ca. 1920.

p.j.'s or **P.J.'s.** Physical exercises: coll.: from ca. 1925. (D. Sayers, *Murder Must Advertise*, 1933). I.e. 'physical jerks'.

p- (or **P-**) **maker.** The male, the female pudend: low: mid-C. 19–20. See pee.

p.o.q.! or **P.O.Q.**! Push (or piss) off quickly: military coll.: 1915; ob. F. & Gibbons After *p.d.q.*

***p.p.**! or **P.P.**! A pickpocket: c. (— 1887). Baumann.—2. Play or pay, i.e. go on with the arrangement or forfeit the money; esp., the money must be paid whether the horse runs or not: mostly the turf: from ca. 1860; slightly ob. H., 3rd ed.

p.p.c. A 'snappish good-bye': middle classes': late C. 19–early 20. Ex *p.p.c.* (i.e. *pour prendre congé*, to take leave) written on a visiting card. (Ware.)—2. Hence, *to p.p.c.*, to quarrel with and 'cut' (a person): Society: from ca. 1880; virtually †. Ware.

P.R., the. See P.G.

p.s. or **P.S.** See o.p., 1.—2. An advance on wages: hatters' (— 1909). Ware. Ex *postscript* written *p.s.* Also, and gen., **x.**—3. Penal servitude: c. or low s. (— 1923). Manchon.

p.S.a. or **P.S.A.** A recreational afternoon organised by a Bible society: ironic coll. (— 1923) by abbr. Ex *pleasant Sunday afternoon*. Manchon.

p's and q's (or **P's and Q's**), **learn one's.** To learn one's letters: coll.; 1820, Combe. Ob. Prob. ex children's difficulty in distinguishing *p* and *q*, both having tails. O.E.D. Cf.:

p's and q's (or **P's and Q's**), **mind one's.** To be careful, exact, prudent in behaviour: coll.: 1779, Mrs. H. Cowley, 'You must mind your *P's* and *Q's* with him, I can tell you' (O.E.D.). Also *peas and cues*; occ. (and ob.) *be on* (or *in*) *one's p's and q's*. Perhaps influenced by *p* and *q*; perhaps cognate with preceding entry; perhaps, as F. & H. suggests, ex 'the old custom of alehouse tally, marking

" p " for pint and ' q " for quart, care being necessary to avoid over- or under-charge '.—2. Grose, 2nd ed., shows that ca. 1786–1830, there was the more dignified sense, ' to be attentive to the main chance '.

p.t. ; P.T. Physical training : naval and military coll. : from ca. 1910. F. & Gibbons.—2. A desirable female : (low) urban, esp. London : C. 20. Ex ' prick-teaser '.—3. A pupil teacher : teachers' coll. : late C. 19–20.

P.V. A variant of *Pav*, q.v. ; extremely ob.

P.W. Abney. A high, feminine hat appearing in 1896 : lower classes' : late 1896–7. Ex *Prince of Wales Abney Cemetery*, the hat being worn with ' three black, upright ostrich feathers, set up at the side . . . in the fashion of the Prince of Wales's crest feathers ' (Ware).

p.y.c. or P.Y.C. A pale yellow candle : the Baltic Coffee-House, London (— 1909) ; † by 1930. Ex ' this establishment persistently rejecting gas ' (Ware).

P.Z.s. Tactical exercises : naval : from ca. 1920. Bowen, ' From the two code flags hoisted as an order '.

pa. A mainly childish abbr. of *papa*, q.v. : (in C. 20, low) coll. : 1811, L. M. Hawkins, ' The elder sat down . . . and answered "Yes, Pa' ! " to everything that Pa' said.' (O.E.D.)—2. Hence, ' the relieving officer of a parish ' : lower classes' (—1909). Ware. Cf. corresponding sense of *daddy*.

pa-in-law. Father-in-law : Society (— 1887). Baumann. See *pa*, 1.

pac. A cap : back s. (— 1859). H., 1st ed.

pace, alderman's. A slow, dignified gait : coll. : from ca. 1580 ; ob. Melbancke, 1583 ; Cotgrave ; 1685, S. Wesley the Elder, ' And struts . . . as goodly as any alderman ' ; Grose. Apperson.

[**pace, go the**, is S.E., as are the following in F. & H. :—**pack**, a harlot ; **pack off and send packing** ; **pad-clinking** (see separate entry) ; **paddle**, to caress ; **paddy-w(h)ack** or **Paddy's watch** ; **padlock** ; **pagan**, a harlot ; **pair**, a flight of steps ; **pale, leap the** ; **palliard** (except as = a straw-sleeping vagabond) ; **palm**, n. and v., in bribery and card-sharping terms ; **palm, bear the** ; **palsy** ; **pan** (or **frying-pan**), **savour of the** ; **Pancake Tuesday** ; **panel, parnel, pernel** ; **panjandrum** and **the Grand** or **Great P.** ; **pannier-man** ; **Pantagruelian** ; **pantile as adj.** ; **pantler** ; **pap**, nipple, breast, and bread sauce ; **pap-head** and **pap-mouth** ; **paper**, money in paper not coin ; **paper-building** ; **paperstainer**, a clerk ; **Paphian** ; **papoose** ; **par, at par** ; **parader** ; **paradise** (euphemistic S.E.) ; **paradise, fool's** ; **parcel-bawd** ; **parrot**, n. and v., **parrot-lawyer**, and **parrote(e)r** ; **parts below, more dear, of shame, and carnal or other parts** ; **partlet** ; **partner, sleeping** ; **passage at arms** ; **past believing, hoping**, etc. ; **past complaining** (due to a misapprehension of Grose's entry at *content*) ; **past master** ; **pasterns** ; **pat**, adj. and adv. ; **pathic**, n. ; **Paul Pry** ; **Paul's walkers** ; **paunch**, v., and **paunch-guts** ; **pay home** ; **pay old scores**—one in his own coin—the last debt to nature ; **peacher** ; **peacock**, to display, and **peacocky** ; **pea(k)-goose** ; **peat**, a young girl, etc. ; **peccavi, cry** (cf. the classical pun : *Peccavi* = I have Scinde) ; **peck**, to pitch, throw ; **peculiar**, a wife ; **peculiar river** ; **ped**, a basket ; **pedescript** ; **Sir Peeler** ; **peep**, speak weakly or shrilly ; **Peep o' Day Boy** ; **peg**, a leg or foot ; **peg**, a step or degree, hence *hoist a peg higher* and *take down a peg* ; **peg**, a text, an excuse ;

peg (at cocks) ; **Pegasus's neck, break** ; **peg(-)tops** ; **pell-mell** ; **pelt**, hurry, rage, a miser ; **pelt**, to hurry ; **pelter**, a miser, a pistol ; **pelting**, angry, paltry ; **pelts, garments** ; **pen, knight of the** ; **Penniless Bench** and **Pierce Penniless** ; **penny** (money), **a pretty penny** ; **penny, at first** ; **penny, turn a** and **an honest** ; **penny in the forehead** ; **penny plain and twopence coloured** ; **penny wise (and) pound foolish** ; **penny-father, -poet, -wedding** ; **pennyworth, a good p., cast pennyworths** ; **pensioner** (Cambridge University) ; **pepper**, v., **peppered**, **pepperer, peppering, peppery** ; **pepper-and-salt** ; **pepper-boxes**, cupolas ; **perform** ; **periodicity-rag** ; **perished** ; **periwinkle**, a wig ; **perk up**, to adorn ; **perkin** ; **perking**, adj. ; **pernickety** ; **perspire**, v.i., to melt away ; **pert** ; **pestle**, a leg, and **pestle-head** ; **pet**, a tantrum, a darling ; **petard, hoist with a or one's own** ; **Peter-see-me** ; **Petronel Flash, Sir** ; **all petticoat terms, except four** ; **pettifogger**, etc. ; **petty**, n. ; **pew**, as in C. 17 literature ; **pfotze** ; **phallus** ; **pharaoh**, faro ; **pheaze, phuze, feeze**, etc. ; **philander**, etc. ; **Philistia, Philistine** ; **phœnix' nest** ; **pi** or **pie** in printing ; **picaroon** ; **piccadill(o)** ; **pick**, to shoot, eat mincingly, pilfer ; **pick a bone** ; **pick and choose** ; **pick a quarrel** ; **pick at** ; **pick fault, holes** ; **pick off** ; **pick-purse** ; **pick-thank** ; **pick the brains of** ; **pickaback** ; **picker**, a petty thief ; **pickle, rod in** ; **pickle(d) herring**, a buffoon ; **picksome** ; **picktooth**, leisurely ; **Pickwickian** ; **picture-hat** ; **piddle**, etc., to trifle, etc. ; **piddler**, a trifler, and **piddling**, trifling, paltry ; **pie**, magpie, a gossip ; **pie, have a finger in the** ; **pie, in spite of the** ; **piece of flesh or goods**, a woman ; **pieces**, money ; **pig**, a person ; **pig-eyed, -faced, -headed** ; **pig together** ; **piggery** ; **piggish** ; **pig, long for** ; **pig for a hog, mistake a** ; **pig is proffered . . .**, when a ; **pig's tail** proverb ; **child's pig, father's bacon** ; **pigs** (or **hogs**) **to market, take one's** ; **pigeon-breasted, -hearted, -livered, -toed** ; **pigeon-pair** ; **pigeon-wing** ; **pigeon's milk** ; **pign(e)y** ; **pike, give the** ; **pikes, pass the** ; **Pilate-voice** ; **pile**, a large sum of money ; **pilgarlic**, an old person ; **pill, gild the** ; **pill and poll** ; **pill-monger** ; **pillicock**, an endearment ; **pillory** ; **pimp**, n. and v., —but see at **pimp**, n. ; **pin**, a trifle ; **pin oneself on, pin faith to, be pinned to** ; **pinch**, a dilemma, hence **at a, and come to the, pinch** ; **pinch**, to reduce ; **pinch at**, to criticise ; **pinchbeck** ; **pinched to the bone** ; **pink**, a beauty, a model, etc., a hunting coat ; **pink**, to pierce, make elaborately ; **pinnace** (of women) ; **pioneer of nature** ; **pip** (on dice or playing-cards) ; **pipe another dance** ; **pipes, the lungs, bagpipes** ; **pipe-merry** ; **pipe(-)clay**, routine ; **piping hot** ; **pirate** (literary, sexual, omnibus) ; **pishery-pashery** ; **the piss proverbs** ; **piss-burnt**, stained with urine ; **piss-bowl, -pot, -prophet** ; **pissing-post and -dale** ; **pissing-clout** ; **pit**, a hole, even as in B.E. ; perhaps **knight of the pit** ; **pit-hole** ; **pit of darkness** ; **pit-a-pat** ; **pitch on** ; **pitcher** proverbs ; **pitcher-man** ; **pitchfork**, a tuning-fork, also to thrust (into a position) ; **pitter-patter** ; **pittle-pattle** ; **placebo** ; **placket** as **shift, petticoat** or **petticoat-slit** ; **placket-racket** ; **plank** (political) ; **plate**, money ; **platform** (political) ; **platter-face** and **-faced** ; **plausible** ; all **play** terms (except the few at **play**, later) ; **pleasure** in all sexual terms except two ; **pledge**, a baby ; **plough**, sexual v. ; **plough** proverbs ; **ploughshare** (sexual) ; **pluck**, to reject at an examination, to deflower ; **pluck-penny** ; **plum**, a good thing ; **plum-porridge** as term of contempt ; **plum-tree** ; **plumb**, adj.-adv.

(as in Milton's ' plumb down he falls '); **plump,** fat ; plump, political v. ; **plump,** adv. ; **plumper** (beautifying and political); **plump-pate ; poach** and **poacher-court ; pocket** (resources) ; **pocket,** adj. ; pocket, v. ; be in—out of—put one's hand in one's—pocket ; carry or have in one's pocket ; pick pocket and to pick pockets ; **pocket-borough, -piece, -pistol ; pocket an affront,** one's horns, pride, etc. ; carry one's passions in one's pocket ; **pocketed ; poem,** fig. ; **poet-sucker ;** all **point** phrases except those noticed later ; points, beauties ; **nine points of the law ; poke,** a bag or pocket ; **poke about—face—nose ; pokerish ; poky ; pole-cat ; poll-parrot ; pollard ; polt ; poltroon ; pommel ; poniard ; pony** (euphem. S.E.) ; **pony,** adj. ; **poop,** to cheat ; all **pop** terms not given later ; **pope-holy,** be or play ; **popinjay ; poplet ; pork,** a pig-headed person ; **porker,** a (young) pig ; **port-able ; portage ; portal to the bower of bliss ; porter** and **porter's knot ; portionist ; portmanteau-word ; pose** and **poser ; possess** (a woman) ; **post,** employment ; **post,** to reject, to publish, raise to the rank of post-captain ; **pillar to post ; deaf as a—kiss the—run the head against a—talk—post ; postman ; postmaster ; pot,** a chamber-pot, the female pudend ; such **pot** terms as are not defined later ; **pot-hooks and hangers ; potheen ; potion** and **potomania ; potter, potterer, pottering ; pouch,** to pocket ; **pound,** a prison ; **pound,** to hammer, to move noisily, and the hunting sense ; **pow-wow ; powder,** fig. ; **prancer,** a dancer ; **prank ; prat,** a trick ; **prate-apace, prating, prattle, prattle-basket** and **-box, prattler, prittle-prattle ; pray-pray fashion ; preach,** fig. v. ; **precision ; presbyteress, presbyterian ; present,** a baby ; **pretty,** as ironic adj. and as = rather ; **price,** v. ; **prick,** a skewer ; **pricked,** sour ; **prickers,** cavalry ; **prickmedenty ; pride, proud** (sexual senses) ; **priest ; be one's priest ; priest's niece ; prig,** a superior person ; **prim,** a wanton ; **prime,** adj. and v. ; **prine-cock-boy ; princock** or **-cox ; princod,** a pin-cushion ; **print, in—out of—quite in ; Priscian's head, break ; privates ; private-stitch** (tailors' j.) ; **privy,** n. ; **privy-hole ; proboscis,** of the human nose ; **procession ; at the head of the procession ; profession, the** (see, however note at **pro,** 2) ; **procto(u)r,** except as c. ; **promoter ; promotion, on,** on approval or trial ; **proof,** the best ale at Magdalen College, Oxford ; **property of one, make ; prosit !,** an academical toast ; **protection, under ; proud** (sexually) ; (except for one sense) **prowler, prowlery, prowling ; Pry** and **Paul Pry ; Pack,** the devil ; **puck-fist** or **-foist ; pudder,** n. and v. (also dial.) ; **pudding,** good luck, profit ; **pudding-head(ed), -hearted, -sleeves ; in pudding time ;** the **pudding** proverbs ; **puddingy ; puddle,** to muddy ; **pudend ; pudgy ; puff,** n. and v., sham, advertise-(ment) ; **puff up ; puffed ; puffer ; puke ; puling ; pull,** a drink, an advantage, an attempt at, rowing exercise ; **pull,** v. (cricket, rowing, racing) ; **pull, long** (over-measure on drink) ; all such **pull** phrases as are not defined later ; **puller-on ; pulpit** as a euphemism ; **pulse, feel one's ; pummel, -er-, -ing ; pump,** n. and v. (artful questioning), make breathless ; **pumps,** dancing-shoes ; **pun ; punch, punchiness, punchy** (of stocky build); **punch,** a blow ; **puncher ; punk, punquette ; punt** (in Rugby football) ; **puny,** n. and adj. ; (of men) **pup, puppy, puppy-headed, puppyish ; purchase** (plunder), **live on p., get in p. ; Puritan ; purl,** a kind of liquor ; **purse,** a prize, the scrotum ; all **purse** proverbs ; all **purse** phrases not recorded later ; **pursive, pursy ; push,** enterprise ; **push,** energy ; **push, put to the ; at push of pike ; puss,** a hare, a woman ; **puss-gentleman,** an effeminate ; **put,** n., in Stock Exchange sense ; all **put** phrases not recorded later ; **putage,** fornication ; **putter-on ; puzzle, puzzle-headed, puzzledom, puzzlement.**

Dial. are : **pack,** familiar, intimate ; **pack, eat the ; pact, spend the ; paiker, paikie ; ped-belly ; pelter,** a rage ; **pen ; pepperidge** or **pipperidge, pay the ; petman ; pitchpole** and **turn a pick-pie,** to turn a somersault ; **pod ; poker** (at Newcastle) ; **poor mouth, make a ; porridge, cook the ; potato-boggle ; pout,** i.e. poult, a young girl ; **preeze ; prial ; prig,** to haggle ; **puddle,** (of a person) pejorative n. and adj. ; **pulling time.]**

pacer. Anything (esp. a horse) that goes at a great pace : coll. (— 1890). *Century Dict.*

paces, show one's. To display one's ability : coll. : from ca. 1870. Ex horses.

Pacifics. Pacific Railway (C.P.R.) shares : Stock Exchange coll. (— 1887). Baumann.

Pack. The ship *Pactolus* : naval (— 1909) ; ob. Ware.

pack, go to the. To go to pieces (fig.) ; lose a leading position : s. > coll. : New Zealand : C. 20. Perhaps ex a trained or a domestic animal going wild, or ex a dog falling back into the pack. Perhaps cf. :

pack, send to the. ' To relegate to obscurity,' C. J. Dennis : Australian (—1916).

pack one's hand. See **pack up.**

pack the game in. To desist ; esp. abandon a way of life : lower classes' : C. 20. Philip Allingham, *Cheapjack,* 1934. Cf. *pack up.*

pack-thread, talk. To speak bawdily in seemly terms : coll. : late C. 18–20 ; very ob. Grose, 2nd ed. (In North Country dial., merely to talk nonsense.) Ex *packing-thread,* used for securing parcels. Cf. *wrapped-up,* q.v.

pack up ; occ. **pack one's hand ;** coll., military (1915) >, by 1920, gen. To retire ; stop working or trying ; to die. Prob. ex *pack* (*up*) *one's kit*(*-bag*). F. & Gibbons. Opp. *carry on,* q.v.

packet. A false report : coll. : mid-C. 18–19 ; mostly Northern. Grose, 1st ed. Cf. *packets !*—2. A (large) sum of money lost or won in betting or speculating : from mid 1920's. (O.E.D. Sup.)—3. Any kind of ship or boat : nautical coll., gen. as an endearment : C. 20. Bowen.—4. A lady : nautical : C. 20. Ibid.

packet, cop or **stop a.** To be wounded, esp. if fatally : G.W. +. Occ. *cop it.* Ex *cop* (q.v.), to catch ; *packet* may be the missile. B. & P.—2. Hence (only **cop a packet**), to have bad luck, meet with trouble : military : 1915 ; ob. F. & Gibbons.

packet or **parcel from Paris.** A baby : Australian and New Zealand : C. 20.

Packet of Fags or **Woodbines, the.** ' The famous five-funnelled Russian cruiser *Askold.* (Also the *Floating Skeleton*) ' : naval : ca. 1914–20. Bowen ; B. & P.

packet-rat. ' A seaman in the old transatlantic sailing packets ' : nautical coll. : C. 19. Bowen.

packet to, sell a. To hoax ; lie to ; deceive : coll. : 1847 (E.D.D.) ; ob. Hardy, 1886, *The Mayor of Casterbridge,* ch. xliii (O.E.D.). Cf. *pup, sell a.*

packets ! An expression of incredulity : mid-C. 19–20 ; very ob. H., 3rd ed. Ex *packet,* 1, q.v.

packfong. Erroneous for *paktong*, Chinese nickel-silver : from 1839. O.E.D.

packing. Food : low (— 1909) ; hence, in G.W., rations. Ware ; F. & Gibbons. Cf. S.E. *stuff oneself with food* and *inside lining*, q.v.

*packing-ken. An eating-house : c. (— 1909). Ware. Ex the preceding.

packing-penny to, give a. To dismiss : coll. : late C. 16–early 19. Jonson. By pun.

packs. Storm-clouds : nautical coll. (— 1887). Baumann.

packstaff. See **pikestaff**.

Pad. A not very gen. abbr. (— 1887) of *Paddy*, q.v. Baumann.

*pad. A path ; a road. Esp. *the high pad*, the highway ; in C. 16–17, occ. *padde*. From ca. 1565 : c. until C. 19, then dial. Harman ; Middleton & Dekker ; Prior ; Scott. Ex O.H. Ger. *pfad*.—2. An easy-paced horse : 1617, Moryson (O.E.D.) : coll. until C. 19, then S.E. Also *pad-nag*, q.v.—3. A highway robber : c. : ca. 1670–1840. Head, B.E., Messink, Byron. Ex next sense. See also **pad, high** and **low**, and **padder**.—4. Robbery on the highway : 1664, Etherege, ' I have laid the danger-ous pad now quite aside ' ; Bee ; Henley & Steven-son : c. until C. 19, then low s. ; very ob.—5. (Ex senses 3, 4.) A street-robber : low : ca. 1820–50. ' Jon Bee.'—6. A bed : ca. 1570–1890 : low s. verg-ing on c. Drayton, Broome, Defoe, Grose, Bran-don. In C. 16–17 also *padde*. Ex the S.E. sense, a bundle of straw, skins, etc., on which to lie.—7. Occ. (— 1874, † by 1920) an itinerant musician. H., 5th ed. Ex sense 3.—8. A walk : c. (— 1839). Brandon. Ex sense 1 of :

*pad, v. To travel on foot as a vagrant : C. 17–20 : c. until C. 19, then mainly dial. Rowlands, 1610, ' O Ben mort wilt thou pad with me ? ' Ex S.E. *pad*, to walk (1553, O.E.D.). Prob. cf. the n., sense 1. See also **pad the hoof**.—2. To rob on foot or on the highway : ca. 1635–1840 : orig., prob. c. ; never better than low s. Ford, 1638, ' One can . . . cant, and pick a pocket, Pad for a cloak or hat.' Cf. *pad, go out upon the*, q.v.—3. V.i., to put handkerchiefs, etc., in one's trousers-seat before being caned : Public Schools' coll : C. 20.

pad, gentleman of the. Also *knight* (ca. 1670–1840), *squire* (ca. 1700–1830) *of the pad*. A high-wayman : C. 18–mid-19 : low s. > low coll. Farquhar. See **pad**, n., 4.

*pad, go (out up)on the. To (go out to) rob on the highway : c. : late C. 17–mid-19. B.E., who notes the variant *go-a-padding* ; Grose. See **pad**, n., 1.

*pad, high. The highway : ca. 1565–1800 ; c. Harman.—2. Hence, C. 17–early 19, a robber on the highway, esp. a highwayman. Head. Contrast :

*pad, low. A footpad : c. : late C. 17–early 19. Ex *pad*, n., 1. Cf. preceding.

*pad, on or **upon the.** (Engaged in robbery) on the highway : c. : late C. 17–early 19 ; prob. low s. after ca. 1790. L'Estrange.—2. Hence, on tramp : C. 19–20, though not with certainty re-corded before 1851, Mayhew. Both senses ex *pad*, n., 1 ; the former, gen. *upon* ; the latter, *on*.

*pad, rum. ' A daring or stout Highway-man,' B.E. : c. : late C. 17–early 19. See **rum, 1, pad**, n., 3, and cf. *pad, high*, 2.

*pad, sit. See :—**pad, stand.** To beg by the wayside : c. : 1859, H. ; 1862, Mayhew ; ob. Properly, while remaining stationary—and stand-ing. Obviously *sit pad* is to beg from a sitting position : recorded in 1851, likewise in Mayhew.

In both, the beggar gen. has a piece of paper inscribed ' I'm starving—blind—etc.' Also *stand Paddy*.

*pad, upon the. See **pad, on the**.

*pad, water. ' One that Robbs Ships in [esp.] the Thames,' B.E. : c. : late C. 17–early 19. See **pad**, n., 3.

pad-borrower. A horse-thief : s. > low coll. : ca. 1780–1840. Grose.

[**pad-clinking.** ' Hobnobbing with footpads,' says F. & H., defining it as c. : Kingsley's note to the sole record, 1865, says ' Alluding to the clinking of their spurs ' (O.E.D.).]

pad-horse. An easy-paced horse : from ca 1630 ; ob. Coll. quickly > S.E. Jonson.

pad in the straw. A hidden danger : coll.: 1530, Palsgrave ; not quite † in dial. Still, *Gammer Gurton's Needle* ; Ray. Ex † S.E. *pad*, a toad.

pad it. To tramp along, esp. as a vagrant : late C. 18–20 : s. > ca. 1840, low coll. > ca. 1890, S.E.

pad-nag. An easy-going horse : from ca. 1650 ; ob. Coll. >, ca. 1810, S.E. 1654, Whitelocke, ' A sober . . . well-paced english padde nagge,' O.E.D.

pad round. To pay excessive attention to a customer : tailors' coll. : from ca. 1870. Ex the S.E. *pad*, (of animals) to walk, etc., ' with steady dull-sounding steps ' (O.E.D.).

pad the hoof. To go on foot : from ca. 1790 (Grose, 3rd ed.) ; cf. O.E.D. date. On *plod o' the hoof* (Shakespeare), *beat the hoof* (mid-C. 17–early 19). Cf. *pad it*, q.v.—2. Hence, to make off, quickly : racing c. : C. 20.

pad the wall. To sit on a comfortable leather seat against a wall, esp. in a restaurant or a bar : coll. : 1936, James Curtis, *The Gilt Kid*.

pad-thief. A horse-thief : late C. 17–early 19 : coll. >, ca. 1750, S.E. Shadwell.

[**padar**, in Wotton, is an unsolved error admitted by Johnson and others. O.E.D.]

*padde. See **pad**, n.—**padden crib** or **ken.** See **padding-crib.** (*Answers*, May 11, 1889.)

*padder. A robber on the highway ; esp a foot-pad : C. 17–20 ; ob. : orig. c. >, in C. 18, low s. ; in late C. 19–20, archaic S.E. Rowlands, Scott. Cf. *paddist*, q.v. Ex *pad*, v., 1, influenced by *pad*, n., 3.—2. See **padders.**—3. (**Padder.**) Paddington terminus (G.W.R.) : Oxford undergraduates' (— 1899). Ware. Ex *Paddington* by process of ' the Oxford-*er* '.

padders. Feet ; shoes or boots : low : from ca. 1825 ; ob. Egan, *Finish to Tom and Jerry*, 1828, ' My padders, my stampers, my buckets, otherwise my boots.'

*paddin-ken. See **padding-crib.** P. H. Emerson in *Signor Lippo Lippi*, 1893.

*padding. Robbery on the highway : c. : ca. 1670–1840. B.E. (see **pad, go . . .**).—2. Short, light articles in the magazines : journalistic coll. (— 1887) ; ob. Baumann notes that the term is used ' in opposition to the serial stories '. (The ordinary, the S.E. sense of padding is : fill-up matter within a story or article.—3. See ' Miscel-lanea ' in Addenda.

*padding, adj. Practising highway robbery : c. of ca. 1670–1840. Eachard, fig. (O.E.D.).

*padding-crib, -ken ; loosely **padden -c. and -k.** A lodging-house for the underworld, esp. for vagrants : c. : from ca. 1835 ; ob. Brandon (both) ; Mayhew, 1851 (-*ken*) ; H., 1st ed. (both). Ex *pad*, v., 1., and n., 5. Brandon distinguishes thus: *p.-c.*, a boys' lodging-house; *p.-k.*, a tramps' lodging-house: a distinction that seems to have been lost as early as the 1850's.

*Paddington fair (day) ; or **P. Fair(-day)**. A hanging (day): c.: late C. 17–early 19. Tyburn was in the parish of Paddington. Ex ' a rural Fair at the Village of that Name, near that Place' (Tyburn), B.E. Cf.:

*Paddington frisk, dance the. To be hanged: c.: ca. 1780–1830. Grose, 1785. Cf.:

*Paddington spectacles. The cap drawn over a criminal's eyes at his hanging: either c. or low s.: early C. 19. Cf. the preceding pair of entries.

paddist. A professional highwayman: ca. 1670–1800: Scots s. >, in C. 18, coll. O.E.D.

paddle. A hand: late C. 19–20: low and ob. ? suggested by *daddle*, q.v.

paddle, v. To drink strong liquor: low: from ca. 1860; ob. ? ex noisy drinking. Hence, *to have paddled*, to be intoxicated.—2. To run away; to abscond: c. (– 1860) >, by 1890, low. H., 2nd ed.; Baumann. Ex S.E. *paddle*, to toddle: cf. post-G.W. s. *toddle*, to depart.

paddle one's own canoe. See **canoe, paddle . . .** Perhaps one might mention the French-teachers' 'gag': *pas d'elle yeux Rhône que nous.* (Such tricks should be collected: cf. η β π, to eat a bit of pie !)

paddler. A paddle-steamer: coll.: from ca. 1890. (O.E.D.)

Paddy. A nickname (cf. *Pat*, q.v.) for an Irishman: coll.: 1780, A. Young, ' Paddies were swimming their horses in the sea to cure the mange,' O.E.D. Ex the very common Irish name, *Patrick*, of which *Paddy* is the Irish diminutive. Also *Paddylander, Paddywhack*, qq.v. Cf.:

paddy. A rage, a temper: coll: 1894, Henty (O.E.D.). Also *paddy-whack*, q.v. Cf. *Irish*, q.v., and see esp. *Words !* at ' Offensive Nationality.'—2. Erroneous for *baddy*: Motley and recent dictionaries. O.E.D.—3. A paddywhack almanac: coll. and dial. (– 1876); † by 1930.—4. A hobby, a fad: non-aristocratic (– 1887). Baumann. Ex *pad*, n., 2.

*Paddy, stand. See **pad, sit.**

paddy-boat. A vessel of the Henderson line from the Clyde to Burma: nautical: C. 20. Bowen. Suggested by S.E. *paddy-boat*, a ship for the carrying of rice: Burma exports much rice.

Paddy Doyle, do. To be a defaulter: naval and military: late C. 19–20. F. & Gibbons.

Paddy Land or **Paddyland.** Ireland. Hence, *Paddylander*, an Irishman. Coll.: from ca. 1820.

paddy over, come (gen. **the).** To bamboozle, ' kid ', humbug: from ca. 1820; slightly ob. Ex *Paddy*, q.v., and the Irishman's reputation for blarney.

Paddy Quick. A stick.—2. Thick. Both rhyming s. (– 1859); the latter, ob. H., 1st ed.

Paddy rammer. A hammer: rhyming s., esp. among urban labourers: late C. 19–20. *John o' London's Weekly*, June 9, 1934.

paddy-row. ' More jackets off than blows struck, where sticks supply the place of fists,' Bee: coll.: from ca. 1820; ob.

paddy wax or **-wax.** A variant (– 1923) of *paddy-whack*, 2. Manchon.

Paddy Wester ; occ. **paddywester.** A bogus seaman carrying a dead man's discharge-papers; a very incompetent or dissolute seaman: nautical: from ca. 1890. Bowen, ' After a notorious board-

ing-house keeper in Liverpool who shipped thousands of green men as A.B.'s for a consideration.'

paddy-w(h)ack, paddyw(h)ack, paddy w(h)ack ; or with capitals. An Irishman (in C. 18–early 19, only if big and strong): coll.: 1785, Grose (*at whack*); cf. O.E.D. date. Humorous on *Paddy*, q.v.—2. Whence, on the analogy of *paddy*, 1, q.v., a rage, a temper: coll.: 1899, Kipling, ' He'll be in a ravin' paddy-wack,' O.E.D.—3. A paddywhack almanac: coll. (– 1886); † by 1910. Cf. *paddy*, 3, q.v.

Paddy's Blackguards. The Royal Irish Regiment (until ca. 1881, the 18th Foot): military: C. 19–20; ob. Also *the Namurs.*

Paddy's Goose. ' The White Swan, a noted flash public house in the east of London,' H., 1864. Mayhew, 1861, fixes it as in High Street, Shadwell. Presumably ex Paddy's notion of a goose.

Paddy's grapes. Potatoes: South Lancashire jocular (–1905). E.D.D. (Sup.). Cf. several of the Irish terms.

Paddy's hurricane. A dead calm: nautical · from ca. 1840: ob. Also *Irishman's h.*

Paddy's Land. Ireland: coll. (– 1864). H., 3rd ed. Also *Paddy Land*, q.v.

Paddy's lantern. The moon: nautical: late C. 19–20. Bowen. Prob. after *parish-lantern*, q.v.

Paddy's lucerne. ' A prevalent type of weed,' Jice Doone: Australian coll. (– 1926). Ex the prevalence of lucerne as fodder.

Paddy's Milestone. ' Ailsa-Craig, just half-way between Greenock and Belfast on the packet route '; nautical: late C. 19–20. Bowen.

paddywester. An occ. form of *Paddy Wester*, q.v.

paddyw(h)ack. See **paddy-w(h)ack.**

padre. A chaplain: naval (1888, *Chambers's Journal*, Jan. 14) and military (– 1900); by 1916, coll. Ex Portuguese (lit. a father) as used, from ca. 1580, in India for any priest or parson (see esp. Yule & Burnell). For the G.W. padre, see esp. B. & P.

pædomancy. Like *pedimancy*, incorrect for *pedomancy*: C. 17–20. O.E.D.

paff ! A coll. interjection (contemptuous): mid-C. 19–20; ob. Hence *piff and paff*, jargon.

page of your own age, make a. Do it yourself: semi-proverbial coll.: Draxe, *Bibliotheca Scholastica Instructissima*, 1633; Ray; Swift. (Apperson.)

Paget's Irregular Horse. The 4th Hussars: military: from ca. 1843; very ob. Ex their slack drill on their return in 1842 from twenty-six years' service in India, and their C.O.'s name. F. & Gibbons.

pagoda-tree, gen. preceded by **shake the.** (To obtain) rapid fortune in India: s.: by 1870, coll.: 1836, T. Hook, ' The amusing pursuit of " shaking the pagoda-tree " once so popular in our Oriental possessions.' Slightly ob. by 1886, † by 1920. App. ex a coin that, owing to the design of a pagoda thereon, was called a pagoda. Esp. W., O.E.D. and Yule & Burnell.

pahny. An occ. variant of *parnee*, q.v. (B. & P.)

paid. Tipsy: ca. 1635–70. Shirley, *The Royal Master*, 1638. (O.E.D.)

' paid ' to, put. ' To regard a matter as finished, as over and done with ': S.E. of an account, coll. in such fig. connexions as ' Oh, don't worry; you can *put paid* to any friendship that ever existed between him and me ; I've found out the sort of fellow he really is ! ' (Lyell): late C. 19–20.

pain !, you give me a. The c.p. form of :

pain in the neck, give one a. To bore intensely ; to irritate : C. 20.

paint. Money : esp. among house-painters (—1866) ; ob. Cf. *brads, sugar,* qq.v.—2. Jam : military : from the 1890's. F. & Gibbons. Ex its inferior quality.

paint, v.i. To drink (something strong) : 1853, Whyte-Melville, ' Each hotel . . . called forth the same observation, " I guess I shall go in and paint " .' Ob.—2. V.t., to make numerous corrections on (a proof) : printers' (— 1909). Ware. Ex resulting appearance.—3. See :

paint a job. To scorch one's work : tailors' : C. 20. See e.g. *The Tailor and Cutter,* Nov. 29, 1928.

paint-brush baronet. An ennobled artist : Society coll. : 1885, *The Referee,* June 28 ; extremely ob. (Ware.) Cf. *gallipot baronet,* q.v.

paint one's eye for him (her, etc.). To give him a black eye : low (— 1887). Baumann.

paint the town red. See **red, paint the town.**

painted edge. A coat-edge in, or of, coloured cloth : tailors' : C. 20. E.g. in *The Tailor and Cutter,* Nov. 29, 1928.

painted mischief. Playing cards : 1879, *The Daily News,* March 8. Ob.

painter. A workman that scorches his job : tailors' : C. 20.

painter stainer. (Gen. pl.) An artist : Society : latter half of 1883. Ex the Lord Mayor's reference, at the Royal Academy banquet, to the Painter Stainers' Company. Ware.

painter, cut one's. To prevent a person's doing harm : late C. 17–mid-18 nautical s. B.E.—2. Hence, to send a person away : nautical s. (— 1785). Grose.—3. (Of oneself) **cut one's** or **the painter,** to depart unceremoniously : nautical (— 1867). Smyth.—4. Hence, to sever one's connexion : gen. coll. (— 1888) >, ca. 1905, S.E. (' The painter being the rope that holds the boat fast to the ship,' Grose.) Occ. *slip the painter,* in senses 3, 4 : from ca. 1865.

painter, let go the. To deliver a (heavy) punch : boxers' (— 1887) ; ob. Baumann. Ex nautical j. Cf. *paint one's eye,* q.v.

painter, what pleases the. A late C. 17–mid-18 c.p. in the world of art and literature : ' When any Representation in the Productions of his or any Art is unaccountable, and so is to be resolv'd purely into the good Pleasure of the Artist,' B.E.

Painter Pug. Wm. Hogarth (1697–1764), the artist. Dawson. (An inimical sobriquet was *the Pensioned Dauber.*)

painting. vbl.n. See **paint a job.**

pair of. *Pair* is coll. (and often humorous) when used of ' the two bodily members themselves, as " a pair of eyes, ears, lips, jaws, arms, hands, heels, legs, wings ", etc ', O.E.D. : late C. 14–20.

pair o(f) compasses. Human legs : London : ca. 1880–1910. Ware. The term arose when the male leg began to be narrowly encased.

pair o(f) drums. See **drums, pair o'.**

***pair o(f) kicks.** Boots ; shoes : tramps' c. (— 1935).

pair of hands. A man : coll. : from ca. 1630. O.E.D.

pair of heels. See **clean pair of heels, show a.**

pair of lawn sleeves. A bishop : coll. : 1844, Macaulay. O.E.D.

pair of oars. A boat rowed by two men : coll. verging on S.E. : C. 17–20.

pair of shears. See **shears.**

pair of shoes, a different or **another.** A different matter : coll. : 1859, Thackeray ; 1865, Dickens. Both have *another.* O.E.D.

pair of spectacles. See **spectacles.**

pair o(f) subs. See **subs, pair o(f).**

pair of wheels. A two-wheeled vehicle : coll. : from ca. 1620. Cockeram. O.E.D.

***pair of wings.** (A pair of) oars : ca. 1790–1890 : c. : Grose, 3rd ed. Ex speed.—2. Sleeves : tailors' : late C. 19–20.

pair off with. To marry : coll. : 1865, Miss Braddon in *Sir Jasper.* Ex S.E. sense, to go apart, or off, in pairs. O.E.D.

pairosaul. A parasol : illiterate pronunciation (— 1887). Baumann.

pajamas. See **pyjamas.**

pakaru. Broken, crushed, smashed : New Zealand military : G.W. Ex Maori *pakaru* (to destroy), common as N.Z. coll. in late C. 19–20. (F. & Gibbons.)

pakeha. A white man : a Maori word colloquially adopted in New Zealand ca. 1850. Perhaps ex a Maori word meaning a fairy ; perhaps a Maori attempt at *bugger,* ' said to have been described by Dr. Johnson (though not in his dictionary), as " a term of endearment amongst sailors " ', a theory app. supported by Morris. (Pronounced as a molossus, the *a*'s being, as always in Maori, given the Continental value.)

pakka. See **pukka.**

***pal.** An accomplice : c (— 1788). Grose, 2nd ed. (*chosen pells, pell* being an occ. C. 18–19 form) ; Vaux, 1812, *pall.* In late C. 19, this sense > low s. —2. Earlier and from ca. 1850 the prevailing sense, a chum, a friend : 1681–82, the Hereford Diocesan Register, ' Wheare have you been all this day, pall ? ' (O.E.D.) : s. >, ca. 1880, low coll. Ex Romany *pal,* brother, mate (cf. c. and Romany *blo(w)en*), ex Turkish Gypsy, *pral, plal,* brother ; ultimately related to Sanskrit *bhratr,* a brother (cf. L. *frater*). W., O.E.D., Borrow, and Smart & Crofton. (Cf. *pally,* q.v.) Hence :

pal, v.i. To associate (*with*) ; become another's ' pal ' (q.v.) : perhaps orig. c. ; certainly, at best, low s. (— 1879) >, ca. 1905, (decreasingly low) coll. Often, esp. in C. 20, *pal in with, pal up* (*to* or *with*) ; in C. 19, occ. *pal on.* ' The Autobiography of a Thief ', in *Macmillan's Magazine,* 1879, ' I palled in with some old hands at the game.'—2. (Gen. **pall**) to detect : c. : 1851, Mayhew ; ob. Perhaps ex *pal,* n., 1, or, more prob., ex the Romany preposition *palal, palla,* after, as in *av palla,* lit. to come after, i.e. to follow, and *dik palla,* to look after, i.e. to watch (Smart & Crofton) : cf. *be after a person,* to pursue him, desire strongly to find or catch.

pal-looral. Drunk : Glasgow (— 1934). Cf. *palatic,* q.v.

palace. An incorrect variant of † *palis,* a palisade, an enclosure. O.E.D.—2. A police-station : policemen's : from ca. 1870 ; somewhat ob. —3. (Palace.) The Crystal Palace : coll. (—1887). Baumann.—4. Hence, the Crystal Palace Association Football team : sporting coll. : from the 1890's.

palampo. A bed-spread, a quilt : Anglo-Indian coll. (— 1864). H., 3rd ed. A corruption of *palempore,* itself of doubtful etymology. Yule & Burnell.

***palarie,** v.i. and t. To talk, speak : vagrants' c. (— 1893) ; ob. P. H. Emerson, ' She used to palarie thick [cant] to the slaveys.' A variant of *Parlyaree*, q.v., influenced by *palaver*, v.

palatic. Drunk : 1885, *The Stage*, 'Sandy told me he last saw him dreadfully palatic ' : theatrical ; very ob. I.e., *paralytic* (q.v.) corrupted.

palaver. A fussy, ostentatious person : Scots coll. : C. 19–20 ; ob. Gen. *old palaver*. Presumably ex :—2. Conversation or discussion, gen. idle, occ. (in C. 19–20) flattering or wheedling ; ' jaw ', q.v. : nautical s. >, ca. 1790, gen. coll. : 1748, Smollett, ' None of your palaver.' Ex S.E. (orig. trade and nautical) sense, a parley, a conference, esp. one with much talk, itself ex Portuguese *palavra* (cf. Sp. *palabra*), used by the Portuguese in parleying with the natives on the African coast. (Partly O.E.D. ; see also Grose, P.) Cf. the v.—3. Hence, business, concern : from middle 1890's. C. Hyne, 1899, ' It's not your palaver . . . or mine.' O.E.D. (Sup.).

palaver, v. To talk much, unnecessarily, or (in C. 19–20) plausibly or cajolingly : from ca. 1730 : s. or coll. > in C. 19–20 definitely coll., latterly almost S.E. Ex the preceding, but until ca. 1775 unrecorded except as *palavering*.—2. Hence, to flatter ; wheedle : from ca. 1780 ; ob. Grose.

*palaver to (a person) **for** (a thing). To ask one for something ; beg it : tramps' c. (— 1859). H., 1st ed. Ex *palaver*, v., 2.

palaverer, occ. **palaverist**. One who palavers ; one given to palavering : from ca. 1785 (ob.) ; coll., in C. 20 almost S.E. Ex *palaver*, v., 1. Cf. :

palavering, vbl.n. and ppl. adj. Copious or idle talk ; very talkative : resp. 1733, 1764 (O.E.D.) : s. or coll. until C. 19, then definitely coll. ; in C. 20, almost S.E. Foote, ' He is a damned palavering fellow.' Ex *palaver*, v.

palayl. Incorrect for *polayl*, poultry : C. 14–16. O.E.D.

pale. Pale brandy : London coll. : mid-C. 19–20 ; ob. Mayhew, 1861, ' A " drain of pale ", as she called it, invigorated her.'

[**pale as** . . . These similes, e.g. pale as *ashes*, *clay*, *death*, are S.E. Apperson.]

Palestine in London. Ca. 1820–50 : low. Egan, 1821, ' That portion of the parish of St. Giles, Bloomsbury, inhabited by the lower Irish.' Cf. *Holy Land*.

palette. A hand : late C. 18–19. Cf. *daddle* and *paddle*, qq.v.

palone or **palon(e)y.** A girl : grafters' : C. 20. Philip Allingham, *Cheapjack*, 1934. Perhaps cf. Sp. *paloma*, a dove. In low theatrical, the form is *polone*.

pall. See pal, n., 1, and v., 2.—2. To detect : c. or low s. : 1859, H. ; † by 1900.—3. To stop, e.g. *pall that !*, stop (doing) that !, and *pall there !*, silence ! : nautical (— 1864) ; ob. H., 3rd ed. ; Baumann. Ex *pall*, properly *pawl*, an instrument used to stop the windlass. See **pawl**, the earlier, more gen. form.—4. To appal ; daunt (as in C. 14–17 S.E.) : nautical (— 1864). Ibid. (Cf. *palled*.) Abbr. *appal*, or ex the nautical order *ease and pall*.

pallad. An † incorrect form of *pallet*, a mattress. O.E.D.

pallaver. See palaver, esp. v., 2. (Grose.)

palled, be. Not to dare to say more : low coll. (— 1864). H., 3rd ed. Ex *appal*, or *pall*, v., 3.

*palliard. A vagrant that lies on straw ; but esp. ' he that goeth in a patched cloke ', Awdeley : c. of ca. 1560–1830 ; ob. by ca. 1750.—2. In C. 17–

early 18, the seventh ' rank ' of the underworld : born beggars affecting hideous sores. B.E. (Other senses, S.E.) Ex Fr. *paillard*, itself ex *paille*, straw. (O.E.D.) Cf. :

palliasse. A harlot : low : C. 19–20 ; ob. Ex *palliasse*, a straw, i.e. cheap, mattress.

palliness. Comradeship ; the being ' pals ' (q.v.) : from ca. 1890. Cf. *palship*, q.v.

pallish. Friendly, ' chummy ' : mostly schools' : 1892 (O.E.D.) ; ob. Ex *pal*, n., 2. Cf. :

pally. Friendly ; ' thick ' : from 1895 or slightly earlier. Ex *pal*, n., 2, q.v. Cf. preceding.

[**palm.** See entry at pace, go the.]

palm-acid or **-oil.** A caning on the hand : schoolboys' : from ca. 1860 ; ob.

palm-soap. Money ; a bribe : low (— 1860) ; ob. H., 2nd ed. On S.E. *palm-oil*, a bribe.

*palmer. A beggar that, under the pretence of collecting ' harp ' halfpence, by palming steals copper coins from shopkeepers : c. (— 1864) ; † by 1920. H., 3rd ed. Contrast *palming*, q.v.—2. A shy fellow : Durham School : from ca. 1870 ; ob.

Palmer is concerned, Mr. A c.p. applied, ca. 1810–50, to a briber or a bribee. Vaux, 1812. Ex the S.E. *palm-oil*, a bribe. Contrast *palm-acid* and cf. *palmistry*.

*palming. The robbing of shops by pairs, the one bargaining, the other palming desirable articles : c. (— 1839) ; slightly ob. Brandon ; H., 2nd ed. Contrast *palmer*, 1.

*palming-racket. ' Secreting money in the palm of the hand ', Vaux : c. (— 1812) ; ob.

palmistry. Bribery : jocular coll. (— 1923). Manchon. Cf. *palm-soap*.

palore. See polore.

Pals, the. The four Service ' battalions of the Liverpool and Manchester Regiments, raised in 1914 ' : military : G.W. (F. & Gibbons.)

palship. Friendship ; being pals : 1896 (O.E.D.) ; ob. Ex *pal*, n., 2. Cf. *palliness*, q.v.

Paltock's Inn or **inn.** A poverty-stricken place : ca. 1578–1610 : coll. almost imm. > S.E. Gosson, ' Comming to Chenas, a blind village, in comparison of Athens a Paltockes Inne '. Presumably ex some wretched inn, the host one Paltock.

pam or **Pam.** The knave of clubs : 1685, Crowne ; ob. Coll. Pope, ' Ev'n mighty Pam, that Kings and Queens o'erthrew.' Abbr. Fr. *pamphile*, a card-game and esp. this card, which, in trumping, ranks highest. W. ; O.E.D.—2. A card-game rather like nap : from ca. 1690 ; ob. Coll. >, ca. 1780, S.E. Addison, in *The Guardian*, 1713, ' She quickly grows more fond of Pam than of her husband.'—3. Lord Palmerston (d. 1865) a nickname by ' telescoping ' : 1854, Smedley, ' It's very jolly to be on those terms with a man like Pam ' ; slightly ob. Also nickname *Cupid*, by the ladies ; *Pumice-Stone*, by his political opponents.

Pamp, (as) snug as old. Very comfortable : lower classes' (— 1887) ; ob. Baumann. Who was Pamp ? The name is prob. fanciful ex *a pampered person*.—2. (**pamp** or **P.**) A Pampero, i.e. a River Plate gale : nautical : late C. 19–20 Bowen.

*pan. A bed : c. : C. 18. Hall, 1708.—2. Money : c. : mid-C. 18–mid-19. Halliwell.—3. **the pan**, the workhouse : tramps' c. (— 1893). P. H. Emerson. The etymologies are extremely obscure, as are the connexions—if any. Perhaps all three are cognate with Romany *pan(d)*, to ' shut, fasten, close, tie, bind, etc.,' Smart & Crofton ; sense 1 may, via dial., derive ex *pan*, a beam of wood.—4. (*Pan.*) Du Toit's Pan : a Kimberley (South Africa) coll. (— 1913). Pettman.—5. The face : lower classes' (— 1935). Perhaps ex *pan, shut one's*, q.v.

pan, v. To catch ; capture : coll., mostly U.S. and Colonial : 1887. O.E.D.

pan, shut one's. To hold one's tongue : from ca. 1830 ; ob. Marryat, in *Peter Simple*, ' Shut your pan.' Ex that part of an † gun or pistol which holds the priming. Cf. S.E. *flash in the pan*. O.E.D.

pan-flasher. A transitory meteor in the world of sport, esp. **in** lawn tennis : sporting coll. : from 1935. Ex S.E. *flash in the pan*.

pan on, have a. To be low-spirited : printers' : from ca. 1860. ? ex Fr. *panne*, a failure, a ' fizzle ', a breakdown, e.g. *pannes de métro*.

pan out, v.i. To turn out ; (of an event) be : coll. : orig. (1871), U.S. ; anglicised ca. 1895, but common in South Africa (the paradise of American mining-engineers) as early as 1891 : witness Pett-mann. *The Referee*, April 7, 1901, ' We do not want to know about . . . the M.C.C.'s big roller . . . or how the members' luncheon pans out as a commercial speculation.' Ex mining (the shaking of gold-bearing gravel in a pan). Thornton.—2. V.t., to yield : Australian (and U.S.) coll. : 1884, *The Melbourne Punch*, Sept. 4, ' The department . . . only panned out a few copper coins.' Ob. O.E.D.

pan-pudding, stand to one's. To hold one's (lit. or fig.) ground : coll. : late C. 17–early 18. Motteux's *Rabelais*. (A heavy pudding, gen. of flour.)

*panam. See **pannam**.

panatrope. A hermaphrodite : from ca. 1910. Michael Harrison, *Weep for Lycidas*, 1934. Ex the S.E. word.

pancake. The female pudend : low : C. 19–20.— 2. The act of descending vertically with the 'plane kept level : aviators' : 1916 or, at latest, 1917. The v. is gen. considered S.E.—3. (Gen. pl.) Ironically substituted for a word that one doesn't accept : coll. : 1914. A. Neil Lyons, *Arthur's*, ' " What was your particular line ? " " Extra gentleman." " Extra pancakes ! " ' (Manchon.) Cf. *my foot !*

Pancridge parson. A term of contempt : C. 17–18. Field, 1612 ; Halliwell. (Apperson.)

pandemonium. A gambling-hell : educated gamblers' (— 1823) ; † by 1900. ' Jon Bee ', who implies a pun on *hell* being the place of *all the devils*. —2. ' The lower deck subalterns' quarters in the old naval troopships ' : naval and military : ca. 1850–1910. Bowen.

pandie, pandy. A stroke from cane or strap on the hand as punishment : coll., mostly school and nursery and mainly Scots : A. Scott, 1805 (O.E.D.). Ex L. *pande palman* or *manum*, hold out your hand ! —2. (pandy) : a ' revolted Sepoy in the Indian Mutiny of 1857–9 ' : coll. : 1857 ; ob. Ex *Pandę*, the surname of the first man to revolt in the 34th Regiment. O.E.D., Yule & Burnell.—3. Hence, an Indian soldier : Regular Army : late C. 19–20 ; ob. B. & P.

pandie, pandy, v. To cane, strap : coll. (mostly school and nursery) : 1863, Kingsley, ' She . . . pandied their hands with canes.' Ex *pandie*, n., 1.

panel, be or **go on the.** To ' place oneself under the care of a panel doctor ' : coll. (— 1927). Collinson.

*panel-crib, -den, -house. A brothel where theft is (deliberately) rife : c. (— 1860) ; ? orig. U.S. Bartlett, 1860 (*panel-house*, low s.). Whence the next two entries.

panel-dodge or **-game.** Theft in a panel-house : low s. > low coll. : resp. 1885, Burton, *Thousand Nights* ; *Century Dict.*, 1890. Ex *panel-crib*, etc., q.v.

panel-thief, -thieving. A thief, theft, in a *panel-crib*, q.v. : low s. (— 1860) > low coll. ; perhaps orig. U.S. (see Bartlett, ed. of 1860).

*panem. See **pannam**.

*pangy bar. Five pounds sterling : c. : from ca. 1919. James Curtis, *The Gilt Kid*, 1936. A bar is £1 ; *pangy* may derive ex Fr. *cinq*, but it is more prob. a corruption of Romany *pansh*, five.

panic. Preparations at full speed on a ship preparing for sea : naval : 1914–18. F. & Gibbons.

panic-party. ' The men whose job it was to leave a Decoy Ship . . . in disorder when a German submarine opened fire ' : naval coll. (1916) >, by 1918, j. Bowen.

panicker. ' A man showing needless anxiety beforehand ' : military coll. : late 1916 ; ob. F. & Gibbons.

panicky ; occ. **-nn-,** a sol. Like, given to, panic : very or excessively afraid or nervous : coll. 1869, *The Echo*, Oct. 12, ' Hence the delays, mystification, and consequent panicky results ', O.E.D. Cf. *wind up, wind vertical, windy* ; also *breeze*.

*pan(n)am ; panem ; pan(n)um. Bread : c. : resp. mid-C. 16–20, C. 17–18, C. 17–20. Harman ; Brome (*pannum*) ; B.E. (*panam*) ; Bee (*panum*) ; Vance. Ex L. *panis* and prob. ex the accusative *panem*, via Lingua Franca. Cf. Fr. s. *panam*, bread, and *yannam*, q.v.

*pannam(, etc.)-bound. Deprived of one's food-, esp. bread-, allowance : prison c. : mid-C. 19–20. H., 1st ed. Ex preceding. Cf. *pannam-struck* and :

*pannam(, etc. ; or **cokey)-fence** or, more gen., **-fencer.** A street pastry-cook : c. : from ca. 1840. Ex *pannam*, q.v., and see **cokey** and **fence**.

*pannam(, etc.)-struck. Starving : c. : C. 19–20 ; ob. H., 2nd ed. Ex *pannam*, q.v.

*pann(e)y. The highway : c. of ca. 1750–1830. John Poulter, 1753, ' I'll scamp on the panney.' Etymology obscure : perhaps ex Romany.—2. A house ; lodgings, rooms : c. of ca. 1785–1880. Grose, 1788 ; Vaux, 1812 ; Egan.—3. Whence *flash pann(e)y*, often simply *panny* (Ware), a brothel ; a public-house frequented by thieves : c. of ca. 1820–1920.—4. A burglary : c. : implied in Grose, 1788 ; ob. Ex preceding sense, via *do a panny*, q.v. Cf. *pann(e)y-lay*, q.v.—5. A fight between two, among more than two, women : low (— 1909). Ware. Cognate with Devonshire *panel*, to hurt, or pain, and Nottinghamshire *panneling*, a severe beating (E.D.D.).

*pann(e)y, do a. To rob a house ; commit a burglary : c. : Grose, 1788 ; Lytton ; ob. Ex preceding entry, sense 2. Cf. *crack a crib*.

*pann(e)y-lay. A burglary : c. : from ca. 1820 ; ob. See **pann(e)y,** 2.

*pann(e)y-man. A housebreaker : c. : C. 19–20 ; very ob. Ex *pann(e)y,* 2.

pannican, off one's. See **pannikin, off one's.**

pannicky. See **panicky.**

pannier. A robed waiter at table in the Inner Temple : coll. : 1823. Origin unknown, says S.O.D. ; but is not the term an abbr. of *pannier man*, ' a servant belonging to the Temple or Gray's Inn, whose office is to announce the dinner ', Grose, 3rd ed., 1796 (= 1790 or 1791) ? W. compares with *boots* and *buttons*, qq.v.—2. ' A bunched-up part of a skirt forming a protuberance behind': cata-chrestic : 1869. O.E.D.

pannier, fill a woman's. To render her pregnant : C. 17–18 : low coll. Cotgrave.

pannikin, off one's. Crazy : Australian : 1910, A. H. Davis, *On Our Selection* ; 1916, C. J. Dennis (O.E.D. Sup.).

pannikin-boss or **-overseer.** An overseer in a small, 'unofficial' way on a station : Australian coll. (— 1897) ; ob. Morris. (In itself, *pannikin* is S.E. ex dial.)—2. Hence, 'a shift boss. A man in charge of a small gang of workmen ', Jice Doone : Australian coll. (— 1926).

pannikin into another shed, roll one's. To seek work with another employer : Australian coll. (— 1902) ; ob. Cf. the preceding entry.

*****pannum.** See pannam.—**panny.** See pann(e)y.

pannyar. 'The old name for the slave trade on the African coast', says Bowen : nautical : ? C. 18–mid. Prob. ex *pannier*, a basket.

panorama. A paramour : sol. : 1889, *The Ref*, Nov. 17. (Ware.)

pansy. A very effeminate youth ; a homosexual : from ca. 1930. Cf. *Nancy* (*boy*). Also *pansy-boy* : from ca. 1930 ; *The New Statesman and Nation*, Sept. 15, 1934, concerning the Fascist meeting in Hyde Park on the 9th Sept., notes that there were, from the crowd, 'shouts about "pansy-boys"'.

pant. See panto.

panta-. Incorrect for *panto-* in *pantacosm*, *pantagamy*, *pantagraph*, *pantameter*, *pantamorphic*, *pantascopic*, *pantatype*, mid-C. 18–20. O.E.D.

pantables, stand upon one's. To stand on dignity : coll. : ca. 1570–1760. G. Harvey, Cotton, Horace Walpole. Moreover, *pantable* is corrupt for *pantofle*, a slipper, a shoe. Other corruptions are *pantacle*, *pantocle*, *pantap(p)le*, *pantaphel*, *pan-top(p)le*, *pantible*. O.E.D.

pantechnicon. A coll. abbr. of *pantechnicon van* (furniture-removing) : 1891. O.E.D.

pantener ; pantoner. Frequent misreadings of *pautener*, rascal, n. and adj. : C. 14–15. O.E.D.

*****panter.** A hart : c. : late C. 17–early 19. B.E. ; Grose, 'That animal is, in the Psalms, said to pant after the fresh water-brooks ' (1785 revised by 1796). —2. The human heart : from ca. 1720 certainly ; possibly from late C. 17 : low s., prob. orig. c. ; slightly ob. A song of ca. 1725, quoted in *Musa Pedestris* ; Grose, 2nd ed., 'Frequently pants in time of danger '.—3. See :

panters. The female breasts : low : C. 19–20 ; ob. Ex *panter*, 2. Cf. *heavers*.

panteys ; in C. 20, gen. **panties.** Pantaloons : ca. 1848–60 : coll. : orig. and mainly U.S. (Burton, *Waggeries*, 1848).—2. Drawers (women's, children's) : 1905 : coll. >, by 1933, S.E. Cf. *pants*, *scanties* and *undies*, and see esp. 'Euphemism and Euphemisms ' in *Words !*

pantile. See pantables.

pantile. 'Erroneously applied to flat Dutch or Flemish paving tiles, and so '—in the pl.—' to the Parade at Tunbridge Wells which was paved with these ', O.E.D. : ca. 1770–1830. Properly 'a roofing tile transversely curved to an ogee shape ' (ib.). Cf. *pantile-house*, *-shop*, q.v.—2. A hat : ca. 1859–90. H., 1st ed. ; Baumann. Ex shape. Cf. *tile*, q.v.—3. A flat cake, jam-covered : schoolboys' : ca. 1863–1920. H., 3rd ed. Ex sense 1.—4. A hard biscuit, esp. one of those carried by Liverpool ships : nautical : from ca. 1880 ; ob. Bowen. Ex sense 1.

pantile(-)house, (-)shop. Ca. 1780–1830 : s. rapidly > coll. : resp. 1785, Grose ; 1796, Grose (hence, 1790 or 1791). 'A Presbyterian, or other dissenting meeting house, frequently covered with pantiles, called also a cock pit ', Grose, 1st ed.

Pantile Park. London's roofs and chimney-pots : jocular coll. : mid-C. 19–20 ; extremely ob. Ware.

pantiler. A Dissenter : coll. : app. ca. 1720–1890, but not recorded before 1863, according to F. & H., 1889 according to the O.E.D. ; it occurs in H., 1860. Ex *pantile*, 1.—2. Hence, a religious prisoner : prison-staff s. : early C. 19. Mayhew, 1856, 'The officers . . . used to designate the extraordinary religious convicts as "pantilers".'

panto. A C. 20 coll. abbr. of *pantomime*. Ware. Occ. (— 1923 : Manchon), *pant*.

pantocle, pantofle, pantople. See pantables.

pantomine. A sol., frequent among even the semi-literate, for *pantomime* : C. 19–20.

pantry. A prize-ring variant (— 1920 ; ob.) of *bread-basket*, q.v. : cf. *meat-safe*, 1. W.

pants. Pantaloons : low coll. : orig. (1842 ; 1846, O. W. Holmes) and mainly U.S. ; ob. Thornton. Cf. sense 4 and *panteys*, 1, q.v.—2. Pantalettes : coll. : orig. (1851), U.S. ; ob.—3. Hence, coll. (in shops, only of men's) for drawers : 1874, H., 5th ed., 'American term for trousers. Here used to represent the long drawers worn underneath '; 1880, *The Daily News*, Nov. 8, 'Pants and shirts sell rather freely,' O.E.D. Cf. *panteys*, 2, q.v.—4. Hence, trousers : orig. (— 1874), U.S. ; low coll., mostly Colonial : late C. 19–20.

pants, got the. See got the pants.

*****panum.** See pannam.

panupetaston. A loose, wide-sleeved overcoat : Oxford University : ca. 1850–80. H., 5th ed., 1874, 'Now out of fashion '. Prob. ex Gr.

*****panzy.** A burglary : c. : (— 1857) ; † by 1900. 'Ducange Anglicus.' A perversion of *panny*, 3.

*****pap.** Paper ; esp. paper money : c. : 1877, Horsley, *Jottings from Jail*, 'A lucky touch for half-a-century '—£50—' in pap '. Ex *paper* influenced by S.E. *pap* : or the other way about. (—F. & H.'s 'emoluments ' is a special application of S.E.)

pap, (e.g. his) mouth is full of. A c.p. applied to one still childish : late C. 18–early 19. Grose, 2nd ed. Ex *pap*, babies' food. Cf. the C. 18 proverb, *boil not the pap before the child be born*.

*****pap-feeder.** A spoon : c. of ca. 1850–90. Mayhew, 1858.

pap with a hatchet, give. To punish as if one were doing a kindness or conferring a benefit : ca. 1589–1719 ; ob. by 1650. Coll. Lyly or Nashe, 1589 ; G. Harvey, 1589 ; D'Urfey, 1719. (O.E.D.) Halliwell's 'to do any kind action in an unkind manner ' perhaps misses the irony.

papa ; (C. 18) **pappa.** Father : from ca. 1680 : S.E. until ca. 1780 : then a childish coll. ; since ca. 1880, ob. except when jocular. Ex Gr. πάπ(π)αs via Fr. ; ultimately cognate with *pap*, a breast (see esp. W., *Adjectives and Other Words*) : cf. *mam(m)a*, q.v. See also **dad, daddy.**

paper. Broadsides and similar publications : coll. (— 1851) ; ob. Mayhew. Cf. *paper-worker*, q.v.—2. Free passes to an entertainment ; collectively, the recipients of such passes : 1870, *Figaro*, July 15, 'The best sort of paper for a theatre is Bank of England notes.' Also *Oxford clink* and *stationery*. Cf. :

paper, v.t. To fill (a theatre, etc.) by means of free passes: before 1879. Webster, *Supplement*, 1879. Ex *paper*, n., 2. Cf. *papery*, q.v.

paper, adj. corresponding to **paper**, n., 2: theatrical (— 1909). Ware. Esp in *paper house*.

paper, reading the. The excuse given for taking a nap: c.p.: from ca. 1880.

paper-boat. Any lightly built vessel, esp. a paddle excursion-steamer: nautical coll.: late C. 19–20. Bowen.

paper-fake. A ' dodge ' or ' lay ' with paper, e.g. selling ballads: Cockney: ca. 1850–80. Mayhew.

*paper-maker. A rag-gatherer, gutter-searcher: c. >, by 1860, low: from ca. 1835; ob. Brandon. —2. One who, pretending to be the agent of a paper-mill, collects rags free and then sells them: c. (— 1839); ob. Brandon.

paper-man. An officer ' who, being employed on the staff ', is ' not available for regimental duty ', *The Standard*, Oct. 24, 1892; prob. it was used some few years earlier: military coll.: ob.

paper-marriage. A Society wedding: from ca. 1890. Ex fees paid in banknotes.

paper medal. See **medal, a putty.**

paper-mill, the. The record office of the Court of Queen's Bench: legal: ca. 1840–1900.

paper-minister. A minister that reads his sermons: Scots coll.: 1854, H. Miller. O.E.D. The E.D.D. records, at 1828, *paper-ministry*, ' a ministry of preachers who read their sermons '.

paper-padded. (Of foot-wear) shod with paper instead of with leather: shoemakers' s. (— 1887) >, by 1910, coll. Baumann.

paper-scull (or **-skull**). A silly or foolish fellow. Also adj. Coll.: late C. 17–early 19. B.E.; Grose, 1st ed. Whence:

paper-sculled (**-skulled**). Silly, foolish: coll.: C. 18–early 19.

paper-stainer. A clerk: coll.: mid-C. 19–20; ob. (As author, S.E.)

paper-worker. A vendor of broadsides: low coll.: from ca. 1850; ob. Ex *paper*, n., 1. Cf. *running stationer*, q.v.

paperer. The issuer of *paper*, n., 2: theatrical: 1879, says Ware. Ex *paper*, v.

*papers, get one's or, more gen., **the.** See **get the papers.**

papery. Occupied by persons with free passes: 1885, *The Referee*, Nov. 8, ' The stalls were partly papery, and partly empty.' Ex *paper*, n., 2.

papescent. Incorrect for *pappescent*: Arbuthnot, 1731; ' Johnson ' and later dictionaries. O.E.D.

*paplar or **papler.** See **poplars.**

papphe. A C. 15 erroneous form of † *pop*, **to** paint (the face) with cosmetic. O.E.D.

pappy. Father: childish coll. (ob. by 1920): 1763, Bickerstaff; 1897, ' Ouida '. Diminutive of *papa*, q.v. O.E.D.—2. A nursery form of *pap*, infants' food: coll.: 1807, E. S. Barrett; ob. O.E.D.

par. Abbr. *paragraph*, esp. of news: journalistic coll.: 1879, W. Black (O.E.D.); Ware, however, dates *par-leader* (a short leading article in one paragraph) at 1875. ' Pink Pars for Pale People ' has long been a feature of *Books of To-Day*. Cf. *para*.—2. An occ. variant of *pa*.

par-banging. ' Tramping, seeking for work ': urban lower classes' (— 1909). Ware. I.e. banging the *pavé*.

par-leader. See **par.**

para. Abbr. *paragraph*, esp. as part of a book,

an article, etc.: book world: C. 20. While *par*, q.v., is used mainly by printers and journalists, *para* is used mainly by authors; some publishers prefer *par*, some *para*.

*parachute. A parasol; umbrella: c. (— 1864) >, by 1873, gen. low s.; ob. H., 3rd ed.

paracide. A C. 16 incorrect form of *parricide*. O.E.D.

parade, burn the. See **burn the parade.**

paradise. The gallery of a theatre: 1864; always felt to be French; ob. by 1910, † by 1930. H., 3rd ed. Fr. *paradis*. Cf. the cognate *the gods* and contrast the Fr. *poulailler*.—2. A grove of trees outside St. John's College at: Oxford: from ca. 1860; ob. (Its Winchester ' notional ' sense, a small garden, is perhaps rather j. than eligible.)

paradise, get or **have a penn'orth of.** To get, have, take a drink, esp. of gin: low: ca. 1860–1915.

parallelipiped, parallelopiped. Incorrect for *parallelepiped*: resp. C. 16–20, C. 17–20. O.E.D.

paralysed. Tipsy: s. verging on coll.: ca. 1890–1920. Ex the effect. Cf.:

paralytic. Drunk: from ca. 1910. Ex preceding entry. Cf. *palatic*, q.v.

paralytic fit or **stroke.** A badly fitting garment: tailors': from ca. 1870; slightly ob. By a pun on that affliction. Cf. *give fits*.

*param, parum. Milk: c.: late C. 16–17. Harman. Also *yarum*, q.v.

paramologia; paramologetic. Incorrect for *paromologia; paromologetic*: C. 17–18. O.E.D.—

paranomasia. Incorrect for *paronomasia*: C. 17–18. O.E.D.

parapet Joe. Any of the numerous German machine-gunners whose pleasure it was to ' play a tune ' along the parapet, *pom-tiddley-om-pom pom-pom* being the usual burst: Australian soldiers'. 1916–18.

paraphanalia, paraphonalia. For *paraphernalia*: C. 17–18. O.E.D.

parasol. A monoplane that, with wings ' raised above the fuselage and over the pilot's head ', gave ' a clear view of the ground ': Air Force coll.: 1915–18. F. & Gibbons.

parcel. The day's winnings; a pocket-book: the turf: late C. 19–20. *The Pink 'Un and the Pelican*, 1898 (former); *The Sporting Times*, April 6, 1901 (latter).—2. Hence, a sum (esp. if considerable) won or lost: C. 20. Esp. *drop a parcel* (Wodehouse, 1923: O.E.D. Sup.). Cf. *packet*, 2.—3. An English girl sold into a brothel abroad: c. or low (— 1887). Baumann.

parcel-finder. One who, for lost packets, goes to the pawnbrokers: pawnbrokers' coll. (— 1887). Baumann.

parcel from Paris. See **packet from Paris.**

parchment. A bluejacket's certificate of service: naval coll.: late C. 19–20. Bowen.

pard. A partner; a chum: orig. (— 1872), U.S.; anglicised ca. 1885, chiefly in the Colonies. A coll. abbr. of *partner* via *pardner*: itself a coll. (— 1887), recorded by Baumann—but orig. U.S.

parding. Pardon: sol., esp. among Cockneys: C. 19–20. Mayhew, 1861.

Paree. Paris: coll.: from ca. 1850. Often *gay Paree*. Ex Fr. pronunciation.

parenthesis, have one's nose in. To have it pulled: ca. 1786–1850. Grose, 2nd ed. Hence, *parenthesis*, the having one's nose pulled: ca. 1820–40. Bee.

parenthesis, iron. A prison : ca. 1810–50. *Lex. Bal.* Cf. *cage*, q.v.

parenthesis, wooden. A pillory : ca. 1810–40. *Lex. Bal.* Cf. *parenthesis, iron.*

parentheses. Bandy legs : printers' : from ca. 1870. Ex the shape : ( ).

pariah brig. A deep-sea native vessel of India : nautical : late C. 19–20. Bowen. Punning *pariah*.

*parings. Illicit clippings of money : c. : late C. 17–mid-19. B.E., Grose. A special application of the S.E. sense. (Grose's *chippings* is an error.)

parings of one's nails, not to give, lose, part with the. To be a miser : semi-proverbial coll. : from ca. 1540 ; in C. 19–20, mostly dial. 'Proverbs' Heywood, Deloney, Mabbe, 'Phraseologia Generalis' Robertson, Northall. (Apperson.)

paripatecian, pyripatition. Incorrect for *peripatetian* : C. 16, C. 17. O.E.D.

*parish-bull, -prig, -stallion. A parson : c. : resp. 1811, *Lex. Bal.* ; 1864, H., 3rd ed. ; F. & H., 1902. Prob. *prig = prick* (q.v.) influenced by *prig*, v., 3, q.v. Cf. the ambiguous C. 17 proverb, *the parson gets the children.* (Apperson.)

parish-lantern. The moon : dial. and s. (—1847). Halliwell. Cf. *oliver*, q.v.

parish pick-axe. A prominent nose : lower classes' (—1909) ; ob. Ware.

parish-rig. 'A poorly found ship or an ill-clothed man ' : Canadian (and Eastern U.S.) nautical : late C. 19–20. Bowen. Ex S.E. *parish-rigged*, cheaply rigged.

parish-soldier. Ca. 1780–1850. 'A jeering name '—prob. coll. rather than s.—' for a militia man, from substitutes being frequently hired by the parish from which one of its inhabitants is drawn.'

parish-stallion. See **parish-bull.**

parishes, his stockings are of (later, belong to) two. A c.p. applied to one whose stockings or socks are odd : ca. 1790–1860. Grose, 3rd ed.

park. A prison : low s. and Northern dial. : ca. 1820–70. 'Jon Bee.' Perhaps ex the privileged circuit round the King's Bench and/or the Fleet Prison.—2. A back yard, a small strip of garden in a town : jocular coll. : from ca. 1890 ; ob.—3. See **Bushy Park.**

park, v. To place, gen. with implication of safety : coll. ; orig. U.S., anglicised ca. 1915. *The Times*, Feb. 1, 1918, 'A policeman " parked " [the] perambulators and mounted guard . . . while the mothers made their purchases ' (W.). Ex military usage, to put in an artillery-, a car-park, via *park a gun*, *lorry*, *car*.—2. V. reflexive (of persons) : to place oneself ; hence, to sit : coll. : from ca. 1920. Both senses are now on the border-line of S.E.

park, down the. (Of a horse that is) losing : Glasgow sporting (— 1934).

*park, in the. See **Bushy Park, at.**

park-paling(s), -railings. Teeth : low : 1811, *Lex. Bal.* (*paling*) ; *railings* from ca. 1860.—2. A neck of mutton : low : from ca. 1880. Ex the appearance.

parker. A very well-dressed man frequenting the parks : low London : mid-C. 19–20 ; ob. Ware.

*parker, v.i. and t. To speak (about) ; ask ; beg : c. : from ca. 1890 ; ob. P. H. Emerson, 1893, 'Have you parkered to the owner for your letties ? ' Ex It. *pargliare*, via Lingua Franca, or a corruption of *Parlyaree*, q.v.

parky ; incorrectly **parkey.** Cold ; chilly. (Only of weather ; in Midland dial., however, it = witty, smart or sharp of tongue.) From 1898 **or a little**

earlier. Prob. ex *perky*, *parky*, characteristic of a park ; cf. dial. *parkin*, ginger-bread.

parleyvoo. Occ. **parlyvoo, parl(e)y-vous, parlez-vous.** The French language : coll. : 1754, Foote, 'A French fellow . . . with his muff and parle-vous ' (O.E.D.).—2. The study of French : coll. : late C. 19–20.—3. A Frenchman : 1815 (O.E.D.) : slightly ob. Cf. Fr. *goddam*, an Englishman : even C. 15 Villon alludes to the oath. Ex *parlez-vous*, do you speak (e.g. French) ?

parleyvoo, adj. French : 1828, Moir. E.D.D.— 2. Loosely, foreign : late C. 19–20. Both coll.

parleyvoo, v.i. To speak French : s. when not jocular coll. : 1765, Foote, 'You know I can't parler vous,' O.E.D. Ex the n., 1, q.v. also for variant spellings.—2. Hence, to speak a foreign language : from ca. 1880 ; ob. Cf. *sling the bat.*— 3. Hence, loosely, to speak : from ca. 1919.

parliament. Erroneous for *parament* or *palliament* : C. 16. O.E.D.

parliament !, kiss my. A rude c.p., based on ' the *Rump* Parliament ' : early Restoration period. Pepys, Feb., 1660, 'Boys do now cry, " Kiss my Parliament " ' (W.).

parliament whiskey. Whiskey on which inland-revenue dues have been paid : Anglo-Irish coll. : from the 1820's. Ware.

Parliamentary press. 'An old custom of claiming any iron, which happens to be in use, for the purpose of opening the collar seam ', Barrère & Leland, 1889. Tailors' : ob.

parlour ; front parlour. The female pudend : low : C. 19–20. Bee. Whence :

parlour and lie backward, let out one's. To be a whore : low : C. 19–20 ; ob. Bee. Cf. *let out one's fore-rooms*, etc., q.v.

parlour into the kitchen, out of the. From good to bad : coll. : late C. 16–17. Florio. Cf. *out of God's blessing into the warm sun*, q.v.

*parlour-jump, v. Ex *parlour-jumping*, q.v. : c. : 1894, Arthur Morrison. O.E.D.

*parlour-jumper. One who specialises in ' parlour-jumping ' : c. : from ca. 1870, says Ware.

*parlour-jumping. Theft from rooms, esp. by entering at the window : c. : from not later than 1879.

parlous. Extremely clever, shrewd, mischievous ; extraordinary : C. 15–20 (ob.) : S.E. until ca. 1840, then dial. and coll. (= ' awful ', terrible). O.E.D.

parly. A Parliamentary train : railwaymen's (— 1887). Baumann.

[**Parlyaree.** The ' Lingua Francal '—but actually as to 90% of its words, Italianate—vocabulary of C. 18–mid-19 actors and mid-C. 19–20 coster-mongers and showmen : (orig. low) coll. verging, after ca. 1930, on S.E. (How long the word itself has existed, I do not know : prob. not before ca. 1850, when the vocabulary was much enlarged and the principal users changed so radically, though itinerant and inferior actors supply the link.) Ex It. *pargliare*, to speak. Cf. *palarie* and see *Slang*, *passim*, and at ' Circus Slang,' and P. Allingham's *Cheapjack*, 1934. E.g. *donah*, *letty*, *madza*, *mungarly*, *nantee*, *omee*, *saltee*, *say*, *tray*, qq.v.]

parlyvoo, parlyvous. See **parleyvoo,** n. and v.

parnee, parn(e)y ; in India, mostly **pawnee.** Water : orig. (— 1862) among strolling actors (Mayhew) ; by 1890, fairly gen. low s., though— witness Yule & Burnell—popular in Anglo-Indian, e.g. in *brandy-pawnee*, q.v., by 1865 ; much used by soldiers—orig. the regulars with service in India—

esp. in G.W. In C. 20, *pawnee* is the most gen. pronunciation, even in England. English usage derives ex Romany *pani, paani, pauni* (Smart & Crofton), itself ultimately the Hindustani *pani*.—2. Rain : Anglo-Indian (— 1859) ; slightly ob. H., 1st ed. (The term is now common in Parlyaree and in the s. of Petticoat Lane.)

parnee or **pawnee, dowry of.** See **dowry**.

parnee(-), but gen. **pawnee(-)game.** Water-drinking, esp. as abstinence from liquor : low : 1893, P. H. Emerson, 'He sticks to the pawnee game.' See **parnee**.

Parnelliament. Parliament : Society : 1886. Ex Parnell's activities. (Ware.)

parrot-cage. See **mouth like a . . .**

parrot and monkey time. A period of quarrelling : ca. 1885–1915. Adopted ex U.S., Ware noting that it 'started from a droll and salacious tale of a monkey and a parrot'. Whence *parroty time*.

parrot must have an almond, the. A c.p. applied to or hinting of incentive, reward, or bribery, very common ca. 1520–1640. Skelton ; Nashe, *Almond for a Parrot*, 1590 ; Shakespeare ; Jonson ; 'Water Poet' Taylor. (Apperson.) Ex parrot's delight in almonds.

parroty time. The same as *parrot and monkey time* : 1886, *The Daily News*, Oct. 12 ; † by 1920. (Ware.)

parsley. The pubic hair : low : C. 18–20 ; almost †. Whence :

parsley-bed. The female pudend : low : from ca. 1600 (see Mabbe quotation in O.E.D.) ; 1659, anon., *The London Chanticleers*, a play ; Ned Ward, 1719. Esp. *take a turn in the parsley-bed*, to coït with a woman ; ob. (In folklore—cf. Mabbe, 1622, and R. Brome in *The Antipodes*, 1640—little girls come from the parsley-bed, little boys from the nettle-bed or from under a gooseberry bush.) Partly Apperson.

parsnips !, (I) beg (your). I beg your pardon ! : low jocular coll. (— 1887). Baumann.

parson. Any minister of religion except a priest : coll. and, except in country districts, gen. pejorative: mid-C. 17–20. South, Hannah More, George Eliot. O.E.D.—2. A sign-post, 'because like him it sets people in the right way', Grose, 1785 : prob. from ca. 1750, mainly dial. ; ob.

parson, v. To marry ; to church after child-delivery : coll. : from ca. 1880.

Parson Bate. Sir Henry Bate Dudley (d. 1824), who, a clerk in holy orders, became a sporting journalist and the editor of *The Morning Post*. Also *the Fighting Parson*. Dawson.

Parson Greenfields. See **Greenfields**.

Parson Mallum !, remember. 'Pray drink about, Sir ! ' : late C. 16–18 : c.p. Like the next, it must have had its origin in some topicality.

Parson Palmer. 'One who stops the circulation of the glass by preaching over his liquor', Grose, 1785 : coll. : C. 18–early 19. Swift, *Polite Conversation*, Dialogue II. An elaboration of *no preaching*—or *dangerous to preach—over your liquor*, as in Aphra Behn, 1682, and app. a semi-proverb, it is a c.p. See esp. Apperson. Cf. preceding.

parsoned, ppl.adj. Married in church or chapel : coll. (— 1886). Esp. *married and parsoned*, duly and legally married : coll. : 1886, Cassell's *Encyclopædic Dict*.

parsoness. A parson's wife : coll., mostly jocular : 1784 (O.E.D.). Cf. :

parsonet. A parson's child : coll., gen. jocular :

1812, G. Colman (O.E.D.) ; ob.—2. A newly fledged or a very unimportant parson : jocular coll. : 1834, Gen. P. Thompson, 'fashionable parsonets'; P. Brooks, 1874, 'parsonettes'. O.E.D.

parson's barn. See **barn, parson's**.

parson's journeyman. A curate : from ca. 1810 ; ob. *Lex. Bal.* An assistant curate does most of the itinerant work of his vicar or rector.

parson's nose. A chicken's or a goose's rump: coll. (— 1864). H., 3rd ed. Cf. *pope's nose* (q.v.) by which it was, to Protestants, prob. suggested.

parson's side, pinch on the. To withhold, cheat him of, his tithes : coll. > almost proverbial. Lyly, 1579 ; T. Adams, 1630 ; B.E. ; Grose. (Apperson.)

parson's week. A holiday from Monday to the Saturday of the following week : Cowper's letter of June 28, 1790, to Lady Hesketh (O.E.D.) ; also, mid-C. 19–20, Monday to Saturday of one week. Coll. : late C. 18–20.

parson's wife, kiss the. To be lucky in horse-flesh : semi-proverbial coll. : late C. 18–mid-19. Grose (3rd ed.) gives a somewhat longer form.

part, v.i. To pay, give, restore : from ca. 1862 : s. >, ca. 1910, coll. H., 3rd ed. ; G. R. Sims, 1880, 'The [people on the] top floor rarely parted before Monday morning.' Ex S.E. *part with*, C. 14–20.

part, for my. Instead of me ; in my place : Cape Province coll. (— 1913). Pettman.

part brass-rags. To quarrel : naval (from ca. 1890) >, by 1900, military. Bowen, 'From the bluejacket's habit of sharing brass cleaning rags with his particular friend '.

partakener. A mistake for *partaker* : mid-C. 16–17. O.E.D., which notes also *partel*, error for *parcel*, and *partial-gilt* for *parcel-gilt*.

parter. A payer or giver of what is due or advisable ; by itself, 'a free, liberal person' (H.) ; a bad payer is *a bad parter*. From ca. 1862: s. >, ca. 1915, coll. H., 3rd ed. Ex. preceding term, q.v.

partial. Crooked ; over-inclined (lit.) : coll. : late C. 18–early 19. Grose, 2nd ed.

partial to. Liking ; fond of : coll. : 1696, Prior, 'Athens . . . where people . . . were partial to verse'; A. Lang, 1889, 'Cold sausage (to which Alphonso was partial)'. O.E.D.

partic. Particular ; esp. as adj. (fastidious): trivial coll. : C. 20. Neil Bell, *The Years Dividing*, 1935.

particular, n. Something very characteristic or especially liked, e.g. *a glass of one's particular*, i.e. of one's favourite drink : s. : C. 19–20. Earliest and mainly in *particular, London*, q.v.—2. A very close friend ; a favourite mistress : dial. (— 1828) >, ca. 1830, coll. ; slightly ob. Gen. P. Thompson, 1830 (O.E.D.).

particular, adv. Especially : low coll. : mid-C. 19–20. 'I want to speak to you awfully particular,' *The Boy's Own Paper*, cited by Baumann, 1887. (The O.E.D., giving an example of 1600, describes the usage as rare and †.)

particular, London. A Madeira wine imported especially for the London market : coll. : 1807, Washington Irving (O.E.D.) : ob. by 1900, † by 1930. Perhaps the origin of *glass of one's particular* (see **particular,** n., 1).—2. Hence, ex the colour, a' London fog : 1852, Dickens : s. >, ca. 1890, coll. Also called *London ivy* (London fog in gen. ; not a particular one) : 1889 ; somewhat ob. Cf. *pea-souper*, q.v.

particular, one's. The favoured gallant of a courtesan : brothel coll. : 1749, John Cleland ; ? ob.

partinger. A partner : jocular (— 1887) ; ob. Baumann.

partners. Two men working together : tailors' coll. (late C. 19–20) verging on j. Cf. *old thirds*, q.v.

partridge. A harlot : low : late C. 17–mid-18. Anon. song of ca. 1700. Cf. *plover*, by which—plus *partridge(-shot)*, case-shot—it was prob. suggested.

parts, play (a person) **any, or one, of one's.** To play a nasty trick on a person : low coll. (— 1887). Baumann, ' Don't play me any of your parts.'

party. A person : mid-C. 17–20 : S.E. until ca. 1760, then coll. (Foote, 1770) ; from ca. 1850, low coll. (Bagehot, 1855, ' A go-ahead party ') ; in C. 20, when not jocular, s. and usually pejorative. (O.E.D. : dates.) Esp. *old party*, an old person. Ex such legal phrases as *guilty party, be a party to*. See notably Alford's *The Queen's English*, 1863.

party-roll. A list of boys going home together : from ca. 1860 : Winchester College coll. > j. (Such terms are a lexicographical problem.)

parvis. ' By some C. 19 writers applied in error to " a room over a church-porch ". App. originating in a misunderstanding of ' a passage in Blomefield's *Norfolk*, 1745, says the O.E.D., q. certainly v.

pas de Lafarge ! No talk about Madame Lafarge (the reputed murderess) : Society : 1840's. Ex Paris. (Ware.) Cf. *Tich !, no*.

pasan(g). Mistaken by Buffon, who has been followed by some English compilers and lexicographers, for the gemsbok, a South African antelope : late C. 18–20. O.E.D.

pasear ; paseo. A walk : U.S. (— 1840), anglicised ca. 1890. Ex Sp. *paseo*, a walk ; *pasear*, to walk. O.E.D. (Sup.).—2. (Only **pasear**.) To walk : id., id. Ibid.—3. (Ex sense 1 ; only **paseo**.) A street, a promenade : 1920. Ibid.

*****pash.** A ' small ' coin ; a ' copper ' : c. (— 1839) ; † by 1900. Brandon.—2. An infatuation ; among school-children, one for a teacher ; at a few English public schools, a homosexual fondness for another boy. C. 20. (Dorothy Sayers, *Unnatural Death*, 1927.) Abbr. *passion*. Cf. *rave*, n., q.v.

pass. A pass-examination : coll. (— 1887). Baumann.

pass. To fail to understand ; have no concern in : coll. : C. 20. Ex euchre, though its post-1910 usage is mainly owing to the bridge formula.—2. See **pass one**.

pass, sell the. See **sell the pass**.

*****pass along.** To send (stolen articles, *the stuff*) to a ' fence ' ; to conceal them : c. (— 1923). Manchon.

[**pass-bank** in B.E. and Grose, like their **passage**, is S.E.]

pass in a crowd, it'll. See **crowd, pass in a**.

pass in one's checks. To die : orig. (— 1872) and chiefly U.S. ; anglicised, esp. in Canada and Australia, ca. 1890. Nisbet, 1892, ' Mortimer . . . passed in his checks . . . unexpectedly.' Also *hand in* ; also, with either v., *chips*, which, however, is rare outside U.S. Ex settling one's accounts at poker.

pass (a person) **one.** To deliver a blow : Australian (— 1916). C. J. Dennis.

pass out. To die : coll. : 1899 (O.E.D. Sup.). Prob. abbr. *pass out of sight*.—2. To lose consciousness through liquor : military (1916) >, by 1919, gen.—3. Hence, or ex sense 1, to faint : from ca. 1920.

pass the buck. To ' tell the tale ' : low (— 1934). Cf. *buck*, conversation.

pass the compliment. To give a gratuity : low coll. : late C. 19–20 ; ob. Perhaps ex (the ? orig. U.S.) *pass the compliments of the day* (cf. next).

pass the time of day. (In passing) to exchange greetings and/or fleeting gossip : coll. and dial. : 1834, A. Parker, ' Two Indians . . . halted . . ., stared . . ., and then civilly passed the time of day.' O.E.D.

passable (traversable, viable ; able to, fit to circulate ; tolerable) and **passible** (sensitive, perceptible) are, from C. 17, often used in error the one for the other. (O.E.D. ; Fowler.)

Passages. Shares in the Cork, Blackrock, & Passage Railway : Stock Exchange (— 1895) >, by 1910, coll. A. J. Wilson, *Stock Exchange Glossary*.

passed is incorrect for *past*, when the latter is a preposition. ' He went passed me.'

passenger. An ineffective member of a racing-boat crew : 1885 (O.E.D.).—2. Hence, such a member of any team or (C. 20) on a business or other staff : 1892 (O.E.D.) : s. >, ca. 1930, coll. Ex travel by ship.—3. A passenger-train : railway-men's coll. (— 1887). Baumann.

passent. An incorrect form of *passant* (esp. in heraldry) : C. 17. O.E.D.

passing-out number. A second-year naval cadet : in the training-ship *Britannia* : late C. 19–early 20. Bowen.

passy. (Of a master) severe ; bad-tempered : Christ's Hospital : ca. 1840–80. Superseded by *vish*, q.v. Ex *passionate*, says Blanch in his reminiscences.

past. Beyond (the power or ability of a person) : coll. : C. 17–20. Beaumont & Fletcher, 1611, ' You are welcome . . . ; but if you be not, 'tis past me | To make you so ; for I am here a stranger.' O.E.D.

past dying of her first child, be. To have had a bastard : coll. : mid-C. 17–18. Ray, 1678.

past praying for. (Esp. of persons.) Hopeless : coll. : mid-C. 19–20.

paste. Brains : printers' : late C. 19–20 ; ob. Ironically ex *paste and scissors*, q.v.

paste, v. To thrash ; implied in 1851, Mayhew, ' He . . . gave me a regular pasting ' ; H., 5th ed. F. & H. suggests ex bill-sticking ; perhaps on *baste* (W.).—2. As a cricket coll., esp. *paste the bowling*, it is recorded for 1924. Lewis.

paste, play for. To play billiards for drinks : billiard-players' (— 1909). Ware, ' Probably from " vino di pasta "—a light sherry '.

paste and scissors. Extracts ; unoriginal padding : journalistic coll. : late C. 19–20. Usually *scissors and paste*, gen. considered as S.E. Ex cutting out and pasting up.

paste-horn. The nose : shoemakers' : 1856, Mayhew ; ob. Ex an article of the trade. See also **old paste-horn.** Cf. *conk, smeller*.

pasteboard. A visiting-card : 1837, T. Hook. Cf. *pasteboard, drop one's*.—2. A playing-card ; playing-cards collectively : 1859, Thackeray.—3. A railway-ticket, esp. a ' season ' : C. 20. *The Daily Chronicle*, Nov. 11, 1901. O.E.D. (all three).

pasteboard, v.t. To leave one's visiting-card at the residence of : 1864, H., 3rd ed. ; ob. by 1900, † by 1920. Ex preceding and following entry, qq.v.

pasteboard, drop, leave, lodge, shoot one's. To leave one's visiting-card at a person's residence :

resp. —1902 ; 1849 (Thackeray) ; 1837 (Hook), ob. ; —1902.

pasteboard-customer. A taker of long credit : trade : from ca. 1860 ; ob. Either ex cards and compliments or ex S.E. *pasteboard*, something flimsy.

pastey is a loose form (Manchon) of *pasty*, n. (q.v.).

pasting, vbl.n. A drubbing : see the quotation at paste, v.

pastry. Collective for : young and pretty women : from ca. 1917 ; slightly ob. Manchon. Ex *jam, jam-tart*, and *tart*, qq.v.

pastural. An occ. C. 17 mistake for *pastoral* ; cf. C. 16 *pastoral(l)* for *pastural*. O.E.D.

pasty. A book-binder : mostly among publishers, booksellers, and their carmen : from ca. 1860 ; ob. H., 3rd ed. Ex the paste used in binding books.

pasty, adj. Of the complexion : S.E.—2. Hence, indisposed : (orig. low) coll. : 1891, Newman, *Scamping Tricks*, ' I feel pasty.'—3. Hence, angry : low coll. : 1892 ; ob. Milliken, in the *'Arry Ballads*, ' Miss Bonsor went pasty, and reared.'

Pat. An Irishman ; often in address : coll. : 1825, Scott (O.E.D.). Ex *Patrick*, the commonest Irish Christian name. Cf. *Patess*, *Patlander*, also *Paddy*, qq.v.—2. (Gen. pl.) A Chinaman : New Zealand c. (— 1932). Prob. suggested by the relevant sense of *John*.—3. Pataudi, the Nawab of : cricketers' : from 1931. *Who's Who in World Cricket*, 1934.

pat (or **Pat**), **on one's.** Alone ; single-handed : Australian and New Zealand : C. 20. C. J. Dennis, 1916. Ex *Pat Malone*, q.v.

Pat and Mike. A ' bike ' : rhyming s. : late C. 19–20. B. & P.

Pat Malone. Alone : Australian and New Zealand rhyming s. : C. 20. Gen *do a thing, go, on one's Pat Malone*, hence *on one's Pat* (hence *pat*).

pat out. (To say) frankly : coll. (— 1923). Manchon. Ex *pat*, opportunely.

patch. The nickname of Sexton, Cardinal Wolsey's domestic jester. T. Wilson, 1553 ; J. Heywood, 1562. O.E.D.—2. Hence, any ' fool ' or jester : ca. 1560–1700 : coll. soon > allusive S.E. Shakespeare.—3. Hence, an ill-natured or bad-tempered person : C. 19–20 : coll. and dial. Esp. as *cross-patch*. Scott, 1830 (O.E.D.).—4. The female pudend : low : C. 19–20 ; ? ob.

patch (up)on, **not a.** Not to be compared with : coll. : 1860, Reade, ' Not a patch on you for looks ' —a very frequent comparison. Anticipated by Daniel Webster, 1850, in *but as a patch on* (W.).

patched like a whaleman's shirt. (Of a sail or garment) patched as much as it can be : nautical coll. : late C. 19–20. Bowen.

patch(e)y. A, gen. the, harlequin : theatrical : from ca. 1860 ; ob. Ex costume.

patchy, adj. Bad-tempered ; fractious : coll. (ob.) and dial. : 1862, Trollope, ' He'll be a bit patchy . . . for a while.' Ex *patch*, n., third sense. O.E.D.—2. Variable in quality : C. 20 : coll. >, by 1930, S.E. E.g. of form in sport. Ex *patch*, a piece.

pate. The head, esp. the part normally covered with hair : C. 13–20 : S.E. until C. 19, then coll. and gen. jocular. Barham, ' His little bald pate '.

*****patent-coat.** An ' inside skirt coat pocket ', Brandon : c. of ca. 1835–90.

patent-digester. Brandy : coll. : from ca. 1835 ; ob. Dickens. Ex its digestive properties.

patent(-)Frenchman. An Irishman : tailors' : from ca. 1870 ; ob.

patent-inside, -outside. ' A newspaper printed [first] on the inside (or outside) only, the unprinted space being intended for local news, advertisements, etc,' F. & H. : journalists' (mostly provincial) : from ca. 1880 ; very ob.

Patent Safeties, the. The 1st Life Guards : military : from ca. 1850 ; ob. Also *the Cheeses, Cheesemongers, Piccadilly Butchers*, q.v., *Royal Blues*, and *Tin-Bellies*, which explains *the P.S.*

pater. A father ; also in address : mostly among schoolboys : 1728, Ramsay ; Miss Braddon, who italicises it. (O.E.D.) Direct ex the L. Cf. *mater*, q.v.

*****pater-cove.** See **patrico.**

paternoster. A fishing-line with hooks and weights at regular intervals : anglers' coll. (in C. 20, j.) : 1849, Kingsley. Abbr. S.E. *paternoster-line.* Ex rosary-beads.

paternoster, devil's. A muttering, grumbling ; a blasphemous exclamation : coll. : late C. 14–20, but ob. by C. 18. (Chaucer ;) Terence in English ; Congreve.

paternoster-while, in a. In a moment (the time needed for a paternoster) ; quickly : from ca. 1360 (ob. by 1890) : coll. bordering on S.E. Paston Letters.

Patess. An Irishwoman : coll. : 1825, Scott (O.E.D.). See **Pat.**

pathetic. Ludicrous : C. 20 coll. (? orig. s.). Contrast *funny*, odd.

patience !, my. An exclamation of surprise : coll. : recorded 1873 (E.D.D.) ; prob. much earlier.

patience on a monument. An extremely patient and long-suffering person : coll. : from ca. 1890. Henley & Stevenson, 1892, use it as an adj. Prob. ex the seeming patience of all statues, as seen in the immediate origin, Shakespeare's ' She sat, like Patience on a monument, | Smiling at grief ' (W.). Often *like . . .*

patience with, have no. To find too hard to tolerate ; be irritated by : coll. : 1855, Thackeray, ' I have no patience with the Colonel,' O.E.D.

Patland. Ireland : C. 19–20. Earlier than, for it is the origin of :

Patlander. An Irishman : 1820, *The Sporting Magazine* (O.E.D.) ; ob. Cf. *Paddy* and *Pat*, qq.v.

*****patrico.** One of the fifteenth ' rank ' of the underworld, a strolling (pseudo-)priest : c. : C. 16–20, but ob. by 1820. Harman, B.E., Grose, Ainsworth.—2. Hence, C. 17–20 (ob. by 1840), any parson or priest : c. B.E. The forms include *patriarch-*(*patriarke-*)*co*, C. 16 rare, as in Awdelay ; *pattering-* or *patring-cove*, C. 16, Copland ; *pater-cove*, late C. 17–19 (e.g. in B.E., Grose, and Lytton), *patri-cove* (*A New Canting Dict.*, 1725), and *patter-cove*, C. 19–20, as in Henley & Stevenson. (A C. 18 song spells it *patrico-coe*.) Prob. ex *pater* + *co*(*ve*).

*****patrin** ; incorrectly **patteran.** ' A gipsy trail, made by throwing down a handful of grass occasionally ', H., 5th ed. : vagrants' c. Whyte-Melville, 1876, in *Katerfelto* ; 1898, Watts-Dunton in *Aylwin* (O.E.D.) ; an extended use appears in ' I don't see any crosses on the roads or leaves to mark the " patrin ",' Walter Starkie in *John o' London's Weekly*, June 23, 1934. Ex Romany *pat(r)in*, a leaf, or (and in C. 20 only) a trail-sign. (The Romany for trails is *patreni* or *patrinaw*. Smart & Crofton.)

*****patring-cove.** See **patrico.**

patriot. Mistakenly (with possessive) as if = up-holder, devotee : mid-C. 17. Weever, 1631, ' A carefull Patriot of the State ' ; 1641, L'Estrange, ' A Patriot of Truth '. O.E.D.

Patriot King, the. Henry St. John, Viscount Bolingbroke (d. 1751). Ex his *Idea of a Patriot King.* (Dawson.)

Patsy. Elias Hendren (b. 1889) : cricketers' nickname : from ca. 1908. In *Good Days,* 1934, Neville Cardus has an essay entitled ' Patsy '.

*patten-ken. A variant (C. 20) of *padding-ken* : see **padding-crib.** Manchon.

pattens, run on. (Of the tongue) to clatter ; go ' nineteen to the dozen ' : ca. 1550–1620. Udall ; (?) Shakespeare. Ex the noise made by clogs.

*patter. Any secret or technical language : S.E. (says O.E.D. ; but prob. orig. c.) of mid-C. 18–20. Cf. *gammon and patter,* q.v. Ex S.E. *patter,* to talk rapidly or glibly.—2. A cheapjack's oratory ; ' jaw ' ; speechifying : from ca. 1780 : c. >, ca. 1840, s. Parker, Vaux, Mayhew.—3. Hence, mere **talk** ; gabble : coll. : 1858, Gen. P. Thompson, ' A patter . . . about religion ', O.E.D.—4. A judge's summing-up ; a trial : c. or low s. : 1857, ' Ducange Anglicus.'—5. The words of a song, a play, etc. : coll. : from ca. 1875. J. A. Fuller-Maitland, 1880, ' Mozart and many other composers often introduce bits of " patter " into buffo solos,' O.E.D.—6. A piece of street literature : low (— 1889). *Answers,* May 11, 1889. Ex sense 2 or 5, or perhaps ex *patterer,* last sense.

patter, v. To talk, speak, esp. as a cheapjack or a conjurer : pedlars' s. (— 1851). Mayhew. Ex :— 2. To talk the secret language of the underworld : c. : from ca. 1780. Parker, *View of Society.* For derivation, see :—3. To speak (some language) : c. : 1812, Vaux. Esp. in *patter flash,* q.v. Ex S.E. *patter,* C. 15–20, to talk glibly, rapidly.—4. To try (a person) in a court of justice : c. of ca. 1810–50. Vaux.—5. V.t., to eat : Australian pidgin English : 1833, Sturt, ' He himself did not patter . . . any of it ' ; ob. App. ex an Aboriginal dialect. Morris.

*patter, flash the. To talk ; esp. to talk s. or c. : c. (from ca. 1820) >, ca. 1880, low s. Prob. ex *patter flash,* q.v. See **patter,** n., 1 and 2, and **flash,** q.v.

*patter, stand—occ. **be in for**—**the.** To stand for trial : c. : from ca. 1810 ; ob. Vaux, Haggart. See **patter,** n., 1. (The legal talk.)

*patter-cove. See **patrico.**

*patter-crib. A lodging-house, or an inn, fre-quented by the underworld : c. : from ca. 1830. H., 3rd ed. See **patter,** n., 1, and **crib,** n.

*patter flash. To talk ; also to talk s. or c. : c. (— 1812) >, ca. 1860, low s. Vaux. Cf. *patter,* v., 2, and cf. *patter, flash the,* q.v.

*patteran. Incorrect form of *patrin,* q.v.

patterer. One who speaks c., low s., or Romany : 1849, Ainsworth (O.E.D.) : c. rapidly > low s. > s. >, by 1900, coll. Ex *patter,* v., 2.—2. Whence, one who ' speechifies ', esp. a cheapjack : s. (— 1851) >, ca. 1890, low coll. Mayhew.—3. A vendor of broadsides, etc. : from ca. 1850 : ob. by 1880 : s. >, ca. 1870, low coll. Esp. *running patterer* (cf. *flying stationer,* q.v.), one always on the move, and *standing patterer,* one selling from a pitch. May-hew. Cf. *patter,* n., last sense.

*patterer, humbox-. A parson : c. : from ca. 1838 ; ob. Serialist Reynolds.

pattering, vbl.n. The pert or vague replies of servants : coll. : from ca. 1690 ; ob. by 1880, † by

1930. B.E., Grose. Ex *patter,* to talk glibly.—2. Talk intended to interest a prospective victim : c. or low s. : 1785, Grose.

*pattering-cove. See **patrico.**

pattern. ' A common vulgar phrase for " patent " ', H., 3rd ed. : sol. : from ca. 1850.—2. Delightful ; brilliant : Anglo-Irish : late C. 19–20. Ware derives it thus : *pattern fair* ex *patron fair,* i.e. *patron saint's fair.*

patty-cake. An error for *pat-a-cake* : late C. 19–20. O.E.D.

pauca ! Speak little ! ; say nothing : (?) c. : late C. 16–17. Baumann. I.e., L. *pauca verba,* few words.

paul. See **pawl.—Paul, rob Peter to pay.** See **Peter to pay.**

Paul Pry. Fred. Byng, a noted Victorian man-about-town. Dawson.

Paulite. A Boer : military coll. in Boer War. J. Milne, *The Epistles of Atkins,* 1902. Ex *Paul (Kruger).* Cf. *Pauly,* q.v.

Pauls. See **milks.—Paul's, old as.** See **old as Charing Cross.**

Paul's betony, St. Incorrect for *Paul's betony* (wood speedwell) : mid-C. 17–20. O.E.D.

Paul's (or Westminster) for a wife, go to. To go whoring : coll. : late C. 16–18. Shakespeare (im-plied : 2nd *Henry IV,* I, ii, 58) ; Ray. Old St. Paul's was a resort of loungers and worse (cf. S.E. *Paul's men, walkers,* loungers).

Paul's pigeon. (Gen. pl.) A pupil at St. Paul's School, London : ca. 1550–1750. Fuller. O.E.D.

Paul's (steeple), old as. See **old as Charing Cross.**

Paul's work. A bungled job ; a ' mess ' : coll. : C. 17. Dekker, ' And when he had done, made Poules work of it ', O.E.D.

Pauly. (Gen. pl.) A follower of Paul Kruger ; a Boer : mostly journalists' : 1899–1900. Ware.

paunch. To eat : coll. : C. 17. Cf. equivalent *pouch* and Scots *paunch,* swallow greedily.

paunches, join. To copulate : low : C. 19–20 ; ob. Cf. *join giblets.*

Pav, the. The London Pavilion theatre or music hall : from early 1860's. In 3rd ed., where also the variant, *the P.V.* ; *The Observer,* April 1, 1934. (In 1934 it went over to ' the pictures '.) Cf. *Met, the,* q.v.—2. (pav.) A sports pavilion : school-boys' : late C. 19–20. Collinson.

paved, have one's mouth. To be hard-mouthed : coll. : C. 18. Swift, ' How can you drink your Tea so hot ? Sure your mouth's pav'd.'

*pavement artist. A ' dealer in precious stones who stands about in Hatton Garden ' (Charles E. Leach : c. (— 1933). Ex S.E. sense.

*pavement twist. See **hard-up** (cigarette).

pavio(u)r's or **pavio(u)rs' workshop.** The street : ca. 1786–1890. Grose, 2nd ed. ; Baumann. Ex *pavio(u)r, paver,* a paving stone, extant in dial. (E.D.D.)

[**pavon.** A ghost word ex misread Old Fr. *panon,* a pennon. O.E.D.]

paw. A hand : coll. : from ca. 1590. Chapman, 1605, ' I . . . layd these pawes | Close on his shoulders ' ; Dryden ; Scott. Jocularly ex *paw,* a foot. Also *fore paw,* the hand ; *hind paw,* the foot : both recorded in 1785 (Grose) and ob.—2. Hand-writing, esp. a signature : coll. : C. 18–20 ; ob. Ex sense 1.

paw, v. To handle awkwardly, roughly, coarsely, indelicately : coll. : 1604, T. M., ' His palm shall be pawed with pence'; Farquhar; Tennyson. O.E.D. Extension of S.E. senses.

paw, adj. Improper; scabrous: ca. 1660–1740: s. >, ca. 1720, coll. Davenant, 'A paw-word'—a stock phrase (gen. unhyphened); Cibber. 'App. a variant of *pah*, " nasty, improper, unbecoming ", adj. use of *pah* ', interjection: O.E.D. Cf. *paw-paw*.

paw-case. A glove: low (— 1864); very ob. H., 3rd ed. Ex *paw*, n., q.v. Cf. *hind paws*, q.v.

paw-paw. Naughty; esp. improper; from ca. 1720 (S.O.D.): s. >, ca. 1820, coll.; slightly ob. Grose, 2nd ed., 'An expression used by nurses, &c., to children '. Ex *paw*, adj.

paw-paw tricks. Naughty tricks: nursery s. > coll.: from ca. 1785. Grose, 2nd ed.—Whence, 2, masturbation: low: C. 19–20. F. & H. Ex preceding.

paw-pawness. Nastiness, impropriety: coll.: 1828 (O.E.D.); ob. Ex *paw-paw*, q.v.

pawked-up stuff. Bad horses or dogs; poor horsemen: sporting (— 1909). Ware. Ex Scottish (and Northern dial.) *pawk*, a trick, an artifice.

pawl. To check, stop, baffle: nautical coll.: from ca. 1820. Ex S.E. *pawl*, to secure or stop by means of a pawl. 2. V.i., to cease, esp. talking: nautical coll. (— 1867). Ex sense 1. Also spelt *pall*, q.v., and, as in Smyth, *paul*. (Esp. *pawl there !*, stop arguing !)

pawl my capstan !, you. You're too good for me !: naval: late C. 19–20; ob. Ware. Cf. *pawl*, 1.

pawler. A final argument: nautical coll.: from ca. 1867. Bowen. Ex *pawl*, 1.

pawn. Mast of trees: incorrect for *pannage*: ca. 1660–1700. O.E.D.—2. A pawnbroker: s. or low coll.: 1851, Mayhew; ob. By abbr. O.E.D.

pawn. To slip away from (a person) and leave him to pay the reckoning: low (prob. orig. c.): ca. 1670–1750. Head, B.E.—2. In error for *palm*: from ca. 1785. Marryat, 1832, ' Pawned them off on me '. O.E.D.

pawnee, pawny. See **parnee**.

paws off(, Pompey) ! Don't paw me about !: lower classes' c.p. (— 1923). Manchon. As though one were talking to Pompey the dog.

pax. See *pax on* . . . !—2. A friend: from ca. 1780: mostly Public Schools'. At first in *good pax*. ' Winchester ' Wrench explains, rightly I think, as a pl. of *pack*, though L. *pax* is clearly operative. Cf.:

pax ! Silence !; truce !: schoolboys' (— 1852). Kipling, in *Stalky & Co.*, 1899, ' *Pax*, Turkey. I'm an ass.' Ex L. *pax*, peace. O.E.D.

pax, be good. To be good friends : mostly Public Schools' : 1781, Bentham, ' We may perhaps be good pax.' See **pax**, 2, and cf. *pax !* and *pax, make*.

pax !, have. An elaboration of *pax !*, q.v.: schoolboys' : from ca. 1860.

pax, make. To form a friendship: Public Schools' : from ca. 1840. See **pax**, 2.

pax on (it !, him !, etc.). Confound it !, etc.: low coll. : ca. 1640–1730. Brome, ' Pax o' your fine Thing '; Addison. Corrupted *pox*, q.v. O.E.D.

paxwax ; occ. **pax-wax, packwax.** The nuchal ligament: from late M.E. : S.E. until ca. 1850, then coll. and dial. A C. 19–20 variant is *paxy-waxy* ; a late C. 17–early 18 one is *fixfax*, which is a sol. (O.E.D.)

pay. A paymaster: naval coll. : late C. 19–20. Bowen. Abbr. *pay-bob* : id. : id. Ibid.

pay, v. To beat, punish: from ca. 1580 : S.E until ca. 1750, then coll. ; from ca. 1820, s. and dial Grose, 1st ed. Cf. *pay over* . . ., *pay Paul* . . . and *pay out*, qq.v.—2. To deliver (e.g. a letter): Anglo-Chinese coll. (— 1864). H., 3rd ed.—3. See entry at **pace, go the**.

pay, be good (etc.). To be sure to discharge one's obligations, esp. one's debts : coll. : 1727, Gay, ' No man is better pay than I am,' O.E.D. ; slightly ob.

pay ?, what's to. What's the matter, trouble ? : coll. : C. 19–20. Ex lit. sense.

pay and no pitch hot or **ready !, the devil to.** A nice mess ! : nautical : late C. 18–19. Grose, 2nd ed. Punningly ex the paying, i.e. smearing, of a ship's bottom with pitch to stop a leak.

pay away. To proceed ; continue (v.i.), the v.t. form being *pay it away*. Coll. : 1670, Eachard (of talking); in C. 19–20, mainly nautical. Cf. *pay it out !*, q.v.—2. To fight manfully : mainly nautical s. (— 1785) >, ca. 1850, coll. ; ob. Grose.—3. To eat voraciously: mainly nautical (— 1785); almost †. Grose.

pay-bob. See **pay**, n.

pay down. ' To send all heavy weights below ' : nautical coll. : late C. 19–20. Bowen.

pay into. To ' pitch into ', to strike or punch vigorously: (low) coll. (— 1887). Baumann. Cf. *pay*, v., 1.

pay it out ! Keep on talking ! : nautical (— 1887). Besant, ' Pay it out. [I don't care]— not . . . a rope's yarn.' Ex paying out a rope.

*pay-off. Punishment; settlement for infringing the rules of the underworld : c. : C. 20. E.g. in John G. Brandon's novel, *The One-Minute Murder*, 1934.

pay off, v. To throw (a thing) away : naval : late C. 19–20. Bowen. Ex paying off a crew.

pay-off line. A printed form that a man receives on being paid-off ; he signs it as a receipt : Public Works' (— 1935). See **line**, n., 6.

Pay-off Wednesday. A schoolboys' term (— 1864 ; ob.) for the Wednesday before Advent. H., 3rd ed., cites also *Crib-Crust Monday* and *Tug-Mutton Tuesday*.

pay on. To pay cash (for a bet) : turf s. verging on coll. : C. 20.

pay out. See **pay it out**.—2. To give (a person) his deserts : coll. : 1863, Cowden Clarke, ' They, in return, (as the vulgar phrase has it,) " pay him out ".' O.E.D.—3. See **paying out**.

pay out the slack of one's gammon. To relate (too) many stories : low (— 1887). Baumann. Prob. nautical at first.

pay over face and eyes, as the cat did the monkey. To give a terrible beating about the head : a low c.p. (— 1860) ; ob. H., 2nd ed. Ex *pay you as Paul paid the Ephesians*, q.v.

pay the bearer. (Gen. as vbl.n.) To cash a cheque against non-existent funds : bank-clerks' : late C. 19–20. Cf. *cash a dog*.

pay the shot. To pay the bill : C. 16–20 : S.E. till C. 19, then coll. ; ob. Hackwood, *Old English Sports*, 1907, ' [They] called for their ale . . . and . . . expected the losers " to pay the shot ".' Apperson.

pay up and look pretty, occ. **big.** Gracefully to accept the inevitable : 1894, Sala (*pretty*) ; *big* is very, *pretty* slightly ob. Cf. *sit pretty*.

*pay with a hook. To steal : Australian c. : from ca. 1870. Brunton Stephens, in *My Chinese Cook*,

1873, 'You bought them ? Ah, I fear me, John, | You paid them with a hook.' ? ex *hook*, to steal.

pay with pen-powder. To write fair promises but fail to pay : semi-proverbial coll. : ca. 1630–80. John Clarke, 1639. (Apperson.)

pay (or **pay debts**) **with the fore-topsail.** 'To slip away to sea in debt' : nautical : mid-C. 19–20. Bowen. The military variant is *with the drum*.

pay you as Paul paid the Ephesians, I will. Explained by the part gen. added : *over the face and eyes and all the damned jaws.* A low c.p. : ca. 1780–1850. Grose. An elaboration of *pay !*, q.v. ; cf. *pay over face and eyes*, the later form of the phrase.

paying out. (Vbl.n. ; as v., very rare.) The use, esp. by an officer, of very forcible language, gen. in fault-finding ; a leg-pull exercised on a young soldier, e.g. 'telling him to go and wash the last post' : military : C. 20. B. & P. Cf. *pay into* and *pay it out*.

pea. The favourite ; one's choice : low : 1888, *Sporting Life*, Dec. 11, 'Sweeny forced the fighting, and was still the pea when "Time !" was called' ; ob. Ex *this is the pea I choose* in thimble-rigging.— 2. The head : c. : from ca. 1840 ; ob. '*No. 747.*' Prob. ex *pea-nut* : cf. the relevant sense of *nut*.

pea, pick (occ. **do**) **a sweet.** To urinate : low (mostly among—or of—women) : from ca. 1860. Punning *pee*, q.v. Cf. *gather violets, pluck a rose*.

pea-ballast. Gravel that will pass through holes of half an inch (or less) : Public Works' coll. : C. 20. Prob. suggested by S.E. *peas*, coals of a small size.

pea-dodger. A bowler hat : Australian (—1935). Cf. *hard-hitter*.

pea-man or **-rigger.** See **thimble-rigger**.

pea-soup. A French-Canadian : Canadian : late C. 19–20. Ex the frequency of that dish on French-Canadian tables : late C. 19–20. John Beames.— 2. Hence, *talk pea-soup*, to talk French-Canadian ; loosely, French : C. 20. Ibid.

pea-souper. A dense yellowish fog : coll. : 1890, J. Payn (O.E.D. Sup.). Ex the next.

pea-soupy. (Esp. of a dense, yellowish fog) resembling pea-soup : coll. : 1860 (O.E.D.).

pea-whacker. A nautical variant (late C. 19–20) of *pea-souper*, q.v.

Peabody. A 'block of houses built under the Peabody Bequest to the poor of London' : lower-classes' coll. (— 1909) ; ob. Ware.

peace. See **piece**.

peacemaker ; matrimonial peacemaker. See matrimonial peacemaker.—As a pistol (Lever, 1841), it is, by the O.E.D., considered—quite rightly, as against F. & H.—to be jocular S.E.

Peacemakers, the. The Bedfordshire Regiment, formerly the 16th Foot : military ; ob. From ca. 1890. From Surinam, 1804, to Chitral, 1895, they missed active service.

peach. A detective ; esp. one employed by omnibus, and formerly by stage-coach, proprietors to check receipts : from ca. 1835 ; ob. F. & H.— 2. An attractive girl or (gen., young) woman : orig. (1870's), U.S. ; anglicised before 1889. Barrère & Leland. Gen. *a regular peach* or *a peach of a girl*. Occ. (mostly U.S.) *a peach from Peachville* : C. 20. Cf. *daisy*, q.v.

peach, v. As v.t., it is S.E. = † to impeach ; extant when it = to divulge, esp. in *peach a word* (1883, O.E.D.) : ob.—2. V.i., to blab : coll. : 1852, Thackeray, 'The *soubrette* has peached to the *amoureux*,' O.E.D. Ex :—3. V.i. to inform

(against a person) ; turn informer : late C. 16–20 : S.E. (as in Shakespeare) in C. 16–17 ; coll. in C. 18–mid-19 (as in Fielding, Hughes) ; s. in mid-C. 19–20. Either absolute or with *against* or (*up*)*on*. Aphetic form of *a-peche*, to appeach (O.E.D.). Cf. *blow the gaff, give the office, put away, snitch, squeal, squeak, tip the wink, whiddle*, qq.v.

peach-perch. A 'flapper-bracket' (q.v.) : motorists' (— 1935). Ex *peach*, n., 2.

peacharino, -erino. An elaboration of *peach*, n., 2 : U.S. (ca. 1907), partly anglicised in 1918.

peaching, vbl.n. Giving of information against a person : turning or being an informer : mid-C. 15–20 : S.E. until C. 18, then coll. till C. 20, when s.

peaching, ppl.adj. See preceding entry. C. 17–20 : S.E. till C. 18, then coll. till C. 20, when s. and ob. Moore, 1818, 'The useful peaching rat'. O.E.D.

peachy. Very pleasant : from middle 1920's ; mostly U.S. (O.E.D. Sup.)—2. See **peechy**.

peacock. A horse with a showy action : racing coll. : 1869. Cf. *peacock-horse*.

peacock, v. To pay (esp. on ladies and gen. brief) morning calls, at which beer was served : Anglo-Indian : from ca. 1850 ; ob. *The Graphic*, March 17, 1883. Prob. ex the spotless clothes worn by the visitors.—2. V.t. and i., to buy up the choicest land so as to render adjoining territory useless to others : Australia : from ca. 1890 ; ob. Ex *picking out the 'eyes'* of the land : punning the *ocelli* on a peacock's feathers. Cf. *peacocking*, q.v.

peacock-engine. 'A locomotive with a separate tender for coals and water', F. & H. : railway : C. 20 ; ob. Ex the ornamental tail of bird and engine.

peacock horse. A horse with showy mane and tail, and with a fine action : undertakers' coll. (— 1860). H., 2nd ed. Cf. *peacock*, n.

peacocking. The practice mentioned in *peacock*, v., 2, q.v.,—than which it is much commoner. 1894, W. Epps, *Land Systems of Australasia*. Morris.

peacocking business. A formal, esp. a ceremonial, parade : military : 1870, *The Daily News*, April 19 (O.E.D.). Ex the gorgeous display of a peacock.

Peacocks, the. Leeds United Football Club : sporting : C. 20. Ex a well-known Leeds United man.

peacock's tail, the. Euclid, Bk. III, proposition 8 : C. 16 coll. Ex the figure. O.E.D.

*peak. Lace : c. (the O.E.D., however, considers it S.E.) : mid C. 17–early 19. Coles, 1676 ; B.E. Grose. Ex S.E. *peak*, a lace ruff.—2. The nose : low : C. 19–20.

Peak, send a wife to the (devil's arse-a-). To send a woman about her business when she proves vexing : ca. 1663–5. Pepys, *Diary*, Jan. 19, 1663. Ex a courtier's wife being sent home to the Peak in Derbyshire. (Apperson.) N.b., *the devil's arse-a-*, or *in the*, *Peak*, earlier *Peak's arse*, is the Peak Cavern (O.E.D.).

peaked. Sickly-looking ; pinched, thin, esp. from illness : from ca. 1830 : mostly coll. till ca. 1920, then always S.E. Ex sharpness of features.

peaked-cap. A police inspector : coll. (— 1923). Manchon.

peaking. Remnants of cloth : drapers, cloth-warehousemen, from ca. 1859. H., 1st ed. Presumably related to *peak*, to dwindle. Cf. *cabbage, makings*, qq.v.

peakish. Rather thin, pinched, sickly : from ca. 1835 : coll. and dial. Perhaps ex *peaked*.

peaky, peeky. Feeble, puny, sickly : coll. and dial. : from ca. 1850. Ruskin, ' A poor peeky, little sprouting crocus ', O.E.D. Suggested by *peaked*, q.v.

peaky (occ. **peeky)-blinder.** A railwayman from Birmingham : railwaymen's : late C. 19–early 20. Ex the peaked caps worn by Birmingham 'toughs' : cf. the entry in the E.D.D.

peakyish. Rather ' peaky ', q.v. : coll. : 1853, ' Cuthbert Bede ' ; ob. O.E.D. Cf. *peakish*.

peal. The peal of the Chapel bell : Winchester College : from ca. 1840 : coll. > j. > S.E. Mansfield.—2. ' A custom in Commoners of singing out comments on Præfects at Cloister-time ', F. & H. : Winchester : mid-C. 19–20 ; ob.—3. Ibid., same period, ob. : ' Cheers given on the last three Sundays of the Hal for articles of dress, etc., connected with going home ', F. & H.

peal, ring (a person) a ; occ. **ring a peal in one's ears.** To scold him : late C. 18–19. Grose, 2nd ed. ; Baumann. Cf. the dial. *be* or *get into a peal*, i.e. a temper. E.D.D.

pealer. Incorrect form of *peeler*, q.v. In C. 20, very rare, very ob.

pear. To appear : C. 14–20 : S.E. till C. 18, then coll. and dial. Gen. *'pear*.—2. To obtain money from both sides, e.g. from police for information, from underworld for a warning : c. : from ca. 1850 ; † by 1915. Ex *pear-making*, q.v.

Pear, the. Louis Philippe : Anglo-Parisians' : 1830–48. Ware. Ex the shape of his head.

*pear-making. To take bounties from more regiments than one : c. : ca. 1810–60. *Lex. Bal.* ? the making of *pairs*, double-crossing.

pearl-diver. An assistant-pantryman in charge of the washing of the saloon crockery : Western Ocean nautical >, by 1930, fairly gen. in proletarian s. : C. 20. Bowen.

pearl in a hail-storm, like a. Impossible to find : non-aristocratic coll. (− 1887) ; slightly ob. Baumann.

pearl on the nail, make a. To drink : coll. : C. 17–18. Ray. Ex the (late C. 16 +) lit. sense, to drop the moisture remaining in a cup, glass, etc., on to one's nail—a drinking custom recorded by Nashe.

pearlies. (The singular hardly exists.) Pearl buttons, esp. on a coster's clothes : from ca. 1885 : low coll. Henley.—2. Hence (fairly gen. in singular), costermongers : low coll. : C. 20.

peas. Abbr. *peas in the pot*, q.v. : from 1895, says Ware.

peas, as like as two. Very similar indeed : late C. 16–20 : coll. >, in C. 19, S.E. In C. 16–17, *as . . . pease* ; Horace Walpole ; Browning, in *James Lee's Wife*, O.E.D.

peas and cues. See p's and q's, mind one's.

peas in the pot. Apt to be amorous : low London rhyming s. on *hot* : from ca. 1890. Ware. See also peas.—2. Also, hot in the gen. sense. B. & P.

pease-field, go into the. To fall asleep : coll. : ca. 1670–1800. Ray. A semi-proverbial pun on *peace*. Cf. *Bedfordshire*, q.v.

pease-kill, make a. (V.t. with *of*.) To squander lavishly : Scots coll. : C. 18–20. Likewise, *a pease-kill* = a very profitable matter. Jamieson ; E.D.D.

peavy. A cant-hook designed for lumber-work on the river : Canadian lumbermen's : C. 20. John Beames. Perhaps a corruption of Fr. *pioche*.

peb. Abbr. *pebble*, 1, in Dennis's sense. First recorded by Dennis, 1916.

pebble. A person or animal difficult to handle : Australia : from ca. 1890 ; slightly ob. ' Boldrewood ', 1890, ' A regular pebble ' (O.E.D.). From ca. 1905, it has, esp. in the big towns, meant rather ' a flash fellow ; a " larrikin " ', C. J. Dennis, 1916. Ex his ' hard-boiled ' ways (cf. *hard nut*). Also *peb*, q.v.—2. A familiar term of address : ca. : 1840–60. Moncrieff, *The Scamps of London*, 1843. Occ. *pebbles*.

pebble-beach, v. To clean out of money : ca. 1885–1905. Marshall in ' *Pomes* '.

pebble on the beach, not the only. (Of persons) not the sole desirable or remarkable one available, accessible, potential : semi-proverbial coll. : C. 20. Lyell.

pebbles. The human testicles : low : C. 19–20 ; very ob. Suggested by *stones*.

pebbles, my. See pebble, 2. Moncrieff, 1843.

pebbly beach, land on or **sight a.** To be very short of money ; faced with ruin : ca. 1885–1905. Marshall in ' *Pomes* ' (*sight a . . .*). Cf. :

pebbly-beached. Penniless—or nearly so. Ca. 1885–1905. Ex *stony-broke*.

pec. Money ; Eton College : C. 19. Ex L. *pecunia*. H., 3rd ed.

peccadilian, -dulian, -duliun. Corrupt forms of *peccadillo* : C. 16. O.E.D.

*peck ; in C. 16–mid-17, occ. **pek.** Food ; ' grub ' : from ca. 1565 : c. until C. 19, then low s. Harman, Jonson, Centlivre, Moncrieff. Cf. *peckage*, q.v. Ex :

*peck, v.i. and v.t. To eat : mid-C. 16–20 : c. until C. 19, then s. till ca. 1860, then coll. Copland ; Egan ; Dickens, ' I can peck as well as most men.' Ex a bird's pecking ; ? cf., however, Welsh Gypsy *pek*, to bake or roast.—2. To pitch forward ; (esp. of a horse) to stumble : coll. (mid-C. 19–20) and dial. : from ca. 1770. Ex † S.E. v.i. *peck*, to incline.

*peck combinations, *peck* being the second member :—**gere-peck,** a turd, C. 17–19 ; **grunting-peck,** pork, C. 17–20, ob. ; **ruff-peck,** bacon, C. 17–19 ; **rum-peck,** good eating, an excellent meal.

*peck, off one's. Off one's appetite : c. : C. 18–19. Cf. *pecker, off one's*, q.v.

peck-alley. The throat : low : C. 19–20. Ex *peck*, n., q.v. H., 3rd ed.

peck and booze or **tipple.** Meat and drink : low (*booze* orig. c.) : C. 18–20, the former ; C. 19–20, the latter. Mrs. Delany, 1732 (O.E.D.). Cf. *bub and grub* and :

peck and perch. Food and lodging : low (? orig. c.) : 1828, O.E.D. ; slightly ob.

*peck-kidg. See peckidge.

*peckage ; occ. **peckidge.** Food ; food-supply : c. : C. 17–18. Rowlands, B.E. Ex *peck*, n. and v., 1.

pecker. The appetite : mid-C. 19–20. Ex *peck*, v., 1. Possibly ex the next sense.—2. Resolution, courage : 1848 (S.O.D.) ; ' Cuthbert Bede ', 1853, ' Keep up your pecker, old fellow.' Perhaps *pecker* implicitly = beak (hence, head), app. ex the alert sparrow (W.).—3. (With an adj.) an eater, esp. *a good* or *rare pecker* : from ca. 1860. Ex *peck*, v., 1. —4. The penis : low : C. 19–20 ; ob.

Peckham, go to. To go to, sit down to, a meal : jocular coll. : C. 19. Bee, 1823 ; Halliwell.—2. **Peckham, all holiday at.** See all holiday.

Peckham Rye. Tie (n. and v.) : rhyming s. : C. 20. F. & Gibbons.

*peckidge. See **peckage.** B.E.'s spelling ; Coles has *peck-kidg.*

peckish. Hungry : 1785, Grose : in C. 18, perhaps c. : C. 19, (orig. low) s. ; C. 20, coll. George Moore, 1894, ' I feel a bit peckish, don't you ? ' Ex *peck,* n.

pecky. Choppy (sea, as in Blackmore) ; (of a horse) inclined to stumble. Coll. : from ca. 1860, though unrecorded before 1864.—2. (Esp. of kisses) like a bird's peck : coll. : 1886, F. C. Philips, ' Flabby, pecky kisses '. O.E.D.

pecnoster. The penis : low : C. 19–20, ob. Ex *pecker,* 4 ; punning *paternoster.*

peculiar. A mistress : coll. : late C. 17–19. B.E., who wrongly classifies as c. ; Baumann. Ex the S.E. sense of the adj. : private. (As = wife, it is S.E.)—2. A member of the ' Evangelical ' party, ca. 1837–8 : coll. nickname at Oxford. Newman. O.E.D.—3. (Of a bowled ball) odd ; peculiar to the bowler : cricket coll. : 1864 ; very ob. Lewis. (Gen. pl.)

peculiar. Mentally deranged : coll. : C. 20. Ex S.E. sense, strange (1888, O.E.D.).

peculiarly. More than usually : coll. : from ca. 1890. Helen Harris, 1891, ' The Arabs regard the spot as peculiarly sacred,' O.E.D. By confusion with S.E. *particularly,* very.

ped. A professional runner, walker : 1863, Anon., *Tyneside Songs* (O.E.D.). Abbr. *pedestrian.*

peddler's French. See **pedlar's French.** (**peddling French** is a rare C. 16 variant.)

pedestrian digits. The legs : schoolboys' : ca. 1890–1910.

*pedigree-man. A recidivist (criminal) : c. – 1923). Manchon. The police can trace him back a long way.

Pedlar. The inevitable nickname of men surnamed Palmer : mostly military : late C. 19–20. Ex the medieval palmers or pilgrims. B. & P.

pedlar's or **peddler's French.** Underworld slang : 1530, Palsgrave : in C. 16, c. or low s. ; C. 17, s. ; C. 18, coll. ; C. 19–20, S.E. but long very ob.—2. Hence, any unintelligible jargon : late C. 17–early 19 : coll. B.E.

pedlar's news. Stale news : coll. : C. 19. Cf. *piper's* or *tinker's news.*

pedlar's pad, occ. **horse, pony.** A walking-stick : from ca. 1780 : coll. (†) and dial. (ob.). Grose, 1st ed. (*p. pony*). Cf. *Penang lawyer,* contrast *Shanks's pony,* qq.v.

pedragal. Incorrect for *pedregal* : from ca. 1850. O.E.D.

pee. A urination : coll., mostly nursery : C. 19–20. Ex :

pee, v. To make water : coll., esp. nursery : 1788, Picken, (of a cat) ' He never pee'd his master's floor.' A softened perversion of *piss.*

pee and kew. See **p and q.**

pee-pee, do. A variant of ' pee ' : children's coll. : late C. 19–20. Manchon. Cf. *pee-wee,* q.v.

pee-wee. Either sexual organ : nursery : C. 19–20. Prob. ex the v., q.v.—2. A small marble : schoolboys' : ca. 1880–1910. ? ex its yellowish colour.

pee-wee. To make water : nursery : C. 19–20. An elaboration of *pee,* v.

peeble. See **phant.**

peechy ; rarely **peachy.** Soon ; presently : Regular Army coll. : late C. 19–20. F. & Gibbons. Hindustani *pichhe.*

peek, v.i. To surrender ; give up : military : C. 20. Ibid. Prob. *peak.*

peeky. See **peaky.**

peel. To undress : v.i., 1785, Grose.—2. Hence, v.t., to strip, 1820, ' Corcoran ' Reynolds. Both pugilistic j. > gen. coll. Ex peeling fruit. Cf. *peeled,* q.v.

peel eggs. To stand on ceremony : s. or low coll. : from ca. 1860 ; ob.

Peel (occ. **peele**) **Garlic.** See **Pilgarlic.**

peel off. ' To obtain money by a Stock Exchange transaction ' : financial : from ca. 1860. Ware.

peel one's best end. To effect intromission : low : C. 19–20.

peeled. Naked : coll. : 1820 (O.E.D.). See **peel** and cf. :

peeled, keep one's eyes. To watch carefully : coll. : orig. (– 1883), U.S.A. ; anglicised ca. 1905. Cf. *keep one's eyes skinned,* also U.S.A.

peeler, Peeler. (Cf. *bobby,* q.v.) A member of the Irish constabulary : 1817, Parliamentary Debates ; † by 1860 as a distinct term.—2. Hence, any policeman : 1829, *Blackwood's Magazine* : s. > coll. Ex Mr. (later Sir) Robert Peel, Secretary for Ireland, 1812–18. O.E.D.—3. One ready to strip for a fight : boxing : 1852, Anon., *L'Allegro.* Ex *peel,* q.v.

*peep To sleep : c. : late C. 17–mid-18. B.E. On *sleep.*

peep-bo. Bo-peep : coll. : from the middle 1820's. 1837, Dickens, ' A perpetual game of peep-bo ', O.E.D. This jocular or perhaps juvenile reversal of *bo-peep* is rare in C. 20.

peep o' day tree. ' Providential stage machinery ', e.g. a tree whereby escapes and/or rescues are effected : theatrical coll. : 1862 ; ob. Ware. Ex such a tree in *Peep o' Day,* an extremely successful piece produced at the Lyceum Theatre in 1862.

peep-by. See **peepy-by.**

peep-o(h) ! (To and by children.) Look at me ! : here I am ! , esp. as one emerges from hiding : coll. : C. 19–20 ; perhaps centuries earlier.

*peeper. A looking-glass : c. : from ca. 1670 ; ob. Coles, 1676. Also, as in B.E., *peepers.* Ex *peep,* v.—2. A spy-glass : c. : late C. 18–early 19. Grose, 1st ed.—3. An eye : from ca. 1690 : c. >, ca. 1750, low s. B.E. Gen. in pl. Cf. *glaziers, glims, ogles.*—4. In pl., spectacles : c. : C. 19–20 ; ob. Jamieson.—5. (Almost always pl.) A policeman : c. (– 1923). Manchon. Cf. sense 2.

peeper, single. A one-eyed person : late C. 18–mid-19 : low (? orig. c.). Grose, 1st ed.

peepers. See **peeper,** 1, 4, 5.—2. **painted peepers, peepers in mourning** : black eyes : C. 19–20 ; ob. Egan, 1818, ' Peepers . . . taken measure of for a suit of mourning ' ; H., 1860, ' Painted peepers . . .' Pugilistic in origin, mainly such in use.

*peeping. Drowsy, sleepy : c. : mid C. 17–early 19. Coles, 1676. Cf. *peepy,* q.v.

peeping Tom. An inquisitive person : 1785, Grose : coll. >, ca. 1850, S.E. Ex the Coventry legend of Lady Godiva.

peepsies. The pan-pipes : street-performers' s., almost j. : late C. 19–20 ; ob.

*peepy. Sleepy : late C. 17–20 : c. >, ca. 1750, s. >, ca. 1820, coll. (ob.) and dial. B.E., Grose. Ex *peep,* q.v. Cf. *peeping,* q.v.—2. Given to peeping : coll. : 1898, M. P. Shiel, ' Peepy little bewitching eyes,' O.E.D.

peepy-by, go to. To fall asleep : from ca. 1840.

Also *go to peep-by* : from ca. 1850 ; **ob.** Both, **coll.** and **dial.** Ex *peepy.* Cf. *sleepy-by !*

peer. To make (a man) a peer ; ennoble : **coll.** : 1753 (O.E.D.).—2. To be circumspect : **c.** : late C. 18–mid-19. Grose, 1st ed. Ex *peery,* adj.

*__peery,__ n. (Gen. **there's a peery.**) A being observed, discovered : **c.** : late C. 18–mid-19. Grose, 1785, ' There's a peery, 'tis snitch, We are observed, there's nothing to be done.' Ex :

*__peery__ ; occ., in C. 17–mid-18, spelt **peerie.** Sly : **c.** : late C. 17–20 ; extremely **ob.** B.E. Ex *to peer.* Cf. *leary,* q.v.—2. Shy, timid, suspicious : from ca. 1670 ; slightly **ob.** in last, † by 1850 in first and second nuance. Coles and B.E. give it as **c.,** O.E.D. as S.E. ; almost certainly, until mid-C. 18, either **c.** or low **s.**—3. Hence, inquisitive : from ca. 1810 (**ob.**) : low. *Lex. Bal* ; H., 2nd ed.

*__peeter.__ See **peter.** Coles's and B.E.'s spelling.

peety. Cheerful : C. 18 : **c.,** says F. & H., but is it ? Perhaps ex *peart.*

peeve. To disgruntle ; to annoy : from ca. 1920 : **coll.** By back-formation ex :

peeved. Annoyed ; cross : 1918 (S.O.D.) : **coll.** Ex *peevish.* Perhaps orig. U.S.

Peg. A **coll.** diminutive of *Margaret* : late C. 17–20. Also **Peggy.**—2. **the Peg** is Winnipeg : Canadian : C. 20. John Beames. Also **the 'Peg,** as in J. Beames, *Gateway,* 1932.

peg. A drink (esp. of brandy and soda-water) : Anglo-Indian : 1860, H., 2nd ed., is app. the earliest record ; 1864, Trevelyan, '. . . According to the favourite derivation, because each draught is a " peg " in your coffin,' O.E.D. ; actually ex *peg* as one of the pins in a drinking-vessel.—2. A blow, esp. a straight or a thrusting one : **s.** and **dial.** : 1748, Smollett.—3. A wooden leg : **coll.** : 1833, M. Scott (O.E.D.).—4. A tooth (esp. a child's) : late C. 16–20 : S.E. till C. 19, then **dial.** and nursery **coll.** O.E.D.—5. A shilling : Scottish **c.** : 1839, Brandon ; Jennings, 1926. Also among New Zealand soldiers in G.W.—6. A cricket stump : **coll.** : 1891, W. G. Grace (Lewis).—7. See **old peg.**—8. A, or the most, telling point in a play : theatrical **coll.** : 1884. Ware, ' Something upon which the actors, or more probably an actor, can build up a scene '.—9. Abbr. *peg-top* : children's **coll.** (— 1923). Manchon.

peg, v. (See **peg it to, peg it, peg it into, peg out, peg up.**)—2. To drive : 1819, Moore, ' I first was hir'd to peg a Hack ' (i.e. a hackney-coach) ; **ob.**—3. (Also with **away, off, along**) to move, or go, vigorously or hastily : **dial.** >, ca. 1855, **coll.** Le Fanu, 1884, ' Down the street I pegged like a madman.'—4. To work persistently, ' hammer ' away : **coll.** : C. 19–20. Esp. *peg away,* q.v., in eating, and *peg along,* q.v.—5. To tipple : 1874, H., 5th ed. Ex *peg,* n., 1.—6. (Gen. **peg up** or **down.**) To copulate, v.t., occ. v.i. : low **coll.** : from ca. 1850.—7. V.t., to fix the market price of : Stock Exchange : from ca. 1880 : **s.** till ca. 1920, then **coll.** ; prob. soon to be S.E. Gen. as *peg up,* l, q.v.

peg, old. See **old peg.**

peg, on the. (See also **pegs, on the.**) Under arrest.—2. Fined ; having had one's pay stopped. Both military : late C. 19–20. Cf. *peg, whip on the,* q.v.

peg, put in the. To stop giving credit : **coll.** ex **dial.** : late C. 19–20. ' A peg of wood above the latch inside . . . effectually locked it,' Dr. Bridge (quoted by Apperson).

peg, put (oneself) on the. To be careful, esp. as to liquor, behaviour, etc. : late C. 19–20 military ; **ob.** Perhaps suggested by the preceding entry as well as by *peg, on the.* Cf. *pin, keep in the,* q.v.—2. **put (another)** . . . To arrest : military : late C. 19–20. See **peg, on the.**

peg, whip on the. To arrest (a person, esp. a soldier) : military : C. 20. Manchon. Ex *peg, on the,* 1.

peg a hack. See **peg, v., 2.**—2. ' To mount the box of a hackney coach, drive yourself, and give the *Jarvey* a holiday ' : **c.** : ca. 1820–50. Egan's Grose.

peg along. To ' hammer ' away : **coll.** : mid-C. 19–20. See **peg, v., 3,** and cf. the equivalent :

peg away, v.i. = **peg away at,** occ. and **ob. on.** Coll. : from ca. 1830. Dickens, 1837, '. . . The breakfast. " Peg away, Bob ", said Mr. Allen encouragingly ' (O.E.D.). Ex ' industrious hammering in of pegs ', W. See preceding entry.

peg down. See **peg, v.,** sixth sense.

peg-house. A public-house : low : from ca. 1920. O.E.D. Sup. Ex *peg,* n., l.

peg into. To hit ; let drive at : **coll.** : from ca. 1880. Ex *peg it into,* q.v.

peg (or nail) (in)to one's coffin, add or **drive a.** To drink hard : from ca. 1860 ; **ob.** Ex the old peg-tankards : cf. *peg lower* and *peg too low,* qq.v.

peg it. A variant, from ca. 1860, of *peg,* v., 2.—2. Inseparable part of :

peg it into. To hit : 1834, Dowling, ' You peg it into him, and pray don't spare him ' : **coll.** ; **ob.** Cf. *peg into* and *peg it,* qq.v.

peg-leg. A person with a wooden leg : (low) **coll.** : C. 19–20. Ex S.E. sense, a wooden leg.

peg-legger. A beggar : Glasgow (— 1934). Either rhyming **s.** or ex the preceding.

peg lower, go a. To drink to excess : **coll.** : C. 19–20 ; very **ob.**

peg out. To be ruined : ca. 1880–1910. Ex :—2. To die : ? orig. U.S. (1855) ; certainly anglicised by 1860. (O.E.D.) Prob. ex retiring from some game (W.).

peg-puff. An old woman dressing young : Scots **coll.** : from ca. 1810 ; **ob.** (Perhaps dial.)

peg too low, a. Tipsy : ca. 1870–1915.—2. Hence, (fig.) depressed : from ca. 1880.

Peg Trantum's, gone to. Dead : from ca. 1690. B.E. ; 1785, Grose ; † by 1860. Occ. *Peg Crancum's* (Ned Ward). Note that in East Anglia, *Peg Trantum* is extant for a hoyden.

peg up. See **peg, v.,** last two senses. (*The Pall Mall Gazette,* April 8, 1882, ' Arbitrarily raising prices . . . " pegging prices up ", it is called.' (O.E.D.)

pegged, be. To be due for trial for some ' crime ' : military : from 1915. M. A. Mügge, *The War Diary of a Square Peg,* 1920.

pegged out, be. To be notorious : low : 1886, *Tit-Bits,* July 31 ; **ob.**

pegger. A hard drinker : ca. 1873–1915 : **coll.** Ex *peg,* a dram, and the v. Cf. :

pegging. Tippling : from ca. 1870 ; **ob.** H., 5th ed. ; Miss Braddon.

peggy. A thin poker bent for the raking of fires : **coll.** : from ca. 1860 ; **ob.** Cf. *curate* and *rector,* qq.v.—2. (Gen. **Peggy.**) ' A hand . . . called upon to do all the odd jobs in a watch ' : nautical : C. 19. Bowen.—3. ' The man who looks after the seamen's and firemen's messes in a modern liner ' : nautical : C. 20. Ibid. Likewise ex his ' feminine ' duties.—4. (Gen. pl.) A tooth : children's **coll.** : late C. 19–20. Manchon. Ex *peg,* n., 4.

Peggy guns. Guns from the gunboat *Pegasus*: German East Africa campaigners': late 1916–17. F. Brett Young, *Jim Redlake*, 1930.

pego. 'The penis of man or beast', Grose: C. 18–mid-19. Ned Ward, 1709. Ex Gr. πηγή, a spring, a fountain.

pegs, on the. (Of an N.C.O.) awaiting trial by court martial: military: from ca. 1908. F. & Gibbons. Because he was *in suspense*. Also, of any rank below that of an officer, *on the peg*: F. & Gibbons.

pegs than square holes, there are always more round. There are always more applicants than jobs: coll.: late C. 19–20; ob. Ex S.E. *round peg in a square hole* (or *square peg . . .*).

*pek. See **peck.**

peke, Peke. A coll. abbr. of *Pekin(g)ese*, sc. *dog* or *spaniel*: from ca. 1910. Rarely *Pek*; occ. *Pekie* (1920: O.E.D. Sup.).

*pelfry. The booty obtained by picking locks: c.: late C. 16–early 17. Greene, 1592. Ex *pelf*.

*pell. See **pal.**

pelt. See entry at **pace, go the.**—2. The human skin: coll. (jocular) and dial.: C. 17–20. Rowley, ca. 1605, 'Flay off her wicked skin, and stuff the pelt with straw.' O.E.D.—3. Hence, a man: Yorkshire and Pembrokeshire s., not dial.: 1882. E.D.D.

pelt, v. See under **pace, go the.**—2. To sew thickly: tailors': from ca. 1860. Prob. suggested by *pelts*, garments made of furry skins.

pelt at, have a. To attempt vigorously, 'have a shot at ': coll. (— 1923). Manchon.

pelter. See **pace, go the.**—2. A heavy shower: coll.: 1842, Barham, 'The rain . . . kept pouring . . . What I've heard term'd a regular pelter.' Ex the weather v.i.—3. Anything large: coll. (— 1892) ex dial. (— 1851); ob. by 1920, † by 1935. Milliken. Prob. ex sense 1. 4. Any person, etc., going very quickly, esp. a horse: coll.: C. 20.—5. A whoremonger: tramps' c.: from ca. 1850; ob.

peltis-hole. A Scots coll. pejorative addressed to women: late C. 16–17. Jamieson. I.e. *pelts-hole*, i.e. tan-pit.

Pemmy. Pembroke College, Oxford: from ca. 1890. (Very rarely, *Pemmer*: see ' *-er*', Oxford '). Collinson.

pempë. An imaginary object for which a newcomer is sent: Winchester College: C. 19–20; ob. Ex πέμπε τὸν μῶρον πρότερον, send the fool further; i.e. keep the idiot moving ! Cf. *strap-oil, squad umbrella*, qq.v.

pemptarchie. Pentarchy: erroneous form: C. 17. O.E.D.

pen. The male member: late C. 16–20 low; ob. (Cf. *pencil*, q.v.) Ex shape of a pen + abbr. *penis*. See next entry.—2. A **penitentiary** ; a prison: low, almost c.: from ca. 1820.—3. A threepenny piece: Colonial, says F. & H.; but which Dominion ?: app. ca. 1890–1910. Origin ?—4. The female pudend: low: mid-C. 19–20. Properly of sows.

pen, have no more ink in the. To be temporarily impotent from exhaustion: low: late C. 16–17. E.g. in Weever's *Lusty Juventus*. Ex *pen*, 1.

pen and ink. A stink: rhyming s.: from ca. 1858. H., 1st ed.—2. Hence, to stink: id.: from ca. 1870.—3. To ' kick up a stink ', i.e. to yell (with pain): Cockney: late C. 19–20.—4. **Pen and Ink,** Gallipoli **Peni**nsula: New Zealand soldiers': in 1915; occ. after. Cf. *Pinch an Inch.*

pen-driver. A clerk; occ. a writer: coll.: from ca. 1885; very ob. Suggested by *quill-driver*, q.v. Cf. the C. 20 equivalent, *pen-pusher.*

pen-gun ; crack like a p.g. To chatter. Scots coll.: C. 19–20. Scott. Occ. *penguin*. (A toy gun made from a quill.)

pen-pusher. See **pen-driver.** (A. H. Dawson, *Dict. of Slang*, 1913.)

penal. A sentence or a term of penal servitude: coll.: from ca. 1890. O.E.D. (Sup.).—2. See **penals**, 2.—3. Also at Shrewsbury, thus in D. Coke, 1906, ' Pens and paper (which is known as " penal " and is sold by " gats ") . . .'

penals. Lines as punishment: mid-C. 19–20: Shrewsbury School s. >, by 1890, coll. >, by 1900, j. Desmond Coke, *The Bending of a Twig*, 1906.—2. Hence, *penal* is a set of 25 lines: from ca. 1870: s. > coll. >, by 1900, j. Ibid.

*penance-board. A pillory: c.: late C. 17–early 19. B.E.; Grose, 1st ed.

Penang lawyer. The stem of a species of palm much used for walking-sticks, hence a walking-stick so made: coll.: from ca. 1860; ob. *Chambers's Encyclopædia*, 1865. Prob. *Penang liyar* (the wild areca), corrupted.—2. Whence a bludgeon: Singapore: from ca. 1870. H., 1874.

*penbank. A beggar's can: c.: C. 18. Bailey. Origin ?

pencil. The male member: low: late C. 19–20. Ex shape. Cf. *pen*, 1. Cf. *pencil and tassel.*

pencil, knight of the. A bookmaker: the turf: 1885, *Punch*, March 7 ; ob. Cf. *penciller*, q.v.

pencil and tassel. A (little) boy's penis and scrotum: lower classes' euphemism: C. 20.

pencil-fever. The laying of odds against a horse certain to lose, esp. after it has at first been at short odds: the turf: from ca. 1872; ob. H., 5th ed. Also *market-fever* and *milk-fever*. Ex the pencilling of the horse's name in betting-books. Whence *penciller*.

pencil-in dates. To make engagements to perform: theatrical coll.: 1896 ; slightly ob. Ware.

pencil, open, lost, and found. Ten pound (sol. for ten pounds sterling): rhyming s.: from ca. 1870 ; ob. Ware.

pencil-shover. A journalist: printers' (—1887): ob. Baumann. On *quill-driver.*

penciller. A bookmaker's clerk: the turf; *The Daily News*, Oct. 24, 1879 (O.E.D.). See **pencil-fever.** Cf. :

pencilling fraternity. Bookmakers, collectively: the turf: from ca. 1890 ; ob.

pendant used catachrestically for *pennon* (mid-C. 16–17), as *pendentive* for architectural *pendant* (from mid-C. 19). O.E.D.

pendulum. The penis: low: C. 19–20 ; ob. Cf. *dingle-dangle*, q.v.

pene(r)th. See **pen(n)e(r)th** and **penn'orth.**

penguin. An aeroplane organically unable to leave the ground ; a member of the W.R.A.F., which consisted of women (mostly ' flappers '), unable to fly: Air Force: 1917; ob. W.; B. & P.; O.E.D. (Sup.). Cf. the *Wrens*.—2. See **pen-gun.**

Peninsular. A veteran of the Peninsular War: coll.: *The Quarterly Review*, 1888, but prob. in use from ca. 1840. Ob. by 1900, † by 1910.—2. (Also called a *moll tooler*, H., 1st ed.) A female pickpocket: c.: (— 1859) ; very ob. H., 1st ed.

*penman. A forger: c.: late C. 19–20. Charles E. Leach, *On Top of the Underworld*, 1933.

*pennam. A rare variant of *pannam.*—***pennel.** See **pinnel.**

pen(n)e(r)th. C. 16–17 forms of *penn'orth,* q.v.

pennif. A five-pound note : back slang : 1862, *The Cornhill Magazine.*—2. Hence, any bank or currency note ; *single-pennif* being a £1 note : c. : C. 20.

penniless bench, sit on the. To be poverty-stricken : coll. : late C. 16–19. Massinger, ' Bid him bear up, he shall not | Sit long on penniless bench.' Ex a certain London seat so named. Cf. S.E. *Pierce Penniless.*

penn'orth, pennorth, pen'orth ; penn'worth. Abbr. *pennyworth :* coll. : resp. C. 17, C. 18–20, C. 18–19 (H.) ; C. 17. O.E.D. Cf. *pen(n)e(r)th* and *penworth,* qq.v.—2. A year's imprisonment, esp. of a convict and mostly in combination : C. 20 : c. >, by 1930, low s. Michael Harrison, *Weep for Lycidas,* 1934, ' Ronnie will get fourteen penn'orth . . . Fourteen years hard.'

pennorth o(f) treacle. A charming girl : low London : 1882–ca. 1912. Ware. Ex *jam.*

pennorth o(f) treason. A copy of a certain notorious London penny newspaper : news-vendors' (— 1909). Ware.

Penns. Shares in the Pennsylvania Railroad : Stock Exchange (— 1895) >, by 1910, coll. Wilson's *Stock Exchange Glossary.*

penny. See the **penny** entries at **pace, go the.**

penny, clean as a. (Very clean : S.E., C. 18.—) Completely : coll. (and dial.) : ca. 1820–1910. Cf. the ' brightness = completeness ' semantics of *clean as a whistle.*

penny, turn and wind the. To make the most of one's money : coll. : late C. 17–18. B.E. An elaboration of S.E. *get* or *turn a* or *the penny,* to endeavour to live, hence to make money.

penny-a-liar. A jocular variation (— 1887 ; ob.), recorded by Baumann, of :

penny-a-liner. A writer of paragraphs at a cheap rate, orig. a penny a line ; hence, a literary hack: 1834, Ainsworth (O.E.D.) : journalistic coll. >, ca. 1905, S.E.

penny(-)awful. An occ. variant of *penny dreadful,* q.v. : ca. 1875–1910. Also, in C. 20, *penny blood* (Manchon).

penny-boy. A boy haunting cattle-markets in the hope of some droving : coll. : C. 19. Because paid a penny a beast. Also *ankle-beater.*

penny(-)buster. A small new loaf, or a large bun or roll, costing one penny : ca. 1870–1910. H., 1874. But a *penny starver* is a stale one or an unusually small one († by ca. 1910) ; orig., however, a *starver* meant a halfpenny loaf, or, occ., a bun : H., 1874.

penny death-trap. A penny paraffin-lamp : low London : 1897–ca. 1915. Made in Germany, these lamps caused numerous deaths. Ware.

penny(-)dreadful. A sensational story or († by 1910) print : coll. : H., 1874 ; *The Pall Mall Gazette,* Nov. 17, 1892, ' A Victim of the Penny Dreadful ', title. Occ. *penny †awful* or (ob.) *horrible ;* cf. *blood and thunder, shilling shocker,* (U.S.) *dime novel.*

penny-farthing. An old-fashioned, very high bicycle with a large and a small wheel : coll. : from ca. 1885 ; ob.

penny for your thought(s). A c.p. addressed to one preoccupied : from ca. 1540. Heywood's *Proverbs,* 1546 ; Greene ; Swift. The *-s* form, which is not found before C. 17, > gen. in C. 18 ;

a penny for 'em belongs to late C. 19–20. (Apperson ; Collinson.)

penny(-)gaff. A low-class theatre, music-hall : 1851, Mayhew ; slightly ob. by 1902 (F. & H.), but still extant. Also *penny-room.* Ex *gaff,* last sense, q.v.

penny gush. ' Exaggerated mode of writing English frequently seen in a certain London daily paper ' : journalistic coll. : ca. 1880–5. Ware.

penny hop. A cheap (country) dance : C. 19. Thus, in C. 20, *a shilling hop.*

penny-horrible. A ' penny dreadful ', q.v. : coll. : 1899, *The Daily News,* June 13 (O.E.D.) ; ob. Cf. *penny awful.*

penny lattice-house. A low ale-house : coll. : C. 18–early 19. Cf. *red lattice.*

*penny loaf. A man afraid to steal : c. (— 1909). Ware. Lit., one who would pre er to live on a penny loaf.

penny locket. A pocket : rhyming s. (— 1909). Ware.

penny or paternoster. Pay or prayers ; only in *no paternoster, no penny* (no work, no pay) : proverbial coll. : mid-C. 16–early 18. Heywood.

penny pick. A cigar : London : ca. 1838–45. Ware derives ex Dickens's Pickwick : ? *pick-wick.*

penny pots. Pimples on a tippler's face : low : from ca. 1850 ; ob.

penny puzzle. A sausage : low : ca. 1883–1914. Ware. Costing a penny, ' it is never found out '.

penny silver, think one's. To think well of oneself : coll. : late C. 16–early 18. Gabriel Harvey ; Breton ; Fuller, 1732. In early quotations, gen. *good silver.* (Apperson.)

penny(-)starver. See **penny buster.**—2. A penny cigar : low (— 1909) ; ob. Ware.

penny to bless oneself with, not a. No, or extremely little, money : from ca. 1540 : coll. >, by 1700, S.E. (Semi-proverbial : see Heywood's *Proverbs.*)

penny-swag. ' A man who sells articles at a penny a lot in the streets ' : Cockneys' (— 1851) ; ob. Mayhew. I.e. a ' swag-barrowman ' specialising in sales at one penny. E.D.D.

penny toff. ' The lowest description of toff—the cad imitator of the follies of the *jeunesse dorée* ' (Ware) : London : ca. 1870–1914.

penny-white. Ugly but rich : coll. : late C. 17–18. B.E. (Rarely of men.)

pennyworth, Robin Hood's. Anything sold at a robber's price, i.e. far too cheaply : coll. : C. 17, and prob. earlier. (O.E.D.). Cf. the C. 19 proverb, *pirates may make cheap pennyworths of their pillage.*

pennyworth out of, fetch one's. To make a person earn his wages, its cost, etc. : coll. : late C. 17–18. B.E. A variation on *a pennyworth for one's penny.*

pen'orth. See **penn'orth.**

pension !, not for a. Not for all the money in the world : lower classes' coll. (— 1887) ; ob. Baumann.

Pension (or Pensionary or Pensioner) Parliament. The Long Parliament of Charles II : coll. nickname. O.E.D.

*pensioner. A harlot's bully : from ca. 1810 : c. > low s. ; ob. Vaux. Prob. an abbr. of the † S.E. *petticoat-pensioner* or *petticoat-squire,* i.e. any male keep.—2. A blind musician that has a regular round : London itinerant musicians' (— 1861). Mayhew (E.D.D.).

Pensioners, the. Chelsea Football Club ('soccer'): sporting : late C. 19–20. Ex Chelsea Hospital for military pensioners. E.g. in P. G. Wodehouse, *Psmith in the City*, 1910.

pensitive is an error for *pensative* : ca. 1570–1650. O.E.D.

***Pent, the.** Pentonville Prison : c. : 1857, *Punch*, Jan. 31.

pentagraph, †pentegraph. Erroneous for *pantograph* : C. 18–20. O.E.D.

***penthouse-nab.** A broad-brimmed hat : c. : late C. 17–early 19. B.E. (*pentice*) ; Grose.

pentile, erroneous for **pantile** (mid-C. 18–20), **pentionary** for **penitentiary** (C. 17), **pentlike** for **pentelic** (C. 16), **pentograph** for **pantograph** (C. 18–20). O.E.D.

penwiper. A handkerchief : from ca. 1860.—2. The female pudend : low : from ca. 1850 ; ob.

penworth, pen'worth. Coll. abbr. of *pennyworth* : C. 16–17, C. 17. Cf. *penn'orth*, etc.

people. In *people say*, etc., it is coll. : C. 19–20. J. H. Newman, in a letter of 1843, ' People cannot understand a man being in a state of doubt.' O.E.D. —2. Coll. too in *my, your* (etc.) *people*, my or your relatives, esp. the members of the family to which one belongs : 1851, Carlyle, ' Mrs. Sterling had lived . . . with his Father's people ' (O.E.D.). Cf. *people-in-law.*—3. Thieves : c. (— 1887) ; ob. Baumann.

people-in-law. One's husband's or wife's relatives, esp. parents, brothers, sisters : coll. : from ca. 1890. (O.E.D.)

pep. Energy : spirited initiative : coll. : 1920 (S.O.D.). Orig. (ca. 1914) U.S. Abbr. *pepper.* Cf. *go* and :

pep up. To infuse (gen. a person) with new life, spirit, courage : coll. : orig. (early 1920's) U.S. ; anglicised ca. 1927. O.E.D. (Sup.). Ex preceding.—2. Hence, to become lively : from ca. 1930. *The Passing Show*, July 15, 1933.

pepin. A C. 17 form of *pippin*, 1.

pepper. (See **pace, go the.**—) 2. V.t., to put in the accents of a Greek exercise : university : from ca. 1880. Ex sprinkling with black pepper.—3. V.t., to humbug, to ' kid ' : from ca. 1870 ; ob. Ex *throw pepper in the eyes of*. The v.i. form is *use the pepper-box.*

pepper, Chili. Incorrect for *chilli* : from ca. 1670 ; now rare. (O.E.D.)

pepper, snuff. To take offence : coll. : C. 17. On *take pepper in the nose*, q.v.

Pepper Alley or **pepper alley.** Rough treatment, esp. hard punching, as in *The Sporting Magazine*, 1820, ' His mug . . . had paid a visit to " pepper alley " ' (O.E.D.) : pugilistic ; ob. Punningly on the name of a London alley. Cf. *gutter lane.*

pepper-box. A revolver : coll. : from ca. 1840–1910. (Revolver invented in 1835.)—2. A ship's lighthouse at the break of the forecastle : C. 19 nautical. Also, a shore lighthouse : late C. 19–20 nautical (now ob.). Bowen. Ex the shape.—3. **the Pepper-Boxes** was a term applied as early as 1860 (H., 2nd ed.) to ' the buildings of the Royal Academy and National Gallery, in Trafalgar-square.' Cf. *the Boilers*, q.v.

pepper-box, use the. See **pepper, v., 2.**

pepper-castor (occ. **-er**). A revolver : 1889 ; ob. (O.E.D.) Suggested by *pepper-box*, q.v.

pepper in the nose, take. To take offence, grow angry : C. 16–mid-18 : coll. till C. 17, then S.E. (Apperson.) Cf. *snuff pepper*, above

pepper on one's nut, have. To be punched on the head : boxers' (— 1887) ; ob. Baumann.

pepper-proof. (Not, of course, immune to, but) free from venereal disease : low coll. : late C. 17–18. B.E. Contrast :

peppered off. ' Damnably Clapt or Poxt ', B.E. : low coll. : late C. 17–18. († S.E. *peppered*.)

pepperminter. A seller of peppermint water : London lower-class coll. (— 1851) ; very ob. Mayhew, cited by E.D.D.

Pepper's Dragoons. The Eighth Hussars : military : C. 19–20 ; extremely ob.

peppy. Energetic : spirited, e.g. work : from ca. 1921. Ex *pep*, q.v. Evelyn Waugh, *Vile Bodies*, 1930 ; in *The Humorist*, July 28, 1934, a typical retired admiral is described as ' addressing peppy letters to the editor of *The Times* ' (Austin Barber). —2. See **pipi.**

pepst. Tipsy : s. or coll. : ca. 1570–90. Kendall, 1577, quoted by Nares. Origin ?

per is sol. (— 1887) for *pro* in *percession* and *perfessor*, for *pre* in *pervent*. Baumann. Cf. *perty*, q.v.

[**per capita.** It is advisable to read Fowler's note thereon.]

per usual(, as). See **usual.**

peraffetted. Incorrect for *paraphed* : from ca. 1660 ; ob. O.E.D.

peram. A sol. variant (— 1923) of *pram*, q.v. Manchon.

perambulator. A costermonger : ca. 1860–1900. Perhaps ineligible : F. & H. not convincing.

percession. See **per.**

perch. A small and gen. high seat on a vehicle : coll. : from ca. 1840.—2. Death : C. 18. Ex such phrases as *knock off the perch, hop the perch.* O.E.D.

perch, v. To die : ca. 1880–1915. *The Sporting Times*, Aug. 3, 1886. Cf. next entry. Ex *hop the perch.*

perch, be off to. To go to bed : from ca. 1860 ; ob. H., 2nd ed.

perch, drop or **fall off** or **hop the ; perch, pitch** or **tip** or **turn over the.** To die : first three, late C. 18–20, all slightly ob. ; the fourth, late C. 16–17, e.g. in Hakluyt ; the fifth, C. 18 (Ozell's *Rabelais*, Richardson) ; the sixth, late C. 16–17 (Nashe). Scott, *The Pirate*, ' I always thought him a—d fool . . . but never such a consummate idiot as to hop the perch so sillily.' Cf. *hop the twig.* (O.E.D.)—2. Also, though rarely *hop the perch*, to be defeated : same periods.

perch, knock off the. To perturb ; defeat ; kill : from ca. 1850. Also *throw over the perch*, C. 16–17, as in Fulwell, 1568 ; *turn over the perch*, C. 17–18, as in facetious Tom Brown ; occ. *give a turn over the.* The second and third senses > coll.

perch, pitch or **tip** or **turn over the.** See **perch, drop . . .**

percher. A dying person : C. 18–19. Bolingbroke, 1714 (O.E.D.). Ex *perch, drop . . ., etc.*— 2. A Latin cross made horizontally against the name of an absentee : Winchester College (— 1891). Wrench. (Remembered in 1839 : O.E.D.)

percisely, percys(e)ly. Precisely : resp. C. 19–20 (? also C. 17–18) ; C. 15–16. Sol. (O.E.D.)

peremptory. Utter, unmitigated ; complete : coll. : late C. 16–17. Ben Jonson. Prob. ex :

peremptory, adv. Entirely, absolutely : coll. : C. 16–17. Jonson. (O.E.D.)

perfect. (Mostly pejorative.) Sheer ; unmitigated ; utter : mostly coll. : 1611, Shakespeare, ' His complexion is perfect gallows.' The phrase *perfect nonsense* is late C. 19–20 coll. O.E.D.—2. Amusing; pleasant, delightful: Society coll.: from ca. 1910. E.g. Denis Mackail, *Greenery Street*, 1925, ' But *rowing*. How perfect ! '

perfect day, a. A day that one has very greatly enjoyed: coll.: 1909 (O.E.D. Sup.). Whence:

perfect day, the end of a. A coll. G.W. c.p. of indefinite meaning; occ. jocularly applied, by soldiers, to one who had very evidently been ' celebrating '. See the editor's *Bakara Bulletin*, 1919, at the end-sketches; Collinson. Imm. ex Carrie Jacobs-Bond's song, *When You Come to the End of a Perfect Day*.

perfect lady. A harlot: from ca. 1880; slightly ob. Origin prob. anecdotal, as Ware says.

perfectly good . . ., a. An indubitably—or, merely, a quite—good, sound, satisfactory something or other: from ca. 1918: s. > coll. Cf. *perfect*, q.v.

perfessor. See **per.**

perforate. To take the virginity of: low: C. 19–20.

perform, v.i. To copulate: low: C. 19–20.—2. To make a (considerable) fuss, to ' go on ': C. 20 : s. > coll.

perform on, v.t. To cheat, deceive: low: from ca. 1870. H., 1874.

performer. A whoremonger: low: C. 19–20; ob.—2. One who is apt to make a great fuss or noise: C. 20 : rare. Ex *perform*, 2.

perger. See *purger.*

pericranium. As the skull or the brain, the word is by the O.E.D. considered S.E.: rather, I think, S.E. in late C. 16–18, but coll. in C. 19–20. Ex anatomical sense, ' the membrane enveloping the skull '.

period, girl of the. A modern girl: Society coll.: ca. 1880–1900. Coined in this strain in a series of articles published by *The Saturday Review*. (Baumann.)

periphery. A big belly: cultured, jocular coll. (— 1923). Manchon. Prob. suggested by *circumference*.

perish, do a. Nearly to die from lack of water: Western Australia (— 1894). Morris. An interesting contrast is afforded by sense 4 of *perisher*.

perishable cargo. Fruit; slaves: nautical: ca. 1730–1800. Bowen. Cf. *live lumber*, q.v.

perisher. A short-tailed coat: from ca. 1880; ob. The C. 20 prefers *bum-freezer*.—2. An extreme, e.g. in drunkenness, betting: 1888, ' Rolf Boldrewood ', ' Then he . . . went in an awful perisher . . . and was never sober day or night the whole [month].' Ob.—3. Hence, pejoratively of a person: 1896, ' Those perishers in the gallery didn't know anything about Shakespeare ' (S.O.D.). Cf. *perishing*, adj., q.v.—4. A ' freeze ', mostly in *do a perisher*, to feel extremely cold: coll.: C. 20. Cf. sense 1 and *perishing*, adv.—5. A periscope: military: 1915; slightly ob. F. & Gibbons. By jocular perversion.

perishing, adj. A gen. pejorative, as in ' Damn the perishing thing ! ': coll.: C. 20. Cf. *perisher*, 3.

perishing. A pejorative intensive adv.: coll.: C. 20. Orig. and esp. (*it's*) *perishing cold*.

periwinkle. The female pudend: low: mid-C. 19–20; ob.

perk ; perks. Perquisites: (the singular, rare, ca. 1890–1910 ;) 1887, *Fun*, March 30, ' The perks, etc., attached to this useful office are not what they

were in the " good old times ".' In Scots, *perks* is recorded as early as 1824 (E.D.D.).

perk up. To recover health or good spirits: coll. and dial.: from ca. 1650. B.E., Barham. Ex † S.E. *perk*, to carry oneself smartly, jauntily. (O.E.D.)

perked. Tipsy: military: C. 20. F. & Gibbons. Prob. ex preceding.

perker. A person constantly seeking ' perks ' (see **perk**): lower classes' (— 1923). Manchon.

perking. ' Any pert, forward, silly Fellow ', B.E.: coll.: late C. 17–mid-18. Ex adj.

Perkins, perkins. Beer: ca. 1860–90: ' dandy or affected shortening ', H., 1864. Ex the better-known s. phrase, *Barclay and Perkins*, perhaps influenced by S.E. *perkin*, weak cider or perry. Cf. *purko*, q.v.

perks. See **perk.**—**Perks, Board of.** Board of Works: jocular: 1889, *The Pall Mall Gazette*, Sept. 27, as title : ' Provincial Boards of Perks '.

perm. A supposedly permanent wave (of the hair): coll.: from ca. 1925.—2. Hence, from ca. 1927, v.t., to subject a person, or a person's hair, to a permanent wave: coll., and gen. in passive.

permanent. A permanent boarder: hotels, boarding-houses : late C. 19–20 : coll.

permanent pug. A ' fighting man around the door of the premises': journalists', printers', tavern-frequenters': late C. 19–20; ob.

perpendicular. A buffet meal; a party at which the majority of the guests have to stand: 1871, ' M. Legrand ', ' . . . An invitation to a Perpendicular, as such entertainments are styled ' (O.E.D.).—2. Coïtion between two persons standing upright : low: mid-C. 19–20. Also a *knee-trembler*, an *upright*. Contrast with a *horizontal*.

perpendicular, do a. See **do a perpendicular.**

perpetrate. To make (e.g. a pun); do (anything treated as shocking): coll.: 1849, C. Brontë, ' Philip induced . . . his sisters to perpetrate a duet.' O.E.D.

perpetration. The doing of something very bad, or atrociously performed: coll.: from ca. 1850. (Gen. a humorous affectation by the narrator.)

perpetual, got the. See **got the perpetual.**

*perpetual staircase. The treadmill: c.: late C. 19–20. Ware. Also *everlasting staircase*.

perralling. Incorrect for *parpalling*: C. 15–18. O.E.D.

persecute and **prosecute** are occ. confused in C. 19–20. Cf. *perspicuous*, q.v.

Perseus. An editor: Society: 1883. Ware. Ex a phrase used by T. H. Huxley.

person. A personage: coll.: C. 20. Esp. in *quite a person* (of a child).

perspicuity, perspicuous. Perspicacious, perspicacity : a cultured sol., i.e. a catachresis : 1584. Rare. O.E.D.—' The two words are sometimes confused in mod. use,' W. Cf. *persecute* and *prosecute*.

perspiry. Full of, covered with, perspiration: coll.: 1860. O.E.D.

persuader. A spur, gen. in pl.: from ca. 1786; ob. Grose, 2nd ed., ' The kiddey clapped his persuaders to his prad, but the traps boned him.'—2. A pistol: 1841, Leman Rede; slightly ob.—3. Hence, any other weapon: from ca. 1845, but anticipated by Marryat in 1833 (' three rattans twisted into one ', to enforce submission).—4. A whip : coachmen's (— 1887). Baumann.—**5.** A 'jemmy' (q.v.) or other burglar's tool: **c.**: from ca. 1850; ob. Cf.:

*persuading plate. C., from ca. 1880; ob. 'An iron disk used in forcing safes: it revolves on a pivot, and is fitted with a cutting point,' F. & H.

persuasion. Nationality, sex; sort, kind; description: 1864 (S.O.D.). 'A dark little man . . . of French persuasion.' Ex *persuasion*, religious belief, opinion. (In C. 20, jocular coll.)

pert as a pearmonger, as. Very cheerful: from ca. 1560: coll. till C. 19, then dial. Harding, 1564; Gay; Swift. Dial. has at least four synonyms, with *pert* spelt *peart*. Apperson.

Perthshire Greybreeks, the. The 2nd Battalion Cameronian (Scottish Rifles)—in C. 19, the 90th (Perthshire Volunteers) Foot—Regiment: military: 1793; ob. F. & Gibbons. Ex the grey trousers formerly worn, white breeches being at this time the usual regulation wear.

pertic'lar, -ler. Particular(ly): adj., low coll.; adv., sol.: C. 19–20. Baumann.

perty; often, illogically, spelt purty. Pretty: sol.: mostly Cockney (and dial.). Baumann.

Perus. Peruvian stocks: financial coll. (—1887). Baumann.

peruse. A 'look round' ashore: nautical coll.: C. 20. Prob. on *cruise* (*ker-ruse*).

Peruvian Jews; Peruvians. Russian and Polish Jews: a Transvaal coll.: from ca. 1898. 'Applied in the first instance to certain Jews from South America, who had failed, under Baron Hirsch's Colonisation Scheme, to make a living there, and who subsequently made their way to the goldfields of South Africa', Pettman.

pervent. See per.

perverted. A Society euphemism for *bu****red*: from ca. 1918. Philip MacDonald, *R.I.P.*, 1933, 'I'm perverted if I know!'

*pester; pester-up. (V.i. and v.t., resp.) To pay; pay up: c.: from ca. 1920. James Curtis, *The Gilt Kid*, 1936. Ex Romany *pesser*, to pay.

pestilent, adv. Extremely: coll.: late C. 17–early 18. B.E. (Earlier, S.E.)

pestle. A leg: coll. verging on S.E.: C. 16–17. Skelton, '[Her] myghty pestels . . . | As fayre and as whyte | As the fote of a kyte'. Cf. *pestle of pork*, q.v.—2. A constable's staff: coll.: early C. 17 Chapman. O.E.D.—3. A penis: low: C. 19–20 ob. Contrast *mortar*, the female pudend.

pestle, v.i. To coït (of a man): low: C. 19–20; ob. Ex *pestle*, n., 3.

pestle, knight of the. See the knight paragraph.

pestle of a lark. Anything very small; a trifle: late C. 16–early 18: coll. >, by 1690, S.E. Fuller calls Rutlandshire 'Indeed . . . but the Pestel of a Lark'. (O.E.D.)

pestle of a portigue. A portague, a C. 16–early 17 Portuguese gold coin worth about £4: jocular coll. (C. 17) verging on S.E. Fletcher, 1622. O.E.D.

pestle of pork. A leg: low coll.: C. 19–20; very ob. Ex dial., where the phrase = the shank end of a ham, etc., or pork cooked fresh

petard. A trick or a cheating at dice. prob. by some kind of bluff or by the use of loaded dice: gamblers' s. (? orig. c.): Restoration period. J. Wilson, *The Cheats*, 1662 (O.E.D.). Prob. ex, or suggested by, *hoist with his own petard*.

Pete Jenkins. An auxiliary clown: circus: from ca. 1860; very ob. Ex Pete Jenkins, who (fl. 1855) planted 'rustics' in the audience.

Peter. A coll. abbr. of *Peter-see-me* (itself ex Peter Ximenes, a famous cardinal), a Spanish wine: C. 17. Beaumont & Fletcher, *Chances*.

*peter. A trunk, portmanteau, bag; (in C. 19–20) a box or a safe: c.: 1668, Head; Smollett; Grose; Lytton; Horsley, 1879; James Spenser, *Limey Breaks In*, 1934, 'A "peter" is a safe made from tool-proof steel and usually has safety linings made from a special sort of cement,'—this being the predominant C. 20 c. sense in Britain. ? origin: perhaps because frequently 'netted' by thieves: in allusion to Simon Peter's occupation. Cf. † S.E. *peterman*, a fisherman. See also Peter to pay Paul. —2. Hence, any bundle, parcel or package; a tramp's sack: c.: from ca. 1810. Vaux; H., 1st ed.; Horsley, 1879.—3. A kind of loaded dice, hence the using of them: c.: ca. 1660–1750. Wilson, *The Cheats*. Prob. the correct form is *petard*, as above: it is F. & H. that lists under *peter*. Wilson's spelling is *Petarrs*.—4. A punishment cell: Australian c.: from ca. 1880; ob.—5. A partridge: poachers': from ca. 1860. H., 2nd ed.—6. The penis: low: mid-C. 19–20; ob. Cf. *John Thomas*.

*peter, v.t. To cease doing, e.g. speaking: low s. (prob. orig. c.): 1812, Vaux; ob. by 1900, † by 1930. Ex *peter, n., 1* : for *peter that ! = stow that !* —2. V.i., (in whist) to call for trumps by discarding an unnecessarily high card: cards (— 1887). Ex *the blue Peter*, which indicates that a ship is about to start. *Notes and Queries*, 7th Series, iv, 356.—3. Hence, v.i. and t., to run up prices: auctioneers': from ca. 1890.—4. See peter out.

*peter-biter. A stealer of portmanteaux: c.: late C. 17–20; ob. Also *biter of peters*, as in B.E. See peter, n., 1. Cf.:

*peter-claimer. The same; esp. a carriage-thief: c.: late C. 19–20. See peter, n., 1.

*peter-claiming. The stealing of parcels and/or bags, esp. at railway stations: 1894, A Morrison, 'From this, he ventured on peterclaiming' (O.E.D.). Ex *peter*, n., 1.

Peter Collins. An imaginary person on whom the green are asked to call for a *green-handed* (or *handled*) *rake*: theatrical and circuses' (— 1889); ob. J. C. Coleman in Barrère & Leland.

*peter-cutter. An instrument for cutting iron safes: 1862, Mayhew. See peter, n., 1.

*peter-drag. See peter-hunting. C.: C. 19–20; ob. See peter, n., 1, and drag.

Peter Funk. A member of a gang operating 'shadily' at public auctions: late C. 19–20. (Manchon.)

Peter Grievous. A fretful child: coll.: mid-C. 19–20; ob.—2. 'A miserable, melancholy fellow; a croaker': from ca. 1850: coll. H., 1874. ? a euphemising of *creeping Jesus*.

peter-gunner. A poor shot with a gun: coll.: C. 17–20; ob. Anon., *The Cold Year*, 1615 (quoted by Nares). Perhaps ex *petre*, saltpetre. Cf.:

Peter Gunner, will kill all the birds that died last summer. A C. 18–mid-19 (? also late C. 17) c.p.: 'A piece of wit commonly thrown out at a person walking through a street or village near London, with a gun in his hand', Grose, 2nd ed. Ex preceding entry.

*peter-hunting. The stealing of portmanteaux, boxes, etc., esp. from carriages: c.: Vaux, 1812; ob. Also *peter-drag* and *peter-lay*. See peter, n., 1. Whence:

*peter-hunting jemmy. 'A small crowbar used in

smashing the chains securing luggage to a vehicle ', F. & H. : c. : from ca. 1810 ; ob. Vaux.

*peter-lay. The same as *peter-hunting*, q.v., and as *peter-drag*. C. 18–20 c. *A New Canting Dict.*, 1725. See peter, n., 1.

Peter Lug. A drinking laggard. Chiefly in *Who is Peter Lug ?*, a c.p. addressed to one who lets the glass stand before him : ca. 1680–1830. B.E. ; Grose, 1st ed.

*peter-man, peterman. One who uses 'unlawful engines in catching fish in the river Thames ', Bailey : late C. 17–early 18 : c. Ex *peterman*, a fisherman.—2. One who specialises in stealing bags, etc., from carriages : from ca. 1810 ; ob. 1812, *The Sporting Magazine* (O.E.D.) ; Anon., *The Story of a Lancashire Thief*, 1863. Ex *peter*, n., 1.

peter out. To cease gradually ; come to an end : U.S. (1854) anglicised as a coll. almost imm. ; by 1930, S.E. H., 1859 (' To run short, or give out '), makes no mention of America ; *The Saturday Review*, Jan. 9, 1892, ' Human effort of all kinds tends to " peter out " ' (O.E.D.). ' Orig. U.S., of stream or lode of ore. ? from Fr. *péter* . . . ; ? cf. to *fizzle out* ', W.

Peter Pipeclay. A Royal Marine : naval : ca. 1820–90. Bowen. Ex his enforced use of pipe-clay. Cf. *pick him up*.

*peter school. A gambling den : New Zealand c. (— 1932). Cf. *peter*, 3.

*peter that ! See peter, v., 1.

Peter to pay Paul, rob ; in C. 17–19, occ. borrow from, as in Urquhart. To take from one person to give to another : C. 15–20 ; proverbial coll. >, ca. 1820, S.E. Barclay, 1548, has *clothe* (surviving till C. 18). Lytton, *Paul Clifford*, ' If so be as your name's Paul, may you always rob Peter [a portman-teau] in order to pay Paul.' Prob. not ex the rela-tions of the two Apostles but ' merely a collocation of familiar names, *Pierre et Paul* being used in Fr. like *Tom, Dick and Harry* in Eng.' : W.

*peterer. (Also peterman : see peter-man.) The same as *peter-man*, 2 : c. of ca. 1840–70. H., 1st ed.

Peterhouse. St. Peter's College, Cambridge : Cambridge University : C. 19–20. Until ca. 1890, s. ; ca. 1890–1920, coll. ; then S.E. Cf. *House*, 3.

*peterman. See peter-man.

*peters, biter of. See peter-biter.

Peter's needle, go or pass through St. (Of children) to be severely disciplined : C. 19–20 semi-proverbial coll. and dial. ? ex the Biblical eye of a needle.

petit(e) degree. Incorrect for *pedigree* : C. 16. O.E.D.

peto. A Society evasion, ca. 1905–14, for *p.t.o.* (please turn over). Ware.

petre. Saltpetre : late C. 16–20 : S.E. until ca. 1860 (though long ob.) ; then technical coll.

Petrol Hussars, the. ' The Armoured-Car force sent to Egypt in 1916 ' : naval, then military : latter 1916–18. ' Most of the officers had served in Hussar Regiments,' F. & Gibbons.

[petticoat. See at pace, go the.]

petticoat, up one's. Unduly, or very, familiar with a woman : low : C. 18–20 ; ob.

petticoat-hold. A life-interest in a wife's estate : coll. : late C. 18–19. Grose, 1st ed.

Petticoat Lane. Middlesex Street, London, E., where, esp. on Sunday morning, congregate many old-clothes and other itinerant dealers, mostly Jews : 1887, Anon., *I.D.B.*, ' Falling back on Pilomet for his expletives.' In Yiddish, *Pilomet* = the initials

(in Hebrew) *P.L.*—2. Hence, ca. 1900–15, Dover Street, Piccadilly, London, the locality favoured by Court milliners. *The Daily Telegraph*, Nov. 9, 1901.

petticoat-merchant. A whoremonger : low coll. : C. 19–20 ; ob. On S.E. *petticoat-monger* or *petti-coat-pensioner*.

pettifogger. See petty fogger.

pettiloon. A pantaloon : coll. : 1858, Whyte-Melville ; ob. Blend of *petticoat + pantaloon*. (O.E.D.)

petting-party. A party at which much caressing is done ; esp. a party held for that purpose : orig. U.S. ; anglicised ca. 1925. Cf. *necking*.

petty. A petticoat : coll. : from not later than 1913. Cf. *nightly*.

petty fogger ; perhaps more correctly pettifogger. A Customs man : nautical, esp. quay-hands' : late C. 19–20 ; ob.

petty-house. A water-closet : coll. : C. 19–20 ; slightly ob. ' Widely prevalent in familiar use ', Murray, 1905. Whence *little house*, q.v.

*petty lashery ; petulacery. Petty theft : c. : late C. 16–early 17. Both forms in Greene.

pettycoat. See petticoat.

pew. A seat, esp. in *take a pew, park oneself in a pew*, etc. : C. 20. P. G. Wodehouse, *A Prefect's Uncle*, 1903, ' The genial " take a pew " of one's equal inspires confidence ' ; Manchon.

pew, stump the. To pay : low : ca. 1820–30. Moncrieff, *Tom and Jerry*, 1823, ' It's every thing now o' days to be able to flash the screens—sport the rhino—show the needful—post the pony—nap the rent—stump the pew.' Prob. *pew* is an abbr. of *pewter*, 1.

pew-opener's muscle. A muscle in the palm of the hand : medical (— 1902). Sir James Brodie, ' because it helps to contract and hollow the palm of the hand for the reception of a gratuity '.

*pewter. Silver : c. (— 1823) ; † by 1900. Egan's Grose.—2. Hence, money, esp. if of silver ; prize-money : low : 1842, Egan, in *Macheath* (O.E.D.).—3. A tankard : mostly London coll. (1839), verging on S.E. ; ob. Abbr. *pewter tankard*.—Hence, 4, a pot sought as a prize : rowing men's (— 1874) ; ob. H., 5th ed.

pewy. (Of country) so enclosed by fences as to form a succession of small fields : sporting (esp. hunting) : 1828 (O.E.D.). Ex the shape of the old-fashioned big, enclosed pews.

pferfy. Incorrect for *furphy*, q.v.—pfiffing. See piffing, 2.

[ph- is notable for the number of incorrect forms : most of which, thanks to the O.E.D., are noted hereinunder.]

phænigm is a spelling error for *phœnigm* : mid-C. 17–mid-19. O.E.D.

[-phagous, -eating, appears in jocular S.E. verging on coll.]

phalerical. Erroneous for *phalarical* : C. 17. O.E.D.

phalucco is a C. 17 error for *felucca*, phan a C. 16 one for *fan*, phane (C. 15–17) for *fane*, phang(ed) (C. 17) for *fang(ed)*, phangle for *fangle* in C. 17, while phantomnation is a ghostword. O.E.D.

phan. See fan, n., 3.

phant ; or fant ; in the North of England, often *peeble*, by evasion. A phantom-glass, i.e. that sheet of plate-glass, which, set obliquely on the stage, reflects from below, or from the side, the illusion known as Pepper's ghost : showmen's (— 1909). Ware.

Phar Lap. A derisive Australian nickname (from 1933) for a person slow in his movements. Ex Phar Lap, a splendid Australian race-horse (its name = ' flash of lightning ') that died of poison in Mexico in 1933.

pharaoh ; occ. **pharoh.** A strong ale or beer : late C. 17–early 19. Gen. as *old pharaoh*, q.v. Prob. ex strength derived from oldness—' old as Pharaoh '.

Pharaoh's Foot. ' The companies of Volunteers raised among European civilians in Egypt in 1915 ' : military : 1915–18. F. & Gibbons. Egypt being ' the Land of the Pharaohs '.

Pharaoh's lean kine, one of. A very thin person : coll. : 1598, Shakespeare, ' If to be fat be to be hated, then Pharaoh's lean kine are to be loved.'— 2. In C. 19–20, with the qualification of looking ' (1) as though he'd run away from a bone-house ; or (2) as if he were walking about to save funeral expenses ' (F. & H.) ; ob.

phase. An error for *prase* : C. 19–20 ; ob.—2. For *faze*, to disturb, perturb : late C. 19–20 ; ob.— 3. An incorrect form of *pasch, pace* (in Easter sense). O.E.D.

phat(e). Incorrect spelling of *fat* = vat : C. 17. O.E.D.

phaune. A wrong spelling of *fawn*, v. : C. 16. O.E.D.

pheasant. A wanton : low : C. 17–19 ; ob. Cf. *plover* and *quail*.—2. See **Billingsgate pheasant.**

pheasantry. A brothel : low : C. 19–20 ; ob. Ex *pheasant*, 1.

phenomena. Incorrect for *phenomenon* : col. : C. 19–20. Agatha Christie, *The Thirteen Problems* 1932, ' The phenomena was not genuine.' Cf. *data* for *datum, strata* for *stratum.*

phenomenon. A prodigy ; a remarkable person, occ. animal, or thing : coll. : 1838, Dickens, ' This is the infant phenomenon—Miss Ninetta Crumbles,' O.E.D.

phi, occ. in Gr. form φ or φι. ' A Phi book . . . is a book deemed by Bodley's Librarian to be of an indelicate nature, and catalogued accordingly, by some dead and gone humorist, under the Greek letter *Phi*', Dorothy Sayers (herself an Oxford ' first ') in *The Passing Show*, March 25, 1933. Until 1931 when proposed alterations to the Library evoked articles in the Press, the term was known to very few persons outside Oxford.

Phil and Jim. (Occ. pronounced *Fillin Jim*.) The Church of St. Philip and St. James : Oxford undergraduates' : from ca. 1885. Ware.

philabeg. An incorrect form of *philibeg*, a barbarous variant of *filibeg*, a kilt.

Philadelphia lawyer. A smart attorney ; a very shrewd person. Esp. in *puzzle* or *beat a P.l.*, to be extremely puzzling, and *be as smart* or *know as much as a P.l.* A U.S. coll. (1803) introduced into England ca. 1860 ; ob. by 1920. H., 1864 ; Hindley. Cf. *bush-lawyer*, q.v.

philander, ' to ramble on incoherently ; to write discursively and weakly ', H., 1874, like the sense, ' to wander about ' (as in Arthur Sketchley, quoted by Baumann), is a half-sol., half-coll. of ca. 1865– 1910. ? influenced by *meander* and *wander.*

philarea. Incorrect for *phillyrea* : C. 17–18. O.E.D.

Philharmonic. Philharmonic Society : coll. : 1862 (O.E.D.).—2. A Philharmonic concert : coll. : from ca. 1875.

Philip. A policeman, mostly in *Philip !*, the

police are coming ! : c. : from ca. 1860 ; ob. Possibly by a punning reference to *fillip*. Whence *Philiper.*

Philip and Che(i)n(e)y. Two of the common people considered typically : coll. : ca. 1540–90. Tusser has *Philip, Hob and Cheyney*. Cf. *Tom, Dick and Harry.*

philipende, philipendula. Incorrect † forms of *vilipend, filipendula*. O.E.D.

Philiper, philip(p)er. A thief's accomplice : c. : 1860, *The Times*, Sept. 5 ; ob. See **Philip.**

Philippi, meet at. To keep an appointment without fail : literary coll. : ca. 1780–1830. Mrs. Cowley, 1782, ' '' At seven, you say ? '' . . . '' Exactly.'' . . . '' I'll meet thee at Philippi ! '' ' Ex Shakespeare's *Julius Cæsar*, IV, iii, where the ghost speaks thus.

Philistine. (Gen. pl.) A drunkard : late C. 17– 18. B.E.

Philistines. (See **pace, go the.**)—2. Earwigs or other such insects : provincial coll., and dial. : late C. 17–20. Ex ' The Philistines are upon thee,' Judges xvi.

phillipine, cheny. Incorrect for *Philip and Cheyney*, an inferior worsted or woollen stuff (C. 17), as, in C. 19–20, is *philippize*, v.i. and t., if = utter a philippic against. O.E.D.

philm. Error for *film* : C. 16–18. O.E.D.

philosella, philly. Incorrect, ob. forms of *filosella, filly.* O.E.D.

philogenesis, -genetic. Errors for *phylogenesis, -genetic* : from ca. 1875. O.E.D.

philomot is wrong for *filemot*. (O.E.D.)

Phineas. ' The wooden Highlander . . . now [1932] the inalienable property of University College, London ' : from ca. 1875. Weekley, *Words and Names.*

phinney. A burial : c. : C. 18 (?–19). C. Hitchin, *The Regulator*, 1718. Origin ?

Phip. A sparrow : coll. and dial. : C. 14–16. Less a contraction of *Philip* (in same sense) than ex the onomatopœia for a sparrow's chirp.

phis. B.E.'s spelling of *phiz*. Cf. *phys*, 1693 (O.E.D.). Both occur also in C. 18.

phiz (phizz), phyz ; physog. (Cf. *phis*, q.v.) Face ; expression of face : *phiz*, etc., is a jocularly coll. abbr. of *physiognomy* ; *physog*, however, is the abbr. of *physognomy*, q.v. Shadwell, 1688 ; Swift, ' Abbreviations exquisitely refined ; as, . . . *Phizz* for Phisiognomy.' But *physog*, q.v., not till C. 19. A *rum phiz* is an odd one : low : late C. 18–20.

phiz-gig. An old woman dressed young : C. 19. —2. ' A pyramid of moistened gunpowder, which, on ignition, fuses but does not flash ', F. & H. schools' : from ca. 1840.—3. See **fiz-gig.**

phiz-maker. A maker of grimaces : C. 18 : coll.

phizog. See **physog** ; also **phiz.**

phlizz. A failure : from ca. 1925 ; ob. Galsworthy, *The Silver Spoon*, 1926. A blend of *flop* + *fizzle.*

phob. A C. 17 error for *fob*, a small pocket. O.E.D.

[**phœnix-man**, a fireman paid by an insurance office : rather S.E. than coll. : C. 18.]

phone, 'phone. N. and v., *telephone* : coll. : n., 1884 ; v., 1900 (O.E.D.). From ca. 1910, gen. *phone* ; now virtually S.E.—2. Hence a telephone-message : coll. : C. 20.

phoney or **phony,** n. Blarney : c. : from ca. 1930. James Curtis, *The Gilt Kid*, 1936. Ex :

*phoney ; occ. phony. Fraudulent, ' shady ', criminal : c. : U.S., anglicised ca. 1920. Edgar Wallace's later works. Ex *fawney*, q.v.

phos, phoss, even foss. Phosphorus : s. >, ca. 1890, coll. abbr. : from ca. 1810.—2. Esp., in c. of early C. 19, a bottle of phosphorus, used by cracksmen to get a light. *Lex. Bal.* ; Vaux. Whence *phossy*, q.v.

phosgene. An anti-gas instructor, *phosgene* being a German poison-gas ; hence, foolish or profane talk (cf. *gas*, q.v.) : military : 1916–18. F. & Gibbons.

phosphorous. A frequent written error for *phosphorus* : late C. 18–20.

phossy, occ. fossy, jaw. Phosphorus necrosis of the jaw : coll. : 1889. O.E.D.

photo. A photograph : coll. abbr. : 1870, Miss Bridgman, ' I should like her photo.'—2. As v. : coll. : 1870, Carlyle.—3. As adj. : likewise coll. (technical) : 1889. O.E.D.

photographic. (Of a face) easily or strikingly photographable : coll. : from ca. 1910.

phrasy ; incorrectly, phrasey. Abounding in or notable for phrases : coll. : 1849. O.E.D.

phrenetic. Erroneous when used for *phrenic* : C. 18–20 ; rare in C. 19–20. O.E.D.

phunt. One pound sterling : grafters' : late C. 19–20. Philip Allingham, *Cheapjack*, 1934. Perhaps derived ex *ponte* (q.v.) and influenced by Ger. *Pfund*.

phusee, phusy. Errors for the *fusee* of a watch. O.E.D.

phut, go. (See also fut.) To come to grief ; fizzle out ; be a failure : coll. : 1892, Kipling (O.E.D. Sup.) ; A. S. M. Hutchinson, 1908. Partly echoic (cf. *phit*), partly ex Hindustani *phatna*, to explode. O.E.D

phuz. Incorrect for *fuzz*, ' loose volatile matter ' : C. 17.—phy ! Wrong for *fie* ; †.—phyllarea (-erea), phyllet, phyllirea. † errors for *phyllyrea* and *filet*. O.E.D.

phyllis, Phyllis. *Syphilis* : medical and military euphemistic coll. rather than s. : from ca. 1910.

phymosis. Incorrect for *phimosis* : C. 17. O.E.D.

phys. See phis.

physic. Sexual attentions ; coïtion : coll. : C. 17–mid-18. Massinger, ' She . . . sends for her young doctor, | Who ministers physic to her on her back ' ; D'Urfey.—2. Medicine : late C. 16–20 : S.E. till ca. 1850, then coll. Mrs. Henry Wood, 1862, ' You'll take the physic, like a precious lamb,' O.E.D.—3. Losses ; wagers, points : gaming : from ca. 1820 ; ob. ' Jon Bee.'—4. Hard hitting : pugilistic : from ca. 1830 ; ob. Cf. *punishment*, q.v.—5. Strong drink : from ca. 1840. Cf. *medicine, poison*, qq.v.

physic, v. To treat, dose, with medicine, esp. with a purgative : C. 14–20 : S.E. till ca. 1850, then coll. Cf. *physic*, n., 2. (O.E.D.)—2. ' To punish in purse or pocket ' : 1821, Egan ; ob. Cf. *physic*, n., 3.

physic - bottle. A doctor : non - aristocratic (— 1909). Ware.

physical jerks. See jerks.

physical torture. A rare variant (1915) of the preceding. F. & Gibbons. Ex *physical culture*.

physicals. Physical powers : coll. : 1824. Rare in C. 20 ; ob. O.E.D.

physicking, n. and adj. Corresponding to *physic*, n., 2., and *physic*, v., 1 and 2 : mid-C. 17–20 : S.E. until ca. 1810, then coll. Bee, 1823, both n. and adj.

physiog. A coll. abbr. of *physiognomy*, q.v. : ca. 1865–1920. Cf. *phiz* and *physog*.

physiognomy. The face or countenance : (low) coll. : C. 17–20 ; ob. Fletcher & Shirley, ' I have seen that physiognomy : were you never in prison ? ' O.E.D. Cf. *physognomy*.

physiognomist. See conjuror.

physog ; occ. phizog, phyzog. See phiz. App. recorded first in the *Lex. Bal.*, 1811. Cf. *physiog*.

physognomy. Physiognomy : sol. : C. 19–20. See physiognomy.

phyz. See phiz ; cf. *physiog, physog* ; note *physiognomy*.

phyzog. See physog.

pi ; gen. pie. A miscellaneous collection of books out of the *alphabet*, q.v. : booksellers coll. : from ca. 1880 ; ob. Ex *printer's pi(e)*.—2. (Only pi.) A pious exhortation : Public Schools' and universities' : 1870, O.E.D.—3. Cf. the adj., whence *pi*, a pious person : late C. 19–20 ; ob. Ex *pious*.

pi, adj. Pious ; virtuous ; sanctimonious : schools' and universities' : 1870, O.E.D., whose first record of the adj., however, is for 1891. Cf. *pi*, n., 2.

pi-gas, -jaw. A serious admonition or talk : schools' and universities' : ? (*jaw*) from ca. 1875 ; -*gas*, ca. 1880–1915. Ex :

pi-jaw. To give moral advice to ; admonish : schools' and universities' : from middle 1880's. Ex *pi*, adj. F. & H., 1902, quoting a glossary of 1891, ' He pi-jawed me for thoking.' Cf. *pi-gas, pi-squash*, and :

pi-man. A pious fellow : from ca. 1900 ; ob. *To-Day*, Aug. 22, 1901. Ex *pi*, adj., q.v., but prob. also containing a pun on *pieman*.

pi-squash. A prayer-meeting ; any similar assemblage : schools' and universities' : from ca. 1910 ; slightly ob. W. Ex *pi*, adj., q.v. Cf. *pi-gas*, q.v.

piache. Mad ; on *stone-mad*, often *stone-piache* : Regular Army's : late C. 19–20. B. & P. (p. 222) ; Ex Hindustani.

pialler. To speak ; speak to : New South Wales and Queensland ' pidgin ' : mid-C. 19–20. R. M. Praed, 1885. (Morris.) Ex an Aboriginal dialect : cf. *yabber*, q.v.

piano. To sing small, take a back seat : Society : ca. 1870–80. Ex musical *piano*, softly. (Ware.)

pianoforte legs. The legs of a bishop in ecclesiastical costume : jocular (— 1923). Manchon. Ex the former draping of the mahogany, therefore *black*, legs of a piano : cf. *ampute one's mahogany*.

piazzas, walk the. (Of prostitutes) to look for men : ca. 1820–70. ' Jon Bee.' Ex the piazzas—wrongly so called—of Covent Garden.—2. Hence, ca. 1870–1910, to walk the streets : likewise of prostitutes.

pibroch is occ. used erroneously as if = bagpipes : from ca. 1720. O.E.D.

pic. A picture : artists' : C. 20. C. E. Montague, *A Hind Let Loose*, 1910.—2. See pics, 1.

Pic, the. The Piccadilly Saloon, London : ca. 1858–90. H., 2nd ed. Cf. *Dilly*, q.v.—2. The Piccadilly Restaurant and Grill Room : C. 20. (Anthony Gibbs, *London Symphony*, 1934.)—3. See Sunday Pic.

picaninny. See piccaninny.

picaro, on the. ' On the make ', prowling for easy money : coll. : C. 18. Smollett, trans. of *Gil Blas*, ' I see you have been . . . a little on the picaro.' Ex Sp. *picaro*, a rogue, via the English *picaroon* (Sp. *picarón*).

Piccadilly Butchers, the. The First Life Guards, says F. & H.; First Horse Guards, says H.; the Life Guards, F. & Gibbons: C. 19–20 military; ob. They were called out to quell the Burdett or Piccadilly Riots of 1810. (Actually, only one rioter was killed.) Cf. *Patent Safeties.*

Piccadilly crawl. A style of walking prevalent in Society in the Eighties. Ob. Cf. *Alexandra limp, Grecian bend, Roman fall*, qq.v.

Piccadilly fringe. 'Front hair of women cut short and brought down, and curled over the forehead': lower classes': ca. 1884–1900. Presumably suggested by *Piccadilly weepers*. Ware states that the 'fashion originated in Paris about 1868'.

[**Piccadilly Patriot, the.** Sir Francis Burdett (1770–1844), politician. Rather a sobriquet than a nickname proper.]

Piccadilly weepers. 'Long carefully combed-out whiskers of the Dundreary fashion', H., 1874. Ob. Because worn by dandies on Piccadilly, London. Cf. *dundrearies*. Cf.:

Piccadilly window. A monocle: London (non-aristocratic): the 1890's; ob. Ware. Because frequently seen in Piccadilly.

piccaninny; occ. **picaninny** or **pickanin(n)y.** A child: coll. bordering on S.E.: 1785, Grose; 1817, 'The little pickaninny has my kindest wishes' (O.E.D.). Orig. applied, in the West Indies and America, to Negro and other coloured children. Ex C. 17 'Negro diminutive of Sp. *pequeño* or Portuguese *pequeno*, small . . .; cf. Port. *pequenino*, tiny. It is uncertain whether the word arose in Sp. or Port. colonies, or in the E. or W. Indies, but it has spread remarkably,' W.

piccaninny, adj. Little: Australian coll.: from 1840's; slightly ob. Morris. Ex preceding.

picey, adj. Mean: Regular Army: late C. 19–20. B. & P. Perhaps ex *pice*, a quarter-anna.

pick. An abbr. (— 1887) of S.E. *pickwick*, a very inferior cigar: Baumann.—2. A toothpick: coll. (— 1890). *The Century Dict.*—3. An anchor: nautical: late C. 19–20. Bowen.—4. A quick-tempered person: Anglo-Irish: C. 20. Cf. *pick on.*

pick, v.i. To eat: 1786, Capt. T. Morris, 'If it wasn't for shame, I could pick till to-morrow at dinner': s. till C. 20, then coll. Ex S.E. sense, to eat daintily.

pick, adj. Chosen; best: coll.: 1819, Lady Morgan; ob. Ex *pick*, choice. (O.E.D.)

pick, take a. To be spiteful: Glasgow (— 1934). Cf. *pick at* and *pick on.*

pick a hole in (a person's) **coat.** To be censorious: coll. verging on S.E.: late C. 16–19. Anon., *Martin Prelate's Epitome*, 1588; Ray; Manning in a letter to Lamb. Apperson. Whence S.E. *pick holes in.*

pick a soft plank! Sleep easy!: a nautical c.p. addressed to 'young seamen sleeping on deck for the first time': mid-C. 19–20; ob. Bowen.—2. Hence, to find an easy job: nautical coll.: late C. 19–20. Ibid.

pick and cut. To pick pockets: low coll. (? orig. s.): C. 17. Shakespeare, *Winter's Tale*, 'I picked and cut most of their festival purses.'

pick-and-dab. A meal of potatoes and salt: Scots coll.: C. 19–20.

pick at. 'To chaff; to annoy', C. J. Dennis: Australian coll. (— 1916). Ex dial. Cf. *pick on.*

pick-axe. 'A fiery mixture of Cape smoke, pontac'—a dark, dry wine medicinally valuable—

'and ginger-beer, in much request in the diamond fields', Pettman: South African: ca. 1870–90. Boyle, *To the Cape for Diamonds*, 1873. Ex its 'brutality'.

pick flies off. To find fault with: tailors': from ca. 1860; ob.

Pick- (or **Picked-**) **Hatch.** See **Pickt-Hatch.**

pick him up and pipeclay him and he'll do again! A bluejackets' c.p. remark on a Royal Marine fallen on the deck, esp. if he fell hard: ca. 1860–1910. Bowen.

pick-it-up. The diamond bird: Australian boys' coll.: from mid-1890's. G. A. Keartland, 1896, gives the origin in this bird's 'treble note'. Morris.

pick-me-up. A stimulating liquid, orig. and mainly liquor: coll.: 1867, Latham, 'To drink home-brewed ale . . . instead of pick-me-ups'.— 2. Hence, any person or thing (e.g. seaside air) with a bracing effect: 1876, 'Ouida' (of a person). O.E.D.

pick on. To gird at; annoy actively: coll.: C. 20. Ex dial. *pick upon*. The O.E.D.'s 'Now *U.S. dial.*' ignores the coll. Eng. usage, which undoubtedly exists, esp. as = pick a quarrel with. Cf. the v. *pick up*, q.v.

pick on, get a. See **get a pick on.**

pick out robins' eyes. To side-stitch black cloth or any delicate material: tailors': from ca. 1860; ob. by 1920.

pick-penny. A miser: coll. bordering on S.E.: C. 18–19. Ex S.E. sense, a greedy amasser or stealer of money.—2. A sharper: coll.: ? C. 17–18. F. & H.

pick the bird. To dissect a corpse: medical students' (— 1923). Manchon.

*pick the daisies (at —— Station). To rob passengers arriving in London by the Continental boat-trains: c.: from ca. 1920.—2. Hence, *pick-up (man)*, a luggage-thief: c. (— 1932). 'Stuart Wood.'

pick-up. A chance (esp. if carnal) acquaintance (gen. female): low coll. (— 1895). Funk & Wagnall's. Ex the S.E. *pick up with*, to make acquaintance with someone casually met.—2. See **pick the daisies,** 2.—3. A recovery of form: lawn-tennis coll.: from ca. 1927. E.g. 'A wonderful pick-up! From 1–5 to 5 games all.'—4. A pick-up match: coll.: late C. 19–20. One in which the opposing sides are chosen by the two captains selecting one player alternately.—5. Hence, a team in such a match: coll.: C. 20. Both 4 and 5 occur in Alec Waugh, *The Loom of Youth*, 1917.

pick up, v. To cheat, grossly deceive (a person): low (— 1860); † by 1900. H., 2nd ed. Ex:— 2. To 'establish contact' with an unwary person: c. (— 1812); ob. Vaux.—3. To meet casually, esp. of a man on the look-out for a girl: late C. 19–20. Cf. preceding entry. Orig. of harlot 'picking up' a man: c. or low: from ca. 1810 (Vaux, 1812. Cf. sense 2.) Cf. the dial. nuances recorded by the E.D.D.—4. To take (a person up) sharply: coll.: C. 20.—5. (Cf. senses 2, 3.) To rob a man thus: he is allured into speaking with a harlot, whose bully then comes up to extort money or who herself decamps after taking his money 'in advance' and perhaps his watch as well: c. (— 1861). Mayhew.

*pick-up man. See **pick the daisies.**

pick up one's crumbs. To be convalescent: coll.: 1580, Lyly; 1754, Berthelson; in mid-C. 19–

20, dial. **I.e. to** put on weight as well as to eat healthily.

pickanin(n)y. See **piccaninny.**

*picker-up. A thief or a swindler ' picking up ' an unwary person : c. (— 1812) ; ob. Vaux. See **pick up,** v.—2. Hence, a harlot : c. : mid-C. 19–20. ob.—3. ' A dealer buying on quotations trickily obtained from a member trapped into giving a wrong price ', F. & H. : Stock Exchange : from ca. 1890.

pickers and stealers. Hands : coll. : C. 17–20 ; slightly ob. Shakespeare, ' So I do still, by these pickers and stealers.' Ex the Catechism ' To keep my hands from picking and stealing ', which dates from 1548–9 (O.E.D.). Baumann considered Shakespeare's use to be s. ; the O.E.D. considers the phrase, at no matter what period, to be S.E.

picking gooseberries ! Goodness knows ! ; doing God knows what ! : a c.p. of early C. 19. John Davis, *The Post Captain,* 1805 (ed. R. H. Case, 1928).

pickle. A predicament, sorry plight, unpleasant difficulty : mid-C. 16–20 : S.E. till C. 19, then coll. Byron, ' The Turkish batteries thrash'd them . . . into a sad pickle ' (O.E.D.). A fig. use of the lit. secondary S.E. sense, pickled vegetables.—2. Hence, perhaps via *rod in pickle,* a mischievous or ob.—a troublesome child ; any person constantly causing trouble : coll. : the former, late C. 18–20 ; the latter, late C. 18–19. Anon., *History of a Schoolboy,* 1788, ' He told Master Blotch he was a pickle, and dismissed him to his cricket.' O.E.D.— 3. Hence, a wild youth or young man : s. or coll. : ca. 1810–40. *Lex. Bal.*—4. A wretchedly produced, cheap book : booksellers' (— 1887) ; ob. Baumann. Esp. one that won't sell.

pickle, v. To humbug ; to ' gammon ' ; C. 19. Perhaps ex nautical S.E. sense, to rub salt or vinegar on the back of a person just flogged.

pickle, in. Venereally infected : low coll. : late C. 17–early 19. B.E., Grose. Ex salivation.—2. Drunk : late C. 17–mid-18. Farquhar (*in that pickle*) ; Vanbrugh. (*Slang,* p. 65.)

pickle, rod in. See **rod in pickle.**

*pickle-herring. A wag ; a merry companion : c. (— 1887). Baumann.

pickle-jar. A coachman in yellow : ca. 1850– 1910.

pickle-manufacturer. A publisher of cheap, badly produced books : booksellers' : ca. 1885– 1914. Baumann. See **pickle,** n., 4.

pickle-me-tickle-me, play. To coït : low coll. : mid-C. 17–18. Urquhart.

pickled. Roguish ; waggish : coll. verging on S.E. : late C. 17–early 19. B.E., Grose. Cf. *pickle,* n., 2.—2. Drunk : from ca. 1930. C.O.D. (1934 Sup.). For semantics, cf. *oiled* and *soused.*

pickles. Dissection specimens (straight) from the operation theatre : medical : from ca. 1860.— 2. As an exclamation, nonsense ! or b*lls ! : from ca. 1850 ; ob. H. Also *all pickles* (Ware).

pickles, case of. A quandary ; a serious break-down : C. 19–20 ; ob.

pickpocket. A ship able to carry but little cargo : nautical : C. 20. Bowen.

Pickt-Hatch (often Pict-, occ. Pick-, and properly **Picked-Hatch**), go to the Manor of, late C. 16–mid-17 ; go to Pickt-Hatch Grange, ca. 1620–40. To go whoring ; to whore : c., says Grose ; more prob. s. or low coll. In Shakespeare's time, specifically a brothelly tavern in Turnmill Street, Clerkenwell ;

hence, from ca. 1620, any brothel or low locality. A pickt hatch, i.e. a hatch with pikes, was a common brothel-sign. Shakespeare, in *Merry Wives* ; Jonson ; Randolph, ' Why the whores of Pict-Hatch, Turnbull, or the unmerciful bawds of Bloomsbury.'

picnic. A rough-and-tumble ; noisy trouble : coll. : from ca. 1895. F. & H. records it at 1898. Prob. ex :—2. ' An awkward adventure, an unpleasant experience, a troublesome job ', Morris : Australian coll. : at least as early as 1896. Ex the U.S. coll. sense, ' an easy or agreeable thing ', *The Standard Dict.* From ca. 1915, mostly *no picnic,* a difficult task, and by 1918 gen. coll.—3. Hence, a detention : Bootham School (— 1925). Anon., *Dict. of Bootham Slang.*

picnicky. As at or as of a picnic : coll. : 1870. O.E.D.

pics (or **pics.**), **the.** The illustrations : journalists' and authors' : C. 20. Neil Bell, *Winding Road,* 1934.—2. Occ. in the singular, of an artist's picture : artists' : C. 20. Ibid. See also **pic, 1.**

Pict-Hatch. See **Pickt-Hatch.**

picture. A portrait, a likeness, of a person : C. 16–20 : S.E. until ca. 1890, then coll. when not affected. O.E.D.—2. A fine example ; a beau-ideal : coll. (— 1870). E.D.D. ; Baumann. E.g., ' a picture of health ' ; often ironical as in ' a pretty picture ', a strange figure (F. & H., 1902).— 3. Hence, a very picturesque or beautiful object : coll. : from ca. 1890. E.g. ' She's a picture.' In Berkshire dial. as early as 1859 (E.D.D.). See also **oil-painting** and **pretty as paint.**

picture, fake a. See **fake a picture.**

picture, not in the. Inappropriate, incongruous ; (in racing) unplaced : coll. : late C. 19–20. Cf. *not in it.*

picture or portrait, King's or Queen's. See **Queen's picture.**

picture-askew. A jocular perversion of *picturesque* : coll. : from ca. 1870. Cf. *finance* and *gust,* qq.v.

picture-frame. See **sheriff's picture-frame.**

picture of, make a. To render (a person) unrecognisable : coll. : C. 20. Manchon. Ex *picture,* 2.

picture-show. A big battle : military : 1915 ; † by 1920. G. H. McKnight, *English Words,* 1923.

pictures. ' A jocular name for the flitches of bacon, &c., when hanging to a ceiling or against a wall ' : South Lancashire s. (— 1905) rather than dial. E.D.D. (Sup.).

pictures, lawful. See **lawful pictures.**

pictures, the. The cinema : coll. : 1915, Thomas Burke, ' Mother and Father . . . go to the pictures at the Palladium near Balham Station ' (O.E.D. Sup.).—2. Hence, an operating-theatre : military : 1916 ; ob. F. & Gibbons. Under ether (e.g.) one sees fantastic things in dream.

piddle. Urine ; occ., the act of making water : coll., mostly nursery : C. 19–20. Ex :

piddle, v. To urinate : late C. 18–20 : coll., esp. childish ; in C. 20, low coll. Grose, 3rd ed. Ex *piss* influenced by *peddle* ; perhaps an unconscious blend.—2. Hence, of rain : low (— 1887). Baumann, ' It piddled buckets.'

pidgin, rarely **pidjun,** often **pigeon** ; occ. **pidjin.** Pidgin- or pigeon-English, ' the jargon, consisting chiefly of English words, often corrupted in pronunciation, and arranged according to Chinese idiom, used for intercommunication between Chinese and Europeans at seaports etc ', S.O.D. :

coll. abbr. >, by 1930, S.E.: from ca. 1855. (By itself, *pidgin*, etc., occurs in 1850). W. gives an excellent official example (see my **um**). A Chinese corruption of *business*, perhaps via *bidginess*, *bidgin*; *pigeon* is an English 'improvement' on *pidgin*. (See esp. Fowler.) Cf. *Beach-la-Mar* and *Lingua Franca*. 2. See **pigeon**, n., 6.

pie. See **pi**, **pie.**—2. See **pye.**—3. A prize, treat, 'easy thing': U.S., s., anglicised ca. 1910. Ex *fruit pie.*—4. Hence, as adj.: from ca. 1912.

pie !, by Cock and. See **cock and (by) pie !, by.**—

pie, find a. See **find a pie.**

pie, like. Zestfully, vigorously: s. verging on coll.: from ca. 1885; ob. Henley, 1887, 'I goes for 'Olman 'Unt like pie.' ? ex zestful eating of pie.

pie, make a. To combine with a view to profit: coll.: ca. 1820–1910. Ex concerted cooking.

pie, put in. See **put in pie.**

pie-ard. A term of abuse in the Regular Army: late C. 19–20. Ex Hindustani for a pariah dog.

pie-can. A fool; a half-wit: lower classes' (— 1923). Manchon. ? cf. *juggins* and *muggins*.

pie-jaw or **piejaw.** Incorrect forms of *pi-jaw*. A. H. Tod, *Charterhouse*, 1900.

pie in the sky. Paradise; heaven: from ca. 1918. Ex the U.S. song, 'There'll be pie in the sky when you die.'

pie on. Very good: New Zealanders': C. 20. Prob. ex Maori *pai ana*.

pie-pusher. A street pieman: low coll. (— 1909). Ware.

pie-shop. A dog: low London: 1842–ca. 1915. Ware.

piebald. V.t., formed (— 1909) ex, and corresponding to *piebald eye*, q.v.

piebald, adj. 'Bloody': euphemistic (— 1923). Manchon. Cf. *ruddy*.

piebald eye. A black eye: low: late C. 19–20. Ware.

piebald mucker sheeny. A low old Jew: East London (— 1909). Ware.

piece. A woman or girl: C. 14–20: S.E. until late C. 18, then (low) coll. and gen. pejorative. Esp. sexually, as in Grose, 3rd ed.: 'A damned good or bad piece; a girl who is more or less active and skilful in the amorous congress'. (Also C. 19–20 dial.) Cf. the Cambridge toast, ca. 1810–30, 'May we never have a piece (peace) that will injure the Constitution.'—2. A half-crown; gen. *two pieces*, *5s.*, or *three pieces*, *7s. 6d.*: racing c.: C. 20. Abbr. *half-crown piece.*—3. A slice of bread: Scottish, esp. Glaswegian, coll.: late C. 19–20.—4. See **piece, the.**

piece, drunken. A drunkard: coll. (— 1923). Manchon.

piece, on. Very much; very quickly: military (other ranks'): from ca. 1930. A man buying many drinks within a very short space of time is said to *get them in on piece*.

piece, (right) through the. For the duration of the War: military coll., mostly New Zealand: 1915; ob. B. & P. Ex sitting through a play.

piece, the. The thing, matter, affair; it: lower classes': late C. 19–20. E.g., 'He'll fight the piece out with you.'

piece of entire. A jolly fellow: ca. 1820–80. Cf. later *bit of all right*.

piece of muslin. A female, esp. a girl: (low) coll.: ca. 1875–1910. Prob. an elaboration of S.E. *piece of goods*: cf. the C. 20 *bit of skirt*.

piece of mutton. A female viewed as a sexual partner: low coll.: C. 17–early 19.

piece of work. A commotion, fuss, disorderly bustle: coll.: 1810, 'He kept jawing us, and making a piece of work all the time,' O.E.D.—2. A person: from ca. 1920. Always pejorative: nearly always preceded by *nasty* ('X is a nasty piece of work'); the reference is either to moral character or to physical appearance, esp. looks, the latter often with an ethical implication.

piece-out. Employment, a job (esp. if temporary), a loan: tailors': from ca. 1860. F. & H.; *The Tailor and Cutter*, Nov. 29, 1928. Ex the S.E. v. sense, 'to enlarge by the addition of a piece': cf. also S.E. *piece-work*.

pieces, all to. Gen. with *be* or *go*. Exhausted; collapsed; ruined: from ca. 1665: coll. till C. 19, then S.E. Pepys, Aug. 29, 1667, 'The Court is at this day all to pieces'; Ray, of a bankrupt.

pieces, fall or **go to.** To be brought to childbed: mid-C. 19–20: s. > coll.

piejaw. See **pie-jaw.**

pieman. The player who cries at pitch-and-toss: from ca. 1850; ob. Ex the real pieman's cry, 'Hot pies, toss or buy, toss or buy'. H.—2. See **pi-man.**

pier-head jump, do a. 'To join a ship at the last moment': nautical: C. 20. Bowen.

piercer. A piercing eye: 1752, Foote, 'She had but one eye . . ., but that was a piercer,' O.E.D.: s. until C. 19, then coll.; slightly ob.—2. A squint-eye says F. & H., 1902; I suspect this to be an error.

piffer. A member of the **P**unjaub **I**rregular **F**rontier **F**orce: military: from ca. 1890. O.E.D. (Sup.). Ex *piff*, a thinned form of *puff*, to blow.

piffing. An † variant of *spiffing*, q.v.: never very gen.—2. N., sub-calibre firing: artillerymen's coll.: from ca. 1925. Also naval gunners', gen. as *pfiffing*: Bowen.

piffle. Very ineffective talk; feeble, foolish nonsense: from ca. 1890: s. ex dial. (C. 19–20) > S.E. ca. 1925. Ex echoic *piff* (W.), though imm. ex the v. *The Saturday Review*, Feb. 1, 1890, '. . . "piffle" (to use a University phrase . . .'. O.E.D.—2. A rifle; to shoot therewith: Charterhouse: C. 20. By perversion.

piffle, v. To talk, to act, in an ineffective, esp. in a feeble, manner: dial. (— 1847) >, ca. 1880, s. >, ca. 1925, S.E. Halliwell. For origin, see the n.—2. See the n., 2.

piffler. An ineffective trifler; a twaddler; 'an earnest futility, i.e. a person with a moral end in view, and nothing to back it but a habit of talking, or writing sentimental rubbish', F. & H.: 1892 (O.E.D.): s. >, ca. 1925, S.E. Ex *piffle*, v.

piffling, adj. Trivial; feebly foolish; twaddling: C. 20: s. >, ca. 1925, S.E. Ex *piffle*, v.

*pig. A sixpence: c.: from ca. 1620; ob. Fletcher, 1622; Grose. Cf. *hog*, q.v.—2. A policeman, a detective; esp. (also *grunter*) a police-runner: c. of ca. 1810–90. Vaux; H., who, in 1873, writes, 'Now almost exclusively applied by London thieves to a plain-clothes man, or a "nose ".'—3. A pressman: printers': 1841, Savage's *Dict.* Cf. *donkey*, q.v.—4. See *hog*, n., Cambridge University sense.—5. A garment completely spoiled: tailors': from ca. 1860; ob. Also *pork.*—6. Hence, goods returned by a retailer to a wholesaler, or by wholesaler to manufacturer: drapers': from ca. 1870.—7. See **Pigs.**—8. A small piece, esp. a bit, i.e. a section, of orange children's, mostly Cockney (— 1887). Baumann —9. A chancre : c. : C. 20. James Curtis, *The Gilt Kid*, 1936.

pig, v.t. To damage or spoil completely : tailors' : C. 20. To treat as a pig would.

pig, bleed like a. To bleed much : coll. : C. 17–20. Dekker & Webster, 1607, ' He bleeds like a pig, for his crown's crack'd.' In C. 17–18, occ. *stuck pig.*

pig, China Street. A Bow Street officer : ca. 1810–30 : c., or low s. *Lex. Bal.* See **pig, 2.**

pig, cold. The pulling of bedclothes off sluggards and leaving them to lie in the cold : coll. : ca. 1780–1870. Grose, 2nd ed.—2. Goods returned from on sale : ca. 1820–80. ' Jon Bee.'—3. A corpse : medical : from ca. 1840 : very ob.

pig, follow like an Anthony. See **Anthony pig.—**

pig, Goodyer's. See **Goodyer's.**

pig, keep a. To occupy the same rooms as another student : Oxford undergraduates' (— 1887) ; ob. Baumann.

pig, long. See **long pig.**

pig, stare like a stuck. To look fixedly or in terror : coll. : 1749, Smollett, ' He stared like a stuck pig at my equipment.'

pig-a-back. A corruption, esp. children's, of *pick-a-back.* See **piggy-back.**

pig and goose, brandy is Latin for. A c.p. excuse for drinking a dram of brandy after eating pig or goose : ca. 1780–1880. Grose, 2nd ed.

Pig and Tinder-Box, the. The Elephant and Castle tavern, London : ca. 1820–90. Egan, 1821, ' Toddle to the Pig and Tinder-Box . . . a drap of comfort there.'

Pig and Whistle Light Infantry, the. The Highland Light Infantry (before ca. 1882, the 71st and 74th Regiments of Foot) : military : mid-C. 19–20 ; ob. The 71st had an Elephant and Hunting Horn badge. (F. & Gibbons.)

Pig and Whistle Line, the. See **Chidley Dyke.**

pig at home, have boiled. To be master in one's own house, ' an allusion to a well-known poem and story ', Grose, 1785 : coll. : ca. 1780–1830.

Pig Bridge. ' The beautiful Venetian-like bridge over the Cam, where it passes St. John's College, and connecting its quads. Thus called because the Johnians are styled pigs ' (Ware) : Trinity College, Cambridge : mid-C. 19–20.

pig by the ear, pull the wrong. To make a mistake : ca. 1540–1870 ; from ca. 1750, also *get the wrong pig* or *sow by the ear.* Coll. Heywood, 1546.

pig-eater. An endearment : C. 19.

pig-faced lady. The boar-fish : Tasmanian coll. : ca. 1840–90. Morris.

pig in a poke. A blind bargain : mid-C. 16–20 : coll. till C. 19, then S.E. A *poke* here = a bag ; indeed, *bag* is occ. substituted.

pig in shit, (as) happy as a. Very happy (though perhaps rather dirty) : low coll., the ordinary coll. form being . . . *in muck.* C. 19–20. Cf. U.S. *pig in clover.*

pig (or sow) in the arse or **tail, grease** or **stuff a fat.** To give unnecessarily, e.g. to a rich man : the *grease . . . arse* form, ca. 1670–1830 ; the *stuff . . . tail,* late C. 18–19 : low coll.

pig in the sun, snore like a. To snore vigorously or stertorously : coll. : mid-C. 19–20. (Manchon.)

pig-iron polisher. An engine-room rating in the : Navy : C. 20. Bowen.

Pig Islander. A New Zealander : Australian coll. : late C. 19–20. Ex the (formerly) numerous wild pigs in rural N.Z.

pig it. Late C. 19–20 coll. form of ob. S.E. *pig,* live filthily together.

pig-jump, -jumper, -jumping. ' To jump . . . from all four legs, without bringing them together ' : a horse that does this ; the doing thereof : Australian : resp. 1893, 1892, 1893. O.E.D.

pig-market. The proscholium of the Divinity School at Oxford : Oxford University : late C. 17–early 18. ' Oxonienses ' Wood, 1681. O.E.D.

pig-meater. A bullock that will not fatten : Australian : 1884, ' Rolf Boldrewood '. Because fit only for pigs' food.

pig-months. Those months in which there is an *r* (September–April) : non-aristocratic : C. 19–20 ; ob. Ware, ' The months in which you may more safely eat fresh pork than in the . . . summer months.'

pig, no good alive,—like a. Selfish ; greedy ; covetous : coll. and dial. : late C. 16–20 ; in C. 19–20, mainly dial. In C. 16–18, gen. *hog,* and nearly always in form . . . *he'll do no good alive.* Apperson.

pig of his or **one's own sow,** (gen. **give one a**). To pay one back in his own coin : semi-proverbial coll. : ca. 1530–1890. ' Proverbs ' Heywood ; Fielding ; Reade. (Apperson.)

pig-on-bacon. A bill drawn on a branch firm not gen. known to be such : commercial : from not later than 1920. O.E.D. (Sup.). Its two signatures are therefore worth, or equivalent to, only one.

pig-poker. A swineherd : coll. and dial. : C. 19.

pig-running. The chasing, in sport, of a short-tailed, well-greased and/or -soaped, preferably large pig : coll. verging on S.E. : ca. 1780–1890. Grose, 1785. The sport is extant.

pig-sconce. A dullard ; a lout : coll. : ca. 1650-1900. Massinger ; Meredith.

pig-sticker. A pork-butcher : low : from ca. 1850.—2. A long-bladed pocket-knife : from ca. 1880.—3. A sword : from ca. 1890. Cf. *porker,* q.v.—4. A bayonet : C. 20 : military. B. & P.

pig-sty. The press-room : printers' : from ca. 1845. Ex *pig,* 3.—2. An abode, a place of business : jocular coll. : from ca. 1880. Ex *pig-sty,* a miserable hovel. Cf. *piggery ; diggings ; den.*

Pig-Tail. A Chinese : 1886, *The Cornhill,* July (O.E.D.) : coll. till ca. 1905, then S.E.—2. (**pig-tail,** or as one word.) An old man : low urban coll. : ca. 1810–45. Ware, ' From the ancients clinging to the 18th century mode of wearing the hair '.

pig-tail, adj. Chinese, as in *pig-tail brigade, party, land* : coll. : late C. 19–20. O.E.D.

Pig-Tails. Shares in the Chartered Bank of India, Australia and China : Stock Exchange : from ca. 1890. Cf. *Kaffirs.*

pig to play on the flute, teach a. To attempt the impossible ; do something absurd : coll. : C. 19. Ray, ed. of 1813, cited by Apperson.

pig-tub. The receptacle for kitchen-refuse : lower classes' (— 1887) ; slightly ob. Baumann.

pig-widgeon, -widgin. A simpleton ; a fool : coll. : ca. 1685–1890. B.E. ; Grose, 1st ed. ; Baumann. An intensive of *widgeon,* fig. used of a fool (— 1741), just possibly influenced by *gudgeon.* Prob. related to S.E. *pigwiggen, -in.*

pig will make a good brawn to breed on, a brinded. ' A red-headed man will make a good stallion,' Ray : a c.p. of ca. 1670–1750. (Apperson.)

pig-yoke. A quadrant ; a sextant : nautical : 1836, Marryat, ' This was the " ne plus ultra " of navigation ; . . . old Smallsole could not do better with his pig-yoke and compasses.' Somewhat ob. Ex the roughly similar shape.

pigage. Erroneous for *pygarg* : C. 17. O.E.D.

pigeon. See **pigeon, fly a blue.**—2. See **pidgin.**—3. Gen. in pl., one of a gang of lottery-sharpers that specialise in insuring tickets : late C. 18–early 19 c. Grose, 3rd ed., where see a full description.—4. Hence, any person hastening with news surreptitiously obtained : c. of ca. 1820–50. ' Jon Bee.'—5. A simpleton ; a dupe : from ca. 1590. G. Harvey, 1893. Esp. in *pluck a pigeon*, to ' fleece ' someone. Cf. *pigeon*, v., 2.—6. (Occ. **pidgin.**) Business, concern, duty, task : from early 1920's. E.g. ' This is *his* pigeon.' (O.E.D. Sup.) Prob. ex *pidgin*, 1.

pigeon, v. See **pigeon the news.**—2. To deceive grossly ; dupe ; swindle : 1675, Cotton ; 1807, E. S. Barrett, ' Having one night been pigeoned of a vast property ', O.E.D., which classifies as S.E. : but surely s. (cf. *pigeon*, n., 5.)

pigeon, fly a blue. To steal lead from a roof, esp. of a church : c. : from ca. 1785 ; ob. Grose, 2nd ed. ; 1823, Bee (*fly the pigeon*).—2. But *fly the b. p.* is nautical s. : to heave the deep-sea lead : 1897, Kipling (O.E.D.).

pigeon, milk the. See **milk.**—**pigeon, Paul's.** See **Paul's pigeon.**—**pigeon, pluck a.** See **pigeon, n., 5.**

pigeon and kill a crow, shoot at a. To blunder deliberately : coll. : from the 1630's ; ob. Apperson.

pigeon-cracking. Same as next, q.v. : 1859, H. ; ob.

pigeon-flying. Stealing lead from roofs on buildings : c. : C. 19–20. Also *bluey-cracking*. H., 1859.

pigeon-hole. A too-wide gap between two words : printers' : 1683, Moxon ; ob. Cf. *rat-hole*, q.v.—2. A small study : Winchester College : from ca. 1850.—3. The female pudend : low : C. 19–20 ; ob.—4. (Extremely rare—?, indeed, existent—in singular.) The stocks ; the instrument confining the hands of a prisoner being flogged : c. : late C. 16–17. Greene, Eachard. O.E.D.

pigeon-hole soldiers. Clerks and orderlies : military coll. : from ca 1870 ; ob. *Echo*, July 1, 1871.

pigeon-holes. See **pigeon-hole,** last sense.

pigeon the news. To send news by carrier-pigeon : s. verging on coll. : from ca. 1820. ' Jon Bee.' Cf. *pigeon*, n., 4.

pigeoner. A swindler or a sharper : 1849 : coll. >, ca. 1900, S.E. Ex *pigeon*, v., 2. (O.E.D.)

pigeons, fly the. To steal coal as one carts it : c. (— 1923). Manchon. Cf. *fly a blue pigeon.*

pigeons with one bean, catch (or **take**) **two.** To ' kill two birds with one stone ' : semi-proverbial coll. : ca. 1550–1700. North's *Dial of Two Princes*, 1557 ; Ray. Apperson.

piggery. A room in which one does just as one wishes and which is rarely cleaned : coll. : C. 20. Prob. suggested by S.E. *snuggery*.

piggot, Piggot ; Pigott. To forge : political coll. : 1889–ca. 1895. ' A reminiscence of the Parnell Commission : the expression was born in the House of Commons, 28th Feb., 1889,' F. & H.—2. Ware shows that it was used also as ' to tell an unblushing lie to ', gen. in the passive ; that there was a n. corresponding to this sense of the v. ; that the term derived from the forger *Pigott*—which is the correct spelling.

Piggy. The inevitable nickname of any man surnamed May : naval and military : late C. 19–20. Bowen.

piggy-back. A nursery and dial. variant of *pick-a-back* : C. 19–20. Also, *pig-a-back* (Manchon).

piggy-stick. The wooden helve of the entrenching tool : military : from 1914. B. & P. Ex the children's game of tip-cat and the stick's usefulness in a ' rough house '.

piggy-wig ; piggy-wiggy. A pet pig ; hence, a humorous endearment : coll. : resp. 1870, Lear ; 1862, Miss Yonge. O.E.D.

pight. The p. tense and p.ppl. of *pitch* used wrongly as a present tense : late C. 16. O.E.D.

pigmˆn. An incorrect † form of *pygmy*. O.E.D.

Pigot, pigot ; properly **Pigott.** See **piggot.**

pigs. Abbr. of **pig's-ear,** 2. P. P., *Rhyming Slang*, 1932.

Pigs. (Gen. with *the*.) The 76th Foot Regiment, in late C. 19–20, the 2nd Battalion of the West Riding Regiment : military : C. 19–20 ; but rare after 1881 and now virtually †. F. & Gibbons. Ex its badge, granted for brilliant service in the Mahratta War (1803–5). Also the *Immortals* and the *Old Seven-and-Sixpennies*, qq.v.

pigs, please the. If circumstances permit : coll. : late C. 17–20 ; ob. Facetious Tom Brown, Lytton. Perhaps orig. Irish ; perhaps a corruption of *pix* (*pyx*), or more prob. ex *pixies*, fairies (W.). See esp. Apperson.

pig's back, on the. In luck's way : Anglo-Irish (— 1903) >, by 1914, gen. (E.D.D.) Perhaps ex a golden amulet in the shape of a pig.

pig's ear. Beer : rhyming s. : late C. 19–20.

pig's-ear or **-lug.** A very large lapel or collar flap : tailors' : from ca. 1860 ; ob.—2. Beer ; rhyming s. : late C. 19–20. B. & P.

pig's eye. In cards, the ace of diamonds : low (— 1864). H., 3rd ed. Ex appearance.—2. **the pig's eye,** the correct thing ; excellent, ' splendid ' : Canadian (— 1932). John Beames. Cf. *the cat's whiskers.*

pig's foot ! See **foot !, my.**

pigs fly, when. Never : coll. : C. 17–20 ; ob. Withals, in his Dict., defines *terra volat* as ' pigs flie in the ayre with their tayles forward.' (Cf. *blue moon, Greek kalends, Queen Dick, three Mondays in a week*, etc.) In C. 19–20, much less common than the S.E. *pigs might fly !*, perhaps !

pig's fry. A tie : from ca. 1880. P. P., *Rhyming Slang*, 1932. Cf. *Peckham rye* and contrast *pig's ear.*

pig's-lug. See **pig's-ear.**

pigs and whistles, go to. To be ruined : Scots coll. : from ca. 1780. Mrs. Carlyle, 1862, uses *make p. and w. of* as = to upset, or perturb, very greatly. In Scots, *pigs and whistles* is fragments. O.E.D.

pigs (occ. **hogs**) **to a fair**—more gen. **a fine—market, bring one's.** To do well ; make a profit : C. 17–20 : coll. >, by 1800, S.E. Rowlands, Urquhart, Murphy (*carry*), Planché. Apperson.

pigs (or **hogs**) **to market, drive one's.** To snore : coll. : C. 18–20 ; ob. (In C. 19–20, mainly dial.) Origin explained in Swift's ' I'gad he fell asleep, and snored so hard, that we thought he was driving his hogs to market.' New Zealanders (late C. 19–20) say *drive the pigs home*, esp. *driving* . . .

pig's(-)whisper. A grunt : low coll. : C. 19–20. Whence :

pig's whisper, in a. Very quickly indeed ; in a very short time : s. > low coll. : implied in Bee,

1823 ; 1837, Dickens, 'You'll find yourself in bed in something less than a pig's whisper '.

pigskin. A saddle : sporting : from ca. 1860. Dickens. Hence :

pigskin, knight of the. A jockey : sporting : 1898, *The Sporting Times*, Nov. 26, 'Riding rings round their crack knights of the pigskin '.

pigsn(e)y ; occ. in pl. (**-yes).** An endearment : C. 14–early 19 : S.E. till C. 18, when (Grose, 1785) low if used to a woman. (But it is extant in several diall. : E.D.D.) Lit., pig's eye, with intrusive or prosthetic *n*.

pigsty. See **pig-sty.—pigtail.** See **pig-tail, n.,** 2.

pijaw. An occ. form of *pi-jaw* (see **pi-gas** and **pi-jaw).**

pike. A turnpike road : coll. and dial. : from ca. 1850. (Mostly U.S.).—2. A toll-bar or -gate : coll. and dial. : 1837, Dickens. Abbr. *turnpike.*—3. The toll paid thereat : coll. : 1837, Dickens, fig. of death. O.E.D.—4. A tramp : c. : from ca. 1860 ; ob. Ex *turnpike road* or perhaps ex *piker*, q.v.

*****pike, v.** To depart : from ca. 1520 : S.E. until 1650, then s. ; in C. 18–20, low s. verging on c. B.E. Ex *pike oneself*, same sense.—2. In C. 18–20 c., to go ; occ. to run : Shirley, *The Triumph of Wit*, 1724 ; Grose, 1st ed.—3. Hence, to die : late C. 17–20 : low s. B.E. All senses often in form *pike off*.

pike, bilk a. To cheat a toll-keeper : low : C. 18–19.

pike, go. To walk ; depart : coll. and dial.: C. 16–17. Cf. *pike*, v., 1.

pike, prior. See **pike I.**

'pike, tip a. To walk ; to depart ; esp. escape, give the slip to : c. : C. 18–mid-19. Song, 1712, 'Tho' he tips them a pike, they oft nap him again.' Cf. *pike off* and *pike on the been*.

pike I ! An interjection implying prior claim or privilege : schools' : C. 19–20 ; ob. ? = I go first. (Cf. *bags* and *bags I* ; and *pledge*.) Also in the form, *prior pike !*

*****pike it.** To go, depart : c. > low s. : late C. 18–20. G. Parker, ca. 1789, 'Into a booze-ken they pike it.' Elaboration of *pike*, v., 1. Cf. :

pike it !, if you don't like it take a short stick and. A London c.p., rhyming variety, of ca. 1870–1900. H., 5th ed. ; Baumann. Ex preceding.

pike-keeper. A toll-keeper : coll. and dial. : 1837, Dickens. Abbr. *turnpike-keeper.*

*****pike off.** To depart ; run away : c. : late C. 17–20 ; ob. In mid-C. 19–20, it is also common in dial.—2. To die : c. : late C. 17–20 ; ob. B.E., both senses : elaborations of *pike*, go, die.

*****pike on the been** (or **bene).** To run away as fast as possible : c. : mid-C. 17–18. Coles, 1676 ; *A New Canting Dict.*, 1725. Origin, meaning of *been* ? Prob. it = *bien, bene*, excellent : hence, run away on a good road, i.e. to good purpose.

*****piked off, ppl.adj.** Clear away, safe ; dead : c. : late C. 17–20 ; ob. B.E.

pikeman. A toll-keeper : coll. and dial. : 1857, 'Tom Brown' Hughes. Cf. *pike-keeper.*

*****piker.** A tramp or a vagrant ; occ. a Gypsy : c. (— 1874) ex dial. (— 1838). Borrow, *Lavo-Lil*, 1874. Ex *pike*, v., 1, or *pike it.*—2. The nose : North Country (mostly Northumberland) low s. : late C. 19–20. E.D.D.—3. Gen. in pl., wild cattle : Australia : late C. 19–20 ; ob. Ex *pike* (*off*), go, depart.

pikestaff. The penis : low coll. : C. 18–20 ; ob. **pikestaff, plain as a.** See **plain.**

*****pikey.** A tramp, a Gypsy : c. (or low s.) and dial. : mid-C. 19–20. Cf. *pike* and *piker*, in the same sense.—2. An incorrect form of *piky*, abounding in pike (fish) : mid-C. 19–20. O.E.D.

pilcher. Shakespeare's *pilcher* is not c., as described by F. & H.—2. A coll. term of abuse : ca. 1600–40. Ben Jonson. Perhaps *pilcher*, a pilchard. (O.E.D.)

pile. A large sum won : Glasgow coll. (— 1934).

pile, v.i. To climb ; get (into a train) : S.E. of a number of persons, but coll. when used of one person : C. 20. D. Sayers, *The Nine Tailors*, 1934, 'He found a train going to London, and he piled into it.' I.e. in a heap or mass.

pile, go the whole. To 'go the whole hog': lower classes' (— 1887). Baumann.

pile, make one's. To make a fortune : coll. : from ca. 1850. Mostly Colonial and U.S. ; *pile* itself (1731) is S.E. Ex idea of a pile of coins.

pile-driver. The male member : low : mid-C. 19–20 ; ob.—2. A heavy blow or hit : sporting coll. (— 1923) >, by 1933, S.E. Manchon.—3. In 'soccer', a low, fast shot keeping about a foot above the ground : sporting : from ca. 1928.

pile-driving. Sexual intercourse : low : mid-C. 19–20. Cf. preceding term.—2. 'Steaming or sailing into a heavy head sea' : nautical : late C. 19–20. Bowen.

pile it on is a coll. form of :

pile on the agony. See **agony.**

pile up. To run (a ship) ashore : nautical coll. : late C. 19–20. Bowen.—2. Hence, to smash (a motor-car) in such a way that it buckles up into a *pile* or heap : motorists' coll. : from ca. 1915. In the G.W., *pile up one's bus* was the airmen's phrase for 'to crash' (F. & Gibbons).—3. Whence, a *pile-up* is a 'crash' : R.A.F. : from ca. 1918.

Pilgarlic(k) ; in C. 18, occ. **Peel(e) Garlic,** as in Grose (1st ed.). Used of oneself ; almost always *poor Pilgarlic* : coll. and dial. : C. 17–20 ; rare after ca. 1880. Anticipated in Skelton ; Beaumont & Fletcher, 'There got he a knock, and down goes pil-garlick '; Echard, 1694 ; Swift, 'They all went to the opera ; and so poor Pilgarlick came home alone '; Grose ; *Punch*, April 21, 1894, 'No ! 'tis Bull is pilgarlic and martyr '; Collinson, 1927, 'The once popular "Everybody's down on poor Pil-garlic " . . .' Ex S.E. sense, a bald head (which resembles a peeled head of garlic). Apperson and O.E.D.—2. See 'Fops' in Addenda.

pilgrim-salve or **pilgrim's salve.** Excrement : coll. : mid-C. 17–early 19. Anon., *A Modern Account of Scotland*, 'The whole pavement is pilgrim-salve.' The O.E.D. considers it euphemistic S.E., but I very much doubt this classification.

pilgrim's staff. The *membrum virile* : low : C. 18–19.

pill. A physician : 1860, H., 2nd ed. : military from ca. 1855 ; † by 1915. Cf. *bolus*, q.v. Also *pills*, 1899, *Cassell's Saturday Journal*, March 15.—2. A ball, esp. a black balloting-ball or a tennis ball : late C. 19–20. Cf. *pills*, 4, and *pill*, v., 1.—3. (Of a person) a bore : 1897, Maugham, '*Liza of Lambeth*, 'Well, you are a pill !'; slightly ob.—4. Punishment ; suffering ; a sentence of imprisonment : low coll. : from the mid-1890's. Ware, 'Endless in application '. Abbr. *bitter pill* ; often 'That's a pill, *that* is !'—5. A drink : from ca. 1899 ; ob.—6. As a cannon-ball or a bullet, *pill* (C. 17–20) is rather jocular S.E. than coll. in C. 17–mid-19, then coll. ; in G.W., also a bomb.—7. (In billiards) see pills, 6.—8. A custom-house officer: nautical (— 1909). Ware, 'Because both are so very searching'. Cf. sense 1.—9. A cigarette: Canadian: C. 20. B. & P.

pill, v. To reject by ballot: 1855, Thackeray, 'He was coming on for election . . . and was as nearly pilled as any man I ever knew in my life.'— 2. V.i., to twaddle, talk platitudinously: university: ca. 1895–1910.—3. To fail (a candidate) in an examination: 1908, A. S. M. Hutchinson (O.E.D. Sup.). Ex sense 1.

*pill and poll, v.t. To cheat (a comrade) of (his 'regulars', q.v.): c.: from ca. 1835. Ex S.E. sense.

pill-box. A small brougham: coll.: 1855, Dickens, referring, however, to a few years earlier; ob. by 1895, † by 1920.—2. A doctor's carriage: ca. 1870–1910. H., 5th ed.—3. A pulpit: jocular coll.: from ca. 1870; ob. (O.E.D.).—4. A soldier's cap: ca. 1890–1910.—5. A small concrete fort: late 1917: military coll. >, by June, 1918, j. F. & Gibbons; B. & P.; Colonel E. G. L. Thurlow, *The Pill-Boxes of Flanders*, 1933. Ex the resemblance of their shape to that of an oblong box for holding pills. For the genesis of the pill-box, see esp. 'Charles Edmonds', *A Subaltern's War*, 1929. —6. the Pill-Box is Harley Street: London taxidrivers': from ca. 1910. (*The Evening News*, Jan. 20, 1936.)

pill-builder. A doctor: nautical: C. 20. Bowen. Cf. *pill-pusher*; contrast:

pill-driver. An itinerant apothecary: coll.: mid-C. 19–20. Ex S.E. *pill-monger, -peddler*. Cf. *pill-pusher*, q.v.

pill-pate. A friar; a shaveling: C. 16 coll. Bacon, 'These smeared pill-pates, I would say prelates, . . . accused him.' I.e. *pilled* or *shaven pate*.

pill-pusher. A doctor: lower classes' (— 1909). Ware. Cf. (? ex) *pill-driver*, q.v.

pill-roller. A pharmaceutical chemist: lower classes': C. 20. James Curtis, *The Gilt Kid*, 1936. Cf. *pill-pusher*.

pill-yawl. 'A Bristol Channel pilot boat': nautical: late C. 19–20. Bowen.

pil(l)icock, pil(l)cock, pillock. The penis: a vulgarism: C. 14–18. Lyndsay, Florio, Cotgrave, Urquhart, D'Urfey.—2. Hence an endearment, addressed to a boy: late C. 16–17: a vulgarism. Florio. Whence:

pil(l)icock (etc.)-hill. The female pudend: low: C. 16–17. Shakespeare, in *King Lear*, puns thus on Lear's *pelican* daughters: 'Pillicock sat on pillicock-hill.'

pilling. The vbl.n. of *pill*, v., 1. Recorded in 1882; but prob. 27 years earlier.

pillionaire. A female occupant of a 'peach-perch' or 'flapper-bracket': motorists' (— 1935). Ex *pillion* + *millionaire*.

pillory. A baker: late C. 17–mid-18. B.E. ? semantics.

pillow-mate. A wife; mistress; harlot: coll.: C. 19–20.

pillow-securities. Safe scrip: financial coll.: ca. 1860–1915. Ware quotes *The Daily Telegraph*, July 8, 1896, '"Pillow securities"—those which do not trouble an investor's dreams at night and which a man need not worry about.'

pillows under folk's, men's, or people's elbows, sew. To give them a false sense of safety or security: coll.: late C. 14–17. The Geneva Bible; Wycherley. O.E.D.

pillowy. Large-breasted: low coil.: C. 20. Ex S.E. sense, soft or yielding; esp. from *pillowy bosom*.

pills. A physician, esp. in Army and Navy: see pill, n., 1.—2. Hence, a medical officer's orderly: military: from 1915. F. & Gibbons.—3. Hence, Pills, the. The Royal Army Medical Corps: military: from ca. 1895; † by 1915. Also *the licensed* or *linseed lancers, poultice-wallopers, rob all my comrades*, qq.v.—4. Testicles: low: late C. 19–20. Ex *pill*, n., 2.—5. Hence (?), shells or bombs: military: esp. in G.W. (F. & Gibbons). See pill, n., 6. —6. Billiards, esp. in *play pills*: 1896, *The Westminster Gazette*, Oct. 28, 'We can play pills then till after lunch, you know.' O.E.D. Cf. *pill*, n., 2.— 7. The inevitable nickname of any man surnamed Holloway: naval and military: late C. 19–20. Bowen. Prob. ex the well-known Holloway's Pills and Ointment. Thomas Holloway (1800–83) was a great benefactor: witness *John o' London's Weekly*, Oct. 30, 1936.

pilot. 'The navigating officer of a man-of-war': naval: C. 20. Bowen.

pilot, sky. See sky pilot. Whence:

pilot cove. A clergyman: (low) Australian: C. 20. C. J. Dennis.

pilot's grog. Additional liquor served in an Indiaman beating up the Hughli under a pilot: nautical coll.: mid-C. 19–early 20. Bowen.

pimgenet, pimgim(n)it. 'A large, red, angry Pimple', B.E.; any pimple, O.E.D.: s. > coll.: late C. 17–18; extant in C. 19 as dial. Cf. the C. 18 c.p. *nine pimgenets make a pock royal*.

Pimlico, walk in. (Of a man) to be handsomely dressed: ca. 1670–1720. Aubrey. The walks called *Pimblico-Path*, near the Globe Theatre, London, were frequented only by well-dressed men. Cf. the C. 19 Devonshire *to keep it in Pimlico*, to keep a house clean and attractive. Apperson.

pimp. A male procurer: C. 17–20. 'The word is app. of low slang origin, without any recorded basis,' *The Century Dict.*; B.E. and Grose still consider as s. or coll., but prob. S.E. by 1660. Perhaps ex Old Fr. *pimpreneau*, a scoundrel (W.).—2. 'A small faggot used about London [and the Southern counties] for lighting fires, named '—orig., Defoe tells us, by the woodmen—'from introducing the fire to the coals,' Grose, 1st ed. Coll.: from ca. 1720; ob., except in Surrey.—3. One who tells tales on others: New Zealand coll.: C. 20. Ex sense 1.

pimp-whisk, from ca. 1700; pimp-whiskin(g), 1638, Ford. A pimp, esp. a notable pimp: s. or low coll, † by 1830.—2. 'Also a little mean-spirited, narrow-soul'd Fellow', B.E.: coll.: late C. 17–mid-18. Obviously *whiskin(g)* is an elaboration or a diminutive of *whisk*, a whipper-snapper.

pimple. A boon companion: late C. 17–early 18. Congreve, 1700, 'The sun's a good Pimple, an honest Soaker.'—2. The head: low: C. 19–20; ob. *Lex. Bal.*; 'Jon Bee'. (With these senses, considered together, cf. C. 20 *old top*.)—3. A hill: lower classes': from late 1890's. F. & Gibbons, '"The Pimple" was a name given to certain noted hills on various fronts' in the G.W.

pimple in a bent. Something minute: coll.: ca. 1580–1650. Stanyhurst, 'I should bee thoght over curious by prying owt a pimple in a bent.' A *bent* is either a grass-stem or a flower-stalk. Cf. *thimble in a haystack*.

pin. See pins.—2. The penis: low coll.: C. 17–20. Glapthorne. Cf. *pin-case, -cushion*.—3. A trifle; almost nothing, as in *not worth a pin, care not a pin*. Perhaps orig. (C. 14) coll., but very soon S.E.—4. 4½ gallons ; the vessel holding it : 1570, O.E.D. : perhaps coll. in C. 16–17, but thereafter, if not from the first, S.E.

pin, v. To seize : 1768, the Earl of Carlisle, ' I am sure they intended to pin my money,' O.E.D. ; ob.—2. Hence, to steal, esp. if rapidly : c. : C. 19–20 ; ob. Cf. *nab, pinch, snaffle*, qq.v.—3. To catch, apprehend : c. (— 1864). H., 3rd ed.—4. To pawn clothes (v.i.) : low : from ca. 1880 ; ob. Ware. Prob. a corruption of *pawn*.—5. To make a ' dead set ' at (a person) : low Australian : from ca. 1920. Christina Stead, *Seven Poor Men of Sydney*, 1934. Ex S.E. *pin down*.

pin, be down. To be indisposed : coll. : C. 19–20 ; ob. Cf. *peg too low*, q.v.

pin, keep in the. To abstain from drinking : from ca. 1835 : dial., and s. >, ca. 1880, coll. Prob. suggested by *pin, put in the*, q.v. O.E.D. and E.D.D. Cf. *peg, put on the*, q.v.

pin, let loose a. To have an outburst, esp. go on a drinking-bout : from ca. 1850 : dial., and s. >, ca. 1880, coll. ; ob. E.D.D.

pin, nick the. To drink fairly : coll. : mid-C. 17–18. Cf. *peg* phrases. In old-fashioned tankards, there were often pegs or pins set at equal perpendicular distances.

pin, put in the. To cease ; esp. to give up drinking : from ca. 1830 : dial., and s. >, ca. 1880, coll. Mayhew. For semantics, cf. preceding entry ; perhaps, however (as the O.E.D. suggests), ex a pin or a peg used for making something fast or for checking motion, the pin being a linch-pin. As a c.p., it = ' put a sock in it ! ', q.v., i.e. close your mouth !, shut up ! : ca. 1860–90. H., 1874.

pin-basket. The youngest child in a completed family : coll. in C. 18–mid-19, then dial. Bailey (folio edition) ; Grose, 1st ed. ; E.D.D.

pin-buttock. A thin or a bony buttock or behind : late C. 16–20 (ob.) : coll. >, ca. 1660, S.E. Shakespeare, *All's Well*, ' The pin-buttock, the quatch-buttock, the brawn-buttock, or any buttock '. Opp. *barge-arse*, q.v., and comparable with S.E. *pin-tail*.

pin-case or **-cushion**. The female pudend : low : C. 17–20 ; ob. See **pin**, n., 2.

pin-money. A woman's pocket-expenses : late C. 17–20 : coll. till C. 19, then S.E. Orig. a settled allowance : see, e.g., Grose.—2. Money gained by women from adultery or occasional prostitution : late C. 19–20 ; slightly ob. Allusion to *pin*, n., 2.

pin out, coming over with the. A military c.p. of 1916–18 addressed to one to or at whom something is tossed or thrown. Ex the withdrawal of pin from a Mills bomb before it is hurled at the enemy.

pin-pannierly fellow. A covetous miser : coll. : ? C. 17. Kennett MS. (Halliwell). One who pins up his panniers or baskets ; one who hates to lose a pin.

pin-splitter. A first-class golfer : sporting : from ca. 1925. Ex the pin bearing the flag.

pin up. To sell (songs) in the street : lower classes' (— 1923). Manchon. Ex affixing music-sheets with drawing-pins.

pinard. Liquor ; wine : Soho (— 1935). Ex French Foreign Legion s. for cheap wine.

pinch. A certainty : racing : from ca. 1885. Marshall, *Pomes, from the Pink 'Un*, 1886–96. ? by confusion with U.S. *cinch*.—2. **pinch, the.** Pilfering during purchase ; exchanging bad for good money, or giving short change : c. : late C. 18–20 ; slightly ob. Grose, 2nd ed.

*pinch, v. To steal : from ca. 1670 : c. until ca. 1880, then also low s. Head, 1673, ' To pinch all the lurry he thinks it no sin ' ; very gen. among soldiers, 1914–18. Ex the pinching movement of predatory fingers. Cf. *make, nab, nick, win*, qq.v.—2. Hence (gen. *pinch . . . for*), to rob (a person) : C. 19–20, ob. ; c. until ca. 1860, then also low s. Vaux.—3. V.i., to pass bad money for good : c. of ca. 1810–60. *Lex. Bal.* Ex sense 1. Cf. *pinch*, n., 2.—4. To arrest : c. : 1860, H., 2nd ed. ; 1861, Mayhew, ' He got acquitted for that there note after he had me pinched.' In C. 20, low s. Similar semantics. Cf. *grab, pull in*, qq.v.—5. To urge (a horse), esp. press it hard ; exhaust by urging : racing coll. : 1737, Bracken, ' It is the vulgar Opinion that a Horse has not been pinch'd . . . when he does not sweat out,' O.E.D.

pinch, on a. A somewhat illiterate variant (— 1887) of *at a pinch*. Baumann.

*pinch, on the. A-stealing, either as at *pinch*, n., 2, or gen. (— 1887). The latter, Baumann.

Pinch an Inch. Gallipoli Peninsula : New Zealand soldiers' : 1915 ; ob. Cf. *Pen and Ink* and *Inch and Pinch*.

pinch-back, -belly, -commons, -crust, -fart, -fist, -gut, -penny, -plum. A miser ; a niggard : all coll. > S.E. : -*back*, C. 17–19 ; -*belly*, 1648, Hexham ; -*commons*, Scott, 1822, ' niggardly pinchcommons ', ob. ; -*crust*, C. 17–18, as in Rowlands, 1602 ; -*fart*, late C. 16–17, as in Nashe ; -*fist*, late C. 16–20, ob. ; -*gut*, a niggardly purser : nautical (— 1867), ex-*pinch-gut*, a miser, mid-C. 17–20, slightly ob.—in C. 19–20, a vulgarism. Cf. *pinch-gut money*, q.v. ; -*penny*, C. 15–mid-18, as in Lyly, ' They accompt one . . . a pynch penny if he be not prodygall ' ; -*plum*, from ca. 1890. O.E.D. : F. & H.

pinch-bottom, -buttock, -cunt. A whoremonger : low coll. : C. 19–20 ; ob. Cf. *pinch-prick*.

pinch-fart. See **pinch-back.**—**pinch-fist.** See **pinch-back.**

*pinch-gloak. A shoplifter : c. : from ca. 1810 ; ob. Vaux. See **gloak** and **pinch, v.**, 1, and n., 2.

pinch-gut. See **pinch-back** and cf. *pinch-gut money*.—2. Hence, a badly fed ship : nautical coll. : mid-C. 19–20. Bowen.

Pinch-Gut Hall. ' A noted House '—? a tavern-brothel—' at *Milend* ',—i.e. Mile End Road, East London—' so Nicknam'd by the *Tarrs*, who were half Starved in an *East-India* Voiage, by their then Commander, who Built (at his return) that famous Fabrick, and (as they say) with what he Pinch'd out of their Bellies ', B.E. Late C. 17–mid-18.

pinch-gut money. ' Allow'd by the King to the Seamen, that Serve on Board the Navy Royal, when their Provision falls Short ; also in long Voyages when they are forced to Drink Water instead of Beer ', B.E. Coll. : from ca. 1660 ; ob. Smyth, who gives it as *pinch-gut pay* (1867).

pinch on the parson's side. See **parson's side.**—**pinch-penny, -plum.** See **pinch-back.**

pinch-prick. A harlot : a wife keen, and insistent, on her conjugal rights : low coll. : C. 19–20 ; ob. Cf. *pinch-bottom*, etc., q.v.

*pinch the regulars. To take an undue share, or keep back part of the booty : c. : C. 19–20. See **pinch, v.**, and **regulars.**

pinch-wife. A churlish, vigilant husband : (rather low) coll. : C. 19–20 ; ob.

*pincher. A thief, esp. a shoplifter : c. : C. 19–20.—2. One who ' indulges in ' the act of *pinch*, **v.**, 3, q.v. : same status, period, and authority.—

3. **Pincher** is the inevitable nickname, mostly naval and military, of any man surnamed Martin : late C. 19–20. Bowen, ' After Admiral Sir William F. Martin, a strict disciplinarian, who was constantly having ratings " pinched " for minor offences '.

*pinching lay. The giving of short change or bad money : c. : late C. 18–20 ; ob. Grose, 2nd ed. Also *the pinch*. See **pinch**, v., 3, and n., 2.

pincushion. See **pin-case**.

Pindaric heights, the. Studying Pindar's *Odes* : Oxford : ca. 1820–70. Egan's Grose, 1823 ; H., 1st ed.

pine-apple. A Mills bomb : military : from 1916. Ex the criss-cross of lines denoting segments. Ex :— 2. Also and esp. a German grenade weighing four pounds : in 1915. F. & Gibbons.—3. Hence, any bomb, if small : from ca. 1920.

pine-apple, on the. On parish relief : lower classes' (— 1935). Sweet but prickly.

piney. An incorrect spelling of *piny* : C. 18–20. O.E.D.

ping. ' To speak in a quick singing high voice ' : sportsmen's : first half of C. 19. Ware, ' From the sharp ping of the old musket '.

pinguecula. An erroneous form and pronunciation of *pinguicula* : C. 19–20. O.E.D. Cf. *pinguetude, -tudinous*, for *pinguitude, -tudinous* (C. 17–20), and *pinguify* for *pinguefy* (C. 16–20). O.E.D.—**pinguin**, erroneous for *penguin* (the bird) : C. 18. O.E.D.

pinhead. A freak in a side-show : circus s. (— 1933). E. Seago, *Circus Company*.

pinion. Opinion : sol. (— 1887), orig. and mainly Cockney. Baumann. Also dial. : 1868 (E.D.D.).

pink, n. See entry at **pace, go the.**—2. See **pink, in the.**—3. See **pink, adj.**, 2.—4. See sense 2 of :

pink, v. Hit with visible effect, or easily and repeatedly : boxing : 1810 (O.E.D.) ; slightly ob. Ex swordsmanship.—2. To detect ; catch in the act : Bootham School (— 1925). Hence, the corresponding n. (Anon., *Dict. of Bootham Slang*, 1925.)

pink, adj. Smart ; exceedingly fashionable : 1818, Lady Morgan, ' It was Lady Cork's " Pink night " ; the rendezvous of the fashionable exclusives,' O.E.D. : † by 1890, except in U.S. Ex † S.E. sense, exquisite.—2. Secret ; as n., a secret telegram : in Government offices during the G.W. Ex the colour of the telegram form. F. & Gibbons. —3. ' B'oody ' : euphemistic (— 1923) ; ob. Esp. *the pink limit*. Manchon. Cf. *ruddy*.

pink, Dutch. Blood : boxing : 1853, Bradley's *Verdant Green*, ' That'll take the bark from your nozzle, and distill the Dutch pink for you, won't it ? ' Ob. by 1910, virtually † by 1930. Ex the S.E. sense (1758).

pink, in the. In excellent health, spirits : from ca. 1910. E.g. Clarence Winchester, 1916 ; B. & P. Ex *in the pink of condition* (of racehorses).

pink !, perish me ; strike me pink ! A mild, lower classes' expletive : C. 20. (Manchon.)

pink spiders (occ. **elephants**). Delirium tremens : late C. 19–20 : mostly low. Ob.

Pink 'Un, The. *The Sporting Times* : from 1880, says Ware, ' from the tint of the paper, and to distinguish it from the Brown 'un, Sportsman.' By ' Sportsman ' he prob. means *The Sportsman's Guide to the Turf*, which commenced in 1880.

pink wine. Champagne : military (— 1909) ; ob Ware. Prob. an evasion.

pinkany, -eny ; variants in -ck- ; also **pink nye,**

pinken eye, etc. (As an endearment) darling, pet : nursery coll. > S.E. : late C. 16–early 17. Nashe, Massinger. Lit. *pink* (a narrow, hence little, hence dear) *eye*. Influenced by *pigsney*, q.v. O.E.D.

pinkie, pinky. Anything small ; orig. and esp. the little finger : Scots coll., mostly among children : C. 19–20. Lit., the little pink one.

pinking dindee. A sweater or mohawk : Irish coll. : C. 18. Grose, 1785. Lit., a ' turkey-cock ' given to pinking with a rapier.

pinko. Tipsy : military : 1916–19. F. & Gibbons. Cf. *blotto* : perhaps *pinko* was derived from pink blotting-paper and then the suffix -o attached.

pinky. See **pinkie**.

pinna, pinner, pinny. A pinafore : resp. C. 19– 20, coll. ; from ca. 1845, coll. († by 1910) and dial. ; from ca. 1855 (G. Eliot, 1859), coll., mostly nursery. (F. & H. confuses this *pinner* with *pinner*, a double-flapped C. 17–18 coif.)

pinnacles. Spectacles, eye-glasses : lower classes' (— 1909). Ware, ' A corruption of " barnacles ".'

*pinnel, occ. pennel. Penal servitude : c. : from ca. 1860 ; ob. By abbr. and corruption of the two defining words. H., 1874, ' As " four-year pinnel ".' Cf. *penal*, q.v.

pinner. See **pinna**.

*pinner-up. A seller of broadside songs and ballads : c. : 1851, Mayhew ; ob. by 1900, virtually † by 1920. Even in 1873, H. could write, ' There are but one or two left now.' Songs were usually pinned-up on canvas against a wall.

pinnock to pannock, bring. To cause ruin : coll. : C. 16–early 17. Huloet, 1552, ' Brynge somethynge to nothynge, as the vulgare speache is, to brynge pynnock to pannock.' Origin obscure.

pinny. See **pinna**. (Cf. the forms *nanny, nanna*.)

pins. (Rare in singular.) Legs : coll. and dial. : 1530, Anon., *Hickscorner*, ' Than wolde I renne thyder on my pynnes As fast as I might goe ' ; 1781, General Burgoyne in one of his sprightly comedies, ' I never saw a fellow better set upon his pins.' Ex the primary sense of *pin* : a peg. Cf. *peg-leg*.

pins, on one's. Alive ; faring well (cf. S.E. *on his legs*) ; in good form : coll. and dial. : from ca. 1810. *Lex. Bal.* ; Vaux.

pins and needles. The tingling that accompanies the restoration of circulation in a benumbed limb : coll. : 1844, J. T. Hewlett (O.E.D.) ; 1876, G. Eliot, ' Pins and needles after numbness.' Ex the feeling of being pricked with those articles.

pin's head in a cartload of hay, look for a. To attempt the impossible : coll. : mid-C. 16–18. Calfhill, 1565. Hence *find a pin's head . . .*, to do wonders. Cf. *thimble in a bottle of hay* or *in a haystack*.

pinsrap. A parsnip : back s. : from ca. 1880.

pint. Praise ; recommendation : tailors' : from ca. 1860 ; ob. A pint is sufficient recommendation ?

pint, the price of a. A sum sufficient to buy a pint of ale or beer : coll. : late C. 19–20.

pint of mahogany. (A glass of) coffee : low (— 1909). Ware. Ex its colour.

pint-pot. (A nickname for) a seller of beer : coll. : ca. 1560–1620. Shakespeare. O.E.D.

pintail. Incorrect for *pintle* (in gunnery) : C. 17– 19. O.E.D.

pints round ! A c.p. request to one dropping his shears : tailors' : from ca. 1850 ; very ob. by 1902, † by 1918. Cf. *pint*, q.v.

pintle. The penis : *pintel* in A.-S., it is S.E. until

ca. 1720, then (dial. and) a vulgarism (ob.) : cf. the degradation of *pizzle* and *prick*.

pintle-bit or **-maid.** A mistress ; a kept whore : low coll. : C. 19–20 ; ob.

pintle-blossom. A chancre : low : C. 18–20 ; ob. Contrast *grog-blossom*.

pintle-case. The female pudend : low : C. 19–20 ; ob. See **pintle.**

pintle-de-pantledy. ' Sadly Scared, grievously put to it ', B.E. at *pit-a-pat* : coll. : mid C. 17–early 19. Skinner, 1671 (E.D.D.) ; Coles, 1676 ; Grose.

pintle-fancier or **-ranger.** A wanton : low : C. 19–20 ; ob. Cf. *pintle-merchant*.

pintle-fever. Syphilis or gonorrhœa : low coll. : C. 19–20 ; ob.

pintle-keek. An inviting leer : low Scots coll. : C. 19–20.

pintle-maid. See **pintle-bit.**

pintle-merchant, -monger. A harlot : C. 18–20 : low. Ob. Cf. Yorkshire *pintle-twister* (E.D.D.).

pintle-ranger. See **pintle-fancier** and cf. *pintle-bit* and *pintle-merchant*.

pintle-smith, -tagger. A surgeon : low coll. : from ca. 1780. Grose, 1st, 3rd edd.

pinurt pots. Turnip tops : back s. (— 1859). H., 1st ed.

piou-piou. A French soldier, esp. a private in the infantry : coll. : C. 20. Direct ex. Fr. : cf. *Poilu*, of which it may be a corruption and than which, from ca. 1912, it has been very much less gen. ; more prob. a perversion of *pied*, reduplicated (cf. *foot-slogger*). See esp. Gaston Esnault, *Le Poilu tel qu'il se parle*, 1919. See *Words !*

pip, preceded by **the.** Syphilis : coll. verging on S.E. : late C. 16–17. Ex the poultry disease.—2. The mark on a playing-card : coll. (— 1874) ; in C. 20, perhaps rather S.E. H., 5th ed., ' The ace is often called " single pip ".'—3. See **pip, get** (or **have) the** and **give the.**—4. A star on the tunic or jacket of a uniform : military : C. 20. Cf. *pipper*, q.v. Hence, ' He is putting up three pips,' he is now a captain (F. & Gibbons).

pip, v. To blackball : clubs' : 1880, Huth's *Buckle.* Prob. suggested by *pill*, v., 1.—2. To take a trick from (an opponent) : cards : from ca. 1885. —3. To hit with a missile, esp. a bullet ; to wound ; to kill : military : 1900 (O.E.D.). Perhaps ex sense 1 or as with a fruit-pip, or ex :—4. To beat, defeat, e.g. in a race : 1891 (O.E.D.). Ex senses 1 and 2.—5. To fail (a candidate) : 1908, A. S. M. Hutchinson.—6. To annoy : from ca. 1915. Ex *pip, give the*, 2, q.v.—7. To die : Harrow School ; C. 20. Arnold Lunn, *The Harrovians*, 1913. Cf. sense 3.

pip, get or **have the.** To be depressed ; (ob.) to be indisposed : coll. : from ca. 1885. Marshall, in *Pomes*, ' It cost a bit to square up the attack ; | For the landlord had the pip.' Ex the poultry disease via the Thackerayan ' The children ill with the pip, or some confounded thing,' 1862. Cf. Devonshire dial. *take the pip*, to take offence : occurring as early as 1746 (E.D.D.)

pip, give the. To depress ; from ca. 1890 : coll.—2. Hence, to annoy or disgust : from ca. 1910 : coll. Whence—perhaps influenced by *pip*, to wound—*pip*, to annoy.

pip, old. See **old pip.**

pip emma. P.m. : military coll. : C. 20. Ex the signalese for *p.m.* Cf. *ack emma.*

pip out. To die : from ca. 1918. Ex *pip*, v., 3. Cf. *conk*, q.v.

pip-pip ! A ' hue and cry after anyone, but generally a youth in striking bicycle costumery ' : low (— 1909). Ex the cyclist's warning by horn. Ware.—2. Good-bye ! : from ca. 1904, one infers from Collinson ; 1920, P. G. Wodehouse ; ob. by 1930. (O.E.D. Sup.)—3. A cry of encouragement : coll. (— 1923). Manchon. Cf. sense 1.

pip-squeak. An insignificant person or object : 1910, E. V. Lucas (O.E.D. Sup.). Echoic.—2. A small German shell of high velocity : military : from Oct., 1914. Ex the sound of its flight. B. & P.—3. Hence, a two-stroke motor-cycle : motorists' : 1923. O.E.D. (Sup.).

Pip, Squeak and Wilfred. The medals (or medal ribbons, 1914–15 Star, War Medal, Victory Medal : military : from ca. 1919. Ex three characters appearing in the children's corner of *The Daily Mirror.*—2. See Addenda.

pipe. The human voice : C. 17–20 : S.E. until late C. 19, then coll. ; slightly ob. Baumann. Ex *pipe*, a bird's note or song.—2. A boot ; esp. a top-boot : low (? orig. c.) : from ca. 1810. Vaux, 1812. Ob. (Extremely rare—? existent—in the singular.) —3. The female pudend : low : C. 19–20.—4. The urethra : late C. 19–20. Abbr. *water-pipe.*—5. A satirical song, ballad, or prose-piece written on paper, which was then rolled up in the form of a pipe and left at the victim's door : Tasmanian coll. : early C. 19. Morris.—6. A good look (*at* . . .) : low : from ca. 1880. Ex *pipe*, v., 4. Manchon.

pipe, v. To talk ; speak : coll. : late C. 19–20. Esp. in *pipe-up*, speak up, as in Whiteing's remarkable novel, *No. 5 John Street* (1899), ' Nance is called to oblige with a song. She is shy . . . But the Amazon brings her forward . . . " Pipe up, yer blessed little fool ".' Ex playing on a pipe. —2. To weep : low : 1797, Mrs. M. Robinson (O.E.D.) ; ob. Ex *pipe an* (or *one's*) *eye*, than which it has been much less gen.—3. To follow, to dog : detectives' s. (— 1864). H., 3rd ed. —4. (Also **pipe off.**) Hence, to watch ; spy : c. : from ca. 1870. H., 1874 ; ' Pomes ' Marshall ; ' Dagonet ' Sims.—5. V.i., to pant, breathe hard from exertion or exhaustion : boxing : 1814. De Quincey, 1827, ' The baker came up piping ' ; Dickens, 1848. Ex *pipes*, the lungs. (O.E.D.)

pipe, Her Majesty's or **the Queen's (tobacco-).** ' The kiln in the great East Vault of the Wine-Cellars of the London Docks, where useless and damaged goods that have paid no duty are burnt : as regards tobacco, a thing of the past, stuff of this kind being distributed to workhouses, &c.', F. & H., 1901 (pub. 1902). Coll. : from ca. 1840. Also, in C. 20, *the King's pipe*, which, like *the Queen's pipe* from ca. 1880, is used only of ' a furnace for burning tobacco-sweepings and other refuse ', O.E.D. : this sense is, in C. 20, S.E.

pipe, take a. To weep : 1818, Hogg ; ob. : Scots coll. Cf. *pipes, tune one's*, and :

pipe an or **one's eye,** occ. **one's eyes.** To weep : 1789, C. Dibdin : nautical s. >, ca. 1860, gen. coll. ' An obscure variation on to *pipe away* . . ., with allusion to the boatswain's whistle,' W. Earliest, *pipe one's eye ; pipe one's eyes*, from ca. 1810, ob. in C. 20 ; *pipe an eye* is loose and rare. (O.E.D.) Cf. *pipe*, v., 2, q.v.

pipe and smoke it !, put that in your. Digest that if you can ! : coll. : 1824, Peake ; Dickens in *Pickwick* ; Barham ; Miss Braddon.

pipe down. To be quiet: nautical coll.: mid-C. 19–20. Bowen. Ex S.E. sense, ' to dismiss by sounding the pipe '.

pipe in (or occ. **with**) **an ivy-leaf.** To busy oneself, either to no purpose or, more gen., as a consolation for failure; to do any silly thing one likes, gen. as *you may go pipe in an ivy-leaf*: coll.: C. 14–20; very ob.,—indeed, rare since C. 17. Semi-proverbial. O.E.D. An ivy-leaf being emblematic of very small value: cf. *rush, straw*.

pipe-layer, -laying. Political intriguer, intrigue: orig. (ca. 1835), U.S.; partly anglicised ca. 1890: coll. Ex a water-supply camouflaging an electoral plot. Thornton.

***pipe off.** See **pipe**, v., 4.—2. To sound or pump (a person): low (— 1923). Manchon.

***pipe on.** To inform against: c.: from ca. 1875; ob. Baumann. See **pipe**, v., 4.

pipe one's eye. A variant of *pipe an eye*.

pipe-opener. (An) exercise taken as a ' breather': coll.: 1879. Ex *pipes*, the lungs. O.E.D. Ware classifies it as a university term and defines it as the ' first spurt in rowing practice—to open the lungs '.

pipe out, put one's. To spoil one's chance, sport, or showing, ; to extinguish: 1720, Ramsay, ' Their pipe's put out ': coll. till C. 19, then S.E. and dial.; ob. O.E.D.—2. Hence, to kill: low: from ca. 1860; ob.

pipe up. See **pipe**, v., 1.—2. Also, to call, shout: same period.

pipeclay. V.t., to put into meticulous order (esp. accounts): 1833, Marryat; 1853, Dickens: nautical coll. >, ca. 1860, gen. coll., >, ca. 1910, S.E. Ex *pipe-clay*, a white cleaning-material.—2. V.i. and t., to hide defects in material or mistakes in workmanship: from ca. 1850. Ex sense 1.

piper. A broken-winded horse: 1785, Grose; 1831, Youatt: s. >, ca. 1825, j. Cf. *roarer*. Connected with S.E. *pipes*, lungs.—2. A detective or spy: c.: from ca. 1850. Esp., ca. 1860–1910, a person employed to spy on the conductor of an omnibus: low. H., 1864.

piper !, by the. A mild, proletarian asseveration (— 1887); slightly ob. Baumann. Ex dial.

piper, drunk as a. Very drunk: 1770, Graves, *Spiritual Quixote*, ' Jerry . . . proceeded so long . . . in tossing off horns of ale, that he became as drunk as a piper ': coll. >, early in C. 19, S.E.; † by 1890. (Dial.: *piper-fou*.)

piper (occ. **fiddler**), **pay the.** To pay the bill, lit. and fig.: 1681, Flatman (O.E.D.); Congreve; Smollett; Brougham; Carlyle: coll. till C. 19, then S.E.

piper's cheeks. Puffed, swollen, or very big cheeks: coll.: late C. 16–17. Withals, 1602.

piper's news. Stale news: Scots coll.: from ca. 1820; ob. Hogg.

piper's wife. A whore: coll.: late C. 18–19. (Mainly Scots.)

pipes. See **pipe**, n., 2.—A boatswain: nautical nickname: mid-C. 19–20. Bowen. Ex the giving of orders by sounding a pipe.

pipes, pack, or **put,** or **shut up one's.** To cease from action, more gen. from speech: coll.: mid-C. 16–18; in C. 18, virtually S.E. Olde, 1556, *put up*; Nashe, *pack up*. While *shut up* is C. 18 and perhaps early C. 19. Ramsay has *poke up*. Ex the ' musical tube '.

pipes, set up one's. To cry aloud; yell: ca. 1670–1800: coll. >, by 1710, S.E. H.M.'s trans-lation of Erasmus's *Colloquies*. Ex *pipe*, the voice. O.E.D.

pipes, take. ' To tickle one vigorously, in the region of the stomach ': Bootham School (— 1925). Anon., *Dict. of Bootham Slang*.

pipes, tune one's. (To begin) to weep or cry: Scots coll. and dial.: late C. 18–20. Jamieson; O.E.D.; E.D.D. Ex *pipe*, voice, and *pipes*, lungs.

pipey. Incorrect spelling of *pipy*: from ca. 1720. O.E.D.

pipi, incorrectly of a cockle: New Zealand: C. 19–20. Morris. Occ. *peppy, pippy*.

piping, n. Weeping, crying: s. >, ca. 1850, coll.: 1779, Seward, ' No more piping, pray'; Marryat, 1837. O.E.D. Ex *pipe*, v., 2, though *piping* is recorded the earlier.

pipkin. The female pudend, esp. in *crack her pipkin*, to deflower a girl or woman: low: late C. 17–early 19. Ned Ward, 1709; Grose. Ex cook's breakages, *pipkin* being a small earthenware pot.—2. The head; pugilism: from ca. 1820; ob. Jones, *The True Bottom'd Boxer*, 1825.—3. H., 1860, gives *pipkin*, the stomach, as Norwich s. (or coll.): perhaps rather dial. Extremely ob.

pipped. Annoyed; wounded: the latter, military: C. 20. See **pip**, v., 4, 3.

-pipper. As in *one-pipper*, a second, *two-pipper*, a first or full lieutenant: military: 1914 or 1915. Ex *pip*, n., 4; cf. *pip*, n., 2.

pippin. A pejorative term of address: ca. 1660–1820. Cotton, 1664, ' Thou'rt a precious Pepin, | To think to steal so slily from me.' O.E.D. Whence: —2. (Gen. **my p.**) An endearment, mostly costermongers': C. 19–20; ob. Cf. *ribstone* and the C. 20 *old fruit*. N.B. Byron called his wife ' Pippin '.

pippin, sound as a. Rosy-cheeked; very healthy: lower classes' coll. (— 1887). Baumann. Ex the apple's ' high-colour '.

pippin-squire. An ' apple-squire ', q.v.: **s.** or coll.: C. 17. Rowlands.

pippy. See **pipi**.—2. Shaky (of stocks): Stock Exchange: from ca. 1890. ? ex *pip, get the*.

pipy. Apt to ' pipe an eye ', q.v.: from ca. 1860: s. >, by 1890, coll.

pique. Erroneous for *peak* (e.g. of a cap): from ca. 1820. O.E.D.

pirate. Gen. pl., ' Naval small craft on any irregular or detached duty ': naval coll.: late C. 19–20. Bowen.

pirler. An occ. form of *purler*.

pisasphalt. Incorrect for *pissasphalt*: C. 17–20. O.E.D.

piscatory. Catachrestic for *piscine*, adj.: from ca. 1760. O.E.D.

pish. Whiskey; any spirituous liquor: military: C. 20. F. & Gibbons. Origin obscure: possibly the word derives ex *piss* (the effect) on *whiskey*.

piso. A miserly or stingy fellow: military: late C. 19–20. F. & Gibbons. Cf. the † Northern dial. *pesant*, ' a stern, hard-hearted miser ' (E.D.D.).

piss, n. Urine: late M.E. + : S.E., but in C. 19–20 a vulgarism. Ex:

piss, v. To urinate: M.E. + : S.E., but considered a vulgarism from ca. 1760. (Because of its " shocking " association, wrongly regarded as low coll. Cf. *arse, cunt, shit*.) Ex Old Fr. *pisser*, prob. echoic. *Ah, si je pouvais pisser comme il parle*, Clemenceau of Lloyd George.

piss !, a. A vulgar Restoration expletive. Etherege, *The Man of Mode*.

piss, do a. To make water : low coll. : C. 19–20. See **piss**, n.

piss, rods in. A prospective punishment, scolding : low coll. : from ca. 1620. Mabbe, 1623 ; Cotton, *Virgil Travestie*, 1678. Ob. Like brine, urine hardens canes.

piss, so drunk that he opened his shirt collar to. Blind drunk : low coll. : C. 19–20 ; ob.

piss-a-bed. The dandelion : coll. verging on S.E. ; also dial. : mid-C. 16–20 ; † by 1900, except in dial. Ex (not its colour but) its diuretic virtues.

piss blood. To toil : low coll. : late C. 19–20. Ex strain of effort. Cf. :

piss bones or **children** or **hard.** To be brought to childbed : low coll. : C. 19–20 ; ob. Cf. the preceding entry.

piss down one's back. To flatter him : low coll. : late C. 18–19. Grose, 3rd ed. ; Baumann.

piss-factory. A public-house : C. 19–20 (ob.): low. Liquor makes rapid urine.

piss-fire. A blusterer : C. 18–19 : (low) coll. and dial. ? ex the old proletarian habit of extinguishing a fire by pissing it out. Cf. the † proverb, *money will make the pot boil though the devil piss in the fire.*

piss in a quill. To agree on a plan : coll. : ca. 1730–1820. North's *Examen*. (O.E.D.)

piss-kitchen. A kitchen maid : low coll. : C. 18–19.

piss-maker. A great drinker : low coll. : late C. 18–19. Grose, 1785 ; Baumann.

piss money against the wall. To squander, waste money, esp. in liquor : late C. 15–19 : S.E. until C. 18, then (low) coll. Grose ; Baumann.

piss more than one drinks. Gen. *pisses . . . he . . .* A semi-proverbial c.p. preceded by *vain-glorious man* and applied to a boaster : late C. 17–early 19. B.E. ; Grose.

piss off. To depart, esp. to depart quickly : low : late C. 19–20. Cf. *p.o.q.*

piss on a nettle. See **nettle, piss on a**, and cf. the proverbial *as surly as if he had pissed on a nettle.*

piss on one's props. To leave the stage for ever : pejorative theatrical (– 1935). See **props.**

piss one's tallow. To sweat : C. 17–20 ; very ob. Urquhart, ' He's nothing but Skin and Bones ; he has piss'd his Tallow.' Ex S.E. sense of a deer thinning in the rutting-season. O.E.D.

piss pins and needles. To have gonorrhœa : low coll. : from ca. 1780. Grose, 3rd ed.

piss-pot. A nickname for a medical man : coll. : late C. 16–17. Ex :—2. A chamber-pot : mid-C. 15–20 : S.E. until mid-C. 18, then a vulg.

Piss-Pot Hall. A tavern ' at Clopton, near Hackney, built by a potter chiefly out of the profits of chamber-pots, in the bottom of which the portrait of Dr. Sacheverell '—who (d. 1724), after a notorious trial in 1710, was suspended, for three years, from preaching—' was depicted ', Grose, 2nd ed. Ca. 1710–1830.

piss-proud. Having a urinal erection : low coll. : late C. 18–20. Grose, 2nd ed., where occurs the c.p. *that old fellow thought he had an erection, but his —— was only piss-proud*, ' said of any old fellow who marries a young wife '. Cf. *morning-pride*, q.v.

piss pure cream. To have gonorrhœa : low : C. 19–20, ob. Cf. *p. pins and needles.*

piss-quick. Hot gin-and-water : low : ca. 1820–60. ' Jon Bee ', 1823.—2. The German trench-gun (smaller than the ' 77 ') ; also the noise (*shish*) of the travelling shell, the shell itself, and even—though

rarely—its explosion. Cf. *pip-squeak*, perhaps a euphemism for *piss-quick.*

piss the less,—let her cry, she'll. A semi-proverbial c.p. : late C. 18–20 ; ob. Supposed to have orig. been addressed by consolatory sailors to their harlots. In Grose, 3rd ed., it occurs in the form *the more you cry, the less you'll p-ss.*

piss (up)on, as good . . . as you would desire to. Excellent ; extremely, as in Tom Brown's ' There are some Quacks as Honest Fellows as you would desire to Piss upon ', 1700 : (low) coll. : late C. 17–early 19. (O.E.D.) Cf. *pissed, as good . . .* and *pot, as good . . .*

piss when one can't whistle. To be hanged : low : from ca. 1780 ; ob. Grose, 1785.

pissed or **pissed-up.** (Very) drunk : low, and military : C. 20.

pissed, as good—occ. as very—a knave as ever. As good a man, etc.—as big a knave—as may be : (low) coll. : C. 18–20 ; C. 18–19. See **pot, as good . . .**, and cf. *piss upon.*

pissed in the sea,—' every little helps ', as the old woman (or lady) said when she. A c.p. applied to urinating in sea or stream, hence to any very small contribution : mid-C. 19–20.

pissed-up. See **pissed.**

pisser. The penis ; the female pudend : low s. or coll. : C. 19–20.—2. Ex the second nuance comes : A girl : low, esp. among New Zealanders : C. 20.

pisser, vinegar-. A niggard ; miser : coll. : C. 18.—2. ? (in C. 17) a sour fellow : cf. Anon.'s *2nd Return from Parnassus*, 1602, ' They are pestilent fellowes, they speake nothing but bodkins, and pisse vinegar.' (O.E.D.)

pisses my goose, such a reason. A very poor reason : C. 18–19 : low coll. Cf. *pisseth . . . goose.*

pisseth, by fits and starts as the hog. Jerkily ; intermittently : coll. : C. 18–19.

pisseth, when the goose. Never. Often preceded by *you'll be good.* Coll. : C. 18–20 ; ob. Cf. *pisses my goose, such a reason.*

pissing, vbl.n. As in *the tin-whiffin is when you can't shit for pissin(g)*, a low rhyming c.p. : ca. 1870–1910.

pissing, adj. Paltry ; brief : coll. verging on S.E. (cf. *piddling*) : C. 16–early 19.

pissing candle. A small make-weight, or any very inferior candle : coll. almost S.E. : C. 18–19. F. & H.

Pissing Conduit. A conduit with a flow resembling a stream of urine, esp. ' one near the Royal Exchange set up by John Wels (Lord-mayor, 1430),' F. & H. : late C. 16–17. Shakespeare, *1st Henry the Sixth*, IV, vi, ' I charge and command that, of the city's cost, | The pissing conduit run nothing but claret wine, | The first year of our reign.'

pissing-while. A very short time ; an instant : coll. : C. 16–mid-19. Palsgrave ; Still, *Gammer Gurton's Needle*, ' He shall never be at rest one pissing-while a day '; Shakespeare ; Ray's *Proverbs.*

pisteology. Incorrect for *pistiology* : C. 20. O.E.D.

pistol. A swaggering bully : coll. >, ca. 1640, allusive S.E. Shakespeare, *Merry Wives*, dramatis personæ, ' Bardolph, Pistol, Nym, sharpers attending on Falstaff.' Cf. Florio's definition of *pistolfo.*— 2. The male member : late C. 16–20 : low coll. verging on euphemistic S.E. ; ob. See esp. Shakespeare, *2nd Henry the Sixth*, II, iv, the play on Pistol's name and *pistol.*

pistol-shot. A drink : ca. 1850–1910. **Cf.** (*drink a*) *slug* and S.E. *pocket-pistol*.

pit.* A breast-pocket ; a fob : c. : from ca. 1810 ; ob. *Lex. Bal.*—2. The female pudend. It is an open question whether *pit* and its variants, *pit-hole* and *-mouth*, *pit of darkness*, and *bottomless pit*, are low coll. or euphemistic S.E. C. 17–19.

pit, fly or **shoot the.** To turn tail : coll. verging on S.E. and indeed, in C. 19, achieving it : ca. 1740–1890. North, *Examen*, 1740 (*shoot*) ; Richardson, *Pamela*, 'We were all to blame to make madam here fly the pit as she did.' As does a cowardly cock in cock-fighting.

pit, knight of the. See the **knight** paragraph.

pit, shoot the. See **pit, fly the.**

pit and boxes (or, in C. 19–20, **back and front shops) into one, lay.** To remove or destroy the division between anus and vagina : from ca. 1780 ; ob. 'A simile borrowed from the playhouse, when, for the benefit of some favourite player, the pit and boxes are laid together,' Grose, 1785.

pit-hole. A grave : lower classes' coll. (— 1887). Baumann.

***pit-man** ; **pitman** (Baumann). A pocket-book carried in the breast-pocket : c. (— 1812) ; † by 1900. Vaux. Ex *pit*, n., 1 + *-man*(*s*), the c. suffix.

pitch. A place of sale or entertainment ; a stand : 1851, Mayhew : showmen's and tramps' s. >, ca. 1870, low coll. >, ca. 1880, coll. >, ca. 1910, S.E. Prob. ex *pitch a tent.*—2. Hence, a sale, a performance : low (showmen's, tramps') : from ca. 1860. Vance, *The Chickaleary Cove*, ca. 1864 ; Hindley, 1876, 'When I had done my pitch and got down from the stage.'—3. A short sleep : low : from ca. 1870 ; ob. H., 5th ed.—4. A talk, chat : 1892, *The Pall Mall Gazette*, Sept. 7 (O.E.D.). Ex *pitch a ᵗale*, q.v.

pitch, v.i. To sit down ; take a seat (and a rest) : late C. 18–20 : coll. ; ob., except in dial. (where *pitch oneself*). Ex S.E. sense, to place oneself. O.E.D.—2. To do business : showmen's and tramps' : from ca. 1880. Henley, 1887, 'You swatchel-coves that pitch and slam.' Like *pitch*, n., 1, this may orig. have been c. Also *do a pitch.*—3. See **pitch a or the fork, a tale.**—4. To utter base coin : c. (— 1874). H., 5th ed.—5. To go to bed for less than the ordinary time ; have a short sleep : esp. among bakers, busmen, etc. : from ca. 1870. H., 5th ed. Perhaps because they pitch themselves down on the bed.

pitch, do a. See **pitch,** n., 2. From ca. 1860. H. ; Hindley ; Henley, 1887, 'A conjuror Doing his pitch in the street.'

pitch, make a. (Of a cheapjack) to attempt to do business : low coll. (— 1874). H., 5th ed.

pitch, queer the. To spoil a sale, a performance : showmen's and cheapjacks' : 1875, Frost, *Circus Life.* See **pitch,** n., 1, 2.—2. Hence, to mar one's plans : coll. : C. 20. *St. James's Gazette*, April 10, 1901, 'Queering the pitch of the Italians.'

pitch a or the fork, a tale. To tell a story, esp. if romantic or pitiful : resp. s., ca. 1859–1920 ; from ca. 1865,—s. until C. 20, then coll. H., 1st ed. (*pitch the fork*) ; Anon., *A Lancashire Thief*, 'Brummagem Joe . . . could patter and pitch the fork with any one' ; *The London Herald*, March 23, 1867, 'If he had had the sense to . . . pitch them a tale, he might have got off.' Cf. *pitch it strong.*

Pitch-and-Fill. Bill = William. Rhyming s. (— 1859). H., 1st ed.

pitch and pay, v.i. To pay on the nail : coll. :

C. 15–mid-19. Tusser ; Shakespeare, *Henry the Fifth*, 'Let senses rule ; the word is "pitch and pay" ; | Trust none' ; Evans, *Yorkshire Song*, 1810. Ex a Blackwell Hall enactment that a penny be *paid* by the owner of every bale of cloth for *pitching.*

pitch-fingers. A pilferer. Whence *pitch-fingered*, thievishly inclined. Coll. : ca. 1840–1920.

pitch-in. A railway collision : Scottish coll. (— 1909). Ware.

pitch in, v.i. To set vigorously to work : coll., chiefly U.S. and Colonial : 1847 (O.E.D.).—2. Hence, to take a hand ; to begin eating : coll. : from ca. 1850. Perhaps ex :

pitch into. To attack energetically, with blows or words (hence, to reprimand) : 1843, De Quincey, 'Both pitched into us in 1843' (= attacked) ;- Dickens, 1852 (with words) ; Grant Allen, 1885 (of eating heartily). Coll. O.E.D.

pitch it. To desist ; leave one's job ; to cease doing something : tailors' : late C. 19–20. *The Tailor and Cutter*, Nov. 29, 1928.

pitch it (too) strong. To exaggerate : from ca. 1870 : s. till C. 20, then coll.

pitch-kettled. Puzzled ; 'stumped' : ca. 1750–1830. Cowper, 'I . . . find myself pitch-kettled, | And cannot see . . . | How I shall hammer out a letter' ; Grose, 2nd ed. Lit., stuck fast, as in a kettle of pitch.

pitch-pole, pitchpole. To sell at double the cost-price : coll. : ca. 1850–90.

pitch the fork. See **pitch a fork.**—**pitch the hunters.** See **hunters.**

***pitch the nob.** See **prick the garter.**

pitch-up. One's family or chums ; a group or crowd : Winchester : from ca. 1850. Hence :

pitch up with. To associate with : Winchester : from ca. 1860.

pitched. 'Cut', q.v. : tailors' : from ca. 1860.

pitcher. The female pudend : low coll. : C. 17–20 ; ob. Wycherley.—2. Newgate Prison : c. : 1812, Vaux ; † by 1850. Also *the stone pitcher* (cf. *jug*).—3. See **snide-pitcher.**

pitcher, bang a. To drain a pot : coll. : C. 19–20 ; ob. Cf. † S.E. *pitcher-man*, a toper.

pitcher, crack a. To take a virginity ; whereas *crack one's pitcher* is to lose it : C. 18–20 ; ob. Coll., almost S.E. See **pitcher,** 1, and cf. :

pitcher, cracked. A harlot still faintly respect-able : coll. : mid-C. 18–mid-19. Smollett.

pitcher that holds water mouth downwards, the miraculous. The female pudend : a conundrum c.p. of mid-C. 18–mid-19. Grose, 2nd ed. (1788).

pitcher-bawd. 'The poor Hack '—worn-out whore—' that runs of Errands to fetch Wenches or liquor,' B.E. : low coll. : late C. 17–mid-18.

pitching, go (a). To turn somersaults : circus (— 1887). Baumann.

pitchpole. See **pitch-pole.**—**pitchy-man.** See **dolly-man.**

pith. To sever (the spinal cord) : medical (— 1909). Ware. Because this lets out the 'pith' or marrow.

***pitman.** An occ. form of *pit-man.*

pitster. One in, a frequenter of, the pit : theat-rical coll. (— 1887). Baumann. Perhaps on *tip-ster.*

pittite. One sitting in the pit at a theatre : coll. : 1807 (S.O.D.). Thackeray. Occ. *pitite.*

Pitt's picture. A bricked-up window : ca. 1787–1800 : political. Done by the poor and the miserly, to save paying Pitt's window-tax. Grose, 2nd ed.

pity the poor sailor on a night like this ! A semi-jocular c.p. *à propos* of a stormy night : late C. 19–20.

Pivot City, the. A nickname—among outsiders, jocular coll. verging on S.E., but in its proud coiners', i.e. in Geelong, eyes actually S.E.—for Geelong in Victoria, Australia : ca. 1860–1910. Morris.

pivoter. A golfer that, in swinging his club, turns his body as on a pivot : golfers' coll. : from middle 1920's. (O.E.D. Sup.)

piz or **pizz.** A young man-about-town : Society : ca. 1760–80. O.E.D. Cf. *puz(z)*.

pize on, upon, of ; pize take it ; etc. Coll. imprecations : C. 17–20. Since ca. 1840, only dial. Cognate, prob., with *pest, pox,* and possibly *poison.* Middleton, Shadwell, Smollett, Scott. O.E.D.

pizzle. The penis of an animal, esp. of a bull : from ca. 1520. Hence, C. 17–20, of a man. S.E. until ca. 1840, then dial. and a vulg. Ex Flemish *pezel* or Low Ger. *pesel,* orig. a little sinew.

pizzle. (Of the male) to coït with : C. 18–20 : low coll. Ex the n.

placable. Catachrestic for : quiet, peaceable ; C. 17–20 ; rare after C. 18. O.E.D.

place. An abode ; a place of business : coll. : mid-C. 19–20.—2. A privy, a w.c. : coll. : C. 19–20 ; ob.—3. **the place,** the privities : low coll. or perhaps euphemistic S.E. : C. 18–20. Sterne, ' You shall see the very place, said my uncle Toby. Mrs. Wadham blushed.'—4. Erroneous for *pleas,* pl. of *plea,* esp. in *common pleas* ; †. O.E.D.

place, v. To identify (thoroughly) ; remember in detail : orig. (ca. 1855) U.S. ; anglicised as a coll. ca. 1880 ; by 1930, virtually S.E. (Thornton).

place, hot. See **hot place.**

place of sixpenny sinfulness. The suburbs ; esp. a brothel there : coll. : C. 17. Dekker.

place-on. A definite or well-established position, e.g. in a queue : Bootham School (— 1925). Anon., *Dict. of Bootham Slang.*

placebo, be at or **go to the school of—hunt (a)— make—play (with)—sing (a).** To play the sycophant, be a time-server or servile : coll. : resp. approx. mid-C. 16–early 17 (Knox) ; 1360–1600 (Langland) ; 1480–1600 (Caxton) ; 1580–1650 ; 1340–1700 (Chaucer, Bacon). Ex the Office for the Dead. Lit., placebo = I shall be acceptable. F. & H. ; O.E.D. ; Apperson.

placent. Catachrestic, as in Charles Reade, for ' propitious '. O.E.D. (Prob. on *complacent.*)

placet. Erroneous for *placit* : C. 17–early 19. O.E.D. E.g. in Bacon and Scott.

placfont. Incorrect for *paktong* : from ca. 1890. O.E.D.

placket. A woman, as sex ; the female pudend : low coll. : resp. C. 17 ; C. 17–18. With second sense, cf. *placket-racket,* the penis (Urquhart), and *placketing and racketing* in James Ray's *The Scene is Changed,* 1932. Ex *placket,* a petticoat-slit or (dress or petticoat) pocket-hole, occ. a chemise.

placket-stung. Venereally infected : coll. : mid-C. 17–18. Ray.

plague. Trouble : coll. : 1818, Scott, ' Deil a . . . body about my house but I can manage when I like . . . ; but I can seldom be at the plague,' i.e. of doing it. (Slightly ob.) O.E.D. Like the next seven entries, ex the weakening of S.E. sense of the respective words.

plague, v. To trouble, bother ; tease, annoy : late C. 16–20 : S.E. until C. 18, then coll. Gay, 1727, ' Husbands and wives . . . plaguing one another ; 1833, Harriet Martineau. O.E.D.

plague ! In ' a plague (up)on, of ', or 'take' : from ca. 1560 ; ob. Coll. verging on S.E. and, after ca. 1720, better considered as S.E. Also *how the,* or *what a, plague !* : late C. 16–18 : coll. > S.E. (O.E.D.)

plagued. ' Plaguily ' : coll. (— 1887). Baumann, ' I'm plagued hard up.'

plaguesome. Troublesome, teasing, annoying : C. 19–20 : S.E. > coll. ca. 1860 ; ob.

plaguily. Exceedingly : coll. : C. 18–20. Swift; Landor, 1828, ' Ronsard is so plaguily stiff and stately,' O.E.D. Ob. by 1850 ; virtually † by 1920. Cf. next two entries.

plaguy. ' Pestilent ' ; ' confounded ' ; excessive, very great : coll. : late C. 17–20 ; ob. Motteux, 1694, ' Women that have a plaguy deal of religion ' ; *Punch,* May 17, 1879, ' A plaguy rise in the price.' O.E.D. Cf. :

plaguy, adv. Exceedingly, very : coll. : from ca. 1740, earlier examples connoting ' a degree of some quality that troubles one by its excess '. Richardson, in *Pamela,* ' I'm a plaguy good-humoured old fellow.' Ob. Ex preceding entry. O.E.D.

plain. Unwatered, undiluted, neat : coll. : from ca. 1850. Only of drinks.

plain as a pack-saddle. Obvious ; very open : coll. : mid-C. 16–mid-18. T. Wilson, 1553 ; Wither ; Ray ; Bailey. (Apperson.)

plain as a packstaff. The more gen. C. 16–17 form (Becon, J. Hall) of :

plain as a pikestaff. Very clear or simple ; beyond argument : late C. 16–20 : coll. >, ca. 1750, S.E. Shacklock, 1565 ; Greene, 1591 ; Smollett ; D'Urfey ; Trollope. (O.E.D.) Cf. preceding and :

plain as a pipe-stem. Exceedingly plain, clear : coll. : late C. 17–18. Ware.

plain as Salisbury. The same : coll. : 1837, Dickens ; curiously adumbrated, as the O.E.D. indicates, in Udall, 1542. Punning *Salisbury Plain.* (By the way, *plain as the sun at noonday* is S.E.) Cf. Shakespeare's *plain as way to parish-church.*

plain as the nose on one's or **your face.** The same : coll. : late C. 17–20. Congreve, ' " As witness my hand " . . . in great letters. Why, 'tis as plain as the nose on one's face.'

Plain Dealer, nickname, whereas *the Plain Dealer* is merely a sobriquet. Wycherley the dramatist (d. 1715), ex his play so named (1674). Dawson.

plain statement. An easy piece of work ; a meal plain to indifference : tailors' : from ca. 1860 ; slightly ob. Ex a statement contrasted with an invoice.

Plains of Betteris. ' The diversion of billiards ', Egan's Grose : Oxford University : ca. 1820–40.

plaister. See **plaster.**

plan, according to. Jocularly and often ironically among soldiers, to mean willy-nilly : 1917–18. Ex Ger. *plangemäss,* a euphemistic misrepresentation in communiqués reporting loss of ground. W. ; B. & P.

'plane, plane. A coll. abbr. of *aeroplane* : 1914 : by 1933, S.E.—2. Erroneously for *plantain* : from ca. 1660. (Perhaps a mere slip of the pen.) O.E.D.

*planet. A candle : c. : 1840, Longfellow ; ob. by 1890, † by 1920. (As source of light.)

plank, v. To put or set down ; deposit : s. and

dial. : 1859 (O.E.D.). Perhaps ex U.S. sense (no. 3), though this may well come ex Eng. dial. Note, however, that, 2, Egan's Grose, 1823, has *plank*, to conceal, and classifies it as Scottish c.,—which suggests that, in this sense, the term is a perversion of *plant*, v., 1, q.v.—3. To table (money) ; pay readily : earliest Eng. record, 1835, Crockett (*plank up*) ; the U.S. dates (see esp. Thornton) are : *plank*, 1824 ; *plank up*, 1847 ; *plank down*, 1850. Both nuances are prob. a fusion of *put on the plank*(*s*) and *plank* as an echoic v. expressing violent action (cf. *plonk*) ; note that Ware has *plank the knife in*(*to*), to stab deeply.

*plánked. Imprisoned : c. (— 1923). Manchon. Ex *plank*, 1.

*plánt. A hiding-place (orig. at a fence's) : c. : from ca. 1787. Grose, 2nd ed. Ex *plant*, v., 1.—2. Hence, hidden plunder or valuables (*the plant*) : c. : from ca. 1810. Vaux, 1812.—3. ' A position in the street to sell from,' H., 1st ed : low : from ca. 1858 ; slightly ob.—4. A swindle or a cleverly planned robbery : c. >, ca. 1890, low s. : 1825, Westmacott (O.E.D.).—5. A spy ; detective : c. : 1812, *Sporting Magazine* (O.E.D.) ; ob.—Hence, 6, a decoy : c. : from ca. 1830 ; ob.—7 A cordon of detectives : c. : 1880 (O.E.D.).—8. Hence, in C. 20 s., ' A plant set to detect motorists travelling at illegal speed,' O.E.D., 1909.—9. Loosely, a trick, a deception : 1889, *Notes and Queries*, ' The dispassionate scholar finds the whole thing a " plant ".' [Senses 1–3 : ex *plant*, v., 1 ; the other senses, by ' hence '.]—10. (Extremely rare in singular.) A foot : (?) low : C. 17–18. Ex † S.E. *plant*, the sole of the foot.

*plánt. To conceal, hide : c. : C. 17–20. Rowlands, *Martin Mark-All*, ' To plant, to hide ' ; Grose. Now esp. Australian, says the O.E.D. in 1909. Ex the planting of a seed, perhaps influenced by sense 2. Cf. *plant*, n., 1, 2.—2. Hence, to hide (esp. horses) until a suitable reward is offered : Australian : 1840, *The Sydney Herald*, Feb. 10.—3. To place or set in position ; to post (a person) : mid-C. 16–20 : S.E. till ca. 1705, then coll. >, by 1780, low coll. J. Drake, 1706 ; Zangwill, 1892. O.E.D.—4. Whence, to achieve, or to assist, sexual intromission : C. 17–20 : low coll. Cf. *plant a man*. —5. To bury : Grose, 1785 ; Mark Twain, *Innocents at Home*.—6. To abandon : s. or coll. : 1821, Byron ; rare and ob. Cf. Fr. *planter là*. O.E.D.— 7. To select a person or a building for a swindle or a robbery : c. : C. 19–20 ; ob.—8. To plan, or devise, or prepare by illegal methods : c. or low s. : 1892, *The Daily News*, May 27, ' The affair was " planted " between two brothers.' O.E.D.—9. To utter base coin : c. : C. 19–20 ; ob.—10. To humbug ; deceive : c. : C. 19–20 ; ob.—11. To dispose cards for cheating : c. : from ca. 1840.—12. (In mining) to salt : c. almost imm. > low s. : from ca. 1850. Reade, 1850.—13. In conjuring, to prepare a trick by depositing an object in the charge of a confederate : coll. : from ca. 1880.—14. To deliver (a punch) ; to drive (the ball) into the goal or ' into ' another player : boxing, football : from 1808 and ca. 1880 resp. : s. >, as to football, coll. in C. 20. —15. Hence, to hit : at certain Public Schools, esp. Marlborough : late C. 19–20. C. Turley, *Godfrey Marten, Schoolboy*, 1902, ' You would plant him every time if you were taught properly.'

*plánt, in. In hiding ; hidden : c. : 1812, Vaux. Ex *plant*, n., 1.

*plánt, rise the. To take up and remove any-

thing that has been hid, whether by yourself or another ', Vaux, 1812 : c. Cf. :

*plánt, spring a. To unearth another's hidden plunder : c. : 1812, Vaux. Cf. preceding.

plant a man. To copulate : coll. : C. 18–19. (Rarely of a woman.)

plant home. To deliver (a, or as a, blow) ; hence, in argument, to make a point, and, in gen., to succeed (*plant it*, or *one, home*). From ca. 1885 : s. till ca. 1910, then coll. A special use of *plant*, v., last sense but one.

*plánt (the) whids and stow them. To be very wary of speech ; purposely say nothing : c. : C. 17– mid-19. Rowlands, Grose. Cf. *stow it !* ; *whids* = words.

*plánt (a person) upon (another). ' To set somebody to watch his motions ' : c. (— 1812) ; ob. Vaux. Merely a special application of *plant*, v., 3, q.v.

Plantago. A nickname given, by their intimates, to the various Plantagenets, Marquises of Hastings, and esp. to the 4th Marquis, fl.—on the turf—ca. 1850–68. Reginald Herbert, *When Diamonds Were Trumps*, 1908.

planter. A blow ; esp. a punch in the face : sporting : from ca. 1820 ; ob. *The Sporting Magazine*, 1821, ' Smith put in a dreadful planter on Powell's throat,' O.E.D.—2. A horse apt to refuse to budge : (orig. Anglo-Indian) coll. : 1864, ' Competition Wallah ' Trevelyan.—3. A stealer and then hider of cattle : Australia : 1890, ' Rolf Boldrewood '. Morris. Ex *plant*, v., 1 ; cf. *plant*, v., 2, and :

planting, adj. Cattle-stealing : Australia : 1890, ' Rolf Boldrewood '. Cf. *plant*, v., 2, *planter*, 3.

plants. See *plant*, n., last sense.

plants, water one's. To shed tears : C. 19. Cf. *water-works, turn on the*.

plasmasome. Incorrect for *plasmosome* : late C. 19–20. O.E.D.

plaster. ' A huge shirt or applied collar ' : nonaristocratic : ca. 1890–1914. Ware. This looks like a corruption of Fr. *plastron*, a (stiff) shirt-front. —2. A mortgage : Canadian : from ca. 1920. John Beames, *Gateway*, 1932, ' We might put a plaster on the house.'

plaster, v. To shatter (a bird) with shot, blow it into a pulp : sporting : 1883, Bromley-Davenport. Cf. quotation at *plasterer*. (O.E.D.)—2. Hence, to shell heavily : military : from 1914. F. & Gibbons.

plaster of warm guts. ' One warm Belly clapt to another ', B.E. : ' a receipt frequently prescribed for different disorders ', Grose, 1785. A late C. 17– mid-19 low coll., almost a (men's) c.p. Cf. the frequent, and often well-meant c.p. advice, *what you need is a woman* : mid-C. 19–20.

plastered. Drunk : from ca. 1916 ; orig. military. Cf. *plaster* and *shot*, adj.

plasterer. A clumsy shot with a gun (cf. *Peter Gunner*, q.v.) : sporting : 1883, O.E.D. Bromley-Davenport, *Sport*, 1885, ' The plasterer is one who thinks nothing of the lives and eyes of the men who surround him, and blows his pheasant to a pulp before the bird is seven feet in the air.' Cf. *plaster*, q.v.

plasterer's trowel and Seringapatam. Fowl and ham : rhyming s. (— 1909) ; ob. Ware.

plate. The amount collected in the *plate* at church : coll. : C. 20.

plate, be in for the. To be venereally infected :

ca. 1780–1850. 'He has won the *heat* . . . a simile drawn from horse racing,' Grose, 1785.

plate, foul a. See **foul a plate.**

plate-fleet comes in, when the. When I make or get a fortune : coll. : ca. 1690–1830. B.E., Grose. The Plate fleet was that which carried to Spain the annual yield of the American silver mines. Cf. the C. 19–20 *when my ship comes in.*

plate it. To walk : from ca. 1890 : rather low, slightly ob. Ex *plates,* q.v.

plate of meat. A street : rhyming s. (— 1857) 'Ducange Anglicus.' Contrast *plates of meat.*

plated butter. A piece of butter genuine superficially, internally lard : low London (— 1823) ; † by 1900. ' Jon Bee.'

plates. Short for *plates of meat,* q.v. : from ca. 1885. Marshall, ' *Pomes* ', ' A cove we call Feet, sir, on account of the size of his plates '.

Plates, New and Old. Stock Exchange s., from ca. 1880, for shares in, resp., the English Bank of the River Plate and the London & River Plate Bank. The latter, † by 1915.

plates and dishes. Kisses : C. 20. P. P., *Rhyming Slang,* 1932. Cf. *hit or miss,* q.v.

plates of meat. Feet : rhyming s. (— 1874). H., 5th ed.

[**platter-faced.** Broad-faced. Despite B.E. and others, it is prob. S.E.]

platters of meat. A variant (— 1923) of *plates of meat.* Manchon.

platinum blond(e). A female with gold-grey hair : coll. : U.S., anglicised by 1933. C.O.D. (1934 Sup.).

play, v. See **play it off** and **play off.**—2. To make fun of : coll. : 1891, Kinglake, in *The Australian at Home,* ' They do love to play a new chum,' O.E.D. Slightly ob.

play a big game. To try for a big success : low (— 1909). Ware.

*****play a cross.** See **play across.**

play a dark game. To conceal one's motive : coll. verging on S.E. : from ca. 1885. Milliken, 1888, ' Bin playing some dark little game ? '

play-actor. A humorous fellow : Glasgow coll. (— 1934).

*****play across ;** occ. **play a-cross or a cross.** Same as *play booty,* q.v. : c. of ca. 1810–70. Vaux.

play artful. To feign simplicity ; keep something in reserve : low coll. : from ca. 1840.

play at push-pin or two-handed put. See **push-pin** and **put, play at** . . .

play camels. To drink too much : to get drunk : Anglo-Indian (— 1909). Ware. Ex a camel's drinking habits.

play diddle-diddle. (V.i.) to play tricks ; **to** wheedle : coll. : C. 16. Skelton.

play for paste. See **paste, play for.**

play it off. To make an end ; the imperative = it's time you finished : s. or coll. : late C. 16–mid-17. See esp. Shakespeare, 1st *Henry the Fourth,* II, iv, ' They call drinking deep, dyeing scarlet ; and when you breath in your watering, then they cry hem, and bid you play it off.' Lit., orig., and gen., however, this is merely a form of *play off,* v., 2, q.v.

play it (too) low ; occ. **play low.** To take (a mean) advantage : s. > coll. : resp. 1892, Zangwill ; *The Referee,* Aug. 15, 1886.—2. V.t., **play or play it (low) down on** : U.S. (1882) anglicised ca. 1890 : s. > coll. Marie Corelli, 1904. O.E.D.

play least in sight, v.i. To hide ; keep out of the way : coll. : C. 17–mid-19. R. West, 1607 ; Grose, 1785. (Apperson.)

play low. See **play it low.**—**play low down (on).** See **play it too low.**—**play marbles.** See **play trains.**

play off ; play with oneself. To masturbate : low : C. 18–19 ; C. 19–20.—2. To toss off or finish (liquor) : late C. 16–mid- or early 17. See quotation at *play it off* ; Dekker, 1607, ' He requested them to play off the sacke and begon.' O.E.D.

play off one's dust. To drink : ca. 1870–1910. (Remove it from one's throat.)

play owings. To live on credit : sporting (— 1909) : s. verging on coll. Ware.

play possum. See **possum.**—**play square.** See **square.**—**play straight.** See **straight.**

play tapsalteerie. To leap backwards ; fall head over heels : Scots coll. : 1826, John Wilson. O.E.D. The Scots adv. *tapsalteerie* (? ex *top* + Fr. *sauter*) = topsy-turvy.

play the ace against the jack. (Of a woman) to grant the favour : low : C. 19–20 ; ob. A figure that, taken from cards, is suggested by *jack* = *John Thomas.*

play the duck. To show oneself a coward : coll. : C. 17. Urquhart.

play the game. To act honourably : coll. : 1889, *The Daily Chronicle,* May 2, 1904, ' Men do not talk about their honour nowadays—they call it " playing the game ",' O.E.D. (Lit., playing to the rules ; cf. *it's not cricket* and *play up,* 1.)

play the game of dockets. To avoid giving a decision, or expressing a definite opinion, by passing on the matter to some other department : civil servants' : C. 20.

play the (giddy) goat. See **goat, play the.**—2. But *play the goat,* in s. or low coll., also = (of the male) to fornicate hard : C. 19–20 ; ob.

play the Jack. To play the knave : coll. : ca. 1560–1700. Golding ; Ray. (Apperson.)

play the whole game. To cheat : ca. 1780–1840. Grose, 1785. Perhaps lit., play every trick one can : as well as one knows.

play to the gallery. To court applause, esp. if cheaply and coarsely : theatrical coll. : from ca. 1890.—2. Hence, chiefly in sport, to adopt spectacular means to gain applause : C. 20 : coll. >. ca. 1930, S.E.

play to the gas, says *The Daily Mail* of March 16, 1899, ' is used in the general sense in reference to small audiences, but strictly it means that an audience was only large enough to render receipts sufficient to pay the bill for the evening's lighting '. Theatrical s. : ca. 1890–1905.

play trains !, run away and. Don't bother me ! ; go away, you (*anything suitable*) ! : a C. 20 c.p. See—at **play with yourself,**—the cruder *run away and play with yourself !,* with which cf. the schoolboy *run away and play marbles !,* itself an exact equivalent of . . . *play trains !*

play up. To do one's best : coll. : from ca. 1895. Newbolt, 1898, ' Play up, play up, and play the game ! ' See also **play the game** : prob. both phrases are taken from the playing-fields, but *play up* may have been suggested by *play up to,* q.v.—2. To be troublesome : coll. : late C. 19–20. Of animals, esp. horses, and persons.—3. To make fun of, to annoy or tease : from early 1920's : coll. >, by 1933, S.E. (O.E.D. Sup.)

play up to. To take one's cue from another ; to humour another, back him up, or to meet him on his own ground ; to flatter : coll. : from ca. 1825. (Implied in) Disraeli, 1826. Cf. *play up,* 1. Ex :— 2. So to act in a play as to assist another actor :

theatrical s. : 1809, Malkin, ' You want two good actors to play up to you,' O.E.D.

play with oneself. See **play off.**

play with (the ease of) a tooth-pick. V.t., to play (one's opponents' bowling) with ease : cricket coll. : 1899, J. C. Snaith ; slightly ob. Lewis.

play with yourself !, run away and : an insulting variant, or perhaps the original, of *play trains*, q.v.

playground. ' Gingerbread slab, or sandwich, served as pudding ' : Bootham School (— 1925). Ex hardness.

playing the harp. Drunk, and going home by the railings : Anglo-Irish : C. 20. Ex the tapping on the railings, here likened to harp-strings.

ple ; plea. Erroneous forms of *please* : C. 15–16. O.E.D.

pleader, a poor. A poor unfortunate devil : lower classes' coll. (— 1923). Manchon. Cf. *artist, client, merchant*, all = a chap, a fellow. *?* ex *bleeder*.

please God we live. God permitting : lower classes' coll. (— 1887). Baumann.

please, I want the cook-girl ! A London c.p. directed at, or said of, ' a youth haunting the head of area steps ' : ca. 1895–1915. Ware.

please, mother, open the door ! A Cockney c.p. spoken admiringly at a passing girl : ca. 1900–14. Ware.

please oneself. To do just as one likes : coll., esp. in *please yourself !* : late C. 19–20. Ex the S.E. sense, to satisfy, esp. to gratify, oneself.

please the pigs ! See **pigs !, please the.**

pleased !, (s)he *will* be. An ironic c.p. : from ca. 1920.

pleased as Punch(, as). Extremely pleased : 1854, Dickens : coll. >, by 1910, S.E. Perhaps ex the early pictures of Punch on the cover of the weekly so named and founded in 1841.

pleasure. ' To go out for pleasure, take a holiday ', O.E.D. : coll. Not before C. 20, except in dial., where it occurs in 1848 (E.D.D.). Esp. as *pleasuring*, n. Ex the S.E. v.i., to have or take pleasure.

pleasure-boat. The female pudend : low : C. 19–20 ; ob.

pleasure-garden padlock. A menstrual cloth : C. 17–early 19. *?* coll. or euphemistic S.E.

pleasuring, vbl.n. See **pleasure.**

pleb or plebs. At Westminster School, a tradesman's son : pejorative : mid-C. 19–20 ; slightly ob. Ex L. *plebs*, the proletariat. Cf. *Volsci*, q.v.—2. (Only as *pleb*.) Any plebeian : 1823, ' Jon Bee '. Cf. U.S. *plebe*, a newcomer at West Point, and :

plebbish ; plebbishness. Plebeian (character or condition) ; caddish(ness) : 1860, O.E.D. See preceding.

plebs. See **pleb, 1.**

pleceman, pliceman ; or p'l.- A policeman : low coll. (— 1887). Baumann.

pledge. To give away. Esp. in *pledge you !*, after you (with that) !, and *I'll pledge it you when I've done with it.* Winchester : C. 19–20. See esp. R. G. K. Wrench, *Notions*, 2nd ed., 1901.

plenipo. A **plenipo**tentiary : coll. : 1687, Dryden ; rare in C. 19–20. Vanbrugh, 1697, ' I'll . . . say the plenipos have signed the peace, and the Bank of England's grown honest.'—2. The male member : low : C. 18–19. Cf. Captain Morris's scabrosity, *The Plenipotentiary*, ca. 1786.

plenipo, v.i. To be or act as a plenipotentiary : coll. : 1890. Rare. O.E.D.

Plenipo Rummer. Poet Prior (1664–1721), ' who

helped to arrange the preliminaries of the Peace of Utrecht (1713) '. See **plenipo**, n., 1. Dawson.

plentitude. Incorrect for *plenitude* : C. 17–20 ; ob. On *plenty*. O.E.D.

plenty, adj. Plentiful, abundant, numerous : C. 14–20 : S.E. until ca. 1840, then coll. Le Fanu, 1847, ' Wherever kicks and cuffs are plentiest ', O.E.D. Ex the n.—Whence *plenty*, adv. = abundantly : coll. : 1842. H. Collingwood, 1884, ' They're plenty large enough.' O.E.D. and E.D.D.

Plenty and Waste. ' Mrs Gore (1799–1861), novelist and dramatist, and her daughter ' (Dawson).

pleo. Incorrect for *pilau* : C. 17–18. O.E.D.

pliceman. See **pleceman.**

plier. A hand : from ca. 1830 : somewhat low. In C. 20, ob.—2. (Gen. *plyer*.) A crutch : c. : mid C. 17–early 19. Coles, 1676 (at *lifter*) ; B.E. ; Grose.—3. A trader : coll. : C. 18–early 19. The idea of plying one's trade is latent in all three senses.

plink-plonk ; plinkety-plonk ; also **blink-blonk.** White wine : facetious military : 1915–18. B. & P. On Fr. *vin blanc*.

ploll-cat. A whore : C. 17. A corruption of † S.E. *pole-cat*, the same. F. & H.

plonk. Mud, esp. that of no-man's land : military : 1916–18. (Hence, *over the plonk*, ' over the top '.) B. & P. Ex the noise made when one draws one's feet from the clinging mire. Cf. Lakeland *plonch*, to walk in mire (E.D.D.)—2. Pinky, cheap port, sold by the quart : Australian : from ca. 1926. Prob. ex *plink-plonk*, q.v.—3. Hence, any kind of wine of no matter what quality : id. : from ca. 1930. Gen. jocularly.

plonk. (Gen. v.i.) To shell : military : 1915 ; slightly ob. F. & Gibbons, ' Suggested by the sound of the impact and burst '.

plot. A C. 17 erroneous form of *plod*. O.E.D.

plough, n. Ploughed land : hunting s. >, ca. 1900, hunting coll. : 1861, Whyte-Melville, ' It makes no odds to him, pasture or plough.' O.E.D. Ex E. Anglian dial., where it occurs in 1787 : E.D.D. —2. Rejecting a candidate in an examination, whether action or accomplished fact : 1863, Charles Reade. O.E.D. (Cf. *ploughing*.) Ex :

plough, v. To reject in an examination : university (orig. Oxford) : 1853, Bradley, *Verdant Green* ; 1863, Reade, ' Gooseberry pie . . . adds to my chance of being ploughed for smalls.' Cf. S.E. **pluck**, concerning which, in relation to *plough*, Smyth-Palmer in his *Folk-Etymology* makes some interesting, by no means negligible suggestions. Cf. *ploughing*.

plough into. To address oneself vigorously to (food) : coll. (— 1923), mostly lower classes'. Manchon. Cf. *pitch into*.

plough the deep. To (go to) sleep : rhyming s. (— 1859). H., 1st ed.

plough with dogs !, I might as well. This is useless, or very ineffective! : C. 17–20 : a c.p. >, by 1700, semi-proverbial ; from ca. 1860, only in dial. (Apperson.)

ploughed, ppl.adj. See **plough**, v.—2. Tipsy : low : ca. 1852–1910. ' Ducange Anglicus.' Cf. *screwed*.

ploughing. A plucking in an examination : university : 1882, Emma Worboise. O.E.D. Ex *plough*, v., and cf. *plough*, n.

plouter. See **plowter.**

plover. A wanton (cf. *pheasant* and *quail*) : c. : C. 17. Ben Jonson.—2. A dupe or a victim : c. :

ca. 1620–40. Esp. *green plover*, as in Jonson and Chapman, 'Thou art a most greene Plover in policy, I Perceive.' Prob. suggested by equivalent *pigeon* (q.v.). O.E.D.

plowed. See **ploughed**.

plowter ; occ. **plouter**. To copulate : low : C. 19–20 ; ob. ? *plough* corrupted or ex *plouter*, *plowter*, to splash about in mire or water (see O.E.D. and E.D.D.).

'ploy, ploy. To employ : dial. (late C. 17–20) and, hence, coll., late C. 19–20. As a n., it is used in the Public Schools for a task.

pluck. Courage : 1785, Grose : boxing s. >, ca. 1830, gen. coll. Scott, in 1827, called it a ' black-guardly ' word, and ladies using it during the Crimean War were regarded with the same shocked admiration as one felt towards those who in the War of 1914–18 used the exactly analogous *guts* ; it is now almost S.E. Ex *pluck*, the heart, lungs, liver (and occ. other viscera) of an animal, hence, ca. 1710, of a person.—2. In photographs, boldness, distinctness of effect : photographic : 1889. O.E.D. Cf. *plucky*, 2.

pluck, against the. Reluctantly : ca. 1785–1850 : **s.** > coll. Grose, 1st ed.

pluck a pigeon. See **pigeon**, n., 5.

pluck a rose. To visit the privy : coll. : C. 18–19. Grose, 1785. Chiefly among women and because the rural w.c. was often in the garden.

pluck Sir Onion or the riband. To ring the bell at a tavern : resp. late C. 17–mid-18, B.E. ; late C. 17–early 19, B.E., Grose, 1st ed. Prob. *riband* refers to a bell-push ; perhaps *onion*, the round ' handle '.

pluck-up fair. ' A general scramble for booty or spoil,' O.E.D. : ca. 1570–1650 : coll.

plucked. Courageous : gen. preceded by *cool-, good-, rare-*, or *well-* ; or by *bad-*. Coll. : 1848, Thackeray (*good plucked*) ; Hughes, 1857 (*bad plucked*) ; 1860, *plucked 'un*. O.E.D. ; H., 2nd ed.

plucked, hard-. Hard-hearted : coll. : 1857, Kingsley ; ob. Cf. *bad-plucked* and *pluckless*.

pluckily. Bravely : coll. >, ca. 1920, S.E. : 1858, Trollope. (But *pluckiness* is S.E.) O.E.D.

pluckless. Faint-hearted : coll. > S.E. : from ca. 1820 ; ob. Ex *pluck*, 1.

plucky. Courageous, esp. over a period or by will-power : coll. >, by 1920, S.E. : 1842, Barham ' If you're " plucky ", and not over-subject to fright ' ; Disraeli, 1826, had ' with as pluck a heart '. O.E.D. Ex *pluck*, 1, q.v. ; cf. *plucked*, q.v.—2. (Of negative or print) bold, distinct : photographic coll. : 1885. O.E.D. Cf. *pluck*, 2.

pluff. A shot from a musket, etc. : coll. : 1828, J. Wilson (O.E.D.). Ex the echoic S.E. (mainly Scots) *pluff*, an explosive emission of air (1663). Cf. *pluffer*, q.v.—2. As adv. or interjection : coll., mainly Scots : 1860. O.E.D. Cf. S.E. *phit*.

pluffer. A shooter, a gunner : coll. (orig. Scots) : 1828, J. Wilson. See **pluff**, 1. O.E.D.

plug, n. A punch ; a knock (occ. fig.) : 1798, Pitt, ' The bill . . . in spite of many Plugs from Sir W. Pulteney, will certainly pass.' O.E.D.—2. A draught of beer : 1816, ' Come, sir, another plug of malt,' O.E.D. Ob.—3. An inferior horse : **s.** >, ca. 1920, coll. : Colonial and—prob. ex—U.S. : 1872, in U.S. Also *old plug*, ob. Ex *plug*, a stop-hole, perhaps influenced by *plug-tobacco*, often inferior and rank. But in Australia, from ca. 1880, a good, steady, though slow horse, and in New Zealand, late C. 19–20, a horse that is ' a good sort '. O.E.D.—4. Hence, an inferior, deteriorated, or

damaged object or person : from ca. 1890.—5. Hence, a workman with irregular apprenticeship : mostly artisans' : from ca. 1875.—6. Any defect : low : from ca. 1895. Ex senses 1, 3.—7. A translation : school and university : 1853, Bradley, *Verdant Green*, ' Those royal roads to knowledge . . . cribs, crams, plugs, abstracts, analyses, or epitomes '. Ob. by 1900, † by 1920.—8. A ' plug-hat ', i.e. a top hat : U.S. (— 1864), partly anglicised ca. 1890 ; Kipling, e.g., uses it in 1891. Prob. because ' the head fits in it like a plug '. O.E.D.—9. A small jam of logs : Canadian lumbermen's coll. : C. 20. John Beames.

plug, v. (Of the male) to coït with : low : C. 18–20. Cf. *plug-tail*, q.v. Ex S.E. sense, drive a plug into.—2. To punch, esp. *plug in the eye* : 1875, P. Ponder, ' Cries of . . . " Plug him ! " . . .', E.D.D. Cf. sense 1.—3. To shoot (v.t.) : 1875, J. G. Holland ; 1888, ' Rolf Boldrewood ', ' If that old horse . . . had bobbed forward . . . you'd have got plugged instead.' O.E.D.—4. To continue, persist, doggedly : 1865, at Oxford (O.E.D.) ; soon gen. ; in C. 20, coll., esp. *plug along*, mainly of walking.—5. ' To labour with piston-like strokes against resistance ' : 1898, G. W. Steevens (that brilliant unfortunate). O.E.D. By 1930, coll.—6. V.t., to try to popularise (a song) by dinning it into the public ear : coll. : 1927. O.E.D. (Sup.).—7. See **plugged**.

plug along or **on.** See **plug**, v., 4.

Plug Street. ' The Flemish village of Ploegsteert near Armentières ' : military coll. : from 1914. F. & Gibbons.

plug-tail. The penis : low : mid-C. 18–mid-19. Grose, 1785.

plugged, ppl.adj. (Of a bidder) silenced at once by a seller : Stock Exchange : from ca. 1919. Ex *plug*, v., 2, or v., 3.

plugger ; **plugging.** An impersonator, -ation, at elections : Canadian coll. : 1897, *The Westminster Gazette*, Dec. 1 (O.E.D.). ? ex *plug*, to insert something closely (as a stop-gap). 2. E.g. a rower, a runner, who ' plugs ' along ; the corresponding effort : coll. : late C. 19–20. Ex *plug*, v., 4.—3. (plugging.) The interposition of advertisement ' gags ' in ' turns ' on the wireless : from 1933. (*The Evening News*, July 13, 1934.)

pluggy. Short and stumpy : dial. (— 1825) >, ca. 1860, coll. Agnes Strickland, 1861, ' A short, pluggy (thick) man, with a pug nose ', O.E.D. Ex S.E. n. *plug*.

Plum. P. F. Warner, who retired from cricket in 1920 : cricketers' : C. 20. By a slurring of his Christian name : *Pelham*.

plum ; in C. 17–18, gen. **plumb.** A fortune of £100,000 : 1689, the Earl of Ailesbury. Steele, ' An honest gentleman who . . . was worth half a plumb, stared at him ' ; Thackeray. Slightly ob. (O.E.D.)—2. Hence, loosely, a fortune : coll. : 1709, Prior, ' The Miser must make up his Plumb,' though here, as in most other instances, the specific sum may be intended. Slightly ob.—3. (? hence) a rich man ; orig. and properly, the possessor of £100,000 ; C. 18–early 19. Addison, 1709, ' Several who were Plumbs . . . became men of moderate fortunes.' (O.E.D.)

plum, give a taste of. To shoot (a person) with a bullet : low : 1834, Ainsworth ; † by 1900. I.e. *plumb*, lead.

plum and apple. Any jam : military coll. : 1915–18. F. & Gibbons. The ranks seldom got anything but plum and apple : a fact satirised by Bairnsfather in his famous cartoon, ' The Eternal Question. " When the 'ell is it going to be strawberry ? " '

plum-cash. Prime cost : pidgin English (— 1864) H., 3rd ed.

plum-duff. Plum-pudding or dumpling : 1840 : coll., orig. nautical, >, ca. 1890, S.E. O.E.D.

plum-pudding. A type of trench-mortar shell : military coll. : 1915–18. F. & Gibbons. Ex its shape and size.—2. A dappled horse : circus-hands' : C. 20. Laura Knight, *The Evening News*, June 19, 1934.

plum-tree !, have at the. A c.p., either semi-proverbial or in allusion to a song : C. 18–19. Punning S.E. *plum-tree*, the female pudend (Shake-speare). Cf :

plum-tree shaker. ' A man's yard ', Cotgrave, 1611, at *hoche-prunier*. C. 17–18.

plumb, n. See **plum.**—2. V.t., to deceive : ca. 1850–1910 : low. ? ex *plumb*, to fathom.—3. V.i (1889) and v.t. (C. 20), to work (properly, in lead) as a plumber : coll. W. S. Gilbert, ' I have plumbed in the very best families.' Ex *plumber*. O.E.D.

plumb, adv. As an intensive : quite ; com-pletely : 1587, Anon., ' Plum ripe ' : coll. >, by 1750, also dial. In mid-C. 19–20, mainly U.S., but wherever used, in this period rather s. than coll. (O.E.D.)

plumbo-solvent. Incorrect for *plumbisolvent* : late C. 19–20. O.E.D.

plumdanes. Incorrect for *plumdamas*, *-is* : late C. 17–20. O.E.D.

plummy. Rich ; desirable ; very good : 1812, Vaux : s. >, ca. 1880, coll. *The London Herald*, March 23, 1867, ' Ain't this 'ere plummy ? ' Ex S.E. *plum*, something good.—2. Big-bellied : lower classes' (— 1923). Manchon. ? ex *plump*, fat.

plump. A heavy fall or sudden plunge : coll. verging on S.E. : from ca. 1450.—2. Hence, a blow (cf. *plumper*, q.v.) : 1763, C. Johnston (O.E.D.) ; 1785, Grose, ' I'll give you a plump in the bread basket ' : s. >, by ca. 1810, coll. Ob. by 1850, † by 1910.

plump, v. To utter suddenly, abruptly ; blurt out : coll. verging on S.E. : 1579, Fulke, ' A verie peremptorie sentence, plumped downe . . .', O.E.D. —2. To come (very suddenly, i.e.) plump ; plunge *in*, burst *out* : coll. bordering on S.E. : 1829, Lamb (O.E.D.).—3. To shoot ; hit hard, punch : 1785, Grose, ' He pulled out his pops and plumped him ' ; † by 1860.

plump, adj. Big ; great ; well-supplied : coll. verging on S.E. : 1635, Quarles, ' Plump Fee ' ; B.E., ' *Plump-in-the-pocket*, flush of Money ' ; Pollok, 1827. O.E.D. Slightly ob.—2. (Of speech) blunt, ' flat ' : coll. verging on S.E. : 1789, Mme D'Arblay, ' She . . . made the most plump inquiries,' O.E.D. Slightly ob. Cf. *plump*, adv., 2, *plumply*, 1, and *plumpness*, qq.v.

plump, adv. With a sudden fall or encounter : late C. 16–20 : coll. verging on and sometimes merging in S.E. : 1610, Jonson (O.E.D.).—2. Bluntly, flatly : 1734, North, ' Refuse plump ' : coll. >, in C. 20, S.E., though still familiar. O.E.D. Cf. *plump*, adj., 2.

plump currant. In good health ; gen. in negative : ca. 1787–1850. Grose, 2nd ed.

plump (a person) **up to.** To inform him oppor-tunely or secretly about (something) : lower classes' (— 1923). Manchon. Ex *plump*, to fatten.

plumper. A heavy blow : 1772, Brydges, ' Gave

me a plumper on the jaw, | And cry'd : Pox take you ! ' † by ca. 1860.—2. An arrant lie : low coll. : 1812 (O.E.D.). Ob.—3. Something that, in its kind, is uncommonly large : coll. : 1881, *Punch*, Oct. 1 (O.E.D. Sup.). Cf. :

plumping. Unusually or arrestingly large : coll. : C. 20. Cf. *plumper*, 3.

plumply. Unhesitatingly ; plainly, flatly : coll. bordering on S.E. : 1786, Mme D'Arblay, ' The offer was plumply accepted,' O.E.D. Slightly ob. Cf. *plump*, v., 1, and adj., 2 ; also *plumpness*.—2. With a direct impact : same status : 1846, O.E.D. Cf. *plump*, n., 1, and *plump*, v., 2.—3. Immediately : sol. (— 1923). Manchon points out that this is a corruption of *promptly* by *plump*, adv.

plumpness. (Of speech) directness, bluntness : coll. verging on S.E. : 1780, Mme D'Arblay. O.E.D.

plunder. Gain, profit : from ca. 1850. Mayhew, 1851, ' *Plunder* . . . a common word in the horse trade.' Ex the S.E. sense of property acquired illegally or ' shadily '.—2. A grafter's stock or goods : grafters' : from ca. 1890. (Philip Alling-ham, *Cheapjack*, 1934.) Perhaps ex sense 1.

plunge, n. A reckless bet : from ca. 1877 : racing s. >, ca. 1890, gen. coll. Ex :

plunge, v. To bet recklessly ; speculate deeply : 1876, Besant & Rice, ' They plunged . . ., paying whatever was asked,' O.E.D. : (orig. and mostly) racing s. >, ca. 1890, gen. coll. Lit., ' go in deep '.

plunger. A cavalryman : military : 1854, Thackeray, ' Guardsmen, " plungers ", and other military men ', O.E.D. Prob. *plunge*, (of a horse), to throw by plunging.—2. A reckless better, gambler, speculator : 1876, ' The prince of plungers ' ; Besant & Rice, 1876 (O.E.D.). Ex *plunge*, to dive.—3. A Baptist : Church s. : C. 19–20. Ex plunging (immersion) in water at baptism. —4. A hypodermic syringe : orig. medical : from ca. 1912. (Gavin Holt, *Drums Beat at Night*, 1932.)

plunging. Reckless betting, deep speculation : 1876 : racing s. > ca. 1890, gen. coll.

plunk. A fortune ; any large sum : 1767, Josiah Wedgwood (O.E.D.) ; † by 1850. Cf. the U.S. *plunk*, a dollar. As it precedes *plunk*, the v., by some thirty years, the word may be ex *plum*, 1, on *chunk* or *hunk*.—2. ' An exclamation expressing the impact of a blow ', C. J. Dennis : orig. (— 1916) and mainly Australian. Echoic : cf. *plonk*.

plurocentral is incorrect for *pluricentral* : C. 20. O.E.D.

plus, adv.-preposition. And a further, undefined quantity : coll. : C. 20. Ex :—Having in addition, having acquired or gained : coll. : 1856, Kane, ' Bonsall was minus a big toe-nail, and plus a scar upon the nose,' O.E.D.

plus a little something some (loosely, the) **others haven't got.** A c.p., jocular and self-explanatory : 1934 +. Ex an early-1934 motor-oil advertisement.

plus-fours. Wide knickerbockers, orig. and esp. as worn by golfers : 1920 : coll. till ca. 1925, then S.E. Ex *a plus* (e.g.) *2 golfer*, or, more prob., ex the fact that, to get the overhang, the length is in-creased, on the average, by four inches. (O.E.D. Sup. ; C.O.D., 1934 Sup.)

plush. The pubic hair : low : C. 19–20. Cf. *fleece*.—2. That over*plus* of gravy which goes to the cook of each mess : nautical (— 1867). Admiral Smyth. Baumann defines it as an overplus of grog : nautical (— 1887) ; slightly ob. The latter is the usual C. 20 sense : see also F. & Gibbons.

Plush, John. A footman : coll. : from ca. 1845 ; ob. Ex *plushes*, such plush breeches as are worn by footmen, + Thackeray's *The Yellowplush Papers*, ' by Charles Yellowplush, Esq.', the former recorded in 1844 (O.E.D.), the latter pub. in 1837.

plush, take. To accept an inferior position or appointment : coll. : C. 20. Manchon. Perhaps ex the plush worn by footmen.

plute. A plutocrat : coll., orig. (ca. 1920) U.S. ; anglicised not later than 1930.

pluviameter. Erroneous for *pluviometer* : late C. 18–20. O.E.D. On L. *pluvia*, rain.

*plyer. See plier.

*Plymouth cloak. A cudgel : 1608 : c. >, ca. 1660, low s. >, ca. 1700, s. ; † by 1830, except historically. Dekker, ' Shall I walk in a Plymouth cloak (that's to say) like a rogue, in my hose and doublet, and a crab-tree cudgel in my hand ? ' The staff, cut from the woods near Plymouth by sailors recently returned from a long voyage, was jocularly supposed to serve as a cloak to those walking *in cuerpo*, i.e. in hose and doublet : Ray's *Proverbs*. Bowen notes that in the old Navy it = ' an officer's or warrant officer's cane '.

pneumatic cavalry. Cyclist battalions : military : 1917 ; ob. B. & P.

po. A chamber-pot : C. 19–20 : coll. >, ca. 1880, low coll. (When, as rarely, written or pronounced *pot*, it is S.E.) Ex the pronunciation of *pot* in Fr. *pot de chambre*.

po, full as a. Extremely drunk : low : C. 20. Cf. *tight as a drum*.

poach. To blacken (the eyes) : boxing s. > gen. ca. 1890 : ca. 1815–1920. Moore, *Tom Crib*, ' With grinders dislodg'd, and with peepers both poach'd '. Ex Fr. *yeux pochés*.—2. V.t., to gain unfairly or illicitly (an advantage, esp. a start in a race) : the turf : from ca. 1891. Ex S.E. sense, to trespass (on).

po'chaise ; po-chay or **po'chay ; pochay.** Abbr. *post-chaise* : coll. : resp. 1871, Meredith ; 1871 (id., *po'chay*) ; 1827, Scott, in *Chronicles of the Canongate*. O.E.D.

poacher. A broker dealing out of, or frequently changing, his market : Stock Exchange coll. : from ca. 1890.—2. **the Poachers.** The Lincolnshire Regiment : military : late C. 19–20. F. & Gibbons, ' In allusion to the regimental march, " The Lincolnshire Poacher ".'

Poacher Court (or **p.c.**), **the.** The Kirk Session : Scots coll. nickname : 1784, Burns ; † by 1903. E.D.D.

poaching country. ' Resort of all who go shooting ', Egan's Grose : Oxford University : ca. 1820–50.

pock. Small-pox ; syphilis : from M.E. : S.E. until C. 19, then dial. and low coll. Gen. *the pock*. Cf. *pox* and *pocky*, qq.v.

pock-nook, come in on one's own. ' As we say in Scotland when a man lives on his own means ', Sir A. Wylie, *Works*, 1821. Late C. 18–20 ; ob. Coll. A *pock-nook* is a sack-corner or -bottom.

pock- (Eng. **poke-**)**pudding.** An Englishman : Scots coll. : C. 18–20 ; in C. 20, jocular. Burt, *Letters*, 1730 ; Herd. Lit., a bag-pudding ; hence, a glutton ; hence . . . In C. 18, also *pock-pud* : E.D.D.

pocket, he plays as fair as if he'd picked your. A c.p. applied, in C. 19, to a dishonest gambler.

pocket and please yourself !, if not pleased put hand in. A mid-C. 17–18 c.p. retort addressed to grumblers. Ray, *Proverbs*

*pocket-book dropper. A sharper specialising in, or adept at, making money by dropping pocketbooks (gen. containing counterfeit) and gulling the gullible : c. : C. 19–20 ; ob. Cf. *drop-game* and *fawney rig*.

pocket-hank(y). A pocket-handkerchief : resp. low coll. and gen. coll. : late C. 19–20. (Manchon.) The longer form also occurs in dial. : 1886 (E.D.D.).

pocket the red. To effect intromission : billiard-players' erotic s. : late C. 19–20.

pocket-thunder. A breaking of wind : low coll. : C. 19–20 ; ob.

pockets to let(, with). Penniless : jocular coll. : ca. 1820–1900. Moncrieff, in *Tom and Jerry*, 1823, ' Clean'd out ! both sides ; look here—pockets to let ! ' ; Baumann.

pocky. A coarse pejorative or intensive : a vulg.: ca. 1598–1700. Jonson, ' These French villains have pocky wits.' Ex S.E. sense, syphilitic. (O.E.D.)

pocta. A member of the Society for Prevention of Cruelty to Animals : coachmen's : ca. 1885–1910. Baumann.

pod. A pillow, a bed. (Lit., a bundle.) C. 18–19 : c. or low s. See pad, n., 5. F. & H. (The term and its definition are both open to suspicion.) —2. (Gen. **Pod.**) The Post Office Directory : commercial (— 1909). Ware.

pod, in. Pregnant : low (— 1923). Manchon.

poddy, n. A ' poddy calf ', i.e. a calf fed by hand : Australian coll. >, by 1930, standard : late C. 19–20. Jice Doone. Prob. ex dial.

poddy, fat ; cf. sense 1 of :

poddy, adj. Obese, esp. as to the waist-line : coll. : 1844, Edward FitzGerald (O.E.D.). Prob. ex dial. *pod*, a large, protuberant abdomen.—2. Tipsy : (low) coll. : ca. 1860–1910. ? ex sense 1. H., 5th ed. Cf. *podgy*, 2.

podge. A short, fat person ; such an animal : dial. and coll. from ca. 1830.—2. Occ. a nickname : from ca. 1840. Cognate with *pudge*, q.v.—3. A special application is : an epaulette, as in Marryat, 1833 : nautical ; † by 1890.

podgy. Squat ; short, stout, and (if of an animal) thick-set : dial. and coll. >, ca. 1905, S.E. : from ca. 1835. Occ., as a n., a nickname. Ex *podge*, 1.—2. A C. 19 variant of *pogy*, q.v.

pody cody ! A low coll. perversion of *body of God !*, an oath : late C. 17–early 18. Perhaps, however, of Urquhart's invention (1693 in his *Rabelais*). O.E.D.

Poet Bun. See Good Friday.

poet's walk ; Poet's Walk. ' The tea served to Upper Club, on half holidays, in River Walk ', F. & H. : Eton College coll. : late C. 19–20 ; ob.

poge, pogh, pogue. See poke, n.—**pogey.** See pogy.

poggle ; puggle or **puggly.** An idiot : Anglo-Indian coll. (— 1886). Ex Hindustani *pagal*, a madman or idiot. Yule & Burnell.—2. Hence, in the Army (late C. 19–20), mad. F. & Gibbons.

poggle (or **puggle**) **pawnee.** Rum ; any spirituous liquor : Regular Army : late C. 19–20. F. & Gibbons. Ex *poggle*, 2.

poggled ; puggled. Mad-drunk ; mad : id. : id. Ibid. Ex preceding.

pogram. A Dissenter ; a (gen. Nonconformist) formalist ; a religious humbug : 1860 ; † by 1902. H., 3rd ed. : ' from a well-known dissenting minister of the name '. (H., 2nd ed.)

*pogy. (Hard *g.*) Tipsy: c. >, in C. 19, low: ca. 1780–1890, but surviving in U.S. c. Grose, 1785; Halliwell, 1847; H., 1st ed. (where spelt *podgy*); Baumann. Etymology problematic: but perhaps cognate with Romany *pogado*, crooked, ex *pog(er)*, to break, or ex *poggle* (or *puggly*), q.v. Cf. *poggle*, perhaps, and certainly *pogy aqua*; cf., too, *puggy-drunk*.

*pogy (or **pogey**) **aqua !** Make the grog strong ! (lit., little water !): c. or low: ca. 1820–1910. 'Jon Bee', 1823; Baumann. Ex Sp. *poca agua*.

poignet. An error, fathered by Scott, for a dagger-handle or -hilt: 1820. O.E.D.

Poilu. A French soldier; gen., a private in the infantry: coll.: late Oct. or Nov., 1914. Direct ex Fr. ('hairy one', i.e. 'he-man', hence 'brave fellow'). For this extremely interesting term, see esp. *Words !* (article on French soldiers' words and phrases). Cf. *piou-piou*, q.v.

point. A point to which a straight run is made; hence, the cross-country run itself: sporting (esp. hunting) coll.: 1875, Whyte-Melville, *Riding Recollections* (O.E.D.).—2. See **points, get,** and **points to, give.**—3. 'The region of the jaw; much sought after by pugilists', C. J. Dennis: coll.: late C. 19–20.—4. A stopping-place, from which on (e.g.) a tram route, fares are reckoned: coll. (1907: O.E.D. Sup.) >, by 1935, S.E.

point, *v.i.* 'To seize unfair advantage; to scheme', C. J. Dennis: Australian: C. 20. Cf. *pointer,* 2.

point, make his or **their.** (Gen. of a fox) 'to run straight to point aimed at': hunting coll.: 1875, Whyte-Melville, ib. Cf. *point,* 1.

point-beacher. A woman of doubtful character in Portsmouth: naval: C. 20. Bowen. Ex a locality.

point blank. White wine: military: 1914; ob. F. & Gibbons. By 'Hobson-Jobson' ex Fr. *vin blanc.* Cf. *plink-plonk.*

point-failure. Failure in examination: Oxford University: ca. 1820–40. Egan's Grose.

point to, show a. To swindle; act dishonourably towards: New Zealand coll.: late C. 19–20. Cf. *points to, give.*

pointer. The penis: low: C. 19–20.—2. A hint or suggestion; a useful piece of information: U.S. (1884) anglicised ca. 1890: coll. But perhaps ex dial., for see the E.D.D. (Pointing what to do.)—3. A schemer; one watchful for mean opportunities: Australian: C. 20. Jice Doone. Ex *point,* v.

points, get. To gain an advantage: 1881 (O.E.D.): coll. variant of S.E. *gain a point* in the same sense. Cognate with:

points to, give. To be superior to, have the advantage of: coll.: from ca. 1880. Ex S.E. sense, to give odds to (an opponent).

pointy. Terse; full of point; pithily economical: C. 20. O.E.D., 1909.

poison. Liquor; a drink of liquor: coll.: adumbrated in Suckling's *Brennoralt,* approached in Lytton's *Pelham,* first indubitably used by the Americans, Artemus Ward and, in 1867, Pinkerton ('Name your poison '), and generalised in England ca. 1885. Marshall, '*Pomes*', '"My favourite poison ", murmurs she, "Is good old gin "'; Milliken, 1888, 'Wot's yer pison, old pal ?' Hence, ca. 1885–90, *nominate your poison,* say what you'll drink.

poison, like. Extremely: gen. in *hate each other* (or *one another*) *like poison*: coll. Palsgrave, 1530, has 'Hate me like poison ', but *hate like poison* > gen. only in C. 19. Barham, 'And both hating brandy, like what some call pison '.

poison-gas. Treachery: meanness: from ca. 1916, but very ob.: coll. verging on S.E. (W., at *gas.*) Ex the use of poison-gas in G.W.

poison-pate(d). Red-haired: coll.: late C. 17–early 19. B.E. (*poison pate,* prob. also *n.*); Grose's *poisoned-pated* should doubtless read *poison-pated.*

poisoned. Pregnant: (? orig. c. >) low s. or coll.: late C. 17–early 19. B.E., Grose. Ex the swelling that often follows poisoning.

poisonous. A coll. intensive adj. (cf. *putrid,* q.v.): from ca. 1905, according to E. Raymond, *A Family That Was* (1929). Edwin Pugh, *Harry the Cockney,* 1912; F. E. Brett Young, *Woodsmoke,* 1924, 'With these Perfectly Poisonous People '—very satirical; Richard Keverne, *The Man in the Red Hat,* 1930, 'He's a poisonous beast. As shifty as they make 'em '; 'Poisonous child ', Graham Shepard, in his country-house novel, *Tea Tray in the Sky,* 1934. Ex S.E. fig. sense, morally corrupting or destructive, of evil influence, or that of deadly as poison.

poisonously. Very, extremely: from ca. 1924. (Cecil Barr, *It's Hard to Sin,* 1935.)

poitry. In late C. 19–20 considered a sol. pronunciation of *poetry.* Orig. due to the Gr. ποίησις, poetry, and ποιητής, a poet.

pojam. A poem set as an exercise: Harrow School: late C. 19–20; ob. A blend: *poem + jam* (or perhaps *pensum,* an imposition, with intensive *j.*).

*poke. Stolen property: c.: from ca. 1850; ob. *The Times,* Nov. 29, 1860; Baumann. Ex *poke,* a bag, pocket, etc.—2. 'A blow with the fist ', Grose, 2nd ed.: from ca. 1787; † by 1920. (The senses, a thrust, push, nudge, poking, are familiar S.E.) Ex the corresponding v.—3. An act of sexual intercourse: low coll.: C. 19–20. Ex sense 2 and v.—4. Hence, a mistress, 'permanent ' or temporary. A *good,* a *bad poke* : a woman sexually expert or clumsy (or cold). Low: C. 19–20. Cf. *push,* q.v.—5. A poke-bonnet: coll. verging on S.E.: from ca. 1840. Hood, ca. 1845, 'That bonnet we call a poke ', O.E.D.—6. A fish's stomach: coll. and dial.: 1773, Barrington (O.E.D.).—7. Money: circus s., or perhaps genuine Parlyaree: C. 20. E. Seago, *Circus Company,* 1933. Prob. ex Fr. *poche,* a pocket.

poke, v. To coït with (a woman): low coll.. C. 19–20. Ex *poke,* to thrust at. Cf. *poke,* n., 3, and *poker,* 2.—2. (With **up**) to confine in a poky place: coll.: 1860, Miss Yonge. Gen. as (*be*) *poked up,* O.E.D.—3. V.i., to project very noticeably: dial. and coll.: from ca. 1828. (O.E.D.)

poke, get the. A Scottish (esp. Glaswegian) variant of *get the sack,* to be dismissed: late C. 19–20. Also in Yorkshire dial., which has the corresponding *give the poke,* to dismiss: E.D.D.

poke a smipe. To smoke a pipe: Medical Greek or marrowskying: ca. 1840–90. See *Slang* at 'Spoonerisms '.

poke bogey. (V.t. with **at.**) To humbug: s. or low coll.: ca. 1880–1910. Cf. S.E. *poke fun.*

poke-bonnet. A bonnet projecting-brimmed: coll. (in C. 20, S.E.): 1820, O.E.D., where the earliest quotation suggests an origin in poking people's eyes out ; more prob. ex *poke*, to thrust forward.—2. Occ. applied to the wearer of one : coll. : late C. 19–20.

poke borak or **borax.** See borak.

poke fly. To show how : tailors' : ca. 1860–1920. See fly, artful.

poke full of plums !, a. An impertinent c.p. reply to *which (is the) way to* (e.g.) *London ?* : ca. 1580–1680. Melbancke, 1583 ; Torriano, 1666. (Apperson.)

poke-hole ; poking-hole. The female pudend : low coll. : C. 19–20 ; ob. Ex *poke*, v., 1.

poke in the eye. See thump on the back.

poke-pudding. See pock-pudding.—**poke up one's pipes.** See pipes, pack . . .

poker. A sword : jocular s. or coll. : late C. 17–20 ; ob. B.E., Grose. Cf. *cheese-toaster*, q.v.—2. The penis : low : from ca. 1810. *Lex. Bal.* Ex *poke*, v., 1.—3. (Also **holy poker**.) An Oxford or Cambridge University bedell carrying a mace before the Vice-Chancellor : university : 1841. Because he carries a mace or ' poker ' (jocular S.E.)—4. A single-barrelled gun : sporting : C. 19. Ex the shape.—5. A clumsy fencer : fencing coll. : C. 19–20 ; ob.—6. A lighterman employed by the Port of London Authority : nautical : C. 20. Bowen.—7. ' A casual labourer in the dockyard timber-trade : Londoners' : from ca. 1850. Mayhew, ' From their poking about the docks for a job ' (E.D.D.).

poker, burn one's. To get a venereal infection : low : C. 19–20 ; ob. See poker, 2. Baumann.

poker !, by the holy. (Occ., ca. 1840–90, the wholly Irish *by the h.p. and tumbling Tom !*) Occ., ca. 1870–1910, *by the holy iron !*) A mainly jocular expletive, of uncertain meaning (cf., however, *old poker*, q.v.) and Irish origin : 1804, Maria Edgeworth (O.E.D.).

poker, chant the. To exaggerate ; to swagger : s. or low coll. : C. 19. ? ex preceding.

poker, Jew's. See Jew's poker.—**poker, old.** See old poker.

poker-breaker. A wife : low : C. 19–20 ; ob. See poker, 2. Cf. Yorkshire *pintle-twister*.

Poker-Face ; orig. **little P.-F.** Miss Helen Wills, now Mrs. Wills-Moody : lawn tennis devotees' nickname : from 1925. (*The Daily Express*, April 28, 1934.) Ex her imperturbability.

poker-pusher. A naval stoker : naval : late C. 19–20. Bowen.

poker-talk. Fireside chit-chat : coll. : 1885, Mrs. Edwardes. Ex the fireside poker.

pokey. A Yorkshire s. (not dial.) term for goods paid for on the ' truck ' system : from ca. 1870. E.D.D.

poking-hole. See poke-hole.

poky drill. Musketry practice without live cartridges : military (other ranks') : from ca. 1915. Ex *poky*, insignificant.

pol ! By Pollux ! : a coll. asseveration : late C. 16–early 17. Nashe, Dekker. O.E.D.—2. **the pol** or **Pol :** see poll, n., 2.

Pol. Econ. Political Economy : undergraduates' coll. : late C. 19–20. O.E.D. (Sup.).

polarch, polarchical, polarchist, polarchy. C. 17–18 incorrections for *polyarch*, etc. O.E.D.

pole. The weekly wages account : printers' : from ca. 1850. ? because affixed to a pole or because it resembles a pole by its length ; or, more prob., a corruption of *poll*, head, i.e. a ' per capita ' account.—2. The male member, esp. when erect : low : C. 19–20 ; slightly ob.

pole, get on the. To verge on drunkenness : low (— 1909). Ware. Prob. ex *pole, up the*, 4.

pole, go up the. To behave circumspectly : C. 20. Ex *pole, up the*, 1.

pole, up the. In good repute ; hence, strait-laced : military : ca. 1890–1910. Perhaps *up the pole = high up*.—2. (Gen. **up a pole :** Manchon.) In difficulties ; e.g. over-matched, in the wrong : low : from ca. 1890. ' Pomes ' Marshall, ' But, one cruel day, behind two slops he chanced to take a stroll, | And . . . he heard himself alluded to as being up the pole.' Perhaps ex *pole*, the part of the mast above the rigging.—3. Hence, half-witted ; mad : low : C. 20.—4. (Rather) drunk : 1896, says Ware.—5. Annoyed, irritated : nautical : late C. 19–20. Bowen.—6. In Australia, ' distraught through anger, fear, etc. ; also, disappeared, vanished ', C. J. Dennis : late C. 19–20.

pole, (with) lead at both ends,—he is like a rope-dancer's. A c.p. applied to a dull, sluggish fellow : ca. 1787–1830. Grose, 2nd ed.

pole-axe. A low jocularity on *police* : ca. 1860–70. H., 2nd ed.

pole-axing. The reducing of wages to the point of starvation : printers' (— 1887) ; ob. Baumann. Cf. *the axe*, q.v.

pole-footed is incorrect for *polt-footed*. Via careless pronunciation.

pole-work. ' Collar-work ', q.v. and which explains it ; a long wearisome business : coll. : from ca. 1870. Ex North Country dial. of late C. 18–20. E.D.D.—2. Sexual intercourse : low : mid-C. 19–20 ; ob. Also *poling*.

poled, ppl.adj. Stolen : New Zealanders' : C. 20.

poley ; polley. (Of cattle) hornless ; lit., polled : English dial. and, from ca. 1840, Australian coll. —2. In Australian coll., from ca. 1880, also a hornless beast.

police-nippers. Handcuffs ; occ., leg-irons : low : mid-C. 19–20 ; ob.

policeman. A fly ; esp. a blue-bottle fly, which inversely = a policeman, esp. a constable. Mostly London (— 1860). H., 2nd ed. ; E. D. Forgues *La Revue des Deux-Mondes*, Sept. 15, 1864.—2. A sneak, a mean fellow, an untrustworthy man : c. (— 1874). H., 5th ed.—3. Hence, a ' squeaker ' or ' squealer ', a betrayer of confederates to the police : c. : C. 20. E.g. in Edgar Wallace, *The Missing Million*.—4. ' Under sail, the member of the watch who keeps on the alert to catch an order and rouse his mates ' : nautical : late C. 19–20. Bowen.

policeman always a policeman, once a. A late C. 19–20 c.p., imputing ' habit is second nature '. Cf. the proverbial *once a captain always a captain* (Peacock, 1831) ; *once a knave and ever a knave* (C. 17) ; and *once a whore and ever a whore* (C. 17–18),—all three cited by Apperson. Cf. the C. 20 *once a teacher always a teacher*, a c.p. on a par with *once a policeman* . . .

policeman's truncheon. A hand-grenade attached to a handle and having streamers to steady its flight : military coll. : 1915 ; ob. F. & Gibbons.

poling. See pole-work, 2.

-polis ; -opolis. The *o* is euphonic ; *-polis* represents the Gr. for a city. Relevant in nicknames, from ca. 1860, of cities or towns, e.g. *Cottonopolis*, Manchester ; *Leatheropolis*, Northampton ; *Porkopolis*, Chicago and, before 1881, Cincinnati.

polish, v. To thrash, to 'punish': ca. 1840–1910. Ex *polish off*, q.v.

polish (or **pick** or **eat**) **a bone.** (Gen. of eating with another.) To make a meal: ca. 1787–1915. Grose, 2nd ed. (*polish*). Contrast:

polish off. Summarily to defeat an adversary: boxing s., 1829 (O.E.D.) >, ca. 1835, gen. coll. = to finish out of hand, get rid of (esp. a meal) quickly. Dickens, 1837, 'Mayn't I polish that ere Job off ?' Ex *polish*, to give the finishing touches to by polishing.—2. Hence, to kill secretly: c. (— 1923). Manchon.

polish the King's iron with one's or **the eyebrows.** 'To be in gaol, and look through the iron grated windows', Grose, 1st ed.: ca. 1780–1840: (prob. c. >) low s.

polite, do the. See **do the polite.**

politician's porridge, carmen's comfort, porter's puzzle, are found in Ned Ward's *The London Spy Compleat*, 1703, as = beer. At the best, they are very rare; at the worst, they merely represent Ward's alliterative ingenuity.

polka, matrimonial. (Gen. **the m.p.**) Sexual intercourse: low coll.: 1842; † by 1920.

poll. A C. 15 incorrect form of *pole*.—2. (Occ. **pol.**) A pass in the examination for the ordinary, not the Honours, B.A. degree. Gen. as *the Poll*, the passmen, and as *go out in the Poll*, to be on the list of passmen. Hence, *poll*, a passman; *occ. poll-man*. Cambridge University s. first recorded ca. 1830, *poll* is prob. ex. Gr. οἱ πολλοί, the many, 'the general run'. Bristed, 1855, 'Several declared that they would go out in the Poll'; J. Payn, 1884, 'I took . . . a first-class poll; which my good folks at home believed to be an honourable distinction.'—3. A wig: C. 18–early 19. Hall, 1708; Grose, 1788. Ex *poll*, the head—4. A woman; esp. a harlot: nautical: from ca. 1860. H., 2nd ed.; P. H. Emerson, 'A poll gave him a bob.'—5. A decoy bitch used in stealing dogs: c.: from ca. 1870.—6. **Poll.** Mary, as a gen. name for a parrot: C. 17–20: coll. soon > familiar S.E. As *Peg = Meg*, Margaret, so *Poll = Moll*, Mary.

*poll, v.** See **pill** and **poll.** From ca. 1835: c., as in Brandon, 1839; P. H. Emerson, 1893, 'He accused us of polling.'—2. To defeat; outdistance: printers' and sporting: from ca. 1870. H., 5th ed.—3. To snub: low: from ca. 1875; ob.

Poll, Captain of the. The highest of the passmen: Cambridge University (see *poll*, n., 2): ca. 1830–90.

poll-man. See **poll**, n., 2.

poll off. To become drunk: low: from ca. 1860; ob. ? ex *poll*, head.

poll on. See **polling on.**

poll parrot, or with capitals. A talkative, gossipy woman: low, mostly London: from ca. 1870. H., 5th ed.

*poll-thief.** A thief; an informer: c.: from ca. 1890. Cf. *poller*, 2.

poll up. To court; live in concubinage with: low: from ca. 1870. H., 5th ed. Cf. *polled up*, living in unmarried cohabitation; in company with a woman: H., 1859. Cf. *molled up*.

pollaky !; or **o(h) Pollaky** (or p.) ! An 'exclamation of protest against too urgent enquiries': a non-aristocratic c.p.: ca. 1870–80. Ex the advertisements of a foreign detective resident at Paddington Green—one *Pollaky* (accented on second syllable). Ware. See also Addenda.

pollenarious, pollenation, polleniferous. Incorrect

for **pollinarious, pollination, polliniferous:** C. 19–20. O.E.D.

*poller.** A pistol: c. of ca. 1670–1750. *A Warning for Housekeepers.* Lit., a plunderer.—2. The same as *poll-thief*. P. H. Emerson, 1893.

polley. See **poley.**

polling on, ppl. or adj. phrase. Reckoning on, assuming; hence, taking advantage of: military: from ca. 1910. F. & Gibbons. Semantics: *counting on*; (electoral) *poll*.

pollrumptious. Unruly or restless; foolishly confident: coll. or s.: from ca. 1860. ? ex *poll*, head + *rumpus*. (Much earlier in dial.)

*polly.** ? a boot, a shoe: from ca. 1890. P. H. Emerson, 1893, 'All I get is my kip and a clean mill tog, a pair of pollies and a stoock, and what few medazas [? *mezadas*] I can make out of the lodgers and needies.'—2. Apollinaris water: 1893, G. Egerton.—3. As a name for a parrot: C. 17–20: coll. soon > familiar S.E.

Polly Hopkins. One Mr. Potts, the principal crammer of pass-men: Cambridge University: ca. 1840–55. H., 2nd ed. Punning Mr. *Hopkins*, a private tutor for the would-be honours-men, and *poll*, n., 2 + οἱ πολλοί.

Polly, put the kettle on, and we'll all have tea. A c.p.: from ca. 1870; ob. Collinson. Ex the song of Grip, the Raven (Dickens).

polone; gen. **palone.** A girl or woman: low theatrical (— 1935). Ex Romany: cognate with *blowen*, q.v.

polony, drunk as a. Exceedingly drunk: London lower classes' (— 1909). Ware derives **ex Fr,** *soûl comme un Polonais* (drunk as a Pole).

polore; palore. Erroneous for **polone.**

polrumptious. A variant of **pollrumptious.**

polty; dolty. Easy: cricketers', ca. 1890–1910. ? cognate with Kentish *polt*, saucy.

Poly, the. The Polytechnic Institute: Londoners' coll.: C. 20.

polyarchy. Catachrestic when = a group of kingdoms: C. 19–20. Southey, De Quincey. O.E.D.

polyglotter. A person that speaks several languages: coll.: 1912. O.E.D. (Sup.).

Polyphemus. The penis: C. 19–20 (ob.) cultured. Via *Monops*, the one-eyed one.

pom. A Pomeranian dog: coll.: C. 19–20. Cf. *peke*, q.v. Aldous Huxley has somewhere remarked that 'there is no inward, psychological contradiction between a maudlin regard for poms and pekes and a bloodthirsty hatred of human beings.'

pom Fritz. A variant, actually the imm. origin of, *Bombardier Fritz*, q.v. (B. & P.)

pom-pom. A Maxim automatic quick-firing gun: 1899: echoic coll. >, by 1905, S.E.

pomatum-pot. A small pot of throat-mixture kept by Gladstone at his side while he spoke in public: society: ca. 1885–90. Ware.

pome. A poem: sol., C. 19–20. Marshall, '*Pomes*' *from the Pink 'Un*, 1886–96; Joyce, *pomes pennyeach*, 1932.

pommy, Pommy. A newcomer from Britain, esp. from England: Australian: from ca. 1910, or a few years earlier. The O.E.D. (Sup.) records it at 1916, but it was current before the Great War. Origin obscure: possibly *pommy* is a corruption of *Tommy*; perhaps an importation by Australian soldiers returning from the Boer War (1899–1902) and amused by *pom-pom* (? *pom-pommy* > *pommy*), —cf. *Woodbines*, the Diggers' name for the Tommies; perhaps a jocularly 'perverted' blend of *Jimmy*, n., 2 (q.v.) + *Tommy*; Jice Doone thinks it a combination of *immigrant* and *pomegranate*, ex ruddy fruit and cheeks; Dr. Randolph Hughes much more pertinently suggests that it derives from '*Pomeranian*, a very superior sort of "dawg"', or from Ger. *Pommer*, the same—there being many German settlers in Australia.

Pompadours, the (Saucy). The (2nd Battalion of the) Essex Regiment (before ca. 1881, the 54th Foot): military: from ca. 1760; ob. Ex the facings of purple, the favourite colour of Madame Pompadour. F. & Gibbons. (The standardised khaki has doomed—indeed already consigned— many of the old regimental nicknames to oblivion.)

pompaginis. See **aqua pompaginis.**

Pompey. Portsmouth: naval: late C. 19–20. Bowen. Perhaps ex its naval prison: cf. Yorkshire *Pompey*, a house of correction (E.D.D.).—2. See *paws off !*—3. Portsmouth Football Club: sporting: C. 20.—4. A temporary lid set on a cask that, in testing, is being fired: coopers' (− 1935). Cf. the Lancashire dial. *pompey*, a tea-kettle.

Pompey (or the black dog Pompey) is on your back ! A c.p. (− 1869) addressed to a fractious child: provincial coll., and dial. Cf. the old South Devonshire *your tail's on your shoulder*. W. Carew Hazlitt.

Pompey's pillar to a stick of sealing-wax. Long odds: coll.: ca. 1815–60. Tom Moore, 1819; Egan's Grose, 1823. Cf. *all Lombard Street to a China orange, Chelsea College to a sentry-box.*

pompil(l)ion. Incorrect for *populeon*, an ointment: C. 17. O.E.D.

pompkin, Pompkinshire. See **pumpkin,** 1, and **Pumpkinshire.**

Pompo. Admiral Heneage: bluejackets': C. 20. Bowen, 'A little pompous'.

['pon for *upon* is perhaps, orig. at least, rather coll. than S.E.—For '*pon my sivvy*, see **sivvy.**]

'pon my life. A wife: rhyming s.: late C. 19– early 20. Ware. More gen. *trouble and strife.*

ponce; pounce-spicer; pouncey. A harlot's bully or keep: (prob. c. >) low s.: resp. 1872, ca. 1890, 1861 (Mayhew). H., 5th ed., 1874, 'Low-class East-end thieves even will "draw the line" at ponces, and object to their presence in the boozing-kens'; Henley, 1887, 'You ponces good at talking tall.' Prob. ex *pounce on*, though possibly influenced by Fr. *Alphonse*, a harlot's bully (W.). Cf. *bouncer, fancy-cove, mack, prosser, Sunday man* or *bloke.*

ponce on. To live on the earnings of (a prostitute): low: late C. 19–20. James Curtis, *The Gilt Kid*, 1936.

poncho. A loose overcoat: 1859, H.; † by 1900. Ex Castilian *poncho*, a military cloak.

Pond, the. The North Atlantic Ocean: from ca. 1830: (mainly nautical) s. >, ca. 1880, gen. coll >, ca. 1905, S.E. Ex the C. 17–19 S.E. sense, the ocean. Occ. *the Big Pond*, as in Haliburton and Sala; also *the Herring Pond*, and even *the Puddle.*

poney. See **pony.**

pong. A stink: low: from ca. 1850. **?** origin; cf. *pong*, v., 1, its prob. origin.—2. Beer: low: from ca. 1860. H., 3rd ed., where spelt *ponge*. Variants *pongelo(w)* (H., 1864), *pongellorum* (F. & H., 1902), these being fanciful endings. Origin obscure: **?** suggested by *parnee (pawnee)*, q.v. Ware, who defines it as 'pale ale—but relatively

any beer', classifies the term as 'Anglo-Indian Army'.

pong, v. To stink: low: from ca. 1850. Cf. n., 1. Prob. ex Romany *pan* (or *kan*), to stink.—2. (Also **ponge.**) To drink (esp. beer): low: from ca. 1870. Less gen. than the n.—3. V.i., to vamp, or amplify the text (of a part): theatrical: from ca. 1890; slightly ob. (O.E.D.). Perhaps cognate with *pong*, a ringing blow, a bang.—4. To perform, esp. to turn somersaults: circus: from ca. 1850. Perhaps via Lingua Franca ex L. *ponere*.—5. Hence, to talk, esp. to 'gas': theatre, music-hall, circus: from ca. 1890. Cf. sense 3.

ponge, pongelo(w), pongellorum. See **pong,** n., 2, and v. 2. But whereas *pongelow* is recorded (H., 1864) as a v., *pongellorum* is not so recorded.

ponging, n. Somersaulting: circus s.: mid-C. 19–20. See **pong,** v., 4.

pongo. A monkey: showmen's: mid-C. 19–20. In S.E., properly 'a large anthropoid African ape'; loosely, indeed erroneously, the orang-outang, 1834. Native name. S.O.D.—2. Hence, a nickname for a marine: naval: C. 20. Coppleston, 1916. (W.)—3. Hence, a soldier: naval: G.W. (F. & Gibbons.)—4. An Australian infantryman: Australians': from 1915. This Australian usage has been influenced by the Aboriginal name for a flying squirrel.

ponk. A rather rare variant of *pong*, n. and v.

ponkey land, in. Weak-minded; silly: military: C. 20. F. & Gibbons. Possibly ex a blend, or even an ignorant confusion, of *poggle* + *wonky*, qq.v.

ponte. A pound (sterling): showmen's, from ca. 1850. Ex It. *pondo*. Cf. *poona.*

pontic. Credit: London s. (− 1823) > Lincolnshire s. (− 1903). Abbr. *upon tick* (see **tick**). 'Jon Bee' and E.D.D. Cf.:

[**pontie,** adv. On credit: low: from ca. 1890; slightly ob. Prob. F. & H.'s slip for *pontic*.]

Pontius Pilate. A pawnbroker: late C. 18–19. Grose, 1785. Why ?—2. The drugget-covering tied to the thwart to prevent chafing: Oxford rowing men's (− 1884); ob. Why ?—3. A provost sergeant: military: C. 20. F. & Gibbons. Cf. *Pontius Pilate's Body-Guard.*

Pontius Pilate, dead as. Quite dead; long dead: coll. (− 1923). Manchon.

Pontius Pilate's Body-Guard or—**Guards.** The 1st Regiment of Foot, after ca. 1881 the Royal Scots, the oldest regiment in the British Army: military (slightly ob.): Grose, 1785, but prob. in spoken use from ca. 1670. Either simply ex their acknowledged antiquity or ex their alleged claim that, had *they* been on guard at the Crucifixion, they would not have slept.

Pontius Pilate's counsellor. A briefless barrister: legal: from ca. 1780; ob. One who, like Pilate, can say, 'I have found no cause of death in him.' Grose, 1785. Cf. Fr. *avocat de Pilate.*

ponto. A pellet kneaded from new bread: school: late C. 19–20. *St. James's Gazette*, March 15, 1900 (Matthew Arnold ponto-pelted at school). **?** origin: possibly connected with the *punto* of ombre and quadrille (the card-game): cf. sense 2.— 2. Punto, at cards: a corruption: 1861. O.E.D.

pontoon. Vingt-(et-)un, the card-game: 1900: military coll. >, by 1910, gen. S.E. A corruption of, more prob. an approximation to, *vingt-un*. S.O.D.

Pony. An 'inevitable' nickname of men surnamed Moore : military : from ca. 1885. F. & Gibbons. Ex ' a well-known sporting character ' : actually ' Pony ' Moore of the Moore & Burgess Minstrels.

pony. A bailiff ; esp. an officer accompanying a debtor on a day's liberty : coll. : C. 18–mid-19.— 2. Money : low : ca. 1810–40. *Lex. Bal.*, Moncrieff (see quotation at *pew, stump the*), Ainsworth. Prob. ex sense 2.—3. £25 : 1797, Mrs. M. Robinson, ' There is no touching her even for a poney,' O.E.D. Perhaps because only a small sum, as a pony is a small horse. (Cf. *pony up*, q.v.) N.B., among brokers, a *pony* is £25,000 of stock, i.e. 25 £1000-shares. Cf. *monkey*, n., 2.—4. A *small* glass of liquor : 1884, in U.S. ; anglicized ca. 1890, chiefly as a small measure of beer. O.E.D.—5. In gambling, a double-headed or double-tailed coin : c. > low s. : late C. 19–20.—6. A crib : schoolboys' (— 1913). A. H. Dawson.—7. Inferior goods: market-traders' (e.g., Petticoat Lane) : C. 20.

pony, post the. To pay : a C. 19 variant of *post the cole* : see **post**, v., 2, and **pony**, 2. (Baumann's *pot the pony* is an error.)

pony (occ. **lady**), **sell the.** To toss for drinks : low : late C. 19–20. Ex *pony*, third and fifth senses. Hence, he who has to pay, *buys the pony.*

pony and trap. See tom-tit.

pony in white. A sum or value of twenty-five shillings : racing c. : C. 20. Ex *pony*, 3 ; *in white*, in silver.

pony up, v.i. and t. To pay ; settle : a mostly U.S. variant and derivative of *post the pony* :1824, U.S. ; partly anglicised ca. 1840 ; ob. by 1920. (O.E.D. ; Thornton.) Prob. ex *pony*, 2.

pooch. See pouch.

poodle. Any dog : (sarcastic) coll. : from ca. 1880 ; slightly ob.—2. (**Poodle.**) The same as **Paul Pry**, q.v. (Dawson.)—3. (Rare in singular.) A sausage : low : C. 20. A. Neil Lyons, *Arthur's*, 1914, ' We fair busted ourselves on poodles and mashed ' (Manchon) ; slightly ob.

poodle-faker. A man, esp. a naval or military officer, that, for the time being rather than habitually, cultivates the society of women : Anglo-Indian, hence military, hence naval : from middle 1920's (? earlier). Hence, *poodle-faking*, vbl.n. O.E.D. (Sup.). In reference to *lap-dogs*.

poodler. A ' womaniser ' or confirmed flirt among cyclists : cyclists' : from ca. 1930. Ex preceding. The opp. is a *blinder.*

***poof.** A male pervert : c. (— 1932) and low. ' Stuart Wood.' Ex *poof !* or *pooh !*. Also spelt *pouffe.* See also **puff**, n., 2.

pooh-pooh. A rifle ; a big gun : New Zealand soldiers' (rare) : in G.W. Cf. *poop*, v., 4.

pooja, puja. (Gen. in pl. form.) Prayers : Anglo-Indian : 1863, Trevelyan in *The Competition Wallah* (O.E.D.). Ex Sanskrit *puja*, worship.

Poole. An excellent suit ; perfect clothing : male society coll. : from ca. 1840. Ex Poole, a leading tailor, at 37–9 Savile Row, London. Messrs Henry Poole & Co. were established in 1823 by James Poole at 171 Regent Street ; their fame has forced them to open a branch in Paris (10 rue Tronchet). Ware ; *The Red Book of Commerce*, 1906 (ed. of 1935).

poon. To prop (a piece of furniture) with a wedge : Winchester College (— 1891). Wrench, *Notions.* Prob. ex L. *ponere*, to place. Imm. ex :— 2. V.i., to be unsteady : ibid. : ca. 1830–70. Wrench, ' Hence you wedged the leg that pooned.'

poona. £1 ; a sovereign : costermongers' : from ca. 1855. H., 1st. ed. ? *pound* corrupted or ex Lingua Franca (cf. *ponte*, q.v.) or, less likely, *pound* influenced by *poonah*, a painting, etc., on the analogy of *Queen's picture* (q.v.).

Poona Guards, the. The East Yorkshires, formerly the 15th Regiment of Foot : military : from ca. 1860. Ex residence in India. Also *the Snappers.*

poonts. The paps : low : from ca. 1870. Etymology obscure.

poop. The seat at the back of a coach : coll. : ca. 1614–80. Ex the poop of a ship. (O.E.D.)— 2. The posteriors : low coll. : from ca. 1640. Ned Ward, ' While he manages his Whip-staff with one Hand, he scratches his Poop with the other,' O.E.D. Ob. Cf. sense 1.—3. A breaking of wind : low coll. : late C. 18–20. Ex poop ; cf. † S.E. *poop*, a short blast, a toot.—4. A foolish person : 1924, E. F. Benson, *David of King's*, ' When we're young we're pifflers, and when we're old we're poops.' Cf. *poop-stick*, q.v.

poop. To coït : C. 17–18 : low coll. Cf. *poop-noddy*, q.v.—2. To break wind : dial. and low coll. : C. 18–20. Bailey, 1721, ' *To Poop*, to break Wind backwards softly '. Ex S.E. *poop*, to make an abrupt sound ; to toot. Occ. *poupe.* (O.E.D.)— 3. Hence, to defecate (L. *cacare*) : (? late) C. 19–20 : low coll., mostly of and by children (E.D.D.).—4. With senses 2 and 3, cf. the military v.i. to fire a gun, i.e. a big gun, *not* a rifle or machine-gun ; (of a gun) to bang : coll. : from not later than 1916. B. & P. Often *poop off* (F. & Gibbons).—5. Hence, v.t., to shoot a person : coll. : from ca. 1930. (Georgette Heyer, *Why Shoot a Butler ?*, 1933.)

poop-downhaul. An imaginary rope : nautical coll. (— 1883). Cf. the operation, equally imaginary, of ' clapping the keel athwart-ships '. Clark Russell's glossary.

poop-noddy. Sexual intercourse : low coll. : C. 17. (Cf. *poop*, v., 1.) Anon., *Wily Beguiled*, ' I saw them close together at poop-noddy.' So F. & H. ; the O.E.D. suggests that it = *conycatching*, occ. *cony-catcher, noddy* being a simpleton.

poop off. See **poop**, v., 4.

poop-ornament. An apprentice : nautical : ca. 1850–90. *The Athenæum*, Feb. 8, 1902, ' Miscalled " a blarsted poop ornament ", the drudge even of ordinary seamen '.

poop-stick. An objectionable fellow, esp. if a soldier : C. 20. P. MacDonald, *Rope to Spare*, 1932, ' " You make me sick ! " he said. " Let a little poop-stick like that walk all over you ! " ' Virtually a euphemism for *shit*, n., 2. Cf. *poop*, n., 4.

pooper. A great wave coming over the stern (formerly called the *poop*) : nautical coll. : late C. 19–20. Bowen.

poor. Unfortunate ; in pitiable condition or circumstances : C. 13–20 : S.E. until ca. 1855, then coll. Mrs Carlyle, 1857, ' He looked dreadfully weak still, poor fellow ! '—2. When said, as from ca. 1785, of the dead person whom one has known, *poor* verges on coll. O.E.D.

poor as a Connaught man. Extremely poor : Anglo-Irish coll. : ca. 1802, Maria Edgeworth.

poor as a rat, as. Extremely poor : a C. 18–20 (ob.) coll. variation of *as poor as a church-mouse.* E. Ward, 1703, ' Whilst men of parts, as poor as rats . . .', with which cf. Hugh Kimber's ' The country is full of hungry men with brains ' (March 1933) ; Marryat, 1834 ; W. De Morgan, 1907. Apperson.

poor creature. (Gen. pl.) A potato : low London : ca. 1820–50. Bee.

poor knight of Windsor. See next : coll. and dial.: C. 19. Scott, *The Bride of Lammermoor*, 1818, has this footnote, ' In contrast . . . to the baronial " Sir Loin ", ' concerning :

poor man (of mutton). The blade-bone of a shoulder of mutton : Scots coll. : C. 19–20. Scott : see preceding entry.—2. (**poor-man.**) As a heap of corn-sheaves, four upright and one a-top, it is prob. dial. : Scots, C. 19–20.

poor man's blessing. The female pudend : low coll. : C. 19–20.

poor man's goose. Bullock's liver, baked with sage, onions, and a little fat bacon : (low) coll. (— 1909). Ware. Cf. *poor man's treacle*. (In Warwickshire dial., it is ' a cow's spleen stuffed and roasted ', E.D.D., 1903.)

poor man's oyster. A mussel : coll. : 1891, *Tit-Bits*, Aug. 8 ; ob.

poor man's side, or with capitals. The poor man's side of the Thames, i.e. South London : a coll. (— 1887 ; very ob.) verging on S.E. Baumann. Opp. *rich man's side*, the North side of the Thames : same period.

poor man's treacle. An onion : (low) coll. : late C. 19–20. *The Century Dict.*

poor Robin. An almanach : coll. : ca. 1660–1760. Ex *Robert* Herrick, who issued a series of so-called almanachs.

poorly. (Always in the predicate, except in *poorly time*, q.v.) In poor health ; unwell : from ca. 1750 : S.E. until ca. 1870, then near-coll. ; in C. 20, coll. O.E.D.

poorly time. The monthly period : lower-class women's coll. (— 1887). Baumann.

pooser. ' A huge, uncouth thing ' : low Northumberland s. (— 1903). Ex dial. *poose* (or *pouse*), to strike. E.D.D. Cf. *whopper*.

poot. A shilling : East London (— 1909). Ware. Ex Hindustani. Oriental beggars were, before that date, common there.

poove ; pooving. Food ; feeding, i.e. grazing for animals : either circus s. or Parlyaree (— 1933). E. Seago, *Circus Company*. Origin ? : perhaps ultimately ex the root *pa*, as in Sanscrit *gō-pas*, a herdsman.

pop. (**Pop.**) A club chiefly of Oppidans : Eton College : C. 19–20. Founded in 1812 ; see e.g. *Etoniana*, 1869. Traditionally derived ex L. *popina*, a cook-shop, the rooms having long been over a confectioner's.—2. A popular concert : coll. : 1862 (O.E.D.). W. S. Gilbert, ' Who thinks suburban hops more fun than Monday Pops '. Cf. *prom*, q.v.—3. (Gen. in pl.) a pistol : C. 18–20 ; ob. Hall, 1714 ; Harper, 1724, ' Two Popps Had my Boman when he was ta'en ' ; Grose ; Marryat. Like the next, ex the sound.—4. A drink that fizzes from the bottle when the cork—' pop goes the cork '—is drawn ; gen. ginger-beer : coll. : 1812, Southey. Occ., but † by 1870, champagne, as in Hood, ' Home-made pop that will not foam.' Cf. *fizz*, q.v.—5. An, the, act of pawning : 1866, Routledge's *Every Boy's Annual* (O.E.D.). Ex *pop*, v., 3.—6. See *pop, in*.—7. As = father, orig. and almost wholly U.S. (1840). Also *poppa* (— 1897), *popper* (— 1901) : likewise mainly U.S. Ex *papa*. (Ware.)—8. Abbr. *poppycock* : 1924, Galsworthy (O.E.D. Sup.).—9. (**Pop.**) Poperinghe, near Ypres : military, esp. officers' : G.W., and after. (F. & Gibbons.)

Pop. See *pop*, n., 1, 9.—2. **the Pop** ; **the Poplolly.** Lady Darlington, notorious and prominent in English society of the 1820's. John Gore, *Creevey's Life and Times*, 1934.

pop, v. To fire a gun : coll. : 1725, *A New Canting Dict.* ; ob.—2. V.t., to shoot : s. or coll. >, in C. 20, S.E. Gen. with *down* (1762) or *off* (1813). O.E.D.—3. To pawn : 1731, Fielding ; Barrie, 1902, ' It was plain for what she had popped her watch,' O.E.D. Cf. *pop-shop* and *pop up the spout*.—4. See **pop off** and **pop the question**.—5. To lose one's temper : tailors' : late C. 19–20.

pop, give (a person) a. To engage in a fight (from ca. 1910) ; to fire at with machine-gun (G.W.) : New Zealanders'.

pop, go. To go to the pawnshop : low (— 1923). Manchon. Ex the lit. sense of the phrase.

pop, in. In pawn : from ca. 1865 : low. The n., only thus. Cf. *pop*, v., 3, and n., 5.

pop !, sure. Certainly ! ; ' sure ! ' : children's (— 1923). Manchon.

pop-eyed. Having bulging eyes, or eyes opened wide in surprise : U.S. (ca. 1820), anglicized by ca. 1910. (O.E.D. Sup.)

pop goes the weasel !, now gen. regarded as a nursery-rhyme tag, was in the 1870's and 80's a proletarian (mostly Cockney) c.p. Ware, ' Activity is suggested by " pop ", and the little weasel is very active. Probably erotic origin. Chiefly associated with these lines—Up and down the City Road | In and out the Eagle, | That's the way the money goes, | Pop goes the weasel ! '

pop it in, v.i. To effect intromission : low coll. : C. 19–20. Contrast :

pop it on, v.t. To ask for more, esp. a higher price : coll. : 1876, Hindley.

pop-lolly. A sweetmeat : cheapjacks' s. or coll. : 1876, Hindley, ' Lollipop and pop-lolly '.

pop off. See *pop*, v., 2.—2. To die : 1764, Foote, ' If Lady Pepperpot should happen to pop off ', O.E.D. Also, but ob. by 1930, *pop off the hooks*, from ca. 1840, as in Barham.

pop-shop. A pawn-shop : 1772, *The Town and Country Magazine* ; 1785, Grose. Ex *pop*, v., 3. (O.E.D.)

pop the question. To propose marriage : 1826, Miss Mitford, ' The formidable interrogatory . . . emphatically called " popping the question ",' O.E.D. : s. >, in C. 20, coll. Rarely, *to pop* († by 1920). Ex S.E. *pop the question*, to ask abruptly.

pop up the spout. Same as *pop*, v., 3 : low : 1859, H., 1st ed. See **spout**.

pop visit. A short visit : society coll. : C. 17–18. Jonson in *The Alchemist*. (Ware.)

pop-wallah. A teetotaller : military : late C. 19–20. F. & Gibbons. Lit., a ginger-beer fellow. See *pop*, n., 4, and **wallah**.

pope. As a pejorative (*a pope of a thing*), as an imprecation (' A pope on all women,' 1620), in *as drunk as a pope*, and in (e.g. *know, read*) *no more than the pope*, i.e. nothing, the term is on the borderland between S.E. and coll. : all these phrases are † except in dial.—2. See **Pope of Rome**.

pope-holy is catachrestic when = popishly devout or holy : C. 17–20 ; ob. O.E.D.

Pope o' Rome. See **trot the udyju**.

pope of Rome. A home ; home, adv. : rhyming s. (— 1859). H., 1st ed. Often abbr. *pope* (Ware, 1909).

poperine pear. The penis : low coll. : late C. 16–mid-17. Shakespeare, *Romeo and Juliet*, in the quarto edition ; passage afterwards suppressed. Ex shape.

pope's eye. The thread of fat, properly 'the lymphatic gland surrounded with fat ', in (the middle of) a leg of mutton : from ca. 1670 : S.E. till C. 19, then coll. Shirley Brooks, 1852, 'The pope's eye on a Protestant leg of mutton '. Presumably *eye* ex its rounded form. (O.E.D.)

pope's (occ. **Turk's**) **head.** A round broom, with a long handle : from ca. 1820 : coll. >, ca. 1890, S.E. ; ob. Maria Edgeworth, in *Love and Law*, ' Run . . . for the pope's head.'

pope's nose. A turkey's, a fowl's rump : coll. : late C. 18–20. Grose, 2nd ed. Cf. *parson's nose*, q.v.

pope's size. Short and fat : trade s. > j. : from ca. 1885 ; ob. Mostly tailors'.

Poplar finance. Maladministration of public funds, esp. by a town-council : political coll. : from ca. 1925. Collinson. Ex the misuse of the relief system in Poplar ca. 1920–5 and with a pun on *popular*.

*****poplars, popler(s), poppelars ;** rarely, **paplar.** Porridge ; esp. milk-porridge : c. : C. 17–early 19. Dekker (*poplars*) ; Middleton (*popler*) ; Grose, 1st ed. (*poplers*). Prob. a corruption of *pap* (for infants, invalids).

popletic, popletical. Incorrect for *poplitic(al)* : mid-C. 16–17. O.E.D.

Poplolly, the. See **Pop, 2.—poppa.** See **pop, n.,** seventh sense.

popped. Annoyed ; esp. in *popped as a hatter*, very angry : tailors' : from ca. 1860. ? = *popped off, apt to pop off*. Cf. *mad as a hatter*.

*****poppelars.** See **poplars.**

popper. A pistol : 1750, Coventry ; ob. : s. > coll. in late C. 19–20, also a rifle or a shot-gun (E. Seago, 1933).—2. See **pop, n, 7.**

popping-crease. A junction station : railway officials' (— 1909). Ware. Punning the cricket term.

poppite. A performer at (1895), a frequenter of (1901), the popular concerts : coll. Ex *pop*, n., 2. O.E.D.

poppy, adj. Popping, exploding : coll. : 1894, Kipling, ' Little poppy shells '. O.E.D.—2. (Of the ground) causing the ball to ' pop ' (itself, j.) : cricket coll. : from 1874. Lewis.

poppy-show. A display, esp. if accidental, of underclothes ; orig. and properly, of red or brown flannel underclothes : low coll. : late C. 19–20. Ex dial. *poppy-show*, a peep-show, a puppet-show (see E.D.D.).

poppycock. Nonsense : U.S. s. (1865, Artemus Ward), orig.—and throughout C. 19—in sense of bombast ; anglicised ca. 1905 ; by 1930, coll. Thornton. ? ex the flower's flamboyancy.

pops or Pops. Father : C. 20, but rare before 1919. (E. M. Delafield, *Gay Life*, 1933, ' Pops says that . . .' and ' My Pops says . . .'

*****pops and a galloper, his means are two.** He is a highwayman : late C. 18–early 19 : c. or low s. Grose, 2nd ed.

popsy. An endearment for a girl : nursery coll. : 1862. Ex S.E. *pop*, similarly used : see the next entry. O.E.D.

popsy-wopsy. A foolish endearment : (mostly nursery) coll. (— 1887). Baumann ; 1892, *Ally Sloper's Half-Holiday*, March 19, ' Bless me if the little popsy-wopsy hasn't been collecting all the old circus hoops and covering them with her old muslin skirts.' Reduplicating *popsy* (' archaic *pop*, darling, short for *poppet* ', W.).

popularity Jack. An officer given to currying favour either with the men or with the public : naval, gen. as nickname : C. 20. Bowen.

por, pore. Sol. pronunciation of *poor* : C. 19–20 (? earlier). Often so printed : e.g. in Frank Swinnerton's quiet masterpiece, *The Georgian House*, 1933, ' Pore old lady ! '

Porch, the. See **Academy, the.**

porgy. See **Georgey-porgy, puddingy pie.**

pork. A spoiled garment ; goods returned by a customer : tailors' : from ca. 1860. Cf. *pig*, n., 5.—2. Women as food for men's lust : low : C. 18–20 ; ob. Cf. *mutton*.

pork, cry. To act as an undertaker's tout : low : late C. 18–mid-19. Grose, 2nd ed. The raven, ' whose note sounds like . . . *pork* ', is ' said to smell carrion at a distance '.

Pork and Beaners. An occ. variant of :

Pork and Beans. Portuguese ; esp. Portuguese soldiers : military : from 1916. Ex vague similarity of sound. Pork and beans : a tinned food frequent in the Army. (F. & Gibbons ; B. & P.) The New Zealanders called them *Pork and Cheese*. (The Portuguese, by the way, called *their* ' gallant allies ' by two names that may be translated ' Beef-Eaters ' and ' the Horses ', as John Gibbons tells me.)

pork-boat. (Gen. pl.) A Worthing fishing-boat : nautical : ca. 1860–1910. Bowen. Cf. the Sussex *pork-bolter*, a Worthing fisherman (E.D.D.).

pork-pie. A coll. abbr. of *pork-pie hat* (a style modish ca. 1855–65) : 1863 ; ob.—2. A ' toreador ' hat, modish in the 1890's : coll. : *The Spectator*, Dec. 26, 1891, ' The bull-fighter's hat known in England as the " pork-pie " ', O.E.D.

*****porker.** A sword : c. of ca. 1685–1740. Shadwell, *The Squire of Alsatia*, 1688, ' The captain whipt his porker out ' ; B.E. Cf. *pig-sticker* ; but *porker* is more prob. a perversion of *poker*, a sword. —2. A Jew : low : ca. 1780–1900. Grose, 1st ed. ; Baumann. Because, traditionally, Jews never eat pork : on the principle of *lucus a non lucendo*. Cf. *porky*, n.—3. A pork-pie : Bootham School (— 1925). Anon., *Dict. of Bootham Slang*.

porky. A pork-butcher ; a Jew (cf. *porker*, 2, q.v.) : low (— 1909). Ware.

porky, adj. Of, concerning, resembling pork ; obese : coll. : 1852, Surtees. O.E.D.

porpoise. A very stout man : late C. 19–20 : coll. >, ca. 1905, S.E.

porpoise, do a. (Of a submarine) to dive nose first at a sharp angle : naval : from 1916. Bowen.

porpoising, vbl.n. ' The movement of an aeroplane when an imperfect " get-off ", or landing, is made ' : Air Force : from 1915. F. & Gibbons. Contrast the preceding.

porps ! porps ! ' The old time whalers' cry when porpoises were sighted ', Bowen : C. 19.

porracious. Incorrect for *porraceous* : C. 17–20. (Adj., leek-green.) O.E.D.

porridge-bowl. The stomach : low : mid-C. 19–20 ; ob. Cf. *bread-basket* and contrast *porridge-hole*.

porridge-disturber. A punch in the belly : pugilistic : from ca. 1815 ; ob.

porridge-hole. The mouth : lower-class Scots' (— 1909). Ware.

Porridge Island. The nickname for ' an alley leading from St. Martin's church-yard, to Round court. chiefly inhabited by cooks, who cut off ready dressed meat of all sorts, and also sell soup ', Grose, 1785 : London coll. : ca. 1780–1830.

porridge-pot. A (heavy) shell : military (not very gen.) : in G.W. (G. H. McKnight, *English Words*, 1923.)

Porridge-Pots. ' Linesmen's satirical mode of naming the Scotch guard [*sic*] ' : military (— 1909) ; ob. Ware. Ex porridge as staple food of Scotland (cf. *porridge-hole*).

Port Egmont fowl. The large Antarctic gull : nautical coll. : C. 20. Bowen. (Port Egmont is in the north-west of the Falkland Islands.)

port for stuffs. ' Assumption of a commoner's gown ', Egan's Grose : Oxford University : ca. 1820–40. The double pun is obvious.

port-hole. The fundament ; the female pudend : low coll. : from ca. 1660 ; ob.

port-holes in your coffin !, you want. A naval c.p. (C. 20) addressed to a man very hard to please. F. & Gibbons.

Port Mahon sailor. An inferior seaman : naval : C. 19. Bowen. ' A perfectly safe port ' in Minorca : Chisholm's Gazetteer.

portable property. ' Easily stolen or pawned values—especially plate ' : coll. : 1885, *The Referee*, June 7. Ware.

portal. A C. 17 incorrect form of *portas*, a portable breviary. O.E.D.—**portatur(e).** Incorrect for *portraiture* : C. 15. O.E.D.

portcullis. A silver halfpenny : coll. bordering on S.E. : late C. 16–early 17. Jonson. Ex portcullis design.

portentious. Portentous : semi-literate sol. : C. 19–20. On *pretentious*.

porthole. See port-hole.—**portigue.** See **pestle of a portigue.**

portmanteau. A ' big high explosive shell, a name introduced during the Russo-Japanese War ' : naval ; ob. Bowen.

portmantle, portmanty. A portmanteau : C. 17–20 : S.E. till C. 19, then resp. dial. and low coll.

portrait. See **Queen's picture.**

portrait, sit for one's. To be inspected ' by the different turnkeys . . . that they might know prisoners from visitors ', Dickens in *Pickwick* : prison : ca. 1835–80.

portreeve. Erroneous when made to = the reeve of a seaport town : C. 17–20. O.E.D.

Portugoose. A Portuguese (soldier) : jocular military, mostly officers' : 1916, John Buchan, *Greenmantle.*

Portug(u)ee. A Portuguese : low coll., largely nautical : 1878, Besant & Rice. O.E.D.—2. Any foreigner except a Frenchman : naval : late C. 19. Bowen.

Portug(u)ee parliament. ' A forecastle discussion which degenerates into all talkers and no listeners ' : nautical : late C. 19–20. Bowen.

Portuguese man-of-war. A nautilus : nautical coll. verging on S.E. : C. 19–20 ; ob.

Portuguese pumping. A nautical phrase (— 1909), of which Ware was unable to discover the meaning. Nor have I ; but I agree with Ware that ' it is probably nasty ' : it refers almost certainly to either defecation (suggested by *pump ship*, q.v.) or masturbation.

pos, poss, poz, pozz. Positive : coll. abbr. : resp. 1711, 1719, 1710 (Swift), 1710 (Swift) : all † by 1860. The most frequent, *poz*, may date from as early as 1706 or 7, occurring as it does in

Polite Conversation ; *poss* (e.g. D'Urfey, ' Drunk I was last night, that's poss ') is rather rare.—2. As adv., positively : coll. : late C. 18–early 19, but adumbrated in Swift.—3. Only *pos* and *poss* (gen. the latter) : possible ; usually in *if poss*. Low coll. : from ca. 1885 ; slightly ob. ' Pomes ' Marshall. —4. (Gen. **poz.**) A certainty : rare coll. verging on s. : 1923, Manchon. Ex sense 1.

posa. A treasurer : Pidgin English (— 1864). H., 3rd ed. A corruption of *purser.*

pose. A puzzling question : children's (— 1923). Manchon. Ex S.E. *poser.* Cf. the † S.E. *pose,* a state of perplexity.

posey. See **posy.**

*****posh.** Money ; specifically, a halfpenny or other coin of low value : c. (— 1839) ; ob. Brandon ; H., 1st ed. Ex Romany *posh,* a half, as in *posh-horri,* a halfpenny, and *posh-koorona,* a half-crown.—2. A dandy : Society s. (— 1897) ; † by 1920. Barrère & Leland, 2nd ed. ? ex sense 1 ; i.e. a moneyed person (cf. *plum,* 1, 3). Or perhaps a corruption of (*big*) *pot.*—3. When, in *The White Monkey,* 1924 (Part II, ch. xii), Galsworthy wrote ' Pity was posh ! '; he was confusedly blending *punk* and *tosh* : all he meant was ' Pity was bosh '.

posh, adj. Stylish, smart ; (of clothes) best ; splendid : military >, by 1919, gen. : 1918, says O.E.D. ; but it appears as Cambridge University s., though as *push* or *poosh,* in 1903, when P. G Wodehouse, in *Tales of St. Austin's,* says of a brightly coloured waistcoat that it is ' quite the most push thing at Cambridge '. Avoided by polite society since ca. 1930. B. & P. Ex *posh,* n., 2 ; or possibly a corruption of Scottish *tosh,* clean, neat, trim.

posh ; gen. **posh up.** (Gen. in passive—esp. *all poshed-up.*) To make smart in appearance ; to clean and polish : military > gen. : from 1917 or 1918. F. & Gibbons ; B. & P. Ex *posh,* adj. ; and, like it, slightly ob.

poshteen, poshtin. Incorrect for *posteen* or *postin* : in C. 19–20 India. Yule & Burnell.

posish ; occ. **pozish.** A position : coll., orig. (ca. 1860) U.S. ; anglicised ca. 1915. (O.E.D. Sup.)

positive. Certainly no less than ; downright ; indubitable, ' out-and-out ' : coll. : 1802, Sydney Smith, ' Nothing short of a positive miracle can make him . . .', O.E.D.

poss. See **pos.**

posse mobilitatis. The mob : coll. : ca. 1690–1850. B.E. ; Grose, 1st ed. On *posse comitatus.*

possible. A coin, gen. in pl. ; money : ca. 1820–50. Esp. the ' Bee '-Egan group.—2. Hence, means or necessaries ; supplies : 1824 (O.E.D.)—3. (Orig. *highest possible.*) The highest possible score, esp. in rifle-shooting : coll. abbr. : 1866 (O.E.D.).

possibly. Catachrestic or, at the least, incorrect for *possible* in such phrases as *if possibly, by all means possibly, soon as possibly* : mid-C. 16–20 ; ob. ; indeed, rare after C. 17. O.E.D.

possie. See **possy.**

possle ; more correctly **postle.** An earnest advocate : lower classes' satirical (— 1909). Ware. I.e. *apostle.*

possum. Opossum : C. 17–20 : S.E. till mid-C. 19, then coll.

possum, play. To pretend ; feign illness or death : orig. U.S. (— 1824) ; partly anglicised ca. 1850. Ex the opossum's feigned death. The variants *to possum, to act possum*, and *to come possum over* have remained wholly U.S. (O.E.D. and Thornton.)

possum-guts. A pejorative, gen. in address: Australian: 1859, H. Kingsley; ob.

possy ; occ. **possie, pozzy.** A *position*; esp. a dug-out, or other shelter: military, mainly Australian and New Zealand: from 1915. B. & P.; F. & Gibbons.—2. Hence, from 1919, mostly in the Colonies, a house, a lodging, etc.; a job. Jice Doone.—3. See **pozzy, 3.**

post. Such mail as is cleared from one receiving-box or as is delivered at one house : coll.: from ca. 1890.

post, v. Often *post up* and gen. in the passive, esp. in the past passive ppl.: to supply with information or news: U.S. coll. (1847) anglicised ca. 1860 ; > S.E. ca. 1880. Prob. ex posting up a ledger. (O.E.D.)—2. 'To summon (a candidate) for examination on the first day of a series': Oxford University : C. 18. Amherst, 1721, 'To avoid being *posted* or *dogged*', O.E.D. (See **dog, v.**) Ex S.E. *post*, to hurry a person.—3. To pay : from ca. 1780 ; ob. Esp. *post the cole*, orig. c., 1781, C. Johnston ; *post the neddies*, c., 1789, G. Parker ; *post the pony*, 1823, Moncrieff,—see **pony ;** *post the tin*, 1854, Martin & Aytoun. After ca. 1870, the term is influenced by *post*, to send by post.

post, bet on the wrong side of the. I.e. on a losing horse : turf coll. (— 1823) ; † by 1900. 'Jon Bee.'

post, between you and me and the (bed- ; in late C. 19–20, often **gate-).** In confidence : coll. >, ca. 1910, S.E. : 1832, Lytton ; Dickens. O.E.D.

post, kiss the. See **kiss the post.—post, knight of the.** See **knight.**

post, make a hack in the. To use, consume, a considerable part of a thing : from ca. 1840 : coll. >, by 1870, S.E. ; ob. O.E.D.

post, on the. Dealing with postage ; applied esp. to the clerk dealing with this : commercial and insurance coll. : late C. 19–20. (M. Harrison, *Spring in Tartarus*, 1935.)

post-and-rail tea. Ill-made tea : from ca. 1850 ; ob. Only Australian. Ex floating stalks and leaves ; the reference being to post-and-rail fences. Morris.

post-chaise. To travel by post-chaise : coll. : 1854, Thackeray. Ob. O.E.D.

post-chay, post-shay. A post-chaise : ob. coll. : 1757, F. Greville. O.E.D. Cf. *po'chaise*, q.v.

post-horn. The nose : ca. 1820–90 : (low) coll. H., 1st ed. Ex noise and shape.

post meridian, n. Incorrect—indeed, sol.—for *post meridiem* : late C. 18–20. O.E.D.

post-mortem. The examination after failure : Cambridge : 1844, *Punch*, 'I've passed the post-mortem at last.' Punning the examination of a corpse.

post-nointer. A house-painter : 1785, Grose ; † by 1850.

Post Office Bible. The London Delivery Book : Post Office : ca. 1880–1920. Cf. :

Post Office Prayer-Book. *The Post Office Guide* : Post Office : from ca. 1880.

post-shay. See **post-chay.**

post te, e.g. *chum* or *hat*. A Charterhouse c.p., from ca. 1870, to indicate disapproval (of, e.g., hat or companion). A. H. Tod, *Charterhouse*, 1900, implies derivation ex a **post te of** (anything), the right to use

a thing after the ' owner ' has done with it (mid-C. 19–20) ; itself ex **post te** (in L., ' after thee ') as in **post te math. ex,** ' May I glance over your mathematical exercise ? '

post the blue. To win the Derby : racing-men's (— 1909). Cf. *post*, v., 3 ; *the blue* is *the blue riband of racing*, the Derby. Ware.

Postage Stamp, the. Any hotel, etc., known as the Queen's Head : taverns' : 1837–ca. 85. Ex the design on stamps. (Ware.)

postie ; occ. **posty.** A postman : coll. (— 1887). Baumann. It is recorded in dial. in 1871 : E.D.D. For form, cf. *goalie*, goal-keeper.

postil(l)ion of the Gospel. A gabbling person : 1785, Grose ; † by 1870.

postle. See **possle.**

postliminary, postliminiate, postliminious, postliminous. Erroneous for *postliminiary* (C. 18–20), *postliminate* (C. 17), *postliminous* (late C. 17–20), *postliminious* (C. 17). O.E.D.

postman's sister, the. An unnamed or secret informant : middle-class coll. : ca. 1883–1914. Ware. Cf. *Jinks the barber.*

postmaster general. The prime minister : a late C. 17–early 19 nickname. Grose, 1785, ' . . . Who has the patronage of all posts and places '.

postor. A praepostor : Shrewsbury School coll. : mid-C. 19–20. Desmond Coke, *The Bending of a Twig*, 1906.

posty. See **postie.—posy.** See **Holborn Hill.**

pot. (The money involved in) a large stake or bet : 1823, ' Jon Bee ' : sporting. E.g. Lever, ' The horse you have backed with a heavy pot.'— 2. Hence, any large sum : coll. : 1870, L. Oliphant, ' Harrie . . . won a pot on the French horse.'—3. Any horse heavily backed, i.e. gen. the favourite : 1823, ' Jon Bee ' ; H., ' Because [he] carries a pot of money '.—4. A prize, orig. and esp. if a vessel (gen. of silver), given at sports and games : 1885, O.E.D.—5. (A) sixpence : medical students' : ca. 1858–1915. H., 2nd ed., 1860, ' A half-crown . . . is a five-pot piece ' ; *Household Words*, June 20, 1885, ' Because it was the price of a pot or quart of " half-and-half " '.—6. A person of importance, gen. as a *big pot* : coll. : 1880, Hardy (O.E.D. Sup.) ; 1891, *The Licensed Victualler's Gazette*, Feb. 9, ' Some of the big pots of the day '. Coll. >, by 1910, S.E. Cf. the naval nuance (— 1909) ; an executive officer.—7. A steward : nautical : ca. 1870–1920.—8. **the pot** or **Pot,** the Canal : Winchester College : from ca. 1840. Hence, *pot-cad,* a sawyer on the Canal ; *pot-gates,* lock-gates ; *pot-houser,* a leap into the Canal from the roof of a house called *pot-house.*—9. Top : back s. (— 1859). H., 1st ed.—10. See **pots.**—11. A woman : c. (— 1857) ; virtually †. ' Ducange Anglicus.'— 12. A stew : nautical coll. : late C. 19–20. Bowen. Abbr. (the inevitable) *pot of stew.*—13. Stomach : Bootham School (— 1925). Anon., *Dict. of Bootham Slang.*—14. A person : in pejorative s. or coll. combinations, as *fuss-pot,* a fussy person, and *swank-pot,* a conceited one : late C. 19–20. Cf. sense 6.

pot. To shoot or kill for the pot, i.e. for food ; to kill by a pot-shot : coll. : 1860 (O.E.D.).—2. V.i. to have a pot-shot, v.t. with *at* : 1854 (O.E.D.) : coll. till C. 20, then S.E. Cf. *pot away,* q.v.—3. To win, ' bag ' : 1900, H. Nisbet, ' He has potted the girl,' O.E.D. Cf. *pot*, v., 1, and *pot*, n., 4.—4. See **pot, put on the.**—5. To deceive ; outwit : mid-C. 16–20 :. S.E. until C. 19, then s., as in Tom

Taylor's *Still Waters*, 1855, 'A greater flat was never potted'; ob.—6. See pot on.

pot, as good a piece as ever strode a. As good a girl as you could find : low coll. : mid-C. 19–20. Cf. *pissed, as good as ever*, and *piss upon* . . ., qq.v.

pot, give moonshine in a mustard. To give nothing : coll. : ca. 1660–1800. Ray.

pot, go to. To be ruined or destroyed ; to get into a very bad condition : mid-C. 16–20 : S.E. till C. 19, then coll. ; in C. 20, low coll. (Whence *go to pot !*, go to the devil : coll. : late C. 17–20.) Orig., *go to the pot*, lit. ' to be cut in pieces like meat for the pot ', S.O.D.

pot, gone to. Dead : C. 19. See preceding entry.

pot, old. See **pot, the old.**

pot, on the. At stool : low : ca. 1810–60. *Lex. Bal.*

pot, put in the. Involved in loss : turf (− 1823) ; † by 1900. Bee.

pot, put on. To exaggerate, e.g. to overcharge : from ca. 1850 ; ob.—2. (Also **to pot.**) To wager large sums : sporting : 1823, ' Jon Bee ' ; ob. See **pot, n.,** 1.

pot, put on the big. To snub ; to be patronising : from ca. 1891 : coll. (Occ., *big* omitted.)

pot, the old. One's father : mostly Australian (− 1916). C. J. Dennis. Abbr. *the old pot and pan*, ' the old man '.

pot, upset the. To beat the favourite : sporting : from ca. 1860. ' Ouida.'

pot and pan. A rather rare form of *old pot and pan*, q.v.

pot and spit. Meat boiled and meat roasted : coll. verging on S.E. : late C. 17–18. B.E. Ex the respective modes of cooking.

pot away, v.i. To keep shooting : coll. : from ca. 1855. Ex *pot*, v., 2.

pot-boiler. Any literary or artistic work done for money : coll. : 1803 (S.O.D.). I.e. something that will keep the pot boiling.—2. Hence, a producer of ' pot-boilers ' : coll. : 1892, G. S. Layard (O.E.D.).

pot-cad. See **pot, n.,** 8.

pot calls the kettle black arse, the. See **black arse.**

pot-faker. A hawker, a cheapjack, esp. in crockery : low : from ca. 1870 ; ob. H., 5th ed.

pot-gates. See **pot, n.,** 8.

pot-hat. In *Notes & Queries*, 1891 (7th Series, xii, 48), we read : ' Until lately . . . always . . . short for "chimney-pot hat", less reverently known as a "tile" ; but at the present time . . . often applied to a felt hat,' the latter—to be precise, a ' bowler '—being, by 1930, slightly ob., the former historical. Coll. : 1798, Jane Austen (O.E.D.).

pot-head. A stupid person : coll. : 1855, Kingsley. O.E.D. App. ex :

pot-headed. Thick-headed, stupid : coll. : More, 1533. O.E.D. Whence preceding entry.

pot-herb is catachrestic when, as by Stevenson in 1882, used as = *pot-plant*. O.E.D.

Pot-Hooks. The 77th Foot, in late C. 19–20 the 2nd Battalion of the Duke of Cambridge's Own (Middlesex Regiment) : military : C. 19–20 ; ob. Ex the similarity of the two 7's to pot-hooks.

pot-hooks and hangers. Shorthand : coll. : C. 19.

pot-house. An easy-going club : clubmen's coll. (− 1909). Ware. Jocular on S.E. sense.—2. (**Pot-**

House, the.) Peterhouse, Cambridge : Cambridge : mid-C. 19–20 ; ob.

pot-houser. See **pot, n.,** 8.

pot-hunter. One who follows sport for profit, lit. for pots : coll. till C. 20, then S.E. : 1874, H., 5th ed. See **pot, n.,** 4. Ex S.E. sense, one who hunts less for the sport than for the prey. Cf. the next entry.—2. In very local c. of late C. 16, the same as a ' barnacle '. Greene, 1592.

pot-hunting. The practising of sport for the sake of the prizes : coll. till C. 20, then S.E. : 1862, *The Saturday Review*, July 7 ; *Good Words*, 1881, ' Some men are too fond of starring or pothunting at " sports ",' O.E.D. Cf. *pot-hunter*, q.v.

pot in the pate, have a. To be the worse for drink : coll. verging on S.E. : ca. 1650–1780. Bracken, in his interesting *Farriery Improved*, 1737, ' An Ox . . . would serve them to ride well enough, if they had only a Pot in the Pate,' O.E.D.

pot joint. In grafters' s. of late C. 19–20, thus in P. Allingham, *Cheapjack*, 1934, ' An enormous number of crockery sellers are Lancashire men, and their great stalls, where they sell all kinds of china by mock auction, are usually called " pot joints ".'

pot o' honey. See **honey,** 2.

pot of all. A leader-hero, a ' demi-god ' : Cockneys' : ca. 1883–1914. Ware.

pot of beer. Ginger beer : teetotallers' (− 1909). Ware.

pot o(f) bliss. ' A fine tall woman ' : taverns' : from ca. 1876 ; ob. Ware.

pot of O is the abbr. of *pot of O, my dear* : rhyming s. for ' beer ' : 1868, says Ware ; ob.

pot on. To be enthusiastic for : non-aristocratic s. (− 1887) >, by 1900, coll. ; ob. Baumann quotes *Punch* : ' When their fancy has potted on pink ' (*Wenn sie sich in Rosa verliebt haben*).

pot walks, the. A c.p. applied to a drinking bout : ca. 1560–1750. (O.E.D.)

pot-walloper. A heavy drinker : coll. : late C. 19–20 ; ob. Ex :—2. A tap-room loafer ; (theatrical) a ' prosser ', q.v. : low : from ca. 1870. —3. A scullion ; a cook on a whaler : s. (− 1860) > coll.—4. A pejorative term of address : 1820 (O.E.D.) : coll. >, ca. 1870, S.E. Ex the S.E. political sense = *potwaller*.—5. Incorrectly (prob. on preceding sense) applied to anything very big and/or clumsy : late C. 19–20. O.E.D. Whence :

pot-walloping. Making vigorous but clumsy movements : catachrestic : 1899 (O.E.D.). Ex preceding, 5.

pot with two ears, make a or **the.** To set one's arms akimbo : coll. : ca. 1670–1760. Cotton, 1675, ' . . . A goodly port she bears, | *Making the pot with the two Ears.*' O.E.D.

pot-wrestler. The cook on a whaler : nautical : from ca. 1840. Cf. *pot-walloper*, 3.

potaquaine is (mid-C. 19–20) erroneous for *potoquane* ; **potaro** (C. 17) for *pedrero*. O.E.D.

Potater, or **Potato.** The French race-horse *Peut-être* : sporting : 1st decade, C. 20. Ware.

potato. A pejorative coll., as in Smollett's ' I don't value [him] a rotten potato,' O.E.D. : ca. 1750–1850. Cf. *potatoes*, q.v.—2. A large hole in fleshings or stockings : coll. : late C. 19–20. Baumann.

potato, hot. See **hot potato.**

potato, the or **the clean.** The best ; the corrector most apposite thing : resp. 1822, 1880. Esp. in *quite* or *not quite the* (*clean*) *potato*. (O.E.D.

potato-box. The mouth (cf. *p.-jaw*, q.v.) : from ca. 1870.

potato-finger. A long thick finger ; a penis ; a dildo : (low) coll. : C. 17–18. Esp. in Shakespeare's *Troilus and Cressida*. Ex supposed aphrodisiac virtues of the sweet potato. (O.E.D.)

potato-jaw or **-trap.** The mouth : resp. 1791, Mme D'Arblay ; 1785, Grose. Orig. Irish. (O.E.D.)

potato-masher (grenade). A German hand-grenade so shaped : military : 1915 ; ob. F. & Gibbons.

potato-pillin' (orig., prob. **peelin'**). A shilling : rhyming s. (mostly workmen's) : C. 20. *John o' London's Weekly*, June 9, 1934. Cf. the more gen. *rogue and villain*.

potatoes. Abbr. of **potatoes in the mould.** P. P., *Rhyming Slang*, 1932.

potatoes in the mould. Cold : from ca. 1870. P. P., *Rhyming Slang*, 1932.

potatoes, small. Nothing much, nothing great : orig. U.S. (1836) anglicised ca. 1860. Cf. *potato*, 1.

potching. The taking of tips from a person that one has not served : waiters' (— 1883). *The Graphic*, March 17, 1883. Prob. = *poaching*. (Ware.)

potecary. An apothecary : sol. (— 1887) ; ob. Baumann. Ex dial. : 1805 (E.D.D.).

potence. A potent or crutch-staff : erroneous : late C. 17–18. O.E.D.—**potential** : C. 17–18 erroneous for *potential*. O.E.D.

potle-bell, ring the. ' To confirm a bargain by linking the little fingers of the right hand ', F. & H. : Scots dial. and coll., mostly among children : C. 19–20.

potomaine. Ptomaine : from ca. 1880 : sol. Cf. *ptomaine*, q.v.

pots or **Potts.** North Staffordshire Railway ordinary stock : Stock Exchange : from ca. 1885. The railway serves the potteries.

pots ; gen. **be pots,** to be mad, or extremely eccentric : from ca. 1925. (Anthony Weymouth, *Hard Liver*, 1936.) Ex *potty* on *bats*, q.v.

pots and pans, make. ' To spend freely, then beg ', Bee, 1823 : ca. 1820–1900. (Baumann.)

potted ; occ. **potted out.** Confined (e.g. in a lodging) : coll. : 1859, *The Times*, July 21 ; ob. by 1890, † by 1920.—2. Dead and buried : from ca. 1860 ; ob. H., 2nd ed. Ex horticulture.—3. (Of a racehorse) favourite, favoured : turf (— 1923). Manchon. Ex *pot*, n., 1.

potted fug. Potted meat : either dial. or local s. : Rugby (town) : from ca. 1860.

potter-carrier. An apothecary : low coll. and dial. form of *pothecary* : ca. 1750–1820. Foote, 1764, ' Master Lint, the potter-carrier '. O.E.D.

Potteries, the. Stoke City Football Club (' soccer ') : sporting : C. 20.

pottery. Poetry : sol. when not a deliberate perversion : C. 19–20.

potting. Shooting ; esp. the taking of pot-shots : coll. : 1884 (O.E.D.). Ex *pot*, v., 2.

pottle. A bottle (of hay) : incorrect : ca. 1730–1850. Fielding. O.E.D.

Potts. See **pots.**

potty. A tinker : lower classes' (— 1909). Ware. Ex his *pots* and pans.

potty, adj. Indifferent ; shaky ; very unpromising (business scheme) : 1860, H. ; rather ob. —2. (Of a stroke) feeble ; clumsy : cricketers' : from 1870. Lewis.—3. Trivial, insignificant : 1899, Eden Phillpotts (O.E.D. Sup.). Ex *potter* (about).—

4. Easy, simple ; safe : 1899 : s. >, by 1930, coll. Ibid.—5. Silly ; crazy : from ca. 1910. Ex sense 1.

pouch. A present of money : 1880, Disraeli : s. >, by 1910, coll. ; ob. O.E.D. Ex sense 1 of the v. (N.B., *pouch* is, by soldiers, almost always pronounced *pooch*. F. & Gibbons.)

pouch, v. To supply the pouch, i.e. the purse or pocket, of ; to tip : s. >, in C. 20, (low) coll. : 1810, Shelley (O.E.D.) ; 1844, Disraeli, ' Pouched in a manner worthy of a Marquess and of a grandfather '. Slightly ob.—2. To eat : low coll. : 1892, Milliken, ' Fancy pouching your prog on a terrace.' Ex S.E. sense, to swallow.—3. To steal : low (— 1923). Manchon. Ex dial., where it dates from C. 18.

*pouch a gun. To carry a revolver : c. : from ca. 1920. Edgar Wallace, *The Squeaker*, 1927. On U.S. *pack a gat*.

pouch-mouth, n. and adj. A ranter ; ranting : coll., somewhat rare : early C. 17. Dekker, ' Players, I mean, theaterians, pouch-mouth stage-walkers.' I.e. *ore rotundo*.

pouchet. A pocket : either coll. or a corruption of *pocket* by Fr. *pochette*. Radcliffe, 1682, ' Did out of his Pouchet three nutmegs produce.' † by 1800.

Poudering-tub. See **Powdering-tub.**

pouf. A would-be actor : theatrical : ca. 1870–1910. Ex *poof !, pouf !*

pouffe. See **poof.**

poulain. A chancre : low coll. : 1785, Grose ; ob. Ex Fr. *poulain*.

poulderling. An undergraduate in his second year : university : C. 17. Anon., *The Christmas Prince*, 1607. ? origin.

*poulterer. A thief that steals and guts letters : c. : C. 19. *Lex. Bal.* ? ex *quill* = a quill pen, perhaps via metaphor of feathers as letters.

poultice. A fat woman : Society : ca. 1880–1900. —2. A ' very high collar, suggestive of a neck poultice, ring-like in shape ' : Society : ca. 1882–1912. Likewise, Ware.—3. See **poultice over.**—4. A bore (person or thing) : Glasgow (— 1934).

poultice-mixer. A sick-bay attendant : naval (— 1909). Ware. Cf. *poultice-wallah*, q.v.

poultice over the peeper. A punch or blow on the eye : low (— 1909). Ware.

poultice-wallah. A physician's, esp. a surgeon's, assistant : military : from ca. 1870. See **wallah** and cf. *poultice-mixer* and :

poultice-wallopers ; also with capitals. Occ. **P. Wallahs.** The Royal Army Medical Corps : military : from ca. 1870 ; ob. Also *the Pills* (see **pills,** 2), *Linseed Lancers*.—2. Occ. in the singular, esp. in the Navy : a sick-bay attendant : late C. 19–20. Bowen.

poultry. Women in gen. : coll. : C. 17–20. Chapman. Hence, *celestial poultry*, angels, ex the wings. Cf. *hen, hen-party*, and contrast *cock*.

*poultry-rig. The ' dodge ' noted at *poulterer*, q.v. : c. : C. 19. *Lex. Bal.*

poultry-show. A ' short arm ' inspection : military : 1915 ; ob. B. & P., ' It had no reference to hens.'

pounce. A variant of *ponce*.

pounce, on the. Ready to leap verbally : Anglo-Irish : 1887, when brought into fashion by E. Harrington, M.P. *The Daily News*, Oct. 10, 1890, ' " On the pounce ", as the irreverent phrase goes.'

pounce-shicer and **pouncey.** See **ponce.**

pound, v. See **pound it** and **pounded.**

pound. Pounds, whether weight or sterling :

S.E. until mid-C. 19, then coll. and dial. 'He's worth a thousand pound if he's worth a penny'; 'That bullock weighs eight hundred pound.' (In combination, however, the uninflected pl. is S.E.: e.g. 'a four pound trout'.)

pound, go one's. To eat something up: military: ca. 1870–1914. Ex the fact that a soldier's ration of bread used to weigh 1 lb., his ration of meat nearly 1 lb. (actually ¾ lb.), as mentioned in *The Pall Mall Gazette*, July 1, 1885 (cited by O.E.D.).

*pound, in for. Committed for trial: c.: C. 19–20; ob. Ex *pound* = prison.

pound, shut (up) in the parson's. Married: 1785, Grose; † by 1860.

pound and pint. 'The bare Board of Trade ration scale': nautical: late C. 19–20. Bowen.

pound-and-pint idler. A naval purser: naval: late C. 19–early 20. Bowen. Ex preceding.

pound it. To bet, wager, as on a virtual certainty, esp. in *I'll pound it*: 1812, Vaux; ob. by 1900, virtually † by 1930. Ex offering £10 to 2s. 6d. at a cock-fight. Dickens, 'I'll pound it that you han't.' Cf. *poundable*, q.v.

pound (of lead). Head. See **bake, n.**

pound-not(e)ish. Stylish; aristocratic; affected of speech or manner: lower classes': from ca. 1930. James Curtis, *The Gilt Kid*, 1936, 'Her pound-noteish voice both annoyed and amused the Gilt Kid.'

pound-text. A parson: coll.: late C. 18–20; ob. Cf. *cushion-thumper*.

pound to an olive(, it's a). It's a certain bet: Jewish coll. (– 1909). Ware. Perhaps ex Jewish fondness for olives.

poundable. (Esp. of the result of a game, the issue of a bet) certain, inevitable; or considered to be such: low (? c.): 1812, Vaux; ob. by 1890, † by 1920.

pounded, ppl.adj. Discovered guilty of impropriety: male Society: ca. 1820–50. Egan, *Life in London*, 1821. Ex the pounding of strayed animals.

pounders. (Rare in singular.) Testicles: coll.: late C. 17–18. Dryden's *Juvenal*, VI, 117.

poundrel. The head: coll.: 1664, Cotton, 'Glad they had scap'd, and sav'd their poundrels'; † by 1830. Origin obscure, though prob. connected with weight.

poupe. See **poop, n.,** 2, and **v.,** 2.

pour. A 'continuous' rain; esp. *a steady pour* (all the morning): coll.: late C. 19–20.

pouter. The female pudend: low: C. 19–20; ob. Cf. *diddly-pout*.

Poverty and Grief. Messrs. Pollock & Gilmour, shipowners: Clydeside nautical: late C. 19–20. Bowen. Ex reputed abstention from pampering their crews.

poverty-basket. A wicker cradle: s. or coll.: ca. 1820–70. Bee, 1823.

poverty-corner, more gen. **p.-junction**; or with capitals. The corner formed by York and Waterloo Roads, London: music-hall and variety artists' (– 1890); ob. *Tit-Bits*, March 29, 1890. There they used to wait to be engaged. Since ca. 1910, it has gen. referred to a corner in the Leicester Square district and is a gen. theatrical coll. Cf. *the Slave Market* of New York.—2. The corner of Fenchurch Street and the approach to the Station: nautical: late C. 19–20. Bowen. (The haunt of out-of-work seamen.)

Poverty Row; Poverty Row picture. See 'Moving-Picture Slang', § 8.

povilion. Erroneous for *pavilion*: late C. 17–18 O.E.D.

powder. (Of a horse) vigour, spirits: turf (– 1923). Manchon. Perhaps ex *gunpowder* + sense 2 of:

powder, v.i. To rush: coll. and dial.: lit., in Quarles, 1632, 'Zacheus climb'd the Tree: But O how fast . . . he powder'd down agen!'; fig., from ca. 1730. O.E.D. Ex the rapid explosiveness of powder.—2. Hence, to spur (a horse) to greater speed: sporting (– 1887). Baumann.—3. V.t., to 'camouflage' the fact that a horse is glandered: horse-copers': from ca. 1860. '*No. 747*', p. 20.

powder, burn bad. To break wind: coll. (– 1923). Manchon. Euphemistic.

powder away, v.i. To perform fine but useless deeds: coll. (– 1923). Ibid. Ex S.E. *powder*, to scatter or sprinkle like powder.

powder-monkey. A boy employed to carry powder from magazine to gun: 1682, Radcliffe, 'Powder-monkey by name': naval coll. till C. 19, then S.E.

powder or shot, not worth. Not worth cost or, esp., trouble or effort: 1776, Foote: coll. till ca. 1850, then S.E.

powdering (one's) hair, be. To be getting drunk: taverns': C. 18–20; extremely ob. Ware, 1909, remarks: 'Still heard in remote places. Euphemism invented by a polite landlord.'

powdering-tub. A salivating cradle or pit, used against syphilis: late C. 16–early 19: humorous S.E. until C. 18, then coll. Shakespeare; Grose, 1st ed.—2. With capitals, 'the Pocky Hospital at Kingsland near London', B.E.: low coll.: late C. 17–mid-18.

power. A large number of persons, number or quantity of things; much: from ca. 1660: S.E. until ca. 1820, then dial. and (low) coll. Dickens, 'It has done a power of work.' O.E.D. Cf. *nation* and:

poweration. A large number or quantity; much: coll.: ca. 1830–1910. Also dial.

powerful. Great in number; in quantity: dial. and low coll.: 1852, in U.S.; anglicised in 1865, by Dickens, 'A powerful sight of notice', O.E.D.—2. Adv., powerfully; exceedingly, very: dial. and, esp. in U.S. (1833, Thornton) and Canada, low coll.: 1835, Washington Irving; Besant & Rice, 1876, 'Rayner seems powerful anxious to get you on the paper,' O.E.D.; *Tit-Bits*, Sept. 17, 1892, 'He's powerful bad, miss.' Ob. as coll. in Great Britain. (The adj. ex the adv., the adv. ex *power*, q.v.)

Powos, the. The Prince of Wales's Own Regiment: late C. 19–20 military; ob. Also known as *the Old and Bold*, q.v., and *Calvert's Entire*.

powwow. A conference of, discussion of plans by, senior officers before a battle, or during manœuvres: military: from ca. 1912. F. & Gibbons. A natural extension of the S.E. sense.

pox. Syphilis: C. 16–20: S.E. until mid-C. 18; then a vulg. That the word was early avoided appears in Massinger's 'Or, if you will hear it in a plainer phrase, the pox', 1631. Often *French pox* (Florio, 'The Great or French poxe'); occ. *Italian, German, Spanish, Indian pox*, also (*the*) *great pox*,—Swift has *the greater pox*; cf. *French gout*. Altered spelling of *pocks*, orig. applied to the pustules of any eruptive disease. (O.E.D.) See also **powdering-tub**. Cf. *pox l*, q.v., and :

pox, v. To infect with syphilis: late C. 17–20:

S.E. until mid-C. 18, then **a** vulg. Amory, 1766, 'She . . . lives . . . to . . . pox the body,' O.E.D. Cf. :

pox ! (Cf. *pox*, n. and v.) In imprecations and irritated exclamations, esp. *a pox of* or *on . . . !*, (*a*) *pox take, a pox !, what a pox !, with a pox !, pox on it !* Late C. 16–mid-19 : S.E. until C. 18, then a vulg. Shakespeare, 1588, 'A pox of that jest '; Fielding, 1749, 'Formalities ! with a pox !' O.E.D.

poxed, poxt, ppl.adj. Infected with syphilis : late C. 17–20 : S.E. until mid-C. 18, then a vulg.

poyson ; poysoned, poyson'd. See **poison, poisoned.—poz, pozz.** See **pos.**

pozish. See **posish.**

pozzy. See **possy**, 1, 2.—2 **Pozzy.** Pozières, a small village on the Somme front, the scene of fierce fighting in the 'Big Push': July, 1916 : mostly among the Australian soldiers.—3. (**pozzy.**) Jam : military : late C. 19–20. B. & P., esp. the 3rd ed. Perhaps ex a South African language, for the natives in S.A. 'used the word, before 1900 at least, to designate any sort of sweetmeat or preserve '; its revival in the G.W. may have been caused by the Posy brand of condensed milk being, in 1914–early 15, often spread on bread when jam ran out. I myself hazard *posset*.

pozzy-wallah. 'A man inordinately fond of jam ': military : C. 20. B. & P. Ex sense 3 of the preceding + *wallah*, q.v.

practicable, n. A door, window, staircase, etc., actually usable in a play : theatrical coll. : 1859, Wraxall. Ex the corresponding theatrical adj. (1838). O.E.D.

practicable, adj. Gullible ; illicitly accessible ; facile : 1809, Malkin. O.E.D. Ex *practicable*, feasible.

practical, n. (Rare in singular.) A *practical* joke ; a trick : 1833, M. Scott. Ob. O.E.D.

practical politician. A public-house, self-appointed orator or spouter : coll. : late C. 19–20.

practice, n., and **practise,** v., are often catachrestically confused in spelling.

practise in the milky way. To fondle a woman's breasts : low cultured coll. verging on, but not achieving, S.E. : C. 17–20 ; ob. Carew, 1633.

*__practitioner.__ A thief : c. : from ca. 1865 ; ob. J. Greenwood, 1869.

*__prad.__ A horse : c. : app. not recorded separately before 1799, but implied in Grose, 2nd ed., 1788, in *prad-lay*. Egan, Dickens, Mayhew, Marriott Watson. Ex Dutch *paard*, a horse (O.E.D.). Cf. *Charing Cross, gee*, *__prancer__ ; and esp. *prod*, 2.

*__prad-cove.__ A horse dealer : c. : from ca. 1820 ; ob. Egan's Grose.

*__prad-holder.__ A bridle : **c.** : 1798, Tufts, *A Glossary of Thieves' Jargon.*

*__prad-lay.__ 'Cutting bags from behind horses '; the stealing of bridles, etc. : c. : 1788, Grose.

*__prad-napper ; -napping.__ A horse-thief ; horse-thieving : c. : C. 19–20 ; ob. H., 2nd ed. See **prad.**

*__pradback.__ Horseback : **c.** (– 1812) ; ob. Vaux. See **prad.**

prae. An occ. variant of *pre*, a prefect. Desmond Coke, *The School across the Road*, 1910.

*__prag, pragge.__ A thief : c. of ca. 1590–1600. Greene, 1592. Prob. ex *prig*, n., and v.

Pragger-Wagger, the. The Prince of Wales : Oxford undergraduates': from ca. 1913 ; ob. Collinson. By 'the Oxford *-er* '.

praise. (The name of) God : a Scots euphemistic coll. : C. 17–early 19. Callander, 1782, ' *Praise be blest*, God be praised. This is a common form still in Scotland with such as, from reverence, decline to use the sacred name,' E.D.D. Ex † S.E. *praise*, 'an object or subject of praise '.

pram. A perambulator (for infants) : (until ca. 1920, considered rather low) coll. abbr. : 1884, *The Graphic*, Oct. 25, ' Nurses . . . chattering and laughing as they push their " prams ".'—2. Hence, a milkman's hand cart : coll. : 1897 (O.E.D.).

prance. To dance, caper, gambol : mid-C. 15–20 : S.E. until ca. 1850, then coll. (O.E.D.).

*__prancer.__ A horse : c. : ca. 1565–1860. Harman, B.E., Grose, Ainsworth. Cf. the S.E. usage : a prancing or mettlesome horse. See also **pranker.** —2. A highwayman : C. 17 : c. >, ca. 1680, low s. Day, Head. O.E.D.—3. Hence, a horse-thief : c. : C. 18–mid-19. Anon., *The Twenty Craftsmen*, 1712, ' The fifteenth a prancer . . . If they catch him horse-coursing, he's nooz'd once for all.'—4. A cavalry officer : military : from ca. 1870 ; ob. H., 5th ed.

*__Prancer, the Sign of the.__ The Nag's Head (inn) : from ca. 1565 (very ob.) : c. >, in C. 19, low s. Harman. Also *the Sign of the Prancer's Poll*, B.E., Grose.

*__prancer's nab__ or **nob.** A horse's head as a sham seal to a counterfeit pass : c. : late C. 17–mid-19. B.E., Grose. Cf. :

*__prancer's poll.__ The same : late C. 17–mid-18. B.E.—2. See **Prancer, the Sign of the.**

*__pranker.__ A horse : c. : late C. 16–17. Greene. Prob. a corruption of *prancer*, 1.

p'raps. Perhaps : coll. abbr. (in C. 19, rather low) : 1835, Hood ; prob. much earlier. (O.E.D.)

*__prat, pratt.__ A tinder-box : c. : late C. 17–early 19. B.E., Grose. ? origin.—2. (Gen. in pl.) A buttock ; a thigh : mid-C. 16–20 : c. >, ca. 1820, low : Harman, Brome.—3. A behind : late C. 16–20 : c. >, in C. 19, low. Rowlands, 1610, ' And tip lowr with thy prat ' ; Marriott-Watson, 1895, ' We ain't to do nothing . . . but to set down upon our prats.' Cf. U.S. c. sense, a hip-pocket.—4. The female pudend : low : C. 19–20.

*__prat,__ v. To go : c. : 1879, Horsley. Connected perhaps with *prat*, n., 3, but prob. with Romany *praster*, to run.—2. Hence, *prat oneself*—or, more gen., *one's frame—in*, to butt in, come uninvited, interfere : low : late C. 19–20.—3. To beat, to swish : late C. 16–20 (ob.) : low. App. ex *prat*, n., 3. Shakespeare, *Merry Wives*, IV, ii.

prat one's frame in. An Australian and N.Z. variant of *prat*, v., 2 : C. 20.

prate-roast. A talkative boy : ca. 1670–1840 : low : Glanvill ; B.E.; Grose (1st ed.), who, by the way, certainly errs when he describes it as c.

pratie, praty. A potato : dial. and Anglo-Irish : 1832, a Scots song (O.E.D.) ; Marryat ; Reade, 1857, has the very rare spelling *pratee*. A slurred abbr. Also see **tater (-ur), tatie.**

*__prating cheat.__ The tongue : c. : ca. 1565–1860. Harman ; B.E.; Grose, 1st ed. See **cheat, a thing.**

*__pratt.__ See **prat, n.**

*__pratting-ken.__ A low lodging-house : c. : from ca. 1860. ' *No. 747*.' Ex *prat*, n., 2. Cf. *kradying-ken*, q.v.

prattle-broth. Tea : late C. 18–mid-19. Grose, 1788. Cf. *chatter-, scandal-, broth*.

*__prattle-cheat.__ See **prattling cheat.**

prattling-box. A pulpit : low : late C. 18–mid-19. Grose, 1785. Cf. *hum-box*.

*prattling-cheat. An occ. variant of *prating cheat*, q.v.

prattling-parlour. A private apartment : ca. 1820–60. Moncrieff, 1821.

*pratts. See **prat**, n.

praty. Talkative : coll. (gen. low) : C. 19–20 ; ob. Ex S.E. *prate*, (idle) talk.—2. See **pratie**.

prawn, silly. A pejorative applied to persons ; gen. *you silly prawn* or *the s.p.* : coll. : from ca. 1905 ; slightly ob. It may date from ca. 1890, for in 1895 W. Pett Ridge, *Minor Dialogues*, has : ' Ah, I expect you're a saucy young prawn, Emma.'

pray with knees upwards. (Of women) to coït : low : 1785, Grose.

prayer-bones. The knees : low coll. : from ca. 1850 ; ob.

prayer-book. A small holy-stone (cf. *bible*, q.v.) : nautical s. >, ca. 1870, nautical coll. (ob.) : 1840, Dana, ' Smaller hand-stones . . . prayer-books . . . are used to scrub in among the crevices and narrow places, where the large holystone [see **bible**] will not go.'—2. See **Post Office Prayer-Book.**—3. (Also **the sportsman's prayer-book**.) Ruff's *Guide to the Turf* : sporting : mid-C. 19–20. Ware. (The *Guide* dates from 1842.)

prayer-book parade. ' A promenade in fashionable places of resort, after morning service on Sundays ', F. & H. : ca. 1880–1920 ; very ob. Cf. *church-parade*, q.v.

prayers, at her last. (Adj. applied **to**) an old maid : late C. 17–mid-19. Ray, Grose. Cf. *lead apes in hell* : see at **apes.**

prayers, say. (Of horses) to stumble : sporting : C. 19–20 ; ob. Cf. *devotional habits.*

prayers backwards, say. To blaspheme ; to curse : coll. : late C. 17–early 19. Ray's *Proverbs* ; Ned Ward, 1706, ' They pray . . . backwards ' ; Nathan Bailey's *Erasmus*, 1725.

pre. A prefect : Public-Schoolboys' : late C. 19–20. Collinson. Also *prae*, q.v.

preach. An act of preaching ; a sermon ; a discourse ; tediously moral talk (cf. *pi-jaw*, q.v.) : C. 16–20. Mrs Whitney, 1870, ' I preached a little preach,' O.E.D. Slightly ob.

*preach at Tyburn Cross. To be hanged : c. or low s. : ca. 1810–60.

preachification. Vbl.n. of next : coll. : 1843, Lockhart (O.E.D.). Cf. *preach*, q.v.

preachify. To deliver a (tedious) sermon ; moralise wearisomely : coll. : 1775, S. J. Pratt (O.E.D.).

preachifying. Tedious moralising : coll. : 1828 (O.E.D.). Ex *preachify*. Cf. *preachification*.

preachiness. The being *preachy*, q.v. : coll. : 1861, O.E.D. Cf. preceding entry.

preaching-shop. A church ; more gen., a chapel : coll. : from ca. 1840. Thackeray. Pejorative on *preaching-house* (1760), Wesley's name for a Methodist Chapel. (O.E.D.).

preachy. Given to preaching ; as if, as in, a sermon : coll. : 1819, Miss Mitford, ' He was a very good man . . . though preachy and prosy,' O.E.D. Whence :

preachy-preachy. Tediously moral or moralising : coll. : 1894, George Moore, ' I don't 'old with all them preachy-preachy brethren says about the theatre.'

precede and **proceed** have been confused since

C. 14. Rather different is the C. 17 erroneous use of *precedential* for *precedented*. O.E.D.

preceptacyon. A C. 17 incorrectness for *precipitation*. O.E.D.

precession and **procession** : occ. catachrestic the one for the other : C. 16–20. (O.E.D.)—2. Moreover, *precession* is a C. 17 erroneous form of the † *presession*. O.E.D.

precious. Egregious ; arrant ; (pejoratively) thorough ; occ. an almost meaningless intensive : coll. : late M.E.–C. 20. Lydgate ; Jonson, 1605, ' Your worship is a precious ass ' ; Darwin, 1836. O.E.D.

precious, adv. Exceedingly ; very : coll. : 1837, Dickens (who, as W. remarks, popularised this use), ' We've got a pair o' precious large wheels on ' ; Baumann, however, implies its use as early as the 1740's. Ex the adj. Cf. *precious few.*

precious coals ! A coll. expletive : ca. 1570–1620. Gascoigne. Prob. ex *precious !* = *precious blood* or *body*, recorded by the O.E.D. in 1560.

precious few. Very few : coll. : 1839 (O.E.D.). Ex *precious*, adv. (q.v.).

Precious John. Prester John : C. 17 sol. Sir T. Herbert, 1634, mentions it. O.E.D.

preciously. Exceedingly ; very : coll. : 1607, Middleton ; Thackeray. O.E.D. Cf. *precious*, adv.

precipitate(ly) and **precipitous(ly)** are often confused : C. 19–20. (E. F. Benson amusingly in *Secret Lives*, 1932.)

precisianist. Incorrect for *precisionist* (a purist) : C. 19–20. Error due to *precisian*. O.E.D.

precognizance, -nization. Incorrect for *preconizance, -ization* : C. 18. O.E.D.

predeceased. Obvious : ca. 1890–1915 ; orig. legal. Ware. Perhaps ex *Queen Anne's dead.*

predicate. Catachrestic for *predict* : from ca. 1620. Similarly *predication* for *prediction*. O.E.D.

predic(k)lement. A predicament : sol., esp. Cockneys' (— 1887). Baumann.

preëmpt. A preëmptive right : Australian coll. : 1890, Rolf Boldrewood. Morris. Ob.

prefector, -ship. Incorrect for *prefect, prefecture* : C. 17–18. O.E.D.

preferable, more. Preferable : an indefensible incorrectness : late C. 19–20. Fowler.

preference. A choice ; e.g. ' Of the two authors, X is my preference ' : coll. : from ca. 1890. By 1935, virtual y S.E.

pregnable. Pregnant : a C. 17 catachresis. O.E.D.

prejaganint. (Too) thrustful, interfering ; having the unfortunate knack of being always in the way : New Zealanders' : from ca. 1912. Perhaps a corruption of *prejudiced.*

prejurie. An † incorrect form of *perjury*. O.E.D.

prelim. A preliminary examination : students' : from ca. 1883.—2. In pl., the pre-text pages of a book, i.e. title-pages, preface, contents-page and, when there is one, the dedication : printers' and publishers' : C. 20. Abbr. *preliminaries*.—3. A preliminary practice or match : sporting : C. 20. O.E.D. (Sup.).

premises. The female pudend : low : C. 19–20. Cf. *lodgings to let.*

premune. A præmunire (= a predicament) : coll. abbr. : ca. 1755–1800. Mrs Lennox, 1758. O.E.D.

prep. Preparation of lessons ; the period of such preparation : school s. : 1862, O.E.D. ; Eden

Phillpotts, in *The Human Boy*, 1899.—2. Abbr. of next : school s. : from 1900 at the latest. Collinson.

prep. school. A preparatory school : school s. : 1899 (O.E.D. Sup.), but prob. earlier.

preposter. Incorrect for *præposter* : mid-C. 18–20. O.E.D.

prescle. Erroneous for *presle* (shavegrass) : C. 18. O.E.D.

Prescott.⋅ A waistcoat : rhyming s. Gen. *Charley Prescott* (— 1859). H., 1st ed.

presence, this. The present document : C. 15–17 catachresis. On *these presents*. O.E.D.

present. A white spot on a finger-nail : coll. : C. 19–20 ; slightly ob. Suggested by S.E. *gift* in the same sense. Supposed to betoken good fortune.

[Present tense for preterite : a common sol. : prob. contemporaneous with the language. Esp. *give* for *gave* (see, e.g. quotation at **reener**), *run* for *ran*. Cf. : 2. Present infinitive for *do(es)*, or *did*, + that infinitive : coll. : mid-C. 19–20. E.g., R. Keverne, *Menace*, 1935, ' "Mr Parry get away all right ? " " Yes. Went off early, as you arranged ".']

presenterer. A whore : low coll. : ca. 1820–70. F. & H. (A presenter of herself.)

preserve (of long bills). A collection of outstanding debts : Oxford University : ca. 1820–50. Egan's Grose.

preservitor. Incorrect spelling of *preservator* : C. 16. (Gen. *-our*.) O.E.D.

President Bob. Robert Spencer, 2nd Earl of Sunderland (1640–1702). Very versatile. (Dawson.)

press, hot. See **hot press**.

press the button. To be the person to make a definite and/or important beginning : coll. (—1931). Lyell.

press the flesh ! Shake hands ! : a c.p. from ca. 1910. A. E. W. Mason, *The Sapphire*, 1933.

pressed off, ppl.adj. Finished : tailors' coll. : late C. 19–20.—2. Hence, asleep : tailors' s. : C. 20.

presumptious. Presumptuous : sol. : late C. 19–20 ; C. 15–18, S.E. ; ca. 1810–70, coll.

preterite, n. and adj. (A) very old (person) : Society : ca. 1870–1900. Ware, ' Especially applied to women '. Cf. *B.C.* and *has been*.

[Preterite misused for present-perfect tense results, mainly, from an aping of ' gangsterese ', orig. and chiefly U.S. ; esp. in ' You said it ' for ' You've said it ' : illiterate coll. : from ca. 1930.]

pretermit is catachrestic when = to cease completely : from ca. 1830. (O.E.D.)

prettification. Rendering finically or cheaply pretty : coll. : from ca. 1855.

prettified, adj. (Made) pretty in a too-dainty or in a cheap way : coll. : from ca. 1851. Ex :

prettify. To make pretty, esp. if cheaply or pettily : to represent prettily : coll. : 1850, Mrs Trollope, ' Your money to prettify your house ', O.E.D.

prettifying. Vbl.n. of preceding, q.v. : coll. : C. 20. Cf. *prettification*.

pretty. (Always the p.) The *fairway* : golfers' coll. : 1907. O.E.D. (Sup.).—2. As the ornamented part of a glass or tumbler, it is S.E.

[**pretty.** This S.E. adj. has, since ca. 1850, had a slightly coll. tinge.—2. The adv. (C. 16–20) has been almost coll. since ca. 1890 : i.e. in sense of ' rather ', ' considerably '. Contrast :]

pretty, adv. Prettily : 1667 (O.E.D.) : S.E. until C. 19, then coll. ; in C. 20, low coll.

pretty, do the or speak or talk. To affect

amiability or courtesy in action or speech : low coll. : from ca. 1890. J. Newman, *Scamping Tricks*, 1891, ' We can talk pretty to each other.'

pretty, sit. To (be very comfortable and) look pretty : coll. : C. 20. Orig. U.S. Ex fowls, esp. chickens, sitting prettily on the nest.

pretty as paint, as. Very pretty : coll. : 1922, E. V. Lucas, ' She's as pretty as paint ' (Apperson). Because like a painting. Cf. *oil-painting* and *picture*, qq.v.

pretty-behaved. Prettily behaved : coll. : late C. 18–20. Cf. *pretty-spoken*.

pretty-boy clip. ' Hair brought flat down over the forehead, and cut in a straight line from ear to ear ' : Society : ca. 1880–1900. Ware.

pretty dancers, the. The Aurora Borealis : Scots coll. : C. 19–20. Cf. *merry dancers*.

pretty-face. A small kangaroo : Australian coll. : from ca. 1885 ; very ob. Morris.

pretty Fanny's way, only. Characteristic : c.p. (in C. 19, a proverb) on *only her* (*his*) *way* : ca. 1720–1900. Ex Parnell, ca. 1718, ' And all that's madly wild, or oddly gay, | We call it only pretty Fanny's way ' (O.E.D.).

pretty-perch. A very neat landing : Royal Air Force's (— 1932). Opp. a *thumped-in landing*.

[**pretty-pretties**, pretty things, knick-knacks, 1875, and **pretty-pretty**, rather too, or prettily pretty, 1897, are given by O.E.D. as S.E. : but orig. they were almost certainly coll.]

pretty-pretty. ' Ornamental work on shipboard ' : nautical coll. : from ca. 1880. Bowen. Ex preceding.

Pretty Royal. H.M.S. *Princess Royal* : naval : C. 20. Bowen.

pretty-spoken. Speaking prettily : coll. : 1809, Malkin. Cf. *pretty-behaved* (12 years earlier).

prettyish. Rather pretty : coll. : 1741, Horace Walpole, ' There was Churchill's daughter, who is prettyish and dances well,' O.E.D.

[**preventative**, despite the opinion of many, is S.E. ; in C. 20, however, *preventive* is preferred. Prob. there has been some confusion with :]

preventitive, n. and adj. Incorrect, C. 17–20, for *preventive*, i.e. preventive. Doubtless due to influence of *preventive* (1639) on *preventative* (1654). O.E.D.

preventive. A preventive officer : nautical : 1870, E.D.D.

previous ; gen. **too previous.** Premature ; hasty : s. >, ca. 1895, coll. : 1885, *The Daily Telegraph*, Dec. 14, ' He is a little before his time, a trifle *previous*, as the Americans say, but so are all geniuses.' Whence :

previousness. The coming too soon or being premature, hasty : coll. : 1884 in U.S. ; anglicised ca. 1890. Ex preceding term, q.v.

*****prey.** Money : c. : late C. 17–early 19. B.E., Grose. Ex S.E. sense.

price —— ?, what. (Occ. admiring, but gen. sarcastic ; in reference to a declared or well-understood value.) What do you now think of —— ? Just consider, look at —— ! : orig. racing (' What odds —— ? '), then gen. : from ca. 1890. P. H. Emerson, 1893, ' What price you, when you fell off the scaffold.'

priceless. (By itself, it =) ludicrous ; extremely amusing. With n., egregious : e.g. ' priceless ass ' (of a person) : s. >, ca. 1935, coll. : from ca. 1906. ' Now a favourite schoolboy word ', W., 1920. Ex S.E. sense, ' invaluable '.

prick. A pimple : coll. : C. 17–18. Jonson, Marston, *et al.*, in *Eastward Ho !*, III, ii, ' I have seen a little prick no bigger than a pin's head . . . swell to an ancome,' i.e. a boil or ulcer ; this is a quibble on sense 3.—2. An endearment : late C. 16–17. (Cf. *pillicock*, 2.) Ex :—3. The penis : 1592 (O.E.D.) : S.E. until ca. 1700 ; in C. 18–20, a vulg. verging, in C. 20, on low coll. Shakespeare ; Robertson of Struan, Hanbury Williams, Burns. Ex basic sense, anything that pricks or pierces. Cf. *cock*, q.v. See esp. Grose, P., and Allen Walker Read, *Lexical Evidence*, 1935 (Paris ; privately printed). (The variant *prickle*, dating from ca. 1550, has always been S.E. : in C. 19–20, literary only.)—4. An offensive or contemptuous term (applied to men only), always with *silly* ; gen. *you silly prick*, occ. *the s. p.* : low : late C. 19–20.—5. A pin : tramps' and beggars' c. (— 1933).

prick-ear or **-ears ;** or with capitals. A Round-head : a coll. nickname : 1642 ; † by 1690. Though influenced by *prick-eared* (or *-lugged*), q.v., *prick-ear* derives mainly ex the fact that ' the Puritan head-gear was a black skull-cap, drawn down tight, leaving ears exposed,' F. & H., or, as B.E. defines *prick-eared fellow*, ' a Crop, whose Ears are longer than his Hair '.

prick-eared, adj. Roundhead : ca. 1640–1700 : coll. verging on S.E. Cf. preceding.

prick for a (soft) plank. ' To find the most com-fortable place for a sleep ' : nautical : late C. 19–20. Bowen.

prick has no conscience. See standing prick.

prick-(in-)the-garter ; also **prick-(in-)the-loop.** A fraudulent game, in which pricking with a bodkin into the loop of a belt figures largely : C. 19. In C. 17–18 called *prick-(in-)the-belt* ; in C. 18 s., *the old nob*. Orig. coll., but almost imm. S.E.

prick-louse ; occ., as in Burns, **prick-the-louse.** (Also nip-louse.) A tailor : coll. : C. 16–20 ; in C. 19–20, mainly dial. Dunbar, L'Estrange. (O.E.D.)

prick-the-garter, play at. To coït : C. 18–19 : low. Ex *prick-in-the-garter*, q.v.

prick-the-louse. See prick-louse.

pricked, with its ears. (Of a horse winning) easily : race-course coll. (— 1932). *Slang*, p. 243.

pricket. A sham bidder : auctioneers' : C. 19–20 ; ob. Cf. *putter-up*.

prickly Moses. See Moses, prickly.

pride-and-pockets. Officers on half-pay : coll. : ca. 1890–1915. P. H. Emerson, 1893.

pride of the morning. A morning erection due to retention of urine : late C. 19–20 (low) coll. Also *morning-pride*. Perhaps suggested by the S.E. and dial. *p. of the m.*, an early morning shower of rain.

*pridgeman. See prigman.

priest, a great. An ineffectual but strong desire to stool : Scots coll. : C. 18–19.

priest-linked. See priest say grace, let the.

priest of the blue bag. A barrister : coll. : from ca. 1845 ; ob. Kingsley, 1849, ' As practised in every law quibble . . . as if he had been a regularly ordained priest of the blue bag '. Cf. *green bag*.

priest say grace, let the. (V.i.) to marry : coll. : C. 17–18. Hence, *priest-linked*, joined in matri-mony : late C. 17–early 19. B.E., Grose.

priest spoke on Sunday, know more than the. To be worldly-wise : coll. : C. 15–20 ; in C. 19–20, mostly dial. Bale, ca. 1540. Apperson.

priestess. A priest's wife : coll. : 1709, Mrs Manley. (O.E.D.)

*prig ; in C. 16–18, often **prigg.** A tinker : c. : 1567 ; † by 1690. Harman. Perhaps ex dial. *prig*, v.i., to haggle about the price ; prob., however, connected closely (see, e.g. **prig, prince**) with :—2. A thief : 1610, Rowlands : c. >, ca. 1750, low s. In C. 19–20, gen. a petty thief. Ex *prig*, v., 1.—3. Hence, a cheat : late C. 17–early 19 : c. >, ca. 1750, s. B.E., Grose.—4. See prig-napper, 2.—5. A fop, coxcomb : late C. 17–early 19. B.E., ' A Nice beauish, silly Fellow, is called *a meer Prig* ' ; Grose, ' a conceited coxcomical [*sic*] fellow '.—6. Hence, a vague pejorative (dislike, contempt) : late C. 17–18 coll. Shadwell, 1679, ' A senseless, noisie Prig,' O.E.D.—7. A religious precisian, esp. a dissenting minister : coll. : late C. 17–mid-18. O.E.D. Facetious Tom Brown, Arthur Murphy. ' Per-haps partly a violent shortening of *precisian* ', W.—Hence, 8, a precisian in manners, a purist in speech, esp. if conceited, didactic, or tedious : coll. >, in C. 19, S.E. : 1753, Smollett (O.E.D.) ; George Eliot, in *Middlemarch*, ' A prig is a fellow who is always making you a present of his opinions.'

*prig ; prigg (as for **n.**). To steal : 1561, Awdelay ; Harman : c. >, in C. 19, low s. In C. 19–20, gen. applied to petty theft. ? a corruption (cf. that in sense 4) of †*prick*, to pin, to skewer.—2. Hence, to cheat, to swindle : low s. : 1819, *The Sporting Magazine*, ' [He] shook hands with me, and trusted I should soon prig the London cocknies,' O.E.D.—3. V.i., to beg, importune : 1714, Wood-row ; G. Douglas, 1901 (O.E.D.) : coll. and dial. Prob. ex *prig*, to haggle.—4. To ride : 1567, Har-man ; B.E. and Grose at *prigging* : c. and dial. ; † by 1850. Cognate with S.E. *prick*, as in Spenser's ' A gentle Knight was pricking on the plaine.'—5. Hence, v.i., to coït : c. : late C. 17–early 19. B.E., Grose : at *prigging*.

*prig, prince. C. of late C. 17–early 19 : B.E., ' A King of the Gypsies ; also a Top-thief, or Re-ceiver General ', i.e. a notable (or important) thief, or a very important ' fence '. Ex *prig*, n., 2.

*prig (or prigging-lay), work on the. To thieve : c. : C. 19–20 ; ob. Cf. :

*prig and buzz, n. and v. : picking of pockets : resp. 1789, G. Parker (*p. and b.*, *work upon the*), ob. ; C. 19–20, ob. Both, c. See buzz and prig, n., 2, and v., 1.

*prig-man. See prigman.

*prig-napper. A thief-taker : c. : late C. 17–early 19. B.E. ; Grose, 1st ed.—2. A horse-stealer : c. : mid C. 17–mid-18. Coles, 1676. This sense leads one to posit an unrecorded *prig*, n., a horse, ex *prig*, v., 4.

*prig-star. A rival in love : c. : mid C. 17–18. Coles, 1676 ; B.E. ; Grose, 1st ed. Ex *prig*, n., 2, or *prig*, v., 1. Obviously, *star* may = *-ster*.—2. Cf. *prigster*, 1 and 2.

*prigg. See prig, n. and v.

*prigger. A thief : c. >, in C. 19, low s. : 1561, Awdelay ; B.E. E.g. *p. of cacklers, prancers*, a poultry-, horse-thief. Ex *prig*, v., 1. (In C. 16, often *priggar*.)—2. A highwayman : C. 17 c. Ex *prig*, to ride ; *prigger* also meaning any rider : c. (or low s.) and dial.—3. Hence, a fornicator : c. (? > low s.) : C. (? 18–)19. Bee, 1823. Ex *prig*, v., 5. Cf. *parish-prig*.

*priggery. Thievery ; petty theft : c. : C. 18–early 19. Fielding, 1743. Cf. *priggism*, q.v.

*prigging, vbl.n. to *prig*, v., q.v. : e.g. B.E. ' Riding ; also Lying with a Woman ' ; Greene, 1591, ' This base villany of Prigging, or horse-stealing '. From ca. 1820, mostly of petty theft; and, as such, low s.

*prigging, adj. Thieving; thievish: from ca. 1567: c. >, in early C. 18, low s. Ex *prig*, v., 1.

*prigging law, lay. Theft; esp. pilfering: c.: resp. late C. 16–17 and C. 19–20; ob. Greene; Maginn, 1829, ' Doing a bit on the prigging lay '. (Prob., despite a lack of examples, the *law* form endured till ca. 1750, when—again prob.—the other arose: see **law** and **lay**.) Ex *prig*, v., 1.

*priggish. Thievish; dishonest: c.: late C. 17–early 19. B.E. Ex *prig*, n., 1.

priggism. Thieving: (c. or) low s.: C. 18. Fielding, 1743, ' The great antiquity of priggism '.

*prigman; occ. **prig-man.** A thief: c. of ca. 1560–1600. Awdelay (*prygman*); Drant, 1567 (*pridgeman*). Ex *prig*, n., 1, or, more prob., v., 1. (O.E.D.)

*prigster. A thief: c. >, by 1840, low s.: C. 19. Ex *prig*, v., 1—2. A vague pejorative : 1688, Shadwell; † by 1750. Ex *prig*, n., 6, in same sense. —3. See **prig-star**, 2 : B.E. and Grose both spell without hyphen : *prigstar*.

prim. ' A silly empty starcht Fellow ', B.E.: late C. 17–19 : low s., by 1750, coll. and dial. Ex both the adj. and the v.

primætiall. An incorrect form of *primitial*: C. 17. O.E.D.

Prime, the. The Prime Minister: from ca. 1919. John Galsworthy, *The White Monkey*, 1924, ' Didn't he think that the cubic called " Still Life—of the Government ", too frightfully funny—especially the " old bean " representing the Prime ? '

prime as a universal approbative adj. ca. 1810–40 is a coll. almost s. Vaux; Bee; Egan's Grose.

prime, adv. Excellently; in prime order : coll.: 1648, Gage, ' Prime good '; C. Scott, *Sheep-Farming*, ' The hoggets will be prime fat by Christmas.' O.E.D.

prime kelter, in. (Of a ship, esp. her rigging) in excellent condition : nautical coll.: C. 19–20. Bowen.

primitive. Unmixed; undiluted: society s. of ca. 1890–1910.

primrose. ' A beverage composed of old and bitter ale mixed ' : West Yorkshire s. (— 1905), not dial.; slightly ob. E.D.D. (Sup.).

primo. The chairman, or master, of a Buffalo lodge : friendly societies': from ca. 1880 : coll. > in C. 20, j. Ex L. *primus*, the first.

primogenial (occ. **-eal**), **-genian, -genious** (occ. **-geneous**). Incorrect for *primigenial, -genian, -genious* : C. 17–18. O.E.D.

*prinado. A sharper, prob. female : c. of ca. 1620–60. Dekker; Brathwait, *Clitus's Whimzies*, 1631, ' His Nipps, Ints, Bungs, and Prinado's . . . ofttimes prevent the Lawyer by diving too deep into his Client's pocket.' Origin obscure : the O.E.D. hazards Sp. *preñada*, pregnant : unmarried pregnant women of the lower classes used to tend to become criminals.

Prince Alberts. ' Burlap wound round the feet when a man's socks are worn out ' : sailing-ships': from ca. 1860; ob. Bowen.—2. Hence, rags worn by swagmen and bushmen in the same way : Australian : C. 20.

*prince prig. See **prig, prince.**

Prince Robert's metal. Incorrect for *Prince Rupert's metal* : late C. 17–20. O.E.D.

Prince's points. ' Shilling points at whist ' :

Society and clubmen's coll. : 1877–1901. H.R.H. (afterwards King Edward VII) argued that ' the best whist-players were not necessarily the richest of men,' Ware.

Princess Pats, the. Princess Patricia's Regiment : Canadian military : G.W., and after. F. & Gibbons (at *colours*).

principate. Incorrect for *principiate* : ca. 1660–1700. O.E.D.

[**principe.** See ' Westminster School slang ', near end.]

princock, -cox. The female pudend : low coll. · C. 16–mid-19. Ex S.E. sense.

princod. ' A round, plump ' person, Grose, 1st ed. : Scots coll. : ca. 1780–1860. Ex S.E. sense, a pincushion. (Possibly, however, it never emerged from dial.)

princum. Nicety of dress, fastidiousness of behaviour : coll. : late C. 17–18. D'Urfey, 1690. A mock-Latin perversion of *prink*, q.v. (O.E.D.) Cf. :

princum-prancum. See **prinkum-prankum.**

Princum Prancum, Mistress (B.E.) or **Mrs** (Grose, 1st ed.). A fastidious, precise, formal woman : coll. : late C. 17–early 19. See **prinkum-prankum**, stressing *prink* rather than *prank*.

prink, n. An act of making (gen. oneself) spruce : coll. : 1895 (O.E.D.). Ex :

prink, v.t. To make spruce; in reflexive, to dress oneself up : coll. : 1576, Gascoigne, ' Now I stand prinking me in the glasse,' O.E.D. The v.i., in the reflexive sense, is also coll. : C. 18–20 (D'Urfey); in C. 19–20, much the more gen. Cognate with equivalent *prank*.

prinked. The ppl.adj. of *prink*, v.t., and = ' all dressed up '. Coll. : 1579, North. (O.E.D.)

prinker. A very fastidious dresser of self : coll. : from ca. 1860. Webster, 1864. Cf. :

prinking. A fastidious adorning, mostly of oneself : coll. : 1699, Farquhar (O.E.D.). See **prink**, v.

prinkle, esp. **prinkled.** To sprinkle; sprinkled : children's sol. : since when ? Manchon. (But I believe Manchon's ' *prinkled in all her finery*, en grande toilette ' is simply an error or, more prob., a misprint for *prinked* . . .)

prinkum-prankum. A prank : coll. : late C. 16–17. Nashe. A reduplication on *prank* with *um* (see **princum**) added to each element. (O.E.D.)—2. (Mostly in pl.) Fine clothes; fastidious adornment : C. 18–early 19 : coll. Here the stress is laid on *prink* (see the v.). See also **Princum Prancum, Mistress.**

print, out of. See **out of print.**

printed character. A pawn-ticket : low s. (? > coll.) : from ca. 1860; ob.

Printing House Square, adj. ' Powerful—crushing, *ex cathedra*, from *The Times* being published in that locality ' : London clubmen's coll. : ca. 1810–80. Ware.

priorily. An incorrect variant of *priorly*, adv.: late C. 18–20; ob. O.E.D.

priscillas. See **pucellas.**

*prison-bug. A man that spends most of his time in prison : c. : from ca. 1920.

prithee. I pray thee; i.e. please ! : coll. : 1577 G. Harvey; †, except as an archaism, by 1880. Addison, ' Pr'ythee don't send us up any more Stories of a Cock and a Bull.' An abbr. corruption. O.E.D.

private business. Additional work done with a tutor : Eton College : late C. 19–20.

Private Leak. 'One whose position cannot be discovered': nautical: late C. 19–20. Bowen. Cf. *up in Annie's room.*

private peace, (I think) I'll make a. See **separate peace.**

private property. The generative organ: low coll.: C. 19–20. Suggested by *privity (-ies), privates.*

privee, n. A private one: Charterhouse: from ca. 1880. A. H. Tod, *Charterhouse,* 1900.

prize, adj. Egregious; esp. 'prize idiot': coll.: C. 20. Ex S.E. sense, first-class.

prize faggots. 'Well - developed breasts in women'; low London (— 1909). Ware. A *faggot* is a kind of rissole.

prize-packet. A novice that pays to play: theatrical: late C. 19–20. *The Globe,* July 27, 1899, 'Another man spent a happy holiday as . . . a prize packet.' Punning S.E. *prize-packet* and, I suggest, *surprise-packet.*

prizer. A prize-winner: coll., somewhat rare: mid-C. 19–20. O.E.D. (Sup.).

pro. A pro-proctor: university (esp. Oxford coll.: 1823, Anon., *Hints for Oxford,* '[Freshmen] cap the Pro's too in the street'; Bradwood, *O.V.H.,* 1869.—2. An actor: theatrical (— 1859). H., 1st ed. (Introduction). I.e. one who belongs to *the* profession, i.e. acting. (N.b., *the profession* is rather j. than coll., though orig. it may possibly have been theatrical coll.)—3. Hence, any professional as opp. to an amateur: e.g. cricketer, 1867; journalist, 1886; golfer, 1887. Coll. O.E.D.—4. In post-War days, esp. of a prostitute whose *profession* is body-vending: as opp. to a notoriously or very compliant 'amateur', esp. an 'amateur' that makes a little extra by sexual 'adventures'. —5. A probationer (nurse): medical: late C. 19–20.

pro-donna. An actress: music-halls': from ca. 1880; ob. Ware. Lit., professional lady.

procesh. A procession: late C. 19–20. (Never as v.; contrast :)

process. To be part of, go along with a procession: coll.: 1814 (O.E.D.). Ex *procession,* on *progress.*

process-pusher. A lawyer's clerk: legal (—1909). Ware. He serves writs.

procession, as applied to a race, esp. a boat-race (above all, one in which there are only two crews), implies 'an ignominious defeat' (*The Graphic,* March 24, 1883): in C. 19, coll.; in C. 20, S.E.

procession, go on with the. To continue (esp. in the imperative): coll.: late C. 19–20; very ob. Displaced by *on with the dance !,* itself somewhat ob. by 1935.

processional. A procession: a catachresis of late C. 19–20. O.E.D.

proclamations, have one's head full of. See **head full of proclamations.**

proctors' dog or bulldog. The orig. of *bulldog,* one of the University police: Oxford and Cambridge University: 1847, Tennyson in *The Princess,* 'He had climbed across the spikes . . . | And . . . breath'd the Proctor's dogs.' O.E.D.

*****proctour,** i.e. **proctor.** Awdelay, 1561, 'Proctour is he, that will tary long, and bring a lye, when his Maister sendeth him on his errand,' i.e. of the 12th of the 25 orders of knaves: c.: mid-C. 16–early 17. Ex S.E. sense, one licensed to beg for a hospital.

prod, n. and v. (Of a man) the act of coïtion; to coït: C. 19–20: low coll. Cf. *poke.*—2. A horse;

esp. an old horse: from ca. 1890. A perversion of *prad,* q.v. (O.E.D.)

prodigious. Prodigiously; very greatly; very: from ca. 1670: S.E. until ca. 1750, then coll.; in late C. 19–20, low coll.; ob. E. de Acton, 1804, 'A prodigious high hill'. O.E.D. Cf. :

prodigiously. Exceedingly; very: coll.: C. 18–20; ob. Swift, 1711, 'It snowed . . . prodigiously.' (O.E.D.)

produce, gen. in imperative. To pay over the money won: two-up players': C. 20. Abbr. *produce the money.*

prof ; often, in C. 19, **proff.** A professor: U.S., 1838 ; anglicised ca. 1860. Thornton.

profession, the. See note at **pro,** 2.

professional. A 'professional examination' (medicine): Scottish universities', mostly medical students': C. 20. (O.E.D.)

profit !, all. A barbers' c.p., indicating that a customer having his hair cut requires no 'dressing' on his hair; gen. said to the customer. C. 20.

proforce, profos. A provost: Scots sol. : C. 18–20. (O.E.D.)

prog. Food in gen.: 1655, Fuller, 'The Abbot also every Saturday was to visit their beds, to see if they had not shuffled in some softer matter or purloyned some progge for themselves'; Swift; Disraeli. Prob. ex corresponding v.—2. Hence, food for a journey, a picnic: coll.: 1813 (O.E.D.)— 3. A proctor (Oxford, Cambridge): undergraduates' s.: C. 20. By perversion. Also *progger* and *proggins.* Cf. sense 1 of the v.—4. A programme: not very gen. coll. (— 1923). Manchon.

prog, v.t. To proctorise: C. 20 Oxford and Cambridge. Ex *prog,* n., 3.—2. To poke about for food ; to forage : C. 17–20 : in C. 17, (low) s.; C. 18, s. > low coll.: C. 19–20, mainly dial. Origin obscure.— 3. To prognosticate: printers': from ca. 1870.

prog-basket. A provision-basket on journey or picnic : coll. : mid-C. 19–20. Ex *prog,* n., 2.

progger. A beggar: late C. 17–20 : s. until ca. 1750 ; then coll. till ca. 1850 ; then dial. (O.E.D.) Ex *prog,* v., 2.—2. (Also **proggins,** which is more gen.) A proctor : C. 20 Oxford, Cambridge. Ex *prog,* v., 1.

progging, n. A proctorial discipline: Oxford, Cambridge : C. 20. Ex *prog,* v., 1.—2. Foraging : mid-C. 17–20: s. >, by 1700, coll.; ob. J. Chappelow, 1715, 'All their . . . progging is for themselves.' O.E.D.

progging, adj. Begging; foraging: from ca. 1620 : s. >, by 1700, coll.; very ob. Ex *prog,* v., 2.

proggins. A proctor : from ca. 1898. See **prog,** n., 3, and cf. *progger,* n., 2. (O.E.D.)

prognostic. An artistic eater : literary, ca. 1900– 10. I.e. *prog,* n., 1 + *gnostic,* one who knows; obviously with pun on S.E. *prognostic.*

proing, vbl.n. Being a professional (esp. actor, showman, singer): coll. (— 1887); slightly ob. Baumann.

[**Projector, the.** John Law, financier (d. 1729). Also *Beau Law* and *the Paper King.* Rather sobriquets than true nicknames.]

proling. See **prowl,** 1. Spelling in B.E. and *A New Canting Dict.*

prom. A promenade, a place for promenading: coll., orig. (1899), U.S.; anglicised by 1910. (O.E.D. Sup.)—2. A promenade concert: 1902, *The Free Lance,* Jan. 4, 1902, 'There is never one of the programmes at the Proms . . . unworthy of the . . . most cultured music lover.' Cf. *pop* and :

promenade. A promenade concert : coll., now verging on S.E. : 1901, *The Westminster Gazette*, Sept. 18. O.E.D. (—Contrary to a wide-spread opinion, *promenade* as used by soldiers is S.E.)

promiscuous. Carelessly irregular ; haphazard ; casual : low coll. : 1837, Dickens ; L. Oliphant, 1883. O.E.D.—2. Casually ; incidentally : 1885, Grant Allen. (O.E.D.) Cf. sense 2 of :

promiscuously. Unceremoniously ; promptly : coll. : C. 17. Rowlands, 1609 (O.E.D.).—2. Casually ; incidentally : coll. : 1812. Leslie Stephen, 1871, ' The stone was dropped promiscuously.' O.E.D.

promise. Declare ; assert with assurance : coll. : mid-C. 15–20. Esp. in *I promise you*, I assure you ; I tell you confidently or plainly. O.E.D.

promo. A promotion : Charterhouse : from ca. 1880. A. H. Tod, *Charterhouse*, 1900. An unexpected, perhaps an undeserved promotion was, ca. 1890–1905, a **Stedman.**

promoss. To talk rubbish ; play the fool : Australia : ca. 1895–1910. ? origin.

promoted. Dead : Oct.–Nov., 1890. Ex the public funeral of Mrs Booth, General Booth's wife, and Salvation Army j. (Ware.)

promoter. A fool-catcher : coll. : ca. 1880–1920. Ex *company-promoter*.

promotion, be on one's. To behave with marriage in view and mind : coll. : 1836 (O.E.D.) ; 1848, Thackeray, ' " Those filthy cigars," replied Mrs Rawdon. " I remember when you liked 'em, though ", replied her husband . . . " That was when I was on my promotion, Goosey ", she said.' Ex *on promotion*, on approval or trial.

promotionitis. The symptoms displayed by officers potentially promotable : naval coll. : C. 20. Bowen.

prompter. A member of the 2nd Form : Merchant Taylor's School : C. 19–20 coll. > j.

prone, at the. Adj.-adv., lying with face down : military coll., esp. of firing position : C. 20.

pronounciation. Pronunciation : sol., written as well as spoken : C. 16–20 : not incorrect until C. 19. Owing to *pronounce, pronounceable*, etc. (Yet I have never heard—or seen—*denounciation*.)

pronto. Promptly ; quickly : U.S., anglicised in 1918, esp. in the Navy and Army. Bowen ; F. & Gibbons. Ex Sp. *pronto*, promptly.

Prooshan, -in. (A) Prussian : low coll. : C. 19–20. Cf. quotation at *Prussian blue*.

Prooshan blue, my. See **Prussian blue.**

prop. See **props**, 2–4.—2. Any stage requisite ; a portable article used in acting a play : theatrical : 1864, H., 3rd ed. Ex *property*. Gen. in pl. : *actor's props*, acting material provided by himself ; *(manager's) props*, articles provided by the manager for stage use. Cf. *props*, n., 4.—3. A breast-pin ; a tie-pin : c. : 1850, Dickens, ' In his shirt-front there's a beautiful diamond prop.' Perhaps ex *prop*, a support ; more prob. ex Dutch *prop*. In C. 20 c., also a lady's brooch : Manchon.—4. The leg : s. and dial. (1793) ; the arm extended : s. only : 1869. See **props**, 3. Hence partly :—5. A straight hit ; a blow : pugilistic and low street : 1874, H., 5th ed., ' A prop on the nose ' ; 1887, *The Licensed Victuallers' Gazette*, Dec. 2, ' Ned met each rush of his enemy with straight props.' Ex *prop*, v., 1.—6. The gallows : Punch and Judy s. verging on j. : from ca. 1860.—7. A proposition, as in

geometry : schools' : 1871, ' M. Legrand ' (O.E.D.). Ex abbr.—8. A propeller : aviators' coll. : from ca. 1915. B. & P.

prop, v. To hit ; knock down : pugilistic and low : 1851, Mayhew, ' If we met an " old bloke " . . . we " propped him ".' Perhaps by antiphrasis ex *prop*, to support, influenced by *drop* ; but cf. *prop*, n., 5.—2. Only in *prop and cop*, a four-handed game in which one says *I prop* (I propose), and another *I cop* (accept) : 1923, Manchon ; ob.

prop, kick away the. To be hanged : low coll. : early C. 19.

*prop-nailer. A stealer of pins or brooches : c. : 1856, Mayhew. Ex *prop*, n., 3.

prop on, put the. To seize an opponent's arm and thus prevent him from hitting : pugilistic : from ca. 1860 ; ob. Cf. *props*, 3.

propaganda. Exaggerated talk ; senseless rumours or information : military coll. : 1916–18. F. & Gibbons. (Comment unnecessary.)

propeller-guards. Ladies' stockings : nautical (officers') : C. 20. Bowen. Punning the technical term + legs as propellers.

propensities, have musical. (Of a horse) to be a ' roarer ' : sporting, esp. journalists' (— 1887) ; ob. Baumann.

proper. (Of things.) Excellent ; admirable : from late M.E. : S.E. >, ca. 1850, coll. >, ca. 1890, low coll.—2. (Of persons.) Respectable ; decorous : 1818, Moore : somewhat, and increasingly, coll. O.E.D.—3. Thorough ; complete ; perfect : C. 14–20 : S.E. till C. 19, then dial. and coll. Miss Yonge, ' Old Markham seems in a proper taking,' O.E.D. Cf. sense 1.

proper, adv. Excellently ; thoroughly ; without subterfuge ; handsomely : an intensive adv. = hard (' Hit him proper ! '), very much : mid-C. 15–20 : S.E. until ca. 1820, then coll. ; since ca. 1880, low coll. ; since ca. 1920, almost a sol. Conan Doyle, 1898, ' " Had 'em that time—had 'em proper ! " said he,' O.E.D.

proper, make oneself. To adorn oneself : low coll. : from ca. 1870. Cf. Fr. *propre*, clean.

proper bit of frock. A ' pretty and clever well-dressed girl ' : London lower classes' : ca. 1873–1910. Ware.

properly. Admirably ; handsomely ; well : C. 14–20 : S.E. until C. 19, then coll. ; in C. 20, low coll.—2. Thoroughly, perfectly ; very : C. 15–20 : S.E. until ca. 1850, then coll. *The Daily News*, March 18, 1896, ' The accused said he got " properly drunk ",' O.E.D.

propers, adj. Rejected, refused : lower classes' (— 1909). Ware implies an erotic connotation.

property, alter the. To disguise oneself : late C. 17–early 19 : coll. >, by 1750, S.E. (Implied in) B.E. ; *A New Canting Dict.*, 1725.

prophecy, the n., and **prophesy**, the v., Often confused in writing : occ. in speech.

prophet. A sporting tipster : journalistic : 1884, *The Pall Mall Gazette*, May 3 (O.E.D.) ; slightly ob. —2. **Prophet, the.** The Cock (tavern) at Temple Bar, London : 1788–ca. 1830 : a London nickname. Grose, 3rd ed. Presumably because a cock announces the dawn.

prop'ly, proply. Properly : slovenly coll. : C 19–20. E.g. Frank Swinnerton, *The Georgian House*, 1933.

propose, v.i. To offer marriage : coll. : **1764,** Gray in his poem *The Candidate*. O.E.D.

proposition. A matter : C. 20 coll. (orig. U.S.); prob. soon to be S.E. 'That's quite a different proposition.' Ex the very closely allied S.E. (orig. U.S.) sense, ' a problem, task, or undertaking . . . a person to be dealt with ', S.O.D. See, e.g., the Fowlers' *King's English.*—2. A *tough proposition* retains its U.S. flavour.

proppy. Like a prop or pole : coll., but rare : 1870, O.E.D.

propriet. To own : journalistic : 1887, *The Referee,* July 31 ; ob. Ware (at *Pink 'un*). Ex *proprietor.*

props. See **prop**, n., 2.—2. Crutches : late C. 18–20. Grose, 2nd ed. I.e. things that support.—3. The arms ; not, as Manchon defines it, fists : low : 1869, *Temple Bar,* vol. XXVI, ' Take off your coat and put up your props to him.' Cf. *prop,* v., 1. Prob. same semantics as for sense 2 ; cf. *prop,* n., 4. —4. (Also *propster.*) The property-man : theatrical : from ca. 1889. Cf. *prop,* n., 2.—5. **(props or Props.)** Shares in the Broken Hill **Proprietary** Company : Stock Exchange (— 1895). A. J. Wilson, *Stock Exchange Glossary.*

props, piss on one's. See **piss on one's props.**—**propster.** See **props,** 4.

pros ; occ. **pross.** A water-closet : Oxford and Cambridge University (— 1860). H., 2nd ed. Abbr. πρός τινα or τὸν τόπον. Cf. the old undergraduate ' wheeze ' : ' When is *pote* used [or, put] for *pros* ? | When the nights are dark and dreary, | When our legs are weak and weary, | When the quad we have to cross, | Then is *pote* put for *pros* ' : doubtless a double pun, for *pote* = (*chamber-*)*pot, pros* = a w.c., and *pote* = Gr. πότε, when ?, *pros* = Gr. πρός, to. Cf. *topos,* q.v.

pros, adj. Proper : low London (— 1887) ; ob. ? ex *prosperous.*—2 Occ. as adv.

Pros' Avenue ; p. a. The Gaiety Bar : theatrical : 1880's. Because a resort of actors. Ware. Cf. *Prossers' Avenue,* q.v.

prose, n. and v. A lecture ; to lecture : Winchester College : from ca. 1860. Ex S.E., a prosy discourse σr ex :—2. Familiar talk ; a talk : coll. : 1805, Mrs Creevey ; ob. by 1890, virtually † by 1930. O.E.D. Ex :—3. **prose**, v. To chat ; gossip : coll. : 1797, Tweddell ; ob. by 1890, † by 1930. O.E.D.—4. A prosy, esp. if dull, person : coll. : 1844, Dickens (O.E.D. Sup.). Ex sense 2.

prosecute. See **persecute.**

prospect. A person more or less likely to take out an insurance policy : an insurance coll. now verging on j. : C. 20. Ex S.E. mining sense, a spot giving prospects of, e.g., gold.

Prosperity Robinson. Fred. Robinson (d. 1859), Viscount Goderich. Ex untimely eulogy of British prosperity. (Also known as *Goosey Goderich.*) Contrast *Adversity Hume* and cf. *Starvation Dundas.* (Dawson.)

pross. One who, to an (itinerant) actor, throws money : low theatrical : 1851, Mayhew ; very ob. Prob. ex *prosperous* : cf. *pros,* adj.—2. Hence, a cadged drink : theatrical : from ca. 1860.—3. A **prostitute** : low (mostly London) : from ca. 1870.— 4. See **pross, on the,** and cf. *prosser* and *pross,* v.— 5. A variant of *pros,* n.

pross, v. To cadge (a meal, a drink) ; occ. v.i. : theatrical : from ca. 1860. H., 3rd ed. Either ex *pross,* n., 2, or *pross,* v., 2. Anon., ca. 1876, ' I've prossed my meals from off my pals.'—2. ' To break in or instruct a stage-infatuated youth ', H., 1st ed. : theatrical : from ca. 1858 ; ob. This sense may

have been influenced by Romany *pross,* to ridicule.

pross, on the, adj. and adv. Looking for free drinks, etc. ; on the cadge : theatrical >, ca. 1890, low gen. s. : from ca. 1860. P. H. Emerson, 1893. —2. Breaking in (and sponging from) a stage-struck youth : theatrical : from ca. 1865.

prosser. A cadger of refreshment, stomachic or pecuniary : theatrical : from ca. 1880. Cf. *Prossers' Avenue* and ' For he don't haunt the Gaiety Bar, dear boys, | A-standing (or prossing for) drinks,' *The Referee,* Nov. 18, 1883.—2. Hence, a loafer, a hanger-on : 1886, *The Cornhill Magazine,* Nov. Senses 1 and 2, prob. ex :—3. A ' ponce ' (q.v.) : low : from ca. 1870. H., 5th ed. Ex *pross,* n., 3.

Prosser's, occ. **Prossers' Avenue.** The Gaiety Bar : theatrical : from ca. 1882. Ex *prosser,* 1, q.v.

prostitute. To prostrate : a C. 17 catachresis. O.E.D.

prostituted. (Of a patent) so long on the market that it has become known to all : commercial coll. (— 1909). Ware.

[**protagonist.** See Fowler.]

protected. Lucky ; uncannily or very lucky : Australian and New Zealand : C. 20, but not gen. before G.W. Prob. *protected by the gods* or *by one's superiors.* Cf. :

protected man. ' A merchant seaman unfit for the Royal Service and therefore free of the press-gang ', F. & H. : naval coll. : ca. 1800–50.

protervious. An incorrect form of †*protervous* : mid-C. 16–17. O.E.D.—**protest.** See **detest.**— **prothesis, prothetic,** are incorrect for the *prosthesis, prosthetic,* of surgery : from ca. 1840. O.E.D.

[**proud.** Feeling very gratified, delighted : S.E. verging on coll. and dial. : C. 19–20. Whence :]

proud, do one. To flatter (ob.) ; to honour ; to treat very generously : coll. : 1819 (O.E.D.) ; 1836, Clark, *Ollapodiana Papers,* 1836, ' I really thought, for the moment, that " she did me proud ".' Cf. ' *the Cull tipt us Rum Prog,* the Gentleman Treated us very High,' B.E. and :

proud, do oneself. To be delighted (ob.) ; to treat oneself well, live comfortably : coll : from ca. 1840. Ex preceding entry.

proud as an apothecary. Very proud or conceited : a C. 17 catach. Apperson. Cf. :

proud as old Cole's dog. Exceeding proud : C. 19 : coll. Southey explains that this animal ' took the wall of a dung-cart and got squeezed to death by the wheel '. Anecdotal origin. (Apperson.)

prov, on the. Out of work and *on the provident* funds of a trade society or union : workmen's : from ca. 1870 ; > ob. on the Dole's arrival.

provencion. An incorrect form of *prevention* : C. 16–17. A C. 17 incorrectness for the same is *provension* : C. 17. O.E.D.

*****provender.** ' He from whom any Money is taken on the Highway ', B.E. : c. of late C. 17–early 19. Ex *provender,* food, a provider thereof.—2. Hence, money taken from a person on the highway : c. : C. 18. *The New Canting Dict.,* 1725.

provender pricks one. One grows amorous : coll. : ca. 1540–1750. Heywood, E. Ward. (Apperson.)

proverbial, the. A fall, smash ; disaster : military : 1916 ; ob. F. & Gibbons. Abbr. *the proverbial gutser* that comes after pride : see **gutser.**

providence. One who appears, or acts, in the

character of Providence : coll. : 1856, Emerson (O.E.D.).

province of Bacchus. Drunkenness : Oxford University : ca. 1820–40. Egan's Grose.

provost. A garrison or other cell for short-sentence prisoners : military coll. (– 1890) >, ca. 1905, S.E. ; ob. Abbr. *provost-cell*.

prow. A bumpkin : naval : ca. 1800–90. ? ex ob. *prow*, good, worthy.

prowl. To womanise : low coll. : late C. 17–20. B.E., as *proling* [sic]. (Like a wild beast for meat : cf. *mutton*, q.v.)—2. To wait for 'the ghost to walk' : theatrical : from ca. 1870 ; ob. See ghost.—3. To go about, looking for something to steal : c. (– 1887). Baumann.

Prowler, Hugh. A generalised (? low) coll. nickname for a thief, a highwayman : mid-C. 16–17. Tusser, ' For fear of Hugh Prowler get home with the rest.'

proxime. Proxime accessit : coll. abbr. (schools', universities') : 1896. O.E.D.

Pru, the. The Prudential insurance company : insurance : late C. 19–20. Collinson.

pruff. Sturdy : Winchester College : from ca. 1870. Ex *proof against pain*. Pascoe, 1881, ' Deprive a Wykehamist of words . . . such as quill . . . pruff . . . cad . . . and his vocabulary becomes limited.'

prugg(e). A female partner ; a doxy : C. 17 : either (low) s. or c. Nares (1822) ; Halliwell (1847). Prob. cognate with *prig* and perhaps with *prog*, qq.v.

prunella, leather and. This misquotation of Pope's *leather or prunella* has been misapplied to mean something to which one is completely indifferent. (Fowler.)

Prunella, Mr ; or **prunella.** A clergyman : late C. 18–mid-19. Grose, 1st ed. Clergymen's, like barristers', gowns were formerly made from this strong (silk, later) worsted stuff.

Prussian blue, my. An endearment : ca. 1815–70, though app. not recorded before 1837, Dickens, ' " Vell, Sammy," said the father. " Vell, my Prooshan Blue," responded the son.' Punning the colour ; ex the tremendous popularity of the Prussians after Waterloo : cf. the old toast, *Prussian blue*. Brewer.

*****prygge.** See prig, n. and v.—*****prygman.** See prigman.—**pr'ythee.** See prithee.

P's and Q's. See imm. after ' p.s or P.S.'—2. Shoes : rhyming s. late C. 19–20. B. & P.

psalm-smiter. A ranting nonconformist ; a street preacher : low : from ca. 1860 ; ob. H., 2nd ed. ? ex *psalm-singing*, noisily religious. Cf. *cushion-smiter* and *-thumper*.

psico-, psicro-. Incorrect for *psycho-, psychro-*. C. 19–20. O.E.D.

Psych. See Sike.

psyche (pronounced *sik*). To subject to psychoanalysis : coll. (– 1927). Collinson. Cf. :

psycho. Psycho-analysis (1921) ; to psychoanalyse (1925) : coll. O.E.D. (Sup.).

psychological moment. (Cf. the misuse of *inferiority complex*.) The critical moment ; *at the p. m.*, in the very nick of time : catachrestic : from ca. 1871. The error arose from the French *moment psychologique*, a confusion of *das psychologische Moment* with *der p. M.*, i.e. the ' momentum ' or factor for the moment of time. Esp. common in journalism. See esp. W., O.E.D., and Fowler.

ptomaine. The pronunciation *toe-mane* was in

1909 condemned by the O.E.D. as illiterate ; but by 1920 (so I infer from W.) it was no worse than coll. ; by 1930, it was S.E., for the orig. correct *toe-may-in* had disappeared,—the author (*horribile dictu !*) has never even heard it. Cf. *potomaine*, q.v.

pu-pu. A variant of *pooh-pooh*.

pub. A public-house (see public, n.) : 1859, H., in his first ed. : s. >, ca. 1890, coll. Anon., *The Siliad*, ca. 1871, ' All the great houses and the minor pubs.'—2. See *P.B.*

pub (always pub it). To frequent ' pubs ' : coll. : 1889, Jerome K. Jerome. Ex preceding. O.E.D.

pub-crawl ; esp. do a p.-c. A liquorish peregrination from bar to bar : from not later than 1910. Hence *pub-crawler*, *pub-crawling* : from ca. 1910.

pubes. An incorrect pl. of *pubis*, a part of the innominate bone : from ca. 1840.—2. Also incorrect for *pubis*, the pubic bone : 1872. O.E.D.

pubis. A mistake for *pubes*, the hypogastric region : from ca. 1680. O.E.D.

public. A public-house : coll. : 1709, a churchwarden's account (O.E.D.) ; ob. Scott, ' This woman keeps an inn, then ? interrupted Morton. A public, in a prim way, replied Blane.' Cf. *pub*, q.v.

public, adj. In, of, a public-house : coll. : mid-C. 18–20. Ex preceding.

public buildings, inspector of. An idler ; a loafer : from ca. 1850 ; ob. Hence, one in search of work : from ca. 1860 ; † by 1930.

public ledger. A harlot : low : late C. 18–20 ; very ob. ' Because like that paper, she is open to all parties,' Grose, 2nd ed. Punning not *The Public Ledger* (of Philadelphia, 1836) but perhaps the Public Register.

public line, something in the. A licensed victualler : coll. Dickens, who, in 1840, originated—or, at the least, gave currency to—the phrase ; prob. on *the public business*.

public man. A bankrupt : ca. 1810–80. *Lex. Bal.*, 1811. Perhaps suggested by † S.E. *public woman* (Fr. *femme publique*), a harlot.

*****public patterer.** A ' swell mobsman ' (see mobsman) who, pretending to be a Dissenting preacher, harangues in the open air to attract a crowd for his confederates to rob : c. : ca. 1860–1910. H., 3rd ed., 1864. See patterer.

public-room men. ' In modern liners, the deck, smoke-room, library and lounge stewards and the like ' : nautical coll. : C. 20. Bowen.

pucellas ; priscillas. Incorrect for *procello* : C. 19–20. O.E.D.

Publican. A nickname for General Booth ' after buying the Grecian Theatre and Tavern in the City Road ' : 1883–ca. 90. Ware.

puck-ball. Erroneous for *puff-ball* : C. 18–20. Ex Bailey's misreading of Kersey. O.E.D.

pucka. See pukka.—**pucker,** adj. See the same.

pucker. Excitement ; (a state of) agitation : coll. : 1741, Richardson (O.E.D.) ; Smollett, 1751, ' The whole parish was in a pucker : some thought the French had landed.' Rare except as *in a pucker*, which Grose, 2nd ed., defines as ' in a dishabille ', a sense † by 1880 ; ' also in a fright ', which is a little too strong. Common, moreover, in dial. ; cf. the Lancashire *puckerashun*, vexation or agitation. Ex the puckering of facial skin. See pucker up.

pucker, v. To talk privately : showmen's s. (perhaps orig. c.) : 1851, Mayhew, ' The trio . . . began puckering . . . to each other in murdered

French, dashed with a little Irish.' **?** a corruption of Romany *rok(k)er* or *vok(k)er*, to talk : cf. *rocker*, q.v.

pucker up. To become angry : coll. : C. 19–20. Ex. n., q.v., and S.E. v., primary sense.

pucker-water. An astringent employed—esp. by ' old experienced traders ', i.e. prostitutes—to counterfeit virginity : low coll. : Grose, 1785 ; † by 1890. Gen., water impregnated with alum. (Cf. post-parturition astringents.) Ex *pucker*, to contract.

*puckering, vbl.n. Private talk : c. and showmen's s. (— 1859). H., 1st ed. Ex *pucker*, v., q.v.

puckerow ; occ. **pukkaroo.** To seize : Anglo-Indian and military (— 1864). H., 3rd ed. Ex Hindustani, where this, as in all the Anglo-Indian *-ow* vv., is the form of the imperative, not of the infinitive. Perhaps cf. *pakaru*, q.v.

pud. A (child's) hand ; an animal's fore-foot : a nursery coll. : 1654, O.E.D. Lamb, 1823, ' Those little short . . . puds.' Origin unknown : but cf. Dutch *poot*, a paw (W.) and the later *pudsy*, plump, chubby.

pudden. Pudding : dial. and low coll. : C. 16–20. And cf. :

pudden, v. C. 17–20. To supply with pudding ; treat with a pudding(-like substance) : low coll.— 2. Esp., in c., to silence a dog by throwing a narcotic ball to it : 1858, Youatt (O.E.D.).

pudden-basin. An illiterate variant of *pudding-basin*, q.v. (B. & P.)

pudden club, put in the. To render pregnant : low : late C. 19–20. James Curtis, *The Gilt Kid*, 1936. See also **pudding, with a bellyful of marrow.**

*pudding. Liver drugged for the silencing of house-dogs : c. : 1877, but prob. much earlier,— see **pudden,** v., in c. sense. Horsley, *Jottings from Jail.* Cf. the old saying ' Pudding is poison when it is too much boiled ' (Swift).—2. Coïtion ; the penis ; the seminal fluid : low coll. : from Restoration days. *Wit and Mirth*, 1682 ; D'Urfey.—3. See **puddings.**—4. An English 60-pound bomb : military : 1916–18.

pudding, give or **make** or **yield the crow(s) a.** To die ; also and orig., to hang on a gibbet : late C. 16–19. Grose, 3rd ed. (*give*) ; Shakespeare, ' He'll yield the crow a pudding one of these days.'

pudding !, not a word of the. Say nothing about it : coll. c.p. of late C. 17–early 18. B.E., at *mum-for-that.*

pudding, ride post for a. To exert oneself for a small cause : coll. : C. 18–19 coll.

pudding, with a bellyful of marrow- ; in the pudding club. Pregnant : low : C. 19–20 ; ob. Cf. *pudding*, n., 2. The latter, esp. as *put in the pudden club*, to render pregnant, is still current : witness James Curtis, *The Gilt Kid*, 1936.

pudding about the heels. Thick-ankled : low coll. : C. 19–20 ; very ob.

pudding for supper, have a hot. See **hot pudding.**

pudding-bag. ' A stocking pennant used as a vane ' : nautical : late C. 19–20. Bowen. Ex shape.

pudding-basin. A British shrapnel-helmet : military : 1915 ; ob. Ex its shape. (F. & Gibbons.)

pudding-bellied. With great paunch : coll. : C. 18–20.

pudding-filler. A glutton : Scots coll. : C. 16–19. Dunbar. See **puddings.**

pudding-house. The stomach, the belly : low : late C. 16–20 ; ob. Nashe. Cf. *bread-basket.*

*pudding-ken. A cook-shop : c. : C. 19–20 ; ob. P. H. Emerson. Cf. *pudding-snammer.*

pudding-sleeves. A clergyman : ca. 1780–1860. Grose, 1st ed. Cf. *prunella*, q.v.

*pudding-snammer. A cook-shop thief : c. (— 1839) ; slightly ob. Brandon.

puddings. The guts : mid-C. 15–20 : S.E. till C. 18, then dial. and low coll. Shakespeare ; Brydges, 1772 ; Grose, 1st ed., ' I'll let out your puddings,' i.e. disembowel you.

puddings and pies. Eyes : rhyming s. (— 1859). H., 1st ed. Later, *mince pies.*

puddle. The female pudend : low : C. 19–20.— 2. **the Puddle** or **puddle,** the Atlantic Ocean : coll. : from ca. 1880. Cf. *the Pond*, q.v.—3. A muddle, a mess : late C. 16–20 : S.E. till ca. 1850, then coll. and dial.

puddle, v. To tipple : low coll. : from ca. 1870 ; ob. ? ex *piddle* on *fuddle.*

Puddle-Dock, the Countess or **Duchess of.** An imaginary aristocrat : coll. : C. 18–mid-19. Swift, ' *Neverout.* I promised to squire the Countess to her box. *Miss.* The Countess of Puddledock, I suppose.' Ex an almost permanent, large and dirty pool in Thames Street, which runs parallel to the river, London, E.C.4.

puddling, adj. A vague pejorative : coll. : 1764, Foote ; ob. Ex *to puddle.* Cf. *piddling.* O.E.D.

pudge. A short squat person ; anything both short and thick : coll. and dial. : 1808, Jamieson. Of obscure origin but prob. cognate with *podge.*

pudsy. A foot : late C. 18–20 : a nursery coll. A diminutive of *pud*, q.v.

pudsy, v. To greet affectionately or with familiarity : coll. : C. 19–20 ; ob. Ex *pudsy*, a term of endearment, esp. to a baby, itself ex *pudsy*, plump.

puff. A decoy in a gambling-house ; a mock-bidder at auctions : resp. 1731 and (—1785). O.E.D.—2. A sodomist : tramps' c. : from ca. 1870.—3. Breath, ' wind ' : s. and dial. : 1827, *The Sporting Magazine* (O.E.D.). Hence, *out of puff*, out of breath : same status and period.— 4. Life ; existence : tailors' > (low) gen. : from ca. 1880. As in *never in one's puff*, never, and as in ' Pomes ' Marshall, ' He's the winner right enough ! It's the one sole snip of a lifetime— simply the cop of one's puff.'

puff and dart. Beginning, commencement : rhyming s. (on *start*) : C. 20. *The Evening Standard*, Aug. 19, 1931.

puff-ball, v.t. In the 1890's, John Masefield tells us in his history (1933) of the *Conway* training ship, ' large cakes of soft bread were moulded in tea at tea-time to the size and similitude of dumplings and then thrust down the victim's neck between his shirt and the skin ' : a mess's punishment of an ' impossible ' member.

puff-guts. A fat man : low coll. : 1785, Grose ; slightly ob.

puff-puff. A locomotive ; a railway-train : nursing coll. : from ca. 1870. Echoic. Cf. *puffer* and *puffing billy.*

puff the glim. Horse-coping s. from before 1890, thus : ' Old horses are rejuvenated by puffing the glim, . . . filling up the hollows . . . above [the] eyes by pricking the skin and blowing air into the loose tissues underneath,' *Tit-Bits*, April 11, 1891. (Verging on c.)

puffer. A steam-engine : coll. : verging on S.E. : 1801 (O.E.D.). Cf. *puff-puff.*—2. A steam barge : nautical coll. verging on S.E. : C. 20. Bowen.

puffin, plump as a. Very plump : coll. > S.E. : C. 19–20. Ex corpulence of young bird. (W.)

puffing Billy or **billy.** A locomotive : coll. : late C. 19–20. Cf. *puff-puff* and *puffer*, qq.v.—2. Hence, a person puffing or much given to puffing : coll. : C. 20.

pug. A boxer : sporting : 1858, Mayhew, 'Known by his brother pugs to be one of the gamest hands in the ring '. Abbr. *pugilist.* Hence *Pug's* or *Pugs' Acre*, that corner of Highgate Cemetery where Tom Sayers and other 'pugs' lie buried.—2. A dog of no matter what breed : coll. : from ca. 1860. See sense 7.—3. A bargeman : coll. : late C. 16–early 17. Lyly, 1591, 'With a good winde and lustie pugges one may goe ten miles in two daies.' O.E.D.—4. A ship's boy : coll. : late C. 16–17. 'Hudibras ' Butler. (O.E.D.)—5. A harlot : coll. : C. 17–early 18. Ned Ward.—6. An upper servant in a large house (etc.) : from ca. 1840. Halliwell.—7. A nickname for a dog or a monkey : coll. : resp. (—1731), Bailey ; 1664. † except in dial.—8. Hence, like 'monkey ', to a child : mid-C. 18–20, but since ca. 1850, † except in dial. O.E.D.—9. A fox ; gen. as a nickname : C. 19–20 : coll. R. S. Surtees, 1858, 'Pug . . . turns tail, and is very soon in the rear of the hounds,' O.E.D. In C. 20, virtually S.E.

pug-nasty. A dirty slut : coll. : late C. 17–early 19. B.E. Ex *pug*, 5. Cf. pug Nancy in Addenda.

*puggard. A thief : c. : C. 17. Middleton, 1611. Ex *pug*, to tug, pull.

puggle, puggly. See poggle.—**puggle pawnee.** See poggle p.—puggled. See poggled.

puggy. A coll. endearment to a woman or a child : C. 17–early 18.—2. A monkey : Scots coll. : from ca. 1820. Ex *pug*, 7.—3. A nickname for a fox : coll. : 1827. Ex *pug*, last sense.

puggy-drunk. Extremely drunk : rather low : late C. 19–20. Prob. ex *pogy* influenced by *poggle* (*puggle*), 2, and with an allusion to *puggy*, a fox (cf. *foxed*, drunk).

pugified. Snub-nosed : coll. : late C. 18–mid-19. Grose, 2nd ed. Cf. S.E. *pug-nosed*.

Pug's or **Pugs' Acre.** See pug, 1.

pug's or **pugs' hole, parlour.** The housekeeper's room in a large establishment : coll. (— 1847). Halliwell (*pugs'-hole*). The latter not till late C. 19.

puja. See pooja.

puker. A good-for-nothing : a Shrewsbury School coll. : C. 19–20. Prob. ex the famous Shakespearian passage beginning : 'The infant Mewling and puking in the nurse's arms '.

pukka ; often, though rare in C. 20, *pucka.* Also *pakka, puckah, pucker* : all rare in C. 20. Certain, reliable ; genuine ; excellent : Anglo-Indian coll. : from ca. 1770. Grant Allen, 1893, 'That's a good word . . . Is it pucker English, I wonder.' In *pukka sahib* (in C. 20, often derisive), it connotes the acme of gentlemanliness.—2. Permanent, as of an appointment : mid-C. 19–20 : coll. Ex Hindu *pakka*, substantial. O.E.D. ; Yule & Burnell.

pukkaroo. See puckerow.

*pull. A mechanical 'catch' or knack ; an ulterior and hidden motive : c. : 1812, Vaux ; † by 1890. Prob. ex pulling of strings and wires.—2. Hence, an illicit trick or manipulation : card-sharpers' c. (— 1861). Mayhew.—3. Ex *have a pull*, i.e. an advantage, *over one*, comes the sense in 'What's the good of having push '—energy—' if

the other chap has the pull ? ', i.e. personal or private influence that one can use for one's advantage : U.S. s. (1889) anglicised ca. 1900 as a coll. ; by 1920, S.E. Thornton ; O.E.D.—4. See pull in. —5. An anxious moment : lower classes' (— 1909) ; slightly ob. Ware. Ex the pull at one's heart.

*pull, v. To arrest : c. : 1811, *Lex. Bal.* Cf. *pull in* and *pull up*.—2. Hence, to raid : c. (— 1871) ; ob. *Figaro*, April 15, 1871.—3. To steal ; occ., to cheat : c. : 1821, Haggart ; Mayhew. † by 1900.

*pull, in. Under arrest : c. of ca. 1810–70. Vaux. Ex *pull*, v., 1.

pull, take a. 'To desist, to discontinue ', C. J. Dennis : Australian : C. 20. In the imperative, occ. *take a pull on yourself !*

pull a kite. To look or be serious : low : C. 19–20 ; ob.

pull a soldier off his mother !, ('pull ' ? He or you) wouldn't. A c.p. directed at laziness or slacking : nautical (from ca. 1880) >, by 1900, military.

pull about. To treat roughly or without ceremony : coll. and dial. : C. 19–20. Ex S.E. sense, to pull this way and that. (O.E.D.).—2. Hence, to take liberties with a woman : low coll. : from ca. 1860. Cf. *pully-hauly*, play at, and *muck about*, qq.v.—3. *Pull oneself about*, to masturbate : low coll. : C. 19–20.

pull-back. A retarding or repressing act or influence : late C. 16–20 : S.E. till C. 19, then coll. and dial.

pull-down. The moustache that succeeded the 'nap ': Society : ca. 1870–90. Ware. Ex its shape.

*pull down, v. To steal from shop doors : c. (— 1839). Brandon.—2. To earn (money) : from ca. 1920. (D. Sayers, *Murder Must Advertise*, 1933.)

pull down the blind ! A c.p. addressed to couples love-making : London lower classes' : from ca. 1880 ; ob. Ware.

pull foot. To decamp ; run hard : coll. : 1818. M. Scott, 'The whole crew pulled foot as if Old Nick had held them in chase ', 1833. O.E.D. Cf. *pull it* and dial. *pull feet* or *hot-foot*, to walk fast (E.D.D.).

*pull in. To arrest : c. >, ca. 1890, low s. : C. 19–20. Implicit in Vaux, 1812, 'To pull a man, or have him pulled is to cause his apprehension for some offence ; and it is then said that Mr. Pullen is concerned.' Cf. *pull*, v., 1, *pull over*, and *pull up*.

pull it. To decamp ; run as fast as possible : coll. : 1804 (O.E.D.). Cf. *pull foot*, q.v.

pull off. To obtain (some benefit) : sporting : 1870 (O.E.D.). Ex sporting j., to win.—2. Hence, to succeed with, or in effecting, something : 1887, Black, 'We haven't pulled it off this time, mother.' O.E.D.

pull . . . on. To cite (something) as an excuse . Canadian (and U.S.) : C. 20. John Beames.

pull one's load. To do all one can : coll., mostly Canadian : late C. 19–20. (Esp. in present perfect.) Cf. the S.E. *pull one's weight*.

pull one's wire. (Of the male) to masturbate : low : late C. 19–20.

pull-ons. A pair of women's drawers that are merely pulled on without fastening : from 1923 or 1924. Coll. : by 1935, virtually S.E. Ex S.E. *pull-on*, n. and adj., (of) a garment that can be pulled on and needs no fastening or tying. Cf. *step-ins*.

pull out. To hurry work in hand : tailors' s. verging on j. : from ca. 1860.—2. To achieve, as in ' He pulled out a special effort ' : C. 20.

pull over. To arrest : low : mid-C. 19–20 ; very ob. Cf. *pull*, v., 1, and *pull up*.—2. **pull** (oneself) **over** (an edible). To eat : London lower classes' : 1886, *The Referee*, June 6 ; very ob. Ware. Cf. *get outside of*.

pull the chocks. To depart : aircraft engineers' : from ca. 1930. *The Daily Herald*, Aug. 1, 1936. Thus is an aeroplane released for flight.

pull-through. A very thin man : military : from ca. 1905. F. & Gibbons. Ex the rifle pull-through.

***pull up.** To arrest : 1812, Vaux : c. >, by 1835, low s. >, by 1870, coll. >, by 1910, S.E. Dickens in *Boz*. Ex the act of pulling up, a checking, a fugitive. Cf. *pull*, v., 1.

***pull up a Jack.** To stop a post-chaise on the highway with a view to robbery : c. of ca. 1810–50. Vaux.

pull up one's boot. To make money : coster-mongers' (— 1909). Ware, ' When a man prepares for his day's work, he pulls on and strings up his boots.' Cf. :

pull up one's socks. See **socks** . . .

pull your ear ! Try to remember ! : lower classes' c.p. of ca. 1860–1910. Ware.

***pulled.** See **pull**, v., 1.—**pulled up.** See **pull up.**

pulled trade. Secured work : tailors' coll. : from ca. 1860.

Pullen is concerned, Mr. See **pull in.**

pullet. A young girl : coll. : C. 19–20 : **ob.** Bee ; H., 3rd ed. Cf. *pulley*, q.v.

pullet, virgin. ' A young woman . . . who though often trod has never laid ', Bee, 1823 : low : ca. 1820–70. Ex *pullet* ; and cf. :

pullet-squeezer. A womaniser that ' likes 'em young ' ; a ' chicken-fancier ' : from ca. 1830 ; somewhat ob. Ex *pullet* ; cf. *pullet, virgin*.

***pulley.** A confederate thief, gen. a woman : c. (— 1859) ; very ob. H., 1st ed. Ex Fr. *poulet*.

pullies. Women's drawers that are pulled on : feminine coll. : from ca. 1932. See quotation at **neathie-set.** Imm. ex *pull-ons*, q.v.

pulling the right string ?, are you. Are you correct ? ; are you going the right way about it ? : cabinet-makers' c.p. : from 1863, says Ware. Ex small measurements being made with string. Cf. *who pulled your chain ?*, q.v.

Pullman Pup, the. The night train running from Leeds to Scotland precedes that much more luxurious one from London to Scotland ; hence this nickname of the former. Railway s. (— 1890) ; ob.

pully-hauly (in Grose, **-hawly**). A rough-and-tumble ; a romp : coll. : late C. 18–19, but in C. 20 surviving in dial. and, as coll., in :

pully-hauly, play at. To romp with women ; esp. to copulate : coll. : late C. 18–20 ; slightly ob. The idea, however, is extant in dial. *pulling and hauling time* and *dragging time* : cf. the † dial. *pulling time*. See Grose, P.

pulp. Nonsense ; excessive sentimentality : Society : 1924, Galsworthy, *The White Monkey* ; ob. (Collinson.)

pulpit. An artillery observation-ladder : military, esp. artillerymen's : from 1915. F. & Gibbons.

pulpit-banger,-cuffer,-drubber,-drummer,-smiter, **-thumper ; pulpit-cuffing, -drubbing,** etc. A ranting parson ; a violent sermon or moral exhortation : coll. bordering on S.E. : late C. 17–20 ; *-drubber* (*-drubbing*), † by 1850 ; *-cuffer* and *-drummer*, very ob.

pulpiteers. A ' Cloister-time ' rearrangement of two upper forms : Winchester (— 1891) : coll. See Wrench's *Winchester Word Book* and cf. *cloisters*.

pulse, a heart-beat, is sometimes construed mistakenly as a pl. (Fowler.)

Pumice-Stone. See **Pam** (Palmerston).

pum-pum. A fiddler : coll. : C. 18–mid-19. (F. & H.) Echoic.

pump. The female pudend : low coll. : late C. 17–20 ; ob. Also (as in Ned Ward) *pump-dale*. —2. The penis : low : C. 18–20 ; ob. Also *pump-handle*.—3. A breaking of wind : Scots low coll. : C. 19–20.—4. A public-house : Scots coll. : C. 19–20 ; ob.—5. A solemn noodle : low : mid-C. 19–20 ; ob.—6. See **pumps.**

pump, v. To coït with (a woman) : low : C. 18–20 ; ob.—2. To urinate : low coll. : C. 18–20 ; ob. except in form *pump ship*.—3. To break wind : Scots low coll. : C. 19–20.—4. To duck under the pump : coll. : late C. 17–mid-18. Esp. as treatment applied to bailiffs, constables, and pick-pockets. B.E.—5. To weep : low : 1837, Marryat, ' And she did pump | While I did jump | In the boat to say, Good bye.' Ob. Partly ex S.E. sense, partly ex *pumps*, n., q.v.

pump, ignorant as a. Extremely ignorant : **coll.** verging on S.E. : late C. 19–20. Manchon.

pump, purser's. See **purser's.**

Pump-and-Tortoises, the ; or the **Pump and Tortoise.** The 38th Regiment of Foot, in late C. 19–20 the South Staffordshire Regt. : military : from ca. 1770 ; ob. Ex their enforced abstemious-ness and physical debility when kept in the West Indies for an appalling number of years in the earlier C. 18. F. & Gibbons.

pump at Aldgate, draught on the. See **Aldgate.**

pump-handle, n. See **pump**, n., 2.—2. V. In greeting, to shake (a hand or person by the hand) as if working a pump : coll. : 1858, R. S. Surtees (O.E.D.). Also v.i.

pump-handler. A hand-shake as in preceding : coll. : J. T. Hewlett, 1844, ' Exchanged the salute for a most hearty old English pump-handler ', O.E.D.

pump is good but your or **the sucker's dry, your.** A c.p. addressed to one trying to pump, i.e. extract information : from ca. 1780 ; ob. Grose.

pump (oneself) **off.** To masturbate : low : C. 19–20 ; ob. Cf. *frig.*

Pump Parliament, the. The Long or Pension Parliament of Charles II of England : nick-name : 1677, J. Verney, ' A little water put into a pump fetches up a good deal,' O.E.D. ; now only historical.

pump ship. To make water : nautical s. (— 1788) >, ca. 1870, gen. gentlemanly coll. Grose, 2nd ed.—2. To vomit : nautical : late C. 18–mid-19. Ibid.

pump-sucker. A teetotaller : low : from ca 1870 ; ob.

pump-thunder. A blusterer : coll. : C. 19–20. —2. Also, without hyphen, a v. ; likewise ob.

pump-water, christened in or **with.** Red-faced : coll. or, in form *he* (*she*) *was christened* . . ., c.p. : late C. 17–mid-19. Ray ; Grose, 2nd ed.

pumped, be. 'To stand drinks all round':
nautical : C. 20 Bowen.

pumper. Any effort that puts one out of breath :
coll. (– 1886). *Cassell's Encyclopœdic Dict.*—2.
Hence, a signal defeat : turf and sports coll.
(– 1923). Manchon.—3. A very boring or wearisome questioner : coll. (– 1923). Ibid. Ex S.E.
pump, to question.

pumping. The vbl.n. of *pump*, v., 4, q.v. Grose.

pumpkin ; pompkin. A man or woman of
Boston : late C. 18–early 19. Grose, 1785, 'From
the number of pompkins raised and eaten' there.
(Whence, perhaps, the orig. and mainly U.S.
some—occ. *big*—*pumpkins*, persons—occ. things—
of importance. Coll. : mid-C. 19–20.)—2. The head :
mid-C. 19–20.

Pumpkinshire ; also Pomp-. 'Boston, and its
dependencies', Grose. See **pumpkin, 1.**

pumps. Eyes : low : 1825, Buckstone, 'Your
pumps have been at work—you've been crying,
girl' : ob. by 1910, † by 1935. Cf. *pump*, v., last
sense.

pun. Punishment : Harrow School : mid-C. 19–
20. Abbr., s. > coll. Cf. *pun-paper.*—2. Pound
or pounds (£) : sol. : C. 19–20. Cf. Northern dial.
pund.

pun (v.i.) **or pun of** (v.t.), at Hertford ; **pun out**
(v.i. and t.), London. To inform (against) :
Christ's Hospital, orig. at the country section :
mid-C. 19–20. Ex dial. *pun*, to pound.

pun-paper. Ruled paper for impositions : Harrow. See **pun, n., 1.**

punce. An occ. variant of *ponce.*

punch (or **P.**) ; **Suffolk punch.** An inhabitant
of Suffolk : coll. nickname (– 1884). Ex the
famous breed of horses.

punch, v. To deflower : coll. : C. 18–19.
Grose implies it in *punchable*, q.v. Ex S.E. *punch*,
to pierce.—2. (Gen. **punch it.**) To walk : c. :
1780, Tomlinson, 'Now she to Bridewell has
punch'd it along' ; Grose ; Haggart.—3. V.i., to
drink punch : 1804, Coleridge (O.E.D.). Never
very gen. ; in C. 20, ob.

punch, cobbler's. Urine with a cinder in it :
low : ca. 1810–60. *Lex. Bal.*—2. See **cobbler's
punch.**

punch a cow. 'To conduct a team of oxen',
C. J. Dennis : Australian : C. 20. Cf. the now
S.E. *cow-puncher.*

Punch and Judy. Lemonade : *English Illustrated Magazine*, June, 1885 ; † by 1920.

punch-clod. A farm-labourer ; clodhopper :
rural coll. : C. 19–20 ; ob.

punch-house. A brothel : coll. : late C. 17–
mid-19. B.E. Ex the S.E. sense, a tavern where
punch may be had, and ex *punch*, v., 1.

*punch it. See **punch,** v., 2. Cf. also *beat it* and
punch outsides.

punch one's ticket. To hit (a man) with a
bullet : from 1899 (ob.), mostly military. J.
Milne, *The Epistles of Atkins*, 1902.

*punch outsides. To go out of doors : c. :
C. 19–20 ; ob. See **punch,** v., 2.

punchable. 'Ripe for man' : (low) coll. : C. 18–
19. *A New Canting Dict.*, 1725 ; Grose, 1st ed.
Ex *punch*, v., 1.

Puncheous Pilate. A lower classes' c.p. (– 1909)
'jocosely addressed to a person in protest [against]
some small asserted authority'. Ware. Punning
Punch and Pontius Pilate.

puncture. To deflower : cyclists' low s. ; ' late

C. 19–20. Ex punctured tyres. Cf. *punctured.*—
2. V.i. and in passive, (of cycle or rider) to get a
puncture : coll. : from ca. 1893. Ex the tyre's
being punctured. (O.E.D.)

punctured. Damaged, fig., as in 'a punctured
reputation' : coll. : C. 20.

pundit ; occ., before C. 20, **pundet.** An erudite
expert : coll. : 1816. *The Saturday Review*,
March 15, 1862, 'The doctors of etiquette and the
pundits of refinement'. (By 1930, virtually S.E.)
Ex Hindi *pandit*, a learned man. O.E.D. ; Yule &
Burnell.

pung. A surreptitious doze while on telephone
duty : Army signallers' : G.W., and after. F. &
Gibbons. Corrupted *bung* : cf. *caulk*, a sleep.

pungo, go. (Of a rubber tyre) to burst : from
ca. 1920. Manchon. Ex *punctured.*

punish. To handle severely, as in boxing (1812) ;
food and drink (1825) ; the bowling, at cricket
(1845) ; a horse (1856) ; a plant (1882) : s. >, in
C. 20, coll. (O.E.D.)—2. To hurt, pain : coll. and
dial. : from mid-C. 19. E.D.D.

punisher. A hard hitter : in boxing, 1814, *The
Sporting Magazine* (O.E.D.) ; at cricket, 1846
(Lewis).—2. A heavy task : coll. : 1827, ibid.,
'Fifty miles' road-work this day . . . a punisher',
O.E.D.—3. A farrier that visits forges and cadges
from his fellows without doing any work or render-
ing any service for the loan : London farriers' :
late C. 19–20.

punishing, adj. Exhausting ; handling severely ;
esp. hard-hitting : s. >, ca. 1850, coll. : 1819,
Moore, 'An eye that plann'd punishing deeds' ;
in boxing, 1820, J. H. Reynolds (O.E.D.) ; in
cricket, 1846 ; *The Field*, Jan. 28, 1882, 'Each
course to-day was of the most punishing kind.'

punishment. Severe handling, orig. that dealt
out by a cricketer or a boxer : s. >, ca. 1890,
coll. : 1846, W. Denison (Lewis) ; 1856, H. H.
Dixon.—2. Pain ; misery : coll. and dial. : from
mid-C. 19. E.D.D.

punk. A punctured tyre : cyclists' : late C. 19–
20 ; ob. Cf. next entry.—2. See **punk and
plaster.**—3. Nonsense, ' bilge ', twaddle : 1927,
Dorothy Sayers, *Unnatural Death*, 'We had to sit
through a lot of moral punk . . . about the prevalence of jazz and the immoral behaviour of modern
girls.' Like the adj., it comes from the U.S.A.
Semantically, it is comparable to *rot*, n.

punk, v. To puncture (a tyre) : cyclists' : late
C. 19–20 ; ob. Cf. the n., 1.

punk, adj. Worthless ; decidedly inferior ; displeasing, ' rotten ' : from ca. 1917, via American
soldiers : low, as in U.S., where, via *punky* (1876),
ex *punk* (touchwood), it originated in late C. 19.
Thornton ; Irwin.

*punk and plaster. Bread and margarine :
tramps' c. (– 1932). F. Jennings, *Tramping with
Tramps.* Ex U.S.—2. In the Army, however, and
as early as 1915, the term meant, food (F. &
Gibbons) ; often simply *punk* (B. & P.). And in
Canada, *punk*, bread, dates from ca. 1900.

punkah one's face. To fan oneself : Anglo-
Indian (– 1909). Ware. Ex the punkah.

punker. A frequenter of *punks* or harlots : ca.
1735–1800. Addison. (O.E.D.)—2. (Also **punkar**)
An incorrect form of *punka(h)* : C. 18. Yule &
Burnell.

punse. The female pudend : Yiddish and low
London : late C. 19–20.

punt. An occ. variant (recorded in 1862 : F. &

H. at *Sheeney*) of *poona*, £1.—2. A promotion in school : Scottish Public Schools' : C. 20. Ian Miller, *School Tie*, 1935. Ex v., 4.

punt, v. To act as a decoy : auctioneers' (— 1891). See **punter**, 1. Prob. ex :—2. To bet upon a race, etc. : 1873, implied in *punter* ; *The Pall Mall Gazette*, Sept. 13, 1887. O.E.D. Ex punting at faro, baccarat, etc.—3. Hence, to be a purchaser, to buy something : grafters' : late C. 19–20. Philip Allingham, *Cheapjack*, 1934. Cf. sense 4 of *punter*.—4. (V.t., gen in passive.) To promote to another form : Scottish Public Schools' : C. 20. Ian Miller. Ex football.

punt-about. An irregular form of football : Charterhouse coll. (— 1900). A. H. Tod. Cf. *shoot-about*.

punter. An auctioneer's decoy or mock-bidder : auctioneers' : from ca. 1880. See esp. *Answers*, April 2, 1891. Prob. suggested by *punting*, q.v.—2. An outsider betting on horses in a small way : s. (— 1874) >, by 1900, coll. >, by 1920, S.E.—3. Hence, a small-scale speculator ' watching the fluctuations in speculative securities' (A. J. Wilson) ; from the early 1890's : s. >, by 1910, coll. >, by 1920, S.E.—4. (Prob. ex sense 2.) ' A grafter's customer, client, or victim ' : grafters' : late C. 19–20. Allingham. Ex *punt*, v., 3.—5. A large mug or tankard (of beer) : jocular public-house term : from ca. 1930. With a pun on sense 2 : ' a big mug '.

punting. (Gen. of an outsider) a betting on horse-races : from ca. 1873. See **punt**, v., 2.

punting-shop. A gambling den : 1874, H., 5th ed. Cf. *punt*, v., 2.

pup. A pupil : school and college s. : 1871, ' M. Legrand '. Jocularly approximated to *pup* = a puppy. Cf. *pupe*, q.v. (O.E.D.)—2. A small, fast Sopwith single-seater 80 H.P. aeroplane : Air Force : 1915 ; now only historical. F. & Gibbons.

pup. To be brought to childbed : low coll. : from ca. 1860. (As a bitch.)

pup, buy a. The opp. to *sell a pup*, q.v. : coll. : from ca. 1920.

pup, in. Pregnant : low coll. : from ca. 1860. As a bitch : cf. *pup*, v.

pup, sell a. To swindle, v.i. Gen. *sell one a pup*. C. >, ca. 1905, gen. coll. : late C. 19–20, though not recorded before 1901, *The Daily Chronicle*, May 4, ' There is a poetical phrase in our language, " to sell a man a pup ",' O.E.D. Cf. *see a man about a dog*.

Pup and Ringer, the. The Dog and Bell, ' a flash public-house ' in London ca. 1860–70. H., 3rd ed.

pupe. A pupil-room : Eton College : mid-C. 19–20. Cf. *pup*, n, 1.—2. One who, to learn acting, is attached to a company : theatrical : from ca. 1920. (*The Passing Show*, April 29, 1933.) Ex *pupil*.

***puppy,** n. and adj. (A) blind (man) : c. > low s. : from ca. 1850 ; ob. Mostly U.S. (e.g. in Matsell). Ex the ' blindness ' of new-born puppies.

puppy-dog. A puppy : children's coll. : late C. 16–20. Shakespeare. (O.E.D.)

puppy-match. A snare : coll. : ca. 1690–1750. J. Smyth's *Scarronides*, ' He . . . might catch | Us Trojans in a puppy-match.' ? ex the stealing of puppies.

puppyism. Affectation or excessive care in costume or posture : Army officers' coll. (— 1923). Manchon. Cf. *doggy*, adj.

puppy's mamma. See **dog's lady**.

pupsie, pupsy. A puppy : a children's coll. : C. 17–20. Cotgrave. Cf. *popsy*. (O.E.D.)

pur- for *pre-* (as in *purtend*) and *pro-* is a sol. ; for *per-*, a spelling sol. Both are mainly Cockney and of C. 19–20. Baumann.

puradventure. Incorrect for *peradventure* : †. O.E.D.

Purby, the. The Pre-Raphaelite Brotherhood : Society : ca. 1850–90. Ware. Ex the initials *P.R.B.*

***purchase.** Stolen goods ; booty : c. : late C. 16–mid-17. Greene ; Shakespeare. (Baumann.) —2. Those from whom it is taken : c. : late C. 16–early 17. Greene, 1592.

***pure.** A mistress, esp. a kept mistress ; a wanton : ca. 1685–1830 : c. >, ca. 1750, low s. : 1688, Shadwell, ' Where's . . . the blowing that is to be my natural, my convenient, my pure ? ' Cf. *purest pure*, q.v. By antiphrasis.—2. A ' pure ' physician, a ' pure ' surgeon. (I.e. the one, not the other ; not a general practitioner.) Medical coll. : 1827, *The Lancet* (O.E.D.).—3. ' Dog's-dung is called pure, from its cleansing and purifying properties,' Mayhew : coll. >, ca. 1905, j. : 1851.

pure, adj. Excellent ; splendid ; very pleasant. (Indeed, a gen. intensive.) Ca. 1675–1900, though ob. by 1850 ; it is, however, extant in several diall. Wycherley, 1675 (O.E.D.) ; Cibber, 1704, ' She looks as if my master had quarrelled with her . . . This is pure ' ; Henley & Stevenson, 1884, ' O, such manners are pure, pure, pure ! ' Cf. *purely*, q.v.—2. See **pure and . . .**

***pure, purest.** ' A Top-Mistress, or Fine Woman ', B.E. ; ' a courtezan of high fashion ', Grose : ca. 1690–1830 : c. >, ca. 1750, (low) s. Ex *pure*, n., 1.

pure and . . . (another adj.). Nice, or fine, and . . . ; also quasi-adverbially, excellently, very well, thoroughly. 1742, Fielding, ' [The hogs] were all pure and fat ' : coll. >, ca. 1840, dial. (O.E.D.)

pure-finder. A street collector of dogs' dung : coll. from ca. 1850 ; in C. 20, j. ; slightly ob. Mayhew, 1851. See *pure*, n, 3.

pure Merinoes. See **Merinoes, pure merinoes**.

purely. Excellently ; very well : 1695, Congreve : s. >, ca. 1750, coll. Hood. O.E.D.

purgatorial list. (Of officers) to be retired : Army officers' jocular coll. (— 1923). Manchon. Ex *purgatory* (between hell and heaven).

purge. Beer : military and low gen. : from ca. 1870. Cf. the barrack-room c.p. rhyme, recorded by F. & H. in 1902, *Comrades, listen while I urge ; | Drink, yourselves, and pass to purge*, ob. by 1925, and :

purge. To dismiss from employment (gen. in passive) : from ca. 1930. Cf. *Pride's Purge*.—2. V.i., to swear, grumble ; worry audibly : military : from 1915. F. & Gibbons, ' The Captain purged no end about it.'

purger or **perger.** A teetotaller ; hence, a pejorative : ca. 1860–1920 : low. Vance, ca. 1864, in *The Chickaleary Cove*, ' My tailor serves you well, from a purger to a swell.' ? one who, to keep himself fit, takes laxatives or purges instead of beer : cf. *purge*, n.

puritan, Puritan. A whore : coll. : C. 18. Prob. ex Puritans' reputed hypocrisy.

purko. Beer : military : ca. 1870–1910. Ex the name of the makers, Barclay, **Perk**ins and Co. Perhaps influenced by *purger* and suggested by *perkin*.

purl. A fall, or a dive, head foremost or head over heels : 1825, *The Sporting Magazine* (O.E.D.) : s. >, ca. 1870, coll. Ex. S.E. *purl*, to whirl or spin round. Cf. *purler* and :

purl, v.i. and v.t. To turn head over heels : coll. and dial. : 1856, Reade. Ex *purl*, n.—2. To dive : Winchester College : late C. 19–20. Wrench. Ex the n.

purler. A headlong fall ; a throw head foremost ; a knock-down blow, esp. a blow that casts one head foremost : coll. : 1867, Ouida, in her best-known story, *Under Two Flags*. Ex *purl*, v. (q.v.), influenced by *purl*, n. Variant *pirler* ; *pirl* is frequent in dial. for the preceding pair of terms.

purple, adj. Glorious ; 'royal': coll., 1894, *The Pall Mall Gazette*, Dec. 20, 'A purple time of it'. Ex the purple of royal robes (cf. *born in the purple*). O.E.D.

purple. Blood : Scottish : 1804, Couper, *Poetry* ; ob. E.D.D. Cf. *claret*.

purpose, a- or **o'.** On purpose : S.E. (gen. *a purpose*) >, ca. 1790, dial. and low coll. (O.E.D.)

purpose as the geese slur upon the ice (or **as to give a goose hay**), **to as much.** Uselessly : semi-proverbial coll. : late C. 17–19, C. 18–20. Cf. *to no more purpose than to beat your heels against the ground* or *wind*.

purposes, for (e.g. **dancing**). For (e.g.) dancing : coll., tautological : late C. 19–20. Cf. *side, on the.*

purse. The female pudend : low coll. : C. 17–20. (Beaumont & Fletcher).

purse, v.i. To take purses ; to steal : late C. 16–17 : low coll. (? orig. s.). Lyly, 1592 (O.E.D.) Beaumont & Fletcher, in *The Scornful Lady*, 'Why I'll purse : if that raise me not, I'll bet at bowling alleys.'

purse, no money in his. Impotent : low : C. 19–20. Ex *purse*, n.

purse a purgation, give a person's. To take money from one : coll. : ca. 1540–80. Heywood ; Bullein. Apperson.

purse-bouncer. A swindler practising the purse-trick : C. 20 : low. O.E.D. records it for 1902.

purse-catcher, -emptier, -lifter, -snatcher. A stealer of purses : s. or coll. verging on S.E. : resp. C. 17, C. 17, late C. 19–20, late C. 19–20. (O.E.D.)

purse-finder. A harlot : low : C. 19–20, ob.
purse-proud. Lecherous ; amorous : low : C. 18–20, ob. See **purse,** n.

***pursenets.** C. of ca. 1608–1830 : 'Goods taken upon Trust by young Unthrifts at treble the Value', B.E. ; Grose, 1st ed. ; but first in Dekker. Cf. the dial. *purse-net*, the movable net in which ducks are snared, and *rabbit-sucker*.—2. Also, though prob. in the singular form : a small purse : ca. 1690–1750 : app. likewise c. B.E.

purser's. Contemptuous or derisive in *purser's dip*, an undersized candle ; *purser's quart* (Smollett), a short quart ; etc. : nautical coll. : C. 18–20 ; slightly ob. Because a purser, i.e. ship's store-keeper and treasurer, was often dishonest. Cf. :

purser's (gen. **pusser's**) **crabs.** 'Navy uniform boots, with toe-caps': naval : late C. 19–20 : Bowen. See **crab-shells.**

purser's (gen. **pusser's**) **dagger.** A service clasp-knife : naval : late C. 19–20. Bowen. Cf. :

purser's (gen. **pusser's**) **dip.** A candle : nautical : mid-C. 19–20 ; slightly ob. Bowen.

purser's (gen. **pusser's**) **dirk.** Same as *purser's dagger* : naval : late C. 19–20. Ibid.

purser's (gen. **pusser's**) **grin.** A hypocritical grin ; a sarcastic sneer : nautical coll. : C. 19–20 ; ob. Esp. in the c.p., *there are no half laughs or purser's grins about me ; I'm right up and down like a yard of pump water.*

purser's grind. A coïtion bringing the woman no money but some consolation in the size or potency of the member : low nautical : mid-C. 19–20.

purser's name. A false name : nautical coll. >, in C. 20, S.E. : C. 19–20 ; ob. Ex false name given to the purser by a passenger travelling incognito. W.

purser's (gen. **pusser's**) **pack.** The Slop Chest : naval coll. : late C. 19–20. Bowen.

purser's pump. A siphon, because prominent in a purser's stores ; a bassoon, 'from its likeness to a syphon', Grose, 1788 : nautical of ca. 1785–1890.

purser's shirt on a handspike(, like a). (Of clothes) ill-fitting : nautical : C. 19–20 ; ob.

purser's (gen. **pusser's**) **stocking.** A meta-phorical article in the Slop Chest : naval : mid-C. 19–early 20. Bowen.

purser's (gen. **pusser's**) **tally.** A name assumed by a seaman, esp. if naval : (naval) coll. : C. 19. Bowen.

purser's (gen. **pusser's**) **yellow.** Naval soap : naval coll. : late C. 19–20. Ibid.

purtend. See **pur-.**

purting glumpot. A sulky person : dial. and low coll. : from ca. 1850. Ex *glum*, gloomy, and dial. *purt*, to sulk.

purty. See **perty.**

Puseum, the. Pusey House in St. Giles's Street, Oxford : Oxford University : late C. 19–20 ; ob. On *museum.*

push. (As enterprise, moral energy, it has, con-trary to frequent opinion, been always S.E. : 1855, O.E.D.)—2. A thronging, a crowd, of people : low s. (perhaps orig. c.) >, in C. 20, gen. s. : 1718, C. Hitchin, 'A push, alias an accidental crowd of people'; Vaux, 1812, 'When any particular sense of crowding is alluded to, they [the underworld] say, the push . . . at the . . . doors ; the push at the . . . match.' Ex the inevitable pushing and jostling. —3. Hence, a gang or a group of convicts, as in Davitt's *Prison Diary*, 1888 ; or a band of thieves, as in Anon., 'No. 747', reference to the year 1845 ; or, in Australia, a gang of larrikins, as in *The Melbourne Argus*, July 26, 1890, and esp. in Morris's dictionary : in C. 19, c. ; in C. 20, low s., as indeed the 'larrikins' sense was from the first. —4. Hence, any company or party, group, associ-ation, or set of people : C. 20. (The U.S. sense (Thornton, 1912), 'a combination of low poli-ticians', derives directly from Australia.)—5. Hence, in G.W. and in post-War military and naval, a military or a naval unit, but esp. a battalion, a battery, or a ship's crew. Cf. military sense of *mob*, n.—6. A robbery ; a swindle ; a dealing out of profits : c. : from ca. 1860 ; slightly ob. H., 5th ed. Not unnaturally ex sense 3.—7. See **push, do a.**—8. Mostly in *give* or *get the push.* A dismissal, esp. from employment : from ca. 1870 : s. >, by 1910, coll. Anon., ca. 1875, 'The girl that stole my heart has given me the push.' Cf. *push, order of the.*—9. See **tidderly push.** (—10. The military sense, 'an attack', is S.E. of a cen-tury's standing.)—11. A foreman : Canadian, esp. among lumbermen : from before 1932. John Beames. Ex his urging the men on.

push, v. See push off and pushed.—2. V.i. (occ.
push on), rarely v.t., to coït (with) : low coll., gen.
of the male : C. 18–20. Robertson of Struan.

push, adj. See posh, adj.

push, do a. See do a push.

push, do a. To coït : low, gen. of the male :
late C. 19–20.—2. See do a push.

push, give or get the. A coll. abbr. (from middle
1920's) of the phrase in :

push, order of the. A dismissal, esp. from employment, and gen. as give or get the o. of the p. :
s. >, by ca. 1910, coll. ' Pomes ' Marshall. An
elaboration of push, n., eighth sense. Cf. order of
the bath.

push, stand the. (Of a woman) to coït : coll. :
C. 18–19. Cf. push, do a.

push a bit of bow back. To have a sleep : Regular Army's : C. 20. B. & P. I.e. bowed back.

push-and-pull. A (little) motor-train that reverses at the termini : railwaymen's (— 1935).

push-bike, s. ; push-cycle, coll. A foot-propelling
bicycle as opp. to a motor-cycle : coll. : resp. from
ca. 1910 and ca. 1904. Cf. derivative :

push-cyclist. A bicyclist, opp. to a motor-
cyclist : coll. : from ca. 1905.

push off. To depart : late C. 19–20. Same
semantics as for shove off : pushing off a boat.—2.
Hence, to begin, v.i., esp. of a game : C. 20.

push one's barrow. To move on, away ; to
depart : mostly costers' : from ca. 1870.

push out the boat. See boat, push out the.
Contrast push the boat out (next entry but two).

push-penny. A coll. variant (— 1903) of shove-
halfpenny.

push-pin, occ. -pike, play at ; play at put-pin.
To coït : low coll. : resp. C. 17–18, late C. 17–18,
and mid-C. 16–mid-18. Rychardes, Misogonus,
1560 ; Massinger, 1623, ' She would never tell | Who
play'd at pushpin with her ' ; Ned Ward, 1707,
' When at push-a-pike we play | With beauty, who
shall win the day ? ' Cf. push, v., 2, push, do a,
and pushing-school.

push the boat out ! Go ahead ! ; I'm all right :
military c.p. in G.W.

*push the brush out. (Of a convict) to attract
the attention of a warder : c. (— 1933). Charles
E. Leach. It is occ. done in this way when the
convict is in his cell.

*push-up, be at the. To work with a gang of
pickpockets : c. (— 1933). Ibid. Cf. push, n., 3, 6.

push up the scale. A rise in salary : lower
classes' coll. (— 1923). Manchon.

pushed. Short of money : coll. : from ca. 1825.
Abbr. pushed for money.—2. Drunk : ca. 1870–
1910. Perhaps ex the tendency to fall ; cf. the
next entry.—3. Bustled : ship-stewards' coll.
(— 1935).

pushed ?, did she fall or was she. A late C. 19–20
c.p. applied to a person stumbling ; also, and orig.,
to a girl deprived of her virginity.

pusher. A fledgling canary unable to feed itself :
ca. 1690–1750. B.E. Perhaps because it pushes
with its bill.—2. A girl, a woman : low. Also
square pusher (q.v.), a virtuous girl. See also
square-pushing. Late C. 19–20.—3. A blucher
boot : shoemakers' : from ca. 1860.—4. A finger
of bread used as a feeding-implement : nursery
coll. : from ca. 1880.—5. An aeroplane with propeller behind the main lifting surface : aviators'
coll. : from 1916. O.E.D. (Sup.)—6. A scene-shifter :
theatrical (— 1935).—7. In pickpocketry, he who

pushes the prospective victim against the actual
thief : c. : late C. 19–20. (Charles E. Leach,
1933.)

Pushful Joe. Joseph Chamberlain (d. 1914). Cf.
his sobriquet among African potentates : Moatlodi,
he who gets things done. Dawson. Also Brummagem Joe, q.v.

pushing daisies. Dead and buried : see daisy-
pushing.

pushing-school. A brothel : low : late C. 17–19.
Ex the S.E. sense, a fencing-school : cf. also push,
v., 2, and push, do a.

*pushing-tout. A thieves' scout or watchman
that brings intelligence of an accidental crowd or
assemblage : c. : C. 18. C. Hitchin, 1718.

pushing up daisies. A variant of pushing daisies,
than which it is more gen.

puss. The female pudend : low : C. 17–20.
Cotton, ' Æneas, here's a Health to thee, | To
Pusse and to good company.' Also, in C. 19–20,
pussy, pussy-cat.—2. A cadet of the Royal Military
Academy : ca. 1820–80. Ex the short jacket with
pointed tail.

puss-in-boots. A swaggerer : military : from
ca. 1908. F. & Gibbons. Ex the fairy tale.

pusser is the inevitable nautical shape of purser :
coll. : C. 20. Bowen. But for combinations, see
under purser.—2. Any wound, sinus, or boil that
freely discharges pus : medical students' (— 1933).
Slang, p. 192.

pusserpock. ' Bad, hard salt-meat ' : : naval
(— 1909) ; ob. Ware. A corruption of purser's
pork, the purser being the purchaser.—2. (Gen. pl.)
A fur : c. (— 1933). Charles E. Leach.

pussy- or Pussey-cat. See next, sense 2.—
pussy. See puss, 1.

pussy-cat. See puss, 1.—2. A Puseyite : Church :
from ca. 1839 ; ob. by 1880, † by 1900. Cf.
Puseum, q.v. Suggested by Puseyite (1838). Occ.
Pussey-cat, as in H.—3. A cat : nursery coll. :
1837, Marryat (O.E.D.).

put. A rustic ; a dolt : 1688, Shadwell ; Grose
(country put, a frequent variant) : s. until ca. 1750,
then coll. until ca. 1830, then S.E. and archaic.
The discrimination of put, a blockhead, and country
put, a bumpkin, is logical : but the distinction
cannot be pressed.—2. Hence, loosely, a chap,
fellow : coll. : ca. 1800–30. Gen. applied, somewhat contemptuously, to elderly persons : cf.
Thackeray in Vanity Fair, I, xi, ' The captain . . .
calls [his father] an old put.'—3. A harlot : ? C. 17–
18 : F. & H., but who else ? ! (Ex Fr. putain, a
whore.)—4. See :

put, do a ; have a put-in. To coït : low coll. :
C. 19 ; C. 19–20 (ob.).

put, play at two-handed. To coït : low : C. 18–
early 19. Cf. push-pin.

put, stay. Remain in position, firm, lit. and fig. ;
to continue to be safe, satisfactory, sober, honest,
faithful, in training, etc. : coll. : from ca. 1915.
Ex U.S. ; Bartlett stigmatised it in 1848 as ' a
vulgar expression '.

put a bung or sock in it. (Gen. imperative.)
To ' shut up ' ; cease being noisy : military :
C. 20. F. & Gibbons. Here, it is the mouth.—2.
(In barracks or hut) to close the door (bung only) :
id. : id. Ibid.

put (or lay) a churl upon a gentleman. See churl.

put a hat (up)on a hen. To attempt the impossible : proverbial coll. : mid-C. 17–mid-19. Ray.

put a new face (or head) on. To disfigure by

punching ; hence, to get the better of : U.S. (— 1870) ; anglicised by 1890 ; † by 1920.

put a poor mouth on (a position). To complain (moaningly) about : Anglo-Irish (— 1884). Ware.

put a sock in it. See **put a bung** . . .

put a steam on the table. 'To earn enough money to obtain a hot Sunday dinner' : lower classes' : from ca. 1860. Ware, 'Refers chiefly to boiled food'.

put a tin hat on. See **tin hat on, put a.**

put across. To achieve ; execute successfully : from ca. 1910 : coll., now verging on S.E. Whence :

put across a beauty. To execute a smart move : coll., mostly New Zealanders' : from ca. 1911.

put along ; gen. **put her along.** To cause (a motor-car) to travel at a high speed : motorists' coll. : 1924, Francis D. Grierson, *The Limping Man.*

put-away. An appetite ; a (considerable) capacity for food or drink : low : late C. 19–20. Ex the v., 1.—2. Imprisonment : late C. 19–20 ; ob. Ex the v., 2.—3. An information to the police : (c. or) low s. : late C. 19–20. Ex the v., 3.

put away, v.t. To eat, drink, gen. in large quantities : 1878, Besant & Rice, 'I never saw a man put away such an enormous quantity of provisions at one time.'—2. To put in gaol : s. >, in C. 20, coll. : 1883 (O.E.D.).—3. To inform against : (c. or) low s. : from ca. 1890 ; app. orig. Australian.—4. To pawn : s. >, ca. 1910, coll. : 1887, *The Daily News*, Oct. 22 (O.E.D.).—5. To kill : coll. : 1847, Anne Brontë (O.E.D. Sup.).

put down. To eat : lower classes', esp. Cockneys' coll. (— 1909). Ware.—2. To cash (a cheque) : c., and police s. : late C. 19–20. Charles E. Leach, *On Top of the Underworld,* 1933.

put down south. See **south.**

put 'em up ! Raise your arms ! : from ca. 1860 : coll.—2. Put up your fists ! : coll. : late C. 19–20. A variant is *stick 'em up !*, in both senses. Contrast *put it up !*

put-in, n. See **put, do a.**

put in, v. To pass (a period of time), gen. at or with the help of some occupation : coll. : C. G. Gibson, 1863 (O.E.D.).—2. See **put the windows in.**

put in a bag. Killed, esp. in battle : military : 1914 ; ob. Ex shot birds put in a game-bag.

***put in a hole.** To defraud : c. : from ca. 1860. A variant of *put in the hole*, q.v. at **hole, put in the.**

put in one's eye, as much as one can. (Virtually) nothing : coll. : late C. 17–early 19. B.E.

put in one's motto. To 'lay down the law' ; butt rashly into a conversation : low coll. : from ca. 1880.

put in pie. To spoil or bungle (a thing), lead (a person) astray : printers' (— 1887) ; ob. Baumann. Ex the jumble of printers' pie.

put in the boot. See **boot, put in the.**

***put in the bucket, garden, hole, pin, squeak, or well.** See at the nn.

put in the pudden club. See **pudden club, put in the.**

put inside. In detention : military coll. : C. 20.

put it across (a person). To punish, get even with, revenge oneself on : coll. : from ca. 1914. (Now verging on S.E.)—2. To deceive, delude, trick, impose on : coll., now verging on S.E. : 1915, Edgar Wallace. O.E.D. (Sup.).—3. See **put across.**

put it in, v.i. To achieve intromission : perhaps rather an S.E. approximation to euphemism than a coll. : when, however, there is no thought, in-

tention or subconscious impulse towards euphemism, it may be considered a coll. and not, from the psychological nature of the case, S.E.

put it on, v.i. To overcharge : C. 20 coll. Ex *put on the price* ; prob. influenced by :—2. V.t. To extract money from (a person) by threats, lying or whining : low London : late C. 19–20. *The People,* Jan. 6, 1895 (Ware).

put it on her. To drive a ship hard in a strong breeze : nautical coll. (sailing-ships') : mid-C. 19–20. Bowen. The *it* = her set of sails.

put it over (a person). See **put it across, 1, 2** : same status and period.—2. See **put over.**

put it there ! Shake hands : coll. : late C. 19–20. Mostly Colonial.

put it up ! Have done ! ; stop ! ; shut up ! : low (— 1859) ; † by 1910. H., 1st ed.

put it where the monkeys put the nuts ! Go to blazes ! : a low c.p. : late C. 19–20. An elaboration of the low familiar S.E. *stick it up your a*** !*

put off. To disconcert, disturb : s. (1909) >, ca. 1930, coll. (O.E.D.)—2. Hence, to annoy, be distasteful to : Bootham School : from ca. 1920. Anon., *Dict. of Bootham Slang,* 1925.

put-on. A deception, subterfuge, excuse : coll. : from ca. 1860.—2. An 'old woman mendicant who puts on a shivering and wretched look' : c. or low (— 1909). Ware.

put on, v. To begin to smoke, as in F. W. Crofts, *Mystery in the Channel,* 1931, 'Dispirited, he sat down on the shore . . ., put on a pipe, and gave himself up to thought' : coll. : C. 20.

put on a boss. To assume a malevolent look : low (— 1909). Ware, 'Squinting suggests malevolence.'

put on a cigar. To assume gentility : lower classes' : mid-C. 19–20 ; ob. Ware.

***put on the bee.** See **bee, put on the.**

put on the flooence (unnecessary spelling) or **fluence.** See **fluence.**—**put on the peg.** See **peg, put on the.**

put on the pot. To give oneself airs : late C. 19–20. Ware. See **pot,** n., 6.

put one's hair in(to) a curl or **put a curl in one's hair.** To make one feel (very) fit : coll. : from ca. 1870 ; slightly ob. H., 5th ed.

put oneself outside. To eat ; occ., to drink : from ca. 1860. Ware. Cf. *get outside.*

***put out.** To kill : c. and low : late C. 19–20. Ware. Ex :

***put out** (a person's) **light.** To kill : c. and low : 1884, *The Graphic,* Sept. 24. Ware.

put over. To knock over with a shot, to kill : Australian : 1859, H. Kingsley ; ob.—2. To cause to be accepted ; to succeed in getting a favourable reception for : orig. U.S. ; anglicised ca. 1920 as a coll., > by 1935 S.E.

put paid to. See **paid to.**

put some jildi into it. To 'jump to it' (q.v.) : military : C. 20. B. & P. See **jildi.**

put stuff on. See **stuff on the ball.**

put that in your pipe . . . ! See **pipe and smoke it.**

put the acid on. To test (man or statement) ; to put a stop to : lower classes' : from ca. 1908. F. & Gibbons.—2. To ask (a person) for a loan : Australian : from ca. 1912.

***put the black on.** V.i. and t. To blackmail : c. : from ca. 1920. Edgar Wallace, passim. Abbr. *blackmail.*

***put the block.** To 'mask' or cover a thief at work : c. (— 1933). Charles E. Leach.

*put the gloves on. To improve (a person): Scots c.: 1868; slightly ob. Ware.

put the hard word on. See hard word.

put the lid on. See lid on.

put the miller's eye out. See miller's eye.

put the nips in. See nips in.

put the pot on. To bet too much money on one horse: sporting: from ca. 1820. See pot, n., 1.

put the strings on. See strings on.

put the traveller on. See tip the traveller.

put the value on. To sign (a canvas): artists' (— 1909); ob. Ware.

put the windows in. To smash them: low urban (— 1909). Ware.

put through. To succeed with (some plan, e.g.) by swindling: low: late C. 19–20; ob. Ex the S.E. (orig.—1847—U.S.) sense, carry to a successful issue. (Thornton.)

put through the hoop. See hoop, put through the.

put to bed. (The journalistic sense is S.E.—2.) To defeat: music-halls' (— 1909); ob. Ware.

put to find. To put in prison: low (— 1909). Ware. (? *fined.*)

put to sleep. See sleep, put to.

put together with a hot needle and burnt thread. To fasten insecurely: ca. 1660–1850: semi-proverbial coll.

*put-up. A laying of information against a fellow-criminal: c. (— 1823); ob. Bee, who implies that *put-up* serves also as n. to *put up*, v., 2, q.v.

put up. To show, achieve, e.g. *a good fight* or, G.W. †, *a good show*: coll.: from ca. 1890. *The Field*, Jan. 30, 1892, 'Pettitt put up a good game.' —2. To plan in advance (a robbery, a swindle, a fraud): c.: from ca. 1810. Vaux.—3. Hence, to preconcert anything devious or underhand or disingenuous: from ca. 1890. ' Barclay put up a job to ruin old Overton,' *The Sporting and Dramatic News*, Aug. 13, 1892 (O.E.D.).—4. See put it up.— 5. To wear: military coll., only as in *pip*, n., 4: C. 20.—6. To charge (a soldier) with a ' crime ': military coll.: C. 20. F. & Gibbons. Cf. the C. 15–16 S.E. sense, to bring (a person) into court on a charge.

*put up a squeak. To give information to the police: c.: from ca. 1920. Edgar Wallace.

put up a stall. To act or speak misleadingly: low: late C. 19–20. F. & Gibbons.

*put-up job. (The chief use of the adj. *put up*.) A pre-arranged crime or deception: as the former, c. (from ca. 1838); as the latter, s. >, ca. 1930, coll. A *put-up robbery* occurs in 1810, a *put-up affair* in 1812 (Vaux). (O.E.D.)

put up one's hat ; put one's hat up. To pay serious court ; often *put your hat up there !*, I see you mean to make one of the family: lower classes': late C. 19–20. Ware.

*put up the fanny. See fanny, put up the.

put (a person) up to. To enlighten or forewarn about ; inform of ; instruct in: coll.: 1812, Vaux.—2. To incite or excite to (some act, to do something) ; to induce, persuade (to do something): coll.: 1824 (O.E.D.).

put wise. See wise, put.

put your head in a bag ! Be quiet: (low) coll.: from ca. 1890. A horse with its head in the nosebag does not trouble about other things.

Putney !, go to. Go to the devil !: from ca. 1840 ; ob. From ca. 1850, occ. *go to Putney on a*

pig, by a typical assonantal addition. Kingsley, 1863, ' Now, in the year 1845, telling a man to go to Putney was the same as telling a man to go to the deuce.' Cf. *Bath, Halifax, Hong-Kong, Jericho.*

putred. Incorrect for *putrid* : C. 16–17. O.E.D.

putrescent. An occ. variant (ca. 1906–13), noted by Collinson, of :

putrid. A pejorative of the *awful* kind: C. 20: s. now verging on coll. *The Sporting Times*, April 27, 1901, ' All beer is putrid, even when it's pure.' Prob. suggested by *rotten* (q.v.) ; cf. *poisonous*, q.v.

putt. See put, n., 1, of which it is a C. 17–18 variant.

*putter-down. A presenter of forged cheques or counterfeit money: c. (— 1933). Charles E. Leach.

*putter-up. One who plans and pre-arranges robberies, frauds, swindles ; esp. ' a man who travels about for the purpose of obtaining information useful to professional burglars ', H., 5th ed. ; also, in C. 20, an instigator to crime: c. >, ca. 1910, low s. and police coll.: 1812, Vaux ; 1933, Charles E. Leach.

*putting the black on. Blackmail. See put the black on.

puttock. A whore ; a greedy person: coll. verging on S.E.: in C. 20, dial.: C. 16–20.

puttun. A regiment: Anglo-Indian, esp. military, coll. (— 1874). H., 5th ed. See Addenda.

putty. Money: mostly (? and orig.) U.S.: mid-C. 19–20 ; ob. Prob. glaziers' at first.—2. A glazier, a house-painter ; in the Navy, any painter rating: from ca. 1820. Bee ; Bowen. Ex frequent use of putty.—3. ' Sticky mud at the bottom of a body of water ': 1880, P. H. Emerson: dial. and s. >, by 1910, coll.

putty, adj. Stupid, idiotic: low (— 1923). Manchon. Perhaps ex *up to putty*, but cf. dial. *putty-brain*, a blockhead, a mental defective (E.D.D.). Perhaps ex *putty cove.*

putty, could not fight. I am, he is, you are, etc., a very poor fighter (with one's hands) ; hence, also of, e.g., an army. Coll.: late C. 19–20. Semantics as in the following entry. Cf. *could not fight his way through a paper bag.*

putty, up to. Of very poor quality ; disappointingly inferior ; (virtually) negligible: C. 20. Mostly Australian, as Jice Doone implies. Either ex the softness of putty or ex the idea in preceding entry.

putty and plaster on the Solomon knob, the. Be silent ! ; the *Master's* coming: a Freemasons' c.p. intimation: from ca. 1870. Masonic punning on Masonic j.

*putty cove or covess. An unreliable man or woman: c. of ca. 1820–90. Egan's Grose. Ex softness of putty.

putty medal. (A satirical recommendation to) a reward for mischief, incompetence, or injury: non-aristocratic coll.: 1856, says Ware, who adds: ' No medal at all '. See also medal, a putty.

puz(z). A young man about town: London Society: ca. 1760–80. O.E.D. Cf. *piz(z).*

puzzle-cause ; *-cove. A lawyer: resp. coll. of ca. 1780–1830, Grose, 1st ed. ; c. or low of ca. 1830–1900, mostly U.S. (Matsell). But while *p.-cove* = any lawyer, *p.-cause* is one ' who has a confused understanding.' Cf. *puzzle-text*, q.v.

puzzle-headed spoon. An Apostle spoon : C. 19 : coll.

puzzle-text. A clergyman ; esp. 'an ignorant, blundering parson', Grose, 1st ed., 1785 : ob. by 1830, † by 1870. Cf. *puzzle-cause*, q.v.

puzzling arithmetic. A statement of the odds : gamblers' coll. (? > j.) : C. 17. Webster, 1613, 'Studying a puzzling arithmetic at the cockpit '.

puzzling-sticks. 'The triangle to which culprits were tied for flagellation' : (prob. c. >) low s. : 1812, Vaux ; † by 1870.

pyah. Weak ; paltry, inferior ; useless : mainly nautical (— 1864). H., 3rd ed. Ex *pariah*.

pye. A contraction of *pariah-dog* : Anglo-Indian military (— 1886). Yule & Burnell.

pygostole. A 'M.B.' coat or waistcoat : Church :

1844 ; † by 1920. (See **M.B. coat**.) Lit. pygostole, i.e. rump-stole, ex Gr. πυγή.

pyjamas, the cat's. The correct thing ; 'just it ' : ca. 1920–7. Ex U.S.

pyjams. Abbr. *pyjamas* : from ca. 1910 : **s.**, >, by 1935, almost coll. Never *pajams*.

pyke off. See **pike**, v. (Thus in Bowen.)

pynacle. Incorrect for *piacle*, expiation : late C. 15 (? –16). Caxton.

pyrage. Incorrect for *pirogue* : C. 17.—**pyrogeneous.** Erroneous for *pyrogenous* : C. 19–20. O.E.D.

pysoe. A close-fisted seaman : nautical : late C. 19–20. Bowen. Cognate with † Scottish *pyster*, to hoard up (E.D.D.).

pyze. A variant of *pize* : see **pize on.**

Q

[In F. & H., at **Q**, there are the following inadmissible terms. 1, S.E. :—q, a coin ; **quab** ; **quaff** ; **quag** ; **quail**, a harlot, yet see entry ; **quaint** ; **quaker(-gun)** ; **qualm**, **qualmish** ; **quantum**, a sufficiency ; **quash** ; **quat** ; **quean** ; **queasy** ; **queed**, the devil ; **queen of holes**, Rochester's euphemism ; **queen's** or **king's ale** ; **queen's** or **king's carriage** or **cushion** ; **Queen's** or **King's English** ; **queen's herb** ; **quickening peg**, a euphemism ; **quid** of tobacco, with corresponding v. ; **quid for quod**, **quid pro quo** and **quidnunc** ; **quietus (est)** ; **quiff** of hair (but see separate entry) ; **quill-driver**, etc. ; **quill** phrases, except the Wykehamist ; **quill-pipes** ; **quillet** ; **quilt**, a fat man ; **quip**, n. and v. ; **quirk** ; **quirky** ; **quiver**, a euphemism ; **quiz**, n. and v. ; **quizzer** ; **quizzify** and **quizzical(ly)** ; **quodling** ; **quot(quean)** ; **quoz**.

2. Dial :—**quavery wavery** ; **Queen Bess** ; **quilt**, v. ; **quockerwodger**.]

q. See letter **Q**.

q, que, cue, kue, not worth a. Of negligible value : coll. > S.E. : C. 16. Skelton, 'That lyberte was not worth a cue.' Ex *q*, half a farthing. —2. See **p and q**, **p's and q's**.

Q.b.b. A Queen's bad bargain : reign of Queen Victoria : coll. Cf. **K.b.b.**, and see **bad bargain**. Also (**K.h.b.** and) **Q.h.b.**, Queen's hard bargain, as in *The Cornhill Magazine*, Feb., 1865. Cf. *Queen's* or *King's bad shilling*.

q (or Q) in a corner. Something not at once seen but brought to subsequent notice : legal : from ca. 1870 ; ob. Perhaps = *query in a corner*, suggested by the old game of *Q in the corner* (prob., puss in the corner).

Q.S. 'Queer Street ', q.v. : non-aristocratic : late C. 19–20 ; ob. Ware.

q.t. (or Q.T.), on the ; or **on the strict q.t.** On the quiet : resp. ca. 1870, 1880. Anon., *Broadside Ballad*, 1870, 'Whatever I tell you is on the Q.T.'

Q.V.R.'s, the. See **Queen Vics, the.**

Qantas ; pedantically **Quantas**. The Queensland and Northern Territory Aerial Service : Australian coll. : from 1933.

***qua* ; qua-keeper.** A prison ; a gaoler : c. of late C. 18–early 19. Tufts (dict. of flash), 1798. I suspect an error for *quad* = *quod*.

quack. A pretended doctor : 1659 (O.E.D.) : coll. till C. 19, then S.E. Abbr. *quacksalver*, q.v. **See esp.** the essay entitled 'Quacks and Quackery '

in my *Literary Sessions*.—2. A duck : late C.19–20. More often, *quack-quack*. Cf. *quacking-cheat*.

quack, v. Play the quack (see **quack**, n., 1) : C. 17–20 : coll. till C. 19, then S.E.—2. To change (the title of a book), v.t. : C. 18 : booksellers'. Centlivre, 1715, 'He has an admirable knack at quacking titles . . . When he gets an old good-for-nothing book, he claps a new title to it, and sells off the whole impression in a week.' Ex *quack*, to palm off as a quack would.

quack, in a. In a mere moment : Scots coll. : from ca. 1840.

quack-quack. A duck : an echoic nursery coll. : recorded 1865 (O.E.D.), but prob.—as indeed with all such words—used much earlier. Cf. *bow-wow*.

quacker. A duck : coll. : C. 19–20. Cf. *quack*, n., 1, and :

quacking-cheat. A duck : c. : from ca. 1565 ; † by 1860. Harman, B.E. ; Grose, 1st ed. See **cheat**.

quacksalver. A pretended doctor : 1579, Gosson : coll. till ca. 1660, then S.E. ; ob. One who sells his salves by quacking (noisy patter). W. Cf. *quack*, n., 1.

***quad.** A prison : c. : late C. 18–20. Also and much more gen. *quod*, q.v. Prob. ex *quadrangle*.— 2. A quadrangle : 1820 (O.E.D.) : Oxford s. >, ca. 1860, gen. coll. Trollope, 'The quad, as it was familiarly called . . .'—3. A horse : low : 1845, ' *No. 747* ' (p. 416) ; 1885, *The English Illustrated Magazine*, April, 'The second rider . . . got his gallant quad over, and . . . went round the course alone.' Abbr. *quadruped*.—4. A bicycle for four : 1888 (O.E.D.). Abbr. *quadruple*.—5. A quadrat : printers' : from ca. 1880 : coll. >, by 1890, j.— 6. Hence, **a** (printer's) joke : printers' : 1884 (O.E.D.).

quadra- is incorrect for *quadri-* : C. 17–20, as **quadri-** is for *quadru-* in the very few words beginning thus (e.g. *quadrumanous* : mostly C. 18. (O.E.D.)

Quads, the. See **Quins, the.**

quædam. A harlot : cultured coll. : late C. 17– 18. Hacket. Lit., a certain woman : cf. *one of those*, euphemistic for 1, harlot ; 2, a homosexual.

quaegemes or **quae-gemes.** A bastard : coll. : C. 18–early 19. F. & H.

Quagger. A student at the Queen's College : Oxford undergraduates': from late 1890's. By 'the Oxford *-er*', and perhaps, as Ware suggests, ex *gooser*, q.v., thus : *gooser*, *goose*, *quack*, *quacker*, *Quagger*. Cf. :

Quaggers. The Queen's College, Oxford : Oxford undergraduates' : late C. 19–20. By 'the Oxford *-er*'.

[**quail**, a harlot, or a courtesan,—C. 17–early 18,— may orig. have been coll. or even s., but it is gen. treated as S.E. : cf., however, *pheasant* and *plover*. C. 17–18. Motteux, 'With several coated quails, and lac'd mutton, waggishly singing'. Ex the bird's supposed amorousness.—It is interesting to note that in U.S. university s. (now ob.), *quail* is a girl student. Thornton.]

quail-pipe. A woman's tongue : late C. 17–19. B.E. ; Grose, 1st ed. ; Baumann.—2. The throat : late C. 17–18 (Dryden, Pope) : on border-line between coll. and S.E., the O.E.D. treating it as the latter. Ex the pipe with which quail are decoyed.

quail-pipe boot. (Gen. in pl.) A rather coll. or illiterate form of *quill-p. b.* : C. 17–18.

quaint. In C. 14–15, *queinte* or *queynte* ; in C. 15–16, also *quaynt(e)*. The female pudend : C. 14–20 : in C. 14–16, a vulg. ; in C. 17–20, dial., now † except in parts of the North Country, where ob. Florio, '*Conno*, a woman's privie parts or quaint, as Chaucer calls it.' If not a mere variant of, certainly cognate with *cunt* : 'Chaucer may have combined Old French *coing* with M.E. *cunte*, or he may have been influenced by the Old Fr. adjective *coint*, neat, dainty, pleasant,' Grose, P., q.v. for fuller discussion.

quaint, adj., as used from ca. 1920 (the practice was on the wane by 1934) to mean amusingly old-fashioned, entertainingly unusual, even occ. as funny in an odd way, is (mostly upper-)middle- and upper-class s. It is less relevant than may at first appear to note that B.E. included *quaint*, 'curious, neat ; also strange' in his glossary, for, so far as we are aware, he had no reason to treat it at all.

quake-breach or **-buttock.** A coward ; dolt ; sot : coll. verging on S.E. : late C. 16–17.

Quaker. A member of the Society of Friends : 1653, H. R., (title) *A Brief Relation of the Irreligion of the Northern Quakers* (O.E.D.) : coll. until ca. 1810, then S.E., but never recognised, though in mid-C. 19–20 often used, by the Society. Orig. a pejorative nickname, ex supposed 'agitations in preaching', Grose.—2. A rope or lump of excrement : low : C. (? 18–)19. H., 3rd ed. Cf. *Quaker*, *bury a.*—3. A conscientious objector (*conchie*) : military coll. : from 1916. F. & Gibbons. Ex the honest attitude of Friends towards war.

Quaker oat ; gen. pl. and more properly, **Quaker Oats.** A coat : C. 20. P. P., *Rhyming Slang*, 1932.

Quaker, bury a. To defecate : low : C. (? 18–)19. See **Quaker, 2.**

Quaker's bargain. A '*yea* or *nay*' bargain ; a 'take it or leave it' transaction : coll. : late C. 18–19. Ex the well-known directness, reliability and integrity of the Quakers, as honourably honest as a well-bred Chinese

Quaker's or **Quakers' burying-ground.** A privy ; a w.c. : low : C. 19. Ex *Quaker*, 2.

***quaking cheat.** A calf ; a sheep : c. of ca. 1560–1850. Harman. See **cheat.**

qualified. Damned, bloody, etc. : euphemistic coll. : 1890, Kipling, 'He was . . . told not to make a qualified fool of himself.' O.E.D. (Sup.).

qualify, v.i. To coït : cultured s. : late C. 19. ? ex *qualify as a man.*—2. To register one's name as

playing football, or as being changed : Bootham School : from ca. 1910. Anon., *Dict. of Bootham Slang*, 1925.

qualify for the pension. To be getting on in years : coll. (— 1927). Collinson.

quality, the. The gentry : late C. 17–20 : S.E. until ca. 1830, then dial. and low coll. Mrs Centlivre notably omits *the* ; A. Trollope, 1857, 'The quality, as the upper classes in rural districts are designated by the lower . . .' Whence :

quality hours, the. Late hours for rising and for eating : lower classes' ironic coll. : mid-C. 19–20. Manchon.

qually. (Of wine) 'Turbulent and Foul', B.E. : late C. 17–mid-18 : coll. rapidly > j. ? *cloudy* corrupted.

quamino or **Q.** A negro on shipboard : nautical : mid-C. 19–20. Bowen. ? ex a Negro name. Cf. *quashee.*

quandary. A state of perplexity ; the difficulty causing it : coll. till C. 19, then S.E. : 1579, Lyly, 'Leaving this olde gentleman in a great quandarie' (O.E.D.). Occ., C. 17–early 18, as a v. : the Rev. T. Adams (d. 1655), 'He quandaries whether to go forward to God, or . . . to turn back to the world.' The O.E.D., concerning the etymology, rejects M.E. *wandreth*, abbr. *hypochondry*, and Grose's and Baumann's *qu'en dirai-je* ? Prob. L. *quam dare* ? or *quando dare* ?, less likely *quantum dare* ?

Quantas. See **Qantas.**

quantum. A drink : from ca. 1870 ; very ob. Baumann. Ex S.E. sense, a sufficiency.

quantum suff. Enough : coll. : C. 19–20 ; slightly ob. J. Beresford, 1806 (O.E.D.) ; 1871, Anon., *The Siliad*, 'I, too, O comrade, *quantum suff.* would cry.' Ex the medical formula in prescriptions : *quant(um) suff(icit)*, 'as much as suffices'.

quaquiner is incorrect for *quaviver* : C. 17–18. O.E.D.

quarrel-picker. A glazier : coll. (? orig. s.) : late C. 17–18. B.E. ; Grose, 1st ed. A pun on *quarrel*, a small pane of glass, ex Old Fr. (cf. *carreau*).

***quarrom(e)** or **-s ; quarron** or **-s.** A or the body : c. of ca. 1565–1830. Harman and Grose, *quarromes* ; Brome and B.E., *quarron* ; Anon., *The Maunderer's Praise . . .*, 1707, *quarrons*. Perhaps ex Fr. *charogne* or It. *carogna.*

quarry. The female pudend : C. 18–19 : coll., bordering on S.E. euphemism.

quart. A quart-pot, esp. as a drinking vessel : Australian coll. : late C. 19–20. Perhaps ex Devonshire usage (1865 : E.D.D.).

quart-mania. Delirium tremens (cf. *gallon-distemper*) : ca. 1860–1910.

quart-pot tea. Billy tea : Australian coll. : Mrs H. Jones, *Long Years in Australia*, 1878 (Morris) ; 1885, Finch-Hatton, *Advance Australia* ; ob. Ex its making in a tin pot holding a quart.

quarter, the ; in address, **Quarter** or **Quarters.** (The) quartermaster sergeant : military coll. : C. 20. (F. & Gibbons.)

quarter bloke, the. The same ; also, the quartermaster : id. : id. (Ibid.)

quarter bloke's English is 'the business-like, itemised English affected by Quartermasters and their assistants' in the Army ; thus *gum boots* > *boots, gum.* Military coll. : from 1916. B. & P.

quarter-decker. An officer with manners (much) better than his seamanship : naval coll. : from ca. 1865 ; slightly ob. Ex deck used by superior officers and/or cabin-passengers. Like the next, recorded first in Admiral Smyth's *Sailor's Word-Book*, 1867. Cf. *queen's parade*.

quarter-deckish. Punctilious : naval coll. : from ca. 1865 ; slightly ob. Ex preceding.

quarter-jack. A quartermaster : military : from not later than 1917. Cf. *quarter bloke* and, for the form, *popularity Jack*.

quarter of a sec !, (wait) a. A Society intensification of *half a sec !* : ca. 1900–14. Ware.

quarter pound bird's eye. A quarter-ounce of tobacco : lower classes' (— 1909) ; † by 1930. Ware.

quarter sessions ! A jocose form of swearing : legal coll. (— 1909). Ware.

quarter-sessions rose. A 'perpetual' rose : gardeners' coll. : from ca. 1880. Ex the Fr. *rose de quatre saisons*, i.e. all the year round.

***quarter stretch.** Three months' imprisonment : c. : (?) from ca. 1815. Ware. See **stretch**, n., 2.

quarter-to-one feet. 'A man who turns out his feet more than [is] usual' : naval : C. 20. F. & Gibbons.

quartered. See **rider**, 2. A coll.

quartereen. A farthing : (low) theatrical and showmen's : from ca. 1850. (Cf. *quatro*, q.v.) Perhaps suggested by U.S. *quarteroon*, a quadroon (Thornton), but more prob. by the It. *quattrino*.

quarterer. Four, esp. in *quarterer saltee*, fourpence : Parlyaree : mid-C. 19–20. Ex It. *quattro*.

quarterfoil or **-foyle.** Incorrect for *quatrefoil* : C. 19, C. 15.—**quartern(e).** Incorrect for *quartan*, adj. : C. 16. O.E.D.

quartermaster's erasmic. Soap for scrubbing floors : military : C. 20. F. & Gibbons. Jocular ex *Erasmic*, the deservedly popular toilet soap.

[**quartern.** See 'Westminster School slang', at end.]

quartern of bliss. A small, attractive woman : low London : from ca. 1882 ; ob. Ware. Cf. *pot of bliss*.

quarters. See **quarter, the.**

quarto ; Mr Quarto. A bookseller ; a publisher : coll. : mid-C. 18–mid-19.

quash ; quash kateer. Resp. good ; very good, pleasant, etc. : Eastern Fronts coll. in G.W. F. & Gibbons. In Arabic, *kwush kethir* = very good.

quashee, -ie ; occ. quassy. A Negro ; above all, a Negro seaman from the British West Indies ; esp. as a nickname : coll. : from ca. 1830. E.g. Michael Scott, 'I say, quashie.' Ex a Negro proper name. O.E.D. ; Bowen.

quat. A contemptuous pejorative applied to a (gen. young, nearly always male) person : early C. 17. Shakespeare, Webster. Ex *quat*, a pimple. (O.E.D.)

quat, go to. To defecate : low coll. : C. 19–20 ; very ob. Ex *quat*, to squat.

[**quatch**, as in Shakespeare's *quatch-buttock*, may be coll. and may = flat.]

quaternity. A quarter = a C. 17 catachresis. O.E.D.

quatro. Four : from ca. 1850 : Parlyaree. Ex It. *quattro*. Cf. *quarterer*.

quaver. A musician : low coll. or s. : from ca. 1860 ; ob. H., 3rd ed.

quean ; incorrectly **queen.** A homosexual, esp. one with girlish manners and carriage : low : late C. 19–20 ; ob. except in Australia. Prob. ex *quean*, a harlot, influenced by *Queenie*, a girl's name, and dial. *queanish*, effeminate. Cf. *queanie*.

Quean Street. See **Queen Street**.

queanie ; incorrectly **queenie.** A ' Nancy ' : late C. 19–20 : Australian. See **quean**.—2. A very good-looking man or boy : military : from ca. 1920.

queen. See **quean**.

Queen Anne—Queen Elizabeth—my Lord Baldwin —is dead. A c.p. retort on old news : coll. : resp. 1722 ; C. 18, e.g. in Swift ; ca. 1670–1710, as in Ray. A ballad of 1722, cited by Apperson, ' He's as dead as Queen Anne the day after she dy'd ' ; Barham. Swift, ' What news, Mr Neverout ? *Neverout*. Why, Madam, Queen Elizabeth's dead.' The first was occ., ca. 1870–1910, elaborated to *Queen Anne is dead and her bottom's cold*. Cf. the Yorkshire *Queen Anner*, ' an old-fashioned tale ; a tale of former times ', E.D.D.

Queen Anne's fan. Fingers to nose : coll. : mid-C. 19–20 ; ob. (Manchon).

Queen Anne's Mansions. ' The combined control tower and fore bridge of the *Nelson* and the *Rodney*, named after the tallest block of flats in London ', Bowen, 1929 : naval : from ca. 1910 ; ob.

Queen Dick. See **Dick**.—2. **Queen Dick, to the tune of the life and death of.** To no tune at all. Grose, 2nd ed. Late C. 18–early 19 coll.—3. Richard Cromwell, Protector in 1658–9. Ex his effeminacy. Dawson.

Queen Elizabeth. See **Queen Anne**.—2. The street-door key : c. : ca. 1860–1910. On *betty*.

Queen Elizabeth's pocket-pistol. ' A Brass Cannon of a prodigious Length at *Dover Castle* ', B.E. : a coll. nickname, ca. 1680–1780. Smollett.

queen (or Queen) goes on foot or sends nobody, where the. A water-closet : low coll. : ca. 1860–1915.

queen of the dripping-pan. A cook : coll. : from ca. 1850 ; ob.

Queen Sarah. The first Duchess of Marlborough (d. 1744). Dawson.

Queen Street, live in ; or **at the sign of the Queen's Head.** To be governed by one's wife : coll. : ca. 1780–1850. Grose, 1st ed.

Queen Vics, the. The Queen Victoria Rifles (9th Battalion London Regiment) : military : late C. 19–20. F. & Gibbons. Also *the Q.V.R.'s*.

queenie. See **queanie**.—2. **queenie !** A ' mock endearing name called after a fat woman trying to walk young ' : Cockneys' : 1884–ca. 1914. Ex *Queenie, come back, sweet*, addressed in a Drury Lane pantomime of 1884 to H. Campbell, who, exceedingly fat, was playing Eliza, a cook. Ware.

Queenite (opp. **Kingite**). A partisan of Queen Caroline, George IV's wife : coll. : † by 1860. Southey, ' He thought small beer . . . of some very great . . . Queenites.'

Queen's. The Queen's College, Oxford : coll. : C. 19–20. Queen's men do not like outsiders—even undergraduates of other Oxford colleges—to use the term.

Queen's bad or **hard bargain** or **bad shilling.** See **Q.b.b.** and **bad bargain**.

Queen's Bays, the. The Third Dragoon Guards : military coll. : from ca. 1840. Since Queen Victoria's death, *the Bays*. Ca. 1767, they were mounted on bay horses, the other heavy regiments—excepting always the Scots Greys—having black horses.

***Queen's bus** or, as in Baumann, **carriage.** A prison van : ca. 1860–1901 : c. (But *the King's bus* did not ' take on '.)

Queen's College. See **college**.

Queen's gold medal. (Gen. **the.**) A shilling : lower classes' (— 1887) ; † by 1902. Baumann.

Queen's head. A postage stamp : (low) coll. : ca. 1840–1901. *King's head*, † by 1910. Moncrieff, *The Scamps of London*, 1843.

queen's or **Queen's parade.** The quarter-deck : naval coll. : ca. 1865–1901. Smyth.

Queen's or **King's picture** or **portrait.** Money ; coins : coll. verging on S.E. : C. 17–20 ; slightly ob. Brome ; Ned Ward, 'Queen's pictures, by their features, | Charm all degrees of human creatures' ; *Judy*, April 27, 1887.—2. A sovereign : C. 19–20 ; ob. Mayhew.

Queen's pipe. See **pipe, her Majesty's.** Orig. **Queen's tobacco-pipe.**

Queen's or **queen's stick.** A stately person : (low) coll. : ca. 1870–1910.

Queen's woman. (Gen. in pl.) A soldier's trull : military coll., bordering on S.E. : ca. 1860–1905. A Royal Commission report of 1871.

*queer, adj. (Orig. opp. to *rum*, excellent, which in C. 19–20 has approximated to *queer* : see **rum.**) Base, criminal ; counterfeit ; very inferior : c. : C. 16–20. First in Scots, 1508 (O.E.D.), as = odd, eccentric, of questionable character, prob. coll. (*not* c.) and soon > S.E., this sense being perhaps independent of the c. (not attested before 1561) ; by 1560 very gen. in Eng. c. Awdelay, as *quire* ; Harman, *quyer*, of liquor ; Dekker, *quier* ; Fletcher the dramatist, *quere* ; B.E., *queere* ; *The Spectator*, *queer*, as in Grose. Origin obscure, but perhaps ex *quire* = *choir* : Awdelay, 'A Quire bird is one that came lately out of prison' : cf. Grose's (1st ed.) definition of *queer-bird*, and see **canary** and **canary bird** ; or, as H. suggests, ex Ger. *quer*, crooked.— 2. Not until C. 19 do the derivative senses occur : drunk, 1800, W. B. Rhodes, 'We feel ourselves a little queer' (in C. 20, gen. *he looks, looked, rather,* etc., *queer*), O.E.D.—3. Hence, unwell ; giddy : s. >, in C. 20, coll. (cf. the Australian *crook*, q.v.) : from ca. 1810, e.g. in Vaux. Cf. *queery*, q.v.—4. Unfavourable, inauspicious : coll. : late C. 19–20.—5. Not honest ; ' shady ' : coll. : late C. 19–20.—6. Shrewd ; alert : c. : late C. 18–early 19. Parker, 1789. But this may merge with preceding sense.—7. Of strange behaviour ; (slightly) mad, orig. (*a bit*) *queer in the head* : coll. : 1840, Dickens. This links with sense 3, but prob. deriving imm. ex *queer in one's attic.* (In gen., cf. the n. and v. ; also the *queer* combinations and phrases.)

*queer, n. Counterfeit money : c. : from ca. 1810. Vaux ; Egan, 1821, 'The dealer in queer '. Cf. *shover of the queer*, a counterfeiter.—2. An inferior substitute for soot : dealers in soot : (low) s. : ca. 1815–70. Egan in *Boxiana*, vol. ii.—3. A hoax, a quizzing : low : late C. 18–20, ob. Ex *queer*, v., 1, q.v.—4. A look : low s. verging on c. : Henley & Stevenson, 1892, 'Have a queer at her phiz ' ; ob.—5. See **queer, tip the,** and **queer, in** and **on.**

queer, v. To ridicule ; to puzzle : from ca. 1790 ; ob. Grose.—2. To hoax ; cheat ; trick ; evade : c. or low s. : late C. 18–20. Anon., 1819, 'There's no queering fate, sirs.'—3. To spoil, ruin : from ca. 1790. Grose, 3rd ed. ; 1812, Vaux : c. >, ca. 1840, low s. Cf. *pitch, queer the,* q.v. E.g. *queer the ogles,* blacken someone's eyes (Grose).—4. Hence, ' to put (one) out ; to make (one) feel queer ', S.O.D. : 1845, W. Cory, 'Hallam was rather queered,' O.E.D. ; Hindley, 1876, 'Consumption was queering him.'

*queer, in. Wrong, e.g. with the police : *ø.* : late C. 19–20.

queer, on the. Acting dishonestly or shadily : low : C. 20.

*queer, shover of the. See **queer,** n., 1. Cf. *queer-shover*, q.v.

Queer, Sir Quibble. 'A trifling silly shatter-brain'd Fellow ', B.E. : late C. 17–mid-18.

*queer, tip (one) **the.** To pass sentence of imprisonment on : c. : from ca. 1820 ; ob.

queer as Dick's hatband. See **Dick's hatband.**

*queer bail. Fraudulent bail : c. : 1785, Grose ; ob. Cf. *straw-bail.*

*queer bird ; in C. 16–mid-17, **quire bird.** One only recently out of gaol but already returned to crime : c. : mid-C. 16–early 19. Awdelay.—2. An odd fellow : from ca. 1840 : s. Cf. *queer cove*, q.v.

*queer bit, cole, money, paper, screens, soft. Base money, *q. paper* and *soft* obviously applying only to notes : resp. c., late C. 18–20 ; late C. 17–20, ob., c. ; C. 19, s. or low coll. ; C. 19–20, low ; C. 19–20, c. (ob. in C. 20) ; mid C. 19–20, c.

*queer bit-maker. A coiner of counterfeit : *c.* : 1785, Grose ; Ware. Cf. *queer cole-maker.*

queer bitch. 'An odd out-of-the-way fellow ', Grose, 1785 ; recorded 1772 ; † by 1870.

*queer bluffer. 'A sneaking, sharping, Cut-throat Ale-house or Inn-keeper ', B.E. ; ' the master of a public house, the resort of rogues and sharpers ', Grose, 1st ed. : c. : late C. 17–early 19. See also **bluffer.**

*queer booze. Poor lap, swipes ; 'small and naughtye drynke ', Harman : c. >, ca. 1750, low s. : ca. 1560–1830. See also **booze.**

*queer bung or **boung.** An empty purse : c. : mid-C. 17–early 19. B.E.

queer card, fellow, fish ; in pl., also **queer cattle.** A person odd in manner, strange in opinion : coll. : resp. C. 19–20 ; 1712, *The Spectator* ; 1772, 'Gods are queer fish as well as men ' ; (gen. of women), 1894, G. Moore—but prob. much earlier—coll. >, in C. 20, S.E. Cf. *odd fellow*, etc.

queer checker. A swindling box-keeper : low theatrical : late C. 18–mid-19. Grose, 2nd ed.

*queer clout. 'A sorry, coarse, ord'nary or old Handkerchief, not worth *Nimming*' (i.e. stealing), B.E. : c. : late C. 17–18.

*queer cole. Counterfeit money : c. : from ca. 1670. B.E. See **queer bit.**

*queer-cole fencer. A receiver, or utterer, of false money : c. : late C. 17–19. B.E.

*queer cole-maker. A counterfeiter : c. : late C. 17–20 ; ob. B.E.

*queer-cove. A rogue : c. : late C. 16–mid-19. Greene (*quire cove*) ; B.E. ; Grose, 1st ed.—2. A strange fellow : low >, by 1900, gen. s. : from ca. 1830. Cf. *queer bird*, q.v.

*queer cramp-rings. Bolts ; fetters : c. (—1567) ; † by ca. 1750. Harman.

*queer cuffin, occ. q. **cuffen** or **cuffing ;** even **cuffin quire** (Elisha Coles, 1676). A magistrate : c. : C. 17–19. Dekker, 'Because he punisheth them belike ' and ' Quier cuffin, that is to say, a Churle, or a naughty man ', which gives the secondary sense, ' a churl ', recorded by B.E. and Grose.

*queer cull. 'A Fop, or Fool, a Codshead ; also a shabby poor Fellow ', B.E. : c. : late C. 17–mid-19 : c. See **cull.**

*queer degen. 'An Iron, Steel, or Brass-hilted Sword ', B.E. ; ' an ordinary sword ', Grose, 1st ed. C. of ca. 1670–1830. Opp. *rum degen*, q.v.

*queer diver. A bungling pickpocket: c.: mid-C. 17–early 19. B.E.

*queer doxy. A jilting jade; an ill-dressed harlot: c.: mid-C. 17–mid-18. B.E.

*queer drawers. ' Yarn, coarse Worsted, ord'nary or old Stockings ', B.E.: c.: late C. 17–18.

*queer duke. A decayed gentleman; a starveling: c.: late mid-C. 17–18. B.E.

*queer 'em or 'um or 'un; queerum. The gallows: c.: ca. 1820–60. Bee, 1823 (queer 'em); Sonnets for the Fancy, 1824, 'The queerum queerly smear'd with dirty black'. ? queer them or queer one.

queer fellow; queer fish. See queer card.

*queer fun. A bungled trick or swindle: c.: late C. 17–18. B.E.

*queer-gammed. Very lame; crippled: c., in C. 20 slightly ob. George Parker, 1789, 'Though fancy queer-gamm'd smutty Muns | Was once my fav'rite man.' See gam.

*queer gill. A shabby fellow: c.: ca. 1800–40. Ainsworth, in Rookwood, 1834, ' Rum gills and queer gills '. See gill and cf. cull.

queer in one's (occ. the) attic. A variant—ca. 1820–1910—of queer, adj., 7. ' Jon Bee ', 1823; Baumann. Ex queer, adj., 3.—2. Hence, perverse, wrong-headed: low (— 1887); ob. Baumann.

*queer it. See queer, v., 3. Cf. pitch, queer the.

*queer ken. A prison: c.: 1608, Dekker; Grose. † by 1850.—2. A house not worth robbing: c.: late C. 17–18. B.E. Here, queer = worthless. Cf.:

*queer-ken hall. A prison: c.: 1610, Rowlands, who spells quirken hall. C. 17; cn queer ken. Prob. genuine c., but Rowlands often ' improved on ' Dekker, who, although he used Harman somewhat à la Molière, prob. knew the underworld intimately.

*queer kicks. ' Coarse, ord'nary or old Breeches ', B.E.: c.: late C. 17–early 19.

*queer money. See queer bit.

*queer mort. ' A dirty Drab, a jilting Wench, a Pockey Jade ', B.E.: c.: C. 17–early 19. Grose (2nd ed.) records only ' a diseased strumpet '. Contrast rum mort, q.v.

*queer nab. A shabby hat, or a cheap one: c.: late C. 17–early 19. B.E., who uncompromisingly defines it as ' A Felt, Carolina, Cloth, or ord'nary Hat, not worth whipping off a Man's Head '.

*queer-ogled. Squint-eyed: c. (— 1887). Baumann.

*queer on or to. To rob; treat harshly: resp. c. and low s.: C. 19–20; ob. Cf. queer, v., 3 and 4.

*queer paper. See queer bit.

*queer peeper. An inferior mirror: late C. 17–18. B.E.

*queer peepers. Squinting or dim-sighted eyes: c. >, by 1830, low s.: C. 18–20; ob. A New Canting Dict., 1725.

*queer place, the. Prison: c.: late C. 19–20. James Curtis, The Gilt Kid, 1936, ' In the queer place '. By euphemism. Cf. queer ken, 1.

*queer plunger. One who works a faked rescue of a drowning man: c.: 1785, Grose. It applies both to the ' victim ' and to the ' rescuer '. In order that the ' rescuer ' ' wangle ' a guinea from a humane society; moreover, the supposed ' suicide ' often got a small sum.

*queer prancer. An inferior or a foundered horse: late C. 17–early 19 c. B.E.; Grose, 1st ed., who

records also ' a cowardly . . . horse-stealer ': c.: late C. 18–early 19.

*queer roost, dorse (or doss) or sleep (up)on the. To live together as supposed man and wife: c.: late C. 18–mid-19. George Parker (dorse).

*queer rooster. A police spy residing among thieves: c.: 1785, Grose; † by 1890.

*queer-rums. Confusing talk: c. of ca. 1820–50. Bee. Lit., bad-goods.

*queer screen. A forged bank-note: c. (— 1812). Vaux; H., 1st ed. Cf. queer soft.

*queer-shover or shover of the queer. See queer, n., 1. From ca. 1870.

*queer soft. See queer bit.

queer stick. A very odd, or incomprehensible, fellow: coll.: late C. 19–20. Cf. dial. rum stick and the c. and dial. rum duke.

*Queer Street, in. In a serious difficulty; very short of money: c. >, ca. 1840, s. >, ca. 1890, coll. >, ca. 1930, S.E.: 1811, Lex. Bal.; 1837, Lytton, ' You are in the wrong box—planted in Queer Street, as we say in London '; Dickens.

queer the pitch. See pitch, queer the.

queer thing, the. ' A basket or sack hoisted in a Grand Banks schooner to recall the dories ': fishermen's: late C. 19–20. Bowen.

*queer to. See queer on.

*queer topping. A frowsy or inferior wig or other head-dress: c.: late C. 17–18. B.E.

*queer wedge. Base gold or, more gen., silver: c.: ca. 1800–60.—2. A large buckle, says Grose, in his 3rd ed.: c.: late C. 18–early 19.

*queer whidding. A scolding: c.: C. 18–mid-19. F. & H. Ex:

*queer whids. Esp. in cut queer whids, to give evil words: c.: 1567, Harman. Ob.

queered. Tipsy: 1822, Scott, ' You would be queered in the drinking of a penny pot of malmsey.' † by 1850. See queer, adj., 2.

queerer. A quizzer, a hoaxer: ca. 1810–50. Colman, 1812, ' These wooden wits, these quizzers, queerers, smokers '. Ex queer, v., 1.

queerish. Somewhat ' queer ', in various senses: coll.: mid-C. 18–20. Also in dial.

*queerly. Like a criminal: c.: late C. 17–early 19. B.E.

*queerum. See queer 'em.

queery. Shaky: low, esp. boxing: ca. 1820–70. Jones, The True-Bottomed Boxer, 1825.

queint(e). See quaint.—queme. See quim.

quencher; frequently a modest quencher. A drink: coll.: 1840, Dickens.

quep, in Scott, is erroneous for guep (= gup). O.E.D.

querier. A chimney-sweep irregularly soliciting custom, e.g. by knocking at the doors of houses: low: from ca. 1858. H., 1859; Mayhew (also gumbler). Cf. knuller.

querry and quetry in Greene's Second Cony-Catching, 1592, are prob. misprints for quarry; nevertheless they are late C. 16 c. and = a surety (to be victimised).

question, ask (a horse) a. To test before racing: the turf: The Licensed Victuallers' Gazette, Nov. 7, 1890, ' A thorough judge of horses . . . and . . . not afraid of asking them a question, like some trainers we know of.'

question, pop the. See pop the question.

*question lay. ' To knock at the Door, and ask for the Gentleman of the House, if a Bed [a-bed] you desire the Servant not to disturb him, but you will wait untill he rises, and then an opportunity to steal something ', C. Hitchin, *The Regulator*, 1718 : c. : C. 18.

queynte. See **quaint.—Quhew.** See **whew, the.**

qui, get the. To be dismissed : printers' : from ca. 1875. Ex *quietus*.

qui-es-kateer ? How are you : Regular Army's (late C. 19–20) and Eastern Front (1915–18). B. & P. Direct ex Arabic.

qui-hi or **-hai** or **-hy.** An Anglo-Indian, esp. of the Bengal Presidency : Anglo-Indian coll. : 1816, Anon., *Quiz* ; Thackeray, 'The old boys, the old generals, the old colonels, the old qui-his . . . paid her homage.' Ex Urdu *koi hai*, ' Is anyone there ? ' —in India a summons to a servant. Yule & Burnell, who cf. (*Bombay*) *duck* and *mull*, q.v.—2. In the Regular Army, *qui-hi* is used (mid-C. 19–20) in its lit. sense. B. & P.

qui tam ; qui-tam, quitam. A solicitor that seeks such a conviction that the resultant penalty goes half to the informer (i.e. the lawyer himself), half to the Crown : also adj., as in Moncrieff, 1843, 'The quitam lawyer, the quack doctor ' ; *qui tam*, as n., app. recorded first in this sense in H., 3rd ed., 1864 ; in C. 20, ob. except as legal s.—2. The adj., however, figures also in the earlier *qui-tam horse*, ' one that will both carry and draw ', Grose, 3rd ed. : legal, † by 1860. Ex the legal action so named ; L., ' who as well '.—3. But *qui tam*, an informer, occurs as early as 1816 in ' Quiz's ' *Grand Master* (O.E.D.) : coll.

Quibble Queer, Sir. See **Queer, Sir Quibble.**

quick and nimble ; more like a bear than a squirrel. A c.p. addressed to one moving slowly when speed is required : C. 18–mid-19. ' Proverbs ' Fuller, 1732 ; Grose, 2nd ed.

Quick Dick. A certain quick-firing British gun on the Western Front : military nickname. F. & Gibbons.

quick-firer. A field-service stereotyped post-card : military : from 1915. Frank Richards, *Old Soldiers Never Die*, 1933. Cf. *whizz-bang*.

quick one. A drink taken quickly : coll. verging on familiar S.E. : from ca. 1910.

quick stick(s). Rapidly ; hurriedly. Esp. in the s. phrase, *cut quick sticks*, to start or depart thus (cf. *cut one's stick*, q.v.) : coll. : from ca. 1860. H., 2nd ed. Occ. *in quick sticks* (Rolf Boldrewood, 1890). The first phrase and the last occur also in various diall. : E.D.D.

quickee. See **quicky.**

quicker than hell would scorch a feather. Promptly : sailing-ship officers' c.p. ' duly impressed on all youngsters ' : mid-C. 19–20 ; ob. Bowen. Cf. *an icicle's chance in hades*.

quick(e)y ; occ. quickee. The act of backing a horse after the result of a race is known : Glasgow sporting (— 1934). Perhaps ex *quick return on one's money*.—2. A fast bowler : cricketers' coll. : 1934, P. G. H. Fender in several articles (e.g. on June 21) in *The Evening News*.

quicumque (loosely **quicunque**) **vult.** A very compliant girl (sexually) : 1785, Grose ; † by 1850. Also an *Athanasian wench*. Ex *quicumque vult salvus esse*, whosoever will be saved, the opening words of the Athanasian Creed (O.E.D.).

*****quid.** A guinea : c. : 1688, Shadwell ; † by 1800. Perhaps L. *quid*, what ?, for ' the wherewithal ': cf. *quids*, q.v.—Hence, 2, a sovereign, or the sum of twenty shillings : low : C. 19–20.—3. A shilling, says Grose, 3rd ed., but this I believe to be

an error.—4. As a pl. = *quids*, sovereigns or £, as in Dickens, 1857, ' " Take yer two quid to one ", adds the speaker, picking out a stout farmer.'— 5. See **quids.**—6. The female pudend : low : C. 19–20 ; ob.

' quid est hoc ? ' ' hoc est quid.' A late C. 18– early 19 punning c.p. : Grose, 3rd ed. As H. explains, the question is asked by one tapping the bulging cheek of another, who, exhibiting a ' chaw ' of tobacco, answers ' *hoc est* ' *quid*. Lit., ' What is this ? This is a quid [of tobacco].'

*****quid-fishing.** Expert thieving : c. (— 1909). Ware. Ex *quid*, 2.

quid to a bloater, (it's) a. (It's) a certain bet : low urban (— 1909) ; slightly ob. Ware.

quidding, vbl.n. The chewing of tobacco : *Conway* training ship (— 1900). John Masefield's history thereof, 1933.

quiddle. ' Custard, or any sauce for pudding ' : Bootham School : C. 20. Perhaps cf. *squish*.—2. To spit : id. : † by 1925, says the anon. *Dict. of Bootham Slang* of that date.

quidlet. A sovereign ; £1 : low : C. 20. Diminutive of *quid*, 2.—2. In pl. = :

*****quids.** Money, or rather cash, in gen. : late C. 17–20 (ob.) : c. >, ca. 1750, low s. B.E. (*quidds*) ; Moore, 1819, ' If quids should be wanting, to make the match good '. Ex *quid*, 1.

*****quids, tip the.** To spend money : c. : late C. 17– 19. B.E., Grose.—2. To lend money : c. : mid-C. 18–mid-19. Grose, 1st ed. See **quids.**

quien. A dog : low (? orig. c.) : mid-C. 19–20 ; ob. Reade, 1861, ' " Curse these quiens," said he.' Origin obscure, but obviously cognate with L. *canis*, Fr. *chien*, a dog. Perhaps ex Northern Fr. dial.

quier. See **queer,** adj., 1.

quiet, on the. Quietly, unobtrusively, secretly : s. >, ca. 1910, coll. : 1860, H., 2nd ed. Whence *q.t., on the*, q.v.

quiet as a wasp in one's nose(, as). Uneasy, restless : coll. : 1670, Ray ; ob.

quiff. ' A satisfactory result : spec. an end obtained by means not strictly conventional ', F. & H. : low : from ca. 1875 ; ob. Esp. as in F. & Gibbons (C. 20 senses) : ' Any specially ingenious smart, tricky, or novel or improvised way of doing anything ' (naval) ; ' in the Army . . . any drill method peculiar to a battalion '. Ex dial. *quiff*, a dodge or trick, a knack, a ' wrinkle ' (E.D.D.).—2. Whence, ' an idea, fancy, movement, suggestion ': Anglo-Indian (— 1909). Ware.—3. As an oiled lock of hair plastered on forehead, the S.O.D. considers it S.E., W. as s., orig. East End of London. Perhaps ex It. *cuffia* ; cognate with *coif*. F. & H., 1902 (first record), says ' military ' ; Ware dates it at 1890.

quiff, v.i. To copulate : C. 18–20 (very ob.) : low. D'Urfey, ' By quiffing with Cullies, three Pound she had got ' ; Grose, 2nd ed., gives as *quiffing*, copulation. Not in O.E.D. ; origin problematic.—2. V.i., to do well ; jog along nicely, merrily : from ca. 1870. Prob. ex the dial. n. *quiff* (see **quiff,** n., 1) ; cf. :

quiff. Smartly dressed (esp. for a particular occasion) : military : from ca. 1908. F. & Gibbons. Ex *quiff*, n., 1.

quiff in the press. To move a breast pocket to the other side : tailors' : from ca. 1870. Cf. the Somersetshire dial. use (E.D.D.).

quiff tack. ' Materials for cleaning harness

equipment ' : military : from ca. 1910. F. & Gibbons. Ex *quiff*, adj.

quiff the bladder. To conceal baldness : low : from ca. 1870. Lit., to coif the bladder-resembling head ; more prob.—cf. *quiff*, n., 1—ex dial. *quiff*, a dodge, a trick.

quiffing. See **quiff, v.**, 1.

quifs. Manoeuvres : military : late C. 19–20 ; virtually †. Ware. Ex *quif*, n., 1 or 2.

quill. To curry favour : Winchester College : C. 19–20. Perhaps ex *jump in quill*, to act in harmony, and *in a* or *the quill*, in concert. Cf. *quilled*.

quill, brother—knight—of the. See **brother** and **knight.**

quill, drive a. See **drive a quill.**

quill-driver. ' Anybody on shipboard doing clerical work ' : nautical coll. : late C. 19–20. Bowen. Ex S.E. sense.

quilled, adj. Pleased : Winchester College : C. 19–20. Prob. ex *quill*, q.v.

quiller, *occ.* **quilster.** A toady : Winchester : C. 19–20. Ex *quill*, q.v.

quim. The female pudend : a vulg. : C. 17–20. Variants, *queme*, *quim-box*, *quimsby*, *quin*, all † except the second, itself ob. Grose, 2nd ed., suggests ex Sp. *quemar*, to burn.—Hence such C. 19–20 compounds as *quim-bush*, *-whiskers*, *-wig*, the female pubic hair ; *q.-stake* or *-wedge*, the penis ; *q.-sticker*, a whoremonger : *q.-sticking* or *-wedging*, and *quimming*, sexual intercourse.

quimsby, quin. See **quim.**

quimp. Slack ; unsoldierly : military : C. 20. F. & Gibbons. Perhaps a corruption of dial. *quim*, pleasant, smooth.

quincentenary. Incorrect for *quingentenary* : late C. 19–20. O.E.D. See also **quint-.**

Quins. Harlequins Rugby Football Club : sporting : C. 20.

Quins, the. The Dionne quintuplets of Canada ; born May 28, 1934 : coll., mainly journalists'. Cf. *the Quads*, the English quadruplets born in 1935.

quinsy, choked by a hempen. Hanged : C. 16–early 19. Grose, 2nd ed.

quint-. Wrongly used in combinations instead of *quinqu(e)*, as in *quintangular* (1787), *quintagenarian* (1844), for *quinquagenarian* (1843), *quintennial* (1871) for *quinquennial*. Likewise, *quinti-* is incorrect for *quinque-* : late C. 17–20. O.E.D.

*quire. See **queer,** adj., 1.

quirk. An Air Force officer while under instruction : Air Force : 1916 ; ob. Cf. *erk*, but ex :—2. A ' B.E.' aeroplane, stable but very slow : Air Force : 1915 ; ob.—3. Hence, ' any freak type, or unusually designed aeroplane ' (F. & Gibbons) : Air Force : from 1917.

*quirken. See **queer-ken hall.**

quirklum. A puzzle : Scots : late C. 18–19. (' A cant term ' in Jamieson = s.)

quis ? Who wants some ? : Public-Schoolboys' : mid-C. 19–20. The answer is *ego !* Collinson. Direct ex Latin.

quisby. An idler : 1837 (O.E.D.) ; † by 1920. Desmond, *Stage Struck*, ' That old quisby has certainly contrived to slip out of the house.' ? ex *quiz*, an eccentric.—2. See **quisby, do.**

quisby, adj. Bankrupt, 1853 ; out of sorts, 1854 ; queer, not quite right, 1887, *Punch*, July 30, ' Arter this things appeared to go quisby.' ? **ex** *quiz*, an eccentric, or ex *quisby*, q.v.

quisby, do. To idle : 1851, Mayhew. Ob. See **quisby,** n.

quisi. Low ; obscene : Anglo-Chinese (— 1864). H., 3rd ed.

quit, to leave off in a very lazy or a cowardly manner, and **quitter,** a shirker, are C. 20 coll. ex U.S. Ultimately ex S.E. *quit*, to cease doing something (in C. 20 U.S.), or ex Anglo-Irish *quit*, to ' clear out '—as in Lover, 1848, ' Quit this minit,' cited by E.D.D.

quitam. See **qui tam.**

quite ! ; quite so ! Yes ! ; no doubt ! ; I agree : coll. : from the mid-Nineties. Cf. Fr. *parfaitement* and our *exactly* and *rather*. (O.E.D. Sup.) The clergyman in Sutton Vane's excellent and most original play, *Outward Bound*, continually says *quite !*

quite a stranger ! See **stranger !, quite a.**

quite too. Too ; esp. *quite too dull*, which Ware quotes in his introduction : orig. and mainly Society : from ca. 1905. Prob. on the earlier *too too*.

quiteish, not. Indisposed : from ca. 1920. Richard Keverne, *Carteret's Cure*, 1926, ' You look a bit not quiteish, eh ? ' I.e. *not quite the thing*.

quitsest. A release, discharge : late C. 16–early 17 : prob. coll. Holinshed. ? ex *quietus est*. O.E.D.

quitter. See **quit.**

quivication. An equivocation : sol. (? orig. nautical) : from before 1887. Baumann.

quiz. (Of arbitrary origin, perhaps on *queer*, adj. ; cf. *quoz*.) An eccentric person : 1782, Mme D'Arblay (O.E.D.) : Oxford s. >, ca. 1830, gen. coll. and, ca. 1860, S.E.—2. Hence, an odd-looking thing : coll. : 1798, Jane Austen ; ob. O.E.D.—3. A monocle : from ca. 1810 : coll. Abbr. *quizzing-glass*, as in Thackeray, 1843, ' The dandy not uncommonly finishes off with a horn quizzing-glass.' Ob. Prob. ex sense 1.

*quiz, v.i. and t. To watch ; play the spy : c. : from ca. 1890. Ex dial.

quockerwodger. A politician acting under an outsider's orders : political (— 1859) ; † by 1887. H., 1st ed. (Introduction) ; Baumann. Ex dial. *quocker-wodger*, a puppet on strings.

*quod or, never in C. 20, **quad.** A prison : late C. 17–20 : c. until ca. 1780, then low s. B.E. ; Fielding ; Tarras, *Poems*, 1804 (*quad*). Gen. *in quod*. Prob. ex *quadrangle*. Cf. :

*quod, v. To imprison : from ca. 1810 : c. >, ca. 1840, low s. Vaux, Tom Taylor. Ex n.

*quod-cove. A turnkey : c. : 1812, Vaux ; † by 1910. Ex *quod*, n. Cf. :

*quod-cull. A prison warder : c. : C. 18. C. Hitchin, *The Regulator*, 1718.

quodded, adj. In prison : low : from ca. 1820. Ex *quodded*, imprisoned. See **quod, v.**

*quodding dues are concerned. It is a case of imprisonment : c. (— 1812) ; † by 1890. Vaux.

quodger ; quodjer. By what law ? : legal : 1864, H., 3rd ed. Ex L. *quo jure.*

quoniam. A drinking-cup of some kind : drinking s. : early C. 17. Healy, 1609, ' A Quoniam is a glasse . . . well knowne in Drink-allia.'—2. The female pudend : low : C. 17–18. ? a learned pun, suggested by *quim* (q.v.), on L. *quoniam*, whereas (all males desire it).

*quota. App. c. for a share (esp. of plunder) : late C. 17–early 18. B.E. Cf. *earnest*, q.v.

quote. A quotation, 1885.—2. A quotation-mark, 1888. Literary, publishing, and printing coll. >, ca. 1910, S.E., but certainly not dignified S.E. (O.E.D.)

quoz. An odd or absurd person or thing : coll. : ca. 1790–1810. Also, as in Mme D'Arblay, as a plural. A jocular perversion of *quiz*, n., 1, q.v.—2. As an ejaculation or a retort, indeed a monosyllabic c.p. : same period. O.E.D.

*quyer. See queer, adj., 1. (A variant spelling of *quire*.)

R

Under **R**, F. & H. has the following ineligibles : S.E. :—rabbit, a pejorative, also a drinking-can, rabble ; rack and manger, rack and ruin ; rack off, to tell ; racket, v. and (except as c.) n. ; racketer, racket(t)y ; play racket and without racket ; raff ; raffle ; raffling-shop ; rag, a ragamuffin, a newspaper ; rag-tag, rag-tag and bobtail ; ragamuffin ; rage, v., and ragerie ; rag(e)man ; ragout ; raid the market ; raillery ; rain proverbs ; rainbow-chase ; rainy day ; raise, to rear ; rake, rakehell, rakehellion, rakeshame ; rake, lean as a ; rake and scrape, rake-down, rake in the pieces, better with a rake than a fork ; rake-kennel and raker, scavenger; rally, in theatrical sense ; ramagious ; ramhead ; rammish ; ramp, a and to wanton ; rampage ; rampager, rampaging, rampageous ; rampallion ; ramrod, penis ; ramshackle ; randan ; range, ranger, to whore, a whoremonger, or a highwayman ; Rangers, military ; rank, as intensive adj. ; rannel ; ransack, ranshackle ; rant, to talk big, etc. ; corresponding ranter, ranting ; rantipole ; rap, n. and v., indicating quickly forcible or explosive action or speech, also a coin ; rapparee ; rapper, a lie (but see entry), and rapping, great or very ; rapscallion ; raree-show(man) ; rascal ; rat, a renegade ; like a drowned rat and smell a rat ; ratten, rattening, ratter ; rattle, a dice-box, a clamour, a scolding, a lively talker ; and the death-rattle ; rattle, to censure or to confuse, irritate ; rattle-baby ; rattle-bag, etc. ; rattle down and up ; rattled, confused ; rattler, constant talker, a smart blow, a snake, anything of notable size or value ; rattling, brisk, lively, and as adv. before e.g. *good* ; rattle-trap, n. and adj., (anything) broken down, curiously mechanical ; raw, a novice, anything raw, a tender point ; the corresponding adj. ; raw-flesh or -head, a spectre ; ready, prepared, and ready-money ; reckon and reckon up ; record, beat or cut or lower the ; recreant ; red, a republican ; all red combinations and phrases not hereinunder ; red-tape, -taper, -tapery, -tapeism, -tapist ; reefer (jacket) ; reefing ; reel, off the, and reel-off, reel-pot ; reflector ; refresher, a fee ; a regular (visitor, etc.) ; relieve ; remainder ; remedy at Winchester School ; renovator ; repartee ; reptile, n. and adj. ; Republican ; respectable ; respond ; Responsions ; resty ; resurrection-man or -woman, and resurrectionist ; revel-dash, -rout ; revenge ; reviver (tailor) ; reward ; rex, play ; rib ; ribald, etc. ; rib-roasting ; rich face ; ride phrases not hereinunder ; rider, coin and ' commercial ' ; riff-raff, etc. ; riggish ; all right combinations and phrases not listed separately ; rigol ; a ring (boxing, racing, etc.) ; ring, come on the ; ring the changes ; riotous living ; ripe, ready ; rip(p)on ; rise and its phrases not done separately ; rivet, v. ; road to heaven or paradise ; roadster ; roarer, roaring ; roaring buckie, drunk, and Meg ; roast proverbs ; roaster ; rob-altar and -pot and -thief ; robe, gentleman of the ; robbery, exchange is no ; Robin Hood terms, etc., not de-

tailed ; rock and phrases, etc., not listed separately ; rocketer ; rod ; rodomontade ; rogerian ; rogue, etc., if not separately ; roister ; Roland for an Oliver ; roll combinations and phrases not done hereinunder ; roller as go-cart and wave ; rolley ; romance, n. and v. ; Romany, etc. (but see note) ; rook, etc., where not defined ; room, leave the ; ro(o)mbelow ; roost, etc., if not defined ; rope, id. ; rosary, the coin ; rosin, to drink ; rosy, favourable, and rosy about the gills ; rouge at Eton ; rough, etc., where not separately ; rough-and-tumble, adj. ; rough music ; roughshod ; round, etc., if not defined ; rouse, rouser, rousing ; roust, roust-about ; rout ; rove, rover ; row in the same boat and row to hoe, a hard ; rowdy, etc., where not defined ; royster ; R's, the three ; rub, etc., where not done separately ; rubber ; rubicon (at cords ; n. and v.) ; ruby and ruck, etc., if not listed ; rudesby ; rug-gown(ed), -headed ; ruff ; ruffian, etc., where not listed ; ruffle, ruffler, id. ; rufty-tufty ; rug (liquor ; tug) ; ruge ; rule of thumb ; rum-blossom or -bud ; rumbling ; rumkin ; rump, etc., if not separately ; run, id. ; runabout, runner, runner-up, running ; runt ; rural ; rush, etc., where not defined ; rustic and rusticate ; rusty-fusty-dusty ; ruttish ; rutter.

Dial. are these :—ramgumption ; rannack ; randy, n. ; randy-dandy ; rap, in a ; rattler, a sound scolding ; rick-ma-tick ; rid the stomach ; ridiculous ; riners ; roaring game ; router ; rudge (= rug, esp. in rug-gown) ; rumgumptious ;

r. Intrusive after another *r*, or as ' Upper rouse-maid, ain't you, at St. Jimes's Palace ? ', W. Pett Ridge, 1898, in his Cockney novel, *Mord Em'ly* : mostly Cockney : C. 19–20 (? from earlier).—2. r l More gen. written *ar l* : mostly Cockney : (? late) C. 19–20. Manchon suggests that it is an abbr. of *right l*, certainly l ; more prob. = *ah l*, i.e. *ah*, *yes l*—3. -r' for -*rt* (as in *star'*) is Cockney : since when ?

r.i.p. (or R.I.P.), let him, her, it, etc. Let him, her, etc., rip ; i.e. don't bother about him, her, etc. : late C. 19–20. Ex the abbr. of *requiescat in pace*, on tombstones. Cf. *rip l, let him* or *her*, q.v.

R.M.D. (separately articulated). Immediate payment : (unexalted) financial coll. : late C. 19–20. Ex *ready money down*.

R.O. See relieving officer.

R.O. workers. Men who ' frame ' a mock auction : showmen's : C. 20. P. Allingham in *The Evening News*, July 9, 1934.

rabbit. A new-born babe, mostly in *rabbit-catcher*, a midwife : low : ca. 1780–1850. Grose, 1785, —2. Political (ob.) as in report of the House of Commons Election Commission, 1866, ' Out of £50 . . . he had paid a number of rooks and rabbits . . . In general . . . " the rabbits were to work in the burrow and the rooks to make a noise at the public meetings.'—3. ' A rabbit, as a horse that runs " in and out " is sometimes called,' 1882, *The Standard*, Sept. 3 : racing ; slightly ob.—4. Hence, an inferior player of any game : C. 20 : s. >, by 1930, coll. Related also to S.E. use of *rabbit* as a pejorative. (The derivative *rabbitry* is too academic and rare to be eligible.)—5. ' Property stolen from the Royal Dockyards, most frequently used in Devonport ' : naval : C. 20. Bowen.—6. Sol. for *rebate* : C. 20. Manchon.

rabbit, v. In imprecations, it = confound, as in Fielding's ' " Rabbit the fellow ! " cries he,' 1742, and Smollett's ' Rabbit it ! I have forgot the degree,' in the same decade. Cf. *drabbit !* (— 1787), and *od*(*d*) *rabbit* : qq.v. The O.E.D. considers *rabbit* an alteration of *rat* in *od rat, drat* ; F. & H.'s *rot it* won't ' fit '.

rabbit or **rabbits, buy the.** To have the worst of a bargain ; to be a dupe : orig. (1825) U.S. ; anglicised ca. 1850 ; very ob. Cf. the C. 16 proverb, *who will change a rabbit for a rat ?*

rabbit, fat and lean like a. A mid-C. 17–early 19 coll. Ray, 1678 ; explained in Swift's *Polite Conversation*, Dialogue I : ' I am like a Rabbit, fat and lean in Four-and-twenty Hours,' a rabbit responding very promptly to food.

rabbit, live. The male member : low : C. 19–20 ; ob. Whence *skin the live rabbit* or *have a bit of rabbit-pie*, to coït : cf. *rabbit-pie*.

rabbit, run the. ' To convey liquor from a public-house ', C. J. Dennis : low Australian (— 1916). Why ?

rabbit-catcher. See **rabbit,** n., 1.

rabbit dies, I hope your. See **hope . . . A** variant is *may your rabbit die !*

rabbit-hunting—or (a) **coney-catching—with a dead ferret, go.** To undertake something with unsuitable or useless means : coll. : ca. 1670–1820. Ray ; Fuller, 1732.

rabbit-pie. A harlot : low : mid-C. 19–20 ; ob. Ex *rabbit, live,* q.v. also for phrase.

rabbit-pie shifter. A policeman : low London : ca. 1870–1920. Barrère & Leland quote a music-hall song of ca. 1870, ' Never to take notice of vulgar nicknames, such as " slop ", " copper ", " rabbit-pie shifter ", " peeler ".'

rabbit-skin ; occ. **cat-skin.** An academical hood : university : from ca. 1850 ; ob. Cf. :

rabbit-skin, get one's. To obtain the B.A. degree: university : from ca. 1850 ; ob. Ex preceding ; the trimming is of rabbit's fur.

*rabbit-sucker. A young spendthrift ' taking up Goods upon Tick at excessive rates ', B.E. : c. of C. 17–early 19. Dekker. Prob. ex Shakespearian sense, ' baby ' rabbits. Cf. *pursenets,* q.v.—2. Also, a pawnbroker ; a tally-man : c. or low s. : ca. 1720–60. *A New Canting Dict.*, 1725.

rabbiter. A side-handed blow on the nape of the neck : Winchester College : from ca. 1875. As in killing a rabbit.—2. In pl., a form of punishment : Charterhouse : C. 19. A. H. Tod, *Charterhouse*, 1900.

rabbits out of the wood !, it's. It's ' splendid ' or sheer profit or a windfall ! : racing c.p. (— 1932). See *Slang*, p. 245, note 15.

rabbit's punch. A cuff on the nape of the neck : pugilistic : from ca. 1920. (*The Daily Telegraph*, Jan. 30, 1936.) Ex one method of killing rabbits. Cf. *rabbiter,* 1, q.v.

rabble. Fun of any sort ; as v.i., to ' rag ' : Bootham School : C. 20. Anon., *Dict. of Bootham Slang*, 1925.

rabsha(c)kle. A profligate : coll. : ? C. 17–18. F. & H. : but who else ? Cf. S.E. *ramshackle.*

race-card, the. The morning sick-report : jocular military : 1915 ; ob. F. & Gibbons. The odds are heavily against the ' entrants '.

Rachel or **rachel,** v. To rejuvenate ; renovate : ca. 1890–5. Ex Madame Rachel, the ' beautiful for ever ' swindler. (The C. 20 is kinder to such impositions.)

rack. A bone, gen. in pl. : slaughterers' coll. >, ca. 1890, j. : 1851, Mayhew.—2. A rib of mutton : Winchester School coll. (— 1870). Ex S.E., a neck of mutton.

rack, stand the. To stand the strain : low : C. 20. James Curtis, *The Gilt Kid*, 1936. I.e. the *racket.*

rack off. To make water : low coll. : late C. 19–20 ; ob. Ex wine-making.

rack-rider. The samlet : Northern fishermen's coll : late C. 19–20. Bowen. Because gen. it appears in bad weather.

rackaback. A ' gormagon ', q.v. : ca. 1785–1850. Grose, 3rd ed.

rackabimus. ' A sudden or unexpected stroke or fall ', Jamieson, who adds that ' It resembles *racket* ' : Scots : late C. 18–19.

*racket. A dodge, trick ; plan ; ' line ', occupation, esp. if these are criminal or ' shady ' : c. (— 1812) >, ca. 1860, low s. >, ca. 1930, gen. s. ; it now verges on coll. Vaux. Ex *racket,* noise, disturbance.—2. Esp. as in *be in a racket,* be privy to an illicit design, and as set forth in Egan's Grose, 1823, ' Some particular kinds of fraud and robbery are so termed, when called by their flash '—i.e. underworld—' names ; as the Letter-racket ; the Order-racket . . . In fact, any game '—i.e., illicit occupation or trick—' may be termed a racket . . . by prefixing thereto the particular branch of depredation or fraud in question.' Whence the various U.S. ' rackets ' : see esp. Irwin. Cf. *racket-man.*— 3. See **racquet.**

*racket, stand the. To take the blame for one's gang : c. (— 1823) >, by 1850, s. >, by 1900, coll. ' Jon Bee.'—2. Hence, to pay the bill, stand the expense : late C. 19–20 : s. >, by 1930, coll.

*racket-man. A thief : c. : from ca. 1850 ; ob. Mayhew. Ex *racket,* 2.

*raclan. A married woman : tramps' c. : from ca. 1830. Brandon. Cf. Romany *rakli,* a girl.

racquet ' is . . . incorrect . . . [The implement used in lawn tennis] is spelt " racket " in all the official books of the various associations, and nearly all the authorities from the early days up to the present time spell it thus. In some mysterious way it has got mixed up with the French spelling " raquette ",' Sir Gordon Lowe, May, 1935, in *Lowe's Lawn Tennis Annual* (1935).

rad. A Radical : political s., in C. 20 coll. : 1831, *The Lincoln Herald,* Jan. 7 (O.E.D.). Disraeli in *Coningsby,* ' They say the Rads are going to throw us over.'—2. A radiator : servants' : from ca. 1905. Francis E. Brett Young, *White Ladies,* 1935, ' The rads are stone-cold.'

Radder, the. The Radcliffe Camera : Oxford undergraduates' : C. 20. Collinson. By ' the Oxford -*er* '.

raddled. Tipsy : late C. 17–18. Motteux. Cf. dial. *raddle,* to do anything to excess ; but more prob. ex *raddle,* to colour coarsely with red.—2. (Of a face) much made-up : pejorative coll. : from ca. 1920. Collinson. Ex *raddle,* red ochre.

rafe or **Ralph.** A pawn-ticket : low ; esp. at Norwich : from ca. 1860 ; ob. H., 2nd ed.

Rafferty rules. No rules at all, esp. as applied to boxing—' M.Q. (and Rafferty) rules ' is the heading of a boxing section in *The Sydney Bulletin* of 1935— hence to a ' rough house ' ; *according to Rafferty rules,* without rule or restraint or, in politics, honour : Australian coll. (— 1914). Ex dial. *raffatory, raffertory, ref(f)atory* : refractory (E.D.D.).

Raffish. Connected with the Royal Aircraft Factory : Air Force : 1915 ; ob.. F. & Gibbons. Punning S.E. *raffish.*

raffle-coffin. A ruffian, lit. a resurrectionist : C. 19 low coll. Corruption of *rifle(-coffin).*

raffs. ' An appellation given by the gownsmen of the university of Oxford to the inhabitants of that place ', Grose, 1785 : coll. : ca. 1780–1920. Cf. *riff-raff.*

rag. (See the S.E. list at beginning of **R.**—) 2. A farthing : c. : ca. 1690–1850. B.E. ; Egan's Grose. Because of so little value.—3. A bank-note : 1811, *Lex. Bal.,* which proves that *rag* also = bank-notes collectively.—4. Hence, money in gen. : from ca. 1810. *Lex. Bal.*—5. A flag : from ca. 1700 : coll. till C. 20, then S.E. Kipling, 1892. Cf. *rag, order of the,* q.v.—6. The curtain : theatrical and show-men's : from ca. 1875.—7. Hence, a dénouement, a ' curtain ' : id. : from ca. 1880.—8. A street tumbler : circus : 1875, *The Athenæum,* April 24.— 9. See **rag, order of the.**—10. The tongue : from ca. 1825. Ex *rag, red,* q.v.—11. Talk ; banter, abuse : :rom ca. 1880. Gen. *ragging.* Cf. :— 12. A jollification, esp. and orig. an undergraduates' display of noisy, disorderly conduct and great high spirits, considered by the perpetrators as excellent fun and by many outsiders as ' a bloody nuisance ' : university >, ca. 1910, very common in the Army and Navy ; by 1930, pretty gen. : 1892, *The Isis,* ' The College is preparing for a good old rag to-night,' O.E.D. ; *The Daily Mail,* March 10, 1900, ' There was keen excitement at Cambridge yester-day when the magistrates proceeded to deal with the last two prosecutions of students arising out of the notorious rag in celebration of the relief of Lady-smith ' ; but in existence from ca. 1860 (O.E.D. Sup.). Ex the S.E. v., to annoy, tease.—13. See **Rag, the,** three senses.—14. See **rags.**

rag, v.t. and i. To question vigorously or jocu-larly ; waylay, or assail, roughly and noisily ; to create a disturbance, hold a ' rag ' (see n., 12) : university : *The Isis,* 1896, ' The difficulty of " ragging " with impunity has long been felt,' O.E.D. ; but implied by Baumann in 1887 and, in the first nuance, recorded by O.E.D. (Sup.) for 1891. Perhaps abbr. of *bully-rag.* Origin : see **rag,** n., 12.—2. Hence, to wreck, make a mess of, by way of a rag : Public Schools' : 1904, P. G. Wode-house, *The Gold Bat,* ' Mills is awfully barred in Seymour's. Anybody might have ragged his study.' In c. (mainly of Norwich) to divide (esp. plunder) : 1860, H., 2nd ed. Prob. ex, or at the least cognate with, the † S.E. sense, to tear in pieces. Also **go rags.**

rag, chew the. To scold, complain ; sulk or brood : low and military, 1888. Ex *rag,* tongue.

rag, dish of red. Abuse : low : from ca. 1820 ; ob. Egan, *Anecdotes of the Turf,* ' She tipped the party such a dish of red rag as almost to create a riot in the street.' See **rag, red.**

rag, have two shirts and a. To be comfortably off : coll. : ca. 1670–1800. Ray.

rag, lose one's. To lose one's temper : Glasgow (— 1934). Ex *rag out, get one's* : q.v.

rag, order of the. (Preceded by **the**). The mili-tary profession : coll. : 1751, Fielding ; slightly ob See **rag,** 5.

rag, red. (Also red flannel.) The tongue : low : late C. 17–20 ; slightly ob. B.E., Grose, Combe, Bruton (1826, ' Say . . . why that red rag . . . is now so mute '), W. S. Gilbert, 1876. See **rag,** n., 10, and cf. *Rag, the,* q.v.

rag, sky the. To throw in the towel : Australian boxing (— 1916). C. J. Dennis.

Rag, the. The Army and Navy Club : naval and military : 1839 (see *The Times Literary Supplement,* June 21, 1934, in its review of Capt. C. W. Fire-brace's *The Army and Navy Club,* 1837–1933,— published in 1934). Ex an officer's description of a meal there as ' a rag and famish affair '. Also *the Rag and Famish.*—2. ' The **Rag**lan ' public-house : London : from ca. 1864. Ex Lord Raglan, the British Commander in the Crimean War. (Near Leather Lane : see esp. Greenwood, *The Seven Curses of London,* 1869.)—3. (Also **the rag.**) The regimental brothel : Indian Army (non-officers') from ca. 1880. Frank Richards, *Old-Soldier Sahib,* 1936.

rag, too much red. Loquacious : low : from ca. 1840. See **rag, red.**

*****rag, win the shiny.** See **shiny rag** . . .

rag, without a ; not a rag (left). Penniless : coll. : late C. 16–20 ; ob. Shakespeare, ' Not a rag of money ', though here *rag* rather = ' scrap ' ; B.E.

rag a holiday, give the red. To be silent : low : from ca. 1850 ; ob. See **rag,** n., 10.

rag about. To fool about : C. 20 : orig. and mainly universities' : Collinson. See **rag,** v., 1.

rag-(and-bone-)shop. A very dirty and untidy room : coll. : from ca. 1880 ; ob. Baumann.— 2. Hence, a woman in rags : lower classes' (— 1923). Manchon. Occ. corrupted to *ragaboneshop.*

Rag and Famish. See **Rag, the,** 1. This form is perhaps ex ' Ensign Rag and Captain Famish, imaginary characters, out of which Leech some years back obtained much amusement ', H., 5th ed., 1874 ; but see **Rag, the.**

rag-bag or **-doll.** A slattern : coll. : from ca. 1862.

rag-box or **-shop.** The mouth : low : from ca. 1890. Kipling, 1892, ' You shut up your rag-box and 'ark to my lay.'

rag-carrier. An ensign : 1785, Grose ; † by 1890. Ex *rag,* n., 5.

rag-fair. An inspection of soldiers' kit-bags, etc. : 1785, Grose ; ob. by 1915 : military. Ex the S.E. sense, an old-clothes market at Houndsditch, Lon-don : which, contrary to F. & H., is certainly S.E.

rag-gorger or **gorgy.** See **rag-splawger.**

rag-mannered. Violently coarse or vulgar ; coll. : C. 19–20 ; ob.

rag money. Bank notes, bills of exchange, etc. : from ca. 1860 : coll. till C. 20, then S.E

rag on every bush,—(oh,) he has a. He is, or is in the habit of, paying marked attention to more than one girl at a time : from ca. 1860 ; ob.

rag out, v.i. To show the white flag or feather : ca. 1880–1910.

rag out, get one's. To bluster (ob.) ; to grow angry : low : from ca. 1880. Explained by the synonymous *get one's shirt out,* 2, and by *rag,* n., 10.

rag-sauce. Chatter ; impudence : low : from ca. 1840. Egan. Ex *rag,* n., 10.

*rag-seeker. See rag-sooker.

rag-shop. See rag-box.—2. See rag-and-bone shop.—3. A bank : c. or low s. : 1860, H., 2nd ed. ; ob. Whence :

rag-shop boss or cove. A banker : from ca. 1865 ; ob.—2. See :

rag-shop cove. A cashier : low : from ca. 1865. —2. See preceding entry.

*rag-sooker, occ. -seeker. C. as in Anon.'s The Tramp Exposed, 1878, ' The ragsooker, an instrument attached to the end of a long pole for removing clothes-pins from the lines, and afterwards dragging the released clothes over the fence.' Cf. *angler.

rag-splawger. A rich man : low (if not orig. c.) : ca. 1858–1900. H., 1st ed., 1859 ; Baumann. Gen. ' used in conversation to avoid direct mention of names '. Also rag-gorger or (Vaux) gorgy : low (perhaps orig. c.) : ca. 1820–1900. See gorger.

rag-stabber. A tailor : from ca. 1870 ; ob. Also stab-rag, q.v. Cf. snip, q.v.

rag-stick. An umbrella, esp. if ' loose and unreefed ' : lower classes' (— 1909). Ware.

rag-tacker. A coach-trimmer : ca. 1820–70.— 2. A dressmaker : ca. 1850–1920.

rag-tailed. Tattered ; of, or like, a ragamuffin : coll. (— 1887). Baumann.

rag-time, adj. Merry : coll. : from 1901 or 1902. —2. Haphazard ; carelessly happy-go-lucky ; farcical : coll. : from ca. 1910. Esp. in a rag-time army : military coll. : from 1915. Cf. Fred Karno's army. B. & P. Cf. the naval coll., from 1915, rag-time navy, esp. of the auxiliary patrol during the G.W. : Bowen. Cf. :

rag-time girl. A sweetheart ; a girl with whom one has a joyous time ; a harlot : all, from 1901 or 1902. Ex rag-time (music) = jazz. Cf. jazz.

rag-trade. The purchasing of false bank-notes, which are then palmed off on strangers : 1843, Marryat : mostly U.S. : ob.—2. Tailoring ; dressmaking ; the dry-goods trade in gen. : from ca. 1880 : coll. Barrère & Leland.

rag-waggon. A sailing-ship : steam or turbine, esp. if Australian (or American) : seamen's pejorative : from ca. 1910. Bowen. I.e. rag, set of sails.

rag-water. Any inferior spirits : late C. 17–early 19. B.E.—2. Esp. gin : ca. 1780–1850. Grose, 2nd ed., ' These liquors seldom failing to reduce those that drink [such spirits] to rags ' : which is not an etymology but a pun.

ragaboneshop. See rag-and-bone shop, 2.

rage, the. The fashion or vogue : 1785, The New Rosciad, ' 'Tis the rage in this great raging Nation, | Who wou'd live and not be in the fashion ? ' Coll. till ca. 1850, then S.E. Cf. go.

rager. An old, fierce ' bullock or cow that always begins to rage in the stock-yard ', Morris : Australian coll. : 1884, ' Rolf Boldrewood '.

ragged. Collapsed : rowing s., says F. & H., 1902 ; but † by 1920.—2. Inferior, wretched (game, form, display) : coll. (— 1887) ; from ca. 1920, verging on S.E. Baumann.—3. (Of time, a period) wretched, unfortunate, ill-starred : coll. (— 1887). Baumann, ' A ragged week '.

ragged-arse, adj. Tattered ; fig., disreputable, ruined : a vulg. : from ca. 1880.

Ragged Brigade, the. The 13th Hussars : military : C. 19–20 ; ob. (In early C. 19, also the 14th Hussars). Ex their tattered uniforms. F. & Gibbons. Also the Evergreens, Green Dragons, and Great Runaway Prestonpans.

ragged robin. A keeper's follower : New Forest s. or dial. : from ca. 1860. (Rare in singular.)

ragged soph. See soph.

ragger. One given to ' ragging ' (see rag, v., 1) schools' (—1923). Manchon.

raggery. Clothes, esp. women's : coll. bordering on S.E. : very ob. Thackeray, 1855, ' Old hags . . . draped in majestic raggery '. Cf. Fr. chiffons.

raggie, raggy. A particular friend (ex the sharing of brass-cleaning rags : Bowen) ; but gen. in pl., as be raggies, to be steady chums : naval (— 1909). Ware implies that it is mildly pejorative.

raggy, adj. Annoyed, ' shirty ' : 1900, G. Swift (O.E.D. Sup.). Ex rag out, get one's.

raging favourite. A coll. variant (— 1887) of a hot favourite. Baumann.

rags. See rag, n., 4.—2. rags, go. See rag, v., c. sense. H., 3rd ed.—3. ' Old lace used for decorative purposes ' : art s. verging on coll. and j. : from ca. 1880 ; ob. Ware.—4. A steward in charge of the linen : nautical : late C. 19–20. Bowen.—5. A low-class harlot : proletarian (— 1935).

rags, flash one's. To display, gen. ostentatiously, one's bank notes : low (? orig. c.) : from ca. 1860.

rags, glad. See glad rags.

rags a gallop, tip one's. To move ; depart, esp. if hastily : low : 1870, Hazlewood & Williams, in Leave It to Me, ' I see ; told you to tip your rags a gallop, and you won't go.' Here tip = give.

rags and bones. The Salvage Corps ; a member thereof ; an officer in charge thereof : military : 1915 ; ob. F. & Gibbons.

rags and jags. Tatters : coll. : from ca. 1860 ; very ob.

rags and sticks. A travelling outfit : showmen's and low theatrical : from ca. 1870. Hindley, 1876, ' Rags and sticks, as a theatrical booth is always termed '.

rah ! A coll. abbr. of hurrah ! : orig. and mainly U.S., anglicised ca. 1910. N.b., rah ! (shouted thrice) forms the termination of the Maori war-cry, now—and since late C. 19—affected by Maori and other New Zealand Rugby teams.

rail-bird. A tout watcher of race-horses being exercised : sporting, esp. turf : from ca. 1890 ; slightly ob. Ex his vantage-point on gate or hurdle. (Ware.)

railings, count the. To go hungry : low : from ca. 1860 ; slightly ob. See also Spitalfields breakfast.

railly. Really : a sol. (or an ignorantly affected) pronunciation (— 1887). Baumann.

railroading. See jarring.

rails. See head rails.—2. rails, dish of. ' A lecture, jobation, or scolding from a married woman to her husband ', Grose, 1st ed. (where misplaced) : late C. 18–mid-19.—3. Railway stocks and shares. Stock Exchange coll. (—1887). Baumann, ' home —s, englische Eisenbahnaktien '.

rails, front. The teeth : low : C. 19–20 ; slightly ob. Also head-rails, q.v.

rails, off the. Not in normal or proper state or condition ; ' morally or mentally astray ' : 1859, Gen. P. Thomson : coll. >, ca. 1910, S.E. Ex railway phraseology. (O.E.D.)

Railway Men, the. Swindon Football Club (' soccer ') : sporting : C. 20. A noted railway junction. Cf. Biscuit Men and Toffee Men.

railways. Red stockings worn by women : railwaymen's (—1909). Ware. Ex red signal.

rain, (know enough to) get out of the. To (be shrewd enough to) look after oneself, e.g. to refrain from meddling : to be common-sensical : coll. : 1848, Durivage, 'Ham was one of 'em—he was. He knew sufficient to get out of the rain'; but anticipated by H. Buttes in 1599 : ' Fooles . . . have the wit to keep themselves out of the raine' (O.E.D.). In Australia, *to keep out of the rain* (C. J. Dennis) : cf. U.S. *go in when it rains.*—2. Hence, *get out of the rain*, 'to absent oneself when there's likely to be any trouble' (Lyell) : coll. : C. 20.

rain, right as. See **right as . . .**

rain-napper. An umbrella : low : ca. 1820–1910. Moncrieff, 1823 ; H., 1874 ; Baumann.

rain trams and omnibuses. A coll. variant (–1923) of *rain cats and dogs.* Manchon.

rainbow. A discoloured bruise : from ca. 1810 ; ob. (O.E.D.) An excellent example of what G. K. Chesterton well names the poetry of slang.— 2. A mistress : ca. 1820–70. Egan, *Life in London,* 1821, 'The pink of the ton and his rainbow.' Because dressed in a variety of colours.—3. A foot-man : from ca. 1820 ; very ob. Egan, ibid., ' It was the custom of Logic never to permit the Rain-bow to announce him.' Abbr. *rainbow, knight of the,* q.v.—4. A pattern-book : ca. 1820–60. Egan, ibid. Ex the variety of colours.—5. A sovereign : costers' : from ca. 1850 ; ob. Perhaps suggested by *rhino,* for *rainbow* is in Costerese pronounced *rinebo* ; perhaps, however, ex rainbow as a sign of better weather—as a sovereign is of better times.— 6. A post-Armistice reinforcement or recruit : mili-tary : late 1918–19. F. & Gibbons, ' As arriving after the storm was over '.

rainbow, knight of the. A footman in livery. Grose, 1785. See **knight.**

rains, the. The rainy season : Anglo-Indian coll. (in C. 20, S.E.) : 1616, Sir T. Roe. Yule & Burnell.

Rainy Day Smith. J. T. Smith (1766–1833) : from 1845, when his fascinating *Book for a Rainy Day* was published ; it was reprinted, with excellent notes by ' John o' London ' (W. Whitten).

raise. A rise in salary : coll. : late C. 19–20. Ex U.S. sense, an(y) improvement (1728 : O.E.D. Sup.).

raise, v.i. To rise : in late C. 19–20 ranked as sol. ' The ball didn't raise an inch.'

raise a barney. See **rise a barney.—raise Cain.** See **Cain.**

raise-mountain. A boaster : coll. : ? C. 17–18. F. & H.

Rajah, the. The Mogul (place of entertainment) : Drury Lane district : ca. 1850–80. Ware.

rake. A comb : jocular : from ca. 1860. Also, *garden-rake* and, ca. 1840–60, *raker* : low, says Ware.

***rake, v.i. and t.** To steal from a letter-box : c. (– 1933). Charles E. Leach. Gen. as vbl.n. (*raking*).

rake-jakes. A blackguard : C. 18–20 ; ob. Rhyming on *jakes,* q.v. Cf. S.E. *rake-kennel.*

rake off. A(n unlawful) profit ; a commission : orig. (1899), U.S. ; anglicised as coll. ca. 1920. Thornton ; O.E.D. (Sup.).

rake out. To coït with (a woman) : low : C. 19–20.

rake the pot. To take the stakes : racing : from ca. 1825. See **pot, n., 1.**

raked fore and aft. Desperately in love : naval : late C. 19–20. Ex damage done by well-directed shelling. (Ware.)

raker. A very fast pace : coll. : 1876 (S.O.D.). Perhaps ex *rake,* (of hunting dogs) to run head down. —2. A heavy bet : sporting : 1869, Bradwood, *The O.V.H.* (O.E.D.) ; 1884, Hawley Smart, in *From Post to Finish* ; 1891, *The Sportsman,* March 25, ' Jennings . . . stood to win a raker . . . over Lord George.' Esp. in *go a raker* (cf. sense 1), to bet heavily or, more gen., recklessly (1869).—3. See **rake, n.—4.** A good stroke : golfers' coll. : 1899 (O.E.D. Sup.).

rakes, carry heavy. To swagger ; put on ' side ' : C. 17 coll. Terence in English, 1614.

***raking.** See **rake, v.**

ral, the. The admiral : naval (– 1909). Ware.

rally-o(h)! Proceed vigorously : *Conway* c.p. of encouragement (– 1891). John Masefield's history of the *Conway* training ship, 1933.

Ralph, ralph. See **rafe.—2.** In printers' s., from ca. 1860, ob. by 1930, ' The supposed author of the tricks played upon a recalcitrant member of a *chapel* (q.v.) ', F. & H.

Ralph Spooner. A fool : coll. : late C. 17–early 19. B.E. ; Grose, 1st ed. In Suffolk dial., *Ralph* or *Rafe* means the same thing (E.D.D.).

ram. An act of coïtion : low : C. 19–20. Cf. S.E. *ram-rod,* the penis. Ex v., 1.—2. A crowd ; a crush : Shrewsbury School : from ca. 1880. (Desmond Coke, *The Bending of a Twig,* 1906.) Ex the force of a battering ram. Cf. v., 2.

ram. To coït with (a woman) : low : C. 19–20. Cf. *poke* and *ride.*—2. V.t., to get (a boy) off a punishment : Shrewsbury School : from ca. 1880. (D. Coke, *The Bending of a Twig,* 1906.)

ram and dam(n). A muzzle-loading gun : jocular coll. : 1866 ; ob. (O.E.D.)

ram booze. See **rum booze.**

***ram-cat ; ram-cat cove.** A man wearing furs : c. : from ca. 1860. Ex *ram-cat,* a he cat.

ram-jam. A surfeit : s. and dial. : from ca. 1885. Ex *ram-jam full,* q.v.

ram-jam, v. To stuff (esp. with food) : from ca. 1885. Ex :

ram-jam full. Packed absolutely full : dial. and (mostly U.S.) s. : 1879, Waugh. O.E.D.

ram-reel. A dance, men only : Scots coll. (in C. 20, S.E.) : C. 19–20. D. Anderson, 1813, ' The chairs they coup, they hurl an' loup, | A ram-reel now they're wantin''. Cf. *bull-dance* and *stag-party.*

ram-rod. A ball bowled along the ground : Winchester School : from ca. 1840. (Also *ray-monder.*) Mansfield. Ex the straightness of its ' flight '.

Ramsammy or r. A Hindu : Southern India. An Indian coolie in Ceylon : Ceylon. This coll. (– 1886) is a corruption of *Ramaswami,* a frequent Hindu surname in Southern India. Yule & Burnell. —2. Whence, in Natal and the Cape, this word is used as a generic name for Indian coolies ', Pett-mann, *Africanderisms,* 1913.

rambounge. 'A severe brush of labour ', Jamie-son : Scots : late C. 18–mid-19. This *ram* is the dial. prefix = strong ; very. Cf. :

rambustious, ramgumption. See **rumbustious, rumgumption.** (Cf. U.S. *rambunctious,* 1854. Thornton.)

ramfeezled. Exhausted, worn out : mostly dial., whence, in C. 1890–1910, coll.

ramiram. Incorrect for *ramizan, ramadan* : C. 19–20. O.E.D.

ramjollock. To shuffle (cards) : C. 19. ? lit.,

jumble well. Also late C. 19–20 Shropshire dial. : E.D.D.

rammaged. Tipsy : Scots coll. (F. & H.) or, more prob., dial. : late C. 18–20. Ex *ramished*.

rammed up, ppl.adj. Crowded ; chock-a-block : Public Schools' : C. 20. Desmond Coke, *The School across the Road*, 1910. Ex *ram*, v., 2.

*rammer. An arm : c. : late C. 18–20 ; ob. Grose, 2nd ed.

ramming. Forceful, pushing : 1825, *The Sporting Magazine*, 'The most ramming . . . cove you ever saw perform ', O.E.D. ; ob. by 1900, virtually † by 1930. Ex *ram*, the animal.

rammo. The former naval evolution, 'Prepare aloft for action ' : bluejackets' : late C. 18–mid-19. Bowen. Ex *ramming a ship*.

rammy. A ' row ', quarrel, altercation : Glasgow (— 1934). Perhaps ex *on the rampage*.

Ramnuggar Boys, the. The 14th (King's) Hussars : military : from 1848 ; ob. In this battle, they bravely encountered tremendous odds. F. & Gibbons. Also *the Emperor's Chambermaids*.

*ramp. A robbery with violence : c. : Vaux, 1812 ; ob. Moncrieff, 1830, 'And ramp so plummy '. Ex *ramp*, to storm, rage, violently, or v.t., to snatch, tear.—2. A swindle : c. >, by 1905, s. : from ca. 1880. G. R. Sims.—3. Hence, a swindle ' depending on an artificial boom in prices ' : 1922. S.O.D.—4. A footpad and garrotter : c. : from ca. 1870 ; ob. Cf. *ramper*.—5. A race-course trickster : c. : from ca. 1860. Also, *rampsman* (H., 1st ed., 1859) and *ramper*, as in H., 5th ed., 1874, and in Runciman's *Chequers*, 1876, 'A man who is a racecourse thief and ramper hailed me affably ' : cf. the quotation at *ramper.*—6. A hall-mark : c. : 1879, Horsley. Ex the rampant lion forming part of the essay stamp for gold and silver (F. & H.).—7. See **ramps.**—8. A parody : a skit : book-world : 1934.—9. A counter (in a shop, etc.) : c. (— 1935). David Hume. One climbs over it.

*ramp, v.t. To thieve or rob with violence : c. (— 1811) >, ca. 1860, low s. *Lex. Bal.* ; Vaux ; H., 1st ed. See **ramp,** n., 1, for origin. Cf. *rank* and *rant*, hereinunder.—2. Esp. to force (a person) to pay an alleged debt : c. : 1897, *The Daily News*, Sept. 3, ' Charge of " ramping " a book-maker ', O.E.D. ; but it must be at least as early as the horse-racing sense of *ramper* (see **ramp,** n., 4).—3. To change the colour of (a horse) : c. (— 1933). Charles E. Leach.

*ramp, on the. Engaged in swindling : c. : late C. 19–20. Manchon. — 2. On a ' spree ' : low (— 1923). Ibid. — 3. Finding fault : Glasgow (— 1934).

rampacious. An illiterate form of S.E. *rampageous*. Manchon.—2. Hence, mad : lower classes' (— 1923). Manchon.

*ramper and ***rampsman.** See **ramp,** n., 5. Cf. *The Daily News*, Oct. 12, 1887, ' " Rampers ", i.e. men who claimed to have made bets to bookmakers, and hustled and surrounded them if they refused to pay ' (O.E.D.). Cf. *ramping.*—2. (**ramper** only.) A noisy, turbulent street-ranger, esp. if a youth : low London (— 1909) ; ob. Ware.

*ramping. The practice described in sense 1 of preceding entry : c. (— 1891) >, by 1905, s.

ramping, adj. and adv. Rampant(ly) : lower classes' coll. (— 1887). Baumann has *ramping mad*.

*ramps. A got-up quarrel or ' row ' to cover a theft or a swindle : c. (— 1923). Manchon. Cf. *ramp,* n., 1 and 2.

ramps, the. A brothel : Regular Army's : late C. 19–20. B. & P. Perhaps ex *rampant* or *on the rampage.*

*rampsman. See **ramper.—ramrod.** See **ram-rod.**

ramrod-bunger. An infantryman : military (— 1923). Manchon.

Rams, the. Derby County ' soccer ' team : sporting : late C. 19–20. Ex the famous breed of Derbyshire rams.

ram's challenge. See **give the ram's challenge**

ram's horn. One who shouts as he talks : coll. (— 1923). Manchon.

Ramsgate Jimmy. Ranjitsinhji (see **Ranji**) : Cockneys' nickname : 1893 ; † by 1930. See esp. Roland Wild, *Ranji*, 1934. By ' Hobson-Jobson.'

*ran-cat cove. See **ram-cat.—ran-tan, on the.** See **rantan.**

rancid. Very objectionable or unpleasant : upper classes' : from ca. 1910. Barry Pain, *Stories in Grey*, 1912, ' Black kid gloves, the most rancid form of gloves ' ; E. F. Benson, *David of King's*, 1924, ' How frightfully rancid ! ' ; John G. Brandon, *The One-Minute Murder*, 1934. Prob. after *putrid*, q.v.

Randal's-man or **randlesman.** A green handkerchief white-spotted : pugilistic (— 1839) ; ob. Ex the colours of Jack Randal, the famous early C. 19 boxer. (Brandon.)

randan. See **rantan.**

random-(or random-)tandem. Three horses driven tandem : from ca. 1870 : coll. >, ca. 1890, S.E. ; ob. Ex :—2. Adv. In that manner in which three horses are harnessed tandem : 1805 : coll. >, by 1870, S.E. Ex S.E. *randan* on *tandem*. Also, as in H., 1860, *random*.

randle. ' A set of nonsense verses, repeated in Ireland by school boys, and young people, who have been guilty of breaking wind backwards, before any of their companions ; if they neglect this apology, they are liable to certain kicks, pinches, and fillips, which are accompanied with diverse admonitory couplets,' Grose, 1785 ; ob. by 1880, † by 1930. Whence :

randle, v. To punish (a schoolboy) for breaking wind : C. 19. Halliwell. Ex preceding.—2. See **randling** which is much commoner than the v. proper.

randlesman. See **Randal's-man.**

randling. The punishment, by hair-pulling, of an apprentice refusing to join his fellows in taking a holiday : mostly at Birkenhead : 1879, *Notes and Queries*. Ob.

random. See **randem-tandem.**

Randy. Lord Randolph Churchill : nickname (— 1887) ; † by 1920. Baumann.

randy. Violent ; esp. sexually warm, lecherous : from ca. 1780 : dial. and coll. ; in C. 20, mainly dial. Burns, 1785 ; *Lex. Bal.*, 1811 ; Halliwell 1847 ; E.D.D. ? ex *rand*, to rave.

randy beggar. A Gypsy tinker : Northern coll. (— 1874) and dial. (— 1806). H., 5th ed. ; E.D.D. Ex preceding.

randy Richard. See **Richard,** 2.

randyvoo. A tavern that is the resort of recruiting sergeants : military (— 1909). Ware.—2. Hence, noise and wrangling : mostly military (— 1909). Ware. Ex *rendez-vous*.

ranger. The penis : low : C. 18–20. Ex *range*, to be inconstant.—2. See **Atlantic ranger.**

Rangers, the. The Connaught Rangers : military coll. (C. 19), now S.E. (F. & Gibbons.)

[**ranging,** n. 'Intriguing, enjoying many Women' is S.E.: not, as B.E. says, c.]

rangling. Misprint in *Lex. Bal.* and Egan's Grose for the preceding.

*rank. To cheat: c. and low s. (— 1864). H., 3rd ed. Prob. *ramp* corrupted, with some influence exercised by U.S. *outrank*, 1842, and *rank*, 1860, to take precedence of (Thornton). Cf. *rant*.

rank and riches; or hyphenated. Breeches: rhyming s.: 1887, 'Dagonet' Sims.

rank and smell. A common person: lower classes': ca. 1870–1905. Ware. Punning *rank*, smelly and (*high*) *rank* + '*swell*'.

[**rank-rider,** highwayman, jockey: S.E., says O.E.D.; c., says B.E.: the former, right.]

ranker. An officer risen from the ranks: 1874, H., 5th ed.; 1878, Besant & Rice, 'Every regiment has its rankers; every ranker his story': coll. till ca. 1915, then S.E.—2. A corruption of *rank duffer*: low London: from ca. 1870; ob. H., 5th ed.

rant. To appropriate forcibly: low (— 1887). Walford's *Antiquarian*. Corruption of *ramp*, v.— 2. To be unduly free with (females): low (— 1887). Ibid. Perhaps ex *ramp*, v., 1, influenced by S.E.; *rantipole*, v.; more prob. a dial. form of *rend* (see E.D.D.).

rantallion. 'One whose scrotum is so relaxed as to be longer than his penis', Grose, 1st ed.: low: ca. 1780–1850. Cognate with, perhaps even a blend of, '*rantipole*' and '*rapscallion*', so closely related to each other in meaning.

, rantan; ran-tan. Also **randan.** A spree: from ca. 1710: coll. >, in C. 19, S.E. except as in the next entry; by itself, *randan* (etc.) is extremely ob. ? ex *at random*.—2. Hence, a riotous person: coll. soon > S.E.: 1809; ob. by 1890, † by 1920. (O.E.D.)

rantan, on the. On the spree; drunk: coll.: from ca. 1760; slightly ob.; since 1853, gen. in the form, *on the ran-tan*. See preceding.

rantipole, ride. Same as *ride St George* (see **riding** . . .). Low: late C. 18–19. Grose, 2nd ed.

rantum-scantum. Copulation, esp. in *play at r.-s.* (Grose, 2nd ed.): low: mid-C. 18–early 19. ? a rhyming combination ex † S.E. *rant*, to be boisterous or noisily gay; cognate with *rantipole*.—2. A wordy and mutual recrimination: low: ca. 1820–95. 'Jon Bee'; Baumann.

Ranzo. 'A native of the Azores, from the number named Alonzo who shipped in the whalers, where "Rueben [*sic*] Ranzo" was a favourite shanty': nautical coll.: mid-C. 19–20. Bowen.

rap, n. See **rap, on the,** and **rap, take the.**—3. A charge; a cause: c.: C. 20. James Curtis, *The Gilt Kid*, 1936, 'That is if they did not do [*arrest*] him on this murder rap.'

rap, v.t. To barter; 'swop': late C. 17–20: s. († by 1850) and dial. B.E.; Grose, 1st ed. Perhaps ex ob. S.E. sense, to transport, remove.—2. V.i., to take a false oath: c.: from ca. 1740; † by 1890. Fielding, in *Jonathan Wild*, 'He [is] a pitiful fellow who would stick at a little rapping for a friend'; Id., *Amelia*, I, ch. X, the footnote establishing the c. origin; Grose, 2nd ed. Perhaps ex *rap (out) an oath*.—3. Also, v.t., to swear (something, *against* a person): 1733, Budgell, 'He ask'd me what they had to rap against me, I told them only a Tankard.' O.E.D.—4. To knock out; to kill: c., esp. Australian > low s.: 1888, Rolf Boldrewood, 'If he tries to draw a weapon, or move ever so little,

he's rapped at that second'; ob. Ex Scots *rap*, 'to knock heavily; to strike', E.D.D.

rap, not care a. To care not at all: 1834: coll. >, ca. 1850, S.E. Ex *rap*, an Irish counterfeit halfpenny.

rap, on the. On a bout of dissipation; slightly drunk: low (— 1893). Milliken, 'The way the passengers stared at me showed I was fair on the rap.'

*rap, take the. To be (punished or) imprisoned, esp. for another: orig. (late C. 19 or first decade of C. 20), U.S.; anglicised ca. 1920: low s. verging on c.

rape. A pear: back s. (— 1859). H., 1st ed.

rapped, ppl.adj. Ruined: from ca. 1870; ob.— 2. (Killed) dead: low (? orig. c.): from ca. 1888. See **rap**, v., last sense.

[**rapper,** an arrant lie: S.E., declares O.E.D.; coll., F. & H. Arising early in C. 17, this sense is prob. best considered as coll. until ca. 1850, then S.E.; in C. 20, it is mostly dial. See esp. Grose, P.]

rapping. Perjury: mid-C. 18–19. 'Ducange Anglicus.' See **rap**, v., 2 and 3.

rare. Excellent, fine, splendid, as applied to comparatively trivial objects; often ironically. Coll.: 1596, Shakespeare, 'Master Bassanio, who indeed gives rare new liveries'; 1878, Mrs. Henry Wood, 'Guy will about die of it . . . Rare fun if he does.'—2. As an intensive: coll.: 1833, Harriet Martineau, 'They put me in a rare passion.' (Both senses, O.E.D.) Cf.:

rare and (another adj.) A coll. intensive: 1848, Mrs. Gaskell, 'We got a good supper, and grew rare and sleepy,' O.E.D.; slightly ob. except in Northern dial.

rarebit, Welsh. Welsh rabbit: this sol. would seem to have been inaugurated by Grose in 1785: 'A Welsh rabbit, bread and cheese toasted, i.e. a Welsh rare bit.' With *Welsh rabbit* cf. *Bombay duck*; for alteration, cf. *catsup* for *ketchup*. (W.)

rarefied. Tamed, subdued: Society: ca. 1855–90. Ware. Ex one *Rarey* (1828–66), a horse-tamer.

rarely or ever. Almost never: a catachresis caused by a confusion of *rarely if ever* and *rarely or never*: 1768, Anon., 'But those schemes . . . rarely or ever answer the end.' O.E.D.

rarified. A frequent error for *rarefied*.

rarze(r). A 'raspberry' (sense 1): theatrical: C. 20. B. & P. (at *raspberry* in 3rd ed.). By 'the Oxford -er'. Also spelt *ras* in its shorter form.

rascal. 'A man without genitals', Grose, 1785: low: ca. 1750–1850. Ex deer.

rasher of bacon. Some fiery liquor: ca. 1750–70. Toldervy, 1756. See quotation at **slug**, n., 1.

rasher of wind. A very thin person: from ca. 1860; slightly ob. Cf. *yard of pump-water*.—2. Any person or thing of negligible account: from ca. 1890. *The Daily Telegraph*, April 7, 1899, 'Lets 'em howl, an' sweat, an' die, an' goes on all the time, as if they was jest rashers o' wind'.

rasp. The female pudend: low: C. 19–20; ob. —2. See **rasp, do a.**

rasp, v.i. and t. To coït (with): low: C. 19–20; ob. Rare compared with:

rasp, do a. To coït: low: C. 19–20. Gen. of the male: for semantics, see **pucker-water**, which not only astringes but roughens and hardens.

rasp, get the. A variant of *berry, get the*.

Raspberries, the. The King's Royal Rifle Corps: military: late C. 19–20. F. & Gibbons. Ex the colour of their (former) facings.

raspberry. A disapproving, fart-like noise, described by F. & H. as stable s., but gen. considered to be theatrical of late C. 19-20. Ex *raspberry-tart*, 1. Cf. *rarzer*.—2. Hence, a gesture or a sign made in disapproval : theatrical : from the middle 1890's.—3. Abbr. *raspberry-tart*, 2 : low, mainly military : late C. 19-20.

raspberry, get or **give the.** To ' get the bird ', to be ' hissed ' ; to ' hiss ' : theatrical : late C. 19-20. Mainly and properly when the disapprobation is shown by a *raspberry*, 1.

raspberry, old. See **old raspberry.**

raspberry-tart. A breaking of wind : low rhyming s. on *fart* : from ca. 1875.—2. The heart : rhyming s. : from ca. 1890. ' Pomes ' Marshall, in the *Sporting Times*, Oct. 29, 1892, ' Then I sallied forth with a careless air, | And contented raspberry-tart.' (In U.S., though now ob., a dainty girl : cf. Eng. *jam-tart*.)

rasper. A difficult high fence : hunting s. (1812) >, ca. 1840, j. >, ca. 1870, S.E. (O.E.D.) Ainsworth, 1834, ' A stiff fence, captain—a reg'lar rasper '.—2. ' A person or thing of sharp, harsh, or unpleasant character ' : 1839, Dickens, ' He's what you may a-call a rasper, is Nickleby.' O.E.D.—3. Anything that, in its own way, is extraordinary ; e.g. a large profit on the Stock Exchange : from ca. 1860.—4. In cricket, a ball that, on leaving the bat, glides ' fiercely ' along the ground (e.g. from a slashing stroke by McCabe): from not later than 1910. Cf. *rasping shorter*.

***raspin, the.** A house of correction ; a gaol : c. : early C. 19. ? lit., the unpleasant thing, perhaps a pun on *grating*, adj., and *gratings*, n. Cf. the † Scots *rasp-house*, as in Scott, 1818 (E.D.D.).

rasping. (High and) difficult to jump : 1829 (O.E.D.) : hunting coll. >, ca. 1870, S.E. Dr J. Brown, 1858, ' You cannot . . . make him keep his seat over a rasping fence.' See **rasper**, 1.

***rasping gang.** ' The mob of roughs and thieves who attend prize-fights ', H., 1864 : c. ; ob.

rasping shorter. The same as *rasper* (last sense), of which it is the earlier form : a cricketing coll. of ca. 1900-20. F. & H.

rasted, adj. and adv. ' Blasted ', of which it is a euphemistic perversion : 1919, J. B. Morton (O.E.D. Sup.).

***rat.** A drunken person taken into custody : c. : late C. 17-early 19. B.E. ; Grose, 1st ed. ? ex idea of a drowned rat or, more prob., ex *drunk as a rat*, q.v.—2. A clergyman : C. 17. ' Microcosmography ' Earle, ' A profane man . . . nicknames clergyman . . . rat, black-coat, and the like.' Prob. current also in C. 18, since Grose puns thus : ' *Rats*. Of these there are the following kinds : a black rat and a grey rat, a py-rat and a cu-rat,' esp. as, in C. 17-early 18, *rat* occ. designated a pirate.— 3. A police spy : c. : from ca. 1850. Ex the gen. term of contempt.—4. An infernal machine for the foundering of insured bottoms : nautical coll. (from ca. 1880) > j. Barrère & Leland.—5. See **rats** and **rats** !—6. In Australia, ' a street urchin ; a wharf labourer ', C. J. Dennis : late C. 19-20.—7. A workman that has not served his time and can, therefore, enter no union : artisans' (— 1909). Ware.—8. A thief : c. : from ca. 1920. E.g. in Edgar Wallace, *The Twister*, 1928.—9. (the **Rat.**) Sir R. Ratcliffe, a C. 15 statesman. Dawson.

rat, v.t. To steal or rob ; to search the body of (a dead man) : military : 1914. F. & Gibbons.—2. See **rat it.**

rat it. ' To run away quickly ', E.D.D. : Berkshire s. (— 1903), not dial.

rat !, rat it ! or **rat me !** A low coll. imprecation : late C. 17-20 ; ob. Vanbrugh, Hoadly, Thackeray, Conan Doyle. Ex *rot*. Cf. *drat !* O.E.D.

rat, do a. To change one's tactics : coll. : from ca. 1860. Ex S.E. *rat*, to desert.

rat, drunk as a. Hopelessly tipsy : coll. : mid-C. 16-17. Boorde, 1542.

rat, smell a. See **smell a rat.**

rat and mouse. A house : rhyming s. : late C. 19-20. B. & P.

rat back-clip. Short hair : lower classes' : ca. 1856-1900. Ware.

rat-catcher. Unconventional hunting dress : hunting people's (— 1930). O.E.D. (Sup.).

rat-firm, -house, -office, -shop. A workshop, etc., where less than full union rates are paid : trades unions' coll. (— 1888) >, in C. 20, S.E.

rat-hole. Too large a gap between printed words : printer's : from ca. 1870.

rat it ! ; **rat me !** See **rat !**—**rat-office.** See **rat-firm.**

rat-shop. A shop or factory that employs non-union workers : lower classes' : from ca. 1910. Manchon. See also **rat-firm.**

rat-trap. A bustle or dress-improver : ca. 1850-80. Cf. *bird-cage*, q.v.—2. The brake on a bicycle : cyclists' (— 1923). Manchon. Cf.—? ex—Fr. *rat-trappe-pédales*.—3. The mouth : lower classes' (— 1923). Manchon.

ratch. An incorrect form of †*rotch* : late C. 17. O.E.D.

***ratepayers' hotel.** A workhouse : tramps' c. (— 1935). Workhouses are maintained out of the rates and taxes.

rather ! (In replying to a question) I should think so ; very decidedly : coll., orig. somewhat low : 1836, Dickens, ' " Do you know the mayor's house ? " inquired Mr Trott. " Rather," replied the boots, significantly, as if he had some good reason for remembering it.' Occ. *rayther*, from ca. 1860 : very affected ; ob. by 1905, † by 1920. Cf. the very genteel *quite*, q.v. Often emphasised as in Denis Mackail, *Greenery Street*, 1925, ' " Rather," said Ian enthusiastically, " Oh, rather ! " '

rather of the ratherest. Slightly in excess or deficit : dial. and coll. : 1787, Grose's *Provincial Glossary* ; 1860, H., 2nd ed. Ob. by 1920, virtually † by 1935.

ratherish, adv. Slightly ; somewhat : coll., orig. U.S. (1862), anglicised ca. 1890. Ob. (O.E.D.).

rations. A flogging : naval and military : ca. 1880-1910. See **iron rations.**

rats. A star : back s. : from ca. 1875. (Not very gen.)—2. See **rats, get.**—3. **the rats**, delirium tremens : from ca. 1865. Ex *rats*, (have or) *see*, q.v.

rats ! A contemptuous retort = ' bosh ! ' : (low) coll. : orig. U.S., but anglicised ca. 1891. ' Pomes ' Marshall, ' One word, and that was Rats ! ' Prob. ex the following :

rats and mice. Dice : from ca. 1870. (P. P., *Rhyming Slang*, 1932.)

rats, get or **have** or **see.** To be out of sorts (rarely with *see*) : 1865, E. Yates, ' " Well . . . old boy, how are you ? " . . . " . . . Not very brilliant . . ." " Ah, like me, got rats, haven't you ? " '—2. To be drunk ; very drunk : from ca. 1865. Likewise ob., very ob.—3. (Rarely *get* or *have*.) To have delirium tremens : low : from ca. 1865.—4. Hence (though not with *get*), to be eccentric : (low) coll. :

from ca. 1880.—5. Hence, from ca. 1885, to be crazy.

rats, give (one) green. To malign; slander: ca. 1860–1910. Perhaps ex *rats : sick 'em !*, a call to a dog . . . Perhaps not.

Rats After Mouldy Cheese. The Royal Army Medical Corps: military: 1915; ob. F. & Gibbons.

rats in the garret or **loft** or **upper storey.** Eccentric; mad: from ca. 1890; ob. Prob. ex *bats in the belfry* and *rats, get* . . ., 3, 4, 5.

rat's-tail. A writ: legal: from ca. 1870. ? ex scroll on cover.

ratses'. Rats', esp. in *ratses' holes* : sol. (—1887). Baumann.

rattat. See **rutat.**

*rattle. A coach: c. late C. 18–early 19. Grose, 1785. Rare except in *rattle and pad*, a coach and horses. More gen. is *rattler*, q.v. : yet cf. *rattle, take.*—2. 'The commander's report of defaulters': naval: late C. 19–20. Bowen. Cf. the † S.E. *rattle*, a sharp reproof.—3. A quarrel: see 'Miscellanea' in Addenda.

rattle, v. To move or work quickly and/or noisily: s. and, from ca. 1850, dial.: late C. 17–20. Esp. in *rattle away* or *off*. B.E., who wrongly classifies as c.—2. (Also **rattle on.**) To strike (a person) in (the, e.g. *ivories*, teeth): c. (— 1923). Manchon.

rattle, be in the. To be a defaulter: naval: C. 20. F. & Gibbons. See **rattle**, n., 2.

rattle, spring the. (Of a policeman) to give the alarm: policemen's (— 1887); ob. Baumann.

*rattle, take. To depart hurriedly: c.: late C. 17–mid-18. B.E., ' *We'll take Rattle*, . . . we must not tarry, but whip away': a quotation that may possibly premise *rattle*, a coach, as early as late C. 17; otherwise we must suppose that *rattle*, v., has been substantivised.

rattle, with a. With unexpected rapidity: turf (— 1909). Coll. (Ware.)

rattle and drive (or hyphenated). Scamped work: workmen's coll. (— 1887). Baumann.

rattle-bag, devil's (Scots **deil's**). A bishop's summons: coll.: from ca. 1725; † by 1900. Scott.

rattle-ballocks. The female pudend: low: late C. 18–20; ob.

*rattle on. See **rattle**, v., 2.

*rattle one's cash. To 'stump up': c. (— 1923). Manchon.

rattled. Very drunk: coll.: late C. 19–20. Lyell. Cf. *floored*.

*rattler. A coach: early C. 17–mid-19 : c. >, ca. 1750, s.: 1630, J. Taylor the Water Poet; B.E.; Grose, 1st ed.; H. Like *rattle*, because it rattles.—2. Hence, a cab ; ca. 1815–1910 : Moore, 1819; Egan, 1821, 'At length a move was made, but not a rattler was to be had.'—3. A train: c. (1845 : ' *No. 747* ') >, by 1874 (H., 5th ed.), low ; in C. 20, mostly a bookmakers' term. Cf. *rattlers*, 2. —4. A bicycle: 1924, D. H. Lawrence (O.E.D. Sup.).—5. (**Rattler.**) The inevitable nickname of men surnamed Morgan: naval and military: C. 20. F. & Gibbons. Ex *Morgan Rattler* (or *r.*), common in dial. in various senses, e.g. anything first-rate (E.D.D.).

*rattler, mace the. To travel, esp. on a train, without a ticket: c.: mid-C. 19–20. (Manchon.)

rattlers. Teeth: s. > low coll.: C. 19–20; ob.— 2. A railway (— 1859); ob. by 1900, † by 1915. H., 1st ed. Cf. *rattler*, third sense.

rattles, the. A or the death-rattle: (low) coll.: from ca. 1820.—2. (With *the* often omitted.) The croup: somewhat coll.: C. 18–20.

rattletrap. The mouth: from ca. 1820. Scott. (O.E.D.)—2. A chatterbox: coll.: 1880, Anon., *Life in a Debtors' Prison*, ' You're as great a rattletrap as ever.' Both senses tend to be low; the former is somewhat ob.

*rattling cove. A coachman: c.: mid C. 17– early 19. Coles, 1676. Cf. *rattle*, n. and v. Cf. :

*rattling mumper. A beggar plying coaches and carriages: c.: mid C. 17–early 19. Coles; B.E.; Grose, 1st ed.

*rattling-peeper. A coach-glass: c.: mid-C. 18. *The Scoundrel's Dict.*, 1754.

ratty. Wretched, miserable; mean: orig. (— 1885), U.S. and Canadian, anglicised ca. 1900. *Blackwood's Magazine*, Nov., 1901, ' Both were pretty "ratty" from hardship and loneliness.' O.E.D. Ex lit. sense, infested with rats.—2. Angry, irritated: from ca. 1906. ? ex U.S.; cf. *rats in the garret* and *rats !*, qq.v. But prob. ex the appearance of a cornered rat.

raughty. See **rorty.**

rave. A strong liking; a craze; a passion: from ca. 1899; ob. by 1910, † by 1930. F. & H., 1901 (pub. 1902), ' X has a rave on Miss Z.' (Cf. *crush*, q.v.) Ex the ob. late C. 16–20 S.E. sense, a raving, a frenzy, excitement (O.E.D.).—2. Esp. of a warm friendship between school-girls: 1919, Arnold Lunn, *Loose Ends*. Cf. *pash*.

raven. A ' small bit of bread and cheese': taverns' (— 1909); ob. Ex the story of Elisha and the ravens. (Ware.)

' Ravilliac, any Assassin ', B.E.: coll.: ca. 1610– 1750. Properly *Ravaillac*. Ex François Ravaillac, who, the assassinator of Henry IV of France, died in 1610.

raw lobster. A policeman: C. 19. In contrast with *lobster*, a soldier.

raw meat. The penis: low coll.: mid-C. 18–20. Anon., *The Butcher* (a song), 1766.—2. A nude (female) performer of the sexual act: low: C. 19– 20; ob.

raw recruit. A nip of undiluted spirits: from ca. 1860; very ob.

raw stock. Coll., from ca. 1925, as in ' Moving-Picture Slang ', § 6 ; q.v.

raw uns or **'uns, the.** The naked fists: pugilistic: 1887, *The Daily News*, Sept. 15, ' This encounter was without gloves, or, in the elegant language of the ring, with the raw uns '; 1891, *Sporting Life*, March 26, ' Even Jean Carney . . . has been obliged to abandon the raw-un's for gloves pure and simple.' Slightly ob. (Here, *raw* = unprotected or uncovered.)

*ray. The sum of 1*s*. 6*d*.: c.: 1861, Mayhew. ? ex or cognate with the already long-† S.E. *ray*, a small piece of gold or gold leaf.

ray-neck. 'A landsman in a clipper packet's crew': nautical: mid-C. 19–20; ob. Bowen thinks that it may represent a corruption of *raw-neck*.

raymonder. See **ram-rod.**—**rayther.** See **rather.**

Razor. Smith, the English right-hand slow bowler prominent ca. 1910–26: cricketers'.

razor, real. ' A defiant, quarrelsome, or bad-tempered scholar': Westminster School: from 1883; ob. Ware.

razor-strop. A copy of a writ: legal: from some date after 1822, when the lit. sense appears (O.E.D.).

razors. Inferior liquor : Regular Army : late C. 19–20 ; very ob. F. & Gibbons. Ex the gripe it produces.

razoo. A small coin ; *razoos*, (human) testicles : New Zealanders' : C. 20. App. a corruption of the Maori *rahu*.

razzle. Abbr. of *razzle-dazzle*, 2. Esp. in *razzle, on the*, on the spree.

razzle-dazzle. 'A new type of roundabout . . . which gives its occupants the . . . sensations of an excursion at sea ', *The Daily News*, July 27, 1891 (O.E.D.) ; † by ca. 1915.—2. A frolic, a spree ; riotous jollity : U.S. (1890, Gunter), anglicised ca. 1895, esp. in *on the razzle-dazzle*, after ca. 1920 gen. abbr. to *on the razzle* and gen. of a drunken spree. Binstead, *More Gal's Gossip*, 1901, ' Bank-holidayites on the razzle-dazzle '. An echoic word expressive of rapid movement, bustle, active confusion, but orig., I think, a reduplication on *dazzle* as in Gunter's ' I'm going to razzle-dazzle the boys . . . with my great lightning change act,' 1890, in *Miss Nobody*.

razzle-dazzle, v. To dazzle : anglicised ca. 1895 ex U.S. ; ob. See preceding, 2. Cf. :

razzle-dazzler, gen. in pl. A sock that dazzles : 1897, *The Daily News*, Aug. 10, ' Two dozen pair of plain socks and half a dozen pair of the sort known as " razzle-dazzlers ",' O.E.D. Ex *razzle-dazzle*, v. Cf. *bobby-dazzler*, q.v.

razzo. The nose : c. : from ca. 1895. Clarence Rook, *The Hooligan Nights*, 1899 ; James Curtis, *The Gilt Kid*, 1936. Prob. fanciful ; cf. *boko*.

re, in the matter of, is considered rather low except in business letters (etc.) or when jocular. The full form *in re* is now ob.

re-dayboo. Re-début : music-halls' coll. : 1899– ca. 1903. Ware. Lit., a first appearance for the second time.

re-raw, occ. **ree-raw.** Esp. *on the re(e)-raw*. A drinking-bout : low : from ca. 1850 ; ob. Dickens, 1854 (O.E.D.). Prob. ex Scots *ree*, excited with drink, + Anglo-Irish *ree-raw*, noisy, riotous.

reach-me-down, adj, 1862 ; **reach-me-downs,** n., 1862. Thackeray ; Besant & Rice. Ready-made, or occ. second-hand, clothes ; in late C. 19–20, often of such, hence of any, trousers : perhaps always S.E. (ex U.S.). Coll. ; in C. 20, S.E. (O.E.D.).—2. Hence, anything improvised : coll. (— 1923). Manchon.

reacher. A beggar that walks always with a female mate : c. : early C. 17. Dekker.—2. A gross exaggeration, a ' stretcher ' : coll. : 1613, Purchas ; † by 1720. (O.E.D.)—3. A blow delivered at one's full reach : boxing : late C. 19–20 ; ob.

reaching !, excuse me. A lower-middle class c.p. uttered when one reaches for something at table : C. 20. Rather ob. Punning *retching*.

read, v.i. Rarely v.t. To steal : c. : Anon., *A Song*, ca. 1819, ' And I my reading learnt betime, | From studying pocket-books, Sirs.' Ex *reader*, 1, q.v.—2. To search (esp. a shirt) for lice : military : 1914 ; ob. F. & Gibbons. The shirt spread on one's knees resembled a newspaper being read in that position.

read and write. To fight : rhyming s. (— 1857). ' Ducange Anglicus.'—2. A flight : id. : ibid. Rare.

read between the lines. To discern the underlying fact or intention : from ca. 1865 : coll. till C. 20, then S.E.

read me and take me. (In reference to riddles) a Restoration c.p. equivalent to *get me ?* or *get me !* Dryden, *Marriage à la Mode*.

[**read of tripe.** Transported for life : rhyming s. (— 1859). H.'s approximation ; † by 1900.]

read the paper. To have a nap : coll. : from ca. 1860.

reader. A pocket-book : c. : 1718, C. Hitchin, *The Regulator* ; Grose, 2nd ed.—2. Whence, a newspaper, a letter, etc. : c. : from ca. 1840.—3. A marked card : c. or gamblers' s. : 1894, Maskelyne, ' The preparation of " faked " cards or " readers ",' O.E.D.

reader-hunter. A pickpocket specialising in pocket-books : c. (— 1812). Vaux. Ex *reader*, 1.

reader-merchant, gen. in pl. ' Pickpockets, chiefly young Jews, who ply about the Bank to steal the pocket-books of persons who have just received their dividends there,' Grose, 2nd ed. : late C. 18–20 ; ob. Ex *reader*, 1, and see **merchant.**

readered. Wanted by the police : c. : from ca. 1845. ' *No. 747* ' (p. 412). Ex *reader*, 2, and the fact of being ' advertised ' in *The Police Gazette*.

readies. Money in bank and/or currency notes : bank-clerks' (— 1935).

Readings. Shares in the Pennsylvania & Reading Railroad : Stock Exchange coll. (— 1895). A. J. Wilson, *Stock Exchange Glossary*.

***ready,* or the ready.** Money, esp. money in hand : c. until C. 19, then low s. till ca. 1870 ; by 1930, rather ob. Shadwell, ' Take up on the reversion . . . ; and Cheatly will help you to the ready ' ; Arbuthnot, 1712, ' He was not flush in ready ' ; Egan, 1821, ' The waste of ready '. Abbr. *ready money*. Often with *rhino* : *ready rhino* (T. Brown, 1697) is adumbrated in Shadwell's *the ready, the rhino* (1688).—2. See **readies.**

ready, v. To pull a horse so that he shall not win : racing : Black, 1887 (O.E.D.).—2. To give, illicitly, a drug to (a person) in order to render temporarily innocuous : c. : C. 20. E.g. in Edgar Wallace, *The Gunner*, 1928. Prob. ex sense 1, whence certainly :—3. To contrive, manipulate, engineer, ' wangle ' : from ca. 1890. ' Pomes ' Marshall, ' He made us all . . . believe he could ready his chance.' (Sense 1 is ex † S.E. sense, prepare, put in order.) Cf. *ready up*, q.v.—4. Hence, to bribe : low (— 1909). Ware.

ready, (at) a good. Thoroughly alert ; occ. dead certain : low (? orig. c.) : from ca. 1890 ; ob. Cf. *spot, on the,* 1.

ready gilt. Money (in hand) : a C. 19 variant of *ready*, n., (' Ducange Anglicus.') For *gilt*, cf. *gelt*.

Ready-Reckoners. The Highland regiments : Army : ca. 1850–90. H., 3rd ed. Ex the legendary Scots aptitude for reckoning money.

ready to drop. (Of a person) exhausted : late C. 19–20 : coll. >, by 1920, S.E. (Lyell)

ready-up. A conspiracy : Australian low s. (— 1926). Jice Doone. Ex :

ready up. To prepare, or contrive, illicitly or not honourably : Australian : 1893, *The Melbourne Age*, Nov. 25, ' A great deal has been " readied up " for the jury by the present commissioners ' (Morris). Prob. ex *ready*, v., 3.

readying, readying-up. Vbl.nn. of *ready*, v., and *ready up*, qq.v.

real, adv. Extremely, very : coll. : from ca. 1880 in England, earlier in Scotland and U.S. ; esp. in *real nice*. Ex *real* as adj. before another adj., esp.

when no comma intervenes (J. Fox, 1718, 'An Opportunity of doing a real good Office', O.E.D.).

real jam. A very delightful person or thing : s. verging on coll. : 1879, Justin McCarthy, 'Real jam, I call her'; *Punch*, Jan. 3, 1885, 'Without real jam—cash and kisses—this world is a bitterish pill.' Earlier, a sporting phrase for anything exceptionally good : from ca. 1870. H., 5th ed.

real Kate. A kind matron : Clare Market, London : ca. 1882–1900. Ware. Ex *Kate*, the charitable queen of the market.

real live. See **live,** adj., 2.

real peacer (or **P.**). A 'dashing' murderer : low coll. : late C. 19–early 20. Ware. Ex Charles *Peace*, the celebrated murderer.

real raspberry jam. The superlative of *jam tart*, a girl : low : ca. 1883–1915. Ware.

real thing, the. The genuine article (fig.) : 1818, Lady Morgan, 'He is the real thing, and no mistake,' O.E.D.

Really Not a Sailor. (A member of) the Royal Naval Air Squadron : naval : G.W. (F. & Gibbons.) Mostly a merchantmen's c.p. : witness W. McFee, *North of Suez*, 1930.

*ream. Genuine ; honest, honourable, aboveboard : an occ. C. 19 c. variant of *rum*, adj. very rare outside London. Mayhew, 1851, 'A "ream" . . . concern'; Baumann. Cf. :

ream-penny, gen. in pl. = Peter-pence. C. 17 : coll. and dial. Ex *Rome-penny*.

ream-pennies, reckon (up) one's. To confess one's faults : coll. : ca. 1650–1700. Ray. Ex *ream-penny,* q.v.

rear, rears, the. The latrine : university : from ca. 1880. Cf. :

rear, v. To visit the latrine ; to defecate : from ca. 1890 : university >, ca. 1905, gen. s. Ex *rear,* n. Cf. :

rear, do a. To defecate : C. 20. Ex preceding pair of entries.

rear-rank private. See **lance-private.**

rear-up. A noisy argument ; a quarrel ; a 'row' : lower classes' : C. 20. F. & Gibbons. Ex :

rear up, v. To become extremely angry : coll. : late C. 19–20. Ex horses.

rearer. The upsetting of a vehicle—the wheel(s) on one side going into a ditch, drain, etc.—so that the vehicle turns underside up : 1827 (O.E.D.); very ob.—2. A battledore : Restoration period.

rebound, catch on the. To get engaged to (a person) after he or she has been refused by another : coll. : from ca. 1908. Ex lawn tennis. (Collinson.)

rec, the. The recreation ground : lower-class, esp. Cockneys' coll. : C. 20. Ernest Raymond, *Mary Leith,* 1931. Cf. *Recker, the,* q.v.

receipt. Recipe : S.E. till C. 20, then considered somewhat sol.—2. Punches received : boxers' : mid-C. 19–20 ; extremely ob. *Bell's Life,* 'He showed strong symptoms of receipt' (Baumann). Cf. *receiver-general,* 2.

receipt of custom (or hyphenated). The female pudend : C. 19–20 ; ob. Cf. Grose's *custom-house goods,* q.v. (Where Adam made the first entry.)

receiver-general. A harlot : C. 19. *Lex. Bal.,* 1811. Ex S.E., a chief receiver of public revenues. —2. 'A boxer giving nothing for what he gets', F. & H. : boxing : from ca. 1860 ; ob.

Recent Incision. The New Cut, properly Lower Marsh, a busy thoroughfare on the Surrey side of the Thames : London jocular coll. of ca. 1859–95. H., 2nd ed. ; Baumann.

recission, -ory. Incorrect forms of *rescission -ory* : C. 17–20. O.E.D.

Recker or **Rekker, the.** The town recreation-ground, where the School sports are held : Harrow : late C. 19–20. Oxford *-er.* Cf. **rec, the,** q.v.

reckernise. See **reckonize.**

reckoning, cast up one's. To vomit : low (– 1788) ; very ob. Grose, 2nd ed. More gen. *cast up one's accounts.*

reckoning, Dutch. A bill that, if disputed, grows larger ; a sharing of the cost or the money, plunder, etc. : coll. : late C. 17–20 ; ob. Swift. See the paragraph on *Dutch.*

rec(k)onize or **-ise.** To recognise : sol. (–1887), esp. Cockneys'. Baumann. Also *reckernise.*

reconnoitre, v.i. To 'scrounge' (q.v.) : military : 1916 ; ob. B. & P.

[**record,** a performance superior to all others of the same kind, dates from 1883 (O.E.D.) : the S.O.D.—quite rightly, I feel sure—gives it as S.E. : *The Times* has always (?) spelt it with quotation marks, as though it considers it to be coll.]

record, smash the. To go one better : coll., esp. in athletics : from ca. 1890. *Break, cut* (†), *lower the record* are S.E.

Recordite, adj. and (gen. in pl.) n. (Of) the Low Church Party of the Anglican Church : a Church coll. : 1854, Conybeare, *Church Parties,* for both adj. and n. ; ob. Ex *The Record,* the party's official organ.

records. (Shares in) the African Gold Recovery Company : Stock Exchange (– 1895). A. J. Wilson's glossary.

recourse. See **resort.**

[**recrudescence.** See Fowler.]

recruit, n. See **recruits.**—2. 'To get a fresh supply of money', Grose, 1785 : coll. Cf. the next two entries.

recruiting service. Robbery on the highway : ca. 1810–40 : s. verging on c. (*Lex. Bal.*) Ex :

*recruits. Money, esp. expected money : late C. 17–early 19 : c. B.E., 'Have you rais'd the *Recruits,* . . . is the Money come in ?' Ex Army.

rector. 'A poker kept for show : *curate* (q.v.) = the work-a-day iron ; (2) the bottom half of a tea-cake or muffin (as getting more butter), the top half being the *curate,* and so forth ', F. & H. : coll. : from ca. 1860 ; ob.

[**rector of the females.** The penis : C. 17–20 ; ob. Either low coll. or, more prob., euphemistic S.E. Rochester.]

*red. A sovereign : c. or low (– 1923). Manchon. Ex the adj.—2. See **reds.**

*red, adj. Made of gold ; golden : C. 14–20 : S.E. till C. 17, then c. See esp. **red clock, kettle, one** or **'un, rogue, stuff, tackle, toy.**

red, paint the town. To have a riotously good time : U.S. (– 1880), anglicised ca. 1890 as a coll. Anon., *Harry Fludyer at Cambridge,* 'Won't he paint the whole place red on Tuesday night !'

red, see. To be in, fly into, a rage : coll. : C. 20. Ex a bull's reaction to red.

red ace ; occ. **red C.** The female pudend : low : mid-C. 19–20.

red and yellow, Tom Fool's colours. A c.p. (semi-proverb) in allusion to brightly coloured clothes : already old in 1874. Ex a jester's parti-coloured dress. Apperson.

red beard. (App.) a watchman or constable :

C. 17 : **?** c. Dekker & Webster, 1607, 'White haires may fall into the company of drabs as red beardes into the society of knaves,' O.E.D.—2. A red marble : London schoolboys' (— 1887). Baumann.

red Biddy. Cheap red wine, also called *crimson dawn* : Glasgow (— 1934). Alastair Baxter.

red breast, redbreast. A Bow Street runner : C. 18–early 19, though app. first recorded by Dickens in 1862. Ex red waistcoat.—See **redbreast.**

red cap (or with capitals). A military policeman : military coll. : G.W. +. B. & P. Cf. :

red cape. A sister in Queen Alexandra's Imperial Military Nursing Service : military coll. : 1915–18. F. & Gibbons.

***red clock.** A gold watch : c. : from ca. 1860. Baumann. Also *red 'un*, q.v. Cf. *red lot.*

red coat. A woman inspector in the Anti-Poison Gas Department : coll. : 1916–18. F. & Gibbons.

red cross. An English ship : nautical coll. : C. 17. Smith, 1626.

red(-)dog. Prickly heat : Anglo-Indian coll. : ca. 1740–1800. Yule & Burnell.

red duster. The Red Ensign : naval : late C. 19– 20. Bowen.

red eel. A term of contempt : coll. : C. 19. F. & H.

red face (or **neck**), **have a.** To be ashamed : Glasgow (— 1934). Ex blushing.

Red Feathers, the. The 46th Foot (in late C. 19–20, 2nd Battalion of the Duke of York's Light Infantry) : military : from ca. 1777 ; ob. Ex an incident of the American War of Independence. F. & Gibbons.

red flag. See **red rag, mount the.**

red flag at the mast-head. In dead earnest : naval coll. : mid-C. 19–20 ; ob. Bowen. Ex a single-flag signal enjoining either ' close action ' or ' no quarter '.

red flannel. The tongue : low : C. 19–20 ; ob. Cf. *red rag*, 1, q.v.

***red fustian.** Red wine, esp. port or claret : c. : late C. 17–early 19. B.E.—2. Porter : C. 19. F. & H.

red hat. A staff officer : military : 1915 ; ob. Ex red tabs. Cf. the more gen. *brass hat*, q.v.

red-headed. Zealous : *Conway* training-ship cadets' : late C. 19–20. John Masefield, *The Conway*, 1933.

red-headed tea and bare-footed bread. Lenten fare : Anglo-Irish : C. 20. Milk in tea and butter on bread being prohibited on the fast-days.

red heart. ' Redheart ' rum ; hence, any rum : London taverns' : ca. 1870–1910. Ware. (Coll. rather than s.)

red herring, a soldier (1853 ; very ob.). Cf. *soldier*, a red herring.—2. See **herring, red.**

red herring ne'er spake word but e'en, Broil my back, but not my weamb or womb (i.e. stomach). A c.p. of ca. 1670–1700. (The *weamb* form is dial.) Ray. (Apperson.)

Red Herrings. Lord Yarmouth (1777–1842). Dawson. Yarmouth is famous for its bloaters.

red hot. ' Extreme ; out-and-out ', C. J. Dennis : coll. > , by 1930, S.E. : late C. 19–20. Not as, e.g., *a red-hot socialist*, but as *that's red hot, that is !*

red-hot treat. An ' extremely dangerous person ' : lower classes' (— 1909) ; ob. Ware.

red incher. A red bull-ant : Australian children's : C. 20. Opp. *black incher*. (Some of these bull-ants are nearly an inch long.)

red ink. Red wine : military : 1914–18. F. & Gibbons.

red ink, in. Having no pay forthcoming : naval : from ca. 1910. Ibid. Ex the notation in the ledger.

***red kettle.** See **red toy.**

Red Knights, The. The 22nd Regiment (in late C. 19–20, the Cheshire Regt.) : military : from 1795, when served with red clothes instead of their proper uniform. Ob. F. & Gibbons.

red lamp. A brothel : coll. : late C. 19–20. Ex U.S. *red light district.*

Red (or **Scarlet**) **Lancers, the.** The 16th (in C. 19, the Queen's) Lancers : military : C. 19–20 ; very ob. They were the only lancers to wear a scarlet tunic.

red lane. The throat : coll. : late C. 18–20. Grose, 1st ed. ; 1812, Colman ; ob. Also in dial.

red-letter man. A Roman Catholic : coll. : late C. 17–early 19. B.E., Grose. Ex *red-letter day* and cf. *red neck*, q.v.

red(-)liner. Ca. 1840–80, as in Mayhew's *London Labour*, II, 564, ' The Red Liners, as we calls the Medicity officers, who goes about in disguise as gentlemen, to take up poor boys caught begging '. **?** ex putting a red line under an offender's name.

***red lot.** Gold watch and chain : c., and low : late C. 19–20. See **red,** adj.

Red Lion Lane. See **lane,** 2.

Red Marines. The Royal Marine Light Infantry : naval coll. : C. 19–early 20. Bowen. Ex their (former) red tunic.

red neck. A Roman Catholic : Northern (esp. Lancashire) coll. and dial. : C. 19.—2. See **red face.**

red Ned. A cheap muscatel wine : Sydneyites' (— 1935). Why *Ned* ?

red-nosed rooter. A port-maintopman : *Conway* cadets' : 1890's. John Masefield, *The Conway*, 1933.

red one. See **red 'un** and cf. *ruddock.*

red petticoat shall pay for it, the lass in the. See **lass in . . .**

red rag. The tongue : late C. 17–20, ob. B.E., Grose, W. S. Gilbert. Cf. *red flannel*.—2. A menstrual cloth : low coll. : C. 19–20. Cf. :

red rag, flash the. To menstruate : low : C. 19–20. Ex *red rag*, 2.

red rag, mount the. To blush : coll. : C. 19–20. Occ. *red flag.*

red ribbon. Brandy : ca. 1820–60. (Contrast *red fustian.*) Egan's Grose.

***red rogue.** A gold coin : c. : C. 17. Fletcher, in *The Mad Lover*. See **red.**

***red-sail** (**yard**) **docker.** A buyer of ' stores stolen out of the royal yards and docks ', Grose, 1st ed. : c. of ca. 1780–1840.

***red shank, red-shank, redshank.** A duck : c. : mid-C. 16–19. Harman, B.E., Grose.—2. A turkey : C. 18. Ex the pool-snipe so named.—3. A woman wearing no stockings : Connaught coll. : ca. 1840–1920. (O.E.D.) Ex the historical S.E. *redshank.*

***red stuff.** Gold articles : c. : late C. 19–20 David Hume.

red tab. A staff officer : military : 1915 ; ob. F. & Gibbons. Cf. the more gen. *brass hat.*

*red tackle. A gold chain: c.: 1879, *Macmillan's Magazine*, 'I touched for a red toy . . . and red tackle.'

*red tape. Red wine: c. of C. 19. Lytton in *Paul Clifford*. Cf. *red fustian*, q.v.

red tie. Vulgarity: Oxford University coll.: ca. 1876–1900. Ware.

*red toy. A gold watch: c.: 1879 (see quotation at red tackle).

red-triangle man. A member of the Y.M.C.A.: military coll.: 1915; ob.. F. & Gibbons. Ex the Association's badge.

*red 'un. The O.E.D. instances *red ones* in C. 16: prob. coll. But *red 'un* is c.: from ca. 1860. Gen., a gold coin and usually a sovereign; occ. an object made of gold (Sims, in *The Referee*, Feb. 12, 1888); e.g. a gold watch: c. (— 1864), as in H., 3rd ed. Cf. *redding*, q.v.

red, white and blue. Cold salt beef: *Conway* cadets': late C. 19–20. J. Masefield, *The Conway*, 1933.

red wings. A staff officer: military: 1915; ob. F. & Gibbons. Cf. *red tabs*, q.v.

redbreast. See red breast.—2. The Redbreasts: the 5th Lancers, i.e. the Royal Irish: military: C. 19–20, ob. Cf. *Red Lancers*.—3. The New South Wales Lancers: 1899 (O.E.D.); †.

redding. A gold watch: c. of ca. 1860–1915. H., 3rd ed. A corruption of *red 'un*, q.v., perhaps influenced by dial. *redding*, oxide of iron, red ochre (E.D.D.).

redemptioner. A man that works his passage: nautical coll.: C. 19. Bowen.

Redfern. A 'perfectly-fitting lady's coat or jacket': Society coll.: ca. 1879–1915. Ware. Ex a celebrated ladies' tailor.

*redge. See ridge. (Brandon; H., 1st ed.)

[Reduplication is 'a common phenomenon of baby speech . . . esp. in imitative words (*bow-wow*, *gee-gee*), and in popular words formed either by rime (*hurly-burly*, *roly-poly*) or by variation of original vowel (*see-saw*, *zig-zag*),' in which last 'the fuller vowel is usually the original,' W.]

redraw. A warder: low back s. (— 1875). Greenwood, in *Low-Life Deeps*, 'Shying a lump of red oakum at the redraw'.

reds. Blushes: coll. and dial.: C. 19–20.—2. The menses: mid-C. 16–20; S.E. till C. 18, then coll.; almost †.

redshank. See red shank.

redundant. Impertinent: City of London: 1899–1900. Ware. Ex a phrase by Horatio Bottomley.

redwop. Powder: back s.: from ca. 1890. Collinson.

ree-raw. See re-raw.

reeb. Beer: back s. (— 1859). H., 1st ed.

*reef. 'To draw up a dress-pocket until a purse is within reach of the fingers', F. & H.: c.: from ca. 1860. Ex nautical S.E.

reef (or two), let out a. To undo a button or so, esp. after a meal: from ca. 1870: nautical > gen. Baumann.

reef taken in, need a. To be drunk: from ca. 1880: nautical > gen.

reefer. A midshipman: nautical: 1829, Marryat. Because, says Smyth, he has to 'attend to the tops during the operation of taking in reefs'. (O.E.D.)

*reek. Money: c.: early C. 19. ? ex *reekpenny*.

Reekie. See Auld (or Old) Reekie.

reel, dance the miller's; dance the reel o' stumpie or of bogie. To have sexual intercourse: low Scots coll.: C. 18–20; ob.

*reeler. A policeman: c. (— 1879); ob. Presumably on *peeler*, q.v.

reeling, n. Feeling (gen. pl.): rhyming s. (— 1909). Ware.

*reener. A coin (less, app., than a florin): tramps' c.: from ca. 1890. P. H. Emerson, 1893, 'The old man never give her a reener.' ? *deaner* corrupted.

reesbin. A gaol: tramps' c., and tinkers' s. verging on c.: 1845, reference in '*No. 747*' (p. 413). Prob. a corruption of *prison* on Romany *stariben* (whence *stir*, q.v.).

ref. A reformer: political (— 1909); ob. Ware.—2. A referee: sporting: C. 20.—3. A reference (as to ability, etc.): commercial: 1907, P. G. Wodehouse, *Not George Washington*.

refresh. A refreshment, esp. of liquor: coll., verging now on s.: from ca. 1884. Ex *refresher*.— 2. A 'horizontal' (meal): C. 20. Manchon.

refresh, v.i. To take refreshments: C. 20. Manchon. Ex the n., sense 1.

refresher. A drink: coll.: 1841, T. Hook (O.E.D.). Cf. the pun in 'As a rule barristers don't object to refreshers,' *Ally Sloper's Half-Holiday*, Aug. 3, 1889. Cf. *pick-me-up*.

reg. duck-egg. An egregious '0': cricketers': late C. 19–20. Ware.

regalio. Incorrect for *regalo*: ca. 1650–1750. O.E.D.

regardless. See got-up regardless.

regimental. A downfall: military: from 1916. Esp. *come a regimental*, 'to be court-martialled and reduced to the ranks'. F. & Gibbons. Sc. *smash*. Cf. *proverbial, the*, q.v.—2. The Regimental. The Regimental as opp. the Company Sergeant-Major: military coll.: C. 20. Ibid.

regimental sports. Coal-carrying fatigue: Regular Army: late C. 19–20; ob. F. & Gibbons.

reg'lar; regler. When not deliberate, the adj. is a sol. form of *regular*: C. 19–20. Baumann. As adv., it is sol.

regular. A drink taken at a fixed hour: coll.: from ca. 1850.—2. See regulars.

regular, adj. Thorough, absolute; perfect: coll.: 1821, Shelley, 'A regular conjuror', O.E.D.; 1850, Smedley, 'A regular sell'; 1888, *The Cornhill Magazine*, March.—2. As adv., C. 18–20: S.E. till C. 20, then sol.

regular Callao. A free-and-easy ship lax of discipline: nautical coll.: late C. 19–20. Bowen.

regularly. Thoroughly; wholly: coll: 1789, 'Regularly dissipated', O.E.D. Cf. *regular*, adj.

*regulars. A division of booty: c.: from ca. 1810. *Lex. Bal.*, Vaux, Moncrieff, 'Gypsy' Carew. Abbr. *regular share(s)*.

regulated, be. 'To go through the Press Gang's perfunctory medical examination': naval coll.: ca. 1750–1840. Bowen.

regulator. The female pudend: low coll.: late C. 18–19. Prob. ex the S.E. sense, a regulating power or principle (1766, O.E.D.).

rehoboam. A shovel hat: coll. of ca. 1845–70. C. Brontë, 1849.—2. A quadruple magnum, a double jeroboam, gen. of champagne: from ca. 1860; ob.

*reign. A period of wrongdoing; a successfully criminal period out of gaol : c. : from ca. 1810. Vaux ; Egan's Grose. Cf. :

*reign, v. To be at liberty, esp. at profitable liberty : Australian c. >, by 1910, gen. c. : late C. 19–20. James Spenser, *Limey Breaks In*, 1934, 'Full-time crooks don't "reign" long.' Ex preceding.

reign of Queen Dick. See Dick, Queen.

reïnstoushment. A reinforcement : Australian military : 1916 ; ob. See stoush.

Rekker, the. See Recker, the.

relations (or **country cousins**) **have come, her.** She is in her menstrual period : lower classes' c.p. : mid-C. 19–20. Manchon (*les Anglais ont débarqué*).

reliever. An old coat usable by all (the workmen) : ca. 1845–1900. Kingsley.

relieving officer (rarely **a**). One's father, because he pays one's debts : 1857, G. Lawrence (O.E.D.). Grenville-Murray, 1883, 'The Relieving Officer, or . . . the "R.O.", was a term of endearment which [he], in common with other young noblemen and gentlemen at Eton, applied to his father.' Slightly ob.

religieuse. A monk : incorrect for *religieux* : C. 18–19. (A Gallicism.) O.E.D.

religion, get. See get religion.

religious. (Of a horse) apt to go down on his knees : late C. 18–mid-19. Grose, 2nd ed. Cf. *devotional habits* and contrast the old West American *religious* applied to horses : free from vice.

religious painter. 'One who does not break the commandment which prohibits the making of the likeness of any thing in heaven or earth, or in the waters under the earth ', Grose, 2nd ed. : ca. 1780–1820. Either a little joke of Grose's or painters' s.,—he was a painter and draughtsman (see Grose, P.).

relish. Coïtion with a woman : low : C. 19. *Lex. Bal.* Cf. *greens*, q.v.

Relish, the. The (sign of the) Cheshire Cheese : late C. 18–mid-19. Grose, 3rd ed.

reluctance, regret or sorrow, is a catachresis : C. 18. O.E.D.

rem-in-re, esp. **be caught with.** Copulation, esp. be taken in the act of : low : from ca. 1860 ; ob. Lit., a thing in a thing.

*remedy. A sovereign (coin) : c. : ? mid-C. 18–early 19. F. & H. Ex the technical S.E. *remedy*, the permissible variation of weight in coins (also called *tolerance*).

remedy-critch. A chamber-pot : late C. 18–early 19. Grose, 2nd ed. A *critch* = any earthenware vessel ; *remedy*, because therewith discomfort is remedied.

remember Belgium ! A c.p. (1915–18) heard, among soldiers, ' with ironic and bitter intonations in the muddy wastes of the Salient ', B. & P. Ex the famous enlistment-poster : cf. *Kitchener wants you*, q.v.

remember I'm your mother and get up those stairs ! A military c.p. of the G.W. (B. & P.)

remember Parson Mallum (or **Meldrum, Malham,** or **Melham**) **!** See Parson Mallum.

remember there's a war on ! See war on.

remi. A holiday : Westminster School : from ca. 1860. Ex *remedy* in that sense.

reminisce. To relate reminiscences, esp. if freely : coll. : from ca. 1880. Ex the jocular *reminisce*, v.i. and t., to recollect, + *reminiscences*.

remnants, a man of. A tailor : coll. (— 1923). Manchon.

removal. A murder : political : 1883–5. Ware. Ex a witness's euphemism in the Phœnix Park assassination case.

rench. To rinse : sol. (— 1859). H., 1st ed. Also dial.

render, v.i. (Of any mechanical thing) to act ; to work properly : naval and military coll. : from 1915. F. & Gibbons. Ex nautical j. *render*, as applied esp. to a rope. 'A rope is said to render or not, according as it goes freely through any place,' R. H. Dana, 1841 (O.E.D.).

*rent. Plunder : c. : late C. 18–mid-19. Implied in Grose's *collector*, q.v.—2. See rents.—3. Money ; cash : lower classes' : late C. 19–20. F. & Gibbons.

rent, collect. To rob on the highway : c. : late C. 18–mid-19. See rent, n., 1 ; also in Bee, 1823. See esp. rent-collector.

rent, pay (someone) **his.** To punish : coll. : C. 14–(?) 16. S. Oliphant's *New English.* (?)

*rent-collector. A highwayman, esp. one who fancies money only : c. : (? late C. 18–)early 19. Bee. Cf. *collector*, *rent*, and *rent, collect.*

rents (in C. 17, **rent**) **coming in.** Ragged ; dilapidated : a punning coll. c.p. of C. 17–mid-18. Withals, 1616, ' " That hath his rent come in " ', O.E.D. ; Swift, *Polite Conversation*, Dialogue I, ' I have torn my Petticoat with your odious Romping ; my Rents are coming in ; I'm afraid, I shall fall into the Ragman's Hands.'

rep. Reputation : coll. : ca. 1705–50 (extant in U.S.). Shippery, ' Upon rep ', O.E.D. ; D'Urfey, ' Dames of rep ' ; Fielding. (See rep, (up)on or pon.)—2. Hence, a man (ob.) or woman († by 1850) of loose morals : coll.: 1747, Hoadly (O.E.D.). Here, *rep* is ex *reprobate* (W.), influenced by *rep*, 1, and suggested by *demi-rep*, q.v.—3. Hence, a worthless or inferior object : coll. : 1786, Wolcot, ' The fiddle . . . though what's vulgarly baptiz'd a *rep* ', O.E.D. Very ob.—4. A repetition (lesson) : school s., esp. at Harrow : from ca. 1860. Anstey. At Charterhouse, esp. : poetry as repetition : late C. 19–20. Cf. *prep*, q.v. : W.—5. A repertory theatre ; gen. *the Rep*, a specific theatre, or *the Reps*, the world of repertory : mainly theatrical : from ca. 1920. See esp. Ivor Brown's ' The " Reps " ' in *The New Statesman*, Dec. 15, 1934.

rep, on or **'pon** or **upon.** On (my) word of honour, lit. on my reputation : coll. : C. 18, though rare after ca. 1750. See rep, 1. Swift, ' Do you say it upon Rep ? '

repairs, no. Reckless ; neck or nothing : from ca. 1880 ; ob. (Gen. of contests.)

reparty. A repartee : Society : 1874–ca. 90. Ware. (Satirical.)

repentance curl. The English society form of the curl known in Fr. as *repentir* : 1863–ca. 90. Ware. [Repetition is a mark of illiteracy—or of a minor intelligence. E.g. this dialogue from Freeman Wills Crofts, *Sudden Death*, 1932, ' It looked bad, that it did ! With all the . . . Very bad, it looked. Hersey wouldn't half be interested, he wouldn't ! ']

reporter. A (hair-trigger) pistol : coll., mostly Irish, verging on S.E. ; † by 1910. Jonah Barrington, 1827. Ex the suddenness of the report.

reposer. A final drink ; a nightcap : coll. : from ca. 1870. (Repose-inducing.)

repository. A lock-up, a gaol : ca. 1780–1830 Grose, 1785.

reprehend for apprehend or occ. represent : sol. : late C. 16–20. (O.E.D.)

republic of letters, the. The Post-Office : ca. 1820–50. Bee. Punning S.E. sense.

repulsive. Unpleasant ; dull : Society : 1930, Evelyn Waugh, *Vile Bodies*, ' Isn't this a repulsive party ? '

reservoir !, au. Au revoir ! : jocular coll. (— 1897) ; ob. Cf. *olive oil !*

residential club. A usual assemblage of idlers, esp. those frequenting the British Museum for warmth or shelter : jocular coll. verging on S.E. ; from ca. 1890 ; ob., as (thanks be !) is the practice.

resin up. To smarten up (a man) at his work : nautical : late C. 19–20. Bowen. Ex resining a fiddle.

resort, resource, recourse : often confused : C. 19–20. See esp. Fowler.

respectively is often used catachrestically, esp. in C. 20. Fowler.

responsible. A sensible actor able to take the lead : theatrical coll. : from ca. 1890. Ware.

respun ; occ. rispin. To steal : tinkers' s., bordering on c. : from ca. 1850. ? origin. Just possibly ex or cognate with Scots *risp*, to rasp, to file.

rest. A restaurant : urban (— 1923). Manchon.

rest, v. To arrest : mid-C. 15–20 : S.E. until C. 19, then dial. and low coll.

rest ?, and the. A c.p. retort on incompleteness or reticence : from ca. 1860.

rest and be thankful, the. The female pudend : C. 19–20 ; ob.

rest camp. A cemetery : military : 1917 ; ob. B. & P. Ex military j.

resting. Out of work : theatre, music-hall : late C. 19–20 : since ca. 1920, coll.

results. News of sports results : journalistic coll. : from ca. 1921.

resurrection-bolly. Beefsteak pudding : preparatory schools' : late C. 19–20. (E. F. Benson, *David Blaize*, 1916.)

resurrection-cove. A body-snatcher : low : ca. 1810–95. Vaux ; Baumann.

resurrection-jarvey. A nocturnal hackney-coach-man : ca. 1820–60. Westmacott (O.E.D.).

resurrection(-pie). A dish made from remains : from ca. 1864 : coll. till C. 20, then S.E. : orig. and esp. a schoolboys' term. H., 3rd ed.

Resurrectionists, the. The Buffs, i.e. the East Kent Regiment : from 1811, when, at Albuera, they rallied after a severe dispersal by the Polish Lancers. Ob. F. & Gibbons.

reswort. Trousers : back s. (— 1874). H., 5th ed.

ret. A reiteration in printing : printers' (— 1874). H., 5th ed.

*retoure. See tour(e).

*retriever. A ' verser ' (q.v.) : local c. of ca. 1592. Greene.

retrogate, retrogation. Incorrect for *retrograde, -gradation* : late C. 16–18. O.E.D.

retsio. An oyster : back s. (— 1874). H., 5th ed.

return home. (Of a convict) to be released on ticket-of-leave : police coll. : C. 20. (Charles E. Leach, 1933.)

returned empty. A Colonial bishop returning to, and gen. taking up a post in, Britain : Church : from ca. 1890. (Much the same sort of feeling

prevails regarding those who, having held professorships in the Dominions, seek for jobs in England.)

reune. To hold a reunion : 1929, E. W. Springs (O.E.D. Sup.).

rev. An engine's revolution : Air Force : 1914. F. & Gibbons. Cf. :

rev, v.i. To circle rapidly in the air : Air Force : 1915. F. & Gibbons. Cf. :

rev up. To increase the revolutions of (an engine) : from ca. 1916 : coll. >, by 1930, S.E. Also v.i., of the engine. O.E.D. (Sup.).

revenge in lavender. A vengeance reserved : coll. bordering on S.E. : late C. 17–early 19. B.E. ; Grose. See lavender and cf. *rod in pickle.*

reverence. See sir reverence.

reverent. Reverend, n. : erroneous use : C. 14–15. W.

reverse. Incorrect for *revess, revesh* (to revest) : C. 14–15 (? 16). O.E.D.

[reversed, as given by B.E. and Grose (a man set on his head by bullies, who thus obtain the money in his pockets), is but a special application of S.E.]

Review. See Magazine.

review of the black cuirassiers. A visitation by the clergy : late C. 18–early 19. Grose, 1785. Ex priestly black and shining crosses and/or crucifixes. Cf. *crow fair.*

reviver. A drink (rarely of non-intoxicants) : orig. Society : 1876, Besant & Rice, ' It was but twelve o'clock, and therefore early for revivers of any sort.' Cf. *refresher*, q.v.

revlis. Silver : back s. (— 1859). H., 1st ed.

rewrite. A virtual re-writing of another person's book : publishers' coll. (— 1933). *Slang*, p. 181. Ex the v.

-rf for -th (e.g. barf for *bath*) is sol., mostly Cockney : C. 19–20. Cf. the equally sol. *orf* for *off* in *off* itself, *cough*, *trough* : Cockney : C. 19–20.

*rheumatic dodge. The gaining of sympathy— and alms—by a pretence of (acute) rheumatism : c. (— 1887). Baumann.

rheumaticky. Afflicted with rheumatism : coll. : from ca. 1850.

rheumatics ; often the r. Rheumatism : late C. 18–20 : coll. : from ca. 1890, considered increasingly low coll. ; indeed, in C. 20, it ranks as a sol. Ex the adj. Cf. *rheumatiz* and *rheumaticky.*

rheumatism in the shoulder. Arrest : low : from ca. 1820 ; ob. Egan's Grose. Esp. *have r. in the s.*, to be arrested.

rheumatiz, r(h)umatiz ; occ. (esp. until ca. 1830) *rheumatise* or *-ize*, or *rheumatis* (Baumann). Rheumatism : dial. and low coll. (in C. 20, a sol.) : 1760, Foote, ' My old disorder, the rheumatise ', O.E.D.

*rhino ; occ. rino, ryno, but not after C. 18. Money : 1688, Shadwell ; B.E. ; Grose ; Barham. C. until ca. 1820, then low s. >, ca. 1870, gen. s. Often *ready rhino* : cf. *ready*, q.v. Origin problematic ; there is prob. some allusion to the size of a rhinoceros : cf. next three entries. C. synonyms are *bit(e)*, *cole*, *gelt*, *loaver*, *lurries*, *pewter*, *quids*, *reek*, *ribbin* ; the s. and coll. synonyms are too numerous to list,—see F. & H. at *rhino* and H. at pp. 61–5.—2. Rhinoceros : coll. abbr. : 1884 (S.O.D.).—3. Cheese : military : from ca. 1910. F. & Gibbons. Ex the all too prominent rind.

rhino-fat. Rich : C. 19. Ex preceding ; suggested by *rhinocerical* ; cf. :

rhinoceral. Rich : from ca. 1860. H., 2nd ed. See rhino ; abbr. cf. :

*rhinocerical. Rich : c. until C. 19, then s. ;
† by 1860. Shadwell, B.E., Grose. As Shadwell
has both *rhino* and *rhinocerical* in 1688, the latter
may well be the origin of the former. See rhino.

rhody, -ie. A rhododendron : 'nursery' and
familiar coll. : C. 20. Cf. *roddy*, q.v.

Rhondda'd, be. (Of things) to be lost : 1918–
early 19 : mostly Army officers'. Ex Lord Rhondda, the food controller (1917) who died for his
country. W.

rhubarb. A loan : dockers' : late C. 19–20.
Bowen. Ex its ruddy length.

rhumatiz. See rheumatiz.

rhyme-slinger. A poet : coll. : from ca. 1850.
[Rhyming slang dates from ca. 1840 ; originated
among Cockneys, where now still commonest ;
eschewed by the middle and upper classes, it had
its apotheosis in the G.W. E.g. *Abraham's willing*,
a shilling ; the second word is often suppressed,
as in *elephant's* (*trunk*), drunk. See my *Slang*,
revised ed.]

ri. See lep.

rib, crooked. A cross-grained wife : coll. : late
C. 18–20, ob. Grose, 2nd ed. (The S.E. *rib*, a
wife, is Biblical in origin and affected esp. by
Scottish poets.)

rib-baste or, much more gen., -roast. To thrash :
coll. : resp. late C. 16–17, late C. 16–20, ob. Occ.
a n., with variant *rib-roasting*, *-basting*. Gascoigne, ' I hope to give them al a rybbe to roste for
their paynes ' ; Smollett, ' He knew he should be
rib-roasted every day, and murdered at last ; ' H.,
1874, ' *Ribroast . . . Old* ; but still in use.' Cf.
next two entries.

rib-bender or -roaster ; occ. rib of roast ; ribber.
A punch on the ribs : boxing : from ca. 1810 ;
the 2nd and 3rd, very ob. Tom Moore has *ribber*,
' Cuthbert Bede ' *rib-roaster*, Hindley *rib-bender*.
Cf. the next entry.—2. A ball rising so high as to
endanger the batsman's body : cricket : 1873 ; ob.
Lewis.

rib-bending or -roasting ; ribbing. The vbl.n.
counterparts of *rib-bender*, etc.

rib-roast, -roaster. See rib-baste and rib-bender.

rib-shirt. A front or dickey worn over a grubby
shirt : lower classes' : from ca. 1880 ; ob. Ware.

rib-tickle ; rib-tickler. To thrash, also *tickle
one's ribs*. A punch in the ribs ; thick soup.
From ca. 1850 ; slightly ob. Cf. *rib-baste* and
-bender.

ribband. See ribbin.—ribber. See rib-bender.

*ribbin ; also ribband, ribbon. Money : c. :
late C. 17–mid-19. B.E. ; Vaux (*ribband*). ? cf.
fat, being ex *ribbing* (cf. *ribs*, q.v.), or ex *ribbon*,
gen. of rich stuff. Cf. :

*ribbin runs thick or thin, the. There is, he
(etc.) has, much or little money : late C. 17–mid-19.
B.E., Grose. See ribbin.

*ribbon. See ribbin.—2. See ribbons.—3. A bell-
pull : c. : late C. 17–mid-18. B.E., ' *Pluck the
Ribond*, . . . ring the Bell at the Tavern.' Ex likeness of ribbon to rope.—4. Esp. *blue ribbon* : gin :
c. : from ca. 1810 ; ob. *Lex. Bal.* Prob. suggested by *satin*, q.v.—5. After ca. 1860, *ribbon*
(but not *blue ribbon*) = spirits in gen. ; ob. H.,
3rd ed. (' Servants' term ').

ribbons. Reins : 1813 (O.E.D.) : sporting coll.
>, ca. 1880, S.E. Dickens in *Pickwick*. Esp. in
handle or † *flutter the ribbons*.—2. Ropes forming the
boundary ; hence, loosely, any boundary :
cricketers' : from ca. 1920. Neville Cardus, *Good

Days*, 1934, ' George Gunn cut it to the ribbons, as
the saying goes.'

*ribby. Destitute ; (of places) poverty-stricken,
squalid : c. : from ca. 1930. James Curtis, *The
Gilt Kid*, 1936. Ex *ribs, on the*, 2.

ribs. (A nickname for) a stout person : coll. :
C. 19–20 ; ob.

*ribs, on the. (Of horse or dog) no good at all :
racing c. : from ca. 1926.—2. Destitute ; down and
out : c. : C. 20. James Curtis, *The Gilt Kid*, 1936.
Cf. *on one's back* and *down on the knuckle* (q.v. at
knuckle).

ribston(e). A Cockney's term of affectionate
address : 1883, Milliken in *Punch*, Oct. 11 ; ob. by
1910, † by 1930. Abbr. *ribston(e) pippin*. See
pippin.

ribuck ! ' Correct, genuine ; an interjection
signifying assent ', C. J. Dennis : (low) Australian :
C. 20. Perhaps—very obscurely !—ex *rybeck*, q.v.
Cf. *jonnick*.

rice-bags. Trousers : a trifle low : ca. 1890–
1910. On *bags*, trousers, q.v.

rice-cake !, for. Public Schools' euphemistic s.
for *for Christ's sake !* : C. 20.

rice Christian. An Aboriginal ' accepting '
Christianity for food : Society coll. : 1895, *The
Referee*, Aug. 11 (Ware) ; ob.

rich. Very entertaining—preposterous, ridiculous—outrageous : mid-C. 18–20 S.E. verging on
coll.—2. Spicy ; indelicate : coll. : from ca. 1860.

rich as a new-shorn sheep. An ironic, semi-
proverbial c.p. of C. 16–mid-18. Churchyard,
Breton, Fuller. (Apperson.)

rich as crazes. Rich as Crœsus : Anglo-Irish
(— 1909). Ware.

rich man's side. See poor man's side.

rich one. The wealthy wife of ' a man who
finds home not to his liking ' : better-class harlots'
coll. (— 1909). Ware.

Richard, Richard Snary, Richardanary. A dictionary : s., low coll., sol. : resp. late C. 18–20,
e.g. in Grose, 2nd ed., an abbr. of *R. S.* ; from ca.
1620, as in ' Water Poet ' Taylor ; C. 19–20 (also
dial.), a corruption of *R. S.* All ob. Cf. *Dick*
(or *dic*), which indicates the semantics.—2. (randy)
Richard. An observation balloon : military ·
1915 ; ob. B. & P.

Richard, get the (ripe). To be ' ragged ', hooted,
or publicly snubbed : military, esp. officers' : 1915 ;
ob. F. & Gibbons. Perhaps suggested by *raspberry, get the*, q.v.

Richard the Third. A bird : rhyming s. : late
C. 19–20. B. & P.

Richardanary. See Richard.

ricing. The throwing of rice over the bride :
middle-class coll. (— 1909). Ware.

rick. A ' gee ' in the grafters' sense (trade accomplice) : grafters' : C. 20. Philip Allingham, *Cheapjack*, 1934. Perhaps ex *rick*, a wrench.

rick(-)ma(-)tick. Arithmetic : school s. and gen.
sol. : C. 19–20. On *'rithmetic*, as in the three R's,
reading, 'riting and 'rithmetic.

ricko. A ricochet : military : from 1914.
B. & P.

rid. Rode : after ca. 1850, gen. considered a
sol. (Cf. dial. *red*.) Baumann.

ride. (Gen. used by women.) An act of coïtion :
low : C. 19–20. Ex *ride*, v. (Cf. the scabrous
smoke-room story of the little boy that wanted
' a ride on the average '.) Esp. in *have* or *get a
ride*.

ride, v. To mount a woman in copulation : v.i. and t. : M.E.–C. 20 : S.E. till ca. 1780, then (low) coll. D'Urfey has *ride tantivy.* Cf. *riding* and *rider*, 1.—2. See **rider,** 2. (3. For relevant phrases not under *ride*, see the second member ; e.g. *ride bodkin.*)—4. To cart : South African coll. : 1897, Ernest Glanville, *Tales from the Veld*, 'I want you to ride a load of wood to the house.' Pettman. —5. To keep girding at : Canadian : C. 20. John Beames. Ex Lancashire dial. *ride*, to be a burden to (E.D.D.).

ride, take (one) **for a.** To take a person in a motor-car and then, at a convenient spot, shoot him dead : U.S. (C. 20), anglicised ca. 1930, often loosely (i.e. in order to thrash). Gordon Fellowes, *They Took Me for a Ride*, 1934. Cf. the old U.S. *ride* (one) *on a rail*, to expel forcibly (Thornton).

ride as if fetching the midwife. To go in haste : coll. : late C. 17–mid-19. Ray.

ride behind. See **rider,** 2.

ride (a man) **down like a main-tack.** To overwork him : nautical coll. : mid-C. 19–20. Bowen.

ride out. To be a highwayman : coll. : C. 17–18. Anon., *The London Prodigal*, 1605. Cf. Chaucer's *riden out*, to go abroad, serve on a military expedition (the description of the knight, in the *Canterbury* Prologue).

ride rantipole. See **rantipole, ride.—ride rusty.** See **rusty, ride.—ride St. George.** See **riding St. George.**

ride the black donkey. To be in a bad humour : coll. : mid-C. 19–early 20. H., 2nd ed.

***ride the donkey.** To cheat in weight (weighing) : c. (– 1857). 'Ducange Anglicus.'

ride the fore-horse. To be early ; ahead of another : coll. : ca. 1660–1840. Etherege ; Scott. (Apperson.)

ride the fringes. To perambulate the boundaries of a chartered district : Irish coll. of ca. 1700–1820. Anon., *Ireland Sixty Years Ago*, 1847. A corruption of *ride the franchises.*

ride the mare. To be hanged : (c. or) low : late C. 16–17. Shakespeare. See **three-legged.**

ride the wild mare. To play at see-saw (Onions) ; hence, I conjecture, to act wildly or live riotously : coll. : late C. 16–mid-17. Shakespeare ; Cotgrave, ' Desferrer l'asne . . . we say, to ride the wilde mare.' Apperson.

rider. An—esp. customary—actively amorous man : low coll. : C. 18–20 ; ob. Ex *ride*, v., q.v. Cf. *riding St. George.*—2. 'A person who receives part of the salary of a place or appointment from the ostensible occupier, by virtue of an agreement with the donor, or great man appointing. The rider is said to be quartered upon the possessor, who often has one or more persons thus riding behind him,' Grose, 3rd ed. Coll. of late C. 18–mid-19.—3. A passenger : cabmen's coll. (– 1887) ; ob. Baumann.

***ridg.** An early variant of :

***ridge** ; occ., in C. 19, **redge.** Gold : c. : from ca. 1660 ; ob. by 1840, † by 1900. Head (implied in *ridge-cully*, q.v.). A *cly full of ridge*, a pocketful of money.—2. Hence, a guinea : ca. 1750–1830. Grose, 1st ed. ? ex *ridge*, a measure of land.

***ridge, thimble of.** A gold watch : ca. 1830–60 : c. Ainsworth, 1834. (O.E.D.)

***ridge-cully.** A goldsmith, lit. a gold-man (see **ridge** and **cully**) : c. : 1665, Head (O.E.D.) ; B.E. ; Grose. Very ob. by 1880. Whence, prob. :

***ridge-montra.** A gold watch : C. 19 (?–20) : c. Egan's Grose. See **ridge** and **montra.**

riding. Adroitness ; ability : sporting (– 1886) ; ob. Ware. Ex a jockey's skill.

riding-hag. A, the, nightmare : coll. : C. 19–20 ; ob.

riding St. George or **the dragon upon St George.** N. and adj. (The position of) the woman being on top in the sexual act : late C. 17–mid-19. B.E. ; *A New Canting Dict.*, 1725 ; Grose, 1785. (This posture was supposed to be efficacious if the parents wanted their child to be a bishop.) A pun on the legend of St. George and the dragon, adumbrated in Fletcher's *Mad Lover.*

riffle. A shuffle ' in which . . . the thumbs " riffle ", or bend up the corners of the cards ', Maskelyne : from ca. 1890 : sharpers' s. verging on c. (O.E.D.) Cf. :

riffle, v. To do this (see the n.) : same period, status and authority.—2. See :

rifle ; in C. 17, often **riffle.** To coït with, or to caress sexually, a woman : coll. verging on S.E. : C. 17–20 ; ob. Prob. ex the S.E. *rifle*, (of a hawk) to tread (the hen).

***rifler.** In ' prigging law ' (horse-stealing), app. he who takes away the stolen horse : c. of late C. 16–early 17. Greene's *Second Cony-Catching*, 1592.

rifting, vbl.n. ' Cleaning gear, harness, etc.' : Regular Army : late C. 19–20. F. & Gibbons. Perhaps ex dial. *rift*, ' to break up (grass-land) with the plough ', O.E.D.

rig. Ridicule, esp. in *run one's rig upon* a person : from ca. 1720 : s. till C. 19, then coll. ; in C. 20, dial. *A New Canting Dict.*, 1725 ; Thackeray.—2. A trick or dodge ; a swindling scheme or method : 1775, Anon., ' I'm up to all your knowing rigs.' Cf. *rig sale*, q.v.—3. A prank ; a mischievous or a wanton act : coll. : from ca. 1720 ; ob. *A New Canting Dict.*, 1725.—4. A (somewhat ' shady ') manipulation of the money-market ; a corner : 1877 (O.E.D.) ; s. >, ca. 1890, coll. (Senses 2–4 follow naturally ex sense 1.)—5. Outfit ; (style of) dress : coll. : mid-C. 19–20. Ex the rig of a ship ; but cf. *rig*, v., 3. Also *rig-out* and *-up*.

rig, v. To play tricks on, to befool : from ca. 1820 : s. >, ca. 1860, coll. ; in C. 20, dial. Ex *rig*, n., 1 and 3.—2. Hence, to manipulate illegally or illicitly : from ca. 1850 : s. >, ca. 1880, coll. ; slightly ob. Cf. *rig the market* and *rig up*, v.—3. To clothe ; supply with clothes : from ca. 1530 : S.E. until C. 19, then coll. ; in C. 20, rather slangy. *The Sporting Magazine*, 1821, ' The gentlemen were neatly rigged, and looked the thing to a T ' (O.E.D.). Cf. *rig out*, v.

rig, run a or **the ; run one's rigs.** To play pranks, even if wanton ones ; run riot : s. >, ca. 1820, coll. : thus, Cowper, 1782, ' He little dreamt, when he set out, | Of running such a rig ! ' ; *r. the r.*, 1797 ; *r. one's rigs*, 1818. O.E.D.

rig-me-role. See **rigmarole.** Only in C. 18.

rig-mutton. A wanton : coll. : C. 17–18. Elaboration of *rig*, a wanton.

rig-my-role or **-roll.** See **rigmarole.** C. 18 only.

rig-out, n. An outfit ; (esp. a suit of) clothes, a costume : coll. : from ca. 1820. Cf. *rig*, n., last sense ; *rig*, v., last sense ; *rig-up* ; and :

rig out, v. To dress ; provide with clothes : from ca. 1610 : S.E. until C. 19, then coll.

rig sale. An auction-sale under false pretences : 1851, *Chambers's Journal.*

rig the market. To engineer the (money-) market in order to profit by the ensuing rise or fall in prices : 1855, Tom Taylor, 'We must rig the market. Go in and buy up every share that's offered ' : in C. 20, coll. Ex *rig*, v., 2, and n., 4.

rig-up, n. An outfit ; (style of) dress : coll. : from ca. 1895 ; ob. Cf. *rig-out*, n.

rig up, v.t. To send (prices) up by artifice or manipulation : commercial s. >, in C. 20, coll. : 1884, *The Pall Mall Gazette*, Feb. 14. O.E.D. Ex *rig*, v., 2.

rigby. See **rigsby**.

rigged. Ppl.adj. of *rig*, v., 2, q.v. : O.E.D. records at 1879, but prob. considerably older.—2. Of v., 3.

riggen (riggin ; properly, **rigging), ride the.** To be extremely intimate : dial. and low coll. : C. 19–20 ; ob. Here *riggen*(, *rigging*) is the back(bone), though the coll. use may have been influenced by sartorial *rigging*.

rigger. A racing boat : Durham School : late C. 19–20. ? ex :—2. Outrigger : coll. abbr. : late C. 19–20.—3. A thimble-rigger : from ca. 1830 : low coll. >, by 1900, S.E.—4. One who ' rigs ' an auction (1859) or the market (1883) : s. >, by 1910, coll. O.E.D.

rigging. See **riggen, ride the.**—2. Clothes : C. 17–20 ; ob. Not c., as B.E. asserts, but s.—3. The vbl.n. of *rig*, v., 3.

rigging, climb the. See **climb the rigging.**—**rigging, ride the.** See **riggen, ride the.**

***rigging, rum.** Fine clothes : c. : late C. 17–18. B.E. ; Grose, 1st ed.

riggmonrowle. An occ. C. 18 form of *rigmarole*, q.v. Foote. (O.E.D.)

right, n. Incorrect for *rite* : late C. 16–20. Shakespeare. (O.E.D.)

right, adj. See **right, all,** 2 ; **right, too** ; **right as . . . ; right enough ; right you are.**—2. Favourably disposed to, trustable by, the underworld : c. : ca. 1865, ' *No. 747* ' has *right screw*, a ' good fellow ' warder.

[**right,** adv. With adjj. (e.g. *right smart*) and advv. (e.g. *right away*) : very : C. 13–20 : S.E. that, in C. 19–20, borders on coll. ; in C. 20, however, archaic.]

right, a bit of all. Excellent ; most attractive, delightful : coll. : from ca. 1870. Often applied by a fellow to a girl, with the connotation that she is very pretty or very charming or, in the sexual act, ardent or expert (or both). Slightly ob. Cf. the mock-French translation : *un petit morceau de tout droit*.

right !, all. Certainly ! ; gladly ! : 1837, Dickens : coll. till C. 20, then S.E. Like next entry, prob. ex c. sense (ca. 1810–50), 'All's safe or in good order *or* as desired ' : *Lex. Bal.* Cf. *right-(h)o*, *rightio* (*righty-o*) *!*, and *right you are !*

right, all, adj. and adv. As expected ; safe(ly) ; satisfactor(il)y : coll. : 1844, Edward FitzGerald, ' I got your letter all right ' (O.E.D.). Ex preceding entry.

Right, Mr ; Miss R. The right person—the person one is destined to marry (i.e. he or she who, before marriage, seems to be the right life-partner) : coll. : Sala, 1860, ' Mr Right ' ; Kipling, 1890, ' Miss Right ' (O.E.D.). Since the G.W., *Miss Right* is increasingly rare. (Collinson.)

right !, that's. I agree : coll. : C. 20. Prob. ex *all right* (as above). Cf. :

right !, too. Most certainly : coll. : from ca.

1910. Often *too bloody right* (cf. *too bloody Irish*) *!* An extension of *right !, all*, q.v.

Right-Abouts, the. The Gloucestershire Regiment : military : from 1801. F. & Gibbons. Also *the Back Numbers* (q.v.), *the Old Braggs*, *the Slashers*, *the Whitewashers*.—2. Rights (of a case), special circumstances : jocular (— 1923). Manchon.

right as . . . There are various coll. phrases denoting that one is quite well or comfortable or secure, that a thing, a job, a prospect, etc., is dependable or quite safe :—**right as a fiddle** (— 1903 ; F. & H.), an ob. corruption of the much earlier *fit as a fiddle* ; **. . . a line** (C. 15–early 17 ; e.g. Chapman) ; **. . . a trivet** (1837, Dickens) ; **. . . anything** (— 1903 ; F. & H. Very gen.) ; **. . . my glove** (1816, Scott ; ob.) ; **. . . my leg** (C. 17–18 ; e.g. Farquhar) ; **. . . ninepence** (1850, Smedley), in C. 19 often *nice as ninepence* (H., 5th ed.) ; **. . . rain** (1894, W. Raymond ; 1921, A. S. M. Hutchinson) ; **. . . the bank** (1890, ' Rolf Boldrewood ', ? on *safe as the Bank of England*). O.E.D. and esp. Apperson.

right as a ram's horn. (Very) crooked : ironic coll. : C. 14–17 (? early 18). Lydgate, Skelton, Ray. Apperson. Cf. the late C. 19–20 coll. *as straight* (occ. *as crooked*) *as a dog's hind leg*.

right away. Immediately, directly : U.S. (— 1842), perhaps ex Eng. dial. ; anglicised as coll. by 1880.

right-coloured stuff. Money : Norfolk s. (— 1872), not dial. E.D.D.

right-down. Downright, outright ; veritable : low coll. (— 1887). Baumann, ' A right-down swindle '. Ex dial., which has also *right-up-and-down* (E.D.D.).

right enough, adj. Esp. in *that's right enough* = that's all right so far as it goes (but it doesn't go nearly far enough) ; or, that's all right from *your* point of view. Coll. : late C. 19–20. Contrast :

right enough, adv. All right, well enough ; esp., all right (or well enough) although you may not at present think so. Coll. : from ca. 1880 ; O.E.D. records it at 1885 in Anstey's *The Tinted Venus*. Cf. preceding entry.

right eye, or hand, itches,—(and) my. A coll. c.p. ; the former denotes prospective weeping, the latter a(n unexpected) heritage or gift of money : C. 18. Swift.

***right fanny.** ' Real, or pathetic, story or tale ' : c. : from ca. 1925. George Ingram, *Stir*, 1933.

right forepart. (One's) wife : tailors' : late C. 19–20. Ex tailoring j.

right-(h)o, right-oh, righto. Very well ! ; certainly ! ; agreed ! : C. 20. Cf. *right you are*, *rightio* (*righty-o*).

right in one's, or the, head. (Gen. preceded by *not*.) (Un)sound of mind : coll. : C. 19–20. Randolph Hughes, in *The Nineteenth Century*, July 1934, ' The meanderings of a man not quite right in the head '. App. orig. dial. : cf. the Scottish *no richt*.

right off, put. To give a violent distaste for a thing, a plan, or dislike for a person : coll. : late C. 19–20.

right sort. Gin : low · ca. 1820–50. ' Peter Corcoran ' Reynolds.

right tenpenny on the cranium, hit. To hit the nail on the head : non-aristocratic jocular coll. : ca. 1890–1915. Ware.

right there !, put it. Shake hands ! : coll. : orig. U.S., anglicised ca. 1905.

right up and down, like a yard of pump-water. 'Straightforward and in earnest': nautical: mid-C. 19–20. Bowen. Cf. *right-down*, q.v.

right you are ! All right !; certainly !; agreed !: s. (– 1864) >, ca. 1920, coll. H., 3rd ed. ; Churchward, 1888, 'Right you are ; I don't think I'll go up,' O.E.D. Prob. the origin of *right-(h)o* and *rightio (righty-o)*, qq.v. ; cf. *right !, all*, q.v.

righteous. Excellent, e.g. 'a righteous day ', a fine one : coll. : from ca. 1860. Contrast *wicked*.

righteous, more holy than. Very holey or tattered : late C. 19–20. Applied to both persons (now ob.) and, always more gen., garments, esp. socks, stockings. (This kind of pun is rare among the upper and upper-middle classes.)

rightio !, righty-o !, righty-ho ! All right !; certainly ; gladly !: from ca. 1920. Ex *right-(h)o l* Dorothy Sayers, *Unnatural Death*, 1927, Lord Peter Wimsey *loquitur* : ' Righty-ho ! Wonder what the fair lady wants.'

righto ! See **right-ho.**

*rights, be to. To have a clear (legal) case against one : c. of ca. 1850–1910. ' Ducange Anglicus.'

righty-o(h) or -ho. See **rightio.**

rigmarole ; in C. 18, occ. **rigmarol.** A string of incoherent statements ; a disjointed or rambling speech, discourse, story ; a trivial or almost senseless harangue : coll. : from ca. 1730. Mme D'Arblay, 1779 (O.E.D.). A corruption of *ragman roll*, C. 13–early 16, a rambling-verse game ; also a list, a catalogue. (Other C. 18 variations are *rig-me-role, -my-roll* or *-role*, and *riggmonrowle*.)— 2. (Without a or the.) Such language : coll. : C.19–20.

rigmarole, adj. (With variant spellings as for the n.) Incoherent ; rambling ; trivially longwinded : coll. : from ca. 1750. Richardson, 1753, ' You must all . . . go on in one rig-my-roll way '; 1870, Miss Bridgman, ' A rigmarole letter'. O.E.D.

rigmarole, v.i. To talk rigmarole : coll. : from ca. 1830. (O.E.D.) Note : *rigmarolery* and *rigmarolic* are too rarely used to be eligible.

rigmarolish. Rather like a rigmarole : coll. : 1827, J. W. Croker (O.E.D.). The adv. (*-ly*) is too seldom used to be eligible.

rigs. See **rig**, n., 1, and **rig, run a.**—**rigs, up to one's or the.** Wide-awake, ' fly '; expert : s. : C. 19–20 ; ob. In late C. 18–early 19, *up . . . rig*, Grose, 1st ed.

rigsby. A wanton ; a romping (lad or) girl: coll. : from ca. 1540. In late C. 17–20, only dial. In C. 16, occ. *rigby*. Ex *rig*, a wanton.

rile. To vex, anger : coll. : U.S. (1825), anglicised ca. 1850, though the consciousness of its U.S. origin remained until ca. 1890 ; the v.i. *rile up*, grow angry, has not been acclimatised in Britain. A later form of S.E. *roil*.

riled, ppl.adj. Vexed, annoyed, angry : see **rile.** —**riling**, annoying, etc. : id.

rim-rack. To strain or damage (a vessel), esp. by driving her too hard in a sea : Grand Banks fishermen's coll. : late C. 19–20. Bowen. Prob. cognate with the Aberdeen *rim-raxing*, a surfeit (-ing) : E.D.D.

rimble-ramble, n. and **adj.** Nonsense, nonsensical : late C. 17 coll. Reduplication on *ramble*.

rinder. An outsider : Queen's University, Belfast : mid-C. 19–20. Ex *rind of fruit*.

ring (gen. with *the*). The female pudend : low coll. verging on euphemistic S.E.,—or is it the other way about ? C. 16–20, but rare after C. 18. Also *black—hairy—Hans Carvel's ring.*—2. ' Money extorted by Rogues on the High-way or by Gentlemen Beggers ', B.E. : c. of late C. 17–early 19. By 1785, it applied to any beggars ; ' from its ringing when thrown to them ', Grose.—3. See **ring, the dead.**—4. A good-conduct stripe : military : C. 20. F. & Gibbons.

ring, v. To manipulate ; change illicitly : from ca. 1785 : perhaps orig. c. ; certainly low s. (See **ring the changes.**)—2. Simply to change or exchange : from ca. 1810 : orig. low, then gen. s. Vaux.—3. Hence, or ex sense 1, to cheat (v.i. ; also *ring it*) : low : late C. 19–20. F. & Gibbons. —4. V. reflexive : c. from ca. 1860, as explained in *The Cornhill Magazine*, 1863 (vii, 91), ' When housebreakers are disturbed and have to abandon their plunder they say that they have rung themselves.'—5. See **ring in.**—6. V.i. (of cattle), to circle about : Australian coll. (– 1884) >, ca. 1910, S.E. ' Rolf Boldrewood.'—7. Even more essentially Australian is *ring*, v.i. and v.t., to shear the most sheep in a day or during a shearing (at a shearing-shed) : from ca. 1895 : coll. A. B. Paterson (*Banjo* as Australians affectionately call him), 1896, ' The man that " rung " the Tubbo shed is not the ringer here.' (Morris.) See **ringer**, 2.—8. See **ring a peal.**—9. See **ring it.**

ring, cracked in the. No longer virgin : late C. 16–20 ; ob. : coll. In C. 16–17, occ. *clipped (with)in the ring*. Lyly ; Beaumont & Fletcher. See **ring, n.**, 1.

ring, go through the. To go bankrupt : commercial : ca. 1840–80. H., 2nd ed. ? ex circus.

ring, have the. To ring true : coll. (– 1923), now verging on S.E. (Manchon.)

ring, the dead. ' A remarkable likeness ', C. J. Dennis ; astonishingly or very similar : Australian : C. 20. Perhaps ' as like as ring is to ring '; prob. suggested by the U.S. *be a ringer for*, to resemble closely.

ring (a person) **a peal.** To scold : coll. : C. 18–mid-19. Grose, 2nd ed., ' Chiefly applied to women. His wife rung him a fine peal ! '

ring bells. A coll. that (dating from ca. 1930) is gen. in the negative, as in Gavin Holt, *Trafalgar Square*, 1934, ' When it comes to pets, snakes don't ring any bells in my emotional system,' i.e. do not appeal to me. Ex the bell that rings when, at a shooting-gallery, a marksman hits the bull's-eye.

*ring-dropper, -faller. One who practises ring-dropping : c. : resp. from ca. 1795 and ca. 1560–1600. Cf. *fawney-dropper*, q.v., and :

*ring-dropping. The dropping of a ' gold ' ring and subsequent prevailing on some ' mug ' to buy it at a fair price for gold : c. : from ca. 1820. Bee.

ring in. To insert, esp. to substitute, fraudulently : from ca. 1810 : orig., perhaps c., certainly at least low s. Vaux. (Notably in gambling.) Cf. *ring*, v., 1.

ring it. The v.i. form of the preceding : low : late C. 19–20.—2. See **ring**, v., 2.—3. To show cowardice : military : from 1915. F. & Gibbons. Perhaps cf. *ring*, v., 6.

ring-man. The ring-finger : from ca. 1480 : coll. till C. 18, then dial. Ascham. (O.E.D.)

ring-money. A wife's allowance from the Government : military : 1914–19. Collinson. Ex showing her marriage-lines ; perhaps with reference to ring-paper.

ring off ! Desist ! ; shut up ! : C. 20 coll. Lyell. Ex telephonic *ring off, please !*

ring-pigger. A drunkard : coll. : ca. 1560–1600. Levins. (O.E.D.)

ring-neck. A jackaroo : Australian coll. : 1898, Morris, ' In reference to the white collar not infrequently worn by a Jackaroo on his first appearance '.

ring-tail. A recruit : military : ca. 1860–1914. Cf. *rooky, snooker*.

ring the changes. See **changes, ring the.**

ringer. A bell : (low) coll. : late C. 19–20 ; ob.— 2. An excellent person or thing, esp. with *regular* : Australian : 1894, *The Geelong Grammar School Quarterly*, April, ' Another favourite [school] phrase is a " regular ringer " ' (Morris). Ex *ringer*, that shearer who does the most sheep.—3. A quick changer of disguises : C. 20 c. Cf. Edgar Wallace's title, *The Ringer*, and *changes, ring the*, 3.

ringie, the. The man that, at two-up, keeps the ring, arranges the wagers, and pays out the winnings : Australian and New Zealand coll. : late C. 19–20.

***ringing castors.** The practice of substituting bad hats for good : c. (— 1812) ; virtually †. Vaux.

rings round, run. To beat hollow : Australian s. (— 1891) >, ca. 1910, fairly gen. coll. *The Argus*, Oct. 10, 1891. Ex sport, prob. ex Rugby, or ex Australian football. Morris. Cf. *circling-boy*, q.v.

rink, get out of one's. To sow wild oats : coll. : from ca. 1870 ; ob. by 1910, † by 1930. Perhaps ex skating ; prob. ex Scots *rink*, ' the sets of players ' forming sides at curling and quoit-playing (E.D.D.).

rinkasporum. An occ. Australian error for *rhyncospora* (a genus of plants) : from ca. 1880.

rino. See **rhino.**

rinse. A wash : coll. : 1837, Dickens, ' " I may as vel have a rinse," remarked Mr Weller ' (O.E.D.). —2. A drink : from ca. 1870 ; ob. Cf. C. 20 *gargle*.

rinse, v.i. To drink, esp. liquor : from ca. 1870. Prob. ex *rinse down* (with liquor).

rinse-pitcher. A toper : coll. : ca. 1550–1640. Bullein. (O.E.D.)

Rio. Rio de Janeiro : coll., mostly nautical : mid-C. 19–20. (W. McFee, *The Beachcomber*, 1935.)

Riot Act (to), read the. To reprove, administer a reproof : coll. : from ca. 1880.

rip. A mild term of reproof : coll. and dial. : C. 19–20. Ex *rip*, a rake, which may be ex *reprobate*. Rarely applied to a female.—2. A quick run, a rush : coll. ex dial. : from ca. 1870 ; ob. in coll. —3. A sword : ca. 1690–1750. Ned Ward, 1700 (Matthews). Proleptic.

rip ! An exclamation : coll. : late C. 16–mid-17. Cf. *rip me !*

rip !, let her. Let her go ! : U.S. (— 1859) anglicised ca. 1875 ; in C. 20, coll.

rip !, let her or **him.** A callous punning on *r.i.p.*, i.e. *requiescat in pace*, let him (her) rest in peace. Late C. 19–20. Cf. *r.i.p. !, let . . .*, q.v.

rip and tear. To be very angry : from ca. 1870 (ob.) : coll. and dial. Prob. on *rip and swear*, an intensive of dial. *rip*, to use bad language, to swear.

rip me ! A low coll. asseveration : mid-C. 19– early 20. Marriott-Watson.

ripe. Drunk : C. 19–20 ; ob. Bee. Either ex *reeling-ripe* (Shakespeare, Tennyson) or ex *ripe*, (of liquor) fully matured, with the occ. connotation of potent, or merely suggested by *mellow*.

ripe Richard. See **Richard, get the.**

rippen. A sol. variant (— 1887) of *rippin'* = *ripping*, q.v.

ripper. A person or thing esp. good : 1838, of a ball bowled extremely well at cricket (Lewis) ; 1851, Mayhew. Prob. ex *ripping*, adj., q.v.—2. In boxing, a knock-down blow : from ca. 1860 ; very ob.— 3. A notable lie : from ca. 1860 ; ob. Cf. *whopper*.— 4. One behaving recklessly ; a rip : 1877 (O.E.D.) ; ob.—5. A longshoreman taking his fish inland to sell : fishermen's : late C. 19–20. Bowen.

ripping, n. A ceremony (involving the ripping of his gown), ' incidental to the departure of a Senior Colleger for King's College, Cambridge ', F. & H. : Eton College : C. 19–20 : s. > coll. > j.

ripping, adj. Excellent ; very fast ; very entertaining : 1826, *The Sporting Magazine*, ' At a ripping pace ' ; 1858, ' Ripping Burton ' (ale). O.E.D. Cf. *rattling, stunning, thundering* (W.).—2. Occ. it verges on the advl., as in ' A ripping fine story ' (Baumann, 1887) and ' A ripping good testimonial ' (Conan Doyle, 1894 : O.E.D.). Cf. :

rippingly. Excellently ; capitally ; splendidly : 1892, Hume Nisbet.

ripstone. An incorrect form of *ribstone* : Dickens in *Pickwick*. O.E.D.

ris ; riz. (E.g. he) rose ; risen : both senses, sol. (— 1887). Baumann.

rise. A rise in salary : coll. >, ca. 1890, S.E. : 1837, Dickens, ' Eighteen bob a-week, and a rise if he behaved himself '.—2. In Australia, ' an accession of fortune ', C. J. Dennis : coll. : late C. 19–20.—3. A fit of anger : Cockney coll. : 1895, H. W. Nevinson, *Neighbours of Ours*. Ex v., 2.

rise, v. To raise, grow, rear : coll. (in C. 20, almost a sol., certainly low coll.) : 1844, Dickens, ' Where was you rose ? ', O.E.D.—2. To listen credulously, often—esp. in C. 20—with the connotation of to grow foolishly angry : coll. : 1856, Whyte-Melville. Ex a fish rising to the bait : cf. *bite*, v., q.v., and the S.E. *get, have*, or *take a rise out of a person*.

rise a barney. To collect a crowd : showmen's : from ca. 1855. H., 1st ed.

rise and shine. (Gen. in imperative.) To get up in the morning : military : C. 20. F. & Gibbons. The imperative is partly c.p., partly j.

rise (or raise) arse upwards. To be lucky : coll. : ca. 1670–1800. Ray. Rising thus from the ground was regarded as lucky.

***rise the plant.** See **plant, rise the.**

risky. Secretly adulterous : Society coll. : ca 1890–1905. ' John Strange Winter.' (Ware.)

rispin. See **respun.**

risy, adj. Apt to, trying to, take a *rise* out of persons : Cockney : C. 20. Esp. ' Don't be risy ! ' (Heard on Aug. 21, 1936.)

Rit, rit. A ritualistic Anglican clergyman : university : ca. 1870–1910. Ware.

rith. Three : back s. (— 1923). Manchon.

ritualistic knee. A sore knee caused by kneeling at prayers : medical coll. : ca. 1840–60. Ware.

river, up the. Reported to the Trade Union officials for speeding : workers' (— 1935). Perhaps ex American c., wherein *sent up the river* = sent to prison.

river hog or **pig.** A lumberman specialising in river work : Canadian lumbermen's : C. 20. John Beames.

River Lea. The sea : rhyming s. (— 1903). F. & H.—2. But orig., and until ca. 1900 gen., tea (— 1859). H., 1st ed. Cf. *Rosy Lee*.

River Ouse. A drink ; a drinking-bout : rhyming s. (on *booze*) : late C. 19–20. B. & P.

river pig. See **river hog.**

river(-)rat. 'A riverside thief : specifically one who robs the corpses of men drowned', F. & H. In the former sense, S.E. ; in the latter, c. : from ca. 1880.

river tick ; gen. **River Tick.** (F. & H. refers us to *tick*, where, however, no reference is made to *r.t.*) Standing debts discharged at the end of one's undergraduate days : Oxford University : ca. 1820–50. Egan's Grose.

rivets. Money : ca. 1890–1910. Prob. suggested by *brads*, q.v.

rivet(t)ed, ppl.adj. Married : app. ca. 1695–1730. Congreve, *The Way of the World*, 1700. (G. H. McKnight, *English Words*, 1923.) Cf. ' the modern *spliced* and *tied up*, the Scottish *buckled*, and the Australian *hitched* or . . . *hitched up* ', *Slang*, p. 64.

riz. See **ris.**

rizzle. ' To enjoy a short period of absolute idleness after a meal ' : provincial s. (not in E.D.D.) : 1890, *Cassell's Saturday Journal*, Aug. 2, ' the newest of new verbs '. Perhaps ex dial. *rizzle*, to dry by the heat of sun or fire, via the notion of sunning oneself.

roach, sound as a. See **sound as . . .**

roach and dace. The face : rhyming s. (— 1874). H., 5th ed.

road. A harlot : coll. : late C. 16–17. Shakespeare.—2. The female pudend : C. (?) 17–20, very ob. : either low coll. or S.E. euphemism. Cf. *road-making*, q.v.—3. Way, manner ; esp. in *any road*, occ. *anyroad* : non-aristocratic, non-cultured coll. : late C. 19–20. In dial. before 1886 ; Australian by 1888 (Boldrewood). P. MacDonald, *Rope to Spare*, 1932, ' Anyroad, sir, to cut a long story short, I gets down to the mill-'ouse.' Ex :—4. Direction ; esp. *all roads*, in every direction : (mostly lower-class) coll. : mid-C. 19–20.

road, gentleman or **knight of the.** A highwayman : C. 18–19 : coll. > journalistic S.E. See the paragraph at **knight.**

road, get the. To be dismissed from employment : Glasgow (— 1934). Prob. suggested by *walking-orders*, q.v.

road, give the. See **give the road.**

road-hog. An inconsiderate (cyclist or) motorist : 1898 (O.E.D.), though, in U.S., as early as 1891, of a cyclist : coll. >, by 1910, S.E.

road-making ; road up for repairs. A low phrase indicating menstruation : mid-C. 19–20. See **road, 2.**

*road-starver. A long coat without pockets : mendicants' c. : ca. 1881–1914. Ware.

roader. ' A parcel to be put out at a roadside station ', *The Times*, Feb. 14 : 1902 : railway coll. O.E.D.—2. A young ' swell ' in the Mile End Road : East London (— 1909) ; † by 1930. Ware.

roadster. A tramp : tailors' : late C. 19–20. Cf. *road, get the.*

roaf. (Cf. *rouf*, q.v.) Four : back s. (— 1874). H., 5th ed. Ex the sol. pronunciation of *four* as *foär* or *foër*.—2. Whence (same period) *roaf gen*, four shillings ; *roaf yanneps*, fourpence.

Roaming. See **Roming.**

roar. (Of horses) to breathe noisily : 1880 (O.E.D.) : coll. >, in C. 20, S.E. Cf. *roarer*, 1.

roar up. To speak abusively to ; shout at : lower classes' : from ca. 1905. F. & Gibbons.

roaratorio. See **roratorio.—roaration.** See **roration.—roaratorious.** See **roritorious.**

roarer. A broken-winded horse : from ca. 1810 : coll. >, ca. 1900, S.E. *Lex. Bal.* Cf. *roar*, v.—2. A riotously noisy reveller or bully : late C. 16–early 18 : coll. D. Rowland, 1586 ; 1709, Steele. Ex *roar*, *rore*, to riot. O.E.D.—3. A noisy or a rousing song : 1837, Marryat : coll., though the O.E.D. considers it S.E.

roaring. The disease in horses noted at *roar* and at *roarer*, 1. From ca. 1820 : coll. >, by 1900, S.E.

roaring, adj. Brisk, successful, esp. in *roaring trade* : from ca. 1790 : coll. >, ca. 1860, S.E. Grose, 3rd ed.—2. Boisterous ; (of health) exuberant : 1848, Thackeray. O.E.D.

roaring, adv. Extremely ; very greatly : lower classes' coll. (— 1923). Manchon.

roaring blade, boy, girl, lad, ruffian. A street bully ; a riotous, noisy, lawless female : C. 17–mid-18 (later, only archaic) : coll. A *roaring blade*, 1640, Humphry Mill ; *r. boy*, 1611, J. Davies (O.E.D.); *r. girl*, 1611, Middleton & Dekker (title) ; *r. lad*, 1658, Rowley, etc. (but current from ca. 1610) ; *r. ruffian*, 1664, Cotton.

roaring forties ; R. F. ' The degrees of latitude between 40° and 50° N—the most tempestuous part of the Atlantic ', F. & H. ; occ. the corresponding zone in the South Atlantic. Nautical coll. ; in C. 20, S.E. From ca. 1880.

roaring ruffian. See **roaring blade.**

*roast. To arrest : c. : late C. 17–early 19. B.E. ; Grose, 2nd ed. Perhaps on *(ar)rest*, via the idea of giving a person a hot time.—2. (Also *roast brown*.) To watch closely : c. : 1888, G. R. Sims, ' A reeler was roasting me brown.' Cf. *roasting*, n., c. sense.—3. To ridicule, to quiz (a person), severely or cruelly : 1726, Shelvocke : >, ca. 1760, coll. ; ob. Cf. *to warm*. (O.E.D.) In C. 20 Glasgow, esp. to pester.—4. In telegraphy, to click off a message so fast that it cannot be followed by (a person ; v.t.) : 1888 (O.E.D.) : telegraph-operators'.

roast, smell of the. To get into prison : coll. : ca. : 1580–1640. Nares.

roast a stone. To waste time and energy : coll. : ca. 1520–1620. Skelton. Apperson.

Roast and Boiled, the. The Life Guards ; military : ca. 1780–1830. Grose, 2nd ed., ' [They] are mostly substantial housekeepers, and eat daily of roast and boiled,' i.e. roast meat and boiled potatoes. Cf. *roast-meat clothes*, q.v.

roast-beef dress. Full uniform : naval coll. (— 1867) : ob. Smyth. Either ex *roast-meat clothes*, q.v., or ex the uniform of the royal beef-eaters.

*roast brown. A C. 20 variant of *roast*, v., 2. Manchon.

roast (h)and an(d) new (or noo). Roast shoulder (of mutton) and new potatoes : eating-house waiters' (— 1909). Ware.

roast meat, cry. To talk about one's good fortune or good luck : coll. : C. 17–early 19. Camden, B.E., Grose, Fielding, Lamb. Northall, 1894, notes that in dial. it also = to boast of women's favours. (Apperson.)

roast meat and beat with the spit, give (a person). ' To do one a Curtesy, and Twit or Upbraid him with it ', B.E. : coll. : ca. 1670–1820.

roast-meat clothes. Sunday or holiday clothes : coll. : late C. 17–mid-19. B.E., Grose.

roast meat for worms, make (one). To kill :

coll. : late C. 16–early 18. Shakespeare. Cf. the jocular S.E. *food for the worms.*

roast snow in a furnace. To attempt the absurd or unnecessary : coll. : C. 19–20 ; ob. Apperson.

roaster. A person burnt to death in a crash : Royal Air Force's (— 1935). By influence of ' the Oxford *-er* '.

roasting, vbl.n. of *roast,* v., in all senses except the first ; sense 2 occurs mostly in *give* (one) *a roasting,* recorded for 1879, and in *get a roasting,* to be very closely watched.

roasting-jack. The female pudend : low : mid-C. 19–20 ; ob. Ex S.E. sense.

Rob All My Comrades. The Royal Army Medical Corps : military, more gen. as c.p. than as nickname : G.W., but rare after 1916. F. & Gibbons.

rob-(o')-Davy. Metheglin : a mid-C. 16–mid-17 coll. variation of *roberdavy.* Taylor the Water Poet.

rob Peter to pay Paul. See **Peter to pay Paul, rob.**

rob the barber. To wear long hair : lower classes' coll. : late C. 19–20. Ware.

rob(-)the(-)ruffian. The female pudend : low coll. : C. 19–20 ; ob.

roba. See **bona roba.**

robe. A wardrobe : furniture-dealers' coll. : late C. 19–20. *The Spectator,* June 7, 1935. Cf. *board,* n., 2 : they may be written *'board* and *'robe.*

Roberdsmen, Robert's men, etc. ' The third (old) Rank of the Canting Crew, mighty Thieves, like *Robin-hood* ', B.E. : c. : C. 16–17. In other than this technical sense, it covers the period C. 14–20 and is S.E., though long archaic. Prob. on *Robert* + *robber.*

Robert ; Roberto. A policeman : coll. : resp. 1870, ca. 1890 ; both ob. Ex Robert Peel. Cf. *peeler.*

robin. See **Robin Redbreast.**—2. A penny : low : from ca. 1890 ; ob.—3. A ' little boy or girl beggar standing about like a starving robin ' : c. and low : late C. 19–20 ; ob. Ware.

Robin Hog. (Prob.) a constable : coll. : early C. 18. O.E.D.

Robin Hood. An audacious lie : coll. : ? C. 18–19. F. & H. Abbr. *tale of Robin Hood.*

Robin Hood, adj. Good : from ca. 1870. P. P., *Rhyming Slang,* 1932.

Robin Hoods, the. ' The 7th (Territorial) Battalion of the Sherwood Foresters ' : military nickname : late C. 19–20. F. & Gibbons. Sherwood Forest was Robin Hood's reputed haunt.

Robin Hood('s) bargain. A great bargain : coll. : C. 18. Cf. *pennyworth, Robin Hood('s).*

Robin Hood's choice. This—or nothing. Coll. : C. 17. (Apperson.)

Robin Hood's mile. A distance two or three times greater than a mile : coll. : ca. 1550–1700. Almost proverbial.

Robin Redbreast ; r. r. A Bow-Street runner : ca. 1840–70. Also *robin* and *redbreast.*

Robin Ruddock. Gold coin : ? late C. 16–mid-18. Manchon. See **ruddock, 1.**

robin's-eye. A scab (sore) : low : mid-C. 19–20 ; ob. Ex shape.

Robinson. See **Jack Robinson.**

Robinson Crusoe. Do so : from ca. 1890. P. P., *Rhyming Slang,* 1932.

roble. An † error for *romble (rumble).* O.E.D.

robustious was, ca. 1740–90, a coll. See esp. Johnson.

Roby Douglas. The anus : nautical : ca. 1780–1850. Grose, 1785, ' One eye and a stinking

breath ' : which indicates an allusion to one so named.

Rochester portion. ' Two torn Smocks, and what Nature gave ', B.E. : late C. 17–early 19. (N.b., *portion* is marriage-portion, *dot* ; *what* = physical charms in gen., but esp. the genitals in particular.) Cf. the C. 18–19 equivalent, a *Whitechapel portion.* Pegge, 1735, cites *R. p.* as a Kentish proverb.

rock. School (opp. to baker's) bread : Derby School : from ca. 1850. Less s. than coll. > j.— 2. A medium-sized stone : Winchester School coll. : from ca. 1860. Perhaps owing to U.S. and Australian use of *rock* as a stone however small.—3. See **Rock, the.**—4. See **rocks.**—5. See sense 2 of :

rock, v. To speak : tramps' c. (— 1893) ; very ob. Abbr. *rocker (rokker),* q.v.—2. V.t. ' To hit with a missile ; . . . also used by children for a hit when playing at marbles ', Pettman : South African coll. (— 1913). Ex Dutch *raken,* to hit, to touch.

Rock, the. Gibraltar : coll. : from ca. 1840. Ex the main feature of Gibraltar.—2. See **Old Steadfast.**

rock-a-low. An overcoat : dial. and (low) coll. (— 1860) ; ob. by 1890, † by 1910. H., 2nd ed. = Fr. *roquelaure.*

rock-nosing. ' Inshore boat work in the old whalers ' : whalers' coll. : ca. 1850–1910. Bowen.

rock of ages. Wages : rhyming s. : C. 20.—2. **by the rock of ages,** relying on sight ; without a measure : tailors' : 1928, *The Tailor and Cutter,* Nov. 29. Cf. :

rock of eye and rule of thumb, do by. To guess instead of measuring precisely : tailors' : from ca. 1860. Presumably *rock* = a movement to and fro.

Rock(-)Scorpion. A mongrel Gibraltarine : naval, military : from ca. 1850. Cf. S.E. *Rock English,* the Lingua Franca spoken at Gibraltar (Borrow, 1842). Ex *Rock, the,* q.v.

rocked. Absent-minded, forgetful : low (— 1812) † by 1900. Vaux. Ex :

rocked in a stone kitchen. A little weak in the head ; foolish : coll. : late C. 18–mid-19. Grose, 2nd ed., ' His brains having been disordered by the jumbling of his cradle ' on the stone floor. Cf. *half-rocked.*

rocker (or **rokker**) ; occ. **rock,** q.v. To speak : tramps' c. : from ca. 1850 ; since ca. 1900, gen. low s. H., 5th ed., 1874 ; C. Hindley, 1876, ' Can you rocker Romany . . . ? ' ; A. Morrison, 1894, ' Hewitt could rokker better than most Romany chals themselves.' Ex Romany *roker* (Sampson's *raker*), to talk, speak, with variant *voker* (cf. L. *vox, vocare*) ; cf. Romany *roker(o)mengro,* lit. a talk-man, i.e. a lawyer.

rocker, off one's. (Temporarily) mad ; extremely eccentric : low : 1897 (O.E.D.). Ex the piece of wood that enables a chair or a cradle to rock.

rocket, off one's. A military perversion (G.W.) of the preceding. F. & Gibbons.

rockiness. Craziness : from ca. 1898. Ex S.E. term influenced by *rocker, off one's.*

rocks. Jewels ; pearls ; precious stones : c. : from ca. 1920. Ex U.S. *rocks,* diamonds.

rocks, on the. Without means : coll. (— 1889) >, by 1910, S.E. Ex stranded ship.

rocks, pile up the. To make money : U.S. (*rocks,* money, 1847), partly anglicised ca. 1895. Kipling uses it in 1897 (O.E.D.). Prob. ex *rock* = a nugget : cf. *rock,* n., 2, and, in C. 20 U.S. c., *rock,* a precious stone.

rocks and boulders. (The) shoulders : rhyming s. : late C. 19–20. B. & P.

rocky. A R.N.R. rating ; a R.N.V.R. rating : naval : resp. ca. 1890–1914 and from ca. 1914. Bowen.

rocky, adj. A vague pejorative : e.g. unsatisfactory (weather), unpleasant or hard (for, on a person) : 1883 (O.E.D.). Ex S.E. *rocky*, unsteady, unstable, tipsy. Hence *go rocky*, go wrong.—2. Penniless—or almost : coll. : 1923, Galsworthy (O.E.D. Sup.). Ex *on the rocks*.

rod. The penis : coll. : C. 18–20. Also *fishing-rod* : C. 19–20 : s. Cf. the Fr. *verge*, which is literary.—2. Incorrect for *rad*, afraid : C. 16. O.E.D.

rod, v.i. and t. To coït (with) : low : C. 19–20. Ex *rod*, n., 1.

rod at, or **under, one's girdle.** With various vv., it implies a whipping, present or past : coll. verging on S.E. : ca. 1579–1620. Lyly, Jonson. O.E.D.

rod in pickle. See **pickle** and **piss.**

rod-maker. 'The man who made the rods used in *Bibling* (q.v.) ', Mansfield, referring to ca. 1840 : Winchester School : coll. > j. ; † by 1920.

roddy. A rhododendron : London lower-class coll. : 1851, Mayhew (E.D.D.). Cf. *rhody*, q.v.

rodger. See **roger, v.**

rodney or **R.** A (very) idle fellow : coll. : ca. 1865–95. Ex dial., where still extant, in the North and Midlands. Cf. the sad declension of *Sawney*.

roe. The semen : low : from ca. 1850 ; ob. Hence, *shoot one's roe*, emit. Ex fish-roe.

rofefil ; occ. **ro(u)f-efil.** A life sentence : back s. (— 1859) of *for life*. H., 1st ed. On *for life*.

***roge, roging.** C. 16–17 forms of *rogue, roguing*, qq.v.

***roger.** A beggar pretending to be a university scholar : c. of mid-C. 16. Copland. Cf. *rogue*.— 2. A goose : c. : mid-C. 16–18. Harman, Grose. Also *Roger* (or *Tib*) *of the buttery* : C. 16–18.—3. A portmanteau : c. : late C. 17–early 19. B.E., Grose. Perhaps a corruption of *poge*.—4. A thief-taker : c. of ca. 1720–60. *A New Canting Dict.*, 1725. ? via postulated *rogue-er*, a taker of rogues.— 5. The penis : from ca. 1650 : perhaps orig. c. Ex the name *Roger* : cf. *dick, John Thomas*.—6. A ram : rural coll. : ca. 1760–1900. Ex the name.— 7. A bull : coll. (— 1785) ; ob. Grose, 1st ed.— 8. See **Roger, jolly**.—9. See **old Roger**.—10. A gas-cylinder : military : 1916. W. Ex the code word therefor (F. & Gibbons).—11. Rum : military : from ca. 1912. F. & Gibbons. Ex a U.S. coon-ditty with the refrain ' O Rogerum ! '—12. ' The naval nickname of the senior officer of each section of the 4th Division of the Home Fleet . . . A contraction of Rozhdestvensky, the Russian Commander-in-Chief ', Bowen : C. 20 ; † except historically.

roger ; often **rodger.** To coït with (a woman) : perhaps orig. c. : 1750, Robertson of Struan, who spells it *rodger* ; Grose, 1st ed., ' From the name of Roger, frequently given to a bull '.

Roger, jolly ; in late C. 19–20, occ. **Roger.** A pirate's flag : 1785, Grose : coll. >, ca. 1850, S.E. Earliest record, 1723, as *old Roger* (W.). (A white skull in a black field ; ironic.)

Roger Gough. Scrub (or brush) bloodwood : Australian coll. : from early 1880's. ' An absurd name ', Morris : either ex the general that won the battles of Sobraon and Ferozeshah, or, as *The*

Australasian, Aug. 28, 1896, suggests, a corruption of an Aboriginal word now lost.

***Roger** (or **Tib**) **of the buttery ;** or **r.** (or **t.**) . . . See **roger**, n., 2.

Rogers. ' A ghastly countenance ' : Society : ca. 1830–50. Ware. Ex *Rogers*, the poet when old, or ex *the Jolly Roger* of the pirates.

***rogue.** A professed beggar of the 4th Order of Canters : c. : mid-C. 16–17 ; then historical. Awdelay implies it in *wild rogue* ; Dekker ; B.E. ; Grose. Whence S.E. senses. Perhaps an abbr. of *roger*, n., 1, of problematic origin, unless a perversion of † *rorer*, a turbulent fellow, on L. *rogare*, to ask.

***rogue,** v. To be a beggar, a vagrant : c. of ca. 1570–1630. Ex the n.

***rogue, wild.** A born rogue ever on tramp or a-begging : c. : ca. 1560–1700. Awdelay.

***rogue and pullet.** A man and woman confederate in theft : c. : mid-C. 19–20.

rogue and villain. A shilling : rhyming s. (— 1857). ' Ducange Anglicus.' On *shillin'*.

rogue in grain. A corn-chandler : ca. 1780–1840. Grose, 2nd ed. Lit., a great rogue. Cf. :

rogue in spirit. ' A distiller or brandy merchant ', Grose, 2nd ed. : ca. 1780–1840. Prob. suggested by *rogue in grain*, q.v., with a pun on *spirit(s)*.

rogue's salute. ' The single gun on the morning of a court-martial ' : naval jocular coll. : late C. 19–20. Bowen.

Rogues' Walk, the. From Piccadilly Circus to Bond Street : Society : ca. 1890–1905. Ware.

rogue with one ear. A chamber-pot : late C. 17–early 18. Randle Holme.

***roguing,** n. Tramping as rogue or vagrant : ca. 1575–1720 : prob. orig. c. Harrison, 1577 (O.E.D.). The c. origin is postulated, for *roguing* is ex *rogue*, n., via the v. Cf. :

***roguishness.** The being a *rogue*, q.v. : late C. 16–early 17 : prob. orig. c.

rogum pogum, or **dragum pogram** (**-um**). The plant goat's beard eaten as asparagus : late C. 18–mid-19 : less s. than dial. and low coll. Grose, 3rd ed., ' So called by the ladies '—ironic, this— ' who gather cresses, &c.'

***roister, royster.** In C. 17–early 18 c., one of a band of ' rude, Roaring Rogues ', B.E.

roker. A ruler (esp. *flat roker*) : stick ; poker : schools' : from ca. 1850. Ex *roke*, to stir a fire, a liquid : Halliwell.

***roker** (rare), **rokker,** v. See **rocker.**

[**role** or (unashamedly Fr.) **rôle** (italicised) is correct, the former being preferable as thoroughly English ; but either *role* (italicised) or *rôle* (without italics) is illogical—and silly.]

roll, n. See **rolls**.—**roll,** v. See the next seven or eight entries.—N., 2. Conceit ; ' side ' ; presumption : Shrewsbury School : from ca. 1890. Desmond Coke, *The Bending of a Twig*, 1906. Also at Harrow : witness A. Lunn, *The Harrovians*, 1913. (Cf. *lift*, a Shrewsbury synonym.) By pun ex the words *roll from side to side*.

roll, be at the top of (a person's). To be heartily scorned by him : Regular Army's : from ca. 1910. Frank Richards, 1933. Perhaps = at the head of the crime-sheet.

roll in every rig. To be up to every trick ; be up-to-date : low : Old Song, 1790, ' We roll in every knowing rig.'

***roll in one's ivories** or **ivory.** To kiss : 1780 Tomlinson in his *Slang Pastoral*, ' To roll in her ivory, to pleasure her eye'. After ca. 1850, always *ivories*. C.; ob. Cf. *ivory, ivories*; e.g. *flash the ivories*.

roll into. To pitch into; to thrash: coll.: Australian (and U.S.): 1890, 'Rolf Boldrewood'. (O.E.D.)

roll me in the dirt (occ. hyphenated). A shirt: rhyming s. (— 1874); † by 1915. H., 5th ed. In late C. 19–20, *dicky* (or *Dicky*) *dirt*.

roll me in the gutter. Butter: rhyming s.: late C. 19–20. F. & Gibbons.

*roll of snow. (A piece of) linen; (bundle of) underclothing: c. (— 1839). Brandon. See **snow**.

roll on(, big ship) !; roll on, duration ! A military c.p. (1917–18) expressive of a fervent wish that the war might end. Manchon. See **duration**; the ship is that which takes one back home.

*roll on, cocoa ! (Ex the preceding phrase and the phrase succeeding the present one.) A prison c.p., esp. as the indication of a desire for the evening meal to arrive: from ca. 1919. James Curtis, *The Gilt Kid*, 1936.

roll on, demobilisation. Engines of the Railway **O**perating **D**epartment plying between 'Pop' and 'Wypers': military: 1917–18. B. & P.

roll one's hoop. To go ahead; be successful (both with a connotation of playing safe): coll.: from ca. 1870; ob.

roll out. To rise (esp. in the morning): coll.: from ca. 1880. Abbr. *roll out of bed*.

*roll the leer. To pick pockets: c.: from ca. 1820; † by 1900. Egan, *Boxiana*, vol. iii, 'The boldest lad | That ever mill'd the cly, or roll'd the leer'.

roll up. A roly-poly pudding: coll.: in C. 20, S.E. and ob.: 1856 (O.E.D.). 1860, George Eliot. Cf. *dog in a blanket*.—2. A meeting: Australian: 1861 (O.E.D.): coll. till C. 20, then S.E.; anticipated in Grose (at *Hussar-Leg*). 'Rolf Boldrewood', 1890, 'As if you'd hired the bell-man for a roll-up'.—3. An order for a 'three-cross double' (q.v.) doubled: Glasgow public-houses' (— 1934).

roll up, v.i. To assemble: Australian s. >, ca. 1910, gen. coll.: 1887, J. Farrell, 'The miners all rolled up to see the fun.' Morris. Cf. *roll-up*, n., 2. —2. Hence, to appear on the scene: coll.: C. 20. (C.O.D., 1934 Sup.)

rolled on Deal Beach. Pitted with small-pox: nautical: late C. 19–20. Bowen. Ex 'the shingly nature of that beach'.

roller. A roll-call: Oxford University: 1883 (O.E.D.). Occ. *rollers*. Oxford *-er*.—2. See: *rollers. The horse and foot (police) patrols: c.: ca. 1810–40. Vaux. Presumably because they rolled along at a great pace.—2. U.S. rolling stock: Stock Exchange: from ca. 1885.—3. See **roller**.

Rollickers, the. The 89th Foot Regiment, later the Royal Irish Fusiliers: from ca. 1830: military; ob. F. & Gibbons. Ex their habits. Also, in 1798 +, known as *Blayney's Blood-Hounds*.

rolling. Smart, clever: low: ca. 1770–1870. ? ex *rolling blade*; cf. *rolling kiddy*.—2. Very rich: coll.: 1905, H. A. Vachell, 'He's going to marry a girl who's simply rolling' (Manchon). Abbr. *rolling in money* (or *wealth*).

*rolling kiddy. A smart thief: c.: ca. 1820–90. Egan, 'With rolling kiddies, Dick would dive and buy'; Lytton.

rolling off a log, (as) easy as. Very easy, easily: U.S. (1847), anglicised as a coll. ca. 1870.

rolling-motion dickey. The three-*wavy*-lined blue

jean collar worn by the Royal Naval Volunteer Reserve before the G.W.: naval: late C. 19–early 20. Bowen.

rolling-pin. The male member: low: mid-C. 19–20. Cf. *roly-poly*, 2.

Rolling Rezzie. H.M.S. *Resolution* of 1889: naval. Bowen.

rolls. A baker: C. 19–20, ob.: coll. Also, but rather S.E. than coll., *master of the rolls*: mid-C. 18–20; slightly ob. Adumbrated by Taylor the Water Poet. (O.E.D.)

Rolls. A Rolls-Royce motor-car: motorists' coll.: from ca. 1925.

rollster. An incorrect form of *roster*: C. **19.** Occ. *rolster*. O.E.D.

roly-poly. Un-deux-cinq (a game): Londoners': ca. 1820–50. Bee.—2. A jam roll pudding: 1848, Thackeray: coll. till ca. 1880, then S.E. Abbr. *roly-poly pudding*, also in Thackeray (1841). Also *roll-up* and *dog in a blanket*.—3. The penis: low: mid-C. 19–20; ob.

rom. See **rum** (adj.).—2. Occ. among tramps, *rom* = a male Gypsy: from ca. 1850. In Romany, *rom* is a bridegroom, a husband; any (adult) male Gypsy: see esp. Sampson.

Roman. 'A soldier in the foot guards, who gives up his pay to his captain for leave to work; serving like an ancient Roman, for glory and the love of his country,' Grose, 1st ed.: military: ca. 1780–1830.

Roman fall. That affected posture in walking which throws the head well forward and puts the small of the back well in; mostly among men, the women favouring the *Grecian bend*, q.v.: coll.: ca. 1868–71. *The Orchestra*, March 25, 1870.

[Romany. The language of the English Gypsies. See esp. O.E.D. and F. & H. It contributes many words to c. and to low s., esp. grafters'.]

Romany, patter. To talk Romany: C. 19–20: low. Vaux; Ainsworth.

Romany rye. A gentleman that talks and associates with Gypsies: mid-C. 19–20: coll. Ex Romany *rai* or *rei*, a gentleman. Popularised by Borrow's *The Romany Rye*, 1857.

*romboyle, or -s. The watch (early police): mid C. 17–18 c. Coles, 1676; B.E.; Grose. Occ. *rumboile, -boyle.*

*romboyle. To make hue and cry; search for with a warrant: c.: late C. 17–early 19. B.E.; Grose, 1st ed. Esp. *romboyled*, wanted by the constables. Whence *rumble*, q.v.

rombullion. See **rumbullion**.—**rombustical, rombustious.** See **rumbustical, rumbustious.**

*rome. See **rum,** adj., 1.—So for combinations, e.g. *rome mort*.

Rome, gone to. See **gone to Rome.** Cf. *return from Rome*, (of bells) to resume ringing after the forty-eight hours' Easter silence: Roman Catholic coll. (— 1890). Ware.

Rome-runner. A person, esp. a cleric, constantly running off to Rome in search of spiritual and monetary profit: coll.: mid-C. 14–15.

*Rome Ville, Romeville ; in C. 16–early 17, often -vyle. Also Rumville. London: c.: mid-C. 16–mid-19. Harman, Dekker, B.E., Grose. Lit., excellent city. See **rum,** c. adj., 1.

*romely. See **rumly.**

Romeo. Robert Coates (1772–1848), a London leader of fashion. Also *Diamond Coates*. He was very gallant, very wealthy. (Dawson.)

*Romeville. See **Rome Ville.—Romford.** See **Rumford.**

Romford. See **Rumford**.

Roming (or **Roaming**) **Catholic.** A sol. pronunciation of *Roman Catholic* : C. 19–20. Dorothy Sayers, *Unnatural Death*, 1927, ' A nice lady . . . a Roaming Catholic or next door to one '.

romp. To move rapidly (and with ease) : racing : from ca. 1890. J. S. Winter, 1891, ' To use the language of the turf, she romped clean away from them,' O.E.D. Cf. **romp away with.**

Romp, Miss. Mrs. Jordan (1762–1816), the actress. She was William IV's mistress when he was Duke of Clarence. Dawson.

romp away with. To win (a race) easily : racing s. : from ca. 1890. In C. 20, it is gen. coll., often used fig. Ex *romp*, q.v. Cf. :

romp home or **in**, v.i. To win very easily : racing s. >, in C. 20, gen. coll. : 1888, ' Thormanby ' (*romp in*) ; *Sporting Life*, March 20, 1891 (*romp home*, fig. of the winner of an athletic half-mile). O.E.D. and F. & H.

ronny. See **rouny**.

roo, 'roo. A rake : Society coll. : mid-C. 19–20 ; ob. I.e. *roué*.—2. A kangaroo : Australian : late C. 19–20. Properly a termination : cf. *kangaroo*, *potoroo*, *wallaroo* (Morris).

Roody Boys. Rue du Bois, near Neuve Chapelle (Flanders) : military coll. : G.W. (F. & Gibbons.)

roof. A hat : 1857, Hughes ; ob. O.E.D.—2. The head : 1897, ' Pomes ' Marshall ; slightly ob.

roof, hit the. See **hit the roof**.

roof-scraper. A spectator at the back of the gallery : theatrical coll. (— 1909). Ware. Cf. :

roofer. A wretched little theatre : lower classes' (— 1923). Manchon.

Rooinek. A British immigrant (1897) ; in Boer War, a British soldier : Boers' nickname : late C. 19–early 20. In Sth. African Dutch, lit. redneck. The name replaced *rooibatje*, red coat. Pettman ; W. ; O.E.D. Cf. *rough neck*, q.v.

*****rook.** A housebreaker's jemmy or ' crow ' (whence *rook*) : ca. 1786–1850. Grose, 2nd ed.—2. As a swindler or a sharper, from ca. 1575, and until C. 19, s. (in C. 18, coll.) ; perhaps orig. c. Cf. *hawk*.—3. A clergyman : 1859, H., 1st ed. ; ob. Ex black clothes.—4. A sloven : tailors' : from ca. 1870 ; ob. ? because his laziness ' rooks ' others of their time.

rook, v. To cheat ; defraud, and defraud of ; charge extortionately : late C. 16–20 : s. (? orig. c.) >, in C. 19, coll.

rookery. A gambling-hell : coll. : 1751, Smollett ; ob. Like the next, ex *rook*, to cheat.—2. A brothel : coll. : 1821, Egan ; ob.—3. A densely populated slum : coll. : 1823, Bee : coll. till. C. 20, then S.E. Ex *rookery*, a colony of rooks.—4. The subalterns' quarters in barracks : military (—1860). H., 2nd ed. Ex the noise.—5. A scolding-match, a row, disturbance : s. > coll. : 1824 (O.E.D.). Also dial. Cf. preceding sense.

rook(e)y ; rookie. A (raw) recruit : military : 1893, Kipling. A perversion of *recruit*, no doubt ; but with a pun on *rooky*, rascally, scampish.

rooking. Vbl.n. of *rook*, v., q.v. : mid-C. 17–20. **room.** See **fore-room**.—*****room(e)**, adj. See **rum**, adj., 1.

roomer. A lodger, esp. if occupying only one room : coll. : anglicised ca. 1875 ex U.S.

Rooshan. A Russian : sol. (— 1887). Baumann.

*****roosher.** A constable : c. : from ca. 1870 ; ob. Either a corruption of *rozzer*, q.v., or ex Scots *'rooser*, *ruser*, a braggart.

roost. A garret : low Scots coll : C. 19–20. Jamieson, 1808. (O.E.D.)—2. A resting-place ; a bed : coll. (— 1860). H., 2nd ed.

roost, v.i. To perch ; seat oneself : coll. : 1816, Scott (O.E.D.). Ex fowls.—2. V.t., to imprison : military : ca. 1870–1910. ? ex *roster*.—3. V.i., to cheat ; v.t., roost over ; also, to take a rise out of a person : low : from ca. 1880 ; ob.

*****roost-lay.** The practice—and art—of stealing poultry : c. : from ca. 1810. *Lex. Bal*.

rooster. The female pudend : low : mid-C. 19–20 ; ob. Where the —— roosts.—2. See **queer rooster**.—3. A member who makes himself heard : Parliamentary : from ca. 1860 ; ob. Ware.—4. An angler keeping to one place : River Lea anglers' (— 1909). Ware.

*****roosting-key.** A lodging-house ; a ' doss-house ' : c. (— 1887). Baumann.

root. Money : coll. (— 1899) ; ob. Abbr. *root of all evil*.—2. (Also **man-root**.) The penis : low coll. : C. 19–20.—3. Whence, a priapism : low : late C. 19–20. Esp. in *have the, get the r*. Cf. *rootle*, q.v.—4. Bottom (of, e.g., a class) : Charterhouse : C. 20.—5. A kick on the posterior : late C. 19–20 ; orig. Public Schools'. Ex :

root, v.t. To kick (a ball, a person) : late C. 19–20. Semantics : *uproot*, *root up*. Perhaps orig. Public Schools' ; Ian Hay, *The Lighter Side of School Life*, 1914, ' We rooted Sowerby afterwards for grinning.'

root, the old. The male member : perhaps rather coll. than s. : C. 19–20.

root, the real. The real thing ; the best or the correct thing (to do) : C. 20 ; slightly ob. Prob. ex *the real root of the matter is* . . .

root-about. Promiscuous football practice : school's (orig. Leys) : late C. 19–20.

root about, v.i. To indulge in such practice : ib. : same period.—2. To search, esp. by rummaging about : dial. and, by C. 20, coll. Ex pigs rooting.

rooter. Anything very good, of prime quality. 1860, H., 2nd ed. E.g. a very smart dress, a brilliant gem.—2. Hence, anything (or any act) very flagrant (e.g. a lie) or brutal (attack, blow, ? orig. kick) : from ca. 1865. Both senses very ob.

rooti. See **rooty**.

rootle, v.i. To coït : low : from ca. 1850 ; ob. Ex S.E. sense, to grub, poke about.—2. Also as n., in *do a rootle* : from ca. 1880. Cf. *root*, n., 2, 3.—3. To go or run about the place : from ca. 1925. Ronald Knox, *The Body in the Silo*, 1933. Ex *root* (*around*) + *tootle* (to go).

rooty ; rooti. Bread : military : in India, from ca. 1800 ; fairly gen. from 1881, when the Army was reorganised. First recorded in 1883, G. A. Sala (a notable slangster) in *The Illustrated London News*, July 7. Ex Hindustani *roti*. (After the G.W., common among tramps as = casual-ward bread. Frank Jennings, 1932.)—2. Hence, food in gen. : military : C. 20. F. & Gibbons.

rooty gong. A long-service medal : Regular Army : late C. 19–20. F. & Gibbons. Ex preceding + *gong*, q.v. Occ. *rooty medal*.

rope, v.t. To hold a horse in check so that it shall not win : racing coll. : 1857, G. Lawrence (O.E.D.) ; in C. 20, S.E. Also, in late C. 19–20, *rope in*.—2. V.i., to hold back in order to lose a race : racing and athletic coll. >, in C. 20, S.E. : 1874, H., 5th ed.

rope, cry (a). To cry a warning : late C. 16–17 :

coll. Shakespeare, 'Winchester Goose, I cry a rope ! a rope ! '; Butler, 1663, 'When they cry rope '. ? Ex hanging rope.

rope, for the. Due, or condemned, to be hanged : police coll. : late C. 19–20. Charles E. Leach.

rope-hooky. (Of hands) with fingers curled in : nautical coll. : late C. 19–20. Bowen. Esp. an old shell-back's, from years of handling ropes.

rope in. See rope, 1.—2. To decoy ; enlist the services of : U.S. (— 1848) anglicised, as a coll., ca. 1890 ; after ca. 1918, S.E. Prob. ex lassoing.—3. Hence, *rope in the pieces*, to make money : coll. : late C. 19–20.—4. (**rope in.**) To arrest : coll. (now verging on S.E.) : from ca. 1920.

rope to the eye of a needle, put a. To attempt the absurd, the impossible : semi-proverbial coll. : C. 19. Apperson.

Rope-Walk (or r. w.), go into the. 'In the law . . . a barrister is said to have gone into the rope-walk, when he has taken up practice in the Old Bailey,' Temple Bar, 1871 ; ob. As Serjeant Ballantine shows in his *Reminiscences*, 1882, when he says, 'What was called the Rope-Walk [at the Old Bailey] was represented by a set of agents clean neither in character nor person', *the rope-walk* meant also a set of shysters battening on Criminal Law ; moreover, he implies that the term dates back at least as early as 1850.

rope-yarn Sunday. A Sunday off : nautical coll. (— 1887) ; slightly ob. Baumann.—2. More correctly, a synonym of *make and mend*, q.v. : nautical coll. : late C. 19–20. Bowen.

ropeable. Angry ; quick-tempered : from ca. 1890 : Australian. Ex *ropeable* (i.e. *wild*) *cattle*.

roper. A hangman : †, says Bee in 1823. See *Mr Roper*.—2. One who 'ropes ' a horse (1870) or, in athletics, himself (1887) : coll. till C. 20, then S.E. See rope, 1 and 2. Occ. (of a horse only), *roper-in*. Dates : O.E.D.

roper-in. See roper, 2.—2. A decoy to a gambling den : U.S. (— 1859), anglicised ca. 1880 : coll. >, ca. 1910, S.E. See rope in.

Roper, Mr ; or **the roper.** The hangman : jocular coll. : ca. 1650–1750. (Cf. *John Roper's window*, q.v.) Charles Sackville, 6th Earl of Dorset. Cf. *Roper's news*, no news, in the Cornish *that's Roper's news—hang the crier !* (Apperson.)

Roper, Mrs. A Marine ; the Marines : naval (— 1868) ; ob. ' Because they handle the ropes like girls, not being used to them ' (Brewer). Cf. the C. 17 S.E. sense of *roper* : one deserving the rope.

Roper, marry Mrs. To enlist in the Marines : naval (— 1864) ; ob. H., 3rd ed. Ex preceding.

Roper's window, John. A rope-noose : ca. 1550–1640 : coll. Huloet (O.E.D.).

ropes, be up to or **know the.** To be well-informed, expert ; artful : coll. (in C. 20, S.E.) : 1840, Dana, 'The captain . . . knew the ropes '; *be up to*, not before ca. 1870 and only in ' artful ' sense.

ropes, on the high. See high ropes.

ropes, pull or **work the.** To direct ; exercise one's influence : coll. (in C. 20, S.E.) : from ca. 1880.

ropes, put up to the. To inform fully ; to ' put wise ' : from ca. 1875 : coll. Ex *ropes, know the*, q.v. Besant & Rice, 1877, have ' You've put me up to ropes '; *up to the* . . . is much commoner, at least in C. 20.

roping, vbl.n. See rope, v.

*****ropper.** A scarf ; a comforter : tramps' c. : 1873, Greenwood. ? *wrapper* perverted, asks

F. & H. : this seems viable, for cf. † Scots *roppin*, to wrap. (E.D.D.)

*****roram.** The sun : c. : late C. 18--mid-19. Tufts. ? ex *Roland*, suggested by *Oliver*, c. for the moon, as F. & H. ingeniously suggests.

roration ; rarely **roaration.** ' An oration pronounced with a loud unmusical voice ', Grose, 1785 ; † by 1890 : jocular coll. or s. As in *roratorio, roar* is punned. Cf. :

roratorio or **roaratorio.** ' *Roratorios and Uproars*, oratorio's and opera's ', Grose, 1785 ; † by 1890. Sometimes sol. (cf. the Northamptonshire *roratory*, an oratorio), sometimes jocular coll. or s. Cf. :

roritorious ; roaratorious. (Jubilantly) noisy : ca. 1820–60. Egan, 1821, 'The Randallites '—i.e. partisans of the great boxer—' were roritorious and flushed with good fortune.' Punning *oratorio* and *uproarious*, and perhaps *notorious*. Cf. the S.W. dial. *rory-tory*, ' loud, noisy, stirring ' (E.D.D.).

rort at. To complain of ; blame fiercely : low : C. 20. (Michael Harrison, *Spring in Tartarus*, 1935, ' It isn't you . . . that I'm rorting at.') Ex *rorty*, q.v.

rortiness ; rarely **rortyness.** The abstract n. of :

rorty ; occ. **raughty.** Of the best ; excellent ; dashing ; lively ; jolly ; sprightly : costers' : from ca. 1860. ' Chickaleary ' Vance, ca. 1864, 'I have a rorty gal '; Milliken, 1893, ' We'd a rare rorty time of it ; ' Whiteing, 1899, ' A right-down raughty gal.' Ware ranks a *rorty toff* as inferior to a *rorty bloke*. W. suggests a rhyme on *naughty*.— 2. Amorous : low : from not later than 1893. Manchon.—3. Likewise ex sense 1 ; always in trouble : military : C. 20. F. & Gibbons.

rorty, adv. to **rorty,** adj., 1 : C. 20. O.E.D. (Sup.).

rorty, do the. To have a good time : costers' (— 1893). Milliken. Ex *rorty*, adj., 1.

rorty dasher ; 2, **rorty toff.** A fine fellow ; 2, an out-and-out swell : costers' : from ca. 1880.

rory ; R. Short for :

Rory o' More. A whore (— 1874 ; ob.) ; a floor (— 1857) ; a door (— 1892). Resp. H., 5th ed. ; ' Ducange Anglicus ' ; ' Pomes ' Marshall, 'I fired him out of the Rory quick.'

Rorys, the. The 93rd Highlanders, later the Argyll and Sutherland Highlanders : military : mid-C. 19–early 20. F. & Gibbons. *Rory* being a common Scottish name.

ros-bif Yorkshee. A red-faced Yorkshireman : in the catering trade, esp. in Italian restaurants : C. 20. Ex the fact that Yorkshiremen expect to find roast beef and Yorkshire pudding even in Italian restaurants.

rosa, sub. See sub rosa.

Rosalie. A bayonet : rare military : 1915–18. B. & P. Adopted from Fr. s., where it was more common among civilians than among soldiers.

*****rosary, the.** A variation of the confidence trick : c. : C. 20. Charles E. Leach.

rosary-counter. A Roman Catholic : Irish Orangemen's (— 1934).

rose. The female pudend ; a maidenhead : C. 18–20.—2. A bitch : showmen's : from ca. 1860. —3. An orange : 1860, H., 2nd ed. ; † by 1915. ? ex the sweet smell.

rose, v. Raised. See rise, v.—2. Risen : S.E. until C. 19, then sol. Baumann.

rose, pluck a. To take a virginity ; (among women) to ease oneself in the open air : both coll.

verging on euphemistic S.E.: **C**. 18–20. Swift (2nd sense).

rose, strike with a feather and stab with a. To punish playfully: coll.: ca. 1888–1914. Ex a music-hall refrain; cf., however, Webster's ' *M*. If I take her near you, I'll cut her throat. *F*. With a fan of feathers,' 1612. Cf. *run through the nose with a cushion*, q.v.

rose, under the. In confidence; ' on the quiet '; secretly: mid-C. 16–20: S.E. >, ca. 1660, coll. >, ca. 1850, again S.E. Dymock, 1546; Grose. Here, *rose* = rose-bush; *sub rosa* is modern, not Classic, L. Grose, 2nd ed., mentions that the rose was ' sacred to Harpocrates, the God of Silence ', as does Sir Thomas Browne.

rose-coloured. ' Bloody ': coll. euphemism (– 1923); ob. Manchon. Also *roseate*: id.; id. Ibid.

Roseberys. London County Council 2½% Stock: money-market: late C. 19–early 20. Ex Lord Rosebery, who was the first Chairman of the Council. Incorrectly *Roseberrys* or *-berries*.

rosebuds. Potatoes: rhyming s. (on *spuds*): late C. 19–20. B. & P.

rosella. A European working bared to the waist: Northern Australia (– 1898). ' The scorching of the skin . . . produces a colour which probably suggested a comparison with the bright scarlet of the parrakeet so named,' Morris.

roses and raptures. A literary c.p. (ca. 1830–90) applied to the *Book of Beauty* kind of publication. Ware.

rosey. See **rosy.**

rosh; roush. To horse-play: Royal Military Academy: from ca. 1880. Hence, *stop roshing !*, be quiet! Perhaps a corruption of *rouse*. .

rosie. A rubbish-tin: nautical, esp. stewards' (– 1935). Perhaps ex the stench.—2. See **rosy.**

rosin. A fiddler: coll.: 1870, *Figaro*, Oct. 31, ' They playfully call me " Rosin " . . . yet I must . . go on with my playing.' Ex the rosin used on violin bows.—2. Fiddler's drink: coll.: mid-C. 19–20; ob. H., 3rd ed. Ex S.E. *rosin*, to supply with, or to indulge oneself in, liquor.

rosin-the-bow. A fiddler: coll (– 1864); very ob. Ex a song so titled. Cf. *rosin*, 1.

Rossacrucian. A follower of O'Donovan Rossa: journalistic: 1885–6. Invented by G. R. Sims, punning *Rossa* and *Rosicrucian*.

rosser. See **rozzer.**—*rost* = *roast*. See **roast.**

rost, turn roast to. From arrogant to become humble: coll.: C. 16. Halliwell. Prob. ex the humbling of a boastful cook, *rost* being rust.

rosy, always preceded by **the.** Wine: 1840, Dickens, ' Richard Swiveller finished the rosy, and applied himself to the composition of another glassful.' Orig. and properly, red wine; cf. Fr. s. *le rosé*, which Kastner & Marks have omitted in their excellent Glossary.—2. Blood: sporting (– 1891); ob. *Sporting Life*, March 25, 1891. Suggested by *claret*, q.v.—3. Good fortune: Cockney (– 1893); Milliken. Ex *rosy*, favourable, of good omen.—4. **(Rosy.)** Abbr. of **Rosy Lee**: esp. among grafters: C. 20. Philip Allingham, *Cheapjack*, 1934.

rosy, do the. To have a ' rosy ', i.e. pleasant, time: Cockney (– 1893); ob. Milliken, ' A doin' the rorty and rosy as lively as 'Opkins's lot '.

rosy, give the. See **give the rosy.**

Rosy Lee. Tea: rhyming s.: late C. 19–20. F. & Gibbons.

rot. Nonsense trash, ' bosh ' (q.v.): s. >, ca.

1920, coll.: 1848, O.E.D.; 1861, H. C. Pennell, ' " Sonnet by M. F. Tupper ". A monstrous pile of quintessential rot.' Like *rotter*, ' app. first at Cambridge ', W. Ex *rot*, dry rot, decay. Also *tommy rot*, q.v., and *dry rot*: coll. (– 1887); † by 1920 (Baumann).

rot, v. To chaff severely: 1890, Lehmann, ' Everybody here would have rotted me to death '; slightly ob. Ex *rot*, n. (O.E.D.)—2. To talk nonsense : 1899, Edén Phillpotts; ob. (O.E.D.)—3. In imprecations: late C. 16–19: coll. Shakespeare, 1588, ' But vengeance rot you all.' Semantics: ' may you go rotten ! ' Also in *rot it !*, C. 17–18, and *rot* (*up*)*on*, C. 17. In *rot um !*, *um* = 'em, them. (Extant, though ob., in dial.)—4. To spoil; mar nonsensically or senselessly: 1908, A. S. M. Hutchinson, ' He was rotting the whole show.' Also *rot up*, as in Desmond Coke, *The House Prefect*, 1908 : orig. Public Schools'.

rot! Nonsense !; bosh !: from ca. 1860. Henley & Stevenson, 1892, ' Oh, rot, I ain't a parson.' Ex the n., q.v.; quite independent of *rot*, v., 3. Cf. *rotten !*

rot about. To waste time from place to place; to play the fool: from late 1890's. Ware.

rot-funk. A panic: cricketers': ca. 1890–1914. Ware.

rot-gut; occ. rotgut. Any unwholesome liquor; esp. inferior weak beer: late C. 16–20: coll. >, by C. 19, S.E. G. Harvey, 1597. Occ. as adj.: C. 18–20. T. Hughes, ' rot-gut stuff '. Grose, 1785, rhymes thus, ' *Rot gut*, small beer, called beer a bumble, | Will burst one's guts before 'twill make one tumble.'

Rot-His-Bone, be gone to. To be dead and buried: late C. 18–early 19. Grose, 1785. Punning Ratisbon. Cf. *be gone to the Diet of Worms.*

rot it !; rot on !; rot um !; rot upon ! See **rot**, v., 3.—For **rot up**, see **rot**, v., 4.

rotan. A wheeled vehicle: 1725, *A New Canting Dict.*; Grose; † by 1870. Prob. c. Ex L. *rota*. Whence, according to Bee, comes *Rotten Row*: which etymology may be correct.

Rothschild. See **come the Rothschild.**

rotten. In a deplorable state or ill-health; ill; worthless; ' beastly ': from ca. 1880. R. L. Stevenson, 1881, ' You can imagine how rotten I have been feeling,' O.E.D.—2. Drunk: Glasgow (– 1934). Proleptic.

[**rotten, bells go.** In C. 20, certainly j.; prob. always j. For those who wish to claim it as unconventional English, I supply two references: E.D.D. at *bell*, n.; R. G. K. Wrench, *Winchester Word-Book*, 2nd ed., 1901, at *peals* and *rotten*.]

rotten ! An expletive corresponding to **rotten**, sense 1: from ca. 1890.

rotten-guts. A person with stinking breath: lower classes' coll. (– 1923). Manchon.

rotten orange ; Rotten Orange, the. A follower of William III : William III himself : Jacobites': 1686–ca. 1700. Ware. Because he was Prince of Orange.

Rotten Row. ' A line of old ships-in-ordinary in routine order ', Smyth, 1867: nautical; ob.—2. A bow: rhyming s. (– 1909). Ware.

Rotten Row, belong to. (Of ships) to be in ordinary: naval: C. 19. Bowen.—2. Whence (likewise of ships) to be discarded as unserviceable: nautical: from ca. 1890; ob. A pun on *Rotten Row*, perhaps via *rotten borough.*

rotten sheep. A useless person (esp. male), a

mean traitor : Fenian : 1889, *The Daily News,* July 3 ; ob. Ex a sheep affected with the rot.

rotter. An objectionable person : 1894, George Moore (O.E.D.). Ex *rot,* n., and *rotten.* (Addenda.)

Rouen, client for. A soldier venereally infected : military coll. : 1915 ; ob. F. & Gibbons. The main venereal hospital was there.

rouf. Four : back s. (— 1859). H., 1st ed.

rouf-efil. See rofefil.

rough, n. A rough rider : coll. : 1899, *The Daily News,* Feb. 23 (O.E.D.) ; ob. Cf. *rougher.*

rough, adj. See rough on.—2. Of food, esp. fish : coarse, inferior, stale : London coll. : from ca. 1850 ; slightly ob. Mayhew, ' The . . . " rough " fish is bought chiefly for the poor.'

rough, a bit of. A woman, esp. if viewed sexually ; low : from ca. 1870.

rough, cut up. See cut up rough.

rough and tough. A (? rhyming) coll. variant of *rough* : ca. 1880–1915. Baumann. = *rough neck,* q.v.

rough and tumble (often hyphenated). A free fight ; a go-as-you-please fight : from ca. 1810 : boxing coll. >, ca. 1910, S.E. (The adj. is S.E.)— 2. The female pudend : low : from ca. 1850. Also *the rough and ready.* Cf. *rough, a bit of,* and *rough malkin.*

rough as a sand-bag. (Of a story) very exaggerated ; (of a person) uncouth or objectionable : military coll. : C. 20. F. & Gibbons. Cf. *rough as bags.*

rough as a tinker's budget (bag). Very rough : ca. 1650–1700. Howell. (Apperson.) Cf. :

rough as bags. (Of persons) very rough or uncouth : Australian coll. : C. 20.

rough as I run it runs. Though I am rough, coarse, ignorant ; it's certainly rough : coll. : late C. 17–mid-19. T. Brown, 1687, ' If you don't like me rough, as I run, fare you well, madam ' ; Ray, 1813, ' Rough as it runs, as the boy said when the ass kicked him.' Apperson.

rough diamond. A person of good heart and/or ability but no manners : from ca. 1750 : coll. till ca. 1880, then S.E. *The Adventurer,* 1753 : Lytton.

rough fam or **fammy** ; occ. hyphenated. A waistcoat pocket : c. : ca. 1810–50. Vaux. In c., *fam* (q.v.) is the hand : ? ex the habit of putting one's thumb in the pocket.

rough house. Disorder ; a quarrel ; a noisy disturbance or struggle : coll. ; U.S. (1887) anglicised ca. 1910.

rough-house, v. To treat roughly : coll., orig. (ca. 1900) U.S. ; anglicised ca. 1914. O.E.D. (Sup.). Ex the n.—2. Hence, to act noisily or violently : coll. : 1920, ' Sapper ' (ibid.).

rough Malkin (or m.). The female pudend : low Scots : C. 16.

rough neck, rough-neck, roughneck. A rough, ignorant fellow : U.S. (1836, a rowdy), anglicised ca. 1910 : coll. Cf. *rooinek,* q.v.

rough on. Hard for ; bearing hardly on : coll. : U.S. (1870, Bret Harte), anglicised ca. 1885 (e.g. Besant, 1887). ? ex *rough luck* (cf. tough luck).—2. Severe on or towards (a person) : coll. : U.S. (1870), anglicised ca. 1890. Hardy, 1895. O.E.D. Cf. :

rough on rats ; gen. it's . . . Rough luck : from ca. 1890. See rough on.

rough-rider's (or -ers') wash-tub. The barrack water-cart : military : ca. 1890–1915.

rough-up. A contest arranged at short notice ;

an informal contest : orig., boxing : 1889, *The Referee,* Jan. 26.—2. Hence, a trial race : esp. turf s. : C. 20. (O.E.D. ; Manchon.)

rougher. A rough-rider (cf. *rough,* n.) : coll. : C. 20 ; ob. (O.E.D.)—2. A rough time ; a severe tackle at Rugby football : Scottish Public Schools' : from ca. 1910. Ian Miller, *School Tie,* 1935. By ' the Oxford-er '.

roughing, vbl.n. A students' ' scragging ' of a university teacher of whom they disapprove : Scottish undergraduates' s. (late C. 19–20) >, by 1920, coll.

roughy. A rough man ; a rough horse, etc. : Australian coll. : C. 20. *What I Know,* by a Philosophic Punter, 1928,—a little-known and amusing book ; Ion L. Idriess, *Flynn of the Inland,* 1932.

round. A shirt collar : 1859, H. ; † by 1910. Perhaps ex trade names *all rounds, all rounders.*—2. ' A bedside dissertation and demonstration of cases in a ward by the senior physician or surgeon to students' ; if the audience consists of qualified practitioners, and if the cases are obscure, it is a *hot-air round* or *shifting dullness* (cf. the technical sense) : medical students' (— 1933). See esp. *Slang,* p. 192.—3. ' Punishment consisting of running round playground ' : Bootham School : C. 20. Anon., *Dict. of Bootham Slang,* 1925.

round, v.i. To peach, lay information : low : from ca. 1859. V.t., *round on.* H., 1st ed. Prob. a development of *round on,* to turn upon and berate.

round. Languid : tailors' : from ca. 1870 ; ob. ? ex *circular padding.*

round, bet. To bet upon—or against—several horses : the turf : from ca. 1820 ; in C. 20, coll. ' Jon Bee ', 1823.

*round-about. A treadmill (invented ca. 1821) : prison coll. rather than s. or c. : from ca. 1823 ; ob. Bee.—2. A female thief's all-round pocket : c. : from ca. 1820. ' Jon Bee ', 1823.—3. A housebreaking tool that cuts out a round piece (about five inches in diameter) from shutter or door : c. : from ca. 1820. Egan's Grose. Occ. *round Robin,* C. 19. —4. A big belly : lower classes' (— 1923). Manchon.

round and square. Everywhere : rhyming s. (— 1903). Not very gen.

round betting. See round, bet.

round dozen. Thirteen lashes with the cat-o'-nine-tails : naval coll. : C. 19. Bowen.

round me houses. The earliest form of *round the houses,* q.v. ' Ducange Anglicus ', 1857. In C. 20, gen. . . . *my* . . .

round mouth, gen. preceded by **the.** The fundament : low : ca. 1810–70. Also *brother r. m.,* esp. in *Brother round mouth speaks,* he has broken wind. *Lex. Bal.*

round-mys. Trousers : rhyming s. (— 1909). Ware. Abbr. *round my houses.*

round o (or **O**). A notable lie : coll. : C. 17. Ex the *oh !* of remonstratory surprise.—2. No runs ; batsman's score of ' O ' : cricket coll. : ca. 1855–65. Reade in 1863 refers to it as ' becoming obsolete ' (O.E.D.).

round one or **un.** A notable lie : mid-C. 19–20 ; ob. H., 5th ed.

round robin. The host : low coll. : mid-C. 16–17. Coverdale, Foxe, Heylin. Cf. *jack-in-the-box,* q.v.— 2. A housebreaker's tool : see round-about, 3.—3. ' A good hearty swindle ', Clarkson & Richardson, 1880 : c.

round shaving. A reprimand : (low) coll. : from ca. 1870 ; ob. Ex dial.

round the bend. Crazy ; mad : naval : mid-C. 19–20 ; ob. Bowen.

round the buoy. See buoy, **round the.**

round the corner. A military c.p. reply to ' How far is it ? ' : 1914 ; ob. B. & P.

*****round the corner, get** (one). Deliberately to annoy an irritable person : c. : ca. 1810–50. Vaux, who notes the variant *get* (one) *out.*

round the corner, wrong (all). Having had something strong to drink : lower classes' : from the middle 1890's ; slightly ob. Ware.

round the houses. Trousers : rhyming s. (1859) on sol. pronunciation, *trousies.* H., 1st ed. An improvement on orig. form, *round me houses.*

round 'un. See **round one.**

*****roundem.** A button : c. : from ca. 1860. H., 3rd ed. A disguising of *round* (cf. *roundy*).—2. Whence, the head : c. (— 1923). Manchon.

rounder. One who peaches : low : 1884 (O.E.D.). Ex *round,* v.—2. A short, close-fitting jacket : coll. : mostly Cockney : from ca. 1890. Milliken, 1893, ' That's me in plaid dittos and rounder.' Ex *round-about* in same sense.

Roundhead. A Puritan : coll. : 1641 ; S.E. by 1800. Ex cropped head. Cf. *square head.*

rounding. A betrayal of one's associates : low : 1864. See **round,** v. ; cf. *rounder,* 1.

*****rounds.** Trousers : tramps' c. : from ca. 1890. P. H. Emerson. Ex *round the houses.*

rounds of the galley. Openly expressed abuse of a seaman by his mess-mates : naval : ca. 1850–1910. Bowen.

*****roundy(-ken).** A watch-house or lock-up : c. of ca. 1825–60. Egan. Lit., round place.

*****rouny.** A potato : c. of ca. 1820–70. Haggart. Also (? misprint), *ronny.* A corruption of *roundy,* a round object : cf. dial. *roundy,* a lump of coal.

*****rouse,** v.i. To fight : c. : 1888, *The Evening Standard,* Dec. 26 ; ob.—2. (Pronounced *rouss.*) To ' grouse ', to scold (v.i.), esp. if coarsely : Australian : C. 20. An Australian c.p. runs : *If a woman caught a louse* (occ. *mouse*) | *In her blouse* [pron. *blouss*], | *Would she rouse ?* Perhaps ex *rouse a person,* to anger him. Constructed with *on* (a person).—3. (Also **roust.**) V.t., ' to upbraid with many words ', C. J. Dennis : Australian : C. 20. Ex sense 2.

rouse and shine (naval, C. 19) ; **rise and shine** (naval and military, C. 20). A c.p. order to get out of bed. Bowen. B. & P.

rouser. A formidable breaking of wind : coll. : C. 18. Swift.—2. A handy man : Australian coll. : C. 20. Lawson, 1902. Ex *rouseabout.*

roush. See **rosh.**—2. See ' Winchester College slang ', § 2, and cf. *housle* (q.v.) for *hustle.*

roust. An act of kind : coll. : làte C. 16–17. Hall, *Satires,* ' She seeks her third roust on her silent toes.' Ex *roust,* a roaring or bellowing.

roust, v.i. To coït : coll. : late C. 16–17. Ex *roust,* n., q.v. ; the corresponding S.E. sense is ' to shout, bellow '.—2. To steal : c. : ca. 1820–80. Haggart. Ex dial. *roust,* to rout out.—3. See **rouse,** 3.

roustabout. A rouseabout or handy man, esp. at a shearing : Australian : 1883 (O.E.D.) : coll. >, by 1905, S.E. Ex U.S. *roustabout,* a deck hand or wharf labourer.

*****router-putters.** Cows' feet : c. : ca. 1820–60. Haggart. Ex *router,* (Scots dial. for) a cow

rovers. Thoughts : Scots coll. : C. 19–20 ; ob. Jamieson. Ex *wandering thoughts.*

row. A disturbance ; a noisy quarrel : 1785, Grose, who says that it was a Cambridge term. S. until ca. 1910, then coll. Esp. in *make a row* (1787, O.E.D.), *kick up a row* (1789, O.E.D.), and *get into a row.* Origin obscure ; W. suggests that it is cognate with *rouse = carouse.*—2. A noise : 1845(O.E.D.) ; s. >, ca. 1910, coll. *Eton School Days,* 1864, ' Chorley cried, Hold your row, will you ? '

row ! ' Shut up ! ' ; ' pax ! ' : Charterhouse : from ca. 1920. Perhaps elliptic for *stow that row*

row, v. To assail roughly : attack (a person or his rooms) : 1790 (O.E.D.) : s. until ca. 1890, then coll. ; ob. Ex *row,* n., 1.—2. V.i., to make a disturbance ; to quarrel : 1797 (O.E.D.).—3. To ' rag ', v.i. : university : ca. 1820–80.—4. To scold severely, to reprimand (v.t.) : from ca. 1810 : s. > coll. ca. 1910. Byron.—5. To criticise harshly or sharply : from ca. 1825 ; in C. 20, coll. (O.E.D.).—6. See **row in the boat.**

Row, the. Goldsmith's Row : C. 17 : coll. Middleton. O.E.D.—2. Rotten Row : from ca. 1810 : coll. ; in C. 20, S.E. Combe, ' Vulgar tradesmen, in the Row '. 3. Paternoster Row : booksellers' coll. : from ca. 1820. ' Jon Bee.'—4. Holywell Street : booksellers' coll. : ca. 1860–80. H., 3rd ed.

row ?, what's the. What's the noise about ? What's the matter or trouble ? ; 1837, Dickens, ' What's the row, Sam ? ' (O.E.D.)

row in. To conspire : low : from ca. 1860. Ware. Ex next entry.—2. To work or enter into association (*with*) : grafters' s. (— 1934). Philip Allingham, *Cheapjack.*

*****row (in the boat).** To go shares (*with*) : c. of ca. 1810–60. Vaux.

row-man. Incorrect for *roundsman,* a peripatetic labourer : from ca. 1830 ; ob. O.E.D.

row up. To reprimand severely : 1845 (O.E.D.) : coll. ; in C. 20, S.E. but ob. ? ex :—2. To rouse noisily : C. 19–20 ; ob. S. >, ca. 1890, coll.

rowdy. Money : from ca. 1840 : low. Ob. Leman Rede (*rowdy*) ; Thackeray (*the r.*). ? ex *ruddy,* n.

rowdy, adj. (Of horse or bullock) troublesome : Australian s. (— 1872) >, by 1900, coll. C. H. Eden, 1872 ; A. B. Paterson, ' And I can ride a rowdy colt, or swing the axe all day.' Extension of S.E. sense. Morris. Cf. *roughy,* q.v.

rowdy-dow. Abbr. of next, q.v., or ex *row-de-dow,* a din. From ca. 1860. H., 2nd ed., ' Low, vulgar ; " not the cheese ", or thing.'

rowdy-dowdy. Noisily rough ; turbulently noisy : from ca. 1850. Reduplication on *rowdy.*

rowing, vbl.n. To *row,* v., esp. in senses 1 and 4.

rowl. Money : low : C. 19. Prob. a corruption of *royal* (*images*), q.v.

rowlock phrase. See **rullock.**

'Roy. ' Fitzroy, a suburb of Melbourne ; its football team ', C. J. Dennis : Australian coll. : late C. 19–20.

royal. A member of the Royal Family : coll. : 1788, Mme D'Arblay (O.E.D.) ; ob.—2. A privileged labourer working regularly enough but not on the staff : dockers' coll. : 1883, G. R. Sims.—3. See **Royals.**—4. See **spread the royal.**

royal, adj. Noble ; splendid ; excellent : coll. : from ca. 1580 ; but not gen. before ca. 1850. E.g. *a royal time.* (O.E.D.)

royal bob. Gin : ca. 1729–70. **Cf.** *royal poverty*, q.v. ? origin.

Royal Goats, the. The 23rd Foot, afterwards the Royal Welch Fusiliers : military : from ca. 1850. F. & Gibbons. Also *the Nanny-Goats.* Ex their goat mascot.

royal image. A coin : mid-C. 18–early 19 : coll. or perhaps S.E. ; coll., however, is *royal images*, money : mid-C. 18–mid-19. On *royal* (*ryal*), the coin ; on the analogy of *King's* and *Queen's picture*, q.v.

Royal N. Royal Navy : naval coll. : from the late 1870's ; ob. E.g. W. S. Gilbert in *H.M.S. Pinafore.*

royal poverty. Gin : ca. 1725–80. N. Bailey. Cf. *royal bob.* Perhaps because, though a ' royal ' drink, gin is apt to lead to poverty.

royal-roast. Roast meat and vegetables for, and on, the lower deck : naval coll. : late C. 19–20. Bowen. Cf. *royal roast and straight bake,* roast meat and baked potatoes : id. : id. F. & Gibbons.

*****royal scamp.** A highwayman that, without brutality, robs only the rich : c. : late C. 18–early 19. Grose, 2nd ed. See **scamp.**

Royal Standbacks, the. ' A regiment imagined by others . . . not to have shewn particular keenness about going into action ' : military coll. : C. 19–20 ; slightly ob. F. & Gibbons.

Royal Tigers, the. The 65th Foot, now the York and Lancaster Regiment : military : from ca. 1823. F. & Gibbons, ' From the " Royal Tiger " badge, granted for distinguished service in India between 1802 and 1822 '.

royally. Splendidly ; excellently : coll. : 1836, E. Howard, ' Royally drunk ', *O.E.D.*

Royals. The Marines : 1797, when they were loyal in the naval mutiny : nautical, esp. naval, coll. ; ob. by 1900, † by 1930. Smyth.

*****royster.** See **roister.**—**rozin.** See **rosin.**

*****rozzer** ; occ. **rosser.** A policeman : c. : from ca. 1870. See **roosher** for possible etymology ; cf., however, Romany *roozlo* (or *-us*), strong.

-rr-. Cockney for *-t a* : C. 19–20. See **gorra** and **norra.**

rub. A rubber in card-games : 1830, ' An occasional rub or two of whist ', O.E.D. : coll. till C. 20, then S.E.—2. A loan (e.g. of a newspaper) : military : ca. 1880–1910. F. & H.

rub, v. See **rub down, in, off, out, rub, to, up.** —2. F. & H. postulates *rub* as a variant of *rub off* and *rub up* ; I doubt its independent existence. —3. As the base of *rub to,* q.v., it occurs in 1737. —4. B.E. and Grose describe *rub,* to go, run away, as c., but it is familiar S.E.

rub-a-dub, n. and v. A ' sub ', to ' sub ' (advance wages) : workmen's rhyming s. : C. 20. *John o' London's Weekly,* June 9, 1934.—2. A ' pub ' ; a club : late C. 19–20. P.P., *Rhyming Slang,* 1932.

rub-a-dub-dub. The club in Crown and Anchor : military rhyming s. : C. 20. B. & P.

rub about. To make a fool of : tailors' : C. 20. *The Tailor and Cutter,* Nov. 29, 1928, ' Took me for a josser. Nothing below the waist, me. I'm not to be rubbed about.' Ex a process in tailoring.

rub and a good cast ! A c.p. warning : ca. 1635–90. Clarke ; Ray. Ex bowls. (Apperson.)

*****rub-down,** n. corresponding to the ensuing v. : c. of late C. 19–20. James Curtis, *The Gilt Kid,* 1936.

rub down. To search (a prisoner) by running the hands over his body : coll. : 1887 (O.E.D.).

More gen., *run the rule over.*—2. To scold, reprimand : from ca. 1895 ; ob.

rub-down, give (a person) **a good.** To thrash : coll. (— 1923). Manchon.

rub in. To emphasise annoyingly ; insist vexatiously or unkindly upon ; remind naggingly of. Esp. as *rub it in. The Daily News,* May 26, 1870, ' Rubbing it in is a well-known phrase amongst the doubtful portion of the constabulary,' esp. as = to give fatal evidence (Ware). Cf. dial. *rubber.*

rub of the thumb, give (a person) **a.** To explain something to ; esp. to show him how to do something : coll. : mid-C. 19–20 ; ob. Ex some trade. Cf. :—2. To show appreciation for good work : tailors' : late C. 19–20. E.g. *The Tailor and Cutter,* Nov. 29, 1928.

rub-off. A copulation : coll. : late C. 17–early 19. Congreve.—2. A masturbation : low : C. 19–20 ; ob. In this sense, *rub-up* is much more gen. Cf. :

rub off, v. In same senses and periods as *rub-off.* —2. See **rubbed off.**

rub out. To kill : orig. (1848), U.S. ; anglicised ca. 1870 : S.E. until C. 20, then coll. Ex erasing. The phrase was used fairly often in the G.W.

rub, rub ! ' Us'd on the Greens when the Bowl Flees too fast, to have it forbear, if Words wou'd do it ', B.E. : a bowling c.p. soon > j. : late C. 17–18.

*****rub to.** (See **rub,** v.) To send, carry off, to (prison) : c. : ca. 1670–1840. Anon., *Warning for Housekeepers,* 1676 ; Grose. Prob. a development of *rub,* to go, to run.

rub-up. See **rub-off,** 2. From ca. 1620 : low coll. Esp. *do a rub-up.* Also *rubbing-up.* Ex :

rub up. The v. corresponding to *rub off,* 2, and *rub-up,* n. Low coll. : C. 17–20. This sense is almost inseparable from :—2. So to caress a person that he or she becomes actively amorous : low coll. : from ca. 1620. Fletcher's *Martial.*

rubacrock ; gen. **rubbacrock.** A filthy slattern : coll. : C. 19–20 ; ob. Ex S.W. dial. ; the word occurs in the famous *Exmoor Scolding,* 1746 (E.D.D.).

rubba(d)ge ; **rubbi(d)ge** ; occ. **rubbich.** Rubbish : C. 19–20. When not dial. (see esp. E.D.D.) it is low coll., verging indeed on sol.

rubbed about, be. (Of a person) to be made a convenience : tailors' : from ca. 1870. Cf. *rub about.*

rubbed-in. ' When a picture is commenced, it is spoken of as being " rubbed in " ' (J. Hodgson Lobley) : artists' coll. : from ca. 1910. Ex the technical sense of the phrase.

rubbed off. Bankrupt and gone, indeed run, away : coll. : late C. 17–18. B.E.

rubbed(-)out. Dead : see **rub out.** ' Of late frequently used in fashionable novels ', H., 1864.

rubbedge. See **rubbadge.**

rubbege. See **rubbadge.**

rubber. A caoutchouc eraser : coll. : late C. 18–20.—2. Some illicit device or swindling trick : c. : early C. 17. Dekker, ' Betting, Lurches, Rubbers, and such tricks '. Prob. connected with the *rubber* of games of skill and/or chance.

*****rubber, fake the.** See **fake the rubber.**

rubber gun. ' A big gun firing at a very long range ' : military : 1917 ; ob. B & P. Esp. a German naval high-velocity shell, which the New Zealanders called *rubber guts.*

rubber(-)neck ; **(-)necking.** A very inquisitive

person ; excessive curiosity or inquisitiveness :
U.S. (— 1900), partly anglicised, esp. in Australia,
ca. 1905 ; slightly ob. Ex ' considerable craning
and stretching ', as though one's neck were made
of rubber : as in *The Pall Mall Gazette*, March 8,
1902.

rubber-neck, v.i. in sense of the n. (q.v.) : 1932,
Dorothy Sayers, *Have His Carcase*, ' She . . . could
not waste time rubber-necking round Wilvercombe
with Lord Peter [Wimsey].'

rubber-up. The agent expressed in *rub up*, **v.**,
q.v. : low coll. : C. 19–20.

rubbich. See **rubbadge**.

rubbing-up. The act in *rub up*, **v.**, q.v. Also
rub-up.

rubbish. Money : low : ca. 1820–60. Egan,
1821, ' She shall stump up the rubbish before I
leave her.' Cf. S.E. *dross* and *filthy lucre*.—2. Luggage, esp. household effects and furniture : Anglo-
Indian military : early C. 19. Ware.

rube ; reub, reuben or **Reuben.** A country
bumpkin : U.S. (middle 1890's) ; anglicised,
among ' movie-fans ', by 1931. O.E.D. (Sup.).
Cf. *hick* (ex *Richard*).

rubiform, in Johnson and later lexicographers, is
erroneous for *rubriform*. O.E.D.

rubigo. The penis : (low) Scots coll. : late
C. 16–17. R. Sempill. ? ex L. *ruber*, red, on L.
rubigo (or *robigo*), rust (on metals), perhaps influenced by L. *prurigo*, lasciviousness.

rubric, in or **out of the.** In, out of, holy orders :
coll. : late C. 17–18. Farquhar. Like *rubigo*, it
is by the O.E.D. considered as S.E. : provisorily,
I believe F. & H. to be right.

ruby. Blood : boxing : 1860, *Chambers's
Journal*; ' Pomes ' Marshall, ca. 1886, ' You'd be
sure to nark the ruby round his gilt.' Cf. *carmine*,
claret, qq.v.—2. See :

Ruby, cross the. To cross the Rubicon : fast
life : early C. 19, when *ruby* was s. for port wine.
Ware.

Ruby Queen. A young nurse or nursing sister
of fresh complexion : military : 1916–18. F. &
Gibbons. Ex the issue tobacco so named.

ruby red. The head : rhyming s. : C. 20 ; ob.
F. & Gibbons. (Not very gen.)

*ruck. A word, or a deposition, that is idiotic :
c. (— 1923). Manchon. Ex sense 1 of the v.—
2. A cigarette-end : lower classes' (— 1923). Ibid.
Perhaps because *rucked up* (S.E. sense).

*ruck, v. To lay information (see also **ruck on**) :
c. >, by 1900, low s. : from ca. 1884.—2. To grow
angry or irritated : low : from ca. 1890 ; ob.
Ex sense 1, or independently ex *ruck* (*up*), as
applied to clothes ; origin of sense 1 is hazy.

ruck (or **rucket**) **along.** To walk quickly : ca.
1900–10 : Oxford University. While *ruck*, prob.
the earlier form, may derive ex dial. *ruck*, to go,
rucket may be an elaboration suggested by *rocket
along*.

*ruck on ; occ. **ruck upon.** To ' split on a pal ' ;
blab about (a person) : c. >, ca. 1900, low s. :
1884, *The Daily News*, ' I told the prisoner that I
was not going to ruck on an old pal.' See **ruck**.

ruck up, v.i. To get angry ; ' blow up ' : lower
classes' (— 1923). Manchon.

ruckerky. Recherché : Society : 1890's. Ware
quotes *The Daily Telegraph* of April 4, 1898.

rucket along. See **ruck along.**

rucktion ; gen. ruction. A disturbance, uproar,
noisy quarrel, ' row ' : dial. (— 1825) >, ca. 1830,

coll. In the pl., trouble, esp. noisy and avoidable
trouble. The C. 19 variant '*ruction*, combined with
Lover's use of the word, points to origin in *insurrection* ; P. W. Joyce, in *English in Ireland*, postulates ' the Insurrection of 1798, which was commonly called " the Ruction ".' (W. ; O.E.D.)

Rudders. The Rudiments of Faith and Knowledge : Oxford undergraduates' : ca. 1895–1905.
Ware. Now *divvers*.

*ruddock. A gold coin : 1567, Turberville :
† by 1750 ; ob. indeed by 1650,—it occurs in
neither B.E. nor Grose. Occ. *red* or *golden ruddock*. Prob. ex *ruddock*, a robin (redbreast) ; cf.
ruddy.—2. In pl., money, gold ; esp. gold money :
late C. 16–17. Also *red* or *golden r*. Heywood,
ca. 1607 (printed 1631), ' They are so flush of
their ruddocks.' Cf. *glistener* and *redge* and *red one*
(or *un*).

*ruddy. A sovereign : c. and low sporting
(— 1887). Baumann has *thirty ruddy*, £30. Ex
colour. Cf. :

ruddy, adj. Bloody ; confounded : euphemistic
s. : from ca. 1905 (see Collinson, p. 26). (Synonymous colour ; rhyme.) Cf. *rose-coloured*, q.v.—2.
Hence, *the ruddy edge*, the utter ' limit ' (— 1923).
Manchon.—3. Adv., as in Maurice Lincoln, *Oh !
Definitely*, 1933, ' I'd have ruddy well . . . locked
the door.'

Ruff. Ruff's *Guide to the Turf* : sporting coll. :
from ca. 1860. (With this title, 1854 ; actually
begun, in its first form, in 1842.)

*ruff, the wooden. The pillory : c. : ca. 1690–
1830. B.E. ; Grose, 1st ed. Punning the neck-
wear.

*ruff-peck. Bacon : c. of ca. 1565–1750. Harman, Dekker, Shirley (1707). ? lit., rough food.

*ruffelar or **-er.** See **ruffler.**

*ruffemans. A variant of *ruffmans*.

ruffer. One who is rough : lower classes'
(— 1909). Ware.

*ruffian. See **ruffin.**—2. In boxing s., a boxer
disregarding science in his desire for victory : ca.
1820–50. Egan's Grose.

*ruffin or **Ruffin** ; also spelt **Ruffian.** The
devil : c. : 1567, Harman (*ruffian*) ; Dekker
(*Ruffin*) ; B.E. (*Ruffin*) ; Grose (*Ruffian*) ; Ainsworth
(*Old Ruffin*). *Ruffin*, the name of a fiend (C. 13–
early 16), influenced by *ruffian*, a cut-throat villain.—
2. Whence, a justice of the peace : c. : ca. 1620–1820.
Fletcher, ca. 1622 (*Ruffin*) ; B.E. (*Ruffin*) ; Grose
(*ruffin*, 1st ed. ; 2nd ed., *ruffian*).

*ruffin, to the. See **nines, to the.**

**ruffin cook ruffin, who scalded the devil in his
feathers.** A c.p. applied to a bad cook : ca. 1780–
1860. Grose, 2nd ed. Prob. influenced by *puffin*,
q.v.

Ruffin's (or **-ans'**) **Hall.** A coll. of ca. 1590–1680,
thus in Blount, 1674, ' So that part of Smithfield
was antiently called, which is now the Horse-
market [in London], where Trials of Skill were
plaid by ordinary Ruffianly people, with Sword
and Buckler.' Nashe, Massinger. (O.E.D.)

Ruffians' Hall, he is only fit for. A c.p. applied
to an apprentice overdressed : London : coll. : ca.
1640–1820. Fuller ; Grose's *Provincial Glossary*.
Ex preceding.

*rufflar. See **ruffler.**

*ruffle, gen. in pl. A handcuff : c. : ca. 1780–
1850. Grose, 1st ed. ; Ainsworth, 1839.

*ruffler ; also ruffelar or **-er, rufflar, ruffleer,
rufler.** A vagabond : c. : ca. 1530–1620. Cop-

land.—2. Esp. one of the 1st or the second order or rank of 'canters': C. 17–18. B.E. and Grose (*1st order*); *A New Canting Dict.* (*2nd*).—3. A beggar pretending to be a maimed soldier or sailor: c. of ca. 1560–1830. Awdelay; Grose, 1st ed. (The term derives ex *ruffle*, to deport oneself arrogantly.)

*ruffmans. A hedge: c. of ca. 1620–1840. Fletcher (1622), Grose. Lit., rough time.—2. Harman and B.E. define it as the wood, a bush; Grose as a wood, a bush, or a hedge: as wood or bush, it is a special application of sense 1: ca. 1565–1840. See -mans.

*rufler. See ruffler.

rufus or Rufus. The female pudend: low: mid-C. 19–20; ob. Ex *rufous*.

rug. See bug.—See rug, at.—Rug. A Rugbeian: Rugby School (— 1892).—See:

*rug, all. Safe; certain: c. > gaming s.: late C. 17–18. B.E., 'It's all Rug, . . . the Game is secured'; Grose, 1st ed.—2. Hence, 'safe' in general: C. 18–early 19: s. Rowe, 1705, 'Fear nothing, Sir; Rug's the Word, all's safe.' O.E.D. Perhaps ex the warmth and snugness afforded by rugs. Cf.:

rug, at. In bed; asleep: low (? c.): ca. 1810–60. Prob. *rug* (of bed) influenced by *all rug*: an interesting clue is offered by the Devonshire *rug*, warm. Cf. *ruggins*, q.v. (Egan's Grose.)

Rugby, real. Cruel: Public Schools' (— 1909); virtually †. Ware. Ex the roughness of Rugby football.

[Rugby School slang:—Its sole (?) remarkable feature is that -*er* which, when introduced among Oxford University undergraduates, > 'the Oxforder', q.v.

rugger. Rugby football: s. (1893, O.E.D.) >, ca. 1920, coll. Ex *Rugby* on Oxford -*er*.

*ruggins; more gen., as in Vaux and in Egan's Grose, Ruggins's. Bed: c. of ca. 1810–70. Lytton, 1828, 'Toddle off to ruggins'. An elaboration of *rug* of bed, influenced by *all rug* and *at rug*; or perhaps merely *rugging* (coarse blanket cloth) pluralised or genitivised (*rugging's*), with *g* omitted.

*ruggy. Safe; withdrawn; secluded: c. (— 1887); ob. Baumann. See rug, all.

ruin. See blue ruin. By itself, rare: 1820, J. H. Reynolds (O.E.D.).—2. (Ruin.) Rouen: military: 1915; ob. B. & P. Prob. because it was the centre for treatment of venereal diseases.

rule of three(, the). Penis and testes: low: C. 18–20. D'Urfey.—2. Hence, copulation, C. 19–20. Other mathematical indelicacies are *addition*, *multiplication*, *subtraction*, all implying the juxtaposition of opponent genitals.

*rule over, run the (occ. a). To search: c. (— 1874) >, ca. 1910, gen. s.; now coll. H., 5th ed.; Horsley; 'Pomes' Marshall, 'Run the rule through all | His pockets.' Cf. *rub down*, which has remained low s., and *frisk*, ob. c. 'No. 747' has it for 1845: (of a pickpocket) to feel over the person of (a prospective victim).

ruler, v. To rap, beat, with a ruler: coll.: 1850, Dickens; ob. O.E.D.

rullock. A rowlock: nautical coll. (— 1887). Baumann, who has *shove one's ear into a seaman's rullock* (to seek a quarrel with a sailor), which is ob.

rully. Really: a coll. pronunciation: late C. 19–20. (D. Sayers, *Murder Must Advertise*, 1933, 'I'm rully very sorry.')

rum, n. A needy rural clergyman in Ireland:

ca. 1720–40. Swift (O.E.D.). Perhaps ex *rum*, adj., 1, as a mark of appreciation.—2. A 'rum', i.e. questionable, person (gen. male): ca. 1800–50. Barham. Ex *rum*, adj., 2. (O.E.D.).—3. An old, hence an unsaleable book: ca. 1810–30. 'Anecdotes' Nichols. Ex *rum*, adj., 2. O.E.D.

rum, v. To cheat: ca. 1810–20. 'He had rummed me,' 1812. Ex *rum*, adj., 2. O.E.D.

*rum, adj. Variants: *rome*, C. 16–18; *room(e)*, C. 17. Excellent; fine, good; valuable; handsome; great: c.: ca. 1565–1910; but comparatively rare after ca. 1810. The sense varies with the n.: see the ensuing list of terms, to many of which there is a precisely contrasted sense afforded by *queer* with the same n.: see queer, adj. Harman, 1567; Jonson; B.E.; Grose; Vaux; H.; Smyth (*rum-gagger*). Quotations are here unnecessary: see the combinations, which illuminate and objectify this strange adj. It may well, as H. suggests, derive from *Rome* (" the glory that was Rome ") as a city of splendid repute and fame; the dial. *ram*, very or strong, is ineligible, for its history does not go far enough back; Romany *rom*, a male (Gypsy) is a possibility, but not so probable as *Rome*. (Cf. *ream*.) Note that in Turkish, 'Roman' is *Rûm*; the Gypsies passed through Turkey,—indeed there is a Turkish Gypsy dialect. Note, too, that L. *Roma* is cognate with, perhaps actually derived ex, that Teutonic radical *hruod* (fame) which occurs in *Roger* and *Roderick*, and in Ger. *Ruhm* (fame), whence *ruhmvoll*, famous: cf. the s. sense of *famous* itself.—2. Either hence, by ironic 'inversion', or ex *Rom*, a Gypsy, used attributively (for the adj. is *Romano* or -*ani*),— *A New Canting Dict.*'s (1725) and Grose's remarks (1785) at *Gypsies*, make it clear that, even so early, the Gypsies had a 'rum' reputation,—comes the sense 'queer, odd, eccentric, strange, questionable, disreputable': such terms as *rum bite, rum bob* (sense 2), *rum bubber*, (esp.) *rum cove, rum cull, rum fun, rum ned*, taken along with those C. 18 strictures on the Gypsies, may have caused the change of sense from excellent, fine, etc., to queer, strange, etc. The earliest record is of 1774, but this sense does not > gen. until ca. 1800, as the O.E.D. points out. The remarkable merging with the c. sense of *queer* (q.v.), of which, from ca. 1820, it is mostly a mere synonym, is due, in part, to the vitality of *queer* itself, for in c. *queer* was more potent after ca. 1790 than *rum* was. H. Kelly, 1774, 'Rum tongue' (language); Grose; Dickens, 1837, 'There's rummer things than women in this world' (O.E.D.); Besant & Rice. Cf. *rummy*.—3. Strangely silly: late C. 17–18. This is an extremely rare sense: I know it only in *rum ned*, where the silliness may reside only in the second member. (N.B. Of the clear instances in Grose, 3rd ed., forty belong to sense 1; three to sense 2; only one to sense 3. And practically all of Grose's terms were already in B.E.: B.E.'s terms, with one exception (*rum ned*, q.v.), are all in sense 1.)

rum, come it. To talk oddly: low: ca. 1820–70. 'Jon Bee', 1823.—2. Hence, to act oddly: low: mid-C. 19–20; ob. Baumann.

*rum beak or beck. A justice of the peace: c.: late C. 17–early 19. B.E. See beak, beck.

*rum bing. See rum bung.

*rum bit or, mostly, bite. A clever trick or swindle: c.: late C. 17–early 19. B.E. See bit and bite.—2. (Only bite.) Hence, a clever rogue: c.: early C. 19. F. & H.

*rum bleating cheat. A (very) fat wether : c. : late C. 17–early 19. B.E.

*rum blowen (C. 19) or blower (late C. 17–18). 'A handsome wench', Grose, 1st ed. ; esp. one 'kept by a particular Man', B.E. See blowen, blower.

*rum bluffer. A jolly inn-keeper or victualler : c. : late C. 17–18. B.E. See bluffer.

*rum bob. 'A young Prentice ; also a sharp, sly Trick, and a pretty short wig', B.E. : late C. 17–early 19, except the third († by 1780).

rum-boile. A variant of romboyle, n. : q.v.

*rum booze, bouse, bouze, buse, buze. (See booze, n.) Good wine (mid-C. 16–19) or other liquor (C. 17–19) : c. Harman ; B.E. ; Grose.

*rum-boozing welts. Bunches of grapes : c. : mid-C. 17–early 19. Coles, 1676 ; B.E. ; Grose. Lit., excellent-liquor lumps or bunches.

rum-bottle. A sailor : naval : ca. 1860–1900. Ware. Ex his fondness for rum.

*rum bub. Very good liquor : c. : late C. 17–18. B.E. at bub.

*rum bubber. 'A dexterous fellow at stealing silver tankards from inns and taverns', Grose, 1st ed. : c. : late C. 17–18. B.E. Ex bub, liquor.

*rum buffer (C. 18–early 19) or bughar, gen. bugher (late C. 17–early 19). A handsome and/or valuable dog : c. B.E. ; Grose, 1st ed. See buffer, bugher.

*rum bung (occ. bing). A full purse : c. : late C. 17–early 19. B.E.

*rum chant or chaunt. 'A song', Grose, 3rd ed. ; 'a good song', Vaux, 1812 : the latter seems to be the correct definition. A late instance of rum, adj., 1.

*rum chub. 'Among butchers, a customer easily imposed on', Grose, 1st ed. : c. : late C. 17–early 19. B.E. For chub, cf. gudgeon.

rum clan is Baumann's misprint for :

*rum clank. A gold or silver cup or tankard : c. : C. 18–early 19. A New Canting Dict., 1725.

*rum clout, wipe, wiper. 'A Silk, fine Cambrick, or Holland Handkerchief', B.E. : c. : late C. 17–19; wipe not before C. 19.

*rum cod. A full purse (esp. of gold) ; a large sum of money : c. : late C. 17–early 19. B.E. ; Grose, 1st ed. Cf. rum bung.

*rum co or coe. A smart lad : late C. 16–early 17. Cf. rum cove.

*rum cole. 'New Money' ; 'Medals, curiously Coyn'd', B.E. : c. : late C. 17–early 19. Grose. See cole. Also, in first nuance, rum gelt.

*rum coll. A rhyme-needed variant, early C. 18, of rum cull, 1.

*rum cove. 'A great Rogue', B.E. : c. : C. 17–mid-18. Rowlands ; Dekker's use stresses rum, rich.—2. Hence, 'a dexterous or clever rogue', Grose, 1st ed. : c. : mid-C. 18–mid. 19. (Cf. cove.) A very operative term : see rum, adj., 2.—3. A 'queer fish' : low : mid-C. 19–20.

*rum cull. 'A rich Fool, that can be easily . . . Cheated . . . ; also one that is very generous and kind to a Mistress', B.E. : c. : ca. 1670–1840. Cf. the U.S. sugar-daddy.—2. A manager : low theatrical : from ca. 1860. Esp. the master of a travelling troop (— 1864). H., 3rd ed. ; ob. Perhaps ex :—3. An intimate friend (gen. in the vocative) : low : ca. 1840–90. Selby, 1844, 'What's in the wind, my rum cull ?'; 1886, Stephens & Yardley.

*rum cully. Elisha Coles's variant (1676) of rum cull, 1.

rum customer. A person, an animal, that it is risky, even dangerous to meddle with or offend · late C. 18–20. Cf. queer cuss.

*rum cuttle. A sword : c. : early C. 17. Rowlands, 1609. A cuttle is a knife.

*rum dab. 'A very Dextrous fellow at fileing, thieving, Cheating, Sharping, &c', B.E. (at dab, not at rum) : late C. 17–early 18 : c.

*rum degen or tol or tilter. A splendid sword ; esp. a silver-hilted or silver-inlaid one : c. : late C. 17–18. B.E., Grose.

*rum dell, doxy, mort. A handsome whore : C. 17–early 19. Jonson (roome mort) ; B.E. (in this sense, dell and doxy) ; Grose (id.).—See separately rum doxy and rum mort.

*rum diver. A skilful pickpocket : c. : C. 18–mid-19. A New Canting Dict., 1725. Also rum file.

*rum doxy. A beautiful woman, a fine wench : c. : late C. 17–early 19. B.E., Grose.—2. A 'light Lady', B.E. : late C. 17–early 18.

*rum drawers. Silk, or very fine worsted, stockings : c. : late C. 17–18. B.E., Grose.

*rum dropper. A vintner (wine-merchant) ; landlord of a tavern : c. : mid-C. 17–18. Coles, 1676 ; Ned Ward (1709) ; Grose.

*rum dubber. A dexterous picklock : c. : late C. 17–18. B.E. ; Grose.

*rum duchess. A jolly, handsome woman : c. : late C. 17–mid-18. B.E. Cf. rum duke, 1.

*rum duke. A jolly, handsome man : c. : late C. 17–18. B.E. ; Grose, who (1785) adds, 'an odd eccentric fellow', or, as he defines at duke, 'a queer unaccountable fellow' : c. : late C. 18–mid-19. Extant in East Anglian dial. in 1903 (E.D.D.).—3. Gen. in pl., 'The boldest and stoutest fellows lately among the Alsatians [see Alsatia], Minters, Savoyards, and other inhabitants of privileged districts, sent to remove and guard the goods of such bankrupts as intended to take sanctuary in those places', Grose : c. : late C. 17–mid-18. B.E. (This is the only one of Grose's rum-terms that we find in dial. : in sense 3.)

*rum fam or fem. A diamond ring : c. : ca. 1850–90. F. & H. See fam.

*rum file. See rum diver : late C. 17–early 19. B.E. ; Grose, 1st ed.

*rum fun. A sharp trick ; a clever swindle : c. : late C. 17–18. Ibid.

*rum gagger. One of those impostors 'who tell wonderful stories of their sufferings at sea, or when taken by the Algerines', Grose, 1st ed. : c. of ca. 1780–1850 ; then nautical s. (witness Smyth, 1867), with the Algerian gambit omitted ; ob.

*rum gelt or gilt. (In B.E. and Grose, rum ghelt.) See rum cole.

*rum gill. A clever thief ; a handsome man : c. of ca. 1820–50. Ainsworth.

*rum glimmer, gen. spelt glymmar (or -er). The chief of the link-boys : c. : late C. 17–18. B.E., Grose. See glim and glymmer.

rum go. A puzzling and not too respectable contretemps ; a mysterious (not merely because wholly unexpected) occurrence or, esp., development of a plot, situation, etc. : from ca. 1850. Thackeray, 1850 (O.E.D.) and George Eliot, 1876 ; rummy go is in Punch, 1841. See rum, adj., 2, and go, n.

*rum going. Fast trotting : c. or low s. : ca. 1820–60. Jones, 1825, The True Bottom'd Boxer.

*rum gut(t)lers. Canary wine : c. : mid-C. 17–18. Coles, 1676 ; B.E. ; Grose. Cf. S.E. *guzzle*.—2. 'Fine Eating ', *A New Canting Dict.*, 1725 : c. : C. 18.

*rum hopper. A drawer at a tavern : c. : late C. 17–18. B.E. One who hops or ' springs to it ' with great alacrity.

rum-jar. A kind of German trench-mortar bomb : military : 1915 ; ob. F. & Gibbons. Ex shape.

rum johnny or Johnny. A native wharf-labourer : Anglo-Indian : C. 19–20 ; ob. Prob. ex *rum*, adj., 2 ; but see Yule & Burnell.—2. A whore : naval and military : mid-C. 19–20. Ex Hindustani *ramjani*, a dancing-girl. Yule & Burnell.

*rum Joseph or joseph. A very good coat or cloak : c. : late C. 17–18. B.E. at *Joseph*.

*rum ken. A popular inn, tavern, brothel : c. of ca. 1810–60. Egan, 1821.

*rum kicks. ' Breeches of gold or silver brocade, or richly laced with gold or silver ', Grose, 1st ed. : c. : late C. 17–early 19. B.E.

*rum kiddy. A clever young thief : c. : late C. 18–early 19. G. Parker, 1781.

[rum kin, postulated by F. & H., is prob. an error on S.E. *rumkin*.]

*rum maund (or mawnd). ' One that Counterfeits himself a Fool' while begging : late C. 17–18. B.E., Grose. See maund. Cf. :

*rum maunder. A late C. 18–19 early form of the preceding. F. & H., where it is defined as ' a clever beggar '.

*rum mizzler. A thief clever at escaping : c. : ca. 1780–1900. Parker, 1781 ; H., 5th ed. ; Baumann. Cf. *needy mizzler* and see mizzle.

*rum mort. See rum dell.—2. A queen ; the Queen : c. : Harman, 1567 (*Rome mort*) ; B.E. ; Grose. † by 1840.—3. Hence, a great lady : c. : late C. 17–early 19. B.E., Grose. See mort.

*rum nab. ' A Beaver, or very good Hat ', B.E. : late C. 17–early 18, the former (Shadwell, 1688) ; until ca. 1830, the latter. See nab, n.

*rum nantz or Nantz. Good French brandy : c. : late C. 17–early 19. B.E., Grose.

*rum ned or Ned. ' A very silly fellow ', B.E. ; ' a very rich silly fellow ', Grose : c. : late C. 17–18. Cf. *rum cull*, 1 ; cf. *rum*, adj., 2.

rum one or un ('un). (Gen. *r. one*) a settling blow, punch : boxing : early C. 19. ' Jon Bee.'—2. (Gen. *r. un*). An odd or eccentric fellow ; a strange-looking animal or object ; a strange affair : from ca. 1825. Dickens. Prob. ironic on :—3. (Only rum un.) A ' stout fellow'; a capital chap : c. : ca. 1820–50. Jones, 1825 ; Moncrieff, 1830, in the vocative. Cf. *rum cull*, last sense.

*rum omee (or omer), occ. rum homer, of the case. See omee, omer.

*rum pad ; Moore writes it *rumpad*. The highway : c. : late C. 17–early 19. B.E., Grose. The v. *rum-pad*, to attack, rob, on the highway, is only ' literary ' c. of late C. 19.—2. A highwayman : an error or a catachresis : C. 17–mid-18. J. Shirley ; *The Scoundrel's Dict.* (O.E.D.)

*rum(-)padder. One of ' the better sort of Highwaymen, well Mounted and Armed ', B.E. : mid-C. 17–early 19 : c. (Coles, 1676.) Ex *rum pad*.

*rum peck. Good food : c. : late C. 17–early 19. B.E. (at *peckidge*) ; Grose ; Moncrieff.

*rum peeper. A silver looking-glass : c. : late C. 17–18. B.E., Grose.

rum phiz or phyz. ' An odd face or countenance '; Grose, 1st ed. : low : from ca. 1780 ; ob.

*rum prancer. A very fine horse : c. : late C. 17–early 19. B.E., Grose.

rum quick is a misprint in Baumann for :

*rum quid(d)s. A large booty ; a great share of spoil : c. : late C. 17–early 19. B.E., Grose.

Rum Row. ' Position outside the prohibited area taken up by *rum-running* vessels ': coll. ; U.S., anglicised before 1927 ; ob. Collinson ; C.O.D. (1934 Sup.)

*rum ruff peck. Westphalia ham : c. : late C. 17–18. B.E. ; Grose. Contrast *ruff peck*, q.v.

*rum slim or slum. Punch : c. : ca. 1780–1890. Parker (*slim*) ; Egan (*slum*) ; H., 3rd ed. (*slim*). ? the ' originator ' of *rum sling*, rum punch (cf. *gin sling*).

*rum snitch. A hard blow on the nose : c. : late C. 17–early 19. B.E., Grose.

*rum squeeze. Copious drink for the fiddlers : c. : id. Ib.

rum start. An odd occurrence : s. and dial. : from ca. 1840 ; slightly ob. as s. Recorded in ' *No. 747* ' as used in 1845.

*rum strum. A long wig, esp. if a fine one : c. : late C. 17–18. B.E., Grose, both at *strum*.—2. A handsome wench or harlot : c. : late C. 17–early 18. B.E. (at *strum*).

*rum tilter ; rum tol (see tol). A *rum degen*, q.v. : c. : late C. 17–early 19. B.E., Grose.

*rum Tom Pat. A clergyman (not a hedge-priest) : c. of ca. 1780–1840. See adam, v.

*rum topping. A rich head-dress : c. of ca. 1670–1810. B.E. ; Grose. Orig. of the style designated by *commode*.

rum touch. See touch, rum.—rum un ('un). See rum one.

*Rum ville or vyle ; Rumville. London : c. : C. 17–19. See Rome Ville.

*rum wipe or wiper. See rum clout and quotation at rummy, adj.

rumble. An (improvised) seat for servants at the back of a carriage : 1808 (O.E.D.) : coll. till ca. 1840 > then S.E. ; ob. Abbr. *rumble-tumble*, q.v.—2. A stage-coach : coll. : ca. 1830–50. This differentiation (F. & H.) is open to dispute.—3. The surreptitious opening of the throttle to enable one to land at the desired spot : Royal Air Force's : from 1932. Perhaps ex sense 2 of :

*rumble, v. To rule *out* unceremoniously, handle roughly : ca. 1810–50. (O.E.D.) Ex *rumboyle*, v.—2. Hence, to test, try ; handle ; examine : c. of ca. 1820–1900. Haggart.—3. Hence, v.i. & t., to detect ; fathom, understand ; low : from ca. 1875. Binstead, 1898, ' I soon rumbled he was in it when I heard . . .' Cf. *tumble to*, by which this sense may have been suggested and has certainly been influenced.

rumble-tumble. See rumble, n., 1. C. 19 : coll. till ca. 1830, then S.E. Ex the noise.—2. Any wheeled vehicle that rumbles : 1806, J. Beresford (O.E.D.) ; † by 1910. Coll. till ca. 1840, then S.E. and dial.

rumbler. Same as rumble, n., 1 : coll. : ca. 1800–20.—2. A hackney coach : ca. 1815–60 : coll. Moncrieff, 1823, ' A rattler . . . is a rumbler, otherwise a jarvey.—3. Hence, a four-wheeled cab : ca. 1860–1910. H., 3rd ed. (' Not so common as *bounder* ').

*rumbler, running. A carriage-thief's confederate : c. : ca. 1820–80. ? ex :

rumbler's flunkey. A footman ; one who, for tips or wages, runs for cabs, etc. : low : ca. 1815–90. Anon., *The Young Prig* (song), ca. 1819. See rumbler, 2, 3.

rumbo. Rum-punch : ca. 1750–1840, then archaic : coll. till C. 19, then S.E. Smollett, 1751, 'He and my good master . . . come hither every evening, and drink a couple of cans of rumbo apiece.' Either fantastic on *rum* or ex *rumbullion*. -–2. A prison : c. of ca. 1720–1830. Also *rumboken* (Harper, 1724). Perhaps ironic on *rum*, adj., 1. *A New Canting Dict.*, 1725.—3. Stolen rope : nautical and dockyard s. (— 1867). Smyth. Cf. *rumbo-ken*, 2.

rumbo, n. and adj. Plenty, plentiful ; sufficiency, sufficient ; good : low : 1870, Hazlewood & Williams ; 1876, Hindley, ' " Chuck rumbo (eat plenty), my lad " ' ; *The Pall Mall Gazette*, Dec. 21, 1895 (horses and carts described as *rumbo*, good). Prob. ex coll. Sp. *rumbo*, liberality, generosity (cf. *rumbosamente*, grandly, liberally), via Lingua Franca.—2. Elegant, fashionable : C. 20. Manchon. Perhaps ex *rumbo* !—3. Successful : theatrical (— 1923). Ibid.

rumbo ! Splendid ! : lower and lower-middle classes' : ca. 1860–1915. Ware : ex Sp. via the Gypsies.

*rumbo-ken. See rumbo, n., 2.—2. A pawnbroker's shop : c. : (?) ca. 1700–1850.

rumbowling. Anything inferior or adulterated : nautical (— 1864). H., 3rd ed. (Occ. as adj.) Prob. a corruption of S.E. *rombowline*.—2. Grog : nautical (— 1885). Ex sense 1, but perhaps influenced by *rumbo* and :

rumbullion, -ian ; occ. rombullion. Rum : ca. 1650–1750 : coll. soon > S.E. ? etymology.

rumbumptious. Obstreperous : coll. : ca. 1786–1895. Grose, 2nd ed. ; H., 5th ed., ' Haughty, pugilistic ' (? quarrelsome). Ex dial. *ram* (see rumbustious) + *bump* on *fractious* ; cf. *rumgumption* on *gumption*. (N.b., *bumptious* is later than *rumbumptious*, *gumption* earlier than *rumgumption*.)

rumbustical ; occ. (†) rombustical. Boisterous, very noisy ; unruly : coll. and dial. : 1795, O.E.D. Prob. on † S.E. *robustic* ex *rumbustious*, q.v. Cf. :

rumbusticate. To coīt with (a woman) : late C. 19–early 20. Ex *rumbustical* on *spiflicate*.

rumbusticator. A moneyed man : ca. 1890–1910. Cf. preceding two entries.

rumbustious ; occ. († in C. 20) rombustious. Same as *rumbustical*, q.v. : coll. : 1778, Foote, ' The sea has been rather rumbustious.' Lytton, 1853, *rambustious*. Prob. a perversion of *robustious* on dial. *ram*, very, strong, and *rum*, adj., 1. (This type of word >, ca. 1840, very gen. in U.S. : cf. *catawampus*, *rambunctious*.)

rumdadum. The posteriors : low (— 1923). Manchon. Echoic.

Rumford (properly, Romford), ride to. To get a new pair of breeches, or an old pair new-bottomed : coll. : ca. 1780–1830. Grose, 1st ed. ; in the 2nd he adds, ' Rumford was formerly a famous place for leather breeches.' But cf. :— *you (one, etc.) may or might ride to Romford (up)on a (this, etc.) knife*, a c.p. imputing bluntness : ca. 1705–1860. Swift, ' Well, one may ride to Rumford upon this knife, it is so blunt ' ; *Notes & Queries*, 1901, referring to ca. 1850–70, ' You might ride to Romford on it.'

Rumford or Romford lion. A calf : coll. : C. 18–mid-19. *A New Canting Dict.*, 1725. More gen. is *Essex lion*, q.v. : calves being very numerous in Essex.

rumgumption. Common sense : coll. (mostly Scots and Northern) : from ca. 1770. A strengthened form of *gumption*, q.v. (The adj. is gen. considered to be dial.)

*rumly. Finely ; excellently ; gallantly ; strongly : c. of ca. 1670–1770. Head ; B.E. In C. 17, often *romely*, as in Rowlands, 1609. Ex *rum*, adj., 1.—2. Oddly ; eccentrically : s. : 1819, Moore, ' Thus rumly floored '. Ex *rum*, adj., 2.

rummage. To caress a woman sexually ; possess her : low coll. : C. 19–20 ; ob. Ex S.E. *rummage*, to disarrange, disorder ; to knock about.

rummagy. Such as may be found, obtained, by *rummaging* in rubbish : coll. : 1899, Baring-Gould, ' The " rummagy " faces ', O.E.D. ; slightly ob.

rummily. Oddly, queerly : 1827, Scott (O.E.D.) : s. >, ca. 1890, coll. Ex *rummy*.

rumminess. Oddness ; singularity : 1899, Eden Phillpotts : s. >, ca. 1920, coll. O.E.D. Cf. :

rummish. Rather odd or peculiar : 1826 (O.E.D.) ; somewhat rare in C. 20. Ex *rum*, adj., 2.

rummy. A Canadian term of address (— 1932). John Beames. Perhaps ex :

rummy, adj. Odd ; singular : 1828, *The Sporting Magazine*, ' A neat, but rather rummy looking blue pony ', O.E.D. Moncrieff's ' rummy Spitalfields wipes ' may mean odd handkerchiefs, but it might be a variant on *rum wipe*, a silk handkerchief.

*rummy, adv. ' Capitally ', excellently, well : c. of ca. 1825–40. Moncrieff, 1830, has ' We chaunt so rummy ' (cf. *rum chant*, q.v.) and ' We frisk so rummy.' Ex *rum*, adj., 1, via some of the *rum combinations.

rumour !, it's a ; often 's a rumour. A military c.p. (1915–18) in retort on ' an opinion expressing a very well-known fact or [on] a statement emphatically (and, usually, disagreeably) true ', B. & P.

Rump. (The R.) The Long Parliament remnant from Dec. 1648 to April 1653 : coll. : 1648.—2. That remnant of the L.P. which, after being restored in May 1659, was dissolved in Feb. 1660 : coll. : 1659. Prob. an anatomical pun. O.E.D.

rump. To flog : ca. 1810–90 : coll. Vaux, 1812.—2. (Of the male) to coït with, esp. dorsally : low : from ca. 1850 ; slightly ob. As v.i. of either sex : cf. *rumper*. Cf. *loose in the rump*, *rumpsplitter*.

rump, he hath eaten the. A semi-proverbial c.p. applied to one who is constantly talking : ca. 1670–1800. Ray.

rump, loose in one's or the. (Of women) wanton : coll. : C. 18–mid-19. D'Urfey.

rump and a dozen. An Irish wager, ' A rump of beef and a dozen of claret ', Grose, 2nd ed. : coll. : late C. 18–mid-19. Also called *buttock and trimmings* (Grose).

rump-and-kidney men. ' Fidlers that Play at Feasts, Fairs, Weddings, &c. And Live chiefly on the Remnants of Victuals ', B.E., who—wrongly, I think—classifies it as c. ; Grose doesn't. (Prob.) coll. : late C. 17–early 19.

rump(-)and(-)stump, adv. Completely ; utterly : dial. and coll. : from ca. 1820 ; ob. Lit., rump and tail; cf. *lock, stock, and barrel*. A rhyming phrase perhaps suggested by (*utterly*) *stumped*. The synonymous *rump and rig* is wholly dial.

Rump Parliament. (See **Rump**.) Not before 1670; soon S.E.

rump-splitter. The penis: low coll.: ca. 1650–1800. Urquhart. Cf. *rump*, v., 2.—Whence, a whoremonger: low: C. 19–20; ob. Cf. *rump, loose in the*, and :

rump-work. Copulation: low coll.: C. 19–20; ob. Cf. *rump*, v., 2, and :

*****rumpad**. See **rum pad**.

rumper. A whore; a whoremonger: low: C. 19–20; very ob. Ex *rump*, v., 2, though partly a pun on *Rumper*, a member of the Rump Parliament.

rumption. A 'rumpus': 1802 (O.E.D.): coll. till ca. 1820, then dial. Prob. ex *rumpus* on *gumption*.

rumpty. One thirty-second of £1 : Stock Exchange: 1887. Cf. *tooth*, q.v.

rumpus. An uproar or, † in C. 20, a riot; a 'row', quarrel: coll.: 1764, Foote, 'Oh, Major! such a riot and rumpus!' Always in collocation with *riot* before ca. 1785; Grose has it in his 2nd ed. Also without article, gen. as riotousness, noise, quarrelling: 1768, O.E.D.; slightly ob. W. suggests a s. use of Gr. ῥόμβος, spinning top, also commotion, disturbance; tentatively, I suggest a fanciful perversion of *rumble*, used, esp. as v., of the noise made by the bowels (C. 16 onwards), for Grose, 1785, says 'There is a rumpus among my chitterlins, i.e. I have the cholick.'—2. A masquerade: c.: ca. 1810–40. Vaux.

rumpus, v. To make a 'rumpus': coll.: 1839, Hood (O.E.D.); ob.

rumtitum. In fine condition, gen. of a bull or a whoremonger: ca. 1810–40. Egan's Grose. Cf. *rumtitum, rumtiddy(-tum)*, in refrains, though these are unrecorded before 1820.

*****Rumville**. See **Rome-Ville**.

*****rumy**. A good girl or woman: tramps' and Gypsy c. (— 1859). H., 1st ed. A perversion of Romany *romeni*, a bride, a wife.

run. To manage: U.S. (1827), anglicised as coll. ca. 1860; in C. 20, S.E.—2. Ran (the preterite tense): a frequent C. 19–20 sol. Cf. *give* for *gave*.—3. To tease, irritate, nag at : Australian coll. (1888) >, ca. 1910, S.E.; rather ob. 'Rolf Boldrewood'. (O.E.D.)—4. To charge with a 'crime': naval (Bowen) and military: from not later than 1915. Ex *run in*, q.v.—5. To arrest: military (C. 20) > gen. s. (— 1931). Lyell. See **run, be**, for it is gen. in the passive.—6. To report (a prisoner) to the governor of a gaol: c. (— 1932). Anon., *Dartmoor from Within*.—7. To go out often with (a person of the opp. sex; gen. of a man with a girl): from ca. 1910. Prob. ex the turf.—8. To let the water run into (the bath): domestic coll. : C. 20. R. Hichens, *The Paradine Case*, 1933, 'Without summoning his valet, [he] went to "run" the bath.'

run-about. From ca. 1890: coll. See **compulsory**.

run, be. 'To be placed in arrest': military : C. 20. F. & Gibbons. Cf. *run*, 4, 5, and *run in*.

run, have a. To take a walk, a 'constitutional': coll.: from ca. 1880.—2. Esp. *have a run for it*, q.v.

run, let it. See **let it run**.

*****run, on the**. Wanted by the police : orig. (late C. 19), c.; by 1925, coll. In c., however, it

implies leaving the usual haunts when one is wanted by the police.

*****run a rule over**. See **rule over**.

run across. To meet by chance : late C. 19–20: coll. till ca. 1905, then S.E.

run as swift as a pudding would creep. To be very slow: coll.: early C. 17. Apperson.

run away and play marbles ! An insulting c.p. rejoinder or dismissal: late C. 19–20. C. H. Bacon, a Sedbergh boy, aptly pointed out, in July 1934, that an exact equivalent occurs in Shakespeare's *Henry V* : where the Dauphin sends the King a present of tennis balls. Cf. :

run away and play trains ! See **trains**.

Run Away, Matron's Coming. Less a nickname for than a military c.p. directed at the Royal Army Medical Corps : G.W., but not very gen. F. & Gibbons.

run big. To be out of training : sporting : late C. 19–20; ob.

run down. The gangway or bridge between stage and auditorium : conjurors' coll. (from ca. 1880) >, in C. 20, S.E.

run (something) fine. (Esp. *run it* or *that fine*.) To leave only a very small margin (gen. of time): coll.: 1890 (O.E.D.).

run for it, have a. To make a fight : coll.: from ca. 1890; slightly ob.

run for one's money, a. An ample *quid pro quo* ; extended liberty; a good time in exchange for one's money : from ca. 18 : racing s. >, ca. 1890, coll. >, by 1930, S.E.

run goods. 'A maidenhead, being a commodity never entered', Grose, 2nd ed.: c. ca. 1786–1840. Punning the nautical sense, contraband.

run in. To arrest: coll. >, in C. 20, S.E.: 1872 (O.E.D.); H., 5th ed.

run of one's teeth or **knife and fork, the**. Victuals free : s., 1841 (in C. 20, coll.); coll. (ca. 1860) >, in C. 20, S.E. Ex *the run*, freedom, *of a place*.

run off one's legs. Bankrupt ; gen. *he is run off his legs*. Coll.: ca. 1670–1760. Ray. (Apperson.) Cf. *run over shoes*.

run on. To run up an account : lower classes' coll. (— 1887). Baumann.

*****run on** (a person), **get the**. To play a dirty trick on (him) : c. (— 1887). Baumann.—2. See **run upon**.

run on, get the. See **run upon** . . .

run one way and look another. To play a double game : coll. : from ca. 1850 ; ob.

run one's face, or **shape, for**. To obtain an article on credit : coll. : orig. (— 1848) and mainly U.S.; anglicised ca. 1880; ob. (O.E.D.; F. & H.)

run one's tail. To be a whore: from ca. 1850. See **tail**.

run out on. To embroider, enlarge on : coll. : late C. 19–20; ob.

run-out, the; often abbr. to **R. O.** A faked auction : grafters' : C. 20. Philip Allingham, *Cheapjack*, 1934. See also **R. O. workers**.

run over him, the coaches won't. He is in gaol. Also *where the coaches . . .*, gaol. A coll. c.p. ca. 1820–70. Cf. *where the flies won't get at it*.

run over shoes ; be run over shoes. To get, be, heavily in debt : coll. : late C. 16–early 17. Apperson.

run rings round. See **rings round**.

run rusty. See **rusty**.—**run the rule over**. See **rule over**.

run the show. To ' manage ' an enterprise, entertainment, etc. : from ca. 1915.

run thin. To back out of a bargain : from ca. 1880 ; ob. Ex dial.

run through the nose with a cushion. To strike playfully : coll. : late C. 17–early 18. Apperson. Cf. *stab with a rose*.

run to. To understand, comprehend : coll. (— 1859). H., 1st ed.—2. To afford, be able to pay : 1859, H. : coll. till C. 20, then S.E. Always in the negative or the interrogative. Ex horse-racing, thus :

run to it !, won't. A sporting c.p. (— 1909 ; ob.) applied to a horse that has insufficient staying power to reach the winning-post. Ware.

run to seed : occ. hyphenated. Pregnant : low coll. : from ca. 1860 ; ob.—2. Shabby : coll. : 1837, Dickens, ' Large boots running rapidly to seed '.

run upon (a person), **get the.** To have the upper hand of ; be able to laugh at : coll, (— 1859) >, by 1890, S.E. ; very ob. H., 1st ed. Also *get the run on*.

Runaway Prestonpans, the (Great). The 13th Hussars : military : 1745 ; ob. Some of their men panic'd in this battle which Sir John Cope lost to the Young Pretender. Also *the Evergreens* and *Green Dragoons ; Geraniums ; Ragged Brigade.*

runned. Run ; ran : sol., esp. Cockneys' (— 1887). Baumann.

*****runner.** A clothes-thief entering a house in the dark : c. : late C. 17–early 18. B.E. Cf. *budge.* —2. A wave : coll. : from ca. 1870 ; ob.—3. A dog-stealer : c. (— 1909). Ware.—4. An exchange clerk : bank clerks' : from ca. 1916.—5. A clerk, or a collector, for a street ' bookie ' : Glasgow (— 1934).

runner-up. A docker ' employed by gangers to liven up the gangs and expedite the work ' : nautical : late C. 19–20. Bowen.

*****runners.** He who ' calls over ' the names of the horses competing or *running* in a race : turf c. (— 1932).

*****running glasier, glazier.** A thief posing as a glazier : c. of ca. 1810–70.

running horse or **nag.** A gleet, a ' clap ' (q.v.) : low : ca. 1780–1860. Grose, 1st ed.

running leather, have shoes of. To be given to wandering or rambling : semi-proverbial coll. : from ca. 1850 ; ob.

running (occ. **flying**) **patterer** or **stationer.** A hawker of books or, more gen., broadsheets, newspapers, about the streets : C. 19, c. > low s. (Mayhew) ; late C. 17–19, coll., as in B.E., Grose, H.

*****running rumbler.** See **rumbler.**

*****running smobble.** ' Snatching goods off a counter, and throwing them to an accomplice, who brushes off with them,' Grose, 2nd ed. : c. of ca. 1787–1840. Cognate with *smabble* (or *snabble*), q.v. ; cf. the next entry ; as *running smabble*, it occurs in 1718, in C. Hitchin, *The Regulator.*

*****running snavel.** A thief specialising in the *kinchin-lay*, q.v. : c. : C. 18. Cf. preceding entry and see **snaffle**, of which *snavel* is a corruption on *snabble.*

running stationer. See **running patterer.**

ruof. Four : back s. (— 1874). H., 5th ed.

Rupert. A kite ; an observation balloon : military, esp. the Air Force : from 1915. F. & Gibbons. By personification. Cf. *Richard*, 2.

rural, do a. To ease oneself in the open air : coll. : C. 19–20 ; ob. Obviously suggested by Swift's *pluck a rose* (see at **rose**).

rural coach. A tutor not attached to a college : undergraduates' (— 1887) ; ob. Baumann.

*****rush.** (See also **rusher.**) A robbery (specifically with violence) of many objects at one rush : c. : from ca. 1785. Cf. U.S. *rush*, a street encounter, which Thornton records at 1860.—2. Hence, any swindle : c. or low s. : from ca. 1840. Cf. *rush*, v., 1 and 2.—3. See ' Moving-Picture Slang ', p. 6.

rush, v.t. To cheat (gen. *rush out of*) ; esp. to charge extortionately : 1885, former ; ca. 1895, latter. From ca. 1910, coll. O.E.D., S.O.D. ; F. & H., ' I rushed the old girl for a quid.' The semantics being : not to give time to think.—2. Hence, to deceive : Glasgow (— 1934).—3. To arrest : c. : from ca. 1890 ; ob. Clarence Rook, *The Hooligan Nights*, 1899.

rush, do a. To back a safe horse : racing : from ca. 1860 ; ob.—2. To lay a dummy bet : bookmakers' : from ca. 1870. I.e., rushing the public into betting on this horse.

*****rush, give it to** (one) **upon the.** To make a violent effort to get in or out of a place : c. : ca. 1810–40. Vaux.

rush, give one the. To sponge on a person all day and then borrow money from him at the finish, ' or pursue some such procedure,' H. : low : from ca. 1860.

rush, roam on the. In horse-racing, to swerve as the finishing spurt begins : sporting : from ca. 1880 ; ob. Cf. *rope*, v., 1.

rush-buckler. A violent bully : coll. : ca. 1530–90. Robinson's More, ' Bragging rush-bucklers.'

*****rush-dodge.** See **rush**, n., 1, and **rusher**, 1.

rush for and **rush out of.** See **rush**, v.

rush-light. Some strong liquor : ca. 1750–80. Toldervy, 1756. See quotation at **slug**, n., 1.

rush one's fences. To be impetuous : ' County ' coll. : C. 20. Ex the j. of hunting.

rush up the frills or **petticoats** or **straight.** To coït with a woman without any preliminary blandishments : low coll. : from ca. 1850 ; ob. The third comes from horse-racing (cf. *rush, roam on the*).

*****rusher**, gen. in pl. ' Thieves who knock at the doors of great houses, in London, in summer time, when the families are out of town, and on the door being opened by a woman, rush in and rob the house ; also house breakers, who enter lone'— unoccupied—' houses by force,' Grose, 1st ed. : c. of ca. 1780–1850. Cf. *rush*, n., 1.—2. A person (gen. male) of a ' go-ahead ' nature or habits : coll. : late C. 19–20 ; ob.

*****rushing-business.** Robbery by adroitness or with apparent fairness : c. : from ca. 1880.

ruskit. Rustic : a late C. 19–20 sol.

*****russia ; R.** A pocket-book : c. (— 1877) ; ob. The reference in ' *No. 747* ' is valid for 1845. Because made of *Russia* (leather).

Russian. A ' difficult ', unruly animal : Australian : 1888, ' Rolf Boldrewood ' ; ob.

Russian Coffee-House, the. The Brown Bear tavern in Bow Street, Covent Garden, ' a house of call for the thief-takers and runners of the Bow-street justices,' Grose, 2nd ed. : ca. 1787–1830. Because the brown bear is a characteristic of Russian fauna.

Russian duck. Muck: rhyming s. (— 1923). Manchon.

Russian law. 'A 100 blowes on his bare shins,' John Day, 1641 : mid-C. 17 coll.

Russian socks. Rags bound about one's feet on a march : French Foreign Legion (— 1935).

Russki. A Russian soldier : military : 1914 ; slightly ob. B. & P. Ex *Russian* + *-ski*, a frequent Russian termination.

rust, n. Old metal : London (— 1884) ; ob. Cf. *rusting* and *rust,* v.—2. Money : low : ca. 1855-1910. Mayhew, 1858, 'There's no chance of nabbing any rust (taking any money).'—3. See **rust, nab the.**—4. See **rust, in.**

rust, v.i. To collect and sell old metal : London (— 1884) ; ob.

rust, in. Out of work : theatrical : 1889 (O.E.D.) ; ob. Punning *rest* (see **resting**) and *rusty.*

***rust, nab the.** To be refractory (orig. of horses) ; hence, take offence : c. of ca. 1780-1890. Grose, 1st ed. ; H., 5th ed. Cf. *rusty.*—2. To be punished : c. : from ca. 1890 ; † by 1850. Cf. *nab the stoop, the teize,* qq.v.—3. See **rust,** n., 2.

rust, take (the) ; also **nab the rust.** (Of horses) to become restive : coll. : 1775, Colman (*take rust*). Ob. (O.E.D.)

rustic. A recruit : military (mostly officers') : from ca. 1925. Ex his 'greenness'.

rustiness. Annoyance (state of) ; bad temper : 1860, Whyte-Melville (O.E.D.) ; ob. Ex *rusty,* adj.

rusting. The frequent vbl.n. of *rust,* v., q.v.

rustle. To bestir oneself, esp. in business : U.S. (— 1872), anglicised ca. 1885 as a coll. But *rustler* (adopted by Morley Roberts in 1887) has not caught on. In C. 20, gen. *hustle,* q.v.—2. Among Canadian soldiers in the G.W., *rustle* and *rustler,* ex the U.S. senses, to steal cattle and cattle-stealer, were the equivalents of *scrounge* and *scrounger.* B. & P.

***rusty.** An informer : c. : 1830, Lytton, 'He'll turn a rusty, and scrag one of his pals ! ' ; † by 1910. Ex :

rusty. Ill-tempered ; annoyed : coll. : 1815, Scott, 'The people got rusty about it, and would not deal.' Esp. *cut up,* or *turn, rusty.* Prob. ex :

rusty (or grub), ride. To be sullen : coll. : ca.

1780-1840. Grose, 1st ed. Ex *reasty,* restive, applied esp. to a horse.

Rusty Buckles. The 2nd Dragoon Guards : military : C. 19-20 ; ob. F. & Gibbons. Also *the Bays.*

rusty guts, rusty-guts ; rustyguts. 'An old blunt fellow,' B.E. : late C. 17-mid-18.—2. Then, though now slightly ob., any 'blunt surly fellow,' Grose, 1785. Both B.E. and Grose consider it a 'jocular misnomer of *rusticus*'.

rut, keep a. To make mischief : coll. : late C. 17-18. ? ex dial. *rut,* friction (itself ex *rub*) ; the O.E.D. considers it ex † *rut,* noise, disturbance, which is the more likely, for dial. *rut* may not date back so far.

rutat ; occ. **rattat.** A potato : back s. on *tatur.* Mid-C. 19-20. H., 1st ed. ; Ware, ' *Ruttat-pusher* (1882). Keeper of a potato car ' (i.e., barrow).

***rutter.** One of a party (gen. numbering four) of swindlers ; he stood at the door : c. : late C. 16 ; Greene.

rux, v. To reprimand, or blame, scold, severely : T: M. Ellis, 1899 (O.E.D.). Prob. ex dial. *rux,* shake ; to tread upon (E.D.D.).

rux. Bad temper ; (a gust of) anger, passion : Public Schools' (— 1934). C.O.D. (1934 Sup.). Either ex Lincolnshire *ruck,* a noise, a racket, or, more prob., ex Kentish *have one's ruck up,* to be angry (E.D.D.).—2. To 'rag', to get up to mischief : Dartmouth Naval College : C. 20. Bowen. Either ex the orig. of sense 1 or ex *rags.*

ry. A sharp trick ; a dishonest practice : Stock Exchange : late C. 19-20 ; ob. It may possibly be a distorted abbr. of *rig,* n., q.v.

ryakonite. Incorrect for *rhyacolite* : C. 19-20. O.E.D.

rybeck. A share : low London (mostly Yiddish) : 1851, Mayhew (O.E.D.).

ryder. A cloak : low : ca. 1870-1910. ? *rider,* that which rides on.

rye. See **Romany rye.**

***rye mort ; rye mush.** A lady ; a gentleman : c. : C. 20. James Curtis, *The Gilt Kid,* 1936. For *rye,* see **Romany rye** ; *mort,* c. for a girl or woman ; and see **mush,** n., 7,—cf. *coring mush* and *tober-mush.*

***ryer.** One shilling and sixpence : turf c. (— 1932). Perhaps a corruption of *kye,* q.v.

***ryno.** See **rhino.**

S

[F. & H. records the following ineligibles under **s**. S.E. :—Sabin or s. ; Sacheverel(l) ; saddle a place, s. one with a thing ; sadly (> dial.) ; safe phrases not done separately ; sail near (etc.) the wind ; St. Martin's evil and St. Lawrence's tears ; for (old) sake's sake, etc. ; salad days or stage ; salamander, anything fire-proof ; sally-port ; salmagundy, the dish ; salt (senses and phrases not treated separately) ; saltimbanco ; sample of sin ; Samson's posts ; sandwich boat ; sandy pate ; sap, ale ; sappate (or -skull) and sap-head(ed) ; sappy, polish ; sard ; sauce, vegetables ; sauce for the goose . . . ; sauce-pate ; sauce, pay, pay an extortionate price ; serve with the same sauce ; saunter ; save-all, a miser ; saw in cords ; say-so ; scabbard (sexually) ; scabilonian ; scabby sheep ; scaffolders ; scalda-

banco ; scamp, a rogue,—to do badly ; scampery ; scandal-proof, lost to shame ; scant of grace ; scape ; scape-gallows, -grace, -shift ; Scaramouch(e) ; scarlet, to wear ; Scarlet Woman ; scatterbrain(ed) ; scattergood, scatterling ; scene and behind the scenes ; sceptre ; schism-monger ; scissors and paste ; scob ; sconce, a fine ; scorpion of the brow ; scoundrel ; scout, watchman, mean fellow ; scraggy ; scramble ; scrape, trouble, a miser, a term at fiddling, and scrape, to bow ; scrape-shoe and -trencher ; scraper, scraping ; scrappy, etc. ; scrat(ch), also dial. ; scratch, adj. and v. ; screecher and screechly ; screw, senses, etc., not listed ; scroyle ; scrub where not hereinunder ; scrunch ; scud, v. ; scal (or skul-)duggery ; scum ; scumber ; scumble ; scurry ; scute ;

scuttle (gait) ; sea phrases, etc., not listed ; **season** ; **see**, etc., not separately ; **see-saw** ; **seedy, seediness** ; **seek-sorrow** ; **seggon** ; **send down** ; **sense** ; **servant** ; **set-down, -off**, and **-to** ; **seven-year** ; **sewer**, sense 3 ; **sex** ; **shab off** ; **get or make shabby** ; **Shades, the** ; **shadow**, n. and v. ; **shadrach** ; **shady spring** and **shaft of Cupid** as sexual complements ; **shag-rag** ; **shake** phrases, etc., not separately listed ; **shaky** ; **shallow** unlisted ; **sham**, id. ; **shamble-legged** ; **shambrogue** ; **shameless** ; **shandry(gan)** ; **shandygaff** ; **shanghai** ; **shank**, etc., not listed ; **shanker** ; **shanty** (hut), n. and v. ; **shap**, also dial. ; **shape**, v. ; **shape-smith** and **in good shape** ; **share, share-penny** ; **shark** unlisted ; **sharp**, id. ; **shatterbrain(ed)** ; **shave**, v. ; **shaveling** ; **shay** ; **sheath** ; **she-familiar** ; **sheep**, etc., if unlisted ; **sheets**, euphemistic ; **shell** (in schools) ; **shell-out**, n. ; **shift**, v., **shifter** and **shiftwork** ; **shin** (up), v. ; **shin-rapper** ; **shindy**, a disturbance ; **shine**, to make an impression, excel, (**cut a**) **shine** and **s.**, a flash ; **shining light** ; **shinner** ; **ship**, except where listed ; **shirk, shirker** ; **shit** terms if unlisted ; **shocker** ; **shoddy** ; all **shoe** phrases, etc., not given later ; **shog, shoot**, etc., when unlisted ; **shooter** ; **shooting-iron** ; undesignated **shop**'s ; **Shoreditch fury** ; **short** terms if unspecified ; **shotten herring** ; **shoulder-clapper, -knot, -pegged**, and **shoulder-of-mutton fist** ; all over bar the shouting ; **shovel**, unspecified **show**'s ; **shrimp** ; **shuffle** ; **shuttle-brain, -head, -wit** ; (**fight**) **shy** ; **sick**, etc., if unrecorded ; **side**, id. ; **siege** ; **sieve** ; unlisted **sight**'s ; **sign-manual** ; **silk-petticoat** and **-stocking** ; **silly** if unnoted ; **silver-cooper** ; **simkin** ; **simple Simon, simpleton** ; (sin) **sinews of war** ; undenoted **sing**'s ; **singlebroth, -soldier**, and **-woman** ; **sink**, a slum, etc. ; **sink**, v. ; (old) **sinner** ; **siquis** (public announcement) ; **sir, Sir John Lack-Latin**, and **Sir Martin Wagstaffe** ; **sirrevence** (as apology) ; **siserara** ; **sister, sisterhood** ; all unspecified **sit**'s are ; **six** (beer) ; **sixes and sevens, set on seven** ; **six-footer, -shooter, six of one** . . . ; **size, sizar** ; **skeet** ; **skeleton** ; **skilly, skilligolee** ; **skimble-skamble** ; **skimmington** ; **skimp** ; **skin** phrases, etc, unrecorded ; **skink** ; **skip** phrases unspecified ; **skipper**, captain ; **skipping** ; **skirry** ; **skirter** ; **skirts, sit upon one's** ; **skit** ; **skittles** phrases ; **skue** ; **skulk** ; unrecorded **sky**'s (including compounds) ; **slabbergullion** ; **slack** (time) ; **slam** (cards) ; **slam-bang** ; **slampam** ; undetailed **slang** terms ; **slangam, slangrill** ; **slapsauce** ; **slapdash** ; **slappaty-pouch** ; unrecorded **slash**, etc. ; **slaughter**, v. ; **sledge-hammer** ; **sleep** ; **sleeping-house, -partner** ; **sleepy** (fruit) and **s.-head** ; unspecified **sleeve**'s ; **sleeveless** ; **slibberslabber** ; **slick** (S.E. > dial. and U.S.) ; unrecorded **slide**'s ; **slim**, adj. ; **slinging** ; **slink**, a bastard ; **slip**, etc., undenoted ; **slit** ; **slither** ; **slive** ; **slobber**, v., and **slobberer** ; **slop**, etc., not recorded ; **slosh**, a drink ; **slouch, slouchy** ; **slow**, n. ; **slowback, -coach, -up** ; **slug(-a-bed)** ; **sluice**, v. ; **slum**, v. ; **slump**, n. and v. ; **slur**, an affront ; **slush**, a drunkard or filthy feeder ; **slut**, etc. ; **sly**, secret ; **smack**, a tang, and **s.**, to kiss ; **smackering** ; **small**'s unrecorded ; **smart**'s, id. ; **smash**, to ruinate ; **smatterer, -ering** ; **smectymnus** ; **smell**, to investigate ; **smell-feast, -smock** ; **smelly** ; **smelt**, a dupe, simpleton ; **smicker, smickering** ; **smickly** ; **smiling** ; **smirk** ; **smiter**, a sword ; **smock**, etc. ; unrecorded **smoke**'s ; **smoother** ; **smouch**, v. ; **smug**, adj. ; **smuggle**, to fondle ; **smulkin** ; **smush** ; **smut**, etc. (obscenity) ; **snack**,

except in games sense ; **snag, snaggler** ; **snail** ; unspecified **snake**'s ; **snap**, id. ; **snarler** ; **snatch** entries unnoted hereinunder ; **sneak**, etc., id. ; **sneck-drawer, -drawing** ; **sneering** ; **sneeze** ; **snickersnee** ; **snigger** ; **snick**'s unrecorded ; **snip-snap, -snipper-snapper** ; **snivel, -ler, -ling**, and **s.-nose** ; **snob**, an inferior, a vulgarian ; **snoozer** ; **snort** ; **snot-gall** ;. **snout**, nose, face, and **snout-fair** ; **snow-ball, snow-broth** ; **snub** ; **snub-nose** ; **snudge** (now dial.), a miser ; **s.-snout** ; **snuff**, etc., except as specified ; **snuffle** (**-r, -s**) ; **snuggery** ; **so !** ; **so-and-so, so-so** ; **soak(er), soaker, soaking** ; **sobersides** ; **sock** (comedy) ; **s.**, to sew up ; **socket** ; unrecorded **soft**'s ; **soiled dove** ; **solace** ; **solid** ; **solution of continuity** ; **song** and **change one's song** ; **sonnikin** ; **sooterkin** ; **sop** and **sop in the pan** ; **sorry** ; **sort, after a** ; **sound**, to examine ; **sour**, adj. ; **sow** ; **spade** and **call a s. a s.** ; **spado** ; **Spain, build a castle in** ; **spaniel** ; **spanker** (nautical) ; **spark** (dandy, lover) and **sparkful, sparkish, sparky** ; **sparrow, mumble a**, and **sparrow-mouth, -tail** ; **speak** phrases, etc., not listed ; **special**, n. ; **speedy man** ; **spell**, a period of work or rest, with corresponding v. ; **spell for** ; **spend-all, s. the mouth, spendings** ; **spew** ; **spick(-and)-span(-new)** ; **spicy, racy**, indelicate ; **spider-shanked, -shanks**, and **s.-web** ; **spigot** ; **spill-good, -time** ; **spin a fair thread** and **s. out** ; **spindle-legs, spindly** ; **spirit, spiriter** ; **spit**'s unrecorded ; **spital** or **spittle** ; **spittoon** ; **splatter-face** ; **splay-foot** ; unspecified **split**'s ; **splodgy** ; **spoil**, id. ; **spoke in one's wheel** ; **sponge**'s unspecified ; **spook, spooky** ; **spoonage** ; all unspecified **sport**'s ; **spot** (sexual) ; **spout, a** pawnbroker's shoot, his shop ; **spout**, v. ; **spouting-club** ; **spouter** ; **sprat** (pejorative) ; **spread** (sexual, v.) ; **spread-eagle** ; **sprig** ; **spring**, except as defined ; **springal** ; **spry** ; **spud** (dwarf, spade) ; **spy** ; **squab**, n., and **s.**, to fall heavily ; **squabash** ; **squabbled** ; **squail(er)** ; **squall** ; all **square**'s not treated separately ; **squarson** ; **squash**, etc., not detailed ; **squat** ; **squatter** ; **squawk** ; **squeak**, n. ; **squeaker**, a young bird ; **squealer**, id. ; all unspecified **squeeze**'s ; **squelch** ; **squench** ; **squib**, a satire, to satirise ; **squin-eyes** ; **squinny** (**-eyed, eyes**), **squint-minded**, and **squintafuego** ; **squire**, etc., undenoted ; **squireen** ; **squiress** ; **squirm**, v. ; **squirt**, a spurt, and **squirts** ; **squishop** ; **stab**, v., and **stab-shot** ; **stable** ; **stack**, n. ; **staff** (**of life**) and other **staff** terms not hereinunder ; **stage-fever** ; **staggerer** ; **stale**'s unrecorded ; **stall**, id. ; **stallion** ; **stamps** (printing) ; undenoted **stand**'s ; **stang, ride the** ; unspecified **star**'s ; **starch, starched** ; **starling** (coin) ; **start-up** ; **starter**, a milksop ; **startler** ; **state of nature** ; unrecorded **stay**'s ; **steam**, energy ; **steel-boy** ; **steenkirk** ; **steeple, s.-fair, -house** ; **stepper** (horse) ; undenoted **stern**'s ; **stew** (pond, brothel), **stewed, stewish** ; **stew in one's own grease, juice**, etc. ; **stibbler** ; **stichel** ; unspecified **stick**'s ; **stickler** ; **stiff**, id. ; **stifler**, a heavy blow ; **stigmatic** ; **stile** phrases ; **stingy** ; **stinkard** ; **stinking fish, cry** ; **stitch-back** and **stitch, go through** ; **stive** ; all undenoted **stock**'s ; (in one's) **stockings** ; **stocky** (build) ; **stodge** (food) ; **stoke** ; unrecorded **stomach**'s ; **stone**, id. ; **stools, fall between two** ; unspecified **stoop**'s and **stop**'s ; (blind) **story** ; untreated **straught**'s ; **strain** ; **stranded** ; **stranger**, a visitor ; unrecorded **strap**'s, including **strapper, strapping** ; **straw**, id. ; all **strawberry** terms ; **streak**, a sequence ; **streamers** ; undescribed **street**'s ; **stretch**, id. ; **stride, take in one's** ; unrecorded **strike**'s ; **string**, id. ; **strip**, v. ;

stroker ; stroller ; strum (v. in music) ; strumpet ;
strut-noddy ; stub, a fool ; study ; unspecified
stuff's ; stuffy, airless ; stump, etc., unrecorded ;
suburb, etc.—but see note on ; succuba, -us ;
suck, etc., where unspecified ; sufferer, a loser ;
sugar, flattery, and sugar-loaf ; suit (complete
series, etc.) ; sulky, n. ; sullen ; unrecorded
summer ; sumpsimus ; unspecified sun's ; Sunday
best, Sunday's fellow ; superannuate ; unrecorded
sure's, including suresby ; surtout ; supercollate ;
swab, etc., unspecified ; swag-belly ; swaining ;
unrecorded swallow's ; swarm ; swash (and -er,
-ing) ; unspecified swear's ; sweat, id. ; sweater, a
jersey ; sweep, etc., undetailed ; sweet, id. ; swill ;
swim, etc., where not detailed ; swine, id. ; swing,
id. ; swinge, id. ; swish, id. ; swobber ; swollen
head.

 Dial. :—Sandgate rattle ; saucebox, the mouth ;
scaff-and-raff ; scallops ; scate ; screed o' drink ;
screw, a stomach-ache ; shrudge ; shack, n. and adj. ;
shackbag, etc. ; shalley-gonahey ; shammock ;
shaney ; shank it ; shard ; sharge ; sherry-mow ;
(do a) shift ; shine, n. ; shinfeast ; shoard ; shot-
pot and, shot-flagon ; side-winder ; sit (of milk), sit a
woman sit in, sit-still nest ; skelper ; skinsmedam ;
skitter-brain ; sky-wannocking ; (on the) skyte ;
slab ; slake ; slam (a sloven), slam(mer)kin and
slammocks ; slamtrash ; slapper ; slive-Andrew ;
sliverly, sliving ; slump, adv. ; smeekit ; smicket ;
smouch (hat) ; smug (snail) ; snaggy ; snifter (a
breath) ; snirp ; snoach ; snob (mucus) ; snook, n.
and v. ; so (pregnant) ; soldier, v., and soldier's
thigh ; sonkey ; sow-child and -drunk (cf. swine-
drunk, S.E.) ; sozzle, a heavy fall ; spiddock-pot
legs ; spitter ; sprug ; squit ; squitters ; stacia ;
stag (a romping girl) ; staggering Bob ; stam-bang ;
stand-further ; stang(e)y ; star-bason ; starf ;
stepmother ; stickit minister ; stifler, a busybody ;
stimble ; stink-a-puss ; (go a good) stitch ; stocky,
irritable ; Stockport coach (properly chaise) ;
strava(i)g ; strunt (liquor) ; stump and rump (perhaps also coll.) ; sumph ; swad (lout, lump) ;
swankey (small beer) ; swattled.]

 'S ; rarely **'s.** A coll. euphemistic abbr. of *God*'
in oaths ; gen. continuous with governing words as
in *'Sblood* and *'Slife* : C. 16–20 ; from mid-C. 18,
only ' literary '.

 's. (Contrast with dial. **s'**, shall.) Is : late
C. 16–20 : S.E. until C. 18, then coll. (though permissible in verse). Richardson, 1741, ' The Devil's
in't if we are not agreed in so clear a case ' (O.E.D.).
Or even = ' it is ' (the *s* forming liaison with
the next word) : coll. : C. 20. E.g., H. C. Bailey,
Mr. Fortune Wonders, 1932, ' You wouldn't
blame your dear boy ! Your only one ! 's too bad.'
—2. Are : sol. : C. 19 (and presumably centuries
earlier)—20. Baumann.—3. Has : coll. : from ca.
1540.—4. Us : late C. 16–20 : S.E. until C. 18,
then dial. except in *let's*, which is coll. Richardson,
1741, ' Let's find him out ' (O.E.D.).—5. As : C. 18–
20 : dial. and, more rarely, coll.—6. As a ; mostly
in *'s matter of fact* : low coll. : late C. 19–20. E.g.
J. A. Bloor in *The Passing Show*, July 7, 1934.—7.
As = ' his ', *'s* has not emerged from formal and,
in C. 19–20, dial. speech.—8. This : coll. : late
C. 19–20. See quotation at *'smorning.*—9. Does :
coll. : late C. 19–20. Neil Bell, *Winding Road*,
1934, ' When's Parliament reassemble, Stephen ? '
Mostly after *when* but not unknown after *how*, as in
' How's he do it ? It beats me ! '—10. See preceding entry.

s-. ' As I write (1917) there is a slang tendency
to say *snice* for *nice*, etc.,' W. See esp. *snice mince
pie.*

 s.a. ; S.A. Sex appeal : from ca. 1929. Agatha
Christie, 1930 ; Dorothy Sayers, *Have His Carcase*,
1932, ' The girl . . . exercising S.A. on a group of
rather possessive-looking males.'

 's luck ! (Pron. *'sluck* ; occ. written so.) Here's
luck ! : coll. : from ca. 1912. Francis D. Grierson,
Murder at Lancaster Gate, 1934.

 s. and b. ; S. and B. An occasional variant
(— 1887 ; very ob.) of *b. and s.* Baumann.

 S.M., the. The company sergeant-major : military coll. : C. 20. (Never in the vocative.) F. &
Gibbons.

 S.O.B. or **s.o.b.** ' Son of a bitch ' : mostly Australian : from ca. 1925. Christina Stead, *Seven
Poor Men of Sydney*, 1934, ' That s.o.b. Montagu
got me the job 'ere, you know.'

 S.O.L. Unlucky : Canadian : C. 20. B. & P.
Euphemistically ' short of luck ', actually ' sh*t,
out of luck '.

 S.O.S. See **same old stew.**

 S.O.S. course. The **S**niping, **O**bservation and
Scouting ' course of training at the Sniping Schools
established in 1916 ' : military jocular coll. : 1916–
18. F. & Gibbons. Prompted by S.E. ' S.O.S. '.

 S.P.Q.R. **S**mall profits, **q**uick **r**eturns : jocular
coll. : C. 20. O.E.D. (Sup.).

 S.R.D. See **seldom reaches destination.**

 S.P.O. A cheap restaurant specialising in
sausages, potatoes and onions : London : from ca.
1925.

 sa. Six : showmen's, mostly Parlyaree : from
ca. 1850. P. H. Emerson, 1893, ' I was hired out
. . . for sa soldi a day.' Ex Lingua Franca.

 sa'. Save, esp. in *God sa' me* : C. 17–mid-19 :
S.E. till ca. 1660, then coll. Shadwell, 1668, ' As
God shall sa' me, she is a very ingenious Woman '
(O.E.D.).

 saam. ' E.g. " Can I come saam ? " " He went
saam " ; meaning " Can I come with you ? "
" He went with them." ' . . . An imitation of the
Dutch idiom,'—*samen*, together—' and is current
in the Midland districts of the Cape Colony,' Pettman : South African coll. : C. 20.

 Sabæan. Incorrect for *Sabian* : C. 18–20.
O.E.D.

 sabe, save, savvy. See **savvy.**

 sable Maria. A variant († by 1920) of *black
Maria*, q.v.

 sabby. A pidgin English variant (— 1864) of
savvy, q.v. H., 3rd ed.

 saccer. The sacrament : Harrow School : late
C. 19–20. By the Oxford-*er.*

 ***sack.** A pocket : c. : late C. 17–mid 19.
B.E. ; Mayhew, 1858.

 sack, v. To ' pocket ', take (illicit) possession of :
coll. : C. 19–20 ; ob. E. S. Barrett, 1807, ' He
sacked the receipts, without letting them touch one
farthing,' O.E.D.—2. To dismiss one from employment or office : from ca. 1840. Gen. in passive.
Ex (*get* and/or) *give the sack.*—3. To defeat (in a
contest, esp. in a game) : from ca. 1820 (orig. Anglo-
Irish) ; rare after ca. 1860. ? *cx sack*, to plunder.
—4. To expel : Public Schools' : from ca. 1880.
Desmond Coke's school stories, *passim.* Ex
sense 2.

 sack, bestow or **confer the order of the.** See **sack,
order of the.**

 sack, break a bottle in an empty. To make a

cheating bet, a hocus wager, ' a sack with a bottle in it not being an empty sack,' Grose, 2nd ed. : coll. : late C. 18–mid-19.

sack, buy the. To become tipsy : s. > coll. : ca. 1720–1840. *A New Canting Dict.*, 1725 ; Grose, 1st ed. Ex *sack*, generic for the white wines formerly imported from Spain.

*sack, dive into a. To pick a pocket : c. : late C. 17–early 19. B.E.

sack, get or **give the.** See **get** or **give the sack.** Cf. :

sack, the order of the. Gen. as *get* or *give* (occ. *bestow, confer*) *the order* . . . A dismissal from employment, a discharge from office, a being discarded by sweetheart or mistress (rarely lover) : from ca. 1860. Yates, 1864, ' I'd . . . confer on him the order of the sack.' See also **give the sack,** and cf. *order of the.*

sack of coals. A black cloud (gen. black clouds) in the Southern Hemisphere : nautical : late C. 19–20. Bowen.

*sacking, prostitution ; **sacking law,** harlotry as practised by the underworld with a view to further gain : c. of late C. 16–early 17. Greene, 1592, 1591 resp. Ex the S.E. v., *sack*, to lay waste.

sacks. Long trousers : Charterhouse : C. 20. On *bags.*

sacks to the mill !, more. Pile it on ! ; there's plenty here ! : coll. : late C. 16–18, then dial. Nashe ; Middleton & Rowley in *The Spanish Gipsie* ; Richardson. (Apperson.)

Sacramentarian, gen. in pl. A Methodist : **an** Oxford nickname : ca. 1733–1810. O.E.D.

sacratil, -tyle. An error for *serratile* : ca. 1540–80. O.E.D.

sacred lamp. A ballet-girl burlesque : theatrical : 1883–ca. 1900. Ware. Ex a cynicism by John Hollingshead (' The sacred lamp of burlesque ').

sacrifice. A(n alleged) loss : coll. >, ca. 1880, S.E. Dickens, 1844, ' Its patterns were last Year's and going at a sacrifice.' Esp. *alarming* or *astounding s.*

sacrifice. To sell, or claim to sell, at less than cost price : from ca. 1850 : coll. >, ca. 1880, S.E. Ex the n.

sad. Mischievous, troublesome, merry, dissipated : late C. 17–20 (ob. except in *sad dog*) : coll. Chiefly of a place (' London is a sad place,' Mackenzie, 1771) and of a person, esp. in *sad dog*, in C. 18–mid-19 a debauched fellow, and thereafter rare except in playful reproach. Farquhar, 1706, ' *S*. You are an ignorant, pretending, impudent Coxcomb. *B*. Ay, ay, a sad dog.'

sad vulgar. A vulgarian : Society : ca. 1770–1820. Ware cites *The St. James's Gazette* of Aug. 17, 1883.

saddle. The female pudend ; woman as sexual pleasure : coll. verging on euphem. S.E. : C. 17–20, but rare since C. 18.—2. ' An additional charge upon the benefits ' from a benefit-performance : 1781, Parker : theatrical, † by 1920.

saddle-back. See **saddleback.—saddle becomes** ... See **saddle suits.**

saddle-leather. The skin of the posteriors : coll. : mid-C. 19–20. Punning S.E. sense.

saddle on the right or **wrong horse, put the.** To blame—occ., to praise—the right or wrong person (loosely, act, thing) : coll. (in C. 20, S.E.) : from ca. 1750. Ex the earlier *set* . . . (1607) and *lay* . . . (1652), both † by 1840. An occ. variant : *place*, mid-C. 19–20, ob. (O.E.D.) Also *s. upon* ...

saddle one's nose. To wear spectacles : coll. : late C. 18–mid-19. Grose, 3rd ed.

saddle-sick. Made ill or very sore by riding : coll. and dial. : late C. 18–20 ; ob. Grose, 1st ed. Cf. *saddle-leather*, q.v.

saddle suits a sow, suit one as a. To suit, become, fit ill ; be very incongruous : coll. : C. 18–19. Swift, who has *become* for *suit*.

saddle the spit. To give a meal, esp. a dinner : coll. : late C. 18–mid-19. Grose, 3rd ed. Ex S.E. *saddle a spit*, to furnish one.

[**saddle up.** To saddle (a horse). Considered by Pettman to be a South African coll. : but it has always, and everywhere, been S.E.]

saddle upon . . . See **saddle on** . . .

saddleback. A louse : C. 19–20 ; ob. (Not in the best circles.)—2. Incorrect for *saddle-bag* (upholstery) : from ca. 1830. W.

saddling-paddock. A place where lovers tend to congregate : Australian (— 1909). Ware. Semantics : *ride, riding.*

safe . . . a. E.g. ' He is a safe second ', i.e. he is sure to obtain second-class honours : coll. : late C. 19–20. (S.O.D.)

safe (and sound), be or **arrive.** To have duly arrived, be at one's destination : coll. : 1710, Swift, ' I send this only to tell that I am safe in London.'

safe as . . ., **as.** Very safe : coll. : none recorded before 1600, thus : **as safe as a church,** 1891, Hardy (not very gen.) ; **safe as a crow** (occ. sow) **in a gutter,** ca. 1630–1730, Clarke, Ray ; **as a mouse in a cheese,** ca. 1670–1750, Ray ; **as a mouse in a malt-heap,** ca. 1630–1700, Clarke, Ray ; **as a mouse in a mill,** ca. 1600–50, Davenport ; **as a thief in a mill,** ca. 1620–1750 (then dial.), Beaumont & Fletcher, Swift ; **as anything,** from ca. 1895, F. & H. (1903) ; **as Chelsea** is dial. ; **as coons,** 1864, † by 1920 ; **as houses,** 1864, Yates ; **as safe,** 1860, Whyte-Melville (O.E.D.) ; **as the bank,** 1862 ; **as the Bank of England,** 1923, J. S. Fletcher ; **as the bellows,** 1851, Mayhew (mostly Cockney, † by 1930). With hearty thanks to Apperson, the ' locus classicus ' for *safe as*, as for so many other coll. similes and semi-proverbial c.pp.

safe card. An alert fellow : from ca. 1870 ; slightly ob. H., 5th ed. Cf. *card*, q.v.

safe un. A horse that will not run, certainly will not (because meant not to) win : the turf : 1871, ' Hawk's-Eye ', *Turf Notes*, ' The safe uns, or " stiff uns " ' . . . horses that have no chance of winning.'

sag. ' To drift off a course ' : nautical coll. : late C. 19–20. Bowen.

sahib. A ' white man ', a thoroughly honourable gentleman : mainly in the Services : late C. 19–20. Since ca. 1925, often derisive of ' Public School ' morals and mentality. Ian Hay, 1915. Ex Arabic and Urdu respectful address to Europeans. W.

saïda ; saïda bint or **girl.** See **bint.**

said. Have said ; esp. in *you said it* : U.S., anglicised ca. 1931 via the ' talkies '. Dorothy Sayers, *Murder Must Advertise*, 1933, ' " The idea being that . . . ? " " You said it, chief ".'

said he. E.g. ' " Do you like that ? " . . . " No," said he frowning ! " ' : a coll. c.p. (— 1927). Collinson. Prob. ex the novelist's trick and the journalist's mannerism.

said than done, no sooner ; 2, (that's) easier. Both these phrases, obvious in meaning, are C. 19–20 coll.

sail about. To saunter about : coll. : late C. 17–mid-18. B.E.

sail in, v.i. To arrive, to enter : coll. : from ca. 1870. Ex S.E. *sail in,* to move in a dignified or a billowing manner.—2. Hence, to begin boldly (to act) : from ca. 1880.—3. Hence the special sense, to begin to fight : 1891, *The Morning Advertiser,* March 30. Cf. :

sail into. To attack, e.g. with one's fists : from ca. 1891.—2. To begin vigorously on (e.g. a meal). Cf. *sail in,* 3.—3. To enter (a building, a room, etc.) : C. 18–20. Tom Brown, 1700, 'From thence I sailed into a Presbyterian Meeting near Covent-Garden,' O.E.D. : cf. *sail about,* q.v.

sailor-teasers. 'Studding sails and flying kites which the sailor disliked intensely' : nautical coll. : C. 19. Bowen.

sailor's blessing. A curse : nautical : from ca. 1880. Cf. *fuck you, Jack, I'm all right* and *sailor's farewell.*

sailor's champagne. Beer : lower classes' jocular coll. (— 1909) ; ob. Ware.

sailor's farewell. A parting curse : nautical, military : C. 20. Cf. *sailor's blessing, soldier's farewell,* and *butler's grace.*

sailor's friend, the. The moon : nautical coll. : mid-C. 19–20. Bowen.

sailor's pleasure. 'Yarning, smoking, dancing, growling, &c.', Clark Russell, 1883 ; ob. As applied to the first three, it is S.E. ; to the last, coll. Cf. *soldier's privilege.*—2. 'Overhauling his sea chest or bag and examining its contents' : nautical : C. 20. Bowen.

sailor's waiter, the. A second mate on a sailing-ship : nautical (— 1840) ; ob. Dana ; Bowen.

sailor's weather. 'A fair wind and just enough of it' : sailing-ships' coll. : C. 19–20. Bowen.

sails. A sail-maker : nautical (— 1840). Dana. Cf. *chips,* q.v.

sails, take the wind out of one's. To nonplus, surprise, gen. unpleasantly : mid-C. 19–20 : coll. (orig. nautical) >, ca. 1905, S.E.

sails like a haystack. See **haystack.**

saint. 'A piece of spoilt timber in a coach maker's shop, like a saint, devoted to the flames,' Grose, 2nd ed. : ca. 1785–1850.—2. (**Saint.**) One belonging to a religious association at Cambridge : a nickname : ca. 1793–1830. They affected a great sanctity and a marked zeal for orthodoxy (see e.g. *Gradus ad Cantabrigiam,* 1803).—3. A member of that party which, in England, instituted and fostered the agitation against slavery : a nickname : ca. 1830–50. O.E.D.—4. An inhabitant of Grahamstown, *the City of the Saints* (q.v.) : South African (— 1913). Pettman.—5. (Gen. pl.) See **Saints.**

[**St** is more logical than **St.,** as the Fowlers indicate. (**S't,** more accurate still, is pedantic.) The same applies to *Bp* (Bishop), *Dr, Mr,* etc.]

St Anthony, dine with. A variant of *dine with Duke Humphrey,* to go without dinner or, loosely, any other meal : 1749, Smollett, translation of *Gil Blas.*

St Alban's clean shave. The clean-shaven face of a high churchman : ecclesiastical : late C. 19–early 20.

St Alban's doves. Two active canvassers of 1869 : political of that year. Ware. Ex their church.

St Anthony pig. See **Anthony.**—**St Anthony's pigs.** See **Anthony's pigs, St.**

St Benedict. See **St Peter.**

St Bernard Croly. The Rev. George Croly (1780–1860), author of *Tales of the Great St Bernard,* 1829. Dawson.

St Francis. See **St Peter.**

St Geoffrey's day. Never : coll. : ca. 1786–1850. Grose, 2nd ed. Cf. *Queen Dick.*

St George, riding and the dragon upon. See **riding St George.**

St George a-horse-back. The act of kind : C. 17–18. Massinger, ca. 1632, omits *St.*

St Giles, dine with. See **dine with St Giles.**—**St Giles's bread.** See **Giles's bread.**

St Giles's carpet. A sprinkling of sand : Seven Dials, London : C. 19. Ware.

St Giles's Greek. See **Giles's Greek, St.**

St Hugh's bones. Shoemaking tools : coll. : C. 17–mid-18 ; then dial., extant in Cheshire. Dekker, 1600 ; E. Ward, 1700. Apperson.

[**St John to borrow.** 'See *borrow* ', F. & H. : but not there. ? = a nut : see E.D.D. at *St John.* Or perhaps a loan or a pledge or surety : see E.D.D. at *borrow.* Prob. there is an error.]

St John's Wood donas. Harlots, courtesans : taverns' : ca. 1880–1912. Ware. Many once lived there.

St Lubbock's day. A bank-holiday : 1871 : coll. ; ob. Ex Sir John Lubbock, the institutor, who brought in an Act in that year. Ware records *St Lubbock,* an orgy or drunken riot : lower London : ca. 1880–1914.

St Luke's bird. An ox, 'that evangelist being always represented with an ox ', Grose, 1st ed. : c. or low : ca. 1780–1850.

St Marget's ale. Water : coll. : 1600, Munday & Drayton ; † by 1800. Cf. *Adam's ale.*

Saint Maritan. A Samaritan : sol., esp. Cockneys' (— 1887). Baumann.

St Martin's lace. Imitation gold-lace : coll. : 1607, Dekker ; H., 5th ed. (Cf. etymology of *tawdry.*)

St Martin's ring. A copper-gilt ring : coll. : C. 17–early 18. Anon., early C. 17, *Plain Percival,* 'I doubt whether all be gold that glistereth, sith Saint Martin's rings be but copper within, though they be gilt without.'

St Martin's the Grand. A hand : rhyming s. (— 1857). 'Ducange Anglicus.'

St Mary's knot, tie with. To hamstring : Scots coll. : 1784, *The Poetical Museum.* (F. & H.)

Saint Monday. Monday : South African coll. (— 1896). Because observed as a holiday by the Malays. Pettman. Ex :—2. Esp. *keep Saint Monday,* to be idle on Monday as a result of Sunday's drunkenness : 1753, *The Scots Magazine,* April, (*title*) 'St. Monday ; or, the tipling tradesmen.' O.E.D.

St Nicholas. See **Nicholas.**

saint of the saucepan. A good cook : coll. verging on S.E. : 1749, Smollett ; ob.

St Old's. St Aldgate's, Oxford : Oxford undergraduates' : late C. 19–20. Collinson.

St Partridge. The 1st September, when the partridge-shooting opens : sportsmen's coll. (— 1923). Manchon.

St Patrick. The best whiskey : coll. : ca. 1650–1850. Ex *drink at St Patrick's well* : coll. : 1648, anon., *A Brown Dozen of Drunkards* ; † by 1850.

St Peter, silence and mortification ; **St Radegonde,** a small cross studded with nails ; **St Benedict,** a hair-shirt ; **St Francis,** the discipline, i.e. the whip or scourge :—Roman Catholic ecclesiastical **s.** : late C. 19–20. Ex incidents recorded in hagiology.

***St Peter's son.** (Gen. in pl.) A general thief, ' having every finger a fish-hook ', Grose, s.v. *fidlam ben*, q.v. : c. of ca. 1780–1840.

St Peter's the Beast. St Peter-le-Bailey : Oxford undergraduates' : from ca. 1890. To rhyme with St Peter's in the East. Ware—whose definition is incorrect.

St Radegonde. See **St Peter.**

St Stephen's hell. No. 15 Committee Room, House of Commons : Parliamentary : in the 1880's. Ware. (See also Addenda.)

St Taur. H.M.S. *Centaur* of 1746 : naval : mid-C. 18. Bowen.

St Thomas a' Waterings, the 'Spital (or 'spital) stands too nigh. A semi-proverbial c.p. derived ex London topography, *waterings* being a pun : C. 17–mid-18 ; e.g. in the anon. play, *The Puritan*, 1607. ' Widows who shed most tears are sometimes guilty of such indiscretions as render them proper subjects for the public hospitals,' Hazlitt. (There is a cynical early C. 17 play dealing with a woman successfully courted at her husband's funeral.)

Saints. ' A football team of St Kilda, Victoria ' (Australia), C. J. Dennis : Australian sporting : late C. 19–20.—2. The Southampton Association Football Club : English sporting : late C. 19–20. Ex *Southamptonites* slurred.

sakes (alive) ! A (low) coll. exclamation : from ca. 1840 : mostly dial. and U.S. (O.E.D.)

sal. A salivation, or treatment for syphilis : 1785, Grose, who adds ' *in a high sal*, in the pickling tub or under a salivation '. † by 1860.—2. A salary : theatrical : 1859, H., 1st ed. ; 1885, *Household Words*, Aug. 29.

sal hatch, or **S.H.** An umbrella : lower classes' (— 1909). Ware. Perhaps ex a proper name : cf. *Mrs Gamp* and † S.E. *sal hatch*, a dirty wench.

sal slappers. A common woman : costers' (— 1909). Ware.

salaams ! (My) compliments (to you, her, etc.) : Anglo-Indian coll., fairly gen. in C. 20 and almost S.E. Ex Arabic for ' Peace (be upon *or* with you).'

salad. After having been wakened, to have another nap : nautical, applied only to officers (— 1877). Cf. the C. 16–early 17 S.E. *pick a salad*, to be trivially engaged.

salad march. A ' march of ballet girls in green, white, and pale amber—from the usual colours of salads ' : late C. 19–early 20 theatrical coll. Ware.

salad oil. Hair-oil : lower classes' (— 1923) Manchon.

salamander. A fire-eating juggler : circus (— 1859). H., 1st ed.—2. A nickname for ' the first type of Sopwith 'plane with armoured fuselage ' : Air Force : mostly 1915. B. & P.

***salamon.** A C. 17–19 form of *salmon*, q.v.

sale, house of. A brothel : coll. : late C. 16–17. Shakespeare in *Hamlet*.

salesman's dog. A shop-tout : ca. 1690–1840. B.E. ; *A New Canting Dict.*, 1725 (*saleman's* . . ., prob. a misprint) ; Grose. On *barker*, q.v.

Salisbury. A civil lie ; a polite evasion : political : ca. 1890–1900. *The Pall Mall Gazette*, March 5, 1890, ' The famous Salisbury about the Secret-Treaty . . . must henceforth be read " *cum grano salis*-bury " !' Ex the statesman.

Sallenger's (or Sallinger's) Round, dance. To wanton ; copulate : coll. : C. 17–early 18. *Sal-*

lenger's Round was an indelicate ballad of ca. 1600 ; lit., *St Leger's*.

Sallies. See **Johnnies.**

Sally. See **Aunt Sally.**—2. (Also **sallow.**) An Australian corruption of Aboriginal *sallee*, acacia. Morris.

***sally, v.** ; **sallying, vbl.n.** These c. terms, valid for 1865 in ' *No. 747* ', are of obscure sense ; it is, however, clear that they refer to some not very skilled ' dodge ' for illicitly obtaining money.

Sally Nixon (occ. **s.n.**). Salenixon (sal enixum) : workmen's : from ca. 1880. O.E.D. (Sup.). By ' Hobson-Jobson '.

Sally Booze. Sailly-la-Bourse, a village on the Western Front : military : G.W. (F. & Gibbons.)

sally-port. The mouth : nautical (— 1923). Manchon. Ex a ship's sally-port.

salmagundy. A cook : coll. : C. 18–early 19. Ex the dish so named.

***salmon** ; occ. **salamon, salomon** or **-an,** and **solomon.** The Mass ; Harman defines as also an altar, a sense not recorded after C. 16. Rare except in *by salmon !*, by the Mass !, the beggar's expletive or oath, or in the C. 18–early 19 *so help me salmon !* : c. of ca. 1530–1830. Copland, Overbury, Moore-Carew, Scott. Prob. a corruption of the Fr. *serment*, an oath.—2. A C. 20 abb. of sense 3 of :

salmon and trout. The mouth : rhyming s. (— 1859) ; ob. H., 1st ed., as *salmon trout*, which is rare after ca. 1870 ; the 5th ed. has *s. and t.*—2. The nose : id. (on *snout*) : C. 20. B. & P.—3. Gout ; a tout : C. 20. P.P., *Rhyming Slang*, 1932.

salmon-gundy. A (rather low) coll., indeed almost sol. form of *salmagundy* : late C. 18–early 19. Grose, 2nd ed. (See also **salmagundy.**)

***saloman, -mon.** The former a frequent, the latter a rare variant of *salmon*, q.v. : resp. C. 17 and mid-C. 16–early 19. Resp., Overbury ; Harman, Middleton, Shirley.

Sal's, sleep at. To sleep at a Salvation Army shelter : lower classes' (— 1923). Manchon.

salt. A sailor ; esp. one of long experience, when often *old salt* (as in Hughes, 1861) : coll. : 1840, Dana, ' My complexion and hands were enough to distinguish me from the regular salt.' Occ., though by 1910, ob. : *salt-water*.—2. (An instance of) sexual intercourse : coll. : mid-C. 17–early 18. Ex *salt*, amorous, lecherous. Cf. :

salt, v.i. To copulate : coll : (?) C. 17–early 18. Ex the S.E. adj. : cf. *salt*, n., 2.—2. V.t., to admit (a freshman) by putting salt in his mouth, making him drink salty water, or practising on him some similar burlesquery : students' : ca. 1570–1650. (O.E.D.)—3. In an invoice or account, to price every article very high, gen. in order to allow a seemingly generous discount on settlement (*salt an account, an invoice*, etc.) : commercial : 1882, Ogilvie. Perhaps directly ex next sense :—4. To insert in the account books fictitious entries with a view to enhancing the value of a business to a prospective buyer : commercial (— 1864). H., 3rd ed. (Gen. *salt a book, the books*, etc.) Prob. suggested by :—5. In mining, to sprinkle or plant an exhausted or a bogus claim with precious dust, nuggets, or gems : orig. (— 1864), of gold in Australia ; of diamonds, ca. 1890 ; of oil, ca. 1900. H., 3rd ed. ; *The Pall Mall Gazette*, Dec. 22, 1894, ' Even experienced mining men and engineers have been made victims by salters.'—6. To introduce secretly into (a meeting) opponents of, or persons to oppose, the speaker : coll. (— 1923). Manchon.

salt, adj. Dear, costly, excessive in amount (of money) : C. 18–20 dial. >, ca. 1850, s. ; as s., slightly ob. H., 2nd ed., ' " It's rather too salt," said of an extravagant hotel bill ' ; F. & H., ' *as salt as fire* = salt as may be.' Also *salty.*—2. Aristocratic ; wealthy : 1868 (O.E.D.) ; slightly ob. **Ex** *the salt of the earth*, a phrase that began ca. 1840 to be used of the great in power, rank, wealth,—a trivial use that, during the G.W., > ob.—3. Drunk : late C. 19–early 20. Abbr. *salt junk,* adj. (q.v.). Ware.

salt, we shan't take. Our box-office returns will be very small : theatrical c.p. (— 1909). Ware, ' We shall not take enough money to pay for salt, let alone bread.'

salt and spoons, come after with. To be slow or dilatory : coll. : late C. 17–18. B.E., ' One that is none of the Hastings ' ; cf. *Hastings* (*sort*), q.v.

salt away. See **salt down.**

salt-beef flag. ' The Blue Peter, in anticipation of the diet ' : nautical : late C. 19–20. Bowen.

salt-beef squire. More usual than *salt-horse squire,* q.v. (F. & Gibbons.)

*salt-box. A prison cell ; esp. the condemned cell at Newgate : c. of ca. 1810–90. Vaux ; Egan's Grose ; H., 2nd ed. Ex (? smallness and) bitterness.

*salt-box cly. A flapped outside pocket : c. : ca. 1810–40. Vaux.

salt-cellar. The female pudend : low : C. 19(?–20). Cf. *salt,* n., 2.—2. (Gen. pl.) A very deep hollow, above the collar-bone, in the female neck : coll. : from ca. 1912. O.E.D. (Sup.)

salt down ; occ., in C. 20, **away.** To put by (money, 1873, or stock, 1897) ; store it away. Ex *salt,* to preserve with salt. O.E.D.

salt eel. A rope's end, esp. in *have* (*a*) *salt eel for supper,* to receive a thrashing : ca. 1620–1830 : naval coll. Mabbe, Congreve, B.E., Smollett, Colman, Grose. (O.E.D.)

salt horse or **junk.** Salted beef : nautical coll. >, ca. 1870, S.E. : resp. 1840 (O.E.D.) ; 1837, Marryat. Whence *salt-horse squire.*—2. A non-specialist naval officer : naval : C. 20. Bowen.

salt-horse squire. A warrant as opp. a commissioned officer : naval : mid-C. 19–early 20. Ware.

salt it for (a person). To spoil or ruin something for : C. 20. Manchon. Ex *salt,* v., 5.

salt junk, adj. Drunk : rhyming s. : ca. 1890–1910. Ware.—N. : see **salt horse.**

salt on one's, its, the tail,—**cast** or **fling** or **lay** or **put** or **throw.** To ensnare, capture : coll. : mid-C. 17–mid-19, C. 18–19, late C. 16–mid-19, mid-C. 19–20, and C. 19–20. Lyly ; ' Hudibras ' Butler, ' Such great atchievements cannot fail | To cast salt on a woman's tail ' (see **tail**) ; Swift (*fling*) ; Lamb, 1806, ' My name is . . . Betty Finch . . . you can't catch me by throwing salt on my tail ' (Apperson) ; Dickens, 1861 (*put*).

salt-pits. A or the store of Attic wit : Oxford University : ca. 1820–40. Egan's Grose. Ex *Attic salt.*

salt-water. See **salt,** n., 1. (Ainsworth, 1839.)—2. Urine : coll. : late C. 17–18. Tom Brown.

Saltash luck. ' A wet seat and no fish caught ' : naval : late C. 19–20. Bowen. Ex *Saltash,* a small town four miles N.W. of Devonport.

salted. Experienced : of horses, coll., 1879 ; of persons, **s.,** 1889. O.E.D.—2. See **salt,** v., 5. :

recorded by O.E.D. in 1886, but doubtless twenty years older.—3. Tipsy : from before 1931, but not very gen. For semantics, cf. the synonymous *corned* and *pickled.*

saltee. A penny : Parlyaree : mid-C. 19–20. H., 1st ed. ; Reade, ' It had rained kicks all day in lieu of saltees.' Also *saulty.* Ex It. *soldi.*

salter. One who salts mines : from ca. 1890. See **salt,** v., 5.

salting, vbl.n. See **salt,** v., 2.—2. See **salt,** v., 5.

salts. Smelling salts : coll. : 1767 ; slightly ob. --2. Epsom salts : coll. : 1772. O.E.D.

salts and senna. A doctor : a nickname from ca. 1860 ; ob. Ex *salts* ; cf. *No. 9.*

salt's pricker. A ' thick roll of compressed Cavendish tobacco ' : naval (— 1909). Ware.

salty. See **salt,** adj., 1 : mostly U.S. (1847, Robb).

salubrious. Drunk : from ca. 1870 ; ob.—2. In reply, esp. to a query as to health, ' Pretty or very well, thanks ! ' : from ca. 1880 ; ob. Perhaps via *scrumptious,* q.v.

salvage. A New Zealand soldiers' synonym of to *make* (steal), *scrounge, souvenir, win* : in G.W. By meiosis.

Salvation Army, the. The Salvage Corps : military : from 1915. (B. & P.) Contrast *salvo.*

Salvation jugginses — rotters — soul - sneakers. Members of the Salvation Army : London lower classes' : 1882–84. Ware.

salve, n. Praise ; flattery : 1859, H., 1st ed. ; rather ob. Cf. S.E. *lip*(-)*salve,* flattery.

salve over. To persuade or convince by plausibility or flattery : coll. : 1862 (O.E.D.).

Salvo. A Salvation Army recreation hut : military : from 1915. F. & Gibbons.

Sam ; occ. **sam.** A Liverpudlian : dial. and s. : from ca. 1840. Perhaps ex *sammy,* 1., q.v. Also and gen. *Dicky Sam* (1864, H., 3rd ed.).—2. Hence, a fool : 1843, Moncrieff, ' I'm a ruined homo, a muff, a flat, a Sam, a regular ass.' Ex *sammy,* n., 1, and adj.—3. See **sam, upon my,** and **sam, stand.**

sam, v. Abbr. (— 1909 ; proletarian) of the next. Ware.—2. To slam (esp. a door) : Lancashire rhyming s. (— 1905) rather than dial. E.D.D. Sup.

sam, or **Sam, stand.** To pay the reckoning, esp. for drinks or other entertainment : 1823, Moncrieff ; 1834, Ainsworth, ' I must insist upon standing Sam upon the present occasion ' ; Henley. Prob. the *sam* is cognate with that of *upon my sam,* and derives either ex *salmon,* q.v., as I prefer, or ex *Samuel,* as the O.E.D. suggests ; H.'s theory of U.S. origin (*Uncle Sam*) is, I feel sure, untenable. Also *stand sammy.*—2. **stand sam to,** to promise (a person something) : C. 20. (Neil Bell, *Andrew Otway,* 1931.)

Sam, uncle. See **Uncle Sam.**

sam !, upon my ; more gen. **'pon my sam !** A jocular asseveration : 1879, F. J. Squires (O.E.D.). See preceding entry for etymology ; it is, however, not improbable that *'pon my sam* is a corruption of dial. *'pon my sang*(*s*), recorded as early as 1860, *by my sang* occurring at least as early as 1790, and *my sang* ca. 1840 (E.D.D.). Cf. *say-so, on my* (*sammy*), q.v.

Sam Hill. Hell, e.g. ' What the Sam Hill ' : Cockney euphemism : C. 20.

Sambo, gen. in address. A Negro : coll. : from

ca. 1860 ; orig. U.S. (Nautically, any Negro rating.) Ex S.E. sense, a Negro with a strain of Indian or European blood.

same, the. The same person : coll. ' in confirming a conjecture as to the identity of a person mentioned by the speaker ' : 1889, *Chatterbox*, Aug. 24, ' " The bushranger, do you mean ? " asked Allan. " The same ".' O.E.D.

same like. Same as ; exactly like : coll., almost sol. : from ca. 1870. W. Pett Ridge, *Mord Em'ly*, 1898 , ' Beef Pudding same like Mother makes '— a cheap eating-house's advertisement.

same o.b. Same old ' bob ' (shilling) : lower classes' c.p. : ca. 1880–1910. Ware. Ex usual entrance-fee.

same old stew. A punning c.p. on the inevitable stew : military : 1915 ; ob. B. & P. With reference to an *S.O.S.* message.

same old 3 and 4. Three shillings and four pence a day wages : workmen's (— 1909) ; † by 1920. Ware.

same time. At the same time : i.e. nevertheless, or, ' but, mark you, . . .' : coll. (mostly in dialogue) ; C. 20. E.g. Freeman Wills Crofts, *Mystery in the Channel*, ' Same time, if we do not learn of her elsewhere, we shall see the skipper of every lugger on the coast.'

same to you with knobs on(, the). See **knobs.**

samey. Monotonous : coll. : from ca. 1920. Ex :—2. Indistinguishable ; the same : schoolboys' : late C. 19–20. Ernest Raymond, *A Family That Was*, 1929, ' The days that followed, becoming " samey " . . ., sank out of memory's sight.'

samkin. An occ., now ob., variant (— 1886) of *simkin*, 2.

Sammy or **sammy** ; occ. **sammy soft** or **S.S.** A fool : from ca. 1830 ; slightly ob. Peake, 1837, ' What a Sammy, give me a shilling more than I asked him ! ' Cf. *Sam*, n., 2, q.v.—2. (**Sammy.** A Hindu idol (e.g. of Siva) : British soldiers' (in India) : late C. 18–20. Ex *Swamy*, ex Sanskrit *suamin*, Lord. Yule & Burnell (at *Swamy*).—3. A South African abbr. of *Ramasammy*, q.v. Pettman, 1913. Also for an Indian pedlar of fruit.—4. An American soldier : a coll. nickname : Oct. 17, 1917. Ex *Uncle Sam*, q.v. (W.)

sammy, v. To clean (equipment, esp. if of leather) : military coll. : C. 20. F. & Gibbons. Ex S.E. *sammy*, to dry (leather) partially. Also *sammy up* : whence *sammying-up*, preparations for guard-duty (B. & P.).

sammy, adj. Foolish : from ca. 1810 ; ob. *Lex. Bal.* Whence the n., 1. Cf. *Sammy Soft.*

sammy (or **S.**), **stand.** A variant of *sam*, *stand*, q.v. : 1923, Moncrieff ; ob.

sammy-house. An idol-temple : British soldiers' (in India) : 1859 (Yule & Burnell). Ex *Sammy*, n., 2.

Sammy Soft (or **s.s.**). A fool : from ca. 1840 ; slightly ob. See **Sammy**, n., 1.

sammy up ; sammying-up. See **sammy**, v.

Sampan. The ship *Sans Pareil* : naval : late C. 18–early 19. Ware.

sample. To caress intimately, or to ' occupy ', a woman for the first time : coll. : C. 19–20. Ex *sample*, to ' obtain a representative experience of '. Cf. :—2. To drink : from ca. 1845. Porter, 1847, ' Old T. never samples too much when on business.' Via ' drink as a test or trial.'

sample-count. A commercial traveller : commercial coll. : 1894, Egerton ; very ob.

sampler. The female pudend : C. 19–20 ; ob. Semantics : needlework.

sam(p)son or **S.** A drink of brandy and cider, with a little water and some sugar : dial. and s. : from ca. 1840 ; ob. Halliwell. Also, mainly dial. and from ca. 1880, *Samson with his hair on*, which denotes a very strong mixture of the same ingredients, as in ' Q ', *Troy Town*, 1888 (E.D.D.).—2. A baked jam pudding : Durham School : from ca. 1870. Both senses ex the sense of power, the second perhaps also ex toughness.

samshoo. Any spirituous liquor : Anglo-Chinese (— 1864). H., 3rd ed. Ex *samshoo*, a specific fiery spirit, rice-distilled.

Samson and Abel. Oxford University : from ca. 1860. ' A group of wrestlers in the quadrangle of Brasenose. [Some said it represented Samson killing a Philistine ; others Cain killing Abel : the matter was compromised],' F. & H., 1903 ; H., 5th ed., 1874.

san fairy (Ann or **Anna).** See **sanfairyann.**

san. A sanatorium : coll. : from not later than 1913. Orig. Public Schoolboys' : witness Ian Hay, *The Lighter Side of School Life*, 1914.

san skillets, or **S.S.** The *sans-culottes* of Paris : proletarian : late C. 18. Ware.

*****San Toys.** Crooks : c. rhyming s. (on *boys*) : C. 20. P. P., *Rhyming Slang*, 1932.

sanakatowmer. A heavy fall ; a violent blow : nautical : late C. 19–20. Bowen. Echoic.

sanatarium, sanatry. Incorrect for *sanatorium*, *sanitary* : mid-C. 19–20.

sanc. A hiding-place (e.g. for pipes) : Dartmouth Naval College cadets' : C. 20. Bowen. Ex *sanctuary.*

sancipees. See **sank.**

*****sand.** Moist sugar : c. of ca. 1810–50. Vaux, Egan's Grose.—2. Money : C. 19. Cf. *dust*, q.v.—3. Constancy of purpose ; courage ; stamina : orig. (ca. 1870), U.S. ; anglicised ca. 1895, but never very gen. and, by 1930, ob. Cf. *grit*, q.v.—4. Salt : nautical : mid-C. 19–20. Bowen.—5. Any sugar : Canadian, and at Bootham School : late C. 19–20. B. & P. Cf. sense 1.

sand, eat. (Gen. of the helmsman) to shorten one's watch by turning the hour-glass before it has quite run out : nautical s. or coll. : ca. 1740–1820. *Memoirs of M. du Gué-Trouin* (properly Du Guay Trouin or Duguay-Trouin), 1743. Ex the sand in the glass.

sand-bag, -boy, -groper, -man, -paper. See these as single words.

sand-storm. ' A soup of boiled maize . . . from its brownish colour ' : military : C. 20. F. & Gibbons.

sand-storm medal. (Gen. pl.) An Egyptian Army decoration : military : late C. 19–20. Ibid.

*****sandbag.** A long sausage-shaped bag of sand used as a weapon : orig. (— 1871) c. ; by 1900 gen. s. and by 1820, S.E. Pocock, *Rules of the Game*, 1895. (It leaves almost no mark ; often employed by soldier deserters or gangsters on Salisbury Plain and on the Etaples dunes during the G.W.) Hence :

*****sandbag,** v. To fell with a sandbag : orig. (— 1890) c. >, ca. 1910, gen. s. >, ca. 1919, S.E. App. both weapon and word—see O.E.D.—were first used in U.S. ' Hence *sandbagger.*

sandbag duff. An Army pudding made from ground biscuit : New Zealanders' : in G.W.

*****sandbagger.** A ruffian using a sandbag as a

weapon : c., orig. (1884) U.S., anglicised ca. 1890 : by 1910, gen. s. ; by 1920, S.E.

Sandbags, the. The Grenadier Guards : from ca. 1855 : military. Ob. Also known as *the Bermuda Exiles, Coal-Heavers, Housemaids' Pets,* and *Old Eyes.*

sandbeef. A sandwich : Anglo-Indian (—1887) ; ob. Baumann.

sandboy (properly **sand-boy**), **as happy** or **jolly** or **merry as a.** Very happy, etc. : resp. late C. 19–20, never very gen. ; 1823, ' Jon Bee ', this being the usual form ; 1841, FitzGerald, ' We will smoke together and be as merry as sandboys ' (O.E.D.). These coll. phrases > S.E. ca. 1850, ca. 1870, ca. 1910.

Sandgroper. (Gen. pl.) A Western Australian : Australians' : C. 20. The State of W.A. consists mainly of sand.

sandman (from ca. 1870, occ. **sandy man) is coming, the.** Addressed to, or remarked of, children showing signs of sleepiness : a nursery coll. : 1861 (O.E.D.). Cf. *dustman,* q.v. Ex rubbing eyes as if sand were in them.

sandpaper. To rub out or off ; to remove : 1889, *Answers,* Feb. 9, ' " Can't do it," said Lancaster, " and I hope to be sandpapered if I try " .' Ob.

sandpapering the anchor. ' Doing unnecessary work aboard ship ' : nautical jocular coll. : mid-C. 19–20. Bowen.

sands, leave or **put a person to the long.** To abandon ; place in a difficulty : Scots coll. of ca. 1670–1700. J. Brown, 1678, ' How quickly they were put again to the long sands (as we say),' O.E.D. Ex *sands,* a desert or perhaps a sand-bank.

sandwich. A sandwich-man : 1864 (H., 3rd ed.) though adumbrated by Dickens ca. 1836 : coll. >, ca. 1910, S.E.—2. One of the two boards carried by a sandwich-man : a catachrestic sense dating from ca. 1880.—3. A gentleman between two ladies : from ca. 1870 (H., 5th ed., 1874) ; ob. Perhaps ex Thackeray's ' A pale young man . . . walking . . . *en* sandwich ' (*Vanity Fair,* 1848). Rather coll. than s.

sandwich, v. To set or insert between dissimilars : from ca. 1860 : coll. >, ca. 1910, S.E.

sandwich board. A police-ambulance stretcher : lower classes' : ca. 1870–1914. Ware.

Sandy. A Scotsman : a coll. nickname (—1785), mostly Scots. Grose, 1st ed. Ex *Sandy,* abbr. *Alexander,* a very gen. Scottish name.—2. **(sandy.)** Gen. pl., ' Thames barge men who dredge for sand in the river ' : nautical coll., esp. Thames-side : late C. 19–20. Bowen.

sandy blight. Ophthalmia : Australian coll. (— 1916). C. J. Dennis.

sandy man. See **sandman is coming, the.**

sanfairyann !, or **san fairy Ann !** It doesn't matter : military c.p. : from late 1914. B. & P ; F. & Gibbons ; Hugh Kimber puts his War novel, *San Fairy Ann,* 1927, thus : ' There is a magic charter. It runs, " San Fairy Ann " .' A perversion of Fr. *ça ne fait rien* (that makes no odds). Variants : *san fairy, san fairy Anna,* and *(Aunt) Mary Ann.*

sang (occ. **sank) bon.** Very good indeed ; as n., a ' nap ' hand at cards : military : 1915 ; ob. F. & Gibbons. Ex Fr. *cinq fois bon.* Cf. *sankey.*

sangaree. A bout of drinking (to excess) : coll. : ca. 1820–70. Halliwell. Ex S.E. sense, a cold drink made of spiced wine diluted.

Sangster. An umbrella : London : ca. 1850–70. Ex the inventor of a special kind. (Ware.)

sanguinary, jocular for *bloody,* is **s.** verging **on**

coll. : C. 20. O.E.D., 1909. Cf. *blood-stained, rose-coloured, ruddy.*

Sanguinary Doubles, the. The Piccadilly Saloon : ca. 1850–62. H., 3rd ed. Because situated at No. 222 (Piccadilly).

sanguinary James. (Cf. *bloody Jemmy,* its origin.) A (raw) sheep's-head : 1860, H., 2nd ed. ; ob.

sanitory is incorrect for *sanitary* : mid-C. 19–20. O.E.D.

sank, sanky, occ. **sancipees** (or **centipees,**—F. & H. erroneously **centipers**). A tailor employed by a clothier in the making of soldiers' clothing : ca. 1780–1870. Grose, 1st ed. Perhaps ex Yorkshire dial. *sanky,* boggy, spongy, but prob. cognate with dial. *sank,* to perform menial offices as servant in a dining-room, itself a variant of *skink,* to wait on the company (see Grose, P.).

sank bon. See **sang bon.**

sank-work. The making of soldiers' clothes : coll. : ca. 1850–1920. Mayhew, 1851 ; Baumann. This word bears a curious resemblance to the C. 14 S.E. *sank,* to bring together ; cf. *blown together,* q.v. ; see, however, remarks at *sank,* whence it derives, and cf. Mayhew's suggestion that the origin resides in Fr. *sang* (Norman *sanc*), blood, in reference to a soldier's work or to the colour of his coat.

sankey. A five-franc note : military : late 1914 ; ob. F. & Gibbons. Ex Fr. *cinq francs.*

Sankey's Horse. The 39th Foot, now the Dorsetshire Regiment : military : C. 18–20. F. & Gibbons. Ex the name of its colonel in the War of the Spanish Succession (1701–13) and a ' tradition that the battalion was mounted on mules for special service.'

sanniferan. Rare for *sanfairyann.*

sans ill-used : see Fowler.—2. Worthless ; useless ; ' dud ' : Bootham School (— 1925). Anon., *Dict. of Bootham Slang.* Ex the Shakespeare quotation. Cf. the Bootham *wet.*

Santa. Santa Claus : coll., mostly of the nursery : from ca. 1880. Cf. *Santy.*

*santar or **-er.** He who, in a trio of thieves working together, carries away the booty : c. : late C. 16–early 17. Greene, 1591. I.e. to sanctuary.

santeit ! See under **geluk !**

Santy. Santa Claus : coll., mostly Canadian : late C. 19–20. (John Beames, *Gateway,* 1932.) Cf. *Santa.*

sap. A fool or a simpleton : 1815, Scott : coll. >, ca. 1900, S.E. Milliken, ca. 1893, ' Sour old sap.' Abbr. *sapskull.*—2. One who works, esp. studies, hard ; a book-worm : schools' : 1798, Charlotte Smith ; 1827, Lytton, ' When I once attempted to read Pope's poems out of school hours, I was laughed at, and called a sap ' ; Goschen, 1888, ' . . . Those who . . . commit the heinous offence of being absorbed in [work]. Schools and colleges . . . have invented . . . phrases . . . such as " sap ", " smug ", " swot ", " bloke ", " a mugster " .' Whence :

sap, v. To be studious or a great reader : schools' : 1830 (O.E.D.), but implied in *sapping.* See also ' Eton slang ', § 3.

sap out. To work up (a subject) ; resolve (a problem or a ' construe ') : Shrewsbury School : from ca. 1880. Desmond Coke, *The Bending of a Twig,* 1906. Cf. *sap,* v.

sapper. One who studies hard : Eton : 1825, Westmacott (O.E.D.). Cf. *sap,* v. and n , 2.—2. A gay, irresistible fellow : music-halls' : late C. 19. Ware. Ex Fr. *sapeur*.

Sappers, the. The Royal Engineers : military coll. : from 1856, when the Royal Sappers and Miners were amalgamated with the Royal Engineers as the Corps of Royal Engineers. F. & Gibbons.

sappiness. Foolishness ; folly : coll. : late C. 19–20. See **sap**, n., 1.

sapping. Hard study : schools : 1825, Westmacott. Cf. *sap*, n., 2, and v.

sappy. (Of a caning) severe : Durham School : from ca. 1870. Ex S.E. sense : vigorous, rich in vitality, perhaps influenced by dial. sense, putrescent. (—As = foolish, *sappy* dates from C. 17 ; certainly S.E. up till ca. 1860 ; by 1870, it seems to have > coll. : see e.g. H., 5th ed.)

Sara. A *Sara*toga trunk : Australian : C. 20. E.g. John G. Brandon, *Th' Big City*, 1931. (Often personified.)

Sarahs ; more gen, **Saras**. Manchester, Sheffield and Lincolnshire Railway deferred ordinary stock : late C. 19–20 (ob.) : Stock Exchange. Prob. on *Doras* and *Coras* and *Floras*. Cf. *Sheffields*.

Sarah's Boots. The *Sierra Buttes* Gold Mining Company's shares : late C. 19–20 : Stock Exchange. Cf. preceding entry.

sarc. (Occ. **sark.**) Sarcasm : schools' : from ca. 1920. Cf. *sarky*, q.v.

sarcky. An occ. form of *sarky*, q.v. John Brophy, *Waterfront*, 1934.

sarcy. A low coll. form of *saucy* : C. 19–20. Moncrieff, 1843. Prob. influenced by *sarcastic* : see **sarky**.

[**sard**, to copulate, C. 10–17, seems to have, in late C. 16, > a vulg.]

Sardine. ' The nickname of the Prince of Wales, son of King George V, when [a few years before the G.W.] he was a naval cadet at Dartmouth,' Bowen.

sardine-box. A prison-van : lower classes' (—1909) ; ob. Ware. (Packed as if with sardines.)

sardine-tin. A clumsy steamer : nautical : late C. 19–20. Bowen.

Sardines. Royal Sardinian Railway shares : Stock Exchange : late C. 19–20.

sardines, packed like. Crowded, huddled : mid-C. 19–20 : coll. till C. 20, then S.E. Ex the close packing of sardines in tins. Occ. *like sardines (in a tin)*. Cf. the U.S. *sardine*, a sailor on a whaling ship.

Sarey Gamp. An elaboration of *gamp*, an umbrella : mid-C. 19 London. Ware.

sarga ; sarge. Sergeant : military coll. ; *sarga* only, *sarge* mostly, in address : C. 20. F. & Gibbons. (Not merely, nor prob. even orig., U.S.)

sargentlemanly. So gentlemanly : satirical low coll. : ca. 1870–1900. Ware.

sark. To sulk : Sherborne School : from ca. 1880. Prob. ex *sarcastic* ; cf. *sarky*.—N. : see **sarc**.

Sarken News, the. The Clerkenwell News : London : 1860–83. Ware.

sarky. Sarcastic : (low) coll. : late C. 19–20. Cf. *sarc* and *sark*.

sarnt. ' A smart and soldierly pronunciation of sergeant ', used only before the surname ; *sarntmajor* can, however, be used without the surname · coll. : C. 20. B. & P.

sartin. Certain : sol. : mid-C. 18–20. Colman, 1762. (O.E.D.) Cf. :

sarvice. Service : low coll. and dial. : C. 18–20. ' Jon Bee ', 1823.

sashy, sas(s)hay. To chassé (in dancing) : sol. : mid-C. 19–20 ; mostly U.S.

sassage. A sausage : either sol. or low, esp. Cockneys', coll. (— 1887). Baumann. Cf. :

sassenger ; sassiger. A sausage : sol., mostly children's : late C. 19–20 ; slightly ob. Baumann.

sasshay. See **sashy**.

sassiety. A jocular form of *satiety* and a sol. form of *society* : both, from before 1887. Baumann.

sat. Satisfaction : universities' : ca. 1860–1900. Ware. (Ex L. *satis*.)—2. A fag : Public Schools' (— 1909) ; ob. Ware. Abbr. *satellite*, a jocular name for a fag.

sat-upon. Repressed, humiliated ; down-trodden : coll. : from ca. 1890. O.E.D. (Sup.).

Satan Montgomery. Robert Montgomery (1807–55), who, at the ripe age of twenty-three, wrote a long poem entitled *Satan*, compounded of piffling pretentiousness. (Dawson.)

sate-poll. A stupid person : low s. > coll. : late C. 19–20. ? = *sated poll* (head).

satin. Gin : from ca. 1860, ob. H., 3rd ed. Ex *white satin*, q.v.

satin, a yard of. A glass of gin : mostly among women (— 1864). H., 3rd ed. Cf. *ribbon* and *tape*, esp. among servants.

sating. (Pronounced *satting*.) Satin : sol. (— 1887). Baumann.

saturated. An occ. variant (— 1931 ; ob.) of *soaked*, very drunk. Lyell.

Saturday nighter. At Harrow, an exercise to be done on Saturday evening : late C. 19–20.

Saturday pie. A ' resurrection ' pie : lower classes' (— 1909) ; ob. Ware.

Saturday soldier. A volunteer : 1890, *The Globe*, Aug. 11 ; ob. Also *cat-shooter*.

Saturday(-)to(-)Monday. A mistress for the week-end : coll. (— 1903) ; very ob.

Saturday-to-Monday Station, the. The Gibraltar naval base, so near England : naval : C. 20. Bowen.

***satyr.** A professional stealer of cattle, horses, sheep : C. 18 c. ' Highwaymen ' Smith, 1714 (O.E.D.). Prob. ex the Roman representation of satyrs as goat-like.

sauce. Impudence, impertinence : coll. and dial. : 1835, Marryat (O.E.D.) ; perhaps much earlier (see **sauce than pig, more**). Ex *saucy*, q.v.—2. A venereal infection : coll. : C. 18–early 19. Vanbrugh.

sauce, v. To charge (a person) extortionately : coll. (or jocular S.E.) : late C. 16–early 17. Shakespeare.—2. To strike ; to thrash : coll : 1598, Jonson ; † by 1750.—3. Hence, in C. 17–18, to reprimand (severely) ; rebuke smartly : coll. Shakespeare. (Extant in dial.)—4. Hence, to address impertinently : low coll. : from ca. 1860. Dickens, 1865, ' Don't sauce me in the wicious pride of your youth.' (All dates, O.E.D.)

sauce, carrier's or **poor man's.** Hunger : mid-C. 19–20 : coll. ; but the latter soon S.E.

sauce, eat ; gen. **to have eaten sauce.** To be saucy : coll. : C. 16. Skelton, who has the variant *to have drunk of sauce's cup*.

sauce than pig, (have) more. (To be) very impudent, impertinent : coll. : late C. 17–18. B.E. Cf. *saucepan runs over*, q.v.

saucebox. An impudent or impertinent person : coll. : 1588, Marprelate's *Epistle* ; ob. Tylney, 1594, ' You, master saucebox, lobcock, cockscomb ' ; Fielding ; Miss Mitford. Cf. *sauce*, n., 1.—2. (Also dial.) ' In low life it also signifies the mouth ' ; H., 3rd ed., 1864 ; recorded, without comment, in the ed. of 1860.

saucepan on the fire, have the. To be desirous of, ready for, a scolding bout : coll. and dial. : mid-C. 19–20 ; almost † as coll. Cf. :

saucepan runs (occ. boils) over, your. You're very saucy : a late C. 17–18 c.p. or coll. B.E. (runs . . .). Cf. sauce than pig.

saucers. Eyes, esp. if wide-opened or very large : coll. : 1864, Mark Lemon, ' I always know when he has been in his cups by the state of his saucers.' Ex S.E. eyes like (or as big as) saucers, saucer-eyes (or -eyed), etc.

saucy. Impudent or rude ; impertinent : coll. : late C. 18–20. Ex C. 16–18 S.E., senses (insolent, presumptuous).—2. Hence, smart, stylish : coll. : from ca. 1830. An East End tailors' broadside advertisement of ca. 1838 runs, ' Kicksies made very saucy.'

saucy box. A ' saucebox ' (1), q.v. : coll. : 1711, Swift ; † by 1780. (O.E.D.)

Saucy Greens, the. The 36th Foot Regiment, now the Worcester Regiment : military : mid-C. 18–20 ; ob. F. & Gibbons. Ex facings of 1742–1881.

saucy jack. An impudent fellow : coll. : ca. 1550–1700. Cf. Jack sauce.

Saucy Pompeys, the. See Pompadours, the.

Saucy Seventh, the (old). The 7th Hussars : military : C. 19–20 ; almost †. Also the Lily-White Seventh, Old Straws, Strawboots, and Young Eyes.

Saucy Sixth, the. The 6th Foot Regiment >, in 1881, the Royal Warwickshires : military : late C. 19–20 ; ob. F. & Gibbons. Also Guise's Geese and the Warwickshire Lads.

saulted. Incorrect spelling of salted, 1, q.v. : from ca. 1880. (O.E.D.)

saulty. See saltee.

sausage ; live sausage. In sexual sense, it is on the marches of coll. and S.E.—2. (sausage or S.). A German : lower classes' : late C. 19–20. Ware ; B. & P. ; Manchon. Suggested by German sausage. —3. A German heavy trench-mortar bomb : military coll. : 1915–18. F. & Gibbons. Ex its shape.

Sausage Hill, go to. ' To be taken prisoner, " Sausage Hill " being generic for a German prison camp ' (F. & Gibbons) : military : 1915–18.

sausage toad. Sausage toad-in-the-hole : eating-houses' coll. : late C. 19–20.

sausanmash. A sausage and mashed potatoes: junior clerks' (— 1909). Ware.

savage, adj. Furiously angry ; unsparing in speech : from 1820's : mostly coll. (O.E.D.)

savage, Savage. (Gen. pl.) A member of the Savage Club : coll. : late C. 19–20. The Observer, Aug. 11, 1935.

savage as a meat-axe. See meat-axe.

savage rabbits, do. To wait in readiness for action ; ' to conceal small concentrations of tanks for local counter attacks against an enemy offensive ' : Tank Corps : Feb., 1918 ; ob. F. & Gibbons, ' From a phrase used by General Elles ' in that month ; Clough Williams-Ellis, The Tank Corps.

save. A piece of economy, a saving : dial. >, ca. 1905, low coll.

save, v.t. To protect oneself, or one's book of bets, by hedging ; to keep (a horse) on one side, not betting against it, thus making it a clear winner for oneself : the turf : 1869. In C. 20, coll.

save ! ; savé ? See savvy.

save-all. One of ' boys running about gentlemen's houses in Ireland, who are fed on broken

meats that would otherwise be wasted,' Grose, 1785 : Anglo-Irish coll. : mid-C. 18–mid-19. Prob. ex the save-all candlestick.

save oneself. To hedge : racing coll. : 1869, Broadwood, The O.V.H., ' Most who received the news at least saved themselves upon the outsider.' See save, v.

save-reverence. See sir-reverence.

Saveloy Square. Duke Place, Aldgate : East London (— 1909). Inhabited by Jews, it rarely sees a sausage. Ware, ' On the lucus a non lucendo principle.'

saver. A prudent covering bet : the turf : from ca. 1890. Nat Gould, 1891, ' I've put a saver on Caloola.' Ex save (oneself), to bet thus.

savers ! Halves ! : boys' : late C. 19–20. Cf. saver, q.v.

savey, savie. See savvy.

saving !, hang. See hang saving.

saving chin. A projecting chin : coll. : ca. 1776–1840. Bridges ; Grose, ' That catches what may fall from the nose.' Cf. the proverb he would save the droppings of his nose, applied to a miser.

savvy ; also sabby, sabe, savey, savie, savvey, scavey. Common sense ; good sense ; gumption : 1785, Grose ; ' Rolf Boldrewood ', 1888, ' If George had had the savey to crack himself up a little.'—Hence, acuteness, cleverness : 1864, H., 3rd ed. Forms : savvy, mid-C. 19–20 ; sabby, q.v. (— 1864) ; sabe, late C. 19–20, now rare ; savey, 1785 ; savie, Scottish, C. 19–20 ; savvey, from ca. 1880 ; scavey, C. 19 Ex Negro-ising of Fr. savoir, to know, or more prob of Sp. sabe usted, do you know ; imm. ex :

savvy ; also sabby, sabe(e) ; savey ; savvey ; scavey. (Resp. C. 19–20 ; mid-C. 19–20 ; C. 18–20 ; C. 19–20 ; C. 18.) V.t. (in C. 20, occ. v.i.), to know : 1785, Grose, ' " Massa me no scavey " '.' For etymology, see end of n.—2. In pidgin English, also to have, to do, etc., etc. : C. 19–20.

saw, held at the (occ. a) long. Held in suspense : coll. : ca. 1730–1830. North's Lord Guilford, 1733, ' Between the one and the other he was held at the long saw over a month.'

saw your timber ! Go away ! : low : from ca. 1855 ; ob. H., 2nd ed. On cut your stick ; a further elaboration is amputate your mahogany.

sawbones. A surgeon : from ca. 1835, Dickens in 1837 saying ' I thought everybody know'd as a sawbones was a surgeon.'

sawder, rare except as soft sawder. Flattery ; soft speech : 1836, Haliburton (O.E.D.) ; Grant Allen, ' I didn't try bullying ; I tried soft sawder.' Perhaps ex solder, n. ; prob. sawder, v. Cf. blarney.

sawder, v. To flatter ; speak softly to : 1834, Lover. Prob on to solder, perhaps influenced by sawdust, for cf. next two entries.

sawdust. Same as sawder, n. : rather low (— 1887). Baumann ; 1893, Milliken, ' True poetry . . . not sawdust and snivel ' ; ob. Either sawder (n.) corrupted or ex sawdust as used, in various sports, to soften a fall.

sawdusty. The adj. of the preceding : low : 1884, Punch, Oct. 11, ' Me doing the sawdusty reglar ' ; ob.

sawmill, the. The operating theatre in a hospital: military : 1915 ; ob. F. & Gibbons.

Sawney ; occ. Sawny. A Scot : a (mainly pejorative) coll. nickname : C. 18–20. Tom Brown ; Gay, ' He sung of Taffy Welch, and Sawney Scot ' ; Henley & Stevenson. Ex Alexander ; cf. Sandy, q.v.

sawn(e)y. A fool; a stupid or very simple (gen., man): late C. 17–20. B.E., Grose. In late C. 19–20, through (non-Scottish) dial. influence, it often = a soft, good-natured fellow. Prob. ex *zany* (in 1567 spelt *zawne* in Edwards's *Damon and Pythias*), though conceivably influenced by *Sawney*, q.v.— 2. Bacon: c. (— 1812). Vaux; Mayhew, who restricts to stolen bacon. ? ex *sawn*, bacon being cut off in slices (rashers). Cf. *sawney-hunter*, q.v.

sawn(e)y, v. To wheedle or whine: coll.: ca. 1805–90. Southey, 1808, 'It looks like a sneaking sawneying Methodist parson.' Ex the adj., perhaps also in part ex, or influenced by the East Anglian *sanny*, 'to utter a whining, wailing cry without apparent cause', E.D.D.—2. To be soft; to fool about: coll.: mid-C. 19–20. Ex n., 1, and adj., 2.

sawn(e)y, adj. Whining, wheedling: ca. 1800–1850. Cf. *sawney*, v., 1.—2. Foolish; softly good-natured or sentimental: s. > coll.: C. 19–20. Rhoda Broughton, 1873 'There is no sawny sentiment in his tone, none of the lover's whine.' Ex *sawney*, n., 1.

*sawn(e)y (rarely **sawny)-hunter.** One who purloins bacon and/or cheese from grocers' shops: 1856, Mayhew, *The Great World of London*. See **sawney,** n., 2.

sax. A saxophone: trivial: from ca. 1910.

saxpence !, bang goes. A c.p. (— 1890) addressed to a person excessively careful about small expenses. Manchon. Popularised by Sir Harry Lauder.

say. Yes: back s. (— 1859). H., 1st ed. (Logically but not actually *sey*.)—2. Six: Parlyaree: mid-C. 19–20. Ware. Ex It. *sei*.

say !; I say ! An introductory interjection; a mere exclamation: coll.: resp., orig. U.S., anglicised ca. 1900; C. 17–20. Beaumont & Fletcher, 1611, 'I say, open the door, and turn me out these mangy companions,' O.E.D.

say. See **ape's paternoster, boh, Jack Robinson, knife, mouthful, nothing, prayers, Te Deum, thing, when.**

say away ! Speak, then !; 'fire ahead !': coll.: mid-C. 19–20. Cf. *fire away.*

say, bo ! A c.p. (term of) address: C. 20. Orig. U.S. (see **bo**).

say for oneself, have nothing to. To be, by habit, silent: coll.: mid-C. 19–20.

say it with flowers ! See **flowers, say it with.**

say nothing when you are dead. Be silent !: c.p. of ca. 1670–1750. Ray.

say-so, on my (sammy). On my word of honour: coll.: mid-C. 18–20 (. . . *sammy* . . . not before ca. 1880); ob. Cf. *sam, upon my.*

say so !, you don't. Expressive of astonishment (occ. of derision) at a statement: coll.: from ca. 1870. (O.E.D.)

sayin(g) were, as the. As one says; as the saying is: lower classes' coll. (— 1923). Manchon.

says, it. The book mentioned, or its author, says: C. 10–20: S.E. until mid-C. 19, then coll. (O.E.D.)

says he. Said he: coll.: late C. 17–20. Congreve. (O.E.D.) Cf.:

says I ; says you. I say; you say: sol. or jocular coll.: late C. 17–20. Dryden, Bage. O.E.D.

says you ! See **sez you !**

'Sblood or **'sblood !** A coll. form of (by) *God's blood !*: late C. 16–mid-18, then archaic. See **'S** and cf. the following more or less coll. oaths: **'Sbobs** (i.e. *Od's bobs*), late C. 17–mid-19 ; **'Sbodikins** (= *God's bodikins*), ca. 1670–1800, then archaic ;

'Sbody (*God's body*), C. 17 ; **'Sbores** (like **'Sbobs**, obscure in meaning), C. 17 ; **'Sbud(s)**, which = **'Sbodikins,** ca. 1670–1760, then archaic. (O.E.D.)

scab. A pejorative applied to persons, a 'scurvy' fellow, a rascal or scoundrel: from ca. 1590; slightly ob. except in next sense ; not after C. 18 applied to women. Occ., as in Lyly, a constable or a sheriff's officer (not after C. 18). Shakespeare, Defoe, Kipling. Ex the skin-disease or the crust forming over a sore: cf. *scurf,* 2.—Hence, a workman refusing to strike, esp. one working while his companions are on strike: orig. (1811), U.S., anglicised ca. 1880. Occ. attributively.—3. Among tailors, a button-hole: from ca. 1870; ob. Ex the shape of a sore-crust.

scab, v. To behave as a, be a, 'scab' (n., 2): C. 20, O.E.D. recording at 1905.—2. See Addenda.

scab coal. See **black coal.**

scab-raiser. A drummer: military: ca. 1850–95. H., 3rd ed. Because one of his duties was to wield the cat-o'-nine-tails, thus raising sores.

scabbado. Syphilis: mid-C. 17–mid-18: coll. verging on S.E. Bailey's *Erasmus,* 1725. Ex S.E. *scab + ado,* a mock-foreign suffix.

scabby. Vile, contemptible, beggarly: C. 18–20: S.E. until mid-C. 19, then coll. Smollett ; Meredith, 1861, 'A scabby sixpence ?' Ex lit. S.E. sense. Cf. *scabby sheep,* q.v.—2. Among printers, unevenly or blotchily printed: from ca. 1870. Ex sense 1.—3. At Christ's Hospital, stingy: mid-C. 19–20. Cf. quotation in sense 1.—4. Pertaining to one who does not employ Union labour: from ca. 1890: Australian s. >, ca. 1910, coll. Ex *scab,* n., 2.

Scabby Liz. Scapa Flow: naval: from 1914. Bowen. A place of which one easily wearies.

scabby neck (or **S.N.**). A Dane; esp. a Danish sailor: nautical (— 1864); ob. H., 3rd ed.

scadger. A mean fellow, a contemptible begger of loans: low: from ca. 1860; ob. Perhaps ex *cadger* (q.v.) on Cornish *scadgan,* a tramp. At Winchester College, a rascal: † by 1901. E. J. K. Wrench.

scaff. A selfish fellow: Christ's Hospital: mid-C. 19–20. (Cf. *scabby,* 3, and *scaly.*) Perhaps influenced by dial. *scaff,* one who wanders idly about, or derived ex † dial. *scaff-and-raff,* the rabble (E.D.D.).

scaffold-pole. A fried potato-chip: low London (— 1909). Ware.

scalawag ; more gen. **scallawag** and (esp. in C. 20) **scallywag ;** occ. **scal(l)iwag, scallowag, skallewag,** but very rarely in C. 20. A ne'er-do-well or disreputable fellow; a scoundrel. (Esp. in C. 20, frequently playful like *rascal.*) U.S. s. (— 1848), anglicised ca. 1860 and >, ca. 1910, coll. Bartlett, 1st ed. ; Haliburton, 1855, 'You good-for-nothing young scallowag' ; *The Melbourne Argus,* 1870, 'Vagrants are now [in Melbourne] denominated scalawags.' The earliest recorded dates (considerably earlier ones prob. occur in unpublished letters) of the various forms are: *scalawag,* 1848; *scallawag,* 1854; *scallywag,* 1864; *scalliwag.* 1891 ; *scallowag,* 1855; *skallewag,* ca. 1870. Origin problematic: I suggest that *wag* (a playful scamp) has, through a lost reduplication *scag-wag,* hence *scagga-wag,* > *scal(l)awag ;* but it is possible that the term = (*scabby* >) *scaly wag,* as applied to 'lean and ill-favoured kine', as in O.E.D. at *scallywag,* p. 3, second quotation ; W. suggests origin in dial. *scall,* skin-disease.—2. Hence, in politics, an impostor or a rascally intriguer : 1864, Sala (O.E.D.) : s. >, ca. 1890, coll.—3. Ex sense 1, in trade-union s., one (rarely of women) who will not work : 1891, in the Labour Commission glossary (O.E.D.) ; ob.

scalawag, etc., as adj., dates in England from ca. 1865. In C. 20, coll.

scald. To infect venereally : coll. : late C. 16–20 ; ob. (Lit., to burn.) Cf. :

scald, adj. ; **scalded.** Venereally infected : coll. : resp. C. 17–18 ; C. 18–20.

scald-rag. A dyer : a C. 17 coll. nickname. ' Water Poet ' Taylor.

scalder. A venereal infection, esp. a ' clap ' (q.v.) : low : from ca. 1810 ; ob. Lex. Bal. Cf. scalding-house, q.v.—2. Tea, the beverage : low: from ca. 1890. Sydney Watson, Wops the Waif, 1892, ' I'm good at a hoperation, I can tell yer, when it's on spot and scalder (which being interpreted, meant cake and tea).' Ex the heat.

[**scalding-house**(, **Cupid's**). A brothel : late C. 16–17 : on border-line between coll. and S.E. Middleton's quotation, cited by F. & H., makes it, however, appear as if the term had no such gen. meaning, though it may have been so used in allusively jocular S.E.]

scaldings ! A warning, esp. among sailors and at Winchester : ' get out of the way ! ' ; ' be off ! ' ; ' look out ! ' : mid-C. 19–20 ; slightly ob. Smyth's Word-Book and Adam's Wykehamica. Ex cry scaldings, to announce loudly that one is carrying scaldings, i.e. boiling liquid. Cf. gangway for a naval officer, q.v.

*****scaldrum.** A beggar : tramps' c. : mid-C. 19–20 ; ob. Prob. ex :

*****scaldrum-dodge.** Tramps' c. of mid-C. 19–20 (ob.), as in Mayhew, 1851, London Labour, vol. i, ' By then Peter was initiated into the scaldrum-dodge, or the art of burning the body with a mixture of acids and gunpowder, so as to suit the hues and complexions of the accident to be deplored.' Practised chiefly by ' schools of shallow coves ', groups of men pretending to have escaped from shipwreck, fire, or similar perils. Prob. a perversion of scald or scalding (nn.).

scale. To mount a woman : coll. : C. 17–20. Wentworth Smith, The Puritan, 1607.—2. To impress ; to astound : low (– 1887) ; ob. Baumann. Perhaps ex S.E. scale, take by escalade.—3. (Also **scale off**.) To run away ; depart hurriedly or furtively ; to disappear of one's own motion : C. 20 : mostly Colonial (esp. Australian). Possibly ex scale in, (of a jockey) to be weighed after a race.—4. To steal (a thing), rob (a person) : New Zealanders' : C. 20. Perhaps ex sense 3.

scale-backed 'un. (Gen. pl.) A louse : low (– 1923). Manchon.

*****scaler.** One who decamps with his mates' share of the loot : New Zealand c. (– 1932). Ex scale, 3.

scaley. See **scaly**.—**scaliwag, scallawag, scalliwag, scallowag, scallywag.** See **scalawag**.

scalp. A charm worn on a bangle : Society : 1896–1914. Ware, ' Given by young men to young girls.'

scalp. To buy very cheap so as to sell at less than ruling price : Stock Exchange coll. >, ca. 1905, S.E. : 1888, The Pall Mall Gazette, Oct. 15, ' . . . " Scalped " the market on a big scale for a small profit per bushel ' (O.E.D.). One who does this is a scalper, which occurs in the same article ;

scalping arose about the same time : both coll. > S.E. not later than 1910.

scaly ; incorrectly **scaley**. Shabby, poor, in poor health : late C. 18–20 ; ob. Southey, 1793 (O.E.D.). Ex S.E. skin-disease sense.—2. Hence, stingy : from ca. 1810 ; like sense 1, slightly ob. Lex. Bal ; Egan, 1821, ' If you are too scaly to tip for it, I'll shell out and shame you.' The sense is very common at Christ's Hospital (cf. scaff, q.v.).— 3. Ex senses 1 and 2, despicable : mid-C. 19–20. Besant & Rice, 1875, ' If I were an author—they are a scaly lot, and thank Heaven I am not one,' O.E.D.

scaly-back. A sailor : nautical : mid-C. 19–20. Bowen. Perhaps suggested by scaly fish, q.v.

scaly bloke. A thin man : New Zealand (–1935). —2. See **scaly**, 2 and 3.

scaly fish. An ' honest, rough, blunt sailor ', Grose, 2nd ed. : late C. 18–19.

scamander. To loaf : 1860, H., 2nd ed., ' To wander about without a settled purpose.' Coll. Cf. (perhaps ex) Yorkshire dial. skimaundering (hanging about), which may—or may not !—derive ex the Classical river Scamander.

scammered. Tipsy : low : from ca. 1840 ; ob. ' Ducange Anglicus ' ; Carew's Autobiography of a Gipsy, 1891—the reference being valid for the year 1845. Perhaps (scuppered on) dial. scammer, to climb or scramble.

*****scamp.** A highway robber : 1781, Messink, ' Ye scamps, ye pads, ye divers.' Ex v., 1, q.v.— 2. Hence, highway robbery (cf. scampery) : 1786 (O.E.D.) ; like sense 1, † by 1840 or, at latest, 1850. —3. A cheat or a swindler : ca. 1805–40 : rather s. than c. Ex sense 1. (Other senses, S.E.)

*****scamp**, v. To be, or go out as, a highway robber : c. : ca. 1750–1840 ; implied, however, as early as C. 16 in scampant, ' used in imitation of rampant in a rogue's burlesque coat of arms ', W. The Discovery of John Poulter, 1753, ' I'll scamp on the panney,' i.e. go out and rob on the highway. Prob. ex scamper.—2. V.t., to rob (a person) on the highway : c. (– 1812) ; † by 1870. Vaux.

*****scamp, done for a.** Convicted (esp. for highway robbery) : c. of ca. 1810–50. Vaux.

*****scamp, go (up)on the.** To rob as occasion offers : c. of ca. 1820–1910. Bee ; Baumann. (Applied to tramps and beggars, not to professional thieves.)

*****scamp, royal.** ' A highwayman who robs civilly,' Grose, 1st ed. : c. of ca. 1780–1840.

*****scamp, royal foot.** A footpad who does this. Ibid. and id.

scamper. To run hastily ; to ' bolt ' : 1687, ' Facetious ' Tom Brown : s. until mid-C. 18, then coll. till ca. 1830, then S.E. (B.E. errs in calling it c.) Either ex scamp, v. of motion, or ex † Dutch schampen, to go away, to escape. O.E.D. ; W.

*****scamperer.** A street ruffian : C. 18–early C. 19 : prob. orig. c. Steele. (O.E.D.)

*****scamping**, adj. Dishonest : ca. 1820–60 : orig., prob. always, c. Bee, 1823, ' Fellows who pilfer in markets, from stalls or orchards, who snatch off hats, cheat publicans out of liquor, or toss up cheatingly—commit scamping tricks.'

*****scampsman.** A highwayman : c. : late C. 18–mid-19. Vaux. Ex scamp, n., 2.

scandahoofian. An occ. form of Scandihoovian, q.v. (John Beames.)

scandal-broth, -potion, -water. Tea : coll. : resp. 1785 (Grose), 1786 (Burns), 1864 (H., 3rd ed.) : all ob. by 1900, † by 1930.

*****scandal-proof.** Adj. applied to ' a thorough

pac'd Alsatian [q.v.] or Minter,' B.E. : prob. c. : late C. 17–mid-18.

*scandalous. A wig : c. : late C. 17–18. B.E., Grose.

Scandihoovian, Scandiwegian. A Scandinavian : West Canadian and nautical : C. 20. Bowen. Cf. *Scowegian.*

scanmag, from ca. 1850 ; *scan-mag,* from ca. 1820 ; *scan. mag.* (or *S.M.*), 1779, Sheridan. Scandal. Abbr. *scandalum magnatum,* an old law term for a scandal of magnates. (O.E.D.)

scanties. A pair of women's knickers : from ca. 1930. Cf. *panties, tighties.* See quotation at **briefs.**

scapa. An occ. form of **scarper.** Cf. *scaper.*

Scaparey. See **Johnny Scaparey.**

scape. A snipe : a coll. nickname : from ca. 1860. Ex flushed snipe's cry.—2. See 2 in :

scape. ' To neglect one's brush,' Bee : artistic : ca. 1820–50.—2. N. and v. (To) escape : S.E. in Shakespeare, but by 1850 it is coll. Baumann.

scaper. An occ. variant of **scarper.** Mayhew. (E.D.D.)

Scarborough warning ; in C. 19, occ. **S. surprise.** A very or too short notice, or none at all : coll. : mid-C. 16–20 ; ob. ' Proverbs ' Heywood, Fuller, Grose, P. H. Emerson. ' In 1557 Thomas Stafford entered the took possession of Scarborough Castle before the townsmen were aware of his approach,' E.D.D.

scarce, make oneself. To retire ; to absent oneself, disappear : coll. : 1749, Smollett, ' It was my fixed purpose to make myself scarce at Seville ' ; Grose, 1st ed. ; 1821, Scott, ' Make yourself scarce— depart—vanish ! '

scare up. To find, discover (e.g. *scare up money*): coll. : from ca. 1850. Ex shooting game.

*scarecrow. C. : 1884, Greenwood, ' The boy who has served [a thief] until he is well known to the police, and is so closely watched that he may as well stay at home as go out.' Ob.

scarehead. A headline in large, thick type meant to arouse attention : journalistic coll. : ca. 1900–1920. Abbr. *scare headline.*

scarf-bolt. Erroneous for *scarp-bolt* : from ca. 1870. O.E.D.

scarlatina. Catachrestic when used of a mild attack of scarlet fever : mid-C. 19–20. Properly, *scarlatina* (C. 19–20) is merely another name for *scarlet fever* (1676). O.E.D.

scarlet. A Mohock or aristocratic street ruffian : coll. or s. : ca. 1750–60. J. Shebbeare, 1755 (O.E.D.). Either ex colour of dress or on *blood.*

scarlet, dye. To drink deep or hard : late C. 16– early 17. Shakespeare.

scarlet beans. See **sow potatoes.**

scarlet countenance, wear a. To be impudent or shameless : coll. : late C. 19–20. Manchon. Ex S.E. *scarlet,* (of an offender) deep-dyed.

scarlet-fever. (A) flirtation with or passion for a soldier : jocular : ca. 1860–1910. Mayhew. With reference to the scarlet uniform.—2. A great admiration for soldiers : jocular (– 1889) ; † by 1910. Barrère & Leland.

scarlet horse. A hired horse : ca. 1780–1840. Grose, 1st ed. Punning *high-red.*

Scarlet Lancers. The 16th Lancers : military : from ca. 1880 ; ob. F. & Gibbons, ' The only British lancer regiment wearing scarlet.' Also *Red Lancers.*

scarlet runner. A Bow Street officer : mid-C. 19. Ex the scarlet waistcoat.—2. A footman : from ca. 1860. Partly ex sense 1, partly ex the vegetable.—3. A soldier : late C. 19–very early 20. Manchon.—4. A battalion despatch-carrier in action : military : 1915 ; ob. F. & Gibbons. Ex his red brassard and his familiar name, *runner.*—5. See **sow potatoes.**

Scarlet Town. Reading, Berkshire : provincial coll. : from ca. 1800 ; very ob. H., 3rd ed. Ex pronunciation.

*scarper. To run away ; v.t. to decamp from : Parlyaree and c. ; as latter, it > low Cockney ca. 1905. Selby, 1844, ' Vamoose—scarper—fly ! ' Ex It. *scappare* via Lingua Franca. See *Slang.*—2. On the stage, it = to leave a play without notice : from ca. 1900.

scarper the letty. To leave one's lodgings without paying : mid-C. 19–20 : Parlyaree >, by 1900, theatrical. Ex *scarper,* 1.

scat ! Go away : coll. : 1869 (O.E.D.). Hence, occ. as jocular v. Mostly U.S. The O.E.D. ingeniously proposes *ss !* *cat* (i.e. a hiss + *cat*) ; 1, a hiss + *get !* There are, however, of the dial *scat* (see E.D.D.) several senses that might easily have originated our term. (But see Adenda.)

scatter, esp. in imperative. To go (away) ; move quickly : coll. : C. 20. Prob. influenced by *scat !*, q.v.

scatter-gun. A shot-gun : coll. ; U.S. (ca. 1870), anglicised ca. 1920. (*The Passing Show,* Dec. 24, 1932.)

scatty. (Not very) mad ; crazy : lower classes' : C. 20. B. & P., 3rd ed. Perhaps ex *scatter-brained* : cf. Derbyshire *scattle* (*scattel*), easily frightened (E.D.D.).

scavenge. To clean up a mess : Public Schools' : from ca. 1920.

scavenger's daughter. An instrument of torture : coll. : C. 17. (Afterwards, merely historical.) *Journals of the House of Commons,* May 14, 1604. On *Skevington's* (or *Skeffington's*) torture, the technical S.E. term being *Skevington's gyves* (1564) or *irons.* Invented ca. 1545 by Leonard Skevington (or Skeffington), Lieutenant of the Tower of London.

scavenging party. In society s. of 1932–34, thus in Ronald Knox, *The Body in the Silo,* 1933, ' " A scavenging party—what on earth's that ? " " Miles, dear, don't be old-fashioned. A scavenging party is when you go round in cars picking up tramps and feeding them fish and chips . . . ; or collecting sandwich-boards and doorscrapers and things like that. All the brightest young people do it." '

scavey. See **savvy.**—***scawfer.** See **scoffer.**

sceau. Incorrect for *seau,* a dish in the form of a pail : mid-C. 19–20. O.E.D. (Sup.).

*scellum. See **skellum.**

scene-rat. A supernumerary in ballet or pantomime : theatrical : from ca. 1880 ; ob.

scene-shifter. ' The nickname of a big gun in action on the Arras sector in 1917 ' : military ; now only historical. F. & Gibbons. Its shells displaced much earth.

scent-bottle. A water-closet : euphemistic s. (– 1887) ; † by 1920. Baumann.

scent-box. The nose : pugilistic : from ca. 1825 ; virtually †. Cf. *smeller.*

sceptre ; in C. 18, occ. **scepter.** A sceptred gold unite : coll. : C. 18–20 ; in mid-C. 19–20, virtually

S.E. In 1736, Folkes writes, 'Sovereigns or
Unites [properly *unites*], vulgarly called Scepters.'
O.E.D.

*scew. See skew.—schack-stoner. See shack-
stoner.

scheme. A collection of the questions likely to
be asked in the various subjects of examination :
universities' : ca. 1775–1810. *The Gentleman's
Magazine*, 1780. (O.E.D.)—2. A practical joke at
Winchester, ca. 1840–1910. Wrench, 'The candle
on reaching a measured point ignites paper, which
by burning a string releases a weight ; this falls on
the head of the boy to be waked.' Cf. old S.E.
scheme, 'a party of pleasure' (Grose), and the
more relevant dial. sense, an amusement.

schemozzle. See shemozzle.—schice(r). See
shice(r).—schickster. See shickster.

schism-shop. A nonconformist place of worship :
Anglican pejorative coll. : late C. 18–20. Grose,
2nd ed. Cf. *heresy-shop*, q.v.

schitt. A goal at football : Winchester : ca.
1830–60. Wrench. Prob. ex *shot*.

schlemozzle. See shemozzle.

*schlenter. Dubious, untrustworthy ; make-
believe : South African (diamond fields) : from ca.
1890 : c. >, by 1900, low s. The Comtesse de
Brémont, *The Gentleman Digger*, 1891.—Whence,
2, as a n. : imitation gold : 1898, *The Cape Argus*,
weekly ed., March 16.—3. (Also n., only in pl.)
Imitation diamonds : 1899, Griffith, *Knaves of
Diamonds*. Senses 2, 3 were prob., at first, c.
Pettman gives no etymology : the term derives
ex Dutch *slenter*, a trick (O.E.D. Sup.).

*schliver. A clasp-knife : c. (or low) : ca.
1820–1910. Bee ; Baumann. Ex *chive*, q.v.

schnorrer. A Jewish beggar : Yiddish coll. :
1892, Zangwill. Ex *schnurren*, to beg. O.E.D.

schofel or -ful. See shoful.

schol. A scholar : Harrow : mid-C. 19–20.—2.
A scholarship : late C. 19–20, ibid. ; in C. 20, gen.
school term. Cf. *schols*, q.v.

scholar. 'In illiterate use, one whom the
speaker regards as exceptionally learned,' mid-
C. 17–20. 'Often merely, one who is able to read
and write,' C. 19–20. O.E.D. Not s. but coll.

scholar as my horse Ball, as good a. No scholar
at all : a coll., semi-proverbial c.p. of ca. 1630–70.
John Clarke, 1639.

scholard, schollard. A scholar : resp. C. 19–20
C. 16–20 : low coll. > ca. 1850, sol. Also in senses
indicated at *scholar*, q.v.

scholion. Incorrect for *scolion* : C. 17–20.
O.E.D.

schols. (Often without article : e.g., *in for
schols*.) A scholarship examination : schools' (orig.
Public Schools') : C. 20. Cf. *schol*, 2, q.v.

school. A number or a group of persons met
together in order to gamble : from ca. 1810 : perhaps orig. c. > low s. ca. 1880. Vaux. Cf.
schooling, 2, q.v.—2. Hence, a 'mob' or gang of
thieves or beggars : mostly c. (in C. 20, however, s.) :
mid-C. 19–20. Mayhew. (The term may apply to
four, three, or even two persons.) See quotation
at scaldrum-dodge.

School Board will be after you !, the. Take
care ! : London lower classes' : ca. 1881–1900.
Ware.

School-Board worrier. A school-inspector : London teachers' (— 1887) ; † by 1920. Baumann.

school-butter. A flogging : C. 17–19. Pasquil's
Jests, 1604 ; B.E. ; Grose, 1st ed. (Apperson.)

school of Venus. A brothel : coll. : late C. 17–
19. B.E. ; Grose, 1st ed. ; Baumann.

School-Street. The University : Oxford University coll. : C. 18–early 19.

schoolgirl complexion, that. A c.p. dating from
ca. 1923 ; P. G. Wodehouse has the phrase in
Ukridge, 1924. Ex the inspired advertisement-
poster by Palmolive Soap. (Collinson.)

schoolie or -y. A naval instructor : naval coll. :
C. 20. Bowen. Ex *schoolmaster*.—2. A school—as
opp. to a house—prefect : Scottish Public Schools' :
from ca. 1880. Ian Miller, *School Tie*, 1935.

*schooling. A term of confinement in a reforma-
tory : c. (— 1879) ; slightly ob.—2. 'A low
gambling party,' H., 1859 : c. >, ca. 1890, low
s. See school, 1.—3. Hence, a, or the, playing
of pitch and toss : c. (— 1888) ; slightly ob.

schoolman. A fellow-member of a 'school'
(q.v.) : c. or low s. : 1834, Ainsworth ; ob.

schoolmaster. (Gen. in training other horses) a
horse good at jumping : stables' coll. : late C. 19–
20. Prob. ex S.E. sense, the leader of a school of
fishes ; esp. of a bull whale.—2. schoolmaster,
bilk the. See bilk.

schooly. See schoolie.

schooner ; frigate ; full master. Among youths,
new-comer ; handy fellow ; passed master in
navigation : naval : late C. 19–early 20. Ware.

schooner on the rocks. 'A cooked joint surrounded by potatoes' : naval : late C. 19–20.
Bowen.

schooner-rigged. Destitute : sailing-ships' : late
C. 19–20 ; ob. Bowen.

s(c)hroff. A banker ; treasurer ; confidential
clerk : Anglo-Indian coll. : mid-C. 16–20. Yule
& Burnell. Ex Arabic.

schwassle-box. See swatchel-box.—science,
blinded with. See blinded with science.—science,
dazzle with. See dazzle.

sciatic. A sciatic nerve : medical coll. : 1919.
E. F. Brett Young, *The Young Physician*.

science, the. Boxing or, as in Dickens (1837)
fencing : from ca. 1830 : s. >, ca. 1870, coll
(O.E.D.) Cf. *profession, the*, q.v.

scientific. A scientist : coll. : 1830, Lyell ; De
Morgan. Slightly ob. O.E.D.

scientifics. Scientific matters : low coll. : ca.
1840–70. Lover. (O.E.D.)

scintillation. Catachrestic for *scintilla*, a fig.
spark : mid-C. 17–20. O.E.D.

scissor-bill. A nagging, gossiping, and otherwise objectionable woman : low (— 1931). O.E.D.
(Sup.). Ex the bird so named.

scissor-grinder. An engine-room artificer :
naval : C. 20. Bowen.

scissorean operation. Gutting a book : literary :
ca. 1890–1915. On *Caesarean operation*.

scissors ! ; oh, scissors ! Indicative of disgust
or impatience : 1843, Selby ; ob. Cf. :

scissors, give (a person). To treat drastically,
pay out : mid-C. 19–20 ; ob. ? ex *cut up*.

scoff. Food : South African coll. : 1856, the
Rev. F. Fleming, *Southern Africa* (Pettman) ;
1879, Atcherley. Ex Cape Dutch : see the v.—2.
Hence, a meal : id. : late C. 19–20. (The term,
ca. 1890, > gen. among tramps and sailors, often
as *scorf*.) Cf. :

scoff ; often scorf ; in South Africa, gen. skoff.
V.t. To eat voraciously : s. (— 1864) and dial.
(1849). H., 3rd ed. Prob. ex dial. *scaff*.—2.
Hence, modified by South African usage (see scoff,

n.), v.t., simply to eat : from ca. 1880 : outside of South Africa, nautical (W. Clark Russell, 1883). —3. Occ., but seldom after ca. 1920, v.i. : late C. 19–20 and rare outside South Africa. But this may be the primary sense, as we see from Lady Barnard's *South African Journal*, 1798, '[The Boer] concludes that the passengers want to scoff (to eat)' : see W.—4. (Ex sense 1.) To seize ; to plunder : 1893, Kipling, 'There's enough [gold-leaf] for two first-rates, and I've scoffed the best half of it,' O.E.D.

*scoffer ; occ. **scawfer.** Gold or silver plate : c. : mid-C. 19–20 ; ob. 'Gypsy' Carew : a reference that is valid for 1845.—2. Hence, a (single) plate : vagrants' c. : C. 20.

scold. A scolding : coll. and dial. : from ca. 1725 ; ob. except in Scots.

scold, v.i. To be constantly uttering reproofs : coll. : mid-C. 18–20.

*scoldrum (dodge). A variant of *scaldrum (dodge).*

scold's cure. A coffin : low : ca. 1810–60. *Lex. Bal.* Esp. *nap the s.c.,* be coffined.

scolicecoid. Incorrect for *scolecoid* : mid-C. 19–20. O.E.D.

scollogue. To live or act dissipatedly, wildly : low (— 1857) ; † by 1900. 'Ducange Anglicus.' Perhaps ex *scalawag,* q.v.

scolopendra. A harlot : ca. 1630–1700. D'Ave-nant. Ex sting in centipede's tail.

scolopendria. Incorrect for *scolopendra,* a centi-pede : C. 17. O.E.D.

sconce. The head ; esp. the crown of the head : 1567, *Damon and Pythias* ; Thackeray. Perhaps ex *sconce,* a fort, or its Dutch original, *schans.*—2. Hence, Wit, sense, judgement, ability : coll. : mid-C. 17–20 ; ob.—3. Occ. the person himself : coll. : ca. 1570–1750. Kendall, 1577 (O.E.D.).— 4. See **sconce, build a.** (— As a fine, *sconce* is S.E.)

sconce, v. To fine, mulct : university (orig.— see Minsheu, 1617—and mainly Oxford) : C. 17–20. Until C. 19, of officials fining undergraduates ; in C. 19–20, of undergraduates fining one of them-selves (gen. a tankard of ale) for a breach of manners or convention. Randolph, 'Honours of Oxford' Miller, Colman the Elder, ' C. Bede.' Perhaps ex *sconce,* n., 1 (via ' so much a head ').—2. (Gen. **sconce off.**) To reduce (the amount of a bill, etc.) : coll. : 1768, Foote ; † by 1910. Occ. *to sconce one's diet,* to eat less : coll. (very ob.) : C. 19–20.—3. V.i. and v.t. to hinder ; get in the way (of) : Win-chester, mainly in games (e.g. a catch at cricket) : late C. 19–20. *The Public School Magazine,* Dec. 1899. Prob. ex preceding sense.

sconce, build a. ' To run a score at an ale-house,' Bailey (1730) ; ' run deep upon tick,' B.E. defining *build a large sconce.* There is often the connotation of lack of intention to pay the account, for Grose, 1785, defines it as ' a military term for bilking one's quarters '. Ca. 1640, Shirley ; Tom Brown ; Goldsmith. † by 1840. Ex *sconce,* a (small) fort.

sconce off ; sconce one's diet. See **sconce,** v., 2.

sconcing is the vbl.n. of *sconce,* v., all senses. Very gen.

[**scone.** Despite many purists, the pronunciation *ecŏn* is equally correct with *scŏn* ; indeed, in C. 16–19, *scon* (or *skon*) was a frequent spelling. The Scottish town, however, is always pronounced with the *o* long.]

scooch. Spirituous liquor(s) : naval and hence,

occ., military : from ca. 1920. Bowen. A cor-ruption of *hooch.*

scoodyn. ' The fouling of a ship's bottom ' : nautical coll. : C. 19–20 ; ob. Bowen. Possibly by antiphrasis ex dial. *scud,* to clean, scrape clean ; but prob. ex Shetlands dial. *scovin,* crust adhering to ' a vessel in which food has been cooked ' (E.D.D.)

scoop. Male hair worn low and flat on the fore-head : military : ca. 1880–90. Ware.—2. See **scoop, on the.**—3. News obtained (and, of course, printed) in advance of a rival newspaper : journa-listic : orig. U.S., anglicised ca. 1890 : s. >, ca. 1920, coll.—4. In the money-market, a sudden reduction of prices enabling operators to buy cheaply and to profit by the ensuing (carefully planned) rise : Stock Exchange : orig. (— 1879) U.S., anglicised ca. 1890 : after ca. 1920, coll.—5. An advantage, a (big) ' haul ', a very successful or, more properly, a lucky stroke in business : 1893, Kipling ; *The Daily Chronicle,* July 27, 1909, ' Her engagement . . . at the Palace is a big " scoop ",' O.E.D. This last sense follows ex nos. 3, 4, which, in their turn, derive ex the S.E. sense, an act of scooping.—6. In singing, the attack on a commencing note ' by way of a chromatic slide from the " fourth " below ' : coll. (— 1911). O.E.D. (Sup.).

scoop, v. (Gen. **scoop in,** occ. **scoop up.**) To obtain (a lot of money), make a big ' haul ' of ; to appropriate in advance : orig. (ca. 1880) U.S., anglicised ca. 1890. Ex S.E. sense, to heap up by means of a scoop.—2. (Occ. **scoop out.**) To get the better of (a rival) by anticipating him or by obtain-ing what he has failed to obtain : journalistic ; orig. U.S., anglicised ca. 1890. Elizabeth Banks, *The Newspaper Girl,* 1902, ' Miss Jackson . . . [is] going to print it in to-morrow's paper, and I shall be scooped,' O.E.D. (—3. As applied to a whale feeding, *scoop* is wholly U.S.)

scoop, on the. On the drink ; engaged in dissipa-tion : 1884 (O.E.D.) ; ob.

scoop in. To persuade (a person) to participate : nautical : from ca. 1915. Hamish Maclaren, *The Private Opinions of a British Blue-Jacket,* 1929.—2. See **scoop, d.,** 1.

scoop out. See **scoop,** v., 2.—**scoop up.** See **scoop,** v., 1.

scoot, occ. **skoot** or **skute.** A scooting (see the v.) : s. and dial. from ca. 1860. Esp. in *do a scoot,* run away, late C. 19–20, and *on the scoot,* on the run (lit. and fig.), 1864.

scoot ; occ.—though, as to the n., very rarely in C. 20—**skoot, skute ; skewt** seems to have re-mained U.S. (Gen. with *about, along, away, off, round,* etc., as adv.) To go (away) hurriedly or with sudden speed : orig. (ca. 1840) U.S. ; angli-cised ca. 1860 : s. until ca. 1910, then coll. *The Quarterly Review,* 1869, ' The laugh of the gull as he scoots along the shore.' Ex the mainly nautical s. *scout,* to dart, move quickly : see **scout,** v., 1.— 2. Loosely, to go, to depart : C. 20. Collinson.

scoot-train. An express train : late C. 19–20 ; ob. Ex *scoot,* n., but see v.

scooter. One who goes with sudden swiftness or hurriedly : dial. (— 1825) and (from ca. 1860) s. >, ca. 1910, coll. See **scoot,** v.—2. A coastal motor-boat : from 1915, when introduced as a defence-measure : naval coll. Bowen. Ex *scoot,* v., q.v.

scóp, scôp. Pedantic errors for *scop,* poet, minstrel : mid-C. 19–20. O.E.D.

scope. A cystoscope (used in examining the bladder): medical students' (— 1933). *Slang*, p. 190.

scorch. A very fast run on (motor-) cycle or motor-car: 1885 (O.E.D.): coll. >, ca. 1905, S.E. Ex:

scorch, v.i. To ride a bicycle, drive a motor-car, etc., at considerable or very great speed: coll. (— 1891) >, ca. 1905, S.E. Implied in n. and in:

scorcher. A furious propeller of cycle or car (etc.): 1885 (O.E.D.): coll. *The Daily Telegraph*, Jan. 7, 1901, 'The police have been keeping a sharp look-out for scorchers.' Ex the v.—2. An exceedingly hot day: coll.: 1874 (O.E.D.). Often *a regular scorcher*.—3. Any thing or person severe, notably eccentric, deplorably hasty; a scathing remark, vigorous attack, etc.: orig. schoolboys': 1885, Hawley Smart.—4. Hence, a sensation-causer, habitual or incidental, deliberate or unintentional: 1899, Conan Doyle (O.E.D.); ob.—5. A rotten potato: green-grocers' (— 1887). Baumann.

scorching, n. Furious riding (of cycle) or driving (of car, etc.): from ca. 1890: coll. till ca. 1905, then S.E. Ex *scorch*, v.

scorching, adj. Very hot; esp., immoral or indelicate: coll.: 1897, *The Referee*, Oct. 24.

scorching your eyes out !, the sun's. A military c.p. at reveille, no matter whether it is summer or winter, clear light or pitch-darkness: C. 20. F. & Gibbons. Prob. suggested by *rise and shine*.

score, n. The gaining of a point or points in games: coll.: from ca. 1840.—2. Hence, a notable or successful 'hit' in debate, argument, or keen business: likewise coll.: from ca. 1890. Cf. the v.—3. Twenty pounds (£20): c.: late C. 19–20. (George Ingram, *Stir*, 1933.)

score, v.i. and v.t. To gain (a success): from ca. 1880: coll. Cf.:

score off. To achieve a success over, make a point at the expense or to the detriment of (gen. a person): coll.: 1882, 'Lucas Malet', 'For once she felt she had scored off her adversary,' O.E.D. Ex scoring at games: cf. the n., sense 1.

scorf. See scoff. (A low variant, more frequent of the v. than the n.)

scorium. A catachrestic singular, ca. 1680–1710, of *scoria* (slag). O.E.D.

scorny; occ. **scorney.** Scornful: low coll.: 1836, Haliburton. Also Cornish dial. E.D.D.

scorp. A late C. 19–20 naval and military abbr. of the next, sense 1. Bowen.

scorpion. A civilian native inhabitant of Gibraltar: military: 1845. Also, from ca. 1870, as in H.M. Field, 1889, 'A choice variety of natives of Gibraltar, called "Rock scorpions ".' (O.E.D.) Ex the scorpions that infest the Rock of Gibraltar. See Rock and cf. *Gib*.—2. A very youthful actor or actress, whose advice and remarks are of little use: theatrical (— 1909). Ware. (There is no sting in his tale.)

Scot. A very irritable or quickly angered person: from ca. 1810; slightly ob. Vaux; Bee, 1823, shows that, orig. at least, it may have been a butchers' term, 'the small Scots oxen coming to their doom with little resignation to fate.'—2. Hence, gen. *scot*, a temper, or passion of irritation: 1859, H., 1st ed. Cf. *scotty* and *scottish*, adj., and *paddy*, n., qq.v.

Scotch or (though very rare in C. 19) **scotch.** (A drink of) Scotch whiskey: from ca. 1885: coll.

>, ca. 1905, S.E. ('Pomes' Marshall, 'He had started well on Scotches ').—2. A leg: abbr. *Scotch peg*, q.v.

Scotch, adj. Mean (of persons); ungenerous (of acts): coll.: C. 19–20. Esp. *be Scotch*, as in 'He's (*or* He must be) Scotch.' (The Scot's, like the Jew's, meanness is actually apocryphal.) Ex following combinations.

Scotch bait. A halt and a rest on one's staff as practised by pedlars: coll.: ca. 1780–1850. Grose, 1st ed.

Scotch bum. A kind of (dress-)bustle: coll.: C. 17. Dekker & Webster.

Scotch casement. A pillory: late C. 18–mid-19.

Scotch chocolate. Brimstone and milk: coll.: ca. 1780–1850. Grose, 1st ed. Cf.:

Scotch coffee. Hot water flavoured with burnt biscuit: from ca. 1860; ob. H., 3rd ed. Orig. and mainly nautical; prob. suggested by *S. chocolate*.

scotch fashion, answer. To reply to a question by asking another (*à la Jésus*): coll.: 1834, Michael Scott, *The Cruise of the Midge*; slightly ob.

Scotch fiddle. The itch: coll.: 1675, Rochester; ob. Also *Welch* (*welsh*) *fiddle*.

Scotch fiddle, play the. 'To work the index finger of one hand like a fiddle-stick between the index and middle finger of the other ': coll.: ca. 1820–1920. H., 2nd ed. To do this ' provokes a Scotchman in the highest degree, it implying that he is afflicted with the itch', H.

Scotch (occ. **Scots**) **Greys** or **greys.** Lice: C. 19–20. Egan's Grose; H., 2nd ed. Punning the regiment. Hence, *headquarters of the Scotch Greys*, a lousy head: from ca. 1820 (ob.): Egan's Grose.

Scotch hobby. A scrubby little Scotch horse: coll.: C. 17–early 19. B.E.

Scotch or (mid-C. 19–20) **Scottish mist.** Rain: coll.: 1589, Anon., *Pap with a Hatchet*; ' Phraseologia ' Robertson, 1681; Grose, 1st ed., 'A sober soaking rain; a Scotch mist will wet an Englishman to the skin '; Scott. (Apperson.)

Scotch navy. The Clan line of steamers: nautical: C. 20. Bowen.

Scotch ordinary. A privy: ca. 1670–1750. Ray.

Scotch peg. A leg: rhyming s. from mid-50's. H., 3rd ed., has it in full, whereas H., 1st ed., only implies it in '*scotches*, the legs '; it occurs, however, in ' Ducange Anglicus,' 1857.

Scotch pint. A bottle holding two quarts: from ca. 1820; ob. Egan's Grose.

Scotch prize. A capture by mistake: coll., mostly nautical (— 1867); ob. Smyth.

Scotch rabbit. A Welsh rabbit (cf. at *Scotch fiddle*): ca. 1740–70. Mrs. Glasse, the C. 18 Mrs. Beeton, gives a recipe in 1747. (O.E.D.)

Scotch seamanship. Seamanship by brute force: nautical coll. from ca. 1890; slightly ob. *St James's Gazette*, April 9, 1900. Cf. *Scotch prize*, q.v.

Scotch tea. See tea.

scotch up. V.i. and t. To follow up (an attack): military coll.: from 1916. F. & Gibbons. Ex *scotching* a snake.

Scotch or occ. **Scottish warming-pan.** A wench: coll.: ca. 1670–1880. Ray; S. Wesley the Elder; Grose. An elaboration of *warming-pan*, 1.—2. A breaking of wind: low: ca. 1810–1910. *Lex. Bal*.

scotchie (or **S.**). A marble with gay stripes: schoolboys' (— 1887). Baumann. In reference to tartan.—2. (Gen. in pl.) A leg: late C. 19–20. E.G. in P. Allingham, *Cheapjack*, 1934. Ex *Scotch peg*.—3. See **Scotchy**.

Scotchman. A florin : South Africa, esp. among the natives (— 1879). (Atcherley, whom Rider Haggard repeats in *Jess*, 1886). Ex that canny Scot who, among the Kaffirs, passed off a number of florins as half-crowns; which may account for a story related in J. Milne's *The Epistles of Atkins*, published in 1902 and dealing with the Boer War. —2. A Scotch fir : coll. : 1901, ' Lucas Malet ' (O.E.D.)—3. The less gen. form of :

Scotchman, the Flying. The Scotch Express from Euston to Edinburgh : coll. : 1874. The abbr. *Scotsman*, rare in C. 20, occurs in 1881. (O.E.D.)

Scotchman hugging a or **the Creole**, often without *a* or *the* before *Scotchman*. A clusia or kind of creeper : West Indian coll. : 1835, M. Scott.

*****Scotchmen.** Lice : c. (— 1887). Baumann. Ex *Scotch greys*.

Scotchy. A coll. nickname for a Scotsman : from ca. 1860. Cf. *Jock*, q.v.

Scotlands. Shares in the Great North of Scotland Railway : Stock Exchange coll. (— 1895); † by 1920. A. J. Wilson, *Stock Exchange Glossary*. Also *haddocks*.

Scots, the. The 26th Foot Regiment (in late C. 19–20, the 1st Battalion Cameronians Scottish Rifles) : military : coll. rather than s. : C. 19–20 ; slightly ob.

Scots Greys. See **Scotch Greys.**

Scotsman's Cinema, the. Piccadilly Circus : Londoners' : from 1933. Ex the numerous electriclight advertisements to be seen there—without admission charge.

Scott !, great. See **great Scott !**

Scottish. Irritable ; easily angered : low : ca. 1810–80. Vaux. Ex *Scot*, 1.

Scottish mist, warming-pan. See **Scotch m., w-p.**

Scotty. A Scotsman : coll. : late C. 19–20. Prob. ex *Scotchy*, q.v.

scotty. Angry ; apt to grow easily annoyed : late C. 19–20. Ex *Scot*, 2, q.v.

scour. A cleansing ; a polishing : coll. : C. 20. ' Give the floor a good scour,' O.E.D. Ex **Scots.**

*****scour ;** often spelt **scow(e)r, scowre.** To decamp, run away, depart hurriedly : ca. 1590–1870 : s. with more than a tinge of c., as have the next three senses. Greene, Shadwell, Grose. Ex S.E. *scour*, to move rapidly or hastily.—2. V.i. to roam noisily about at night, smashing windows, waylaying and often beating wayfarers, and attacking the watch : ca. 1670–1830. Shadwell, Prior.—3. Hence, v.t., to ill-treat (esp. the watch or wayfarers) while street-roistering : ca. 1680–1750. Dryden, ' Scowring the Watch grows out of fashion wit.'—4. V.t ' to roister through (the streets)': ca. 1690–1830. Grose.—5. To wear, esp. in *scour the cramp-ring(s)* or *darbies*, to wear, i.e. to go or lie in chains : ca. 1450–1840 (*cramp-rings* not before mid-C. 16, *darbies* not before late C. 17) : s. >, ca. 1560, c. Awdelay, B.E., Egan's Grose. Ex *scour*, to cleanse by rubbing. (Ex this sense comes *scouring*, n., q.v.)—6. To coït with (a woman): ꜿoll. : C. 17–19. (All dates, O.E.D.)

*****scourer,** often **scowrer.** One who behaves as in *scour*, 2, q.v. : s. verging on c. : ca. 1670–1830. Wycherley. Cf. *hawkabite, mohock, mum, nicker, tityre-tu*, qq.v.—2. Hence, a night-thief : c. : late

C. 17–18. Anon., *The Gentleman Instructed*, ca. 1700, ' [In London] he struck up with sharpers, scourers, and Alsatians.'

*****scouring.** (An) imprisonment : c. . 1721, Defoe ; † by 1820.—2. Adj. to *scour*, v., 2–4, q.v.

scours. A purge : coll. (— 1923). Manchon. Ex S.E. *scours*, diarrhœa.

scouse. Any kind of stew : *Conway* cadets' coll. : from ca. 1880. John Masefield, 1933. Abbr. *lobscouse*, q.v.

scout. A college servant at Oxford (cf. the Cambridge *gyp*): Oxford University : C. 18–20 : coll.till ca. 1850, then S.E. Hearne, 1708 (O.E.D.); Grose, 1st ed. ; ' Cuthbert Bede.' Prob. ex the military, just possibly (W.) ex the † cricket, sense. —2. A member of the watch : c. of mid C. 17–early 19. Coles, 1676 ; Shadwell, 1688 ; Haggart, 1821. Ex † *scout*, a watchman.—3. See **scout, good.** Cf. :—4. A detective : Glasgow (— 1934).

scout, v.i. To dart ; go, move, suddenly and swiftly : mid-C. 18–early 19 : orig. and mainly nautical. Captain Tyrrell, 1758 ; Anon., *Splendid Follies*, 1810, ' Sponge was actually obliged to scout out of the room to conceal his risible muscles,' O.E.D. Ex Swedish *skjuta*, v.i., to shoot (W.). Cf. *shoot*, v., q.v.—2. See **scout on the lay.**—3. ' To shoot pigeons outside a gun-club enclosure,' F. & H. : coll. : from ca. 1880. Ex S.E. pigeonshooting sense of the n.

scout, good. (Occ., *scout* is used independently = a fellow.) A good, a trustworthy or helpful person : U.S., anglicised ca. 1920. Cf. the Scottish *scout*, a term of contempt.

*****scout-cull.** A watchman : c. : C. 18. C. Hitchin, *The Regulator*, 1718.

*****scout-ken.** A watch-house : c. of ca. 1810–40. Vaux. Ex *scout*, n., 2.

scout-master, scoutmaster. A schout (Dutch chief magistrate) : catachrestic : ca. 1650–1700. O.E.D.

*****scout on the lay.** To go searching for booty : c. : late C. 18–19. See c. **lay.**

scowbank, n. (1861). See **scowbanker.**—2. V., to loaf : dial. (— 1868) >, ca. 1880, s. ? etymology. (E.D.D.)

scowbanker ; also **skow-,** occ. **skull-** and, ca. 1890–1910, **showbanker.** A loafer, a tramp : mostly Australian (— 1864) ; by 1910 slightly, by 1930 very ob. H., 3rd ed. Prob. ex *scowbank*, v., q.v.—2. ' An outside paper-maker, one who has not served seven years to the trade ': papermakers' (— 1909). Ware, who spells it *skalbanker*.

scowbanking, n. Loafing : see **scowbank, v.**

Scowegian. (Pron. *Scow-wegian*.) A Scandinavian : West Canadian and nautical : late C. 19–20. Bowen. Ex *Scandinavian* + *Norwegian*. Cf. *Scandihoovian*.

scow(e)r. See **scour.**—**scowre(r).** See **scour, v.,** and **scourer.**

*****scrag.** A person's neck : c. : from ca. 1750; slightly ob. ? ex *crag*, Scottish *craig*, the neck.—2. The gallows : C. 19 c. Ex *scrag*, v. 1, or abbr. *scrag-squeezer*, q.v.—3. At Shrewsbury School (— 1881), a rent across a paper signifying ' no marks '. Perhaps ex *scrag*, to handle roughly.—4. A very rough tackle at Rugby football (cf. *scrag*, v., 4) : Public Schools' : C. 20. (P. G. Wodehouse, *Tales of St. Austin's*, 1903, ' There's all the difference between a decent tackle and a bally scrag like the one that doubled Tony up.')

*scrag, v.t. To hang by the neck : from ca. 1750 (slightly ob.) : c. until ca. 1840, then s. Toldervy (O.E.D.) ; Tomlinson ; Grose ; Barham.—2. Hence, to wring the neck of : from ca. 1820. ' Jon Bee.'—3. To garotte : c. or low s. : mid-C. 19–20.—4. To manhandle, properly (as in Rugby football), to twist the neck of a man whose head is conveniently held under one's arm : late C. 19–20. Kipling, Stalky & Co., ' Don't drop oil over my " Fors ", or I'll scrag you.' (*I'll scrag you* has > a vague threat and c.p., esp. among schoolboys.) Ex dial.

*scrag a lay. ' To steal clothes put on a hedge to dry,' Tufts : c. : late C. 18–early 19. Cf. *snow*, q.v.

*scrag-boy. A hangman : c. : from ca. 1780 ; ob. Ex *scrag*, n., 1 and v., 1.

*scrag-'em fair. A public execution : c. of ca. 1810–50. *Lex. Bal.* ; Bee. Ex *scrag*, v., 1.

scrag-hole. The gallery : theatrical (– 1909) ; ob. Ware. Ex the craning of scrags or necks.

*scrag-squeezer. A gallows : ca. 1820–1900 : c. Henley, 1887, Villon's *Straight Tip*, ' Until the squeezer nips your scrag.' Ex *scrag*, n., 1.

*scragged. Dead by hanging : c. : mid-C. 18–20 ; ob. Grose, 1st ed.

*scragger. A hangman : c. or low s. : 1897, P. Warung. O.E.D.

*scragging. An execution : C. 19–20 : c. >, ca. 1880, low s. ; slightly ob. Ex *scrag*, v., 1.

*scragging-post. A gallows : c. : from ca. 1810 ; slightly ob. Vaux.

*Scragg's Hotel. The workhouse : tramps' c. : from ca. 1880 ; ob. *The Daily Telegraph*, Jan. 1, 1886.

scram ! Clear out ! : U.S. ; anglicised, among devotees of the cinema, by 1930. Perhaps ex *scramble* (v.) : cf. South Cheshire *scramble*, ' to get away ; with a notion of fear or stealth ' (E.D.D.).

*scran ; occ., though—except in dial.—very rare in C. 20, skran. A reckoning at a tavern or inn : c. of ca. 1710–1740. In *Bacchus and Venus*, 1724, ' Frisky Moll's Song ' by Harper. App. this sense, without leaving any record that I have found, survived until 1903, when listed as low s. by F. & H. ; by 1930, virtually †. ? etymology.—2. ? hence (or perhaps cognate with *scrannel* : W.), food, esp. broken victuals : s. (– 1785) and dial. (– 1808) ; in mid-C. 19, the word verged on c. (witness ' Ducange Anglicus,' 1857). Grose, 1st ed., ' *Scran*, victuals.'—3. Hence, refuse (of food) : mostly dial. (– 1808) and, as s., † by 1910.—4. Ex sense 2, a meal : from ca. 1870 : mostly military.—5. Bread and butter : military : C. 20. B. & P.—6. See scran to, bad.—7. See scran, out on the.

scran, v.t. To provide with food : c. (in C. 19–20, low s.) : from ca. 1740 ; slightly ob. (This entry seems to show that *scran*, n., 2 existed half a century before our earliest record.)—2. V.i. to collect broken victuals : c. (? orig. dial.) >, ca. 1880, low s. : from the 1830's. H., 1st ed. Ex *scran*, n., 2.—3. V.i. to eat a meal, to take food : military : C. 20, esp. in G.W. Ex *scran*, n., fifth sense.

*scran, out on the. Begging for scraps of food : c. (– 1864). H., 3rd ed. Prob. ex *scran*, v., 2. Cf. *scranning*.

*scran-bag. A receptacle for scraps of food : c. : from ca. 1850. Burn, *Autobiography of a Beggar-Boy*, 1855 (O.E.D.). Ex *scran*, n., 2.—2. Hence, a haversack : military (– 1864). H., 3rd ed.—3.

A receptacle for the impounding of articles carelessly left about : nautical : late C. 19–20. Bowen.

*scran-pocket. A c. variant (– 1887) of *scran-bag*, 1 ; ob. Baumann.

scran to, bad. Bad luck to ——! : Anglo-Irish coll. : from ca. 1840. Lever, P. H. Emerson. Perhaps ex *scran*, n., 2, q.v. Cf. *cess*, q.v.

*scrand. An occ. variant of *scran*, n.

*scranning, vbl.n. A begging of scraps of food : Scots dial. (– 1839), whence c. (– 1859), as in H., 1st ed. Ex *scran*, v., 2 ; cf. *scran, out on the*.

scrap. A blow, a punch : c. of early C. 17. Rowlands in *Martin Mark-All*. Cf. sense 3, of independent origin.—2. (In C. 18–19, occ. scrapp.) An intention, design, plot, always either vile or villainous : ca. 1670–1830 : either c. (see Grose, 1st ed.) or low s. E.g. in B.E. (at *whiddle*). ? ex *scrape*.—3. ? hence, a struggle, scrimmage, fisti-cuffs (the predominant C. 20 sense) : from ca. 1873. H., 5th ed. (In G.W., a battle.) Cf. U.S. *scrape*, a rough encounter, 1812 (Thornton).

scrap, v.i. To fight, esp. with the fists (– 1874). H., 5th ed. Ex *scrap*, n., 3.—2. To scrimmage (– 1891). O.E.D.—3. Ex sense 1, v.t. to box with : 1893, P. H. Emerson, ' I was backed to scrap a cove bigger nor me.'

scrap, do a. See do a scrap.

scrap-up. An occ. variant of *scrap*, n., 3 : Barrère & Leland.

scrape. A shave : jocular coll. (– 1859). H., 1st ed. Cf. v. and *scraper*.—2. Cheap butter : 1859, H., 1st ed.—3. See scrape, bread and.—4. Short shrift : coll : 1899, *The Pall Mall Gazette*, April 5, ' From the French adventurers he was only likely to get what schoolboys call scrape.'

scrape, v.i., v.t., and v. reflexive. To shave : jocular coll. : from ca. 1770.

scrape, bread and. Bread with but a smear of butter : orig. schools' : coll. : 1861 (O.E.D.) ; 1873, Rhoda Broughton, ' Happiness thinly spread over their whole lives, like bread and scrape ! ' Ex S.E. *scrape*, a thin layer.—2. Hence, short commons : coll. : from ca. 1865.

scrape !, go. Go away ! : contemptuous coll. : early C. 17. Cotgrave.

scrape the enamel. To scratch the skin by falling : cyclists' : from ca. 1890 ; ob.

scraped 'em off me putties ! A ranks' c.p. directed against the Staff : G.W. military. B. & P. The allusion is to *sh*t*, n., 2.

scraper. A barber : pejorative coll. : from ca. 1790.—2. A razor : jocular coll. : from ca. 1860. See scrape, v.—3. As a cocked hat (1828, Moir), coll. verging on S.E. (E.D.D.)—4.—4. A ' short one to two-inch whisker, slightly curved ' : Society : ca. 1880–90. Ware.

scrapers, take to one's. To make off : Anglo-Irish : from ca. 1820. Here, *scraper* = a foot, esp. a heel ; cf. *scrape* with one's feet.

scraping-castle. A water-closet : low : ca. 1850–90. H., 1st ed.

scrapings, be away to. To be doomed or done for or dead : lower classes' : C. 20.

scrapings of his nails !, he wouldn't give you the. A semi-proverbial, coll. c.p. (– 1887), applied to a very mean person ; slightly ob. Baumann.

scrapp. See scrap, n., 2.

scrapper. A pugilist ; any fighter, whether with fists or weapons : from ca. 1870. H., 5th ed.

scrapping. Fighting or boxing : from ca. 1890. See scrap, v., and cf. scrapper.

scrappy. A farrier : Regular Army : late C. 19–20. F. & Gibbons. Ex the scraps of iron or hoof he leaves about.

Scratch. Gen. and orig. *Old Scratch.* The devil : coll. : 1740 (O.E.D.) ; Amory, 1756 (*Scratch*). In late C. 19–20, mostly dial. Ex *scrat*, a goblin, on *scratch.*

scratch. A competitor starting from *scratcn* in a handicap contest : coll. : 1867 (O.E.D.).—2. In billiards, a fluke : coll. : from ca. 1890.—3. Generic for genuine bank- and currency- notes : c. (— 1935). David Hume. Contrast *slush.*

scratch, bring to the,—come (up) to the or **toe the.** To bring oneself or another to the requisite point, lit. or fig. ; to do, or cause to do, one's duty : coll. >, ca. 1890, S.E. : resp. 1827, Scott ; 1834, Ainsworth ; 1857, ' Cuthbert Bede.' Ex the line drawn on the ground or floor to divide the boxing-ring.

scratch, no great. Of little value or importance : orig. (1844), U.S., anglicised ca. 1858 ; slightly ob. H., 1st ed. Lit., not very painful.

scratch a beggar before you die, you'll. You will die a beggar : a semi-proverbial c.p. of ca. 1630–1800. Clarke, Ray, Fuller. (Apperson.)

scratch-down. ' The public scolding of a man by a woman ' : low (— 1909). Ware.

scratch it. To depart ; make off : low (— 1923). Manchon.

scratch-me. A lucifer match : London's lower classes' (— 1909). Ware.

scratch my breech and I'll claw your elbow. Let us indulge in reciprocal flattery : C. 17–19 : a semi-proverbial c.p. Cf. *ca me, ca thee,* and S.E. *scratch me and I'll scratch thee.*

scratch one's arse with, not a sixpence to. Penniless : low coll. : mid-C. 19–20 ; ob.

scratch one's wool. To puzzle ; wonder greatly : tailors' : from ca. 1870. On S.E. *scratch one's head* ; and see **wool,** hair.

scratch-platter. See **tailor's ragout.**

scratch-rash. A scratched face : artisans' (— 1909). Ware. Cf. *gravel-rash,* q.v.

scratch with, not a sixpence to. Penniless : coll. (— 1931). Lyell. Ex *scratch one's arse . . .,* q.v.

scratched. Tipsy : C. 17 c. or s. ' Water-Poet ' Taylor, 1622.

scratcher. A lucifer match : proletarian (— 1909). Ware. Cf. *scratch-me.*—2. A paymaster, or his clerk : naval : late C. 19–20 ; ob. Ware, ' From the noisy times of quill pens.'—3. A bed : low Glasgow (— 1934). For the semantics, cf. *flea-bag.*

Scratchland. Scotland : ca. 1780–1890. Grose, 1st ed. Cf. *Scotch fiddle,* q.v.

scratchy. (Of a batsman) lacking sureness and confidence in his strokes : cricket coll. : 1904, P. F. Warner (Lewis).

scream. An extremely ridiculous or funny person or thing : 1915 (S.O.D.) : s. >, by 1935, coll. Often *a perfect s.* An abbr., with modification of sense, of *screamer,* 2 and 3.

scream. To turn King's evidence : low : from the early 1920's. O.E.D. (Sup.) Cf. *squeal.*

screamer. An animate or inanimate of exceptional size, intensity, attractiveness : orig. U.S., anglicised in 1850 by Frank Smedley. Runciman, 1888, ' She's a screamer, she's a real swell.' (O.E.D.) —2. A startling, exaggerated, or extremely funny book, story, etc. : 1844, Dickens (O.E.D.).—3. Hence, one who tells exaggerated or very funny stories : 1849, Albert Smith (O.E.D.).—4. ' A thief

who, robbed by another thief, applies to the police,' F. & H. : c. : from ca. 1890.—5. An exclamation-mark (cf. *Christer* and *shriek-mark*): from ca. 1920 and mostly among printers, authors, journalists, typists, and copy-writers. D. Sayers, *Murder Must Advertise,* 1933, ' Capital N, capital P, and screamer.'

screaminess. The quality of being *screamy,* q.v. : coll. : from ca. 1880.

screaming. Splendid ; excellent : orig. theatrical (— 1859). H., 1st ed. Ex *screamer,* 1, q.v.

screaming gin and ignorance. Bad newspaper-writing : sporting reporters' : 1868–ca. 80. Ware.

screaming ostrich. A ' super bird ', an exceptionally marked hissing by the audience : theatrical (— 1935). See **bird** in this sense.

screamy. Apt to scream ; (of sound) screaming ; fig., very violent, exaggerated, or unseemly in expression ; (of colour) glaring : coll. : in 1882, *The Spectator* describes two of Swinburne's sonnets as ' thoroughly unworthy and screamy '. O.E.D. Cf. *scream* and *screamer* (2), qq.v.

*****screave.** See **screeve.**

screech. Whiskey : low : from ca. 1880 ; ob. ? ex its strength, or possibly ex its tendency to make females [*sic*] screech. See also **screigh.**

screecher. A street singer : showmen's : C. 20. P. Allingham in *The Evening News,* 9 : vii : 1934.

screed. Ca. 1870–90 a journalistic coll. (later S.E.) for ' an illogical or badly written article or paper upon any subject,' H., 5th ed.—2. Hence, a picture execrably painted : artists' (— 1887) ; ob. Baumann.

*****screen.** A bank or currency note ; esp. if counterfeit : from ca. 1810 : c. Vaux. (Cf. *screen, queer,* q.v.) Ca. 1820–50, it often meant esp. a £1 note (cf. *screeve,* n., 2), as in Egan, 1821. The word, which may be a witty perversion of *screeve* (q.v.), was ob. by 1900, virtually † by 1930.

*****screen, queer.** A forged note : c. (— 1812). Vaux, Lytton, Ainsworth. See **screen.**

*****screen-faking.** The forging of notes : c. : 1830, Moncrieff. See **screen.**

*****screeve** (1801) ; also **screave** (1821), **scrieve** (from ca. 1850), **scrive** (1788). Any piece of writing : 1788 ; Scots s. or coll.—2. Whence, a banknote : (mainly Scottish) c. : ca. 1800–1890. *The Sporting Magazine,* 1801, ' The one-pound screeves ' ; Haggart.—3. A begging letter, a petition, a testimonial : c. : from ca. 1810. Vaux, Mayhew. (From ca. 1890, letter is the predominant sense.)—4. A drawing in chalk on the pavement : c. : from ca. 1855. Ex *screeve,* v., 2 ; and see **screeving.** (Dates, mainly O.E.D.) The etymology is not so simple as it looks : prob. ex. dial. *scrieve,* to write, or ex the Dutch *schrijven* ; ultimately ex L. *scribere* ; cf. :

*****screeve ;** occ. **scrieve.** V.t. to write (esp. a begging letter, a petition) : c. and East-End s. : mid-C. 19–20. ' *No. 747* ', reference 1845 ; Mayhew, 1851. Ex It. *scrivere* via Lingua Franca ; perhaps imm. ex *screeve,* n., 1–3.—2. Whence, v.i. draw on the pavement with chalk ; to do this as a livelihood : c. : 1851, Mayhew.

*****screeve, fake a.** See **fake a screeve.**

*****screeve-faker.** The same as *screever,* 1, q.v. : ca. 1850–1910.

*****screever ;** occ. **scriever.** One who, for a living, writes begging letters : c. : 1851, Mayhew. Ex *screeve,* v., 1, q.v.—2. A ' pavement artist ' : c. and East-End s. : implied by Mayhew in 1851 (see quotation at **screeving**) and recorded by H. in 1859.

Punch, July 14, 1883, ' Here is a brilliant opening for merry old Academicians, festive flagstone screevers, and ". distinguished amateurs " '.

Screeveton. The Bank of England : low (— 1903) ; ob. Ex *screeve*, n., 2.

screeving. Vbl.n. of *screeve*, v., 1 and 2. Mayhew, 1851, ' By screeving, that is, by petitions and letters ' ; ibid., ' Screeving or writing on the pavement.'

screigh ; occ. **skreigh**. Whiskey : Scottish s. : C. 19–20. Lexicographer Jamieson (E.D.D.). I.e. a screech : proleptic usage.

screw. A skeleton key : c. : 1795, Potter ; slightly ob.—2. ? hence, a turnkey or prison warder : 1821, Egan : c. until ca. 1860, then low s.—3. A robbery effected with a skeleton key : c. of ca. 1810–90. Vaux.—4. **the screw**, the doing of this, esp. as an occupation : c. : ca. 1810–80. Vaux. —5. An old or otherwise worthless horse : 1821 (O.E.D.) ; ' Nimrod ' Apperley, 1835, ' Mr Charles Boultbee, the best screw driver in England.' Coll. >, ca. 1890, S.E. Perhaps by the semantic process illustrated by *rip* (see W.) or orig. of a race-horse that can, by ' screwing ', be made to gain a place (O.E.D.)—6. Wages, salary (— 1859). H., 1st ed. —7. Hence (?), a dram, a ' pick-me-up ' : 1877. Cf. 7, *a*, a bottle of wine : Anglo-Irish (— 1827) ; ob. Barrington (E.D.D.).—8. See **screw, female.**—9 (Whence, or more prob. ex *screw*, v., 3), an act of copulation : C. 19– 20 : low.—10. Whence, a woman *qua* sexual pleasure : low : late C. 19–20.—11. See **screws, the.**

screw, v. To break into (a building) by using a skeleton key : c. : from ca. 1810. Vaux ; Arthur Morrison. See **screw**, n., 1, 2, and 3.—2. Hence, v.i. to burgle ; also, to keep watch for one's burglar-confederate : c. : C. 20. Charles E. Leach, 1933. Also, v.t., to look at : grafters' : C. 20. Allingham.—3. To copulate with (a female) : low (— 1785). Grose, 1st ed.

screw, all of a. Very crooked or twisted : coll. — 1887). Baumann. Perhaps influenced by *askew*.

screw, fake a. See **fake a screw.**

screw, female ; occ. simply **screw**. A harlot : resp. ca. 1780–1850 (Grose, 1st ed.) and ca. 1720– 1870 (*A New Canting Dict.*, 1725).

screw, under the. See **under the screw.**

screw-jaws. A wry-mouthed person : coll. (— 1788) verging on S.E. ; ob. Grose, 2nd ed.

screw loose, a. A phrase indicative of something wrong : from ca. 1820 : s. until ca. 1840, then coll. till ca. 1880, then S.E. Egan, 1821 ; Dickens ; Trollope. Ob. in this gen. sense.—2. Hence, (slightly) crazy or mad, gen. as *have a screw loose* : coll. : from ca. 1870.

screw one's nut. To ' dodge a blow aimed at the head ' : London lower classes' : from the early 1890's. *The People*, Jan. 6, 1895 (Ware). A double pun—on *nut* and on *screw*.

screw-thread, drunken. A defective spiral ridge of a screw : a technological coll. : from ca. 1850. Ronalds & Richardson, *Chemical Technology*, 1854. O.E.D.

screw up, v.i. To force one into making a bargain : coll. : late C. 17–mid-19. B.E. Ex S.E. sense, to tighten up with a screw.—2. To garotte : c. : 1845 (p. 419 of ' *No. 747* ') ; ob.

screwed. Tipsy : 1838, Barham, ' Like a four-bottle man in a company screw'd, | Not firm on his legs, but by no means subdued.' S. >, ca.

1870, coll. >, ca. 1910, S.E. For semantics, cf. *tight*. Cf. *screwy*, 2, and *blind, blotto, corned, elevated, fuzzy, lushy, muzzy, paralysed, scammered, squiffy, three sheets in the wind, up a tree, wet*. F. & H. gives a magnificent synonymy ; H., in the Introduction, a good one.

screwed on right or **the right way, have one's head.** To be shrewd and businesslike ; be able to look after oneself : coll. : mid-C. 19–20.

screwed up. Vanquished : Oxford and Cambridge undergraduates' : late C. 19–early 20. Ex ' the ancient habit of screwing up an offender's door,' Ware.—2. (Also *screwed up in a corner*.) Penniless : artisans' (— 1909). Ware, ' Without money—can't move.'

screwer or **screwman.** Occ. variants (C. 20 : Edgar Wallace, *Sooper Speaking*, has the latter ; ' Stuart Wood ', the former) of *screwsman*.

screwing. A house- or shop-breaking : c. : from ca. 1810. See **screw**, v., 1.

screws, the. Rheumatism : coll. and dial. : mid-C. 19–20. Ex instrument of torture.

screwsman. A thief using a skeleton key : c. (— 1812). Vaux. Ex *screw*, n., 1–3. In C. 20, esp. a petty house-breaker : ' Stuart Wood ', *Shades of the Prison House*, 1932.

screwy. Mean, stingy : 1851, Mayhew, ' Mechanics are capital customers . . . They are not so screwy,' coll. >, ca. 1890, S.E. Ex S.E. *screw*, a miser.—2. Drunk (cf. *screwed*, q.v.) ‹ 1820, Creevey (O.E.D.) : coll. >, ca. 1890, S.E. ; ob. —3. (Of horses) unsound : 1852, Smedley, ' It's like turning a screwy horse out to grass,' O.E.D. : coll. >, ca. 1890, S.E. Ex *screw*, n., 4, q.v.—4 Crazy, mad ; (very) eccentric : lower classes' (— 1935). Perhaps ex sense 2.

scribbler's luck. ' An empty purse and a full hand,' *The Pelican*, Dec. 3, 1898 : coll. of ca. 1890–1915.

scribe. See **one-eyed scribe.**—2. A bad writer : journalistic : ca. 1870–90. Ware.—3. Any clerical rank or rating : naval coll. : C. 20. Bowen.

scrieve. See **screeve.**

scrim. An abbr. (— 1923) of both *scrimshank* (n. and v.) and *scrimshancer*.

scrimmage. A free-fight, scuffle, or confused struggle : coll. : 1780, Johnson (*skrimage*) ; 1826, Fenimore Cooper (*skrimmage*) ; 1844, *The Catholic Weekly Instructor* (*scrimmidge*) ; 1859, H , 1st ed. (*scrimmage*). Ex S.E. sense, a skirmish, prob. via dial. (O.E.D.)

scrimshander. See **scrimshaw.**

scrimshank ; occ. **skrim-**. A shirking of duty : military : C. 20. Ex :

scrimshank ; occ. **skrim-**. V.i. to shirk work : military (— 1890). Barrère & Leland ; Kipling, 1893. Prob. a back-formation from *scrimshanker*, q.v.

scrimshanker ; occ. **skrimshanker**. A shirker : military (— 1890). Barrère & Leland. *Tit-Bits*, April 26, 1890, ' Besides the dread of being considered a skrimshanker, a soldier dislikes the necessary restraints of a hospital.' Etymology obscure : perhaps a perversion of *scowbanker*, q.v. The importance of the subject may be gauged from the fact that in 1843 there appeared a book entitled *On Feigned and Factitious Diseases, chiefly of Soldiers and Seamen*.

scrimshanking ; **skrim-**. Vbl.n. and ppl. adj. ex *scrimshank*, v., q.v.

scrimshaw (work) ; occ. **scrimshander, -y, mostly**

U.S. Small objects, esp. ornaments, made by seamen in their leisure : nautical : from ca. 1850 : s. >, ca. 1880, coll. >, ca. 1910, S.E., as the v. has prob. always been. Etymology unknown, though the word is prob. either ex, or influenced by, the surname *Scrimshaw*. W. ; O.E.D.

scrip. A small (gen. written-upon) piece of paper : from ca. 1615 : S.E. until ca. 1680, then c. till early C. 19, then dial. ; in c., esp. in *blot the scrip*, it occ. = a bond. B.E., Grose. ? ex *scrap* : cf. the famous *mere scrap of paper*. (In its commercial sense, despite Grose, 2nd ed., *scrip*, having originated as an obvious abbr., has prob. always been S.E.)

scrip-scrap. Odds and ends : coll. : C. 19–20. Reduplication on *scrap*.

***scripper.** He who, in a swindle, keeps watch : c. : late C. 16–early 17. Greene, describing ' high law '. ? etymology, unless ex † Scots *scrip*, to jeer.

***scrippet.** Prob. a misprint for, rather than a variant of, the preceding : id. Ibid.

[**scripturience** is a variant of S.E. *scripturiency* and lies on the borderland between literary s. and literary j. : late C. 19–20 ; very ob. Ware ; and see esp. *Slang*, p. 178.]

***scrive.** See **screeve, n.**

***scroby**, or **claws**, (for breakfast),—**be tipped the.** ' To be whipt before the justices,' Grose, 1st ed. : c. (orig. at least) of ca. 1780–1850. The C. 18 form is *be tipped the scroby* ; *claws* came ca. 1810, *for breakfast* (rare with *scroby*) was added about the same time ; from ca. 1850 († by 1890), the term survived as *get scroby* (H., 1st ed., 1859, ' to be whipped in prison before the justices '). See **tip**, v. ; with *claws* cf. *cat-o'-nine-tails* ; *scroby* is a mystery unless perchance it = *scruby*, scurvy, here used fig. (cf. *do the dirty on*).

scroo(d)ge. See **scrouge, v.**

scroof. A sponger : c. or low (— 1823) ; † by 1890. Egan's Grose. A variant form of *scruff*, scurf, hence anything worthless.

scroop. To skirt very closely ; to rub : coll. (— 1923). Manchon. Ex S.E. *scroop*, make a scraping sound.

***scrope.** A farthing : c. of ca. 1710–1820. Hall ; Grose, 2nd ed. ? origin.

scroudge. See **scrouge, v.**

scrouge ; occ. **scrowge.** A crush ; a crowd : low coll. : 1839. C. Keene, 1887, ' I went to the Academy " Swarry " last night—the usual scrouge.' O.E.D. Ex :

scrouge, the earliest and gen. form ; also **scroo(d)ge** (C. 19–20), **scroudge** (C. 19–20), **scrowge** (C. 19–20), **skrouge** (C. 19–20), and **skrowdge** (C. 18). V.t. to crowd ; to inconvenience by pressing against or by encroaching on the space of : low coll. : mid-C. 18–20. Ex *scruze*, to squeeze, ' still preserved, at least in its corruption, *to scrouge*, in the London jargon ', Johnson, 1755. (O.E.D.)—2. V.i. in same senses : from ca. 1820. Egan. (The vbl.n. *scrouging* is fairly gen.)

scrounge. Esp. in *do a scrounge*, to go looking for what one can ' find ' ; to take it : military : 1914 or '15. Ex the v.—2. A ' scrounger ' : from ca. 1916.

scrounge, v.t. To hunt for ; cadge, to get by wheedling ; to acquire illicitly ; hence, to steal ; also v.i. : military in G.W. ; from ca. 1920, fairly gen. Ex dial. *scrunge*, to steal (esp. apples) or ex dial. and coll. *scrouge*, q.v., of which, clearly, *scrunge* may be a variant ; cf. *skrump*, q.v. The

S.O.D. records at 1919 ; W. quotes *The Westminster Gazette* of Jan. 1920 ; but the soldiers used it from the early days of the War. See esp. B. & P.

scrounge on. To sponge on : U.S. (— 1911) >, by 1918, anglicised. (O.E.D. Sup)

scrounger. One who does ' scrounge ' (see the v.) : military : from 1915.

scrounging. Vbl.n. and ppl.adj. of *scrounge*, v. : military : 1914 or '15.

scrouperize. To coït : a rather literary coll. : mid-C. 17–early 18. Translations of Rabelais. Cf. later S.E. *scroop*, to scrape.

scrovie, -y. A useless hand shipped as an able-bodied seaman : nautical : late C. 19–20. Bowen. Cognate with S.E. *scruffy* : cf. *scroof*.

scrowge. See **scrouge, v.**

scrub. ' One who pays not his whack at the tavern,' Bee : public-house coll. : ca. 1820–60. Ex *scrub*, a shabby fellow.—2. Handwriting : Christ's Hospital : mid-C. 19–20. Ex sense 2 of :

scrub, v. To drudge : coll. : late C. 19–20. Ex scrubbing floors, steps, etc.—2. V.t. to write fast : Christ's Hospital : mid-C. 19–20. Ex L. *scribere*.—3. See **scrubbing-brush**, 2 : low coll. : C. 20.

scrub and wash clothes. ' A substitute expression in reading aloud for a word suddenly come upon which the reader cannot pronounce ' : naval coll. : late C. 19–20. F. & Gibbons.

scrub-dangler. A wild bullock : ca. 1885–1920. Cf. *scrubber*, 1.

scrub her (gen. **'er**). To sponge off the big odds on one's [bookmaker's] board : turf c. (— 1932). Cf. *scrubbing-brush*, 2.

scrubbed. See **get scrubbed.**

scrub(b)ado. The itch : mid-C. 17–early 19 : coll. on † S.E. *scrub*, the same.

scrubbed-hammock face. ' A miserable-looking person ' : naval : C. 20. Bowen, ' The naval hammock . . . does not look at its best when wet.' Hence, *have a scrubbed-hammock face*, to look gloomy (F. & Gibbons).

scrubber. An animal living in the scrub : Australian coll. >, ca. 1900, S.E. : 1859, H. Kingsley in *Geoffry Hamlyn*; F. D. Davison, *Man-Shy*, 1934.—2. Hence, a person living there : 1890, ' Rolf Boldrewood '.—3. An outsider ; in university circles, ' one who will not join in the life of the place ' (cf. the Oxford *smug*) : Australian : 1868 ; slightly ob. Morris. Ex sense 1, as is :—4. Any ' starved-looking or ill-bred animal ' : Australian coll. (— 1898). Morris. Cf. the Australian j. *scrub-bull*, an inferior bull or bullock. —5. See **dry scrub.**

scrubbing. A flogging of four cuts : Winchester : ca. 1840–1900. Mansfield, ' The ordinary punishment was called scrubbing.' Ex gen. coll. of ca. 1810–50, often in sense of defeat (O.E.D.).

scrubbing-brush. The pubic hair : low : mid-C. 19–20.—2. An ' outside ' horse or dog that ' scrubs ' or beats the favourites : turf c. (— 1932). *Slang*, p. 246.

Scrubs, the. The convict prison at Wormwood Scrubs : c. (— 1916) >, by 1923, low s. E.g. in Manchon, 1923 ; George Baker, *The Soul of a Skunk*, 1930 ; Anon., *Dartmoor from Within*, 1932.

scruey. See **screwy**, 2. Thackeray, 1855.

scruff. Newfoundland s. of ca. 1860–1900. *Figaro*, Nov. 25, 1870, quoting from *The Montreal News*, on ' Codland Habits ' : ' The best society is called " merchantable ", that being the term for fish of the best quality ; while the lowest stratum is " scruff " or " dun ".' Ex ob. S.E. *scruff* applied to anything valueless or contemptible.

scruff, v. To hang : C. 19 coll. Ex *scruff*, the nape of the neck.

scrum. A scrummage in Rugby football : 1888 (O.E.D.) : coll. till C. 20, then S.E.

scrum, v. To scrimmage : C. 20 : Rugby Football coll. >, ca. 1920, S.E. Ex n.

scrumdolious. ' Scrumptious ', of which it is an elaboration ; late C. 19–20. (J. B. Priestley, *Faraway*, 1932.)

scrummy. ' Scrumptious ' (whence it derives) : from ca. 1906, on the evidence of Collinson (p. 24) ; 1918, Galsworthy (O.E.D. Sup.).—2. An occ. corruption of *crummy*, lousy : New Zealand soldiers' in G.W.

scrump. See **skrimp.**

scrumptious. First rate, excellent, ' glorious ' : coll. : 1859, H., 1st ed. ; 1865, Meredith, ' Hang me, if ever I see such a scrumptious lot,' O.E.D. Ex U.S. coll. sense, stylish (of things), handsome (of persons).—2. The sense ' fastidious, hard to please ' is by the O.E.D. queried as U.S. only : perhaps orig. U.S. (whence the O.E.D.'s quotation, 1845), but app. current in England ca. 1855–75, for the life-time edd. of H. define the word as ' nice, particular, beautiful.' Prob. ex dial. sense of mean, stingy ; sense 1, therefore, as W. points out, may have been influenced by *sumptuous*.

scrumptiously. The adv. of the preceding : coll. : from not later than 1880.

scruncher. A glutton : coll. : from ca. 1860. Ex *scrunch*, to bite *crushingly*.

scruntch. An illiterate form of (to) *scrunch* : 1851, Mayhew.

scud. A fast runner : schools' : 1857, Hughes in *Tom Brown*, ' I say . . . you ain't a bad scud ' ; ob. Ex *scud*, to move quickly.—2. Hence, a fast run : from ca. 1870 ; slightly ob.

scuddick, the gen. form ; also **scuddock, scurrick, scuttick** (mostly dial.), **skiddi(c)k** (id.), and **skuddick.** An extremely small sum or coin, amount or object : s. and dial. : from ca. 1780 (E.D.D.) ; in C. 20, only dial. ' Jon Bee,' 1823, ' Used negatively ; " not a scuddick " . . . " Every scuddick gone " ; " she gets not a scuddick from me ".' Perhaps ex † S.E. *scud*, refuse ; more prob. ex dial. *scud*, a wisp of straw, despite the fact that this sense is not recorded until 1843 (O.E.D.),—many dial. terms were almost certainly existent ' ages ' before their earliest appearance in print.—2. In c. of ca. 1820–60, a halfpenny : only in form *scurrick*. Egan's Grose, 1823 ; Moncrieff, 1843.

*scuff. A(ny) crowd : c. : from late 1870's. *Macmillan's Magazine*, 1879 (XL, 501), ' This got a scuff round us ' : ' Dagonet ' Sims in *The Referee*, Feb. 12, 1888. Ex more gen. S.E. sense, a noisy crowd.

*scuffle-hunter. One who hangs about the docks on the pretence of looking for work but actually to steal anything that ' comes his way ' : c. and nautical s. from ca. 1790 ; ob. Colquhoun's *Police of the Metropolis*, 1796 ; Bowen.

scuffy. Inferior, contemptible : Christ's Hospital (— 1887). Baumann. Prob. ex *scurfy*.

*scufter. A policeman : Northern c. (cf. *bulky*) : ca. 1855–90. H., 2nd ed. Ex either *scuffe*, to throw up dust in walking (cf. dial. *scuff*, to shuffle), or, more likely, *scuff*, to buffet.

scug ; also (very rare in C. 20) **skug.** An untidy or ill-mannered or morally undeveloped boy ; a shirker at games ; one ' undistinguished in person, in games, or social qualities ' : Eton and Harrow : from ca. 1820. Westmacott, 1825, refers it to *sluggish* ; perhaps, however, ex Scots and Northern *scug* (*skug*), a pretence ; ex Yorkshire and Lancashire dial. *scug*, scum ; but possibly *scadger*, q.v. See esp. ' Eton Slang ', § 2.

scuggish ; scuggy. Adj. to the preceding.

scull. The head of a college : university (— 1785) ; ob. by 1864 (see H., 3rd ed.), † by 1890. Grose, 1st ed. Cf. *scull-race* and *Golgotha*, qq.v.— 2. ' A one horse chaise or buggy,' Grose, 1st ed. (also *sculler*) : ca. 1780–1830.—3. See **sculls.**

scull-race. An examination : University : ca. 1810–70. Ex *scull*, 1, q.v.

scull-thatcher. A wig-maker : coll. (— 1785) ; ob. Grose, 1st ed.—2. Whence, a hatter : C. 19–20 ; ob.

sculler. See **scull,** 2.

scullery-science. Phrenology : jocular coll. : ca. 1830–60. Chorley, 1836. Punning *skull*.

sculling around. (Of a person) wandering aimlessly ; (of a thing) left lying about : nautical : C. 20. Bowen. Ex leisurely rowing.

sculls. A waterman plying sculls : coll. : C. 18–20. Cf. *oars*.

sculp. A piece of sculpture : coll. : 1883, *The Daily News*, Jan. 18. (Ware.) Cf. :

sculp, v.t. To sculpture : from ca. 1780 : S.E. until ca. 1880, then (gen. jocular) coll. R. L. Stevenson, 1887.—2. Hence, v.i. : coll. : 1889, W. E. Norris ; 1893, Kipling, ' Men who write, and paint, and sculp.' O.E.D. (Rather S.E. than ' unconventional ' is *sculpt*, which, recorded for 1864, is very rare in C. 20. See O.E.D.)

*scum. Enough : c. of ca. 1720–50. *Street Robberies Considered*, 1728. ? etymology.

scupper. To take by surprise and then massacre : military : 1885 (the Suakin Expedition). W.—2. Hence, to kill : military : late C. 19–20. B. & P. ? ex *cooper* (q.v.), to ruin.

scuppered. Killed, dead in battle : naval, hence military : late C. 19–20. Ex preceding.—2. Sunk : naval : C. 20. Bowen.—3. Scattered ; demoralised : naval and military : C. 20. F. & Gibbons.

scurf. A mean, a ' scurvy ' fellow : ca. 1850–1915. Mayhew, 1851, ' " There's a scurf ! " said one ; " He's a regular scab," cried another.' Cf. *scab*, n., 1.—2. A ' scab ' as in *scab*, n., 2, q.v. : from ca. 1850.—3. Also, an employer paying less than the standard wage : from ca. 1850. Like sense 2, first in Mayhew.

*scurf, v. To apprehend, arrest : c. of ca. 1810–50. Vaux. ? ex S.E. *scruff*.

*scurrick. See **scuddick.**

scuse or **'scuse.** (Esp. in *'scuse me !*) To excuse : late C. 15–20 : S.E. until C. 19, then (when not, as occ., deliberately humorous) coll. verging on illiteracy. T. E. Brown, 1887, ' 'Scuse me, your honour.' O.E.D.

scushy. Money : Scottish : late C. 18–mid-19. Shirrefs, *Poems*, 1790. E.D.D. Origin ?

scut. The female pudend or pubic hair : coll. : late C. 16–20 ; ob. Ex *scut*, a short upright tail, esp. of hare, rabbit, deer. (Implied in Shakespeare, Cotton, Durfey, and several broadsides, but not, I believe, defined as the pudend before Grose, 1st ed.) Also, the behind : C. 18. Ned Ward, 1709

(Matthews).—2. A person ; occ. a number of persons : coll. and dial., either jocose or pejorative : from early 1890's. O.E.D. (Sup.). Ex S.E. sense.

scutter. To go hastily and fussily or excitedly or timorously : coll. and dial. : from ca. 1780. Mrs. Delany, 1781, ' She staid abᵗ 24 hours, then scutter'd away to Badminton.' The vbl.n. is frequent, the ppl. adj. rare. O.E.D. Prob. ex *scuttle* on *scatter*. Imm. ex dial. (1777 : E.D.D.).

scuttick. See **scuddick.**

scuttle. An undignified withdrawal : political : 1884 (O.E.D.) ; slightly ob. Ex :

scuttle, v.i. To withdraw with unseemly haste from the occupation, or the administration, of a country : political : 1883, Lord Randolph Churchill in a speech delivered on Dec. 18 ; slightly ob. Ex S.E. sense, ' to run with quick, hurried steps.' O.E.D.—2. V.i. to shout in order to attract the attention of the masters to one's being roughly treated : Christ's Hospital : mid-C. 19–20 ; ob. Whence *scuttle-cat*, one who does this : † by 1903. —3. To deflower : orig. nautical : mid-C. 19–20. Whence *scuttle a ship*, to take a maidenhead.—4. To stab : c. : from ca. 1860 ; ob.—5. To go ; to depart : schoolboys' s. (from ca. 1906) now verging on coll. Collinson. Cf. S.E. *scuttle away.*—6. See **scuttle a nob.**—7. See **scuttling**, 2.

scuttle, do a back. To engage in an act of sodomy : low : late C. 19–20.

scuttle, on the. On a bout of drinking or a round of whoring : from ca. 1870 ; slightly ob. Cf. preceding entry and see **scuttle**, v., 3.

scuttle a nob. To break a head : pugilistic : from ca. 1810 ; ob. Randall.

scuttle a ship. See **scuttle**, v., 3.—**scuttle-cat.** See **scuttle**, v., 2.

scuttle-mouth. A small oyster in a very large shell : costermongers' : 1848, though first recorded in vol. I (1851) of Mayhew's *London Labour.*

scuttled, ppl.adj. Captured : military : 1914 ; ob. G. H. McKnight, *English Words*, 1923.

scuttler. An advocate of ' scuttle ' (see the n.) : political : 1884 (O.E.D.) ; ob.

scuttling. The policy implied in *scuttle*, v., 1 : political : 1884 (O.E.D.) ; ob.—2. As street-fighting between youthful ruffians, *scuttling*, like *scuttle* the v. (1890) and the n. (1864), is gen. considered S.E. : perhaps orig. coll. or dial.—see E.D.D.

'sdeath !, 'sdeynes !, 'sdiggers ! Abbr. *God's death !, deynes* or *dines !*, and *diggers !* : resp. C. 17–18, then archaic ; early C. 17 (Jonson) ; late C. 17. (O.E.D.) All coll. except perhaps the first, which should perhaps be considered S.E. ; all may be euphemistic, though this is to underestimate the power of colloquialism, which is at least as great as that of euphemism.

'sdheart. See **'sheart.—se.** See **sey.**

'se. Are : sol. : C. 19–20. Baumann, ' If they'se left to theirselves.'—2. See **Addenda.**

sea ?, who wouldn't sell a farm and go to. A nautical c.p. spoken when something unpleasant or extremely difficult has to be done : mid-C. 19–20. Bowen.

sea-blessing. A curse ; curses : jocular nautical coll. : late C. 19–20. Bowen.

sea-boot face, have a. To look gloomy : naval : C. 20. F. & Gibbons. Cf. *scrubbed-hammock face*, q.v.

Sea-Boots, the. ' The naval name for the old

turret-battleships " Hero " and " Conqueror ", which had . . . the upper works bunched aft ' : early C. 20. Bowen.

sea-coal. Money : C. 19, mainly nautical. On *sea-cole* = sea-kale.

sea-cook, son of a. A term of abuse : nautical coll. : 1825 (O.E.D.). M. Scott, 1836, ' You supercilious son of a sea-cook.'

sea-coot. A seaman, esp. if of fresh water or scant ability : nautical (— 1887) ; ob. Baumann ; Manchon. Prob. ex preceding, with a pun on (*silly*) *coot.*

sea-crab. A sailor : nautical : ca. 1780–1890. Grose, 1st ed. ; ' Jon Bee,' 1823 ; Baumann. Cf. *scaly fish*, q.v.

sea-galloper. A special correspondent : naval coll. : C. 20 ; ob. *The Army and Navy Gazette*, July 13, 1901, ' These sea-gallopers—to use Lord Spencer's historical designation.'

sea-grocer. A purser : a nautical nickname : from ca. 1860 ; ob. Smyth, 1867.

sea-lawyer. A shark ; esp. a tiger-shark : coll. nickname : from ca. 1810. *Lex. Bal.* (N.B., *sea-attorney*, the ordinary brown shark, is a mere derivative—and S.E.)—2. A grey snapper : id. (— 1876). O.E.D.—3. Ex sense 1 a captious and argumentative, or a scheming, fo'c's'le hand : nautical coll. : 1848, C. C. Clifford (O.E.D.) ; Smyth, 1867. (Cf. *bush-lawyer*, q.v.) Whence *sea-lawyering*, such behaviour : mid-C. 19–20.

Sea-Orphan. H.M.S. *Seraphim* : naval : C. 20. Bowen. By ' Hobson-Jobson '.

sea-pheasant. A bloater or a kipper : nautical : late C. 19–20. Bowen.

sea-pork. The flesh of young whales : id. : id. Ibid.

sea-rover. A herring : mostly London (— 1890). Gen. in *a doorstep and a sea-rover*, a slice of bread and a herring, and *doorsteps and (a) sea-rover*, a herring sandwich, as in Whiteing's *No. 5 John Street*, 1899.

sea-toss. ' A toss overboard into the sea ' (Century Dict.) : coll. : late C. 19–20.

sea-wag. An ocean-going vessel : nautical : late C. 19–20 ; ob.

sea William. A civilian : naval : ca. 1800–50. Marryat. (Ware.)

seagly. See **Sedgley curse.**

seagull. ' An old sailorman retired from the sea ' : nautical : late C. 19–20 ; ob. Bowen. —2. Chicken : Royal Naval College, Dartmouth : C. 20. Ibid.

seal. A preacher's convert : ecclesiastical : ca. 1850–80. Conybeare, 1853. Either ex *set one's seal to* or ex *under (one's) seal.* Cf. *own*, q.v.

seal, v. To impregnate (a woman) : C. 19–20 ; ob. Cf. *sew up.*

sealer. ' One that gives Bonds and Judgments for Goods and Money,' B.E. : c. : late C. 17–early 19. Shadwell, Grose. Also known as *squeeze-wax.*

seals. Testicles : C. 19–20 ; ob. Because they seal a sexual bargain.

seam. See **white seam.**

seam-squirrel. A louse : military : from 1914. F. & Gibbons. Body-lice make for the seams of one's clothes.

seaman if he carries a millstone will have a quail out of it, a. A mid-C. 17–mid. 18 semi-proverbial c.p. alluding to the ingenuity displayed by sailors as regards meat and drink. Ray.

seaman's disgrace. A foul anchor: nautical coll.: late C. 19–20. Bowen.

sear; sere. The female pudend: coll.: late C. 16–17. Partly ex *sear*, the touch-hole of a pistol, and partly ex *light* (or *iickle*) *of the sear* or *sere*, wanton.

*****search.** (Of a pickpocket) to rob (a person): c.: C. 20. David Hume.

search me ! or **you can** (or **may**) **search me !** *I* don't know: c.p.: C. 20 (U.S., anglicised by 1910); slightly ob. by 1935. (So.—*but you won't find it.*)

searcher. A searching question, an embarrassing problem: coll. (— 1923). Manchon.

seaside moths. Bed vermin: middle classes' (— 1909); ob. Ware.

seasoner. A person in the fashion: coll. (— 1923). Manchon.

seat. A rider: sporting coll. (— 1887). Baumann. Ex *have a good seat* (*in the saddle*).

seat of honour, shame, vengeance. The posteriors; jocular coll. (in C. 20 ob.): resp. 1792, Wolcot (adumbrated in Bailey's *Erasmus*, 1725); 1821, Combe, and rare ; 1749, Smollett,—likewise rare. Ex the fact that ' he was commonly accounted the most honourable that was first seated, and that this honour was commonly done to the posteriors ' (Bailey).

seat of magistracy. ' Proctor's authority ', Egan's Grose: Oxford University: ca. 1820–50.

*****seat, hot.** See **hot seat.**

Seats Bill. Redistribution (of Seats) Bill : political coll.: 1884. Baumann.

Sebastianist. A Mr Micawber, one who believes that something good will turn up some day: coll. (late C. 19–20) among the English Colony at Lisbon. Ex the Portuguese. In 1578, King Sebastian was defeated in Morocco and never again heard of: but half Portugal, refusing to credit his death, believed that he would return ánd lead them to victory.

sec. A second: coll.: from ca. 1880. Orig.— ca. 1860 (Ware)—a mere abbr.—2. A secretary: coll. (— 1923). Manchon.

seccetary or **-try.** Incorrect pronunciation of *secretary* : C. 18–20.

second; third. Second mate; third mate: nautical coll.: mid-C. 19–20. Often in address, as in ' Go easy, third ! '

second dickey. The second mate: nautical: late C.·19–20. Bowen.

second fiddle. See **fiddle.**

second greaser. ' Second mate under sail ': nautical: late C. 19–20. Bowen.

second-hand sun. Refracted sunlight: poor peoples' coll. (— 1909). Ware.

second-hand woman. A widow: Army in India: 1859–ca. 1900. Ware.

second-liker. A second (e.g. drink) like—the same as—the first: taverns' : 1884 ; slightly ob. Ware.

second mate's nip. ' A full measure of liquor ': nautical coll. : late C. 19–20. Bowen.

second over the head. Rather worse than the first : *Conway* cadets': late C. 19–20. John Masefield, *The Conway*, 1933.

second peal. See **peal.**

second picture. The ' tableau upon the rising of the curtain to applause, after it has fallen at the end of an act, or a play ': theatrical coll.: 1885. Ware.

second-timer. A prisoner convicted for the second time : coll. : late C. 19–20.

seconds up ! Second helpings available : Canadian Army cooks' c.p. in G.W. (B. & P.)

secret, in the grand. Dead: coll.: from ca. 1780 ; ob. Grose, 1st ed. Cf. *join the great majority* and contrast :

*****secret, let into the.** Swindled, e.g. at horse-racing, sports, games : late C. 17–early 19 : c. >, ca. 1730, s. B.E., Grose. Contrast preceding entry.

sect. Sex: C. 13–20 : S.E. until C. 19, then coll. until ca. 1850 ; then low coll. till C. 20, when sol. unless deliberately humorous. Cf. *persuasion*, q.v.

Sedgley (occ. **Seagly**) **curse.** A semi-proverbial coll. of ca. 1620–1840. Fletcher, ca. 1625, ' A seagly curse light on him, which is, Pedro ' the feind ride through him booted, and spurd, with a Sythe at's back '; Ray ; Defoe ; Scott. Ex a town in Staffordshire ; but I cannot improve on Apperson's ' I know not why '.

see, v.i. To coït : low s. verging on c., for it is a prostitutes' word : C. 19–20 (? ob.). Also *see stars lying on one's back.*—2. Saw (in all persons, both numbers): sol. : C. 19–20. Cf. *seed* and *seen.* —3. To bet (a person) ; call his bluff : cotton-factors' (— 1909). Ware. Ex the v. *see* in the game of *poker*.

see, I. I agree or understand (as comment on an explanation or an argument): coll. : C. 19–20.

see a man or, occ., **a friend**(, **go and**). To have a drink : late C. 19–20 (Lyell), as is *see a man about a dog*, loosely in same sense, properly to visit a woman sexually.

see about it, I'll. A coll. evasion : mid-C. 19–20.

see and (another v.) To take care to (do something): coll.: from ca. 1760 ; slightly ob. Mrs F. Sheridan, ca. 1766, ' David . . . told me he'd see and get me another every jot as pretty,' O.E.D.

see as far into a millstone (or **milestone**) **as** . . . See **millstone, look.**—see **candles.** See **see stars.**

see (a person) **coming.** To impose on ; esp., to charge too much : coll. : late C. 19–20. Gen. in some such phrase as ' He saw you coming,' i.e. saw you were gullible and so took advantage of you. Perhaps ex the Fr. *voir quelqu'un venir*, see one's drift.

see him (**her,** etc.) **damned** or **further** or **hanged** or **to hell** or **the devil first, I'll.** I certainly don't or won't agree to his proposal, etc. : coll. : resp. 1631, Heywood ; mid-C. 19–20 ; 1596, Shakespeare; C. 19–20. (O.E.D.)

see home. See **home, see.**

see London. See **show London.**

see off. To ' tell off ', reprimand, scold severely . from ca. 1912. Ernest Raymond, *The Jesting Army*, 1930. Cf. *see home*, q.v. at **home, see.**

see one's aunt. To defecate : euphemistic s. > coll. : mid-C. 19–20 ; ob.

see-otches. See **seeo.**

see stars or **spots** or **candles.** To be dazed : coll. : resp. late C. 19–20 (*The Century Dict.*, 1891), mid-C. 19–20, and mid-C. 18–mid-19. Smollett, 1749, ' He . . . made me see more candles than ever burnt in Solomon's temple '; Galsworthy, *The White Monkey*, 1924, ' " *Per ardua ad astra*," " Through hard knocks we shall see stars." '

see stars lying on one's back. See **see,** 1.

see the breeze. To enjoy the fresh air (on a heath): Cockneys': ca. 1877–1900. Ware. Cf. *taste the sun*, q.v.

see the devil. To become drunk : mid-C. 19–20 ; ob.

see the king. To be very experienced, knowing, alert : ca. 1870–90. H., 5th ed. An English modification of the orig. U.S. *to have seen the elephant* (see **elephant**).

see things. To experience hallucinations : coll. : late (? mid) C. 19–20.

see through. To ' get through ' (a meal) : coll. : 1863 (O.E.D.) ; slightly ob.

seed, see'd. Saw : (dial. and) sol. : C. 18–20. Foote, 1752 (O.E.D.)—2. Seen : id., id. Pegge, *Anecdotes of the English Language,* ' The common people of London . . . will say, for instance,—" I see'd him yesterday " ; and " he was see'd again to-day." ' (O.E.D.)—3. seed in lawn tennis is S.E.

seed, run to. See **run to seed**.

seed-plot. The female pudend : C. 19–20 (ob.) : coll. verging on S.E.

seedy. Of a ' shady ' character : low : ca. 1780–1910. G. Parker, ' A queer procession of seedy brims and kids ' ; Baumann. Ex *seedy,* shabby. (In other senses—shabby, almost penniless, in poor health—perhaps orig. coll. ; but the O.E.D. does not think so.)

seedy(-boy). A Negro : Anglo-Indian coll. : mid-C. 19–20. Also *sidi(-boy).* Ironically ex Urdu *sidi,* my lord.

seek others and lose oneself. To play the fool : coll. : late C. 16–17. Florio.

Seeley's pigs. Pig iron, orig. and properly in Government dockyards : nautical : ca. 1870–1910. H., 5th ed. Ex Mr Seeley, the M.P. for Lincoln, who revealed that some of the yards were half-paved with iron pigs : cf. the use in the G.W., of boxes of ammunition and bully-beef as trench-flooring,—for which, however, there was often justification.

seem to, cannot or **could not.** See **cannot seem to**.

seems to me. Apparently : coll. : 1888, ' John Strange Winter,' ' Seems to me women get like dogs—they get their lessons pretty well fixed in their minds after a time,' O.E.D.

seen dead with, (he, I, etc.) **would not be. I** detest (properly a person, loosely a thing) ; it, he, etc., is disgusting : coll. : late C. 19–20. Lyell.

seen the elephant. See **elephant**. (Ware's sense was not adopted.)

seen. Saw (all persons, both numbers) : sol. : late C. 18–20. Cf. *see* (2), *seed.*

seeo (occ. **see-o**). Shoes : back s. (– 1859). H., 1st ed. (Instead of *seohs.*) Baumann records the form *see-otches.*

*seer. An eye (gen. *the seer*) : c. (– 1785) > low s. ; very ob. Grose, 1st ed. Cf. :

sees. The eyes : c. or low s. : from ca. 1810. *Lex. Bal.* ; Moore, 1819, ' To close up their eyes—alias, to sew up their sees,' in a boxing context. Cf. *seer* and *daylights.*

seething. (In surgery) a seton : low coll. (latterly, sol.) : C. 19–20. O.E.D.

segnotic. Incorrect for *stegnotic* (ca. 1670–1750), as *seisant* (C. 17) is for *sejant.* O.E.D.

seldom reaches destination. A c.p. parallel with *soon run dry,* q.v. (B. & P.)

Selborne's Light Horse. Short-service ratings under Lord Selborne's scheme : naval : G.W. Bowen. Ex discipline of certain Light Horse units in the Boer War.

self, be. (E.g. *be himself.*) To be in one's normal health or state of mind : coll. : 1849,

Macaulay ; *The Daily News,* May 23, 1883, on a cricket match, ' Mr Grace was all himself.' Also, late C. 19–20 (very rarely of things), *to feel like* (e.g. *one-)self.* Cf. *be one's own man* or *woman* : see **own**.—2. Hence, of things, be in its usual place : mid-C. 19–20.—3. **self and company** (or **wife,** etc., etc.) is jocular coll., excusable only as a jocularity : late C. 19–20. O.E.D. ; Fowler.

sell. A successful deception, hoax or swindle (the latter rare in C. 20) : 1850, Smedley. Ex the v.—2. Hence, a planned hoax, deception, swindle : from ca. 1860.—3. Ex sense 1,—a (great) disappointment : 1860, H., 2nd ed. ; 1874, Mrs H. Wood, ' It's an awful sell . . . no hunting, and no shooting, and no nothing.'

sell, v. To take in, deceive ; impose on, trick, swindle (these more serious senses being somewhat rare in C. 20) : C. 17–20. Jonson, 1607, *Volpone,* ' When bold, each tempts the other again, and all are sold ' ; Smedley ; ' Rolf Boldrewood '. Prob. ex *sell,* to betray (a person, cause, party, or country). —2. See **sold out** and **sold up**.

sell (a person) **a pup.** See **pup, sell a**.

*sell (a person) **blind.** To deceive or swindle utterly : c. (– 1887). Baumann.

sell-out. A contest for which all the seats are sold : sporting coll. : from ca. 1930. G. Simpson, in *The Daily Mail,* Dec. 1, 1934, ' The interest in McAvoy's fight with Kid Tunero . . . is so great that . . . the match is a sure sell-out.'

sell the pass. To give away an advantage to one's opponent(s) : coll. : C. 20. Ex mountain warfare.

seller ; sellinger. A selling race (one in which the winner must be auctioned) : sporting coll. : from ca. 1921. O.E.D. (Sup.)

selopas. Apples : back s. (– 1859). H., 1st ed. (A few back s. terms are only in the pl. : cf. *pinurt pots, seeo, spinsrap, starps, stoob,* qq.v.)

s'elp (loosely, **selp**). So help, esp. in *s'elp me God* : C. 14–20 : S.E. until C. 19, then coll. ; in C. 20, almost a sol. Kipling, 1888, ' S'elp me, I believe 'e's dead,' O.E.D. Cf. *swelp* and :

s'elp me Bob (bob) ! So help me God ! : low coll. : from ca. 1840. Barham ; J. Payn ; ' Pomes ' Marshall. Cf. preceding entry and *s'elp my greens.*

s'elp me never ! ' May God never help me if I lie now ' (Ware) : low (– 1909). Ware.

s'elp my greens ! So help me God ! : low coll. : ca. 1850–1910. Mayhew. Obviously *greens* (q.v., however) jocularly varies *Bob,* which itself euphemises or perverts *God.* See preceding three entries and **swelp** and **swop my Bob** !

semi-bejan. See **bejan**.

semi-quotes. Single (instead of double) quotation-marks : coll. : world of books, esp. and orig. printing : late C. 19–20. See **quotes**.

seminary. The female pudend : mid-C. 19–20 ; ob. Punning *seminary,* a school, college, etc., and *semen = liquor seminale.*

semolella. Incorrect for *semoletta,* a variety of semolina : mid-C. 19–20. O.E.D.

semper. A Winchester term explained by Mansfield (1866) in reference to ca. 1840 as ' A very common prefix ; *e.g.* a boy was said to be semper continent, tardy . . . if he was often at Sick House, or late for Chapel . . . An official who was always at the College meetings went by the name of Semper Testis.' Ex L. *semper,* always. (The s., coll., and j. at Winchester, even more than at Westminster, abound in Latinisms : both schools have always been rightly famous for the excellence of the teaching given in the Ancient Classics). See also 'Winchester College slang ', § 6.

senal pervitude. Penal servitude : cheap urban witticism : ca. 1900–14. Ware. In addition to the switch-over of initial letters, there is a glancing pun on *senile*.

send. See Coventry, daylight, flea in (one's) ear, and the next ten entries.

send for Gulliver! A Society c.p. (1887–ca. 95) on 'some affair not worth discussion. From a cascadescent incident ' in Part I of *Gulliver's Travels* (Ware).

send for Mary Ann! An occ. variant of *san-fairyann*, q.v. (F. & Gibbons.)

send (a person) for yard-wide pack-thread. To despatch on a fool's errand : coll. : ca. 1800–60. Apperson.

send in. To drive in : ca. 1810–60. *Lex. Bal.*, 'Hand down the jemmy and send it in ; apply the crow to the door, and drive it in.'

send it down, David! See David !, send it down.

send me!; or simply **send!** An 'exclamation of surprise, amusement, annoyance, etc.' : Bootham School : C. 20. Anon., *Dict. of Bootham Slang*, 1925. Perhaps abbr. *send me to blazes!*

send-off. A God-speed : coll. : orig. (1872), U.S. ; anglicised ca. 1875.—2. Hence, a start in life, in business, etc. : 1894, A. Morrison, 'A good send-off in the matter of clothes.'—3. Occ. as adj. : 1876, Besant & Rice, 'A beautiful send-off notice.'

send round. C. 20. coll. *a*, v.t. to send to some-one near-by ; *b*, v.i. to send a message to a neigh-bour. (O.E.D.)

send round the hat. See hat, send round the.

send up. To commit to prison : orig. U.S. (1852) ; anglicised by 1887, when Baumann re-corded it without comment on its American origin. *The Westminster Gazette*, April 30, 1897, 'Two prisoners . . . occupied the prison-van . . . Burns was being " sent up " for wife-beating, and Tanna-hill for theft,' O.E.D. : s. >, ca. 1910, coll. >, ca. 1920, S.E.—2. (Gen. in passive.) *En masse* to scoff at and mock : upper- and middle-class coll. (— 1931). Lyell, '*He was sent up* unmercifully by half the room.' Ex the Public School j., to send (a boy) to the headmaster for punishment.

sender. A severe blow : from ca. 1890 ; ob, Perhaps ex *send spinning*.

seneschaunce. Incorrect for *seneschalsy*, a sene-schal's territory (C. 16) ; *senical* for *sinical* (C. 17–18). O.E.D.

senior. See junior.

Senior, the. The United Service Club in Lon-don : naval and military : C. 20. Bowen.

sensation. Half a glass of sherry : Australian : ca. 1859–1890. (O.E.D.) Prob. ex sense 3, though this is recorded later.—2. In England, a quartern of gin : 1859, H., 1st ed. ; † by 1920.—3. A (very) small quantity, esp. of liquor, occ. of food, rather rarely of other things : mid-C. 19–20 : coll. Lit., just so much as can be perceived by the senses ; cf. the French *soupçon*.

[**sensational**, adopted from U.S.A. ca. 1870, is, in its exhaustion by journalists and crude authors, on the border-line between S.E. *cliché* and s. Ware.]

sense, it stands to. It stands to reason, it's only sensible : coll. : 1859, George Eliot (O.E.D.). Ex † *it is to (good) sense on it stands to reason.*

sensual ; -ity. ' Obstinately self-willed ' ' self-willed obstinacy ' : catachrestic : ca. 1520–90. O.E.D., which also notes *sententiary* wrongly used by Lytton for a sententious discourse.

sent. Sent to prison : lower classes' coll. : late C. 19–20. *The People*, March 20, 1898. (Ware.)

sent ashore. Marooned : nautical coll. : late C. 19–20. Bowen.—2. Dismissed from the service : naval : C. 20. Ibid.

sent for, be. To be done for ; to be dead (*has been sent for*) or dying, doomed to die (*is sent for*) : C. 20, esp. in the Army.

sent to the skies. Killed, murdered : lower-middle class's (— 1909) ; † by 1920, the G.W. intervening. Ware.

sent up, be. See send up, 2.—**sententiary.** See sensual.

Sentimental Club, the. The Athenæum : liter-ary : ca. 1890–1915. Is this prompted by a jealousy that imputes to the members a ' mushy ' anecdotage ?

sentimental hairpin. ' An affected, insignificant girl ' : Society : ca. 1880–1900. Ware.

sentimental journey, arrive at the end of the. To coït with a woman : from ca. 1870 ; very ob. F. & H. says ' common ' (i.e. used by the lower classes) : should not this be read as ' cultured ' ? Ex the conclusion of Sterne's *Sentimental Journey*, ' I put out my hand and caught hold of the *fille-de-chambre's* ——. FINIS.' The unworldly postulate ' hand ' ; the worldly, ' c*** ' : to those who know their Sterne, *verb. sap.*

sentiments!, them's my. That's what I think about it : jocular c.p. : C. 20. (Galsworthy, *Swan Song*, 1928.)

sentinel. A candle used at a wake . Anglo-Irish coll. : mid-C. 19–20. Punningly : because it keeps watch.

sentry, on. Drunk : rather low : ca. 1885–1914. Ex *on sentry-go* : but why ? Perhaps home-service sentries are tempted to take a tot too many in the laudable desire to keep out the cold on night-duty.

sentry-box, Chelsea Hospital to a. See Chelsea Hospital.

*separate ; but extremely rare in the singular. A period of separate confinement in prison, esp. during the first year of a sentence : from ca. 1860 : prison c. >, ca. 1890, low s. >, ca. 1920, coll. *The Cornhill Magazine*, 1862, vol. vi, p. 640 ; Anon., *Five Years' Penal Servitude*, 1877. Abbr. *separate confinement*.

separate between. Catachrestic for *distinguish between* or, occ., *separate* (one thing) *from* (another) : ? before C. 20. E.g. Freeman Wills Crofts, *Mystery in the Channel*, 1931, ' He had . . . to separate between what was essential and what was acci-dental.'

separate (or, occ., private) peace, I'll make a or I think I'll make a. A wistfully jocular soldiers' c.p. of 1917–18. B & P.

*separates. The period (often three months) served in a local prison by one condemned to penal servitude before he begins that servitude : c. (— 1932). ' Stuart Wood ', *Shades of the Prison House.* Ex *separate*, q.v.

Sepoy. Any Indian foot-soldier, esp. an infantry-man : Regular Army coll. : late C. 19–20. B. & P.

septa- is incorrect for *septua-* in *septuagenary*, etc. ; *septual*, for *septal*. O.E.D.

septic. Sceptic : jocular : C. 20. (The author first heard it in 1912.)—2. Unpleasant ; objectionable : from ca. 1930. (H. A. Vachell, *Moonhills.* 1934.) Suggested by *poisonous*, q.v.

sepulchre. A large, flat cravat : London middle classes : ca. 1870–85. Ware. Ex the ' sins ' it covered.

seraglietto. 'A lowly, sorry Bawdy-house, a meer Dog-hole,' B.E. : coll. : late C. 17–18. A diminutive of :

seraglio. A brothel : coll. : late C. 17–early 19. B.E., Grose. Ex *seraglio*, a harem, though *seraglio* itself was orig. incorrect when used for *serai*, a Turkish palace. (The term > gen. ca. 1750 with Mrs Goadby, ' the great Goadby ', who kept an excellent house in Berwick Street, Soho : Beresford Chancellor, *Pleasure Haunts of London*.)

serang. See **head serang.**—**sere.** See **sear.**— **serene, -eno.** See **all serene, -eno.**

serg(e). See **sarga, sarge.**—2. A tunic : Regular Army : C. 20. B. & P.

sergeant. See **come.**—2. A commander : naval : C. 20. Ex ' the similarity of his three gold stripes to a Marine sergeant's chevron ' (Bowen). Contrast *major*.—3. **sergeant !, kiss me.** (Occ. **kiss me, corporal !,** if a corporal is deputising for a sergeant.) A military c.p. of C. 20. Meant to annoy and gen. uttered during the sergeant's final rounds of barracks, tents, etc. Either derisive of nursemaids' invitations or, less prob., reminiscent of Nelson's *kiss me, Hardy*.

Sergeant Kite or **Snap.** A recruiting sergeant : allusive coll. : from ca. 1850. H., 3rd ed. : ob. by 1900 ; † by 1920.

sergeant-major. A fat loin of mutton: butchers': late C. 19–20. Ex the usual plumpness of sergeant-majors, with whom the cooks and the quarter-master's staff know that it pays to stand well.—2. ' A large piece of mutton in the rib part ' : butchers' (— 1889). Barrère & Leland, ' From the white stripes like sergeant's stripes.'—3. A zebra : South African : C. 20. Pettman, ' On account of its very distinct stripes.'—4. In the game of crown and anchor, the crown : military : C. 20. Often *the* (*good*) *old sergeant-major*. F. & Gibbons ; B. & P.— 5. In c., dating from ca. 1840 but now ob. : ' a large cold-chisel . . . for cutting through metal plates ', p. 422 of ' *No. 747* ', *The Autobiography of a Gipsy*, 1891,—the reference valid for 1845.—6. (Also **sergeant-major's.**) Tea ; orig., strong tea esp. if good, then tea drunk between meals : military : from ca. 1910. B. & P. (The S.M. could get tea almost whenever he desired it.)

sergeant-major's brandy and soda. A gold-laced stable jacket : military : ca. 1885–1914. Barrère & Leland.

sergeant-major's tea. Tea with sugar and milk ; esp. tea laced with rum : military : from 1915. F. & Gibbons. Ex *sergeant-major*, 6.

sergeant-major's wash-cat. A new kit : cavalry : ca. 1885–1910. Barrère & Leland.—2. A troop's store-man : ca. 1885–1914. Ibid. ? because he supplied a basin.

Sergeant Snap. See **Sergeant Kite.**

Seringy. The Blackwall frigate *Seringapatam* : naval : mid-C. 19. Bowen.

serpent, stung by a. Got with child : coll. : C. 19–20 ; ob.

serpent by the tail, hold a. To act foolishly: coll. : C. 19–20 ; ob. Ray, 1813.

Serpentiners. Those who like (?) to bathe in the Serpentine when it is icy : from ca. 1925.

serpently. (Only in dialogue.) Certainly : jocu-

lar : ca. 1930–35. Dorothy Sayers, *Murder Must Advertise*, 1933.

serræform. Rare error for *serriform*, C. 19. O.E.D.

serried. Serrated : catachresis : C. 19. Ibid.

serve. A service in lawn tennis : coll. : C. 20. Ex the v.

serve, v. To treat in a specified—and, gen., unpleasant or inequitable—manner : C. 13–20 : S.E. until 1850, then—except in formal contexts—coll. (O.E.D.)—2. To rob, thus ' I served him for his thimble,' I robbed him of his watch : c. : from ca. 1810 ; ob. Vaux.—3. To convict and sentence : c. : from ca. 1810 ; ob.—4. To injure, wound, treat roughly : c. : ca. 1810–90. Vaux. Cf. *serve out and out* and *serve out*.—5. To serve a term of imprisonment : criminals' coll. (rather than c.) : late C. 19–20. Ware.—6. ' To impose a punishment ' : Bootham School coll. : late C. 19–20. Anon., *Dict. of Bootham Slang*. Cf *service*.

serve (a person) **glad.** See **glad, serve.**

serve-out. An issue (of, e.g. clothes) : naval coll. : C. 20. Cf. *fit to bust a double ration serve-out of navy-serge*.

serve out, v. To take revenge on, to punish ; retaliate on (a person) *for* . . . : from ca. 1815 : boxing s. >, ca. 1830, gen. coll. *The Sporting Magazine*, 1817, ' The butcher was so completely served out, that he resigned all pretentions to victory,' O.E.D. By ' an ironic application of nautical *serve out* (*grog*, etc.) ', W.—2. To smash (a fence) : hunting s. : 1862 (O.E.D.).

***serve out and out.** To kill : c. of ca 1810–90. Vaux. Cf. *serve out*.

serve out slops. To administer punishment at the gangway : naval : ca. 1830–90. Bowen. Cf. *serve out*, 1, q.v.

serve right. Coll. only in (*and*) *serve* (e.g. *you*) *right !*, and *serves* (e.g. *you*) *right !*, which indicate satisfaction that someone has got his deserts : from ca. 1830. Dickens, 1837, ' Workhouse funeral— serve him right,' O.E.D.

serve the poor with a thump on the back with a stone. To be a miser : semi-proverbial coll. : ca. 1670–1750 ; Ray.

serves you right ! See **serve right.**

Servia(n). An incorrect form, very gen. until 1914, of *Serbia(n)* : C. 19–20. Ex native *Serb*. ' Perhaps due to some vague association between *Slavs* and *serfs*,' W.

service. An imposition : Bootham School : late C. 19–20 ; ' practically obsolete ', says the anon. *Dict. of Bootham Slang*, 1925.

service about, sling one's. See **sling one's service about.**—**service-book, to have eaten one's.** See **teethward.**

***service lay.** The ' dodge ' by which one hires oneself out as a servant and then robs the house : c. : C. 18. C. Hitchin, *The Regulator*, 1718.

-ses, for **-s,** the sign of the pl., is frequent in illiterate speech : C. 19 (? earlier)–20. Mayhew, 1861, ' You wants to know if them rowses is common.'

sessions. To commit (one) to the sessions for trial : 1857, Mayhew. O.E.D.

sessions ! Well, I'm blowed ! : late C. 19–20 ; ob. Ex dial. *sessions*, a fuss, disturbance, argument, difficulty, task (E.D.D.).

set. Abbr. *dead set* (see **set, dead**) : 1829, *The Examiner* (O.E.D.) : s. >, ca. 1860, coll. >, ca. 1900, S.E.

set, v. To sit, be seated : C. 13–20 : S.E. until C. 19, then low coll. ; in C. 20, sol. except in dial.— 2. To sit, lie, in fig. senses : C. 15–20 : S.E. until C. 19, then low coll. ; in C. 20 (except in dial.), sol. Anon., 1803, ' A disappointment that ought not to set very heavily on her mind,' O.E.D.—3. V.t., to fix on as prey or victim ; to watch with a view to robbing ; make a set at : from ca. 1670 : perhaps orig. c., as also in late C. 19–20 Australian. Gay, in *The Beggar's Opera*, 1727, ' There will be deep play to-night at Marybone, . . . I'll give you the hint who is worth setting.' O.E.D.—4. ' To attack ; to regard with disfavour,' C. J. Dennis : low Australian (— 1916). Cf. *set, dead,* 3, q.v., and *set, have.*

set, adj. ; gen. **all set.** Ready and willing ; thoroughly prepared : coll. : C. 20 : mostly Australian. Prob. ex S.E. sense, carefully arranged in advance.—2. Cf. the late C. 17–18 *all set* applied to ' desperate fellows, ready for any kind of mischief ' (Duncombe).—3. See **set, have.**

*****set, dead.** Esp. in *make a dead set at.* ' *Dead Set,* a Term used by Thief-catchers when they have a Certainty of seizing some of their Clients,' *A New Canting Dict.,* 1725 : † by 1850.—2. Also, ca. 1780–1860, ' a concerted scheme to defraud a person by gaming ', Grose, 1st ed. : like sense 1, it is c.— 3. The extant senses—a determined onslaught, an incessant attempt, and (in sport) an abrupt stop—date from ca. 1820, derive from those two c. senses, and are gen. considered S.E. : prob., however, they were orig. coll.

set, have (a person). ' To have [him] marked down for punishment or revenge,' C. J. Dennis : low (esp. in Australia) : C. 20. Cf. *set,* v., 4, and *set, dead,* qq.v.—2. To get the better of ; take at a disadvantage : low : C. 20. F. & Gibbons.

set about. To attack, set upon : coll. : 1879, Horsley, ' He set about me with a strap till he was tired,' O.E.D.

set back. To cost (a person) so much : U.S., anglicised by 1932, via ' the talkies '. (O.E.D. Sup.)

set-down. A sit-down meal : tramps' c. (— 1932). F. Jennings, *Tramping with Tramps.*

set (something) **in a crack.** To settle (a matter) quickly ; e.g. *set a bet in a crack,* to wager smartly at two-up ; *be set in a crack,* (of persons) to be comfortably placed (lit. or fig.), to be very pleased with circumstances : New Zealanders' : from the 1890's. Perhaps ex the idea of doing a thing as sharply as the crack of a whip.

set jewels ; gen. as vbl.n., **setting jewels.** To purloin the best parts of a little-known (esp. if clever) book for incorporation in a new work by another author : literary coll. : 1873, when originated by Charles Reade *à propos* of a flagrant instance published at Christmas, 1872 ; ob. H., 5th ed. ; Baumann.

set-me-up, often preceded by **young.** One who sets himself up to be somebody : often pejoratively : late C. 19–20. Ian Hay, *David and Destiny,* 1934.

set-out. A set or display of china, plate, etc. : coll. : 1806, J. Beresford.—2. (Of food) a ' spread ' : coll. : 1809, Malkin.—3. A ' turn-out ', i.e. a carriage ' and all ' : a mainly sporting coll. : from ca. 1810.—4. A person's costume or manner of dressing (cf. *rig-out,* q.v.) ; an outfit, equipment : coll. : from ca. 1830.—5. A public show or performance ; ' an entertainment for a number of people ' ; a party : coll. : 1818, Lady Morgan.—6. Hence, a company or a set of people : from ca. 1850 : coll.

(—As a beginning (1821), *set-out* is rather S.E. than coll.) O.E.D.—7. A to-do or fuss : (low) coll. late C. 19–20. D. Sayers, *Murder Must Advertise,* 1933, ' Coo ! that was a set-out, that was.'

set the hare's head to the goose giblets. To balance matters, to give as good as one gets : coll. : C. 17–early 18. Dekker & Webster.

set the swede down. To have a (short) sleep : military : from ca. 1910. F. & Gibbons. Ex the resemblance of a large Swede turnip to a man's head. Cf. *couch a hogshead.*

set-up. Bearing, carriage, port : coll. (slightly ob.) : 1890, T. C. Crawford.

set up, v. To sit up late : late C. 17–20 : S.E. till C. 20, then coll. ; in C. 20,—except in dial.— it is sol. Cf. *set,* v., 1.

set-up, adj. Conceited : coll. and dial. : mid-C. 19–20.

set up for, be. To be well supplied with : coll. : 1863, Mrs Henry Wood, ' I'm set up for cotton gownds,' O.E.D. Ex S.E. *set up,* to establish or to equip in business, etc.

setaceous. Incorrect for *cetaceous,* C. 17–18 ; *setateous,* for *setaceous,* C. 19. O.E.D.

sets-off, -out, -to. Incorrect for *set-offs, -outs, -tos,* nn. : C. 19–20. Even *-off's, -out's, -to's* are catachrestic.

setta ; occ. **setter.** Seven ; sevenpence : Parlyaree (— 1859). H., 1st ed. Ex It. *sette.*

*****setter.** See **setta.**—2. An enticer to liquor or gambling ; a confederate of swindlers or sharpers : c. : late C. 16–17. Greene, 1592 ; ob. Ex the dog.—3. Hence, a person used by criminals to watch intended victims : c. : from ca. 1640 ; ob. *Memoirs of John Hall.* (O.E.D.)—4. Hence, ' a Sergeant's Yeoman, or Bailiff's Follower, or Second, and an Excise-Officer to prevent the Brewers defrauding the King', B.E. : c. of late C. 17–early 19. Grose, 1st ed. Also *setting-dog* (B.E.).—5. A police spy ; an informer to the police : from ca. 1630 : S.E. until ca. 1850, then c. and low s. Barrère & Leland. (O.E.D.)—6. A runner-up of prices : late C. 17–20 (ob.) : mostly among auctioneers.—7. Only in combination, as in ' a long four setter ' (Sir Gordon Lowe, in *Lowe's Lawn Tennis Annual,* 1935), i.e. a four-set match : lawn tennis coll : from 1933.

setter, clock-. One who, to shorten a spell of duty, tampers with the clock : nautical coll. : mid-C. 19–20 ; slightly ob.—2. Hence, a ' sea-lawyer ' : late C. 19–20 (ob.) : nautical.

*****setting-dog.** See **setter,** 4.—**setting jewels.** See **set jewels.**

settle. To stun, finish, knock down : C. 17–20 : S.E. until ca. 1750, then coll. Grose, 1st ed. ; Dickens ; Kipling. (O.E.D.)—2. To give (a person) a life-sentence : c. : mid-C. 19–20. Ca. 1850–70, it also = to transport as a convict, as in ' Ducange Anglicus ' and H., 1st ed. Cf. *winded-settled,* q.v.

settle (a person's) hash. See **hash, settle one's.**

settlement-in-tail. An act of generation : legal : C. 19–20 ; ob. (Pun.)

settler. A parting drink : mid-C. 18–20 ; ob. M. Bishop, 1744 (O.E.D.). Because it is supposed to ' stabilise ' the stomach.—2. A crushing remark : coll. : from ca. 1815.—3. A knock-down blow : coll. : 1819, Moore, ' He tipp'd him a settler.'— 4. Hence, any ' finisher ' whatsoever : from ca. 1820 : coll.

Settler's Bible, the. *The Grahamstown Journal* :

South Africans' from ca. 1860 ; ob. Pettman. Cf. *saint*, 4, and *City of the Saints*, qq.v.

seven, all in the. To be expected ; (as) a matter of course : military coll. : C. 20. F. & Gibbons, ' In allusion to the soldier's term of service [seven years] with the Colours.'

seven, be more than. To be wide-awake ; knowing : coll. : from ca. 1875 ; slightly ob. A music-hall song of ca. 1876 was entitled *You're More Than Seven* ; Gissing, 1898. Occ. *more than twelve*.

Seven and Sixpennies, the. The 76th Foot (the 2nd Battalion Duke of Wellington's) : military : C. 19–20. F. & Gibbons, ' From the figures of the number, and . . . seven and sixpence, a lieutenant's pay per diem.'

seven bells out of a man, knock. To knock him out ; give him a thrashing : nautical : late C. 19–20. Bowen.

Seven Dials raker. A harlot ' who never smiles out of the Dials ' ; London costers' (– 1909) ; very ob. Ware.

*****seven(-)pennorth ; sevenpence.** Seven years' penal transportation : c. of ca. 1820–70. Egan (*sevenpence*) ; Bee and H. (1st ed.) (*seven pennorth*). —2. **(seven-penn(y)worth.)** Seven days' confinement to barracks : military : C. 20. F. & Gibbons.

seven-sided animal. (U.S. variant, C. 19, *s.-s. son of a bitch*.) ' A one-eyed man or woman, each having a right side and a left side, a foreside and a backside, an outside, an inside, and a blind side,' Grose, 2nd ed. : low jocular, also Somersetshire dial. : ca. 1785–1890. H., 5th ed.

seven-times-seven man. A ' hypocritical religionist ' : proletarian-satirical (– 1909) ; ob. Ware. Perhaps *seven-times-seven* is meant to rhyme *heaven*.

seven ways for Sunday, looking. See **looking seven ways** . . .

seven years are the worst, the first ; often prefaced with **cheer up !** A military c.p. of late 1915–18. B. & P., ' Usually either Job's comfort to a grouser or a whimsical encouragement to oneself.'

sevendible. Very ' severe, strong, or sound ' : Northern Ireland : mid-C. 19–20. ' Derived from sevendouble—that is, sevenfold—and . . . applied to linen cloth, a heavy beating, a harsh reprimand, &c.,' H., 3rd ed. Coll. rather than s., as in the adv. *sevendibly* : same period (E.D.D.).

sevener. A criminal sentenced to seven years : coll. : from the 1890's.

*****sevenpence.** See **seven(-)pennorth.**

several is occ. used very loosely as in the following excerpt from an academic foreword of 1929 : ' We are also indebted to Professor [——] for reading through our manuscript and making several helpful suggestions, most of which we have adopted.' Admittedly common in dial., but elsewhere it is catachrestic.

severe. Excellent ; very large or strong or hard to beat : orig. (1834) U.S. (esp. Kentucky), anglicised ca. 1850. De Quincey in 1847 refers to it as ' Jonathan's phrase.' O.E.D.

severe dig or **prod.** A reprimand from a senior (officer) : military coll. : from 1915. B. & P.

severely. Greatly, excessively : coll. : mid-C. 19–20. Whyte-Melville. Ex *severe*, q.v.

Seville, learn manners in. To learn respectable though somewhat childish manners : coll. (– 1923). Manchon. By a pun on *civil*.

sewed in his blanket. Dead and buried : naval and military : C. 20. F. & Gibbons.

sew up. To impregnate (a woman) : coll. C. 19–20 ; ob.—2. See **sewed up**, 1–8.

sew up a person's stocking. To silence, confute : coll. : 1859, C. Reade ; ob.

sewed(-)up ; occ. **sewn up.** Pregnant : coll. (not upper nor middle class) : C. 19–20 ; slightly ob.— 2. Exhausted : from ca. 1825 (orig. of horses ; not till 1837 of persons) : as in Dickens's *Pickwick* ; Smedley, 1850, ' I thought she'd have sewn me up at one time—the pace was terrific ' : slightly ob.— 3. Cheated, swindled : 1838, Haliburton (O.E.D.). —4. At a loss, nonplussed, brought to a standstill : 1855, Smedley ; 1884, Clark Russell ; slightly ob. —5. Severely punished ; esp. with ' bunged-up ' eyes : boxing : from ca. 1865 ; ob.—6. (Ex senses 2, 7.) Sick : late C. 19–20 ; slightly ob.— 7. Drunk : 1829, Buckstone, ' This liquid . . . will sew him up ' ; ob.—8. Grounded : nautical coll. : mid-C. 19–20. Also *sued up*.

sewer. The Metropolitan and Metropolitan District Railways : late C. 19–early 20 : London.

sewer, common. An indiscriminate tippler : coll. bordering on S.E. : C. 19–20.—2. The throat : mid-C. 19–20 ; ob. Cf. *red lane*, q.v.

sewers. East London Railway shares : Stock Exchange : ca. 1895–1910. Cf. **sewer.**

sewn up. A variant of *sewed up* (q.v.), esp. in senses 4, 6, 7.

sexa. Incorrect for *sex(i)*- in a few scientific terms : late C. 19–20. O.E.D.

Sexton Blake. The provost sergeant : military : 1915 ; ob. F. & Gibbons. Ex a detective of fiction popular early in the century.

sexy. A sexual offender, esp. against children : police coll. : from ca. 1910.

sey ; occ. **se.** Variants of *say*, q.v. : mid-C. 19– 20 ; *se* † by 1920.

sez you ! ; occ. **says you !** A derisive c.p. : orig. U.S., anglicised ca. 1930. John Brophy, *English Prose*, 1932. See also **says.**

'sflesh !, 'sfoot !, 'sgad ! Coll. euphemisms for *God's flesh !, foot !*, and *Egad !* : C. 18, C. 17, C. 18. (O.E.D.)

[**sh** for **ts**, as in *thash* for *that's*, is one of the commonest devices for representing the blurred speech of drunk persons. Truncations are common (cf. *ri* for *right*, as in ' All ri, ol' man '), as is the omission of a syllable in trisyllabics or longer words, and of two syllables in long words. Cf. the thickening effect of a cold in the head.]

shab. A low fellow : 1637, Bastwick ; 1735, Dyche & Pardon, ' *Shab*, a mean, sorry, pitiful Fellow, one that is guilty of low Tricks, &c ' ; 1851, Borrow. Ex *shab*, a sore. Cf. *scab*, n., 1, q.v.

shab, v.i. To play low or mean tricks : mid-C. 18–19 ; extant in dial. Johnson. Ex *shab*, n.— 2. V.t., to rob ; perhaps rather, to cheat or to deceive meanly : coll. : ca. 1780–1800. W. Hutton, 1787. O.E.D.—3. V.i., to run away : tramps' and Gypsies' c. : C. 19–20. Smart & Crofton. Cf. much older S.E. *shab off*, to sneak away.

shab-rag. Shabby, damaged, very worn : from ca. 1760 : s. till mid-C. 19, then dial. T. Bridges (O.E.D.). Ex *shab*, n. The n., C. 19–20, is solely dial. Cf. :

shab(a)roon ; also **shabbaroon** (C. 18–19), **shabberoon** (C. 17–18). A ragamuffin ; a mean, shabby fellow ; an otherwise disreputable or a mean-spirited person : late C. 17–mid-19. B.E. ; Ned Ward ; Halliwell. Ex *shab*, n., on *picaroon* (O.E.D.).

shabby, cut up. See **cut up rough.**

Shabby Woman, the. The statue of Minerva at the portal of the Athenæum : literary : ca. 1860–1910. Ex *shabby*, stingy, ' for since the Athenæum Club was established, no member has ever afforded the simplest rites of hospitality to a friend ', H., 3rd ed. (All that has been changed !)

shabroon. See **shab(a)roon.**

shabster, listed by F. & H. as a variant of *shab*, n., is not in the O.E.D., nor is it supported by quotation in F. & H., nor have I seen it elsewhere. Prob. genuine, but rare and of ca. 1850–1905.

shack. A misdirected or a returned letter : Post Office : late C. 19–early 20. Perhaps ex *shack*, ' grain fallen from the ear, and available for the feeding of pigs, poultry, etc.' (O.E.D.), or ex dial. *shack*, a vagabond, a worthless fellow. F. & H.

shack-per-swaw. Everyone for himself : London's East End and gen. London sporting (— 1864) : † by 1930. H., 3rd ed. A corruption of Fr. *chacun pour soi.*

shack-stoner ; occ. **schack-s.** A sixpence : low s., perhaps c. : ca. 1890–1910. P. H. Emerson, *Signor Lippi*, 1893. ? ex *six-stoner.*

*****shackle-up.** A meal of stew or broth : vagrants' and tramps' c. : C. 20. James Curtis, *The Gilt Kid*, 1936. Ex *shackles*, 2 : q.v.

shackles. Remnants and scrapings of meat in a butcher's shop : lower classes' (— 1923). Manchon. Prob. ex *shackle*, abbr. *shackle-bone*, a knuckle-bone.—2. Stew ; meat-soup : military : C. 20. F. & Gibbons.

shadder. A, or to, shadow : sol. pronunciation : C. 19 (? earlier)–20.

shade. A very small portion or quantity added or taken away : coll. : mid-C. 19–20. Ex *shade*, ' a tinge, a minute qualifying infusion ' (O.E.D.).

*****shade**, v. To keep secret : c. : late C. 19–20 ; ob. Ex *shade*, to hide.

shadow. A new boy in the care of one who is not new (the ' substance ') and learning the ropes from his temporary guardian : Westminster School : from ca. 1860. Wm. Lucas Collins, *Public Schools*, 1867.

shadow never grow (occ. **be**) **less !, may your.** May you prosper : a Persian phrase introduced to England by Morier in 1824 and, ca. 1880, generalised as a coll. *The Referee*, Jan. 2, 1887. (O.E.D.)

shadwoking. A ' grotesque rendering of shadowing ' : Society : ca. 1900–14. Ware.

shady. Uncertain, unreliable, inefficient ; unlikely to succeed : 1848, Clough (of a tutor), ' Shady in Latin,' O.E.D. : coll. ; though perhaps orig. university s.—2. Hence, disreputable ; not quite honest, not at all honourable : coll. : 1862, *The Saturday Review*, Feb. 8, ' Whose balance-sheets are " shady ",' O.E.D.

Shady Groves of the Evangelist, the. St. John's Wood, London : London : ca. 1865–1910. Punning *shady*, 2 ; once a haunt of harlots and *demi-mondaines.*

shady side of, on the. Older than : 1807, W. Irving, ' The younger being somewhat on the shady side of thirty,' O.E.D. : coll. >, ca. 1910, S.E.

shaft or a bolt of it, make a. To determine that a thing shall be used in one way or another : late C. 16–20 : coll. till ca. 1660, then proverbial S.E. ; in C. 19–20, merely archaic. Nashe, 1594 ; Isaac D'Israeli, 1823. (Apperson.)

shaft(e)sbury ; S. A gallon-potful of wine with cock : s. > coll. : late C. 17–early 19. B.E. ;

Grose. Presumably ex the Dorsetshire town of Shaftesbury.

shag. A copulation ; also, copulation generically : C. 19–20. Ex :—2. A performer (rarely of a woman) of the sexual act, esp. in ' *he is but bad shag* ; he is no able woman's man ', Grose, 2nd ed. : late C. 18–mid-19. Ex the v., 1, q.v.—3. ' Any coat other than an " Eton " or " tails " is a " shag " ', R. Airy, *Westminster*, 1902 (O.E.D.) : Westminster School : late C. 19–20. Ex *shaggy.*

shag, v.t. To coït (with a woman) : late C. 18–20. Very gen. among soldiers in G.W. Grose, 2nd ed. Prob. ex † *shag*, to shake, toss about. Cf. n., 1, 2.—2. Whence perhaps, v.i., to masturbate : Public Schools : certainly ca. 1900 and prob. many years earlier. Cf. :

shag, adj. Exhausted, esp. after games : Marlborough College : C. 20. Perhaps ex *shag*, v., 2, q.v. (A thin and weedy dog that, ca. 1919–23, haunted the college precincts, was known as *Shagpak* or *Shagphat*, as Mr A. B. R. Fairclough, formerly of the Alcuin Press, tells me.)

shag, wet as a. Very wet indeed : a mainly rural coll. : from ca. 1830. Marryat (O.E.D.). Ex *shag*, a cormorant.

shag back. To hang back ; refuse a fence : hunting coll. : from ca. 1870.

shag-bag. A poor, shabby fellow ; a worthless fellow : coll. : late C. 17–20 ; slightly ob. B.E. Ex *shake-bag* on *shag-rag*, via cock-fighting.

shag-bag, adj. Shabby ; worthless ; inferior : coll. : 1888 (O.E.D.). Ex preceding.

shagger. A ' dud ' boy : Public Schools' : C. 20. Perhaps ex *shag*, v., 2.

shags, go. To get extremely tired : schoolboys' : C. 20. Cf. *shag*, adj.

shake. A harlot : low London (— 1860). H., 2nd ed. ; ob. Ex Northern dial.—Whence (or ex *shake*, v., 1), 2, a copulation : from ca. 1860 ; ob.—3. See **shakes, no great.**—4. Abbr. *milk-shake*, *egg-shake*, etc. : coll. (— 1903) : ? orig. U.S.—5. Generic for instantaneous or very rapid action : from ca. 1815 : by C. 20, coll. Esp. *in a shake* (late C. 19–20), *in the shake of a hand* (1816), *in a brace* (1841) or *a couple* (1840) *of shakes*, *in two shakes* (from ca. 1880), *in the shake of a lamb's tail* (1903) or jocularly, from ca. 1905, *of a dead lamb's tail.*—6. Hence, a moment : (? late C. 19–) C. 20. E. Nesbit, 1904, ' Wait a shake, and I'll undo the side gate,' O.E.D.—7. Hence also, *a great shake*, a very fast pace (— 1903).—8. See **shakes, the.**

shake, v.t. To coït (with a woman) : coll. : ? C. 16–20 ; ob. In late C. 19–20, rare except in *shake a tart.* Halliwell, ' This seems to be the ancient form of *shag*, given by Grose ' (see **shag**, v., 1).—2. ? hence, v. reflexive, to masturbate : C. 19–20. Cf. *shag*, v., 2.—3. V.t., to rob (a person) : low s., or perhaps c. : C. 19–20. *Lex. Bal.* ; in C. 20, mainly Australian. Cf. the C. 15–16 S.E. *shake* (a person) *out of* (goods, etc.).—4. (? hence) to steal : from ca. 1810 : c. >, ca. 1880, low s. Vaux ; H. Kingsley, 1859, ' I shook a nag, and got bowled out and lagged.' In C. 20, almost wholly Australian. See also **shook.**—5. See **shook on.**—6. See **shake an elbow.**—7. See :

shake ! Shake hands : from ca. 1890 ; mainly U.S. Often *shake on it !* (Other forms are very rare, except for, e.g., ' Well satisfied, they shook on it.')

shake a cloth in the wind. To be hanged : late C. 18–mid-19. Grose, 2nd ed.

shake a fall. To wrestle : C. 19–20 ; ob.

shake a flannin. To fight : navvies' : ca. 1870–1914. Ware. A *flannin* is a flannel shirt or jacket.

shake a leg. (Gen. in imperative.) To hurry : coll. (mainly military and nautical) : late C. 19–20. Anstey, 1892, ' Ain't you shot enough ? Shake a leg, can't yer, Jim ? ' Ex S.E. *shake a foot, leg,* etc., to dance.

shake a loose leg. To go ' on the loose ' : coll. : mid-C. 19–20.

shake-bag. The female pudend : low : mid-C. 19–20.

shake-buckler. A swashbuckler or bully : coll. nickname : mid-C. 16–mid-17. Becon.

shake (a person's) **fleas.** To thrash : low : C. 19. Ware.

*shake-glim. A begging letter, or petition, on account of fire : ca. 1850–90. Cf. :

*shake-lurk. The same, only for shipwreck : c. of ca. 1850–1900. Mayhew, 1851. See **lurk, a** dodge or ' lay ' ; and cf. *lurker.*

shake one's shambles. See **shambles . . .**

*shake one's toe-rag. To decamp : vagabonds' and beggars' c. (— 1909). Ware. Cf. *toe-ragger.*

shake-out. A ' sudden revulsion and following clearance—due to panic ' : Stock Exchange coll. : from ca. 1880. Ware.

shake the bullet or **red rag.** See **bullet** and **red rag.**—2. To threaten to discharge a person : tailors' : from ca. 1870 ; slightly ob.

shake the (occ. **one's**) **elbow.** To dice : C. 17–20 (ob.) : coll. >, ca. 1800, S.E.

shake the ghost into. To frighten (a person) greatly : mid-C. 1920 ; ob.

shake the gum out of a sail. To test new canvas for the first time in bad weather : nautical coll. : late C. 19–20. Bowen.

shake up, v.i. To masturbate : C. 19–20 ; ob. Cf. *shag,* v., 2.—2. V.t., to hurry : nautical coll. : late C. 19–20. Bowen. Ex S.E. *shake up,* to rouse with, or as with, a shake.

shake your ears !(, go). C.p. advice to one who has lost his ears : ca. 1570–1790. G. Harvey, 1573 ; Shakespeare ; Mrs F. Sheridan, 1764. (Apperson.) Cf. the modern crudity *get the dirt out of your ears !,* wake up !

shaker. A hand : low coll. : mid-C. 19–20 ; ob. —2. A shirt : from the 1830's : c. >, ca. 1870, low s. Brandon ; Snowden ; H., 1st ed.—3. An omnibus : busmen's : from ca. 1870 : rather ob. Cf. *bone-shaker.*—4. A beggar that pretends to have fits : c. (— 1861). Mayhew.

shakes, in a brace or **couple of.** See **shake, n.,** 5.

shakes, no (occ. **not any**) **great.** Nothing remarkable or very important or unusually able or clever : from ca. 1815 : coll. till C. 20, then familiar S.E. Moore, 1819, ' Though no great shakes at learned chat.' Ex dicing.

shakes, the. Any illness or chronic disease marked by trembling limbs and muscles : coll. : from the 1830's. O.E.D.—2. Hence, delirium tremens : coll. : from ca. 1880. *The Cornhill Magazine,* June, 1884, ' Until she is pulled up by an attack of delirium tremens, or, as she and her neighbours style it, a fit of the shakes.'—3. Hence, extreme nervousness : coll. : C. 20.

*shakes ?, what. What's the chance of stealing anything : c. (— 1859). H., 1st ed.

Shakespeare-navels. A ' long-pointed, turned-down collar ' : London youths' : ca. 1870–80. Ware. Precisely why ?

shakester. See **shickster.**—**shaler.** See **sheila.**

*shaller dodge. See **shallow dodge.**

*shallow. A hat : c. of ca. 1810–40. Vaux.— 2. See **shallow brigade, cove, dodge, mort, scriver.** Perhaps ex dial. *shalleygonahey, shallegonaked* (i.e. shall I go naked ?), used chiefly of insufficient clothing (E.D.D.).

*shallow, do the ; go shallow. To practise the ' shallow dodge ' (q.v.) : c. (— 1887). Baumann (*go shallow*) ; P. H. Emerson (both forms). The earliest shape of the phrase is *go on the shallows,* H., 1st ed. Cf. *run shallow.*

shallow, lily-. A white whip-hat, i.e. a low-crowned one : fashionable s. : ca. 1810–40.

*shallow, live. To live in discreet retirement, when wanted by the police : c. : from ca. 1870 ; slightly ob. Contrast *shallow, do the.*

*shallow, run. To practise the ' shallow dodge ' : c. (— 1893). *The Ripon Chronicle,* Aug. 23, 1893, ' By running shallow I mean that he never wears either boots, coat, or hat, even in the depths of the most dismal winter.' A synonym of *do the* (or *go*) *shallow.*

shallow brigade. Perhaps merely a more or less literary synonym for *school of shallow coves* (see **s. cove**). Mayhew, 1851.

*shallow cove ; s. fellow. C. 19–20 tramps' c. (first recorded in 1839 and now ob.), as in Brandon and in Mayhew, 1851, ' He scraped acquaintance with a " school of shallow coves " ; that is, men who go about half-naked, telling frightful tales about shipwrecks, hair-breadth escapes from houses on fire, and such like . . . calamities.' Also a *shivering Jemmy,* q.v. Cf. :

*shallow dodge. The capitalising of rags and semi-nudity : c. : 1869, Greenwood, ' A pouncing of the exposed parts with common powder blue is found to heighten the frost-bitten effect.'

*shallow fellow. See **shallow cove.**

*shallow mort or **mot(t).** A female practiser of the ' shallow dodge ' : 1842, *The Edinburgh Review,* July (*mott*) ; H., 1st ed. (*mot*). O.E.D. Cf. *shallow cove,* q.v.

*shallow screever, scriver, etc. A man who, very meagrely dressed, sketches and draws on the pavement : c. (— 1859). H., 1st ed. See **shallow** and **screever, n.**

*shallows, go on the. See **shallow, do the.**— **shally-shally.** See **shilly-shally.**

sham. A trick or hoax, an imposture, a fraud : 1677 : orig. s., it had by 1700 > S.E. The same with the corresponding v., also in Wycherley in 1677. Prob. ex *shame,* n. and v. : cf. *cut a sham,* ' to play a Rogue's Trick ', B.E. (who wrongly, as I think, classifies this phrase, along with the simple n., as c.), late C. 17–18, and *upon the sham,* fraudulently (late C. 17 only), and *put a sham upon,* to ' sell ', to swindle ; ca. 1680–1830,—all three, by the way, s. only for a year or two before being made S.E.— 2. Hence, a false testimonial, certificate, or subscription list : c. : from ca. 1840 ; ob. ' *No. 747.*' —3. As false sleeve or shirt-front, prob. always S.E. —4. **Champ**agne : 1849, Thackeray. Cf. the early C. 20 album c.p. : ' A bottle of champagne for my real friends ; of real pain for my sham friends.' Occ. (— 1874) *shammy,* as in H., 5th ed. : very ob. The more gen. C. 20 term is *fizz.*

sham, v. To ply with, or treat oneself to, champagne : rare : from ca. 1820. Byron. (Baumann.) Cf. *cham,* n., 3.

*sham Abra(ha)m. See **Abra(ha)m.**

sham-legger. A man that offers to sell very cheaply goods that are very inferior : low s. (mostly London) of ca. 1870–1910.

sham the doctor. To malinger : military : from the 1890's. F. & Gibbons.

[**shamateur,** contrary to gen. opinion, is S.E. and it dates from ca. 1900. O.E.D. (Sup.).]

shambles, shake one's. (Gen. in imperative.) To be off : late C. 17–mid-18 : either low s. or perhaps, orig. at least, c. B.E.

shambly. Shambling, lurching : nautical coll. : late C. 19–20. W. E. Llewellyn has described sailors thus : ' Their hands were in a grab half-hook [i.e. as though grasping a grapnel], always, and their shoulders shambly.'

shame. Anything very ugly, painfully indecent, disgracefully inferior : coll. : 1764, Gray, ' His nose is a shame ' ; 1815, Scott, ' Three [hens] that were a shame to be seen.' O.E.D.

shame, the last. Imprisonment ; prison : coll. (— 1923). Manchon. Euphemistic.

shaming. Shameful ; ' shy-making ' : Society : ca. 1929–34. Evelyn Waugh, *Vile Bodies*, 1930, ' How too shaming.'

shammy. See **sham,** n., last sense.

shamrock. A prick with a bayonet : military : ca. 1850–1905. Ware.—2. See **puff and dart.**

shamrock, drown the. To drink or go drinking on St Patrick's Day, properly and nominally in honour of the shamrock : 1888, *The Daily Telegraph*, March 22, but prob. in spoken use many, many years earlier : coll. till ca. 1910, then S.E.

*****shan(d).** Base or counterfeit coin : c. (— 1812) ; very ob. Vaux. Ex dial. *shan*, paltry. Cf. *sheen*, q.v.

[**shandy,** for *shandygaff*, is on the border-line between coll. and S.E.]

shanghai. To stupefy and then put on a vessel requiring hands : nautical s. (orig. U.S.) >, in C. 20, coll. : 1871 (U.S.) and 1887 (England). Ex *Shanghai* as seaport, or perhaps as propelled from a *shanghai* or catapult (*shanghai*, to shoot with a shanghai, is not recorded before C. 20). O.E.D.

Shanghai gentleman. One definitely not a gentleman : naval (— 1909). Ware.

Shank-End, the ; hence **Shankender.** The Cape Peninsula ; an inhabitant thereof : South African jocular coll. : late C. 19–20. Pettman. Cf. the *heel* of Italy.

Shanks'(s) mare, nag, naggy, pony. One's legs as conveyance : coll. (in C. 20, S.E.) : resp. 1795 (S. Bishop) ; *nag*, 1774 (Ferguson), and *naggy*, 1744 (an anon. Scottish song, W.), the former being mostly, the latter wholly Scots) ; *pony*, 1891, *The Globe*, June 5. (O.E.D.) Jocular on *shanks*, the legs, and gen. as *ride S. m.* (or *n.*, or *p.*).

shanky. ' Thrifty ; close-fisted ' : military : C. 20. F. & Gibbons. Perhaps ex one who walks (see preceding entry) when the ordinary person would ride or go by bus or train.

Shannon, to have been dipped in the. To be anything but bashful, the immersion being regarded as a cure competely effectual and enduring against that affliction : coll. : ca. 1780–1880. Grose, 1st ed.

shanny. Idiotic, silly ; mad : Cockneys' (— 1887). Baumann. Ex Kentish dial.

*****shant.** A quart or a pot ; a pot of liquor (esp. *shant of gatter*, a pot of beer) : mid-C. 19–20 : c. and low s. Mayhew, 1851 ; P. H. Emerson, 1893. ? etymology : cf. *shanty* and *shanty-liquor*, qq.v.

sha'n't (less correctly, **shan't**). Shall not : coll. :

1664, S. Crossman, ' My Life and I shan't part ' ; 1741, Richardson (*shan't*) ; 1876, Black, ' He sha'n't marry Violet ' (app. earliest record of this form). O.E.D.—2. As a n., 1850, Smedley, ' A sulky, half-muttered " shan't " was the only reply,' O.E.D. : likewise coll.

sha'n't ! A somewhat uncouth and gen. angry or sullen form of :

sha'n't !, I. I shall not (do so) : a coll. peremptory refusal : C. 18–20.

sha'n't be long !, now we. It's all right ! : a c.p. of ca. 1895–1915. *The Daily Telegraph*, Sept. 8, 1896 ; Maugham, *Liza of Lambeth*, 1897, ' Now we shan't be long ! she remarked.' Ware derives it from ' railway travellers' phrase when near the end of a journey '.

shanty. A public-house ; a ' sly-grog shop ' ; showmen's s. (prob. from ca. 1850) >, by 1860, Australian coll. ; in C. 20, virtually S.E. H. Lawson, 1902, ' They got up a darnse at Peter Anderson's shanty acrost the ridges.' Prob. ex Fr. *chantier* ; nevertheless, derivation direct ex *shant* (q.v.) is not impossible : cf. senses 3 and 4.—2. Hence, a brothel : nautical : from ca. 1890. F. & H.—3. A quart of liquor, esp. of beer or ale : 1893, P. H. Emerson. Prob. ex *shant*, q.v.—4. Beer-money : 1893, P. H. Emerson, ' Any shanty in your sky-rocket.' Prob. sense 3 is slightly earlier than, and the imm. source of, sense 4.

shanty, v. To drink often, habitually, at a ' shanty ' (sense 1) : 1888 : Australian coll. >, ca. 1905, S.E. ' Rolf Boldrewood ', 1888, ' The Dalys and us shantying and gaffing.' *The Century Dict.*

shanty-bar. The bar in a ' shanty ' (sense 1) : late C. 19–20 : Australian coll. >, ca. 1920, S.E. H. Lawson, 1902, ' Throwing away our money over shanty bars,' O.E.D.

shanty-keeper. One who keeps a ' shanty ' (sense 1) : 1875 : Australian coll. >, ca. 1920, S.E. Cf. preceding and ensuing entry. Morris.

shanty(-)liquor. Sly-grog-shop drink : Australian coll. >, ca. 1920, S.E. : 1886, H. C. Kendall, ' He'll . . . swig at shanty liquors,' O.E.D. Ex *shanty*, 1.

shanty-man. An electrician : circus-men's (— 1932). Edward Seago, *Circus Company*. Prob. suggested by *juice*, electricity : cf. *shanty*, n., 3.

shap. See **shapo.**

shape, spoil a woman's. To get her with child : coll. : late C. 17–20 ; ob. Facetious Tom Brown, ' The . . . king who had spoil'd the shape . . . of several mistresses.' By an indelicate pun.

shape, travel on one's. To live by one's appearance, to swindle : coll. : C. 19.

shape for you !, there's a. A c.p. in respect of an extremely thin person or animal : mid-C. 19–20 ; very ob. Cf. :

shapes. An ill-made man often in vocative : late C. 17–mid-19. B.E.—2. Hence, a very tightly laced girl : ca. 1730–1910. Dyche & Pardon, Halliwell, O.E.D.—3. ' An ill-made irregular Lump of Flesh, &c,' Dyche & Pardon : ca. 1730–1830.—4. ' The meat ingredient of a meal, especially breakfast : usually the same but in a different shape : rolled for sausages, in a ball for faggots, or round and flat for rissoles ' : military : C. 20. B. & P.

shapes, cut up or show. To frolic ; exhibit flightiness : mid-C. 19–20 ; ob. H., 1st ed. Cf. :

shapes, show one's. To ' turn about, march off ', B.E. : late C. 17–mid-19.—2. ' To be stript, or made peel at the whipping post,' Grose, 1st ed. :

mid-C. 18–early 19.—3. To come into view : coll. :
1828, Scott ; ob. (O.E.D.)

shapes and shirts. Young actors' term, ca. 1883–
1900, for ' old actors, who swear by the legitimate
Elizabethan drama, which involves either the
" shape " or the " shirt "—the first being the cut-in
tunic ; the . . . shirt being independent of shape.'
Ware.

*****shapo**, rare ; gen. **shappeau** or **shappo** ; rarely
shop(p)o ; less rarely **shap**. A hat : late C. 17–
early 19 : c. B.E., ' *Shappeau*, c. or *Shappo*, c. for
Chappeau,'—properly Fr. *chapeau*—' a Hat, the
newest Cant, *Nab* being very old, and grown too common ' ; Grose, 2nd ed., has *shappo* and *shap*, in
1st ed. only *shappo* ; C. Hitchin, 1718, has
shap.

share that among you ! A soldiers' c.p. (from
1915) on hurling a bomb into an enemy trench or
dug-out. B. & P.

*****shark**. A pickpocket : c. of C. 18. J. Stevens,
1707 ; Grose. (O.E.D.)—2. (? hence) a customs
officer : ca. 1780–1880. Grose, 1st ed.—3. See
sharks.—4. (Also *black shark* : Baumann.) A
lawyer : nautical coll. : 1840, Marryat (O.E.D.)—
5. A recruit : military : ca. 1890–1910. ? on
rooky, a rook being a shark.—6. A sardine : jocular
nautical : late C. 19–20. Bowen. Cf. *whale*.—
7. A professional punter : bookmakers' (— 1932).
Slang, p. 241.

shark-baiter. A too venturesome swimmer :
Australian coll. (— 1935).

shark out. To make off ; decamp slyly : dial.
(— 1828) >, by 1880, low coll. Manchon.

sharks, the. The press-gang : 1828, D. Jerrold ;
† by 1900.

shark's mouth. ' An awning shaped to fit round
a mast ' : nautical coll. verging on j. : late C. 19–20.
Bowen.

sharp. A swindler ; a cheat : coll. : 1797, Mrs
M. Robinson (O.E.D.) ; Vaux ; Maskelyne's title
for a most informative book, *Sharps and Flats*.—
2. Hence, an expert, connoisseur, actual or would-
be wise man : coll. : 1865, *The Pall Mall Gazette*,
Sept. 11, ' " Sharps " who advertise their " tips " in
the sporting journals,' O.E.D. Ex *sharp*, alert.—
3. (Gen. in pl.) A needle : c. : late C. 19–20.
Ex S.E. *sharps*, one of three grades of needles,
including the longest and most sharply pointed.

Sharp come in yet ?, has Mr. A traders' c.p.
addressed by one (e.g.) shopman to another ' to
signify that a customer of suspected honesty is
about ' : from ca. 1860. H., 3rd ed. Cf. *two-pun-
ten*, q.v.

sharp and blunt. The female pudend : late C. 19–
20 rhyming s. on *cunt*.

sharp as the corner of a round table. Stupid :
coll. (lower classes') : from ca. 1870 ; ob. Prob. by
opposition to S.E. *sharp as a needle* or *razor* or †*thorn*.

sharper's tools. Fools : rhyming s. : late C. 19–
20. (As = dice, it is S.E.)

*****sharping omee.** A policeman : c. and Parlyaree :
ca. 1850–90. H., 1st ed. See **omee**.

*****sharpo.** See **go on the sharpo**.

Sharp's Alley bloodworms. Beef sausages ; black
puddings : ca. 1850–1900. Ex a well-known
abattoir near Smithfield. H., 1st ed.

sharp's the word and quick's the motion. A c.p.
implying that a person is ' very attentive to his own
interest ', Grose, 2nd ed. : late C. 18–20 ; slightly
ob. Ex *sharp's the word*, an enjoining of promptitude.

sharpy. A derisive coll. nickname for a person
self-consciously alert : late C. 19–20.

sharry. A charabanc : low coll. : 1924 (O.E.D.
Sup.). Imm. ex *chara*.

s'hart. See '**sheart**.

shat. A tattler : ca. 1709–20. Steele in *The
Tatler*, No. 71, 1709. O.E.D.

shattered ; shattering. Nervy, nervous ; tiresome, upsetting, boring, unpleasant : Society :
from ca. 1925. Agatha Christie, *The Murder at the
Vicarage*, 1930, ' I feel shattered ' and ' Life's very
shattering, don't you think ? ' ; E. Waugh, *Decline
and Fall*, 1928, 'My dear, how too shattering for you.'

shave. A narrow escape : 1834, R. H. Froude
(O.E.D.) : coll. >, ca. 1860, S.E. Ex S.E. sense,
' a slight or grazing touch '.—2. Hence, passing an
examination by a ' shave ' : university (orig.
Oxford) : 1840, Theodore Hook (O.E.D.) ; slightly
ob.—3. A definitely false, or at the least, an unauthenticated report : military : 1813, Capt. R. M.
Cairnes (O.E.D.), so that Sala was wrong when, in
1884, he implied that the term arose (instead of
saying that it > gen. popular) during the Crimean
War, though he may have been right when he said
that as = a hoax, it arose then ; the latter nuance,
unless applied to a deliberately false rumour, was
† by 1914. ' From a barber's shop, the home of
gossip ' (B. & P.). Cf. *latrine rumour*, q.v.—4. ' The
proportion of the receipts paid to a travelling company by a local manager ', F. & H., 1903 : C. 20
theatrical. Ex *shaved-off*.—5. 'A money consideration paid for the right to vary a contract, by extension of time for delivery or payment, &c.', F. & H. :
orig. U.S. ; anglicised ca. 1900.—6. A drink :
proletarian : ca. 1884–1914. Ware. Perhaps ex
the excuse of going for a shave.—7. A customer for
a shave : barbers' coll. : 1895, W. Pett Ridge. So
too *hair-cut, shampoo, singe*.

shave. To deprive a person of all his money or
goods ; to charge him extortionately : late C. 14–
20 : S.E. until C. 19, then coll. verging on s. Cf.
shaving the ladies, q.v.—2. Hence, to steal (v.t.) :
late C. 16–mid-18. D'Urfey, ' The Maidens had
shav'd his Breeches,' O.E.D.

shave through, v.i. Abbr. *just shave through* :
from ca. 1860 : university coll. >, ca. 1890, S.E.
H., 2nd ed. A variant is *make a shave* : see **shave,
n.**, 2.

shaver. A fellow, chap ; also a joker, a wag :
late C. 16–20 : coll. From ca. 1830 (though *young
shaver* occurs as early as 1630) only of a youth, and
gen. preceded by *young* or *little*, very often depreciatively,—except that, at sea, *old shaver* = a man
throughout C. 19 (see, e.g. H., 5th ed.). Marlowe,
1592, ' Sirrah, are you not an old shaver ? ' . . .
Alas, sir ! I am a very youth ' ; 1748, Smollett, ' He
drew a pistol, and fired it at the unfortunate
shaver ' ; Dickens ; P. H. Emerson. Ex *shaver*,
one who shaves (for barbers have always been
'cute, knowledgeable fellows) ; or perhaps ex
shaver, an extortioner (esp. *cunning shaver*).—2
Very rarely applied to a woman : prob. only in
C. 17, e.g. Cotton, 1664, ' My Mother's a mad
shaver, | No man alive knows where to have her.'
(This instance may, however, be merely an extension of the C. 17 coll. *mad shaver*, a roysterer.) Cf.
the C. 20 sporting women's use of *chap* in address or
application to women.—3. A short jacket : late
C. 19–early 20 : lower classes. Because it gen. fits
close ; cf. *bum-freezer, -perisher*.

shaving. A defrauding, whether process or completed act : C. 17–20. Dekker. (O.E.D.) Hence *shaving terms*, the making all the money one can : C. 19–20.

shaving-brush. The female pubic hair : from after 1838 ; ob.

shaving-mill. An open boat, sixteen-oared, of a type used as privateers in the war of 1812 : Canadian. Bowen.

shaving the ladies. A drapers' phrase for overcharging women : 1863, ' Ouida ', ' We have all heard of an operation called shaving the ladies ' ; ob. Ex *shave*, n., 1.

shavings. Illicit clippings of money : late C. 17–20 : c. >, ca. 1750, s. >, ca. 1800, coll. >, ca. 1860, S.E. B.E. ; Grose, 1st ed.

shawl. A greatcoat : jocular military : C. 20. F. & Gibbons.

shawly. An Irish fisherwoman, esp. of Dublin : Anglo-Irish : late C. 19–20. (F. Tennyson Jesse, *Many Latitudes*, 1928.) Ex the great shawl they wear.

shay sho (or so) !, you don't. A jocular form of ' really ! ' : C. 20. Ex tipsy distortion of *say* and perhaps influenced by *so say*, q.v. Also *I should shay sho* or *so !*, certainly, as in Ian Hay, *David and Destiny*, 1934, ' I should shay sho ! Go right ahead **!** '

She. Queen Victoria : Society's nickname : 1887–88. Ware. Ex Rider Haggard's *She*, published early in 1887 : it was so popular that Andrew Lang and W. H. Pollock, in the same year, parodied it as *He*.

she. A woman : mid-C. 16–20 : S.E. until mid-C. 19 then coll. ; in C. 20, low coll. when not jocular.—2. (Also **shee.**) A plum pudding : Charterhouse : late C. 19–20 ; † by 1923. A. H. Tod, *Charterhouse*, 1900. Cf. *he*.—3. Her : C. 16–20 : S.E. until late C. 17 then coll. ; ca. 1750–1810, low coll. ; from ca. 1840, sol. Foote, 1752, ' The fat Cook . . . fell out at the Tail of the Waggon ; so we left she behind,' O.E.D.

she didn't seem to mind it very much. A proletarian ironic c.p. intimating jealousy : ca. 1885–1900. Ware.

she-dragon. A termagant or a forbidding woman, esp. if elderly : from the 1830's : coll. bordering on, in C. 20 >, S.E.—2. A kind of wig, says F. & H. : ? early C. 19 : prob. coll.

she-flunkey. A lady's maid : coll. (lower classes') : from ca. 1875.

she has (or she's) been a good wife to him. An ironic proletarian c.p. ' cast at a drunken woman rolling in the streets ' (Ware) : from ca. 1905 ; not wholly †.

she-house. A house under petticoat rule : late C. 18–mid-19. Grose, 1st ed.

' She ' is a cat's mother. A c.p. addressed to (esp.) a child constantly referring thus to his mother : mid-C. 19–20 ; slightly ob.

she-lion. A shilling : from ca. 1780 ; very ob. Grose 1st ed. By a pun.

she-male, n. and adj. Female : orig.—ca. 1880—London lower classes' > by ca. 1912 fairly gen. jocular. Ware. Pairing with *he-male*, q.v.

*she-napper. A female thief-catcher ; a bawd, a pimp : late C. 17–mid-19 : c. > ca. 1750 low s. B.E. ; Grose 1st ed.

she-oak. Native ale : Australian (1888), hence New Zealand ; ob. Cf. *shearer's joy*. Ex the Australian tree so named : quite ! but why ? (Morris.) Whence :

she-oak net. A net spread under the gangway to catch seamen drunk on ' she-oak ' : nautical : late C. 19–20 ; ob. Bowen.

she-school. A girls' school : C. 19–20 (ob.) : coll. Cf. *she-house*.

she thinks she's wearing a white collar ! She's putting on ' side ' ! : a W.A.A.C.'s c.p. : 1917–18. B. & P. Among the ' Waacs ', a white collar was worn by N.C.O.'s.

she will go off in an aromatic faint. A Society c.p. of 1883–ca. 86, ' said of a fantastical woman, meaning that her delicate nerves will surely be the death of her ' (Ware).

sheaf. Incorrect for *sheath* : late C. 17–20 ; rare in C. 19–20. (O.E.D.)

shearer's joy. Colonial beer : Australian coll. : 1892, Gilbert Parker. Cf. *she-oak* q.v. Morris.

shears, there's a pair of. They're very like : coll. : C. 17–18. Ex the more gen. *there goes* or *went but a pair of shears between* (e.g.) *them*.

'sheart ; occ. **s'heart, shart, s'harte,** incorrectly (C. 18) **'sdheart.** A coll. euphemism for *God's heart !* : late C. 16–18. Occ. *s'hart*. O.E.D.

sheath !, by my. A trivial oath : coll. : ca. 1530-50. Heywood, More. O.E.D.

sheave-o, sheaveo, sheavo or **sheevo.** A drunken bout ; a free-fight : nautical. F. & Gibbons ; Manchon. A late C. 19–20 derivative of :—2. An entertainment : naval : C. 19–20. Indeed, F. & Gibbons records it for 1798 thus : ' Sir John Orde gave a grand chevaux ' (letter of Lieut. Charles Cathcart, May 6). See *chevoo*.

sheba. An attractive girl or woman ; esp. as the counterpart of *sheikh* (sense 1) : from 1926, and mostly American. Ex the Queen of Sheba, reputedly alluring.

shebang. As a hut, room, dwelling, shop, it has remained U.S. ; but derivatively as a vehicle (Mark Twain, 1872) it was anglicised in the late 1890's ; the debased sense, a thing, matter, business (— 1895 in U.S.) esp. in *the whole shebang*, is not, in C. 20, unknown in the British Empire. Prob. ex Fr. *cabane* (De Vere).

shebo. Navy soap : naval : C. 20. Bowen. ? ex the Queen of Sheba, because so rich (in colour).

sheckles. See **shekels.** (The form given by Ware.)

she'd. She would : coll. See **'d.**

shed. To give ; give away (something of little value) ; drop, let go : coll. : 1855, Dickens, ' Would shed a little money [for] a mission or so to Africa.' O.E.D.

shed a tear. To make water : mid-C. 19–20.—2. (? hence by antiphrasis) to take a dram, hence—from ca. 1860—any drink : 1864, H., 3rd ed. ; 1876, Hindley, ' I always made time to call in and shed a tear with him.' Less gen. and very ob.

shedduff. A middle-class corruption (— 1909) of *chef-d'œuvre*. Ware.

shee. See **she,** 2.—**sheela(h).** See **sheila.**—**sheele.** See **'le.**

*sheen. Counterfeit coin : c. (— 1839). Brandon ; H., 1st ed. Occ., from ca. 1880, as adj. Ex *shan(d)*, q.v., very prob. (cf. Brandon's and H.'s designation as Scottish) ; but perhaps influenced by :

sheeny (gen. **S.**) ; occ. **sheeney, -nie,** or **shen(e)y.** A Jew : 1824 (O.E.D.) : in C. 20, opprobrious (witness S.O.D.) ; in C. 20, inoffensive (witness H., 5th ed., 1874 = 1873). Thackeray, 1847, ' Sheeney and Moses are . . . smoking their pipes before their lazy shutters in Seven Dials.' From ca. 1890, occ.

as adj., as in *The Licensed Victuallers' Gazette*, Jan. 23, 1891, ' " Don't like that Sheeney friend of yours," he said.'—2. Hence, a pawnbroker : mid-C. 19–20.–-3. A dark-coloured tramp : tramps' c. (— 1932). F. Jennings, *Tramping with Tramps.*— 4. A very economical, money-careful man : military : C. 20. F. & Gibbons. W. risks the guess that *sheeny* may derive ex Yiddish pronunciation of Ger. *schön* beautiful, used in praising wares ; very tentatively, I suggest that the term arose from the *sheeny*, i.e. glossy or brightly shiny, hair of the average ' English ' Jew : cf. *snide and shine*, q.v.

sheeny or **S.** ; etc. Adj. See **sheeney, n., 1.**—2. Fraudulent (person) ; base (money) : late C. 19–20. A rare sense, due prob. to *sheen*, q.v.

sheep. A second-classman : Aberdeen University : 1865, G. Macdonald.

sheep by moonlight, keep. To hang in chains : late C. 18–mid-19. A. E. Housman's note to *The Shropshire Lad* (1898), ix. (O.E.D.)

sheep-guts, old. A term of contempt : coll. : C. 19–20 ; ob.

*sheep-shearer. A cheat or swindler : c. : late C. 17–mid-18. B.E.

*sheep-walk. A prison : c. of ca. 1780–1840. Messink, 1781.

sheep-wash. To duck : Winchester : from ca. 1890. Ex sheep-dipping.

sheep's head, all jaw,—like a. A c.p. of a very talkative person : late C. 18–20 ; ob. Grose, 2nd ed. See jaw, n.

sheep's head,—two heads are better than one even if one is only a. A c.p. aimed at the second party to a plan, etc. ; often in retort to the trite *two heads are better than one.* C. 20 (? late C. 19–20).

sheep's tail. Sheep's-tail fat : South African coll. (— 1888). Pettman.

sheepskin-fiddle. A drum : ca. 1810–60. Whence *sheepskin-fiddler*, a drummer (*Lex. Bal.*).

sheer-cloath is incorrect for *cerecloth* ; † **shehide** for *shahi.* O.E.D.

Sheer Nasty ; Sheer Necessity. Sheerness : naval : late C. 19–20. Bowen. (Naval men go there only when necessary.)

sheet, on the. Up for trial ; ' crimed ' : military coll. : from ca. 1905. F. & Gibbons. See **sheet it home to.**

sheet-alley or **-lane.** Bed : mid-C. 19–20 ; ob. Cf. *Bedfordshire* and *blanket fair*, and Baumann's (*go*) *down sheet lane into Bedfordshire*, to go to bed.

sheet in the wind or (less gen. and, by 1930, slightly ob.) **wind's eye, a.** Half drunk : 1840, Dana, in adumbration ; 1862, Trollope, ' A thought tipsy—a sheet or so in the wind, as folks say,' O.E.D. ; R. L. Stevenson, 1883 (*wind's eye*). S. >, ca. 1890, coll. ; now virtually S.E. Ex *three sheets in the wind*, q.v. below.

sheet it home to (a person). To prove something against him : coll. (— 1923). Manchon. Perhaps ex entry of person's name on a charge-sheet.

sheet of tripe. A plate of tripe : low urban (— 1909). Ware.

sheets, between the. In bed : from ca. 1860 : coll. now verging on S.E.

sheets in the wind, three. Drunk : 1821, Egan ; 1840, Dana : mainly sporting s. >, ca. 1860, coll. >, ca. 1930, S.E.

sheevo. See sheave-o.

Sheffield handicap. A sprint race with no defined scratch, the virtual scratch man receiving a big

start from an imaginary ' flyer ' : Northern coll. and dial. : late C. 19–20 ; ob.

Sheffields ; Sheffs. Shares in the Manchester, Sheffield and Lincolnshire Railway : Stock Exchange (— 1895) : resp. coll. and s. A. J. Wilson, *Stock Exchange Glossary.* Cf. *Saras.*

sheikh ; often incorrectly **sheik.** A ' he-man ' : from 1925. Collinson ; *Slang.* Lit., Arabic for a chief ; Miss Edith Maude Hull's best-seller *The Sheikh*,—for its sales were, lit. and fig., phenomenal,—appeared in 1924.—2. Hence, a lover, a girl's ' young man ' : from ca. 1926 ; mostly U.S. (O.E.D. Sup.)

sheila or **-er** ; occ. **shiela(h)** or **sheela(h).** A girl : Australian, hence New Zealand : late C. 19–20. The *-a* form has, in G.W. and after, been much the more gen. ; presumably influenced by the female Christian name. A perversion of English dial. and low s. *shaler* (Brandon, 1839 ; H., 1st ed.).

shekels ; occ. **sheckles.** Coin ; money in gen. : coll. : 1883, F. Marion Crawford, but prob. used at least a decade earlier,—cf. Byron's anticipation of 1823. Ex *shekel*, the most important Hebrew silver coin.

shele. See 'le.

*shelf. An informer ; esp. one who has himself participated in the crime : Australian c. (— 1926). Jice Doone. Because he very effectually puts a criminal there. Cf. *shelfer.*

shelf, off the. See sense 4 of :

shelf, on the. In pawn : C. 19–20. *Lex. Bal.* ; H., 1st ed.—2. Under arrest : military : from ca. 1870 ; ob.—3. Transported : ca. 1850–70 : c.—4. Dead : from ca. 1870. Whence *off the shelf*, resurrected (gen. as *take off the shelf*) : C. 20. (—5. As applied to old maids and unemployed or involuntarily retired persons, it is S.E.

*shelfer. An informer to the police : New Zealand c. (— 1932). Ex *shelf*, q.v.

shell. An undress, tight-fitting jacket : military : from ca. 1880. *St. James's Gazette*, Dec. 22, 1886, ' Tunics and shells and messing-jackets and caps.' Abbr. S.E. *shell-jacket* (1840, O.E.D.).— 2. The female pudend : C. 19–20 : coll. verging on euphemistic S.E.—3. See shells.—4. A hearse : lower classes' (— 1923). Manchon (' corbillard des pauvres ').

she'll. She will : coll. : C. 18–20. Cf. *he'll*, q.v.

shell, old. See old shell.

shell-back. A sailor of full age, esp. if tough and knowledgeable : nautical coll. (— 1883). Perhaps for the reason given by W. Clark Russell in *Jack's Courtship* (1883), ' It takes a sailor a long time to straighten his spine and get quit of the bold sheer that earns him the name of shell-back.'

shell out. To disburse ; pay (out) : coll. : C. 19–20. Maria Edgeworth, Tom Moore, Headon Hill. Scott, in 1816, has *shell down*, but this form is very rare. Ex *shell*, remove a seed from its shell (etc.).— 2. As v.i., to hand over what is due or expected, pay up : coll. from ca. 1820. Egan, 1821.—3. To club money together, gen. as vbl.n. : ca. 1820–50. Egan's Grose.—4. **shell** (a person) **out**, to pluck him at cards or dice : low (— 1923). Manchon. Ex senses 1, 2.—5. V.t., ex sense 1, to declare : a rare coll. of ca. 1860–1910. Mrs Henry Wood. (O.E.D.)

shell-proof, n. and adj. (A) boastful or foolhardy (fellow) : military : 1915 ; ob. F. & Gibbons. Cf. *bomb-proofer.*

*shell-shock. Cocoa : c. : from ca. 1918 (Michael Harrison, *Spring in Tartarus*, 1935.)

shell-shock bread. Bread arriving, impaired, to those in the front line : New Zealand soldiers' : 1916–18.

shell with name on it. See **bullet** . . .

shelling peas, as easy as. Very easy : coll. : C. 19–20. (O.E.D.)

shells ; occ. shels. Money : cf. of ca. 1590–1620. Greene. (Cf. the use made of cowries.)

s'help. See **s'elp.** (1904, O.E.D.) ; cf. *s'welp.*—**shels.** See **shells.**

[Shelta is ' a kind of cryptic Irish spoken by tinkers and confirmed tramps ; a secret jargon composed chiefly of Gaelic words disguised by changes of initial, transposition of letters, back-slanging and similar devices,' F. & H. Discovered in 1876 by Leland, who published his account of it in his *Gypsies*, 1882 : considerable attention has been paid to its since the Gypsy Lore Society started in 1889, its Journal in 1890. (See, e.g. **toby.**)]

shelter-stick. An umbrella : Cumberland s. (— 1904), not dial. E.D.D.

shelve, gen. v.t. To hold over part of (the weekly bill) : printers' coll. : from ca. 1870. Contrast *horsing*, q.v.

shemozzle ; occ. **shimozzel, s(c)hlemozzle, even chimozzle.** A difficulty or misfortune ; a ' row ' : from late 1880's : East End, orig. (esp. among book-makers) and mainly. *The Referee*, Dec. 1, 1889, *schlemozzle* ; Binstead, 1899, *shlemozzle* ; Anon., *From the Front*, 1900, *chimozzle* ; J. Maclaren, 1901, ' If Will comes out of this shemozzle.' Ex Yiddish (Ware).—2. Hence, loosely, ' an affair of any sort ' (F. & Gibbons) : lower classes' and military : C. 20.

shemozzle (etc.), v. To make off, decamp : orig. (ca. 1901) and mostly East End, >, by 1914, fairly gen.

shenan(n)igan or -in ; occ. **shenan(n)iken, shi-** (with either ending), and, nautical, **shenanecking** (Bowen). Nonsense, chaff ; (the predominant C. 20 sense :) trickery, ' funny ' games : orig. (ca. 1870), U.S. ; anglicised ca. 1890. R. Barr, 1902, ' If I were to pay them they might think there was some shenanigan about it.' Perhaps fantastic on the Cornish *shenachrum*, a drink of boiled beer, rum, sugar, and lemon ; but much more prob. the base is *nenan(n)igan* (etc.) and the origin the East Anglian and Gloucestershire *nanna(c)k, nan(n)ick*, to play the fool, with imm. origin in the vbl.n. *nannicking* (etc.) : E.D.D. It has, however, been suggested by Mr A. Jameson (of Sennen) that the term derives from the Erse *sionnach* (pronounced *shinnuch*) : cf. Anglo-Irish *foxing*, hiding or malingering.—2. Hence, as v.i. and t. : late C. 19–20.

shenan(n)i(c)ker. A shirker : from the middle 1890's. Ex preceding, 2.

shen(e)y. See **sheeny.**

shepherd. ' Every sixth boy in the cricket-bill who answers for the five below him being present,' F. & H. : Harrow : late C. 19–20.

shepherd, v.t. To shadow ; watch over (e.g. a rich relative, an heiress, a football or hockey opponent) : 1874, H., 5th ed., ' To look after care-fully, to place under police surveillance ' : s. >, ca. 1910, coll. See esp. Barrère & Leland. Perhaps ex the tending of sheep. (O.E.D.)—2. To follow (a person) in order to cheat or swindle him, or else to get something from him : from ca. 1890 : Aus-tralian s. >, ca. 1920, coll. Morris.—3. To force (the enemy) into a difficult position : military s. (Boer War) >, ca. 1915, coll. ; by 1930, almost S.E. *The Daily Telegraph*, April 2, 1900, ' Cronje was

shepherded with his army into the bed of the Modder by a turning movement.'

shepherd pie. Incorrect for *shepherd's pie* : C. 20. Seen on the ' Special Lunch ' label attached to the Hart Street (London) branch of the Express Dairy's eating-houses on June 4, 1935.

shepherd's plaid. Bad : from ca. 1870. P. P., *Rhyming Slang*, 1932. Contrast *Robin Hood*, q.v.

sherbet. (A glass of) any warm alcoholic liquor, e.g. a grog : s. (— 1890) ex catachresis. (Not among the upper classes.) Barrère & Leland. Cf. :

sherbet(t)y. Drunk : 1890, *The Licensed Vic-tuallers' Gazette*, Feb. 8, ' By the time one got to bed Tom was a bit sherbetty ' ; ob. Ex *sherbet*, q.v.

sheriff's ball. An execution : ca. 1780–1850. Grose, 1st ed. Whence :

sheriff's ball and loll out one's tongue at the com-pany, dance at the. To hang (v.i.) : ca. 1780–1850. Grose, 1st ed. Cf. *go to rest in a horse's night-cap* (ibid.), and a variant of the entry-phrase : *dance on nothing at the sheriff's ball* (Grose in his *Olio*).

sheriff's basket or **tub.** A receptacle set out-side a prison for the receipt of charity for the prisoners : resp. late C. 16–mid-17 (Nashe) and ca. 1630–60 (Massinger). O.E.D.

sheriff's bracelets. Handcuffs : ca. 1780–1850. Grose, 1st ed. Cf. :

sheriff's hotel. A prison : ca. 1780–1850. Grose, 1st ed. Cf. :

sheriff's journeyman. A hangman : early C. 19. *Lex. Bal.* Cf. :

sheriff's picture-frame. The hangman's noose : ca. 1780–1850. Grose, 1st ed. ; Egan.

sheriff's posts. ' Two painted posts, set up at the sheriff's door, to which proclamations were affixed,' O.E.D. : late C. 16–mid-17. Jonson.

sheriff's tub. See **sheriff's basket.**—**sherk.** See **shirk.**

Sherry. The English dramatist Sheridan : from ca. 1770. (The title of an important review in *The Observer*, Oct. 8, 1933.)

sherry ; shirry. A scurry ; a rapid or furtive departure : from ca. 1820 ; even in dial., very ob. Haggart, 1821, ' The shirry became general—I was run to my full speed,' O.E.D. Ex the v.—2. A sheriff : low (— 1859) ; ob. H., 1st ed., at *tip the double.*—3. Cheap ale : taverns' : late C. 19–early 20. Ware.

sherry, v. (Also **sherry off.**) To run away (esp. hastily) : 1788, Grose, 2nd ed. In C. 19–20, often *shirry* (as in Haggart, 1821) and, from ca. 1850, † except in dial. The O.E.D., prob. rightly, sug-gests ex *(to) sheer (off)* ; less likely, a perversion of Fr. *charrier*, to carry off ; less likely still, though not impossibly, ex an offensive-nationality idea, *sherry* the wine being from *Xeres* (now Jerez) in Spain.

sherry, go to. To die : circus-workers' (— 1887). Baumann. Ex *sherry*, n. and v.

sherry-cobbler. A cobbler made with sherry : coll. : 1809 ; ob. ' Ouida.' (Thornton.)

sherry-fug. To tipple sherry : university : ca. 1870–1915. (Cf. *fug*, q.v.)

sherry off. See **sherry,** v.

Sherwood Foresters, the. The 45th Regiment ; from ca. 1881, the 1st Nottinghamshire Regiment : mid-C. 19–20 : military coll. >, by 1910, S.E. (Dawson.)

shet for **shut, shettered** for **shuttered** : sol. pro-nunciation seen in other words as well : C. 19 (? earlier)–20. Ware.

shevoo. A party, esp. in the evening : C. 20 : mostly Australian. Prob. ex Fr. *chez vous* : cf. *sheave-o*, q.v.

shevvle. C. 1860–90, as in *The Daily News*, Dec. 2, 1864, ' This is a term recently introduced as a genteel designation for cat's meat, and evidently derived from *cheval*, French for horse, as mutton from *mouton*, &c.'

*shew a leg. To run away : c. (— 1823) ; † by 1900. Egan's Grose.—2. (Gen. in imperative.) To rise from bed : mid-C. 19–20 : nautical >, ca. 1910, military. Lit., show a leg from under the bed-clothes. John Masefield, *The Conway*, 1933, notes that the full call on that training ship has, from before 1891, been : ' Heave out, heave out, heave out, heave out ! Away ! | Come all you sleepers, Hey ! | Show a leg and put a stocking on it.' Cf. *rise and shine*.

shew-leg day. A windy day : London coll. (— 1887) ; ob. Baumann.—2. A very muddy day : London coll. : ca. 1880–1925. Ware. Often pron. *shulleg-day*.

*shice ; occ. **chice, schice, shise.** Any worthless person or thing : c. of ca. 1860–1910. Rare. Prob. ex :—2. Nothing, as *work for shice* : c. or low s. (— 1859). H., 1st ed.—3. Counterfeit money : c. : 1877, Anon., *Five Years' Penal Servitude*, ' I ascertained while at Dartmoor that a very large " business " is done in shise.' Either ex *shicer*, 1, q.v., or direct ex Ger. *Scheisse*, excrement, or ex the v., sense 1.—4. ' An unprofitable undertaking. A wash-out. " To catch a shice " = to have an unremunerative deal ' : grafters' : late C. 19–20. Philip Allingham, *Cheapjack*, 1934.

*shice, v. To deceive, defraud, leave in the lurch, betray ; v.i., to ' welsh ' : c. : from ca. 1860. Baumann. Ex n., 2.—2. To befoul : low (— 1887). Baumann.

shice, catch a. See shice, n., 4.

*shice (chice, schice, shise), adj. No good : c. or low s. (— 1859). H., 1st ed. at *chice*, ' The term was first used by the Jews in the last century.' ? ex Ger. *Scheisse*. (See also **shish**.)—2. Whence (or directly ex *shice*, n., 3, q.v.), spurious, counterfeit : c. : 1877, ' Two shice notes ' (source as in n., 3).— N.B. : Senses 1 and 2 have variants *shicery*, *shickery*.—3. Drunk : low : late C. 19–early 20. Presumably ex sense 1 influenced by *shicker*, adj., q.v.

shicer ; occ. **schicer, shiser,** and, in sense 2, rarely **skycer.** An unproductive claim or (gen. gold-) mine : Australia : 1855, *The (Melbourne) Argus*, Jan. 19 : s. >, ca. 1880, coll. >, ca. 1910, S.E. (The occ. spellings are, in this sense, merely illiterate and, in any case, very rare.) Either ex *shice*, adj., 1, or n., 2, qq.v., or—as W. suggests—direct ex Ger. *scheisser*, a voider of excrement ; or, just possibly, ex *shicery*, q.v.—2. (? hence, or ex *shice*, adj., 1) A worthless person (the predominant, and virtually the only C. 20, sense) ; a very idle one ; a mean, sponging man ; a humbug : low (— 1857). 'Ducange Anglicus ' ; H., 1st ed. Also *shyster* (H., 1874).—3. A welsher or defaulter : Australian racing : from mid-1890's. Morris. Ex sense 1 or 2—or both.

shicery. Bad ; spurious : c. or low s. : from ca. 1860 ; very ob. F. & H., giving no illustration. Either ex *shicer*, 2, or a perversion of *shickery*, q.v.

shick. Drunk : low Australian : C. 20. C. J. Dennis. Abbr. *shickered*, q.v.

shicker. Intoxicating liquor : C. 20 : mostly Australian. C. J. Dennis. Much less gen. than its origin :

shicker, v.i. ; occ. **schicker, shikker, shikkur.** To drink liquor ; get drunk : C. 20 (prob. from late 1890's : cf. next entry) : mostly Australian and not gen. considered respectable. ? ex Arabic, as is the tradition in Australia and New Zealand, or, as is more prob., a derivation and corruption of *she-oak*, q.v. No ; ex Hebrew *shikkur*, drunk, as is :

shicker, etc. Adj., drunk : from late 1890's. (? ex the v.) Binstead, 1899, ' She comes over shikkur and vants to go to shleeb.' Cf. :

shickered ; **shick.** Tipsy : C. 20 (? also very late C. 19). Ex *shicker*, v. Cf. 2 in :

shickery ; rarely **shikerry.** (Cf. *shicery*, q.v.) Shabby, shabbily ; bad, badly : c. or low s. : 1851, Mayhew, ' The hedge crocus is shickery togged.' ? ex *shice*, adj., 1.—2. Occ., in late C. 19–20 (though very ob. by 1935), drunk. Perhaps ex *shicker*, adj. Cf. *shick* and *shickered*.—3. Spurious : see shice, adj.

shi(c)ksel. A nice Gentile girl : Jewish coll. : mid-C. 19–20. A diminutive of *shiksa* : see sense 2 of :

shickster ; occ. **shickser, shiksa, shikster, shickster,** and († by 1903) **shakester.** A lady : 1839, Brandon, *shickster* ; 1857, Snowden (*Magazine Assistant*, 3rd ed.), *shikster* ; 1859, H., 1st ed., *shakester* and *shickster* ; 1899, Binstead, *shiksa*.—2. Hence, any (Gentile) woman or girl : mostly Jewish and pejorative : late C. 19–early 20. Contrast *shicksel*, q.v.—3. A Gentile female servant : among Jews : late C. 19–20.—4. A none-too-respectable girl or woman : mid-C. 19–20 : low. Carew, *Autobiography of a Gipsy*, 1891, p. 414, ' As I was leavin' the court, a reg'lar 'igh-flying shickster comes up,' refers to mid-C. 19 ; cf. H., 3rd ed., ' A " gay " lady.' Possibly the term derives ex *shice*, adj., 1 : that *shickster* is, in any case, from Yiddish is a virtual certainty ; that senses 1 and 4 may orig. have been c. is a possibility, as appears also in :

*shickster-crabs. Ladies' shoes : tramps' c. (— 1864) ; ob. H., 3rd ed.

shie. See shy, v.—**shielah** (Jice Doone). See sheila.—**shier.** See shyer.

shif. Fish : back s. (— 1859). H., 1st ed.

shift, v.t. To dislodge (a body of the enemy) : coll. : 1898.—2. To murder : 1898.—3. (The operative origin of senses 1, 2) to dislodge from its back, i.e. to throw (of a horse its rider) : coll. : 1891.—4. To eat ; more gen. to drink : s. (1896) >, ca. 1910, coll. All four senses, O.E.D.—5. To change (clothing) : nautical coll. : C. 20. Bowen. Ex dial.

shift, do a. To stool : low : from ca. 1870 ; slightly ob.

shift-monger. A young man-about-town : taverns' : ca. 1881–90. Ware. Ex stiff shirt-front of evening dress.

shift yer barrow ! Move on ! : Glasgow, mostly lower classes' (— 1934).

*shifter. A sly thief ; a sharper : ca. 1560–1640 : c. >, ca. 1600, s. or coll. Awdelay, Florio, Withals. Prob. ex S.E. *shift*, to use shifts, evasions, expedients, though this is recorded not before 1579 (O.E.D.).—2. ' An alarm, an intimation, given by a thief to his *pall*,' Vaux : c. of ca. 1810–40. Because it causes him to shift.—3. A drunkard : from ca. 1896 ; ob. Ex *shift*, v. (above).

Shiftesbury. See Old Tony.

[*shifting. A warning ; esp. an alarm conveyed by the watching to the operating thief : c. : from ca. 1820 ; ob. Cf. *shifter*, 2. This may be a F. & H. error.]

shifting ballast. Landsman—esp. soldiers—aboard : nautical : late C. 18–mid-19. Grose, 1st ed.

shifting dullness. See **round**, n., 2.

shifty cove. A trickster : from ca. 1820 (ob.) : low. See **cove** ; cf. *shifter*, 1.

shig. A shilling : Winchester : from ca. 1840 ; ob. Mansfield. Cf. *shiggers*, q.v.—2. Hence, *shigs*, money, esp. silver : East End : from ca. 1860. H., 3rd ed.

shiggers. White football shorts costing 10s. : Winchester : mid-C. 19–20. Ex *shig*, 1.

shigs. See **shig**, 2.

shikerry. See **shickery.—shikker, -ur.** See **shicker.—shiksa, shikster.** See **shickster.—shiksel.** See **shicksel.**

shillen ; shillin'. Whereas the latter is merely a pronouncing coll., the former is a sol. (— 1887). Baumann.

shilling, take the Queen's or **King's.** To enlist in the Army : C. 18–20 : coll. >, by 1830, S.E. Also, though not in C. 20, *take the shilling*.

shilling(-)dreadful († in C. 20), **shocker.** A (short) sensational novel sold at one shilling : coll. >, ca. 1905, S.E. : 1885, *The Athenæum*, Nov. 14, ‘Mr R. L. Stevenson is writing another shilling-dreadful’ ; *s. shocker*, July, 1886 (O.E.D.). The earlier term is on the analogy of *penny dreadful*, q.v. ; the latter, due to desire for variation. Cf. *thriller* and *yellow-back qq.v.*

shilling tabernacle. A Nonconformist tea-meeting at one shilling per head : lower classes' (—1909) ; ob. Ware.

shilling emetic. ‘A pleasure boat at a seaside-resort’ : nautical (officers') : C. 20. Bowen.

shilling to ninepence, bring a. See **ninepence to . . .**

shilly-shally. To be undecided ; to hesitate ; vacillate : 1782, Miss Burney : coll. till ca. 1850, then S.E. Ex the n. (1755, Shebbeare), itself ex the adj. (1734, Chesterfield), in its turn ex *stand shill I, shall I* (Congreve, 1700), earlier *stand shall I, shall I* (Taylor, 1630) ; *shilly-shally* as n. and (in C. 20, ob.) adj., orig. coll., both > S.E. early in C. 19. F. & H.; O.E.D.

shim ; shim-plough. Catachrestic for *skim, skim-plough* : C. 19–20. O.E.D.

shimmey (1837, Marryat) ; more gen. **shimmy** (1856, H. H. Dixon, O.E.D.). A chemise : coll. ; not, as the O.E.D. asserts, merely dial. and U.S. Whence *shimmy-shake*, q.v.—2. The game of *chemin de fer*, of the first two syllables of which it is a corruption : Society : late C. 19–20. (A. E. W. Mason, *The Sapphire*, 1933, ‘I think we ought to play a little at the shimmy table.’)

shimmy-shake. A kind of fox trot popular in 1920's : coll. > S.E.

shimozzel, -le. See **shemozzle**.

shin. A kick on the shin-bone : (esp. London) schoolboys' coll. (— 1887). Baumann.

shin-plaster. A bank-note : U.S., anglicised ca. 1860 ; ob. H., 3rd ed.

*****shin-scraper.** A treadmill : c. : 1869, J. Greenwood, ‘On account of the operator's liability, if he is not careful, to get his shins scraped by the ever-revolving wheel.’ † by 1920.

shin-stage, (take) the. (To go) a journey on foot, not by stage-coach : non-aristocratic coll. : mid-C. 18–mid-19. Ware. Cf. *Shank's mare*.

shinan(n)igan or **-in** or **i(c)kin.** See **shenan(n)igan**.

shindy. A spree or noisy merrymaking : from ca. 1820. Egan, 1821, ‘The Jack Tar is . . . continually singing out, “What a prime shindy, my mess mates ”.’ Either ex ‘ the rough but manly old game of “ shinty ” ’ (J. Grant, 1876) or, more prob., ex sense 3, which therefore presumably derives ex *shinty*.—2. A (rough) dance among sailors : nautical (— 1811). *Lex. Bal.* ; Smyth.—3. See **shines** (cf. *shindy*, 1, 2). (The sense, a row or a commotion, from the 1840's, is gen. considered S.E., but it may orig. have been coll. Ex sense 1 or sense 3.)

shine. A fuss, commotion, row : coll. : from ca. 1830. Dickens, 1852. Esp. *make* (or *kick up*) *a shine*. Perhaps ex *shine*, brilliance, influenced by *shindy*, 1. Hence, boasting ; chaff(ing) ; esp. *no shine*, honestly, sincerely, genuinely : tailors' : mid-C. 19–20. E.g. *The Tailor and Cutter*, Nov. 29, 1928.—3. Money : from ca. 1840 : (? c. >) low s. Egan, 1842. ? ex *shiners* (q.v.). Cf. *shiney*, *shino*.—4. See **shine to, take a**.

shine, adj. Good ; likable, e.g. ‘ A shine chap ’ : New Zealanders' : C. 20. Ex brightness as opp. obscurity.

shine, v.i. To raise money, or display it : late C. 19–20 ; ob. Ex *shine*, to excel.—2. **shine up to,** see **shine to, take a**.—3. Cf. *shiner*, 4.—4. See **shines like . . .**

shine, shyin', adj. ‘ Excellent ; desirable ’, C. J. Dennis : low Australian (— 1916). Ex brightness : cf. *dazzler*.

shine, cut a. To make a fine show : coll. : 1819 (O.E.D.). Occ. († in C. 20), *make a shine*.

shine !, rise and. See **rise and shine !**

shine from or **out of, take the.** To deprive of brilliance ; to surpass, put in the shade : coll. : 1818, Egan, *Boxiana*, I, *out of* ; 1819, Moore, *from*, which is † in C. 20. (O.E.D.)

shine-rag, win the. To lose ; be ruined ; London, ca. 1850–1910. Mayhew. Occ. *shiney-rag*, as in H., 1st ed., ‘Said in gambling when any one continues betting ’ after the luck sets in against him.

shine to, take a. To take a fancy to or for : coll. : U.S. (— 1850), adopted ca. 1890 by Australians, who occ., in C. 20, use *shine up to*. Cf. dial. *shiner*, a sweetheart, one's flirt.

shiner. See **shiners**.—2. A mirror ; esp. a card-sharpers' : from ca. 1810 : perhaps orig. c. Vaux. —3. A clever fellow : coll. and dial. : from ca. 1820. Halliwell.—4. A boaster : tailors' : from ca. 1860. Cf. *shine*, v., 3.—5. A silk hat : coll. : 1867, F. Francis (O.E.D.).—6. A stone so built into the wall of a house that its thick end is outward : South African : 1881, Douglass, *Ostrich Farming*.—7. A diamond : South African : 1884, *The Queenstown Free Press*, Jan. 15. Pettman. Cf. *shiners*.—8. (**Shiner.**) The inevitable nickname of any man surnamed Green or Wright, Black or White, Bryant (Bryant & May's matches) or Bright : naval and military : late C. 19–20. F. & Gibbons.

shiners. Money ; coins, esp. guineas and/or sovereigns : 1760, Foote, ‘To let a lord of lands want shiners, 'tis a shame.’ Occ. in singular as a gold or, less gen., a silver coin : C. 19–20 : Surr, 1806 (O.E.D.) ; ‘ Pomes ’ Marshall. Cf. *shine* (n., 2), *shindy*, *shino*.—2. Jewels : C. 20. (D. Sayers, 1934.) Ex *shiner*, 7.—3. A cleaning-up parade ; something highly polished : military : from ca. 1920.

Shiners, the. The 5th Foot Regiment >, in late

C. 19, the Northumberland Fusiliers : military : since the Seven Years War, in which they shone with ' spit and polish '. F. & Gibbons.

shines. Capers ; tricks : U.S. (1830), anglicised ca. 1860 : coll. Cf. *shindy* with its sense-history very similar to that of *shine*, *shines*, nn.—2. ? hence, copulation between human beings : from ca. 1870.

shines like a shitten barn door, it. It shines most brilliantly : a low coll. of C. 18–mid-19. Swift, *Polite Conversation*, ' Why, Miss, you shine this morning like a sh— barn-door ' ; Grose, 3rd ed.

shiney, properly **shiny.** Money ; esp. gold nuggets : 1856, Reade ; very ob. Cf. *shiners*, *shino*.—2. **(Shiney.)** The East, esp. India : Regular Army's : late C. 19–20. B. & P. Ex the brilliant sunlight. Cf. *Sweatipore*, q.v.

shiney-rag. See shine-rag.

shingle. Incorrect for *single* (tail of roebuck or deer) : from ca. 1660. O.E.D.

shingle short, have a. To have a ' tile loose ', to be mentally deficient : from ca. 1850 : Australian s. >, ca. 1910, gen. coll. Mundy, 1852 ; Mrs Campbell Praed, 1885. (O.E.D.)

shingle-splitting. The bilking of creditors by retiring to the country : Tasmanian : 1830, *The Hobart Town Almanack* ; † by 1900. Here, *shingle* = a piece of board. Morris.

shingle-tramper. A coastguardsman : naval coll. (— 1867) ; ob. by 1900, † by 1920. Smyth. Because he constantly walked the shingle of the (pebbly) shore.

shining saucepan and rusty pump. A nautical c.p. (late C. 19–20) applied to a happy ship. Bowen.

Skinkin-ap-Morgan. A Welshman : a coll. nickname : mid-C. 17–mid-18, when *Taffy* (q.v.) > gen. A broadside ballad of ca. 1660 (see Farmer's *Musa Pedestris*) has : ' With Shinkin-ap-Morgan, with Blue-cap, or Teague [q.v.], | We into no Covenant enter, nor League.'

Shinner. A Sinn Feiner : coll. : 1921. O.E.D. (Sup.). Ex pronunciation (*shin fāner*).

shino. An ob. variant of *shiny*, q.v. : from ca. 1860. On *rhino*, q.v. Cf. *shiners*, *shinery* ; see also **shine,** n., 2.

shins, break (one's). To borrow money (cf. U.S. *shinner*, *shinning*) : late C. 17–20 ; slightly ob. B.E. Ex the old Russian custom of beating on the shins those who have money and will not pay their debts (see O.E.D.).

shins, clever. See clever shins.

shiny, adj. See Shiny Seventh.

shiny, the. See shiney. Cf. *shine* (n., 2), *shiners*, *shino*.

shiny rag, win the. See shine-rag.

Shiny Seventh, the. The 7th Battalion City of London Regiment : military : late C. 19–20. F. & Gibbons. Ex ' the always brightly polished brass buttons of their tunics, in contrast to the dark metal buttons worn by the other three battalions with which they were brigaded under the Territorial System.'—2. Also, the 7th Hussars and the 7th Royal Fusiliers : military : mid-C. 19–early 20. ' " Shiny " is the normal nickname of all regiments bearing the number Seven,' R. J. T. Hills, 1934.

Shiny Tenth, the. The 10th Royal Hussars : military : late C. 19–20. (R. J. T. Hills, *Something about a Soldier*, 1934.) Formerly *the China Tenth*, q.v.

ship. A body of compositors working together : printers' coll. : 1875, Southward's *Dict. of Typo-* graphy (O.E.D.). Abbr. *companionship.* Cf. *stab*, q.v.—2. See ship, old.—3. See ship, out of a.

ship, v.t. To pull out of bed, mattress on top : Sherborne School : from ca. 1860.—2. To turn back in a lesson : Shrewsbury School : from ca. 1860. Both are prob. ex *ship* (*off*), to send packing.—3. To drink (v.t.) : nautical coll. (— 1887). Baumann. Lit., take on board.—4. (Ex sense 1.) To turn upside down, to ' rag ' : Oxford undergraduates' : C. 20. Alec Waugh, *The Baliols*, 1934, ' Aesthetes . . . whose rooms are shipped on bump-suppers.' And in the same author's *The Loom of Youth*, 1917, as Public School s.

ship, old. A jocular coll. address to a sailor : orig. and mostly nautical to a former *ship*-mate : mid-C. 19–20 ; ob. Cupples, *The Green Hand*, 1849 (O.E.D.) ; Bowen.

ship, out of a. Out of work : theatrical : ca. 1880–1910. Ware (at *whispering gallery*).

ship a swab. To receive a sub-lieutenant's commission : naval : mid-C. 19–early 20. Bowen. The ' swab ' was the single epaulette conferred by this rank.

ship blown up at Point Nonplus. (Indicates that a man is) plucked penniless or politely expelled : Oxford University : ca. 1820–50. Egan's Grose. *Point Nonplus* is a punningly imaginary geographical feature.

ship for a ha'porth of tar, lose (or spoil) a. Erroneous for *lose a sheep . . .* : mid-C. 19–20. ' Tar is used to protect sores or wounds in sheep from flies, and the consequent generation of worms,' Apperson ; *tar* being the cause of the error. (The proverb dates from late C. 16.)

ship-husband. A sailor seldom on shore and even then anxious to return to his ship : nautical coll. : from ca. 1840 ; ob. Marryat, 1842. Punning the now ob. *ship's husband*, an agent that looks after a ship while it is in port.

ship in full sail. (A pot of) ale : rhyming s. (— 1857). ' Ducange Anglicus.'

ship-mate with, be. To have personal knowledge (of a thing) : nautical : late C. 19–20. Bowen, ' E.g. " I've never been shipmate with single topsails ".'

Ship of Troy, the. A variant of (*the*) *Horse of Troy*, q.v. F. & Gibbons.

ship one's land-face. To revert to one's sea-going attitude : nautical : late C. 19–20 ; ob. Bowen. With hard-case skippers a significant c.p. was *fetch me a bucket of water to wash off my land-face* : a hint to the crew of squalls ahead.

ship's. Naval cocoa or tobacco : naval coll. : C. 20. Bowen.

ship's cousin. A rating or apprentice berthed aft, but working with the men : nautical : late C. 19–20. Bowen. Prob. suggested by S.E. *ship's husband*.

ship's lungs. Dr Hall's patent bellows for ventilating men-of-war : naval coll. : late C. 19–early 20. Bowen.

shipwrecked. Tipsy : East London (— 1909). Ware. Cf. :

shipwrecky. Weak ; ' shaky ' : mid-C. 19–20 : coll. (not very gen.). Hughes, 1857. O.E.D.

shiralee ; shirralee. A swag or bundle of blankets, etc. : Australian : from ca. 1880 ; ob. Ex an Aboriginal word. Cf. *bluey*, q.v. Morris.

shirk. (As used at Eton, j. = S.E.—) At Winchester, from ca. 1860, *shirk in* is to walk, instead of plunging, into water, while *shirk out* is to go out without permission. Cf. *shirkster*.

shirk, in its orig. sense, ' shark, sharper ', ' needy parasite ' and ' to live as a parasite ' (C. 17–18), may have been coll. or s. or even c. Also **sherk**, **shurk**. A variant of *shark*.

shirkster. One who shirks : Winchester : from ca. 1860. Ex *shirk*, q.v.

shirralee. See **shiralee.—shirry.** See **sherry, n.** and **v.**

shirt. See **boiled shirt** and **historical or illustrated s.**

shirt, fly round and tear one's. To bestir oneself : coll. : C. 19–20 ; ob.

shirt, lose one's. To become very angry : from ca. 1865. Ex *shirt out . . .*, q.v.

shirt !, that's up your. That's a puzzler for you ! mid-C. 19–20 ; ob. F. & H.

*shirt, up my (your, etc.). For myself, to my account (etc.) : c. (— 1923). Manchon. Cf. ***watch, my.**

shirt collar. (The sum of) five shillings : rhyming s. (on *dollar*) : from ca. 1850 ; ob. *Everyman,* March 26, 1931. *Oxford scholar* is more usual.

shirt does !, do as my. Kiss my a**e ! : low c.p. : C. 18–20 ; ob. D'Urfey.

shirt-front wicket. A cricket-pitch that looks glossy and is extremely hard and true : Australian cricketers' coll. (— 1920) >, by 1934, S.E. (Lewis.)

shirt full of sore bones, give one a. To beat him severely : coll. : C. 18. Thomas Fuller, *Gnomologia,* 1732. (Apperson.)

shirt in the wind. A piece of shirt seen through the fly or, much more gen., through a hole in the seat : late C. 19–20 ; ob. Gen. *flag in the wind.*

shirt on, bet or (in C. 20, much more gen.) **put one's.** To bet all one's money on, hence to risk all on (a horse) : from ca. 1890. The O.E.D. records *bet* at 1892, *put* at 1897.

shirt out, get or **have** (a person's). To make or become angry : from middle 1850's. ' Ducange Anglicus ' (*have*) ; H., 1st ed. (*get*). Ex the dishevelment caused by rage. Cf. *shirty*, q.v.

shirt-sleevie. A flannel dance : Stonyhurst : late C. 19–20. ' The costume is an open flannel shirt and flannel trousers,' F. & H.

shirtey. Incorrect for *shirty*, q.v.

shirtiness. The n. (late C. 19–20) formed from *shirty*, q.v.

shirtsleeves and shirt-sleeves is a lower classes' c.p. (ca. 1900–12) distinguishing the poor from the rich, hard work from luxury. Ware.

shirty. Angry (temporarily) ; ill-tempered (by nature) ; apt to become quickly angered : from late 1850's. H., 1st ed. ; Maugham, 1897, *Liza of Lambeth,* ' You ain't shirty 'cause I kissed yer ? ' Ex *shirt out,* q.v.

shise, shiser. See **shice, shicer.**

shish. A late C. 19–20 variant of *shice*, adj., 1, and the v., qq.v. Perhaps on *shit(ty)*.

*shish joint. A ' shady ' bookmaker and assistant : turf c. (— 1932). Also *knocking-joint.*

*shisher. A variant of *shicer*, 3 : C. 20. *Slang,* p. 246.

shit, shite. Excrement ; dung : late C. 16–20 (earlier as diarrhœa, a sense † by C. 15) : S.E., but in C. 19–20 a vulgarism. As n., *shite* is in C. 19–20 comparatively rare except in dial. As excrement, prob. ex the v., common to the Teutonic languages : cf. *shice, shicer,* qq.v. I.e. it is ultimately cognate with *shoot.*—2. As a term of contempt applied to a person (rarely to a woman), it has perhaps always, C. 16–20, been coll. ; in C. 19–20, it is

a vulgarism. In C. 19–20, esp. *a regular shit,* in late C. 19–20 *an awful s.* Cf. *shit-house,* q.v.—3. (Gen. subjectively.) A bombardment, esp. with shrapnel : G.W. military. B. & P. Cf. *shit, in the,* 2.— 4. Mud : military : G.W., and prob. before, as certainly after. B. & P.—N.B., 5, many compounds and all proverbs (even Swift's *shitten-cum-shites*) from n. and v. are S.E., but where they survive (e.g. *shit-breech*) they survive as vulgarisms : they (e.g. *shit-fire,s.-word*) do not here receive separate definition unless (e.g. *shit-sack*) in a specifically unconventional sense : all those which are hereinunder defined have always been coll. or s. See Grose, P., and A. W. Read, *Lexical Evidence,* 1935 (Paris ; privately printed), for further details. —6. ' Before the war [of 1914–18], didn't you sportsmen call everybody who didn't hunt and shoot by a very coarse name, which we can change euphemistically into—squirts ? ', H. A. Vachell, *The Disappearance of Martha Penny,* 1934.

shit, shite, v. To stool : C. 14–20 : S.E., but in C. 19–20 a vulgarism ; at the latter stage, *shite* is less gen. than *shit*. See n., 1.—2. To vomit : low coll (— 1887). Baumann.

shit ! ; rarely **shite !** An exclamation : rather low coll. than a vulgarism : C. 19 (? earlier)–20 Cf. Fr. *merde !*

sh**, in the. In trouble : low coll. : mid-C. 19– 20. Often *land* (another) *in the sh**.*—2. Hence, in G.W. military, in the mud and slush ; in mud and danger ; in great or constant danger.

sh**, stir- ; also **sh**-hunter.** A sodomist : low : C. 19–20. F. & H.

sh**, only a little clean. A derisive c.p. addressed to one bedaubed or self-fouled : C. 19–20. In Scottish, gen. *. . . clean dirt.*

sh**-bag. The belly ; in pl., the guts : low : mid-C. 19–20. F. & H.

sh** cinders !, go and eat coke and. A low, derisively defiant c.p. of late C. 19–20 ; ob. (A good example of popular wit.)

sh** 'em !,—soldiers (! or ?), **I've.** C. 20 military c.p. derisive of another unit. Prob. suggested by the proverb, applied to the mean, misshapen, ridiculous : *He* (etc.) *looks as though the devil had shit him flying.*

sh**-hole. The rectum : low coll. : C. 19–20.

sh**-house. A C. 20 variant of *sh**,* n., 2, q.v. Cf. *sh**-pot,* q.v.

sh**-hunter. See **sh**, stir-.**

sh** in your teeth ! A retort on disagreement : C. 18–mid-19 : coll.

sh** it in silver, swallow a sovereign and. A semi-proverbial c.p. indicative of the acme of convenience : C. 19–20 (ob.) vulgarism.

sh** or bust with (e.g.) him, it's. He loves bragging : low coll. : late C. 19–20. Key : ' He's all *wind.*'

sh**-pot. A thorough or worthless humbug (person) ; a sneak : low s., and dial. : mid-C. 19–20 ; ob.

sh**-sack. A Nonconformist : 1769, Granger's *Biographical History of England,* concerning Wm. Jenkin ; this coll. term may have arisen in late C. 17 ; † by 1860. Grose, 2nd ed., repeats Granger's anecdotal ' etymology '.

sh**-shark. A nightman : low : mid-C 19–20 ; ob.

sh**-shoe (occ. **s.-shod**). ' Derisive to one who has bedaubed his boot,' F. & H. : a low coll. of mid-C. 19–20 ; very ob. Cf. *sh**, only a little clean.*

sh through one's or the teeth.** To vomit : low : late C. 18–mid-19. Grose, 2nd ed., gives the following c.p., (*Hark ye, friend,*) *have you got a padlock on your a*se, that you sh*te through your teeth ?*

sh to a shovel, like.** Very adhesive(ly) indeed : low coll. : mid-C. 19–20.

shite. See **shit,** n. and v.—**shitten door.** See **shines like . . .**

shitters. Diarrhœa : dial. and low coll. : C. 19–20.

shittle-cum-shaw, shittle (or shiddle)-cum-shite, shittletidee. Occ. as nn. in allusion, often as exclamations : both contemptuous : C. 19–20 (ob.) dial. and low coll. reduplications on *shit and shite*, app. influenced by *shittle*, fickle, flighty.

Shitten Saturday. Easter Saturday : (dial. and) schools' : from ca. 1855 ; ob. H., 2nd ed. Ex *Shut-in Saturday*, for on it Christ's body was entombed.

shivaree. (Much) official talk : 1926, Galsworthy, *The Silver Spoon*, concerning a law-suit, ' Next came the usual " shivaree " about such and such a case, and what would be taken next, and so on.' For the etymology, see :

shivaroo. A spree ; a party : Australia : 1888, *The* (*Sydney*) *Bulletin*, Oct. 6, ' Government House shivaroos ' ; slightly ob. On Fr. *chez vous* (cf. *shevoo*) ex U.S. *shivaree*, a noisy serenade, itself a corruption of *charivari*, itself echoic.

shiver my timbers ! See **timbers !, shiver my.**

shivering Jemmy (occ., in late C. 19–20, **James**). A beggar that, on a cold day, exposes himself very meagrely clad for alms : low, mostly London (— 1860). H., 2nd ed. Perhaps ex *s. J.*, dial. for *shivering grass*. Cf. *shallow cove* and see **shallow dodge.**

shivers, the. The ague : coll. : 1861, Dickens, in *Great Expectations* (O.E.D.).—2. Hence (often *cold shivers*), horror, nervous fear : coll. : from ca. 1880. In C. 20, both senses are S.E. Cf. :

shivery-shakes. The same ; chills : coll. : mid-C. 19–20. Whence :

shivery-shaky. Trembling, esp. with ague or the cold : coll. : mid-C. 19–20. Anon., *Derby Day*, 1864, ' He's all shivery-shaky, as if he'd got the staggers, or the cold shivers.'

shlemozzle. See **shemozzle.**—***shlenter.** Occ. variant of *schlenter*.—***shliver.** An occ. variant of *chiv(e)*, a knife. Manchon, 1923.—**shoal.** See **shool.**

shoal-water off, in. E.g. ' In shoal-water off the horrors,' on the brink of delirium tremens ; ' near ' in any fig. sense : nautical coll. : late C. 19–20 ; ob. Bowen.

shock-absorber. An observer (opp. the pilot) : Air Force : from 1915. F. & Gibbons.

shocker. See **shilling shocker,** which, from 1890, it occ. displaces. Coll. > S.E.

shocking. Extremely shocking or disgusting or objectionable : coll. : 1842, Browning, ' Shocking | To think that we buy gowns lined with Ermine | For dolts . . .,' O.E.D., but doubtless in spoken use a decade earlier at least. Cf. *shockingly*.

shocking, adv. Shockingly : low coll. : 1831, ' " Vot a shocking bad hat ! "'—the slang Cockney phrase of 1831, as applied to a person : in 1833, Sydney Smith describes New York as ' a shocking big place '.' O.E.D.

shockingly. Extremely or very, esp. in pejorative contexts : 1777, Miss Burney, ' Dr Johnson

. . . is shockingly near-sighted,' O.E.D. Cf. *shocking*, adj.—2. Shockingly ill : coll. : 1768, Goldsmith, ' You look most shockingly to-day, my dear friend,' O.E.D.—3. Hence, from ca. 1880, ' abominably ', very badly. W. G. Marshall, ' Shockingly paved,' O.E.D.

Shocks. Choques, a small Fr. town near Bethune : military : G.W. (F. & Gibbons.)

shod, come in hosed and. To be born to a good estate : coll. : C. 19–20, ob. Cf. *be born with a silver spoon in one's mouth.*

shod (all) round, be. To know all about married life : coll. : C. 18–early 19. Swift, in *Conversation*, I, ' " Mr Buzzard has married again . . ." " This is his fourth wife ; then he has been shod round." '—2. ' A parson who attends a funeral is said to be shod all round, when he receives a hat-band, gloves, and scarf : many shoeings being only partial,' Grose, 2nd ed. : late C. 18–mid-19.

***shoddy-dropper.** A seller of cheap serge : New Zealand c. (— 1932).

shoe (or S.). Always *the*—. A room in Southgate Debtors' Prison : C. 19.—2. A tyre, esp. of a motor-car : garages' s. : from ca. 1920. Richard Blaker, *Night-Shift*, 1934.

shoe-buckles, not worth. Worthless : coll. : late C. 17–18. Ray.

shoe is on the mast, the. ' If you like to be liberal, now's your time ' : a c.p. of C. 19 : sailors' > gen. lower classes'. In C. 18, ' when near the end of a long voyage, the sailors nailed a shoe to the mast, the toes downward, that passengers might delicately bestow a parting gift.' (Ware.)

***shoe-leather !** Look out ! ; be careful ! : c. : mid-C. 19–20 ; ob. ' Ducange Anglicus ' ; H., 1st ed. Perhaps cf. Warwickshire dial. *s.-l.*, a kicking (E.D.D.).

shoe pinches him, his. He is drunk : coll. : C. 18. Franklin's *Drinker's Dict.*

shoe the cobbler. ' To tap the ice quickly with the fore-foot when sliding,' F. & H. : coll. : from ca. 1840 ; ob. Cf. *cobbler's knock*, q.v.

shoe the goose. To undertake or do anything futile or absurd : coll. : C. 15–18. Hoccleve, Skelton, Breton. By late C. 18, it has > a proverb, gen. in form *shoe the goslings*, usually, however, applied to a busybody smith. Apperson.—2. To get drunk : coll. : C. 17. Cotgrave. Extant in Shropshire and Herefordshire diall. (E.D.D.).

shoe the horse. To cheat one's employer : lower classes' (— 1923). Manchon. Perhaps ex :

shoe the (wild) colt. To demand an initiation-fee from one entering on office or employment : dial. (— 1828) and coll. ; very ob. as the latter. Punning *colt*, a greenhorn. F. & H. favours *wild*, Apperson omits it.

shoemaker. The large Antarctic gull : nautical (—1867). Bowen. Perhaps jocular on its scientific name, *skua antarticus.*

shoemaker's pride. Creaking boots or shoes : dial. and coll. : mid-C. 19–20. Cf. :

shoemaker's stocks, be in the. To be pinched by strait shoes : ca. 1660–1910. Pepys, 1666 (O.E.D.); Ray, 1678 ; B.E. ; Grose. Cf. *shoemaker's pride.*

shoes, die in one's. To be hanged : ca. 1690–1910 : S.E. until C. 19, then coll. Motteux ; Barham ; H., 5th ed. (O.E.D.)

shoes, make children's. To be occupied absurdly or trivially ; (to be made) to look ridiculous : coll. : late C. 17–19 ; in C. 19, mainly dial. Behn, 1682, ' Pox ! shall we stand making children's shoes all the year ? No : let's begin to settle the nation, I say, and go through-stitch with our work.' Cf :

shoes, make feet for children's. To coït : late C. 18–mid-19. Ex preceding.

shoes are made of running leather, my, your, etc. I, you, etc., am—are—of a wandering disposition, or very restless : semi-proverbial coll. : from ca. 1570 ; ob. Churchyard, 1575 ; Hone, 1831. Apperson.

shoesmith. A cobbler : jocular coll. : C. 19–20 ; ob. On S.E. sense, a shoeing-smith.

shoey. A shoeing-smith : military : late C. 19–20. F. & Gibbons.—2. (**Shoey.**) The ' inevitable ' nickname of men surnamed Smith : military : late C. 19–20. F. & Gibbons.

***shoful** (1854, but implied for ca. 1850 by Carew's *Gipsy*) ; occ. **schofel**(l) (1839), **schoful** (1859), **shofel** (1839), **shofle** (1862), **shouful** (— 1914), (? only in sense 4) **shovel** (1864) ; often **showfull** (1851). (Only in sense 1 as an adj.) Counterfeit money : Brandon, 1839 ; 1851, Mayhew ; Carew's *Autobiography of a Gipsy*. Yiddish almost imm. > Cockney s. verging on c., which indeed it may orig. have been—as Smythe-Palmer, 1882, says it was. Ex Yiddish *schofel*, worthless stuff, ex Ger. *schofel*, worthless, base, ex Yiddish pronunciation of Hebrew *shaphel* (or *-al*), low, as the O.E.D. so clearly sets forth. (Also **shoful money** : cf. *shoful-man*, q.v.)—2. A low-class tavern : low : ca. 1850–1910, and perhaps never very gen. Mayhew, 1851. Prob. directly ex the adj. *schofel* (see sense 1) with *place* or *tavern* suppressed.—3. A humbug, an impostor : ca. 1860–90. H., 3rd ed. See sense 1.—4. (Often spelt *shofle*, occ. *shovel*.) A hansom cab ; among cabmen, a ' shoful ' cab, according to Mayhew (*London Labour*, iii, 351), is one infringing Hansom's patent : 1854, *Household Words*, vol. viii. (O.E.D.) ; ob. by 1910, virtually † by 1930. There is little need to suppose with the O.E.D., that this sense may have a distinct origin, though H., 3rd ed., suggests the similarity of a hansom to a shovel or a scoop, and his successor in the 5th ed. cites (*à titre de curiosité*) a friend's ' shoful, full of show, ergo, beautiful—handsome—Hansom.'—5. See :

shoful (jewellery). Sham jewellery : 1864, H., 3rd ed., but prob. a decade older. Here, *shoful* may be adj. or n. (see **shoful,** 1) : cf. *shoful money.*

***shoful-man.** A counterfeiter of coins, notes, etc. ; occ. = *shoful-pitcher* : c. : 1856, Mayhew.

***shoful(-)money.** Counterfeit money : c. : from the 1850's. See **shoful,** 1.

***shoful(etc.)-pitcher.** A passer of counterfeit money : c. (— 1839). Brandon (*schofels-*) ; H., 1st ed. (*shoful*).

***shoful-pitching.** Passing of counterfeit money ; c. (— 1857). ' Ducange Anglicus ' ; H., 2nd ed. : but the reference in Carew's *Autobiography of a Gipsy* is to some twelve years earlier than in ' Ducange Anglicus '.

shoful pullet. ' A " gay " woman ', H., 2nd ed. : low (? c.) : ca. 1860–90.

***sholl.** (Gen. v.t.) To crush the wearer's hat over his eyes : c. : from ca. 1860 ; ob. H., 3rd ed. ? ex *shola* (*hat*), a sola topee.

shoo to a goose, cannot say. To be timid, bashful : from ca. 1630 : coll. till C. 19, then S.E.—with *boh* much more frequent.

***shook,** ppl. (adj.), itself sol. Robbed ; lost by robbery : c. of ca. 1810–80. Vaux, 1812, ' I've been *shook* of my *skin*, I have been robbed of my purse.' See **shake,** v., 3 and 4, and cf. next entry.

—2. A synonym, ca. 1810–50, of *rocked*, q.v. Vaux.

***shook ?, have you.** Have you succeeded in stealing anything ? : c. of ca. 1810–80. See **shake,** v., 4, and cf. *shook.* Vaux.

shook on. (Sense 1, gen. of a man ; 2, of either sex.) In love with, or possessed of a passion for : Australian : 1888, ' Rolf Boldrewood', ' He was awful shook on Madge ; but she wouldn't look at him.'—2. Having a great fancy for (a thing) : 1888, Boldrewood, ' I'm regular shook on the polka.' Cf. the very Australian *crook*, ill.

shook-up ; esp. **reg'lar s.u.** Upset ; nerveracked : low coll. : late (? mid) C. 19–20.

shool ; Shool. A church or chapel : East London : from ca. 1870. Ware. Ex the Jews' term for their synagogue.

shool ; occ. **shoole** (Grose, 2nd ed.) or **shoal** (C 19) ; often **shule** (C. 18–20) To go about begging, to sponge, to ' scrounge ' : dial. and s. : from 1730's. Smollett, 1748, ' They went all hands to shooling and begging ' ; Lover, 1842. Perhaps ex *shool*, a shovel, via dial. *shool*, to drag the feet, to saunter.—2. Hence, to skulk : dial. and s. : from ca. 1780 ; ob. Grose, 1st ed.—3. To impose on (a person) : 1745, Bampfylde-Moore Carew (O.E.D.). Ex sense 1.—4. To carry as a ' blind ' : 1820, Clare : dial. and s. ; ob. O.E.D.

shooler or **shuler ;** occ. **shoolman.** A beggar, vagabond, ' scrounger ', loafer : 1830, Carleton, ' What tribes of beggars and shulers,' E.D.D. ; F. & H. (*shoolman*).

***shoon.** A fool ; a lout : c. of late C. 19–20 ; ob. ? on *loon.*

shoot. Amount, number : see **shoot, the whole.** —2. Dismissal, esp. in *get* or *give* (a person) *the shoot* : C. 20.—3. See **Shoot, the.**

shoot, v.i. (Also **shoot a bishop.**) To have a wet dream : low : from ca. 1870 ; ob.—2. V.t., to unload : railway : 1872, *The Echo*, July 29 ; slightly ob. Prob. on *shoot rubbish.*—3. To give utterance to : 1929. Ex *shoot* !, q.v.—4. See phrases hereinunder.

shoot ! Go ahead ; speak ! : from ca. 1925. Ex the cinema : in making a film, *shoot !* = use your camera now : orig. U.S.

Shoot, the. The Walworth Road station : London : late C. 19–20 ; ob. Because ' a large number of workpeople alight there ', F. & H. ; punning *rubbish-shoot.*

shoot, the whole. The entire amount or number or price, etc. : 1884 (O.E.D.) or perhaps from as early as 1880 (Ware) : s. >, ca. 1920, coll. Occ. *the entire shoot* (? first in 1896). Hence, *go the whole shoot* (— 1903), to risk everything. Suggested by *whole shot.* Cf. *shooting-match*, q.v.

shoot ?, will you. Will you pay for a (small) strong drink ? : Australian c.p. : ca. 1900–14.

shoot a man. Gen. as vbl.n., *shooting a man*, the common practice of jobbers who, guessing whether a broker is a buyer or a seller, alter their prices up or down accordingly : Stock Exchange (— 1935).

shoot a paper-bolt. To circulate a false or unauthenticated rumour : coll. (— 1923). Manchon.

shoot-about. See **shootabout.**

shoot-and-scoots. A gen. military synonym of *imshee artillery*, q.v. : 1915–18.

shoot between or **(be)twixt wind and water.** To coït with a woman : coll. : late C. 17–20 ; ob. Implied in Congreve, 1695.—2. To infect venereally : late C. 17–early 19. B.E., Grose. Gen. in the passive, punning the S.E. sense, 'to receive a shot causing a dangerous leak '.

*shoot-fly. The snatching theft of watches : c. (— 1933). Charles E. Leach.

shoot in the eye. To do (a person) a bad turn : coll. : late C. 19–20.

shoot in the tail. To coït with (a woman) ; to sodomise : low : mid-C. 19–20.

shoot into the brown. To fail : Volunteers' : ca. 1860–1915. Ware. Ex rifle-practice, at which the poor shot misses the target, his bullet going into the brown earth of the butt.

shoot off one's mouth. To talk ; esp. to talk boastfully or indiscreetly ; to tell all one knows (cf. *spill the beans*) : orig. (1887) U.S. and = talk abusively ; anglicised, thanks to the ' talkies ', in 1930–31 ; in Canada, by 1925. Cf. *say a mouthful, spill the beans.*

shoot one's linen. To make one's shirt cuffs project beyond one's coat cuffs : coll. : 1878, Yates, in *The World*, Jan. 16. Cf. *shoot your cuff*, q.v.

shoot one's lines. To declaim vigorously : theatrical : from ca. 1870.

shoot one's milt or **roe.** To ejaculate seminally : low : mid-C. 19–20.

shoot one's mouth off. A variant of *shoot off one's mouth*. Dorothy Sayers, *Murder Must Advertise*, 1933. Also, as H. Wade, *Constable Guard Thyself*, 1934, *shoot one's mouth.*

shoot one's star. To die : late C. 19–20 ; ob. Ex evanescent shooting stars.

shoot (out) one's neck. ' To butt into a conversation with an unwarranted air of authority ; to make a long speech where either brevity or silence is indicated. Often with an implication of boasting or exaggeration ' : military : from 1915. B. & P. Of American origin.

shoot over the pitcher. To brag of one's shooting : coll. : C. 19.

shoot that ! Oh, be quiet ! : late C. 19–20. Possibly ex such Americanisms as *shoot that hat !*— 2. Stop talking (about), as in *shoot the shop !* : late C. 19–20.

shoot the amber. (Of a motorist) to increase speed when the amber light is showing, in order to pass before the red (' stop ') light comes on : motorists' : from late 1935.

shoot the cat. See **cat, shoot the.**—2. ' To sound a refrain in the infantry bugle call to defaulters' drill, which, it is fancied, follows the sound of the words " *Shoot the cat—shoot the cat* ",' F. & H. : military : late C. 19–early 20.

shoot the crow. To depart without paying : 1887, *Fun*, June 8 ; ob. Cf. *burn.*

shoot the moon. See **moon, shoot the ;** also **shove the moon.**

shoot the sitting pheasant. ' To injure or destroy the life or reputation of one who is entirely helpless to defend himself, and therefore has no chance ' : coll. (— 1931) now verging on S.E. Lyell, ' To shoot at a bird, except when it's in flight, is the height of unsportsmanship.'

shoot up the straight, do a. To coït with a woman : low : mid-C. 19–20. Cf. *do a rush . . .* and *shoot in the tail.*

shoot (a person) up with. Not to do something that someone wishes done ; to do something other than what was desired : military : from ca. 1925.

shoot your cuff ! ' Make the best personal appearance you can and come along ' (Ware) :

lower classes' : ca. 1875–90. The semantics are those of *shoot one's linen*, q.v.

shootable. Suitable : sol. when not jocular : from ca. 1830. (O.E.D.)

shootabout. An irregular form of football : schools', esp. Charterhouse : late C. 19–20. Also *shoot-about*, as in A. H. Tod, *Charterhouse*, 1900. Cf. *punt-about* and *run-about.*

shooter. A gun or pistol ; esp. a revolver : resp. 1840, 1877 : s. >, ca. 1910, coll. O.E.D.—2. A shooting-stick : printers' : from ca. 1860. Prob. on sense 1.—3. A black morning coat as distinguished from the tail coat worn by the Fifth and Sixth Forms : Harrow : from ca. 1870. Hence, more gen. = any black morning coat : C. 20. O.E.D. (Sup.).

shooter's hill. The ' mons veneris ' : low : late C. 19–20 ; ob. Punning *Shooter's Hill*, London.— 2. Whence *take a turn on Shooter's Hill*, to coït.

shooting a man. See **shoot a man.**

shooting-gallery, the. The front line : military : 1914–18. The metaphor exists also in Ger. military s.

shooting-match, the whole. The whole thing, affair, etc. : from ca. 1915. (R. Blaker, *Night-Shift*, 1934.) Ex *the whole shoot* by influence of the G.W.

Shop, always preceded by **the.** The Royal Military Academy : Army : mid-C. 19–20. Kipling. A special use of :—2. **(shop.)** A place of business ; where one works : coll. : 1841, Thackeray. An extension of the basic sense (a building, a room, where things are sold).—3. Often, Oxford or Cambridge University : from ca. 1840 : s. >, ca. 1880, coll. ; slightly ob. Clough in his *Long Vacation Pastoral*, ' Three weeks hence we return to the shop ' ; Thackeray, 1848. Esp. *the other shop*, which is often used of a rival (chiefly, the most important rival) establishment of any kind.—4. Linked with the preceding sense is the jocular one, place—any place whatsoever. (Thus, in political s., the House of Commons, as in Trollope's *Framley Parsonage*, 1861 ; among small tradesmen, one's house or home, as in H., 5th ed. ; among actors, the theatre, from ca. 1880, says Ware.) Mid-C. 19–20. Cf. *shop, all over the*, q.v.—5. Hence, in racing, a ' place ' (1st, 2nd, or 3rd) : from ca. 1870. H., 5th ed.—6. An engagement, ' berth ' : theatrical : 1888, Jerome K. Jerome, ' Being just before Christmas . . ., there was no difficulty in getting another shop,' O.E.D. From twenty years earlier in dial. : see the E.D.D. (Also gen. s. : 1898, W. Pett Ridge, *Mord Em'ly*.—7. (Cf. sense 1.) **the Shop.** Stock Exchange s. >, ca. 1900 coll. >, ca. 1910 j., as in *The Rialto*, May 23, 1889, ' The latest name for the South African gold market is the Shop.'—8. **(the shop.)** The promoting interest behind an issue of stock : Stock Exchange (— 1935).—9. **(shop.)** A prison : c. : late C. 17–18. B.E. ; Grose. Cf. *to shop* in c.—10. ? hence, the mouth : dial. and s. : from ca. 1860. Whence *shut your shop !*, be silent ! —11. (Certainly ex ' prison ' sense.) A guard-room : military : mid-C. 19–20 ; ob. by 1914, virtually † by 1930.—12. A causing to be arrested : c. : from ca. 1920. Edgar Wallace, e.g. in *A King by Night*, 1925.. Ex :

*shop, v. To imprison : late C. 16–20 : S.E. until mid-C. 17, coll. till late C. 17, then c. B.E., Grose.—2. To put (an officer) under arrest in the guard-room : military (— 1864). H., 3rd ed.—3. To lay information on which a person is arrested :

c.: mid-C. 19–20. Frequent in Edgar Wallace's detective novels. Ex sense 1.—4. Whence, or directly ex sense 1, to kill: c.: late C. 19–20. F. & H. Perhaps influenced by *ship*, to send packing.—5. To dismiss (a shop-assistant): from ca. 1860; ob. H., 3rd ed. Prob. ironically on S.E. *shop*, to give a person work (1855, O.E.D.).—6. **be shopped, get a shop**: to gain 1st, 2nd or 3rd place: the turf: from ca. 1870. H., 5th ed. (*get a shop*; the other from ca. 1890). Ex the corresponding n. —7. (Gen. in passive.) To engage a person for a piece: theatrical (— 1909). Ware. Ex *shop*, n., 6.

shop, all over the. Much scattered, spread out, dispersed; erratic in course: 1874 (= 1873), H., 5th ed., 'In pugilistic slang, to punish a man severely is "to knock him all over the shop", i.e. the ring, the place in which the work is done'; 1886, *The Pall Mall Gazette*, July 29, 'Formerly, the authorities associated with our fisheries were "all over the shop", if a vulgarism of the day be permissible,' O.E.D.: coll. >, ca. 1910, S.E. Ex *shop*, n., 4.

shop, come or **go to the wrong.** 'To come (go) to the wrong person or place to get what one requires': coll.: late C. 19–20. Lyell. See **shop, n., 4.**

shop, get a. See **shop, v., 6.**

shop, shut up. To cease talking: mid-C. 19–20. Cf. *shop*, n., penultimate sense.—2. **shut up** (a person's) **shop.** To make him cease; to kill him: late C. 19–20; ob.

shop, sink the. To refrain from talking shop: coll.: late C. 19–20. Prob. on *sink the ship*. (This sense of *shop* is excellent S.E.; in many ways preferable to *jargon*, except where a technical term is indispensable.)

shop, top of the. 'No 99 in the game of "Crown and Anchor"': military: C. 20. F. & Gibbons.

shop-bouncer. Mid-C. 19–20; ob. H., 1st ed.: low s., bordering on c. A variant of *shop-lift*, q.v. Ex:

*shop-bouncing.** Shoplifting: c. (— 1839). Brandon.

*shop-lift.** A shop-thief; esp. one who, while pretending to bargain, steals goods from the shop: ca. 1670–1830: c. until ca. 1700, then S.E. Head, 1673; B.E. See **lift.**

*shop-lifter.** The same: 1680, Kirkman (O.E.D.): c. or s. until C. 19, then coll. till ca. 1840, then S.E. Cf. *shop-lift.* (Perhaps always S.E.: *shop-lifting*.)

shop-masher. A very well, or much, dressed shop-assistant: lower classes': ca. 1885–1910. Baumann.

*shop-mumper.** A beggar operating in shops: c. (— 1887). Baumann.

shop-officer. A professional soldier: military coll. (— 1923). Manchon. Prob. ex *shop*, n., 1.

shop-pad. A shop-thief: C. 18: s. > coll. Dunton, 1705 (O.E.D.). See **pad, n.**

shop-'un. A preserved as opp. to a fresh egg: coll.: 1878, dramatist Byron, 'I knows 'em! Shop-'uns! Sixteen a shilling!'

shopkeeper. An article still, after a long time, unsold: 1649, G. Daniel, who uses the frequent variant *old shopkeeper*. (O.E.D.)

*shopper.** He who causes the arrest of a malefactor: c.: C. 20. Edgar Wallace.

shoppie. See **shoppy.—shop(p)o.** See **shappo.**

shoppy. A shop-girl or, less often, -man: coll.: C. 20 (H. A. Vachell, *Martha Penny*, 1934).

shore boss. 'The steward's name for the superintendent steward': nautical coll.: C. 20. Bowen.

shore loafer. Any civilian: bluejackets' pejorative coll.: late C. 19–20. Bowen.

shore saints and sea devils. A nautical (mid-C. 19–20; ob.) c.p. applied to such sailing-ship skippers as were lambs with the owners and lions with the crew. Cf. *ship one's land-face*, q.v. Bowen.

Shoreditch, the Duke of. A mock-title: coll. verging on S.E.: ca. 1547–1683. See esp. Ellis's *History of Shoreditch*, p. 170.

Shores. Lake Shore & Michigan Railroad shares: Stock Exchange coll.: late C. 19–20. A. J. Wilson, *Stock Exchange Glossary*, 1895.

short. A card (any below the 8) so tampered-with that none above the 8 can be cut, thus reducing the chances of an honour's turning up to two to one: gaming: mid-C. 19–20. (Not to be confused with *shorts*, short whist.)—2. The same as *short, something*, q.v.: coll.: 1823, Egan's Grose. Cf. *short*, adj.—3. A short excerpt; a short film or musical composition: coll.: from not later than 1927.

short, adj. Undiluted: coll.: from ca. 1820. See n., 2, and **short, something.**—2. A cashier's 'Long or short?' means 'Will you have your notes in small or large denominations?', *short* because thus there will be few notes, *long* because many, or because the former method is short, the latter long: bankers' > gen. commercial coll.: from ca. 1840.— 3. 'A conductor of an omnibus, or any other servant, is said to be short, when he does not give all the money he receives to his master,' H., 3rd ed.: from ca. 1860; ob. Cf. *short one*, q.v.

short, bite off. To dismiss, or refuse, abruptly: tailors': from ca. 1870. Prob. ex the habit of biting instead of cutting thread or cotton.

short, something. (A drink of) undiluted spirits: coll.: from ca. 1820. Either because, as Egan (1823) suggests, 'unlengthened by water' or, as O.E.D. proposes, ex short name—e.g. 'brandy', not 'brandy and water'.

short, the long and the. See **long and the short.**

short and sweet, like a donkey's gallop. A coll. elaboration of *short and sweet*: late C. 19–20: coll. and dial. Apperson.

short and thick, like a Welshman's prick. A low c.p. applied to a short person very broad in the beam: mid-C. 19–20.

short-arm inspection. An inspection 'conducted periodically . . . to detect symptoms of venereal disease': military: from ca. 1910. B. & P. With a pun on pistols.

short-arse driver. An artillery driver: artillerymen's: from ca. 1910. Irrespective of height.

short circuit. Gastro-enterotomy: medical: C. 20. Richard Ince, *Shadow-Show*, 1932, 'The pleasant little major operation they call . . . facetiously "a short circuit".'

short cock. Cheese: Yorkshire s. (— 1904), not dial. E.D.D.

short hairs, have by the. See **hairs, have by the short.**

short(-)head. A horse that fails by a short head: racing coll.: 1883, J. Greenwood, 'That horribly anathematised short head.'

short home, come. To be put in prison: coll.: C. 17–18. Ex S.E. sense, to fail to return (orig. and esp. from an expedition).

short(-)length. A small glass of brandy: coll. (Scots, esp. Glasgow): 1864, *The Glasgow Citizen*, Nov. 19, 'The exhilarating short-length.'

short-limbered. Touchy: late C. 19–early 20. Cf. *short-waisted*.

short of a sheet. Mentally deficient: late C. 19–20; ob. Cf. *shingle short*.

short(-)one. A passenger not on the way-bill: coaching: ca. 1830–70. Because the way-bill is short of this passenger's name: C. *short*, adj., 3.—2. See **short 'un**.

short(-)stick. (Occ. collective.) A piece, or pieces, of material of insufficient length: drapers': from ca. 1860. *Once a Week*, 1863, viii, 179.

short time. A visit to a prostitute for one copulation only: low coll.: late C. 19–20. Hence:

short-timers. An (amorous) couple hiring a room for an hour or two: low: C. 20. Manchon.

short 'un. A partridge: poachers' (— 1909). Ware derives ex 'the almost complete absence of tail feathers'. Contrast *long 'un*, and see **tall 'un.**

short-waisted. Irritable; touchy: esp. among tailors: from ca. 1870. Cf. *short-limbered*.

***shortening**, vbl.n. Clipping coins (as a profession): c.: ca. 1865; ob. '*No. 747*.'

shorter. A coin-clipper: low s. verging on c.: 1857, Borrow's *Romany Rye*.

shorthorn; mechanical cow. A Maurice Farman biplane, either without (*shorthorn*) or with (*m. cow*), long front skids: Air Force nicknames: 1913; now only historical. O.E.D. (Sup.).

shorts. Short-dated securities: money-market coll.: from ca. 1930. O.E.D. (Sup.).

Shorty is an inevitable nickname of men surnamed Wright: military: C. 20. F. & Gibbons.

Shot. (Always—or virtually—*the Shot*.) Aldershot: Regular Army: from ca. 1880. F. & Gibbons.

shot. Amount due for payment; one's share thereof: late C. 15–20: S.E. until late C. 18, then coll. Grose. Cf. *shoot, the whole*, q.v.—2. A corpse disinterred: body-snatchers' s. > j.: 1828, *The Annual Register*; ob. by 1900, virtually † by 1930. App. ex *a good shot for the doctors*. O.E.D.—3. A meridional altitude ascertained by *shooting the sun*: nautical (— 1867). Smyth.—4. An extremely hard cake, tart, etc.: coll (— 1923). Manchon.—5. Hence, something difficult to tolerate or believe: id. Ibid.—6. Money: low (— 1923). Ib.—7. A photograph taken with cinematograph camera: coll.: U.S. (ca. 1923), anglicised by 1925. O.E.D. (Sup.). —8. A dram (of spirits): coll.: U.S., anglicised by 1932. Ibid.—9. A dose (of a drug): 1929. Ibid. —10. A stroke with cane or strap: Harrow School: late C. 19–20. Arnold Lunn, *The Harrovians*, 1913.

shot, v. To make a weak-winded horse seemingly sound: horse-dealers' (— 1874). H., 5th ed. By dosing with small shot to 'open his pipes'.

shot, adj. Tipsy: from ca. 1870. Ex being wounded by a shot. Cf. the U.S. *shot in the neck*, perhaps the imm. origin, and *shot-away*, and *overshot*.

shot! Look out, a master's coming!: Royal High School, Edinburgh: late C. 19–20. Abbr. *good shot!*; gen. 'shot, sir!': late C. 19–20: coll. >, by 1920, S.E. (Collinson.)

shot, be. 'To make a disadvantageous bet which is instantly accepted,' F. & H.: the turf: from ca. 1880.—2. To be photographed: photographers' coll.: from ca. 1885.

shot, do a. See **do a shot**.

shot, hot. See **hot shot**.

shot, like a. Very quickly; immediately: coll.: 1809, Malkin (O.E.D.).—2. Hence, very willingly, unhesitantly: coll.: late C. 19–20.

shot, pay the. v.i. and t. To coït (with a woman): coll.: C. 17–19. F. & H. quotes two C. 17 broadside ballads. Ex *pay the shot*, to pay the bill or one's share of it, now coll. (see **shot**, n., 1.).

shot at dawn, to be. A jocular military c.p. (1915; ob.) applied to a person in trouble. F. & Gibbons. Ex death at the hands of a post-court-martial shooting-squad.

shot-away. Tipsy: nautical: late C. 19–20. Bowen. Cf. *shot*, adj.

shot-bag. A purse: 1848, Durivage, 'Depositing the "tin" in his shot-bag'; slightly ob. Ex *shot*, money, as in *shot in the locker*.

shot between or **(be)twixt wind and water.** See **shoot between** . . .

shot-clog. A simpleton tolerated only because of his willingness to 'pay the shot': mid-C. 19–20; ob. Cf. *shot-ship*, q.v.

shot down, ppl.adj. Beaten in an argument: aircraft engineers': from ca. 1918. *The Daily Herald*, Aug. 1, 1936. Ex 'planes being shot down in G.W.

shot first, I'll see (him, her, gen.**) you.** Damned if I'll do it!: low coll.: 1894, 'John Strange Winter' (O.E.D.). A variant of:

shot if ——, I'll (or may I) be. Mildly imprecatory or strongly dissenting: low coll.: 1826, Buckstone, 'He, he, he! I'll be shot if Lunnun temptation be onything to this.' H., 1st ed., has the ob. variant, *I wish I may be shot if ——*. Cf. *shot first* . . .

shot in the eye. An ill turn: coll.: late C. 19–20; slightly ob. *Pearson's Magazine*, Sept., 1897, 'Getting square with the millionaire who had done him such an unscrupulous shot in the eye.'

shot in the giblets or **tail.** Pregnant: low: mid-C. 19–20.

shot in the locker, not a. Destitute of money, ideas, or anything else: naval coll.: mid-C. 19–20. Bowen.

shot of. A mid-C. 19–20 Cockney variant of *shut of*, q.v. H., 2nd ed.

shot on the post, be. To have a competitor pass one as one easies for, or wearies at, the finish: athletics coll.: 1897. Ex—2. The same of horses in racing: adumbrated in 1868: coll. (By 1920, both senses were S.E.) O.E.D.

shot-ship. 'A company sharing and sharing alike,' F. & H.: printers': from ca. 1875.

shot-soup. Inferior pea-soup: nautical: late C. 19–20; ob. Ex peas like bullets.

shot 'twixt . . . See **shot between** . . .

shot up the back, be. To be put out of action or detected: military: C. 20. F. & Gibbons.

shotter. See **fly-balance.—shouful.** See **shoful.**

should say (suppose, think), I. I'm very much inclined to say, etc.; I certainly do say, etc.: coll.: 1775, C. Johnston, 'I should rather think he has a mind to finger its finances,' O.E.D.

shoulder, v.i. and t. To take passengers without entering them on the way-bill, thus defrauding the employer: coaching: ca. 1820–70. 'Jon Bee', 1823; cf. his *Picture of London*, 1828 (p. 33). —2. Hence, v.t., of any servant embezzling his master's money: from ca. 1860. H., 2nd ed.; ob. Both senses very frequent as vbl.n.

shoulder (or, more gen., **shoulders), narrow in the.** Not good at taking a joke: coll. (— 1923). Manchon.

shoulder, over the (left). See **left (shoulder), over the.**

shoulder, slip of the. (Of the woman 'victim') seduction : coll. : C. 19.

shoulder-feast. A dinner for the hearse-bearers after a funeral : ca. 1810–60. *Lex. Bal.*

*shoulder-sham. A partner to a 'file', q.v. : c. : late C. 17–early 19. B.E.

shoulder-stick. A passenger not on the way-bill, i.e. one whose fare goes into the pockets of driver and guard : coaching : ca. 1825–70. Cf. *short one.*

shouldering. See **shoulder.**

shouldology ; sleeveology. Discussion of shoulders and sleeves by : tailors : C. 20. Cf. *collarology.*

shout. 'A call to a waiter to replenish the glasses of a company : hence, a turn in paying for a round of drinks. Also, a free drink given to all present by one of the company ; a drinking party,' this last being rare : Australian, hence New Zealand ; by 1903 (indeed, long before that : see H., 3rd ed., 1864), fairly gen. : 1863, H. Simcox, 'Many a "shout" they're treated to.' O.E.D. and Morris. Ex *shout*, v.i.—2. Hence, one's turn to entertain another : from ca. 1885. E.g. 'It's my shout this time.' Baumann.

shout, v. To stand drinks to the company, hence to even one person : v.i., 1859, H. Kingsley ; v.t., to pay for drinks for (a person, persons), hence for (say) 'smokes', 1867, Lindsay Gordon ; hence, late C. 19–20, to entertain (a person, persons). Australian, hence New Zealand ; by 1864—witness H., 3rd ed.—well-known in England. (Morris ; O.E.D.) Ex shouting to the waiter to fetch drinks.

shout, go on the. To embark on a bout of drinking ; to drink to excess : from ca. 1890 : orig. Australian ; by 1905, gen. Kipling (O.E.D.). See **shout**, n., and cf. next two entries.

shout, stand (a). To pay for drinks all round : 1887, 'Hopeful', 'There is a great deal of standing "shout" in the Colonies,' O.E.D. See **shout**, n., 1.

shout oneself hoarse. To get drunk : gen. s. (— 1903). Punning lit. sense of the whole phrase and the s. sense of *shout*, v. (q.v.).

shout the odds. See **odds, shout the.**

shout up. To address vigorously by way of warning : coll. : from ca. 1930.

shouter. One who 'shouts' : 1885, Douglas Sladen (O.E.D.). See **shout**, v. Cf. :

shouting, vbl.n. (Issuing) an 'all-in' invitation to drink. See **shout**, v. 1.

*shov. A knife : c. (— 1909). Ware. Ex *chiv(e)* on **shove.**

shove, n. See **shove, the** and **on the** ; also *shove in the eye* and *the mouth.*—2. A coïtion : coll. : C. 18–20. Ned Ward, 1707. Esp. in *give* (a woman) *a shove.* Cf. *shove*, v., 2, and *push.*—3. Empty talk ; self-glorification : coll., at first (ca. 1880) low urban, but by 1887 (at latest), gen. ; † by 1920. Prob. ex :—4. Energy ; initiative : (low) coll. : from the 1870's ; ob. Presumably suggested by equivalent *push.*

shove, v.t. To thrust, put, carelessly or roughly or hurriedly into a place, a receptacle : familiar S.E. often merging into coll. : 1827, Scott, 'Middlemas . . . shoved into his bosom a small packet.' Also *shove aside* (1864) or *away* (1861). O.E.D.—2. Gen. v.t. To coït (with) : coll. : C. 17–20 ; ob. —3. See vbl. phrases here ensuing.

shove, be on the. To keep moving, to move : coll. : late C. 19–20.

shove, get and **give the.** See **shove, the.**

shove, on the. On the move ; moving : coll. : late C. 19–20. Milliken, 1893, 'There's always some fun afoot there, as will keep a chap fair on the shove.'

shove, the. A dismissal : 1899, Whiteing in *No. 5 John Street*, has both *get the shove* and *give the shove*, to be dismissed, to dismiss. Cf. *push, get* or *give the.*

shove along. See **shove off.**

shove for. To go to ; make a move towards : coll. : 1884, Mark Twain, 'Me and Tom shoved for bed.' Cf. *shove, be on the*, and *shove off.*

shove-halfpenny. A gambling game akin to shovel-board : 1841, *Punch*, Nov. 27, 'The favourite game of shove-halfpenny' : s. >, ca. 1910, coll. On the † *shove-groat*, *slide-groat*, and *shove-board* (later *shovel-board*).

shove in (a thing). To pawn it : low coll. : late C. 19–20. Ware.

shove in one's face. To put in one's mouth : low coll. : late C. 19–20. A. A. Milne, *Two People*, 1931, (self-made millionaire *loquitur*) 'For years . . . I used to say, "Here, shove that in your face," whenever I offered anybody a cigar.'

shove in the eye, etc. A punch in the eye, etc. : coll. : late C. 19–20. Whiteing, 1899, 'Mind your own bloomin' business, or I'll give yer a shove in the eye.'

shove in the mouth. A drink : 1811, *Lex. Bal.* ; ob.

shove off. To depart : coll. : C. 20. Ware. Ex nautical sense, prob. on *push off*, q.v. Cf. *shove along* : coll. (— 1923) : To make one's way quietly. Manchon.

shove on. To lay a bet of so much on (a horse) : turf coll. : late C. 19–20. Manchon.

shove the moon. To slip away with one's goods without paying the rent : low : 1809, G. Andrewes, slang-lexicographer ; † by 1880. Cf. *moon, shoot the.*

*shove the queer, the article being occ. omitted. To pass counterfeit money : c. : mid-C. 19–20 : ? orig. U.S. Matsell. See **queer**, n.

*shove the tumbler. To be whipped at the cart's tail : c. : late C. 17–early 19. B.E. ; Hall's *Memoirs*, 1708, 'Those cast for Petit-larceny shove the tumbler' ; Grose. A *tumbler* is a cart.

*shove-up. Nothing : c. or low s. of ca. 1810–60. Ex † *shove-up socket*, a 'gadget' enabling a candle to burn right out. (Vaux.)

shovel. A hansom cab. See **shoful, 4.**—2. An engineer in the Navy : nautical : ca. 1855–70. Because they were rough and ignorant. *Century Dict.*

[shovel, bloody. Generic for unnecessarily coarse speech : C. 20. Ex the chestnut of the bishop who, to a workman asserting that he always called a spade a spade, replied that that was all right but that he thought the workman usually called it a bloody shovel.]

shovel, or fire-shovel, he or **she was fed with a.** A c.p. applied to a person with a very large mouth : ca. 1780–1850. Grose, 1st ed. (*fire-shovel*).

shovel, put to bed with a. To be buried : coll. : from ca. 1780 ; very ob. Grose, 1st ed. In C. 19, occ. *with a spade.*

shovel !, that's before you bought your. That is one against you ; that settles your hash : coll. : ca. 1850–1910.

shovel-engineer. An artificer engineer : naval coll. : from ca. 1910. F. & Gibbons.

*shover. A passer of base coin : c. : orig. U.S. : anglicised ca. 1890. Abbr. *shover of the queer*.—2. (Also shuvver.) A chauffeur : jocular coll. : 1908 (S.O.D.).

*shover of the queer. The same : c. : U.S., anglicised ca. 1870. *Figaro*, Feb. 20, 1871, ' A saloon . . . headquarters of all the counterfeiters and shovers of the queer in the country.' See queer, n.

show. Any public display (a picture-exhibition, a play, a fashionable assembly or ceremony, a speech-making, etc.) : coll. : 1863, Sala. O.E.D. Ex *show*, an elaborate spectacle.—2. Hence, a matter, affair, ' concern ' : 1888, Rider Haggard, in the Summer Number of the *Illustrated London News*, ' Their presence was necessary to the show.' —3. A group or association of persons. Mostly in *boss the show*, and implicatively in *give the show away*, qq.v.—4. A fight, an attack : G.W. military, but not, I think, before 1915. Ex sense 1. (Cf. *show, put up a*.) B. & P.

show, v.i. In boxing, to enter the ring as a combatant : boxing coll. of ca. 1813–50, the O.E.D.'s latest example being of 1828.—2. Hence, to appear in society or company ; at an assembly, etc. : coll. : 1825, Westmacott, ' He *shows* in Park ' ; 1898, Jean Owen, ' If the king was in the cabin . . . no subject might show on deck.' O.E.D. In C. 20, this sense is ob., *show up* being much more gen. : *show up*, likewise coll., occurring first in W. Black's *Yolande*, 1883 (' Don't you think it prudent of me to show up as often as I can in the House . . . so that my good friends in Slagpool mayn't begin to grumble about my being away so frequently ? ') and meaning also to ' turn up ' for an appointment.—3. To exhibit oneself for a consideration : coll. : 1898, *The Daily News*, April 2, ' He got a living by " showing " in the various public-houses,' O.E.D.

show, boss or run the. To assume control ; act as manager : 1889, *boss* (perhaps orig. U.S.) ; in C. 20, often *run*. See show, n., 2, 3.

show, do a. To go to a public entertainment : coll. : from ca. 1906. See show, n., 1.

show, put up a. To give some, gen. a good, account of oneself. Usually defined as *a (very) good, a bad (or rotten) show* : from 1915, orig. military. See show, n., last sense.

show, run the. See show, boss the.

show, steal the. To gain most of the applause ; greatly to outshine other performers : music-hall and variety s. : C. 20. *The New Zealand Free Lance*, late June or early July 1934 (reprinted in *Everyman*, Aug. 24, 1934), in an article entitled ' The Star Turn ', represents a British Lion batsman saying to an Australian Kangaroo bowler, ' It seems we've stolen the show, Aussie.'

*show, there's another. A ' tic-tac ' (q.v.) has signalled new odds : turf c. (— 1932).

show a leg ! See shew a leg.

show a point to. See point to.

show away, give the. To blab, confess ; to expose the disadvantages or pretentiousness of an affair, esp. one in which a group is concerned : 1899, Delannoy, £*19,000*, ' I didn't want to give the show away ' : s. >, by 1930, coll. (Lyell.)

show (him) London. To hold one, upside down, by the heels : schools' : from ca. 1880. Opp. *see London*, to be thus held ; also, to hang by the heels from a trapeze, a horizontal bar, etc.

show kit. To go sick : military coll. : from

1915. F. & Gibbons. If, as a result, one left one's unit, certain equipment was, in certain circumstances, handed in at the quartermaster's stores.

show-leg day. See shew-leg day.

show off, v.i. To act, talk, ostentatiously or in order to attract attention to oneself : coll. : from ca. 1790. Gilbert White ; D. C. Murray. O.E.D. Frequently as vbl.n.

show-up. An exhibition (of work) : coll. : 1930. O.E.D. (Sup.) Prob suggested by Fr. *exposé* and *exposition*.

show up, v. See show, v., 2. Esp. of a released convict reporting once a month to the police : c. (— 1933). Charles E. Leach.—3. To report (a boy) : Charterhouse : C. 20. E.g., ' I'll show you up.'

showbanker. See scowbanker.—showed. Shown : sol. : C. 19–20. Baumann.

showful(l) and compounds. See shoful.

showing, a front. A short-notice parade : military : late C. 19–20 ; ob. Because while one might possibly pass muster in front, at the back . . .

[Showman, The. For this ' gag '-recitation, see B. & P., 3rd ed., pp. 271–72.]

[Showmen's s. is an ' odd mixture of rhyming slang, Yiddish and Romany [and Italian and cant],' P. Allingham in *The Evening News*, July 9, 1934. Cf. ' Grafters' slang ', q.v.

*shrap. Wine used in swindling : very local c. of ca. 1592. Greene, *The Black Book's Messenger*. Prob. ex † *shrap(e)*, a bait, a snare.—2. Shrapnel : military coll. : from 1914. F. & Gibbons.

shrapnel. French currency notes of low denomination : New Zealanders' : in G.W. They were often holey, as though punctured with shrapnel.

shred(s). A tailor : late C. 16–early 19. Jonson, *shreds* ; Massinger & Field, B.E., and Grose, 1st ed., *shred*. O.E.D. Cf. :

shreds and patches. A tailor : coll. : C. 18–20 ; ob.

shrewd head. A New Zealand and Australian variant (C. 20) of :

shrewdy. A shrewd, esp. a cunning, person ; a trickster : coll. : late C. 19–20. Mostly military and Australian. (F. & Gibbons.)

Shrewsbury clock, by. A coll. phrase lessening or even cancelling the period of time—or the fact—mentioned : late C. 16–20 ; ob. Shakespeare ; Gayton, ' The Knight that fought by th' clock at Shrewsbury ' ; Mrs Cowley, 1783 ; Stevenson, 1891. Apperson.

shriek. An exclamation-mark : coll. : 1864, Dean Alford ; ob. Whence shriek-mark.—2. An alarmed, surprised, or reproachful outcry : coll. : 1929 (O.E.D. Sup.).—3. A ' scream ' (q.v.) : coll. : 1930, E. Bramah (ibid.).

shriek-mark. An exclamation-mark : authors', typists' coll. : C. 20. Cf. *Christer*.

shrieking sisterhood. Women reformers, hence female busybodies : journalistic coll. : ca. 1890–1910. Milliken, 1893, ' This yere shrieking sisterhood lay ain't 'arf bad.'

shrift !, he hath been at. An ecclesiastical c.p. of C. 16 : applied to one who has been betrayed he knows not how. Tyndale, *The Obedience of a Christian Man*, 1528. The implication is that the priest to whom he confessed has betrayed him.

shrimp. A harlot : ca. 1630–70. Whiting, 1638, in *Albino and Bellama*.

shroff. See schroff.

shrubbery. (Gen. the female) pubic hair : coll. : late C. 19–20.

shtumer. See stumer.

shucks ! Nonsense ! ; *I* don't care ! : coll. : 1885 (O.E.D.) : U.S. partly anglicised ca. 1900. Ex *shuck*, typifying the worthless, itself orig. (and still) a husk or shell.

shuffer. A chauffeur : from ca. 1905. (Milward Kennedy, *Death to the Rescue*, 1931.)

shuffle, v.t. To feign, as in *shuffle asleep*, pretend to be asleep. Whence *shuffler* : mid-C. 19–20. Ex S.E. sense, act evasively.

*shuffler. (App.) a drinker ; prob. one who ' wangles ' or ' scrounges ' drinks : Brathwait, 1652. Always with *ruffler* and *snuffler*. O.E.D.

shule, shuler, shuling. See shool, shooler, shooling.—shulleg-day. See shew-leg day.

'shun ! Attention ! : military coll. (from the middle 1880's) >, ca. 1910, j. Cf. *hipe*, q.v.

shunt. To move aside (−1859) ; to kill (−1909) : railwaymen's coll. H., 1st ed. ; Ware. Ex lit. sense. —2. To shift the responsibility of (a thing) on to another person : coll. (− 1923). Manchon. —3. See :

shunt, v. ; shunter. The v. is app. unrecorded before 1908 (O.E.D.). The n. : ' One who buys or sells stock on the chance of undoing his business, on one of the provincial Stock Exchanges, at a profit,' Atkin in *Home Scraps*, 1887 : Stock Exchange coll. : from ca. 1885. Ex railway terminology. Also *shunting*, C. 20.—2. An able organiser : C. 20. S.O.D. Likewise ex railway sense.

*shurk. A variant of *shark*. See shirk.

*shut-eye. Sleep : tramps' c. (from not later than 1915) >, by 1925 at latest, gen. jocular. On Jan. 13, 1934, the incorrigible K.G.R.Browne speaks of ' A spot of shut-eye.'—2. Hence, a deception, a trick, a swindle : Glasgow (− 1934).

shut it ! Be silent ! ; stop that noise ! : from mid-1880's. ' Pomes ' Marshall, ca. 1890, ' Oh, shut it ! Close your mouth until I tell you when'

shut of, be or get. (See also shot of.) To be free from, rid of : late C. 16–20 : S.E. until C. 19, then coll. ; in late C. 19–20, low coll. Rolf Boldrewood, 1888, ' Father . . . gets shut of a deal of trouble . . . by always sticking to one thing ' ; R. L. Stevenson, 1891, ' What we want is to be shut of him.' In active mood from ca. 1500, whence this passive usage. Cf. dial. *be shut on*, as in Mrs Gaskell's *Mary Barton*, 1843, and *shut*, a riddance.

shut one's lights off. To commit suicide ; whence, loosely, to die : from ca. 1929. (Lyell.)

shut up. To end (a matter) : coll. : 1857, Dickens, ' Now, I'll tell you what it is, and this shuts it up,' O.E.D.—2. (Gen. in imperative : cf. *shut it !* and *shut your face, head, mouth, neck !*) To cease talking ; stop making a noise : 1853, ' C. Bede ' (O.E.D.) ; Mursell, *Lecture on Slang*, 1858, ' When a man . . . holds his peace, he shuts up ' ; Maugham, 1897. S. >, ca. 1890, coll. Ex S.E. sense, to conclude one's remarks. The C. 17 equivalent was *sneck* (or *snick*) *up !*, q.v.—3. V.i. ' To give up, as one horse when challenged by another in a race,' Krik, *Guide to the Turf*. (*Krik* being the pseudonymn of B. Reid Kirk, *Amicus Equus* . . . *And a Guide to Horse Buyers*, 1884) : racing coll. (? orig. s.). Cf. *shut up*, adj.—4. Hence, to stop doing something (no matter what) : low : C. 20.

shut up, adj. Completely exhausted : ca. 1860–1900. H., 3rd ed.

shut-up house. ' The land headquarters of the local Press Gang ' : naval coll. : late C. 18–mid-19. Bowen.

shut up shop. See shop, shut up.

shut up shop-windows, have. To be bankrupt : coll. : mid-C. 1675–1850. Ray, 1678 (Apperson). Cf. *shutters, put up the*, 2.

shut up, you little . . . See what did you do . . . ?

shut up your garret ! Hold your tongue ! : low (− 1909). Ware. Cf. :

shut your face, head, neck, rag-box ! Be quiet ! ; Stop talking : low : from mid-1870's : perhaps (except for last, which occurs in Kipling, 1892) orig. U.S., for *shut your head !* is recorded first in Mark Twain in 1876 and this appears to be the earliest of these phrases ; *shut your neck* is in Runciman, *Chequers*, 1888 ; *shut your face*, from before 1903. All on the analogy of *shut your mouth !*, which, though admittedly familiar, is yet S.E. Cf. *shut it !* and *shut up*, 2, qq.v.

shuts. As n., a hoax, a ' sell ' ; as interjection, ' sold again ! ' Christ's Hospital : from ca. 1860. Cf. *done !*

shutter, gen. pronounced *shetter*. To convey a ' drunk ' on a shop-shutter to the police-station, the police carrying him : low Cockney (− 1909) ; very ob. Ware.

*shutter-racket. The practice of stealing from a building by boring a hole in a window-shutter and taking out a pane of glass : c. of ca. 1810–60. Vaux.

shuttered (often pron. *shettered*). In a state of complete ignominy : low (− 1909). Ware. Perhaps ex sense 2 of :

shutters, put up the. To ' bung up ' the eyes of one's opponent : boxing : mid-C. 19–20 ; slightly ob.—2. To stop payment, announce oneself bankrupt : coll. : mid-C. 19–20. Ex S.E. sense, to close a shop for the day. Cf. *shut up shop-windows*.

shutters up, got the. See got the shutters up.

shuttle-bag, swallow the. To get husky-throated : (? dial. and) coll. : mid-C. 19–20.

shuvly-kouse. A public-house : low urban (− 1909) ; virtually †. Ware, ' This phrase spread through London from a police-court case, in which a half-witted girl used this phrase.'

shy. A quick and either jerky or careless (or jerkily careless) casting of a stone, ball, etc. : coll. : 1791, Brand (O.E.D.). Ex v., 1, q.v.—2. Hence, A ' go ', attempt, experiment, chance : coll. : 1823, Egan's Grose ; 1824, Egan (vol. iv of *Boxiana*), ' I like to have a shy for my money.' —3. Fig., a ' fling ', a jibe or sarcasm (*at* . . .) : 1840, De Quincey, ' Rousseau . . . taking a " shy " at any random object,' O.E.D.—4. The Eton Football sense, orig. (1868) coll., soon > j.—5. A thrower, esp. in cricket : coll. : 1884 (O.E.D.)

shy, v. (In late C. 19–early 20, occ. *shie*.) V.i., to throw a missile jerkily or carelessly or with careless jerkiness : coll. : 1787, Bentham, ' A sort of cock for him . . . to shie at,' O.E.D. Perhaps ex *shy(-)cock*, q.v.—2. Hence, v.t. : To throw, toss, jerk : coll. : lit., 1824, Egan ; fig., Scott, 1827, ' I cannot keep up with the world without shying a letter now and then.'

shy, adj. Short, low (of money) : low : 1821, Haggart, ' Although I had not been idle during these three months, I found my blunt getting shy.' † by 1900.—2. Whence *shy of*, short of (money ;

hence provisions, etc.) : Australia : late C. 19–20. Cf. U.S. *shy, shy of*, lacking, short of (O.E.D., 799, § 6, b), a usage perhaps influencing, but not originating, the Australian.—3. Disreputable ; not quite honest : 1849, Thackeray, 'Mr Wagg . . . said, "Rather a shy place for a sucking county member, ay, Pynsent ?" ' ; 1864, H. J. Byron, 'Shy turf-transaction.' S. >, ca. 1900, coll. ; by 1930, ob. Prob. ex S.E. sense, timid, bashful.—4. ? hence, doubtful in quantity and/or quality : 1850, Thackeray, 'That uncommonly shy supper of dry bread and milk-and-water ' ; Mark Lemon, 1865, ' Her geography is rather shy, and I can make her believe anything,' O.E.D. Rare in C. 20, virtually † by 1935.

shy, coco-nut. An amusement (and its means) consisting in throwing balls at coco-nuts : 1903 (S.O.D.) : coll. >, ca. 1920, S.E.

shy(-)cock. A wary person, esp. one who keeps indoors to avoid the bailiffs : 1768, Goldsmith (O.E.D.) ; Grose, 1st ed.—2. Hence, a cowardly person : 1796, F. Reynolds (O.E.D.). Both senses † by ca. 1850, the latest record being of 1825 (F. & H.). Prob. ex lit. sense, a cock not easily caught, one that will not fight.

shy-making. Alluded-to by Somerset Maugham in *Cakes and Ale*, 1930, thus, ' Popular adjectives (like " divine " and " shy-making "),' this adj., used lit., was nevertheless ob. by 1934. It was coined, or rather first recorded, by Evelyn Waugh.

shyer ; shier. One who throws as in *shy*, v. (q.v.) : coll. (— 1895). O.E.D.

shyin'. See **shine**, adj.

shyster. An unprofessional, dishonest, or rapacious lawyer (1856) ; hence, anyone not too particular as to how he conducts business (1877) ; hence (— 1903), a generic pejorative : U.S., anglicised resp. ca. 1890, 1900, 1905. Either ex *shy*, adj., 3, or ex *shicer* : cf. next sense. Thornton, F. & H., O.E.D.—2. A duffer, a vagabond,' H., 3rd ed. : from ca. 1860. This sense, independent of U.S. *shyster*, is a variant of *shicer*, 2, q.v.

si quis. A candidate for holy orders : from ca. 1860 ; ob. H., 3rd ed. Ex the public notice of ordination, so named because it began *Si quis*, if any . . .

***sice.** Sixpence : c. : ca. 1660–1850. Tatham, 1660 (O.E.D.) ; *Covent Garden Drollery*, 1672 ; B.E. ; Grose ; Lytton. Ex *sice*, the six in dice.

sich, sitch. Such : sol. and dial. : C. 19 (? earlier) –20. Baumann.

sick. Disgusted ; exceedingly annoyed or chagrined : 1853, Surtees, ' How sick he was when the jury . . . gave five hundred pounds damages against him,' O.E.D. Ex *sick* (of), thoroughly weary (of), prob. via *sick and tired* (of).—2. (Of a ship) ' in quarantine on suspicion of infectious disease ' (Bowen) : nautical coll. : C. 20.

sick, enough to make a horse. See **sick as a cat**.

sick, knock (a person). To astound, ' flabbergast ' : coll. (— 1923). Manchon. Ex *sick*, 1.

sick, the. See **sicks, the**.

sick as a cat, cushion, dog, horse, rat,—as. Very sick or ill indeed : coll. verging on S.E. : resp. 1869, Spurgeon ; ca. 1675–1800, Ray, Swift ; late C. 16–20, G. Harvey, Garrick, Mrs. Henry Wood ; ca. 1680–1830 (Meriton, 1685 ; Sterne ; Grose), then coll. ; late C. 19–20, ob. (F. & H.). As a horse does not vomit, to be *as sick as a horse* connotes extreme discomfort. Northamptonshire dial. is

logical in that it applies the phrase to a person ' exceedingly sick without vomiting ' (Miss Baker, 1854).

sick-bay moocher. A malingerer : *Conway* cadets ' : from before 1891. (John Masefield, *The Conway*, 1933.) See **moocher**.

sick friend, sit up with a. (Of a man) to excuse oneself for absence all night from the conjugal bed : from ca. 1880 ; slightly ob. Cf. *see a man about a dog* (at **dog**).

sick-list, on the. Ill : coll. : C. 20. Ex *s.-l.*, an official list of the sick.

sick man (or **S.M.**) **of Europe, the.** ' Any reigning sultan of Turkey ' : political nickname (coll. verging on S.E.) : 1853, when used by Nicholas I of Russia to Sir George Hamilton Seymour, the English Ambassador at St Petersburg ; slightly ob. (Ware.)

sick of the fever burden. To be ' bone ' lazy : coll. : C. 16–17. E.g. in Fulwood's *Enemy of Idleness*, 1593, ' You have the palsey or eke the fever burden ' ; Ray. (Apperson.) Cf. *sick of the Lombard fever*.

sick of the idle crick and the belly-work in the heel. As preceding : coll. : ca. 1670–1750. Ray, 1678, thus : *sick o'th'idle crick, and the belly-work i' th' heel*, therefore prob. orig. Northern dial. Derisive, presumably, of an illness alleged to excuse idleness. Cf. :

sick of the idles. Exceedingly lazy ; idle without the will to work : coll. : 1639, John Clarke ; Ray, 1670. Ob. by 1850, but not yet †. Cf. preceding two entries and :

sick of the Lombard fever. The same : coll. : ca. 1650–1720. Howell, 1659 ; Ray, 1670. (Apperson.) Cf. *sick of the fever burden*.

sick of the simples. See **simples, be cut for the**.

sick up, v.i. and t. To vomit : low coll. : late (? mid-) C. 19–20.

sickening. Unpleasant ; inconvenient ; (of persons) rude : Society coll. : from ca. 1920. Denis Mackail, *Greenery Street*, 1925, ' " Just a little demonstration of two men telephoning to each other. Twenty seconds by the clock." " Don't be sickening, Ian," [said Felicity].'

sicker, the. The medical officer's report : military, mostly officers' : from 1914. F. & Gibbons. I.e. *sick* + ' the Oxford-*er* '.

sickrel. ' A puny, sickly Creature,' B.E. : late C. 17–early 18. O.E.D. says that it is c. : but B.E. does not so classify it. Pejorative on *sick* : cf. *cockerel* on **cock**.

sicks (occ. **sick**), **the.** A feeling of nausea. Esp. in *give one the sicks*, to get on a person's nerves : late C. 19–20. (Compton Mackenzie, *Water on the Brain*, 1933, *the sick* ; John Brophy, *Waterfront*, 1934, *the sicks*.)

sid down. A low, slovenly form of *sit down*, esp. in the imperative, which is occ. written *siddown*, as, e.g., in James Curtis, *The Gilt Kid*, 1936. The *t* has been blunted by the *d* of *down*.

siddown ! See **sid down**.

side. Conceit, swagger ; pretentiousness. Earliest and often *put on side*, to give oneself airs, to ' swank '. Hatton, 1878 ; ' Pomes ' Marshall. Ex *side*, proud, or more prob., as W. suggests, by a pun on *put on side* at billiards.

***side !** Yes : Northern c. (— 1864) ; ob. H., 3rd ed. ? on It., Sp. *si*, yes.

side, on the (e.g. **cool**). Rather cool : 1923, A. J. Anderson : coll. >, by 1933, S.E. (Collin-

son; O.E.D. Sup.)—2. Often tautological, **as in**
the musical side, music. Cf. *purposes*, q.v.

side, over the. See **over the side.**

side about. To put on ' side ': Public Schools':
C. 20. (P. G. Wodehouse, *Mike*, 1909.)

side-boards. A shirt-collar : low (— 1857) ; † by
1900. ' Ducange Anglicus '. Prob. the same collar
as that defined at **sideboard.**—2. See **sideboards.**

side-kick. A close companion ; a mate, occ. an
assistant, on a job : Canadian and Australian : from
not later than 1914. Ex the *side-kicker* of U.S.A.,
where, since 1920, *side-kick* has been the more
frequent ; *side-kicker* is occ. heard in England, as
e.g. in P. MacDonald, *Rope to Spare*, 1932. Cf.
offsider, q.v.

side-lever, gen. in pl. Hair growing down the
check at the side of the ear : C. 20. (Author first
heard it in 1923.) Cf. *side-wings, side-boards,* and
the U.S. *side-burns.*

side-lights. Eyes : nautical : late C. 19–20.
Bowen.

**side-pocket, wanted as much as a dog (or toad)
wants a.** A c.p. applied to one who desires something unnecessary : late C. 18–20 ; ob. Grose,
1st ed., *toad* (at *toad*) ; *dog* in Grose, 2nd ed.,
where also the variant *as much need of a wife as a
dog of a side-pocket,* applied to a debilitated old
man. Quiller-Couch, 1888, ' A bull's got no more
use for religion than a toad for side-pockets.'
Occ. *monkey*, unrecorded before 1880 and † by
1930 ; very rarely *cow*, as in Whyte-Melville, 1862.
(Apperson.)

side-scrapers. ' Side-wings ', ' side-levers ', qq.**v.**:
London middle classes': ca. 1879–89. Ware.

side-sim. A fool : C. 17 coll. Nares records for
1622. ? opp. *Sim subtle*, a crafty person or a
subtle one. *Sim* = Simon. Cf. *simple Simon.*

side up with. To compare, or compete, with :
1895, *Punch*, Feb. 23 (O.E.D. Sup.); ob.

side-wings. Whiskers : late C. 19–20 ; ob.
Contrast *side-lever, side-boards.*

sideboard. A ' stand-up ' shirt-collar : 1857,
' Ducange Anglicus '; ob. Gen. in pl. (H., 1st
ed., shows that the term was applied to the collars
of ca. 1845–55.)

sideboards. Whiskers : from ca. 1890 ; very ob.
Cf. *side-wings* ; contrast *side-lever.*—2. See **side-
boards** (above).

'sides. Besides ; moreover ; late C. 16–20 :
S.E. until C. 19, then coll. and dial.

sidey. See **sidy.**—**sidi-boy.** See **seedy-boy.**

sidledywry. Crooked : late C. 18–early 19. Grose,
2nd ed. Ex *sidle* + *awry.*

sidy ; occ.—but incorrectly—**sidey.** Conceited ;
apt to ' swank it ' : 1898 (O.E.D.) : s. >, ca. 1910,
coll. ; ob. Ex *side,* q.v.

sif, siff. See **syph.**

*sift, v.t. ; occ. v.i. To steal small coins, i.e.
such as might be conceived of as passing through a
sieve : thus F. & H. (1903) ; but in 1864, H. says
that it = to purloin ' the larger pieces, that did not
readily pass through the sieve !' It appears,
however, that F. & H. is right, for in H., 1874, we
find ' To embezzle small coins, those which might
pass through a sieve—as threepennies and four-
pennies—and which are therefore not likely to be
missed.'

sig. A signaller : C. 20 military (esp., G.W.).
Also in *sig* (signalling)-*station.*

sigarneo. A loose form of *sirgarneo.* See **Sir
Garnet.**

sigh. Incorrect for *sith* : C. 16. O.E.D.

sighing Sarah. See **Whistling Willie.**—2. A shell
that ' sighs ' in its distant flight : military : 1915 ;
ob. (G. H. McKnight, *English Words*, 1923.)

sight. A multitude or a (great) deal : late
C. 14–20 : S.E. until mid-C. 18, then coll. (in C. 20,
virtually s.). Sheridan & Tickell, 1778, ' They
wear . . . a large hat and feather, and a mortal
sight of hair,' O.E.D.—2. As adv. : coll. >, ca.
1890, s.: 1836, T. Hook ; 1889, Grant Allen,
' You're a sight too clever for me to talk to.'
O.E.D.—3. An oddity, often pejoratively (' You've
made yourself a perfect *or* regular sight ') : late
C. 17–20 : S.E. until C. 19, then coll. Cf. *fright*,
q.v.—4. An opportunity or chance. Esp. *get
within sight*, to near the end, and *get within sight of*,
to get anywhere near. Coll. : late C. 19–20.—5.
' A gesture of derision : the thumb on the nose-tip
and the fingers spread fan-wise : also *Queen Anne's
fan.* A *double sight* is made by joining the tip of
the little finger (already in position) to the thumb
of the other hand, the fingers being similarly
extended. Emphasis is given by moving the fingers
of both hands as if playing a piano. Similar actions
are *taking a grinder* . . . or *working the coffee-mill*
. . .; *pulling bacon* . . .; *making a nose* or *long
nose ; cocking snooks*, &c,' a passage showing
F. & H. to advantage. (The custom seems to have
arisen in late C. 17 : see the frontispiece to the
English *Theophrastus*, 1702, and cf. *The Spectator*,
1712, ' The 'prentice speaks his disrespect by an
extended finger.') T. Hook, 1836, ' Taking a
double sight,' O.E.D.; Dickens, 1840, ' That peculiar form of recognition which is called taking a
sight ' ; cf. H., 2nd ed., at *sight.*

sight, v. ' To tolerate ; to permit ; also, to see ;
observe,' C. J. Dennis : Australian : C. 20.

sight, put out of. To consume ; esp., to eat :
coll. : from ca. 1870. Cf. *get outside of.*

sight, take a. See **sight**, n., 5.

*sighter. A minute dot on a card : card-
sharping c. (— 1894). O.E.D.—2. See **fly-balance.**

sights, take. To have a look, to glance ; v.t. with
of: low : C. 20. Philip Allingham, *Cheapjack*,
1934.

sigma (phi). Syphilis : coll. medical euphemism
(— 1933). *Slang*, p. 193. Ex Gr. letters written
on the patient's certificate.

sign of a house or **a tenement to let.** A widow's
weeds : 1785, Grose ; ob. by 1900, virtually † by
1930. In American low s., *a house for rent* (Irwin).

sign of the cat's foot, live at the. To be hen-
pecked : C. 19–20 ; very ob.

sign of the feathers, the. A woman's best good
graces : mid-C. 19–early 20.

sign of the five, ten, fifteen shillings, the. An
inn or tavern named The Crown, Two Crowns,
Three Crowns : late C. 18–20 ; ob. Grose, 2nd ed.

sign of the horn, at the. In cuckoldom : C. 19–
20 ; very ob.

sign of the prancer, the. See **prancer.**

sign of the three balls, the. A pawnbroker's :
C. 19–20 : coll. >, ca. 1910, S.E.

sign on the dotted line. See **dotted line.**

[Signalese is the use of *Ack* for *A*, *Beer* for *B.*,
etc. See, e.g., *o pip* and *pip emma*.]

signboard. The face : from ca. 1870 ; very ob.
Cf. *dial*, q.v.

signed all over. (Of a good picture) clearly
characteristic of its creator : artists' (— 1909).
Ware.

signed servant. An assigned servant : Australian coll. : ca. 1830–60. Morris. Ex that convict system under which convicts were let out as labourers to the settlers.

significant. Attractive, esp. as being in the forefront of modernity : art s. verging on j. : from ca. 1920. A vogue-cheapening of *significant*, very expressive or suggestive, perhaps influenced by *significant*, important or notable.

Sike or **Psych** (pron. *sike*), **the.** The Society for Psychical research : from middle 1880's. Baumann.—2. A member thereof : id. Ibid. (Also *sike*.)

*sil. See silver-beggar.

silence. To knock down, to stun : implied in 1725 in *A New Canting Dict.* (at *silent*).—2. Hence, to kill : C. 19–20.

silence in the court, the cat is pissing. A c.p. addressed to anyone requiring silence unnecessarily : ca. 1780–1850. Grose, 1st ed. Cf. :

*silence-yelper. An usher in a court of law : c. (— 1909). Ware. I.e. ' silence ! '-yelper.

silencer. A blow that knocks down or stuns : C. 19–20. Ex *silence*, 1.

*silent. Murdered : c. (— 1725). *A New Canting Dict.* Cf. *silence*, 2.

silent beard. The female pubic hair : coll. : late C. 17–early 19. T. Brown (d. 1704) : *Works*, ii, 202.

silent deaths. A night patrol, armed with daggers, lurking in No Man's Land to surprise German patrols : military : 1915–18. F. & Gibbons.

silent flute. The male member : late C. 18–mid-19. Grose, 2nd ed.

[**silent match,** one that makes no noise on being struck, is classified by Baumann as c. : but a S.E. term does not > c. simply because it is used by criminals.]

silent Percy or **Susan.** A type of German high-velocity gun, and its shell : military : 1914–18. F. & Gibbons ; B. & P.

silk. A Q.C. or K.C. : 1884 (O.E.D.) : coll. till ca. 1905, then S.E. Abbr. *silk-gown*, a Q.C. : 1853, Dickens, ' Mr Blowers, the eminent silk-gown.' A Counsel's robe is of silk ; a Junior Counsel's, stuff.—2. A bishop : ecclesiastical : late C. 19–early 20. The apron is of silk.

silk, carry or **sport.** To ride in a race : turf coll. : 1884, Hawley Smart. Ex the silk jacket worn by jockeys.

silk, obtain, receive, take. To attain the rank of Counsel : legal coll. >, ca. 1905, S.E. : *obtain*, very rare before C. 20, and perhaps always S.E. ; *receive*, 1872, *The Standard*, Aug. 16 ; *take*, 1890, *The Globe*, May 6. Contrast :

silk, spoil. To cease being Counsel ; esp. on promotion : legal coll. >, ca. 1900, S.E. : 1882, *Society*, Nov. 4, ' Ere long he " spoiled silk " (as the saying is), and was made a Serjeant.' ? ex *despoil oneself of*.

silk facings. A beer-stained coat-front : tailors' : C. 20.

silk-gown. See **silk**, 1.

silk-port. ' Assumption of a gentleman commoner's gown ' : Oxford University : ca. 1820–60. Egan's Grose, 1823. (Pierce Egan added a fair amount of Oxford s. to Grose.)

*silk-snatcher. A thief addicted to snatching hoods or bonnets from persons walking in the street : c. of ca. 1720–1840. *A New Canting Dict.*, 1725 ; Grose, 1st ed

silks and satins, support one's. To parade, or prank oneself out in, silk and satin : modistes' coll. (— 1887) ; slightly ob. Baumann.

silkworm. ' A woman given to frequenting drapers' shops and examining goods without buying ' : coll. : C. 18. Steele, 1712, in *The Spectator*, No. 454. (O.E.D.)

sillikin. A simpleton : 1860, G. A. Sala (O.E.D.). Since ca. 1920, ob. Cf. :

silly. A silly person : coll. : 1858, K. H. Digby, ' Like great sillies,' O.E.D.

silly, adv. Sillily : C. 18–20 : S.E. until mid-C. 19, then (low) coll. and dial.

silly, knock. To infatuate : coll. : from ca. 1890. (Lit., to stun, stupefy.)

silly (or **S.**) **Billy.** A clown's juvenile butt : coll. : ca. 1850–1900. Mayhew, 1851, ' Silly Billy . . . is very popular with the audience at the fairs.'—2. Hence, gen. affectionately, a ' silly ' (q.v.) : coll. : late C. 19–20. Cf. *silly Willy*.—3. William Frederick (1776–1834), Duke of Gloucester. Dawson. —4. William IV (d. 1837). Ibid.

silly season. In Great Britain, the months of August and September, when—owing to recess of Parliament and to other prominent persons' being on holiday—there is a shortage of important news, the lack being supplied by trivialities. (Such a periodical as *The Times Literary Supplement*, however, welcomes August–mid-September for the working-off of arrears : the authors and publishers concerned feel perhaps less enthusiastic.) 1871, *Punch*, Sept. 9, ' The present time of the year has been named " the silly season ",' O.E.D. : coll. till ca. 1910, then S.E. Whence :

silly-seasoner, -seasoning. A typical silly-season article or story (1893) ; the writing and publishing of such matter (1897). Still coll. O.E.D.

silly Willy. A simpleton : coll. : C. 17 (? till C. 19). Cf. *silly Billy*, 2. (Also dial. : mid-C. 19–20.)

sillybrated ; occ. **silly brated.** Celebrated : sol., mostly Cockneys' (— 1887). Baumann.

*silver-beggar or **-lurker.** C. : *s.-b.*, 1859, Sala ; *s.-l.* (H., 3rd ed.) from ca. 1860 ; both ob. ' A tramp with *briefs* (q.v.) or *fakements* (q.v.) concerning bogus losses by fire, shipwreck, accident, and the like ; guaranteed by forged signatures or *shams* (q.v.) of clergymen, magistrates, &c., the false subscription-books being known as *delicates* (q.v.). Also ' from ca. 1870—' *sil* = (1) a forged document, and (2) a note on " The Bank of Elegance " or " The Bank of Engraving ",' i.e. a counterfeit banknote ; likewise ob. F. & H.

silver bullets. ' Money contributed to the war loans ' : journalistic coll. verging on j. : 1916–18. Collinson.

silver-cooped. (Of a naval seaman) deserting for the merchant service : nautical coll. : late C. 18–early 19. Ex the bounties offered to the crimps. Bowen.—2. Hence, (of any merchant seaman) ' shipped through the crimps ' : nautical coll. : C. 19. Ibid.

silver fork. A wooden skewer, used as a chopstick when forks were scarce : Winchester : † by 1870.

Silver Fork School, the. A school of novelists stressing the etiquette of the drawing-room and affecting gentility : literary coll. of ca. 1834–90. The school flourished ca. 1825–50 and included Disraeli, Lytton, Theodore Hook, Lady Blessington, Mrs Trollope. Four-pronged silver or electroplated forks, though known long before, ousted the steel two-prongs only ca. 1860.

silver hell. A low-class gaming saloon or den: coll.: from ca. 1840; ob. Moncrieff, 1843, ' He's the principal partner of all the silver hells at the West End.' Only or mainly silver was risked.

silver hook, catch fish with a. To buy a fish (or several fish) to ' conceal unskilful angling ', as F. & H. delicately say: anglers': C. 19–20; ob. Perhaps on the proverbial *angle with a silver* (or *golden*) *hook*, to get things by bribery, or only through paying for them.

silver-laced. Lousy: low s. (? orig. c.) of ca. 1810–1910. *Lex. Bal.*; Baumann. Ex the colour of lice.

silver pheasant. A beautiful society woman: from ca. 1920; ob. Manchon. (See **bird.**) Cf. *silver-tail*, q.v.

silver spoon in one's mouth, born with a. Born rich: C. 18–20: coll. till ca. 1850, then S.E. Motteux, 1712; Buckstone, 1830, ' Born . . . as we say in the vulgar tongue, with . . .' Anticipated by John Clarke in 1639, *born with a penny in one's mouth.* (Apperson.)

silver-tail; silver-tailed, n. and adj. (A) " swell ": Australian bushmen's coll. (— 1890); ob. Opp. *copper-tailed,* democratic. A. J. Vogan, *The Black Police,* 1890. (Morris.)

Silver-Tailed Dandies, the. The officers of the 61st Foot Regiment: ' a Peninsular War nick-name, in allusion to the elaborate silver embroidery on the tails of their coats', F. & Gibbons.

silver-wig, A grey-haired man: coll. (— 1923). Manchon.

silvers or **S.** Shares in the India Rubber, Gutta Percha, and Telegraph Company: Stock Exchange: ca. 1890–1915. Ex the works at Silvertown.

silvoo play ! Please ! G.W +. (Gavin Holt, *Drums Beat at Night,* 1932.)

Sim. ' A follower of the late Rev. Charles Simeon,' H. (2nd ed.): ca. 1850–60. The Rev. Charles, d. 1836, was 54 years Vicar of Holy Trinity, Cambridge. Abbr. *Simeonite* (1823).—2. Hence, and far more widely at Cambridge University, a quiet, religious (esp. if evangelical) man: ca. 1851–70, then only historical. Bristed, 1851.

simkin or **simpkin**; or with capitals in sense 1. The fool in (comic) ballets: theatrical coll. of ca. 1860–1920. Mayhew, 1861 (O.E.D.). Ex *simkin,* a fool.—2. (simkin; occ. **samkin.**) Champagne: Anglo-Indian coll. (1853); slightly ob. H., 3rd ed. Ex native pronunciation.

simon (or **S.**) A sixpence: c.: late C. 17–19. B.E.; Grose, 1st ed.; H., 5th ed. Prob. by a fancy on the name: since *tanner, 6d.,* is unrecorded before 1811, *simon* cannot derive from ' the old joke . . . about St Peter's banking transaction, when he " lodged with one Simon a tanner " ' (*Household Words,* June 20, 1885), but *tanner* may well have come from *Simon* in this connexion.—2. A trained horse: circus: from ca. 1850; ob. Is this a pun ? On what ?—3. A cane: King Edward's School, Birmingham: ca. 1850–90. Ex Acts ix, 43.

Simon Pure (occ. Simon- or simon-pure), **the** or **the real.** The real or authentic person or, from ca. 1859 (H., 1st ed.), thing: coll.: *the real S.P.,* 1815, Scott; *the S.P.,* 1860, W. C. Prime (O.E.D.). Ex *Simon Pure,* a Quaker who, in Mrs Centlivre's *A Bold Stroke for a Wife,* 1717, is, for part of the play, impersonated by another character; see esp. Act V,

scene 1.—2. Its use as an adj. is mainly, as it certainly was orig. (Howells, 1879), American.

*Simon soon gone. In Awdeley, *Simon soone agon,* ' He, that when his Mayster hath any thing to do, he will hide him out of the way ': c. of ca. 1560–90.

simp. A simpleton: coll.; U.S. (— 1916), partly anglicised—owing to the ' talkies '—by 1931. (O.E.D. Sup.)

simper like a furmity-kettle. See furmity-kettle.

simpkin. See simkin.

simple infanticide. Masturbation: pedantic coll. or s.: late C. 19–20.

simple-lifer. One who leads ' the simple life ': 1913 : coll. >, by 1930, S.E. Collinson ; O.E.D. (Sup.).

*simpler. A simple or foolish man much given to lust : c. of late C. 16–early 17. Greene, 1592 ; Rowlands, 1602. O.E.D. I.e. *simple + er.*

simples, be cut for (in C. 17–early 18 of) **the.** To be cured of one's folly : mid-C. 17–20 : s. (not c.) until ca. 1820, then mainly, and in C. 20 nothing but, dial. Apperson records it for 1650 ; B.E. ; Swift ; Grose, 1st ed. In C. 18 often in semi-proverbial form, *he must go to Battersea, to be cut for the simples,* as in Grose, 1st ed., where also the corrupt variant, . . . *to have their simples cut,* for at Battersea *simples* (medicinal herbs) were formerly grown in large quantities. Cognate is the C. 18 semi-proverbial *sick of the simples,* foolish : coll.

simpson ; occ. incorrectly, **simson.** Also with capital. Water used in diluting milk : dairymen's : 1871, *The Daily News,* April 17, ' He had, he stated on inquiry, a liquid called Simpson on his establishment.' Ex the surname *Simpson,* that of a dairy-man who, in the late 1860's, was prosecuted for such adulteration.—2. Hence, inferior milk : 1871, *The Standard,* May 11, Police Report, ' If they annoyed him again he would christen them with Simpson, which he did by throwing a can of milk over the police.'—3. Almost co-extensive is the sense, ' That combined product of the cow natural and the " cow with the iron tail "', *The Standard,* Dec. 25, 1872. See also **Simpson, Mrs** ; cf. *chalkers* and *sky-blue,* and next entry.—4. A milkman : mostly London (— 1887) ; † by 1910. Baumann.

simpson or **S.** ; incorrectly **simson.** To dilute (milk) with water : 1872, *The Times,* Dec. 24. Ex n., 1, q.v. Also *Simpsonise,* gen. v.t.

Simpson, Mrs. The (village) pump : mostly among dairymen (— 1874). H., 5th ed. Also *Simpson's cow* and :

Simpson-pump. A pump as a means of diluting milk : dairymen's : from ca. 1879. *Punch,* Jan. 31, 1880. Cf. preceding entry.

Simpsonise, -ize. Gen. v.t., to dilute milk with water : dairymen's : 1871, *The Echo,* Dec. 13 (O.E.D.). Ex *simpson,* n., 1 ; cf. *simpson,* v.

Simpson's cow. See **Simpson, Mrs** : dairymen's (— 1903).

simulate. See at dissolute.

Sims' circus. 'The American flotilla of destroyers sent over first on America coming into the War ': naval : 1917–18. F. & Gibbons. Ex Admiral Sims, commanding the U.S. navy during the G.W.

sin. (E.g. ' It's a sin that *or* to . . .') A shame ; a pity : C. 14–20 : S.E. until C. 19, then coll. (O.E.D.) Cf. :

sin, like. Very vigorously ; furiously : late C. 19–20. Here, *sin* = the devil.

Sinbad. An old sailor : nautical : ca. 1860–1910. Ex the legendary figure.

since leads often to a catachrestic use of tense. It is obviously incorrect to write ' He is a notability since he has written that book '; less obviously incorrect is 'He has been a notability since he has . . .', the logical (and correct) form being, ' He has been a notability since he wrote . . .'

since Caesar was a pup. Since long ago (or before): Canadian (— 1932). John Beames.

since when I have used no other   A c.p. applied to any (gen. domestic) article : from ca. 1910. Collinson. Ex the witty Pears' Soap advertisement of a tramp (' Twenty years ago I used your soap, since when I have used no other '). Cf. *good morning, have you* . . .

sines. (Generic for) bread, whereas *a sines* is a small loaf : Winchester : from ca. 1870 ; † by 1915. Perhaps a pun on *natural sine*(s) and *sign*(s).

sing like a bird called the swine. To sing execrably : coll. : ca. 1675–1750. Ray, 1678 ; Fuller, 1732. (Apperson.)

*sing out. C. of ca. 1810–40. Scott, 1815, in a note to *Guy Mannering*, ch. xxviii, says, ' To sing out or whistle in the cage, is when a rogue, being apprehended, peaches against his comrades.' (N.B., the phrase is not *sing out in the cage*.) Cf. :

*sing out beef. To call ' Stop thief ' : c. of ca. 1810–40. *Lex. Bal.* (More gen. *cry beef* or *give (hot) beef*.) Possibly a rhyming synonym.

sing placebo (or P.). See placebo.

sing small. To make less extravagant or conceited claims or statements : coll. : 1753, Richardson, ' I must myself sing small in her company ' ; Grose, 1st ed. ; Clement Scott, 1885. Perhaps suggested by S.E. *sing another*, or *a different, tune*, to speak, act, very differently, though it may follow naturally ex C. 17–early 18 *sing small*, to sing in a small voice : cf. Shakespeare's ' Speaks small like a woman.'

[sing-song. Perhaps orig. coll., but prob. always S.E.]

single-peeper. A one-eyed person : ca. 1780–1850. Grose, 1st ed. On *single-eyed*.

single-pennif. A five-pound note : back s. on *finnup* (q.v.) : from ca. 1850. Also, in C. 20 c., a £1 note.

single-ten or singleten. See senses 1, 2 of :

singleton. ' A very foolish, silly Fellow,' B.E., where spelt *single-ten* : late C. 17–early 19. Grose, 1st ed. Prob. ex † S.E. *single*, (of persons) simple, honest, on *simpleton*, but possibly ex *single*(-)*ten*, the 10 in a card-suit, thus : the ' 10 ' is below and next to the knave and—by the age-old juxtaposition of fools and knaves—is therefore a fool.—2. ' A nail of that size,' says B.E. puzzlingly ; Grose, who likewise has *singleten*, is no clearer with ' a particular kind of nails '. Late C. 17–early 19. Possibly an obscure allusion to the single ten in cards : cf. sense 1.—3. ' A cork screw, made by a famous cutler of that name [*Singleton*], who lived in a place called Hell, in Dublin ; his screws are remarkable for their excellent temper,' Grose, 1st ed. : coll. : ca. 1780–1830.

singular or plural ?   A hospital c.p. inquiry when eggs appear on the diet-sheet : military : 1915–18. B. & P.

singulary. Singular, odd, strange : sol. (— 1887). Baumann. Perhaps influenced by *leary*.

sinister, bar. Incorrect for *bend sinister* (occ. *baton sinister*).

Sinjin's (or -un's) Wood. St. John's Wood : London satirical : 1882–ca. 1900. Ware. Ex the pronunciation of the English surname *St John* as *Sinjun*.

sink. A toper : coll. : mid-C. 19–20 ; ob. Cf. *sewer, common*.—2. the sink. The throat : mid-C. 19–20.—3. A heavy meal : Leys school : late C. 19–20. Cf. *stodge*.—4. Hence, a glutton : ibid. : late C. 19–20.—5. the sink (or S.). The Royal Marine office in a battleship : naval : late C. 19–20. Bowen.

sink, v. To ' lower ' or drink : from ca. 1926. Gavin Holt, *Drums Beat at Night*, 1932, ' Let's go out and sink a few beers. We can talk at the pub.'

sink, fall down the. To take to drink : late C. 19–20 : ? rhyming s.

sink me !   A coll. imprecation : 1772, Bridges, ' But sink me if I . . . understand ' ; very ob. Prob. orig., and mainly, nautical.

*sinker. A counterfeit coin : c. (— 1839). Brandon. Gen. in pl., bad money, ' affording a man but little assistance in keeping afloat ', H., 3rd ed.—2. A small, stodgy cake (of the doughnut kind) : late C. 19–20. Gen. in pl.—3. A shilling : tramps' c. (— 1932). F. Jennings.

sinks. The five : dicing coll. (— 1860). H., 2nd ed. Ex Fr. *cinq*.

sinner. A publican : coll. : from ca. 1860 ; ob. Ex Luke xviii.

sip. A kiss : London's lower classes' : ca. 1860–1905. Ware. Ex the bee sipping : cf. that popular early C. 20 song in which the male warbles, ' You are the honeysuckle, I am the bee.'

sip. To make water : back s. (— 1903) on *piss*, q.v.

sip, do a. See do a sip.

sipper. Gravy : low : late C. 19–20. ? ex dial. *sipper-sauce* (ex C. 16–17 S.E. *sibber-sauce*), sauce, influenced by *to sip*. Cf. *jipper*, q.v.

Sir Cloudesley. A choice drink of small beer and brandy, often with a sweetening and a spicing, and nearly always with lemon-juice : nautical : late C. 17–mid-18. B.E. (at *flip*) spells it *Clousley*. Ex *Clowdisley* Shovell (1650–1707), knighted in 1689 for naval services, esp. against pirates.

Sir Garnet ; often all Sir Garnet. All right : whether as predicate or as answer to a question : from ca. 1885. ' Pomes ' Marshall, ' And the start was all Sir Garnet, | Jenny went for Emma's Barnet.' In C. 20 often corrupted to (*all*) *sirgarneo*. Both forms were slightly ob. by 1915, very ob. by 1935. Ex *Sir Garnet* (later Viscount) Wolseley's military fame. (Wolseley, 1833–1913, served actively and brilliantly from 1852 to 1885.)

Sir Harry. A privy ; a close-stool. Esp. in *go to*, or *visit, Sir Harry* : C. 19–20 : coll. and (in C. 20, nothing but) dial. ; app. orig. dial. H., 2nd ed. Cf. *Mrs Jones*. Cf. *Sir John*, 2.—2. Whence, constipation : lower classes' (— 1923) ; ob. Manchon.

Sir Jack Brag. General John Burgoyne (1722–92), notable dramatist as well. Dawson.

Sir Jack Sauce. See Jack Sauce.

Sir John. See John, Sir. (By itself, *sir*, a parson, is † S.E.)—2. A close-stool : coll. (C. 19) and dial (C. 19–20) ; ob. Cf. *Sir Harry*, q.v.

Sir Oliver. See Oliver.—Sir Petronel Flash. See Petronel.—sir reverence. See sirreverence.

Sir Roger, (as) fat as. A real Falstaff in girth and weight : lower classes' coll. : ca. 1875–1900. Baumann. Ex Sir Roger Tichborne of the famous lawsuit.

Sir Sauce. See Jack Sauce.

*Sir Sydney. A clasp-knife : c. of ca. 1810–50.

Vaux. Why ? : unless Sydney, Australia, already had a notorious underworld.

Sir Thomas Gresham, sup with. To go hungry : C. 17 coll. Hayman, 1628, ' For often with duke Humphrey [q.v.] thou dost dine, | And often with sir Thomas Gresham sup.' Sir Thomas Gresham, 1519–79, founded the Royal Exchange and was a noted philanthropist.

Sir Timothy. ' One that Treats every Body, and pays the Reckonings every where,' B.E. : col: late C. 17–early 19. Prob. ex a noted ' treater '.

' sir ' to you ! A c.p. of mock dignity : C. 20. P. G. Wodehouse, *The Pothunters*, 1902 ; H. A. Vachell, *Vicar's Walk*, 1933.

Sir Tristram's knot. A hangman's noose : coll. : mid-C. 16–early 17. Wm. Bullein. Prob. ex some famous judge or magistrate.

Sir Walter Scott. A pot (of beer) : rhyming s. (— 1857) ; ob. ' Ducange Anglicus.'

siretch. See sirretch.—**sirgarneo ; all sirgnareo.** See Sir Garnet ; cf. *sigarneo*.

Sirlogical Gardens. Zoological Gardens : Cockney sol. (— 1887). Baumann.

sirname. Incorrect for *surname*.

sirrah may orig. (C. 16) have been coll.

sirretch. A cherry ; more properly, cherries : back s. (— 1859). H., 1st ed., where spelt *siretch* and defined as cherries. The ' logical ' *seirrehc* is impossible, the former *e* is omitted, *hc* reversed, and *t* interpolated to make the *ch* sound unequivocal.

sirreverence ; frequently *sir-reverence*. Human excrement ; a lump thereof : late C. 16–20 : S.E. until ca. 1820, then mainly (in C. 20, nothing but) dial. In late C. 18–mid-19, a vulgarism. Grose. Ex *save* (via *sa'*) *reverence*, as an apology.

sis ; often **siss.** Sister : coll. : gen., term of address : orig. (— 1859), U.S. ; anglicised before 1887 (Baumann). (The O.E.D. dismisses it as ' U.S.' ?) Cf. *sister* and :

sissie, sissy ; occ. **Cissy, cissy.** An effeminate boy or man ; hence a passive homosexual : late C. 19–20 ; ob. in latter sense (cf. *pansy*, q.v.). Ware declares it to have originated in 1890 as a Society term for an effeminate man in Society ; the O.E.D. (Sup.) that it was orig. U.S. s.,—but is this so ? Ex *sissy*, sister, as form of address orig. (— 1859) U.S. but anglicised before 1887 : coll. : cf. *sis*.

sister. A term of address to any woman : (low) coll. : orig. U.S. ; anglicised, ca. 1925, chiefly among journalists, but not yet at all gen.—2. **sister of the Charterhouse.** See Charterhouse.—3. Sister [in charge of] Children's [Ward, etc.], Sister Theatre, etc. : medical coll. : C. 20. See *Slang*, p. 193.

sister Susie. ' A woman doing Army work of any sort. Primarily a Red Cross worker ' : military : 1915–18. F. & Gibbons, ' From a war-time popular song, " Sister Susie's sewing shirts for Soldiers ".'

sit. An engagement (for, in, work) : printers' : 1888, Jacobi (O.E.D.). Abbr. *situation*. But that it has always been also gen. is shown by Baumann (1887).

sit, v. To hang (on a branch) ; lie, rest (on the ground) : South African coll. : C. 20. Ex Cape Dutch *zetten*, to lie, to rest. Pettman.

*sit, be at the. ' To travel by buses and trams for the purpose of picking pockets,' G. R. Sims in *The Referee*, Feb. 17 : 1907 : c. (O.E.D.)

sit down. To land : aviators' coll. : from the middle 1920's. O.E.D. (Sup.).

sit-down-upons. Trousers : 1840, J. T. Hewlett (O.E.D.) ; ob. Cf. *sit-upons*.

sit her down. (Of an aviator) to land : Royal Air Force's (— 1935). The *her* is the 'plane.

sit-in-'ems. Trousers : jocular (— 1887) ; ob. Baumann. Cf. *sit-down-upons*.

sit longer than a hen. See sitting breeches.

sit-me-down. One's posterior : semi-nursery, semi-jocular : late C. 19–20. Cf. :

sit-me-down-upon. A C.20 jocular variant of the preceding. Dorothy Sayers, *Clouds of Witness*, 1926, ' He's left the impression of his sit-me-down-upon on the cushion.'

sit on or (rare in C. 20) **upon.** To check ; snub or rebuke : 1864. H., 3rd ed. (*sit upon*). Often as *sat upon*, squashed, ' pulled up '.

sit on the splice. See splice, sit on the.

sit still. (Of the Aborigines) to be peaceful : South African coll. : 1852, Godlonton, *The Kaffir War*, 1850–51. Pettman.

sit up, make one. ' To make one bestir oneself, to set one thinking, to surprise or astonish one,' Pettman, who wrongly regards it as esp. South African : coll. (— 1887). Baumann.

sit up and take notice. To take (a sudden) interest : coll. ; orig. (1889) U.S., anglicised by 1900. (O.E.D. Sup.)

sit up and take nourishment. To be convalescent : coll. : from 1915, and orig. among officers in military hospitals. On the analogy of the preceding.

sit upon. See sit on.—2. (Only in pl. : *sit-upons*.) Trousers : 1841, J. T. Hewlett,; ob. Suggested by *sit-down-upons*, q.v. Contrast *sit-me-down*.

sitch. See sich.

sith-nom, sithnom. A month : back s. (— 1859). H., 1st ed.

sitiwation. A situation : Cockney sol. (— 1887) ; ob. Baumann.

sitter. A sitting-room : Harrow (from ca. 1890) >, by 1902, Oxford University undergraduates'. Charles Turley, *Godfrey Marten, Undergraduate*, 1904. The term has > gen. in bed-sitter. Cf. *brekker*, *rugger*, *soccer* ; see ' -er ', Oxford '.—2. In cricket a very easy catch : 1898, *Tit-Bits*, June 25, ' Among recent neologisms of the cricket field is " sitter ". So easy that it could be caught by a fieldsman sitting.' W. J. Lewis, *The Language of Cricket*, 1934.—3. An easy mark or task (1908). Ex shooting a sitting bird. S.O.D. Senses 2 and 3 > coll. ca. 1930.—4. (Cf. senses 2, 3.) A certainty : C. 20. Hence *for a sitter*, certainly, assuredly : Arnold Lunn, *The Harrovians*, 1913.

sitting(-)breeches on, have one's ; in C. 19, occ. **wear one's sitting breeches.** To stay long in company : coll. : ca. 1870–1910. Grose, 1st ed. From ca. 1880, *sit longer than a hen*. Cf. the Yorkshire *sit eggs*, to outstay one's welcome : E.D.D.

sitting drums. One's working-trousers : tailors' : C. 20.

sitting on their hands. (Of an audience) that refuses to clap : theatrical : from ca. 1930.

*sitting-pad. Begging from a sitting position on the pavement : c. (— 1859) ; ob. H., 1st ed. See *pad*, n.

sitting-room. The posteriors : late C. 19–20 jocular ; slightly ob. (Cf. *sit-me-down*, q.v.) Prob. ex the smoke-room story of ' only a pair of blinds for her sitting-room ' in connexion with a pair of drawers. Cf. the mid-C. 16–early 18 *sitting-place*, the posterior, the rump.

situation. A 1st, 2nd, or 3rd place : 1871

(O.E.D.) : racing coll. >, ca. 1905, S.E. 'Thormanby,' *Men of the Turf*, ca. 1887, 'The three worst horses, probably, that ever monopolised the Derby "situations".'

siv(v)ey or **sivvy, 'pon my !** On my word of honour ! : low : mid-C. 19–20 ; slightly ob. H., 1st ed. ; J. Greenwood, 1883. Not *asseveration*, but prob. *davy*, corrupted, or, as Baumann implies, *soul*.

siwash. A mean and/or miserable seaman : Nova Scotian (and U.S.) nautical : late C. 19–20. Bowen, 'The Siwash is described as the meanest type of Indian.'

six. A privy : Oxford University : ca. 1870–1915. ? origin.

six-and-eightpence. 'The usual Fee given, to carry back the Body of the Executed Malefactor, to give it Christian Burial,' B.E., who classes it as c. : more prob. coll. : late C. 17–mid-18.—2. A solicitor or attorney : coll. : 1756, Foote ; Baumann. † by 1910. Because this was a usual fee. Cf. *green bag*.

six-and-tips. Whiskey and small beer : Anglo-Irish coll. : ca. 1780–1850. Grose, 1st ed. An elaboration of †*six*, six-shilling beer.

Six-and-Two's, the. The 62nd Foot, now the Wiltshire Regiment : military : C. 19–20. F. & Gibbons. Ex the figures of the number.

six-by-four. 'Bumf' (q.v.) : Army officers' : 1915 ; slightly ob. B. & P., 'The dimensions in inches of the Army Article.'

six-cylinder hat. A large, non-regulation cap affected by many despatch-carrying cyclists : military : 1915 ; ob. F. & Gibbons.

six feet and itches. Over six feet : lower classes' (— 1909) ; ob. Ware. Ex *inches* written as *ichs*.

Six Mile Bridge assassin. (Gen. pl.) A soldier : Tipperary : late C. 19–early 20. Ware, 'Once upon a time certain rioters were shot at this spot, not far from Mallow.'

six-monther. A third-term cadet in the old training-ship *Britannia* : naval coll. : late C. 19–early 20. Bowen.

six-monthser. A very severe stipendiary magistrate : police coll. (— 1909). Ware. I.e. one 'who always gives, where he can, the full term (six months) allowed him by law.'

six-o-six ; gen. written '606'. Salvarsan, a remedy for syphilis : medical, hence military coll. : from ca. 1910. B. & P.

six of everything, with. Respectably married : work-people's coll. (— 1909). Ware. Applied only to the girl : her trousseau contains six of everything.

six-on-four, go. 'To be put on short rations' : naval : late C. 19–20. Thus, a *six-on-four* is a supernumerary borne on a warship : Bowen, 'Supposed to have two-thirds rations.'

six pips and all's well ! Six o'clock and all's well ! : c.p. : from 1933. Referring both to the radio time-signal and to the nautical *six bells and all's well*.

six-pounder. 'A servant maid, from the wages formerly given to maid servants, which was commonly six pounds [per annum, plus keep],' Grose, 1st ed. : coll. : ca. 1780–1850.

six-quarter man ; three-quarter man. A superior —an inferior—employee : cloth-drapers' (— 1909). Ware, 'There are two widths of cloth—six quarter and three quarter.'

six upon four. Short rations : nautical coll. :

1838, Glascock in *Land Sharks and Sea Gulls* ; ob. Because the rations of four had to suffice for six. See also **six-on-four, go.**

six-water grog. Grog in which water : grog :: 1 : 6. Nautical coll. : 1834, Marryat. In mid-C. 19–20, often *six-water*.

***sixer.** Six months' hard labour : c. or low s. : 1869, 'Pomes' Marshall, 'I see what the upshot will be, | Dear me ! | A sixer with H.A.R.D.'—2. A sixth imprisonment : 1872 (O.E.D.) : low s. rather than c.—3. The six-ounce loaf served with dinner : prison c. (— 1877).—4. Anything counting as six : orig. (1870) and mainly in cricket : coll. H. A. Vachell, *The Hill*, 1905, 'Never before in an Eton and Harrow match have two "sixers" been hit in succession,' O.E.D. (This is that novel which did for Harrow what E. F. Benson's *David Blaize* did in 1916 for Winchester, which the author 'disguises' as *Marchester*.)—5. 'A naval cadet at the beginning of his second year' : naval : C. 20. Bowen. ? because he has *six* terms ahead of him.

sixes. Small hook-curls worn by men ; composed of forehead hair, they are plastered to the forehead : military : ca. 1879–90. Ware. Ex shape. If Manchon has not erred, the term app. > *number sixes* and an underworld term, still extant though ob.

sixpences, spit. See **spit sixpences.**

sixpenny. A playing-field : 1864, *Eton School Days* : Eton College ; ob.

sixpenny, adj. Inferior, cheap ; worthless : coll. : ca. 1590–1630. Esp. *sixpenny striker*, a petty footpad (as in Shakespeare's *1st Henry IV*).

sixth-forming. A caning by the prefects assembled in the sixth-form room : Public Schools' coll. : late C. 19–20. Desmond Coke, *The School across the Road*, 1910.

sixty. A British 60-pounder gun : military coll. : from ca. 1910. B. & P.—2. *Sixty* is the 'inevitable' nickname, in the Regular Army (esp. on Egyptian service), for men surnamed Hill : from ca. 1919. Ex Hill Sixty, a famous locality on the Western Front in the G.W. ; cf. *Jebbel*, q.v.

sixty, like. Very vigorously or rapidly : orig. (1848) U.S., anglicised ca. 1860. H., 2nd ed. ; O.E.D. ? abbr. *like sixty to the minute* or *like sixty miles an hour*. Cf. *forty*, q.v.

sixty per cent. A usurer : coll. : 1853, Reade ; slightly ob. Cf. Fletcher, 1616, 'There are few gallants . . . that would receive such favours from the devil, though he appeared like a broker, and demanded sixty i' th' hundred.'

sixty-pounder. A suet-dumpling : military : 1915–18. (Sidney Rogers, *Twelve Days*, 1933.)

size ; gen. **size up.** To gauge, estimate ; to regard carefully (in order to form an opinion of) : coll. : orig. (1847), U.S. ; anglicised ca. 1890. Marriott-Watson, 1891, *size* († by 1930) ; Newnham Davis, 1896 (O.E.D.), *size up*. Cf. the rare S.E. *size down*, v.t., to comprehend.

size of (a thing), **the.** What it amounts to : coll. : from the middle 1880's. E.g. 'That's about the size of it.' O.E.D. (Sup.). Ex dial. : E.D.D.

sizes. Short rations : naval : C. 20. Bowen. Ex *six-on-four, go.*

skalbanker. See **scowbanker.—skallewag.** See **scalawag.**

skate. A troublesome rating : naval : from ca. 1920. Bowen. Ex U.S.

skater. An N.C.O.'s chevron : Regular Army : late C. 19–20 ; ob. F. & Gibbons. Perhaps because its wearer 'skates on thin ice '.

skates, put on (one's) ; get one's skates on. To hurry ; evade duty ; desert : military (from not later than 1916) >, by 1919, gen. F. & Gibbons.

*skates(-)lurk. ' A begging impostor dressed as a sailor,' H., 1st ed. : c. ; † by 1903. Perhaps = *skate's lurk*, a fish's—hence a ' fishy '—trick ! (Bowen has *skate-lurker*.)

skeary, skeery. Terrifying ; (mostly U.S.) timorous : low coll. : C. 19–20. Blackmore.

skedaddle. A hasty flight ; a scurry : coll. : with article, 1870, Mortimer Collins ; without, 1871, *The Daily News*, Jan. 27. O.E.D. Ex :

skedaddle ; occ. (though not in C. 20) **skeedadle**, v.i. (Of soldiers) to flee : orig. (1861), U.S., anglicised ca. 1864. H., 3rd ed., ' The American War has introduced a new and amusing word.' Prob. of fanciful origin, though H.'s ' The word is very fair Greek, the root being that of " *skedannumi* ", to disperse, to " retire tumultuously ", and it was probably set afloat by some professor at Harvard ' is not to be dismissed with contempt.— 2. Hence, in gen. use, to run away, decamp, hastily depart : coll. : 1862 ; Trollope, 1867, O.E.D.—3. Also ex sense 1, (of animals) to stampede or flee : 1879, F. Pollock. O.E.D.

skedaddler ; skedaddling. One who ' skedaddles ' (1864, O.E.D.) ; the act (— 1898).

skeery. See skeary.

skeeter. A mosquito : coll. : orig. (1852), U.S. ; then, ca. 1870, Australian ; then ca. 1880, English, —but it is still comparatively rare in Britain.

Skeffington's daughter. See scavenger's daughter.

skein. A glass of beer : military : C. 20. F. & Gibbons. Origin ?

skein of thread. Bed : from ca. 1870. P. P., *Rhyming Slang*, 1932.

*skelder, v.i. To beg, esp. as a wounded or demobilised soldier : c. : late C. 16–mid-17, later use (esp. in Scott) being archaic. Ben Jonson.— 2. V.t., to cheat, defraud (a person ; obtain (money) by begging : c. : late C. 16–mid-17. Ben Jonson. Perhaps Dutch *bedelen* perverted.

*skeldering, vbl.n. and ppl.adj. of *skelder* : late C. 16–mid-17 c. Ben Jonson, who, I surmise, introduced it from Holland ; cf. *skellum*.

skeleton. ' A typical sentence, not to exceed sixty words ; no word therein to be of more than two syllables,' as an old journalist defines it : journalists' coll. : C. 20.

skeleton army. Street-fighting or -brawling : London : late 1882–3. Ware. Ex the Skeleton Army ' formed to oppose the extreme vigour of the early Salvation Army ' (Ware).

skelington. A sol. (and a dial.) form of *skeleton* : C. 19–20. E.D.D.

skel(l)um ; scellum. A rascal, villain : perhaps orig. coll., but certainly very soon S.E. Coryat, D'Urfey. Ex Dutch or Ger. *schelum*.

skelter. A quick ruin, a rush, a scamper : dial. (— 1900) >, by 1920, coll. O.E.D. (Sup.). Ex *helter-skelter*.

skerfer. A punch on the neck : boxing : from ca. 1880 ; ob. Ex *scruff*.

skerrick. A small fragment : 1931, I. L. Idriess, ' Not a skerrick of meat on it ' (O.E.D. Sup.). Ex *scurrick* (see scuddick). Also in dial.

*sket. A skeleton key : c. : from ca. 1870. By telescoping *skeleton*.

sketch. A person whose appearance offers a very odd sight (cf. *sight*, 3, q.v.) : coll. : from ca. 1905. E.g. ' Lor', what a sketch she was ! '—2. A small

amount ; a drop (of liquor) : 1894 (O.E.D.) ; very ob. Cf. :

sketchy. Unsubstantial (meal) ; flimsy (building, furniture) ; imperfect : coll. : 1878, O.E.D.

skettling. Full-dressing : naval officers' (— 1909). Ware. Perhaps a pun on *scuttling*.

Skevington's daughter. See scavenger's daughter.

*skew ; occ. **scew.** A cup or wooden dish : c. of ca. 1560–1830. Awdelay, Brome, B.E., Grose. ? etymology.—2. At Harrow School, from ca. 1865, a hard passage for translation or exposition ; also, an entrance examination at the end of term (that at the beginning of term is a *dab*). F. & H. ; O.E.D. Ex *skew*, v., q.v.—3. In back s. (— 1859) : see kews.

skew, v.t. To fail in an examination : gen. as *be skewed* : 1859, Farrar in *Eric, or Little by Little* ; 1905, Vachell. O.E.D.—2. Also v.t., to do (very) badly, fail in (a lesson) : likewise Harrow (— 1899). Occ. v.i.: late C. 19–20 : Lunn, *The Harrovians*, 1913. Perhaps ex *skew at*, look at obliquely, esp. in a suspicious way.—3. App. only *be skewed*, to be caught or punished : schools' (— 1923). Manchon. Ex sense 1.

skew-fisted. Ungainly, awkward : coll. : late C. 17–18. B.E.

skew-gee. Crooked ; squinting : low coll. : late C. 19–20. Ex *on a*, or *the*, *skew*, slantwise (1881). Cf. *skewvow*.—2. Hence, a squint : low coll. : C. 20.

skew-the-dew. A splay-footed person : low late C. 19–20 ; ob. Cf. *skewvow*.

skew-whiff, adj. and adv. Crooked(ly) ; askew : dial. and coll. : 1754 (S.O.D.).—2. Hence, tipsy : C. 20. See fog-bound.

skewed. See skew, v., 1 and 3.

skewer. A pen : from ca. 1880 ; ob. Ex shape.

skewgy-newgy. A composition of caustic used to keep decks clean : yachtsmen's : 1886, *St. James's Gazette*, April 7, ' The mysterious name.' Very ! : unless it be perchance a reduplicated perversion of *caustic*.

skewings. Perquisites : gilders', from ca. 1850. Ex *skew*, to remove superfluous gold leaf. ' Analogous terms are *cabbage* (tailors') ; *bluepigeon* (plumbers') ; *menavelings* (beggars') ; *fluff* (railway clerks') ; *pudding*, or *jam* (common),' F. & H. See those terms.

skewvow. Crooked : coll. or s. : ca. 1780–1880. Grose, 1st ed. (An elaboration of *skew*, a slant, or possibly a jocular perversion of *skew-whiff*, q.v.) Whence *skew-gee* and *skew-the-dew*, qq.v.

Ski. See Sky.

skid, n. See skiv.

skid, v. To go ; to depart : mostly jocular, esp. schoolboys' : C. 20 ; ob. Collinson. Cf. *scoot* (sense 2) and *scuttle*.

skid, put on the. To act, speak, cautiously : coll.: 1885, *Punch*, Jan. 31. Ex *skid*, a chain or block retarding a wheel. Also (*s*)*he might put the skid on* is a coll. semi-c.p. applied to a talkative person, occ. with the addition *with advantage to us, you, his listeners* : from ca. 1870 ; ob. H., 5th ed.

skiddi(c)k. See scuddick.—**skiddoo.** See skidoo. —**skie.** See sky (v.).

skidoo, skiddoo. To make off, to depart : 1907, Neil Munro (O.E.D. Sup.). Ex *skedaddle*.

skied ; **skyed.** (Of a picture) hung on the upper line at the Exhibition of the Royal Academy : artistic coll. >, ca. 1900, S.E. : 1864, H., 3rd ed., at *skyed*. Opp. *floored*, q.v.

skiff. (Presumably) a leg : low s. of ca. 1890–1910. *The Morning Advertiser*, April 6, 1891, 'To drive an "old crook" with "skinny skiffs".' ? origin : perhaps cognate is dial. *skiff*, to move lightly, skim along ; ? cf. also † dial. *skife*, to kick up one's heels.

Skiff Skipton. Sir Lumley *Skeffington* (1771–1850), dandy and playwright. Dawson.

skiffle. A great hurry ; among tailors, a job to be done in a hurry ; low coll. or s. : late C. 19–20. With this thinning of *scuffle*, cf. that of *bum* in *bim* (q.v.) ; the word exists also in West Yorkshire dial.

skilamalink. Secret ; 'shady' : East London : late C. 19–20 ; ob. Ware, 1909, remarks : 'If not brought in by Robson, it was re-introduced by him at the Olympic Theatre, and in a burlesque.' Origin ?

skill. 'A goal kicked between posts' : football : ca. 1890–1920. F. & H. This being the result of skill.

skillet. A ship's cook : nautical : from ca. 1880 ; ob. Ex the cooking-utensil.

Skilligareen. An extremely thin person : lower classes' (– 1923). Manchon. Perhaps, by slurring, ex S.E. *skin-and-bones*.

Skillingers, the. The 6th (Inniskilling) Dragoons : military : mid-C. 19–20 ; very ob. Also known as *the Old Inniskillings*.

skilly. Gruel ; oatmeal soup : 1839, Brandon : low s. >, ca. 1890, coll. >, ca. 1920, S.E. Abbr. *skilligolee*, perhaps on *skillet*, often, in dial., pronounced *skilly* : W.—2. Hence, a fount-carrying his own lead : printers' : ca. 1870–1910. It was unpopular with compositors, for it lent itself to ill-paid piece-work.—3. 'Tea or coffee supplied to messes' : *Conway* cadets' : late C. 19–20. John Masefield, *The Conway*, 1933.

*****skim.** C. : 1869, *The Daily News*, July 29, 'They thought it contained his skim (money)' ; ob. Perhaps the 'skim' of milk, i.e. cream.

*****skimish.** Drink ; liquor : tramps' and beggars' c. (– 1933). W. H. Davies in *The New Statesman*, March 18 of that year. Origin ?

Skimmery. St. Mary's Hall : Oxford University : ca. 1853–1910. Whence *Skimmeryman*, as in *Verdant Green*. By slurred pronunciation of *St Mary*.

*****skin.** A purse : c. of ca. 1810–80. Vaux, Haggart, Mayhew. Because made of skin. Hence, a *queer skin* is an empty one.—2. ? hence, and ? ca. 1830–60, a sovereign. F. & H. Perhaps partly by rhyming suggestion of 'sovrin'.—3. See **skins**.—4. A horse ; a mule : military : from the late 1890's. F. & Gibbons.—5. An official explanation required for any discrepancy : Post Office telegraph-messengers' (– 1935). Perhaps ex *skin*, v., 7. Among railwaymen, it = a report.

skin, v.t. At cards, to win from a person all his money : 1812, Vaux.—2. Hence, to strip (of clothes, money) ; to fleece : 1851, Mayhew. In C. 20, almost coll. Cf. *skin-game* and *skin the lamb*, qq.v.—3. To steal from : c. or low s. : 1891, *The Morning Advertiser*, March 21, 'Sergeant Hiscock . . . saw him skinning the sacks—that is, removing lumps [of coal] from the tops and placing them in an empty sack.'—4. To shadow, esp. just before arresting : c. : from ca. 1880 ; ob.—5. In gaming, to 'plant' (a deck of cards) : from ca. 1880.—6. To lower (a price or value) : 1859, H., 1st ed. ; ob.—7. Also *skin alive*. To thrash : orig. (– 1888), U.S. ; anglicised ca. 1895. Headon Hill, 1902, 'I'd

have skinned the 'ussy if I'd caught her prying into my grounds.'

skin, in a bad. Angry : ill-humoured : late C. 18–mid-19. Grose, 3rd ed. Prob. suggested jocularly by S.E. *thin-skinned*.

skin, in his, her, etc. An evasive reply to a question as to a person's whereabouts : coll. : C. 18–20. Swift, *Polite Conversation*, Dialogue I. Cf. *there and back*.

skin, next of. Next of kin : military : C. 20. F. & Gibbons.

skin-a-guts. A proletarian variant (– 1923) of S.E. *skin-and-bones*, a very thin person. Manchon. Cf. *skin-and-grief*.

skin a razor. To drive a hard bargain : coll. : from ca. 1870 ; ob.

skin alive. See **skin**, v., last sense.

skin and blister. A sister : rhyming s. : late C. 19–20. F. & Gibbons.

skin-and-grief. A variant of *skin-and-bones*, (a) skinny (person) : lower classes (– 1887) ; ob. Baumann.

skin and whipcord, all. Extremely fit ; with not a superfluous ounce of fat : coll. : (U.S. and) Colonial : from ca. 1880 ; slightly ob.

skin-coat. The female pudend. Esp. in *shake a skin-coat*, to coït : mid-C. 17–18.—2. Skin. Only in *curry one's skin-coat*, to thrash a person : C. 18–mid-19.

skin-disease. Fourpenny-ale : low : ca. 1880–1914.

skin-game. A swindling game : 1882. Ex *skin*, v., 1, 2.—2. Hence, a swindle : C. 20. Cf. :

skin-house. A gambling den : from ca. 1885 ; ob. Suggested by *skin-game*.

skin-merchant. A recruiting officer : coll. : late C. 18–mid-19. Burgoyne, 1792. A cynical reflection on the buying and selling of skins ; cf. *gun-fodder*.

skin of one's teeth, by or (C. 16–17) **with.** Narrowly ; difficultly : mid-C. 16–20 : S.E. until C. 19, then coll. Orig. a lit. translation of the Hebrew.

skin of the creature. A bottle (containing liquor) : Anglo-Irish : mid-C. 19–20. See **creature.**

skin off your nose !, here's to the. Your good health ! : mostly military : from ca. 1910 ; virtually †. F. & Gibbons.

skin out. To desert (v.i.) : naval : C. 20. Bowen.

skin the cat. 'To grasp the bar with both hands, raise the feet, and so draw the body, between the arms, over the bar,' F. & H. : gymnastics : 1888 (U.S.).

skin the lamb. Lansquenet (the game of cards) : 1864, H., 3rd ed. ; ob. A perversion of *lansquenet*.—2. V. When an outsider wins a race, the bookmakers are said to 'skin the lamb' : 1864, H., 3rd ed. Lit., fleece the public. Also, from ca. 1870, *have a skinner*, ob. by 1930.—3. Hence, to concert and/or practise a swindle : from ca. 1865.—4. Also to mulct a person in, e.g. blackmail : from ca. 1870.

skin the live rabbit. To retract the prepuce : low : late C. 19–early 20.

skin-tight. A sausage : (lower classes') coll. : from ca. 1890 ; ob.

skin-the-pizzle. The female pudend : low : mid-C. 19–20. See **pizzle.**

Skinflinteries, the. The Museum of *Economic* (by 1903, Practical) Geology, in Jermym Street, London, W.1 : ca. 1889–1910. *The Daily Telegraph*, May 11, 1889.

Skindles. A restaurant at Poperinghe : military : 1915 ; ob. F. & Gibbons. Ex the fashionable resort at Maidenhead.

skinful, to have got a or **one's.** To be extremely drunk : low coll. (— 1923). Manchon. Cf. *tight* and *got all* (or *more than*) *one can carry.*

skinned, keep one's eyes. See **eyes skinned, keep one's.** See also **peeled.**

skinned rabbit. A very thin person : coll. : from ca. 1870 ; slightly ob.

skinner. Mayhew, 1856, ' " Skinners ", or women and boys who strip children of their clothes,' in order to eye lustfully their nakedness : low s. verging on c. ; ob.—2. **skinner, have a.** See **skin the lamb,** 2. (Here, *skinner* may be a punning corruption of *winner* ; the whole phrase, however, is prob. a light-hearted perversion of *skin the lamb*, as H., 5th ed. (1874) suggests. Hence, a *skinner* has by 1893 > = a result very profitable to the ' bookies ' (O.E.D.), as it had, in essence, been twenty years earlier.)—3. A driver of horses : Canadian : late C. 19–20. Cf. *skin*, n., 4. (John Beames.)—4. See.

skinners. Mental torture ; terrible anxiety : low urban (— 1909) ; slightly ob. Ware. Because it ' flays ' one.

skins. A tanner : coll. : ca. 1780–1860. Grose, 1st ed.

skint. Very short of or wholly without money : jocular, lower classes' and military : C. 20. F. & Gibbons. I.e., *skinned.*

skip. A dance : Anglo-Irish coll. : late C. 19–20. Cf. *hop*, q.v.—2. A portmanteau ; a bag, a valise : grafters' : C. 20. Philip Allingham, *Cheapjack*, 1934. One ' does a skip ' with it.—3. See ' Shortenings ' in Addenda. At Scottish Public Schools it = captain : C. 20 : witness Ian Miller, *School Tie*, 1935.

skip, v. To make off (quickly) : C. 15–20 : S.E. until ca. 1830, then coll. (mostly U.S.) with further sense, to abscond. Marryat, *King's Own*, 1830.— 2. Hence, to die : late C. 19–20. Often *skip out.* Savage, *Brought to Bay*, 1900.

skip-kennel. A footman : coll. : ca. 1680–1840. B.E. ; Grose, 1st ed.

skip-louse. A tailor : coll. : 1807, J. Beresford ; ob. Cf. *prick-louse.* (O.E.D.)

*****skipper** ; in C. 16–mid-17, often **skypper.** A barn : c. : mid-C. 16–19 ; but after late C. 19, only in *skipper-bird*, q.v. Harman, 1567 ; B.E. ; Grose, 1st ed. As H. suggests, prob. ex the Welsh *ysgubor* (a barn), of which the *y* is silent, or, as O.E.D. proposes, ex Cornish *sciber* (the same).—2. Hence, a ' bed ' out of doors : tramps' c. : late C. 19–20.—3. The devil : C. 19. ? ex *skipper*, a captain.—4. A master, a boss : coll. : late C. 19–20. Ex *skipper*, captain : cf. coll. sense of *captain*.—5. A military captain : naval (— 1909), hence military (mostly officers') coll. in G.W., and for a few years before. Always *the skipper* and not *Skipper So-and-So.*—6. One who is retreating : c. (— 1909). Ware. Cf. *skip*, v., 1.

*****skipper** ; gen. **skipper it.** To sleep in a barn or hay-rick, hence under, e.g. a hedge : c. : mid-C. 19– 20. ' *No. 747* ', p. 413, valid for 1845 ; Mayhew, 1851, ' I skipper it—turn in under a hedge or anywhere.' Ex *skipper*, n., 1. Cf. *hedge square* and :

*****skipper-bird.** Mid-C. 19–20 c., as in : Mayhew, 1851, ' The best places in England for skipper-birds (parties that never go to lodging-houses, but to barns or outhouses, sometimes without a blanket).'

Also *keyhole-whistler.* Ex *skipper*, n., 1, and v., qq.v.

skipper's daughter. A crested wave : from ca. 1888 : coll. >, ca. 1910, S.E.

skipper's doggie. A ' midshipman acting as captain's A.D.C. ' : naval : C. 20. F. & Gibbons.

[**skirry.** A run or scurry : either coll. or familiar S.E., as is the v. : resp. 1821, Haggart (who also has the v.) and 1781, George Parker. Ex *scurry.*]

skirt. A woman : mid-C. 16–20 : S.E. until late C. 19, then s. Hence, a *light skirt* is a loose woman : late C. 19–20 (Manchon).—2. **the skirt,** women in gen. ; women collectively : late C. 19–20. Hyne, 1899. Cf. :

skirt, v.i. To be a harlot : late C. 19–20, ob. Cf. *skirt, flutter a.*

skirt, a bit of. A woman, a girl : late C. 19–20. Not necessarily pejorative. Hence :

skirt, do a bit of. To coït with a woman : late C. 19–20. Ex preceding.

skirt, flutter a. To be a harlot : late C. 19–20 : coll. Ob.

*****skirt-foist.** A female cheat : c. of ca. 1650– 1700. A. Wilson, ca. 1650.

skirt-hunting. A search, ' watch-out ', for either girls or harlots : coll. : late C. 19–20. (James Spenser, *Limey Breaks In*, 1934.)

skit. Beer : military : from the 1890's. F. & Gibbons. Ex S.E. *skit*, a small jet of water.—2. A large number ; a crowd ; esp. in pl., lots (*of*) : coll. : 1925, A. S. M. Hutchinson. O.E.D. (Sup.). Cf. U.S. *scads* in same sense.

*****skit.** (Gen. v.t.) To wheedle : c. : late C. 18– mid-19. Grose, 2nd ed. Prob. ex S.E. *skit*, to be skittish, to caper.

skite. A boaster ; boasting : Australian : late C. 19–20. Abbr. *blatherskite* ; or possibly ex Scottish and Northern dial., a person viewed with contempt ; cf. also *skyte.*—2. A motor-cycle : 1929. O.E.D. (Sup.). Perhaps ex the abominable noise it makes.

skite, v.i. To boast : Australia : C. 20. Ex *skite*, n., 1.

skiter. A boaster : Australian : C. 20. C. J. Dennis. Ex preceding.

skitter. A person : pejorative : C. 20. Perhaps ex *mosquito.*

*****skitting-dealer.** A person feigning dumbness : C. 19 c. Ex † *skit*, to be shy.

skittle. Chess played without ' the rigour of the game ' : coll. : mid-C. 19–20. O.E.D. (Sup.).—2. Also as v.i. : id. : id. Ibid.

skittles. Nonsense : coll. : 1864, *The Orchestra*, Nov. 12, ' *Le faire applaudir* is not " to make oneself applauded ", and " joyous comedian " is simply skittles.' Perhaps ex *not all beer and skittles.*—2. Hence, an interjection : coll. : 1886, Kipling, ' " Skittles ! " said Padgate, M.P.'

skiv (1858, O.E.D.) ; **skid** (1859, H., 1st ed.). A sovereign (coin). ' Fashionable s.', says H. ; ob. by 1910, virtually † by 1930. ? on *sov.*

skive, v.i. To evade a duty : military : from 1915. F. & Gibbons. ? ex Lincolnshire *skive*, to turn up the whites of the eyes (E.D.D.).

skivvy ; occ. **skivey.** A maid servant, esp. a rough ' general ' : from ca. 1905. Ex *slavey*, q.v.

skivvy ! A naval asseveration or exclamation (— 1909). Ware. Ex Japanese.

skolka, v.t. and i. To sell or bargain : Murmansk and North Russia forces' : 1918–19. F. & Gibbons. A Russian word meaning ' how many ? '

or 'how much ?' Vbl.n., *skolkering*. (Applied esp. to illicit traffic in food and rum between our men and the natives.)

skoff. See **scoff.**

skoosh or **skosh.** A sweetheart: military: C. 20. F. & Gibbons. Possibly cognate with dial. *scouse, scousse,* etc., to frolic.

skoot. See **scoot.—skowbanker.** See **scowbanker.—skower.** See **scour.**

skran. See **scran.**

skreak, skreek. To creak: sol., mostly Cockneys': mid-C. 19–20. Baumann.

skreigh. See **screigh.**

skrim. See **scrim.—skrim(m)age.** See **scrimmage.**

skrimp, skrump or **scrump,** v.i. and v.t. To steal apples: dial. and provincial s.: late C. 19–20. In James Spenser, *Limey Breaks In,* 1934, it appears as Birmingham s. (C. 20) in the gen. sense : to rob orchards. Cognate with *scrounge,* q.v.—2. Hence, to ' scrounge ': Regular Army: late C. 19–20.

skrimshank, -er. See **scrimshank, -er.—skrip.** A c. spelling of *scrip,* q.v.

skrouge, skrowdge. See **scrouge, v.—skrump.** See **skrimp.**

skrunt. A whore: Scots dial. >, by 1890, coll.: mid-C. 19–20.

skuddick. See **scuddick.—skug.** See **scug.**

skulker. ' A soldier who by feigned sickness, or other pretences evades his duty, a sailor who keeps below in time of danger ; in the civil line, one who keeps out of the way, when any work is to be done,' Grose, 1st ed.: 1785 : coll. till ca. 1830, then S.E.

skull ; skull-race, -thatcher. See **scull,** etc.

Skull and Crossbones, the. The 17th Lancers : military : mid-C. 19–20 ; ob. Ex the regimental badge. Also *Bingham's Dandies,* (the) *Death or Glory Boys,* (the) *Gentlemen Dragoons,* and (the) *Horse Marines.*

skullbanker. See **scowbanker.**

skull's afly !, my. I'm awake, alert, shrewd ! : C. 19. Cf. *fly,* adj.

skunk. A mean, paltry, or contemptible wretch : coll.: orig. (1841), U.S. ; anglicised ca. 1870. H., 5th ed., 1874 ; *The Referee,* June 1, 1884, ' The bloodthirsty and cowardly skunks.' Ex the stink-emitting N. American animal.

skunk, v. To betray ; leave in the lurch : London school-boys' (— 1887). Baumann. Ex preceding.—2. Whence (?), not to meet a bill of exchange : commercial (— 1923). Manchon.

skunk-haul. A very small catch of fish : Grand Banks fishermen's : C. 20. Bowen. Cf. *skunk,* n.

skutcher. A synonym of *snozzler,* q.v. : New Zealand (— 1935). Fanciful in origin.

skute. See **scoot.**

Sky ; occ. **Ski.** An outsider : Westminster School (— 1869). Ex the *Volsci,* a tribe traditionally inimical to Rome ; the Westminster boys being *Romans.*—2. Hence, though recorded earlier, ' a disagreeable person, an enemy ' (H., 2nd ed.) : ca. 1860–1910.

*sky. A pocket : c.: 1893, P. H. Emerson ; Edgar Wallace ; Charles E. Leech. Abbr. *sky-rocket,* q.v.—2. A tackle at football : Harrow School : C. 20. Arnold Lunn, *The Harrovians,* 1913. Ex v., 3.

sky, v. To throw up into the air ; esp. *sky a copper,* as in the earliest record : 1802, Maria Edgeworth.—2. Hence, with pun on *blue* (v.), to

spend freely till one's money is gone : from ca. 1885. ' Pomes ' Marshall, ' With the takings safely skyed.' Ob.—3. To throw away ; at football, to charge or knock down : Harrow : from ca. 1890. F. & H., 1903 ; Vachell, 1905. Ex sense 1.—4. See **skied.** Coll. >, ca. 1910, S.E.

sky-blue. Gin : perhaps orig. c. : 1755, *The Connoisseur ;* Grose, 3rd ed. † by 1859.—2. Thin or watery milk : late C. 18–20 : S.E. until ca. 1850, then coll. H., 1859. Ob. Cf. *simpson,* n., and *chalkers.*

sky falls,—we shall catch larks, if or when the A semi-proverbial c.p. retort on an extravagant hypothesis : late C. 15–20 ; ob. Cf. *if pigs had wings . . .* See esp. Apperson, who quotes Heywood (1546), Randolph (1638), Bailey (1721), Spurgeon (1869), G. B. Shaw (1914), and others.

*sky-farmer. A beggar who, equipped with false passes and other papers, wanders about the country as though in distress from losses caused by fire, hurricane, or flood, or by disease among his cattle : c. : 1753, John Poulter. † by 1850. As Grose, 1st ed., suggests, either because he pretended to come from the Isle of Skye or because his farm was ' in the skies '.

sky-gazer. A sky-sail : nautical : from ca. 1860 ; ob. On nautical *sky-scraper.*

sky-high. Very high indeed : coll. : 1818 (Lady Morgan), adv. ; 1840, adj. O.E.D.

sky-lantern. The moon : coll. : ca. 1840–70. Moncrieff, 1843.

sky-light ; skylight. An eye : nautical · 1836, Michael Scott ; ob.

sky . . . limit. See **limit, the sky is one's.**

sky-line. The top row of pictures at an exhibition : artistic coll. (— 1911). Webster. Suggested by *skied,* q.v.

sky-parlour. A garret : 1785, Grose : coll. >, ca. 1840, S.E. Also (in Baumann) *sky-lodging* : lower classes' coll. (— 1887) ; slightly ob.

sky-pilot. A clergyman, esp. if working among seamen : low (— 1887 ; Baumann) > nautical s. (1888, Churchward) > by 1895 (W. Le Queux, in *The Temptress*) gen. s. >, by 1910, gen coll. Because he pilots men to a heaven in the skies. Cf. *pilot-cove,* q.v.—2. Hence, loosely, an evangelist: from before 1932. *Slang,* p. 245.

sky-rocket ; occ. **skyrocket.** A pocket : rhyming s. : 1879, J. W. Horsley. Cf. *sky,* n.

sky-scraper ; occ. **skyscraper.** A high-standing horse : coll. : 1826, Hone (O.E.D.) ; ob. Like the following senses, it derives ex the nautical *sky-scraper,* a sky-sail.—2. A cocked hat : nautical : ca. 1830–90.—3. The penis : low : from ca. 1840. —4. An unusually tall person (gen. of a man) : coll. : 1857, ' Ducange Anglicus '.—5. In cricket, a skied ball : coll. : from ca. 1890 ; slightly ob.—6. A rider on a ' penny-farthing ' bicycle : ca. 1891–1900. *The Daily News,* March 7, 1892, ' . . . Often derisively styled " sky-scrapers ",' O.E.D.

sky the towel. To give in, yield : boxers' (from ca. 1890) >, by 1910, soldiers' coll. F. & Gibbons.

sky the wipe. A variant of *rag, sky the,* q.v. (Australian : C. J. Dennis.)

sky-topper. A very high person or thing (e.g. house) : coll. (— 1923). Manchon. A variant of *sky-scraper.*

skycer. See **shicer.—skyed.** See **skied.**

Skying a Copper. Hood's poem, *A Report from Below,* ' to which this title was popularly given until it absolutely dispossessed the true one '

(Ware).—2. Hence, 'making a disturbance—upsetting the apple-cart': lower classes': ca. 1830–50; Hood dying in 1845. (Ware.)

[**skylark**, n. and v.; derivative **skylarker, skylarking**. Perhaps orig. nautical coll. (as F. & H. supposes), but soon S.E.; prob. (see O.E.D.) always S.E.]

***skylarker**. A housebreaker that, both as a blind and in order to spy out the land, works as a bricklayer: c.: from ca. 1850; ob.

skylight. See **sky-light.**—***skypper**. See **skipper**, n., 1.

skyrocket. See **sky-rocket.**—**skyscraper**. See **sky-scraper**.

skyte. A dayboy: Shrewsbury School: from ca. 1840. Pascoe, 1881. Gen. in pl.: Desmond Coke, *The Bending of a Twig*, 1906, 'Are not the despised Day Boys called Skytes—" Scythians " or " outcasts " ?' Cf. the Westminster *Sky*.

slab. A milestone: low: ca. 1820–1910. 'Jon Bee', 1823; Baumann. Abbr. *slab of stone*.—2. A bricklayer's boy: ca. 1840–90. Ex dialect.—3. A portion; a tall, awkward fellow: both Australian: late C. 19–20. C. J. Dennis.

slabbering-bib. A parson's, lawyer's, neck-band: late C. 18–mid-19. Grose, 2nd ed. Lit., a slobbering-bib. (F. & H., wrongly, *slabbering-bit*.)

slack. The seat (of a pair of trousers, gen. mentioned): coll.: mid-C. 19–20. Prob. ex *slacks*, q.v.—2. A severe or knock-down punch: boxing: C. 19. Ex Jack Slack, a powerful hitter. Also *slack un*. Cf. *Mendoza* and *auctioneer*.—3. Impertinence, decided 'cheek': dial. (1842) >, ca. 1870, s. >, ca. 1910, coll. T. Hardy, 1876, 'Let's have none of your slack.' (O.E.D.) Abbr. *slack-jaw*.—4. A 'spell of inactivity or laziness': coll.: 1851, Mayhew (O.E.D.). Ex *slack period* or *spell*.

slack, v. To make water: late C. 19–20. Ex relaxation. See *slack off*.

slack, hold on the. To be lazy; avoid work: nautical (— 1864); ob. H., 3rd ed. Ex the loose or untautened part of a rope.

slack and slim. Slender and elegant: non-aristocratic (— 1887); slightly ob. Baumann.

slack in stays. Lazy: nautical coll.: late C. 19–20. Bowen, 'From the old description of a ship which is slow in going about.'

slack off. See **slack, v.—slack un**. See **slack**, n., 2.

slack out. To go out: Public Schools': C. 20. (E. F. Benson, *David Blaize*, 1916.)

slacken your glib! Shut up!: low (— 1887). Baumann.

slacker. A shirker; a very lazy person: coll.: 1898 (O.E.D.). Cf. *slackster*.

slacks. Trousers (full length): 1824: coll. >, ca. 1905, S.E. Surtees. (O.E.D.) In C. 20, applied esp. to an English soldier's trousers.—2. Pilfered fruit: late C. 19–20: greengrocers' s. >, by 1920, j.

slackster. A 'slacker' (q.v.): C. 20 coll.; ob. *The Daily Chronicle*, Nov. 6, 1901, 'There are "slacksters ", as the slang of the schools and universities has it, in all professions.' O.E.D.

slag. A coward; one unwilling to resent an affront: late C. 18–early 19. Extant, however, in showmen's s.: Neil Bell, *Crocus*, 1936. Grose, 2nd ed. Corruption of *slack(-mettled)*.—2. A (watch)-chain, whether of gold or of silver: c.: (— 1857); ob. 'Ducange Anglicus'. Perhaps a perversion of *slack* (hanging slack).—3. A rough: grafters':

late C. 19–20. (P. Allingham, *Cheapjack*, 1934.) Ex dial.

***slagger**. A brothel-keeper: c. or low (— 1909). Ware. Prob. a corruption of *slacker*: cf. *slag*, 1.

***slam**. A variant (— 1887) of *slum*, n., 2, 4, 5.—2. An attack; esp. *the grand slam*, the big attack: military: 1915; ob. Frank Richards, *Old Soldiers Never Die*, 1933. Ex bridge.

slam, v. To brag; esp. among soldiers, to simulate tipsiness and brag of numerous drinks: from ca. 1880. Cf. *slum*, v. Perhaps ex:—2. To 'patter'; talk fluently: itinerant showmen's: from ca. 1870. Henley, 1884, 'You swatchel coves that pitch and slam.' According to H., 5th ed., ex 'a term in use among the birdsingers'—presumably dealers in singing birds—' at the East-end [of London], by which they denote a certain style of note in chaffinches.'

slam-bang shop. A variant (Bee, 1823; † by 1910) of *slap-bang shop*: see **slap-bang**.

slam-slam. To salute: Anglo-Indian (— 1909). Ex *salaam*. (Ware.)

slammer, slamming. (Anything) exceptional; a 'whopper', whopping: from ca. 1890; ob.

***slaney**. A theatre: c.: from ca. 1880. Ex *slum*, to act.

slang. The special vocabulary (e.g. cant) of low, illiterate, or disreputable persons; low, illiterate language: 1756, Toldervy (O.E.D.): c. >, ca. 1780, s. >, ca. 1820, coll. >, ca. 1850, S.E. Likewise, the senses 'jargon' (1802), 'illegitimate colloquial speech' (1818), i.e. what now we ordinarily understand by 'slang' (1818), and 'impertinence' or 'abuse' (1825), began as s. and > S.E. only ca. 1860. (Earliest dates: O.E.D.) The etymology is a puzzle: the O.E.D. hazards none; Bradley, Weekley, Wyld consider that cognates are afforded by Norwegian *slenja-keften*, to sling the jaw, to abuse, and by several other Norwegian forms in *-sleng*; that *slang* is ultimately from *sling* there can be little doubt,—cf. *slang the mauleys, sling language* and *sling the bat*, qq.v.; that it is an argotic perversion of Fr. *langue* is very improbable though not impossible. (See esp. the author's *Slang To-Day and Yesterday*, revised edition, 1935, at pp. 1–3.) All the following senses, except the last two, derive ultimately ex sense 1.—2. Nonsense; humbug: ca. 1760–90. Foote, 1762.—3. A line of work; a 'lay' or 'lurk': c. of ca. 1788–1800. G. Parker.—4. A warrant or a licence, esp. a hawker's: from ca. 1810: c. >, ca. 1850, s. Vaux; H., 3rd ed.—5. A travelling show: showmen's (— 1859). H., 1st ed. Ob.—6. Hence, a performance or 'house' in a show, e.g. a circus: showmen's: 1861, Mayhew. Cf. *slang-cove* and *-cull*.—7. (Gen. in pl.) A short measure or weight: London, mostly costermongers': 1851, Mayhew.—8. (Ex Ger. c. *schlange*, a watch-chain, or Dutch *slang*, a snake: O.E.D.) A watch-chain; any chain: c.: from ca. 1810. Vaux.—9. See **slangs**, 1.

slang, adj. Slangy: 1758: c. >, ca. 1780, s. >, ca. 1820, coll. >, ca. 1850, S.E. Ex *slang*, n., 1.—2. (Of persons or tone.) Rakish, impertinent: ca. 1818–70: s. > coll. Ex sense 1.—3. (Of dress.) Loud; extravagant: coll.: ca. 1830–70.—4. (Of measures, weights,) Short, defective: costers': 1812, Vaux.—5. Hence, adv., as in Mayhew, 1851, 'He could always "work slang " with a true measure,' O.E.D.; ob.

slang, v.i. To remain in debt: University s. of ca. 1770–1800. See (?) Smeaton Oliphant (*à propos*

of tick), *The New English*, at II, 180. F. & H.—
V.i.—2. To exhibit at (e.g.) a fair: 1789, G.
Parker; † by 1860.—3. V.i. and t., to cheat,
swindle, defraud: 1812, Vaux. Also *slang it*
(Mayhew, 1851).—4. To fetter: c. of ca. 1810–50.
Lex. Bal.; Vaux. Implied in *slanged*, q.v., and
prob. ex *slangs*, 1.—5. V.i. to use slang; rail
abusively: 1828, Lytton: s. > coll.; slightly ob.
—6. V.t. to abuse, scold, violently: 1844, Albert
Smith (O.E.D.); in C. 20, coll. Cf. *slanging*, q.v.

*slang, boy of the. A C. 19 variant of *slang-boy*,
q.v.

*slang, on or upon the. At one's own line of
work: c. of ca. 1788–1850. G. Parker.

slang, out on the. Travelling with a hawker's
licence: 1864, H., 3rd ed.

slang-and-pitcher shop. A cheapjack's van or
stock-in-trade: mid-C. 19–20. Ex *slang*, a hawker's licence, + *pitcher*, q.v.

*slang-boy. (Gen. pl.) A speaker of (under-
world) cant: late C. 18–mid-19. G. Parker, 1789.
Also *boy of the slang*.

slang-cove, -cull. A showman: *cull*, c. or showmen's s. of ca. 1788–1850 (G. Parker, 1789); cove,
showmen's s. of mid-C. 19–20 (Mayhew, 1851).

*slang-dipper; -dropper. A *slang-dipper* is 'one
who gilds metal chains for the purpose of selling
them as gold.' A *slang-dropper* is the man 'who
disposes of them, as he usually does so by pretending
to pick [one] up in the street under the nose of his
victim, [whom] he immediately asks to put a value
on it': c. (— 1935). David Hume. See **slang**,
n., 8.

slang it. To use false weights: low: mid-C. 19–
20. Cf. *slang*, n., 7 and v., 3.

slang the mauleys. To shake hands (lit., sling
the mauleys): late C. 18–20: low London. G.
Parker, 1781. Of *mauley* (q.v.), the hand, the
dial. form is *mauler*: E.D.D.

slang-tree. A stage; a trapeze: resp. itinerant
actors' and showmen's: mid-C. 19–20. Ex *slang*,
a travelling show. Cf. *slang-cove* and:

slang-tree, climb (up) the. To perform; make
an exhibition of oneself: showmen's: resp. mid-
C. 19–20 and late C. 19–20.

[slang-whang, -er, -ery, -ing. Prob., as O.E.D.
indicates, always S.E.]

*slanged, ppl. adj. In fetters: c.: 1811, *Lex.
Bal.* Cf. *slangs*, 1, and *slang*, v., 4.

slanger. A showman: circus-men's (— 1933).
Edward Seago, *Circus Company*. Prob. ex *slang*,
n., 5.

slanging, vbl.n. Exhibiting (e.g. a two-headed
cow) at fair or market: showmen's s. verging on
c.: late C. 18–19. G. Parker, 1789. Ex *slang*,
v., 1.—2. Abuse; violent scolding: mid-C. 19–20:
s. >, ca. 1880, coll. >, ca. 1910, S.E. Lever,
1856 (O.E.D.). Ex *slang*, v., 6.—3. Singing:
music-halls': ca. 1880–1900. Ware derives it
ex 'the quantity of spoken slang between the
verses.'

slanging-dues concerned, there has or have been.
A low London c.p. uttered by one who suspects
that he has been curtailed of his just portion or
right: ca. 1810–50. Vaux.

*slangs. Fetters; leg-irons: c.: from ca.
1810; ob. Vaux. Cognate with *slang*, a watch-
chain or any chain whatsoever. Cf. *slanged*, q.v.
—2. the slangs. A collection of travelling shows;
the travelling showman's world or profession:
showmen's: prob. from ca. 1850, though app. the

first record occurs in T. Hood the Younger's *Comic
Annual*, 1888 (p. 52). Ex *slang*, a travelling show.

slangular. Belonging to, characteristic of, slang
(highly colloquial speech): jocular S.E. verging on
coll.: 1853, Dickens. On *angular*. (Likewise,
slanguage, which, however, is definitely, S.E.:
1899. Cf. *Slango-Saxon*, from ca. 1920: a word
condemnatory of the slangy tendency of English.)

slangy, flashy or pretentious (ca. 1850–90), and
(of dress) loud, vulgar (ca. 1860–1900), may orig.
have been coll. Cf. *slang*, adj., 2, 3.

slant. A chance; an opportunity (e.g. of going
somewhere): 1837, *Fraser's Magazine*, 'With the
determination of playing them a slippery trick the
very first slant I had,' O.E.D. Ex nautical *slant*,
a slight breeze, a favourable wind, a period of
windiness.—2. A plan designed to ensure a particular and favourable result (or scene of operations for
that result): Australian: 1897, P. Warung;
slightly ob. (O.E.D.)—3. A sidelight (*on*); a
different or a truly characteristic opinion (*on*) or
reaction: U.S., anglicised ca. 1930. Via *angle*
(*on*).

*slant, v. To run away: c.: from ca. 1899. Ex
dial. (Graham, 1896), to move away, itself ex
slant, to move, travel, obliquely (O.E.D., § 3, a).
—2. (V.i.) to exaggerate: from ca. 1900; ob.
Prob. ex *slant*, 'to diverge from a direct course.'
—3. In racing, to lay a bet (v.i.): from ca. 1901.

slanter. 'Spurious; unfair,' C. J. Dennis:
Australian (— 1916). Ex *on the slant*: cf., however,
s(c)hlenter, q.v.

slantindicular (1855, Smedley); occ. slanting-
(1840, J. T. Hewlett) or slanten- (1872, De Morgan).
Slanting, oblique; neither perpendicular nor horizontal: jocular coll., orig.—1832—U.S. (see esp.
Thornton). O.E.D.—2. Hence, fig.: from ca.
1860.—3. Occ. as n. and adv. Ex *slanting* on
perpendicular. Cf.:

slantindicularly, etc. Slantingly, obliquely:
1834, De Quincey: jocular coll. (O.E.D.). Though
recorded earlier than the adj., it must actually be
later.

slaoc. Coals: back s. (— 1859). H., 1st ed.

*slap. Plunder, booty, 'swag': c.: late C. 18–
early 19: mainly Anglo-Irish. ? ex *slap*, a blow.
—2. Make-up: theatrical: 1860, H., 2nd ed.; ob.
'Pomes' Marshall, 1897, 'You could just distin-
guish faintly | That she favoured the judicious use
of slap.' Perhaps ex the dial. version of *slop*;
perhaps, however, as Ware suggests, ex 'its being
liberally and literally slapped on.'

slap, v. Gen. *slap along*. To move, walk,
quickly: from ca. 1825: coll. and (in C. 20,
nothing but) dial. ? ex *slap*, i.e. bang, *a door*.

slap, adj. Excellent; first-rate; in style:
from ca. 1850; ob. Mayhew, 1851, 'People's got
proud now . . . and must have everything slap.'
Abbr. *slap-up*.

slap, adv. Quickly, suddenly, unexpectedly:
coll.: 1672, Villiers; Sterne. Also *slap off* (Reade,
1852, 'Finish . . . slap off') and † *slap down* (1865,
Dickens). Lit., as if with a slap.—2. With vv. of
motion: coll.: 1676, Etherege (*slap down*); 1766,
Mrs F. Sheridan; 1890, 'Rolf Boldrewood.'—3.
With vv. of violent collision or impact: coll.:
1825. Meredith, 1861, 'A punch slap into Old
Tom's belt.'—4. Directly; straight: coll.: 1829,
Marryat, 'I . . . lay slap in the way'; Barham,
'Aimed slap at him.' All senses: mainly O.E.D.
—5. Precisely: coll.: 1860, H., 2nd ed. '"Slap
in the wind's eye," i.e. exactly to windward.'

slap at, have a. To engage in a fight with; to attempt: coll.: late C. 19–20.

slap-bang, whether adj., adv., or n. (except in its c. sense), is almost certainly S.E.; but *slap-bang shop,* which 'lived' ca. 1780–1850, is prob.—until C. 19, at least—coll., while its abbr., *slap-bang* (in 'Ducange Anglicus'), is c. In 1785, Grose, who gives a secondary sense that is indubitably coll. or even s., defines it thus: '*Slap-bang shop,* a petty cook's shop where there is no credit given, but what is had must be paid down with the ready'— i.e. with cash—'slap-bang, i.e. immediately. This is a common appellation for a night cellar frequented by thieves, and sometimes for a stage coach or caravan': with the latter, cf. the later, long †, *slap-bang coach.*

slap down and slap off : see **slap,** adv., 1 and (**s. d.** only) 2.

slap-up. A battle; an attack : New Zealanders': in G.W. The word persists, both in N.Z. and— though less gen.—in Australia, for a fight of any sort.

slap-up, adj. Excellent; superior, first-rate; grand : 1823, Bee, who says that it is Northern but does not distinguish between persons and things; 1827, *The Sporting Magazine,* 'That slap-up work, *The Sporting Magazine*' (O.E.D.); of persons, certainly in 1829, 'slap-up swell' (Thackeray, 1840, has 'slap-up acquaintances'): both, s. >, ca. 1860, coll.; in England, ob. since ca. 1905. Or *bang-up,* q.v.

*****slash.** An outside coat-pocket : c. (— 1839). Brandon; H., 1st ed. Abbr. *slash pocket.* Ex *slash,* a vertical slit for the exposition of the lining or an under garment of a contrasting or, at the least, different colour.

*****slash,** v.i. To cut a person across the face with a razor : c. (— 1933). Esp. as vbl.n. Charles E. Leach, *On Top of the Underworld.*—2. V.t. To deprive (an accomplice) of his share : c. (— 1933). Ibid. Cf. *carve up,* q.v.

slasher. Any person or thing exceptional, esp. if exceptionally severe : from ca. 1820 : coll. Cf. *ripper,* q.v.—2. A man in charge of a 'fleet' of steam or petrol locomotives : Public Works' (— 1935).

Slashers, the. The 28th Regiment of Foot (now the Gloucestershire Regiment) : military : during and since the American War of Independence. James, *Military Dict.,* 1802. Ex an attack delivered, at the Battle of White Plains in 1776, with their short swords : F. & Gibbons. Also *the Old Braggs* and *the Right-Abouts.*

slashing. Exceptionally vigorous, expert, successful, brilliant, notable : from ca. 1820 : coll. till C. 20, then S.E. Dickens, 'A slashing fortune,' 1854. Cf. *slasher.*

slashing, adv. Very; brilliantly : coll.: from 1890's; slightly ob. F. & H., 1903, 'A slashing fine woman; a slashing good race; and so forth.' Ex *slashing,* adj.

*****slat.** A sheet : c.: a mid C. 17–mid-18 variant of *slate,* n., 1, q.v. Coles, 1676; B.E.—2. A half-crown : c.: a late C. 18–early 19 variant of *slate,* n., 2. Grose, 2nd ed.—3. See **slats.**

*****slate.** A sheet : c.: 1567, Harman; 1622, Fletcher; Grose, 1st ed. : † by 1840, and prob. ob. a century earlier. ? origin, unless a perversion of *flat* (even, level) : cf. Ger. *Blatt.* Cf. *slat,* 1.—2. A half-crown : c.: late C. 17–18. B.E. ? origin. Cf. *slat,* 2—3. As in Andrew Lang, 1887 (earliest

record), ' " Slate " is a professional term for a severe criticism,' O.E.D. : book-world coll. >, ca. 1905, S.E. ; by 1930, slightly ob. Ex :

slate. To criticise severely : coll. : 1848, Alaric Watts ; Blackmore ; Saintsbury ; Kipling ; Kernahan. Ex :—2. To abuse ; reprimand or scold severely : 1840 : s. (orig. political) >, ca. 1870, coll. Ex :—3. To thrash ; beat severely : ca. 1825–70, then very rare : app. orig. Anglo-Irish. If this sense is earlier than the next but one, then it may well derive ex the Scottish and Northern *slate,* ' to bait, assail, or drive, with dogs,' esp. since this hunting term was used fig. at least as early as 1755.—4. Hence, as a military coll., to punish (the enemy) severely : 1854, in the Crimea ; ob. by 1914,—I, for instance, never heard it used during the G.W.,—and by 1930 virtually †.—5. (Perhaps the originating sense : presumably ex covering a roof with slates.) To ' bonnet ', knock his hat over the eyes of (a person) : 1825, Westmacott ; H., 3rd ed. Ob. by 1890, † by 1930. As v.i. in form, *fly a tile.*—6. (Perhaps ex the military sense.) To bet heavily against (a horse, a human competitor) : sporting : from early 1870's ; slightly ob. H., 5th ed. (1874)—7. In medical s., gen. in the passive, to prophesy the death of (a patient) : late C. 19–20. Ware. Ex putting his name on a slate : see the author's *Slang.* (For all except the last two senses, dates from O.E.D.)

slate, on the. ' Written up against you ' : lower classes' coll. : late C. 19–20. Ware.

slate loose or **off, have a.** To be mentally deficient : s. >, ca. 1900, coll. : *loose,* 1860, H., 2nd ed. ; *off,* 1867, Rhoda Broughton (O.E.D.). The latter, ob. Cf. *shingle short* and *tile loose,* qq.v., and dial. *have a slate slipped.*

slated, ppl.adj. See **slate,** v., esp. in senses 1, 2. Cf. *slating.*—**slated, be.** To be expected to die. See **slate,** v., last sense.

[**slater,** a wood-louse, is, in New South Wales, ess coll. than a survival ex English dial.]

Slater's pan. A coll. nickname for the gaol at Kingston, Jamaica : West Indies : late C. 18– early 19. Grose, 2nd ed. Ex the deputy provost-marshall.

slating, vbl.n. See **slate,** v., esp. in senses 1, 2, 4. —2. Adj., little used.

slats. The ribs : U.S., whence Australian (— 1916) and Canadian. C. J. Dennis ; John Beames. Ex shape.

slaughter. A wholesale dismissal of employees : lower classes' (— 1935). Also a *work-out.*

*****slaughter-house.** A gaming-house where men are employed to pretend to be playing for high stakes : sharpers' c. : 1809 (O.E.D.) ; ob.—2. A shop where, at extremely low prices, goods are bought from small manufacturers (glad of a large turn-over even at a very small profit) : 1851, Mayhew. One would, if it were not for the libel laws, name several firms that buy thus. Cf. *slaughterer.*—3. A factory paying miserable wages : operatives' (— 1887). Baumann.—4. The Surrey Sessions House : c. (— 1909). Ware.—5. ' A particularly hard sailing ship with a brutal after-guard ' : nautical : late C. 19–20 ; slightly ob. Bowen.

slaughterer. A vendor buying very cheaply from small manufacturers : 1851, Mayhew. Cf. *slaughter-house,* 2.—2. ' A buyer for re-manufacture : as books for pulp, cloth for shoddy, &c.': late C. 19–20 commercial. F. & H.

slaughterman. A manufacturer paying very low wages : (esp. furniture) operatives' (— 1887). Baumann. Cf. *slaughter-house*, 3.

slave-driver. A stern taskmaster or master : coll. : from ca. 1840.

slave one's life (coll.) **or guts** (low coll.). To work extremely hard : late C. 19–20. Manchon.

slaver. 'One engaged in the "white slave traffic",' C. J. Dennis : Australian : C. 20.

slavey. A male servant : coll. : ca. 1810–60. Vaux, Thackeray. Ex *slave*.—2. A female servant : coll. : ca. 1810–70. Vaux.—3. Esp. a hardworked 'general' : 1821, Egan ; P. H. Emerson. Cf. *skivvy*.—4. A servants' attic : London students' (— 1887) ; ob. Baumann.

slawmineyeux. A Dutchman : nautical : ca. 1860–1910. Ex Dutch *ja, mynheer* (yes, sir).

slay. At Shrewsbury School, from ca. 1890, as in Desmond Coke, *The Bending of a Twig*, 1906, ' " Slays " are spreads [feasts], ambitious beyond all imagining, ordered from the Shop.' Cf. the adj. *killing*.

***sleek-and-slum shop.** ' A public house or tavern where single men and their wives resort,' Bee : c. of ca. 1820–90. See **slum**, a room.

***sleek wife.** A silk handkerchief : c. (— 1823) ; † by 1920. Egan's Grose.

[**sleep, put to.** To kill : a euphemism that is, rather, familiar S.E. than coll.]

sleep-drunk. Very drowsy ; 'muzzy' : coll. : from ca. 1870 ; ob. Ex heavy awaking.

sleep on bones. (Of children) to sleep in the nurse's lap : coll. : C. 19–20 ; ob.

***sleep with Mrs Green.** To sleep in the open : New Zealand tramps' c. (— 1932). · I.e. on the green grass. Cf. *Star Hotel*.

sleeper. A player too much favoured by his handicap : lawn tennis (— 1923). Manchon.

sleeping. Slow-witted : Glasgow (— 1934). Cf. *slept in*, q.v.

sleeping near a crack, (I, he, or **you) must have been.** A c.p. reply to an inquiry as to how a male has caught a cold : lower and lower-middle classes' : late C. 19–20. (Ernest Raymond, *Mary Leith*, 1931.) An innuendo in respect of the anatomical *crack*.

sleeping-partner. A bed-fellow : jocular coll. : mid-C. 19–20.

sleepless hat. A hat with the nap worn off : ca. 1860–1905. H., 3rd ed. ; Baumann. Cf. :

sleepy. Grose, 2nd ed., has this punning c.p. : *the cloth of your coat must be extremely sleepy ; for it has not had a nap this long time* : late C. 18–early 19. Whence *sleepless hat*, q.v. ; cf. *wide-awake*.—2. Repaid, recompensed : low (— 1923). Manchon.

Sleepy Queens, the. The 2nd Foot Regiment (ca. 1880–1901, the Queen's Royal Regiment) : military : from ca. 1850 ; very ob.

sleepy-seeds. The mucus forming about the eyes in sleep : nursery : late C. 19–20. Suggested by *sand-man* (q.v.) and *sleepy sickness*.

sleepy-walker. A sleep-walker : lower classes' coll. (— 1887). Baumann.

sleeve-board. A word hard to pronounce : tailors' : from ca. 1870. Ex hardness.

sleeveology. See **shouldology**.

sleever. An order taken by a ' commercial ' on a good day but held up for the next day, to preclude reporting a blank day to his employers : commercial travellers' : late C. 19–20. I.e. an order ' up one's sleeve.'

slender in the middle as a cow in the waist, as. Very fat : C. 17–20 (ob.) : coll. till C. 19, then dial. Burton, 1621 ; Fuller, 1732 ; Evans, *Leicestershire Words*, 1881. Apperson.

slep. See **-p**.

slept in (he, she, etc.). A Glasgow c.p. (— 1934) = too late ; not quick enough.

slewed ; occ. **slued.** Tipsy : coll. : 1834, M. Scott (*slewed*) ; Dickens, 1844 (*slued*). Ob. Ex *slew*, to swing round.—2. Hence, beaten, baffled : coll. : late C. 19–20. (O.E.D.)

Slice. The same as *Silly Billy*, 3.—2. (**slice.**) A slice of bread and butter : coll. : C. 20. (Anon., ' Down and Out ' in *The Week-End Review*, Nov. 18, 1933.)

slice, take a. ' To intrigue, particularly with a married woman, because a slice of [*sic*] a cut loaf is not missed,' Grose, 2nd ed. : coll. : mid-C. 18–mid-19. Ex the C. 17–20 proverbial *it is safe taking a shive* (in C. 18–19, occ. *slice*) *of a cut loaf*, as in Shakespeare's *Titus Andronicus*. Apperson.

***slice of fat.** A profitable robbery : c. (— 1887). Baumann.

slice off. To settle part of (an old score) : military (— 1909) ; very ob. Ware.

slick. ' A fine result or appearance ' : Conway cadets' : C. 20. John Masefield, *The Conway*, 1933. Ex the adj.

slick, v. To despatch rapidly, get done with : coll. : 1860, H., 2nd ed. ; ob. Ex *slick*, to polish : cf. *polish off*, q.v.—2. See ' Eton slang ', § 2.

***slick-a-dee.** A pocket-book : Scots c. (— 1839) ; ob. Brandon ; H., 1st ed. On *dee*, the same.

'Slid ! Coll. abbr. *God's lid*, a late C. 16–17 petty oath. O.E.D.

slide. (Esp. in the imperative.) To decamp : coll. : U.S. (— 1859) anglicised ca. 1890. Whiteing, 1899, ' Cheese it, an' slide.' Occ. *slide out*. Ex *slide*, to move silently, stealthily.

slide up the board or **the straight, do a.** (Of a man) to coït : low : from ca. 1870. Cf. *rush up the straight*.

slider. An ice-cream wafer : Glasgow (— 1934). Alastair Baxter.

sliders. A pair of drawers : coll. : late C. 17–mid-18. J. Dickenson, 1699.

'Slife ! God's life ! : C. 17–18 coll. Preserved only in period plays and Wardour Street novels. By abbr. Cf. *'Slid*, q.v., and :

'Slidikins. A petty oath : coll. : late C. 17–18. Ex *'Slid* on *'Sbodikins*. (O.E.D.)

'Slight ! God's light ! : a late C. 16–17 oath : trivial coll. O.E.D.

slightly-tightly. Bemused (not drunk) with liquor : fast life : ca. 1905–14. Ware. Perversion of *slightly ' tight '*.

sligo, tip (someone) the. To warn by winking ; wink at : 1775, S. J. Pratt, ' I tips Slappim the sligo, and nudges the elbow of Trugge, as much as to say, . . . I have him in view,' O.E.D. Prob. on *sly* : *o* is a common s. suffix.

***slim.** Rum (the drink) : c. : 1789, G. Parker ; † by 1850. ? *rum* perverted.

slime, v.i. To ' cut ' games ; to loaf : Durham School : late C. 19–20. Ex S.E. *slime*, to crawl slimily.—2. To sneak along : Felsted : late C. 19–20. Whence *do a slime*, to take a mean or crafty advantage. Cf. :—3. To move, go, quietly, stealthily, or sneakingly : Harrow : late C. 19–20. Howson & Warner, 1898, ' His house-beak **slimed**

and twug him.'—4. Hence, to make ' drops ' at racquets : Harrow : from ca. 1900.

slime, do a. See **slime, 2.**

slimy. Deceitful ; treacherous : coll. : C. 20. Ex *slimy*, vile.

sling. A draught of, ' pull ' at a drink, bottle : 1788 (O.E.D.) ; † by 1903, prob. by 1860, perhaps (cf. W.) by 1830. Cf. *go.*

sling. To utter : coll. : C. 15–20. (O.E.D.) See **sling language** and cf. sense 3.—2. To distribute or dispense : s. (— 1860) >, ca. 1890, coll. H., 2nd ed., ' *Sling*, to pass from one person to another.'—3. Hence, to give (as in ' Sling us a tanner '): low (— 1887) >, by 1910, low coll. Baumann.—4. To do easily : from ca. 1864 : s. >, ca. 1900, coll. Mainly in *sling ink*, etc.—5. To use (e.g. slang) ; relate (a story) : from ca. 1880 : s. >, ca. 1910, coll. Mrs Lynn Linton, ' I am awfully sorry if I slung you any slang,' O.E.D. See **sling a yarn** and **sling slang.**—6. To abandon : C. 20 : mostly Australian. H. Lawson, 1902, ' Just you sling it [liquor] for a year,' O.E.D.—7. For c. usage, see **sling one's hook**, 2, and **sling the smash.** In c., moreover, *sling* = to throw away : late C. 19–20 : cf. *sling*, to abandon.—8. See **sling a snot.**—9. V.i. to sleep in a hammock : *Conway* cadets': late C. 19–20. John Masefield, *The Conway*, 1933. Abbr. *sling one's hammock.*

sling !, let her. See **sling yourself !**

sling a book, poem, an article. To write one : from ca. 1870 : s. >, 1900, coll. Cf. *sling ink*, q.v.

sling a cat. To vomit : low : mid-C. 19–20 ; ob. Cf. *cat, jerk the.*

sling a daddle. To shake hands : low : from ca. 1870. Cf. *slang the mauleys.*

sling a foot. To dance : coll. : from ca. 1860 ; ob.

sling a hat. To wave one's hat in applause : coll. : from 1830's ; ob.

sling a nasty part. To act a part so well that it would be hard to rival it : orig. and mainly theatrical : from ca. 1880. Ex :

sling (or jerk) a part. To undertake, to play, a role : theatrical : from ca. 1880.

sling a pen. See **sling ink.**

sling a pot. To drink (liquor): from ca. 1870 : coll. rather than s.

sling a slobber. To give a kiss ; hence, to kiss : low (— 1909). Ware. Ex *sling*, v., 3 (q.v.) and *slobber*, which, very low s. for a kiss, dates from late C. 19.

sling a snot. To blow one's nose with one's fingers : low : from ca. 1860. Also, from ca. 1870, simply *sling* (v.i.): ob. H., 5th ed.

sling a tinkler. To ring a bell : from ca. 1870 ; ob.

sling a yarn. To relate a story : C. 20 : s. >, ca. 1930, coll. Cf. *sling language*, q.v.—2. Hence, to tell a lie : 1904, *The Strand Magazine*, March, ' Maybe you think I am just slinging you a yarn,' O.E.D.

sling about, v.i. To idle ; to loaf : from ca. 1870 ; in C. 20, coll.

sling ink ; occ. **sling a pen.** To write : from ca. 1864 : s >, ca. 1900, coll. Orig. U.S. and app. coined by Artemus Ward.

sling language or **words.** To talk : mid-C. 19–20 : s. >, ca. 1900, coll. Cf. *sling*, v.,1, *sling a yarn*, 1, and *sling the bat.*

sling-next. The two cadets sleeping on either side of oneself : *Conway* cadets' : late C. 19–20. John Masefield, *The Conway*, 1933. See **sling, v., 9.**

sling off, v.i. To utter abuse or cheek or impertinence.—2. V.t. with *at*, to give cheek to, to jeer at, to taunt. Both : late C. 19–20. See *Slang*, 2–3.

sling (a person) **one in the eye.** To punch one in the eye, gen. with the implication of blackening it : 1899, Whiteing.

sling one's body. To dance vigorously : London lower classes' (— 1909). Ware. I.e. sling it about.

sling one's Daniel ; sling one's hook. To make off ; decamp : *Daniel*, 1873, J. Greenwood ; *hook*, 1873 or 1874 (H., 5th ed.). The origin of neither is clear ; the latter may be nautical, though Ware derives it from mining-procedure. Cf. *sling yourself !*

sling one's hammock. To get used to a new ship : naval coll. : late C. 19–20. Bowen.

sling one's hook. See **sling one's Daniel.**—2. In c., to pick pockets : from the 1870's. Anon., 1877, *Five Years' Penal Servitude.* O.E.D.

sling one's jelly or **juice.** To masturbate : low: from ca. 1870.

sling one's service about. To boast : military coll. : C. 20. F. & Gibbons. Lit., to talk much of one's length of service.

sling over. ' To embrace emphatically ': Society: ca. 1905–14. Ex U.S., says Ware.

sling round on the loose. To act recklessly : from ca. 1875 ; in C. 20, coll. Possibly an elaboration of *sling about*, q.v.

sling (a person) **slang.** To abuse, scold violently : from ca. 1880 : s. >, ca. 1910, coll. See **sling, v., 5.**

sling the bat. To speak the vernacular (esp. of the foreign country, orig. India, where one happens to be) : military : late C. 19–20. Kipling, 1892. See **bat.**

sling the booze. To stand treat : low : from ca. 1860. Cf. *sling*, v., 2.

sling the hatchet. To talk plausibly : military : late C. 19–20. F. & Gibbons.—2. See **hatchet, sling the.**

sling the language. To swear fluently : lower classes' (— 1903) ; ob.—2. To speak a foreign language : military : from 1915. Cf. *sling the bat.*

sling the lead. See **lead, sling the.**

*sling the smash. To smuggle tobacco to prisoners : c. : from the 1870's. Anon., 1877, *Five Years' Penal Servitude.* O.E.D. Cf. *sling*, v., 2.

sling type. To set type : printers' s. (— 1887) >, by 1910, coll. ; ob. Baumann.

sling words. See **sling language** and contrast **sling the language, 2.**

sling yourself ! or **let her sling !** Bestir yourself ! get a move on ! : low : from ca. 1880 ; the former is very ob. Cf. *sling one's Daniel.*

slinger. (Gen. pl.) A piece of bread afloat in tea or coffee ; a dumpling, a sausage : low (— 1889) >, by 1910, military. Barrère & Leland ; F. & Gibbons.—2. (**Slinger.**) An inevitable nickname of all men surnamed Woods : naval and military : late C. 19–20. Bowen. Cf. *Lac(k)ery.*

slink. A sneak, skulker, cheat : dial (—1824) >, ca. 1830, coll. *The Examiner*, 1830, ' Such a d—d slink,' O.E.D. Ex *slink*, an abortive calf, etc.

slink, v.i. To abort : low (— 1923). Manchon. Same origin as the preceding.

slinky. Sneaky, mean, sly, furtive : dial. and coll. : late C. 19–20. Ex *slink*, q.v.—2. Hence, (of a person's gait) stealthy : late C. 19–20.—3. Hence, (of gait) slyly smooth ; glidingly and unobtrusively sensuous or voluptuous : C. 20. Senses

2, 3 have been influenced by *slink*, to move stealthily.

slip. A counterfeit coin : ca. 1590–1630 : perhaps orig. c., as its use by Greene suggests. Origin doubtful. The derivative *nail up for a slip*, to try and find wanting (late C. 16–early 17), may, orig. at least, have been coll.—2. A slash-pocket in the rear-ward skirt of a coat : ca. 1810–40. Vaux.—3. A Royal Air Force coll. (— 1932), abbr. of *side-slip*, ' a method of losing height quickly without gaining speed '.

slip, v.i. ; gen. be slipping. To weaken, physically ; go downhill, fig. ; lose grip, ground, status, etc. : coll. : C. 20. Ex one's foot slipping.

slip at, let. To rush violently at a person and then assault him vigorously : coll. (— 1860). H., 2nd ed. Cf. :

slip into. To begin punching (a person) vigorously, gen. with the connotation that the person ' slipped into ' receives a sound beating : low coll. (— 1860). H., 2nd ed. Cf. preceding entry.—2. To set about a thing, a task, with a will, vigorously : low coll. (— 1887). Baumann.

slip it across or **over** (a person) To hoodwink ; to befool : from ca. 1912. B. & P.

slip off the hooks. See hooks.

slip one's breath, cable, wind. To die : resp. 1819, Wolcot (O.E.D.) ; 1751, Smollett, ' I told him [a doctor] as how I could slip my cable without direction or assistance ' ; 1772, Bridges. Orig. nautical s. ; by mid-C. 19, gen. coll. In post-G.W. days, *slip one's breath* and *wind* are never heard ; they > † ca. 1910.

slip-slops. ' Soft ' drinks : C. 18. Ned Ward, *The Whole Pleasures of Matrimony*, 1714 (cited by W. Matthews).

slip up. To swindle ; to disappoint : Australian : 1890, *The Melbourne Argus*, Aug. 9, ' I'd only be slipped up if I trusted to them,' O.E.D. Ex *slip*, to elude, evade, stealthily ; give the slip to.—2. **slip a girl up**, to render her pregnant unexpectedly or by trickery : lower classes' (— 1923). Manchon.—3. v.i. To make a mistake, to fail : mid-C. 19–20 ; U.S. anglicised ca. 1910 as a coll. variant of *make a slip*. O.E.D. ; Lyell.

slipper. A sixpence : tailors' (— 1909). Ware. Because it slips into corners and cracks.

Slipper-Slopper, old Mother. A little old woman : coll. (— 1923). Manchon. She slip-slops along.

*slippery. Soap : c. (— 1839) ; slightly ob. Brandon.

slippery, adj. Quick : coll. : late C. 19–20. Prob ex :

slippy. Quick ; spry, nimble : dial. (— 1847) >, ca. 1880, coll. Esp. *look slippy* (Runciman, 1885) and *be slippy* (Rolf Boldrewood, 1889). Coulson Kernahan, 1902, ' We must look slippy about it . . . It's lucky I haven't far to go.' Ex *slippy = slippery* in its fig. as well as lit. senses. O.E.D.

*slither. Counterfeit money : c. (— 1929). O.E.D. (Sup.).—2. A rush, a great hurry : 1915, Edgar Wallace (O.E.D. Sup.). Ex :

slither, v.i. To hurry (away) : low (— 1889). Barrère & Leland. Ex *slither*, to *slide* : cf. *slide*, q.v. Imm. ex dial. : E.D.D.

sloan. To hamper, obstruct, baulk : lower classes' : 1899 only. Ex jockey Sloan's trick—learnt from Archer—of slanting his horse across the track and thus obstructing the other riders. Ware.

slobber. Ink badly distributed : printers' coll. : from ca. 1870.—2. See *sling a slobber*.

slobber, v. To fail to grasp (the ball) cleanly in fielding : cricket coll : 1851, Pycroft ; † by 1890. Lewis. For semantics, cf. *butter* in its cricketing sense.

slobber-swing. A complete circle on the horizontal bar : circus s. verging on j. (— 1933). E. Seago.

slobberation. Kissing ; esp. (lit.) sloppy kissing : low coll. (— 1923). Manchon. Cf. *sling a slobber*.

*slobberings. Money, esp. cash : c. (— 1923). Manchon.

slobgollion. ' An oozy, stringy substance found in sperm oil ' : whalemen's : from ca. 1880. Clarke Russell. Perhaps a perversion of *slumgullion* (q.v.) on *slob*, mud, ooze.

slockdolager ; slogdollager. See sockdolager.

slog. (A period of) hard, steady work : coll. : 1888 (O.E.D.). Ex v., 6.—2. A hard punch or blow ; (at cricket) a hard hit : coll. : 1867 (Lewis) ; as a ' slogger ' (sense 3), it appears also in 1867 (ibid), but is rare. Ex v., 1 ; cf. v., 4.—3. A large portion, esp. of cake : Public Schools' : late C. 19–20.

slog, v.t. To punch, hit, hard : coll. : 1853, Bradley in *Verdant Green* ; v.i., not before 1888. Cf. *to slug*.—2. Hence, to thrash, chastise : 1859, H., 1st ed.—3. Hence, fig., attack violently : coll. : 1891, *The Spectator*, Oct. 10, ' They love snubbing their friends and slogging their enemies,' O.E.D.— 4. (Ex sense 1.) To make runs at cricket by hard hitting : v.i. and v.t. : coll. : resp. early 1860's (H., 3rd ed.) and in 1867 (Lewis).—5. V.i., to walk heavily, perseveringly : coll. : 1872, Calverley (O.E.D.). Prob. ex sense 1. Cf. *foot-slogger*, q.v.— 6. V.i. To work hard and steadily, often with *away*, v.t. with *at* : coll. : 1888, *The Daily News*, May 22, ' I slogged at it, day in and day out,' O.E.D. Ex sense 1.—7. V.i., to steal fruit, esp. apples : school-children's : from ca. 1880. (Neil Bell, *Crocus*, 1936.) Cf. *scrounge*, v.

slog on, have a. To work hard or hurriedly or both : 1888.

slogdollager. See sockdologer. (Manchon.)

slogger. Gen. in pl. A trial or 2nd division rowing-race : Cambridge : ca. 1852–80. In etymology, prob. cognate with ensuing senses ; H., 1860, proposes *slow-goers*, but this seems unlikely. Cf. the Oxford *toggers*, q.v.—2. A deliverer of heavy blows: coll. : 1857, T. Hughes, ' The Slogger pulls up at last . . . fairly blown.' Ex *slog*, v., 1.—3. At cricket, a hard hitter : coll. (— 1864). H., 3rd ed. —4. A (hard) punch : pugilistic (— 1887) ; ob. Baumann. Ex sense 2 reinforced by sense 3.—5. A slung shot (as a weapon) : c. : 1892 (O.E.D.).

slogging, vbl.n. (cricket ; 1860 : Lewis) and ppl. adj. See **slog, v.**, various senses.

'Slood. A variant of *Slud*, q.v.

*sloop. A neckerchief : c. (— 1933). Charles E. Leach. Perhaps because '*s a loop*.

sloop of war. A whore : rhyming s. (— 1859). H., 1st ed. † by 1874 : H., 5th ed., has ' *Rory o' More*, the floor. Also to signify a whore.'

sloosh. A wash, a sound of washing : from ca. 1905. (O.E.D. Sup.) Ex *sluice*.—2. Hence, *sloosh* or *slooshy*, v.i. and v.t., to wash : 1907, W. De Morgan (ibid.).

slop. A policeman : abbr. of back s. (— 1859) *esclop* (properly *ecilop*, police) ; ob. H., 1st ed. Already in the 2nd ed. (1860), H. writes ' At first *back slang*, but now general.'—2. A tailor : from ca. 1860 ; ob. Cf. *slops*.—3. At Christ's Hospital,

pejorative for a person : mid-C. 19–20. Cf.
Nashe's ' slop of a ropehaler ' (1599).

slop-feeder. A tea-spoon : low (? orig. c.) :
from ca. 1810. Vaux. Ex *slop*(*s*), tea.

slop-made. Disjointed : Australian coll.
(— 1909) ; very ob. Ware. Presumably ex
sloppily made.

slop-pail. A man doing housework : low coll.
(— 1923). Manchon.

slop trade. Trade that is ' no class ' : tailors'
coll. : mid-C. 19–20.

slop-tubs. Tea-things : c. >, ca. 1870, low :
from ca. 1820 ; ob. Egan's Grose. Cf. *slop-feeder*.

slope. A running-away, making-off ; escape :
coll. : U.S. (— 1859) anglicised ca. 1880. Esp. *do a
slope* : coll. and dial. : from ca. 1890. Ex :

slope, v. To make off ; run away, decamp :
coll. : orig. (1839) U.S., anglicised ca. 1857 (see
' Ducange Anglicus '). Song-writer Vance ;
' Pomes ' Marshall. Either ex *let's lope !* as H.,
1st ed., proposes, or ex *slope*, to move obliquely.—
2. With adv., esp. *off* (1844, Haliburton) and occ.
home(*ward*), the latter in Mayne Reid, 1851 : coll. :
orig. U.S., anglicised by 1860.—3. (Ex sense 1.)
' To go loiteringly or sauntering,' 1851. S.O.D.—
4. (Likewise ex sense 1.) V.t., to leave (lodgings)
without paying : 1908 (O.E.D.). Ex *slope*, 1,
influenced by dial. *slope*, to trick, cheat. O.E.D.—
5. In c. of early C. 17 (e.g., Rowlands, 1610), to lie
down to sleep ; to sleep. (Cf. *slope*, v.t., to bend
down). It replaced *couch a hog's head*.

slope, do a. See **slope,** n.

Sloper's Island (or i.). A weekly-tenement neighbourhood : London : from ca. 1870. Esp. ca.
1870, ' the Artisans' Village near Loughborough
Junction, originally in the midst of fields ; now in
the centre of a densely populated neighbourhood,'
F. & H., 1903. Ob. by 1910, † by 1930. Prob. ex
sloper, one who decamps.

sloping billet. A comfortable job for a married
naval man : naval : C. 20. Bowen. I.e. with
many opportunities to be ashore with one's family :
? ex *sloping roofs*.

slopper. A slop-basin : Leys School : late C. 19–
20. See ' -*er*, Oxford '.

slopping-up. A drinking bout : low : from ca.
1870 ; ob.

sloppy. Very sentimental : coll. : late C. 19–20.
Ex *sloppy*, feeble, infirm. Cf. *slushy*.

slops, tea still in the chest, is to be considered
either s. or low coll. (— 1859). H., 1st ed. Ex
slops, (weak) tea as beverage.—2 A synonym of
ales, q.v.—3. Subjects other than Classics or Mathematics : Cambridge University (— 1923). Manchon.

slosh. Slush (liquid mud) : dial. and Cockney
coll. (— 1887). Baumann.—2. A drink ; drink in
gen. : from the middle 1880's.—3. Hence, tea :
schoolboys' s. (C. 20) ex dial. (— 1899) E.D.D.—
4. Nonsense, esp. if sentimental : from ca. 1920.
(Denis Mackail, 1933.) Ex *slush + bosh*.

slosh. V.t., to hit, esp. resoundingly : from not
later than 1915. E. M. Forster, in *Time and Tide*,
June 16, 1934, ' Sir Oswald Mosley . . . sends them
[his followers] to slosh the Reds.' Prob. ex S.E.
slosh, to splash about in mud,—influenced by dial
sloush, v.t., to sluice,—via U.S. *slosh around*, explained by ' Major Jack Downing ' in 1862 as ' jest
goin rite through a crowd, an mowin your swath,
hitten rite an left everybody you meet ' (Thornton).

slosh around. To strut about ; take one's

'swanky ' ease : lower classes' (—1923). Manchon.
Cf. preceding.

slosher. A school boarding-house assistant :
Cheltenham College : late C. 19–20. ? ex U.S.
slosh, to move aimlessly about.

sloshiety paper. A gushing Society periodical :
journalistic : 1883–ca. 1890. Ware. Punning
society + sloshy, slushy.

sloshing. The vbl.n. of *slosh*, v. ; esp. a thrashing : from ca. 1916. Lyell.

sloshy. Emotional, excessive in sentiment :
orig. at Harrow : A. Lunn, *The Harrovians*, 1913 ;
1924, E. F. Benson, in his delightful Cambridge
novel, *David of King's*, ' " Positively his last appearance," said David. Rather theatrical, but not
sloshy . . ." ' ; 1933, *The Daily Mirror*, Oct. 26,
' " Sloshy talk ".' Ex *sloppy + slushy*.—2. Very
moist : preparatory schools' : from ca. 1910. E. F.
Benson, *David Blaize*, 1916, ' Sloshy buttered toast.'

slouch at, no. Rather or very good at : U.S.
(1874) partly anglicised in late 1890's. F. T. Bullen,
1898, ' He was no " slouch " at the business either,'
O.E.D. Ex *slouch*, a lout, a clumsy fellow.

slour. To lock (up) ; fasten : c. (— 1812) ; ob.
by 1890, virtually † by 1930. Vaux ; Ainsworth ;
H., 3rd ed., classifies it as prison c. ? origin unless
perchance a perversion of *lower*.—2. Also, to button
(up) a garment : esp. in *sloured hoxter*, an inside
pocket buttoned up : 1812, Vaux, *slour up* ; the
simple v. is unrecorded before 1834 in Ainsworth's
Rookwood.

sloured is a variant (— 1923) for *slowed*, q.v.
Manchon.—2. See *slour*, 2.

slow. Old-fashioned ; behind the times : 1827,
The Sporting Times, ' Long courtships are . . .
voted slow,' O.E.D. (The Winchester sense
' ignorant of Winchester *notions* ', dating from ca.
1880, is a variant.)—2. Hence, (of things) tedious,
dull, boring : coll. : 1841, Lever (O.E.D.)—3. (Of
persons) hundrum ; dull, spiritless : 1841, Lever
(O.E.D.).—4. Hence, sexually timid : late C. 19–20.
' If there's anything a woman hates, it's a slow
man ' : heard by the author late in 1914, the
aphorist being a virtuous, lively and intelligent
middle-aged woman, speaking *en tout bien, tout
honneur*.

slow as molasses in winter. See **molasses.**

slowed. Imprisoned ; in prison : c. (— 1859) ;
ob. by 1890, † by 1920. H., 1st ed. Ex *slow*,
retard, but perhaps influenced by *slour*, 1, q.v. : cf.
late C. 19–20 *slower*, to check.

slowpoke. A dull or (e.g. socially or sexually)
slow person : Australian : C. 20. Christina Stead,
Seven Poor Men of Sydney, 1934. Perhaps a
corruption of *slowcoach*.

slows, troubled with the. Slow-moving : sporting : from ca. 1870. Perhaps orig. U.S. and punning U.S. *slows*, milk-sickness.

slubberdegullion. A dirty and/or slobbering
fellow ; a sloven ne'er-do-well : from ca. 1615 ; ob.
Perhaps orig. coll., which (witness B.E. and Grose,
who wrongly spells it *slubber de gullion*) it may have
remained till C. 19. On *slubber* (later *slobber*) : cf.
tatterdemalion : W.

'sluck. See **'s luck !**

'Slud ! A C. 17–18 oath : coll. variant of
'sblood ! Jonson, Fielding. O.E.D.

slued. See **slewed.**

slug. An unascertained kind of strong liquor :
1756, Toldervy, ' Tape, glim, rushlight, white port,
rasher of bacon, gunpowder ; slug, wild-fire, knock-

me-down, and strip me naked'; † by 1790. (O.E.D.)
--2. ? hence, a dram, a drink : 1762, Smollett,
'. . . That he might cast a slug into his bread-room.'
(Since ca. 1880, only U.S.) Hence, *fire a slug*, to
take a drink of potent liquor, as in Grose, 1st ed. :
ca. 1780–1840.—3. A set-back ; a (great) disappointment : coll. : late C. 19–20. Ex dial. *slug*,
a defeat. Cf. :

slug, v.t. To strike heavily : dial. (— 1862) soon
> coll. *The Echo*, March 8, 1869, 'He has several
times been told by unionists on strike that he would
be "slugged" if he went on as he was going,'
O.E.D. Perhaps ex dial. *slug*, a heavy blow, recorded thirty years earlier. Cf. *slog*, v., 1, q.v., and
slug, n., 3.

slug, fire a. See slug, n., 2.

sluice. The female pudend : low coll. : late
C. 17–20 ; ob. 'Facetious' Tom Brown.—2. The
mouth : low : from ca. 1830 ; ob. Prob. ex *sluice*,
a channel, influenced by † *sluice*, a gap ; but perhaps imm. ex :

sluice-house. The mouth : low : 1840, Egan ;
very ob. Cf. *sluice*, 2.

sluice one's or **the bolt, dominoes, gob,** or **ivories.**
To drink heartily : low : resp. mid-C. 19–20 (H.,
3rd ed.), idem, late C. 18–20 (Grose, 2nd ed.) and
mid-C. 19–20. All slightly ob. Cf. *sluice*, 2, and :

sluicery. A public-house : low : ca. 1820–90.
Egan's Grose ; H., 1st ed. Contrast *sluice-house*.—
2. Hence (?), a drinking-bout : low (— 1923).
Manchon.

***sluicing.** Pickpocketry in public wash-places :
c. : from ca. 1920. E.g. in Edgar Wallace, *Room
13*.

Sluker. An inhabitant, esp. a harlot, of the
Parish of *St Luke*, London : Cockney (— 1909).
Ware. Cf. *Angel*, q.v.

***slum.** A room : c. : ca. 1810–50. Vaux.
? origin, unless Bee is right in deriving it ex *slumber*.
—2. Nonsense, gammon, blarney : c. : ca. 1820–
1910. Egan's Grose cites, from *Randall's Diary*,
'And thus, without more slum, began '; H., 5th
ed. Prob. ex sense 4.—3. Hence, Romany : c. of
ca. 1821- 50. 'Jon Bee', 1823, 'The gipsey
language, or cant, is slum.'—4. A trick or swindle :
c. : 1812, Vaux ; 1851, Mayhew. Cf. *slum, fake
the*, and *slum, up to*, q.v.—5. ? hence, a begging
letter : c. : 1851, Mayhew, 'Of these documents
there are two sorts, "slums" (letters) and "fakements" (petitions).' Ob.—6. Hence, any letter :
prison c. (— 1860). H., 2nd ed. Ob.—7. (? ex
slum, a begging letter) An innuendo, a discreditable insinuation : c. (— 1864). H., 3rd ed. ; † by
1900.—8. A chest ; a package (e.g. a roll of counterfeit notes) : c. (— 1859) ; ob. H., 1st ed., ' "He
shook a slum of slops ", stole a chest of tea.' Perhaps ex sense 4.—9. In the language of Punch and
Judy showmen (partly c., partly Parlyaree), the
call : from ca. 1860. Cf. *slum-fake* and *slumming*,
2, qq.v.—10. Sweetmeats for coughs : market-
traders' (e.g. Petticoat Lane) : C. 20.—11. Abbr.
(1908 : O.E.D.) of *slumgullion*, q.v.

***slum.** To talk nonsense ; speak cant : c. of ca.
1820–80. Cf. *slum*, n., 2.—2. Hence, v.t., to trick,
cheat, swindle : c. (— 1859). H., 1st ed., in
variant form, *slum the gorger*, 'to cheat on the sly,
to be an eye servant,' which is †—prob. since late
C. 19.—3. Hence, v.t., to hide ; to pass to a confederate : c. (— 1874). Implied in H., 5th ed.
though already implied in *slumming*, 1, q.v.—4.
V.i., to hide : c. (— 1923). Manchon.—5. V.t., to

do hurriedly and/or carelessly : coll. (1865) >, ca.
1900, S.E. (O.E.D.). Perhaps suggested by *to slam*
(a door), influenced by *slum*, a poverty-stricken
neighbourhood.—6. V.i., to enter, or haunt, slums
for illegal or rather for illicit or immoral purposes :
University s. : Oxford, ca. 1860 ; Cambridge, ca.
1864 (H., 3rd ed.) : ob. by 1910, virtually † by 1935.
—7. Hence, 'to keep to back streets in order to
avoid observation', Barrère & Leland : University
s. (— 1897) ; ob.—8. Hence, from ca. 1899, to
keep in the background : gen. coll. ; ob.—9. V.i.,
to act : low theatrical : from ca. 1870 ; ob. Cf.
slumming, 2.

slum, cough. Cough-lozenges : grafters' : C. 20.
Philip Allingham, *Cheapjack*, 1934. Also *slum* :
see slum, n., 10.

***slum, fake the.** To do the trick ; effect a
swindle : c. : mid-C. 19–20.

***slum, up to.** Alert ; knowing : c. (— 1823).
Egan's Grose. Ex *slum*, n., 4.

slum-box. A (typical) house in the slums : coll.
(— 1923). Manchon.

slum-fake. The coffin in a Punch and Judy show:
showmen : from ca. 1860. Cf. *slum*, the call, and
slumming, 2.

***slum-scribbler.** One who employs penmanship
for illicit ends, e.g. for begging-letters : c. (— 1861).
Mayhew.

slum shop, sleek-and-. See sleek-and-slum shop.

slumber in. Public Schools' s. of late C. 19–20,
as in P. G. Wodehouse, *Tales of St Austin's*, 1903,
'To slumber in is to stay in the house during school
on a pretence of illness.'

slumber-suit. Pyjamas : derisive : from ca.
1924. Ex drapers' j.

slumgullion. 'Any cheap, nasty, washy beverage,' H., 5th ed. : from ca. 1870 ; ob. Perhaps a
fantasy on *slub* (= *slob*) and the *gullion* of *slubberdegullion* (cf. *slobgollion*, q.v.) ; certainly fanciful.
(As a watery stew or hash, it is U.S.)

slumguzzle, v.t. To deceive : anglicised ca. 1910.
Ex U.S.

slummery. Gibberish ; 'ziph' : ca. 1820–50 :
low s., perhaps orig. c. 'Jon Bee', 1823, 'Dutch
Sam excelled in slummery—"Willus youvus
givibus glasso ginibus".'

***slumming,** vbl.n. Passing counterfeit money :
c. (— 1839) ; ob. Brandon. Perhaps ex *slum*, v.,
1.—2. Acting : low theatrical : from ca. 1870 ; ob.
Miss Braddon, 1872, 'The gorger's awfully coally on
his own slumming, eh ? ' Cf. *slum*, the call, and
slum-fake, q.v.—3. 'The secreting of type or sorts,'
Jacobi : printers' s. (— 1888). Ex *slum*, v., 2,
q.v.

slummock, improperly -**uck** (v.t. and i.). To
clean carelessly, imperfectly ; to dust : coll.
(— 1923). Manchon. A back-formation from
S.E. *slummocky*, slovenly.

slummy. A servant girl : low : late C. 19–20.
? ex *slummy*, careless, influenced by *slummy*, from
a slum neighbourhood. Cf. *slavey*.—2. One who
lives in a slum : coll. : late C. 19–20. (Pat
O'Mara, *The Autobiography of a Liverpool Irish
Slummy*, 1934).

Slumopolis. Slum London : jocular coll.
(— 1887); ob. Baumann. On *Cottonpolis*.

slung. (Of a picture) rejected : artists' and art-
students' (— 1909). Ware. Prob. suggested by
hung.

slung out on hands and knees. Dismissed :
tailors' : from ca. 1870. ; ob.

slung sword, ship one's. To be promoted to warrant officer : naval : late C. 19–20. Bowen.

slur. A method of cheating at dice : ca. 1640–1750 : perhaps orig. s. or coll., but soon j. (therefore S.E.). Ex *slur*, to make a die leave the box without turning (Nash, 1594 : O.E.D.).

slush. Food : nautical : late C. 19–20. Ex nautical S.E. *slush*. Cf. *slushy*, n.—2. 'Coffee and [? or] tea served in a common coffee-house' : low urban (— 1909). Ware.—3. Counterfeit paper money (esp. notes) : c., orig. U.S., anglicised in 1924 by Edgar Wallace (O.E.D. Sup.). Ex the inferiority of slush. (—4. As = sickly sentiment, *slush* is familiar S.E.)

slush-bucket. A foul feeder : coll. : ca. 1780–1850. Grose, 1st ed. (Extant in dial.)

slusher. A cook's assistant at shearing time on a station : Australian coll. >, ca. 1910, S.E. *The Melbourne Argus*, Sept. 20, 1890. Cf. *slushy*, 2. (Morris.)—2. One who (prints and) circulates counterfeit paper-money : c. : 1924, Edgar Wallace, *Room 13*. Ex *slush*, 3.

slushy. A ship's cook : nautical coll. (— 1859). H., 1st ed. Ex *slush*, refuse fat of boiled meat. Cf. *slush*, 1.—2. Hence, influenced by *slusher* (q.v.), a cook's assistant at a shearing : Australian coll. : 1896, A. B. Paterson, in *The Man from Snowy River*, 'The tarboy, the cook, and the slushy . . . with the rest of the shearing horde.' Morris. In C. 20, *slushy* is much more gen. than *slusher* (sense 1).

slushy, adj. Extremely sentimental : C. 20. Ex *slushy*, washy, rubbishy. Cf. *sloppy*, q.v.

sly. Illegal, illicit : earliest and mainly in *sly grog*, Australian s., 1844 (O.E.D.),—*sly grog-selling, seller, shop*. Mayhew, 1851, 'sly trade '. Ex *sly*, secret, stealthy. Cf. *sly, on the*, and *sly, run*, qq.v.

sly, on or **upon the.** Private(ly), secret(ly), illicit(ly) : 1812, Vaux : coll. >, ca. 1870, S.E. Mayhew, 1851, 'Ladies that liked a drop on the sly,' O.E.D.

sly, run. To escape : low s. (? c.) : late C. 18–early 19. F. & H., whose quotation long anticipates the sporting sense : (of a dog) to run cunningly.

sly-boots ; ca. 1730–1830, occ. **sly-boot.** A sly or crafty person : coll. : ca. 1680, Lord Guilford was thus nicknamed (North, *Lives of the Norths*, p. 169). Esp.—see B.E. and Grose—a person seemingly simple, actually subtle or shrewd. In C. 19–20, often jocular and hardly if at all pejorative. Cf. † *sly-cap*, a sly or a cunning man (Otway, 1681), and the much more gen. *smooth-boots*, late C. 16–early 18.

sly grog. See **sly.**—**sma'am.** A variant, mainly dial., of *smarm*, q.v.

*smabble or **snabble.** To despoil, knock down, half-skin : arrest : c. of ca. 1720–1840. *A New Canting Dict.*, 1725. See **snabble.**

smabbled or **snabbled.** Killed in battle : ca. 1780–1840. Grose, 1st ed. Ex *smabble.*

smack. A liking or fancy : tailors' coll. : from ca. 1870. 'He had a real smack for the old 'un,' F. & H. Cf. C. 14–mid-17 S.E. *smack*, enjoyment, inclination (for a place).—2. A 'go' : coll. : 1889, *The Pall Mall Gazette*, 'I am longing to have a smack at these Matabeles,' O.E.D.—3. Hence, an attempt (*at*) : coll. : late C. 19–20. Manchon. Prob. ex dial. : see E.D.D. Hence :

smack, at one. At the first attempt ; (all) at the one time : coll. : late C. 19–20. Ex senses 3, 2 of the preceding.

smack at, have a. See **smack, n.**, 2.

smack(-)smooth. Perfectly even, level, smooth : 1755, Smollett (O.E.D.) : coll. until late C. 19, then dial. Ex *smack*, vbl.adv.—2. As complement, with semi-advl. force : ' so as to leave a level surface ' : 1788, Dibdin.—3. Hence, adv. : smoothly ; without hindrance : C. 19–20 : like sense 2, coll. till C. 20., then mainly dial. H. Martin, 1802, 'A tour . . . went on smack smooth,' O.E.D.

smack-up. A fight : New Zealanders' : from ca. 1906.—2. Hence, a battle : id. : in G.W.

smacked up, be. To come off worst in a fight of any kind : New Zealanders' : C. 20.—2. Hence, in G.W., to be wounded : id. Also *be smacked.*

smacker. A peso : South American English : late C. 19–20. C. W. Thurlow Craig, *Paraguayan Interlude*, 1935, ' " I will give you a thousand beautiful smackers for your church . . ." 'Mac took out a thousand peso bill and handed it to me.' —2. £1, note or coin : Australian : from ca. 1929. Christina Stead, *Seven Poor Men of Sydney*, 1934.

smacker, (go down) with a. (To fall) ' smack ' : lower classes' coll. (— 1887). Baumann.

*smacking-cove. A coachman : c. : mid C. 17–early 19. Coles, 1676 ; B.E. ; Grose, 1st ed. Ex whip.

small, n. See **smalls**, 2.—**small, sing.** See **sing small.**

small and early ; (or hyphenated). An evening party, few-personed and early-departing : 1880, Lord Beaconsfield (O.E.D.) : coll. till C. 20, then S.E. ; slightly ob. Adumbrated in Dickens, 1865, 'Mrs Podsnap added a small and early evening to the dinner.'

small arm, one's or **the.** The penis. Esp. in *small-arm inspection*, a medical inspection, among men, for venereal disease : military : from ca. 1910. Ex *small arms*, revolvers and rifles. See esp. B. & P. (3rd ed., 1931).

small beer of, think. (Gen. with **no.**) To have a low opinion of (persons, mostly oneself) : coll. : 1825, Westmacott (O.E.D.) ; Thackeray ; Lytton. Ex *small*, i.e. weak or inferior, *beer*. Also *small coals* and *small things*, qq.v. ; cf. *potatoes, small*, q.v.

small cap O. A second-in-command ; an under overseer : printers' : from ca. 1870 ; ob. Lit., a *small capital letter O*, i.e. a capital in a word all of equal-sized capitals, as OVERSEER.

small cheque. A dram ; a (small) drink : nautical : from ca. 1880 ; ob. Cf. *knock down a cheque*, spend all in drink : see **knock down . . .**

small coals . . . A ca. 1860–90 variant of *small beer . . .*, q.v. H., 2nd ed.

small cuts. A small pair of scissors : tailors' : late C. 19–20.

small fry. See **fry.**

small-gang, v.t. To mob : low : mid-C. 19–20 ; ob. Mayhew, 1851 (O.E.D.).

small jeff. A small employer : tailors' : late C. 19–20. Cf. *flat-iron jeff*, q.v.

small-parter. A player of small parts : theatrical coll. : C. 20. (*The Passing Show*, June 24, 1933.)

small pill. A diminutive football (used on runs) : Leys School : late C. 19–20.

small potatoes. See **potatoes.**

small things of, think. A variant of *small beer . . .*, q.v. : coll. : 1902, *The Pall Mall Gazette*, Sept. 19, ' Vogler '—the South African cricketer (googly bowler)—' had reason to think no small things of himself.' Cf. *small coals.*

smalls. The Responsions examination : Oxford

University coll. : ca. 1841, as E. A. Freeman (1823–92) shows in his article in *The Contemporary Review*, vol. li, p. 821 ; Bristed, 1852 ; 'Cuthbert Bede ', 1853 ; Hughes, *Tom Brown at Oxford*, 1861. Perhaps, as the O.E.D. points out, ex *in parviso* (or *-siis*). At Cambridge, the corresponding term is *little-go*, q.v.—2. 'Towns not boasting a regularly built and properly appointed theatre,' *The Ardrossan Herald*, Sept. 11, 1891 : theatrical coll. : from ca. 1890. F. & H., however, in 1903 defines thus, implying a singular : 'A one-night performance in a small town or village by a minor company carrying its own "fit-up".' Hence *do the smalls*, to tour the small towns : theatrical coll. : C. 20.

smarm ; occ. **smalm**, v.i. To behave with fulsome flattery or insincere politeness : coll. : from not later than 1915. Ex :—2. *smalm*, *smarm*, coll. (late C. 19–20), to smooth down, as hair with pomade. S.O.D. The word prob. represents a blend : ? '*smarten* with *cream*'.

smarmy. Apt to flatter fulsomely, speak toadyingly or over-politely or with courteous insincerity : coll. : from ca. 1915. Ex :—2. *smarmy*, (of hair) sleek, plastered down : coll. : C. 20.—3. Also as adv. in both senses, esp. 1.

smart. A very elegant young man about town : (London) Society : ca. 1750–80. O.E.D.

smart, adj. Rather steep (ground) : mid-C. 17–20 : S.E. until late C. 19, then coll. (ob.) and dial. O.E.D., and esp. E.D.D. Cf. *steep* (price).

smart Alec. A know-all, an offensively smart person : coll. ; orig. (ca. 1870), U.S., anglicised by 1930. (O.E.D. Sup.) Also *smart Alick*.

smart as a carrot(, **as**). Gaily dressed : 1780 : coll. until mid-C. 19, then dial.,—which it had been since 1791 at least. Grose, 2nd ed., *as smart as a carrot new scraped*. (Apperson.)

smart as be damned(, **as**). Extremely smart in appearance : coll. : C. 20. (F. Brett Young, *Jim Redlake*, 1930.) See also the *like* paragraph and the *be damned* entry.

smart as threepence. Smartly dressed : lower classes' coll. (— 1887) ; ob. Baumann.

smarty. A would-be clever, cunning, or witty person : U.S. (1880), anglicised—as a coll.—ca. 1905, chiefly as an impertinent and esp. in Australia and New Zealand.—2. A fashionable person ; one in the swim : coll. : from ca. 1930. E. F. Benson, *Travail of Gold*, 1933, 'Social smarties.'

smash. Lit. and fig., a heavy blow : coll. and dial. : 1779, O.E.D. In 1780, it was used like *smack*, 2, q.v.—2. Mashed vegetables, esp. turnips : ca. 1780–1830. Grose, 1st ed., 'Leg of mutton and smash, a leg of mutton and mashed turnips, (*sea term*).' Cf. modern *mash*, mashed potatoes.—3. Counterfeit coin : c. : late C. 18–20 ; slightly ob. Potter, 1795. Cf. *smash*, v., 2, and *smash-feeder*, q.v. ? because it 'smashes' acceptors.—4. Loose change : c. : mid-C. 19–20 ; rhyming s. on *cash*. F. & H.—5. Tobacco : c. : from late 1880's. Cf. *sling the smash*, q.v. ? because it breaks regulations.

*****smash**, v. To kick down stairs : c. : late C. 17–early 19. B.E. ; Grose, 2nd ed. Prob. imitative (O.E.D.).—2. To pass, occ. to utter (counterfeit money) : c. : from ca. 1810. *Lex. Bal.*,—but see **smasher**, 4. Cf. *smashing*, adj.—3. To give change for (a note, a coin) : from ca. 1810 : either c. or low s. ; ob. Vaux.—4. To beat badly : pugilistic coll. : from ca. 1820.—5. V.i., to go bankrupt ; be *ruined* : coll. : 1839, Hood (O.E.D.). Occ. *smash up* : not before 1870's ; very rare in C. 20.—6. Esp. *smash*

a brandy-peg, to drink one : military : from ca. 1880. Ware cites *The Daily News*, May 7, 1884.—7. To break burglariously into (a house, etc.) : c. : from ca. 1920. E.g. in Edgar Wallace, *We Shall See !*, 1926.

smash ! ; smash me ! ; smash my eyes ! A coll. and dial. imprecation : ob. in C. 20 : resp. 1819 (mostly North Country dial.) ; 1894 ; 1833, Scott. O.E.D. H., 3rd ed., defines *smash-man-Geordie* as 'a pitman's oath' in Durham and Northumberland : cf. *Geordie* and *smasher*, last sense, qq.v.

smash, go (to). Variant of *smash*, v., fifth sense : coll. : mid C. 19–20. H., 1st ed.

*****smash a load.** To get rid of twenty counterfeit coins : c. (— 1933). Charles E. Leach.

*****smash-feeder.** A silver or a Britannia-metal spoon : c. : resp. ca. 1839–59 and ca. 1859–1910. (The best imitation shillings were made from Britannia metal. Ex *smash*, n., 3.

smash me ! ; smash my eyes ! See **smash !**

smash the teapot. To break one's pledge of abstinence : urban lower classes' (— 1909) ; ob. Ware.

smashed, adj. Reduced in rank : naval (—1909). Ware.

smasher. Anything very large or unusually excellent ; (in post-G.W. s., often it = an extremely pretty girl) : 1794 (E.D.D.). Ob.—2. Hence, a crushing reply, a very severe article or review : coll. : 1828, *Blackwood's Magazine*, 'His reply . . . was a complete smasher,' O.E.D. Slightly ob.—3. Hence, a heavy fall (1875) or a damaging or settling blow (1897) : coll. O.E.D.—4. A passer (1795, Potter) or, less gen., an utterer (1796, O.E.D.) of false money, whether coin or note : c. : late C. 18–20. Ex *smash*, n., 3, or it may argue an existence for *smash*, v., 2, at least sixteen years before the app. earliest record.—5. Hence, a base coin or, says F. & H., forged note : c. : mid-C. 19–20 ; very ob. Mayhew, 1851.—6. A North Country seaman : nautical (— 1883). Clark Russell. Prob. ex *smash !*, q.v.—7. 'A soft felt hat with a broad brim,' Pettman : South African coll. : from ca. 1885. Pettman.—8. A receiver of stolen goods : c. (— 1929). O.E.D. (Sup.) ; Charles E. Leach, *On Top of the Underworld*, 1933. Prob. influenced by senses 4 and 5.

*****smashing.** The passing or uttering of false money : c. (— 1812). Vaux. Ex *smash*, v., 2.

*****smashing**, adj. Counterfeit : c. : 1857, Borrow. —2. Engaged in 'smashing' : c. : 1899, O.E.D.—3. Excellent ; the adj. corresponding to *smasher*, 1 : C. 19–20.

smatteract. As a matter of fact : shorthand typists' : C. 20.

smawm. A variant, mainly dial., of *smarm*, q.v.

*****smear.** A house-painter : c. : late C. 17–mid-18. *Street Robberies Considered*, ca. 1700. Ex the rough work of many painters.—2. Hence, a plasterer : ca. 1720–1820 : c. >, ca. 1750, s. *A New Canting Dict.*, 1725 ; Grose, 1st ed.

*****smear-gelt.** A bribe : ca. 1780–1840 : c. or low s. Grose, 1st ed. Ex Ger. *gelt*, payment ; with *smear*, cf. *grease a person's palms*.

*****smeer.** An incorrect spelling of *smear*, q.v.

smell. To make smelly ; fill with offensive odour : coll. : 1887. O.E.D.—2. (Gen. with negative.) To approach at all, be even compared with, in ability : from ca. 1915. E.g. 'Fleetwood-Smith can't '—rarely 'doesn't '—' smell Grimmett as a batsman' ; ' "Are you as good as he is at batting ? " "No ; can't smell him "." Ex *smell*, to detect, have an inkling of. Cf. *smell at*, q.v.

[**smell a rat.** Ca. 1780–1830, it was, to judge from Grose (all edd.), c. : not, however, that one lexicographer connotes irrefragable certainty.]

smell at, get a. (Only in interrogative or negative.) To get a chance at ; to approach : (low) coll. (— 1887). Baumann. Cf. *smell*, 2, q.v. Ex olfactory inaccessibility.

smell one's hat. To pray into one's hat on reaching one's pew in church : jocular coll. (—1887). Baumann.

smell-powder. A duellist : coll. : ca. 1820–60. Bee. Cf. *fire-water*.

*****smeller.** A garden : c. : early C. 17. Rowlands. Prob. ex *smelling cheat*, 1, q.v.—2. The nose : late C. 17–20 : c. >, ca. 1750, s. B.E. ; Grose, 1st ed. ; Walker, 1901, *In the Blood*, 'I tipped 'im one on the smeller as soon as 'e said it.' Cf. *smellers*, 1, q.v.—3. Hence, a blow on the nose : boxing : from early 1820's. 'Jon Bee.' Cf. *noser*.—4. Hence, in late C. 19–20, fig. : a grave set-back. In April, 1931, a well-known novelist told the author that he had got ' a rap on the smeller of a criticism ' from a certain London periodical.—5. Anything exceptional in the way of violence, strength, etc. : coll. : 1898, Kipling, 'Good old gales—regular smellers ' (O.E.D. Sup.) Cf. *snorter*.—6. A sneaking spy ; a Paul Pry : late C. 19–20 ; slightly ob. *The Century Dict.*

smeller, come a. To have a heavy fall (lit. or fig.) : low : late C. 19–20. Manchon. Cf. *smeller*, 3 and 4.

smellers. Nostrils : 1678, Cotton, 'For he on smellers, you must know, | Receiv'd a sad unlucky blow.' Prob. ex *smeller*, a feeler, e.g. of a fly.—2. As a cat's whiskers', it may orig. (1738) have been coll,—Grose, 1st ed., clearly classifies it as coll. or s.,—but from ca. 1850, at latest, it has certainly been S.E.

*****smelling cheat** or **chete.** A garden ; an orchard : c. : 1567, Harman ; B.E. ; Grose, 1st ed. † by 1830 ; ob. as early, prob., as 1700. Lit., a smelling, i.e. fragrant, thing.—2. A nosegay : C. 17–early 19 (prob. ob. by 1750) : c. B.E. ; Grose, 1st ed. It seems likely that after C. 16, the predominating sense of *smelling cheat* is nosegay, for in 1610 Rowlands writes, 'Smellar, a garden ; not Smelling cheate, for thats a Nosegay.'—3. The nose, says F. & H. : but this I believe to be an error caused by confusion between *smeller* and *smelling cheat*.

smelly. 'Shady ', dishonourable, illicit : low (— 1923). Manchon. Prob. after *fishy*.

*****smelt.** A half-guinea : c. of ca. 1630–1830, but ob. as early, prob., as 1750. Shirley, 1635 (O.E.D.); Shadwell ; Grose, 1st ed. Not impossibly an *s* perversion—*s* perversions are fairly common in English c. and s. (cf. the prefix-use of *s* in Italian)—of *melt* (v. as n.) : the ' melt ' or melting-down of a guinea. Cf. *smish* for *mish*, qq.v.

smelts, westward for. (Esp. **go westward . . .**) On the spree : semi-proverbial coll. : early C. 17. Dekker & Webster. Lit., in search of ' conies ', male or female, a *smelt* being a simpleton.

smiff-box. The nose : pugilistic : ca. 1860–90. H., 3rd ed.

Smiffield. Smithfield (Market), London : Cockney (— 1887). Baumann.

smifligate ; smifligation. Ob. variants of *spiflicate, -ation* : 1839, Dickens (O.E.D.).

*****smiggins.** A barley soup, a (cold) meat hash : prison c. : ca. 1820–80. Knapp & Baldwin, *The*

Newgate Calendar, vol. iii, 1825 (O.E.D.) ; Brandon. A nickname, perhaps ex a warder named Higgins. (C. etymologies are heartbreaking.)

smile. A drink of liquor, esp. of whiskey : U.S. (1850), anglicised ca. 1870 : s. till C. 20, then coll. Jerome K. Jerome, 1889 (O.E.D.). Cf. :

smile, v.i. To drink (liquor, esp. whiskey) : U.S. (1858), anglicised ca. 1870.

smile !, I should. A lot I care ! : c.p. : 1891 (O.E.D.). Cf. *worry !, I should*.

smile like a brewer's horse. To smile delightedly or broadly : coll. : C. 17. Howell, 1659. A brewer's horse thrives on its food and the circumambient odour of hops.

smilence ! Silence : non-aristocratic (— 1909); ob. by 1920, † by 1930. Cf. *smole* (Ware).

smiler. A kind of shandy-gaff : 1892, *The Daily News*, Nov. 16 ; ob. O.E.D.

smirk. ' A finical, spruce Fellow,' B.E. : late C. 17–early 19. Ex the v.

*****smish.** A shirt : c. : from ca. 1810 ; ob. Vaux. Perversion of *mish*, q.v., or via *s(e)miche = chemise* (Baumann).

smit. In love : mid-C. 19–20 coll., jocular on archaic past ppl.

smite. To obtain money from (a tutor) : University : ca. 1780–1830. Grose, 1st ed. ? ex *smite hip and thigh*. Cf. *rush* and *sting*, qq.v.

*****smiter.** The arm : c. : ca. 1670–1815. Coles, 1676 ; B.E. ; Grose, 1st ed.

Smith. See **Duleep.**

Smith, Mr. Mussolini : from ca. 1924 among British residents on the Italian Riviera, esp. at Bordighera. By euphemism.

Smith !, what an O. What a grim laugh ! : non-aristocratic : ca. 1835–50. Ware. Lit., ' what an " O. Smith " ! ' ex the cavernous laugh of one O. Smith, a popular actor of villains' parts.

smithereens ; smithers. Small pieces or fragments : coll. and dial., orig. Anglo-Irish : from ca. 1840 ; the latter, only dial. after ca. 1890. S. C. Hall, 1841, 'Harness . . . broke into smithereens '; Halliwell, 1847, ' *Smithers*, fragments, atoms.' Actually, *smithers*, of obscure etymology but perhaps cognate with *smite*, is the earlier, *-een* being (as in *colleen*) an Irish diminutive suffix. Esp. *go*, and *blow, to smithers*, and *blow, break, knock, split to* or *into smithereens*, and (rare in C. 20) *go to smithereens* ; cf. *all to smithereens*, all to smash. O.E.D. ; E.D.D.

Smithfield bargain. A bargain or deal in which the purchaser is taken in : coll. : ca. 1660–1830. 'Cheats ' Wilson, 1662 ; Richardson, 1753. Adumbrated in Shakespeare's *2nd Henry IV*, Act I, Sc. 2. Ex the horse and cattle (now the great meat) market.—2. Hence, ca. 1770–1840, a marriage of convenience, with money the dominant factor : coll. Grose, 2nd ed. Cf. Breton, 1605, ' Fie on these market matches, where marriages are made without affection.'

smoak, -y. C. 17–18 spelling of *smoke, smoky*, qq.v.

smock. Of all the numerous phrases in F. & H. and O.E.D.—' usually suggestive of loose conduct or immorality in, or in relation to, women,' O.E.D.— only two are to be considered ; these may possibly be coll. and certainly the latter is not s. :—**smock-alley** (Ned Ward), the female pudend ; **smock-pensioner**, a male keep. Cf. *skirt*, q.v.

smoke. A cigar, cigarette, or pipe : 1882 (O.E.D.) : coll. >, ca. 1910, S.E.—2. **Smoke, the**, 1864, H., 3rd ed. ; **the big S.** (— 1897); **the great S.**

(— 1903). London : tramps' s. >, ca. 1900, gen. coll. Cf. *Auld Reekie*, Edinburgh.—3. **smoke, Cape.** See **Cape Smoke.**—4. (Also **smoke-on** : ex *have a smoke on*.) A blush : Scottish Public Schools' : from ca. 1885. Ian Miller, *School Tie*, 1935.

smoke, v. To ridicule, make fun of : late C. 17–mid-19 : coll. >, ca. 1800, S.E. Ned Ward, in *The London Spy*, ' We smoak'd the Beaus . . . till they sneak'd off one by one ' ; Miss Burney ; Keats. Perhaps ex *smoke*, to suspect (a person).—2. As a specific nuance of this : ' to affront a Stranger at his coming in,' B.E. : late C. 17–18.—3. To coït with (a woman) : C. 17–19.—4. V., to blush : Public Schools' : from ca. 1860. Farrar in *St Winifred's*, 1862 (O.E.D.). Cf. the C. 16 *smoke*, to fume, be very angry.—5. To decamp : low Australian : from ca. 1890. Morris. Ex *smoke along*, to ride at great speed.

smoke, Cape. See **Cape Smoke.—smoke, in.** See **in smoke.**

smoke, like. Rapidly : ca. 1806, an Irish lady's-maid writes of the Russian postillions that ' they drive like smoke up the hills ' (*The Russian Journals of Maria and Katherine Wilmot*, 1803–1808, edited by J. H. M. Hide ; 1833, M. Scott : coll. till ca. 1870, then S.E. Ex the manner in which smoke disperses in a high wind.

smoke, the great. See **great smoke** and **smoke, n., 2.**

smoke-boat. A steamer : sailing-ships' pejorative : late C. 19–20 ; ob. Bowen.

smoke, gammon, and spinach,—all. See **all smoke . . .**

smoke-ho ; -oh ; smoko. A cessation from work in order nominally to smoke, certainly to rest : coll. : 1897, Frank Bullen ; H. Lawson, 1900. O.E.D.

smoke-jack. An inspector of factories, esp. of their chimneys : lower classes' (—1923). Manchon.

smoke-on. See **smoke, n., 4.**

smoke-stack. A steamer : sailing-ship seamen's pejorative coll., as is their *steamboat man* for a sailor therein : from not later than 1885.

smoker. A chamber-pot : low : mid-C. 19–20 ; ob. Ex steam arising therefrom in cold weather.—2. A voter : Preston s. or coll. : ca. 1800–1832. See Halliwell. Because every man that used the chimney of his cottage had a vote.—3. A steamer : coll. : ca. 1825–50. O.E.D. Cf. *puffer*.—4. One who blushes : Public Schools' : 1866 (O.E.D.). Ex *smoke*, v., 4.—5. A sultry day : low coll. (— 1887) ; slightly ob. Baumann. Cf. sense 1.

Smokes, the (great). An occ. variant (— 1923) of *smoke*, n., 2. Manchon.

smoking. Vbl.n. of *smoke*, v., esp. 1, 4.—**smoko.** See **smoke-ho.**

smoky. Jealous : s. or coll. : late C. 17–mid-18. B.E., who is, I think, wrong in classifying it as c. Ex *smoky*, suspicious.—2. (**Smoky.**) The inevitable nickname of men surnamed Holmes : military : C. 20. F. & Gibbons. With a jest on smoky homes.

smole, n. and v. Smile ; esp. in (*he*) *smoled a smile* (or *smole*) : jocular >, by 1900, non-aristocratic (— 1909) ; slightly ob. ' Invented ' by F. C. Burnand, ca. 1877, in *Punch*, says Ware. Cf. *smilence !*

smoodge, v.i. To flatter, wheedle, speak with deliberate amiability : Australian : late C. 19–20. Ex *to smoothe.*—2. Hence, to make love, pay court : Australian : C. 20. C. J. Dennis (*smooge*). Hence,

smoodger, the agent, and *smoodging*, the action. Prob. ex ob. S.E. *smudge*, v.t., to caress, and dial. *smudge*, to kiss, to yearn for, *smudge after*, to begin to pay court to : on dial. *smouch*, to kiss.

smoot, n. and v. See **smout.**

*smooth white. A shilling : c. and low : late C. 19–20 ; ob. (F. & H.)

'smorning. This morning : coll. : late C. 19–20. Dorothy Sayers, *Murder Must Advertise*, 1933, ' " When's he coming ? " " 'Smorning ".'

smother. A hiding-place for stolen goods ; an overcoat folded over a pickpocket's arm to mask his movements : c. (— 1933). Charles E. Leach.—2. Trade s., mid-C. 19–20, as in Mayhew, 1851, ' A " lick-up " is a boot or shoe re-lasted, and the bottom covered with a " smother " . . . obtained from the dust of the room.' O.E.D.—3. ' A fur coat or overcoat ' : grafters' : C. 20. (P. Allingham, *Cheapjack*, 1934.) Prob. ex the warmth it gives.

*smother, v.t. To cover up ; to hide : New Zealand c. (— 1932). Cf. n., 1, q.v.

smother (or **s'm'other**) **evening !** A c.p. of cynical refusal : music-halls' : 1884–5. Ware. Ex one of the great Arthur Roberts's songs ; it was thus titled and themed.

smother a parrot. To drink, neat, a glass of absinthe : Anglo-French : ca. 1900–14. Ware. Like so many parrots, absinthe is—or was—green.

smouch. ' Dried leaves of the ash tree, used by the smugglers for adulterating the black, or bohea teas,' Grose, 1st ed. : ca. 1780–1840 : perhaps orig. c. or s., despite the O.E.D.'s assumption that it is S.E.—2. See :

Smous, Smouse ; Smouch, Smoutch. A Jew : *Smouse*, 1705 (Bosman) ; *Smous*, 1785 (Grose, who restricts it to a German Jew) ; *smouch*, 1765 (C. Johnston) ; *Smoutch*, 1785 (Cumberland). The -*s*, -*se*, forms are rare in C. 19 ; both -*s(e)* and -*ch* forms are † by 1880, except as archaisms. Why the O.E.D. should treat *smou(t)ch*—an alteration of *smous(e)*—as S.E., and *smous(e)* as s., I cannot see : both, I believe, are s., *smous(e)* coming direct ex the Dutch *smous* (identical with German-Jewish *schmus*), patter, profit, Hebrew *schmuoss*, news, tales (O.E.D. ; W.) ; Sewel, 1708, proposed derivation ex *Moses*,—cf. *Ikey*.—2. Hence, in South Africa, an itinerant (esp. if Jewish) trader : coll. : *smou(t)ch*, 1849 ; *smouse*, 1850, but anticipated fifty years before. Also *Smouser* : 1887 (Pettman) ; *smousing*, itinerant trading, from mid 1870's, is another South African coll. O.E.D. ; Pettman.—**smousing.** See **Smous, 2.**

smouse, v.i., corresponding to *Smous(e)*, n., 2. Pettman. **smousing.** See **Smous, 2.**

smout ; smout. A compositor seeking occasional work at various houses : printing (— 1888). Jacobi. While *smoot* is, in C. 20, more gen., *smout* is recorded the earlier. Ex :

smout ; smout, v.i. To work on occasional jobs at various houses or even at one if it is not one's regular place of employment : printing : from ca. 1680 : in C. 20, *smoot* (app. unrecorded before 1892) is the more gen. Moxon. In C. 17–18, v.t. as *smout on* (a firm). O.E.D. Perhaps ex Dutch *smutte*, to slink : cf. dial. *smoot*, to creep, and *smoot after*, to court (a girl) furtively (E.D.D.).

Smoutch. See **Smous.**

smudge. A photograph : grafters' : from ca. 1920. Philip Allingham, *Cheapjack*, 1934. Ex blurred effect seen in many cheap photographs.

Smudger. One of several 'inevitable' nick-names (cf. *Shoey*) of men surnamed Smith : mili-tary : C. 20. F. & Gibbons.

smug. A blacksmith : C. 17–18 : perhaps c. Rowlands, 1609 ; Ned Ward ; Grose. Prob. ex C. 16–27 *smuggy*, grimy, smutty, dirty.—2. **Smug-gling** : Anglo-Chinese (— 1864). H., 3rd ed. Cf. *smug*, v., 1, and *smug-boat*, qq.v.—3. A (quiet and) hard-working student ; esp. (at Oxford) one who takes no part in the social life of the place : Univer-sity : 1882 (O.E.D.) ; ob. See quotation from Goschen at **sap**, n., 2, and cf. *scrubber*, 3, q.v. ; Ex *smug*, consciously respectable.—4. Hence, an unpleasant, unhealthy boy to be avoided : school-boys' (— 1923). Manchon.—5. A person affectedly clean : coll. (— 1923) Ibid. Ex the S.E. sense, a self-satisfied person.

*****smug, v.** To steal ; run away with : 1825, T. Hook (O.E.D.) : c rapidly > low s. Perhaps ex *smuggle* : cf. *smug-boat* and *smugging*, 2, qq.v.—2. To hush up : 1857, *The Morning Chronicle*, Oct. 3. 'She wanted a guarantee the case should be smugged' ; prob. orig. c. ; by 1900, s. ? ex sense 1 or ex *smug*, to smarten up.—3. (? hence) to arrest, imprison : c. : from mid-1880's. J. W. Horsley, *Jottings from Jail*, 1887, 'Then two or three more coppers came up, and we got smugged, and got a sixer each.'—4. V.i., to copy ; to crib : from ca. 1860 ; ob. Perhaps ex sense 2.—5. To work hard : university : from ca. 1890. Ex *smug*, n., 1, q.v.

smug-boat. A boat carrying contraband ; esp. an opium boat off the Chinese coast : nautical coll. (— 1867) Smyth. Ex *smuggle* ; cf. *smug*, v., 1. and :

*****smug-lay.** The 'dodge' of selling (almost) worthless goods on the ground that they are valuable contraband : c. of ca. 1810–50. *Lex. Bal.* Ex *smuggling*.

smugging. See **smug**, v.—2. (In pl.) **smuggings !** Mine ! : schoolboys' s. (— 1859), shouted at the conclusion of a game, when (e.g. at top-spinning or marbles) it was lawful to purloin the plaything. H., 1st ed. ; in 1825, Hone notes that this practice is called *smugging*. Ex *smug*, v., 1.

smuggle, gen. v.t. To sharpen (a pencil) at both ends : schools : late C. 19–20 ; ob. Cf. the late C. 17–18 *smuggle*, to caress.

smuggle the coal (or cole). 'To make people believe one has no Money when the Reckoning is to be paid,' Miége, 1687 ; † by 1750. See **cole**.

smuggler. A pencil sharpened at both ends : schools' : see **smuggle**. Esp. at Winchester.

*****smuggling-ken.** A brothel : c. of ca. 1720–1830. *A New Canting Dict.*, 1725 ; Grose, 1st ed. Pun-ning *smuggle*, to caress, and *smuggle*, to 'contra-band '.

*****smut.** A furnace ; a copper boiler : c. (—1811) >, ca. 1840, low s. ; † by 1890. *Lex. Bal.* As a furnace, app. † by 1859 : witness H., 1st ed. Ex *smut*, soot.

Smut !, ditto, brother. See **brother Smut.**

smuvver. See **-uvver**.

snab. See **snob**, 1.

*****snabble.** To arrest : c. : 1724, Harper, 'But fileing of a rumbo ken, | My Boman is snabbled again ' ; † by 1790. Gen. as *snabbled*.—2. To rifle, plunder, steal ; knock down, half-stun : c. of ca. 1720–1840. *A New Canting Dict.*, 1725 ; Grose. Also *smabble*, q.v. ; cf. *snaffle*.—3. Hence, to kill, esp. in battle : c. : mid-C. 18–early 19. Grose,

1st ed. Cf. *smabbled*, q.v.—4. Gen.v.t., to copulate : low s. : late C. 18–early 19. F. & H.

snack. A racquets ball : Winchester : from ca. 1860 ; ob. (—2. It is possible that *snack*, a share, esp. in go *snacks*, be partners,—cf. *go snicks*,—may orig. have been c. : see B.E.)

*****snaffle.** 'A Highwayman that has got Booty,' B.E. : c. : late C. 17–18. Perhaps ex *snaffle*, a bridle-bit ; but prob. allied with *snaffle*, v., 1, q.v.— 2. Talk uninteresting or unintelligible to the others present : coll. : from ca. 1860 ; almost †. H., 3rd ed. Perhaps because such conversation acts as a snaffle ; more prob. ex East Anglian *snaffle*, to talk foolishly.—3. Hence, (a) secret talk : c. (— 1923). Manchon.

*****snaffle.** To steal : 1724, Harper, 'From priggs that snaffle the prancers strong ' ; Grose : c. >, ca. 1840, dial. and low s. Cognate with *snabble*, q.v. Cf. *snaffle*, n., 1, *snaggle*, and *snavel*.—2. To seize (a person) ; arrest : c. (— 1860) >, ca. 1890, low s. H., 2nd ed. Ex *snaffle a horse*.—3. To 'appro-priate ', to seize a thing for oneself : mostly mili-tary : from the middle 1890's. (O.E.D. Sup. ; B. & P.) Ex sense 1.—4. To catch or cut off (in the air) : Air Force : from 1915. F. & Gibbons. Ex sense 2.

*****snaffler.** A thief, only in *snaffler of prancers* (horses) : from ca. 1780 : c. >, ca. 1840, dial. and low s. Grose, 1st ed. Ex *snaffle*, v., 1.—2. A highwayman : ca. 1786–1840 : c. Grose, 2nd ed. Cf. *snaffle*, n., 1.—3. As = one who arrests, very rare : C. 19.

*****snaffling lay.** Highway robbery as a trade : c. : mid-C. 18–early 19. Fielding, 1752, 'A clever fellow, and upon the snaffling lay at least.' Ex *snaffle*, v., 1 ; cf. *snaffle*, n., 1, and *snaffler*, 2.

snag. 'A formidable opponent,' C. J. Dennis : Australian coll. : ·C. 20. Ex *snag*, an obstacle.

snag-catcher. A dentist : low : from ca. 1880 ; very ob. Ex angling.

*****snaggle**, v.i. and t. To angle for geese as a means of stealing them : either c. or low s. : from late 1830's ; ob. Often as *snaggling*, vbl.n. Brandon ; H., 1st ed. Prob. a corruption of *sniggle* (as in eel-fishing) and perhaps cognate with *snabble* and *snaffle*, 1, qq.v.

snaggle-tooth. A proletariat woman, esp. if a shrew, with an irregular set of teeth : urban lower classes' coll. (— 1909). Ware.

snail(e)y. A bullock with horn slightly curled, like a snail's : Australian coll. : from ca. 1880. ' Rolf Boldrewood ', 1884. Morris.

'Snails ! God's nails ! : a coll. petty oath : late C. 16–early 19. O.E.D.

snail's gallop, go a. To go very slowly indeed : semi-proverbial coll. >, ca. 1850, dial. : from ca. 1545. ' Proverbs ' Heywood ; Ray, 1670 ; N. Bailey, 1725 ; Colman, Jr., 1803 ; Combe, 1821 ; Brogden's *Lincolnshire Words*, 1866. Apperson.

snaily. See **snailey**.

snake. A skein of silk : tailors' : from ca. 1870 ; ob. Ex shape.

*****snake.** To steal (something) warily : c. : from ca. 1885. Ex dial.

snake, give (a person) a. To vex, annoy : low (— 1887) ; ob. Baumann.

snake-charmer. A bugler ; a Highland piper : military : late C. 19–20 ; ob. F. & Gibbons. Ex music played to charm snakes.

snake in the grass. A looking-glass : rhyming s. (— 1859). H., 1st ed.

snake-headed. ' Annoyed ; vindictive,' **C. J.** Dennis : Australian : C. 20. (Australia abounds in snakes.)

snake-juice. Whiskey : Australian : from ca. 1890. C. J. Dennis. Ex *see snakes.*

snake-tart. Eel-pie : mid-C. 19–20 ; ob. Cf. *dove-tart.*

snake the pool. To take the pool : billiards : from ca. 1880.

***snakes.** .A prison-warder's felt-shod shoes or slippers : c. (– 1923). Manchon. So he snakes along silently.

snakes, a caution to. (Something) very surprising, odd, eccentric, or unusual : 1897, ' Pomes ' Marshall, ' Her Sunday best was her week-day worst, | 'Twas simply a caution to snakes ' ; ob. Cf. *caution* (q.v.), which, prob., it merely elaborates.

snakes !, great. A coll. imprecation : 1897, F. T. Bullen ; slightly ob. Orig. U.S. (*why in snakes* occurring in 1891 in *Scribner's Magazine*). O.E.D.

snakes, see. To have delirium tremens : U.S. ; anglicised as coll. ca. 1900. Earlier form, *have* or *have got snakes in one's boots,* remained U.S.

***snakesman.** Only in *little snakesman,* q.v. Cf. *sneaksman.*

***snam.** To steal ; esp. to snatch (from the person) : c. : from ca. 1835. Brandon. Origin ?

***snam, (up)on the.** Thus engaged : c. : mid-C. 19–20. Cf. **snam.**

***snap.** A share : c. : from ca. 1560 ; ob. Awdelay, 1561. Also *snaps,* as in *go snaps,* to go shares (cf. *snack,* q.v.) : late C. 18–20 : Pegge, ca. 1800 ; H., 1st ed., spells it *snapps,* q.v. Cf. *snick,* n., q.v.—2. (A synonym of *cloyer,* q.v.) A sharper, cheat, pilferer ; esp. a thief claiming a share in booty (cf. **sense** 1) : c. : late C. 16–early 17 for ' cloyer ' nuance ; ca. 1620–1720 for ' sharper ' senses : former in Greene, latter in Fletcher and L'Estrange. In Ned Ward, 1731, *brother snap* is a sharking lawyer : C. 18 s.—3. Affair, business ; easy job : see **snap, soft,** and **snap away, give the.**— 4. Energy : U.S. (1872), anglicised ca. 1890 : coll. >, ca. 1910, S.E. Doyle, 1894, ' A young . . . man with plenty of snap about him,' O.E.D. Cf. *go, pep, vim,* qq.v.—5. An engagement (for work) : theatrical : from ca. 1890. Cf. *snapps,* q.v.

***snap, v.i.** To go shares with sharpers or thieves : early C. 17 c. Field, 1609. O.E.D. Cf. *snap,* n., 1 and 2 ; also *snack, snick* (n.).

***snap, on the.** On the look-out for something to steal : c. : mid-C. 19–20. Cf. *snapper-up of unconsidered trifles* and *snap,* 2, q.v.—2. Hence, looking out for occasional work : from ca. 1890 : s. >, ca. 1910, coll.

snap, soft. An easy matter, business, project ; a profitable affair ; an easy job ; occ. a pleasant time : s. >, ca. 1910, coll. : from ca. 1885 ; orig. U.S. (1845). In C. 20, often simply *snap,* esp. in *it's a snap.*

snap away, give the. To blab ; ' blow the gaff ' : low s. : from ca. 1870.

snap out of it ! Go away quick ! : low : U.S., anglicised ca. 1925.

***snap the glaze.** To break shop-windows or show-case glasses : c. : ca. 1780–1840. Grose, 1st ed.

***snappage.** A share in booty : c. : early C. 17. Rowlands. Cf. *snap,* 1, and *snappings.*

snapped, ppl. adj. Abrupt, sudden, unexpected : coll. : 1893, Leland. O.E.D.

***snapper.** An accomplice ; a sharer (in booty) :

c. : ca. 1530–50. Cf. *snap,* n., **1.**—2. A taker of snapshot photographs ; the taker of the snapshot in question : from ca. 1908 : coll. now verging on S.E.

snapper-rigged. (Of a ship) poorly rigged and found ; (of a man) poorly clothed : East Canadian (and U.S.) nautical : late C. 19–20. Bowen.

Snappers, the. The 15th Foot, now the East Yorkshire, Regiment : military : 1777 in the American War. F. & Gibbons : owing to lack of ammunition, the men snapped their musket locks in order to befool the enemy. Also known as *the Poona Guards,* ob.

***snapping.** A share in booty : c. : late C. 16– early 17. Greene, 1591. Cf. *snap,* n., 1, *snappage, snapper,* and *snapps.*

***snapps.** A variant of *snap,* n., 1, q.v. H., 1st ed., ' " Looking out for *snapps* ", waiting for windfalls ' ; H., 2nd ed., 1860, adds ' or odd jobs '. Cf. *snap,* 5, q.v.

snappy. Smartly intelligent ; energetic ; lively ; pointed (story) coll. : 1873.—2. Whence, smart (of dress) ; neatly elegant : coll. : 1881 ; ob. O.E.D.

snappy !, make it. Look lively ! ; be quick ! C. 20 : coll. (orig. U.S.). Cf. *snap out of it !,* q.v

snare. ' To acquire ; to seize ; to win,' C. J. Dennis : Australian : late C. 19–20. Ex *snaring* animals.

snarge. An ugly or an unpleasant person : lower classes' and military : C. 20. F. & Gibbons. Perhaps ex *snitch,* 3, + *nark* (s. sense).

snarl. An ill-tempered discussion ; a quarrel : tailors' : C. 20. (*The Tailor and Cutter,* Nov. 29, 1928.)

snarls, bunch of. A disagreeable man : id. : id. (Ibid.)

snatch. A hasty or illicit or mercenary copulation : coll. : C. 17–20. ' Melancholy ' Burton, ' I could not abide marriage, but as a rambler I took a snatch when I could get it.'—2. Hence, ultimately, though imm. ex Yorkshire dial. : the female pudend : late C. 19–20. Cf. the next term.—3. Hence, girls viewed collectively as ' fun ' : from ca. 1930. Peter Chamberlain, ' Yet another couple of " snatch ".'

snatch-blatch. The female pudend : ca. 1890– 1915. On *snatch,* 2.

***snatch-cly.** A pickpocket, esp. one who snatches from women's pockets : c. : late C. 18–19. Grose, 2nd ed. ; Baumann. See **cly.**

snatcher. One who, when hire-purchasers fail to pay instalments, seizes (part of) the furniture : trade : from ca. 1920. (*The Daily Telegraph,* Oct. 19, 1934.) Abbr. of an assumed *furniture-snatcher.*

***snavel, n.** See **running snabble** and cf. *running smobble.*—2. V., to steal, esp. by snatching or by pocket-picking : c. : from ca. 1850. ' Jon Bee.' A corruption of *snabble* or of *snaffle* (v., 1), or perhaps a fusion of both.

'Snayles ! A C. 16–17 variant of *'Snails !,* q.v.

***sneak ;** in late C. 18–19, gen. **the sneak.** The practice, or a specific act, of creeping in stealthily with a view to robbery ; a theft thus effected : c. : late C. 17–20 ; ob. Esp. in *sneak, (up)on the,* q.v.— 2. Partly hence, a stealthy departure or flight : c. : from ca. 1810. Vaux.—3. A pilferer, a stealthy enterer with a view to theft : from ca. 1780 : s. >, ca. 1830, coll. >, ca. 1880, S.E. Grose, 1st ed.— 4. See **sneaks.**

***sneak, v.t.** To steal from (a place) after stealthy entry : c. : from ca. 1810 ; ob. Vaux. Prob. ex

sneak, go upon the, q.v. Cf. sense 4 and *sneak,* n., 1.
—2. To escape from (a person) by stealth : c. :
from ca. 1810 ; extremely ob. Vaux. Cf. *sneak,*
n., 2.—3. To walk about looking for something to
steal or pilfer : c. : from ca. 1820 ; ob. Bee.—4.
To filch ; steal furtively, stealthily : coll. : 1883
(O.E.D.). Ex sense 1.—5. To tell tales (v.i.) :
schools ' : 1897, *The Daily News,* June 3, ' Sneaking,
in the ethics of the public school boys, is the un-
pardonable sin,' O.E.D. ; by 1930, coll. Ex *sneak,*
to be servile.

sneak, area. See **area sneak.—sneak, evening.**
See sneak, evening.

*sneak, give it to (a person) **upon the.** See sneak,
v., 2. Vaux.

*sneak, **go upon the.** To slip into houses whose
doors are left open and there steal : c. : late C. 18-
20 ; ob. Ex *sneak, upon the,* q.v.

*sneak, **morning.** The practice of ' going out
early to rob private houses or shops by slipping in
at the door unperceived,' Vaux : c. : from ca. 1810 ;
ob. Ex :—2. In late C. 18–20, the person doing
this : c. Grose, 1st ed., where also *evening sneak,*
one given to pilfering in the evening, also (in C. 19–
20) the doing of this.

*sneak, **upon** or (in C. 19–20) **on the.** Stealthily :
c. : late C. 17–20. B.E., Vaux. Mainly in reference to robbery (see **sneak,** n., 1), but see also **sneak,
give it . . . the.**—2. Prowling for booty : c. : from
ca. 1820. Cf. *sneak,* v., 3.

*sneak, **upright.** A thief preying on potboys,
whom he robs of the pots as they are engaged in
collecting them : c. : late C. 18–20 ; ob. Grose,
1st ed.

sneak-cup. Erroneous for *sneak-up,* a sneak or
skulker : late C. 16–17. O.E.D.

*sneak **on the lurk.** To prowl about for booty :
c. : from ca. 1820 ; ob. An elaboration of *sneak,*
v., 3, q.v. See **lurk.**

sneaker. ' A large cup (or small basin) with a
saucer and cover,' esp. for drink : e.g. a *sneaker of
punch* : from ca. 1710 : perhaps orig. s., soon >
coll. ; by 1830, S.E. Yule & Burnell.—2. (Gen.
pl.) A variant of *sneak* (at *sneaks*) : coll., orig.
(— 1891) U.S. ; anglicised by 1920. Manchon.

*sneaking-budge.** A lone-hand thief or robber :
c. : late C. 17–early 19. B.E. ; Grose, 1st ed. Cf.
sneak, n., 1, and v., 1, and see **budge.**—2. Fielding
incorrectly uses it to mean pilfering or stealing, n.
and adj.

*sneaks.** C. from ca. 1870 as in James Greenwood's *In Strange Company,* 1873, ' Sneaks . . .
are shoes with canvas tops and india-rubber soles.'
Ex *sneak,* n., 2.

'Sneaks ! God's neaks !, a coll. petty oath :
early C. 17. Marston. Properly, *neaks* should be
neakes or *neaques* = *nigs.* A variant of the oath
occurs in Fletcher, 1619, ' I'll . . . goe up and
downe drinking small beere and swearing 'odds
neagues.' O.E.D. Cf. '*Snigs* !, q.v.

*sneaksman.** A stealthy thief, cowardly pilferer :
c. : from ca. 1810. Vaux. Properly, one who goes
' upon the sneak ', q.v. Ex *sneak,* n., 1, but perhaps
influenced by *snakesman,* q.v.—2. Hence, a shop-
lifter : c. : mid-C. 19–20. H., 1st ed.

sneck up ! ; **snick up !** Go hang ! : late C. 16–17
coll. ; extant in dial. ' Women of Abingdon '
Porter, 1599 ; Shakespeare ; dramatist Heywood.
Lit., latch ! Cf. *shut up* !, q.v., and the Derbicism
put a sneck before one's snout, to watch one's speech,
to say little or nothing.

sneerg. Greens : back s. (— 1859). H., 1st ed

sneeze. The nose : from ca. 1820 ; very ob.
' Jon Bee.' Ex *sneezer,* 2.

sneeze at. To underrate, disregard, scorn : coll. :
1806, Surr (O.E.D.) ; Combe, 1820, ' A . . . dame
. . . who wish'd to change her name, | And . . .
would not perhaps have sneezed at mine.' In C. 20,
mainly in *not to be sneezed at* : see **sneezed at.**

*sneeze- or snuff-lurker.** A thief that operates
after disabling his victim with snuff, pepper, or any
similar unpleasantness : c. : from ca. 1859 ; ob.
H., 1st ed., *sneeze-lurker.* As = snuff, *sneeze,* once
S.E., is now dial. Cf. *snuff,* 1, and :

*sneeze- or snuff-racket, give it** (to a person) **on
the.** To do this : from ca. 1820 ; slightly ob. See
sneeze-lurker.

sneezed at, not to be. Not to be underrated, dis-
regarded, despised : coll. : 1813, Scott ; 1891, Nat
Gould. O.E.D. Ex *sneeze at.*

*sneezer.** A snuff-box : c. of ca. 1720–1880. *A
New Canting Dict.,* 1725, ' *Cog a Sneezer,* Beg a . . .
Snuff-box ' ; Vaux. Ex *sneeze,* snuff.—2. The
nose : 1820 (O.E.D.). Cf. *snorter,* last sense.—3.
Hence, a pocket-handkerchief : low (— 1857) ; ob.
' Ducange Anglicus.'—4. A drink, esp. a dram of
something strong : from ca. 1820 : dial. >, ca.
1835, s. J. T. Hewlett, 1841, ' He knew he should
get a sneezer of something short for his trouble ' ;
Dickens. O.E.D. Lit., enough to make one
sneeze. Cf. *snifter,* 1.—5. Something exceptionally
good or bad, big or strong or violent, in some
specified respect : s. >, in late C. 19, coll. : 1820,
a blow (dial. >, ca. 1840, s.) ; a gale, 1855 (mainly
nautical ; a very well-bowled fast ball, late C. 19–20
(cricket) ; in 1836, Haliburton speaks of ' a regular
sneezer of a sinner ' ; a martinet (military s. of
—1903). O.E.D. ; F. & H. Cf. preceding sense,
snorter, 2, and *snifter,* 2.—6. A mouth-gag : c. :
from ca. 1890. Clarence Rook, *The Hooligan
Nights,* 1899. Ex sense 3.

sneezes (or s.), like. Vigorously, intensively ;
remarkably : lower-class coll. : C. 20. Dorothy
Sayers, *Strong Poison,* 1930. Perhaps *Sneezes* is a
euphemism for *Jesus* and, oddly yet—ins.—possibly,
the phrase = *like the devil.*

*sneezing-coffer.** A snuff-box : c. of ca. 1810–
50. Vaux. Cf. *sneezer,* 1.

Sneezy. The second month in the French
Republican Calendar : late C. 18–early 19. Ex (*le
mois*) *brumaire,* the foggy month.

*snell.** A needle : c. ; hawkers' s. : from ca.
1845. Ex Scots *snell,* sharp.

*snell-fencer.** A needle-hawker : id. : id.
Carew, *Autobiography of a Gipsy.*

*snib.** A petty thief : c. : ca. 1605–1840.
Dekker ; Egan's Grose, where it is described as
Scotch cant. O.E.D. ? cognate with snib, to check.

snib, v. To coït with (a woman) : low Scots :
from ca. 1810. Prob. ex *snib,* to fasten (a door) ;
cf. *snib a candle,* snuff it.

snice mince-pie, it's a. A c.p. : from ca. 1916 ;
ob. Suggested by the sibilance of *a nice mince-pie,*
esp. when preceded by *it's.* See **s-.**

snick. A share : s. and dial. : from ca. 1720.
At Winchester, *go snicks* (— 1891), to go shares. A
variant of *snack,* q.v.

snick, v. To slip, cut, across or along (a road)
suddenly or quickly : coll. : 1883 (O.E.D.). Ex
snick, v.i., to cut, snip, esp. crisply.

snick-fadge. A petty thief : c. : mid-C. 19–20
Ex S.E. *snick off.*

snick up ! See **sneck up !**

snicker. A glandered horse : late C. 18–early 19. Grose, 3rd ed. Cf. *snitched*.

*__snicking.__ A surreptitious obtaining : c. or low s. : ca. 1670–1750. Head, 1673 (O.E.D.). See **snick**, n., and cf. *snack*, *snap* (v.), and *snicktog*.

__snickle__, v.i. To inform, peach : c. : mid-C. 19–20 : mostly U.S. Matsell. Prob. ex the now dial. *snickle*, to snare.

snicks, go. See **snick, n.**

*__snicktog.__ To go shares : c. : late C. 19–20 ; ob. Perversion of *snick*, n. Cf. *snack* (esp. as *go snacks*), *snap*, n., 1, and v., *snick* (esp. *go snicks*), and *snicking*, qq.v.

*__snid.__ A sixpence : mainly Scots c. (— 1839) ; ob. by 1900, virtually † by 1930. Brandon.

*__sniddy.__ See **snide**, adj.

snide. An occ. form of *snid*, q.v.—2. (Occ. __snyde.__) Anything spurious, esp. base coin or sham jewellery : c. (in C. 20, low) : implied in *snide-pitcher*, q.v., as early as 1862, but by itself unrecorded before ca. 1885, except in H., 5th ed., 1874, ' Also . . . as a [n.], as, " He's a snide ", though this seems but a contraction of *snide 'un* ' ; perhaps, however, the reference in ' *No. 747* ' at p. 416 is valid (as = base metal) for 1845. Origin obscure. Cf. *schlenter*, q.v. ; prob. ex Yiddish.—3. Hence, a contemptible person : c. >, by 1890, low : see quotation from H. for sense 2.—4. ' The business of passing counterfeit half-crowns and other imitation silver coins ' : c. : from ca. 1920. James Spenser, *Limey Breaks In*, 1934. Abbr. *snide-pitching*, q.v.

*__snide ; snyde,__ adj. Spurious, counterfeit, sham, bogus : c. : 1862, ' " Snyde witnesses ", ' O.E.D. ; but the reference in Carew's *Autobiography of a Gipsy*, p. 418, points to 1845.—2. Hence, mean, contemptible : c. : from ca. 1870. H., 5th ed. ; ' Pomes ' Marshall, ' His pockets she tried, | Which is wifely, though snide.' Both senses also in forms *sniddy* and *snidey* : late C. 19–20.—3. Hence, loosely, wrong, incorrect : C. 20. David Esdaile in *The Daily Mirror*, Nov. 18, 1933, ' Slang is snide . . . the antithesis of correctitude.'

snide and shine (or **S. and S.**). A Jew, esp. of East London : East London Gentiles' (— 1909). Ware. For *shine*, cf. *sheeny*.

*__snide lurk.__ The passing of counterfeit money : c. : from ca. 1845. ' *No. 747.*'

*__snide-pitcher.__ A passer of base money : c. : 1862 (O.E.D.). See **snide**, n., 2.

*__snide-pitching.__ The passing of counterfeit money : c. : 1868, Temple Bar, ' Snyde-pitching is . . . a capital racket.' See **snide**, n., 2 ; cf. *snide-pitcher*.

*__snide shop.__ An agency for the selling of counterfeit notes : c. : from ca. 1920. E.g. in Edgar Wallace, *Mr Reeder*.

snider. See **snyder.**—2. A sly fellow, a spy, a connoisseur : c. (— 1923). Manchon. Prob. ex *snide*, adj.

*__snidesman.__ A ' snide-pitcher ' (q.v.) : c. : 1897, Arthur Morrison. O.E.D.

*__snidey.__ See **snide**, adj.—2. Snappish, irritable : Glasgow (— 1934).

snie ; occ. **sny.** A hole filled with water ; a hidden pool, even if large : Canadian coll : C. 20. John Beames. Origin ?

sniff, v.i. To drink (strong liquor) : from ca. 1920. (Michael Harrison, *Weep for Lycidas*, 1934.) Cf. :

sniffler ?, will you have a. Will you take a drink ? : Anglo-Irish c.p. (— 1935). Perhaps influenced by *snifter*, 1.

sniffy. Scornful, disdainful ; occ. ill-tempered : coll. and dial. : from ca. 1870. Lit., apt to sniff in contempt. Cf. *sneeze at*, q.v.

snifter. A dram : low : from ca. 1880 ; ob. Prob. ex U.S. *snifter* (1848), a small drink of spirits : Thornton. Cf. *sneezer*, 4.—2. Any thing or person excellent, or very big or strong : late C. 19–20. Ex dial. *snifter*, a strong breeze. Cf. *sneezer*, last sense, and *snorter*, 2.

snifter, adj. (Very) good or satisfactory : C. 20. F. & Gibbons. Ex sense 2 of the n.

snifty-snidey. Supercilious, disdainful : Lancashire s. (— 1904), not dial. E.D.D. Cf. *sniffy* and *snidey*, 2. : qq.v.

snig. To steal ; pilfer : 1892, Kipling (E.D.D.). Ex dial.

sniggered if (e.g. you will), **I'm.** A mild asseveration (— 1860). Very ob. H., 2nd ed., ' Another form of this is *jiggered*.' Cf. :

'Sniggers ! A trivial oath : coll. : ca. 1630–1890. Rowley, Smollett, Haliburton (O.E.D.). Whence perhaps *sniggered*, q.v. Cf. :

sniggle, v.i. To wriggle ; creep stealthily : dial. (— 1837) >, ca. 1900, coll. Ex *snuggle*.—2. Whence, to get (something) *in* surreptitiously : dial. (—1881) >, ca. 1900, coll. O.E.D.

sniggy. Mean, penurious : C. 20 ; ob. E.D.D. Prob. ex Yorkshire dial.

'Snigs ! *God's nigs*, a trivial oath : coll. : ca. 1640–90. (O.E.D.) More prob. a variant than an abbr. of *'Sniggers !*, q.v. Cf. *Sneaks !*, q.v.

*__snilch,__ v.i. ; rarely v.t. To see ; to eye : c. of ca. 1670–1850. Coles, Grose (1st ed.). ? origin.—2. Hence, to examine closely, to feel suspiciously : c. : mid-C. 19–20 ; ob. Manchon.

snip. A tailor ; often as a nickname : late C. 16–20 : s. >, in C. 18, coll. Jonson, Grose, Trollope. In late C. 19–20, the inevitable naval and military nickname of all men surnamed Taylor or Parsons. Ex *to snip*, to cut, in tailoring.—2. A swindle or cheat : low (— 1725) ; † by 1840. *A New Canting Dict.*, 1725. Cf. the v.—3. A good tip : racing : from ca. 1890. ' Pomes ' Marshall.—4. Hence, a bargain ; a certainty ; an easy win or acquisition : 1894 (O.E.D.—5. Hence, an easy job : C. 20. B. & P.—6. See **snips.**

snip, v.t. To cheat : low : ca. 1720–1840. *A New Canting Dict.*, 1725. Cf. *snip*, n., 2, q.v.

snip-cabbage or **-louse.** A tailor : resp. C. 18–early 19 (E. Ward, 1708) ; from ca. 1820 (Bee, 1823). Both are very ob. For former, cf. trade sense of *cabbage*.

snipe. A lawyer : from ca. 1860. H., 2nd ed. Prob. ex :—2. A long bill, esp. among lawyers, whose bills are often tragi-comic in their length : from ca. 1855. H., 2nd ed. Ex the long-billed bird.—3. See **snipes.**—4. (Gen. in pl.) A cigarette-end : vagrants c. : C. 20. W. A. Gape, *Half a Million Tramps*, 1936. Cf. the v., 2.

snipe, v. F. & H.'s ' to fire at random into a camp' is prob. an error.—2. To pilfer : low (— 1923). Manchon. Prob. ex shooting.

Snipe, the. Madame de Lieven, prominent in English society of the 1820's. *The Creevey Papers*.

*__snipes.__ A pair of scissors : c. : from ca. 1810 ; ob. Vaux.—2. Second-mortgage bonds in the New York, Lake Erie, and Western Railway :

Stock Exchange (— 1895). A. J. Wilson, *Stock Exchange Glossary.*

snippy. Snappy; captious: coll.: C. 20. Ex dial. Lit., cutting. (E.D.D.)

snips. Handcuffs: low: from ca. 1890. Ex *snip*, adv. denoting sound. O.E.D.

snish. Ammunition: military: from ca. 1905. F. & Gibbons. Ex Scots and Northern dial. *snish* (more gen. *sneesh*), snuff.

*****snitch.** A fillip on the nose: c.: ca. 1670–1750. Coles, B.E. Also *snitchel*: same status, period and authorities.—2. The nose: late C. 17–20: c. >, ca. 1830, dial. and low s. B.E. at *snite.*—3. Hence (cf. *nose*, n.), an informer, esp. by King's evidence: only (? first in *Lex. Bal.*) in *snitch, turn*, q.v.—4. See **snitches.**

*****snitch,** v.i. To peach, turn King's evidence: c.: C. 19–20. Vaux, Maginn. Prob. ex the n.; perhaps cognate with *snilch*, q.v. Cf. *to nose.*—2. V.t. To inform against: c.: C. 19–20; rare, the gen. form being *snitch upon.* O.E.D.—3. To purloin: 1933, Dorothy Sayers, *Murder Must Advertise*, 1933, 'He . . . snitched other people's ideas without telling them.'

*****snitch, turn.** To turn King's evidence: c.: from ca. 1780. Grose, 1st ed. Cf. *nose*, n.

*****snitchel,** n. See **snitch,** n., 1.—2. V.t. **to** fillip on the nose: c.: late C. 17–early 18. B.E.

snitched, ppl.adj. Glandered: horse-dealers' s. (— 1876). Hindley. Cf. *snicker*, q.v.

*****snitcher.** A member of a set of bloods: ca. 1760–80. *The Annual Register*, 1761. O.E.D. ? origin.—2. One who peaches; an informer: c.: 1827 (O.E.D.); John G. Brandon, *The One-Minute Murder*, 1934. Ex *snitch*, v., 1.—3. In pl., handcuffs; or strings used therefor: c. (— 1860). H., 2nd ed. Cf. *snitches.*—4. A detective: c. (— 1923). Manchon. Ex sense 2.—5. A person or thing remarkably good, strong, attractive, etc.: New Zealand (— 1935). Perhaps influenced by *snifter.*

*****snitches.** Handcuffs: c.: from ca. 1870. A corruption of *snitcher*, 3.

*****snitching.** The art and practice of peaching; turning King's evidence: C. 19–20: c.

*****snitching-rascal.** A variant of *snitcher*, **2.** Vaux. († by 1890.)

*****snite his snitch.** 'Wipe his Nose, or give him a good Flap on the Face': resp. late C. 17–20 (c. >, in C. 19, low s.; B.E.) and late C. 17–early 19 (c.; Grose, 1785). By itself *snite* is S.E. > dial.

*****sniv.** To hold one's tongue: c.: ca. 1810–50. Ex *snib*, to fasten.—2. *sniv !* See **bender !** C. of ca. 1810–40. Vaux.

sniveller. A toadying seaman: nautical: late C. 19–20. Bowen.

snizzle. To fornicate: lower classes' (— 1923). Manchon. Origin ? Possibly cognate with dial. *sniggle* (see E.D.D., at *sniggle*, v., 2).

snob. A shoemaker, cobbler, or an apprentice thereto: from ca. 1780: s. >, ca. 1800, coll. and dial. In Scots coll., C. 19–20, *snab.* Grose, 1st ed. ? etymology. Cf. *snobber.*—2. Hence, in the Navy, 'a man earning extra money by repairing shipmates' boots in spare time': late C. 19–20: coll. F. & Gibbons.—3. A townsman: Cambridge University: ca. 1795–1870. Perhaps ex sense 1. Cf. the corresponding *cad.*—4. Among workmen, a 'blackleg' or 'scab': coll.: from ca. 1859; very ob. Abbr. *snobstick*, q.v.

snob, v.i. and t. 'To sloven one's work,' F. & H.: tailors': from ca. 1870; ob.

snob-shop. 'The regimental boot repairer or maker's workshop': military coll.: late C. 19–20. F. & Gibbons. See **snob**, n., 1.

snobber. A shoemaker, cobbler: coll.: 1900 (O.E.D.). Ex *snob*, n., 1.

snobbery. Slovenly work; slack trade: tailors': from ca. 1870; ob. Cf. *snob*, v. Whence, *hide the snobbery*, to conceal bad workmanship, inferior material.

snob's boot. A sixpence: tailors': from ca. 1870; ob. Cf. *snob's duck.*

snob's cat, full of piss and tantrums,—like a. A low c.p. applied to a person: ca. 1820–50. 'Jon Bee.'

snob's duck. 'A leg of mutton, stuffed with sage and onions,' F. & H.: tailors': from ca. 1870; ob. See **snob**, n., 1, and cf. *snob's boot.*

snobstick. A non-striker, a 'scab': workmen's coll. (— 1860); ob. H., 2nd ed. Prob. a corruption of *knobstick*, q.v., as H., 2nd ed., suggests.

snodder. One who dislikes spending: grafters': C. 20. Philip Allingham, *Cheapjack*, 1934. Ex Yiddish.

snoddy. A soldier: low: ca. 1890–1914. A corruption of *swaddy*, q.v.

snoodge. See **snooze.**—**snook.** See **snooks, cock.**

snooker. A freshman at the Royal Military Academy: R.M.A.: 1872 (O.E.D.). Prob. ex *snook*, a variant of *snoke*, to sneak about (v.i.).

snooker, v. To delude, trick, 'best', 'be too much for': from 1914 at latest. (O.E.D. Sup.) Ex the game: cf. S.E. *euchre.*

snooks. 'The imaginary name of a practical joker; also a derisive retort on an idle question—*Snooks !*,' F. & H.: from ca. 1860; ob. H., 2nd ed.

snooks, cock; occ. **cock a snook;** also **cut a snook, cut snooks.** To make the derisive gesture described at *sight*, 5: coll.: (resp.)—1903; 1904; 1879;—1903. F. & H.; O.E.D. Origin obscure. 'Cf. Fr. *faire un pied de nez*, Ger. *eine lange nase machen.* Perhaps name *Snook-s* felt as phonetically appropriate (cf. *Walker*),' W.

snookums. A trivial endearment; esp. applied to a lap-dog: coll.: 1928. O.E.D. (Sup.) Cf. *diddums.*

snoop ; gen. **snoop around.** To pry; go about slyly: orig. (ca. 1830) U.S.; anglicised as a coll. ca. 1905; by 1935, gen. considered virtually S.E. Ex the Dutch *snoepen.* Thornton. Hence *snooper*, *snooping*, one who does this, and the action; also *snoopy*, adj.: all anglicised ca. 1920.—2. Hence v.t. *snoop*, to 'appropriate', steal on the sly: coll.: 1924, Galsworthy, *The White Monkey.*

snoose. See **snooze.**

snooty. (Of persons) unpleasant; cross, irritable; supercilious: Society and near-Society: from ca. 1930. (Denis Mackail, *Summer Leaves*, 1934.) Perhaps on *snoopy* (see preceding entry) but ex *snorty*: cf. Lancashire *snoot*, v.i. to sneak, hang round. Adopted ex the U.S.A.; used in Canada from ca. 1920.

*****snooze ;** occ. **snoose** (ob.); in late C. 18–early 19, occ. **snoodge.** A sleep; esp. a nap or doze: 1793 (O.E.D.): c. >, by 1820, s. >, ca. 1840, coll. Ex *snooze*, v.—2. Whence, a lodging; a bed: c.: from ca. 1810; ob. Vaux; Brandon.

*****snooze,** v.; occ. **snoose** († in C. 20) and **snoodge** (late C. 18–20: Grose, 2nd ed.: since ca. 1850, illiterate). To sleep: 1789, George Parker: c. >, ca. 1810, s. >, ca. 1840, coll. Grose, 1788, 'To snooze with a mort [wench] . . . *Cant.*'—2.

Hence (in late C. 19–20, the prevailing sense), to doze, take a nap : from ca. 1840 : coll. Thackeray, 'Snooze gently in thy arm-shair, thou easy bald-head.' Etymology problematic : the word may have been suggested by 'sleep', 'nap', and 'doze'.

*snooze-case. A pillow-slip : low (— 1864) ; slightly ob. H., 3rd ed. Ex *snooze*, n., 2.

*snooze-ken. A variant of *snoozing-ken*, q.v.

snoozem. Sleep ; a sleep : low : 1838, Beckett, *Paradise Lost* ; ob. by 1900, † by 1930. An elaboration of *snooze*, n., 1.

snoozer. One who 'snoozes' : coll. : O.E.D., 1878 ; prob. half a century earlier.—2. 'One of those thieves who take up their quarters at hotels for the purpose of robbery' : c. : mid-C. 19–20. Mayhew.

snoozing, n. and adj. See **snooze, v.** From ca. 1810. Cf. :

*snoozing(-)ken. A brothel : c. (— 1811). *Lex. Bal.* See **snooze, v.** Also, according to F. & H., a lodging-house, bed-room, bed. Occ. *snooze-ken*.

snoozle, v.i. To nestle and then sleep ; to nuzzle : resp. ca. 1830, 1850 : coll. and dial. Perhaps, as W. suggests, ex *snooze* + *snuggle* + *nuzzle*.—2. Hence, v.t. to thrust affectionately, nuzzle : coll. and dial. : 1847, Emily Brontë. O.E.D.

*snoozy. A night-constable : c. of ca. 1820–60. Egan's Grose. Ex *snooze*, v., 1.

snoozy, adj. Sleepy ; drowsy : coll. : 1877 (O.E.D.) See **snooze, n.,** 1.

snork. To surpass ; cap (another) in argument, repartee ; do the whole of (an examination paper): Shrewsbury School : late C. 19–20. Perhaps ex :—2. A rebuff, a setback : id. : from ca. 1880. Desmond Coke, *The Bending of a Twig*, 1906. Perhaps cf. dial. *snork*, a snort.—3. Whence, *snorks !*, a term of defiance : id. : from ca. 1885. Ibid.

snorter. A gale ; a strong breeze : 1855 (O.E.D.) : s. >, ca. 1890, coll. Cf. *sneezer* 5, q.v.—2. Anything exceptional, esp. in size, severity, or strength : 1859, J. Lang, 'The Commander-in-Chief . . . certainly did put forth "a snorter of a General Order,"' O.E.D. : s. >, ca. 1890, coll. Cf. *snifter*, 2.—3. A blow, punch on the nose : from ca. 1873. H., 5th ed. Cf. *sneezer*, 5, q.v.—4. The nose : from ca. 1880. Cf. *sneezer*, 2. Baumann defines it as the mouth and classifies it as boxing s. : I do not know it in this sense, but he may well be right : he almost always is !

snorting. The ppl.adj. corresponding to *snorter* 2 ; esp., excellent : late C. 19–20.

snorty. Irritable, irritated ; peevish ; captious : 1893, Kate Douglas Wiggin, 'She found Mr Gooch very snorty, very snorty indeed,' O.E.D. Ex *snort contemptuously*. Cf. *snotty*, adj., 2.

snossidge. A sausage : London's lower classes' : ca. 1890–1900. Ware.

snot. Nasal mucus : C. 15–20 : S.E. until C. 19, when dial. and a vulgarism. Cognate with *snite*, q.v.—2. Hence, a term of contempt for a person : C. 19–20 : s. when not dial. ; ob. except in dial.—3. A gentleman : Scots c. (— 1839) ; ob. Brandon.

snot, v.i., v.t., and v. reflexive. To blow the nose : late C. 16–20 : mostly dial. ; in C. 19–20, also (though very ob.) a vulgarism. Ex *snot*, n., 1.

snot-box. The nose : low coll. : mid-C. 19–20 ; ob. Ex *snot*, n., 1.

snot-rag. A pocket-handkerchief : low : late C. 19–20. Cf. *snot-box* and *snotter*.

snotted, ppl.adj. Reprimanded : c. : late C. 19–20 ; ob. Prob. a perversion of *snouted*, rooted up as with the snout ; perhaps on *snotty*, adj., 2.

snotter. A dirty, ragged handkerchief : low : from ca. 1820 ; ob. Bee. Ex *snot*, mucus.—2. The nose : low : from ca. 1830 ; very ob.—3. A handkerchief-thief : c. : mid-C. 19–20 ; ob. H., 1st ed.—4. A midshipman : nautical (— 1903). F. & H. Perhaps influenced by nautical *snotter* (a short rope spliced at the ends). More gen. *snotty*, q.v.

*snotter-hauling. The thieving of handkerchiefs : c. : mid-C. 19–20. Ex *snotter*, 3.

snottery. A C. 20 Glasgow variant of *snotty*, adj., 2.

snottie. See **snotty, n.—snotties' nurse.** See **snotty, n.—snottily.** Adv. of *snotty*, adj., 2, q.v.

snotting. A reprimand : tailors' : 1928, *The Tailor and Cutter*, Nov. 29. Cf. *snotty*, adj., 2.

snottinger. A handkerchief : low : from ca. 1860 ; ob. H., 2nd ed. Ex *snot*, n., 1, on *muckinger*, q.v. Cf. *snot-rag*, and *snotter*, 1.

snottle-box. The nose : low : mid-C. 19–20 ; ob. Cf. *snot-box*.

snotty ; occ. **snottie.** A midshipman : nautical (— 1903). F. & H. ; Kipling, 1904 (O.E.D.). Prob. ex *snotty*, adj., 2, not *snotty*, adj., 1 ; 'Taffrail', however, derives it ex the buttons worn by midshipmen on their sleeves, whence arose the jest that the buttons were there to prevent them from wiping their noses on their sleeves (cited by F. & Gibbons). Hence, *snotties' nurse*, a naval officer detailed to look after the midshipmen. Bowen.

snotty, adj. Filthy ; mean, contemptible : late C. 17–20 : S.E. until C. 19, then dial. and s. Ex *snot*, n., 1. Cf. S.E. *snotty-nosed*.—2. Angry, short-tempered ; apt to take offence ; very proud ; proudly conceited : dial. (— 1870) >, ca. 1880, s. Prob. ex sense 1.

*snout. A hogshead : c. of ca. 1720–1800. *A New Canting Dict.*, 1725. Ex a hog's nose.—2. Tobacco : c. (— 1896 : O.E.D.). 'Stuart Wood.' ? origin.—3. Among hawkers, a cigar : late C. 19–20. Ex sense 2 and (?) shape.—4. A betrayer ; an informer to the police : c. : from ca. 1920. Edgar Wallace ; Charles E. Leach. Cf. *nose*, q.v.—5. Hence, a detective : low Glasgow (— 1934).

snout. 'To bear [a person] a grudge,' C. J. Dennis : military and Australian : C. 20. Ex *pigs*.—2. Whence *snouted*, 'treated with disfavour', id. : ibid. : id.

snout-piece. The face : coll. : C. 17–19. 'Melancholy' Burton, 1621.

*snouting, vbl.n. Giving information to the police : c. : from ca. 1920. Edgar Wallace.

snouty. Overbearing ; haughty ; insolent : coll.: 1858 (O.E.D.) ; somewhat ob. Cf. *sniffy*.

Snow. See **snowy,** 2.

*snow. Linen ; esp. linen hung out to dry or bleach : c. (— 1811). *Lex. Bal.* ; H., 1st ed. Ex whiteness. Also occ. *snowy*.—2. Cocaine : U.S. ; anglicised ca. 1920 as c. >, ca. 1930, s. Edgar Wallace, *passim* ; Irwin. Ex colour.—3. Silver ; silver money : military : C. 20. F. & Gibbons. Cf. the c. adj. *white*, of silver.

*snow, sweeping the. A variant (— 1935) of *snow-dropping*. David Hume.

snow-broth. Cold tea : 1870, Judd ; ob. Ex *snow-broth* : melted snow.

*snow-dropper or -gatherer. A linen-thief : c. :

from ca. 1810, though *snow-dropper* is unrecorded before 1864, *-gatherer* before 1859. Ex *snow*, 1.

*snow-dropping. Linen-thieving : c. : from ca. 1810 ; recorded, 1839. Cf. *snow-dropper*.

snow rupee. A genuine rupee : Southern Indian coll. (— 1886). Ex Telegu *tsanauvu*, authority, currency, by process of Hobson-Jobson. Yule & Burnell.

snowball. A Negro : from ca. 1780 ; ob. Grose, 1st ed. Ironic nickname.

'Snowns. A trivial oath : late C. 16–early 17 ; coll. abbr. *Od's nouns*. O.E.D.

*snowy. Linen ; esp. that hung out to dry : c. (— 1877). Ex *snow*, 1.—2. (Snowy.) An inevitable nickname of men with flaxen or bleached hair : lower classes' : late C. 19–20. Also, in Australia, for men surnamed Baker : C. 20. (Cf. *Dusty* Miller.) Also, there, of Aboriginals : late C. 19–20. In the second and third nuances, often *Snow*.

snozzler. Any person or thing remarkable for excellence, skill, strength, etc. : New Zealand (— 1935). Prob. suggested by such terms as *snifter* and *bobby-dazzler*, of which pair it may be a blend.

snub-devil. A clergyman : ca. 1780–1900. Grose, 1st ed. ; Baumann.

snubber. A reprimand : Public Schools' (— 1909). Ware. Prob. by ' the Oxford *-er* '.

*snudge. One who, to steal later, hides himself in a house, esp. under a bed : c. (— 1676) ; † by 1840. Coles ; B.E. ; Grose, 1st ed. A special development ex *snudge*, to remain snugly quiet.

Snuff. Charles Stanhope (1780–1851), Lord Petersham, who concocted the Petersham snuff-mixture. Dawson.

*snuff, v.i. To blind (esp. a shopkeeper) with snuff and then, all being well, steal his goods : c. : from ca. 1810 ; ob. Vaux.—2. See snuff it, snuff out.

snuff, beat to. To defeat utterly : coll. : 1819 (O.E.D.) ; ob.

snuff, give (a person). To rebuke, reprimand, scold : coll. : 1890, Anon., *Harry Fludyer*, ' He rather gave me snuff about my extravagance, but I was prepared for that.'—2. Hence, to punish : coll. : 1896, Baden-Powell (O.E.D.).

snuff, in high. In ' great form ' ; elated : coll. : 1840, Dana ; slightly ob. O.E.D.

snuff, up to. Alert ; not easily tricked ; shrewd : coll. : 1811, Poole, ' He knew well enough | The game we're after : zooks, he's up to snuff.' Lit. of one who knows to what dangerous uses snuff can be put. Egan's Grose adds : ' Often rendered more emphatic by such adjuncts as " Up to snuff and twopenny," " Up to snuff, and a pinch above it." '

snuff-box. The nose : 1853, ' Cuthbert Bede ' ; ob. O.E.D.

snuff it. To die : s. (— 1874) >, ca. 1900, coll. H., 5th ed., ' Term very common among the lower orders of London . . . Always to die from disease or accident.' Ex *snuff out*, q.v.

*snuff-lurker. See sneeze-lurker.

snuff out, v.i. To die : s. (— 1864) >, ca. 1900, S.E. H., 3rd ed. Prob. ex snuffing out a candle. Cf. *snuff it*.

*snuff-racket. See sneeze-racket and cf. *sneeze-lurker*.

snuffers. The nostrils : ca. 1650–1750 : s. and dial. Cleveland. O.E.D.

snuffy. Drunk : low : from ca. 1820 ; ob. Bee, 1823 ; H., 3rd ed. Perhaps ex *snuffy*, apt to take offence, displeased, angry.

snug. A bar-parlour at inn or ' public ' : from ca. 1860 : s. (ob.) and dial. Ex *snug*, comfortable ; cf. S.E. *snuggery*.

snug, v. To coït with : C. 19–20 ; ob. Ex *snug*, to make comfortable : cf. euphemistic *ease*. 2.—Also v.i. : C. 19–20 ; ob. Prob. ex *snug down*, to nestle.

snug, adj. Drunk : low : late C. 19–20 ; very ob. Cf. euphemistic *comfortable*.

snug as a bug in a rug. Very snug, cosy, comfortable : coll. : from ca. 1760. See quotation at *mopus*, 3. Apperson.

*snug, all's. All's quiet : c. of ca. 1720–1840. *A New Canting Dict.*, 1725 ; Grose, 1st ed. Cf. the † S.E. *snug*, secret, concealed, private. Cf. :

snug as a pig in pease-straw. Very comfortable (-bly) : coll. : ca. 1635–70. Davenport, 1639, ' He snores and sleeps as snug | As any pigge in pease-straw.' Apperson. Cf. *snug as a bug in a rug*.

snug's the word ! Say nothing of this ! : coll. : C. 18–19 ; ob. by 1860. Congreve, Maria Edgeworth, Lover. O.E.D. Cf. *snug, all's*, q.v.

snurge. ' To get out of doing some unpopular job ' : nautical : C. 20. Bowen. Prob. ex dial., *snudge*, to sneak, to sulk, curry favour (E.D.D.).

sny. See snie.—*snyde. See snide.

snyder ; snider. A tailor : coll. : C. 17–20 ; ob. F. & H., an early C. 17 quotation ; H., 2nd ed. Ex Ger. *Schneider*, tailor ; prob. imported by soldiers.

so. Tipsy : coll. : from ca. 1820. Ex *so-so*, 1.—2. Menstruating : women's euphemistic coll. : mid-C. 19–20.—3. Homosexual : from ca. 1890. Thus ' a *so* man ' is a homosexual, ' a *so* book ' a Uranian novel, poem, etc. Cf. The Venetian *così*.

so, adv. Very : as a mere counter of vague emphasis, it is admittedly S.E. ; yet it has a coll. tinge.—2. Tautologically in intensifications, it is a proletarian coll. : (?) mid-C. 19–20. ' It gets on my nerves, so it does ! ' ; ' A well-doing young man, so he is ' (both in MacArthur & Long, *No Mean City*, 1935).

so, ever. See ever so.

so and so ; So and So. Senior Ordnance Store Officer : military : ca. 1890–1914. Ware.

so as ; so's. So that ; in order that : catachrestic : late C. 19–20.

So Brien or S'O'Brien (or -an). The Australian steamship *Sobraon* : nautical : late C. 19–early 20. Ware.

so glad ! A c.p. of ca. 1847 (introduced by the French King) and of 1867–68 (from a song in W. Brough's *Field of the Cloth of Gold*) : mostly London. Ware.

so is your old man ! A c.p. from ca. 1900 ; ob. ; often *so's* . . . (John G. Brandon, 1931 ; *Slang*, p. 280.)

so long ! Au revoir ! : coll. : 1865, F. H. Nixon. Cf. Ger. *so lange* (O.E.D.), but more prob., as W. suggests, the term is a corruption of *salaam*, though Ware's suggested derivation ex the Hebrew *Selah* (God be with you) is not to be wholly ignored.

so say. Say so. Esp. *you don't so say* : c.p. : C. 20. Cf. *shay so*.

so-so. Drunk : coll. : 1809, Malkin.—2. Menstruating : women's euphemistic coll. : mid-C. 19–20.

so sudden !, this is. A jocular c.p. applied to an unexpected statement or offer : from ca. 1910. Ex the reputedly usual reply of a girl to a proposal of marriage. (Collinson.)

so very human was. ca. 1880–84, applied in so many ways that *The Daily News*, Oct. 27, 1884, could speak of it thus : ' In the slang of the day, " so very human." ' (Ware.) Rather a c.p. than s.

soak. To ply with liquor : coll. : 1822, Banim (O.E.D.). In C. 20, gen. in passive. Ex *soak*, to saturate. (N.b., *soak*, v.i. to drink heavily, is S.E.) —2. Hence, to spend in drink : coll. : C. 20.—3. To pawn : 1882, G. A. Sala, ' Soak my gems.' O.E.D.—4. V.i. gen. as *soak it*, to be lavish of bait : anglers' coll. : late C. 19–20.—5. To charge (a person) an extortionate price ; to tax heavily : orig. (late 1890's) U.S. ; anglicised by 1914. O.E.D. (Sup.)—6. Hence (?), to catch (a person) out, ' have him set ', give (him) unpleasant work : military : from 1915. F. & Gibbons. Esp. in passive, as ' I was soaked for a fatigue.'—7. To borrow money from : from ca. 1925. Dorothy Sayers, *Have His Carcase*, 1932, ' Poor, but not mercenary or dishonest, since he refused to soak Mrs W.' Ex senses 5 and 6.

soak, in ; come out of soak. Drunk ; to regain sobriety : low coll. (— 1887). Baumann. Ex S.E. *soak*, a heavy drinking-bout.

soak one's clay or **face.** To drink ; esp. to drink heavily : resp. C. 19–20 (slightly ob.) and C. 18. Barham, 1837. Cf. *soak*, 1. O.E.D.

soaked. Tipsy ; very drunk : see **soak**, 1. Cf. *saturated*.

soap. Flattery : 1859, H., 1st ed. ; ob. In C. 20, gen. *soft soap*, q.v. Ex the v.—2. Cheese : Royal Military Academy (— 1903) ; ob. F. & H. —3. Girls collectively : ca. 1883–1900. Ware. Ex the more gen. *bits of soap*, girls, esp. harlots and near-harlots.—4. ' A hard worker ; one who curries favour ' : Bootham School : C. 20. Anon., *Dict. of Bootham Slang*, 1925. Cf. the synonymous *sap* and *soft soap*.

soap, v.t. To flatter ; address ingratiatingly : 1853, ' Cuthbert Bede ' ; ob. Cf. *soft-soap*, v.—2. ' To work hard ; to curry favour ' : Bootham School : C. 20. Anon., *Dict. of Bootham Slang*, 1925. Cf. *sap*, to study hard, and *soft-soap*, v.

soap ?, how are you off for. A c.p. senseless question : 1834, Marryat ; 1886, Baring Gould (O.E.D.). Ob. by 1910, † by 1935. Origin obscure,—but then the origin of almost every c.p. is obscure !

soap, soft. See **soft soap**, n. and v.

soap-and-baccy pay(master). An accountant officer of the Victualling Branch : naval : C. 20. Bowen.

soap and bullion. Soup-and-bouilli : nautical (— 1883) ; ob. Clark Russell. Partly a play on words and partly because of its nauseating smell. Also *hishee-hashee*.

soap and water. Daughter : rhyming s. : late C. 19–20. F. & Gibbons.

soap-crawler. A toady : ca. 1860–1910. Ex *soap*, n., 1.

soap over, v.t. To humbug : low (— 1857) ; ob. ' Ducange Anglicus.' Cf. *soft-soap*.

soap-suds. ' Gin and water, hot, with milk and lump sugar,' Bee : low : ca. 1820–70.

soaps. Shares in A. & F. Pears : Stock Exchange (— 1895). A. J. Wilson, *Stock Exchange Glossary*.

soapy. Unctuous ; ingratiating ; given to ' soft soap ' : 1865 (O.E.D.). Cf. *Soapy Sam*.—2. (Of fits) simulated, or caused by, chewing or eating soap : 1886, *The Daily News*, Dec. 13. O.E.D. Cf. cordite-chewing in C. 20.

soapy Isaac. See **suet(t)y Isaac**.

Soapy Sam. Bishop Wilberforce : ca. 1860–73. Ex his unctuous manner. Samuel Wilberforce, 1805–73, became Bishop of Oxford in 1845, about which time diarist Greville described him as ' a very quick, lively, and agreeable man '.

sob-stuff. Intentional and, gen., excessive sentimentality (to appeal to the emotions—and often the pocket) : orig. (ca. 1919) U.S. ; anglicised, by 1921, as a coll., now verging on S.E. (O.E.D. Sup. ; Lyell.)

sober as a judge on Friday (, as). Very—oh, so very slightly—tipsy : coll. (— 1923). Manchon. His work for the week ends on Friday. Elaboration of the dial. *sober as a judge* (1864 : E.D.D.).

sober-grudge fight. A fight arising out of a long-standing quarrel : Canadian coll. (— 1932). John Beames.

sober-water. Soda-water : punning coll. : from ca. 1873 ; ob. H., 5th ed.

soc, Soc. A trades-union man : printers' : ca. 1870–1910. Ex *Society*.

soccer. See **socker**, 3.

social E. A middle-class evasion of *social evil* (prostitution) : coll. : ca. 1870–1905. Ware.

society. A workhouse : artisans' (— 1909). Ware. Evasive.

[**Society Clown, the.** George Grossmith, the actor : rather a sobriquet than a nickname. Ex his book, *A Society Clown*. (Dawson.)]

society journalist. A contributor to *The Society Journalist* : journalists' : ca. 1875–78. Ware.

Society-maddist. A person that, not born in Society, spends much time and money to get there : Society : ca. 1881–95. Ware.

socius. A companion, a chum : Winchester : C. 19–20 ; ob. Ex the school precept, *sociati omnes incedunto*. Cf. the occ., cultured use, since mid-C. 19, of *socius* as a comrade, itself perhaps ex the ecclesiastical term.—2. Whence, v.t., to accompany : ibid. : mid-C. 19–20 ; ob.

sock. A pocket : c. : late C. 17–mid-18. B.E. —2. As used by Shadwell in *The Squire of Alsatia*, 1688, in Act I, Sc. 1, it seems to = a small coin (cf. *rag*) : prob. c.—3. A blow, a beating : late C. 17–20 : c. >, ca. 1850, low s. ; † as a beating, except in *give* (one) *socks*. B.E. at *tip* ; H., 3rd ed. Cf. *sock*, v., 1.—4. Eatables ; esp., dainties : Eton : 1825, C. Westmacott (O.E.D.). Perhaps ex *suckett*, dainty.—5. ? hence : credit : low (— 1874). H., 5th ed.

sock, adv. Violently : (low) coll. : late C. 19–20. Charles Turley, *Godfrey Marten, Undergraduate*, 1904, ' One of you 'as 'it Susan sock in the eye.'

*****sock.** To hit ; strike hard ; drub, thrash : late C. 17–20 : c. >, ca. 1850, s. B.E. ; Kipling, 1890, ' We socks 'im with a stretcher-pole.' Origin obscure.—2. Hence, to ' give it ' *to* a person : 1890, Kipling, ' 'Strewth, but it socked them hard !'—3. V.i., to deliver blows : 1856 (O.E.D.). E.g. ' Sock him one on the jaw ! ' Ex sense 1. Cf. *sock into*, q.v.—4. To treat one to ' sock ' (see the n., 4) : Eton (— 1850). O.E.D.—5. Hence, to give (one something) : Eton (— 1889). A mere extension of this occurs in the upper and upper-middle classes' *sock*, to offer, as in Evelyn Waugh, *A Handful of Dust*, 1934, ' I'll sock you to a movie.'—6. Cf. **v.i. to buy, to eat, ' sock ' :** Eton : 1883, Brinsley Richards, ' We . . . socked prodigiously.'—7. ? hence, v.i., to get credit : low : late C. 19–20 ; ob. F. & H. Cf. *sock*, n., last sense. —8. To win : Winchester College : late C. 19–20. Wrench. Cf. *sock*, n., 3.

sock, give (one). To beat or thrash soundly ; 1864, H., 3rd ed. ; ob., the C. 20 preferring *give* (one) *socks*, recorded by O.E.D. at 1897. Ex *sock*, n., 3. Cf. *sock*, v., 1 and 2, and *sock into*.

sock, on. ' On tick ' : see **sock,** n., 5. (Baumann.)

sock a boot into. To take advantage of the misfortunes of (a person) : lower classes' : C. 20. F. & Gibbons. See **sock,** v., 1 and 2 ; prob. imm. an elaboration of *sock into*, q.v.

sock in (or **into**) **it !, put a.** Be quiet ! ; stop talking, *it* being the offender's mouth : from ca. 1910 : military (esp. in G.W.) >, by 1920, gen. B. & P. Cf. *wood in it, put a bit* (or *piece*) *of*.

sock into. To hit vigorously ; pitch into : 1864, H., 3rd ed. Ex *sock*, v., 3. Australia, in C. 20, has the variant *sock it into* : C. J. Dennis.—2. See **sock in it.**

sock (a person) **one.** To hit him hard : from not later than 1915. Ex *sock*, v., 1 and 2.

sock-shop. The tuck-shop : Eton : mid-C. 19– 20. Ex *sock*, n., 4.

sockastic. Sarcastic : sol. : mid-C. 19–20.

sockdologer (1830), **-ager** (— 1848), rarely **-iger** (1842) ; occ. **sog-** (1869) or **slock-** (1838) or **slog-** (1862) ; also **stock-** (1864, H., 3rd ed.). Occ. **-ll-**. A very heavy blow ; a ' finisher ' : U.S., anglicised, to some extent, ca. 1870 ; ob. A fanciful, assonantal elaboration of *sock*, a blow (see **sock,** n., 3, and cf. v. 1), influenced by *doxology*, ' regarded as final ' (W.).—2. Hence, anything exceptional : U.S. (1869), partly anglicised ca. 1890 ; slightly ob. *Blackwood's Magazine*, Feb. 1894 ; ' The pleasant remembrance of the capture of a real sockdologer ' (large fish), O.E.D.

socker. A sloven, lout, simpleton, fool : coll. : 1772, Bridges, ' The rabble then began to swear, | What the old socker said was fair ' ; ob. Also *sockie* (ob.) and *sockhead*, †.—2. A heavy blow : low : from ca. 1870. Ex *sock*, v., 1.—3. Also *soccer*. Association football : from ca. 1890 : orig. Harrow School ; by 1903, gen. The O.E.D. records *socker* at 1891, *soccer* at 1895 ; in C. 20, usually *soccer*. By truncated *assoc.* + Oxford *-er*. Cf. *rugger*.—4. One who strikes hard : low : from not later than 1930. O.E.D. (Sup.) Ex *sock*, v., 1.

socket, burnt to the. Dying : late C. 17–18 : coll. >, ca. 1700, S.E. Ray.

socket-money. ' Money demanded and spent upon marriage ' B.E. : late C. 17–18. Perhaps ex *socket*, the female pudend.—2. Hence, ' money paid for a treat, by a married man caught in an intrigue,' Grose, 1st ed. : mid-C. 18–mid-19. Bridges, 1772. Cf. dial. *socket-brass*, hush-money. —3. Also, ' a whore's fee, or hire,' Grose, 1st ed. : late C. 18–mid-19.—4. Ex senses, 2, 3 : hush-money : from ca. 1860 ; ob. H., 3rd ed. Cf. :

socketer. A blackmailer : ca. 1860–1910. H., 5th ed. Ex *socket*, last sense.

socketing. A variant (ca. 1810–50) of *burning shame*, 2. ' Jon Bee '.

sockhead ; sockie. See **socker, 1.**

socks, hot. See **hot socks.**

socks, old. See **old socks.**

socks, pull up one's. To brace oneself for, to make an effort : from early 1920's. R. Blaker, 1922. Ex that significant preparation for action.

sod. A **sod**omist : low coll. : mid-C. 19–20 ; ob.—2. Hence, a pejorative, orig. and gen. violent : late C. 19–20. Often used in ignorance of its origin : cf. *bugger*.—3. A **sod**den damper : Australian : from ca. 1910. (Ion L. Idriess, *Lasseter's Last Ride*, 1931.) Prob. influenced by Scots *sod*, a bap.—4. At Charterhouse, it is, in C. 20, applied to a person, esp. another school-boy, doing anything dirty, e.g. spewing.

sodduk. (Soft) bread ; *Conway* cadets' : from before 1880. John Masefield, *The Conway*, 1933. Prob. a slurring of *soft tack*.

sodger. See **soger** and **soldier,** n., 1.

Sodgeries, the. The Military Exhibition, Chelsea Barracks, in : 1890 : London. Ex *sodger* on *Colinderies, Fisheries*, etc. Ware.

Sodom. London : literary coll. : C. 19. Ex *Sodom*, generic for any very corrupt place.—2. Wadham College, Oxford : from ca. 1870 ; very ob. H., 5th ed. Rhyming.

sods, odds and. See **odds and sods.**

soft. A weakling ; a very simple or a foolish person : dial. (— 1854) >, by 1860, coll. George Eliot, 1859 (O.E.D.). Cf. *softy*, q.v.—2. Banknotes (as opp. to coin) : c. (— 1823). Egan's Grose ; H., 1st ed. Also *soft-flimsy*, from ca. 1870. Cf. U.S. *soft*, adj. applied to paper money as early as ca. 1830.

soft, adj. Half-witted : coll. (and dial.) : 1835, Marryat, ' A good sort of chap enough, but rather soft in the upper-works ' ; adumbrated by Miss Burney in 1775. O.E.D. Ex *soft*, ' more or less foolish, silly or simple.'—2. (? hence). Foolishly benevolent or kind ; constantly helping others without thinking of one's own advantage or interests : coll. : 1890, ' Rolf Boldrewood ', ' He . . . did a soft thing in bringing those other chaps here,' O.E.D. Ex *soft*, compassionate.—3. Easy, idle, lazy : coll. : 1889, *The Daily News*, Oct. 12, ' People crowd into literature [*sic*], as into other " soft " professions, because it is genteel ' ; 1905, H. A. Vachell, ' You wanted a soft time of it during the summer term,' O.E.D. Ex *soft*, involving little effort or no work.—4. Broken in spirit : 1898, Sir G. Robertson (O.E.D.) : coll., Anglo-Indian >, by 1910, gen. Ex *soft*, physically weak, lacking in stamina.

soft, a bit of hard for a bit of. Copulation : low : mid-C. 19–20.

*****soft, do.** To utter counterfeit notes : c. : from ca. 1870. See **soft,** n., 2.

soft ?, hard (arse) or. Third class or first ? : low coll. : late C. 19–20.

soft ball. Lawn tennis : Royal Military Academy, Woolwich : late C. 19–20 coll.

soft down on. In love with : low coll. : from ca. 1870. Elaboration of *soft on*.

*****soft-flimsy.** See **soft,** n., 2.

soft horn. A donkey, lit. or fig. : coll. : from ca. 1860 ; ob. H., 3rd ed. Because an ass's ears, unlike horns, are soft.

soft is your horn. You've made a mistake : c.p. : ca. 1820–50. Bee.

soft number. An easy task or job : mostly military : from ca. 1910. F. & Gibbons. Perhaps ex music.

soft on or **upon.** In love with ; sentimentally amorous for : 1840 : S.E. >, ca. 1880, coll

'Rolf Boldrewood,' 1888, ' I . . . thought she was rather soft on Jim,' O.E.D.

soft-roed. Tender-hearted : non-aristocratic London coll. (— 1887) ; slightly ob. Baumann. Ex fish-roe.

soft sawder, n. See **sawder.**—2. V.t. and i. (gen. hyphenated) : to flatter : coll. : 1843, Haliburton ; Hickie's *Aristophanes*, 1853. O.E.D. Ex *soft sawder*, n. (see **sawder**). Cf. :

soft sawder to order. An elaboration of *soft sawder*, n. : 1883, *Entr' Acte*, April 7 ; ob.—2. Ware records the sense ' clothes made to order ' and implies existence ca. 1883–1900.

soft-sawderer. A flatterer : coll. : mid-C. 19–20. Ex *soft-sawder*. Cf. :

soft soap. Flattery ; ' blarney ' : U.S. (1830), anglicised ca. 1860. T. Hughes, 1861, ' He and I are great chums, and a little soft soap will go a long way with him.' Ex *soft soap*, potash soap, on *soft sawder*.

soft-soap, v. To flatter : U.S. (1840), anglicised ca. 1870. Ex the n.

soft tack. See **soft tommy.**

soft thing, a. A very obliging simpleton : coll. : mid-C. 19–20. Ex *soft*, adj., 1.—2. A pleasant, an easy, task ; an easy contest or win : coll. : from ca. 1890. Ex *soft*, adj., 3, q.v.

soft to, do the. To flatter, to ' blarney ' (a person) : coll. (— 1923). Manchon.

soft tommy. Bread, as opp. to biscuits : nautical coll. (— 1864). H., 3rd ed. ; 1878, W. S. Gilbert, ' I've treacle and toffee, and excellent coffee, | Soft tommy and succulent chops.' Also *soft tack* (H., 1859), which has its corresponding *hard tack*. See **tommy.**

softie ; properly **softy.** A silly, very simple, or weak-minded person : coll. and dial. : 1863, Mrs Gaskell, ' [Nancy] were but a softy after all.'

sog. A sovereign (coin) : schools' : late C. 19–20 ; very ob. Ex *sov*, q.v.

soger, sojer ; sodger. A soldier : coll. and dial. : C. 15–20.—2. If applied to a sailor, it constitutes a grave, disgracing pejorative, for it connotes shirking and malingering : nautical coll. (— 1840). R. H. Dana in *Before the Mast* ; cf. Clark Russell in *Sailor's Language*, 1883.—3. See **soldier,** n., 1. —4. Gen. *sodger* : a big cross made on an examination-paper to indicate a glaring error : Winchester (— 1839). Wrench. Cf. *percher*.—5. For *Sogeries*, see **Sodgeries.**

soger ; occ. **sodger** or **sojer.** To shirk and/or malinger ; to pretend to work : mainly nautical (— 1840) ; in C. 20, coll. Dana. Also *soldier*.

solar. Sola (topee) : orig. (— 1878) a sol. spelling. Yule & Burnell. Ex Hindustani *shola*.

solay, v. Error for *splay* (a fish) : C. 18–20 ; ob. O.E.D.

sold, ppl.adj. Tricked : see **sell,** v. Cf. :

sold again and got the money ! A costermonger's c.p. on having successfully ' done ' someone in a bargain : ca. 1850–80. H., 1st ed. Ex *sell*, v. Cf. :

sold like a bullock in Smithfield, ppl.adj. Badly cheated or duped : almost a c.p. : ca. 1810–50. Vaux. Cf. preceding entry.

sold out. Bankrupt : coll. (— 1859) ; ob. H., 1st ed. Cf. :

sold out, be. To have sold all one's stock (*of* some article) : coll. : late C. 19–20. Perhaps on the analogy of S.E. *be sold up*, to have had part or all of one's goods sold to pay one's creditors. Cf. preceding entry.

soldier. A red herring : from ca. 1810 : sailors' and seaports '. *Lex. Bal.*, 1811. Also *sodger, soger*. —2. A boiled lobster : ca. 1820–1910. Both ex red uniform.—3. An inferior seaman : nautical coll. : from ca. 1835 ; ob. Cf. *sojer*, n., 2.—4. A forest kangaroo : Australian coll. >, ca. 1920, S.E. : from the late 1890's. ' Rolf Boldrewood ' (O.E.D)—5. (Gen. **Soldier.**) ' The senior Royal Marine officer on board. *Young Soldier*, his subaltern ' : naval : late C. 19–20. Bowen.—6. An upright (often, in j., termed a ' runner ') of 9 inches by 3, gen. used as a support for ' shuttering ' : Public Works' (— 1935). They are usually placed at intervals, edge on to the shuttering : and thus they resemble a rank of soldiers.

soldier, v. See **sojer,** v. ; but this form began by being coll., and in C. 20 is S.E.—2. V.i., to clean one's equipment ; doing routine work or fatigues : military : 1885 (O.E.D.) : s. >, ca. 1915, coll.—3. V.t., to use temporarily (another man's horse) : Australian (— 1891) ; ob. *Century Dict.*

soldier, old. See **old soldier.**—2. An empty bottle : ca. 1880–1910. Cf. *dead marine*, q.v.—3. **old soldier, come the.** See **come the old soldier.**

soldier on. To persevere against peril and/or hardship : military coll. : esp. 1916–18. Often as a c.p. in form *soldier on, chum* (B. & P.).

soldier-walking. 'Any operations by bluejackets on land ' : naval : late C. 19–20. Bowen. Cf. *soldier*, n., 5.

Soldiers, the. Aldershot Football Club (' soccer ') : sporting coll. : C. 20.

soldiers !, oh. A proletarian exclamation : from ca. 1880 ; ob. by 1909, † by 1918. Ware.

soldier's bite. A big bite : coll. and dial. : C. 19–20.

soldier's bottle. A large bottle : coll. : late C. 17–early 19. B.E. ; Grose, 1st ed.

soldier's breeze. A variant, dating from the early 1890's, of *soldier's wind*, q.v. : coll. >, by 1910, S.E.

soldier's farewell, a. ' Go to bed ! ', with ribald additions and/or elaborations : military (— 1909). Ware. Cf. *sailor's farewell*, q.v.—2. Also (in G.W., and after) = ' Good-bye and bugger (*or* fuck) you ! ' M. Lincoln, *Oh ! Definitely*, 1933, ' " Good-bye . . . ! " he yelled . . . " Soldier's farewell ", he said amiably.'

soldier's friend. A rifle : military coll. : late C. 19–20. F. & Gibbons. Cf. the Ger. *soldier's bride*.—2. ' The metal polish used for cleaning brass buttons, etc.' : military coll. : C. 20. Ibid.

soldiers ?, I've shit 'em ! A c.p. ' expression of contempt for another unit (especially if slovenly) ' : military : from ca. 1912. B. & P. Contrast *scraped 'em off me putties.*

soldier's joy. Masturbation : low coll. : ca. 1850–1910.

*****soldier's mawnd.** A sham sore or wound in the left arm : c. : late C. 17–mid-18. B.E. Cf. *mason's mawnd*, q.v.—2. Hence, ' a pretended soldier, begging with a counterfeit wound, which he pretends to have received at some famous siege or battle,' Grose, 1st ed. : c. : mid-C. 18–early 19.

soldier's mast. A pole mast without sails, ' during the transition period from sail to steam in the Navy,' Frank C. Bowen : nautical coll. : mid-C. 19.

soldier's pomatum. A piece of tallow candle : late C. 18–mid-19. Grose, 2nd ed.

soldier's privilege. Complaining : G.W. military coll. See **grouse** ; see **sailor's pleasure**

soldier's supper. A drink of water and a smoke : coll. : 1893 (O.E.D.). Ware, 'Nothing at all—tea being the final meal of the day.' Cf. *subaltern's luncheon.*—2. As a c.p. (e.g. *a soldier's supper to you !*), 'piss off and go to bed ' : esp. in Glasgow (— 1934). Cf. *soldier's farewell.*

soldier's thigh. An empty pocket : dial. and s. : mid C. 19–20 ; ob. E.D.D.

soldier's wind. A fair wind either way, a beam wind : 1833, Marryat (O.E.D.) : nautical coll. >, ca 1890, j. Kingsley, Clark Russell.

sole-slogger. A shoemaker : lower classes' (— 1887) ; ob. Baumann recalls Shakespeare's 'surgeon to old shoes '.

[Solecisms have received more attention in these pages than in those of any other dictionary. It is, indeed, a curious fact that whereas catachrestic usages are almost adequately treated in the O.E.D. and in Webster, solecisms are not. Catachreses may be defined as solecisms of the literate : but why should the mistakes of the less literate be ignored ? The usual answer, that solecisms are obvious and catachreses are not so obvious, seems a trifle snobbish ; certainly it is unsatisfactory.]

solemnc(h)oly. Excessive seriousness : coll. : from ca. 1860. This blend of *solemn + melancholy* is an extension of the jocular S.E. adj. coined in America in 1772 (O.E.D. Sup.). A ludicrous perversion is *lemoncholy*, q.v.

solfa. A parish clerk : late C. 18–mid-19. Grose, 2nd ed. Ex intoning responses.

solid. (Of time) complete, entire : C. 18–20 : S.E. until ca. 1890, then coll. 'Rolf Boldrewood ', 1890, 'I walked him up and down . . . for a solid hour.' (O.E.D.)—2. Severe ; difficult : Australian (— 1916) and gen. coll. C. J. Dennis.—3. Adv., solidly : low coll. : mid-C. 19–20. As = severely : C. 20.

solitary. Solitary confinement : 1854, Dickens (O.E.D.) : prison s. >, by 1900, coll.—2. 'A whale cruising by himself, generally an outcast and savage bull ': nautical coll, : late C. 19–20. Bowen.

***sollomon.** See solomon.

Solly. The Marquess of Salisbury : comic papers': ca. 1880–1900. Baumann.

solo. A solitary walk (without a 'socius ', q.v.) : Winchester : from ca. 1870.

solo player. 'A miserable performer on any instrument, who always plays alone, because no one will stay in the room to hear him,' Grose, 1st ed. : jocular coll. of ca. 1780–1850 punning the lit. sense.

***solomon.** A late C. 17–early 19 variant of *salmon*, q.v.

solomon-gundy. A mid-C. 18–19 coll. form of *salmagundy*. Cf. *salmon-gundy.*

sols and obs. See ob and sol.

solus. An advertisement on a page containing no other advertisement : advertising coll. (from ca. 1926) verging on j.

some. Both as adverb of quantity and as an intensive adjective—equivalent respectively to *much*, or *very*, and *great*, *lovely*, etc.—*some* was originally, and still is, an Americanism that has contributed laudably to the gaiety of nations and enabled the English to take their pleasures less sadly. As an adjective, e.g. *some girl !*, it is a 20th century importation (rare before the G.W.) into England, but as an adverb, e.g. *going some*, it was known at least as early as 1890 in Britain. In America, the earliest examples are ' I hunt some and snake a little ', 1834, or in a slightly different

sense, 'He stammers some in his speech ', 1785 ; and ' She's some woman now, that is a fact ', 1848. Nevertheless, the Americans prob. adopted both the adj. and the adv. from English dial. : see E.D.D. Cf. the French, ' Ca, c'est quelque chose ' and the next entry. (O.E.D. and Supplement ; Ware ; Thornton ; Weekley ; Fowler.)

some, and then. And many, or much, in addition : U.S. (ca. 1913), anglicised by 1919. O.E.D. (Sup.). Prob. a mere elaboration of the Scots *and some*, and much more so, as in Ross's pastoral poem, *Helenore*, 1768, and as in the ' She's as bonny as you, and some ' of lexicographer Jamieson (E.D.D.).

some hopes ! It is *most* unlikely : a c.p. dating from ca. 1905. B. & P. Cf. *what hopes !*

some say ' Good old sergeant ! ' A c.p. spoken or shouted by privates within the sergeant's hearing ; gen. one added (often affectionately), *others say* 'F**k *the* (*old*) *sergeant !* ' : military : from ca. 1890. B. & P.

some when, adv. Some time : Society c.p. : ca. 1860–70. Ware.

something, adv. with adjj. An intensive, esp. with *cruel* (*s. cruel* = cruel or cruelly) : dial. and low, in C. 20 sol., coll. : mid-C. 19–20. E.g. ''E suffered something cruel '—or, frequently, 'something think cruel '; 'the heat was something frightful '.—2. As in 'the something something ' (the bloody bastard), 'the something horse ' (the bloody horse) : a coll. euphemism : mid-C. 19–20 ; in C. 20 use, gen. considered S.E.—3. Hence as v. in past ppl., *somethinged* = damned, etc. : 1859 (O.E.D.).

something damp. See damp.

something good. A good racing tip : s. (from ca. 1890) >, ca. 1920, coll.—2. Hence, a profitable affair, a safe but not generally known investment, venture, etc. : coll. : C. 20. E.g. 'I'm on something good.'

something in the City. See City, something in the.

something short. See short, something.

something the cat's brought in. See like something.

something to hang things on. An infantryman's jocular coll. description of himself : G.W. F. & Gibbons, 'In allusion to the paraphernalia of his heavy marching order kit.'

somethinged. See something, 3.

somethink, n. and adv. Something : sol. : C. 19–20 ; mid-C. 19–20. Cf. *something*, and see -ink.

somewhere in France was, in 1914–18, often put to jocular uses or to senseless variations and thus > a c.p. B. & P., 'The heading of most Western-Front soldiers' letters home.'

somewheres. Somewhere ; approximately : dial. and low coll. : mid-C. 19–20. 'It's somewheres along of fifty quid,' F. & H. ; R. L. Stevenson, 1883, 'I know you've got that ship safe somewheres,' O.E.D. Cf. the frequent sol. *anywheres* and the rare *nowheres*.

son. In such phrases as *son of Apollo*, a scholar (late C. 17–mid-19), *son of Mars*, a soldier (C. 16–19), *son of Mercury*, a wit (id.), *son of parchment* (id. : B.E., by a slip, has *parclement*), *son of prattlement*, a barrister (C. 18–mid-19), and *son of Venus*, a wencher (late C. 17–mid-19) are—except for *son of Mars*, perhaps always S.E.—coll. verging on, and in C. 19 being, S.E. : *prattlement* is in *A New Canting Dict.*, 1725 ; the first, third, fourth, and sixth in B.E.—2.

son of wax, a cobbler, C. 19, is coll.—3. See *son of a* . . .

son, every mother's. See **mother's son, every.**

son of a bachelor. A bastard : coll. bordering on S.E. : late C. 17–20 ; ob. Ray.

son of a bitch or **whore.** (Lit., a bastard, hence) a pejorative for a man, a fellow : coll. : C. 18–20 : the former in *The Triumph of Wit*, 1712, the latter, ca. 1703, in ' Facetious ' Tom Brown.

[**son of a dunghill** and **son of a shoemaker**, pejorative : S.E., not coll.]

son of a gun. ' A soldier's bastard ', Bee, 1823 ; but, as gen. pejorative (increasingly less offensive), it dates from early C. 18 : see **gun, son of a.**

son of a sea-cook. See **sea-cook.**

son of a sow or **sow-gelder.** A pejorative for a man, a fellow : coll. verging on S.E. : C. 17–mid-19. Chapman has *sow-gelder*.

son of the white hen. A lucky person (properly male) : C. 17–18 : coll. Jonson, 1630 ; *Poor Robin's Almanack*, Feb., 1764. Ex Juvenal's *gallinae filius albae*. Apperson.

song about, nothing to make a. Very unimportant : coll. : mid-C. 19–20.

song do not agree, his morning and evening. He soon tells another story for one told even recently : late C. 18–19 : coll. >, ca. 1830, S.E. Grose, 2nd ed. An elaboration of *change one's*, or *sing another*, *song*.

sonkey. A lout : c. or perhaps only low (—1887). Baumann. Cf. *sawney* and *sukey* for both form and sense.

sonnie ; properly **sonny.** A coll. term of address to a boy or to a man younger than oneself, though not if the addressee is old or middle-aged : O.E.D. records at 1870, but prob. existing a decade earlier. In Australia, the *-on-* is occ. pronounced as in the preposition, as Morris remarked, citing A. B. Paterson's rhyme of *sonny* with *Johnnie*.

*sonny. To catch sight of, to see, to notice : c. : 1845, in ' *No. 747* ' ; app. † by 1900. Cf. *granny*, to understand.

sooer. See **soor.—sook(e)y.** See **sukey, 4.**

sool. To set (a dog) on : Australian coll. : from ca. 1890. Morris. Also *sool on* : C. 20. Prob. ex dial. *sowl*, to handle roughly, or *sowl into*, to attack fiercely (E.D.D.).—2. Hence (as of a dog a cat), to worry : id. : 1896, Mrs Parker, ' "Sool 'em, sool 'em " . . . the signal for the dogs to come out.'

soon run dry. An occ. military c.p. (1915–18) on rum-jars, on which were stamped the initials *S.R.D.* (service rum diluted). B. & P.

sooner. A shirker : naval (— 1935). Ex *sooner dog*, one that would sooner feed than fight : from before 1914.

sooner, adv. Better, as in ' You had sooner go,' you had better go, you would do well to go : lower classes' coll. (— 1923). Manchon. Ex S.E. *sooner*, ' more readily as a matter of choice ' (O.E.D.).

sooner dog. See **sooner, n.**

soonish. Rather soon ; quite soon ; a little too soon : 1890 (E.D.D.) : coll. and dial.

soop. An occ. variant (from ca. 1910 ; e.g. in John G. Brandon, *The One-Minute Murder*, 1934) of :

sooper. A variant (— 1909) of *super*, n., 1–5. Ware.

soor ; occ. **sooer.** An abusive term : Anglo-Indian (— 1864) and Regular Army's. Ex Hindustani for a pig. H., 3rd ed.

soor dook. See **sour dook.**

Soos. Shares in the Minneapolis, St Paul, & Sault Ste Marie Railroad : Stock Exchange coll. (— 1895), *Sault* being pronounced *soo*. A. J. Wilson's glossary.

soot. A foolish variant spelling of *suit* : mid-C. 19–20.

soot-bag. A reticule : c. (— 1839) >, by late 1850's, low s. Brandon ; H., 1st ed.

so'p. Esp. in *so'p me bob !*, a variant of *s'elp* . . ., q.v. : Cockney : 1898, W. Pett Ridge.

sop. A simpleton ; a milk-sop : from ca. 1620 : S.E. until ca. 1850, then coll. ; ob. H., 1st ed.

soph, Soph. A sophister : coll. : mid-C. 17–20 : mainly Cambridge ; ob. at Oxford by 1720, † by 1750. O.E.D. records at 1661 ; D'Urfey, 1719, ' I am a jolly soph.' Partly ex *sophomore*, which since C. 18 is solely U.S. Cf. *Harry Soph.*

sopped through. Sopping-wet : lower classes' coll. (— 1887). Baumann.

soppy. Foolishly sentimental, ' soft ' · coll. : 1919. Manchon. (Cf. *wet.*) Lit., wet with sentiment.—2. Hence, *be soppy on*, to be foolishly fond of (a person) : coll. : from ca. 1924.

soppy boat. Gen. pl. ' Nickname for Folkestone fishing craft ' : nautical : mid-C. 19–early 20. Bowen. Ex their wetness.

Sopwith pup. A Sopwith aeroplane : Air Force : 1914–18. B. & P.

sore. Incorrect for *sire*, an † variant of *sir*, n. O.E.D.

sore, get. ' To become aggrieved,' C. J. Dennis : coll. (esp. Australian and U.S.) : late C. 19–20.

sore finger, dressed up like a. Too elaborately dressed : Australian : from ca. 1912.

sore fist. A bad workman : tailors' : from ca. 1870 ; ob. ? ex *write a poor hand*, to sew badly, likewise tailorese.

sore-head. A curmudgeon : Australian : late C. 19–20. C. J. Dennis.

sore leg. A German sausage : military : ca. 1880–1915.—2. A plum pudding : low London : from ca. 1880 ; ob. Prob. ex *spotted dog*.

sorra. Dial. and, to some extent, coll. form of *sorrow* : C. 19–20.

sorrow ! Sorry ! : late C. 19–20 : orig. and mainly jocular, and mostly Society. E.g., F. Morton Howard in *The Humorist*, Feb. 3, 1934, ' Oh, sorrow, uncle ! Sorrow—sorrow ! ' Ex *sorrow* as an imprecation (cf. *sorrow on* . . . *!*). The O.E.D.'s C. 15 instance of *sorrow = sorry* is inoperative ; this use was prob. rare.

sorrowful tale. Three months in gaol : rhyming s. (— 1859) ; ob. H., 1st ed.

sorry. ' Mate, pal, chum. Usually in vocative and chiefly among Yorkshire and Lancashire troops ' : military in G.W. and after (as, doubtless, before). From dial. ; perhaps ultimately ex *sirrah*. B. & P.

sorry ! I am sorry ! : C. 19–20 : coll. >, by 1850, S.E.

sort, a bad or **a good.** A bad, a good, fellow or girl, woman : coll. : from ca. 1880. In C. 20, *bad sort* is rare except as *not a bad sort*. J. Sturgis, 1882, ' They cursed and said that Dick was a good sort ', O.E.D. Cf. Fr. *espèce (de)*.

sort !, that's your. A term of approbation, gen. of a specific action, method, occ. thing : 1792, Holcroft ; H., 3rd ed. Ob. by 1910, virtually † by 1935. By ellipsis.

sort of ; a sort of. In a way ; to some extent ; somehow ; one might say : dial (— 1790) >, ca

1830, coll. : *a sort of*, ob. by 1890, † by 1930 ; *sort of*, app. not before ca. 1830. Thackeray, 1859, ' " You were hurt by the betting just now ? " "Well ", replied the lad, "I am sort of hurt ".' Orig. and mainly U.S. is *sorter* (1846), orig. *a sorter* (as in Marryat's *American Diary*, 1839) ; cf. Thornton, *passim*. See also kind of, kinder.—2. Hence, merely modificatory, deprecatory, or tautological : C. 20. E.g. Denis Mackail, *Summer Leaves*, 1934, ' Wissingfield's our sort of village ', i.e. (simply) our village.

sort of, these. E.g. 'These sort of cases ' for ' this sort of case ', i.e. ' such cases ' : mid-C. 16–20 : S.E. >, by 1887, somewhat catachrestic >, by 1920, coll. Baumann. In ' These sort of things are done by conjurers ' (well-known novelist) there is a confusion between ' This sort of thing is done . . .' and ' These sorts of things are done . . .'

sort-out. A fight, a mellay : workers' (— 1935). Ex what the combatants do after the fight.

sorter. See sort of. Occ. *sorter kinder* : C. 20.

sorts, all. Coll. >, in late C. 19, idiomatic S.E. is the phrase as used in these two examples from the O.E.D. : 1794, Mrs Radcliffe, ' There they were, all drinking Tuscany wine and all sorts ' ; 1839, Hood, ' There's a shop of all sorts, that sells everything.'

sorts, of. Inferior ; unsatisfactory : coll. : C. 20. E.g. ' He's certainly a writer—of *sorts*.' Ex the ob. *of sorts*, of various kinds.

sorts, out of. Dispirited ; slightly unwell : from ca. 1620 : S.E. until mid-C. 19, then coll. In C. 19, it received an unconventional impetus from printers.

sorty. Similar : coll. : 1885 ; ob.—2. Mixed : coll. : 1889, ' A " sorty " team.' (Both O.E.D.)

so's. See so is.

soss(-)brangle. A slatternly wench : low coll. and dial. : late C. 17–19. Grose, 2nd ed. ; E.D.D. Cf. *soss*, a slut (in mid-C. 19–20, dial.).

sosseled, sossiled ; sossled. See sozzled.

sossidge is frequent but unnecessary, for *sausage* should, in ordinary dialogue anyway, be pronounced precisely thus. Ware has *sossidge-slump*, decline in popularity of Germans consequent on the Kaiser's telegram to Kruger in 1896 : political : 1896–7.

sot, v. Sat : sol., esp. among Cockneys : C. 19–20. Mayhew, 1861.

sot-weed. Tobacco : coll. : C. 18–early 19. T. Brown, 1702 ; Grose.

sou or souse, not a. Not a penny ; penniless : coll. : *not a sou* from ca. 1820 (Byron) ; *not a souse*, ca. 1675–1820, as in D'Urfey, 1676. Ex the French coin, orig. of considerably higher value than 5 centimes. In C. 19 and occ. (though ob.) in C. 20, *not a sous* : see sous.

sou oneself. To wound oneself deliberately : military : 1917–18. Ex *s.i.w.* (self-inflicted wound) pronounced as one word.

souji-mouji. ' Any cleansing composition ' (Merchant Service coll., C. 20) ; even canvas and sand used for cleansing (naval coll., C. 20). Properly ' one special preparation '—a trade name. Bowen. —2. Hence, fig., from ca. 1905, as in ' " There are no sailors to-day ", says [Conrad], " only Suji-Muji men " . . . Mere washers of paint. Deckhands on modern ships wash and chip paint, morning, noon and night,' James Hanley in *The Spectator*, Jan. 26, 1934.

soul, be a. To be a drunkard, esp. on brandy : coll. or s. : late C. 17–mid-18. B.E. ' *He is a*

Soul, or loves Brandy ' Ex *soul*, a person, + Fr. *soûl*, tipsy (as in Mathurin Régnier, d. 1613). Cf. *soul in soak*, q.v.

soul !, bless my ; 'pon my, etc. A mild asseveration : coll. and dial. : the former, C. 19–20 ; the latter, C. 15–20, but S.E. till C. 19.

soul, have no. To lack sensibility or gen. decency or emotional force : coll. : 1704, Swift (O.E.D. Sup.).

soul above, have a. To care not about, be indifferent or indifferently superior to (something) : coll. : 1899, G. B. Burgin (O.E.D. Sup.).

soul-and-body lashing. ' Under sail, a piece of spun yarn tied round the waist and between the legs to prevent a man's oilskins blowing over his head when aloft ' : nautical : late C. 19–20. Bowen. Because a matter of life and death.

soul-case. The body : late C. 18–20 ; ob. by 1900. Grose, 3rd ed.

soul-doctor, -driver. A clergyman : resp. late C. 18–mid-19, late C. 17–early 19. B.E. ; Grose, 1st ed. (both). On *soul-chaplain* or *-priest*. (In U.S., ca. 1818–49, an Abolitionists' name for an overseer of slaves. Thornton.)

soul-faker. A member of the Salvation Army : lower classes' : 1883–ca. 85. Ware, ' Before their value was recognised.'

soul in soak. Drunk : nautical : ca. 1820–1910. Egan's Grose. Lit., soaking drunk : see soul, be a, and soak.

soul-smiter. A sensational novel (of the sentimental sort) : book-world coll. (— 1923) ; ob. Manchon. The 1930's prefer to speak of ' a sloppy thriller '.

souldier's mawnd. B.E.'s spelling of *soldier's mawnd*, q.v.

*sound. Gen. *sound a cly*, to ' try ' a pocket : c. : C. 19. *Lex. Bal.*—2. V.i., to knock or ring to see if the occupants of a house to be robbed are at home : c. (— 1933). Charles E. Leach, *On Top of the Underworld*. Cf. *drum*, v.

sound as a bell, roach, trout. Perfectly sound or healthy : coll. bordering on S.E. : resp. 1576 (1599, Shakespeare) ; 1655, T. Muffett, but in late C. 19–20, † except in dial ; from late C. 13, also in Skelton, but in C. 19 mainly, and in C. 20 only, dial. (Dial., by the way, has also, from mid-C. 19, *sound as an acorn*.) Apperson.

sound egg. A very ' decent ' fellow : C. 20. Denis Mackail, in *The Strand Magazine*, April, 1934, ' Another and infinitely superior sex still remained, full of stout fellows, sound eggs, and great guys.'

sound on, be. To have orthodox or well-grounded views concerning : coll. : orig. (1856) U.S., anglicised ca. 1890.—2. Hence, to be both intelligent on and reliable in (a given subject) : coll. : from ca. 1900. E.g. ' He's very sound on the little-known subject of psychopaedics.'

sounder. Catachrestic when, in C. 18, used of a wild boar's lair and when, in C. 19–20, applied to a boar one or two years old, or when, as by Grose in 1785, it is used, in the pl. form !, for a herd of any swine. Properly, *sounder* is a noun of assembly for a herd of wild swine.

soup. (Collective from 1856, simple from ca 1890.) Briefs, a brief, for prosecutions given to junior members of the Bar (esp. at Quarter Sessions) by the Clerk of the Peace or Arraigns, to defend such poor prisoners as have no choice, at two guineas a time : legal s. >, ca. 1910, coll. *The Law Times*, 1856, ' But will soup so ladled out . . . support a barrister in the criminal courts ? '—2. Hence (both collective and simple), the fee paid for such briefs or such a brief : 1889, B. C. Robinson : s. >, ca. 1910, coll. O.E.D.—3. Bad ink : printers' : from ca. 1870. Ex its thickness or intrusive clots.—4. A fog : coll. : C. 20 ; ob. except in *pea-souper*.—5. Melted plate : c. : late C. 19–20 ; ob. If of silver, also *white soup*.—6. Nitro-glycerin : c. (— 1905). Prob. orig. U.S. In New Zealand c. (— 1932), gelignite.—7. ' Any material injected into a horse with a view to changing its speed or temperament,' Webster, 1911 : low s., orig. and mainly U.S. (—8. Rare, though prob. to be considered coll., is *soup*, a picnic at which ' a great pot of soup is the principal feature,' *Century Dict.* : from ca. 1890 ; ob.)—9. See ' Moving-Picture Slang ', § 6.

soup, in the. In a difficulty ; in trouble : coll. : orig. U.S. (1889), anglicised ca. 1895. *The Pall Mall Gazette*, Nov., 1898, ' Of course he knows we're in the soup—beastly ill luck,' O.E.D.

*****soup, white.** See soup, 5.

*****soup-shop.** A house (see fence, n.) for the disposal of stolen plate : c. : 1854 (O.E.D.). Punning the S.E. sense. F. & H., ' Melting-pots are kept going, no money passing from fence to thief until identification is impossible.'

*****souper.** A ' super ', i.e. a watch : c. : mid-C. 19–20 ; ob. ' Ducange Anglicus ' ; H., 1st ed. See super, 6.—2. A cadger of soup-tickets : coll. : from ca. 1875. Ex *souper*, a Roman Catholic converted to Protestantism by free soup or other charity.—3. See pea-souper.

soupy. Vomitingly drunk : low (— 1909). Ware.

*****sour.** Base silver money, gen. made of pewter : c · 1883, J. Greenwood. Cf. :

*****sour, plant the.** To utter base silver coin : c. : from ca. 1833. See sour.

sour ale (dial. only, **milk**) **in summer, mend like.** To get worse : (dial. and) coll. : late C. 17–early19 ; extant in dial. E.D.D.

sour apple-tree, be tied to the. To be married to a bad-tempered husband : semi-proverbial coll. : late C. 17–18. Ray ; Bailey. (Apperson.) Via *crab-apple*.

sour cudgel, a. A severe beating : coll. : C. 17. Withals, 1608.

*****sour-dook ;** Scottish **soor dook.** Buttermilk : c. (— 1932). T. B. G. Mackenzie in *The Fortnightly Review*, March, 1932. Adopted from Scots.

sour on. To form a distaste or dislike to : U.S. (1862), anglicised as a coll. ca. 1895. *The Daily News*, Nov. 13, 1900, ' Dan soured on Castlereagh boys . . . forthwith,' O.E.D. Ex *be sour towards*.

*****sour-planter.** An utterer of base silver coin : c. : from ca. 1885. Ex *sour, plant the*. Cf. *shover*, q.v., and see snide, n. and adj.

*****sours, swallow the.** To conceal counterfeit money : c. (— 1887). Baumann.

sous. As a sou in *not a sous*, it is a C. 19–20 coll. that, though ob. by 1880, is not quite † by 1937. W. quotes Barham, ' Not a sous had he got, not a guinea or note ' and *The Daily Chronicle*, May 15, 1918, ' He had not given a sous since the war began.'

souse. A getting drunk : from late 1920's. (O.E.D. Sup.)

souse. To drink to intoxication : from ca. 1920. (O.E.D. Sup.) Ex *souse*, to drench.

souse, not a. See sou, not a, and cf. *sous*.

souse, sell. To be sullen, surly ; to frown : C. 17 coll. Cotgrave.

souse-crown. A fool : coll. : late C. 17–early 19. B.E., Grose. Ex *souse*, a thump

soused. Tipsy : coll. : mid-C. 19–20. Ex *soused*, soaked in liquor. Cf. *sozzled*.

soush. A bouse : back s. (— 1859). H., 1st ed. Additional *s*, euphonic.

south, put down. Lit., to put into one's pocket ; hence, to put away safely, to bank, not to spend : late C. 19–20. Cf. *trouser*, q.v., and :

south, dip. To put one's hand in one's pocket for money, esp. if it is running low : New Zealanders' : C. 20.

[**South-Easter.** Itself S.E., it has three coll. synonyms : see table-cloth.]

south jeopardy. The terrors of insolvency : Oxford University : ca. 1820–40. Egan's Grose, 1823. Ex *jeopardy*, danger,+some topical allusion.

south-paw ; occ. **southpaw.** A left-handed boxer : pugilistic : U.S., anglicised in : 1934, *The Daily Telegraph*, Sept. 21, concerning Freddie Miller, ' He is, in boxing parlance, a " southpaw ".' Ex U.S. baseball s. (— 1918).

*****south sea or S— S—.** Any strong distilled liquor : c. of ca. 1720–50. *A New Canting Dict.* (1725), where also *south-sea mountain*, gin : c. of ca. 1721–1830 (also Grose, 1st ed., where confusingly printed as ' SOUTH SEA, mountain, gin '). Prob. ex the South Sea Bubble (1720).

South Spainer. ' A North Country ship in the Spanish trade ' ; nautical coll. : late C. 19–20. Bowen.

southerly buster. See buster, 6.—**southpaw.** See south-paw.

Souths. Shares in the London & South-Western Railway : Stock Exchange coll. (— 1895) ; † by 1930. (A. J. Wilson's glossary.)

souvenir. (Gen. pl.) A shell : military : 1915 ; ob. (G. H. McKnight, *English Words*, 1923.)

souvenir, v. To take illicitly : military : 1915 ; ob. B. & P. Ex *s.*, to pick up as a souvenir. (Cf. the jocular S.E. senses in the O.E.D. Sup.)

sov. A sovereign : coll. : 1850, *The New Monthly Magazine*, ' As to the purse, there weren't above three or four sovs in it.' Also *half-sov.* (O.E.D.)

sovereign, for a. Assuredly ; ' I'd bet on it ' : coll. (— 1923). Manchon.

sovereign's not in it, a. A nautical c.p. (— 1909) applied to a person with jaundice. Ex the sufferer's dark yellow. Ware.

Sovereign's parade, the. ' The quarterdeck [officers'] of a man-of-war in ' C. 18–early 19 : naval. Bowen.

sow, as drunk as a. A C. 19–20 (ob.) variant of *David's sow . . .*, q.v.

sow-belly. Salt pork : naval and military : from ca. 1870 ; ob. In Canada, any pork.

sow by the ear, get the right, wrong. See ear, get the . . .

sow in or on the arse, grease a fat. See grease a fat . . .

sow potatoes (or **scarlet-runners**, etc.) **on his neck, you could or might.** A lower classes' c.p. (— 1887 ; ob.) applied to a man with a dirty neck. Baumann.

sowar. An Indian cavalryman : Regular Army coll. : late C. 19–20. B. & P. By the extension of a Hindustani word. Opp. *Sepoy*, q.v.

sowcar. A Regular Army term of abuse : late C. 19–20. Ex Hindustani for a miser.

*****sowr.** To beat severely : c. : ca. 1720–50. *A New Canting Dict.*, 1725. ? = *sour*.

sow's baby. A sucking pig : late C. 17–20. B.E. ; Grose, 1st ed.—2. Sixpence : c. (— 1859). H., 1st ed. Because smaller than a *hog* (a shilling).

sow's ear, come sailing in a. A coll. of ca. 1670–1770 (Ray, Fuller). Apperson does not explain the phrase ; ? = to prosper.

sozzled ; occ. (rare after ca. 1920) **sossled** ; rarely **sosseled** (virtually † in C. 20). Tipsy : late C. 19–20. 'Pomes' Marshall, 1897, 'She was thick in the clear, | Fairly sossled on beer' ; Norah James in *Sleeveless Errand*, 1929 (*sozzled*). Prob. ex dial. *sozzle*, to mix in a sloppy manner (O.E.D., E.D.D.) : cf. dial. *sozzly*, sloppy, wet, and, more significantly, U.S. *sozzle*, to render moist (Thornton).

spaces, the wide open ; occ. the vast open spaces, This once serious phrase has, since ca. 1925, >, for the irreverent, something of a derisory c.p. (Cf. Collinson, p. 89.)

spad. A type of single-seater biplane : Air Force coll. : 1916–18. F. & Gibbons. Ex the initials of the Société pour Aviation et ses Dérivés.

spade. A Negro : low : from ca. 1920. Ex the colour of the card-suit.

spadge. To walk : Christ's Hospital : ca. 1820–80. ? origin. Whence *spadge*, an affected or mincing manner of walking : ibid. : from ca. 1880.

spadger. A sparrow : dial. (recorded, 1862, as *spadger-pie*) >, ca. 1880, coll. (orig. provincial). Occ. adj. By dial. corruption rather than fanciful change.

spalme. An † incorrect form of *psalm*, as *spalter* of *psalter*. O.E.D.

spalpeen. A low fellow ; a mean one ; a scamp or rascal : Anglo-Irish coll. >, ca. 1905, S.E. : 1815, Maria Edgeworth, 'The spalpeen ! turned into a buckeen, that would be a squireen,—but can't,' neatly illustrative of the Celtic diminutive suffix -*een* (properly, *in*) ; the radical is of uncertain meaning. The imm. source is S.E. *spalpeen*, a casual farm labourer.—2. Hence, a youngster, esp. a boy : coll. : 1891. Bram Stoker (O.E.D.) ; by 1920, virtually S.E.

spandau or **S—.** Generic for the latrines at Ruhleben internment camp, 1914–18. Ex the 'mushroom' munition-town of Spandau.

spang. Entirely ; exactly ; fair (e.g. in the centre) ; straight and with impetus : coll. : C. 20, mostly Colonial. Ex U.S. *right spang* (1843), wholly, exactly, fair (e.g. in the centre), ex *spang*, irresistibly or with an impetus, a spring, a smack, itself ex Scottish and Northern *spang*, to leap, bound. (Thornton ; E.D.D.)

spange, adj. and, occ., adv. New ; dressy, smart : R.M.A., Woolwich : from ca. 1880. 'A spange uniform,' a new one ; 'You look spange enough.' F. & H. Perhaps ex Northern dial. *spanged*, variegated.

*spangle. A seven-shilling piece : c. (— 1811) ; † by 1903. *Lex. Bal.* ; Egan's Grose. Ex its brightness.—2. A sovereign : theatrical : ca. 1860–1905. Ware.

spangle-guts, -shaker. A harlequin : theatrical : from ca. 1870. Ex spangled costume.

Spaniard. Gen. pl. 'Brighton fishing boats, from a colony of Spanish fishermen in that town' (Bowen) : nautical : C. 19.

Spanish (or **s.**) : gen. **the S.** Money ; esp. ready money, and again esp., in coin : from ca. 1786 ; ob. Grose, 2nd ed. ; Barham, 1837, 'Bar its synonyms Spanish, blunt, stumpy and rowdy.' Elliptical for *Spanish coin* or *gold*.

Spanish, adj. As a pejorative, common in coll. and s. ca. 1570–1750 and by no means rare until well on into C. 19. Ex commercial and naval rivalry (cf. *Dutch*, q.v.). See ensuing terms and, esp., 'Offensive Nationality' in my *Words !*

Spanish, walk. See **chalks, walk one's.**

Spanish coin. 'Fair words, and compliments,' Grose, 1st ed. : ca. 1780–1850. Ultimately ex Spanish courtesy derided ; imm. ex *Spanish money*.

Spanish fag(g)ot. The sun : 1785, Grose ; † by 1850. Ex heretic-burnings.

Spanish gout, needle, pox. Syphilis : coll. : resp. late C. 17–early 19 (B.E. ; Grose, 3rd ed.) ; early C. 19 ; C. 17–early 19. *French*, *Italian*, similarly used.

Spanish mare, ride the. To sit astride a beam, guys loosed, sea rough, as a punishment : nautical : ca. 1840–80. F. & H.

Spanish money. 'Fair Words and Compliments,' B.E. : coll. : late C. 17–18. Cf. *S. coin.*

Spanish padlock. 'A kind of girdle contrived by jealous husbands of that nation, to secure the chastity of their wives,' Grose, 2nd ed. : ca. 1786–1850.

Spanish pike. A needle : coll. : 1624, Ford,' A French Gentleman that trayls a Spanish pike, a Tailor ' ; † by 1700.

Spanish plague. Building : dial. and coll. : late C. 17–mid-18. Ray.

Spanish pox. See **Spanish gout.**

Spanish trumpeter ; also **King of Spain's trumpeter.** An ass braying : ca. 1780–1850. Grose, 1st ed. The clue is *Don Key.*

Spanish worm. A nail met in a board while sawing : carpenters' coll. (— 1785) ; † by 1860. Grose, 1st ed. Ex shape.

spank. A resounding blow, esp. with the open hand : coll. and dial. : from ca. 1780. Grose, 1st ed. ; in cricket, 1873 (Lewis). Ex *spank*, v., 1.—2. Hence, the sound so caused : coll. and dial. : 1833, H. Scott (O.E.D.).—3. A robbery effected by breaking a window-pane : c. of ca. 1810–50. Vaux. See **spank,** v., 4.—4. See **spanks.**

spank, v. To smack, slap, with the open hand : coll. (— 1727, N. Bailey) and dial. Echoic (cf. *spang*).—2. Hence, to crack (a whip) : coll. (rare and ob.) : 1834, M. Scott (O.E.D.).—3. To bring down, insert, slappingly : coll. and dial., mainly the latter : 1880, Tennyson, ' 'An 'e spanks 'is 'and into mine.'—4. To rob (a place) by breaking a window-pane (*spanking a glaze* is the c. term) : c. (— 1812). Vaux. Cf. *spank*, n., 3.—5. V.i., to fall, drop, with a smack : coll. : 1800, Hurdis, ' The sullen shower . . . on the . . . pavement spanks,' O.E.D. ; slightly ob.—6. V.i., of a boat pounding the water as it sails along : coll. (— 1891).—[The next group derives ultimately ex *spank*, to slap, to make a spanking sound, etc., influenced by dial. *spang* (see **spang** above).]—7. To move quickly and briskly ; to ride, drive, smartly or stylishly at a smart trot or a graceful canter : dial. (— 1807) >, by 1811, coll. *Lex. Bal.* ; Thackeray, 1860, 'A gentleman in a natty gig, with a high-trotting horse, came spanking towards us.' Frequently with *along* (first, 1825, in dial.) ; and esp. of a ship bowling along.—8. Hence, v.t., to drive (horses) with stylish speed : coll. : 1825, Westmacott (O.E.D.) ; 1840, Thackeray, ' How knowingly did he spank the horses along.' Slightly ob.

spank, adv. With a smack : coll. : 1810 (O.E.D.) ; rare, ob. Ex *spank*, v., 5.

*spank, upon the. By employing spank (n., 3): c.: C. 19. Vaux.

*spank a (or the) glaze. See glaze, spank a, and cf. spank, v., 4.

spanker. A gold coin; gen. in pl. as = ready money, coin: prob. c. (1663, Cowley) >, ca. 1730, s.; † by 1830. Grose, 1st ed. Prob. ex † dial. spank, to sparkle. Cf. spanks, q.v.—2. Any thing or person unusually fine, large, or excellent: coll. and dial.: 1751, Smollett (concerning 'a buxom wench'), ''Sblood, . . . to turn me adrift in the dark with such a spanker.' Ex spanking, adj., 1, q.v.—3. Hence, a resounding blow or slap: coll.: 1772, Bridges; Meredith, 1894, 'A spanker on the nob,' O.E.D.; in cricket, 1877 (Lewis).—4. A horse that travels with stylish speed: coll. and dial.: 1814, Scott (E.D.D.). Ex spank, to trot (etc.) smartly.

spanking. A (good) beating, esp. with the open hand: coll. and dial.: mid-C. 19-20. H., 1st ed. Ex spank, v., 1.

spanking, ppl.adj. Very large, fine, smart, showy; excellent: coll. and dial.: from early Restoration days. Fanshawe, ca. 1666; Bridges, 1772, 'A table . . . a spanking dish.' Esp. of girls (— 1707): cf. spanker, 2, q.v.—2. Hence, though influenced by the v. of motion, (of a horse) rapidly and smartly moving: coll. and dial.: 1738 (O.E.D.).—3. Hence, (of persons) dashing: coll.: C. 19-20; ob.—4. (Of a breeze) brisk: coll.: mid -C. 19-20.—5. (Of pace) rapid; esp. smartly and vigorously rapid: coll.: 1857, T. Hughes, 'The wheelers in a spanking trot, and leaders cantering,' O.E.D.

spanking, adv. Very: coll. (— 1887). Baumann, 'A spanking fine dinner.' Ex dial.

spankingly. Rapidly; esp. with smart rapidity: coll.: C. 19-20.

*spanks. Coin (gold or silver): c.: ca. 1720-1840. A New Canting Dict., 1725. Ex spanker, 1.

spanky. Smart; showily smart: from ca. 1870; slightly ob. Ex spanking, adj., 1.

spar. A dispute: coll.: 1836 (O.E.D.). Ex spar, a boxing-match.

sparagrass. See sparrow(-)grass.

Sparagras, the. That express freight train which 'takes Asparagus during the Season from Worcester to Crewe': railwaymen's: from ca. 1905. The Daily Telegraph, Aug. 15, 1936. Cf. the Spud.

spare, adj. Idle; loafing: low: from ca. 1919. James Curtis, The Gilt Kid, 1936. Ex:

spare, look. 'To be idle: not engaged on any particular job': military coll.: from 1915. F. & Gibbons. Cf. dial. spare, dilatory.

spare general. An overbearing or conceited superior below the rank of general: sarcastic military coll.: from 1915. F. & Gibbons. Cf. spare parts, q.v.

spare me days! 'A pious ejaculation,' C. J. Dennis: Australian coll.: C. 20.

spare parts. A person either incompetent or unsuitable: military: from 1915. F. & Gibbons. I.e. not actually in use.

spark. See spark, bright.—2. A diamond: c. (— 1874). H., 5th ed. Cf. spark-prop. Ex S.E. spark, a small diamond, orig. diamond spark.—3. Hence, in pl., other precious stones: c.: C. 20. Manchon, 1923; Charles E. Leach, 1933.

*spark, v. To watch closely: Australian c. (— 1901).

spark, bright. Ironic for a dull fellow: coll.

verging on S.E.: late C. 19-20. Cf. S.E. gallant spark; ex spark, a beau, via gay spark.

spark, have a. To be a youth, or man, of spirit: Conway cadets': from before 1890. John Masefield, The Conway, 1933. Ex the cliché, have no spark of courage.

spark in one's throat, have a. To have a constant thirst: 1785, Grose; but adumbrated in Scots ca. 1720. Ex the proverbial the smith had always a spark in his throat (Ray, 1678); cf. Spurgeon, 1880, 'He is not a blacksmith but he has a spark in his throat.'

spark out; gen. pass spark out. Utterly; to become unconscious through liquor, to faint, to die: pugilistic: C. 20. James Curtis, The Gilt Kid, 1936. Ex dial. spark out, utterly extinguished (E.D.D.).

*spark prop. A diamond breast-pin: c.: from the middle or late 1870's. Ex spark n., 2.

sparkle. A diamond: low (— 1923). Manchon. Prob. ex a confusion of spark, n., 2, and sparkler, 2: for there is no connexion with the S.E. sparkle (a diamond) of late C. 15-early 18 (O.E.D.).—2. Hence (?), generic for jewellery: c. (— 1935). David Hume.

sparkler. A bright eye (gen. in pl.): mid-C. 18-20: S.E. until 1850, then coll.; in C. 20, s.—2. A sparkling gem; esp. a diamond: from ca. 1820: S.E. until mid-C. 19, then coll.; in C. 20, virtually s.

sparks. (Nickname.) A wireless operator: from ca. 1916. F. & Gibbons. Ex electrical sparks.—2. The torpedo officer: naval: from ca. 1915. Bowen.—3. The X-ray department: medical students' (— 1933). Slang, p. 193.

sparks, get the. To set the aim of a machine-gun on an enemy trench after dark 'by firing into the wire-entanglement and noting where the sparks fly off as the bullets cut the wire': machine-gunners' coll.: 1915-18. F. & Gibbons.

sparm-fish. A sperm-whale: nautical coll. (— 1887). Baumann.

sparrer. A boxer: coll.: 1814, 'Rival sparrers,' O.E.D.—2. Hence, from ca. 1860, a sparring partner: coll. This is virtually the sense in Thackeray and Shaw (O.E.D.).—3. A sol. form, C. 19-20, of sparrow.—4. (Properly sparrow.) A find in a dust-bin, e.g. silver spoon or thimble: dustmen's (— 1895). Ware. Cf.:

sparrow. Gen. in pl.: beer, or beer-money, given to dustmen: 1879 (O.E.D.). Perhaps ex the colour of these birds and these men.—2. A milkman's secret customer (gen. in pl.): milkmen's (— 1901). O.E.D. Why? —3. (Sparrow.) The ship Spero: nautical sol. or perhaps rather nickname: C. 19. Ware.—3. See sparrer, 4.

sparrow-catching, n. Walking the streets in search of men: low: from ca. 1880.

sparrow-fart, at. At daybreak: dial. >, ca 1910, coll.; popularised by G.W.

sparrow(-)grass; sparagrass. Asparagus: mid-C. 17-20: S.E. until early C. 19, then dial. and coll.; by 1870, low coll. or, rather, sol. 'Cuthbert Bede', in 1865, 'I have heard the word sparrowgrass from the lips of a real Lady—but then she was in her seventies,' O.E.D.

sparrow-mouthed. (Of a person) having a large mouth: lower-class coll. (— 1923). Manchon.

sparrow-starver. A collector of dung from off the streets: lower classes' (— 1923). Ibid.

spasm. The verse of a song, stanza of a poem: jocular coll.: late C. 19-20. Ex stanza + the agony caused by much amateur singing.

spassiba ! Thanks ! : military coll. in North Russia in 1918–19. F. & Gibbons. Direct ex Russian.

spat, a quarrel, a smart blow, a smacking sound,—all C. 19–20,—is, when not U.S., rather dial. than coll.—2. See **spats.**

spat, v. To cane : Public Schools' : from ca. 1910. Francis Beeding, *Take it Crooked,* 1932. Ex the preceding, sense 1.

spatch(-)cock. A fowl killed, dressed and either grilled or broiled at short notice : orig. (— 1785) Anglo-Irish, but from ca. 1850 mainly Anglo-Indian : coll. >, ca. 1860, S.E. Grose, 1st ed. ; R. F. Burton, *Goa,* 1851 (O.E.D.). Either abbr. *dispatch-cock,* or corrupted *spitchcock* (? *spit-cock*) : W.

spatch(-)cock, v. To insert, interpolate : orig. military coll. >, almost imm., gen. S.E. : 1901, General Redvers Buller, *The Times,* Oct. 11, ' I therefore spatchcocked into the middle of that telegram a sentence in which I suggested it would be necessary to surrender.' Ex the n.—2. Hence, to modify by interpolation : military coll. >, by 1902, gen. S.E. : 1901, Oct. 24 ; 1901, Nov. 16, *The Speaker,* ' Generals spatchcock telegrams and receive dismissal,' O.E.D.

spats. Those stream-lined covers over landing-wheels which are in aircraft designed to reduce air-resistance : aviators' : from 1934. *The Daily Telegraph,* Feb. 9, 1935.

speak, v. See **speak at the mouth, to, with.**—2. To pay court : lower classes' (— 1909). Ware.

*****speak, make a** (gen. **good** or **rum**). To make a (gen. good) haul, get a (good) ' swag ' : c. (— 1811) ; † by 1860. *Lex. Bal.* Ex *speak to,* q.v.

speak, that would make a cat. See **cat speak.**

speak at the mouth. To say one's say : ca. 1870–1910. Ex North Country dial.

speak brown to-morrow. To get sun-burnt : Cockney : 1877–ca 1900. Ware. Cf. *taste the sun.*

speak-easy. A shop or café where liquor is illicitly sold : U.S. (late 1880's), anglicised by 1925. (O.E.D. Sup.). One speaks softly in ordering it. Cf. *speak-softly shop.*

speak French. See **French, speak.**

speak like a mouse in a cheese. See **mouse in a cheese.**

*****speak to.** To rob (person, place) ; to steal : c. : 1799 (O.E.D.) ; 1812, Vaux ; † by 1860. A variant of *speak with,* q.v.—2. See **spoke,** or **spoken, to.**

speak to, not to. Not to see or know at close quarters : jocular coll. : from ca. 1925. Richard Blaker, *Night-Shift,* 1934, of a motor-car, ' I've never seen one like this before—not to speak to.'

*****speak with.** C. of ca. 1720–1810, as in *A New Canting Dict.,* 1725, ' I will never speak with any thing but Wedge or Cloy, I'll never steal, or '—the basic sense—' have to do with '—a nuance † by 1785—' any thing but Plate, or Money ' ; Grose, 1st ed. (to rob, steal). Cf. *speak to,* 1.

*****speak-softly shop.** A smuggler's house : c. or low (— 1823) ; † by 1890. Bee.

speakie. A ' talkie ' : coll. : 1928–9. O.E.D. (Sup.). (In the sense of a stage-play, the word did not catch on at all.)

speaks the parrot ! See **parrot, speaks the.**

*****speaky.** Booty ; capture of booty : c. (—1887). Baumann. Ex *speak, make a,* q.v.

Spearmen, the Delhi. The 9th Lancers : military : from middle 1850's (ob.). Coll. verging on journalistic S.E. Ex Indian Mutiny.

spec. A commercial venture : orig. (1794), U.S. ; anglicised ca. 1820 as s. >, ca. 1890, coll. Bee, 1823. Abbr. *speculation.* Cf. *spec, on,* q.v.—2. Hence, ' a lottery, conducted on principles more or less honest, the prize to be awarded according to the performance of certain horses,' J. Greenwood, 1869 : racing (mostly London) ; ca. 1850–65.—3. A good or enjoyable thing or a pleasant occasion : Winchester s. (— 1891). Perhaps rather from *special* or from *speculation* influenced by *special.* Cf. *spec, on,* 2.—4. **Spec, the.** The Speculative Society : Edinburgh advocates' coll. : late C. 19–20.—5. See **specs.**

spec, on. On chance ; as, or at, a risk ; esp. on the chance of getting something or of making a profit : 1832, Marryat (O.E.D.) : s. >, ca. 1890, coll. See **spec,** 1.—2. At Winchester, on a pleasant occasion or outing : from before 1891. Wrench.

speci. Abbr. *specimen* : s. (— 1923) rather than coll., for it is infelicitous. Manchon.

special, adv. In a special way ; especially, particularly : C. 14–20 : S.E. until early C. 19, then coll. (in C. 20, almost sol.). Helps, 1851, ' A case came on rather unexpectedly . . . and I was sent for " special " as we say.' O.E.D.

specimen. A person : from middle 1850's : derogatory, coll. if with *bright, poor,* etc., s. if alone. Thoreau, 1854, ' There were some curious specimens among my visitors,' O.E.D. Ex such phrases as *specimens of the new spirit abroad,* via such as *strange specimen of the human race* (Dickens, 1837). Cf. *spess,* q.v.

speck, v. To exult ; to show oneself confident of a victory : at certain Public Schools, esp. at Shrewsbury : late C. 19–20. Desmond Coke, *The House Prefect,* 1908, ' Look at the joy of the beastly County [players] ! " They're specking horribly," the watchers say.' Ex *expect.*

Speck, the. Tasmania : Australian Continentals' : C. 20. Because Tasmania is so small compared with Australia.

*****specked wiper.** A coloured handkerchief : c. : ca. 1690–1890. B.E. ; Grose, 1st ed.

speckle-belly (or **S.**). A Nonconformist, a Dissenter : provincial s. (— 1874) ; slightly ob. H., 5th ed., ' A term used in Worcester and the North, though the etymology seems unknown in either place.' Perhaps ex the tendency of the lower middle class to wear coloured waistcoats : cf. *specked wiper,* q.v.

speckled. Of a mixed nature, appearance, character, merit ; motley : coll. : 1845, S. Judd, ' It was a singularly . . . speckled group ' (of persons). O.E.D.

speckled potato. A spectator : C. 20. A jocular perversion of *spectator.* Ob.

speckled wipe. Variant, early C. 19, of *specked wiper.* Egan's Grose.

specks. (App. never in singular.) Damaged oranges : costers' coll. : 1851, Mayhew ; H., 1st ed. Ex the markings caused by mildew, etc.—2. See **specs.**

speckt. Erroneous for *specht, speight* (green woodpecker) : C. 16–17. O.E.D.—2. See **specked wiper.**

specs ; also **specks.** Spectacles for the sight : dial. (orig. and mainly *specks* ; 1807, Hogg) >, ca. 1830, coll. (mainly *specs*). Barham, 1837, ' He wore green specs with a tortoise-shell rim ' ; R. D. Blackmore, 1882, ' Must have my thick specks,' O.E.D.—2. Since 1900 (when used by P. F

Warner), and also as *pair of specs*, an occ. abbr. of *spectacles*. Lewis.

spect. To expect : sol. (— 1887). Baumann.

spectable. Respectable : id. Ibid.

spectacles. (Cf. *specs*, 2, q.v.) Two scores of 0 by a batsman in the one match : cricket coll. >, ca. 1910, S.E. : 1865, Wanostrocht, ' The ominous " spectacles " have been worn by the best sighted men ' ; 1885, P. M. Thornton ; 1898, Giffen ; W. J. Lewis, 1934. Abbr. *pair of spectacles*, same meaning : 1862. Lewis records the rare v., *be spectacled*, as early as 1854. Ex ' 0—0 ' in statistics.

spectacles-seat. The nose : 1895, Meredith, in *The Amazing Marriage* (O.E.D.) ; ob.

speech. ' A tip or wrinkle on any subject. On the turf a man will wait . . . until he " gets the speech ", as to whether [a horse] . . . has a good chance. To " give the speech " is to communicate any special information of a private nature,' H., 5th ed. : mainly racing : from ca. 1872. Since ca. 1920, largely superseded by *dope*, q.v.

Speecher (or **s.**). The speech-room : Harrow : from ca. 1890. Influence of ' Oxford-*er* '.—2. Hence, speech-day : ibid. (— 1903). F. & H. ; Vachell, 1905.

speechless. Extremely drunk : coll. : 1881, Besant & Rice (O.E.D.).

speed-cop. A policeman observing the speed of motorists : coll., orig. (ca. 1924) U.S., anglicised by 1929. (O.E.D. Sup.)

speed-merchant. One who cycles or, esp., motors at high speed : U.S. ; anglicised ca. 1920. Cf. *road-hog*, q.v. (The forms *speed-bug* and *speed-hog* are hardly eligible, for they have not ' caught on '.)—2. Whence, from ca. 1926, a very fast bowler : cricketers'. In this compound, *merchant* = chap, fellow.

speedo. A speedometer : motorists' : from ca. 1920. (*The Passing Show*, July 21, 1934.)

speedy. Living a loose life ; apt to be amorous : jocular coll. (— 1923). Manchon. Punning *fast*.

***speel.** To decamp : Northern c. (— 1839) ; ob. by 1910, virtually † by 1930. Brandon ; H., 1st ed. Ex *speel* (Scottish and Northern dial.), v.i., to clamber, (of the sun) to mount. Cf. *speel the drum*, q.v.—2. See **spiel.**

***speel-ken.** See **spell-ken.**

***speel the drum.** To make off for, or to, the high-way, esp. with stolen property : c. (— 1859) ; very ob. H., 1st ed. Ex *speel*, 1.

speeler. See **spieler.**—**spefflicate.** See **spificate**—**speiler.** See **spieler.**

speg, adj. Smart : Winchester ; † by 1903. F. & H. Perhaps ex *spick and span.*

spell. An incorrect spelling : coll. : C. 18–20.—2. Hence, a mode of spelling a word : coll. : C. 19–20. *The Monthly Magazine*, 1801, ' Why should this spell (as school children say . . .) be author-ised ? ' O.E.D.—3. A playhouse, a theatre : c. (— 1812) ; ob. Also as adj. Both in Vaux, 1812. Abbr. *spell-ken*, q.v.

***spell.** To advertise ; put in print : c. (—1864) H., 3rd ed. Esp. *spelt in the lear*, advertised-for in the newspaper, hence ' wanted '. Ob.—2. To be spelt : coll., esp. children's (— 1877). Baumann, ' How does it spell ? '

spell-binder ; spellbinder. A ' spiller of rhetorical dope ' (Allan M. Laing) : journalistic coll. (from ca. 1920) verging on rank j.

***spell-ken** or **spellken** ; occ. **speel-ken** (— 1860). A theatre : o. of ca. 1800–90. Jackson, ca. 1800, as quoted by Byron in *Don Juan*, note to XI, 19 ; Vaux. Ex Dutch *spel* (Ger. *spiel*), play ; cf. *spieler*, q.v., and † S.E. *spill-house*, a gaming house.

spell-oh ; occ. **spell-ho** or (in C. 20) **spell-o.** A rest : *Conway* training-ship, and Australian, coll. : late C. 19–20. Henry Lawson, 1900, ' Bill . . . was having a spell-oh under the cask when the white rooster crowed,' O.E.D. Ex *spell-oh*, a call to cease work or to rest.—2. Allotted work : on the *Conway* : from before 1891. (John Masefield, *The Conway*. 1933.)

***spelt in the lear.** See **spell,** v.

spencer. A small glass of gin : low London : 1804 (O.E.D.) ; † by 1880.

spend, (up)on the. Spending : late C. 17–20 : S.E. until late C. 19 then coll. (rarely *upon*). *The Saturday Review*. Dec. 17, 1904, ' The Government is " on the spend ",' O.E.D.

spending departments, the. War Office and Admiralty : Parliamentary jocular coll. (— 1887) ; † by 1920. Baumann.

spendulicon(s) is a low perversion (— 1923) of *spondulicks*, q.v. Manchon.

spirrib. A wife : London lower-middle classes' (— 1909) ; slightly ob. Ware. Corruption of *spare rib*.

speshul if pronounced with accent on first syllable is unnecessary, for that is precisely how *special* is pronounced ; if, however, with accent on the second, it is sol.—2. As n., it meant, in 1884–5—the time of the Soudan War—a lie. Ex the news-vendors' cry. (Ware.) Cf. *British official*, q.v.

spess. A specimen : Felsted School : 1899, *The Felstedian*, July, ' Others . . . calling out . . . " frightful spesses ", which word is specimens.' Cf. *speci*, q.v.

spew-alley. The female pudend : low : C. 19.—2. The throat : low coll. : mid-C. 19–20 ; ob. Cf. *gutter lane* and *red lane*.

spew her caulking or **spew (the) oakum.** ' A ship spews oakum when the seams start,' F. & H. : nautical coll. (from ca. 1860) >, ca. 1890, in Young's *Nautical Dict.*, 1863.

***spice.** C. of ca. 1800–50, thus : *a spice*, a foot-pad ; *the spice*, footpad robbery. Vaux. ? ex *spice of adventure* or *danger*. See **spice, high toby.**

***spice,** v.t. To rob : c. (— 1811) ; † by 1850-*Lex. Bal.* Cf. the n.—2. Gen. in full, *spice the soot*, to mix ashes and earth in with soot : chimney-sweepers' s. : 1798, O.E.D. ; ob.

***spice, high toby.** Highway robbery : c. : late C. 18–mid-19. Jackson, ca. 1800, as quoted by Byron in his notes to *Don Juan*, xi, ' On the high toby spice flash the muzzle.' See **spice, n.**

***spice-gloak.** A footpad : c. of ca. 1810–60. Vaux. Ex *spice*, n.

spice island. The rectum ; a privy : low : ca. 1810–50. *Lex. Bal.*—2. Whence, applied to : any filthy, stinking vicinity : low coll. : ca. 1810–70. Ibid. Punning the Spice Islands.

***spicer.** A footpad : c. : ca. 1820–60. F. & H. Ex *spice*, v., 1.

spicy. Spirited ; energetically lively : 1828, ' A remarkably spicy team,' O.E.D. ; *Puck*, 1844, ' The milliners' hearts he did trepan, | My spicy, swell small-college man.' Ob. Perhaps ex † Scottish *spicy*, proud, conceited.—2. Hence, smart-looking ; neat : 1846, T. H. Huxley, ' The spicy oilcloth . . . looks most respectable,' O.E.D. Cf. *spicy*, adv.—3. Hence, handsome : 1868, Whyte-Melville, (of a horse) ' What a spicy chestnut it is.'—4. Sexually

'luscious' or attractive : low coll. : from ca. 1870.
Ex *spicy*, highly flavoured.

spicy, adv. Smartly : low : 1859, Meredith,
'He've come to town dressed that spicy,' O.E.D.
Ex *spicy*, adj., 2, q.v.

spicy, cut it. To act the beau, the dandy : lower
classes': from ca. 1880. Manchon. Ex *spicy*,
adj., 2.

*spider. A wire pick-lock (of considerable
utility): c. : 1845 in '*No. 747* '; † by 1920.—2.
Claret and lemonade : ca. 1890–1915. Ex :—3. A
drink of brandy and lemonade : Australian : 1854,
The Melbourne Argus ; ob. by 1900, † by 1930.

spider, swallow a. To go bankrupt : coll. : mid-
C. 17–18. Howell, 1659 ; Ray ; Berthelson, 1754.
Gen. *he has, you have,* etc., *swallowed a spider.*
Apperson.—2. See 'Moving-Picture Slang ', § 3.

spider-brusher. A domestic servant : 1833, T.
Hook (O.E.D.); ob. by 1890, † by 1930.

spider-catcher. A very thin man : late C. 17–
mid-18. B.E., whose *for* is, I think, obviously a
misprint for *of* in 'a Spindle for a Man '.—2. A
monkey: coll. and dial.: ca. 1820–70. Halliwell.

spider-claw, v.t. To grasp and stroke (the *testes*) :
low : late C. 19–early 20. (As F. & H. gives no
date, this is a mere guess.)

spider-web. (Gen. pl.) Wire-entanglement:
military, but not very gen. : 1915 ; † by 1920.
G. H. McKnight, *English Words,* 1923.

spidereen. Nautical, ca. 1860–1915 : 'an
imaginary vessel figuring in an unwilling reply :
"What ship do you belong to ? " "The *spidereen*
frigate, with nine decks, and ne'er a bottom,'
F. & H. (H., 3rd ed.)

*spiel. A hard-luck story : tramps' c. (— 1932).
'Stuart Wood.' Ex sense 2 or 3 of the v.—2. A
grafter's patter : late C. 19–20. (P. Allingham,
1934.)

*spiel, v. See **speel.**—2. To talk glibly, plausibly;
to patter : mostly Australian : from ca. 1870.
Perhaps a back-formation ex *spieler*.—3. Hence, to
'tell the tale ' : tramps' c. (— 1932). 'Stuart
Wood.'

spieler ; occ. **speeler** or **speiler.** A gambler, esp.
a card-sharper ; a professional swindler : Australia
and New Zealand : 1886, *The New Zealand Herald,*
June 1, 'A fresh gang of " speelers " are operating
in the town,' O.E.D. Ex Ger. *spieler,* player, esp.
at cards, a gamester.—2. Hence, a glib and crafty
fellow : Australia : from ca. 1905.—3. A 'weaver
of hard luck stories ': tramps' c. (— 1932). 'Stuart
Wood.' Cf. *spiel,* v., 3.—4. A gambling-den : c. :
from ca. 1925. Charles E. Leach.—5. A ' barker ':
grafters': C. 20. Cf. senses 2, 3. (P. Allingham,
1934.)

spierized, be. To have one's hair cut and sham-
pooed : Oxford University : ca. 1870–1910. H.,
5th ed. Ex *Spiers,* a barber in 'the High '.

Spierpon orchestra. The orchestra of Spiers and
Pond : Society coll. : 1885–ca. 1900. Ware.

spif. See **spiff,** adj., 2.

spiff, n. See **spiffs.**—2. A 'swell ': from ca.
1873 ; ob. by 1910, † by 1930. H., 5th ed. Abbr.
spiffy, but imm. ex *spiff,* adj., 2.

spiff, v.t. Only in past ppl. passive : see **spiffed.**
—2. V.t., to pay, or allow, commission as to (say)
half-a-crown on (a named article) : trade : from ca.
1890. *The Ironmonger,* Sept. 19, 1891, 'A "job "
chandelier . . . may be " spiffed ", say 1*s.,* but a
more unsaleable one should bear a higher sum,' i.e.

carry a higher commission. O.E.D. Ex *spiffs,* q.v
Cf. *spiff,* adj.

spiff, adj. Esp. *s. stores,* one where 'spiffs ' are in
force, and *spiff system* (recorded by O.E.D. at 1890),
the procedure of paying commission to the assistants : from ca. 1889. Ex *spiffs,* q.v.—2. (The form
spif is almost wholly dial.) Smartly dressed ;
dandified ; in good spirits or health ; excellent,
superior : dial. (— 1862) >, ca. 1870, s. >, ca. 1890,
coll. ; ob. F. & H. has : 'Awfully spiff,' 'How
spiff you look ', ' " How are you ? " " Pretty
spiff ".' ? abbr. *spiffy,* q.v. ; cf. *spiffing,* q.v.

spiffed, ppl.adj. Smartly dressed ; tricked *out* ;
very neat ; spruce : 1877, W. S. Gilbert (O.E.D.) ;
ob. See **spiff,** v., 1, and cf. *spiffing* and *spiffy,* qq.v.
—2. Tipsy : mainly Scottish (— 1860) ; ob. H.,
2nd ed. Perhaps ex *skew-whiff,* or even ex *squiffed*
(q.v.) influenced by *skew-whiff.* Cf. *screwed* and
squiffy.

[**spiffin is** by Baumann wrongly distinguished
from :]

spiffing ; occ., though rarely in C. 20, **spiffin.** (In
dial., *spiving.*) First-rate, excellent ; (of, or as to,
dress) fine, smart, dandified, spruce : dial. and s. >.
ca. 1900, coll. : 1872, 'The vulgar Pupkins said . . ,
"It was spiffing ! " '; G. Moore, 1884. Perhaps ex
dial. (— 1865) *spiffym,* n., work well done. O.E.D.,
which relates *rattling, ripping, topping,* Cf. *spiff,*
adj., 2, and *spiffy,* qq.v., and the dial. *spiffer* (1882),
anything exceptional or very large, fine, good.—2.
Hence, adv. ; ob.

spifflicate, etc. See **spiflicate,** etc.

spiffs ; occ., esp. in C. 20, in the singular. Trade
(esp. drapery) s. as in H., 1859 : 'The percentage
allowed . . . to [assistants] when they effect sale
of old fashioned or undesirable stock.' (Cf. *spiff,*
v., 2, and adj., 1.) Prob. cognate with dial. *spiffyn* :
see **spiffing.**

spiffy. Smart, in the fashion ; fine (in appearance) ; spruce ; first-rate, excellent : coll. and dial.:
1860, H., 2nd ed. Recorded before *spiff,* adj., 2,
but prob. ex this adj., which may have existed in
dial. (where earliest in print) some years earlier than
1860. Cf. also *spiffing,* for it is certain that *spiff,*
n., 2, *spiff,* v., 1, *spiff,* adj., 2, *spiffed,* 1, and *spiffy*
form a semantic and presumably a phonetic group,
and I suspect that the trade group,—*spiff,* n., 1,
spiff, v., 2, *spiff,* adj., 1, *spiffs,* and dial. *spiffyn* (see
spiffing etymology),—is cognate and ultimately ex
the same radical ; that root, prob., is either an
echoic v.—cf. *biff*—with some such sense as to hit
(hard), hence to startle or astonish, or an adv. of the
spang kind—cf. its use in dial *spiff and spack bran
new,* quite new (E.D.D.).

spiflicate (— 1785) ; often **spifflicate** (1841,—in
dial.) and, mainly Cornish dial., **spefflicate** (1871) :
s. that, ca. 1870, > coll. 'To confound, silence, or
dumbfound,' Grose, 1st ed., 1785 ; hence, to handle
roughly, treat severely, to thrash, O.E.D., 1796 ;
hence, to crush, destroy, kill, as in Moore, 1818,
'Alas, alas, our ruin's fated ; All done up, and
spificated !' (O.E.D.) ; hence, as in 'Jon Bee ',
1823, to betray (a thief) to the intended victim or to
the police,—a very ob. sense ; and, ex the first or
the third nuance, to do something mysterious (and
unpleasant) to, often as a vague threat to children,—
a sense dating from ca. 1880 or at latest 1890, the
author hearing it first, as a child, ca. 1900. In C. 20,
the last is the prevailing signification, the first
nuance being very ob. In C. 20, it is often fig. :
to ruin, to destroy, as in D. Sayers, *Have His*

Carcase, 'It completely busts up and spifflicates the medical evidence.' Etymology : O.E.D., ' Prob. a purely fanciful formation. Cf. *smifligate*, v.' ; W., ' ? Fanciful formation on *suffocate*. Cf. dial. *smothercate*,' which word blends, or perhaps, confuses *smother* and *suffocate* ; H., 3rd ed., ' A corruption of [" stifle "], or of " suffocate " ' ; E.P., very diffidently, ' Ex *spill*, to spoil by injury or damage, to render useless, to destroy the value of (a thing),— as in O.E.D., 600, § 5, c,—on the analogy of either *castigate*, the *f* being perhaps due to the influence of *stifle* or even of *smother* (in both of which the vowels are obviously inoperative on a problematic *spilligate*) or, more prob., merely arbitrarily intrusive as are so many elements of unconventional vocables ; or, preferably, ex *spill*, as above, + *stifle*, the dial. form of *stifle*, +, or with ending on the analogy of, *castigate*, or ex *spill* + *stifle* + ending as in *fustigate*, to cudgel. Cf. the later *smifligate*, q.v., and the (app. much later) dial. *tussicated*, intoxicated.'

spiflicating, ppl.adj. Castigatory ; crushing : coll. : 1891, Meredith, ' You've got a spiflicating style of talk about you,' O.E.D. Rare and ob. Cf. :

spiflication. The being ' spiflicated ', the action of ' spiflicating ' ; severe punishment ; complete destruction : (mostly jocular) coll. : mid-C. 19–20 ; slightly ob. Sir Richard Burton, 1855, ' Whose blood he vowed to drink—the Oriental form of threatening spiflication.' Ex *spiflicate*, q.v. Ronald Knox, in *The Body in the Silo*, 1933, uses it (p. 296) for ' suffocation '.

spiffification. A sol. form of *spiflication* : late C. 19–20. Due to *-ifli-*.

[**spigot, brother, knight, man, son of the** S.E. clichés verging on coll. : from ca. 1820 ; Scott has the second and third. A tapster ; an alehousekeeper. O.E.D.]

spigot-sucker. A tippler : coll. : C. 17–18. Cotgrave. Ex the vent-hole peg of a cask.—2. A mouth-whore : low : C. 19–20 ; ob. Ex physiological spigot.

***spike.** A casual ward : tramps' c. : 1866, *Temple Bar*, xvi, 184. Ex the hardness of beds, fare, and treatment.—2. Hence, the workhouse : (low) s. : 1894, D. C. Murray, ' To sleep in the workhouse is to go "on the spike",' O.E.D. Cf. *spiniken* (*-kin*), q.v.—3. An Anglican High Church clergyman : ecclesiastical : late C. 19–20. (The O.E.D. records it at 1902, but Mr R. Ellis Roberts clearly remembers it in the middle and late 1890's.) Ex *spiky*, 1, q.v.—4. A bayonet : military : late C. 19–20.—5. A needle : lower classes' (— 1923). Manchon.—6. **Spike.** The inevitable nickname of all (male) Sullivans : naval and military : late C. 19–20. Bowen. In areas where Irish potatohoers were working, tramps used frequently to assume the name on entering the *spike* (sense 1).

spike, v. (Of an editor) to reject (a news-item, etc.) : journalistic : 1908, A. S. M. Hutchinson, *Once Aboard the Lugger*.

spike, get the. To become annoyed or angry : low : 1895 (E.D.D.). Cf. *get the needle* in the same sense. Ex *spike*, n., 5. Also, in C. 20, *have the spike* (E.D.D.).

spike-bozzle. To demolish : Air Force (orig. Naval) : 1915 ; ob. Ex *to spike* (a gun) + a fanciful ending.—2. Hence, to do away with, supersede : Air Force and military : from ca. 1918. O.E.D. (Sup.).

Spike(-)Park. The grounds of a prison ; hence, from ca. 1860, the Queen's Bench Prison : 1837, Dickens (O.E.D.) ; H., 3rd ed. (secondary sense) ; both † by 1890.

***spike-ranger.** A continual tramper from casual ward to casual ward : c. : from ca. 1897.

spiky. ' Extreme and uncompromising in Anglo-Catholic belief or practice ' : orig. and mainly Church : 1881 (S.O.D.). Ex the stiffness and sharpness of opinions and attitude. Cf. *spike*, 3.— 2. **Spiky.** A variant of *spike*, 6. F. & Gibbons, ' From the celebrated prize fighter.'

spill. A small fee, gift or reward, of money : 1675, Crowne (O.E.D.) ; B.E. ; Grose, 1st ed. † by ca. 1840. Constructed with *of* (e.g. *a spill of money*): C. 18–early 19. Prob. ex *to spill* ; cf. *a splash*, a small quantity, of liquid.—2. A fall ; a tumble, esp. from a horse : from ca. 1840 : coll. >, ca. 1890, S.E. Barham. Ex *spill*, v., 1.—3. A drink : ca. 1890– 1914. Ware.

spill, v. To cause to fall from vehicle (from ca. 1706 or 7) or from horse (— 1785) : coll. : resp. Swift and Grose.—2. Hence, from a boat, a box, etc., etc. : coll. : mid-C. 19–20. (O.E.D.)—3. V.t. To confess, divulge : c. (— 1932) now verging on low s. ' Stuart Wood ', *Shades of the Prison House*. From U.S.

spill and pelt. ' The practical fun at the end of each scene in the comic portion of a pantomime ' : theatrical : from ca. 1830. Ware. Ex things deliberately spilt and hilariously thrown.

spill milk against posts. A phrase, says Ware used in ' extreme condemnation of the habits of the man spoken of ' : lowest class (— 1909).

spill the beans. To blab ; to divulge, whether unintentionally or not, important facts ; to confess ; to lay information : U.S., anglicised by : 1928, D. Sayers, *The Ballona Club*, 1928. ; J. Brophy, *English Prose*, 1932. Orig., to ' make a mess ' of things. Cf. *mouthful* and *shoot off one's mouth*, qq.v.

***spill the works.** A c. variant, from ca. 1929, of the preceding. E.g. in John G. Brandon, *The One-Minute Murder*, 1934.

Spillsbury, come home by. To have a ' spill ', lit. or fig. : coll. : late C. 17–18. Hacket's *Life of Williams*, 1692. Cf. *Clapham, Peckham*, qq.v.

[**spilt** in *Lex. Bal.*, Egan's Grose, Baumann, Manchon, is a misprint for *spill*, n., 1.]

spilt milk, cry over. To indulge vain regrets : 1836, Haliburton ; 1860, Trollope ; 1900, Dowling : coll. >, ca. 1900, S.E. In mid-C. 19, *spilt water* offered a feeble rivalry. (O.E.D.)

spilter. Incorrect for *spiller* (branchlet on deer's horn) : mid-C. 17–20. O.E.D.

spin. A brisk run or canter ; a spurt : coll. >, by 1890, S.E. : 1856 (O.E.D.) ; 1884, *The Field*, Dec. 6, ' After a short undecided spin, Athos took a good lead.' Ex *to spin* (*along*).—2. A spinster : Anglo-Indian coll. : 1872, ' A most unhappy spin,' O.E.D. Ware dates it from 70 years earlier.— 3. A chance, esp. a fair chance, as in ' Give a chap a spin, can't you ! ' : C. 20 Australian. Ex *to spin a coin*, to decide (e.g. a bet) by spinning a coin.

spin, v.t. To fail in an examination : mostly military colleges (— 1859) and esp. the R.M.A., Woolwich. H., 1st ed. ; mostly in passive, as in Whyte-Melville, 1868, ' Don't you funk being spun ? ' Ex *spin*, to cause to whirl.—2. Hence, v.i., to be failed in an ' exam ' : 1869 (O.E.D.) ; rare. Cf. :

spin, get a. The same as *spin*, v., 2 : same period ; ob.—2. To be given a (fair) chance : C. 20 Australian. See **spin**, n., 3.

spin, go for a. To go for a drive in a motor-car ; occ. on a motor-cycle or in its side-car : coll. : from ca. 1905. Cf. *spin*, n., 1.

spin, go into a flat. See **go into a flat spin.**

spin, up for a. (Of an N.C.O.) ' brought up for a reprimand for some minor offence ' : military : from 1915. F. & Gibbons. Cf. *spin*, v., 2.

spin a cuff. To ' bore a mess with a long, pointless story ' : naval (— 1909). Ware. Cf. :

spin a cuffer ; spin a dippy. To tell an improbable story ; a probable one : naval : late C. 19–20. Bowen. See **cuffer** ; the *dippy*, used only in this phrase, may possibly derive ex *dippy*, crazy.

spin a twist. See **twist, spin a.**—**spin a yarn.** See **yarn, spin a.**—**spin-house.** See **spinning-house.**— **spin street-yarn.** See **street-yarn.**—**spin-text.** See **spintext.**

spin the bat. To speak vigorously, very slangily : the Army in India : mid-C. 19–early 20. Ware. Perhaps ex *spin a yarn* + *sling the bat*, qq.v.

spinach (occ. spelt **spin(n)age**), **gammon and.** Nonsense ; humbug : coll. : 1850, Dickens, ' What a world of gammon and spinnage it is, though, ain't it ! ' ; ob. ' The words *gammon* and *spinage* are part of the refrain to the song, " A frog he would a-wooing go "," O.E.D. Cf. *gammon*.

spindle. The penis : (low) coll. : C. 19–20 ; **ob.** Cf. S.E. *spindle side*.

spindles, make or **spin crooked.** (Of a woman) so to act as to make her husband a cuckold : coll. : late C. 16–17. Florio.

***spiniken, -kin.** See **spinniken.**

spink. Milk : R.M.A., Woolwich : from ca. 1890 ; slightly ob. ? origin if not a perversion of *drink* nor ex *spinked cattle* nor ex Fifeshire *spinkie.*

spinn-house. Incorrect for *spin-house* (see **spinning-house).**—**spinnage.** See **spinach.**

***spinniken,** loosely **-kin.** A workhouse : c. (— 1859). H., 1st ed.—2. **Spinniken, the.** St Giles's Workhouse : c. (— 1864). H., 3rd ed. Cf. *the Lump*, that of Marylebone, and *the Pan*, that of St Pancras, both in H., 3rd ed. ; note, however, that by 1874, these two terms were ' applied to all workhouses by tramps and costers ', H., 5th ed. Ex *ken*, a place, on *spin-house* (see **spinning-house).**

spinning. Rapid : coll. : 1882, *Society*, Dec. 16, ' The Cambridgeshire enjoyed a spinning run,' O.E.D. ; slightly ob. Ex *spinning*, gyrating.

spinning-house ; spin-house. Both ex *spin-house*, a house of correction for women, on the Continent (ex Dutch *spinnhuis*, cf. Ger. *spinnhaus*) : the former, a house of labour and correction, esp. for harlots under University jurisdiction : Cambridge : C. 19 : perhaps always S.E., but prob. orig. coll. ; the latter, a workhouse : C. 18–mid-19 coll., as in Brand's *History of Newcastle* (1702), where spelt *spinn-house.* Cf. *spinniken.* O.E.D. and F. & H.

spinning-out. Loquacious : lower classes' coll. (— 1887). Baumann, ' A spinning-out sort of chap.'

spinsrap. A parsnip ; parsnips : back s. (— 1859). H., 1st ed. Also *spinsraps.*

spinster. A harlot : coll. : ca. 1620–1720. Fletcher, 1622 ; Fuller, 1662, ' Many would never be wretched spinsters were they spinsters in deed, nor come to so public and shameful punishment.' Cf. *spindles, make* or *spin crooked*, q.v.

spintext ; spin-text. A clergyman : late C. 17– 20 : coll. (in earliest examples, a nickname or an innuendo-surname) >, ca. 1830, S.E. ; very ob. Congreve, 1693, ' Spintext ! Oh, the fanatick one-eyed parson ! ' Because he spins a long sermon from the text ; cf. the spider-spinning lucubrations of medieval (and a few modern) philosophers.—2. Esp. a prosy one : C. 18–20 ; ob. Vicesimus Knox, 1788, ' The race of formal spintexts, and solemn saygraces is nearly extinct.'

Spion Kop. Monkey Island : nautical of first decade, C. 20. Bowen. Ex the unpleasantness of Spion Kop as a military experience in the Boer War and the island's ' unpleasantness in bad weather '.— 2. City Road : London taxi-drivers' : C. 20.

[**spirit**, to kidnap (for export to the American plantations), ca. 1665–1800, may orig.—to judge by B.E. and Grose—have been coll. See Grose, P.]

spirit of the troops is excellent !, the. A military c.p. (late 1916–18) ' taken from newspaper blether and used in jocular, and often in bitterly derisive irony ', B. & P.

spiritual. A sacred song ; a hymn : coll. (since ca. 1920, S.E.) : 1870, ' " Negro Spirituals ", T. W. Higginson, in *Army Life.* (O.E.D.) Abbr. *spiritual song.*

spiritual case. ' The lower-deck term, probably unintentional at first [i.e. orig. a sol.], for spherical case shot ' : naval : ca. 1840–1900. Bowen.

spiritual flesh-broker. A parson : coll. : late C. 17–early 19. B.E. ; Grose, 1st ed.

spiritual whore. A woman infirm of faith ; esp. as a C. 16 ecclesiastical c.p., *she is a spiritual whore* (Tyndale, 1528). Cf. S.E. *go lusting* or *whoring after strange gods.*

spirity. Spirited ; energetic ; vivacious : from ca. 1630 : coll. till C. 19, then dial. (O.E.D.)—2. Ghostly : supernatural : jocular coll. (— 1887). Baumann.

spirter. See **spurter.**

spiry. Very distinguished : 1825, T. Hook (O.E.D.) ; ob. by 1890, † by 1930. Ex height.

spit ; gen. **the very** or, in C. 20, **the dead spit of.** A speaking likeness (of) : 1825 (O.E.D.) : coll. >, ca. 1890, S.E.—but still rather familiar. Mayhew, 1851, ' the very spit of the one I had for years ; it's a real portrait '. Ex such forms as ' As like an urchin, as if they had been spit out of the mouths of them,' Breton, 1602, and ' He's e'en as like thee as th' had'st spit him,' Cotton. Cf. Fr. *c'est son père tout craché.*—2. A (distinguished or remarkable or attractive) manner of spitting : coll. : C. 20. (Henry Wade, *Constable Guard Thyself*, 1934.)

spit, v. ' To foraminate a woman ', F. & H. : v.t. : coll. : C. 18–20 ; ob.—2. To leave (visiting-cards), gen. *at* So-and-so's : coll. : 1782, Mme D'Arblay ; ob. O.E.D.

spit, put four quarters on the. To have sexual intercourse : low : C. 19. Cf. *make the beast with two backs* and *spit*, v., 1.

spit alley (or **S.A.**). ' The alleyway in which the junior officers' cabins are situated ' (in a man-of-war) : naval : late C. 19–20. Bowen.

spit and a drag, a. A smoke on the sly : naval : late C. 19–20. Ibid. Ex *spit and drag*, a cigarette : rhyming s. (on *fag*) : late C. 19–20. B. & P.

spit and a draw. A proletarian variant (— 1935) of the preceding.

spit and a stride, a. A very short distance : Fletcher, 1621 (Apperson) ; 1676, Cotton, ' You are now . . . within a spit, and a stride of the peak,'

O.E.D.; Scott, 1824. Coll. until early C. 19, then dial.

spit and polish. Furbishing; meticulous cleaning: naval and, esp., military: from ca. 1860 or perhaps even earlier, though unrecorded before 1895 (O.E.D.): coll. >, ca. 1920, S.E. Cf. *elbow-grease.* Hence, *the Spit-and-Polish Navy* is the C. 20 coll. (naval) term for the Victorian Navy : Bowen.—2. In G.W., any officer exigent of the spick-and-span was likely to be dubbed ' (Old) Spit-and-Polish or Shine ' by the (gen. rightly) exasperated soldiery.

spit and polish ; no wonder . . . See **clean and polish.**

spit-and-scratch game. A hair-pulling fight: lower classes' coll. : C. 20. A. Neil Lyons, *Arthur's*, 1914. (Manchon.)

spit and shine. See **spit and polish,** 2.

spit brown. To chew tobacco : nautical coll. : late C. 19–20. Bowen.

spit button-sticks. (Gen. as vbl.n. *spitting . . .*) To use forcible language : Regular Army : C. 20. B. & P. A button-stick was a ' gadget ' used in button-polishing.

spit-curl. A curl lying flat on the temple : U.S. (– 1859) ; anglicised ca. 1875 as a coll., chiefly among costers : cf. *agg(e)ravators.*

spit one's guts. To tell or confess everything : low s. verging on c. : from not later than 1931.

spit out. To confess ; gen. as *spit it out !* : coll. : C. 20. Lyell. Ex S.E. *spit out,* to utter plainly, bravely, or proudly.

spit sixpences or **white broth.** To expectorate from a dry, though healthy, mouth : resp. coll. (1772, Graves, ' Beginning to spit six-pences (as his saying is) ' and s. (late C. 19–early 20).

Spitalfield(s) breakfast. ' A tight necktie and a short pipe ' ; i.e. no breakfast at all : East End (– 1864). H., 3rd ed. Ex the poor district in East London. Cf. *Irishman's dinner* and *soldier's supper,* qq.v., as well as *dine with Duke Humphrey,* q.v., and the c.p. (– 1874 ; ob.) *I'll go out and count the railings,* ' the park or area railings, mental instead of maxillary exercise,' H., 5th ed.

spitcher. To sink (an enemy submarine) : naval : from 1916. (O.E.D. Sup.) Perhaps a perversion of *spiflicate.* Cf. *spike-bozzle.*

spite Gabell. To cut off one's nose to spite one's face : Winchester : from ca. 1820. Mansfield ; Wrench. Ex the inadvisability of trying to get a rise out of him. Dr. Henry Gabell (1764–1831) was head master of the College from 1810 to 1823.

Spithead nightingale. A boatswain or his mate : nautical coll. : late C. 19–20 ; ob.

splarm. To smear : Dulwich College : C. 20. Collinson. App. a blend of Scottish *spla(i)rge,* to bedaub, + *smarmy.*

splash. Ostentation ; a display thereof ; a dash ; a sensation : coll. : esp. in *cut* (1806) or *make* (1824) *a splash.* (O.E.D.) Cf. *cut a dash.* Ex noisy diving or swimming.—2. Hence, without article : coll. : late C. 19–20 ; rare. *The Westminster Gazette,* Dec. 5, 1899, ' That last speech . . . ' caused enough splash for some time to come,' O.E.D.—3. Face-powder : 1864, H., 3rd ed. ; very ob. Cf. *slap* in the same sense.—4. A small quantity of soda-water (added to whiskey, etc.) : coll. (– 1927). Collinson.

splash, v.i. To be actively extravagant with money : coll. : from ca. 1912. Ex *splash,* n., 1, + *splash money about.* Whence *splasher.*—2. V.t., **to** expend : Australian (– 1916). C. J. Dennis.

***splash,** adj. Fine, elegant, fashionable, distinguished : c. (– 1887) >, by 1920, low s. Baumann ; Manchon. Ex *splash,* n., 1.

splash-up, adj. and adv. (In) splendid (manner) ; ' tip-top ' : lower classes' (– 1887) ; ob. Baumann. Cf. *bang-up.*

splasher. A person very extravagant with money. coll. : from ca. 1919.—2. A piece of oil-cloth protecting the wall against the splashing from a wash-hand bowl : domestic coll. (now verging on S.E.) : late C. 19–20. E.g. R. H. Mottram, *Bumphrey's,* 1934. Ex the S.E. *splasher* on vehicles.

Splashers, the. The 62nd Foot Regiment, in late C. 19–20 the Wiltshires : military : from ca. 1850 ; ob. Ex their dashing manner.

splashing, adj. and adv. ; **splashy,** adj. Fine(ly) ; splendid(ly) : ca. 1885–1920. Baumann,' A splashing (fine) feed.' Cf. *splash,* n., 1.

splathers !, hold your. Be silent ! : tailors' : from ca. 1870 ; ob. Prob. ex Yorkshire *splather,* noisy talk (E.D.D.). Whence :

splatherer. A loquacious person ; **a braggart** : tailors' : from ca. 1875 ; ob.

splatterdash. A bustle ; an uproar : late C. 19–20 ; ob. ? ex *splutter + dash.*

splendacious, splendidious, splendidous, splendi-ferous. Very splendid, remarkably fine, magnificent ; excellent : resp. 1843, *Blackwood's,* ' Some splendacious pattern in blue and gold ', O.E.D., which notes forms in *-aceous* (Thackeray, 1848) and *-atious,* all slightly ob. and all coll. ; C. 15–20, being S.E. until C. 19 (rare before 1880 ; now ob.), then coll. ; *splendidous,* S.E. in C. 17, is rare in coll. and now extremely ob. ; *splendiferous,*—loosely *-erus,* S.E. in C. 15–16 for ' abounding in splendour ', was in C. 17–early 19, like *splendidious,* ' subterranean ' in usage, and, like *splendacious,* it arose again in 1843 (Haliburton's ' Splendiferous white hoss,' O.E.D.), to be more gen. in U.S. than in Britain. All four are, in mid-C. 19–20, jocular in tendency.

splice. A wife : ca. 1820–1930. Ex *splice,* to marry.—2. Marriage ; a wedding : 1830, Galt ; 1876, Holland, ' I'm going to pay for the splice,' O.E.D.

splice, v. To join in matrimony : gen. in passive, as in the earliest instance : 1751, Smollett, ' Trunnion ! Trunnion ! turn out and be spliced, or lie still and be damned.' Ex lit. nautical sense.—2. Hence, to coït. : low : C. 19–20.—3. At Winchester College (– 1903), to throw or fling.

splice, sit on or **(upon) the.** To play a strictly defensive bat : cricket s. >, by 1935, coll. : from ca. 1905. Lewis. As if to sit on the shoulder of the bat.

splice the main-brace. See **main-brace, splice the.**

spliced(, get). (To get) married : late C. 18–20. Ainsworth, 1839. Ex *splice,* v., 1.

spliced, with main-brace well. Drunk : orig. nautical. See **main-brace.**

splicer. A sailor : lower classes' coll. : late C. 19–20. Manchon. Ex the S.E. sense, one (gen. a sailor) who splices, or specialises in splicing, ropes.

***split.** A detective, a police spy, an informer : c. (– 1812). Vaux. Ex *split,* v., 2, q.v. Cf. *split (up)on.*—2. See **splits.**—3. A drink of two liquors mixed : coll. : 1882, *Society,* Nov. 11, ' The " nips ", the " stims ", the " sherries and Ango sturas ", the " splits " of young Contango,' O.E.D. —4. A split soda : coll. : 1884 (O.E.D.) ; but *a soda split* occurs in H., 5th ed., 1874.—5. Hence, a half-size bottle of mineral water, 1896. O.E.D.— 6. A half-glass of spirits : coll. (– 1903).—7. In the same semantic group as senses 3–6 : **a split bun or roll** : coll. : 1905 ; and **a split vote**, 1894. O.E.D. —8. See **split, like.**—9. A harlot's bully : c. (— 1909). Ware. He splits her earnings with her. —10. 'A division of profits' : low (— 1919). O.E.D. (Sup.).—11. A ten-shilling currency-note : low : C. 20. (The half of a £1 note.)

split, v.i. To copulate : low : C. 18–20.—2. To turn informer, give evidence to the police : c. (— 1795) >, ca. 1850, low s.—3. Hence, to betray confidence, give evidence injurious to others : 1840, Dickens, but prob. a decade earlier. See also **split about** and **split on.**—4. Hence, v.t., to disclose, let out : 1850, Thackeray, 'Did I split anything ?', O.E.D.—5. V.i., to act vigorously : coll. : U.S. (ca. 1848), anglicised ca. 1870 : ob. Prob. ex :—6. V.i., to move, esp. to run, walk, gallop, etc. : coll. : 1790, R. Tyler, 'I was glad to take to my heels and split home, right off,' O.E.D. ; 1888, Adam Lindsay Gordon, *Poems*, 'We had run him for seven miles or more, | As hard as our nags could split.' Also *split along* and *go like split.*—7. V.i., to divide, or share in, profits : low (— 1919). O.E.D. (Sup.). Cf. *split*, n., 10.

split, (at) full. At full speed : coll. : U.S. (middle 1830's), anglicised ca. 1865. 'Rolf Boldre-wood,' 1890, 'In saddle and off full-split,' O.E.D. Cf. :

split, like ; esp. **go like split.** (To go) at full speed : coll. : U.S. (ca. 1848), partly anglicised ca. 1870, but never so gen. as *full split.*

split, make all. To cause, make, a commotion : coll. : late C. 16–17. Shakespeare.

split about. To divulge ; esp. to the police : 1836, *The Annual Register.* O.E.D.

split along. To move very fast : coll. : C. 19–20. See **split,** v., sixth sense.

split-arse, adv. A low variant (— 1923) of *(at) full split*, full speed. Manchon.

split-arse cap. The (former) R.F.C. cap, rather like a Glengarry : Air Force : 1915–ca. 1920. B. & P.

split-arse mechanic. A harlot : low : C. 19. Cf. *split-mutton*, 2.

split-arse merchant. A merely reckless flyer ; a fine 'stunt' flyer : Air Force : from 1915. B. & P. Cf. :

split-arse turn. A flat turn, without banking ; it is caused by using the rudder instead of rudder and ailerons. Royal Air Force's (— 1935).

split-arsing. 'Stunting low and flying near the roofs of billets or huts' : Air Force : from 1915. B. & P. See also **split-hairing** and **splitassing.**

split asunder. A costermonger : rhyming **s.** (— 1859) ; ob. H., 1st ed.

split-cause. A lawyer : coll. (— 1785) ; ob. by 1870, † by 1910. Grose, 1st ed.

split chums. To break friendship : *Conway* cadets' : from before 1891. John Masefield, *The Conway*, 1933. Cf. *part brass-rags*, q.v.

Split Crow, the. The Spread Eagle, tavern and sign. : from ca. 1780 ; ob. Grose, 1st ed., '. . . Two heads on one neck, gives it somewhat [this] appearance.'

split fair. To tell the truth : mid-C. 19–20. See **split,** v., 2.

split-fig. A grocer : coll. : late C. 17–early 19 ; then dial. B.E. ; Grose, 1st ed. Cf. *nip-cheese.*

split-hairing. A euphemism for *split-arsing.* (B. & P.)

[Split infinitives : see Fowler.]

split-mutton. The penis : low : ? C. 17–19.—2. Women in gen. ; a woman as sex : low : ? C. 18–20 ; ob. See **mutton** ; cf. *split-arse mechanic.*

split my windpipe ! 'A foolish kind of a Curse among the *Beaux*,' B.E. : coll. : late C. 17–mid-18. Also *split me* : C. 18–early 19 (Cibber, Thackeray : O.E.D.).

***split on** or **upon.** To inform the police about (a person) : c. (— 1812) >, ca. 1840, low s. >, ca. 1870, gen. s. Vaux (*upon* ; *on* app. unrecorded before 1875, O.E.D.). See **split,** v., 2, and cf. *split about* and *split fair.*

***split out.** V.i., to part company, to separate : c. : from ca. 1875 ; ob.

split pea. Tea : rhyming s. (— 1857). 'Du-cange Anglicus.' Rare ; † by 1900.

split pilot. A variant of *split-arse merchant* : from 1932.

***split-up.** A division of booty : c., and low : C. 20. James Curtis, *The Gilt Kid*, 1936.

split-up. A lanky person : from ca. 1875. Ex (*well*) *split-up*, long-limbed, itself (Baumann) s. from ca. 1870, prob. suggested by *splits*, q.v.

split soda. 'A bottle of soda water divided between two guests. The "baby" soda is for one client' : tavern coll. : from ca. 1860. Ware.

***split upon.** See **split on.**

split with. To break off acquaintance with ; to quarrel with : 1835, G. P. R. James (O.E.D.) : s. >, ca. 1910, coll. In C. 20, occ. absolutely, *split*, as in 'For good reasons, we don't wish to split.'

splitacer. A 'stunting' aviator : Air Force : from 1918. (O.E.D. Sup.) Ex *split-arse.* Cf. *split-arse merchant.*

splitassing. A euphemism of *split-arsing*, q.v. (B. & P.)

splits, the. In dancing or acrobatics, the act of separating one's legs and lowering oneself until, right-angled to the body, they extend flat along the ground : 1851, Mayhew (ii, 569) : coll. >, ca. 1890, S.E., though rare and ob., in the singular, as in Mayhew, iii, 1861.—2. The police : grafters' : late C. 19–20. Philip Allingham, *Cheapjack*, 1934. Ex *split*, n., 1.

splitter of causes. A lawyer : coll. : late C. 17–18. B.E. Cf. *split-cause.*

splodger. A country lout : coll. (— 1860). H., 2nd ed. Ex *splodge*, to trudge through mud and/or water.

splosh. Money : low : 1893, Gus Elen, 'Since Jack Jones come into that little bit o' splosh' ; ob. ? ex *splash* ; prob. cognate with *splosh*, adv. (q.v.). 2. An abrupt, resounding fall into water ; a 'quan-tity of water suddenly dashed or dropped' : dial. (1895) >, by 1910 at latest, coll. E. M. Stooke (E.D.D.) ; Collinson. Echoic.

splosh, adv. Plump : coll. >, ca. 1920, S.E. : 1891, Anon., *Harry Fludyer*, 'Such larks when you heard the ball go splosh on a man's hat.' Echoic.

splutter. A 'shindy' or 'dust' ; a scandal : low (— 1923). Manchon. Ex C. 19–20 dial.

spo. A spot : Charterhouse : C. 20. Cf. *squo* for the form.

Spoff. Spofforth, the great Australian bowler : cricketers' nickname : 1898, Giffen. (Lewis.)

spoffish. Fussy, bustling, officious : 1836, Dickens ; 1935, Ivor Brown in *The Observer*, Aug. 11. Very ob. Perhaps suggested by *officious* or *fussy* ; obviously, however, derived ex or cognate with *spoffle*, q.v. ; cf. *spoffy.*

spoffle, v.i. To fuss or bustle : from ca. 1830 ;

very ob. Ex East Anglian dial. *spuffle*, to fuss, bustle; be in a flurry or great haste (Forby's glossary, ca. 1825). E.D.D. Cf. *spoffish*, *spoffy*.

spoffskins. A harlot: low: ca. 1880–1910. Perhaps ex:

spoffy. The same as, and ex, *spoffish*, q.v.: 1860, H., 2nd ed.; ob.—3. Hence, n.

spogh. V.i., 'to show off, make a display': South African coll.: 1871, Dugmore, *Reminiscences of an Albany Settler*. Ex Dutch *pochen*, to boast. Pettman.

*****spoil** in New Zealand c. (— 1932) has the specific sense: stolen property.

spoil, v. In boxing, to damage, injure, seriously: sporting: 1811 (O.E.D.); very ob. Egan, 1821, has *spoil one's mouth*, to damage the face.—2. To prevent (a person) from succeeding, to render (a building, etc.) unsuitable for robbery: c. (— 1812); ob. Vaux.—3. Hence, in seashore-nautical s., as in R. C. Leslie, 1884, ' "Spoil a gent " is used . . . in the sense of disgusting him with the sea and so losing a good customer,' O.E.D.

spoil-bread. A baker: coll.: from ca. 1860; ob. Cf.:

spoil-broth. A cook: same status and period. Cf. next two entries.

spoil-iron. A smith: coll.: from ca. 1780; ob. Grose, 1st ed. Cf.:

spoil-pudding. A long-winded preacher: ca. 1785–1850. Grose, 2nd ed.

spoil the shape of. See **shape, spoil one's.**

spoiling salt water. A sea-cook's job: nautical coll.: mid-C. 19–early 20. Bowen.

spoke. Spoken: in C. 19–20, coll. (latterly, low coll.) when neither dial. nor jocular (e.g. ' English as she is spoke ').—2. See **spoken to.**

spoke-box. The mouth: jocular coll.: 1874, Anon., *The Siliad*; ob.

*****spoke to.** See **speak to.**

Spokeshay. Shakespeare: jocular Australian: C. 20. By perverted reversal: perhaps on *spoke-shave.*

*****spoken,** illiterately **spoke, to.** Robbed; stolen: see **speak to.**—2. In a bad way (gen. physically); dying: c. (— 1812); ob. Vaux. Lit., warned.

*****spoke(n)** to the crack, hoist, screw, sneak, etc. Robbed or stolen in the manner indicated by the nn., q.v.: c.: C. 19.

spok(e)y. A wheelwright: military: C. 20. F. & Gibbons. Ex the spokes of a wheel.—2. **(Spokey.)** An ' inevitable ' nickname of men named Wheeler or Wheelwright: id.: id. Ibid.

spondoolic(k)s, -ix ; spondulacks ; spondulicks (the most gen.), **-ics, -ix.** Money; cash: U.S. (1857), anglicised ca. 1885: resp. — 1903, 1902; — 1903; 1863, ca. 1870, and 1857. G. A. Sala, Dec. 8, 1883, derives it, by ' enlarged vulgarisation ' (or perversion and elaboration), from *greenbacks*, its orig. signification; ' Pomes ' Marshall. Thornton.

sponge, v.t. To throw up the sponge on behalf of (a defeated person or animal); gen. *to be sponged*, to have this happen to one: 1851, Mayhew (O.E.D.); ob. Cf.:

sponge, chuck or throw up the. To give in; submit: coll.: resp. from ca. 1875 and 1860 (H., 2nd ed.). Rolf Boldrewood, 1889 (*chuck*); ' Captain Kettle ' Hyne, 1899. Ex boxing, where this action signifies defeat.

spoof. A nonsensically hoaxing game: 1889 (O.E.D.). The name and the game were invented by Arthur Roberts the comedian (1852–1933).—2.

Hence, a card game in which certain cards, occurring together, are called ' spoof '; 1895 (O.E.D.).—3. Ex sense 1 : humbug; hoaxing : 1897 (O.E.D.); an instance of this (— 1903).—4. A theatrical variation (ca. 1896–1914) of *oof*, money. Ware.

spoof, v.t. To hoax; humbug: 1895, 'I "spoof" him—to use a latter-day term,' *Punch*, Dec. 28 (O.E.D.). Ex n., 1, q.v.—2. Hence, v.i., to practise hoaxing or humbugging, gen. with present ppl. (' You're not spoofing, are you ? '): from ca. 1920.

spoof, adj. Hoaxing; humbugging: 1895, A. Roberts, ' My " spoof French " has often been the subject of amusement,' O.E.D.—2. Hence, bogus, sham : C. 20.

spoofer. One who ' spoofs ': see **spoof, v.** From ca. 1910 ; by 1935, almost coll.

spooferies, the. A sporting club—or, generically, sporting clubs—of an inferior kind : ca. 1889–1912. Ware. Ex *spoof*, n., 1. Cf. the coll. *spoofery*, cheating (1926 : O.E.D. Sup.).

spook. An artillery signaller : artillerymen's jocular s.: from 1915. F. & Gibbons.

spoon. A simpleton, a fool : 1799 (O.E.D.): s. >, ca. 1850, coll.; ob. Vaux, 1812, ' It is usual to call a very prating shallow fellow a *rank spoon.*' Ex its openness and shallowness, but imm. **ex** *spoony*, n., 1.—2. A sentimental, esp. if silly, fondness : in pl., 1868; in singular, from ca. 1880. Slightly ob. Ex *be spoons on* or *with*, q.v.—3. Hence, a sweetheart : 1882 (O.E.D.); slightly ob.— 4. Hence, a flirtatious person ; a flirtation : C. 20. —5. At *spoons*, H., 3rd ed. (1864) gives several terms that, used by a certain firm in 1861–62, he thought might > gen. commercial s.: but they didn't.

spoon, v.i. To make love, esp. if very sentimentally and, in addition, rather sillily : 1831, Lady Granville (O.E.D.). Prob. ex *spoon*, n., 1.— 2. Hence, to flirt : C. 20.—3. V.t. To court, to make love to, in a sentimental way : 1877, Mrs Forrester (O.E.D.); ob. Cf. *spoon on.*—All senses are frequent as vbl.nn. in the same status ; but derivatives not listed here are not much used and are rather S.E. than ' unconventional '.

spoon, come the. To make ridiculous, too sentimental love : from ca. 1890 ; ob.

spoon, feed with a. To corrupt by bribing : coll. (— 1923). Manchon.

spoon about, v.i. To run after women ; play the gallant : C. 20. Ibid. See **spoon, v.** 2.

spoon and gravy. Full-dress evening clothes (men's) : C. 20 ; ob. (Mr R. Ellis Roberts vouches for its use in 1903.)

spoon in one's mouth, born with a silver. See **silver spoon.**

spoon in the wall, stick one's. To die : coll.: mid-C. 19–20 ; virtually † by 1930. H., 5th ed., 1874.

spoon on. Same as *spoon* v., 3 : from ca. 1880; ob. Ex *spoon*, v., 1.

[Spoonerisms : see *Slang*, pp. 279–80. Ex the Rev. W. A. Spooner (1844–1930) of Oxford.]

spoon-victuals. (Of a batsman) getting under a ball : Cambridge cricketers' : 1870's. Lewis. An elaboration of *spoon* (in cricket j.).

spooney, spoony. A simpleton, a fool : 1795, Potter ; ob. Cf. *spoon*, n., 1.—2. Hence (— 1812), adj. Vaux.—3. Sentimentally in love, foolishly amorous : 1836, Marryat (O.E.D.); in 1828 with (*up*)*on*,—' I felt rather spoony upon that vixen,'

O.E.D. Ex *spoon*, v., 1.—4. Hence, one thus in love or thus amorous : 1857, ' C. Bede ' (O.E.D.).

spoons, fill the mouth with empty. To go hungry : coll. : late C. 17–18. Ray.

spoons on (1863) or **with** (− 1860 ; † by 1910), **be.** To be sentimentally, esp. if sillily, in love with (a girl ; very rarely the converse). H., 2nd ed. Prob. ex *spoon*, n., 1.—2. Also (of a couple) *it's (a case of) spoons with them*, they are sentimentally in love : from ca. 1863 ; ob.

spoony. See **spooney.**—2. Adv., foolishly or sentimentally, esp. in *spoony drunk*, sentimentally drunk, as in the *Lex. Bal.*, 1811 ; ob.

spoony stuff. ' Weak, sentimental work, below contempt ' : London theatrical : ca. 1882–1915. Ware.

sporran. The pubic hair : late C. 19–20 low. Ex S.E. *sporran*.

sport. A ' good sport ', either one who subordinates his or her own personality or abilities to the gen. enjoyment ; or, of women only, one who readily accords the sexual favour : coll. : C. 20. Hence, *be a sport !* = don't be a spoil-sport ! Abbr. *a good sport*, ex *sport*, a sportsman : cf. *sporty*, q.v.

sport, v. (Thanks mainly to O.E.D., but by no means negligibly to F. & H.) To read (a book, an author) for *sport* : ca. 1690–1710. T. Brown, ' To divert the time with sporting an author.'—2. To stake (money), invest (it) riskily : ca. 1705–1860 : s. >, ca. 1750, coll.—3. Hence, to lay (a bet) : ca. 1805–50.—4. Prob. ex senses 2, 3 : to treat (a person) with food, etc. ; to offer (a person) the hospitality of (wine, etc.) : ? elsewhere than, 1828–30, in Lytton, **as** e.g. ' I doesn't care if I sports you a glass of port.' Cognate, however, is : to provide as in *sport a dinner, a lunch*, etc. : from ca. 1830.— 5. Ex sense 2 : v.i., to speculate or bet : ca. 1760–1820. ' Chrysal ' Johnston.—6. V.t. to spend (money) extravagantly or very freely or ostentatiously : 1859, H. Kingsley ' I took him for a flash overseer, sporting his salary.'—7. To exhibit, display, in company, in public, gen. showily or ostentatiously : from ca. 1710 (esp. common ca. 1770–1830) : s. >, ca. 1830, coll. Steele, 1712 ; J. H. Newman, ' A man . . . must sport an opinion when he really had none to give.'—8. Hence, to display on one's person ; esp. to wear : s. (1778) >, ca. 1890, coll. ' Pomes ' Marshall, ' She sported her number one gloss on her hair | And her very best blush on her cheek.'—9. To go in for (smoking, riding, billiards, etc, etc.) ; to maintain (e.g., a house, a carriage) : from ca. 1805 : s. >, ca. 1900, coll.—10. To shut (a door), esp. to signify ' Engaged ' : orig. and mainly university. Ex *sport oak* or *timber* : see **oak, sport.** Cf. *sport in*, q.v.—11. (Perhaps hence by metaphrasis :) to open (a door) violently, to force (it) : ca. 1805–20.—12. See vbl. phrases here ensuing.

sport, old. See **old sport.**

sport a baulk. See **baulk.**

sport a report. To publish it far and wide : mid-C. 19–20 ; ob.

sport a right line, be unable to or **cannot.** To be drunk : ca. 1770–1800. Oxford University. Because of inability to walk straight.

Sport and Win. Jim : rhyming s. (− 1859) ; ob. H. 1st ed.

sport in. To shut (one) in by closing the door : 1825, Hone, ' Shutting my room door, as if I was " sported in " ' ; ob. Cf. *oak, sport.*

sport ivory or **one's ivory.** To grin : from ca. 1785 ; ob. Grose, 2nd ed.

sport literature. To write a book : 1853, Mrs Gaskell ; ob.—very ob. !

sport oak. See **oak, sport.**

sport off. To do easily, as if for sport : late C. 19–20 ; ob. Cf. *sport*, v., 1.

sport silk. To ride a race : the turf (coll.) : 1885, *The Daily Chronicle*, Dec. 28. Ex the silk jacket worn by jockeys.

***sport the brown.** C., from ca. 1875 ; as in Anon's *Five Years' Penal Servitude*, 1877, ' If a man wishes to see the governor, the doctor, or the chaplain, he is to " sport the broom ", lay his little hairbroom on the floor at the door, directly the cell is opened in the morning,' O.E.D.

sport timber. The Inns of Court variation of *sport oak* : from ca. 1785 ; ob. Grose, 2nd ed.

sported oak or **door.** Same as *sporting door*, q.v. : from ca. 1870.

sporter. A wearer (of something showy, notable) : coll. : late C. 19–20.—2. **The Sporter** is *The Sportsman* : Public Schools' of ca. 1900–14. P. G. Wodehouse, *A Prefect's Uncle*, 1903.

sportiness. Sporty characteristics or tendency : coll. : 1896, *The Daily Chronicle*, Oct. 31 (O.E.D.).

sporting, adj. Like, natural to, a ' sport ', q.v. : C. 20.—2. See :

sporting action. At Winchester College, ' an affected manner, gesture or gait, or a betrayal of emotion,' F. & H. : from ca. 1870. Cf. *sport*, v., 7.

sporting chance. A slight or a problematic chance : coll. : from mid-1890's : sporting >, almost imm., gen. ; by 1935, virtually S.E. Mary Kingsley, 1897, ' One must diminish dead certainties to the level of sporting chances along here,' O.E.D.

sporting door. A door closed against intruders : university : from ca. 1850 ; ob. Bristed, 1852 (O.E.D.). Also *the oak*. See **sport,** v., in corresponding senses.

sportings. Clothes worn at the exeat : Charterhouse (− 1900). Tod's *Charterhouse*, 1900.

Sports Ship, the. The S.S. *Borodine* : naval coll. : G.W. (F. & Gibbons). It was supply-ship and entertainment ship to the Grand Fleet at Scapa Flow.

sportsman for liquor. ' A fine toper ' (Ware) : sporting : ca. 1880–1910.

sportsmanlike. Straightforward ; honourable : coll. : 1899, E. Phillpotts (O.E.D.).

sportsman's gap. The female pudend : low : C. 19–20. (Cf. S.E. *sporting-house*, a brothel, and *sporting-piece*, a plaything.) Ex gaps in hedges.

sportsman's prayer-book, the. See **prayer-book,** 3.

sportsman's toast. For this allusive coll., see **pointer and stubble.**

sporty. Sportsmanlike ; sporting ; generous : 1889 (O.E.D.) : s. >, ca. 1920, coll.

Spo's, the. The School Sports meeting : Charterhouse : C. 20. For the form cf. *spo* and *squo*.

s'pose. Suppose, esp. in *s'pose so !* : coll. : C. 19–20. Baumann.

sposh. Excellent : mainly theatrical : from ca. 1929 ; ob. A. A. Milne, *Two People*, 1931, ' Sposh . . I should adore to.' Perhaps a blend of *spiffing* + *posh*.

spot. A drop of liquor : coll. : 1885, D. C. Murray, ' A little spot of rum, William, with a squeeze of lemon in it.' In C. 20 Anglo-Irish coll., it has a specific sense : a half-glass of whiskey. Ex *spot*, a small piece or quantity. Cf. Fr. *larme*.—2. Hence, a small amount of. Gen. *a spot of . . .*, e.g. lunch, hence of rest, work, pleasure, music, etc. C. 20, but common only since ca. 1915 : s. >, ca. 1930, coll. Dorothy Sayers, *Have His Carcase*, 1932.—3. A cake : low : from ca. 1890 ; ob. See quotation at **scalder**, 2.—4. A person—usually a man—employed by an omnibus company to watch, secretly, its employees : 1894 (O.E.D.) : coll. >, ca. 1910, j. Ex *spot*, to detect.—5. Hence, any detective : low (— 1923). Manchon.—6. See **spots on burnt**.—7. A worn patch on the pitch : cricketers' coll. : C. 20. Neville Cardus, *Good Days*, 1934, concerning the third test match, 'It is the duty of all loyal subjects to talk about "a spot " in loud voices so that the Australians will hear.'

*spot, v. To note (a person) as criminal or suspect : c. : 1718 (O.E.D.) ; 1851, Mayhew, 'At length he became spotted. The police got to know him, and he was apprehended, tried, and convicted.' Perhaps ex † *spot*, 'to stain with some accusation or reproach.'—2. Hence, to inform against (a person) : c. : 1865, Dickens (O.E.D.) ; rare in C. 20.—3. (Prob. ex sense 1 :) to guess (a horse) beforehand as the winner in a race : orig. turf >, ca. 1890, gen. coll. : 1857, *The Morning Chronicle*, June 22, 'Having met with tolerable success in spotting the winners.'—4. Hence, to espy ; mark, note ; recognise, discover, detect : coll. : 1860, O. W. Holmes.—5. Whence, prob. : to hit (a mark) in shooting : coll. : 1882, Bret Harte (O.E.D.). Although the earliest record of this, as of the preceding sense, is U.S., there is perhaps no need to postulate an American origin for either ; cf., however, H., 1864, 'Orig. an Americanism, but now gen.'—6. (Ex spotting winners.) To gamble, v.t. and v.i. : low : from ca. 1890 ; ob. F. & H.—7. To pick out the best of (the land) for one's farm or station : New Zealand (— 1898). Morris. Cf. the Australian *peacock* and *pick the eyes out*.—8. Hence, to look for (a building) to break into : c., (— 1933). Charles E. Leach, *On Top of the Underworld*.—9. (Gen. **spot at**.) To jeer (at) ; make fun (of) : South African coll. (— 1906). Ex Dutch *spotten*, to mock or jeer. Pettman.

*spot, be in a. To be in a very difficult or dangerous position or condition : c. : from ca. 1930. James Curtis, *The Gilt Kid*, 1936. Perhaps ex *be put on the spot*.

*spot, on the. Alert ; quite certain : 1887, Henley, 'Palm and be always on the spot' : low, if not orig. c. Hence, *off the spot* : uncertain, not alert (in S.E., inexact, irrelevant).—2. A C. 20 U.S. c. sense, anglicised ca. 1930 as s. rather than as c. : in the place (and position) pre-arranged for one's murder. The rapidity of the anglicising, once it started, was largely owing to the popularity of Edgar Wallace's play (*On the Spot*), an excellent 'thriller', and of the ensuing novel (1931). Merely a special application of the S.E. sense, 'at the very place or locality in question '. See esp. Irwin.

spot, put on the. To determine and arrange the murder of : U.S., anglicised by 1930. Ex *spot, on the*, 2.

spot, soft. 'An easy, comfortable, or desirable berth, thing, or circumstance,' F. & H. : late C. 19–20 ; slightly ob. Ex Northern dial. *spot* (— 1877), a place of employment, a job (E.D.D.).

spot, vacant ; gen. **have a vacant spot**. To be half-witted : from ca. 1890 ; slightly ob. Cf. *shingle short, tile loose*.

spot at. See **spot**, v., 9.

spot-joint. A booth for the presentation of a form of amusement popular at fairs : grafters' : C. 20. Philip Allingham, *Cheapjack*, 1934.

Spot Ward. Joshua Ward (1685–1761), quack doctor. Ex 'a birth-mark on his face ' (Dawson).

spots off or **out of, knock**. See **knock spots**.—**spots, see**. See **see stars**.

spots on burnt(, e.g. two). (E.g. two) poached eggs on toast : low (— 1923). Manchon.

*spotted, ppl.adj. Known to the police : c. (— 1791). Tufts. Ex *spot*, v., 1.

*spotted covey. A c. variant (— 1923), noted by Manchon, of :

spotted Dick. A suet pudding made with currants or raisins : 1849, Soyer, *The Modern Housewife* (O.E.D.) : coll. >, ca. 1890, S.E. Ex the raisins that, on the surface, give the pudding a spotty appearance. Cf. the next three entries.

spotted dog. The same : from ca. 1865 : coll. that had by 1920 > S.E. Prob. *dog* puns *dough*, as Ware suggests.—2. Among soldiers, a sausage or a saveloy : from ca. 1885 ; very ob. Ex the legend. Cf. *spotted mystery*.

spotted donkey ; **spotted leopard**. The same as *spotted Dick* : resp. schools' (— 1887), ob. (Baumann) ; low urban, from ca. 1880 (Ware).

spotted duff. A coll. variant (from ca. 1870) of *spotted Dick*. Ware.

spotted mystery. Tinned beef : military : from ca. 1880 ; ob. An elaboration on *mystery*, a sausage, and on *potted* (*mystery*). Cf. *spotted dog*, 2.

spotter. A variant of *spot*, n., 3 ; an informer (see **spot**, v., 2) ; a detective whose job it is to unmask beggars : all in Manchon and therefore from before 1923 : the first, s. ; the second, c. ; the third, police coll.—4. He who 'spots' a likely victim for a 'mob' to rob : police s. : C. 20. Charles E. Leach.

spousy. A spouse ; gen., husband : jocular coll. : ca. 1795–1820. (O.E.D.) On *hubby*.

spout. A large mouth, esp. if mostly open : lower classes' coll. (— 1909). Ware.—2. A showman's 'palaver ' or patter : showmen's : from ca. 1880. Neil Bell, *Crocus*, 1936. Cf. v., 2.

*spout, v. To pawn : c. (— 1811). *Lex. Bal.* From ca. 1850, (low) s. ; in C. 20, ob. Hughes, 1861, ' The dons are going to spout the college plate.' Ex *spout*, a pawnbroker's shoot, which, despite F. & H., is S.E.—2. To talk (without any such modification as characterises S.E.) : c. (— 1933). Charles E. Leach.

spout, in great. In high spirits ; noisy : late C. 18–mid-19 ; then dial. Grose in his *Provincial Glossary*, 1787. Perhaps ex *spout*, to declaim.

spout, up the. In pawn : coll. (— 1812). Vaux ; Barham. See **spout**, v.—2. Hence, imprisoned ; in hospital : low (— 1823) ; ob. Bee.—3. Hence, in a bad way (1853) ; bankrupt (— 1854), this being mainly dial. O.E.D.—4. Pregnant with child : low : late C. 19–20. Often in form, *to have been put up the spout*.—5. (Of a bullet) in the rifle-barrel and ready to be fired : military : from 1914. B. & P.

spout Billy. To make a living by reciting Shakespeare in tap-rooms : low coll. (— 1823) ; ob. by 1900, † by 1930. Bee. (Poor William !) Also *spout Bill*. Cf. *swan-slinger*, q.v.

spout ink. To write books, etc. : coll. : from ca. 1880 ; ob. Cf. *sling ink*.

sprag. 'To accost truculently,' C. J. Dennis: Australian (— 1916). Possibly ex *snag* + *rag* (v.t.); prob. ex dial. *sprag*, to put the brake on.

sprained one's ankle, to have. See **ankle.**

sprang. Tea; any drink: military: C. 20. F. & Gibbons. A corruption, prob. of Southern dial. *sprank*, a sprinkling, a slight shower (E.D.D.).

spraser, spras(e)y. A sixpence: grafters': C. 20. Philip Allingham, *Cheapjack*, 1934. Perhaps ex *sprat*, 1, on *Susie (Suzie).* A variant is *sprowsie.*

sprat. A sixpence: low s. (— 1839) >, ca. 1880, gen. s.; slightly ob. Brandon. Prob. ex its smallness and that of the fish.—2. A sweetheart: low: from ca. 1870; ob. Cf. fig. use of *bloater, duck, pippin.*

sprat-weather. A dark winter's-day: fishermen's coll. (— 1887); ob. Baumann; Bowen. Such weather is suitable for the catching of sprats.

sprats. Personal effects; furniture: low: from ca. 1880; ob. Cf. *sticks.*

sprawne. A prawn: sol.; or, at best, illiterate coll.: mid-C. 17–mid-18.

***spread.** A saddle: c.: late C. 18–mid-19. Tufts. Cf. S.E. *spread*, a coverlet.—2. ? hence, a shawl: low (— 1859); ob. H., 1st ed.—3. Butter: c. (— 1811) >, ca. 1840, low s.; slightly ob. *Lex. Bal.*; H., 3rd ed., 'A term with workmen and schoolboys.' Because spread, but prob. influenced by *bread*. Cf. *spreader*, q.v.—4. An umbrella: ca. 1820–50. Egan's Grose.—5. A banquet; an excellent or a copious meal: coll.: from ca. 1820. 'Pomes' Marshall, 1897, ' 'E didn't even give me an invite | To 'is New Year's spread.'—6. Hence, among sporting men, a dinner: from ca. 1870. H., 5th ed.—7. An option : Stock Exchange: late C. 19–20; ob. Prob. suggested by *straddle*.—8. Gen. **middle-aged spread**, q.v.—9. See **do a spread.**—10. 'A herbalist who sells a mixture of dried plants. He spreads these herbs out in front of him and lectures on the health-giving value of each'; *work the spread*, ' to graft as a herbalist ': grafters': late C. 19–20. Philip Allingham, *Cheapjack*, 1934.

spread, do a. See **do a spread.**

spread it thick, thin. To live expensively, poorly: coll. (— 1923). Manchon. Ex spreading butter thick or thin.

spread oneself. To make every effort, esp. monetary; to do one's very best, ' damn the expense ! ': orig. (1832) U.S., in sense of making a display; anglicised ca. 1890 as a coll.; by 1920, S.E.

***spread the royal.** (Gen. as vbl.n.) To give evidence against confederates: c. (— 1935). David Hume. Ex ' turn *King's* evidence.'

***spreader.** Butter: c.: early C. 17. Rowlands. Cf. *spread*, 3.

[**spreame.** An error (? a nonce-error) for *sperm*: C. 16. O.E.D.]

'Sprecious, Sprecious, S'pretious. A coll. oath: C. 17. Jonson. Abbr. *God's precious*. O.E.D.

spree. A boisterous frolic; a period of riotous enjoyment: Scots dial. (1804, Tarras) >, by 1810, coll. Origin problematic; but W.'s provisional identification, via early dial. variant *spray*, with *spreagh, spreath*, foray, cattle-raid, ex Gaelic *spréidh*, cattle, may well be correct.—2. Hence, a drinking bout, a tipsy carousal: coll.: 1811, *Lex. Bal.* Cf. *spree, on the.*—3. Hardly distinguishable from senses 1, 2: ' rough amusement, merrymaking, or sport ; prolonged drinking or carousing ;

indulgence or participation in this,' O.E.D.: Scots dial. (— 1808) >, ca. 1820, coll. Occ. without article, as in Frank Bullen, 1899, 'A steady course of spree.' (O.E.D.; E.D.D.)—4. A conceited person : Winchester College : from ca. 1870 ; ob. Pascoe, *Public Schools*, 1881. Ex adj.

spree, v.i. To carouse ; have, take part in, a spree: coll.: mid-C. 19–20. Mrs Gaskell, 1855 (O.E.D.) Ex n., 1, 2. Whence *spreeing*, vbl.n. and, occ., adj.

spree, adj. Befitting a Wykehamist; smart: Winchester: from ca. 1860; ob. Perhaps ex *spree-mess*, q.v.—2. Conceited: ibid.: from ca. 1870. This sense is applied only to juniors; used of acts, it = ' permissible only to prefects, or those of senior standing ', Wrench. Ex dial.; cognate with S.E. *spry* and *spruce.*

spree, on a. Enjoying oneself: coll.: 1847 (O.E.D.). Ex *spree*, n., 1. Cf. :

spree, on or **upon the.** E.g. *go on the spree.* Having a riotous time, esp.—and in C. 20 almost solely—on a drinking bout: coll.: 1851, Mayhew, who has the † *get on the spree* ; H., 1st ed., ' " Going on the spree ", starting out with intent to have a frolic.' Ex *spree*, n., 1, 2, and cf. *spree, on a.*

spree-mess. A feast, esp. in the form of a ' spread ' at tea-time, raised by subscription or given by departing boys and always held at the end of the half-year : Winchester College : ca. 1840–60. Mansfield. Ex *spree*, n., 1, 2, 3.

spreeish. Fond of or frequently sharing in ' sprees ': coll.: 1825, C. Westmacott (O.E.D.).— 2. Slightly intoxicated: coll (— 1888). See **spree,** n., 2.

spress or **'spress.** Express; express train: sol.; or rather, low coll. (— 1887). Baumann.

spring. V.i., to offer a higher price: 1851, Mayhew (O.E.D.); or, by 1890, † by 1930. Whence *spring to*, q.v.—2. To give; disburse; buy (a certain amount): coll.: 1851, Mayhew, ' It's a feast at a poor country labourer's place when he springs sixpenn'o.th of fresh herrings '; 1878, J. F. Sullivan, *The British Working Man*, 'Wot's 'e sprung ? ' (how much money has he given ?). Ex *spring, to* cause to appear. Contrast *rush*, to charge extortionately.—3. Hence, to afford to buy : late C. 19–20. Cf. *spring to*, q.v.

***spring a partridge.** To entice a person and then rob or swindle him: c.: late C. 17–mid-18. B.E. In *A New Canting Dict.*, 1725, collectively as *spring partridges.* Ex *spring partridges*, to cause them to rise.

***spring-ankle warehouse.** ' Newgate, or any other gaol,' Grose, 1st ed.: c. of ca. 1780–1840: Anglo-Irish. A sprained ankle = disablement = imprisonment.

spring at one's elbow, have a. To be a gamester: coll.: latish C. 17–mid-18. Ray, 1678. (Apperson.) Cf. the *to raise one's elbow* of drinking.

spring fleet. N.E. coast collier brigs going into the Baltic trade in the slack coal season ; nautical coll.: late C. 19–early 20. Bowen.

spring-heeled Jack. A rocket-propelled torpedo: naval: very late C. 19–very early 20. Bowen.

spring like a ha'penny knife, with a. Floppy; with no resilience: lower classes' (— 1909). Ex ' deadness ' of such a knife. Spare.

***spring the plant.** See **plant, spring the.**

spring to. To be able to pay or give; to afford: coll.: 1901, Anon., *Troddles and Us*, ' It's seven pound fifteen, and we can spring to that between us.'

Ex *spring*, 1, q.v.—2. Hence, to be able to accomplish : coll. : 1903, F. & H.

spring to it ! Look lively ! : coll. : from 1918 or 1919, esp. among ex-service men. Ex the military order. Cf. *wait for it !*, q.v.

[**Springboks**, South Africans, is journalese.]

*****springer.** A ' dark ' horse so much an outsider that no odds are quoted until just before the race : turf c. (— 1932). Ex springing a surprise.

springer-up. A tailor selling cheap, ready-made clothes : mid-C. 19–20 ; ob. Mayhew, 1851 ; H., 1st ed., ' The clothes are said to be " sprung up ", or " blown together ".'—2. Hence, an employer paying ' famine ' wages : lower classes' : C. 20. Manchon.

Springers, the. The 10th Foot, from ca. 1881 the Lincolnshire, Regiment : military : mid-C. 19–20. —2. Also, from 1777, the 62nd Foot (*the Splashers*), now the Wiltshire Regiment. F. & Gibbons. Ex a compliment passed by General Burgoyne in the American War.

sprinkle. To christen : jocular coll. : mid-C. 19–20.

sprook ; sprooker. See **spruik.**

sprout wings. To become angelic, extremely upright, chaste, etc. : C. 20 jocular coll.

spowser. A costermongers' variant (— 1935) of :

sprowsy, -ie. A sixpence : nautical, c., low : C. 20. G. Orwell, 1933. See **spraser.**

*****spruce.** A field : c. (— 1933). Charles E. Leach, *On Top of the Underworld*. Perhaps **ex** spruce growing there.

spruce, v.i. To tell lies or ' tall stories ' ; v.t., to deceive thus : military : from 1916. F. & Gibbons. Prob. a corruption of *spruik*, q.v.—2. Hence, *sprucer*, one who does any, or all, of these things : from 1916. Cf. *spruiker* in :

spruik. ' To deliver a speech, as a showman ' : Australian : C. 20. C. J. Dennis. Presumably ex Dutch *spreken*, to speak.—2. Whence *spruiker*, a plausible ' spouter ' : id. : id. Hence, a platform speaker : Australian (— 1926). Jice Doone.

sprung. Tipsy : low s. >, in C. 20, coll. : from ca. 1825 ; ob. Often as in Judd, 1870, ' Ex-Corporal Whiston with his friends sallied from the store well-sprung.' Either ex *spring*, to moisten (in C. 19–20, only in dial.), or, as the O.E.D.'s earliest quotation tends to show, ex *sprung*, split or cracked, *masts*.

sprung-up, adj. See **springer-up.**

spud. A potato : dial (— 1860) >, by 1868, s. Possibly ex *Spuddy*, the nickname for a seller of bad potatoes (Mayhew, 1851), but prob. *spud* is the earlier. Perhaps an Anglo-Irish corruption of *potato* via *murphy*, q.v. : cf. *Spud*, the inevitable nickname of any male Murphy and occ. of anyone with an Irish name (F. & Gibbons). W., however, proposes a s. ' application of *spud*, weeding instrument ', and pertinently compares the etymology of *parsnip*. Possible also is the *spud* adduced in the etymology of :—2. A baby's hand : dial. and nursery : mid-C. 19–20 ; ob. Halliwell. ? a corruption of *pudsy*, pudgy, or simply a special application of *spud*, a stumpy person or thing.

Spud, the. A fast goods-train carrying potatoes to London : railwaymen's : C. 20. *The Daily Telegraph*, Aug. 15, 1936. Cf. *the Sparagras* and *the Flying Pig*, and see **the Bacca.**

spud run. The bringing-off, in the duty cutter, of the weekly supply of potatoes : *Conway* cadets' (— 1917) ; ob. John Masefield, *The Conway*, 1933.

spud-adjutant. An orderly corporal : military : C. 20. F. & Gibbons : ex ' his duty in superintending the party carrying rations (potatoes) from the cook-house '. Cf. *spud-practice.*

spud-barber. A man on cook-house fatigue, esp. potato-peeling : military, esp. New Zealanders' in G.W.

spud-hole. A detention cell : military : C. 20. B. & P.

spud-practice. Peeling potatoes : military coll. : C. 20. F. & Gibbons. Cf. *spud-peelers*, men detailed for cook-house fatigue : id. : id. B. & P.

spuddy. See **spud,** 1.—2. A seller of baked potatoes : costers' : late C. 19–20.

spun. See **spin,** v., 1.—2. Exhausted, tired out : 1924 (S.O.D.).—3. Checkmated ; at a loss : C. 20. E.g. Miles Burton, *To Catch a Thief*, 1934, policeman *loquitur*, ' We know our way about . . . the underworld . . . But when it's a case . . . of the overworld, as one might say, then we're spun.'

spun from the winch. (Of a story that has been) invented : nautical : C. 20. Bowen. Punning *yarn.*

spun-yarn major. A lieutenant-commander : naval : C. 20. Bowen.

spun-yarn trick. (Gen. pl.) An unfair trick : naval coll. : late C. 19–20. Ibid. Ex the unfair use of spun yarn in competitive evolutions.

spunk. Mettle, spirit ; pluck : 1773, Goldsmith, is preceded by Bridges, 1772, ' Whether quite sober or dead drunk, | I know, my dear, you've too much spunk ' ; Grose. App. coll. >, ca. 1800, S.E. >, ca. 1850, coll. >, ca. 1890, s. : cf. the quotations and remarks in F. & H., O.E.D., and W., who derives it ex Gaelic *spong*, tinder : cf. phonetically and contrast semantically *punk*, q.v.—2. Hence, the seminal fluid : C. 19–20. Cf. *mettle*, q.v.—3. As in :

spunk-fencer. A match-seller : c. or low s. (— 1839). Brandon. Ex dial. *spunk*, a match.

spunky. Spirited ; plucky : dial. (Burns, 1786) >, ca. 1800, coll. Lamb, 1805, ' Vittoria Corombona, a spunky Italian lady,' O.E.D. ; 1819, Moore, ' His spunkiest backers were forced to sing small.'

*****spur.** To annoy : c. : from ca. 1875 ; ob. Whence :

*****spur, get the.** To be annoyed : c. : from ca. 1880. Cf. *needle*, q.v.

spur in one's head, have got a. To be (slightly) drunk : ca. 1770–1800 : orig. and mainly jockeys'. *The Gentleman's Magazine*, 1770. O.E.D.

[Spurious words :—See ' Ghost words '.]

spurlos versenkt. Disappeared ; gone completely : naval and military coll. : latter 1917 ; ob. F. & Gibbons. In Ger., lit. ' sunk traceless ' : ex a Ger. official despatch concerning recommended treatment of Argentine ships.

Spurs, the. Tottenham Hotspur Football Club : sporting : late C. 19–20.

spurs, dish up the. To cause guests to feel that it is time for them to depart : coll. (— 1923). Manchon. I.e. spurs to speed them on their way.

spurt. A small quantity : s. (— 1859) and dial. >, ca. 1890, dial. only. H., 1st ed. Prob. **ex** *spurt*, a brief effort, a short run, etc.

spurter. A blood-vessel severed in an operation : medical students' (— 1933). *Slang*, p. 193. It spurts blood.

*****spy** in c. of C. 20 is thus mentioned in Edgar Wallace, *Angel Esquire*, 1908, ' It may mean policeman, detective, school-board official, rent collector, or the gentleman appointed by the gas company to extract pennies from the gas meters.'

Spy, Black ; b.s. See black spy.

*spying. A vbl.n. corresponding to *spy*, q.v.

squab, v.i. To squeeze by : King Edward's School, Birmingham : late C. 19–20. Prob. ex *squab*, to squeeze flat, influenced by sense of *squash*.—2. (Gen. as **squob.**) V.i. and v.t., to treat thus : ' With foot on wall or desk, and back against the victim who is similarly treated on the other side, or pressed against the opposite wall,' F. & H. : ibid. : id.

squab up, v.i. and v.t. To push : ibid., id.

squabash. A crushing blow ; to crush, defeat : resp. 1818, Prof. Wilson, and 1822 : s. >, ca. 1860, coll. >, ca. 1910, S.E. ; ob. A blend of *squash* + *bash*. Cf. Scottish *stramash*. W.

squabble. (Of type) to be or get mixed : printers' (— 1887). Baumann.

squad. A squadron : naval (— 1887). Baumann. (This is independent of the S.E. use in late C. 17.)

squad, halt ! Salt : military rhyming s. : late C. 19–20. F. & Gibbons.

squaddy. An occ. perversion of *swaddy* : rare before C. 20. George Ingram, *Stir*, 1933.

squalino. To squeal : ca. 1818–60. (O.E.D.) Ex *squall* + *squeal* ; fanciful suffix.

*squall. A voice : c. of ca. 1720–60. *A New Canting Dict.*, 1725.

square, n. See the adj., which it merely substantivalises.—2. Here, however, it may be noted that, in the underworld, all just and honest practices and actions are called *the square*, as opp. to *the cross* : from ca. 1810. *Lex. Bal.* Cf. fig. *straight.*—3. A square dance : ball-room coll. : ca. 1890–1914. Ware.

square, v. To settle (a matter) satisfactorily : coll. : 1853, Dickens, ' I have squared it with the lad . . . and it's all right,' O.E.D. Ex *square*, to equalise, to balance (accounts).—2. Hence, to satisfy or win over, esp. by bribery or compensation ; to get rid of thus : s. >, ca. 1910, coll. : 1859, Lever, ' The horses he had " nobbled ", the jockeys squared, the owners " hocussed " ' ; 1879, T. H. Huxley. Specifically, *square his nibs* is to give a policeman money : H., 1st ed.—3. Hence, to get rid, or dispose, of by murder : 1888 (O.E.D.). Cf. *square, get.*—4. See **square at, square it, square round, square up, square up to.**

square, adj. Only in (*up*)*on the square.* (Predicatively.) Free from duplicity ; just ; straightforward, upright : from ca. 1680 : S.E. until ca. 1830, then coll. ; by 1860, s. Cf. :

square, adv. Justly ; honestly ; straightforwardly : late C. 16–20 : S.E. until ca. 1840, then coll. ; in C. 20, s. Mayhew, 1851, '. . . I wished to do the thing square and proper,' O.E.D.—2. Solidly, (almost) unanimously : coll. : 1867 (O.E.D.) ; mostly U.S.—3. Correctly, duly : coll. : 1889, ' Rolf Boldrewood ', ' Here they were married, all square and regular, by the Scotch clergyman,' O.E.D.

square, be on the. To be a Mason : mid-C. 19–20.

square, be pushed off the. To be excused, or dismissed from, recruits' preliminary drill : Regular Army coll. : C. 20. F. & Gibbons. The *square* is the barrack-square.

square, on or **upon the.** See **square,** n., 2.—2. On the tramp : beggars' and tramps' c. (— 1926). F. Jennings, *In London's Shadows.*—3. Engaged in

squad-drill : military coll. : late C. 19–20. B. & P. I.e. on the barracks-square.

square, straight down the crooked lane and all round the. A late C. 19–early 20 c.p. : ' A humorous way of setting a man on his word,' F. & H.

square, turn. To reform, and get one's living honestly : from ca. 1850. H., 1st ed.

square at (1827, De Quincey ; ob. by 1890, † by 1920) ; **square up to** (from ca. 1850). To take up a boxing stance against (a person) : coll. till ca. 1880. then S.E. Ex *squaring one's shoulders.*

square an' all ! ' Of a truth ; verily,' C. J, Dennis : (low) Australian : C. 20.

square bit, piece, (rarely **tack.** A sweetheart : military : from not later than 1916. F. & Gibbons ; B. & P. Ex :—2. **square bit, piece, pusher,** a respectable girl or young woman : low and military : from not later than 1914. Ibid. Here, *bit* and *piece* = a girl or a woman. For *pusher* see **square-pushing.**

square clobber, square cove, square crib. Here, *square* = respectable, reputable : C. 19–20 : coll. (though *clobber* and *crib* are not coll.). Vaux. A variation of *square*, honest, honourable, etc., applied to the implied activities.

Square Drinks, the. See **Diamond Drinks.**

square dinkum is an occ. variant of *fair dinkum*, itself an intensive of *dinkum* (q.v.), genuine, honest, straightforward : from ca. 1910. G. & Gibbons. *A square dinkum bloke* is the highest Australian praise for any man.

square-face ; squareface. Gin ; schiedam : 1879 (O.E.D.). Mostly South African. Ex ' the square bottles in which it was retailed in all parts of South Africa,' Pettman.

square-head ; squarehead. A Scandinavian or, esp. in G.W. and after, a German : coll. : late C. 19–20. Ex shape of head.—2. Earlier, a free immigrant : Australia : ca. 1870–90.—3. In c., an honest man : mid-C. 19–20 ; ob.

square it. To act, esp. to live, honestly : 1873 (O.E.D.) : coll.

square-mainsail coat. A frock coat : nautical, esp. naval : late C. 19–20. Bowen.

square number. An easy billet : naval : C. 20. Ibid., ' the " number " refers to the station bill in which every man's job is entered.'

square off. To placate (a person) : Australian : from ca. 1905.

square peg in a round hole, a. See **peg in . . .**

square piece. See **square bit.**

square-pusher. A decent girl : lower classes' (— 1902) >, by 1915, almost exclusively military. Lit., a ' square ' or respectable ' pusher ' or girl. F. & H. (at *pusher*) ; B. & P.—2. In pl., civilian boots : military : 1914–18. B. & P., 3rd ed.

square-pushing. An instance, or the habit, of ' walking out ' with a girl or young woman : military : from ca. 1885. Ex the military practice of strolling with nursemaids and other maids round the square, or perhaps by back-formation ex the preceding. See also **pusher.** B. & P. Frank Richards considers (wrongly, I think) that the phrase originated ' in the care that men took to get their knapsack to look properly square before parading in full order ' : *Old-Soldier Sahib*, 1936.

square round. To make room : Winchester coll. : mid-C. 19–20. Wrench. Ex dial. sense, ' to sit so as to widen the circle and make room for others ' (E.D.D.).

square-rigged. Well-dressed : from ca. 1850

(ob.); coll., orig. and mainly nautical. Ex the lit. S.E. sense. Cf. *rig-out*, q.v., and :

square tack. See **square bit.**

square (the) yards. To settle a score, esp. to take vengeance : from ca. 1835 (ob.) : nautical. Dana, 'Many a delay and vexation . . . did he get to " square the yards with the bloody quill-driver " ' ; Bowen.

square-toes. See **old square-toes.**

square up. To pay (a debt) : coll. : 1862, Mrs Henry Wood, ' I can square up some of my liabilities here,' O.E.D. Ex *square*, v., 1.

square up to. See **square at.**

squaresel. A square-sail : nautical coll. (—1887). Baumann.

squarum. A lapstone : shoemakers' : from ca. 1860. H., 3rd ed. I.e. *a square one*.

squash. A scrimmage or rough scrum : school football s. : from middle 1850's.

squash, v. To silence or snub (a person) crush-ingly : coll. : from ca. 1900.

squash ballad. A ballad ' prompting war and personal devotion ': pacifists' : 1896–1910. Ware. ? ex sentiment.

squashed fly or, gen., **flies.** A sandwich biscuit with currants : children's : late C. 19–20.

squat. A seat : London lower classes' (— 1909). Ware. Also *do a squat*.

squatter. A kind of bronze-wing pigeon : Aus-tralian coll. nickname : from ca. 1870. Morris.

squattez-vous ! Sit down ! : from late 1890's. Kipling's *Stalky*, ' Be quick, you ass ! . . . Squattez-vous on the floor, then ! ' Cf. *twiggez-vous*.

*squawl. A variant of **squall.**

*squeak. A criminal that, apprehended, informs on his colleagues : c. (— 1795) ; ob. by 1850, † by 1880. Cf. *squeak*, v., 1, and *squeal*.—2. A piece of information to the police : c. : C. 20. Edgar Wallace. Esp. *put in the squeak*, to turn informer : c. (— 1935). David Hume. Ex :

*squeak. To turn informer : c. : C. 18–20 ; ob. *A New Canting Dict.*, 1725 ; Ainsworth. Cf. *squeal*. Ex :—2. To confess (v.i.) : s. : late C. 17–20 ; ob. In C. 10–20, rare except as in sense 1. Dryden, 1690, ' Put a civil question to him upon the rack, and he squeaks, I warrant him.' In construction, *squeak on* (a person), as in Edgar Wallace, *Room 13*.

*squeak, put in the. See **squeak,** n., 2.

*squeak beef. To cry ' Stop thief ! : c. : late C. 17–early 19. B.E. ; Grose, 1st ed.

*squeak on. The v.t. form of *squeak*, v., 2, q.v.

squeak than wool, more. See **wool, more squeak than.**

squeaker. A pot-boy : ca. 1670–1830. Coles, 1676 ; Egan's Grose.—2. A child ; esp. a bastard : from ca. 1670. Coles, B.E., Grose. Cf. *squealer*, 2. —3. A youngster : nautical : mid-C. 18–19. Bowen, who notes that in the training-ship *Conway* it designates a mizzen-top cadet (late C. 19–20). John Masefield, however, in his history of the *Conway* (1933), defines it as ' a small, noisy cadet ', —not that the definitions are mutually exclusive ! Comparable is the late C. 19–20 Public School sense, a boy in the lowest form (e.g. in Ian Hay, *David and Destiny*, 1934.)—4. A blab ; an informer, esp. to the police : C. 19–20. Cf. *squeak*, v.—5. A foxhound : sporting : 1828 (O.E.D.).—6. A pig, esp. if young : coll. : from ca. 1860.—7. A heavy blow : 1877 (O.E.D.) : s. >, ca. 1890, coll. ; ob. Ex effect.— 8. See **squeakers.**—9. An Australian coll. name

' applied to various birds from their cries ' : 1848, J. Gould, *The Birds of Australia*. (Morris).—10. A cicada : South African coll. (mostly juvenile) : from the 1890's. Pettman. It's ' cry ' is hardly a squeak.—11. A tapioca pudding : nautical : late C. 19–20. Bowen.

squeaker, stifle the. To get rid of a bastard : late C. 17–20 ; ob. B.E.—2. Hence, in C. 19–20, to procure abortion. Both senses, low s. ; almost c.

Squeaker, the. *The Speaker* : journalists' : 1890's. Ware. It was the Radical mouthpiece.

*squeakers. Organ pipes : c. : late C. 18–20 ; ob. Grose, 2nd ed.

*squeal. An informer : Scots c. (— 1823) ; ob. Egan's Grose. Cf. *squealer*, 1.—2. Bacon : late C. 19–20. ' Hamadryad ' in *The Saturday Review*, April 21, 1934, ' The farme.'s land, crops, pigs and squeal.'

*squeal, v.i. ; v.t. with **on.** To turn informer : c., orig. (— 1864), North Country ; but in late C. 19–20 mainly U.S. H., 3rd ed. Cf. *squeak*, v., 1.

*squealer. An informer : c. (— 1864). H., 3rd ed. Ex *squeal*, v.—2. An illegitimate baby : low s. (— 1864). H., 3rd ed. Cf. *squeaker*, 2.—3. A noisy small boy : Wellington (the English public school) : late C. 19–20. Cf. *squeaker*, 3.—4. A pork sausage : tramps' c. : C. 20. (W. A. Gape, *Half a Million Tramps*, 1936.)

squealer, v.i. To behave as a noisy lower-form boy : Wellington College : C. 20. C.O.D., 1934 Sup.

squeege. Squeeze (n. and v.) : (in C. 20, low) coll. : late C. 18–20.

squeegee band. ' An improvised ship's band ' : nautical : C. 20. Bowen. Ex the sound made by the squeegee when vigorously used.

squeek, squeeker. B.E.'s spelling of *squeak*, *squeaker*, qq.v.

*squeeze. The neck : c. (— 1812) ; ob. Vaux. Also *squeezer*. Ex squeezing by the gallows-rope.— 2. Hence, the rope itself : c. : from ca. 1830 ; ob.— 3. Silk : c. (— 1839). Brandon. Also as adj. from ca. 1870. Ex squeezeability into very small space.—4. Hence, a silk tie : c. : 1877 (O.E.D.).— 5. Work, esp. in a crowd, e.g. stealing at a theatre : c. (— 1864) ; ob. H., 3rd ed. Perhaps ex :—6. A crowded assembly or (social) gathering : coll. : 1799, Mrs Barbauld, ' There is a squeeze, a fuss, a drum, a rout, and lastly a hurricane, when the whole house is full from top to bottom,' O.E.D.— 7. An escape, esp. if a narrow one : coll. : 1875 (O.E.D.) ; ob. Ex *squeeze by* or *past*.—8. A strong commercial demand or money-market pressure : coll. : 1890 (O.E.D.) : trade and Stock Exchange.— 9. An illegal exaction : Anglo-Chinese coll. : from ca. 1880. Yule & Burnell.—10–12. Without date or quotation, F. & H. gives the following three s. senses : a hard bargain (from ca. 1870) ; hence, a Hobson's choice (ca. 1880–1920) ; a rise in salary (ca. 1890–1910), this last because of the difficulty of obtaining it.—13. An impression : police coll. : C. 20 ; G. D. H. and M. Cole, *Burglars in Bucks*, 1930 ; Richard Keverne, *Menace*, 1933, ' Parry's " squeeze " of the key to the Bruges warehouse.'

squeeze. To bring into trouble : 1804 (O.E.D.) ; ob. by 1890, † by 1920.

squeeze, at (1897) or **upon** (1892 ; ob.) **a.** At a pinch : coll. O.E.D.

squeeze-box. A ship's harmonium : naval (— 1909). Ware, ' From the action of the feet.'

squeeze-crab. A morose or a peevish man : low — 1887). Baumann.

squeeze-em-close. Sexual intercourse : coll. : mid-C. 19–20.

squeeze-wax. A surety : C. 18–early 19. Grose, 1st ed. Ex sealing.—2. An accommodating sort of fellow : c. (— 1923). Manchon.

squeezable. Easy to make speak : lower classes' coll. (— 1923). Manchon.

*squeezer. The hangman's noose : c. : from ca. 1830 ; ob. ' Father Prout ' Mahoney.—2. Hence, the neck : c. of ca. 1840–90. Cf. *squeeze*, n., 1.

squelcher. A heavy blow, crushing leading article, etc. : coll. : 1854, ' Cuthbert Bede ', ' There's a squelcher in the bread-basket ' ; 1876, Besant & Rice (editorial). O.E.D.

squib. An apprentice ' puff ', getting half the salary of a ' puff ' (one who, at a gaming-house, receives money with which, as a decoy, to play) : ca. 1730–1830 : c. > s. > coll.—2. A gun : 1839, G. W. R. Reynolds (O.E.D.) ; almost †.—3. A sweet in the form of a squib : coll. : mid-C. 19–20. Mayhew. O.E.D.—4. (Gen. pl.) A head of asparagus : London (mainly costers') : from ca. 1850. Mayhew. Ex shape.—5. A paint-brush ; gen. pl. (— 1864). H., 3rd ed.—6. In Christ Church (Oxford) s., any member of the University not privileged to belong to ' the House ' : ca. 1860–70.—7. A professional punter : turf c. (— 1932). Ex his often ' pyrotechnic ' gains.

squiffed. Tipsy : late C. 19–20 ; ob. Prob. ex *squiffy*, q.v.

squiffer. A concertina : rather low : 1911, George Bernard Shaw (O.E.D. Sup.), but prob. dating from ca. 1890, for it was orig. a nautical term (Bowen). Perhaps a perversion of *squeezer* : cf. dial. *squidge* for *squeege*.—2. ' By a process of excusable exaggeration, an organ-bellows, or even the organ itself. By a characteristic confusion of ideas, a person who blows an organ ', Ian Hay (in *David and Destiny*, 1934) : Public Schools'.

squiffy. Slightly drunk : from ca. 1873. H., 6th ed.—2. Hence, drunk in any degree : from ca. 1880. Kipling, 1900, ' I never got squiffy but once . . . an' it made me horrid sick,' Prob. ex *skew-whiff*, perhaps on *swipey*, q.v.

[**squigly,** squirmy and wriggly, is rather S.E. than coll.]

squilde. A ' term of street chaff ' : London proletariat : 1895–96. A blend of a Christian and a surname. (Ware.)

squillagee. An unpopular seaman : nautical : C. 20. Bowen. Ex nautical *squillagee*, a small swab ; itself a diminutive of *squeegee*.

squinsy. See **hempen squinsy**.

squint. ' A man who hangs about the market with a paltry order, and who will not deal fairly ' : Stock Exchange (— 1909). Ware. Cf. Fr. *louche*.

squint, v. To lack (anything material) : tailors' : from ca. 1870 ; ob.

squint-a-pipes. A squinting person : from ca. 1786 ; † by 1870. Grose, 2nd ed.

squint is better than two finesses, one. A c.p. addressed, in bridge, to one's partner, to warn him that the opponents are trying to see his hand : from ca. 1925, and mostly Anglo-Irish.

squinters. The eyes : boxers' and low : from ca. 1860 ; ob. Baumann.

Squinting Jack. John Wilkes (1727–97), writer-politician. Ex his deformity. Dawson.

squire. A title prefixed to a country gentleman's surname and thus forming, very often, part of his appellation : mid-C. 17–20 : S.E. until C. 19, then coll. (O.E.D.) Cf. *squire, the*, q.v.

squire, stand. To stand treat : coll. : ca. 1780–1850. Grose, 1st ed. Cf. :

squire, the. ' A Sir Timothy Treat-all,' B.E. : late C. 17–early 19. Sometimes amplified to *squire of the company*, as in Grose, 1st ed. Cf. preceding entry.—2. A simpleton or a fool : late C. 17–mid-18. B.E., who adds : ' *A fat Squire*, a rich Fool.' Cf., perhaps abbr. of *squire of Alsatia*.

Squire Gawk(e)y. Richard Grenville (1711–79), 1st Earl Temple, the statesman. ' Ridiculously awkward ' (Horace Walpole). Dawson.

squire of Alsatia. See **Alsatia**.—**squire of the company.** See **squire, the**, 1.

squire of the gimlet. A tapster : jocular coll. : ca. 1670–1800.

squire of the pad. See **pad**.

squire of the placket. A pimp : jocular coll. : ca. 1630–1800. D'Avenant. O.E.D. With these *squire* terms, cf. the much larger *knight* group.

squirish. Of ' One that pretends to Pay all Reckonings, and is not strong enough in the Pocket,' B.E. : late C. 17–mid-18. Ex *squire, the*, 1, q.v.—2. Foolish : same period. B.E. See **squire, the**, 2.

squirl. A flourish in writing : dial. (ca. 1840) >, before 1900, coll. (O.E.D. Sup.) Prob. ex *squiggle* and *twirl*.

squirm. A small objectionable boy : Public Schools : from ca. 1880 ; ob. Cf. *squirt*.

squirrel. A harlot : late C. 18–mid-19. Grose, 2nd ed., ' Because she, like that animal, covers her back with her tail. *Meretrix corpore corpus alit*.'

squirt. A paltry person ; a contemptible person, esp. if mean or treacherous : coll. : U.S. (— 1848), anglicised ca. 1875 ; common also in dial. Cf. *squit*.—2. Hence, at Public Schools, an obnoxious boy : from ca. 1880. Cf. *squirm*, q.v.—3. A doctor ; a dispensing chemist : from late 1850's ; slightly ob. H., 1st ed. Ex *squirt*, a syringe.—4. Champagne : low : from ca. 1870 ; ob. Ware, ' Suggested by its uppishness.' Cf. *fizz*.—5. A water-pistol : mostly boys' : from ca. 1900. Collinson.—6. Hence (?), a revolver : Australian c. (— 1926) >, by 1930, low s. (Jice Doone) ; in N.Z c. by not later than 1932. It sprays with bullets. 7. The cheapest (and worst) beer : low : from ca. 1920. Ex its effect : cf. *squitters* and *belly-vengeance*, qq.v.

squirt, v.i. To blab : low coll. : C. 19. Prob. ex excremental sense.

squirt, do a squeeze and a. (Of the male) to coït : low : C. 19–20. Also *squirt one's juice*.

squirt a mouldy. See **mouldy**, 2.

squish. Marmalade : university (— 1874), hence Public Schools'. H., 5th ed. Ex *squishy*, soft and wet, or *squish*, v.i., to squirt out splashily or gushingly.—2. At Winchester, from ca. 1880, also and mainly, it = weak tea.—3. Nonsense : 1912 (O.E.D. Sup.) ; ob. Ex senses 1, 2—esp. 1. Cf *slush*.

squit. In same sense as, and prob. cognate with, *squirt*, n., 1, q.v. : dial. (— 1825), partly colloquial-ised ca. 1880 (cf. Anstey, 1889, ' He's not half a bad little squit,' O.E.D.) and by 1920, > s. Esp. a small cadet (*Conway* s. : late C. 19–20,—witness John Masefield's history of the *Conway*, 1933), and used, in gen., esp. of a small man, as in G. D. H. and M. Cole, *The Great Southern Mystery*, 1931, ' Little squit of a chap.'

squitters. Diarrhœa : mid-C. 17–20 : S.E. till C. 19, then dial. ; in late C. 19–20, also schoolboys' **s.** Cognate with *squirt*.

squivalens. Extras ; perquisites : Australian : ca. 1870–1910. R. D. Barton, *Reminiscences of an Australian Pioneer*, 1917. Perhaps ex *equivalents*.

squiz. 'A brief glance,' C. J. Dennis ; a sly glance : (low) Australian. Ex *squint* + *quiz*. (Cf. *swiz*.)

squo. Racquets played with a soft ball : Charterhouse : from ca. 1880. Also in *squo-ball* and *-court*. By a slurring of *squash*, that game. (A. H. Tod.) Hence, *squo off*, to snub (a person) : ibid. : C. 20. By a pun : cf. *squash*, v.

squob ; squob up. See **squab, squab up.**

[**squooch** in Manchon is dial.—more gen. *squa(i)ch.*]

sres-wort ; sreswort. Trousers : back **s.** (—1859). H., 1st ed. See :

sret-sio ; sretsio. Oysters : back **s.** (— 1874). H., 5th ed., where, of *spinsrap, sret-sio, sres-wort, starps, stools, storrac, stun,* and *stunlaw,* qq.v., it is said that ' all these will take the *s,* which is now [i.e. there] initial, after them, if desired, and, as may be seen, some take it doubly.'

St. See **saint, Saint.—st, 'st.** Shall : orig. and properly dial., but occ. illiterate coll. : late C. 16– mid-18. Cotton, 1670, ' Hee st give me Kisses half a score,' O.E.D. Gen. written as in *we'st* = *we'll*.

stab, 'stab. Establishment, as in *on (the) stab,* in regular work at a fixed wage, as opp. to occasional piece-work : printers' (— 1864). H., 3rd ed.

stab, v.i. S. or coll. (? orig. c.), ca. 1670–1780, as in Cotton's *Complete Gamester* : ' Stabbing, . . . having a smooth box and small in the bottom, you drop in both your dice in such a manner as you would have them sticking therein . . . the dice lying one upon another ; so that, turning up the box, the dice never tumble . . . by which means you have bottoms according to the tops you put in.'

stab at, have or **make a.** To attempt, endeavour, have a shot at : coll., orig. (ca. 1907) U.S., anglicised ca. 1929. O.E.D. (Sup.).

stab in the thigh. To coït (with a woman) : coll. : C. 19–20.

stab-rag. A (regimental) tailor : military : from ca. 1840. *Punch,* 1841 ; H., 3rd ed. ; O.E.D. (Sup.). Also *rag-stabber* : mid-C. 19–20. Cf. *prick-louse.*

stab yourself and pass the bottle ! Help yourself and pass the bottle : a theatrical c.p. (— 1864) ; very ob. H., 3rd ed. Ex dagger-and-poison melodrama.

stabbed with a Bridport dagger. See **Bridport dagger.**

stable-companion. A member of the same club, clique, etc. : coll. : C. 20. Ex lit. sense, a horse from the same stable.

stable Jack. A cavalryman : infantrymen's (—1909) ; ob. Ware.

stable-mind. Devotion to horses : Society (—1909) ; ob. Ware. By a pun.

stable-my-naggie, play at. To coït : C. 19–20 ; ob.

stack. To shuffle (a pack of cards) in a dishonest manner : C. 20 : coll. >, by 1930, S.E. Ex U.S. (late C. 19).—2. Hence, to take an unfair advantage : from ca. 1905 : coll. >, by 1933, S.E.

stacks (of the ready). Plenty of money : coll. : late C. 19–20. F. & H. In the singular, *stack,* a quantity, is S.E. (unrecorded before 1894 : O.E.D.).

—2. Hence, *stacks* = much, as in *stacks of fun* (cf. *heaps of fun*) : C. 20. O.E.D. (Sup.).

staff. (Gen. **the.**) Staff-sergeant : Regular Army coll. : C. 20. F. & Gibbons. Cf. *major, the.*

staff, the worse end of the. (Gen. preceded by *have.*) The disadvantage : coll. : ca. 1530–1890. One of the Coventry Plays, 1534 ; J. Wilson, *The Cheats,* 1664 ; North, 1740. (Apperson.) Whence *wrong end of the stick.*

staff-breaker or **-climber.** A woman : low : C. 19–20. Ex such literary euphemisms as *staff, staff of life,* and *staff of love.* Cf. allusive S.E. *lance.*

staff crawl. An inspection tour of the trenches by a general and his staff : military coll. : 1915–18. F. & Gibbons.

staff naked. Gin : low (— 1857) ; † by 1920. ' Ducange Anglicus.' Perhaps a mere misprint for **stark-naked,** q.v.

Stafford court, be tried or **have a trial in.** To be (severely) beaten, greatly ill-used : coll. : early C. 17. Cotgrave. (Cf. the late C. 14–early 15 *clad in Stafford blue,* blue-bruised by beating : either coll. or merely jocular S.E.) Prob. ex :

Stafford law. ' Club ' law ; violence : coll. : late C. 16–mid-17. Occ., as in ' Water-Poet ' Taylor, *Stafford's law.* Punning *staff.* Cf. preceding entry.

Staffordshire Knots, the. The 80th Foot—now the South Staffordshire—Regiment. Military : C. 19–20. Their badge, adopted in 1793, is a knotted cable ; prob. suggested by *Stafford('s) knot,* a knot resembling that used heraldically in the badge of the Stafford family. (F. & Gibbons.)

*****stag.** An informer : c. (— 1725) >, ca. 1820, low s. ; virtually †. *A New Canting Dict.,* 1725 ; Grose ; Ainsworth. Ex the animal ; cf. *stag, turn,* q.v.—2. A professional bailsman or alibi-provider : c. of ca. 1820–90. ' Jon Bee.' Perhaps ironically on ' noble beast '.—3. Any such applicant for shares as intends to sell immediately at a profit or, if no profit quickly accrues, is ready to forfeit the deposit money : commercial : 1846, Thackeray (O.E.D.). Perhaps ex sense 1.—4. Hence, an irregular outside dealer : commercial : 1854 (O.E.D.).—5. A shilling : low s. (— 1857) ; ob. ' Ducange Anglicus ', 1st ed. ; Henley, 1887. Cf. *hog.*—6. See **stag-dance, -month, -party, -widow.**—7. See **stag, in.**— 8. Sentry-go : military : late C. 19–20. B. & P. Prob. ex sense 1.

*****stag,** v.t. To observe, watch, detect : late C. 18–20 : c. >, ca. 1850, low s. (Also, from ca. 1820, as v.i. ' Jon Bee.') Grose, 3rd ed. ; H. Kingsley, 1859. Ex *stag,* n., 1.—2. Hence, v.i., to turn informer (*against*) : c. : from late 1830's. W. Carleton, 1839 (O.E.D.). Cf. *stag, turn,* q.v.—3. To be severe towards (a person) ; to cripple (him) financially ; refuse a loan to : from ca. 1810. *The Daily News,* July 13, 1870, ' A man refusing . . ., his line was . . . " stagged ", and when he went for an advance it was resolutely refused,' O.E.D. Ex sense 1.—4. V.i. and v.t., to beg (money) ; dun (a person) : low s., perhaps orig. c. (— 1860) ; ob. H., 2nd ed.—5. V.i., to deal in shares as a ' stag ' (see **stag,** n., 3 and 4) : commercial : mid-C. 19–20. Often *stag it,* as in Thackeray, 1845.—6. To cut ; mostly in *stag off* : Canadian, esp. lumbermen's (— 1932). John Beames. Ex Midlands dial. *stag,* ' to cut a hedge level at the top ' (E.D.D.)

stag, in. Naked : C. 17 coll. Dekker, 1602. ? ex a stag's colour.

*****stag, turn.** To impeach one's accomplices : c. (— 1785) >, ca. 1840, low **s.** Grose, 1st ed., ' From a herd of deer who are said to turn their horns against any of their number who is hunted.'

stag-book. A book containing (gen. only) the names of bogus shareholders : commercial : 1854, *Household Words* (O.E.D.). See **stag,** n., 3.

stag-dance. A dance with only men present : U.S. (— 1848), partly anglicised ca. 1870. Cf. *bull-dance* and see *stag-party*.

stag-mag. A stage-manager ; to stage-manage : theatrical : from ca. 1880.

stag-month. The month of a woman's lying-in : from ca. 1870 ; ob. Cf. the C. 18 *gander-month*, q.v. ; cf. also the next two entries.

stag-party. A party of men : U.S. (1856), anglicised ca. 1870. Cf. *stag-dance*.

stag-widow. A man whose wife is lying in : from ca. 1870. Cf. *stag-month*.

*stage ; always **the s.** The privilege-period of a convict's imprisonment ; gained by a certain number of good-conduct (or remission) marks : c. (— 1932). Anon., *Dartmoor from Within*. I.e. the final stage.

stage, v. To do or accomplish, esp. if unexpectedly or very effectively or effectually : mainly sporting : from ca. 1920. E.g., Crawford was, in the Wimbledon semi-finals, 1934, said to have staged a come-back against Shields after being two, and very nearly three, sets down. Cf. s. use of *show*.

[**stager,** old. A veteran ; a person (occ. an animal) of experience : late C. 16–20 : either coll. > S.E. or always S.E. Cf. Old Fr. *estagier*, an inhabitant or resident.]

*stagger. A spy ; a look-out : c. (— 1859) >, ca. 1880, low s. H., 1st ed. Ex *stag*, v., 1.—2. An attempt : dial. (— 1880) >, ca. 1890, s. Esp. in telegraphers' s. (— 1895), 'a guess at an illegible word in a telegram,' Funk & Wagnall.—3. See **staggers.**

stagger, v. To go : among young men-about-town : from ca. 1908. P. G. Wodehouse ; Dorothy Sayer's Lord Peter Wimsey novels. Hence, *stagger off* (e.g. to bed), to depart.

stagger, do a. See **do a stagger.**

stagger out, to depart : 1909, P. G. Wodehouse, *Mike*.

stagger-juice. Strong liquor : Australian : 1907 (O.E.D.) ; slightly ob. Also, in gen. low s., *staggering juice* (Manchon).

staggers, get the. To lose one's touch, temporarily lose one's skill ; to be making mistakes : sporting : 1933, *The Passing Show*, July 15. Ex the next.

staggers, the. A drunken fit : coll. : C. 19–20. Ex *have the staggers*, to be unable to walk straight.

staggery. (Of an animal) affected with staggers (1778) ; (of a person) apt to stagger ; unsteady (1837, Dickens). Coll. O.E.D.

stagging, vbl.n. ; ppl.adj. See **stag,** v., the fifth sense. Kinglsey, 1849 : both.

Stagyrite is incorrect for *Stagirite* : C. 18–20. (O.E.D.).

Stahlhelmer. A member of the Stahlhelm (the Ger. organisation of Steel Helmets) : coll. : 1928 (O.E.D. Sup.).

Staines, be at. To be in pecuniary difficulties : ca. 1810–50. Vaux. Also, *be at the Bush*, in reference to the Bush Inn at Staines.

stair-steps, -steppers. Children at regular intervals, as one sees by (e.g.) their height : coll. : both in C. R. Cooper, *Lions 'n' Tigers*, 1925. O.E.D. (Sup.).

*stairs without a landing, the. A treadmill : c. : ca. 1880–1910. J. Greenwood, 1884, 'He's lodging now at Coldbaths Fields—getting up the stairs without a landing.' Cf. *everlasting staircase*.

stajum. Stadium : sol., mostly Cockney and Australian (— 1916). C. J. Dennis.

*stake. A booty acquired by robbery, a ' swag ' ; if large, *a prime* or *a heavy stake* : c. (— 1812) >, ca. 1850, low s. ; ob. Vaux.—2. Hence, same period, a valuable or desirable acquisition of any kind is a *stake*. Vaux.

stake one's lot. To gamble all : Glagsow coll. (— 1934).

stakes, the ——. The [specified] ' line ', way of life : coll. : C. 20. As in James Curtis, *The Gilt Kid*, 1936, ' Both men looked as if they might be on the Jo Roncing stakes ' (q.v. at *Joe Ronce*). Prob. ex racing j.

stalding is incorrect for *scalding* : C. 16–17. Holinshed. O.E.D.

*stale. A thief's or sharper's accomplice, gen. acting as a decoy : ca. 1520–1650 : S.E. >, ca. 1590, c., as in Greene and ' Water-Poet ' Taylor. Ex *stale*, a decoy-bird. An early form of *stall*.

stale bear or **bull.** A ' bear ' having long been short of, a ' bull ' having long held, stock : Stock Exchange coll. : from ca. 1890.

stalk, the. The gallows in Punch and Judy : showmen's : mid-C. 19–20.

stalk a judy. To follow (and accost) a woman : low : late C. 19–20. Cf. :

stalk the streets. (Of either sex) to look for sexual satisfaction : late C. 19–20 ; ob.

stalky. Clever, cunning ; cleverly or cunningly contrived : schoolboys' : ca. 1895–1900. Thus in Kipling's school-story. (O.E.D. Sup.) I.e. good at stalking.

*stall. A pickpocket's helper, who distracts the victim's attention : c. : from ca. 1590. Greene, 1591 ; Dekker. (Also *stallsman*.) Ex *stall*, a decoy-bird. Cf. *stale*, q.v.—2. Hence, the practice, or an act, of ' stalling ', i.e. thus helping a pickpocket : c. : from ca. 1810. Vaux, ' A violent pressure in a crowd, made by pickpockets.'—3. Hence, a pretext—or its means—for theft or imposition : from ca. 1850 : c. >, ca. 1910, low s. Mayhew.—4. Hence, any pretext or excuse ; esp. a playing for time : from ca. 1855. H., 1st ed. Cf. *stall-off*, n.

*stall, v. To screen (a pickpocket or his thieving) : c. : from ca. 1590. Greene, 1592 ; Head ; ' Ducange Anglicus '. Ex *stall*, n., 1, q.v. Also *stall off*, q.v., and cf. *stall up*.—2. V.i., to make excuses, allege pretexts, play for time : from ca. 1870. Ex *stall*, n., 3.—3. V.i., to play a role : theatrical : from ca. 1860. H., 2nd ed. Perhaps suggested by preceding sense.—4. V.i., to lodge, or to stay the night at, a public house : from ca. 1855 ; slightly ob. H., 1st ed. Prob. ex dial. (in Shakespeare, S.E.) *stall*, to dwell.—5. V.i., to travel about : c. : ca. 1840–90. ' *No. 747*.' Perhaps the imm. origin of sense 4.—6. See **stall one's mug** and **stall to the rogue.**—7. V.i., to hang about : grafters' : late C. 19–20. (P. Allingham, 1934.) Ex senses 2 and 4.

*stall, chuck (one) a. The same as *stall*, v., 1 : c. : from ca. 1880. J. Greenwood in *The Daily Telegraph*, Dec. 30, 1881, republished in 1884.

*stall, make a. To effect a robbery as in *stall up*, q.v. : c. (— 1812). Vaux.

stall, put up a, v.i. To mislead, to deceive, to

hoodwink : lower classes' (late C. 19–20) and military (C. 20). F. & Gibbons. Ex *stall*, n., 4.

*stall-off. An act of ' stalling off ' ; an evasive trick or story ; a pretence, excuse, or prevarication : c. (−1812). Vaux ; Mayhew. (O.E.D.) Cf. :

*stall off, v. See **stall**, v., 1 : c. : from ca. 1810. Vaux.—2. Hence, to avoid or get rid of evasively or plausibly : c. (− 1812) >, ca. 1850, s. Vaux ; H., 1st ed. ; Sala (O.E.D.).—3. Hence, to extricate, free, get off (a person) by trickery or other artifice : c. (− 1812) >, ca. 1860, s. ; ob. Vaux.—4. Hence, or ex sense 2, to keep the mastery, maintain superiority, over (a competitor, be it horse, as orig., or man) : sporting : 1883 (O.E.D.). Frequently *stall off the challenge of* (another horse in the race).

stall one's mug. To depart ; esp. hurriedly : c. : mid-C. 19–20 ; ob. Gen. *stall your mug !*, a sharp order. ' Ducange Anglicus ', 1857 ; H., 1st ed. Prob. ex *stall off*, v., 2, q.v.

stall-pot. (Gen. pl.) The occupant of a stall-seat : theatrical (− 1909). Ware.

*stall to the rogue ; occ. to the order of rogues. To instal (a beggar) in roguery, appoint him a member of the underworld : c. : ca. 1565–1840, but archaic after C. 17. Harman, B.E. By itself, *stall* is rare ; Fletcher, 1622, has ' I . . . stall thee by the Salmon '—by the beggar's oath—'. . . To mand on the pad.'

*stall up. To hustle, after surrounding, a person being robbed : c. (− 1812). Vaux, who specifies the method whereby the victim's arms are forced up and kept in the air. Cf. *stall*, v., 1.

*stall-whimper. A bastard : c. (− 1676) ; † by 1840. Coles, Grose.

staller. A person constantly, or very good at, making excuses or playing for time : from ca. 1870. Ex *stall*, n., 3, via v., 2.

*staller-up. One who acts as in *stall up*, q.v. : c. : from ca. 1810. Vaux.—2. Hence, any accomplice of a pickpocket : c. : from ca. 1820.

*stalling. The ' ordination ' and/or actual ' ordaining ' of a beggar : c. (− 1688) ; † by 1850. Randle Holme. See **stall to the rogue.**

*stalling-ken. Also, in C. 16, *staulinge, stawling-* ; in C. 17, *stawling-, stuling.* A house, office, or room for the reception of stolen goods : c. : ca. 1565–1840, but archaic after ca. 1750. Harman, B.E., Grose. Here, *stalling* simply = placing.

*stallsman ; incorrectly, **stalsman.** See **stall**, n., 1. : c. (− 1839) ; ob. Brandon ; H., 1st ed.

stalume. Incorrect for *stallion* : C. 16. O.E.D.

*stam flash. To talk the s. of the underworld : c. : late C. 17–early 19. B.E. ; Grose (1st ed.), who repeats B.E.'s misprinted *flesh.* See **flash**, n. ; *stam*, unrecorded except in this phrase and ignored by the O.E.D., is prob. cognate with A.-S. *stemn*, a voice, via the *stefne* (*steven*) of M.E., which has occ. examples in *-m-* or *-mn-* ; its imm. source is prob. either Ger. *stimmen*, to make one's voice heard, to sing (cf. the lit. meaning of *to cant*, particularly significant for our phrase), or the corresponding Dutch v., *stemmen.*

stammel. ' A brawny, lusty, strapping Wench ', B.E. : late C. 16–early 19. Deloney, 1597 (O.E.D.) ; Grose, 1st ed. Perhaps = ' wearer of a stammel '—coarse woollen—' petticoat,' O.E.D. The form *strammel* does not occur before C. 18 and is gen. applied to an animal.

*stammer. An indictment : c. of ca. 1820–60. Egan's Grose. Ex its effect.

*stamp. See **stamps.**—2. ' A particular manner

of throwing the dice out of the box, by striking it with violence against the table,' Grose, 2nd ed. : from ca. 1770 : dicing coll. >, by 1830, j. ; ob.

stamp-and-go. A chanty ' sung for a straight pull along the deck ' : nautical : late C. 19–20. Bowen.

stamp-crab. A heavy walker : late C. 19–early 20 ; ob. On *beetle-crusher.*

*stamp-drawers. Stockings : c. : C. 17–early 19. See **drawers** and **stamps.**

stamp-in-the-ashes. Some fancy drink : early C. 16. Cf. *swell-nose.*

*stampers. Shoes or boots : c. : from ca. 1565 ; ob. Harman ; B.E. ; Grose ; Egan, 1828, ' My padders, my stampers, my buckets, otherwise my boots.' Cf. *stamps*, 2.—2. Hence, feet : c. : ca. 1650–90. Brome, Head. Cf. *stamps*, 1.—3. Carriers : c. : from ca. 1670. Coles ; B.E. ; *The Sporting Magazine*, 1819, ' Coster-mongers, in all their gradations, down to the Stampers,' O.E.D. ; † by 1860. Hence, in late C. 17–18, *deuseaville stampers*, county or country carriers : B.E.

*stamps. Legs : c. : ca. 1565–1840. Harman, Grose. Because with them one stamps. Cf. *stampers*, 2.—2. Hence, shoes : c. (− 1812) ; ob. Vaux. Cf. *stampers*, 1.—3. Types, esp. in *picking up stamps*, composing : printers' s. (− 1875). O.E.D. Cf. *stamp*, a die.

stan. To stand : sol. : C. 19–20. Michael Harrison, *Spring in Tartarus*, 1935, ' A sharp word of command bit like acid into the lush half-silence. Company : fohm-*fowers !* Stan-*nat* ease ! '

stand. A thief's assistant that keeps watch : c. of ca. 1590–1640. Greene ; ' Water-Poet ' Taylor. (O.E.D.) Ex standing on watch : cf. *standing.*—2. An *erectio penis* : low coll. : C. 19–20. Ex the v. —3. A mouth-whore : low (? rather, c.) : late C. 19–20.

stand, v. To make a present of ; to pay for : coll. : 1835, Dickens, ' [He] " stood " considerable quantities of spirits-and-water ', O.E.D.—2. Hence, to pay for the drinks of (a person, or persons) : coll. : 1894 (O.E.D.).—3. To make stand ; set upright, leave standing ; set firmly in a specified place, or position : 1837, Dickens : coll. >, ca. 1870, familiar S.E. E.g. ' stand a child in the corner.'— 4. See **stand in** and **stand up** ; also see **pad, patter, racket, sam, treat,** and **velvet.**

' **stand always !** ', as the girl said. A c.p., mid-C. 19–20 (ob.), with a punning reference to priapism. Ex the physiological S.E. sense of *stand.*

stand at ease ! Cheese : military rhyming s. : late C. 19–20. F. & Gibbons.

stand bluff or **buff.** To swear it is so ; to stand firm ; to take the consequences : late C. 17–20 ; *bluff*, † by 1900 ; *buff*, ob. ' Hudibras ' Butler ; Fielding ; Sheridan, 1777 (*bluff* : ? earliest record) ; Scott. See **buff.**

stand for. To endure, tolerate ; agree to : U.S. (middle 1890's), anglicised as a coll. in early 1920's. O.E.D. (Sup.).

stand (one) in. To cost (a person) so much, the sum gen. being stated : C. 15–20 : S.E. until ca. 1850, then coll. ; in C. 20, fashionable s. when not dial. Thackeray, 1848, ' It stands me in eight shillings a bottle,' O.E.D.

stand-off. Stand-offish : Australian coll. (− 1916). C. J. Dennis.

stand on me for that ! You can take my word for it ! : sporting c.p. : from before 1932. *Slang*, p. 242.

stand on one's hind legs. To show temper: coll.: late C. 19–20.

stand on the stones. See **stones, stand on the.**

stand one's hand. To meet the bill (esp. for the company's refreshment or entertainment): coll.: from ca. 1880. H. Nisbet, 1892, ' I used to see her . . . " standing her hand " liberally to all . . . in the bar,' O.E.D. Cf. *stand shot*, q.v.

***stand pad** or (derivatively) **Paddy.** (Of a pedlar) to sell from a stationary position: tramps' c.: resp. C. 18–20 and late C. 19–20. Ex *pad*, a road.

stand ready at the door. To be handy for use: coll.: mid-C. 19–20 ; ob. Ex spade, axe, saddle and bridle, whip, gen. standing there.

stand right under ! Clear out ! : nautical coll. (— 1887). Baumann. Ex nautical j. *stand from under*.'

stand sam. See **sam, stand.**

stand shot ; rarely **stand the shot.** Same as *stand one's hand*, q.v. : coll. : from ca. 1820. V.t. with *to*. Cf. *stand sam* and S.E. *stand treat*.

***stand the patter.** See **patter, stand the.**

stand to, boys !, the Jocks are going over. A c.p. jocularly directed at ' kilties ' : 1916–18. B. & P. The ' Jocks ' were extremely popular with women, Australians, journalists.

stand to sense. See **sense, stand to.**

stand-up. A dance : low coll. : 1851, Mayhew, ' It was a penny a dance . . ., and each stand-up took a quarter of an hour,' O.E.D.—2. A meal or a snack taken standing : coll. (1884 : O.E.D.) >, ca. 1910, S.E. Cf. *perpendicular*.—3. An act of copulation done standing : low coll. : mid-C. 19–20. Also a *perpendicular* or *knee-trembler*.

stand up, v.i. To shelter from the rain : coll. and dial. : 1887, ' Mark Rutherford ' ; 1908, G. K. Chesterton, ' Hoping . . . that the snow-shower might be slight, he . . . stood up under the doorway.' O.E.D.—2. V.t., to keep waiting ; to deceive : c. : from ca. 1925. J. Curtis, *The Gilt Kid*, 1936, ' He didn't want Maisie to think that he was standing her up.'

stand up in. To be wearing at that moment : coll. : C. 20. ' I can't very well stay the night, I've only the things I stand up in.'

stand-up prayers. Divine Service under makeshift conditions : naval coll. : 1914–18. F. & Gibbons.

stand-up seat, have a. To (be obliged to) stand, e.g. in a train : jocular coll. : C. 20.

stand up with. To dance with : coll. : 1812, Jane Austen, ' If you want to dance, Fanny, I will stand up with you ' ; ob.—2. To act as bridesmaid or groomsman for : mid-C. 19–20 ; ob. by 1910, † by 1935.

standard. (A person's) height : catachrestic for *stature* : C. 19–20. O.E.D.

***stander.** A criminal's, esp. a thief's, sentinel : early C. 17 c. Rowlands, 1610.

***standing.** A thieves' station : c. : 1548, Latimer ; † by 1590.

standing, take. To accept composedly, endure patiently or without fuss : coll. : 1901, *The Free Lance*, April 27, ' Like a philosophical American, he took it standing, merely remarking . . .' Ex taking a high jump without a run up.

***standing bridge.** A thief's or thieves' sentinel : c. : late C. 17–early 19. B.E., ' The Thieves Scout or Perdu ' ; Grose. Cf. *sneaking bridge* ; see **bridge.**

standing part. ' The original structure of anything that has since been embellished, even down to a much-patched pair of trousers ' (Bowen) : nautical coll. : late C. 19–20. Ex the nautical j. senses.

standing patterer. One of those men ' who take a stand on the curb of a public thoroughfare, and deliver prepared speeches to effect a sale of any articles they have to vend ' (esp. broadsides), H., 1st ed. : London s. (from ca. 1850), ob. by 1890, † by 1910 ; The Metropolitan Streets' Act, 1867, made it very difficult for them. Contrast *flying stationer* and cf. *paper-worker*.

standing prick has no conscience, a. A low c.p. (mid-C. 19–20) that, from its verity and force, has >, virtually, a proverb.

standing room for (a man), make. To receive him sexually : low : late C. 19–20. Whence *understandings*, a woman's conquests ; ob.

standing ware. A variant of *stand*, n., 2, q.v. : mid-C. 19–20.

stang(e)y. A tailor : low : late C. 18–20 ; ob. Grose, 1st ed. (also *twangey*) ; H., 2nd ed. (Cf. *prick-louse*.) Ex the needle : cf. *stang*, an eel-spear. —2. A person under petticoat government : rural (— 1860). H., 2nd ed. Ex the custom of *riding the stang*, where *stang* = a pole.

[**stangs,** says Manchon, is c. for ' chains ' : but is not this an error for *slangs ?* See **slangs, 1.**]

stap my vitals ! A coll. exclamation or asseveration : late C. 17–20 ; ob. Ex Lord Foppington's pronunciation, in Vanbrugh's *The Relapse*, 1696, of *stop*. In late C. 19–20, occ. affectedly, *stap me !* (O.E.D.)

staph. Staphylococcus, a common type of bacteria : medical students' (— 1933). *Slang*, p. 190. Cf. *strep*.

Star. (Always **the Star.**) The Star and Garter inn at Richmond : coll. (— 1864). H., 3rd ed.

***star.** A ' starring the glaze ' ; *the star*, this practice : c. (— 1812) ; ob. Vaux, ' A person convicted of this offence, is . . . *done for a star*.' See **star the glaze.**—2. One who ' shines ' in society ; a very distinguished person : mid-C. 19–20 : mostly coll.—3. Hence, in late C. 19–20, a famous actor or actress, esp. the most prominent one in any given play or film : coll. Ex *to star*, 2, q.v.—4. ' An article introduced into a sale after the catalogue has been printed : marked in the official copy by a *star*,' F. & H. : auctioneers' : from ca. 1880.—5. In reference to the badge worn by first offenders : prison s. : 1882 (O.E.D.). E.g. *star-class prisoners*. —6. Hence, a prisoner of the ' star ' class : coll. : 1903, Lord W. Neville (O.E.D.).

star, v. See **star the glaze.**—2. V.i., to act the leading part in a play : 1824 (O.E.D.) : coll. >, by 1860, S.E. Also, from 1825, *star it* : same status.— 3. Hence v.t., as in *star the provinces*, to tour there as the ' star ' of a dramatic company : 1850, Thackeray, ' She . . . had starred the provinces with great éclat,' O.E.D. : coll. till ca. 1870, then S.E.

star and garter !, my ; gen. **my ss. and gg.** A coll. expression of astonishment : 1850, R. G. Cumming, ' My stars and garters ! what sort of man is this ? ' (O.E.D.) Cf. *stars !, my*, q.v.

star-back. An expensive seat : circus s. (— 1933). Edward Seago, *Circus Company*. I.e. a seat with a back, not a mere plank.

star company. A company with one star, and the rest mere nobodies : theatrical coll. : ca. 1884–1914. Ware.

star-gazer. A penis in erection : C. 18–20 ; ob.— 2. A hedge whore : from ca. 1780 ; ob. Grose, 1st ed.—-3. A horse that, in trotting, holds its head well up : late C. 18–mid-19. Grose, 1st ed.—4. An imaginary sail : nautical : from ca. 1865 ; ob. Smyth ; Clark Russell. Prob. suggested by nautical *sky-scraper*.

star-gazing on one's back, go. (Of a woman) to coït : low : mid-C. 19–20. Ex *star-gazer*, 2, q.v.

*****Star Hotel, sleep in the.** To sleep in the open : New Zealand tramps' c. (— 1932). Cf. *sleep with Mrs Green*.

star it. See **star**, v., 2.

*****star-lay.** Robbery by breaking windows : c. : from ca. 1810 ; ob. *Lex. Bal.*, Egan's Grose, Baumann, misprint it as *star lag*. Ex *star the glaze*.

*****star man.** A prisoner on first conviction : c. and police s. (— 1933). Charles E. Leach. Ex the official mark against his name.

Star of the Line, the. The 29th Foot—in late C. 19–20, the Worcestershire—Regiment : military : C. 19–20 ; ob. F. & Gibbons. Ex the ' eight-pointed " Garter Star ", worn as a special distinction on the greatcoat straps.'

star of the movies, the. The No. 9 pill : military : 1917 ; ob. B. & P. It caused one to move briskly to the latrine.

*****star-pitch.** A sleep(ing) in the open : tramps' c. : from ca. 1870. Cf. *Hedge Square* and *do a starry* (see at **starry**) and *Star Hotel* . . .

*****star the glaze.** ' To break and rob a jeweller's show glass,' Grose, 2nd ed. : c. : from ca. 1786 ; ob.—2. Hence, to smash any window (or show-case) and steal the contents : c. : C. 19–20 ; ob. Ex *star*, to mark or adorn with a star. Cf. *star*, n., and *star-lay*, qq.v.

starboard fore-lift(, give a person a shake of one's). The right hand : nautical : mid-C. 19–early 20. Bowen.

starbowlines. The starboard watch : nautical : mid-C. 19–20 ; ob. Bowen. Cf. *larbowlines*, q.v.

Starch Johnny. John Crowne (d. 1703), the dramatist. Dawson.

starch out of, take the. (Of a woman) to receive sexually : low : mid-C. 19–20. Ex the S.E. sense, to abase or humiliate.

starcher. A stiff white tie : late C. 19–20 ; ob. Ex † *starcher* (starched cravat).

starchy. Drunk : from ca. 1870 ; ob. (Not upper-class s.)

stare, as like as one can (or could). Very like in appearance : coll. : 1714, Gay, ' A fine child, as like his dad as he could stare ' ; Jane Austen. Ob. O.E.D.

stare-cat. An inquisitive neighbour, esp. if a woman : women's : orig. U.S., anglicised ca. 1902. Cf. *rubber-neck*, q.v., and *copy-cat*.

stare like a dead (1694, Motteux) or **a stuck** (1720, Gay) **pig.** To gape and stare in utter astonishment or dismay : coll. : the former, rare and † by 1800 ; the latter (G. Parker, 1789 ; Joseph Thomas, 1895), actively extant, but considered, in C. 20, as slightly vulgar. Apperson, who cites the Cheshire *stare like a choked throstle* and *like a throttled cat* or *earwig*.

starers. Long-handled eye-glasses ; a lorgnette : coll. (society > by 1900, gen.) : 1894, Anthony Hope, *The Dolly Dialogues*.

staring-quarter. An ox-cheek : late C. 18–mid-19. Grose, 1st ed. In dial., a ' staring quarter ' is a laughing-stock.

stark-naked. (Neat or raw) gin : low : 1820, J. H. Reynolds (O.E.D.) ; almost †. Cf. *strip-me-naked*. q.v.—2. Occ. any unadulterated spirit :

from late 1850's. H., 2nd ed.—3. Hence, adj. : unadulterated : mid-C. 19–20. All senses derive ex the notion of resultant poverty.

starkers ; starko. Stark-naked : from ca. 1910 : resp. Oxford University s. and low coll. Manchon. I.e. *stark* + ' the Oxford-*er* ' with ' familiar plural-isation ', and *stark* + the lower-class suffix *o* (as in *wido*).

starling. See **brother starling.**—2. A marked man : police : from ca. 1890. Because ' spotted ' or starred, marked with an asterisk for future reference.

starn, n. Stern : nautical coll. (— 1887). Baumann. Ex dial.

starps. Sprats : back s. (— 1859). H., 1st ed. See *sret-sio*.

*****starrer.** See **angler.**

*****starry, do a.** To sleep in the open : tramps' c. : C. 20. Cf. *star-pitch*.

stars, see. See **see stars.**

stars !, my. Good heavens ! : coll. : 1728, Van-brugh & Cibber, ' My stars ! and you would really live in London half the year, to be sober in it ? ', O.E.D.—2. **stars and garters !, my.** See **star and garter.** Cf. :

stars out ! A *Conway* cadets' c.p. expressive of incredulity : ca. 1900. John Masefield, *The Conway*, 1933.

start. The brewer's procedure whereby he empties several barrels of liquor into a tub and thence conveys it, through a leather pipe, down to the butts in the cellar : late C. 17–mid-18. B.E.—2. A prison : from ca. 1820 ; ob. C. >, ca. 1860, low s. Ex *Siart, the*, 1, q.v.—3. A surprising incident or procedure : 1837, Dickens (*queer start*). Often *rum(my) start* : mid-C. 19–20 : cf. *rum go*. O.E.D. Ex the start of surprise.—4. See **Start, the,** 2 and 3.

start, v.t., as in the *Gentleman's Magazine*, 1825, ' " I started him." To start is to apply a smart word to an idle or forgetful person,' O.E.D. In short, to make him jump by startling him.

*****Start, the.** Newgate prison : c. : mid-C. 18–19. Also, in late C. 18–19, *the Old Start*, as in Grose, 2nd ed. Perhaps because Newgate represented the beginning of a personal ' epoch ' ; but cf. Romany *stardo*, imprisoned,—it is therefore ultimately cognate with *stir*, a prison.—2. Hence, the Old Bailey : c. : mid-C. 19–20. Mayhew. Likewise, *the Old Start*.—3. London : tramps' c. >, ca. 1870, low s. ' *No. 747* ', reference valid for 1845 ; Mayhew, 1851 ; H., 5th ed. (status). Also without article : mid-C. 19–20 (ob.), as in ' Gypsy ' Carew's *Autobiography* and ' Ducange Anglicus '. ' The great starting point for beggars and tramps,' H., 2nd ed.

start in, v.i. ; v.t. with **on.** To begin work, one's job (on or at) : coll. : U.S. (— 1892), anglicised ca. 1900. E.g. ' I start in, Monday.'

start on. To tease, jest at, bully : coll. : late C. 19–20.

start tack or sheet. See **tack or sheet.**

*****starter.** A question : c. : late C. 17–early 18. B.E. Because apt to make one start in surprise or dismay. Cf. *start*, n., 3., and v.—2. A laxative : lower classes' (— 1923). Manchon.

Starvation ; Starvation Dundas. Henry Dundas, first Viscount Melville (1742–1811). On March 6, 1775, Dundas, in a famous speech on American affairs, introduced *starvation* ; which word > thence-forward a nickname that survived until some years after his death. H. Walpole, April 25, 1781, 'Starvation Dundas, whose pious policy suggested that the devil of rebellion could be expelled only by fasting '; W. Mason, in 1782, was app. the first to use the shorter name.

starvation, adv. Gen. *starvation cheap*, as in Kipling, 1892 (the adv.'s first appearance in print): coll. Lit., so as to cause starvation ; hence, excessively, extremely.

starve, do a. To be starving : (mostly lower classes') coll. : from ca. 1910 at the latest.

Starve'em, Rob'em, and Cheat'em. Stroud, Rochester, and Chatham : naval and military : ca. 1780–1890. Grose, 1st ed. ; H., 3rd ed. Cf. *the London Smash'em and Do-for-'em*, the old London, Chatham, and Dover Railway.

Starving Fifty or **Hungry Half Hundred.** 'The R.N.R. officers admitted into the Supplementary List of the R.N., in 1913 ': naval. Bowen. Cf. *Hungry Hundred*, q.v.

***stash.** To stop, desist from : c. (— 1811) >, ca. 1840, low s. >, ca. 1870, s. *Lex. Bal.*, 1811, 'The cove tipped the prosecutor fifty quid to stash the business '; Vaux ; 1841, Leman Rede, 'Stash your patter '—shut up !—' and come along.' Prob., as W. suggests, ex *stow + squash* : cf. Vaux at *stash*. Perhaps, however, it blends *stop + squash* : Chignell. —2. Hence, to quit (a place) : 1889, 'Rolf Boldrewood ', 'The rest of us . . . stashed the camp and cleared out,' O.E.D.—3. See next three entries.

stash it. Specifically, 'to give over a lewd or intemperate course of life,' H., 1859 ; ob.—2. **stash it !** Specifically, be quiet ! : ibid. See **stash, l.**

***stash the glim.** To cease using the light ; to extinguish it : c. (— 1823) >, ca. 1840, low s. ; † by 1890. 'Jon Bee ', 1823. Cf. *douse the glim.* Ex *stash*, 1.

stash up. To terminate abruptly, as in the earliest record (H. G. Wells' *Tono Bungay*, 1909), 'She brought her [piano-]playing to an end by— as schoolboys say—"stashing it up ",' O.E.D. Ex *stash*, 1. Among dockers, from ca. 1920, *to have stashed the game up* is to have stopped the job : *The Daily Herald*, late July or early Aug., 1936.

state. A dreadful state, esp. of untidiness, confusion, dirtiness : coll. : 1879, F. W. Robinson, 'Just look what a [dirty] state I am in ! ' O.E.D. ; C. 20, 'The house *is* in a state ! '—2. Agitation, anxiety, state of excitement : coll. : 1837, Marryat (O.E.D.) ; W. E. Richards, in *The Humorist*, Aug. 18, 1934, 'When I reached the station, my wife was in what is known in domestic circles as " a state ".'

state, lie in. To be 'in bed with three regular harlots ', Grose, 1st ed. : ca. 1780–1850.

State frighters. 'Those who foolishly fear any infringement of their own State-rights ': Australian (— 1935).

[State nicknames, U.S.A., are very little known in the British Empire. The best lists are those in F. & H., vol. 6, 1903, at *State Nicknames* ; Thornton's *American Glossary*, 1912, *passim* ; and Harvey's *Oxford Companion to English Literature* in the latest edition.]

state of elevation, in a. A coll. >, in late C. 19, S.E. ; very ob. As in Smollett, 1749, 'We drank hard, and went home in a state of elevation, that is half-seas over.'

state tea. A 'tea at which every atom of the

family plate is exhibited ': Society : ca. 1870–1914. Ware, 'Probably suggested by State ball.'

state-the-case man. 'A pressed seaman whose protests were strong enough to bring an Admiralty order that he should be given a chance to state his case ': naval coll. : ca. 1770–1840. Bowen.

Stater. A member of the Irish Free State Army : Anglo-Irish coll. : from 1922.

states can be saved without it. A 'political, hence cultured, c.p. expressive of ironic condemnation : ca. 1880–90. Ware.

states of independency. The 'frontiers of extravagance,' Egan's Grose : Oxford University, ca. 1820–40.

station—see 'Westminster School slang '—is on the border-line between coll. and j.

station-jack. A meat pudding used on stations : Australian coll. : 1853. (Morris.)

stationery. Free passes : theatrical : from ca. 1880 ; ob. Ex synonymous *paper*, q.v.—2. Cigarettes : C. 20 ; now rare.

stationmaster's hat. 'The cap with gilt peak worn by commanders and above ': from ca. 1916 : naval officers'. Bowen.

statiscope. Incorrect (C. 20) for *statoscope*; *statory* (C. 17), for *statary.* O.E.D.

***staulinge-, stawling(e)-ken.** See **stalling-ken.**

stay. A cuckold : ca. 1810–50. *Lex. Bal.* ? because he stays his hand.

stay. To lodge or reside regularly or permanently : standard Scots (C. 18–20) >, in late C. 19, Colonial, esp. South African, Australian, and New Zealand. (O.E.D.)

stay, come to. To become permanent, established, recognised, regularly used : coll. : orig. (1863, Abraham Lincoln), U.S. ; anglicised in late 1890's. *The Athenœum*, April 13, 1901, 'Lord Byron as a letter-writter has come to stay.'—2. Hence, (of merchandise, etc.) to secure a position in public favour as fulfilling a general need : coll. : 1903, *The Referee*, Feb. 8, 'No one with half a grain of sense could . . . question the autocars' many merits, nor their having come to stay and become a great power in the land.'

stay and be hanged ! A lower-middle class c.p. of C. 19–early 20 : 'Oh, all right ! ' Ware.

stay out. To stay in, esp. because on the sick list : Eton College (— 1857). See esp. Brinsley Richards's and 'Mac' 's memoirs of Eton. By antiphrasis.

stay put. See **put, stay.**

stay-tape. A tailor : coll. : ca. 1780–1850. Grose, 1st ed. Ex the frequency with which that article figured in tailors' bills. Cf. :

stay-tape is scorched, one's. One is in bad health: tailors' : late C. 19–20. E.g. in *The Tailor and Cutter*, Nov. 29, 1928.

stay with. To keep up with (a competitor, a rival, in any contest) : U.S. (1887) ; anglicised, as a coll., ca. 1920.

staying. For a day, a week, etc., as in 'They have staying visitors ': non-aristocratic coll. (— 1887). Baumann.

Staymaker, the (old). Sir Alex Thomson, Chief Baron of the Exchequer in 1815–17. Dawson, 'From his habit of checking witnesses.'

staysel. A staysail : nautical coll. (— 1887). Baumann.

'stead for **instead** is coll. in late C. 19–20. O.E.D.; Baumann.

steady. A steady admirer, wooer, of a girl (rarely

vice versa) : U.S. (ca. 1899) ; anglicised by 1907 ; by 1930, coll. O.E.D. (Sup.).

steady, the Buffs ! A c.p of adjuration or of self-admonition : mid C. 19–20 : military and, in C. 20, naval. Of anecdotal origin.

steal. A thieving ; a theft ; a thing stolen : Scots (− 1825) >, ca. 1890, coll. ; since ca. 1920, rare except in U.S. *The Saturday Review*, July 26, 1890, ' This is an audacious steal from " In a Gondola " ! ' O.E.D.

steal a manchet or **a roll out of the brewer's basket** ; gen. **have stolen . . .** To be tipsy : coll. : ca. 1670–1820. Ray, 1678, *manchet* ; Fuller, 1732, *roll*.

steal the show. See show, steal the.

stealers, the ten. The fingers : first half of C. 17. Davenport, 1639 (O.E.D.). Ex Shakespeare's *pickers and stealers*, q.v.

steam. A trip or excursion by steamer : coll. : 1854, Kingsley (O.E.D.). Ex nautical usage as in *a few hours' steam away.*—2. A dish cooked by steaming : coll. (orig. military) : 1900 (O.E.D.) ; by 1930, > rare. Cf. *steaming.*—3. The phrases *get (one's) steam up*, to start, and *put the steam on*, to try or begin to work hard, are S.E. verging on coll. Baumann, 1887.—4. Cheap, fiery liquor (esp. ' plonk '—Australian brand) : Australian, esp. Sydney, c. : from ca. 1930.

steam, v.t. To convey on any steam-propelled vessel : coll. : 1901 (O.E.D.)

steam, keep up the. See steamer.

steam ahead, away. To put on speed : coll. : 1857, T. Hughes, ' Young Brooke . . . then steams away for the run in,' O.E.D. ; *ahead* not before late C. 19. Ex the motion of a railway engine or of a steamer.—2. Hence, to progress rapidly, to work vigorously : coll. (− 1911). C.O.D.

steam antics. See antics.

steam boatswain or **bo'sun.** An artificer engineer in the Navy : C. 20. Bowen.

steam builders. Shares in the Dublin & Liverpool Steam Building Company : Stock Exchange (− 1895). A. J. Wilson's glossary.

steam-bus. A steam pinnace or launch in the : Navy : C. 20. ' Taffrail ', 1916.

steam-engine. A potato-pie : Lancashire s. (− 1864) ; ob. H., 3rd ed. Prob. ex the steam it emits when properly served at table.

steam-kettle. A steamer : sailing-ships' pejorative : mid-C. 19–20 ; ob. Bowen. A C. 20 variant is *steam-pot* (Manchon).

steam on the table, have. To have ' a boiled joint—generally steaming, on Sunday ' : workmen's : late C. 18–20. Ware.

steam-packet. A jacket : rhyming s. (− 1857). ' Ducange Anglicus.'

steam-pot. See steam-kettle.

steam-roller. A man that is ' sure—but very slow and usually too late ' : military : 1915 ; ob. B. & P. Ex *the Russian steam-roller*, a journalistic term applied to the Russian Army in 1914–15.

steam tug. A ' mug ', a simpleton or easy dupe : low : rhyming s. : C. 20.

steam-tugs. (Bed-)bugs : from ca. 1890. P. P., *Rhyming Slang*, 1932. Contrast *steam-tug.*

steamboat man. See smoke-stack. Virtually †.

steamboating, n. ' Cutting simultaneously a pile of books which are as yet uncovered ' : bookbinders' s. (− 1875) >, by 1890, coll. >, by 1910, j.

steamed-up. Tipsy : Glasgow (− 1934). Because heated.

steamer. A tobacco-pipe. A *swell s.*, a long one. Ca. 1810–50. *Lex. Bal.*, 1811 ; Bee, 1823, ' " Keep up the steam or steamer," to smoke indefatigably.'—2. A ' mug ' : turf c. (− 1932). Ex *steam tug*, q.v. (See *Slang*, p. 241.) Also gen. c. : witness James Curtis, *The Gilt Kid*, 1936.

steamer in one, have a. To be the worse for drink : naval : from ca. 1910. F. & Gibbons. Ex the stertorous breathing.

steaming. A steamed pudding : military (− 1903). Cf. *steam*, n., 2.

*Steel, the. Coldbath Fields prison, London : c. from ca. 1810. *Lex. Bal.*, 1811 ; J. Greenwood, *Dick Temple*, 1888. Virtually † by 1910. Abbr. *Bastille.*—2. Hence (gen. *the steel*) any prison or lock-up : c. >, ca. 1900, low s. : 1845, ' *No. 747* ', p. 413 (*steel*) ; 1889, Thor Fredur, ' He pitched into the policeman, was lugged off to the steel, . . . and got a month ' ; but adumbrated in *Lex. Bal.*, 1811. Cf. *chokey*, *quod*, *limbo*, *stir.*—3. A rare c. sense, viable only ca. 1835–60, is that given by Brandon and ' Ducange Anglicus ' : the treadmill.

Stedman. See promo.

steel-bar driver or **flinger.** A tailor ; esp. a journeyman tailor : resp. ca. 1850–90 (' Ducange Anglicus ') ; ca. 1780–1890 (Grose, 1st ed.). Prob. *steel bar*, a needle, is also s. of same period ; Grose, ibid.

steel jug. A shrapnel-helmet : military, but not very gen. : 1916 ; ob. B. & P. Cf. *tin hat.* (First used on Aug. 12, 1915.)

steel-nose. Some kind of strong liquor : mid-C. 17. Whitlock's *Zootomia*, 1654. O.E.D.

steel-pen coat. A dress coat : coll. : 1873 (O.E.D.) ; ob. Ex the resemblance between the split nib and the divided coat-tail.

Steelbacks, the. The 48th Foot (in late C. 19–20, the 1st Battalion of the Northamptonshire) Regiment ; the 57th Foot, in late C. 19, become the 1st Battalion of the Middlesex Regiment : military : resp. mid-C. 18–20 and C. 19–20. Either ex the weighty packs they carried or with reference to *steelback*, Alicant wine, in some connexion with the Peninsular War ; or, best of all, ex adj. phrase *steel to the (very) back*, very robust, trustworthy, or brave, as in *Titus Andronicus*, IV, iii

Steenie. George Villiers, Duke of Buckingham (1592–1628). ' Given by James I . . . from his fancied resemblance to the head of S. Stephen at Whitehall ' (Dawson). For a brilliant character-sketch, see Evan John, *Charles I*, 1933.

steep. Excessive, resp. of price, fine or damages, taxes, and figures ; hard to believe, exaggerated, esp. of stories : U.S. (1856), anglicised ca. 1880. Baumann, ' This sounds very steep ' ; *The Westminster Gazette*, April 22, 1895, ' This is rather a steep statement,' O.E.D. Cf. *stiff* (price) and *tall* (story).

steer. A piece of information ; mostly *give a steer* : nautical : from ca. 1870. F. & H.

steer a trick. To take a turn at the wheel : nautical : mid-C. 19–20.

steer small. To exercise care : from ca. 1860 : nautical coll. >, by 1900, j. Ex S.E. sense, ' to steer well and within small compass ' (Smyth).

steerage, the. The gun-room : naval : C. 20. Bowen.

steerage hammock. A long meat roly-poly (meat-pudding) : nautical : late C. 19–20. Ibid.

steever. See stiver.—***steevin.** A rare variant of *stephen.* Bee, 1823.

stems. Legs : low : from ca. 1860 ; **ob. H.,** 2nd ed. (Despite F. & H., not coll.)

stenog. A shorthand writer : office coll., orig. (ca. 1905) U.S. ; anglicised ca. 1920. (O.E.D. Sup.) Abbr. *stenographer*.

step. Gen. *a good step* (Sterne, 1768) or *a tidy step* (Blackmore, 1894) ; occ. *a goodish step* (— 1888). A walking distance : dial. and coll. : mid-C. 18–20. O.E.D.—2. A stepfather or stepmother : coll. : late C. 19–20.—3. A step-brother or -sister : coll. : C. 20. (G. Heyer, *Why Shoot a Butler ?*, 1933).

step. To depart, make off, run away : coll. : mid-C. 19–20, though adumbrated as early as C. 15. The variant *step it* occurs both in Mayhew, vol. III, and in H., 1st ed.—2. Hence, to desert : military : from ca. 1870.—3. To clean one's own doorstep or others' doorsteps : coll. : 1884 (O.E.D.) ; slightly ob. Ex *doorstep*.

step !, mind the. A c.p. ' look after yourself ! ' to a parting visitor : from ca. 1880. Ware. Ex lit. admonition, perhaps orig. to a drunkard.

step off. To die : 1926, Edgar Wallace (O.E.D. Sup.) Cf. *step out*.

step on it. To hurry : from ca. 1929. (O.E.D. Sup.) Ex :

step on the gas. See **gas, step on the.**

step out. To die : low : U.S., anglicised in late C. 19. Cf. *pop off*.

step up to. To pay court to (a girl) : lower classes' coll. (— 1923). Manchon.

*****stephen ;** gen. **steven.** Money ; esp. ready money : c. and low s. : ca. 1810–50. *Lex. Bal.,* ' Stephen's at home ; i.e. he has money ' ; Ainsworth. Perhaps suggested by *stever* = stiv(v)er.— 2. Esp. in *Stephen's at home*, the money's there or ready.

*****stepper.** A treadmill : prison c. : mid-C. 19–20 ; ob. Mayhew. Cf. *everlasting staircase*.—2. See **steppers.**—3. A doorstep-cleaner, esp. a step-girl : coll. : 1884 (O.E.D.). Ex *step*, v., 3, q.v.—4. A trotting horse : Cockneys' : 1899, C. Rook, *The Hooligan Nights*.

steppers. The feet : 1853, *Household Words*. Cf. *stampers*, 2, and *stepper*, 1.

*****stepping-ken.** A dance-hall : late C. 19–20 : orig. c. and mostly U.S.

steps. ' Thick slices of bread and butter, overlaying each other on a plate ' : London lower classes' : mid-C. 19–20 ; ob. Ware. Cf. *doorstep*.

*****steps, up the.** Committed for trial : c. (— 1933). Charles E. Leach. Ex going into the dock.

stereo. Stale news : printers' coll. : from late 1880's. Ex *stereotype*.

stereo, adj. Stereoscopic : from ca. 1875 : coll. ; now verging on S.E. (O.E.D.)

sterics, the. Hysteria : a low coll. abbr. of *hysterics* : 1765, Foote. O.E.D.

sterling. Persons born in Great Britain or Ireland : Australian coll. : ca. 1825–1910. Peter Cunningham, 1827. Gen. in juxtaposition to the complementary *currency*, q.v.

stern. The buttocks, esp. of persons : late C. 16–20 : mostly jocular, and since ca. 1860 gen. considered a vulgarism. Furnivall, 1869, ' We don't want to . . . fancy them cherubs without sterns.'

stern, bring (a ship) down by the. To over-officer (a ship) : nautical coll. : from ca. 1835. Dana. Officers slept towards the stern.

stern-chaser ; -post. Resp. a sodomite, a penis :

nautical : mid-C. 19–20.—2. (*s.-chaser* only.) A leg : nautical (— 1923). Manchon.

stern galley. Posteriors : *Conway* cadets' : from before 1887. John Masefield, *The Conway*, 1933.

Steve. A gen. term of address, esp. in *believe me, Steve !* : C. 20, and mostly Australian. Cf. the generic use of *George* and *Jack*. For terms of address, see my essay in *Words !*

Steve !, come on. See **come on, Steve !—Steve ?,** **got me.** See **got me(, Steve)** ? Also *I've got you, Steve !*

*****steven.** See **stephen.—stever.** See **stiver.**

stew. (Great) alarm, anxiety, excitement : 1806, J. Beresford (O.E.D.) : coll. >, ca. 1905, S.E. In late C. 19–20, esp. *be in an awful stew*.—2. A state of perspiration or overheating : coll. : from ca. 1890. Ex *stew*, to remain in a heated room (etc.). Cf. :

stew, v.i. To study hard : orig. and mainly school s. : 1866, *Every Boy's Annual*, ' Cooper was stewing over his books,' O.E.D. See **stew, n.,** 2 ; cf. :

stew-pot. A hard-working student : gen. derisory : from ca. 1880. Ex *stew*, v. ; the pun on the kitchen utensil was perhaps suggested by *swot*.

stewed. (Not very) drunk : s. (— 1874 ; virtually †) synonym with *corned*, *pickled* and *salted*. H., 5th ed.

stibber-gibber, adj. Given to telling lies : mid-C. 16 : ? c. Awdelay, 1561. ? origin.

stick. See **sticks.**—2. A sermon : late 1750's-early 1760's. ? because wooden.—3. A dull, stupid, awkward, or (in the theatre) incompetent person : C. 19–20 : S.E. until mid-C. 19, then coll. Via *wooden*.—4. Quasi-adverbially as an intensive of alliterative phrases ; esp. in *stick*, *stark*, *staring* (*wild*, 1839, Hood ; *mad*, 1909, W. J. Locke). O.E.D.—5. Gen. **the stick,** esp. *give* (a child) *the stick* ; (in C. 20) *get the stick*, to be caned. A beating with a stick : coll. : 1856, Charlotte Yonge. O.E.D.—6. A crowbar or jemmy : c. : from ca. 1870. Horsley, *Jottings from Jail.*—7. A candle-stick ; a candle : silversmiths' : resp. coll. and s. : late C. 19–20.—8. A badly printed ink-roller : printers' : from ca. 1870.—9. A mast : nautical coll. : C. 19–20.—10. Gen. **the stick.** A venereal disease : low : from ca. 1880.—11. A variant form of *sticker*, 4 (q.v.) : 1863 ; ob. Lewis.—12. See **board, n.,** 3.

stick, v.t. (Of the man) to coït with : low : C. 19–20.—2. V.t. (Mostly of persons) to continue long, remain persistently, in one place : C. 19–20 : coll. until late C. 19, then S.E. Of a cricketer, as early as 1832 (see *sticker*, 4).—3. V.t., to put up with (things), tolerate (persons) : 1899, ' He could not " stick " his mother-in-law,' *The Daily News*, Oct. 26 (O.E.D.). Also *stick it*, to continue, without flinching, to do something : the phrase was used by soldiers in the Boer War (1899–1901), as J. Milne, *The Epistles of Atkins*, 1902, makes clear. In the G.W., one often heard " Stick it, lads ! " ' Appears to be a . . . variation on to *stand it*,' W.—4. To bring to a stand(still) ; incapacitate from advance or retirement : coll. : 1829, Scott, in the passive as in gen. ; *The Westminster Gazette*, July 14, 1902, ' The climber may easily find himself " stuck " on the face of a precipice,' O.E.D.—5. Hence, to nonplus ; puzzle greatly : coll. : 1884, *The Literary Era*, ' You could not stick me on the hardest of them,' O.E.D.—6. To cheat (a person) out of money or in dealing ; impose illicitly upon : 1699 ; slightly ob. *Blackwood's Magazine*, 1843, ' They think it ungentlemanly to cheat, or, as they call it, "stick" any of their own set.' Sometimes, esp. in the underworld, to desert : mid-C. 19–20 ; esp. *stuck by a pal*. Also, *stick with*, to saddle (a person) with (anything unpleasant, sham, or worthless), e.g. with an inferior horse : 1900. O.E.D.—7. To settle (a matter) ; gen. *stick a point* : from ca. 1890 ; ob. Lit., make it stick : cf. *stay put*.—8. To persuade to incur expense or loss ; ' let in ' *for* : coll. : 1895, J. G. Millais, ' [He] publishes his work (at his own expense) and sticks his friends for a copy,' O.E.D.—9. See stick it in or on, stick out, stick with, etc.—10. See stuck on.—11. See sticked, be.—12. (Cf. sense 2.) Of a horse : to refuse to start, to jib, to be obstinate : South African coll. (— 1891). Pettman. Cf. *sticks*, 6, q.v.

stick, as close or full as (ever) it (he, they, etc.) can or could. This coll. phrase expresses crowding or repletion : 1776, G. Semple, ' Piles . . . driven in as close together as ever they can stick ' ; 1889, ' Rolf Boldrewood ', ' She . . . was . . . as full of fun . . . as she could stick,' O.E.D. Slightly ob.

stick, be high up the. To be eminent in one's profession or at one's work : ' So high up the stick, they have no time . . . to answer inquiries,' Sir C. Morgan, 1818 ; † by 1890. O.E.D.

stick, cut one's. A variant (Barham, Dickens, De Quincey, Thackeray, Kingsley, Boldrewood), ob. in C. 20, of *cut one's sticks* : see cut . . . sticks.

stick, every. See (furniture) sticks.

stick, fire a good. To be an excellent shot : shooting coll : from ca. 1840. The *stick* is the gun or rifle ; suggested by *play a good stick*.

stick, get the. To be, as the most smartly turned out man, excused guard-duty and made the guard's orderly : Regular Army coll. : late C. 19–20. F. & Gibbons. See also stick wallah.

stick, give some. See give some stick.

stick, have the fiddle but not the. To have the means but not the sense to use them properly : coll. : C. 19. Cf. :

stick, play a good. (Of a fiddler) to play well : 1748, Smollett (O.E.D.) ; ob. Ex *stick*, a violin bow.—2. Hence, to perform, or play one's part, well at anything : coll. : C. 19–20.

stick, shoot for the. To shoot with a view to a good bag, not merely for pleasure : sporting coll. : 1834 (O.E.D.). Ex a tally-stick.

stick, the wrong or right end of the ; gen. preceded by have or get. To have the advantage or the disadvantage in a contest or a bargain : coll. : 1890, ' Rolf Boldrewood ' ; by 1920, virtually S.E. Cf. *staff, worse end of the*.—2. Hence, in C. 20, *to have got hold of the wrong end of the stick* is either to have misunderstood a story or to be ignorant of the facts of a case : still coll.

stick, up the. (Very) eccentric ; crazy, mad : workers' (— 1935). Ex synonymous *up the pole*.

*stick a bust. To commit a burglary : c. (— 1899). Ware.

stick a pin there ! Hold hard : coll. : C. 18. C. Hitchin, *The Regulator*, 1718.

stick and bangers. A billiard-cue and balls : sporting : late C. 19–20. Ware.—2. Whence, in C. 20, a man's sexual apparatus. Ibid.

stick and lift, v.i. To live from hand to mouth : low : from ca. 1870 ; ob.

stick-and-string man. ' The old type of seaman, generally applied by a junior with a touch of envy ' (Bowen) : nautical : late C. 19–20 ; ob.

stick-at-it. A persevering, conscientious person : coll. : 1909, H. G. Wells (O.E.D. Sup.).

stick away, v.t. To hide (an object) ; v.i., to go into hiding : South African coll. : late C. 19–20. Hicks, *The Cape as I Found It*, 1900. Pettman. Cf. S.E. *stick* (a thing) *out of the way*.

*stick-flams. A pair of gloves : c. : late C. 17–19. B.E., Grose, Baumann. Perhaps a corruption of *stick(-on-the)-fams* (lit., stick-on-the-hands).

stick for drinks. To win the toss to decide who shall pay for them : late C. 19–20. An elaboration of *stick*, v., 5, q.v. ; cf. ibid., 8.

stick, frozen on the. See frozen on the stick.

stick-hopper. A hurdler : athletic coll. : late C. 19–20 ; ob. See (athletic) sticks.

stick in it, with a. (Of a drink, esp. tea or coffee) with a dash of brandy : C. 19–20. In late C. 19–20, only Colonial and U.S. Cf. Fr. *du café avec*.

stick-in-the-ribs. Thick soup (like glue) : from ca. 1870 : not upper-class.

stick it. See stick, v., 3, and cf. *stick it out*.

stick it in or on, v.i. To charge extortionately. V.t. *stick it into* or, occ., *on to* : s. >, ca. 1880, coll. : 1844, Dickens, ' We stick it into B. . . . and make a devilish comfortable little property out of him,' O.E.D. See stick, v., 5, and cf. *rush*.—2. stick it into (a person) is also, in Australia, to ask, esp. if surprisingly or abruptly, a person for a loan : C. 20.

stick it out. To endure and go on enduring : coll. : 1901, ' Lucas Malet ', ' It would be ridiculous to fly, so she must stick it out,' O.E.D. A variant of *stick it* : see stick, v., 3.

stick it up. To cause a charge to be placed against one's name, orig. (1864) in a tavern-score, hence (also in 1864) in gen.—i.e. to obtain credit— as in *stick it up to me* !, put it on my account ! Coll. Both in H., 3rd ed.

stick-jaw. A pudding or, as predominantly in C. 20, a sweetmeat that is very difficult to chew : coll. : 1829, Caroline Southey (O.E.D.). Occ. as adj. : late C. 19–20 : coll.—2. Something extremely boring : lower classes' (— 1923). Manchon. Cf. *sticking-plaster*, q.v.

*stick man ; stickman. The accomplice of a pair of women engaged in robbing drunken men ; to him they entrust their booty : c. (— 1861) ; slightly ob. Mayhew.

stick on. See stick it in.—stick on the price, to increase it : coll. : mid-C. 19–20. H., 1st ed., ' *stick on*, to overcharge, or defraud.'

stick one's spoon in the wall. See spoon in the wall.—stick oneself up. See stick up to be.

stick out. V.i., to be conspicuous ; esp. too conspicuous : mid C. 17–20 : S.E. until mid C. 19, then s. (mainly U.S.). *The Daily Chronicle*, Dec. 3, 1902, ' " Of her " is all very well . . ., but when it occurs too often it " sticks out ", as Mr Henry James would say,' O.E.D. Esp. *it sticks out a mile*, it's obvious : used absolutely or with *that*.—2. See stick it out.—3. To persist in demanding (e.g. money) : coll. : v.i., 1906 ; v.t. with *for*, 1902. O.E.D.—4. Hence, (v.t. with *that*) to persist in thinking : coll. : 1904, R. Hichens, ' Do you stick out that Carey didn't love you ? ' Also *stick* (a person) *out*, to maintain an opinion despite all his arguments : coll. : from ca. 1905. O.E.D.

*stick-slinger. One who, gen. in company with harlots, robs or plunders with violence : c. (— 1856). Mayhew. Cf. *bludger*, q.v.

stick to. To remain resolutely faithful to ; or, despite all odds, attached to (a person or a party) :

C. 16–20 : S.E. until ca. 1860 ; thereafter, coll. ; ca. 1800–60, however, it was familiar S.E. H., 2nd ed., 1860 ; ' Mrs Alexander ', 1885, ' But I should have stuck to him through thick and thin,' O.E.D.

stick-up. A stand-up collar : from ca. 1855 (ob.) : coll. >, by 1890, S.E. ' Ducange Anglicus ', 1857.

stick up. See **stick up for**—to—to be—and **stick it up.**—2. V.i., to stand firm in an argument : coll. : 1858, Darwin, ' I admired the way you stuck up about deduction and induction,' O.E.D.—3. (V.t.) In Australia, to stop and rob (a person) on the road : 1846, J. L. Stokes : coll. >, by 1880, S.E. Ex making the victim stick up his hands. Morris.—3a, Hence, to rob (a bank, etc.) : 1888, Boldrewood : coll. >, by 1890, S.E. Morris.—4. Hence, to demand money from (a person) : 1890, Hornung : Australian coll. >, by 1910, S.E.—5. To stop : 1863 : Australian coll. >, by 1890, ' standard '. Morris.—6. To pose or puzzle : 1896 : Australian coll. Morris.—7. To increase (the price or, in games, the score) : ca. 1875–1920. C. Sheard, in his song, *I'm a Millionaire*, ca. 1880, ' Though some stick it up, now I'll pay money down ' ; F. & H., 1903, ' *To stick up tricks (points, runs, goals, &c.)* = to score.'—8. In cricket, to cause (a batsman) to play strictly on the defensive : coll. : 1864, Pycroft (Lewis). Cf. **stick, v., 4,** q.v.

stick up for. To champion (a person) ; defend the character or cause of : coll. : U.S. (1837) >, almost imm., British. H., 1859 ; Thackeray, 1862 ; Anstey, 1882, ' " Why, you are sticking up for him now ! " said Tom . . . astonished at this apparent change of front.' Cf. **stand up for.**

stick up to. To oppose ; esp. to continue offering resistance to : coll. : from ca. 1840 : dial. till ca. 1860, then coll. H., 2nd ed. ; Baumann ; *The Contemporary Review*, Feb., 1889, ' If there is no one who dare stick up to [the head boy], he soon becomes intolerable,' O.E.D.

stick up to be ; occ. **stick oneself up to be.** To claim to be : coll. : 1881, Blackmore, ' I never knew any good come of those fellows who stick up to be everything wonderful,' O.E.D.

stick wallah. A man scheming ' get the stick ' (see **stick, get the**), esp. one who habitually aims at this : Regular Army : late C. 19–20. F. & Gibbons. Perhaps ex S.E. *button-stick.*

stick with. See **stick, v., 6.**

stickability. The ability to preserve and/or endure : coll. : from ca. 1920. O.E.D. (Sup.).

sticked(, be). (To be) caned : Wembley County School : from ca. 1925.

sticker. A commodity hard to sell : coll. : 1824, Dibdin (O.E.D.). Cf. *shop-keeper*, q.v., and see **sticky, adj., 2.**—2. Hence (— 1887), a servant that a registry office has difficulty in placing. G. R. Sims. —3. A lingering guest : coll. (— 1903). F. & H.— 4. A slow-scoring batsman hard to dislodge : cricket coll. : 1832, Pierce Egan, in his *Book of Sports* ; 1888, A. G. Steel ; 1903, W. J. Ford ; 1934, W. J. Lewis's *Language of Cricket.*—5. ' A pointed question, an apt and startling comment or rejoinder, an embarrassing situation,' F. & H. : coll. : 1849, Thackeray (O.E.D.). Ex *stick*, v., 5.— 6. A sticking knife, fishing spear, gaff : coll. : 1896, Baring-Gould (O.E.D.).—7. A *two-*, *three-*, *four-sticker* is a two (etc.)-masted ship, esp. a schooner on the Canadian and American coast : nautical coll. : late C. 19–20. Bowen.—8. A good worker : Glasgow (— 1934).—9. A supporter of a

mob-' king ' : Glasgow c. : C. 20. MacArthur & Long, *No Mean City*, 1935.

sticker-up. One who warmly or resolutely defends (always *for* something) : coll. : 1857, Borrow in *Romany Rye* (O.E.D.). Ex *stick up for.*—In Australia :—2. A rural method of cooking meat by roasting it on a spit : 1830, *The Hobart Town Almanack* : coll. >, by 1870, S.E. Morris.—And, 3, a bushranger : 1879, J. W. Barry : coll. >, by 1890, S.E. ; ob. (Morris.) Ex Australian *stick up*, q.v. Cf. *sticking-up.*

stickiness. The n. ex all senses of *sticky*, adj. : q.v. (Compton Mackenzie, 1933, ' The stickiness of the Treasury.')

sticking-parade. See **stuck, be.**

sticking-plaster. An extremely boring visit (made by another person on oneself) : from ca. 1920. Manchon. Ex its adhesiveness. Cf. *stick-jaw, 2,* q.v.

sticking-up. The action of stopping (person or vehicle) on the road and robbing him or it : 1855, *The Melbourne Argus*, Jan. 18 : coll. >, by 1890, S.E. Ex Australian *stick up* (v.). Cf. *sticker-up,* last sense.

stickler. Erroneous for *sticker*, a gatherer of sticks for firewood : mainly lexicographical, Cowel (1607) having misread a passage in a Roll of 1422 and Todd (1818) and others following him. O.E.D.

*stickman. See **stick man.**

*sticks. (Rare in singular.) Pistols : from ca. 1786 : c. >, ca. 1840, s. ; ob. by 1859 (H., 1st ed.) ; † by 1914, except in still extant *shooting-stick* (1890). Grose, 2nd ed. Whence, *stow your sticks !*, hide your pistols. Ex shape.—2. Household furniture : from ca. 1810 : s. until C. 20, then coll. *Lex. Bal.* ; ' Jon Bee '. Abbr. *sticks of furniture.* The singular is rare and, in C. 20, ob. : 1809, Malkin, *every stick*, app. the only form (O.E.D.).—3. Legs : 1830, Marryat (O.E.D.).—4. The stumps : cricket coll. (in C. 20, S.E.) : from ca. 1840. Lewis.— 5. Hurdles : athletic coll. : from mid-1890's. Cf. *stick-hopper.*—6. A horse that will not move ; one that won't pull : South African coll. (— 1891). Bertram Mitford. Ex Cape Dutch *steeks*, used in the same way.—7. Hence, likewise South African coll. (— 1913), a person either obstinate or obstructive. Pettman. Cf. *stick, n., 3.*—8. A drummer : military (— 1909). Ware. In the Navy, also of a bugler : C. 20. Bowen.—9. A ship's derricks : London dockers' (— 1935). Perhaps by the suggestion of rhyme.

sticks, (as) cross as two. Very angry : coll. : mid-C. 19–20 ; ob. H., 1st ed.

sticks, beat (1820)—rarely **knock** (Thackeray, 1840 ; † by 1930)—**all to.** Utterly to overcome, clearly or completely to surpass : coll. Barham, ' They were beat all to sticks by the lovely Odille.' (O.E.D.) Cf. S.E. *in bits.*

sticks, cut one's. To make off : see **cut . . . sticks** ; cf. *stick, cut one's.*

sticks, go to. To be ruined : coll. : ca. 1842, Carlyle. Emphatically, *go to sticks and staves*, as in *Susan Ferrier*, 1824. Kingsley, 1855, has the variant *go to noggin-staves*, † by 1920. Lit., be smashed.

sticks, in quick. Immediately ; very quickly or rapidly : 1872, Besant & Rice, ' You won't pay her any more attentions, for you shall come out of this place in quick sticks ' ; ob. by 1915, virtually † by 1935. Prob. a fusion of *sticks*, legs, and *cut one's sticks.*

stick(s), up. To set up a boat's mast : nautical s. : *stick*, 1845, rare in C. 20 ; *sticks*, from not later than 1888 (Clark Russell). Occ. fig. Ex *stick*, a mast.

stick's end, keep (a person) **at the.** To treat with reserve : coll. : 1886, Stevenson (O.E.D.) ; ob. Cf. *wouldn't touch* (*him, it*) *with a barge-pole*.

sticks to, hold the ; hold sticks with. ' To compete on equal terms with ' : resp., dial. (ca. 1817) >, ca. 1860, coll. ; and coll. (1853, Reade). O.E.D. Both are, as coll., rare in C. 20. Perhaps ex single-stick.

sticky. (Not to be confused with S.E. *stické*, a game that, fusing racquets and lawn tennis, had a vogue ca. 1903–13.) Lawn tennis in its first decade or perhaps its first three lustres : sporting and social. Ex *sphairistiké*, the game's original designation : invented, like its object, in 1874 by Major Wingfield. *The Saturday Review*, June 30, 1934 ; E.P., Christmas card, 1934.—2. Sealing-wax : from late 1850's. H., 1st ed.—3. Sticking-plaster : lower and lower-middle class coll. : late C. 19–20.

sticky, v. To render sticky : coll. : 1865, Mrs Gaskell, ' I was sadly afraid of stickying my gloves,' O.E.D. Not a common word.

sticky, adj. (Of persons) wooden, dull ; awkward : 1881, Mrs Lynn Linton (O.E.D.). Ex *stick*, a dull person.—2. (Of stock) not easy to sell : Stock Exchange : 1901, *The Times*, Oct. 24 (O.E.D.) : s. >, by 1920, coll. Cf. *sticker*, 1, q.v.—3. (Of persons) not easy to interview ; unpleasant and/or obstinate ; difficult to placate : from ca. 1919. Ex :—4. Of situation, incident, work, duty : unpleasant ; very difficult : 1915 (' A sticky time in the trenches ' : O.E.D. Sup.) ; T. S. Eliot, in *Time and Tide*, Jan. 5, 1935, ' [St Thomas of Canterbury] came to a sticky end.' This sense derives prob. ex senses 1 and 2 + S.E. (? orig.—1898—coll.) *sticky*, (applied to troops) apt to hesitate in obeying commands (O.E.D., adj., 2, 949, § 2, b).—5. See :

sticky at or on, be. To be ' potty ' on (a member of the opposite sex) : lower classes' (— 1923). Manchon. Ex *stuck on*, q.v.

sticky-back. A very small photograph with gummed back : from ca. 1910. A. H. Dawson, *Dict. of Slang*, 1913.

sticky-beak. An inquisitive person : Australian (— 1926). Jice Doone. Ex a bird that, in searching for food, gets its beak sticky.

sticky dog. A sticky wicket : cricketers' : from ca. 1930. (P. G. H. Fender, in *The Evening News*, June 19, 1934.)

sticky Jack. A field-service green envelope (unopened by one's own unit) : military : from 1915. F. & Gibbons. One gummed it down.

***stievel.** A fourpenny piece : old c., says Baumann. But this may be a confusion with *stiver*, q.v.

***stiff.** Paper, a document ; esp. a bill of exchange or a promissory note : c. (— 1823). Egan's Grose. (In ' *No. 747* ' (a reference valid for 1845), an announcement-bill,—a nuance app. † by 1900.) Hence, *give* (one) *the stiff*, to give (one) either of these documents ; *take the*, or *do a bit of, stiff*, to accept a bill or a promissory note.—2. A forged bank-note : c. : late C. 19–20 only.—3. Ex sense 1, a clandestine letter : c. : late C. 19–20. Griffiths, *Fast and Loose*, 1900.—4. A hawker's licence : London c. or low s. : from ca. 1890.—5. A corpse : U.S. (— 1859), anglicised ca. 1880. Medical students *carve a stiff* (dissection). Abbr. *stiff 'un*, 1, q.v.—6. ? hence, a horse certain not to run or, if

running, not to win : the turf : from ca. 1880. Abbr. *stiff 'un*, 2.—7. A wastrel ; a penniless man : 1899, *The Daily Chronicle*, Aug. 10 (O.E.D.). Perhaps orig. South African. Because cramped by lack of money.—8. Esp. in Australia (ex U.S.), a term of contempt (though often jocular), as *you stiff !, the big stiff* : C. 20.—9. ' An unlucky man : one always in trouble ' ; military : from ca. 1910. F. & Gibbons.—10. An unskilled dock-hand : workingmen's : 1914. O.E.D. (Sup.). Prob. ex preceding sense.—11. Money : low : 1930, Belloc (O.E.D. Sup.). Prob. ex sense 1.

stiff, adj. Closely packed : late C. 17–20 : S.E. until C. 19, then coll., but only in *stiff with*, densely crowded with : 1907, ' There seemed . . . more yachts than ever, and the water was " stiff " with masts and rigging,' O.E.D.—2. Certain to win : (esp. Australian) turf : late C. 19–20. Prob. ex *stiff 'un*, 2, by antiphrasis.—3. Hence (of an event), certain to be won : sporting : 1912, *Punch*, Aug. 21, ' He ought to have this event absolutely stiff at the next Olympic Games ' (O.E.D. Sup.).—4. Penniless : Australian : C. 20. Ex *stiff*, n., 7, q.v.—5. ? hence, unlucky : mostly Australian and New Zealand : from ca. 1910. Contrast *tinny*.

stiff. Greatly. Only in *bore* (one) *stiff* : coll. : from ca. 1910. (Cf. the U.S. *scared stiff*.) Lit., to death.

stiff, bit of. See *stiff*, n., 1.

stiff, bookmaker's. ' A horse nobbled at the public cost in the bookmakers' interest,' F. & H. : the turf : from ca. 1880. See *stiff*, n., 6.

stiff, cut up. See *cut up nasty*. Thackeray, ca. 1885.

stiff and stout, the. A *penis erectus* : low : mid-C. 17–20 ; ob. Urquhart.

stiff-arsed. Haughty ; supercilious : low coll. : mid-C. 19–20. Ex *stiff-rumped* : cf. *stiff-rump*, q.v., and *stiff in the back*.

stiff as a poker. (Gen. of posture) very stiff coll. : 1797, Colman, Jr.

***stiff-dealer.** A dealer in *stiff*, n., 1, q.v. : c. : from ca. 1820. ' Jon Bee.'

stiff-fencer. A hawker of writing paper : London low : from ca. 1850. Ex *stiff*, n., 1.

stiff in the back. Resolute ; firm of character : coll. : late C. 19–20. ' Anthony Hope ', 1897, ' Are you going to let him off ? . . . You never can be stiff in the back,' O.E.D.

stiff-lifter. A body-snatcher : Yorkshire s. (— 1904), not dial. E.D.D. Ex *stiff*, n., 5.

stiff one. See *stiff 'un*.

stiff or hard ? By promissory note or in hard cash ? : commercial : from ca. 1860.

stiff-rump. A person haughty or supercilious ; an obstinate one : C. 18–early 19. Addison & Steele, 1709 (O.E.D.). Cf. *stiff-arsed* and *stiff in the back*.

stiff 'un ; occ. stiff one. A corpse : 1823, Egan's Grose (*one*) ; 1831, *The Annual Register* (O.E.D.). Also *stiffy*, q.v.—2. A horse certain not to win : the turf : 1871, ' Hawk's-Eye ', ' Safe uns, or stiff uns.' Also *stiff*, n., 6 ; cf. *dead 'un* and *stumer*, qq.v.

stiff upper lip, carry or have or keep a. To be firm, resolute ; to show no, or only slight, signs of the distress one must be feeling : coll. : resp. 1837, ob. ; 1887, very ob. ; and 1852. App. orig. U.S., for the earliest examples of *carry* and *keep* are American.

stiffen. To kill : 1888.—2. Hence to prevent (a horse) from doing its best : the turf : 1900, *The*

Westminster Gazette, Dec. 19. O.E.D. both senses.
—3. Hence, to buy over (a person) : low Australian
(— 1916). C. J. Dennis. Mostly as passive ppl.

stiffen it !, God. A low oath : late C. 19–20.
Eden Phillpotts, *Sons of the Morning*, 1900 (E.D.D.).
Lit., render it useless, destroy it ; but gen. as a
vague and violent expletive. Cf. *stiffen*, 1.

stiffener. A pick-me-up drink : 1928, Dorothy
Sayers (O.E.D. Sup.). In Glasgow, it is used of
any heavy drink. Now coll.

stiffy. A corpse : late C. 19–20. See **stiff**, n., 5,
and **stiff 'un**, 1.—2. A horse that is losing : Glasgow
sporting (— 1934). Cf. *stiff 'un*, 2.

***stifler.** Always *the s.* : the gallows : c. : 1818,
Scott ; ob. Hence, *nab the stifler*, to be hanged ;
queer the stifler, to escape hanging.—2. A camouflet :
military : 1836 : s. >, ca. 1915, coll.

still. A still-born infant : undertakers' : from
ca. 1860. H., 3rd ed.

still and all. Nevertheless : coll. : C. 20.
K. G. R. Browne, 1934, in *The Humorist*, ' Still and
all . . . the average politician does no great harm
to anybody.'

still going strong. See **Johnny Walker**.

still he is not happy ! A c.p. applied to one whom
nothing pleases, nothing satisfies : ca. 1870–75.
Ware quotes *The Daily Telegraph*, July 28, 1894, as
attributing it to a phrase often spoken in a Gaiety
burlesque of 1870.

still sow. ' A close, slie lurking knave,' Florio :
coll. : late C. 16–mid-17. Ex the proverb, *the still
sow eats up all the draff* (Apperson).

***stilting.** ' First-class pocket-picking,' J. Green-
wood, 1884 : c. ; ob. by 1930. ? a perversion of
tilting, or a pun on *stilting*, the action of stilt-
walking.

Stilton, the. The correct thing : 1859, Hotten ;
virtually †. A polite variation of *cheese*.

stim. A stimulant, gen. of liquor : Society :
1882 ; ob. by 1910, † by 1930.

stimulate, v.i. To drink alcoholic stimulants :
C. 19–20 : S.E. until mid-1830's, then coll. (mostly
U.S.) ; except in U.S., † by 1930.

***sting.** To rob ; to cheat : c. (— 1812) ; † by
1903. Vaux.—2. Hence, to demand or beg something, esp. money, from (a person) ; to get it thus :
late C. 19–20. Cf. *put the nips in*.—3. (Also ex
sense 1.) To swindle, often in a very mild way and
gen. in the passive voice : late C. 19–20. Lyell.—
4. *sting oneself*, to get stung, is coll. and surprisingly
old : 1663, Tuke, ' I've touch'd a nettle, and have
stung my self,' O.E.D.—5. (Gen. in passive.) To
snub : Charterhouse : C. 20.

sting-bum. A niggard : late C. 17–early 19.
B.E. ; Grose. The O.E.D. gives *sting-hum* ; there
is no such term : B.E.'s *b* is irrefutable.

stingareeing. ' The sport of catching *Stingrays*,
or *Stingarees* ' : New Zealand coll. : 1872, Hutton &
Hector, *The Fishes of New Zealand*. (Morris.)

stinger. Anything that stings or smarts : late
C. 16–20 : S.E. until C. 19, then coll., in such senses
as a sharp, heavy blow (1823, Bee) or the hand that
deals it (1855, Browning),—something distressing,
such as a very sharp frost (1853, Surtees),—a
trenchant speech or a pungent (or crushing) argument, as in late C. 19–20. O.E.D. and F. & H.—
2. A bowsprit : Canadian (and U.S.) nautical :
C. 20. Bowen. Perhaps because it is bitterly cold
work on it in the winter.

stinger, fetch a. See **fetch a stinger**.

stingo. Strong ale or beer : from ca. 1630 ; **ob.**

except in the trade name, *Watney's stingo nips*.
Randolph, ca. 1635 ; Ned Ward, 1703 ; Bridges,
1774 ; ca. 1840, Barham (*styngo*) ; 1891, Nat Gould,
' Host Barnes had tapped a barrel of double stingo
for the occasion,' O.E.D. Ex its ' bite ' + Italianate *o*. Cf. *bingo*.—2. Hence, as adj. (C. 19–20)
and, 3, fig. energy, vigour (late C. 19–20 : coll.).

stingy. (Of, esp. nettles) having a sting : coll. :
late C. 19–20. (O.E.D.)

***stink.** A disagreeable exposure ; considerable
alarm : c. (— 1812) >, ca. 1850, low s. >, ca. 1910,
gen. s. Vaux ; Mayhew.—2. Hence, a ' row ' : late
C. 19–20.—3. **big** or **little stink**, a high- or low-
powered boat : Conway cadets' : C. 20. J. Masefield, *The Conway*, 1933.

stink, v.t. To smell the stink of or from : Public
Schools' : C. 20. (E. F. Benson, *David Blaize*,
1916.)

stink, kick up a. See **pen and ink**, 3 ; cf. *stink*, 2.

stink, like. A variant of *like stinking hell*,
desperately hard or fast or much : from not later
than 1915. Ex *stinking hell !*, a C. 20 asseveration.
(D. Sayers & R. Eustace, *The Documents in the Case*,
1930, ' Toiling away like stink.')

stink-bomb. A mustard-gas shell : military
coll. : 1917 ; ob. F. & Gibbons.

stink-car. A motor-car : ca. 1900–10. *The
Sporting Times*, April 27, 1901. Prob. ex *stinker*, 4,
on the analogy of *stinkard*.

stink-finger, play at. To grope a woman : low :
mid-C. 19–20.

stink for a nosegay, take a. To err egregiously,
be very gullible : coll. : late C. 18–mid-19. Malkin,
Gil Blas, 1809.

stink-pot. See sense 3 of **stinker**.—2. An objectionable fellow : late C. 19–20.

stink of money. To be ' lousily ' or ' filthily '
rich : middle and upper classes' (— 1929). The
C.O.D., 2nd ed. (With thanks to O.E.D. Sup.)

stinker. A stinkard, or disgusting, contemptible
person : C. 17–20 : a vulgarism. In C. 20 Glasgow
it is applied esp. to a liar.—2. A black eye : c.
(— 1823) ; † by 1910. Egan's Grose. Cf. sense 5.
—3. Any of the ill-smelling petrels, esp. the giant
fulmar : nautical coll. (— 1896). Also *stink-pot*
(— 1865). O.E.D.—4. Anything with an offensive
smell : a vulgarism : 1898, a motor-car († by 1920 ;
cf. *stink-car*) ; 1899, a rank cigar—former in O.E.D.;
the latter in C. Rook, *The Hooligan Nights* ;
a cigarette made of Virginia tobacco (from before
1923 : Manchon).—5. A heavy blow : C. 20 Public
Schools'. Perhaps a corruption of *stinger*, q.v.
Cf. *come a stinker*, q.v.—6. Hence, a very sharp or
an offensive letter, a stinging criticism, a pungent
comment or a crushing argument : from ca. 1916, it
being orig. military.—7. Anything (very) difficult
to do : from ca. 1924. Lyell. Prob. ex senses 5
and 6.—8. See **Stinker** in Addenda.

stinker, come a. To come a ' cropper ', lit. or
fig. : from before 1923. Manchon. Cf. *stinker*,
n., 5.

stinkeries. A set of cages for a (silver-)fox farm :
middle-class rural : from ca. 1920. (Evelyn
Waugh, *A Handful of Dust*, 1934.)

stinkibus. Bad liquor ; esp. rank, adulterated
spirits : C. 18. Ned Ward, 1706 ; Smollett, 1771
(*stinkubus*). Spurious-Latin suffix on *stink* ; cf.
stingo.

stinking. Disgusting ; contemptible : C. 13–20 :
S.E. until C. 19, then a vulgarism. Cf. *stinker*, 1.—
2. (Of a blow, criticism, repartee, etc.) sharp : C. 20.

See **stinker**, 5, 6.—3. Extremely drunk : Society : from ca. 1929. (Evelyn Waugh, *A Handful of Dust*, 1934.)

stinking, adv. A late C. 19–20 Scots (somewhat uncouth) coll., as in *I'd be stinking fond*, i.e. foolish, *to do it*, I should never think of doing it, I'd certainly not do it. O.E.D.

stinking hell ! ; like stinking hell. See **stink, like.**

stinking Yarra ! See **Yarra, stinking.**

stinkious. Gin : C. 18. F. & H. Perhaps ex *stinkibus*, q.v.

stinkman. A student in natural science, esp. in chemistry : schools' and universities' (— 1923). Manchon. Ex *stinks*, 2 and 1. More gen. and properly *stinksman* or *stinks man*.

Stinkomalee. London University : ca. 1840–70. Ex *stink* on *Trincomalee* : Theodore Hook thus alluded to some topicality affecting that town and to the cow-houses and dunghills that stood on the first site of the University.

stinks. Chemistry : universities and Public Schools' : 1869 (O.E.D.). Ex the smells so desired by youth.—2. By 1902, also Natural Science : ibid. Cf. *tics*.—3. In late C. 19–20, a teacher of, lecturer on, Chemistry : Public Schools'. Cf. :

stinks (O.C.), or **O.C. Stinks.** A gas officer ; a gas instructor : military : from 1916. F. & Gibbons.

stinky. A farrier : military : from ca. 1870. Ex burning of hair or hooves.

stipe. A stipendiary magistrate : rural : from ca. 1859. H., 2nd ed.

stir. An illiterate form of *sir* (in address) : Scots : 1784, Burns ; ob. O.E.D. Cf. the slightly later Scottish *stirra*, sirrah.—2. A prison : mid-C. 19–20 : c. >, ca. 1900, low s. Mayhew, 1851, ' I was in Brummagem, and was seven days in the new " stir " ' ; 1901, *The Referee*, April 28, ' Mr . . . M'Hugh, M.P. . . ., has gone to stir . . . for a seditious libel.' Abbr. Romany *stariben, steripen* (Crofton & Smart) : cf. also Welsh Gypsy *star*, to be imprisoned, and *stardo*, imprisoned, and see **Start, the.** (Much nonsense has been written about this word.)—3. A crowd : low : late C. 19–early 20. Ex *stir*, bustle, animation : cf. *push*.—4. Stew : military : late C. 19–20. B. & P. Ex the cooking-operation.

stir on, have plenty of. To be wealthy : late C. 19–early 20.

stir up. ' To visit on the spur of the moment ' : lower classes' (— 1909). Ware.

Stir-Up Sunday. The last Sunday before Advent : dial. (— 1825) >, ca. 1860, coll. H. 2nd ed. The appropriate collect begins ' Stir up, we beseech Thee, O Lord ' ; but, as the O.E.D. observes, ' the name is jocularly associated with the stirring of the Christmas mincemeat, which it was customary to begin making in that week.'

*****stirabout.** A pottage of maize and oatmeal : prison c (— 1887). Baumann.—2. Any ' pudding or porridge made by stirring the ingredients—generally oatmeal or wheat-flour—when cooking ' : lower classes' (— 1909). Ware. Ex dial.

stirrup-oil. A beating, esp. with a strap : jocular coll. (— 1676) bordering on S.E. : ob. except in the All Fools' Day practical joke. Lexicographer Coles. Prob. suggested by *stirrup-leather*, an instrument of thrashing. Cf. *strap-oil*.

stirrups, up in the. See **up in the stirrups.**

stitch. A tailor : coll. : from late C. 17 ; very ob. B.E. Cf. *stitch-louse*.—2. ' Also a term for

lying with a woman,' Grose, 1st ed. : low : late C. 18–20 ; ob.

stitch-back. Beer ; strong liquor : ca. 1690, B.E. ; E. Ward, *History of the London Clubs* ; † by 1800.

stitch-louse. The same : 1838, Beckett ; ob Ex *stitch* on *prick-louse*. Cf. :

stitch off. To refrain from, have nothing to do with a thing ; in the imperative, it = ' keep off it ! ' : tailors' : late C. 19–20. Ex tailoring j.

stitches, or S—. A sail-maker, esp. on board ship : nautical, gen. as nickname : mid-C. 19–20.

stitches, man of. The same as *stitch-louse* : mid-C. 19–20 coll. Cf. preceding two entries.

stiver. A small standard of value ; esp. in *not a stiver*, not a penny : coll. : mid-C. 18–20. Ex *stiver*, a small Dutch coin. Other spellings : *stu(y)ver*, C. 18 ; *stuiver*, C. 19 ; *ste(e)ver*, late C. 19–20, when the usual form ; Yiddishly, *shtibbur*. O.E.D ; F. & H.

stiver-cramped. Needy : coll. : ca. 1780–1850. Grose, 1st ed. See **stiver.**

stiver's worth of copper. A penny : East London : late C. 19–20. Ware.

stivvy. A domestic servant : Bootham School : from ca. 1918. Anon., *Dict. of Bootham Slang*, 1925. A corruption of *skivvy*.

stivvy blug. A boot-boy : Bootham School : ca. 1910–20. Ex preceding. Cf. :

stivvy's blag. A boot-boy : id. : from ca. 1920. Ex preceding.

stizzle. To hurt : Tonbridge School : from ca. 1880. ? ex *stodge*, v., 1, q.v.

stoater. See **stoter.**

stock. A stock of impudence ; esp. *a good stock* : coll. : late C. 18–mid-19. Grose, 2nd ed. Also absolutely : ' cheek '.—2. As in *live stock*, q.v.—3. Repertory (n.) ; esp. *in stock* : theatrical coll. : C. 20. (M. Lincoln, *Oh ! Definitely*, 1933). Ex *stock piece*.

stock, v. To arrange (cards) fraudulently—i.e. to ' stack ' them—may orig. (— 1864) have been s. H., 3rd ed. The O.E.D. classifies *stocking*, such manipulation, as s. : 1887.

stock-bubbling, n. Stock-broking : money-market s. (— 1923). Manchon. Ex causing stocks and shares to rise and fall.

*****stock-buzzer.** A pickpocket of handkerchiefs : c. (— 1861). Mayhew.

*****stock-drawers.** Stockings : c. : mid-C. 17–early 19. Coles, 1676 ; B.E. ; Grose, 1st ed. See **drawers.**

[Stock Exchange terms. The various terms occur *passim*. For a list, see F. & H. at *Stock Exchange Terms* and my *Slang* at this section, which includes also some gen. remarks on the subject.]

stock in, take. Esp. *large*, etc., *stock in*, rarely *of*. To be interested in, have faith in, consider important : coll. : 1878, Anon., ' Taking large stock in Natural Selection,' O.E.D.

stock-in-trade. The privities : coll. : late C. 19–20. Punning the lit. sense.

stock of, take. To scrutinise (gen. a person) with interest, curiosity, suspicion : coll. (— 1864). H., 3rd ed. Ex S.E. sense, to evaluate, assess.

Stockbrokers' Battalion, the. ' The 10th Battalion of the Royal Fusiliers, raised for the War among members and clerks of the Stock Exchange in Aug., 1914 ' : military coll. : 1914 ; ob. F. & Gibbons.

stockdol(l)ager. See **sockdologer.** H., 2nd ed.

stocking. A store of money : gen. *a fat* or *a long stocking* : dial. (— 1873) >, ca. 1875, coll. >, ca. 1905, S.E. S. R. Whitehead, 1876, 'She had a "stocking" gathered to meet the wants of an evil day,' O.E.D. Ex a stocking used in preference to a bank.—2. See **stock**, v.

***stocking crib.** A hosier's shop : c. : ca. 1810–60. Vaux. Ex *crib*, n., 3.

stocking-foot(er). A projectile approaching noiselessly : military : 1915–18. F. & Gibbons. It comes in *stocking feet*.

stodge. Heavy eating ; gorging : mostly schools' : 1894, Norman Gale, concerning a bowler at cricket, ' Your non-success is due to Stodge.' Ex *stodge*, 'stiff farinaceous food ', and see **stodging**. O.E.D.—2. Hence, a heavy meal : mostly schools' (— 1903). F. & H.—3. At Charterhouse, the crumb of new bread (— 1903) ; (F. & H.). Cf. sense 1.—4. Stodgy notions : 1902, Elinor M. Glyn (O.E.D.). Ex senses 1, 2.—5. Any food : (gunroom) naval : from ca. 1905. Bowen. Ex senses 1 and esp. 2.

stodge, v.t. To hurt : Tonbridge School (– 1903). F. & H. Cf. *stizzle*.—2. V.i., to work steadily (*at* something, esp. if wearisome, dull, or heavy) : coll. : 1889 (S.O.D.). Prob. ex :—3. See **stodging**.—4. To trudge through slush or mud ; to walk heavily : dial. (— 1854) >, ca. 1910, coll. O.E.D. (Sup.).

stodged, ppl.adj. Crammed with food : dial. and coll. : from ca. 1870. Cf. *stodging*.

stodger. A gormandiser : s. or coll. : late C. 19–20. Cf. *stodge*, n., 1.—2. A dull and/or spiritless person : coll. : from not later than 1904. O.E.D. (Sup.). Whence *stodgery*, the behaviour, or an action, characteristic of such a person (coll. : 1920, Warwick Deeping).—3. (the **Stodger**.) H.M.S. *Warspite* : naval : C. 20. Bowen. Prob. ex sense 2.—4. A penny bun : Charterhouse (— 1900). A. H. Tod.

stodging, vbl.n. and ppl.adj. Gormandising : coll. : late C. 19–20. Ex *stodge*, v.t., to gorge (oneself or another) with food ; often in passive : dial. (— 1854) >, by 1860, coll. ; the O.E.D., which considers it to have been always S.E., records *stodge* as v.i. only in 1911,—but it occurs in Baumann (*sich satt essen*) in 1887. Cf. *stodged*.

[**stogy,** a coarse cigar, may, orig. in England (ca. 1890), have been coll. Ex *Conastoga*, U.S.A.]

stoke ; gen. **stoke up.** V.i., to eat ; nourish oneself : coll. : C. 20. Ex stoking an engine.

stokers. ' Smuts and cinders flying from a ship's funnels at high speed ' : nautical : C. 20. Bowen.

stole. Stolen : sol. : C. 19–20. (D. Sayers, *The Nine Tailors*, 1934.)

***stoll.** To understand (e.g. *stoll the patter*) : North Country c. : from ca. 1860. H., 3rd ed. ? a corruption of *stall*, to place, used fig.—2. V.i., to tipple : low s. : from ca. 1880 ; ob. Whence *stolled*, tipsy. ? origin : perhaps cognate with rare Norfolk *stole*, to drink, swallow (E.D.D.).

Stolypin's necktie. ' The final halter ' : political : 1897–ca. 1914. Ware. Ex a formerly well-known Russian functionary.

stomach, hot. See **hot a stomach**.

stomach on one's chest, (have got) a. (To have) something lying heavy on one's stomach : jocular coll. (— 1887). Baumann.

stomach thinks my throat is cut, my. See **throat is cut.**

[**stomach-timber** is rather a nonce-variation of *belly-timber* than an eligible coll. Recorded by F. & H. for 1820 ; certainly † by 1900.]

stomach-worm gnaws, the. I'm hungry : ca. 1785–1850. Grose, 2nd ed.

stomjack, or **stom Jack.** Stomach (n.) : nursery sol. (— 1887). Baumann.

stone. See **stones.** Cf. *stone-fruit*, q.v.—2. **stone, kill two birds with one.** See **birds**.—3. A diamond : South African s. (1887) >, by 1915, coll. (O.E.D. Sup.)—4. **the stone.** Diamonds : late C. 19–20 : gem-dealer's coll. verging on j. A gem-trade proverb runs. ' When the stone goes well, all goes well.' Carl Olsson in *The Passing Show*, Jan. 13, 1934.

stone and a beating, give a. To beat easily : racing s. (— 1885) >, by 1900, sporting coll. Ex racing and athletics j., *stone* being a stone-weight. (Ware.)

stone-brig. See **stone-doublet.**

stone-broke ; ston(e)y-broke. (Almost) penniless ; ruined : resp. from before 1887 (Baumann) and now rare ; 1894, Astley. The link between the two forms is provided by R. C. Lehmann's *Harry Fludyer*, 1890, ' Pat said he was stoney or broke or something but he gave me a sov.'

stone cold, have (a person). An intensive of *cold, have*, q.v. (Lyell.)

stone(-)doublet, jug, pitcher, tavern ; brig, frigate. A prison ; orig. and esp. Newgate : *-doublet*,—the exemplar,—B.E. ; Motteux, 1694 ; † by 1850 ; *-jug*,—in C. 19, the commonest, whence *jug*, q.v.,—late C. 18–19, Grose, 3rd ed., and Reade, 1856 ; *-pitcher*, ca. 1810–60 ; *-tavern*, late C. 18–mid-19, Grose, 3rd ed. ; *-brig* and *-frigate* are both nautical (mainly naval), C. 19, the latter recorded by Frank C. Bowen. Dial. has *stone-house* and, in 1799, U.S. has *stone jacket*.

stone-fruit. Children : low C. 19–20 ; ob. Ex *stones*, q.v. ; punning lit. sense.

stone-ginger, a. A certainty : Aucklandites' (N.Z.) : from ca. 1910 ; ob. By 1930, however, it was gen. : James Curtis, 1936. Ex a horse that won virtually every hurdle-race for which it was entered.

stone-jug ; stone-pitcher ; stone-tavern. See **stone-doublet**.—2. (stone-jug.) A fool, an easy dupe : low rhyming s. (— 1923) on *mug*. Manchon.

stone lakes. Stone-mad : low, esp. among grafters : C. 20. Philip Allingham, *Cheapjack*, 1934. See **lakes**.

stone ship. A War-time ferro-concrete ship (mostly they were tugs and barges) : nautical coll. of G.W. (Bowen.)

stone the crows ! An Australian expletive : coll. : C. 20. Ion L. Idriess, *Flynn of the Inland*, 1932.

stone under weight or **wanting, two.** Castrated : punning coll. : 1785, Grose (*under weight*, the *wanting* form not before C. 19) ; ob.

stone (up) in the ear, take a. To play the whore : late C. 17–mid-18. Shadwell, 1691 (O.E.D.) ; ' Facetious ' Tom Brown. Cf. *stone-priest* and *stones*.

stone-wall ; stonewall. Parliamentary obstruction ; a body of Parliamentary obstructionists : 1876 : Australian >, by 1898, New Zealand political s. Morris. Cf. the C. 16–17 proverb, *it is evil running against a stone wall* (Apperson) and :

stone-wall ; gen. **stonewall.** To play stolidly on the defensive : cricket s. (1889) >, by 1920, coll. Lit., to block every thing as though one were a stone wall ; but imm. ex S.E. *stonewall*, a cricketer doing this (1867 : Lewis).—2. In politics, v.i. and v.t., to obstruct (business) by lengthy speeches and other retarding tactics : Australian s. (from ca. 1880) >, ca. 1900, fairly gen. Ex the n. Morris.

stone wall as anyone, able to see as far through a. See **see through a stone wall.**

stone(-)waller ; stone(-)walling, n. and adj. One who stonewalls (in sport, ca. 1890 ; in politics, ca. 1885) ; the act or practice of doing this and the corresponding adj. (in cricket, ca. 1895 ; in politics, 1880).—2. (**stone-waller.**) A certainty : Glasgow sporting (— 1934).

stone wanting, two. See **stone under weight.**

stone winnick, gone. Muddled ; out of one's wits : military : from 1914. F. & Gibbons. See **winnick.**

stones. Testicles : C. 12–20 : S.E. until ca. 1850, then—except of a horse—a vulgarism. Cf. *stone-fruit* ; *stone (up) in the ear, take a.*—2. Diamonds : South African s. (1887, *South African Sketches*, by Ellis) >, by 1920, coll. Pettman.

stones, on the. On the street, i.e. destitute : coll. (— 1923). Manchon.

stones, stand on the. Gen. *standing on the stones*, omitted from the list of those ' wanted ' (for work) : dockers' : from ca. 1930. (*The Daily Herald*, late July or early Aug., 1936.)

stonewall. See **stone-wall.—stoney.** See **stony. —stoney-broke.** See **stony-broke.**

'stonish. To astonish : in C. 19–20, gen. coll. and mostly nursery.

stonkered, be. To be put out of action : military : 1914 or 1915 ; ob. F. & Gibbons. Perhaps ex dial. *stonk(s)*, the game of marbles, on *scuppered.*

stonnicky. A rope's end as an instrument for the inculcation of naval smartness : training-ships' : ca. 1860–1910. Bowen. Perhaps cognate with *stunner.*

stony ; less correctly, **stoney.** (Almost) penniless, ruined : from ca. 1890. For earliest record, see **stone-broke.** For semantics, cf. *hard-up.* Cf. :

stony- (occ. **stoney-)broke.** The same : see **stone-broke.**

stoob(s). Boots : back s. (— 1859). H., 1st ed. See **sret-sio.**

*stook.** A pocket-handkerchief : c. (— 1859). H., 1st ed. ; 1893, P. H. Emerson (*stoock*). Prob. ex Yiddish : cf. Ger. *Stück* (O.E.D. Sup.). Hence, *stook-buzzer* or *-hauler*, a pickpocket specialising therein.

*stool pigeon.** An informer : c., orig. U.S. ; anglicised by 1916. Edgar Wallace, *passim.*—2. Hence, a Secret Service agent : military : 1917 ; ob. B. & P.

*stoolie or -y.** A spy upon criminals : c. : from ca. 1920. E.g. in John G. Brandon, *The One-Minute Murder*, 1934. Prob. ex the preceding.

stool's foot in water, lay the. To prepare to receive a guest or guests : coll. : ? C. 18–mid-19. F. & H.

*stoop.** Always *the stoop.* The pillory : c. of ca. 1780–1840. George Parker ; Grose, 1st ed. (at *nab*). Whence *nab* (*nap*) *the stoop*, to be pilloried ; *stoop-napper*, one in the pillory : both c. : same period. Ex the position therein enforced.—2. Catachrestic when used of a porch or a veranda : late C. 18–20. Canada (and U.S.). O.E.D.

*stoop,** v.i. To become a victim to crook or criminal : c. : late C. 16–early 17. Greene.—2. To

set (a person) in the pillory : c. of ca. 1810–40. Vaux. Ex n., 1.

*stooping match.** ' The exhibition of one or more persons in the pillory,' Vaux : c. : ca. 1810–40.

*stop.** A police detective : c. (— 1857) ; app. † by 1903. ' Ducange Anglicus.' Ex action.

stop, v. To receive (a wound) ; only in *stop (a nasty* or *a Blighty) one, stop a packet* : military : from 1915. Ex familiar S.E. *stop a bullet.* (B. & P.) Cf. *cop a packet.*

stop a pot. ' To quaff ale,' C. J. Dennis : (low) Australian : C. 20.

stop a blast. To be reprimanded by a superior : military : from 1916. F. & Gibbons. See **stop,** v.

stop a packet. See **packet** and **stop,** v.

stop and look at you (them, etc.). An occ. variant of *get up and look at you*, q.v. : 1926, J. B. Hobbs (Lewis).

stop-gap. The last-born child : lower classes' (— 1923). Manchon.

*Stop-Hole Abbey.** The chief rendezvous of the underworld : c. : late C. 17–early 19. B.E. It was at some ruinous building in London.

stop me and buy one ! A c.p. of 1934–6 ; (?) ob. Ex the Wall's Ice Cream slogan.

stop my vitals ! ' A silly Curse in use among the Beaux,' B.E. : coll. : late C. 17–18. Often *stap my vitals !*, q.v.

stop one. See **stop,** v.

*stop one's blubber.** A *New Canting Dict.*, 1725, ' *I've stopt his Blubber* . . . I've done his Business. He'll tell no Tales, &c.' : c. : C. 18.

stop out, v.t. To cover (one's teeth) with black wax to render them invisible to the audience : theatrical coll. : from ca. 1870. Ex etching.

stop thief. Beef : rhyming s. (1859, H.) ; orig. (— 1857), stolen meat, as in ' Ducange Anglicus ', but not after 1870 at latest.

stop ticking. To cease being of importance ; **to die** : from ca. 1930. Ex a watch.

stop up. To sit up instead of going to bed : coll. : 1857, Mrs Gaskell. (O.E.D.)

stopper. Something that brings to a standstill or that terminates : s. (1828, Egan in *Boxiana*) >, in late C. 19, coll. Esp. in *clap a stopper on* (' that jaw of yours ', Marryat, 1830), † by 1910, and in *put a* or *the stopper on*, to cause to cease (Dickens, 1841) : both s. >, ca. 1890, coll. O.E.D.—2. Whence, a brake : motor-racers' : from ca. 1925. (Peter Chamberlain.)

stopper, v.t. To stop : 1821, Scott, ' Stopper your jaw, Dick, will you ? ', O.E.D. Cf. *stopper*, n., 1830 quotation. Ex lit. nautical sense.

stopping, hot. See **hot-stopping.**

stopping oyster. See **oyster.**

stops !, mind your. Be careful : coll. : 1830, Marryat, ' Mind your stops . . . or I shall shy a biscuit at your head.' Ex an injunction to a child reading aloud. O.E.D.

store. ' A bullock, cow, or sheep bought to be fattened for the market ' : 1874 : Australian coll. >, by 1900, ' standard '. Morris. Also (but S.E.) : *store-cattle.*

storey, upper. See **upper storey.**

storrac. Carrots : back s. (— 1859). H., 1st ed. See **sret-sio.**

stort. A cormorant : incorrect for *scart.*

story, for the *storey* of a building, is not incorrect, though slightly frowned on in England ; but *storey* is preferable, if only to differentiate the sense.

story. A lie : a coll. euphemism : ca. 1697,

Aubrey ; Barham. Chiefly in *to tell stories* and *what a story !*—2. Whence, a ' story-teller ' : low coll. and among children ; esp. as *you story !*, you liar ! : 1869. O.E.D.—3. story, upper. See upper storey.

story-teller. A liar : euphemistic coll. : 1748, Richardson, ' Wicked story-teller ', O.E.D.

*stosh. A variant of *stash.*

*stoter ; occ. stotor ; also stoater and stouter. A sharp, heavy blow : late C. 17–early 19 : c. >, ca. 1800, low s. : Motteux, 1694, *stoater* ; B.E., *stoter* ; *stouter*, 1769. Only H. and F. & H. record *stotor.* O.E.D. Ex :

*stoter, v. To fell heavily ; hit hard : c. : 1690, D'Urfey ; B.E., ' *Stoter him*, or *tip him a Stoter*, settle him, give him a swinging Blow ' ; † by 1750. Ex Dutch *stooten*, to push or knock. (O.E.D.)

stouch. An occ. variant of *stoush*, q.v.

stoupe. To give up (v.i.) : c. : C. 18–early 19. Halliwell. Ex *to stoop.*

stoush, n. A fight ; v.t., to fight, esp. to beat in a fight (anything from fisticuffs to a great battle) : Australian : C. 20. C. J. Dennis. Prob. cognate with *stash*, q.v. ; cf. dial. *stashie, stushie*, an uproar, a quarrel (E.D.D.).

stoush-up. A variant of the preceding n. : Australian : from ca. 1910.

stout, ca. 1670–1770, was s. for strong beer. Swift ; Johnson.

stout across the narrow. Corpulent : coll. : C. 20 ; ob. Anon., *Troddles*, 1901.

stout fellow. A reliable, courageous, and likable fellow : coll. : C. 20. B. & P. Abbr. *stout-hearted fellow.* See the quotation at *sound egg.*

*stouter. See stoter.

stouts, Stouts. (Ordinary) shares in Guinness : Stock Exchange : late C. 19–20. A. J. Wilson, *Stock Exchange Glossary.*

stove, v. ' Incorrect nautical use of incorrect past of *stave* as present ' : C. 19–20. W.

stove-pipe (hat). A top hat, a ' chimney-pot ' : mid-C. 19–20 (ob.) ; U.S. >, ca. 1865, English. In late C. 19–20, coll. Ex shape.

stove-pipes. Trousers : 1863 (O.E.D.) ; ob. by 1920, † by 1935.

*stow, v.i. To cease talking, to ' shut up ' : c. (— 1567) ; ob. by 1820, † by 1850. Harman, ' Stow you, holde your peace ' ; B.E., ' *Stow*, you have said enough ' ; Grose, 3rd ed., ' *Stow you*, be silent.'—2. Hence, v.t., to desist from : c. (— 1676) >, ca. 1800, low s. >, ca. 1850, gen. s. Coles, 1676, ' *Stow your whids*, . . . speak warily ' ; stow (*one's*) *jabber*, 1806 ; *stow* (*one's*) *mag*, 1857 ; ' Ouida ', 1882, ' " Stow that, sir," cried Rake, vehemently.' Ob. Prob. ex S.E. *stow*, ' to place in a receptacle to be stored or kept in reserve ', O.E.D. (whence several of the dates). Cf. *stash*, q.v., and :

*stow faking ! ; stow it ! Stop doing that !, gen. as a warning in the underworld : c. : resp. ca. 1810–1900 ; C. 19–20, ob. Vaux. See stow. Cf. :

*stow magging and manging ! Be silent ! ; lit., stop talking ! : c. of resp. ca. 1810–80, ca. 1820–80. Vaux ; Bee (. . . *magging*). See mag, v., and mang. Bee, 1823, has the variant *stowmarket !*

stow on their edges. To save money : Merchant Service : C. 20. Bowen.

Strad. A Stradivarius violin : coll. : 1884, Haweis, *Musical Life* (O.E.D.).

Strada Reale Highlanders. The 75th Foot Regiment, in late C. 19–20 the 1st Battalion of the Gordon Highlanders : military : 1812 ; † by 1910. In 1812, the Regiment formed the Main Guard of the Governor's residence in the Strada Reale, Valetta.

straddle is the C. 20 Stock Exchange s. (from ca. 1920, coll.) for the operation in which, ' when a broker executes an order to buy grain deliverable in a certain specified month, executing at the same time an order to sell the same quantity and description deliverable in another specified month, he shall be at liberty to carry out both transactions for one brokerage,' 1902 : quoted by the O.E.D. (F. & H. confuses the English with the U.S. term, of which *spread-eagle* is a synonym.) Occ. as v.i.

straddle, v.i. ' In Sports and Gaming to play who shall pay the Reckoning ', Dyche & Pardon, 1735 ; † by 1820.—2. See end of sense 1 in the preceding entry.

straddle-legged patents. ' Patent reefing gear ' (Bowen) : nautical coll. : C. 20.

straemash is a mainly dial. variant of *stramash*, q.v.

strafe ; occ. straff. A fierce assault : military : from 1915. *Blackwood's*, Feb., 1916, ' Intermittent strafes we are used to,' O.E.D. Ex the v.—2. Hence, a severe bombardment : military : from late 1915. Cf. *hate*, n., q.v.—3. Hence, a severe reprimand : 1916 : military >, by 1919, gen. See esp. B. & P.

strafe (occ. straff), v. To attack fiercely ; to bombard : military : from 1915. *The Times Literary Supplement*, Feb. 10, 1916, ' The German are '—but after 1916 they were not—' called the Gott-strafers, and strafe is becoming a comic English word,' O.E.D. Ex the Ger. salutation and toast, *Gott strafe England*, ' may God punish England ! '— 2. Hence, to punish ; to damage : military : from early 1916.—3. Hence, from mid-1916, to swear at, to reprimand severely : military >, by 1918, gen. See B. & P.—4. Hence also, strafe it !, ' shut up ! ' : id. : 1917–19. F. & Gibbons.

strafer ; strafing. The agential and the vbl.nn. of the preceding.

stragger. A stranger : Oxford University undergraduates' : late C. 19–20. (O.E.D. Sup.) By ' the Oxford *-er* '.

straggling money. A sailor that overstays his furlough : nautical (— 1887). Baumann. Because he has money left.

straight, n. See the adj. and *in the straight, on the straight.*—2. (Also straighter.) A cigarette of Virginia tobacco : from ca. 1920. Manchon. Ex *straight-cut.*

straight, adj. (Of an utterance) outspoken ; (of a statement) unreserved, certain : coll. (— 1887). Baumann. Hence, *straight talk*, (a piece of) plain speaking : 1900.—2. Of persons or their conduct : honest, honourable ; frank : coll. : 1864 (O.E.D.). In C. 16–mid-17, this sense was S.E., but ' the present use . . . is unconnected.'—3. Hence, (of any person) steady, (of a woman) chaste : coll. : 1868, Lindsay Gordon, *keep* (one) *straight*, the chief usage.—4. (Of accounts) settled : coll. : C. 17–20. —5. See straight face.—6. ' Often absent-mindedly confused with *strait* ', W.

straight ! Honestly ! ; it's a fact ! : low coll. : 1890, Albert Chevalier ; 1897, ' Pomes ' Marshall, ' " If that isn't a good 'un," the bookie cried, " I'll forfeit a fiver, straight." '

straight, in the. A rare form of *straight, on the*, behaving reputably or like a good citizen : from late 1890's. Edgar Wallace, 1900, ' O the garden it is lovely—That's when Jerry's on the straight ! ',

O.E.D. Ex lit. sense, along a straight line.—2. (Only **in the straight**.) Near the end : racing coll. > gen. : 1903, *T.P.'s Weekly*, Jan. 2, 'Good, I'm in the straight now . . . Thank Heaven that's done.' Ex coming up the straight of a race-course and making the final effort.

straight, lay (a person). To operate on : medical students' (— 1923). Manchon.

straight, out of the. Dishonest ; illicit, illegal : late C. 19–20.

straight arm. See **make a straight arm**.

straight as a dog's hind leg. Crooked : jocular coll. : late C. 19–20. Cf. Swift's 'Straight ! Ay, straight as my leg, and that's crooked at knee' (Apperson). Contrast :

straight as a loon's leg. Absolutely straight : nautical coll. : late C. 19–20. Bowen.

straight as a pound of candles. Very straight : coll. : 1748, Smollett, ' My hair hung down . . . as . . . straight as a pound of candles ' ; ob. Cf. the (C. 19) Cheshire *straight as a yard of pump water*, applied to a tall, thin man, and Ray's (C. 17–18) *straight as the backbone of a herring*, which may have been coll. before being proverbial S.E. (Apperson.) —2. Hence, very honest : coll. : C. 19–20 ; extremely ob.

straight bake. A roast joint : naval : C. 20. Bowen. Cf. *straight rush*.

*straight-cut. A respectable girl ; a girl in no way connected with the underworld : c. : from ca. 1920. James Curtis, *The Gilt Kid*, 1936. An elaboration of *straight*, honest, virtuous.

straight drinking. 'Drinking without sitting down—bar-drinking ' : London taverns' : ca. 1860–1905. Ware.

straight face ; also **keep one's face straight.** (To do) this as a restraint from laughing : coll. : 1897, *The Spectator*, Sept. 25, ' An expressive vulgarism . . . " with a straight face ",' O.E.D.

straight griff or **griffin.** See **griff, griffin**.

*straight line, get on the. To get on the right scent or track : c. (— 1887). Baumann.

straight off the turnips. See **turnips, straight off the**.

straight rush. A prepared joint taken to the galley for roasting : naval : C. 20. Bowen. Cf. *straight bake*.

*straight screw. A warder that traffics with the prisoners : c. : C. 20. George Ingram, *Stir*, 1933.

straight-set, v.t. To defeat in the minimum number of sets (i.e. in *straight sets*) : lawn-tennis coll. : 1935, *The Daily Telegraph*, April 4. Hence, such a match is called a *straight-setter* : lawn-tennis s. : June, 1935.

straight tip. See **tip, straight**.

straight-up, adj. Correct ; the truth : low : from ca. 1925. James Curtis, *The Gilt Kid*, 1936, ' Maisie was the only girl he had ever loved. That was straight-up.'

straight up and down the mast. (Of weather) calm : Irish nautical (— 1909). Ware.

straight wire, the. The genuine thing ; esp., authentic news : Australian : from ca. 1910.

*straighten. To bribe, try to bribe (a police officer) : c. : from ca. 1920. Edgar Wallace, *passim* ; Charles E. Leach. I.e. straighten him out.

straighten up, v.i. To become honest or honourable : s. (ca. 1906) >, ca. 1930, coll. Ex lit. sense, to assume an upright posture.

straighter. See **straight, n., 2**.

*Straights (occ. **Streights**), **the.** Jonson, 1614 :

† by 1700 : prob. c Perhaps ex *strait*, adj., or *straits*, n. Gifford, 1816, ' These Streights consisted of a nest of obscure courts, alleys, and avenues, running between the bottom of St Martin's Lane, Half Moon, and Chandos Street ' ; they were ' frequented by bullies, knights of the post, and fencing masters '. Cf. *the Bermudas*.

strain hard. To tell a great or hearty lie : coll. : late C. 17–18. B.E.

strain one's taters. To make water : low : from ca. 1880 ; ob. Ex the colour of water in which potatoes have been washed or strained.

Straits, the. The Mediterranean : nautical : C. 20. Bowen. Ex the S.E. sense, the Straits of Gibraltar.

*stram, the. (Harlots') street-walking : c. >, ca. 1900, low s. ; ob. : 1887, Henley, ' You judes that clobber for the stram '. ? ex U.S. *stram*, to walk some distance (1869), influenced by *strum*, v. (q.v.), or *strumpet*.

stramash ; also **straemash**, very rare outside of dial. A disturbance ; a rough-and-tumble : dial. (— 1821) >, ca. 1835, coll. Barham, ca. 1840, former sense ; Henry Kingsley, 1855, ' I and three other . . . men . . . had a noble stramash on Folly Bridge. That is the last fighting I have seen.' Ex Northern and Scottish *stramash*, to break, crush, destroy, itself perhaps ex *stour* (a disturbance) + *smash* : W.

stram(m)el. See **stammel** and **strommel**.

strammer. Anything exceptional, esp. in size or intensity, and *stramming*, huge, great, are dial. >, ca. 1850, coll., but, after ca. 1910, very ob. as coll. Ex dial. *stram*, to bang or strike : it is therefore one of the numerous ' percussive ' intensives.

stranger. A guinea : low (— 1785). Grose. Ex rarity.—2. A sovereign : from ca. 1830 : low >, in C. 20, tramps' c. F. Jennings, *Tramping with Tramps*, 1932.

stranger !, quite a ; often preceded by **well !** A coll. c.p. addressed to a person not seen for some time : C. 20. (R. Blaker, *Night-Shift*, 1934.)

strangle-goose. A poulterer : ca. 1780–1900. Grose, 1st ed. ; Baumann.

*strangler. A neck-tie : c., and low : C. 20. J. Curtis, *The Gilt Kid*, 1936.

strangullion. Sol. or catachrestic for *strangury* : Palsgrave, 1530 ; Phillips, 1678. Whence, via *strangury*, the confusion worse confounded of *strangurion* : mid-C. 16–early 17. O.E.D.

strap. A barber : mid-C. 19–20 ; by 1920, virtually †. H., 3rd ed. Ex † *strap*, a strop, + (Hugh) *Strap*, a barber in Smollett's *Roderick Random*, 1748.—2. Credit : dial. (— 1828) >, ca. 1880, s. Esp. *on strap*, occ. *on the strap*. Slightly ob.

*strap, v.i. To lie with a woman, esp. as vbl.n. *strapping* : c. : late C. 17–19. B.E., Grose. Prob. ex *strapping* (*wench, youth*, etc.).—2. To work, esp. if energetically, v.t. with *at* : from ca. 1810 ; ob. *Lex. Bal.* Also with *away* (1849), and *to* (both v.i. and v.t. : mid-C. 19–20).—3. V.t., to allow credit for (goods) : dial. (— 1862) >, ca. 1890, s. Ex *strap*, n., 2.—4. Hence, *strap it* (gen. as vbl.n.), to get goods on credit : Glasgow : C. 20.

strap-'em, oil of ; **strap-oil.** Often preceded by *a dose of*. A thrashing with a strap : C. 19–20. Halliwell, 1847, ' It is a common joke on April 1st to send a lad for a pennyworth of strap-oil, which is generally ministered on his own person.' On *stirrup-oil*, q.v.

strap-hang, v.i. From ca. 1910. By back-formation ex :

strap(-)hanger. A passenger compelled, or occ. choosing, to hold on to a strap in omnibus, train, etc. : from ca. 1904 : s. >, ca. 1930, coll. *Punch*, Nov. 8, 1905 ; in 1934, Norah James published a novel entitled *Strap-hangers*. Cf. the S.E. port-manteau word, *strapeze* or *trapeze*.

strap-oil. See strap 'em.

strap up. 'To wash up the saloon table gear. A steward is said to be " *on the Crockery Strap-up* " ' : Bowen : nautical : C. 20. Prob. because so many articles have then to be firmly secured.

*straping. See strapping. B.E.'s spelling (? a mere misprint).

strappado. Catachrestic when = a punishment by blows, as in mid-C. 17–18, as also it is when = to beat with a strap (mid-C. 17). O.E.D.

strapped, ppl.adj. (Of goods, etc., had) on credit : Glasgow : C. 20. See strap, v., 3 and 4.

strapper. A very energetic or an unremitting worker : 1851, Mayhew, 'They are all picked men . . . regular " strappers ", and no mistake,' O.E.D. Ex strap, v., 2.

*strapping, vbl.n. Lying with a woman : c. : late C. 17–19. B.E., Grose.

strapping it, vbl.n. See strap, v., 4.

straps. Sprats : a modified rhyming (or, perhaps, back) s. that is low urban (— 1909). Ware.

strata, singular with pl. *stratas* : catachrestic : C. 18–20. Cf. *data, phenomena*.

Strata Smith. Wm. Smith (1769–1839), the geologist and engineer. Dawson.

straw, v.i. To do as in *strawer*, 1, q.v. : London : mid-C. 19–20 ; ob.

straw, one's eyes draw. Grose's variation of *straws*, 2, q.v. ; *straw* is rare.

straw, pad in the. See pad in the straw.—**straw-bail.** See bail.

straw and t'other serves the thatcher, one eye draws. He (she, etc.) is half asleep : coll. : late C. 18–mid-19. Grose, 2nd ed. An elaboration of *straws*, 2, q.v.

straw-basher. A boater, a straw hat for man or boy : 1930. (O.E.D. Sup.) Prob. suggested by *hard-hitter*.

straw-chipper. A barber : low : ca. 1820–50. Moncrieff, 1823. Cf. *nob-thatcher*.

Straw House. The Sailors' Home, Dock Street, London : nautical : mid-C. 19–20. Bowen, 1929, mentions that ' a century ago seamen were [there] given a sack of straw for their bed.'

straw in her ear, wear a. To seek re-marriage : C. 20. Manchon.

straw-yard. See strawyards.

strawberry. A ' brandy-blossom ' or liquor-caused face-pimple : low (— 1887). Baumann.

Strawboots ; Old Strawboots. The 7th Dragoon Guards ; also the 7th Hussars : military : resp. from ca. 1830 and ca. 1760 ; ob. Also *the Straws* ; as well as *the Black Horse* and *the Virgin Mary's Guard* (both — 1879), applied only to the Dragoons. ' Tradition says from these regiments having been employed to quell agricultural riots ', F. & H. : this is correct only of the Guards ; the Hussars prob. got their name from straw used as foot-protection in the Seven Years War (F. & Gibbons).

strawer. London s. > coll (now almost †) of mid-C. 19–20, as in Mayhew, 1851, ' The strawer offers to sell any passer by . . . a straw and to give

to the purchaser a paper which he dares not sell . . . political, libellous, irreligious, or indecent.' Ex *straw*, v.—2. A straw hat : schools' (— 1903). Cf. *strawyard*, 2.

strawing, vbl.n. See straw, v., and strawer, 1.

straws. Straws : see Strawboots.—2. straws, draw, gather, or pick. (Of the eyes, not the person) to show signs of sleep : late C. 17–20 (ob.) : coll. >, by 1850, S.E. Motteux (*draw*), Swift (*draw*), Grose (*draw straw*), Wolcot (*pick*), J. Wilson (*gather*). (O.E.D.) Both *gather* and *pick* are virtually †. Cf. *straw and . . .*, q.v.

strawyard. See strawyards.—2. A (man's) straw hat : coll. : late C. 19–20 ; ob. (By 1929, † in the Navy : Bowen.)

strawyard bull, like a. A jocose reply (often amplified by *full of fuck and half starved*) to ' How do you feel *or* How are ȳou ? ' : low c.p. : from ca. 1870 ; ob.

strawyarder. A longshoreman acting as a sailor : nautical : mid-C. 19–20 ; slightly ob.—2. Esp. (— 1903), a ' scab ' on shipboard duty during a strike.

strawyards, the. Night shelters (refuges, homes) for the destitute : the London poor : mid-C. 19–20 ; ob. Mayhew, 1851.

streak. A very thin person : mostly Australian and New Zealand : C. 20.

streak ; occ. **streek.** To go very fast : 1768, ' Helenore ' Ross, ' [She] forward on did streak ' ; H., 1st ed. Gen. *streak off* (*like greased lightning* : 1843, Carleton) ; occ. *streak away*, as in *The Field*, Sept. 25, 1886. S. >, in late C. 19, coll. Prob. ex flashes of lightning. The form *to streak it* is U.S.

streak, like a. With exceeding swiftness : late C. 19–20. I.e. like a streak of lightning. Also *like streaks* : C. 20. See streak ; cf. :

streak away. See streak.

streak down. To slip or slide down ; to descend : s. (— 1889) >, by 1920, coll. App. mostly South African. (Pettman.) Cf. *streak*, v., q.v.

streak of lightning. A glass, gen. of gin, occ. of other potent spirit : mid-C. 19–20 ; very ob. Ex its sudden effect.

streak of misery. A tall, thin, miserable-looking person : coll. : late C. 19–20.

streaks, like. See streak, like a.

streaky. Bad-tempered, irritated ; irritable : from late 1850's ; ob. H., 2nd ed. Perhaps suggested by U.S. *streaked*, disconcerted, annoyed (1834 : Thornton). — 2. Changeable ; variable : coll. : 1898, Bartram (of courage, weather) ; 1899, A. C. Benson (of additions to a building) : 1903 (of runs at cricket). O.E.D.

stream-line. A tall, thin man : military : from 1917. F. & Gibbons. Cf. :

stream-line(d). Slim and graceful (of persons) : from ca. 1932. Ex stream-lined motor-cars, designed to offer small resistance to the atmosphere.

Stream's Town ; or **s.t.** The female pudend : low : ca. 1820–90.

streek. See streak, v.

street, down or **up.** Towards or in the lower or the upper end of the street : low coll. : 1876, Miss Braddon. O.E.D.

Street, Easy. See Easy Street.—**Street, Grub.** See Grub Street.—**street, key to the.** See key.—**street, man in the.** See man in the street.

street, not in or **not up my** (**his**, etc.). That's not my concern ; not my strong point ; not my method :

C. 20 (*in* is now ob.): **s.** >, by 1930, coll. F. & H. (*in* only).

street, not in the same (constructed with **be** and either **as** or **with**). (To be) far behind (lit. or fig.); much inferior to: s. >, ca. 1910, coll.: 1883, Mrs Kennard, comparing two race-horses.

street, not the length of a. A small interval: s. (1893, O.E.D.) that, like preceding entry, was orig. sporting; cf. *streets ahead*, q.v.

Street, Queen. See **live in Queen Street.—Street, Queer.** See **Queer Street.**

Street, the. Wall Street as money-mart: from ca. 1860: coll. >, ca. 1910, S.E.: U.S., anglicised ca. 1890. Cf. *'Change, on*, q.v.—2. The money-market held outside the Stock Exchange after 4 p.m.: Stock Exchange coll.: C. 20.—3. See **G.P.**

street, up one's. One's concern: see **street, not in my.**

*****street-chanting.** The practice of singing in the streets for a living: c. (— 1887). Baumann.

*****street-ganger.** A beggar: c.: late C. 19–early 20. Baumann, 1887.

street-knocker, grin like a. To 'grin like a Cheshire cat': coll.: from the 1830's. Baumann. Prob. ex its brightness.

street-pitcher. A vendor or a mendicant taking a station (or 'pitch') in the street: from late 1850's; slightly ob. H., 1st ed., who adds the specific sense († by 1890) of the 'orator' advertising various activities (e.g. ballad-singing) and, where relevant, selling illustrative broadsheets or booklets.

street-yarn, spin. To walk about idly, gossiping from house to house: coll.: mid-C. 19–20; U.S., anglicised ca. 1870; ob.

street-yelp. A c.p. of the streets: lower classes' 1884; ob. Ware.

streets, be in the. A lower-classes' coll. variation (— 1887) of *walk the streets*, to be a prostitute. Baumann.

streets ahead (of) or better (than), be. To be far ahead (of) in a race: from ca. 1895.—2. Hence, to be much superior (to): 1898 (O.E.D.). Both s. >, ca. 1920, coll. Also absolutely. Occ. *streets better off.*

Streights, the. See **Straights.**

Strelits (C. 17) and **Strelitz** (C. 17–20) incorrect as pl. O.E.D.

strength of it or this or that or the other, the. The 'real'—i.e. the hidden or ulterior or most important —meaning or significance (of some act or thing specified or implied), as in 'What's the strength of him (*or* his) coming here?': coll., perhaps first in Australia, where it is much used: C. 20. F. & Gibbons. Cf. C. 15–early 17 S.E. *strength*, the tenor or import (of a document).

strenuous. Excited; angry: upper classes': from ca. 1930. See the quotation at *crashing bore.* Ex the S.E. sense.

strep. Streptococcus, a common type of bacteria: medical students' (— 1933). *Slang*, p. 190. Cf. *staph.*

streperous. Abbr. *obstreperous*, q.v. Cf. † S.E. *streperous*, noisy.

strestell, strestulle. Illiterate forms of *trestle*: C. 16. O.E.D.

*****stretch.** A yard (length): c. (— 1811); † by 1920. *Lex. Bal.*; Vaux, 'Five . . . stretch signifies five . . . yards.'—2. A year's imprisonment, esp. with hard labour: c.: from ca. 1810. Vaux; Haggart, Horsley, Edgar Wallace. Ex sense 1 + *a long stretch.* Thus *one, two, three (four*, etc.) *stretch* = two (etc.) years' imprisonment, as in Hag-

gart, 1821, and J. Greenwood, 1888. See also *quarter stretch.*

stretch, gen. v.i.; occ. in late C. 19–20, *stretch it.* To exaggerate; tell lies: coll.: from ca. 1670. D'Urfey, Grose. Cf. *strain*, q.v.—2. V.i. and t., to outstay (one's furlough): naval coll.: C. 20. Ware; Bowen.

stretch leather, v. See **leather**, n., 2, and cf. *leather-stretcher.*

stretch off the land, a. A sleep: nautical: late C. 19–20. Bowen. Ex a ship lying at anchor near land.

stretch one's legs according to the coverlet. To adapt oneself to (esp. one's financial) circumstances: late C. 17–18: coll. >, by 1750, S.E. Bailey, 1736. Ex the very old proverb, *whoso stretcheth his foot beyond the blanket shall stretch it in the straw.* Apperson.

stretched, has had his breeches. (The boy) has received a thrashing: lower-class coll.: mid-C. 19– 20. Ware.

stretched of one's mess. See **mess, lose the number of one's.**

stretcher. A University-*Extension* student: university: late C. 19–20; ob.—2. A layer-out of corpses: Anglo-Irish coll.: late C. 19–20. Ware.— 3. A long journey, or stretch of road: coll.: C. 20. Manchon.—4. A large *membrum virile*: low coll.: 1749, John Cleland.

stretcher, hang over the. To eat too much; put on weight: low (— 1923). Manchon.

stretcher-fencer. A vendor of trouser-braces: low: mid-C. 19–20. H., 1st ed. Ex:

stretchers. Trouser-braces: low: mid-C. 19– 20. Cf. preceding entry.—2. Laces: tramps' c. (— 1935). Because they, too, stretch.

stretching. 'Helping oneself at table without the help of servants': coll.: from ca. 1895. Ware.

stretching-bee, -match. A hanging: low: resp. ca. 1820–80 and ca. 1820–1910. 'Jon Bee'; H., 2nd ed.

stretchy. Stretchable, elastic: coll.: 1854 (O.E.D.)—2. Hence, too easily stretched, too elastic: coll.: from mid-1880's.—3. Inclined to stretch one's limbs or to stretch and yawn; sleepy: coll.: from ca. 1870. Cf. the C. 17 proverb, *stretching and yawning leadeth to bed.*

'Strewth! God's truth!: low coll. when not deliberately jocular: 1892, Kipling, ' 'Strewth! but I socked it them 'ard.'

strict Q.T., on the. See **Q.T.**

*****stride-wide.** Ale: c.: ca. 1570–1620. Harrison's *Description of England*, 1577.

strides. Trousers: theatrical (— 1904). Ex dial., where it occurs as early as 1895 (E.D.D.). In which one strides; cf. *stride* in C. 19 tailoring j. (O.E.D., 1122, col. 3, § 4, c).—2. Hence, women's drawers: Colonial: from ca. 1919.

*****strike.** A sovereign (coin) or its equivalent: c.: ca. 1786–1920. Grose, 2nd ed.—2. A *stike* or *stick*, a measure of quantity in small eels: incorrect: from ca. 1670. O.E.D.—3. In curses: mid-C. 19– 20 coll.—4. A watch: c. (— 1909). Ware. On the *lucus a non lucendo* principle.

*****strike**, v.t. and v.i. To steal; to rob: c. of ca. 1565–1750. Harman, Greene, B.E.—2. Hence, v.i., to borrow money: c.: C. 17–early 19 (perhaps until late C. 19). Mynshul, 1618 (O.E.D.); B.E. Esp. as vbl.n., *striking.*—3. Hence, v.t. and v.i., to ask (a person) suddenly and/or pressingly *for* (a loan, etc.): low: mid-C. 18–20; slightly ob. Fielding,

1751, '. . . Who in the vulgar language, had struck, or taken him in for a guinea ', O.E.D. Cf. *sting*, 2.—4. V.i., to beg (also *strike it*) : (low) Australian : from late 1890's ; slightly ob. as *strike*.—5. Semantically ex sense 1 : to open, as in *strike a jigger*, to pick a lock, to break open a door : c. (— 1857). ' Ducange Anglicus.'—6. As in Baumann's ' How warm you strike in here ! ', the connotation is of timely and most welcome arrival : lower classes' coll. (— 1887). Cf. *bash into*, q.v.

strike, make a. To be successful ; lucky : coll. : from ca. 1860. Ex *strike*, ' the horizontal course of a stratum ' (of gold, etc.).

strike a bright. To have a bright idea : tailors' and lower classes' (— 1909) ; ob. Ware. Cf. *brain-storm*.

*strike a hand. (Of a thief) to be successful on a given occasion : c. : late C. 16–early 17. Greene, 1592. Cf. *strike*, v., 1.

*strike a jigger. See **strike**, v., 5.

strike a light. To run up a tavern score : see **light**.—2. **strike a light !** A mild expletive : coll. : from ca. 1880. Cf. *strike me blind !*—3. To commence a piece of welding : sheet-metal workers' : C. 20. *The Daily Herald*, Aug. 11, 1936.

strike all of a heap. See **heap**.

strike-fire. Gin : 1725, G. Smith on distilling (O.E.D.) ; very ob.

strike-me-blind. Rice : nautical (— 1904) ; slightly ob. Bowen, ' From the old superstition that its eating affected the eyesight '.

strike me blind ! A (gen. proletarian) expletive : coll. : 1704, Cibber. Also *strike me dumb !* (1696, Vanbrugh ; † by 1890) ; . . . *lucky !* (1849, Cupples) ; . . . *silly !* (— 1860 ; very ob.) ; . . . *pink !*, mid-C. 19–20 ; . . . *ugly* (C. 20 : Manchon) ; and *strike me !*, late C. 19–20. (O.E.D.) These imprecations may be constructed with *if* or *but*. Cf. *strike a light*, 2, and the Australian *strike me up a gum-tree !* (from ca. 1870 : H., 5th ed.), occ. in C. 20 varied by *strike me up a blue-gum !*

strike-me-dead. Small beer : naval : from early 1820's ; ob. Cf. *strike-fire*.—2. Bread : military rhyming s. : from ca. 1899. F. & Gibbons.—3. Head : rhyming s. : C. 20. B. & P.

strike me lucky !—pink !—silly !—up a gum-tree ! See **strike me blind !** For the first, see also **lucky !**, **strike me.**

strike oil. See **oil, strike.**

strike—or give me the bill ! Mind what you're about : coll. : ca. 1660–1750. Walker, 1672. Ex injunction to man clumsy with this weapon. (Apperson).

*striking, vbl.n. See **strike**, v., 1 and 2.

strill. A lie with intent to cheat : North Country c. (— 1864) ; ob. H., 3rd ed. Origin ?

string. A subject argued out ; an argument (or logical résumé) ; a commodious test of syllogisms : Oxford University : C. 18. Amherst, 1721 ; the O.E.D. records it also at 1780. Rarely in singular. Ex *string*, a continuous series.—2. A hoax ; a discredited story : printers' : from ca. 1890. Prob. ex *on a string*.—3. A surgical ligature : medical students' (— 1933). *Slang*, p. 193.

string, v. See **string on.**

string, brother of the. See **brother** paragraph.

string, feel like going to heaven in a. To feel utterly and confusedly happy : coll. : C. (? 18–)19. Lit., so happy that one would willingly die a martyr ; in late C. 16–18, *go to heaven in a string* (applied orig. to Jesuits hanged temp. Elizabeth) meant,

simply, to be hanged, as in Greene and Ned Ward (O.E.D.).

string, go to heaven in a. See preceding entry.

string, on a. Esp. *have* or *have got* (one) *on a string*, to hoax, befool : coll. : from ca. 1810. Bee ; ' Pomes ' Marshall, ' You can't kid me . . . they've been having you on a string.' Ex *lead in*, or *have in* or *on, a string*, to have completely under control. Cf. *string on*.—2. Hence, *have* (or *keep*) *on a string*, ' to keep a person in suspense for a long time ' : coll. : late C. 19–20. Lyell.—3. *get* (one) *on a string* or *line*. See **line, get one on a.** Vaux.

String of Beads. Leeds : railwaymen's rhyming s. : C. 20. *The Daily Herald*, Aug. 5, 1936.

string on. To befool, to ' lead up the garden path ', as, e.g. ' You can't string *him* on ! ' : from ca. 1810. Vaux. (Whence U.S. *string*, to humbug.)

stringer. A ball difficult to play : cricket (— 1904) ; † by 1930. F. & H. Perhaps ex *string on*, q.v.—2. In pl., handcuffs : 1893, Kipling (O.E.D.) ; ob.

stringing up. A strong admonition, severe reprimand : 1925, F. Lonsdale (O.E.D. Sup.).

strings on, put the. To hold (a horse) back in a race, to ' rope ' him : turf : ca. 1860–1900. *Fraser's Magazine*, Dec., 1863.

stringy-bark. Australian (ob. by 1915) as in A. J. Vogan, *Black Police*, 1890, ' Stringy-bark, a curious combination of fusil [*sic*] oil and turpentine, labelled " whisky ".' Ex the :—2. Adj. Rough or uncultured ; also (and orig.) rustic, belonging to the ' bush ' : Australian coll. >, ca. 1900, S.E. (slightly ob.) : 1833, *The New South Wales Magazine*, Oct. 1, concerning inferior workmanship, ' I am but, to use a colonial expression, " a stringy-bark carpenter ".' Morris.

*strip. To rob (a house or a person) ; esp. to steal everything in (a house) ; to swindle (a person) out of his money : late C. 17–mid-18 : c. B.E., whose phrases are of the ' *strip the ken*, to gut the house ' order, i.e. with direct object and no further construction. Ex *strip . . . of*, to plunder . . . of.

strip a peg. To buy ready-made, or second-hand clothes : 1908 (O.E.D. Sup.) ; slightly ob.

strip-bush. ' A fellow who steals clothes put out to dry after washing ' : either c. or low s. (— 1864) ; ob. H., 3rd ed.

strip-me-naked. Gin : from ca. 1750. Toldervy, 1756 ; Grose, 3rd ed. Cf. *stark-naked*, q.v.

*stripe. ' One who is no longer a first offender ' : c. (— 1933). George Ingram, *Stir*.

striper, two—two and a half—three. A lieutenant ; lieutenant-commander ; commander, R.N. : naval coll. : C. 20. F. & Gibbons. Ex the indications of rank. Cf. *one-pipper*, q.v.

stripes ; old s. or O.S. A tiger : jocular coll. : resp. 1909, 1885. O.E.D.—2. (Also **stripey.**) A sergeant of Marines : naval, esp. as a nickname : late C. 19–20. Bowen. Ex his badge of office.

stripped. (Of spirits) unadulterated ; neat : mid-C. 19–20. ; ob.

strippers. ' High cards cut wedge-shape, a little wider than the rest, so as to be easily drawn in a crooked game ', F. & H. : gaming coll. : from mid-1880's. See esp. Maskelyne, *Sharps and Flats*, 1894. Ex the manner of stacking, with a pun on impoverishment.

*stripping law. The (jailers') art and/or practice of fleecing prisoners : c. : late C. 16–early 17. Greene. Cf. *lay, n.*

strive. To write with care : Christ's Hospital :

from ca. 1870. Ex L. *scribere*, to write, via *to scrive*, q.v., on *strive*, to try very hard.

strode a pot, as good as ever. See **pissed, as good as ever**.

stroke, take a. (Of the male). To coït : low coll. (— 1785) ; ob. Grose, 1st ed.

***strolling mort**. A pretended-widow beggar roaming the country (often with a ' ruffler '), making laces, tape, etc., and stealing as chance favours her : c. (— 1673) ; † by 1830. Head ; B.E. ; Grose, 1st ed. In C. 17, often *strowling m*.

***strommel** (ca. 1565–1840) ; also **strummel** (C. 16–19), very common ; **stramel** (C. 18) and **strammel** (C. 18–19) ; **strommell** (C. 17–18) and **stromell** (C. 17) ; and **strumil** (C. 18, rare). Straw : c. of ca. 1565–1830. Harman, B.E., Grose (1st ed.), Scott. Perhaps via Anglo-Fr. ex Old Fr. *estramer* : cf. *stramage*, rushes strewn on a floor. O.E.D.—2. Hence, hair (prob. orig. of straw-coloured hair) : c. (— 1725) ; † by 1850, except in Norfolk (H., 1st ed.). *A New Canting Dict.*, 1725 ; Vaux ; Ainsworth, ' With my strummel faked in the newest twig ', done in the newest fashion. Cf. *strum*, n., 1, and :

***strommel- or strummel-faker**. A barber : c. of ca. 1810–40. Ex *strommel*, 2. (Implied in Vaux.)

***strommel- or strummel-patch**, n. A very contemptuous epithet for a person : late C. 16–early 17 c. Jonson, 1599, ' The horson strummell patch '. O.E.D. Ex *strommel*, 1.

strong. (Of a charge or payment) heavy : coll. : 1669 (O.E.D.) ; ob.

strong, be going. To be vigorous or prosperous : coll. : 1898, *Punch*, Oct. 22, ' And though, just now, we're going strong, | The brandy cannot last for long,' O.E.D. Ex horse-racing.

strong, come it. See **come it strong** ; cf. *go it strong*, below.

strong, come out. To speak or act vigorously or impressively ; to ' launch out ' : coll. : 1844, Dickens (O.E.D.). Cf. be *going strong*, above, and :

strong, go it. To act recklessly or energetically : coll. : from ca. 1840. Cf. :

strong, pitch it. To exaggerate ; tell a ' tall ' story : coll. : 1841, Hood (O.E.D.).

strong man, play the part of the. To be whipped at the cart's tail : low : ca. 1780–1840. Grose, 1st ed., ' I.e. to push the cart and horses too.'

strong on. Laying great stress on : coll. : 1883, ' Strong on the proprieties ', O.E.D.

strong on, go. To uphold or advocate energetically and/or emphatically : coll. : 1844, Disraeli, ' " We go strong on the Church ? " said Mr Taper,' O.E.D. ; ob.

strong silent man. This cliché has, since the early 1920's, > a virtual c.p. to the sarcastic. (Cf. Collinson.) Ex popular fiction.

stronger house than ever your father built, you'll be sent to a. You'll go to prison (someday) : C. 17 semi-proverbial coll. Apperson.

strongers. Any powerful cleanser such as spirits of salts : naval officers' : C. 20. Bowen. Ex *strong* by ' the Oxford -*er* '.

strongle. A strongyle (*stroṅ-djil*) : illiterate pronunciation : from mid-1880's. (Thread-worm.) O.E.D.

strook is, in mid-C. 19–20, sol. for *struck*. Baumann.

Strop Bill, the. South African coll. (— 1913) for ' a bill introduced into the Cape Parliament, which had it passed would have allowed a farmer to punish

his servants for misconduct by flogging ', Pettman By 1930, virtually †.

strow. Incorrect for † *frow, frough*, adj. O.E.D.

***strowling mort**. See **strolling mort**.

struck. Bewitched : dial. and coll. : 1839, J. Keegan (O.E.D.). In composition, *struck with*. Cf. *struck so*.

struck comical, be. To be very astonished : low coll. (— 1891). Cf. *struck*.

struck on. (Low) coll. form of *struck with*, charmed by (orig. a person—of the opposite—gen. female—sex) : from early 1890's. (O.E.D.)

struck so. Struck motionless in a particular posture or grimace : from ca. 1850 : low coll. Mayhew. Ex *struck*, bewitched. (O.E.D.)

struck with. See **struck**.

strade. A stock of mares : incorrect for *stud* : J. Kersey, 1702, and later. O.E.D.

strue. To construe or translate : schools' coll. : late C. 19–20.—2. Hence, a ' construe ' : Shrewsbury School coll. : from ca. 1890. (Desmond Coke, *The Bending of a Twig*, 1906.)

struggle and strain. A train : rhyming s. : late C. 19–20. B. & P.

struggle-for-lifer. A struggler for life : s. or coll. (— 1895). Ex biological *struggle for life*, though imm. ex Daudet's *struggle-for-lifeur* (1889).—2. Hence, one who, thus struggling, is none too scrupulous in seeking success : 1899 ; ob. O.E.D.

struggle with, I (etc.) **could**. I could do with, I'd gladly take (e.g. a drink) : lower classes' coll. (— 1887) ; ob. Baumann.

struguël. A, to, struggle : sol. when not, as occ. in C. 20, jocular (cf. *loverly*) : C. 19–20. Ware.

***strum**. A wig : late C. 17–early 19. B.E. ; Egan's Grose (' Cambridge '). Ex *strommel*, q.v. A *rum-strum* is a long one.—2. A *strum*pet ; a wench (if *rum*, then handsome) : c. : late C. 17–early 19. B.E.—3. See **stram**.

strum, v.i. and v.t. To have intercourse (with a woman) : low : from ca. 1780 ; ob. Grose, 1st ed. Semantically, to play a rough tune (on her). Possibly suggested by a pun on *strum*, n., 2, q.v.

***strummel, s.-faker, s.-patch**. See **strommel**, etc.

strunt. The male member : C. 17. Middleton, in *Epigrams and Satyres*, 1608. Ex S.E. and dial. *strunt*, the fleshy part of an animal's tail

strut like a crow in a gutter. See **crow in a gutter**.

'Struth ! ' An emaciated oath ', C. J. Dennis : low : late C. 19–20. (*God's truth !*) Also *'Strewth*, q.v.

stub (or **stubb**). See **stubbs**.—2. ' The lower part of a rainbow ' (Bowen) : nautical coll. : mid-C. 19–20 ; ob. An extension of the S.E. sense.

stub. To kick (a football) about : Felsted : late C. 19–20. Ex *stub one's toe*.

stub-faced. Pitted with small-pox : late C. 18–19. Grose, 2nd ed., where the phrase *the devil run over his face with horse stubs* (horseshoe nails) *in his shoes*.

stubb. See **stub, n**.

stubble. The female pubic hair : low : C. 18–20. Whence, *shoot over the stubble* (or *in the bush*), to ejaculate before intromission, and *take a turn in the stubble*, to coït (both, C. 19–20), and *pointer and stubble*, q.v.

***stubble it !** ; **stubble your whids !** Hold your tongue : c. : resp. late C. 17–19 (B.E. and Lytton) and ca. 1810–50 (Lytton). Prob. ex *stubble*, v.t., to clear of stubble.

Stubborns, the (Old). The 45th Foot Regiment,

now the Sherwood Foresters : military nickname :
from ca. 1840. F. & Gibbons. Ex a passage in
Napier's *Peninsular War*, bk. viii, ch. 2, referring to
them at the battle of Talavera as a 'stubborn
regiment '.

*****stubbs.** Nothing : c. of ca. 1810–1900. Vaux ;
Baumann. Ex *stub*, the end (of, e.g., a cigar).

stubs in his shoes. See **stub-faced.**

stuck. See **fly-stuck.**—2. Adversely affected ;
left in an unenviable position ; penniless ; grossly
deceived ; utterly mistaken : from ca. 1863. H.,
3rd ed. Cf. *stuck in*, q.v.

stuck, be. To be confirmed ; *sticking-parade*,
Confirmation : Charterhouse : C. 20. I.e., fixed in
one's Faith.

stuck, dead. Utterly ruined or flabbergasted ;
wholly disappointed : low : from ca. 1870.

stuck away. In pawn : Glasgow (− 1934).
Euphemistic. Cf. *upstairs* (adj.), q.v.

stuck by. Deserted or grossly deceived or imposed on by (esp. one's pal) : low : from ca. 1880.

stuck for. Lacking ; at a loss how to obtain :
from ca. 1870. Esp. *stuck for the ready*, penniless.
Cf. *stuck* and *stuck, dead*, qq.v.

stuck in (e.g. one's calculations). Mistaken ;
also, at a loss concerning : from ca. 1870. Prob. an
elaboration of *stuck*, q.v.

stuck in the mud. Cornered, baffled, nonplussed,
stalemated : from ca. 1880.

stuck into it !, get. Work hard ! ; don't dally ! :
military : from 1916. B. & P., 'The metaphor is
from digging ' (a clayey trench).

stuck on. Enamoured of (gen. a man of a
woman) : late C. 19–20 : rare among upper classes.
Ex U.S. sense, captivated with (things).

stuck on one's lines. To forget one's speech(es) :
theatrical coll. : mid-C. 19–20. Mayhew, iii.

stuck pig. See **stare like a stuck pig.**

stuck-up. Unjustifiably ' superior ' ; offensively
conceited or pretentious : coll. : 1829 (O.E.D.).—
2. See **stick up**, v., 8.

stuck-up marm. See **lady marm.**

stuckuppishness. The n. of *stuck-up* : coll. : 1853
(O.E.D.).

studding-sails on both sides(, with). With a girl
on each arm : nautical : late C. 19–20 ; ob. Bowen.

studify, v.i. To study : illiterate coll. : 1775, T.
Bridges (O.E.D.) ; † by 1850.

studnsel, stunsail or **-sel.** Nautical coll. (− 1887)
for *studding-sail*. Baumann.

study. To take care and thought for the convenience, desires, feelings of (a person) ; esp., to
humour (him) : coll. : mid-C. 19–20. Dickens,
1852 ; Mrs Carlyle, 1858, ' With no husband to
study, housekeeping is mere play'. Ex *study the
advantage, convenience, feelings, wishes, of* (a person).
O.E.D.

study up, v.t. To study for a special purpose :
coll. : from ca. 1890.

stuff. Medicine : C. 17–20 : S.E. until mid-C. 18,
then coll. Moore, 1819, ' It isn't the stuff, but the
patient that's shaken.' Also (ob. by 1890) *doctor's
stuff*, recorded in 1779 (O.E.D.). Ex *stuff*, ' matter
of an unspecified kind '.—2. Money, esp. cash:
adumbrated by Bridges, 1772 ; definite in Sheridan,
1775, ' Has she got the stuff, Mr Fag ? Is she rich,
hey ? ' ; Nat Gould, 1891. Slightly ob. Perhaps
ex *stuff*, household goods, hence personal effects.—
3. Whiskey, always *the stuff* (Croker, 1825) or *good
stuff* (1861, Meredith) : coll. O.E.D. Prob. ex
sense 1.—4. Stolen goods (*stuff* or *the stuff*) : c.

and low **s.** : 1865, *The Daily Telegraph*, Nov. 5.
O.E.D.—5. ? hence, ' contraband ' smuggled into
gaol : c. : C. 20. Esp. tobacco (− 1904).—6.
Hence (?), drugs ; esp. cocaine (*the stuff*) : c. :
C. 20.—7. Men as fighting material : coll. : 1883,
The Manchester Examiner, Nov. 24, ' The army of
Ibrahim included a good deal of tougher stuff than
the ordinary fellah of Egypt,' O.E.D. ; by 1930,
virtually S.E.—8. ' Copy ' ; one's MS. : coll.,
journalistic and authorial : 1898 (U.S.) ; certainly
anglicised by 1915, at the very latest. (O.E.D.)—
9. Shell-fire ; gen. with adj., as *heavy stuff*, heavy
shells or shell-fire : military coll.: from 1914. B. & P.
—10. An anæsthetic ; *give stuff* is to anæsthetize at
an operation ; *do stuffs* is to take a course in the
administration of anæsthetics : medical (− 1933).
Slang, p. 193.—11. Often employed as a coll. (mid-
C. 19–20) to connote vagueness in the speaker's
mind or intention, or to imply ignorance of the
precise term or name, as, e.g., in Christopher Bush,
The Case of the April Fools, 1933, ' Made his escape
down the creeper stuff '.—12. See ' Moving-Picture
Slang ', § 6.—13. See **stuff to give the troops.**

stuff, v.t. ; **stuff up.** To hoax, humbug, befool
(cf. *cram* in same sense) : ? orig. (1844) U.S., in
form *stuff up* ; English by 1859 as *stuff*, as in H.,
1st ed. Slightly ob. Prob. ex *stuff* (a person) *with*.
—2. Hence, v.i., ' to make believe, to chaff, to tell
false stories ', H., 1st ed. ; ob. by 1890, † by 1900.
—3. V.i., to be or to live in a stuffy atmosphere or
place ; to be inside when one could be in the open
air : late C. 19–20. E. Raymond, *Child of Norman's
End*, 1934, ' Here's that boy stuffing indoors again,'
when he was reading a book.

stuff,—and. And such dull or useless matters :
coll. : late C. 17–20. J. Lewis, ca. 1697, ' You
pretend to give the Duke notions of the mathematics, and stuff ' ; 1774, Goldsmith, ' Their
Raphaels, Corregios [*sic*], and stuff ' ; 1852, Thackeray. Slightly ob. O.E.D.

stuff, bit of. See **bit of stuff.**—**stuff, do one's.**
See **do one's stuff.**—**stuff, give.** See **stuff, n., 10.**—
stuff, good. See **stuff, n., 3.**

stuff, hard. Money in coin : low (− 1923).
Manchon. Ex *stuff*, n., 2.

stuff, hot. See **hot stuff.**—**stuff, know one's.**
See **do one's stuff.**

stuff on the ball, put. To make the ball break :
cricketers' : ca. 1880–1905. For *stuff* we now say
work and for *put* we prefer *get* : S.E.

stuff to give the troops !, that's the. That's the
idea ; that's what we want : coll. : orig. (1916)
military >, by 1919, gen. coll. Since 1917, often
that's the stuff to give 'em ! ; since ca. 1920, often
that's the stuff !, which may have been the original
(for it is recorded in U.S. in 1896 : O.E.D. Sup.), the
others mere elaborations. Among soldiers, since
ca. 1917, occ. *that's the giv to stuff 'em !* B. & P.

stuffata. Incorrect for *stufata* : mid-C. 18–early
19. O.E.D.

stuffed monkey. ' A very pleasant close almond
biscuit ' : Jews' coll., mostly London : from ca.
1890. Zangwill. (Ware.)

stuffed shirt. A pompous fool : upper and middle
classes' : from ca. 1920.

stuffing. Superfluous matter included to fill the
required space : journalistic coll. (− 1904) >, ca.
1920, S.E. Cf. *stuff*, n.

stuffing out of. See **knock the stuffing out of.**
But there are variants : *beat . . .* (1887, very ob.)
and *take . . .* (1906, Lucas Malet) : coll. O.E.D

stuffs, do. See stuff, n., 10.

stuffy. Angry, irritable; sulky; obstinate, 'difficult': U.S., anglicised ca. 1895 as a coll.; authorised by Kipling, 1898 (*get stuffy*). Cf. *sticky*, adj., 3. (O.E.D.)—2. Hence, secretive: schools' (— 1923). Manchon.—3. (Also ex sense 1.) Easily shocked; strait-laced: from ca. 1925. Galsworthy defines it in 1926, in *The Silver Spoon*.

stug. Guts: back s.: late C. 19–20 (R. H. Mottram, *Bumphrey's*, 1934.)

stugging. The rolling motion of a ship that is stranded: nautical coll.: mid-C. 19–20. Bowen. Cognate with *stog*, to walk heavily.

***stuling-ken.** See stalling-ken.

stumble. See truckle-bed.

stumer; occ., in C. 20, **stumor**; rarely **stumour** (Manchon). 'A horse against which money may be laid without risk', H., 5th ed., where spelt *shtumer*; racing s.: from ca. 1873. This sense and this spelling were both ob. by 1904 (F. & H., vol. vii, indirectly) and by 1935 virtually †. In Glasgow sporting s., however, it is still applied to a horse that is losing. The word probably derives from Yiddish; but ? cf. Swedish *stum*, dumb or mute.— 2. Hence, a forged cheque or a worthless one (an 'R.D.'): 1890, *Blackwood's* (*stumer*). O.E.D.— 3. Hence, or direct ex sense 1, a counterfeit bank-note or a base coin: 1897, 'Pomes' Marshall (see quotation in next sense).—4. Hence (often as adj.), a sham; anything bogus or worthless: 1897, 'Pomes' Marshall, in a poem entitled *The Merry Stumer*, 'Stumer tricks . . . stumer stake . . . stumer note . . . stumer cheque'; 1902, *The Sporting Times*, Feb. 1, 'He . . . had given her as security a stumer in the shape of an unfinished history of Corsica.'—5. Hence, a 'dud' shell: military: from 1914. F. & Gibbons.—6. A 'dud' person: from not later than 1913. Manchon. Perhaps orig. at Harrow School, for it appears in Arnold Lunn's *The Harrovians*.

stump. A leg: S.E. except in the pl., when (in C. 19–20, at least) coll., esp. in *stir one's stumps*, to walk or dance briskly: C. 17–mid-18, *bestir . . .*, as in Jonson and B.E.; mid-C. 17–20, *stir . . .*, as in Anon., *Two Lancashire Lovers*, 1640; 1774, Bridges, 'Then cease your canting sobs and groans, And stir your stumps to save your bones'; 1809, Malkin; 1837, Lytton.—2. Money: low s.: ca. 1820–50. Egan's Grose. Ex *stump*, a small piece. Cf. *stumpy*, q.v.—3. See stump with (us).

stump, v. To walk: from late 1850's. H., 1st ed. Gen. *stump it*, which in Lytton, 1841, means to decamp, a sense very ob. and rare. Ex *stump*, to walk clumsily.—2. To beggar, ruin: dial. (— 1828) >, by 1830, s. Esp. in passive, to be penniless, as in T. Hook, 1836, and 'Pomes' Marshall, 1897, 'In the annals of the absolutely stumped'. Ex *stump*, to truncate, or perhaps (H., 1860) ex cricket. —3. To challenge, esp. to a fight. Canadian (— 1932). John Beames. Perhaps ex sense 2. —4. See stump up.

stump, pay on the. To disburse readily and/or promptly: coll.: late C. 19–20.

stump, up a. In a difficulty: U.S. (late 1820's), anglicised by 1919. O.E.D. Sup. I.e. 'up a tree'.

stump it. See stump, v., 1.

stump up, v.t. To pay down, disburse: 1821, Egan (see quotation at rubbish); 1881, Blackmore. Rare. Ex *stump up*, to dig up by the roots. Cf. *plank down*.—2. Hence, v.i., to pay up; to disburse money, 'fork out': 1835, Dickens, 'Why don't you

ask your old governor to stump up ? '—3. To exhaust (a horse) by strain: 1875, Reynardson (O.E.D.): coll. > , by 1900, S.E.

stump with (e.g. us), it's a case of. A variant (— 1923) of *be stumped* (see stump, v., 2). Manchon.

stumped, adj. See stump, v., 2.

stumper. Small cricket: Tonbridge School (— 1904). At Harrow, *stumps*: coll. By 1919, it was gen. and S.E. Ex *stump-cricket*.

stumps. See stump, n., 1.—2. See stumper.—3. it's (a case of) stumps with (us). (We) are lost, ruined: low (— 1887). Baumann. Ex *stump*, v., 2.—4. See 'Body' n Addenda.

stumpy. Money: low: 1828 (O.E.D.); 1835, Dickens, H., 5th ed. Ob. Ex *stump*, n., 2, which was perhaps suggested by *short of blunt* (money).— 2. A stumpy person; gen. as nickname: coll. and dial.: mid-C. 19–20. Ex adj.—3. Whence, 'a Thames sailing barge without a topmast': nautical coll.: from ca. 1870. Bowen.

stun. Nuts: back s. (— 1859). H., 1st ed. See sret-sio; cf. *stunlaw(s)*.—2. Stone (weight): sol. or, at best, low coll. (— 1887). Baumann. Cf. *pun*.

***stun,** v. To cheat, swindle, as in *stun out of the regulars*, to defraud or deprive (a man) of his 'rightful' share of booty: c.: late C. 19–20; ob. Ex lit. sense of *stun* and perhaps influenced by *sting*, 1, q.v.

stung, be. See sting.

stunlaw(s). Walnuts: back s. (— 1859). H., 1st ed. See sret-sio.

stunned. Tipsy: from ca. 1910: New Zealanders' and, by 1933 at latest, Glaswegians'. Ex effects of liquor.

***stunned on skilly, be.** To be sent to prison and compelled to eat skilly: c. (— 1859); † by 1900. H., 1st ed. Cf. *stun*, v.

stunner. An exceedingly attractive woman (Albert Smith, 1848) or thing (1848, Thackeray, of the performance of a play); a person excellent *at* doing something (Thackeray, 1855, of a cook) or a thing excellent in quality or remarkable in size (from ca. 1875): coll. O.E.D. and F. & H. Cf. *stunning*.

stunners on, put the. To astonish; confound: low (— 1859). H., 1st ed. Ex *stunner*.

stunning. Excellent, first-rate; delightful; extremely attractive or handsome: coll.: 1849, Dickens (of ale); 1851, Mayhew (of a ring); of a girl, from not later than 1856, F. E. Paget, 'The most stunning girl I ever set my eyes on'. (O.E.D.) Ex *stun*, to astound; cf. *stunner* and *stunners on*, qq.v.—2. Hence, clever, knowing: low coll. (— 1857); † by 1900. 'Ducange Anglicus.'

stunning Joe Banks. 'Stunning' *par excellence*: low London: ca. 1850–80. Ex *stunning*, q.v. + Joe Banks, a noted public-house keeper and 'fence' (fl. 1830–50), who, despite the lowness of his customers, was notoriously fair in his dealings with them. H., 2nd ed.

stunningly. The adv. of *stunning*, q.v.: coll.: mid-C. 19–20.

stunsail, stunsel. See studnsel.

stunt. An item in an entertainment: coll.: 1901, *The Westminster Gazette*, Jan. 31, 'There will be many new "stunts" of a vaudeville nature,' O.E.D. Ob. Ex U.S. *stunt*, an athletic performance, any (daring) feat, 1895, itself perhaps ex Ger. *stunde*, an hour (O.E.D.), or, more prob., ex Dutch *stond*, a lesson (W.).—2. Hence, an enterprise undertaken to gain an advantage or a reputation : coll. : from ca. 1912. H. G. Wells in *Mr Britling*, 1916, ' It's the army side of the efficiency stunt,' W.—3. Hence, any enterprise, effort, or performance : coll. : 1913, Rupert Brooke (O.E.D. Sup.).—4. Hence, from ca. 1920, a dodge, a (political, commercial or advertising) trick or novel idea : coll. E.g. ' The economy stunt ' ; ' He's a bit too fond of stunts.' Manchon.—5. Ex sense 1 or 2, or both : an attack or advance ; a bombing-sortie : military coll. : from late 1915. (O.E.D. records it for April, 1916.)

stunt, adj. in first four senses of the n. (q.v.) : coll.

stunt, v.i. To do some daring or very showy feat, esp. in aviation : coll. : orig. (1915), military. Ex *stunt*, n., 1 and 2.—Ex n., 2 (q.v.), to undertake such an enterprise, esp. with a tinge of the sense in n., 4 : coll. : from ca. 1921.

stunter. The agent of the preceding : coll., now verging on S.E.

stunting, vbl.n. See **stunt**, v. J. S. Phillimore, 1918, ' Poets are a flying corps . . . In prose the stunting genius is less indispensable,' W.

stupe. A fool : 1762, Bickerstaffe, ' Was there ever such a poor stupe ? '; Blackmore, 1876 (O.E.D.). Coll. >, ca. 1900, dial. Ex :

stupid. A stupid person : coll. : 1712, Steele; 1860, George Eliot. Ex adj.—2. Bacon : Westmorland and Warwickshire s. (— 1904), not dial. E.D.D.

stupid, adj. Very drunk : euphemistic, mostly Anglo-Irish, coll. : late C. 19–20.

stupified, stupify, stupifying. Stupefied, stupefy, stupefying : very common misspellings : C. 17–20.

*****sturaban or -bin.** A variant of *sturiben*, q.v. Resp. H., 1st ed., and Baumann.

*****sturdy beggar.** A beggar that rather demands than asks, esp.—or rather, only—if of the 5th (in C. 18, the 50th) Order of beggars : c. : C. 16–18. B.E. An underworld application of the other world's gen. description.

*****sturiben** or **-bin** ; occ. **sturaban** or **-bin**. A prison : c. : ca. 1855–1925, *stir* being the usual C. 20 word. A corruption of Romany *stariben* (*steripen*). See **stir**.

*****stush.** A variant of *stash*, q.v. (Baumann.)

style, cramp one's. To prevent one from doing, or being at, one's best ; to handicap or check one : upper-class coll. : C. 20 (certainly from not later than 1916). F. & Gibbons ; Lyell. Ex athletics or racing.

stymied, adj. Awkwardly placed ; nonplussed : from ca. 1920 : sporting coll. >, by 1933, S.E. Ex golf ; golf sense ex *stymie*, a person partially blind (W.).

styria. A *stiria*, ' a concretion . . . resembling an icicle '. Incorrect : c. 1660–1750. O.E.D.

styx ; Styx. A urinal : Leys School (— 1904). F. & H. Ex the gloomy river.

sub. A subordinate : coll. : late C. 17–20 (slightly ob.), but uncommon before Herbert Spencer's use of it in 1840.—2. A subaltern (officer) : coll. : mid-C. 18–20. Thackeray, 1862, ' When we were subs together in camp in 1803.'—3. A subject : coll. : 1838, Beckett, ' No longer was he heard to sing, | Like loyal subs, " God save the King ! " '; very ob. except in U.S.—4. A subscriber : coll. : 1838, Hood (O.E.D.). Rare and virtually †.—5. A substitute : cricketers' coll. : 1864. Lewis.—6. A subscription : coll. (— 1904).—7. An advance of

money, esp. on wages : coll. : 1855. Ex *subsist money* (1835). O.E.D.—8. A submarine : naval and Air Force coll. : from 1914. (O.E.D. Sup.)—9. All : Anglo-Indian (— 1864). H., 3rd ed.

sub, v.i. To pay, or receive, a ' sub ' (the seventh sense) : coll. : from early 1870's. H., 5th ed.—2. From late 1890's, to pay (a workman) ' sub '. O.E.D.—3. V.i. and v.t., to sub-edit : coll., orig. and mainly journalistic : from ca. 1890.— 4. V.i., to act as a substitute (*for* somebody) : coll. : from late 1870's. (O.E.D.)—5. To subscribe : late C. 19–20. A. Lunn, *The Harrovians*, 1913, ' A few men . . . subbed together to buy a few books.'

sub-beau. ' A wou'd-be-fine ', B.E. : coll. : late C. 17–mid-18. Also *demi-beau*.

sub-fusc. The 1931–6 variation of *dim* (insignificant, lacking character), q.v. : Oxford University. This, however, is a revival, for the term existed in 1864, *Fun*, May 21, ' Anon I saw a gentle youth (no ' *sub fusc* ' undergrad). | ' *Toga virilis* ' he had none, no mortar-board he had ' (F. & H.). It existed at Harrow School in first decade of C. 20 : Lunn, *The Harrovians*, 1913. Lit., *sub-fusc, subfusc, subfusk* = dusky ; sombre (lit. and fig.).—2. Hence, (of dress) modest, of quiet colour : ibid. : from ca. 1932. D. Sayers, *Gaudy Night*, 1935, ' I notice that we are both decently subfusc. *Have* you seen Trimmer in that frightful frock like a canary lampshade ? '

sub-line. A printed form enabling a man to get an advance of wages : Public Works' (— 1935). See **sub**, n., 7, and **line**, n., 6.

sub on one's contract. To raise a loan, using contract as a proof of ability to repay : theatrical : late C. 19–20. See **sub**, v., 1.

[**sub rosa.** Secretly, surreptitiously : when used seriously it is S.E. (though, in C. 20, a rank cliché) ; when jocularly, it at least verges on coll. : mid-C. 17–20.]

subaltern's luncheon. A glass of water and a tightening of one's belt : coll. : late C. 19–20 ; ob. A. Griffiths, 1904, ' The traditional " subaltern's luncheon ",' O.E.D.

subby. A sub-warden : Oxford undergraduates' : from ca. 1870. Charles Turley, *Godfrey Marten, Undergraduate*, 1904.

subduplicate ; subtriplicate. Subduple ; subtriple : catachrestic : mid-C. 17–20. Hobbes. (O.E.D.)

subjec(k). Subject : sol. (— 1887). Baumann. Cf. *objec(k)*.

subject. Kind, sort : catachrestic : late C. 19–20. George Ingram, *Stir*, 1933, ' Roberts shared in all the contraband—many and various in subject— that Smith managed to get hold of.'

sublime, when ironical, is coll. : late C. 19–20. E.g. ' sublime conceit '.

sublime rascal. A lawyer : ca. 1820–80. H., 3rd ed.

subordination. Subornation : catachrestic : ca. 1640–1700. On the other hand *subsidary* for *subsidiary* is merely erroneous : ca. 1628–1700. O.E.D.

subs, pair o'. A pair of shoes : Glasgow lower classes' (— 1934). Perhaps Cf. *sub.* n., 5.

subsee. Vegetables : Regular Army's : late C. 19–20. B. & P. Ex Hindustani.

substance. See **shadow**.

substract, -tion. To subtract ; subtraction : mid-C. 16–20 : S.E. until mid-C. 19, then sol.

subtle as a dead pig. Very ignorant or stupid : coll. : ca. 1670–1720. Walker, 1672 ; Robertson, *Phraseologia Generalis*, 1681. Apperson.

suburb. The following phrases may be coll. verging on S.E. or wholly S.E. ; they belong to ca. 1590–1680 :—**suburb-garden**, a keep's lodging, or a private ' harem ' ; **suburb-humour**, blackguardly humour ; **suburb justice**, ' money is right ' ; **suburb-trade**, harlotry ; **suburb** (wanton) **tricks** ; **suburb wench** (occ. **drab** or **sinner**), a harlot ; **suburban roarer**, a brothel bully ; **house in the suburbs**, a brothel ; and **minion of the suburbs**, a male keep.

succedaneum, a remedy, is a C. 18 catachresis ; **succeedaneum** a C. 18–20 error. O.E.D.

successfully. Successively : sol. (Grose, 3rd ed., suggests that it is Anglo-Irish) : late C. 18–20. (In several dialects, it = *excessively*. E.D.D.) The O.E.D. example is irrelevant.

such, pron. This, that, these, those, it, them : sol. : mid-C. 19–20. E.g. ' If you have leisure, don't waste such.'—2. Also adj. This, that, these, those : id. : id. E.g. ' At such election ' for ' at that election '. Fowler.

such, adj. An intensive, the criterion being vague and/or ignored : coll. : mid-C. 16–20. Udall, ca. 1553, ' Ye shall not . . . marry . . . Ye are such . . . an ass ' ; 1900, W. Glyn, '. . . Where we stayed the night at *such* an inn ! ' O.E.D.—2. See **such**, pron., 2.—3. See **no such**.

such, as. Accordingly or consequently ; thereupon : (rather illiterate) coll. : 1721. W. Fowler, 1814, ' [She] motioned for me to come to her Highness. As such she addressed me in the most pleasant manner possible.' Ex *as such*, in that capacity. O.E.D.

such a dawg ! A theatrical c.p. (1888–ca. 1914) applied to a tremendous ' masher '. Ware.

such a few ; such a many. So (very) few ; so (very) many : coll. : from ca. 1840 ; ob. Thackeray, 1841, ' Such a many things in that time ', O.E.D.

such a much. So much . . . a ; to so great an extent a : catachrestic : late C. 19–20. P. G. Wodehouse, *A Prefect's Uncle*, 1903, ' That is why . . . Rugby is such a much better game than Association.'

such a reason my goose pissed or **pissed my goose.** A c.p. retort on anyone making an absurd excuse, giving an absurd reason : late C. 18–mid-19. Grose, 3rd ed.

such a thing as . . . !, there is. Look out for —— ! : a coll. threat : late C. 19–20. Ex the hint that since this thing exists, it must be considered. O.E.D.

such . . . who. Such . . . as : catachrestic verging on sol. : C. 19–20. E.g. John Rhode, *The Hanging Woman*, 1931, ' Such of my acquaintances who care to submit themselves to my experiments . . . come to visit me here.'

*****suck.** Strong drink : c. : late C. 17–early 19. B.E., Grose. Hence, *rum suck*, excellent liquor. Ex *suck*, a small draught or drink.—2. A breast-pocket, says F. & H.; open to doubt.—3. A disappointing or deceptive incident, event, or result : U.S. (1856), anglicised ca. 1890. Gen. *suck-in*, orig. U.S. ; anglicised ca. 1880. Ex *suck in*, v.—4. A toady : university : from ca. 1860 ; ob. H., 2nd ed. Ex *sucker*, q.v.—5. See **sucks**.

suck. The homosexual v. (i. and t.) and occ. n. : low coll. : C. 19–20. See esp. Allen Walker Read,

Lexical Evidence from Folk Epigraphy, 1935 (Paris ; privately printed).

suck-and-swallow. The *pudendum muliebre* : low : C. 19–20. Cf. *sucker*, 4.

suck-bottle, -can, -pint, -pot, -spigot. A confirmed drunkard or tippler : coll. verging on S.E. : resp. mid-C. 17–mid-18 (Brome), C. 19, C. 17–19 (Cotgrave), C. 19–20 (ob.), and late C. 16–17.

suck-casa. A public-house : low : mid-C. 19–20. H., 1st ed., where it is spelt *cassa*. Ex *suck*, n., 1 + *casa*, q.v.

suck-egg. A silly person : dial. (– 1851) > s. (– 1890). Barrère & Leland.

suck eggs, teach one's grandmother to. See **grandmother to . . .**

suck-in, n. See **suck**, n., 3.—2. V., to deceive ; to cheat : dial. (– 1842) >, by 1850, s. (orig. U.S. ; re-anglicised, as s., in late C. 19). Ex *suck in*, to engulf in a whirlpool.

suck one's face. To drink : low coll. : late C. 17–mid-18. B.E.

suck one's forefinger. To suck it and then, with it, draw a line round one's neck as a form of oath : lower classes' coll. (– 1923). Manchon.

suck-pint, -pot, -spigot. See **suck-bottle.**

suck the monkey. See **monkey.**

suck the mop. To be the victim of an omnibus ' nursing ' exploit : ca. 1870–80. H., 5th ed. See *nurse*, v., in omnibus sense.—2. ' To wait on the cab-rank for a job ' : cabmen's (– 1889) ; ob. Ware.

suck the sugar-stick. See **sugar-stick.**

suck up to. To insinuate oneself into another's favour ; to toady to : schoolboys' s. (– 1860). H., 2nd ed. ; Kipling, 1900, ' That little swine Manders . . . always suckin' up to King ' ; Dorothy Sayers, 1932.

sucker. A parasite or sponger : U.S. (1856) ; partly anglicised ca. 1890.—2. A greenhorn ; a simpleton : coll. : U.S. (1857), partly anglicised ca. 1895. Thornton.—3. Hence, in C. 20, among tramps, one who gives money (*not* always derisive : F. Jennings) ; and among criminals, a prospective victim (Charles E. Leach).—4. The *membrum virile* : low : C. 19–20 ; ? ob.—5. A baby : lower classes' coll : C. 19–20. Bee ; Manchon.

suckey. See **sucky.**

sucking Nelson. A midshipman : nautical coll. : from ca. 1820 ; ob. Lit., immature N.

suckles is a jocular coll. spelling (? first printed in Galsworthy's *Swan Song*, 1928) of *circles* : as in *the best suckles*.

sucks. Sweetmeats : coll. : 1858, T. Hughes. (Lit., things to suck.) Also, collective singular, as in *a knob of suck* (1865). O.E.D. Cf. *suction*, 4.

sucks ! An ' expression of derision ' : Bootham School : C. 20. Anon., *Dict. of Bootham Slang*, 1925. Cf. *suck in*, q.v. Also, and from ca. 1890, at other schools. Often *sucks to you*. E. F. Benson, *David of King's*, 1924, has *sucks for* ——!, that's a disappointment for so-and-so !

suckster, suckstress. An irrumator, -trix : low coll. : C. 19–20 ; ob.

*****sucky.** Rather drunk : late C. 17–19 : c. >, ca. 1750, low s. B.E. (*suckey*) ; Grose ; Baumann. Ex *suck*, n., 1, q.v.

suction. The drinking of (strong) liquor ; drinking : 1817, Scott (O.E.D.).—2. Hence (– 1887 ; nautical, says Baumann), strong drink.—3. The phrases *power of suction*, capacity for ' booze ' (Dickens, 1837) ; *live on suction*, to drink hard

(— 1904).—4. Sweetmeats : Winchester : late C. 19–20. Wrench. Cf. *sucks.*

sudden !, this is so. See **so sudden.**

sudden death. A decision by one throw (not, e.g., by two out of three) : 1834, Maginn.—2. Hence, a decision by one game, as in lawn tennis when the set-score is 5-all : C. 20 : s. >, by 1930, coll. (Collinson).—3. A fowl served as a spatchcock : Anglo-Indian : 1848 (Yule & Burnell).—4. A crumpet or a Sally Lunn : university (— 1874) ; ob. H., 5th ed.—5. Coffee : Cockneys' : late C. 19–20 ; ob. E. Pugh, *The Cockney at Home*, 1914.

sudding. Sudden : sol. : C. 19–20. Likewise *suddingly.*

suds. Ale : military : C. 20. F. & Gibbons. Bubbles on ale likened to soap-suds.

suds, in the. In a difficulty ; perplexed : from ca. 1570 : S.E.' until C. 18, then coll. ; in C. 19–20, s. ; very ob. Swift ; Grose, 1st ed.—2. Fuddled ; slightly drunk : ca. 1765–80. (O.E.D.)

Suds, Mrs. A washerwoman : coll. (— 1923). Manchon.

sued up. See **sewed up.**

*****suet(t)y Isaac.** Suet pudding : c. (— 1904) ; ob. Also *soapy Isaac.* Ex sallowness.

Suez canals. Suez Canal shares : Stock Exchange coll. (— 1887). Baumann.

suffer much ?, do you. A c.p. of mock pity : late C. 19–20 ; ob.

sufferer. A tailor : low : from ca. 1855 ; ob. H., 1st ed. ? ex patience.

suffering a recovery. Getting over a drinking-bout : Australian coll. euphemism (— 1935).

suffering cats ! An agonised c.p. directed at bad, or very shrill, singing : from ca. 1870. Ex caterwauling.

*****suffler.** A (seeming) drunkard taking part in *versing law* (swindling with false gold) : c. : late C. 16–early 17. Greene.

Suffolk bang. An inferior, excessively hard cheese : nautical coll. : C. 19. Bowen.

Suffolk punch. See **punch**, n.

Suffolk stiles. Ditches : coll. : mid-C. 17–early 18. Fuller, 1662. Cf. *Essex stiles.*

suffisticate. A C. 17 incorrectness for *sophisticate.* O.E.D.

sufi, a Mohammedan mystic, is often confused with *sophy*, a Persian monarch. O.E.D.

sugar. Money : low : 1862, *The Cornhill Magazine*, Nov., ' We have just touched for a rattling stake of sugar at Brum.' Ex *sugar and honey*, q.v. —2. A grocer : lower classes' (— 1909). Ware. Ex a principal commodity.—3. North(wards) : Wood Wharf (West India Dock, London) dockers' (— 1935). E.g. ' a little more sugar, Tom (*or* Bill *or* Jack) ! ', called by the piler to the driver of the electric gantry. Ex the fact that the *North* Quay of the West India Dock is regarded as ' the natural home for *sugar* storage.' (Very local, this : but included for the light it throws on the origin of s.)— 4. Gen. **a sugar.** A cube or lump of sugar : coll. : C. 20.—5. A term of address to a girl : from ca. 1930. Ex U.S. (J. Curtis, *The Gilt Kid*, 1936.)

sugar, v.i. To shirk while pretending to row hard : Cambridge University rowing (— 1890). Barrère & Leland.—2. To tamper with (food) ; to fake (accounts) ; to give a specious appearance of prosperity to : from ca. 1890. (O.E.D. Sup.) Prob. suggested by ' cooking ' accounts and ' salting ' mines.—3. Hence, to dupe (a person) : low (— 1923). Manchon. Cf. :—4. **sugar** (a person's)

milk for him. To harm a person under the pretext of doing his work : workmen's (— 1923). Manchon.

sugar and honey. Money : rhyming s. (— 1859). H., 1st ed. Cf. *sugar,* n.

sugar-basin ; sugar-stick. The female, the male, pudend : low : resp., mid-C. 19–20 ; late C. 18–20 (Grose, 2nd ed.). Ob. Whence *suck the sugar-stick*, sexually to take a man.

sugar-boat. See **captured** . . .

sugar candy. Brandy : rhyming s. (— 1859) ; ob. H., 1st ed.

sugar daddy. An oldish man spending lavishly on a young woman : U.S., anglicised, via the ' talkies ', ca. 1931. Cf. *sugar*, n. 1, q.v.

sugar (for the bird), little bit of. A premium, a bonus ; an unexpected benefit or acquisition : low : 1897–ca. 1910. Ware.

sugar (a person's) **milk for him.** See **sugar**, v., 4.

sugar on, be. To be much in love with (a person) : non-aristocratic (— 1887) ; † by 1930. Baumann. Punning *be sweet on.*

sugar-shop. ' A head centre of bribery ', electioneering (— 1909) ; ob. Ware. Ex *sugar*, n., 1.

sugar-stick. See **sugar-basin.**

Sugar-Stick Brigade, the. The Army Service Corps : military (— 1904) ; † by 1915.

sugar up. To flatter (a person) : coll. (— 1923). Manchon.

sugared !, I'm or **I'll be.** I'm damned ! ; it connotes (profound) astonishment or (great) perplexity : from ca. 1890. Anon., *Troddles*, 1901. Euphemistic for *b****red.*

sugarer. A funker ; a shirker, esp. at rowing : C. 20. O.E.D. (Sup.). Ex *sugar*, v.i.

suicide. Four horses driven in a line : Society and sporting : ca. 1860–1900. H., 3rd ed.

suicide club (or **S.C.**), **the.** Machine-gunners, battalion stretcher-bearers, or, esp., bombers : military coll. : late 1915 ; ob. F. & Gibbons. Because theirs was dangerous work.

suicide club, join the. ' To undertake any dangerous duty' : naval coll. : 1915 or 1916 ; ob. Bowen. Cf. the preceding.

*****suit.** ' Game ', ' lay ' ; method, trick ; pretence ; imposition : c. of ca. 1810–50. Vaux.—2. A watch and seals : c. of ca. 1830–90. Ainsworth. Ex S.E. *suit*, a complete set.

suit, birthday. See **birthday suit.**

*****suit, upon the.** In the (specified) manner : see **suit**, 1. Vaux.

*****suit and cloak.** A ' good store of Brandy or any other agreeable Liquor, let down Gutter-lane ', B.E. : c. : late C. 17–early 19.

suit of mourning. A pair of black eyes : ca. 1820–80. Egan's Grose.

*****suite.** See **suit**, 1.—**suji-muji.** See **souji-mouji.**

sukey. A kettle : low (— 1823) ; ob. Bee. ? origin : cf. Welsh Gypsy *šukar*, to hum, to whisper. —? hence, 2, a general servant or ' slavey ' : from ca. 1820 ; ob. Ex *Sukey*, a lower-class diminutive of *Susan*, a name frequent among servants.—3. Hence, *sukey-tawdry*, a slatternly woman in fine tawdry : ca. 1820–50. Bee.—4. Perhaps hence, a simpleton : mid-C. 19–20.

sulphur. Pungent or lurid talk : 1897 (O.E.D.) : s. >, by 1920, coll. Slightly ob. Because sulphurous. Cf. sense 2 of :

sultry. Indelicate : 1887, Kipling, ' **Sultry**

stories ' (O.E.D.) : **s.** >, by 1920, coll.—2. Hence (of language), lurid : 1891, ' Sultry language ', O.E.D. : s. >, by 1910, coll. Cf. *sulphur*.—3. Uncomfortable, lively, ' hot ' : 1899, Conan Doyle, ' I shall make it pretty sultry for you,' O.E.D.

sum. An arithmetical problem to solve which one must apply a rule ; such a problem solved : coll. : C. 19–20. Dickens, 1838, has ' Sums in simple interest ', O.E.D. (I think that its use in New Zealand and Australia has never been classifiable as other than standard.)

sum ! Adsum ! : Public Schools' coll. : mid-C. 19–20.

sumfin(g) ; sumpfin(g). Something : sol. : C. 19–20. Cf. *summat*.

sumjao. To warn, correct, coerce : Anglo-Indian coll. : 1826. Ex Hindustani. Yule & Burnell.

summat. As ' somewhat ', it is low coll. (prob., ex the dial. use) ; as ' something ', it is sol. : both, C. 19–20. Baumann.

summer-blink. A gleam of sunlight on a day of bad weather : nautical coll. : C. 20. Bowen.

summer-cabbage. An umbrella : low (— 1823) ; ob. Egan's Grose. Cf. *greens*, q.v.—2. A woman : F. & H. ; but is this so ? If correct, of ca. 1850–1900.

summerhead. A sun-umbrella : Anglo-Indian coll. : 1797 (O.E.D.). Corrupted *sombrero*.

summin. Something : sol. : C. 19–20. (Ernest Raymond, *A Family That Was*, 1929.) Cf. *sumfin(g)* and *sup'n*, qq.v.

summons. To summon legally : late C. 18–20 : S.E. till C. 20, then a sol.

sumpfin(g). See **sumfin(g).**

sumpsy. An action of *assumpsit* : legal : from ca. 1860. H., 3rd ed.

sun, have been in the ; have, or have got, the sun in one's eyes. To be drunk : resp. 1770 (O.E.D.) and 1840, Dickens, *have* ; *have got* not before ca. 1860. Also *have been standing too long in the sun* (— 1874). Cf. *sunshine*. Ex sun-dazzle or -drowsiness.

sun, taste the. See **taste the sun.**

sun-arc. A cinema coll. : from ca. 1927. See ' Moving-Picture Slang ', § 3.

sun-dodger. A heliographer : military : 1900, *Illustrated Bits*, Dec. 22. Via *sun-signalling*.

sun-dog. A mock sun : nautical coll. verging on S.E. : from ca. 1630.

sun is scorching your eyes out, the. See **scorching your eyes out.**

sun over the foreyard, get the. To drink before noon : nautical (— 1904). Bowen defines *sun over the foreyard* as ' the time by which a drink is permissible ' ; gen. *the sun is over the foreyard*. Cf. *sun, have been in the.*

sunburnt. Having many (orig. and esp., male) children : late C. 17–early 19. B.E. ; Grose, 1st ed. Punning *son*.—2. ' Clapped ' : ca. 1720–1890. *A New Canting Dict.*, 1725. Punning *burnt*.

Sunday. To spend Sunday (*with* a person) : Society coll. (— 1909) ; ob. Ware.

Sunday, look both or nine or two ways for. See **look . . .**

Sunday-afternoon courting-dress. (Of servant-girls) best clothes : lower classes' coll. (— 1887). Baumann.

Sunday clothes on, the old man has got his. A low c.p. indicating an *erectio penis*. In allusion to *starched*

Sunday face. The posteriors : low : from ca. 1860 ; ob.

Sunday flash togs. (Of men) best clothes : low (— 1880). Ware.

Sunday girl. A week-end mistress : ca. 1890–1915.

Sunday-go-to-meeting clothes and **togs.** Sunday clothes : resp. coll. (C. 20) and s. (1894, Baring-Gould : O.E.D.).˙ By jocular amplification of *Sunday clothes*. Cf. *Sunday-afternoon courting-dress*, q.v.

Sunday man. ' One who goes abroad on that day only, for fear of arrests ', Grose, 1st ed. : from ca. 1780 ; ob. : coll. >, ca. 1850, S.E.—2. A prostitute's bully : low : from ca. 1880. Because he walks out with her on that day.

Sunday-mopper. An employee that, to increase his earnings, does others' Sunday work : workmen's (— 1923). Manchon.

Sunday out(, one's). A domestic servant's monthly or alternate Sunday free : from late 1850's : coll. till ca. 1920, then S.E. (Orig. a servants' term.)

Sunday Pic, the. *The Sunday Pictorial* : journalists' coll. : C. 20.

Sunday promenader. See **once-a-week man.**

Sunday saint. One who, having been dissolute all the week, turns respectable and sanctimonious on Sunday : coll. : from ca. 1870. Cf. *Scottish Sunday face.*

Sundayfied. Suitable to Sunday ; in Sunday clothes : coll. >, by 1920, S.E. : 1899 (O.E.D.).

Sundayish. Rather like, or as on, Sunday : 1797 : coll. >, by C. 20, S.E. (O.E.D.)

Sundays. See **month of Sundays.—Sundays come together** or **meet, when two.** Never : semi-proverbial coll. : from ca. 1610 ; ob. except in dial. : Haughton, 1616 ; Ray. Cf. Shropshire *the first Sunday in the middle of the week* and *Tibb's Eve, St*, q.v. (Apperson.)

Sunderland fitter. The Knave of Clubs : jocular North-Country coll. (— 1847). Halliwell.

sundowner. A tramp habitually arriving at a station too late for work but in time to get a night's shelter and a ration : Australian coll. >, by 1910, S.E. : 1875, Miss Bird ; 1926, Jice Doone, ' The word is now almost obsolete, swaggie being the term almost universally in use.' (See esp. Morris.) Hence :

sundowning. This practice : Australian coll. : from ca. 1890. Kinglake.

Sunlight !, don't worry—use. A c.p. of the 1920's. Collinson. Ex a famous advertisement by Sunlight Soap.

sunny bank. A good fire in winter : coll. : late C. 17–early 19. B.E. ; Grose, 1st ed. Ex the warmth, with pun on *banking a fire*.

sunny south. The mouth : rhyming s. : 1887, *The Referee*, Nov. 7.

sun's high lad. A smart fellow : tailors' : 1928, *The Tailor and Cutter*, Nov. 29. An elaboration of *bright lad.*

Sunshades ; or **s.** The *Sunehales* Extension of the Buenos Aires and Rosario Railway Company shares : Stock Exchange : late C. 19–early 20.

sunshine, have been in the. To be drunk : 1857, George Eliot. As early as 1816 in ɔial. : E.D.D. See **sun, have been in the.**

sunspottery. The science of solar spots ; astronomers' (— 1887). Baumann.

sup. A supplement : coll. (— 1923). **Manchon.**

sup(e). A variant of *super*, 1 (H., 1st ed.), 3 (1824, O.E.D.), 4 (— 1904, F. & H.), and 6 (— 1904, F. & H., esp. *supe and slang*, watch and chain), qq.v.

super. A supernumerary : 1853, 'Cuthbert Bede' (O.E.D.) : theatrical s. >, ca. 1880, coll.—2. A supernumerary on a ship, i.e. a supercargo : nautical s. (1866) >, ca. 1890, coll.—3. Ex senses 1 and 2, a supernumerary in gen. : coll. : from ca. 1880.—4. A superintendent of a station : Australian s. (1870, Lindsay Gordon) >, ca. 1900, coll. Morris.—5. A police superintendent, esp. in address : coll. : mid-C. 19–20.—6 (Also **souper.**) A watch : c, : from late 1850's. Ware derives it from *soup-plate*, hence *souper*, hence *super*. Cf. *super, bang a*, and *super-screwing*.

super, v. To be a 'super', sense 1 ; often as vbl.n., *supering* (1889, O.E.D.)—2. See **super list**.

super, adj. Superficial (in measurement ; gen. after the n.) : trade coll. : 1833, T. Hook, ' At so much per foot, super ', O.E.D.—2. Superfine : trade coll. : from ca. 1840. Bischoff, *Woollen Manufacture*, 1842 (O.E.D.).—3. Extremely strong, capable, intelligent : from ca. 1910. (See esp. Fowler.) Ex *superman*. Cf. *wizard*, q.v.—4. Hence, excellent, ' swell ' : from ca. 1925. R. Keverne, *The Man in the Red Hat*, 1930, ' He was staying at the " Beach ". Very super.'

*****super, bang a.** To steal a watch by breaking the ring : c. : late C. 19–20. H. Hapgood, 1903 (O.E.D.). See **super,** n., last sense.

super list, be on the. To be marked for supersession (Turley) ; more gen., **be supered,** to be superseded : at certain Public Schools : from the 1880's. Charles Turley, *Godfrey Marten, Schoolboy*, 1902, ' " I have been in Lower Fourth exactly four terms," he went on, " and my people are getting sick, and Sandy says I shall be ' supered ' in a term or two."

*****super-screwing.** Watch-stealing : c. (— 1859). H., 1st ed. Ex twisting handles off. See **super,** n., last sense, and **super, bang a.**

*****super-super bastard.** A mean, bullying, tyrannical fellow : c., and low s. : from ca. 1910. James Spenser, *Limey Breaks In*, 1934, ' This warder was another of the variety known amongst prison populations as super-super bastards.'

supercede. To supersede : C. 15–20 : S.E. until C. 19, then incorrect. (O.E.D.)

supercharged, ppl.adj. Intoxicated : aircraft engineers' : from ca. 1926. *The Daily Herald*, Aug. 1, 1936.

supered, be. See **super list.**

Superfine Review, The. *The Saturday Review* : literary : ca. 1863–1910. Thackeray-coined.

supernacular. (Of liquor) excellent : 1848, Thackeray (O.E.D.) ; ob. Ex :

supernaculum. A liquor to be drained to the last drop ; excellent liquor ; excellent anything : C. 18–20 ; ob. W. King, 1704, ' Their jests were *Supernaculum* ' ; Grose, 1st ed. (' Good liquor '). Ob. Ex the adv., q.v. Cf. *supernacular*.—2. Hence, a draught that utterly empties cup or glass : 1827, Disraeli (O.E.D.).—3. A full glass : mid-C. 19–20 ; like sense 2, ob.

supernaculum, adv. ; occ., C. 16, **-nagulum,** **-neg-,** and, C. 17, **-nacullum, -nagullum.** To the last drop : late C. 16–20 ; ob. Nashe, 1592, ' Drinking super nagulum, a devise of drinking new come out of France ' ; B.E. ; *The Edinburgh Review*, 1835. Ob. Ex the practice of placing one's upturned glass on the left thumb-nail, to show that not a drop has been left : a mock-L. translation of the

Ger. *auf den nagel* (*trinken*). Cf. Fr. *boire rubis sur l'ongle* (W.).—2. Often elliptically, as in Cotton, 1664, and fig., as in Jonson, 1598, ' [Cupid] plaies super nagulum with my liquor of life.'

supersnagative. First-rate ; ' splendid '; excellent : Australians' and New Zealanders' : from ca. 1890 ; ob. Perhaps ex *superfine* on *supernacular*, q.v., but prob. fanciful on *superlative*.

superstitious pie. A minced or a Christmas pie : a Puritan or Precisian nickname : late C. 17–mid-18. B.E. Because, by Puritans, made some weeks before Christmas.

sup'n ; supp'm, supp'n. Something : illiterate slurring, esp. in New Zealand (— 1935). Ex dial.

*****supouch.** An inn-hostess ; a landlady : c. : late C. 17–18. B.E., Grose. ? origin, unless ex *sup*, n. + (*to*) *pouch*.

supped all one's porridge, have. No longer to suffer with one's teeth : lower classes' coll. (— 1923). Manchon.

supper, give the old man his ; supper, warm the old man's. To confer the act of kind ; to sit, skirts raised, before the fire. Low : late C. 19–20.

supper, set one his. To perform a feat that another cannot imitate, let alone surpass : coll. (— 1891). J. M. Dixon's dictionary of idiomatic English.

supple is often, by the illiterate, confused with *subtle*. (Desmond Coke, *The School across the Road*, 1910.)

supple both ends of it. To abate a priapism : low Scots : late C. 18–20.

Supple Twelfth, the. The 12th Lancers : military : from the Peninsular War ; slightly ob. F. & Gibbons.

supp'm, supp'n. See **sup'n.**

suppose or **I suppose.** Nose : rhyming s. See **I suppose.** (Manchon has the abbr.)

suppose or **supposing,** introductory of a proposal or a suggestion, is coll. : resp. 1779 and late C. 19–20. R. Bagot, 1908, ' By the way, supposing you were to drop " uncle-ing " me ? ' O.E.D.

Surat. An adulterated or an inferior article : coll. (mostly Lancashire) : 1863, *The Times*, May 8 ; ob. *Surat* cotton is inferior to American.

surbeaten, surboted, surbutting. Incorrect for *surbated*, id., *surba*(*i*)*ting* : C. 17. O.E.D.

sure ! Certainly ! ; with pleasure ! ; agreed ! : coll. : early C. 18, in England, whence it fled to the U.S. ; re-anglicised ca. 1910. Farquhar, in *The Beaux' Stratagem*, 1707 (cited by G. H. McKnight, *English Words*, 1923).

sure !, be ; I am sure ! ; you may be sure ! At end of sentence, these phrases when asseverative are coll. : 1830, N. Wheaton, ' To all my inquiries . . . I only received for answer—" I don't know, I'm sure ", O.E.D.

sure, for. As certain ; for certain ; indubitably : late C. 16–20 : S.E. until late C. 19, then coll. Stevenson, 1883, ' Desperate blades, for sure ', O.E.D.

sure !, to be. Of course ! : mid-C. 17–20 : S.E. until late C. 19, then coll.—2. Often concessively : admitted ! ; indeed ! : coll. : mid-C. 19–20.

sure !,—well, I'm ; well, to be sure ! I *am* surprised : coll. : 1840, Thackeray, ' " Well, I'm sure ! " said Becky ; and that was all she said,' O.E.D. ; *well, to be sure !*, app. not before late C. 19.

sure and . . ., be. (Only in infinitive or imperative.) To be careful to ; not to fail to : coll. : from ca. 1890. ' Be sure and look ! '

sure as . . ., as. Very sure. Of these phrases, prob. only those are coll. of which the criterion-member or the gen. tone is familiar S.E. or coll. Thus, **(as) sure as the Creed** or **one's creed** is S.E., as is **(as) sure as fate** or **death ;** but **(as) sure as a gun** (B. & Fletcher, 1622 ; Steele, 1703 ; Meredith, 1859) is coll., as are **sure as eggs** (Bridges, 1772), **sure as eggs is eggs** (Goldsmith), **sure as God made little apples** (late C. 19–20 ; orig. dial.), **sure as the devil is in London** (mid-C. 18), and the following in Ray, 1670, **as sure as check,** or **Exchequer pay** (ca. 1570–1620), **as sure as a juggler's box** (ca. 1650–1740), and **as sure as a louse in bosom** (late C. 17–18), or, late C. 17–mid-18, **in Pomfret.** (Apperson.)

sure card. See card, sure.

sure find. One who is sure to be found : coll. (— 1933). S.O.D.

sure-fire. Certain ; infallible : coll. ; U.S. angli-cised ca. 1918. (D. Sayers, *Murder Must Advertise*, 1933, ' He thought it was a sure-fire mascot.')

sure I don't know !, I'm. As asseverative tag, it is coll. : mid-C. 19–20.

sure thing ! The same as *sure !*, q.v. : coll., orig. (1896) U.S. ; anglicised not later than 1910. (O.E.D. Sup.)

surely, with second syllable stressed, either = ' is it not so ? ' or as a vague intensive, is a sol. when not dial. Dickens, ' And so it is, sure-ly,' O.E.D.

surely me. A proletarian variation of *to be sure !,* sense 1 : from ca. 1880. Ware (at *cupboardy*).

surf. An actor or musician or scene-shifter, who combines night-work at the theatre with some daily work outside : theatrical : from late 1850's. H., 1st ed. ? pun on *serf.*—2. Hence, a parasite, toady, sponger : low (— 1887) ; ob. Baumann.

surgeon's bugbear. Adipose tissue : medical (— 1933). *Slang*, p. 193. Because, when cut, it bleeds in a way difficult to check.

surly as a butcher's dog, as. Extremely surly : coll. : late C. 17–20 ; ob. Ray ; Spurgeon, 1869. Because the animal gets so much meat to eat. Apperson, who gives also the Cheshire *surly as a cow's husband.*

surly boots. A grumpy, morose fellow : coll. verging on S.E. : C. 18–20 ; ob. E.g. Combe, 1812. Cf. :

surly chops. A nautical variant of the preceding : coll. (— 1887). Baumann.

[**Surly Sam.** Dr Johnson : rather sobriquet than nickname ; *Ursa Major* is likewise sobriquet. Dawson.]

Surprisers, the. The 46th Foot Regiment, now the Duke of Cornwall's Light Infantry : mili-tary : ' dating from the American War, with special reference to the surprise of the enemy at White Plains in September, 1777 ', F. & Gibbons. Cf. *Red Feathers, the.*

surquedry, -idry. Excess or surfeit : cata-chrestic : late C. 16–17. O.E.D.

surtout. See wooden surtout.

surveyor of the highway(s). A person reeling drunk : late C. 18–mid-19. Grose, 2nd ed.

surveyor of the pavement. A person in the pillory : late C. 18–mid-19. Ibid.

surveyor's friend, the. Whitewash : naval : C. 20. Bowen. Ex ' the amount used for marking points on shore '.

sus. ' The remains of the Praefects' tea, passed on to their valets in college ' : Winchester College : late C. 18–19. Wrench. Ex dial. *sus(s)* or *soss,* hog-wash.—2. (N. and adj.) A being *suspected* ;

suspected ; (on) suspicion : c. : from ca. 1920. James Curtis, *The Gilt Kid*, 1936, ' What you nick me for ? Sus ? ' Cf. *suspect,* below.

sus. per coll. Hanged by the neck : ca. 1780–1850. Grose, 1st ed. Ex *suspensus per collum* (F. & H. ; or *suspensio . . .,* W. ; or *suspenda-tur . . .,* O.E.D.), the jailor's entry against a hanged man's name. Cf. :

susancide. Self-murder : half-wits' jocular (— 1909). Ware. Ex *Susan + suicide.*

*****susie.** A sixpence, whether coin or value : turf c. (— 1932). Perhaps *Susie* : by personification suggested by *bob,* a shilling. More prob. ex dial. *suse,* six : cf. the Lancashire *susepence,* sixpence (E.D.D.).

Susie. See sister Susie.

*****suspect, for.** For being a suspicious character ; on suspicion of crime : c. : from ca. 1920. J. Curtis, *The Gilt Kid*, 1936, ' He got nicked for suspect.' Cf. *sus,* 2.

suspence or **suspense, in deadly.** Hanged : ca. 1780–1860. Grose, 1st ed.

suspicion. A very small quantity ; a minute trace : 1809, Malkin (O.E.D.) : coll. >, ca. 1880, S. E. Trollope, 1867, ' He was engaged in brushing a suspicion of dust from his black gaiters.' Ex Fr. *soupçon* ; cf. Fr. *larme* and *spot,* n., 1.

suspish. Esp. *under suspish,* under suspicion (by the police) : Australian : from ca. 1925. Cf. *ambish* for *ambition.*

Sussex weed(s). Oaks : Southern (esp. Sussex) coll. : C. 20. A. S. Cooke, *Off the Beaten Track in Sussex,* 1911, ' Among the " Sussex weed " '. (Apperson.)

sustension. Incorrect for *sustention* : late C. 19–20. (O.E.D.)

sut. Satisfactory ; fortunate : tailors' : from ca. 1870. ? corruption of *sat(isfactory).*—2. As an exclamation, it = ' good ! ' or ' serve you right ! ' : late C. 19–20. E.g. in *The Tailor and Cutter,* Nov. 29, 1928.

*****sutler.** ' He that Pockets up, Gloves, Knives, Handkerchiefs, Snuff and Tobacco-boxes, and all the lesser Moveables ', B.E. : c. of late C. 17–early 19. Ex military sense.

suttenly, suttingly. Certainly : sol. (and dial.) : C. 19–20.

suzie. A variant of *susie.*

s'velp me. A Cockney variation († by 1920) of *s'welp,* q.v. (Baumann.)

swab. A naval officer's epaulette : nautical jocose or pejorative : 1798, *The Sporting Magazine* (O.E.D.) ; Marryat. Ob. Ex the shape of a *swab,* anything for mopping up.—2. A spill ; a spilling : Bootham School (— 1925). Ex :

swab, v. To spill ; to splash : Bootham School : C. 20. Anon., *Dict. of Bootham Slang,* 1925. Ex swabbing a deck.

swab-betty. ' A woman who washes floors, etc.' : Bootham School (— 1925). Ibid. Ex the pre-ceding.

swabber, swobber. (Gen. pl.) In whist, the Ace of Hearts, Knave of Clubs, and the Ace and Deuce (2) of Trumps : late C. 17–early 19 : coll. >, by 1750, S.E. First recorded in B.E. Prob. ex S.E. sense.

swack. A deception, whereas *swack-up* (H., 3rd ed.) is a falsehood : mid-C. 19–20.—2. Also v.t., *swack up,* to deceive. All : Christ's Hospital : from ca. 1860. Perhaps cognate with Scottiah *swack,* supple, smart, or *swack,* a whack.

*swad. A soldier : diak., and c, >, mid-C. 19, s. :
C. 18–20 ; ob. in s. by 1910. *The Memoirs of John
Hall*, 1708 ; Grose, 2nd ed. ; Smyth, 1867, ' A
newly raised soldier '. In late C. 19–early 20, esp. a
militiaman. Perhaps ex *swad*, a bumpkin, a lout.
Cf. *swadkin* and *swaddy*, qq.v., and :

swad-gill. A soldier : low s. (– 1812) and dial. ;
† in s. by 1860. Vaux, who spells it *swod-gill*. Ex
swod, q.v., + *gill*, a fellow.

*swadder. A pedlar : c. of ca. 1565–1750.
Harman, B.E. In C. 18, esp. of a pedlar given to
robbery with violence : *A New Canting Dict.*, 1725.
Perhaps cognate with *swad* as a term of abuse. Cf.
swaddler, 4., q.v.

swaddie. See swaddy.

swaddle. To beat soundly ; to cudgel : coll. : ca.
1570–1840. Ca. 1570, Anon., ' Thy bones will I
swaddle, so have I blisse ' ; Dryden ; B.E., ' I'll
Swaddle your Hide ' ; Scott. Ex *swaddle*, to
bandage.

swaddler. A Methodist : a coll. (mainly Anglo-
Irish) nickname from ca. 1745. C. Wesley, *Journal*,
Sept. 10, 1747, where the anecdotal origin is given
(O.E.D.) ; Grose ; *The Academy*, May 11, 1889.—
2. Hence, a Methodist preacher, esp. in Ireland :
coll. : C. 19.—3. Any Protestant : Anglo-Irish
coll. : from ca. 1870. H., 5th ed.—4. (Often
swadler.) A member of the 10th Order of the
underworld : c. of late C. 17–early 19. B.E. ;
Grose, 1st ed., ' who not only rob, but beat, and
often murder passengers '. Ex *swadder*, q.v., on
swaddle, q.v.

swaddling, vbl.n. See swaddle, v.—2. Method-
ism ; conduct (supposed to be) characteristic of
Methodists : coll. : mid-C. 18–early 19. See
swaddler, n., 1.—3. Adj., Methodist : coll. : mid-
C. 18–20 ; ob. In C. 19–20, Protestant in gen. :
likewise coll.

swaddy ; swaddie, swoddy. A soldier : low >,
ca. 1860, naval and military s. : C. 19–20. Vaux,
1812 ; Smyth, 1867, ' A discharged soldier ', with
which cf. Smyth on *swadkin*, q.v. Ex *swad*, n., q.v.
Among soldiers, in late C. 19–20, gen. of a private
and esp. as a term of address : see chiefly B. & P.
Cf. U.S. *swatty*.

*swadkin. A soldier : c. (1708, John Hall) >,
ca. 1850, dial. and naval s. (– 1867) ; as latter, ob.
Grose, 2nd ed. ; Smyth, ' A newly raised soldier '.
Diminutive of *swad*, q.v. Cf. *swad-gill* and *swaddy*.

*swadler. See swaddler, 4.

*swag. A shop : c. (– 1676) ; ob. Coles, B.E.,
Grose. ? origin. (Cf. *swag-shop*, q.v.) Hence, a
rum swag is a shop full of rich goods (B.E.) : † by
1850.—2. Imm. ex *swag-shop*, q.v. : one who keeps
a ' swag-shop ' ; s. (? low) : 1851, Mayhew.—3.
Any quantity of goods, esp. a pedlar's wares or a
thief's booty, esp. as recently or prospectively
obtained : c. (– 1811) >, ca. 1850, low s. >, by
1890, gen. s. in the wider sense, any unlawful gains
or acquisition. *Lex. Bal.* ; Vaux, who, like the
preceding glossarist, notes the nuance, ' wearing-
apparel, linen, piece-goods, &c.' as, in a robbery,
distinguished from ' plate, jewellery, or more portable articles '—† by 1900 ; Dickens, 1838, ' " It's
all arranged about bringing off the swag, is it ? "
asked the Jew. Sikes nodded ' ; ' Pomes ' Marshall ; Edgar Wallace, *passim*. Perhaps ex dial.
swag, a large quantity ; prob. ex the *swag* or bag in
which the booty is carried.—4. Imm. ex *swag-shop*,
or the origin of *swag-shop* and therefore ex *swag*, 1 :
trade in small, trivial, or inferior articles : from ca.

1850. Mostly in combination (see, e.g., swag-shop) ;
when by itself, it is gen. attributive, as in Mayhew,
1851, ' The " penny apiece " or " swag " trade ',
O.E.D.—5. A tramp's (hence, miners' and others',
bundle of personal effects : 1852, Samuel Sidney,
The Three Colonies of Australia, ' His leathern overalls, his fancy stick, and his swag done up in a
mackintosh ' ; 1861, McCombie, *Australian Sketches* ;
1902, *The Pall Mall Gazette*, July 2, ' The unmarried
shearer, roaming, swag on back, from station to
station '. Coll. >, ca. 1880, S.E. Ex sense 3, which
Cunningham notes as established in Australia before
1827. See esp. Morris. Whence :

swag, v.i. Gen. as *swag it*, q.v.—2. V.t., to rob,
plunder : c. (– 1887). Baumann. Ex n., 3.

swag-barrow. A coster's cart, esp. one carrying
small or trashy articles (see swag, 4) : low s. : from
ca. 1850. Also, *swag-barrowman*, a coster, or
another, carrying on such trade. Both in Mayhew,
1851 ; ob.

*swag-chovey bloke. A marine store dealer : c.
(– 1839) >, ca. 1870, low s. : late C. 19–20 ; ob.
Brandon. See swag, 4 ; *chovey* is a shop.

*swag in. To cause to enter secretly : c.
(– 1923). Manchon.

swag it. To carry one's ' swag ' (5) : 1861,
McCombie : coll. >, ca. 1890, S.E. Morris.

swag-man ; swagman. A man in the ' swag-
trade ' or keeping a ' swag-shop ' : from ca. 1850.
Mayhew, 1851. Gen. *swag-man*.—2. A man travelling with a swag (5) : Australian : 1883, Keighley :
coll. >, ca. 1890, S.E. Gen. *swagman*. Also
swagsman, q.v.

*swag of, a. ' Emphatically a great deal ',
Vaux : c. of ca. 1800–50. Ex *swag*, n., 3.

swag-shop. A shop specialising in trivial or
trashy articles, very cheap : mid-C. 19–20 : lower-
class London. Mayhew, 1851. See swag, 1 and 4.
Cf. :

swag-trade. The trade in *swag*, 4, q.v. : mid-
C. 19–20. Mayhew.

swagger. A swagger-cane or -stick : military
coll. (– 1887). Baumann. I.e. a stick carried for
swagger or show.—2. In Australia, hence in New
Zealand, one who carries a ' swag ' (5) : 1855, *The
Melbourne Argus*, Jan. 19 (O.E.D.) : coll. >, ca.
1880, S.E. Cf. *swag-man*, 2, and *swagsman*.
(Morris.)

swagger, adj. Smart, fashionable ; ' swell ' ;
rather showy or ostentatious : (orig. Society) s. >,
ca. 1930, coll. : 1879, *The Cambridge Review*
(O.E.D.) ; 1897, ' Ouida ', ' Lord, ma'am, they'll
. . . take the matches away from their bedrooms,
but, then, you see, ma'am, them as are swagger can
do them things.' Ex S.E. *swagger*, superior and/or
insolent behaviour. (The v. is likewise S.E. Note,
however, that from ca. 1920 the n. has had a coll.
tinge.)

swagger-cane or -stick. An officer's cane or
stick for parade-ground appearance ; a private's or
non-com.'s walking-out stick or short cane : military coll. : resp. 1889, 1887 (O.E.D.). Ex *swagger*,
adj., q.v. ; cf., however, *swagger*, n., 1.

swagger-dress. Walking-out dress : military
coll. : C. 20. On *swagger-cane*.

swagger-pole. A variant, from ca. 1920, of
swagger-cane. Suggested by : *swagger-stick*. See
swagger-cane.

swaggery. A non-aristocratic variant (– 1887 ;
slightly ob.) of *swagger*, adj. Baumann.

swaggie, swaggy. A man carrying a ' swag ' (5) as

a habit : Australian (gen. humorous) coll. : 1892, E. W. Hornung (Morris) ; 1902, Henry Lawson (O.E.D.). Ex *swag-man*, 2, q.v.

swagman. See **swag-man.**

swagsman. The same as *swaggie*, q.v. : 1879, J. Brunton Stephens : coll. >, ca. 1890, S.E. Ex *swag-man*, 2, q.v.—2. In c. (— 1859), an accomplice who, after a burglary, carries the plunder. H., 1st ed. ; Barrère & Leland. Ex *swag*, n., 3, q.v. Also, a ' fence ' : c. (— 1904). F. & H.—3. An occ. variant of *swag-man*, 1, q.v. F. & H.

swain. A theatrical term of contempt : 1912, A. Neil Lyons, *Clara*, ' They're a silly set o' swain, the General Public ' (Manchon) ; ob. Ex the sense of yokel. Or ex affected pron. of *swine*.

swak. A superscription of *S.W.A.K.*, ' sealed with a kiss ', often found on sailors' and soldiers' letters to sweethearts ; occ. *S.W.A.N.K.* (. . . *nice kiss*) : military and naval : C. 20. F. & Gibbons.

swaller. An illiterate form of, i.e. a sol. for, *swallow*.

swallow. Capacity (for food) : late C. 16–20 : S.E. until ca. 1850, then coll.—2. Esp. as a mouthful : from ca. 1820 : S.E. until ca. 1890, then coll. These two senses are sometimes indistinguishable, as in the c.p., ' What a swallow ! ', which may refer to one act of swallowing or to appetite. Ex *swallow*, the throat or gullet.

swallow, v. To prepare (a part) hastily : theatrical : 1898 (O.E.D.). Ex *swallow the cackle*.

swallow, have a spiral. To have a taste for liquor : from ca. 1920. Manchon.

swallow a gudgeon. To be gulled : coll. : 1579, Lyly ; Dekker & Webster, 1607 ; Fuller, 1732 ; Halliwell. † by 1900. Ex fig. *gudgeon*. Apperson.

swallow a sailor. ' To get drunk upon rum ' : ports' and harbours' (— 1909). Ware.

swallow a spider. See **spider,** 3, and **spider, swallow a.**

swallow a stake. See **swallowed a stake ;** the earlier *to have eaten a stake* is recorded by Palsgrave in 1530 but, app., was † by 1700.

swallow a tavern-token. To get drunk : coll. : late C. 16–18. Jonson, *Every Man in His Humour*, ' Drunk, sir ! you hear not me say so : perhaps he swallowed a tavern token or some such device.' Cf. *tavern-fox*.

swallow my knife ?—you say true, will you. I doubt it ! : a c.p. applied esp. to an impossible story : from ca. 1890 (ob.) : not aristocratic.

swallow-tail. A dress-coat : coll. : 1835, Frith, ' I should look a regular guy in a swallow-tail,' O.E.D. Ex *swallow-tailed coat*.

swallow the anchor. See **anchor, swallow the.**

swallow the cackle. To learn a part : theatrical (— 1890). Barrère & Leland.

swallowed a stake and cannot stoop, he (she) has. A c.p. applied to a very stiff, upright person : from ca. 1660 ; ob. L'Estrange, 1667 ; Fuller, 1732. Apperson. Cf. at *swallow a stake*, q.v.

swan-slinger. A Shakespearian actor : theatrical (— 1904) ; ob. Ex the phrase, *to sling the Swan of Avon* (late C. 19–20 ; ob.). Cf. *spout Billy*, q.v.

swank. Showy or conceited behaviour or speech ; pretence : dial. (— 1854) >, ca. 1904, s. *The Daily Chronicle*, April 17, 1905, ' What he said is quite true, barring the whisky—that is all swank,' O.E.D. ; Ware, 1909, records analogous senses, ' small talk, lying ' as printers' s. Dates make it appear that the n. derives ex the v., but, dial.

records being notoriously incomplete, the reverse may be true : in either case, *swank*, as Baumann suggests, derives prob. ex Ger. *Schwang* as in *in S. sein* (or *gehen*), to be in the fashion.—2. See **swak.**—3. (Ex sense 1.) The tricks one plays ; one's ' game ' : Cockneys' : from ca. 1890. C. Rook, *The Hooligan Nights*, 1899.—4. Hence, flattery, ' blarney ' : id. : id. Ibid., ' I . . . calls 'im a rare toff an' a lot of old swank of that kind.'

swank, v. To behave showily or conceitedly ; to swagger ; to pretend (esp. to be better than, or superior to, what one is) : dial. (— 1809) >, ca. 1870, s., though not gen. till ca. 1901. H., 5th ed., ' *Swank*, to boast or " gas " unduly ' ; A. McNeill, 1903, ' To see . . . your sons swanking about town with Hon. before their names '. For the most viable etymology, see the preceding entry : but one cannot ignore these possibilities :—Perhaps ex *swing* (the body) via either Scottish *swank*, agile (O.E.D.) or *swagger* (E.D.D.) ; or simply a perversion of *swagger* (W.).—2. To work hard : Public and military school s. (— 1890). Barrère & Leland. Perhaps ex *swat* + *swank*.

swank, adj. ' Swanky ' (q.v.) : from ca. 1917 ; ob. Ex *swank*, n., or *swank(e)y*.

swank-pot. A variant (— 1923), noted by Manchon, of :

swanker. One who behaves as in *swank*, v., 1 and 2 : same period and status. Cf. *swanking*, the vbl.n. of *swank*, v., q.v.

*swank(e)y. Inferior beer : c. (— 1859.) H., 1st ed. ; Baumann. Prob. ex Ger. *schwank*, feeble.

swank(e)y, adj. Showy ; conceited ; pretentious ; pretentiously grand : dial. >, ca. 1910, s. The O.E.D.'s earliest record is of 1912. Ex *swank*, v., 1.

swankiness. The rather rare abstract n. ex *swanky* : from ca. 1914.

swanking, n. See **swanker.** — 2. Adj. ' Swank(e)y ' : rare and only of persons : C. 20 ; ob.

swannery, keep a. To make out that all one's geese are swans : coll. (— 1785) ; ob. by 1890, † by 1930. Grose, 1st ed.

Swans, the. The **Swans**ea Town Football Club : sporting : C. 20.

swap, swop. An exchanging ; an exchange : coll. >, ca. 1850, s. : resp. ca. 1625 (Purchas) and 1682 (Flatman). O.E.D. Ex *swap*, an act of striking (esp. the hands as a sign of a bargain made) ; or more imm. ex the v. Cf. *swap*, *get the*.—2. Esp. in *get a swap (swop)*, to fail to effect a sale : drapery and kindred trades' (— 1935).—3. Also, in the same trades, a synonym of *tab*, n., 6.

swap, swop, v.t. To exchange (*for* something else, or a thing *with* somebody else) : coll. >, ca. 1850, s. : resp. 1594, Lyly, ' Ile not swap my father for all this', and 1624, Quarles, ' . . . That for his belly swopt his heritage ', O.E.D. A ' low word ', says Johnson ; ' Irish cant ', says Egan (1823). Orig. a horse-dealer's term ex *swap* (strike) *a bargain*.—2. See **swap away** or **off.**—3. V.i., to make an exchange : coll. >, ca. 1850, s. : 1778, Miss Burney ; 1885, Jerome K. Jerome, ' I am quite ready to swop,' O.E.D. Ex sense 1.—4. V.t., to dismiss from employment : 1862, *Macmillan's Magazine*. O.E.D. Cf. *swap*, *get the*.—5. V.i., to change one's clothes : 1904, D. Sladen. O.E.D. Ex sense 1.

swap or **swop, have** or **get the.** To be dismissed from employment : from before 1890. Barrère & Leland. Ex *swap*, v., 4, q.v.

swap away or **off.** V.t., to exchange : coll. >,

ca. 1850, s. : resp. 1589, R. Harvey, 'He swapt away his silver for Copper retaile,' and from ca. 1860 ; the latter, orig. and mainly U.S. O.E.D. Ex *swap*, v., 1.—2. *swap* (or *swop*) *off* only. V.t., to cheat : orig. (1830, J. C. Harris) and mainly U.S. ; partly anglicised ca. 1910.

swapper, swopper. One who exchanges : late C. 17–20 : coll. >, ca. 1850, s. Ex *swap*, v., 1.— 2. Gen. *swapper*. Anything very big, a 'whopper' (esp. of a lie) : s. and dial. : from ca. 1700. Ex *swap*, to strike.

swapping. An exchanging, an exchange ; barter : coll. >, ca. 1850, s. : 1695, J. Edwards (O.E.D.). Ex *swap*, v., 1, q.v. Cf. *swapper*, 1, and *swap*, n.

swapping, swopping, adj. Very big : coll. >, ca. 1850, s. : mid-C. 15–20. Middleton, 1624, 'Swapping sins '. Ex *swap*, to strike ; cf. *swapper*, 2, and *whopping*.

swarbout is an occ. C. 16 variant of *sworbote*, q.v. [**swarmy** in Lyell is an error for *smarmy*.]

swarry ; occ. **swarree, swarrey.** A *soirée* or social evening : coll., in C. 20 considered somewhat sol. : 1837, Dickens, 'A friendly swarry '; 1848, Thackeray (*swarrey* : O.E.D.).—2. H., 5th ed., ' A boiled leg of mutton and trimmings ' : is this a mistake founded on the Dickens passage (and repeated by F. & H.), or, as H. says, a resultant therefrom ?

swash-bucket. A slattern : proletarian coll. : from ca. 1870 ; ob. Ex *swash-bucket*, a receptacle for scullery refuse (ex *swash*, pig-wash). In dial. as early as 1746 for ' a farm-house slattern ' (E.D.D.).

swat. A (smart or heavy) blow : dial. (— 1800) >, ca. 1840, s. or coll., but never very gen. Halliwell. ' Babe ' Ruth, the baseball player, has, since ca. 1920, been known in the U.S. as *the Sultan of Swat*. Ex next entry.—2, 3, 4. See **swot.**

swat, v. To strike smartly : dial. (— 1796) >, before 1848 (Bartlett), U.S. ; reimported into England before 1904 (witness F. & H.) as a coll. Esp. in *swat that fly* (1911, W.).—2. See **swot.**

swatchel. Punch, in Punch and Judy : showmen's (esp. and orig. P. & J. showmen) : mid-C. 19–20. Perhaps cognate with *swatch*, a sample or specimen, ex *swatch*, a sample piece of cloth ; possibly, as the O.E.D. (Sup.) suggests, ex *schwätzeln*, the frequentative of *schwatzen*, to tattle. Hence *swatchel* (occ. *schwassle*)-*box*, the Punch and Judy show or, more correctly, the booth ; and *swatchel-cove*, a Punch and Judy man, or, esp., the patterer. Other terms, all from ca. 1850 and to be consulted separately, are :—**buffer,** the dog *Toby* (recorded in 1840), and **buffer-figure,** the dog's master ; **crocodile,** the demon ; **darkey** or **D.,** the Negro ; **filio,** the baby ; **(the) frame,** the street arrangement or ' pitch ', etc. ; **(the) letter cloth,** the advertisement ; **Mozzy,** Judy ; **nobbing-slum,** the bag for collected money ; **peepsies,** the pan-pipes ; **(the) slum,** the call ; **(the) slum-fake,** the coffin ; **the stalk** (occ. **prop),** the gallows ; **tambour,** the drum ; **vampire,** the ghost ; **vampo** or **V.,** the clown :—F. & H. Despite its Italian origin, Punch and Judy vocabulary contains far more c. and/or low s. than Italian words.

sway (away on) all top-ropes. See **top-ropes.**

swaying the main with an old mess-mate(, I've been). The bluejackets' c.p. explanation of a bibulous evening ashore : from ca. 1860. Bowen.

swear. A formal oath : mid-C. 16–20 : S.E. until ca. 1870, then coll. Eden Phillpotts, 1899, ' We swore by a tremendous swear,' O.E.D. ; ob.— 2. Hence a profane oath ,a ' swear-word '; a fit of swearing : coll. : 1871, C. Gibbon, ' A good swear is a cure for the bile,' O.E.D.—3. A harsh noise made esp. by a cat, occ. by a bird : coll. : 1895 (O.E.D.). Ex :

swear, v.i. (Of a canine or feline or, occ., a bird) to make a harsh and/or guttural sound : from late C. 17 : S.E. until C. 19, then coll. The O.E.D. gives, at 1902, an example of a locomotive ' swearing '.

swear at. (Mostly of colours) to clash with : coll. : 1884, *The Daily News*, Nov. 10, ' Two tints that swear at each other ', O.E.D. Ex Fr. *jurer*.

swear by. To accept as authoritative, have (very) great confidence in : coll. : 1815, Jane Austen ; 1890, G. A. Henty, ' His fellows swear by him.' Ex *swear by*, to appeal to (a god). O.E.D.

swear by, enough to. A very small amount or slight degree : mid-C. 18–20 : coll. >, in mid-C. 19, s. On (*just*) *enough to mention.*

swear like a cutter (C. 17–20 ; ob.), or **a lord** (C. 16–17), or **a tinker** (C. 17–20 ; ob.), or **a trooper** (1727). To swear profusely : coll. soon > S.E. Apperson.

swear off. To renounce : lower classes' s. (— 1887) >, ca. 1900, gen. s. >, ca. 1920, coll. Baumann. ? *swear oneself off.*

swear through an inch or **a two-inch board ; . . . a nine-inch plank ;** and see quotation in sense 2. To back up any lie : coll. : resp. 1678, Ray ; 1728, Earl of Ailesbury (O.E.D.) ; from ca. 1800, app. Nelson's variation of the other forms, according to Clark Russell in 1883. Dickens, in 1865, has ' That severe exertion which is known in legal circles as swearing your way through a stone wall,' O.E.D. Cf. the Cheshire semi-proverbial ' Oo'd swear the cross off a jackass's back,' *oo* being ' she '.—2. These phrases are also indicative of vigorous bad language, as in R. Franck, 1658, ' It's thought they would have sworn through a double deal-board, they seem'd so enrag'd,' Apperson.

swear-word. A profane oath or other word : coll. ; orig. U.S., anglicised ca. 1880. Cf. the U.S. *cuss-word*.

[Swearing. See ' Cursing '.]

swearing-apartment. The street : taverns' (— 1909). Ware. Prob. ex the barmaids' exclamatory question, ' If you want to swear, why don't you go out into the street ? '

Swears. Ernest Wells, founder and member of the Pelican Club : nickname : from middle 1890's ; almost †. Ex his literary pseudonym. Ware.

sweat. Hard work ; a difficult task ; something requiring painstaking trouble : C. 14–20 : S.E. until C. 20, then s., esp. in *an awful sweat*. (O.E.D. Sup.)—2. A long run taken in training : Public Schools' : late C. 19–20. (E. F. Benson, *David Blaize*, 1916.)

sweat. To lighten (a—gen. gold—coin) by friction or acid : coll. (— 1785) >, ca. 1850, S.E. Grose, 1st ed. Ex *sweat*, to cause to perspire.—2. To deprive of : from ca. 1784, as in Anon., *Ireland Sixty Years Ago*, 1847, ' [In] 1784 . . . " sweating " him, i.e. making him give up all his fire-arms.' Cf. S.E. *sweating*, a ruffianly practice of the Mohocks (q.v.).—3. Esp. to ' fleece ', to ' bleed ' : from ca. 1840 low s. H., 2nd ed. ; Smyth, 1867 (see *sweat the purser*).—4. V.i. and v.t., to squander (riches) : from late 1850's. H., 2nd ed. Ex *sweat*, to give off, get rid of, as by sweating.—5. Hence, v.t., to spend (money) : from ca. 1860.—6. Hence, to remove some of the contents of : 1867, in Conington's

Horace, ' He'd find a bottle sweated and not rave,' O.E.D.—7. To unsolder (a tin box, etc.) by applying fire or a blow-pipe: c. (— 1909). Ware. Cf. senses 1, 6.—8. Perhaps ex sense 1 : v.t., to pawn: low s. (orig., prob. Anglo-Irish): from ca. 1800 ; † by ca. 1880.—9. To force (a person) to do something: Winchester : mid-C. 19–20. Wrench.—10. Hence, v.i., to be engaged in compulsory work: ibid. : late C. 19–20. Wrench. Cf. the n., 1.

sweat, all of a. (Of a street, pavement, etc.) like a bog ; slushy : coll., esp. London (— 1887). Baumann.

sweat, be in a. To be at pains (*to* do something): lower-class coll. (— 1923). Manchon.

sweat, old. See **old sweat.** (' A very old expression ', F. & Gibbons.)

sweat-box. A cell for prisoners waiting to go before the magistrate : low s. : from ca. 1875, though unrecorded before 1888 (Churchward's *Blackbirding* : O.E.D.). In C. 20 U.S., *sweat-box* is the application of third-degree methods.

sweat-gallery. (Coll. for) fagging juniors : Winchester : from ca. 1865 ; ob. Ex *sweater*, 2.

sweat on the top line ; be sweating . . ., the more gen. form. ' To be in eager anticipation ' or ' on the eve of obtaining something much wanted ' : military : C. 20. F. & Gibbons. Ex the game of House : a player with four or five numbers on the top line anxiously awaits the call of one more number to win.

sweat one's guts out. To work extremely hard : (mostly lower-class) coll. : late C. 19–20. Lyell.

sweat-rag. A pocket-handkerchief : Australia : C. 20. Lawson, 1902 (O.E.D.).

sweat the purser. To waste Government stores : naval : late C. 19–20. Bowen.

sweater. An occupation or act causing one to sweat : coll. : 1851, Mayhew, ' The business is a sweater, sir,' O.E.D.—2. A servant : Winchester : from ca. 1860. Cf. *sweat-gallery*, q.v.—3. A broker working for very small commissions, thus depriving others of business and himself of adequate profit : Stock Exchange coll. : from ca. 1870.

sweating. See **bending,** 2 ; also **sweat on . . .**

Sweatipore. India : Army officers' : from ca. 1920. A pun on *paw* (hand) and *pores* of the hand, and also on such names of military stations as *Barrackpore*. Cf. *the Shiny* (at *shiny*, 2).

swede. See **set the swede down.**

sweep. A sweepstake : coll. (1849) >, ca. 1905, S.E. Kipling. (O.E.D.)—2. A scamp, a disreputable : from ca. 1850. F. & H., ' You dirty sweep '. Ex (*chimney-*)*sweep*.—3. (Also **bogey.**) Mucus (esp. hardened mucus) that can easily be extracted from the nostrils : domestic and nurses', chiefly Scottish : late C. 19–20. Cf. :

sweep, v. To chimney-sweep for : low coll. : 1848, Thackeray, ' The chimney-purifier, who had swep' the last three families ', O.E.D. Cf. *-p*'.

sweeper. A train that, following a through train, calls at all stations : Australian coll. (— 1908) >, ca. 1915, S.E. Because it ' sweeps up ' all passengers.—2. A sweepstake : Harrow and Oxford : late C. 19–20. Arnold Lunn, *The Harrovians*, 1913. By ' the Oxford *-er*'.

*sweeping the snow. See **snow, sweeping the.**

Sweeps, the. The Rifle Brigade : military (— 1879) and prob. as early, at least, as 1850, for the black facings date from the Brigade's inception in 1800 and *sweep* = chimney-sweep dates from 1812. (F. & H. ; **O.E.D.**)

sweeps and saints. Stockbrokers and their clientèle : City of London : mid-C. 19–20 ; ob. Ware, ' From the First of May (Sweeps' Day) and the First of November (All Saints' Day) being holidays on the Exchange '.

sweep's frill. ' Beard and whiskers worn round the chin, the rest of the face being clean shaven ', F. & H. : 1892, *Tit Bits*, March 19. Cf. :

sweep's-trot. A loping amble : coll. : 1842, Lover (O.E.D.) ; ob.

*sweet. Gullible ; unsuspicious : c. (— 1725) >, in late C. 19, low s. *A New Canting Dict.*, 1725.— 2. Clever, expert, dexterous : c. (— 1725). Ibid. Cf. *sweet as your hand.*—3. In the speaker's opinion, attractive, very pleasant : coll. : 1779. Fanny Burney, 1782, ' The sweetest caps ! the most beautiful trimmings ', O.E.D. Cf. *nice*, q.v., and Fr. *mignon.*

sweet as a nut, adj. and adv. Advantageous(ly) ; with agreeable or consummate ease : coll. : late C. 19–20.

*sweet as (or 's) your hand. ' Said of one dexterous at stealing ', Grose, 1st ed. : c. (ob.) of C. 18–20. *A New Canting Dict.*, 1725.

sweet craft. See **craft,** 2.—**sweet damn all.** A mild synonym (Lyell) of :

sweet Fanny (rare) or **sweet Fanny Adams** or **sweet F.A.** See **F.A.** and **Fanny Adams.**

(Sweet) Lambs, the. The 1st Madras European Regiment, now the Royal Dublin Fusiliers : mid-C. 18–mid-19 ; during the Indian Mutiny, *Blue Caps* took its place. Perhaps ex *Kirke's Lambs.* q.v. F. & Gibbons. (—2. For *the Lambs*, see **Lambs, the.**)

sweet-lips. A glutton ; a gourmet : (low) coll. : from ca. 1870 ; ob.

sweet on, be. ' To coakse, wheedle, entice or allure', B.E. : late C. 17–18. The O.E.D. considers it S.E. ; B.E. classifies it as c. ; prob. coll., as, I think, is the mid-C. 18–20 sense, to be very fond of, enamoured with (one of the opposite sex).

sweet-pea, do or **plant a.** (Of, and among, women) to urinate, esp. in the open air : mid-C. 19–20. Prob. suggested by *pluck a rose.*

sweetbread. A bribe ; a timely reward of money : coll. : ca. 1670–90. Hacket, 1670, ' A few sweetbreads that I gave him out of my purse '.

*sweeten. A beggar, says F. & H. : is this so ? If correct, c. : presumably C. 18.

*sweeten. To decoy, draw in ; swindle : c. : late C. 17–early 19. B.E., Grose.—2. V.i., see **sweetening,** 1.—3. V.t., to allay the suspicions of (a victim) : C. 18 : c. or low s. E.D.D.—4. To bribe ; give alms to : late C. 18–20 : c. >, ca. 1850, dial. and low s. Haggart, former nuance ; Egan's Grose, latter. Prob. ex sense 1.—5. To contribute to (the pool), increase the stakes in (the pot, at poker) : cards : from 1896. Cf. *sweetening.*—6. V.i., to bid at an auction merely to run up the price : orig. and mainly auctioneers' (— 1864). H., 3rd ed. Cf. *sweetener.*—7. V.t., to increase (the collateral of a loan) by furnishing additional securities : financial (— 1919). O.E.D.

sweeten and pinch. Occ. v., gen. n., ca. 1670–1720, as in Anon., *Four for a Penny*, 1678 : to get money, by politeness and considerateness, from a man about to be arrested. Bum-bailiffs' s.

*sweetener. A decoy ; a cheat or a swindler : c. : late C. 17–early 19. B.E. ; Grose, 1st ed. Ex *sweeten*, v., 1.—2. A guinea-dropper : c. : same period. B.E., Grose. Ex *sweetening*, 1.—3. One who, at an auction, bids only to run up the price : auctioneers' (— 1864). H., 3rd ed.—4. A temporary officer (gen. first mate) replacing his predecessor, who is in hiding : nautical, with esp. reference to the Atlantic clipper packets : ca. 1850–1910. Bowen.—5. See :

*sweeteners. The lips : c. or low s. : from ca. 1860. Esp. *fake the s.*, to kiss.

*sweetening. Guinea-dropping, i.e. the dropping of a coin and consequent swindling of a gullible finder : c. : from ca. 1670 ; † by 1870. *The Country Gentleman's Vade Mecum*, 1699.—2. The vbl.n.—both the action and the concrete result—of *sweeten*, v., 5.—3. That of *sweeten*, b., 6.—4. That of *sweeten*, v., 4.

sweetheart. A tame rabbit : (sporting and dealers') coll. : from late 1830's. Blaine's *Encyclopædia of Rural Sports*, 1840 (O.E.D.). Ex winning ways of such rabbits.

sweetheart and bag-pudding. A c.p. applied to a girl got with child : C. 17–early 18. Day, *Humour out of Breath*, 1608 ; Ray, 1670.

sweetie. A sweetmeat : dial. (— 1758), and coll. (from ca. 1820) >, ca. 1890, S.E. W. Havergal, 1824, ' Baby . . . was satisfied with a bit of sweetie ' ; Thackeray, in 1860, has ' Bonbons or sweeties ' ; the pl. is much the more gen. (O.E.D.) —2. A sweetheart : coll. : from ca. 1920 ; much earlier in U.S. Ultimately ex dial.

sweetmeat ; occ. sweet-meat. The male member ; a mere girl who is a kept mistress. Both senses are low and date from mid-C. 19.

*sweetner. See sweetener, 1, 2, of which it is a frequent variant.

swell. A fashionably or smartly dressed person (*a heavy* being an ' ultra' *swell* : 1819, O.E.D.) ; hence, though rare before ca. 1820, a (very) distinguished person, a lady or gentleman of the upper classes : s. (— 1811) >, in late C. 19, coll. *Lex. Bal.*, 1811 ; Bee, 1823, of nob and swell, ' The latter makes a show of his finery ; . . . the nob, relying upon intrinsic worth, or bonâ-fide property, or intellectual ability, is clad in plainness.' Byron ; Thackeray. Usually of men, and prob. ex *swell, cut a*, q.v.—2. Hence, one who has done something notable or who is expert *at* something : s. >, in late C. 19, coll. : 1816, Moore (O.E.D.), but not gen. before ca. 1840 ; Barham, ' No ! no !—The Abbey [Westminster] may do very well | For a feudal nob, or poetical " swell " ' ; the Eton usage.—3. See swells.

swell, adj. Stylishly dressed : from ca. 1812. E.g. in Egan's Grose. Prob. ex n., 1.—2. Hence, from ca. 1820, gentlemanly (Byron, 1823) or ladylike ; of good social position (Disraeli, 1845).—3. (Of things) stylish, very distinguished : from ca. 1811. Vaux.—4. Hence, excellent, whether of things (e.g. *a swell time*) or of persons considered as to their ability (e.g. *a swell cricketer*) : not before mid-C. 19 and—except in U.S.A.—slightly ob. All four senses were orig. s. (1–3, indeed, were low s. for a decade or more) ; they > coll. only in late C. 19.

swell, v. To take a bath : Winchester : from ca. 1860 ; ob. Ex *swill.*—2. See swell it.

swell, cut a ; do the swell. To swagger : resp. ca. 1800–40, as in *The Spirit of the Public Journals* 1800, ' Our young lords and . . . gentlemen " cutting a swell " as the fashionable phrase is ', O.E.D.; and mid-C. 19–20 (ob.), as in Baumann. (Cf. *swell*, n., 1.) Ex *swell*, arrogant behaviour.

swell (or itch) ?, does your nose. (Gen. completed

by *at this* or *at that*.) Are you angry or annoyed ? : coll. : C. 19.

swell, rank. ' A very " flashly " dressed person . . . who . . . apes a higher position than he actually occupies ', H., 1st ed. ; ob. by 1900, † by 1920. Ex *swell*, n., 1, first nuance.

swell about. See swell it.

swell fencer. A street vendor of needles : low London (— 1859) ; † by 1920. H., 1st ed.

swell-head. Conceit : coll. : C. 20. Prob. ex *swelled head*, q.v.—2. Hence, a conceited person : coll. : C. 20.—3. As = an important person, it is U.S.—4. A drunken man : low : late C. 19–early 20.

swell-headed. Conceited ; puffed with pride : coll. : 1817, Cobbett, ' The upstart, . . . swell-headed farmer can bluster . . . about Sinecures,' O.E.D.

swell hung in chains, a. A much-bejewelled person : low : mid-C. 19–20 ; ob. H., 2nd ed.

swell it. To play or ape the fine gentleman : low (— 1887) ; ob. Baumann. Ex *swell*, n., 1. In C. 20, also *swell about* (Manchon).

*swell mob. That class of pickpockets who, to escape detection, dress and behave like respectable people : 1836, Marryat (O.E.D.) ; c. >, by 1870, low s. Ex *swell*, adj., 1 and 2.—2. In C. 20 c., ' the " kite " men, the confidence artists, and . . . fashionably dressed young men who lie in wait for gullible strangers ', Edgar Wallace in *The Double*, 1928.

*swell-mobsman. One of the ' swell mob ' : c. (— 1851) >, by 1870, low s. Mayhew ; Hotten, 3rd ed., ' Swell mobsmen, who pretend to be Dissenting preachers, and harangue in the open air for their confederates to rob '.—2. See preceding entry, sense 2.

swell-nose. Strong ale : early C. 16. Anon., *De Generibus Ebriosorum*, 1515.

Swell Street, be (— 1812) or live (— 1904) in. To be a well-off family man of good social standing : low : from ca. 1810 ; ob. Vaux. By 1864—see H., 3rd ed.—*Swell Street* had > the West End (London).

swelldom. The world of ' swells ' (n., all senses) : coll : 1855, Thackeray ; ob.

swelled head. Excessive conceit, pride, or vanity : coll. : 1891, Kipling (O.E.D.).—2. Perhaps only one of Grose's jokes, and at most a piece of military punning s. of late C. 18–early 19 : ' A disorder to which horses are extremely liable . . . Generally occasioned by remaining too long in one livery-stable or inn, and often rises to that height that it prevents their coming out of the stable door. The most certain cure is the *unguentum aureum* . . . applied to the palm of the master of the inn or stable,' 2nd ed. Cf. *oat-stealer*, q.v.

swelled-headedness. ' Swelled head ', sense 1, q.v. : coll. : 1907, E. Reich, ' The Germans are afflicted with the severest attack of swelled-headedness known to modern history,' O.E.D.

swelled nose. See swell ?, does your nose.

swellish. Dandified : 1820 (O.E.D.) : s. >, in late C. 19, coll. Ex *swell*, n., 1, q.v.—2. Gentlemanly ; distinguished : from ca. 1830 : idem.

swellishness. The n. of *swellish*, in sense 2, q.v. : coll. : late C. 19–20.

swellism. The style (esp. in dress) or the social habits of a ' swell ', in sense 1, rarely in other than the first nuance, q.v. : 1840 (O.E.D.) : s. >, by ca. 1870, coll. ; ob. Cf. :

swellness. The being a ' swell ', esp. in sense 2

and never in the first nuance of sense 1 : coll. : 1894, T. H. Huxley, 'My swellness is an awful burden,' O.E.D. ; ob. Cf. *swellishness* and *swellism*, qq.v.

swells. Occasions—e.g. Sunday church-services —on which surplices are worn : Winchester : from ca. 1860. Ex *swell*, adj., 3, q.v.

swelp, s'welp. (God) so help : as in Whiteing, 1899, 'Swelp me lucky, I ain't tellin' yer no lie ! ' Also *swelp me !* (— 1887) ; *swelp me* or *my bob !* (— 1904) ; *swelp me davy* (— 1887) ; *swelp my greens* or *taters !* (id.), with which cf. the (— 1895) dial. *bless my taters !* (E.D.D.) and the earlier (1864, H., 3rd ed.) *s'elp my tater !* See also **s'elp !, s'elp me bob !, s'elp my greens !** (1864, H., 3rd ed.) ; likewise *s'help !* Ex *so help* (*me, God !*)

swelter. Hot, hard work : lower classes' (— 1887). Baumann. Cf. :

swelter, do a. To perspire profusely : 1884. Ex S.E. *swelter*, a state of perspiration. O.E.D.

Swensker. A Swede : nautical coll. : mid-C. 19–20. Bowen, 'A corruption of Svenske '.

***swi.** Two-up, the gambling game : New Zealand c. (— 1932). Perhaps *swi* = *twi*(*ce*).

swift. A fast-working compositor : printers' (— 1841). Savage's *Dict. of Printing.*

swift, adj. Apt to take (sexual) liberties with, or to accept them from, the opposite sex : coll. : late C. 19–20. Suggested by *fast*. Cf. *speedy*.

swig ; in C. 16, also **swyg.** Liquor : coll. : mid-C. 16–20 ; very ob.—has been so since early C. 19. Udall, 1548 (O.E.D.). `Etymology unknown : W. proposes Scandinavian *svik*, a tap.—2. Hence, a ' pull ' ; a (copious) draught : coll. >, in late C. 18, s. : from ca. 1620. Middleton & Rowley, ' But one swig more, sweet madam ' ; Ned Ward ; Marryat ; Whiteing. Also, in C. 17, *swigge*.—3. At Oxford University (orig. and esp. Jesus College), toast and (spiced) ale, or the bowl in which it is served : from ca. 1825. Hence, *Swig Day*, the day (? St David's) it is ritualistically served.

swig ; in C. 18, occ. **swigg.** V.i. To drink deeply, eagerly, or much (esp., strong liquor) : mid-C. 17–20 : coll. >, in early C. 19, s. Ex n., 1.— 2. V.t., with either the liquor or its container as object : coll. >, in early C. 19, s. : resp. 1780, ' Slang Pastoral ' Tomlinson, ' To swig porter all day ', O.E.D., and 1682, in *Wit and Drollery*, ' I . . . swigg'd my horn'd barrel,' this latter nuance being ob.

swig, play at. To indulge in drink : coll. : late C. 17–18. Ex *swig*, n., 2.

Swig Day. See **swig**, n., 3.

swigged. Tipsy : mid-C. 19–20 : rather proletarian.

swigging, vbl.n. (1723) and ppl.adj. (1702). See **swig**, v., 1. (O.E.D.)

***swigman ;** in C. 16, also **swygman.** ' One of the 13th Rank of the Canting Crew, carrying small Haberdashery-Wares about, pretending to sell them to colour their Roguery ', B.E. ; Awdelay, 1561, says that he ' goeth with a Peddlers pack '. C. of ca. 1560–1800. Prob. ex *swagman*, despite the fact that *swag*, a bulgy bag, is recorded only in early C. 14.

swiling, n. Sealing : Newfoundland nautical coll. : late C. 19–20. Bowen. By corruption.

swill. A bath : Shrewsbury School coll. : mid-C. 19–20. Desmond Coke, *The Bending of a Twig*, 1906.

'Swill. A coll. euphemism for (*by*) *God's will* : C. 17. Marston. O.E.D.

swill, v.i. ' To wash at a conduit by throwing water over the body ' : Winchester College coll. : C. 19–20. Wrench. Cf. the Shrewsbury n. and *get swilled*.

swilled, get. To take a bath : Shrewsbury School coll. : mid-C. 19–20. (D. Coke, *The Bending of a Twig*, 1906.)

swim. A swimming, i.e. a dizzy, feeling : dial. and coll. : 1829, Ebenezer Elliott (O.E.D.).—2. A plan or enterprise, esp. a tortuous or a shady one : 1860, Sala (O.E.D.) ; slightly ob.

swim, give one's dog a. To have the excuse of doing something or, esp., a reason for something to do : South African and Australian coll. An English approximation is *take one's dog for a walk*.

swim, how we apples. See **apples.**

swim, in the. Whereas *in the swim with*, in league with, has always, it seems, been S.E., *in the swim*, lucky, very fortunate, is coll. and ob. : in 1869, *Macmillan's Magazine* (the earliest record, by the way) explained that it derives ex *swim*, a section of river much frequented by fish. By 1864, *in a good swim* = in luck, doing a good business (H., 3rd ed.) ; by 1874, *in the swim* = in the inner circle, movement or fashion ; popular : a sense that, from coll., >, ca. 1900, S.E.—2. In c. (— 1860) : a long time out of the hands of the police. H., 2nd ed.

swim, out of the. The opp. to *in the swim*, except that it has no c. sense : 1869. Rare in C. 20.

***swim for it, make (a man).** To cheat (a pal) out of his share of booty : c. : late C. 19–20.

swim in golden grease, lard, oil. To receive many bribes : C. 17 coll. Jonson.

swim like a brick. See **brick, like a.**

***swimmer.** A counterfeit (old) coin : c. : late C. 17–early 19. B.E. ; Grose, 1st ed. Why ?— 2. A guard-ship : c. (— 1811) ; † by 1860. *Lex. Bal.* ; Vaux. Cf. S.E. *swimmer*, an angler's float.— 3. A half-push stroke : cricketers' (— 1909). Lewis.—4. A swimming-suit : coll. : 1929 (O.E.D. Sup.).

***swimmer,** v. To cause (a man) to serve in the Navy instead of sending him to prison : c. (— 1812) ; † by 1860. Vaux. Gen. *be swimmered*. Ex *swimmer*, n., 2.

***swimmer, have a.** A variant of the preceding term : 1811, *Lex. Bal.*

swindge, swindging. See **swinge, swingeing.**

swindle. A lottery ; a speculation, a toss for drinks : 1870, *Legal Reports* ; slightly ob. Ex lit. S.E. sense.—2. Something other than it appears to be, a ' fraud ' : coll. : 1866 (O.E.D.). Cf. sense 1.— 3. Any transaction in which money passes : from ca. 1870, as in *what's the swindle ?*, what's to pay ?, which may coll. have been U.S., in *why don't you pay him his swindle ?*, his price, and in *let's have a swindle !*, let's toss for it ; all three phrases are ob., the third only slightly so.

swindle, v.i. To practise fraud : 1782 ed. of Bailey's *Dict.* : s. >, ca. 1820, S.E. A backformation ex *swindler*, q.v.—2. Hence, v.t., esp. with *out of* : C. 19–20 : s. >, ca. 1820, S.E. Sydney Smith, 1803 (O.E.D.).

***swindler.** A practiser of fraud or imposition for gain ; a cheat : ca. 1762 : c. >, ca. 1790, s. >, ca. 1820, S.E. E.g. in Foote, 1776 ; Grose, 1st ed., but ' dictionaried ' first in the 1782 ed. of Bailey. Ex Ger. *schwindler*, a cheat ; cf. *schwindeln*, to be extravagant or giddy. In England picked up from and applied orig. to German Jews in London ;

much used, too, by soldiers during the Seven Years War. See esp. F. & H., O.E.D., and W.

swindling, n. and adj. ex *swindle*, v., 1, date from late C. 18 ; by 1820, S.E.

swine, go the complete (or **entire**). A London coll. variation (— 1887) of *go the whole hog* ; ob. Baumann.

swine, sing like a bird called a. See **sing like** . . .

swine-up. A quarrel : lower classes' : ca. 1880–1915. Ware, ' Suspected to be of American origin '. Ex pigs' bad temper.

*swing. (Always **the s.**) The gallows : c. or low **s.** : ? late C. 18–mid-19.

swing, v.i. To be hanged : s. >, in C. 18, c. > s. >, in late C. 19, coll. : 1542, Udall, *swing in a halter* ; *swing* by itself, app. not before C. 18 ; Dickens in *Boz*, ' If I'm caught, I shall swing.'—2. Hence, v.t., to put to death by hanging : from ca. 1815 ; ob. and, at all times, rare.—3. See next four entries.— 4. To control (a market, a price, etc.) : commercial coll. : late C. 19–20 ; slightly ob. Cf. *swing it*.

swing Douglas or **Kelly.** To use the axe : Australian coll. (— 1935). Ex two well-known makes of axe.

swing for you if you don't (agree, do it, etc.) **!, I'll.** A c.p. threat : proletarian : ca. 1820–90. H., 3rd ed. See **swing,** v., 1.

swing it. To wangle successfully, get something by trickery ; to shirk or malinger, esp. if successfully : from late 1890's. Prob. ex **swing,** v., 4.

swing it down the line. To get a (good) job away from the front line : military : 1915–18. F. & Gibbons.

swing it on, v.t. To deceive slyly, to impose on, do (one) a bad turn : C. 20 : mostly Australian. Prob. ex *swing*, v., last sense, though imm. ex *swing it*, q.v.—2. To malinger successfully with, as in *swing it on a sore foot* : military : from 1915. B. & P. (at *swinging the lead*).

swing (a matter, business) **over one's head** or **shoulders.** To manage easily ; find well within one's powers : commercial : from ca. 1890. Cf. S.E. *swing*, scope.

swing-tail. A hog : low : ca. 1786–1860. Grose, 2nd ed. Contrast *swish-tail*.

swing the lead. See **lead, swing the.**

swing the monkey. To strike ' with knotted handkerchiefs a man who swings to a rope made fast aloft ', Clark Russell : nautical coll. : from ca. 1880.

swinge ; in C. 16, occ. **swynge** ; in C. 16–18, **swindge.** To copulate with (a woman) : ca. 1620–1750. Fletcher, 1622 ; Dryden, 1668, ' And that baggage, Beatrix, how I would swinge her if I had her here.' Ex *swinge*, to castigate.—2. See all senses of :

swinge off. To toss off (a drink) : ca. 1525–1660. Also *s. up* (Skelton, 1529). ? cf. *punish*, q.v.—2. To infect with (severe) gonorrhœa : late C. 17–18. Gen. passive, *be swinged off*, as in B.E. Perhaps suggested by *clap*, q.v.—3. Occ. as variant of *swirge*, q.v. : late C. 17–early 18. Miège.

swingeing, swinging (pron. *swindjing*) ; in C. 17–19, occ. **swindging.** Very effective, great, large, esp. of a lie : coll. >, by 1700, s. : late C. 16–20, but rare since mid-C. 19. Greene, Motteux, Grose (2nd ed.), Dickens.—2. Hence, adv. : hugely : 1690, Dryden (O.E.D.) ; 1872, C. D. Warner, ' A . . . swingeing cold night '. Cf. S.E. *strapping*, adj. and adv.

swing(e)ingly. Very forcibly ; hugely : coll. > by 1700, s. : 1672, Dryden, ' I have sinned swing-

ingly, against my vow.' Archaic. Ex *swing(e)ing*, q.v.

*swinger (pron. *swindjer*). A rogue, a scoundrel : Scottish c. (? > low s.) of C. 16–mid-18. Dunbar ; A. Nicol, 1739. Prob. ex Flemish. O.E.D.—2. Something very effective or large (of a blow, not before 1830's) : from 1590's, but rare since ca. 1850 : coll. >, by 1700, s. Ex *swinge*, to beat. Cf. *whopper*. —3. Hence, esp. a bold or rank lie : ca. 1670–1820. Eachard, 1670, ' Rap out . . . half a dozen swingers.'—4. A box on the ears : Charterhouse coll. (— 1890). Barrère & Leland.—5. In pl., testicles : low : C. 19–20. (Pron. as in *swing*.)

swinging, adj. See **swingeing.**—**swingingly.** See **swingeingly.**

swinging. A hanging : from late C. 16 : s. >, in late C. 19, coll. Percivall, 1591, ' Swinging in a halter ' : R. L. Stevenson. O.E.D. Ex *swing*, v., 1.

swinging ball game, the. The ' cobbler '—see last sense of **cobbler** : grafters' coll. : C. 20. Philip Allingham, *Cheapjack*, 1934.

*swinging the stick ; or, **the bludgeon business.** A robbery committed with brutal violence and a life-preserver or bludgeon : c. (— 1861). Mayhew.

swink. See ' Winchester College slang ', § 5.

swinny. Drunk : low : late C. 19–20. Ex dial. *swinny*, giddy, dizzy.

swipe ; occ. **swype.** A heavy blow ; in golf and cricket, a stroke made with the full swing of the arms : C. 19–20 : coll. (? orig. dial) >, ca. 1920, familiar S.E. Perhaps ex *sweep* ; perhaps sibilated *wipe*, a blow (H.).—2. Hence, one who does this : coll. : 1825, Westmacott, ' A hard *swipe*, an active field, and a stout bowler ', O.E.D. ; † by 1900.—3. A term of reproach or scornful condemnation : from ca. 1920. O.E.D. (Sup.). : ' Cf. *swipes* [bad beer].'

swipe, v.i. and t. ' To drink hastily and copiously ; . . . at one gulp ' : low s. (— 1823) and dial. (— 1829) >, ca. 1860, coll. >, ca. 1890, s. ; in C. 20, also of food. Egan's Grose. Often *swipe off*. ? ex *sweep off*.—2. The sporting v.i. (1857) is coll. >, ca. 1890, S.E. T. Hughes, 1857, ' The first ball of the over, Jack steps out and meets, swiping with all his force.' The v.t. not before ca. 1851. F. & H. and Lewis.—3. At Harrow : to birch (v.t. : from) ca. 1880. A sense-blend of *swish*, to birch, and *swipe*, v., 2.—4. To appropriate illicitly ; steal ; loot : U.S. (— 1890), anglicised ca. 1900, when used by Kipling ; fairly gen. in G.W., and in England always mostly a military term.

swiper. A heavy drinker : 1836, F. Mahony (O.E.D.) : coll. >, by 1890, s. Ex *swipe*, v., 1, q.v. —2. The cricketing sense dates from the early 1850's (e.g. in F. Gale, 1853) : coll. >, in late C. 19, S.E. Ex *swipe*, v., 2. (Lewis.)

swipes ; occ. **swypes.** Small beer : from ca. 1786 : coll. >, in late C. 19, s. Grose, 2nd ed. Cf. *swipe*, v., 1, which it inconveniently precedes by thirty years or more.—2. Hence, any beer : from ca. 1820. Scott ; Hood, ' Bread and cheese and swipes ', O.E.D.—3. A potman : ca. 1810–50. Ex sense 1.

swipes, purser's. Small beer : nautical : ca. 1786–1870. Grose, 2nd ed. See **swipes.**

swipey. (Not very) tipsy : coll. : 1844, Dickens, ' He's only a little swipey, you know.' Never gen. and, by 1900, ob. Ex *swipes*, q.v. Cf. *squiffy*.

swiping is the vbl.n. of *swipe*, v., 2 ; also **blind swiping** : coll. : 1879, W. G. Grace. Lewis.—2. A birching, esp. by a monitor : Shrewsbury School :

from ca. 1880. (Desmond Coke, *The Bending of a Twig*, 1906.) Cf. *swipe*, v., 3.

swish, v. Very rare except as *swished*, q.v.

swish, adj. Smart; fashionable: C. 20; ob. Ex dial. *swish*, the same: cognate with dial. *swash*, gaudy or showy.

swish ! Oh, is that all ? ! : ironic (— 1923). Manchon.

swish-tail. A pheasant, ' so called by the persons who sell game for the poachers ', Grose, 3rd ed. : ca. 1790–1870.—2. A schoolmaster : late C. 19–20 ; ob. On *bum-brusher*.

swished, ppl.adj. Married : low (? orig. c.): ca. 1810–80. Vaux ; H., 1st ed. Cf. *switched*.

Swiss admiral. A pretended Naval officer : naval coll. : from ca. 1870 ; ob. Ex the Fr. *amiral suisse*, a naval officer employed ashore : cf. the allusive S.E. *Swiss navy*.

switch. To copulate with (a woman): 1772, Bridges, ' Paris . . . longs to switch the gypsy ' ; ob. Cf. *swinge*, v., 1, q.v. : many old vv. of coïtion are sadistic.

switch off ! Stop talking !, ' shut up ! ' : C. 20 : s. >, by 1930, coll. Manchon. Ex disconnecting a 'phone and/or turning off an electric light.

switched, ppl.adj. Married : low (— 1864). H., 3rd ed. Prob. suggested by *swished*, q.v. Presumably cognate with *switch*, q.v.

switchel. To have sexual intercourse : Restoration period. Cf. *switch*, q.v.

swive, v.t. and i. To copulate (with a woman); hence *swiver*, *swiving*, and *the Queen of Swiveland* (Venus). Excellent S.E. that, dating from late C. 14, >, early in C. 17, a vulgarism ; † since ca. 1800, except as a literary archaism and in several diall.

swivel-eye. A squinting eye : coll. : 1864, H., 3rd ed. ; 1865, Dickens ; ob. Ex :

swivel-eyed. Squint-eyed : coll. : 1781, C. Johnston ; Grose, 1st ed. Perhaps suggested by Sheridan's ' T'other [eye] turned on a swivel ', 1775. O.E.D.

swivelly. Drunk : late C. 19–20 ; very ob. Ex *swivel* on *squiffy*, q.v.

swiver. See **swive.—Swiveland, Queen of.** Ibid.

swiz ; occ. **swizz.** A ' fraud ' ; great disappointment : late C. 19–20 schoolboys'. Prob. an abbr. of *swizzle*, recorded in the same sense by A. H. Dawson in 1913 ; the longer form being perverted *swindle*.

swizzle. Intoxicating drink, whether a specific cocktail or strong liquor in gen. : s. >, ca. 1850, coll. : from not later than 1791, for it appears in the 3rd ed. of Grose, where, moreover, it is said that at Ticonderoga, in North America, the 17th (English) Regiment had, ca. 1760, a society named The Swizzle Club ; 1813, Colonel Hawker, ' The boys . . . finished the evening with some . . . grub, swizzle, and singing,' O.E.D. Slightly ob. ? a corruption of *swig* (W.) or cognate with the U.S. *switchel*, which, however, is recorded later and may be ex *swizzle* ; perhaps *swizzle* derives ex *swig* or *guzzle* or even on dial. *twizzle*, v.t., turn round quickly.—2. See **swiz.**

swizzle, v.i. To tipple : s. and dial (— 1847) >, ca. 1880, coll. ; ob. Halliwell. Ex *swizzle*, n., 1.— 2. V.t., to stir (drink) with a swizzle-stick : 1859, Trollope (O.E.D.) : s. >, ca. 1880, coll. Prob. ex sense 1 but strongly influenced by *twizzle* (see end of *swizzle*, n., 1). Whence the next entry.—3. V.i corresponding to n., 2 ; whence *swizzler*, a swindler, as in Neil Bell, *Crocus*, 1936.

swizzle-stick. A stick for stirring drink to a froth : coll. : 1885 (O.E.D.).

swizzled. Tipsy : from ca. 1850. Ex *swizzle*, v., 1, q.v.

swizzy. A s. variant of *swizzle*, n., 1, and v., 1.

swob ! ' Swelp me bob ! ' (q.v.) : low (— 1923). Manchon. Cf. *swop me bob !*

swobbers. See **swabber.**

swod-gill. See **swad-gill.—swoddy.** See **swaddy.** Thus spelt, rare in C. 20.

Swolks ! See **'Swounds !**

swollen head, have a. To be tipsy : coll. : late C. 19–20 ; ob.

swop. See **swap.** So too for derivatives.

swop me bob or **Bob !** A perversion of *s'elp* (via *swelp*, q.v.) *me bob !* : 1890, P. H. Emerson (E.D.D. : *my*). See also at **s'elp** and cf. *swob !* A variant (— 1923) is *swop me Dick(e)y* : Manchon.

sworbote (or **S.**) **!, God.** A coll. corruption of *God's forbote !* : ca. 1580–1620. O.E.D.

sword, ship one's slung. See **slung sword.**

*sword-racket. Enlisting in various regiments and deserting after getting the bounty : c. of ca. 1810–50. *Lex. Bal.*

sworder. A ship engaged in catching *sword*-fish : nautical coll. : late C. 19–20. Bowen.

swore for *sworn* is sol. in C. 19–20. Baumann.

sworn at Highgate. See **Highgate.**

swosh. Nonsense ; drivel : 1924, Galsworthy, *The White Monkey*, ' And anyway sentiment was swosh '. It lived only ca. 1923–5. A blend of *swindle* + *bosh* (or perhaps *tosh*).

swot, swat. Mathematics : ca. 1845–95 : military. Also, a mathematician. (Rarely *swat*.) Perhaps ex a R.M.A. professor's pronunciation of *sweat* (v.).—2. Hence, (hard) study : Public Schools' (— 1881) and universities'. Perhaps imm. ex v.—3. One who studies hard : 1866 (O.E.D.). Ex second nuance of sense 1.

swot ; occ. **swat**, v.i. To study hard : from ca. 1859 : Army >, ca. 1870, gen. at the universities (H., 5th ed.). H., 2nd ed. Ex *swot*, n., 1. Hence *swot (swat) up*, to work hard at, esp. for an examination ; to ' mug up ' : rare before C. 20.

swot, in a. In a rage : Shrewsbury (school) : late C. 19–20. Corruption of *sweat*.

swotter. A ' swot ' (sense 3) : mostly schools' (— 1919). O.E.D. (Sup.)

'Swounds ! A coll. euphemism for *God's wounds !* : 1589, Nashe ; † by 1650. Cf. the very rare perversion of *'Swounds* : *Swolks !*, recorded by Swift in his *Polite Conversation*. O.E.D.

swret-sio. The earliest form (— 1859) of **sret-sio,** q.v. H., 1st ed.

swyg. See **swig**, n.—***swygman.** See **swigman.** —**swynge.** See **swinge.—swype.** See **swipe.—swypes.** See **swipes.**

sybil, Sybil. Incorrect for *sibyl, Sibyl* : from inception (C. 14). But very common.

Sydney-bird, -duck, or -sider. A convict : Australian : ca. 1850–90. (In C. 20, a *Sydney-sider* is merely a native or inhabitant of Sydney.) Ex the convict settlement.

syebuck. A sixpence : low : ca. 1780–1850. G. Parker, 1781. Ex *sice*, 6 ; the *buck* may be a mystifying suffix suggested by *hog*, a shilling.

syl-slinger. An actor that mouths his words : theatrical (— 1913) ; ob. A. H. Dawson, *Dict. of Slang* (1913).

'sylum, sylum. An asylum : sol. (— 1887.) Baumann. Also in dial.

sylvan. Incorrect though very gen. for *silvan*: from inception (C. 16).

sympathy. A man's intimate caressing of a woman : C. 20. Ex that indelicate definition of sympathy which arose from Byron's ' A fellow-feeling . . .'

symptom, symptomatic. Catachrestic for *symbol*, *symbolic* : C. 17, C. 19. Cf. the catachrestic use of *synchronous* for ' uniform in speed ' and —*ly* for ' at a uniform speed ' : late C. 18–20. O.E.D.

Synagogue, the. A shed in the N.E. corner of : Covent Garden : from 1890. Covent Garden is almost wholly run by Jews. (Ware.)

syntax. A schoolmaster : coll. of 1780–1860. Grose, 1st ed. Cf. William Combe's *Tour of Dr Syntax*, 1813. Ex grammar. Cf. *gerund-grinder*, q.v.

syph ; incorrectly **siph.** Syphilis : coll. : late C. 19–20. Contrast *clap*, q.v.

syrup. Money : dispensing chemists' (— 1909). Ware. Cf. *brads*.

T

[In F. & H. are, under **T**, the following ineligibles, whether S.E. or dial. S.E. :—**T, to a** ; **t-beard** ; **tabarder** ; **tabernacle** ; **tables, turn the** ; **tag-end** ; **tag, rag, and bobtail** ; **tag-rhyme, -tail** ; unrecorded **tail's** and **tailor's** ; **take** and derivatives, etc., id. ; **talesman** ; unrecorded **talk**, etc. ; **tall**, id. ; **tallow-face(d)** ; **tally-men** ; **tame** unlisted ; **tan, smell of the** ; **tandem** (bicycle) ; **tannikin** ; **tanquam** ; unrecorded **tantivy** ; **tantony**, etc. ; unrecorded **tap's** ; **tar**, id. ; **target** ; **tarse** ; **tart**, adj. ; **Tartar**, except as c. ; **Tartuffe** ; **taste** if unlisted ; **tatterdemalion** ; unrecorded **tattle** ; **tattoo** ; **taut** ; **taverned** and **taverner** ; undefined **taw's** ; **tawdry** ; **tawny-coat** and **-moor** ; **tea-party** ; **team** ; unlisted **tear's** ; **tease, on the** ; unrecorded **teeth**, etc. ; **teetotal** ; **tell**, etc., where unrecorded ; **temple of Venus** ; **ten-in-the-hundred** ; **tent** ; **tenterbelly** ; **tenterhooks** ; **tercel gentle** ; **termer** ; **terrae filius** ; **terrible boy** ; unrecorded **that** and **thatch** ; **theta** ; unlisted **thick's** ; **thief** (one sense is dial.), etc., unrecorded; **thimble**, id. ; **thin**, id. ; **thing**, etc., id. ; **thirding** ; undefined **thirteen**, and **thirty** ; **Thomas Courteous** ; **thorns, on** ; **thorough-stitch** ; **thread's** unrecorded ; **three**, id. ; **Thresher, Captain** ; **throat** when undefined ; **throttle**, id. ; **through**, id. ; **throw**, id. ; **thrum**, id. **thug** ; unrecorded **thumb's** and **thump's** ; **thunder, steal one's** ; **thwack(er)** ; **tib** (also dial.) ; **tick and toy** ; **ticker** (horse and stock-indicator) ; unrecorded **ticket's** ; unrecorded **tickle's** ; **tidy**, n. ; **tie**, to marry ; **tiffity-taffet(t)y**, etc. ; **tigerkin** ; unlisted **tight's** ; **tim-whisky** ; **timber-mare, timbered** ; **timbrel** ; **Timothy tear-cat** ; **tingle-tangle** ; unrecorded **tinker's** ; **tin-pot**, adj. ; unrecorded **tip**, etc. ; **tipper** ; **tippet** ; **tipple**, v., and its derivatives ; **tiry** ; **tit, a horse, and** other unlisteds ; **titivil** ; **titter-totter** ; **tittup**, n. ; **tivy** in hunting ; **toad, toady**, etc. ; **to-do** ; **toast** (pledged person, etc.) ; **tobaccanalian**, etc. ; **toby** (jug) ; **toddle** ; **toddy** ; undefined **toe's** ; **token**, except in phrase ; **told you so** ; **Toledo** ; **toll** ; undefined **Tom's** ; **tomahawk** ; **tompion** ; **tongs**, if unrecorded ; **tongue**, etc., id. ; **tonish** ; **tonner** ; **too too** ; unrecorded **tool's** ; **tooth**, id. ; **top** (etc.), id. ; **tope**, etc. ; **topsy-turvy** ; **torch-race** ; **Torpids** ; **torturer of anthems** ; **tosher** (a boat) ; unrecorded **coss**, etc. ; **tostication** ; unlisted **tot's** ; **totter** ; **tottery** ; unrecorded **touch**, derivatives and phrases; **tough**, id. ; **tour** ; **tousle** ; **tow, in** ; **tower**, n. (fashion in head-dress) ; **towhead** ; **towering** ; unlisted **town**, etc. ; **toy** (except c. sense) ; **tprot** ; **trace** ; unrecorded **track's** ; **train** ; **tramp**, etc. ; **trang(r)am** ; **transcribbler** ; **transfisticated** ; **translate** ; **translator** ; **trap**, etc., unrecorded ; **trash** (worthless, and n.) ; **trat** ; unrecorded **travel**, etc. ; **tray (trey) ace** ; **treacle sleep** ; **tread, treading**, etc., where unrecorded ; **treason** ; **treasure** ; **treat, a** round of drinks ; **treating** ; unrecorded **tree's** ; **tremble(r)** ; **trench(er)** ; **trial** ; **triangle** ; **tribe** ; **tribune** ; **tribute** ; unlisted **trick's** ; **tried virgin** ; **trig** where undefined ; **trillibub** ; **trilli** ; unlisted **trim**, etc. ; unrecorded **tripe's** ; **trivet** ; **trolloll** ; **trollop** ; **trolly-lolly** ; **tronk** ; unrecorded **trot's**, esp. **old trot** ; **trouble**, id. ; **trounce** ; **trowel** ; unlisted **true's** ; **trumpery** ; **trumpet** ; unrecorded **trunk's** ; **trut** ; **truth** ; **try**, etc., unrecorded ; **tub**, id. ; **tucker-in** ; unlisted **tuft's** ; **tug**, id. ; (Anglo-Indian) **tum-tum** ; **tumble**, etc., id. ; **tun** (vessel) ; **tup**, etc., id. ; **turf**, id. ; **turk, Turk**, id. ; **turn**, id. ; **tush** ; **tussle** ; **tut** ; **tut-work** ; **tutivillus** ; **twaddle** unrecorded ; **twang** (etc.), id. ; **twatter-light** ; **twattle** ; **tweague** and **tweak**, id. ; **tweedle-dum** ; **twelvepenny** ; **twenty** ; **twice** ; **twiddle** ; **twilight** ; **twinklers** ; **twittle-twat** ; **twire**, v. ; **twish** ; unrecorded **twist's** ; **twit** ; **twitteration**, **twitters** ; **twitter-light** ; **twittle(-twattle)** ; **two-handed**, adroit ; **twopenny** (beer ; adj.) ; **Tyburn**, etc.,—but see note on ; **tyg** ; **tympany**.

Dial. :—**tacker, tacket, tagster, tangle, tantara-bobs, tap-peckle, tatterwag(g)s, tatterwallop(s), Tavistock grace, Teignton squash, thrapple, tim-doodle, timothy, tinger, tinkler, tisty-tosty, tittle-goose, toby-trot, todge, tolsery, tom-toe, tom-trot, tommy** (a simpleton), **toot, tootledum-pattick, torril, tossy-tail, totty-headed, trail-tongs, traneen, tranklements, trapes** (a slattern), **tray-trip, treacle-wag, trim-tram, trollybags, trub, tuel, tumptsner, tussey, tussicated, tutting, twank, twanking, twitcher, twitter.**]

't. That, esp. *so't*, so that (e.g. one did so-and-so) : sol. and dial. : mid-C. 19–20. O.E.D. (Sup.). —2. It ; as in ' If't comes to that, he doesn't know ' : slovenly coll. : late C. 19–20.

t'. To : slovenly coll. : ? since early C. 19. Esp. as in Neil Bell, *The Years Dividing*, 1935, ' Anna ought t've had her results by now.'

T, marked with a. Known as a thief : coll. : late C. 18–mid-19. ' Formerly convicted thieves were branded with a " T " in the hand,' F. & H.

t. and o. ; **T. and O.** Odds of two to one : sporting : from ca. 1880 ; ob. Ware.

t.b. ; loosely **t.-b.** (or **T.-b.**). Tuberculosis : coll. (orig. medical) : C. 20.—2. **t.b.** or **T.B.** Top boy : London schools' coll. (— 1887). Baumann.

T.G. See **temporary gentleman.**

t.G.i.F., or **T.G.I.F.** A c.p. among non-resident teachers in secondary schools : C. 20. ' Thank God it's Friday ! '

T.P. See **Tay Pay.**

t.t. ; occ. **tee-tee.** Teetotal ; a teetotaller : late C. 19–20.

t.w.k. Too well known : Army in India : mid-C. 19–20. Ware.

ta ! ; rarely **taa !** Thanks ! : coll., orig. and mainly nursery : 1772, Mrs Delany, ' You would not say " ta " to me for my congratulation,' O.E.D. Ex a young child's difficulty with *th* and *nks.* Cf. :

ta-ta ! Good-bye ! ; au revoir ! : coll., orig. and chiefly nursery : 1837, Dickens, ' " Tar, tar, Sammy," replied his father,' O.E.D. Perhaps suggested by Fr. *au 'voir.*—2. Hence (also **tata**), a hat : theatrical (— 1923). Manchon.

ta-ta's (or **-tas**), **go** ; **go for a ta-ta.** (Of a child) to go for a walk : (proletarian) nursery coll. : late C. 19–20. Ex *ta-ta !*, q.v.

Tab(, the). The Metropolitan Tabernacle in Newington Causeway : London : late C. 19–20. Baumann.—2. **Tab.** A Cantab or Cambridge University man : coll. : from ca. 1910. S.O.D.—3. **tab.** (Gen. pl.) An ear : tailors' : from ca. 1870. —4. An old maid ; loosely, any oldish woman : theatrical (— 1909). Ware. Abbr. *tabby*, 1.—5. A staff officer : military : 1917 ; ob. F. & Gibbons. Ex his red tabs. Cf. *brass hat*, which is much more usual.—6. A customer that, after giving an infinity of trouble, buys precisely nothing : drapers' and hosiers' (— 1935). Perhaps ex *tab*, v.—7. A cigarette : Northern : from ca. 1920. Also among grafters : witness P. Allingham, *Cheapjack*, 1934.

tab, v.i. (Of a customer) to give much trouble : drapery and kindred trades' (— 1935). Perhaps cf. *tab*, n., 4 ; perhaps ex *keep (a) tab.* Whence *tabber*, a customer hard to please.

tab, drive. ' To go out on a party of pleasure with a wife and family ', Grose, 1st ed. : ca. 1780–1830. Perhaps ex *tabby*, an old maid.

tab, keep (a) ; keep tabs. (V.t. only with *on.*) To keep watch, a check (*on*), a note of the doings (of a person) : coll. : U.S. (from ca. 1880) anglicised ca. 1905. The form *keep tabs* is rare and specifically British. Not ex *tab*, a label or ticket, for this arises later, but perhaps by abbr. ex *tablet.*

tab-nabs. Cakes and/or pastries : nautical, esp. stewards' (— 1935). Prob : because they are mostly for the saloon—not for the crew or the steerage.

tabber. See **tab**, v.

tabby ; occ. **tabbie.** An old maid : coll. (in C. 20, S.E.) : 1761, G. Colman, ' I am not sorry for the coming in of these old tabbies, and am much obliged to her ladyship for leaving us to such an agreeable tête-à-tête ' ; Grose, 1st ed., ' Either from *Tabitha*, a formal antiquated name ; or else from a tabby cat, old maids being often compared to cats ' ; Rogers.—2. Hence, a spiteful tattler : coll. : from ca. 1840. In C. 20, S.E. Cf. *cat*.—3. Loosely, any woman ; mostly in *tabby-party*, a gathering of women : coll. (— 1874). H., 5th ed.—4. In C. 20, esp. in Australia, often ' girl ', sweetheart.

tabby meeting. The May meeting of the evangelical party at Exeter Hall : London : London : ca. 1890–1905. Ware. Ex its old-maidishness.

tabefical is incorrect for *tabifical*, consumptive : C. 17. O.E.D.

table-cloth, the. A white cloud topping Table Mountain : South African, esp. Cape Town coll. >, ca. 1880, S.E. : from mid-1830's. In *Addresses to the British and South African Association, 1905*, we read that ' *South-easters* are of three kinds— (1) " Table-cloth " [also as n. : 1898] . . ., (2) " Blind " . . ., (3) " Black " south-easters ' : all these are coll. Pettman.

table-part. A role ' played only from the waist upwards, and therefore behind a table ' : theatrical coll. : C. 19–20. Ware.

tabloid. ' A small Sopwith biplane of high speed and rapid climbing powers ' : Air Force : 1917 ; ob. F. & Gibbons. Ex its ' concentrated excellencies '.

tabs. See **tab**, 3 ; **tab, keep (a).**

tace is Latin for a candle ! Be quiet ; it'd be better for you to stop talking ! : coll. : 1688, Shadwell, ' I took him up with my old repartee ; Peace, said I, *Tace is Latin* for a candle ' ; Swift ; Fielding ; Grose, 2nd ed. ; Scott ; then in dial., occ. *cat for candle.* The pun is double : L. *tace* = be silent ! ; a candle is snuffed or otherwise extinguished. Cf. *brandy is Latin for a goose*, q.v. (Apperson.)

tach. A hat : back s. (— 1859). H., 1st ed. Via *tah* aspirated.

tachs. A fad : Tonbridge School : from ca. 1880. Ex *tache*, a trait, now dial. ; cf. the Somersetshire *tetch*, a habit or gait.

tack. Foodstuff, esp. in *soft tack*, bread, and *hard tack*, ship's biscuit : orig. (ca. 1830), nautical. Marryat, *soft tack*, 1833 (O.E.D.). Cf. *tackle*, victuals, which is rather later. Prob. a sailor's pun on either *tackle*, cordage, or *tack*, a ship's (change of) direction, or ex dial. *tack*, cattle-pasture let on hire. The O.E.D. considers it S.E. ; more prob., I think, nautical s. >, ca. 1860, coll. and then perhaps, in C. 20, S.E. Cf. *tommy*, q.v.—2. Hence, food (esp. cooked food) in gen. : coll. : late C. 19–20. Lyell, ' What a filthy looking restaurant ! What ever [*sic*] sort of *tack* do they give you in this place ? ! '—3. A feast in one's study : Sherborne School : from ca. 1870.—4. Tact : sol. : mid-C. 19–20. See also **tact.**

tack, on the. Teetotal : military : late C. 19–20. F. & Gibbons. Ex *tack*, 1. Cf. *tack wallah.*

tack-on. The act of adding something ; the thing added : coll. : 1905 (O.E.D.)

tack or sheet, will not start. Resolute ; with mind firmly made up : nautical coll. : late C. 19–20. Bowen. Ex nautical j.

tack together. To marry : jocular coll. : 1754, Foote ; ob.

tack wallah. A teetotaller : military : late C. 19–20. B. & P. Cf. *tack, on the* (q.v.).

tacked, have or **have got** (a person). From ca. 1870, but † by 1920 : ' When a man has another vanquished, or for certain reasons bound to his service, he is said to have " got him tacked ",' H., 5th ed. Cf. *taped*, q.v.

tackies. Rubber-soled sand-shoes : Eastern Province (South Africa) coll. (— 1913). Pettman. Prob. ex the marks left on, e.g., moist soil by the corrugations.

tacking, n. ' Obtaining end by roundabout means ' : lower classes' (— 1909). Ware. Ex nautical j., perhaps with a glance at *tact.*

*tackle. A mistress : c. : 1688, Shadwell ; B.E. ; Grose. † by 1830. Prob., like the next, ex *tackle*, instruments, equipment.—2. Clothes : c. >, ca. 1840, nautical s. : late C. 17–19. B.E., ' *Rum-tackle*, . . . very fine Cloth[e]s ' ; Grose, 1st ed. ; H., 1st ed. Cf. *rigging.*—3. Orig. (Grose, 2nd ed.) *a man's tackle*, = the male genitals : late C. 18–20 ; ob.—4. Victuals : s. : 1857, T. Hughes, ' Rare tackle that, sir, of a cold morning ', O.E.D. ; slightly ob. In dial., it dates from mid-C. 18 : witness E.D.D. Prob. suggested by *tack*, q.v.—5. A watch-chain, a *red t.* being a gold chain : c. : from late 1870's. Ex *tackle*, cordage, and frequently in combination with *toy*, a watch.

tackle, v. To lay hold of; encounter, attack, physically: coll.: orig. (— 1828), U.S., anglicised by 1840 at latest. Perhaps ex *tackle*, to harness a horse, influenced by *attack*.—2. Hence, to enter into a discussion, etc., with (a person), approach (a person on some subject): coll.: 1840, Dickens (O.E.D.); 1862, Thackeray, 'Tackle the lady, and speak your mind to her as best you can.'—3. Hence, to attempt to handle (a task, situation), or to understand or master (a subject); attack (a problem): coll.: 1847, FitzGerald (O.E.D.).—4. Hence, v.i., with *to* (1867, Trollope), to set to; or *with*, to grapple with (from late C. 19 and mainly dial.): O.E.D. and E.D.D.—5. V.t., ex senses 1 and 3: to fall upon (food), begin to eat, try to eat: coll.: 1889, Jerome K. Jerome, 'We tackled the cold beef for lunch,' O.E.D.

tacks. An artist's paraphernalia: artists' (— 1909). Ware. Ex *tack*, equipment.

tact (sol., tack) !,—**and that, Bill, is.** A C. 20 c.p. based on the chestnut of the plumber explaining to his assistant that 'tact is when you find her ladyship in the bath and you get away quickly saying "Beg pardon, my lord".' Occ. *and that is what they call tack.*

taddler. A sausage: low (— 1923). Manchon. Perhaps *tiddler* corrupted or perverted.

tadger, tadging. See **teaich-gir.**

Tadpole. A party-hack: political: middle 1880's; ob. Collinson. Gen. in the phrase *Tadpoles and Tapers.* Coined by Disraeli.

taepo. See **taipo.**

taf; taffy. Fat, adj.; fatty, n.: back s., 'near' back s.: from late 1850's. H., 1st ed. The latter is very ob.

taff. A potato: Christ's Hospital: from ca. 1860. ? ex *tatie* or *tatur*.—2. (**Taff.**) A C. 19–20 abbr. (noted by Bowen) of :

Taffy. A Welshman: a coll. nickname dating from ca. 1680 though adumbrated in Harrison's *England*, where a Welshman is called a 'David'. Popularised by the old nursery-rhyme, 'Taffy was a Welshman, Taffy was a thief' (see interestingly the **v.** *welsh*). Also an 'inevitable' nickname of anyone with a Welsh name or accent: lower classes': mid-C. 19–20. Ex a (supposed) Welsh pronunciation of *Davy.* Cf. *Paddy* and *Sawney*.—2. **taffy.** See **taf.**

Taffy's Day. St David's Day (March 1): late C. 17–20. B.E. See **Taffy.**

tag. A lower servant, so called because he assists another (cf. S.E. *tag after*, to follow servilely): servants' s. (— 1857) > coll. Cf. corresponding *pug.* O.E.D.—2. An off-side kick: Winchester: from ca. 1840. Mansfield.—3. An actor: from ca. 1860; virtually † by 1900, † by 1910. Ex tags of speeches. Cf. :—4. The last line of a play, whether in prose or in verse: theatrical coll.: late C. 19–20. It is, Alfred Atkins tells me, considered unlucky to speak it at rehearsals.

Tag, der. See **der Tag.**

tag along. To go along; to go: C. 20. (James Spenser, *Limey Breaks In*, 1934.) Perhaps ex *tag* (oneself) *on to a person and go along with him.* Cf. :

tag around with. To frequent; follow about: C. 20. D. Sayers, 1933, 'He used to tag around with that de Momerie crowd.'

taihoa ! Wait a bit !: New Zealand coll.: from ca. 1840. Direct ex Maori. Morris.

tail. The posteriors; fundament: C. 14–20: S.E. until ca. 1750, then (dial. and) coll.; in late C. 19–20, low coll.—2. The penis; more gen., the female pudend: mid-C. 14–20: S.E. until C. 18, then coll.; in C. 19–20, low coll.—3. Hence, a harlot: ca. 1780–1850; but extant in Glasgow. Grose, 1st ed., 'Mother, how many tails have you in your cab ? how many girls have you in your nanny house ?' Other derivatives—prob. not coll. before late C. 17 or early 18, all ob. except those marked †, and all drawn from F. & H.—are these :—Penis, †tail-pike, -pin, -pipe, -tackle, -trimmer, and ††tenant-in-tail, which also = a whore; pudend, **tail-gap**, -gate, -hole. Also tail-feathers, pubic hair; †tail-fence, the hymen; †tail-flowers, the menses; †tail-fruit, children; tail-juice (or -water), urine or semen; tail-trading, harlotry; **tail-wagging** or -work, intercourse; cf. †*make settlement in tail*, go *tail-tickling* or *-twitching, play at up-tails all*, and, of women only, *turn up one's tail, get shot in the tail*; *hot* or †*light* or *warm in the tail*, (of a woman) wanton; but †*hot-tailed* or *with tail on fire* = venereally infected. These terms are not results of F. & H.'s imagination: most of them will be found in one or other of the following authors: Langland, Chaucer, Shakespeare, Rochester, Motteux, Ned Ward, Tom Brown, C. 18 Stevens and Grose.—4. 'The train or tail-like portion of a woman's dress': late C. 13–20: S.E. until C. 18, then coll. Bridges, 1774, 'Brimstones with their sweeping tails'. (O.E.D.)—5. A sword: c.: late C. 17–early 19. B.E.; Grose, 1st ed.

tail, v.i., to coït: C. 18–20; ob.—2. V.t., to follow, as a detective a criminal: coll.: late C. 19–20. Perhaps ex Australian sense, *tail* (drive or tend) sheep or cattle.

tail, be—gen. **shall or will be**—**on a person's.** To look for, to pursue, a person with a view to punishing or severely scolding him: C. 20.

tail, cow's. A rope's end frayed or badly knotted: nautical coll.: from ca. 1860. Whence *hanging in cow's* (or *cows'*) *tails*, of an ill-kept ship.

tail, get (one) **on the ; get on the tail of** (someone). To attack an opponent in the rear: Air Force coll.: from 1915. F. & Gibbons.

tail !, kiss my. A contemptuous retort: C. 18–20; very ob.

tail, make settlement in, and **tenant-in-tail** (see **tail,** n., 2) constitute an indelicate pun on the legal S.E. *tail* (ex Fr. *taille*, assessment), limitation as to freehold or inheritance. K.W., 1661, has *tenure in tail* (O.E.D.)

tail, she goes as if she cracked nuts with her. A semi-proverbial c.p. applied to a frisky woman: C. 19–early 20.

tail, top over ; tail over top. Head over heels: coll.: C. 14–20 (ob.): S.E. until mid-C. 18, then coll. See **tail,** n., 1.

tail-block. A watch: nautical (— 1864); ob. H., 3rd ed. Ex lit. nautical sense.

tail-board. The back-flap of a (gen. female) child's breeches: low: from ca. 1870. Ex the movable tail-board of a barrow, cart, van, etc.

***tail-buzzer.** A pickpocket: c. (— 1859); ob. H., 1st ed. Ex *tail*, the breech, + *buz*, to steal. Orig., it would seem, of a thief specialising in removing articles from hip-pockets. Cf. :

***tail-buzzing.** That kind of pickpocketry: c.: from ca. 1845. 'No 747.'

***tail-drawer.** A sword-stealer, esp. from gentlemen's sides: c.: late C. 17–early 19. B.E.; Grose, 1st ed. at *tayle drawers.* Ex *tail*, n., last sense.

tail in the water, with. Thriving, prosperous : coll. : ca. 1850–1910. F. & H.

tail is up the turd is out,—as hasty as a sheep, as soon as the. A low, mostly rural, c.p. of ca. 1860–1920.

tail of, get on the. See **tail, get on the.**

tail off. To run or go off ; to retire, withdraw : coll. : 1841, F. E. Paget, 'Mrs Spatterdash . . . tailed off at last to a dissenting chapel,' O.E.D., which cites from Rider Haggard (1885) the occ. variant *tail out of it*. Ware, 'From the tails of birds and animals being last seen as they retreat '.

tail-pulling. 'The publication of books of little or no merit, the whole cost of which is paid by the author ', F. & H. : publishers' : from late 1890's ; ob. In contradistinction to the honourable publication of books of considerable merit and—to say the least of it—inconsiderable saleability. The former is practised only by sharks and amateurs, the latter by all.

tail-tea. 'The afternoon tea following royal drawing-rooms, at which ladies who had been to court that afternoon, appeared in their trains ': Society : 1880–1901. Ware.

tail-twisting. The act of twisting the British lion's tail : political : 1889 (O.E.D.). Whence the rare *tail-twist*, v.i., and *tail-twister*.

*****tail up.** A C. 20 c. variant of *tail*, v., 2. Edgar Wallace.

tail will catch the chin-cough, (e.g.) his. A c.p. applied to one sitting on the ground esp. if it is wet : ca. 1670–1800. Ray, 1678.

tailer. An exclamation on falling, or sitting, unexpectedly on one's behind : late C. 16–early 17. Shakespeare, *Midsummer Night*, II, i. Ex *tail*, n., 1, whence also :—2. Such a fall : C. 19–20 ; very ob.

tailor, v.t. To shoot at (a bird) so as to miss or, gen., to damage : sporting : 1889, *Blackwood's Magazine* (O.E.D.). Ex tailor's slashes.—2. V.i., to have dealings or run up bills with tailors : coll. : 1861, T. Hughes (O.E.D.) ; very ob. and never common.

tailor, the fag-end of a. A botcher : coll. : late C. 16–17.

tailoring, do a bit of. To ' sew up ', q.v. : from ca. 1860 ; ob.

tailor's ragout. ' Bread sopt in the oil & vinegar in which cucumbers have been sliced ', Grose, 3rd ed. (at *scratch platter*) : ca. 1790–1850. See **cucumber.**

tailor's wound. A bayonet wound in the back : jocular military coll. (— 1923). Manchon. Such a wound being likened to the prick from a tailor's needle.

tails. A tail-coat, as opp. a jacket : coll. : 1888. —2. Esp. a dress-suit, and properly the coat only : C. 20 coll.—3. Batmen completing a party of horsemen of high rank : New Zealand soldiers' : in the G.W. Opp. *the heads*, those in authority : ex the game of two-up.

tails, charity. A tail-coat worn by a Lower School boy taller than the average : Harrow School : from 1890's. Ex *tails*, 1.

tails of the cat. A nautical coll. variant (—1887 ; ob.) of *cat-o'-nine-tails*. Baumann.

tails up, in good spirits, often in the imperative ; **tails down,** the reverse. C. 20 coll. (esp. military) on the verge of S.E. Ex the behaviour of dogs. F. & Gibbons.—**Tails Up.** Air Marshall Sir John Salmond : Air Force : from 1918. Ibid. Ex a statement made by him.

taint, 'tain't ; also **'tan't.** It is not : so!. : C. 19–20. See **ain't.**

taipo ; occ. **taepo.** A vicious horse ; as name for a dog : New Zealand coll. : mid-C. 19–20. Perhaps ex Maori : but see Morris.—2. Among Maoris, a s. term for a theodolite, ' because it is the " land-stealing devil " ' (Morris). Ex *taepo*, Maori for a goblin.

Tait. A moderate clergyman : Church coll. : ca. 1870–80. Dr Tait, Archbishop of Canterbury (d. 1882), tried in vain to reconcile all parties in the Church of England. (Ware.)

taj. ' Ripping ' ; luscious : boys' : ca. 1900–12. Ware. Ex *Taj Mahal.*

take. See ' Moving-Picture Slang ', § 6.

take, v.i., To be taken : coll. and dial. : 1674, †*took with child* ; 1822, *took ill*, the gen. form ; occ. as in 1890, *took studious*, jocular. Ex *be taken ill*, etc. O.E.D.—2. V.t., followed by *to do* : to require (a person or thing of a stated ability, capacity, or nature) to do something : coll. : 1890, *The Field*, March 8, ' Any ignoramus can construct a straight line, but it takes an engineer to make a curve,' O.E.D.—3. V.i. To be a good (*well*) or bad (*badly*) subject for photographing : coll. (orig. photographers') : 1889, B. Howard, ' The photographers . . . say a woman " takes " better standing,' O.E.D.—4. V.i., to hurt : Charterhouse : late C. 19–20. Ex a disease or an injection *taking*, i.e. taking effect.

take ! All right ; all correct ; certainly ! : Canadian : C. 20. B. & P. Perhaps a perversion of *jake* ; but cf. *take eight !*

take a Burford bait. To get drunk : C. 19 coll. ex C. 18–20 dial. Orig., to take a drink : coll. : ca. 1630–1780. ' Water-Poet ' Taylor, 1636 ; Fuller, 1662 ; 1790, Grose in his *Provincial Glossary*. Apperson.

take a carrot ! I don't care ! : a low c.p. (— 1887) ; slightly ob. Baumann.

take a dagger and drown yourself ! A theatrical c.p. retort : ca. 1860–1910. Ex old coll. phrase = to say one thing and do another, as in Ray, 1678.

take-a-fright. Night : rhyming s. (— 1859) ; slightly ob. H., 1st ed.

take a hair of the same dog. See **hair.**—**take a pew.** See **pew.**—**take a pick.** See **pick, take a.**—**take a running jump.** See **go and take.**

take a sight. (Gen. as vbl.n.) As skipper, to engage a hand without knowing him : nautical (Canadian) : C. 20. Bowen.

take a stagger. A more gen. form (— 1935) of *do a stagger*, q.v.

take a toss. To ' fall for ' a person : coll. : C. 20.—2. As in Cecil Barr, *It's Hard to Sin*, 1935, ' In her set, the word adultery was not often mentioned. One went in off the deep end about somebody ; one took a toss, one even dropped a brick : one slid off the rails.' Ex hunting.

take a trip. To give up a job : tradesmen's (— 1909). Ware : ' Followed by movement searching for a new situation '.

take a tumble (to oneself). See **tumble, take a,** and **tumble to.**

take a wrong sow by the ear. See **sow.**

take an earth-bath. See **earth-bath.**

take an oath. To take a drink : late C. 19–early 20. Cf. *taking it easy.*

take and . . . (Gen. imperative.) To go and (do something) : lower class coll . C. 20. Manchon. Ex dial.

take and give. To live, esp. as man and wife : rhyming s. (— 1909). Ware.

*****take beef.** To run away : c. (— 1859) ; ob. H., 1st ed. Cf. *cry beef*, q.v.

take (one's) **Bradlaugh.** To take one's oath : 1883–ca. 85. Charles Bradlaugh was 'intimately associated with the Affirmation Bill ' (Ware).

take care of. To arrest : police coll. (— 1909). Ware. By meiosis.

take care of dowb. To look after ' No. 1 ' : political, ca. 1855–60. Ware. ? cf. dial. *dowb* = dial. *daub* = *dab*, an expert.

take charge. See **charge, take.**

take corner-pieces off. See **take off corner-pieces.**

take-down. A gross deception ; a swindle, trivial or grave : coll. : C. 20. Ex v., 2, q.v.—2. Hence, a thief, a cheat : Australian : from ca. 1910. Jice Doone.

take-down, v.t. To deceive grossly ; to swindle : coll. (orig. Australian) : 1895, *The Melbourne Argus*, Dec. 5, ' [The defendant] accused him of having taken him down, stigmatised him as a thief and a robber.'—2. In Australian sporting s., ' to induce a man to bet, knowing that he must lose . . . To advise a man to bet, and then to " arrange " with an accomplice (a jockey, e.g.) for the bet to be lost . . . To prove superior to a man in a game of skill ', Morris : from ca. 1895. From ca. 1920, coll.

take (one) **down a peg** or **take a peg lower.** See **peg.**

take eight ! You've won ! : a military c.p. of C. 20. F. & Gibbons. Ex points obtained at some game or other.

take (a person's) **eye.** To be appreciated by (a person) : tailors' coll. : C. 20. E.g. *The Tailor and Cutter*, Nov. 29, 1928.

take (a person) **for.** To impose on to the extent of (getting) ; to ' sting ' for : low : C. 20. James Curtis, *The Gilt Kid*, 1936, ' Good kid that Molly even if she had taken him for a oncer ' (£1).

take gruel. To die : lower classes' (— 1909). Ware. Ex gruel as staple food in long illness among the poor.

take gruel together, we or **they.** We or they live together as man and wife : 1884, *The Referee*, Dec. 14 ; † by 1890. Ware. Ex a euphemism in a police-court case late in 1884.

take his name, sergeant-major(, take his name) ! An Army c.p. : C. 20, though not gen. before the G.W. Ex the actual order so worded.

take-in. A (gross) deception, a swindle : 1778, Fanny Burney ; H., 1st ed., ' Sometimes termed " a dead take in " ' (†). Ex the v.—2. Hence, a person that, intentionally or not, deceives one : coll. : 1818, *Blackwood's*, ' There are . . . at least twenty take-ins . . . for one true heiress,' O.E.D. : — 3. Hence, occ. as adj. = deceptive : late C. 19–20. —4. A man that takes a woman in to dinner : coll. : 1898 (O.E.D. Sup.).

take in. To deceive, impose on, swindle : coll. : 1725, *A New Canting Dict.* ; 1897, ' Pomes ' Marshall, ' He was " dicky ", She was tricky— | Took him in, and cleared him out.' On *draw in.*—2. To believe or accept as ' gospel ' : coll. : 1864, ' The Undergraduates took it all in and cheered . . .', O.E.D.

take (a thing) **in snuff.** See **snuff.**

take in your washing ! A nautical c.p. ' order to a careless boat's crew to bring fenders, rope's ends, etc., inboard ' : late C. 19–20. Bowen.

take it. See **take the biscuit.**

take it out, v.i. ' To undergo imprisonment in lieu of a fine ', C. J. Dennis : low (? c.) Australian : C. 20.

take it out of that ! Fight away ! : London : ca. 1820–60. Bee, ' Accompanied by showing the elbow, and patting it '.

take-off. A mimic ; a mimicking, caricature, burlesque : coll. : from ca. 1850. Ex :

take off. To mimic, parody ; mock : coll. : 1750, Chesterfield (O.E.D.) ; 1766, Brooke, ' He . . . perfectly counterfeited or took off, as they call it, the real Christian.'

take off corner-pieces or **take corner-pieces off.** To beat or manhandle (esp. one's wife) : low urban (— 1909). Ware.

take on. To show emotion ; grieve, distress oneself greatly : C. 15–20 : S.E. until early C. 19, then coll. and dial. Whyte-Melville, 1868, ' There's Missis walking about the drawing-room, taking-on awful ' : that it had, ca. 1820, > a domestic servants' word appears from Scott, 1828, ' Her sister hurt her own cause by taking on, as the maid-servants call it, too vehemently.'—2. To become popular, ' catch on ' : 1897, ' Ouida ' (O.E.D.).—3. V.t., to engage (a person, or army) in a fight, a battle : coll. : C. 20. C. J. Dennis.

take on with. To take up with (a woman) : proletarian coll. (— 1923). Manchon. Ex dial.

take one's hook. To decamp ; run away : New Zealanders' : C. 20. Ex *sling one's hook.*

take one's last drink. See **last drink.**

take one's teeth to. To begin eating (something) heartily : coll. : late C. 19–20.

take (e.g. energy) **out of** (a person) is S.E., but *take it out of* (him) is coll. when = to tire or exhaust him (1887) and when = to exact satisfaction from, have revenge on him (1851, Mayhew). Baumann ; F. & H. : O.E.D.

take sights. See **sights, take.**

take that fire-poker out of your spine and the (or those) **lazy-tongs out of your fish-hooks** (hands) ! A nautical c.p. of adjuration to rid oneself of laziness : late C. 19–20.

take the air. To fly : Air Force jocular coll. : from 1916. F. & Gibbons.

take the aspro. An Australian variant of *take the cake* : 1934 ; ob. Suggested by *Aspro* advertisements, esp. slogans.

take the biscuit. A variant (— 1923) of *take the bun.* Manchon notes also *take it.*

take the bun. See **bun, take the.** A lower-classes' variant of ca. 1900–14 is *take the kettle* (Ware).

take the cake. See **cake, take the.**

take the can back. To be reprimanded ; see **carry the can (back)** : nautical and military : late C. 19–20. Bowen. Perhaps ex illicit usage of its contents.—2. To be held responsible for a mishap : railwaymen's : from ca. 1919. *The Daily Herald*, Aug. 11, 1936.—3. To be imposed on : road-transport workers' : from ca. 1925. Ibid. Cf. *carry the can*, q.v.

take the count. See **count . . .**

take the Huntley and Palmer. See **Huntley and Palmer.—take the kettle.** See **take the bun.**

take the number off the door. A c.p. of ca. 1895–1915, applied to a house where the wife is a shrew. Ware, ' The removal of the number would make the cottage less discoverable.'

*****take the stripes out.** To remove, with acid, the

crossing on a cheque : **o.** (— 1933). Charles E. Leach.

take the tiles off (the roof), enough (or **sufficient**) **to.** Extremely extravagant(ly) : Society : ca. 1878–1910. Ware.

take too much. To drink too much liquor ; drink liquor very often indeed : coll. verging on S.E. : late C. 19–20. Perhaps orig. euphemistic.

take to one's land-tacks. To go ashore for a spree : nautical : late C. 19–20. Bowen.

take-up. A point at which a passenger gets in : coachmen's and cabmen's coll. (— 1887) ; ob. Baumann.

take up savings for. To do without (a thing) : nautical : C. 20. Bowen.

take your washing in, Ma ; here come(s) the (name of unit). A military c.p. addressed, on the line of march, by one unit to another : late C. 19–20. B. & P.

*****taker** is a contemporaneous variant of *taker-up*, q.v. Greene, 1591. (In *Barnard's law*, q.v.)

taker-in. The agent of *take in*, v., 1 : coll. (— 1887). Baumann.

*****taker-up.** He who, in a gang of four swindlers, breaks the ice with, and ' butters up ', the prospective victim : c. of ca. 1590–1620. Greene, 1591.

taking. Attractive, charming, captivating : C. 17–20 : S.E. until early C. 19, then coll. Cf. *taky*.

taking any (occ. with object expressed), **not to be.** To be disinclined for : ca. 1900–10. *The Daily News*, March 10, 1900, ' In the language of the hour, "nobody was taking any".' Perhaps orig. of liquor. Now, and long, *not having any*.

taking it easy. Tipsy : ca. 1880–1914. Perhaps ex *take one's ease in one's inn*, to enjoy oneself as if at home.

taky. ' Taking ', q.v. : coll. ; in C. 20, ob. : 1854, Wilkie Collins, ' Those two difficult and delicate operations in art technically described as " putting in taky touches, and bringing out bits of effect " ', O.E.D. correcting F. & H.

tale, pitch a. To spin a yarn : coll. : late C. 19–20.

tale !, tell that for a. A c.p. indicative of incredulity : from ca. 1870.

tale, tell the. To tell a begging-story ; to make love : C. 20.—2. To tell an incredible or a woeful tale ; from ca. 1910. (Esp. among soldiers.)—3. Hence, to explain away (gen. one's own) military offences and delinquencies : military : from ca. 1914. B. & P.

tale-pitcher. A ' romancer ' : coll. : from ca. 1890. Ex *tale, pitch a*.

talent, the. Backers of horses as opp. the bookmakers : sporting coll. >, ca. 1910, j. : from the early 1880's. Clever because they make a horse a favourite.

Taliano. An Italian : mostly lower classes' : C. 20. Ex It. *Italiano*.

talk. To talk about, discuss : late C. 14–20 : S.E. until ca. 1850, then coll.—2. (Of a horse) to roar : stable s. (— 1864) > coll. H., 3rd ed.—3. See **talking** and **talks**.

talk big or **tall.** To talk braggingly or turgidly : resp. coll., 1699, L'Estrange (O.E.D.) ; and s. (— 1888), orig. U.S. Coulson Kernahan, 1900, ' Public men who talk tall about the sacredness of labour '. Cf. **tall**, 1 and 2.

talk by a bow. To quarrel : London lower classes' : ca. 1860–82. Ware.

talk it out. See **talker**, 2.—**talk nineteen to the dozen.** See **nineteen** . . .

talk the hind leg off a bird (Apperson), **cow, dog, donkey** (Baumann), **horse** (mainly dial.), **jackass**, etc. ; or **talk a bird's** (etc.) **hind leg off.** To wheedle, to charm ; to talk excessively, often with implication of successful persuasion : coll. : Cobbett, 1808 (' horse's hind leg ') ; Beckett, 1838, ' By George, you'd talk a dog's hind leg off.' In C. 20, often *talk the leg off a brass pan* (dial.) or *saucepan* (not *brass s.*).

talk through one's hat. See **hat, talk** . . .—**talk through (the back of) one's neck.** See **neck, talk** . . .

talk to. To rebuke, scold : coll. : 1878, W. S. Gilbert (O.E.D.). Ex lit. sense.—2. To discuss as being likely to reach (a certain figure or price) : Stock Exchange coll. : from ca. 1920. ' Securitas ' in *Time and Tide*, Sept. 22, 1934, ' Local loans are up to the new high level (post-war) of 93$\frac{11}{16}$, and are being talked to 100.'

talkee-talkee house, the. Parliament : London jocular (— 1887). Baumann. Cf. *talky-talk*.

talker. A horse that ' roars ' : stable s. : from ca. 1870. Ex *talk*, v., 2.—2. From ca. 1860, as in Howson & Warner, *Harrow School*, 1898, ' Then followed solos from those who could sing, and those who could not—it made no difference. The latter class were called talkers, and every boy was encouraged to stand up and talk it out.'

talkie, talky. (Gen. pl.) A moving picture with words : 1928 (S.O.D.) : coll. >, by 1935, S.E. On *movie*, q.v.

talking !, now you're. Now you're saying something arresting, important, amusing : coll. : from ca. 1880. O.E.D. (Sup.).

talks, money. Money is might, influence : coll. : from ca. 1910. (O.E.D. Sup.) Prob. ex preceding.

talky-talk. Idle or pointless or trivial talk : coll. : C. 20. (O.E.D. Sup.) Cf. *talkee-talkee house*, q.v.

tall. (Of talk) grandiloquent, high-flown : coll. : 1670, Eachard, ' Tall words and lofty notions ', O.E.D.—2. Hence, extravagant ; exaggerated : U.S. (1844, Kendall) : anglicised, esp. as *tall talk* (Baumann) or *tall story*, in the eighties ; by 1920, coll.—3. (Very) large or big or (of speed) great or (of time) long : U.S. (ca. 1840) ; anglicised ca. 1860. ' " Very tall " scoring ' (in cricket), 1864 (Lewis) ; H., 5th ed. ; ' Pomes ' Marshall, 1897, ' Her cheek was fairly " tall ".' Ex sense 1 or, more prob. (despite contradictoriness of earliest records), ex sense 2.—4. ? hence, excellent ; first-rate : orig.—ca.1840—and mainly U.S. Baumann, 1887, ' We had a tall time (of it)—*wir hatten lustige Tage*.' (Often hardly distinguishable from preceding sense.)

tall, to talk. See **talk big.**

*****tall-men, tallmen.** Dice so loaded as to turn up 4, 5 or 6 : c. of late C. 16–early 17. Kyd, 1592 (O.E.D.). Cf. *highmen*.

tall order. See **order.**

tall ship is catachrestic when applied to a steamer : C. 20. Bowen.

tall 'un. A ' pint of coffee, half a pint being a short 'un ' : urban lower classes' : late C. 19–20. Ware.

tall-water man. A blue-water (or deep-sea) seaman : nautical coll. : C. 20. Bowen.

tallow, piss one's. See **p. one's t.**

tallow-breeched. With fat behind : C. 18–mid-19. Cf. :

tallow-gutted. Pot-bellied : low coll. : C. 18–mid-19.

tally. A name : nautical : C. 20. Bowen. Ex *tally*, a mark, label, or tab.

tally, v.t. To reckon (*that* . . .) : coll. : 1860 (O.E.D.) ; ob. Ex *tally*, to count.

tally, live (rarely *on*). To live in concubinage : chiefly mining districts (— 1864). H., 3rd ed. Ex *tally*, a corresponding half or part of anything. Whence :

tally-husband or -man. A man living thus : from 1870's. On :

tally-wife or -woman. A woman living thus : resp. early 1860's (H., 3rd ed.) and late 1880's. Like preceding, mostly Northern. See **tally, live.**

tallywag ; occ. **tarriwag.** The penis : late C. 18–20 ; ob., except in Derbyshire and Cheshire dial.— 2. Gen. in pl., the testicles : resp. late C. 18–20 (Grose, 1st ed.) and C. 17–20 (' Water-Poet ' Taylor ; Grose ; Beckett, 1838). ? origin, unless ex *tally*, the corresponding half, + (to) *wag*, v.i., an etymology that fits sense 1, since this sense derives ex sense 2.

tam ; tammy. A tam-o'-shanter : from mid-1890's : coll. >, by 1900, S.E.

Tam of the Cowgate. Sir Thomas Hamilton, noted mid-C. 16 Scottish lawyer. Dawson.

tamarinds. Money : dispensing chemists' (— 1909). Ware. For semantics, cf. *syrup*, q.v.

tamaroo. Noisy : Anglo-Irish (— 1909). Ware. Cf. Erse *tormánać*, noisy.

tamasha. Anything entertaining or exciting ; an entertainment, a display : Regular Army : late C. 19–20. F. & Gibbons. Ex Hindustani.

tame cat. ' A woman's fetch-and-carry ' : coll. : from ca. 1870 ; ob. Ex S.E. sense.

tame jolly. See **jolly,** n. (naval sense).—**tammy.** See **tam.**

*****tamtart.** A girl : c. : 1845, in ' *No. 747* '. **A** perversion of *jam tart* or possibly its original.

tan ; tan one's hide. To beat severely ; to thrash : resp. s., mid-C. 19–20 (H., 1859) ; and coll., mid-C. 17–20. Mrs Henry Wood, 1862, ' The master couldn't tan him for not doing it.' Ex *hide*, human skin, + *tan*, to treat it.—2. Hence, to overwork (a means of livelihood) : grafters' : C. 20. Philip Allingham, *Cheapjack*, 1934.

tandem. ' A two wheeled chaise, buggy, or noddy, drawn by two horses, one before the other ', Grose, 1st ed. : s. >, ca. 1820, coll. >, ca. 1850, S.E. Prob. university wit, ex *tandem*, at length, so frequent in L. classical authors (esp. Cicero).—2. A pair of carriage horses thus harnessed : 1795, W. Felton (*tandum*, an erroneous form : O.E.D.) : s. >, ca. 1820, coll. >, ca. 1850, S.E—3. Ex sense 1, influenced by sense 2, as adv. : one behind the other : 1795 (O.E.D.) : same evolution of status.— 4. As adj., long : Cambridge University : ca. 1870–90. Ware, ' Used in speaking of a tall man '.

Tangerines or Tangierines, the. The 2nd Foot Regiment >, in late C. 19, the Queen's (Royal West Surrey).—2. The 4th Foot > the King's Own (Royal Lancaster Regt.). Both, military : ? C. 17–20 ; ob. These regiments were raised to defend Tangiers, part of the dowry of Charles II's wife.— 3. See :

Tangier. ' A room in Newgate, where debtors were confined, hence called Tangerines ', Grose, 3rd ed. : c. or low s. of ca. 1785–1840.

tangle-foot. Whiskey : U.S. (— 1860), partly anglicised ca. 1900. Ex effect.

tangle-monger. One ' who fogs and implies everything ' : Society : ca. 1870–1905. Ware.

tank. Incorrect abbr. of *copped tank* : late C. 17–

early 18. O.E.D.—2. A safe : New Zealand c. (— 1932). Ex its resemblance to a small cubic tank.—3. A wet canteen : Regular Army : late C. 19–20. F. & Gibbons.

tank, v. To cane : King Edward's School, Birmingham : from ca. 1870. Ex dial. *tank*, a blow.

tank up. To drink much liquor : U.S. (ca. 1900), anglicised ca. 1916, esp. in the Army. O.E.D. (Sup.) ; F. & Gibbons. Cf. *tanked*.

tankard, tears of the. Liquor-drippings on a waistcoat : coll. : ca. 1670–1830. Ray, 1678 ; B.E., and Grose at *tears*. (Apperson.)

tanked. Tipsy : from early 1917. Prob. ex *tank*, n., 3 ; perhaps suggested by *canned*, q.v., though the term may have originated among soldiers with the floundering of the tanks in the mud of Flanders and Picardy in late 1916–early '17. (' Tanks first went into action at Pozières ridge, Sep. 5, 1916,' W.)

tanker. A steamer fitted for carrying tanks of oil : 1900 : coll. >, by 1930, S.E. (O.E.D. Sup.)

tanky. The foreman of the hold, ' which ooks like a tank ' (Ware) : naval (— 1909).—2. The navigator's assistant : naval : from ca. 1912. Bowen. Because responsible for the fresh water.

tanned, ppl.adj. Beaten (severely), thrashed : perhaps as early as 1860. Ex *tan*.

tanner. A sixpence : low (— 1811) >, ca. 1870, gen. s. *Lex. Bal.* ; Dickens, 1844. Etymology problematic : H., 1st ed., suggests Gypsy *tawno*, young, hence little ; in 2nd ed., L. *tener*. But see the note at *simon*, 1.—2. Whence *tannercab*, a sixpenny cab (1908, O.E.D.) and *tannergram*, a telegram (when, early in 1896, the minimum cost was reduced from 1*s.* to 6*d.*) ; both terms † by 1920, the telegram-rate having been raised to ninepence during the War and to one shilling in 1920. The return, in 1936, of the sixpenny telegram has not revived the term.

tanner and skin. Money : tanners' : ca. 1855–1900. H., Introduction.

tanning. A thrashing : mid-C. 19–20. Ex preceding, q.v. Cf. *tanned*.

tanny. A mid-C. 19 variant of *teeny*. H., 1st ed.

tansnear. B.E.'s misprint for *transnear*.

[**'Tant, Tantest.** ' Mast of a Ship or Man, Tall, Tallest ', B.E. This cryptic entry should read : ' *Tant, Tantest.* Of a Ship's-mast or of a Man : Tall, Tallest.' It is a nautical adj., gen. spelt *taunt*.]

'tan't. See **taint.**—**tantadlin, tautaublin.** See **tantoblin.**—**tantarum.** See **tantrum.**

Tantivy. A post-Restoration true-blue Tory or High Churchman : ca. 1680–1740, but esp. ca. 1681–89. G. Hickes, *The Spirit of Popery*, 1680–1 ; B.E., '. . . Or Latitudinarians a lower sort of Flyers, like Batts, between Church-men and Dissenters ' ; Swift, 1730. Ex a caricature representing High Church clerics ' riding tantivy ' to Rome, and partly ; a satire on the hunting parson and squire. O.E.D., F. & H.—2. (*tantivy.*) Incorrect as imitative of the sound of a horn : C. 18–20. Ex *tantivy* as imitation of galloping feet. O.E.D.—3. Likewise as imitative of flourish of a horn : from ca. 1780. Grose, 1st ed.

Tantivy-Boy ; **t.-b.** Same as *Tantivy* (1), q.v.: ca. 1690–1710. Motteux ; B.E.

tantoblin ; **tantadlin** (**tart**). A lump of excrement : s. and dial. : resp. 1654, Gayton : 1785. Grose (*t. tart*). † by ca. 1840. Ex *tantablin*, etc., a tart or round pasty : extant in dial. In C. 17. occ. *tantaublin.*

tantrems. 'Pranks, capers, or frolicking', H., 1st ed. : coll. or s. : ca. 1850–1910. Ex *tantrums*, q.v., + the dial. senses of the same + the occ. dial. spelling *tantrim*. (H. thought *tantrem* distinct from :)

tantrum ; occ., though in C. 20 very ob., **tantarum ;** in H., 1st ed., **tantrem.** (Gen. in pl.) A display of petulance ; a fit of anger : coll. : 1748, Foote, 'I am glad here's a husband coming that will take you down in your tantrums' ; Grose, 1st ed. ; Reade. Possibly, as H., 2nd ed. (though actually of *tantrems*), suggests, ex the *tarantula* (1693, O.E.D.), properly *tarantella* (not till 1782 ?), a rapid, whirling Italian dance ; but perhaps rather ex the cognate *tarantism*, that hysterical malady which expresses, or tends to express, itself in dancing frenziedly, for *tarantism*, recorded ca. 1640, might easily be corrupted to *tant(a)rums*, the singular not appearing before C. 19. Less prob. ex *trantran*, a tantara, for it does not occur in C. 18. Much, much less prob. ex :—2. (Frequent in singular.) The penis : 1675, Cotton in *The Scoffer Scofft* ; app. † by 1800. Possibly cognate with North Country *tantril* (a vagrant, a Gypsy), recorded as early as 1684 (E.D.D.); cf. the later G.W. dial. *tantrum-bolus*, a noisy child, —which, however, is presumably ex *tantrum*, 1.— 3. See **tantrems**.

tanyard, the. The poor-house : Caithness s., not dial. : ca. 1850–80. Pejorative. E.D.D., 'Very common for some years after the Poor Law Act, 1845. The paupers had the greatest aversion to indoor relief and called the Poorhouse by this name.'

taoc, toac ; tog (not properly back s.) A coat : back s. (— 1859). H., 1st ed., has also *toac-tisaw*, a waistcoat ; F. & H., 1904, adds *taoc-ittep*, a petticoat. The correct form, *taoc*, app. appears first in H., 3rd ed., 1864 ; and H., 1874, notes that ' " Cool the *delo taoc* " means, " Look at the old coat," but is really intended to apply to the wearer as well.'

tap. A **tap**-house or -room : s. (— 1725) >, early in C. 19, coll. *A New Canting Dict.*, 1725 ; T. Hughes, 1857.—2. ' Liquor drawn from a particular tap ' : from ca. 1620, though not certainly recorded before 1832 ; fig., however, used in 1623, 'A Gentleman of the first Tappe ' (cf. *of the first water*). O.E.D., both senses.—3. A wound : military : from 1915. F. & Gibbons.—4. A sunstroke : Regular Army's : C. 20. Cf. *doolally tap*.

tap, v.i. To spend, pay up, freely : ca. 1712–20. Addison ; Steele. Semantics, ' to " turn on the tap " of gifts ', O.E.D.—2. V.t., to broach, in these s. senses : *tap a guinea*, to change it (Grose, 2nd ed.), † by 1890 ; *tap a house*, to burgle it (late C. 19–20, ob.) ; *tap a girl*, to deflower her (Grose, 2nd ed.),—in C. 19–20, often *tap a judy* ; *tap one's claret* (1823, ' Jon Bee '), to make one's nose bleed, *tap by* itself occurring in Dickens, 1840 (O.E.D.) but ob. by 1900, † by 1930 ; *tap the admiral*, see **admiral**.—3. To arrest ; also *tap* (one) *on the shoulder* (implied in Grose, 1st ed., ' a tap on the shoulder, an arrest ') : coll. ; resp. † by 1890, and ob.—4. See **tap for**.

tap, do the. To win at cards : military : late C. 19–20. F. & Gibbons. Prob. ex :

tap, get the. To obtain the mastery : tailors' : from ca. 1870.

*tap, on the. Begging for money : c. (— 1933). Charles E. Leach. Cf. :

tap (a person) **for.** To ask (him) for (money) : C. 20. Suggested by *sting*, 2 ; ex *tap*, to hit,— therefore contrast *tap*, **v.**, 1, q.v.

tap-lash. A publican : coll. : ca. 1648–1750. Ex *t.-l.*, inferior beer.

tap on the shoulder, n., and v. See **tap, v.**, third sense.—**tap one's claret.** See **tap, v.**, 2.

tap the Admiral, he would. He'd do anything for a drink : naval : late C. 19–20. Bowen, ' From the old naval myth that when Lord Nelson's body was being brought home seamen contrived to get at the rum in which it was preserved '. Cf. *tap*, v., 2, q.v.

Tap-Tub, the. *The Morning Advertiser* : ca. 1820–80 : book-world. Bee, 1823, ' Because that print catcheth the drippings of yesterday's news, and disheth it up anew ' ; H., 1864, ' So called by vulgar people [because it] is the principal organ of the London brewers and publicans. Sometimes termed *The Gin and Gospel Gazette*.'

*tape. Strong liquor : c. (— 1725) >, ca. 1840, (low) s. *A New Canting Dict.*—2. Occ. gin : from ca. 1820 ; H., 1859, having ' *tape*, gin,—term with female servants ', and Egan's Grose quoting from Randall's *Scrap Book*. Gen., however, *white tape* (1725) is gin, as occ. is †*Holland tape* (1755) and rarely †*blue t.* (1785, Grose) ; *red tape* (1725) is brandy ; loosely (as in Grose, 1st ed.), *red*, *white*, *blue t.*, any spirituous liquor. For semantics, cf. *ribbon*, q.v.—3. Sending messages by ' tic-tac men ' (q.v.) : turf : ca. 1885–1910. MS. note in B.M. copy of H., 5th ed.

tape-worm. An official collecting prices of stock for transmission on the *tape* : Stock Exchange : not before 1884. Punning the parasite. Cf. *ticker*, an account.—2. A speculator constantly watching the price-tape : id. : from not later than 1923. Manchon.

taped, be ; gen. **have** or **have got** (one) **taped.** In these phrases, *taped* = sized-up ; detected ; so seenthrough as to be rendered incapable of harm, mischief, etc. : orig. (1916), military >, ca. 1920, gen. B. & P. ; Lyell. Ex *tape*, to measure (something) with a tape—on *tacked*, *have one*, q.v.—with esp. reference to the Engineer-laid tapes along which the Infantry lay waiting for the signal to attack when there was no trench or sunken road convenient as a jumping-off place.—2. Hence, from ca. 1920, *taped* often = arranged, or settled, as in Ronald Knox, *The Body in the Silo*, 1933, ' Let's get the whole thing taped.' Also *taped up* (G. D. H. & M. Cole, 1927).

Taper. A ' seeker after profitable office ' : political : 1897, *The Daily Telegraph*, April 27 ; ob. Ware. Ex *red tape*. Cf. *Tadpole*, q.v.

taper, v.t. To give over gradually ; v.i., to run short : from late 1850's. H., 1st ed. Ex :

taper, adj. (Of supplies, money) decreasing : 1851, Mayhew (O.E.D.); ob. Lit., (becoming) slender (cf. *slender chance*). Cf. also the later *thin* (*time*, etc.). See, too, **taper, run** : Addenda.

taper off, v.i. To leave off gradually ; esp. to lessen gradually the amount and/or strength of one's drink : coll. : from ca. 1870 ; ob. Ex *taper*, v., q.v.

tapes, on the. Ready to commence : military coll. : from 1916. F. & Gibbons. For semantics see **taped, be**.

tapis, on the. Possible ; rumoured : diplomatic coll. (— 1909) verging on S.E. Ware.

tapped. Eccentric ; slightly mad : military : C. 20. B. & P. Cf. *cracked* and S.E. *touched*.

tapper (C. 19) ; **shoulder-tapper** (ca. 1780–1910). A bailiff ; a policeman. Grose, 1st ed. ; F. & H. Prob. on much earlier *shoulder-clapper*, q.v. Ex *tap*, v., 3.—2. One who broaches casks of wine or spirits and drinks therefrom with a straw : low coll. (— 1923). Manchon.—3. A beggar : Glasgow (— 1934). Ex *tap for*. Also tramps' c. (— 1936). W. A. Gape, *Half a Million Tramps*.

tapping, vbl.n. Begging : Glasgow (— 1934). Ex *tap for*.

tappy, on the. Under consideration : mid-C. 19–20 : low coll. Ex Fr. *tapis*, carpet, imm., however, ex the S.E. (*up*)*on the tapis*.

taps. The ears : ? mid-C. 18–mid-19. Because they tap conversation. F. & H.

Tapsky. Lord Shaftesbury. Cf. *Shiftesbury* ; see **Old Tony.** Dawson.

tar. A sailor : coll. : 1676, Wycherley, ' Dear tar, thy humble servant ' ; Dibdin in *Tom Bowling*, 1790 ; Macaulay, 1849. Abbr. *tarpaulin*, q.v. Cf. *tarry-breeks*.

tar, lose a ship. . . See **sheep, lose a.**

tar-box. A heavy shell, with esp. reference to its burst (see the more gen. **coal-box**) : military : 1915–18. F. & Gibbons.

tar-brush. A tarboosh : among wanderers, esp. in India (— 1886). Ex Hindustani ex Persian *sarposh*, lit. head-cover. Yule & Burnell.

tar out. To punish, ' serve out ' : coll. : ca. 1860–1910. H., 3rd ed. Cf. S.E. *tar on*, but perhaps suggested by *tar and feather*. Cf. :

tar out of, beat the. To thrash soundly : from ca. 1920. Michael Harrison, *Spring in Tartarus*, 1935.

tar-tar. A rare † variant of *ta-ta*, q.v.

taradiddle. See **tarradiddle.**

taradiddler. A fibber : 1880 (O.E.D.) : s. >, by 1900, coll. ; ob. Ex preceding.

tarantula. Incorrect for, but perhaps orig. form of, *tarantella*.

tardy. Late with, at, in doing ; e.g. ' I was tardy task,' I was late with my work : Winchester College : mid-C. 19–20. Also *tarde*.

tare an' ouns ! An Anglo-Irish oath : C. 19–20. Ware. Corruption of *tears and wounds* (*of Christ*).

tare and tret. ' City bon-ton for—a Rowland for an Oliver ', Bee : ca. 1820–50. Ex *t. and t.*, ' the two ordinary deductions in calculating the net weight of goods to be sold by retail ', O.E.D.

taring. See **tearing.** C. 17–early 18.

tarmac, on the. ' Detailed for flying duty ' : Air Force : from 1915. F. & Gibbons. Ex ' the tarmac . . . laid down in front of a hangar '.—2. Hence, *tarmac* = any landing ground : R.A.F. (— 1935). Less gen. than synonymous *deck*.

tarnal. ' Confounded ' : dial. >, early in C. 19, low coll. ; mostly U.S. Ex *eternal*.

tarnation, n., damnation ; adj., adv., ' confounded(ly) ' : late C. 18–20 : rather illiterate coll. and mostly U.S. Ex *damnation* (cf. *darnation*), the adj. and adv. being influenced by *tarnal*.

tarp or **Tarp.** An ecclesiastical (Anglican) c.p., of ca. 1920 onwards, ' used of those ministrants who take the Ablutions immediately after the Communion instead of after the Blessing ' (R. Ellis Roberts, in private letter of Oct. 18, 1933). I.e. ' take Ablutions in right place '.

tarpaulin ; occ., though not after ca. 1850, **tarpawlin.** A sailor : coll. : 1647, Cleveland ; Bailey, 1725 ; Stevenson, 1893 (O.E.D.) ; Frank C. Bowen, 1930, ' A practical seaman, particularly applied when appointments went by favour rather than by merit.' In C. 20, only archaic ; ob., indeed, by 1870. Tar much used by sailors. Cf. *tar* and *tarry-breeks* ; also *Jack tar*.

tarpaulin muster. A forecastle collection of money, esp. to buy liquor : nautical coll. : late C. 19–20. Bowen. The money is thrown on to a tarpaulin.

tar(r)adiddle. A lie, esp. a petty one : from ca. 1790 : s. >, in mid-C. 19, coll. ; by 1930, slightly ob. Grose, 3rd ed. (*tara-*). On *diddle*, the *tar(r)a-* being problematic : cf. *tarrywags* (at *tallywag*) and *tara !*, an exclamation used by Dryden. Hence : **tar(r)adiddle**, v.i. To tell fibs : coll. (— 1916). O.E.D.—2. V.t., to hoax, impose on, bewilder, by telling lies : s. >, by late C. 19, coll. ; by 1930, ob. : 1828, *The Examiner*, ' His enemies . . . squibbed . . . and taradiddled him to death,' O.E.D. Cf. the ob. dial. *taradiddled*, puzzled, bewildered.

tarriwag. See **tallywag.**

tarry-breeks, -jacket, -John. A sailor : coll. jocular nicknames : resp. orig. (1785, Forbes), Scottish ; 1822, Scott (O.E.D.) ; 1888, Stevenson (ib.) : second and third, † by 1930 ; first, ob. by 1920. According to Bowen, ' a naval ranker officer ' in C. 17. Cf. *tar* and *tarpaulin*, qq.v.

tars or **Tars.** Shares in the Tharsis Copper Mining Company : Stock Exchange (— 1895). A. J. Wilson's glossary.

tart. A girl or woman (but if old, always *old tart*) : from early 1860's. Orig. endearingly and of chaste and unchaste alike ; but by 1904 (F. & H.) only of fast or immoral women,—a tendency noted as early as 1884 (Ware) ; by 1920—except in Australia (where, from before 1898, it = a sweetheart and where it is still applied also to any girl)— only of prostitutes. H., 3rd ed. (1864), ' *Tart*, a term of approval applied by the London lower orders to a young woman for whom some affection is felt ' ; *The Morning Post*, Jan. 25, 1887 ; Baumann, 1887, ' My tart—*mein Schätzchen* ' ; in late 1880's, the occ. diminutive *tartlet* (Barrère & Leland) : ' Pomes ' Marshall, 1896 ; above all, F. & H. ; B. & P. Ex the idea of sweetness in a woman and a *jam-tart* : cf. *sweetness* as a term of address.—2. The young favourite of one of the older boys ; not necessarily a catamite : Scottish Public Schools' : C. 20. Ian Miller, *School Tie*, 1935. Whence *tarting*, this practice.

*tartar ; T. (Properly *Tatar*. ' The *r* was inserted in mediæval times to suggest that the Asiatic hordes who occasioned such anxiety to Europe came from hell (Tartarus), and were the locusts of Revelation ix,' *The Century Dict.*) A thief, strolling vagabond, sharper : c. : 1598, Shakespeare, ' Here's a Bohemian Tartar ' ; B.E. ; † by 1780. Abbr. *Tartarian*, q.v.—2. An adept : from ca. 1780 ; ob. Grose, 1st ed., ' He is quite a tartar at cricket, or billiards.' Ex *to catch a Tartar*. Cf. *hot stuff*, q.v.

*Tartar, catch a. ' Said, among the Canting Varlets, when a Rogue attacks one that he thinks a Passenger, but proves to be of [the 59th order of rogues], who, in his Turn, having overcome the Assailant, robs, plunders, and binds him,' *A New Canting Dict.*, 1725 : c. : C. 18. Ex *tartar*, 1.

*Tartarian. A strolling vagrant ; a thief ; a sharper or swindler : c. : though prob. from 1590's, not recorded before 1608, *The Merry Devil of Edmonton* ; † by 1690. Nares. Ex *Tartarian*, a native of Central Asia, the home of a warlike race.

tarting. See **tart, 2.**

tartlet. See **tart, 1.** (After ca. 1910, rare and ' literary '.)

tassel. An undergraduate : university s. of ca. 1828–40. Because his cap has a tassel. Cf. *tuft*, q.v.—2. See **pencil and tassel.**

Tassy, Tassie. (Pronounced *Tazzy*.) Tasmania : Australian coll. : from ca. 1890.—2. Hence, in C. 20, a Tasmanian. Cf. the two senses of *Aussie*.

taste, a, adv. A little ; slightly : coll. : 1894, Hall Caine, ' Nancy will tidy the room a taste,' O.E.D. (Cf. *a bit* used adverbially.) In Anglo-Irish, it dates from the 1820's (E.D.D.).

taste of the creature. See **creature.**

taste the sun. To enjoy the sunlight : Cockneys' : ca. 1877–1900. Ware. Cf. *see the breeze.*

taster. ' A portion of ice-cream served in a [*taster* or] shallow glass ' : coll. : from ca. 1890. Ware.

tastey ; properly **tasty.** Appetising : from ca. 1615 : S.E. until mid-C. 19, then coll. Buckle, ca. 1862, ' A tasty pie '.—2. Hence, pleasant, attractive : from mid-1790's : S.E. until mid-C. 19, then coll. ; ob. except where it merges with senses 1 and 4.—3. Elegant : from ca. 1760 : S.E. until ca. 1870, then coll. ; rare in C. 20.—4. Hence, of the best : late C. 19–20 : coll. verging on s. ' Pomes ' Marshall, ' He's fond of something tasty . . . me and him was spliced last Monday week.'—5. (Ex sense 1.) Sexually alluring, ' spicy ' : from 1890's : s. rather than coll. ; slightly ob. Whiteing, 1899, ' Nice and tastey, observes my friend . . . as he points to a leg that seems to fear nothing on earth . . . not even Lord Campbell's Act.'

tasty-looking. Appetising : coll. : from mid-1860's. Ex *tasty*, 1, q.v.

*****tat.** See **tats.**—2. A rag ; esp. an old rag : c. : 1839, Brandon ; 1851, Mayhew. Hence, *milky tats*, white rags or linen (Brandon). Ex *tatter*.—3. Abbr. *tattoo*, a pony (esp. for polo) : Anglo-Indian coll. (1840) >, by 1910, S.E. Yule & Burnell. Also *tatt*.

*****tat,** v.i. To gather rags, be a rag-gatherer : c. : 1851, Mayhew. Prob. ex *tat*, n., 2.—2. V.t., to thrash, flog : low s. (— 1812) ; † by 1890. Vaux. Ex dial. *tat*, to pat or tap.

*****tat-box.** A dice-box : c. (— 1859). H., 1st ed. Ex *tats*, q.v. Cf. :

*****tat-monger** ; **tatogey.** A sharper using loaded dice : c. : resp. late C. 17–20, ob. (Shadwell, 1688, and Grose, 1st ed.) ; late C. 19–20 (F. & H.). Ex *tats*, q.v. ; but what is the second element of *tatogey* ? Perhaps *bogey* or it may be F. & H.'s mistake.

*****tat-shop.** A gambling-den : c. (— 1823). Egan's Grose. See *tats*.

tata. See **ta-ta** !, 2, and **ta-ta's, go.**

tater, 'tatur. A potato : dial. and low coll. : C. 19–20. Cf. *tatie*, *tatto*.

tater (etc.), **on for a.** Fascinated ; esp. of a man by a barmaid : lower classes' (— 1909). Ware. I.e. ready for a *tête-à-tête*.

tater !, **s'elp my.** The earliest form (— 1860) of *taters !*, *s'welp my* : see **swelp.** H., 2nd ed. A variation is *s'elp my greens !* For hidden sense, see **strain one's taters.**

tater, settle a person's. To thrash him : proletarian (— 1923). Manchon.

tater-and-point. A meal of potatoes : low coll. : mid-C. 19–20. See **point.**

tater-skying. A game in which one throws potatoes up in the air and returns them, with a toss from the top of one's head, to one's opponent : proletarian coll. (— 1923). Manchon.

tater-trap. The mouth : low : 1838, Beckett ; 1856, Mayhew. See **tater.**

taters, settle one's. To settle one's hash : low s. (and Shropshire dial.) : late C. 19–20 ; ob. On *settle one's hash*. Contrast *tater, settle*. . .

taters, strain one's. See **strain one's taters.**—**taters** !, **s'welp my.** See **tater, s'elp my,** and **swelp.**

tatie, 'tato. A potato : dial. and low coll. : C. 19–20. Cf. *tater*, q.v.

taties in the mould. Cold (adj.) : rhyming s. : late C. 19–20. *John o' London's Weekly*, June 9, 1934.

*****tatler.** See **tattler.**—**'tato.** See **tatie.**

tatol. A tutor in Commoners : Winchester College : from ca. 1870. It looks like a corrupted-ending blend of ' *tutor* ' and ' Commoners ', perhaps punning (a) *tattle*.

*****tats, tatts.** Dice ; esp. false dice : c. : 1688, Shadwell ; Grose, 1st ed. ; Henley, 1887, ' Rattle the tats, or mark the spot.' Perhaps ex *tat*, to touch lightly : cf. *tat*, v., 2.

*****tats and all** ! Same as *bender !*, q.v. : c. : ca. 1810–50. Vaux. Ex preceding : cf. *some hopes !*

*****tat's-man** ; **tatsman.** A dicer, esp. if sharping : c. : 1825, Westmacott (O.E.D.). Ex *tats*.

tatt. See **tat,** n., 3.—*****tatt-box, -monger, -shop.** See **tat-box,** etc.

Tattenham Corner. ' The narrow water-way entrance into the Firth of Forth from May Island to Inchkeith, where German submarines constantly lurked, always passed by the British Fleet at full speed ' : a Grand Fleet nickname : 1915 ; now only historical. F. & Gibbons. The allusion is to a famous corner on a famous English race-course.

*****tatter.** A rag-gatherer : c. : from ca. 1860. Ex *tat*, v., 1. Also *tatterer* ; from the early 1890's.

*****tatter,** v.i. To collect rags ; be a rag-gatherer : c. : from ca. 1860. ? ex *tat*, n., 2.—2. As a variant of *totter*, it is incorrect—and rare.—3. V.t., in *tatter a kip*, to wreck a brothel : 1766, Goldsmith ; † by 1830.

*****tatterdemal(l)ion.** ' A tatter'd Beggar, sometimes half Naked, with Design to move Charity, having better Cloaths at Home ', *A New Canting Dict.*, 1725 : c. : C. 18. Ex lit. S.E. sense.

*****tatterer.** See **tatter, n.**

tattie. A potato : dial. and low coll., mostly Scots : C. 19–20. Cf. *tatie*.

*****tattle.** An occ. C. 18–mid-19 variant, as in *A New Canting Dict.*, 1725, of :

*****tattler** ; occ. **tatler.** ' An Alarm, or Striking Watch, or (indeed) any ', B.E. : c. : 1688, Shadwell ; slightly ob. The origin is explained by B.E.'s definition. Hence, *flash a tattler*, to wear a watch (late C. 18–20), and *speak to a tattler* (1878) or *nim a t.* (— 1859), to steal one.

tatto. A potato : dial. and low coll., mostly Scots : C. 19–20. Cf. *tattie*.

*****tatts.** See **tats.**—**tatty tog.** See **tog, n.**—**tatuette.** A rare error for *tatou*, an armadillo. O.E.D.—**tatur.** See **tater.**

taut hand. A first-class working rating that gives no, or very little, trouble : naval : late C. 19–20. Bowen. Ex *t.h.*, a strict disciplinarian. Opp. *bird* (naval sense).

tavarish. A comrade : North Russia Expeditionary Force coll. F. & Gibbons. Direct ex Russian.

Tavern, the. New Inn Hall : Oxford University : 1853, ' Cuthbert Bede ' ; exceedingly ob., for the

Hall did not survive the century of its foundation. By pun and ex its buttery open throughout the day.

tavern-bitch has bit him in the head, the. He is drunk : C. 17. Middleton, 1608 (Apperson). Prob. the first form of :

tavern-fox, hunt a. To get drunk : coll. : 1630, ' Water Poet ' Taylor ; † by 1700. On *swallow a tavern-token,* q.v., but ex *tavern-bitch* . . .

taw, I'll be one—or a marble—(up)on your. A threat (= ' I will pay you out ! ') derived ex the game of marbles, *taw* being the large and gen. superior marble with which one shoots : coll. : resp. from late 1780's and early 1800's ; † by 1890, except among schoolboys. Grose, 2nd ed. : Vaux ; H., 5th ed.

tax-collector. A highwayman : a ca. 1860–90 variant of *collector,* q.v.

tax-fencer. A disreputable shopkeeper : low London : 1878 ; ob. Ware. Ex avoidance of taxes.

tax-gatherer. See gather the taxes.

taxes, the. The tax-collector : coll. : 1874, W. S. Gilbert (O.E.D.).

taxi ; occ. **taxy,** rare after 1909. Abbr. *taximeter* : 1907 (O.E.D.) : coll. and ob.—2. Abbr. *taxi-cab* : 1907 (ibid.) : coll. >, ca. 1933, S.E. (Late in 1934, the latter sense was received into standard Fr.)

taxi. To go by taxi-cab : coll. : from ca. 1915. Ex *taxi,* n., 2.

taxi(†taxy)-driver, -man. A driver of a taxi-cab : resp. coll. (1907) >, ca. 1934, S.E., and coll. (1909), id. O.E.D. Ex *taxi,* n., 2.—2. (**taxi-driver.**) An aeroplane pilot : Air Force : from 1915. F. & Gibbons.

taxi-duty, on. (Of the destroyers of the Dover Patrol) ' employed ferrying politicians, etc., across to France ' : naval : 1916–18. Bowen.

Tay Pay. T. P. O'Connor : nickname in late C. 19–20 ; ob. Ex Irish pronunciation of *T. P.*

*tayle ; *tayle-drawer. See tail, n., last sense, and *tail-drawer.*

tea. A spirituous liquor : from ca. 1690. Sometimes defined : *cold tea,* brandy (1693) ; *Scotch tea,* whiskey (1887). Ex the colour. O.E.D.—2. Urine : 1716, Gay ; implied by Grose, 1st ed., in *tea-voider* ; † by 1860.—3. See ticket, be a person's.

tea, v.t. To supply with, or entertain at, tea : coll. 1812, Sir R. Wilson.—2. Hence, to drink tea, have one's tea : coll. : 1823 (O.E.D.) ; Dickens, 1839, ' Father don't tea with us.'

tea and a wad. See wads, 2.

tea-and-toast struggle. A Wesleyan tea-meeting : lower classes' coll. (— 1909). Ware. On *tea-fight.*

tea and turn out. A proletarian c.p. of ca. 1870–1905 applied to absence of supper. Ware.

tea-blow. A taxi-cab rank where refreshments can be obtained : taxi-drivers' : from ca. 1926. Ex *blow,* n., 8.

tea-boat. A cup of tea : nautical : late C. 19–20. Bowen.

tea-bottle. An old maid : lower middle classes' (— 1909). Ware. Ex fondness for tea.

tea-cake or **-cakes.** ' A child's seat or fundament ' : Yorkshire s. (— 1904), not dial. E.D.D.

Tea-Chest, the. H.M.S. *Thetis* : naval : early C. 20. Bowen. Ex attempted substitution of tea for rum.

tea-chop. A Chinese tea lighter (boat) : nautical coll. : ca. 1860–1900. Bowen.—2. Pl., the Chinese watermen loading the tea clippers : id. : id. Ibid.

tea-cup and saucer. A very respectable, middle-class play : theatrical : 1880–ca. 95. Baumann.

tea-fight. A tea-party : 1849, Albert Smith (O.E.D.) : s. >, ca. 1880, coll. Occ. *tea-scramble* (C. 20 : Manchon) and *tea-shine,* q.v.

tea-kettle groom. A groom that has to work also in the kitchen, etc. : low (— 1887). Baumann.

tea-kettle purger. A total abstainer : London lower classes' (— 1909). Ware. Punning *tee-totaller.* Cf. *tea-pot.*

tea in China. See China, not for all the tea in.

*tea-leaf. A thief : c. (from ca. 1905) >, by 1930, low s. Edgar Wallace.

*tea-man, teaman. A prisoner entitled to a pint of tea, instead of gruel, every evening : c. : from ca. 1870 ; ob.

tea-party. See Boston tea-party, q.v.—2. Hence, a lively proceeding : 1903 (O.E.D.).

tea-party ribbons. ' The multi-coloured ribbons on some (usually non-combatant) officers' breasts ' : Army officers' : from 1916. B. & P. (Cf. C. E. Montague's ' Honours Easy ' in *Fiery Particles.*)

tea-pot. Same as *tea-kettle purger,* q.v. : same period and status. Ware.—2. A tea-party : universities' : ca. 1880–1900. Ware.

tea-pot lid(ding). To ' kid ' (pretend) ; ' kidding ' : rhyming s. : late C. 19–20. *John o' London's Weekly,* June 9, 1934.

Tea-Room Party. A group of forty-eight Radicals in : Parliament : 1866. (Coll. rather than s.) They met in the tea-room. Ware.

tea-scramble. See tea-fight and :

tea-shine. A ' tea fight ' (q.v.) : coll. : 1838, Mrs Carlyle (O.E.D.) ; † by 1890.

tea-spoon. £5000 : commercial : the 1860's and '70's. H., 3rd to 5th edd.

tea-tree oneself ; be tea-treed. See ti-tree oneself.

tea-voider. A chamber-pot : ca. 1780–1890. Grose, 1st ed. See *tea,* n., 2.

tea-wad. A cup of tea and bun(s) : military (— 1935). See wad, a bun.

tea-wag(g)on. An East Indiaman : nautical coll. of ca. 1835–90. Dana. Because these ships carried tea as a large part of their cargo.

tea with, take. To associate with : Australian : 1888, Boldrewood.—2. Hence, esp. to engage with, encounter, in a hostile way : 1896, Kipling, ' And some share our tucker with tigers, | And some with the gentle Masai (Dear boys !), | Take tea with the giddy Masai.' Cf. *tea-party,* q.v.

teach-guy. A late, rare form of *teaich-guy* (see teaich-gens).

teach iron to swim. To perform the impossible : coll. verging on familiar S.E. : C. 16–20 ; ob.

teach your grandmother to suck eggs. See grandmother to.—**teacher always a teacher, once a.** See policeman always.

teacher !, please. (With upraised hand.) A c.p. indicating that the speaker wishes to make a remark ; *thank you, teacher,* a c.p. connoting irony or derision towards someone permitting condescendingly or explaining pompously. Both : C. 20.

teaer, teaing. One who takes tea ; the taking of tea, or the corresponding adj. : coll. : resp. 1892, 1874, 1852 (Surtees) : O.E.D. Ex *tea,* v., 2. Often written *tea-er, tea-ing,* or *tea'er, tea'ing.*

Teague ; in C. 17, occ. **Teg,** in C. 18 **Teigue.** An Irishman : coll. nickname : 1661, *Merry Drollery* (*Teg*) ; Swift, 1733 ; 1900, Stanley Weyman (O.E.D.) ; extremely ob., and since ca. 1870 nearly archaic. An English 'transcription' of the Irish name *Tadhg*, pronounced (approximately) *teeg*. Cf. *Paddy, Sawney, Taffy*, qq.v.—2. In Ulster, a Roman Catholic : coll. (— 1904). E.D.D.

Teagueland ; Teaguelander. Ireland ; an Irishman : coll. : late C. 17–19. B.E., Grose. Ex *Teague*.

teaich-gens. Eight shillings : back s. (— 1859). H., 1st ed. Also *teaich-guy* (ib.), by perversion of *gens*, and *theg-gens* (id.). Contrast :

teaich-gir (pronounced *tadger*). Right : back s. (— 1874). H., 5th ed. ; Ware spells it *teatchgir*. Hence *tadging*, tip-top, excellent, ' splendid ' : late C. 19–20 ; ob. F. & H.

teaing. See **teaer**.

team, teamer, teaming. Incorrect (mid-C. 17–20) for *teem*, to unload, etc. O.E.D.

tear. A boisterous jollification : U.S. (1869, Bret Harte) ; partly anglicised ca. 1890, but by 1930 very ob. in Britain. Cf. S.E. *full tear*.

tear, v.i. To move violently ; rush (*about*) : coll. : 1599, Massinger (O.E.D.) ; Dickens, 1843, ' And now two smaller Cratchits . . . came tearing in.' Perhaps ex *tearing through obstacles*, as the O.E.D. suggests.

tear, shed a. See **shed a tear**.

tear and ages (1841, Lever) or **wounds,** occ. **'oun's** (1842, Lover). Anglo-Irish coll. interjections of astonishment. Cf. dial. *tear*, a passion ; *ages* may = *aches*. O.E.D.

tear-arse. Cheese : proletarian and military : C. 20.—2. One works devilish hard : proletarian (— 1923). Manchon.—3. An excitable man : tailors' : 1928, *The Tailor and Cutter*, Nov. 29.

tear Christ's body ; tear (the name of) God. To blaspheme : coll. >, by 1550, S.E. : C. 14–mid-17.

tear 'em up. To delight the audience : music-halls' : from ca. 1920. M. Lincoln, *Oh ! Definitely*, 1933, ' A number . . . that simply " tore 'em up ".'

tear it. See **torn it**.

tear one's seat. To attempt too much : tailors' : from ca. 1870. Cf. *tear-arse*, 2.

tear-pump, work the. To weep : late C. 19–20 ; ob. On *water-works, turn on the*, q.v. See also **pump,** n., for earliest form.

tear the end off. To finish ; to finish with : coll. (— 1923). Manchon.

tear the tartan. (Gen. as vbl.n.) To speak in Gaelic : Glasgow (— 1934). Alastair Baxter.

tear-up. A stir, a commotion : coll. : mid-C. 19–20. Baumann.

tear up for arse-paper. To reprimand severely : New Zealand soldiers' : in the G.W. (B. & P.)

tearing. Violent ; passionate ; roistering ; rollicking : coll. : 1654, Gayton, ' Some tearing Tragedy full of Fights and Skirmishes ' ; 1869, J. R. Green, ' I am in such tearing spirits at the prospect of freedom ' ; ob.—Hence, 2, grand ; ' splendid ', ' ripping ' : late C. 17–20 ; rare since mid-C. 19. O.E.D.—3. (Of work) exhausting : coll. (— 1923). Manchon.

tears of the tankard. See **tankard**.

teary. Tearful : late C. 14–20 : S.E. until mid-C. 19, then coll.

tease ; teaze, very rare in C. 20. One given to teasing ; one playfully irritating another : coll. : 1852, Dickens, ' What a teaze you are,' O.E.D. Ex the v.

*tease, teaze ; occ. **teize.** To whip, flog : c. : ca. 1810–80. Vaux. Ex :

*tease (but gen. **teaze** or **teize**), **nab** or **nap the.** To be flogged ; esp. to be whipped privately in gaol : c. : ca. 1780–1840. Grose, 1st ed. Prob. ex *tease*, the act of teasing. Cf. sense 4 of :

teaser ; teazer, very rare in C. 20. Something causing annoyance ; a ' poser ' : coll. : 1759, Franklin (O.E.D.) ; of a difficult ball in cricket, 1856 (Lewis).—2. Hence, in boxing s. (1812, O.E.D. ; ob.), an opponent hard to beat.—3. ' An old horse belonging to a breeding-stud—" though devoid of *fun* himself, he is the cause of it in others "',' Bee : turf : ca. 1820–70.—4. A flogging or whipping : c. or low s. : from ca. 1830. Ex *tease*, v., q.v. Cf. *teasing*.—5. A preliminary advertisement (specifying neither article nor advertiser, or, loosely, specifying only the one or the other), prior to an advertising campaign : advertising (esp. publicity) coll. : from ca. 1920.

*teasing. A flogging : c. of ca. 1820–80. Ex *tease*, v. ; cf. *teaser*, fourth sense.

teasy. (Of persons) teasing ; (of things) irritating : coll. : from ca. 1907. Rare. O.E.D. Ex dial.

teatchgir. See **teaich-gir**.

teatotal. Incorrect for *teetotal* : from the 1830's

*teaze. See **tease,** n., v., and phrase ; **teazer,** see **teaser**.

teazle. The female pudend : low : C. 19–20 ; ob. Ex *teasel*, a plant.

tec ; 'tec. A detective : 1886, *The Echo*, Dec. 4 ; 1899, Whiteing. Occ. *teck* (Baumann).—2. (**tec** or **tech,** gen. preceded by **the**.) A **tech**nical college or institution : from ca. 1910 : s. now verging on coll. O.E.D. (Sup.).

tec ; 'tec, v.t. To watch as a detective does : C. 20 ; rare. Ex n.

tech. See **tec,** n., 2.—**teck.** See **tec,** n., 1.

Teddies. ' One of the names for the U.S. troops on first landing in France ; disliked by the Americans equally with " Sammies "[, which, however, survived], and soon dropped ' : military : 1917–early 1918. F. & Gibbons. Ex ' Teddy ' Roosevelt (d. 1919).

teddy bear. A shaggy goatskin or fur coat ' issued for winter wear in the trenches in 1915 ' : military : late 1915–early 1916. F. & Gibbons. Ex the plaything.

Teddy Hall. St Edmund Hall, Oxford : Oxford University (— 1874). H., 5th ed.

Teddy my godson. An address to a simpleton : Anglo-Irish coll. : from ca. 1780 ; ob. Grose, 1st ed.

Teddy Woodbine. See **Woodbine, Teddy**.

Teddy's hat. The crown in the game of Crown and Anchor : military : 1902 ; ob. F. & Gibbons, ' With reference to King Edward VII '.

tee-tee. See **t.t.**

teejay. A new boy : Winchester College : from ca. 1870 ; ob. Abbr. *protégé*. Also *tejé*, 1st syllable as Eng. *tee*, 2nd as in Fr. Wrench.—? Hence, as v.

teek ; tique. Mathema*t*ics ; arithme*t*ic : Harrow : from ca. 1880 ; ob. Ex a French master's pronunciation of the relevant syllable.

teeming and lading, n. ' Using cash received to-day to make up cash embezzled yesterday ' (Alfred T. Chenhalls) : accountants' : C. 20. Lit., unloading and loading.

teeny ; teeny-tiny ; teeny-weeny. Tiny : resp., dial. (— 1847) >, ca. 1860, coll. ; coll., 1867, ob. ; coll., 1894, Baring-Gould. Ex child's pronunciation. (O.E.D.)

teeth. See **tooth** for phrases, etc., not herein-under.—2. (Only in pl.) A ship's guns : nautical : 1810 (O.E.D.) ; slightly ob. ? ex *show one's teeth.*— 3. The dental department of a hospital ; medical coll. (— 1933). *Slang*, p. 193.

teeth, draw. See **draw teeth.**

teeth, fed up to the (back). See **fed up.**

teeth upwards, go to grass with. To be buried : late C. 19–20 ; ob.

teeth well afloat, have one's or the. To be tipsy : from ca. 1870 ; ob.

teethward (properly **teeth-ward**), **be clerk to the.** A coll. of late C. 16–early 17 as in Hollyband's, i.e. Claude Desainliens's, *Dictionarie French and English*, 1593, ' He is clarke to the teethward, he hath eaten his service book ; spoken in mockage by [? of] such as maketh shew of learning and be not learned.'

***Teetotal Hotel(, the).** A prison : c. : from ca. 1880 ; ob.

teetotically. Teetotally : non-aristocratic jocular : 1890's. Ware. A perversion, silly enough ; but with a less foolish glance at *theoretically.*

teetottler. A teetotaller : jocular : ca. 1885–1900. Baumann.

Teg, Teigue. See **Teague.**—***teize.** See **tease**, n., v., and phrase.—**tejé.** See **teejay.**

tejious ; tejus. Tediously ; hence, extremely, as in *tej(io)us bad, good, quick,* etc., etc. : sol. : from ca. 1860 ; ob. as an intensive. Ex Kentish dial.

***tekelite.** A defaulting debtor : ca. 1830–50 : c. of the Debtors' Prison in Whitecross Street, London. ? ex ' *Tekel* : weighed in the balances, and found wanting ', Daniel v. 27. O.E.D.—2. **the Tekelites.** The Whigs : 1683–ca. 1700. ' First given currency by Sir Robert L'Estrange ', Dawson.

tekram. A market : back s. : from 1860's. Ware.

teleometer. Catachrestic for *telemeter* : from ca. 1890. By confusion with *telometer.* (O.E.D.).

telescope. To silence (a person): Australian : ca. 1890–1910. ? ex telescoped carriages.

telist ; telt. A telegraphist : telegraphists' coll. (— 1923). Manchon. Ex these two words written as official abbr.

tell, hear. To hear (something) spoken of ; absolutely, as in ' So I've heard tell ', so I've heard. C. 13–20 : S.E. until mid-C. 19, then coll. and dial. Stevenson, 1896, ' I asked him if he had ever heard tell of . . . the house of Shaws,' O.E.D. See also **hear.**

tell-a-cram. A telegram : jocular (— 1923). Manchon. Lit., tell-a-lie.

tell me !, don't ; never tell me ! I can hardly believe it ! ; don't be silly ! : coll. : resp. mid-C. 18–20, slightly ob. ; and C. 17–20, extremely **ob.** Shakespeare in *Othello* ; Foote (*don't* . . .). O.E.D.

tell me the old, old story ! A c.p. (often, too, a chant sung in unison), in retort on rumours of good times or on specious promises : military : 1915 ; ob. But it was in use in Sydney at least as early as 1905 : often whistled. B. & P., ' The first line of a Nonconformist hymn '.

tell mother ! Tell me ! : a C. 20 c.p. E.g. Somerset Maugham, *The Casuarina Tree*, 1926, ' " What is it, old man ? " she said gently [to her husband]. " Tell mother." '

tell off. To scold, blame, rebuke severely : coll. (— 1919). Perhaps ex the military sense. (O.E.D. Sup.)—2. Hence, to sentence (an incriminated per-

son) : c. : from ca. 1920. George Ingram, *Stir*, 1933.

tell on, tell of : see **of** in sense of *on.*

tell one his own. To tell him frankly of his faults or mistakes : coll. : C. 16–20 ; ob. Horman, 1519 (O.E.D.). Cf. *give a piece of one's mind.*

tell that to the marines ! See **marines.**—**tell the tale.** See **tale, tell the.**

tell the world !, I'll. I say so openly or emphatically : U.S. ; anglicised in 1930 or 1931 as a coll.

tell you what, I'll ; in C. 19–20, often **I tell you what ;** in mid-C. 19–20, occ. **tell you what** (Baumann). I'll tell you something ; this is how it is : coll. Shakespeare, Tennyson ; Violet Hunt, ' I tell you what, Janet, we must have a man down who doesn't shoot—to amuse us ! ' O.E.D.

teller. A well-delivered blow : boxing s. : 1814, *The Sporting Magazine* (O.E.D.) ; 1834, Ainsworth, ' Ven luckily for Jem a teller | Vos planted right upon his smeller.' Ob. Lit., something that tells, makes a mark.

teller of the tale. He who ' tells the tale ' (see **tale, tell the,** 1) : mostly low : C. 20.

telling, that would be or that's. See **tellings.** App. from ca. 1830.

telling-off. A scolding ; a reprimand : coll. (— 1923). Manchon. Ex *tell off,* q.v.

telling you !, I'm. There's no argument necessary or possible : coll. : C. 20. Prob. abbr. ' I'm not arguing ; I'm *telling* you.' Contrast *tell me !, don't,* q.v.

tellings, that's. A c.p. reply to a question that one should, or does, not wish to answer : from ca. 1835 ; slightly ob. Marryat, 1837, ' " Where is this . . ., and when ? " " That's tellings," replied the man,' O.E.D. A playful coll. or perhaps, orig., a sol. for ' *That's telling* ' = *that would be telling,* phrases that are themselves—at first, though not now—somewhat trivially coll.

tellywag. A telegram : Public Schools' : C. 20. (E. F. Benson, *David Blaize*, 1916.) In dial. as early as 1867 (E.D.D.).

telt. See **telist.**

temperature, have a. To be feverish : coll. : from late 1890's. E. F. Benson, 1904, ' He has . . . had a temperature for nearly a week,' O.E.D. Abbr. *have a temperature higher than one's usual.*

tempest. A confused or crowded throng or, esp., assembly : Society coll. soon > S.E. : ca. 1745–80. Smollett, 1746, in a note on *drum,* says : ' There are also drum-major, rout, tempest, and hurricane, differing only in degrees of multitude and uproar.'

tempestive and **tempestuous, temporal** and **temporary,** are in C. 19–20 catachrestic if used one for the other of its pair ; in C. 17, the interchange of the latter two words was permissible. Likewise with the derivative nn.

temple. From ca. 1860 at Winchester College, as in Pascoe, 1881 : ' On the last night of term there is a bonfire in Ball Court, and all the temples or miniature architectural excavations in " Mead's " wall are lighted up with candle-ends.'

Temple of Bacchus. ' Merry-making after getting a liceat ', Egan's Grose : Oxford University : ca. 1820–50.

***temple-pickling.** The ducking, under a pump, of bailiffs, detectives, pickpockets, and other unwelcome persons : London c. or low s. : late C. 17–18. B.E. ; Grose. Lit., a pickling within the limits of the Temple.

temporary gentleman. An officer for the duration

of the War or until demobilised : Regular Army pejorative coll. : 1916 ; ob. Manchon, who notes the occ. abbr. *t.g.* (or *T. G.*). The term caused much justifiable resentment.

temporise. To extemporise (v.t.), lit. and fig. : catachresis : late C. 19–20. (O.E.D.)

tempory. A frequent sol. for **temporary.**

ten. To play lawn **tennis** : 1906, P. G. Wodehouse, *Love among the Chickens* ; Collinson.

ten-bob squat. A (seat in a) stall : theatrical (— 1909). Ware.

ten bones. (One person's) fingers and thumbs, esp. in a coll. oath : C. 15–19.

ten commandments. The ten fingers and thumbs, esp. of a wife : mid-C. 15–20 ; ob. Heywood, ca. 1540, 'Thy wives ten commandments may serch thy five wyttes' ; Dekker & Webster, 1607 ; Scott ; H., 3rd ed., 'A virago's fingers, or nails. Often heard in a female street disturbance.' (Apperson.)

[**ten-in-the-hundred,** a usurer : perhaps orig. coll.; certainly soon S.E.]

ten (gen. **10**) **wedding.** A wedding at which (? and after) the wife = 1, the husband = 0 : non-aristocratic (— 1909) ; ob. Ware.

ten-to-two. A Jew : low rhyming s. : C. 20.

ten toes. See **Bayard of ten toes.**

*****ten penn'orth.** A sentence of ten years : c. : C. 20. George Ingram, *Stir*, 1933.

ten-pennyworth. The punishment designated ' 10 A ' : naval : C. 19. Hence, in C. 20, of the modern substitute. Bowen.

ten-stroke. A complete victory : billiard-players' (— 1909). Ware. Ten being the highest stroke.

ten-to-four gentleman or **toff.** A (superior) Civil servant : jocular coll. (— 1887). Baumann.

tena koe ? How do you do ? : coll., North Island of New Zealand : late C. 19–20. Ex Maori (lit., 'that is you'). Morris. Cf. *taihoa*, q.v.

tenacious. Obstinately averse from any action : catachresis : mid-C. 18–early 19. O.E.D.

tenant at will. ' One whose wife usually fetches him from the alehouse,' Grose, 2nd ed. : ca. 1786–1840. Orig., a legal pun. Cf. :

tenant for life. A married man, because he is hers for life : ca. 1810–1900. *Lex. Bal.*

tenant-in-tail. See **tail, make settlement in.—tenantcy.** Incorrect for **tenancy.**

*****tench.** A penitentiary : c. : mid-C. 19–20 ; ob. F. & H. record it as used specifically (*the Tench*) of the Hobart Town Penitentiary (1859) and of the Clerkenwell House of Detention (not in C. 20). Abbr. *'tentiary*, q.v. (Morris). Cf. *steel* and *stir*, qq.v.—2. The female pudend : low s. : mid-C. 19–20. ? ex sense 1, or a pun on the fish.

tendency ; tendent. Incorrect in C. 18 for *tendancy*, care, attention ; in C. 17 for *tendant*, attentive, giving service or attention. O.E.D.

[**tender Parnel** or **Pernel,** a mistress, a well-educated and delicate creature, is on the borderland between coll. and S.E., which latter it probably is, as also is *as tender as Parnel*(*l*), *who broke her finger in a posset drink*, with variants. The former in B.E., and long before ; the latter in Ray and Grose (1st ed.). Cf. the S.E. *tender as a parson's leman.*]

tenderfoot. A greenhorn ; any raw, inexperienced person : U.S. coll. (recorded ca. 1880, but implied in 1861 : Thornton) >, ca. 1890, Colonial coll. >, ca. 1905, S.E. Ex the tender feet characteristic of one unused to hardship.—2. Hence, a

tramp always looking for conveyance along the road : tramps' c. (— 1932). F. Jennings, *Tramping with Tramps.*

tenement to let. A ' house to let ', q.v. : ca. 1790–1850. Grose, 3rd ed.

tenip. A pint : back s. (— 1859). H., 1st ed. With *e* harmoniously intrusive.

tenner. A £10 note : coll. : 1861, T. Hughes. Cf. *fiver.*—2. (A sentence of) ten years' imprisonment : c. (1866, O.E.D.) >, ca. 1890, s. >, ca. 1910, coll.

tennis. Lawn tennis : catachresis >, ca. 1920, S.E., but to be deprecated on the score of ambiguity. *St James's Gazette*, Aug., 1888, ' It is melancholy to see a word which has held its own for centuries gradually losing its connotation. Such a word is " tennis ", by which nine persons out of ten to-day would understand the game of recent invention,' O.E.D. Invented in 1874 as sphairistiké, the game assumed its present form in 1877. See **sticky.**

tennisy. Addicted to, fond of, lawn tennis : coll. : 1890 (O.E.D.).

tenny. Detention : Stationers' Company School at Hornsey : C. 20. Words, esp. nicknames, in -*y* are very noticeable there, it seems.

tenpence, up a tree for. See **up a tree.**

tenpence to the shilling (only). Weak in the head : s. (— 1860) >, ca. 1900, coll. H., 2nd ed. Cf. S.E. *tenpenny*, cheap, hence inferior.

tens, dressed to the. An occ. variant (— 1923) of *dressed up to the nines.* Manchon.

[**Tense, wrong use of.** This matter is, at least in detail, ineligible here : the two 'loci classici' are the Fowlers' *The King's English* and H. W. Fowler's *Modern English Usage.* Note, however, the errors in ' It is a long time since he has (or, had) come here ' for *came here* ; ' I didn't seem to have had any wish to eat ' for *have any wish* . . . ; ' He had departed when I had arrived ' for *when I arrived.* See also at *have* and *had* and *of* at ' Preterite misuse . . .' (The best training for correct use of tense is perhaps a sound knowledge of Latin prose.)

tent. An umbrella : Anglo-Irish (— 1904). E.D.D.

Tenth don't dance, the. A military, gibing c.p. directed at the 10th Hussars in 1823–ca. 1840. It originated in 1823, when the officers, at a ball in Dublin and after much experience of London and Brighton society, declined to be introduced to the ladies, on the plea that ' the Tenth don't dance '. F. & Gibbons.

'tentiary. A penitentiary : low coll. : mid-C. 19–20. Morris at **tench.**

'tention. Attention : Canadian (and U.S.) coll. : late C. 19–20. (John Beames.)

tenuc. The female pudend : back s. : from ca. 1860. F. & H. ' Eased ' *tnuc.*

tenure in tail. See **tail, make settlement in.**

ter for v. ending in *t* + *to* is a ' constant ' of sol. speech, esp. in Cockney : virtually immemorial. E.g. *oughter*, ought to, and *wanter*, want to (do something).

term-trotter. One who keeps the terms merely for form's sake : Oxford University : ca. 1780–1820. Vicesimus Knox, 1782. O.E.D. Cf. *trotter*, 2, q.v.

terms (with), on, often preceded by **get.** (To get) on an equal footing (with) : sporting : 1887, Sir R. Roberts (O.E.D.). Ex lit. sense, on friendly terms. —2. Hence, in cricket : (of a side) having made a score comparable with their opponents' : 1897 (O.E.D.).

terps. An interpreter : military : G.W., and after. (F. & Gibbons.) Suggested by *turps*, q.v.

terra firma. (A) landed estate : jocular coll. : late C. 17–early 19. B.E. ; Grose, 1st ed.

terræ filius. A Master of Arts acting as the orator making a satirical and humorous speech at the Encænia : Oxford University (improperly at Dublin) : ca. 1650–1750 : perhaps orig. s., but certainly soon j. Ex *t. f.*, a son of the earth, hence a man of unknown origin. (O.E.D.)

terras incognitas. Pl. of *terra incognita* : C. 19–20 : catachresis. (O.E.D.)

terrible as a mere intensive is coll. ; gen. = very large or great ; excessive. From ca. 1840. Dickens. 1844, ' She's a terrible one to laugh,' O.E.D. Cf. *awful, filthy, foul, frightful, terrific, tremendous.* Cf. :

terrible, adv. Greatly ; very : late C. 15–20 : S.E. until C. 20, when gen. considered sol. ' She took on (something) terrible,' she was greatly distressed. Cf. :

terribly. A frequent intensive (= excessively, extremely, very, very greatly) : mid-C. 19–20 : coll. Trollope, Jowett. Ex *terribly*, very severely or painfully. (O.E.D.) Cf. *awfully.*

Terrier ; terrier. A member of the Territorial Army : coll. : 1908 (O.E.D.). Punningly.

terrific ; terrifically. Excessive, or very severe or great ; extremely, excessively, frighteningly : coll. : in 1809, J. W. Croker describes the extent of business as ' terrific ', and in 1859 Darwin admits that the corrections in his *Origin of Species* are ' terrifically heavy '. O.E.D.—2. Hence, ' great ' ; very : Society : from ca. 1920. Dennis Mackail, *passim.*

terror. A ' holy terror ' : coll. : 1889 (O.E.D. Sup.).

Terry. (Gen. pl.) Same as *Terrier*, q.v. : 1907–? 10. (O.E.D.)

terse. Abrupt in manner : Society coll. : from ca. 1928. (Maurice Lincoln, *Oh ! Definitely*, 1933.) Suggested by ' terse style ' and ' short-tempered '.

test. A test match ; properly one of a series (gen. three or five) of such representative matches : from 1908 : coll. >, by 1913, S.E. Orig. of cricket matches, both the full term and the abbr. were by 1924 applied to football matches—and in 1932 to lawn-tennis matches—between two countries ; *international* is also used in much the same way—often very loosely. Also as adj. : of a player in such a match. In 1905, Mr ' Plum ' Warner wrote : ' Until the year 1894 no one had ever heard of a " Test " match,' *The Westminster Gazette*, Aug. 19 (W.).

testament. Testimony : catachresis going back to mid-C. 15. (O.E.D.)—2. See bible, 2.

tester. A sixpence : definitely in 1613 (O.E.D.), but prob. earlier by some twenty years : s. >, by 1700, coll. ; by 1850, ob., by 1890 †, except as an archaism. Farquhar, Swift, Grose (1st ed.), Lamb, H. Ex *tester*, a debased teston and *teston*, orig. worth a shilling but by 1577, at latest, only sixpence.

testify. See detest.

testugger. A ' testamur ' or certificate : Oxford undergraduates' (– 1899). Ware. By ' the Oxford *-er* '.

*testy. A c. form of *tester* (sixpence) : C. 19. See cat on testy dodge. This form virtually proves the *tester* origin of *tizzy*, q.v.

Tetbury portion. A c**t and a ' clap ' (q.v.) : ca. 1780–1850. Grose, 2nd ed. Cf. *Rochester portion, Whitechapel p.*, and *Tipperary fortune*, qq.v.

*teviss. A shilling : costers' s. and tramps' c. (– 1859) ; ob. H., 1st ed. Perhaps *shilling > shill* ' backed ' to *llihs > lihess > lehiss > teviss.*

texts. ' Various passages learnt by heart before breakfast by the Schoolroom forms ' : Bootham School coll. verging on j. : late C. 19–20. Anon., *Dict. of Bootham Slang*, 1925.

th'. There, esp. in *th' is* . . ., there is : C. 19–20 : dial. and, esp. in Canada and U.S.A., low coll.—2. The : this slovenly coll. is, apart from being in several diall., esp. characteristic of Australian speech ; this usage is implied by John G. Brandon in his amusing ' thriller ', *Th' Big City*, 1930. Pronounced *thĕ* with great rapidity.

Thames butter. Very bad butter : London's poorer classes' : ca. 1870–5. Ware. Ex a journalist's attack on a Frenchman that was making ' butter ' out of Thames mud-worms.

Thames on fire, set the. Earliest in Foote, ca. 1770, as *set fire to the Thames* ; in Wolcot, 1788, we find *burn the Thames* : both these forms were † by 1850. The present form arose ca. 1786, being first recorded in Grose, 2nd ed. Gen. in negative : to do nothing wonderful ; never to make one's mark : coll. >, by 1860 at latest, S.E. A similar phrase has been applied to the Liffey and the Spree, and W. quotes Nigrinus, ca. 1580, ' Er hat den Rhein und das meer angezündet,' he has set fire to the Rhine and the sea. The proposed derivation ex *temse*, a sieve, is unauthenticated ; in any case, it is *prima facie* improbable. See esp. Apperson, O.E.D., Skeat.

than. Then : C. 14–20 : in C. 14–17, S.E. ; in C. 18–20, dial. and in C. 19–20, a sol. more frequent than the O.E.D. admits.—2. (After *hardly* or *scarcely*) when : catachrestic : mid-C. 19–20. Froude, 1864, ' He had scarcely won . . . the place . . ., than his health was found shattered,' O.E.D. By confusion with *no sooner . . . than.* —3. See than in Addenda.

than, like. (In comparisons.) Such as : catachresis : ca. 1590–1600 (? later). Warner, 1592 ; Anon., 1595, ' Then '—see than, 1—' which the like was never heard before '. O.E.D. Cf. :

than, so (far, good, much, etc.), in comparisons. So . . . as : catachresis : C. 17–20. G. Blackwell, 1602, ' I can blame none so much . . . then '—see than, 1—' Mr Collington ' ; Mandeville, 1723. O.E.D. Cf. *then,* 2, and *than, like.*

thank God we've got a navy ! See navy !, thank God.

thank the mussies ! Thank the Lord ! : lower classes' : ca. 1870–1914. Ware. Ex *mercy.*

thank you for those few kind words ! A semi-ironic c.p. (– 1933). *Slang*, p. 133.

thank you, teacher ! See teacher !, please.

thankee ! ; occ. **thanky** (Baumann). Thank you ! : illiterate coll. verging on sol. : from ca. 1820. Dickens, 1848, ' Thankee, my Lady ', O.E.D. Corruption of *thank ye !* Cf. :

thanks ! (1) thank you : coll. : late C. 16–20. Ex *my thanks to you*, etc. Likewise *many* or *best thanks*, rare before C. 19, though Shakespeare has *great thanks.* (O.E.D.)

thanks, be nicely. To be slightly drunk : coll. (– 1923). Manchon. Ex the reply, ' Nicely, thanks ! '

thanks be ! (May) thanks be given to God : coll. : late C. 19–20. Also in Cornish dial.

thanky ! See thankee !

*thary, v.i. and v.t. To speak (to) : tramps' c. ;

from ca. 1845; ob. *Gipsy* Carew, 1891, 'I grannied some of what you were a-tharyin' to your cousin.' App. ex Romany. Cf. *rocker, rok(k)er*, q.v.

that, pronoun, in 'anticipatory commendation by way of persuasion or encouragement (esp. to a child)', O.E.D.: which, illustrating by 'Come along, that's a good boy!', implies that it is a coll. of late C. 19–20, ex the *that* of commendation for something already done, as in Shakespeare's 'That's my good son' (*Romeo and Juliet*).—2. Representing a statement already made and gen. coming first in its own clause, as in ' *That* I will,' I shall do that all right!: coll.: mid-C. 14–20. Shakespeare, '"Was there a wise woman with thee?" "Ay, that there was,"' O.E.D.—3. The omission of the relative *that* (cf. *which, who*) is an 'elemental' of coll. speech and is recorded as early as C. 13; but it occurs frequently also in S.E. and often justifiably—indeed, advisably—on the score of euphony. No one would classify as coll., or object to, Tennyson's 'To put in words the grief I feel' (O.E.D.), but one might well condemn as slovenly, and prob. no one would describe as other than coll., such a sentence as ' This is the book you'll find the passage I spoke to you about in.'—4. The same applies to the conjunctive *that*. The omission occ. leads to ambiguity: this is prob. why the French never omit *que*.—5. Redundant *that* is catachrestic: almost immemorial. E.g. ' I only hope that when we have personal servants, sir, that they'll do the same thing,' John G. Brandon, *The One-Minute Murder*, 1934.

that, adv. So; so very: mid-C. 15–20: S.E. until late C. 19, then dial. and coll.; in these days, it is considered rather sol. Boldrewood, 1888, ' He was that weak as he could hardly walk,' O.E.D.

that, all ; and all that (= and all such things). These phrases used to be ' perfectly good English ', but since late 1929, when Robert Graves's notable War-book appeared, or mid-1930, when Albert Perceval Graves's *To Return to All That* somewhat modified that picture, they have been so coll. as to verge on s. Cf. *things, . . . and*, q.v.

that, as. ' As how ', i.e. that: sol. (— 1887). Baumann, ' I can't say as that I'm first-class.'

that, at. (Estimated) at that rate or standard; even so; even so acting; in that respect; also; unexpectedly, or annoyingly, or indubitably; in addition; and, what's more; yet, however; in any case, anyway: U.S. s. (from 1840's), anglicised ca. 1885; by 1900, coll. Keighley Goodchild, 1888, ' So we'll drain the flowing bowl, | 'Twill not jeopardise the soul, | For it's only tea, and weak at that.' Perhaps ex ' cheap, *or* dear, at that price' (O.E.D.). But this phrase is so confusing to a foreigner and so little used in the Dominions, that other instances of its chameleonic use are required :— Charles Williams, *The Greater Trumps*, 1932, ' "Try me and let me go if I fail. At that," she added with a sudden smile, " I think I won't fail " '; Ibid., ' The nearest village to his grandfather's, Henry told them, and at that a couple of miles away.'

that !, come out of. Clear out !: late C. 19–20. Lit., come out from inside or shelter.

that, of ; esp. **something of that** (sc. **sort**). See **of**, preposition, 6.

that moan's soon made. That grief is easily consoled : Scots coll. (— 1885). Ware.

that there (thing, etc.). See **there, that, and of. this here.**

that won't pay the old woman her ninepence. A Bow Street Police Court c.p. (— 1909 ; ob.) in condemnation of an evasive act. Ware.

thatch. See **thatched, be well.**

thatch-gallows. A worthless fellow : coll. : ca. 1785–1850. Grose, 2nd ed.

thatched, be well. To have a good head of hair : jocular coll. verging on s. (— 1874). H., 5th ed. Ex *thatch*, a head of hair, esp. if thick : itself coll. : from ca. 1630 (O.E.D.). Cf. *Tatcho* hair-tonic punningly named by G. R. Sims ex the Romany for ' genuine '.

Thatched Head. An Irishman : pejorative coll. nickname : C. 17. Beaumont & Fletcher.

thatched house under the hill, the. The female pudend : low coll. or s. : ca. 1770–1850. Used as a title by Stevens in 1772.

that's a cough-lozenge for him ! He's punished : a proletarian c.p. of ca. 1850–90. Ex an advertisement for cough-lozenges. (Ware.)

that's up against your shirt ! That's a point against you ! : lower classes' c.p. of ca. 1900–14. Ware. Perhaps ex stains on a white shirt.

that's where you spoil yourself ! A non-aristocratic c.p. directed at a smart person overreaching himself : 1880–1. Ware.

that's right ! Yes ! : low coll. : late C. 19–20. Ex S.E. formula of approval.

that's the stuff. See **stuff to give . . .**

that's where you want it. See **want it, it's up there you.**

the is coll. when it is used for *my*, as in, esp. and earliest, *the wife*, rarely *the husband*, often *the mater* and *the pater* or *governor* (1853), rarely *the mother* and almost never *the father* ; only occ. of other relatives. Not recorded before 1838 (O.E.D.), but perhaps arising a score of years earlier. (O.E.D. for dates.)—2. In Oxford s., as in *the Broad*, Broad Street, and *the Turl*, Turl Street : late C. 19–20. 3. See **th'**, 2.—4. See :

the wrongly ' cased ' and ' typed '. There is a distressingly frequent tendency among printers and journalists, hence in the book-world, to put the *The* of titles, whether of periodicals or of books, into lower case and roman type. Thus, ' *The Daily Mail* ' is reduced to ' the *Daily Mail* '. A title is as much an entity as the name of a person : we do not write ' john Smith ' ; nor do we, if we adopt the italic mode, write ' Punch ' for ' *Punch* ' ; nor should we write ' the *Times* ' for ' *The Times* '. It has been advanced that in all such titles of periodicals as commence with *The*, the first element may be assumed ; but if it were assumed, it would be omitted. Admittedly it is dropped in colloquial speech : a journalist, if asked on which newspaper he works, may reply ' *Daily Mail* ',—that is, if he does not shorten it to ' *Mail* ' ; but such an omission is a coll. If, however, he has a due regard for the dignity of his newspaper, he will, in reply, give the full title, and say ' *The Daily Mail* ' not ' the *Daily Mail* '. In book-titles there is still less excuse for describing Arnold Bennett's ' *The Card* ' as ' the *Card* '. We do not treat the *A* of titles in this cavalier fashion : there is no more reason why, e.g. *The Window*, edited by Bertram Ratcliffe and myself in 1930, should be referred to as ' the *Window* ' than that Barrie's *A Window in Thrums*, 1889, should be referred to as ' a *Window in Thrums* '.

the spirit of the troops is excellent. See **spirit.**

*****theatre.** A police court : c. (— 1857) ; almost †.

'Ducange Anglicus.' Because there the prospective prisoner assumes a part unnatural to him.—2. The pronunciation *the-ā'ter* is in the British Empire (? except Canada) considered, in late C. 19–20, to be incorrect and almost illiterate. Baumann.

Theatre Royal, amen. A church : low (— 1909); ob. Ware. Precisely why ? Perhaps it was orig. theatrical : touring players perform frequently at Theatres Royal.

Theatre Ship, the. S.S. *Gourko* : naval coll. : 1915–18. F. & Gibbons. Ex dramatic performances given thereon. Cf. *Sports Ship*, q.v.

theatrical. (Gen. pl.) An actor or actress : stage coll. (— 1859). H., 1st ed. I.e. *theatrical person* or *people*.

theca- is incorrect for *theco-* in such words as *thecospore* : C. 19–20. O.E.D.

theg. Eight, as in *theg gen*, *8s.*, and *theg yanneps*, *8d.* Rhyming s. (— 1859). H., 1st ed. See also **teaich** (occ. **teach** or **teaitch**).

their, them, they for singular (*he* or *she*, etc.) : a common error. E.g. Agatha Christie, *The Murder of Roger Ackroyd*, 1926, ' It was rather like a jig-saw puzzle to which everyone contributed their own little bit of knowledge.' Esp. after *anyone*, *everyone* (or *-body*), *nobody*.

theirn. Theirs : (dial. and) sol. : C. 19–20. Baumann. Cf. *theirselves*.

their's, like **her's,** and esp. **it's,** possessive pronouns, is in C. 20 considered a sol. if written thus with an apostrophe.—2. The enemy's : military coll. : C. 20. Cf. *ours*.

theirselves, themselves, is, in late C. 19–20, gen. considered a sol., except, naturally, where an adj. intervenes, as in *their very selves* (cf. the *your good selves* beloved of commerce). Cf. *theirn*, q.v.

them, adj. Those : late C. 16–20 : S.E. until C. 18, then dial. and coll. ; in C. 19–20, sol. The O.E.D. gives two excellent examples : ' It was a rare rise we got out of them chaps,' Thackeray, 1840, and ' Them ribbons of yours cost a trifle, Kitty,' Lover, 1842. Cf. *they*, q.v.—2. (As pronoun.) They ; those (in the nominative, before *who*) : late C. 15–20 : S.E. >, ca. 1700, dial. and (low) coll. : in C. 19–20, sol. E.g. ' Them as does this ain't no good.' Cf. *they*, 2, q.v.—3. (Pronoun in the objective.) Those : S.E. >, in early C. 19, (low) coll. ; in C. 20, sol. E.g. ' I don't like them who say one thing and do another.'—4. Their : sol. : C. 19–20. Baumann.—5. After *as* and *than* and after *is*, *are*, *were*, etc., *them* is a very frequent coll. (mid-C. 17–20), but, except exclamatorily, is grammatically incorrect. The O.E.D. quotes ' It was not them we wanted,' 1845,—which as compared with the absolute ' It was not them ' (e.g. at the theatre) has some justification since *them* represents *they whom*.

them's my sentiments ! See **sentiments.**

then. Than : C. 14–20 : S.E. until C. 19, then coll. ; in late C. 19–20, definitely a sol. This is the counterpart of *than*, 1, q.v.

then comes a pig to be killed ! A c.p. expressive of disbelief : lower-middle and lower classes' : ca. 1900–14. Ware, ' Based upon the lines of Mrs Bond who would call to her poultry—" Come, chicks, come ! Come to Mrs Bond and be killed." '

then the band began to play ! See **band played.**

then the band played ! That was the end of it : c.p. (— 1909) ; ob. Ware. Ex music played at end of a function, a celebration.

theogonist is catachrestic when = one born of God. C. 19–20. (O.E.D.)

there. When a relative clause follows *there* (*is* or *are*, *were*, etc.), the relative pronoun is often omitted. This usage is, in C. 19–20, S.E. verging on coll. Wordsworth, 1806, ' But how he will come and whither he goes, | There's never a scholar in England knows.' O.E.D.—2. *there* + singular v. + pl.n. is a grammatical error, as in Agatha Christie, *The Thirteen Problems*, 1932, ' There remains the other three.' Perhaps, in part, ex the influence of Fr. *il y a*, *il y avait*, etc.

there, all. Shrewd ; alert ; smart. *not all there* : mentally deficient. Coll. : 1864, Mrs Gatty (O.E.D.). The negative phrase sometimes = dishonest, or criminal, as in Anon., 1877, ' He stayed . . . doing the grand and sucking the flats till the folks began to smoke him as not all there.' Whence:

there, be. ' To be on the *qui vive* ; alive ; knowing ; in one's element ', F. & H. : coll. (— 1890).

there, get. See **get there.**

there, have (a person). To ' pose ' **or** ' stump ' him : coll. : late C. 19–20.

there, that. That, as in Richardson, 1742, ' On leaving . . . Mrs B.'s . . . house, because of that there affair ', O.E.D. : dial. and illiterate coll. Occ. *that 'ere* (C. 19–20) ; in U.S., *that 'air*.

there and back. A c.p. reply to an impertinent or unwelcome inquiry ' where are you going (to) ? ' : late C. 19–20.

there first. A thirst : rhyming s. : late C. 19–20. B. & P.

there'll ; there're, there's. There will (be) ; there are, is : coll. : C. 19–20. Baumann.

there you are ! A coll. variation of the *there you go !* of surprise, disgust, or approval : app. not before C. 20 ; app. unrecorded before 1907.

there you are then ! A rather foolish, stop-gap c.p. of C. 20 ; gen. in greeting.

therefore is incorrect when used for *therefor* : C. 19–20.

there's. There is : coll. : C. 18–20.—2. There are : sol. : C. 18–20. Baumann.

there's (h)air ! There's a girl with a lot of hair ! : London streets' c.p. of ca. 1900–12. Ware. But also *there's 'air—like wire*, which is self-explanatory (Collinson).

(there's) no — about it ! A coll. c.p., from ca. 1920, thus : ' You *must* do it ! '—' There's no must about it ! ' Michael Arlen in *The Green Hat* (cited by Collinson).

therm is incorrect for the ' term ' of a pedestal : C. 18–20. O.E.D.

these kind or **sort of.** Incorrect for *this kind* (or *sort*) *of* : C. 16–20. Cf. *those kind*, and *sort of*, *these*, qq.v.

they. Them : mid-C. 17–20 : S.E. until mid-C. 18, then (dial. and) coll. ; in C. 19–20, a sol. Cf. *them*, 2, q.v.—2. ' Those ', adj., as in ' I don't like they things ' : late C. 13–20 : S.E. until C. 17, then (dial. and) coll. ; in C. 19–20, sol. Cf. *them*, 1.

they say, where **they** is indefinite and may refer to one person. It is said : coll. verging on S.E. : C. 17–20.

they've opened . . . See **tin !, they've opened another.**

*thick. A synonym of *stiff*, n., 1, by which it was prob. suggested : c. of ca. 1820–50. Egan's Grose. —2. A blockhead ; a foolish person : coll., mostly schools' ; ob. T. Hughes, 1857, ' What a thick I was to come ! ' Ex *thick*, stupid.—3. Cocoa :

(mostly London) street s. : from ca. 1870 ; ob. Ex the consistency of cocoa as usually made.—4. Coffee : c. (— 1923). Manchon.—5. Porter, which is said to be ' a decoction of brewers' aprons ' : rather proletarian : from ca. 1870 ; ob.

thick, adj. In close association ; familiar ; intimate : coll. : ca. 1756, Bishop Law, ' " Yes," said he, " we begin . . . without my seeking," to be pretty thick,' O.E.D. ; Barham ; G. Eliot. And see the thick as . . ., as phrases. Ex *thick,* close.— 2. Excessive in some unpleasant way ; intolerable, unmanageable ; unjust : from early 1880's, the O.E.D. recording it in 1884. ' " It's a bit thick ", he said indignantly, " when a man of my position is passed over for a beginner . . .",' Horace Wyndham, 1907 (O.E.D.) : this being the predominant C. 20 sense. Perhaps ex S.E. *lay it on thick,* to exaggerate, to flatter fulsomely.—3. Hence, indelicate ; esp. in *a bit thick,* rather indecent : from ca. 1890 ; slightly ob. F. & H., 1904.—4. Hence (?), noisy and/or bibulous, esp. the latter : from ca. 1891. W. Pett Ridge, *Minor Dialogues,* 1895, ' " I was out at a smoker last night." " Thick ? " " Thick isn't the word " '—5. See dead thick in the Addenda.

thick, adv. Densely : coll. : late C. 19–20. ' The syrup runs thick,' O.E.D.

thick, got 'em. Very drunk : from ca. 1890 ; slightly ob. ' Pomes ' Marshall, 1897, ' I've got 'em thick, he said . . . And . . . went upstairs to bed.' The *'em* is generic : cf. got *'em,* q.v.

thick and thin. Unshakable devotion to a party or a principle : political : 1884, *The Pall Mall Gazette,* Feb. 14, ' The hidebound partisans of thick and thin ', O.E.D.—2. Hence, gen. hyphenated, as adj. in same sense : 1886, J. Payn (O.E.D.) : political and journalistic. Both n. and adj. little used after ca. 1901 ; by 1935, virtually †.

thick as . . ., as. Similes—all coll.—elaborating *thick,* adj., 1, q.v. :—as glue, C. 19–20 ; as inkleweavers, late C. 17–20 (ob.), as in B.E., Cowper, Scott,—ex their working so close together ; as *peas in a shell,* late C. 18–19,—cf. as *three in a bed ; as thieves,* C. 19–20, as in Theodore Hook, 1833, and Dr. L. P. Jacks, 1913, ex the confidential and secret manner of thieves conferring ; *as three in a bed,* C. 19–20, as in Scott, 1820, but since ca. 1870 only in dial.,—ex the close-packed discomfort. (O.E.D. and Apperson.) Dial. has many synonyms, e.g. *thick as Darby and Joan, Dick and Laddy, Harry and Mary, herrings in a barrel, two dogs' heads,* and (also a C. 19–20 coll.) *thick as thick* : see esp. E.D.D.

thick ear. (Gen. *give one a t. e.*) An ear swollen as the result of a blow : low coll. : late C. 19–20. Ware. (Often in threats.)

*****thick one ;** gen. **thick 'un.** A sovereign ; a crown piece : both, c. (— 1859) >, almost imm., (low) s. ; the latter sense, † by 1920. H., 1st ed. ; ' House Scraps ' Aitken ; B. L. Farjeon. Hence, *smash a t. u.,* to change it.

thick starch double blue. A ' rustling holiday dress for summer ' : middle classes' : ca. 1905–14. Ware. Ex its over-laundered state.

thick upon one, bear one's blushing honours. To have the red face of a drunkard or of one who, at the least, drinks much : jocular coll. : (— 1923). Manchon. With a pun on the trite S.E. phrase.

Thicker. Thucydides, as a text : Harrow : from ca. 1890. See ' *-er,* Oxford '.

thickest part of his thigh . . . See humdudgeon.

Thicksides. Thucydides : Public Schools' : from ca. 1880. P. G. Wodehouse, *Tales of St Austin's,* 1903, ' I'm going to read Pickwick. Thicksides doesn't come within a mile of it.' Cf. *Thicker,* q.v.

thief. A horse failing to run to form : racing : 1896 (O.E.D.).

thief and a murderer, you have killed a baboon and stole his face,—you are a. A c.p. of vulgar abuse : ca. 1780–1830. Grose, 1st ed.

thief in a mill, safe as a. See safe as.

*****thieved, be.** To be arrested : c. : from ca. 1925. James Curtis, *The Gilt Kid,* 1936.

Thieves, the Murdering. The Army Service Corps : military : 1857–60. Ex ' the Military Train ', as the Corps was then known. Also nicknamed *the London Thieving Corps,* 1855–7, and *the Moke Train,* 1857–60. For C. 20 names, see Ally Sloper's Cavalry ; cf. Linseed Lancers, the A.M.C.

thieves' cat. A cat-o'-nine-tails with knots : nautical (— 1867) ; ob. Smyth. Because it was used as a punishment for theft.

Thieves' Kitchen, the. The Law Courts : London satirical : 1882–ca. 90. Ware.—2. The City Athenæum Club : City of London jocular (— 1923). Manchon (' cercle des financiers de la Cité ').

[**thieves' Latin,** as a term, is S.E. It is often used—orig. by Scott, in 1821—as a synonym for *cant* as used in this dictionary : the ' secret ' language of criminals and tramps. Cf. *St Giles' Greek.*]

thieving hooks. Fingers : low (— 1887). Baumann.

thieving irons. Scissors : C. 19. F. & H. ? because used for cutting purses.

*****thimble.** A watch : c. (— 1811). *Lex. Bal.*—2. Hence *thimble-twister,* a watch-thief (— 1859), as in H., and *t. and slang,* a watch and chain (— 1901).

thimble, knight of the. A tailor : jocular coll. : 1812 (O.E.D.). See knight.

Thimble and Bodkin Army. The Parliamentary Army in the Civil War : a coll. nickname at the time ; recorded by O.E.D. for 1647. Ex the smallness of Roundhead gifts to the cause as compared with Royalists' munificence.

*****thimble-crib.** A watchmaker's shop : c. : ca. 1810–60. Vaux. Ex *crib,* n., 3.

thimble-rig. A sharping trick with three thimbles and a pea : s. (1825, Hone) >, ca. 1850, coll. >, before 1890, S.E.—2. Hence, from ca. 1830, *thimble-rigger,* such a sharper. See rig, n.

*****thimble-twister.** See thimble, 2. The vbl.n. is *thimble-twisting* (— 1845 : ' *No. 747* ').

*****thimbled.** Owning or wearing a watch : c. (— 1812). Vaux. See thimble.—2. Arrested ; laid by the heels : c. of ca. 1820–40. Bee. ? by a pun on *thimble* = a watch = the watch = the police.

thin. To deceive, dupe, ' catch out ', swindle : from ca. 1922. Manchon. Cf. :

thin, adj. Disappointing ; unpleasant : distressing. Gen. *(have) a thin time,* to go through hardship, spend a disappointing holiday, have a thoroughly disagreeable or distasteful experience. From ca. 1922. Mainly ex S.E. *thin,* feeble (as in *thin story*), slight, almost worthless, but partly proleptic (' enough to make one thin '). Cf. *slender, taper,* and contrast *thick,* adj., 4, q.v.

thin as a rasher of wind. See rasher of wind.

thin-gut. A very thin person ; a starveling : C. 17–20 : S.E. until C. 19, then (low) coll. ; so ob. as to be virtually †.

Thin Red Line, the. The 93rd Foot Regiment,

afterwards the Argyll and Sutherland Highlanders :
military : from ca. 1855. Ex an incident in the
Crimean War ; whence the vague S.E. sense of the
phrase. (The Army was reconstituted in 1881.)

thin 'un. A half-sovereign : from ca. 1860 ;
almost †. On *thick 'un*, q.v.

thing. ' Thingamy ', e.g. *Mrs Thing* : low coll. :
C. 20. Heard in the street, May 3, 1935.—2.
Phrases : see **any old thing, good thing, old thing,
a thing or two**, and **know a thing or two**.—3. See
thing, the, and **things**.

thing, the. (Always in predicate). That which
is suitable, fitting, fashionable ; the correct thing ;
(of a person) fit, in good form or condition : coll. :
1762, Goldsmith, ' It is at once rich, tasty, and
quite the thing ' ; 1775, Mme D'Arblay, ' Mr Bruce
was quite the thing ; he addressed himself with great
gallantry to us all alternately,' O.E.D. ; 1781,
Johnson (of a procedure), ' To use the vulgar
phrase, not the thing ' ; 1864, Meredith (of health),
' You're not quite the thing to-day, sir,' O.E.D.,—
in C. 20, gen *feel the thing* or *not quite the thing*.—2.
Hence, the requisite, special, or notable point :
coll. : 1850, Thackeray (O.E.D.) ; M. Arnold, 1873.
' [A state church] is in itself . . . unimportant.
The thing is to re-cast religion.'—3. See **things, the**.

thing-a-merry. See **thingumajig**.—**thingamobob.**
See **thingumbob**.—**thingamy**. See **thingummy**.—
thing'em. See **thingum**. — **thing'em bob**. See
thingumbob.—**thing-o-me(-my)**. See **thingummy**.

things. Personal effects carried with one at a
given time ; impedimenta : coll. : C. 17–20 ; e.g.
in 1662, J. Davies, ' We . . . went to the Custom
House to have our things search'd,' O.E.D. Ex
things, possessions, goods.—2. Clothes : coll. :
from ca. 1630, as in Sheridan, 1775, ' I suppose you
don't mean to detain my apparel—I may have my
things, I presume ? '—3. Hence, esp. such garments, etc., as, in addition to her indoor dress, a
woman dons for going out in : coll. : 1833, T.
Hook, ' Take off your things—and we will order
. . . tea,' O.E.D.—4. Implements or utensils ;
equipment : if the kind is specified, then coll. :
C. 18–20. ' The kitchen things ' is recorded by
O.E.D. at 1738. Cf. sense 1.—5. Base coin : c. of
mid-C. 19–20 ; ob. Ex contemptuous use of *things*.

things, . . . and. And other such things ; *et
cetera* : coll. : 1596, Shakespeare, 'Ruffs and cuffs,
and fardingales, and things ' ; 1920, Denis Mackail,
What Next ?, ' We've had such tremendous fun and
things.' Cf. *that, all*, q.v.

things, no great. (Predicatively.) Nothing
much ; mediocre ; very ordinary : coll. and dial. :
1816, ' Quiz ', ' " The Governor ",—He's no great
things . . ., Sir,' O.E.D. ; slightly ob.

*****things, the.** Base coin : c. (— 1839) ; virtually
†. Brandon.

thingstable. ' Mr Thingstable, Mr Constable, a
ludicrous affectation of delicacy in avoiding the . . .
first syllable in the title of that officer, which in
sound has some similarity to an indecent monosyllable,' Grose, 1st ed. ; † by 1830. (Cf. *rooster* for
cock.)

thingum ; in C. 19, occ. *thing'em*. ' Thingummy '
(q.v.) : coll. : 1681, Flatman, ' The Thingum in the
Old Bailey ', O.E.D. : from mid-C. 19, only in dial.
Cf. *thing* + *um*, a meaningless suffix. Prob. earlier
than :

thingum thangum. ' Thingummy ' (q.v.) : coll. :
1680, Otway ; † by 1800. Reduplicated *thingum*.

thingumajig (occ. **thingermajig, thingummijib** (or

-jig), **thingymyjig**, etc.), often hyphened **thingum-a-
jig** ; **thingumary**, occ. **thingummarie**, also **thing-a-
merry**. A ' thingummy ' (q.v.) : coll. : *-jig*, 1876,
' Lewis Carroll ' ; *-ary* (etc.), 1819, and ob. by 1930 ;
the rare *thing-a-merry*, occurring in 1827, is † by
1890. Elaborations of *thingum*, q.v. O.E.D. Cf. :

thingumbob ; occ. **thingamobob, thing'em bob,
thing(-)em(-)bob, thingumebob, thingummybob.** A
' thingummy ' (q.v.) : coll. : resp. 1751, Smollett,—
cf. Grose, 1st ed., ' A vulgar address or nomination
to any person whose name is unknown ' ; 1870 ;
C. 19–20 ; 1778, Miss Burney ; 1832, Lytton ; mid-
C. 19–20 and due to a confusion with *thingummy*.
Ex *thingum*, q.v. + a senseless suffix. (O.E.D. ;
F. & H.) Cf. *thingummy*.—2. In pl. : see senses 3,
4, of **thingummy**.

thingumitum. An occ. C. 20 variant (Manchon)
of :

thingummy ; often **thingam(m)y** ; rarely **thing-
o-me** or *-o'-me* or *-o-my* ; fairly often **thingummie**
or **-umy**. A thing or, occ., a person one does not
wish to, or cannot, specify, or the name of which one
has forgotten : coll. : resp. 1819 ; 1803 ; 1796,
thing-o'-me, perhaps a nonce-use, as prob. also is
thing-o-me in late 1790's ; *thing-o-my*, rare, is of
early C. 19 ; *-ummie*, from ca. 1820 ; *-umy*, H.,
1864. Thackeray, 1862, ' What a bloated aristocrat
Thingamy has become.' Ex *thingum*, q.v., +
diminutive *y* or (*ie*) or, less prob., ex *thing* + *of me*
(= mine). O.E.D. ; F. & H. ; W. Cf. *thingumajig*
and *thingumbob*.—2. The penis or the pudend :
euphemistic coll. : C. 19–20.—3. In pl., the testicles : *thingumbobs* in Grose, 1st ed. ; *thingummies*
(etc.) not till C. 19 ; *thingumajigs* not before ca.
1880, nor *thingumaries* before ca. 1820.—4. (Also in
pl.) Trousers : lower classes' (— 1909). Ware.

think. An act or period of thinking : dial. (from
ca. 1830) >, ca. 1840, coll. Ex v.—2. An opinion :
coll. : 1835, Lady Granville, ' My own private
think is that he will . . .,' O.E.D.—3. Sol. for
thing, esp. in *anythink* (q.v.), *nothink*, and *somethink*.

think !, I don't. This c.p. (which is rather s. than
coll.) reverses the ironical statement it follows :
1837, Dickens, ' " Amiably-disposed . . ., I don't
think," resumed Mr Weller, in a tone of moral
reproof,' O.E.D. In late C. 19–20, it often elicits
the dovetail, *you don't look as if you do* or *I didn't
suppose you did* ; and in C. 20 one occ. substitutes
fink (*à la* Cockney) for *think*.

think !, only ; **think !, you can't.** Phrases
exclamatory and/or intensive of that which follows : 1782, Mme D'Arblay, ' You can't think how
I'm encumbered . . . ! ' ; 1864, Mrs Carlyle, ' Only
think ! I get . . .' O.E.D.

think ?, what or **who do you.** Phrases, esp. if
parenthetical, ushering in a surprising statement :
coll. : 1616, Jonson, ' 'Mongst these . . ., who do
you think there was ? Old Banks . . .,' O.E.D.

think about breakfast. See **breakfast, think
about**.

think and thank. Thank you ! ; thanks, gratitude : Yiddish (— 1909). Ware, ' Translated from
the first words of the ordinary Hebrew morning
prayer '.

think small beer of oneself. See **small beer**.

think-tank, have bubbles in one's. To be crazy :
motorists' : ca. 1908–15.

think to do (something). Think of doing : coll. :
C. 20. Gen. in past, as ' Did he think to close the
door, I wonder.' O.E.D. ; Fowler. Ex † Scottish.

think up. To invent, or to compose, by taking

thought ; esp. by racking one's brains, to hit upon, to devise : U.S. coll. (1885) anglicised ca. 1900. E.g. 'Things look bad ; I must think up some stunt.' Possibly, to bring up to the surface of one's mind by hard thinking.

thinker. An actor playing a 'thinking part' : theatrical coll. : 1886. (O.E.D.)

thinking, to my. In my opinion : from late 1870's : S.E. until ca. 1920, then coll. On the very much older *in my thinking.*

thinking part. A role in which one says very little or nothing : theatrical coll. : 1898, *The Daily News*, March 12 (O.E.D.). Because in such a part, an actor has plenty of time for thought.

thinks he holds it, he. He's a vain conceited fellow : from ca. 1870 : a sporting c.p. > gen. ca. 1875 ; ob. Ware. Presumably *it* is the prize.

thinks I. (Parenthetically) I think : sol. or, at best, low coll. (— 1887). Baumann.

third. See **second.**

[Third person for first or second singular is a 'constant' of sol. speech : immemorial. E.g. John Rhode, *The Hanging Woman*, 1931, 'I never opens none of the ground-floor windows.']

thirsty. Causing thirst : late C. 16–20 : S.E. until C. 19, then coll.

***thirteen clean shirts.** Three months' imprisonment : prison c. : late C. 19–20 ; slightly ob. I.e. at the rate of one shirt a week.

thirteen to the dozen, talk. An occ. C. 20 variant (Manchon) of *talk nineteen to the dozen.*

thirteenth juryman. 'A judge who, in addressing a jury, shows leaning or prejudice' : legal (— 1895). Ware.

thirtyish. Approximately thirty years of age : coll. : from the early 1920's. O.E.D. (Sup.).

this. The present ; now in office : coll. : 1785, Boswell, 'This Mr Waller was a plain country gentleman,' O.E.D. (Sup.).—2. This . . . now fashionable or recently invented (or introduced) : coll. : C. 20. The O.E.D. instances, in 1916, 'What do you think of this wireless telegraphy ?'

this child. I ; myself ; I myself : orig. (— 1842), U.S., at first esp. among Negroes ; partly anglicised, mostly in the Colonies, late in C. 19. (Thornton.)

this here. Emphatic, esp. if contemptuous, 'this' : see **here, this.**

this is all right ! Everything is wrong ! : non-aristocratic c.p. of ca. 1896–1905. Ware.

this is the life. A c.p. dating from several years before, but popularised by soldiers in, the G.W. Mencken alludes to it in his admirable *American Language*. Also, *it's a great life !*

thistle-down. Children apt to wander, esp. on moor or heath : Anglo-Irish coll. (— 1909). Ware. Cf. the Devonshire dial. *thistle-seed*, Gypsies.

thistle-whipper. A hare-hunter : hunting : 1801 O.E.D.). Contemptuous.

thoke. A rest, esp. in or on one's bed ; an idling : Winchester (— 1891). Wrench. Prob. ex *thoky*, q.v., not as at Winchester but as in dial.

thoke, v. To lie late in bed ; to idle : Winchester (— 1891). Ex n.

thoke on or **upon.** To look forward to : ibid. ; id. Elaboration of preceding.

thoker. 'A piece of bread soaked in water and toasted or baked in the ashes' : Winchester College : mid-C. 19–20. Wrench. Ex *toasted + soaked.*

thokester. An idler : ibid. ; id. Ex *thoke*, v., q.v.

thoky. Idle : Winchester College (— 1891). Ex dial. *thoky*, earlier *thokish*, sluggish, lazy.

thole ; tholl. † incorrectnesses for *toll*, as is Scottish *thoil(l)*. O.E.D.

Thomas, John ; man Thomas. The penis : resp. C. 19–20 ; C. 17–mid-19, recorded in Grose, 1st ed., but implied in Fletcher's *Monsieur Thomas* in 1619. Cf. *Dick.*

Thomasina Atkins. A 'Waac' (q.v.) : journalistic coll. : 1917 ; † by 1920. F. & Gibbons.

Thomond's cocks, all on one side—like Lord. Applied ironically to a group of persons nominally in agreement, actually likely to quarrel : late C. 18–early 19. Grose, 2nd ed. Lord Thomond's cock-tender shut in one room a number of birds due to fight, the next day, against another ' team ' ; result, internecine warfare.

thornback. An old maid : late C. 17–early 19. B.E. ; Facetious Tom Brown ; Grose, 1st ed. A pun on *maid*, the female young of the *thornback* (ray, skate).

Thorny. A Thornycroft motor-truck : coll., mostly Australian : from ca. 1920. Ion L. Idriess, *Lasseter's Last Ride*, 1931.

thorny wire. A quick-tempered person : Anglo-Irish : C. 20.

Thorough. Sir Thomas Wentworth (1593–1641), 1st Earl of Strafford. Dawson, 'From his giving the name to a scheme of his which was to make England an absolute monarchy '.

thorough bass. Catachrestic when = a deep or loud bass. Mid-C. 18–20. O.E.D.

thorough churchman. ' A person who goes in at one door of a church, and out at the other without stopping ', Grose, 1st ed. : ca. 1780–1850. A pun on †*thorough*, through.

thorough cough. A simultaneous cough and crepitation : late C. 17–mid-19. B.E.

thorough-go-nimble. Diarrhœa : 1694, Motteux ; Grose ; since mid-C. 19. Ob., except in dial. —2. Hence, inferior beer : ca. 1820–60. Scott, 1822 (O.E.D.).

thorough good-natured wench. ' One who being asked to sit down, will lie down ', Grose 1st ed. : ca. 1780–1880.

thorough passage. ' In at one Ear, and out at t'other ', B.E. : late C. 17–mid-19. Cf. *thorough churchman* and *thorough-go-nimble*, qq.v.

those, one of. See **one of those.**

those kind or **sort of** (e.g. *men, things*). Loose, indeed catachrestic, for *this* . . . : mid-C. 16–20. The error is generated in illogical minds by the pl.n. following *of.* Cf. *these kind* . . .

thou. A thousand ; esp. £1000 : coll. : 1869 (O.E.D.). Ware dates it from 1860. Cf. *sov.*

though. (As adv., gen. at end of phrase.) For all that ; nevertheless ; however, yet : C. 9–20 : S.E. until mid-C. 19, then coll. Browning, 1872 ; Anstey, 1885, 'I've lost [the note]. She told me what was inside though.' O.E.D. Cf. the enclitic use of *however* and even the very awkward *but.*—2. Clumsily used, i.e. as a non-adversative, conjunction : stylistic or logical error rather than catachresis : immemorial. Fowler.

thought did !, you know what. A c.p. to 'I *think* . . .'; late C. 19–20. If the other asks *What ?*, one adds *Ran away with another man's wife.* A softening of the late C. 18–mid-19 form recorded in Grose, 2nd ed. : ' *What did thought do ? Lay in bed and besh*t himself, and thought he was up* ; reproof to anyone who excuses himself for any breach of positive orders, by pleading that he thought to the contrary.' Cf. the curious *thing* proverb (no. 1) in Apperson, p. 625.

thou'rt. Thou art ; thou wert : coll. : C. 16–20 ; in C. 19–20, only as archaism. Baumann.

thousand a year !, another (ten). A drinking pledge : coll. : mid-C. 19–20 ; very ob.

thousand-miler. A black twill shirt : nautical : C. 20. Bowen. Prob. because often worn for a thousand miles without being changed.

thousand pities ; or, towns and cities. A woman's breasts : rhyming s. (on *bubs and titties*) : late C. 19–20.

thousand strokes and a rolling suck(, a). A nautical c.p. applied to a leaky ship : from ca. 1870. Bowen. Her pumps require many strokes and suck—an indication that she is dry—only when the ship rolls.

thrash one's jacket or the life out of one. To thrash ; to thrash severely : coll. : resp. 1687 (T. Brown), in C. 20 almost † ; from ca. 1870. O.E.D.

thread the needle. To coït with a woman : C. 19–20 ; ob.

three. A Rugby three-quarter : sporting coll. : C. 20. (O.E.D. record : 1905).—2. A third-term cadet in : the training-ship *Britannia* : late C. 19–early 20. Bowen.

three !, the cube of. An Oxford toast of 1705–6. Thomas Hearne, in his *Reliquiæ*, ' The great health now is . . ., . . . 27, . . . the number of the protesting lords.' In reference to a political incident of the day.

three acres and a cow. A satirical c.p. (1887–ca. 89) directed at baseless or excessive optimism. Ware. (Cf., however, Collinson who notes that it was revived ca. 1906.)

three and sixpenny thoughtful. A ' feminine theory novel ' : Society : ca. 1890–8. Ware. Satirical of, e.g., Mrs Craigie and Mrs Humphry Ward.

three balls. See **uncle Three Balls.**

three B's. Brief, bright, brotherly : ecclesiastical (— 1909). Ware. In reaction against the somnolence of so many services in Victorian days.

three cold Irish. See **Fenian.**

three-cornered. (Of a horse) awkwardly shaped : coll. : 1861, Whyte-Melville (O.E.D.).

three-cornered constituency. A house where one person's ' vote ' gives victory to either wife or husband : Society : ca. 1870–1914. Ware. Ex boroughs in which one voted for two of the three members returned.

three-cornered scraper. A cocked hat : nautical (— 1864) ; † by 1900. H., 3rd ed.

three-cornered tree. See **three-legged mare.**

three-cross double (or treble). A glass of beer, a half-glass of rum, and a gill of red wine : Glasgow public-houses' (— 1934). Cf. *roll-up*, q.v.

three dark-blue lights was a 1916–18 military c.p. : thus would peace be announced ; i.e. never, since such a light would be virtually invisible against a night sky. B. & P.

three-decker. A pulpit in three tiers : coll. nickname ; 1874 (O.E.D.) ; ob.—2. ' A sea pie or potato pie with three layers of meat and crust or potato ' : nautical coll. : late C. 19–20. Bowen.

three decks and no bottom. An ocean liner : sailing-ship men's c.p. : late C. 19–20. Bowen.

three draws and a spit. (Occ. hyphenated.) A cigarette : low : late C. 19–20 ; ob.

three-er. Something counting for three, esp. in

cricket : coll. : from the early 1890's. O.E.D. (Sup.).

three F's, the. Fuck, fun, and a foot-race : low : ca. 1882–1914. Punning the three demands of the Irish Land League, Free Sale, Fixity of Tenure, and Fair Rent.

*three-handed. Three (adj.) : c. (— 1933). Charles E. Leach.

three ha'porth of Gorde(1)pus. A street arab : London (— 1909) ; ob. Ware. Ex Cockney form of *God help us !*

three is an awkward number. A c.p. (1885–6) paraphrasing *two are company* ; *three, not.* Ex Lord Durham's nullity-of-marriage law-suit (1885). Ware.

three-island ship. ' A steamer with forecastle, bridge deck and poop ' : nautical coll. : C. 20. Bowen.

three-legged mare, stool. The gallows ; in C. 17–18, esp. that at Tyburn : resp. 1685, T. Brown, and Grose, 1st ed.,—† by 1850 ; and late C. 17–mid-19, as in B.E. Also *three-cornered tree*, 1654, but † by 1800 ; *mare with the three legs*, Ainsworth, 1834, and rare ; *(the) three trees*, late C. 16–mid-17, as in Breton. Also *(the) triple tree*, *(the) Tyburn tree*, qq.v. ' Formerly consisting of three posts, over which were laid three transverse beams ', Grose, 1785.—2. *comb one's head with a three-legged* (or *a joint-*) *stool.* Gen. as threat, *I'll comb your head*, etc. : coll. : late C. 16–18, then in dial. Shakespeare (*noddle*).

three L's. Look-out—lead—latitude : nautical coll. : C. 19. Bowen.

three-man breeze. A stiff breeze : sailing-ships' : late C. 19–20. Ibid. A pun on *catamaran*, from whose crew such a breeze sent several men ' out on to the weather outrigger '.

three more and up goes the donkey ! See **donkey !, a penny . . .**

three nines agreement. A lease for 999 years : house-agents' coll. (— 1927). Collinson.

three-o ; two-o. Third officer ; second officer : nautical : C. 20. Ex the abbrr. *3 o.* and *2 o.*

three-op packet. A passenger ship carrying three operators : ' nautical ' wireless operators' : from ca. 1925. Bowen.

three-out. A glass holding the third of a quartern : coll. : from ca. 1836. Dickens in *Sketches by Boz.*

three-out brush. A drinking-glass shaped like an inverted cone and therefore rather like a painter's brush esp. when dry : taverns' (— 1909). Ware.

three parts seven-eighths. Tipsy : nautical : C. 20. Bowen. Prob. ex *three sheets in the wind.* In F. & Gibbons it is . . . *five-eighths.*

three-piece bamboo. A three-masted ship : pidgin and nautical : from ca. 1870 ; slightly ob. Bowen.

three planks. A coffin : lower classes' coll. (— 1909). Ware.

three-pointer on the deck. A heavy fall : aircraft engineers' : from ca. 1925. *The Daily Herald*, Aug. 1, 1936. I.e. a falling flat. Cf. :

three-pricker. A perfect landing, with the two wheels and the tail-skid simultaneously on the tarmac : Royal Air Force : from 1932.

three-quarter man. See **six-quarter man.**

three-quarters of a peck, often abbr. *three-quarters* and by experts written ' ¾ '. The **eck :** rhyming s. (— 1857). ' Ducange Anglicus.'

three sheets in the wind. See **sheets.**

three sixty-five ; gen. written ' 365 '. Eggs-and-bacon : commercial travellers' : late C. 19–20. Because eaten for breakfast every day of the year. On slates in commercial hotels may be seen the legend ' 7 (*or* 7). 365 ', which means ' Call me at 7 (*or* 7.30) ; eggs-and-bacon for breakfast.'

three skips of a louse ; not three skips of a louse. (Of) no value ; not at all : coll. : 1633, Jonson, ' I care not I, sir, not three skips of a louse ' ; † by 1850. Hence, *for three,* etc. : very easily, or with very little provocation, as in Murphy, 1769, ' I'd cudgel him back, breast and belly for three skips of a louse ! ' ; † by 1850. Cf. *for tuppence* (s.v. *tuppence*).

three slips for a tester(, give). (To give) the slip : coll. : ca. 1625–1700. F. Grove, 1627 ; Anon., ca. 1685, ' *How a Lass gave her Love Three Slips for a Tester* [part of a ballad title], and married another three weeks before Easter.' Lit., (to give) three counterfeit twopennies for a sixpence. Apperson, as also for the preceding.

three S's !, mind your. A naval c.p. rule for promotion : late C. 19–20. Bowen. I.e. be sober, silly [simple ; not offensively intelligent], and civil.

three steps and overboard. See **fisherman's walk.**

three-stride business. The taking of only three strides between hurdles, this being the ' crack ' style : athletics coll. : late C. 19–20.

Three Tens, the. The 30th Foot Regiment ; after 1881, the (1st Battalion of the) East Lancashire Regt. : military : C. 19–20. Also *the triple X's.*

three to one (and sure to lose), play. (Of a man) to coït : low : late C. 18–20, ob. Grose, 2nd ed. (*though* for *and*). Physiological arithmetic.

three trees. See **three-legged mare.**

three (in late C. 19–20, often **two**) **turns round the long-boat and a pull at the scuttle** characterises, among sailors (— 1867 ; ob.) the activities of an artful dodger, ' all jaw, and no good in him ', Smyth. Also *Tom Cox's traverse,* ' up one hatchway and down another ', Smyth ; likewise ob. This *traverse* dates from (not later than) 1835, when Dana first heard the phrase. Bowen makes the *two turns* phrase mean also : ' Under sail, killing time.'

three-up. A gambling game played with three coins : only if three heads or three tails fall is the toss operative : coll. >, ca. 1900, S.E. : 1851, Mayhew (O.E.D.) ; H., 1st ed.

three vowels. An I.O.U. : ca. 1820–1920. Scott, 1822 (O.E.D.). Cf. *vowel,* q.v.

three-wheeler. A tricycle : sporting coll. (— 1887) ; ob. Baumann. Cf. *tri.*

Three X's, the. Same as *Three Tens,* q.v.

threepence, smart as. See **smart as threepence.**

threepence more . . . See **donkey !**

threepenny bit or upright. A coïtion with a whore, price 3*d.* : low : mid-C. 19–20 ; late C. 18–20. Grose, 2nd ed., applies it to the ' retailer of love '.

threepenny masher. A young man ' of limited means and more or less superficial gentlemanly externals ' : non-aristocratic : ca. 1883–90. Ware.

threepenny shot. A beef-steak pudding, globe-shaped : artisans' (— 1909). Ware.

threepenny upright. See **threepenny bit.**

threepenny (pronounced *thruppenny*) **vomit.** Fish and chips : low Glasgow (— 1934).

threp, thrip ; *threp(p)s, thrups. Threepence ; a threepenny bit : in C. 17–18, c., but in C. 19–20, (low) s. : resp. late C. 19–20 ; id. ; late C. 17–mid-

19 ; from late 1850's. B.E., *threpps* ; H., 1st ed., *thrups* ; *thrip* existed in U.S. as early as 1834 (Thornton) for a coin intermediate between a nickel and a dime. Ex popular pronunciation of *threepence* ; the *s* arises ex the ' suffix ' *-ence*. Cf. *thrums,* q.v.

threshold. A lintel : catachrestic : C. 19–20. Clare ; Harriet Martineau. O.E.D.

thrill. A ' thriller ', whether fiction or non-fiction : ca. 1886–1905. Ex its effect.

thrilled. Pleased ; content ; quite satisfied : Society coll. : from ca. 1915. E.g. Denis Mackail, passim. Cf. *thrilling.*

thriller. A sensational play (1889) or, esp., novel (1896) : s. >, by 1920, coll. ; by 1935, virtually S.E. (O.E.D.) Cf. *awful, dreadful,* as nn., and *shocker.*

thrilling. Pleasing ; pleasant ; suitable, apt : Society coll. : from ca. 1915. Cf. *thrilled,* q.v.

thrip. See **threp.**

thrips. Incorrectly treated as a pl., with erroneous singular *thrip.* The genus of *Thripsidæ,* or an insect belonging thereto ; catachrestically of one of the *Jassidæ* (leaf-hoppers). Late C. 18–20. O.E.D.

throat, have a. To have a sore throat : coll. : late C. 19–20. Cf. *temperature.*

throat a mile long and a palate at every inch of it, wish for a. Applied to a ' healthy ' thirst : mid-C. 19–20 ; slightly ob. ' A modern echo of Rabelais ', F. & H. : see Motteux's *Rabelais,* V, xlii. Cf. the C. 20 *what wouldn't I give for a thirst like that !* and *I wouldn't sell my thirst for a fortune* or *a thousand* (*quid*), etc.

throat (is) cut, one's belly thinks one's. One is extremely hungry : 1540, Palsgrave : a semi-proverbial c.p. ; in mid-C. 19–20 mostly rural. (Apperson.)

throats, cut one another's. To compete ruinously : coll. : from 1880's. Cf. *cut-throat.*

Throstles, the. The West Bromwich Football Club (' soccer ') : sporting : C. 20. Perhaps because their ground is in Hawthorn Road ; thrushes like hawthorn hedges.

***through, be.** To be acquitted : c. of ca. 1810–50. Vaux, *be through it, through the piece.* Ex lit. S.E. sense.

through a woman, go. To coït with her : low coll. : C. 19–20. Often, more vulgarly, *go through a woman like a dose of salts* : C. 20.

through-shot, adj. Spendthrift : coll. : late C. 19–20 ; ob. ? ex going through one's money much as a shot goes through paper.

through the lights. (Of a punch) that is an upper-cut : low, and boxing (— 1935).

***through the piece.** See **through, be.**

throw. ' He threw me with a stone ' = he threw a stone at me. This South African Midlands coll., of late C. 19–20, like *throw wet* (q.v.), shows Dutch influence ; Pettman aligns Ger. *Er warf mir ein Loch in den Kopf,* he threw a stone at me and cut my head open.—2. To throw away, i.e. lose deliberately, a game, a set in order to obtain service or to conserve energy : lawn tennis coil. : from 1933, or early 1934. *Lowe's Annual,* 1935.—3. To bring as wages : lower-class Glaswegians' : C. 20. MacArthur & Long, *No Mean City,* 1935, ' His job " threw him " forty-eight shillings for the week of forty-eight hours.'

throw a chest. See **chest, throw a.**

throw a levant. To make off : mid-C. 19–20. Ex *levant,* to abscond.

throw a party. To give a party : U.S. ; anglicised ca. 1925. Prob. ex such U.S. phrases as *throw* h ave) *a fit* : cf. *chuck a dummy*, q.v.

throw at a dog, not a (this, that, or the other) to. Gen. preceded by *have*. No — at all : coll. : from ca. 1540, for it is implied in Heywood, 1546 ; 1600, Day, ' I have not a horse to cast at a dog ' ; Swift, ca. 1706, ' Here's miss, has not a word to throw at a dog ' ; 1884, Stevenson & Henley. Slightly ob. Apperson.

throw back. ' To revert to an ancestral type or character not present in recent generations ' : coll. >, ca. 1920, S.E. : 1879. Also fig., as indeed is the earliest recorded example. (The n. has always been considered S.E.) O.E.D.

throw-down. A defeat : 1903 (O.E.D.). Ex *throw-down*, a fall in wrestling.

throw-down, v. To be too much for, to floor : 1891, Anon., *Harry Fludyer*, ' These blessed exams. are getting awfully close now ; but I think I shall floor mine, and Dick's sure to throw his examiners down.' Also of the ' exam.' itself and the papers constituting it. Perhaps ex throwing down a wicket at cricket.

[**throw in the towel** is rather sporting j. than coll. See **sponge, chuck up the**.]

throw it up against, at, or **to one.** To reproach or upbraid one with : coll. (*to* : low coll.) : 1890, *The Universal Review*, Oct. 15 (O.E.D.).

throw me in the dirt. A shirt : rhyming s. (— 1857) ; † by 1900. ' Ducange Anglicus.' The modern form is *Dicky dirt* : much C. 20 rhyming s. retains something—actual word or semantic essence—of the discarded form : *daisy recroots* and *German flutes*, both = ' boots ', afford a particularly interesting example.

throw mud at the clock. To despair much or utterly : lower classes' (— 1909). Ware, ' Means defy time and die '.

throw-off. A depreciative remark or allusion : C. 20. Manchon. Ex sense 2 of :

***throw off.** To boast of booties of the past : c. of ca. 1810–60. Vaux, who notes also :—2. ' To talk in a sarcastical strain, so as to convey offensive allusions under the mask of pleasantry, or innocent freedom ' : c. (— 1812) >, by 1860, s. in sense, to be depreciative (*at* a person).—3. To deduct (so much) from (a stated sum) : lower classes' (— 1923). Manchon. Perhaps suggested by *cast accounts.*—4. To vomit : coll. : C. 20.

throw-off practice. ' Gunnery practice where an actual ship is used as the target ' : naval coll. : C. 20. Bowen.

throw one's weight about. See **weight about**.

***throw over the bridge.** (Gen. ppl.adj., *thrown* . . .) To swindle as in *bridge, v., Vaux.

throw snot about. To weep : low : 1678, Ray ; ob. See **snot**.

***throw the feet.** To hustle ; to beg : tramps' c. and low s., orig. (— 1900) U.S. Ex a horse *throwing his feet*, lifting them well.

throw the hammer. To obtain money under false pretences : low military (— 1909). Ware. Of erotic origin.

throw up. To abandon hope completely : from ca. 1929. A. A. Milne, *Two People*, 1931, ' When it became definitely mottled, there was really nothing for a girl to do but to " throw up ". Perhaps ex *throw up the sponge.*

throw up one's accounts. To vomit : from ca. 1760 ; ob. C. Johnston, 1763 (O.E.D.). A variant of *cast up one's accounts.*

throw up the sponge. See **sponge, chuck up the**.

throw wet. To dash water upon : Cape Midlands (Sth. Africa) coll. : C. 20. ' A literal rendering of the Dutch *nat gooien* ', Pettman. Cf. *throw*, q.v.

throw with. See **throw**.

throwed. Threw ; thrown : sol. : C. 19–20. Baumann.

thrum, n. See **thrumbuskins**.

thrum, v.t. To thrash (a person) : C. 17–mid-19. Dekker. The vbl.n. (a beating,) is recorded in 1823 Ex strumming a musical instrument. O.E.D.—2 To coït with (a woman) : C. 17–early 19. Florio, 1610 ; Brydges, 1762.

***thrumbuskins, thrummop ; thrum(m)s.** Threepence : c. : *thrum(m)s*, late C. 17–19 ; the other two forms (Vaux, 1812) are elaborations and rare. B.E. has *thrumms*, Grose *thrums* ; H. (all edd.) the latter. A corruption of *threepence* : cf. *thrups* (at *threp*). Dial. has *thrum*, a commission of 3*d.* per stone on flax : E.D.D. Cf. :

***thrummer.** A threepenny bit : c. or low s. (— 1859) ; † by 1910, except among grafters : witness P. Allingham, *Cheapjack*, 1934. Ex preceding.

***thrum(m)s.** See **thrumbuskin.**—**thruppenny.** See **threepenny.**—**thrups.** See **threp.**

thruster. One who, in the field, thrusts himself forward or rides very close to the hounds : hunting s. >, ca. 1920, coll. : from 1885. Ex usual sense. (O.E.D.) Also *thrusting*, n. and adj.

thumb. To drain (a glass) upon a thumb-nail (see **supernaculum**) : coll. : ? C. 18–mid-19. F. & H. gives this term without quotation ; the O.E.D. has it not.—2. To possess (a woman) : C. 18–19. In C. 20, only in *well-thumbed (girl)*, ' a foundered whore ' (F. & H.). Ex *thumb*, to handle, paw, perhaps influenced by *fumble* and *tumble*.

thumb, as easy as kiss my. Exceedingly easy : coll. : from ca. 1890.

thumber. A sandwich ; a slice of bread and meat eaten between finger and thumb : low (mostly London) : late C. 19–20 ; ob.

thumby ; occ. thummie, -y. A little thumb ; a pet-name for the thumb : coll. : from ca. 1810. W. Tennant, 1811 (O.E.D.). Rare in C. 20.

thumby. ' Soiled by thumb-marks ' : coll. : from late 1890's. (O.E.D. Sup.)—2. Clumsy : coll. : 1909 (O.E.D. Sup.). Ex *all thumbs*.

thumbs up !, occ. preceded by **put your.** Be cheerful : C. 20. Ex the gesture that spared the life of gladiators at Rome. Cf. *tails up !*

thump. An occ. late C. 19–20 variant of *thumper*, 2. Manchon.

thump ! ' I *don't* think ' ; it's,—as is,—very improbable : an ejaculation of dissent modifying the preceding statement : military in G.W. See esp. Ernest Raymond's fine War-novel, *The Jesting Army*, 1930. Hence, among the lower and lower-middle classes, as in Ernest Raymond, *Mary Leith*, 1931, ' Call me a business man ! Am I ? *Thump !* I'm going in for gardening.'

thump, v. To defeat ; to lick, thrash (severely) : coll. : 1594, Shakespeare ; 1827, Scott, ' We have thumped the Turks very well.' Ex *thump*, to strike violently. O.E.D. Cf. *thrum*, v., 1.—2. To coït with (a woman) : s. or coll. : C. 17–20 ; ob. in C. 19–20. Shakespeare in *Winter's Tale*, ' Delicate burthens of dildos and fadings, " jump her and thump her ".' Cf. *thrum*, v., 2, *knock*, and Klüge's proposed etymology of *fuck*.

thump,—thatch, thistle, thunder and. ' Words to

the Irish, like the Shibboleth of the Hebrews ',
Grose, 2nd ed. : Anglo-Irish of mid-C. 18–mid-19.
A cross between an (and esp. an) incantation and
a c.p.

**thump on the back with a stone, this is better than
a.** A c.p. ' said on giving any one a drink of good
liquor on a cold morning ', Grose, 2nd ed. : ca. 1786–
1850. Cf. the C. 20 *it's better than a kick on the
pants* and the mid-C. 19–20 *it's better than a poke in
the eye with a sharp stick*.

thumped-in. (A landing that is) badly effected,
necessitating the use of the engine : Royal Air
Force's : from 1932.

thumper. Anything unusually big : coll. : 1660,
Tatham punningly of a dragon's tail. Cf. *whacker*,
whopper, the semantics being that it ' strikes ' one.—
2. Hence, esp. a notable lie : 1677, W. Hughes ;
Swift ; J. R. Green, 1863. F. & H., and esp. O.E.D.

thumpers. Dominoes (game) : showmen's s. :
mid-C. 19–20. Ex noise made in falling.

thumping. Unusually large, heavy, or, of a lie,
outrageous : coll. : 1576, Fleming, ' He useth great
and thumping words ' ; Grose, 2nd ed., ' A thumping boy ' ; of a lie, app. not before C. 19, though
applied to commendation as early as 1671. (O.E.D.)
Cf. *thumper*, q.v.

*****thumpkin.** A hay-filled barn : c. : late C. 19–
20. ? etymology. Cf. *skipper*.

thunder ! ; **by thunder !** ; (what, where, who,
etc.) **in thunder ?** ; **thunder and lightning !** ;
thunder and turf ! Imprecatively, exclamatorily,
intensively used as s. (*thunder and turf*) or coll. (the
rest) : resp. C. 18–20 (Steele) ; C. 19–20 ; mid-
C. 19–20 ; late C. 19–20, ob. ; and ca. 1840–70
(Barham, Lover). Cf. the German imprecations
and U.S. *thunderation !*

thunder and lightning. See preceding.—2. Gin
and bitters : C. 19–20 ; ob. Ex the effects.—3.
Treacle and clotted cream ; bread thus spread : s.
and dial. (– 1880). Miss Braddon ; E.D.D. The
O.E.D. notes that sense 1 approximates to the dial.
sense (brandy-sauce ignited) ; W. implies that sense
2 arises ex the colours, *black* (of thunder and treacle),
yellow (of lightning and cream),—cf. *pepper and salt*.

thunder-mug. A chamber-pot : low : C. 18–
mid-19. Ex noise therein caused.

thunderbolt. A meteorite or meteoric stone :
catachrestic : C. 19–20. O.E.D.

Thunderbomb, the ; or *H.M.S. Thunderbomb*.
An imaginary ship of fabulous size : nautical coll. :
ca. 1828, Buckstone in *Billy Taylor*, ' Straightway
made her first lieutenant | Of the gallant Thunder-
bomb ' ; † by 1915. Cf. *Swiss Navy*, q.v.

Thunderer, The. *The Times* newspaper : journalistic s. (1840, Carlyle) >, ca. 1880, coll. Anon.,
The Siliad, 1874, ' If a small cloud in the East
appear, | Then speaks The Thunderer, and all men
hear ' ; many critical notices in Jan., 1935 (notably
in *The Times Literary Supplement*, Jan. 3). Ex its
Olympian utterance and pronouncements + Jove
(*Iuppiter tonans*) and his thunderbolts. Legend
(see Pebody's *English Journalism*) has it that it was
the writing (1830–40) of Edward Sterling (' Vetus ')
which gave *The Times* this name—orig. applied to
Sterling himself.

thundering. Very forcible or violent : coll. :
adumbrated in Hall, 1597, ' Graced with huff-cap
terms and thundering threats ' ; 1618, T. Adams,
' He goes a thundering pace ' ; 1632, Lithgow, ' A
thundering rage ', O.E.D. Ex the noise made
thereby or in that manner.—2. Hence, as an inten-

sive : very large or great ; excessive : 1678, Cotton,
' A thundering meal ' ; of a lie, app. not before
mid-C. 18.—3. Hence, as adv. : from not later than
1743 in Hervey's *Memoirs*, ' A thundering long
sermon ' ; 1852, Dickens, ' A thundering bad son '
(O.E.D.). S. >, by 1900, coll. Cf. :

thunderingly. Excessively : 1885, C. Gibbon,
' It's thunderingly annoying,' O.E.D., but prob.
much earlier, for Thornton records it, for U.S., in
1839 : s. >, by 1900, coll. Ex lit. S.E. sense, but
not very gen. Ex *thundering*, 2.

thunderstorm, like a dying duck (or pig) in a. See
dying duck.

thusly. Thus : U.S. (1889) >, by 1893, English :
coll. ; mostly jocular. (O.E.D.) Cf. :

thusness. The state or condition of being thus :
jocular coll. : U.S. (1867, Artemus Ward) >
anglicised ca. 1883. S.O.D.—2. Esp. *why this thusness ?*, a pleonastic ' why ? ' : 1888, Fergus Hume,
' Why all this thusness ? ', O.E.D.,—which records
the simpler form in the same year. Slightly ob.—
thank Heaven !

thuzzy-muzzy. Enthusiasm : London lower
classes' : ca. 1890–1912. Ware. Ex *enthusiasm*
on *muzzy*.

ti-ib ! Good ; all right ! : military on the
Eastern Fronts (G.W., and before). F. & Gibbons.
Arabic *tay-ib*.

ti-toki. A mixed drink of beer, lemonade and
raspberry : New Zealanders' : C. 20. Ex Maori.

ti-tree. Erroneous for *tea-tree* : New Zealand :
mid-C. 19–20. Worse still, *ti-tri*. Morris, whom
see at p. 463.

ti-tree oneself ; be ti-treed. To take shelter from
artillery fire : New Zealand soldiers' : in G.W. Ex
Maori custom of retreating to the bush at time of the
Maori War. See preceding entry.

tib. A bit : back s. (– 1859). H., 1st ed.
Hence *tib fo occabot*, a little tobacco.—2. A goose :
c. : late C. 18–early 19. Abbr. :

*****tib o(f) the buttery.** A goose : c. : ca. 1620–
1830. Fletcher, B.E., Grose. Broome, 1641,
' Here's grunter and bleater with tib of the butt'ry, |
And Margery Prater, all dress'd without slutt'ry.'

tib out, v.i. To break bounds : schools', mainly
Public and esp. Charterhouse : 1840, J. T. Hewlett
(O.E.D.) ; 1855, Thackeray. Also *tibble* : late
C. 19–20. Etymology obscure : perhaps ex *tip*
(*oneself*) *out*, to get out by giving a tip.

Tibb's Eve (or Evening ; properly **Tib's), St.**
Never : coll., mainly Anglo-Irish (– 1785) ; long
ob., except in dial. Grose, 1st ed. Cf. *blue moon*,
S.E. *Greek kalends*, and *Queen Dick*.

tibby. A cat : late C. 18–mid-19. Grose, 3rd
ed. Ex *tabby* + dial. *tib(by)-cat*, a female cat.—2.
The head : low : from ca. 1865 ; ob. Esp. in
phrases signifying ' to take unawares ', as in Vance,
ca. 1866, ' For to get me on the hop, or on my
tibby drop, | You must wake up very early in the
mornin'.' ? a corruption of Fr. *tête* mispronounced.

tibby drop. Hop : rhyming s. : late C. 19–20.

Tib's. See **Tibb's Eve.**

tic-tac ; tick-tack. Gen. *t.-t. man* (1899), occ. *t.-t.
telegraphy* (1905) : O.E.D. N. and adj., (characteristic of, concerned with) the system of ' telegraphy '—
actually, signalling with the arms—used by bookmakers communicating a change in the odds or
some significant information to outside bookmakers :
sporting. Occ. as v., to signal thus : 1907 (O.E.D.
Sup.) : likewise coll. >, by 1935, S.E. Ex the
onomatopœia representing an alternating ticking (as

of a clock), perhaps influenced by *tape*, n., 2. Hence, *tick-tacker*.—2. See :

tic-toc or **-tac**. A signaller : military : 1914 ; ob. F. & Gibbons. In the *-tac* form, ex *tic-tac*, 1 ; it was suggested by ' the sound of the telegraphic instrument '.

ticca. See **ticker**, 3.

tice. A ball ' something between a half-volley and a Yorker ' ; cricketers' : from ca. 1840 ; ob. Lewis. I.e. an *enticer*.

'tice, v. To entice, decoy ; gen. in passive : lower-class coll. : C. 19–20. Mayhew, 1861. Also in dial.

Tich. A nickname given to any small man : C. 20. E.g. ' Tich ' Freeman, Kent's googly bowler. Ex little Tich, the comedian.

Tich !, no. No talk about the Tichborne case ! : Society : 1870's. Ware (at *pas de Lafarge*).

Tichborne's Own. The 6th Dragoon Guards : military : from ca. 1872 ; ob. Sir Roger Tichborne, of the famous trial (1871–4), served therein in 1849. Also *the Wagga-Wagga Guards*, q.v.

tick. An objectionable or meanly contemptible person, though rarely of a female : C. 17–20 : S.E. until mid-C. 19 or so ; ? ' submerged ' for years ; in C. 20, s. (Lyell.) E.g. ' That awful little tick ! ' Ex the insect parasite.—2. Credit, trust ; reputed solvency : coll. >, in C. 19, s. : 1668, Sedley, ' I confess my tick is not good, and I never desire to game for more than I have about me ' ; 1901, *The Sporting Times*, Aug. 17, 'During my late Oxford days, I got put up to at least twenty different ways of getting tick.' Ex (*up*)*on tick*, esp. *run on tick*, q.v. five entries later.—3. Hence, a score or reckoning, a debit account : coll. >, ca. 1800, s. ; in C. 20, ob. : 1681, Prideaux (Dean of Norwich), ' The Mermaid Tavern [at Oxford] is lately broke, and our Christ Church men bear the blame of it, our ticks, as the noise of the town will have it, amounting to 1500*l*. ' ; Thackeray, 1862.—4. A watch : c. of ca. 1780–1800. Parker, 1789. Cf. *ticker*, 2, q.v. Ex the sound.—5. A second, moment ; properly and etymologically, the time elapsing between two ticks of the clock : coll. : adumbrated by Browning in 1879, but not gen. before the late 1890's. Esp. *in a tick* or (1904, Jerome K. Jerome) *in two ticks*, and *to the tick*, with meticulous punctuality (1907, Phyllis Dare of theatrical fame). O.E.D.

tick, v.i. To buy, deal, on credit : coll. >, ca. 1800, s. (in C. 20, ob.) : 1648, Winyard (O.E.D.). Ex *tick*, *run on*, q.v.—2. Hence, to run into debt : 1742, Fielding (O.E.D.) ; ob.—3. V.t., to have (an amount) entered against one : coll. >, ca. 1800, s. ; ob. : 1674, S. Vincent (O.E.D.) ; ca. 1703, T. Brown, ' Pretty nymphs . . . forced to tick half a sice a-piece for their watering.'—4. V.i., to grant credit ; supply goods, etc., on credit : coll. >, ca. 1800, s. ; in C. 20, rare : 1712, Arbuthnot, ' The money went to the lawyers ; counsel won't tick.'— 5. Hence (v.t.), to grant credit to (a person) : 1842, ' Nimrod ' Apperley, ' He never refused a tandem, and he ticked me for a terrier at once,' O.E.D. ; ob. —6. V.i., to grumble : military : from 1916 or 1917. F. & Gibbons. Prob. ex *tick off*, 2.—7. See **tick off** ; **tick up**.

tick, buy on the never. To buy ' on tick ' : lower classes' (— 1923). Manchon. With allusion to a clock.

tick, full as a. See **full as a tick**.—**tick, go (on)**. See **tick, run upon**.

Tick, River. Oxford University, ca. 1820–40, as in

Egan's Grose (1823) : ' Standing debts, which only discharge themselves at the end of three years by leaving the Lake of Credit, and meandering through the haunts of 100 creditors.'

tick, run (up)on, v.i. To buy on credit ; run up a debt or into debt : 1642 (O.E.D.) : coll. >, ca. 1800, s. A variant is *go on tick* (1672, Wycherley) or *go tick* (1861, Hughes) : O.E.D. Thus (*up*)*on tick*, on credit,—though, despite the dates, this prob. preceded *run on tick*, for we find (*up*)*on ticket* (on note of hand) a generation or so earlier : *ticket* being abbr. to *tick*.

tick being no go. No credit given : low (— 1857). ' Ducange Anglicus.' See **tick**, n., 2.

tick-down ; **tick-off**, n. See **mark-off**.

tick off, v. To identify : coll. : C. 20. Ex *tick off a person's name on a list*.—2. Hence, from ca. 1916 (orig. military), to reproach, upbraid, blame ; esp. to reprimand. ' I ticked him off good and proper.' Partly influenced by *tell off*, q.v.

tick-off, work the. A *tick-off* is a fortune-teller ; gen. in *work the tick-off*, to practise fortune-telling : grafters' : late C. 19–20. Philip Allingham, *Cheapjack*, 1934, ' Dates from the time when grafters working this line sold cards on which were printed various . . . statements.'

Tick-Offs' Gaff, the. Hull Fair : grafters' : late C. 19–20. Philip Allingham, *Cheapjack*, 1934. Fortune-tellers have always flourished there. See **tick off, work the**.

tick over, v.i. To come ; to act, function : from ca. 1930. F. Keston Clarke, in *The Humorist*, July 28, 1934, of water-divining, ' How shall I know when the influence is ticking over ? ' Ex motoring j.

tick-tack. Sexual intercourse : coll. : mid-C. 16–20. Weaver, *Lusty Juventus*, ca. 1550. Ex the onomatopœia.—2. See **tic-tac**.

tick-tack, done in a. Quickly done : low coll. (— 1887). Baumann.

tick-tacker, one practising such telegraphy as that mentioned in the tic-tac entry : 1912 (O.E.D.).

tick up, v.t. To put to account : late C. 19–20. Ex *tick*, v., 3.—2. V.i., to run into debt : late C. 19– 20 ; ob. Elaboration of *tick*, v., 2.

*ticker. A fraudulent debtor by profession : c. of mid-C. 18. Recorded in title of Anon., *The Thief-Catcher*, 1753 (O.E.D.). Ex *tick*, v., 1 and 2. —2. A watch : c. (1823, ' Jon Bee ') ; before 1864 (see H., 3rd ed.), ' street ', i.e. low, s. >, by 1890, gen. s. Ex the noise : cf. Fr. *tocante* and *tick*, n., 4. Rarely and (I consider) improperly, a clock : the O.E.D. records an instance in 1910.—3. ' Any person or thing engaged by the job, or on contract ' : Anglo-Indian coll. (— 1886). Properly *ticca* (ex Hindustani). Yule & Burnell.—4. The heart : low (in U.S., c.) : late C. 19–20. Because it keeps the body's time.—5. An account ; an invoice or a statement : from ca. 1910 : esp. among publishers. Ex S.E. *ticker*, a stock-indicator.

ticket. A certificate : nautical s. (late 1890's) >, ca. 1920, coll. Chiefly *captain's* or *mate's ticket*. Ex *ticket*, a licence.—2. See **ticket, the**.

ticket, be a person's. To appeal to one, be of his kind : from ca. 1920. (Evelyn Waugh, *A Handful of Dust*, 1934.) Often abbr. to *tea* (properly *t*),—see Evelyn Waugh, ibid.,—but cf. *cup of tea*, q.v.

ticket, be on the straight. To live respectably : lower classes' (— 1923). Manchon.

[**ticket, get one's**. See **ticket, work one's**.]

ticket, have the run of the. To buy on credit, run

up debts : late C. 19–20 ; very ob. An elaboration of *tick*, n., 2 and 3, qq.v.

ticket, the. The requisite, needed, correct, or fashionable thing to do. Esp. *that's the ticket* : 1838, Haliburton (O.E.D.) ; 1854, Thackeray, ' Very handsome and . . . finely dressed—only somehow she's not—she's not the ticket, you see.' (See also **very cheese, the.**) Perhaps ex *the winning ticket*.—2. Hence, the plan or procedure ; the job, on (or in) hand : 1842, Marryat, ' What's the ticket, youngster—are you to go abroad with me ? '

ticket ?, what's the. What's the price ? : late C. 19–20 ; very ob.

ticket, work one's (occ. **the**). To obtain one's discharge from the Army by having oneself adjudged physically unfit : from late 1890's : s. >, ca. 1910, coll. (The phrase *get one's ticket*, to be, in the ordinary way, discharged from the service, is military j.) Wyndham, *The Queen's Service*, 1899, ' It is a comparatively easy matter for a discontented man to work his ticket.'

ticket for soup !, that's the. You've got it—be off ! : c.p. of ca. 1859–1910. Cf. *ticket, the*, sense 1, which it elaborates. H., 2nd ed., ' [From] the card given to beggars for immediate relief at soup kitchens '.

ticking. The taking of goods on credit : mid-C. 18–20. See **tick**, v., 1, 2.

***ticket man.** A distributor of tickets for a meal and/or a bed : tramps' c. (— 1933). Cf. *slice*, 2, q.v. for ' authority '. Cf. *ticketer*, q.v.

ticket of leave. A holiday ; an outing : lower classes' : ca. 1870–1900. Ex S.E. sense. (Ware.)

***ticketer.** One who hands out, or checks, cards in a casual ward : tramps' and beggars' c. (— 1887). Baumann.

tickey, tickie ; tickey-nap. See **ticky ; ticky nap.**

ticking, ppl.adj. of *tick*, v., 1, 2, etc. (qq.v.) : 1673, Wycherley (sense 1). O.E.D.

tickle. To puzzle (a person) : coll. (— 1874) ; ob. H., 5th ed. Ex dial : cf. *tickler*, 1, q.v.—2. To steal from, to rob, as in *tickle a peter*, to rob the till : New Zealand c. (— 1932). Perhaps ex *to tickle trout*. See **sere** and **tail**.—3. F. & H.'s *tickle-faggot*, *-gizzard*, and *-piece* are almost certainly S.E. nonce-words.

tickle-pitcher. ' A Toss-pot, or Pot-companion ', B.E. : coll. : late C. 17–early 19.—2. ' A lewd Man or Woman ', *A New Canting Dict.*, 1725 : low C. 18. A pun on the fig. sense of *pitcher*.

tickle-tail. A wanton ; the penis : ? S.E. or low coll. : C. 17–20 ; ob.—2. A schoolmaster ; his rod : coll. (— 1785) ; ob. Grose, 1st ed. Cf. *tickle-toby*.

tickle-text. A parson : from ca. 1780 ; very ob. Grose, 1st ed.

tickle-Thomas. The female pudend : low : C. 19–20. Cf. *Thomas, John*, q.v.

tickle-toby. A rod or birch : coll. : 1830, Bentham (O.E.D.).—2. A wanton ; the penis : ? C. 17–19. F. & H. See **tickle**, 2, and cf. *tickle-pitcher*, 2, and *tickle-tail*.

tickle your tail !, I'll. A jocular coll. threat of punishment : late C. 19–20. Ex S.E. *tickle*, ironic for ' to chastise '.

tickler. A thing (occ. person) hard to understand or deal with ; a puzzler or ' teaser ' (q.v.) : dial. (— 1825) >, ca. 1840, coll. ; ob.—2. A strong drink : low : late C. 19–20. Manchon.—3. The penis : low : C. 19–20.—4. (Tickler.) Jam : military : late 1915 ; ob. Ex Tickler's jam, the usual brand. Also *Tickler's*.—5. Hence, a hand-grenade

made from a jam-tin : military : 1915 ; ob.—6. A short-service rating introduced under Lord Selborne's scheme : naval : 1903–ca. 10. Bowen. Likewise ex the jam, introduced into the Navy at about the time of the scheme (1903).—7. A cigarette ' made from the monthly issue of naval tobacco ' : naval : from ca. 1910. Bowen. Ex effect on one's throat.—8. Hence, a cigarette-smoker : naval : from ca. 1912. Ibid.—9. See **Kruger's tickler.**

Tickler's. See preceding, sense 4.

Tickler's artillery. Hand-grenades (see preceding, 5) ; those who used them : military : 1915 ; ob. B. & P.

tickling his ear. See **guardee-wriggle.**

***tickrum.** A licence : c. : ca. 1670–1830. Coles ; Grose, 1st ed. A corruption of *ticket*.

ticks. Debts, obligations : sporting (— 1887) ; ob. Baumann. Ex *tick*, n., 2.

ticky, tickey, or **tickie** ; occ. **tiki, tikki, tikkie.** A threepenny piece : South African coll. : from ca. 1850. Etymology obscure : perhaps ex a native attempt at *ticket* (O.E.D.) or at *threepenny* ; perhaps —though much less likely—suggested by Romany *tikeno, tikno*, small, little ; prob., however, as Pettman ably shows, ex Portuguese, hence Malayan, *pataca* († Fr. *patac*).

ticky, adj. Verminous : military coll. : C. 20. F. & Gibbons. Ex Lancashire dial. : E.D.D.

ticky nap. A game of nap(oleon) with a ' ticky ' stake for each trick : late C. 19–20 : South African. Pettman. See **ticky, n.**

tidderly push, and. And the rest of it ; and so on : a c.p. (— 1923) ' used to replace any statement . . . considered . . . too long or too involved to be expressed in full ' (Kastner & Marks, at the Fr. equivalent, *et patati et patata*). Manchon.

tidd. A children's abbr. (late C. 19–20) of *tiddler*, 1, q.v. (Collinson.)

tiddipol. ' An overdressed fat young woman in humble life ', Halliwell : provincial : C. 19. Cf. :

tiddivate, tidivate. See **titivate.**

tiddle, v.i. To fidget, potter : S.E. until ca. 1830, then dial. and coll. : 1748, Richardson ; slightly ob. —2. V.t., to advance slowly or by small movements (e.g. a ball, a wheelbarrow) ; *tiddle a girl*, to master her very gradually : coll. : mid-C. 19–20. Perhaps ex dial. *tiddle*, to tickle, possibly influenced by *diddle* ; much more prob. by a development of sense ex S.E. (in C. 19–20, dial. and coll.) *tiddle*, to pamper, to fondle excessively.

tiddle-a-wink. See **tiddlywink.**—**tiddlebat.** See **tittlebat.**

tiddler. A stickleback : nursery coll. : 1885 (O.E.D.). Ex *tittlebat, tiddlebat*, the popular form. —2. A feather(-brush) for tickling : C. 20. Notably used on Mafeking night, whence dates the name. Ex *tiddle*, to tickle.—3. ' Thingamy ', ' thingummy-bob ' : lower classes' : 1912, A Neil Lyons, ' Clara, steady on with that tiddler ! ' (Manchon.)

tiddl(e)y. See **titley.**—**tiddlewinks, tiddleywink.** See **tiddlywink.**

tiddlies, run. To run over unsafe ice : provincial : mid-C. 19–20.

tiddling. A vbl.n. ex *tiddler*, 1, q.v. : nursery coll. : C. 20.

tiddly, n. See **titley.**—2. Adj., drunk : late C. 19–20 : low. Ex *titley*, n.—3. Little : dial. and nursery coll. : C. 19–20.—4. Hence (?), particularly smart : naval : late C. 19–20. Bowen.

Tiddly Chats ; Tiddly Quid. H.M. ships *Chatham*

and Royal *Sovereign* : naval : C. 20. Bowen. The *tiddly* is prob. that of *tiddly*, 4.

tiddlywink ; also **tid(d)leywink**, **tiddle-a-wink**. An unlicensed house (pawnbroker's, beer-shop, brothel, etc.) : 1844, J. T. Hewlett (O.E.D.). Perhaps ex *titley*, q.v. + *wink* (cf. *on the sly*). Also *kiddlywink*.—2. Pl. only ; with variant *tiddlewinks* : knick-knacks of food : 1893, J. A. Barry (O.E.D.). Perhaps influenced by *tiddly*, adj., 2, q.v.—3. A drink : rhyming s. (— 1909). Ware.—4. (In pl.) A sickly, very thin child : lower classes' (— 1923). Manchon. Ex the adj.

tiddlywink, v.i. To spend imprudently or with unsanctioned excess : Australian : 1888, Boldrewood, ' He's going too fast . . . I wonder what old Morgan would say to all this here tiddley-winkin', with steam engine, and wire fences ' ; ob. Ex the n. ; rare except in the form of the vbl.n.

tiddlywink, adj. Slim, puny : from ca. 1863 ; ob. H., 3rd ed. Not because *tiddlywinks* is considered a feeble, futile game, for it is recorded later, but ex *tiddlywink*, n., 1. Occ. *tillywink*.

tiddlywinker. A cheat ; a trifler : resp. 1893 (O.E.D.), ca. 1895. Ultimately ex *tiddlywink*, n., but imm., though nuance 2 is perhaps influenced by *tiddlywinks*, ex :

tiddlywinking, adj. Pottering ; trifling : 1869 (O.E.D.). Ex *tiddlywink*, n., 1.

tiddlywinks. See tiddlywink, n., 2 and 4.

tiddy. Small, tiny : dial. (— 1781) ; by 1860, coll., esp. nursery coll. O.E.D. (Sup.). Perhaps ex a confusion of *tiny + little*.

tiddy iddy. A reduplication of *tiddy*, q.v. : 1868, W. S. Gilbert (O.E.D. Sup.).

Tiddy-Poll. George Temple, C. 18. Dawson.

tiddyvate, tidivate. See titivate.—**tidlywink**. See **tiddlywink**.

tidy. Fairly meritorious or satisfactory ; (of a person) decent, nice : coll. : 1844, Dickens, ' For a coastguardsman . . . rather a tidy question ', O.E.D. Ex † S.E. *tidy*, excellent, worthy.—2. (In amount, degree) considerable : coll. : 1838, Dickens, ' At a tidy pace ', Dickens (O.E.D.). Hence, *a tidy penny*, very fair earnings, etc. Cf. sense 1, and the adv.

tidy, v.t., often with **up**. To make orderly, clean, etc. : from ca. 1820 : in serious contexts, familiar S.E. ; in trivial, coll. Ex *tidy*, in good condition, clean.—2. Hence, v.i. : coll. : 1853, Dickens, ' I have tidied over and over again, but it's useless.'—3. Also ex sense 1 : *tidy away* or *up*, to stow away, clear up, for tidiness' sake : coll. : 1867 (O.E.D.).

tidy, adv. Pretty well ; a good deal ; finely, comfortably : dial. and low coll. : 1824 (O.E.D.) ; 1899, Whiteing, " ' Was you knocked about much . . . ? " " Pretty tidy." '

tie. See **tye**.—2. The need of constant attendance (e.g. on invalids or children) ; restraint, or deficiency, of freedom : coll. and dial. : C. 20.—3. Thigh : London tailors' (— 1909). Ware. (Only as applied to a leg of mutton.)

*tie it up. See tie up, v., 1.

tie one's hair or **wool**. To puzzle (a person) : tailors' : from ca. 1870.

tie-mate. A particular friend : naval coll. : mid-C. 18–early 19. Bowen.

tie-o(h). See **tyo(h)**.

tie-up. A knock-out blow, a ' settler ' : boxing : 1818 (O.E.D.). Ex lit. sense (cf. cricket j.).—2. ? hence, a conclusion : 1829 (O.E.D.) ; rather ob.—

3. An obstruction, stoppage, closure : from late 1880's : coll. >, by 1920, S.E.

*tie up, v. To forswear : c. : mid-C. 19–20 ; ob. E.g. *tie up prigging*, to live honestly. Ex the parallel s. sense, to desist, to desist from,—a sense recorded by O.E.D. for 1760 (Foote).—3. To knock out : boxing : from ca. 1810. Vaux. Cf. *tied-up*, 1.—4. To join in marriage : coll. >, ca. 1910, s. : 1894, Astley (O.E.D.).—5. To get (a woman) with child : low : C. 19–20 ; ob.

tie up your stocking ! No heel-taps ! : Oxford University : late C. 19–20 ; ob. Ware.

tie with St Mary's knot. See **St Mary's knot**.

tied-up. Finished, settled : orig., boxing (— 1859). H., 1st ed.—2. Costive : from ca. 1870. —3. See tie up, v., 4.—4. Hanged : low (— 1923). Manchon.

tied with the tongue that cannot be untied with the teeth, a knot. See knot tied with the tongue.

tiego. Vertigo : sol. or low coll. : C. 17. Massinger, 1634. O.E.D.

tier. Incorrect spelling of *teer* : C. 19–20. O.E.D.

'ties, be in one's. To have reached the age of twenty : coll. (— 1923). Manchon. Abbr. *twenties*. (By the way, *in his sixties* and *in the 'Sixties*, etc., etc., are S.E.—not, as is sometimes stated, coll.)

tiff. Liquor, esp. if thin or inferior : from ca. 1630 ; ob. by 1870, † by 1930 : coll. >, ca. 1750, s. Corbet, ca. 1635 (O.E.D.) ; Fielding ; Scott. Perhaps of echoic origin.—2. Hence, a small draught (rarely of other than diluted liquor, esp. punch) : coll. (— 1727) >, ca. 1750, s. Bailey ; Scott.—3. A slight outburst of temper or ill-humour : coll. (— 1727). Bailey ; Thackeray, 1840, ' Numerous tiffs and quarrels ' ; ob. Etymology problematic, but possibly ex (the effects implied by) sense 1 ; cf., however, echoic *huff* and *sniff*.—4. Hence, a slight quarrel, a briefly peevish disagreement : coll. : 1754, Richardson.—5. Ex sense 1 : a gust of laughter, etc. : coll. : 1858, Carlyle (O.E.D.). Rare and ob.

*tiff, v.i., occ. t. (The rare form *tift* occurs only in sense 3.) To lie (with a woman) : c. : late C. 17–early 19. B.E. ; Grose, 1st ed. Cf. the rare or ' nonce ' *tiffity-taffety girls*, harlots (late C. 16), and the C. 15 (? later) *tiff*, to be idly employed.—2. V.t., to drink, esp. slowly or in sips : ca. 1769–1850. Combe, 1811, ' He tiff'd his punch, and went to rest.' Ex *tiff*, n., 2, q.v.—3. V.i., to have a tiff, be peevish or pettish : coll. (— 1727). Bailey ; 1777, Sheridan, ' We tifted a little before going to church, and fairly quarrelled before the bells had done ringing ' ; slightly ob. Ex *tiff*, n., 4.—4. To have, eat, lunch : Anglo-Indian coll. (1803, Elphinstone : Yule & Burnell) >, ca. 1850, S.E. But much the earliest record I have seen is this, dated Sept. 23, 1712, from Bencoleen in Sumatra : ' At 12 I tiff, that is eat . . . some good relishing bit, and drink a good draught ' : *The Letter Books of Joseph Collett*, ed. by H. H. Dodwell, 1933. Abbr. of the v. implicit in *tiffin*.

tiffic(k)s. Odds and ends of iron (e.g. screws) : nautical (— 1923). Manchon. Origin ? (? error.)

tiffin. A lunch, esp. if light : Anglo-Indian coll. (1800 : O.E.D.) >, ca. 1830, S.E. Ex *tiffing*, q.v. Esp. Yule & Burnell.—2. Hence, in New Zealand : a snack and a drink (gen. tea) at 10.30 or 11 a.m., as a rest from work : late C. 19–20 : rare coll.

tiffing. ' Eating, or drinking out of meal times ', Grose, 1st ed. : ca. 1780–1830. Ex *tiff*, v., 2, q.v.

Whence *tiffin*, q.v. It occurs in 1784 as *triffing* (Yule & Burnell).

tiffish. Apt to take offence ; peevish : coll. (— 1855). Rare. Ex *tiff*, n., 3. (O.E.D.)

tiffy. An engine-room ar*tif*icer : nautical : from late 1890's. F. T. Bullen, 1899 (O.E.D.).—2. Hence, any artificer or fitter : mechanics' : C. 20. (R. Blaker, *Medal without Bar*, 1930.)

tiffy, adj. In a tiff : coll. : 1810 (O.E.D.). Ex *tiff*, n., 3.—2. Hence, apt to take offence : coll. (— 1864). H., 3rd ed.—3. Hence, faddy : from ca. 1880 ; ob.

tift. See tiff, v., 3.

Tiger, or **the Tiger.** Edward, 1st Baron Thurlow (d. 1806), Lord Chancellor. Dawson.—2. Mr Joseph Chamberlain : political : 1895 till his death. —3. Clemenceau : political : C. 20.—4. (Tiger only.) E. J. Smith, Warwickshire's wicket-keeper from 1904 to 1930. *Who's Who in World Cricket*, 1934.—5. See Tigers.

tiger. A smart-liveried boy-groom : 1817 (O.E.D.) ; Lytton, ' *Vulgo* Tiger ' ; ob. by 1880, † by 1930. Ex livery.—2. Hence, any boy acting as outdoor servant : from ca. 1840 ; id.—3. ' The steward who acts as personal servant to the captain of a liner ' : nautical : C. 20. Bowen. Ex sense 1. —4. A vulgarly overdressed person : 1827, Scott (O.E.D.) ; 1849, Thackeray. Ob. by 1860, † by 1890. Ex a tiger's bright colours. Cf. sense 1.— 5. Hence, a parasite, rake, swell-mobsman : ca. 1837–60.—6. Streaky bacon : navvies' : from ca. 1890. Ex the streaks.—7. A convict that tears to pieces another convict's yellowish suit : c. : from late 1890's. Ex the ' ferocity ' of the act + the colour of the suit.—8. A leopard : South African catachresis (— 1852). Pettman.—9. A jaguar : South American Englishmen's catachresis : from ca. 1880. Ex American usage.—10. Tough-crusted bread : schoolboys' : ca. 1870–1905. Ware. Ex its powers of resistance.—11. A formidable opponent, esp. at lawn tennis : coll. (— 1934). C.O.D., 3rd ed., Sup. Opp. *rabbit*, 4.

Tiger Bay. A certain well-known sailors' quarter in London, before 1887 ; Mayhew delimits it as Brunswick Street (East End) ; Cockneys' : ca. 1820–90. Baumann. Ex their wild goings-on. Also ex the fact that ' Tiger Bay . . . is full of brothels and thieves' lodging houses,' Mayhew, 1861.

[**Tiger Earl, the.** See **Earl Beardie.** Sobriquet *r*ather than nickname.]

tiger, hot. See hot tiger.

*****tiger-hunter.** A mat-mender, the trade gen. being learnt in gaol : c. (— 1932). ' Stuart Wood ', *Shades of the Prison House.* Prob. ex rugs of tiger-skin.

tigerish. Flashy ; loudly dressed : ca. 1830–70. Lytton, 1853, ' Nothing could be more . . ., to use a slang word, *tigrish*, than his whole air. Ex *tiger*, 4. (The n., *tigerism*, may perhaps be considered s. or coll. : in sense of *tiger*, 1, mainly in 1840's ; of *tiger*, 4 and 5, rarely after 1830's. O.E.D.)

Tigers, the. The 17th Foot, now the Leicester-shire, Regiment ; also, the 67th Foot, now the Hampshire, Regiment : military : from the late 1820's. Ex the Royal Tiger badges granted in, resp., 1825 and 1827. F. & Gibbons.—2. The Leicester Rugby Football Club : sporting : C. 20. *The News Chronicle*, Feb. 25, 1935.—3. Hull City Football Club (' soccer ') : id. : id. Ex their colours.

tight. Hard, severe, difficult : coll. : 1764, Foote (O.E.D.) ; ob. except in *tight squeeze* (Haliburton, 1855 ; after U.S. *tight spot*), *place* (mentioned in 1856 as an Americanism), and *corner* (1891). O.E.D., F. & H., Thornton. Cf. *tight fit*, q.v.—2. (Of a contest) close ; (of a bargain) hard : U.S. coll. (ca. 1820) anglicised ca. 1860.—3. (Of a person) close-fisted : coll. (— 1828). Mostly U.S.—4. (Of money) hard to come by ; (of the money market) with little money circulating : 1846, *The Daily News*, Jan. 21, ' In Paris money is " tight " also, and discounts difficult,' O.E.D.—5. Tipsy : 1843 in U.S. (O.E.D. Sup.) ; 1853, Dickens's article in *Household Words*, Sept. 24 (see *Slang*) ; H., 1st ed. ; Kipling. Cf. *screwed*, (lit. screwed tight, hence) drunk.—6. Cramped ; over-worked ; meticulous : artists' : from ca. 1890. Occ., in C. 20, as adv. (O.E.D.) Cf. *tired*.—7. (Of balls) in contact, (pockets) with small openings : billiards (— 1909). Supplement to *The Century Dict.*—8. (The Winchester usage is in line with S.E.)

tight !, blow me. See blow, v., 3. (Ex blowing up bladders, balloons, etc.)

tight !, hold. Stop !, don't move ! ; steady ! : coll. : from ca. 1910. Ex bus-conductor's adjuration.

tight junior. See junior.

tight, sit. To sit close, stay under cover ; not to budge : coll. : from mid-1890's.—2. Cf. the C. 18 sense : to apply oneself closely to : 1738 (O.E.D.).

tight-arsed. (Of women) chaste : low coll. : late C. 19–20.—2. Stingy : C. 20.

tight as a drum. Extremely drunk : 1908, A. S. M. Hutchinson, *Once Aboard the Lugger*.

tight boots, sit in. To be ill at ease with one's host : semi-proverbial coll. (— 1855). H. G. Bohn's *Handbook of Proverbs.* (Apperson.)

tight cravat. The hangman's noose : coll. : late C. 18–mid-19.

tight fit, a. Coll. when used of things other than clothes : late C. 19–20.

tighten, v.i. To tight-lace : (not aristocratic) coll. : 1896 (O.E.D.) ; slightly ob.

tighten one's galabieh. See galabieh.

tight(e)ner. A hearty meal ; occ. a large amount (of liquor) : low coll. : 1851, Mayhew. Hence, *do a* or *the tightener* ; the latter in J. E. Ritchie's *Night Side of London*, 1857.

tighties. Women's drawers that fit very tight : feminine coll. : from ca. 1933. See quotation at *neathie-set*.

tightified. (Rendered) tight ; close-fitting : (low) coll. : C. 20. (Compton Mackenzie, 1933.)

tightner. See tightener.

tightness. Tipsiness : from some time in 1853–64. See tight, 5.

tigress. A vulgarly overdressed woman : 1830's. On *tiger*, 4, q.v.

tigser, n. ' A slang juvenile epithet used when a person is in quick motion . . . " Go it, tigser " ' : West Yorkshire s. (— 1904), not dial. Prob. ex dial. *tig*, ' to run hither and thither when tormented by flies, &c.'

tike, gen. **tyke** ; **T.** A Yorkshireman : coll. nickname : C. 18–20. E. Ward, 1703 (Matthews). Ex *Yorkshire tyke*, q.v. In Yorkshire, *tyke* very gen. for a dog.

*****tike (tyke)-lurking.** Dog-stealing : c. (— 1859). H., 1st ed. Also *buffer-lurking*.

tik(k)i, tikkie. See ticky.

tilbury. (A) sixpence : ca. 1790–1850. Grose,

3rd ed., ' From its formerly being the fare for crossing over from Gravesend to Tilbury fort.' Cf. *tizzy*.

tile. A hat : 1823, Egan's Grose. Esp. ca. 1850–1900, a dress-hat ; extant as *tile-hat*, esp. in Glasgow, where it is also called a *tum hat*. Ex *tile* as part of roof ; cf. *thatched, be well*, q.v.

*tile-frisking, n. Stealing hats from lobbies and halls ; c. of ca. 1823–80.

tile-hat. See **tile.**

tile loose, (have) a. (To be) slightly crazy : from mid-1840's. Ex *tiles loose on roof* ; cf. *tile* and a *shingle short*, q.v.

tiled, adj. Hatted : 1792, *The Annual Register* (O.E.D.). Cf. *tile*, q.v.

*tiled down. Under cover ; esp., out of the way, hidden : c. : 1845 in ' *No. 747* ' ; app. † by 1900. Lit., under the tiles.

*tiler. A shoplifter : c. of ca. 1650–80. ? ex L. *tollere.*

tiles, (be or go) on the. (To be or go) on the loose ; esp. a-drinking or on sexual adventure : low (— 1857) >, ca. 1910, gen. ' Ducange Anglicus ' ; Baumann. Ex the procedure of cats.

till. The female pudend : low : C. 19–20. Suggested by *money(-box)*, q.v.

*till-boy. An assistant tampering with the cash in his master's till : c. (— 1864). H., 3rd ed. Perhaps on :

*till-sneak. A thief specialising in shop-tills : c. : from ca. 1860.

till the cows come home. See **cows come . . .**

tilladum. ' A slang word for to " weave ". . . . Hence **tilladumoite,** . . . a handloom weaver ', E.D.D. : Lancashire : from ca. 1860. The former occurs in James Staton, *Rays fro' th' Loominary*, 1866 ; the latter in Staton's *Bobby Shuttle un his woife Sayroh*, 1873.

tiller soup. That rough treatment with a tiller by (the threat of) which a coxswain encourages his boat's crew : nautical : late C. 19–20. Bowen. Cf. *belaying-pin soup.*

till(e)y, easy as. Very easy : ? C. 18–19. Lit., easy as saying :

till(e)y-vally ; tully-valy, etc. Nonsense ! : trivial coll. of ca. 1525–1890. Skelton, Scott. Vaguely onomatopœic in origin : cf. *tush !*

tillywink. See **tiddlywink.** (H., 3rd ed.)

tilter. A sword or rapier : 1688, Shadwell ; † by 1840. Ex *tilt*, to take part in a tourney or jousting.

timber. Wooden gates, fences, hurdles, etc. : hunting : 1791, ' G. Gambado ' (O.E.D.).—2. A wooden leg ; hence, any leg (1862, Whyte-Melville). O.E.D.—3. The stocks : from ca. 1850. Douglas Jerrold the First. Cf. *timber-stairs*, q.v.—4. A wicket, the wickets : cricket coll. : 1861 (Lewis). Cf. *timber-yard*, q.v.—5. See **timbers.**—6. See **timber merchant.**—7. (Timber.) A variant of *Lackery*, q.v. (F. & Gibbons.)

timber, bowl for. See **bowl for timber.**

timber, small. Lucifer matches : (mostly London) street s. : from ca. 1859. Cf. *timber-merchant.*

timber, sport. See **sport timber.**

timber-jumper. A horse good at leaping gates and fences : hunting : 1847, Thackeray, ' I never put my leg over such a timber-jumper,' O.E.D.

timber-merchant. A street match-seller : (London) streets' (— 1859) now verging on c. : H., 1st ed. Ware, 1909, records *timber* (gen. pl.), a lucifer match, as low s.

timber-stairs. The pillory : mid-C. 18–early (? mid-)C. 19. In Herd's collection of songs

(O.E.D.). Cf. *timber*, 3, q.v. Cf. also the *tree* synonymy.

timber-toe. A wooden leg : from ca. 1780 ; ob. Implied in Grose, 1st ed., where *timber-toe* is a person with a wooden leg, a sense reappearing in Hood. The variant *timber-toes* is C. 19–20, and, from ca. 1870 in the East End of London, it also = a person wearing clogs, as in H., 5th ed.

timber-toed. Having a wooden leg or legs : from ca. 1810. See preceding.

timber-toes. See **timber-toe.**

timber-topper. The same as, and ex, *timber-jumper* : hunting : 1883 (O.E.D.).

Timber-Town, H.M.S. The camp at Groningen (Holland) ; Royal Naval Division coll. : dating from the fall of Antwerp in the G.W. (F. & Gibbons mentions that many R.N.D. men were interned there.)

timber-tuned. Heavy-fingered ; wooden in movement : late C. 19–20 ; ob.

timber-yard. One's wickets ; more precisely, the place where one's wickets stand : cricket : 1853, Cuthbert Bede, ' Verdant found that before he could get his hand in, the ball was got into his wicket . . . and . . . there was a row in his timber-yard ' ; virtually †.

timbered up to one's weight, not. Not in one's style : coll. : mid-C. 19–20 ; ob.

timbers. The wickets : cricketers' coll. (— 1877). Lewis. Esp. in *shiver one's timbers*, to scatter the wickets and stumps. Cf. *timber*, 3, and *timber-yard* ; contrast *bowl for timber*, q.v.—2. Worked wood in gen., e.g. escritoires, cabinets, elaborate tables : artistic : ca. 1880–1914. Ware.

timbers !, my ; dash my t. ! ; shiver my t. ! Nautical s. exclamations : resp. 1789, Dibdin, ' My timbers ! what lingo he'd coil and belay,' O.E.D. ; mid-C. 19–20, rare and hardly nautical ; and 1835, Marryat (see **shiver . . .**).

time. In boxing sense ; see **time of day**, 5, and **time, knock out of.**—2. (The time spent in) a term of imprisonment : rare except in *time, do*, q.v.—3. Among cab-drivers of ca. 1863–1910, the hours are used to denote the amount of a fare. ' To express 9*s.* 9*d.* they say " it is a quarter to ten " ; if 3*s.* 6*d.*, half-past three ; if 11*s.* 9*d.*, a quarter to twelve,' H., 3rd ed.—4. See **times.**

*time, do. To serve a term in prison : 1865 (O.E.D.) : c. >, by 1890, s. H., 5th ed., ' Sometimes stir-time (imprisonment in the House of Correction) is distinguished from the more extended system of punishment . . . called " pinnel (penal) time " ' ; Nat Gould, 1898, ' If it had not been for me you would have been doing time before this.' Hence *timer*, a convict, in such combinations as *first, second, third timer*, a prisoner serving for a first, etc., stretch : c. (— 1887). Baumann.

time, hot. See **hot time.**

time, in no ; in less than no time. Very soon, immediately ; (very) quickly : coll. : resp. 1843, Borrow : 1875, Jowett—but prob. a decade or even two or three decades earlier. (O.E.D.)

time, knock out of. ' So to punish an opponent that he cannot come up to the call of time ', F. & H. : boxing : from ca. 1870 ; slightly ob.

time, on. Punctual(ly) : coll., orig. (1878) U.S. ; anglicised ca. 1890 ; by 1930, virtually S.E.

time, short. A single act of copulation as opp. to ' a night of it ' : low, coll. rather than s. : C. 19–20. ? orig. a prostitutes' term.

time for, have no. ' To regard with impatient

disfavour ', C. J. Dennis : (? orig. Australian) coll. : late C. 19–20. I.e. 'have no time to spare for'. Cf. the S.E. *have no use for.*

time of day. 'The time as shown by the clock' is S.E., but the derivative 'a point or stage in any course or period' is coll. : 1687, T. Brown ; 1699, Collier, 'The favour of a prince was not . . . unreputable at that time of day,' O.E.D.—2. Hence, *give one,* or *pass, the time of day,* to greet a person, to exchange greetings : resp. C. 17–20, mid-C. 19–20 : S.E. until late C. 19, then coll. and dial. ; *give one . . .* is ob. as a coll. Whiteing, G. R. Sims. —3. The prevailing state of affairs ; the present state of the case : coll. : 1667, Poole ; slightly ob. O.E.D. Ex sense 1.—4. Hence, 'what's what' ; the right or most fashionable way of doing something ; the latest dodge : from ca. 1820. 'Jon Bee', 1823, 'In the island (Wight) every good joke is "the time o' day"' ; more clearly in Dickens, 1838, 'Pop that shawl away in my castor . . . ; that's your time of day.' Esp. in *fly to the time of day,* 'fly', alert, 'knowing' (1828, Maginn ; ob.) ; *put one up to the time of day,* to initiate a person (1834, Ainsworth) ; *know the time of day* (adumbrated in Bunyan, 1682, but not at all gen. before ca. 1895), to know 'what's what',—' Ouida ', 1897, ' "She knows the time o' day," said the other,' O.E.D. ; *that's your time of day !,* well done ! (1860, H., 2nd ed.).—5. *(give one) the time of day,* (to administer) a knock-out blow : boxing : late C. 19–20 ; slightly ob.

time on, mark. See **mark** . . .

***timer.** See **time, do.**

times, behind the. Old-fashioned ; having only such knowledge (esp. of method) as is superannuated : mid-C. 19–20 : coll. >, by 1930, S.E. Cf. :

times go, as. As things are at present : coll. : 1712, Steele (O.E.D.).

Times Lit., The. *The Times Literary Supplement* : book-world coll. : from 1901.

Timmie. The gymnasium : certain schools' : late C. 19–20. (Geoffrey Dennis, *Bloody Mary's,* 1934.)

timmynoggy. A term for almost any time- or labour-saving device : naval : ca. 1850–95. Bowen. Ex dial. *timmynoggy,* 'a notched square piece of wood ; used to support the lower end of the "vargood"' or long spar serving as a bowline, itself ex dial. *timmy,* the stick or bat used in the game of rounders : E.D.D. Cf. *gadget,* q.v.

timothy. A brew, or a jorum, of liquor : Scottish : 1855, Strang (O.E.D.). Ex the proper name (? of a brewer or a noted publican).—2. The penis, esp. a child's : either dial. or provincial s. (— 1847). Halliwell. The personification of penis (*Dick, man* or *John Thomas*) and of pudend (*Fanny*) would make an interesting but unpublishable essay.

timp. See **tymp.**

tin. Money, cash ; orig. of small silver coins, so apt to wear thinly smooth and thus assume a tinny appearance : prob. from early C. 19, but not recorded before 1836, in Smith's *The Individual* ; 'Pomes' Marshall. Cf. *brass.*—2. See **Tins.**—3. See **tins, on the.**

tin, v. To dismiss or supersede (gen. an officer) : military : 1916 ; ob. B. & P. Perhaps ex *put the tin hat on.*

tin !, they've opened another. A depreciatory military c.p. (1915–18) 'frequently heard . . . among the men . . . with reference to some newly arrived draft, or officer', F. & Gibbons. Prob. ex tinned sardines.

tin-arsed. See **tinny, 2.**

Tin Bellies, the. The 1st and 2nd Life Guards : military : from 1821. F. & Gibbons. Ex the cuirass.

tin bread. Biscuit : military : from 1914. B. & P. Ex the container and the hardness of Army biscuits.

Tin Duck. H.M.S. *Iron Duke* : naval : 1914–18. Bowen.

tin fish. A torpedo : naval : from not later than 1916. F. & Gibbons.

tin gloves. A criss-cross of blisters methodically made by a bully on the back of a victim's hand : Winchester : ca. 1840–60. Mansfield.

tin hat. A helmet : theatrical : C. 20. W.—2. Hence, a soldier's steel helmet : from late 1915.—3. A staff officer : military : 1917. Much rarer than *brass hat* ; † by 1913.

tin-hat, adj. Drunk : Anglo-Port Said (— 1909). Ware. Often *tin hats* (F. & Gibbons).

tin hat on, put a or **the.** To finish in a manner regarded as objectionable by the speaker : from 1916 : mainly military. On *put the lid on,* ex *tin hat,* n., 2.—2. (V.i.) To 'talk big' : Glasgow (— 1934).

tin-hatted. A nautical variant of *tin-hat,* adj. Bowen.

tin Lizzie. H.M.S. *Queen Elizabeth* : naval : 1914 ; ob. Bowen.—2. A Ford motor-car : from ca. 1915. Occ. *Lizzie.*—3. Hence, any (cheap) motor-car : from ca. 1920.

tin-opener. A bayonet : dating from the Boer War (1899–1901) : military. F. & Gibbons. Ex its chief use.

tin pirate. A German submarine : naval : 1916 ; ob. F. & Gibbons. Cf. *tin fish,* q.v.

tin-pot. An ironclad : naval : from ca. 1880 ; ob. Contrast :

tin-potter. A malingerer : nautical (— 1867) ; ob. Smyth. Ex *tin-pot,* inferior.

tin-tab. The carpenter's shop : Dulwich College : late C. 19–20. Cf. :

tin tabernacle. An iron-built or tin-roofed church : 1898, William Le Queux, *Scribes and Pharisees,* V, 54 : s. >, by 1930, coll. Cf. *dolly-shop* and similar amenities.

tin tacks, come (or get) down to. An occ. coll. variant (dating from middle 1920's) of *brass tacks . . .,* q.v. (O.E.D. Sup.) Both are rhyming s. on *facts.*

tin tack. A sack : from ca. 1870. P. P., *Rhyming Slang,* 1932.

Tin Tacks and Onions. Mount Tintwa Inyoni : Boer War military. J. Milne, *The Epistles of Atkins,* 1902.

tin tank. A bank : from ca. 1880. P. P., *Rhyming Slang,* 1932.

tin town. A hutment of corrugated iron : military coll. : from 1915. B. & P.

tin-type !, not on your. Certainly not ! : a c.p. of late C. 19–20 ; † by 1930, except in Australia : witness Christina Stead's brilliantly realistic novel, *Seven Poor Men of Sydney,* 1930. Ex an old-fashioned type of photograph. Perhaps with a pun on *not on your life !,* certainly not.

tin-wedding (day). The tenth anniversary of a wedding : coll. : 1876 (O.E.D. Sup.). Punning *golden* and *silver* weddings.

tinge. A commission allowed to assistants on the

sale of outmoded stock : drapers' (— 1860). H., 2nd ed. Cf. *suspicion*, q.v.

tink. 'A tinker ; a disreputable vagabond' : Scots coll. : mid-C. 19–20. E.D.D. By abbr.

tink-tinky. See **tinky.**

***tinkard.** A begging tinker : c. of ca. 1560–1620. Awdelay.

tinker. To batter : boxing : 1826, *The Sporting Magazine*, 'Tom completely tinkered his opponent's upper-crust,' O.E.D. ; almost †. Ex *tinker*, v.t., mend tinker-wise.

tinker, swill like a. To tipple unstintedly : coll. : late C. 17–early 19. Motteux.

tinkerman. Incorrect for *trinkerman* : C. 17–18. O.E.D. Occ. *tinklerman*, equally wrong : C. 19.

tinker's budget or **news.** Stale news : coll. and dial. : mid-C. 19–20.

tinker's curse (or cuss) or damn. See **curse.**

tinker's mufti. A dress half military, half civilian : military coll. (— 1923). Manchon. Tinkers frequently wear very odd garments.

tinkler. A bell : (low) coll. : 1838, Dickens, 'Jerk the tinkler'.

tinkling-box. A piano : South Lancashire s. (— 1904), not dial. E.D.D.

tinky. A South African juvenile coll. variant (— 1899) of *tink-tinky*, itself orig. (the 1890's) coll. for the bird properly known as *ting-ting*. Ex its cry, *tink, tink, tink*. (Pettman.)

tinman. A rich man, esp. a millionaire : sporting : from ca. 1880 ; ob. Ware. Ex *tin* ; cf. *tinny*, adj., 1.

tinned air. Artificial ventilation : nautical : from ca. 1910. Bowen.

***tinny ; tinney** (Bee). A fire : c. : C. 19. Vaux. Hence *tinny-hunter* (ibid.), a thief working after fires.

tinny, adj. Rich : 1871, *Punch*, Oct. 14 (O.E.D.). Ex *tin*.—2. ? hence, lucky : Australia and New Zealand : C. 20. Occ. *tin-arsed*. Cf. *protected*.

tins, on the. On the scoring-board : cricketers' coll. : C. 20. O.E.D. (Sup.). Ex the tin plates on which the numbers are painted.

Tins, the. The Composite Regiment of Household Cavalry : military : 1915–18. F. & Gibbons. Cf. *Tin-Bellies*, q.v.

tinter. See **barrel tinter.**

Tiny is an inevitable nickname of very big or tall men : lower classes' : late C. 19–20. Contrast *Tich*, q.v.

***tip.** 'The tip . . . money concerned in any dealings or contract . . . ; synonymous with *the dues*', Vaux : c. of ca. 1810–50. Cf. v., 8, 9.—2. Special information conveyed by an expert, private knowledge, esp. as to investment in the money market and to racing ; a hint for an examination : from ca. 1840 : s. >, by 1900, coll. *The Quarterly Review*, 1886, 'It should be the first duty of consuls to keep the Foreign Office promptly supplied with every commercial tip that can be of use to British trade.'—3. Hence, something 'tipped' to win, to prosper ; esp. a horse : 1873, Besant & Rice (O.E.D.).—4. Hence, a special device, a 'wrinkle' : from the 1880's : s. >, by 1910, coll.—5. Hence, at Felsted School, from late 1880's, a false report ; hence, ibid., from early 1890's, a foolish mistake in translating. *The Felstedian*, Feb. 3, 1890, 'Some one ventured to suggest that it was all a beastly tip.'—6. See phrases.—7. A draught of liquor : c. (— 1700) soon > s. ; † by 1840. B.E., Swift. Prob. abbr. *tipple*.—8. Drink in gen. : c. (— 1700)

soon > s. ; † by 1830. B.E. Certainly ex *tipple*, q.v.

tip, v. To render unsteady, esp. to intoxicate, mostly in the passive : C. 17–early 18. Camden, 1605 (O.E.D.) Ex *tip*, to tilt or incline.—2. (Often **tip off.**) To drink off : late C. 17–20 : c. until mid-C. 18, then s. ; from mid-C. 19, only in dial. B.E. Ex tipping the glass or bowl in order to drain it.—3. To die : rare except in C. 19–20 dial. and in *tip off* (late C. 17–20 : c., as in B.E., > s. by 1730 ; in C. 19–20, dial.), *tip over the perch* (1737, Ozell) or *tip the perch* (C. 19–20, in the same sense.) (The *perch* phrases are ob. in C. 20.) Partly O.E.D.—4. To give ; pass : C. 17–20 : c., by 1730, s. Rowlands, 1610, 'Tip me that Cheate, Give me that thing.' Esp. of money, as in Rowlands, 1610 ; Head ; B.E. ; Grose. Perhaps ex *tip*, to touch lightly ; the Romany *tipper*, to give, is a derivative.—5. Hence, to lend (esp. money) : c. : late C. 17–20. B.E.—6. Hence (of a person in the presence of others), to assume the character of : from ca. 1740 ; ob. For its most frequent use, see **tip the traveller.**—7. Often almost synonymous with 'do' or 'make' (cf. *fake*, q.v.) : late C. 17–20 : c. >, early in C. 18 though not in certain phrases, (low) s. See, e.g., *tip a nod*(1), *stave*, *yarn*, and *tip the grampus*.—8. To earn : C. 17–18 : c. >, by 1730, (low) s. Rowlands, 1610 ; Bridges, ca. 1770, 'This job will tip you one pound one.' Ex *tip*, to give, and cognate with :—9. To give a 'tip' or present of money to,—whether to an inferior in recognition of a service or to a child or school-boy or -girl : s. >, early in C. 19, coll. : 1706–7, Farquhar, 'Then I, Sir, tips me '—ethic dative—' the verger with half a crown.' Ex sense 4.—10. Hence, v.i., in same sense : 1727, Gay, 'Did he tip handsomely ?' : s. >, early in C. 19, coll.—11. To indicate by a secret wink : 1749, Fielding, 'I will tip you the proper person . . . as you do not know the town,' O.E.D. Ex *tip the wink*, q.v.—12. To give private information, a friendly hint, about : from early 1880's : s. >, by 1910, coll. Esp. to indicate a horse as a probable winner, a stock as a profitable investment. Ex *tip*, n., 2, q.v. ; perhaps cognate with preceding sense of the v.—13. Hence, to supply (a person) with ' inside ' information : from ca. 1890 : s. >, by 1910, coll.—14. Hence, v.i., to impart such information : s. (— 1904) >, by 1910, coll.

tip, miss one's. To fall ; fail at a jump : showmen's : from ca. 1850. (In late C. 19–20 circus s., to miss the word indicating that one is due to do something. Barrère & Leland.) Dickens, 1854.—2. Hence, to fall, fail, in gen. : 1869, H. J. Byron, 'Mr Topham Sawyer missed his own tip as well as his victim's, and came down a cropper on a convenient doorstep.' Lit., to fail in one's expertise : see **tip,** n., 2, q.v. Cf. *fall down*, q.v.

***tip, stand the.** See **tip, take the.**

tip, (gen. the) straight. Genuine or valuable ('inside') information, esp. and orig. as to a horse : s. >, by 1900, coll. : from late 1860's, to judge by H., 5th ed. (1874) ; 1871, *Punch*, Aug. 26 (O.E.D.). Because direct from owner or trainer ; influenced by *straight*, honest.—2. Hence, the horse or the stock so recommended : from ca. 1880 : s. >, by 1905, coll.

***tip, take the.** C. of C. 19–20, as in Vaux, 1812, '. . . To receive a bribe in any shape ; and they say of a person who is known to be corruptible, that he will *stand the tip*.' Ex *tip*, a gratuity : a sense that the O.E.D. (rightly, I believe) classifies as S.E.

tip, that's the. That's the right thing : from ca. 1860. H., 3rd ed. Ex *tip*, n., 1.

***tip a copper.** To sky a coin : c. or low s. : mid-C. 19–20.

***tip a** (gen. one's) **daddle, a** (gen. one's) **fin, the fives, the gripes in a tangle.** To shake hands ; with *to* expressed or implied, to shake hands with or extend one's hand to be shaken : c. or low s. : resp. late C. 18–20 (Grose, 1st ed.), mainly nautical (− 1860 : H., 2nd ed.), late C. 18–20, late C. 18–early 20. See **daddle ;** the third and fourth occur in Anon., *Ireland Sixty Years Ago*, 1847 ; *tip the gripes* (grips) *in a tangle* is Anglo-Irish and rare.

***tip a mish.** ' To put on a shirt ', F. & H. : c. : C. 18–20 ; ob. The definition is suspect, for the normal sense is to give, lend, it.

tip a moral. To give ' the straight tip ' : racing : late C. 19–20. See **tip, straight,** and **moral,** a ' moral ' certainty.

tip a nod (to). To recognise (a person) : low : mid-C. 19–20.—2. The same as *tip the wink*, q.v. : 1861, Dickens (O.E.D.).

tip a rise. To befool : low : from ca. 1880. See **rise.**

tip-a-runner. The game of tip and run : coll. : 1805 ; ob. Lewis.

tip a settler, a *sock. To land (a person) a knock-out blow, a heavy blow : low : resp. 1819 (Moore) and late C. 17–20 (B.E. : c. > low s.).

tip a stave. To sing a song : 1881, R. L. Stevenson, *Treasure Island.*

tip a yarn. To relate a story : low : from ca. 1870.

tip all nine. To knock down all the skittles at once : from ca. 1780. Grose, 1st ed. Perhaps ex *tip*, to touch ; cf. *tip*, v., 1.

tip and run, n. and v. ' Used during the Great War of German naval dashes at seaside resorts ', W. Ex the *tip* (hit lightly) *and run* of cricket.

tip-book. A literal translation ; any other book likely to be especially useful in an examination : schools' : 1845 (O.E.D.). See **tip,** n., 4.

tip-merry. Slightly drunk : C. 17. Ex *tip*, n., last sense.

tip off. See **tip,** v., 2. B.E.—2. To die : late C. 17–20 : c. until ca. 1720, then (low) s. ; in C. 19–20, dial. B.E. Cf. *tip*, v., 3, q.v.—3. Whence, to kill : low (− 1928). O.E.D. (Sup.).—4. A variant of *tip*, v., 12 : from ca. 1910.

tip one's boom off. To depart hastily : nautical : from ca. 1855 ; slightly ob. H., 2nd ed. Cf. *shove off*, q.v.

***tip one's legs a gallop.** To make off ; decamp hastily : c. (− 1823) ; ob. Egan's Grose.

tip over the perch. See **tip,** v., 3. (Cf. C. 19–20 dial. *tip over*, to swoon.)

tip-slinger. A race-course tipster : Australian : C. 20. Jice Doone.

tip the double. To give the slip : low : 1838, Wright, *Mornings at Bow Street,* ' In plain words he tipped them the double. he was vanished.'

tip the grampus. To duck a man (for sleeping on watch) : nautical : from ca. 1860 ; ob. Also *blow the grampus.* Contrast :

tip the lion. To press a man's nose against his face and then either, as in Steele, 1712 (O.E.D.), bore out his eyes with one's fingers, or, as in Grose (1st ed.) and gen., ' at the same time to extend his mouth with the fingers, thereby giving him a sort of lionlike appearance ' ; † by 1850.

tip the little finger. To drink : Australian : late C. 19–20 ; ob.

tip the long 'un. ' To foraminate a woman ', F. & H. : late C. 19–20 low.

tip the nines. (Of a sailing-ship carrying too much sail in dirty weather) to be ' driven right under ' (Bowen) : nautical : late C. 19–20 ; ob.

tip the rags (occ. **legs**) **a gallop** or **the double.** To decamp : low : resp. C. 19–20 and mid-C. 19–20 (H., 1st ed.). Cf. *tip the double.*

tip the red rag. See **red rag, tip the.**

tip the traveller. To exaggerate, to romance, as a traveller is apt to do : 1742, Fielding (O.E.D.) ; Smollett ; Grose. App. ob. by 1860 and † by 1930. Variant of *play the traveller.* Cf. the C. 16–18 proverb, *a traveller may lie by authority* (Apperson). —2. Hence (variant : *put the traveller*, C. 19 : Manchon), with *upon*, to impose upon ; befool : implied in 1762 in Smollett ; † in C. 20.—3. Grose, 1st ed., has *top the traveller*, but this is prob. a misprint.

tip the velvet. See **velvet.**

tip the (occ. C. 18–19, **a**) **wink.** To warn, signal to, with a wink : 1676, Etherege (O.E.D.) ; Dryden ; Pope ; Grose. S. >, by 1850, coll. Cf. *tip the nod.*

tip-top. The very top ; fig., the acme : coll. : 1702, S. Parker (O.E.D.). Ex *top* strengthened by *tip*, extremity, or, as O.E.D. suggests, reduplicated *top.*—2. Hence, occ. as collective singular, the ' swells ' : coll. : mid-C. 18–mid-19. Thackeray, 1849, ' We go here to the best houses, the tiptops', O.E.D.

tip-top, adj. At the very top ; excellent ; ' splendid ' : coll. : before 1721, Vanbrugh, ' In tip-top spirits ' ; G. Eliot. Ex the n., 1.

tip-top, adv. Excellently ; ' splendidly ', ' toppingly ' : from ca. 1880. Ex preceding.

tip-topper. A ' swell ' : 1837, Thackeray (O.E.D.) ; ob. Other forms (*tip-topping*, etc.) are too little used to qualify as unconventional : they're merely eccentric.

tip-toppedest. See **tippest-toppest.**

tip up. To hand over, ' fork out ', esp. money : low (− 1859). H., 1st ed.—2. To hold out : low and nautical (− 1887). Esp. as in Baumann, *tip up your fist* (or *fin*), reach or give (me) your hand !, shake hands ! Cf. *tip a daddle*, q.v.

tipper. One who gives a gratuity : 1877 (O.E.D.) : coll. >, by 1900, S.E.—2. A tipster : mostly racing : from ca. 1890. Cf. *tip*, n., 2.

Tipperary fortune. Breasts, pudend, and anus : Anglo-Irish (− 1785) : ob. Grose, 1st ed., ' Two town lands, stream's town, and ballinocack, said of Irish women without fortune.' Cf. at *wind-mill* ; see **Rochester, Tetbury, Whitechapel portion ;** also **Whitechapel fortune.**

Tipperary lawyer. A cudgel : Anglo-Irish : mid-C. 19–20. Cf. *Plymouth cloak.*

tippest-toppest. Absolutely ' tip-top ' : jocular (− 1887) ; ob. Baumann (also *tip-toppedest*).

tippet ; hempen t. (Marlowe) ; **St Johnstone's t.** (Scott) ; **Tyburn t.** (Latimer, 1549). A hangman's rope : mid-C. 15–early 19 : jocular coll. verging on S.E. (O.E.D.).

tipping, n. See **tip,** v.—2. Adj. Excellent, ' topping ' : dial. (− 1887) > school s. before 1904. Prob. ex *topping* on *ripping.*

tipple. Liquor : late C. 16–20 : coll. >, by 1700, s. Ex the v. Occ. of non-intoxicants : mid-C. 19–20.—2. A drinking-bout : ? C. 18–20. F. & H.

tipple, v.t. To disarrange (beds) : Bootham

School : C. 20. Anon., *Dict. of Bootham Slang*, 1925. Perhaps a perversion of S.E. *tip-up*.

tippling-ken. A tavern : low : C. 18. Ned Ward, *A Vade Mecum for Maltworms*, 1715. (His *tippling-office*, however, is prob. a nonce-word. W. Matthews, in *Notes and Queries*, June 15, 1935.)

tipply. Unsteady : coll. : 1906 (O.E.D.). Lit., apt to tipple over.—2. Hence, drunk : from ca. 1910. (Miles Burton, *Murder at the Moorings*, 1932.)

tippy. Extremely fashionable ; ' swell ' : 1810 (O.E.D.) ob. by 1900, † by 1935, except in Glasgow. Cf. the U.S. *tippy* (occ. *tippee*), an exquisite of 1804–5 (Thornton). Ex :—2. **the tippy.** The height of fashion ; the fashionable thing to do : ca. 1794–1812. Ex *tip*, the very top. O.E.D.— 3. Extremely ingenious ; very neat, smart, effective : 1863, M. Dods, ' A tippy little bit of criticism ' ; ob. Perhaps ex *tip*, n., 1.—4. Unsteady : coll. : from mid-1880's. Lit., likely to tip over. Cf. *tipply*, q.v. *The Century Dict.*—5. Generous with *tips* (of money) : servants' and subordinate staffs' : C. 20. E.g. John G. Brandon, *Th' Big City*, 1931.

tipster. One who gives ' tips ', orig. in racing (1862) and by 1884 in gen. : coll. >, by 1900, S.E. See *tip*, n., 2. (O.E.D.)

tiptop. See **tip-top.**

tique. See **teek.**

tire to death. To tire to exhaustion : coll. : resp. mid-C. 16–20, 1740. (O.E.D.)

tired. (Of a picture, or rather of the painting thereof) overworked : artists' : C. 20. Virtually synonymous with the longer-established *tight* (sense 6). Also *hard*. (J. Hodgson Lobley, R.B.A.)

tired, be born. To dislike work ; occ. as ' an excuse for assumed apathy or genuine disinclination ', F. & H. : from late 1890's. Whiteing, 1899. Occ. *be tired*.

tired, make (a person). See **you make me tired.**

tiresome. Troublesome, annoying, unpleasant : coll. : 1798, Charlotte Smith, ' The tiresome custom you have got of never being ready ' (O.E.D.).

tirly-whirly. The female pudend : Scots : late C. 18–20 ; ob. Burns. Reduplicated *whirly*. Lit., ' a whirled figure, ornament, or pattern ' : cf. lit. senses of *tirly*.

Tirps. Von Tirpitz, Admiral-in-Chief of the German Navy : naval : 1914 ; ob. F. & Gibbons. Contrast *terps* and *turps*.

tirret, tirrit. A fit of temper, occ. fear ; an ' upset ' : coll. ; orig. illiterate for *terror*, perhaps influenced by dial. *frit*, frightened : late C. 16–20. Shakespeare.

'tis. It is : coll. when not poetical,—at least after ca. 1850. Baumann.

'Tiser or **'Tizer, The.** *The Morning Advertiser* : journalistic (— 1860). H., 2nd ed. ('*Tizer*) ; Anon., *The Siliad*, 1874, ' The Victualler's anger, and the 'Tiser's rage ' ; † by 1920.

tish. A partition ; esp. a cubicle : Public Schools', universities' (— 1904).

tissey. An occ. variant of *tizzy*, q.v. ; † by 1900

tisty-tosty. Twistigrab (a game) : C. 20 ; ob. W. J. Lewis, *The Language of Cricket*, at *googly*. Ex dial. *tisty-tosty*, a cowslip-ball, hence adj. ' round like a ball ' (E.D.D.).

tit. A girl or young woman (in mid-C. 19–20, often, in low s., of a harlot) : from end of C. 16 ; S.E. until C. 18, then coll. until C. 19, then s. ; from late C. 19, low s. and possibly influenced by *titter*, q.v. Grose, 1st ed. ; T. Creevey, 1837, ' [Lady

Tavistock] thinks the Queen a resolute little tit,' O.E.D. Ex *tit*, a (small) horse : cf. *jilly*, q.v.—2. The female pudend : low : C. 18–20 ; ob. Abbr. *tit-bit*, *titmouse*, in same sense (C. 17–18) ; the former occ. = the penis, as in Urquhart, 1653.—3. A sol. spelling and pronunciation of *teat* : prob. from C. 17 or even earlier.—4. A student at Durham University : Durham townsmen's : late C. 19–20. Also '*Varsity tit.* Ex *tit* applied to persons.—5. A horse : c. : 1834, Ainsworth ; Charles E. Leach. Earlier in dial.

tit-bit. See *tit*, 2.

Tit-Bits. The R.F.C. weekly communiqué : Air Force : 1915–18. F. & Gibbons. Punning the popular weekly.

tit-fer (gen. **titfer**) ; **tit-for-tat.** A hat : the short form being an obvious abbr. (C. 20) of the second, which is rhyming s. of late C. 19–20. F. & Gibbons ; B. & P.—2. (tit-for-tat.) ' Too bloody right ' (q.v.) : military : 1914 ; ob. B. & P.

tit willow. A pillow : from ca. 1870. P. P., *Rhyming Slang*, 1932.

titch. A flogging : Christ's Hospital : mid-C. 19–20. ? ex *tight breeches* by blending, or ex dial. *titch*, touch.—2. Hence, occ. as a v. F. & H.

titery. See **tittery.—titfer.** See **tit-fer.**

tith. Tight : coll. and dial. : ca. 1615–30. Rare except in dramatist Fletcher. O.E.D.

Titire-Tu. See **Tityre-Tu.**

titivate, tittivate ; occ. **tiddivate, tidi-, tiddyvate.** To put finishing or additional touches to (one's toilet, oneself) : coll. : resp. 1805, 1836, 1824, 1833, 1823. E.g. Dickens in *Boz*, ' Regular as clockwork —breakfast at nine—dress and tittivate a little ', this quotation illustrating and affording the earliest example of the v.i. used as v. reflexive. Perhaps ex *tidy* with a quasi-Latin ending on *cultivate* : O.E.D. ' Or fanciful elaboration of synonymous dial. *tiff*, Fr. *attifer*, " to decke, . . . adorne " (Cotgrave) ' : W. Also with †*off* or *up*.—2. Hence, v.t., to treat gently : lower classes' (— 1923). Manchon.

titivated, -ating, -ation, -ator. Obvious derivatives ex *titivate* : C. 19–20. Coll.

titley ; gen., and in C. 20 almost always, **tiddly,** occ. **tiddley.** Intoxicating liquor : low (— 1859). H., 1st ed. (*titley*). Prob. ex *tiddlywink* (q.v.), a public-house.—2. Hence, a drink : low : from ca. 1870. Baumann. In C. 20, gen. a little drink (Manchon).

titley ; tiddly. Drunk : low : app. unrecorded before C. 20, though *on the tiddl(e)y*, intoxicated or in a fair way of becoming intoxicated, appears in *Punch* in 1895 (O.E.D. Sup.). If thus late, then ex the n., but if earlier than *tiddlywink* (q.v.), then perhaps a corruption (? orig. dial.) of *tipsy*.

titley (or **tiddley**) **and binder.** A drink of beer and a piece of bread-and-cheese (cf. *binder*, 1) : public-house phrase : C. 20. (Desmond Ryan, *St Eustace and the Albatross*, 1935.)

titmouse. See *tit*, n., 2. Ex *titmouse*, fig. = a small thing.

titotular bosh. Absolute nonsense : orig. and mainly music-halls' : 1897–8. Ware. Punning *teetotal*.

*****tit's back, as fine a fellow as ever crossed.** A very fine fellow : either c. or low (— 1887). Baumann. See *tit*, 1.

*****titter.** A girl or young woman : criminals' and tramps' c. (— 1812) >, by 1900, low s. Vaux ; H., 1st to 3rd ed. ; Henley, 1887, ' You flymy titters full of flam.' Either ex *titter*, a giggle, or ex

Scots *titty*, a sister, or again, ex dial. *titty*, a breast : the third possibility is perhaps the likeliest, for *titty*, sister, is mainly a child's word, unless we consider that dial. *titty*, a girl, has been influenced by *titty*, a breast.

tittery. Gin : C. 18. Perhaps ex *titter*, to giggle : Bailey. Occ. *titery, tityre.*

Tittery-tu. See Tityre-tu.

tittie. See titty.—**tittivate.** See titivate.

tittle. To whisper ; to gossip : late C. 14–20 : S.E. until late C. 18, then coll. and dial. ; in C. 20, mainly dial. Prob. echoic.

tittlebat. A somewhat illiterate, mainly London, coll. form of *stickleback* : C. 19–20. E.D.D. and W. Also *tiddlebat, tittleback.* (Slovenliness generates many such popular corruptions.)

tittup ; occ. **titup.** As n., eligible only in *the tit(t)up*, the thing : *that's the t.*, that's the thing ; *the correct t.*, the correct thing : low : late C. 19–20 ; ob. Ex *tit(t)up*, a horse's canter, itself echoic.

tittup, v.i. To toss for drinks : nautical : C. 20. S.O.D. Ex *tittup*, to canter. Cf. :

tit(t)uppy. Unsteady, shaky : coll. : 1798, Jane Austen. Rarely of persons, and in C. 20 mainly dial. Ex *tit(t)up*, a horse's canter.

titty ; occ. **tittie.** A sister ; a girl or young woman : Scots coll. (mostly among children as ' sister ') : from ca. 1720. Ramsay, Burns, Scott. Perhaps ex child's pronunciation of *sister.* O.E.D. Cf. *titter*, q.v.—2. A or the breast, esp. the human mother's : nursery coll., and dial. : from ca. 1740. (In dial., occ. *tetty.*)—3. A diminutive of *teat* (cf. *tit*, 3, q.v.) : coll. : C. 19–20.—4. Hence, a dummy *teat* : coll. (— 1927). Collinson.—5. A kitten, a cat ; also in address : nursery coll., and dial. : C. 19–20. Clare, 1821 (O.E.D.). Ex child's pron. of *kitty.*

titty and billy (or -ie and -ie). Sister and brother : Scots coll. : C. 19–20. Ex *titty*, 1, q.v.—2. Hence, *be titty-billy* (or *-ie*), to be intimate : Scots coll. (— 1825). Jamieson.

titty-bag ; -bottle. Resp., a small linen bag containing bread sprinkled with sweetened milk, given by some nurses to their charges ; a bottle (of milk) with teat attached : children's : C. 20. Manchon.

tityre. See tittery.

titup. See tittup.

Tityre-tu ; also **Titire-Tu, Tytere (or -ire)-tu, Tittery tu, tittyry.** A member of a band of rich and leisured roughs of ca. 1620–60 : a coll. nickname > S.E. The O.E.D. records the name in 1623 (J. Chamberlain) ; ' Water-Poet ' Taylor ; Herrick. Ex the opening words of Virgil's *First Eclogue.*

tius. A suit (of clothes) : back s. (— 1909). Ware restricts it to East London.

tiv(v)y. The female pudend : low : C. 19–20 ; ob. ? ex dial. *tiv(e)y*, activity.

'Tizer, The. See 'Tiser.

tizzy ; occ. **tizzey, tissey.** A sixpence : resp. 1804, 1809, and († in C. 20) 1829. Moncrieff, 1823, ' Hand us over three browns out of that 'ere tizzy.' O.E.D. ; F. & H. Prob. a corruption of *tester*, q.v., via *tilbury*, q.v. See also *testy.* Cf. *swiz* for *swindle* (W.).

tizzy-poole. A fives ball : Winchester : from ca. 1870. Because it used to cost 6*d.* and be sold by a head porter named Poole. Cf. the Harrow *tizzy-tick*, ' an order on a tradesman to the extent of 6*d.* a day ', F. & H. : mid-C. 19–20.

tizzy-snatcher. An assistant-paymaster : naval : C. 20. F. & Gibbons. Ex *tizzy*, q.v.

to, preposition. At (as in *to home*) ; in (a place, as in ' He lives to London ') : S.E. until mid-C. 18, then dial. and (mostly U.S.) coll.,—in England, it is, as a coll., illiterate, as indeed it is throughout the Empire, except Canada.—2. (After *to be* and in *all to bits* or *pieces*) in, into : coll. : C. 18–20. Vanbrugh, ca. 1720, ' The glasses are all to bits,' O.E.D.—3. The very pregnant use of *to* (in speech, gen. emphasised) as in ' There's more *to* the Bible than there is to *The Sheik*,' ' There's something to Shakespeare ' is a C. 20 coll. (? earlier than 1915) prob. derived ex *to it*, q.v.—4. Used at the end of phrase or clause and = ' to do ', etc., it is rare before C. 19, but a very frequent coll. in late C. 19–20. ' I went because I had to.' O.E.D.

to, adv. Expressing contact as in *shut a door to* : M.E.–C. 20 : S.E. until mid-C. 19, then coll. (O.E.D.)—2. ' Expressing attachment, application, or addition ' : C. 15–20 : S.E. until C. 19, then coll. ' We ordered the horses to ', 1883 (O.E.D.) ; C. W. Thurlow Craig, 1935, ' We threw the coat to ', i.e. on to the body.

to, conjunction, is sol. : late C. 19–20. E.g. ' Wait to I see you.' Rare. (Also in dial.)

to it, that's all there is. There is nothing to add, do, or say : coll. (orig. U.S.), anglicised ca. 1910. Cf. *to*, 3, q.v. In these cognates, (*is*) *to* = (is) notable, good, significant (in it, etc.). Possibly the pregnancy of this *to* originated in the *to* stated or implied in the ethic dative.

to-night's the night ! A c.p. of late C. 19–20 ; ob.

to rights. See rights, to.—**toac.** See taoc.

to the nines, *to the ruffian. To an extreme or superlative degree : for *to the nines*, see *nines* ; *to the ruffian* is c. of ca. 1810–50 : Vaux.

toad. A German hand-grenade, shaped rather like one : military coll. : 1915 ; ob. F. & Gibbons. —2. ' A piece of hot toast put into their beer by college men ' : Winchester : C. 19. Wrench.

toad-in-the-hole. A sandwich-board : mostly London (— 1864) ; † by 1920. H., 3rd ed. Ex the meat dish so named.—2. Hence, occ., the man carrying it : late C. 19–early 20. Manchon.

toad is of feathers, as full of money as a. Penniless : coll. : ca. 1785–1900. Grose, 2nd ed. ; Baumann. Prob. suggested by :

toad of a side-pocket, as much need of it as a. See side-pocket.

toad on a chopping-block, (s)he sits like a. (S)he sits badly on a horse : coll. (— 1785) ; † by 1920. Grose, 1st ed. A picturesque simile as applied to a side-saddle. (In Lincolnshire dial. : *. . . on a shovel* : E.D.D.)

toast. A toper ; (*old toast*) a lively old fellow fond of his liquor : coll. : ca. 1668–1800, but ob. by 1730. L'Estrange, B.E., Grose. Ex such phrases as *ale and toast.*

toast, (had) on. Swindled : from ca. 1885. *St James's Gazette*, Nov. 6, 1886, refers to *had on toast* as ' a quaint and pleasing modern phrase '.—2. Hence, *on toast* = cornered : from early 1890's.— 3. Hence, in C. 20 : compliant, extremely willing to help, servile, at one's mercy.

toast your blooming eye-brows ! Go to blazes ! : lower classes' c.p. of ca. 1895–1915. Ware.

toasting-fork, -iron. A sword : jocular coll. : 1596, Shakespeare, and Grose, 1st ed., have *t.-iron*, which is ob. by 1880, † by 1914 ; *t.-fork* dates from ca. 1860 and occurs in *Tom Brown at Oxford*, 1861. Cf. *cheese-toaster* (and the † S.E. *toaster*), likewise derived ex its most gen. use.

toasty. Warmly tinted : artists' : from mid-1890's. Lit., (burnt) brown.

tobacco, make dead men chew. To keep the names of dead men on the books : naval : late C. 18–early 19. John Davis, *The Post Captain*, 1805.

Tobacco Browne. Isaac Hawkins Browne (1705–60), wit and poet ; author of parodies entitled *A Pipe of Tobacco*. (Dawson.)

tobacco chart. Gen. pl., ' the . . . inaccurate charts that could formerly be bought from any ship chandler at a low price ' : nautical : ca. 1840–90. Bowen. Perhaps as sold at the price of an ounce of tobacco, or because they were tobacco-stained.

tobacco-pipe curls. Corkscrew curls worn by costers and Gypsies : (esp. London) lower classes' (— 1887) ; ob. Baumann. Ex the curve of such a pipe.

tobaccy. Tobacco : lower classes' coll. : from the 1870's if not earlier. W. S. Gilbert, *H.M.S. Pinafore*, ' I've snuff and tobaccy and excellent jacky.' (*Slang*, p. 101.)

tobby. A deck boy : nautical : late C. 19–20. Bowen. ? ex *toby*, n., 5 : because always at hand.

*tober. A road : tramps' c. and Romany, the former in 1845 in ' *No. 747* '. See *toby*, 3.—2. Hence, a circus-field : Parlyaree (?) and circus s. (— 1933). E. Seago, *Circus Company*.—3. Among grafters, it is a fair-ground or market ; hence, one's pitch thereon or therein : C. 20. Philip Allingham, *Cheapjack*, 1934.

tober-mush. A market-inspector : market-traders' (e.g. Petticoat Lane) : C. 20. Ex preceding + *mush*, n., last sense : cf. *coring mush* and *rye mush*. Cf. also :

tober omee (or **omey** or **homee** or **homey**). A toll-collector : grafters' : late C. 19–20. Philip Allingham, *Cheapjack*, 1934. Cf. *tober-mush*.

toby. The buttocks : from ca. 1675. Esp. in *tickle one's toby*, to beat him on the buttocks. Ex the proper name.—2. Hence, the female pudend, as in Cotton, ca. 1678. Ob.—3. (Always **the toby.**) The highway : c. (— 1811). *Lex. Bal.*, Lytton, Ainsworth, Hindley ; ob., the gen. C. 20 term being *drum*. Also, fig., robbery on the highway : 1812, Vaux. Cf. *toby man*, q.v. Ex Shelta *tobar*, a road, itself perhaps a ' deliberate perversion of Irish *bothar*, road ', W. Occ. *tober*. Cf. the v. and the phrases.—4. Hence, a pitch : showmen's : from ca. 1890. *The Standard*, Jan. 29, 1893, ' We have to be out in the road early . . . to secure our " Toby ".'—5. **Toby**, the dog in a Punch and Judy show : 1840 : coll. very soon > S.E. : see *swatchel*. ' The dog in [The Book of] Tobit . . . is probably the eponym of " Dog Toby " of " Punch and Judy " ' (Sir Paul Harvey).—6. A lady's collar : Society coll. : ca. 1882–1918. Ex ' the wide frill worn round the neck by Mr Punch's dog ' (Ware).—7. Hence (?), a steel helmet : military : from late 1915. F. & Gibbons.—8. A tramp : c. : C. 20. George Orwell, *Down and Out*, 1933. Ex senses 3, 4.

*toby, v.t. To rob (a person) on the highway ; hence, *done for a toby*, convicted for highway robbery : c. of ca. 1810–50. Vaux (v. and phrase).

*toby, high (or **main**). Highway robbery by a mounted person ; that of footpads being *the low toby*. C. of ca. 1810–50. Vaux. See *toby*, n., 3.—2. Also (*high toby* only), the highway itself.

*toby, high spice ; high toby spice. The highway viewed as the locality for robbery : c. (— 1812). Byron, 1812 (*h.t.s.*) ; Hindley, 1876 (*h.s.t.*). Ex *toby*, n., 3.

*toby, ply or **ride the.** To practise highway robbery : c. of ca. 1812–70. Ex *toby*, n., 3, and cf. *toby, high.*

*toby concern or **lay.** The practice of highway robbery : c. : 1811 (*lay*) ; † by 1880. ' Ducange Anglicus ' and H. 1st ed., have *toby consarn.*

*toby gill ; high toby gloak ; toby man. A highwayman : c. : from ca. 1810 ; † by 1880. Vaux, 1812, has all three. (Romany : *tober kov*, cove.) Cf. :

*toby man, high and **low.** A highwayman and a footpad : c. : ca. 1810–80. *Lex. Bal.*, 1811. Ex *toby*, n., 3, and cf. *toby gill*, etc.

*toby spice. See *toby, high spice*, and **spice.*

toe emma. A trench mortar : military : from 1915. Ex signalese for *t m*.—2. Hence, a *travelling medical board* : Australian : from 1916. Such a board ' shot ' soldiers into the trenches.

toco, toko. Chastisement : from ca. 1820 ; ob. Bee, 1823, ' If . . . Blackee gets a whip about his back, why he has caught toco.' Hence, *to give* (a person) *toco*, to thrash him, as in Hughes, 1857, ' Administer toco to the wretched fags '. Perhaps ex (the dative or ablative of) Gr. τόκος, interest, as the O.E.D. suggests ; or ex Hindustani *tokna*, to censure, via the imperative *toco*, as Yule & Burnell pertinently remarks ; or, as I diffidently propose, ex some Negro or Polynesian word : cf. Maori *toko*, a rod (Edward Tregear's Dict., 1891). Cf. :

toco for yam, get or **nap.** To be punished ; among sailors from ca. 1860, to get paid out. Bee records this (the *get*), prob. the orig., form in 1823. On the analogy of a stone for a loaf of bread, and, presumably, at first a treatment meted out to slaves. See *toco*.—2. By 1874, *toco for yam* had come to mean ' a Roland for an Oliver ' (H., 5th ed.) ; ob.

Tod is the ' inevitable ' nickname of any man surnamed Sloan (after the famous jockey) or Hunter (cf. the surname *Todhunter*) : naval and military : late C. 19–20. F. & Gibbons.

tod ; toddy. A foppishly or gaily dressed person (rarely female) : West Yorkshire s. (— 1904), not dial. E.D.D. I.e. dial. *tod*, a fox.

tod, adj. Alone ; esp. *be on one's tod*, to be, or to work, alone : grafters' : from ca. 1895. Philip Allingham, *Cheapjack*, 1934. Prob. ex a lost *Tod Sloan*, rhyming s. arising ca. 1894 : cf. *Tod.*

[**toddle**, to go, walk, depart, is, by the O.E.D., considered S.E. ; but its C. 20 use, esp. in the upper and upper-middle classes (see, e.g., Dorothy Sayers's *Lord Peter Wimsey* novels), seems to me to be coll.]

toddy, -ie. In address to a child of 1–3 years : coll. : ? mid-C. 19–20. Such a child toddles rather than walks ; cf. dial. *toddy*, little, and familiar S.E. *toddles*, a toddling child.—2. See *tod*, n.

toddy-blossom. A ' grog-blossom ', q.v. : C. 19–20 ; ob. Ex *toddy*, the beverage.

toddy-stick. A muddler : low : mid-C. 19–20. On *stick* used pejoratively.

todge. To smash (to a pulp) : provincial : C. 19–20. Ex dial. *todge*, stodge.

toe, v.t. To kick : low : from ca. 1860 : coll. >, ca. 1910, S.E.

toe, have or **hold by the.** To hold securely : coll. : mid-C. 16–mid-17. Chronicler Hall and Bishop Hall. O.E.D. Cf. *short hairs*, q.v.

toe, kiss the Pope's. Respectfully to set one's lips to the golden cross on the Pope's right sandal : 1768, the Earl Carlisle : s. >, ca. 1890, coll. (O.E.D.)

toe, turn on the. To turn (a person) off the ladder

in hanging: late C. 16–early 17. Nashe, 1594 (O.E.D.).

[toe-and-rag is Manchon's error for *toe-rag*, q.v.]

toe-face. An objectionable or dirty fellow: low (— 1923). Manchon.

toe-fit-ti(e). To tie a string to (a boy's) toe and haul him out of bed: Public Schools', esp. Winchester and Felsted: ca. 1870–1900. *The Felstedian*, Nov., 1881, ' "To fit-ti", in reference to verbs of the third conjugation transferred from the similarity of sound to the schoolboy's toe.'

toe-nail poisoning. Ptomaine poisoning: jocular: from 1934.

toe-path. An infantry regiment: cavalrymen's: ca. 1890–1914. Ware. Punning *tow-path*.

toe-rag. A beggar: provincial s. (— 1909). Ware. Perhaps ex *toe-ragger*, q.v.—2. 'A London docker who works bulk grain ex-ship': nautical: C. 20. Bowen.

toe-rag, shake one's. See shake one's toe-rag.

toe-ragger, -rigger. A term of opprobrium: Australia and New Zealand resp., as in *Truth* (the Sydney one), Jan. 12, 1896, ' "A toe-ragger" is Maori . . . The nastiest term of contempt was *tua rika rika*, or slave. The old whalers on the Maoriland coast in their anger called each other *toe-riggers*, and to-day the word in the form of *toe-ragger* has spread throughout the whole of the South Seas.' Morris.

*toe-rags. Those windings of cotton-wool about the ball of the foot and the toes which, to displace socks, prevent blistering: tramps' *v.* : C. 20. E.g. in F. Jennings, *Tramping with Tramps*, 1932.

toes, claw one's. To indulge oneself: coll. : mid-C. 15–early 16. O.E.D.

toes, cool one's. To have to wait: coll. : ca. 1660–1700. Brathwait, 1665 (O.E.D.). Cf. *to cool* (or *kick*) *one's heels*.

toes, on old. Aged; in old age: coll. : C. 15. O.E.D. Cf. *old bones*.

toe's length, the. Almost no distance: coll. : from ca. 1820 ; ob. (O.E.D.)

toes of, step or tread on the. To vex ; give umbrage to: coll. : mid-C. 19–20. Robert Browning, 1868 (O.E.D.). Ex lit. sense.

toes up. (Lying) dead: 1851, Mayhew (O.E.D.) ; slightly ob. Cf. :

toes up, turn one's. To die: 1860, Reade, 'Several arbalestiers turned their toes up.' In C. 20, occ. elaborated to *turn one's toes up to the daisies* (Manchon). Cf. *toes up*, and 'die' synonymy in *Words* !

toey. A 'swell': New South Wales: late C. 19–20 ; ob. ? corruption of :

toff. A 'swell' ; a 'nob' (well-to-do person): proletarian: from 1850's ; slightly ob. Ca. 1868, there was a music-hall song entitled *The Shoreditch Toff*, by Arthur Lloyd ; Whiteing, 1899. Ex *tuft*, via *toft*, q.v.—2. Hence, a man of fortitude and courage: late C. 19–20 ; slightly ob. *The Daily Telegraph*, Sept. 16, 1902, 'He held out his wrists to be handcuffed, and exclaimed, "Now I'll die like a toff".'—3. A 'brick', a person behaving handsomely : 1898 (O.E.D. ; slightly ob.

toff, v. Esp. *be toffed up*, to be dressed like a 'toff': low: 1928 (O.E.D. Sup.).

toff bundle-carrier. A gentleman accompanying a prosperous serio-comic from hall to hall on her evening 'rounds': theatrical: ca. 1870–1900. Ware. Ex *toff*, 1.

*toff-omee. The superlative of *toff*, 1: c. (— 1909). Ware.

toff-shoving. 'Pushing about well-dressed men in a crowd': London roughs': ca. 1882–1900. Ware.

*toffee. Tobacco: c. (— 1932). 'Stuart Wood.' Ex its colour.

toffee, not for. Not at all; by no manner of means ; not in any circumstances: uncultured: late C. 19–20. Hugh Walpole, *Vanessa*, 1933 ; 'That fellow X. can't bat for toffee,' of a Test cricketer in 1934.

toffee-apple. A trench-mortar stick-bomb: military coll. : 1915–18. F. & Gibbons, 'From . . . the apples dipped in toffee [and] sold under the name at English country fairs'.

Toffee Men, the. Everton Football Club ('soccer') : sporting : C. 20. Ex *Everton toffee*.

toffee-nosed. Supercilious ; too proud ; conceited : lower classes' : C. 20 ; ob. F. & Gibbons. With pun on *toffy*.

toffee-scramble. A toffee-making: schoolboys' coll. : C. 20. Anon., *Troddles*, 1901.

toffer. A fashionable whore: low: ca. 1860–1914. H., 2nd ed. Cf. :

tofficky. Showy ; vulgarly dressy: low: ca. 1860–1910. H., 2nd ed. Ex *toff*, 1.

toffish ; toffy. Stylish ; 'swell' : resp. from ca. 1873, when *toffishness* occurs in Greenwood's *Strange Company* ; 1901, Jerome K. Jerome (O.E.D.) ; *toffy*, ob., ex *tofficky*.

toft. A variant, prob. the imm. source of *toff*, 1, q.v. : ca. 1850–1910. Mayhew, 1851 ; H., 1st ed. If not *toff* debased—and the dates seem to preclude this—then *tuft* corrupted.

*tog. A coat: late C. 18–20 : c. >, ca. 1820, low s. Tuft, 1798, 'Long tog, a coat' ; Andrewes, 1809, 'Tatty tog, a gaming cloth' ; Vaux, 1812, 'Tog, a coat'. O.E.D. Ex *toge*, q.v., or, less prob., *tog(e)man(s)*, a cloak.—2. See toge and togs.—3. See taoc.—4. A week's wages on piece-work : tailors' : C. 20. Perhaps ex sense 1.

tog, v. First as past ppl. *togged*, dressed, 1793, *to tog* being recorded not before 1812. Vaux, 'To *tog* is to . . . put on clothes ; to *tog* a person, . . . to supply them with apparel.' Low s. verging on c. Ex *toge*.

tog, long. See tog, n.—**tog, tatty.** See ibid.

tog, upper. An overcoat: c. of ca. 1810–50. Vaux. Cf. *togger*, 1. Ex *tog*, n.

tog-bound. Having no good clothes: lower classes' (— 1909). Ware.

tog-fencer. A tailor: London proletariat: ca. 1870–1915. Ware.

tog it ; t. out ; t. up. V.i., to dress smartly: proletarian: resp. 1844, 1869, 1903. O.E.D.—2. As v.t., *tog out* occurs in 1820 in *The London Magazine* (I, 25), 'He was always togged out to the nines,' and *tog up* in 1894 (O.E.D.).

tog-maker. A low-class tailor: proletarian: late C. 19–20. Prob. ex *togs*.

tog up. See tog it.

toga play. An Ancient-Classics drama: theatrical coll. (— 1909) ; ob. Ware. Ex the ancient Roman male garment.

*togamans. See togemans.

*toge. A coat: c. : late C. 17–18. B.E. Ex *togemans* on S.E. *toge* (= *toga*).

*togeman(s) ; togman. A cloak ; a (loose) coat ; rarely, a gown (B.E.) : c. of ca. 1565–1840, but ob. by 1800 if not indeed by 1750. Harman, 1567, all three forms ; *togeman*, very rare after 1700, *togman* app. not later than 1700 ; Grose, 1st ed., *togmans*, 2nd ed., *togemans* ; Bee, the rare *togamans*. Ex Roman *toga*, perhaps in its Fr. form (*toge*), + the c. suffix *-mans*, q.v. Cf. *tog, toge, togs*.

togey. A knotted lanyard used disciplinarily or bullyingly : in the training-ship *Britannia* : late C. 19–early 20. Bowen. Prob. ex *toco* ; cf. *toko, take*.

togged, togged out or **up ; togged up to the nines.** See resp. **tog, v.,** and **tog it.**

togger. Perhaps only in *upper togger*, an over-coat : low s. of ca. 1820–50. Egan, 1823, 'And with his upper togger gay, | Prepared to toddle swift away.' Ex *tog*, n., 1, q.v.—2. A boat in the Torpids : Oxford University : from mid-1890's. Ex *Torpid*, via 'the Oxford *-er*', on Cambridge *slogger*. (Occ. as adj. : F. & H., 1904.)—3. In pl., gen. *T*, the Torpids, i.e. the races themselves, the competition as a whole : ibid. : C. 20.—4. At Harrow (also *Torpid*), a boy not yet two years in the School : from ca. 1896. F. & H.

toggery. Clothes : s. (1812, Vaux) >, ca. 1890, coll. Moncrieff, 1823, 'This toggery will never fit —you must have a new rig-out.'—2. Hence esp., official or vocational dress : from ca. 1825 ; slightly ob. Marryat, 1837, has *long toggery*, landsmen's clothes : cf. *togs, long*.—3. Hence, (a horse's) harness : from late 1850's ; slightly ob. H., 1st ed. —4. Hence, loosely, one's 'gear' or belongings : from late 1850's ; ob. H., 1st ed.

*****toggy.** A cloak ; a coat : c. : ca. 1815–1910. Ex *tog*, n., 1, on *toggery*, or perhaps imm. ex †*toggy*, *tuggy*, an overcoat for the arctic regions.

togies. See **togy.**

*****togman.** See **togman(s).** The *togmans* of Grose, 1st ed., is a confusion, as also, prob., is Baumann's *togomans*.

*****togs.** Clothes : c. (— 1809) >, ca. 1825, low s. >, ca. 1860, gen. s. ; in C. 20, usually jocular coll. G. Andrewes's Dict. ; Dickens ; Blackmore. Ex *tog*, n., 1, q.v.—2. In phrases,—chiefly these two :

togs, long. Landsmen's clothes : nautical s. >, ca. 1890, coll. : 1830, Marryat, 'I retained a suit of "long togs", as we call them,' O.E.D. ; Dana. Prob. on *long clothes*. Cf. at *toggery*, 2, and the derivative :

togs, Sunday. One's best clothes : London and nautical s. (— 1859) >, by 1904, gen. H., 1st ed. ; Smyth ; F. & H. Ex *togs*, q.v. ; cf. *togs, long*.

togy. (Gen. pl.) A knotted rope's-end 'carried about hidden by elder boys to beat their fags with' : Public Schools' : from ca. 1870 ; ob. Ware. Prob. ex *toco*, q.v. Also *togey*, q.v.

toheno ; occ. **tohereno.** Very nice : late C. 19– 20 : costers'. Lit., *hot one* reversed.

*****toke.** (Dry) bread : low s. (— 1859) verging, orig., on c. H., 1st ed. Perhaps *tuck* (food) or (*hard* and *soft*) *tack* corrupted.—2. Hence, food in gen. : low s. and c. : from ca. 1875. Anon., *Five Years' Penal Servitude*, 1877, 'What in prison slang is called his toke or chuck.'—3. A loaf of bread, esp. a small loaf of bread served in prison : (mostly prison) c. : late C. 19–20. 'Stuart Wood', 1932 ; 'James Spenser', 1934.—4. (Prob. ex 1.) A piece, portion ; lump : rare and low : from early 1870's ; ob. H., 5th ed.

toke, v. To idle, 'loaf' : Leys School : late C. 19–20. Ex *thoke*, v. : q.v.

token, Tom-fool's. Money : late C. 17–mid-18. B.E. Contrast '

token, the. Venereal disease, esp. in *tip one* (gen. male) *the token*, to infect venereally : low : from ca. 1780 ; very ob. Grose, 1st ed. Ex *token*, a blotch or discoloration indicative of disease, esp. the plague. (*the tokens*, the plague, is S.E.)

toko. See **toco.**

toko, take. 'To take four dozen lashes in the old Navy without crying out' (Bowen) : ca. 1840–90. Ex *toco for yam*, q.v.

tokon. A rare variant (— 1923) of *toco*, q.v. Manchon.

tol. A sword : c. of late C. 17–18. B.E. ; Grose, 1st ed. Abbr. *Toledo*, a sword there made. Hence, *rum tol*, a gold- or silver-hilted sword ; *queer tol*, a brass- or steel-hilted one, i.e. an ordinary one. —2. A share ; a *lot* (of . . .) : back s. (— 1859). H., 1st ed.

tol-lol. Intoxicated : Yorkshire and Notting-hamshire : from ca. 1890. E.D.D.—2. See :

tol-lol(l) ; **tol-lollish.** Pretty good : resp. from middle 1790's and late 1850's ; ob. Mrs A. M. Bennett, 1797 ; H., 2nd ed., has both ; W. S. Gilbert, 'Lord Nelson, too, was pretty well— | That is, tol-lol-ish !' F. & H. ; O.E.D. By the re-duplication of the first syllable of *tolerable*.—2. As adv., tolerably : from late 1850's. H., 2nd ed.

told, be. To obtain one's colours in a school team : Tonbridge : late C. 19–20.

told out. Exhausted : coll. : 1861, Whyte-Melville, of a horse. Lit., counted out. O.E.D.

tole. Told : sol. : C. 19–20. Cf. *stole* for *stolen*.

tolerable. In fair health : coll. : 1847, C. Brontë, 'We're tolerable, sir, I thank you.'—2. As adv. (= tolerably) : from ca. 1670 : S.E. until late C. 18, then coll. and dial.

tolerably. (Predicatively, of health.) Pretty well : coll. : 1778, Mme D'Arblay (O.E.D.).

tollcester. Incorrect for *tollsester* : C. 17. O.E.D.

*****tol(l)iban rig.** 'A species of cheat carried on by a woman, assuming the character of a deaf and dumb conjurer', Grose, 2nd ed. : c. : ca. 1786–1850. Ex *rig*, a trick, + *toloben* (q.v.), *tol(l)iban*, the tongue.

tolly. A candle : Public Schools' : mid-C. 19–20. (Cf. *tolly up*, q.v.) Ex *tallow*. Hence, *the Tolly*, a tapering spire at the back of the Close of Rugby School : Rugby : late C. 19–20. Barrère & Leland. *The Athenæum*, June 16, 1900.—2. A flat instru-ment (e.g. a ruler) used in caning : Stonyhurst : late C. 19–20. ? ex sense 1, or ex L. *tollere*. Esp. *get the tolly* (Manchon).

tolly, gen. **tolly up.** To work by candle-light after the extinction of the other lights : Harrow School (— 1889). Barrère & Leland. Ex *tolly*, n., 1.

tolly-shop. A prefect's room (where caning is done) : Stonyhurst : late C. 19–20. Ex *tolly*, n. 2nd sense. Cf. *tolly-ticket*, a good-conduct card : ibid. : id. Because it ensured against caning, except for a particularly serious offence.

tolly up. See **tolly, v.**

toloben. The tongue : c. : late C. 18–20. Hence, *toloben rig*, fortune-telling. Cf. *tolliban rig*. Also occ. spelt *tollibon* or *tullibon*. (I am, however, unconvinced about *toloben* being the tongue : it is vouched-for only by F. & H., and I think that there may be a confusion with Romany *tullopen* or *tulipen* (Smart & Crofton), or *tulipen* (Sampson), fat, lard, grease, a sense that, if extended to 'paint' for the face, might well explain *toloben-rig*, fortune-telling, and possibly also *tolliban-rig* as above.)

Tom, the big bell at Christ Church, Oxford, is S.E.,

but *after Tom*, after hours, is a Christ Church coll. (— 1874). H., 5th ed.—2. **tom, long.** See **long tom.**—3. **tom, old.** Gin : c. or low s. (— 1823) ; ob. Bee. Occ. (— 1887), merely *tom* or *Tom*, as in Baumann.—4. Inevitable nickname of all men named King : naval and military : late C. 19–20. Bowen. Ex Tom King, the famous C. 18 highwayman.—5. (Either *tom* or *Tom*.) A girl : Australian : C. 20. C. J. Dennis. Prob. ex :—6. 'A masculine woman of the town' (harlot) : low London : mid-C. 19–20.—7. A woman 'who does not care for the society of others than those of her own sex' : Society : ca. 1880–1914. Ware.—8. A tomato : C. 20 : a trade abbr. >, by 1925, a lower class coll. —9. (Cf. sense 4.) On the music-halls it is a frequent nickname for men surnamed Collins : C. 20. Ex 'the frequency of *Tom Collins* on the old 'vaudeville bills' (Douglas Buchanan). Cf. *Jumper* and *Lottie*, qq.v.

Tom-a-Styles or **-Stiles.** Anybody, esp. in law, with *John-a-Nokes*, q.v., as his opponent : ca. 1770–1830 : coll. >, by 1800, S.E. G. A. Stevens, 1772, 'From John o' Nokes to Tom o' Stiles, | What is it all but fooling ?' ; Grose, 1st ed. (*Tom-a-Stiles*). Occ. *John-a-Stiles.* See *Words !*

Tom and funny. Money : rhyming s. (— 1909) ; ob. Ware.

Tom-and-Jerry days. The Regency (1810–20) ; also, the reign of George IV : coll. : ca. 1825–60. Ex Tom and Jerry in Pierce Egan's *Life in London*, 1821, with a continuation in 1828. The v., *Tom-and-Jerry*, to behave riotously (1828), is rather S.E. than coll., but *Tom-and-Jerry* (— 1864) or *T.-and-J. shop* (— 1874), a low drinking-shop, is coll. ; † by 1910. The latter elaborates *jerry-shop*, a low beerhouse, recorded in 1834. H., 3rd and 5th edd. ; F. & H. ; O.R.D.

Tom and Tib. See **Tom, Dick, and Harry.**

Tom Astoner. A dashing or devil-may-care fellow : nautical : from ca. 1860 : ob. Smyth. Ex *to astonish* or perhaps abbr. *astoniser* ; Ned Ward, however, has, in 1706, *Tom Estenor*, which may pun a surname (O.E.D.).

*****Tom Bray's bilk.** 'Laying out ace and deuce at cribbage', Vaux, 1812 : ca. 1810–60 : prob. orig. c. > (low) gaming s. ? ex noted sharper.

*****Tom Brown.** 'Twelve in hand, in crib', Vaux : ca. 1810–60 : ? c. > s.

Tom Cony. A simpleton or very silly fellow : coll. : late C. 17–early 19. B.E., who spells it *Conney* ; Grose, 1st ed.

Tom Cox. A shirker ; one who talks much, little does : naval : mid-C. 19–20. Cf. :

Tom Cox's traverse. See **three turns.** Cf. *sojering*, q.v.

Tom, Dick, and Harry. The common run of men (and women) : coll. soon > S.E. : *T., D., and H.*, app. not before ca. 1815, but Lindsay, in 1566, has *Jack and Tom*, *Tom and Tib* is frequent in C. 17, *Jack, Tom, Will, and Dick* in 1604 (James I *loquitur*), *Tom, Jack and Dick* in 'Water-Poet' Taylor, 1622, *Tom and Dick* occurs in C. 18, *Tom, Dick, and Francis* in Shakespeare (1596), *Dick, Tom, and Jack* in 1660 (A. Brome), *Jack, Tom, and Harry* ca. 1693 (T. Brown), and *Tom, Jack, and Harry* in 1865. F. & H. ; O.E.D. ; Apperson (above all), and my *Words !* Cf. *Tom Tiler.*

Tom-doodle ; rarely **-a-doodle.** A simpleton : popular coll. : C. 18–20 ; ob. Ned Ward, 1707, 'That . . . Tom-doodle of a son . . . talks of nothing but his mother.'

Tom Double. A double-dealer, a shuffler : coll. : C. 18–mid-19.

Tom Drum's entertainment. The (very) rough reception of a guest : coll. : ca. 1570–1640. Holinshed. Also *John* (Shakespeare), *Jack* ('Water-Poet' Taylor). Possibly ex an actual person's name ; more prob., a pun on *drum*.

Tom farthing (or **F.**). A fool : coll. (1689, Shadwell) >, early in C. 18, S.E. ; ob. by 1910, † by 1930. F. & H. Pejorative *farthing*. Cf. *Tom-doodle*.

Tom Fool than Tom Fool knows, more know. A semi-proverbial c.p. of C. 18–20 ; ob. Defoe ; F. & H., 'A sarcastic retort on failing to recognise, or professing to be unacquainted with, a person saluting'.

Tom Long. A person long a-coming or 'tiresomely' so in telling a tale : coll. (? > S.E.) : from ca. 1630 ; ob., except in dial., which in C. 19–20 it mainly is. W. Foster, 1631, 'Surely this is Tom Long the carrier, who will never do his errand,' O.E.D., but this is preceded by 'Proverbs' Heywood, 1546, 'I will send it him by John Long the carrier,' i.e. at some vague date, and by Cotgrave, 1611, 'To stay'—in C. 18–20, gen. *wait*—'for John Long the Carrier : to tarry long for that which comes but slowly.' In his *Phraseologia Generalis*, 1681, W. Robertson has *Tom Long the carrier* ; in late C. 17, B.E. has *come by T. L. the c.*, 'of what is very late, or long a coming', and Grose, 1st ed., much the same phrase. Apperson.

Tom-noddy. A stupid, a foolish, person : coll. (— 1828) >, by 1860, S.E.

*****Tom o' Bedlam.** A madman, esp. if discharged from Bedlam and allowed to beg : c. and s. : C. 17–early 19. B.E., Grose. Cf. *Abram-man*.

Tom Owen's stop. 'The left-hand open, scrawling over the antagonist's face, service with the right', Bee : pugilistic : ca. 1820–40. Ex a boxer.

*****Tom Pat.** A parson or hedge-priest : c. : late C. 17–early 18. *Street Robberies Considered*. A *rum Tom Pat* is a clerk in holy orders, i.e. a genuine cleric. App. *Pat = patrico*, q.v.—2. A shoe : c. : C. 19–20 ; ob. (In Romany, a foot.)

Tom Pepper. A liar : nautical s. (— 1867) >, by 1890, coll. Smyth. In sailors' folk-lore, 'Tom Pepper' was the seaman who was kicked out of Hell for lying' (Bowen).

Tom Quad. The big quadrangle at Christ Church, Oxford : Oxford University coll. : late C. 19–20. Ex *Tom*, the great bell at Christ Church.

Tom Right. Night : rhyming s. (— 1857) ; ob. 'Ducange Anglicus.'

tom-rot. A variant (— 1887 ; † by 1920) of *tommy-rot*, q.v. Baumann.

Tom Tailor. A tailor in gen. : coll. >, by 1890, S.E. : 1820, Scott (O.E.D.).

Tom Tell-Troth (**Truth**). An honest man : coll. resp. C. 17 and C. 18–20 (ob.). *Tom True-Tongue*, C. 14, is the generator ; *Tom Truth*, mainly C. 16 (e.g. Latimer), the imm. generator. O.E.D. ; F. & H. ; Apperson.

Tom Thacker. Tobacco : rhyming s. (on *bacca*) : late C. 19–20. B. & P.

Tom Thumb. Rum : rhyming s. : late C. 19–20 F. & Gibbons.

Tom Tiler or **Tyler.** Any ordinary man : coll. : ca. 1580–1640. Stonyhurst, 1582. Cf. *Tom, Dick, and Harry.*—2. Hence, a henpecked husband : id. : early C. 17.

tom-tit. To defecate : rhyming s. (late C. 19–20)

on *sh*t*. B. & P. Also *pony and trap* (same period)
on *crap* (Ibid.).

tom-tom. A Chinese gong : catachrestic : from
late 1830's. Also *tam-tam*. O.E.D.

Tom Topper(s) or **Tug.** A ferryman ; any river
hand : low London : from ca. 1860 ; ob. H., 3rd
ed. ('*Topper* . . . From a popular song, entitled
"*Overboard he vent*"'), for both ; *Tug* presumably
from that vessel, though perhaps imm. ex 'the
small stage-play', H., 5th ed.

Tom Tripe. A pipe : rhyming s. (— 1859) ; † by
1900. H., 1st ed. The C. 20 term is *cherry ripe*,
q.v. Cf. *Tommy tripe*, q.v.

Tom Tug. A fool : rhyming s. (— 1874) on *mug*.
H., 5th ed.—2. See **Tom Topper**.—3. A bed-bug :
rhyming s. (— 1909). Ware. Contrast sense 1.

Tom Turdman. A nightman : low : from ca.
1700 ; ob. E. Ward, 1703 (Matthews) ; Grose,
1st ed.

Tom Tyler. See **Tom Tiler**.

tomahawk is catachrestic when used of a knob-
kerry : late C. 17–20. O.E.D.—2. A policeman's
baton : urban, esp. Cockneys' (— 1909) ; slightly
ob. Ware.

tomall(e)y. Incorrect when = *tamal*, a South
American dish : mid-C. 19–20. O.E.D.

Tomasso di Rotto or **tomasso di rotto.** Tommy-
rot : middle-class youths' : ca. 1905–14. Ware,
'Italian shape', i.e. an Italianising of *Tommy Rot*.

*tomato-can tramp. A tramp that, to sleep, will
curl up anywhere : tramps' c. (— 1932). Frank
Jennings. Even an old tin suffices as a pillow.

tombstone. A pawn-ticket : low (— 1864). H.,
3rd ed.—2. A projecting tooth, esp. if discoloured :
C. 20.

tombstone-style. An advertisement (rarely of
other matter) so 'displayed', i.e. composed, that it
resembles a monumental inscription : printers'
coll. : from ca. 1880.

tomjohn ; Tomjohn. A tonjon : Anglo-Indian
(— 1886). Yule & Burnell. By Hobson-Jobson.

tommy, as applied to goods (mainly food) supplied to workmen in lieu of wages, is S.E. ; so too,
according to the O.E.D., it is as the soldiers' and,
from ca. 1860, the lower classes' word for (orig.
brown) bread. The latter I hold to be s. in C. 18–
early 19, coll. in mid-C. 19–20, as are *soft* (or, 1811,
white) *tommy*, bread as opp. to biscuit (Grose, 2nd
ed.), and *brown tommy* (*Lex. Bal.*, but prob. much
earlier) ; as used by workmen for food or provisions
in gen., from ca. 1860 (H., 3rd ed.), it is a coll. that
in 1914–18 was the prevailing sense among soldiers
(B. & P.). Perhaps by a pun : *brown George* (q.v.)
suggesting *brown Tommy*, with alternative *Tommy
Brown*, whence *Tommy*, whence *tommy*. See esp.
Grose, P. But note that in Bedford (and elsewhere) *tommy* = loaves of bread distributed by
charity on St *Thomas*'s Day (21st December), for
hundreds of years : this, which prob. explains the
orig. of a puzzling word, I owe to Mr R. A. Parrott
of Bedford.—2. A sham shirt-front : Dublin University (— 1860) ; ob. H., 2nd ed. ; F. & H.
Prob. on equivalent *dickey* ex Gr. τομή, a section.—
3. (Gen. in pl.) A tomato : low : from ca. 1870.—
4. *Tommy*. 'Tommy Atkins', a private British
(specifically, non-Colonial) soldier : 1893, Kipling
(O.E.D.) : coll. >, by 1915, S.E. *Tommy Atkins*
occurs in Sala in 1883 ; coll. >, by 1895, S.E. Ex
Thomas Atkins, a specimen name for signature on
attestation-forms and in pay-books since early
C. 19. See *Words !* for further details.—5. A

prostitute's bully : low (— 1923). Manchon.—6
A frequent term of address to a young boy whose
name is unknown to the speaker : coll. (— 1887).
Baumann. Cf. *George* and *Jack* addressed to a man
in these circumstances.

tommy (or **T.**), v. See **Tommy Tripe**.

tommy or **Tommy, hell and.** An elaboration of
hell in intensives or asseverations : from ca. 1885.
In P. MacDonald, *R.I.P.*, 1933, we find a variation :
'Where the devil and Tommy did I put that corkscrew ?' Cf. *hell and spots*, q.v. The *tommy* is
perhaps ex *tommy-rot* ; the capital *T*, on *my eye and
Betty Martin* : ? cf. *yo, Tommy !*, q.v.

*tommy !, that's the. That's right : c. (—1887).
Baumann. Prob. ex *tommy*, 1.

tommy and exes. Bread (see **tommy**, 1), beer,
and 'bacca : workmen's (— 1909). Ware. Here
exes = *extras*.

Tommy Atkins. See **tommy**, 4.

tommy-axe. A tomahawk : Australian coll. :
late C. 19–20. Not certainly a corruption (by
Hobson-Jobson) of *tomahawk* ; perhaps on *tommy*
as applied to a small tool or instrument, e.g. a spade,
—with which cf., in military j., *tommy bar*, 'a bent-
wire spanner used to unscrew the bases of Mills
bombs.'

[**Tommy Brown's, in.** The entry in the first
edition is grotesquely erroneous and it arose from
too ingenious interpretation.]

Tommy Dodd. In tossing coins, either the winner
or the loser, by agreement ; the mode of tossing :
from ca. 1863 ; ob. : rather proletarian. H., 3rd
ed. Ca. 1863 there was a music-hall song, 'Heads
or tails are sure to win, Tommy Dodd, Tommy
Dodd.' Rhyming on *odd*.

Tommy, make room for your uncle ! A c.p. addressed to the younger man (men) in a group : from
ca. 1883. Ware. Ex a popular song.

Tommy o' Rann. Food : rhyming s. (— 1859) on
scran. H., 1st ed.

Tommy Pipes. Nickname for a boatswain—
'because he pipes or whistles all hands'. Naval :
ca. 1850–1910. Ware.

Tommy Rabbit (or **r.**). A pomegranate : rhyming s. (— 1909). Ware.

tommy-rot. (See also **tom-rot**.) Nonsense ; as
exclamation, 'bosh !' : s. >, ca. 1900, coll. : 1884,
George Moore, 'Bill . . . said it was all "Tommy
rot",' O.E.D. Perhaps ex *tommy*, goods supplied
instead of wages ; though Manchon's theory that it
is a euphemism (via the Tommies' former scarlet
uniform) for *bloody* is not ridiculous. Cf. *tommy* in
Hell and Tommy (or *h. and t.*), q.v. at *tommy, hell
and*.—2. Occ. as v.i., to fool about ; v.t., to humbug : rare : late C. 19–20.

Tommy-Shop, the. The Royal Victualling Yard :
naval (— 1923). Manchon. An extension of S.E.
tommy-shop.

Tommy tit. 'A smart lively little fellow', Grose,
1st ed. : coll. : mid-C. 18–19.

Tommy-toes. (Little) toes : London children's
(— 1887). Baumann.

Tommy Tripe. To observe, examine, watch :
rhyming s. (— 1874) on *pipe*, v. H., 5th ed. Occ.
abbr. *Tommy* or *tommy*, as in 'Tommy his plates (of
meat)', look at his feet !

Tommy Tucker. Supper : from ca. 1860. P. P.,
Rhyming Slang, 1932. Suggested by the nursery
rhyme, 'Little Tommy Tucker sang for his supper.'

Tommy Waac. (Gen. pl.) A 'Waac' (q.v.) :
1917. F. & Gibbons. Cf. *Thomasina Atkins*.

tommyrotic. Nonsensical : literary coll. >, by 1920, S.E. : from mid-1890's ; ob. Whence, likewise ex *tommy-rot* (q.v.) on *erotic* : *tommyrotics*, obscenity, esp. foolish obscenity : coll. (− 1904) >, by 1920, S.E. ; ob.

ton. (Rare in singular.) Much ; plenty : coll. : from early 1890's. E.g. Barrie, 1911, ' " I say ! Do you kill many [pirates] ? " "Tons." ' O.E.D. —2. Gen. **the ton.** The fashion ; fashionable Society : from late 1760's : coll. (mostly Society) until ca. 1840, then S.E. ; ca. 1815–25, it verged (witness ' Jon Bee ') on s. Ex Fr. *ton*.

ton for ton and man for man. ' The fair division of prizes between two ships sailing in company ' : naval c.p. verging on j. : C. 19. Bowen.

ton of bricks, like a. See **bricks.**

tone, t'one ; tother, t'other. (Whether pronouns or adjj.) The one ; the other : S.E. until C. 18, then coll. and dial. ; in C. 20, *t'one* as coll. is slightly illiterate. Often in juxtaposition, *t'one . . . t'other.* N.B., *tother day* in † S.E. = the next day, occ. the preceding day ; as = a few days ago, it arose in C. 16 and was S.E. until C. 18 ; then coll. and dial.

toney. See **tony,** n. and adj.

tongs. Forceps : dental and medical : from ca. 1870.

tongs, pair of. A tall thin person : low : from ca. 1880 ; ob. Ex the two thin ' legs '.—2. Whence, in sarcastic address or comment, *tongs !*—3. **touch with a pair of tongs.** See **touch with . . .**

tongue, v.t. To talk (a person) down : low (− 1860) ; ob. H., 2nd ed. Ex the ob. S.E. sense, to attack with words, to reproach.

tongue, give (a lick with) the rough side of one's. To scold, abuse : coll. : 1820, Scott (O.E.D.) ; ob. Cf. dial. *give a person the length of one's tongue* (E.D.D.).

tongue, have a. To be sarcastic and/or ironic : non-aristocratic coll. : from ca. 1880. Charles Turley, *Godfrey Marten, Schoolboy*, 1902, ' " He had a tongue ", as servants say, and could be sarcastic.' Ex *have a sharp tongue.*

tongue, lose one's. To fall very, be long, silent : coll. : 1870, Dickens (O.E.D.).

tongue, and a little older than my teeth,—as old as my. A c.p. reply to *how old are you ?* : late C. 18–20 ; ob. Grose, 2nd ed.

tongue enough for two sets of teeth(, with ; to have). Applied to an exceedingly talkative person : ca. 1786–1870. Grose, 2nd ed. Cf. *tongue-pad, tongue too long for one's teeth,* and *tongued,* qq.v.

tongue in another's purse, put one's. To silence : ca. 1540–1620. ' Proverbs ' Heywood.

tongue is well hung, his (etc.). He is fluent, ready, glib of speech : coll. : C. 18. Swift ; Berthelson's Dict., 1754. Apperson. Cf. *tongue-pad,* q.v. Perhaps also coll. are the C. 18 semi-proverbial *your tongue is made of very loose leather* (' Proverbs ' Fuller, 1732) and the semi-proverbial C. 16–17 *her (your, etc.) tongue runs on pattens* (' Proverbs ' Heywood ; Davies of Hereford), both recorded by Apperson, who notes the analogous *his* (etc.) *tongue runs on wheels* (mid-C. 15–20 ; in mid-C. 19–20, dial.) enshrined by Swift.

tongue of the trump, the. The best or most important thing or person : Scots coll. : from ca. 1870. In a Jew's harp, the tongue is the steel spring by which the sound is made.

tongue-pad. A talkative person, esp. if smooth and insinuating : late C. 17–20 : s. until late C. 19, then dial. B.E. ; Grose in 1st ed., adds : ' A

scold ', a sense † by 1850. On *foot-pad.* Cf. the **v.** —2. See ' Rogues ' in Addenda.

tongue-pad. To scold, v.t. ; v.i., to chatter : resp. mid-C. 17–20, C. 19–20 ; both dial. in C. 20. J. Stevens, 1707 ; Scott, the v.i. in 1825. Whence *tongue-padder = tongue-pad,* n., and vbl n., *t.-padding.* O.E.D.

tongue-pie, get or give. To be scolded ; to scold : lower classes' (− 1923). Manchon.

tongue runs nineteen to the dozen, one's. See **nineteen to the dozen.—tongue runs on pattens** or **wheels, one's.** See **tongue is well hung.**

tongue to, call (a person) **everything one can lay one's.** To scold, abuse, violently : coll. and dial. : late C. 19–20. Cf. *tongue-pad,* n., l, 2nd nuance.

tongue too long for one's teeth or **mouth.** Either *have a . . .* or, more gen., as in Reade, 1859, ' Hum ! Eve, wasn't your tongue a little too long for your teeth just now ? ' To be indiscreet or too ready to talk : mid-C. 19–20 ; ob. Prob. ex *tongue enough . . .,* q.v. ; cf. the C. 17 proverb, *the tongue walks where the teeth speed not.*

tongued. Talkative : low (− 1860) ; ob. H., 2nd ed. Cf. *tongue enough,* q.v.

tonic. A halfpenny : ca. 1820–50. Egan's Grose. ? origin : cf., however, *tanner.*—2. A drink, esp. if taken as an appetiser : late C. 19–20. Cf. *medicine.*

tonk. At cricket, to hit a ball into the air : Charterhouse and Durham (schools) : late C. 19–20. Cf. *tonkabout,* the corresponding n. Ex the mainly Midland dial. *tank,* n., a blow ; v., to strike.— 2. Hence, gen. in passive, to defeat utterly : from ca. 1920. E.g. Galsworthy, *The Silver Spoon,* 1926, ' He seems to enjoy the prospect of getting tonked.'

tonkabout. The hitting of catches at cricket-practice : Charterhouse (− 1900). A. H. Tod. Ex preceding term, sense 1.

tonquin bean. A tonka bean : incorrect : from late C. 18. (W.)

tontine. A slate club : from ca. 1870 : a catachresis. O.E.D.

tony ; in C. 18, occ. **toney.** A fool, a simpleton : mid-C. 17–early 19. Gayton, 1654 (O.E.D.) ; but it must be a few years earlier, for the rare v., *tony,* to befool or swindle, is recorded ca. 1652. B.E. ; Grose. Ex *Ant(h)ony.*—2. **Tony,** abbr. of *Antonio.* A Portuguese (soldier) : military coll. : 1916 ; ob. F. & Gibbons.

tony ; loosely, **toney.** Adj., stylish, ' swell ' ; high-toned : coll., orig. (− 1886), U.S. >, in 1890's, Australian and New Zealand. H. Lawson, 1901. (O.E.D.) Ex *high tone,* or possibly ex ob. *ton-ish, tonish* (itself ex *ton,* fashion).

tonygle, in Harman, merely = *to niggle.* See **niggle,** in sexual sense.

too. Very ; extremely : C. 14–20 : S.E. until early C. 19, then coll.—esp. as an emotional intensive among non-proletarian women. The O.E.D. has, at 1868, ' How too delightful your expeditions must have been.' Cf. :

too, only. As mere intensive : coll. : late C. 19–20. (O.E.D.) ? ex preceding.

too all-but. A London society c.p. of 1881–2. Ware, ' Resulting out of *Punch's* trouvaille " too-too ".'

too (bloody) Irish ! Of course ! : lower classes' : C. 20. B. & P. Also *too bloody right !*

Too Damn Good(s), the. The 2nd Dragoon Guards : military : late C. 19–20. Ware, ' From the regimental indication **on** the shoulder-straps : 2 D.G.'

too many cloths in the wind. Tipsy : late C. 19–20. Bowen. On *three sheets in the wind*.

too many (gen. **too much**) **for.** Sufficient to overcome or quell ; too able or strong, i.e. more than a match, for : coll. : *much*, 1832 ; 1861, Dickens, ' Mr Juggers was altogether too many for the Jury, and they gave in.' O.E.D. Catachrestic is *too many* applied to things, as in A. Neil Lyons, *Arthur's*, 1914, ' This job is one too many for me ' (Manchon).

too much !, this is. A c.p. retort or comment : from mid-1860's. F. & H. suggests that it echoes *Artemus Ward among the Shakers* (ca. 1862).

too much of a good thing. Excessive ; intolerable : coll. : 1809, Sydney Smith, ' This (to use a very colloquial phrase) is surely too much of a good thing,' O.E.D. An elaboration of *too much*, but perhaps prompted by the literal sense, as in Shakespeare's *As You Like It*, IV, i, ' Why then, can one desire too much of a good thing ? ' Apperson. Cf. preceding entry.

too much with us. Excessively boring ; an intolerable nuisance : Society c.p. : 1897–9. Ware. Ex the Wordsworthian *the world is too much with us.*

too numerous to mention. Angrily drunk : London : 1882–ca. 90. Ware. Prob. *uttering curses too*, etc.

too right ! Certainly ! ; ' rather ! ' : Australian : from ca. 1910. Jice Doone. See also **too bloody Irish.**

too-too (see **too all-but**) was in 1881 a Society c.p. Cf. the derivative *too utterly too* (1883) and *too utterly utter* (late C. 19–20 ; ob.) : also Society c.pp.

toodle-em-buck. The game of Crown and Anchor : Canadian : C. 20. B. & P.

toodle-oo ! See **tootle-oo !**

took. Taken : sol. : C. 19–20. Baumann. Cf. *shook.*

tool. The penis : mid-C. 16–20 : S.E. until C. 18, then coll. ; in C. 19–20, s. unless the context definitely renders it archaic S.E. (O.E.D.)—2. A whip : ca. 1820–90. Ex *tool*, to drive.—3. ' A small boy employed to creep through windows, etc., to effect entry ' : c. : ca. 1840–1910. 1845 in ' *No. 747* ' ; H., 3rd ed. ; F. & H. Cf. *tool*, v., 4.— 4. See **tools.**—5. A run ; to run : Charterhouse : late C. 19–20. Ex *tool*, v., 3.

tool, v.t. To drive : 1812, *The Sporting Magazine* (O.E.D.) ; 1849, Lytton, ' He could tool a coach ' ; 1899, Whiteing. Ex instrument for effect.—2. Hence, as in Jessop, 1881, ' The high-stepping mare that tools him along through the village street.' Rare.—3. (Ex sense 1.) V.i., to drive, to go or travel, esp. *along* : 1839 (O.E.D.).— 4. Gen. v.i., to pick pockets : c. (— 1859) ; slightly ob. H., 1st ed. Prob. ex *tool*, n., 3, q.v.—5. To murder (v.i.) : Society : ca. 1845–1900. Ex a metaphor by De Quincey. (Ware.)—6. See n., 5.

tool, dull or **poor.** An inferior workman : late C. 17–20 ; in late C. 19–20, dial. B.E. ; H., 1st ed. Cf. *a poor* (occ. bad) *workman blames his tools.*—2. Hence, (*poor tool*) a shiftless person : C. 18–20 ; latterly dial.

tool, grind one's. (Of the male) to coït : low : mid-C. 19–20.

tool about or **around.** To do nothing in particular : upper classes' : from ca. 1910. Francis Iles, *Before the Fact*, 1932, ' " What are you doing with

yourself ? " " Me, eh ? Oh, tooling round, you know. Nothing much." ' Ex coaching, perhaps on *fool around*. Cf. :

tool off. To depart : 1881, *Punch*, Dec. 17 (O.E.D. Sup.) ; ob. Ex *tool*, v., 3.

***tooler.** A burglar, a pickpocket : c. (— 1859). H., 1st ed. See **tool**, n., 3, and v., 4.—2. Hence, *moll-tooler*, a female thief or pickpocket.

Tooleries, the. Toole's Theatre : theatrical : 1885–ca. 87. Ware. Ex *Toole* on *Colinderies* and *Fisheries*, qq.v., with a pun on the *Tuileries* of Paris.

Tooley Street tailor. A conceitedly bumptious fellow : mostly London : ca. 1870–80. H., 5th ed., ' The " three tailors of Tooley Street " are said to have immortalised themselves by preparing a petition for Parliament—and some say, presenting it—with only their own signatures thereto, which commenced, " We, the people of England ".' How *do* such yarns arise ?

***tools.** The hands : c. : mid-C. 19–20 ; ob.—2. Pistols : possibly c. : id.—3. As = housebreaking implements, merely a specific application of gen. S.E. sense.—4. ' Knives, forks and spoons ' : nautical : late C. 19–20. Bowen.

***tools, fixed for the.** Convicted for possessing a burglar's tools : c. of ca. 1820–1910. Egan's Grose. Cf. *tool*, v., 4, and *toby*, v.t. (analogous *done . . .*).

tooniopperty or **tuniopperty.** Opportunity : centre s. (— 1923). Manchon.

***toosh.** A sovereign, coin or value : c. (esp. tramps') : from before 1935. Ex *tusheroon*.

toot. Money : naval : C. 20. F. & Gibbons. Origin ? Cf. *hoot*.—2. A chap, a fellow : Canadian (— 1932). John Beames. Perhaps ex Fr. *tout homme.*

toot, at (occ. **on**) **the.** Immediately ; at high speed : military : from 1915. Ex *tout de suite* (pron. *toot sweet*), whence also the military c.p., *the tooter the sweeter*, the sooner the better. B. & P.

toot-sweeter. A high-velocity shell : military : 1915 ; ob. F. & Gibbons. Ex preceding.

tooth. See **teeth ;** and the following compounds and phrases :

tooth, have an aching. To have a desire, a longing (*for*) : coll. : late C. 16–20 ; in C. 19–20, mostly dial. Lodge, 1590 ; North, 1742 ; 1887, Parish & Shaw, *Dict. of Kent Dialect*. (Apperson.)—2. (*have . . . at* a person.) To be angry with : coll. : C. 18. N. Bailey, 1730.

tooth, have cut one's eye. To be ' knowing ' : a (— 1860) variant of *teeth, have cut one's eye.* H., 2nd ed.

tooth, high in. Bombastic : low : from the 1870's ; ob. Baumann.

tooth, long in the. See **long in the tooth.**

tooth, old or **up in the.** (Esp. of old maids) aged : from ca. 1860. H., 2nd ed., ' *Stable term* for aged horses which have lost the distinguishing mark in their teeth.'

tooth-brush. A tooth-brush moustache, so named because, at most one and often only a half-inch laterally, and short and bristly vertically, it closely resembles the hairy part of a small tooth-brush : coll. : from 1915.

tooth-carpenter. A dentist : low : ca. 1880–1920. Cf. *tongs*, q.v.

tooth-drawer, like a. Thin : coll. : mid C. 17–18. Ray. Prob. ex, not *tooth-drawer*, a dentist, but †*tooth-drawer*, his instrument.

tooth-music. (The sound of) mastication : from ca. 1786 ; ob. Grose, 2nd ed.

toothache. A priapism : low : late C. 19–20. Orig. *Irish toothache.*—2. A knife *has the toothache* if the blade is loose : schoolboys', mostly Colonial : id.

toothachy. Having, characteristic of, toothache : coll. : 1838, Lady Granville (O.E.D.).

toother. A punch on the mouth : boxing : from ca. 1890 ; slightly ob.

toothful. A drink : jocular coll. : from ca. 1920. E. F. Benson, *David of King's,* 1924. Cf. Scottish *toothful,* to tipple.

toothpick. 'A large stick. An ironical expression', *Lex. Bal.* : London : ca. 1810–50.—2. A very narrow fishing-boat with pointed prow : mainly nautical : 1897, Kipling. O.E.D. Ex shape.—3. A sword : military : ca. 1898–1913. Cf. *cheese-toaster* and *toasting-fork,* qq.v.—4. A bayonet : military : from 1914. F. & Gibbons.

toothpick brigade, crutch and. Foppish 'men about town' : London society : ca. 1885–1905. Ex :—2. Hangers-on at stage doors, esp. at the Gaiety : London society : ca. 1884–5. 'They affected, as the badge of their tribe, a crutch-handled stick and a toothpick,' F. & H.

toothy-peg. A tooth : nursery coll. : 1828, Hood, ' Turn we to little Miss Kilmansegg, | Cutting her first little toothy-peg.' By itself, *toothy,* a child's tooth, is less common : lit., a little tooth. [**tooting-tub,** in F. & H., is U.S. ; his 'authority' is Wesley Brooke.]

tootle. Twaddle ; trashy verbiage : university : 1880's. Ex *tootle,* an act of tooting on a horn ; cf., however, dial. *tootle,* silly gossip (E.D.D.). (—2. Hence, *tootle,* to write twaddle : university and journalistic : ca. 1883–94. O.E.D.)

tootle, v. To go ; esp. *tootle off,* to depart : dial. (C. 19–20) form of *toddle* >, in late 1890's, U.S. and reintroduced, as s. or coll., ca. 1920. P. G. Wodehouse, *passim.* Prob. on *toddle.*—2. See **tootle,** n., 2.

tootle-oo ! ; loosely, **toodle-oo !** Good-bye ! : from ca. 1905, according to Collinson ; the O.E.D. (Sup.) records it at 1907. Ob. Perhaps ex *tootle,* v., 1, q.v., or ex *tootle-too,* to toot frequently or continuously.

tootsie, tootsy ; tootsie (or **-y)-wootsie.** A child's, a woman's small, foot : playful or affectionate coll. : resp. 1854, Thackeray (O.E.D.) ; ca. 1890. The form *tootsicum* is a facetious ' literary ' elaboration. On *foot,* but ex *toddle* : W.

Top. See **Topsy.**

top. See **old top.**—2. Abbr. *top gear* in motoring ; gen. on *top,* very rarely—and, by 1930, †—*on the top* : 1906, *on the top* ; 1909, *on top.* O.E.D.—3. In c., a dying speech : ca. 1830–80. H., 1st ed. (Also known as a *croak.*) Ex the c. *top,* to behead.—4. In earlier c., a cheating trick whereby one of the dice remained at the top of the box : gaming : ca. 1705–50. *The Tatler,* No. 68, 1709. O.E.D. Ex the specific gaming sense of the v.—5. (Gen. pl.) Counterfoil of a divided **warrant** : accountants' coll. (C. 20) verging on j.

*top, v.i. To cheat, esp. at cards : c. >, by 1750, low s. : ca. 1660–1820. Etherege, B.E., Grose. V.t. with *on, upon.*—2. ? hence, v.i. and v.t. (the latter, gen. *top upon*), to insult : late C. 17–early 19 : c. >, by 1750, low s. B.E., Grose.—3. (Likewise ex sense 1.) To impose or foist (a thing) *on* : ca. 1670–1750. O.E.D.—4. To behead, to hang : c. :

C. 18–20, in C. 20, mostly in the passive. Implied in *topping cheat, t. cove,* and *topman* or *topsman,* though not separately recorded before 1811 (*Lex. Bal.*).—5. (Gen. v.i.) To break in, through skylight or roof trap-door : c. (— 1933). Charles E. Leach.—6. See **top a clout, top off, top up,** and other v. phrases.

top, a little bit off the. Some of the best : coll. : late C. 19–20 ; ob.—2. Slightly crazy : from ca. 1897 ; ob.

top, go over the. To leave one's own trench and join in the attack on the enemy : military coll. : from 1916. The *top* is both the top of the trench and the open ground between the trenches. B. & P.—2. Hence, to do something dangerous and/or notable (e.g. getting married) : from 1919. Collinson ; Lyell (' take the plunge ').

top, off one's. Insane : mostly Australian : C. 20. C. J. Dennis, 1916.

top, old. See **old top.**—**top, on.** See **bet on top.**

top, on the. Above trench-level in the front-line area : military coll. : in the G.W.

top, over the. See **over the top.**—2. Whence, in trouble ; ' crimed ' : military : 1916–18. F. & Gibbons. Cf. *top, go over the,* 2.

*top a clout (a handkerchief) or other article is to draw a corner or an end to the top of the pocket in readiness for removal at a favourable moment : c. (— 1812) ; slightly ob. Vaux.

top-diver. ' A Lover of Women. *An Old Top-diver,* one that has Lov'd *Old-hat* in his time ', B.E. : low : late C. 17–early 19. Grose.

top drawer, out of the. (Mostly in negative.) Well-bred ; gentlemanly, ladylike : coll., by 1935 verging on S.E. : C. 20. Gen. *come out of . . .* H. A. Vachell, 1905 (O.E.D.).

top drawing-room. An attic or garret : London lower-classes' jocular (— 1909). Ware.

top-dressing. The hair : jocular coll. : from ca. 1870. James Brunton Stephens, 1874. An elaboration of *top* (as in the barber's ' You're getting a little bald on the top, sir '), with a pun on *t.-d.,* a fertilising manure.—2. ' An introduction to a report : usually written by an experienced hand and set in larger type ', F. & H. : journalistic : from ca. 1870. H., 5th ed. Cf. fig. use of *window-dressing.*

*top-fencer, -seller. A seller of last dying speeches : ca. 1830–70 : resp. c. and (low) s. Ex *top,* n., 3.

*top-gob. A pot-boy : c. (— 1857) ; ob. ' Ducange Anglicus.' Complete back s. would be : *top-yob.*

top-hat. A tall or high hat (esp. as for formal occasions) : coll. : from ca. 1880. Miss Braddon, 1881 (O.E.D.). Suggested by *topper,* 2, q.v.

top-hat party. Ratings enlisted for the War only : naval : 1915–18. Bowen. Cf. *duration,* q.v.

top-heavy. Drunk : coll. : from ca. 1675 ; ob. Ray, 1678 ; B.E. ; Bailey, 1736 ; Grose ; Hone, 1825. (Apt to topple.) Apperson.

top-hole, adj. Excellent ; ' splendid ', ' topping ' : 1908, E. V. Lucas, ' A top-hole idea,' but adumbrated by Conan Doyle, 1899, as *up to the top-hole,* though this may be considered a variant († by 1930, and, indeed, ob. by 1915). O.E.D. On *top-notch.*

top-joint (pron. jint). A pint (of beer) : rhyming s. (— 1857) ; ob. ' Ducange Anglicus.' Cf. *top-o'-reeb,* q.v.

top-knot ; topknot. The head : from 1860's. E.D.D. Cf. *top-piece.*

top lights !, blast your. Blast your eyes : nautical : from ca. 1790 ; ob. Grose, 3rd ed.

top line, sweat on the. See **sweat on** . . .

top-lofty, toplofty ; toploftical. Haughty ; ' high and mighty ' ; highfalutin : coll. : resp. mid-C. 19–20 and 1823 ; both slightly ob. (O.E.D.)

top-o'-reeb. A pot of beer : back **s.** (— 1859). H., 1st ed.

top of Rome. (A) home : rhyming **s.** (— 1857) ; ob. ' Ducange Anglicus.'

top of the bill. First-rate ; the best of all : coll. : C. 20 (1934, ' " She's wonderful," I breathed. "Marvellous. Top of the bill, in fact." ') Ex theatrical and music-hall advertisements, ' stars ' being at the top. Cf. S.E. *top-liner.*

top of the house (or **shop**). No. 99 in the game of House : C. 20 : coll., now verging on j. F. & Gibbons ; B. & P. Also, esp. among soldiers with service in India, *top of the bleeding bungalow* (Frank Richards, *Old-Soldier Sahib,* 1936).

top of the morning (to you) !, the. A cheery greeting : orig. and mainly Anglo-Irish : coll. verging on S.E. : 1815, Scott (O.E.D.).

top of the shop. See **top of the house.**

top of the world, (sit) on. (To be) prospering, prosperous ; esp. to be it and show it, to be very confident and high-spirited : U.S., anglicised ca. 1930. Cf. *sit pretty,* q.v.

top off or **up.** To finish off or up ; to conclude : coll. : both from ca. 1835, Newman in 1836 having *up,* Dana *up* (printed 1840, known earlier). O.E.D. —2. To put the finishing touch to : coll. : from ca. 1870. Both senses derive ex *top* (or *top up*), to put the top on, to crown.—3. (Only **top off.**) ' To knock down ; to assault ', C. J. Dennis : Australian c. > low s. (— 1916).

top (occ. **top up**) **one's fruit, punnet,** etc. To place the best fruit at the top of one's basket, punnet, etc. : garden-produce market : from mid-1880's. O.E.D. Cf. *toppers,* which prob. suggested it.

top-piece. The head : from 1830's : coll. and dial. Cf. *top-knot.* E.D.D.

top-ropes, sway away on all. To live extravagantly or riotously : nautical coll. of ca. 1810–1900. Ex fig. *sway* (incorrectly *swing*) *on all t.-r.,* to go to all lengths. (O.E.D.)—Hence, 2. (*sway all top-ropes.*) To give oneself airs : nautical : late C. 19–20 ; ob. Bowen.

top-sawyer. A collar : tailors' : from ca. 1870 ; ob.—2. The sense, ' the best man ; one in a superior position', may orig. (— 1823) have been **s.** > coll. >, by 1860, S.E. Egan's Grose. Ex the timber trade, where he ' who works the upper handle of a pit-saw ' gets a much higher wage than those beneath him. (O.E.D.)—3. Hence, the favourite (horse) : turf coll. (— 1923). Manchon.

top-sawyer, play. To coït : mid-C. 19–20 ; ob. Cf. *tops and bottoms.*

top-seller. See **top-fencer.**

top-shuffle. ' To shuffle the lower half of a pack over the upper half without disturbing it ', F. & H. : gaming s. (— 1904) > j.

top . . . tail. See **tail, top** . . .

top the officer. ' To arrogate superiority ', Smyth : nautical : 1833, Marryat. O.E.D.

top traverse, off one's. ' Off one's head. Acting crazily ': military : 1916 ; ob. F. & Gibbons. By elaboration of *top,* head.

top up. See **top one's fruit.**—2. See **top off.**

top upon. See **top,** v., 1 and 2.

top with the best of luck !, over the. An officers' and sergeant-majors' c.p. to the men as they leave the trench in attack : 1916–18. B. & P. Cf. *top, go over the.*—2. Hence, from 1919, often fig. among ex-service men ; ob.

top-yob. A pot-boy : back **s.** (— 1859) ; ob. H., 1st ed.

top your boom ! Go away ! : a nautical c.p. addressed to a man, esp. ' when he has forced his company where he was not invited ' : late C. 19–20. Bowen.

*toper. A street ; a highway : c., mostly tramps' (— 1923). Manchon. A corruption of *tober* (see **toby,** n.).

topman. A hangman : C. 17. (In C. 19, *topsman,* q.v.) Cf. *top,* v., 4.

topos. A variant of pros, n. : English undergraduates' (— 1884) ; ob. Ex Gr. τόπος, a place.

Topper. The inevitable nickname of men surnamed Brown : military : C. 20. F. & Gibbons. Orig. prob. anecdotal.

topper. A thing or person excellent or exceptionally good in his or its kind : coll. : 1709, *The British Apollo,* of a bowl of punch compared with other drinks (O.E.D.). Slightly ob. Lit., at the top.—2. A top-hat : s. (1820) >, by 1860, coll. ' Pomes ' Marshall, 1897, ' A most successful raid | On a swell's discarded topper.'—3. A (violent) blow on the head (or ' top ') : 1823, Bee ; 1834, Ainsworth ; ob.—4. See **toppers.**—5. A cigar- or cigarette-end ; a dottle : mostly London and mostly low (— 1874). H., 5th ed. ; Cassell's *Encyclopædic Dict.,* 1888.—6. A tall, thin person : low : from 1890's ; ob. F. & H.—7. A public hangman : c. : C. 20. Edgar Wallace, in *Big Foot,* 1927, speaks of ' Mr Topper Wells—public executioner of England '. Ex *top,* v., 4.—8. A sovereign (coin) : tramps' and beggars' c. (— 1926). Frank Jennings, *In London's Shadows.* Prob. ex sense 1.

topper, v. To knock on the head ; to kill thus : from late 1860's ; slightly ob. E. Farmer, 1869 (O.E.D.). Ex *topper,* n., 3, q.v.

topper-hunter. A scavenger (and seller) of ' toppers ' (*topper,* 5). H., 5th ed., 1874.

Toppers. Top Schools : at Shrewsbury : late C. 19–20. Desmond Coke, *The Bending of a Twig,* 1906. By ' the Oxford *-er* '.

toppers. Large, fine fruit (esp. if strawberries) luring one from their display-point at basket- or punnet-top : 1839, Mogridge (O.E.D.). Because they are at the top. Cf. *top one's fruit,* q.v.

topping. A lower-class coll. variant (— 1923) of the preceding. Manchon. An extension of the S.E. sense, a top layer.

topping, adj. In c., only in *topping cheat* and *cove* and *fellow,* qq.v.—2. Excellent in number, quantity, or quality ; ' tip-top ' : from ca. 1820 : coll. >, ca. 1890, s. Galt, 1822 (O.E.D.) ; Clough, 1860, ' Shady in Latin, said Lindsay, but topping in Plays and Aldrich.' Ex *topping,* eminent.—3. Hence, as an adv. : mid-C. 19–20.

*topping cheat ; t.-c. A gallows (gen. *the t. c.*) : c. : mid C. 17–early 19. Coles, 1676 ; B.E. Grose. Ex *cheat, chete,* a thing ; and cf. *top,* v., 4, and :

*topping cove or **fellow.** A hangman : resp. c., mid C. 17–mid-19 (Coles, B.E. and Grose) ; (low) **s.,** late C. 18–mid-19 (B.E.). The latter puns the lit. sense, a preëminent person. Cf. *topping cheat* and *topsman,* qq.v.

topping man, as opp. *topping fellow* (in lit. sense), is a rich man : prob. the s. of a London social class or convivial set : ca. 1788–1800. Grose, 3rd ed.

toppy. Tipsy: coll.: ca. 1880–1915. O.E.D. Cf. *top-heavy*, q.v.—2. Stylish; (too) showy: from ca. 1890: coll. >, by 1920, low coll. (by 1930, ob.) and dial. O.E.D. Perhaps suggested by *topping*, 2, q.v.

tops and bottoms, play at. To copulate: mid-C. 19–20; ob. Anatomical pun.

topsail, pay one's debts with the. (Of a sailor) to go to sea having left his debts unpaid: nautical: ca. 1785–1850. Grose, 2nd ed., who adds, ' So soldiers are said to pay off their scores with the drum; that is, by marching away '; same period, but chiefly military.

topsel. A coll. nautical variant (— 1887) of *topsail*. Baumann.

topside. Fig., on *top*; in control: coll.: from late 1890's. O.E.D.

*topsman. A hangman: from early 1820's: c. >, by 1860, low s. Ex *top*, v., 4, on *headsman*. (O.E.D.) Cf. *topping-cove* and *topman*.

Topsy. William Morris. ' At Oxford [1853–6] he was given the nickname of " Topsy ", after the character in *Uncle Tom's Cabin*, owing to his conspicuously thick mop of hair, and later he was always known as " Topsy " or " Top " to his intimates,' Montague Weekley, in his biography of William Morris, 1934.

topsy-boosy. Drunk: low: from ca. 1890; ob. Reduplicated *boosy*. Cf. *toppy*, 1.

tora-loorals. Feminine bust, esp. if somewhat exposed: theatrical (— 1909); ob. Ware. Perhaps ex *dairies* via dial. *tooral-ooral* (merry with drink), itself ex *truly rural* used as a test for drunkenness (E.D.D.).

torche-cul. Toilet-paper: coll.: late C. 17–mid-19. B.E.; Grose, 1st ed. Direct ex the Fr. Cf. *bum-fodder*, the English equivalent.

tore. Torn: sol.: C. 19–20. Baumann. Cf. *wore*.

tormentor. (In a theatre) the first wing; a door therein: theatrical s. > coll.: mid-C. 19–20, though not recorded before 1886 (O.E.D.). Because often a nuisance.—2. An instrument (cf. *tickler*, q.v.) devised to annoy at fairs: coll.: from ca. 1890.—3. A flatterer: low: late C. 19–20. Suggested by *back-scratcher*.—4. See **tormentors**.

tormentor of catgut. A fiddler: coll. (— 1785); very ob. Grose, 1st ed. Because the violin-strings are made of catgut. Also *catgut-scraper*.

tormentor of sheepskin. A drummer: ca. 1810–1900. *Lex. Bal.*; Baumann. Cf. preceding.

tormentors. Riding-spurs: 1875, Whyte-Melville (O.E.D.). Cf. *persuaders*.—2. A cook's big forks: nautical (— 1887). Baumann. (Rather rare in singular.)

torn it !, that's. That has spoiled it, ruined everything: s. (orig. low): 1909, ' Ian Hay ' (O.E.D. Sup.). Rare in other parts of the v. Cf. the Northern proverbial *the swine's run through it*, of anything—orig. and esp. a marriage—ruined by bad luck, and *tear one's seat*, q.v.

torpedo Jack. A torpedo lieutenant: naval coll.: C. 20. F. & Gibbons. Cf. *torps*.

Torpid. See **togger**, 4.

torps. A *torpedo* officer; often as nickname: naval: C. 20. Bowen. Cf. *chips* and *sparks*.

torrac. A carrot: back s. (— 1859). H., 1st ed. Whence the indelicate c.p. retort (— 1904), *ekat a torrac*: cf. *banana !, have a.*

torrefication; torri-. Incorrect for *torrefaction*: mid-C. 18–20. O.E.D. Cf. *torrify* for *torrefy*: C. 17–20. Ibid.

tortoise-shell. The pronunciation *torte(r)-shell* is coll.; both *s*'s should be sounded.

tortious. Tortuous: sol.: late C. 17–20. By confusion with legal *tortious*.

tortuous. Malign (†); wrongful: catachresis: late C. 16–20. O.E.D. Confused with S.E. *tortious*.

torture-truck. A hospital trolley (bearing lancets, fomentations, etc., etc.): military: 1915; ob. B. & P.

Tory. (Despite F. & H., all senses are S.E. except these two :—) One of those who, in 1679–80, opposed the exclusion of James from the English crown: a nickname in use among the Exclusioners; rare after C. 17. Cf. *Tantivy* and see esp. Roger North's *Examen*, II, v, § 9. F. & H.; O.E.D. Ex *Tory*, a rapparee or outlaw and itself ex an Irish word = ' a pursuer '. Cf. *whig*, q.v.—2. Hence, a *Conservative*: coll.: from ca. 1830, when *Conservative* superseded *Tory* as the official and formal name for a member of the traditionalist party. (The same holds of *Tory* used as an adj.)

Tory Rory. A London nickname given, ca. 1780–1845, to ' those who wore their hats fiercely cocked ' (Ware).

tosh. The penis: schoolboys': from 1870's. W. ? ex *tusk*; more prob. ex dial. *tosh*, ' a tusk; a projecting or unseemly tooth ', E.D.D.—2. A hat: modified back s.: ca. 1875–1900. The correct *tah* > *ta-h*, *ta-aitch*, *tosh*.—3. (Also *tosh-can* or *-pan*.) A foot-pan, a bath: Public Schools' (— 1881). Pascoe, *Life in Our Public Schools*. Perhaps a perversion of *wash*; possibly cognate is Romany *tov*, to wash. Cf. *tosh*, v.—4. Nonsense: 1892, *Oxford University Magazine*, Oct. 26, ' Frightful tosh '. Perhaps *bosh* (q.v.) perverted; cf., however, dial. *toshy*, ' over-dressed '; *tawdry*, E.D.D. Often as an exclamation.—5. Hence, very easy bowling: cricketers': 1898 (Ware).—6. A pocket: c.: C. 19–20; ob. Ware, ' Prob. a corruption of French *poche*.'—7. A mackintosh: a synonym of *mac(k)*: C. 20; rare. A. H. Dawson.

tosh, v.t. To splash, throw water over: Public Schools' : 1883, J. P. Groves (O.E.D.). Ex *tosh*, n., 3, q.v.—2. Hence, v.i., to bath: ibid.: C. 20.

tosh-can, -pan. See **tosh,** n., 3.—**tosh-pond,** the bathing pond: Royal Military Academy: from 1880's. Ex *tosh*, n., 3.

tosh-soap. Cheese: Public Schools' (— 1904). F. & H. Ex *tosh*, n., 3.

*tosher. One who, in the Thames, steals copper from ships' bottoms: c. (— 1859). H., 1st ed. For etymology, cf. *tosh*, n., 3. Hence *toshing*, such theft: c. (— 1867). Smyth.—2. ' A non-collegiate student at a university having residential colleges ': undergraduates' (— 1889); † by 1919. Ex *unattached*: see ' *-er*, Oxford '. Cf. *brekker*.

tosheroon. A variant of *tusheroon*.

toshy. Rubbishy: 1902, Belloc, ' Toshy novels ' (O.E.D.). Ex *tosh*, n., 4.

toss, v. Incorrect for *toze* (in mining): C. 19–20. O.E.D. So *tosser* for *tozer*.

toss, argue the. See **argue the toss.**—**toss, take a.** See **take a toss.**

toss in the towel. An Australian coll. variant of *rag, sky the*. C. J. Dennis.

toss it up airy. To ' show off ', put on ' side ': lower classes' (— 1923). Manchon.

toss-off. An act of masturbation: low coll. (— 1785). Grose, 1st ed. Presumably ex:

toss-off, v.i. and v. reflexive. (Gen. of the male.) To masturbate: low coll.: from ca. 1780.

toss-up. An even chance : coll. : 1809, Malkin, ' It is a toss up who fails and who succeeds : the wit of to-day is the blockhead of to-morrow.' Ex *toss-up*, the ' skying ' of a coin.

tossaroon. See **tusheroon.**

tossed. Drunk : C. 19–20. Ex *tossed*, disordered, disturbed, but perhaps influenced by Scots *tosie*, *-y*, slightly intoxicated, occ. in form *tosy-mosy*.

tosser. A penny used in pitch-and-toss : Glasgow (– 1934).—2. Also, any coin, esp. a sovereign : from ca. 1910. M. Harrison, *Spring in Tartarus*, 1935.

tossy. Proud, haughty, supercilious : proletarian coll. (– 1923). Manchon. An extension of the rare S.E. sense, pert or contemptuous.

tost. See **toast.** (B.E.'s spelling.)—2. A corruption of *toss* (v.) : C. 17. O.E.D.

tostificated. Drunk : late C. 19–20 ; ob. Elaboration of dial. *tosticated* (i.e. corrupt *intoxicated*).

tot. The sum-total of an addition, an addition sum : coll. : from 1870's. Perhaps imm. ex *tot-up*, n., q.v. ; ultimately ex *total*, less prob. ex L. *totum*, the whole. Cf. *tots*, *long*, q.v.—2. A very young or small child : dial. and coll. : 1725, Ramsay. Cf. Danish *tommel-tot*, Tom Thumb (O.E.D.). Gen. *tiny* or *wee tot*.—3. ? hence, a (very) small drinking-vessel, esp. a child's mug or a tin mug : dial. (– 1828) >, by 1840, coll. O.E.D.—4. (Perhaps ex sense 2 ; prob. ex sense 3.) A very small quantity, esp. of liquor : dial. (– 1828) >, by 1850, coll., as in Whyte-Melville, 1868, ' He . . . often found himself pining for . . . the camp-fires, the fragrant fumes . . ., and the tot of rum.'—5. A bone ; hence, anything worth taking from a dustbin or a refuse-heap ; but esp. a rag, as in *The Gilt Kid*, 1936 : dust-heap pickers', hence rag-and-bone men's : from early 1870's. H., 5th ed. Perhaps on *tat*, a rag, = the suggestion coming from the juxtaposition in *rag-and-bone*. Hence *tot-picker* (– 1874) or *-raker* (– 1904) or *-hunter* (– 1909), and *totter* (– 1891), such a scavenger, esp. if illicit, and *totting* (– 1874), such scavenging : H., F. & H., Ware, O.E.D.—6. See **tote**, n., 2.

tot, v.t. To add (orig. *together*) to ascertain the total of : coll. : ca. 1760, H. Brooke ; slightly ob. Ex *total* or *tot* as abbr. *total* (or *totum*) : cf. *tot*, n., 1.— 2. Hence, *tot up*, to ascertain (esp. expeditiously) the total of : from mid-1830's. O.E.D.—3. Hence, vbl.n. *totting-up*, *totting* : coll. : resp. ca. 1820, 1860. —4. Hence, v.i., to amount ; often constructed with *to*. Coll. : 1882, Besant, ' I . . . wondered how much it would tot up to,' O.E.D.—5. To drink drams : mid-C. 19–20. Ex *tot*, n., 4.

to't. To it : when not poetical, it is, in mid-C. 19–20, coll.

tot-book. A book containing (long) addition sums to be worked out : coll. : late C. 19–20. Cf. *long tots*. Ex *tot*, n., 1.

tot-hunter, -picker or **-raker.** See **tot**, n., 5.

Tot-hunting. ' Scouring the streets in search of pretty girls ' : low (– 1909). Ware. Cf. *Tottie*, 2, q.v.

tot-sack. A bag ; esp. a sand-bag containing rations for a number of men : military : 1914 ; ob. F. & Gibbons. Prob. ex *tot*, n., 4, rather than ex sense 5.

tot-up. An adding-up : coll. : 1871 (O.E.D.).— 2. V. : see **tot**, v., 2, 4.

tote ; occ. **tot.** A hard drinker : ca. 1870, a music-hall song entitled *Hasn't Got over It Yet*, ' As

well we'd another old chum, | By all of his mates called the Tote, | So named on account of the rum | He constantly put down his throat.' Perhaps punning *tote*, total, and *tot*, n., 4 ; perhaps ex :—2. (Occ. **tot.**) A total abstainer : low coll. : prob. from late 1860's, but not irrefutably recorded before 1887 (O.E.D.). The music-hall song *Toper and Tote*, ca. 1889, has : ' You'll always find the sober Tote | With a few pounds at command.' F. & H.—3. A totalisator : from ca. 1890 : Australian coll. >, ca. 1901, gen. British coll. Kinglake, 1891 (O.E.D.). Cf. *tote-shop*.

***tote**, v.t. A variant of *tout*, v., 2 : c. (– 1887). Baumann. Cf. *toter*.—2. To carry : U.S. (ca. 1676) >, ca. 1910, partly anglicised as a coll. Thornton. The origin of this obscure word is not impossibly *tole*, *toll*, v.t., ' to pull, drag, draw physically ', recorded by O.E.D. for C. 15–17 ; the earliest example of *tote* may be a scribal error (for it occurs in an official document) and there exist no, or very few, other examples before mid-C. 18. But W., prob. rightly, suggests the Old Fr. *tauter* (as defined in Cotgrave).

***toter.** A C. 17 variant of *touter*, a spy : c. : 1633, Jonson.

tother, t'other. See **tone, t'one,** which cf.

tother, one with. Copulation : ? C. 18–20 ; ob. Rather coll. than s.

tother from which, tell. (Gen. in negative). To distinguish between two persons or things : coll. : late C. 19–20. Baumann, 1887. A jocular manipulation of *tell one from the other*.

tother school. One's former school ; any school not a Public School : Winchester coll. : mid-C. 19– 20. Cf. *totherun*, q.v.—2. As adj., unbecoming because alien to Winchester : id. : from ca. 1860. Cf. *non-licet*. Wrench.

tother-sider, or as one word. A convict : coll. of Victoria, Australia : ca. 1860–1905. With reference to Sydney, where stood the earliest penal settlement : also *Sydney*(-bird or)-*sider*. The rivalry between Melbourne and Sydney, esp., now takes, and has long taken, the form of an exchange of our *'Arbour !* and *stinking Yarra !*—2. One from the other side of Australia, esp. a Westralian : late C. 19–20 : Australian coll. >, by 1925, S.E.

totherun. A preparatory school ; a private school : Charterhouse : late C. 19–20. I.e. the *other one* (one's former school). Cf. *tother school*, q.v.

toto. A hippopotamus : pet-name coll. (– 1916). O.E.D. (Sup.). A manipulated abbr.—2. A louse : military : 1916–18. F. & Gibbons. Adopted, not very gen., ex Fr. military s., where it shared the honours with *gau* (see the glossaries of Dauzat and Déchelette).

tots, long. Very long addition sums : coll. : late C. 19–20. Ex *tot*, n., 1.

Tots, the Old. The 17th Lancers : military : from ca. 1870 ; ob. Perhaps ex the regimental badge of skull and crossbones, which certainly engendered the synonymous *Death and Glory Boys*.

totter. See **tot**, n., 5.

totter-arse. A seesaw : provincial : from ca. 1870. Ex dial. *t.-a.*, a person walking unsteadily (E.D.D.).

Tottie ; occ. **Totty.** A Hottentot : coll. : 1849, E. E. Napier (O.E.D.).—2. The ' inevitable ' (or inseparable) nickname of men surnamed Bell : military : C. 20. F. & Gibbons. Origin prob. anecdotal : see remarks at **Nicknames.**—3. *tottie*, rarely *totty*. A high-class whore : from ca. 1880. Ex

Dot, Dorothy, or *ex tottie, -y*, a little child : perhaps influenced by *titty*, q.v.

Tottie all-colours. A brightly dressed young woman (of the streets): low London (— 1909). Ware. Cf. :

Tottie one-lung. ' An asthmatic, or consumptive young person who, for good or bad, thinks herself somebody ': low urban (— 1909). Ware. See **Tottie, 3**.

totting. See **tot, n., 5.**—2. See **tot, v., 3**. Also *totting-up* : ibid.

totting, go. To collect (rags and) bones : low (— 1887). Baumann. See **tat, v**.

Tottle. Aristotle : schools' (— 1923). Manchon. Cf. *Thicker*.

Totty. See **Tottie**.

touch. Anything that will, at a stated price, interest customers at (about) that price : from ca. 1710 : coll. >, in mid-C. 19, s. Swift, 1712, ' I desire you to print in such a form, as in the booksellers' phrase will make a sixpenny touch '; Sir Erasmus Philipps, in his *Diary*, Sept. 22, 1720, ' At night went to the ball at the Angel. A guinea touch '; H., 3rd ed. (1864), ' Sometimes said of a woman to imply her worthlessness, as, " Only a half-crown touch ".' Lit., something that will *touch*, appeal to.—2. At Eton (— 1864), a present of money, a ' tip '. H., 3rd ed. Cf. sense 5.—3. A theft, esp. by pocket-picking : low s. bordering on c. : 1888, ' Rolf Boldrewood '. O.E.D. (In C. 20 c., an illicit haul.)—4. Hence, the obtaining of money from a person, e.g. by a loan : from ca. 1890. —5. Hence, the sum of money obtained at one time, esp. by cadging or theft : low : C. 20.—6. ' Manner ; mode ; fashion ', C. J. Dennis : Australian coll. : C. 20. Cf. sense 1.—7. Cognate is the English low s. sense (— 1923), ' sort of thing ', as in ' Don't come that touch on (or with) me ! ' Manchon.—8. ' In these rounds or . . . " walks ", we have our " touches "—regular places of call where we pick up letters and, in certain cases, leave them,' from ' You're in My Bag ! ' by a Postman, in *The Passing Show*, Dec. 24, 1932.

touch. To receive (money), draw (it) : mid-C. 17–20 : S.E. until C. 19, then coll. ; in C. 20, s. Cf. Fr. *toucher de l'argent*.—2. ? hence, to steal : c. : late C. 18–20. Holman, 1796, ' I could not go abroad without her, so I touch'd father's cash.' In C. 20 c., often v.i., ' to make a haul or bring off a coup ' (Charles E. Leach). Cf. sense 4.—3. To approach (a person) *for* money, to get from (a person) the money one asks (*for*) : coll. : 1760. C. Johnston, 1760, ' I am quite broke up ; his grace has touched me for five hundred,' O.E.D. In late C. 19–20, for things other than money.—4. To rob (a person : *for*, of the article concerned) : c. : mid-C. 19–20.—5. Hence, in Australian c. or low s. (— 1904), to act unfairly towards, to cheat, to swindle. F. & H.—6. The sense ' to arrest ', ca. 1780–1850, may, as the O.E.D. has it, be S.E. ; or it may, as Grose, 1st ed. implies, be coll. or s.—7. To rival, compare with, equal (in ability) : coll. : 1838, Dickens, ' Wasn't he always top-sawyer among you all ? Is there any one of you that could touch him, or come near him ? ' Ex *touch*, to reach, get as far as.

touch, rum. An odd or eccentric fellow : 1804–6 T. Creevey. O.E.D. Perhaps *touch* here = a ' contact ', a person whom one meets or deals with. —2. Hence, a very strange affair : from ca. 1807 ; very ob. Cf. *queer start* (see **start**).

touch bone and whistle. ' Any one having broken wind backwards, according to the vulgar law, may be pinched by any of the company till he has touched bone (i.e. his teeth) and whistled,' Grose, 2nd ed. Often in the imperative. From late 1780's to mid-C. 19.

touch bun for luck. See **bun**.

***touch-crib.** A brothel : c. or low s. : C. 19–20 ; ob. Ex euphemistic S.E. *touch*.

touch for. See **touch, v., 3, 4**.—3. To get, incur, catch (gen. something unpleasant) : from ca. 1910.

touch-hole. The pudend : low coll. : C. 17–20 ; ob. Punning a fire-arm's vent.

touch lucky. To have a stroke of luck : non-aristocratic coll. : C. 20. F. & Gibbons. Cf. *touch*, v., 1.

touch me. A shilling : from ca. 1880 ; ob. Abbr. *touch me on the nob*, a ' bob ', rhyming s. of ca. 1870–90. F. & H., 1904, has *touch-my-nob*, a bastard or composite form. The *touch-me* forms are recorded in a MS. note in the B.M. copy of H., 5th ed.

touch of Caruso. ' A turn or two astern on the engines ' : nautical (officers') : from ca. 1910 ; ob. Ironic ex the great singer.

touch of the tar-brush, a. A pejorative c.p. applied to ' the naval officer who is primarily an efficient seaman ' : mid-C. 19–20. Bowen. Ex the constant use of tar on a ship.

touch off (someone) **for.** A variant, mostly Colonial, of *touch*, v., 3 : late C. 19–20. A. Cecil Alport, *The Lighter Side of the War*, 1934, ' I touched him off for a fiver.'

touch out, v.i. ' To evade a duty by trickery ' : military : 1915 ; ob. F. & Gibbons. Cf. *touch*, v., 5.—2. (V.t. with *for*.) Whence, to be lucky : military : from 1916. B. & P.

touch pot, touch penny. A semi-proverbial c.p. = No credit given : from ca. 1650, ob. by 1880, † by 1935. Gayton, 1654 ; Graves, 1772 ; Scott, 1822. Cf. Swift's ' He touch'd the pence when others touch'd the pot,' 1720. Apperson.

touch-trap. The penis : low coll. opp. *touch-hole*, q.v.

touch up. To caress intimately in order to inflame (a person to the sexual act) : coll. : C. 18–20. —2. To coït with (a woman) : late C. 18–mid-19. Grose, 1st ed.—3. Reflexively, to masturbate : C. 19–20. All senses ex *touch up*, to stimulate.

touch with a pair of tongs, not to. (Gen. I, etc., would not.) To touch on no account : coll. : from 1630's. Clarke, 1639 ; Fuller, 1732 ; 1876, Blackmore. (Apperson.) Cf. . . . *with a barge-pole*.

touch with death. Narrowly to escape death : military coll. : from 1915. F. & Gibbons. I.e. to touch death.

touched, (slightly) insane, is, despite gen. opinion, S.E. It abbr. *touched in the head*, ex S.E. *touch*, to affect mentally, to taint.—2. (Of vegetables, fruit) beginning to go bad ; defective : green-grocers' coll. (— 1887). Baumann.

toucher. A(n instance of) close contact, a tight fit : dial. (— 1828) >, by 1840, coll. Thus *to a toucher*, exactly. E.D.D.—Hence, 2, *as near or nigh as a toucher*, almost, very nearly : 1840, J. T. Hewlett (O.E.D.) ; H., 1st ed. Slightly ob. Orig. a coaching term, ex touching without disaster : H., 5th ed.

touching. Bribery ; the obtaining of money, esp. by theft or begging : resp. C. 18–19 (C. D'Anvers, 1726) ; late C. 19–20 (Arthur Morrison, 1896). O.E.D. Ex *touch*, v., 2, 3.

touching-up. A caning : Public Schools' : late C. 19–20. (P. G. Wodehouse, *Tales of St Austin's*, 1903.)—2, 3, 4. Vbl. n. of *touch up*, q.v.

touchy. 'Descriptive of a style in which points, broken lines, or touches are employed, as distinguished from firm unbroken line work', F. & H. : artistic s. (ca. 1820) >, ca. 1850, coll. >, ca. 1910, S.E.—2. Adv., rather : Christ's Hospital : from ca. 1860. E.g. *touchy a lux*, rather a good thing. Ex *touch*, a small amount of, a 'suspicion'.

tough, v.t. To support, bear, face up to (esp. a difficulty, a hardship) : Canadian : from ca. 1905. John Beames, *An Army without Banners*, 1930. Prob. ex U.S. *tough it*, to rough it.

tough. Morally callous and/or commercially unscrupulous : also n. From ca. 1910 : coll. Ex two U.S. senses : *tough*, criminal, vicious, and *tough*, a rough, esp. a street bully.—2. Unfortunate ; severe : from ca. 1928. P. G. Wodehouse, 1929, ' " Tough ! " ' You bet it's tough. A girl can't help her appearance '.' (O.E.D. Sup.). Ex U.S. *tough luck*.

tough, make it. To raise difficulties ; take excessive pains : coll. : late C. 19–20 ; ob.

tough as a jockey's tail-end—as old Nick—as shoe-leather. Anglo-Irish phrases (the first, s. ; the other two, coll.) applied to a person who is a 'hard case ' : resp. C. 20, late C. 19–20, and mid-C. 19–20.

tough as an old lanyard knot. Exceedingly tough (whether meat or seaman) : nautical coll. : late C. 19–20. Bowen.

tough as tacker. Exceedingly tough : lower classes' coll. (— 1909). Ware. Perhaps S.W. dial. *tacker*, something insuperable.

tough gut, or **tough-gut.** A tough, i.e. hardy, fellow : Canadian men's (— 1932). John Beames.

tough 'un. A 'thumping ' lie ; execrable pun : low (— 1887). Baumann.—2. See **tough**, adj., 1.

*tough-yarn. 'A long story ', Egan's Grose : c. (— 1823) ; † by 1890, by when it meant a 'tall story ' : nautical (Bowen).

Toughs. See **Old Toughs, the.**

toupee. The female pubic hair : mid-C. 18–20 ; very ob. By ribald jest on lit. sense.—2. A merkin : mid-C. 18–mid-19. Both, occ., *lady's low toupee*.

*tour ; also **toure, tower, towre.** To watch closely ; spy on : c. of ca. 1565–1650. Harman, 1567. Prob. unconnected with S.E. *twire* (v.i. only), to peer, peep. Possibly—as Grose (1st ed., at *touting*) suggests—cognate with later c. *tout*, v.i. and t. (q.v.) ; more prob. with *tower*, to fly up, as a hawk does, in order to (have the advantage of and then) swoop down on the prey.

tout. (Also *toute* ; *towte*, C. 15–16.) The posteriors or rump : C. 14–20 : S.E. until C. 15, then † ; revived by 'Thousand Nights ' Payne as literary s.—2. A thieves' 'look-out man ' : c. : 1718, C. Hitching (*toute*, a C. 18 variant) ; ob. except as a spy (C. 20 : c.). Ex *tout*, v., 1.—3. Hence, 'a look out house, or eminence ', Grose, 1st ed. : c. of ca. 1780–1850.—4. As a solicitor of custom for tradesmen, etc., and 5, as a racing touter, *tout* is mid-C. 19–20 : both may orig. have been s. or coll., but the former was S.E. by 1880, the latter by 1910, at latest.—6. A watching or spying : c. (— 1812) ; ob. Vaux, ' *A strong tout*, is strict observation, or eye, upon any proceedings, or persons.' Esp. in *keep tout* (— 1812) or, occ., *keep the tout* (1834, Ainsworth : O.E.D.), to keep watch, esp. in an illicit activity. Ex sense 3.

*tout, v.i. To be on the look-out, to watch very carefully : c. of mid C. 17–mid-19, and in C. 19 only in literary revival. Coles, B.E., Grose. Ex C. 15–17 S.E. *tout*, to peep or peer. Cf. *tour*, q.v.— 2. V.t., to watch, spy on : mid C. 17–20 : c. until C. 19, then low s. until mid-C. 19, then s. with esp. reference to a racing tout's activities. Coles, B.E., Vaux.—3. The racing sense (from ca. 1812) may orig. have been s., but is gen. considered as S.E. ; the same applies to *tout*, v.i., to seek busily for trade (from ca. 1730). O.E.D.

*tout, keep (the) and **tout, strong.** See **tout, n., 6.**

tout droit. See **bit of.**—**toute.** See **tout, n.**

*touter. A thieves' look-out man : c. or low s. : 1844, Dickens (O.E.D.) ; ob. A rare variant of *tout*, n., 2, q.v.

*touting (or tooting)-ken. A tavern, a beer-shop ; a tavern-bar : c. (— 1676) ; † by 1850. Coles, B.E., Grose. Ex *toot*, *tout*, to drink copiously. (O.E.D.)

touzery or **towzery gang, the.** Mock-auction swindlers : London low : from ca. 1870 ; ob. H., 5th ed. 'They hire sale-rooms, usually in the suburbs, and advertise their ventures as . . . "Important Sales of Bankrupts' Stock ", etc.,' F. & H. Perhaps ex *touse* (-ze), horse-play, a ' row ', or *touse* (-ze), to abuse or maltreat.

tow. (At hare and hounds) a long run-in : Shrewsbury School (— 1881). Pascoe. Ex slow motion of towing a ship.—2. Money : low : from ca. 1880 ; ob. Perhaps because, like *tow*, it ' burns ' so quickly.

*tow, v. See **tow out.**—***tow-line, get in a.** See **line, get in a.** Vaux, 1812.

*tow out. To decoy ; to distract the attention of (a person) and thus assist a confederate in robbery : c. of ca. 1810–50. Vaux.

Tow-Pows, the. The Grenadier Guards : military (— 1864) ; ob. H., 3rd ed. Ultimately ex the busbies they wear.

tow-rag. The female breast : West Yorkshire s. (— 1905), not dial. E.D.D.

tow-row. A grenadier : military : ca. 1780–1860. Grose, 1st ed. Why ? : *row* is prob. a misprint for *pow*, head (see **Tow-Pows**) ; cf., however, *tow-row*, adj.—2. A noise : dial. > (low) coll. : from ca. 1870. Reduplicated *row*, a disturbance. Cf.

tow-row, adj. Drunk (? and disorderly) : C. 18. Steele, 1709. On *row*, disturbance.

*tow-street. To ' get (a person) in a line ', i.e. to decoy him : c. (— 1823) ; † by 1890. Egan's Grose.

towards you, I looks. See **looks towards.**

towel (rare) ; oaken towel. (Esp. *rub one down with an oaken towel*, to cudgel or beat him.) A stick or cudgel : resp. 1756 (Toldervy) and 1739. Ob. Ex *towel*, v.—2. **lead** (rarely **leaden**) **towel.** A bullet : 1812, J. & H. Smith, ' Make Nunky surrender his dibs, | Rub his pate with a pair of lead towels ' ; ob. by 1900, virtually † by 1930.

towel, v. To cudgel ; to thrash : J. Dunton, 1705 (O.E.D.). For semantics, note the gen. ridiculed *dry-rub* etymology of *drub*.

towel, sky the. See **sky the towel.**

towelling. A drubbing or thrashing : 1851, Mayhew, ' I got a towelling, but it did not do me much good.' Ex preceding. Cf. *towel*, n., q.v.

*tower. Clipped money : c. of C. 18–early 19. *A New Canting Dict.*, 1725 ; Grose, 1st ed. Ex, and gen. in, *they have been round the Tower with it*, ' that Piece of Money has been Clipt ', B.E. : a late

C. 17–early 19 c.p. of the underworld. App. Tower Hill and, in fact, the whole neighbourhood of the Tower of London were rough, for cf. *Tower-Hill play*.

*tower, towre, v. See **tour**.

Tower Bridge, the. 'The huge pit-head mine structure at Loos': late 1915–18. F. & Gibbons. Ex a fancied resemblance to the Tower Bridge in London.

Tower Hill, preach on. To be hanged: C. 16. Skelton in *Magnificence*. Tower Hill was long the place of execution in London. Cf. *Tyburn* phrases.

*Tower-Hill play. 'A slap on the Face and a kick on the Breech', B.E.: c.: late C. 17–18. Grose, 1st ed. Cf. *tower*, n., q.v., and :

Tower-Hill vinegar. The headsman's block : C. 16–17. Ex *Tower Hill, preach on.*

town or **Town,** as in **go to, leave, t.** or **T.** London : coll. : C. 18–20.—2. (*town.*) A halfpenny : rhyming s. (— 1909) on *brown*, n. Ware.

*town, in ; town, out of. See **in town** and **out of town.**

town-bull, a wencher, is rather S.E. than coll. or s., but perhaps *as lawless as a town-bull* (a notable wencher : late C. 17–early 19) and *roar like a town-bull*, to bellow (late C. 18–mid-19) are coll. (B.E. ; Grose.) Cf. Ray, 1678, *then the town-bull is a bachelor*, i.e. 'as soon as such an one', Apperson : a c.p. † by 1850.—2. A harlot's bully : low (—1923). Manchon.

town-lout. A scholar living at home in the town : Rugby School : from ca. 1860 ; ob. H., 3rd ed. Cf. *town(e)y.*

town red, paint the. See **red.**

towner. A s. variant of S.E. *townee* : ca. 1885–1915. F. & H.

towney, towny. Alien to the school : Christ's Hospital : from ca. 1860. Contrast- *housey*, peculiar to the Hospital.—2. A fellow-townsman (or woman) : in U.S., 1834 ; in England, 1865 (O.E.D.). Cf. Fr. *mon pays(e)*.—3. A town-bred person, esp. a Londoner : coll. : 1828, Peter Cunningham (O.E.D.).—4. **towny,** adj. Townish : coll. : 1837 (O.E.D.).—5. **towneys,** properly *townies.* Clothes more suitable to town wear than are the school's blue garments : Christ's Hospital : from ca. 1860.

towns and cities. See **thousand pities.—towre.** See **tower.**

*towre. See **tour.—towzery gang.** See **touzery gang.**

tox. To intoxicate, gen. in ppl.adjj., *toxed, toxing* : 1630's. Heywood. O.E.D.

toxy. In*tox*icated : from ca. 1905 ; very ob. A. H. Dawson, *Dict. of Slang*, 1913. Ex Scottish.

*toy. A watch : c. (— 1877) ; slightly ob. Horsley, *Jottings from Jail*, 1877. Hence, *toygetter, -getting,* a watch-snatcher (Arthur Morrison, 1896 : O.E.D.), watch-stealing ; *toy and tackle,* a watch and chain (see **tackle,** n.) ; a *red toy* is a gold watch (see **red,** c. adj.), while a *white toy* is a silver one.

toy-box. The engine-room : naval (not very gen.) : C. 20. Bowen.

toy-time. Evening preparation : Winchester : from ca. 1860. Ex :

toys. A bureau, esp. in the form of desk and bookcase combined : Winchester : from ca. 1860. Ironically ex *toy*, a trinket or knick-knack.

tra-la-la ! Good-bye ! : c.p., — slightly contemptuous and not too polite,—of ca. 1830–90. Ware, 'The phrase took its rise with a comic singer

named Henri Clarke, whose speciality was imitating Parisians.' This being so, Clarke almost certainly knew the Fr. s. sense of *tra-la-la* (the posterior) : cf., therefore, *kiss my* ——.

traces, kick over the. See **kick.**

trachitis. Incorrect for *tracheitis* : from ca. 1840. O.E.D.

trachy. Tracheotomy : medical students' (— 1933). *Slang*, p. 190.

track. Sol. for (*a*) *tract* ; likewise for †*tract*, v.— 2. (Also *trag.*) A quart : back s. (— 1859). H., 1st ed. Thus : trauq > traq > *trag* or *trak* > *track*.

*track, v. See preceding, 1.—2. **track up the dancers,** to go, esp. if quickly, upstairs : c. (—1671) ; † by 1850. Head, B.E., Grose. Ex † S.E. *track*, to go.

track, inside. The truth : sporting s. > coll. : from ca. 1880 ; ob. Cf. *have the inside running,* i.e. an advantage, and *inside information,* valuable ' tips '.

track with. To woo : Australian (— 1916). C. J. Dennis. Cf. *walk out with.*

tractile. Tractive : catachresis : 1839. O.E.D.

tractor. 'A 'plane with frontal propeller' (B. & P.) : Air Force : from 1915.

trade. An act of trading ; an exchange ; in politics, a private arrangement : U.S. s. (1829 : Thornton) anglicised ca. 1890 as coll > , by 1920, S.E.—2. *the trade* is prostitution : late C. 18–19. Cf. *trader*, q.v.—3. In G.W., *the trade* = the submarine service : naval coll. (W.) : from 1915.

trade, v. To exchange, 'swap' : U.S. coll. anglicised ca. 1885. Baumann.

trade-mark. A scratch on the face ; esp. in *draw, leave,* or *put one's trade-mark on one* or *one's ace* or *down one's face,* to claw the face. Chiefly of women : (low) coll. : from early 1870's. Anon. music-hall song, *Father, Take A Run !,* ca. 1875.

trader. A harlot : ca. 1680–1820. Radcliffe, 1682, *she-trader,* a variant. Also *trading dame,* as in Cotton, 1678. Cf. *the trade* at **trade,** n., 2.

Trades Union, the. The 1st Dragoon Guards : military : ca. 1830–1914. At one time many of the officers were—*horribile dictu !*—sons of tradesmen (cf. the snobbery and arrogance of *temporary gentlemen* in G.W.). F. & Gibbons, however, derive it ' from the K.D.G.'s being constantly employed in suppressing Trade Union disturbances in Lancashire and the Midlands between 1825–34 '.

trading dame. See **trader.**

trading justices. Such low fellows as, ' smuggled into the commission of the peace ', live ' by fomenting disputes, granting warrants and otherwise retailing justice ', Grose, 3rd ed. : coll. : ca. 1785–1840.

trady. Belonging to, characteristic of, trade : coll. : 1899 (O.E.D.).

traffic. A whore : c. of late C. 16–early 17. Greene, 1591 (*traffique*). Ex the large amount of business she plies.—2. Wireless messages sent or received : wireless operators' (esp. at sea) coll. : from ca. 1926. Bowen.

Traffy. The *Trafalgar* (ship) : naval (— 1909) ; ob. Ware.

trag. See **track,** n., 2.

tragedy Jack. A heavy tragedian : pejorative theatrical : from ca. 1875 ; ob.

trail. A befooling : rare coll. : 1847, C. Brontë (see next entry) ; ob.

trail, v. To quiz or befool : coll. : from ca. 1845. C. Brontë, 1847, ' She was (what is vernacularly termed) trailing Mrs Dent ; that is, playing on the ignorance ; her trail might be clever, but . . . decidedly not good-natured ' ; Coulson Kernahan, 1900, ' To see the Ishmaelites " trail " a sufferer from " swelled head " is to undergo inoculation against that fell malady.' Ex *trail*, to draw (a person) out or on.

*trailer. One who rides a horse away and sells him afar off : c. : late C. 16–early 17. Greene, 1592.—2. A prowling cab-driver : London coll. ca. 1870–1905. E.D.D.

traily. Slovenly ; weak, languid : dial. (−1851) >, by 1860, coll. O.E.D.

train. To consort : coll. : from ca. 1880 ; slightly ob. Cf. *tag about (with)* and the C. 17 S.E. *train*, to walk in a notable's retinue.—2. (Also **train it.**) To travel by train : coll. (− 1887). Baumann (*train it*) ; 1888, *The Pall Mall Gazette*, April 2 (O.E.D.).

trains !, go and play ; also . . . **with yourself !** Also *run away and play trains !* A derisive c.p. of dismissal : C. 20. Cf. *run away and play marbles !*, q.v.

traipse. See **trapes.**

traitors at table, there are. A c.p. applied to a loaf of bread turned the wrong side upwards : mid-C. 17–19. Ray, 1678, ' Are there traitors at the table that the loaf is turned wrong side upwards ? '

tram. A tramway car : coll. (1879) >, ca. 1905. S.E. (O.E.D.) Cf. :

tram. To travel by mining-district tramroad : coll. : 1826 (E.D.D.).—2. Hence, by tram-car : likewise coll. : from ca. 1880,—see **tram**, n. Also *tram it* (1904, E. Nesbit : O.E.D.). Cf. *train*, 2.

tram-fare. Twopence : London streets' : 1882–ca. 95. Ware.

tram-lines. The 4½ ft.-wide area on each side of a (doubles) lawn-tennis court : sporting : from ca. 1929. Esp. *down the tram-lines*, i.e. more or less straight along this strip of the court.

tramp. A journey on foot ; a long, tiring, or arduous walk or march ; a ' hike ' : coll. : 1786, Burns ; 1898, J. Hutchinson, ' Exhausted by a long tramp in hot weather '. O.E.D. Ex *tramp*, to walk, to walk steadily.

tramp, v. To go on a walking excursion, a ' hike ' : coll. : mid-C. 19–20. Also *tramp it*.—2. To proceed as a tramp : coll. (− 1891). *The Century Dict.*—3. To drive out of or into some stated condition by *tramping*, vigorous walking : coll. : 1853, Kane, ' Tramping the cold out of my joints ', O.E.D.—4. To make a voyage by tramp steamer : coll. : 1899 (O.E.D.).—5. Hence, v.t., to run (such a steamer) : coll. : 1899, likewise in Cutcliffe Hyne (ibid.).—6. To run over (e.g. an animal) ; to smash (e.g. a gate) : South African coll. (− 1913) >, by 1930, ' standard '. Influenced by ' the Cape Dutch *trap*, to ride or drive over ', Pettman.

tramping the ties. Trespassing on the railways : Canadian : late C. 19–20. O.E.D. (Sup.). The *ties* are the sleepers of a railway track.

*trampler. A lawyer or attorney : c. of ca. 1635–50. Middleton. Perhaps because he tramples on others ; prob. ex †*trample*, to act as an intermediary.

trampolin. A double spring-board : circus : mid-C. 19–20. Ex *trampolin*, performance on stilts.

transcendent, -ly ; transcendental, -ly. Occ. confused : a late C. 19–20 catachresis.

transfer. To steal : Society : ca. 1895–1915. Ware. On *convey*. Cf. :

translate the truth. To lie evasively : Society c.p. : 1899. Ware. Ex a phrase used, by a Parisian newspaper, of Delcassé, the French cabinet-minister, in connexion with the Muscat incident.

translated. Intoxicated ; very drunk : Society : 1880's. Ware derives it ex Shakespeare's ' Bless thee, Bottom, thou art translated.'

translators. A pair of re-made boots and shoes : (low) London : mid-C. 19–20 ; ob. Mayhew, 1851. Ex *translator*, a cobbler, esp. of old shoes.

transmogrify ; occ. **transmografy, -aphy, -riphy , -migrafy ; -mugrify.** To change, alter ; esp. to metamorphose utterly or strangely : coll., humorous >, ca. 1700, rather low : resp.,—1700, but implied in 1661 ; 1656, 1688, 1671 ;—1725 ; 1786. Always v.t. and orig. of persons only. S. Holland, 1656 ; B.E. (-*mogrify*) ; *A New Canting Dict.*, 1725 (-*mogrify, -migrafy*) ; Burns (-*mugrify*) ; Barham ; Mary Howitt, ca. 1888. In C. 20, ob. The Dictionary of 1725 asserts that *transmigrafy* is the correct form : if so, *transmigrate* prob. supplies, via illiterate corruption, the etymology.—2. The derivatives *transmogrification, transmogrifier*, are much less frequent : resp., K.W., 1661, ' To the botchers for transmogrification ', and 1676. O.E.D. (chiefly) ; F. & H.

*transnear. To come up with (a person) : c. : late C. 17–early 19. B.E., where it is misprinted *tansnear* ; Grose, 1st ed. Perhaps on C. 17 S.E. *transpear*, the word prob. = to cross (e.g. a street) in order to approach.

transpire. To happen : catachrestic : U.S. (− 1804), anglicised ca. 1810 ; recorded by Webster, 1828. Rife in journalism. Properly, *transpire* = to ' leak out '. See esp. O.E.D., W., and Fowler.—2. (Of time) to elapse : likewise catachrestic, but rare : ca. 1820–40. O.E.D.

transport tale. A false rumour ; a ' tall ' story : infantrymen's pejorative coll. : from 1915. F. & Gibbons. Cf. *latrine rumour.*

trap. Trickery, a deceitful trick ; fraud. Esp. in *understand trap*, to be wide-awake or, esp., alert to one's own interest. (Anon., 1679, *Counterfeits*, III, i, ' You're deceiv'd in old Gomez, he understands trap ' ; 1821, Scott : Apperson) ; *smell trap*, to suspect danger, as of a thief ' spotting ' a detective (J. Greenwood, 1869) ; and *be up to trap* (in dial. before 1828,—see Apperson ; but recorded as coll. in 1819 by O.E.D. ; H., 1860). Low s. ; very ob. except in the third phrase. Cf. *trap is down, the*. Ex lit. S.E. influenced by *trapan, trepan*, a trick on stratagem.—2. A sheriff's officer, policeman (in Australia, ca. 1860–90, a mounted one), detective : c. or low s. : 1703, Ned Ward ; 1838, Dickens ; 1895, Marriott-Watson. Slightly ob., except in South Africa, where it has, since the early 1880's, been esp. used both of an exciseman and of an I.D.B. detective (Pettman). Ex *trap*, to catch.—3. A smallish, sprung carriage ; in Britain, esp. an gig, but in Australia and New Zealand a four-wheeled carriage : from ca. 1805 : coll. >, by 1900, S.E. Perhaps ex *rattle trap*.—4. See **traps.**—5. The mouth : low : from ca. 1780 as *potato-trap*, q.v., the simple form being of mid-C. 19–20. (O.E.D. Sup.)—6. A mould used in coining counterfeit : c. (− 1929). O.E.D. (Sup.).—7. (Prob. ex sense 1.) A go-between employed by a pickpocket and a whore working together : c. : C. 18. C. Hitching, in *The Regulator*, 1718, destribes the procedure.

trap is down !, the. The trick, or attempt to ' do '

me, has failed; it's no go!: a c.p. of ca. 1870–1910. Ex *trap*, 1, q.v., with an allusion to the fallen door of a trap for birds, etc.

trap-stick. The penis: ca. 1670–1900. Cotton; 'Burlesque' Bridges. Ex the lit. sense.—2. In pl., the legs; esp. thin legs: ca. 1780–1850. Grose, 1st ed., 'From the sticks with which boys play at trap ball'.

*****trapan**; **trepan** in these senses is rare and not earlier than ca. 1680. 'He that draws in or wheedles a Cull, and Bites'—swindles—'him,' B.E.: c. of ca. 1640–1830. Prob. ex (*to*) *trap*, with a c. disguise-suffix (cf. *-mans*).—2. Hence, a deceitful or fraudulent trick or stratagem: (orig. low) s.: ca. 1660–1830.

*****trapan, trepan, v.** To ensnare, beguile, inveigle, swindle: c. or low s. (– 1656) >, by 1750, (low) s.; ob. Blount, B.E., Grose. Ex *trapan*, n., 1.

trapes; occ. **trapse**; often **traipse**. A slovenly or slatternly female: coll. and (in late C. 19–20, nothing but) dial.: ca. 1673, Cotton, 'I had not car'd | If Pallas here had been preferr'd; | But to bestow it on that Trapes, | It mads me'; the other two forms, C. 19–20, though *trapse* is almost †. Ex *trapes*, v., 1, q.v.—2. (Same origin.) A going or wandering in listless or slovenly fashion; a wearisome or disagreeable tramp: coll. and dial.: 1862, Mrs Henry Wood, 'It's such a toil and a trapes up them two pair of stairs.'

trapes; traipse. (In C. 18–20, occ. *trapse*. Dial. has many variants, varying from *traaps* to *trapus* and *traipass*.) To walk untidily, listlessly, aimlessly; gad about: coll.: 1593, Bilson implies it in 'This trapesing to and fro', O.E.D.; 1710–11, March 2, Swift, 'I was traipsing to-day with your Mr Sterne,' ibid. Perhaps cognate with †*trape* (to walk idly to and fro), which prob. derives ex medieval Dutch *trappen*, to tread (O.E.D.).—2. Hence, to trail, or hang, along or down: coll.: from ca. 1770; from late C. 19, only in dial.— 3. (Ex sense 1.) V.t., to tramp over, tread or tramp (e.g. the fields): 1885, Hall Caine. O.E.D.

trapesing, traipsing. N.: see **trapes**, v., 1.—2. Adj., 1760, Foote, *trapsing*: idem.

trapezihedron. Incorrect for *trapezohedron*: 1828, Webster. O.E.D.

trapish. Slovenly; slatternly: coll.: C. 18. Rowe, 1705 (O.E.D.). Ex *trapes*, n., 1, q.v.

trapper. A horse used in a 'trap' (q.v., sense 3): coll.: from early 1880's. 'Cf. *vanner*, *busser*, *cabber*, etc., on the model of "hunter",' F. & H.

trappiness. The n. of *trappy*, q.v.: coll.: 1885, *The Field*, Dec. 26.

*****trapping.** Blackmail: c.: late C. 17–mid-18. Anon., *A Country Gentleman's Vade Mecum*. A special development from *trap*, to ensnare. Cf. *trapan*, n., 2.

trappy. Treacherous; trickily difficult; i.e. lit. or fig. containing a trap or traps: coll.: 1882, *The Daily Telegraph*, Nov. 13, 'The fences might have been increased in size, however, without being made trappy'; in cricket, of the ball: 1887 (Lewis).

traps. Personal effects; belongings; baggage: coll.: 1813 (O.E.D.). Abbr. *trappings*.—2. Hence, in Australia, a 'swag' (q.v.): from late 1850's. H., 2nd ed

trapse. See **trapes**.

trash. (Contemptuously: cf. *dross*, *filthy lucre*.) Money: ca. 1590–1830. Greene, ca. 1591; 1809, Malkin. As the O.E.D. remarks, Shakespeare's

'Who steals my purse, steals trash' was prob. an operative factor.

trav. Travelling money: Felsted School: late C. 19–20.

travel. To admit of, to bear, transportation: coll.: (Dec.) 1852, Beck's *Florist*, 'Not . . . good plants for exhibition, as they travel badly', O.E.D. —2. To go, move, fast: coll.: 1884, of a dog, 'How he travels,' E.D.D.; 1904, F. & H., 'The motor travelled along, and no mistake.'

travel on one's props. To leave luggage with the railway company as security against the travelling facilities granted, money lacking for the fares and freight, by the company: theatrical: late C. 19–20.

travel out of the record. To wander from the point: coll.: from mid-1850's; ob. Dickens in *Little Dorrit*. Cf. *off the map*.

travel the road. To take to highway robbery: euphemistic coll.: C. 18–mid-19. Farquhar, in *The Beaux' Stratagem*, 1707. Cf. sense 1 of:

traveller. A highwayman: coll.: C. 18–mid-19. Cf. preceding.—2. A tramp: from ca. 1760: coll. till late C. 19, then dial.; ca. 1840–80, common among tramps (H., 1st ed.), and often = an itinerant hawker. Goldsmith (O.E.D.); Mayhew.—3. Esp. in Australia: 1869, 'Peripatetic Philosopher' Clarke: coll. >, by 1900, S.E.; ob.—4. Also *traveller at His* or *Her Majesty's Expense*. A convict sent abroad: ca. 1830–1910. H., 2nd ed., the longer form.—5. 'A thief who changes his quarry from town to town', F. & H.: c.: from ca. 1830; ob. Brandon. Cf. senses 1, 2.—6. A Gypsy: low: ca. 1865, in 'No. 747'.—7. A sermon delivered, by the one preacher, on different occasions and in various places: coll.: orig. (ca. 1890) and mainly ecclesiastical, esp. among theological students. (O.E.D.)—8. A walking ganger, a man in charge of a section of the job on which are working gangs of navvies under the charge of ordinary gangers, or gangs of bricklayers, etc.: Public Works coll. (– 1935).

traveller, tip the. See **tip the traveller**. (Occ. *put the traveller*: Manchon.)

traveller's tale or **talent.** Exaggeration; romancing: ca. 1820–50. Ex preceding.

travelling circus. A group of machine-gunners moving from point to point; a staff tour of inspection of the trenches: military: 1915–18. F. & Gibbons. Cf. *circus*, q.v.

['Travelling language' is a C. 18 term—it occurs, e.g. in Bampfylde-Moore Carew—for the s. of vagabonds and, to a less degree, of criminals.]

travelling piquet. A coll. name, ca. 1785–1840, for 'a mode of amusing themselves, practised by two persons riding in a carriage, each reckoning towards his game '—app. 100 points—'the persons or animals that pass by on the side next them, according to the following estimation', which ranges from 'a man or woman walking', 1' to 'a parson riding a grey horse, with blue furniture; game.' Grose, 3rd ed.

travelling scholarship. Rustication: jocular coll., Oxford and Cambridge University: from early 1790's to mid-C. 19. *The Gentleman's Magazine*, 1794, p. 1085, 'Soho, Jack! almost presented with a travelling scholarship? very nigh being sent to grass, hey?'

Travelling Tinkers, the. The 30th Regiment (Lancashires): military (– 1909) Ware.

traverse. See **cart, traverse the**, and **Tom Cox's traverse.—traviata.** See **come the traviata**.

trawl, trawl-net ; troll, troll-net. In C. 18–20, occ. confused. (O.E.D.)

*tre-moon. An occ. variant of *tree-moon*.

*tray, trey. Three, whether as number or set : c. >, ca. 1910, low s. : from mid-1890's. Ex *tray, trey,* the 3 at dice or cards.—2. Hence (also *tray-, trey-bit*), a threepenny piece : low : 1907 in O.E.D. ; but prob. several years earlier.—3. **tray soddy mits,** threepence halfpenny : Parlyaree and low London : late C. 19–20. Here, *soddy* = It. *soldi* (see **saltee**) and *mits* = It. *mezzo,* a half (see **madza**).—4. In pl. (*trays*), infantrymen : military : 1915 ; ob. F. & Gibbons. Ex their usefulness for carrying things. Cf. *something to hang things on* and *Christmas tree.*— 5. See **tree-moon.**

tray bon for the troops. (Very) good ; of a girl, attractive : military : 1915. B. & P. Ex Fr. *très bon ;* see also **troops.**

tray beans. See **trez beans.—tray-bit.** See **tray,** 2.—**tray jake.** See **jake.—trays.** See **tray,** 4.

treacle. Thick, inferior port : from ca. 1780. Ex thick sediment.—2. Love-making, as in *treacle moon,* a honeymoon : coll. : 1815, Byron ; ob. Ex sweetness.

treacle-factory. A training-ship : naval : late C. 19–20. Bowen. Ex the heavy ' incidence ' of molasses.

*treacle-man. A ' beautiful male decoy . . . pretended young man of the housemaid and the real forerunner of the burglar ' : c. : from ca. 1880. Ex *treacle,* 2.—2. Hence, a ' commercial ' touting sewing-machines, etc., to women : commercial travellers' : late C. 19–20. Ware.—3. He who makes the smartest sales : drapers' assistants', (— 1909). Ware.

Treacle Town. Bristol : (low) coll. : from ca. 1870. Ex the sugar-refineries.—2. Macclesfield : coll. and, esp. Cheshire, dial. : from ca. 1880. Ex a hogshead of treacle bursting and, for a time, filling the gutters (F. & H.) : but Dr Bridge, *Cheshire Proverbs,* 1917, doubts this.

tread, chuck a. (Of the male) to coït : low : from ca. 1860. Cf. *treadle.*

tread on the gas. See **gas, step on the.**

treader. (Gen. pl.) A shoe : low : from ca. 1880 ; ob.

treadle, treddle. A whore : low : ca. 1630–1890. Ford, 1638 ; Halliwell. By a pun on the lever so named + *tread* (copulate with).

treason-monger. A dynamiter : political : 1885–86. Ware.

treasure. (Of a person) a ' gem ' or ' jewel ' : coll. : 1810, Lady Granville (O.E.D.). A certain lady calls all her maid-servants, irrespective of quality, ' treasures '.

treasury, the. The weekly payment : theatrical (— 1874). H., 5th ed. (Introduction, p. 60.)

treat. Something very enjoyable or gratifying ; the pleasure therefrom or the delight therein : coll. : 1805, E. Dayes. Rarely of a person (1825, Lady Granville). O.E.D. Esp. *a fair treat.*—2. Anything, anybody, objectionable or a great nuisance : low ironic coll. : from 1890's. F. & H.—3. **a treat,** adv. : most gratifyingly ; very well indeed : low coll. : 1899, *The Daily News,* May 8, ' This air makes yer liver work a treat,' O.E.D. Often ironically or vaguely it = extremely : C. 20, low coll.—4. **do a treat.** To suit admirably : low coll. (— 1904). F. & H., ' " It does me a *treat* " = " That's O.K. ; real jam, and no error." ' All senses : ultimately

ex *treat,* entertainment offered by another person, but senses 2–4 derive imm. ex 1.

treat, a. See preceding, 3.—**treat, do a.** Ibid, 4.

treble-seam. A three-seamed leather cricket ball : cricket s. (1897, *The Globe,* July 1) >, ca. 1920, coll. ; slightly ob. (O.E.D.)

Treble X's, the. The 30th Foot Regiment >, ca. 1880, the 1st Battalion of the East Lancashire Regiment : military : mid-C. 19–20 ; ob. Ex ' XXX ' in Roman numerals. Also *the Three Tens* and *the Triple X's.*

trecoil. Treacle : Bootham School (— 1925). Anon., *Dict. of Bootham Slang.*

treddle. See **treadle.**

*tree. Only as in *treewins* and *tree-moon,* qq.v.

tree, v. To put in a difficulty ; drive to the end of one's resources : orig. (1818 : Thornton) U.S., anglicised in the 1850's as a coll. >, by 1880, S.E. Henry Kingsley, 1859, ' It's no use . . . you are treed,' O.E.D. Ex treeing an animal. Cf. *tree, up a.*

tree, bark up the wrong. See **bark.**

tree, lame as a. Extremely lame : lower classes' coll. (— 1887). Baumann. Perhaps ex the noisy walking of a man with a wooden leg.

tree, up a. Cornered ; done for ; in a serious difficulty ; penniless : coll. : U.S. (1825), anglicised ca. 1840, Thackeray in 1839 having ' Up a tree, as the Amercans say.' Ex a hunted animal taking refuge in a tree. Also *up the tree* (Baumann) and *up a tree for tenpence.*

*tree-moon. Three months' imprisonment : c. : mid-C. 19–20. ' *No. 747* ' (= year 1845). Also *trey* (or *tray) of moons,* often in C. 20, abbr. to *tray* or *trey.*

Tree of Knowledge. ' The tree under which books, etc., are piled in the interval between morning school and [lunch],' F. & H. : Charterhouse : from ca. 1860 ; ob. by 1900, † by 1920. Punning the lit. sense.

treer. ' A boy who avoids organised sports, but plays a private game with one or two friends. [Presumably because played at the trees by the side of the ground] ', F. & H. : Durham School : ca. 1850–90.

*treewins. Threepence : c. : late C. 17–20 ; ob. B.E. Cf. *treswins,* q.v. Ex **win,* n.

trek. To depart : from ca. 1890 : coll., orig. and mainly South African. Ex *trek,* to journey by ox-wagon, hence to migrate,—itself ex Dutch.

tremble, (all) in a or all of a ; (up)on the tremble. Trembling, esp. with emotion : coll. : resp. 1719, ca. 1760 (Henry Brooke) ; 1800 (Lamb). O.E.D.

trembly. Tremulous ; quivering : coll. : 1848, Dickens, ' So trembly and shaky ', O.E.D.

tremendous. As a mere hyperbole or intensive (= astounding ; immense) : coll. : 1812, Southey, ' A tremendous change has been going on.' O.E.D. Cf. *awful, terrible.*—2. Extraordinary as regards some quality stated in the context : from ca. 1830. George Eliot, 1866, ' A tremendous fellow at the classics '. O.E.D.

tremendously. Very greatly, extremely, excessively : coll. : mid-C. 19–20. Ex *tremendous,* 1, q.v. D. Mackail, *Greenery Street,* 1925, ' So frightfully and *tremendously* proud.'

trench-mortar. A bed-pan : military : from 1915. B. & P.

*trepan. See **trapan.**

*treswins. Threepence : c. (— 1725) ; ob. *A New Canting Dict.,* 1725. Cf. *treewins,* q.v.

Trew John. See **Trudjon.**

*trey. See tray.—*treyn(e), treyning-cheat. See trine, v., 2, and trining cheat.

trez (occ. tray) beans. Very well (adv.); very good or pleasant : military : 1916 ; ob. B. & P. Ex Fr. *très bien*. Cf. *Fray Bentos*, q.v.

tri. A tricycle : coll. : C. 20. Cf. *three-wheeler*, q.v.

Triangle Dinks, the. See Diamond Dinks.

triangles ; gen. the triangles. Delirium tremens : low (— 1864) ; very ob. H. 3rd ed. A perversion of *tremens*, prob. on *the trembles* and perhaps also with an allusion to the percussive musical instrument ; H., however, suggests that it is because, during 'd.t.'s', one sees everything 'out of the square'. Cf. *heeby-jeebies, jim-jams, jitters*, and *willies*.

triantelope ; occ. triantulope. A tarantula : an Australian coll. and popular corruption of that word : 1846, C. P. Hodgson, *Reminiscences of Australia*. On *antelope*.

*trib. A prison : c. : late C. 17–early 19. Abbr. *tribulation*, as remarked by B.E., who implies a more gen. sense in ' *He is in Trib*, . . . he is layd by the Heels, or in a great deal of trouble.' Grose, 1st ed. Cf. :

tribulation. 'The condition of being held in pawn' ; ca. 1660–1780. Dryden. (O.E.D.)

trichi, -y ; occ. tritchie, -y. A Trichinopoli cigar : 1877, Sir Richard Burton. Yule & Burnell.

*trick. A watch : c. of late C. 18–mid-19. Tufts, 1798. Ex *trick*, a small, esp. if cheap, toy or ornament, a trinket.—2. A person, esp. a child, that is alert and amusing : Australian and New Zealand coll. : late C. 19–20.

trick, do the. To effect one's purpose, do what is necessary or desirable : coll. (— 1812) >, by 1870 or so, S.E. Vaux ; Egan's Grose.—2. Hence (absolutely), to get a woman with child : low coll. : from ca. 1830.

trick and a half. 'A master-stroke of roguery', F. & H. : coll. : C. 19. A development ex *a trick worth two of that* (not coll. but S.E.).

*trickar ; properly tricker. A device for opening a window : c. : late C. 16–early 17. Greene, 1592. ? cf. *jigger*.

trickett. A long drink of beer : New South Wales : ca. 1895–1910. Ex Trickett, that champion sculler who knew that 'beer's best for an A1 nation.' Morris.

trickle. To go : jocular coll. : 1920, P. G. Wodehouse (O.E.D. Sup.) ; ob. Cf. *filter*.—2. See trickle, n., in Addenda.

tricks, bag of. See bag of tricks.

tricks, been playing. Pregnant : euphemistic coll. : C. 19–20 ; ob.

tricks ?, how's. How are you ; how are things going ? : C. 20. (Michael Harrison, 1935.) Ex cards.

trickum legis. A quirk or quibble in the law : jocular : ca. 1790–1850. Grose, 3rd ed. Lit., a trick of the law, -*um* pointing the jest at Law Latin.

tricky. Unexpectedly difficult, needing careful handling or cautious action ; catchy, risky : coll. : 1887, Saintsbury, ' One of the tricky things called echo sonnets ', O.E.D. (By 1935, virtually S.E.)

trier ; tryer (try-er). A player that perseveres in the attempt to win : cricket s. (1891) >, ca. 1905, gen. sporting coll. *The Century Dict*.

trifa. See tripha.—triffing. See tiffing.

*trig. A piece of stick or paper left in the front door ; if still there the next day, it practically shows

that the house is unoccupied. The act is, *to trig the jigger* (door) : c. (— 1812). Vaux. Ex *trig*, brake, a sprag.—2. A hurried walk, a tramp : from ca. 1880 : dial. and coll. Cf. v., 1, q.v.—3. Trigonometry : coll., esp. schools' and universities' : from not later than 1908 and prob. from mid-C. 19.

trig, v. Grose, 2nd ed., ' *To trig it*, to play truant ' : from late 1780's ; slightly ob. Ex (S.E. > dial.) *trig*, to walk quickly : whence also *trig*, n., 2, q.v.—2. See trig, n., 1.—3. V.i. To pull the trigger of a camera in taking a snapshot : from ca. 1925. Collinson.

trig-hall. Open house ; Liberty Hall : late C. 18–20 : dial. and (low) coll., the latter † by 1900. Grose's *Provincial Glossary* ; F. & H. Ex North Country dial. *trig*, to stuff, to cram, to fill up (esp. the stomach). (E.D.D.)

trigging, lay a man. To knock him down : ca. 1785–1850. Grose, 3rd ed. Perhaps ex the v. *trig* of ninepins ; or ex *trig*, v., 1, q.v.

trigonometry ; gen. commit t. Trigamy : jocular : C. 20.—2. Occ. bigamy (cf. *eternal triangle*).

trigry-mate ; gen. trigrymate. ' An idle She-Companion', B.E. : late C. 17–20 : s. >, early in C. 19, dial. Grose, 1st ed. Ex *trig*, to walk briskly. (The form *trigimate* is dial.)—2. Hence, an intimate friend : C. 19–20 : coll. > dial. Halliwell.

trike. A tricycle ; to ride a tricycle : (low) coll. : 1885 (O.E.D. Sup.) ; 1901, *The Pall Mall Gazette*, May 15, ' The commercial " trike " is, perhaps, the least supportable of the various tyrannies on wheels which it is the perambulating Londoner's lot to endure.' On *bike*, q.v. ; cf. Fr. and English *tri*. Hence, *triker*, the rider of one, and *triking*, such cycling : coll. : from late 1880's. Barrère & Leland.

trilby. A ' woman's exquisite foot ' : Society : 1894–ca. 96. Ware. Ex Du Maurier's *Trilby*.—2. A trilby hat : coll. : 1897, *The Daily News*, Feb. 6 (O.E.D. Sup.). Same source.

Trilbys. Pig's feet or trotters : West Yorkshire s. (— 1905), not dial. E.D.D. Cf. *Trilby*, 1.

trilithonic. Trilithic : erroneous form : from the 1830's. O.E.D.

trill. The anus : ? late C. 17–mid-19. Halliwell. ? ex crepitation : cf. *ars musica*.

*trim. To cheat ; to fleece : C. 17–20. Dekker ; implied by B.E. in ' *Trimming*, c. Cheating People of their Money ' ; Edgar Wallace, 1928 (O.E.D. Sup.) ; c. >, by 1720, s. Prob. ex *trim*, to thrash ; cf. :

trim one's jacket. To thrash a person : coll. : 1748, Smollett (O.E.D.). An elaboration of S.E. *trim*, to thrash, with perhaps an allusion to *trim*, to decorate (a hat) or dress (hair : cf. *dress down*, q.v.).

trim the buff. (Absolutely.) To deflower, or merely to coït with, a woman : 1772, Bridges, ' And he . . . has liberty to take and trim | The buff of that bewitching brim,' i.e. harlot ; ob. Ex *buff*, the human skin ; and cf. *trim one's jacket*.

trimmer. A person who, a thing which, *trims* or thrashes, lit. or fig. : e.g. a stiff letter, article, review ; a strict disciplinarian ; a redoubtable competitor, fighter, runner (human or animal) ; a severe fight, blow, run, etc. ; an especially well-delivered ball at cricket : coll. : 1776, Foote, of a severe leading article ; 1804, Nelson, of a letter—as, in 1816, Scott ; 1827, *The Sporting Magazine*, of a hound ; 1832, P. Egan, ' At last a trimmer Dick sent down,'

—cf. 1882, 'Clean bowled by a trimmer', F. & H.; O.E.D.; Lewis. Cf. the adj. in:

*trimming, n. See trim, v.—2. Adj. Excellent, 'rattling': coll.: 1778, the Earl of Carlisle, 'Such trimming gales as would make . . . a landsman . . . stare'; 1825, *The Sporting Magazine*, of a run with hounds; slightly ob. Cf. preceding entry. O.E.D.

trimmingly. To a notable extent; excellently: coll.: 1789, A. C. Bowers, 'I had the gout trimmingly,' O.E.D.; ob. Ex *trimming*, adj., q.v.; cf. *trimmer.*

trimmings. Masked alcohol: tradesmen's: 1897, *The Daily Telegraph*, Jan. 18. Ware.

trincum; gen. **trinkum**; occ. **trinkrum.** A trinket: from mid-1660's: S.E. until C. 19, then coll. (very ob.) and dial.: resp. C. 18–20, C. 17–20, late C. 19–20. Scott, 1819 (O.E.D.). Merely *trinket* with 'Latin' *-um* for *-et.*—2. For reduplicated forms, see **trinkum-trankum.**

*Trine. Tyburn: c. of mid-C. **17–18.** Coles, 1676. Ex sense 2 of:

*trine. To go: c. of C. 17–mid-19. Fletcher 1622; Scott. A survival from S.E. *trine*, to go, to march (C. 14–16), itself of Scandinavian origin. (O.E.D.)—2. V.i. and t., to hang: c. of ca. 1560–1840, but, like sense 1, ob. as early, prob., as mid-C. 18. Harman, B.E., Grose. Also *tryne*, C. 16–17, and *treyn(e)*, C. 17. Perhaps, as the O.E.D. observes, ex a shortening of *trine to the cheats*, to go to the gallows, to be hanged.

tringham trangham, tringum-trangum. See **trinkum-trankum.**

*trining, treyning, tryning. An execution by hanging: see **trine**, v., 2.

Trinity. Trinity College: Oxford and Cambridge coll.: mid-C. 18–20.

trinity (or **Trinity**) **kiss.** 'A triple kiss—generally given by daughters and very young sons, when going to bed, to father and mother': Society: ca. 1870–80. Ware.

trinkety; incorrectly **trinketty.** Of little importance or value: (rare) coll.: 1817, Scott. O.E.D.

trinkum. See **trincum.**

trinkum-trankum; also **tringham trangham, tringum-trangum.** A trinket (C. 18–20); a whim or fancy (late C. 17–early 19): s. >, early in C. 19, mainly dial. B.E., *tringum-trangum*, 'a Whim, or Maggot'; 1702, Steele, *tringham trangham*, as adj.; 1718, Motteux, *trinkum-trankum*. Reduplicated *trinkum* (see at **trincum**). Mostly O.E.D.

*trip. A harlot; a thief's woman: c.: from mid-1870's; slightly ob. Horsley, *Jottings from Jail*, 1877. ? ex *tripping* motion.—2. Hence, an affectionate term of address: lower classes' (— 1923). Manchon. Cf. Fr. *cocotte.*—3. (Trip.) Tripos: Cambridge University coll.: from ca. 1920. (O.E.D. Sup.)

tripe. Utter nonsense; very inferior writing, singing, acting, etc. etc.: from ca. 1890: coll. verging on S.E. Crockett, 1895, 'A song . . . worth a shopful of such "tripe",' O.E.D. Ex the *tripe* as typical of inferior food, etc.—2. See **tripes.**—3. An occ. abbr. of *tripe-hound*, 1. F. & Gibbons.—4. Tissues for microscopic examination: medical students' (— 1933). *Slang*, p. 193. Also *meat.*

tripe, bag of. A term of opprobrium for a person: low coll. or perhaps rather a vulgarism: C. 19–20. Cobbett, 1822 (O.E.D.). Suggested by *tripes*, q.v. Cf.:

tripe, blooming six feet of (or **six blooming feet of**).

A tall, solid policeman: low urban: from ca. 1880; ob. Ware.

Tripe, Mr Double. A (very) fat man: low: ca. 1780–1850. Grose, 1st ed.

tripe, up to. Worthless; thoroughly objectionable: lower classes': C. 20. F. & Gibbons. Ex *tripe*, 1.

tripe-hound. A naval nickname for 'the Sopwith triplane used for a short time by the R.N.A.S.': during the G.W. (Bowen.) The *tripe* puns '*tri*-plane', whereas *hound* is a reference to the fact that it behaved like a bitch. Imm. ex:—2. A foul, an objectionable fellow: lower classes': C. 20. Manchon.

triper is an East London corruption (— 1909) of *tripha*, q.v. Ware.

tripes; **tripe.** (Very rare, after C. 18, in the singular.) The intestines; the paunch containing them: mid-C. 15–20: S.E. until mid-C. 18, then coll.; in mid-C. 19–20, low coll. Grose, 1st ed. (*tripe*; *tripes* implied); Hood, 1834, 'I'm as marciful as any on 'em—and I'll stick my knife in his tripes as says otherwise.'

tripes and trillibubs or **trullibubs.** A jeering nickname for a fat man: ca. 1780–1880. Grose, 1st ed. Lit., the entrails (of an animal). Cf. *tripe, bag of*, and *Tripe, Mr Double*, qq.v.; see also **tripes.**

tripha or **trifa**, ritually unclean (opp. *kosher*), is Hebrew; it can be considered as s. only when it is loosely applied by Gentiles to things other than food.

*triple tree. A gallows: c. of ca. 1630–1750, then only archaical. Randolph, ca. 1834; Brome, 1641; T. Brown, ca. 1700. Ex the three parts.

Triple X's, the. See **Treble X's, the.**

Tripoly, come from. To vault, tumble; perform spiritedly: s. (— 1847); † by 1890. Halliwell. Ex performances of Moorish dancers.

*tripos. The intestines; the paunch: c. (— 1887). Baumann. On *tripes* (see **tripe**).

tripos pup. An 'undergrad' Cantab doing Honours: Cambridge undergraduates' (— 1887); ob. Ware.

tripper. An excursionist: coll.: 1813, 'Trippers to the seaside for a week'. Also *cheap tripper*, one who goes on a cheap trip: coll.: 1872. O.E.D.

*tripper-up. One who *trips* and then robs a person: c.: from mid-1880's. *The Daily Chronicle*, Nov. 18, 1887.—2. A woman preying on drunken men: c.: C. 20. J. Sweeney, *Scotland Yard*, 1904 (O.E.D.).

*tripping-up. The criminal practices in *tripper-up*, 1 and 2, qq.v.

trippist. A 'tripper' (q.v.): coll.: 1792 (O.E.D.); rare in C. 20; virtually † by 1930.

Tristram's knot, Sir. A halter: esp. in *tie Sir Tristram's knot*, to hang: coll.: ? C. 17–19. F. & H.

tritchie, -y; or **T.** See **trichi.**—***tritrace.** See **troll.**

triumph, ride. To go helter-skelter or full tilt: ca. 1760–1850: coll. bordering on S.E. Sterne, 1761. Presumably abbr. *ride in triumph.*

triumpherate, -ery. Incorrect for *triumvirate*, *triumviry*: C. 17; late C. 16–17. Shakespeare has both. By confusion with *triumph*. O.E.D.

Troc, the. The Trocadero: 'formerly Music Hall, now [1904] Restaurant', F. & H.: orig. and mostly London: from late 1880's. Cf. *the Cri, the Pav*, qq.v.

trochulus, troculus are incorrect for *trochilus*: C. 18, C. 17–20. O.E.D.

troffy. See **trophy, 2.**

Trojan. A roysterer, boon companion, a dissolute : C. 17–mid-18. Kemp, 1600 ; adumbrated in Shakespeare, 1588. Ex the fame of Troy.—2. Hence, a good fellow : coll. : from ca. 1660, though adumbrated in Kemp (as in 1) ; ob. Butler, 1663, ' True Trojans ' ; Scott, 1827, ' Trusty as a Trojan ', *true* and *trusty* being the usual epithets : cf. *trusty trout*, q.v. O.E.D.—3. A brave, plucky, or energetic person (rarely of a woman) ; gen. in *like a Trojan*, very pluckily or, in C. 20 always, energetically : coll. : 1838 (in *Fraser's Magazine* ; 1841, in book form), Thackeray, ' He bore . . . [the amputation] . . . like a Trojan ' ; 1855, Dickens, ' He went on lying like a Trojan about the pony ' (Apperson). Cf. *like a trooper* (at *trooper*).

*troll occurs in four phrases in Awdelay, 1561, as c. of ca. 1550–80 :—**troll and troll by**, one who, esteemed by none, esteems nobody,—perhaps ex C. 14–17 *troll*, to saunter or ramble ; **troll hazard of trace**, one who follows his master ' as far as he may see him ',—cf. *trace = track*(*s*), n. ; **t. h. of tritrace**, ' he that goeth gaping after his master ', in reference to *trey-trace*, of obscure origin but connected, allusively, with *try-*[*to-*]*trace* ; and **troll with**, one who, a servant, is not to be known from his master.—2. See **trawl.**

trollop. A woman, respectable, or otherwise : Oxford University and underworld coll. : from ca. 1923.

trollywags. Trousers : low : from ca. 1870 ; very ob. ? on *bags*, q.v.

tromboning, go. To coït : low : from late 1880's. By anatomical analogy. Cf. *flute.*

troop. To march, walk, pass, in order : late C. 16–20 : S.E. until mid-C. 20, then coll., though only just coll., as the O.E.D. makes quite clear.

troop away, off, etc. To depart : coll. : 1700, T. Brown, ' I thought 'twas time to troop off to an eating-house,' O.E.D.

*trooper. A half-crown : c. : late C. 17–early 19. B.E. ; Grose. (? a ' brave ' coin, or because it frequently formed part of a trooper's pay.)

trooper, like a. Much ; hard ; vigorously : coll. : 1727, *swear like a trooper*, the most frequent use ; the O.E.D. records *eat like a trooper* in 1812, *lie* . . . in 1854 ; but in C. 20, anything but *swear* is ob. Cf. *Trojan*, 3, q.v., and see also **swear like a cutter.**

trooper's horse, you will die the death of a. A jocular c.p. = ' You will be hanged ' : ca. 1780–1850. Grose, 1st ed., ' That is with your shoes on '.

troops, the. We, us ; I, me : military : from 1914. Esp. in *that's the stuff to give the troops*, that is what I (we) want or enjoy.

trooso. A sol. spelling of *trousseau* : late C. 19–20. (Francis Beeding, *The One Sane Man*, 1934.)

trophy. A convert : Salvation Army j. >, by 1920, coll. Manchon.—2. A dull-witted recruit : military : from ca. 1910. F. & Gibbons. Ex sergeant-major's irony. Also *troffy* (B. & P.).

tropical. (Of language) blasphemous ; obscene : from ca. 1920. Ex *tropical*, very hot.

trork. A quart : back s. (— 1874). H., 5th ed. Variant of *track* (*trag*), q.v.

tros ; tross. Sort : back s. (— 1859 in form *trosseno* : H., 1st ed.). Thus *trosseno*, lit. ' one sort ', is used for a ' bad sort ' (of day, coin, etc.), as also is *dabtros*, the more precise form of ' bad sort '.

trossy. Dirty; slatternly; slovenly : lower

classes' : late C. 19–20. F. & Gibbons. Perhaps ex preceding.

trot. A child learning to run : coll. : 1854, Thackeray, ' Ethel romped with the . . . rosy little trots.' (Cf. *toddles*.) Hence, in late C. 19–20, *trottie*, a toddling child.—2. Hence, a small and/or young animal : coll. : from 1890's.—3. A walk ; e.g. *do a trot* : from ca. 1875 : London lower-classes' coll. >, ca. 1910, gen. Ware.—4. A succession of heads thrown at two-up : Australians' and New Zealanders' : late C. 19–20. I.e. *trot* = a run.—5. See **trots.**

*trot. ' To steal in broad daylight ' : c. : from ca. 1860. F. & H.—2. To walk with short, quick steps in a small area : coll. : 1863, Mrs Cowden Clarke, ' She . . . will keep her husband trotting,' O.E.D.—3. See **trot out—round** (or **to**)—and **up.**

trot, lie as fast as a dog can. To be a persistent liar : coll. : C. 19–20 ; ob.

trot it out ! Lit., show it : see next, sense 1.—2. Hence, speak ! : confess ! : from ca. 1890. Cf. *spit it out !* and *cough it up !*

trot out. To bring out (a person, hence an opinion, etc.) for inspection and/or approval ; hence, to exhibit : coll. : 1838, Lytton (O.E.D.) ; 1888, Christie Murray, ' They would sit for hours solemnly trotting out for one another's admiration their commonplaces.' Ex the leading out of a horse to show his paces.—2. Hence, to spend, as in *trot out the pieces* : (low) coll. : mid-C. 19–20.—3. Cf. *trot out a song*, to sing one : from ca. 1870. This *trot* is generic for *do* and it occurs in such phrases as *trot out a speech*. Equivalent also is *trot it out !* (q.v.), where the connexion with sense 1 is obvious. —4. To walk out with (a woman), lover-wise : 1888, ' John Strange Winter ' (O.E.D.). Esp. *trot out a judy* : low s. See **judy.** Cf. the analogous *trout round*.—5. **trot out one's pussy** (or **feed** it), to receive a man sexually : low : mid-C. 19–20. See **pussy.**

trot round, to. To escort or conduct round or to a place : from the middle 1890's. ' Seton Merriman ', 1898, ' Perhaps you'll trot us round the works,' O.E.D. Prob. a development from *trot out, 4*, q.v.

trot the udyju, Pope o' Rome. To side-track or dismiss one's wife or other woman : low urban (mostly London) : late C. 19–20. In transposed s., *udyju* is *judy* (woman, girl), while *Pope o' Rome* is rhyming s. for *home*. (Ware.)

trot-town. A loafer, an idler : London coll. (— 1887) ; ob. Baumann.

trot up. To bid against (a person), run up (a price) : auctioneers' s. (— 1864) >, ca. 1910, coll. H., 3rd ed. Cf. S.E. *trot*, to draw a person out, or on, in conversation in order to make him a butt.

trots. (Very rare in singular.) Feet : low London (— 1909). Ware. Ex *trotters*.—2. (Rare in singular.) Policeman : lower classes' : mid-C. 19–20 ; slightly ob. Because so much ' on the go ' or *trot.* Ware.

trotter. A tailor's assistant who touts for orders . Oxford and Cambridge (— 1860). H., 2nd ed.—2. One who goes, without residence, to Dublin for a degree : Dublin University : from ca. 1880.—3. A day-student : Durham University : from ca. 1890. O.E.D.

trotter-boxes, gen. **-cases.** Boots ; shoes : low : mid-C. 19–20 ; 1820, Hood (O.E.D.), and Dickens in 1838,—*boxes* is vouched for by F. & H. ; both are

ob. Also *trotting-cases*: from late 1850's; **ob.** H., 1st ed.

trotters. The human feet: jocular coll. verging on S.E.: late C. 17–20. B.E. has *shake your trotters !*, be gone ! ; C. 19–20 variants are *move your trotters !*, and, nautical, *box your trotters*, but the earliest remains gen. Cf. :

trotters at B(e)ilby's ball, shake one's ; sometimes with addition of **where the sheriff pays the fiddlers.** To be put in the stocks: low s. bordering on c. : ca. 1780–1840. Grose, 1st ed., 'Perhaps the Bilboa's ball, i.e. the ball of fetters : fetters and stocks were anciently called the bilboes.' At *Beilby's ball*, however, see another interpretation.

trottie. See **trot,** n., 1, and **trotty.**—**trotting-cases.** See **trotter-boxes.**

trotty ; occ. **trottie.** (Adj.) Of small and dainty make or build : coll. : 1891, 'Lucas Malet' (O.E.D. Sup.). Ex *trot*, n., 1.

trouble. Imprisonment ; arrest. Mostly in (*be*) *in trouble*, (be) in gaol : coll. in C. 16, s. in C. 19–20 : recorded ca. 1560 (in Cavendish's *Wolsey*), but app. then rare until C. 19. Cf. *get into trouble*, to be fined, arrested, imprisoned, transported : from ca. 1820. Prob. euphemistic.—2. As, certainly, is *trouble*, unmarried pregnancy : coll. : 1891, Hardy (O.E.D.)

trouble. To trouble oneself ; to worry : coll. : 1880, Justin McCarthy ; W. C. Smith, 1884, 'Do not trouble to bring back the boat.' O.E.D. Ex *trouble oneself*, to take the trouble.

trouble and strife. A wife : rhyming s. : late C. 19–20. Cf. the C. 16 proverb, *he that hath a wife hath strife.*

troubled with corns, that horse is. I.e., foundered : c.p. : C. 19–20 ; ob.

troubled with the slows. (Of swimmer or boat) defeated : aquatics (— 1909). Ware.

trouser, trowser. A Jack of all trades : East London : from ca. 1895. Ware. Ex the 'comprehensiveness' of trousers.

trouser, v. To put (money) into one's trouser-pocket, hence to pocket (it) : from ca. 1890.—2. Hence, to earn : cabmen's (— 1892). *Labour Commission Glossary*, 1892. O.E.D. Cf. *put down south*, which *trouser*, 1, may have suggested.

(trousers) !, not in these. See **boots !, not in these.**

trousies. Trousers : sol. : mid-C. 19–20. Baumann. (Implied in *round my* or *the houses*.)

trout. Orig. and gen., *trusty* (ca. 1661) or *true* (1682) *trout*, a good fellow (cf. *Trojan*, 2), a trusted servant or a confidential friend ; Shadwell has *your humble trout*, your humble servant. S. of ca. 1660–1830 ; extant, however, in *old trout*, q.v. B.E. ; Grose ; O.E.D. Contrast (*poor* and *queer*) *fish*. Perhaps suggested by the alliteration of *true Trojan* (later, *trusty Trojan*).

trouting, n. Catching trout : anglers' coll. : 1898, *The People*, April 3 (Ware.)

trowser. See **trouser,** n.

truck. A hat : nautical (— 1864) ; ob. H., 3rd ed., 'From the cap on the extremity of a mast', whence also, at least prob., is *truck-gutted.*

***truck,** v. ; frequent as vbl.n., **trucking.** Of obscure meaning ; I hazard the guess that it signifies : by legerdemain, to keep buying things with more or less the same coins ; or, to steal certain more useful or valuable articles while getting change for the purchase of lesser articles. C. of mid-C. 19–20 ; † by 1910. '*No. 747*.'

truck-gutted. Pot-bellied : nautical (— 1860) slightly ob. H., 2nd ed.

***trucking.** See **truck,** v.

truckle (or **trundle-**) **bed, stumble at the.** To mistake the chambermaid's bed for one's wife's : semi-proverbial coll. : ca. 1670–1750. Ray, 1678.

trucks. Trousers : low (— 1859) ; slightly ob. H., 1st ed. Prob. ex *truck*, (collective for) small, miscellaneous articles of little value and/or lowly use.

truculent. Base ; mercenary : catachrestic : from 1820's. Ex *truck*, intercourse, + *truckle*, v. O.E.D.

Trudjon. A variant of *Trojan* : sol. (— 1887). Baumann (also *Trew John*).

True. A member of the Whig Party : late C. 17 coll. nickname.

true as that the candle ate the cat or as (that) the cat crew and the cock rocked the cradle. I.e. untrue, false : a semi-proverbial coll. or c.p. : mid-C. 16–18 : 1666, Torriano, the former ; 1732, Fuller, the latter. Apperson, who also quotes *that's as true as [that] I am his uncle* (Ray, 1670).

True Blue. See **Blue, True.**

true for you ! An Anglo-Irish c.p. of assent to another's statement : from early 1830's. O.E.D. (Sup.). Direct ex Irish.

true inwardness. Reality ; quintessence : literary j. verging on s. : from ca. 1890 ; ob. Ware.

truepenny, n. and adj. An honest fellow ; true, genuine : coll. : both from ca. 1590 ; in C. 19–20, ob., except in the earlier *old truepenny* (C. 16–20), a hearty old fellow, a staunch friend, an honest man : dial. in C. 19–20. Ex a *true* or genuine coin of that denomination.

truff, v. To steal : North country c. (— 1864). H., 3rd ed. Ex C. 18 (?–mid-19) Scots *truff*, to obtain deceitfully, pilfer, steal.

***truff.** A purse : c. : C. 18. C. Hitching, *The Regulator*, 1718. Perhaps by a pun on † S.E. *truff*, a truffle.

***trugging-house, -ken, -place.** A brothel : the first and third are c. or low s of ca. 1590–1620,— Greene has both ; the second, c. of (?) C. 17—only F. & H. records it. Ex *trug*, a whore, esp. a dirty one.

truly, yours. I ; myself : jocular coll. bordering on and, in C. 20, > S.E. : 1860, Sala (O.E.D.) ; 1866, Wilkie Collins, 'Yours truly, sir, has an eye for a fine woman and a fine horse.' Contrast *your nibs*.

trump. A very good fellow, a 'brick' : coll. : 1819 (O.E.D.) ; in Barham as a term of address (*my t.*), a usage † in C. 20. Adumbrated by T. Brydges in 1762, 'I . . . Shall make him know I'm king of trumps.' Egan's Grose, 'One who displays courage on every suit'.

trump, v. To break wind : low coll. : C. 18–20 ; very ob. D'Urfey. Hence the vbl.n., *trumping*, and *trumper*, the agential n. ; the latter is rare. O.E.D.

trump, tongue of the. See **tongue of . . .**

trump of the dump, the. Anyone in authority : New Zealanders' : in G.W.

trumpery insanity. Temporary insanity : a c.p. directed at the frequency of this verdict in cases of suicide : ca. 1880–1900. Baumann.

trumpet-cleaning, gone. Dead : Regular Army : late C. 19–20 ; ob. F. & Gibbons. Perhaps ex a martial vision of a job in the heavenly orchestra.

Trumpet Moore. Moore the poet, who blew his own. Dawson.

trumpeter as an endearment = 'dear boy'. (Low) coll. of ca. 1870–1900. Baumann.

trumpeter, King of Spain's or **Spanish.** A braying ass : ca. 1780–1850. Grose, 1st ed. (*K. of Spain's t.*). Ex the pun, *Don Key :: donkey*. Cf. :

trumpeter, for he smells strong,—he would make a good. A c.p. applied to one with fetid breath, *for he smells strong* being occ. omitted : ca. 1785–1850. Grose, 2nd ed., where the second member is *for he has a strong breath*. Ex the pun, *strong breath :: good lungs*. Cf. preceding.

trumpeter is dead, his (her, etc.**).** A c.p. applied to a person boasting or to a confirmed braggart : from ca. 1725 ; ob. Franklin, 1729 ; Grose, 2nd ed., in the orig. form, *his . . . dead, he is therefore forced to sound his own trumpet*, which supplies the 'etymology' ; but cf. also *trumpeter, King of Spain's*, q.v.

trumpety. Trumpet-like ; blaring : coll. : 1822, *The Examiner*. O.E.D.

trumps, turn up. To turn out well, prove a success : coll. : 1862, W. W. Collins (O.E.D.). Ex games of cards. Cf. *trump*, above.

truncheon. Stomach : West Yorkshire s. (— 1905), not dial. E.D.D., 'He filled his truncheon.'

trundle, the ob. coll. n. (1869 : Lewis) of :

trundle, v.t. and i. To bowl : cricket coll. : 1849 ; cf. *trundler*, bowler, 1871, and *trundling*, n., bowling, 1861. Lewis. 'Orig. the ball was trundled along the ground.' Cf. *wheel 'em up* and contrast *trundling bowler*.—2. See **let 'em trundle !**

trundler. See preceding.—2. In pl., peas : c. : ca. 1670–1830. Coles, 1676 ; B.E. ; Grose, 1st ed. Presumably because they roll along the ground. Cf. :

trundling. See **trundle,** v.—2. **trundling bowler** : one who, bowling fast, makes the ball bound three or four times : cricketers' coll. : 1851 ; † by 1890. Lewis.

*trundling-cheat. A wheeled vehicle, esp. cart or coach : 1630, Jonson ; † by 1700. Ex *trundle*, v.i., to roll along, + **cheat, chete*, q.v.

trunk. A nose : late C. 17–20. B.E. ; Grose, 1st ed. Esp. in phrases (see next two entries).—2. In pl. (also **T-**), shares in the Grand Trunk of Canada : Stock Exchange coll. (— 1895). A. J. Wilson's glossary.

trunk ?, how fares your old. A c.p. jeer at a big-nosed man : ca. 1690–1850. B.E. ; Grose, 1st ed. In allusion to an elephant's trunk.

trunk, shove a. 'To introduce oneself unasked into any place or company', Grose, 1st ed. : low : ca. 1780–1890.

trunkmaker-like. With more noise than work : ca. 1780–1840. Grose, 1st ed.

trunkmaker's daughter,—all round St Paul's, not forgetting the. A book-world c.p. applied to unsaleable books : late C. 18–early 19. *The Globe*, July 1, 1890, 'By the trunkmaker was understood . . . the depository for unsaleable books,' O.E.D. ; and St Paul's, then as now, was famed as a book-selling district.

trunks, live in one's. To be at a place for so short a time that it is not worth while to unpack ; to live in a confined space, esp. a ship's cabin : coll. (— 1931). Lyell.

Trunks. See **trunk,** 2.

trusted alone, he may be. He is very experienced

or shrewd : ca. 1820–50. Egan's Grose. Rather sarcastic, the implication being that he may be so trusted to go anywhere without danger to himself.

trusty. An overcoat : Anglo-Irish coll. : 1804, Maria Edgeworth. I.e. trustworthy garment.

trusty Trojan. See **Trojan,** 2.—**trusty trout.** See **trout.**

try. An attempt ; an effort : coll. verging on S.E. : from ca. 1830.

try, v.i., with **across, after, in,** etc. ; also v.t. To search (a place) to find (e.g. game) : coll. : v.i., 1810, *The Sporting Magazine*, ' He bid the other defend-ants try across the Six Acres ' ; v.t., late C. 19–20. O.E.D.

try a fresh needle ! ' Shut up ! ' : Charterhouse : from ca. 1910. Ex gramophones : cf. *switch off !*

try and (do something). To try to do something : 1686, J. Sergeant, 'They try and express their love to God by thankfulness,' O.E.D. : coll. now verging on S.E. (see Fowler).

try back ! A c.p. addressed to a person boasting : ca. 1820–60. Bee.

try it on. To make an attempt (to outwit, to impose on a person) : from ca. 1810 both in this s. sense and in c., where it = to live by theft. Vaux. Both as v.i., the more gen., and as v.t. (Thackeray, 1849, ' No jokes . . . ; no trying it on me,' O.E.D.). Hence, *coves that* or *who try it on*, professional thieves : c. : from ca. 1812.—2. See next two entries.

try it on a, gen. **the,** dog. To experiment at the risk or expense of another, esp. a subordinate or a wife : from ca. 1895 : theatrical s. (as in *The Daily Telegraph*, Feb. 4, 1897) >, ca. 1905, gen. coll. Ware. Ex *matinée dog* (q.v.), though ultimately ex experimenting with meat on a dog or with poisons on animals. In the film industry, it = to put a picture (not yet publicly shown) into a programme unannounced in order that its effect on the audience may be noted by the producers, who afterwards may make any alterations they think advantageous : coll. : from ca. 1920. Prob. ex the theatrical sense (C. 20), to take a new play to the provinces before London production : likewise coll.

try it on with. The usual v.t. form of *try it on* in s. sense : from ca. 1820. Esp. *try it on with a woman*, to attempt her chastity : 1823, 'Jon Bee'.

try-on. An attempt, orig. and gen., to 'best' someone ; e.g. an extortionate charge, a begging letter : from ca. 1820. Bee, 1823 ; H., 5th ed. Ex *try it on*, q.v.—2. Whence *up to the try-on* : see **up to the cackle.**

try-out. A selective trial : coll. : U.S. (— 1900), anglicised ca. 1910.

tryer. See **trier.**—**tryne.** See **trine.**

tu quoque. The female pudend : late C. 18–early 19. Grose, 2nd ed. Possibly suggested by *pu(dendum)* and *twat* ; or a disguising of the latter.

tub. A pulpit : from ca. 1640 (O.E.D. records it in 1643) : coll. >, ca. 1850, S.E. ; ob. Whence the coll. (verging on s.) terms, *tub-drubber* (ca. 1703, T. Brown ; very ob.), *-man* (ca. 1640–70), *-pounder* (rare ; ca. 1820–1910), *-preacher* (1643 ; very rare in C. 19–20), and, the commonest, *-thumper* (from ca. 1660 ; Grose, 1785, ' a Presbyterian parson ') ; also *tubster* (coll. : ca. 1680–1720). Likewise, *tub-thumping* (app., not before ca. 1850 : H., 1st ed.), etc. Ex the tub from within which popular, and esp. Nonconformist, clergymen used, in the open air, to preach, but also, and in several instances, independently ex the humorous likening of a pulpit to a tub. F. & H.; O.E.D.—2. A bath; the practice of having a bath, esp. on rising: coll.: 1849 (O.E.D.); 1886, *The Field*, Feb. 20, 'A good tub and a hearty breakfast prepared us for the work of the day.' Ex *tub*, a bath-tub.—3. A seatless carriage, an open truck: (low) coll.: ca. 1840–70. H. S. Brown, *Autobiography*, 1886 (O.E.D.).—4. ' A chest in Hall into which *dispars* (q.v.) not taken by the boys were put ', F. & H.: ca. 1840–70. Perhaps rather j. than s. or coll., as prob. also are *tub-mess* and *prefect of tub*: see Farmer's *Public School Word-Book*.—5. A (very) fat person: low coll.: from mid-1890's. Cf. *tubby*, q.v.—6. A cask or keg of spirit, holding about four gallons: smugglers' s. (– 1835) >, by 1860, coll.; ob. O.E.D. Ex *tub*, a varying measure of capacity.—7. An omnibus: c. (– 1933). Charles E. Leach, *On Top of the Underworld*.—8. **the Tub.** See **Academy, the.** The allusion is to the tub of Diogenes.

tub, v.t. To wash, bathe, in a tub: coll.: 1610, Jonson.—2. Hence v.i., to bath in a tub, esp. on rising: coll.: 1867 (O.E.D.).—3. To train (oarsmen) in a 'tub', i.e. a fool-proof practice boat: rowing s., orig. and esp. at the two older universities: 1883; the v.i., to practise rowing in a 'tub', dates from 1882. (Dates, O.E.D.) Whence *tubbing*, vbl.n. to both v.t. and v.i. (from 1883) and *get tubbed*, to be thus coached.—4. (Of a tug) to make (a ship—esp. a big ship) fast to a buoy: nautical coll.: late C. 19–20. Bowen.

tub, in the. See **in the tub.**

tub-drubber, -man. See **tub, n., 1.**

tub-men. 'Landsmen employed during the second, or secret, period of smuggling to receive the contraband from the luggers and carry it inland': ca. 1830–80: s. >, by 1860, coll. See **tub, n., 6.** (Bowen.)

tub-mess. See **tub, n., 4.**

tub-pair. A practice boat for two oarsmen: (orig. Oxford and Cambridge college) rowing s. >, ca. 1920, coll.: 1870 (O.E.D.). See **tub**, v., 3 and 4.

tub-pounder, -preacher, -thumper, -thumping. See **tub, n., 1.**

tubbichon. A non-cultured corruption of Fr. *tire-bouchon*, the lone corkscrew ringlet of back hair worn in front of the left shoulder (a fashion introduced by the Empress Eugénie): 1860's. Ware. Cf. *zander*, q.v.

tubbing. See **tub**, v., 3, 4.—2. Imprisonment: c.: late C. 19–20; ob. Why ?

tubby. Fat (person): as adj. (1835), S.E.; as nickname (mid-C. 19–20), coll.—2. The latrine-attendant: Christ's Hospital: from ca. 1870. Ex one so nicknamed.

tube. The tunnel in which runs an underground electric train: coll.: from ca. 1895.—2. Hence (often *the Tube*), abbr. *tube-railway*: coll.: 1900.—3. Hence, *the Twopenny Tube*, the Central London Railway (opened in): 1900: coll. (The inclusive fee (cf. the Paris *Métro*) was abolished not later than 1915.) O.E.D.

tube, v.i.; also **tube it.** To travel by 'tube': coll.: 1902 (O.E.D.). Ex n., 2.

tube-train. 'A shell passing high overhead and making a heavy rumbling sound ': military: 1915; ob. F. & Gibbons.

tuber. A race-horse with a *tube* inserted in the air-passage: turf: 1922 (O.E.D. Sup.).

tubs. A butter-man: low (– 1864); ob. H., 3rd ed. Ex butter in tubs.

tubster. See **tub, n., 1.**

tuca. Incorrect for *tuça* (gen. spelt *tuza*): late C. 18–20. O.E.D.

tuck. A hearty meal, esp. (orig. and mainly in schools) of delicacies: 1844, J. T. Hewlett. Also, in C. 19 more gen., *tuck-out*, 1823; occ. in C. 19, very often in C. 20, *tuck-in*, 1859, H., 1st ed. (Cf. *tucker*, q.v.) F. & H. and O.E.D. ? ex *tuck*, a fold or pleat: *tuck-out*, the earliest form, suggests a meal that removes a tuck or a crease from one's waistcoat or trousers-top; but prob. imm. ex the v., 2 and 3, qq.v.—2. Hence, food; esp. delicacies (e.g. pastry, jam): orig. and mainly school s.: 1857, Hughes, 'The Slogger looks rather sodden, as if he . . . ate too much tuck.'—3. Appetite: dial. and provincial s.: from the 1830's. Halliwell.

*****tuck**, v. To hang (a person): c. of late C. 17–19. B.E. But gen. *tuck up*: from mid-1730's: c. rapidly > (low) s.; in C. 20, ob. Richardson, 1740, 'The hangman asked the poor creature's pardon, and . . . then calmly tucked up the criminal.' Ex *tuck*, to put away in a safe place.—2. To eat, occ. to drink: v.t., 1784, Bage, 'We will . . . tuck up a bottle or two of claret '; hence, v.i., eat a lot or greedily, 1810; *tucking-in, tuck into* occurring in 1838 in Dickens. (Mostly O.E.D.) The simple v. is less frequent than the prepositional combinations. Etymology: prob. as in sense 1.—3. Ex 2, v.i. sense: to distend (another or oneself) with food: 1824, 'Comfortably tucked out ', O.E.D.; † by 1900. Rare, esp. in simple form.—4. Prob. ex sense 1: to hang (a bell) high in the stock: 1860 (O.E.D.): bell-makers' and bell-ringers', perhaps coll. rather than s. Abbr. *tuck high (in the stock).* Gen. *tuck up.*

*****tuck-'em fair.** An execution: c. (– 1700) >, in mid-C. 18, low s. B.E.; Grose. Parker, 1789, 'We went off at the fall of the leaf at Tuck'em Fair.' Ex *tuck*, v., 1. Also *Tuck-up Fair*, q.v.

tuck-hunter. An assiduous feast-seeker: 1840, A. Bunn. Ex *tuck(-out)*, n., 1.

tuck-in, tuck in ; tuck-out, tuck out. N.; v. See **tuck**, n., 1 ; v., 2.

tuck-man. A moneyed partner: commercial: from ca. 1880; ob. Ex *tuck*, n., 2.

tuck-parcel. A hamper from home: Charterhouse: ca. 1860–1920; ob. by 1904 (F. & H.). See **tuck**, n., 2, and cf. :

tuck-shop. A (mainly school) pastry-cook's shop: from mid-1850's. Hughes, 1857, 'Come . . . down to Sally Harrewell's . . . our schoolhouse tuck-shop.' Ex *tuck*, n., 2.

tuck up. See **tuck**, v., 1.—2. See **tuck**, v., 2.—3. See **tuck**, v., 4.—4. **tuck-up fair** or **T.-up F.,** the gallows: c. (– 1864); ob. H, 3rd ed. On *tuck-'em fair*, q.v.

tucked away. Dead and buried: Australian coll.: C. 20. C. J. Dennis.

tucked-up. (Of dog or horse) thin-flanked from hunger or fatigue: from early 1840's: dial. and s. Ex *tuck*, a pleat.—2. Hence, exhausted: dial. >, by 1890, s. Kipling, 1891 (O.E.D.). Cf. U.S. *tuckered out* (see Bartlett or Thornton).—3. Cramped, hindered, for lack of space or time: coll.: 1887 (O.E.D.). Ex sense 1.

tucker. Rations, orig. of gold-diggers: Australian, hence from ca. 1860, New Zealand: 1858, *The Morning Chronicle*, Aug. 31, 'Diggers, who have great difficulty in making their tucker at digging '; slightly ob.—2. Hence, by ca. 1870, food, as in Garnet Walch, 1874: Australian >, by 1875 or so, New Zealand.—3. Hence, *earn* (1883) or *make one's* *tucker,* **to** earn either merely or at least enough to pay for one's board and lodging : orig. Australian, then New Zealand. Like 1 and 2, it is in C. 20 fairly gen. Colonial. Ex *tuck,* n., 2, or v., 2. Cf. *grub* and *scoff,* qq.v.

tucking-in, vbl.n. See **tuck,** v., 2.

tuefall, -fold. Incorrect for *to-fall* (n.) : 1846, onwards : mid-C. 17–mid-19. O.E.D.

tuft. A titled undergraduate : 1755, in *tuft-hunter,* one who, at Oxford or Cambridge, toadies to the young noblemen ; *t.-h.* > gen. and S.E. in mid-C. 19 ; *tuft* is very ob. Ex the *tuft* or gold tassel worn on their caps by aristocratic students. Whence *tuft-hunting* : from 1780's ; by 1850, S.E.

tug. A Colleger : Eton (— 1881). Pascoe's *Life in Our Public Schools,* 1881. Ex the *toga* worn by Collegers to distinguish them from the rest of the school, says F. & H. ; perhaps rather ex dial., where *tug* is to work hard, and (*a*) *tug,* arduous labour (see E.D.D.).—2. An uncouth person ; esp. if dirty and/or none too scrupulous : late C. 19–20. Perhaps ex *tug,* adj.—3. (**Tug.**) The inevitable nickname of all male Wilsons : naval and military : late C. 19–20. Bowen. Even Admiral Sir A. K. Wilson, V.C., was named thus by his bluejackets. Possibly ex adj., 1 : at Winchester, *Tug* Wilson would be in contradistinction to, e.g., Sturt-Wilson. —4. (Gen. pl.) A tug-of-war match : Harrovian coll. : late C. 19–20. Arnold Lunn, 1913.

tug, v. To eat (greedily) : proletarian (— 1923). Manchon. Ex tugging with one's teeth.

tug, adj. Stale, vapid ; common, ordinary : Winchester : from ca. 1880. The origin is mysterious, unless perchance it is cognate with the dial. terms mentioned in *tug,* n., 1.—2. Whence *tug-clothes,* one's everyday clothes ; *tug-jaw,* dull talk ; and *tugs,* stale news.

Tug-Button Tuesday. See **Pay-Off Wednesday.**

tug-mutton. A whoremonger : C. 17. 'Water-Poet' Taylor. Ex *mutton,* q.v.—2. A glutton : provincial s. (— 1847) ; ob. Halliwell. The rhyming is prob. accidental.

tugger. A participator in a tug-of-war : 1909 (O.E.D.) : coll. >, by 1935, virtually S.E. Ex *tug,* v.i., to pull.

tuggery. College at Eton ; esp. in *try for tuggery,* to try to pass on to the foundation at Eton as a King's Scholar : Eton (— 1883). Brinsley Richards, *Seven Years at Eton,* 1883. Ex *tug,* n., 1.

tugs. See **tug,** adj., 2 and n., 4.

tui. Tuition : Winchester : late C. 19–20. Wrench. On *remi.*

tulip. A bishop's mitre, or the figure of one : from late 1870's ; by 1930, coll. Ex the shape. O.E.D.—2. **my tulip** (H. ; 1st ed.), my fine fellow, occurs mostly in *go it, my tulip !,* a London street c.p. of the 1840's–50's. F. & H. : 'An echo of the tulipomania of 1842 '. Note, however, that *tulip* has since C. 17 been used of a showy person.

tulip-sauce. Kissing ; a kiss : cheaply jocular (— 1904) ; very ob. Punning *two lips.*

***tullibon.** See **toloben.**

tum (1868, W. S. Gilbert) ; **tum-tum** (— 1904). Variants of *tummy,* q.v.: coll., esp. nursery. (O.E.D. Sup ; F. & H.)

tum-hat. See **tile.**

tumbies. Ablutions : Oxford University : 1853, 'Cuthbert Bede ' ; ob. Ex *tubbing* (*tub,* v., 1).

tumble, n. See **tumble, do a** and **take a.**—2. A failure : c. : from ca. 1910. James Curtis, *The Gilt Kid,* 1936.

tumble, v.i. To move stumblingly or hastily, rush, roll along : late C. 16–20 : S.E. until C. 19, then coll. E.g. Lever, 1843, 'Tumble into bed, and go to sleep as fast as you can,' O.E.D. See also **tumble in** (v.) and **tumble up.**—2. To understand, perceive, something not obvious, something hidden ; v.t. with *to* : low : from ca. 1850. Mayhew, 1851, of long or highfalutin words, 'We can't tumble to that barrikin.' Either, as W. suggests, ex *understumble,* to understand, or perhaps, as the O.E.D. implies, ex *tumble on,* chance on (a thing).—3. (Always **tumble to.**) Hence, to assent to, agree with, form a liking for : from early 1860's. Mayhew. Rather rare, and, after G.W., slightly ob.—4. (Of values, prices, stocks.) To fall rapidly in value : 1886 (O.E.D.) : commercial s. >, ca. 1920, coll. Ex lit. sense ('fall to the ground ').—5. Abbr. (C. 20) of *tumble down the sink,* q.v. J. Phillips's *Dict. of Rhyming Slang,* 1931.

tumble, do a. (Of a woman) to lie down to a man : low : C. 19–20. Cf. S.E. *tumble,* to handle with rough indelicacy.

tumble, take a. 'To comprehend suddenly ', C. J. Dennis : Australian : late C. 19–20. Cf. *tumble,* v., 2.

tumble-a-bed. A chambermaid : a harlot : coll. (? C. 18–) C. 19. Ex v. phrase.

tumble along. See **tumble,** v., 1.

Tumble-Down Dick. See **Queen Dick, 3.** Because Protector for less than a year. Dawson.

tumble down the sink. A drink ; to drink : rhyming s. : late C. 19–20. B. & P.

tumble-in. An act of copulation ; to copulate : low : C. 19–20.—2. Also, to go to bed : coll. : from ca. 1840. Ex *tumble into bed* : see quotation in **tumble, 1.**

tumble to, v.i. To set-to vigorously : coll. : mid-C. 19–20 ; slightly ob. See **tumble, 1.**—2. V.t., to understand : see **tumble,** v., 2.—3. See **tumble,** v., 3.

tumble to oneself, take a. To take oneself to task ; to realise one's own faults : low (— 1904). Ex *tumble,* 2, q.v.—2. To go steady, be cautious : from ca. 1905.

tumble to pieces. To be brought to bed with child and to be safely delivered of it : low : from ca. 1870. H., 5th ed.

tumble up. To rise in the morning : coll. : from ca. 1840. Prob. ex :—2. To come up on deck : nautical coll. : from ca. 1830. Ex *tumble,* 1.

***tumbler.** A decoy for swindlers or card-sharpers : c. : C. 17–early 19. Jonson, 1601 (O.E.D.) ; B.E. ; Grose. Prob. ex *tumbler* (dog), a lurcher.—2. A cart : c. : ca. 1670–1830. Head, B.E., Grose. Esp. in *shove the tumbler,* q.v. Ex a cart's lumbering motion + *tumbril.*—3. One of a class or band of London street ruffians that set women on their heads : C. 18 : prob. s. > coll. >, by 1800, archaic S.E. Steele, 1712.—4. A worthless horse : the turf (— 1904). Because it tumbles about ; cf. *screw,* racing n.

tumbling down to grass, n. and adj. Breaking up, failing, going to the bad : non-aristocratic : 1884–ca. 90. Ware 'From the fact of land going out of cultivation, 1875–85 ' (shades of 'Peter Porcupine ' !).

tumlet. A tumbler (glass) : domestic Anglo-Indian 'pidgin ' (— 1886). Yule & Burnell.

tummy. Stomach : coll. : 1868, W. S. Gilbert (O.E.D. Sup.). Prob., orig., a children's corruption of *stomach.* Cf. *tum* and *tum-tum.*—2. Hence, *tummy-tickling,* copulation, and *tummy-ache* : the former s.; the latter, coll.—3. 'A chronic though perhaps slight abdominal pain' (*Slang*, p. 193): medical (— 1933).

tump. Rubbish; nonsense: from ca. 1930. D. L. Murray, *The English Family Robinson*, 1933, 'Did you ever read such tump as our parish magazine?' Perhaps ex *tush* + *dump*.

tun. A tippler: low: mid-C. 19–20; ob. Abbr. *Lushington*, q.v.; but also punning *tun*, a arge cask.

tund; tunder; tunding. To beat (a boy) with a stick, as punishment (1871); he who does this (1876); such a beating (1872): Winchester School: from ca. 1870. *Punch*, ca. 1890, Confession by a Wykehamist, 'I like to be tunded twice a day, | And swished three times a week.' (Dates: O.E.D.) Ex L. *tundere*, to beat.

tune; gen. **tune up.** To beat, thrash: from ca. 1780; C. 19–20. Both slightly ob. Grose, 2nd ed., 'His father tuned him delightfully: perhaps from fetching a tune out of the person beaten, or . . . the disagreeable sounds on instruments when tuning.'

tune the (old) cow died of, the. A grotesque or unpleasant noise: jocular coll.: 1836, Marryat. Ex an old ballad. Apperson adduces Fuller's *that is the old tune upon the bag-pipe*, 1732.—2. Hence, advice or a homily instead of alms: from ca. 1880; ob. F. & H.

tuney; gen. **tuny.** Melodious: coll.: 1885 (O.E.D.). Often pejorative.

tuniopperty. See **tooniopperty.**

tunker. A street preacher: ca. 1850–1910. A corruption of *Dunker*, a German baptist.

*tunnel, v.i. **; go tunnelling.** To catch partridges at night: poachers' c.: mid-C. 19–20. '*No. 747*.'

tunnel-grunters. Potatoes: low: late C. 19–20; ob. ? because so filling.

Tunnels, the. The Opéra-Comique Theatre: theatrical: 1885–ca. 90. Ware, 'From the several subterranean passages leading to this underground theatre'. (It was 'swept away by Strand improvements'.)

tuny. See **tuney.** Hence, *tuniness*: coll.: C. 20. O.E.D.

tup. A young bullock: Smithfield and drovers' term, says H., 3rd ed.: an error that had disappeared by the 5th ed.—2. But *a stray tup on the loose*, a man questing for a woman, is s. (— 1904). F. & H.—3. So is *venison out of Tup Park*, mutton: late C. 17–mid-18. B.E.

tup. Arrested; in gaol: low London, esp. in the Woolwich district (— 1909). Ware. I.e. 'locked up'.

tuppence. Twopence: C. 17–20: S.E. until C. 19, then coll. So the adj. *tuppenny* (with which cf. *twopenny*, q.v.).

tuppence, for. Very easily: coll.: late C. 19–20. R. H. Mottram, *Bumphrey's*, 1934, 'I'm all heavy with that stuff. I could go to sleep for tuppence.' Lit., very cheaply.

tuppence on the can. Slightly drunk: lower classes': C. 20. Ernest Raymond, *The Jesting Army*, 1930. Ex public-house j.

tuppenny, n. See **twopenny.**

tuppenny-ha'penny. Inferior; insignificant: urban coll. (— 1909). Ware. The S.E. form (*twopenny-halfpenny*) is much earlier.

Tupper. 'A commonplace honest bore': Society coll.: ca. 1842–90. Ware. Ex the *Proverbial*

Philosophy (1838–42; revised and augmented up till 1867) of Martin Tupper (1810–89).

tuppy. (Of an animal) worn out; almost worthless: Australian: 1910, A. H. Davis, *On Our Selection*. Origin?: possibly ex *tuppenny*.

turd. A lump of excrement: C. 11–20: S.E., but in mid-C. 18–20 a vulgarism. Cuthbert Shaw, in his vigorous literary satire *The Race*, 1766, spells it *t—d*. Ex A.-S. *tord*, from a Germanic radical: cf. L. *tordere*.

turd, chuck a. To evacuate: low: C. 19–20. See preceding.

turd, he will never sh*t a seaman's. He will never make a good seaman: nautical: from ca. 1790; very ob. Grose, 3rd ed.

turd, not worth a. Utterly worthless: C. 13–20; in C. 18–20, a vulgarism.

turd for you !, a. 'Go to hell and stay there,' F. & H.: low: mid-C. 19–20. Cf. the low *turd in your teeth* (Jonson, 1614; anticipated by Harman, 1567), and the late C. 16 insult *goodman Turd*. See **turd.**

turd-walloper. A night-soil man: low: C. 20.— 2. Hence, a man on sanitary fatigue: military: from ca. 1910. B. & P.

turds for dinner, there were four; gen. amplified thus: **stir t., hold t., tread t.,** and **must-t.** 'To wit, a hog's face, feet, and chitterlings, with mustard': Grose, 3rd ed.: a low late C. 18–early 19 rebus-c.p.

turf. The cricket pitch, the field being *long grass*: Winchester School: from ca. 1860.—2. (Always with *a* or *the*.) The cricket field: Felsted School: from 1870's. *The Felstedian*, Nov., 1881, 'There are (or were) six cricket pitches on turf.'—3. Prostitution: low: ca. 1870–1905. Ware, 'From loose women being on parade'. Whence *turfer*, a harlot: low: ca. 1875–1910.—4. A kick; to kick: Charterhouse: late C. 19–20.

turf, v. To send (a boy) to bed at bed-time: Derby School: from ca. 1880. Perhaps cognate with sense 3, q.v.—2. To chastise: Marlborough School: from ca. 1880. Cf.:—3. *turf out.* To kick out; to expel: from ca. 1912. Manchon. Perhaps pregnant for *put out on the turf*, i.e. outside. —4. See n., 4.

turf, on the. Adj. and adv. applied, from ca. 1860, to a harlot: low. H., 2nd ed. Because, as a race-horse the turf, so she walks the streets.

turf out. See **turf,** v., 3.—**turfer.** See **turf,** n., 3.

Turk, not to have rounded Cape. Still to regard woman solely as an instrument of pleasure: coll. (— 1923). Manchon. Ex the Turks' reputation in sexual matters.

turkey. A Royal Marine Light Infantryman: naval: from ca. 1870; ob. Ex the scarlet tunic. (Bowen.)

turkey, head over. See **head over turkey.**

turkey-buyer. A 'toff' (sense 1), a banker, an important person: Leadenhall Market: late C. 19–20. Ware, 'Because it requires more than twopence to buy gobblers'.

turkey-cock, turn (or go) as red as a. To blush violently: coll., mostly provincial and Colonial: from ca. 1860.

turkey-merchant. A driver of turkeys: late C. 17–mid-18. B.E. A pun on *Turkey merchant*, one trading with Turkey (and/or the Levant).—2. Hence, a poulterer: mid-C. 18–mid-19, though it survived till ca. 1880 (see H., 1st–5th edd.). Grose, 1st ed.—3. Ex senses 1, 2: a chicken-thief: c.: 1837, Disraeli, in *Venetia*; ob.—4. A dealer in contraband silk : c. (— 1839). Brandon. Cf. origin of sense 1.—5. An ' extensive financier in scrip—a City plunger ' : London-financial : from ca, 1875 ; ob. Ware.—6. A bag : Canadian, esp. lumbermen's : C. 20. John Beames.

turkey off. To decamp : New Zealanders' : C. 20.

turkeys to market, be driving. To be unable to walk straight : semi-proverbial coll. (— 1869). W. Carew Hazlitt.

Turkish. Turkish tobacco : 1898.—2. Turkish delight : 1901, Fergus Hume. (O.E.D.) Both coll.

Turkish medal. A button undone or showing on one's fly : Eastern Front military : 1914 ; ob. B. & P. After *Abyssinian medal.*

Turkish Shore, the. Lambeth, Southwark, and Rotherhithe : low London : late C. 17–early 19. B.E. ; Grose, 1st ed. Ex the barbarous treatment likely to be had there : cf. S.E. *Turkish treatment,* sharp dealing, and *young Turk.*

Turl, the. Turl Street, Oxford : Oxford under-graduates' : late C. 19–20. Cf. *the Broad.*

turmyntyne. Turpentine : C. 15 ; *termentyne,* C. 16 : corrupt forms. O.E.D.

turn. A hanging from the gallows : rare coll. : C. 17–18. Shakespeare in *Measure for Measure,* IV, ii, 62 ; ' Hudibras ' Butler. Abbr. *turn-off.* (Not c., as F. & H. states ; the O.E.D. considers it S.E.)— 2. A momentary nervous shock of fear or other emotion : coll. (nowadays rather proletarian,—not that it's the worse for that !) : 1846, Dickens, ' What a hard-hearted monster you must be, John, not to have said so, at once, and saved me such a turn.' Ex *turn,* an attack of illness or faintness.— 3. An act of copulation : low : C. 19–20. (Cf. C. 17 S.E. *turn-up,* a whore.) 'Hence,' says F. & H., ' *to take a turn* (or *to turn a woman up*) = to copu-late : see **ride** : also to *take a turn among the cab-bages, up one's petticoats* (or *among one's frills*), *in Abraham's bosom, in Love Lane, Bushey Park, Cock Alley, Cupid's Alley, Cupid's corner, Hair Court, on Mount Pleasant, among the parsley, through the stubble,* or *a turn on one's back* (of women) ' ; the *Cupid* phrases may be literary euphemisms ; *Bushey Park* and *Mount Pleasant* are confined to London.—4. See **turns.**

turn, v. See **turn down, in, on, out, up, turned over.**

turn a horse inside out. To school (a bucking horse) by ' slinging up one of [his] legs, and lunging him about severely in heavy ground ' : Australian coll. : ca. 1850–80. The Rev. J. D. Mereweather, 1859. Morris at *buck-jumping,*

turn an honest penny. To be a pimp, a harlot's bully : low (— 1923). Manchon. Ironic.

turn copper. See **copper, come.**

turn down. To toss off (a drink) : coll. : from ca. 1760 ; very ob. Henry Brooke. Lit., turn it down one's throat.—2. To reject (an application) ; curtly say *no* to (a request, suggestion, invitation) ; refuse to accept (a suitor for one's hand) : U.S. (from ca. 1890), anglicised, esp. in the Dominions, ca. 1900.

turn-in. A night's rest : coll. : from ca. 1830. (O.E.D.) Ex :

turn in. To go to bed : 1695, Congreve : coll., nautical till mid-C. 19, then gen. Theodore Hook, 1837, ' Jack " turned in ", as the sailors say,' O.E.D. Ex turning into one's hammock. Cf. *turn out,* v.—2. V.t. To abandon, to desist from doing : C. 20. **?** ex *turn* (i.e. hand) *in one's resignation,*

where *turn in* may represent yet a third sense : coll. and dating from late C. 19. Cf. *turn up,* v., 1, q.v.

turn it in. To die : military : from 1914. F. & Gibbons. Ex *turn in,* v., 2. Cf. :

turn it up. See **turn up,** v.

turn on. To put (a person) *to do* something : coll. : from early 1890's.

turn-out. An interval : theatrical coll. : 1851, Mayhew, ' The 'Delphi was better than it is. I've taken 3s. at the first turn-out ! '

turn out, v.i. To rise from bed : coll. : 1805, W. Irving (O.E.D.) ; R. H. Dana, 1840, ' No man can be a sailor . . . unless he has lived in the fo'castle with them, turned in and out with them.' Prob. suggested by *turn in,* 1, q.v.—2. V.t., as in *turn out one's hand,* to show it, esp. at cards : coll. (— 1904). F. & H. Ex *turn out,* to empty (e.g. one's pockets).

turn over. ' A book to dip into rather than read ' : journalistic coll. : 1885, *The Saturday Review,* Dec. 26 ; but Ware dates it from 1880.—2. ' A transference of votes from one party to another ' : political : 1895 (O.E.D.).—3. V., see **turned over, be.**—4. To cross-question, examine severely : c. (— 1930). O.E.D. (Sup.).

turn-round pudding. Porridge or a ' slop ' pud-ding much stirred : lower-classes' coll. (— 1909). Ware. Cf. *stir-about pudding.*

turn the best side to London. See **side to London, turn one's or the.**

turn the corner. (Gen. as vbl.n. *turning . . .*) To round the Grand Banks on the trans-Atlantic passage : nautical coll. : C. 20. Bowen.

turn the tap on. ' To be ready with tears ' : lower-class urban : 1883, *The Daily Telegraph,* Feb. 8 (Ware).

turn-up. A sudden departure : low : from late 1850's ; ob. H., 1st ed. Prob. ex *turn up,* v., 2.— 2. ' An unexpected slice of luck ', H., 5th ed. : racing coll. >, in C. 20, S.E. : from ca. 1870. Ex *to turn up lucky.*—3. An acquittal : c. : from ca. 1820. Ex *turn up,* v., 3 (Ware).

turn up, v.t. To renounce, abandon (person or thing), cease dealing with (a tradesman), ' throw up ' (a job) : from ca. 1620 : S.E. until C. 19, then s. Vaux ; Holten, 1859, ' I intend *turning it up,* i.e. leaving my present abode or altering my course of life.' Frequently *turn it up !* = ' oh !, stop that ', ' stop doing that ' or ' talking '.—2. Whence, v.i., to quit, to abscond, to run away : low (— 1859). H., 1st ed., ' " Ned has *turned up,*" i.e. run away.' Esp., to throw up one's job. (Gen in passive.)— 3. To acquit, discharge or release (an accused or im-prisoned person) : low s. or, more prob. (at first, anyway), c. : from ca. 1810. Vaux. Ex S.E. *turn up,* to turn (esp. a horse) loose.—4. To stop and search ; to arrest (a criminal) : c. : from ca. 1890. H., 3rd ed. (Cf. *turned over,* 3.) Perhaps ironic ex preceding.—5. To chastise : Marlborough School : from ca. 1880. Ex lit. sense, the punishment being on the posteriors.—6. See **turn,** n., 3.—7. To hand out a share of stolen goods : c. : mid-C. 19–20 ; ob. ' *No. 747.*'

turn up a trump. To have a piece of monetary luck : coll. (— 1812). Vaux.

turn up crabs. See **crabs, come off.—turn up one's toes** or **one's toes up.** See **toes up, turn one's.**

turn up sweet. As in *to turn up a flat sweet,* to leave a ' pigeon ' in good humour after ' plucking ' him : c. : from ca. 1810. Vaux.

*turned over, be. To be acquitted for lack of evidence : c. : from ca. 1820. Cf. *turn up*, v., 3, q.v.—2. Whence, to be remanded : c. : from ca. 1830.—3. ' To be stopped by the police and searched ', F. & H. : c. : from ca. 1850. H., 1st ed. ; Horsley, *Jottings from Jail*, 1877, ' What catch would it be if you was to turn me over ? ' Cf. *turn up*, v., 4, q.v.

*turner out. A coiner of base money : c. (— 1859). H., 1st ed. Ex *turn out*, to produce, to manufacture.

*turning-tree. A gallows : either c. (F. & H.), s., or even coll. : ca. 1540–1660. Hall, in his chronicle of Henry VIII, ca. 1548, ' She and her husband . . . were apprehended, arraigned, and hanged at the foresayd turnyng tree.' Cf. later S.E. *turn off*, to hang.

turnip. An old-fashioned, thick, silver watch : 1840, E. Fitzgerald (O.E.D.). Ex its resemblance to a small turnip. In Anglo-Irish, it means—since ca. 1920, at least—a five-shilling Ingersoll. Also called a *frying-pan* ; cf. *warming-pan*, 2.—2. An affectionate term of address, gen. *old turnip* : coll. (— 1923) ; ob. Manchon. Cf. *old bean.*

turnip !, one's head to a. A fanciful bet : late C. 17–19. Motteux's *Rabelais*, V, ii. Cf. *(all) Lombard Street to a China orange.*

turnip, tickle one's. To thrash on the posteriors : late C. 16–mid-17. There is a pun on *turn-up*. O.E.D. Cf. *turnips, give one*, q.v.

turnip-pate, -pated. White- or very fair-haired : coll. : late C. 17–18 (B.E.) ; late C. 18–20 (Grose, 1st ed.) ; ob. Ex colour.

*turnip-tops, cut. To steal a watch with its chain and adjuncts : c. (— 1887). Baumann. Ex *turnip*, q.v.

*turnips, get or **(k)nap ; give turnips.** To abandon (a person), heartlessly or unscrupulously ; to be thus abandoned : c. (— 1812) >, ca. 1830, low s. ; extremely ob. Vaux (*give* and *nap*). Punning *turn-up* in its lit. sense : cf. *turnip, tickle one's*, q.v.—2. Whence *to get turnips*, to be jilted : from ca. 1830. On Suffolk dial., *give*, or *get, cold turnips*, to jilt, be jilted.

turnips, straight off the. Applied to one who is a country bumpkin or very green : New Zealanders' (— 1932).

turnover. Incorrect for *turnour*, a turner or small copper coin : C. 17. O.E.D.

turnpike-man. ' A parson, because the clergy collect their tolls at our entrance into and exit from the world,' Grose, 1st ed. : coll. : ca. 1780–1850.

*turnpike-sailor. A beggar pretending to be a distressed sailor : tramps' c. : ca. 1835–1900. Brandon, 1839 ; Mayhew, 1851 ; H., 5th ed., ' A sarcastic reference to the scene of their chief voyages.'—2. Hence, ' any lubberly seaman ' : nautical : from ca. 1890 ; ob. Bowen.

turnups is a variant (Ware) for *turnips*, 2.

turpentine, talk. To discuss painting : coll. : 1891, Kipling (O.E.D.) ; slightly ob. Ex painters' use of oil of turpentine (catachrestically : *spirit of turpentine* : mid-C. 17–20) in mixing colours.

turpin. A kettle : Yorkshire s. (— 1847). Halliwell ; E.D.D. ? ex *Dick Turpin.*

turps. Turpentine : from ca. 1820 : coll., workmen's and painters' >, ca. 1880, gen. (e.g. photographers' and housewives'). By abbr. ; *-s*, collective. O.E.D. (Contrast *terps* and *Tirps*, qq.v.)

turret rat. ' A sweeper in a ship's turret ' : naval : C. 20. Bowen.

turtle. Turtle-soup : restaurant and hotel staffs' coll. (— 1887). Baumann.

turtle doves. (A pair of) gloves : rhyming s. (— 1857). ' Ducange Anglicus.' Also *turtles*. P. H. Emerson, in *Signor Lippo Lippi*, 1893, ' A long-sleeve cadi on his napper, and a pair of turtles on his martins finished him.'

turtle-frolic. A feast of turtle : coll. : 1787 (O.E.D.). Ob. ; never gen.

turtle-soup. Sheep's-head broth : workmen's (— 1909). Ware. Cf. *City sherry.*

tusheroon. A crown piece (5s.) : low London (— 1859). H., 1st ed. Also called a *bull* or a *cartwheel*, ex its size. But H. errs, I believe : he should mean half-a-crown, for *tusheroon* and its C. 20 variant *tossaroon* (2s. 6d.) are manifest corruptions of Lingua Franca *madza caroon.*

*tuskin. ' A country carter or ploughman ', Grose, 1st ed. : either c. or provincial s. : ca. 1780–1840. Cognate with, possibly ex, dial. *tush*, the broad part of a ploughshare, and *tush*, v.t., to drag or trail (E.D.D.).

tussle. To argue (v.i.) : coll. (— 1859) >, somewhere about 1890, S.E. H., 1st ed. Ex *tussle*, to struggle.

tussocker. A ' sundowner ' (q.v.) : New Zealand : from mid-1880's ; slightly ob. V. Pyke, 1889, in *Wild Will Enderby* (Morris). Prob. because he loitered in the *tussocks*, till *dusk* (perhaps also operative).

tutoring. ' Trench-instruction to new troops ' (B. & P.) : 1915–18 : military coll. verging on j.

*Tuttle ; Tuttle Nask. The bridewell in *Tuttle* Fields (London) : resp. C. 19, late C. 17–19. See ***nask**, a prison. (' Closed in 1878 ', F. & H.)

tuz I. ' Bags I ! ', ' Faints ! ', qq.v.v. : Felsted School : mid-C. 19–20. Perhaps ex *(to) touse*, for cf. dial. *tuzel, tuzzle*, to tousle (E.D.D.).

tuzzy-muzzy ; occ. **tuzzi-muzzy** (or as one word). The female pudend : from ca. 1710 : (low) s. >, early in C. 19, dial. Ned Ward, 1711 ; Bailey ; Grose, 2nd ed. ; Halliwell. Ex *t.-m.*, a posy, nosegay, or garland. O.E.D. ; F. & H.

twachel, -il, -ylle ; twatchel. The pudend : mid-C. 17–early 19. App. a diminutive of *twat*, q.v., influenced by *twachylle = twitchel*, a passage.

twaddle. (S. of ca. 1783–5 for) ' perplexity, confusion, or anything else ', Grose, 2nd ed. ; earliest in Grose, 1st ed., in the Preface. Ex *twaddle*, prosy or gabbling nonsense,—itself recorded only in 1782 (O.E.D.) and prob. ex *twattle*, idle talk. Cf. *bore*, n., which it for a while succeeded.—2. ' A diminutive person : ? ca. 1820–80. F. & H., the sole authority. ? cognate with dial. *twaddle*, to walk feebly.

twait. See **twat**.

*twang. To coït with (a woman) : c. : C. 17–18. Baumann.

twanger. Anything very fine or (e.g. a lie) large : dial. and s. : from ca. 1870 ; very ob. as s. For semantics, cf. *twanging* entries.

twang(e)y. A tailor : North Country : ca. 1780–1850. Grose, 1st ed. ? a musical pun, or a phonetic relative of *stang(e)y*, q.v.

twanging. Excellent : coll. : 1609, Jonson (O.E.D.) ; † by 1700. Cf. *twanger* and :

twanging, go off. To go well : C. 17 coll., as is *as good as ever twanged*, as good as may be : resp. Massinger and Ray. The latter phrase, with complementary *the worst that ever twanged*, arose, however, ca. 1540. Cf. *go off with a bang* of a great success.

twankey. Gin : from late 1890's : tea-trade. Ex *twankey*, green tea. O.E.D.

'twas. It was : C. 17–20 : C. 17–18, coll. and S.E. ; C. 19–20, dial. and archaic. (O.E.D.) But when emphasised violently, it is still coll., as in ' " It wasn't there at all."—" '*Twas*, I tell you ! " '

twat ; in C. 18, occ. twait. The female pudend : mid-C. 17–20 : perhaps always a vulgarism ; certainly one in C. 18–20 ; very far from being †. R. Fletcher, 1656 ; Tom Brown, ca. 1704 (O.E.D.) ; Bailey ; Browning, in *Pippa Passes*, by a hairraising misapprehension,—the literary world's worst ' brick '. Origin obscure, but cf. *twachylle* = *twitchel*, a passage, and dial. *twatch*, to mend a gap in a hedge.—2. As v., erroneous for *troat*, to bellow ; † by 1800. O.E.D.

*twat-faker ; twat-masher. A prostitute's bully : resp. c. (— 1923) and low s. (id.). Manchon.

twat-rug. ' The female pubic hair ', F. & H. : low (— 1904).

twat-scourer. A surgeon ; a doctor : low s. (not a vulgarism, this) : C. 18. Bailey, 1727 (*t.-scowerer*). See twat, 1.

twatchel. See twachel.

twattle ; twattling, ppl.adj. To sound ; sounding : a vulgarism : C. 17–18. Florio, 1611 (the adj.) ; Cotton, 1664 (the v.). Ex *twattle*, to talk idly, to babble.—2. Whence *twattling strings*, a vulgarism for the *sphincter ani* : mid-C. 17–18. Implied in Cotton (as above). O.E.D.

tweak ; tweake, C. 17 only. A whore : C. 17–18. Middleton, 1617. Ex *tweak*, a twitch, or the v.— 2. A whoremonger : ? C. 18–early 19. Halliwell. —3. An adept at sport : Shrewsbury School : from ca. 1885. Desmond Coke, *The Bending of a Twig*, 1906.

tweak, v. ' To hit with a missile from a catapult ' : 1898, Kipling, ' Corkran . . . "tweaked" a frisky heifer on the nose.' O.E.D. Ex :

tweaker ; occ. tweeker. A catapult : from early 1880's. Ex S.E. (*to*) *tweak*.

twee. Dainty ; chic ; pleasing : coll. : 1905 (S.O.D.) ; ob. Ex *tweet*, affected or childish *sweet* : coll. : late C. 19–20.

*tweedle. ' A Brummagem ring of good appearance used for fraudulent purposes ', F. & H. : c. : late C. 19–20. ? ex *tweedledum and tweedledee*.

tweedledum sir. (Gen. pl.) A musical composer made baronet or knight : Society : ca. 1860–90. Ware. Cf. *gallipot baronet*.

tweeker. See tweaker.

tween(e)y, tweenie. A between-maid : coll. : from 1880's. For semantics, cf. *twixter*.

tweer. See twire.—tweet. See twee.

*twelve. A shilling : c. (— 1839) ; ob. Brandon. Cf. *twelver*, q.v.

twelve, after. Adv. and advl.n. From noon to 2 p.m. : Eton coll. (— 1861) > j.

twelve, more than. See seven, more than.

twelve apostles ; or T.A. The last twelve in the Mathematical Tripos : Cambridge University : from ca. 1820 ; ob.—2. Hence, the first twelve students : Stonyhurst : from ca. 1880.

*twelve godfathers. A jury : c. (— 1864) > low s. ; ob. H., 3rd ed., ' Because they give a name to the crime . . . Consequently it is a vulgar taunt to say, " You will be christened by *twelve godfathers* some day before long." '

twelve o'clock ! It's time to be moving : artisans' c.p. : ca. 1890–1914. Ware. Ex noon, break-off time.

twelve-pound actor. A healthy child born in ' the profession ' : theatrical (— 1909). Ware.

twelver. A shilling : c. >, in C. 19, low s. : late C. 17–19. B.E. ; Grose, 1st ed. ; H., 2nd ed. Ex the twelve pence.

twencent. Up-to-date, very modern : society : 1900–1 ; it died of inanition. Ex ' *twentieth century* '. L. M. de la Motte Tischbrook's letter in *John o' London*, Oct. 21, 1933.

twenty-firster. A coming-of-age ; a celebration thereof : university, orig. (— 1912) Oxford. O.E.D. (Sup.).

twenty-in-the-pounder. One who, on liquidation, pays 20 shillings in the £ : non-aristocratic coll. (— 1909). Ware.

twenty-two and twenty-two. Football : Winchester School coll. : ca. 1880–1910. This was the variety played with 22 a side.

twerp. An 'unpleasant or objectionable or foolish or ' soft ' person (rarely female) : from ca. 1910. F. & Gibbons ; Percy Brown, *Blind Alleys*, 1934.

*twibill. A street ruffian : c. : C. 17. F. & H. Ex *twibill*, a two-edged axe, perhaps suggested by the obvious pun, ' doubly sharp '. (Perhaps an error.)

twice-laid. A hash-up of fish and potatoes : low (— 1864) ; ob., except as nautical s. H., 3rd ed. ; Bowen defines it as ' any sea dish that is cooked for the second time ' and derives it ex ' the old name for rope made of the best yarns of an old rope '.

twicer. A printer working, or professing to work, at both press and case : printers' pejorative : from ca. 1880. Jacobi, 1888.—2. One who goes to church twice on Sunday : late C. 19–20. (The O.E.D.'s quotation of 1679 is either a nonce-use or connotes rarity.)—3. Something doubly, hence very, forceful or valuable : low : 1857, Mayhew, ' He expressed his delight . . . "Here's a start ! a reg'lar twicer ! " ' ; ob. O.E.D.—4. One who asks for two helpings ; hence, one who persistently tries to get more than his due : Australian : C. 20 ; esp. in G.W.—5. Hence (?), a cheat, a liar : mostly commercial : C. 20.—6. A widow or widower remarrying : lower classes' : C. 20. F. & Gibbons. —7. See :

twicers. Twins : lower classes' : mid-C. 19–20. Ware.

twicest (pron. *twȳst*). Twice : sol. : C. 19–20. Also *twict* and *twicst*.

Twickenham. A torpedo : naval : C. 20. Bowen. Did this arise in some pun about *twigging 'em* or *twitting 'em* ?

twiddle-diddles. Human testicles : low : from ca. 1786 ; ob. Grose, 2nd ed. A reduplication of *twiddle* (v.) with a pun on *diddle* (v.).

twiddle-poop. An effeminate-looking fellow : late C. 18–mid-19. Grose, 2nd ed. Cf. preceding entry and see poop.

twig. Style, fashion, method : low s. (— 1811). *Lex. Bal.* Esp. *in twig*, handsome or stylish ; cleverly (Vaux, 1812). Often *in good* or *prime twig* (both : Vaux). Hence *out of twig*, disguised, esp. in *put* (*oneself* or *another*) *out of twig* ; out of knowledge : low s. (— 1812). Vaux. ? etymology. Perhaps ex v.i. *twig*, to do anything vigorously.— 2. Hence, condition ; fettle, spirits : low s. : 1820, Randall's *Diary*, ' In search of lark, or some delicious gig, | The mind delights on, when 'tis in prime twig ' ; ca. 1840–70, very gen. in the boxing world. Both sets of senses were ob. by 1860, † by

1900.—2. The Headmaster : Marlborough : ca. 1850–90. Ex *twig*, the rod or birch.

*twig, v. To disengage ; to sunder : c. : ca. 1720–1840. *A New Canting Dict.*, 1725, has *twig the darbies*, to knock off the irons or handcuffs. Prob. cognate with *tweak*.—2. To watch ; inspect : 1764, Foote, ' Now, twig him ; now, mind him ; mark how he hawls his muscles about ' ; slightly ob. Possibly suggested by *twig*, to beat, to reprove, but more prob., as W. suggests, cognate with dial. *twick*, to pinch (esp. in s. sense, to arrest), to nip (cf. S.E. *tweak*).—3. Hence, to see, recognise, perceive : 1796, Holman, ' He twigs me. He knows Dicky here.'—4. Hence to understand : 1815, ' Zeluca ' Moore, ' You twig me—eh ? ', O.E.D.—5. Hence, v.i., to comprehend : 1833, Michael Scott (O.E.D.) ; 1853, Reade, ' If he is an old hand he will twig.' Cf. *twiggez-vous*, q.v.

twig, hop the. See hop.—twig, in and out of. See twig, n., 1, 2.

twig, measure a. To act absurdly : coll. : ca. 1670–1750. Ray.

twig and berries. A child's penis and testicles : lower-class euphemism : C. 20. Cf. *pencil and tassel*.

twig the fore (or the main). ' To look over the fore-mast (or main) to see that all the sails are furled and the yards properly squared ' : nautical : late C. 19–20. Bowen. Ex *twig*, v., 2.

twigger. An unchaste, even a lascivious person ; esp. a whore or near-whore : ca. 1590–1720. Marlowe & Nashe in *Dido*, 1594 (O.E.D.) ; Motteux, 1694. Prob. ex *twigger*, (of a ewe) a prolific breeder, itself ex *twig*, to act vigorously.—2. Hence, a wencher : C. 17, and much less gen. F. & H.

twiggez-vous ? Do you understand ? : from ca. 1898 ; virtually †. Kipling, in *Stalky & Co.*, ' " Twiggez-vous ? " " Nous twiggons." ' (But *nous twiggons*, we understand, has not ' caught on '.) Ex *twig*, v., last sense, on Fr. *comprenez-vous*, do you understand. Cf. *squattez-vous*, q.v., and *compree* : resp. for form and for sense.

twiggy ? ; twiggy-vous. Variants of the preceding. Pre-War, says Collinson.

twigs, hop the. To walk with crutches : nautical (— 1923). Manchon. Contrast *hop the twig* (at hop).

*twine. To give false change : c. : late C. 19–20. Ex (S.E. > dial.) *twine*, to twist, wring, with a pun on *wring*.

*twinkler. A light : c. : late C. 19–20. Cf. *twinkler*, a star.

twinkling. See bed-post.

twire. A glance ; esp. a leer : 1676, Etherege, ' Amorous tweers ', *tweer* only in C. 17 ; 1719, D'Urfey (O.E.D.) ; † by 1750. Ex v.i. *twire*, to peer, look round cautiously, peer. Cf. *tour(e)*, *tower*, *towre*.

*twirl. A skeleton key : c. : from ca. 1877. Horsley, *Jottings from Jail*. Because a burglar twirls it as he uses it. Also, in C. 20, *twirler*.—2. A warder : prisoners' c. (— 1933). George Ingram, *Stir*. Ex his bunch of keys.

*twirl, on the. (Adj. and adv.) A-thieving professionally : c. : C. 20. James Curtis, *The Gilt Kid*, 1936. Ex twirling the locks of safes.

twiss. A chamber-pot : ca. 1777–1830 : Anglo-Irish. Richard *Twiss* (1747–1821) published in 1776 his *Tour in Ireland* in 1775, which, understandably, was very unpopular in Ireland : whereupon there were manufactured some of these utensils with his portrait at the bottom, which bore the rhyme, ' Let everyone ——— | On lying Dick Twiss.' (Earlier in the century, Sacheverell had been similarly execrated.)

twist. A drink of (gen.) two beverages mixed : late C. 17–20 ; ob. In B.E., tea and coffee ; by 1725, also brandy and eggs ; by 1785, brandy, beer and eggs (Grose) ; by 1823, *gin-twist*, gin and hot water, with sugar and either lemon or orange juice (' Jon Bee ') ; in 1857, ' Ducange Anglicus ' defines *twist* as brandy and gin ; but from ca. 1860, by far the commonest is *gin-twist.* Ex one thing twisted in with another.—2. An appetite, esp. a hearty one : from early 1780's ; slightly ob. Grose, 1st ed. Ex *twist*, v., 1, q.v.—3. ' A stick spirally marked by a creeper having grown round it : also *twister* ', F. & H. : Winchester School coll. : from ca. 1860. Perhaps ex a *twist* of tobacco.

twist, v.i. and t. To eat ; esp. to eat heartily : from ca. 1690 ; ob. B.E. (v.i.) ; Motteux, 1694 (v.t. : O.E.D.). Also *twist down*, v.t., to eat heartily : from ca. 1780. Grose, 1st ed. Perhaps ex twisting pieces off loaves, cakes, etc. Cf. *twist*, n., 2.—2. In passive, to be hanged : from ca. 1720 ; very ob. *A New Canting Dict.*, 1725. Ex twisting as one swings on the rope.—3. To swindle, to cheat : Australian : from not later than 1914. Perhaps by back-formation ex *twister*, 5.

*twist, at the. Adj. and adv. (By) double-crossing : c. (— 1933). Charles E. Leach, *On Top of the Underworld.*

twist, spin a. A naval variation († by 1929) of *spin a yarn* : latish C. 19–early 20. Baumann, 1887 ; Bowen. Suggested by ' spin a *yarn* '.

twist one's sleeve-lining. To change one's opinions or attitude : tailors' : late C. 19–20.

*twist the book (on). To turn the tables (on a person) : c. : from early 1920's. Edgar Wallace. Cf. *twister*, 6.

twister. A very hearty eater : 1694, Motteux (O.E.D.) ; from mid-C. 19, only in dial. Ex *twist*, v., 1.—2. Anything that puzzles or staggers one, a gross exaggeration, a lie : from ca. 1870.—3. See *twist*, n., 3.—4. A sound thrashing ; a grave anxiety, a ' turn ', as in ' It gave me a twister ' : low (— 1887). Baumann.—5. A ' shady ' fellow, a swindler, a crook ; a shuffler, a prevaricator ; a person of no decided opinions : low : from not later than 1912 in Australia, not later than 1914 in England.—6. One who cannot be tricked or swindled : c. : from ca. 1920. See esp. Edgar Wallace, *The Twister*, 1928. Ironic ex sense 5, or direct ex *twist the book*, q.v.

twistical. Rather twisted ; fig., tortuous, devious : coll. : 1815, D. Humphreys (O.E.D.) ; ob. except in U.S. Ex *twist* on, e.g., *comical*.

twisting. A scolding ; a thrashing : 1833, Marryat (O.E.D.) ; ob.—2. A grief ; (a cause of) anxiety : coll. (— 1923). Manchon.

twitchers. Tight boots : Lancashire coll. (— 1904). E.D.D. Ex the dial. sense, ' pincers '.

twitchet(t)y. Nervous, fidgety : low coll. (— 1859). H., 1st ed. Ex *twitchy*.

*twittoc. Two : c. (— 1785) ; † by 1860. Grose, 1st ed. By perversion of *two*.

twixter. ' Either a lady-like young man, or a man-like young woman ' : low London (— 1909) ; slightly ob. Ware. Cf. *tween(e)y*. Ex *betwixt and between*.

twizzle, v.i. To spin (rapidly) : dial. (— 1825) >, ca. 1880, coll. Prob. ex dial. *twistle*, v.t., to twirl. O.E.D.—2. Hence, v.t., to rotate; to shape by twisting: dial. (— 1854) >, ca. 1885, coll. 'My friends . . . began twizzling up cigarettes,' C. Keene, 1887. O.E.D.

two. Two pennyworth (of spirits): 1894, G. A. Henty; ob. O.E.D.

two, adj. Only as in two fools, exceedingly foolish, is it coll. Donne's ' I am two fools, I know, | For loving, and for saying so | In whining poetry ' is not an example,—for he means that he is two different kinds of fool or a fool on two different counts,—but it is relevant, for it supplies the semantic link. (Lit., doubly foolish.)

Two and a Hook, the. The 29th Foot (now the Worcestershire) Regiment: military: C. 19. F. & Gibbons, ' Suggested by the numerical figures'.

two and a kick. See kick, n., 2.

two-backed beast, the; do the . . . Two persons in coitu; to coït: low coll.: C. 17–18. E.g. in Othello, I, i, 117; Urquhart's Rabelais, 1653.

two brothers alive and one married (i.e. as good as dead !). A music-halls' c.p. of 1897–8. Ware.

two buckle horses. Tuberculosis: stables' jocular (— 1909); ob. Ware.

two-by-three. ' A species of Canteen cake': military: from 1915. F. & Gibbons. Ex its size, 2″ × 3″ (× ca. 1″).

two-ender. A florin: Cockneys': C. 20. (The Evening News, Jan. 20, 1936). Also grafters': witness P. Allingham, Cheapjack, 1934.

two ends and the bight of (a thing). The whole of (something): nautical coll.: late C. 19–20. Bowen. Cf.:

two ends and the middle of a bad lot. (Of a person) utterly objectionable: middle classes' (— 1909); ob. Ware. Perhaps ex preceding.

two-eyed steak. A (Yarmouth) bloater: low: 1864 (O.E.D.). Cf. Glasgow magistrate. The O.E.D. has the rare variant (now †), t.-e. beef-steak.

two feet one backyard. A jocular middle-class c.p. applied to very large feet: C. 20. Punning ' Three feet (make) one yard.'

two-fisted. Clumsy: coll. and dial.: from late 1850's. Cf. two-handed, 2, q.v.—2. ' Expert at fisticuffs ', H., 1864, is a coll. variant of two-handed, ambidextrous.

two five two, be put on the. To be ' crimed ': military coll.: from ca. 1912. F. & Gibbons. The crime-sheet was officially known as Form 252.

Two Fives, the. The 55th Foot Regiment; from ca. 1881, named the Border Regiment: military: C. 19–20; ob. F. & Gibbons. Cf. Two Fours.

two-foot rule. A fool: rhyming s. (— 1859). H., 1st ed.

Two Fours, the. The 44th Foot Regiment; from ca. 1881, the 1st Battalion of the Essex Regiment: military: C. 19–20; ob. F. & Gibbons. See Two Sevens.

two F's, the. A fringe (on the forehead) and a follower (or followers) worn by maidservants: middle classes': ca. 1880–95. Ware.

two-handed. (Seldom of things.) Big; strapping: coll.: ca. 1685–1910. B.E.; Grose, 1st ed.; Lamb, 1830 (O.E.D.). Prob. ex t.-h., requiring or entailing the use of both hands.—2. Awkward, clumsy: ca. 1860–1920. H., 3rd ed., ' A singular reversing of meaning '. Perhaps on two-fisted, q.v.

two-handed put. ' The amorous congress ', Grose, 2nd ed.: ca. 1780–1840.

two (he)arts in a pond. Two bullocks' hearts in a

two-sectioned dish: lower classes' (— 1909). Ware.

two inches beyond upright. A non-aristocratic, non-cultured c.p. applied, ca. 1900–14, to a hypocritical liar. Ware, ' Perversion of description of upright-standing man, who throws his head backwards beyond upright '.

two ladies on bikes. The figure of Britannia on the obverse of the two pennies: two-up players', esp. New Zealanders': C. 20. I.e. when both turned up tails; the ' heads ' betters call them the two bastards on bikes.

two-legged tree. The gallows: low: C. 19.

two-legged tympany or tympany with two heels, a baby, is rare except in have a t.-l. t., to be got with child, and be cured of a tympany with two heels, to be brought to child-bed: coll.: ca. 1579–1850. Tarlton, 1590; Ray. (O.E.D.; F. & H.) Ex tympany, a tumour.

two-nick. A female baby: printers': from ca. 1870. Anatomical wit.

two-o. See three-o.

two of that. Something much better, esp. as in Hugh Walpole, Vanessa, 1933, ' [Mr. Childers] had forestalled the Conservatives, . . . but Gladstone knew two of that ': coll.: late C. 19–20. Abbr. a trick worth two of that.

two-pip artist, merchant, or wallah. A first lieutenant: military: from ca. 1915. B. & P. Lit., a fellow with two stars. A 2nd lieutenant is a one-pipper.

*two poll one. Swindled by two confederates: c. (— 1812); † by 1850. Vaux. Perhaps poll = upon.

two pun ten. See two upon ten.

Two Red Feathers, the. A variant of the Red Feathers, q.v. (F. & Gibbons.)

Two Sevens, Sixes, Tens, Twos, the. Resp., the 77th Foot Regiment, from ca. 1881 the 2nd Battalion of the Duke of Cambridge's Own Middlesex Regiment; the 66th Foot, from ca. 1881 the 2nd Battalion of the (Princess Charlotte of Wales's) Royal Berkshire Regiment; the 20th Foot, from ca. 1881 the Lancashire Fusiliers; and the 22nd Foot, from ca. 1881 the Cheshire Regiment: military: C. 19–20; very ob. Nicknames on numbers are common in the Army: cf. Two Fours, Two Fives, and the vocabulary of the game of House. (F. & Gibbons.)

two shoes (or T.-S.); gen. little t.-s. (Gen. in address to) a little girl: nursery coll.: C. 19–20, though I find no earlier record than 1858, George Eliot in Mr Gilfil's Love Story, ' He delighted to tell the young shavers and two-shoes . . .' Ex the heroine of The History of Little Goody Two-Shoes, 1766.

Two Sixes, the. See Two Sevens.—two slips for a tester. See three slips for a tester, give.

two-sticker. A two-master: nautical coll.: 1884 (O.E.D.). Ex stick, mast.

two Sundays come together, when. See Sundays come . . .

Two Tens, the. See Two Sevens.

two thieves beating a rogue. ' A man beating his hands against his sides to warm himself in cold weather; also called Beating the Booby, and Cuffing Jonas ', Grose, 2nd ed.: coll.: ca. 1780–1850.

Two-to-One, Mr. A pawnbroker: low (—1823); † by 1890. ' Jon Bee.' Cf. next two entries.

two to one against you. Very much against your

getting your pledge back : lower classes' c.p. of ca.
1890–1915. Ware. Ex the pawnbroker's sign :
two balls over one. Cf. :

two-to-one shop. A pawnbroker's : ca. 1780–
1840. Grose, 1st ed., ' Alluding to the [arrange-
ment of the] three blue balls, [in] the sign of that
trade, or perhaps from its being two to one that the
goods pledged are never redeemed.' Cf. preceding
two entries.

two-topmaster. A ' fishing schooner or coaster
with both masts fitted with top-masts. As a rule
the main top-mast only is carried ' (cf. *bald-headed*) :
Canadian (and U.S.) nautical coll. : late C. 19–20.
Bowen.

two turns round the long-boat . . . See **three
turns . . .**

two twos, in. In a moment ; immediately : s.
(1838, Haliburton : O.E.D.) >, ca. 1890, coll.
Lit., in the time taken to say *two* twice.

Two Twos, the. See **Two Sevens.**

two-up school. A gambling den or group : (low)
Australian : late C. 19–20. C. J. Dennis. See
school ; *two-up*, itself s., ex tossing up two coins or
ex the ' heads ' and ' tails ' of one coin.

two upon ten, or **two pun ten.** Abbr. **two eyes
upon ten fingers,** this is a trade c.p. dating from
early 1860's or late 1850's. H., 3rd ed., ' When a
supposed thief is present, one shopman asks the
other if that *two pun*' (pound) *ten* matter was ever
settled . . . If it is not convenient to speak, a
piece of paper is handed to the same assistant bearing
the to him very significant amount of £2 : 10 : 0.'
Cf. *John Orderly* and *Sharp*(, *Mr*), qq.v.

**two white, two red, and (after you with the black-
ing-) brush !** ; hence, **after you(, miss,) with the two
two's and the two b's !** A London streets' c.p.
directed at the excessive use of cosmetics : 1860's.
Ware. I.e. two dabs of red, two of white, and a
brush to make up the eyebrows.

two with you ! A c.p. ' suggesting a twopenny
drink ' : taverns' : ca. 1885–1914. Ware.

two-year-old, like a. In a very lively manner ;
vigorous(ly) : coll. : C. 20. (Galsworthy, 1928.)
Ex race-horses.

twoer. Anything comprised by, or reckoned as,
two : coll. : 1889, a hit for two runs at cricket
(O.E.D.) ; a florin, as in Clarence Rook, *The
Hooligan Nights*, 1899 ; a hansom cab (ca. 1895–
1910).

twofer. A harlot : low : late C. 19–20. Ex *two.*

twoops. (A) twopenny ale : ca. 1752–60. The
O.E.D. records it at 1729. Ex *two* + *p*(enny) + *-s*,
the collective suffix as in *turps.*

twopence more . . . See **donkey !** — ***twopenn'orth of rope.** See **twopenny-rope.**

twopenny ; tuppenny. The head : low (—1859) ;
ob. H., 1st ed. Rhyming s. ; G. Orwell, 1933,
explaining it thus : ' Head—loaf of bread—twopenny loaf—twopenny.' Cf. *loaf*, q.v.—2. Hence,
tuck in your twopenny (or *tuppeny*), at leap-frog, is
used fig., stop !, or stop that !, as in the song *The
Lord Mayor's Coachman*, ca. 1888.—3. (**twopenny.**)
A professional pawner,—one who acts as intermediary between pawnbroker and client : low London : ca. 1870–1915. ' The usual fee being twopence ', F. & H.—4. A term of affectionate address :
lower classes' (— 1923). Manchon.

twopenny damn, not to care a. To care not at all :
coll. : ca. 1820–90. Cf. *not to care a hoot, a tinker's
curse,* etc.

Twopenny Damn, The. *The St James's Gazette* :

literary : ca. 1880–1910. ' On account of its strong
language concerning Mr Gladstone and the " latter-
day Radicals " ', F. & H.

***twopenny hangover.** A place where tramps may
sleep, sitting in a row on a bench with—stretched
before them—a rope on which they may lean :
tramps' c. (— 1933). George Orwell, *Down and
Out in Paris and London*

twopenny hop. A cheap dance : coll. : from ca.
1850 ; ob. by 1904 (witness F. & H.), but not
absolutely † by 1935. Mayhew, 1851 ; H., 1st ed.
See **hop.**

***twopenny-rope.** ' A [low] lodging-house : one
in which the charge is (or was) twopence : sacking
stretched on ropes served as a shakedown. *To have
twopenn'orth of rope* = to " doss down " in such a
place : Fr. *coucher à la corde*,' F. & H. (1904) : from
ca. 1870. H., 5th ed. Ob., if not indeed † : see
***rope** and cf. *twopenny hangover*, q.v.

Twopenny Tube. See **tube**, n., 3.

twopenny upright. A C. 19 variant of *threepenny
upright* (see **threepenny bit**).

Twopenny Ward. Ca. 1600–40, part of one of
the London prisons was thus named. Jonson, 1605,
Eastward Ho, V, i, ' He lies in the twopenny ward.'
Perhaps *twopenny* here, as it certainly did from 1560
(O.E.D.), = ' worthless ' ; or perhaps the initiation-
fee was twopence.

twug. Harrow form of *twigged* (past ppl. passive), caught. Ex *twig*, v., 3.

Twyford, my (his, etc.) name is. I know (he
knows, etc.) nothing of the matter : a semi-proverbial c.p. of ca. 1690–1830. Motteux, 1694,—
Charles Whibley refers to this in his essay on
Rabelais ; Fuller, 1732. Apperson. For origin,
see the Addenda.

[**Tyburn.** The *Tyburn* phrases are on the border-
line between coll. and S.E. : the status of all such
allusive topographical terms cannot be determined
arbitrarily. The following are the chief.—**Tyburn
blossom,** a young thief, who will prob. ripen into a
gallows-bird (ca. 1785–1840 : Grose, 2nd ed.) ; **T.
check,** a halter (ca. 1520–80 : Skelton) ; **T. collar,**
' the fringe of beard worn under the chin ', H., 2nd
ed., 1860 (ca. 1860–80. Synonymous with *Newgate
frill* or *fringe*. Cf. *T. top*) ; **T. collop** (? : C. 16) ; **T.
face,** a hangdog look (Congreve, 1695) ; **T. fair (jig,
show, stretch),** a hanging (mid-C. 16–early 19) ; **T.
tippet,** a halter (mid-C. 16–mid-19 : Latimer ;
Egan) ; **T. top** or **fore-top,** ' a wig with the foretop
combed over the eyes in a knowing style ', Grose,
2nd ed. († by 1850), with variant *Tyburn-topped wig*
(1774, Foote) ; **T. Tree,** the great Tyburn gallows
(1727, Gay ; † by 1850). Also **preach at T. cross,** to
be hanged (1576, Gascoigne), with such variants as
dance the T. jig (1698, Farquhar) or **a T. hornpipe on
nothing** (late C. 18–mid-19),—cf. *dance the Paddington frisk*,—**fetch a T. stretch** (Tusser, 1573), **dangle in
a T. string** (1882, J. Walker : ' literary '), **put on a
T. piccadill** (' Water-Poet ' Taylor) or **wear T.
tiffany** (1612, Rowlands). Tyburn gallows, the
place of execution for Middlesex from late C. 12 till
1783, stood where the present Bayswater and
Edgware Roads join with Oxford Street ; from 1783
until 1903, the death penalty was exacted at Newgate Prison. F. & H. ; O.E.D. Cf. :]

Tyburnia. ' A name given ', ca. 1850, ' to the
district lying between Edgware Road and Westbourne and Gloucester Terraces and Craven Hill,
and bounded on the south by the Bayswater Road,
and subsequently including (Hotten [3rd ed.]) the

Portman and Grosvenor Square districts: facetiously divided by Londoners'—on *Arabia Felix* and *Arabia Deserta*—'into "Tyburnia Felix", "Tyburnia Deserta", and "Tyburnia Snobbica": it soon fell into disuse,' F. & H.: it was still current in 1874 (witness H., 5th ed.), but † by 1880. See preceding entry.

[**tye**; in late C. 19–20, always, and often thus much earlier, **tie**. A necktie: according to H., 1st ed. (1859), it was, ca. 1820, s. (? rather coll.); but the evidence of the O.E.D. rather belies this ' ranking '.]

*tye, v. See **tie it up.**—**tyke.** See **tike.**—***tyler.** See **tiler** and **Adam Tiler** (or t.).

tymp; occ. **timp.** A tympanist, whether a drummer or a player of the tympan: musical: late C. 19–20.

tympany, two-legged or **with two heels.** See **two-legged tympany.**

tyo, tyoh; occ. **ty-o(h), tie-o(h).** Tired: children's and lovers' coll: C. 20.

type has, since the G.W., been increasingly used very loosely for ' kind ', ' category ', ' character ', ' nature '.

type-lifter or **-slinger.** An expert compositor:

printers': from ca. 1870.—2. Occ., a slovenly workman printers' (— 1904). F. & H. Cf. *typo.*

typewriter. A fighter, boxer: rhyming s.: from ca. 1920. J. Phillips, *Dict. of Rhyming Slang*, 1931.

typewriters (no singular); **typewriting.** Machine guns; their fire: New Zealanders': in G.W. Ex the crisp tapping.

typhoid. A case of typhoid, a typhoid-patient: medical coll.: 1890 (O.E.D.).

typhus, ' not to be confused with typhoid fever ', Dr Charles Singer, *The Observer*, May 6, 1935.

typo. A compositor: printers': orig. (1816), U.S.; anglicised ca. 1860; slightly ob., *comp* being, in C. 20, much more gen. Thornton; Mayhew, 1861. Either abbr. *typographer* or imm. adopted from France.—2. A typographer, esp. if expert: printers' (— 1887). Baumann.—3. Adj., typographic: 1891 (O.E.D.); comparatively rare.

tyre. A very gen., but until ca. 1930, usually considered incorrect spelling, of *tire* (of wheel): late C. 18–20.—2. As also is *tyro* for *tiro*, a beginner: C. 17–20.

tzing-tzing. Excellent; ' A1 ': low: ca. 1880–1900. ? ex *chin-chin* !, q.v.

U

[F. & H. has the following ineligibles; S.E.:— **ugly**'s here unrecorded; **ultimate favour**; **umble-pie**; **unbaked**; **unconscionable**; **uncouth, unkissed**; **uncular**; **under, lie**; **under a cloud**; **under-spur-leather**; **underfellow**; **under-stair**; **undisgruntled**; **unfortunate**; **unicorn** (coin); **unlicked cub**; **unlock the lands**; **unpaved** (castrated); **unready**; **unrig** (plunder; dismantle); **unspeakable**; **unto, go in**; **untrimmed**; **unwashed, the** (great); **unwashed**, adj.; **unrecorded up**'s and phrases; **upper-stock**; **uppish** (proud; tipsy); **upsitting**; **upskip**; **upsodown**; **upstart**; **upsyturvy**; **uptails-all**; **upways**; **urchin**; **urinal**; **use**, n. and v.; **utter.**

Dial.:—**ugly** (a beating); **uzzard.**]

U.B.D'd ! You be damned !: euphemistic coll. (— 1923). Manchon.

U bet ! A written jocularity (*The Referee*, Oct. 14, 1883) for *you bet* !

U.P.; gen. **it's all U.P.** (It is) all ' up ', finished, remediless: 1823, Bee, ' " 'Tis all up " and " 'tis U.P. with him," is said of a poor fellow who may not have a leg to stand upon '; Dickens, 1838, ' It's all U.P. there, . . . if she lasts a couple of hours, I shall be surprised,' O.E.D. The spelt pronunciation of *up*; perhaps suggested by—

U.P.K. spells (May) goslings. ' An expression used by boys at play to the losing party,' *The Gentleman's Magazine*, 1791 (I, 327). Here, *U.P.K.* is *up pick*, ' up with your pin or peg, the mark of the goal ', Brand, 1813. At some time before 1854, the phrase had > *U.P. spells goslings*, indicative of completion or attainment, also of imminent death; from ca. 1840, only in dial. Evans, *Leicestershire Words*, 1881, says: ' Meaning, as I always understood, " it is all up with him, and the goslings will soon feed on his grave." ' Apperson.

uckeye. All right, esp. exclamatorily: Regular Army: late C. 19–20. F. & Gibbons, ' A perversion of the Hindustani word *uchcha*.'

'ud. A variant of *'d* (had, would): coll.: C. 19–20. Rarely so written. Cf. *ull*, q.v.

Uds ! Alone or in combination (e.g. *Uds niggers* !), a trivial coll. oath common in late C. 16–17. A perversion of *Ods*. O.E.D.

udyju. See **toot the udyju Pope o' Rome.**

Ugger, the. The Union: Oxford undergraduates' (— 1899). Ware. By ' the Oxford *-er* '.

-ugger. Cf. *-agger*, q.v., and see esp. ' Harrow slang '. E.g. *memugger* and *testugger*.

uglies, the. Delirium tremens: low: from ca. 1870; ob. Perhaps on *horrors*.

ugly; **Mr Ugly.** As term of address: mid-C. 19–20. Ex (an) *ugly* (person).—2. (**ugly.**) A bonnet-shade: Society: 1850's. Ware.

ugly, adj. Thick: lower-class coffee-houses': from ca. 1860; ob. Ware.

ugly, come the. To threaten: from ca. 1860. Cf. S.E. *ugly customer*.

ugly, cut up. See **cut up** (rough, etc.).—**ugly** !, **strike me.** See **strike me blind** !

ugly as sin. Extremely ugly: coll.: 1821, Scott: 1891, Stevenson. Apperson, who cites the prob. prototype, *ugly as the devil*, 1726, Defoe.

*ugly man; **uglyman.** He who, in garrotting, actually perpetrates the outrage: c. (— 1904). F. & H. Suggested by the synonymous *nasty man*, q.v.

ugly rush. Forcing a bill to prevent inquiry: Parliamentary (— 1909). Ware.

ugmer. See **hugmer.**

Uhlan. A tramp: tailors': ca. 1870–1910. Ex Franco-Prussian War.—2. (**Uhlan, the.**) Lord Randolph Churchill: Parliamentary nickname: 1883–ca. 85. Ware. Ex his dashing methods.

'ull. A variant of *'ll* (shall, will): coll.: C. 19–20. Rarely written thus. Cf. *'ud*, q.v., and esp. *'ill*.

ullage(s). Dregs in glass or cask: from ca. 1870. H., 5th ed. Lit., the wastage in a cask of liquor.—2. Whence (*ullage*) a useless thing or incompetent person: naval: late C. 19–20. F. & Gibbons.

ulster. See wooden ulster.

ultramarine. ' Blue ' in its s. senses : ca. 1890–1914.

ultray. Very : coll. corruption of *ultra* : ca. 1890–1910. F. & H.

ululation. ' First night condemnation by all the gallery and the back of the pit ' : journalistic : ca. 1875–90. Ware.

um, 'um. Them : C. 17–20 : S.E. until ca. 1720, then coll.—increasingly low and increasingly rare—and dial. Cf. '*em*, q.v. See what-d'ye-call-'em. —2. The : ' pidgin ' : C. 19–20. See W. at *pidgin*.

umberella. An umbrella : sol. (— 1887). Baumann.

umble-cum-stumble. To understand (thoroughly) : lower classes' (— 1909). Ware. Ex *under comestumble*, q.v.

umbrella. Very long or thick hair : jocular (— 1887) ; ob. Baumann, ' He has a regular umbrella.'

umbrella, been measured for a new. Dressed badly ; hence, embarked on a course of doubtful wisdom : c.p. : from ca. 1895 ; ob. Only his umbrella fits.

umpire ?, how's that. What do you say to that ? ; ' what price —— ? ' : coll. : from ca. 1880 ; ob. Ex the appeal at cricket.

um(p)teen, umpty, nn. ; um(p)teenth, umptieth, adjj. An undefined number ; of an undefined number : C. J. Dennis, (and heard by editor in) 1916 : G.W. military, to disguise the number of a brigade, division, etc. ; orig. signallers' s., says F. & Gibbons. Whereas *umpty*, *umptieth*, are ob. and were never very gen., *umpteen(th)* is still common, though rather in the sense of ' (of) a considerable number ', as in *for the umpteenth time*, a change of sense implicit from the beginning. Ex *um*, a non-committal sound aptly replacing an unstated number, + *-teen* ; the later *umpty*, *-ieth*, ex the same *um* + *-ty* as in *twenty*, *thirty*, etc. Possibly *um* represents *any*. Perhaps cf. :

umpty iddy, feel. To feel indisposed : military : from 1915. F. & Gibbons. Perhaps a perversion of *feel* ' *any old way* '.

umpty poo. Just a little more : military : 1915 ; ob. Ibid. Ex Fr. *un petit peu*.

umses (or U-). The ' boss ' : tailors' : C. 20. See, e.g., *The Tailor and Cutter*, Nov. 29, 1928. Cf. *himses*, q.v.

un, 'un. One : coll. form preserving what was orig. the correct pronunciation : C. 19–20. W. ; B. & P. ; O.E.D. (Sup.) ; Manchon.—2. And : slovenly coll. : C. 19–20.

un- is properly prefixed to words of Germanic origin. In C. 18 the C. 14–17 (esp. C. 17) vacillation between *un-* and *in-* (*im-*) before words of Latin origin was terminated in favour of the more logical *in-* (*im-*) before such words, *un-* disappearing altogether or being retained to convey a sense different from that of an accepted *in-* (*im-*) form ; a number of absolutely synonymous doublets, however, remain (e.g. *unalienable*, *inalienable*), though the literate tendency is to discard the *un-* form ; note that *unable*, *uncourteous*, etc., have not been changed,—largely because these words have ' passed through older French ' and, perhaps, partly because, in that transition, their Latinity has > less obvious. (Mostly O.E.D.)

unan. Unanimous : (mostly) upper classes' : C. 20. (John G. Brandon, *West End*, 1933.)

unappropriated blessing. An old maid : cultured jocular coll. (— 1923). Manchon.

unattached. (Of a member of the legislation) whose vote can never be counted on by any party : Parliamentary coll. : mid-C. 19–20. Ware. [Unattached participles :—See Fowler.]

unauthordox. See authordox.

unbeknowns ; -nst, adj. and adv. Unknown ; without saying anything : resp., rare, mainly dial., mid-C. 19–20 ; and coll. (in C. 20, low coll.) and dial., mid-C. 19–20. T. H. Huxley, 1854, ' I hate doing anything of the kind " unbeknownst " to people,' O.E.D. Ex *unbeknown* on the slightly earlier dial. *unknownst*.

*unbetty. To unlock : c. (— 1812). Vaux. Ex *betty*, a picklock.

unboiled lobster. See lobster, unboiled.

unbounded assortment of gratuitous untruths. ' Extensive systematic lying ' : a Parliamentary c.p. of late 1885–mid-86. Ware, ' From speech (11th Nov., 1885) of Mr Gladstone's at Edinburgh '.

uncertainty. A girl baby : printers' : from ca. 1870. Opp. *certainty*, a boy baby. Cf. also the complementary *one-nick* and *two-nick*.

uncle ; gen. my, his, etc., uncle. A pawnbroker : 1756, Toldervy (O.E.D.) ; Grose, 1st ed. ; Hood ; Dickens. Hence, *uncle's*, a pawnbroker's shop · Grose, 1st ed. (*mine uncle's*). Prob. ex the legend of rich or present-giving uncles.

uncle, Dutch. See Dutch uncle.

uncle, he has gone to visit his. A c.p. applied to ' one who leaves his wife soon after marriage ', Grose, 1st ed. ; † by 1900.

uncle, if my aunt had been a man she'd have been my. A c.p. addressed derisively to one who makes a ridiculous surmise : ca. 1670–1850. Ray.

uncle, my. See uncle.

uncle, your. I ; myself : non-aristocratic : late C. 19–20 ; slightly ob. In C. 20, very often just *uncle*. Cf. *yours truly*, I, myself.

uncle (or U.) Antony to kill dead mice, helping. Wasting one's time ; idling : coll. C. 20. C. Lee, *Our Little Town*, 1909. (Apperson.)

uncle Charlie. (In) heavy marching-order : military : from 1914. F. & Gibbons. Cf. *Charlie*, military sense.

Uncle Fred. Bread : C. 20. P. P., *Rhyming Slang*, 1932.

Uncle George. King George III : a coll. nickname : C. 19–20 ; latterly, only historical. Marryat, 1829 (O.E.D.). Cf. *Farmer George*.

Uncle Jeff. Admiral Sir Geoffrey Phipps Hornby (1825–95) : naval : 1869–95. Bowen.

uncle Ned. Bed : rhyming s. : late C. 19–20. F. & Gibbons.

uncle over, come the. A variant of ' come the *Dutch uncle* ' (q.v.).

Uncle Sam. The U.S. government or people : ' usually supposed to date back to the war of 1812 ' (F. & H.), this coll. nickname has, in C. 20, > S.E. Perhaps facetiously ex the letters *U.S.* Thornton ; Albert Matthews ; F. & H.

uncle Three Balls. A lower-classes' variant (— 1887) of *uncle*, q.v. Baumann.

Uncle Willie. Silly : from ca. 1870. P. P., *Rhyming Slang*, 1932. Contrast *Uncle Fred* and *Uncle Ned*.

uncle's, mine or my. See uncle.—2. A privy or w.c. : ca. 1780–1850, *aunt* (q.v.) succeeding. Cf. the Fr. *chez ma tante* (used also in sense 1).

uncling. See go uncling.

uncommon. Uncommonly, very much : (C. 20, low) coll. and dial. : from ca. 1780.

Uncrowned King, the. Parnell : political nickname : 1881–91. Ware, ' The crown . . . that of Ireland, from one of whose kings, like most Irish leaders, C. S. Parnell [1846–91] was descended.'

unction. See blue unction.

***under,** n. Sexual intercourse : **o. :** C. 20. James Curtis, *The Gilt Kid*, 1936.

under. Under (the influence of) a narcotic : medical coll., now verging on S.E. (R. Blaker, *Night-Shift*, 1934.)

under, down. In the Antipodes : 1899 (O.E.D.) : coll. >, by 1920, S.E.

under-cart. Under-carriage of a 'plane : Royal Air Forces' : from 1932.

***under-dubber** or **-dubsman.** A warder other than the chief warder : c. : C. 19. *Lex. Bal.* See **dubber** and **dubsman.**

under-grounder. A bowled ball that does not rise : cricket coll. : 1873 ; ob. Lewis.

under hatches. Dead and buried : nautical coll. : mid-C. 19–20. Bowen.

under one, do all. To do it all at one ' go ' : low (— 1887). Baumann.

under or over. ' Under the grass ', dead, or ' over the grass ', alive, but divorced or being divorced : Society, esp. Anglo-American : ca. 1860–1914. Ware. (Applied to widows in reference to their husbands.)

under-petticoating, go. To go whoring or copulating : low : ca. 1870–1920.

under-pinners. The legs : coll. : from late 1850's ; ob. Cf. *understandings.*

under sailing orders. Dying : nautical coll. : mid-C. 19–20. Bowen. Cf. *under hatches*, q.v.

***under-shell.** A waistcoat, as *upper-shell* is a coat : c. : C. 19.

under the arm. See arm, under the.

under the belt. In the stomach : coll. : 1815, Scott.

under the crutch. See crutch, under the.

under the influence. Tipsy : coll. : C. 20. Abbr. *under the influence of liquor.*

***under the screw, be.** To be in prison : c. (— 1864) ; ob. H., 3rd ed.

under the sea. ' In sail, lying to in a heavy gale and making bad weather of it ' : nautical coll. : late C. 19–20. Bowen.

undercome(-con- or **-cum-)stumble ; under-stumble.** To understand : illiterate or jocularly perversive coll. : resp. (low) coll. and dial., mid-C. 19–20, ex dial. *undercumstand* ; ca. 1550, Anon., *Misogonus*, ' You unde[r]stumble me well, sir, you have a good wit,' with *stumble* substituted for *stand.* Cf. *tumble*, v., 2, q.v., and *umble-cum-stumble*, q.v.

underdone. (Of complexion) pale or pasty : ca. 1890–1915. Ware. It partly superseded *doughy*, q.v.

undergrad. An undergraduate : coll. : 1827 (O.E.D.) ; after ca. 1914, rarely used by university men or women.—2. Hence, a horse in training for steeplechasing or hunting : the turf : late C. 19–20 ; ob.

undergraduette. A girl ' undergrad ' : s. >, by 1930, coll. : 1919, *The Observer*, Nov. 23, ' The audience was chiefly composed of undergraduates and undergraduettes,' W.

undershoot. To fail to land at the intended spot : Royal Air Force's : from 1932.

understandings. Boots, shoes : from ca. 1820 :

coll. >, by 1874, s. ; ob. H., 5th ed., ' Men who wear exceptionally large or thick boots, are said to possess good understandings.'—2. Hence, legs ; occ., feet : 1828 (O.E.D.). Cf. the pun in *Twelfth Night*, III, i, 80.—3. See standing room.

undertake, v.i. To be a funeral-undertaker : coll. (— 1891). *Century Dict.*

undertaker's squad, the. Stretcher-bearers : military : 1915 ; slightly ob. F. & Gibbons.

undies. Women's, hence occ. children's, under-clothes : (orig. euphemistic) coll. : 1918, ' Women's under-wear or " undies " as they are coyly called ', *Chambers's Journal*, Dec. (O.E.D.) ; 1934, *Books of To-Day* (Nov.), ' I like my daily paper, | But one thing gets me curl'd, | And that's the morning caper | Of London's " undie "-world,'—with which cf. the quotations at *briefs* and *neathie-set.* Perhaps on *nightie* or, more prob., *frillies*, q.v. ; cf. the ob. S.E. *unders*, in same sense.

undigested Ananias. A triumphant liar : ca. 1895–1914. Ware quotes *The Daily Telegraph*, June 24, 1896.

***undub.** To unlock, unfasten : c. of ca. 1810–50. Vaux. See *dub up.

undy. The rare singular of *undies* : 1928, A. P Herbert (O.E.D. Sup.).

unearthly hour, time. A preposterously early hour or time : coll. : 1865 (O.E.D.).

unfair. Unfairly : sol. : C. 19–20. Ware.

unfledged. (Of persons) naked : jocular coll. (— 1923). Manchon. Extended from ' feather-less '.

Unfortunate Gentlemen. The Horse Guards, ' who thus named themselves in Germany ', Grose, 1st ed., where a topical origin is alleged : military : ca. 1780–1840.

ungrateful man. A parson : ca. 1780–1830. Grose, 1st ed. Because he ' at least once a week abuses his best benefactor, i.e. the devil '.

ungly. Incorrect for *ugly* (adj. and adv.) : C. 15–early 16. O.E.D.

ungodly. Outrageous ; (of noise) dreadful : coll. : 1887, Stevenson (O.E.D.). Cf. *infernal*, *unholy.*

ungryome. (One's) hungry home : lower classes' coffee-houses' sol. (— 1880). Ware.

unguentum aureum. A bribe ; a tip : ca. 1780–1840. Grose, 1st ed. Lit., golden ointment : it cures surliness, reluctance, tardiness, and negligence.

ungummed. Disrated or reduced in rank ; dismissed ; superseded : military : 1915 ; ob. F. & Gibbons. Ex Fr. *dégommé.* Also *unstuck.*—2. See unstuck, come.

unhealthy. (Of area) exposed to gun-fire ; unsafe. G.W. military coll. W. ; B. & P.

unhintables. See unmentionables.

unholy. Awful ; outrageous : coll. : 1865, Dickens (O.E.D.). Whence, prob., *ungodly*, q.v.

unhung for unhanged (of persons) is in C. 20 considered almost a sol.

uni ; gen. **the Uni.** A, one's own, university : Australian coll. : C. 20.

unicorn. A carriage (or coach) drawn by three horses, two wheelers abreast and a leader : s. (— 1785) >, by 1820, coll. >, by 1850, S.E. ; ob. Grose, 1st ed. Ex the unicorn's single horn compared with the leader out in front.—2. Hence, a horse-team thus arranged : from ca. 1860 : coll. >, almost imm., S.E.—3. Hence, two men and a woman (or vice versa) criminally leagued : c. : from ca. 1870 ; ob.

Union, the. The workhouse : lower classes' coll. (— 1887). Baumann.

Union Jack. The Union Flag : coll. (C. 19–20) >, ca. 1930, S.E. (W., in 1921, could still describe it as ' incorrect '.)

Unions. Shares in the Union Pacific Railroad : Stock Exchange coll. (— 1895). A. J. Wilson, *Stock Exchange Glossary.*

unique(ly) is often catachrestically used to mean ' excellent(ly) ' : C. 19 (? 18)–20.

United Kingdom of Sans Souci and Six Sous. ' Riddance of cares, and, ultimately, of sixpences ', Egan's Grose : Oxford University : ca. 1820–40.

Univ. University College, Oxford : Oxford University coll. : mid-C. 19–20.

***universal staircase.** The treadmill : c. : ca. 1850–1910. Mayhew. Also *everlasting staircase.*

unkinned. Unkind : Society : 1884–early 85. Ware. Ex Wilson Barrett's substitution, in *Hamlet*, of *unkin'd* for *unkind.*

unkermesoo (or **-zoo**). Stupid : tailors' : C. 20. A fanciful word.

unload, v.i. and t. To drop (bombs) on the enemy : Air Force jocular coll. : from 1915. F. & Gibbons.

unlocked, to have been sitting in the garden with the gate. To conceive (esp. a bastard) child : a virtual c.p. : late C. 19–20 ; ob. With a pun on *garden.*—2. To have caught a cold : ca. 1890–1910.

unmentionables. Trousers : coll. : U.S., anglicised, as a coll., in 1836 by Dickens ; slightly ob. The chronology of these semi-euphemisms (all ob. in C. 20) is : *inexpressibles,* prob. 1790 or 1791 ; *indescribables,* 1794 ; *unexpressibles* and *unspeakables* (both, 1810 ; rare) ; *ineffables,* 1823 ; *unmentionables,* 1830 ; *unexplicables,* 1836 ; *unwhisperables,* 1837 ; *innominables,* ca. 1840 ; *indispensables,* 1841 ; *unutterables,* 1843 ; *unhintables* (— 1904). Calverley satirised the group when, in his *Carmen Sœculare,* he described the garment as *crurum non enarrabile tegmen,* ' that leg-covering which cannot be told ' (W.). See also **inexpressibles.**

unmonkeyable. (Of a person or thing) that one cannot play tricks with : coll. (— 1923). Manchon.

***unpalled.** Single-handed : c. : ca. 1810–90. Vaux. Lit., without a ' pal ', q.v. (But only of one who has been deprived of his pals.)

unparliamentary. Obscene : coll. : from ca. 1870. H., 5th ed. (Other nuances, S.E.)

unpaved. Rough ; inflamed with drink : low : ca. 1870–1910. F. & H.

[**unpleasantness, the late.** The war of 1914–18 : from Dec., 1918 : a mildly jocular understatement that some consider S.E., and others (including myself), coll. It may be noted that it was employed in U.S. as early as 1868 in reference to the American Civil War : O.E.D. (Sup.).]

unrag. To undress : Yorkshire and Gloucestershire s. (— 1905), not dial. E.D.D. Ex *unrig,* q.v., on *rags,* clothes.

unrelieved holocaust. A Society c.p. of 1883 applied to even a minor accident. Ware. Ex the phrase used by a writer in *The Times* to describe the destruction, in 1882, of the Ring Theatre in Vienna and of a circus at Berditscheff in Russia, both accompanied by a heavy loss of life.

[**unrig,** to undress, is a coll. verging on, prob. achieving the status of, S.E. : late C. 16–20 ; in late C. 19–20, dial. except where jocular.]

unrove his life-line, he (has). He is dead, he died : nautical coll. (— 1883). Clark Russell.

uns. See **we-uns** and **you-uns.**

unshop. To dismiss (a workman) : lower classes' (— 1923). Manchon.

***unslour.** To unlock, unfasten, unbutton : c. : ca. 1810–50. Vaux. See **slour** and cf. *unbetty* and *undub.*

unspit. To vomit : low (— 1887). Baumann.

unstick, v.i. To leave the ground as one begins a flight : Air Force : from 1916. F. & Gibbons.

unstuck, come. The vbl. form of *ungummed* (q.v.) or *unstuck.* B. & P.—2. Hence, to go amiss ; to fail : from ca. 1919. E.g. Dorothy Sayers, *The Five Red Herrings,* 1931, ' The plan came rather unstuck at this point.'

unsweetened. Gin ; properly, unsweetened gin : low : from ca. 1860 ; ob.

***unthimble ; unthimbled.** To rob of one's watch ; thus robbed : c. : ca. 1810–80. Vaux. See **thimble.**

untwisted, adj. Ruined, undone : coll. : late C. 17–early 19. B.E. ; Grose, 2nd ed.

unutterables ; unwhisperables. See **unmentionables.**

unyun. Unnecessary for *onion,* except when pronounced *un-yun'.* Baumann.

up, v. To rise abruptly, approach, begin suddenly or boldly (to do something) : coll. and dial. : from ca. 1830. Lover, 1831, ' The bishop ups and he tells him that . . .' From ca. 1880, gen. *up and* ——, as in ' You have the . . . insolence to up and stand for cap'n over me ! ' O.E.D.—-2. See **up with.**—3. See **upped** (Addenda).

up, adj. Occurring ; amiss : as in ' What's up ? ', What's the matter ?, or, when *up* is emphasised, What's wrong ? Mid-C. 19–20 : coll. rather than s. Albert Smith, 1849 (O.E.D.) ; Jeaffreson, 1863, ' I'll finish my cigar in the betting room and hear what's up.' Prob. ex *up to* (as in ' What are you up to now, you young rascal ? '). A C. 20 variant is *(it's all) up the country (with* a person) : Manchon.

up, adv. At or in school or college ; on the school or college roll ; in the capacity of pupil or student : coll. : from mid-1840's. Gen. implies residence, but often as in ' X was up in your time— 1925–8.' Prob. abbr. *up there.*—2. On horseback ; riding : 1856, H. Dixon (O.E.D.) ; ' Sydney Howard Up in the Derby ' was a cinema title in 1933–4.

up, preposition. In coïtion with (a woman) : low : late (? mid-)C. 19–20.—2. See ' Westminster School slang.'

up-a-daisa, up-a-dais(e)y. See **ups-a-daisy.**

up a tree. See **tree.** A proletarian intensive (mid-C. 19–20 ; ob.) is *up a tree for tenpence,* penniless (Ware).

up against. Confronted by (a difficulty) : coll. : U.S. (1896, George Ade : O.E.D. Sup.) >, by 1914, anglicised. Esp. in the phrase *up against it,* in serious difficulties : 1910, *Chambers's Journal,* April, ' In Canadian phraseology, we were " up against it " with a vengeance ! ', O.E.D. See also Fowler. Cf. :

up against a (or the) wall. Sentenced to death : military : from 1916. F. & Gibbons. (It was there usually, that such a soldier was shot.)

up against you !, that's. What do you say to that ? : coll. : late C. 19–20.

up and ——. See **up,** v.

up and do 'em. To begin spinning the pennies : two-up players' coll. : C. 20.

up-and-down job. An engineer's, a trimmer's job ' in a reciprocating-engined, as opposed to a turbine, steamer ': nautical coll. : from 1904. Bowen.

up and down : mind the dresser. A c.p. used when dancing in a farmer's house : Anglo-Irish : C. 20.

up-and-down place. ' A shop where a cutter-out is expected to fill in his time sewing ', F. & H. : tailors' : from ca. 1870 ; ob. Ex *up-and-down*, fluctuating, changeable.

up-and-downer. A violent quarrel : lower classes' : late C. 19–20. P. MacDonald, *Rope to Spare*, 1932. Ex changing positions of participants.

up at second school, be. ' To go to any one for work at 10 or 11 o'clock ', F. & H. : Harrow School (— 1904) : coll. > j.

up-foot. (To get or rise) to one's feet : low coll. (— 1887). Baumann, ' [I] up-foot and told him.'

up-hander. A soldier surrendering : military coll. : 1916 ; ob. Manchon. Ex the gesture of surrender

up in. Well informed on, clever at, practised in : coll. : 1838, Dickens : 1885, Anstey, ' I did think Potter was better up in his work.' O.E.D.

up in Annie's room. See **Annie's room.**

up in one's hat. Tipsy : low : ca. 1880–1910. Cf. *screwed.*

up in the stirrups. Having plenty of money : low (— 1812) ; ob. Vaux, ' " In swell-street " ',— see swell street. Ex riding.

up jib or the stacks or (the) stick(s). To be off ; pack up and go : from ca. 1860 ; ob. The first is nautical, the others non-aristocratic. H. Kingsley, 1865, ' I made them up stick and take me home.' Cf. :

up killick. To run away : nautical : late C. 19– 20. Bowen. Ex nautical **j.** *up killick*, to weigh anchor.

up on oneself, be. To be conceited : mostly Cockney : late C. 19–20.

up one's sleeve, it is (was, etc.) six pots. He (etc.) is (was, etc.) drunk : mid-C. 19–20 ; ob. Ware.

up or down. Heaven or hell : lower and lower-middle classes' euphemistic coll. : mid-C. 19–20. Ware.

Up School. Upper School (' the great school-room ', Ware) : Westminster School coll. : mid-C. 19–20.—2. **up-school**, detention, may be coll. rather than j. : see ' Westminster School slang '.

up-stage. Haughty, supercilious ; conceited : theatrical coll. (from ca. 1920) >, by 1933, gen. S.E. (O.E.D. Sup.) Ex *play up-stage*, a foremost role.

up-stairs. Up in, up into, the air : aviators' coll. : from 1918. O.E.D. (Sup.).

up-tails all. See **uptails all.—up the country.** See up, adj.—**up the pole.** See pole, up the.—**up the spout.** See spout.—**up the stick.** See stick.— **up the tree.** See tree, up the.—**up the weather, go.** See weather, go down or up the.—**up there.** See want it.

up to. Before, as in Trollope, 1862, ' She told me so, up to my face,' O.E.D. ; coll. ; ob. ? ex *looking up to.*—2. Obligatory (up)on ; (one's) duty ; the thing one should, in decency, do : coll. : U.S. (1896, George Ade the inimitable : O.E.D. Sup.), anglicised ca. 1910. *The East London Dispatch* (South Africa), Nov. 10, 1911 ; C. J. Dennis, 1916 ; Hugh Walpole, 1933. Orig. in poker, as Greenough & Kittredge remark.

up to a thing or two, be. To ' know a thing or two ' : coll. : 1816 (O.E.D. Sup.).

up to blue china, live. To spend all, or more than, one's income : ca. 1880–1915. Ex *blue china* as a sign of gentility.

up to Dick, dictionary. See **Dick, dictionary.**

up to much, not. (Rather) incapable ; (of things) inferior : (dial., from ca. 1860 ; hence) coll. : 1884, Sala, ' The shoes were not, to use a vulgarism, " up to much ",' O.E.D.

up to putty. See **putty.—up to slum, snuff.** See **slum, snuff.**

up to the or **one's cackle, gossip,** or **try-on.** Alert, shrewd, experienced : low : resp. C. 19, late C. 18–mid-19 (G. Parker, 1781), mid-C. 19–20 (ob.). See also the nn. and cf. *snuff, up to.*

up to the knocker, nines. See **knocker, nines.** A rare variant is *up to the door.*

up to trap. Shrewd ; alert : see **trap**, n., in sense of sagacity. It occurs in David Moir's *Mansie Wauch*, 1828 (E.D.D.).

up with. To raise (esp. one's arm) ; to lift or pick up : coll. : 1760, Henry Brooke, ' She ups with her brawny arm.' Cf *up*, v.

up you go with the best of luck ! ' The M.O.'s valediction when sending you up the line after hospital ' (B. & P.) : c.p. of the G.W.

upards or **up'ards.** Upwards : sol. : C. 19–20. Mayhew, 1861.

***uphills.** Dice so loaded as to turn up high numbers : gaming c. (— 1700) >, s. ; † by 1840. B.E. ; Grose, 1st ed. Opp. *low men*, q.v.

upon. See (the) cross, (one's) say-so, (my) sivvy, (the) square, (the) suit.—2. (Adv.) Gen. *all upon*. Almost : sol. (— 1923). Manchon, ' The button's all upon off,' almost detached.

upper-and-downer. A wrestling-match : lower classes' (— 1909). Ware. Cf. *up-and-downer*, q.v.

***upper-ben** or **benjamin.** A great-coat : c. >, ca. 1840, low s. : late C. 18–20 ; ob. Grose, 2nd ed. (*u. benjamin*) ; H., 1st ed. (id.). App., *upper ben* (Vaux) is C. 19–20. The term *benjy*, stated by H., 3rd ed., and by F. & H. to be a synonym, is also applied to a waistcoat (H., 1st ed.). A great-coat was orig. termed a *joseph*, ' but, because of the preponderance of tailors named *Benjamin*, altered in deference to them ', H., 5th ed. (Vaux, 1812, has also *upper tog* : see **tog, upper.**)—2. In pl., trousers : low : ca. 1850–80. ' Ducange Anglicus.'

upper-crust. The head (not, as F. & H. says, the skin) : boxing : from ca. 1825 ; ob. Egan. Ex *u.-c.*, the top crust of a loaf of bread.—2. Hence, a hat : ca. 1850–1910.—3. The higher circles of society ; the aristocracy : coll. : orig. (mid-1830's), U.S. ; anglicised ca. 1890, but in England already ob. by 1920, and virtually † by 1930. Cf. *upper ten*, q.v.

Upper Crust, Mr. ' He who lords it over others ', Bee : low : ca. 1820–40. Whence, perhaps, *upper-crust*, 3.

upper lip, stiff. See **stiff upper lip.—upper loft.** See upper storey.

***upper shell.** A coat : c. : C. 19. Cf. *under-shell*, q.v.

upper sixpenny. A playing field at the College : Eton : mid-(? early) C. 19–20.

upper storey or **works.** The head ; the brain : resp. 1788, Grose, ob., and from ca. 1770, both Smollett and Foote using it in 1771–4. Occ., ca. 1859–1910, *upper loft* (H., 2nd ed.). All of architectural origin, *loft* prob. being suggested by *bats in the belfry* : cf. *unfurnished in the upper storey* (or *th* *garret*), empty-headed, a nit-wit,—a phrase given by Grose, 2nd ed., as *his upper storey* or *garrets* [*is*,] *are unfurnished*; *wrong in his upper storey*, however, indicates lunacy (H., 5th ed.).

upper ten, the. The upper classes; the aristocrats: coll.: orig. U.S. and in the form *the upper ten thousand* (1844); in England the longer form (ob. in C. 20) is recorded in 1861, the shorter a year earlier. 'Usually referred to N. P. Willis'—an American journalist well known in England—' and orig. applied to the wealthy classes of New York as approximating that number', F. & H. Cf. *upper crust*, q.v.—2. Hence *upper-tendom*, the world of the upper classes: orig. (1855) and mainly U.S.: likewise coll.—Also, 3, *upper-ten set*, servants employed by 'the upper ten': these servants' (— 1909). Ware.

upper works. See **upper storey.**

uppers, (down) on one's. In (very) reduced, in poor, circumstances; occ., having a run of bad luck: U.S. (— 1891) coll., anglicised ca. 1900. Orig. *on one's uppers*; *down* being, app., unrecorded before 1904 (F. & H.). Ex shoes so worn that one walks on the uppers.

uppish. Having, at the time, plenty of money: ca. 1678–1720. B.E. The earliest sense of the word, which is otherwise, despite Swift's condemnation of the 'cock-a-hoop' sense, S.E.

uppy. (Of a stroke) uppish: cricketers' coll.: 1851; † by 1900. Lewis.

upright. A drink of beer strengthened with gin: 1796, *The Sporting Magazine* (O.E.D.); ob.—2. The sexual act performed standing, a 'perpendicular': late C. 18–20. See **threepenny bit.**

upright, go. A c.p. (late C. 17–early 19) defined by B.E. as 'Said by Taylers and Shoemakers, to their Servants, when any Money is given to make them Drink and signifies, bring it all out in Drink, tho' the Donor intended less and expects Change or some return of Money'.

*upright man. The leader of a band of criminals or beggars: c.: mid-C. 16–early 19. Awdelay, 1561; Middleton; B.E., 'Having sole right to the first night's Lodging with the *Dells*' (q.v.); Grose, 1st ed., 'The vilest stoutest rogue in the pack is generally chosen to this post.' Perhaps because he carries a short truncheon. See esp. Grose, P.

uproar. An opera: ca. 1760–1830. G. A. Stevens, 1762, has it in the form *opperore*; Grose, 1st ed., *uproar*. Cf. *roaratorio*, an oratorio.

ups-a-daisy !; upsi- or **ups(e)y-daisy !; up-a-daisa, -daisy, -daisey, -dazy.** A cry of encouragement to a child to rise, or as it is being raised, from a fall, or to overcome an obstacle, or when it is being 'baby-jumped': C. 18–20 ⁘ S.E. until mid-C. 19, then coll. and dial. Resp., mid-C. 19–20; id.; and mid-C. 19–20, mid-C. 18–20, id., and C. 18. An elaboration on *up*, perhaps influenced (via *lackadaisy*) by *lack-a-day !* O.E.D.

Ups and Downs, the. The 69th Foot Regiment, from ca. 1881 the 2nd Battalion of the Welsh Regiment: military: C. 19–20; ob. Ex the fact that the number can be read upside down. (F. & Gibbons.) See also **Agamemnons.** Frank Richards, however, in *Old-Soldier Sahib*, 1936, explains the nickname more satisfactorily when he refers to 'the 2nd Welsh Regiment, who started as a mixed battalion of old crocks and young recruits, then fought for some time as marines, and at the finish, after nearly two hundred years of service, were officially converted into Welshmen'.

[**upsee** (occ. **upse, upsie, upsey, upzee,** but properly **upsy**) **Fre(e)ze,** i.e. **Friese**; hence **upsy Dutch**; hence **upsy English.** After the Frisian, Dutch, English fashion, orig. and esp. of modes of drinking: late C. 16–17: perhaps orig. coll., but gen. considered S.E. Ex Dutch *op zijn*, on his, hence in his (sc. fashion). O.E.D.; F. & H.]

upset the apple-cart. See **apple-cart.—upsidaisy.** See **ups-a-daisy.**

upshot. A riotous escapade, drunken frolic: ca. 1810–40. *Lex. Bal.* (preface).

upsides with (a person), **be.** To be even or quits with; to be (more than) a match for: (orig. Scots; from mid-C. 19, also English) dial. and coll.: from the 1740's. O.E.D.; E.D.D.—2. Hence, on a level with: coll.: from ca. 1880. Variant, *be upsides of*, to be alongside of: 1894 (O.E.D.).

upstairs. (For the adv., see **up-stairs.**) A special brand of spirits: London public-house: late C. 19–20. Because usually kept on a shelf. The brand, etc., varies with the house. F. & H., 'A drop of upstairs '.

upstairs, adj. In pawn: Glasgow (— 1934). Euphemistic. Cf. *stuck away.*

upstairs, kick (a person). To thrust (e.g. an unpopular statesman) into a higher office: political coll. (— 1887). Baumann.

upstairs out of the world, go. To be hanged: jocular coll.: late C. 17–18. Congreve, 1695, 'By your looks you should go,' etc.

upsy-daisy. See **ups-a-daisy.**

uptails (up-tails) all, play at. To coït: ca. 1640–1750: coll. rather than s. Herrick. Ex the name of a song and its lively tune.

*uptucker. A hangman: c. (— 1864); ob. H., 3rd ed. Ex *tuck*, v, 1.

upwards of, correct as 'rather more than ', is catachrestic (and dial.) when = 'rather less than ': late C. 19–20. Esp. E.D.D.

urger. A race-course tipster: Australian (— 1926). Jice Doone. Cf. *tip-slinger.*

Uriahites. The 3rd Battle Squadron of the Grand Fleet: naval officers': 1914; ob. Bowen. Is there a pun on *striking all of a Uriah Heap ?* No; the reference is to that Uriah whom David, with sinister intent, set 'in the forefront of the battle' (F. & Gibbons)

Urinal of the Planets, the. Ireland: literary coll.: late C. 17–mid-19. B.E., 'Because of its frequent and great Rains, as *Heidelberg* and *Cologne* in *Germany*, have the same Name on the same Account '. Cf. *England's umbrella*, q.v.

urjee. A (humble) petition: Anglo-Indian coll. (— 1886). Corruption of *urz(ee)*. Yule & Burnell.

us. We: a frequent sol. in mod. English. Cf. *we uns*, q.v.—2. In the predicate, after some part of the v. *to be*, it is, however, merely coll. and dial.; if any emphasis is laid, it is almost S.E.: C. 19 (prob. earlier)–20. ' "Who's there ?" "It's us "' is coll., but ' "It wasn't you ", "It was *us*, we tell you "' borders on S.E.—3. Me; to me: dial. and (low) coll.: recorded in 1828, but prob. considerably older.

[**use, the.** Ware's definition is incorrect, the term, moreover, is S.E.]

*use at (a place). To frequent: c.: from mid-1870's. Horsley, *Jottings from Jail*, 1877, 'I got in company with some of the wildest people in London. They used to use at a pub. in Shoreditch.' Ex dial. *use about, round.*

use for, have no. To consider superfluous or

tedious or objectionable : coll. : orig. (1887), U.S. ; anglicised ca. 1900. Cf. *have no time for*, q.v.

use to (do something). To be accustomed to do it, in the habit of doing it : M.E.–C. 20 : S.E. until mid-C. 19, then coll. ; in C. 20, almost a sol. (N.B., the past tense, *used to*, is, however, still S.E.) E.g. ' I didn't use to do that,' ' He hadn't used to do it,' are now illiterate coll.

use up. See towards end of next entry.

used up. Killed : military : mid-C. 18–mid-19. Grose, 1st ed., ' Originating from a message sent by the late General [John] Guise, on the expedition '— ca. 1740—' at Carthagena, when he desired the commander-in-chief, to order him some more grenadiers, for those he had were all used up ' ; actually, of the 1,200 attacking the castle of St Lazar, a half were, within a couple of hours, killed or wounded.—2. Hence, broken-hearted ; utterly exhausted (1840) ; bankrupt : mid-C. 19–20 : the second nuance being coll. bordering on S.E. ; the other two, s. ; all three nuances are ob. H., 1st ed. ; Calverley, 1871, ' But what is coffee but a noxious berry | Born to keep used-up Londoners awake ? ' The O.E.D. records *use up*, to tire out, as a coll. at 1850 : app. ex *used up*, utterly exhausted.

useful. Very good or capable ; (extremely) effective or effectual : from ca. 1929. E.g. ' He's a pretty useful boxer.'

Ushant-eyed. ' A man with a fixed eye. Ushant lights were once one fixed and the other revolving ' (Bowen) : nautical coll. : C. 20 ; ob.

Ushant Team, the. The Channel Fleet blockading Brest during the Napoleonic Wars : naval coll. of that period. Bowen.

***usher !** Yes ! : c. : from 1870's ; ob. Horsley, *Jottings from Jail*, 1877. Prob. ex Yiddish *user* (it is so), as F. & H. proposes ; possibly suggested by *yessir !*

usher of the hall, the. The odd kitchen-man : Society : ca. 1880–1910. Ware.

using the wee riddle. (Vbl.n.) Pilfering : Clyde-side nautical : late C. 19–20. Bowen, who gives an anecdotal explanation.

usual, as per. As usual : coll. : 1874, W. S. Gilbert. Occ., later, *per usual*. (O.E.D.) Ex, and orig. jocular on, the commercial use of *per*, perhaps influenced by Fr. *comme par ordinaire* (W.).

usual, his, her, my, our, their, your. His (etc.) usual state of health : coll. : from mid-1880's. Annie S. Swan, 1887, ' Aunt Susan is in her usual,' E.D.D.

util. Only in *util actor*, that actor who can take almost any part : theatrical (— 1909). Ware.

utter in affected use is S.E. except when it occurs in such a phrase as s. *the blooming utter*, the utmost (Henley, 1887) ; even *utterly utter*, which the O.E.D. records at 1882, is S.E., but *quite too utterly utter* (F. & H., 1904) is coll.

-uvver is, in illiterate speech, found for *-other* where the *o* is pronounced *ŭ* ; especially in Cockney. E.g. *bruvver* (q.v.), *muvver*, *smuvver*. Certainly C. 19–20, probably from centuries earlier.

V

[Under *v*, F. & H. has the following ineligibles ; S.E. :—vagaries ; vagrant ; vain-glorious ; vanner ; vantage loaf ; vapour ; varlet ; varmint, n. ; varying (a Winchester ' vulgus ') ; veal, vealy ; veck ; velvet-cap, -jacket, -pie ; velveteen ; venturer ; Venus ; verdant ; vessel ; view-point ; viewy ; villadom ; violento ; virago ; virgin-knot, -treasure ; virginhead ; visor-mask ; vixen ; volant ; voluntary ; vulgus,—but see entry. Dial.: —victuals, in one's.]

v for **th.** E.g. *farver* for *father*. Sol., mostly Cockney : C. 19–20. P. G. Wodehouse, *The Pothunters*, 1902, ' Go in at 'im, sir, wiv both 'ands.'

v for **w** is an indication of Cockney birth or influence. Recorded first in Pegge, 1803, it must have arisen considerably earlier ; genuine examples, in fact, of this change, as of *w* for *v*, occur in the *Diary* (1550–63) of Henry Machyn, as W. points out in *Adjectives and Other Words*. This *v* for *w* is a change which ' recent investigators have been unable to verify as still existent ', O.E.D., 1928. (American writers often err in using it in the speech of post-War Cockneys.) Dickens, 1837, ' Ve got Tom Vildspark off . . . ven all the big vigs . . . said as nothing couldn't save him,' O.E.D. Cf. the converse *w* for *v*.

V, make. To make horns (the first and second fingers being derisively forked out) as an implication of cuckoldry : coll. : early C. 17. Chapman.

V. and A., the. The Royal yacht the Victoria and Albert : naval coll. : C. 20. F. & Gibbons.—2. The Victoria and Albert Museum : museum-world coll. : late C. 19–20.

V.C. Plucky : London : ca. 1881–90. Ware.

I.e. deserving of the Victoria Cross.—2. **V.C. mixture.** Rum : military : from 1915. F. & Gibbons. Because of the Dutch courage thereby imparted.

V.R. Ve (i.e. we) are : a London, esp. Cockneys', c.p. at the time of Queen Victoria's Diamond Jubilee (June, 1897). Punning *V.R.*, Victoria Regina. Cf. *Jubileeve it*, q.v.—2. In ' evasive reference to the prison van, which, in the reign of Victoria, bore these initials on each side ' : lower classes' : ca. 1850–1901. Ware. Also *vagabonds removed* : ibid. : id.

vac. A vacation : university and, though less, school coll. : C. 18–20. Often with capital initial. White, *West End*, 1900, ' Fork out . . . I'll pay you back in the Vac.'

***vacation.** An imprisonment ; a prison : tramps' c. (— 1932). Frank Jennings, *Tramping with Tramps*.

vag, on the. ' Under the provisions of the Vagrancy Act ', C. J. Dennis : Australian and to some extent, English (and U.S.) : late C. 19–20.

vagabonds removed. See **V.R.**, 2.

vain, take one's name in. To mention a person's name : coll. : C. 18–20. Swift, ' Who's that takes my name in vain ? '

vakeel. A barrister : Anglo-Indian coll. : mid-C. 19–20. H., 3rd ed., 1864. Properly a representative. Ex Urdu *vakil*, Arabic *wakil*. Yule & Burnell.

vainglorious man. See **piss more . . . valley.** See **cascade.**

valoose. Money : soldiers' (Eastern front and Egypt) : C. 20 ; esp. in G.W. Ex Arabic. B. & P., ' The soldiers' usual reply to beggars and touts in Egypt was *Mafeesh valoose.*'

vally. A valet : illiterate coll. : C. 18 (? earlier)–20. Cf. Scots *vallie.*

vamos, vamoss, vamoos, vamoose, vamoosh, vamose, vamous, varmoose. To depart, decamp, disappear : U.S. coll. (ca. 1840), anglicised as s. : 1844, Selby, in *London by Night,* 'Vamoose—scarper—fly ! ' The forms *vamoss* (C. 20), *vamous* (H., 1st ed.) and *varmoose* (1862) are rare, while *vamoosh* (Baumann) or *vamosh* (Manchon) is illiterate, and *vampose* or *vampoose* is incorrect—but rare after the 1850's. Ex Sp. *vamos,* let us go.—2. As v.t., to disappear from, the word has not caught on in England.

***vamp.** A robbery : c. : mid-C. 19–20 ; ob. Perhaps ex *vamp,* v., 1, q.v.—2. See **vamps.**—3. A woman that makes it her habit or business to captivate men by an unscrupulous display of her sexual charm : coll. : 1918 (O.E.D. Sup.). Abbr. *vampire.*

vamp, v. To pawn : late C. 17–19 : c. >, by 1780, low s. B.E. ; Grose, 1st ed. ; H., 3rd–5th edd. Ex *vamp,* to renovate.—2. (V.t. and i.) To attract (men) by one's female charms ; to attempt so to attract (them) : coll. : 1927 (O.E.D. Sup.). Ex *vamp,* n., 3, q.v.—3. To eat : military : 1914 ; ob. F. & Gibbons. Possibly ex the S.E. musical sense influenced by horses' *champing.*

***vamper.** A thief ; esp. one of a gang frequentnig public-houses and picking quarrels ' with the wearers of rings and watches, in hopes of getting up a fight, and so enabling their " pals " to steal the articles ', H., 3rd ed., 1864. Cf. *vamp,* n., 1.—2. (Gen. in pl.) A stocking : c. : late C. 17–early 19. B.E. ; Grose, 1st ed. ' Perhaps an error for *vampeis* or *vampeys* ', O.E.D. Cf. *vamps* q.v.

vamping, n. and adj. of *vamp,* v., 2, q.v.

vampire. The ghost in Punch and Judy : showmen's : mid-C. 19–20. See **swatchel.** Cf. *vampo.* —2. A person insufferably boring or wearisome : from ca. 1860 ; very ob. Ex lit. sense. (Occ. *vampyre.*)

vampo. The clown (see **vampire,** 1) : id. : id. : ? ex Lingua Franca. See **swatchel.**

vampo(o)se. See **vamos.**

vamps. Refooted stockings : London (— 1859). H., 1st ed. Ex lit. S.E. sense.

van. (Ad)vantage : lawn tennis : C. 20.

Van, Madam. See **Madam Van.**

van blank (or **blonk**). White wine : military coll. : G.W. (F. & Gibbons.) A mispronunciation of Fr. *vin blanc.*

van blank (or **blonk**) **anglee.** Whiskey : military : G.W. (F. & Gibbons.) Ex preceding.

***van-dragger.** ' One who steals parcels from vans ' (David Hume) : c. : C. 20.

van John. A s. corruption of *vingt-et-un* : orig. and mainly university : 1853, ' Cuthbert Bede ', ' " Van John " was the favourite game ' ; ob.

Van Neck, Miss or **Mrs.** ' A large-breasted woman ', Grose, 2nd ed. : low : late C. 18–early 19. Because she is well to the fore.

vandemonianism. Rowdyism : Australian coll. : ca. 1860–90. Morris. Ex *Vandemonian,* an inhabitant of Van Diemen's Land (Tasmania), esp. as applied to a convict resident there in early C. 19 ; suggested partly by *demon.*

vandook. A corruption of *bandook,* q.v. : Regular Army : late C. 19–20. F. & Gibbons.

vantage. Profitable work : printers' coll. : late C. 17–18. Moxon. Cf. *fat,* printers' n.

vardi or **-ie.** See **vardy.**

***vardo.** A waggon ; *vardo-gill,* a waggoner : c. (— 1812) ; † by 1900. Vaux. Ex Romany *vardo* (or *wardo*), a cart. (Sampson's *verdo*).—2. Hence, a caravan : grafters' : from ca. 1880. (P. Allingham, *Cheapjack,* 1934.)

vardo, v.t. To see, look at, observe : Parlyaree and low London (— 1859). H., 1st ed., ' *Vardo the cassey* [gen. *casa, carsey, case*], look at the house ' ; H., 5th ed. (1874), ' This is by low Cockneys gen. pronounced *vardy.*' Cf. *dekko,* q.v. ; perhaps ex Romany *varter,* v.t., to watch ; note, too, that since in Romany *v* and *w* are nearly always interchangeable, there may be a connexion with *ward* (esp. in *watch and ward*).

vardy. A verdict ; an opinion : C. 18–20 coll. and (in C. 20, nothing but) dial. Swift has *vardi,* an occ. C. 18 form,—and *vardie* occurs in C. 18–20 ; Grose, 2nd ed. ; H., 3rd ed. Ex †*verdit,* verdict. (O.E.D.)—2. See **vardo,** v.

varicose. A varicose vein ; (collectively with pl. v.) one's varicose veins : coll. : C. 20.

varjus. Verjuice : Cockney (— 1823) ; **ob.** ' Jon Bee.' Cf. *clargy* and *sarvice.*

varment, varmint. ' A sporting amateur with the knowledge or skill of a professional ' : mainly sporting : ca. 1811–40. Byron, 1823, ' A thorough varmint, and a real *swell,* | Full flash, all fancy ', O.E.D. Perhaps ex dial. *varment,* a fox.—2. Hence, spruce, natty, dashing : ca. 1811–80 ; extant in dial., though ob. even there. *Lex. Bal.*—3. Hence, *varment* (more gen. *varmint*) *man,* a ' swell ' : Oxford and Cambridge University : ca. 1823–40. Anon., *Alma Mater,* 1827.—4. Vermin : low (— 1823) ; ob. Egan's Grose.

varment, varmint, adj. See n., 2 and 3.—2. Knowing, cunning ; clever : dial. (— 1829) soon > s. ; in C. 20, only dial. Trelawny, 1831 (O.E.D.). Ex *varment,* a fox.

varmentish ; varmentey. The adj. and n. of *varment,* n., 1 and esp. 3 : ca. 1811–30. *The Sporting Magazine,* 1819, ' Nothing under four horses would look " varmentish ",' O.E.D.

varmint-man. See **varment,** n., 3.—2. One who writes themes for idle undergraduates : university : ca. 1840–1900. Perhaps ex sense 1.

varnish. Bad champagne : Society : ca. 1860–1905. Ware.

***varnisher.** A coiner of counterfeit sovereigns . c. (— 1864) ; ob. H., 3rd ed. Because this finishing touch often gave an effect of varnish.

varsal ; 'varsal. Universal, whole ; mostly in *in the varsal world* : illiterate coll. (1696, Farquhar : O.E.D.) >, in C. 19, dial.—2. Hence, single : ca. 1760–1820, then dial. ; rare and ob. Scott.—3. Hence, adv. : extremely : 1814, ' A varsal rich woman ', O.E.D. : rare coll. and dial. ; ob. Cf. *versal,* q.v.

varsity, V. ; 'varsity, 'V. University College, Oxford : Oxford University coll. : mid-C. 19–20.—2. Orig. university coll., now gen. coll. for *university* : from ca. 1845. Dorothy Sayers, in *The Passing Show,* March 25, 1933, ' Nobody says " undergrads " except townees and journalists and people outside the university. . . . Stick to " University ". " Varsity " has somehow a flavour of the 'nineties.'—3. As adj. : 1863 (O.E.D. Sup.) ; 1864, Tennyson. Whether as n. or adj., the term, in its wider sense, has not always been approved at the two older English universities. Ca. 1640–1700, *Versity :* likewise coll. W. ; O.E.D.—4. **varsity tit.** See **tit,** 4.

vaseline. Butter: Royal Military Academy: late C. 19–20. Cf. *grease.*

vast of, a. A great amount (e.g. of trouble) or number: dial. (1794: E.D.D.) > also, by 1900, proletarian coll. Manchon.

vatch. (To) have: back s., esp. butchers': late C. 19–20.

Vaughan, the. The School library: Harrow coll.: late C. 19–20. Ex Dr Vaughan (1816–97), the famous headmaster of Harrow.

vaulting-school. A coll. or s. (? orig. c.) variation of *v.-house*, a brothel: ca. 1605–1830. H. Parrot, 1606 (O.E.D.); B.E.; Grose.—2. Hence, ' an Academy where Vaulting, and other Manly Exercises are Taught ', B.E.: c. or s.: late C. 17–early 19. Grose.

've. HAVE: coll. (*he've*, e.g., is sol.): C. 19–20. Rather rare in the infinitive, as in A. Fielding, *Death of John Tait*, 1932, ' My road sense seems to've deserted me for the time being.' Often intrusive: see **of,** v., and **have,** v.

veal will be cheap, calves fall. A jeering c.p. addressed to a spindle-legged person: from ca. 1670; ob. Ray, 1678. Cf. *mutton dressed as lamb.*

veg. Vegetable(s): eating-houses' coll.: mid-C. 19–20. E.g. ' Meat and two veg '. Ex abbr.

vegetable breakfast. A hanging: low jocular: late C. 19–early 20. The meal consists of an artichoke (punning *hearty choke*) and ' caper sauce ' (q.v.).

Vein-Openers, the. The 29th Foot Regiment, from ca. 1881 the 1st Battalion of the Worcestershire Regiment: military: late C. 18–20; very ob. F. & Gibbons, ' The first to draw blood ' in the American War.

*velvet. The tongue; ' especially the tongue of a magsman ', H., 5th ed. : in gen., late C. 17–20, c. >, by 1800, low s. (B.E., Grose); in particular sense, from ca. 1870, low s. Ex its texture. See **velvet, tip the.**

velvet, on. In an easy or advantageous position: 1769, Burke (O.E.D.): S.E. rapidly > sporting coll., Grose, 1st ed., having ' *to be upon velvet*, to have the best of a bet or match ' ; esp. as = sure to win. Hence the next two entries.

velvet, play on. To gamble with winnings: gaming s. (in C. 20, coll.): from ca. 1880. Ex *velvet, on*, q.v.; perhaps influenced by :

velvet, stand on. ' Men who have succeeded in their speculations, especially on the turf, are said to stand on velvet,' H., 5th ed., 1874.

*velvet, tip the. ' To Tongue a Woman ', B.E.: late C. 17–20 : c. >, by 1800, low s. Grose, 1st ed. See **velvet** and **tip,** v., 4, 6.—2. To scold : low : ca. 1820–50. Bee.

[**velvet !, to the little gentleman in.** This C. 18 Anglo-Irish Tory and Roman Catholic toast verges on the coll., *the little* . . . *velvet* being that ' mole which threw up the mound causing Crop (King William [III]'s horse) to stumble'. Grose, 3rd ed.]

vemon ; vemynous. Venom ; venomous : incorrect forms : C. 15. O.E.D.

Venetian cramps. ' Peculiar and ritualistic variation of " cramps " (used in various bedroom ceremonies)' : Bootham School : from before 1900. Anon., *Dict. of Bootham Slang*, 1925.

vengeance. See **whip-belly.**

venerable monosyllable. The female pudend : ca. 1785–1840. Grose, 2nd ed. See **monosyllable.**

venial. Venal : catachrestic : late C. 19–20. E. F. Benson employs it cleverly in *Secret Lives*, 1932.

venter, n. and v. (To) venture : sol., esp. Cockneys' (— 1887). Baumann.

ventilator. ' A play, player, or management that empties ' a theatre : theatrical (— 1904). F. & H. Neat wit on the lit. sense.

ventually. Eventually : (low coll. or) sol. (— 1887). Baumann.

venture-girl. A poor young lady seeking a husband in India : Anglo-Indian : ca. 1830–70. Ware.

venture it as Johnson did his wife, and she did well,—I'll. A semi-proverbial c.p. implying that it sometimes pays to take a risk : ca. 1670–1800. Ray, 1678 ; Fuller, 1732. Apperson.

Venus is occ. used catachrestic for *Venice* : C. 17–20. E.g. *Venus sumach.* O.E.D.

Veranda(h), the. The gallery of the old Victoria Theatre : London : late C. 19. Ware.

verb-grinder. A (pedantic) schoolmaster : coll. : 1809, Malkin ; ob. On *gerund-grinder*, q.v.

Verey. See **Véry.**

*verge. A gold watch : c. : late C. 19–20. F. & H. Ex a *verge* (*watch*).

verites ; V. At Charterhouse, a boarding-house : mid-C. 19–20 ; ob. ' A corruption of *Oliverites*, after Dr Oliver Walford, 1838–55 ', F. & H.

vermilion. To besmear with blood : sporting : 1817 (O.E.D.) ; virtually †.

verneuk ; verneuker ; verneukerie. To swindle, cheat, deceive ; one who does this ; such behaviour : South African coll. : resp. 1871, 1905, 1901. Direct ex Cape Dutch. Pettman.

Verry. See **Véry.**

versal, 'versal. Universal, whole ; gen. with *world* : illiterate coll. : late C. 16–19. Shakespeare ; Sheridan.—2. Hence, single : id. : 1709, Mrs. Manley, ' No versal thing '. O.E.D. Cf. *varsal*, q.v.

*versing law. Swindling with counterfeit gold : c. of ca. 1590–1620. Greene. Ex :—*verse*, v.i. and v.t., to practise fraud or imposition (on) : id. Ibid. Cf. :—*verser.* A member of a band of swindlers : c. : ca. 1550–1620. ? ex *verse*, to overthrow, upset.

Versity. See **varsity.**

vert ; 'vert. A pervert or convert to another religion (esp. Roman Catholicism) : coll. : 1864, *The Union Review*, May number. W., however, thinks that it may have originated, ca. 1846, with Dean Stanley.—2. Occ. as v.i. : coll. : 1888.

vertical. A plant living on the side of a perpendicular rock-face : gardening s. (— 1902) >, ca. 1910, coll. O.E.D.

vertical breeze or gust. See **wind vertical.**

*vertical care-grinder. A treadmill : c. (—1859) ; almost †. H., 1st ed. Known also as the *everlasting, horizontal,* or *universal staircase.*

verticle is a C. 17 incorrectness for *vertical*, n. and adj. O.E.D.

very at end of phrase or sentence is coll. (—1887). Baumann, ' And when it is faded, that looks ugly, very.'

Véry or **Vérey ; Verey ; Verry.** Incorrect for *Very* (*flare, light, pistol*) : from 1915.

very cheese, the ; the very ticket. Correct ; requisite : Glasgow : C. 20. Ex *the cheese, the ticket.*

very famillionaire. Characteristic of the patronage shown by rich men : Society : 1870's. Ware. Ex *familiar* + *millionaire.*

very froncey. Very pronounced ; vulgar : Society : ca. 1870–1905. Ware. Ex *très français*, very French.

very ' oh my !' Smug : Glasgow (— 1934)

very well. An intensification of *well*, adj. (q.v.). Ware.

vessel. The nose : sporting : ca. 1813–30. *The Sporting Magazine*, LXI (1813), ' There d—n your eyes, I've tapped your vessel,' O.E.D. Cf. *tap one's claret.*

vest, lose one's. To get angry : low : ca. 1890–1910. A mere elaboration of *get one's shirt out*, q.v. ; cf. *shirty.*

Vestas ; vestas. Railway Investment Company deferred stock : Stock Exchange (— 1895). A. J. Wilson, *Stock Exchange Glossary.*

[**vestat.** Is this a ghost word ? F. & H., at *rorty*, quotes *The Chickaleary Cove* (ca. 1864) : ' The vestat with the bins so rorty '.]

vet. A veterinary surgeon : coll. : 1864, H. Marryat (O.E.D.).—2. Whence, *the vet*, the medical officer : military : from 1914. F. & Gibbons.

vet, v. To cause (an animal) to be examined by a ' vet ' (q.v.) : coll. : from ca. 1890. Ex *vet*, n , 1.—2. Hence, to examine, occ. to treat, (a person) medically : coll. : 1898, Mrs Croker (O.E.D.).—3. Hence, to revise (a manuscript) : a book-world coll., orig. and mainly publishers' : from ca. 1910.—4. Also, to sound, or ask questions of (a person), in order to discover his abilities or opinions : coll. : from ca. 1920. Richard Keverne, *The Havering Plot*, 1928, ' I brought you here so that I might " vet " you. I do things like that—and then trust my instinct.'

vex. (So much the) worse, as in *vex for you* : Christ's Hospital : from ca. 1860. Perhaps ex L. *pejus* (pronounced—one may presume—*peddjus*), but more prob. simply an abbr. of *vexing* or *vexation.*

vic ! Cave ! : Felsted School : from ca. 1870. Hence, *Keep vic*, to watch against official intrusion. Perhaps from L. *vicinus*, near, or even L. *vigil* or the imperative of *vigilare*, to watch.—2. The Victoria Theatre : London (— 1859). H., 1st ed.—3. Queen Victoria : London streets' (— 1860) ; ob. H., 2nd ed.—4. The Princess Royal : Society : early C. 20. Ware.—5. Victoria Station : London streets' (— 1887). Baumann.

Vic, the Old. This coll. for the Old Victoria Theatre has, since ca. 1925, been virtually S.E.

vicar of St Fools, the. (Implying) a fool : a semi-proverbial coll. : mid-C. 16–17. Heywood, 1562 ; Nashe, 1589 ; Howell, 1659, and Ray, 1670, omit the *Saint* (Apperson.) Sc. *Church* ; by punning ' topography '.

vice-admiral of the narrow seas. See *seas.*

vice (or Vice), **the.** The Vice-Chancellor, -President, etc. : coll. (— 1887). Baumann.

Vice-Chancellor's court. ' Creditor's last shift ', Egan's Grose : Oxford University : ca. 1820–50.

Vice-Chuggins, the. The Vice-Chancellor : Oxford undergraduates' : late C. 19–20. Charles Turley, *Godfrey Marten, Undergraduate*, 1904. Cf. *Wuggins*, Worcester.

Viceroy, the. Sarah Jennings, 1st Duchess of Marlborough. Ex her influence with Queen Anne. (Dawson.)

Vics, the. A variant of *the Queen Vics*, q.v. (F. & Gibbons.)

victual. A ' feed ' (not a school meal) ; to eat, feed : Bootham School : C. 20. Anon., *Dict. of Bootham Slang*, 1925. Ex S.E. *victuals.*

victualler ; victualling-house. A pander ; a house of accommodation : late C. 16–17 : resp., Shakespeare, *2nd Henry IV*, Act II, sc. iv ; and Webster, *A Cure for a Cuckold.* Because a tavern-

keepers' trade often cloaked intrigue and bawdry. Cf. *bagnio*, q.v.

victualling department or **office.** The stomach : boxing > gen. s. : resp. 1878 (O.E.D.) and 1751, Smollett ; both are ob. By a pun on that Government office which victuals the Navy. Cf. *bread-basket* and *dumpling-depot.*

***view the land.** To examine in advance the scene of a crime : c. (— 1887). Baumann.

viewy. Designed, or likely, to catch the eye ; attractive : 1851, Mayhew ; ob. Hence, *viewiness*, display : theatrical (— 1923). Manchon.

vigilance. ' A crude periscope consisting of a mirror affixed to the top of a stick ' : military : late 1914 ; ob. B. & P.

***vile, ville, vyle.** A city, a town : c. : in combination from 1560's ; by itself, app. not before C. 19. *Romevil(l)e, -vyle, Rum-*, London : mid-C. 16–20 ; *deuce-a-vile, deuseaville, daisyville*, the country : mid-C. 17–20. By itself, ' *No. 747* ' (valid for 1845) ; H., 1st ed., 1859, ' Pronounced *phial*, or *vial*.' Ex Fr. *ville.*

vile, adj. As a mere intensive (cf. *foul*) = ' unpleasant ', ' objectionable ' : coll. : C. 20.

vill ; V. Felsted village : Felsted School : mid-C. 19–20. Prob. independent of poetic S.E. *vill*, a village, and of preceding entry.

village (or V.), **the.** London : sporting coll. : from ca. 1820 ; slightly ob. Westmacott, 1825 (O.E.D.) ; H., 3rd ed., which adds : ' Also a Cambridge term for a disreputable suburb of that town, generally styled " *the* village " ' ; the reference holds for the 1860's–70's.—2. **Hardware Village,** Birmingham : from early 1860's ; ob. H., 3rd ed.

village blacksmith. A performer or actor not quite a failure, his engagements never lasting longer than a week : music-halls' and theatrical (—1909) ; ob. Ware. Ex Longfellow's poem, ' *Week in, week out*, from morn till night . . .'

***village butler.** A petty thief ; esp. an old thief ' that would rather steal a dishclout than discontinue the practice of thieving ', Potter, 1795 : c. of ca. 1790–1850. F. & H. misprints it as *v.-bustler.*

villain as ever scuttled a ship, I'm as mild a. A c.p. applied to oneself in jocular reproach : coll. (— 1904). Prob. on S.E. *I'm a bit of a villain myself, but* ——

***ville.** See *vile.*

villian. Villain : sol. (— 1887). Baumann. In C. 20, often jocular among the educated : as, e.g., in K. de B. Codrington's notable, unknown novel, *The Wood of the Image*, 1934 (p. 28).

vim. Force ; energy : U.S. (adv., 1850, † ; n., early 1870's), anglicised : ca. 1890 : coll. >, ca. 1910, S.E. Either echoic or ex L. *vis* (accusative *vim*), energy, strength. Cf. *pep*, q.v.

vin. Wine : Australian soldiers' : in G.W. Ex Fr. *vin blanc.*

vin blink. French white wine : New Zealand soldiers' : 1916–18. Ex Fr. *vin blanc.*

***vincent.** A dupe in a betting game : c. : ca. 1590–1830 ; though prob. ob. in C. 18–19. Greene ; Grose. Etymology obscure : ? ironic ex L. *vincens*, (being) victorious. Whence ?

***vincent's** (or V.) **law.** The art and practice of cheating at a betting game, esp. bowls or cards : c. : same period and history as preceding. Greene ; Grose, 1st ed. Here, *law* = lay = line of criminal activity.

***vinegar.** A cloak : c. : late C. 17–early 19. B.E. ; Grose, 1st ed. Perhaps because it is worn in *sharp* weather. Cf. the semantics presumably operative in :—2. ' The person, who with a whip in his hand, and a hat held before his eyes '—cf. the man that, in a public conveyance, pretends to sleep while women are strap-hanging—' keeps the ring clear at boxing matches and cudgel playings ', Grose, 1st ed. : sporting : ca. 1720–1840. *A New Canting Dict.*, 1725.

ving blong. French white wine (' vin blanc ') : military : from 1914. Frank Richards, *Old Soldiers Never Die*, 1933.

vintage. Year of birth : U.S. (— 1883) >, by 1890, English. Ware. Ex *vintage*(-year) of wines.

violently. Showily, ' loudly ' (e.g. dressed) : coll. : 1782, Mme D'Arblay ; ob. O.E.D.

violet ; garden-violet. An onion ; gen. in pl. as = spring onions eaten as a salad.—2. Pl., sage-and-onion stuffing. Both, proletarian-ironic : from ca. 1870 ; slightly ob.

violets, Brits's. An East African campaign term of 1917–18, as in F. Brett Young, *Jim Redlake*, 1930 : ' Doomed horses . . . fed till they dropped, and became, in their noisome end, what the soldiers called " Brits' violets ".' Brits commanded a contingent of Boers in German East Africa.

vir-gin. See **man-trap.**

virgin. A cigarette made of Virginia tobacco : smokers' (— 1923). Manchon.—2. A mixture of *vermouth* and *gin* : topers' (— 1923). Ibid.—3. A term of reproach among chorus-girls : from ca. 1920.

Virgin Mary's (Body-)guard, the. The 7th Dragoon Guards : military : mid-C. 18–20 ; ob. ' They served under Maria Theresa of Austria, temp. George II,' F. & H. See also **Strawboots.**

Virgin of the Limp, the. See **Lady of the Limp.**

virgins ; V. Virginia New Funded Stock : Stock Exchange : late C. 19–20 ; ob.

virgins' bus, the. The last bus running from Piccadilly Corner westward : lower classes' : ca. 1870–1900. Ware. Its chief patronesses were prostitutes.

virgin's dream, the. See **maiden's prayer.**

virtue. ' Smoking, drinking, whoring. When a man confesses to abstention from tobacco and intoxicating liquors he is perversely said to have no virtues,' F. & H. : non-aristocratic : ca. 1880–1915.

virtue rewarded. A c.p. in reference to occupants of prison-vans (bearing *V.R.* on their sides) : lower classes' : ca. 1870–1901. Ware. Cf. *V.R.*, 2, and *vagabonds removed.*

vish. Angry ; cross : Christ's Hospital : from ca. 1890. Abbr. *vicious* in this sense. It superseded *passy* (abbr. *passionate*), q.v.

visitation. An over-long visit or protracted social call : coll. : 1819 (O.E.D.). Ex the length of ecclesiastical visitations.

vittles. ' An accountant officer, R.N., borne for victualling duties ' : naval : C. 20. Bowen.

vitty. Fitty, i.e. fitting, suitable ; neat : late C. 16–20 : S.E. until C. 18, then s. († by 1900) and dial. (O.E.D.).

viva. A viva-voce examination : university coll. : from ca. 1890. Whence ?

viva, v.t. and, rarely (C. 20), v.i. To subject, be subjected to, a ' viva ' : id. : 1893 (O.E.D.). Ex preceding.

Vlam. Vlamertinghe, in Flanders : military coll. : G.W. Cf. *Pop*, Poperinghe. (F. & Gibbons.)

vocab. A vocabulary ; a glossary or dictionary :

Charterhouse (— 1904) >, by 1920, gen. Public School coll.

***vodeodo.** Money, cash ; booty : c. : from ca. 1930. James Curtis, *The Gilt Kid*, 1936. This has the appearance of being a rhyming fantasy on *dough*, money, possibly suggested or influenced by Romany *vongar*, money.

voetsak ! (To a dog) go away ! : South African coll. (— 1877). Prob. ex Dutch *voort seg ek !*, away, I say ! Pettman. Sometimes *footsack !*

***voil.** A rare form (Egan's Grose, 1823) of *vile*, n.

voise. A vase : sol. : mid-C. 19–20.

voker, v.t. To speak : tramps' c. and low s. (— 1859) ; ob. H., 1st ed. This is the orig. form of *rocker*, q.v. Cf. L. *vocare.*

vol, adj. Voluntary : Harrow School (— 1904). F. & H.

voluptious. Illiterate for *voluptuous* : C. 19–20.

[**Voluminous Prynne.** Wm. Prynne (1600–69), insatiable Puritan pamphleteer. Dawson.]

volunteer knee-drill. ' Abject adulation ' : Society and middle classes' (— 1909 ; † by 1920). Ware, ' Outcome of volunteer movement '.

von. One : see ' **v** for **w** '.

vote. To propose, suggest : coll. : 1814, Scott (O.E.D.). Only with *that* . . .

vote for the alderman. See **alderman, vote for the.**

vote khaki. To plump for the Liberal Unionists : 1900–1. Ware.

vouch. An assertion or formal statement : C.17–20 : S.E. until C. 19, then coll. : ob. (O.E.D.)

***voucher.** One of those who ' put off False Money for Sham-coyners ', B.E. : c. of ca. 1670–1720. Head. (He ' vouches for ' the counterfeit.) —2. (Gen. in pl.) A receipt clerk : bank-clerks' coll. : C. 20. Cf. *ledger.*

voucher, force the. To elicit money from the betting public and then abscond : sporting (— 1874). H., 5th ed.

voulez-vous squattez-vous ? Will you sit down ? : theatre gods' : from ca. 1820. ' Started by Grimaldi ', says Ware. Cf. *twiggez-vous.*

vowel. To pay (a winner ; indeed, any creditor) with an I.O.U. : C. 18–19. Steele, ' I am vowelled by the Count, and cursedly out of humour,' O.E.D. Ex either spoken formula, or written statement of, ' I.O.U.'

vowel-mauler. An indistinct speaker : not upper classes' : ca. 1880–1910.

voyage, Hobbe's. An act of coïtion : late C. 17–18. Vanbrugh, 1697, ' Matrimony's the spot . . . So now I am in for Hobbe's voyage ; a great leap in the dark.' Ex some lost topical allusion, unless it be a jeer at *Hob*, a country bumpkin.

***voyage of discovery.** ' Going out stealing ' : c. (— 1857) ; † by 1920. ' Ducange Anglicus.'

***vrow-case.** A brothel : c. : (prob.) late C. 17–mid-19. F. & H., who app. deduce it, justifiably (I think), from B.E.'s *case-fro*, ' a Whore that Plies in a Bawdy-house '. Ex Dutch *vrouw*, a woman, + *casa*, *case*, a house, shop, etc.

[**Vulgarization.** See Fowler.]

[**vulgus.** A Latin or, occ., Greek verse exercise : C. 19–20 : O.E.D. considers it S.E. : W., Public School s., ' for earlier *vulgars* ' (C. 16), ' sentences in [the] vulgar tongue [i.e. English] for translation into Latin '. See esp. R. G. K. Wrench, *Winchester Word-Book*, 2nd ed., 1901.]

Vun O'Clock. See **General One O'Clock.**

W

[Under **w**, F. & H. has admitted the following ineligibles ; S.E. :—**wabble** (or **wobble**) ; **waddle** ; **waddler** and **waddy** ; **wade** (act of wading) ; **waders** ; **wafer-woman** ; **wag's** here unrecorded ; **waggle** (to wag) ; **waggoner** ; **wagtail** ; **waistcoateer** ; **waister** ; **wait**, etc. ; unrecorded **walk's** ; do., **wall** ; **wamble-cropped** ; **wand** ; **wanion** ; unrecorded **want's** ; do., **war** ; **wardrobe** ; **ware** ; **warling** ; **warm's** unlisted ; **wash**, id. ; **waspish** ; **waste-time** ; **waster** ; **watch's** unrecorded ; **water**, id. ; **Watling Street** ; **way's** unrecorded ; **weak**, id. ; **weapon** ; **wear's** unlisted ; **weather**, id. ; **weave**, v. ; **wedge's** unlisted ; **wedlock** ; **wee** ; unrecorded **weed's** ; do., **week's** ; **weeper**, except as side-whisker ; **wegotism** and **weism** ; **weight** (lust) ; **well at a river, dig a** ; **Wellington** ; **Welsh ambassador** and **wig** ; **welt** ; **wench** ; **Westralia** ; **wet's** unrecorded ; **wether-headed** ; **whalebone**, **white as** ; **wharl** ; unrecorded **what's** ; **whay-worm** ; unrecorded **wheedle's** ; do., **wheel's** and derivatives ; **whelp**, n. ; **wherret** ; **whetstone, give the** ; unrecorded **whiff's** ; **whiffle** ; **whim's** and **whimling** ; **whimper** ; **whine** ; unrecorded **whip's** (including derivatives) ; **whirligig** ; **whirrit** ; unlisted **whiskey's**, etc. ; do., **whisper** ; do., **whistle** ; do., **white** and derivatives ; **Whitsun ale** ; **whittled** ; **whore's** undefined ; **why**, id. ; **wicket** ; **wide's** unrecorded ; **widgeon** ; **widow's man** ; **wild**, id. ; **willow** ; **willy-nilly** ; **wind's** unrecorded ; **window**, id. ; **wine** ; **wing** (to wound slightly) ; **wipe's** unrecorded ; **wire-puller** ; **wishy-washy** ; **wisp** ; **wittol** ; **wobble** ; unrecorded **wolf**, etc. ; do., **woman** ; **woodcock** (a simpleton) ; **woodman** (a wencher) ; unrecorded **wool's** ; **word and a blow, a** ; **work, make** ; **world** ; **worricrow** ; **wretch** and **wretchcock** ; **writerling** ; **writings** ; **wrong's** unlisted.

Dial. :—**wabbler** ; **wallop** (v. of agitation) ; **wapper-eyed** ; **weather-dog** ; **westy-head** ; **whack** (appetite) ; **whang** (a beating), **whangby**, **whanger** ; **what-like** and **-nosed** ; **whelk** (2, 3) and **whelking** ; **whennymegs** ; **whid** (a falsehood or exaggeration ; a quarrel or dispute) ; **whid, to tell lies** ; **whimmy** ; **whindle** ; **whipper** (anything excellent) and **whippy** ; **whisk-telt** ; **whistle-jacket** ; **whizzer** ; **widdy-waddy** ; **wooden sword, wear the** ; **wringle-gut** ; **wry-not.**]

w. A w.c. : late C. 19–20, non-aristocratic coll. ; ? orig. euphemistic. Always *the w.* E.g. in F. Brett Young, *Jim Redlake*, 1930.

w elided. ' In the unstressed second element of a compound, (w) tends to be elided in coll. speech . . . In some cases a mere vulgarism (. . . *back'ard, forrad, allus* for *always*),' O.E.D. : throughout mod. English.

w for r. Orig. and properly caused by a physical defect or, as in baby-talk, by immaturity, this feature has sometimes been a mere (fashionable) affectation ; the former, since time immemorial ; the latter, not before the 1830's. ' " Gwacious heavens ! " said his lordship,' O.E.D. Frequently in *wubbish*.

w for v. A Cockney habit arising in C. 16 (see ' **v** for **w** ') ex South-Eastern dial. ; very common in earlier half of C. 19, but † in C. 20. Foote, 1763, ' Yes, werry like Wenus ' ; the Dickensian Weller. American writers often err in using it of C. 20 Cockneys.

W.F.'s. Wild cattle : Tasmania : ca. 1840–80. Fenton, *Bush Life in Tasmania Fifty Years Ago*, 1891, ' The brand on Mr William Field's wild cattle '.

W.G. Dr William Grace (1849–1915), the great cricketer : cricketers' nickname. See esp. Bernard Darwin's delightful biography.

w.h. or **W.H.** A whore : euphemistic coll. (— 1887) ; ob. Baumann.

W.H.B., the. The ' Wandering Hand Brigade ', those who are apt to take liberties with women : late C. 19–20.

W.M.P. We accept the invitation : naval coll. verging on j. : late C. 19–20. I.e., with much pleasure.

W.P. ; **w.p.** Abbr. (— 1860) of *warming-pan*, 3, q.v. H., 2nd ed. ; ob.

W.P.B. To put into the waste-paper basket (*w.p.b.*, itself coll. : 1884) : coll. : from ca. 1930.

W. Two ; **W.2.** ' Satirical description of the Emperor William II . . . on his telegram to . . . Kruger on [Jan. 1] 1896 ' : only in that year.—Hence, 2, ' of any military-looking man stalking town ' : 1896–7. Ware.

Waac. A member of the Women's Auxiliary Army Corps : coll. : 1917, *The Times*, Nov. 19. (O.E.D. Sup.). Cf. *Wraf* and *Wren*, qq.v. Also spelt *Wack* : which is perhaps s.

wabbler. See foot-wabbler and **wobbler.—wack.** A mainly dial. form of *whack*, q.v.—**Wack** is also a variant form of *Waac*, q.v.

wad. A gunner : naval : mid-C. 19–20. Ware ' A survival from the days of muzzle-loading cannon '.—2. In the C. 20 underworld, it specifically = a roll of bank-notes. Charles E. Leach.—3. See wads, 1.—4. A fortune : C. 20. Cf. sense 2.

wad-scoffer. A bun-eater : esp. a teetotaller : military : from ca. 1904. F. & Gibbons. See **wads**, 2. Also *wad-shifter* : Regular Army : from ca. 1910. Frank Richards.

waddle ; orig. and gen. **waddle out** ; often extended to **waddle out lame duck** or **w.o. of the Alley.** To become a defaulter on the Exchange : Stock Exchange : 1771, Garrick, ' The gaming fools are doves, the knaves are rooks, Change-Alley bankrupts waddle out lame ducks ! ' ; Grose, 1st ed. ; 1860, Peacock (*waddle off*, rare) ; † by 1900. See **lame duck.**

waddy. A walking-stick : Australian coll. (— 1898). Ex lit. Aboriginal sense, a club. Morris.

wade. A ford : coll. : C. 19–20. Ex *wade*, an act of wading.

wadge, wodge. A lumpy mass or bulgy bundle : dial. (— 1860) >, ca. 1880, coll. Ex *wad* on *wedge*. O.E.D.—2. Hence, late C. 19–20, adj. *wodgy*.

wadmarel (C. 19 : nautical), **wadmus** (C. 18). Corruptions of *wadmal* (a woollen cloth). O.E.D. ; Bowen.

wads. A gunner : naval, esp. as a nickname : from ca. 1890. Bowen. Ex the use he makes thereof.—2. (Very rare in singular.) Buns ; occ., small cakes sold at a canteen : military : C. 20. F. & Gibbons. Ex shape ; also ex ' What doesn't fatten, fills.' Hence, *tea and a wad* = a snack, esp. that at the 11 a.m. break : Royal Air Force's (— 1935).

Waff. The West African Frontier Force : military coll. : G.W. Cf. *Waac.*

waffle. Nonsense; gossip(ing); incessant or copious talk: printers' (— 1888). Jacobi. Ex dial. *waffle*, a small dog's yelp or yap. Cf. *waffles* and :

waffle, v. To talk incessantly; printers': from ca. 1890. Ex *waffle*, to yelp.—2. To talk nonsense : from ca. 1890 : Durham School >, by 1910 or so, gen. Perhaps ex sense 1; cf., however, the n.—3. See **woffle.**

waffles. A loafer; a sauntering idler: low (— 1904); ob. F. & H. Cf. *waffle.*

Wafricans. West African stocks and shares : Stock Exchange : C. 20. *The Westminster Gazette,* Feb. 7, 1901, anathematises it as 'language murdered to the disgust of the purist'. Prob. on the analogy of *Westralian.*

wag, n. See **wag, hop the.**—2. V., to play truant; often *wag it*: mid-C. 19–20. Dickens, 1848 (O.E.D.). Ex:—3. **wag,** to go, to depart: late C. 16–20 : S.E. until C. 19, then coll.—4. V.t., gen. in negative. To stir (e.g. a limb): late C. 16–20 : S.E. until mid-C. 19, then coll. F. Harrison, 'I . . . declined to ask him . . . to wag a finger to get me there,' O.E.D. Cf. :—5. V.i., to move one's limbs : C. 13–20 : S.E. until mid-C. 19, then coll.; ob. Whyte-Melville, 1860 (O.E.D.).

wag, hop the ; play the wag ; play the Charley-wag. To play truant : 1861, Mayhew, the first two; 1876, Hindley, the third, which is very ob. Ex *wag,* v., 1, q.v.,—perhaps with a pun on lit. sense of *play the wag,* to be amusingly mischievous, to indulge constantly in jokes. In C. 20, often *wag it* (Manchon).

wag one's bottom. To be a harlot : mostly Cockney : late C. 19–20.

wagabone, n. and adj. Vagabond : C. 19. G. R. Sims, 'His wagabone ways' (Baumann). See 'w for v '.

Wagga-Wagga Guards, the. See **Tichborne's Own.** Wagga-Wagga in N.S.W. was frequently mentioned at the trial. F. & Gibbons.

wagger-pagger-bagger. A waste-paper-basket : Oxford University : from ca. 1905. Cf. *the Pragger-Wagger,* q.v., and see '-er, the Oxford'. Collinson; *Slang.*

waggernery ! O(h) agony !: lower Society : 1880's. Ware. The pun is specifically on *Wagner,* much ridiculed in that decade.

waggle. To wield (a bat, stick, oar): jocular coll.: C. 20. Ex lit. sense.—2. To overcome : low (— 1904); ob. except in U.S. F. & H. Cf. 1.

waggley ; gen. **waggly.** Unsteady; 'having frequent irregular curves' : coll. : 1894, E. Banks, 'Even in [the path's] most waggly parts', O.E.D. Lit., waggling.

waggon. 'In the old guardships, the place where the supernumeraries slung their hammocks': nautical : ? ca. 1840–90. Bowen.—2. A bunk (bed) : ships' stewards' (— 1935).—3. An omnibus : busmen's : from ca. 1928. *The Daily Herald,* Aug. 5, 1936.

waggon, on the. See **water-waggon.**

***waggon-hunter.** A brothel-keeper's tout visiting the inns at which the stage-coaches stopped : c.: 1760–1840. O.E.D.

***waggon-lay.** 'Waiting in the street to rob waggons going out or coming into town, both commonly happening in the dark', Grose, 3rd ed. : c. : late C. 18–mid-19.

wagon. See **waggon.**

wahine. A woman : New Zealand coll. : late C. 19–20. Direct ex Maori. Cf. *lubra.*

waipiro. Intoxicating liquor : id. : id. Straight from Maori.

waistcoat. See **wesket.**—2. **fetid waistcoat.** 'A waistcoat of a flaunting and vulgar pattern', F. & H.: ca. 1859. So 'loud' that it 'stinks to heaven'.

waistcoat piece. 'Breast and neck of mutton—from its resemblance to . . . half the front of a waistcoat not made up': tailors' (— 1909). Ware.

wait. To postpone (a meal) for an expected person : coll. : 1838, Dickens, 'It's a trying thing waiting supper for lovers,' O.E.D. Cf. *wait about.*—2. To wait at; only in *wait table,* to wait at table : servants' coll. (— 1887). Baumann.

wait about or around, v.i. To 'hang about': coll. : resp. 1879, Miss Braddon : 1895, orig. and mostly U.S. (O.E.D.)

wait and see ! A c.p. dating from March–April, 1910, when Asquith used it in reference to the date to be assigned for the reintroduction of Lloyd George's rejected budget. See esp. my anthology, *A Covey of Partridge.*—2. Hence, a French match : military : 1914–18. They often failed to light.

wait for it ! Don't be in too much of a hurry : military coll. : C. 20. Ex the order given in fixing bayonets.

wait till the clouds roll by ! A c.p. inducive of optimism : 1884; by 1915, a proverb. Ware, 'From an American ballad '.

waive and wave (esp. *w. away*) are occ. confused : C. 19–20.

waked. Awoke : in late C. 19–20, this is gen. considered sol. Baumann.

waler ; orig. **W.** A (cavalry) horse imported from New South *Wales* into India : 1849 (O.E.D.) : Anglo-Indian coll. >, ca. 1905, S.E. An advertisement in *The Madras Mail,* June 25, 1873 : 'For sale. A brown waler gelding '.—2. Hence, a horse imported into India from any part of Australia : from early 1880's. Yule & Burnell, 1886 ; *The Melburnian,* Aug. 28, 1896.

walk. To depart of necessity ; to die : mid-C. 19–20 : resp. coll. and s. Trollope, 1858 (latter sense). Ex *walk,* to go away. (O.E.D.)—2, v.t. To win easily : Public Schools' coll. : from ca. 1895 (P. G. Wodehouse, *A Prefect's Uncle,* 1903.) Abbr. *walk off with.*

walk, cock of the. See **cock.**

***walk, go for a.** To go to the separate cells ('separates') : c. : from ca. 1920. George Ingram, *Stir,* 1933.

walk, on the. (Of bank clerks and/or messengers) taking money round to other banks and to business-houses : commercial : C. 20.

walk, the ghost doesn't. See **ghost walks.** *Household Words,* 1853.

walk around, gen. **round.** To beat easily : coll., U.S. (Haliburton, 1853) anglicised ca. 1890. Cf. the synonymous *run rings round.*

walk down one's throat. To scold, abuse : late C. 19–20. Ex *jump* . . .

walk into. To attack vigorously : coll. : 1794, Lord Hood (O.E.D.).—2. Hence, to scold or reprove strongly : coll. : from 1850's.—3. To eat, drink, much or heartily of : 1837, Dickens (O.E.D.) ; id., 1840, 'Little Jacob, walking . . . into a home-made plum cake, at a most surprising pace.'—4. To 'make a hole in' one's money : 1859, Henry Kingsley (O.E.D.).—5. See :

walk into one's affections. To win a person's love or affection effortlessly and immediately : coll. : 1858 (O.E.D.).—2. Jocularly for *walk into*, 1 and 2, q.v. : 1859, H., 1st ed. ; also for *walk into*, 3 (Baumann, 1887).—3. Hence ironically, to get into a person's debt : from ca. 1860 : ob. H., 3rd ed.

walk it. To walk (as opp. to riding) : coll. : 1668, Pepys (O.E.D.).—2. (Of race-horse or dog) to win easily : turf : C. 20. Ex *walk*, 2.

walk, knave, walk ! A coll. c.p. taught to parrots : mid-C. 16–17. 'Proverbs' Heywood, 1546 ; Lyly ; 'Hudibras' Butler ; Roxburgh, *Ballads*, ca. 1685. (Apperson.)

walk one's chalks. See **chalks, walk one's.**

walk out, v.i. and n. (To have) an affair : Society : from ca. 1930. (Evelyn Waugh, *A Handful of Dust*, 1934.) Ex dial. v.t. *walk out*, to take one's fiancée out.

walk out with the bat. To achieve victory : Society : ca. 1880–1900. Ex a cricketer 'carrying' his bat. (Ware.)

walk round. To prepare oneself to attack or be attacked : lower classes' (— 1909). Ware. Ex dogs' circling.—2. See **walk around.**

walk Spanish. See **chalks, walk one's.**

*****walk the barber.** To lead a girl astray : c. (— 1859). H., 1st ed. (Anatomical.)

walk the chalk. 'To walk along a chalk line as a test of sobriety' : military (— 1823) >, by 1850, gen. 'Jon Bee.' See also **chalk, able to walk a.**—2. Hence, by 1845 at latest, to keep oneself up to the moral mark.

walk the pegs. In cheating at cribbage, to move one's own pegs forward or one's opponent's back : low s. >, ca. 1870, s., >, ca. 1900, coll. > 1920, S.E. : 1803 (O.E.D.). Lit., to make walk.

walk up (against) the wall. See **wall, crawl . . .**

walk up Ladder Lane and down Hemp Street. To be hanged at the yard-arm : nautical : C. 19. Cf. note at **hemp, hempen.**

walked off, be. To be led to prison : proletarian (— 1923). Manchon.

walked out, the lamp (has). The lamp has gone out, went out : jocular (— 1887) ; ob. Baumann.

Walker ! orig. and properly **Hook(e)y Walker !** 'Signifying that the story is not true, or that the thing will not occur', *Lex. Bal.*, 1811 ; *Walker* is recorded by Vaux in the following year.—2. Hence, be off ! : late C. 19–20.—3. As n., in, e.g., 'That is all (Hooky) Walker' : late C. 19–20. Ex sense 1, which derives perhaps ex 'some hook-nosed person named Walker', O.E.D.

walker. A postman : ca. 1860–1910. H., 3rd ed. Ex an old song entitled *Walker the Twopenny Postman.*—2. See **walkers.**—3. See preceding entry. —4. A coll. abbr. of *shop-walker* : (—)1864, H., 3rd ed.

Walker, my (or his, etc.) **name's.** I'm (he's, etc.) off : late C. 19–20. Ex *Walker*, 2, q.v.

walker !, that's a. A C. 20 variant of *Walker !*, 1. Manchon.

walkers. The feet : C. 19. Pierce Egan, 1832 (O.E.D.). ? ex †*walkers*, legs.

walking cornet. An ensign of foot : military (— 1785) ; † by 1890. Grose, 1st ed.

*****walking distiller.** See **distiller.**

walking-go. A walking-contest : coll. : C. 19–20 ; very ob. O.E.D.

*****walking mort.** A tramp's woman : c. : early C. 19. On *strolling mort.*

walking Moses ! See **Moses !**

walking-orders, -papers, -ticket. A (notice of) dismissal : U.S. (1830's) ; partly anglicised, esp. in the Colonies, in C. 20. Jocular.

*****walking poulterer.** One who hawks from door to door the fowls he steals : c. of ca. 1785–1840. Grose, 2nd ed.

walking speaking-trumpet. A midshipman engaged in passing orders : jocular naval coll. : C. 20. Bowen.

walking stationer. 'A hawker of pamphlets, &c.', Grose, 2nd ed., 1788 : (? orig. c. >) low s. ; ob. by 1870, † by 1900.

walking-stick. A rifle : Anglo-Irish : 1914 ; ob. (Orig. either euphemistic or secretive.)

walkist. A walker : sporting (esp. athletics) coll. (— 1887) ; ob. Baumann.

wall, crawl or **walk up the** ; in *Lex. Bal.*, 1811, also as **walk up against the wall.** 'To be scored up at a public house', Grose, 1st ed. : public-house (— 1785) ; † by 1850. Ex the mounting bill written up, in chalk, on the wall.

wall, up against the. In serious difficulties : military : from 1916. F. & Gibbons. Ex *up against a wall*, q.v.

wall and it will not bite you !, look on the. A jeering c.p. addressed to one whose tongue has felt the bite of mustard : ca. 1850–1910.

wall as anyone, see as far into a brick. See **see as.**

wall-eyed. Inferior, careless (work) ; irregular (action) : from the 1840's ; ob. by 1890, virtually † by 1930. Halliwell, 1847. The C. 20 equivalent for 'inferior' is *cock-eyed*. Ex *wall-eyed*, squinting.

wall-prop, be a ; **make wall-paper.** C. 20 variants (Manchon) of (*be a*) *wallflower*, q.v. below.

wallabies ; **W.** Australians : coll. : from ca. 1908. Mostly in sporting circles and esp. of teams of Australians. O.E.D. (Sup.).

wallaby, on the. On tramp : Australian s. >, ca. 1910, coll. : 1869, Marcus Clarke. Abbr. *on the wallaby-track.* In the 'bush', often the only perceptible track. Morris.

[**wallah**, in Anglo-Indian (hence in Army) compounds—e.g. *competition wallah*,—is simply a chap, a fellow : late C. 18–20. Only in certain (mostly, jocular) compounds (e.g. *amen-wallah, base-wallah*) is it eligible ; these will be found in their alphabetical place. Ex Hindustani *-wala*, connected with. See esp. Yule & Burnell.]

walled. (Of a picture) accepted by the Royal Academy : artists' : 1882 ; ob. Ware.

wallflower. A second-hand coat, exposed for sale : low London : 1804 (O.E.D.) ; ob. For semantics, cf. next sense.—2. Orig. and gen., a lady keeping her seat by the wall because of her inability to attract partners : coll. : 1820, Praed, 'The maiden wallflowers of the room | Admire the freshness of his bloom.'—3. Hence, any person going to a ball but not dancing, whatever the reason : coll. : from 1890's. *The Free Lance*, Nov. 22, 1902, 'And male wall-flowers sitting out at dances | Will reckon up their matrimonial chances.'

wallop ; occ. **wallup.** A clumsily ponderous, noisily brusque or violent movement of the body ; a lurching : coll. and dial. : 1820, Scott (O.E.D.). Ex *wallop*, v., 1, q.v.—2. A resounding, esp. if severe, blow : coll. (— 1823). 'Jon Bee.' Cf. v., 3.—3. Hence, the strength to deliver such a blow : boxing : from ca. 1910. *Varsity*, Feb. 24, 1914

'[He] has a prodigious "wallop", but no great amount of skill.'—4. Liquor: c.: from ca. 1930. James Curtis, *The Gilt Kid*, 1936, 'He could not stand his wallop as well as he had been able to.' Ex its potency.

wallop, occ. **wallup**, v.i. To move with noisy and ponderous clumsiness; to lurch, flounder, or plunge: dial. (early C. 18) >, ca. 1815, coll. (Scott, 1820: cf. n., 1). Ex *wallop*, to gallop; the word is echoic. O.E.D.—2. V.i., to dangle, to flap or flop about: recorded by O.E.D. in 1822, but prob. in fairly gen. coll. use as early as 1780: see **wallop in a tow** or **tether**.—3. V.t., to belabour, thrash: dial. (— 1825) >, in 1830's, coll.—4. Hence, fig., to get the better of: coll.: from ca. 1860. Meredith, 1865 (O.E.D.).

wallop, go (down). To fall noisily and heavily: coll.: and dial.: mid-C. 19–20.

wallop (or **wallup**) **in a tether or tow.** To be hanged: Scots coll.: from ca. 1780; slightly ob. Burns, 1785 (O.E.D.). Cf. *wallop*, v., 2, q.v.

walloper. One who belabours or drubs; that with which he does it—e.g. stick or cudgel: coll.: from ca. 1820. (E.D.D.) Ex *wallop*, v., 3, q.v.— 2. A hotel; drinking-den: c.: from ca. 1930. J. Curtis, *The Gilt Kid*, 1936. Ex *wallop*, n., 4.

walloping, n. and adj., to **wallop**, v. (q.v.): coll. Cf. *walloper*,—2. Also as adv., though it may be merely a reinforcing adj., as in Hyne, 1903, 'I came upon a walloping great stone.'

Wallsy. A Wall's Ice-Cream man: coll.: from ca. 1925. James Curtis, *The Gilt Kid*, 1936.

wallup. See **wallop**, n. and v.

wallwort is occ. applied incorrectly to the wall pellitory, the pellitory of Spain, and the comfrey: mid-C. 16–20. Properly *sambucus ebulus*. O.E.D.

Wallyford. 'The usual run on a wet whole school-day' (about 3½ miles): Loretto coll.: late C. 19–20.

walnut, shoulder. To enlist as a soldier: coll.: 1838, D. Jerrold; † by 1900. Cf. *brown Bess* and the coll. use of *mahogany*.

walnut-shell. A very light carriage: 1810 (O.E.D.); ob. Cf. *cockle-shell* (boat).

Waltham's calf, as wise as. Very foolish: coll.: ca. 1520–1830. Skelton; Grose, 3rd ed. Perhaps suggested by *the wise men of Gotham*, who 'dragged the pond because the moon had fallen into it' (Charles Kingsley). Apperson.

waltsom(e). Incorrect for *wlatsome*, detestable: late C. 14–16. O.E.D.

waltz; esp. **waltz hither and thither, (a)round** or **about.** To move in light or sprightly or nimble fashion; to buzz round or fuss about: from ca. 1870: resp. coll. and s. (The O.E.D.'s example of 1862 is S.E.)

waltz into. To attack, 'walk into' (a person): coll. (— 1923). Manchon.

waltz Matilda; gen. as vbl.n., *waltzing Matilda*, carrying one's swag: Australian: from ca. 1910. Ex the song *Waltzing Matilda*.

wamble; C. 18–20, **womble.** A rolling, or a feeling of uneasiness or nausea, in the stomach: C. 17–20: S.E. until mid-C. 18, then coll. and dial. As coll., ob. except in *the wombles*, a sensation of nausea. Ex *wamble*, to feel nausea.—2. Hence, milk fever: coll. and dial.: C. 18–20; ob.—3. A rolling or staggering movement or gait, esp. in (up)on the *wamble*, staggering, wobbly or wobbling: coll. (ob.) and dial.: from ca. 1820. Ex *wamble*, v.i., to roll about as one walks.

wamble (or, C. 18, **womble-)cropped** or **-stomached.** Sick at the stomach: resp. mid-C. 16–20, but in C. 19–20 only U.S. and until mid-C. 18, S.E.; C. 16–?, so prob. not late enough to be eligible. See **wamble**, 1; cf.:

wamblety (or **womblety-)cropped.** Suffering, in the stomach, the ill effects of a debauch: late C. 17–early 19. B.E.; Grose. A variant of preceding. (In U.S., fig. uncomfortable.)

wames thegither, nail twa. To coït: Scots: C. 17 (?)–20. Lit., *wame*, belly.

wa'n. Wasn't: sol.: late C. 19–20. ''Bout five to ten, wa'n it, Sam ?', *Time and Tide*, Nov. 24, 1934.

wan-horse chaise. A one-horsed chaise: a Hyde Park Corner joke, ca. 1820–30. Bee, 1823.

wand. Incorrect for *wan* (sail of windmill): mid-C. 18–20. O.E.D.

wander. To lead astray; fig., to confuse, bewilder: coll.: from mid-1890's. (O.E.D.)

wander ! Go away !: ca. 1880–1905. Ware, who classifies it as street s.

wangle. A 'wangling'; some favour illicitly obtained: from 1915: orig. military. Ex the v.— 2. Hence (— 1935), a swindle.

wangle, v.t. To arrange to suit oneself; contrive or obtain with sly cunning, insidiously or illicitly; to manipulate, to 'fake': printers' s. (— 1888) >, before or by 1911, fairly gen.; in G.W., a very common soldiers' word; since G.W. very gen. indeed. Jacobi, 1888; esp. B. & P., Esp. *wangle a job, wangling leave* (of absence).—2. Hence as v.i.: 1920 (O.E.D. Sup.).—3. To persuade (one) to do something: 1926 (ibid.). Possibly ex dial. *wangle*, to shake, as W. suggests; perhaps (O.E.D.) ex *waggle*; in either case, perhaps influenced by *wanky*, q.v.

wangler. One who 'wangles' (see preceding): from ca. 1910. Edgar Wallace, in *Private Selby*, 1912, 'A wangler is . . . a nicker, a shirker, a grouser—any bloomin' thing that talks a lot an' don't do much work,' W.—2. Hence, from ca. 1915, a schemer (cf. *wangle*, n.).

wangling. The n. ex *wangle*, v. (q.v.): from ca. 1915. Cf. *wangler*.

wank. See **wonk**.

wanker. A bloater: Felsted School: 1892, *The Felstedian*, Oct.; ibid., June, 1897, 'He sniffs, 'eugh, wankers again.' Ex *stinker* (via *stwanker*).

wanky, wonky. Spurious, inferior, wrong, damaged or injured: printers' (— 1904) >, by 1914, gen. 'A *wanky* tanner = a *snide* (q.v.) sixpence,' F. & H. Prob. ex dial. *wankle*, unsteady, precarious; delicate in health; sickly. In East Anglian dial., *wanky* is 'feeble': E.D.D.—2. Hence, nervous, jumpy: Air Force: from 1915. F. & Gibbons.

wannegan. A store: Canadian: C. 20. John Beames. Ex a Red Indian word.

wa'n't; warnt (q.v.). Was not: coll. (1702, Vanbrugh) >, in mid-C. 19, low coll.; also dial. Via *wasn't*.

want an apron. To be out of work: workmen's (— 1909); ob. Ware, 'The apron off'.

want doing, it will; it wants or **wanted doing.** It will, does, or did need doing: mid-C. 16–20: S.E. until late C. 19, then coll. 'Seton Merriman', 1898, 'Roden is a scoundrel . . . and wants thumping,' O.E.D.

want in; want out. To wish to enter; to wish to go out: from ca. 1840: coll. of Scotland,

Northern Ireland, and U.S. Abbr. *want to go in* or *out.* (O.E.D.)

want it !, it's up there (with a tap on one's forehead) **you ;** or **that's where you want it.** You should use your brains ! : a lower-class and military c.p. : from ca. 1908. B. & P.

want-to-was(s)er, n. and adj. (An athlete or a pugilist) hopeful but past his prime : Canadian : C. 20. John Beames.

wanted. A wanted person (whether advertised for in the Situations Vacant, or sought by the police) : coll. : 1793, W. Roberts, 'I design to publish a list of Wanteds, solely for the use of your Paper,' O.E.D. In the police sense, the adj. app. arises ca. 1810—Vaux has it ; the comparatively rare n., 1903 (O.E.D.)

wants his liver scraping ! Applied, as a c.p., to a superior in an evil temper : military : from 1914. B. & P.

***wap.** To copulate (gen. v.i.) : c. : C. 17–early 19. Rowlands, 1610 ; B.E. ; Grose, 1st ed. Ex *wap* (*down*), to throw (down) violently : cf. *knock*, to coït with (a woman). Whence, *wappened*, deflowered, wanton. Cf. *wap-apace.*—2. See **whop,** v.

***wap-apace, mort.** A woman experienced in copulation : c. : late C. 17–early 19. B.E., Grose. See **wap** and cf. the c.p. *if she won't wap for a win, let her trine for a make,* ' If she won't Lie with a Man for a Penny, let her Hang for a Half-penny,' B.E. : same period.

wap-John. A gentleman's coachman : sporting : ca. 1825–50. O.E.D.

wapper. See **whopper.—wapping.** See **whopping.**

***wapping-dell, -mort.** A whore : c. : C. 17–18. Resp. Rowlands, Dekker. See **wap.**

waps(e), wops(e). A wasp : sol. and dial. : C. 18–20. Esp. in pl., owing to the difficulty of pronouncing *wasps.*

war. Was : (dial., prob. from C. 17) and sol. (C. 19–20). Baumann.

war !, (anyway,) it's winning the. A bitterly ironic military c.p. of the G.W., apropos of something disliked : 1915. F. & Gibbons.

war !, it's a great. An ironic military c.p. : G.W. (not before 1915).

war and strife. Rare for *trouble and strife,* q.v. (B. & P.)

war 'awks ! ; war orks ! ; warrocks ! ; worracks (-ocks) ! See **warorks !**

war-baby. An illegitimate born during the G.W. : late 1916 ; ob. Ex the S.E. sense, a child that is born, during a war, while its father is on active service.—2. A young soldier, esp. if a subaltern : military : 1917–18. F. & Gibbons.

war-caperer. A privateer : naval coll. : (?) C. 18–early 19. Bowen.

war-cry. A mixture of *stout* and *mild* ale : taverns' : 1882–ca. 86. Ware derives it from *The War Cry,* the periodical of the Salvation Army, which ' spoke stoutly and ever [?] used mild terms '.

war-hat or **-pot.** A spiked helmet : military (— 1904) ; ob. by 1915, † by 1918.

War House, the. The War Office : General Staff's and Generals' : 1915 ; ob. B. & P.

war on !, there's a. A military c.p. = ' hurry up ! ' or palliating a refusal : 1915–18. F. & Gibbons. Occ. preceded by *remember.*

war-paint. One's best or official clothes, with jewels decorations, etc. : coll. : 1859, H. Kingsley, ' Old Lady E— in her war-paint and feathers ',

O.E.D. Ex lit. sense.—2. Hence, make-up : theatrical : late C. 19–20.

warbler. A singer that, for pay, liquor, or other benefit, goes to, and sings at meetings : low : from ca. 1820 ; ob.

warbling on the topmost bough, be left. To be left with one's stocks and shares and unable to sell them : jocular Stock Exchange (— 1923). Manchon.

ward-room joints as lower-deck hash. ' Officers' conversation or information which finds its way forward ' : naval : C. 20. Bowen.

ware skins, quoth Grubber, when he flung the louse into the fire. A semi-proverbial c.p. of ca. 1670–1770. Ray, 1678 ; Fuller, 1732 (*Grub for Grubber, shins for skins*). Apperson.

warehouse. A fashionable pawn-shop : Society (— 1904) ; ob. Whence :

warehouse, v. To pawn (an article) : Society (— 1904) ; ob. Cf. n. Perhaps ex :—To put in prison : 1881, *Punch,* Feb. 12 (O.E.D.). Cf. *jug,* v.

warm. An act of warming, a becoming warm : mid-C. 18–20 : S.E. until mid-C. 19, then coll. Esp. in *get* or *have a warm, give a warm.*

warm, v. To thrash : s. (— 1811) and dial. (— 1824) >, by 1850, coll. *Lex. Bal.* ; ' Cuthbert Bede ', 1853. Also *warm one's jacket* : cf. *dust one's jacket.*—2. Hence, to berate, ' call over the coals ' : coll. : from ca. 1870. H., 5th ed. Cf. the semi-c.p. *I'll warm yer,* a vague Cockney threat.

warm, adj. Rich : from ca. 1570 : S.E. until late C. 18, then coll. Grose, 1st ed. Ex *warm,* comfortably established or settled. (O.E.D.)—2. Of an account or bill : exorbitant. Coll. : from ca. 1890 ; ob. Cf. *hot.*

warm as they make them. Sexually loose : coll. (— 1909). Ware. Cf. *hot stuff* and :

warm bit. Such a woman : low : 1880 ; slightly ob. Ware.

warm corner. ' A nook where birds are found in plenty ', Ware, who by *birds* means harlots : sporting and Society (— 1909). Punning S.E. sense.

warm flannel. Mixed spirits served hot : public-house (— 1823) ; † by 1900. Cf. *hot flannel.*

warm member or **'un.** A whore ; a whore-monger : low : mid-C. 19–20 ; ob. Ex *warm,* amorous, prone to sexual desire and practice.—2. (Only **w. m.**) A very energetic, pushful person : ca. 1895, *Keep it Dark* (a music-hall song), ' Dr Kenealy, that popular bloke, | That extremely warm member, the member for Stoke.'

warm shop or **show.** A brothel : low (— 1923). Manchon. Cf. *hot stuff* in its sexual sense.

warm-sided. (A ship, a fort) mounting heavy batteries : naval coll. (— 1904). F. & H. Because such a ship can supply a warm reception.

warm sun, out of God's blessing into the. See **out of.**

warm the wax of one's ear. To box a person's ear : low : ca. 1860–1915. H., 3rd ed. An elaboration of *warm one's jacket* (see **warm,** v.).

warm with, adj. and n. (Spirits) warmed with hot water and sweetened with sugar : coll. : 1840, T. A. Trollope (O.E.D.), the n. ; 1836, Dickens, the adj. Contrast *cold without.*

warmed-up corpse, feel like a. To feel half-dead : low (— 1923). Manchon.

warmer. A smart person : Glasgow (— 1934). Cf. *hot,* expert.

warming-pan. A female bed-fellow : from the Restoration ; ob. Esp. *a Scotch warming-pan* : see

Scotch w.-p. D'Avenant, B.E., Grose.—2. A large, old-fashioned watch, properly of gold (a silver one being a *frying-pan*) : late C. 17–20 ; very ob. B.E. ; H., 3rd–5th edd. Ex size : cf. *turnip*.— 3. A locum tenens, esp. among the clergy : from mid-1840's ; slightly ob. The abbr. *W.P.* is rare for any person other than ' a clergyman holding a living under a bond of resignation ', F. & H. : clerical (— 1864). H., 3rd ed. Now only historical, the practice having been made illegal.

warming the bell. ' Having one's relief turned out early ' : nautical : late C. 19–20. Bowen. (The bell that sounds the hours.)

warnt. See **wa'n't**. But also = ' were not '.

warorks or **warrocks** ! ; **war orks** ! ; **war 'awks** ! Ware hawks !, i.e. look out for yourself : sol. : mid-C. 19–20. Baumann.

*warp. The criminal confederate who watches : c. : late C. 16–early 17. Greene. *?* *watch* corrupted.

warrab. A barrow : back s. (— 1859). H., 1st ed.

warrant officers' champagne. Rum and ginger-ale mixed : naval jocular coll. : C. 20. Bowen.

warrant you, I or **I'll.** I'll be bound : coll. : late C. 18–20.

warrantee. Guarantee : catachrestic : mid-C. 17–20 ; ob. (O.E.D.)

*warren. A brothel ; a boarding-school : c. > low s. : late C. 17–early 19. B.E., Grose. Jocular. Cf. *cunny-warren*, q.v.—2. ' He that is Security for Goods taken up, on Credit, by Extravagant young Gentlemen ', B.E. : c. : C. 17–18. Dekker, B.E., Grose. By sense-perversion—or perhaps merely, as the O.E.D. holds, by misapprehension, of *warren*, a variant of *warrant*.

warrigal. A worthless man : Australian bush-slang (— 1898). Ex Aboriginal for ' wild ' (orig. ' a dog '). Morris.

warrocks ! See **warorks** !

wars, have been in the. To show signs of injury, marks of ill or hard usage : coll. : 1850, Scoresby (O.E.D.). Ex a veteran soldier's scars.

wart. A youthful subaltern : 1894, ' J. S. Winter ' (O.E.D.) : s. >, by 1930, coll.—2. A naval cadet : naval : C. 20. Bowen.—3. An objection-able fellow : upper classes' : from ca. 1919. Ex senses 1 and 2. Perhaps abbr. *wart-hog*.—4. The single star of a 2nd lieutenant : military : from 1914. F. & Gibbons.

Warwicks. (At cards) sixes : Regular Army : late C. 19–20. F. & Gibbons. The Warwickshire Regiment used to be the 6th Foot.

Warwickshire Lads, the. The 6th Foot—after 1881, the Royal Warwickshire—Regiment : military : late C. 18–20 ; ob. F. & Gibbons. Partly ex the song, *Ye Warwickshire Lads and Lasses*.

was for *were* is a frequent sol. : cf. *is* for *are*. See esp. O.E.D. at *be*, p. 717, col. 2.

was-bird. A ' has-been ' : C. 20. Cf. *never-waser*.—2. Hence, an elderly man eager to enlist : G.W. (F. & Gibbons.)

wash. An act of ' washing ' : printers' (—1841). Cf. v., 2. O.E.D.—2. A fictitious sale of securities (by simple transference, therefore to the brokers' profit) : Stock Exchange (— 1891). *The Century Dict.* Cf. v., 3.—3. School tea or coffee : Durham School (— 1904). Because of its weakness.—4. Nonsense ; drivelling sentiment : from ca. 1905. Perhaps orig. Harrovian : witness Arnold Lunn, 1913 ; Georgette Heyer, *Why Shoot a Butler*, 1933, ' The Public School spirit, and Playing for the Side, and

all that wash '. Prob. abbr. *hog-wash* on *bilge* and *slush*.—5. Garage s., from ca. 1920, as in Richard Blaker, *Night-Shift*, 1934, ' Hales went . . . through the workshop to the " wash ", where finished jobs were left, ready for collection or delivery.'

wash, v. To bear testing or investigation ; prove to be genuine : coll. : 1849, C. Brontë, ' That willn't wash, Miss,' O.E.D. ' As good fabrics and fast dyes stand the operation of washing ', F. & H.—2. To punish, to ' rag ' (a fellow workman for falsehood or misconduct) by banging type-cases on his desk, or (among tailors) by swearing and cursing loudly : printers' s. (— 1841) >, by 1900, gen. craftsmen's. Savage's *Dict. of Printing*. Presumably ex the notion of purification. Among tailors, there is, in C. 20, a secondary nuance, gen. as vbl.n. *washing*, a reprimand by the ' boss ' (as in *The Tailor and Cutter*, Nov. 29, 1928).—3. To do or practise ' wash ' as in n., 2 : Stock Exchange : as v.t., app. unrecorded before 1895, but as v.i. implied in the vbl.n. as in : 1870, Medbery, *Men and Mysteries of Wall Street*, ' Brokers had become fear-ful of forced quotations. Washing had become a constant trick before the panic, and bids were now closely scrutinised.' Perhaps ex *one hand washes the other* (O.E.D.) ; perhaps ex *take in one another's washing*. Cf. :

wash about, v.i. (Of stocks and shares) to be in (rapid) circulation : Stock Exchange coll. (— 1923). Manchon.

wash-boards. White facings on the early uni-forms : naval : late C. 19–early 20. Bowen.

wash-deck boatswain. ' A non-specialist war-rant officer ' : naval : C. 20. Ibid.

wash-house ghost. Toasted bread : military : C. 20. B. & P.

wash one's face in an ale-clout. To take a glass of ale : coll. : ca. 1540–90. ' Proverbs ' Heywood. Ex putting one's face far into the jug, etc.

wash one's or **the head without soap.** To scold a person : coll. : ca. 1580–1620. Barnaby Rich, 1581. Apperson.

wash one's ivories or **neck.** To drink : low : 1823, Moncrieff (*ivories*) ; *neck* (— 1904). On the †*wash one's brain, head*, etc., to drink wine. Cf. *sluice one's ivories* (*Punch*, 1882) and *sluice one's bolt*, q.v.

wash-out. A failure (thing or person) ; a dis-appointment or ' sell ' ; a cancellation : used in the Boer War (J. Milne, *The Epistles of Atkins*, 1902). Perhaps ex *w.-o.*, a gap or hole caused by violent erosion, but much more prob. ex :—2. In shooting, a shot right off the target : military : app. from ca. 1850, if not earlier. Ex pointing out of shots on the old iron targets by the application of paint or, gen., some kind of wash.

wash-pot. A hat : universities' : ca. 1880–1910. F. & H. Ex the shape.

wash-up. A scrubbing and sterilising of the hands before an operation : medical coll. (— 1933). *Slang*, p. 193.

washed-out. (Severely) wounded : military (not very gen.) : 1915 ; ob. G. H. McKnight, *English Words*, 1923.

washer-dona. A washerwoman : low London : from ca. 1860 ; ob. Ware.

washical. What do you call it ? : illiterate : ca. 1550–1600 Still, *Gammer Gurton's Needle*. Per-haps ex *what shall I call it ?*

washing, n. Ex *wash*, v., 2, 3 : resp. 1825, 1870 (both earlier than v.).

washing the tiles, vbl.n. Pouring out the Mah Jong tiles : Mah Jong players' : from late 1923 ; ob. (Agatha Christie, *The Murder of Roger Ackroyd*, 1926.)

*washman. A beggar with sham sores : c. of ca. 1550–80. Awdelay, 1561. Prob. because the sores will wash out.

wasn't. Was not : coll. : C. 17–20. Cf. *isn't* and *won't.*

wasp. A venereally diseased harlot : ca. 1785– 1850. Grose, 2nd ed., '. . . Who like a wasp carries a sting in her tail.'

waste, cut to. 'To apportion (time) wastefully' : sporting : 1863 ; very ob. Ex tailoring sense, 'to cut (cloth) in a wasteful manner'. O.E.D.

waste, house of. 'A tavern or alehouse where idle people waste both their time and money', Grose, 1st ed. : literary coll. : ca. 1780–1850. Cf. :

waste-butt. A publican : coll. (— 1823) ; † by 1890. Egan's Grose.—2. An eating-house : jocular c. of ca. 1880–1915. Baumann.

waste of ready. Esp. gambling : Oxford University : ca. 1820–50. Egan's Grose. I.e. *the ready,* cash.

Wat ; occ. **wat.** A hare : late C. 15–20 : coll. till C. 19, then dial. A familiar use of the proper name : cf. *Ned* for a donkey.

*watch, his (her, my, etc.). Himself, etc. : c. : ca. 1530–1690. Copland, ca. 1530 ; Harman ; Dekker. Cf. *his nibs, watch and seals,* and perhaps *dial* (face), for semantics.—2. **Paddy's watch.** See **Paddywhack.**

watch and seals. A sheep's head and pluck : low (— 1860) ; ob. H., 2nd ed. But earlier as *watch, chain and seals* : 1811, *Lex. Bal.*

watch it !, I'd. Certainly not ; I certainly won't ! : low c.p. (— 1923). Manchon.

watch out, v.i. To be on one's guard ; to look out : U.S. coll. (1880's), anglicised ca. 1905 ; by 1930, S.E.—2. The n., as in *keep a watch-out,* dates from ca. 1910 and, though still coll., is not very gen.

watcher. 'A person set to watch a *dress-lodger*' (q.v.) : low : from 1860's. Greenwood, *The Seven Curses of London,* 1869.—2. One spying for bribery : electioneering coll. (— 1909). Ware.

watcher . . . ? What do you . . . ? : sol. : C. 19–20. Dorothy Sayers, *Clouds of Witness,* 1926, ' Watcher mean . . . ? '

*watchmaker. Gen. pl. 'The idle and dissolute, who live in Calmet's-buildings, Oxford-street' : c. (— 1839) ; † by 1880. Brandon. Cf. :

*watchmaker (in a crowd). A thief that special- ises in stealing watches : c. : mid-C. 19–20. H., 1st ed., *watchmaker* ; 5th ed., *w. in a crowd.* Prob. ex preceding entry.

water. Boating, aquatics : Westminster School coll. (— 1881). Pascoe, *Our Public Schools.*—2. Additional nominal capital created by 'watering' (see **water,** v., 2) : U.S. coll. (1883) anglicised ca. 1885 ; by 1900, S.E. *St James's Gazette,* June 14, 1888.

water, v. To entertain freely, to 'treat' : ca. 1740–60. (O.E.D.) Water costing nothing.—2. To increase (the nominal capital of a company) by the creation of shares that, though they rank for interest, carry no corresponding capital : U.S. coll. (1870) anglicised ca. 1880 ; by 1900, S.E. Occ. *water up* (1899). F. & H. ; O.E.D. I.e. weaken by dilution.

water, between wind and. See **shot between wind and water.—water, hot.** See **hot water.—water, over the.** See **over the water.**

water, make a hole in the. To drown oneself suicidally : 1853, Dickens (O.E.D.).

water, the malt's above the. He is drunk : semi- proverbial c.p. : ca. 1670–1770. Apperson. Cf. the proverbial and equivalent *the malt is above wheat with him* (mid-C. 16–early 19).

water-barrel. See **water-butt. — water-box, -course, -gap, -gate.** The female pudend : low : C. 19–20. Cf. *water-engine, waterworks.*

water bewitched. Very thin beer : coll. (—1678) ; ob. Ray. (Unholy influence at work.)—2. Hence, weak tea : coll. : C. 18–20. Swift ; Grose ; Dana. —3. Occ. of both (1699, T. Brown) ; † by 1800. O.E.D.—4. Occ. of punch (1785), occ. of coffee : dial. (— 1825) and (as for broth) coll. In all four senses, occ. *water damaged* : C. 19–20 coll. ; ob.

water-bobby. A water-policeman : lower classes' (— 1887). Baumann.

water-bottle. A total abstainer : lower class urban (— 1909). Ware. Cf. *water-waggon,* q.v.

water-bruiser(, gen. **rare old).** A tough (and old, hard-working) shore-man : nautical (— 1909). Ware.

water-butt, occ. **-barrel.** The stomach : lower classes' : late C. 19–20.

water-can, Jupiter Pluvius has got out (or **put,** or **turned, on) his.** A coll. c.p. for ' It is raining ' ; applied mostly to a heavy shower. From ca. 1870 ; ob.

water-carnival, the. ' Cleaning down a warship after coaling ' : naval : C. 20. Bowen.

water-cart, v.i. To weep : 1921, W. de Morgan (O.E.D. Sup.) ; ob. Ex the n.

water-cart, on the. An occ. variant of *water- waggon, on the,* q.v.

water-colours, wife in. See **wife.—water-course.** See **water-box.**

water-dog. A Norfolk dumpling : from ca. 1860 ; ob. H., 3rd ed.

water-dona. A washerwoman : low urban, esp. London (— 1909). Ware. Also *washer-dona,* q.v.

water-engine. ' The urinary organs male or female ', F. & H. : low : late C. 19–20.

water-funk. A person shy of water : schools' : 1899, Kipling ; now coll.

water-gap, -gate. See **water-box.**

water-grass. Water-cress : Anglo-Irish sol. : C. 18–20. O.E.D.

Water-Gunners, the. The Royal Marines : mili- tary : ca. 1870–1914. H., 5th ed. Because they are ' amphibious '.

water in one's shoes. A source of discomfort or annoyance : C. 18 coll. North, ca. 1740, ' They caressed his lordship . . . and talked about a time to dine with him ; all which (as they say) was " water in his shoes ".' Abbr. *as welcome as water in one's shoes,* very unwelcome : mid-C. 17–20 : coll. till late C. 19, then dial. only. Apperson.

water-logged. Dead-drunk : coll. (— 1923). Manchon.

water-mill. The female pudend : low (— 1811). *Lex. Bal.*

water of life. Gin : from early 1820's ; ob. Egan's Grose ; H., 2nd ed. App. on Fr. *eau-de-vie* (brandy).

water one's horse at Highgate. See **Highgate.— water one's nag.** See **nag.**

water one's plants. To weep : jocular coll. : ca

1540–1880; in C. 19, dial. only. Udall; Lyly; Swift. On S.E. *water one's eyes*, to weep. (Apperson.)

*water-pad. A thief operating on the water, esp. on the Thames: c.: late C. 17–early 19. B.E.; Grose. The . S.E. (nautical) variant is *water-rat* (Clark Russell).

water-scriger. 'A doctor who prescribes from inspecting the water of his patients', Grose, 3rd ed.: late C. 18–early 19. A *scriger* is presumably *scrier* (or *scryer*), one who (de)scries. Cf. † S.E. *water-caster*.

*water-sneak, the. 'Robbing ships . . . on a . . . river or canal, . . . generally in the night': c. of ca. 1810–90. Vaux.—2. Hence, *water-sneaks-man*, such a thief: c. (— 1823); † by 1900. Egan's Grose.

water the dragon. See **dragon**; cf. *nag*, *water one's*.—**water up.** See **water**, v., 2.

water-waggon, on the. Teetotal for the time being: U.S. (— 1904), anglicised by 1908. From ca. 1915, often *on the waggon*.

Waterbury watch. Scotch: C. 20. P. P., *Rhyming Slang*, 1932.

Wateries, the. The Naval Exhibition at South Kensington: coll.: ca. 1886–1910. Cf. the *Col-inderies* and the *Fisheries*, qq.v.

Waterings, the, 'Spital stands too nigh St Thomas à. Copious weeping sometimes produces an illness: proverbial c.p.: late C. 16–17. This place, near a brook used for watering horses, stood near London, and on the Canterbury road, and, as it was the Surrey execution-ground until the C. 17, the name is often employed allusively in C. 16–mid-17, as in Jonson, 1630, 'He may perhaps take a degree at Tyburn . . ., come to read a lecture | Upon Aquinas at St Thomas à Waterings, | And so go forth a laureat in hemp circle.'

waterloo (or **W.**). A halfpenny: London: ca. 1830–75. Ware. Ex the former toll (a halfpenny) paid to cross Waterloo Bridge.

Waterloo day. Pay-day: military: from ca. 1870; ob. Cf. *Balaclava day.*

waterman; (not in 2, 3) **watersman.** A blue silk handkerchief: c. or low (—1839); very ob. Because worn (light or dark) by friends of Cambridge and Oxford at the time of the boat-race. Brandon. —2. An artist in water-colours: 1888 (O.E.D.): s. >, by 1920, coll.—3. One possessing (expert) knowledge of boating: coll.: 1912 (O.E.D.).

waters. Paintings in water-colour: coll.: 1909, *The Daily Chronicle*, June 4 (O.E.D.).

waters, watch one's. 'To keep a strict watch on any one's actions', Grose, 3rd ed.: coll.: late C. 18–early 19. Ex *urinospection.*

water's man, watersman. See **waterman**, 1.

waterworks. The urinary organs: low: mid-C. 19–20; ob.—2. **waterworks, turn on the.** To weep: coll.: mid-C. 19–20. Ex jocular S.E. *waterworks*, tears. Cf. *watery-headed.*—3. (**the waterworks.**) Rain: 1931, Dorothy Sayers, *The Five Red Herrings*, 1931, 'You'd think they turned on the water-works yesterday on purpose to spoil my sketching-party.'

watery-headed. 'Apt to shed tears', Grose, 1st ed.: ca. 1780–1890.

waun(d)s! An illiterate form of *wounds!*: C. 17–18. (O.E.D.)

wave a flag of defiance. To be drunk: low: ca. 1870–1915.

wavy (or **W.**) **Bill.** A R.N.V.R. officer in a ship

for training: naval: C. 20. Bowen. Cf. *wavy navy.*

wavy in the syls. 'Imperfect in one's lines': theatrical (— 1904); ob. F. & H. Lit., unsteady in one's syllables (cf. *syl-slinger*, q.v.).

wavy navy, the. The Royal Naval Volunteer Reserve: C. 20. Bowen, 'Seldom heard afloat'.

wavy rule, make. To be rolling-drunk: printers': from ca. 1880. Ex the rule or line that waves thus : ~~~.

wax. A rage; esp. *be in a wax*: 1854, 'Cuthbert Bede', 'I used to rush out in a fearful state of wax,' O.E.D. ? ex *waxy*, q.v., or, as W. suggests, 'evolved ex archaic to *wax wroth*'.

wax, close as. Extremely mean or secretive: 1772, Cumberland (O.E.D.): coll. >, by 1850, S.E. Because impermeable to water and perhaps because sticky.

wax, lad or man of. See *lad of wax.*

wax, my cock of. A shoemakers' term of address (— 1823); ob. 'Jon Bee.'

wax, nose of; gen. **have a**, to be very impressionable: London (— 1823); † by 1900. 'Jon Bee.'

wax-pot. A person apt to be 'waxy' (q.v.): coll. (— 1923). Manchon. Ex *wax*, q.v., or *fuss-pot.*

waxed, be (well). To be (well)known: tailors': from ca. 1870. 'So-and-so has been well *waxed*, i.e. We know all about him,' F. & H.

waxed, have (a person). A military variant (G.W. and after) of *have someone cold* (F. & Gibbons.) And Cockney: E. Pugh, 1906. Ex the preceding.

waxiness; waxy. Angriness, proneness to rage; angry: resp. (—)1904 and 1853, Dickens. Although *waxy* is recorded earlier than *wax*, the latter may have arisen the earlier; yet, semantically, the transition from lit. *waxy* to fig. *waxy* is not difficult: cf. *sticky*, adj.—2. **waxy** is also a nickname (ob. in C. 20) for a cobbler: 1851, Mayhew (O.E.D.). Ex his frequent use of *wax*.—3. A saddler: military: C. 20. F. & Gibbons.

waxy-homey. An actor that blacks up with burnt cork; a 'nigger-minstrel': theatrical: C. 20. The *homey* = a man.

'way. Away: coll. (U.S., 1866,) anglicised late in C. 19. Esp. in *'way back.*

way, be up her. To be *in coitu* with a woman: low: late C. 19–20. Always in an innuendo: punning neighbourhood.

way, in a. In a state of vexation, anxiety, distress: dial. and coll.: mid-C. 19–20. (O.E.D.)

way, in a kind or **sort of.** A modifying tag: coll.: mid-C. 19–20.

way, in the (e.g. *fish*). Engaged in (e.g. the fish-trade): lower classes' coll.: late C. 19–20; slightly ob. Manchon. 'He's in the grocery way.' Now, *way* is gen. replaced by *line.*

way, pretty Fanny's. See *pretty Fanny's way.*

way, that; gen. **a little**, or **rather, that way.** 'Approximating to that condition': coll.: mid-C. 17–20. Dickens, 1837, ' "I'm afraid you're wet." "Yes, I am a little that way ",' O.E.D. Cf. :

way, the other; gen. **all, quite, very much the other way.** Diverging from a stated condition: coll.: mid-C. 19–20. Trollope, 1858, 'They are patterns of excellence. I am all the other way,' O.E.D. Cf. *way, that.*

way down, all the. See **all** . . .

*way for, be out of the. To be in hiding from police wishing to arrest one for (such and such an offence): c. (— 1812); ob. Vaux.

way of, (being, doing, etc.), by. In the habit of, giving oneself out as, having a reputation for, or making an attempt (esp. if persistent or habitual) at (being or doing something): coll.: 1824, Miss Ferrier, 'The Colonel was by way of introducing him into the fashionable circles'; 1891, *The Saturday Review*, July 18, concerning *by way of being*, '. . . And this with an implied disclaimer of precise knowledge or warranty on the speaker's part.' O.E.D.—2. In C. 20, the phrase is often used almost as if = as it were, ' in a sort of way '; and, in post-War days, *is* (or *are*, etc.) *by way of being* is, only too often, a careless or an affected synonym of *is* or *are* (etc.).

way of all flesh(, gone the). Dead : lower and lower-middle classes' coll. (— 1909). Ware. Contrast with the S.E. sense—as in ' Erewhon ' Butler's novel.

way of life, the. Prostitution : low London (— 1823); ob. ' Jon Bee.'

ways about it (or that), no two. (There can be) no doubt of it : U.S. coll. (1818 : Thornton) anglicised ca. 1840 ; by 1880, S.E.

ways for Sunday, look both or nine or two. See look . . .

wazz ; wozz, v.i. and v.t. To accompany (another messenger) unofficially on delivery : Post Office telegraph-messengers' (— 1935). Perhaps ex *wangle* : cf. *swiz* ex *swindle*.

Waz(z)a or, loosely, Wazzer, the battles of the. Two Australian brushes with the police, 1915, in the Wazza, a low, native quarter of Cairo : Australian military : 1915 ; ob. B. & P.

we. Us : C. 16–20 : S.E. until C. 18, then sol.

we do see life ! A C. 20 c.p., with which cf. *this is the life*. Adopted, in 1931, as a title by the Rev. Desmond Morse-Boycott. Often *we ain't got much money but* . . .

we had one and (or but) the wheel came off. A military c.p. (C. 20) expressive of feigned helpfulness or droll regret .or ' gamin ' comment on words not understood.

we uns. We : low coll. : late C. 19–20. Orig. U.S. ; cf. *you uns*.

weak brother, sister. An unreliable person: religious s. : mid-C. 19–20.

weak in the arm(, it's). A public-house c.p. (— 1909 ; ob.) applied to a ' half-pint drawn in a pint pot '. Ware.

weaken !, it's a great life if you don't. A military c.p. of 1915–18.

weanie, -y. See weeny. (Influenced by dial. *weanie*, a very young child.)

wear. To tolerate, put up with : Regular Army : C. 20. F. & Gibbons.

wear a revolver-pocket. To carry a revolver : low : ca. 1880–1914. Ware.

wear a straw in her ear. See straw in her ear.

wear-arse. A one-horse chaise : ca. 1785–1830. Grose, 2nd ed. Ex jolting.

*wear it. To be under ' the stigma of having turned a *nose* ', Egan's Grose : c. of ca. 1820–50. Ex :

*wear it upon. To inform against, try to best (a person) : c. : ca. 1810–50. Vaux. *It* is the nose : for semantics, cf. *nose*, a spy.

wear the bands. To be hungry : low s. : ca. 1810–40. Vaux.

*wear the broad arrow. To be a convict : c. —· 1909). Ware.

wear the head large. To have a headache from alcoholic excess : lower-middle class (— 1909). Ware.

wear the leek. To be Welsh : lower and lower-middle classes' (— 1909) : coll. rather than s. Ware.

weary. Drunk : proletarian : ca. 1870–1920. Cf. dial. *weary*, sickly, feeble. (Curiously enough, the Old High Ger. *wuorag*, drunk, is cognate with A.-S. *werig*. W.)

weary Willie. A long-range shell passing high overhead and, app., slowly : military : 1915–18. F. & Gibbons.

weasel, be bit by a barn. To be drunk : ca. 1670–1700. Head.

Weasel, the. Robert Cecil, Earl of Salisbury (1563–1612). James I called him *the Little Beagle*. Dawson.

weather, go up the ; go down the wind. To prosper ; to fare ill, be unfortunate : coll. : resp. early C. 17 and C. 17–20 ; in mid-C. 19–20, dial. only. Breton, both ; Pepys ; Berthelson, 1754 ; Scott, 1827. Also, *go down the weather*, to become bankrupt : C. 17. O.E.D. and Apperson.

weather-breeder. A fine, bright day : nautical (— 1887). Baumann.

weather-lorist. A meteorologist : jocular (— 1923). Manchon.

weather-peeper. (One's) best eye ; a good look-out : nautical (— 1909). Ware. Cf. S.E. *keep one's weather-eye open*.

weather-scupper. ' It is an old joke at sea ', writes Clark Russell, in 1883, ' to advise a greenhorn to get a handspike and hold it down hard in the weather-scuppers to steady the ship's wild motions.' Coll. ; slightly ob.

weaver's bullock. A sprat : East-Londoners (— 1880) ; ob. E.D.D. Cf. *two-eyed steak*, q.v.

*weaving. ' A notorious card-sharping trick, done by keeping certain cards on the knee, or between the knee and the underside of the table, and using them when required by changing them for the cards held in the hand ', H., 3rd ed. : 1803 (O.E.D.) ; prob. c. > gaming s.

weaving leather aprons. An evasive c.p. reply to an inquiry as to what one has been doing lately : low (— 1864). H., 3rd ed., ' *See* newspaper reports of the trial for the gold robberies on the South-Western Railway.' (Similarly, to an inquiry as to one's vocation, *I'm a doll's-eye weaver* : low (— 1874). H., 5th ed.) Equivalent c.p. replies are *making a trundle for a goose's eye* or *a whim-wham to bridle a goose* : low (— 1864). H., 3rd ed.

weazling. The act of depriving a comrade of his tip : low (— 1923). Manchon. Ex that pleasant creature, the weasel.

web-foot. (Pl. web-foots.) A dweller in the Fens : coll. nickname : from ca. 1760 ; very ob. (O.E.D.)

webs. (A sailor's) feet : naval : C. 20. F. & Gibbons. Cf. the preceding.

wedding. The ' emptying a necessary house ': London (— 1785) ; † by 1850. Grose, 1st ed.

wedding, you have been to an Irish. A c.p. addressed to one who has a black eye : ca. 1785–1850. Grose, 2nd ed., '. . . Where black eyes are given instead of favours '.

*wedge. Silver, whether money or plate, but mostly the latter ; hence, occ., money in general : c. (— 1725). *A New Canting Dict.*, 1725 ; Grose, 2nd ed., ' *Wedge*. Silver plate, because melted by the receivers of stolen goods into wedges ': H.

1st-5th edd.—2. **the wedge,** the last student in the classical tripos list : Cambridge University (— 1852) : coll. > j. Also the *wooden wedge.* On †*wooden spoon,* the last man in the mathematical tripos, + T. H. *Wedgwood,* who, last in the classical tripos in 1824, was to be a famous etymologist. O.E.D., F. & H.—3. A Jew : back s. (— 1859). H., 1st ed. Lit., *wej.*

*****wedge, flash the.** To 'fence the swag', to deposit stolen goods with a receiver : c. : mid-C. 19–20. See *****wedge,** 1.

*****wedge-bobb.** The same as *wedge-lobb,* q.v. ' Ducange Anglicus ' : but *w.-bobb* I suspect to be a misprint.

*****wedge-feeder.** A silver spoon : c. (— 1812). Vaux. See **wedge,** 1. Cf. :

*****wedge-hunter.** A thief specialising in silver plate and watches : c. : mid-C. 19–20. F. & H. See **wedge,** 1.

*****wedge-lobb.** A silver snuff-box : c. (— 1812). Vaux. See **wedge,** 1. Cf. :

*****wedge-yack.** A silver watch : c. : mid-C. 19–20 ; slightly ob. Ex *wedge,* 1.

Wee Free Kirk, the. The Free Church of Scotland minority after the majority, in 1900, joined with the U.P. Church to constitute the United Free Church. Hence, from 1904, *Wee Frees* and, from 1905, *Wee Kirkers,* the members of that minority. Coll. nicknames. O.E.D.

wee-jee ; wejee. A chimney-pot : ca. 1864–90. H., 3rd ed. Etymology obscure ; the word may be a perversion of *wheeze,* a gag, though this origin fits only sense 3, which is perhaps the earliest.—2. Hence, a (chimney-pot) hat : late C. 19–early 20 : lower classes', as are senses 1 and 3.—3. Anything extremely good of its kind ; esp. a clever invention : from ca. 1860 ; ob. H., 3rd ed.—4. Hence, a hand pump : N.E. Coast colliers' : late C. 19–20. Bowen.

Wee-Wee. See **Wi-Wi.**

wee-wee. A urination ; esp. *do a wee-wee* : nursery coll. : late C. 19–20. Perhaps ex *water* on *pee.*—2. Also, in C. 20, as v.i.

weed. A cigar, a cheroot : coll. : 1847, Albert Smith (O.E.D.). Ex *weed,* tobacco.—2. A hatband : low (— 1864) ; † by 1920. Perhaps ex the vague resemblance of its shape to that of a large cigar.—3. A leggy, ill-compacted, and otherwise inferior horse : 1845 (O.E.D.) ; Lever, 1859. Perhaps ex *weedy,* 1, q.v.—4. Hence, a thin, delicate, weak and soon-tiring person : 1869, A. L. Smith (O.E.D.).

*****weed,** v. To pilfer or steal part of, or a small amount from : c. (— 1811) ; slightly ob. *Lex. Bal.* Vaux. Hence, *weed a lob,* steal small sums from a till ; *weed a swag,* to abstract part of the spoils unknown to one's pals and before the division of that spoil : both in Vaux. Ex *weed,* to remove the weeds from. Cf. :

*****weeding dues are concerned.** An underworld c.p. (ca. 1810–80) used when a process of ' weeding ' (see **weed,** v.) has been applied. Vaux.

weedy. (Of horses, dogs) lank, leggy, loose-limbed, weak and spiritless : coll. : 1800, *The Sporting Magazine* ; 1854, Surtees, ' He rode a weedy chestnut,' O.E.D. Lit., like a weed.—2. Hence (of persons), lanky and anaemic ; weakly : coll. : 1852, Surtees (O.E.D.).

week, inside of a. From Monday to Saturday : coll. : C. 19–20.

week, knock into the middle of next. To knock

out (lit. or fig.) completely : pugilistic s. (1821, Moncrieff) >, by 1900, gen. coll. O.E.D.

week, parson's. See **parson's week.**

week, when two Sundays come in a ; also **(in) the week of four Fridays.** Never : coll. : C. 19–20 ; mid-C. 18–early 19. H. Brooke, 1760 (O.E.D.)

week-ender. A week-end mistress : from 1880's : coll. Ex lit. sense.—2. A week-end holiday : likewise low coll. : from ca. 1895. Oxford *-er.*

weekly-accompts. The small square white patches on the front, to right and left, of a middy's collar : ca. 1815–70. Vaux, 1819 (O.E.D.) ; Bowen. Now *mark of the beast,* q.v.

week's (or **month's**) **end, an attack of the.** Lack of funds, according as one is paid one's wages or salary every week or every month : jocular coll. : ca. 1890–1915. F. & H.

wee'l, weele, wee'll. See **we'll.**

weelikies. Sausages : Glasgow (— 1934).

weenie, weeny ; weany (rare) and **weny** (C. 18 dial. only). Tiny : dial. (— 1790) >, by 1830, coll. Ex *wee* on *teeny.*—2. (Rarely other than *weenie !*) A telegraph clerks' warning that an inspector is coming : C. 20. F. & H., 1904. ? ex *warning.*

weep Irish. To shed crocodile tears ; feign sorrow : coll. : late C. 16–mid-18. Fuller, 1650 ; Mrs Centlivre. Ex the copious lamentations of the Irish at a keening. Apperson.

weeper. (Gen. pl.) A long and flowing side-whisker, such as was ' sported ' by ' Lord Dundreary ' in the play *Our American Cousin* : coll. : from ca. 1860 ; ob. Ex *Dundreary weepers* (1859), later *Piccadilly weepers.* E. A. Sothern played the leading part ; in 1858, the piece was hardly a success ; in 1859–60, it was the rage.—2. (Gen. pl.) An eye : late C. 19–20. Cf. *peeper.*—3. A sentimental problem-novel : journalists' : from ca. 1925. Neil Bell, *Winding Road,* 1934.

Weeping Cross (or **weeping cross**), **return (home)** or, more gen., **come home by.** To fail badly ; be grievously disappointed : from early 1560's ; ob. Bullein (1564), Gosson, Lyly, playwright Heywood, Grose, Spurgeon, William Morris (1884). Ex a place-name employed allusively. Nares, F. & H., O.E.D., Apperson.

weeping willow. A pillow : rhyming s. : late C. 19–20. F. & Gibbons.

weeze. See **wheeze,** n., 5 ; **weezy,** see **wheezy,** adj.

Weg. Gladstone : political nickname : 1885–6. Ware. Ex his initials and ' given in memory of Mr Wegg ([Dickens's] *Our Mutual Friend*), who was a great sayer of words ' : *o tempora, o oratores !*

*****weigh.** See **weight, let him . . .**

weigh, under. Under way : erroneous : from ca. 1780. Ex *weigh anchor.* (O.E.D.)

*****weigh forty.** See **weight, let him alone . . .**

weigh in. To start ; in imperative, go ahead ! : sporting : late C. 19–20. (P. G. Wodehouse, *The Pothunters,* 1902.) Cf. :

weigh in with. To produce (something additional), introduce (something extra or unexpected) : coll. : 1885, *The Daily News,* Nov., ' The journal " weighs in " with a prismatic Christmas number,' Ware. Ex a jockey *weighing in,* being weighed before a race.—2. Hence, *weigh in,* v.i. to appear (on the scene) : sporting coll. : from ca. 1920.—3. To ' stump up ' or ' fork out ' : low (— 1923). Manchon.

*****weigh out.** To give in full (one's share) : c. : late C. 19–20. Ware cites *The People,* Jan. 6, 1895, and derives the term from 'the distribution of stolen plate melted down to avoid identification'.

weigh up. To appraise: coll.: 1894 (O.E.D.). Cf. *weigh*, to consider.

weighed off, be. 'To be brought up before an officer and punished': military: C. 20. F. & Gibbons.

weighing the thumb, n. 'Cheating in weight by sticking down the scale with the thumb': low (— 1896). Ware.

weight, (a bit) above one's. (A little) beyond one's class, too expensive, fashionable, highbrow, or difficult: coll., orig. (ca. 1910) racing. Ex a horse's handicap of weight.

weight, let him alone till he weighs his. A police c.p. to the effect that a criminal is not yet worth arresting, for his offences are so small that no reward attaches to them, whereas a capital crime will produce a big reward: ca. 1810–40. Vaux, who notes that *weigh forty* (of a criminal) is to carry a £40 reward for capture.

weight about, throw one's. To boast, swagger, unduly stress one's authority: military: from ca. 1910. F. & Gibbons. Prob. ex boxing or circus.

weird (frequently, by the way, misspelt *wierd*). Odd; unusual; wonderful: from the middle 1920's, and mostly upper classes'.

Welch, welcher, welching. For these three terms see **Welsh.**—**welcome, and.** See and **welcome.**—**welcome as water in one's shoes.** See **water in** . . . Cf. S.E. *welcome as snow in harvest* and contrast *welcome as the eighteen trumpeters*, very welcome indeed: coll.: ca. 1610–40. Apperson.

we'll ; wee'l(l). We will: coll.: resp. C. 17–20; late C. 16–17. In late C. 16–early 17, occ. *weele, we'le, wele.* O.E.D.

well. To pocket: low (— 1860); virtually †. H., 2nd ed.; id., 5th ed., 'Any one of fair income and miserly habits is said to " *well it* ".' Lit., to put as into a well: cf. *put down South.* But imm. ex, 2, c. *well*, to put (money) in the bank: 1845, in '*No. 747*'. Ex :—3. *well = put in the well*, q.v.: c.: from ca. 1810 ; slightly ob. *Lex. Bal.* (In late C. 19–20, low s.)

well, adj. Satisfactory, very good, capital: Society coll.: ca. 1860–1900. Ware.

***well, put** (one) **in the garden or the.** To defraud (an accomplice) of part of the booty forming his share: c. (— 1812); ob. Vaux. Cf. preceding entry. A variant is *put* (one) *in a hole.* A person down a well is at a disadvantage.—2. Hence, to inconvenience or get the better of : mid-C. 19–20; ob. (except . . . *hole*).

well away, be. To be rather drunk: coll.: C. 20. Lyell.—2. To prosper, be doing splendidly: coll.: from ca. 1912. 'He's well away with that girl.' Orig. sporting: ex a horse that has, from the start, got well away.

well down in the pickle. (Of a ship) heavily loaded: sailing ships' coll.: late C. 19–20. Bowen. The *pickle* is 'the briny'.

well-gone. Much in love; fatally or very severely wounded: New Zealand coll.: resp. from ca. 1913 and from ca. 1915.

well fucked and far from home. See **Barney's bull.**

well hove ! Well played !; well done !: proletarian coll. (— 1923). Manchon.

well-hung. (Of a man) large of genitals: low (— 1823); ob. Egan's Grose.

well in. An Australian variant of *well off*, well

to do: 1891, 'Rolf Boldrewood': coll. >, by 1910, S.E.

well-to-do's, the. Those who are well-to-do: coll.: C. 20. The equivalent S.E. is *the well-to-do.*

well-sinking. Making money: Anglo-Indian: late C. 18–20; ob. Ware. Ex excavating for treasure.

well to live, be. To be rather drunk: coll.: ca. 1610–1700; then dial. Ray, 1678. Ex *well to live* (*in the world*), prosperous.

well under. Drunk: Australian: from ca. 1916. Prob. an abbr. of *well under water.*

'well, well,' quoth she, 'many wells, many buckets.' A proverb-c.p. of C. 16 (Heywood, 1546) that may have suggested the C. 20 catch, ' "Have you heard the story of the three wells ? " "No ; what is it ? " "Well, well, well ! " '

well, you *said* **you could do it !** A c.p. reply to a 'grouse': Army officers': G.W., and after.

welly. Almost: C. 17–20: coll. till C. 18, then dial. Ex *well nigh.* O.E.D.

Welsh, welsher, welshing; in C. 19, often -ch-. To swindle (one) out of the money he has laid as a bet (orig. and properly at a race-course); he who does this ; the doing : racing s. >, ca. 1880, coll. >, ca. 1900, S.E.: resp. 1857, 1860, 1857 (O.E.D.). Perhaps ex the old nursery-rhyme, *Taffy was a Welshman, Taffy was a thief*: W.; my *Words !*

Welsh bait. A foodless, drinkless rest given a horse at the top of a hill: coll.: C. 17–20 ; very ob. T. Powell, 1603 (O.E.D.). Ex *bait*, food. For pejorative *Welsh*, see *Words !* at 'Offensive Nationality '.

Welsh Camp. The late C. 17–early 18 nickname for a field between Lamb's Conduit and Gray's Inn Lane, where, late in C. 17, ' the Mob got together in great numbers, doing great mischief,' B.E.

Welsh comb. The thumb and four fingers: coll. or s.: ca. 1785–1840. Grose, 2nd ed. Contrast *Jew's harp.*

Welsh cricket. A louse : late C. 16–early 17. Greene.—2. A tailor : ? C. 17. F. & H. Prob. via *prick-louse* (a tailor), q.v.

Welsh ejectment. By unroofing the tenant's house: ca. 1810–50. *Lex. Bal.*

Welsh fiddle. The itch: late C. 17–early 19. B.E., Grose. Also *Scotch fiddle*, q.v. Cf. the synonymous dial. *Welshman's hug* (E.D.D.).

Welsh goat. A Welshman: nickname: mid-C. 18–mid-19. Lord Hailes, 1770.

Welsh mile, long and narrow,—like a. Either thus or as *like* . . . *mile*, applied to anything so shaped: coll.: ca. 1785–1850. Grose, 2nd ed. Ex *Welsh mile*, a mile unconscionably long : cf. the equally S.E. *Welsh acre.*

Welsh Navy. Holt's Blue Funnel Line : nautical : C. 20. Bowen. Ex its numerous executive officers from Wales.

Welsh parsley. Hemp ; a halter : coll. or s. : ca. 1620–50. Fletcher. O.E.D.

Welsh rabbit. This dish, incorrectly spelt *W. rarebit* (Grose, 1785), is recorded by that eccentric poet John Byrom (O.E.D.) in 1725 : orig. coll., it had, by 1820, > S.E. Even in C. 18 (see Grose) the Welsh were reputed to be fervid cheese-fanciers. For semantics, cf. *Bombay duck*, q.v.

Welshman's hose, turn (something) **like a ; make a W. h. of ; make like a W. h.** To suit the meaning of (a word, etc.) to one's purpose : coll. : ca. 1520–1600. Skelton.

welsher. See **Welsh.**

Welshie, -hy. Nickname for a Welsh person : coll. : C. 19–20. Ex adj.

*welt. Only in B.E.'s ' *rum-boozing-Welts*, bunches of Grapes ' : late C. 17–18 c. The phrase, lit., = excellent drinking bunches (or, perhaps, grape-bunches).—2. A blow : coll. : late C. 19–20. C. J. Dennis. Ex the S.E. *welt*, to flog.

welter. Anything unusually big or heavy of its kind : dial. (— 1865) >, by ca. 1890, coll. Kipling, 1899, ' He gave us eight cuts apiece—welters—for—takin' unheard-of liberties with a new master.' O.E.D., F. & H. Ex *welt*, to thrash.

wench, from Old English *wencel*, a child, is facetious and university-witted where once it was serious but used only in addressing an inferior (as in Shakespeare's *The Tempest*, ' Well demanded, wench ') and where, orig., it meant simply a girl : the facetious usage is coll., whereas the other two are S.E. A similar degradation of words is seen in *damsel* and the French *maîtresse*, *amie*, and *fille*.

we'n't. Will not : coll. : C. 18. Shebbeare, 1754 (O.E.D.). Cf. *willn't*, won't.

went. Gone : sol. : C. 19–20 (? earlier). Prob. unrelated to *went*, p.ppl. of *wend*.

were. Was : sol. : C. 17 (? earlier)–20. Cf. *are* for *is* and the quotation at *which*, 3.

weren't. Were not : coll. : C. 17–20. Cf. *aren't*, *isn't*, *wasn't*, *won't*.

wesket, weskit. A waistcoat : coll. bordering on sol. : C. 19 (? earlier)–20.

west, go. See go west.

west-central or **West Central.** A water-closet : London (— 1860) ; ob. H., 2nd ed. Ex *W.C.*, the London district, and *w.-c.*, a water-closet.

Western Ocean relief. ' An overdue relief at the end of a watch ' : nautical : C. 20. Bowen. In sailors' j., the *Western Ocean* = the Atlantic.

Westerns. Shares in the Great Western Railway : Stock Exchange coll. (— 1895). A. J. Wilson's glossary.

Westminster brougham. See **Whitechapel brougham.**

Westminster wedding. ' A Whore and a Rogue Married together ', B.E. : low London : late C. 17–early 19. Prob. ex the late C. 16–early 19 proverb, *Who goes to Westminster for a wife, to Paul's for a man, or to Smithfield for a horse, may meet with a whore, a knave and a jade* (Apperson).

Westminster Palace of Varieties. The Admiralty : sea-going naval officers' : C. 20. Bowen.

[Westminster School slang. In his interesting *Westminster*, 1902, Reginald Airy discourses thus :— ' Westminster has a fairly large repertoire of words and phrases peculiar to the school. In the first place, a Westminster never goes " to " a part of the school, but always " up " or " down ". Thus a boy will talk of going " up-fields ", " down-school ", etc. Nor does he use the preposition " in " : e.g. he leaves his books " down " college. To be " out of school " is to be ill. " Up-school " also serves as a name for " detention ". [All these uses are rather j. than either s. or coll.] The college servant is in all cases " John "—a name now applied to any school servant. A " ski " [q.v.] is the word for a cad . . . To work is to " muzz "—a " muzz " being one who works hard, corresponding, even in the delicate opprobrium underlying the name, to the Eton " sap ". A " greeze " is a scrum or crowd, and compulsory games are known as " station " [ex *stationary*]. In many cases words are shortened : e.g. the Debating Society is Deb. Soc., etc. A boy is " tanned " by a monitor, but " handed " by the headmaster. A half-holiday is " late play ", a whole holiday " a play ". [Both these terms are j.] , . . [At Grant's] a study is known as a " Chiswick ". Several words are peculiar to college : milk is known as " bag ", sugar as " beggar " : a new gown is a " bosky ", and the pendent sleeve of a gown a " bully ", while any coat other than an " Eton " or a " tails " is a " shag ". When the monitors meet to interview a culprit, they hold a " case " [ex the legal term]. An inkpot was until lately known as a " dip " . . . : a novel is " a bluebook ". The monitors in college are Mon. Cham. (short for Monitor of Chambers and pronounced Monsham), Mon. Stat. (Monitor of Station), and Mon. Schol. (Monitor of School). [These three terms are j.] . . . For other words, a ball is called a " blick ", prize compositions are sent up on " principe " paper, while ordinary foolscap sheets are called " quarterns " ' ; the second and the third of these terms are j.—Cf. the entries at ' Eton ', ' Harrow ', ' Winchester '.]

Westo. A Devon or Cornish ship or seaman : nautical coll. : late C. 19–20. Bowen. Ex *West Country*.

Weston !,—my oath, Miss. See **my oath, Miss Weston !**

Westphalia. The backside : trade (— 1904) ; ob. Ex Westphalia hams.

westward for smelts. See smelts.

wet ; occ. **whet** (Ned Ward). Liquor : late C. 19–20. Ex *heavy wet*, q.v., or next sense.—2. A drink : coll. : 1703, Steele ; 1879, Brunlees Patterson, *Life in the Ranks*, ' Many are the . . . devices . . . to obtain a wet or reviver, first thing in the morning '.—3. A dull, stupid, futile or incompetent person : from ca. 1930. (D. L. Murray, *The English Family Robinson*, 1933.) See wet, adj., last sense.

wet, v.t. See wet the other eye and whistle, wet one's.—2. V.i., drink a glass of liquor : coll. . ca. 1780–1910. O.E.D. (Sup.).

wet, adj. Showing the influence, or characteristic, of drink ; connected with liquor : coll. : 1592, Nashe ; 1805, *wet bargain* ; 1848, Thackeray, ' A *wet night* ', a frequent phrase. O.E.D. ; F. & H., where also *wet goods*, liquor, and *wet hand* or *wet 'un*, a toper,—both of late C. 19–20.—2. Hence, having drunk liquor ; somewhat intoxicated : coll. : 1704, Prior ; 1834, Coleridge, ' Some men are like musical glasses ;—to produce their finest tones, you must keep them wet,' O.E.D. Perhaps ex :—3. Prone to drink too much : coll. : from 1690's. B.E., Grose. Cf. *wet*, n., 2.—4. (Of a Quaker) not very strict : 1700, T. Brown. Hence, of other denominations : likewise coll. : from ca. 1830 ; ob. Perhaps suggested by Grose's (2nd ed.) *wet parson*, a parson given to liquor ; indeed, this sense links with sense 3, for B.E. has ' *Wet-Quaker*, a Drunkard of that Sect '. —5. ' Of women when secreting letch-water ' : low coll. : mid-C. 18 (? earlier)–20. ' Burlesque Homer ' Bridges, addressing cheap or inferior harlots, ' Or else in midnight cellars ply | For twopence wet and twopence dry '. Cf. *wet bottom*.—6. See wet, get.—7. ' Soft ', silly, dull, stupid, ' dud ' : C. 20 ; unheard by me before 1928, except in *talk wet*, q.v. Anon., *Dict. of Bootham Slang*, 1925 ; Bowen. Perhaps ex sense 2 ; perhaps ex *wet goose*, q.v. (Rarely of things, occ. of occasions.)

wet, all. All wrong ; esp. ' You're all wet ' : New Zealanders' (— 1934).

wet, get. ' To become incensed, ill-tempered .

C. J. Dennis: Australian (— 1916). Perhaps ex *wet*, adj., 1 and 2.

wet, heavy. Malt liquor : 1821, Egan, ' Tossing off the *heavy wet* and spirits ', O.E.D. Cf. *wet*, n., 1, and *wet*, *twopenny*.

wet,——is. Thus ' Coffee is wet ', i.e. something to drink, ' a drink, anyway ! ' : coll. c.p. (— 1923). Manchon.

wet, talk. See talk wet in the Addenda.

wet, twopenny. A drink costing twopence : C. 19–early 20. See wet, n., 2.

wet a line. To go fishing : anglers' coll. (—1909). Ware.

wet all her self, to have. Of a Grand Banks fishing schooner ' when she has filled up with fish, used all the salt . . . brought out, and turns for home ' : fishermen's coll. : late C. 19–20. Bowen.

wet as a shag. See shag, wet as a.

wet-bed. One who, esp. while asleep, wets his bed : coll. : C. 20. (James Spenser, *Limey Breaks In*, 1934.)

wet behind the ears. Ignorant, untrained, inexperienced ; youthful : military : C. 20. B. & P. A boy seldom dries himself behind the ears.

wet bob. See bob.

wet bottom, get a ; do a wet 'un ; do, have or perform a bottom-wetter. (Of women) to have sexual intercourse : low coll., s., s. : C. 19–20. Cf. :

wet dream. An amorous dream accompanied by sexual emission : coll. : C. 19–20,—and prob. from at least a century earlier.

wet goose. A poor simple fellow : rural : mid-C. 19–20. Cf. *wet*, adj., 6.

wet hand. A drunkard : coll. (— 1904). F. & H. ; Manchon. See wet, adj., 1.

wet one's mouth, weasand, or, gen., whistle. See whistle, n.

wet Quaker. ' A man who pretends to be religious, and is a dram drinker on the sly ', H., 2nd ed. : ca. 1860–1910. Ex *wet*, adj., 3, 4, qq.v.

wet the (or one's) neck. To be a drunkard : low : ca. 1820–50. Egan's Grose.

wet the other (1745) or **t'other** (1840) **eye.** To take one glass of liquor after another : s. >, by 1850, coll. ; ob. O.E.D. for dates.

wet-thee-through. Gin : low : ca. 1820–60. Egan's Grose.

wet triangle, the. The North Sea : political coll. : from ca. 1905 ; ob. Collinson.

wet 'un. See wet, adj., 1, and wet bottom.—2. A diseased beast : slaughterers' (— 1864). H., 3rd ed. Cf. *wet*, adj., 6, and *wet goose*, qq.v.—2. (Gen. pl.) A tear (*lacrima*) : low : from ca. 1870 ; ob. Ware.

wetter. A wetting, soaking, by rain : coll. : 1884 (not '85), D. Sladen (O.E.D.).—2. A ' wet dream ' (q.v.) : low (— 1923). Manchon.

we've. We have : coll. : mid-C. 18–20. Cf. *I've, you've, they've*.

Wewi. See Wi-Wi.

whack ; in C. 19, occ. **wack.** A heavy, smart, resounding blow : from 1730's : dial. >, ca. 1830, coll. Barham, Mayhew. Prob. echoic. (O.E.D.) —2. Hence, its sound : coll. : mid-C. 19–20. Thackeray (O.E.D.).—3. A (full) share : c. (— 1785) >, by 1800, s. >, by 1880, coll. Grose, 1st ed. Esp. in *take* (1830), *get* or *have one's whack*, and in *go whacks* (— 1874). ? ex the sound of the physical division of booty.—4. Hence, fig. : mid-C. 19–20. Walch, 1890, ' My word ! he did more than his whack.'—5. See whack-up, n.—6. See whack at.—7. Anxiety ; dilemma : from ca. 1925.

David Frome, *That's Your Man, Inspector*, 1934, ' I was in a frightful whack . . . I thought I was blotto.'—8. Hence, a rage ; a bad state of nerves : from ca. 1925. David Frome, *The Body in the Turl*, 1935.

whack, v. To strike with sharp, resounding vigour : coll. and dial. : 1721, Ramsay (O.E.D.). Also as v.i., esp. in *whack away* (mid-C. 19–20), as in *The Daily Telegraph*, Feb. 21, 1886, ' The Flannigans and the Murphys paid no heed to him, but whacked away at each other with increasing vigour.' Prob. echoic ; cf. *whack*, n., 1.—2. Hence, to defeat in a contest or rivalry : coll. : from 1870's.—3. To bring, get, place, put, etc., esp. in a vigorous or violent manner : from C. 17 'teens : dial. >, in late C. 19, coll., as in Kipling, 1897, ' They whacked up a match,' O.E.D. Prob. ex sense 1.—4. To share or divide : c. (— 1812) >, by 1860, s. >, by 1910, coll. Vaux, who spells it *wack* ; J. Greenwood, 1888, *A Converted Burglar*, ' The sound, old-fashioned principle of " sharing the danger and whacking the swag "'. Also *whack up*. Ex *whack*, n., 3, q.v.—5. See whack it up.—6. To sell illicitly : military : from ca. 1910. Prob. suggested by the synonymous *flog*.

whack ! An interjection politely = ' You lie ! ' : printers : from ca. 1870. Ex *whacker*. Cf. *thump !*

whack, adv. With a ' whack ' (n., 1, q.v.) : coll. : 1812, H. and J. Smith (O.E.D.). Cf. :

whack at, have or **take a.** To attempt ; to attack : coll. : U.S. (1891) >, before 1904, anglicised. F. & H. Perhaps ex tree-felling.

whack it out, v.i. To defend or support successfully : proletarian (— 1923). Manchon.

whack it up, v.i. To coït : low : mid-C. 19–20 ; ? ob. Cf. *whack*, v., 1, 3, 4.—2. V.t. To deal severely with (a prisoner) : c. (— 1933). G. Ingram, *Stir*.

whack one's own donkey. See donkey, whack one's own.

whack out. To distribute (e.g. rations) equitably : military : C. 20. B. & P.

whack-up. A division of accounts : coll. : 1885 (O.E.D.). Elaborating *whack*, n., 3.

whack up, v. See whack, v., 3 and 4, qq.v. : coll. : from ca. 1880.—2. See whack it up and :

whack up to. To cause a ship to attain such and such a speed : nautical coll. (— 1923). Manchon. Cf. *whack*, v., 3.

whacked ; whacked to the wide (sc. *world*). Utterly exhausted : late C. 19–20. Ex *whack*, v., 1.

whacker. Anything unusually large ; esp. a ' thumping ' lie (cf. *whopper*, q.v.) : coll. and dial. (— 1825). *The Sporting Times*, in 1828, describes certain fences as whackers, as T. Hughes does caught fish in 1861. Ex *whack*, v., 1. (O.E.D.)

whacking. A thrashing : coll. (— 1859). H., 1st ed. Ex *whack*, v., 1.—2. Hence, a defeat in a contest : coll. : late C. 19–20.—3. A division or sharing : from ca. 1850 : (low) s. >, by 1900, coll. Mayhew. Ex *whack*, v., 4.

whacking, adj. Unusually big, large, fine, or strong : coll. : 1819, Thomson (E.D.D.) ; H., 1st ed. Often *whacking great*, occ. *w. big*. Ex *whack*, v., 1 ; cf. *whacker*.

whacks, go. See whack, n., 3.

whacky. A person acting ridiculously or fooling about : tailors' (— 1904) F. & H. Ex Yorkshire dial. *whacky*, a dolt.

whale. A codfish : Cheltenham College : late C. 19–20. Because a large fish.—2. A sardine :

Royal Military Academy : from ca. 1870. Because so small.—3. (Always in pl.) Anchovies on toast : rather proletarian : from ca. 1880. Cf. sense 2.

whale, go ahead like a. To forge ahead ; act, speak, write vigorously : coll. : from 1890's. F. & H. Ex the majesty of a whale's movements.

whale, old. See **old whale.**

whale !, very like a. A c.p. applied to an improbability, esp. a preposterous assertion : from 1850's ; ob. H., 1st ed. ; in 2nd ed., *very like a whale in a tea-cup*. Ex Polonius's phrase when, in III, ii, 392–8, he is doing his best to approve Hamlet's similes.

***whale and whitewash.** Fish and sauce : tramps' c. (— 1932). F. Jennings, *Tramping with Tramps*.

whale of a . . ., a. ' No end of a . . .' : coll. : U.S. (— 1913), partly anglicised ca. 1918. Ex the whale's huge size.

whale on . . ., a. Greatly liking, having a great capacity for, expert at : coll. : 1893, Justin McCarthy, ' He was not . . . a whale on geography,' O.E.D. ; rather ob. For semantics, cf. preceding entry. Also, occ., *whale at* and *for*.

whaler. A sundowner : Australian coll. : ca. 1890–1910. *The Sydney Morning Herald*, Aug. 8, 1893, ' The nomad, the whaler, it is who will find the new order hostile to his vested interest of doing nothing.' (He didn't.) Ex his cruising about. (Morris.) He who travels up and down the banks of the Murrumbidgee River is a *Murrumbidgee whaler*, which some authorities consider to be the ironic original.

whales. See **whale, 3.**

Whaley. The Whale Island Gunnery School (Portsmouth) : naval : C. 20. Bowen.

whang. A ' whanging ' sound or blow : dial. (— 1824) and, from ca. 1860, coll. Ex :

whang, v.t. To strike heavily and resoundingly : coll. : C. 19–20. Ex dial. (C. 17–20). Echoic.— 2. V.i. (of, e.g., a drum), to sound (as) under a blow : coll. : 1875, Kinglake (O.E.D.).

[**whangam, whangdoodle.** An imaginary animal : rather nonce-words than coll.]

Whanger ; Cod-Whanger. A Newfoundland fish-curer : nautical (— 1867). Smyth. Precisely why ? (Also in lower case.)

whap, whapper (Grose, 1st ed.). See **whop, whopper.**

wharf-rat. A thief prowling about wharves : mid-C. 19–20. Perhaps orig. U.S.

wharp is incorrect for *warp* (silt, n.) : C. 18–20. O.E.D.

what. Who, that ; which : C. 10–20 : S.E. until C. 19, then sol. and dial. Esp. *all what*, C. 16–20 : same status. F. & H., ' If I had a donkey what wouldn't go ' ; J. B. Morton, *The Barber of Putney*, 1919, ' If I sat down to write a book, I'd want to shove in all what I saw,' O.E.D.—2. At what, as in ' What time do you start ? ' : coll. (— 1887). Baumann.—3. The : sol. : C. 19–20. Baumann, ' What one I 'ave I'll keep.'—4. See next two entries.

what ! (more precisely **what ? !**) ; occ. **eh what !** A questioning interjection or expletive, gen. at the end of a phrase or sentence : coll. : 1785, Mme D'Arblay, ' [George III] said, " What ? what ? "— meaning . . . "it is not possible. Do you think it is ?—what ? " ' ; not very gen. before mid-C. 19 ; 1914, Neil Lyons, ' It's a bit too literary for me. What ? . . . You had it at school, I dare say What ? ', O.E.D. This enclitic *what* is an infallible characteristic and hall-mark of the upper-middle

and upper class (males much more than females) and it is confined to Great Britain ; the lower and lower-middle classes, and all Colonials and most Americans, find it very odd, affected, and, at first, a little disconcerting (esp. in the explosive form common among, e.g., Army officers) in its app. senselessness ; actually, it is a modifier (often deliberate) of abruptness, insolence, or audacity. Cognate with, and perhaps ex the next term.—2. Abbr. *what cheer* (l.v. at **cheer !, what**) : Cockneys' : from ca. 1880. H. W. Nevinson, *Neighbours of Ours*, 1895.

what ? What is it ? ; what did you say ? : coll. : recorded by the O.E.D. for 1837, Dickens, ' " What's your name ? " " Cold punch," murmured Mr Pickwick . . . " What ? " 'demanded Captain Boldwig ' ; but prob. a half, even a full century earlier. Arising naturally ex *what* connoting ' ellipsis, esp. of the remainder of the question ', as in ' " I'm so frightened ! " " What at, dear ?—what at ? ",' Dickens, 1837 (O.E.D.).

[**what, (and) the Lord knows**, marches between coll. and S.E. Cf. *what all*.]

what, but. But that ; that . . . not : coll. : from ca. 1560. Googe, 1563 (see quotation at *what's what*) ; Arthur Murphy, 1753, ' There hardly arose an Incident, but what our Fellow-Traveller would repeat twenty or thirty Verses in a Breath.' Almost always with actual or implied negative ; in late C. 19–20, mostly *not but what*. O.E.D.—2. Except what ; which (occ. who) . . . not : as in Charlotte Smith's ' Not one of these insinuations but what gathered something from malevolence ', 1796. O.E.D. Cf. *what, than* : q.v.

what !, I('ll) tell you, as prefacing a proposal, is coll. : mid-C. 19–20. ' I'll tell you what, we'll row down,' 1872 (O.E.D.). Ex the same phrase as = let me tell you !

what ?, or, used as a final, yet wholly indefinite, ' alternative in a disjunctive question ' : mid-C. 19–20 ; mostly, and in conversation nearly always, coll. Edward FitzGerald, in a letter, 1842, ' Have you supposed me dead or what ? ' O.E.D.

what, than. The *what* is a sol. and dial. redundance when it is used after that *than* which ushers in a clause : C. 19–20. Scott, 1818, ' I think I laughed heartier then than what I do now.' O.E.D.

what a life ! A c.p. expressive of disgust : late C. 19–20.

what a many. How many : sol. : mid-C. 19–20. Baumann cites ' If you knew what a many they're of them ' from J. Greenwood.

what a tail our cat's got ! A lower classes' c.p. directed at a girl (or woman) ' flaunting in a new dress ', the rear skirt of which she swings haughtily : mid-C. 19–20 ; ob. Ware (*tale*—obviously a misprint).

what about a (small) spot ? ; what is it ? ; what'll you have ? See **how will you have it ?**

what all, . . . and I don't know. And various others unknown or unmentioned ; and, in addition, all sorts of things : coll. : mid-C. 19–20. Dickens, 1859, ' There's . . . and . . . and I dunno what all.' O.E.D. Cf. *who all*, q.v.

what-call ; what-call-ye-him. A variant (resp. early C. 17, late C. 15–early 17 : O.E.D.) of the *him* part of *what-d'ye-call-'em* (etc.).

what cheer ! See **cheer !, what.**

what did Gladstone say in (e.g.) **1885 ?** A political hecklers' c.p. of late C. 19–20. For the most part, merely obstructive.

what did you do in the Great War, daddy ? A

military c.p. (1917–18, and after) used 'scathingly in times of stress'. B. & P. Ex a recruiting-poster. In late 1917–19, the phrase had many variations, and several c.p. replies, the most popular being *shut up, you little bastard ! Get the Bluebell and go and clean my medals*, which is devastating.

what do you know ? What is the news ? ; is there any new development ? : c.p. : from ca. 1917.

what do you know about that ? ! A c.p. expressive of surprise : non-aristocratic and non-cultured : from ca. 1910.

what do *you* think ? 'What is your general opinion of things ? ' : a middle-class c.p. introduced in 1882 by a comic singer ; † by 1915.—2. From ca. 1912, it = ' Well, of *course* ! '—3. See **think, what do you?**

what do you want ?—I am on it. A military c.p. reproach to a constant grumbler : late C. 19–20.

what-d'ye-call-'em (occ. um), her, him, it ; less frequently **what-do-you-call-'em,** etc. A phrase connoting some thing or person forgotten, considered trivial or not to be named, or unknown by name : coll. : C. 17–20. Shakespeare, *As You Like It*, ' Good even, good Master What-ye-call't ; how do you, sir,'—a late C. 16–17 variant ; Ned Ward ; Smollett ; Dibdin ; Dickens ; etc., etc. The Shakespearian form has an alternative in *-you-* and a mid-C. 19–20 variant : *what-you-may-call-it* (Dickens, 1848). Cf. Cotton's satirical ' Where once your what shal's cal'ums—rot um ! It makes me mad I have forgot um.' O.E.D. ; F. & H.

what-er. See **whatter.**

what ever ; loosely **whatever.** Emphatic *what ?* : C. 14–20 : S.E. until C. 19, then coll., as in F E. Paget, 1856, ' Whatever in all the world was that ? ', O.E.D.—2. Hence, as interrogative adj. : coll. : late C. 19–20. O.E.D.

what for ; **what-for.** Trouble ; a great fuss, e.g. *raise what-for*, to ' raise Cain ' : C. 20. (David Frome, *The By-Pass Murder*, 1932.) Ex *what for, give one.*

what (e.g., do you do that) **for ?** ; **what for** (by itself) ? Why : coll. : mid-C. 19–20.

what for, give one. To punish or hurt severely : from ca. 1870. Du Maurier, 1894, ' Svengali got " what for ",' O.E.D. Ex *what for ?*, why : ' to respond to [one's] remonstrant *what for ?* by further assault ', W.—2. Hence, to reprimand, reprove severely : from 1890's. F. & H.

what ho ! As greeting or expletive, it is (orig. low) coll. : mid-C. 19–20. Ballantyne, 1864, ' What ho ! Coleman . . . have you actually acquired the art of sleeping on a donkey ? ', O.E.D. ; 1898, ' Pomes ' Marshall, ' Where 'e let me in for drinks all round, and as I'd but a bob, I thought, " What ho ! 'ow am *I* a-going on ? " ' (Cf. the semi-coll. *what cheer !*) Orig., a S.E. formula to attract a person's attention.

what ho ! she bumps. A satirical c.p. applied to ' any display of vigour—especially feminine ' : London (1899) >, by 1914, gen. ; slightly ob. Ware derives it from ' a boating adventure . . . A popular song made this term more popular.'

what hopes ! ; what a hope you've got ! I don't like your chance ! : lower classes' and military : C. 20. B. & P.

what me ! ' A frequent greeting among soldiers ' (B. & P.) : from ca. 1912. (A c.p.)

what next, and next ? A c.p. contemptuous of audacious assertion : ca. 1820–1905. Ware.

what-o(h). A variant of *what ho !*—2. Thus,

' She is a what-oh ', a lively or fast piece : proletarian coll. (— 1923). Manchon.

what one. See **what,** 3.

what Paddy gave the drum. A sound thrashing : orig. (ca. 1845), Irish military >, ca. 1900, gen. ; ob. Ware.

what price . . . ? See **price, what.**

what shall we do, or go —ing ? Shall we go —ing ?, as in D. Sayers, *The Nine Tailors*, 1934, ' " What shall we do, or go fishing ? " " I'm on ; we can but try ".'

what the Connaught men shot at. Nothing : Anglo-Irish (— 1883). Ware.

what the devil. An intensive of *what* : coll. : C. 20. E.g. E. Phillips Oppenheim, *The Bank Manager*, 1934, ' What the devil concern is it of yours, anyway ? '

what will you liq ? What will you drink : middle-class c.p. of ca. 1905–15. Ware. Ex *liquor*; punning *lick.*

what-ye-call-it, what-you-may-call-it. See **what-d'ye-call-'em.**

what you can't carry you must drag ! A nautical c.p. applied to clipper ships carrying too much canvas : late C. 19–20 ; ob. Bowen.

whatcher ! A nautical variation of (S.E.) *what cheer ?* Ware.

whater. See **whatter.—whatever.** See **whatever.**

what's bit or **biting** or **crawling on** or **eating you ?** What's the matter ? : military (1915) >, by 1920, gen. c.p. B. & P. Ex scratching for lice. (Anticipated in 1911 in U.S.)

what's-his-name, -her-, -its-, -your- ; whatsename. Resp. for a man (or boy ; loosely, thing), woman (or girl), thing, person addressed, or ambiguously for any of the first three of these, with name unknown, forgotten, to-be-avoided, or hardly worth mentioning : coll. : resp. late C. 17–20 (Dryden), C. 19–20 (Scott), from 1830's (Dickens), mid-C. 18–20 (Foote), and mid-C. 19–20 (Reade) ; app. Marryat, in 1829, is the first to apply *what's-his-name* to a thing ; *what's-their-names* (G. A. Stevens) is rare. O.E.D. Cf. *what-d'ye-call-'em,* q.v.

what's matter ? What's the matter ? : lower classes' coll. : C. 20. E.g. Pett Ridge, 1907.

what's-o'clock, know. See **o'clock.** Cf. *time of day* and *what's what.*

what's-o-names. An exceedingly illiterate form (— 1887) of *what's-his-name.* Baumann.

what's the big idea. See **idea ?, what's the big.**

what's the dynamite ? ; what's the lyddite ? What's the ' row ' ? : Society : resp. 1890–9 and 1899–1900. Ware. The former ex dynamiters' activities in the 1880's, the latter ex the Boer War.

what's the mat ? What's the matter ? : Public Schools' : from ca. 1880 ; ob. Ware.

what's the matter with your hand ? A military c.p. (from 1914) to one lucky enough to be holding an article of food. B. & P.

what's what ; orig. and gen. preceded by **know, tell w. w.** belonging to C. 17–20, **understand w. w.** to C. 18–20, and **guess, show** and **perceive w. w.** to C. 19–20. ' To have [etc.] knowledge, taste, judgment, or experience ; to be wide-awake . . ., equal to any emergency, " fly " (q.v.) ', F. & H. : coll. : C. 15–20. E.g. Barnaby Googe, 1563, ' Our wits be not so base, | But what we know as well as you | What's what in every case.' See also **o'clock and time of day.**

what's yer fighting weight ; . . . Gladstone weight ? I'm your man if you want to fight ! : Cockneys' : ca. 1883–1914 ; 1885–6 (ex politics). Ware.

what's-yer-name. An illiterate form (— 1887) of *what's-his-name*. Baumann. Cf. *what's-o-names*.

what's your poll to-day. How much have you earned to-day ? : printers' : from ca. 1870. Ware, ' From numbers on a statement of wages '.

what's yours ? See **how will you have it ?**

whatsename, whatsiname ; occ. **whatsername.** Slurred *what's-his-name* (etc.), q.v.

whatsomever. Whatever, whatsoever (adjj.): C. 15–20 : S.E. until C. 19, then dial. and increasingly illiterate coll. The forms *whatsom(e)dever*, *whatsumdever*, mid-C. 19–20, are sol.

whatter (occ. **what-er** or **whater**), **a.** A what, a what-did-you-say : C. 20. ' " Yesterday I saw a dinosaurus, Jim." ' ' " You saw a—a whatter, Bill ? " '

whatty ; occ. **whaty.** The same as *whatter* : low : late C. 18–mid-19. Ware derives it from an anecdote about George III, whose English was not perfect.

wheadle ; wheedle. As a wheedler, prob. S.E. from the beginning, but as a sharper it is prob. c. : ca. 1670–1830, but ob. by 1720. Wycherley, 1673 ; B.E. Whence, *cut a wheadle* (*wheedle*), ' to Decoy, by Fawning and Insinuation ', B.E. : c. of ca. 1690–1830. Ex :

wheadle, whed(d)le (C. 17), **wheedle, v.** In its usual senses, it may, orig., have been s., as *The Century Dict.* suggests, ex Ger. *wedeln*. Blount records it in 1661.—2. ' Whiddle ' in its c. sense (q.v.), of which it is a variant : c. of ca. 1700–20. (O.E.D.)

wheedle the tire off a cart- (or **cart's**) **wheel, can or be able to.** To be extremely persuasive : non-aristocratic coll. (— 1887). Baumann.

wheel. A 5-shilling piece : C. 19. Extant in New Zealand, however, for the sum of five shillings. —2. A dollar : late C. 18–early 19. Tufts. Both, however, mainly as *cart-wheel*, q.v.

wheel, v. To ' cycle ' : coll. : 1884 (O.E.D.) ; rare after G.W. Cf. *wheeler*.—2. (Of the police) to convey (a ' drunk ') in a cab to the police station : low (— 1909) ; † by 1920. Ware (at *barrered*).

wheel, grease the : To coït : low : mid-C. 19–20 ; ob.

wheel, keep a cart on the. To keep an affair alive : semi-proverbial coll. (— 1887) ; ob. Baumann. In Yorkshire dial. it is *keep cart on wheels*.

wheel-band in the nick. ' Regular Drinking over the left Thumb ', B.E. : drinking : late C. 17–early 19. Grose, 1st ed. Contrast and cf. *supernaculum*.

Wheel 'Em Along. The captured French warship *Ville de Milan* : naval : early C. 19. Bowen. By ' Hobson-Jobson '.

wheel 'em up. To bowl : cricket coll. : late C. 19–20. Cf. *trundle*, q.v.

wheel-man or **-woman** ; or as one word. A cyclist : coll. : 1874 (*-man*) ; ob. Also, for the former, *knight of the wheel* ; very ob. coll. Cf. *wheeler*, q.v.

***wheel-of-life.** The treadmill : prison c. : ca. 1870–1910. Cf. *everlasting staircase*.

wheelbarrow, as drunk as a. Exceedingly drunk : coll. : ca. 1670–1750. Cotton, 1675, where he gives the occ. variant . . . *as a drum* (not, as F. & H. has it, *as . . . the drum of a w.*).

wheelbarrow, go to heaven in a. To go to hell : coll. : ca. 1615–90. T. Adams, 1618. ' In the

painted glass at Fairford, Gloucestershire, the devil is represented as wheeling off a scolding wife in a barrow,' F. & H.

wheeled, adj. or ppl. Conveyed in a cab : lower classes' : late C. 19–early 20. Ware.

wheeled up, be. ' To be brought before an officer for an offence ' : military : C. 20. F. & Gibbons Cf. preceding.

wheeler. A cyclist : coll. (— 1887). Baumann. Rare after G.W.—2. (**Wheeler.**) Inevitable nickname of men surnamed Johnson : military : C. 20. F. & Gibbons.

wheeling, n. See **wheel, v.**—**wheelman.** See **wheel-man.**

wheels, grease the. To advance money for a particular purpose : coll. (in C. 20, virtually S.E.) : 1809, Malkin. Thus ensuring easier running.

wheeze. A theatrical ' gag ', esp. if frequently repeated : circus and theatrical s. (in C. 20, coll. and fairly gen.) : from early 1860's. Ex the act of wheezing : perhaps because clowns often affect a wheezy enunciation. In Lancashire dial. as early as 1873 is the sense, ' an amusing saying ; a humorous anecdote ' (E.D.D.).—2. Hence, a catch phrase, esp. if often repeated ; an ' antiquated fabrication ' (W.) : 1890, *The Spectator*, May 17 (O.E.D.).—3. Hence, a frequently employed trick or dodge : from ca. 1895. Like sense 2, s. >, ca. 1920, coll.—4. A ' tip ' (information) ; gen. *the wheeze*, esp. in *give* (a person) *the wheeze* (cf. *give the whisper*,—see **whisper**, n.) : C. 20 : c. >, by 1930, low s. Cf. the v., which is the possibly imm. origin.—5. Anything remarkable : Seaford Preparatory School : from ca. 1930 Ex senses 3, 4. Also *weeze*.

***wheeze, v.** To give information, to peach : c. (— 1904). F. & H. Cf. n.

wheeze, crack a. ' To originate (or adapt) a smart saying at a " psychological " moment ', F. & H. : from ca. 1895 ; rather ob. See **wheeze**, n., 2.

wheezer. A phonograph : music-halls' : 1897–8. Ware.

Wheezy. The French Revolution month, Vendémiaire (late Sept.–mid-Oct.) : journalistic : ca. 1890–1910. Ex the colds so often contracted during this period. (F. & H.)

wheezy ; occ. **weezy,** adj. Remarkable, very fine : Seaford Preparatory School : from ca. 1930. Ex *wheeze*, n., 5.

whelk. The female pudend : proletarian Cockney : from ca. 1860. Anatomical. Whence the innuendo-c.p., comically threatening, *I'll have your whelk* : 1870's.—2. A sluggish fellow : Cockneys' : late C. 19–20. Manchon. Cf. Fr. *mollusque*.

whelp. To be delivered of a child : low coll. : late C. 19–20 ; ob. Cf. *pup*, which is far from being ob.

when. Lo ! ; see now ! ; then, mark you ! : coll. (— 1887). Baumann, ' When up comes a chap with a basket on his shoulder '.

when !, say. Orig. a c.p. with 'dovetail' *Bob !* (or *bob !*) ; by 1920, S.E. *Modern Society*, June 6, 1889, ' " Say when," said Bonko . . . commencing to pour out the spirit into my glass. " Bob ! " replied I.' The dovetail was † by 1920.

when Adam was an oakum-boy in Chatham Dockyard. Indefinitely long ago : ca. 1860–1900. H., 3rd ed. Cf. :

when Christ was a child. The same : C. 20.

when ever ; loosely **whenever.** In questions, an emphatic form of *when* : from ca. 1710 : S.E. until mid-C. 19, then coll. E.g. 'When ever did you arrive, old man ?'

when father says Turn, we all turn. A c.p. of ca. 1906–8. Ex a political picture-postcard. Collinson.

when hens make holy-water. Never : coll. c.p. : C. 17. See the quotation at *Never-mass*.

when it's at home. A derisive tag implying contempt or incredulity : coll. : C. 20. Best explained by a quotation : Dorothy Sayers, *Have His Carcase*, 1932, ' Hæmophilia. What in the name of blazes is that, when it's at home ?'

when the (bloody) Duke (or Dook) puts his (bloody) foot down, the (bloody) war will be bloody well over. A 62nd Division c.p. of the G.W. Ex the Divisional sign, a pelican with upraised right foot. F. & Gibbons.

when you were cutting bread and jam. A variant of *before you came up*, q.v.

where, with *from* or *to* at end of sentence. The coll. equivalents of *whence* and *whither* : mid-C. 18–20 for both, no doubt. Henry Brooke, 1760, ' I must go suddenly, but where to ?' ; Dickens, 1835 (*where . . . from*). O.E.D.

where are you (a-)going to (—can't yer) ? ! Stop pushing ! : low London : from ca. 1880 ; slightly ob. Ware.

where did that one go ? A military c.p. (1915–18) in reference to a shell-burst (near-by). B. & P. Short for ' Where did that one go to, Herbert, | Where did that one go ?', which comes from a popular War-time song.

where did you get that hat ? See **hat ?, where did you get that.—where do flies go . . . ?** See **wintertime.**

where did you get the Rossa ? I.e. the borrowed plumes : 1885 only. Ware. Ex a New York police trial.

where ever ; loosely **wherever.** In questions, an emphatic form of *where* : C. 13–20 : S.E. until C. 19, then coll. (O.E.D.). Cf. *what ever* and *when ever*, qq.v.

where Maggie wore the beads. See **Maggie.**

where the chicken got the axe. See **chicken . . .**

where the flies won't get it. (Of liquor) down one's throat : c.p. : orig. (— 1909), U.S. ; anglicised by 1912. Ware.

where the whips are cracking. See **whips are . . .**

whereas, follow a. To become a bankrupt : commercial and legal : late C. 18–mid-19. Grose, 2nd ed., where also the synonymous *march in the rear of a whereas*.

-wheres. See **somewhere.**

where's George ? A c.p. applied to any person unexpectedly absent : 1935–36. Ex Messrs Lyons' advertisement-pictures of a vacant stool, etc.

where's the war ? A c.p. directed at a street wrangle : London streets' : 1900–1. Ex scattered fighting in Boer War. (Ware.)

wheresomever. Wherever ; more properly, wheresoever : sol. (— 1887). Baumann.

wherewith ; wherewithal. ' The necessary ', esp. money : resp. rare coll. († by 1910) and dial. ; coll., as first in Malkin, 1809, ' How the devil does she mean that I should get the wherewithal ? . . . Does she take me for . . . treasurer to a charity ?'

whern(e). Incorrect for *wherve* (written *wherue*) = *wharve*, n. : mid-C. 16–17. O.E.D.

wherry-go-nimble. Diarrhœa : lower class (— 1904). F. & H. If *wherry* is not a corruption of *Jerry*(*-go-nimble*), it seems almost senseless.

whet. See **wet,** n.—**whet one's whistle.** See **whistle, wet one's.—whether-go-ye.** See **whither . . .**

Whetstone(s) Park deer or **mutton.** A ' Whetstone whore ' : London fast life : ca. 1670–1700. Ex *Whetstones Park*, ' a Lane betwixt Holborn and Lincolns-Inn-fields, fam'd for a Nest of Wenches, now de-park'd ', B.E. : the district was notorious at least as early as 1668. See esp. Grose, P.

whetting-corn(e). The female pudend : ? C. 17–mid-19. Halliwell. Lit., grindstone.

whew, the. Sir H. Maxwell, in *Notes and Queries*, Dec. 10, 1901, says that in C. 15 the influenza was app. known as ' the Whew ' just as, in C. 20, it is known as ' the Flue '. (Mainly Scots) coll. and gen. spelt *Quhew*.

whiblin. This C. 17 word (unrecorded later than 1652) is explained by F. & H. as a eunuch and, in c., a sword ; by the O.E.D. as perhaps ' thingumbob '. Perhaps ex *whibble + quiblin*.

which, ' in vulgar use, without any antecedent, as a mere connective or introductory particle ', O.E.D. : C. 18 (and prob. earlier)–20. Often it is wholly superfluous ; often, however, it = for, because ; very often it = besides, moreover ; and, occ., it = although. Swift, 1723, *Mary the Cook-Maid's Letter*, ' Which, and I am sure I have been his servant four years since October, | And he never call'd me worse than sweetheart, drunk or sober,' O.E.D. ; J. Storer Clouston, 1932, ' So now they goes and dresses up as Sir Felix, which he were become a knight, and no one could tell them apart from one another,' an example less pregnant than these two in Dorothy Sayers, *Unnatural Death*, 1927 : ' Ironsides . . . a clerk on the Southern, which he always used to say joking like, " Slow but safe, like the Southern—that's me " ' ; ' I believe the gentleman acted with the best intentions, 'avin' now seen 'im, which at first I thought he was a wrong 'un.' Ex pleonastic *which*, as in Locke's ' Provisions . . . which how much they exceed the other in value, . . . he will then see ' (O.E.D.).— 2. Incorrectly with *and*, where the one or the other is unnecessary : catachrestic : C. 17 (prob. earlier)– 20. Gilbert White, ' This is their due, and which ought to be rendered to them by all people ', O.E.D. Perhaps ex Fr. idiom, though the same usage is common also in S.E.—3. What : sol. : C. 19 (? earlier)–20. E.g. Agatha Christie, *Why Didn't They Ask Evans ?*, 1934, ' " You were with her some time, weren't you ? " " Were I which, ma'am ? " '

which way, every. See **every which way.**

***whid ; widd(e).** A word : c. (— 1567) ; slightly ob. Harman, B.E., Grose, Reade. See phrases. Either ex A.-S. *cwide*, speech, as the O.E.D. suggests, or a perversion of *word*.—2. In pl., speech : c. : contemporaneous with 1. See phrases. —3. In singular, speech : c. (— 1823) >, by 1860, low. Bee, ' " Hold your whid," is to stow magging '. —4. ' A word too much ', H., 3rd ed. : mid-C. 19– 20 ; ob. : s. ; closely linked with dial. *whid*, a lie, an exaggerated story.—5. Hence, in c. verging on low s., talk, patter, jocular speech, jest : likewise only in pl. Hindley, 1876, *The Life of a Cheap Jack*, ' The whids we used to crack over them.'—6. A broken-winded horse : horse-copers' c : mid-C. 19– 20. ' *No. 747.'* I.e. a ' roarer ' : cf. *whid*, 3.

***whid,** v.i. To talk cant : Scots c. (— 1823). Egan's Grose. Ex n., 1, 2.

***whid, crack a.** See **crack a whid.**

*whid, cut the (Ainsworth); **cut whids.** To talk, speak : c. : resp. C. 19 (rare) and mid-C. 16–20. Mostly implied, as to *cut whids*, in *cut bene whids* and *c. queer w.*, qq.v.

whidd, whidde. See whid, n. and v.

*whiddle ; in C. 18, occ. **wheadle (wheedle),** q.v. at v., 2, and whidel, whidle, and **widdle** ; see also **whittle.** V.i. and v.t. To tell ; to peach, to impeach : from the Restoration ; ob. The O.E.D. records it at 1661 ; not gen., I think, before the 1680's or 90's ; B.E. ; Grose ; Vaux. Perhaps ex *whid*, n., 1, 2.—2. Hence, to enter into a parley, esp. if nefarious : c. (— 1725). *A New Canting Dict.* ; H., 2nd ed. ; ob.—3. Hence, to ' hesitate with many words ', H., 1st ed. : mid-C. 19–20 ; ob. Either c. or low s. : cf. *whid*, n., 3.—4. See **Oliver.**

*whiddle beef. To cry ' thief ! ' : c. : late C. 17–mid-19. B.E., Grose.

*whiddler. An informer to the police ; a blabber of the gang's secrets : c. : late C. 17–20 ; ob. B.E., Grose. Ex *whiddle*, v., 1.

*whids, cut. See whid, cut the. Mostly in *cut bene* (or *bien) whids*, to speak fairly, kindly, or courteously, and *cut queer whids*, to speak roughly or discourteously, or to use blasphemous or obscene language : c. : resp. (? only) C. 19 and rare (1821, Scott ; 1861, Reade, ' Thou cuttest whids ') ; and, both *bene* and *queer*, mid-C. 16–mid-19. See **whid,** n., 1 and 2.

whiff, v.i. To smell unpleasantly : 1899, Kipling (O.E.D.). Ex corresponding n.

whiff, adj. Stinking, malodorous : low (—1923). Manchon. More usually *whiffy* (1905 : O.E.D.) : gen. s.

whiffing, vbl.n. Catching a mackerel with hooked line and a bright object : nautical : C. 19. Bowen. Perhaps ex *whiff*, a flat-fish, etc.

whifflegig. Trifling : coll. : 1830, H. Lee, ' Whiffle-gig word-snappers ', O.E.D. Presumably ex (mainly dial.) *whiffle*, to talk idly. Cf. *whiffmagig*.

whiffler. One who examines candidates for degrees : Oxford and Cambridge : ca. 1785–1830. Grose, 2nd ed. Ex the official sense.

whiffles. ' A relaxation of the scrotum ', Grose, 1st ed. : ca. 1780–1850.

whiffmagig. A trifler ; a shifty or contemptible fellow : 1871, Meredith (O.E.D.) ; ob. A variant of *whiffler* in these senses. Cf. *whifflegig*, q.v.

whiffs and a spit, take two. To smoke a little, have a short smoke, a pull : lower classes' coll. (— 1923). Manchon.

whiffy. See whiff, adj.

Whig. The opp. of *Tory*, q.v. In the second sense, i.e. an opponent to *Tory* = a Conservative, the word dates from 1689, prob. began as s. and soon > coll. and then S.E. ; ca. 1850, it was superseded by *Liberal*. Ultimately ex *Whiggamer, Whiggamore*. F. & H. ; O.E.D.—2. An irresolute person ; a turncoat : middle-classes' : 1860–9. Ware. Ex the Whigs' temporising at that period.

Whig College, the. The Reform Club : political nickname : ca. 1845–1910. *John Bull*, April 29, 1848, ' The Whig College, commonly called the Reform Club '.

Whigland. Scotland : ca. 1680–1830. Flatman, B.E., Grose. Because the ' home ' of Whigs. Whence *Whiglander* (gen. pl.), a Scotsman : same period.

while, quite a. A considerable time : coll. : C. 20. Elinor Glyn, 1905 (O.E.D.).

whiles, when not deliberately archaic and

' literary ', is, in late C. 19–20, considered a somewhat illiterate coll. for *while*. Baumann.

whilk, giddy. A light-headed, silly girl : Cockneys' (— 1923). Manchon, who misspells it *wilk*. A corruption of *whelk*.

whim ; whim-wham, The female pudend : C. 18 ; C. 18–20, ob. Lit., fanciful object.

Whimsicals, the. A group of Tories temp. Queen Anne : coll. nickname : 1714, Swift (O.E.D.).

*whiners. Prayers, esp. in *chop the whiners*, to pray : c. : C. 18–20 ; ob. *A New Canting Dict.*, 1725 ; 1830, Bulwer Lytton. Ex *whine*, v. : lit., therefore, words that whine.—2. Whence, speech, ' gab ', esp. in *chop whiners*, to talk : low : mid-C. 19–20 ; ob. *Punch*, Jan. 31, 1857.

whinn. An occ. C. 19 spelling of *win*, n., 1, ' Jon Bee.'

whip. Money subscribed by a mess for additional wine : naval and military coll. (— 1864). Ex *whip*, now *whip-round* (H., 5th ed., 1874), an appeal for money.—2. A compositor quick at his work : printing (— 1904). F. & H. Cf. *whip*, a coachman.—3. A bustle, busyness : nautical coll. (— 1923). Manchon. Cf. S.E. v., *whip around* (v.i.).

whip, v. To drink quickly ; gen. *whip off* ; occ. in late C. 17–18, *whip up*. C. 17–20 ; slightly ob. Deloney, B.E., Grose. (O.E.D.)—2. Gen. *whip through*. To pierce with a sword, esp. in *whip through the lungs* : late C. 17–mid-19. B.E.—3. To swindle (v.t.) : c. : late C. 19–20 ; ob. Cf. military *flog* and *whip off*.

whip, drink or **lick on the.** To receive a thrashing : coll. : C. 15–16. Resp. Gascoigne and *The Townley Mysteries.*

whip, old ; gen. **the old whip.** One's ship ; nautical (— 1887). Baumann. Perhaps rhyming.

whip-arse. A schoolmaster : coll. : C. 17. Cotgrave. Cf. *bum-brusher.*

whip-belly ; w.-b. vengeance. Thin weak liquor, esp. ' swipes ' : C. 19–20 ; C. 18–19. Swift ; Grose, 2nd ed., with variant *pinch-gut vengeance* ; Halliwell (*whip-belly*).

whip-cat. Drunken : s. or coll. : late C. 16–early 17. See whip the cat, 1.—2. N., a tailor as in *whip the cat*, 4 : 1851, Mayhew (O.E.D.)

whip-handle. An insignificant little man : Scots : C. 17. Urquhart.

whip-her-jenny. See whipperginnie.

*whip-jack. A beggar pretending to be a distressed, esp. a shipwrecked, sailor : c. : ca. 1550–1880. Ponet, ca. 1550 ; B.E. ; Grose ; H., 2nd–5th edd. The semantics are not very clear. Cf. *turnpike sailor.*

whip off. See whip, v., 1. B.E. gives *whip off*, to steal, as c. : but surely it is no worse than familiar S.E. Cf. *whip*, v., 3.

whip-round. See whip, n., 1. Coll. >, by 1920, S.E.

whip-sticks ; or **W.-S.** The Dunaberg-*Witepsk* shares : Stock Exchange (— 1904).

whip-the-cat. An itinerant tailor : mid-C. 19–20 : Scots s. >, by 1900, coll. E.g. in C. Murray, *Hamewith*, 1910. Ex sense 4 of :

whip the cat. To get intoxicated : ca. 1580–1820. Implied by Stonyhurst in 1582 ; Cotgrave, 1611 ; ' Water-Poet ' Taylor, 1630 ; *The Gentleman's Magazine*, 1807. (See esp. Apperson.) Synonymous with *jerk, shoot, the cat*.—2. To play a practical joke : late C. 17–early 19. Implied in B.E. and Grose. See esp. F. & H.,—3. To be extremely mean : dial. (— 1825) >, ca. 1860, s. ; ob.—4. To work as an itinerant tailor (hence, carpenter, etc.), by the day, at private houses : dial. (— 1825) >, by 1840, s. or, rather, coll. H., 1st ed.—5. **To vomit** : low : mid-C. 19–20. E.D.D. Cf. 1.—6. To idle on Monday : workmen's (— 1897). Barrère & Leland. Cf. *keep St Monday*. Ex :—7. To idle at any time : workmen's (— 1823) ; ob. Bee.

whip the devil or **the old gentleman round the post.** To achieve illicitly or surreptitiously what can be accomplished honourably or openly : coll. : late C. 18–20 ; ob.

whip through ; whip up. See **whip**, v., 2 and 1 resp.

whipper-in. The horse that, at any moment of the race, is running last : racing s. (from ca. 1890) >, by 1930, coll. Ex hunting. F. & H., 1904, gives *whipping-boy* in the same sense.

whipping-boy. See preceding.

whips. Abundance : Australian (— 1916). C.J. Dennis. Suggested by *lashings*, q.v.

whips are cracking, where the. The front line : New Zealanders' : in G.W. Ex the activity of cattle-mustering.

[**Whipshire.** Yorkshire : late C. 17–early 19. B.E. ; Grose, 1st ed. I'm none too sure that this should not, in B.E., read *Whigshire* and that Grose has not copied B.E., for in the former, *Whip-shire* imm. follows *Whig-land*.]

whirligig. A ' gadget ', a ' what-d'ye-call-it ' : coll. (— 1923). Manchon. Cf. *jigger*.

whirligigs ; whirlygigs. Testicles : late C. 17– early 19. B.E. Ex lit. sense.

whishler. A ring-master : circus : mid.-C. 19–20. ? ex *whish* / (a warning).

whisk. A whipper-snapper ; (often of a servant) ' a little inconsiderable impertinent Fellow ', B.E. : ca. 1625–1830. Ford, 1628 (O.E.D.) ; Brome, ca. 1653 ; Grose. Perhaps ex *whisk*, a hair-like appendage.

whisker ; in C. 17–18, occ. **wisker.** Something excessive, great, very large ; esp. a notable lie : 1668, Wilkins (O.E.D.) ; B.E. ; Grose. In mid-C. 19–20, mainly dial. Ex *whisk*, to move briskly.

whisker, the mother of that was a. A c.p. retort on an improbable story : ca. 1850–1900. Cf. *the dam of that was a whisker*, the mainly dial. synonym, applied, however, esp. to a big lie : see **dam of** . . .

whisker-bed. The face : 1853, ' Cuthbert Bede ', ' His ivories rattled, his nozzle barked, his whisker-bed napped heavily.' Ob. in C. 20.

whisker-splitter ; in C. 18, occ. **wisker-.** A man given to sexual intrigue : ca. 1785–1840. Grose, 2nd ed. Cf. the more gen. *beard-splitter*.

whiskerando ; occ. **-os.** A man heavily whiskered : jocular coll. : from ca. 1805 ; ob. Thackeray, ' The . . . whiskerando of a warrior '. Ex *Whiskerandos*, a character in Sheridan's comedy, *The Critic*, 1779. Hence, *whiskerandoed*, (heavily) whiskered : 1838, Southey.

Whiskeries (or **Whiskeyries**), **the.** The Irish Exhibition in London in : 1888 : mostly Londoners'. Ware quotes *The Referee* of June 10, 1888. On *Colinderies, Fisheries*, etc.

whiskers. A ' whiskerando ' (q.v.) ; often loosely of any man, as in the jocular greeting, ' Hallo, Whiskers ! ' : mid C. 19–20. Cf. :

whiskers, all my. Nonsense : from ca. 1920. Dorothy Sayers, *Clouds of Witness*, 1926, ' All that stuff about his bein' so upset . . . was all my whiskers.' On *all my eye*.

whiskers (on it), **have.** (Of a story, an idea) to be

well-known, known for years, old : jocular coll. : from ca. 1925. (Dorothy Sayers, *Gaudy Night*, 1935).

whiskery. (Heavily) whiskered : coll. (in C. 20, S.E.) : from ca. 1860. Ex *whiskers*, q.v.

whiskey-. See **whisky-.—Whiskeyries.** See **Whiskeries.**

whiskeys or **whiskies.** Shares in the Dublin Distillers' Company : Stock Exchange (— 1895). A. J. Wilson's glossary.

whiskin. A pander : ca. 1630–50. Brome, 1632. Cf. *pimp-whisk(in)*. O.E.D.

whisking. (Of persons) briskly moving ; lively ; smart : coll. : from ca. 1610 ; ob. by 1860, virtually † by 1920. Middleton & Dekker, 1611, ' What are your whisking gallants to our husbands ' ; Carlyle, 1824. Ex *whisk*, to move briskly. O.E.D.—2. Great, very big ; excessive : s. (— 1673) >, by 1750, coll. >, by 1830, dial. Head ; Grose. Cf. *whisker*, q.v.

whisky bottle. A Scotch drunkard : Scots (— 1909). Ware. Ex the typically Scottish drink.

whisky-frisky. Flighty ; lightly lively : rare coll. : 1782, Miss Burney. Cf. *whisking*, 1.

whisky jack ; C. 19–20, also **whiskey jack ;** C. 18, **whiskijack ;** all three may be hyphenated. ' A popular name for the common green jay of Canada ' : Canadian coll. verging on S.E. : from ca. 1770. Also *whisk(e)y john*, or, as for *whisky jack*, with capitals. The earlier is *whisky john*, a corruption of Red Indian *wiskatjan*. O.E.D. (In all the two-word forms, the second element may be capitalled.)

whisky-stall. (Gen. pl.) A stall-seat at, or near, the end of a row, enabling the occupant to go out for a drink without inconvenience to himself or his neighbours : journalistic : 1883–ca. 1914. Ware.

Whiskyries, the. See **Whiskeries.**

whisper. ' A tip given in secret ' ; esp. ' *give the whisper*, . . . to give a quick tip to any one ', H., 5th ed., where also *the whisper at the post*, an owner's final instructions to his jockey ' : racing : from early 1870's. Cf. *wheeze*, n., 4, q.v.

whisper, v.t. To borrow money from (a person) ; esp. borrow small sums : from ca. 1870 ; ob. H., 5th ed. Ex the whisper with which such loans are usually begged.—2. V.i., to make water : preparatory schools' : from ca. 1920. Echoic.

whisper, angel's ; gen. **the a. w.** The call to defaulters' drill or extra fatigue duty : military : from 1890's. Wyndham, *The Queen's Service*, 1899. —2. Loosely, reveille : from ca. 1910. F. & Gibbons.

whisper, (in a) pig's. See **pig's whisper.**

whisperer. A petty borrower : from ca. 1870 ; ob. H., 5th ed. Ex *whisper*, v., q.v.

whispering-gallery. The old Gaiety Bar : theatrical : 1883–ca. 90. Ex whispered request for loans and ex the Whispering Gallery of St. Paul's. Ware.

whispering syl-slinger. A prompter (*syl* = *syllable*) : theatrical : late C. 19–20 ; ob.

whispering Willie. A type of big naval gun used by the Germans : East African campaign of the G.W. (F. Brett Young, *Jim Redlake*, 1930.)

whister-clister, -snefet, -snivet. A cuff on the ear or the side of the head : resp. late C. 18–mid-19 (Grose, 1st ed.), then dial. ; C. 16 (Udall) ; C. 16 (Palsgrave : O.E.D.). Perhaps a reduplication of *whister*, that which ' whists ' or puts to silence even so, *-clister* may pun *clyster*, an enema, while *-snefet, -snivet* may be cognate with the vv. *snite*, *snivel.* Perhaps orig. dial., as the Palsgrave locus indicates; certainly dial. are the variants *whisterpoop* (C. 17–20, *whistersniff* (C. 19–20), and *whistertwister,*—which last (C. 18–19) is certainly a punning reduplication.

whistle. The mouth or the throat : jocular coll. : by itself, C. 17–20. Ex *wet* (incorrectly *whet* : C. 17–20) *one's whistle,* to take a drink : late C. 14–20, likewise jocular coll. Chaucer, in *The Reeve's Tale,* ' So was hir joly whistle wel y-wet '; Walton ; Burns ; Marryat (*whet*).—2. A flute : late C. 19–20. —3. An abbr., as in J. Curtis, *The Gilt Kid,* 1936, of :

whistle and flute. A suit (of clothes) : rhyming s. : late C. 19–20. B. & P.

whistle and ride. To work and talk : tailors' (— 1904). F. & H. Presumably ex a rider's whistling as he journeys.

whistle-belly vengeance. Inferior liquor, esp. bad beer : 1861, Hughes, ' Regular whistle-belly vengeance, and no mistake ' ; in C. 20, mainly (Lancashire) dial. Cf. *whip-belly* (*vengeance*), which prob. suggested *whistle-b. v.*

whistlecup. A drinking-cup fitted with a whistle, the last toper capable of using it receiving it as a prize : public-house coll. : from ca. 1880. Also, a cup that, on becoming empty, warns the tapster : id. : id.

whistle-drunk. Exceedingly drunk : mid-C. 18. Fielding's *whistled-d.* is prob. a misprint.

whistle for. To expect, seek, try to get, in vain ; to fail to obtain, go without ; have a very slight chance of obtaining : coll. : 1760, C. Johnston, ' " Do you not desire to be free ? " " Aye ! . . . but I may whistle for that wind long enough, before it will blow,' which indicates the origin, for sailors have for centuries whistled hopefully when becalmed.—2. Hence, *shall I whistle for it ?,* a c.p. that is ' a jocular offer of aid to one long in commencing to urinate ', F. & H. : late C. 19–20 ; ob.

*****whistle in the cage.** See **sing out.**

whistle off. To go off, to depart, lightly or, esp., suddenly : coll. : from the 1680's (Shadwell) ; ob. by 1860 ; † by 1930. O.E.D.

whistle psalms to the taffrail. (Gen. as vbl.n.) To give good advice unwanted and unheeded : jocular nautical : coll. : late C. 19–20. Bowen.

whistle up the breeze. A jocular variant of (H., 3rd ed., 1864, at) *raise the wind,* † by 1890.

whistled drunk. See **whistle-drunk.**

*****whistler.** A bad farthing : c. of ca. 1810–50. Vaux. Ex the false ring it gives.—2. A ' roarer ' (q.v.) or broken-winded horse : from early 1820's : coll. >, by 1890, S.E.—3. An unlicensed vendor of spirits : 1821, Moncrieff (O.E.D.) ; Dickens, 1837 : very ob. Ex *whistling-shop,* q.v.—4. A chance labourer at the docks : East Londoners' : from ca. 1880. Ware quotes *The Referee* of March 29, 1885. Ex whistling for work.—5. A revolver : low (— 1923). Manchon. Ex *whistler,* a bullet.—6. Something big : coll. (— 1923). Manchon. (Recorded in dial. for 1895 : E.D.D.)

whistling. Adj. to *whistling-shop,* q.v.

Whistler, adj. ' Misty, dreamy, milky, softly opalescent [in] atmosphere—from . . . pictures painted by [this] artist . . . Came to be applied to ethics, æsthetics, and even conversation, where the doctrines enunciated were foggy ' (Ware) : Society coll. : 1880's.

whistling-billy (or Billy). A locomotive : (children's) coll. : from ca. 1870 ; ob. H., 5th ed. Cf. *puffing-billy.*

whistling-breeches. Corduroy trousers: unaristocratic : late C. 19–20 ; ob. Ex the swishing sound that they are apt to make as one moves.

Whistling Percy. ' A German 9-inch naval gun of flat trajectory, captured at Cambrai in Nov., 1917— from the sound made by its shell in flight. (Whistling Willie, Whistling Walter, etc., were names similarly given to various other enemy guns and shells.)' F. & Gibbons.

whistling psalms . . . See **whistle psalms.**

whistling-shop. A room in the King's Bench Prison where spirits were sold secretly and illicitly : c. of ca. 1785–1840. Grose, 2nd ed. The signal indicative of ' open shop ' was a whistle.—2. Hence, an unlicensed dram-shop : (low) s. : 1821, Moncrieff (O.E.D.) ; Dickens, who, in 1837, also has ' whistling gentleman ' (see **whistler,** 3). Very ob.

Whistling Willie and **Sighing Sarah** were Boer cannon firing on Ladysmith from Umbalwana : military : 1900. J. Milne, *The Epistles of Atkins,* 1902.

*****Whit** ; often **Whitt,** occ. **Witt.** Newgate Prison.—2. **the whit(t).** Any prison : c. : ca. 1670–1840. Anon., *A Warening for Housekeepers,* 1676, ' O then they rub us to the whitt ' ; Coles and B.E. (Newgate) ; Grose. Perhaps suggested by the *git* of *Newgate* as gen. pronounced : cf., however, *Whittington's College,* q.v.

*****white,** n., only in *large* (or *half-bull*) *white,* a half-crown, and *small white,* a shilling : counterfeiters' c. (— 1823). ' Jon Bee.'—2. See **whites.**—3. See (3) of :

white, adj. Honourable ; fair-dealing : U.S. s. (— 1877), anglicised ca. 1885 ; by 1920, coll. Ex the self-imputed characteristics of a white man. Cf. *white man,* q.v.—2. Hence as adv. : U.S. s. (— 1900) anglicised ca. 1905 ; by 1930, coll. E.g. *act white, use* (a person) *white.*—3. As n., ' a true, sterling fellow ', C. J. Dennis : mostly Australian (— 1916).

white-apron. A harlot : coll. : ca. 1590–1760. Satirist Hall ; Pope. Ex dress.

white-ash breeze. The breeze caused by rowing : boating (— 1904) ; slightly ob. F. & H., ' Oars are gen. made of white ash.' Imm. ex *white ash,* an oar : coll. : mid-C. 19–20.

*****white-bag man.** A pickpocket : c. (— 1923). Manchon. Why ?

White Bear, the. Archbishop Whately (1787–1863), very unceremonious with opponents. Dawson.

White Brahmins. ' Excessively exclusive persons ' : among Europeans in India : from ca. 1880 ; ob. Ex an extremely exclusive religious sect. Ware.—2. Also, among the educated Indians, the English : coll. : from ca. 1880 ; ob. Ibid.

white broth, spit. See **spit white broth.**

white choker. A white tie : lower-class : from ca. 1860 ; slightly ob.—2. Hence, a parson : id. : from ca. 1890 ; ob.

*****white coat.** A hospital attendant in prison : c. (— 1932). Anon., *Dartmoor from Within.*

white eye. Strong, inferior whiskey : military (— 1874) ; ob. H., 5th ed. Orig. U.S. ; so named because ' its potency is believed to turn the eyes round in the sockets, leaving the whites only visible ', H.

white feather, show the. To maintain ' sufficient pressure of steam in the boilers to keep a white feather of steam over the safety valves ' : nautical : C. 20. Bowen.

white friar. A speck of white (froth, scum) floating on a (dark-coloured) liquid : from 1720's : coll. >, in C. 19, dial. Swift, 1729. O.E.D.

white Geordie. A shilling : Ayrshire : 1897, Ochiltree (E.D.D.).

white-haired boy is an Australian and New Zealand variant of the next entry : late C. 19–20. Whence *you must have white hairs*, a New Zealand c.p. to a man getting an unexpected favour : C. 20.

white-headed boy ; usually *my, her* (etc.) **w.-h. b.** Favourite ; darling : 1820 : coll. ; orig. Irish >, by 1890, fairly gen. Melmoth ; Hall Caine (O.E.D.). Ex the very fair hair of babies and young children. Cf. *snowy*, q.v., and † S.E. *white* (i.e. favourite) *boy* and *son*.

white horse. (Indicative of) cowardice : Anglo-Irish coll. : C. 18–20 ; ob. Ware, ' From the tradition that James II fled from the battle of the Boyne on a white horse '.

white-horsed in, be. To obtain a job through influence : tailors' (— 1904). F. & H. Perhaps ex buying a ' boss ' drinks at an inn, (a) white horse being a frequent sign, hence name, of an inn.

white jenny. ' A foreign-made silver watch ', says F. & H., ascribing it to H. : but where in H. is it ?

white lace. See white ribbon.

white lapel. A lieutenant : naval : ? ca. 1860–1910. Bowen. Ex a feature of his uniform.

*white lot. A silver watch and chain : c. : from ca. 1860. Ex *white*, for centuries an epithet applied to silver. Cf. **white wool*, q.v.

white magic. ' Very beautiful fair women ' : Society : ca. 1875–1905. Ex lit. S.E. sense.—2. The Roman Catholic ritual : Protestants' coll. (— 1909). Likewise, Ware.

white man. An honourable man : U.S. s. (1865), anglicised ca. 1887 ; by 1920, coll. Nat Gould, 1898, ' There goes a " white man " if ever there was one . . . That beard [is] the only black thing about him.' See white, adj. ; cf. *sahib*, q.v.

white man's burden, the. Work : jocular coll. : from ca. 1929. Punning the S.E. sense.

white man's hansom woman. A coloured mistress : West Indian : mid-C. 19–20 ; ob. Clearly, there is a pun on *hansom cab* and *handsome*.

White Moor ; gen. pl. A Genoese : coll. nickname : C. 17. Ex a very uncomplimentary proverb recorded by Howell in 1642 : too rough on the Moors.

white nigger. A term of contempt for a white man : Sierra Leone Negroes' coll. : from ca. 1880. Ware quotes *The Daily News* of June 20, 1883. Cf. the American Negroes' *poor white trash*.

white poodle. A rough woolly cloth : tailors' : ca. 1850–80. Ex poodle's coat.

white port. Some kind of strong liquor, prob. gin (cf. *white ribbon . . .*) : ca. 1750–90. Toldervy, 1756. See the quotation at *slug*, n., 1.

*white prop. A diamond scarf-pin : c. (— 1859). H., 1st ed. Cf. *white lot.*

white ribbon, satin, tape, wine, wool ; also **w. lace.** Gin : low : resp. C. 19–20 ; C. 19–20 ; from ca. 1720 (*A New Canting Dict.*, 1725) ; 1820 (Randall's *Diary*) ; from ca. 1780 (Grose, 1st ed.) ; mid-C. 19–20,—occ. merely *lace* or its synonym *driz*. H., 1st ed., describes *w. satin* and *w. tape* as women's terms, as, also, was *lace*. All are ob. ; in fact, *white wine* and *w. wool* did not survive beyond C. 19 ; *white satin* may well endure, however, because of the

trade name, *White Satin Gin*. See also at **ribbon** and **tape.**

white sergeant. A ' breeches-wearing ' wife, esp. and orig. as in the earliest record : Grose, 1st ed., ' A man fetched from the tavern . . . by his wife, is said to be arrested by the white sergeant.' † by 1890 or soon after ; H., 3rd–5th edd., has it. Ex the martial bearing of this hardly less formidable ' woman in white.'

White Sheet. Wytschaete, in Flanders : military coll. : G.W. (F. & Gibbons).

*white soup. Silver plate melted down to avoid identification : C. (— 1887). Ware.

white-stocking day. The days on which sailors' women-folk presented their half-pay notes to the owners : N.E. Coast : late C. 19. Bowen.

*white stuff. Articles in silver : c. : late C. 19–20. David Hume. Cf. *red stuff.*

white swelling, have a. To be big with child : late C. 18–mid-19. Grose, 1st ed., in Corrigenda. Ex the medical *white swelling*, a watery tumour. Cf. *tympany.*

white tape, wine, or wool. Gin. See **white ribbon.** Baumann's *white taps* is an error.

*white 'un (or **un**). A silver watch : c. (—1874). H., 5th ed. Cf. :

white wine. See white ribbon.

white wings. A dinner-table steward : ship-stewards' (— 1935). Ex dress.

*white wool. Silver : c. : late C. 17–mid-18. B.E. Cf. *white lot*, q.v.

Whitechapel ; **w.** An upper-cut : pugilistic (— 1860) ; ob. H., 2nd ed. ; 3rd ed. (1864) has :—2. That procedure in tossing coins in which two out of three wins : London ; ob.—3. The murder of a woman : (East) London : ca. 1888–90. Ware. Ex numerous woman-murders in Whitechapel in 1888. —4. A lead from a single card : card-playing coll. (— 1899) ; slightly ob. O.E.D. Ex *Whitechapel play*, q.v.

Whitechapel beau. One who, as Grose (1st ed.) so neatly phrases it, ' dresses with a needle and thread, and undresses with a knife ' : ca. 1780–1840. Cf. the entries at *St Giles* and *Westminster*, and *Whitechapel oner.*

Whitechapel breed, n. and adj. (A person) ' fat, ragged, and saucy ', Grose, 1st ed. : low : ca. 1780–1850.

Whitechapel brougham ; also **Westminster b.** A costermonger's donkey-barrow : low London (— 1860) ; ob. H., 2nd ed. Occ. *Chapel cart.* On S.E. *Whitechapel cart.*

Whitechapel fortune. ' A clean gown and a pair of pattens ' : low London : 1845 in ' Gipsy ' Carew, 1891 (i.e. ' *No. 747* ') ; H., 3rd ed. A euphemistic of *Whitechapel portion*, q.v.

Whitechapel oner. ' A leader of light and youth in the Aldgate district—chiefly in the high coster interests ' : East London (— 1909). Ware. Cf. *Whitechapel beau.*

Whitechapel play, n. and adj. Irregular or unskilful play, orig. and gen. at cards : coll. : 1755, *The Connoisseur* (O.E.D.).—2. Hence, in billiards (whence, in any game), unsportsmanlike methods : mid-C. 19–20.

Whitechapel portion. ' Two torn Smocks, and what Nature gave ' : low (mostly London) : late C. 17–mid-19. B.E., Grose. Cf. *Rochester* or *Tetbury portion*, and *Tipperary* or *Whitechapel fortune.*

Whitechapel province. ' A club or brotherhood under the government of a prætor ', Grose, 3rd ed.

London club life : late C. 18–early **19**. Punning Roman provincial government : in C. 18 (e.g. in D'Urfey, 1719), *prætor* was occ. used of a mayor.

Whitechapel shave. 'Whitening judiciously applied to the jaws with the palm of the hand', Dickens, 1863, in *The Uncommercial Traveller*; ob. Cf. *Whitechapel beau*.

Whitechapel warriors. Militia or volunteers of the Aldgate district : East London : from ca. 1860 ; ob. Ware.

whitechokery. The upper classes : lower classes' : ca. 1870–1700. Ware. Ex the white *choker* (see **choker**, 1).

Whitehall, he's been to. He looks very cheerful : military c.p. of ca. 1860–1905. Ware. Ex extension of leave obtained at Whitehall.

whiter. A white waistcoat : Harrow School. (— 1904). Ex *white* by ' Oxford -*er* '.

*****whites.** Silver money : c. (— 1887). Baumann. Ex *white*, n. (q.v.).

whitewash. ' A glass of sherry as a finale, after drinking port and claret ', H., 3rd ed. : from ca. 1860 ; ob. (Cf. *whitewasher*, q.v.) Ex colour—and use.

[**whitewash**, the bankruptcy v., may orig. (mid-C. 18) have been coll.]

whitewash-worker. A seller of ' a liquid alleged to replate silverware at home ', P. Allingham in *The Evening News*, July 9, 1934 : grafters' : C. 20.

whitewasher. A glass of white wine (e.g. sherry) taken at the end of a dinner : 1881, J. Grant (O.E.D.). Ex *whitewash*, n.

Whitewashers, the. The 61st Foot Regiment ; from ca. 1881, the (2nd Battalion of the) Gloucestershire Regiment : military : mid-C. 19–20 ; ob. Ex liberal use of pipe-clay at the time of the Indian Mutiny. F. & Gibbons.

whither-go-ye. A wife : ca. 1670–1830. Ray, 1678, has *how doth your whither-go-you ?*, i.e. your wife ; B.E. (misprint *whether . . .*) ; Grose. Ex this question so frequently asked by wives.

Whitt ; **whitt.** See **Whit.**

Whittington Priory. Holloway Prison (for debt) ; debtors' : ca. 1860–1910. Ware. Ex proximity to Highgate (associated with Whittington).

Whittington's College. Newgate Prison : ca. 1785–1840. Grose, 2nd ed. ; in G.'s *Provincial Glossary*, 1790 : *he has studied at Whittington's College*, he has been imprisoned at Newgate ; there, G. adds that Newgate was rebuilt in 1423 by Whittington's executors. Ex the famous Lord Mayor of that name, but perhaps suggested by *Whit*, q.v.

*****whittle.** To give information, to ' peach ' ; to confess at the gallows : from 1720's : c. >, by 1850, low s. ; ob. Swift, 1727 ; H., 5th ed. A variant of *whiddle*, q.v.

whiz, whizz. ' Buz, or noise, interruption of tongues ' : (low) London : ca. 1820–90. Bee.—2. Pocket-picking : c. : from ca. 1920. Chas. E. Leach.

whiz !, hold your. Be quiet ! ; ' shut up ! ' : low (— 1887) ; ob. Baumann. Ex sibilant *whi*spering.

*****whizz.** To be actively a pickpocket : c. : from ca. 1920. Cf. *buz* in the same sense. Ex his speed.

whizz-bang. A shell fired from a light field-gun, esp. the German ·77 ; rarely the gun : military : from 1914. B. & P. One only just heard, if at all !, the whizz of its flight before one heard the bang of the explosion.—2. Hence, the stereotyped field postcard (soon censored) : id. : from 1915. Ibid.

*****whizz-boy.** A pickpocket : c. : C. 20. Margery

Allingham, *Policemen at the Funeral*, 1931. Also among grafters : witness Philip Allingham, *Cheapjack*, 1934. Cf. :

*****whizz-game.** The jostling of persons by one criminal to enable another to pick their pockets : c. : from ca. 1920. (James Spenser, *Limey Breaks In*, 1934.)

*****whizz-man** ; **whizzer.** A pickpocket : c. : from ca. 1920. ' Stuart Wood ', both forms. Ex *whiz*, n., 2.

*****whizz-mob.** A gang of pickpockets : c. : C. 20. Also among grafters : witness P. Allingham, *Cheapjack*, 1934. See **whiz**, 2.

who is catachrestic, both when it is preceded by redundant *and* and when *he, she, they*, etc., follows dundantly in the relative clause : C. 16–20. (O.E.D.)

who and whom. As *who* is often, and increasingly, used, in coll. speech (and more and more in writing), for *whom*, i.e. as the objective after a v.t. or a preposition, so *whom* frequently occurs for *who*. But while ' Who I'm giving this book to isn't your concern ' will, I believe, soon be almost ' universal ' (such is the force and linguistic cogency of speech-habits), there is, for this very reason, perhaps, less —much less—excuse for, and far less cogency in, the condonation and esp. in the authorisation of such barbarisms as ' I don't know whom will be there,'— a phrasal type arising from illogical confusion with such a sentence as ' I don't know whom to thank '. Perhaps the commonest cause of ' *whom* for *who* ' is the parenthesis, actual or virtual : the writer forgets the real subject, as in *The Daily Mail*, Dec. 28, 1935, ' Mr Cornelius . . . told a *Daily Mail* reporter that at 2 a.m. yesterday he was aroused by calls for help from a woman, whom he later learned was Lady . . .', *he later learned* causing all the trouble.

who all, and I don't know. And other persons unnamed : coll. : from ca. 1840 ; rare. Cf. *what all*, q.v. The *who all* may be owing to the influence of some such phrase as *and I don't know who else at all* or . . . *what others at all*, or to a confusion of both these phrases.

who are yer (you) ?—who are you ? An offensive inquiry and its truculent answer : c.pp. of London streets : from 1883 (Ware).

who did yer (you) say ? A c.p. ' levelled at a person of evident, or self-asserting importance, and uttered by one friend to another ' : London streets' : 1890's. Ware.

who pawned her sister's ship ? A Clare Market (London) c.p. of ca. 1897–9, directed offensively at a woman. Ware proposes *shift* corrupted.

who pulled your chain ? A military c.p. snub (1914 ; slightly ob.) ' for anyone intruding into a conversation '. Ex the pulling of a lavatory-chain + *shit*, n, 2.

who shot the dog ? A c.p. directed ill-naturedly at volunteers : London streets' : 1860's. Ware.

who took it out of you ? A c.p. connoting a dejected or washed-out look in the addressee : low London (— 1909). Ware.

who ? who ? Government, the. The Ministry of : 1852 : Society. Ware. Ex the aged Duke of Wellington's inquiries as to who they were.

who wouldn't . . . See **sea ?, who . . .**

whoa-Ball ; incorrectly **whow-ball.** A milkmaid : late C. 17–early 19. B.E., Grose. Prob. = *whoa !* + *Ball*, a common name for a cow, as Grose suggests. Cf. *Whoball's children*.

whoa, bust me ! A low London exclamation of ca. 1850–1910. Ware.

whoa, carry me out ! See **carry me out.**

whoa, Emma ! An urban lower-classes' c.p. directed at a woman 'of marked appearance or behaviour in the streets': ca. 1880–1900. Ware, who gives it an anecdotal origin. 'Quotations' Benham has the form *whoa, Emma ! mind the paint.* —2. Whence, a non-aristocratic warning, to a person of either sex, to be careful : from ca. 1900 ; ob.

whoa, Jameson ! A c.p. constituting 'an admiring warning against plucky rashness': non-aristocratic, non-cultured : 1896–7. Ex the Jameson Raid. (Ware.)

Whoball's children, he is none of John. 'You cannot easily make him a fool,' Terence in English, 1598 : a semi-proverbial c.p. of C. 17. See **whoa-Ball.**

whoever. Whomsoever : catachrestic : C. 16–20.—2. In perplexity or surprise, an emphasised *who* ; properly, two words (cf. *whatever*) : coll. : mid-C. 19–20. R. G. White, 1881, says that it is 'mostly confined to ladies'. O.E.D.

whole boiling, hog, etc. See the nn.

whole-footed. (Of persons) unreserved, free and easy : from 1730's : s. >, ca. 1760, coll. >, ca. 1820, dial. North, ca. 1734. Ex *whole-footed*, 'treading with the whole foot on the ground, not lightly or on tip-toe', O.E.D.

whole hog, go the. See **go the whole hog.**

[**whole-hogger** is political j. rather than coll.]

wholeskin brigade. A military unit that has not yet been in action : Boer War military. Ware.

whom. See '**who** and **whom**'.

whom else is incorrect for *who else* in such a sentence as this in A. Berkeley, *Panic Party*, 1934, 'She carried half a dozen stewards, three cooks, a pantryman, and heaven only knew whom else as well.'

whomever, whomsoever. Occ. catachrestically for *whoever, whosoever* : C. 14–20. (O.E.D.)

whoopee, n. ; esp. **make whoopee,** to enjoy oneself, rejoice hilariously : coll. : U.S. (from ca. 1927) anglicised by 1933 at latest. F. Keston Clarke in *The Humorist*, July 21, 1934, 'Sitting on molehills and counting grasshoppers isn't my idea of rural whoopee.' Ex *whoop with joy.*

whooper-up. A noisy, inferior singer : music-halls' and theatrical (— 1909) ; ob. Ware.

whop ; whap, C. 19–20 ; **whapp,** C. 15. A bump, heavy blow, resounding impact : (in C. 20, somewhat low) coll. : C. 15–20. H. G. Wells, 1905, '. . . Explained the cyclist . . . "I came rather a whop ",' O.E.D. Cf. :

whop, v., C. 18–20 ; **whap,** C. 16, 19–20 ; occ. **wap, wop,** C. 19–20. To strike heavily, thrash, belabour : (in C. 20, low) coll. : mid-C. 16–20. Dickens, 1837, ' "Ain't nobody to be whopped for takin' this here liberty, sir ?" said Mr. Weller,' O.E.D. Ex *whop* (spelt *whapp*), to cast violently, take or put suddenly.—2. Hence, to defeat (utterly) ; to surpass, excel greatly : coll.; in C. 20, low coll. From the 1830's. Thackeray, 'Where [his boys] might whop the French boys and learn all the modern languages.'

whop-straw ; Johnny Whop-Straw. A clodhopper, a rustic : (low) coll., ex dial. : C. 19–20. Clare, 1821 (O.E.D.) ; H., 2nd ed.

whopper ; whapper ; wopper ; wapper. Something, some animal or person, unusually large in its kind : (in C. 20, low) coll. : from ca. 1780. Grose, 1st ed. (*whapper*) ; Marryat, 1829 (*whopper*) ;

Surtees, 1854 (*wopper*) ; Walker, 1901, ' " Blime, she's a whopper ! " says Billy.' Ex *whop*, v.—2. Hence, a 'thumping' lie : (low) coll. : 1791, Nairne (O.E.D.).—3. A person that 'whops' : (low) coll. : late C. 19–20.

whopper-jawed. Incorrect for *wapper-jawed* : mid-C. 19–20. O.E.D.

whopping. A severe beating, thrashing, defeat : (low) coll. : C. 19–20. Ex *whop*, v.

whopping, adj., C. 19–20 ; **whapping,** C. 18–20 ; **wapping,** C. 17–20 ; **wopping,** mid-C. 19–20. Unusually large or great : coll.; in C. 20, low.—2. Rarely, 'terribly' false (tales, etc.), 'terribly fine' (persons) : id.; same period. Ex *whop*, v. Cf. *whopper.*

whore is, in mid-C. 19–20, considered a vulgarism ; *harlot* is considered preferable, but in C. 20, archaic ; *prostitute*, however, is now quite polite.—2. Hence, a term of opprobrium even for a man : coll. : late C. 19–20. Gen. pronounced *hoor* or *hoo'-er.*

whore-pipe. The penis : low (— 1791) ; † by 1890. Grose, 3rd ed.

whore's bird than a canary bird, he sings more like a. He has a strong, manly voice : c.p. : late C. 18–early 19. Grose, 2nd ed. A *whore's bird* is a debauchee.

whore's curse. 'A piece of gold coin value five shillings and threepence, frequently given to women of the town by such as professed always to give gold, and who before the introduction of those pieces, always gave half a guinea', Grose, 1st ed. : (mostly London) coll. : mid-C. 18.

whore's get. An indivisible phrase used mostly as a pejorative term of address : nautical (—1885) ; ob. Ex *get*, n., 2, on *whore's son.*

who's. A frequent written sol. for *whose* : ? since C. 16.

who's your lady friend ? A c.p. : from ca. 1910. Ex a popular song.

whow-ball. See **whoa-Ball.**

whoy-oi ! A 'cry used by coster-class upon sight of a gaily dressed girl passing near them. Also the cry of welcome amongst London costermongers', Ware, 1909. Whence *hoy !*

whuff, n. and v. A or to roar or bellow (e.g. like, or like that of, a rhinoceros) : coll. — 1887). Baumann.

whump. See **wump.**

why, for. See **for why.**

Whyms. Members of the Y.M.C.A. : clubmen's : ca. 1882–1905. Ware. By 'telescoping of these initials '.

Wi(-)Wi ; occ. **Wee(-)Wee,** or **Wewi** ; etymologisingly, **Oui-Oui.** Also, the singular form is often used as a pl. A Frenchman : New Zealand and hence, to some extent, Australia : 1845, E. J. Wakefield ; 1859, A. S. Thomson, 'The Wewis, as the French are now called' ; 1881, Anon., *Percy Pomo* (*Weewees*). Morris. Ex the Frenchman's fondness for *oui ! oui !* (and *non ! non !*) : cf. *Dee-Donk*, q.v.

wibble. Bad liquor ; any thin, weak beverage : (? mainly provincial) s. or coll. (— 1785) ; ob., except in the provinces. Grose, 1st ed. ; F. & H., 1904. ? cf. :

wibble-wobble. Unsteadily : coll. (— 1847). Halliwell. A 'reduplication of *wobble* (with vowel-variation symbolising alternation of movement : cf. *zigzag*) ', O.E.D.—2. Whence as v., to move unsteadily ; to totter, oscillate, vibrate : from ca. 1870 and likewise coll. Whence :

wibblety-wobblety. Unsteady : coll. and dial. : from mid-1870's. Ex preceding.

wibbly. A C. 20 abbr. (unrecorded before 1914) of :

wibbly-wobbly. Unsteady ; apt to ' wibble-wobble ', q.v. : coll. : C. 20.

wibling's witch, or **W. W.** The four of clubs : C. 18–19. Grose, 1st ed., ' From one James Wibling, who in the reign of King James I, grew rich by private gaming, and who was commonly observed to have that card, and never to lose a game but when he had it not '.

***wicher-cully,** etc. See **witcher.**

wicked. Very bad, ' horrid ', ' beastly ' : coll. : C. 17–20. T. Taylor, 1639, ' It is too well known what a wicked number of followers he hath had ' ; Horace Walpole, ' They talk wicked French.' O.E.D. Cf. :

wickedly. Very badly ; horridly : coll. : C. 18–20. Sterne. Ex preceding. (O.E.D.)

Wickedshifts. Lord Brougham : ca. 1828–50. John Gore, *Creevey's Life and Times,* 1934.

***wicket.** A casement : c., or perhaps merely catachrestic : mid-C. 17–early 19. Coles.

wicket-keep. A wicket-keeper : coll. verging on S.E. : 1867. Lewis. Abbr. *wicket-keeper.*

Wickham. A Wickham's fancy : coll. (anglers') : from ca. 1910. (O.E.D.)

Wicklows. Shares in the Dublin, Wicklow, & Wexford Railway : Stock Exchange coll. (— 1895). A. J. Wilson, *Stock Exchange Glossary.*

widda, widder, widdy. A widow : dial. and low coll. : C. 19–20.—2. Hence, **the widdy.** The gallows : Scots : ? C. 19. Cf. *widow,* 3, q.v. : ? pun on *widdy,* a halter.

widdle. See **whiddle.**—**widdy.** See **widda.**

wide. Immoral ; lax : mid-C. 16–20 : S.E. until late C. 19, then coll.—2. Alert, well-informed, shrewd : 1877, Horsley, *Jottings from Jail.* Abbr. *wide-awake.* It verges on c. Cf. :

wide, to the. Utterly ; esp. in *done* or *whacked to the wide,* utterly exhausted : coll. : from ca. 1912. Very gen. among soldiers in G.W. (F. & Gibbons.) I.e. to the wide world : for all to see.— 2. *done* or *dead to the wide,* utterly drunk : C. 20. Lyell.

wide at or **of the bow-hand** (i.e. the left). Wide of the mark : coll. : late C. 16–mid-17. Shakespeare, Dekker, Webster. (Apperson.) Ex archery.

wide-awake. Sharp-witted ; alert : s. (1833) >, ca. 1860, coll. Dickens. (O.E.D.)

wido. Wide-awake, alert : low (— 1859) ; virtually †. H., 1st ed. Cf. *wide,* 2.

widow. As title to the name : mid-C. 16–20 : S.E. until C. 19, then mainly dial. and uncultured coll.—2. ' Fire expiring's call'd a widow,' *The British Apollo,* 1710 : C. 18–20 ; ob. Cf. S.E. *widow's fire.* O.E.D.—3. (Always **the widow.**) The gallows : ? C. 18–mid-19. Ex Fr. *la veuve.*— 4. An additional hand dealt in certain card-games : late C. 19–20 : s. >, by 1920, coll.—5. (**the Widow.**) Queen Victoria : military coll. : 1863–1901. Ware, ' In no way disparaging '.—6. (**the widow, the W.**) Champagne : 1899, Guy Boothby, ' A good luncheon and a glass of the Widow to wash it down ', O.E.D. ; Ware, however, states that it dates from forty years earlier. Ex *Veuve Clicquot.*

widow, grass. See **grass widow.**

widow bewitched. A woman separated from her husband : coll. (1725) >, in mid-C. 19, mainly dial. Bailey ; Mrs Gaskell. Cf. *grass widow,* q.v.

Widows, the. The Scottish Widows' Society : insurance coll. : late C. 19–20. Cf. *the Pru.*

widow's mite. A light : rhyming s. : late C. 19–20. B. & P.

[**widow's weeds** has, in F. & H., a wholly erroneous entry.]

***wife.** A leg-shackle : (mostly prison) c. : from ca. 1810. *Lex. Bal.* ; H., 2nd ed. Ex clinging.

wife, all the world and his. Everybody : jocular coll. : C. 18–20. Swift.

wife as a dog of a side-pocket, as much need of a. See **side-pocket.**

wife cries five loaves a penny, one's. She is in travail : a semi-proverbial c.p. of ca. 1670–1758. Ray, 1678. (Apperson.) I.e. she cries out, pain-racked.

wife in water-colours. A mistress or concubine : ca. 1780–1840. Grose, 1st ed. Easily fading colours : bonds quickly dissolved.—2. Hence, in C. 19, a morganatic wife.

wife out of Westminster. A wife of dubious morality : London coll. : C. 18–20 ; very ob., Ware in 1909 remarking : ' Sometimes still heard in the East of London '. Ex the proverb cited at *Westminster wedding,* q.v.

wifeish. Incorrect for *wifish* : C. 19–20.

wifey, wifie, rarely **wif(e)y.** Endearment for a wife : coll. : from ca. 1820. Properly, little wife, but gen. used regardless of size.

wiffle-woffle. An arrogant fellow : low (—1923). Manchon. Perhaps because he gives one :

wiffle-woffles, the. A stomach-ache ; sorrow ; melancholy, the dumps : mainly proletarian (— 1859) ; ob. H., 1st ed. Cf. *colly-wobbles* (sense), *wibble-wobble* (form).

wifflow gadget. The same as *hook-me-dinghy,* q.v. : nautical : late C. 19–20. Bowen. See also **gadget.**

wify. See **wifey.**

wig. A severe scolding or reprimand : 1804, Sir J. Malcolm (O.E.D.) : s. >, by 1890, coll. ; slightly ob. Cf. *wigging,* much more gen. in C. 20. Perhaps ex a *bigwig's* rebuke.—2. Abbr. *bigwig,* a dignitary : coll. (rare after ca. 1870) : 1828 (O.E.D.). —3. A penny : Ayrshire s. (— 1905), not dial. E.D.D., Sup. Perhaps because it was the usual price of a *wig,* a bun or a tea-cake.

wig, v. To scold ; rebuke, reprimand, reprove severely : s. (1829, *The Examiner*) >, ca. 1860, coll. Ex *wig,* n., 1, or *wigging,* q.v. Cf. Fr. *laver la tête* : W.—2. To move off, go away : North Country c. (— 1864). H., 3rd ed. Whence ?

wig !, dash my ; my wig ! See **wigs.**

wig-block. The head : coll. (— 1923). Manchon.

wig-faker. A hairdresser : low London : late C. 18–19. Ware.

wig, oil (a person's). To make him drunk : coll. (— 1923). Manchon.

wig-wag, v., n. and adv. To wag lightly ; such wagging : coll. : late C. 16–20. (O.E.D.) Reduplicated *wag.* Adj., *wig-waggy* : C. 20.—2. Hence, n. and v., (to transmit) a message by signalling ; the message ; the flag : military : from 1914. F. & Gibbons.

Wigan is national joke, esp. in *come from Wigan* to be a thorough urban provincial : from ca. 1920 : c.p.

wigannowns. A man wearing a large wig : ca. 1785–1830. Grose, 1st ed.

Wiggie. See **Wiggy.**

wigging. A scolding; a severe rebuke, reproof, reprimand : s. (1813) >, by 1850, coll. Barham, 'If you wish to 'scape wigging, a dumb wife's handy.' Ex *wig*, n., 1.

Wiggins, Mr. 'Any mannerist of small brains and showy feather,' Bee : London (— 1823); † by 1900.

wiggle. A wriggle; esp. in *get a wiggle on*, to hurry : Canadian : C. 20. John Beames. Ex :

wiggle, v. To waggle, wriggle : C. 13–20 : S.E. till C. 19, then coll.—2. Hence the n. : coll. : late C. 19–20.—3. The same applies to simple derivatives.—4. See wiggle-waggle, 2.

wiggle-waggle, adj. (1778); hence v. and n., both from ca. 1820. Vacillating; to move (v.i. and t.) in a wiggling, waggling way : coll. O.E.D.—2. To strut about : coll. (— 1923). Manchon. Also *wiggle*.

wiggly ; wiggly-waggly or **-woggly.** The adj. of *wiggle*, q.v. : coll. : C. 20. Ex dial.

Wiggy. The inseparable nickname of men surnamed Bennett : naval, military : C. 20. F. & Gibbons; Bowen. Origin presumably anecdotal.

wig(s) !, dash my ; wig(s) !, my. Mild imprecations : coll. : resp. 1797 (1812); 1891 (1871). Morris, 1891, 'I am writing a short narrative poem. My wig ! but it is garrulous,' O.E.D. Perhaps ex dashing one's wig down in anger.

wigsby. A man wearing a wig : jocular coll. (— 1785). Grose, 1st ed., has also *Mr Wigsby*; *wigster* occurs ca. 1820. All three were ob. by 1880, and by 1920 they were †. Cf. *rudesby*, a rude person, and *wigannowns*, q.v.

*wild. A village : tramps' c. (— 1839). Brandon; H., 2nd ed. Cf. S.E. *vill*, c. *vile*, q.v —2. **the Wild.** 'The extreme Evangelical party in the Church of Scotland' : nickname : from late 1820's. O.E.D.

wild, adj. See 'Moving-Picture Slang', § 6.

wild-cat. A rash projector, risky investor (1812); a risky or unsound business-undertaking (1839) : U.S. coll., anglicised ca. 1880; slightly ob. —2. Hence, adj., risky, unsound (business or business enterprise); hence, reckless or rash : coll., orig. (1838) U.S., anglicised ca. 1880. Ex the American wild-cat; it 'dates from U.S. period of " frenzied finance " (1836),' W.

wild-catter, -catting. A person engaging in, an instance or the practice of, 'wild-cat' business : coll. : U.S. (1883), anglicised ca. 1900. See preceding entry.

*wild dell. A 'dell' (q.v.) begotten and born under a hedge : c. : ? C. 17–early 19.

wild-fire. Some strong liquor; perhaps brandy : ca. 1750–80. See quotation at slug, n., 1.

wild goose. A recruit for the Irish Brigade in French service : military : mid-C. 17–18. M. O'Conor, *Military History of the Irish Nation*, 1845. Ex *wild-goose chase.*—2. Hence, the Irish Jacobites self-exiled on the Continent in 1691 and later : a late C. 17–mid-18 nickname. (O.E.D.)

Wild Indians, the. The Prince of Wales's Leinster Regiment (Royal Canadians) : military : from the 1870's; ob. Ex the Canadian expression of loyalty at the time of the Mutiny. F. & H.

Wild Irishman, the. 'The evening mail train between Euston and Holyhead,' F. & H. : journalistic, hence fairly gen. from ca. 1870. H., 5th ed. Cf. *Flying Scotsman.* Ex conventional phrase.

Wild Macraes, the. The 72nd, now the Seaforth, Highlanders : from 1777, when the regiment was

raised, the Clan Macrae providing the majority of the recruits. F. & Gibbons.

wild mare, ride the. See ride the wild mare.

*wild rogue. A born or thorough-paced thief : c. : late C. 17–early 19. B.E.

wild squirt. Diarrhœa : low coll. (— 1785); **ob.** Grose, 1st ed.

wild train. A train not on the time-table, hence ' not entitled to the track ' as is a regular train : railwaymen's (— 1904). F. & H.

wilderness. A windlass : nautical (not very gen.) : late C. 19–20. Bowen.

wilful murder. The card-game known as ' blind hookey ' : from ca. 1860; ob. H., 3rd ed.

Wilhelm II much. A bit too much of the Kaiser ! : Society : 1898. Ware. Ex his many activities.

wilk. See whilk.

Wilkie Bards. A pack of cards : rhyming s. : C. 20. F. & Gibbons. Ex Wilkie Bard, comedian and ' card '.

will. Unemphasised ' shall ' in the first person : coll., but in C. 20 verging on S.E. Discussion is here supererogatory : see esp. Fowler's *Modern English Usage.*

Will-o'-the-wisp. (Gen. pl.) A shell with flight difficult to follow : Army officers' : in G.W.

will you shoot ? Will you pay for a small drink of spirits ? : Australian taverns' (— 1909); **ob.** Ware.

William, an acceptance, occurs esp. in *meet sweet William*, to meet a bill on its presentation : commercial (— 1864). H., 3rd ed. Punning *bill.*—2. Weak tea : lower classes' (— 1923). Manchon.

William, the people's. Gladstone : journalistic and political nickname : 1884–ca. 90. Baumann. Ex his Christian name.

William Bon Chrétien. Incorrect for *Williams'(s) Bon Chrétien* (pear) : late C. 19–20. O.E.D.

Willie. A (child's) penis : Cumberland and Westmorland s. (— 1905), not dial. E.D.D. (Sup.)

Willie, Big and Little. The Kaiser and the Crown Prince : coll. : 1914; ob. B. & P. Ex *Wilhelm.*— 2. Hence, nicknames for all sorts of things, e.g. guns : military : late 1914–18. Ibid.

Willie, Willie !, o(h). A c.p. of ' satiric reproach addressed to a taradiddler rather than a flat liar ' : non-aristocratic : 1898–ca. 1914. Ware. Cf. :

Willie, Willie—wicked, wicked ! This c.p. of ca. 1900–14 constitutes a ' satiric street reproach addressed to a middle-aged woman talking to a youth.' Ware derives it ex a droll law-suit.

willies, the. (Cf. *wiffle-woffles*, perhaps its origin.) A feeling of nervousness, discomfort, vague fear : U.S. (1900), anglicised ca. 1925. (O.E.D. Sup.)

willin', willing. (Of persons) ' strenuous, hearty,' C. J. Dennis : Australian coll. verging on S.E. : late C. 19–20.

willn't ; willot. Will not : coll. : C. 19. (See wash, v., 1.) Cf. *won't*, q.v.

willock-eater. (Gen. pl.) An Eastbourne fishing-boat : nautical : late C. 19–20. Bowen. A willock is a guillemot, a not very edible bird.

willow. ' Poor, and of no Reputation,' B.E. : late C. 17–early 19. Lit., willowy.

Willy Arnot. Good whiskey : Shetland Islands s. (1897), not dial. E.D.D. Perhaps ex a well-known landlord.

willy-nilly. Undecided : catachrestic : 1883, Galton. Confused with *shilly-shally.* O.E.D.

willywaws. Squalls in the Straits of Magellan;

but also light, variable winds elsewhere : nautical : late C. 19–20. Bowen. Perhaps ex *whirly-whirly*.

wilt. To run away, to ' bunk ' : London : from ca. 1880 ; ob. Ex *wilt*, (of flowers) to fade, to grow limp. Cf. *fade out*, q.v., and the ob. C. 20 ' gag ', ' *wilt thou (be my wedded wife) ?* ' *and she wilted*.

wimmeny-pimmeny. Dainty, elegant : lower-classes' coll. (– 1887) ; slightly ob. Baumann. Echoic.

wimp. A (young) woman, a girl : from ca. 1920 ; ob. Manchon. Perhaps ex *whimper*.

*win, wing, winn, whin(n), but gen. the first or the third. A penny : c. (– 1567) : resp. C. 17–20, late C. 19–20 (mostly in Ireland and hence U.S.), C. 17–20, C. 19–20. Harman, Dekker, B.E., Grose, Vaux (*Winchester* ; † by 1900), ' Jon Bee ' (who defines as a halfpenny), H., Flynt (*wing*). Perhaps abbr. *Winchester*.—2. (**win,** and for senses 3, 4.) A victory : (sports and games) coll. : from ca. 1860. (O.E.D.) —3. A gain ; gen. pl., (mostly monetary) gains : coll. : from ca. 1890. Perhaps abbr. *winning(s)*.— 4. Success of any fig. kind : coll. : C. 20. C. J. Dennis.

*win, v. To steal : c. : from late C. 17. B.E., Grose. In the Army, 1914–18 (and after), s., with the extension : to gain not quite lawfully or officially. Galsworthy, *Swan Song*, 1928, ' " How are you going to get the money ? " " Win, wangle, and scrounge it ".' Cf. *(to) make*, q.v., and, in Fr. c., the exactly synonymous *gagner*. The n. *winnings* may, as = ' plunder, goods, or money acquired by theft ' (Grose, 2nd ed.), be c. : C. 18–20.

winable. Incorrect for *winnable* : C. 18–20. Miss Anna Porter, 1807. O.E.D.

*Winchester. See **win,** n., 1.

[Winchester College slang is the richest and most interesting of all the Public School slangs : cf. the entries at ' Eton ', ' Harrow ', ' Rugby ' and ' Westminster '. Many terms will be found in these pages, but it is to be remarked that in the Winchester ' notions ' it is extremely difficult, in many instances, to distinguish between technicalities (j.) and slang or colloquial terms. The ' locus classicus ' is R. G. K. Wrench's *Winchester Word-Book*, 1891 ; the second edition—the only one possessed by the British Museum—followed in 1901. But a very good short account appears in R. Townsend Warner's *Winchester*, 1900,—from which this abridgement :—

' " Notions ", or the school language. . . . Complicated as the language of Winchester is, there is no consciousness of anything like affectation or pedantry in using it. To a new-comer, after a week of two, notions seem the only possible words for certain meanings . . . As they are the last forgotten, so they are the first learnt lesson of Winchester. A new man must learn, for instance, that the article is seldom found in Winchester grammar, especially in the names of places. . . .

2. Another tendency is the pluralization of words . . . *Hills, meads, crockets* (cricket). The last word also is an example of the fondness of strengthening vowels in the middle of words, such as *cropple*, meaning to " pluck " or " plough " (from *cripple*), and *roush* for a rush or rapid stream of water.

3. A less ancient tendency of Winchester talk is to drop the final " tion " . . ., lengthening the vowel then left final ; thus " *examinâ* " [*examinah*] for " examination " . . . [Wrench dates it from ca. 1850.]

4. Apart from their often respectable antiquity, notions also differ from ordinary school slang in that many of them are not merely the language of the boys, but are part of the official language of the school used by and to masters also. Thus in answer to a Don (master) asking a man why he was " tardy up to books at morning lines " [late in school at first lesson], it would be quite proper to reply that " junior in chambers sported a thoke " [the junior in his dormitory overslept himself instead of waking the others in time].

. . . .

5. Many notions are simply old English words which have been dropped out of common use. For instance, to *firk* is the notion for to send or to send away. And we find this sense . . . in " Morte Arthure " . . . Again, a Winchester man who says he finds it " an awful *swink* (hard work) to do mathematics " [is using an excellent old English word] ; and should he . . . pursue his mathematical labours till he got a headache, he would naturally say it *works* (hurts), thus using the language of . . . Malory : " myn hede *werches* so ". If his head got worse he might have to go *continent* . . . to sickhouse or a *continent* room. The word *continent* here means " keeping within doors " [as in Shakespeare]. And if he got worse the doctor might forbid him to " *come abroad* " (the notion for being allowed out again after " going continent "), [thus employing the language of Sir Thomas More].

6. *Latin words.*

These are either bodily imported into use or slightly altered or contracted . . . This is a common practice of all schools, but . . . particularly prevalent at Winchester, where . . . the talking of Latin was [once] a regular institution.

Half-remedy, commonly *half-rem,* " half holiday ". From *remedium.*

To *tund,* " to beat with a ground-ash ". From *tundo.*

Semper, " always ", used as an adjective.

Non-licet, " not allowed ".

. . . A ball is still called a " pill ", which is simply *pilum* anglicised, while the notion for a stone is a " rock " [via L. *saxum* : cf. U.S. usage]. . . . Other Latin-formed words are evidently perpetuated from the Latin of the statutes, or early school rules. Thus to *socius,* meaning to go in company with another . . ., is a relic of the early rule that scholars must always go in company, " sociati ". . .

7. *Names of people perpetuated as words* . . .

Barter [q.v.] . . .

John Des paper, a special kind of paper introduced at Winchester for mathematics by John Desborough Walford, the first regular mathematical master.

Bill Brighter [q.v.] . . .

8. *Notions surviving as names of places.*

[Technicalities, these.] . . .

9. *Notions commemorating old school customs.*

[E.g. (perhaps), *brock, brockster,* qq.v.] . . .

' Prefects' writing-tables are still called " washing-stools " in college, because the tables were originally provided to stand basins on for washing. [This, clearly, is a technicality.] ']

Winchester goose. A bubo : mid-C. 16–17. Bacon (1559), Shakespeare, Cotgrave. The brothels in Southwark were, in. C. 16, under the Bishop of Winchester's jurisdiction : F. & H.—2. Hence a person infected therewith ; hence, an objectionable person : C. 17. All three senses, also *Winchester pigeon*.

winchin'. Courting; courtship : Glasgow (C. 20). I.e. *wenching* in favourable sense : cf. † Scots *winchie*, a young woman.

wind. The stomach : boxing : 1823 (O.E.D.). Dickens, 1853. A blow thereon ' takes away the breath by checking the action of the diaphragm '.

wind, by the. Short of money : nautical : late C. 19–20. Bowen.

wind, carry the. To be mettlesome, or high-spirited : sporting (— 1904) ; ob. F. & H., ' Properly of horses tossing the nose as high as the ears.'

wind, go down the. See **weather, go up the.**

wind, in the. See **in the wind.**

*****wind, lagged for one's.** See **winder, nap a.**

wind, raise the. See **raise the wind.**—**wind, sail near** (or **close to) the.** See **sail.**—**wind, slip one's.** See **slip the wind.**—**wind, thin as a rasher of.** See **rasher of wind.**—**wind and water, shot between.** See **shot between.**

wind-bag. A wind-jammer : nautical : late C. 19–20. Bowen.—2. See **windbag.**

wind do twirl (or hyphenated). A girl : rhyming s. (— 1859) ; in C. 20, †. H., 1st ed.

wind enough to last a Dutchman a week. More wind than enough : (orig. nautical) coll. : from the 1830's ; ob. Dana. Cf. *Dutch*, q.v.

wind fight. A false alarm : military : 1915 ; ob. F. & Gibbons. Cf. *windy.*

wind-jammer. A sailing vessel : U.S. s. (1899) anglicised almost imm. ; by 1930, coll. *The Athenæum*, Feb. 8, 1902.—2. A player on a wind instrument : theatrical (— 1904). F. & H. Perhaps influenced by U.S. *wind-jammer*, a talkative person.—3. An unpopular officer, esp. if inspecting : military : C. 20. F. & Gibbons ; and esp. if sparing of furlough : naval : C. 20. Bowen.

wind-mill. The fundament : low (— 1811) ; ob. *Lex. Bal,* ' She has no fortune but her mills,' a low c.p. : i.e. ' wind-mill ' and ' water-mill '.

wind one's cotton. To cause trouble : pro-letarian (— 1860) ; ob. H., 2nd ed.

wind-pudding. Air : low : from 1890's. Whence *live on w.p.*, go hungry.

wind-stick. An aeroplane control-lever : Air Force coll. : from 1916. F. & Gibbons.

*****wind-stopper.** A garrotter : c. : late C. 19–20. Cf. *ugly man*, q.v.

wind up. To render (a race-horse) fit to run : racing : from ca. 1870. (O.E.D.)

wind up, get or **have** (**got) the.** To get frightened or alarmed : to be so : military : 1915. After G.W., it > gen. Ian Hay, 1915 (O.E.D. Sup.) ; P. Gibbs, (late) 1916, ' It was obvious that the blinking Boche had got the wind up.' Perhaps ex the early days of aviation, when wind, if at all strong, pre-cluded flight.—2. Whence *wind up*, nervousness, anxious excitement : from not later than 1918.

wind up, put the. To scare or greatly frighten (a person) : 1916 : military > , by 1919, gen. C. Alington, 1922 (O.E.D.). Ex preceding.

wind up the clock. To coït with a woman : educated : from ca. 1760 ; ob. Perhaps ex a mildly pornographic passage in *Tristram Shandy*.

wind vertical ; with vertical breeze. ' Wind up ', i.e. frightened, very nervous : military, mostly officers : from 1916. B. & P. Also *suffer from a vertical breeze* or, occ., *gust*, to be ' windy ' (F. & Gibbons). See **wind up, get the.**

windbag. A mystery packet : grafters' : C. 20 Philip Allingham, *Cheapjack*, 1934. The contents are worth little more than those of an empty bag.— 2. See **wind-bag.**

windbag man. A seller of sealed envelopes : grafters' : from ca. 1910. P. Allingham in *The Evening News*, July 9, 1934. See preceding term.

*****winded-settled.** Transported for life : c. (— 1859) ; ob. H., 1st ed. Ex pugilism.

winder. A knock-out blow (lit. or fig.), some-thing that astounds one, an effort that breathes one : coll. : 1825, Westmacott (O.E.D.). Cf. *winder, nap a*, q.v.—2. A window : sol. and dial. : C. 19–20,— and prob. centuries earlier.

*****winder, nap a.** To be transported for life : c. of ca. 1810–60. Vaux, who has also *be lagged for one's wind.*—2. To be hanged : c. (— 1859). See **winder.** —3. In boxing, to receive a blow that deprives one of breath : mid-C. 19–20.—4. Hence, to receive a shock, a severe set-back : low : from ca. 1860.

*****winding-post, nap the.** To be transported : c. of ca. 1820–60. Egan's Grose. Cf. *winder, nap a.*

windjammer. See **wind-jammer.**—**windmill.** See **wind-mill.**

windmill J.P. An ill-educated J.P. : New South Wales : ca. 1850–80. Because presumed to indicate his name with a cross : on maps, X = a wind-mill.

windmills in the head. Empty projects : coll. : late C. 17–19. B.E., Grose, Spurgeon. Ex the windmill-tilting of Don Quixote. (Apperson.)

window. A monocle : lower classes' : from ca. 1860 ; slightly ob. Ware.

window, goldsmith's. A rich working in which the gold shows freely : gold-mining s. (orig. and mainly Australian) > , ca. 1920, coll. Boldrewood, 1891.

window-blind. A sanitary towel : low (— 1904). F. & H.

window-dressing. ' Manipulation of figures and accounts to show fictitious or exaggerated value ' : commercial coll. > , ca. 1920, S.E. Ex lit. sense.

*****window-fishing.** Entry through a window into a house : c. : late C. 19–20.

window-pane. A monocle : jocular coll. (— 1923). Manchon. Cf. *window*, q.v.

window-peeper. An assessor and/or collector of the window-tax : coll. : ca. 1780–1860. Grose, 1st ed. This tax was removed in 1851 (O.E.D.).

windsel. A nautical variant of windsail : coll. (— 1887). Baumann.

windstick. See **wind-stick.**

windward passage, one who navigates or uses the. A sodomite : low (— 1785) ; ob. Grose, 1st ed.

windy. Conceited, over-proud : C. 17–20 : S.E. until mid-C. 19, then Scots coll.—2. Afraid or very nervous ; apt to ' get the wind up ' : (? late) 1915 : military > , by 1919, gen. Hankey, 1916 (O.E.D.). Ex *wind up, get the*, q.v.—3. Applied to any place likely to induce fear : military : from 1916. There were various ' Windy Corners ' on the Western Front. F. & Gibbons.

windy wallets. ' A noisy prater, vain boaster, romancing yarnster,' F. & H. : C. 19–20 ; ob. Ex dial.

wine. To drink wine, orig. and mainly at an undergraduates' wine-party : coll. : 1829, C. Wordsworth (O.E.D.).—2. Hence, to treat (a person) to wine : coll. : from early 1860's.—3. Whence *dine and wine*, the entertainments being separate or combined : coll. : 1867 (O.E.D.).

wine-bag. A toper specialising in wine : (low) coll. : late C. 19–20. Cf. :

winer. One who habitually or excessively drinks wine : coll. : C. 20. Cf. :

winey. Drunk ; properly, drunk with wine : low (— 1859). H., 1st ed.

*****wing.** A quid of tobacco : prison c. : 1882, J. Greenwood, *Gaol Birds*.—2. See **win**, n., 1.—3. (Gen. pl.) An arm : nautical : ca. 1820–1910. Egan's Grose ; Baumann.—4. A sandwich-man's boards : c. (— 1932). F. Jennings.

wing, v.t. ' To undertake (a part) at short notice and study it in the " wings ",' F. & H. : 1885, *The Stage*, Aug. 31.

wing, hit under the. Tipsy : 1844, Albert Smith (O.E.D.) ; ob. Lit., disabled as a bird shot there.

wings, have one's. To be qualified to fly alone : Air Force coll. : from 1916. B. & P. An observer had only one ' wing ' on his tunic.

winger. A steward at table : nautical : C. 20. Bowen.—2. Hence, a sneak, an underhand fellow : naval : from ca. 1915. Bowen.

winger, do a. To take an unfair advantage in a bargain : naval and military : from ca. 1916. F. & Gibbons.

wingers. Long, flowing whiskers : military : ca. 1900. Ware.

wingy. A man ' minus ' a *wing* (arm) : New Zealanders' : in G.W. Cf. *limby*, q.v.

Winifred !, O(h). A c.p. expressive of disbelief : lower and lower-middle classes' : 1890's. Ware, ' From St Winifred's Well, in Wales ' and its reputedly marvellous cures.

winick. See **winnick**.

wink, n. Rare in singular. See **winks.—wink, tip the.** See **tip**, v.

wink the other eye. Flippantly to ignore a speech, warning, etc. : coll. : late C. 19–20.

winkers. The eyes : from early 1730's : S.E. until C. 19, then coll. ; by mid-C. 19, s. Cf. the dial. *winkers*, eye-lashes.—2. (Also, occ., *flanges*.) Long, wavy or flowing whiskers : ca. 1865–80. Ware. Ex a horse's blinkers.

winking, as easy as. With (consummate) ease : coll. : C. 20. Ex :

winkin(g), like. Very quickly or suddenly : coll. : 1827, Hood, ' Both my legs began to bend like winkin'.' Lit., in the time it takes one to wink. —2. Hence, vigorously ; ' like one o'clock ' : coll. : 1861, Dickens, ' Nod away at him, if you please, like winking.' Cf. *winky, like*.

winkle, v.t. To steal : lower classes' : from ca. 1910. Perhaps ex *wangle*. (F. & Gibbons.)—2. Hence, to capture (individual soldiers) by stealth : G.W. (Ibid.)

winkle-fishing, n. Putting fingers in nose : proletarian (— 1923). Manchon.

winkle-pin. A bayonet : military, esp. Cockneys' : G.W., and after. F. & Gibbons. It serves this useful purpose.

winkler. One who ' winkles ' (sense 2) : G.W. (F. & Gibbons.) Vbl.n., *winkling*.

winks. Periwinkles : streets (mostly London) : mid-C. 19–20.—2. **winks, forty.** See **forty**.

winky, like. A variant of *like winking* (above) : 1830, Lytton ; 1902, Begbie. O.E.D.

Winlaton shag. ' A slang name for an inhabitant of Winlaton [in Durham] ' : Durham s. (— 1892). E.D.D.

*****winn.** See **win**, n., 1.

winner. A thing—e.g. a play—that scores a suc-

cess : from ca. 1912. Ex *winner*, a horse that wins.—2. Hence, from ca. 1920, something esteemed to be certain to score a success. (But many a publishing ' winner ' is a ' flop '.)

Winnie. Quinine : military : from 1914. B. & P.

*****winnings.** See **win**, v.—**wins.** See **win**, n., 2.

Winnick. (See also **stone winnick**.) Crazy ; mad, in any degree : military : 1915 ; ob. B. & P. Ex the lunatic asylum at Winick, Lancashire.

Winston's pet. ' A colossal long range gun made at Sheffield . . . just before the Armistice, but never used ' : naval : late 1918–19. Bowen. Ex Mr. Winston Churchill.

winter-campaign. Riot(ing) ; a drunken ' row ' : 1884–5. Ex dynamiters' winter activities. Ware.

winter-cricket. A tailor : ca. 1785–1890. Grose, 2nd ed.

winter-hedge. A clothes-horse : proletarian (— 1904) ; ob. F. & H.

*****winter-palace.** A prison : c. (— 1887) ; slightly ob. Baumann. A shelter for necessitous criminals.

winter-time ?, where do flies go in the. A C. 20 c.p. from a popular song. In *The Spectator*, Sept.13, 1935, a Swanage hotel begins its advertisement thus : ' Where do flies go in the winter-time ? Quite frankly, we don't know, BUT . . . we shall be very much surprised if it is as comfortable there as at . . .'

winter's day, short and dirty,—he is like a. A late C. 18–mid-19 c.p. Grose, 2nd ed. Cf. the dial. *winter Friday*, a cold, wretched-looking person.

wipe. An act of drinking : coll. : late C. 16– early 17. Rowlands (O.E.D.). Cf. *swipe*.—2. A handkerchief : low : 1789, George Parker ; Henry Kingsley. Cf. earlier *wiper*.

wipe, v. To strike ; to attack, with blows or taunts : C. 16–20 : S.E. until C. 19, then s. and dial. Cf. *swipe*, v., q.v.

wipe (a person) down. To flatter ; to pacify : low (— 1860). H., 2nd ed.

wipe (a person's) eye. In shooting, to kill a bird that another has missed : sporting : from ca. 1820. Cf. sporting sense of next entry.—2. Hence, to get the better of : from late 1850's. H., 2nd ed.—3. A variant of *wipe the other eye*, q.v.—4. To give him a black eye : 1874, R. H. Belcher, ' Cheeky ! it's Sunday, or else I'd wipe your eye for you,' O.E.D.

wipe (a person's) nose. To cheat, defraud, swindle : C. 15–mid-18.—2. The same as *wipe a person's eye*, 1, q.v. : sporting : from ca. 1840. Surtees.

*****wipe-drawer.** A C. 19 variant of *wiper-drawer*, q.v. Baumann.

*****wipe-hauling.** The filching of handkerchiefs from owner's pockets : c. : 1845 in ' *No. 747* ' ; ob. Ex *wipe*, n., 2.

wipe the other eye. To take another drink : from ca. 1860. H., 3rd ed., in form *wipe one's eye*, to take, or to give, another drink : a public-house, esp. an old toper's, term.

wipe up. To steal : military : from ca. 1908 ob. F. & Gibbons.—2. To arrest : c. (— 1935). David Hume.

wipe your chin ! A c.p. addressed to a person suspected of lying : Australian : from ca. 1905. (To prevent the ' bulsh ' getting into the beer he is probably drinking.)

*****wiper.** A handkerchief : 1626, Jonson ; B.E. ; Grose. In C. 19–20, *wipe* (n., 2).—2. A weapon ; ? an assailant : C. 17–20 ; ob. Conan Doyle

(O.E.D.)—3. A severe blow or reply (or taunt) : **s.** > coll. : from mid-1840's ; slightly ob. Cf. S.E. *wipe*, a blow, a sarcasm.

*wiper-drawer. A handkerchief-stealer : c. : late C. 17–18. B.E. ; Grose, 1st ed. See **wiper, 1.**

Wipers. Ypres in Flanders : military : from 1914. Prob. ex the ' Wypers ' (properly Ypre) Tower at Rye : itself coll. of late C. 19–20. B. & P.—2. Hence *Wipers Express*, the German 42 centimetre shell (approximately 16 inches) first notably used at the Second Battle of Ypres.

wire. A telegram : coll. : 1876 (O.E.D.). Ex *by wire*, recorded in 1859. Cf. the v.—2. An expert pickpocket : c. : 1845, in ' *No. 747* ' ; 1851, Mayhew. Ex the wire used in removing handkerchiefs from pockets. Cf. *wirer*.

wire, v.i. and t. To telegraph : coll. : 1859, *The Edinburgh Review*, April, ' Striving to debase the language by introducing the verb " to wire ", ' O E D. Cf. *wire*, n., 1, q.v.—2. Hence, to telegraph to (a person, a firm) : coll. : 1876 (O.E.D.).—3. V.i. and t., to pick pockets (of persons) : c. : 1845, in ' *No. 747* '. Ex *wire*, n., 2.—4. See phrasal vv. ensuing.

wire, give (a person) **the.** To warn secretly : low (pre-War) and military (G.W.) ; ob. F. & Gibbons. Ex *wire*, n., 1.

wire, on the. See **hanging on the wire.**

wire, pull one's. See **pull one's wire.**

wire away (1888) is rare for *wire in*, q.v.

*wire-draw. ' A Fetch or Trick to wheedle in *Bubbles* ' : c. : late C. 17–mid-18. B.E. Ex the corresponding v., which is S.E.

wire in (− 1864), rarely **wire away.** To set-to with a will. H., 3rd ed. ; H., 5th ed., ' In its original form, " *wire-in*, and get your name up ", it was very popular among London professional athletes,' but, at the very beginning, it derives perhaps ex wiring off one's claim or one's future farm. Whence *wire into*. Cf. :

wire in and get your name up ! Have a shot at it ! : 1862–ca. 1914. Ware, ' Originally very erotic.'

wire into (a meal, etc.). To set about eagerly, vigorously : 1887, Baumann. Ex *wire in*.

*wire, the. A c. variant of *the straight wire*, genuine information : from ca. 1918. James Curtis, *The Gilt Kid*, 1936.

*wirer. A pickpocket using a wire (see **wire, n.,** 2) : c. (− 1857) ; ob. ' Ducange Anglicus.'

wireman. A telegraphist : coll. (− 1923). Manchon.

wise as Waltham's calf. See **Waltham's.**

wise-crack. A smart, pithy saying : U.S. coll., anglicised by 1932. Also *wisecrack*.

wise (to). Aware (of) ; warned (about). Esp. *be* (or *get*), or *put* a person, *wise* (*to*) : U.S. coll. (ca. 1900), anglicised ca. 1910. Cf. :

wise up, v.i. To ' get wise ' ; v.t., to ' put (a person) wise ' : U.S. (C. 20), anglicised ca. 1918, but ' Australianised ' by 1916 (C. J. Dennis) : Buchan, 1919 ; Wodehouse, 1922. Ex preceding. (O.E.D.)

Wiseacres' Hall. Gresham College, London : a mid-C. 18–mid-19 nickname. Grose, 2nd ed. The hit is at members of the Royal Society.

wish, I. Incorrect form, as is *I wist*, of *iwis*, certainly : C. 16–20. O.E.D.

wisker. See **whisker.—wisker-splitter.** See **whisker-splitter.—wist, I.** See **wish, I.**

*Wit. See ***Whit.**

wit as three folks, he has as much. Orig. and often self-explanatorily *he has . . . folks, two fools and a madman* : c.p. of late C. 18–mid-19. Grose, 3rd ed. Cf. the C. 17–18 proverb *he hath some wit but a fool hath the guidance of it* ; cf. too the witticism apocryphalised in Einstein, ' Only four persons understand Relativity ; I'm not one of them ; and of the other three, two are dead and the third in a lunatic asylum.'

*witch-cove. A wizard : c. : C. 18–19. Baumann.

*witcher ; occ. **wicher.** Silver : c. : mid-C. 17–early 19. Coles, 1676 ; B.E. ; Grose. Hence, *witcher-bubber*, a silver bowl (all three) ; *w.-cully*, a silversmith (ibid.) ; and *w.-tilter*, a silver-hilted sword (ibid.). Perhaps a corruption of *silver* influenced by *white*.

with. See **throw.—2.** Another South African coll. (− 1913) is *with* as in ' Can I come with ? ', i.e. with you. Ex influence of Cape Dutch *sam*, together. Pettman.

with and without. See **warm with : cold without.** From 1830's. (Rare alone.)

with his hat off. See **hat off.**

without. (By ellipsis of the gerund.) Not counting : 1871, George Eliot, ' My father has enough to do to keep the rest, without me,' O.E.D.—2. (By ellipsis of the object, except as opp. *with*) : C. 14–20, S.E. until C. 19, then coll. Newman, 1834, ' [He] was afraid to tell me, and left Oxford without,' O.E.D.—3. (As conjunction.) If . . . not ; unless : C. 14–20 : S.E. until C. 18, then coll. ; in late C. 19–20, sol. Johnson, 1755, ' Not in use, except in conversation.' (O.E.D.)

without any. Without liquor (for a stated period) : lower classes' coll. : from ca. 1890. Ware.

*Witt, the. See **whit.—wittles.** See ' **w for v** '.—**Wiwi.** See **Wi-Wi.**

wizard, adj. Excellent, first-rate : from ca. 1924. (' Ganpat ', *Out of Evil*, 1933, ' A perfectly wizard week ! ') Ex *wizard*, magical.

wobble like a drunken tailor with two left legs. (Of a ship) to steer an erratic course : nautical c.p. : late C. 19–20. Bowen.

wobble-shop. A shop where liquor is sold unlicensed : c. or low (− 1857) ; ob. ' Ducange Anglicus.' Cf. *whistler*, 3, and *whistling-shop*, qq.v.

wobbler or **wabbler.** (See **foot-wobbler**.) Rare in simple form : military (− 1874). H., 5th ed.—2. ' A boiled leg of mutton, alluding to the noise made in dressing it,' Bee : ca. 1820–50.—3. A horse that, in trotting, swerves from side to side : racing (− 1897). Barrère & Leland.—4. A pedestrian ; a long-distance walker : sporting (− 1909). Ware. Cf. sense 1.—5. An egg : low Cockney : from ca. 1880. Clarence Rook, *The Hooligan Nights*, 1899.

Wobbly Eight, the. The British Third Battle Squadron : naval : 1914–15. Bowen.

wodge, wodgy. See **wadge.**

woe betide you (him, etc.). You'll be getting into trouble : coll. : mid-C. 19–20. Ex † S.E. sense. (O.E.D.)

woefuls, got the. See **got the woefuls.**

woffle. To eat ; drink : low (− 1823) ; † by 1890. Egan's Grose. Perhaps cognate with Northamptonshire dial. *waffle*, to masticate and swallow with difficulty (E.D.D.).—2. V.i. and t., ' To mask, evade, manipulate a note or even [a] difficult passage ' ; music-halls' and musicians' (− 1909). Ware. Ex *waffle*, to yelp : cf. *waffle*, **v.**, 1.—3. Hence, more gen. : from ca. 1920. G. Heyer, *Death in the Stocks*, 1935.

Woggins. Worcester College : Oxford undergraduates' : C. 20. Collinson. Also **Wuggins.**

wog (or **W.**). A lower-class babu shipping-clerk : nautical : late C. 19–20. Bowen.

wolf, see a. (Of a woman) to be seduced : coll. : C. 19–20 ; ob. Ex the fig. sense, to lose one's voice.

*wolf in the breast. An imposition consisting of complaints, by beggar women, of a gnawing pain in the breast : c. : mid-C. 18–early 19. Grose, 3rd ed. Cf. medical *lupus* and :

wolf in the stomach, have a. To be famished : coll. : late C. 18–20 ; ob. Grose, 1st ed. Cf. *stomach worm*, q.v. Ex the old proverb, *a growing youth has a wolf in his belly.*

Wolfe's Own. The 47th Foot Regiment ; from ca. 1881, the (1st Battalion of the) Loyal North Lancashire Regiment : military : from ca. 1760 ; ob. The black worn in the gold lace commemorates Wolfe. In late C. 19–20, occ. *the Wolves*. (F. & Gibbons.)

Wolfland. Ireland : coll. nickname : late C. 17–early 18. O.E.D.

wollop. See **wallop.**

wolly. (Gen. pl.) An olive : East Londoners' (— 1909). Ware. Ex the street cry, *Oh ! olives !*

Wolves, the. See **Wolfe's Own.**—2. The Wolverhampton Wanderers : sporting : late C. 19–20. Cf. *Spurs, the.*

woman and her husband, a. A c.p. applied to ' a married couple, where the woman is bigger than her husband,' Grose, 2nd ed. : late C. 18–mid-19.

woman of, make an honest. To marry : jocular coll. : C. 20. Ex lit. sense, to marry a woman one has seduced or lived with. (Collinson.)

woman of all work. ' A female servant, who refuses none of her master's commands,' Grose, 2nd ed. : ca. 1785–1840.

[**woman of the town.** Orig.—witness *A New Canting Dict.*, 1725—it may have been c.]

woman-who-did or **-diddery.** A popular novel with sexual interest : book-world, resp. coll. and s. : very late C. 19–20 ; virtually †. Manchon. Ex Grant Allen's *The Woman Who Did*, 1895.

womble, womblety. See **wamble, wamblety.**

won, stolen, etc. See **win, v.**

wonder !, I. I doubt it, can't believe it, think it may be so : coll. : 1858, *Punch*, ' What next, I wonder ! ', O.E.D.

wonder !, the. Coll. abbr. of *in the name of wonder* : 1862 (O.E.D.).

wonder !, I shouldn't. I should not be surprised (*if*, etc.) : coll. : 1836, Dickens, ' " Do you think you could manage . . . ? " " Shouldn't wonder," responded boots.' O.E.D.

wonk. A useless seaman ; a very inexperienced naval cadet : naval : from ca. 1917. Bowen. Ex *wonky.*

wonk, all of a. Upset, very nervous : 1918 (O.E.D. Sup.) ; ob. Ex :

wonky. See **wanky.—wonner.** See **oner.**

won't ; C. 17–18, occ. **wont.** Will not : coll. : mid-C. 17–20. Earlier *wonnot.* (O.E.D.)

won't you come home, Bill Bailey ? A c.p. of the first decade, C. 20. Collinson. Ex the popular song.

won't run to it ! See **run to it !, won't.**

wood. Money : London drinking s. (— 1823) ; † by 1890. ' Jon Bee.' Ex liquor from the wood.— 2. A variant of *Woods*, q.v.—3. *wood, the.* The pulpit : 1854. Thackeray (O.E.D.). Implicit in :

wood, look over the. To preach : late C. 18–mid 19. Grose, 2nd ed. Sc. *of the pulpit.*

wood, look through the. To stand in the pillory : id. Ibid.

wood-butcher. A carpenter : aircraft artificers' : from 1915. F. & Gibbons. See **wood-spoiler**, q.v.

Wood in front, Mr and Mrs. A theatrical c.p. (C. 20) = a bad house, i.e. empty seats.

wood in it !, put a bit of. Shut the door ! : military : C. 20. F. & Gibbons. Also *put a piece of wood in the hole !,* which appears also in Yorkshire dial.

wood-sour is incorrect for *wood-sear* : C. 19. O.E.D.

wood-spoiler. A ship's carpenter : naval (— 1909). Ware.

Woodbine. A Tommy : Australian and New Zealand soldiers' : G.W. Because the Tommies smoked so many Wild Woodbine cigarettes. B. & P. Cf. *Woods* and :—2. Any cheap cigarette : coll. : from ca. 1917.

Woodbine, Teddy. Edward Prince of Wales : Australian and N.Z. soldiers' : G.W. B. & P.

Woodbines, the Packet of. See **Packet of Woodbines.**

woodcock. A tailor presenting a long bill : from ca. 1780 ; ob. Grose, 1st ed. Cf. *snipe*, q.v.

Woodcock's Cross, go crossless home by. (P.) To repent and be hanged. Without *crossless*, the phrase app. = to repent. (Cf. *Weeping Cross*, q.v.) Coll. : C. 17.

woodcock's head. A tobacco-pipe : coll. : 1599, Jonson ; † by 1700. Early pipes were often made in the likeness of a woodcock's head. F. & H.

*wooden. One month's imprisonment : c., and grafters' s. : C. 20. Philip Allingham, *Cheapjack*, 1934. Prob. abbr. of postulated *wooden spoon = moon* = month.

wooden casement ; w. cravat. A pillory : jocular : ca. 1670–1720. Contrast *hempen cravat.*

wooden doublet. See **wooden surtout.**

wooden fit. A swoon : proletarian : late C. 19–20. F. & H.

wooden gods. The pieces on a draughts-board : London : ca. 1820–1910. Bee ; Baumann.

wooden habeas. A coffin : ca. 1780–1850. Grose, 1st ed., ' A man who dies in prison, is said to go out with a *wooden habeas*'. Cf. *wooden surtout*, contrast *wooden casement*, and see esp. Grose, P. ; cf. also dial. *get a wooden suit*, to be buried.

wooden horse. A gallows : mid-C. 16–17 : s. soon > coll. D'Urfey. Apperson. Whence, prob. :

wooden-legged mare. The gallows : ? C. 18–mid-19. Cf. *three-legged mare*, q.v.

wooden overcoat. A coffin : a variant (mostly mid-C. 19) of *wooden surtout*, q.v.

*wooden ruff. Same as *wooden casement*, q.v. : c. : late C. 17–early 19. B.E.

wooden spoon. The person last on the Mathematical Tripos list : Cambridge University coll. : C. 19–20. Ex the spoon formerly presented to him. *Gradus ad Cantabrigiam*, 1803.—2. The Parliamentary usage mentioned in H., 3rd ed., is derivative : he whose name appears the least frequently in the division-lists. From ca. 1860 ; ob.—3. A fool : Society : ca. 1850–90. Ware. Ex sense 1.—4. In C. 20 sporting coll., a ' donkey ' or consolation prize for being last.

wooden surtout. A coffin : from ca. 1780. Grose, 1st ed. : H., 3rd ed., ' Generally spoken of as a wooden surtout with nails for buttons ' ; ob. Cf. *wooden doublet, w. habeas, w. overcoat,* or *w. ulster,* the earliest being *w. doublet* (1761 : O.E.D.), likewise the first to disappear ; the latest is *w. ulster* (Ware, 1909).

wooden wedge. ' The last name in the classical honours list at Cambridge,' H., 2nd ed. : Cambridge University coll. (— 1860). See **wedge,** 2. Cf. *wooden spoon.*

woodman. A carpenter : coll. and dial. : late C. 19–20. Cf. *chips.*

***woodpecker.** ' A Bystander that bets,' B.E. : c. : C. 17–early 19. Dekker, 1608, shows that he is an accomplice betting to encourage novices or fools.

Woods. A Wild Woodbine cigarette : military (1914) >, by 1919, lower classes'. B. & P. Also *wood.*

***wool.** Courage, pluck : c. (— 1860) >, ca. 1870, pugilistic s. (witness H., 5th ed.) ; slightly ob. H., 2nd ed., ' You are not half-*wooled,* term of reproach from one thief to another.' Prob. ex jocular S.E. *wool,* hair : see **wool-topped un.**

wool, v.t. To pull a person's hair : U.S., anglicised in late 1860's. Le Fanu. (O.E.D.)—2. To ' best ' (a person) : low (— 1890). Barrère & Leland. Ex *pull (the)wool over the eyes of.*

wool, more squeak than. More noise than substance ; much talk with little result ; semi-proverbial coll. : from ca. 1730 ; ob. (O.E.D.) On *great* (or *much*) *cry and little wool* (proverbial S.E.).

***wool-bird.** A sheep : orig. (— 1785), c. >, early in C. 19, low s. Grose, 1st ed. ; H., 2nd ed., ' wing of a *woolbird,* a shoulder of lamb '. Also *woolly-bird,* q.v.

***wool-hole.** A workhouse : tramps' c. (—1859) ; ob. H., 1st ed. ; also in ' printing ' Savage, 1841, where, further, one learns that the term was orig. printers' s. ex a lit. and technical sense.

wool on !, keep your. Don't get angry ! : 1890, Barrère & Leland. Cf. *woolly,* adj. Ex *keep your hair on.*

wool on the back. Money, wealth : commerical : 1909. O.E.D. (Sup.).

wool-topped un. A plucky fellow : boxing : *ca.* 1870–1900. H., 5th ed., where also *a reg'lar woolled un,* a very plucky fellow. See **wool,** n.

woolbird. See **wool-bird.**—***woolled.** See **wool,** n.

woollies, the. An occ. variant of *the willies* ; esp. *give* (a person) *the woollies* : Army officers' : from Feb., 1935 ; ob.

woolly. A blanket : coll. : from early 1860's ; ob. H., 3rd ed. (Mod. sense, S.E.)

woolly, adj. In a bad temper : from early 1860's; ob. H., 3rd ed. Perhaps the ' originator ' of *keep your wool on.*

woolly bear. Any large, hairy caterpillar, but esp. the larva of the tiger-moth : coll., mainly children's : 1863, Wood ; much earlier in dial. as *woolly boy.* O.E.D. Ex resemblance to the children's plaything.—2. A shrapnel shell (giving off white smoke) : military : G.W. (F. & Gibbons.)

***woolly bird.** A variant of *wool-bird,* q.v. : c. : ca. 1810–50. Vaux.

woolly crown. ' A soft-headed fellow,' Grose, 1st ed. : ca. 1690–1850. B.E.

woolly Maria. An occ. variant of *woolly bear,* 2.

woop woop. The country districts : New South Wales jocular coll. (—1926). Jice Doone. Satirising the Australian Aboriginal names, so often

reduplicatory.—2. Hence *woop,* a rustic simpleton : from ca. 1915 : popularised in 1919 ; by 1935, ob.

wooston. Very, as in ' A wooston jolly fellow ' : Christ's Hospital : late C. 19–20. Ex *whoreson.*

woozy. Fuddled (with drink) ; muzzy : U.S. (1897), anglicised by Conan Doyle (O.E.D.) in 1917. ? ex *woolly* + *muzzy* (or *dizzy* or *hazy*).—2. Dizzy : Canadian : C. 20.

Wop. An Italian : from ca. 1931, via the ' talkies '. Ex U.S. *Wop,* an Italian immigrant in North America. ? etymology.

wop, wopper. See **whop, whopper.**—**wops(e).** See **waps(e).**

worb. An odd-job youth in a circus : Australian : C. 20. Perhaps a corruption of *yob.*

word. To warn or to prime (a person) : C. 20 s. >, ca. 1935, coll. Prob. ex *give* (a person) *the word,* to indicate the password.—2. In Australia (—1916), ' to accost with fair speech ', C. J. Dennis.

word !, my. Indicative of surprise or admiration : coll. : 1857, Locker (O.E.D.).

word, one . . . See **one word . . .**

word, the. ' The right word for the right thing ' : hence, the thing to be done : coll. Shakespeare, Congreve, W. S. Gilbert. O.E.D.

word-grubber. ' A verbal critic ' ; one who uses ' jaw-breakers ' in ordinary conversation : late C. 18–mid-19. Grose, 2nd ed. Cf. *word-pecker.*

word of mouth, drink by. ' I.e. out of the bowl or bottle instead of a glass,' Grose, 2nd ed. : drinkers' : late C. 18–mid-19. Extant in dial.

word-pecker. A punster : ca. 1690–1840. B.E.; Grose, 1st ed. Punning *woodpecker.*

words. A wordy dispute or quarrel : coll. : late C. 19–20. Agatha Christie, 1934, ' What is called in a lower walk of life " words ".'

wore. Worn : sol. : C. 19–20. Baumann.

work. (Esp. of a vendor or beggar) to go through or about (a place) in the course, and for the purposes, of one's business or affairs : 1834, Colonel Hawker, of a hound ; 1851, Mayhew, of an itinerant vendor ; 1859, H. Kingsley, of a parson. O.E.D.— 2. To obtain or achieve, to get rid of, illicitly, deviously, **or** cunningly : 1839, Brandon, *Dict. of Flash.* Esp. ' Can you work it ? ' ' I think I can work it for you.'—3. Hence (of an itinerant vendor) to hawk : 1851, Mayhew.—4. See ' Winchester College slang ', § 5.

work !, good. See **good work !**

***work back.** To recover (stolen property) : c. : mid-C. 19–20. ' *No. 747.*'—2. To use up ; finish : coll., esp. military : C. 20. F. & Gibbons.

work cut out, have (all) one's. To have enough, or all one can manage, to do : coll. : 1879, H. C. Powell (O.E.D.). Ex *cut out work for* (a person), which may, orig., have been a tailoring phrase.

***work-bench.** A bedstead : c. : ca. 1820–50. Egan's Grose.

work for a dead horse. See **dead horse.**

work from magpie to mopoke. See **magpie to mopoke.**

work it (up you) ! Go to the devil with it : low, mostly Australian : C. 20. Also in other grammatical moods.

work off. To kill ; esp. to **hang** : 1840, Dickens (O.E.D.) : slightly ob. Lit., to dispose of.—2. See ' Eton slang ', § 2.

work one's fists. To be skilful in boxing : pugilistic (— 1874) ; ob. H., 5th ed.

work-out. A wholesale dismissal of employees: lower classes' (— 1935). Also *slaughter.*

*work the bulls. To get rid of false crown-pieces : c. : ca. 1839–1910. Brandon, 1839 ; H., 2nd ed.

*work the halls. (Gen. as vbl.n.) To steal from hall-stands, having called as a pedlar : c. (— 1935). David Hume.

work the mark. To handle or operate mail-bag apparatus : (mail-train) railwaymen's : from ca. 1926. *The Daily Herald*, Aug. 5, 1936. Ex the Government mark on the bags.

work the oracle. To achieve (esp. if illicitly or deviously) one's end in a skilful or cunning manner : orig. (— 1859), low s. >, by 1930, coll. H., 1st ed. See work, 2.

workhouse. A hard, ill-found ship : nautical : C. 20. Bowen.

*works, give (a person) the. To manhandle ; to kill, esp. by shooting : c. : (C. 20) U.S. anglicised ca. 1930 as s.

Works, the. Glamorganshire : from the late 1880's : South-Welsh s. >, by 1905, coll. The E.D.D. cites ' Allen Raine ', *A Welsh Singer*, that late-Victorian best-seller which appeared in 1897. Prob. ex the numerous factories there.

workus. A workhouse : sol. : C. 19–20. Usually *the workus*, generic.—2. A Methodist chapel : Anglicans' : ca. 1840–1914.

world. Knowledge of the fine world : Society : ca. 1790–1820. John Trusler, *Life*, 1793, ' That . . . is a proof of your want of world.—No man of *Ton* ever goes to the Theatre, for the amusements of that Theatre.' Ex S.E. *the world*, fashionable society.

world, dead to the. Utterly drunk : s. verging on coll. : C. 20.

world, tell the. See tell the world.

world and his wife, all the. See wife, all the world and his, with which cf. the Fr. *tout le monde et son père* (W.).

world to a China orange, (all) the. An occ. variant (— 1887) of *Lombard Street to a China orange*. Baumann.

worm. ' The latest slang term for a policeman ', H., 1864 ; extremely ob. (Manchon wrongly classifies it as c.)

worm, v.i. and t., esp. in *worming*, ' removing the beard of an oyster or muscle ' [*sic*], H., 1st ed. : mostly lower-class London (— 1859). Ex crustacean—or oyster's beard—likened to a worm.

worm-crusher. A foot-soldier : military : from 1890's ; ob. Cf. *mud-crusher*.

worm-eater. A skilful workman drilling minute holes in bogus-antique furniture to simulate worm-holes : cabinet-makers' (— 1909). Ware.

worms. ' A line cut in the turf as a goal-line at football ' : Winchester College : from ca. 1880. Wrench. Ex the worms so discovered.

Worms, be gone to the Diet of. To be dead and buried : ca. 1780–1830. Grose, 1st ed. A companion pun (Worms, ' the Mother of Diets ' + *worms' meat*) is *to be gone to Rot-his-bone* (i.e. Ratisbon).

worn't. Weren't, wasn't : sol. (— 1887). Baumann. Cf. *warn't*, q.v.

worrab. A barrow : back s. : from the 1860's. Ware.

worracks (or -ocks) ! See warorks !

worries the dog. See dog, he worries the.

worriment. Worry : lower-classes' coll. : late C. 19–20. (Dorothy Sayers, *Unnatural Death*, 1927, ' Such a state of worriment.')

worrit ; occ. -et. Anxiety, mental distress, or a cause of these : (low) coll. : 1838, Dickens. Ex next.—2. A person worrying himself or others : id. : 1848, Dickens. O.E.D.

worrit, v.t. To worry, distress, pester : (low) coll. : 1818, Lamb. A corruption of *worry*, perhaps on dial. *wherrit*, to tease. (O.E.D.)—2. Hence v.i., to worry, to display uneasiness or impatience : id. : 1854, Wilkie Collins. O.E.D.

worriting, n. (1857) and adj. (1845) of *worrit*, v O.E.D.

worry !, I should. I'm certainly not worrying, nor shall I worry about *that !* : coll. (orig. U.S.) : C. 20. Cf. *I should smile !*, and the analogous *not half*.

worse end. See staff, the worse end of the.

worse for, it would be none the. It would be improved by : coll. : C. 20.

worse in gaol (jail), there are. A c.p. (C. 20) indicating that the person referred to might be worse. Cf. *pass in a crowd*.

worsen, adj. and adv. Worse : from ca. 1630 , dial. and sol. : 1634, Heywood ; Dickens. ? ex *worse'n*, worse than. O.E.D. Also, occ., *wors'n*.

worser, adj. Worse : late C. 15–20 : S.E. until C. 18, then (esp. in C. 19–20) either ' literary ' and, in C. 20, affected, or, in C. 19–20, dial. and low coll. —in C. 20, increasingly sol. Dickens, 1837, ' You might ha' made a worser guess than that, old feller.' Also, sol., *wusser* : 1845, Disraeli.—2. Hence, adv. Worse : mid-C. 16–20 : S.E. until early C. 18, then ob. ; in C. 19, low coll. ; in C. 20, sol. Dickens, 1835, ' Your . . . wife as you uses worser nor a dog.' Also, from 1840's, *wusser* : sol. O.E.D.

worserer. Worse : sol. when neither dial. nor jocular,—as the latter, s. : 1752, Foote, ' Every body has a more betterer and more worserer side of the face than the other.' Ex *worser*. O.E.D. Also *wusserer* as in *wusserer and wusserer*. Cf. :

worsest. Worst : sol. (— 1887). Baumann. Cf. *worser* and *worserer*.

worst than. Worse than : sol. : C. 19–20. (Frank Richards, 1933.)

worth . . ., not. See bean, cent, curse, dam, fig, louse, rap, turd, etc.

worth a guinea a box. A c.p. applied to any small, cheap, yet good or useful article : from ca. 1920. Ex the considerably older slogan of Beecham's Pills.

worth a plum, be. To be rich : coll. : ca. 1710– 1800. G. Parker. (Apperson.) Ex *plum*, £100,000.

worth it. (Predicatively.) Worth while : coll. : late C. 19–20.

worthy has, among Public Schoolboys and hence the upper classes, been, since the G.W., much used as the concomitant of both ' decent fellow ' and ' stout fellow ' ; although this usage approximates to that in S.E., yet it may well be classified rather as s. than as coll., for it is glib and somewhat vague. It is also applied to things : e.g. of a remark, one says ' That is not worthy ' instead of ' not worthy of you '.

wot. What : sol. and dial. as written, but extremely gen. as pronounced.

wotchere(o). A proletarian slurring (from ca. 1880 ; ob.) of *what cheer (oh) !* Ware.

would. Should : catachrestic : mid-C. 18–20. Mrs S. Pennington, 1766, ' I choose rather that you would carry it yourself,' O.E.D.

would, I. I advise, recommend, you to : coll. : late C. 16–20. Shakespeare, 1591, ' I would resort

to her by night,' O.E.D. Cf. *wouldn't*, *I*, q.v.
Short for *I would, if I were you*. See:

would !, you ; occ. he (etc.) **would !** Abbr. *you*
(etc.) *would go and do that, curse you !* or *that's the
sort of thing you* would *do*. Coll. : C. 20. Often a
mere cliché or c.p.

wouldn't, I. I advise you *not* to : coll. : (?
earlier than) mid-C. 19–20. The O.E.D. instances
' I wouldn't go skating to-day ; the ice isn't safe.'
On *would*, *I*, q.v.

wounds (e.g. **by Christ's wounds !**) occurs in oaths
of mid-C. 14–mid-18, and as a self-contained interjection (abbr. *God's wounds !*) of C. 17–early 19 ;
occ. in C. 19, *wouns !*

wow, be a ; rare except in **it's a wow.** To be a
great success or most admirable, ' really ' excellent :
U.S. (1927), partly anglicised by 1929, esp. in
theatrical s. Prob. ex a dog's bark : cf.' *howling
success* ' and :

wow-wow. A children's variant of *bow-wow*, a
dog : coll. (— 1887). Baumann.

wow-wow ! ; bow-wow ! A Slade School c.p. of
the late 1890's, as in R. Blaker, *Here Lies a Most
Beautiful Lady*, 1935, ' " Wow—wow—wow—" she
gurgled ; for ' bow-wow ' or ' wow-wow ' was
currency in her circle at that time, to denote quiet
contempt of an adversary's bombast.'

wowser. A person very puritanical in morals ; a
spoil-sport ; one who neither swears, drinks (in
especial), nor smokes : from ca. 1895 : Australian
s. >, by 1930, coll. Perhaps ex *wow*, a bark of
disapproval, + euphonic *s* + agenital *er* ; cf. the
Yorkshire *wowsy*, ' an exclamation, esp. of surprise ',
E.D.D.

wozz. See **wazz.—Wozzer.** See **Wazzer.**

wrack for **rack**, vv. A frequent confusion ; e.g.
in (*nerve-*)*wracked* for *-racked* : C. 16–20.—As, in
late C. 16–20, *wrack* is frequently used for *rack*, n.

Wraf. A member of the Women's Royal Air
Force : from 1917 : (mainly military) coll. Cf.
Waac and *Wren*, qq.v.

wraith(e). Incorrect for *rathe* (a cart-shaft) :
C. 19–20. Cf. *wrag* for *rag*. O.E.D. But these mis-
uses of *wr-* for *r-* are too numerous to be profitably
recorded in greater detail than (*ipse dixit !*) I have
given here : see O.E.D. *passim*.

Wrangler's Hall. The House of Commons :
literary and journalistic coll. : ca. 1820–50. Bee.

wrap-rascal. A red cloak : late C. 18–early 19.
Grose, 2nd ed. An extension of S.E. *w.-r.* (a loose
overcoat or a surtout), perhaps influenced by
roquelaire.

wrapped-up, esp. in *all nicely wrapped up*, in seemly
language, and *not even wrapped-up*, crudely expressed : coll. : late C. 19–20. Ex *pack-thread*,
talk.

wrapt ; wrapture. Rapt, rapture : incorrect
forms : resp. late C. 18–20 ; C. 17 (O.E.D.).

wrapt up in the tail of his mother's smock, he was.
A c.p. applied to ' any one remarkable for his success
with the ladies ', Grose, 1st ed. : ca. 1780–1850.
(Female fondling of male children increases their
latent sexuality : it didn't need Freud to tell us this :
this has been folk-lore for centuries.) Ex *be
wrapped in his mother's smock*, to be born lucky.

wrapt up in warm flannel. ' Drunk with spirituous
liquors,' Grose, 1st ed. : ca. 1780–1830. ? cf. the
' drapery ' terms for gin (see **white ribbon**).

wreak is ' sometimes erron[eously] used by mod.
writers as though it were [the] pres[ent] of *wrought*
(see *work*) ', W., who quotes *The Times*, Oct. 6,

1918, ' The damage they have wreaked must be
repaired to the uttermost farthing.'

wreath of roses. A chancre : lower classes'
euphemism : C. 20. *Slang*, p. 191.

wrecking. The ruining, by ' shady ' solicitors, of
limited companies : financial coll. : 1880–4. Ware.

wren. A harlot frequenting Curragh Camp :
military : 1869, J. Greenwood, who adds, ' They
do not live in houses or even huts, but build for
themselves " nests " in the bush.'—2. (Gen.
Wren.) A member of the Women's Royal Naval
Division : from 1917 : coll., mostly (Army and)
Navy. Cf. *Waac* and *Wraf*, qq.v.

*wrest ; wrester. A picklock (the thieves' tool) :
c. : late C. 16–early 17. Greene, 1592. Ex S.E.
wrest, v.

wriggle navels. To coït : C. 18–20 ; ob. Prob.
later than and suggested by *wriggling-pole*, q.v.

wriggle off. To depart : Londoners' : ca. 1860–
90. Ware.

wriggling-pole. The penis : (late C. 17 or early)
C. 18–20 ; very ob. D'Urfey.

*Wright, Mr. A warder ' going between ' a
prisoner and his friends : prison c. : C. 19–20 ; ob.
Punning *wright*, an artificer, and *right*, adj. Cf.
Right, Mr. q.v.

*wrinkle. A lie, a fib. : c. (— 1812) ; ob. Vaux.
—2. A cunning or adroit trick, device, expedient ;
a smart ' dodge ' : orig. and often *put* (a person) *up
to a wrinkle* (or *two*), as in Lady Granville, 1817
(O.E.D.) : s. >, by 1860, coll. Cf. the C. 15–17
wrinkle, a tortuous action, a cunning device, a trick ;
the link is perhaps supplied by sense 1, or by such a
repartee as occurs in Swift's *Polite Conversation*, I,
or, most prob., by *wrinkle more . . .* , q.v.—3.
Hence, a helpful or valuable hint or piece of information : sporting s. (1818 : O.E.D.) >, by 1870, coll.

*wrinkle, v. To tell a lie : c. (— 1812) ; ob. Vaux.
Prob. ex *wrinkle*, n., 1.

wrinkle-bellied. (Gen. of a harlot) having had
many children : low coll. : late C. 18–20. Grose,
3rd ed., ' Child bearing leaves wrinkles.' Cf. :

wrinkle more in one's arse, have one (or **a**). To
get one piece of knowledge more than one had,
' every fresh piece of knowledge being supposed by
the vulgar naturalists to add a wrinkle to that part ',
Grose, 2nd ed. (cf. H., 2nd ed.) : low : ca. 1786–
1880. Here, perhaps, is the origin of *wrinkle*, n.,
2 and 3, previously considered so problematic.
Cf. preceding entry.

*wrinkler. A person prone to telling lies : c.
(— 1812) ; ob. Vaux. Ex *wrinkle*, v.

wrist-watch. Contemptible : naval : ca. 1900–
13. Bowen. Considered effeminate.—2. High
class ; aristocratic : military : ca. 1905–20. E.g.
' He talks pukka wrist-watch ' ; ' Oh, he's pukka
wrist-watch, he is ! '

writ, when not deliberately ' literary ', is, in late
C. 19–20, gen. considered a sol. Baumann.

writ-pusher. A lawyer's clerk : legal (— 1909).
Ware. Cf. *process-pusher*.

write a poor hand. See **sore fist.—write home
about.** See **nothing to . . .**

write-off. A complete aeroplane-crash : Air
Force : from 1914. F. & Gibbons. The machine
could be written off as useless.

write one's name across another's face. To strike
him in the face : sporting : ca. 1885–1912. Ware.

write one's name on (a joint). ' To have the first
cut at anything ; leaving sensible traces of one's
presence on it,' H., 2nd ed. : from late 1850's.

written, not enough. Insufficiently revised for style : authors' coll. : from ca. 1870 ; ob. Ware.

wrokin. A Dutch woman : ? C. 17–19. F. & H. Perhaps Dutch *vrouw* corrupted.

wrong end of the stick, the. See **stick, wrong end** . . .

wrong fount. An ugly human face : printers' (— 1933). *Slang*, p. 181. Ex the technical term.

wrong in the upper storey. Crazy : mid-C. 19–20. Cf. *wrong in the head*, itself coll. (and dial.) : from ca. 1880—perhaps rather earlier.

[Wrong number. See *e.g.* Fowler, *Modern English Usage*. See, *e.g.* **their**, above.]

wrong side, get up (occ. **out of bed**) **on the** or **the.** To rise peevish or bad-tempered : coll. : C. 19–20. To do this, lit., is supposed to be unfortunate. Scott, 1824 ; A. S. M. Hutchinson, 1921. (Apperson.)

wrong side of the hedge, be or **fall on the.** To fall from a coach : coll. : ca. 1800–80. Ware.

wrong un (or **'un**). A 'pulled' horse : racing s. (1889, *The Sporting Times*, June 29) >, by 1910, (low) coll.—2. Hence, a welsher or a whore, a base coin or a spurious note, etc. : from ca. 1890 : s. >, ca. 1910, (low) coll.—3. (Perhaps suggested by 1.) A horse that has raced at a meeting unrecognised by the Jockey Club : racing s. (— 1895) ; by 1920, racing coll.—4. The wrong sort of ball to hit : cricketers' s. (1897) >, by 1920, their coll. Lewis.

wrong with, get in. See **get in wrong with.**

wrong with ?, what's. What's the objection to ? ; why not have ? : coll. : from early 1920's. Ronald Knox, 1925, ' I want to know what's wrong with a game of bridge ? ', O.E.D.

wronk. Wrong : sol. : C. 19–20. Frank Richards, *Old Soldiers Never Die*, 1933. Cf. *anythink*.

wroth of reses. A wreath of roses : theatrical : ca. 1882–1914. Ware, ' Said of a male singer who vocalises too sentimentally.' A Spoonerism.

wrought shirt. See **historical shirt.**

*wroughter. In the three-card trick, he who plays the cards, the trickster being a ' broadpitcher ' : c. : from (? late) 1860's. B. Hemying, 1870, in his *Out of the Ring*, includes these terms in ' The Welshers' Vocabulary '. O.E.D. ? because *wrought*-on : cf. *wrought-up*, excited.

wrux. A rotter : a humbug : Public-Schools' : from ca. 1875. Perhaps ex dial. (*w*)*rox*, n., and v., (to) decay, rot.

*wry mouth and a pissen (C. 19 pissed), **pair of breeches, a.** A hanging : ca. 1780–1850 : either c. or low s. Grose, 1st ed. Cf. :

*wry-neck day. A day on which a hanging occurs or is scheduled to occur : c. : ca. 1786–1860. Grose, 2nd ed. Prob. suggested by preceding.

Wuggins. See **Waggins.**

wump ; occ. **whump.** A hard blow : coll. (— 1931). Lyell. Perhaps a blend of *whack* (or *wallop*) + *clump* (or *thump*).

wur. Was : sol. (— 1887). Baumann. More gen. *were*.

wurl ; yurse. Defective pronunciation of *well* and *yes*, esp. in emphasis or reflection : C. 19–20. As in Ernest Raymond, *The Jesting Army*, 1930, ' Many casualties in the battalion ? *Wurl*, no—not too bad.' See also **yurse.**

wushup, your (etc.). Your worship : C. 19–20 : orig. and gen. sol., but, as often are *wuss* and *wusser*, it may also be jocular s. Also *your wash-up.*

wuss. Worse : sol. : C. 19–20. For *wusser*, adj., see *worser*.

wusser. A canal boat : bargees' (— 1904). ? *water* perverted.—2. Adj., adv. ; see **worser.**

wusserer. See **worserer.**

wuzzy is an occ. variant of *woozy*, q.v.

wylo ! Be off : Anglo-Chinese (— 1864). H., 3rd ed.

*wyn. See **win, n., 1.—Wypers.** See **Wipers.**

X

X or **×.** ' The sign of cheatery, or *Cross*, which see,' Bee, 1823. Cf. *X division*, q.v.—2. See **p.s.**, 2. **-x** for **-xed**, esp. in *fix*' and *mix*' : sol. : C. 19–20. ' Wheatex mix fruit pudding,' an Express Dairy menu label, Feb. 4, 1936.—2. Also *x* occurs for *xt* in (esp. Cockney) illiterate speech : since when ? W. Pett Ridge, *Minor Dialogues*, 1895, ' " 'Eaven bless our 'Appy 'Ome " . . . ain't so dusty for a tex'.'

X or **letter X, take** (a person). To secure (a violent prisoner), thus : ' Two constables firmly grasp the collar with one hand, the captive's arm being drawn down and the hand forced backwards over the holding arms ; in this position the prisoner's arm is more easily broken than extricated,' F. & H. : c. and police s. : from early 1860's. H., 3rd ed.

*X division. Thieves, swindlers ; criminals in gen. : c. (— 1887). Baumann. Ex *X*, q.v.

X-chaser. ' A naval officer with high theoretical qualifications ' : naval : from ca. 1920. Bowen.

X-legs. Knock knees : coll. verging on S.E. : mid-C. 19–20. Ex shape when knocking.

X.Y.Z. The Y.M.C.A. : New Zealanders' : in G.W. A skit on the initials.

xaroshie. Very good ; quite correct : military (North Russia) : 1918–19. F. & Gibbons. Direct ex Russian ; gen. pronounced *sharoshie*.

xawfully. Thanks awfully : slovenly coll. : from ca. 1919. D. Mackail, *The Young Livingstones*, 1930, ' " Good-bye, old thing. Good luck, and all that." " Xawfully." '

Xmas. Christmas : low coll. when uttered as *Exmas*, coll. when (from ca. 1750) written ; earlier *X*(*s*)*tmas* was not pron. The *X* = *Christ* (cf. scholarly abbr. *Xianity*), or rather the *Ch* thereof—Gr. X (khi).

xonalite. Incorrect for *xonotlite* : from late 1860's. O.E.D.

X's ; more gen. as pronounced—**exes.** Expenses : 1894, Louise J. Miln (O.E.D.). Perhaps orig. theatrical, as the earliest quotation suggests. —2. (Often *X-es*.) ' Atmospheric or static interference with wireless ' : wireless-operators', esp. on ships : from ca. 1926. Bowen.

*X's Hall. The Sessions House, Clerkenwell : c. : mid-C. 19–20. Ware. Ex *Hicks*, a judge.

xyphoid. Incorrect for *xiphoid* : mid-C. 18–20. O.E.D.

Y

[In y, F. & H. includes certain ineligibles; thus, S.E.:—Yahoo (or y.); yankee (or Y.), excellent; unrecorded yap's; yard, yards (Durham and Harrow Schools), and under one's yard; Yarmouth coach; yea-and-nay; year('s)-mind; unlisted yellow's; Yiddisher; yokel; yoop; York and yorker; you-know-what; young and young thing. Dial.:—yaff; yaffle (n.); yank (v.), yanker, yanking; yanks (leggings); yanker; yankie; yap (a cur); yawney and y.-box; yeack; yellow slipper.]

'y. (Properly ye' or yer.) You: (low) coll.: C. 19–20. J. B. Priestley, Faraway, 1932, ' Y'see, you know about the island.'

y-, sol. for h-, is most common among Cockneys: C. 19–20' and prob. from much earlier. E.g. yere for here, beyond for behind.

-y or -ie (C. 14–20); occ. -ey, C. 17; -ee, C. 17–18. As a diminutive and endearing suffix, it has a coll. tendency and savour, as, e.g., has -ish. In diminutives (and for proper names), -y and -ie are almost equally common, but in pet-names and other endearments, -ie is much the more gen.—2. At Manchester Grammar School, -y is used thus:—
-mathy, mathematics; chemmy, chemistry; -gymmy, gymnastics, etc.: mid-C. 19–20.

Y.M.; Y.W. (Pronounced wy em, wy double you.) The Young Men's and the Young Women's Christian Association, frequently abbr. Y.M.C.A., Y.W.C.A.: coll.: C. 20. Cf.:

Y Emma. The Y.M.C.A.: military: from 1915. In signalese, m > Emma. Cf. preceding.

ya-inta! Hallo!: Eastern Fronts' military in G.W. (F. & Gibbons.) Ex Arabic.

yabber. Talk (1874); to talk (1885), v.i. esp. if unintelligibly: Australian ' pidgin'. Ex Aboriginal. Morris.

yabbie. A fresh-water crayfish: Australian coll.: late C. 19–20. Ex Aboriginal.

yachting, go. To break leave: naval (mostly officers'): C. 20. Bowen. Here, yachting = on pleasure bent.

*yack; rarely yac. A watch: c.: app. late C. 18–very early 19 (Vaux, 1812, declaring it †) and revived ca. 1835, for we find it in Brandon, 1839, and Mayhew, 1851, ' At last he was bowled out in the very act of nailing [stealing] a yack.' Perhaps a perversion, by a modified back s., of watch: cf. the process in yadnab. Sampson, however, more convincingly derives it ex Welsh Gypsy yakengeri, a clock, lit. ' a thing of the eyes' (yak, an eye). (See also at christen and church.)

yack-a-poeser. ' A cup of tea flavoured with rum': military: from 1914. F. & Gibbons. Whence ?

yacka, -er. See yakker.

yad. A day; yads, days: back s. (— 1859). H., 1st ed.

yadnab. Brandy: slightly modified back s. (— 1859). Ibid.; but H., 5th ed., has yadnarb, which is close enough. The impossible yd- has >yad-.

*yaffle, v.i. To eat: from ca. 1786: c. >, ca. 1820, low s. († by 1850) and dial. Esp. as vbl.n., yaffling (Grose, 2nd ed.). Perhaps cognate with dial. yaffle, to yelp, to mumble.—V.t., to snatch, take illicitly, pilfer: low: late C. 19–20. Perhaps a perversion of snaffle.

yah-for-yes folk. Germans and Dutchmen: nautical coll.: late C. 19–20. Bowen. Ex Ger. ja, yes.

yah, pron. See yer.

yah! A proletarian cry of defiance: coll.: C. 17–20. Possibly implied in Swift's Yahoos.

yahoo, n. and adj. (A man that is) considered mad, crazy, or extremely eccentric: tailors': C. 20. The Tailor and Cutter, Nov. 29, 1928.

yakker; occ. yacka, yacker, yakka. (Correctly yakka.) To work; work at: Australian ' pidgin': late C. 19–20. Ex Aboriginal. Morris.—2. Whence as n., hard toil: idem: C. 20. C. J. Dennis.

yakmak is incorrect for yashmak: mid-C. 19–20. So is yaknack. O.E.D.

yallah! Go on!: get on with it!: Eastern Fronts' military coll.: G.W. Ex Arabic. (F. & Gibbons.)

yallow. Yellow: sol. and dial.: C. 17–20. Sir W. Mure (C. 17), 'Yellow curls of gold,' O.E.D. The U.S. prefers yallah, yaller. Cf. yeller, q.v.

yam. Food: nautical (— 1904). F. & H. Presumably ex:

yam, v.i. and t. To eat; orig., to eat heartily: low and nautical: from ca. 1720. A New Canting Dict., 1725; William Hickey (1749–1809), in his Memoirs, ' Saying in the true Creolian language and style, " No! me can no yam more ",' W. H., 3rd ed., ' This word is used by the lowest class all over the world.' It is a native West African word (Senegalese nyami, to eat): W., after that extraordinary scholar, James Platt. The radical exists also in Malayan.

yam-stock (or Y.-S.). An inhabitant of St Helena: nickname: 1833, Theodore Hook (O.E.D.).

yan. To go: Australian ' pidgin' (— 1870). Ex Aboriginal. Morris. Cf. yakka.

Yank. Yankee (n. and adj.): coll.: 1778 (O.E.D.: in orig. U.S. sense, C. 19–20 for ' (an) American '; the adj. Yank (of the U.S.), app. not before the 1830's, as in Hurrell Froude. Abbr.:

Yankee; occ. Yank(e)y. Orig. (early 1780's) among the English, this nickname for any inhabitant of the United States (other and earlier senses being U.S.), was coll.; in C. 20, it is S.E. The theories as to its etymology are numerous (see, e.g., O.E.D. and W.'s Romance of Words): the two most convincing, —and the latter (blessed by both W. and the O.E.D.) seems the better,—are that Yankee derives ex U.S. Indian Yangees for English, and that it derives ex Jankee, Dutch for ' little John' (Jan), this Jankee being a pejorative nickname for a New England man, esp. for a New England sailor.

Yankee main tack, lay (a person) along like a. (Gen. as a threat.) To knock a man down: naval: late C. 19–early 20. Ware. A Yankee main tack is a direct line.

Yankee heaven; Yankee paradise. Paris: coll.: resp. ca. 1850–80; from 1880. Ware. Cf. (? ex) the saying, ' All good Americans go to Paris when they die.'

Yankeeries, the. The American and American-Indian display at Earl's Court Gardens: Londoners': 1887; soon †. Ware. On Colinderies and Fisheries.

Yankees. American stocks, shares, securities: Stock Exchange: from mid-1880's. E. C. Bentley,

Trent's Last Case (but it wasn't), 1913, ' A sudden and ruinous collapse of ' Yankees ' in London at the close of the Stock Exchange day.'

*yannam. Almost certainly a misprint for *pannam*, q.v.

yap. A countryman : low s. verging on c. : and mostly U.S. : from 1890's. F. & H. Perhaps ex dial. *yap*, a half-wit.—2. A chat : from ca. 1928. Ex sense 2 of :

yap, v. To pay : back s. (— 1859). H., 1st ed., where it occurs in the form *yap-poo*, to pay up ; in H., 5th ed., it is *yap-pu*. Cf. *yappy*.—2. To prate, talk volubly : coll. : late C. 19–20. C. J. Dennis. Ex *yap*, to speak snappishly.

yappy. Foolishly generous ; foolish, soft : from ca. 1870. H., 5th ed. Ex *yap*, v., i : q.v. Or it may rather derive ex Yorkshire *yap*, a foolish person.

yapster. A dog : low (— 1798) ; ob. Tufts. Cf. S.E. *yapper*.

y'ar, y'are. Ye are ; you are : sol. (— 1887). Baumann.

*yaram. See **yarrum.**

Yard, the. Scotland Yard, headquarters of the London police : coll. : in C. 20 verging on S.E. : 1888, A. C. Gunter (O.E.D.). The C. 20 name is New Scotland Yard.

yard-arm, clear one's. To prove oneself innocent ; to shelve responsibility as a precaution against anticipated trouble : nautical : late C. 19–20. Bowen.—2. Hence, *look after one's own yardarm*, ' to consider one's own interests first ' (F. & Gibbons) : naval : C. 20. Cf. :

yard-arms, square yards with. To settle accounts ; finish, or finish with, a (troublesome) matter ; have it out with (a person) : naval : C. 20. F. & Gibbons.

yard of clay. A long clay pipe, a ' churchwarden ' : from ca. 1840 : coll. >, by 1880, S.E. *Punch*, 1842 (O.E.D.).

yard of pump-water. A tall, thin person : low : late C. 19–20.—2. See **purser's grin.**

yard of satin. A glass of gin : 1828, W. T. Moncrieff ; ob. See **satin.**

yard of tin. A horn : jocular coaching and sporting coll. : mid-C. 19–20 ; ob. Reginald Herbert, *When Diamonds Were Trumps*, 1908.

yardnarb. Brandy : from ca. 1880. Ware. The back s. *ydnarb > yardnarb* for the sake of ' euphony '. See also **yadnab.**

y'are. See **y'ar.**

yark. To cane : Durham School : mid-C. 19–20. A dial. form of *yerk*.

Yarmouth ; gen. quite **Yarmouth.** Mad : naval : C. 20. Bowen. Ex the naval lunatic asylum there.

Yarmouth bee. See **Yarmouth capon.**

Yarmouth bloater (or **B.**). A native of Yarmouth : coll. : 1850, Dickens. Ex lit. sense, Yarmouth being famous for its herrings. Cf. :

Yarmouth capon. A herring : jocular s. > coll. : from ca. 1660 ; ob. Fuller ; B.E. ; Grose, 1st ed. ; J. G. Nall, *Great Yarmouth*, 1886, ' In England a herring is popularly known as a Yarmouth capon.' Also, ca. 1780–1850, a *Norfolk capon*. (Apperson.) Cf. also *Glasgow magistrate*, q.v. Occ. *Yarmouth bee* : mid-C. 19–20 ; ob. F. & H.

Yarmouth mittens. Bruised hands : nautical : from ca. 1860 ; ob. H., 3rd ed. Ex hardships of herring-fishing.

yarn, orig. (— 1812) and often in **spin a yarn** (nautical s. >, ca. 1860, gen. coll.), to tell a—gen. long—story, hence from early 1830's to ' romance '.

A story, gen. long, and often connoting the marvellous, indeed the incredible : nautical s. >, ca. 1860, gen. coll. Vaux, Reade. Ex the long process of yarn-spinning in the making of ropes and the tales with which sailors often accompany that task (W.). Occ. *a sailor's yarn*.—2. Hence, a mere tale : coll. : 1897, Hall Caine, '.Without motive a story is not a novel, but only a yarn,' O.E.D. Cf. the journalistic sense of *a good yarn*, a story that is not necessarily true—indeed, better not.

yarn, v. To tell a story : nautical s. (— 1812) >, by 1860, gen. coll. Vaux ; 1884, Clark Russell, ' Yarning and smoking and taking sailors' pleasure.' Ex preceding. Hence *yarning*, n. and adj. : from 1840's, and prob. earlier.—2. A C. 19 Cockney pronunciation of *earn*. Bee. (But *yearn* is more gen. : Baumann.)

yarn a hammock. To make it fast with a slippery hitch so that the occupant will fall to the deck : naval : late C. 19–20. Bowen.

yarn-chopper, -slinger. A prosy talker ; a fictional journalist : from ca. 1880 ; ob.

yarn-spinner, -spinning. A story-teller ; story-telling : coll. : ca. 1865. Ex *yarn*, n.

yarning, n. and adj. See **yarn,** v.

Yarra ! ; **Yarrah !**, stinking. An offensive c.p. addressed by Sydneyites to Melbournites : C. 20. Cf. *our 'arbour !*

yarraman. A horse : Australian (— 1875). Ex Aborigine. Morris.

*yarrum (C. 17–20) ; **yaram,** rare C. 17 spelling ; **yarum,** frequent C. 16–18 spelling. Milk ; esp. *poplar(s) of yar(r)um*, milk-porridge : c. : from 1560's. Harman, Dekker, B.E., Grose (1st ed.). One of the small group of c. words in *-um* (or *-am*),—cf. *pan(n)um* or *-am*,—*yarum* is of problematic origin ; but I suspect that it is a corruption of *yellow* (illiterately *yallow*)—n.b. the colour of beastings—with *-um* substituted for *-ow* : cf. Italian waiters' *chirroff* for *chill off* and, possibly, Welsh Gypsy *ydro*, an egg (Sampson).

yas. Yes : (dial. and) sol. : C. 19–20. Baumann.

yaw-sighted. Squinting : nautical coll. : 1751, Smollett (O.E.D.). Ex *yaw*, a deviation from one's direct course, esp. if from unskilful steering.

Yaw-Yaw. A Dutchman : nautical (— 1883). Clark Russell. In C. 20, often a Baltic seaman : Bowen. Lit., yes, yes !—2. (**yaw-yaw.**) See **haw-haw,** of which it is an occ. variant. Baumann.

yawn(e)y. A dolt : rare (— 1904) ; ob. I.e. the adj. made n., on *sawney*. (Much earlier in dial.)

ye gods and little fishes ! A lower and lower-middle class c.p. indicative of contempt : ca. 1884–1912. It then > a gen. derisive or jocular exclamation. Ware, ' Mocking the theatrical appeal to the gods.'

Yea-and-Nay man. A Quaker : coll. verging on S.E. : late C. 17–early 19. B.E., Grose. Ex Quakers' preference for plain answers.—2. Hence, ' a simple fellow, who can only answer yes and no ', Grose, 1st ed. : ca. 1780–1850. Contrast dial. *yea-nay*, irresolute (E.D.D.).—3. Hence, a very poor, ' dumb ' conversationalist : mid-C. 19–20 ; ob. H., 2nd ed.

Yeaps. The predominant Cockney pronunciation of **Ypres** : G.W. (B. & P.) Cf. *Eeps*.

year. As a pl., it was S.E. until late C. 18, when it > coll. ; from ca. 1890, it has been considered—and in C. 20 it certainly is—a sol. when it does not happen to be dial.

year'd, 'tis. A semi-proverbial coll. applied to 'a desperate debt ', Ray : ca. 1670–1750.

-yearer. A pupil in his first, second, etc., year : Public School coll. : late C. 19–20. Alec Waugh, *The Balliols*, 1934, 'He was a third yearer at a public school.'

yearn. See **yarn, v.,** 2.

yegg. A travelling burglar or safe-breaker : U.S. c., anglicised by 1932, as s., among cinema-'fans'. Irwin ; C.O.D., 1934 (Sup.). Possibly ex Scottish and English dial. *yark* or *yek*, to break.

yeh. Yes : Cockney : since when ? I.e. *ye'*, clipped form. E.g., like sense 2, in Julian Franklyn's novel, *This Gutter Life*, 1934.—2. You : Cockney : C. 19–20. A variant of *yer*.

yeknod. See **yerknod.**

yell-play. 'A farcical piece . . . where the laughter is required to be unceasing' : theatrical coll. (— 1909). Ware.

yeller. Yellow : illiterate (i.e. sol.) and dial. : C. 19–20. Cf. *yallow*, q.v.

yelling. The rolling of a ship : nautical coll. : C. 19. Bowen. Ex the resultant noise.

yellow. A variant of *yellow-hammer*, 2, q.v. : from ca. 1870 ; ob. H., 5th ed.—2. See **yellows.**

yellow, v. To make a 'yellow admiral' of : nautical coll. : 1747 ; ob. O.E.D.—2. Hence, to retire (an officer) : nautical coll. : 1820, Lady Granville (O.E.D.).

yellow, adj. Cowardly, though perhaps not app. so ; coll. : from ca. 1910. Orig. U.S. ; prob. ex *yellow* as applied to a writer on the *yellow press* (1898).—2. *A New Canting Dict.*, 1725, asserts that *yellow*, jealous, was orig. a c. term : this is prob. correct.

yellow, baby's. (Mainly infantine) excrement : nursery coll. : C. 19–20.

yellow admiral. An officer too long ashore to be employed again at sea : naval : C. 20. Bowen. Cf. *yellowing*.

yellow-back (a cheap, sensational novel) is, by some, classified as s. or coll., but prob. it has always been S.E.

Yellow-Banded Robbers, the. The 13th Foot Regiment, later the Prince Albert's Somersetshire Light Infantry : military : C. 19–20 ; ob.

Yellow Belly, or **y.b.** A native of the fens, orig. and esp. the Fens in Lincolnshire ; 'also known in Romney Marshes, Kent' (E.D.D.) : from the 1790's. Grose, *Provincial Glossary*, 1790 ; id., *Vulgar Tongue*, 2nd ed., 1788. Ex the frogs, which are yellow-bellied, or perhaps, as Grose holds, 'an allusion to the eels caught there '.—2. A half-caste : nautical (— 1867). Smyth. Esp. a Eurasian : Anglo-Indian : from ca. 1860. (George Orwell, *Burmese Days*, 1935.)—3. A knife-grinder : Yorkshire s. (— 1905), not dial. E.D.D. Perhaps ex the yellowish leather apron.

yellow boy. A guinea or, in C. 19–20, a sovereign : from the Restoration : c. >, in C. 18, s. Wilson, *The Cheats*, 1662 (O.E.D.) ; Grose ; Dickens. Ex its colour : cf. Welsh Gypsy *melano*, yellow, hence a sovereign (Sampson).

Yellow Cat, the. The Golden Lion, 'a noted brothel in the Strand, so named by the ladies who frequented it ', Grose, 1st ed. : low : ca. 1750–80.

yellow fancy. A yellow silk handkerchief, white-spotted : pugilistic : from the 1830's. Brandon.

yellow fever. Gold-fever : Australian jocular coll. : 1861, M'Combie, *Australian Sketches*.—2. Drunkenness : Greenwich Hospital (— 1867) ; ob.

Smyth. Sailors there punished for drunkenness used to wear a parti-coloured coat, in which yellow predominated.

*yellow gloak. A jealous man, esp. a jealous husband : c. of ca. 1810–70. Vaux, 1812 ; H., 1st ed. Cf. *yellow house* ; see **gloak.**

yellow-hammer. A gold coin : ca. 1625–50. Middleton, Shirley. (Cf. *yellow boy*.) Ex the colour of the bird and the metal.—2. A charity boy in yellow breeches : C. 19–20 ; slightly ob.

yellow hose or **stockings, he wears.** He is jealous : coll. : C. 17–18. Dekker ; Bailey.

yellow jack (or **J.**). Yellow fever : nautical : 1836, E. Howard (O.E.D.). Ex the yellow jack or flag displayed at naval hospitals, and from vessels in quarantine to indicate a contagious disease.

yellow-jacket. A wasp : Canadian coll. : mid-C. 19–20. (John Beames.)

yellow-man. A yellow silk handkerchief (cf. *yellow fancy*, q.v.) : pugilistic and sporting : ca. 1820–80. *The Sporting Magazine*, 1821 (O.E.D.) ; 'Jon Bee ' ; H., 2nd–5th edd.

yellow peril ; or with capitals. A Gold Flake cigarette : from ca. 1910. Ex the yellow packets, with a pun on journalistic *y.p.*, the Chinese menace.

yellow plaster. Alabaster : provincial coll. : from ca. 1870. ? suggested by rhyme.

yellow silk, n. Milk : rhyming s. : late C. 19–20. B. & P.

yellow-stocking. A charity boy : London : C. 19–20.

yellowing. 'The passing over of captains in a promotion to flag rank' : naval : C. 20. Bowen. Cf. *yellow admiral*, q.v.

yellows (or **Y.**). Pupils at the Blue Coat School : London (— 1887). Baumann. Ex *yellow-stocking*.

yelper. A town-crier : low : from early 1720's ; ob. *A New Canting Dict.*, 1725 ; 'Jon Bee ', 1823. —2. A wild beast : low : from ca. 1820. Egan's Grose.

yen(n)ep. A penny : back s. (— 1859). H., 1st ed. Whence, e.g. **yenep-a-time,** a penny a time (a term in betting) ; **yenep-flatch,** 1½d. : both ibid.

yen(n)ork. A crown (-piece) : back s. (— 1859) ; ob. H., 1st ed.

yeoman of the mouth. An officer attached to His (Her) Majesty's pantry : jocular nickname : late C. 17–early 19. B.E., Grose.

yep ! Yes ! : 1897, Kipling (O.E.D.) : low coll. ex dial. and U.S. *The Humorist*, Jan. 27, 1934, 'Should Americanisms be banished from the English Language ?' Yep.' Cf. *nope*, no !

yer. You ; your : sol. and dial. : C. 19–20. Also *yah* and (for *you* only) *yez*.—2. Yes : sol. : C. 19–20.

yere. See **y-.**

yerknod ; properly **yeknod ;** loosely, **jirk-nod.** A donkey : back s. (— 1859). H., 1st ed.

yere they come. See **here they come.**

yers ; yerse. Yes : sol. : C. 19–20. Cf. *yurse*, q.v.

yerself. Yourself : sol., esp. Cockneys' : C. 19–20. Baumann.

yes of it, make. See **make yes of it.**

yes, she gave me. See **out ?, does your mother . . .**

yes'm ; yessir ! An illiterate 'collision' of *yes, sir !* and *yes, ma'am !* C. 19–20.

yes man, yes-man, yesman. One who cannot say 'no' : coll. : from 1933. C.O.D., 3rd ed. Sup, 1934 ; Margaret Langmaid, *The Yes Man*, published in Aug., 1935. Ex American *yes man*, a private secretary, an assistant (film-)director, a parasite.

yes, we have no bananas ! A c.p. of ca. 1924–28. Collinson. Ex the song.

yest. S. abbr. of *yesterday*: ca. 1720–1870. *A New Canting Dict.*, 1725. Cf.:

yesty. Yesterday: sol.: C. 19–20. Mayhew, 1861.

yez. See **yer.** Mostly Anglo-Irish, as in Maria Edgeworth.

y'iln. Scoundrel; (affectionately) scamp; often *y'iln elkalb*, lit. son of a dog: among soldiers in Egypt: C. 20. B. & P. Ex Arabic.

Yid ; loosely **Yit** (ob.). A Jew; orig. (– 1874) and properly, a Jew speaking *Yiddish*. H., 5th ed., both forms. Also *Yiddisher*, recorded by Barrère & Leland, 1890: coll. *Yiddish* + agential-*er*.

[Yiddish is technically a kind of German, not of Hebrew; but it is often, rather loosely, used as = ordinary spoken Hebrew.]

Yiddisher. See **Yid.**

Yiddle. A Jew; esp. a Jewish boxer: mainly pugilistic: from ca. 1930. An elaboration of *Yid.*

yimkin. Perhaps: Eastern Fronts' military coll. in G.W. (F. & Gibbons.) Ex Arabic.

yis. Yes: sol. (– 1887). Baumann. Cf. *yas*, q.v.

Yit. See **Yid.**

yo, Tommy ! 'Exclamation of condemnation by the small actor [i.e. in minor theatres]. Amongst the lower classes it is a declaration of admiration addressed to the softer sex by the sterner,' Ware, 1909. Perhaps this *Tommy* is related to that in *hell and Tommy* (see **Tommy, hell and**).

yob. A boy: back s. (– 1859). H., 1st ed.—2. Hence, a youth: from ca. 1890. 'Pomes' Marshall, ca. 1897, 'And you bet that each gal, not to mention each yob, | Didn't. care how much ooftish it cost 'em per nob.'—3 ? hence, a lout, a stupid fellow (rarely girl or woman): low (orig. East End): C. 20. F. & Gibbons. Perhaps influenced by:

yock. A fool, a simpleton: grafters': C. 20. Philip Allingham, *Cheapjack*, 1934. Ex Yiddish.—2. An eye: c.: C. 20. James Curtis, *The Gilt Kid*, 1936. Prob. ex Romany.

yog. A Gentile: East London back s. (on *goy*): C. 20. Whence *yock*, q.v.

yokuff. A large box, a chest: c. (– 1812) >, ca. 1850, low. Vaux; H., 1st ed. Prob. a perversion of *coffer.*

yolly. A post-chaise: ca. 1840–1900 at Winchester College. Ex *yellow*, a colour frequent in these vehicles: cf. † *yollow*, yellow.

yonker. See **younker.**—**yooman.** See **yuman.**

york. 'A look, or observation,' Vaux: c. or low: ca. 1810–80. Ex:

*york, v. To stare impertinently at: c. (– 1812); † by 1880. Vaux. Perhaps ex *Yorkshire bite*, 1, q.v.—2. V.i. and t., to look (at), to examine: low: ca. 1810–50. Ibid.—3. V.i., to rain: Bootham School: C. 20. Anon., *Dict. of Bootham Slang*, 1925. York is apt to be wet.

*York Street is concerned ; there is Y.S. concerned. Someone is looking (hard): c. or low: ca. 1810–60. Vaux. Cf. *york*, n. and v.

Yorks. Shares in the Great Northern Railway: Stock Exchange (– 1895). A. J. Wilson, *Stock Exchange Glossary.* The line passes through York and is now the L.N.E.R.

Yorkshire[1] orig. implied boorishness, but the connotation of cunning, (business) sharpness, or trickery appears as early as 1650. Variations of the latter senses occur in certain of the ensuing phrases, all of which have, from coll., >, by late C. 19, S.E. (See also **north**, 1.)

Yorkshire, n. Sharp practice; cajolery: mid-C. 19–20: coll. (> S.E.) and dial.

Yorkshire, v.t. 'To cheat, to take a person in, to prove too wide-awake for him': from ca. 1870. Ex *come* (or *put*) *Yorkshire on* (or *over*) a person. F. & H.

Yorkshire bite. A very 'cute piece of overreaching: 1795 (O.E.D.).—2. Hence, a particularly sharp and/or overreaching person: 1801 (O.E.D.). See **bite** and **Yorkshire**[1].

Yorkshire carrier, confident as a. Cocksure: C. 18–20; ob. Ward, 1706. See **Yorkshire**[1].

Yorkshire compliment. 'A gift useless to the giver and not wanted by the receiver,' F. & H.: mid-C. 19–20; ob. H., 5th ed. See **Yorkshire**[1]. Also, mainly dial., a *North-Country compliment.*

Yorkshire estate. Money in prospect, a 'castle in Spain'; esp. in *when I come into my Yorkshire estates*, when I have the means: mid-C. 19–20; ob. H., 2nd ed. See **Yorkshire**[1] and cf. *Yorkshire compliment.*

Yorkshire hog. A fat wether: 1772, Bridges, 'A pastry-cook | That made good pigeon-pie of rook, | Cut venison from Yorkshire hogs | And made rare mutton-pies of dogs'; Grose, 1st ed.; extremely ob. Cf. *Cotswold lion* and see **Yorkshire**[1].

Yorkshire Hunters, the. 'A regiment formed by the gentlemen of Yorkshire during the Civil War': military nickname: 1640's. F. & H. Yorkshire, a famous hunting county.

Yorkshire on (upon), put, C. 18–20; **come Yorkshire on** (C. 19–20), more gen. **c. Y. over**, app. first recorded in Grose, 1785. To cheat, dupe, overreach, be too wide-awake for (a person). The antidote is to *be Yorkshire too*, which phrase, however, is rare outside of dial. (E.D.D.), though Wolcot has it in 1796 (Apperson). See **Yorkshire**[1] and cf. *Yorkshire*, v.

Yorkshire reckoning. A reckoning, an entertainment, in which each person pays his share: mid-C. 19–20. H., 3rd ed. Cf. dial. *go Yorkshire*, to do this. See **Yorkshire.**[1]

Yorkshire tike or, gen., **tyke.** A Yorkshireman: coll. nickname: mid-C. 17–20. Howell, 1659; B.E.; Grose. *Northern tike* (rare) occurs in Deloney ca. 1600 (Apperson). See **tike** for improving status of this term.

Yorkshire too, be. See **Yorkshire upon, put.**—**Yorkshire upon . . .** See **Yorkshire on . . .**

Yorkshire way-bit. A distance greater than a mile: coll.: ca. 1630–1830. Cleveland, 1640. In the earliest record, *Y. wea-bit.* Apperson.

you and me. Tea: rhyming s.: C. 20. F. & Gibbons. Prob. suggested by *Rosy Lee.*

you are another !; you're another ! You also are a liar, thief, rogue, fool, or what you will: a c.p. retort (coll., not s.): C. 16 (? earlier)–20. Udall; Fielding; Dickens, '"Sir," said Mr Tupman, "you're a fellow." "Sir," said Mr Pickwick, "you're another"'; Sir W. Harcourt, 1888, 'Little urchins in the street have a conclusive argument. They say "You're another".' A variant, late C. 19–20 (? ob.), is *so's your father !* In mid-C. 19–20, the orig. phrase is almost meaningless, though slightly contemptuous. F. & H.

you are (or you're) slower than the second coming of Christ ! A drill-sergeants' c.p.: C. 20. B. & P.

you bet. See **bet** and **betcher.**

you'd be far better off in a home ! A military c.p. to a man in misfortune : 1915 ; ob. B. & P.

you *have* grown a big girl since last Christmas ! A non-aristocratic c.p. addressed to girl or woman : C. 20. (R. Blaker, *Night-Shift*, 1934.)

you'll be a long time dead ! See dead, you'll be a long time.

you'll get yourself disliked. A satirical, proletarian c.p. addressed to anyone behaving objectionably : from ca. 1878 ; now virtually S.E.

you make me tired ! You bore me to tears : a c.p. introduced from U.S.A. in 1898 by the Duchess of Marlborough, 'a then leader of fashion ' (Ware).

you may have broke your mother's heart—(but) you (bloodywell) won't break mine ! A military c.p. (C. 20), orig. and mostly drill-sergeants'. B. & P. Cf. *you shape* . . .

you must. A crust : rhyming s.: late C. 19–20. B. & P.

you pays your money and you takes your choice ! You may choose what you like : c.p.: late C. 19–20. Ex showmen's patter.

you said it. See said.

you shape like a whore at a christening ! A lower classes' and military (esp. drill-sergeants') c.p. to a clumsy person : from the 1890's, if not indeed considerably earlier. B. & P., 3rd ed.

youlie. See yowlie.

you-uns. You : low : late C. 19–20. Ex U.S. Cf. rarer *we uns*.

you would ! See would !, you.

young. (Of inanimates) small, diminutive, not full-sized : mid-C. 16–20 : S.E. until, after virtually lapsing in C. 17–early 19, it >, ca. 1850, coll. and jocular, as in Hornaday's ' Such a weapon is really a young cannon,' 1885. O.E.D.—2. the night's young yet, it is still early : coll.: C. 20. Often *yet* is omitted, rarely is *day* (etc.) substituted for *night*.

Young Bucks, the. The 14th Foot, now the Prince of Wales's Own West Yorkshire Regiment : ' from 1809, when the battalion, till then known as the Bedfordshire Regiment, exchanged County titles and depôts with the 16th Foot, the hitherto Buckinghamshire Regiment ', F. & Gibbons. Opp. *Old Bucks*, q.v.

Young Buffs, the. The 31st Foot Regiment ; from ca. 1881, the (1st Battalion of the) East Surrey Regiment : military coll. nickname : mid-C.18–20 ; ob. At the battle of Dettingen, George II, ' through the similarity of the facings, mistook it for the 3rd Foot (or Old Buffs) ', F. & H.

young Charley. See charley, n., 6.

Young Cub, the. Charles James Fox (1749–1806). Also *Carlo Khan*. Dawson.

Young Eyes, the. The 7th (Queen's Own) Hussars : military : mid-C. 19–20.

young fellow (or feller) me lad. A semi-jocular term of address : coll.: mid-C. 19–20.

Young Fusiliers, the. The 20th Foot Regiment (now the Lancashire Fusiliers) : military : ' a Peninsular War nickname ', F. & Gibbons. Because then only recently formed.

young gentleman, or man, lady or woman are coll. when addressed in ' reproof or warning to persons of almost any age ' : from ca. 1860. O.E.D.

young hopeful. See hopeful.

young kipper. A very poor meal : East End of London : C. 20. Punning the Jewish holy day, *Yom Kippur*.

young lady. A fiancée : low coll. when not jocular : 1896, George Bernard Shaw (O.E.D.). Cf.

young man and *young woman*.—2. See young gentleman.

young man. A sweetheart or lover ; a fiancé : coll. (in C. 19, always low ; in C. 20, often jocular) : 1851, Mayhew, ' Treated to an ice by her young man —they seemed as if they were keeping company,' O.E.D. Cf. *young woman*.—2. See young gentleman.

young one or un (or 'un). A child ; a youth (rarely a girl) : low coll.: C. 19–20 ; *Lex. Bal.*, 1811, ' A familiar expression of contempt for another's ignorance, as " ah ! I see you're a young one " ' ; this nuance is ob. As a young person, *young one* (or *'un*) may not precede the 1830's ; the O.E.D. cites Egan at 1838. Opp. an *old un*, an old man, a father. See un, 'un.

Young Soldier. See soldier, n., 5.

young strop. (Gen. pl.) A newly joined ordinary seaman : nautical : C. 20. Bowen. Perhaps because he does not often need to strop his razor.

young thing. A youth 17–21 years old : masculine women's coll. (— 1909). Ware. (The gen. sense is S.E.)

young 'un. See young one.

young woman. A sweetheart ; a fiancée : coll. (see young man) : 1858 (O.E.D.). On *young man*.— 2. See young gentleman.

youngster. A child, esp. a boy ; a young person (gen. male) not of age : coll.: 1732, Berkeley (O.E.D.). By natural extension of orig. sense.

[younker, earlier yonker, may always be S.E., though H., 2nd ed., ' *younker*, in street language, a lad or a boy ', causes one to doubt it.]

your. You're : sol. spelling and pron.: C. 19 (? earlier)–20. Cf. *youre*, q.v.

your crowd, wasn't it . . . See Emden.

*your nabs ; your nibs ; *your watch. See nabs, nibs and watch, n. Contrast *yours truly*.

your wheel's going round !, often preceded with hey ! and a pause. C. 20 street-wit c.p. directed at person on bicycle or in motor-car.

youre ; you're. Your : a sol. pronunciation : C. 19–20 ; cf. *your*. (J. Jefferson Farjeon, *Old Man Mystery*, 1933, ' Silk stockings . . . like you're young man appreciates '.)—2. you're as = *you are* is coll. : C. 18–20.

you're another ! See you are another !

you're off the grass ! You haven't a chance : cricketers' : ca. 1900–14. Ware. I.e. outside the field.

you're telling me ! I know that : American c.p. anglicised by 1933 : see indignant letter in *The Daily Mirror*, Nov. 7 of that year ; an advertisement in the agony column of *The Daily Telegraph*, Sept. 14, 1934.

you're the top ! A c.p. of approval : 1935. Ex the comedy, *Anything Goes*.

yourn ; your'n (C. 19–20). Yours : late C. 14– 20 : dial. and, C. 19–20, low coll.

your's. Yours : sol.: throughout Mod. E.

yours and hours. Flowers : rhyming s.: late C. 19–20. B. & P.

yours to a cinder. A non-aristocratic c.p. ending to a letter : late C. 19–20. (F. Brett Young, *Jim Redlake*, 1930.) Prob. orig. in the (coal-)mining centres.

yours truly. See truly, yours.

yourself !, be. Pull yourself together ! : a U.S. c.p., anglicised by 1934. C.O.D., 3rd ed., Sup.

yous ; occ. youse. (Pron. *yews*.) You : sol. :

late (? mid-) C. 19–20. Lit., *you* + *-s*, the sign of the pl. With this illiteracy, cf. *you-uns* and the nearly as reprehensible *your*, q.v.

yowlie or **-y.** A member of the watch; a policeman : Edinburgh s. : C. 19–20; ob. Jamieson, 'A low term' that prob. derives ex 'their youling or calling the hours'. Occ. *youlie*.

*yoxter. 'A convict returned from transportation before his time', H., 3rd ed. : c. of ca. 1860–90. Origin ?

y'see. You see : coll. (— 1887). Baumann.

yum. Yes : slovenly coll. : mid-C. 19–20. (A. A. Milne, *Two People*, 1931.)

yum-yum. Excellent ; first rate : orig. (— 1904) and mostly low. Ex *yum-yum !*, an exclamation of animal satisfaction (with, e.g., exquisite or delicious food).

yuman ; yooman. Human : sol. : C. 19–20. (G. D. H. and M. Cole, *The Murder at Crome House*, 1927, 'Shouted at us as if I wasn't a yooman being'.)

yurse. See **wurl.** Ernest Raymond, *The Jesting Army*, 1930, ' " We're *for* it, boys, if you arst me. . . . *Yurse*," he concluded with rich appreciation, " that means we're for it." '

yus(s). Yes : Cockney : C. 19 (? earlier)–20. Julian Franklyn, *This Gutter Life*, 1934, *passim*.

Z

[At **z**, F. & H. has the following ineligibles :— S.E. : *zany.* Dial. : *zemmies-haw* ! ; *zoty*.]

'Z. The *'S* of oaths : see *'S.* Cf. *Zooks* and *Zounds.*

zackly ; zactly. Exactly : resp. sol. and low coll. (— 1887). Baumann. But *zackly* is also dial.

zad ; mere zad. A bandy-legged and/or crooked-backed person : ca. 1720–1840. *A New Canting Dict.*, 1725. Cf. *zed, crooked as the letter*, q.v.—2. Occ. of a thing : same period.

zantho- is incorrect for *xantho-* : mid-C. 19–20. O.E.D.

zarnder. The same as a *tubbichon*, q.v. : London lower classes' : ca. 1863–70. Ware. Owing to its adoption by Princess (later Queen) Ale*x*andra.

zarp ; gen. Zarp. A policeman : the Transvaal : 1897, *The Cape Argus*, weekly ed., Dec. 8 ; ob. An anagram ex *Zuid Afrikaansche Republick Politie*, the South African Republic Police. Pettman.

zat ? How's that ? : cricketers' coll. : late C. 19–20. K. R. G. Browne, in *The Humorist*, Jan. 27, 1934, describes cricket as 'a game that consists chiefly of standing about in *dégagé* attitudes and shouting "Zat ? " at intervals '.

'Zbloud, 'Zbud, 'Z'death. See **'Sblood, 'Sbud, 'Sdeath.** Likewise *'Zfoot = 'Sfoot.*

zeb. Best : back s. (— 1859). H., 1st ed. Modified *tseb.*

zed, crooked as the letter. Very crooked : coll. (— 1785) >, ca. 1840, dial. Grose, 1st ed. See also *zad.*

zed (gen. **zedding**) **about.** To zigzag, to diverge : society : ca. 1883–1900. Ware. Perhaps punning *gad(d)ing about.*

Zedland. The South-Western counties of England : s. or perhaps coll. : from 1780's ; very ob. Grose, 2nd ed. There, dialectally, *s* is pronounced as *z*. (Also *Izzard Land*, dial. ; cf. literary *Unnecessarians.*)

zep ; rarely **zepp.** (Gen. with capital.) A Zeppelin airship : coll. : 1915, Jessie Pope, *Simple Rhymes*, 'The night those Zeps bombarded town,' O.E.D.

Zep, v.t. 'To drop bombs on from a Zeppelin' : somewhat rare coll. : heard in 1917 ; 1920, W. J. Locke (O.E.D.).

Zepp in a smoke screen. (Gen. pl. : **Zepps** . . .) Sausage and mashed potatoes : orig. (1918) military >, by 1920, gen. lower-class s. Margery Allingham, *Look to the Lady*, 1931. Cf. :

zeppelin(s) in a fog. Sausage(s) and mashed potatoes : naval : from ca. 1917. Bowen. The

military form (1917 at latest), now ob., is . . . *in a cloud* (F. & Gibbons).

Zero and **zero hour** are military j. ; but **zero**, to learn, experimentally, the peculiarities of (one's rifle), is marksmen's and snipers' coll. (now verging on j.) : from ca. 1912. B. & P., 3rd ed.—2. A water-closet : Bootham School : from ca. 1916. Anon., *Dict. of Bootham Slang*, 1925.

*ziff. A young thief : c. (— 1864). H., 3rd ed. ? *thief* perverted.—2. A beard : Australian (— 1926). Jice Doone. Why ?

*zig, catch the. See **catch the zig.**

zigzag. Tipsy : military : from 1916. F. & Gibbons ; B. & P. From Fr. s., ex the zigzag course taken by a tipsy man.

Zionist. A member of the Zion Mule Corps, 'a dreadful smelly lot of cut-throats, collected from Syria or somewhere to act as transport . . . Not bad,' as Ernest Raymond remarks in *The Jesting Army*, 1930 : military in 1915 (Gallipoli campaign) then historical.

zip. An echoic word indicative of the noise made by (say) a bullet or a mosquito in its passage through the air : coll. : 1875, Fogg. O.E.D.—2. Hence, force, impetus, energy, spirit : coll. : from ca. 1914. Cf. *vim.*—3. Hence, adj., as in *zip* (lightning) *fastener* : 1925 (S.O.D.) : coll. >, by 1930, S.E. Also *zipper*, n. : from ca. 1926 : coll. >, by 1930, S.E.

zip, v.i. To make a *zip* sound : coll. : from ca. 1880.

[Ziph. That ancient linguistic aberration which consists in saying, e.g., *shagall wege gogo* for *shall we go*. See *Slang*, p. 278.]

ziphoid. Incorrect for *ziphioid* : from ca. 1870 ; likewise *ziphoide* for *xiphoid* : C. 19–20. O.E.D.

zipper. See **zip,** n., 3.

zippy. Lively, bright ; energetic, vigorous : coll. : 1923, P. G. Wodehouse (O.E.D. Sup.). Ex *zip*, n., 2.

Zlead(s), Zlid ; Z'life. Minced oaths : coll. : C. 17–18. I.e. *God's lids, life*. O.E.D.

znees ; zneesy. Frost ; frosty or frozen : ca. 1780–1840, but perhaps covering a period as great as C. 18–mid-19. Grose, 1st ed. Perhaps a S.W. England coll. ; app.—witness E.D.D.—it is not dial. Perhaps ex *sneeze, sneezy*, which are, however, unrecorded in these senses. Cf. :

znuz. A variant of *znees*, q.v. Grose, 1st ed.

Zoo ; zoo. The Zoological Gardens, London (N.W.1) ; elsewhere, as already in the O.E.D.'s earliest example : Macaulay, ca. 1847, ' We treated the Clifton Zoo much too contemptuously.' The *zoō* has been telescoped to one syllable.—2. The Montreal immigration hall for those immigrants who wish to return to their own country ; Canadian : from ca. 1929. Ex the variety of dress and language.

Zooks ! ; Zookers ! ; Zoodikers ! (rare) ; **'Zoonters !** Oaths and asseverations : coll. : C. 17–mid-19. (O.E.D.).

zoom. An abrupt hauling-up and forcing-up of an aeroplane when it is flying level : aviation. Also, and slightly earlier, a v.i. Both, 1917 : *The Daily Mail*, July 19 (O.E.D.). Ex *zoom*, ' to make a continuous low-pitched humming or buzzing sound ' (O.E.D.). See also B. & P.

zouave, play the. To show off, to swagger : not very gen. military coll. : 1915 ; ob. F. & Gibbons. Ex the dashing zouaves' fiercely military bearing.

zouch. A churl ; an unmannerly fellow : C. 18. *Street Robberies Considered*, 1728. Perhaps ex *ouch*, the exclamation.

'Zounds ! An oath or asseveration : late C. 16–20 : coll. until C. 19, then archaic S.E. except when dial. Euphemistic abbr. *by God's wounds.* Cf. *Zooks !*

Zulu Express, the. A certain Great Western afternoon express train : railwaymen's at the time of the Zulu War (1879). Ware. Prob. because it ran to ' Zummerzett '.

zylo- is incorrect for terms in *xylo-* : C. 19–20. O.E.D.

SUPPLEMENT

A

a or 'a. Sense 2 (see *Dict.*) exists independently as far back as late C. 16. Thus Middleton & Dekker, *The Roaring Girl*, 1611: 'I love to lye aboth sides ath bed my selfe.'—7. Of: coll.: late C. 16–20. Ibid., 'Why 'twere too great a burden, love, to have them carry things in their minds, and a' ther backes.'

A.A. of the G.G. (see *Dict.*) is not in gen. use.

A.B. (p. 1) prob. goes back to very early C. 19. It occurs in W. N. Glascock, *Sailors and Saints*, 1829, at I, 21, and still earlier in *The Night Watch*, 1828, at II, 121. (Moe.)

A.B.C.—3. A crib: Rugby Schoolboys': ca. 1880–1910. Ex the letters forming **cab**, n., 4.

A.B.F. A final 'last drink': since ca. 1915. I.e. an absolutely bloody final drink.

AC–DC or A.C.–D.C. (of a man) both heterosexual and homosexual: adapted, 1959, from U.S.A. A pun on Electricity's '*A.C.* or *D.C.*'—alternating current or direct current.

A/C Plonk. Aircraftman, 2nd Class (A.C.2): R.A.F.: since early 1920's. *The New Statesman*, Aug. 30, 1941; Jackson. Ex **plonk**, n., 1 (p. 640).

a cooloo. All; everything: since ca. 1925; R.A.F., esp. regulars with service in the East, whence the term came. Jackson. Probably from Arabic *cooloo*, all; in Army, since ca. 1914.

A.K. Canadian signallers' s. for the s. *arse over kettle* (Canadian: C. 20): 1914–18.

à la… In the fashion of; in such-or-such a way or manner: coll.: late C. 19–20. 'He denied that he was trying to bring his entire family into politics *à la* So-and-So'. Such frequent use of the Fr. locution is certainly eligible; it owes its tardy inclusion here to the prompting of Mr Barry Prentice, my copious, generous, invaluable helper from Rodd Point, New South Wales.

A over T. See **arse over tip.**

A.P. The right procedure, the correct thing to do: Royal Naval College, Dartmouth: since ca. 1930. Granville. I.e. Ádmiralty pattern.

aap (or arp). See **zol.**

aar. See **ar.**

ab. An Aboriginal: Aus.: ca. 1870–1920; displaced by **abo** (p. 2). Alexander Macdonald, *In the Land of Pearl and Gold*, 1907, at p. 249.

Abadan. A 'driver using much oil' (*Railway*, 3rd, 1966): railwaymen's: since ca. 1960. Abadan, a town in S.W. Iran, is one of the world's chief oil-refining and -shipping centres.

abandonment. Bankruptcy of a railway company: financiers' and brokers': ca. 1880–1905. B. & L.

Abbeville Kids, the. Focke-Wulf pilots (or pilots and 'planes): R.A.F.: 1942; ob. by 1946. Partridge, 1945, 'Our airmen first met them over or near Abbeville and … like the Dead End Kids of cinematic fame, they have no very rosy future'.

Abbott's teeth. A ca. 1820–40 variant of **Ellenborough's teeth** (*Dict.*). Pierce Egan, *Life in London*, 1821. Cf. **Abbott's Priory** (*Dict.*).

abdabs, don't come—or, **give me**—**the old.** Don't tell me the tale: C. 20, esp. in 1939–45. Origin? By itself, *abdabs* was, in World War II, used occasionally for 'afters'.

abdabs, the screaming. An attack of *delirium tremens*: since late 1930's. Since ca. 1942, *abdabs* has been more gen. than *hab-dabs*.

abdar. A teetotaller: Anglo-Indian: from ca. 1870. B. & L. Ex Hindustani for a water-carrier.

abe, on one's. Indigent, very short of money: Australian: C. 20. B., 1942. Disguised rhyming s.

Aberdeen booster. See *Scotsman's fifth* at 'Hauliers' Slang'.

Abergavenny. A penny: rhyming: since ca. 1880. Rather: C. 20 and, by 1960, †.

abfab. 'They then looked real "abfab" (absolutely fabulous), another of our bodgie words' (Dick): Australian teenagers': since ca. 1955.

*abishag. Illegitimate child of a mother seduced by a married man: c.: from ca. 1860; slightly ob. B. & L. Ex Hebrew for 'the mother's error'.

abnormality; abnormeth. 'A person of crooked ways, an informer, a deformed or humpbacked person': sol.: resp. from ca. 1880 and ca. 1840–80. B. & L. By confusion of *abnormal* and *enormity*.

abominable 'no'-man, the. One who persists in failing to conform: since ca. 1955. A pun on 'the abominable *snow*-man'.

abortion, as in 'That hat's an abortion'—ludicrous, or very ugly: Australian: since late 1940's. (B.P.)

about as high. See **high as three pennyworth** …

*Abraham suit, on the. Engaged in any begging-letter dodge that will arouse sympathy: c.: from ca. 1860: ob. B. & L.

abram, v. To feign sickness: ? ca. 1840–90. *Sinks*, 1848. Perhaps rhyming s.

abroad.—2 (p. 2). Read: ca. 1810–90. *The London Guide*, 1818.

absoballylutely; absobloodylutely. Absolutely, utterly: late C. 19–20; C. 20. The former occurs in W. L. George, *The Making of an Englishman*,

1914 (p. 299), and both were, by 1940, rather ob. (With thanks to Mr R. W. Burchfield.)

absolute, an. An absolute certainty: coll.: C. 20; ob. Pugh. Cf. *moral*.

Aby, Aby, Aby my boy! Chanted, usually with the rest of the song: a Jew-baiting c.p.: ca. 1920–39.

Abyssinia! I'll be seeing you!: since mid-1930's. Michael Harrison, *Vernal Equinox*, 1939. By a pun.

ac. Accumulator: electricians': C. 20. Partridge, 1945.

Academite (p. 3): much earlier in W. N. Glascock, *Sailors and Saints*, 1829, at I, 167. Moe.

Academy.—4. A lunatic asylum: ca. 1730–90. Alexander Cruden in a pamphlet of 1754.

*acceleration. Starvation; esp. *die of acceleration*: vagrants' c.; from ca. 1880; ob. B. & L. Also **accelerator**, a Union relieving officer: id.: id. Ex refusals 'to give food to the dying outcast'.

accidentally on purpose (p. 3). Often *accidentally done* . . .

*accommodator. One who negotiates a compounding of felonies or other crimes: c.: from ca. 1870: ob. B. & L.

according to Hoyle. Correct; correctly: coll.: late C. 19–20. Ex Edmond Hoyle's *The Polite Gamester*, 1752; soon titled *Mr Hoyle's Games of Whist* . . . , 12th edition, 1760; then as *Hoyle's Games Improved*, 1786; in C. 19, there appeared innumerable re-editings, improvements, enlargements, abridgements. Cf. *according to Cocker* (p. 3).

ace, n.—3. A flagship or other 'key' vessel: Naval: since ca. 1930. Ex card-games.—4. Thomas Skeats, barrow-boy *loq.* (as reported in the *Daily Mail*, July 24, 1963), 'One bad peach—we call it an "ace"—turns the whole lot bad. We say, "Get that bleedin' ace out" ': barrow boys': since ca. 1920. (Also applied to any other fruit.) A singleton.

ace, adj. Excellent; 'star': coll.: from ca. 1932. *The Daily Express*, April 20, 1937, speaking of an orchestra: 'London's ace players improvising hot numbers'. John Winton, *H.M.S. Leviathan*, 1967, of its Naval—esp. its Fleet Air Arm—use, writes, 'The word "ace" meant anything superlative, desirable, well planned or well executed. "Dank" was its antonym and "fat" almost its synonym, meaning satisfied, ready, in a good or advantageous position.'

*ace, on one's. Alone: Aus. c.: since ca. 1930. Sidney J. Baker, *The Drum*, 1959. A *single* 'spot' on a playing card.

Ace, the. A flagship or other 'key vessel'; the escort *guards the ace*: Naval: 1939–45. (P-G-R.)

ace high. As high as possible: coll.: from ca. 1925. Alice Campbell, *Desire to Kill*, 1934, 'Ace-high in public esteem'. Ex. Adopted from U.S.

Ace, King, Queen, Jack. A jocular, non-Catholic description of the sign of the Cross: late C. 19–20.—2. A widow's pension: Naval: since ca. 1930. (P-G-R.)

acid. 'Heavy sarcasm; scornful criticism', Granville: Naval: C. 20. Cf. **acid, come the** (p. 3 end).—2. L.S.D., the psychedelic drug: Canadian: since 1966. (Leechman.) By 1967, also British, as in Alan Diment, *The Dolly Dolly Spy*, 1967. Whence, **acid-head**, a user thereof: Diment, 1967. Both of these terms occur also in Peter Fryer's 'A

Toz of "Zowie"' in *The Observer* colour supplement of Dec. 3, 1967.

acid, come the.—2. To wax sarcastic: Cockneys': C.20. *The Evening News*, March 7, 1938.

acid drop. A rating that's always either arguing or quarrelling or complaining: Naval: since ca. 1900. Granville.

acid (or squeaks) in, put the. See **put the acid in.**

acid on, put the.—2. To ask for a rise in wages: Australian and New Zealand: C. 20. B., 1942.

ack, n. An airman, especially an A.C.1 or an A.C.2: Cranwell (R.A.F. College): ca. 1920–30. (Group-Captain A. Wall, letter of March 3, 1945.) —2. Assistant: Army: 1940 +. Ex the initial.

ack, v. To acknowledge, e.g. a letter: Civil Service and gen. clerical: C. 20.

ack ack. Anti-aircraft (fire) guns: ca. 1939: signalese. Hence, *Ack-Ack*, A.A. Command: H. & P., 1943. *The Reader's Digest*, Feb. 1941, 'To avoid the "ack-acks" (anti-aircraft guns)'.

ack adj. Assistant adjutant. Army: 1940 +. (P-G-R.)

Ack and Quack. The A. & Q. (Adjutant and Quartermaster) Department: Army: since ca. 1925. (P-G-R.)

ack-Charlie. To *arse*-crawl; an *arse*-crawler; Services', esp. Army: since ca. 1939. Ex the signalese for *A.C.* (P-G-R.)

ack emma. Air mechanic: R.F.C. (1912–18), and R.A.F. (April–Dec. 1918). Jackson. The rank became, in Jan. 1919, aircraftman.

ack Willie. Absent without leave: Australian soldiers': 1939–45. (B., 1943.)

ackermaracker. Tea (the beverage): low: since ca. 1920. James Curtis, *They Drive by Night*, 1938. Origin? The form (acker-mar-acker) suggests *tea* reversed and distorted from *aet* to *ack*; *ack* elaborated to *acker*; and, with a swift *mar* interpolated, *acker* repeated.

ackers. A variant of *akkas*, q.v. at *akka*.

ackle. Esp. in 'It won't ackle': work, function: R.F.C.-R.A.F.: 1917–19. Ex *act*.

acquire. To steal; to obtain illicitly or deviously: Army euphemistic coll.: 1939–45. (P-G-R.)

acro. An acrobat: circus people's: late C. 19–20.

act, bung on an. See **bung on an act** below.

act bored, superior, etc. To behave as if bored, superior, etc.: Canadian, originally (ca. 1920) sol., but by 1955, coll. (Leechman.)

act Charley More. To act honestly; to do the fair thing. Naval: C.19–20. Granville. Charley More was a Maltese publican whose house sign bore the legend 'Charley More, the square thing'.

act the angora. To play the fool: Australian: C. 20. B., 1942. Elaboration of . . . *goat*.

act your age! Behave naturally, not as if you were much younger!: since ca. 1920.

acting dicky, 1 (p. 4), goes back to 1806: John Davis, *The Post-Captain*. (Moe.)

acting Jack. An acting sergeant: police: C. 20. (*The Free-Lance Writer*, April 1948.)

acting scran. 'Food substituted for that promised on the mess menu' (P-G-R.): Naval officers': since ca. 1920.

active tack. Active service: Guardsmen's: 1939+. (Roger Grinstead, *They Dug a Hole*, 1946.)

ad (p. 4), occurs two years earlier, *i.e.* in 1852, in

Household Words, V, 5/2. (With thanks to Mr R. W. Burchfield, editor of the new *O.E.D. Supplement*.) Mr Burchfield's team has now traced it back to 1841, when, on May 1 in *Britannia*, Thackeray used it. Cf. **advert** below.

ad(-)lib. To speak without a script, or to add extemporaneously to a script; in music, to improvise: coll.: adopted, in early 1930's, ex U.S. (Cf. **ad lib**: p. 4.)

Adam.—2. In full, *Adam and Eve*, to leave: rhyming s.: late C. 19–20. *The* (Birmingham) *Evening Despatch*, July 19, 1937. Also, to depart (hurriedly): rhyming s. on *leave*: since ca. 1920. (Franklyn, 2nd.)

Adam, not to know (someone) from. Not to know at all: coll.: mid-C. 18–20. *Sessions*, Feb. 1784 (p. 400).

Adam and Eve. *See* **Adam**, 2, above, and **Adam and Eve on a raft.**

Adam and Eve Ball. A Cinderella dance: since ca. 1925.

Adam and Eve on a raft (*Dict.*). Properly two poached eggs on toast, one egg being alone on a raft. In Canada, it is 'firmly entrenched as "short order" restaurant slang'. Leechman (1959).

Adam was an oakum-boy in Chatham Dockyard, when. See **when Adam . . .** in *Dict.*

Adamatical. Naked: C. 20. 'This', remarks one of my correspondents, 'is Standard English, but I can find no dictionary giving this definition'; neither can I, but then I classify it as jocularly erudite coll.—probably on the analogy of such words as *problematical* and *sabbatical*.

Adamising. A cadet's being lowered naked on to the parade ground at night, he being able to return only by presenting himself to the guard: Sandhurst: ca. 1830–55. Mockler-Ferryman, 1900.

add up, it doesn't. It fails to make sense: coll.: C. 20. An elaboration of **add** (p. 4). Atkinson.

*adept. A pickpocket; a conjuror: c.: C. 18. —2. An alchemist: c.: mid-C. 17–18. B. & U.

adj. (or **A.**), n. Adjutant; esp. *the Adj.*, one's adjutant: Army officers': C. 20. Blaker. Hence:

adj. (or **A.**), v. Army officers' s., from ca. 1910 as in Blaker, ' "Yes," said the Colonel. "You're all right. That's why I want you to Adj. for me." '

Adji, the, is the R.A.F.'s shape of **adj.** Partridge, 1945.

Adjie. An Adjutant: Australian: C. 20. B., 1942.

adjutant's at. 'A blonde member of the Auxiliary Territorial Service': Army: 1939–45. (P-G-R.)

Admin. Administration; administrative: Services' coll.: 1939 +. (P-G-R.)

Admiral.—2. One's Admiral is one's father: Eton: ca. 1800–50. (*Spy*, 1825.)

Admiral, the. The Officer-in-charge of R.A.F. Air/Sea Rescue boats. (H. & P.)

Admiral Browning. Human excrement: Naval: ca. C. 20. Personified colour.

admiral of the narrow seas (*Dict.*) goes back to before 1650: see 'Tavern terms', § 7.

Admiral's broom. 'Used humorously to give the Navy an equivalent of the Field Marshal's baton' (A. B. Petch, Aug. 22, 1946): coll.: C. 20. In March 1967 Mr Ramsey Spencer writes, 'This goes back to the Dutch Admiral Martin Tromp (the elder), who beat the English Fleet under Blake at

the Battle of Dungeness in Nov. 1652. The *Encyclopedia Britannica* says that the statement that he sailed up the Channel with a broom at his masthead in token of his ability to sweep the seas is probably mythical. I think it was Newbolt who wrote a song called "The Admiral's Broom" about the turn of this century.'

Admiral's Mate, the. 'A boastful, know-all rating': Navy: C. 20. Granville. Ironic.

Admiralty brown. Toilet paper: Australian Naval: since ca. 1910. Issue and colour.

Admiralty clown. A Naval physical-training instructor: Naval: since ca. 1945.

Admiralty-made coffin. An *A*rmed Merchant Cruiser; collectively, such ships formed *the Suicide Squadron*: Naval: late 1939–45. Many were sunk during the first two or three years of World War II. (Granville.)

*Adonee. God: c.: ? ca. 1550–1890; B. & L., vaguely classifying as 'old cant'. Ex the Hebrew.

Ados. *A*ssistant Director of Ordnance Services: military, not after 1942. (H. & P.)

adrift (p. 5), in the 'absent without leave' nuance, has, since ca. 1920, been current among R.A.F. regulars.—2. (Of a knot) undone: Navy: C. 20. Granville.

advert (p. 4 at **ad**) 'was used by J. Blackwood in 1860 (*Letters of George Eliot*, 1954, III, 244)': R. W. Burchfield in *The New Statesman*, March 17, 1967.

aerated, esp. as 'Don't get aerated!'—excited or angry: since ca. 1930. (A. B. Petch, April 1966.)

aerial coolies. Those airmen who dropped supplies to the Chindits in Burma: Army and R.A.F.: 1943–5. (P-G-R.)

aerial ping-pong. Australian Rules Football: Sydneysiders': since ca. 1950. Mostly in ref. to the game in Victoria. (B.P.)

aeroplanes. A bow tie: Australian: since ca. 1938. B., 1942.

Ætna. 'A small boiler for "brewing" ': Winchester: from ca. 1860; ob. B. & L.

affair.—2. Male or female genitals: C. 19–20; if used euphemistically, it is ineligible, but if used lazily the term is s.

affluence of incohol, esp. **under the . . .** The influence of alcohol: jocularly intentional spoonerism: Australian since late 1950's. (B.P.) But Australia owes it to 'the legion of North Country comedians who have used the phrase in their "drunk" sketches for years': David Holloway in *The Daily Telegraph* on Feb. 23, 1967.

affluent society, the. In 1958 Professor J. K. Galbraith published his book so titled and almost immediately the phrase became a c.p., both in Britain and in the U.S.A. By some people, the *un*-thinkers, it has been held to synonymize 'the welfare state'; by many, to be basically optimistic, whereas, in the fact, the book is only mildly so. (William Safire, *The New Language of Politics*, New York, 1968.)

affygraphy, to an (p. 5). The phrase *in an affygrafy*, as Dr Leechman has pointed out, may have been influenced by (*in*) *half a jiffy*. It occurs much earlier in *The Night Watch* (II, 85), 1828. (Moe.)

Africa speaks. Strong liquor from South Africa: Australian and New Zealand: C. 20. B., 1941 and 1942. In *The Drum*, 1959, B. defines it as 'cheap fortified wine'.

African. 'A tailor-made cigarette' (Baker, *The Drum*, 1959): Aus.: since late 1940.

African harp. See **fish-horn**.

aft. Afternoon as in 'this aft'. Mostly lower-middle class: C. 20. Also Canadian: since ca. 1910. (Brian Moore, *The Luck of Ginger Coffey*, 1960.)

aft, carry both sheets. To walk around with both hands in trouser pockets: Navy: C. 20. Granville. By a technical pun.

aft, get. To be promoted from the lower-deck to the rank of officer: Naval coll.: C. 19–20. Granville, 'The officers' quarters are in the after-part of the ship'.

aft through the hawse-hole. (Of an officer) that has gained his commission by promotion from the lower-deck: Navy: mid-C. 19–20. Granville. See **hawse-holes . . .**, p. 381.

aft, to be taken. To go, as a defaulter, before the Commander: Naval coll.: C. 20. Granville.

after. Afternoon: Aus.: C. 20. (Cf. *afto*) H. Drake Brockman, *The Fatal Days*, 1947, 'Did you see Mr Scrown this after, Les?'. A much earlier example occurs in Edward Dyson, *Fact'ry 'Ands*, 1906. (With thanks to Mr R. W. Burchfield.)

after Davy. See **Alfred Davy** (*Dict.*).

after game, come the. To say, 'I told you so': Australian coll.: since ca. 1925. B., 1942.

after his end (or **hole**), **he is** or **was**, etc. A workmen's c.p., applied to a man 'chasing' a girl: C. 20.

after you, Claude—no, after you, Cecil! A c.p. since ca. 1940; by the end of 1946 slightly ob. Ex the B.B.C. programme 'Itma'. E.P. 'Those Radio Phrases' in the *Radio Times*, Dec. 6, 1946, an article reprinted in *Words at War: Words at Peace*, 1948.

after you, Claude. The Canadian version—by May 1959, slightly ob.—is *after you, my dear Alphonse—no, after you, Gaston*. (Leechman.)

after you with (the thing). A jocular rejoinder to *fuck the . . .!*: c.p.: C. 20.

after you with the trough! A c.p. addressed to someone who has belched and implying that he is a pig and has eaten too fast: North Country: since ca. 1930. (David Wharton.)

afterbirth. Rhubarb: Australian soldiers': 1939–45. B., 1943.

afto. Afternoon: Australian: since ca. 1920. B., 1942.

Ag and Fish. See **Min. of Ag.** below.

-age. A beatnik suffix, as in *dressage* (clothes)—*understandage* (understanding)—*workage* (employment): since ca. 1959. (Anderson.)

agent. To act as literary agent for (an author or his work): authors' coll.: since ca. 1930. (E. C. R. Lorac, *Death before Dinner*, 1942.)

agents, have one's. To be well-informed: Army and Air Force: since ca. 1939. Rohan D. Rivett, *Behind Bamboo*, 1946; E. P., *Forces' Slang* (1939–45), 1948. With an allusion to secret agents.

Aggie. Sense 1 occurs earlier in 'Taffrail'.

aggie. A marble made of agate—or of something that, in appearance, resembles agate: children's: since ca. 1880. *The Manchester Evening News*, March 27, 1939.

Aggie-on-a-horse. H.M.S. *Weston-super-Mare*: Navy: C. 20. Granville. 'Weston' evokes the 'Aggie' implicit in:—

Aggie Weston's. The Agnes Weston Sailors' Home: nautical: late C. 19–20. Cf.:—

Aggie's. A Sailor's Rest House: Navy: C. 20. 'These Rest Houses were founded by the late Dame Agnes Weston—the "Mother of the Navy"—at Portsmouth and Devonport' (Granville). See **Aggie** (p. 6) and cf. entry preceding this one.

aggranoy or **agronoy; aggrovoke** or **agrovoke.** To annoy; to irritate: Australian: since ca. 1920. B., 1942. The former, however, is also Cockney of ca. 1880 +. Blend of *aggravate*, *annoy* and *provoke*.

aggy. 'A grouser': Naval: C. 20. Perhaps ex 'agony column'.

Agincourt. Achicourt, near Arras: 1914–18 military. Blaker.

agreement, three nines. See **three nines agreement** (*Dict.*).

agricultural one. See **do a rural.**

aid of ?, what's this (occ. **that**) **in.** Esp. of something unexpected or surprising: what does this mean?—why?—a reference to *what* precisely?: c.p.: since ca. 1916. Originating, I believe, in those Flag Days which began during the war of 1914–18.

aidh. Butter: Shelta: C. 18–20. B. & L.

Ailsa (p. 6). More probably from Ailsa Craig, an island in the Firth of Forth.

ainoch. Thing: Shelta: C. 18–20. Ibid.

ain't ain't grammar. A c.p. used jocularly in correcting someone saying *ain't*: since ca. 1920.

ain't it a treat. A street: rhyming s.: from ca. 1870. Pugh (2): 'Bits of him all up an' down the ain't-it-a-treat as fur as the old "Glue Pot".'

air, in the. Without support: Army coll.: 1940 +. (P-G-R.)

air, lay on. To obtain, to provide, air support: Army, mostly, but also R.A.F.: 1940–45. (P-G-R.)

air, on the. By radio or wireless: since ca. 1935: coll.>, ca. 1955, familiar S.E. 'I heard it on the air.'

air and exercise.—4. A short term in gaol: Australian: C. 20. B., 1942. Ex 2.

air commode. Air Commodore: R.A.F. s.: since ca. 1925. Jackson. By the 'Hobson-Jobson' process.

air disturber. A telegraphist rating: Navy: since ca. 1930. Granville.

Air House, the. The Air Ministry: R.A.F. officers': since ca. 1919. Jackson. On the analogy of the **War House.**

air pie and a walk round. A clerk's lunch: from ca. 1880.

Air Works, the. The Royal Air Force: R.A.F.: since ca. 1935. 'Not contemptuous' (Atkinson).

airing, take an. To go out as a highwayman: C. 18. Anon., *A Congratulatory Epistle from a Reformed Rake upon Prostitutes*, 1728.

airmaids. Crew of the Air/Sea Rescue boats. H. & P.

airmen of the shufty. Airmen of the Watch (in the Watch Tower on the Station): R.A.F.: since ca. 1938. Jackson. See **shufty.**

airs and graces.—2. Braces (for trousers): not very common rhyming s.: C. 20.

Airships, their. The Air Council: R.A.F.: 1947 +. 'Peterborough' in *The Daily Telegraph*, Sept. 11, 1947. A skit on the Navy's *their Lordships*, the various 'Lords' at the Admiralty.

Airy-fairies. (Large) feet: Cockney: C. 20.

The Evening News, Nov. 20, 1937. Cf. **airy-fairy** in *Dict.*

airyard matey. A civilian mechanic in a Naval Air Station: Naval: 1940 +. (P-G-R.)

ajay. An amateur journalist: schools of authorship and journalism: since ca. 1920.

akka (p. 7). Indeed, since 1914–18 and perhaps since late C. 19. In the pl. *akkas*, it = money, 'cash'; in this sense it reached the regulars in the R.A.F. by 1925 at the latest (Jackson).—2. Hence, a Palestinian piastre: Services: since ca. 1920.

ala kefak, I'm. 'I'm easy' (see *easy*, adj., 2): Army, in Near and Middle East: since ca. 1940. Arabic.

alarm and despondency. War-time depression: 1940 +. Ex speech by Sir Winston Churchill, K.G. Esp (to) *spread a. and d.* In reference to early 1942: 'I was pressed to return urgently to the theatre of my operations and to prepare myself to spread "alarm and despondency" (an expression that was just then coming into fashion),' Vladimir Peniakoff, *Private Army,* 1950: Army, hence the Navy and the R.A.F., mostly among officers; since 1945, reminiscent and usually jocular. 'Popski' records (p. 128) that on May 18, 1942, 'a message came on the wireless for me. It said: "SPREAD ALARM AND DESPONDENCY".'

alarm bird. Kookaburra: Australian. C. 20.

albatross. A hole played in 3 under bogey: golfers', adopted in 1933 ex U.S. (cf. 'birdie', 1 below, and 'eagle', 2 below, bogey). *The Evening News,* Aug. 13, 1937.

Albert the Great. Albert Chevalier, the London music-halls' brightest male star of ca. 1891–1910: since ca. 1892. Prompted by *Albert the Good,* Queen Victoria's Consort.

alberts. 'Toe-rags as worn by dead-beats and tramps of low degree', B., 1942: Australian: C.20. Worn instead of socks; with pun on **albert** (p. 7).

alc. Alcohol: from ca. 1930. (Not very gen.)

alderman.—6. A prominent belly: ca. 1890–1940. So many aldermen used to have one.

alderman's eyes. (House) flies: rhyming s.: since ca. 1890; by 1960, ob. (Franklyn 2nd.)

Aldershot ladies. A double four at darts: darts players': C. 20.—2. A forty-four (44: two 4's) at tombola—or house (housey-housey), a military version of lotto—or bingo, a social version of house: resp. C. 20; C. 20; since ca. 1950. A double 4, via the rhyming allusion *two whores—Aldershot ladies* (of easy virtue).

Alec.—2. Hence, a dupe, esp. a swindler's dupe: Australian: since ca. 1925. B., 1942. Ironically derived from *smart Alec.*

alemnoch. Milk: Shelta: C. 18–20. B. & L.

alert! 'Officer or N.C.O. approaching' (H. & P.): Services: since ca. 1939. Ex the air-raid warning.

Alex.—2. Field Marshal Lord Alexander, C.B., D.S.O., M.C. (etc.): 1940 +. This very great general, far less famous than he deserves to be, always commanded the respect and affection of his men.—3. A fool, a dupe: Australian: since ca. 1930. (Margaret Trist, 1946.)

'alf a mo' (p. 8). Extant: cf. B., 1943.

Algy. Seaweed, sludge or refuse in Swan River, Perth: West Australian: C. 20. B., 1942. The pun is on *algae.*

Ali. Inevitable nickname of men surnamed *Barber*: C. 20. (L. J. Cunliffe, *Having It Away,* 1965.) Ex '*Ali Baba* and the Forty Thieves'.

alibi.—2. Hence, merely an excuse: since ca. 1935. A slovenliness from the U.S.

Alice (p. 8) comes from 'Alice, where art thou?' because hard to find. (Alexander McQueen.)

Alice.—2. *The Alice*: Alice Springs: Australian coll.: late C. 19–20. Archer Russell, *A Tramp Royal in Wild Australia,* 1934.

Alice Springs, via. 'Where have you been all this time? Did you go *via* Alice Springs?' = by a devious route: Australian since ca. 1945. This town—Nevil Shute's *A Town Like Alice,* 1950—is, roughly, in the centre of Australia. (B.P.)

Alick. Variant (B., 1943) of **Alec**, 4.

alive and kicking; all-alive-o. Rather, since ca. 1840, the latter. Mayhew, I, 1851. The former goes back to early C. 19. It occurs in, e.g., W. N. Glascock, *Sailors and Saints,* 1829, at II, 22, 'And there she [a ship] is, all alive and kicking.' Moe.

alive or dead. Head: rhyming s.: ? late C. 19–20. (Franklyn, *Rhyming.*)

all about, adj. phrase in the predicate. Alert; very efficient: mostly Navy: C. 20. (John Irving, *Royal Navalese,* 1946.)

all ballsed-up. Bungled; confused; wrong: Australian: adopted, ca. 1944, ex U.S. servicemen. Cf. **balls-up** below.

all behind, like a fat woman, or **like Barney's bull.** See **Barney's bull** and **fat woman.** But also, in brief, *all behind,* applied esp. to fat-bottomed charwomen all behind with their work: C. 20.

all behind in Melbourne. 'Broad in the beam': West Australian: C. 20. B., 1942.

all bum. A street c.p. applied, ca. 1860–1900, to a woman wearing a large bustle. B. & L.

all callao (or **callo**), on p. 8, comes perhaps ex *alcohol.*

all cando (p. 8). Perhaps from *all white,* rhyming s. for *right*; by pun on L. *candid*us, white.

all chiefs and no Indians; occ. elaborated to *. . . like the University Regiment.* All officers and no Other Ranks: Australian c.p.; the longer, mostly Sydneyites': since ca. 1940. (B.P.)

all clear. A c.p. indicating that officers and N.C.O.s have gone: Services: since 1939. H. & P. Cf. **alert.**

all day, or **yes, all day.** A c.p. reply to a query about the date: C.20. 'Is today the 10th?'—'(Yes,) all day'.

all dolled up like a barber's cat. Dressed resplendently: Canadian: C. 20. (Leechman.)

all done by—or **with-mirrors,** often preceded by *it's.* A c.p. uttered when something clever has been done: since ca. 1920. It presumably originated among stage magicians.

all dressed up and nowhere to go (p. 8). The American form would, of course, have been *. . . no place . . .*

all ends up. See **ends up, all** (*Dict.*).

all for it, be. To be entirely in favour of it; hence, over-keen. Naval coll.: C. 20; by 1925, at latest, general coll.

all g.y. All awry or askew: since ca. 1942.

all hot and bothered. Very agitated, excited, or nervous: coll.: from ca. 1920. *The Times,* Feb. 15, 1937, in leader on this dictionary. Ex the physical and emotional manifestations of haste.

all in a pucker. Agitated. See **pucker** (*Dict.*).

all jam and Jerusalem. A derogatory c.p., directed at Women's Institutes: since ca. 1925. Ex the combination of refreshments and piety.

'Perhaps not so much "piety", as the fact that

Blake's "Jerusalem" is sung at every meeting—probably less from pious intentions than as a signature-tune. And not the refreshments, but the jam-making contests. This is from personal observation; my wife was a member, and I have addressed W.I. meetings a couple of times.' (Ramsey Spencer, March 1967.)

all jelly. See jelly.

all K.F.S. All correct and complete: R.N.A.S.: 1914–18. (S/Ldr. R. Raymond, letter of March 24, 1945.) I.e. knife, fork and spoon.

all kind. All kinds: sol.: C. 19–20. Walking in London, W.C.2, on April 7, 1937, I saw a horse-driven cart bearing the legend, *All kind of old iron wanted.*

all laired (or **mockered**) **up.** Flashily dressed: Australian: late C. 19–20. (Cf. lair and mockered.) Also . . . *lared* . . .

all languages. Bad language: coll.: ca. 1800–40. *Sessions*, Dec. 1809.

all manner. All kinds of things, 'things' usually being made specific to suit the context: lower classes' coll.: from ca. 1870. Nevinson, 1895, 'Through its bein' a boy, there didn't seem nothink necessary to call it. So we called it all manner, and out of all its names', etc.

all mouth. See all jaw (*Dict.*).

all my eye and Betty Martin (p. 9). In *The Phoenician Origin of Britons, Scots, and Anglo-Saxons*, 1914, Dr L. A. Waddell derives the phrase from *o mihi, Brito Martis*, 'Oh (bring help) to me, Brito Martis'. She was the tutelary goddess of Crete, and her cult was that of, or associated with, the sun-cult of the Phœnicians, who so early traded with the Britons for Cornish tin. (I owe the reference to Mr Albert B. Petch.)

All Nations. See Bell and Horns.

all-nighter. 'Prostitutes still classify their clients as "short-timers" and "all-nighters"' (John Gosling & Douglas Warner, *The Shame of a City*, 1960): late C. 19–20.

all of a hough (p. 9). Sense 2 occurs, as *all of a hoo*, in W. N. Glascock, *The Naval Sketch-book*, II, 1829, and as *all ahoo* in *The Night Watch* (II, 85), 1828. (Moe.)

all of a tiswas (or **tizwas**). Very much excited; utterly confused in mind; since early 1940's, esp. in R.A.F. Cf. tizzy, n., 2 (below).

All Old Crocks; or Angels of Christ. Army Ordnance Corps: military: 1914–18. An elaboration of the official abbreviation, *A.O.C.*

all on one's lonesome. See lonesome.

all on the go. Intensified *on the go*, q.v. in *Dict.* at go, on the.

all out, 1 (p. 9), goes back to C. 14. (O.E.D.)

all over, be. To be dead: lower-class coll.: 1898, Edwin Pugh, *Tony Drum.*

all over the auction. 'All over the place': Cockney and Australian: since ca. 1910. (K. S. Prichard, *Haxby's Circus*, 1930.)

all parts bearing an equal strain. A Naval c.p. =All's well; no complaints: since ca. 1930. Granville.—2. Lying down (comfortably): jocular: since ca. 1945. (Peter Sanders.)

all pills! See pills!, all.

all pissed-up and nothing to show. A working-class c.p. directed at one who has spent all his wages, or winnings, on drink: since ca. 1910.

all plopa. Quite right; correct: pidgin: mid-C. 19–20. B. & L.

all revved-up. See revved-up below.

all right. Virtuous: coll.: late C. 19–20. W. B. Maxwell, *Hill Rise*, 1908.

all right for you. Ironical to those worse off than oneself: Services: since 1940. H. & P.

all rounder, 2 (p. 9). Also in J. B., *Scenes from the Lives of Robson and Redpath*, 1857.

all same. All the same; like; equal: pidgin: mid-C. 19–20. B. & L.

all serene. Earlier in *Sessions*, April 8, 1952: policeman *loq.*, 'He said, "It is all serene"—that means calm, square, beautiful'. 'In Spanish towns, a night-watchman was employed in each street to prevent thieving and to call the hours and the state of the weather, in that climate for much of the year "sereno"—from which familiar call he got his name. His modern counterpart has the house-door keys for his street, so that he can admit residents returning home after the concierge has gone to bed, and who call for his services by clapping their hands....Could Gibraltar (captured by us in 1704, thanks to the foresight of S. Pepys) be the channel through which "all serene" reached Eng., especially as Eng. night-watchmen of the period were used to calling e.g. "One o' the clock, and all's well"?' (Ramsey Spencer, March 1967.)

all(-)shapes. 'Lacking regularity of form. The lino-layer says the room is all-shapes, hence he must cut a lot to waste; the electrician fitting numerous short lengths of conduit at odd angles says the wall is all-shapes' (Julian Franklyn): coll.: late C. 19–20.

all smart. Everything's all right: Army: C. 20; ob. by 1940, virtually † by 1945.

All Souls' Parish Magazine. *The Times*: University of Oxford: ca. 1920–40. Christopher Hobhouse, *Oxford*, 1939, says that the Editor and his associates, who were Fellows of the College, often met there in order to discuss policy.

all standing, brought up. Unable to deal with a situation: Naval coll.: C. 19–20. Granville.

all-standing, sleep (or **turn-in**), is recorded as early as 1818 (*sleep*) and 1806 (*turn in*): resp. Alfred Burton and John Davis. (Moe.) The origin is explained in this quotation from Frederick Chamier, *The Life of a Sailor*, 1832, at II, 296: 'This awoke me . . . As I had my clothes on, having turned in "all standing", like a trooper's horse, I was on deck on a second': a horse can sleep standing up.

all taut. Prepared for anything: Naval: C. 20. Granville. Ex:—2. Everything ready: Naval coll.: late C. 19–20.

all that, not. Mostly with 'bad' or 'good', as in 'Seen a lot of people lately, and my memory isn't all that' (good), E. C. R. Lorac, *Death Came Softly*, 1943: working-class, esp. Cockney, coll.: since ca. 1910.

all that jazz. All that sort of thing: c.p.: since ca. 1958. Orig., among jazz-lovers.

all the . . . In the game of House, 'double numbers such as "fifty-five", are called thus: "all the fives"', Michael Harrison, *Reported Safe Arrival*, 1943: late C. 19–20: coll., almost j.

all the better for seeing you! A c.p. reply to 'How are you?': late C. 19–20.

all the go (p. 10) goes back to ca. 1780. Charles Dibdin in *The Britannic Magazine* (I, No. 3, p. 34), 1793, 'Thus be we sailors all the go'. (Moe.)

all the shoot is an occ. variant of *the whole shoot*, q.v. at shoot, the whole in *Dict.*

all the traffic will bear, often preceded by *that's*,

a c.p., relating to fares: Canadian: adopted, ca. 1948, ex U.S.; by 1955, also English. Said to derive from a U.S. magnate's cynicism. (Leechman.)

all the year round. A twelve-months' prison sentence: Australian: since ca. 1925. (B., 1943.)

all there. Also applied to 'one with his whole thought directed to the occasion, *totus in illis*, as Horace says, and so at his best' (*Notes and Queries*, April 24, 1937): coll.: from ca. 1885.

all things (or everything) to all men and nothing (or not anything) to one man. A c.p. aimed at prostitutes or at promiscuous women: since ca. 1940.

all tickettyboo. See tickettyboo.

all tits and teeth. (Of a woman) having protrusive breasts and large teeth: a low c.p.: C. 20.—2. (Of a woman) having an artificial smile and considerable skill in mammary display: a low, mostly Cockney, c.p.: since ca. 1910. 'I have sometimes heard this amplified: ". . . like a third-row chorus girl", i.e. one who can neither sing nor dance, and who depends upon the display of her exceptional physique to keep her on the stage' (Ramsey Spencer, March 1967).

all to cock. Utterly confused, all mixed up. Services': since ca. 1925. (P-G-R.)

all U.P. See **U.P.** in *Dict.*

all-upper. 'A punter who bets "all-up" on a number of races': Australian: since ca. 1910. (B., 1943.)

all up with. The nuance 'utterly exhausted, virtually defeated'—e.g. in boxing—occurs in *Boxiana*, I, 1818. *It's all up* occurs in vol. III, 1821. The sense 'doomed to die' appears in *Sessions*, July 3, 1843. The former nuance occurs in, e.g., W. N. Glascock, *Sailors and Saints*, 1829, at I, 186, 'Well, you know, 'twas bad enough afore —But 'twas not all up with us.' (Moe.)

all wet. 'Silly, foolish' (S. J. Baker, *The Drum*, 1959): mostly Aus.: since ca. 1920.

all wind and piss. A contemptuous c.p.: (probably) C. 19–20. Ex the semi-proverbial C. 18–20 *like the barber's cat, all . . .*

all wool and a yard wide. Utterly good and honest (person): late C. 19–20. Ex drapery.

all ye in: 'Schoolboys' call when school is going in from play or when players in game must gather' (Atkinson): C. 20.

allacompain. Variant of alacompain (p. 7).

allee samee (p. 10). More accurately: 'identical with' or 'similar to' or 'like'. It originated on the China coast.

alleluia. See hallelujah.

alleluia! 'A call to shut the tap when boiler washing' (*Railway*, 2nd): railwaymen's: since ca. 1920.

alleviator (p. 10) was still extant in Australia during the 1940's. (B., 1943.)

alley.—3. A two-up school: Australian: C. 20. (B., 1943.)

alley, (right) up one's. One's concern, applied to what one knows or can do very well: coll.: since ca. 1905. Deliberate variation of . . . *street*.—2. Hence, since ca. 1910, applied to something delightful.

alley up. To pay one's share: Australian: C. 20. B., 1942. Ex the game of marbles.

allez oop! Up with you: C. 20. (Pamela Branch, *The Wooden Overcoat*, 1951.) 'Also used by acrobats when one of them has to be thrown high. First heard in childhood, ca. 1895' (Leechman).

alligator. See 'Canadian'. 3. Later: rhyming s.: C. 20. (Franklyn, *Rhyming*.)—4. A horse: Australian: since ca. 1925. (B., 1943.)

alligator bull. 'Nonsense, senseless chatter' (B., 1942): Australian: since ca. 1920. There are no alligators in N. Australia: cf. **bull**, n., 12 (*Dict.*).

allo. All; every: pidgin Eng.: mid-C. 19–20. '*O* is added to many words in pidgin in an arbitrary manner,' B. & L.

allow me! Allow me to congratulate you: Rugby Schoolboys': from ca. 1880.

all's quiet in the Shipka Pass or **on the Western Front.** See **Western Front.**

*ally-beg. Comfort of a bed; a comfortable bed: c.: C. 18–20; ob. B. & L. Prob. = 'pleasant little bed'.

Ally Pally. Alexandra Palace, London (was H.Q. of television): 1937 +. Earlier is the sense 'Alexandra Park race-course'.

ally slope, do an. To make off: C. 20. Eustace Jarvis, *Twenty-Five Years in Six Prisons*, 1925. A fusion of ally and **Ally Sloper's Cavalry** (see p. 10).

Ally Sloper's Cavalry (p. 10). The name *Ally Sloper* probably contains a pun on Fr. *allez!*, go, and E. *slope*, to make off, to go away.

Alma Gray. A threepenny piece: Australian: C. 20. B., 1942. Rhyming on **tray**, 2 (p. 908).

almighty. Grand; impressive: proletarian coll. verging on sol.: mid-C. 19–20. Nevinson, 1895, makes a Shadwellite describe a picture having 'somethink almighty about it'.

almighty dollar, the (p. 10) occurs earlier in Alfred R. Smith, *To China and Back*, 1859 (p. 44). (Moe.)

almond. Penis: mostly Cockneys': from ca. 1890. An abbr. of **almond rock**, rhyming s. for the same since ca. 1880: on **cock**.

alone on a raft is one poached egg on toast, *Adam and Eve on a raft* (p. 4) is two: C. 20.

Alphabetical. Nickname for anyone with more than two initials to his surname: Services': since ca. 1930. (P-G-R.)

Alphonse. A 'ponce': rhyming s.: C. 20. Jim Phelan, *Letters from the Big House*, 1943.

Alps, the. The 'Carlisle to Stranraer line' (*Railway*, 3rd): railwaymen's: since late 1940's. It has some steep gradients.

altitude, grabbing for.—2. Orig., however, striving for height: R.A.F.: since ca. 1925. In 1939–45 it was used with the connotation 'in order to gain an advantage in an aerial combat': Partridge, 1945.

Altmark, the. 'A ship or a Shore Establishment in which discipline is exceptionally severe': Naval: 1942 +. Granville, 'From the German Prison Ship of that name'.

always in trouble like a Drury Lane whore. A late C. 19–20 c.p. 'stigmatising either self-pity or successive misfortunes to an individual' (Atkinson).

am and **is** used jocularly. 'There are some jocular and ungrammatical uses of these, as "There you is", "There you am" and "That am so"' (A. B. Petch, April 1966): since ca. 1930. Cf. used to was below.

amateur, or **enthusiastic amateur.** A girl that frequently, promiscuously copulates 'for love': coll.: since ca. 1916.

ambidextrous. Both hetero- and homosexual: since ca. 1935. Cf. **AC-DC** above.

ambulance chasers. A disreputable firm of

solicitors specialising in accident claims: adopted ca. 1940 from U.S.A.

ameche. See 'Canadian'. Adopted from U.S. where current since early 1945. Ex a film in which that actor (pron. am-ee-chee) appeared in 1944–45. The film portrayed the life of Alexander Graham Bell, inventor of the telephone.

ameri-can. An *American* petrol *can*: Army: 1942–45. Punning *American* and formed after **jerrican.** (P-G-R.)

American Workhouse, the. The Park Lane Hotel, London: taxi-drivers': since 1917. Herbert Hodge, *Cab, Sir?*, 1939. Ironic: palatial, it caravanserai's many rich Americans.

ammiral. See **admiral** (*Dict.*).

ammunition.—2. A sanitary pad or towel; such pads or towels collectively: feminine: since ca. 1940. Cf. the 1939–45 c.p., adopted from the song, 'Praise the Lord and pass the ammunition'.

Amorous Military Gentlemen on Tour. The personnel of AMGOT: military and political: 1945–7.

amp.—2. An 'amputee': Canadian (medical and hospital): since ca. 1946.—3. An ampère: electricians' coll.: since ca. 1910.

'Ampsteads or 'Ampstids, i.e. *Hampsteads*. See **Hampstead Heath** (p. 370). '*Ampstids*' is the 'deep Cockney' form. (Michael Harrison, letter of Jan. 4, 1947.)

*****ampster or amster or Amsterdam.** A confidence trickster's confederate: Australian: since ca. 1925. B., 1942. Short for some rhyming s. term? Perhaps, however, in ref. to Amsterdam as a market for stolen jewellery and for precious stones.—No! It rhymes on *ram*, 3, as Franklyn, *Rhyming*, has noted.

amput. See 'Prisoner-of-War slang', 12.

amscray. To depart, make off: Australian: adopted, ca. 1944, ex U.S. servicemen. (Ruth Park, *A Power of Roses*, 1953.) American centre s. on *scram*.

an cetera. Et cetera: sol.: late C. 19–20. Blaker. Cf. *et cet*, q.v.

analken. To wash: Shelta: C. 18–20. B. & L.

analt. To sweep (with broom): id.: id. Ibid.

anarchists. 'Matches, especially wax vestas' (B., 1942): Australian: C. 20. Apt to 'blow up'.

anarchists.—2. (As *the anarchists*.) Battalion or brigade or divisional bombers (mortar-throwers): Army: 1915–18. Ian Hay, *Carrying On*, 1917.

anarf = *an'alf* = *a half*, i.e. ten shillings, the half of £1: London's East End: since ca. 1945. Likewise, *arfundred* = £50. (Richard Herd in *The Evening News*, Nov. 12, 1957.)—2. 'Also a halfpenny. I was told of it in London while at home on leave in 1917. Somebody was told the bus fare was "one anarf"—that is, three ha'pence' (Leechman).

anca. A man; a husband or sweetheart: low: C. 19. Price Warung, *Tales*, 1897 (p. 58). Ex Greek *anèr*.

anchor. 'A parachutist who waits overlong before jumping' (Jackson): R.A.F.: since ca. 1930. As though he were anchor-prevented from sailing the empyrean.—2. Also *old anchor*. A pick: Navy: 1868, Tom Taylor, *The Ticket of Leave Man*. Ex shape.—3. See 'Hauliers' slang'. Has, since ca. 1950, been gen. s. in Australia—and always in plural. (B.P.)

anchor, drop the. To apply the brakes: busmen's: from ca. 1930. The Regional wireless

programme, Nov. 23, 1936. See also **anchors** in the *Dict.*

anchor one's stern. To sit down: Naval: C. 20. Granville. See **stern**, p. 828.

anchors!, soon commoner than the orig. **whoa, anchors!**, a request to the driver of a vehicle to stop; hence to a speaker to stop, so that a point may be dealt with: R.A.F.: since late 1940's.

ancient and modern. A hymn-book, as in 'Lend me your ancient and modern': coll.: C. 20. Ex *Hymns, Ancient and Modern*.

Ancient and Tattered Airmen. The Air Transport Auxiliary pilots' name for themselves: 1939 +.

ancient mariners.—2. 'Seagulls, said to possess the souls of dead mariners' (P-G-R.): Naval: late C. 19–20.

Ancient Military Gentlemen on Tour. Variant of **Amorous Military Gentlemen on Tour.**

and omitted. A post-W.W.II colloquialism. Dr Douglas Leechman, in April 1967, comments thus: 'An Americanism that has spread deep into Canada. "Go feather your nest." "Come see Jimmy swim." "Go tell him hello." "Come have a drink."'

and all that (p. 12) seems, ca. 1810–30 (if not for a much longer period), to have been coll., to judge by its use in *Boxiana*, IV, 1824, at p. 74.

and like it! 'A naval expression anticipating a grouse and added to any instruction for an awkward and unwanted job,' H. & P.: since ca. 1930.

and no flies. And no doubt about it: low c.p. tag: ca. 1840–60. Mayhew, I, 1851.

and no messing about. A low intensive: since ca. 1930. 'You can lose half a streatch remishion and no messing about' (Norman). Cf. *and no error*, q.v. at *mistake, and no*, on p. 524.

and no mogue (p. 13). Probably *mogue* represents the Fr. *moquerie*: cf. the synonymous Fr. *moque* (C. 15–16). More prob., as Mr H. R. Spencer of Camberley, Surrey, has proposed, ex the German underworld and Gypsies' *mogeln* (long *o*, which would phonetically explain the -*ue*) —coming into Eng. via Yiddish.

and one, or simply **one, for the road.** A C. 20 (orig. commercial travellers') c.p., applied to the last of several drinks I.e. to keep one warm on the journey.

and then some. See **some, and then** in the *Dict.*

and you too! A C. 20 c.p. addressed to a person suspected of silent recrimination, insult unexpressed. In the Forces it has, since ca. 1915, presupposed an unvoiced *fuck you!* Sometimes shortened to *and you!*

Andrew. Sense 4. not always *the Andrew*: 'Taffrail' has 'Terms . . . heard every day in "Andrew", as the bluejacket calls the Navy.'—1. (p. 13). In the original Greek, it signifies 'man'.

Andrew, the. The Royal Navy: Naval: since ca. 1860. (P-G-R.) Cf. *Andrew*, 2, on p. 13.

Andrew Mack. The frigate *Andromache*: Naval: 1834, W. N. Glascock, *Sketch-Book*, 2nd Series, II, 62. (Moe.) A good example of 'Hobson-Jobson'.

Andrew Millar (or -**er**), 2 (p. 13). 'A notorious Press-gang "tough" who shanghaied so many victims into the Navy that the sailors of the period thought it belonged to him' (Granville).

Andy McNish. Fish: C. 20. Franklyn, *Rhyming*, 'Either raw or fried'.

angel. Sense 3 is earlier than I had supposed: it occurs in 'Taffrail' (Feb. 1916).—5. (Also *angie*.)

Cocaine: Australian: since ca. 1925. B., 1942.

angel suit. A variant of **angel's suit** (*Dict.*).

Angelica (p. 13). Slightly earlier in *Sinks*, 1848.

angels as used by the R.A.F., in ref. to height, is j., not unconventional: and *angel upward*, 'to gain height' (*The Reader's Digest*, Feb. 1941), if ever (1940–1) current, soon gave way to S.E. *climb* and s. *to go* (or *come*) *upstairs*.

Angels of Christ. See **All Old Crocks.**

*****angie.** Cocaine: Australian c.: from ca. 1925. Why?—2. See **angel,** 5.

angler.—3. See **lens louse.**

Anglo-Indian back, have an. (Of a girl) to have dead leaves adhering to the back of her dress as she returns from a stroll: Canadian: since ca. 1908.

angora. See **act the angora.**

angry man; up with the angry men or **where the angry men are; see an angry bullet.** A serviceman, esp. a soldier, in a battle area; in the battle area; to do service in one: among Australian servicemen in New Guinea: 1942–5. (B., 1953.) This could form the source of *the angry young men* of whom, since ca. 1957, one has heard far too much.

anguish, be. To be objectionable or deplorable or extremely boring: smart set and B.B.C. 'types': ca. 1946–57. Prompted by 'a *pain* in the neck'?

animal. A policeman: low: from ca. 1919.

[Animals. In early C. 18 s. and coll., the following terms occur in Ned Ward and are duly listed in Dr W. Matthews's valuable article: Horses were *hobbies* (1709), *scrubs* (1709) and *tits* (1703), all these perhaps always S.E.; a dog was nicknamed *Towzer* (1703), a rabbit *Puss* (1722). A flea, we may note, was called a *gentleman's companion* (1709).]

Annie.—2. An Anson aircraft, 'now used as a Trainer' (H. & P., 1943). Sgt-Pilot Rhodes, letter of Sept. 1942, 'The Anson is "limping Annie" from the uneven engine note, or just "Annie" for short.' Jackson, 1943, '*Annie, Old Annie*, the A. V. Roe "Anson" Bomber and Trainer, now obsolescent. Sometimes called "Old Faithful".' (The name *Anson* constitutes a pun on the latter part of 'A. V. Roe *and Son*'.)—3. H.M.S. *Anson*: Naval: since ca. 1940. Granville.

Annie Laurie. See **whistler, 8–2.**

Annie Laurie. A three-ton lorry: ca. 1914–20. Franklyn, *Rhyming.*—2. See **whistles, 8.**

annual.—2. A bath (the immersion): Australian: C. 20. B., 1942. Ironic.

anonski; esp. in 'I'll see you *anonski*': Australian c.p. of ca. 1930–60. After **cheerioski** above. (B.P.)

another clean shirt oughta (or **ought to**) **see ya** (or **you**) **out.** You look as if you might die at any time: New Zealand c.p.: since ca. 1930. Gordon Slatter, *A Gun in My Hand*, 1959.

another county heard from! 'A c.p. used when one of a company breaks wind or interjects something': Canadian: since ca. 1930. 'Ex the receiving of election results from various counties' (Leechman).

another fellow's. A c.p. applied to anything new, not by the possessor but by some wag: ca. 1880–1910. B. & L.

another good man gone! A c.p. referring to a male engaged to be married: late C. 19–20.

another little drink won't do us any harm. Since ca. 1920, a c.p. Ex a popular song.

another one for the van! Someone else has gone mad: Cockney c.p.: since ca. 1920. The *van* being the ambulance.

another pair of sleeves, that's. That's another matter: Australian: since ca. 1925. (B., 1943.)

another push and you'd have been a Chink (or **Nigger).** A c.p. used by workmen in a slanging match or by youths bullying boys in a factory: C. 20. Imputing a colour-no-objection promiscuity in the addressee's mother.

answer is a lemon, the. It prob. had its origin in an improper story.

answer the bugle. To fall in with the defaulters: Naval coll.: late C. 19–20. (John Irving, *Royal Navalese*, 1946.)

answer to a maiden's prayer. An eligible young bachelor: jocular coll.: C. 20.

Anthony Eden. A black felt hat in the upper Civil Service style: coll.: since ca. 1936. Of the kind favoured by the Rt Hon. Anthony Eden.

anti-wank, adj. Anti-tank: Army rhyming s.: 1940–5. (P-G-R.)

antipodes. Backside: since ca. 1840; but ob. by 1920, very rare by 1960. (Francis Francis, *Newton Dogvane*, 1859.)

ants in one's (male or female) **pants, have.** To be excited, restless: an Americanism adopted in England in 1938, but not gen. until 1942.

anxious (or **inquirers') meeting.** A meeting, after a revivalist address, of those who are *anxious* for salvation. Such a person occupies the 'anxious seat'. Ca. 1880–1910. Of U.S. origin. B. & L.

any.—2. Not any, nothing; none: Naval: C. 20. Ex the abbreviation *N.E.*, **not** eligible for pay. (Communicated by Captain R. J. B. Kenderdine, R.N.)

any amount. Much; a *large* amount: coll.: C. 20. 'Have you any sugar?' 'Any amount.'

any God's quantity. Many; very many; coll.: late C. 19–20. 'Any God's quantity of cocked hats and boleros and trunkhose': James Joyce, *Ulysses*, 1922.

any more for any more? Anyone want more food?: Services', esp. Army, c.p. (indeed, a consecrated and deeply revered phrase): late C. 19–20. (P-G-R.)

any more for the Skylark? A jocular c.p.: C. 20. Ex the invitation of pleasure-boat owners at the seaside.

any plum? See **plum pied.**

any Wee Georgie? Any good?: Australian rhyming s.: since ca. 1920. B., 1942. On 'Wee Georgie Wood', the popular comedian.

anything, like (p. 15). Esp., vigorously. The phrase *like anything* has prob. existed since mid-C. 18: it occurs in, e.g. *Sessions*, July 1766 (trial of Joseph Turner).

anything on two legs, he'll fuck or **shag.** An admiring tribute to a reputedly spectacular potency: mostly a Services' c.p.: late C. 19–20.

Anzac picket, be on (the). To be 'dodging the column' at the Anzac Hostel, El Kantara, Egypt. Australian soldiers': 1940–2. B., 1942.

Anzac tile. An Army biscuit: military: 1915–18.—2. Hence, any very hard biscuit: since 1919; by 1967, ob. (*TV Times*, May 27, 1967.) Cf. **Anzac wafer** on p. 15.

Anzac wafer (p. 15). Also Australian soldiers'. B., 1942.

ape.—2. £50; also £500: Australian: C. 20. B., 1942. Suggested by monkey, 2 (*Dict.*).

'apenny dip. A ship: rhyming s.: since ca. 1860. 'Obsolescent, but heard occasionally in Dockland' (Franklyn, 2nd).

(Aphæresis; Aphesis. The former is the suppression or removal of a letter or a syllable from the beginning of a word; the latter, 'the gradual and unintentional loss of a short unaccented vowel at the beginning of a word' (O.E.D.), being therefore a special class of word within the class determined by aphæresis. The process is common in all unconventional speech, as, indeed, it is also in dial. E.g. '*lo!* for *hullo!*, '*less* for *unless*, '*cept* for *except*: frequently it results, almost imperceptibly, from hurried or slovenly speech. Occ. the process is carried still further, as in the '*Loo* for *Woolloomooloo*, but, in such instances, it cannot be described as either unintentional or imperceptible. Aphæresis is opp. to abridgement, in which the first syllable (as in *et cet* for *et cetera*) or the first two syllables (as, esp., in rhyming s.) are retained. Both aphæresis and abbr. may usefully be contrasted with blends or portmanteau words, with 'telescopics' (reductions from single words), and with anagrammatic words.)

app. Apparatus: chemists' (not druggists') and chemical students': from ca. 1860.

apple, adj. used predicatively. Agreeable, pleasant; eminently suitable; 'all right': Australian: since early 1950's. Noted by Nino Culotta in *Aussie English*, 1965. Short for, and derived from, English rhyming s. *apples and rice*, nice—esp., very nice.

apple and pip. To urinate: late C. 19–20. Rhyming on *sip*, back-s. for *piss*. (Franklyn, 2nd.)

apple daddy. 'Merchant Navy s. for dried apple rings soaked and cooked in a pastry case, and issued as a pudding on Tuesdays and Thursdays to the apprentices, bosun, etc. Considered a great delicacy, they were liable to be stolen from the galley by ordinary seamen, if they were left unattended while soaking': nautical: C. 20. (Ramsey Spencer.)

apple fritter. A bitter (ale): rhyming s.: late C. 19–20.

apple pie. Sky: since ca. 1940; rare since 1946. (Franklyn, *Rhyming*.)

apple-pips. Lips: rhyming s., mostly theatrical: C. 20. (Franklyn, *Rhyming*.)

apple-polishing. Toadying: Canadian: C. 20. Before giving the apple to teacher, a pupil—sometimes ostentatiously—polishes it.

apple-sauce. Impudence: mostly lower middle class: late C. 19–20. An elaboration of sauce, n., 1 (*Dict.*).

apples, 2 (p. 15), doesn't predominate over the full term; yet fairly common. (Witness Lester.)

apples a pound pears. A c.p., derisive of barrow boys, who often use strange cries, thought by some customers to be misleading: since ca. 1930.

apples and rice. 'Oh ve-ry nice, oh ve-ry apples and rice,' Michael Harrison, *Reported Safe Arrival*, 1943: rhyming s.: late C. 19–20.

apples swim (pp. 15–16). Not unsolved: see how we apples swim! on p. 411. The phrase has been known in Germany since C. 16, both in the Latin *Nos poma natamus* and in the German *Da schwimmen wir Apfel, sagte der Rossapfel und schwamm mit den echten*, Look at us apples swim-

ming, said the ball of horse-dung, swimming with the genuine apples. (Communicated by Dr K. Spalding, M.A., Ph.D.)

application. A name: Anglo-Irish sol.: from ca. 1870. B. & L.

appointment. In boxing: see keep one's appointment.

'Appy Day. A pessimistic and inveterate 'grouser': Naval: C. 20. Granville. Ironic. See happy (p. 374).

apricock (-) water. Apricock, i.e. apricot, ale: 1728, Anon., *The Quaker's Opera*.

April fools. Tools: rhyming s.: late C. 19–20. —2. Stools: mostly public-house rhyming s.: since ca. 1910.—3. (Football) pools: rhyming s.: since ca. 1930. (All: Franklyn, *Rhyming*.)

April Showers. Flowers: rhyming 2.: C. 20. (Franklyn, ibid.)

apron. The tarmac surround of a hangar: R.A.F.: since ca. 1930. Jackson.—2. 'The neck fold of a merino ram' (B., *The Drum*, 1959): Aus. sheepfarmers': C. 20.

aqua fluminis filtrata (lit., 'filtered river-water'): an Australian pharmaceutical chemists' variant of aqua pompaginis (p. 16). B.P.

Aqui, the. The *Aquitania*: seamen's coll.: 1914–50, then reminiscent.

ar (or aar) is a Cockney form of the *ou* (*ow*) sound: C. 19–20. E.g. *Sarf*, South.

Arba Rifles, the. 'A force of Pioneers, pressed into service as front-line troops, at the time of the German break-through near Kasserine (in Tunisia)': Army in North Africa: W.W.II. Ex the Souk el Arba. (P-G-R.)

arch is a variant of ark (boat).—2. archbishop: clerical: late C. 19–20.—3. As for 2, always the a. Headmaster: Tonbridge School: late C. 19–20.

Arch Tiffy, the. The Warrant Engineer: Naval: since ca. 1920. Granville. See tiffy, 1 (*Dict.*).

archbeak or archbeako. Headmaster: some English preparatory schools: C. 20. See, e.g., the novels of Anthony Buckeridge.

*Archbishop Laud, often shortened to *Archbishop*. Fraud: rhyming: since ca. 1945—by 1965, also low s. Robin Cook, *The Crust on Its Uppers*, 1962.

Archbishop of Cant, the. Any Anglican archbishop; not necessarily Canterbury: since the late 1930's.

Archie.—2. A young station hand, learning his job: Australian rural: C. 20. B., 1942. Cf. the *Archibald* entries in the *Dict.*—3. Field Marshal Earl (Archibald) Wavell, strategist, statesman and writer: Army: 1940 +.

are there any more at home like you? A c.p., addressed to a pretty girl: since ca. 1910. Ex a musical comedy: the song is 'Tell me, pretty maiden, are there . . . ?'—from *Floradora*, 1900.

are there no doors in your house? A c.p. to one who fails to close the door: C. 20.

are you happy in your work? Ironic c.p. to someone engaged in a dangerous, difficult or dirty job: Services, esp. R.A.F.: since ca. 1940. H. & P.

are you keeping it for the worms? A c.p. addressed to a female rejecting sexual advances: Canadian: since ca. 1945. Here, 'it 'is the hymen.

are you kidding? Are you joking?—or derisively and ironically exclamatory; Surely you're not serious?: c.p.: since ca. 1945. Suggested by the American c.p., *no kidding?* Probably the origin of *you must be joking,* I find it difficult to believe you: since ca. 1960.

arena rat. A 'fan' or an *habitué* or an idler hanging about ice-hockey arenas: Canadian sporting circles': since 1957. (Leechman.)

ari-a-mo. A cigarette: 1914–15, esp. in the Army.

arfundred. See **anarf.**

argufy. Earlier: 1726, trial of Hester Jennings in *Select Trials, from 1724 to 1732,* pub. in 1735. In *Hodgson's National Songster,* 1832, is an old song entitled 'What Argufies Pride and Ambition?'

Ari. Short for **Aristotle** (*Dict.*), which, by the way, occurs in *The* (Sydney) *Bulletin,* Aug. 7, 1897.

Aris. A curtailed form of *Aristotle* (p. 17), a bottle: C. 20. (Lester.)

arisings. Left-overs (as of food): Naval: C. 20. 'Bartimeus.' Ex official **arisings,** residues proving proper use of expendable stores.

arith. Arithmetic: schoolboys': mid-C. 19–20.

Arithmetician. See 'Tavern terms', § 3, *d*.

arm, having a good. See **having a good arm.**

arm, on the. See **not off** below.

arm, under the, 2 (p. 17). By 1940, low s. (Norman.) Implication: it stinks.

Armies. 'Name given generically to *Armament* ratings': Naval: since ca. 1920. Granville.

Armstick or **Armitist, the.** A sol., mostly Cockney, for the Armistice (Nov. 11, 1918): late 1918 +.

army!, thank God we have an. See **thank God . . .**

Army, the. The Salvation Army: coll.: C. 20.

Army and Navy. Gravy: rhyming s.: C. 20. (Franklyn, *Rhyming.*)

Army Form blank. Toilet paper: Army officers': 1939–45. (P-G-R.)

Army left (or **right**)! Drill-instructors' c.p. to one who took the wrong turning: Army: since ca. 1925. (P-G-R.)

Army Tank, usually in pl. An American serviceman: Australian prisoners-of-war in the Far East: 1942–5. (*The* (Sydney) *Sun,* Sept. 22, 1945; B., 1953.) Rhyming on *Yank.*

aromatic bomb. Atomic bomb: Army officers': late 1945–6, then decidedly ob. *The People,* Sept. 2, 1945. By a pun.

aroo! Good-bye!; so long: Australian: late C. 19–20. B., 1942. Ex *au revoir.*

*arp. See **zol.**

arrever is a low Cockney pronunciation of *however.* Clarence Rook, *The Hooligan Nights,* 1899.

arrival. 'The safe landing of an aircraft,' H. & P., 1943; more accurately, 'a poor landing, likely to have been troublesome. Thus ''Bill's made an arrival'',' Jackson, rather later in the same year.

arrow, in good. In good form: dart-players' s. verging on coll.: from ca. 1880. Peter Chamberlain. Punning *dart.*

'Arry. The familiar form of *Aristotle* (p. 17): C. 20 (Franklyn, *Rhyming.*)

'Arry's gators. Thank you: Australian: since ca. 1943. A 'Hobson-Jobson' of Japanese *arrigato.* (Edwin Morrisby, Aug. 30, 1958.)

arse, n.—2. Impudence: Aus.: since ca. 1940. Nino Culotta, *Cop This Lot,* 1960, 'He laughs and

says . . . a man would need plenty of arse to pinch another man's book.' I think so too.

arse, v.—3. 'One of the blokes said, ''Arse her''—a lorry—''up here''. I backed her up against one of the Railway arches' (John Gosling, *The Ghost Squad,* 1959): low: C. 20.

arse!, my; my foot! Expressions of marked incredulity; intense negatives: low: since ca. 1880, ca. 1860, resp. ' ''More like ten past (eight o'clock).'' ''Ten past, my arse'',' Ernest Raymond, *A Song of the Tide,* 1940. Cf. *like fuck!,* s.v. **fuck.**

arse, pain in the. See **you give me . . .**

arse about face, often preceded by *it's* or *you've got it.* Back to front; all wrong: low coll.: late C. 19–20.

arse a-peak or **arse about face.** Topsy-turvy: resp. Army and Navy: C. 20.

arse bandit. Synonym of **arse king:** low: C. 20.

arse brigand. Another synonym of **arse king:** low: C. 20.

arse-crawl. V.i., to toady: low coll.: late C. 19–20. Gerald Kersh, *The Nine Lives of Bill Nelson,* 1942. Cf. **arse crawl** (p. 18).

arse-end Charlie 'is the man who weaves backwards and forwards above and behind the Squadron to protect them from attack from the rear,' Richard Hillary, *The Last Enemy,* 1942: R.A.F.: 1939 +. Synonymous with **tail-end Charlie,** 2.

arse for dust, unable to see (someone's). A low c.p., applied to a swift departure: late C. 19–20.

arse from a hole in the ground, (he) doesn't know his. He's extremely ignorant: Canadian: C. 20. Cf. *arse from . . .* (p. 18).

arse-hole. Anus: a coll. vulgarism: C. 19 (? 18)–20.

arse-hole, v. To dismiss from a job; to discard (someone) as too old: low Australian: since ca. 1920. 'When yuh get a bit old aud yuh can't keep up . . . , they'll arseole yuh' (Dick).

arse-hole, I (or **he,** etc.) **don't** (or **doesn't**) **give an** or **a cat's.** A Naval c.p. assertion, either of bravado or of imperturbability: C. 20.

arse-hole bandit. A variant of **arse bandit:** low: C. 20.

arse-hole crawler; often simply *crawler.* A sycophant: low: late C. 19–20.

arse-hole is bored or punched, he doesn't know if his. He's a complete fool: c.p.: since ca. 1910. Presumably it originated in the engineering workshops. The original form seems to have been (often, it still is) '. . . . bored, punched or countersunk'. Among Canadian Army officers, 1939–45, it ran: 'That guy don't know if his ass-hole was drilled, dug, seamed, bored or naturally evaginated.' Now usually . . . *punched or bored.*

arse-hole of the world. See **you know . . .** The Persian Gulf and Lower Irak; hence, Baghdad is said to be *up the . . .*

arse-hole set fire! A c.p. exclamation: low: since ca. 1920.

Arse-hole Square. Boyish and youthful wit in parroted reply to 'Where?': mostly Cockneys': late C. 19–20.

arse-hole to breakfast time, from. All the way; all the time: low: late C. 19–20.

arse-holes has, since ca. 1940, been short for *pissed as arse-holes,* extremely drunk: low: late C. 19–20.

arse-holes to breakfast time. Upside down;

utterly confused: most unsatisfactory: Cockney: late C. 19–20. Thus 'Them ahses built all . . .' or 'Take no notice of him—he's always . . .'

arse-holey. Obsequious: low: C. 20.

arse in a sling, get one's. See **eye in a sling** . . . below.

arse king. A notorious sodomite: low: since ca. 1910.

arse of the ship, the. The stern: Naval: mid-C.19–20. Granville.

arse or one's elbow, not to know whether one's on one's. To be utterly incompetent or bewildered: coll.: C. 20.

arse over ballocks. A low Cockney synonym (C. 20) of **arse over tip.**

arse over kettle. A Canadian form (C. 20) of:—

arse over tip. Head over heels: C. 20. In military circles, often in the form **A over T.** (Correct, therefore, the supposition at end of **arse over turkey** in *Dict.*)

arse over tit. The Australian form of the preceding: since ca. 1910. Cf. **tit,** 9, below, and:

arse over tits; arse over tock (or tuck). Variants of **arse over tip:** since ca. 1920, perhaps earlier.

arse party, the. Those who, in any ship, are known to be homosexuals: Naval: since ca. 1920.

arse-perisher. See **bum-freezer,** 2.

arse-polishing. An office job: R.A.F.: 1939 +. (P-G-R.)

arse up with care. Applied, as adj. or as adv., to a thorough mess, a real bungle, chaos: low: C. 20.

arse upwards (p. 18). Cockneys pronounce it *arsuppards,* whence the punning *Mr R. Suppards,* a very lucky fellow: C. 19–20 pronunciation; C. 20 pun.

arse-wiper. A workman that toadies to the boss; a servant to the mistress: low coll.: C. 20.

arse-wise, adj. or adv. Inept; preposterous; awry: low coll.: C. 20.

arsey. (Very) lucky: Australian, since ca. 1935 (B., 1953.) Ex *tin-arsed,* q.v. at *tinny,* adj., 2 (p. 888).

arso. Armament Supply Officer: Naval: 1939 +. (P-G-R.)

art of memory. See 'Tavern terms', § 3, *d.*

artful fox (p. 18). *Not* a wooden case, but a *theatrical* box.

Arthur. Arsine gas. H. & P.—2. A simpleton, a dupe: mock-auction promoters': since ca. 1946. Perhaps ex Arthur regarded, by the ignorant, as a 'sissy' name.

artic (p. 18), for *arctic,* goes back to C. 14. Yet perhaps it isn't an error at all, but a true variant pronunciation, common in Old and Medieval French and even in Late and Medieval Latin.— 2. See **Queen Mary.**

artichoke.—2. A dissolute, debauched old woman; Australian low: C. 20. B., 1942.

article, 2 (p. 18). Examples heard by me during the 1950's: *nosey article,* inquisitive; *sloppy article; toffee-nosed article.*—3. A woman exported to the Argentine to become a prostitute: white-slavers' c.: C. 20. A. Londres, *The Road to Buenos Ayres,* 1928.—4. A chamber-pot: domestic coll.: mid-C. 19–20. It probably arose, as a euphemism, from 'article of furniture'. Note the story of that bishop, who, to another, complained that his house

contained forty bedrooms, to which his guest replied, 'Very awkward, for you have only Thirty-Nine Articles'.

artificial, n. Usually in pl., artificial manures: gardening coll.: C. 20.

artillery, one's. One's revolver: Army officers': 1939–45. Ex U.S.? (P-G-R.)

artist.—3. (Specialisation of sense 1.) A specialist, an expert: since ca. 1918.—4. 'One who indulges in excesses, e.g., "bilge a.", "booze a.", "bull a." ' (B., 1942): esp. in Australia: since ca. 1920.

arty, n. Artillery: Australian soldiers': 1939 +. Lawson Glassop, *We Were the Rats,* 1944.

Arty Bishops, the. See **Bishops, the.**

arty roller. A collar: Australian rhyming s.: since ca. 1910. (Baker, *The Australian Language,* 1945.)

arvo. Afternoon: Australian: C. 20. B., 1942. Cf. *afto.* Notably in *s'arvo,* this afternoon: C. 20. (B., *The Drum,* 1959.)

Aryan; non-Aryan. Non-Jewish; Jewish: catachreses (of Hitlerite origin) dating, in England, from 1936. This is a particularly crass and barbarous misusage of a useful pair of complementaries.

as easy as shaking the drops off your John, often preceded by *it's.* It's dead easy: an essentially masculine c.p.: since ca. 1945. Not susceptible to the ludicrous ineptitude of ignorant girls saying 'It gets on my wick', occasionally affected by provocative girls pretending to be innocent.

as ever is (p. 18). Rather is it mid-C. 19–20. Edward Lear (d. 1888) once wrote, ca. 1873, 'I shall go either to Sardinia, or India, or Jumsibob-jigglequack this next winter as ever is.'

as-is. Feminine knickers: since ca. 1920; ob. Joan Lowell, *Child of the Deep,* 1929.

as large as life and twice as natural. A c.p.: C. 20. Ex waxworks?

as much use as my arse, often preceded by *you're.* A low abusive c.p.: late C. 19–20.

as muck. See **muck, as.**

as per use. See **use, as per.**

as rotten. (The score) as written: Australian musicians': C. 20. B., 1942.

as the actress said to the bishop or **as the bishop said to the actress.** A c.p. of innuendo, added to an entirely innocuous remark to render it scabrous, as in 'It's too stiff for me to manage it—as the actress said to the bishop': certainly in use in the R.A.F., ca. 1944–47, and probably of earlier date; by 1967, slightly ob., but likely to survive for some years. Whence:—

as the girl (or the soldier) said: especially, *as the girl said to the sailor.* An end-c.p., to soften a double (esp. if sexual) meaning: since ca. 1919. Cf. the C. 20 *as the monkey said,* ending a smoke-room story. Based upon a prototypical story about someone coming into money. See the preceding.

as what. See **what, as.**

ash beans and long oats. A thrashing: London streets': C. 19. Augustus Mayhew, *Paved with Gold,* 1857, 'Give him with all my might a good feed of "long oats" and "ash beans".'

Ash Wednesday. The day G.H.Q. Cairo was filled with burning documents on the approach of Rommel.

ashcan. That's no good, that shot: cinema: since ca. 1925. *The Evening News,* Nov. 7, 1939.

—2. Hence, wasted time: Services: since ca. 1939. H. & P.—3. A depth charge: orig. its container (ex its appearance): Naval: 1939 +. Granville. —4. See **put a jelly on the ashcan.**

ashcat; usually in pl. An engineer, mostly on destroyers: Naval: since ca. 1935. Less gen. than *plumber.*

Ashes, the. To *Dict.* entry add, from Mr Basil de Sélincourt's review of the first ed. of this work —in *The Manchester Guardian,* Feb. 19, 1937: 'I hoped to find that the victorious Australian team had burned their stumps after the last game of the rubber, and kept the proceeds in an urn in their committee-room.'

Ashmogger, the. The Ashmolean Museum: Oxford undergraduates' (—1920); little used after 1940. Marples, 2.

Ashtip, Mrs. See **Greenfields.**

ask. 'A jockey is said to "ask" . . . a horse when rousing him to greater exertion': turf: from ca. 1860. B. & L.

ask me (or **my**) **behind** is a mid-C. 19–20 variant of **ask my** (or **me**) **arse,** as on p. 19.

ask me foot (occasionally **elbow**)! An Anglo-Irish euphemism (C. 20) for *ask me arse!*

ask silly questions and you'll get silly answers; since ca. 1950, often simply *ask silly questions;* occ., *ask a silly question and you'll get a silly answer* (very nearly shortened). A c.p. form, current in late C. 19–20, of the old proverb, 'Ask no questions and you'll be told no lies'.

ask yourself! Be reasonable! Australian c.p.: since ca. 1925. B., 1942.

askew (p. 19). Perhaps rather from Old-Medieval–Early Modern Fr. *escuelle,* a cup.

asparagus bed. A kind of anti-tank obstacle; military: since ca. 1939. H. & P.

aspect. Aspic: sol.: late C. 19–20. Pugh (2): 'Truffle in aspect'.

aspi or **aspy.** An aspidistra: non-aristocratic, non-cultured: C. 20. A modern wit has summarized his life of toil, ending in straitened circumstances, in the epigram: *Per ardua ad aspidistra.*

Aspro. A vocalising of *S.P.R.O.,* Services Public Relations Officer: Army: 1941 +. (P-G-R.)

aspro. A professional male homosexual: low: since ca. 1940. A correspondent suggests derivation from *arse 'pro'.*

ass, 3 (p. 19). Hence also Canadian.—4. Female pudend: low Canadian: late C. 19–20.

ass about. A post-1918 variant of **arse about** (p. 18). American influence.

Assistance, the. National Assistance: poorer classes' coll.: since ca. 1945.

astern of station. 'Behindhand with a programme or ignorant of the latest intelligence' (Granville): Naval coll.: since ca. 1920.

astronomer.—2. See 'Tavern terms', § 3, *d.*

astronomical. (Esp. in statistics and in sums of money) huge, immense: cultured coll.: since ca. 1938. In ref. to stellar distances and times, and owing much to the vogue of the popular works on astronomy by Eddington and Jeans.

asty! Go slowly! take your time! take it easily!: Army and R.A.F.: C. 20. Jackson. Ex Hindustani, the opposite of 'jildy' (see **jildy,** p. 439).

At. A member of *the Ats* or Auxiliary Territorial Service: orig. (1939) military. H. & P. Cf. **Waff.**

[**at the Inn of the Morning Star.** (Sleeping) in the open air: coll., rather literary, verging on S.E.: from ca. 1880; ob. Suggested by Fr. *à la belle étoile.*]

Ath, the. The Athenaeum Club: the world of learning, and that of clubs: C. 20.

atom-bombo. Cheap but very potent wine: Australian: since 1945. (B., 1953.) A pun on S.E. *atom bomb* and s. *bombo,* 2.

atomaniac; usually *atomaniacs.* People that would like to use the atom bomb on those they dislike: 1945 +.

atramentarius. See 'Stoneyhurst Slang'. Lit. the 'Latin' word = filler of ink-stands.

Ats, the. See **At.**

Atsie (or **-sy**). An affectionate variant of *At:* Army: 1939 +. (P-G-R.)

Attaboy. An Air Transport Auxiliary 'plane or member: 1940 +, Jackson. Suggested by the initials and punning **attaboy** (p. 20).

atterise or **-ize.** To staff with A.T.S. or a proportion of A.T.S.; 'to man static gun sites with mixed batteries', H. & P., 1943: military (orig. jocular). Cf. **waaferise** and:—

Attery. Living quarters occupied by *Ats:* since 1941. H. & P. See **At.**

Attorney General. See 'Tavern terms', § 4.

Augis. Incorrect for Augeas (of the Augean stable); e.g. in Carlyle, *Latter-Day Pamphlets.*

Auguste. A minor circus-clown, a 'feed' to the Joey or Chief Clown: circus: late C. 19–20. Prob. from one so named.

Auk, the. General Sir Claude Auchinleck, G.C.B., G.C.I.E., D.S.O.: Army: since ca. 1938.

aunt, the. The women's lavatory: upper-class feminine: since ca. 1920. Ex **aunt, go to see one's** (p. 20).

Aunt Fanny, (e.g. *my* or *his*). Indicates either disbelief or negation: since ca. 1930. Monica Dickens, *Thursday Afternoons,* 1945, 'She's got no more idea how to run this house than my Aunt Fanny.' A euphemistic elaboration of *fanny,* n., 9.

Aunt Fanny, (you're) like. A disparaging c.p., addressed to someone either clumsy or inexperienced with tools: workmen's: C. 20.

Aunt Maria.—2. A fire: rhyming s.: very late C. 19–20. Variant of **Anna Maria** (p. 14). Franklyn 2nd.

aunt Mary Ann. An occ. variation of **san fairy ann** (*Dict.*): military: ca. 1915–19.

Auntie or **Aunty.** The British Broadcasting Corporation: since ca. 1945; by 1965, slightly ob. Short for *Auntie B.B.C.* Ex its respectability.—2. A mature man kindly—but from suspect tendencies—disposed towards younger men and boys: since ca. 1950 (? much earlier). In e.g., Laurence Little, *The Dear Boys,* a novel, 1958.

Auntie!, don't be. Don't be silly: Aus.: since ca. 1920. Prompted by 'Don't be Uncle Willie!' (B., *The Drum,* 1959.) Cf. **Uncle Willie,** 1, in *Dict.*

Auntie (or **auntie**) **Ella.** An umbrella: rhyming s., 'used almost exclusively by women, at the suburban Cockney level' (Franklyn 2nd): since ca. 1946.

Auntie Flo. The Foreign Office: Civil Service, esp. the Diplomatic: C. 20. Shane Martin, *Twelve Girls in the Garden,* 1957.

Auntie (or **auntie**) **Nellie.** Belly: rhyming s.: C. 20. Franklyn 2nd.

Aussie rules. Australian football: Australian coll.: late C. 19–20. B., 1942. Played under Australian rules.

Austin Seven. A 'Class B Midland freight locomotive' (*Railway*, 3rd): since ca. 1950 (?). Ex appearance.

Australian cigs. During the cigarette shortage of late 1939–45, cigarettes kept under the counter: ca. 1940–45, then historical. By a pun on *down under*.

Australian grip (p. 21) may, as B., 1953 (p. 250), suggests, be a ghost-word: he has seen no record, outside dictionaries, nor heard it used; come to that, neither have I.

Australian surfing slang and colloquialism. The terms cited in the Supplement come notably from four sources: J. R. Westerway ('The Surfies') in *The* (Sydney) *Bulletin* of March 30, 1963; a brief, unsigned article ('Language of Their Own') in the *Sun-Herald* of Sept. 22, 1963; Dick Dennison, 'The World of the Surfies'—a valuable article, with a glossary, containing, however, much that is sheer jargon (technicalities); and the comments, and several additions, made by Mr Barry Prentice, who sent me the articles.

As a sport, surf-board riding became extremely popular soon after World War II; it erupted as a passion, a rage, a cult, almost a way of life, among teenagers, in 1960–61. All its jargon and some of its slang have been imported from Hawaii.

Australorp. The Australian 'utility type of Black Orpington fowl' (B., *The Drum*, 1959): Aus. coll.: since ca. 1930. A blend of *Austral*ian *Orp*ington'.

autem, a church (p. 21). Perhaps essentially 'altar': cf. Old Fr.–MF.–modern Fr. *autel*: with *-em* substituted for *-el*. In c. of C. 16–18, *-am* and *-em* and *-om* and *-um* are common suffixes. (Developed from a suggestion made by Alexander McQueen.)

auto.—2. An automatic revolver: from ca. 1915. *The Pawnshop Murder*.

'ave a Jew boy's. Weight: jocular Cockney: from ca. 1910. Punning *avoirdupois* and often directed at a fat man.

Ave Maria. A fire: rhyming s.: late C. 19–20. More usually *Anna Maria*.

aviate. To fly, esp. to fly showily, ostenta-

tiously: R.A.F.: since 1938 or 1939 in the latter nuance, since ca. 1936 in the former; jocular and resp. mildly or intensely contemptuous. Jackson. Ex *aviator*.

[**avile** is Randle Holme's misprint (or error?) for *a vile* or *a ville*, q.v. at **vile** in *Dict.*]

avit. See 'Prisoner-of-War Slang', 12.

aw for *ar* (or *a* with Continental value) is a mark of Cockney speech. E.g. *pawst* for *past*, pawse for *pass*, *claws* for *class*.

aw shucks! 'The conventional U.S. and American expression of yokel embarrassment. "Aw shucks! I couldn't say that to a lady!"'': since ca. 1910—and, as used by others than yokels, often jocular and always a c.p. (Leechman.)

away for slates or **away like a mad dog.** (Adj. and adv.) Departing hastily: Liverpool: C. 20.

away racing. Absent at a race-course: coll., in London's East End: since ca. 1945. (Richard Herd, Nov. 12, 1957.)

away with the mixer! Let's go ahead; now we're going ahead: c.p.: since ca. 1946. A concrete-mixer?

away the trip. Pregnant: Scottish working-classes': C. 20.

awful people, the; Mr Cochran's young ladies in blue. The police, as in 'Then the awful people arrived': cultured: since ca. 1945, by 1960, the latter slightly ob.

'Awkins (p. 21). Read: 'Sir Henry Hawkins'.

awkward as a Chow on a bike. 'Extremely awkward in behaviour. *Chow* denotes Chinaman' (B., *The Drum*, 1959): Aus.: since ca. 1925.

awri (pron. *aw-ri*). All right: sol.: C. 19–20.

axe my arse, you can. A verbal snook-cocking: low: mid C. 18–20; by 1967, slight ob.

axle-grease. Money: Australian: since ca. 1925. (B., 1943.)—2. Thick hair-oil; Brilliantine: mostly Australian schoolchildren's and teenagers': since late 1930. (B.P.)

'ay is for 'orses. A variant of **hay is** . . . below.

Ayrab, a genoowine Bedoowine. 'A Bedouin Arab. A jocular elaboration of the American pronunciation of Arab' (Peter Sanders, 'Beddo, Blue and Gaberdine Swine' in the coloured supplement of *The Sunday Times*, Sept. 10, 1967): British servicemen's, esp. soldiers', in North Africa, 1940–43.

B

b.—4. See bee—S. A euphemism for *bastard*, n. and adj., and also for *bloody*, adj.: Australian: since ca. 1920. 'You'd think the b. lion'd sleep sometimes': H. Drake Brockman, 'Life Saver' (1939) in *Sydney of the Bush*, 1948.

B.A. See **sweet B.A.**

b. and m. A mixture of brown ale *and* mild bitter: spivs': since late 1940's. (*Picture Post*, Jan. 2, 1954, article on young spivs.)

B.B.—3. A 'bum boy', q.v.: low: C. 20.—4. A bust bodice: feminine coll.: since ca. 1920.—5. A bitter and Burton: public houses': late C. 19–20. *The Fortnightly Review*, Aug. 1937.

B.B.C., talk. To talk politely, to speak in a clear, precise and cultured manner: coll.: since ca. 1930. Berkeley Gray, *Mr Ball of Fire*, 1946.

*b.d.v. or **B.D.V.** A picked-up stump of a cigarette: tramps' c.: from ca. 1920. Lit., a bend-down Virginia; punning *B.D.V.*, a brand of tobacco. Also called a *stooper*.

B-flat homey; B-flat polone (or poloney). A fat man, a fat woman, esp. in a side-show: partly parlary, wholly fair-ground: late C. 19–20. (Sydney Lester.)

B.H. 'Bung-hole', i.e. cheese: Army: since ca. 1918.

B.O.! Run away (and stop bothering me)! since ca. 1955. Abbreviation of *bugger off*.

B.O.L.T.O.P. Put at the end of a letter with 'kisses': coll.: C. 20. Better on lips than on paper. Cf. **S.W.A.K.**

B.Q. Before queues: since 1944. Fred Bason's *Second Diary*, 1952.

b.s. (p. 22) 'goes back at least to 1908 in British Columbia' (Leechman).

B.Y.T. 'Bright Young Things' or the younger set: ca. 1946–51.

baa-lamb.—3. a tram: C. 20. Rhyming.—4. A euphemism for *bastard*: since ca. 1918.

bab. See **baba** (*Dict.*).

babbling brook.—2. A criminal: Australian rhyming s. (on S.E. *crook*): C. 20.—3. As adj., unwell: Australian rhyming s. on synonymous Australian s. *crook*: since ca. 1920.

Babes, the. Charlton Athletic Association Football Club: sporting: from ca. 1925. It is the youngest London club.

baby, 2, was not unknown in English fast, sporting circles of ca. 1895–1910: witness Binstead's *More Gals' Gossip*, 1901.

baby, burying the. See **burying the baby.**

baby, hand over the. See **hand over the baby.**

baby, have a. To be much shocked or nonplussed or flabbergasted: middle-class: since ca. 1930. Cf. *have kittens* (see **kittens, having**).

baby, hold the. See **holding the baby** (*Dict.*).

baby bonus. A maternity allowance: Australian coll.: since ca. 1945. (B.P.) 'Common in Canada also; Family Allowance Act passed in 1944' (Leechman).

baby couldn't help it. Minced meat and brown sauce: Marlborough College: since ca. 1920.

baby-pulling. Obstetrics: medical students': since ca. 1880.

baby's bottom, like a. Smooth, esp. of face after shaving: coll.: C. 20.—2. Hence, expressionless; characterless: since ca. 1930. (Atkinson.)

baby's head (p. 23). Specifically a steak-and-kidney pudding—and not confined to sailors.

baby's leg. Meat roll; marmalade roll; roly-poly pudding: Regular Army: late C. 19–20. Michael Harrison, *Reported Safe Arrival*, 1943. Cf. **baby's head** (*Dict.*). Also at girls' schools: *teste* Berta Ruck, 1935.

baby's pap. A cap: rhyming s.: mid-C. 19–20; but rare since ca. 1920. (Franklyn, *Rhyming*.)

bacca, bacco, backy (p. 23), should all be dated much earlier: *bacco*, for instance, is recorded in *bacco-box* as early as 1793 in 'The Token', a poem by Charles Dibdin, on p. 249 of *The Britannic Magazine*, I, No. 8. (Moe.) *Bacca* occurs in John Wight's *Mornings at Bow Street*, 1824, and the form *back(e)y* in Wight's *More Mornings at Bow Street*, 1827.

Both *backy* and *backey* occur in *The Night Watch* (II, 131 and 159) of 1828. (Moe.)

baccy (p. 23 at **bacca**) occurs in Fredk Marryat, *The King's Own*, 1830 (p. 135 of the 1896 edition). Moe.

bacca- or **bacco-chew.** A chewing tobacco: coll.: prob. late C. 18–20. Ex an unidentified British source, *The Port Folio* of Aug. 28, 1805, quotes an anonymous song, *Dustman Bill*, thus:

> Cries he, 'My Wenches, ever dear,
> Whate'er be your opinions,
> I love ye better both, d'ye hear,
> Than bacco-chew or onions.'

(Moe.)

bach.—2. (Cf. sense 1: p. 23.) 'Camelford's residence was not in a boarding-house, but what is generally known in the Antipodes as a "bach" (or a "batch", if you prefer to maintain fiercely that the word is derived, not from the first syllable of the word "bachelor", but from the idea of a number of similar things being grouped together)'— Frank Arthur, *The Suva Harbour Mystery*, 1941: Australian, New Zealand, Fijian: C. 20.

bach, v. (p. 23). An early Australian example occurs in Edward Dyson, *The Gold Stealers*, 1901, 'Here he "batched", perfectly content with his lot.'

Bachelor: Bachelor of Law. See 'Tavern terms', § 3, *b*.

Bachelor Creek. See **Dodd's Sound.**

bacher. Variant of **batcher** (p. 23).

back, n. A water-closet: domestic: late C. 19–20. From the days of backyard privies.

back, get on (someone's). To bully; to urge on: Aus.: since ca. 1925. (B., *The Drum*, 1959.)

back!, that's what gets up my. That's what angers me: c.p.: since ca. 1930.

back about, be on (someone's). To reprimand concerning, speak sternly to about (something): Australian: since ca. 1910. '"You know bloody well you're supposed to re-stock as soon as you run low on anything," said Billy. "The doc was on your back about this before"' (Jon Cleary, *Back of Sunset*, 1959).

back board. A distant signal: railwaymen's: C. 20. (*Railway*, 3rd, 1936.) Cf. **back stick** below.

back double. A back street: Cockney: late C. 19–20. Gerald Kersh, *Night and the City*, 1938. Ex double, n., 4 (*Dict.*).

back duck (usually in pl.). A piece of fried bread: Naval (lower-deck): C. 20. Granville. Ironic.

back garden. 'The end pages of a magazine, devoted to advertisements inserted between columns of "spill over" from articles and stories in the front of the "book"' (Leechman): Canadian publishers' and journalists': since ca. 1910.

back-hander.—4. A tip or bribe made surreptitiously: since ca. 1915. Back-handedly.

back-handing. See **back-hand** (*Dict.*) and contrast **backhanding** (ibid.).

back in circulation is applied to a female jilted or divorced or widowed and therefore free from a male tie: col.: since ca. 1945.

back o' me hand to ye!, the. An Anglo-Irish retort: c.p.: late C. 19–20. Euphemistic?

back of one's arse, on the. Australian variant of 'on one's back' (p. 23).

back-room boy. Usually pl., . . . *boys*, inventors and theoretical technicians, working for one of the combatant Services: journalistic j. (1941)>, in 1943, a gen. coll.—in 1943–5, mostly Services'. They worked out of the limelight and often literally in back-rooms or back-washes.

***back scratched, have one's.** To be flogged: c.: from ca. 1870. Orig. of the cat o' nine tails.

back-scuttle.—2. Hence, v. and n.: (to commit) sodomy: low: late C. 19–20.

back shift. Late turn (of duty): railwaymen's coll.: C. 20. *Railway*, 3rd.

back slang. The earliest reference I've seen occurs in G. W. M. Reynolds's *Pickwick Abroad*, 1839, p. 587 (footnote).

back stick (G.W.R.); **back 'un; brown one** or **'un; ginger one.** A distant signal: railwaymen's: C. 20. (Harvey Sheppard, *Dictionary of Railway Slang*, 1964.)

back-swap, n. and v. To cry off a bargain; the crying-off: coll. verging on s.: 1888, Fothergill, *Leverhouse*, ' "Then it's agreed?" . . . "Yes, no back-swaps." ' E.D.D. Lit., to go back on a 'swap'.

back teeth are afloat, one's; or . . . **are floating.** A c.p., implying a strong desire to urinate: C. 20; by 1960, slightly ob.

back to it, it's got a. I'm lending it to you, but you must return it: Londoners' c.p.: C. 20.

back to the cactus. Back to duty after leave: Australian Naval c.p., dating from the 1930's. This reference to the prickly pear of the Australian outback occurs, for instance, in a story written in 1944 by Dal Stivens and included in his *The Courtship of Uncle Henry*, 1946.

***back to the war.** Used by Tommies returning to the Line after a spell in back areas: c.p.: W.W. I. (A. B. Petch, April 1966.)

back-up. A 'chain' copulation with one girl: Australian teenage gangsters': adopted, ca. 1945, ex U.S. (Dick.)—2. A second helping of food: Australian, esp. W.A.: C. 20. Ex **back up**, v. (p. 24). Tom Ronan, *Only a Short Walk*, 1961.

back-up, or **horn, pills.** Aphrodisiacs: low: since ca. 1910.

backblock, adj. Of the backblocks or 'The bush': Australian coll.: since ca. 1920. (B., 1943.)

backblocker or **backblockser.** One who lives in a remote rural area: Australian coll.: since ca. 1920. (B., 1943.) Also (*backblocker*) New Zealand coll., as in Jean Deranney, *Dawn Beloved*, 1928.

***backer-up; backing-up.** 'The accomplice of a woman who *works a ginger* on a client—i.e. robs him—is a *backer-up*, and the practice is called *backing-up*' (B., 1943): Australian c.: since ca. 1920.

backhouse flush. A very poor hand: Canadian poker players': since ca. 1955. 'Fit only for the privy' (*backhouse*, American and Canadian). Leechman.

backing dog. 'A sheepdog that will run across the backs of sheep to aid mustering or droving' (B., *The Drum*, 1959): Aus. rural coll.: late C. 19–20.

backward in coming forward (p. 25) is much earlier: it occurs, for instance, in Francis Francis, *Newton Dogvane*, 1859.

backwards—the way Molly went to church; or with *backwards* omitted. Backwards; *not* having gone: Anglo-Irish: C. 20.

backyard, adj. Small; insignificant; 'operating on a shoe-string': Australian coll.: since ca. 1925. 'A backyard publishing company.' (B.P.)

bacon and eggs. Legs: Australian: C. 20. B., 1942. Rhyming s.: cf. **ham and eggs** (*Dict.*).

bacon bonce. 'A dull fellow, one whose reactions are slow like those of a country yokel' (The Rev. P. M. Berry, as reported in *The Daily Telegraph* of June 4, 1958): Borstal, but also gen.: C. 20.

bacon-hole. Mouth: mostly R.A.F.: since ca. 1940. Cf. *cake-hole*.

bacon-tree. A pig: Lancashire jocular coll.: 1867, Brierley, *Marlocks*; slightly ob. Because a pig is 'growing bacon', E.D.D.

bad, taken (p. 25). Rather, since ca. 1840. *Sessions*, April 1851.

bad dog. An unpaid debt: Australian: since ca. 1945. (B., 1953.)

bad manners to speak when one's (more often **your) arse is full, it's.** A proletarian c.p. addressed to one who noisily breaks wind in company: C. 20.

bad mixer. See **mixer** (*Dict.*).

bad patchville. A period of bad luck: racing: since ca. 1960. Dick Francis, *Nerve*, 1964, ' "Pay no attention," he said. ". . . It's bad-patchville, that's all.' The *-ville*, a very popular suffix in the U.S., was adopted in the late 1950's. *Ibid.*, ' "Strictly doomsville, us." '

bad shilling.—2. A remittance man: Australian coll.: late C. 19–20. Cf. **bad halfpenny** (*Dict.*).

bad show. See **show, bad.**

bad trot. A *run* of bad luck: Australian: since ca. 1925. (Jon Cleary, *You Can't See round Corners*, 1949.)—2. A 'rough spin' or 'raw deal': Australian: C. 20. Ex the game of two-up. (B.P.)

bad types. Service personnel not keen on their work; als◆ objectionables: R.A.F. H. & P., 1943. See **types**, 2.

bad 'un (p. 25) occurs in W. N. Glascock's *The Naval Sketch-book*, II, 1826. (Moe.)

bad week, one's. The week of one's period: feminine coll.: late C. 19–20. 'It's my bad week, darling—as if you didn't know!': any wife to any husband, or, so far as that goes, any mistress to any lover. Not necessarily euphemistic.

bad with, get in. To get into bad odour with (e.g. the police): coll.: C. 20. Edgar Wallace, *Elegant Edward*, 1928.

baddy. A bad, an evil, person: mostly school-children's: since late 1950's.

badger, v. (p. 26), occurs in Grose, 1785.

badger-bag (p. 26) occurs in W. N. Glascock, *The Naval Sketch-Book*, I, 1825, as 'old Badger-bag's track', glossed by Glascock thus: 'A name given by Jack [=sailors] to Neptune, when playing tricks on travellers upon first crossing the Line'. (Moe.)

*badger-game. A form of blackmail, based upon timely arrival of 'injured husband'; Canadian c.: adopted, ca. 1910, ex U.S. (See *Underworld*.)

badster. A bad one (any living thing): Australian coll.: since ca. 1925. Jean Devanney, *By Tropic Sea*, 1944, 'He'—a mate—'was a badster, a soul killer.' After *youngster, oldster*, etc.

Baedeker is a coll. shortening of *Baedeker raid*, a raid on a place of historic interest rather than of military importance: 1942–4. Jackson. See esp. my *Name into Word*, 1949.

Baedeker Invasion, the. The invasion of Sicily during World War II: Army coll. Ex the booklets issued, beforehand, to the troops. (P-G-R.) Cf. the preceding entry.

baffle. Elaborate Field Security measure(s): military, esp. Royal Corps of Signals: since 1939. H. & P.

bag, n.—4. A parachute: orig. (ca. 1930) R.A.F.; by 1944 also military. H. & P. Pejorative? Ex its shape while it is unopened.—5. A woman, esp. a middle-aged or elderly slattern ('that old bag'); in certain contexts, a slatternly prostitute or part-time prostitute. I don't recall my having heard it before ca. 1924, but suspect that it goes back to the 1890's or even to the 1880's.

bag. v.—4. To dismiss or discharge (a person): 1848, *Chaplain's Report of Preston House of Correction*; 1895, W. Westall, *Sons of Belial*; rather ob. Cf. **sack.**—5. To shoot down (a 'plane): R.A.F.: 1939+. Jackson. I.e., to add to one's game bag.

bag, come the. To 'try it on'; to attempt something irregular; to bluff: Army: since ca. 1935. Ex horse's nose-bag.

bag!, get a. An Australian and New Zealand cricket spectators' c.p. to a fielder missing an easy catch: late C. 19–20.

*bag, hold the. See **hold the bag.**

bag, in the. (Of a situation, a plan, etc.) well in hand; fully arranged; a virtual certainty; Services: since ca. 1925. H. & P. Ex game shooting.—2. Hence, easy: Army: since ca. 1935.—3. *Be in the bag*, to be taken prisoner: Army: 1941+.—4. (Of a horse) not intended to run: Australian: racing: C. 20. B., 1942.

bag, pull one out of the. See **pull one out of the bag.**

bag, put in the. Taken prisoner (cf. **bag, in the,** 3): 1914–18, 1939–45: Army officers' > gen. Army. John Buchan, *Mr Standfast*, 1918.

bag, the. Money: Scottish, esp. Glasgow lower classes': late C. 19–20. MacArthur & Long.

bag, well, that's the. A publishers' representatives' c.p., addressed to the bookseller as they leave his office: C. 20. Stephen Mogridge, *Talking Shop* (bookshop), 1950.

bag of bones.—2. A 'bush pilot' aeroplane: Canadian: since ca. 1942. (Leechman.)

bag of coke. Australian (C. 20) for *bushel of coke.*

bag of nails, a. A state of confusion: Australian: C. 20. B., 1942. Higgledy-piggledy.

bag of snakes.—2. A pendulous breast: Australian ca. 1910–60. Perhaps the origin of sense 1, q.v. at **snakes, bag of,** below.

bag on the bowline (p. 26) occurs in Glascock's *The Naval Sketch-book*, 1825–26.

bag shanty. A brothel: Naval (lowerdeck): C. 20. Cf. *bag*, n., 5.

bag-swinger. A bookmaker: Australian: since ca. 1930. B., 1943.—2. See **swing a bag.**

*baggage man. He who, in a team of purse-snatchers, runs off with the booty: c.: C. 18. James Dalton, *A Narrative*, 1728.

bagged, adj. Imprisoned: Australian: since ca. 1925. (B., 1943.)

bagged, have one's wind. To be winded: Public Schools': from ca. 1880. E. H. Hornung, *Raffles*, 1899, 'Bunny, you've had your wind bagged at footer, I daresay; you know what that's like?' Ex **bag**, v., 2: q.v. in *Dict.*

baggies. 'Oversize boxer trunks, long in leg' (*Pix*, Sept. 28, 1963): Australian surfers': since ca. 1955.

bagman.—3. A tramp: Australian coll.: late C. 19–20.

Bagman's Gazette, The, or **The Drover's Guide.** An imaginary periodical quoted as the source of a rumour: Aus.: since ca. 1920. (Baker, *The Drum*, 1959.)

bago, the. Lumbago: Naval, but also gen.: C. 19–20. In, e.g., W. N. Glascock, *Sketch-Book*, 2nd Series, 1834, at II, 71. Moe.

bags, rough as (p. 27): also, since ca. 1918, New Zealand. (Gordon Slatter, 1959.)

bags of brace. 'Drill bombardier's exhortation to his squad,' H. & P.: Royal Artillery: since ca. 1920. Ex the idea of bracing oneself to make a special effort.

bags of bull; bags of panic. Excessive spit and polish and/or parading; very pronounced nervousness: R.A.F.: since ca. 1938. Partridge, 1945. See **bags of** (*Dict.*).

bahut atcha. Very good; also as exclamation: Anglo-Indian: mid-C. 19–20. Direct ex Hindustani.

baijan. See **bejan** (*Dict.*).

Bailey, the. The Old Bailey (the Central Criminal Court, London): police coll.: mid-C. 19–20.

bail-up. The n. of the v.: see p. 27.

bail up, v.—2. To corner or accost (a person): Australian: C. 20. (B., 1943.)

bails, the. The milking shed: Australian coll., esp. dairy-farmers': late C. 19–20. 'John is not in the house; he must be down at the bails.' Ex the *bail* that holds the head of a cow that is being milked. (B.P.)

baist (properly **baste**) **a snarl.** To work up a quarrel: tailors': from ca. 1860. B. & L.

bait.—4. A sexually very attractive girl: teenagers': since late 1950's. Variants: *bedbait, jailbait, johnnybait.* (*The Sunday Times*, Sept. 8, 1963.)

bait-layer. A station cook: rural Australian: since ca. 1925. (B., 1943.)

Bajan (pron. *Bay jun*). A Barbadian: B.W.I. coll.: late C. 19–20. For *'Badian*, aphetic for *Barbadian*. Dr Leechman compares *Cajun*, a person of French-Canadian descent living in southeast U.S., esp. Louisiana.

bake.—3. Hence (?), a bore, a nuisance: R.A.F. in India, ca. 1925–35. (Group-Captain Arnold Wall, letter of March 5, 1945.) Cf. the R.A.F. **bind**, n. and v.—4. A disappointment: Naval: since ca. 1920. Granville.

*bake up, v.; **bake-up,** n. See **stove up.**

baked and **mashed.** Baked—mashed—potatoes: domestic and (cheap) restaurants' coll.: late C. 19–20. (Julian Symons, *The Gigantic Shadow*, 1958.)

baker's dozen.—4. A cousin: rhyming s.: late C. 19–20. (Franklyn, *Rhyming*.)

Bakespeare, as in 'It was written by Bakespeare.' A literary or near-literary c.p., used to settle a tedious argument: since ca. 1930. A blend of *Bacon* + Sh*akespeare*.

bakester. See **bake,** v., in *Dict*.

bakey or **bakie.** A baked potato: low coll.: late C. 19–20. Jim Phelan, 1943.

baking-spittle. The human tongue: Yorkshire and Lancashire s., not dial.: from ca. 1890. Ex *b.-s.*, 'a thin spade-shaped board with a handle, used in baking cakes', E.D.D.

balance. (Of a bookmaker) to cheat (v.i.): Australian: C. 20. Hence *balancer, balancing*. B., 1942.

Balbo. 'A large formation of aircraft, so called after the famous flight, Dec. 1930, of the Italian Air Armada from Italy to South America, led by the late Marshal of that name,' H. & P., 1943. See esp. my *Name into Word*, and cf. **Immelmann** (*Dict*.).

balcony. Female breasts, esp. when displayed as a bulging ridge: Australian since late 1940's. Perhaps suggested by the Fr. *elle a du monde au balcon*.

bald.—2. Bad: itinerant entertainers': C. 20. Sydney Lester has 'Bad, *Bald; coteva*'.

bald as a bandicoot. Utterly bald: Australian coll.: since ca. 1910. (B., 1943.)

bald-headed. (See *Dict*.). It is perhaps worth noting that the popularly ascribed origin of the phrase *go bald-headed at it* is the Marquess of Granby's dashing charge at Warburg (1759), 'when his wig fell off and his squadron followed the bald but undaunted head of their noble leader' (*The Army Quarterly*, July 1937).

bald-headed prairie. Great treeless and shrubless plains: Canadian coll.: since ca. 1880. (Leechman.)

balderdash, poppycock and piffle! Nonsense: Australian cultured c.p.: since ca. 1955. A euphemism for *balls*!

baldober or **baldower** (p. 28). Better: *baldover*, as pronounced. German c. has, presumably via Yiddish, taken it ex Hebrew compound of *bal* (= *baal*, master, lord, owner) + *dovor* (word). Dr L. Stein.

Baldy. Nickname for a bald-headed man: coll.: C. 19–20. Cf. **curly.**

baldy. See **boxer.**—2. Usually in pl. *baldies*, white Hereford cattle: Australian rural: C. 20. (Jean Devanney, *By Tropic Sea*, 1944.)—3. An artist's model denuded of pubic hair: painters' and sculptors': since ca. 1950.

baldy! I refuse (cf. English schoolboy's 'fain I'): N.Z. juvenile: late C. 19–20. B., 1941. No hairs on one's head: nothing to offer.

bale out. To make a parachute descent from a 'plane: R.A.F. coll. (—1939) > j. by 1942. Jackson. Prob. an intransitive development of 'to bale out (a boat)': as a boat is emptied of water, so is an aircraft of its crew.—2. Hence, to depart hurriedly from a tank or a self-propelled gun: Army: since ca. 1940. (P-G-R.)—3. To 'ditch' the weight-belt and rise to the surface as quickly as possible: skin divers': since ca. 1950. Ex sense 1.

Bales, a little drive with. Imprisonment, or the going there: London streets': ca. 1880–1900. Ex that policeman who at one time superintended 'the Black Maria'. B. & L.

Balkan tap. 'A man suffering from Balkan Tap was easily recognized: he was gentle, foolish, indifferent, usually smiling, with a Lotus eater's philosophy, and he was almost incapable of performing the most ordinary duties' (C. E. Vulliamy in his delightful autobiography, *Calico Pie*, 1940): Macedonian campaigners', W.W. I.—On the analogy of the much older, better-known **doolally tap** (see *Dict*.).

ball.—2. See **ball o'chalk,** 2.

ball, have a. To have a thoroughly good time: Canadian, Australian, English; adopted ca. 1935, 1950, 1955, resp., ex U.S.

ball, have got the. To have the advantage: tailors': from ca. 1860. B. & L. Ex ball games.

ball, on the. Alert; esp., ready to grasp an opportunity: coll.: since ca. 1925. Ex ball-games.

ball, real gone. A superlatively good party or dance or reception: bodgies': since ca. 1950. (Dick.)

ball and chain. A wife: Canadian: C. 20. From U.S. Ex convicts' gyves.—2. One's girl friend: S. Africa: c. and low s.: since ca. 1920.

ball-bearing mousetrap. An ungelded male cat: Australian jocular: since ca. 1950. (B.P.)

ball-bearings in one's feet, have. To be habitually restless. Since ca. 1930: R.A.F.; by 1942, also Naval.

ball-dozed. Drunk; fuddled or muddled: Australian: since ca. 1942. (B., 1943.) Prompted by *bull-dozed*.

ball (o'chalk). To talk: rhyming s.: C. 20. *The Evening News*, Nov. 13, 1936.—2. See **penn'orth of chalk.**

ball of fire (p. 28). Slightly earlier in J. Burrowes, *Life in St George's Fields*, 1821.—2. As *the Ball of Fire*: the 2nd New Zealand Division: Army in North Africa: 1941–3.—3. A notably energetic and effectual person (usually male); often sarcastically in negative: Canadian: adopted, ca. 1930, ex U.S. (Leechman.)

ball of muscle (, be a). Energetic: very lively. Australian: since ca. 1930. (B., 1943.)

ball of spirit, be a. (Esp. of a horse) to be very high-spirited: Australian: since ca. 1918. (K. S. Prichard, *Working Bullocks*, 1926.)

ball(-)off, n. and v. (To commit) masturbation: men's low: C. 20.

ball-trap. An at times unexpectedly collapsible seat, esp. in an aircraft: R.A.F.: since ca. 1940. Also, since ca. 1945, Australian civilian for tractor seats, etc. (B.P.)

Ballarat lantern. Candle set in bottle neck: Australian: late C. 19–20. Ex mining days.

ballast, carry. See **carry** . . .

ballock. To reprimand, reprove, scold: c.: from ca. 1910; by 1920, low s. *Ballocking*, vbl n. With pun on *balls* and *bawl*. Hence:—

ballock, drop a. See **drop a** . . .

ballock drill. Custard and rhubarb: Naval (lower-deck): C. 20. See **rhubarb**.

ballock-naked. (Of both men and women) stark-naked: low: C. 20.

ballocker. A radar testing-device that resembled an ordinary light-bulb at the end of a long stick: R.A.F.: ca. 1941–5. If you don't 'see' the origin, I can't very well explain it.

ballocks.—Sense 1, parson, may be at least a century older, for in 1684 the Officer Commanding the Straits Fleet always referred to his chaplain as Ballocks. (Arthur Bryant, *The Saviour of the Navy*, 1938.)—3. (Usually *bollocks*.) Muddle, confusion; an instance thereof: Army: since ca. 1915.

ballocks, v. To spoil or ruin (a thing or plan): Australian: C. 20. (Sidney J. Baker, letter.)

ballocks about. To play the fool, esp. in horseplay; to be indecisive: low: C. 20.

ballocks in brackets. A low term of address to a bow-legged man: C. 20. W. L. Gibson Cowan, *Loud Report*, 1937.

ballocks'd. Thwarted; in a dilemma: low: C. 20. Cf. **ballocks, v.**

***ballocky**, adj. Naked: c., and low: from ca. 1905. Compare *Ballocky Bill the Sailor*.

balloon.—2. A high and easy catch: cricketers': from ca. 1925. J. C. Masterman, *Fate Cannot Harm Me*, 1935, 'And then like an ass I missed a balloon this afternoon—just in front of the pavilion too.'

balloon car, usually **balloon**. A saloon bar: C. 20. (Franklyn, *Rhyming*.)

balloonatic.—2. Hence, 'anyone on the strength of a Balloon Command unit or squadron', Jackson: R.A.F.: 1940+. Partridge, 1945. The term was also, during W.W.I, applied—usually in the plural—to the free-balloonists. (Mr William Phillips of the Inner Temple, himself a free-balloonist.)

balls, have (got) someone by the. To have utterly in one's power, esp. of women over men: low: late C. 19–20. (G. Kersh, 1944.)

balls-ache. See **you give me** . . . *A balls-aching talk* is a tedious disquisition: since ca. 1918.

balls, bees and buggery! A synonym—and probably the origin—of *balls, picnics* . . . c.p.: late C. 19–20.

balls chewed off, have one's. To be (severely) reprimanded or taken to task: low: C. 20.

balls in an uproar, get one's. To become unduly excited: Canadian Army: 1914–18.

balls on him like a scoutmaster (, he has). A low New Zealand c.p., dating from ca. 1930 and based upon the scurrilous ideas, popular among the ignorant, that scoutmasters are active homosexuals. Canadian also.

balls, picnics and parties! A c.p. exclamation, from ca. 1925. A punning elaboration of **balls!** (*Dict.*).

balls to that lark! Nothing doing: New Zealand c.p.: since ca. 1920. (Slatter.) An elaboration of *balls to that!*, common to all the Commonwealth countries and current since late C. 19. Cf. **balls to you!** on p. 29.

balls to you, love. A variant of *balls to you*: C. 20. Influenced by working-men's contempt of the white-collar class and by their ignorance of the ardours of lawn tennis.

balls-up. A 'mess', a bungling, confusion: low: since ca. 1910. (Angus Wilson, *A Bit off the Map*, 1957.)

ballum rancum (p. 29). Earlier in Dryden's *Kind Keeper*, 1677–8. Cf. *ballers* in Pepys's Diary, May 30, 1668.

bally (p. 29). Rather, since ca. 1840. *Sessions*, April 1851.

Bally Ruffian, the. H.M.S. *Bellerophon*: Naval: mid-C. 19–20. (Neil Bell, *Crocus*, 1936.)

ballyhoo of blazes (p. 29). Dating since ca. 1880, it occurs in Rudyard Kipling's *Captains Courageous*, 1897.

Balmainiacs. Balmain footballers: Sydney-siders: C. 20. (B., 1943.)

balmy breeze. Cheese: (not very common) rhyming s.: C. 20. (Franklyn 2nd.)

balmy stick dates back to ca. 1880. (B. & L.)

Balt. 'This was the most common term for New Australians from about 1946 to 1952 and will be found in the Australian literature of the period. It was based on the mistaken belief that they came mainly from the Baltic countries' (B.P., 1963).

Balt and **Mary.** A Baltimore—a Maryland—aircraft: airmen's: World War II.

bamboo. Inside information; a rumour: Army: 1940+. Ex makeshift aerials. Cf. **jungle wireless**.

bamboo, three-piece. See **three-piece bamboo** (*Dict.*).

bamboo present. See 'Prisoner-of-War Slang', 15.

bambora. 'The spot of light reflected by a mirror held in the hand' (Dr H. W. Dalton): Anglo-Irish: C. 20. Origin?

ban.—2. (Mostly in pl. *bans*.) A banana: greengrocers': since ca. 1910.

banana. A £1 note: Australian: since ca. 1945. (B., *Australia Speaks*, 1953.) Sweet and acceptable.—2. A surf board with a raised front: Australian surfers': since late 1950's. (B.P.)

banana balancer. An officer's steward: a Wardroom waiter: Naval: C. 20. Granville.

banana boat. An invasion barge: military: 1943+. H. & P. Humorous.—2. An aircraft carrier: R.A.F.: 1941+. Partridge, 1945.

banana van. A 'bogie carriage on wooden frame sagging in the middle' (*Railway*, 3rd): railwaymen's: since ca. 1950.

bananas and cream?, do you like. A c.p. addressed to girls by dirty-minded youths and = Do you 'do it'?: since ca. 1920.

banchoot (or **barnshoot**); **beteechoot.** In Hindustani, *choad* is a male copulator; *ban*, pron. *bahn* (*barn*), is 'sister'; *betee*, 'daughter'. Hence *banchoad*: *beteechoat* = copulator with sister, daughter; hence, a deadly insult.

band. A prostitute: Australian: since ca. 1920. B., 1942.

Band of Hope. Lemon syrup: Australian: C. 20. Baker. Ex name of the Temperance Society. —2. Soap: rhyming s.: late C. 19–20. (Len Ortzen, *Down Donkey Row*, 1938.)

bandabust. A variant (especially among R.A.F. regulars) of **bundabust** (*Dict.*). Jackson.

bander. Soap: Australian: C. 20. Baker. Truncated rhyming s.

bandicoot, poor as a. Extremely poor: Austra-

lian coll.: late C. 19–20. In *The Drum*, 1959,
S. J. Baker lists also the foll. self-explanatory
phrases: *bald as a bandicoot, bandy as a . . .,
barmy as a . . ., lousy . . ., miserable . . .,* and
not the brains of . . .

bandicooting. 'The practice of stealing tuber-
ous vegetables, especially potatoes, out of the soil
without removing the tops' (B., 1943), i.e. with the
tops left: Australian: since ca. 1920. As bandi-
coots do.

bandit. Elliptical for **one-armed bandit** (below):
Australian: since late 1950's. (B.P.)

[**bandit.** An enemy aircraft: orig. a code word,
then j.—not s. Jackson.]

bandmaster, the. A pig's head: Naval (lower-
deck): C. 20. Granville.

bandstand. A cruet: R.A.F. since ca. 1920:
adopted from the Army (C. 20). Ex the 'iron-
work' surrounding one.—2. 'In Ack Ack the Command post of a gun position,' H. & P.: since 1939.
—3. 'The circular gun platform in small escort
vessels' (Granville): Naval: 1939 +.

bandwagon, hop—or, in Britain, mostly **jump-
on the.** To join a majority, once it's known to be
a majority; to favour someone only after the
public has made him or her a favourite: adopted,
ca. 1960, ex U.S.; by 1966, coll. (*The Sunday
Times*, colour section, July 8, 1962, article by
Wallace Reyburn.) In his excellent *The Changing
English Language*, 1968, Brian Foster cites *The
Sunday Times*, Feb. 13, 1955, and *The Times
Educational Supplement* of a few days later.
Perhaps, therefore, it would be better to back-date
the adoption to ca. 1955. See, too, William Safire,
The New Language of Politics, 1968.

bandy, n.—2. A bandicoot: Australian: since
ca. 1910. (B., 1953.)

bandy chair. A Banbury chair, i.e. a seat
formed by two persons' crossing of hands: Cockneys': from ca. 1880.

bane, the. Brandy: low: late C. 19–20; ob.
Pugh (2), ' "You give me a drop o' the bane," said
Marketer; "an' don't be so 'andy wi' your
tongue." ' Suggested by **ruin**, 1 (*Dict.*).

bang, an intensive, as in 'the whole *bang* lot':
mostly Australian: late C. 19–20. (B., 1943.)

bang, n.—6. A brothel: low Australian: since
ca. 1920. B., 1942.—7. (Ex 2.) A stir or considerable movement in stocks and shares, esp.
downward: Stock Exchange: ca. 1810–70. *Spy*,
II, 1826.

bang, v., 3 (p. 31): very common, esp. among
manual workers, in Australia, where also used
intransitively. (B.P.) Also common still in
Canada. (Leechman.)

bang, adv. Noisily and suddenly; suddenly;
immediately;—also, entirely, utterly: coll.: late
C. 18-late 19. *The Night Watch*, 1828, at II, 117.
(Moe.)

bang, have a. To make an attempt (*at*): Services': since ca. 1939. (P-G-R.)

bang like a hammer on a nail or **like a rattlesnake** or **like a shit-house door; go pop like a paper
bag; ride like a town bike.** To copulate vigorously; *bang* referring to men, and *pop* and *ride* to
women: low Australian: esp. Sydney: *bang*, C.
20; *ride* since ca. 1925; *pop* since ca. 1950.

bang alley (p. 31); *bangalay* actually is Aboriginal.

bang-bag. A case for cordite: Australian Naval:
since ca. 1925. (B., 1943.)

bang, bang, you're dead! A children's c.p.,
since ca. 1960. Ex overmuch televiewing of
'Westerns'.

bang-box. The turret of a 6-inch gun: Australian Naval: since ca. 1925. (B., 1943.)

bang(-)on. Everything is all right: correct:
R.A.F. bomber crews': since 1940. H. & P.
I.e. bang on the target. As 'dead accurate,
strikingly apposite', it was adopted by civilians
in 1945. (Nicholas Blake, *Head of a Traveller*,
1948.)

bang-seat. 'A crew member's seat in a jet aircraft (but recently developed for helicopters)—
which, for emergency escape, is blown from the
aircraft by an explosive charge (which, incidentally, the seat occupant does not hear)'—as a
flight lieutenant informs me, late in 1961.— Since
the mid-1950's: orig., Fleet Air Arm, hence gen.
aeronautical.

bang-stick. A rifle: partly marksmen's, partly
Services': since ca. 1925. Cf. *shooting-iron*.

bang-tail. See 'Harlots'.—2. Usually pl. *bang-
tails*, cattle, 'whence *bang tail muster*, a periodical
counting of herds' (B., *The Drum*, 1959): Aus.
rural: since ca. 1930. Contrast the American
bangtail, a horse, esp. a racehorse. Now mostly
written as one word.

bang to rights. Applied, predicatively, to a
'fair cop', a justified charge, a perfect case against
somebody: underworld; London's East End,
police: since ca. 1930, at latest. (Richard Herd,
Nov. 12, 1957; Frank Norman, *Bang to Rights*,
1958.) An elaboration, an intensive, of '(caught)
to rights' or *in flagrante delicto*.—2. 'An expression
of satisfaction, as in "Now we've got everything
bang to rights, we can lay off for a bit and have a
smoke" ' (Julian Franklyn, in a letter, 1962): since
the late 1940's.

bang-up.—4. To lock up, esp. of a warder a cell:
prisons': C. 20. (Norman.)—5. 'A frieze overcoat
with high collar and long cape' (P. W. Joyce,
English As We Speak It in Ireland, 1910): Anglo-
Irish: late C. 19–20.

bang water. Petrol: Canadian (also *firewater*):
since ca. 1920. H. & P.

banger.—4. A sausage: nautical, esp. Naval:
C. 20. ('Taffrail', *Mystery at Milford Haven*,
1936.)—5. Elliptical for *cattle-banger*. (B., 1943.)
—6. A bomb: R.F.C.–R.A.F.: 1917–18. V. M.
Yeates, *Winged Victory*, a novel, 1934.—7. (Also
cracker and **fog.**) A detonator: railwaymen's:
C. 20. (*Railway*.)—8. A motorcar that 'bangs'
(is noisy): motorists': since ca. 1930.—9. A
derelict car: motorists': since ca. 1955.
Sense 4 occurs earlier in 'Bartimeus', *A Tall
Ship*, 1915.

banger, drop a. See **drop a ballock.**

bangers and red lead. Tinned sausages-and-
tomato-sauce: mostly the Services': since ca.
1925.

bangotcher (strictly *bang-gotcher*). A Wild West
film: Australian juvenile: since ca. 1946. (B.,
1953.) 'Bang! Got you!'

Bangkok bowler. See 'Prisoner-of-War Slang',
15.

bangs banagher, it. That beats everything:
Anglo-Irish c.p.: mid-C. 19–20. Rolf Boldrewood, *My Run Home*, 1897 (p. 190), in a passage
dealing with a period ca. 1860. Cf. *banagher* (p.
37) and P. W. Joyce, *English As We Speak It in
Ireland*, 1910, p. 192.

bangtail. See **bang-tail**, 2, above.

banian or **banyan**, 2 (p. 31): much earlier in *The Night Watch*, 1828 (II, 57). (Moe.)

banjax. To ruin, to defeat, to destroy: Anglo-Irish: C. 20. (Desmond O'Neill, *Life Has No Price*, 1959.) Cf.:

banjaxed. Broken, smashed, out of order: Anglo-Irish intensive: since ca. 1920. Blend of '*banged* about' + '*smashed*'?

banjo.—2 (p. 31). Also English builders'. (Communication from a master builder: Dec. 5, 1953.)—4. A sandwich: c., and low: from ca. 1919.—5. A shoulder of mutton: Australian: since ca. 1920. B., 1942.—6. A fireman's shovel: railwaymen's: since ca. 1945. (*Railway*, 3rd.) Cf. sense 2 on p. 31; orig. an American tramps' term.—7. A 'disc signal repeater with black line and white background' (*Railway*, 3rd): railwaymen's: since ca. 1955. Ex the musical instrument.—8. A frying pan: Aus.: since 1959.

banjo box. A wooden box for washing alluvial metal: Australian miners': late C. 19–20. Sarah Campion. *Bonanza*, 1942. Ex shape.

bank, n.—3. The issuing of pocket money: Public Schools: late C. 19–20. (Ernest Raymond, *Tell England*, 1922.)

bank, on the. Subsisting on bank loans: Aus. coll.: C. 20. F. B. Vickers, *First Place to the Stranger*, 1955. 'Chris Cotter came over to Jingiddy on train days and saw the farmers who were "on the bank" then, instead of as before touring round the farms.'

banker.—3. An 'assisting locomotive' (*Railway*, 3rd): railwaymen's coll.: C. 20.—4. 'The man who holds a stock of forged notes for those who give them out or try to do so' (A. B. Petch, April 1966): fringe-of-underworld: C. 20.

banker, come down a. '(Of a river) to become flooded' (B., *The Drum*, 1959): Aus. coll.: late C. 19–20. Cf. **banker**, 1, on p. 32.

banks. Rag shops: Australian: C. 20. B., 1942. Cf. **rag shop**, 3 (*Dict.*), the origin.

banshee wail. An air-raid warning: coll.: 1940+.

banter is described by Swift in *A Tale of a Tub*, 1704, as an 'Alsatia phrase'.

bapper. A baker: Scottish coll.: mid-C. 19–20; ob. E.D.D. Pejoratively ex *bap*, a bread-cake.

Bappo. A Baptist: Australian: since ca. 1925. (B., 1953.) B., *The Drum*, 1959, compares **Congo, Metho, Presbo**—qq.v. below.

baptized. Drowned: Australian: since ca. 1830. Brian Penton's novels, *passim*. Ironic.

bar, n., 2. Earlier in J. W. Horsley, *I Remember*, 1912.—3. An excuse; a yarn, a 'tale': Regular Army, but esp. in the Guards: since ca. 1910. Gerald Kersh, *Bill Nelson*, 1942, 'He had a good bar though, it was on his pass. He'd been trying to get some geezer out of a shelter'; Roger Grinstead, 1943 and 1946, records *soft bar* (a persuasive story), *cakey bar* (a downright lie) and *to spin the bar*. Ex *debar(ring)*?—4. See:

Bar Abbas and **Bar Jonas.** The two coffee-bars, in the Vatican, for the immured Cardinals and their subordinates: the English-speaking Cardinals': since ca. 1950.

bar (or **bar on**), **have a.** To have an erection: low: C. 20. Ex hardness.

bar, over the. Half-drunk; fuddled: nautical: ca. 1810–70. *Sessions*, April 6, 1843.

bar of (person or thing), **unable to stand a.** To detest: Australian: since ca. 1920. (Margaret Trist, *Now That We're Laughing*, 1945; Ruth Park, *Poor Man's Orange*, 1950.)

bar of chocolate, get a. See **chocolate** . . .

bar steward. A bastard: jocular, mostly Londoners': from ca. 1929. Euphemistic or polite.

barbary. Difficult in a tough way: Army in N. Africa and N.W. Europe: 1942–5. A *barbary bugger* was a tough and bloody-minded officer or non-com; (of the enemy) 'They're a bit barbary tonight' (harassing fire, etc.). Perhaps ex 'the Barbary Coast', influenced by *barbarous*; but cf. next.

Barbary (or **bobbery**) **wallah.** An ill-tempered person: Army and R.A.F. regulars': late C. 19–20. Jackson. Prob. from **bobbery** (p. 73), influenced by *Barbary pirates*. 'Used esp. by and to English-speaking Irakis' (Atkinson).

barbed-wire blues (or **fever**). Prisoner-of-war camp despondency or disgust: prisoner-of-war: 1941–5. The former is an adaptation of George Gershwin's famous title *Rhapsody in Blue.*

barber.—2. See **barber a joint.**—3. A hotel-keeper: Australian: since ca. 1925. A gossip.—4. A tramp: Australian: since ca. 1930. (B., 1943.)

barber, she couldn't cook hot water for a. See **she couldn't** . . .

barber?, who robbed the. See **he's a poet.**

*barber a joint. To rob a bedroom while the occupant sleeps: c.: C. 20. Also *barber*, one who does this.

barber-shop harmony. 'Said derisively of male quartettes. From at least 1909' (Leechman): Canadian coll. By 1962, Standard English. (Professor F. E. L. Priestley, letter of Oct. 12, 1965.)

barber's cat, 2 (p. 32). Often *like a barber's cat, all wind and piss*: late C. 19–20.

barbly. Babble; noise: pidgin: from ca. 1860. B. & L. Cf. **bobbery** (*Dict.*).

Barcoo buster. 'A westerly gale in mid or south Queensland' (B., *The Drum*, 1959): C. 20.

Barcoo challenge. Either of two methods of indicating that one is challenging for the day's tally at sheepshearing: Aus. rural: ca. 1890–1940. (*The Drum.*)

Barcoo rot. Gallipoli sores: Australian soldiers': 1915. Ex the literal Australianism.

Barcoo vomit. '*Barcoo rot*: Land scurvy. *Barcoo vomit*, another old bush sickness' (*The Drum*): Aus. rural: C. 20.

Bardia Bill. The 6-inch gun that, in 1941, bombarded Tobruk pretty regularly: Services: 1941, then ob. Granville. Cf. **Asiatic Annie.**

bardies. See **starve the bardies.**

bare-belly. 'A sheep without wool on its belly or inner portions of its hind legs' (B., *The Drum*, 1959): Aus. rural coll.: mid C. 19–20.

bareback riding; or **roughriding.** Coïtion without contraceptive: male: C. 20.

bared, be. To be shaved: low: ca. 1860–1910. B. & L.

barge, n.—6. Hence, the crowd in a R.A.F. mess: since ca. 1916. Duncan Grinwell Milne, *Wings of Wrath.*—7. A straw hat: Cranbrook School: C. 20. Cf. the S.E. *boater.*

barge, v., 1, survives as **barge at**, to argue roughly with: Cockneys': late C. 19–20.

barge the point. To 'argue the toss': C. 20. (*The Pawnshop Murder.*) Cf. **barge**, v., 1 (*Dict.*).

bargeman (p. 32) goes back to ca. 1800. (W. N. Glascock, *Sailors and Saints*, 1829.) (Moe.)

bark, n.—4. An objectionable fellow; a very severe one: Cockneys': from ca. 1910. Ex *bastard* with allusion to dog's bark or snarl.

bark and growl. A trowel: rhyming s.: since ca. 1870. (D. W. Barrett, *Navvies*, 1880.)

bark up the wrong creek. An occ. C. 20 variant of **bark up the wrong tree** (*Dict.*).

barkey, 2 (p. 34). Also *barky*, as in W. N. Glascock, *The Naval Sketch-Book*, II, 1826: which obliges us to date the term back to ca. 1810 or even earlier and to derive sense 1 from sense 2; there it is glossed as 'Jack's fancy phrase for a favourite ship'. Clearly a diminutive of Naval *bark* or *barque.*

barking, adj. Raving mad: since ca. 1965. John Welcome, *Hell Is Where You Find It*, 1968, 'She had something, that girl. She's mad, that's the worst of it. Bonkers, barking, round the bend.' Ex dogs suffering from rabies?

barking belly. A 4-inch anti-aircraft gun: Australian naval: 1939–45. (B., 1943.)

barmaid. A C. 20 Harrow term, thus in Lunn: 'He put on the double collar popularly known as the "barmaid", the monopoly of three-yearers.'

barmaid's blush. 'A drink of port and lemonade, or rum and raspberry' (B., 1942): Australian: C. 20. Ex its vivid colour.—2. That special shade of pink paint which, used on invasion craft, was suggested by Lord Louis Mountbatten and therefor known, semi-officially, as *Mountbatten pink*: Services': ca. 1943–5. (P-G-R.)

barmpot. A person slightly deranged: since ca. 1950. *The Sunday Times*, July 14, 1963 (competition). A blend of *barmy + potty.*

barmy (p. 34). Perhaps its popularity was assisted by the County of Kent lunatic asylum at *Barming.*

Barn dance, the; also **the scramble.** Pedestrians scurrying across a street diagonally as soon as the indicator says 'Go' or 'Cross': at crossings where all traffic halts. Australian and New Zealand: since ca. 1950. The former was named after Commissioner Barnes—Traffic Commissioner of New York City—the inventor of the buzz crossing; origin of latter, obvious.

barn-stormer.—3. One who, ca. 1919–22, did acrobatics, wing-walking, etc., on aeroplanes; also, any pilot who put on a show for the small-town people of the country: Canadian. (Leechman.)

Barnaby Rudge. A judge: rhyming s.: C. 20. (Franklyn, *Rhyming.*)

Barnet. This abbr. of **Barnet Fair** (q.v. *in Dict.*) prob. dates from ca. 1880. See the quotation at **Sir Garnet** (*Dict.*).

barney, n., 4 (p. 35, top). Also common in Australia and New Zealand: late C. 19–20. B., 1941. Much earlier in *Sessions*, July 1877, and orig. Cockney.

barney, v. To argue (*about* something): Australian: C. 20. B., 1942.

barney, bit of. A scuffle, fight or heated argument; esp. rowdyism in a public-house: late C. 19–20. An elaboration of **barney,** n., 6 (*Dict.*).

barney, do a. To prevent a horse from winning: turf: from ca. 1870. B. & L. See **barney,** n., 4 (p. 35).

Barney Moke. A pocket: rhyming s. (on *poke*): originally (−1941), c.; by 1950, low s.

barney over (something). To quarrel about it: Aus.: C. 20. (*The Drum*, 1959.) Cf. **barney,** v., above.

Barney's bull, like.—2. *All behind like Barney's bull*: late; delayed: Australian: since ca. 1920. Baker. Cf. sense 1 (p. 35).

barns. Shorts; trousers: Marlborough College: since ca. 1920.

barnshoot (*Dict.*). See **banchoot.**

Baron.—2. 'Anything free in the Navy is said to be "on the Baron" or "Harry Freemans",' Granville: C. 20. Jocular.

baron.—2. A recognised businessman, or boss, among the prisoners: prison c.: since ca. 1930. (Norman.)—3. One who has money: beatniks': since late 1950's. (Anderson.)

Baron, the. Lord Hawke: cricketers': since the late 1880's: ob. by 1940. Major Martin Blades Hawke (1860–1938), captain of Yorkshire in 1883–1910; succeeded to the title in 1887.

barrack, n. A piece of 'barracking': Australian: C. 20. (Vance Palmer, *The Passage*, 1930.)

barrack ranger. A seaman, that in R.N. Barracks is awaiting draft to a ship: Navy: since ca. 1920. Granville.

barrack-rat. (Gen. pl.) Indian Army, non-officers', from ca. 1880, as in Richards, 'Children born in Barracks were referred to as "barrack-rats": it was always a wonder to me how the poor kids survived the heat, and they were washed-out little things.'

barrack-room lawyer. A soldier professing to know military law: Army coll.: late C. 19–20.— 2. Hence, a confirmed 'grouser': Army: since ca. 1910. (P-G-R.)

Barrack (or Barrick) Stove, the. Aden: Services': since ca. 1950. A very hot station. (Peter Sanders.)

barracking (p. 35). Note, however, that the very able journalist, Guy Innes, says, in a private letter of March 1, 1944, 'I have always understood, and indeed believe, that this word originated from the widespread description in Melbourne of the rough teams that used to play football on the vacant land near the Victoria *Barracks* on the St Kilda Road as *barrackers.*'

barracks (p. 35) occurs in W. N. Glascock, *The Naval Sketch-Book*, II, 32, 1826, and therefore goes back to very early C. 19. (Moe.)

barrage, get a. On the drill-ground or square, to obtain a very smart response to an order; *have a barrage taken off*, to be 'put through it' on the parade ground: Army: since ca. 1919. The sound-effect resembles that of a gun barrage.

barrel, back to the. See **barrel of butter** below.

barrel, have (someone) **over a.** To have him at a grave disadvantage: adopted, ca. 1950—earlier in Canada—ex U.S.

barrel, right into (or **right up**) **one's.** Decidedly one's interest, concern, business: Australian: C. 20. B., 1942.

barrel-fever.—2. Hence, delirium tremens: Australian: C. 20. (B., 1943.)

barrel of butter. A small rock just awash in the middle of Scapa Flow; hence, *back to the barrel*, back to the anchorage in the Flow: Naval: since ca. 1910. (Granville, Aug. 10, 1962.)

barrel of fat. A hat: Australian rhyming s.: C. 20. (Franklyn 2nd.)

barren Joey. A prostitute: N.S.W., low: C. 20. B., 1942.

barrister. See 'Tavern terms', § 3, *d*.

barrow. A 'Black Maria': Australian: C. 20. B., 1942.—2. 'To the bus conductor your ticket is a "brief" and his vehicle a "tub", "kite" or "barrow" ' (*The Evening News*, April 27, 1954).— 3. (Mostly in the Cockney pron., *barrer*.) A motor car: esp. in the secondhand-car business: since ca. 1955. Prob. ex sense 2—which, by the way, goes back to ca. 1945.

barrow, into one's. Occ. variant of **barrel, right into one's.**

barrow, right up one's. Synonymous with **barrell, right . . .**, above. (B., 1959.)

bars. Handlebars: cyclists' coll.: late C. 19–20.

bart. A girl: Australian: since ca. 1920; 'now practically obsolete', says Baker in 1943. Origin obscure, unless—as Julian Franklyn has suggested —it rhymes on *tart*.

base over apex is a refined version of **arse over tip**: from ca. 1925.

bash, n. Brutality: Australian: since ca. 1925. (B., *Australia Speaks*, 1953.)—2. A long—esp. if fast and arduous—ride: cyclists': since ca. 1930. 'The Brighton bash' = London to Brighton and back.—3. An attempt; esp. in *have a bash* (*at* something): since ca. 1935.—4. A lively visit or experience or time: Canadian: since ca. 1955. *Daily Colonist*, April 2, 1967. 'The party of 48 chartered a bus for a night on the town including a bash at the Old Forge.' (Leechman.)—5. A copulation: low: since ca. 1930. Mervyn Jones, *The New Town*, 1953.

*bash, v.—2. To flog: since ca. 1860. B. & L. —3. V.i., to ply as a prostitute: C. 20: c. >, by 1930, low s. Gerald Kersh, 1938. Ex **bash, go on the** (*Dict.*).—4. To sell (personal possessions or Red Cross gifts): prisoners-of-war: 1939–45. (Guy Morgan, *Only Ghosts Can Live*, 1945.) Prompted by the synonymous *flog*, 3 (p. 288).—See *bash it*.

bash; bash it; give it a bash. 'To indulge in a bout of heavy drinking' (B., 1953): Australian: since ca. 1935. Gavin Casey, *The Wits Are Out*, 1947, 'A man's gotta drink. . . . But you can't bash it all the time, the way he does, if you want to get anywhere.'—2. To live gaily, have a good time: general: since ca. 1940. (Jack Trevor Story, *Mix Me a Person*, 1959, has 'bash it around'.)

bash, go on the. To indulge in a drinking-bout: New Zealand: since ca. 1930. (Slatter.) Cf. *bash it* at *bash; bash it* above.

bash, have a. To make an attempt; to help; to take part: since ca. 1925.

*bash, the. Smash and grab: c.: from ca. 1920.

bash it up you! Run away and stop bothering me: Australian (esp. in the Services): since ca. 1940. (B., *Australia Speaks*, 1953.)

bash on. To 'carry on', bravely and doggedly: originally, soldiers' (1940); then, by 1946, general. Hence, by 1942, attribute, as in 'the bash-on spirit', as in *Leader Magazine*, March 4, 1950.

bash the bishop. See **bishop, flog the.**

bash up. To 'beat up', to assault, someone: Australian since ca. 1945. (B.P.)

Basher. The nickname of any pugilist who is a slugger rather than a skilled boxer: mostly sporting: late C. 19–20. Cf. **basher,** 1 (p. 36).

basher.—3. Also, 1925+, at Rugby.—4. A Physical Training Instructor: Services: since ca. 1920. H. & P.—5. See **gravel-basher** and **square basher.** Echoic.—6. '*Buster* or *basher* is very common for mechanics, as in *compass basher*, *instrument basher*,' Sgt-Pilot F. Rhodes, letter of Sept. 20, 1942: R.A.F.: since ca. 1930.—7. Indeed *basher* has often, since 1941, meant little more than 'fellow', 'chap'. Partridge, 1945. Ex the accumulated influence of senses 4–6.—8. A fornicator: R.A.F.: since ca. 1935. Yet another sexual sadism.—9. A bamboo hut: Army (mostly S.E. Asia): 1942+. Ex bamboo used as a weapon.— 10. A hoodlum: Australian: since ca. 1920. (B., 1943.)

bashing, n. See next entry.—2. The loud, vigorous, cheerful playing of dance music: an engagement at which such music is demanded: dance bands': since ca. 1930.—3. Prostitution: low: C. 20. Gerald Kersh, *Night and the City*, 1938. See **bash it.**—4. Short for *bashing the bishop*: low: since ca. 1920. The full phrase may have arisen as an alliterative variant of *box the Jesuit* (p. 87).—5. In *get*, or *take, a bashing*, to suffer heavy losses: Services': 1939–45, and after. (P-G-R.)

bashing-in; bashing-out. A flogging at the beginning (-in*) or at the end (*-out*) of a 'ruffian's term of imprisonment': c.: from ca. 1870. B. & L. Ex **bash,** v., 2. Moreover, *bashing* exists independently.

basic English. 'Plain' English, esp. as used by workmen not averse from vulgarity and obscenity: since ca. 1935. (A. B. Petch, March 1966.)

Basil. A fat man: Liverpool: from before 1952.

Basil dress. Ensa uniform: since ca. 1940. Ensa's director: Basil Dean.

basin of gravy. A baby: rhyming s.: C. 20.

basinful, a. Of trouble, hardship, labour, etc.: C. 20. Hence, *get one's basinful*, to receive a severe —esp., a fatal—wound: mostly Army: 1914–18; 1939–45. Gerald Kersh, *Clean, Bright and Slightly Oiled*, 1946, 'Poor old Pete got his basinful somewhere near Hell-fire.'

basinful, have a. To make an attempt; to agree to do so, as 'I'll have a basinful, if you like': Services': since ca. 1939. (P-G-R.)

basinful of that, I'll have a. A c.p. aimed at anyone using a long or a learned word: since ca. 1910.

*basis. The woman a pimp intends to marry when he retires from business: white-slavers' c.: C. 20. (A. Londres, 1928.)

basket, 4 (p. 36): also otherwise than in vocative, as 'That basket So-and-So'.

*basket, with a kid in the. Pregnant: c.: C. 19. B. & L.

bastard brig. See **schooner orgy.**

bastard from the bush. The C. 20 Australian equivalent of **Ballocky Bill the Sailor** (p. 29). Ex a poem by Henry Lawson (1867–1922). (B.P.)

baste a snarl. See **baist a snarl.**

baster. A house thief: Australian low: C. 20. B., 1942.

Basutes. Native troops from Basutoland: Army: 1940+. (P-G-R.)

bat, n.—7. Hence, a sale: grafters': Aug. 28, 1938, *News of the World*.—8. 'A whip carried by a horse-rider. Also *mop* and *stick*' (B., *The Drum*, 1959): Aus.: since ca. 1930.

B

bat, v. Military, mostly officers', from late 1914, as in Blaker, ' "That fellow Jackman that Reynolds has produced from his section to 'bat' for you is rather an object, isn't he?" ' Ex **bat** (*Dict.*), n., 4: q.v. Contrast **bloke,** v.

bat an eyelid, doesn't or don't. (She, etc.) show(s) no emotion at something either startling or shocking: coll.: C. 20. Cf. the S.E. *bat the eyes.*

bat for. To make one's price at (such or such a sum): showmen's: C. 20. *Night and Day,* July 22, 1937. 'Most crocus bat for a dena . . . or . . . a two ender . . . but to "bat 'em for a straight tosh" is something to be proud about,' Phillip Allingham in a letter, 1937.

bat house. A brothel: Australian low: C. 20. Baker.

bat on a (very) sticky wicket. To contend with great difficulties: coll.: since ca. 1948. (*National News Letter,* Jan. 24, 1952.) Ex cricket.

bat out of hell, go like a. As a civilian coll., it is at least as early as 1908. (Leechman.)

bat the breeze. To chatter, to talk: Australian soldiers': since ca. 1939. (B., 1943.)

batch, n.—2. A small cottage; a shack; Australian: since ca. 1920. B., 1942. Ex **bach,** v. (*Dict.*).

batcher. One who lives alone: Australian: C. 20. Baker.

batchy (p. 37). Also, since ca. 1910, Naval.— 2. 'The nickname for anyone surnamed Payne' (Granville): esp. Naval: since ca. 1910. Proleptic.

bate up. A sexual copulation: low: C. 20. Origin obscure.

Bath bun. A son: rhyming s.: late C. 19–20.

bath-tub. Nacelle of the F.E. aeroplane: R.F.C.–R.A.F.: World War I, then historical. (Frederick Oughton, *The Aces,* 1961.)

bath-tub cabbage. 'Cabbage boiled until it is tasteless and almost colourless, as served in schools and boarding-houses' (Peter Sanders): since ca. 1920.

bathers. A bathing costume: Australian coll.: C. 20. Baker.

bathing beauty. Blancmange: Naval (lower-deck): since ca. 1930. Granville.

Bats. Deck-landing officer in an aircraft carrier: Navy: since ca. 1938. Granville, 'From the bats he carries.'

Bats. British *A*merican *T*obacco Company *s*hares: Stock Exchange: since ca. 1930.

batter. To practise copulation: low: since ca. 1920. Gerald Kersh, *Night and the City,* 1938. Ex **batter, go on the** (p. 37).

Battersea'd. (Of the male member) treated medically for venereal disease: ca. 1715–90. *Select Trials at the Old Bailey,* 1743 (Dublin, vol. 2), trial of George White in 1726, 'Mine is best, yours has been Battersea'd.' The semantic clue is afforded by **simples** (p. 770).

batting and bowling, adj. and n. Participating in both hetero- and homosexual acts: very British: since ca. 1950. Cf. **ambidextrous** above.

*****battle,** v.i. To 'get by' on one's wits': v.t., to obtain, esp. if deviously, the use of: Australian c. (since ca. 1919) > by 1940, low s. Hence, **battler,** one who 'gets by' on odd jobs and alone; a tramp; a hawker; both v. and n. occur in Kylie Tennant's fine novel, *The Battlers,* 1941. The v. occurs earlier in Ion M. Idriess, *The Yellow Joss,*

1934. Ex the influence of the war of 1914–18. A *battler* is also 'a hard-up horse trainer . . . a broken-down punter' (Baker).

battle, on the. An Australian synonym of 'on the batter', engaged in prostitution: low: since ca. 1920. Lawson Glassop, *We Were the Rats,* 1944.

battle-axe. See **old battle-axe.**

battle blouse. A battledress tunic: Army: 1939+. (P-G-R.)

battle buggy. A jeep: Army: 1943+; by 1950, slightly ob.

battle cruiser. A public-house: rhyming s. (on *boozer*): since ca. 1940. Franklyn, *Rhyming.*

battle dress. Pyjamas: R.A.F.: 1940+. Sgt. Gerald Emmanual, letter of March 29, 1945. Ex amorous 'combat'.

battle of the bulge, the. The struggle against 'middle-aged spread': since 1945. Ex the World War II battle so named.

Battle of Waterloo. A stew: rhyming: mid-C. 19–20.

*****battle the rattler.** To travel on a railway without paying: Australian c.: since ca. 1920.

*****battle the subs.** To hawk goods in the suburbs: since ca. 1920: Australian c. > by 1940, low s. Baker.

battle wag(g)on. A battleship: Navy since ca. 1925, R.A.F. since ca. 1930. H. & P.—2. An expensive motor-car: Army since ca. 1940. H. & P.

*****battler.** A gangster handy with his fists and fond of using them: Glasgow c. and low s.: late C. 19–20. MacArthur & Long. Cf. the S.E. sense. —2. See **battle.**—3. A prostitute working independently of brothel or ponce: Australian c.: since ca. 1925. (B., 1953.)—4. A variant of *battle waggon,* 1: Naval: since ca. 1930. (P-G-R.)

[**battlin(g) finch** is j.—unrecorded by O.E.D.— not s. nor coll. See B. & L.]

batty, n.—2. A batman or batwoman: Services: since ca. 1925. H. & P.

batty-fagging. A thrashing: smugglers': C 19. John Davidson, *Baptist Lake,* 1896. Cf. **batty-fang** in *Dict.*

baulk at (p. 38) goes further back by a hundred years; it occurs in W. N. Glascock, *Sailors and Saints,* 1829. 'Such . . . was the redoubted wight . . . As he never baulked at anything, he assumed a familiarity of manner and tone . . .' (Moe.)

bawl out. To upbraid vigorously: Canadian coll.: adopted from U.S. ca. 1910. (Leechman.) Hence a *bawling-out.*

Bay, the.—2. The orig. form of **Babsky** (*Dict.*) was *the Bay of Biscay,* often abbr. to *the Bay.*—3. Long Bay Gaol, Sydney: Australian coll.: C. 20. B., 1942.—4. The Hudson's Bay Company; its stores; a specific store: Canadian coll.: since ca. 1860 (?). Leechman.—5. Botany Bay: Aus. coll.: early and mid C. 19. (B., 1959.)

bay, the. The sick-bay: Naval coll.: mid-C. 19–20. Hence, *bay man,* a sick-bay attendant: Naval coll.: late C. 19–20.

bay-window, adj. Smart, fashionable: lower-middle class: since ca. 1910. (S. P. B. Mais, *Caper Sauce,* 1948.)

Bays, or **Baze, the.** The Bayswater Road (London, W.2): low s., and c.: C. 20. Norman.

bazaar.—2. a public-house bar: rhyming s.: late C. 19–20. (Franklyn, *Rhyming.*)

bazooka. See **high,** adj., 5, below.

be a devil! or **Oh, come on, be a devil!** A merry invitation to be generous or mildly audacious, as in 'Oh, come on, Billy! Be a devil and buy yourself a beer' or 'Be a devil—*or* a real devil—Joe, and kiss the girl': since ca. 1945. This expresses a thought pattern; cf. the idea in '"Come on, have another tomato juice," Ron invited. "Live it up"': Lilian Jackson Braun, *The Cat Who Could Read Backwards*, 1966.

be a good girl and have a good time! A c.p. addressed to someone—not necessarily female—leaving for a party: Canadian: since ca. 1930. The c.p. answer is 'Well, make up your mind!'

be-damned. See also **like a** in these Addenda.

be good! (p. 39). The longer form has, since ca. 1945, been often extended to *and, if you can't be careful, buy a pram*.

be-in. A rally: coll.: since ca. 1966. *Daily Colonist* (Victoria, B.C.), March 28, 1967, 'In Vancouver, some 1,000 "hippies" turned out over the week-end in what they called the first be-in in Canada.'

be my guest. A c.p. addressed to someone wishing to borrow something not valuable enough to be worth returning: since ca. 1950.

be on. To watch; to look at (someone) and see, or understand, what he is doing: Aus.: since ca. 1930. Nino Culotta, *Cop This Lot*, 1960, 'The barman . . . pointed to us. "Be on 'im," Joe said. "Dobbin' us in."'

be your age! Stop being childish!; Use your intelligence!: a c.p. adopted from U.S. in ca. 1936.

beach, take the. To go ashore: Naval: late C. 19–20: 'Taffrail', *The Sub*, 1917.

beach, the. Land as opposed to sea: Services: since ca. 1939: H. & P.

beach-bash, whence the n. *beach-bashing*. To lie on the sand, esp. nocturnally and amorously: Australian servicemen's: 1939–45. (B., *Australia Speaks*, 1953.)

beach bunny. A usually non-surfing girl addicted to watching the surfers surfing: Australian surfers': teenagers': since ca. 1960. Also called a *femlin*, a *female* gremlin. Regarded as a hanger-on. (B.P.)

beachcomber. See **beach-comber** (*Dict.*), of which it is the usual C. 20 form and of which an earlier record is E. J. Wakefield, *Adventure*, 1845. —5. A white man living with an Eskimo woman: Canadian Arctic: heard, there, by Dr Douglas Leechman in 1913; by 1960, slightly ob.

beacher. A quick 'run ashore': Naval: since ca. 1920. (P-G-R.)

beacon. A red nose: mostly Cockneys': from ca. 1890. Cf. **danger light** and **strawberry, 2**.

beagle. A steward: Australian Naval: since ca. 1925. (B., 1943.)

beak, n., 2. Also at Harrow and Rugby.

Beaky, n. Nickname for any person, esp. a man, with a big, sharp nose: Cockney: mid-C. 19–20. A. Neil Lyons, *Arthur's*, 1908.

beam, off the; on the beam. Failing to understand; fully understanding: R.A.F.: since ca. 1938; by 1943 also civilian. Ex that wireless beam which, in bad visibility, guided one to the airfield.

beam-ends (p. 39) occurs esp. in *on his beam-ends* and as early as in John Davis, *The Post-Captain*, 1806. (Moe.)

beamer. A fast, esp. a very fast, ball so delivered by the intimidatory bowler that it bounces

head-high and causes, or should cause, the batsman to duck: cricketers': since ca. 1956. 'Right on the beam'; form suggested by *seamer*.

bean, n.—5. The penis: low: late C. 19–20. Ex the *glans penis*?

bean, v. To hit (someone) on the head: since ca. 1916. Vernon Loder, *Choose your Weapons*, 1937. Ex **bean**, n., 2 (*Dict.*).

beanie. 'A tight-fitting cap, often made from the crown of an old felt hat. The edge is cut, by the exhibitionists, into a zig-zag. Worn by adolescents' (Leechman): Canadian: since ca. 1946(?). Perhaps because it fits as snug as a bean-pod does the beans; also, there is a reference to s. *bean*, the head.

beano.—3. Communion: Cheltenham: since ca. 1915. Marples.—4. A bayonet: Shrewsbury: 1938 +. Marples.

beans, give (p. 39). Prob. from the phrase cited as **ash beans**.

bear a fist. To bear a hand, to help: nautical coll. (—1806); † by 1890. John Davis, *The Post-Captain*, 1806. (Moe.)

bear fight. A rough and tumble in good part: Society coll.: from ca. 1880. B. & L.

bear pit; beerage; brickyard. Steerage: ships' stewards': C. 20. Dave Marlowe, *Coming Sir!*, 1937.

bearded lady, the. A searchlight with diffused beams: since 1939. Berrey, 1940.

beardie. Any man with beard or long hair: Australian coll.: C. 20.—2. A ling: Aus. fishermen's: C. 20. Nino Culotta, *Gone Fishin'*, 1963.

beardy. A male beatnik: since ca. 1959. (Anderson.)

bearings. The stomach: Australian: C. 20. (B., 1943.)

beast. A girl; a young lady: beatniks': since ca. 1960. (Anderson.)

beast with two backs, make the (p. 40), was originally, it would seem, a translation of Rabelais's *faire la bête à deux dos*.

beastly (p. 40) prob. goes back to very early C. 19. It occurs in, e.g., W. N. Glascock, *Sketch-Book*, 2nd Series, 1834, at II, 183, '. . . beastly bad Buccalow [salt-fish]'. Moe.

beastly, the. The time: Public Schools' and Universities': ca. 1880–1918. (Ernest Raymond, *Tell England*, 1922.)

beat, n.—4. A shortening of **Beatnik**: since late 1950's. Rachel & Verily Anderson, 'Square's Guide to the Beats'—in *The Housewife*, May 1961.

beat, the. The musical rhythms of jazz: Canadian jazz-musicians' and -lovers' coll.: adopted, ca. 1950, ex U.S. *The* (Victoria) *Daily Colonist*, April 16, 1959, article 'Basic Beatnik', speaks of 'the Beat fraternity'. (Cf. Norman D. Hinton, article 'Language of Jazz Musicians', in *The American Dialect Society*, Nov. 1958.) The term is a specialisation of the conventional musical sense of *beat*. Cf. **Beatnik**.

beat daddy-mammy (p. 41). 'This is still used in U.S. among people learning to play the drum. They actually say these words while they practise with small drumsticks on a *pillow*' (Alexander McQueen, July 3, 1953).

beat it (p. 41) has, in Canadian usage and since the late 1950's, sometimes been elaborated as *put an egg in your hat and beat it!* (Douglas Leechman records having heard it on Dec. 25, 1961.)

*beat it upon the hoof. To walk; to tramp: c.:

ca. 1680–1760. Anon., *The Post Boy robbed . . .,* 1706.

beat on, have a. To have an erection: low: C. 20. Cf. **bar, have a.**

beat one's gums. To be loquacious: Canadian: adopted, ca. 1945, ex U.S.

beat-out. Exhausted: col.: 1860, H., 2nd ed.; † by 1910.

beat the bag, or **pants, off.** To defeat ignominiously: since ca. 1920.

beat the clock; occ., **beat the gong.** To cease duty before the prescribed time; Services, esp. the R.A.F.: since ca. 1930. Cf. **clock in,** etc., on p. 160.

beat the gun. Of a female: to have intercourse with one's fiancé, esp. if she becomes pregnant by him: Australian: since late 1940's. Ex athletics. (B.P.)

beat the tracks. To walk, esp. a long way and over rough ground: Australian coll.: C. 20. Archer Russell, *A Tramp Royal in Wild Australia,* 1934.

beat-up, n. Ground strafing; hence a lively visit to 'the local' or a good party in the Mess: R.A.F.: since 1940. H. & P. From U.S.; imm. ex:—

beat up, v. 'To stunt-fly, at low level, about (a place)': Partridge, 1945. R.A.F.: since 1940. Adopted from American fliers.

beat up for one's brass-hat. (Of a Lieutenant-Commander, R.N.) to seek promotion to Commander: Naval: C. 20. (P-G-R.)

beat up one's chops. See **Jive.**

beaten at the post. 'Men going on leave would get down to Boulogne [or Calais] and even across the Channel when word would come that all leave had been cancelled and that they were to return to units' (A. B. Petch, April 1966): coll. and s., resp.: W.W. I. Prompted by racing's *beaten,* or *pipped, at the post.* Not, by the way, unheard in W.W. II. See also **pipped on** (or **at**) **the post,** below.

beater.—2. Earlier: prob. from ca. 1860. Abbr. **dew-beaters** (*Dict.*).

beating, or **lashing, up.** 'A Lieutenant-Commander is thought to be beating-up for his "brass-hat" (promotion to Commander) when he becomes particularly "taut-handed" and pays great attention to his job,' Granville: Navy: C. 20. Ex beating up against the wind?

Beatnik. 'Generic term coined by the San Francisco press for members of the Beat fraternity living in North Beach area and abhorred by all Beatniks': article 'Basic Beatnik' (or language of the Beatniks), sub-titled 'A Square's Guide to Hip Talk', in *The* (Victoria) *Daily Colonist,* April 16, 1959. Apparently the term arose in 1957 or perhaps in 1956. Ex *beat, the,* as above + *-nik,* a pejorative suffix adopted from Yiddish.

beats, the.—4. A debt-shirker: Australian coll.: C. 20.

Beattie and Babs. Body lice: since ca. 1930. Rhyming on *crabs.* (One of the penalties of a wide and deserved popularity.)

Beatty tilt is a variant of *Beatty angle,* that at which a cap is worn with a slight tilt to starboard: Naval: since ca. 1915. A characteristic of Earl Beatty.

Beau. A Beaufighter aircraft: R.A.F.: since 1940. Jackson.

beaut. A beauty: Australian: C. 20. (K. S. Prichard, *The Black Opal,* 1921.) Hence, since

ca. 1920, also an adj., as in 'It's a beaut day'. Cf. the entry on p. 41. Perhaps does not, after all, come from the U.S., but rather, esp. as an Australianism, from Cockney, as in Marjory Hardcastle, *Halfpenny Alley,* 1913, concerning a young child, ' "Ain't 'e a *bute?* " answered 'Tilda proudly'.

beautiful and . . . ; or, **lovely and . . .** A C. 19–20 Cockney synonym of **nice and** (p. 559) in the sense of 'very'; they also = 'satisfactorily'. Julian Franklyn, in a communication of early 1939, adduces the examples, ''E 'ad 'is barf beautiful an' quick; and so 'e should 'a' done, the wa'er was lovely an' 'ot'; 'My neighbour's baby is lovely an' quiet, since I hit it beautiful and hard.'

beautiful but dumb is a Canadian (ex U.S.) c.p., foisted, since ca. 1943, on far too many 'dizzy blondes' less stupid than they seem. (Leechman.)

'I suggest a date rather earlier than 1943, since I remember in early 1940, about the time I was commissioned, a Services' security poster showing a very luscious blonde, surrounded by attentive officers of all three Services; the caption was: "She's not so dumb; careless talk costs lives."

'Regarding "dumb" (p. 248), the queried revival in U.S. as slang is probably a transfusion from S. Ger. "dumm"—stupid. It has been estimated that there are 15 million Ger. immigrants in the Mid-West of the U.S.' (Ramsey Spencer, March 1967.)

beautifuls. In address, Beautiful: feminine: since ca. 1920. Cf. **ducks,** 2 (*Dict.*).

beauty! Thank you! = non-cultured Australian, esp. Sydneysiders': since late 1940's. Perhaps *beautiful.* (B.P.)

beaver, 2 (p. 41), perhaps existed as early as 1907 in England.

Beaver, the. Lord Beaverbrook: journalistic: since ca. 1918. (Sydney Moseley, *God Help America!,* 1952.)

beaverette. 'A light armoured-car,' H. & P., 1943: military.

beazel. A girl: since ca. 1930 (P. H. Wodehouse). An arbitrary formation—prob. euphemistic for *bitch.*

becall. To reprimand; abuse; slander: Cockney coll.: from ca. 1880. Clarence Rook, *passim.*

because the higher the fewer! See 'Cockney catch-phrases . . .'

because why? Why?: illiterate coll.: C. 19–20 (? earlier).

beckets, pockets (cf. p. 41), occurs in John Davis's *The Post-Captain,* 1806. (Moe.)

bed and breakfast; half a crown; Southend. 26: darts players': C. 20. Resp. ex tariff; '2/6'; fare from London. (*The Evening News,* July 2, 1937.)—2. **bed and breakfast only.** A cardboard box container for a parachuted pigeon: R.A.F.: mid-1944–45.

bed and breakfast, take (or **get**) **more than.** To share the bed as well as the board of one's landlady or her daughter: Australian: since ca. 1930. (B.P.)

bed-down, n.; **bed down,** v. A going to bed; to go to bed: Services coll.: since ca. 1920. H. & P. Horses are 'bedded down' for the night.

bed-filling. 'Lying down after dinner to rest and digest': Regular Army's: ca. 1880–1914. B. & L.

bed-house. A house of assignation: low: ca. 1880–1910. Ibid.

bed-launching, n. 'Overturning the bed on the sleeping occupant': Sandhurst coll.: from ca. 1830. Ferryman-Mockler, 1900.

bed-post, in the twinkling of a, goes back rather earlier. (Glascock, *Sketch-Book*, II, 1826.)

bed-rollers. Youths, or young men, travelling the country during summer and sleeping rough: since ca. 1950. Ex the bed-rolls they carry.

bed-springs. See **fish-horn.**

bed-tick. The American national flag, the Stars and Stripes: nautical: mid-C. 19–20. Pejorative of the colour-scheme and allusive to the coverings of mattresses. (H. L. Mencken, in *The Saturday Review of Literature*, April 10, 1937.)

bedbait. See **bait,** 4, above.

Beddo. A Bedouin: Services' (North Africa): 1940+. (P-G-R.)

beddy-byes. Sleep; *beddy-byes!*, go to sleep!: nursery: C. 19–20.

Bedford = Bedfordshire (as in *Dict.*): see **wooden hill.**

Bedourie shower. See **shower,** 5, below.

bedworthy. (Of a woman) sexually desirable: upper- and middle-class coll.: since ca. 1925.

bee. A slangy euphemism for *bugger*: since ca. 1920. (Ngaio Marsh, *Swing, Brother, Swing*, 1949, 'The old bee'.) But also for *bastard*.

beech. 'A railway (or station) marked down for closure is said to be "due for beeching". A railway (or station) closed is "beeched"; and axed personnel are described as "on the beech" ' (a pun on *on the beach*): Sean Fielding, letter to Press, some date in Feb. 1964. Current in late 1963–65, but already ob. so soon as by the end of 1965.

Beecham. A bill (list of performers): theatrical: late C. 19–20. Cf. **Beecham's** on p. 42.

***Beecham's pill.** A simpleton; a dupe: Australian c.: since ca. 1920. (B., 1953.) On synonymous *dil(l)*.

Beecham's pills: often shortened to *Beechams*. Rhyming s. for 'testicles', mispronounced *testikills*: late C. 19–20. Probably suggested by the synonymous s. *pills*.

beef. 'An alternative term for the famous "*bind*" [*Dict.*], but only applicable to the crime itself, of boring one's colleagues by retailing shop-news and stale information,' H. & P., 1943; Services. Adopted from U.S.—As 'a complaint', *beef* has been common in Canada since early C. 20.

beef, v. (p. 42). Hence in general use since ca. 1942; in Canada, since ca. 1920.

beef-bag. A shirt: Australian: since ca. 1860; by 1940, ob. 'Tom Collins', *Such is Life*, 1903.

beef-chit. The Wardroom menu: Navy: since ca. 1920. Granville.

beef-heart.—2. Hence, a breaking of wind: low rhyming s.: C. 20. (Franklyn, *Rhyming*.)

beef-screen, the. The meat stores: Navy: since ca. 1920. (Wilfred Granville, letter of Jan. 7, 1947.) Ex the screen to keep the flies off?

beef to the heels. 'A derisive description of a girl's thick ankles, which run from calf to heel in one sad, straight line' (Leechman): Canadian: since ca. 1910. Cf. **Mullingar heifer** (*Dict.*).

beefcake. See **cheesecake.**

***beefment, on the.** It dates from ca. 1880. B. & L.

***beefsteak.** A harlot in the service of a pimp: white-slavers' c.: C. 20. A. Londres, 1928.

beehive. A fighter-escorted close formation of bombers: R.A.F.: since 1940. H. & P. The box-like formation of bombers is the hive, and the fighters buzz around it.—2. Five; esp., £5: since ca. 1920: c. >, by 1940, s. Rhyming. (Robin Cook, *The Crust on Its Uppers*, 1962.)

been robbing a bank? A c.p., addressed jocularly to a person in funds: C. 20.

beer, v. (p. 43). Current in Australia ca. 1860–1900. Sidney J. Baker, in letter of 1946.

beer barrel. A Brewster 'Buffalo' aircraft: R.A.F.: ca. 1941–45. Jackson.

beer-beer. A balloon barrage: since 1939. H. & P. Ex signalese: cf. **ack ack.**

beer-bottle label or simply **beer label.** Coat-of-arms on Warrant-Officer's sleeve: R.A.F.: since ca. 1930, ob. by 1950.

beer, bum and bacca. The reputed pleasures of a sailor's life: c.p.: C. 20. Clearly *bum* = normal sexual intercourse: cf. **bot, work one's,** below.

beer is best is a c.p. arising in 1936 ex the brewers' slogan. *The Pawnshop Murder*: 'Sterling blokes these, all of whom agreed . . . with Mr Pennington that, in moments of relaxation, Beer is Best.'

beer-lever. 'Part of the controls of an aircraft,' H. & P.: R.A.F.: since 1930. Cf. synonymous **joy stick** (*Dict.*).

beer-off. A public-house off-licence department: coll.: C. 20. *The Nottingham Journal*, March 15, 1939, 'Children and beer-off ' (caption).

beer to-day, gone to-morrow. A c.p. of 1941+. Parody of 'here to-day (and) gone to-morrow'.

beer-up. A drinking bout: Australian coll.: C. 20. B., 1942.

beerage. See **bear-pit.**

bees. Money: late C. 19–20. Short for **bees and honey** (*Dict.*).

beetle, n. A Volkswagen car: Australian: since ca. 1955. Ex shape. (B.P.)

beetle, v. To go; to fly: R.A.F.: since ca. 1939. Jackson: 'So we beetled back to base' or 'Let's beetle off to the coast': Wodehousian term.

beetle bait. Treacle: Australian soldiers': 1914+. Baker.

beetle juice. Betelgeux—a star used in astral observation: R.A.F. aircrews': since 1938. Jackson. By folk etymology.

beezer.—2. 'Chap'; fellow: Public Schoolboys': from ca. 1920. Nicholas Blake, *A Question of Proof*, 1935. Prob. ex *bugger* + *geezer*.—3. (Capital B.) *B.S.A.* motor-car: since ca. 1920, esp. at Cambridge.

beezer, adj. Excellent: most attractive: since ca. 1935. Ex *bonzer*?

before breakfast. See **breakfast . . .**

before-time. Formerly, previously, of old: pidgin: from ca. 1860. B. & L.

beg yer pardon. A garden: rhyming s.: late C. 19–20.

beg your pudding (or **pudden**)**!** I beg your pardon: lower-middle-class jocular: from ca. 1890.

beg yours! I beg your pardon: Australian coll.: since ca. 1920. (B.P.)

Begats, the (or italicised or 'quoted'). The Book of Genesis: middle-class: since ca. 1870.

beggar boy's ass.—2. Money: rhyming s. (on *brass*): late C. 19–20. Franklyn, *Rhyming*.

beggar for work. A constant hard worker: coll.: late C. 19–20. Also *he* (or *she*) *deserves a medal*: c.p.: since ca. 1915.

beggar my neighbour, on the. On the Labour (Exchange)—drawing unemployment benefit therefrom: rhyming s.: since ca. 1925. (Franklyn, *Rhyming*.)

beggar on the coals. A small damper: New Zealand and Australian: ca. 1850–1900. B., 1941. Also *bugger* . . .

beggar (or, more often **bugger**) **one's contract.** To spoil something: render it useless or nugatory: Army, 1914–18.

begnet. A Scottish shape of **bagonet** (p. 26). Regular Army: C. 19–20.

begum. A rich widow: Anglo-Indian: mid-C. 19–20; ob. B. & L. A derivation from the S.E. sense, a lady of royal or other high rank in Hindustan.

behave is short and coll. for *behave yourself* (p. 45): since ca. 1870. Mostly nursery ('Behave, miss, or I'll smack you') and lower-class.

behind like Barney's bull, all. See **Barney's bull.**

behind the behind. A semi-coll., semi-c.p., reference to sodomy: since ca. 1930.

behind the eight-ball. In an extremely difficult position; at a grave disadvantage: Canadian: adopted, ca. 1945, from U.S. Ex snooker. By 1960, also English. (Wallace Reyburn, article in colour section of *The Sunday Times*, July 8, 1962.)

bejan (p. 45). An early form of Fr. *bec jaune*, an ignorant person, was *béjaune*.

belay.—3. To cancel, as in 'Belay that last order!': Naval: C. 20. Granville. Ex sense 2.

belcher, 1 (p. 45) occurs earlier in *The Port Folio*, May 16, 1807, at p. 310, and Oct. 17, 1807, at p. 247. (Moe.)

belfa. See 'Harlots'. Origin?

believe. Belief: sol.: late C. 19–20. Henry Wade, *Heir Presumptive*, 1935. ''T's my believe that she's looking for a shop.'

believe (you) me! A conventional, vaguely emphatic c.p.: C. 20.

Belinda. 'A frequent nickname for barrage balloons' (P-G-R.): Services' (esp. Army): 1940–45.

bell, warm the. To put the clock on or relieve the watch early: Naval: C. 20. 'Taffrail', *The Sub*, 1917; Granville.

Bell and Horns. 'Brompton Road cab-shelter is the "Bell and Horns" and Kensington High Street shelter "All Nations" . . . I think named after forgotten pubs,' Herbert Hodge, *Cab, Sir?*, 1939: taxicab drivers': since ca. 1920.

bell-topper. Current in New Zealand as early as 1853 (B., 1941).

bellier. A punch to the belly: pugilistic coll.: ca. 1810–1930. *Boxiana*, III, 1821.

bellowdrama. Melodrama: jocular coll.: late C. 19–20. Rhyming.

bellows.—2; belt, n.—2; **belt tinker.** A very roughly made garment: tailors': from ca. 1870.

bells. Bell-bottomed trousers: Naval (lower-deck) coll.: C. 20. (P-G-R.)

belly. Underside of the fuselage of an aircraft: R.A.F.: since ca. 1925; by 1940, coll. and by 1945, j. Here the 'plane is soft, least protected, most vulnerable.—2. 'Wool shorn from a sheep's belly' (B., 1959): Aus. rural coll.: late C. 19–20.

belly-bumper (p. 46). 'In an old collection of dances and tunes in my library, printed about 1703, one of the dances is entitled The Maiden's Blush, or Bump her Belly. It is to be danced "long way, for as many as will". A sort of Roger de Coverley

affair, with a romping lilt,' Alexander McQueen, July 3, 1953.

belly button. Navel: lowish: mid-C. 19–20.

belly-button is playing hell with my backbone, my I'm damned hungry: c.p., mostly lower-middle class: since ca. 1910.

belly-buster. A bad fall = a clumsy dive into water: Australian coll.: late C. 19–20.—2. Specifically, a dive in which the entire front of the body hits the water at the same time: late C. 19–20.

belly flop (or **flopper** or **flapper,** a dive wherein one falls on one's belly: coll.: since ca. 1870) is, 2, the still-slang variant (since ca. 1930) of **belly landing.** Partridge, 1945.

belly-flopping. Sense 1 was used at Bisley before 1914–18 'to indicate the manœuvre of taking running aim at a target and "bellyflopping" for the purpose of cover as one draws nearer one's objective' (*The Sunday Times*, Johannesburg, May 23, 1937). These nuances drive ex *belly-flopping*, bad diving: swimming coll.: from ca. 1880.

belly-go-round. A belt: St Bees: 1915+. Marples, 'Suggested by merry-go-round'.

belly-grunting. A severe stomach-ache: Australian: since ca. 1920. (B., 1943.)

belly landing. 'A landing with the undercarriage up, when it is impossible to get the wheels of the 'plane down,' H. & P.: R.A.F.: since ca. 1918; by 1945, official j. Ex **belly-flopping.**

belly like a poisoned pup's, have a. To be potbellied: C. 20. (T. Washington-Metcalf, 1932.)

belly muster. Medical inspection: Royal Naval College, Dartmouth: C. 20. Granville.

belly-up (*Dict.*) is still extant, though ob.

belly up! belly up to the bar, boys! 'Drinks on the house!' Canadian c.p.: C. 20. (Leechman.)

Belsen. An army camp, if discipline were strict: Army: 1943–45. (P-G-R.) 'May I cast doubt on the date 1943? It was not until this notorious camp was overrun in 1945 that the name became current. I doubt if many Britons had heard of the place before then, and so the famous newsreels of its horrors made a tremendous impression.' (Ramsey Spencer, 1967.)

belt, n.—2. A copulation: low: late C. 19–20.—3. A prostitute: low Aus.: since ca. 1925. (B., *The Drum*, 1959.) Cf. **endless belt** and **belt,** v.

belt, v. (Of the male) to coït with: low: mid-C. 19–20. Cf. synonymous **bang** (*Dict.*). Hence n.

belt, get the. To be jilted: low: since ca. 1925. Complementary to *belt, give the* (p. 46).

belt, give a. To thrash; to overcome, to defeat: Australian: since ca. 1910. Dymphna Cusack, *Southern Steel*, 1953, 'Must have given eighty a belt' (be past his eightieth year). Cf. the n. *belt* (p. 46).

belt, (have) under the. To have one's credit: Australian: since ca. 1930. Ex a good meal eaten. (B.P.)

belt along. To rush along; to travel very fast: mostly teenagers': since ca. 1945. Perhaps cf. **belting, 2** (p. 46).

belt one's batter. To coït with a woman: low: C. 20. But also, to masturbate, with synonym *pull one's pad.*

belt up! Shut up!: R.A.F.: since ca. 1937. After ca. 1950, also office- and shop-girls'. (Gilderdale.) Ex tightening one's belt. By 1960 a fairly, and by late 1966 an entirely, general phrase.—2. To thrash with a belt; hence, to 'beat up' (someone): Australian: since ca. 1925. (Dick.)

Belvedere. A handsome fellow: Londoners': ca. 1880–1905. B. & L. Ex Apollo Belvedere.

Belyando spew. 'A rural sickness' (B. 1959): Aus.: late C. 19–early 20.

bembow. Variant of **bumbo**, 2 (*Dict.*). 'A Swaker of Bembow a piece,' *Sessions*, June 28–July 1, 1738, trial of Alice Gibson.

Bems, the. The *B.E.M.s*, or bug-eyed monsters of science-fiction writers: since ca. 1960. Patrick Moore, *Survey of the Moon*, 1965.

ben, n.—5. 'The "bens" or lockers' (W. N. Glascock, *Sailors and Saints*, 1829): Naval: ca. 1805–50. (Moe). Ex S.E. *ben*, an inner room.

Ben Flake (p. 47). Obsolete since ca. 1910.

bencher.—2. See 'Tavern terms', § 3, *d*.

bend, n. An appointment: a rendezvous: Anglo-Irish: C. 20. 'He has a bend with a filly'; 'I must make a bend with the doctor.' Ex the slight bow made at the meeting.—2. A drunken bout: C. 20. James Joyce, *Ulysses*, 'I was with Bob Doran, he's on one of his periodical bends.'

bend, v.—2. To deflect a result from the straight by deliberately losing a match: Association footballers': since ca. 1950. In the English popular newspapers of October 1960 there was much talk of players '*bending* matches' and of 'matches being *bent*'.

bend an ear! Listen to this!; pay attention: Air Force: 1939 +. Punning on *lend an ear*.

bend down for. To submit to *effeminatio*: euphemistic coll.: late C. 19–20.

bend one's back. To work hard: Australian coll.: C. 20. (Vance Palmer, *Separate Lives*, 1931.)

bend one's (or the) elbow too much. To drink to excess: since ca. 1905: coll., by 1940, familiar S.E.

bend over backwards. To try very hard, as in 'You needn't bend over backwards to please the children': since the late 1920's.

bend to. See **bend** (*Dict.*).

bended knees. Cheese: rhyming s., mainly theatrical: C. 20. (Franklyn, *Rhyming*.)

bender.—8. A lazy tramp: Australian: C. 20. B., 1942.—9. A cigarette: R.A.F.: since ca. 1938. Ex the frequently crumpled packets.—10. Such a squad instructor as gave his squad a hard time: Army: since ca. 1939. (P-G-R.)

bender, spin a. To tell a tall story: Naval: late C. 19–20. Granville. See **bender**, 7 (p. 47).

benders, on one's. 'Weary, not picking one's feet up' (Jackson): R.A.F.: since ca. 1930. Lit., on one's knees: cf. senses 2, 3 of **bender** (p. 47).

bending drill. 'Defecation in the open': Army in North Africa: 1940–43. (Peter Sanders in *The Sunday Times* magazine, Sept. 10, 1967.) 'Also "going for a walk with a spade".'

bends, the.—2. 'The "bends" and acute alcoholism are very much alike in effect . . . [The former comes] from working in a tunnel under terrific air pressure. "Bends" are one of the snags compressed air workers—or "sand hogs"—encounter,' *Answers*, Feb. 10, 1940.

bene flake in B. & L. is an error for **bene feaker** (*Dict.*).

Bengal Lancers. Toughs armed with razor-blades and addicted to assault with robbery:

Australian: since ca. 1930. B., 1942. (See *Underworld.*)

Benghazi cooker; occ. duke's stove. Sand saturated with oil, a paste of sand and oil, within a tin or can or metal drum; used as a field cooker in North Africa: 1940–3.

Benghazi Handicap, the. 'The confusion that was the retreat to Tobruk in 1941—we always called it the Benghazi Handicap—has rarely been equalled,' Lawson Glassop, *We Were the Rats*, 1944: 7th Aus. Inf. Division's name for it: 1941 +. Back from Benghazi, Glassop refers, ibid., to it as also *The Benghazi Derby*. The forward movements were known as *Benghazi Stakes*, (P-G-R.)

bengo. See 'Prisoner-of-War Slang', 7.

benny. Benzedrine, esp. when taken as a drug: mostly teenagers': adopted, ca. 1950, ex U.S. It is a mild stimulant and comparatively cheap. Also see 'Minor Drugs'.

benny, have a. (Unwittingly) to wet one's bed at night: military (not officers'): from ca. 1890. Richards. Origin? Perhaps *benny* = *Benjamin*, a little one; the minor contrasted with the major physical need.

bent, n. A male pervert: low: since ca. 1945. (Angus Wilson, *A Bit off the Map*, 1957.)

bent.—2. (Of a person) crooked, criminal; (of a thing) stolen: c.: from ca. 1905.—3. Suffering from 'the bends' (see **bends, the, 1**, on p. 47): divers' (pearl or skin or other): since ca. 1945. 'He is bent, poor bugger!'—4. See **flatter**.

*****bent, go.** To turn criminal; (of things) to get stolen: c.: since ca. 1910.—2. Hence, (esp. of a girl) to become faithless: prison c.: since ca. 1920. (Norman.)

ber-lud; ber-luddy. Jocular intensives of *blood*, *bloody*: late C. 19–20. Ex mock horror.

berge. A spy-glass or telescope: Naval: ca. 1810–60. Captain Glascock, *Land Sharks and Sea Gulls*, 1838. Ex a proper name?

bergoo. See **burgoo** (*Dict.*).

berk. Short (—1939) for:—

Berkeley.—3. (Ex 1.) A fool: low: since ca. 1930. Axel Bracey, *Flower on Loyalty*, 1940. Cf. **cunt, silly** (p. 198).

berker. A brothel: Army in North Africa (1939–45). Ex the ill-famed street of Cairo: the Sharia el Berker. (P-G-R.)

Berkshire Hunt. The female pudend: rhyming s.: ? mid-C. 19–20. Franklyn, *Rhyming*, believes it to form the original of the synonymous **Berkeley Hunt** (p. 48) and the *Berkeley* form to be accidental.

berley. Variant spelling of *burley*. (B., 1943.)

Bernardo. Bernard Darwin (b. 1876), golfer and delightful writer: golfers' and cricketers': C. 20. Sir Home Gordon, *The Background of Cricket*, 1939. With a pun on Dr Barnardo's Homes.

besom, drunk as a. See **drunk as a besom**.

best burned (or burnt) pea. Coffee: Naval officers': 1834, W. N. Glascock, *Sketch-Book*, 2nd Series 1834, at II, 175. (Moe.) Ex a coffee-bean's resemblance to a burnt pea.

*****best, give in.** See **give in best**.

best of British luck to you !, the. An ironic c.p., meaning exactly the opposite: since ca. 1944: orig. Army, but by 1955 fairly, and by 1960 quite, general.

bester.—2. A fraudulent bookmaker: Australian: since ca. 1910. (B., 1943.)

bet a pound . . . See **I wouldn't bet** . . .

bet both ways. To back a horse for a win, also for a place in the first three: C. 20: turf s. >, by 1920, coll.; now verging on j. Hence *both ways* is used as adj. and adv. of such a bet.

bet like the Watsons. To bet heavily on horses: Australian racing coll.: since ca. 1925. (Lawson Glassop, 1949.) Ex some famous investors of that name.

bet on the blue, with rhyming variant **bet on the Mary Lou.** To bet 'on the nod', i.e. on credit: Australian racing: since ca. 1920 and ca. 1930. (Lawson Glassop, *Lucky Palmer*, 1949.) Ex 'in the *blue* ink' as opposed to 'in the *red* ink'.

bet on the coat. To lodge a dummy bet with a bookmaker as an inducement for others to bet: Australian sporting: since ca. 1925. (Lawson Glassop, *Lucky Palmer*, 1949.)

bet one's eyes. To watch a contest without laying a wager: Australian sporting: C. 20. B., 1942.

beteechoot. See **banchoot.**

better, v.—2. To re-lock (a door): c. of ca. 1810–50. Egan's Grose, 1823. Ex *betty*, a picklock.

better for your asking, no or **none the;** or **never the better for you.** A c.p.: the 1st, late C. 19–20; the 2nd, late C. 18–20, but slightly ob. by 1960; the 3rd, late C. 17–18, occurring in, e.g., Swift, *Polite Conversation*, 1738.

better pickers than fighters, often preceded by *they're.* 'Used in reference to the type of soldier who frequented the French brothels whenever he had money' (A. B. Petch, March 1966): W.W. I.

better than a dig in the eye . . . (*Dict.*). Also and preferably, **better than a poke in the eye with a sharp stick.**

better than a drowned policeman (*Dict.*). Also and—at least at Cambridge—earlier, **better than sleeping with a dead policeman.**

better than a kick in the ass with a frozen boot. A Canadian c.p.: C. 20. Cf. the entries immediately preceding and following this one.

better than a slap in the belly with a wet fish. A naval c.p. of the same sense as **better than a dig . . .**: from ca. 1890.

betters-off. 'Our betters': the well-to-do: coll.: since ca. 1925. Berta Ruck, *Pennies from Heaven*, 1940.

betting on the black. See **black-marketeer.**

Betty Lea (or **Lee**). Tea: rhyming s.: a C. 20 variant of (Rosie or) **Rosy Lea** (or **Lee**) on p. 707. First (?) recorded by the late John Lardner in *Newsweek*, Nov. 21, 1949.

between-agers. Children aged 10–12: coll.; since ca. 1962. After *teenagers.*

between the flags is a coll. phrase applied to steeplechase riding: sporting: from ca. 1860.

between the two W's. See **W's.**

bev. A shortening of **bevvy** (p. 50); cf. **bevali** below. All three occur on p. 8 of Sydney Lester's *Vardi the Palarey,* (?) 1937.

bevali is an occ. variant (from ca. 1885) of **bevie,** n., 2 (*Dict.*). B. & L.

Beveridge. The social-insurance scheme of Sir William Beveridge: coll.: 1945 +.

bevie (or **bevvy**) **casey.** A public-house: mid-C. 19–20. *News of the World,* Aug. 28, 1938. Lit., a beer-house; therefore cf. *bevie* (p. 56) and *casa* (p. 130).

bevie-homey (p. 50). Sense 2 is the earlier: probably mid-C. 19–20.

bevor. A wedge of bread obtainable between dinner and supper: Charterhouse (school): late C. 17–19. Probably cf. *bever,* 1 (p. 49).

bewer (*Dict.*) derives, says Leland, ex Shelta.

Bexley Heath. Teeth: rhyming s.: late C. 19–20. (Sydney Lester.) Sometimes shortened to *Bexleys.*

beyonek. An occ. C. 20 form of **bianc** (p. 50).

bi. Biology; also attributively, as in *bi lab*: medical students': C. 20.

biargered. A C. 20 variant of **beargered** (p. 40) —and still widely used in 1937 (Sydney Lester).

bib in, push or **put** or **stick one's.** To busybody, to interfere: Aus.: since late 1940's. *The Drum,* 1959.

Bible, the. A Service Manual: Naval: C. 20. Granville.—2. Hence (?), 'the "book of words" about any particular subject' (Granville): Naval: since ca. 1925. Also the *Child's Guide.*—3. The Railway Rule Book: railwaymen's: since ca. 1920. (*Railway.*)

Bible bosun, the. A ship's chaplain, or even the Chaplain of the Fleet: Naval: since ca. 1910. (John Winton, *H.M.S. Leviathan,* 1967.) Cf. **sin bosun** below.

Bible-puncher. A chaplain: Army and Navy (C. 20) >, ca. 1935, also R.A.F. Cf. **Bible-pounder** (p. 50).—2. Hence, a pious airman: R.A.F.: since ca. 1930. Jackson. Cf. **Bible-thumper** (p. 50).

bibler.—2. One's *Bible oath*: low: ca. 1815–1900. *History of George Godfrey,* 1828.

Biblical neckline. A low neckline: Australian raffish: since ca. 1946; by 1965, ob. 'Lo and behold!' (B.P.)

biblio. A bibliographical note (usually on the reverse of the title-page) in a book: book-world coll.: since ca. 1920.

bicarb. Bicarbonate of soda: coll.: late C. 19–20.

biccy or **bikky.** Biscuit: nursery and domestic coll.: from ca. 1870. Blaker.

***bice** or **byce.** £2: c., and low: C. 20. Cf. Fr. *bis,* twice.

bicycle. A prostitute: low, esp. teenagers': since ca. 1940. Something often 'ridden': cf. **town bike** below.

bicycle bum. A seasonal worker that cycles from job to job: Australian: since ca. 1920. B., 1942.

bicycle(-)face. A strained expression caused by nervous tension in traffic: coll., esp. among motorists and cyclists: since ca. 1942. *Cycling,* Sept. 11, 1946.

biddy, n.—5. A (female) schoolteacher: Australian children's: since ca. 1925. Baker.

bidgee. Good: Australian pidgin: C. 19–20. John Lang, *The Forger's Wife,* 1855.

Bidgee, the. Murrumbidgee River—or region: Australian coll.: since ca. 1860.—2. Hence (?), *bidgee,* a drink consisting mainly of methylated spirits: Australian low: since ca. 1920. Baker.

bif. A Bristol Fighter ('plane used in 1916–18): ca. 1916–20, then ob. Jackson.

Biff. A frequent nickname for a Smith: C. 20. It rhymes with the Cockney pronunciation: *Smiff.*

biff, v., 3. Also **biff off,** go off, depart. E.g. in Ian Hay, *Housemaster,* 1934. n. and v.—4. Short for **biffin** (*Dict.*), friend, mate: since ca. 1945.

biff-up. Smartness on parade: Services', esp. Army: since ca. 1925. (P-G-R.)

biffer. A signal-exercise in morse or semaphore: Naval: since ca. 1910. (Granville.)

biffs. A caning or a strapping: Australian schoolboys': since ca. 1920. B., 1942. Ex **biff**, 1 (*Dict.*).

biffy, n. A water-closet, esp. if a backyard privy: Canadian: C. 20.

biffy. 1, adj. Drunk. C. 20. Perhaps a perverted blend of *tipsy* + *squiffy*, or of *bosky* + *squiffy*.

big bad wolf. A threatening or sinister person: coll.: since ca. 1935. Ex a popular song.

big(-)ballocks. A self-important man: low (−1954).

Big Ben (p. 51). As the 'clock' the term is a loose derivative: originally and still strictly, the bell there.—2. Ten: rhyming s.: C. 20.—3. Hence, esp. the sum of ten pounds. (Franklyn, *Rhyming*.)

Big Bertha.—2. 'Banking engine at Lickey Incline. Now withdrawn' (*Railway*, 3rd): railwaymen's: ? ca. 1950–64.

big blow. A hurricane: Australian fishermen's and sailors' coll.: C. 20. (Jean Devanney, *By Tropic Sea and Jungle*, 1944.)

big cats, the. See **cat**, n., 12.

big cheese, the. 'The boss': Canadian: C. 20; by 1959, slightly ob. (Leechman.)

Big City, the. Berlin: R.A.F.'s Bomber Command: 1941+. Ex the coll. English sense 'London'.

big conk, big cock (or **cunt**). A c.p. that—verging upon the status of a proverb—implies that the possession of a large nose entails also that of a large sexual member or part: low. late (? mid-) C. 19–20.

big deal! A contemptuous c.p., applied to a plan or a deal worthy only of contempt: Canadian: since ca. 1945. (Leechman.) Also, since middle 1940's, Australian, with variant (since ca. 1950) *big thrill!*, applied rather to a personal service than to a commercial proposition. (B.P.)

big dig.—2. *The Big Dig* is the cutting of the Panama Canal, ca. 1904–13; engineers' (and Americans'): since ca. 1905; since ca. 1915, merely historical in Britain. Cf. **dig**, n., 5.

big dish, the. A big win: Australian racetracks' and two-up players': since ca. 1930. (Lawson Glassop, *Lucky Palmer*, 1949.)

big dog with a brass collar, the. The most important person in a business: ca. 1880–1910. B. & L.

big drink.—3. A heavy fall of rain: Australian: since ca. 1910. Baker.

big eats. A good meal: Services: since ca. 1925. H. & P.—2. See 'Prisoner-of-War Slang', para 1.

big end; big-end bearing. The human posterior: Australian: esp. mechanics': since ca. 1930. (B.P.)

big fellow. Big, large; much: Australian pidgin: mid-C. 19–20. E.g. 'big fellow water'. B. & L.

big front. (A fellow with) new or good clothes: Canadian carnivals: since ca. 1910.

***big gates, the.** Prison (generic); a prison: c.: late C. 19–20.

big gun (*Dict.*) seems to have been anglicised before 1897.—2. A large surf-board, for use in heavy surf: Australian surfers': since ca. 1960. (B.P.)

big head.—2. A conceited fellow: since ca. 1940. Cf. the U.S. coll. sense, 'conceit; egotism'.

big hit. To defecate: Australian rhyming s. (on *shit*): since ca. 1920. Franklyn, *Rhyming*.

big house, the.—2. Penitentiary or prison: Canadian: since ca. 1925; also in Britain since ca. 1935. Ex U.S.

Big Lizzie is recorded by 'Taffrail'. Also *Lizzie*.

big man, big prick—little man, all prick. A tribute to virility, in lit. sense; fig. 'apostrophizing dolts, dupes or dunderheads' (Laurie Atkinson, Sept. 11, 1967): c.p.: C. 20.

big noise.—2. Hence, a 4,000-lb. bomb: R.A.F.: late 1941–42. Cf. **block-buster**.—3. As an extension of sense 1 (p. 51), *the big noise* = 'the boss': Canadian (−1910), hence English (−1918). Leechman.

big-note. To speak highly of; to exaggerate the worth of: Australian: since ca. 1935. (Cf. the quotation at *bust* below.)

Big O, the. H.M.C.S. *Ontario* (scrapped in 1959): Canadian Naval: since ca. 1939 (?). Leechman.

big on, esp. *very* . . . (Very) keen on; Australian: since ca. 1940. (B.P.)

big shit. A c.p. of derision, directed at someone called 'a big shot': since ca. 1910.

big shot has, since 1935 in England, been, as from much earlier in U.S., applied also to a person successful in any big way.

big side (p. 51)—now mostly written *bigside*—derives rather ex 'the fact that early games of Rugby football were played with sides of any numbers, often the whole school participating': D. F. Wharton, who left Rugby School in 1965 and who adds 'The term is still in use' and, concerning *big-side run*, notes that 'These are no longer run'.

Big Smoke, the.—2. Sydney: Australian, esp. N.S.W.: since ca. 1919. (D'Arcy Niland, *The Big Smoke*, 1959.) Ex *smoke*, 2, on pp. 788–9.

Big Snarl (or **Stoush**), **the.** The War of 1914–18. Australian soldiers': 1919+. B., 1942.

big stuff.—2. Heavy vehicles, e.g. tanks: Army: since ca. 1930. (P-G-R.)—3. In the Navy, a battleship or an aircraft carrier; or collectively: since ca. 1939 (ibid.).—4. In the Air Force, heavy bombs: since ca. 1941 (ibid.).—5. In all three Services, Very Important Persons: since ca. 1944 (ibid.).

big time, in the. Operating on a large scale: Australian, adopted, ca. 1945, ex U.S. (B.P.) 'In the old days of vaudeville, "big time" meant the more important circuits . . . Others, less important, were "small time"' (Leechman): Canadian and U.S.

big truck. A nickname for a man generously sexed: Liverpool: C. 20.

big twist. 'An outstanding success, an occasion for the expression of pleasure' (B., *The Drum*, 1959). Cf. **curl the mo** below.

big un. See **big one** (*Dict.*).

big way, in a. Very much: coll.: since ca. 1935. 'I've had him in a big way'—I can no longer stand him, I've no more use for him. (P-G-R.)

big wig.—2. Esp., a head of a College: Oxford: ca. 1818–60. *Spy*, 1825.

bigger and better (p. 51) is, in Australia, usually *bigger, better and brighter*. (B.P.)

bigger the fire, the bigger the fool, the. The more noise, the less sense: Australian c.p.: C. 20. Orig. bushwhackers'. (B.P.)

bigger they are, the harder they fall, the; occasionally *the taller they are, the further they fall.* A c.p. of defiance and fearlessness towards one's superiors: late C. 19–20; very common in Army of 1914–18. It probably originated in the boxing-booths. (Julian Franklyn.) Usually attributed to Bob Fitzsimmons (1862–1917) before his fight with James J. Jeffries, a much heavier man, on July 25, 1902.

biggy, as in '*Biggy Smith*' (Smith major), is a C. 20 Christ's Hospital term. Marples.

bight job. An unpopular officer or N.C.O.: Australian: soldiers': 1919+. B., 1942, 'Might become "shark bait" when the transport is crossing the Great Australian Bight?'

bightie. An Australian spelling of **bitey** below.

bike, n.—2. Short for **town bike** below. (B., 1959.) Variant: *office bike.*

bike or bike it. To cycle: coll.: C. 20. (Miles Franklin, *Old Blastres*, 1931.)

bike, get off one's. To become annoyed; angry: Australian: since ca. 1930. B., 1942; Lawson Glassop, 1944.

bile yer can! (p. 52) is, in full, *awa' an' bile yer can!*

bilge. V.i., to talk nonsense: from ca. 1921; very slightly ob. *The Pawnshop Murder.*

bilge artist. A pointless chatterer or airy-nothinger: Australian: since ca. 1920. Baker.

bilingual. A jocular coll., used since ca. 1944, thus: 'He's bilingual—speaks both English and American.'

bilk, n., 3 (p. 52): earlier, Anon., *A Congratulatory Epistle from a Reformed Rake,* 1728, at p. 30.

Bill.—2. Inevitable nickname, esp. in the Services, of men surnamed Sikes, Sykes. Ex the character in Dickens's *Oliver Twist.*

bill, the. '"The Bill" is the Metropolitan Police cab-driver's licence, as distinct from the ordinary County Council driving licence. . . . It is also called the "brief" and the "kite"; but the "bill" is the more common name. It is a large red piece of foolscap (hence "the kite"), well bespattered with legal phrases (hence, I suppose, "the brief")': Herbert Hodge, *Cab, Sir?,* 1939: taxi-drivers': since 1910.

Bill Arline. See **s'elp me** . . .

Bill Bailey (*Dict.*). Ex the late C. 19–early 20 popular song, 'Won't You Come Home, Bill Bailey?'. The cross-ref. on p. 52 should be *won't you.*

bill fish. 'A waterman who attends the youngest boys in their excursions,' *Spy,* 1825: Eton: ca. 1815–60.

Bill Jim (p. 52). Current since ca. 1880, as Sidney J. Baker tells me.

bill-o! A note of warning, whether physical or moral: Cockney schoolboys': C. 20. 'Probably a perversion of *below!,* a cry of warning used in the Navy (and the rigging yards) when men aloft were about to drop something onto the deck—sometimes *below, there!*' (Julian Franklyn, letter, 1962.)

billabonger. A tramp keeping to the outback, esp. the Northern Territory: Australian coll.: C. 20. (Tom Ronan, *Vision Splendid,* 1954.)

billed, ppl. adj. Detailed (esp. in orders) for a piece of work; briefed: R.A.F.: 1939+. Jackson. Ex the theatrical *billed* (*to appear*).

billy, 3 (see p. 53), is, says Baker, 1941, 'from the Australian aboriginal *billa,* water',—7. Sense of

'billy-goat' prob. goes back to ca. 1890 or even a decade earlier. It occurs in, e.g., Edward Dyson, *The Gold Stealers,* 1901.

Billy, the. The *Royal William,* flag-ship at Spithead: Naval: ca. 1815–30, then historical only. Alfred Barton, *The Adventures of Johnny Newcome,* 1818. (Moe.)

Billy Blue, 1 (p. 53). Both this and *Coachee* occur in Captain Glascock's *Land Sharks and Sea Gulls,* 1838.

Billy Browns, the. The Grenadier Guards: Regular Army: C. 20. Why?

Billy Bunter. See 'Hauliers' Slang'.

billy-bunting, recorded by E.D.D. for 1851, is prob. an error for **billy-hunting** (*Dict.*).

Billy Button (p. 53), sense 2. Obsolete since before 1940.

Billy Ducker. A shag cormorant: Welsh coast, esp. fishermen's: late C. 19–20. A *ducking* bird. (Wilfred Granville.)

Billy Gorman. A foreman; rhyming s.: since ca. 1870. (D. W. Barrett, *Navvies,* 1880.) Cf. the later—in C. 20, predominant—*Joe O'Gorman.*

Billy Muggins. A mainly Australian elaboration of **muggins,** 1 (*Dict.*): C. 20. B., 1942.

Billy Noodle. A fellow that imagines all the girls to be in love with him: Australian: since ca. 1920. Baker.

billy-o!, go to. Go to the devil!: Australian coll.: C. 20.

billy-o, I will—like. A mild synonym for *like hell I will,* I certainly won't: since ca. 1910.

Billy Prescott. A C. 20 variant of **Charley Prescott** (p. 141). Franklyn 2nd.

***Billy Ricky.** The casual ward at *Billericay* in Essex: tramps' c.: C. 20. See esp. W. A. Gape, *Half a Million Tramps,* 1936, pp. 134–5.

Billy Ruffian (p. 53). The *Bellerophon* of the Napoleonic Wars was, by the seamen, called *the Billyruffin*: Glascock, *Sketch-Book,* I, 1825.

Billy Stink. 'A native fire-water which we called Billy Stink. One could get it cheap in the bazaars, and it was a sort of wood-alcohol, I believe, though I never cared to sample it myself. Its effect on most drinkers was terrible': Indian Army: from ca. 1880. Richards.

billycock gang, the. The clergy: navvies': ca. 1870–1910. (D. W. Barrett, 1880.) Ex their hats.

bim. The posteriors: Scottish Public Schools coll.: C. 20. Ian Miller, *School Tie,* 1935. A thinning of *bum.*—2. Hence, bottom of the class or in an examination: Scottish schools': since ca. 1910. Bruce Marshall, *Prayer for the Living,* 1934.

bim, v. To cane, properly on the bottom: English preparatory schools': since ca. 1920. (Ramsey Spencer, March 1967.) Cf. sense 1 of preceding.

***bimbo.** A fellow, chap, 'guy': adopted by 1938 (witness James Curtis, *They Ride by Night*) from U.S. as c.; by 1945, low s. Ex It. *bimbo,* short for *bambino,* 'a child': cf. **kid,** n., 2 (*Dict.*). —2. The female posterior: since ca. 1950. Ex **bim** (above).

bimph. Toilet paper: Public Schools': late C. 19–20; but since 1920, *bumph* much commoner, Marples. Cf. **bim** and **bumf** (p. 107).

bin.—2. 'Living quarters in which the rooms are very small,' H. & P.: Services: since 1920.—3. 'In a Naval mess, a space curtained off' (P-G-R.): Naval: C. 20.

Bin, the. The Headmaster: Rossall: C. 20. Marples.

binco. A light; a paraffin flare; hence, occ., a magnesium flare: nuances 1, 2 (Edward Seago, *Sons of Sawdust*, 1934), late C. 19–20; nuance 3, since ca. 1920. A corruption of It. *bianco*, white: from the whiteness of the illumination they afford: cf., therefore, **bianc** (p. 50), which, by the way, should be dated mid-C. 19–20.

bind (n. and v.: *Dict.*) 'must be the most used of all Air Force slang expressions', H. & P., 1943; see esp. Partridge, 1945. Whence *bind* (someone) *rigid*: since before 1939; also, though little used after 1940, *bind stiff*. Perhaps ex the ill temper arising from being *bound* or constipated, but prob. ex garage 'It's binding somewhere'—as applied to an engine vaguely out of order.—2. Hence, of persons or things: to be tedious, to be a nuisance; to complain and grumble overmuch ('He binds all day'): since ca. 1925.—3. (Ex 1 and 2.) (Of a person) to be, with sickening frequency, 'in the know': since ca. 1930. Partridge, 1945.—4. To work; esp., hard at one's studies: R.A.F. (mostly officers'): since, ca. 1935. Hence, as n., a tour of duty.

binder, 3. Also a drink, as in A. Binstead, *Gal's Gossip*, 1899; cf. **swing o' the door**. I.e. *binder* as at **titley and binder** (*Dict.*).—5. One who grumbles and moans more than is held permissible: R.A.F.: since ca. 1925. Partridge, 1945.—6. A last drink at a party: Naval: since ca. 1920. Granville. Cf. **one for the gangway**.

binder, have a. See **toe-biter**.

binders. Brakes: R.A.F.: since ca. 1925. Jackson.—2. 'Fibres that grow from one staple to another and hold a sheep's fleece together' (B., 1959): Aus. rural coll.: late C. 19–20.

bindi- (or **bindy-**) **eye.** 'One of the burr-like flower-heads of the Bogan Flea (*Calotis hispidula*) and other varieties of Calotis' (B.P.): Australian, mostly children's, late C. 19–20. Cf. **jo-jo** below.

binding, adj. Given to 'moaning': R.A.F.: since 1925. Partridge, 1945. Ex **bind**, 2, above. —2. Boring; tedious: R.A.F.: since ca. 1920. Ex **bind**, v., 1 (p. 54).

bindle.—2. A blanket-roll or swag: Canadian; adopted, ca. 1890, ex U.S. (Niven.) A thinning of S.E. *bundle*—cf. **jingles** below.

*bindle stiff. A hobo: Canadian c.: since ca. 1910. Ex U.S.

*bines. Spectacles: c.: since ca. 1930. 'Clocking me over the top of his bines' (Norman).

[***bing**, n. A liquor shop: c.: C. 19. What is B. & L.'s authority for this?]

bing up. To brighten, to polish (furniture, metal, etc.): furniture and curio-dealers': C. 20. H. A. Vachell, *Quinney's*, 1914.

binge up. To enliven (a person): C. 20; ob. H. A. Vachell, *Quinney's*, 1914.

binged. Very eccentric; mad: Charterhouse School: since ca. 1920. Ex *binged*, drunk.

bingey or **bingy** (hard *g*): Penis: Anglo-Irish nursery: late C. 19–20. Origin?

bingo, like. Very quickly; low: C. 20. Margery Allingham, *Sweet Danger*, 1933. Ex *like billy-o*, confused with *like winking*.

bingo'd or **bingoed.** Drunk: Society and undergraduates': since late 1920's. Ex **bingo** (*Dict.*).

binjey. Variant of **bingy** (or **bingey**) on p. 54. *The Drum*, 1959.

binni; binni soobli. Small; a boy (lit., little man): Shelta: C. 18–20. B. & L.

Binnie Hale. A tale: rhyming s.: since ca. 1940; by 1959, slightly ob. Ex the famous entertainer. (Franklyn, *Rhyming*.)

binns. Glasses = spectacles; *dark binns*, dark glasses: C. 20: c. >, by ca. 1930, s. (Robin Cook, 1962.) Perhaps ex *binoculars* influenced by *binnacles*.

binocs. Binoculars: New Zealand and elsewhere: since ca. 1945. (Fiona Murray, *Invitation to Danger*, 1965.)

bint.—3. One's girl friend; (e.g. *lush bint*, a very attractive girl) (H. & P.): since ca. 1920; but esp. 1939–45, among Servicemen. *The New Statesman*, Aug. 30, 1941. An elevation of **bint**, 1 (p. 54). Nevertheless, even in 1939–45 it was often pejorative: witness, e.g., Jackson.

bint, v. Mostly in *go binting*, to seek a female companion, esp. as a bedmate: Regular Army in Egypt: C. 20. Ex **bint**, n. (p. 54).

bio. The cinema: South African: since late 1940's. Shirley Milne, *Stiff Silk*, 1962, 'My sister has gone to bio'—to the cinema. Short for *bioscope* used as a deliberate archaism: *bioscope* was a very early synonym of 'cinematograph'.

bionc. A shilling; parlary: mid-C. 19–20. (Sydney Lester, 1937.) A variant of **bianc** (p. 50).

Bip, the. The Bishop: aristocratic and upper-middle class: since ca. 1920. (Margery Allingham, *The Beckoning Lady*, 1955.) By conflation.

birch, n. A room: 1893, P. H. Emerson's *Signor Lippo*. Short for **birch room** (*Dict.*).

birch broom (p. 54) has, since ca. 1920, been little used. Such brooms are now rare. (Franklyn, *Rhyming*.)

Birch Island. The Abbey Ground: Westminster School: ca. 1720–1850. *Spy*, II, 1826.

Birchington Hunt. An occasional variant of *Berkshire* (or *Berkeley*) *Hunt*.

bird, n., 7: earlier in 'Taffrail'.—Sense 3 is short for *bird-lime*.—8, sweetheart (girl), had, by 1920, become fairly general, although still uncultured.—10. A turkey, as in 'We're going to have a bird for Christmas': domestic coll., mostly lower-middle class: late C. 19–20.—11. A certainty, esp. *(make a) dead bird of*, a complete certainty, make quite sure of something: Australian: since ca. 1910. (B., 1943.)—12. 'I did not want my "bird" (crook who is not known but suspected) to get any idea that the police were on his track' (A. F. Neil, *Forty Years of Man-hunting*, 1932): police s.: C. 20.

Sense 3 (p. 54); since ca. 1940, generic for a prison-sentence.—7 (p. 54): much earlier in W. N. Glascock, *Sailors and Saints*, 1829. (Moe.)

bird, go like a. Of, e.g., a motor car: to 'fly along': coll.; mostly Australian: since ca. 1945. (B.P.)

bird, have the. See **have the bird**.

bird-cage.—7. The position and situation of the huntsmen when they find themselves encircled by wired fences and hedges and can escape only by retreat or by crowding the gateways: hunting: C. 20. (Sir William Beach Thomas, *Hunting England*, 1936.)—8. The Wrens' quarters at a Naval establishment: Naval: since ca. 1939. (P-G-R.)—9. A 'signal box built up in girders or gantry'; also, a 'wire-trellised road vehicle' (*Railway*): railwaymen's: C. 20.

bird-dog on the trail, like a. In relentless pursuit of a person or a thing. '"Oh, Jack will find one. He's like a . . ."' (Leechman): Canadian coll.: since ca. 1930.

bird of, make a (dead). To make sure of: Australian: C. 20. B., 1942.

Bird Sanctuary, the. The Wren Headquarters: Naval: 1939 +. Formerly they occupied Sanctuary Buildings.

bird-watcher and **-watching.** One given to the practice—the practice itself—of watching the girls, orig. in a park: jocular: since late 1940's. Ex **bird,** n., 8, on p. 54.

birdie.—2. Time: C. 20. Ex **bird-lime** (Dict.). —3. An aircraft: Australian soldiers' (in Korea): ca. 1951–53. (A. M. Harris, The Tall Man, 1958.)

bird's-eye (p. 55) prob. goes back to ca. 1810; and its original, bird's-eye wipe, to ca. 1800.

bird's nest. A Wren's cabin in the Wrennery at a Naval establishment: Naval: since ca. 1940.

birdseed; birdsong. See 'Prisoner-of-War Slang', 4.

Birdy. General Birdwood: Australian soldiers': in 1914–18. (C. E. McGill, 'Those Medical Officers' in The Bakara Bulletin, 1919.)—2. The nickname given in Nov. 1936 by Australians to R. W. V. Robins, the brilliant Middlesex and England all-round cricketer. Also Birdie.

birl. A variant of **burl.** D'Arcy Niland, The Shiralee, 1955, 'I'm going to give Eucla a birl.' Perhaps suggested by whirl rather than by hurl: cf. the Canadian take a whirl at (something), to attempt it, current since ca. 1925. A blend of bash (attempt) + whirl?

Birmingham, the; esp. going up the Birmingham, travelling up the M.1: motorists': since ca. 1960. (I.T.V., Aug. 13, 1963.)

Birmingham Fusiliers. 'About this time [1902] the Cockneys and Welsh [in the Royal Welch Fusiliers] grew fewer, and the Midlanders more numerous, until in 1914, the Battalion was sometimes jokingly known as the Birmingham Fusiliers,' Richards': military.

birp. A variant spelling of **burp** below.

Birrelling, n. Writing chatty, pleasant, app. shallow essays: literary?: from ca. 1890; ob. Cf. **Birreligion** in Dict.

birthday occurs in the late C. 19–20 fair-ground or Sunday-market patter, 'Look here, it's my birthday, I'll give you a treat and sell it cheap.'

birthday, give (something) **a.** To clean thoroughly, e.g. a room: London women's: C. 20.

birthday suit (p. 55) has, in Canada, remained far more general than in the altogether. (Leechman.) Still very common in Australia also. (B.P.)

bis. Pron. bice, q.v.

biscuit, take the. See **take the biscuit** (p. 862).

biscuits and cheese. Knees: rhyming s.: C. 20; esp. in R.A.F., 1939–40, and as biscuits. Franklyn 2nd.

bish.—3. (Ex sense 1; cf. **bishop**). A chaplain: Naval: since ca. 1930. Granville.

bish, v. To throw: Australian: since ca. 1920. B., 1942. Cf. **biff.**—2. To officiate in the absence of the chaplain: Services: since ca. 1939. (P-G-R.)

bishop, n.—6. A chaplain: Services: since ca. 1925. Jackson. Mainly jocular. n.—7. A broken-down sign-post: mostly East Anglian: (?) mid-C. 19–20. Because—cf. parson, n., 2 (p. 607) —it neither points the way nor travels it.

bishop, flog the. (Of men) to masturbate: low: late C. 19–20. Also bash the bishop (esp. Army). Ex resemblance of glans penis either to episcopal mitre or, more probably, to chess bishop.

Bishop of Fleet Street, the. Mr Hannen Swaffer: journalists': since ca. 1935. On him has descended the mantle of the late James Douglas, self-appointed regulator of the public morals. Cf. **Pope.**

Bishops, the; also **the Arty Bishops.** Archbishop's Park. Lambeth Road, London: Cockney's: C. 20.

Bishopsgate — Cripplegate — the Workhouse. Three London clubs: The Athenæum—the Senior Services—the Union: taxicab drivers': since the 1920's. ('Peterborough' in The Daily Telegraph, Dec. 13, 1949.) The first has many bishops; the second, many aged Service dignitaries; the third puns on modern union for workhouse.

bisom. An unruly child: Australian: C. 20. (B., 1943.) Ex fig. S.E. besom.

bit, n., 8 (p. 56). The coll. a bit of a(n) . . ., rather or . . ., prob. goes back at least seventy years earlier and may have been adopted ex American usage. Colonel Moe quotes from The Port Folio of Nov. 28, 1807 (p. 342):

'Thou, as a bit of a philosopher,
Art friendly, CURTIS, to the slackened rein
Of speculation.'

It appears in W. N. Glascock, The Naval Sketch-Book, II, 307, 1826, as 'a bit of a boy'—a mere boy. n.—11. A jemmy: Australian c.: C. 20. B., 1942. n.—12. The sum of 12½ cents: Canadian coll.: mid-C. 19–20. Adopted from U.S. (Leechman.)

bit, have a. (Of a male, whether human or other animal) to copulate: lower-classes: late C. 19–20. Cf. **do a bit,** 2, in the Dict.

bit-and-bit, n. and v. The practice whereby each rider in a bunch or a breakaway takes a turn at the front, so sheltering and setting the pace to those behind: racing cyclists: since about 1920.

bit by a barn weasel. See 'Tavern terms', § 8.

bit hot, that's a. That's unreasonable, unfair, unjust: Australian: since ca. 1910. Baker.

bit lit, a. Slightly drunk: since ca. 1925. A catchy elaboration of lit or lit up on p. 486.

bit of . . . occurs frequently in s. terms for 'girl, woman' regarded sexually, hence for 'copulation': cf. bit of crumb or cuff or fluff or jam or muslin or raspberry or skirt or soap or stuff, all recorded on p. 56, and several entries here. Add: bit of cunt or homework or share or tickle or tit: the 2nd and 3rd, Services', since mid-1890's; 1st, low, since 1870 at latest; the 4th low, since ca. 1925; the 5th, since ca. 1920.

bit of a brama. See **brama** . . .

bit of all right, a (p. 56). It occurs, e.g., in Alexander Macdonald, In the Land of Pearl and Gold, 1907, '"That's a bit of all right," said the guard, cutting off a piece of the stem and putting it into his mouth.'

bit of barney. See **barney, bit of.**

bit of black velvet. See **black velvet.**

bit of Braille. A racing tip: Australian sporting: since ca. 1930. (B., 1953.)—2. Hence, a tip-off: Australian c.: since ca. 1935. After ca. 1945, usually simply Braille. (B., 1953.)—3. A synonym of the 2nd F in 'the **four F method**' (below); low Australian: since the late 1930's. (B.P.)

bit of cush. A light, or an easy, job or duty: Army: since ca. 1925. Ex *cushy* (p. 200). P-G-R.

bit of hollow. See **hollow**, n.

bit of muslin (p. 56). Earlier in 'The Cadger's Ball' (*Labern's Popular Comic Song Book*, 1852) and in T. W. Moncrieff, *Tom and Jerry*, 1821.

*****bit of nifty; bit of under.** See **nifty** and **under.**

bit of no good, do a. To do harm: jocular coll.: since ca. 1910.

bit of nonsense. A (temporary) mistress: Society: C. 20. Alec Waugh, *Jill Somerset*, 1936. —2. ''A nice bit of nonsense,'' commented Louis, meaning a piece of villainy that had all the makings of a walk-over' (James Barlow, *The Burden of Proof*, 1968): c.: since ca. 1950.

bit of parchment. A convict's certificate of freedom: Australian policemen's: ca. 1825-70. John Lang, *Botany Bay*, 1859.

*****bit of Spanish.** A natural wig (i.e. one made of human hair): c.: C. 18. James Dalton, *A Narrative*, 1728 (p. 13).

bit of string with a hole in it, I've (or I've got) a. A facetious c.p., in reply to a request for something else: C. 20.

bit of stuff, 1 (p. 56): much earlier, as 'a very smartly dressed man', in George R. Gleig, *The Subaltern's Log-Book*, 1828 (II, 164). Moe.—3. A boxer: pugilistic: ca. 1810-50. *Boxiana*, I, 1818.

bit of the other, a. Sexual intercourse: low: since ca. 1930. Contrast *the other*, q.v. at **other, the,** on p. 592.

bit off, to have a. To copulate with; also absolutely: Cockney: C. 20. Cf. *bit, have a.*

bit on the cuff, a. Rather 'thick'—rather excessive, severe, etc.: Australian and New Zealand: since ca. 1930.

bit (-) player. A stage actor with a part in pictures: theatrical and cinematic coll.: since ca. 1930.

bit tight under the arms, a. A jocular c.p., applied to a pair of trousers much too big: C. 20.

bitch; bitching-up. A toady, toadying, to a master; one who makes up to another boy, and the corresponding vbl. n.: Charterhouse: from ca. 1910. Cf. the underworld sense of **bitch**, n., in the *Dict.*

bitch, v.—4. To complain in a bitchy manner: Canadian: since ca. 1925 (?). Leechman.

bitch up. An intensive of *bitch*, v., 3 (p. 57): late C. 19-20.

bitching, adj. A violent pejorative: Australian: mid-C. 19-20. Tom Ronan, *Moleskin Midas*, 1956, ''Wouldn't that be a bitchin' joke?'' Perhaps orig. a euphemism.

bitching, adv. Another violent pejorative: Australian: mid-C. 19-20. Tom Ronan, ibid., 'But he'd manage it somehow. He bitchin' well had to.'

bitchy. (Properly of women.) Spiteful; slanderous: coll.: since ca. 1910. (Angus Wilson, *A Bit off the Map*, 1957.)

bite, n. With sense of 1, cf. Ger. *Bitz*, also the compound *Weiberbitz*.—8. A loan of money: Australian low: C. 20. B., 1942. n.—9. A confidence trick; any easy-money racket: Australian c.: since ca. 1920. (B., 1953.) Cf. sense 2 on p. 57.—10. A simpleton; a dupe: Australian c.: since ca. 1930. (B., 1953.)

bite, I'll; I'll buy it. See **I'll bite.**

bite (someone's) **name.** See **name, bite.**

bite one off. To take, have, a drink of strong liquor: public-houses': since ca. 1910.

bite one's grannam (*Dict.*) goes back to 1650: see 'Tavern terms', § 8.

bitey, often spelt **bightie.** Anything that either bites or stings, e.g. a mosquito or even a chicken, or cuts or otherwise injures, e.g. broken glass or electricity. Australian nursery coll.: since ca. 1910 (? earlier). 'Keep away from that plug. Bitey!' (B.P.)

bits. Pleasant or pretty 'pieces' of scenery: photographers' and artists' coll.: C. 20.

bits and bats. Knick-knacks: rhyming s.: C. 20. Perhaps suggested by '*bits* and pieces'.—2. Hence, esp. in the underworld, small pieces of jewellery: since ca. 1910.

bitser. Anything made of 'bits and pieces': hence a mongrel (e.g. dog): Australian: since ca. 1910. B., 1942.

bitter-gatter. Beer and gin mixed: Cockney and military (not officers'): from ca. 1870. Richards.

bitter weed. 'An acidulous, grumbling type,' Granville: Naval: since ca. 1925.

bitty, adj. In bits and pieces; not in flowing narrative, but in imperfectly connected incidents: coll.: since ca. 1935.

bitumen blonde. 'An aboriginal girl or woman' (B., 1943): Australian: since ca. 1930.

bivvy, n.—4. A small, i.e. a one- or a two-man, tent: Army officers': 1940 +. (P-G-R.) Cf. *bivvy*, n., 2 (p. 58).

biyeghin. Stealing; theft: Shelta: C. 18-20. B. & L.

biz, the. The 'profession'; theatrical or film business: late C. 19-20.

bizzo. Business: Australian teenagers', esp. surfers': since ca. 1950. (B.P.) Ordinary s. *bizz* + the ubiquitous Australian suffix -o (adopted ex Cockneys).

blabber-mouth (or one word). One who cannot keep a secret; but also, one who talks too much: coll.: adopted ca. 1944 (earlier in Canada) ex U.S.

black.—3. 'A black mark for doing something badly,' H. & P.: Services': since ca. 1935. 'A glaring error is a "black", "I have put up a black" they will say,' Hector Bolitho in *The English Digest*, Feb. 1941. The phrase *put up a black* is R.A.F. officers', the R.A.F. other ranks saying, 'I've boobed' (Jackson, 1943).—4. A black-currant: fruit-growers' coll.: mid-C. 19-20. —5. A blackguard: fast life: ca. 1805-50. *Spy*, II, 1826. n.—6. As *the black* it also means 'the black market': since ca. 1942. Whence *on the black*, engaged in black-market activities: since ca. 1943.

black, in the. See **red, in the,** 2.

black and white duck. A magpie: Australian jocular: C. 20. (B., 1943.)

black art.—3. (*the b.a.*) The printers' trade: printers' jocular: ? mid-C. 19-20.

black as a cunt. Badly in need of a wash, esp. after coal fatigue: military in 1914-18.

black as the ace of spades, as. Utterly black or dark: coll.: late C. 19-20.

black as Toby's arse. Pitch-black, usually of a dark night: Canadian: since ca. 1910.

black-beetle. In Thames-side s., from ca. 1860; thus in Nevinson, 1895, 'At last a perlice boat with two black-beetles and a water-rat, as we calls the Thames perlice and a sergeant, they pick me up.'—2. A priest: lower classes': C. 20. Ex black clothes.

black bourse. 'In the Service it covers the out-of-hours' sale of cigarettes for example,' H. & P.: since 1939. Lit., black-market.

black box.—2. Instrument that enables navigator to see through or in the dark: R.A.F.: since ca. 1942. (Radar.) Partridge, 1945.—3. (Prob. ex sense 1.) A hocus-pocus apparatus or piece of an apparatus: since ca. 1945.

black boy (p. 58). Rather until ca. 1860. *Sinks*, 1848.

Black Button Mob, the. Any Rifle Regiment: Army: C. 20.

*black cap. See **white sheep.**

black chums. African native troops: Army: 1940–45. Also *old black man.*

black coat.—2. A waiter: Australian: since ca. 1920. (B., 1943.)

black-coated workers. Prunes: Dalton Hall, Manchester: since ca. 1945. *The Daltonian*, Dec. 1946. With a pun on *work.* Rather, gen. Midlands s.—and it goes back to ca. 1910.

black draught, give (someone) **the.** To administer the *coup-de-grâce* to a sailor dangerously ill: nautical: since ca. 1870. Visualised as a black medicine given as a purge. See also Irwin and *Underworld.*

black five. Class V of a certain type of locomotive: railwaymen's coll.: ? ca. 1930–50. (*Railway.*)

Black Friday, in Labour Party circles, is the day on which the General Strike of 1926 broke up.

black gang, the. 'The "black gang"—that small army of "slags" and "mobsmen" who prey particularly on the grafter [one who 'works a line' at fair or market: a cheapjack, fortune-teller, and so forth] and the bookmaker. It was the first of the hurdles I had to overcome,' Captain R. Marleigh-Ludlow in *News of the World*, Aug. 28, 1938: c.: since ca. 1910. Ex *black* (*mail*): they levy it, or, on its not being paid, beat up the refuser.—2. Stokers': Australian sailors': since ca. 1920. (Dymphna Cusack, *Southern Steel*, 1953.)

Black Hole, the, as 'punishment cell', occurs in Nathaniel Fanning, *The Adventures of an American Navy Officer*, 1806 (p. 23), in reference to the year 1778. (Moe.)

Sense 2 on p. 59 occurs slightly earlier in George R. Gleig, *The Chelsea Pensioners*, 1829, at I, 52. (Moe.)

black jack.—6. (B—J—.) The ace of spades: coll.: from ca. 1860.—7. (Cf sense 1.) A tin pot for boiling tea: Australian: C. 19–20; ob. B., 1942.—8. Treacle: Australian: C. 20. Baker.

black joke (p. 59). A scholarly wit has pertinently asked, 'Something to be cracked?' The term occurs earlier in *The Harlot Unmasked*, a song, ca. 1735.

Black Josephs, the. The Sisters of St Joseph: Australian Catholics' coll.: C. 20. Ex their habit. (B.P.)

black-legged, adj. Swindling: c. of ca. 1790–1850. (Anon. ballad, *The Rolling Blossom*, ca. 1800.) Moe.

black magic. The original form of **black box,** 2. (P-G-R.)

black man kissed her. Sister: rhyming s.: C. 20. But not at all general. (Franklyn, *Rhyming.*)

black marketeer. An illegal bookmaker quoting

his own prices: Australian sportsmen's: since ca. 1946. (B., 1953.) His customer is said to be *betting on the black.*

Black Michael. Sir Michael Hicks-Beach (later, Lord St Aldwyn), sometime Chief Unionist Whip: Parliamentary: ca. 1879–1906. (D. 1916, aged 79.)

*black ointment. 'Pieces of raw meat' (B. & L.): c.: from ca. 1870. Perhaps ex idea of meat poultice for a black eye. (Alexander McQueen.)

black-out, n., and **black out,** v. (To experience) 'a temporary loss of consciousness before pulling out of a power dive', H. & P.: R.A.F. coll. > by 1943, j. Ex the blackness that affects one's sight and that into which the pilot lapses.—2. A coffee without milk: Cape Town University: 1940 + ; ob. Prof. W. S. Mackie in *The Cape Argus*, July 17, 1946.

Sense 1 has, since the late 1940's, widened to mean simply 'to faint' and been extended far beyond the fighting Services.

black-out gong, the. The Defence Medal: since 1945.

black-outs. A Waaf's winter-weight knickers: W.A.A.F.: 1940 + . Jackson. Of Navy blue: cf. **twilights.**—2. In the Navy, a Wren's ditto: since ca. 1918. Granville.

*black peter. A solitary-detention cell: Australian c.: since ca. 1920. Cf. *peter*, n., 4, on p. 620. Hence, to *black-peter*, to put into one. (Kylie Tennant, *The Joyful Condemned*, 1953.)

black princes. 'Locomotive cleaners' (*Railway*, 3rd): railwaymen's: since ca. 1950 (?). They get so dirty that they look like the Black Prince in his armour—or like Negro princes—or, as likely as not, like both.

black show. An 'unfortunate business', a 'discreditable performance', R.A.F. officers': since ca. 1936. Jackson.

black stump, back— or **this side—of the.** In the country: Australian: since ca. 1930 (? earlier). 'Probably ex the bushman's habit of giving such directions' (B.P.). Cf. *back of Bourke* or *Booligal* —cf. **mulga** (p. 542) and **mulga madness** (below)— **the sticks** (below) and **woop woop** (p. 964).

black Sukey. See **black Sal** (*Dict.*).

Black Troops. Dominions Air Forces personnel: self-named: 1940–45. Ironic. (P-G-R.)

black varnish. Canteen stout: Naval: since 1920. Granville.

black velvet, a bit of. *Coïtus* with a coloured woman: military: late C. 19–20. Hence, *black velvet*, such a coloured woman: general: C. 20.

Black Watch, the.—2. Hence, stokers': Naval: C. 20. Granville. Ironic.

black, white, or brindle. Lit., 'of no matter what colour', but = 'of any kind whatsoever': Australian coll.: late C. 19–20. (B.P.)

blackbird and thrush (p. 58). Barrett's book appeared in 1880.

blackers. 'He opened bottles and began mixing stout and champagne in a deep jug. "Blackers"? They had always drunk this sour and invigorating draught,' Evelyn Waugh, *Put Out More Flags*, 1942: originally, University of Oxford: since ca. 1910. Ex its colour; by process of 'the Oxforder'. Cf. the synonymous **black velvet** (p. 60.)

blacketeer. A *black*-market racketeer: journalists' coll.: 1945 + .

blackfellows', or the dog, act. A government

order that can, by publicans, be invoked against drunkards: Australian public-house 'society': since ca. 1920. (B., 1953.)

blackfellow's delight. Rum: Aus.: C. 20. (B., 1959.)

Blackie is, in late C. 19–20, the inseparable nickname of men surnamed Bird. Ex the songster that is the *blackbird.*—2. And of men surnamed Ramsey. Why?—3. *Blackies:* see **blacky.**

blacksmith. 'An incompetent station cook' (B., 1941): New Zealand and Australian rural: late C. 19–20.

blackwash. To blacken (someone's character): since ca. 1925. Prompted by S.W. *whitewash.*

blacky (or **-ie**). A blacksmith: Naval coll.: since ca. 1925. Granville.—2. a blackbird: coll.: mid-C. 19–20.—3. A black duck: Australian: C. 20. (Dal Stivens, *The Gambling Ghost*, 1953.)

bladder of fat (p. 61) 'does not seem to have survived the 1914–18 war' (Franklyn, *Rhyming*).

bladder of lard.—A playing card: rhyming s.: C. 20. (Franklyn, *Rhyming*.)

Bladder of Lard, the; often shortened to *Bladder.* New Scotland Yard: since ca. 1925: orig. c.; by ca. 1935, gen. Cockney rhyming s. (John Gosling, *The Ghost Squad*, 1959.)

Blades, the (p. 61). That entry needs amplification and modification. Sheffield Wednesday, in late C. 19 and early C. 20, 'used to be called "The Blades" and their rivals . . . Sheffield United . . . "The Cutlers". Both were very appropriate. Now, however, Wednesday are known as "The Owls". . . . The district in which the Wednesday ground is situated is divided into localities known as Hillsborough and Owlerton. In 1907 there was first published in the city the *Sports Special* and the cartoonist fastened on the first three letters of Owlerton and in his sketches depicted Wednesday as an Owl. His cartoons appeared regularly year after year . . . until the crowd cried, "Play up the Owls." Further, Sheffield United have been nicknamed "The Blades" and "The Cutlers" has died out,' R. A. Sparling 'Football Teams' Nicknames'. (? in *Answers*), Feb. 16, 1946.

bladhunk. Prison: Shelta: C. 18–20. B. & L.

*****blag,** n. A watch-, or a bag-snatching: c.: since ca. 1920. (Norman.)—2. A North Country grammar schools' term of abuse: since ca. 1955. *New Society*, Aug. 22, 1963. (Ex *black*-guard, pron. *blaggard?*)—3. A piece of bluff; a tall story: since ca. 1945: c. >, by 1960, s. Ex the Fr. *blague*, as in *sans blague.* Hence, v., to bluff, to 'con'. Both n. and v. occur in, e.g., Robin Cook, *The Crust on Its Uppers*, 1962.

blag, blog, blug. A manservant: Rugby: late C. 19–20. Marples. Ex *blackguard?*

blagger. 'It is the job of the Blagger to invite, persuade or trap people into the [Bingo] parlour' (John Holliday's article 'Bingo!' in the *Sunday Telegraph*, Aug. 18, 1963): bingo organizers', hence players': since ca. 1954. Ex the underworld sense, 'he who, in a "team", does the talking', a thieves' 'con man', dating since ca. 1930. Bournemouth *Evening Echo*, April 20, 1966. Cf. the Fr. *blagueur.*

blah, n. (p. 61). Or, of course, merely echoic.

blah, adj.—2. Blind drunk: since ca. 1930. (Somerset Maugham, *Up at the Villa*, 1941—pron. *blàs*, as if French.)

blame. Fault, responsibility: proletarian coll.:

mid-C. 19–20. Georgette Heyer, *A Blunt Instrument*, 1938, 'It isn't my blame'.

Blamey's Mob. The A.I.F.: Australian soldiers': 1940–June 1941. B., 1942. Ex the name of their C.-in-C.

blanchies or blonchies. Females employed in French laundries: Tommies': W.W. I. Ex Fr. *blanchisseuses.* (A. B. Petch, April 1966.)

blankard. Bastard: Australian: C. 20. B., 1942.

blanket drill. Sleep, esp. 'get in some blanket drill', to sleep: R.A.F.: since ca. 1930. Jackson.—2. Hence, copulation; masturbation: since ca. 1935.

blanket show, the. Bed. Esp. to children, 'You're for the blanket show': domestic: late C. 19–20.

blankety blank. The Company or the Battalion C.O.'s language: Army: 1914–18. See **blankety** (p. 61).

blankety-blank verse. Blank verse: jocular coll.: since ca. 1925.

Blanks. 'A rare word used for whites or Europeans by themselves' (B. & L.): Anglo-Indian; † by 1920. Ex Fr. *blanc.* Also South African: C. 20.

blarney, tip the. To 'blarney' (v.i.): ca. 1810–90. Alfred Burton, *Johnny Newcome*, 1818. (Moe.)

blast, n.—2. 'To receive a blast is much the same as "stopping a bottle", a good "ticking-off",' Granville: Naval: C. 20.—3. A party: teenagers': since ca. 1961; by 1966, ob. (*The Sunday Times*, Sept. 8, 1963, correspondence columns.)

blast, v., 1 (p. 62): recorded, ex an English source, in *The Port Folio*, May 16, 1807 (p. 313), 'Mrs Bassett . . . insisted upon some liquor, would not quit the house without it, and began to blow up the hostess and blast the rose (sign of the Rose)'. (Moe.)—2. To go raving mad: beatniks': since ca. 1959. (Anderson.)

blast off, v.i. (Of a car, esp. if a racing car) to start: Australian: since ca. 1960. (B.P.) 'Ex the launching of a space rocket' (Leechman).

blasted pack-mules, the. Tommies carrying heavy loads referred thus to themselves: 1914–18; occasionally revived in 1939–45.

blatherskite (see p. 63) has been current in Australia since ca. 1870. Sidney J. Baker, private letter.

blatty. See **Blighty** (*Dict.*).

blazes, like (p. 62), goes back to 1818: Alfred Burton, *Johnny Newcome.* Moreover, *as blazes*— as an intensive—prob. goes back to very early C. 19 or even to late C. 18. It occurs in, e.g., W. N. Glascock, *Sailors and Saints*, 1829 (p. 184), '. . . as black as blazes'. (Moe.)

bleacher.—2. A cad: Tonbridge: late C. 19–20. Marples. Euphemism?—3. A (reprehensible) girl or woman: ? ca. 1790–1860. *The Night Watch*, 1828 (II, 99), 'That she-devil, Sophy, though as worthless a bleecher as ever stepped in shoe-leather . . .' and, on p. 104, 'The next was an old bleecher of a woman'. (Moe.) Origin?

bleachers, the. The cheap covered seats at a stadium: Australian: since ca. 1945. (B.P.) Adapted ex U.S. sense, 'the cheap uncovered seats at a baseball stadium'.

blear. When lost, to fly about in search of a landmark: Australian airmen's: ca. 1940–5. B., 1943.—2. (Prob. the source of sense 1.) To stroll;

to wander slowly yet purposefully: Cambridge undergraduates': 1920's. 'Let's blear down to the Festival.' Perhaps cf. Yorkshire dial. *blear*, to go about in the cold.

bleat, n.—2. A feeble grumble; also v.: Army: since ca. 1930.

bleater.—3. A Cockney variant of **bleeder**, 4. (*Dict.*): late C. 19–20. In e.g., A. Neil Lyons, *Clara*, 1912.

bleecher. See **bleacher**, 3, above.

bleed, n.—2. A 'blood', a 'swell': Tonbridge: since ca. 1870. Marples. I.e. **blood**, n., 2 (p. 66), thinned.

bleed, v.—6. (Probably ex sense 4: p. 63.) 'To apply blow-lamps to resinous knots to cause resin to flow. This helps to prevent blistering' (a master builder, Dec. 5, 1953): builders': late C. 19–20.

bleed like a (stuck) pig. See **pig**, **bleed** . . . on p. 627. The longer form is still current—and the more usual—in Australia. (B.P.)

bleed one's turkey; drain one's radiator. (Of men) to urinate: Canadian: resp. since ca. 1925 and since ca. 1940. Neither is very common.

bleeder. 4 is earlier in *Sessions*, April 26, 1887. —6. 'There are numerous instances where veins enter and run distinctly through reefs . . . in cases of this sort veins are called "bleeders",' Tom Kelly, *Life in Victoria*, 1859: Australian gold-miners': mid-C. 19–20.

bleeding, adv. (From the adj., p. 63.) Intensive: approximately 'much' or 'very': since ca. 1870. *Sessions*, Jan. 8, 1884, 'If you don't bleeding well let me go.'

Blenburgher. A Blenheim bomber aircraft: R.A.F.: 1940 +; ob. Jackson. A blend of *Blenheim* and (ex the resemblance to a gigantic sausage) *hamburger*.

Blenheim Pippin, the (p. 63). The notion of the victim's shortness was caused entirely by caricaturists; actually he was 5 ft 9½ in. (Winston Churchill, *Thoughts and Adventures*, 1932, p. 28.)

bless 'em all! A Services (esp. Army) c.p., used derisively when one was particularly annoyed by, or 'fed up' with, one's superiors: since ca. 1917. Ex a famous song of the British Army in 1914–18. (P-G.R.)

bless your (little) cotton socks! Thank you!: a middle-class c.p., dating from ca. 1910; by 1960, archaic. Also in the form *bless your little heart and cotton socks*. Moreover, the two phrases often express no more than affection.

blew, v.—3. A variant of **blue**, v., 6: c.: mid-C. 19–20. B. & L.

blimey Charley! A c.p. used to blow off pent-up emotions: New Zealand and Australian: C. 20. B., 1941. In Australian, also *blimey Teddy!*

Blimey O'Reilly! Synonymous with, and presumably deriving ex, **Blind O'Reilly** below: since ca. 1920.

blimp (p. 64). Shortt prob. 'telescoped' it ex '*B*-type airship *limp*'. Whence:—2. *Blimp*, a retrograde, moronic Army officer (hence, civilian), pompous and inelastic: since ca. 1938. Aided and imm. generated by David Low's cartoon-type, Colonel Blimp.

blind, n.—6. 'A grenade that did not explode and had to be disposed of by other means' (P-G.R.): Army coll.: 1939–45. 'Prob. a direct borrowing from Standard military Ger. *Blindganger*—a "dud" shell' (H. R. Spencer).

blind, adj.—4. Pejorative (C. 20) as in ' "I don't

want a blind word out of either of you",' James Curtis, *They Ride by Night*, 1938.—5. (Cf. preceding sense.) Complete; utter: Anglo-Irish coll.: late C. 19–20. Desmond O'Neill, *Life Has No Price*, 1959, ' "I never thought to see the day when a blind stranger wud turn a gun on me in me own mountains . . ." '.

blind, move in the. See **move in the blind**.

blind along, v.i. To drive (very) fast: since ca. 1925. Ex **blind**, v. 2 (p. 64).

blind as Chloe. See **Chloe**.

***blind baggage**. On a train it is a baggage car, as in the quotation: Canadian tramps': C. 20. 'At each end of the coach,' says W. A. Gape, in *Half a Million Tramps*, 1936, 'is a curtained-off part which is used for passing from one coach to another on a corridor train. This is known as the "Blind". The "Blind" facing the back end of the engine is unused, and so provides a small space which affords a good foothold and good protection from the wind.' See esp. *Underworld*.

blind bit of notice, not to take a. To be oblivious: C. 20.

blind country. 'Closed-in country of colourless type and of little worth' (B., 1959). Aus. coll.: C. 20.

blind date. An arrangement to meet an unknown member of the opposite sex: adopted, ca. 1942, ex U.S.: by 1960, coll.

blind drunk (p. 64) goes back to late C. 18: see quotation at **nab the bib** below. Also in *The Night Watch*, 1828.

blind fart. A noiseless but particularly noisome breaking of wind: low: late C. 19–20.

blind Freddie would see it or even **blind Freddie wouldn't miss it**. Australian c.p., imputing the obvious: since ca. 1930. (B., *Australia Speaks*, 1953.)

Blind Half Hundred, the.—2. By some of the troops in 1914–18 it was applied to anti-aircraft batteries: they seemed to be firing 'blind' and at random.

blind hookey (p. 64) prob. goes back much further, to judge by *The Night Watch*, 1828 (II, 147), ' . . . the blind-hookey system' (reckless gambling).

Blind O'Reilly! A coll. expletive: mostly Army: C. 20. Gerald Kersh, *Bill Nelson*, 1942. 'The moment the place opens, in they dash. Blind O'Reilly! it's like a gold rush.' Ex some legendary figure, some obscure piece of folklore. 'He was, they say, a Liverpool docker trade-unionist ca. 1910' (Frank Shaw).

blind out. To obliterate with paint or distemper: builders' coll.: C. 20. Hence, *bug-blinding*, a rough distempering of cellars or slum property: builders': C. 20. (A master builder: Dec. 5, 1953.)

***blind pig**. A speakeasy: Canadian (from U.S.A.): since ca. 1921: c. until ca. 1929, then s. —as in G. H. Westbury, *Misadventures in Canada*, 1930. In Australian, 'a house or shop where liquor may be bought after hours' (B., 1942).

blind stabbing. Blind flying: Australian airmen's: since ca. 1940. (B., 1943.) Cf. *stab*, n. 2.

blind staggers. Excessive tipsiness: Australian: C. 20. Baker.

blind with science. To explain away an offence, etc., by talking at length and very technically, in the hope that one's interlocutor may be so bemused that he will not pursue the matter: Army: 1940 +. Cf. **blinded with science** (p. 64).

blinded with science (p. 64) comes ex boxing: 'it arose when the scientific boxers began, ca. 1880, to defeat the old bruisers' (Julian Franklyn).

blinder.—3. (Mostly in pl.) A bad cigar; a rank cigarette: Cockneys': C. 20.

blinders, adj. and n. Blind drunk; a being very drunk indeed: Oxford undergraduates': since ca. 1930. Marples, 2.

blindy-eyes and **goat-heads.** Large thorns: Australian juvenile: since ca. 1925. (B., 1953.)

blink, 3 (p. 64). Also, since ca. 1918, Australian.

blink, on the. Out of order; esp. applied to mechanism: R.A.F.: 1942+. Adopted from U.S.—2. Acting as a look-out man in e.g., a burglary: Australian c.: since ca. 1920. (B., 1943.)

Sense 1 was adopted, ca. 1944, in Australia, where, by 1950, it was gen. s. usage. (Culotta.)

blind-pickings. Cigarette butts picked up from gutter or pavement: Australian low: C. 20. B., 1942. Cf. **blink,** 3 (*Dict.*).

blinks.—3. Eyes: Cockneys': from ca. 1870. Graham Seton, *Pelican Row*, 1935.

blip.—2. 'The projection of light seen in a cathode-ray tube' (John Bebbington): electricians' (since ca. 1930), hence R.A.F. (since ca. 1939). Related to the echoic *bleep*, the sound made by Asdic; both senses were, by 1960, common among civilian flying personnel.—3. A snub: schools', esp. girls': 1930's. (Angela Thirkell, *Summer Half*, 1937.) Echoic?

blister, n.—3. Flat protuberance which, on an aircraft, lies above and below the fuselage and encloses a gun position: R.A.F.: since ca. 1925: coll. >, by 1942, j. H. & P. **n.**—4. A police-court summons: c. (−1903) >, by 1944, low s. It stings a professional's pride. (See *Underworld*.) —5. A mortgage: Australian: C. 20. Vance Palmer, *Legend for Sanderson*, 1937.—6. Sister: Australian rhyming s.: since ca. 1920. 'Not very common' (B.P.); a rare form of rhyming s.

blithered. Tipsy: Australian: since ca. 1910. (K. S. Prichard, *The Black Opal*, 1921.)

blitz. A bombing by aircraft; hence, v., to air-craft-bomb (a place): 1940, esp. in *the London blitz* (Sept. 1940–May 1941). 'The word that has received the greatest currency at home and abroad is *blitz*, as noun and verb,' Lester V. Berrey ('English War Slang') in *The Nation*, Nov. 9, 1940. Ex Ger. *Blitz*, lightning, and *Blitzkrieg*, that lightning warfare which Germany conducted in April–June 1940.—2. Derivatively, a severe reprimand, to reprimand severely: 1941, orig. military: cf. **strafe,** n., 3, and v., 3, in *Dict.*—3. 'The spring-clean which takes place when important officials are expected,' H. & P.: Services: since late 1941.—4. Hence, the brief, thorough, intensive campaign, as by the police, to enforce a law or a regulation: since ca. 1945.

blitz, solid lump of. 'A large close-flying formation of enemy aircraft' (Partridge, 1945): R.A.F.: since 1940. See prec.

blitz buggy. An ambulance; but also any *fast* transport vehicle: orig. R.A.F.: 1941. H. & P. By 1944 its 'ambulance' sense was, in the R.A.F., almost official.—2. See 'Canadian'.

Sense 1, as 'a fast utility truck or lorry', reached Australia ca. 1944. Jock Marshall & Russell Drysdale, *Journey among Men*, 1962 (p. 81), 'The drivers often found it hard to get their big blitz-buggies between the trees and the termite-hills.'

blitz flu. Influenza caused by, or arising, during 'the Blitz': 1940. Berrey. See **blitz.**

blitz it. To 'get a move on': Cape Town University: 1940+; ob. *The Cape Argus*, July 4, 1946.

blitz-ridden. 'Damaged beyond repair,' H. & P.: since 1941: ob. by 1946. See **blitz.**

blitz wag(g)on. An Australian variant of **blitz buggy** in its secondary sense: since ca. 1941. Kylie Tennant, *The Honey Flow*, 1956, where also in elliptical form *blitz* (since ca. 1945).

bloater.—2. A torpedo: Naval: since ca. 1915. —3. A person, usu. male, both gross and unfair: South African: since ca. 1940. (James Tregay, letter of April 28, 1963.)

bloater, my. Also as vocative to a man's male friend: Cockneys': from ca. 1880. B. & L.

bloats, the. Bloated plutocrats: since ca. 1890; obs. by 1930 and † by 1950. (Maxwell Gray, *The Great Refusal*, 1906.)

blob, n.—4. Also as term of abuse; e.g. 'You ugly blob!': late C. 19–20. **n.**—5. A fool: Australian: since ca. 1925. (B., 1943.)—6. (Usually in pl.) A mine-net float: Naval: 1939+. (P.-G.-R.)—7. A gonorrhœal ulcer: low and Forces': C. 20.—8. The indicative v., esp. as used in advertising: since ca. 1930.—9. An incompetent: Australian: since ca. 1910. Tom Ronan, *Only a Short Walk*, 1961. A cypher, a 'nothing': a nonentity.

blob, be on; be blotty. (Of men) to be much excited, sexually: low: C. 20.

blob-stick. 'A stick with paper- or cloth-covered end used by the instructor to show where shots fell on the ground during miniature-range practice. The practice itself' (P.-G.-R.): Royal Artillery coll.: C. 20.

block, v.—5. To stand (someone) a drink: low, ca. 1830–90. *Sessions*, Aug. 1864.—6. To get the better of; to fool: Aus.: since ca. 1930. Mary Durack, *Keep Him My Country*, 1955. '''Take this boy Job—look at his features, and smart—you can't block him! Smartest race in the world, the Jews.'''

block, do one's (p. 65), to become angry: since ca. 1918, also New Zealand. (Slatter.)

block-buster. A heavy bomb of great flattening power: R.A.F. and journalistic coll.: 1942+. Jackson.

block of ice. (Of a bookmaker) to abscond: low rhyming s.: C. 20. Franklyn, *Rhyming*. On s. *shice*, to abscond. Hence:—

*block of ice mob. Welshers: c.: C. 20. F. D. Sharpe, 1938. Rhyming *shice mob*: see **shice, the.**

block on, put the; the block goes on. To put a stop to (something); something is stopped, or comes to an end: low: since ca. 1920. (Norman.)

blocked. Much-exhilarated by drugs: drug addicts', esp. teenagers': since ca. 1950.

blocker-man. A foreman: Liverpool, esp. dockers': C. 20. Ex **blocker,** 1, on p. 65. (Frank Shaw.)

blocks. '''I'm just about two-blocks, Jack'' is as much as to say, ''I'm fed up to the teeth.'' When two blocks of a purchase are drawn together, they cannot move any further,' Granville: Naval: since ca. 1930. Cf. **chocker.**

blog. A servant-boy in one of the houses: Rugby Schoolboys': from ca. 1860. A perversion of *bloke*—2. Hence, a common boy of the town: id.: C. 20. Cf.:—

blog, v. To defeat: Rugby Schoolboys': C. 20.

bloke, n. (p. 66). The nuance 'a cabman's customer' occurs in *Sessions*, Oct. 1848. The word *bloke* is a common term among cabmen—5. 'The commander—the second in command—is "the bloke"': Naval: C. 20. 'Taffrail.'

bloke, v. To be that officer whom a specified batman tends: military: from ca. 1910. Blaker, 'The Major was to "bloke" permanently for Riding.' Ex *bloke*, a batman's word for the officer he tends. Contrast **bat**, v.: q.v.

blokery. 'The male sex in general and bachelors in particular,' B., 1941: N.Z. and Australian: C. 20. See **bloke** in *Dict*.

blokey. A familiar form of *bloke*, 1 (p. 66): ca. 1835–90. *A Comic English Grammar*, 1841. (Dr Niels Haislund.)

blonchies. See **blanchies** above.

blonde job. 'A fair-haired member of the W.A.A.F.' (H. & P.): R.A.F.: since 1940.

Blondie or **Blondy**. The inseparable nickname of any fair-haired man: Naval: since ca. 1925. (P-G-R.)

blonk on, have a. To be wearing a dull, stupid look: since ca. 1930. Perhaps ex *blonked*, a variant of *blanked* (p. 61).

blood, v.—2. To cause to bleed: Australian: C. 20. Leonard Mann, *Mountain Flat*, 1939, 'He heard the elder Galton boy say to Willy Sigbi, "I'll blood yer snout" . . .'

blood alley. A white, or whitish, marble streaked with red: Australian and New Zealand children's: late C. 19–20. Adopted ex common English dialect.

Blood and Guts. General Patton of the U.S. Army: 1944 (d. 1945). A real warrior!—2. As *the* . . ., it means the Red Ensign of the Merchant Navy: nautical: C. 20. (P-G-R.)

blood back, get one's. To avenge a relative, a friend, by shooting down the enemy aircraft responsible for his death: R.A.F.: since 1940. H. & P.

blood (-) bath. A big battle with heavy casualties: since ca. 1917. Copied from the Germans, who called the Battle of the Somme (1916), 'The Blood Bath'.

blood brothers. Two pals that have been on active service together: coll.: 1940 +.

blood chit. 'A ransom note supplied to pilots flying over possibly hostile territory in the East . . . Sometimes called "gooly chit"' (Jackson): R.A.F.: since ca. 1920, by 1944, j.—2. Hence, since ca. 1925, 'any written authorisation supplied to any individual to cover him' (Jackson). Lit., a chit or note that saves his blood or life.

blood hound. A Bow Street officer: ca. 1815–40. *Sessions*, Dec. 1819 (p. 75).

blood in their boots. See **boots, blood in their**.

blood nose. ' "Blood nose" is Australian for bleeding nose' (S. H. Courtier, *Gently Dust the Corpse*, 1960): coll.: dating from ca. 1930.

blood-stained angels (or **niggers**). Essendon footballers: Melbournites': since ca. 1910. (B., 1943.) Ex the colour of their jerseys?

blood-sucker (p. 66) goes back to ca. 1810 or earlier: it occurs in *The Night Watch*, 1828, II, 121, 'Every bloodsucker and skulker caught toko'. (Moe.)

blood ticket. That 'chit' from a (usually civilian) doctor which testifies to a rating's illness that has caused him to overstay his leave: Naval: since ca. 1930. (P-G-R.)

blood-tub. A theatre 'specialising in the worst forms of blood-and-thunder melodrama, and generally gives two shows a night': Londoners': from ca. 1885; extant. Applied orig. to a popular theatre in N.W. London.—2. A variant (R.A.F.) cited by Jackson ('flying or earthbound'), of:—

blood wag(g)on. An ambulance: originally and mainly R.A.F.: since ca. 1939. H. & P.

bloodhouse. A public-house notorious for brawls: Australian: since ca. 1910. (Dymphna Cusack, *Southern Steel*, 1953; Kylie Tennant, *The Honey Flow*, 1956.)

blood's worth bottling, yer (your) or **his**, etc. See **yer blood's** . . . below.

bloody, adj. (p. 66), must be dated to ca. 1780, at least. *Sessions*, May 1785 (p. 772), 'The prisoner, Fennell, swore an oath if he had a knife he would cut his bloody fingers off.'

bloody, adv.—3. Elliptical for *bloody well*, itself eligible as an intensive stop-gap adv. dating from late (? mid-) C. 19: lower-middle and lower classes': C. 20. 'I don't care what you think! I won't bloody do it!'—'If he doesn't want a ride, he can bloody walk!'

Bloody Mary.—2. Tomato juice and vodka: pubs' and clubs': since ca. 1944.

bloody-minded. Obstructive, deliberately 'difficult', pig-headed, vindictive: coll. since 1930.—2. Hence (?) 'rebellious in consequence of some injustice,' Granville: Naval: since ca. 1930. The noun, *bloody-mindedness*, has existed since the early 1930's.

bloodying, n. Cursing and swearing: mostly Services: since ca. 1937. (P-G-R.)

bloomer.—2. A town where business is (very) poor: circusmen's: C. 20. 'It's a "bloomer" to be there.'—3. A 'McConnell 2-2-2 locomotive with 7 ft. driving wheels (LNWR)': railwaymen's: since ca. 1950 (?). *Railway*, 3rd.

blossom. A 'poetic' variant of either **bloss** (p. 67) or **blowen** (p. 68). It occurs in the anon. ballad, *The Rolling Blossom*, ca. 1800: low: ca. 1790–1850. (Moe.)

blot, the. The anus: low Australian: since ca. 1930. 'He gave me a kick up the blot' (Dick).

blotch. Blotting-paper: Scottish Public Schools': late C. 19–20. Ian Miller, *School Tie*, 1935. Also in Yorkshire dial.—2. A term of abuse: from ca. 1925. Ian Hay, *Housemaster*, 1936.—3. Food: Anglo-Irish: since ca. 1945. Nigel Fitzgerald, *The Student Body*, 1958, 'Let's all go out and eat. You know even the smell of a cork makes me woozy and I must have blotch.'

blots. See 'Colston's'.

blotto. Strong liquor: Army: 1914–18. Ex the adj.

blouse or **blousy suit**. A singleton: card-players': C. 20. 'He holds only a blouse (or a blousy suit).' Perhaps *blouse* derives from the other, and that other = *bloody louse* suit.

blouse suit. See **green suit**.

bloused. 'I had only the King (or any other card) bloused' = I had only a singleton King: Australian card-players': C. 20. (Dr J. W. Sutherland, Jan. 21, 1941.) Ex prec.

blousy suit. See **blouse**.

blow, n.—10. A stroke with the hand shears: Australian shearers': since ca. 1920. (B., 1943.) —11. A crater caused by demolition charges in a road; the corresponding v. *blow* = 'to blow up': Army coll.: since ca. 1940. (P-G-R.)

blow, v., 3 (p. 67): earlier in W. N. Glascock, *The Naval Sketch-Book*, I (p. 113), 1825. Moe. —7. Esp., to abscond on bail. Since ca. 1943, *blow*, to depart, has been ordinary s.—10. To smoke (a pipe): since ca. 1840; ob. *Sessions*, March 1848. 'I could . . . blow my "bacca" '; Henry Mayhew, *The Great World of London*, 1856. Short for **blow a cloud** (*Dict.*).—11. To supercharge (car or aero engine); ppl. adj., *blown*: since ca. 1925. Cf. **blower,** 7.

blow, get a. See **blow,** n., 4 (*Dict.*).

blow a reed. To have (too) much to say: Army: C. 20.

blow cold; usually *be blowing cold*, to be cooling off in sexual ardour: coll.: since ca. 1910.

blow-down (someone's) **ear.** To whisper to him: low: C. 20. F. D. Sharpe, *The Flying Squad*, 1938.

blow great guns (p. 67) must be back-dated to very early C. 19, to judge by what is either the orig. form or an elaboration, *blow great guns and muskets*, which occurs in Fredk Chamier, *The Life of a Sailor*, 1832, at II, 33. Also **blow blunderbusses,** as in W. N. Glascock, *The Naval Sketch-Book*, 2nd Series, 1834, at II, 175. Moe.

blow-hole. A very talkative person: Australian: since ca. 1920. (B., 1943.)

blow-in, n. A newcomer, esp. as still unaccepted: Australian: C. 20. B., 1942. Ex the v. (see *Dict.*).—2. A chance, or a casual, visitor: Australian: C. 20. (B., 1943.) Vince Kelly, *The Shadow*, 1955.) One who has 'blown in'.

blow job. The woman of a pair engaged in 'soixante-neuf' would be 'doing a blow job': low: C. 20.—2. A jet aircraft, as opposed to a *piston job*: R.A.F.: since ca. 1960.

blow me down! An expletive, orig. nautical: C. 19–20.

blow off. To break wind: ? mostly Naval: C. 20. Common also as a euphemism among women.

blow one's bags. To boast: Australian, ? mostly W.A.: C. 20. (Tom Ronan, *Only a Short Walk*, 1961.) Ex *bag*pipes. Cf. S.E. *blow one's own trumpet*.

blow one's cap. A beatnik variant of **blow one's top:** since ca. 1959. Also *blow one's lump.*

blow one's top. To explode with anger: adopted, ca. 1943, ex U.S. servicemen.

blow one's wig. See **jive.**

blow-out.—3. A lengthening of the odds: Australian racing: since ca. 1925. (B., 1953.)—4. A puncture: cyclists' coll.: adopted, ca. 1930, from U.S.

blow the bloody ballet! A philistine c.p. addressed to amateurs of ballet as shown on TV: since early 1950's. (A. B. Petch, March 1968.)

blow three horns and a bugle. 'It's going to blow three horns and a bugle to-night, if I'm any judge of weather, and we may have to beat out to sea for shelter': Australian nautical: C. 20. 'Rann Daly' (Vance Palmer), *The Enchanted Island*, 1923.

blow-through, n.—2. A waggon that, lacking brakes, has pipes to ensure a braking system: railwaymen's: C. 20. (*Railway*.)

blow through. (Of a man) to copulate: low: late C. 19–20. Cf. the derivative n. on p. 68. —2. To depart, esp. if hurriedly: Australian since

ca. 1920. 'It's six o'clock. I'll blow through.' Dick and B.P. Cf. **shoot through** below.

blow-up, n., 4. A quarrel, 'row' or trouble: earlier in *Sessions*, June 1837.

blow up, v. 2 (p. 68) occurs earlier in Sir George Simpson's *Journal of Occurrences in the Athabasca Department*, 1820 *and* 1821, 'Mr Clarke gave him what is vulgarly called "a good blowing up" ': p. 17 of Hudson's Bay Record Society Publication, No. 1, issued in 1938. (Dr Douglas Leechman.)— v., 3. Earlier in passage cited at **blast,** v., 1, above.—6. v.i., 'to call the men to work; used by foremen and gangers' (B. & L.): coll.: from ca. 1870.—7. V. (Of a 'plane) to crash-land and catch fire: R.A.F.: since ca. 1930. Sgt-Pilot F. Rhodes, letter of Sept. 20, 1942.

blowbag. A boastful windbag: Aus.: since ca. 1925. Xavier Herbert, *Capricornia*, 1939. A blend of *blow hard* and *windbag*. Cf. **blow one's bags** above.

blowed, be (p. 68). Earlier in 'I am *blowed* if I appeer ageenst him unless I am drogged in': *Sessions*, 1827. Still earlier in James Henry Lewis, *Lectures on the Art of Writing*, 7th ed., 1816, 'It'll be all dickey wee me, I'm blowed if it won't!' (Moe.)

blower, 5 (p. 68). Hence in gen. Forces' use by 1939 (H. & P.) and in general civilian use by 1936 at latest. In 1939–45, applied also to a broadcast system, e.g. the Tannoy.—7. An aircraft supercharger. R.A.F.: since ca. 1935. Jackson. Current since ca. 1925 in motor-garage s.—8. An air-raid siren: mostly A.R.P. workers': 1940 +. *The New Statesman*, Aug. 30, 1941.—9. A deserter from the Armed Forces: since ca. 1941. *The (London) Star*, Jan. 25, 1945. Ex **blow,** v.—10. Hence, as in 'When Lord Hewart asked, "What is a blower?", he was told he was a man who "blew money back to the course" and saved bookmakers from heavy losses': *The Evening News*, July 12, 1939: racecourse s.: since ca. 1930.—11. A broken-winded horse: Australian coll.: late C. 19–20. (B., *Australia Speaks*, 1953.)

blowie or blowy. A blowfly: Australian: since ca. 1910. Gaven Casey, *Downhill is Easier*, 1945, ' "What d'y mean, the flies found it?" . . . "There was clouds o' blowies." '

blowing (p. 68): 1871, *Knocking about*, by C. J. Money. (B., 1941.)—2. A variant of **blowen** (p. 68).

blowing bubbles, n. The curses uttered by the victims of wildcat schemes and shady company-promotions: since ca. 1930. In short, *frothing at the mouth* with rage.

blown. See **blowie.**

blown, adj. Of a motor, esp. a racing car: supercharged: (racing) motorists': since early 1950's.

blown out. See **left sucking the mop.**

blowpiped, adj. Sent to another job: London docks: since ca. 1945. *The New Statesman*, Dec. 31, 1965, article by R. C. Hall.

blubber-boiler. A variant (from ca. 1860) of **blubber-hunter** (*Dict.*). B. & L.

blubberation. Weeping: coll.: 1912, *Rejected Addresses*; ob. by 1890, † by 1920.

bludgasite. A 'bludger': Australian: 1939–45, (B., 1943.) A blend of *bludg*er + par*asite*.

bludge, n. An easy job: Australian: since ca. 1920. John Cleary, *The Long Shadow*, 1949, 'He was happy in his job, it was a good bludge.' Ex senses 3 and 4 of the n.—2. See **come the bludge on.**

—3. (Ex sense 1.) An easy life: a period of loafing: Australian: since ca. 1920. (Dick.)

bludge.—2. To be a harlot's bully: Australian: Leonard Mann, *A Murder in Sydney*, 1937. Ex sense 1.—3. Hence, to ask for, to 'scrounge': Australian low: since ca. 1910. Lawson Glassop, *We Were the Rats*, 1944, 'Probably a Free Frenchman bludging a lift.'—4. (Ex 2.) To *bludge on*, to impose or sponge on: Australian: since ca. 1910. B., 1942.—5. To have an easy life: to loaf for a while: Australian: since ca. 1920. (Dick.) Cf. preceding.

bludger.—3. A sponger: Australian low s.: C. 20. B., 1942. Ex **bludge**, v., 4.

bludget. A female thief that lures her victims: Australian ephemeral: ca. 1925–39. (B., 1943.)

bludging. The vbl n. of **bludge**, v., esp. in senses 3 and 4.

blue, n.—8. Maltese beer: Services?: since ca. 1935. Ex the blue label of the most general make. —9. A summons: Australian: C. 20. B., 1942. Ex colour of paper.—10. Hence (?), a mistake; a loss: Australian: since ca. 1920.—11. Variant of **bluey**, 3 (*Dict.*): C. 20.—12. A brawl: Australian low: C. 20. Lawson Glassop, *We Were the Rats*, 1944.—13. As *the blue*, it = the desert; esp. *in the blue*: Army in North Africa: 1940–3. (P-G-R.) Sense 7 (p. 69) goes back to ca. 1805 or even a decade or two earlier; it occurs in W. N. Glascock, *Sailors and Saints*, 1829. (Moe.)

blue, v.—7. To fight or attack (someone): Australian since ca. 1925. B., 1942.

blue, bet on the. See **bet on** . . . above.

blue, bit of. 'An obscene or libidinous anecdote' (B. & L.): from ca. 1870.

blue, by all that's (p. 69): earlier in W. N. Glascock, *Sailors and Saints*, 1829. (Moe.)

blue, drive. To drive 'all out': motor-racers': from ca. 1920. Peter Chamberlain. Cf. *till all is blue*, q.v. in *Dict.*, at **blue, till all is.**

blue, get into a; turn on a blue. To become involved in, to start, a fight: Australian: since ca. 1920. (Culotta.)

blue, in the.—4. Out of control: Australian: since late 1920's. B., 1942. Cf. senses 1, 3 (p. 69).

blue, into the. With no horizon whatsoever: Mediterranean skin divers': since ca. 1955. (Wilfred Granville, letter of March 11, 1964.)

blue, till all is, 2 (p. 69): earlier in John L. Gardner, *The Military Sketch-Book*, II (p. 28), 1831. Moe.

blue, till the ground looks. See 'Tavern terms', § 2; cf. **blue, till all is,** p. 69.

blue, true (*Dict.*): cf. end of § 2 in 'Tavern terms'.

Blue at the Main, the. The Port Admiral: Naval coll.: C. 19. In, e.g., W. N. Glascock, *Sketch-Book*, 2nd Series, 1834, at II, 40. Moe.

Blue Bags, the. The Newtown footballers: Sydneyites': since ca. 1910. (B., 1943.)

Blue Bits. The blue-backed periodical *Chemistry and Industry*: since ca. 1946. Pun on 'Tit *Bits*'.

blue blazes: Hell: from ca. 1870. B. & L. Ex blue flames from brimstone.—2. Spirituous liquors: non-aristocratic: from ca. 1875. Ibid.

blue bottle, 2 (p. 69). Revived ca. 1840. G. W. M. Reynolds, *The Mysteries of London*, 1846.

blue-caps, the. Service police: since ca. 1930. H. & P.

blue-chin. An actor: Australian: C. 20.

B., 1942. As he shaves towards evening, so, during the day, he's unshaven.

blue chips. Coal: proletarian: mid-C. 19–20: ob. by 1940. James Bent, *Criminal Life*, 1891.

blue-domer. An officer that absents himself from church parade: military: ca. 1890–1910. H. A. Vachell, *Phœbe's Guest House*, 1939, 'God could be worshipped best under the blue dome of his own heaven.'

blue duck.—2. A failure; a frustration, a disappointment: Australian: since ca. 1930. (B., 1942.)

blue-eye. A favourite of authority: R.A.F.: since ca. 1935. Ex **blue-eyed boy** (p. 70).

blue fever—a ring of roses—Spanish football. Lower-deck names, since ca. 1945, for V.D.

blue flash. A '25,000 volt A.C. electric locomotive' (*Railway* 2nd): railwaymen's: since ca. 1955.

Blue Flue Boats. Ships of the Blue Funnel Line: H.M.S. *Conway*: C. 20. (Granville.)

blue job. A policeman; also the Navy: R.A.F.: since ca. 1939. H. & P. Cf. **brown job.**

blue light. Sense 2 derives ex the fact that, in the Indian Army, a blue light is the symbol of temperance. Kipling, in 'Bobs', a poem on Lord Roberts (appearing in *The Pall Mall Gazette* in Dec. 1893), speaks of him as 'Bluelight Bobs'.—3. A Warrant Gunner: Naval: since ca. 1920.—4. A wild rumour: Army in North Africa: 1940–3. Keith Douglas, *Alamein to Zem Zem*, 1947, 'Fantastic rumours, called blue lights, began to circulate.'

blue light, 2 (p. 70): earlier in W. N. Glascock, *The Naval Sketch-Book*, II (p. 152), 1826. Moe.

blue-light clinic. A V.D. clinic: Australian coll.: C. 20.

blue-light outfit. Anti-V.D. kit supplied to armed services: Australian coll., since ca. 1930. (B.P.)

blue lights, shit. To feel exceedingly afraid: Services: 1940 +. Cf. **blue funk** (p. 70).

blue moon (p. 70). Nearly forty years earlier in J. Burrowes, *Life in St George's Fields*, 1821.—2. A spoon: rhyming s.: late C. 19–20.—3. To 'spoon': ca. 1890–1930.

blue-nose certificate. That entry on a rating's Service Certificate which states that he has served north of the Arctic Circle: Naval: 1939–45. (P-G-R.)

blue one. A green signal light: railwaymen's: C. 20. (*Railway*.)

Blue Orchids. See **College Boys.**

blue pencil. Used to take the place of an unprintable word or phrase: coll.: since ca. 1920. Ex editors' use of blue pencil for corrections and deletions.

Blue Peter.—3. Long Service and Good Conduct Medal: Naval: C. 20. Granville.

blue pill, 2 (p. 70): earlier in W. N. Glascock, *The Naval Sketch-Book*, I (p. 173), 1825. Moe.

blue ruin.—2. A volume of Bohn's series of translations from the Greek and Latin classics: Universities' and Public Schools': ca. 1880–1914. Jocularly ex the 'gin' sense. (Marples, 2.)

blue-shirt. An owner; a manager: Australian rural: since ca. 1920.—2. Hence, a slacker: since 1925. (B., *Australia Speaks*, 1953.)

Blue Sisters, the. Members of the Little Company of St Mary: Australian Catholics' coll.: C. 20. (B.P.)

blue streak. 'Blue Pullman de luxe' (*Railway* 2nd): railwaymen's: since ca. 1920.

blue-tongue. A station roustabout: Australian: since ca. 1920. (B., 1943.)

Blue Train, the. 'The train from "Alex" into the desert, eventually . . . as far as Tobruk. There was probably a greater concentration of hangovers on this train then anywhere else on earth' (Peter Sanders in *The Sunday Times* magazine, Sept. 10, 1967): Army in North Africa: 1940–43. Ex blue, n., 13, above.

Bluebell or, rather, **bluebell.** 'Metal polish, regardless of any brand name' (Granville): Naval coll.: since ca. 1910. Ex the brand name *Bluebell*.

Bluebell Line, the. That part of the Lewes-East Grinstead line, Southern Railway, which is noted for the bluebells visible from the trains: railwaymen's and users' coll.: C. 20. (*Railway*, 3rd.)

bluebird. A (pretty) 'Waaf': R.A.F.: since ca. 1941. Partridge. Ex Maeterlinck's *The Blue-bird* of happiness.—2. A wave that has not broken (a 'greenie'): Australian surfers': since ca. 1960. (B.P.)

bluebottle. See blue bottle (*Dict.*).

blued.—2. Despondent; in low spirits: ca. 1850–1900. Conway Edwardes, in Act I of his comedy, *Heroes*, 1876, 'What's the matter? Feel blued?' (Moe.)

blues.—6. A coll. variant of *best blues* or walking-out uniform of blue serge: Naval: late C. 19–20. (P-G-R.)

Bluey. The Near East—Egypt, Palestine, etc.: Army: 1940–45. Ex 'the *blue* Mediterranean'.

bluey, 2 (p. 71), is also, since ca. 1920, Australian. (Vince Kelly, *The Greedy Ones*, 1958.)—6. A man that drinks methylated spirit: c., esp. tramps': C. 20.

blueys (or **blueies**). See 'Minor Drugs'.

blug. See blag.

bluggy occurs earlier in American Habberton's *Helen's Babies*, 1876.

blunderbuss.—3. A baby-carriage: Canadian: since ca. 1925 (?). A pun on *blunder* and *bus*. (Leechman.)

blunt end, the. 'Landlubber's term for the stern of the ship. See sharp end,' Granville: C. 20.

blunted (p. 71) survived until ca. 1910.

blurb was invented by Frank Gelett Burgess, the American humorist: A. H. Holt, *Phrase Origins*, 1936. 'I have always, subconsciously, related [it] to *blab* and *burble*' (Leechman).

bly-hunker is also spelt *bly-hunka* and is prob. of Shelta origin.

bo (p. 72). Perhaps, as Leechman suggests, ex bor, q.v. at p. 81.—2. In Australia, since ca. 1930, used occ. for any tramp. (Alan Marshall, *These Are My People*, 1946, 'I pulled up a bo.'—3. 'Wardroom mode of address for the Bosun' (Granville): Naval: since ca. 1910.

Perhaps not orig. U.S., after all, for it seems to have been a common vocative among British seamen of the Napoleonic Wars. It occurs frequently in W. N. Glascock's works, notably *The Naval Sketch-Book*, I, 1825, and *Sailors and Saints*, 1829; e.g. in the latter: ' "You may say *that*, bo," said a third' (I, 210) and ' "Never mind that, bo," cried Cheerly, the captain's coxswain, (II, 183) and with preceding 'my' at least three times. (Moe.) Therefore *not* ex *hobo*; Dr Douglas Leechman's conjecture may well be the best.

bo-chuffed. See chuffed.

Bo Joe. A variant of bo, 2 (above): since early 1930's. Either by elaboration of *bo* or by rhyming s. on hobo (p. 394). B.P. Also *bo-jo*, and prob. a corruption of bozo below, as B.P. tells me on Jan 26, 1966.

bo-peep (p. 72). Fifty years earlier in D. W. Barrett, *Navvies*, 1880–3.—3. The stocks: ca. 1760–1850. One's head peeps out.—4. A look: Australian: since ca. 1920. (Lawson Glassop, *Lucky Palmer*, 1949.)

boab. A baobab tree: Australian: C. 20. Jack Marshall & Russell Drysdale, *Journey among Men*, 1962, p. 116, 'We camped in a clump of young boabs.'

board, n.—4. 'The use of *board* for the floor of a shearing shed is also slang, whence comes *a full board* and *boss-over-the-board*,' B., 1941: New Zealand and Australian rural: since ca. 1880; by 1910, coll. *Over the board* occurs in Archer Russell, *Gone Nomad*, 1936.—5. As in 'The board's against me' (the signal is 'No'): Canadian railwaymen's coll.: C. 20. But also, by ca. 1945, British. (*Railway*, 3rd.)

Board of Trade. A 'bench seat in Hyde Park, from the amorous activity for which the locality is notorious. (Noted July 26, 1960)': since the 1940's. Cf. trade, n., 6, below.

board shorts. Shorts descending almost to knees: Australian surfers' coll.: since ca. 1955. (*The Bulletin*, March 30, 1963.)

board the beef in the smoke. To eat dinner: nautical, esp. Naval: ca. 1790–1860. Moe has found it in 1806.

board you! Pass the bottle on: nautical (—1890); ob.

boarding-house reach is that implied in *reaching!*, **excuse me** (p. 690): Canadian jocular coll.: C. 20. (Leechman.)

boat.—2. A motor-car used for races: motor-racers': from ca. 1928. Peter Chamberlain. Punning *motor-boat*.—3. A submarine (usually pl.): Naval: since ca. 1920. Granville.—4. A builder's cradle: builders' jocular: C. 20. n.—5. Short for *boat race*.

boat, be on the. To have been drafted overseas (but *not* yet on the troopship): Forces', esp. R.A.F., coll.: 1939–45.

boat-happy. Excited—often so as to become distrait—at the idea of going back home on a demobilisation ship: Army: 1945–6.

boathook. An 8-foot pole with spitted end, used by the London Fire Brigade: C. 20.

boat race. Face: rhyming s.: since ca. 1946. Often shortened to *boat*. (Both are in Norman.)

Boats. The Boats Officer: Naval (ward-room) coll.: C. 20. (P-G-R.)

boats. Boots, esp. if they are (very) large: non-U jocular: C. 20.

boat's left, the. You've 'had it': Naval c.p.: since ca. 1910. (P-G-R.) The boat taking men ashore.

Boatsville. The Admiralty building in Whitehall, London: orig., and mainly, Fleet Air Arm: since ca. 1930.

boatswell. An Admiral: Naval lowerdeck: since ca. 1930. (Wilfred Granville, April 22, 1962.) Boat 'swell'?

bob. To strike, slap, push sharply, punch: C. 20. Gerald Kersh, *Bill Nelson*, 1942, 'I bob him in the stomach and he fell flat.' Cf. bonk,

bob, n.,—2 (a shilling), goes back more than twenty years earlier than the authority cited on p. 72; it occurs in *Sessions*, June 1789.

bob, v.—2. To be subservient to authority; to be punctilious (and often a shade anxious) in observation of the regulations; hence *bobber*, one who is this or who does this, and *bob on*, to be very respectful towards one's superior: Army, esp. in the Guards regiments. See, e.g., Roger Grinstead, *Some Talk of Alexander*, 1943, and *They Dug a Hole*, 1946. Ex S.E. *bob*, to curtsey.—3. Hence, esp. to dither: since ca. 1939. (P-G-R.)

Bob, old blind. Penis: Lambeth Cockneys': C. 20. Personification.

bob, shift one's. To exchange places: Naval: ca. 1805–50. In W. N. Glascock, *The Naval Sketch-Book*, II, 1826. (Moe.)

bob a nob.—2. Hence, hair-cutting: since ca. 1930; † by 1947.

bob and sock, the game of. Boxing: boxing journalists': since the 1930's. Ex *bob*, to duck one's head, and *sock* to punch hard.

bob down—you're spotted! A c.p. (from ca. 1920): 'Your argument (excuse, etc.) is so very weak that you need not go on!'

bob(-)hole door. A 'wagon door constructed to half open' (*Railway*, 3rd): railwaymen's: C. 20. So that an employee may 'bob in or out'?

Bob Hope. A flying bomb: July–Oct. 1944. *Daily Express*, Aug. 14, 1944, ' "When you hear them coming," I was told, "you bob, hope for the best." ' A pun on the name of the famous American comedian.

bob-in. A voluntary subscription: Australian coll.: late C. 19–20. (B., 1943.) A shilling a head into the kitty.

bob it! See **bob!** in *Dict.*

bob, line and sinker,—lock, stock and barrel. See **lock, stock and barrel, bob, line and sinker.**

bob on. See **bob,** v., 2.

Bob Short; Dumb Dick; Fat Jack. 'And here the unprofessional reader is apprised of "Jack's" propensity to designate people by appellations totally opposite to their characteristics and personal appearance'—footnoted, 'Thus a tall tar is frequently designated " *Bob Short*"—a lean one " *Fat Jack* "—a talkative topman, " *Dumb Dick*" ' (Wm Nugent Glascock, *The Naval Sketch-Book*, 2nd Series, 1834, at I, 58): Naval ratings': C. 19. Moe.

Bob Squash. A wash, to wash (oneself): rhyming s.: C. 20.—2. Hence, the lavatory division of a public convenience: since ca. 1930. 'A pickpocket is said to be "working the Bob" when he specializes in removing wallets from the jackets of people washing their hands' (Franklyn 2nd).

bob tail: bob-tail. See **bobtail** (*Dict.*).

bob to a gussie. 'To ingratiate oneself with an officer' (Jackson): Services: since ca. 1930. See **bobbing.**

bob under. To sing small: Services': C. 20. (P-G-R.)

bobber.—4. A filleter of fish: fishing trade s.: C. 20. It now verges on coll. (The Regional wireless programme of Nov. 23, 1936.) Ex S.E. *bob*, to tap.

bobbers. A fringe of pieces of cork or wood worn on a hat to keep the flies away: Australian: late C. 19–20. B., 1942.—2. Female breasts: North

Country: since ca. 1945. John Wainwright, *Edge of Destruction*, 1968.

bobbery (p. 73) is, however, current in C. 20 Australia. (Vance Palmer's novels, *passim*.)

bobbin!, that's the end of the. That's the end of it!; that's finished!: non-aristocratic coll. c.p. verging on proverbial S.E.: mid-C. 19–20; ob. B. & L., '. . . When all the thread is wound off a *bobbin* or spool. . . . It rose from the refrain of a song which was popular in 1850.'

bobbing. An attempt to curry favour with a superior: Services, since ca. 1930. H. & P. Ex curtseying.—2. See **dry bobbing.**

bobby, 1 (p. 73). My earliest record for it is *Sessions* (Surrey cases), June 1844.—3. A 'poddy' calf: Australian: C. 20. B., 1942. By corruption. —4. A signalman: railwaymen's: C. 20 (*Railway*). Ex sense 1 on p. 73.

bobby, v. To serve, to be, to be occupied as, a policeman: police force coll.: since the 1930's. Hence the n., *bobbying*. Both occur in John Wainwright, *The Worms Must Wait*, 1967. Ex *bobby*, a policeman.

bobby, swallow. See **swallow bobby.**

bobby dazzler (p. 73), a dazzling person: by 1890, s. in Britain; by 1900, s. in Australia, where usually *a real bobby dazzler*. (B.P.)

'In the heyday of Cycling Clubs the police would lie in wait for their dusk return. Those without lights got in the middle, those with the new-fangled very bright acetylene lamps rode on the outside, their lamps were the Bobby Dazzlers' (John A. Yates, letter of Sept. 8, 1966): a pun on *Bobby, bobby*, a policeman. *Se non è vero è ben trovato*.

bobby peeler. A policeman: ca. 1850–70. B. & L. See **bobby** (*Dict.*).

bobby-soxer. A teenage girl rigidly adhering to teenage conventions: adopted, ca. 1959, ex U.S.: by 1965, coll. Ex *bobby socks*, white cotton socks. Cf. quotation at **greatest, the,** above.

bobby's job. An easy job: coll.: C. 20. Ex a common misapprehension.

Bob's-a-dying. Idling; idling and dozing: nautical: ? ca. 1790–1850. Wm N. Glascock, *Sailors and Saints*, 1829 (I, 179), 'Nothing but dining, and dancing, and Bobs-a-dying on deck from daylight till dark'. (Moe.)

Bob's your uncle. Everything is perfect: c.p.: from ca. 1890; slightly ob. 'You go and ask for the job—and he remembers your name—and Bob's your uncle.' 'Still going strong in Australia' (B.P., 1965).

Bocker. See **Bokker.**

bockety. Distorted or deformed: Anglo-Irish, esp. Dubliners': C. 20. (Dr H. W. Dalton.)

bod. A body, i.e. a real person, a person actually available: R.A.F.: since ca. 1935. Jackson. Note *odd bod*, unattached or 'spare' man: orig. Services', then gen. s.

Bod, the. The Bodleian Library: Oxford undergraduates': C. 20. (Marples, 2.) Cf. *Bodder* (p. 74).

bodge. Paper: Christ's Hospital: C. 20. Marples. Ex *bumf?*—2. A bodgie: Australian non-bodgies': since early 1950's. (Dick.)

***bodger.** See sense 2 of **bodgie.**—2. As *Mr Bodger*, it means a confused or inefficient man: Australian: the 1950's. (B., 1953.)

Bodger or **Bidge, the.** The Headmaster: Rugby: late C. 19–20. Marples. *Bodger* corrupts *boss*, and *bidge* thins and shortens *bodger*. 'First applied to Dr James, headmaster 1895–1909.' (Marples.) 'The latter is no longer used' (D. F. Wharton, letter of Oct. 24, 1965).

bodgie or **-gy**. 'Boy with crew-cut and zoot-suit, playing juke-box in milk-bar' (*The Sunday Chronicle*, Jan. 6, 1952): Australian: ca. 1950–60. Cf. *widgie*.—2. 'Anything worthless, such as a fake receipt' (B., 1953): Australian c.: since ca. 1950. Also *bodger*.—3. Hence also, misfits or unclassifiables: since ca. 1952. (B., 1953.)

Sense 1 is still current, as in Dick, but slightly ob. The word app. comes from U.S. teenage s. for a young male jitterbug wearing his hair long and curly, and a sports jacket too large for him: W. & F. record it for 1952 and say that it was, by 1960, archaic, but they don't essay an etymology. My guess is that it doesn't come from Eng. Lakeland dial. *bodgy*, fat, puffy, but is a back-formation from *bodgies*, itself a distortion of 'the *boys*' or, more prob., *boysies* (cf. **boysie** on p. 87). Another guess: **widgie** (below) ex *widgies*, an analogous distortion of 'the *wimmen*' (women)—prompted by *bodgies*.

bodier (p. 74). A little earlier in *Boxiana*, II, 1818.

bodies, the (p. 74) occurs earlier in Major John André's poem, *The Cow Chase*, New York, 1780, London, 1781, with the *Bodies* footnoted thus: 'A cant'—here, fashionable slang—'appellation given amongst the soldiery to the corps that had the honour to guard his Majesty's person'.

body, v. To punch (one's opponent) on the body —i.e. the trunk: pugilistic coll.: ca. 1805–70. *Boxiana*, II, 1818.

[Body, the. 'Ward frequently uses a number of slang terms, some of them vulgar, for various parts of the body. The following . . . occur fairly often in his works': esp. in London: 1700–25. The head was *noddle* (1703); eyes were *peepers* (1722); breasts, *bubbies* (1703) and *dumplings* (1709); feet, *pettitoes* (1709) and the rare *pedestals* (1703); a hand was a *paw* (1700); the nose, *beak* (1715) or *handle of one's face* (1703); tongue, *clapper* (1700); the behind, *bum-fiddle* (1709), *scut* (1709), *tail* (1703) or *toby* (1703); a face, *fiz* (1700); teeth were *stumps* (1709—but is this correct?); entrails, *puddings* (1703). Matthews.]

body (-) and (-) soul lashing. 'A piece of rope tied belt-wise round an oilskin which a messmate can grab if a man is in danger of falling overboard,' Granville: Naval: C. 20. But also, in the old sailing-ship days, to keep water out of legs and sleeves of oilskins.

body-bag. A shirt: low: ca. 1820–70. *Sinks*.

body-basher or **panel-beater**. A garage owner, or the garage itself: Australian motorists': since ca. 1950. (B.P.)

body-binder. A 'waistcoat' or perhaps a 'broad belt': ca. 1810–40, esp. in boxing circles. *The Plymouth Telegraph*, (? March) 1822, 'Bartlett entered first, and *doffed* the *castor* from his *nob*, his *blue bird's-eye* from his *squeeze*, and his *body-binder* from his *bread-basket*'.

body-snatcher, 8. Also R.A.F.: since ca. 1939 H. & P.—10. A surgeon addicted to operating on seamen: Australian Naval: 1939–45. (B., 1943.)

body(-)strike. See **fly(-)strike** below.

boff, have a. To hit out: cricketers': since ca. 1955. *The Sunday Times*, July 9, 1961, Ian Peebles, 'May, with a raincloud at his back and

victory just round the corner, had a boff'. Echoic; cf. **biff** on p. 51.

boffer. See **boffing**.

boffin. Usually *the boffins*, the inventors working for the advancement of aviation: R.A.F. Dating since before the war of 1939–45, it > gen. in the Services only in 1944 (W/Cdr Robin P. McDouall, letter of March 27, 1945). A fanciful name of the Lewis Carroll type, yet with a glance at 'baffle' (the *bafflings* = the baffling fellows = those who baffle the enemy) and perhaps at 'The Boffin Books'—a delightful series for children.—2. In the Navy, any officer over 40 years of age: since ca. 1940. Granville.

boffing, vbl n.; **boffer**. Masturbation; one who indulges in a specific instance: low: since ca. 1930.

bog, n., 1 (p. 74). Earlier in *Spy*, 1825; orig., Oxford University.—3. (Short for *bog-wheel*) a bicycle: Marlborough College: C. 20.

bog, v.—2. To work hard at a manual job: Australian: since ca. 1925. Gavin Casey, *The Wits are Out*, 1947, 'Bogging underground on the goldfields'.

*bog(-)gang. A party of convicts detailed for the work defined at **bog**, 2 (*Dict.*): same period. B. & L.

bog-in, n. A hearty meal: Australian: C. 20. (Jon Cleary, *The Climate of Courage*, 1954.) Ex the v.

bog in, v.i. To eat (heartily): to work energetically: Australian: late C. 19–20. B., 1942.—2. To get started: Australian: since ca. 1910. (Culotta.)

bog man. A term of abuse in the Army, esp. in the Guards: since ca. 1930. Cf. **shit**, n., 2 (*Dict.*).

bog off. To depart; to take off: Air Force: since ca. 1937. Charles Graves, *Seven Pilots*, 1943.

Bog-Trotter, 3 (p. 74): the entry in B.E., however, clearly indicates that, as 'any Irishman whatsoever', the term had existed since late C. 17.

bog up. To make a mess of; to do incompetently; hence the n. *bog-up*: Services: 1939+. (P-G-R.)

bog(-)wheel. A bicycle: Cambridge undergraduates': ca. 1924–40. Its wheels are—like the gap in a water-closet seat—round. Cf. **bog**, n., 1 (p. 74).

bogey.—An aircraft suspected to be hostile: R.A.F.: 1939–45. (P-G-R.)

Bogey, Colonel. See **Colonel Bogey**.

boggart, be off at, with *Meredith* occ. added. To be, or go, off at full tilt or, fig., impetuously: Midlands: late C. 19–20. Ex Midlands dial. (of a horse) *take (the) boggart*, take fright. A *boggart* is, of course, a bogey or hobgoblin or ghost. (Richard Merry.)

boggi (pron. *bog-eye*). 'Handpiece of a shearing machine' (B., 1959): Aus. rural: C. 20. Origin?

bogh. To get; hold; make (esp. a person) work: Shelta: C. 18–20. B. & L.

bogie. A bathe: Australian: since ca. 1815. Alex. Harris, *The Emigrant Family*, 1849. Ex Aboriginal.—2. Hence, a swimming-hole; a bath: Australian: late C. 19–20. (B., 1943.)

Sense 1, † by 1950; sense 2, now usually *bogie-hole*. (B.P.)

bogies. Dissatisfied customers: mock-auction s. See **bogy**, n., 8, on p. 75.

bogs. See **bog**, n., in *Dict.*

bogus, n. One who is detected in a pretence, a bluff, a sham: Services: since ca. 1935. H. & P. Ex the adj. (p. 75).

bogy, 7. See **bogie.**—9. An aircraft suspected to be hostile: R.A.F.: 1939 +.—10. See last sense of **sweep,** n., in *Dict.*

bogy, make a. To make a mistake: Regular Army: late C. 19–20; ob. by 1946. See **bogy,** n. 5 (p. 75).

Bohunk (or b-). 'As a Polish or Slavic labourer [it] was a familiar to me in 1910 in British Columbia' (Leechman): Canadian: C. 20. Probably adopted from U.S.: Mitford M. Mathews records it for 1903 and explains it as a modified blend of *Bohem*ian + *Hung*arian.

boil, n. A teenager whose sex is not immediately discernible, because of long hair and clothing so much alike: since ca. 1962. Ex '*boy* and *girl*'—with a pun on 'pain in the neck'.

boil-over. A series of horse-races in which the favourite loses: Australian sporting: ca. 1870–1910.

boil up, n. An argument: a quarrel: Australian: C. 20. B., 1942.

boiled, adj. Tipsy: Australian: since ca. 1918.

boiled dog (p. 75) is also, since ca. 1918, Australian.

Boiled Rabbit. St Clement's Church, Oxford: Oxford undergraduates': ca. 1830–90. Because of its peculiar architecture. (Geoffrey Faber, *Oxford Apostles*, 1953.)

boiled rag. A stiff shirt: Australian: since ca. 1910. Baker.

boiler.—3. A hat: Public Schools': ca. 1880–1915. Talbot Baines Reed, *The Fifth Form at St Dominic's*, 1907—4. 'A well-used woman of forty or over' (Robin Cook, 1962): since ca. 1925: c. >, by 1960, low s.

boiler-buster. A boiler-maker: Naval: C. 20.

boiler-clean. A boiler-cleaning: Naval coll.: C. 20.

boiler-creepers. Dungarees: Naval: C. 20. Worn by engineers and stokers in the engine-room.

boiler-maker. A mixture, half of draught mild and half of bottled brown ale: public-houses': since ca. 1920.

boiler-plate. Matter already set, on stereotyped plates, for filling up pages of a newspaper: Canadian printers': C. 20.

boiling.—2. Short for *boiling, the whole* (p. 75): coll.: since ca. 1930. Jackson.

boiling, the whole (p. 75). Earlier in 'A Real Paddy', *Real Life in Ireland*, 1822.

boils, heads on 'em (or them) like. An Australian two-up players' c.p. that, dating from before 1914, is applied to a run of heads. (Lawson Glassop, *Lucky Palmer*, 1949.)

boing! This imitation of the noise made by a suddenly released spring, became, ca. 1955, a Canadian c.p., used on any occasion, no matter how inappropriate. (Leechman.) By 1950, also British, with variant *boink*. Cf. **doing** and **kerdoying,** both below.

Bojer or Boojer. A Boer; esp. a Boer soldier: English soldiers': in the South African War.

*bok. A girl. South African c.: C. 20. *The Cape Times*, May 23, 1946. Afrikaans.

bokker or bocker. A bowler hat: Australian: since ca. 1920. B., 1942. Ex **boxer,** 2 (*Dict.*).

boko, adj. Blind in one eye: Australian: C. 20. B., 1942.

Boley or Boly. A Bolingbroke aircraft:

R.C.A.F.: 1940–5. Canadian form of the Blenheim.

bollicks or bollocks. See **ballocks.**

bolo. ' "What's Bolo?" "Cock-eyed; anything not correct in the Coldstream Guards is Bolo" ', Gerald Kersh, *They Die with Their Boots Clean*, 1941. Prob. ex *bow-legged*.

Bolshie.—2. Hence, since ca. 1930 and usually small *b'd*, a synonym of **bloody-minded;** pigheaded; obstructive and deliberately difficult; esp. in the Forces: 1939 +. Without political significance.

bolt, n.—3. (Or *Bolt.*) A non-Latin European: Australian, esp. teenagers': since late 1940's. 'Our boys hated these dagoes and bolts that were coming out here' (Dick). Perhaps 'those who *bolt* from their own country'.—But Mr Barry Prentice (April 1, 1967) thinks this to be 'almost certainly a misprint for **Balt**' above.

bolt upright. An emphasis-tag: mostly Cockneys': from ca. 1880. E.g. 'I'll be damned, bolt upright.' Mr Ramsey Spencer reminds me, in March 1967, that this occurs in *The Canterbury Tales* (The Reeve's Tale):

'. . . I have thries as, in this short night swived the millers doughter bolt-upright'.

bolted. See **mill, been through the.**

bolters, have not the. Of person or racehorse, to have no chance of winning the race or the contest: Australian sporting: since ca. 1920. B., 1942. Ex *bolt*, to run away. Better written *bolter's*, i.e. a bolting horse's chance; B., 1959, compares **Buckley's chance,** q.v. both below and on p. 101.

Boly. See **Boley.**

bomb. In address, a bombardier: military (esp. R.A.): since ca. 1920. H. & P. n.—2. 'An old car or motorcycle' (B., 1953): Australian: since ca. 1945. Noisy. In *The Drum*, 1959, B. defines it as 'any old car, but esp. a car made in the 1930's'.

bomb, v. To dope (a horse): Australian sporting: since ca. 1945. (B., 1953.)

bomb, go like a, esp. in 'It has gone, *or* it went, like a bomb', as in ' "A sort of Grand tour, wasn't it, with Robbie?"—"Sort of. Seeing the world and brushing up my Arabic . . . Oh, it all went like a bomb" ' (Mary Stewart, *The Gabriel Hounds*, 1967). It began, in the late 1950's, for cars with a fine turn of speed and a very rapid acceleration; by early in the 1960's it was being applied to expeditions, visits, parties, love affairs, what have you. Ex the explosion of (large) bombs.

bomb, make a. To make 'a packet' or become rich: low: since ca. 1945. (Norman.)

Bomb Alley. The Straits of Messina: Naval and Merchant Naval from mid-1940 to mid-1943, then only historical.—2. The enemy-held strip of coast between Tobruk and the British lines in Egypt: 1941–3.

bomb-happy. With nerves gone, through exposure to bombing: Army: 1940 +. (Lawson Glassop, *We Were the Rats*, 1944; W/Cdr Robin P. McDouall, letter of April 12, 1945.) Contrast the R.A.F. *flak-happy*. Also as n., a person with bomb-shattered nerves.

bomb-sight buglet. A bright-eyed gremlin, addicted to dazzling the bomb-aimer: R.A.F.: 1940–5. (P-G-R.)

bomb-up. 'To load an aircraft with bombs' (Jackson): R.A.F. coll.: since 1939; at latest by 1944, j.

Bombay bowler. A service-issue topee: R.A.F.: since ca. 1925. (Sgt Gerald Emanuel, letter of March 29, 1945.) Alliterative—and, well, Bombay *is* hot. The Sergeant, however, says, 'Because usually jettisoned at Bombay, port of entry into India, by reason of its uncomfortable weight.'

Bombay fizzer. 'A small tumbler of water with a teaspoonful of sherbet in it,' Richards: Indian-Army coll.: from ca. 1880.

Bombay fornicator. A type of chair (capacious and comfortable): R.A.F.: since ca. 1925; slightly ob. by 1950.

Bombay runner. A large cockroach often encountered in the lands and islands of the Indian Ocean: nautical, esp. Naval: late C. 19–20. (Granville.)

bomber. A newspaper: journalistic: since ca. 1930.

bomber boy. Any member (though esp. the pilot) of a bomber crew: R.A.F. coll.: since 1939. Jackson.

bombie. See **bommie** below.

bombo.—2. Wine: Australian: since ca. 1930. (B.P.) Cf. **bumbo**, 2, on p. 107.—3. Whisky: Australian: C. 20. B., 1942. Ex **bumbo**, 2 (*Dict.*). —4. Cheap wine, esp. if much fortified: Australian: since ca. 1919. (B., 1943.)

bommie, orig. **bombie**. A bombora, i.e. a 'submerged reef beyond the beach breakers' (*The Bulletin*, March 30, 1963): Australian surfers': since late 1950's.

bomper. The 'stamp' on dockers' Dock Labour Board cards, with corresponding v. *bomp on*: Merseyside: since middle 1940's. (*Picture Post*, Dec. 3, 1949.) Ex a dial. variant of *bump* and *bumper*.

bona, adj.—2. Beautiful: prostitutes', esp. London: C. 20. Ex sense 1 on p. 77.

bona, adv. Very: parlyaree: since ca. 1860. (P. H. Emerson, *Signor Lippo*, 1893.) Ex the ad. —see p. 77.

bond-hook or **bondhook.** A variant of **bundhook** (p. 104).

Bondi (tram), go through—or **travel**—**like a.** To travel very fast; hence, to decamp hastily; hence, 'to leave a task or obligation on a sudden whim' (B., *The Drum*, 1959): Aus., esp. N.S.W.: C.20. Cf. **go through** and **shoot through** below.

bone, n.—3. *The bone* is the *penis erectus*: Cockneys': mid-C. 19–20.—4. A dollar: C. 20. Nourishing.

bone, v.—2. To interrogate (a suspect): police and fringe-of-underworld: C. 20. *Evening Echo* (Bournemouth), April 20, 1966. Ex sense 1 on p. 77.—3. To bring bad luck to; to jinx: Aus.: C. 20. Ex S. E. *point a bone*, an Aboriginal practice. B., 1959.

bone boots. To get a patent-leather finish on one's Service boots: Regular Army coll.: C. 20.

bone dome. A crash helmet: esp. in aviation: since ca. 1935.

bone-head (or one word). A boxer: R.A.F. since ca. 1935. Jackson. He needs it or he would not be one.

bone in the mouth, carry a (p. 77). But perhaps the predominant form is *have*—occ., *have got*—*a* (or *the*) *bone in her mouth*, as in Wm Maginn, *Tales of Military Life*, 1829, at I, 327, '"Bless you, Ma'am, she has only got the bone in her mouth—

she is spanking away like a young whale, at nine or ten knots an hour"'. (Moe.)

bone in the throat (etc.). These phrases occur also in the form *in one's throat* (etc.).

bone out. To survey (a stretch of rail) in order to adjust the level; hence, *boning rods*, survey (or siting) boards: railwaymen's: C. 20. (*Railway*.)

bone-shaker.—2. Hence, 'any old vehicle which passengers find uncomfortable,' H. J. Oliver (see **Bovril**): coll.: C. 20.

bone up on. To study (a subject) because the information will soon be needed: Canadian (ex U.S.): since ca. 1910. Either ex *bone* used for polishing shoes or ex the *Bohn* translations of the Classics.

bone with, have a. To have a quarrel with, a grudge against, someone: Australian coll.: C. 20. D'Arcy Niland, 1958. For *have a bone to pick with*.

Bone Yard, the. Neuve Chapelle, after the bloody battle fought there in 1915: Tommies': 1915–18. (A. B. Petch, 'It was hardly possible to dig anywhere without disinterring bones.')

bone-yard.—2. 'White water in front of a wave' (*Pix*, Sept. 28, 1963): Australian surfers': since ca. 1960.

boned. Tipsy: Society (since ca. 1937) and Services officers' (1939 +). Mary Fitt, *The Banquet Ceases*, 1949. Wits *boned* (stolen) away.

boner. 2 (p. 78), occurs esp. in *pull a boner*, to commit one.

bones and hair. Buenos Aires: mostly nautical: late C. 19–20.

bong.—2. Dead: Australian pidgin: from ca. 1860. B. & L. Ex Aborigine.

bong.—3. See **Quego**.

bonk, n.—2. The n.—from 1920—corresponding to

bonk, v.—2. Hence, to hit (v.t.) resoundingly: mostly Public Schools': from 1919.

Bonk! Bang!: coll., mostly Cockneys': C. 20. Echoic. Whence **bonk**, v., in *Dict.* and Addenda.

bonk, the; bonked. (The state of being) devoid of energy: cyclists': since ca. 1945. Cf. (*hunger*) *knock*, *sag*, *sags*.—Hence *bonk-bag*, a small food bag, slung from the cyclist's shoulder.

bonker, stone-wall. A 'stone' (= absolute) certainty: since ca. 1930.

bonkers. Slightly drunk, light-headed: Naval: since ca. 1920. Granville. Perhaps cf. **bonk**, v.i. (*Dict.*).—2. Hence, eccentric; crazy: Naval: since ca. 1925; by ca. 1946, fairly general. Often in the intensive form, *stone fucking bonkers*. 'Since "that speech" by Mr Quintin Hogg, in Oct. 1964, now usually "stark staring bonkers" = "quite mad"': Peter Sanders, mid-1965.

bonny Dundee. A flea: theatrical rhyming s.: C. 20. (Franklyn, *Rhyming*.)

bono (h)omee (or **ommy**). Husband: parlary: mid-C. 19–20. (*John o' London's Weekly*, Feb. 4, 1949.) For the elements, see *bono*, good (p. 78), and *omee* (p. 587): cf. archaic S.E. *goodman*, husband.

bontoger, bontogeriro, bonzerino, bonziorie. Elaborations of **bonza** (*Dict.*): C. 20. B., 1942. Add: *bontoser* (Dal Stivens, 1955).

bony. Good: Christ's Hospital: late C. 18–20. Marples: ex Latin *O bone!*, Oh, good man!

bonzer (*Dict.*). 'Formerly widely used. The word is now rare': B., *The Drum*, 1959.

boo-boo. The human bottom: children's: late 19–20. Nicholas Blake, *The Sad Variety*, 1964, 'No use sitting around on your boo-boo, brooding'. Reduplication of *bottom*.—2. See **booboo** below.

booai or **booay** (pron. *boo-eye*). Remote rural districts: New Zealand: C. 20. 'Corruption of Puhoi, the name of a settlement' (Keith Sinclair, 1959); but perhaps a pejorative from Maori *puhoi*, slow, dull, phlegmatic. Also, since ca. 1910, Australian for 'the open bush', as in D'Arcy Niland, *The Shiralee*, 1955, where it is written *boo-eye*.

Of the N.Z. use, Harold Griffiths says, 'Heard very frequently out here in such expressions as "(way) out in the boo-ay" (far from the towns—in the backblocks) and also "(all) up the boo-ay" (completely off the track—especially with knowledge, an opinion, etc.)': letter of March 19, 1959.

The fig. *up the booai*, lost, utterly wrong, has been common since the late 1940's. (Slatter.)

boob, n.—Sense 2, on p. 79: also, by 1920, gen. Australian. (Jock Marshall & Russell Drysdale, *Journey among Men*, 1962, at p. 132.)—3. A blunder; a *faux-pas*: since ca. 1935. Ex the corresponding v.

boob. To blunder. Army and Air Force: since ca. 1930. R. M. Davison, letter of Sept. 26, 1942; H. & P.: cf.—and see—**black**, n., 2. Usually v.i., but occ. v.t., as in the R.A.F. *boob a landing*, to land clumsily.

boobies. A woman's breasts: since ca. 1920. In, e.g., Henry Miller, *Tropic of Cancer*, 1934. Ex *bubbies*, q.v. at **bubby** on p. 99.

booboo (or **boo-boo**); esp. in *make a booboo*. A blunder: mostly Australian: adopted, ca. 1959, ex U.S. Perhaps ex **boob**, v., above—or ex a baby's cry of pain or frustration. (B.P.) 'About 1950 there was a (briefly) very popular song "Knees up, pat him on the po-po", on the subject of baby-care, but this may be more closely related to Ger. s. "Popo"—the backside. In baby-French, "popo" expresses the need to use a chamber-pot, just as "dodo" refers to sleep and "bobo" to pain or hurt.' (Ramsey Spencer, 1967.) The term occurs in Hugh Atkinson, *Low Company*, 1961.

boobs, the or **one's.** The female breasts: predominantly feminine: since ca. 1960. '*The Observer* of Feb. 11, 1968, interviewing a girl emerging from Fortnums, on the subject of "see-through blouses", quoted her as saying that she wouldn't put her boobs on show for anyone' (communicated by Ramsey Spencer). As *bubbies* > *boobies* (see below), so *bubs* > *boobs*.

booby hatch. A lunatic asylum: Canadian (ex U.S.): C. 20.

booby-hutch, 3 (p. 79). Earlier in *Reed's Weekly Journal*, June 4, 1720.

bood. A bedroom; a sleeping-cubicle: girls' Public Schools': C. 20. (R. C. Hutchinson, *The Answering Glory*, 1932.) Ex *boudoir*.

boodgeree! All right; good: Australian: since ca. 1910. (B., 1943.) Ex Aborigine: cf. *budgeree*, on p. 101.

boodler. A man, esp. a politician, on the make: Australian: since ca. 1920. (Vance Palmer, 1948.)

boody. A snake: Australian: C. 20. (B., 1943.) Ex Aborigine.

booey or **bouie.** A piece of nasal mucus: non-cultured Australian domestic: since ca. 1920. Ex *Fr. boue*, mud, filth. (B.P.)

boofhead. A fool; a very gullible person: Australian: since ca. 1930. (B., 1943.) Ex **buffle-head** (p. 102). The corresponding adj. is *boofheaded*, as in L. W. Lower, *Lennie Lower's Sidesplitters*, 1945.

book, n.—5. A newspaper, a magazine: illiterate coll.: since ca. 1880.—6. But, since ca. 1920, it has been a Canadian publishers' and printers' coll. for an issue, as in: 'My July book is still only half-finished.' (Leechman.)

book, be with. (To be) engaged in writing a book: authors': since ca. 1930. On (be) *with child*, pregnant.

book, on the. In the prompt corner; on duty as prompter: theatrical coll.: C. 20. (Dulcie Gray, *No Quarter for a Star*, 1964.) The 'book of words'—the text of the play.

book, put in the. To enter a man's name in the charge book: Army coll.: since ca. 1910. (P-G-R.)

book all right but doesn't know what page he's on, He's in the. He's right but he doesn't know why: Australian, c.p.: since ca. 1925. B., 1942.

'book!' he says; and can't read a paper yet. A c.p. of ca. 1890–1914, addressed to one who has explosively broken wind.

book of (the) words. A catalogue: jocular coll.: from ca. 1880.—2. A libretto: id.: from ca. 1890.—3. A set of printed or typewritten instructions: C. 20. (Warwick Deeping, *Mr Gurney . . .*, 1944.)

book one's seat. To pad one's trousers with newspapers or a book before going to be caned: schoolboys': since ca. 1945.

booked for kingdom come. Facing certain death; on one's death-bed: coll.: C. 20; orig. railwaymen's.

bookie (or **-ky) boy** (or **bhoy**). A bookmaker: Australian: since ca. 1920. (B., 1943.)

bookmaker's pocket. See **book-maker** (*Dict.*).

bookra (a better spelling). See **bukra** in *Dict.*

books, the. The works of reference: coll.: C. 20. 'Oh, look it up in the books.'

Boom. Lord Trenchard: since ca. 1918. Ex his booming voice.

boom, n.—2. 'Pushing, by vigorous publicity, a person, game, or book': from ca. 1890: coll. till ca. 1905, then S.E. There was, e.g., a Trilby boom in 1896–97.

boom-boom. A soldier: children's, esp. Cockneys': from ca. 1916. Echoic. Moreover, 2, **boom boom** is a Pidgin term (Pacific Islanders', Thailanders', Koreans' and what have you) for rifle fire, cannon fire; a rifle, a cannon; fighting or to fight, war. For instance in prisoner-of-war camps in the Far East, 1942–5, *boom boom yashe* means 'a rifle rest'—see 'prisoner-of-war Slang'. 7. So widely is *boom boom* accepted as echoically precise that little children all over the world use it.

boom off. To fight off; scare away: Naval: 1934–5. Echoic of heavy gunfire.

boom off, top one's (p. 80): prob. from fifty years earlier, to judge by the synonymous *top one's boom* in Alfred Burton, *The Adventures of Johnny Newcome*, 1818. Moe.

boom or bust is a Canadian c.p. (late C. 19–20)—applied to 'western towns, mines and other such enterprises as are subject to varying fortunes' (Leechman.)

boomer.—4. Hence, anything extraordinary: Australian: C. 20. (Authority as for **Bovril.**)—5. An itinerant worker on the railways, usually a 'brakie' or a 'brass-pounder': Canadian railwaymen's: since ca. 1910. (Leechman.)—6. A (very) large wave: Australian coll.: since ca. 1910. (Culotta.)

boomerang. 'Something, esp. a book, that one would like to receive back' (B.P.): Australian: since ca. 1930.

booming. Large: Australian: from ca. 1860; ob. B. & L. Perhaps ex **boomer,** 2 (*Dict.*).

boomps-a-daisy! Domestic and nursery c.p. to a child that has knocked its head or falls over: late C. 19–20. Suggested by *ups-a-daisy!*

boon companion (*Dict.*): cf. § 2 of 'Tavern terms'.

boong. See **Quego.**—2. Hence, 'any dark-skinned person': B., *The Drum*, 1959.

boong-moll. A coloured, esp. a Negro, pathic: Australian low or c.: since ca. 1930. (Dymphna Cusack and Florence James, *Come in Spinner*, 1951.)—2. A prostitute favouring dark-skinned men: Australian c.: since ca. 1935. (B., 1953.)

*boop, v.; usually as vbl n., *booping*, making a fuss about a trifle: Services: since ca. 1935. H. & P. A blend of echoic *boo* + *weep*.

boost, n.—3. A supercharging; additional pressure: R.A.F. coll.: since ca. 1925. Jackson, 'I gave her [an aircraft] all the boost I had'; he cites the corresponding v. Ex sense 1.

boost, be in high or low. (Of persons) to be in good or bad form: Coastal Forces' (Naval): 1940–5. In ref. to engines.

boot-faced. Wearing a miserable or downhearted or thwarted expression: R.A.F.: since ca. 1930. Ex the appearance of an old boot with sole parting from upper. (R.A.F. officer, April 10, 1962.) Whence, by 'the Oxford-*er*', the variant *booters*, with elaboration *Harry Booters*.

Boot Hill. A graveyard: Canadian miners': C. 20. Adopted from U.S.

boot in, put the (p. 80). Note the comment made at **buturakie.**

booters. See **boot-faced** above.

bootie (or -y). Beautiful: Society girls': ca. 1840–80. Diprose's *Book about London*, 1872. Cf. nursery *bootiful* or *booful.*

bootlace. Thin twist tobacco: C. 20: orig., c.; by 1940, s. (L. W. Merrow Smith & J. Harris, *Prison Screw*, 1962.)

bootlaced. Branded. N. Queensland cattlemen's: since ca. 1910. (Jean Devanney, *Travels*, 1951.)

bootlaces. 'The narrow strips of flesh carved off a sheep especially when opening up the neck of a fleece by a rough shearer are *bootlaces*,' B., 1941: Australian and New Zealand rural: late C. 19–20.

boots, blood in the (or their); more often sand in the(ir) boots. 'Used derisively of Desert types who threw their weight about in non-combat areas or, more gallingly, in non-desert operational areas' (Colonel A. L. Gadd, letter of April 20, 1949): Army: 1943 onwards; after 1945, only historical. The reference—made mostly by officers about officers—is to 'veterans' of North Africa.

boots, it (or that) didn't (or doesn't) go into his (or my or your, etc.). There is (or was) an effect, certain though not obvious: c.p., mostly Cockneys': C. 20. I.e. did go elsewhere.

boots and all. Thoroughly, utterly: Australian coll.: C. 20. Vance Palmer, *Let the Birds Fly*, 1955, 'It's boots and all. . . . Boots and all for both of us.'

boots up, hang one's. To give up playing football, either at end of season or finally: footballers' coll.: C. 20. (Atkinson.)

bootsy. A 'boots' at a large, the porter at a small, hotel: since ca. 1950. (A. B. Petch, March 1966.)

booze artist. A heavy drinker; a drunkard: Australian: since ca. 1920. H. Drake Brockman, *Hot Gold*, 1940. Perhaps adopted ex Canada, where current since ca. 1905. (Leechman.)

booze Naffy. Such a N.A.A.F.I. issue as included beer and spirits: Army: 1939–45.

booze the jib (p. 81). The variant *booze up one's jib-stay* occurs in W. N. Glascock, *The Naval Sketch-Book*, I, 1825. (Moe.)

booze-out. A meal, esp. a good 'feed': Naval: from ca. 1870; ob. B. & L.

booze-up. A drinking bout: low: late C. 19–20. *Sessions*, Oct. 26, 1897.

boozed up (p. 81). Recorded in Australia in 1891. (Sidney J. Baker, letter.)

Boozelier. A Fusilier: Regular Army: C. 20. A blend of *booze* (p. 81) and *Fusilier.*

boozician. Synonymous with and prompted by **boozington** (p. 81); Australian: ca. 1890–1940. (B., 1943.) A blend of *booze* and *magician.*

boozing school. A military coll., dating from ca. 1880. 'A boozing school generally consisted of three or four men who pooled their pay, one of them acting as treasurer. They allowed themselves so much for tobacco or cigarettes and so much for a monthly visit to the women in the Bazaar: the remainder was spent on beer. Only one basin was used between a school; it held a quart and each man took a drink in his turn from it, and each in turn walked to the bar with it when it wanted refilling. When money ran short they would borrow money right and left and sell any kit they did not want and also some that they did. Genuine boozing schools always paid their debts. . . . After they had paid their debts they would decide among themselves whether they would continue with the boozing school or not. After being on the tact'—teetotal—'for about six months they would start boozing again with a capital of two hundred rupees.' This passage, in Richards, refers to the Indian Army of the first decade of the C. 20: but the practice, though now less usual, applies elsewhere, with an equivalent of a corresponding capital sum.

boozle. Sexual intercourse: since ca. 1945. Noel Coward, *Pomp and Circumstance*, 1960.

bop. A blow, a punch: Aus.: adopted ex U.S. ca. 1945. Nino Culotta, *Cop This Lot*, 1960.

borachio (p. 81). Influenced perhaps by Borrachio's speech, 'I will, like a true drunkard, utter all to thee': Shakespeare's *Much Ado.*

boracic. ' "You boracic?" she asked.—She meant boracic lint—skint' (Hank Hobson, *Mission House Murder*, 1959)—that is, very short of money: rhyming s.: since ca. 1945. Often pron. *brassic.*

borax.—2. Cheap furniture: Canadian salesmen's: since ca. 1920. (Leechman.)

bore, n., 2 (p. 82), prob. dates from ca. 1750; seems to have, orig., been University of Oxford s.;

and occurs in 'A Familiar Epistle' on p. 366 of *The Gentleman's Magazine*, May 1784:

> 'No books but magazines we read,
> At barbarous Latin shook our head,
> And voted Greek a boar' (*sic*).

There is, however, some evidence for finding the origin of *bore* in *boar*: R. B. Sheridan, letter of Sept. 1772 (Sotheby's catalogue, H. Y. Thompson library sale): Sir William Weller Pepys, letter of 1774: with thanks to Derek Pepys Whiteley, Esqre. If this be correct, *boar* connotes uncouthness and ignorance in speech or action.

bore war, the. Concerning Nov. 1939, Dudley Clarke, in *Seven Assignments*, 1948, writes: 'The "phoney war" was giving way to the "bore war", and at the War Office we started to resign ourselves to a long winter at our desks': Nov. 1939–April 1940, then merely historical. Punning on *boring*, tedious, and *the Boer War*. Also *the Great Bore War*, as in Evelyn Waugh's *Put Out More Flags*, 1942.

Borehole. See 'Prisoner-of-War Slang'.

boretto-man. See 'Rogues'.

born in a barn?, were you. A c.p.—notably Canadian—directed at someone who leaves the door open: late C. 19–20. Of the same order as the semi-proverbial *was your father a glazier?*

born with a pack of cards in one hand, a bottle of booze in the other, and a fag in his (or her) mouth. A c.p. directed, since ca. 1955, at a not uncommon type of man or woman. (Petch.)

born with the horn. A coarse c.p., applied to a lecher: late C. 19–20. A rhyme on **horn**, 4 (p. 405).

born yesterday, not. Esp. 'I wasn't born yesterday' (not a fool): c.p. late C. 19–20.

borrow, v.—2. See **chopper**, 9, below: since ca. 1950.

borrow and beg. An egg: rhyming s.: late C. 19–20. Franklyn, *Rhyming*.

bos-eyed. See **boss-eyed** (*Dict.*).

bose, boatswain, on p. 82, goes back to early C. 19, to judge by W. N. Glascock, *The Naval Sketch-Book*, 2nd Series, 1834, at II, 65. Moe.

bosh, n.—6. Such a game between two houses as does not count towards a cup: Rugby School: C. 20. 'They are usually of low quality' (D. F. Wharton): cf. sense 1 on p. 82.

Sense 3 (p. 82) is also fairground and circus s., as is *bosh-faker*. Witness, Sydney Lester.

bosh lines, the. (The) marionettes: showmen's: from ca. 1855. B. & L. Lit., violin strings.

bosie.—2. A single bomb dropped from the air: Australian airmen's: ca. 1940–5. (B., 1943.) Cf. sense 1: p. 82.

bosom. A bosom friend: C. 20. A. Neil Lyons, *Simple Simon*, 1914.

bosom clasper. A very emotional cinematic film: since ca. 1935. (James Agate in the *Daily Express*, Aug. 14, 1943.)

boss, n.—6. As *the boss*, jocular for one's wife: Australian: since ca. 1920. 'I was hoping that you would ring. The boss has been on my back about it.' (B.P.)

boss-cockie.—2. Hence, 'top dog': since ca. 1920.

boss(-)crusher. One who organises a group seeking to 'cash in' on 'crush' betting: since ca. 1920. (B., 1953.) See **crush** (bet).

boss-hostler. Superintendent of livestock: circusmen's: C. 20.

boss one's own shoes. To manage one's affairs

by oneself or personally: U.S., anglicised ca. 1880; ob. B. & L. See **boss, v.**, 1 (*Dict.*).

boss over the board. See **board, n.**, 4.

boss up. App. ex South Africa. Francis E. Brett Young, *Pilgrim's Rest*, 1936, 'She was always breaking in on their trivialities, getting things done, "bossing them up", as they called it on the Reef' on the Rand.—2. Hence, v.i., to work hard: South African: C. 20. Brett Young, *op. cit.*

bossaroo. A 'boss kangaroo': Australian coll.: from ca. 1870. B. & L.

bossooks, I'll give him, them, etc. A minatory c.p.—a threat to settle a score, to exact vengeance, etc.: late C. 19–early 20. (Laurie Atkinson.) Perhaps of dial. origin.

Fossy. A common Canadian name for a cow: (?) late C. 19–20. Ex *boss-eyed?*

bostruchizer (p. 83). Also 'to *bostruchize*'. (Article by Sir A. West in *The Nineteenth Century*, April 1897.)

bosun. See comment at **sin bosun**.

bosun's nightmare, the. The experimental sweep used against magnetic mines: Naval: late 1939–early 1940. (P-G-R.)

bot, n.—4. A man ever on the move and, like the rolling stone, unable to gather moss: Australian: since ca. 1920. Ex sense 1 (p. 83).—5. (One's) bottom: mostly domestic: late C. 19–20.—6. A sponger: Australian: since ca. 1920. (B., 1943.) Ex, sense 2.

bot, v. To borrow money; (usually *bot on*) to sponge or impose on (others): Australian and New Zealand: since ca. 1925. B., 1941. Ex sense 1 of the n.—see p. 83.

bot, have the. To feel unwell: to be moody: querulous: New Zealand: since ca. 1930. B., 1941. Also Australian: B., 1943. Ex **bot, n.**, 2 (*Dict.*).

bot, work one's. To coït: low: C. 20. ' "Is she working?"—"Yes, her bot." ' I.e. bottom.

bot about, v.i. To move restlessly from one place to another: Australian: since 1920.

bot-fly.—2. A sponger or a scrounger: since ca. 1920. B., 1942.

botanise, v.i. To go to Botany Bay as a convict: 1819, Scott, in a letter; † by 1890.

Botany Bay.—5. To run away: Australian rhyming s. (–1945). Baker, *The Australian Language*.

Botany Bay coat-of-arms. Broken nose and black eye: Australian convicts': ca. 1820–55. (B., 1943.)

both ways; bet both ways. See **bet both ways.**

Botherams. A nuance of sense 1, 'a noisy party': Nov. 15, 1836, *The Individual*; † by 1890.

botheration, 2—*botherment* (p. 83)—occurs in C. P. Clinch, *The Spy*, 1822 (II, vii): an American source, but prob. implying an earlier British source. (Moe.)

bottle, n. A share of money: showmen's: 1893, P. H. Emerson.—2. A reprimand, a dressing-down; especially, *get a bottle*, to be reprimanded: Navy: since ca. 1920. H. & P. Short for 'a bottle of acid': Granville.—3. A wireless valve, cathode-ray tube: R.A.F.: since ca. 1935. (Sgt Gerald Emanuel, March 29, 1945.) Ex shape.—4. *The bottle*, the hip pocket: 1938, E. D. Sharpe, *The Flying Squad* Mostly in *off the bottle*, pickpockets' c. for '(removed) from a rear trouser pocket': Franklyn 2nd. Cf. **bottle, the,** below.—5. Short for *bottle and glass,* arse: low: C. 20. (Robin Cook, 1962,)—6. 'Spirits, guts, courage . . . It's the worst that could be said about you, that you'd lost your bottle' (Tony Park, *The Plough Boy,* 1965): Teddy boys' and teenage gangsters': since late 1940's.

Sense 1 rather = money taken, after a 'turn', by showmen and other entertainers, as in ' "What's the bottle, cull?" . . . "How much have we taken, pal?" ': Sydney Lester, *Vardi the Palarey,* 1937.

bottle, v.—3. See **rim.**—4. To coït with (a woman); to impregnate: low: C. 20.

Sense 1 (p. 83) means, among showmen and other entertainers, 'to approach (someone) for a contribution'. (Sydney Lester, 1937.)

bottle, no. No good; not 'classy': since ca. 1920. Short for *no bottle and glass,* no 'class', itself current throughout C. 20. (John Gosling, *The Ghost Squad,* 1959.)

bottle, on the.—2. Engaged in pocket-picking: c.: C. 20. (*The Yorkshire Post,* latish May 1937.)

***bottle, the.** Pickpocketing: c.: C. 20. Cf. **the shake.** F. D. Sharpe, *The Flying Squad,* 1938.

bottle and glass. See **bottle, no,** and **bottle, n.,** 4, both above; C. 20: rhyming on *arse.*

bottle-arsed. Printing type 'so long used that the base is no longer a solid rectangle, and so the type will not stand in a galley without being tied' (Leechman): Canadian printers': C. 20.

bottle fallen out; e.g., **has your . . .,** Are you afraid?: low: since ca. 1940. Cf., *bundle, drop one's,* on p. 108.

bottle-holder, 2 (p. 84) occurs earlier in Walter Scott's *The Antiquary,* 1816. (O.E.D.)

bottle-o. A dealer in, collector of, empty bottles; hence, *bottle-o's rouseabout* (or *roustabout*), a person of no account: Australian: resp. since ca. 1910, 1920. Baker. In bottle-collectors' street cries, *botto* = bottle.—2. In games of marbles, a green taw: New Zealand children's: C. 20. (Ruth Park, *The Witch's Thorn,* 1952.)— 3. A glass sphere taken from a soft-drink bottle and used as a marble: Australian children's: ca. 1910–50. (B.P.)

bottle o(f) beer. Ear: rhyming s.: C. 20. (Franklyn 2nd.)

bottle of cola. A bowler hat: rhyming: C. 20; by 1950, ob.

bottle of fizz, the. Rhymes whiz, n., 2 (p. 953).

bottle of sauce. A horse: rhyming: late C. 19–20.

bottle of Scotch. A watch: rhyming: since ca. 1910.

Bottle of Whisky, the. The Polish destroyer *Blyskawika:* Naval 'Hobson-Jobson': ca. 1940–2.

bottle-oh's (or **o's**) **rouseabout.** A nobody: Aus.: since ca. 1920. (*The Drum,* 1959.) Ex *bottle-o,* 1, above.

bottle the field. Odds of 2 to 1: racing, esp. bookmakers': C. 20. (*The Sunday Telegraph,* May 7, 1967.)

bottle the tot. To pour one's daily tot of rum into a bottle and save it up for special occasions: Naval coll.: 1939–45.

Bottle-Trekker, 'ex *Voor-trekker,* was a usual name for a Dutchman, owing to their habit of taking a bottle of water to the latrine with them instead of toilet paper' (R. H. Panting): cf.

'Prisoner-of-War Slang' (below), para. 9, where, strictly, it belongs.

bottled.—2. Tipsy: Society: since ca. 1930. Peter Traill, *Half Mast,* 1936.

bottled sunshine. 'Scottish service (esp. Army) name for beer,' H. & P.: since ca. 1930.

bottler.—2. Expression of high praise or deep delight: New Zealand juvenile: C. 20. B., 1941. But also Australian (−1943): witness B., 3rd edition, with variant *bottling.*—3. A sodomite: low: since ca. 1930. Cf. *bottle,* v., 4.—4. A non-seller (motor car): secondhand-car dealers': since ca. 1950. Anthony Cowdy in the coloured supplement of *The Sunday Times,* Oct. 24, 1965.— 5. Esp., *bloody bottler,* a 'real hard case': New Zealand: since ca. 1945. Cf. sense 2.

bottler, adj.; also **bottling.** Superlatively good: Aus.: since ca. 1920. (B., 1959.) Ex **bottler,** 2, above.

botto. See **bottle-o.**

bottom-drawer. There is an earlier reference in S. P. B. Mais, *A Schoolmaster's Diary,* 1918.

***bottom road, the.** A road leading (esp. from London) to the South Coast of England: tramps' c.: C. 20. W. A. Gape, *Half a Million Tramps,* 1936.

bottom-scratchers. A break-off group from a diving club: skin divers': since the late 1950's. 'Interested only in spear fishing (crabs, lobsters, etc.), they *scratch* the sea's bottom' (Wilfred Granville, letter of March 11, 1964).

botts, the. See **bots** (*Dict.*).

bouie. See **booey** above.

boulder(-)holder, occ. preceded by *over-shoulder.* A brassière: Australian raffish: since ca. 1955. 'Used by the same people who use **flopper stopper,** q.v.' (B.P.)

bounce, v. 1.—6. (Of a cheque) to be returned, as worthless, by the bank on which it has been drawn: adopted ca. 1938 from U.S.—7. To attack (suddenly, unexpectedly): Air Force: 1939 +. Brickhill & Norton, *Escape to Danger,* 1946, 'About 12,000 feet they were bounced from above by three 109's.'—8. To dismiss (a person), reject (a play): adopted, ca. 1940, from U.S.

bounce, put (someone) **in the.** To accost, esp. for a loan of money. Australian: since ca. 1930. (D'Arcy Niland, *The Shiralee,* 1955.)

bounce, the grand. Dismissal (from a job); rejection (of a manuscript): adopted, ca. 1940, from U.S.

bounce the ball. To test public opinion or senti-ment; test the stock market: New Zealand political coll.: since ca. 1920. B., 1941. Ex the preliminaries usual among footballers.

bound rigid. Bored stiff: see **bind.**

bounge; bonge. See **bung,** n., 3 (*Dict.*).

***bouquet.** A payment in pesos: white-slavers' c. (Argentine): C. 20. Albert Londres, *The Road to Buenos Ayres,* 1928, 'A "bouquet" always means pesos.'

bovine heart. A human heart that has, through disease, grown as large as that of an ox: medical coll. (from ca. 1860) >, by 1910, j. B. & L.

bovine puncher. A bullock driver: jocular Australian: ca. 1925–50. (B., 1943.)

Bovril. 'A few years ago most young men here [in Sydney] said "Bovril" whenever they found anything unimpressive, and University students certainly made good use of the song, "It all sounds like Bovril to me"', H. J. Oliver in *The Bulletin of the Australian English Association,*

July 1937. Prob. a euphemism for *ballocks* or *balls* used exclamatorily; prompted by bull shit. —2. 'I'm not having my house turned into a Bovril' (the house being a 'public'): since ca. 1930. S. P. B. Mais, *Caper Sauce*, 1948.

bovrilise. To omit all inessential matter from an advertisement: copywriters' coll.: since ca. 1935. Ex *bovril*, 'the best of the meat'.

Bovvy. Bovington Camp, depot of the Royal Armoured Corps: ca. 1939–45.

*****bow, on the.** 'I got in on the bow'—without paying: C. 20: c. >, by 1945, low s. F. D. Sharpe, 1938.

Bow and Arrow War, the. See **Farmers' Strike** below.

bow and quiver. Liver (the bodily organ): rhyming: C. 20. Cf. **cheerful giver** below.

bow catcher (p. 86) occurs in *The Saturday Evening Post*, Dec. 21, 1822—quoting a British source. (Moe.)

*****bow the crumpet** or **duck the scone** or **nod the nut.** To plead guilty in a law-court: Aus. c.: since ca. 1930. *The Drum*, 1959.

bow wave. A tyro sailor: Canadian Naval: since ca. 1920. H. & P.—2. In the R.N., a cap with a bow-wave effect; esp. at the R.N.C. Dartmouth: C. 20. Granville.

bow-wow.—3. *The Bow-wow* = the Brigade Warrant Officer (B.W.O)—the R.A.O.C. representative at a Brigade H.Q.: Army: since 1939.

bow-wow, on the. Australian shape of **bow, on the.**

*****bower.** A prison: C. 20: Australian c. >, by 1940, low s. B., 1942. Ironic.

bower bird. A petty thief: Australian: C. 20. Ex preceding. (B., 1943.) Cf.:

bower-birdin(g). Picking up odds-and-ends for one's own camp or use: N.T., Australia: since ca. 1925. (B., 1953.)

bowl. A period of bowling: cricketers' coll.: C. 20. Ex ob. S.E. *bowl*: a delivery of the ball.

bowl off. To die: 1837, Dickens; † by 1900. E.D.D.

bowl-over, n. A brawl; a fight: Australian: C. 20. B., 1942. Cf. the v.: p. 86.

bowler hat, get a, is the Navy's shape of **b.h., be given a** (p. 86). Granville.

bowler hat, get—or **be given**—**a golden.** To accept an offer of retirement: Army officers': since late 1950's. Such retirement = *take a golden bowler*. Ex the very favourable terms offered by the War Office at the time when it drastically reduced the number of its officers. Cf. a retiring Company Director's *golden handshake*. (Peter Sanders.)

*****bowler(-)hat boys, the.** 'They were always very well dressed and visited houses of old people living alone and by posing as officials from banks, rating authorities, police departments and so on, gained access. They worked in teams of three or four' (Bournemouth *Evening Echo*, April 20, 1966): c. and police s.: since ca. 1963. Cf. **prop game** below.

bowler-hatted, be. To be returned to civil life: Services: since ca. 1918. H. & P. See **bowler hat** (*Dict.*); vbl n., *bowler-hatting*.

bowler's double. 100 wickets + 100 runs in a season: cricketers': since ca. 1930. Humorous, on S.E. *cricketer's double*, 100 wickets + 1,000 runs in a season.

bowling green. A fast line: railwaymen's:

since ca. 1920 (?). *Railway*, 3rd. The 'going' is smooth.

bows down. Be quiet; esp. stop talking: Naval: since ca. 1925. H. & P.

bows under, be. To be extremely busy: Naval: C. 20. (P-G-R.)

bowser king. An N.C.O. in charge of a bowser (towed petrol tanker): R.A.F.: since ca. 1930. Jackson.

bowsprit.—2. Penis: low nautical: ca. 1820–80. Cosgrave, *Irish Highwayman*, 1889.

bowsy. A low guttersnipe: Anglo-Irish: C. 20. Probably ex the adj. *boozy* (p. 81).

bowyang or **boyang;** by corruption, **boang.** A labourer; workman: Australian: C. 20. Kylie Tennant, *The Battlers*, 1941. Ex *bowyangs*, bands worn about the trousers—above the knee.

box, n.—6. An abdominal protector: Marlborough College (and elsewhere): C. 20.—7. A man's room: Dalton Hall, Manchester: since ca. 1919. *The Daltonian*, Dec. 1946.—8. As *the box*, it is short for **black-box,** 2, q.v.—9. A 'mess' (*make a box of*): Australian: since ca. 1920. (B., 1943.) —10. Female genitals: low English and Australian: C. 20.

box, v., 6. Earlier in 'Tom Collins', *Such is Life*, 1903. It is also New Zealand usage: *teste* G. B. Lanchester, *Sons o' Men*, 1904.—7. Also *box on, box along*: to get along *with* a person on give-and-take terms: since ca. 1920.—8. Elliptical for **box clever:** since ca. 1930. (Atkinson.) Cf. **box on** (p. 87).

box, be in a.—2. Hence, to be in a state of confusion: New Zealand: C. 20. B., 1941.

box, bring to, is the active form of **box, be in a** (p. 87). In W. N. Glascock, *The Naval Sketch-Book*, I, 1825. (Moe.)

box, on the.—2. Hence, drawing Friendly Society benefits: *go on the box*, to have recourse to them: C. 20. Francis Brett Young, *Dr Bradley Remembers*, 1938. I.e. the box containing the Society's funds.—3. Appearing on the television screen, as in 'Wilson was on the box last night': since late 1950's.

box, out of the. Unusual: Australian, mostly rural: since ca. 1920. Jean Devanney, *Travels*, 1951, '"But you mustn't run away with the notion that I'm anything out of the box in back-country conditions."'—2. Hence, very special; exceptional; unusually favourable: Australian: since ca. 1920. (S. H. Courtier, *A Corpse Won't Sing*, 1964.) Also New Zealand, since ca. 1930. (Slatter.)

box clever. To use one's head, be a 'shrewdy': since ca. 1925. James Curtis, *The Gilt Kid*, 1936.

box egg. A 'bad egg'; one who doesn't amount to much: since ca. 1930.

box kippers, unable to. See **kippers.**

box-lobby puppy. A 'cheap' would-be man of fashion, a step above an *upper-box Jackadandy*, who is usually an apprentice or a shop-assistant: described by *The London Chronicle* of Nov. 20–23, 1783: apparently ca. 1770–1800.

box of, make a. To muddle: Australian: C. 20. B., 1942.

box of birds, a. Fighting-fit: New Zealand troops': 1939–45. J. H. Fullarton, *Troop Target*, 1943. Singing with health and happiness.—2. Hence, general as *box of birds* and in nuance 'fit and very happy': 1945+. (Ngaio Marsh, *Swing*

Brother, Swing, 1949.) In Australia, *feel like a box of birds,* very happy. (B., 1953.)

box of dominoes (p. 87) is much older. It occurs in *The New Monthly Magazine* at some date before Feb. 1822, as 'A blow in the mouth is a mugger; and if in addition to this, an injury should be done to the teeth, it is called a rattling of the box of dominoes'. (Moe.)

box of sharks, the. A phrase 'indicative of vast surprise. "She nearly gave birth of the box of sharks!" Cf. **baby, have a** and **having kittens'** (Leechman): Canadian: since ca. 1955.

box of toys. Noise: rhyming: late C. 19–20. Len Ortzen, 1938.

box of tricks. A tool box—or any similar receptacle: Australian: C. 20. (B.P.)

Box of Tricks. Euston Station: taxi-drivers': Sept. 13, 1941, *The Weekly Telegraph.* Ex its shape.

box off. To fight with one's fists: Naval: ca. 1805–50. Glascock, *Sketch-Book,* I, 1825. (Moe.)

box office. (Of an actor) a success: theatrical and cinematic coll.: since ca. 1925. 'Now, at last, she's box office.'

box on with. To punch; to fight with: Australian: since ca. 1920. (D'Arcy Niland, *Call Me . . . ,* 1958.) Cf. *box on*: p. 87.

box open. A 1939–45 shortening of *box open, box shut!* see p. 87).

box the wine bin. To leave the table after drinking but little: fast life: ca. 1815–40. *Spy,* II, 1826.

box-up, v. To muddle, confuse: Australian: C. 20. Baker.—Hence also n. (P-G-R.)

boxa. Variant spelling of **boxer,** 1 (*Dict.*): B., 1942.

*boxed in, be. To have entered a house, esp. if single-handed: c.: from ca. 1860. B. & L.

boxed-up, adj. In prison; gaoled: New Zealand: C. 20.—2. Thoroughly confused: Australian: since ca. 1930. (B.P.)

boxer, 1 (p. 87). In two-up, the *boxer* looks after the apparatus and *the guts* or money staked by the two principal betters; *ringie* takes care of operations inside the ring of side-betters: since ca. 1910. George Baker, article ' "Two-Up" Down Under' in *The Strand Magazine,* Dec. 1949. He adds that the pennies used are *bun pennies* (early Victorian), *veiled queens* (late Victorian), *baldies* (Edward VII); notes that the laying of a stake on one result *opens the guts.* If both pennies come down heads or tails, the assembly cries 'He's *headed* them' or 'He's *tailed* them'. The spinner must now spin successfully thrice before he can *drag* or take any winnings from the *guts;* uses *grouter bit* or a run of successes; defines *caser* as 'sum of five shillings', *flag* as 'pound', *spin* as 'five pounds' and *brick* as 'ten pounds'.—Cf. the entries *bun,* 2 (p. 108)—*caser* (p. 130)—*grouter* (p. 357)—*guts,* 6 (p. 363)—*ringie* (p. 706)—*spin* (below). The best description ever written of a two-up session is that made by Lawson Glassop in *Lucky Palmer,* 1949, at pp. 167–176.

boy, 3. Binstead, in the 1890's, asserted that '*the* boy' was incorrect; nevertheless, it does occur.

boy, on. See **on boy.** Cf. *cut boy,* to fail to attend to one's duties 'on boy': Harrow School: from ca. 1890. Lunn.

boy friend, the; the girl friend. Orig. and still used to imply an illicit sex relationship (whether hetero or not); mostly Londoners': from ca. 1920. Ex U.S. (Cf. S.E. *gentleman friend* and *lady friend.*)—2. Hence, without any pejorative implication: orig. and mainly Londoners': from ca. 1925.

boy in a (or **the**) **boat.** Clitoris: low: late C. 19–20.

Boy Scout's leave. A brief shore-leave: Australian Naval: 1939–45. (B., 1943.)

boys, the (p. 87): earlier in *The Night Watch* (II, 113), 1828. (Moe.)—3. '. . . The boys, as all stage hands are called, regardless of age' (Dulcie Gray, *No Quarter for a Star,* 1964): theatrical coll.: C. 20.

boys, white-bearded. The Army's technological 'bright boys': 1939–45. (P-G-R.)

boys on ice. Lice: rhyming s.: late C. 19–20. (Franklyn, *Rhyming.*)

bozo. A fellow: Australian: adapted, ca. 1935, ex U.S.. (Jean Devanney, *By Tropic Sea and Jungle,* 1944.) Of unknown origin.

bozzimacoo! Kiss my —!: low Yorkshire: ca. 1850–1910. (Oliver Onions, *Good Boy Seldom.*) A corruption of *baise mon cul.*

bra. A brassière: feminine: common since ca. 1934 and, ca. 1940, superseding *bras.* Since ca. 1950, coll.

bra is a girl's best friend, a; occ. preceded by *square shape or pear shape:* Australian feminine c.p.: since early 1950's.

Brab. A Brabazon aircraft: aircraft industry: 1945 +; general public, 1949 +.

brace and bits. Nipples; loosely, breasts: low rhyming s., little used in Britain: C. 20. Mostly American. (Franklyn, *Rhyming.*)

brace of shakes, in a (p. 87). Earlier in *Boxiana,* III, 1821.

braced. Hearty; in excellent spirits: Marlborough College coll.: since ca. 1920.

braces, talk through one's. To talk nonsense: Australian: since ca. 1920. Baker.

Braddles. Don (properly Donald George) Bradman, born Aug. 27, 1908: Australian: since 1927 when he first played for N.S.W. Probably the greatest batsman the world has ever seen. Also called *The Don.* (Much more fully on p. 1047 of 2nd edition.)

brag rags. Medal ribbons: Naval: since ca. 1920. Granville.

brahn. Brown ale: Cockney coll.: mid-C. 19–20.

brahn, hawk one's, is the correct form of *brawn, hawk one's,* on p. 89; it is pure Cockney, and valid only in the latter sense.

brain basil (or **Basil**). A clever boy: Oxford schoolboys': C. 20. (James Morris, *Oxford,* 1965.)

brain child. A new idea one's proud of; one's own invention: since ca. 1945: s.>, by 1960, coll.

brain-fever. The bird known as the Pallid Cuckoo: Australian: since ca. 1910. (B., 1943.)

brains.—2. As *the brains,* 'the boss', it was Canadian: ca. 1905–40. (Leechman.) Since ca. 1935, *the brain.*—3. Traffic Control: railwaymen's: since ca. 1930. (*Railway.*)

Brains Trust, the. The Central Trades Test Board: R.A.F.: since ca. 1938. E. P., in *The New Statesman,* Sept. 19, 1942. Unlike the B.B.C's Brains Trust they ask, not answer, questions.—2. Such specialists as rangefinders and surveyors: Royal Artillery: 1939 +.

brainstrains. 'Oxford to Cambridge via Bletchley line' (*Railway*, 3rd): railwaymen's: since late 1940's.

brakey. A brakesman: Canadian railwaymen's: C. 20. W. A. Gape, *Half a Million Tramps*, 1936. Ex U.S. (1887: O.E.D., Sup.). Recorded earlier in Niven and prob. dating back to ca. 1890.

brama, a bit of a. A 'good chap', though a trifle wild and unintelligent: Army: 1940 +. Cf. **brama** (*Dict.*).

branch. A branch pilot Diploma: nautical: since ca. 1820. Captain Glascock, *Land Sharks and Sea Gulls*, 1838.

branch cag(g). See **cag.**

branch out. To become very fat: Australian: since ca. 1925. (Ruth Park, *A Power of Roses*, 1953.)

branches everywhere. Jam containing string (or twigs) and, on the tin, the manufacturers' confession, *branches everywhere*: jocular, mostly domestic: since ca. 1930.

brandy; brandy coatee. A cloak; raincoat: Anglo-Indian: C. 19–20; ob. B. & L. A hybrid.

brandy-snap. A scab (on nose or cheek or chin), from a blow or punch: Australian: since ca. 1925. (B., 1943.)

brandy ticket, be sent with a. To be sent to hospital with one's bad character set forth on the ticket that accompanies one thither. Naval: ca. 1800–60. Captain Glascock, 1838. I.e. *branded* ticket.

bras. A brassière: feminine: since ca. 1910. W. B. M. Ferguson, *Somewhere off Borneo*, 1936. By 1950, †. (Always, of course, pronounced *brah*.)

brass, n.—5. '*Brass:* the Officers, also *Gold Braid*,' Granville: Naval (lower-deck): C. 20. Cf. **brass-hat** (p. 89). n. A Canadian (ex U.S.) variant, 1939 +, is *top brass*.

***brass,** v. Corresponding to **brass,** n., 3 (p. 89): Australian: since ca. 1910. (B., 1943.)—2. Hence, to defraud: since ca. 1920. (Lawson Glassop, 1949.)

brass, adj. Fashionable; smart: raffish London: since ca. 1950. 'Some of them were speaking in French because it was the brass thing to do' (James Barlow, *The Burden of Proof*, 1968). Ex 'the *brass*', the 'heads'.

brass, carry. To have an important rank: Army: 1939–45. (P-G-R.)

brass band. An occ. rhyming term for hand: C. 20. Cf. **German bands** (p. 322).

brass candlestick, (his) face has been rubbed with a. A c.p. applied to an impudent person: from ca. 1870. In elaboration of **brass,** 2 (*Dict.*).

***brass man.** A confidence trickster: Australian c.: since ca. 1930. (B., 1953.)

brass-monkey weather. Bitterly cold weather: Australian: since ca. 1920. Ex *cold enough to freeze the balls off a brass monkey*, q.v. at **monkey, cold enough . . .,** on p. 528. (B.P.)

brass off.—2. To reprimand severely: Services: since ca. 1939. H. & P.

brass-pounder. A telegrapher-agent: Canadian railwaymen's: since ca. 1925. (Leechman.)

brass up occurs earlier in Pugh (2).

brassed has, since 1944, often been used in abbreviation of the next, as *cheesed* can be used for *cheesed off*. But one cannot use *browned* for *browned off*.

brassed off. Disgruntled, fed up: Services, orig. (?): Royal Naval since ca. 1927; general since ca. 1939. *The Observer*, Oct. 14, 1942; H. & P. Sometimes a synonym of *browned off*; sometimes regarded as a shade milder. Cf. **brass off** (p. 89): perhaps from brass-polishing in ships. For *brassed off, browned off* and *cheesed off*, see esp. Partridge, 1945, or *Forces' Slang*, ed. Partridge, 1948.

brassic. See **boracic** above.

brassy. A friend or close companion: Naval: since ca. 1920. H. & P. Cf. **part brass rags** in *Dict.*

brasted. Blasted: sol.: mid-C. 19–20. Pugh (2): 'I'll do as I brasted well like.'

brats. Collective for a deep-sea trawler's crew below skipper and mate: deep-sea trawlers': C. 20. (L. Luard, *All Hands*, 1933, and *Conquering Seas*, 1935.)

Braunhaus. 'British Rail Headquarters' (*Railway*, 3rd): railwaymen's: since ca. 1955 (?). A pun on 'Brown' and 'brown'?

brawny-buttock. See 'Epithets'.

bread. Money: mostly Teddy boys', drug-addicts', teenagers': as such, adopted ca. 1955, ex U.S.; but, basically, the shortening of **bread and honey,** and therefore, orig., English, not U.S. (Ian M. Ball in the *Sunday Telegraph*, Jan. 21, 1962.) Also used by hippies and Flower People: Peter Fryer in *The Observer* colour supplement of Dec. 3, 1967.

bread and cheese.—3. A, or to, sneeze: rhyming: late C. 19–20. Len Ortzen, *Down Donkey Lane*, 1938.

bread and honey. Money: rhyming s.: C. 20. Much less common than **bees and honey** (p. 43). Franklyn 2nd.

bread and lard, adj. Hard: rhyming s.: C. 20. Franklyn 2nd adduces 'Gorblimey! ain't that bread an' lard, eh?'

bread and solitary confinement: prisoners' coll.: late C. 19–20. Jim Phelan, *The Big House*, 1943. I.e. bread and water.

bread-bag, stomach, is an occ. variant of **bread-basket** (*Dict.*): 1834, W. N. Glascock, *Sketch-Book*, 2nd Series, at I, 33. Moe.

bread barge.—2. 'A wooden keg fitted with brass bands and a circular wooden lid, in which the mess ration of bread was kept' (*Daily Colonist*, Victoria, B.C., June 19, 1960): Canadian Navy: ca. 1900–25.

bread-snapper. A child: Glasgow lower classes' from ca. 1880. MacArthur & Long. Suggested by S.E. *bread-winner*.

Breadfruit. Nickname of Admiral William Bligh (1754–1817) of H.M.S. *Bounty.* (*The D.N.B.*)

break, n.—4. Esp. in *give* (someone) *a break*, to give him a chance, an opportunity, a slight advantage: Canadian (ex U.S.) coll.: since the late 1920's. (Leechman.)

break, v.—3. (Usually in the present perfect tense; applied only to events that are exciting or important.) To happen: journalists' coll.; adopted ca. 1930 ex U.S. Christopher Bush, *The Monday Murder*, 1936, '"Anything broken?" Tuke said. "Nothing much," Ribbold told him. "Everything still slack as hell." '—4. V.i., to cost: v.t., *break for*, to cost someone so much: Australian: C. 20. B., 1942.—5. V.t., to change a coin or a bank or currency note: since ca. 1920.

break a bit off. To defecate: Public Schools' jocular: since ca. 1920. The reference is to a hard stool.

break into pictures. To get on the cinematic screen: coll.: since ca. 1925.

break it big. To win a lot of money, esp. at gambling: Australian: C. 20. (Tom Ronan, *Vision Splendid*, 1954.)

break it down! Stop talking like that! stop talking! change the subject!: Australian: since ca. 1920. Lawson Glassop, *We Were the Rats*, 1944. —2. Hence 'to *break it down*', to cease: since ca. 1920. (Jon Cleary, *The Sundowners*, 1952.) Also, since ca. 1935, New Zealand. (Slatter.)

break it up! Disperse! Or Get moving and keep moving: Canadian official c.p. (adopted ex U.S.): since ca. 1930. (Leechman.)—2. 'A couple embracing may be told to "break it up"' (A. B. Petch, April 1966): jocular rather than minatory: since ca. 1935.

break loose. 'When the show breaks loose' = when the battle begins: Army: 1940+. (P-G-R.)

break-o'-day drum. 'A tavern which is open all night' (B. & L.): low: from ca. 1860.

break one's egg; crack one's egg. Variants (ca. 1870–1905) of **break one's duck** (*Dict.*). B. & L.

break one's neck. To long to make water: coll.: since ca. 1918. 'Don't know about *you*, but *I'm* breaking my neck!' Not orig. euphemistic; it shortens *be breaking one's neck for a piss*: C. 20.

break-out, n. A spree: Australian: C. 20. Baker.

break surface. To wake from sleep: Naval: since ca. 1925. Granville, 'From the submarine service'.

break the sound barrier. To break wind: orig. (ca. 1960) and mostly Canadian. 'Neat and almost inevitable' (Leechman).

break the tea-pot. 'He has broken the tea-pot' = he has abandoned abstinence in favour of the wet canteen: mostly Army (−1900); ob. by 1940, † by 1960. (*The Regiment*, vol. viii, p. 288, year 1900.)

break-up, 1 (p. 91) may be very old: cf. 'That the School Master shall before the accustomed time of breaking-up of the school (as they call it) twice a year . . .': Popeson's Rules for Bungay Grammar School, Suffolk, ca. 1600.

break(-)up.—3. A person, thing, situation extremely amusing: Australian: since ca. 1925. B., 1942.

break van. A van (Naafi or Y.M.C.A.) driven around a Station at 'break' or recess period of a quarter of an hour, morning and afternoon: R.A.F. (hence also W.A.A.F.) coll.: since ca. 1935. Jackson.

breakaway, the. Those competitors who have established a substantial lead: racing cyclists' coll.: since ca. 1925. Contrast *bunch*, n., 2. —2. A person broken up, whether physically or mentally: Australian coll.: since ca. 1910. (K. S. Prichard, *Tornado*, 1929.)

breakfast, I could do it (or that) **before.** That's easy: c.p. (? orig. and mainly Australian): C. 20.

breast, v. To approach, to accost: Australian: since ca. 1930. (B., 1943.)

breast-pocket kind of place. A small shop: tailors' coll.: mid-C. 19–20. B & L.

breath that would knock you down. Fetid breath: coll.: late C.19–20.

breathe down (someone's) **neck.** To be very close to someone, as in 'The cops were breathing down my neck': jocular coll.: since ca. 1930.

C

(Cf. the allusive title of John Pudney's delightful collection of short stories titled *It Breathed Down My Neck*, 1946.)—2. Hence, to 'keep after' someone for, e.g., the completion of a job: since late 1940's.

breathed on. (Of a car or its engine), 'converted, often by professionals, to give greater power and speed' (David Mann, Jan. 10, 1963): since middle 1950's. Cf. **souped up** below.

breed. A half-breed: Canadian coll.: mid-C. 19–20. Bod Dyker, *Get Your Man*, 1934.

breeding-wagon. A caravan: Midlands (s., not dial.): since ca. 1930.

breeze, three-man. See **three-man breeze** (*Dict.*).

breeze through (a task). To do it quickly and unfalteringly: Australian: since the late 1940's. (B.P.)

brek. Breakfast: certain Public Schools: late C. 19–20.

brew, n., 3 (p. 92). Hence, in the Army and Navy of late C. 19–20: tea. Cf. the Royal Australian Navy's *the brew's wet* or *she's wet*, the tea has been made. (Senior Commissioned Bo'sun L. D. M. Roberts, M.B.E., letter of June 27, 1951.)

brew-can. Army tin used for making tea: Army: since ca. 1925. Ex **brew,** n. and v. in *Dict.*

brew-up, n. Corresponding to next.

brew up, v.i. To make tea: Army: since ca. 1925.—2. Hence, to catch fire: Army: 1940–5. 'Tank brewed up and his driver's killed,' Keith Douglas, *Alamein to Zem Zem*, 1947.

brewer's asthma; brewer's goitre. Shortness of breath; a large paunch: Australian drinking s.: since ca. 1925. (B., 1953.)

brewer's horse (*Dict.*): cf. the phrase in 'Tavern terms', § 2.

brewer's jockey. A brewer's van-driver's self-appointed assistant: Australian: C. 20. Baker.

Brian O'Flynn has, in C. 20, ousted **Brian O'Linn** (p. 92). Often *Brian*, sometimes even *Bri*. (Franklyn, *Rhyming*.)

brick, n., 3 (p. 92). As 'a loaf of bread': 1848, *Sinks*: but that was low s., † by 1900.—5. A shell: Navy and Army: 1939–45. (P-G-R.) 'That gun throws a pretty hefty brick.'—6. The sum of £10: Australian sporting: since ca. 1920. (Glassop, 1949.)

brick, drop a. I am credibly informed that this phrase arose among a group of third-year undergraduates of Trinity College, Cambridge, in the May term, 1905; that it soon > University s.; and that it spread very rapidly. The guarantor's account of the origin of the phrase is this: H. S. was Sergeant-Major of the Trinity College Company of the University Volunteers—a pre-Territorial force renowned neither for discipline nor for efficiency. Whilst leading his company—small in numbers—along Trumpington Road on a route march, H. S. had to give an order, the road being under repair and building operations in progress on one or both sides. This H. S. did, in his best form and voice. Result: (1) on the troops, *nil*; (2) on the builders, *some in alarm dropped their bricks*. The order was repeated with the same result. H. S. told us that after that he felt that each time he gave an order he too was going to drop a brick—hence the phrase meaning to 'make a mistake'. In a few days the phrase was all over Cambridge and in a few months had gone round the world and returned to us.

brick in the hat, have a. To be intoxicated: non-aristocracy: from ca. 1870. B. & L. Semantics: top-heavy.

Bricks. See **Bricks and Mortar.**

bricks.—3. 'Projectiles, usually of heavy metal,' Granville: Naval: since ca. 1924. In the Army, any shell: since ca. 1930. By meiosis. So, too, at Woolwich Arsenal: *The Daily Mail,* Aug. 16, 1939.

bricks, shit; usually *shitting bricks,* considerably frightened, (very) much afraid: Army: 1940 +. Cf. **drop one's guts.**

Bricks and Mortar; often simply *Bricks.* The Air Ministry Works and Buildings Department: R.A.F.: since ca. 1930. H. & P.

bricks and mortar (p. 92): prob. since the 1890's. Leonard Merrick, *The Position of Peggy Harper,* 1911, has *bricks and mortar manager.*—2. A daughter: rhyming: C. 20.

Bricky. The Rt. Hon. Winston Churchill: mostly workmen's: since ca. 1920. Ex his bricklaying hobby. See **bricky, n.,** 1 (p. 92).

bricky (p. 94) occurs earlier in D. W. Barrett, *Navvies,* 1880.

brickyard. See **bear-pit.**

Brid. Bridlington, a Yorkshire holiday-resort: C. 20.

*****bride.** A girl; esp., one's best girl or one's mistress: C. 20: c. until ca. 1930, then Cockney s. (G. Ingram, *Cockney Cavalcade,* 1935) and, by 1940, Forces' s. Cf. **wife.** 3.

bride and groom.—2. A room: rhyming s.: C. 20. Franklyn 2nd declares both sense 1 (p. 92) and sense 2 to be † by 1960.

bridge, n.—4. An introduction, a form of approach: Australian: since ca. 1925. (B., 1943.) It bridges a gap.—5. Hence, a plausible excuse or story: Aus.: since ca. 1930. (B., 1959.)

Bridge of Sighs, the. St John's Bridge, Cambridge: University of Cambridge: late C. 19–20. Ex its resemblance to the famous bridge in Venice. Hence, in C. 19, also *Bridge of Grunts* and, derivatively, *Pig Bridge.* (Marples, 2.)

bridge widow; bridge widower. A wife, or a husband, often left alone by a bridge-fiendish partner: since early 1920's. On analogy of **golf-widow.**

bridger. A bridge player: mostly Society: since ca. 1925.

bridle-string; hence **bridle.** Fraenum: low: late C. 19–20.

brief.—9. (Ex sense 1.) See **bill, the**

brief, hand in one's. To give notice to an employer: domestic servants': C. 20. (Eric Horne, *What the Butler Winked At,* 1923.)

briefs, 2 (p. 93) has, since ca. 1950, been applied also to men's underpants.

*****briffin.** Bread and dripping: tramps' c.: C. 20. (By telescoping.) W. L. Gibson Cown, *Loud Report,* 1937.—2. Hence, a girl: likewise tramps' c.: from ca. 1920. Ibid. Regarded as 'a necessity of life'.

Brigg's (or **Briggs'**) **Rest;** esp., **Brig's rest.** A vest: rhyming s., esp. among convicts: C. 20. (Franklyn 2nd.) Perhaps a pun on **brig, the** (p. 93).

*****brighful.** A pocketful: c.: from ca. 1880. Pugh (2). Ex **brigh** (*Dict.*).

bright bastard. A 'smart Alec': Australian: since ca. 1910.

bright boy is an Army variant (1945 +) of **wide boy.**

bright eyes (or **bright-eyed**) **and bushy-tailed.** A Canadian c.p., signifying 'alert and active—and ready for anything': since ca. 1955. In May 1959, Dr Douglas Leechman writes, 'Incorporated in a current popular song, but I first heard it about 1956.' Probably ex the habitual aspect of such creatures as squirrels. Colonel Albert Moe tells me that he first heard it in 1933, and frequently since.

bright in the eye is recorded much earlier by B. & L.

brighten one's outlook. To have one's windows cleaned; to clean the lenses of one's glasses: jocular coll.: since ca. 1920.

brightener. A dash of gin or brandy added to a soft drink: public-houses': C. 20. George Robey, *An Honest Living,* 1922.

Brighton Pier. Strange; ill: rhyming (on *queer*): mid-C. 19–20.—2. Hence, since ca. 1940, homosexual.

Brighton sands. Hands: rhyming s.: C. 20. 'Seldom heard': Franklyn 2nd.

brights, clean the. To clean and polish the brass and copper accessories and ornaments, and the silver ornaments: domestic coll.: mid-C. 19–20.

brilliant is short for the next: 1821, *Boxiana,* III, 'Full of *heavy wet* and Booth's *brilliant*'.

brilliant stark-naked. See **stark-naked** (*Dict.*).

brindle. A half-caste: Australian: C. 20. (Vance Palmer, *Legend for Sanderson,* 1937.)

bring anything with you? or, in full, **did you . . .** A Canadian c.p. of ca. 1950–60. Meaning, 'Have you any narcotics on you?' (Leechman.)

bring-'em-back-alive (**So-and-So**). A big-game hunter that caters for zoos: C. 20.

bring it away. To effect an abortion: coll.: C. 20.

bring-me-back-alive. 'A member of an Australian anti-aircraft unit,' B., 1942: Diggers': 1940 +.

bring off. (Of a girl) to induce an orgasm in (a man); less often, (of a man) in a girl: coll.: probably since C. 16. In C. 20, to be classified as (familiar) S.E., even though the expression is completely ignored by the standard dictionaries: cf. the next, which it complements.—One of the most remarkable *lacunae* of lexicography is exhibited by the failure of the accredited dictionaries to include such terms. One readily admits that the reason for these omissions is excellent and that a very difficult problem has thereby been posed. The result is that students of Standard English (British and American) are obliged to seek the definitions of Standard words either in dictionaries of slang, such as, for the U.S., Berrey & Van den Bark's *Thesaurus* and, for Britain and its Dominions, Farmer & Henley's *Slang and Its Analogues* (meagre for the Dominions, and out of print since ca. 1910) and this dictionary of mine, or in encyclopedias and specialist glossaries of sex—where, probably, they won't find many of the words they seek.

bring on. To excite sexually: coll.: probably since C. 16. (In C. 20, familiar S.E.—yet unrecorded by the standard dictionaries.)—2. Hence, to delight, to please (someone) very much: Korean front: ca. 1954–55. Cf. *bring off.*

bring on the dancing girls! Let's watch, or do, something more exciting, *this* is a crashing bore: c.p.: since ca. 1930. Ex Eastern potentates, bored with their guests, ordering the dancers to appear.

bring one's heart up. To spew: coll.: late C. 18–20. Cf. quotation at **heart up** . . . below.

bring the house down. See **bring down the house** (*Dict.*).

brinkmanship. The practice of seeing just how far one can go in a situation already hazardous: adopted, ca. 1961, ex U.S.: coll. >, by 1964, S.E. On the very *brink* of the precipice.

brinny. A stone: Aus.: C. 20. (B., 1959.) Ex an Aboriginal word?

Bris. Brisbane: Australian coll.: C. 20. (Cecil Mann, *The River*, 1945.)

Brisfit. A Bristol fighter: R.F.C. and early R.A.F.: ca. 1915–19. Jackson.

Brish. British: Australian (esp. Sydney): since ca. 1943. Ex a drunken pronunciation of *British.* (Elisabeth Lambert, 1951.)

Brissie. Brisbane: Australian coll.: C. 20.

Bristol hog. A (male) native of Bristol: late C. 18–mid 19. *The Night Watch* (I, 314), 1829. Moe.

Bristols. The female breasts: C. 20. Rhyming: *Bristol Cities* on *titties.*

*britch. (Gen. **the britch.**) The C. 20 form of **brigh** (*Dict.*), but specifically a side trousers-pocket. Cf. **outer.**

Britcom, adj. *Brit*ish *Com*monwealth of Nations: among the United Nations forces in Korea: ca. 1951–55. It hovers between j. and coll.

British was, at Oxford, in ca. 1910–14, the pejorative adj. corresponding to **hearty** (p. 383).

British Ass, the. The British Association for the Advancement of Science; scientific coll.: from ca. 1870.

British Brainwashing Corporation. The. The British Broadcasting Corporation: since the late 1950's. A reference to veiled-propaganda programmes.

British warm. A short, thick overcoat worn by (senior) officers: Army coll.: C. 20.

Britons never shall be slaves—not willingly; . . . wage slaves. These are c.p. adaptations of 'Britons never, never shall be slaves'; since ca. 1925.

Brits. British Israelites: C. 20.

brits up, have the. To be alarmed, afraid: Australian: C. 20. B., 1942. Rhyming s.

Brixton shuffle, the. 'Old lags . . . walk with a curious clipped gait . . . known as "The Brixton shuffle". It is a product of the prison exercise yard, where prisoners . . . had to avoid treading on the heels of the man in front' (John Gosling, *The Ghost Squad*, 1959): police s.: since ca. 1920.

broach, on the. 'Stocking the bars with wines, spirits, and barrels of beer,' Dave Marlowe, *Coming, Sir!*, 1937: ships' stewards': C. 20. Ex the broaching of casks.

broad, n.—3. A girl, esp. one readily available: Canadian: adopted, ca. 1925, ex U.S. (Perhaps ex '*broad* in the beam'.)—4. Backside: Australian: since ca. 1940. (A. M. Harris *The Tall Man*, 1958: 'What about the blokes sitting on their broads in Seoul?')

broad, hit (or **hot**) **that.** ' "Hit that broad" and "hot that broad" are orders to light up and to focus a floodlight,' *The Evening News*, Nov. 7, 1939: cinema: since ca. 1930. For *broad*, see 'Moving-Picture Slang', para. 3.

Broad Fourteens, the. Part of the North Sea off Ymuiden: nautical coll.: mid-C. 19–20.

*broadsman.—2. An exponent of the three-card

trick: c.: since ca. 1920. Stanley Jackson, *An Indiscreet Guide to Soho*, 1946.

Brock's benefit (p. 95). Hence, in the Navy since 1939, 'any pyrotechnic display of gunfire' (Granville); esp. 1939–45. 'Bomber slang for a particularly large display of enemy searchlights, flares, and ack-ack fire' (H. & P., 1943); in 1940–1, the spectacular aspect of a heavy German air raid: E. P., 'Air Warfare' in *The New Statesman*, Sept. 19, 1942.

broke.—2. Dismissed from the Service: Naval officers' coll.: late C. 19–20.

broke for. In need of, esp. *broke for a feed*, hungry: Australian coll.: C. 20. B., 1942.

broke to the wide. Penniless: coll.: since ca. 1910. A variant of *broke to the world* (p. 95)—prompted by the S.E. *the wide, wide world.*

Broken Hill. A silver coin: Australian: since ca. 1920. (B., 1943.) Ex a famous silver-lead-mining centre.

broken knees, have. (Of a woman) to have been seduced or devirginated: lower classes': C. 19–20; ob. B. & L. Cf. **broken-kneed** (*Dict.*).

broken-mouth. An old sheep: Aus. rural coll.: late C. 19–20. (B., 1959.)

broken-square. See **fusilier.**

brokko. A lower-deck name or nickname for a spotty-faced messmate: Naval: since ca. 1920. (P-G-R.)

brolley.—2. A parachute: R.A.F., esp. pilots': since ca. 1930. Sgt-Pilot John Beard, D.F.M., in Michie & Graebner's *Their Finest Hour*, 1940. Derivatively, *brolly hop*, a parachute jump from an aircraft: H. & P.

bromide (p. 95) was 'coined' by Gelett Burgess, who did truly coin *blurb.*

bronchittics. Bronchitis: sol.: from ca. 1870. Nevinson, 1895.

bronza or **bronzer** is the predominant post-1950 form of **bronza,** s.—2. Hence, backside: low Australian: since ca. 1925. (D'Arcy Niland, *The Big Smoke*, 1959.)

bronze.—3. Impudence: 1821, Pierce Egan, *Life in London*: app. † by 1850. Cf. synonymous *brass.*—4. A penny: Australian: since ca. 1920. Baker. Cf. **copper.**—5. Anus: Australian: since ca. 1920. Hence the variant *bronzo*, since ca. 1935. (B., 1953.)

bronzer. See **bronza.**

bronzewing. See **copper-tail.**

bronzie; usually in pl. See 'Prisoner-of-War Slang', 8.

bronzo. See **bronze, 5.**

broom squires. See esp. Eden Philpotts, *The Broom Squires*, 1932.

broom-tail; hence often **broomie.** A mustang (esp. a mare) with a short bushy tail: Canadian coll.: adopted, ca. 1920, ex U.S.

broomie. A boy that keeps his shearing floor swept clean: Australian rural coll.: C. 20. Baker. The N.Z. sheep-shearer's definition is 'the sweeper on the shearing board'. *Straight Furrow* (the official organ of the Federated Farmers of New Zealand), Feb. 21, 1968. (Thanks to Mr Harold Griffiths.)

broseley (p. 96) should rather be dated 'ca. 1815–90'. (*The Virginia Literary Museum*, June 17, 1829, p. 7, col. 2.) Moe.

brothel(-)creepers. Suède shoes: Army (mostly officers') and Navy: 1939 +. Cf. **creepers** (*Dict.*). —2. Hence, since 1940 in Army and R.A.F., those short, suède, desert boots made with rubber soles made from old 'run-flat' tyres and manufactured in Egypt for use in the desert. (Peter Sanders, who adds 'Completely silent'.)

Brothels. Brussels: Army: late 1944–5. (John Prebble, *The Edge of Darkness*, 1947.)

brother! A mild exclamation, esp. of surprise: Australian: adopted, ca. 1943, ex U.S. (B.P.)

brother on one's back, have a (or one's). To be round-shouldered: R.A.F.: since ca. 1925. (Sgt Gerald Emanuel, letter of March 29, 1945.)

brought up all standing. See **all standing.**

brought up with a round turn. To be suddenly or unexpectedly checked: Naval coll.: C. 19–20. (P-G-R.)

brow, the. The gangway: Naval: C. 20. (P-G-R.)

brown, n.—4. An error or blunder: R.A.F.: since ca. 1935. Partridge, 1945. Also *brown show.* Less discreditable than a *black.*—5. Often *a bit of brown,* an act of sodomy, *brown* or *the brown* being generic: ? mid-C. 19–20. Ex:—6. The anus: low: mid-C. 19–20. With senses 5 and 6, cf. *good old Brown:* a C. 20 Canadian c.p. implying sodomy: with a pun on the surname as well as on the common noun.

brown do. Earlier in *Boxiana*, IV, 1824, 'He is then said to be "cooked" or "done brown" and "dished".'

brown, do a. To commit sodomy: low: late C. 19–20.

brown, into the, 2 (p. 96), goes back a further thirty years or so: cf. John Mayer, *The Sportsman's Directory*, 7th edition, 1845, 'Always aim at one particular bird, not firing at random at the whole covey, or into the brown of them.' (Dr D. Pechtold.)

brown-back. A ten-shilling currency note: C. 20. Contrast **green-back,** 3.

brown bag, n.; **brown-bag,** v., whence **brown-bagger.** Hard work, with no social or sporting life; to live this sort of life; one who does it: Imperial College, London (−1940). Ex the little brown bags these students are reputed to carry. (Marples, 2.)

brown Bessie (C. 17) is a variant of **brown Bess,** 1 (*Dict.*). B. & L.

brown bomber. A car warden: Australian: since ca. 1935. 'They wear a brown uniform. I believe that Joe Louis—"the Brown Bomber"— was top boxer at the time these policemen were introduced' (B.P.).

brown food. Beer: Services', but rarely R.A.F. and mostly in the Navy: since ca. 1925. H. & P. Ex colour and (former) substantiality of beer.

brown-hatter. A male homosexual: Naval: since ca. 1910. (Walter Baxter, *Look Down in Mercy*, 1951.) By 1945, at latest, common in the other Services and, by 1950, among civilians. Also *brownie.*

Brown Job, the. The Army; a *brown job,* a soldier: R.A.F. since ca. 1920 (H. & P.) and Naval since 1939 (Granville). From the colour of the uniform; see **job,** n., 8.

brown Joe.—2. To know: Australian rhyming s. (−1945). Baker, *The Australian Language.*

Brown Josephs (coll.), or **Brown Joeys** (s.), **the.** The Sisters of St Joseph (a group different from *the Black Josephs*): Australian Catholics' coll.: C. 20. (B.P.)

brown(-)nose; brown(-)tongue. A sycophant: C. 20. Cf. **bum sucker** (*Dict.*).

Brown Nurses, the. Our Lady's Nurses: Australian Catholics' coll.: C. 20. (B.P.)

brown off. To cause a man to be browned off: Army since 1920; R.A.F. since ca. 1928. H. & P. —2. To treat brusquely, send about one's business; to warn for a duty ('I'm browned off for guard duty to-night'): former nuance (Army) since ca. 1930; latter (Army and Naval) since ca. 1938 (Granville). James Curtis, *You're in the Racket Too,* 1937; a Service example occurs in Gerald Kersh, 1941. Wrongly posed by Berrey thus 'to brown off, to be bored, fed up': in this sense it is always *to be browned off.*

brown one. See **back stick** above.

brown-out Romeo. A man given to molesting females in darkened streets: Australian: 1941–45. (B., 1943.) Ex *brown-out,* a partial black-out.

brown shell; gen. pl. An onion: proletarian: mid-C. 19–20. B. & L.

brown show. See **brown,** n., 4.

brown Titus; brown typhus. Bronchitis: sol.: mid-C. 19–20. B. & L.

brown(-)tongue. See **brown(-)nose.**

brown type. An Army officer; R.A.F.: since ca. 1938. H. & P. Cf. **brown job** and see **type,** 2.

brown Windsor. Soap—any soap whatsoever: R.A.F.: since ca. 1935. Jackson. Windsor soap issued to R.A.F. is brown. *The Daily Mail,* Sept. 7, 1940; Hector Bolitho, *The Listener,* late 1941; Michie & Graebner, *Lights of Freedom,* 1941.

browned off. (Extremely) disgruntled: depressed: disgusted: Regular Army since ca. 1915; adopted by the R.A.F. ca. 1929. H. & P., 1943. Prob. ex cookery: see Partridge, 1945, or *Forces' Slang,* ed. Partridge, 1948. Cf. **brassed off** and **cheesed off,** q.v., and note Ronald Bottrall, *Farewell and Hail,* 1945, 'Girls browned off in Roedean' (the first appearance in true literature). But *browned off* could have been suggested by *brassed off.* A well-known, extremely well-informed R.A.F officer writes: 'I rather think the references are to brass buttons, which, if left uncleaned, first develop a harsh yellow or brassy effect and later go brown. I remember hearing a Regular R.A.F. N.C.O. complain that an airman's buttons were "brassed off". It was obvious that for him this was the *mot juste* and far from being a joke' (letter of 1949). Nevertheless, the predominant Army opinion, from at least as early as 1940, is that the phrase was originally sodomitic.

browned up. Despondent: Cockney: C. 20. Naomi Jacobs, *The Lenient God,* 1937. Cf. prec. entry.

brownie, 3, a copper coin, is extant in Australia. (Cusack.)—8. See **brown-hatter.**—9. A cake or other confection: Canadian coll. (adopted ex U.S.): C. 20.—10. A bad mark: C.P.R.: since ca. 1908. Introduced by one *Brown.* (Leechman.)

brownie box. A superintendent's carriage: Canadian railroadmen's: C. 20. So called because that's where 'brownies' are issued: see preceding, sense 10. (Leechman.)

browning, n. Sodomy: low: late C. 19–20.

browsing and sluicing. Eating and drinking: ca. 1920–40. (P. G. Wodehouse.)

bruiser, 1 (p. 97). In *Sport in England,* 1949, Norman Wymer records (p. 131) an example occurring in May 1742.

brumbie.—2. A poor hand about which its

holder tries to bluff: Australian card-players':
since ca. 1920. (B., 1953.)

Brummagem button. A self-nickname affected
by natives of Birmingham: mid-C. 19–20. Cf.
the **Brum** and **Brummagem** entries in the *Dict.*

Brummagem screwdriver. A hammer: Midlands: C. 20. (Richard Merry.)

Brummie (or **-my**). A familiar form of *Brum*
(see **brum,** n., 5: p. 97).

Brummy boy. A youth or man from Birming-
ham: esp. Regular Army. C. 20. Gerald Kersh,
They Die with Their Boots Clean, 1941. Cf.
Brums, 3 (*Dict.*)

brunch (p. 98) 'was first suggested by Guy
Beringer in 1895 in the pages of the long since
defunct *Hunter's Weekly.* My authority for this is
Punch . . . 1st August 1896' (William Phillips,
letter of Dec. 17, 1963): therefore the term has to
be back-dated to 1895. Moreover, it > coll.,
not ca. 1930 but ca. 1905.

brung. Brought: sol.: C. 19–20. E.g. E. W.
Hornung, 1899, 'We don't sweat to know 'ow you
brung it orf.'

brush, n., 5 (p. 98). Also, *a bit of brush,* coïtion
—hence, a girl: low: since late 1930's. (Dick.)

brush, three-out. See **three-out brush** (*Dict.*).

brush-off. A snub; *give* (someone) *the brush-off,*
to snub: adopted, ca. 1943, ex U.S. As if
brushing dust from one's clothes.

brusher, give (p. 98). Since ca. 1930, usually
give a brusher: B., 1942.

Brussel sprout. A Boy Scout: rhyming s.:
since ca. 1910. (Franklyn, *Rhyming.*)—2. (Often
simply *Brussel.*) A racecourse tout (a watcher of
horses in training): racing rhyming s.: C. 20.
The famous Racing Correspondent known as 'The
Scout' is, in racing circles, called 'The Brussel':
Franklyn 2nd.

brutal and licentious soldiery. An Army officers'
c.p. dating from the Boer War (1899–1901). Prob.
ex some politician's speech.

'No; earlier! Dating certainly from 1891:
Kipling, *Life's Handicap.* Put ironically into the
mouth of Private Mulvaney, satirising a Victorian
civilian attitude to the Regular Army not yet
extinct in 1967' (Ramsey Spencer).

bruvver. With the song quoted on p. 98, Mr
Jack Lindsay compares Martial, xi, 66:

> Et delator es et calumniator,
> et fraudator es et negotiator,
> et fellator es et lanista. Miror
> quare non habeas, Vacerra, nummos;

which he suggests might be translated somewhat
after this fashion:

> You're a pimp, you deal in slander,
> You're a cheat, a pervert, pander,
> And gladiator-trainer. Funny,
> Vacerra, that you have no money!

There is, too, an interesting adumbration in the
anon. ballad or song. *The Joviall Crew,* 1670:

> A Craver my Father,
> A Maunder my Mother,
> A Filer my Sister,
> A Filcher my Brother,
> A Canter my Unckle,
> That car'd not for Pelfe;

> A Lifter my Aunt, a Beggar my self;
> In white wheaten straw, when their bellies were full,
> Then I was begot, between Trinker and Trull.
> *And therefore a Beggar, a Beggar I'le be,*
> *For none hath a spirit so jocond as he.*

An even closer adumbration, as Professor A. W.
Stewart once reminded me, occurs in Goethe's
Faust, Part I (published in 1808), in Marguerite's
song in the course of the Prison Scene:

> Meine Mutter, die Hur'
> Die mich umgebracht hat!
> Mein Vater, der Schelm,
> Der mich gessen hat!
> Mein Schwesterlein klein
> Hub' auf die Bein'
> An einem kühlen Ort;
> Da ward ich ein schönes Waldvögelein;
> Fliege fort, fliege fort!

Postscript. On Aug. 31, 1968, Mr Robert Clairborne of N.Y.C. writes 'Re the charming song
'Why Should We Be Pore'', you may be interested
in a U.S. parallel (prob. of student origin; from
internal evidence, ca. 1925–30). To the tune of
"My Bonny Lies Over the Ocean":

> My mother she works in a cat-house,
> My father makes counterfeit gin,
> My brother sells hop narcotics on the corner,
> My God, how the money rolls in!'

Bryant and May. (Mostly in pl.) A light ale:
public-houses': from ca. 1920. Via *light* from
Bryant & May's matches.

Brylcreem Boys, the. The R.A.F.: Army
(since ca. 1939: H. & P.) and Naval lower-deck
(since ca. 1940). Granville, 'From the advertisement which depicts an airman with immaculately
Brylcreemed hair.'

B's, three. See **three B's** (*Dict.*).

bubbery (p. 98). Earlier in *The London Guide,*
1818.

bubble, n.—2. Short for **bubble and squeak,** n.,
2, below: C. 20. (Robin Cook, 1962.)

bubble, v.—2. To blub: Edinburgh undergraduates' (since ca. 1920) and Sherborne School
(since ca. 1915).

bubble and squeak, n.—2. A Greek: rhyming s.:
from ca. 1870.—3. A magistrate: rhyming s.
(on *beak*): late C. 19–20.

bubble and squeak, v.—2. To inform to the
police: underworld rhyming s. on the synonymous 'to squeak' (p. 819): C. 20. Franklyn 2nd.

bubble(-)dancing. 'Pot washing in the cook-
house,' H. & P.: Services: since ca. 1920.—2.
Hence, washing one's irons and, at some stations,
also one's plate: R.A.F.: 1939–45.

bubble in, put the. To give the game away,
esp. to expose a racket: dockers' rhyming s.:
C. 20. Ex *bubble and squeak,* 4, as above. Also
put in the bubble.—2. Hence, to cause trouble:
since ca. 1920. As *trouble* rhymes with *bubble,* and
sneak with *squeak,* so *bubble and squeak* prob.
combines both of these sounds and both of these
senses.

bubbler. A drinking fountain: Australian coll.:
since ca. 1945.

Bubbles and Squeaks. Greeks and Cypriots
collectively: Teddy boys' : since ca. 1949. (*The*

Observer, March 1, 1959.) So many of them own or manage or man restaurants. Cf. *bubble and squeak*, 2, above—the immediate source.

bubbly. 'Taffrail' defines sense 2 as 'rum'.

bubbly bosun. 'That rating who serves the mess tots of rum from the "fanny" [see **fanny**, n., 2, on p. 266], usually a different member of the mess every day' (Granville): Naval: since ca. 1910. Cf. **bubbly**, 2 (p. 99, and above).

Buck appears earlier in 'Taffrail'.

buck, n.—14. A dollar: Canadian: late C. 19–20; adopted ex U.S.—15. A rough fellow: Liverpool: since the 1920's. Cf. the U.S. *buck mate*.

buck, v.—5. To boast: C. 20 (ob. by 1940), esp. in the Services 1914–18.

buck, give it a; have a buck at (something). To make an attempt: Australian: since ca. 1920. Baker. Ex the language of the rodeo. Cf. *trick at* below.

buck against the tiger. To be up against too great odds: C. 20. Contrast **buck the tiger** (*Dict.*).

buck as if he had a belly full of bed-springs. (Of a horse) to buck violently and repeatedly: Australian rural: since ca. 1930. (Baker.)

buck at is the New Zealand version of *buck against* (p. 100): C. 20. Jean Devanney, *Bushman Burke*, 1930, 'Terrible shacks . . . a decent dog would "buck at".'

Buck Guard. Guard duty at Buckingham Palace: Army. C. 20. Cf. **Jimmy guard.**

Buck House. Buckingham Palace: Society: C. 20. (*The Listener*, March 10, 1937.)

buck jumper. A 'Great Eastern Tank Engine. Six-wheel coupled' (*Railway*, 3rd): railwaymen's: (?) ca. 1945–60.

buck-passing. The 1946-and-after form of **passing the buck.** Ex **pass the buck,** 2.

buck private. An ordinary private with no stripes at all: Canadian soldiers': 1914–18.

buck sergeant. A full sergeant: Army: 1939+. (P-G-R.)

buck the tiger (p. 100). Both *American Speech*, 1943, and C. E. Funk, *A Hog on Ice*, 1950, mention that a colour print of a Bengal tiger indicates that faro is played on the premises.

bucket. n. (p. 100). Also cheapjacks': C. Hindley, *The Life of a Cheapjack*, 1876.

bucket and pail. A gaol (jail): rhyming s.: C. 20. Mostly London's dockland: Franklyn 2nd.

bucketing. A hard task enforced on one: lower class: C. 20 (W. L. George, 1914.)

buckets. Boots: fast life: ca. 1820–50. Pierce Egan, *Finish*, 1828. One 'pours' one's feet into them.

buckets, (simply) throwing up. See **throwing up buckets.**

buckle, n.—3. Condition, state; mood; Australian: ca. 1850–1910. Rolf Boldrewood, *Robbery under Arms*. By confusion of *fettle* with *fetter*?:—see sense 1 of **buckle** (*Dict.*, p. 100).—4. (Also *buckle me.*) Figure 2 in House: late C. 19–20. Michael Harrison, 1943. Truncated form of rhyming s. *buckle-me* (or *my*)-*shoe*.

buckle, v., 2 (p. 101), has been current in Australia throughout C. 20. (Hugh Atkinson, *Low Company*, 1961.)

Buckley's chance (p. 101). William Buckley died in 1856, therefore prob. since 1856. See esp. Marcus Clarke, 'Buckley, the Escaped Convict' in *Stories of Australia in the Early Days*, 1897. In

1959, Sidney J. Baker records the variant *two chances—mine and Buckley's.*

bucko mate. A Merchant Navy first mate given to enforcing discipline with his fists: nautical: since ca. 1905. Cf. *bucko* on p. 101.

bucks. Short for **buckshee** (*Dict.*): mostly Army: since before 1929.

Bucks hussar. A cigar: rhyming s., mainly theatrical: late C. 19–20. (Franklyn, *Rhyming*.)

buckshee bombardier. An N.C.O. with rank, carrying no additional pay: Diggers': 1939+, B., 1942.

budge, n.—4. A promotion: Sherborne School: mid-C. 19–20. Alec Waugh, *The Loom of Youth*, 1917, 'I think I had better get a "budge" this term.' Also at Harrow School: Lunn.

*budge, the sneaking. See **sneaking budge,** 2 (*Dict.*).

budgets (rare in singular). Bottled commodities, esp. toilet articles and patent medicines: fairgrounds': C. 20. (W. Buchanan-Taylor, *Shake It Again*, 1943.)

budgie (or **-y**). A budgerigar: Australian and British coll.: late C. 19–20. Baker.

budgy (p. 101) goes back to—at least—the 1830's. The American *Spirit of the Times*, June 20, 1840 (p. 192, col. 3), app. refers to an English source in the quotation, 'What budgy brutes you all are'.

budli-budli, or **-ly.** Sodomy: low, esp. in India: C. 20. Ex Urdu *badli* (usually pron. *budly*), 'change'.

buff, n.—5. A buffalo: big-game hunters': since ca. 1870. Also, in C. 20, Australian.—6. A corporal: R.A.F.: since ca. 1919. Jackson. Adopted from the Army, where, however, *orderly buff* used to mean Orderly Sergeant: in the R.A.F. *orderly buff* = Orderly Corporal.—7. A stoker; esp. *a second-class buff*, second-class stoker: Naval: C. 20: Granville.—8. One who, protesting that he has been swindled, threatens to go to the police: Canadian carnivals': C. 20. Ex **buff,** v., 2 (*Dict.*). n.—9. An anal escape of wind: Oundle School: C. 20. Echoic. 'Has now reached Rugby School' (D. F. Wharton, 1965).—10. An enthusiast of, or for, e.g. football or fires or Ned Kelly: Australian, adopted, ca. 1944, ex U.S.; also Canadian since ca. 1940.

buff, v., 1 (p. 102), occurs also in *buff well*, to appear to advantage when (almost) stripped: sporting, esp. boxing: prob. since ca. 1810 or even 1800.

buff up. See **shroff up.**

buffalo. To out-bluff or out-wit, to circumvent; to overawe: Canadian: since ca. 1920; by ca. 1945, coll. Ex U.S., where it originally denoted 'to hunt buffalo'.

buffalo navigator. A bullock driver: Australian jocular: ca. 1930–50. (B., 1943.)

*buffar. Dog-like: c. (–1688). Randle Holme. See **bufe** (*Dict.*).

buffer, 1 (p. 102). In late C. 19–20 circus s., it denotes a performing dog, as in:

> Risley kids and slanging buffers,
> Lord alone knows how they suffers.

'Risley (? Riseley) kids' are the children used in foot juggling. (With thanks to David Creswell.) —9. A petty officer: Naval: C. 20. *Weekly Telegraph*, Oct. 25, 1941. He acts as a buffer between officers and men.—10. A boatswain,

whence *buffer's mate* and *chief buffer's mate*:
Naval: late C. 19–20. Ex sense 6 (*Dict.*).

buffers. Female breasts: low: late C. 19–20.

Buffs!, steady the. See **steady the Buffs!**

buffy (or **-ey**). 'Old Buffy' . . . does not mean
anything offensive, just the same as 'Old fellow':
Sessions, Oct. 30, 1845: low s.: ca. 1825–70. Ex
buffer, 3 (*Dict.*)?

buffy, v. To polish (esp. one's buttons): R.A.F.:
since ca. 1930. (P-G-R.)

Bug. A Bugatti car: since ca. 1920 among
motorists.

bug.—7. An old car, rebuilt and remodelled,
race-car fashion: Canadian: ca. 1919–39. (Leechman.)—8. An imperfection in a mechanical device
or invention: Canadian: adopted, ca. 1945, ex
U.S. (Leechman.)—9. A key operated from side
to side: Canadian and Australian telegraphists':
since ca. 1910.—10. A fault, or a delay, on a
new enterprise: Australian: since late 1940's.
(B.P.)—11. An inciter, esp. to homosexuality: c.:
C. 18. James Dalton, *A Narrative*, 1778, 'A Man
who was what they called a *Bug* to the *Mollies*,
. . . picking 'em up, as if to commit . . . Sodomy.'

bug, v.—5. To fit a building or a room with
hidden microphones or transistors: adopted,
1962, ex U.S.—6. To get on (someone's) nerves:
adopted, in late 1950's, ex U.S. (Nicholas Blake,
The Sad Variety, 1964.)

Bug, the. The Natural History Museum:
Rugby Schoolboys': ca. 1880–1910. 'Now any
library, e.g. *the Temple Bug* = the Temple Reading
Room' (D. F. Wharton, Oct. 24, 1965).

bug and flea. Tea: rhyming s., esp. in Army of
1914–18: C. 20; by 1940, †. Franklyn 2nd.

bug-blinding. See **blind out.**

bug box. A 'small four-wheeled passenger
carriage' (*Railway*, 3rd): railwaymen's: C. 20.

bug(-)dust. Small coal: railwaymen's: since
ca. 1920. (*Railway.*)

bug house. A second-rate cinema: South
Africa: since ca. 1920. Cyrus A. Smith, in letter
of July 17, 1946. Cf. **flea pit, 3.**

bug-house. Mad; very eccentric: Anglicised,
as rather low s., by late 1936. For its usage in
U.S., see Irwin. Adopted by Canada in early C.
20. (Niven.)

bug nest: A hat: Guards Depot at Caterham:
1914–18. *John o' London*, Nov. 3, 1939.

bug-out. See **swan.**

bug over. See **bug,** v., 3 (*Dict.*).

bug-rake. A hair comb: Australian juvenile:
since ca. 1930.

bug-rum. Bay rum: Naval (lower-deck): C.
20. (P-G-R.) Cognate: *bug-run*, the parting in a
man's hair: id.: id.

bug-trap. A Naval Auxiliary vessel, or any
tramp steamer: Naval: 1939–45. (P-G-R.)

bug-walk.—2. A hair-parting: low: ca. 1890–
1914.

bug wash. Hair oil: Felsted School (and elsewhere): since ca. 1925. Marples. Cf. **bug walk**
(p. 103) and **bug nest** (above).

bug(-)whiskers. 'The result of an abortive
attempt to grow a "set",' Granville: Naval:
since ca. 1925. Ex Cockney s. of C. 20.

bugger, n.—3. A person (usually male) very
energetic or very skilful; esp. in *a bugger to work—
drive—drink*—what have you: Canadian: since
ca. 1925. (Leechman.) Cf. the Eng. **beggar to
work** above.

bugger, v., 1, and **bugger!** as in *Dict.* The
expletive use is recorded at a very much earlier
date: *Sessions*, Dec. 1793, p. 86, 'She said, b**st
and b-gg-r your eyes, I have got none of your
money.'

bugger in the coals. 'A thinnish cake spreckled
[*sic*] with currants and baked hastily on the glow-
ing embers,' William Kelly, *Life in Victoria*, 1859:
Australian: ca. 1830–90.

bugger it. A variant of **bugger!** (*Dict.*).

bugger me dead! An Australian expression of
surprise: since ca. 1940.

bugger off. To depart, to decamp: low: late
C. 19–20. Cf. *fuck off* and *piss off* in *Dict.* By
late 1950's—see, e.g., Nancy Mitford, *Don't Tell
Alfred*, 1960—no longer low.

bugger on the coals. See **beggar on the coals.**

bugger one's contract. See **beggar** and cf. **contract, mess up the** (*Dict.* and Addenda).

buggered if I know! Sorry, I just don't know:
Australian: C. 20.

buggerizing (or **connivering**) **about.** Aimlessly
wandering or pottering: Australian: since ca.
1935. (B., 1953.)

buggeranto. See 'Rogues'.

buggerlugs (p. 103). Not—in Liverpool, at
least—necessarily offensive; so a Liverpudlian
assured me in 1952.—2. Those little tufts of hair
which are sometimes seen on men's cheekbones:
Naval: C. 20.

buggeroo. An admiring description of a 'card'
or 'character': non-aristocratic: since ca. 1945.
The U.S. suffix *-eroo* has been blended with
bugger.

bugger's grips. The short whiskers on the cheeks
of Old Salts: Naval (lower-deck): C. 20. Also
bugger grips. In *H.M.S. Leviathan*, 1967, John
Winton writes, 'Tufts of biscuit-coloured hair
grew on his cheeks in what were called in the
Service "bugger's grips"'.

buggers-in-the-coals is the late C. 19–20 form of
bugger in the coals. (B., 1943.)

buggery, adj. A strong pejorative, subjective
epithet: low: from ca. 1870; ob.

buggie. A bugbear; a bogey: jocular when
not merely illiterate: since ca. 1925.

buggy. 'Caboose; passenger car; box car' (a
magazine article, 1931): Canadian and U.S. railroadmen's: C. 20.—2. A motor-car: since ca.
1945. (John Creasey, *Battle for Inspector West*,
1949.) Cf. *blood-waggon.*

bugle. Nose. Canadian: C. 20. Perhaps ex
'blow the *bugle*'.

bugle, on the. Malodorous: Australian: since
ca. 1930. Cf. **bugle** above.

Bugs. Synonym of **Bats:** Naval: since ca.
1939. (Granville.) With a pun on **bats,** adj.
(p. 37).

bugs, n.—3. Biology: schools': since ca. 1935.
(*New Society*, Aug. 22, 1963.) Cf. sense 2 on p. 103.

bugs, adj. A 'conflation' of **bug-house** (above):
Canadian (ex U.S.): C. 20. (Niven.)

build. See **milk,** v., 6.

build up, n. & v. 'To describe most favourably
in advance of an appearance. "He gave her a
terrific build-up." Movie personalities are
"built-up" for their audiences in many and
strange ways.' (Leechman.) Since ca. 1925:
a coll. that, by 1955 at latest, was familiar S.E.

built for comfort. (Of a man) stout; (of a
woman) agreeably plump: C. 20.

built like a brick shit-house, he's. Very well made: low Canadian: C. 20.

bukra (p. 103). It had been a Regular Army word since ca. 1880. In 1939–45 it was revived by troops in Egypt: see, e.g., Lawson Glassop, *We Were the Rats*, 1944.

bulge on, have (got) the. An earlier example is in E. H. Hornung, *Raffles*, 1899: 'We had the bulge before; he has it now: it's perfectly fair.'

bulk-monger. A prostitute consorting with male thieves, esp. pickpockets: C. 18. *A Congratulatory Epistle from a Reformed Rake . . . upon Prostitutes*, 1728.

bull, n.—15. (Cf. sense 6, p. 104.) 'Washings of a sugar bag,' Peter Cunningham, *Two Years in New South Wales*, 1827: Australian: ca. 1815–70. Ex **bull the cask** (*Dict.*).—16. A South Seas Islander; esp., a Torres Islander: Australian: C. 20. Vance Palmer, *Legend for Sanderson*, 1937.—17. An elephant: circusmen's: C. 20. Short for '*bull* elephant'.—18. A policeman: Canadian (ex U.S.): C. 20. Niven.

bull, v.—6. To brag; talk nonsense: Australian: since ca. 1925. Baker. Ex the noun. Hence, *bull artist.*—7. To put something across (one's superior officer): Army: 1939–45. Cf. sense 2, p. 104.

bull, peddle the; hence **bull-peddler.** To talk nonsense or 'hot air'; one who does this: Canadian: since ca. 1945. Cf. *bull-shit* on p. 105.

bull, shoot the; bull-session. One does the former at the latter: Canadian: since ca. 1919. See *bull-shit* (p. 105).

bull, sweat like a. To perspire freely: coll., mostly Cockneys': from ca. 1880. Perhaps ex cattle, apt to sweat profusely when confined in a market pen.

Bull, the. General Allenby, famous on the Eastern Front 1914–18: military: C. 20. Ex physique and voice. (C. S. Forester plays on this nickname by transferring it, in his masterly novel, *The General*, 1937, to a Western Front army-commander and changing it to *the Buffalo*.)

bull and boloney. Idle talk; hot air: Guards Division: since ca. 1938. See the elements.—2. Hence, spit and polish *plus* window dressing: Army: 1939 +.

bull ants. Trousers: Australian rhyming s. (on *pants*): since ca. 1930. Franklyn 2nd.

bull-ants, to feel as if (or though) one will (or would) give birth to. To feel much out of sorts, ill: Australian: C. 20. B., 1942.

bull artist, bullshit artist. Synonyms of **bull-shitter**, than which, by 1960, they were commoner: since ca. 1916. All three, Australian; the 1st, also New Zealand, also with derivative sense, a smooth talker, esp. of a travelling salesman, as in Slatter.

bull chilo. See **cow chilo**.

bull dance (p. 104) should be back-dated to early C. 19; it occurs in, e.g., Fredk Chamier, *The Life of a Sailor*, 1832, at II, 38. (Moe.)

bull-dogging. See **steer-decorating**.

Bull Dogs, the. Footscray footballers: Melbournites': C. 20. (B., 1943.)

bull-dozed. Muddled; tipsy: Australian: since ca. 1935. B., 1942. Ex **bull-doze** (*Dict.*).

bull-dust or -fodder. Nonsense: Australian: since ca. 1919. (B., 1943.) By ca. 1940, also English.

bull-dust, v. To talk nonsense; esp., to 'kid': Australian: since ca. 1920. ' "Fairdinkum?" '

said Ritchie. "Or are yuh bull-dustin'?" ' (Dick.) Ex the n.

bull fiddle. A bass viol: Canadian: C. 20. (Leechman.)

bull-fuck. Custard: Canadian railroad-construction crews': since ca. 1910.

bull it through. To accomplish something—esp. an outdoor task—by sheer strength rather than by skill and planning: Canadian coll.: C. 20. (Leechman.)

bull-juice. Condensed milk: mostly nautical: since ca. 1920. Robert Harbinson, *Up Spake the Cabin-Boy*, 1961.

bull-moose. See **moose**.

bull of the woods. A foreman: Canadian railwaymen's and lumbermen's: since ca. 1910. (Leechman.)

bull-session. See, **bull, shoot the**.

bull-shit.—2. Hence (also in forms *bulsh* and esp. *bull*), 'excessive spit and polish' or attention to detail; regimentalism: Services: since ca. 1916. Hence, *bull-shit morning*, that morning on which the C.O.'s inspection takes place: Services: since ca. 1920.

bull-shitter. A boaster; one addicted to empty talk: since ca. 1915, esp. among Australians. Ex **bullshit, 1** (p. 105).

bull the tea. To put soda into it to make it more potent: New Zealand rural: C. 20. B., 1941.

*****bull trap.** A crook impersonating a policeman in order to extort money from amorous couples: Australian c.: since ca. 1930. B., 1942.

Bullabananka; also Bullamakanka and Willa-makanka; esp. in phrase *back of Bullabananka* (etc.), 'back of beyond': Australian coll.: since ca. 1935. Cf. **black stump . . .** above and **woop woop** (p. 964). B.P.

bullamakau. Bully beef: Australian soldiers': 1939–45. (B., 1943.) By a pun.

bulldoze. To ride roughshod over (someone); to force; to cow, to bully: adopted, ca. 1959, ex U.S.

bulldozer. A 'locomotive for shunting coaches and taking them to termini for outgoing trains' (*Railway*): railwaymen's: since ca. 1945.

bulldozing around. An aimless wandering or prowling around: Australian (at first, soldiers'): since ca. 1940. (B., 1953.)

bulled, adj. 'It was decided to give the camels and horses "bulled" water, brackish and pure water mixed' (K. S. Prichard, *Kiss on the Lips* p. 232), 1932): Australian: C. 20. Perhaps ex *bull* the cash (p. 105).

bulled(-)up, adj. Dressed as if for parade: Army: since ca. 1943. Leslie Thomas, *The Virgin Soldiers*, 1966. Ex *bull*, spit-and-polish: see **bull-shit, 2**, below.—2. Hence, 'tarted up' or ostentatiously embellished: since ca. 1945. Len Deighton, *Only When I Larf*, 1968.

buller.—2. A cow on heat, the adj. being *bulling*: Australian rural coll.: C. 20. (B., *Australia Speaks*, 1953.)

bullet.—2. (Gen. pl.) A hard, round, sweet: school-children's coll.: C. 20. From dial. and ex hardness.—3. An ace: Australian poker-players': since ca. 1918. (B., 1953.)

bullet fever, the. Self-inflicted wound(s): military: ca. 1770–1830. *The Diary of a British Soldier. May 5th, 1793 to Nov. 4th, 1795*, in the California State Library. (Communicated by S. H. Ward.)

bullet-proof. See cast iron.

bullets. Peas: Army and lower-deck Navy: C. 20. (P-G-R.)

bullgine is preferred by 'Taffrail' to *bulgine* or *bull-jine*, qq.v. in *Dict.*

bullivant. A large, clumsy person: Cockney: since ca. 1880: by 1940, slightly ob. A blend of *bull* + *elephant*. (L. H. Perraton, letter of May 28, 1938.)

bullo. Nonsense; airy or empty talk: Aus.: since late 1940's. (B., 1959.) Bull, n., 12 ('bull-shit') + the ubiquitous Aus. suffix -*o*.

bullock, n. Sense 3 occurs earlier in 'Taffrail'.

bullock, v.—3. To do (very) heavy manual work: Australian coll.: late C. 19–20. Like a 'bullocky' (p. 105). Kylie Tennant, *Lost Haven*, 1947.—4. To force (one's way): Australian coll.: C. 20. Vance Palmer, *The Passage*, 1930.

bullock puncher (p. 105). App. since ca. 1840. In, e.g., Tom Kelly, *Life in Victoria*, 1859.

bullock-waggon. Cheap, empty talk: Australian: since ca. 1925. B., 1942. Punning *bull*, nonsense. Archer Russell, 1934.

bullocker. A bullock-team driver: Australian coll.: C. 20.—2. Hence, a gang foreman: since ca. 1925. (B., 1943.)

bullock's (or bullocks') blood. 'Strong ale and rum—extremely costive' (Michael Gilbert, *The Doors Open*, 1949): public-house: since ca. 1920. He-man stuff.

bullocky (p. 105). Also a New Zealand usage. Both in New Zealand and in Australia, prob. since ca. 1840 or 1850.

bullocky's joy. Treacle; golden syrup: Australian: C. 20. (B., 1943.)

bulls.—2. *The bulls*, the police: Australian, adopted, ca. 1944, ex U.S. (Dick.)

bull's eye.—7. 'Glass used in old Lancashire and Yorkshire [Railway] hand lamp' (*Railway* 2nd): railwaymen's: ca. 1890–1925.

bull's wool.—3. Nonsense; meaningless talk; ballyhoo: New Zealand and Australia: since ca. 1920. (Niall Alexander, letter of Oct. 22, 1939; B., 1942.) Prob. ex sense 1 (p. 105).—4. The coarse wool used in Army socks: soldiers': since ca. 1880. (Kipling, *Plain Tales from the Hills*, 1888, and *passim*.)

bullshit is the more usual post-1920 way of writing bull shit (Add. and on p. 105).

bullshit, v. To 'kid' (someone) in such a way that an argument ensues: esp. Forces: since ca. 1925.

bullshit and bang-me-arse. 'Bullshit' + a little Patton-like showmanship: Army in N.W. Europe: 1944–5.

bullshit baffles brains. An Army officers' c.p.: 1939–45. Others' bullshit, the speaker's brains.

Bullshit Castle. Air Force H.Q.: New Zealand airmen's: 1939–45. (Slatter.)

Bully, The. *The* (Sydney) *Bulletin*: Australian coll.: C. 20. (B., 1943; Jean Devanney, 1944.)

bully-beef.—2. A chief (esp. warder): low rhyming s., esp. in prisons: since ca. 1919. (Norman.)—3. adj. Deaf: Scottish rhyming s. (on pron. *deef*): since ca. 1945. Franklyn 2nd.—4. See corned beef below.

bully for you! (p. 106): very common in Australia in C. 20. (B.P.)

Bully Ruffian—Eggs and Bacon—Polly In-

famous. The warships *Bellerophon—Agamemnon —Polyphemus*: Naval 'Hobson-Jobson': late C. 18–early 19. (*The Gentleman's Magazine*, Feb. 1796; quoted by Carola Oman in her *Nelson*, 1947.)

bully-splog. 'A desert dish—a ragoût of bully beef and crushed biscuits' (Peter Sanders in *The Sunday Times* magazine, Sept. 10, 1967): Army in North Africa: 1940–43.

bulsh. See bullshit above.

bum, v.—2. (p. 106): but later in Renton Nicholson, *An Autobiography*, 1860, at p. 226.— Sense 4 should be renumbered 5.—6. To come: to go: Aus.: since ca. 1920. Norman Lindsay, *Saturdee*, 1933, "'Know what you are?" he said sternly. "A stinkin' young skite. Come bummin' in here skitin' about knockin' girls you get a hidin'.'"—4. (Ex sense 2: p. 206.) To cadge: since ca. 1944. 'Can I bum a cigarette off you?'— example given by Wallace Reyburn in *The Sunday Times*, July 8, 1962.

bum, adj., was used in the fast and sporting sets of London, ca. 1885–1905, in the sense of disreputable.

bum, have a bit of. To coït with a woman: lower class: late C. 19–20.

bum, on the. See on the fritz.

bum-bags.—2. Men's bathing trunks; since ca. 1910.

bum-boy.—2. One who gets the dirty jobs to do: C. 20.

bum-brusher.—2. A batman: Australian Army: 1939+. Baker.

bum-creeper.—2. A toady: since ca. 1918.

bum-fluff. That unsightly hair which disfigures the faces of pubescent boys; these unfortunate youths are often advised to *smear it with butter and get the cat to lick it off*: Cockneys': late C. 19–20. —2. Hence (?), empty talk: Australian: C. 20. B., 1942.

bum-fodder (p. 107): prob. since ca. 1650. In 1660 an anon. (? Alexander Brome's?) verse satire on the Rump Parliament bears this arresting title: 'Bumm-Fodder; or, Waste-Paper proper to wipe the nation's rump with, or your own'.

bum freezer.—2. Hence a Midshipman's round jacket: Naval: C. 20. Granville records the variant arse-perisher.—3. The short white jacket worn by doctors in hospitals: medical: C. 20.

bum-fuck. Digital massage of prostate via anus and rectum, as diagnostical and therapeutic procedure in treatment of gonorrhœa: low: C. 20.

bum-fucker; corn-holer; gooser. A pederast: low Canadian: C. 20.

bum-licker. A toady: low coll.: C. 20.

bum (one's) load. To boast: Anglo-Irish, and Guardsmen's: since ca. 1930. Also, in R.A.F., *bum one's chat* (Atkinson): 1939+.

bum numb, adj. With posteriors partially paralysed from sitting on a hard seat or too long in one position: Public Schoolboys': C. 20.

bum-starver. A short coat: from ca. 1920. Oliver Onions, *The Open Secret*, 1930.

bum steer; esp. *give* (someone) *a bum steer*, to give bad advice or information or directions: Canadian: since ca. 1925. Also Australian, since ca. 1944.

bum-sucking: arse-crawling, q.v. Mid-C.19–20.

bum-tags. Synonymous with clinkers, 2 (p. 160): low: C. 20.—2. Hence, synonymous with bum-sucker (*Dict.*): low: since ca. 1910.

bumble jar. By 1930, however, the predominant Naval sense was gramophone. Granville.

bumble someone's rumble. See **rumble someone's bumble.**

bumblebug. An early (? the original) nickname for the flying bomb; soon superseded by **doodlebug:** mid-1944.

Bumblebus. Wildcat Aircraft of the Fleet Air Arm: Naval: World War II.

bumbo, 2 (p. 107). Earlier in *Sessions*, 1738, where it is spelt **bumbow.**

bumf (p. 107).—2. Hence, any collection of papers in which one is not interested: since ca. 1945.—3. At Rugby School, any piece of paper, e.g. a test paper (cf. **topos bumf**): late C. 19–20. *The bumfs* = the daily Press. (D. F. Wharton, 1965.)

bumf, v.—3. (Ex sense 3 of the n.) To give a test: Rugby School: C. 20. (D. F. Wharton, 1965.)

bumf, pink. A Confidential Signal pad: Naval: since ca. 1920. Granville. See **bumf,** n. (p. 107).

bumfleteer. See **bumphleteer.**

bummer.—6. A sodomite: low: C. 20. A *graffito* noted on May 1967, a correspondent tells me.

bump, n. An uneven landing; bumpy flying: R.A.F. coll.: since ca. 1919; by 1940, almost j. (H. & P.)—2. Hence any landing of an aircraft: coll.: since ca. 1930. Jackson. See **three months' bumps.**

bump, v.—5. To fight successfully: Australian: 1940+. B., 1942.—6. To polish (a wooden floor) with a 'bumper': Services': since ca. 1925. (P-G-R.)

bump across. To meet by chance: Australian: C. 20. Baker.

bump off.—2. Hence to dismiss (someone) from employment: since ca. 1940.

bumped or **pipped, get.** To be torpedoed by U-boat or even by E-boat: Naval: 1939–45.—2. Of N.C.O.s: to get reduced in rank: Army: 1939+.

bumper.—5. A cigarette end: Australian: since ca. 1920. B., 1942. Ex '*butt*' + '*stump*' + *er.*—6. An amateur rider in steeplechases: racing: since ca. 1930. His hindquarters tend to *bump.*

bumper, adj. Excellent: coll.: C. 20. Ex **bumper,** n., 3 (p. 108).

bumper, not worth a. Utterly worthless: Australian: since ca. 1930. Ex **bumper,** n., 5, above.

bumper-shooter. A picker-up of cigarette-ends: Australian: since ca. 1940. (B., *Australia Speaks*, 1953.)

bumper-sniping. The task of picking up cigarette butts: Australian soldiers': 1939–45. (B., 1943.)

bumper-up. A dockyard labourer: C. 20.—2. A pickpocket's assistant: Australian c.: since ca. 1920. (B., 1943.)—A prostitute's handyman: Australian c.: since ca. 1925. Also *bumper-upper* or *candy-bag*. (B., 1953.)

bumpers. Female breasts: Australian motorists': since ca. 1950. Cf. **buffers** above.

bumpers, ride. To ride in steeplechases: racing: since ca. 1925. (John Welcome, *Wanted for Killing*, 1965.) Cf. **bumper,** n., 6.

bumph is an occ. variant of **bumf** (*Dict.*).

bumph hunt. Variant of **bumf** hunt. See **bumf,** n. (p. 107).

bumphleteer. An aircraft (or its crew or a member thereof) engaged in pamphlet-dropping: R.A.F.: Sept. 1939–April 1940, and then the scene was changed, the war ceasing to be either 'phoney' or funny. (Jackson.)

bumping, n. Delaying or obstructing a bill: Parliamentary: since ca. 1920. Sir Alan Herbert, *Mild and Bitter*, 1936.

***bumping-off.** A murder: c.: from ca. 1932. *The Pawnshop Murder*. From U.S. and ex **bump-off** (*Dict.*).

bumps. See **three months' bumps.**

bum's rush (p. 108) is, more precisely, that method of forcible ejection which consists in the application of one hand to the seat (often a grasping of trouser-slack), the other to the neck, and the ensuing propulsion. Common to bar-tenders and police. It occurs in Liam O'Flaherty, *The Informer*, 1925.

bun, 5, is recorded by B. & L., 1889, as 'the latest synonym for *tart*', and not as specifically Glaswegian.—6. A bowler hat: New Zealand: C. 20. B., 1941. Ex the shape.—7. See **boxer.**

bun in the oven, have a. To be pregnant: low: C. 19–20.

bun on, get a. To become intoxicated: lower class: C. 20; ob. W. L. George, *The Making of an Englishman*, 1914.

bun penny. An early Queen Victoria penny showing her with hair in a bun: coll.: late C. 19–20.

bun rush. Tea (the meal): Royal Naval College, Dartmouth: C. 20. Granville.

bun shop. A Lyons Corner House: London taxidrivers': since ca. 1910. Herbert Hodge, 1939.

bun(-)trap. The mouth: low—or, at any rate, strictly non-U: C. 20. Cf. **cake-hole** below.

bun-worry.—2. (Ex sense 1: p. 108).—A jollification; a hilarious occasion; a fooling about: New Zealand and Australian: late C. 19–20. It occurs, e.g., in G. B. Lancaster's novels.

bunce. For an additional sense, see **kelp.**—4. Sheer, or almost sheer, profit; something for nothing: since ca. 1920. Ex sense 1 in its C. 20 nuances. Common, after ca. 1930, in Australia. (B., 1953.)

bunch, n.—2. The main group in a race, apart from *the breakaway*: racing cyclists' coll.: since ca. 1925.

bunch, v. (p. 108). Dr Leechman doubts its authenticity.

bunch of bastards. A tangled rope: Naval lowerdeck: since ca. 1946.

bunch of dog's meat. 'A squalling child in arms' (*Sinks*, 1848): low: ca. 1825–70.

bunch of fives (p. 108). Earlier in *Boxiana*, III, 1821. It has the Australian, esp. Sydney, variant *bunch of five*. (B.P.)

buncle or **bunkle.** A carbuncle: (dial. and) semi-literate coll.: late C. 19–20.

bund.—3 (prob. ex 1). A wall or barbed-wire fence marking the perimeter of a Station: R.A.F.: since ca. 1925. Jackson. From Persia and India.

bundle, n. See **job,** v., 4.

bundle, v.i. To fight with one's fists: low: C. 20. Brendan Behan, *Borstal Boy*, 1958, ' "Oh, so you want to bundle, you Irish bastard?" said Hanson. "Come on, then." ' Cf. **bundle up** below. Also as n.—also in Behan.

bundle, drop one's or **the** (p. 108).—2. Hence,

in New Zealand, to give birth: low: since ca. 1920.

bundle, go a. In solo whist, to bid *abundance*: ? esp. Merseyside: late C. 19–20.

bundle of socks. The head: Australian rhyming s. (on 'think-*box*'): late C. 19–20. Baker, *The Australian Language*.

bundle on, go a. See 'Jazz Slang'.

bundle on, go the. See **go the bundle on**.

bundle up. To attack (someone) in force: low: 1824, J. Wight, *Morning at Bow Street*, 'He was bundled up or enveloped, as it were, in a posse of charleys'; † by 1900.

bundo. Arrangement (whether singular or collective), as in 'What's the bundo?' or 'I've made a bundo for this evening': Regular Army, esp. in India: late C. 19–20; by 1960, slightly ob. Hindustani *bandobast*.

bundook (p. 109) has, since ca. 1920, been much in use by the R.A.F. (Jackson.)

Bundy, punch the. To register one's arrival or departure on a time-recording clock: Australian workmen's coll.: since ca. 1935. Ex the clocks formerly made by Messrs. W. H. Bundy. (B.P.)

bung, n.—7. A poke, blow, punch: low: late C. 19–20. A. Neil Lyons, *Hockey*, 1902, 'Only yesterday, said he, I got another bung in the eye'. Echoic: cf. sense 3 of the v.—8. A bungalow: since ca. 1920.—9. A bribe, esp. to the police: low: since ca. 1930. (Norman.)

bung, v.—5. To pay protection money to (someone): low: since ca. 1925. 'Sergeant Connor. He's one of them slime-sniffers [the Vice Squad]. Every girl in Bayswater bungs to him if she wants to stay on the game.' Bill Turner, *Sex Trap*, 1968.

bung, adj.—2. Ruined; bankrupt; *go bung*, to fail, to go bankrupt, to die: Australian: since ca. 1910. (B., 1943.)—2. Hence, spurious, illegal; grossly inadequate: since ca. 1925. (B., 1943.)

bung, flog the. See **flog** . . .

bung (someone) **a toffee.** To do him a favour, esp. if considerable: London's East End: since ca. 1947. (*The Evening News*, Nov. 12, 1957, article by Richard Herd.)

bung-eye. An ocular inflammation caused by flies: Australian coll.: late C. 19–20. (Sarah Campion, *Bonanza*, 1942.)

bung(-)hole. See **bung,** n., 6 (p. 109). Both *bung* and *bung hole* are also Naval of C. 20: Granville.—2. Hence (via *bread and cheese*), bread; military since ca. 1925. (H. & P.) Constipating.

bung it! Stow it!: low: late C. 19–20. Pugh (2).

bung it in; often shortened to *bung it*. Gin (the drink): rhyming s.: since ca. 1920. Michael Harrison, letter of Jan. 4, 1947.

bung it on. To spend lavishly in, e.g., catering; to 'put on a good show' (party, reception, etc.): Australian since ca. 1918. (B.P.) Ex **bung on side**.

bung on an act. 'To swear luridly, give way to temper, complain at length' (B., 1959): Aus.: since ca. 1920.

bung on side. To put on 'side', to show off: low Australian coll.: since ca. 1910. (Kylie Tennant, 1953.)

bung-ons. Gifts: mock-auctions': since ca. 1930. Cf. **bung,** v., 2, on p. 109, and **bung it on** above.

bung up and bilge free. By 1920, sense 1 (p.

109) was coll.; by 1930, j.—2. Hence, of a sailor enjoying a rest or sleep: Naval: since ca. 1910. Granville.—3. A Naval c.p. (late C. 19–20) for *femina in coitu*. Ex the description of the correct position for a rum cask.

Bungay!, go to (p. 109). In C. 19 in Suffolk there was the phrase *go to Bungay for a bottom*—or *to get new-bottomed*, applied to repairs for wherries.

bungdung. A large cracker; a firework: Australian: since ca. 1920. (B., 1943.) Echoic. 'Formed on *bundook*?' (Leechman.)

bunged. Tipsy: South Africa: since ca. 1935. Prof. W. S. Mackie in *The Cape Argus*, July 4, 1946. Cf. **bung-eyed** (*Dict.*).

bunged up. Damaged, stove-in, clogged: coll.: late C. 19–20.

bunger. Ponga (a New Zealand plant): New Zealand: since ca. 1860; slightly ob. by 1926. B., 1941. By 'Hobson-Jobson'.

bungie (p. 109). Also and orig. *ingie-bungie*, the *ingie* referring to *ink*.

Bungs. See 'Prisoner-of-War Slang', 8.

Bungy. Naval nickname for anyone named Williams: C. 20. Granville. Also a fairly common nickname of men surnamed Edwards or Edwardes: C. 20. Why?

bungy.—2. Punger, plant and flower: New Zealand coll.: late C. 19–20. (Jean Devanney, 1928.)

bungy-eye. A variant of *bung-eye*.

bungy (or -ie) man (p. 109). After ca. 1925, often shortened to *bungy* (or -*je*). Granville.

bunk, n.—3. Hence 'a small Corporals' Barrack Room usually just outside the Men's Barrack Room. It contains their bunks or beds; the Corporals *bunk down* (or "kip" or sleep) there,' Partridge, 1945: R.A.F. coll. (since ca. 1925) >, by 1944, j.—4. 'Freight or passenger train on Wallingford or Abingdon branches' (*Railway* 2nd): railwaymen's: ? ca. 1920–50.—5. A Canadian term of disapproval for anything disliked or unwanted: since ca. 1920. Ex sense 1.

bunk, v.—5. A synonym of **double-dink** below. (B., 1959.)

bunk off. Australian variant of **bunk,** v., 1 (*Dict.*): C. 20. B., 1942.

bunk over, v.i. To cross: coll.: C. 20. E.g., 'bunk over to see a person'.

bunk-up, n.; less gen. **bunk up,** v.t. Assistance, to assist, in climbing: Cockneys': C. 20. '"Can you give us a bunk-up?" "Yus, I'll bunk you up, Bill."'—2. To *have a bunk-up*, to have casual sexual intercourse: Forces': 1939+.

bunk-wife. A landlady: St Andrews University students': C. 20.

Bunker. A fairly common nickname of men surnamed Lewis or Lewes: C. 20. Why?

bunkle. See **buncle**.

bunny.—5. A dupe: Australian c. and low s.: C. 20. Ex senses 1, 2. n.—6. One who stupidly talks too much: Teddy boys': since ca. 1954. (Gilderdale, 2.)—7. A talk, a chat: low: since ca. 1945. (Norman.) Ex the verb.—8. Someone not fully alert (not 'with it'): Australian: since ca. 1925. Hence, *the bunny*, 'Mr Muggins' or the willing horse. (B.P.).—9. A sanitary towel: women's: since ca. 1920. Perhaps cf. sense 4 (p. 110).—10. A pilotman: railwaymen's: since ca. 1945. *Railway*, 3rd.—11. A waitress at a Playboy Club: raffish: since late 1950's. She is costumed like a rabbit.

bunny, v. To talk, to chat: low: since ca. 1945. (Norman.) Ex rabbit, v., 3.

Buns. C. T. Thornton (1850–1929), famous Eton and, in 1869–72, Cambridge cricketer: cricketers': Sir Home Gordon, *The Background of Cricket*, 1939.

bunter's tea. Strong liquor (? gin): ca. 1715–60. Anon., *The Quaker's Opera*, 1728. 'Quaker. . . . What hast thou got? *Poorlean*. Sir, you may have what you please, Wind or right Nanty or South-Sea, or Cock-my-Cap, or Kill-Grief, or Comfort, or White Tape, or Poverty, or Bunter's Tea, or Apricock-Water, or Roll-me-in-the-Kennel, or Diddle or Meat Drink-Washing-and-Lodging, or Kill-Cobler, or in plain English, Geneva.'

bunts (see bunting-tosser, p. 110) is far from being ob.: *Weekly Telegraph*, Oct. 25, 1941.

bunyip. A humbug, an imposter: Australian: since ca. 1860. Tom Collins, *Such is Life*, 1903. The bunyip is a fabulous Australian animal.

bupper (*Dict.*) occurs also as *buppie, bups, bupsie*, both as bread and butter in gen. and as a slice thereof in particular.

burble (p. 110) occurs in H. C. Bailey, *Rimingtons*, 1904.

Burdett Coutts, often shortened to *Burdetts*. Boots: rhyming s.: since ca. 1925. Ex the name of the well-known bankers.

burg(h)er. A Hamburg(h)er: adopted in 1942 from the U.S.

[Burglars' tools in late C. 17–18 are: *bess* (q.v.) or *betty* (q.v.), *crow* (prob. always S.E.) and *jack* (ditto); the first two are in B.E., the last three in Ned Ward (1714, 1703, 1703). Matthews.]

burk. To avoid work: New Zealand: ca. 1880–1920. (G. B. Lancaster, *Sons o' Men*, 1904, 'I'll exchange. . . . But I won't burk, see?' Rhyming with *shirk*?

burk(e). A misspelling of *berk*. (Gerald Kersh, *Faces in a Dusty Picture*, 1944: *burke*.)

Burke. *Burke's Peerage:* bookmen's and librarians' coll.: mid-C. 19–20.

burke, v., 1. It occurs in *Sessions*, 1832, or nearly forty years earlier than the *Dict.* recording.

Burker. A body-snatcher: ca. 1830–50. In, e.g., W. Chadwick, *Reminiscences of a Chief Constable*, 1900. See burke (p. 111).

burking. Vbl n. of burke (*Dict.*).

burl; esp. in *give it a burl*. To give something a chance; make an attempt: low Australian: C. 20. Kylie Tennant, *Foveaux*, 1939. Perversion of *hurl*? By 1950, no longer low—if, indeed, it ever was! (B.P.) Cf. the Canadian and English *give it a whirl*.

burley. Nonsense, humbug: Australian: C. 20. Baker. Origin? B.P. thinks that the orig. form was *berley*; so does Webster's 3rd edition—which defines the term as 'ground bait'. Therefore burl above, as in 'give it a *burl*', is prob. a variant of *berl*, itself short for *berley*. If a fisherman uses *berley*, he is, after all, trying to catch a fish.

Burlington Bertie. A fop, a dude: since ca. 1909; ob. by 1940, † by 1960. Ex Vesta Tilley's famous song, *Burlington Bertie from Bow*, ca. 1908.—2. Hence, since ca. 1912, any young fellow who dresses up in his leisure or even at work; by 1960, †.

Burlington Hunt. A faulty, not very common, deformation of Berkshire (or Berkeley) Hunt. (Franklyn, *Rhyming*.)

Burma Road. Rice: Army in the Far East: 1942+. Rice is the staple Burmese food.—2. Hence, in 1943–5, in Service messes in Irak and Persia, 'as an exclamation at frequent rice' (Atkinson).

Burmese stocking. In Indian Army s., from ca. 1886, as in Richards, concerning the natives of Upper Burma: 'At a very early age the males were tattooed around the legs with rings of what looked like grinning devils. This was called "the Burmese stocking" and was supposed to avert illness and enchantment.'

burn, n. A 'showing-off' burst of fast driving: Australian motorists': since late 1940's. A motorist 'burns' his tyres. (B.P.) Cf. burn off below.—2. A thrill, as in 'We came up by car for a burn' (Dick): Australian teenagers'; since ca. 1950.

burn, v.—2. To smoke (tobacco): late C. 19–20. Hence also n., as in:—

burn, have a. To have a smoke: Naval: C. 20. Granville. By 1950, also fairly general low s. (Norman.)

burn, twist a. To roll a cigarette: Australian Naval: since ca. 1918. (B., 1943.) Cf. preceding.

burn off, v.i. To drive very fast, esp. if 'showing off': Australian motorists': since late 1940's. (B.P.)

burn the grass. See grass.

burn-up, n. esp. *have a burn-up*, to race in a car or on a motor cycle: mostly teenagers': since ca. 1955. They 'burn up' the road.—2. A marked blush: Rugby School: since late 1950's. (David Wharton.)

burn up, v. To blush; to become very much embarrassed: Rugby School: since late 1950's. (David Wharton.)

burn-up, the. 'One of the most ingenious of confidence tricks' (John Gosling, *The Ghost Squad*, 1959), involving a gang of three or four: adopted, ca. 1946, ex U.S.

burnt.—3. Short for burnt cinder (p. 111).

buro, on the. Out of work and drawing the dole: Glasgow coll.: from ca. 1921. MacArthur & Long. I.e. *bureau*. Or perhaps *on the Borough*.

burp. Esp. of a baby, to eructate; also v.t., to cause (a baby) to belch: late C. 19–20 (? very much earlier): coll. >, by 1920 at latest, S.E. Hence, *burp at both ends*, to pass wind from throat and anus simultaneously: Australian s.: since ca. 1930. (B.P.) Oddly, this word didn't reach the dictionaries until the 1930's. Echoic—cf. gurk (p. 362).

Also, derivatively, n.: C. 20. Both v. and n. have alternative spelling *birp*. Early in 1967, Dr R. L. Mackay, M.D., resident there for some forty years, remarks that, 'in Wolverhampton, *birp* is used in the conversation of the uppermost classes, *rift* by the middle class, and *belch* by the remainder, which may include some public schoolboys'. Note that whereas *belch* is, of course, S.E., *rift* was—and is—a very widespread Northern and Midland dial. term.

Burriis. The. The Burma Rifles: war of 1939–45. Cf. Rajrifs, Rajputana Rifles.

burry. An Aboriginal: Australian: since ca. 1910. (B., 1943.) Ex the burrs in his beard?

Burse, the. The Bursar: colleges' and schools': late C. 19–20.

burst, n.—5. A succession of bullets fired by a

machine-gun: C. 20.: coll. >, by 1941, j. Jackson.

burst, v.—3. To close (v.i.): see gaff street.

burst into flames. See what do you expect me to do?

burster, 1 (p. 112). Earlier in *Sinks*, 1848, as a loaf of bread. See twopenny burster.

Burton, gone for a. See gone for a Burton.

bury it. See dip one's wick.

burying the baby. A c.p. indicative of profit made out of the knowledge of a discreditable or even a guilty secret: from ca. 1910. Ex 'A knows where B buried the baby' and profits accordingly. (*The Times Literary Supplement*, March 20, 1937.)

bus, n., 5 (p. 112). 'Used now very rarely,' Jackson, 1943: indeed it was, by flying officers, rather frowned upon in 1917–18, its vogue having ended for them.—7. (Ex sense 2.) An omnibus volume: book-world: since ca. 1940. E.g., *the Birmingham bus*—a book of stories by George A. Birmingham; orig., jocular.

bus-boy. 'One whose duty it is to clear tables in a restaurant' (Leechman): Canadian: adopted, ca. 1935, ex U.S. Perhaps ex French s. *omnibus*, a kind of apprentice in the restaurant business.

bus-conductor. A sub-conductor, R.A.O.C. (a technical W.O.1): Army: since ca. 1947.

bus(-)driver. A bomber pilot: R.A.F.: since early 1940. 'So called because he is usually on a well-beaten route,' H. & P. See bus, n., 5 (*Dict.* and prec. entry).

bush, n.—3. Pubic hair: low (mid-C. 19–20) after being a literary euphemism. Whence, by facetious derivation, Bushy Park (*Dict.*).—4. Hence, a girl or young woman: Australian: since ca. 1920. B., 1942.—5. (Also cf. 3.) A moustache: Australian: since ca. 1925. Baker. Ex *bushy moustache?*—6. The suburbs: Australian urban: since ca. 1930. (B., 1943.) Ex the Australian sense of S.E. *bush*.

bush, adj. Rough and ready: inferior: Australian coll.: late C. 19–20. Esp. in bush lawyer (*Dict.*). In New Zealand also; esp., *bush carpenter* (or *carpentry*): since ca. 1910. (Niall Alexander, letter of Oct. 22, 1939.)—2. Hiding in 'the bush': Australian: since 1910. Ion M. Idriess, *Man Tracks*, 1935, 'Paddy and Yankee were still "bush" on their *pinki* [walkabout], staying bush for a long long time.'

bush, go.—2. Hence, to escape from gaol and disappear: Australian c.: since ca. 1910. B., 1942. Also *take to the bush*. Ex Aboriginals that revert to the savage state.—3. To seek the peace—the solitude—of the bush: Australian coll.: C. 20. (K. S. Prichard, *Working Bullocks*, 1926.)

bush, up the. Out in the country: Australian coll.: C. 20. B., 1942.

bush ape. Usually in the pl. A worker in the country. Australian coll.: C. 20. B., 1942.—2. A fruit picker: South Australian: C. 20. Baker.

bush artillery. Men not normally considered as fighting men (cooks, clerks, etc.) who manned all sorts of guns during the siege of Tobruk. (Australian.)—2. 'Captured Italian guns manned by odds and sods in the siege of Tobruk' (Peter Sanders, *The Sunday Times* magazine, Sept. 10, 1967): Army in North Africa: W.W. II.

bush Baptist. A person of either dubious or no religious denomination: Aus.: late C. 19–20. I remember hearing it during W.W. I; B., 1959.

*bush bunny. A simpleton; a dupe: Australian c.: since ca. 1920. (B., 1953.)

bush carpenter. A rough-and-ready carpenter: Aus. coll.: C. 20. (B., 1959.)

bush dinner; bushman's hot dinner. Resp., 'mutton, damper and tea' and 'damper and mustard': Australian coll.: late C. 19–20. B., 1942.

bush fire, full of. (Very) energetic; high spirited; (very) plucky: Australian: C. 20. Baker.

bush(-)league, adj. Second-rate: Canadian, adopted, ca. 1930, ex U.S. Ex the leagues of minor baseball teams. (Leechman.)

bush radio or bush wireless are post-1930 forms of *bush telegraph*. (B., 1943.)

bush scrubber.—2. a rural prostitute: Australian: C. 20. Baker.

bush-tail, adj. Cunning: Australian coll.: C. 20. Baker.

bush telegram or telegraph. Unfounded report or rumour: Australian coll.: C. 20. Baker. An early Australian occurs in Ion M. Idriess, *Man Tracks*, 1935.

bush up. To confuse or baffle: Australian: C. 20. Baker. Cf. bush, v., 2 (*Dict.*).

Bush Week; esp. in *What do you think this is—Bush Week?*, 'a c.p. used when someone has proposed something very "fishy"' (B.P.): Australian: since ca. 1945. (It occurs in, e.g., Lawson Glassop, *Lucky Palmer*, 1949.) Sometimes *or Christmas* is added. The time of the local agricultural and pastoral show, when the 'city slickers', esp. the 'con men', fleece the rustics. There is, by the way, no such thing as a *Bush Week*. (B.P.)

bushed.—2. Amazed: Marlborough College: since late 1920's.—3. 'Suffering from mild or serious mental derangement caused by long solitude in the bush. Once a very common and serious trouble, especially among trappers and prairie farmers' wives. Now much mitigated by the wireless which provides human contact even if only mechanically. "Harry's been alone for a couple of years now. He must be pretty well bushed."'—A Canadian coll.: (?) late C. 19–20. (Leechman.)

bushed, be (cf. bush, v., 2, on p. 112, and bushed, 3, above): since ca. 1920, the predominant Australian sense has been 'to have lost one's bearings'. (B.P.)

bushel bubby (p. 112). Cf. the witty Fr. c.p.: 'Elle a du monde au balcon'.

bushel of coke. A 'bloke': rhyming s.: C. 20. Franklyn, *Rhyming*.

bushfire blonde. A red-head: Australian: since ca. 1925. (B., 1943.)

bushies. People living in the outback or 'bush': Australian: since ca. 1925. (B., 1953.)

bushman's clock. A kookaburra: Australian coll.: late C. 19–20. The laughing jackass.

bushman's hot dinner. See bush dinner.

bushranger.—2. Hence, a petty swindler; an unethical opportunist: Australian: since ca. 1910. Baker.

bushwa. A polite Canadian variant of *bull-shit*: since ca. 1916.

bushwhackers. Commandos that went to Rangoon, just before its fall, to do salvage work: Australian: 1942. (O. D. Gallagher, *Retreat in the East*, 1942.)

business.—6. Defecation, faeces; esp. in *do one's business*: nursery coll.: mid-C. 19–20. Cf., semantically, *do a job for oneself*.

business, on the. See business girl, a.

business, quite a. Something unexpectedly difficult to do, obtain, etc.: coll.: late C. 19–20. See business (p. 112).

business, three-stride. See three-stride business (*Dict.*).

business as usual, despite difficulty and danger, was a c.p. of W.W. I; in the 1930's it became ironic; in W.W. II, if used at all, mostly literal; since then, a condemnation of complacency. (William Safire, *The New Language of Politics,* 1968 —an entertaining and valuable book.)

business end, the. For sense 2, an earlier example is in E. H. Hornung, *Raffles,* 1899: 'The business ends of the spoons'.

*business girl, a. Prostitutes' favourite description of themselves: i.e. harlots' c.p.: from ca. 1921. Likewise, **on the business** is favourable, whereas *on the bash, batter, game,* are pejorative for 'engaged in prostitution, esp. at the moment'.

busk, 2, dates (esp. as vbl n. *busking*) back to the 1850's in the sense, to play, sing, dance in public-houses.

*busker. As a nuance of sense 1: among tramps, in C. 20, a *busker* is a man that plays an instrument in the street.

*busnapper. A policeman: Australian c.: C. 20. Baker. A napper or capturer of those who are engaged in 'the buzz' (see buzz, n. 2: p. 116).

buso, go. See 'Prisoner-of-War Slang', 6.

buss, adv. Only: Regular Army: C. 20, virtually † by 1946. Thus, 'He had his coat on buss'—he was wearing only his coat.

bussie or **bussy.** A bus-worker: coll.: since ca. 1940. *Reynolds,* Nov. 18, 1945.

bust, n., 2 (a burglary), survives in Australian c., a sin ' "Mortman the bustman!" Rene sneered. "Listen to him big-note himself. He's going to do a bust",' Kylie Tennant, *The Joyful Condemned,* 1953.—3. A police search or raid: drug addicts', hippies', Flower People's: adopted, in late 1950's, ex U.S. (*The Observer* colour supplement, Dec. 3, 1967.)

bust a frog! 'Well, I'm damned!': Cockneys': mid-C. 19–20; by 1940, ob.

bust (a policeman's) **beat.** To commit a crime on it: police: since ca. 1910. (*The Free-Lance Writer,* April 1948.)

bust the rut. To blaze a trail: Northern Territory, Australia: since ca. 1925. (Ernestine Hill, *The Territory,* 1951.) Baker, 1959, prefers *bust a rut.*

Buster. 'A name for anybody whose real name may or may not be known to the speaker. Usually but not necessarily pejorative. "Now listen here, Buster, this means trouble!" ' (Leechman): Canadian: adopted, ca. 1920, ex U.S.

buster, go in a. To spend regardless of expense: mostly Cockneys': from ca. 1885; ob. Anstey, *Voces Populi,* vol. II, 1892.

*bustle, on the. Cadging; engaged in the sly acquisition of small objects: Australian c.: since ca. 1920. (B., 1943.)

*bustman. See bust above.

busy as a one-armed paper-hanger, as. Bustlingly, or excessively, busy: New Zealand: since ca. 1939. (Slatter.) 'Common in Canada also,' says Dr Leechman, who cites the lengthened . . . *with the itch.*

busy foot, have a. (Of a horse) to be speedy: Australian: since ca. 1920. Baker.

but, conj. at end of sentence, precisely as *however* is often thus used in informal speech: Aus.: since ca. 1935. Nino Culotta's novel, *Cop This Lot,* 1960, contains many examples, as ' "Yer gettin' enough to eat, ain't yer?"—"Gettin' enough, matey. Dunno the bloody names, but." '

Butch. A nickname given to boys by fathers proud of their own muscles and virility and desirous of the same qualities in their offspring: Canadian coll.: adopted, ca. 1920, ex U.S. Ex S.E. *butcher.* (Leechman.)

butch, n. An obviously active, as opposed to a passive, male homosexual: American, adopted, ca. 1950, by English-speaking homosexuals everywhere. It occurs in, e.g., Evelyn Waugh, *The Ordeal of Gilbert Pinfold,* 1957.—2. Hence, a Lesbian; loosely, a masculine sort of woman: homosexuals' (both sexes'): since ca. 1945. Cf. dike below.

butcher, n., 1 (p. 114), is extant among Australian poker-players.—5. A (careless) barber: Australian, esp. Sydney: since ca. 1945. (B.P.)— 6. A medical student: University of Sydney undergraduates': C. 20. (B.P.)—7. 'A small glass of beer'—a South Australian term, equivalent to the *pony* or *lady's waist* of N.S.W.

Butcher, the. William Augustus, Duke of Cumberland (1721–65): from 1746. On account of his severity towards the fugitives of the Young Pretender. The taunt was not wholly merited.

butcher's. Noon: low (parlyaree): 1893, R. H. Emerson, *Signor Lippo.*

butcher's apron. A blue-and-white striped blazer; at a certain Scottish Public School: late C. 19–20. Ian Miller, *School Tie,* 1935. Ex the colouring.—2. The ribbon of the United Nations medal for active service in Korea. Ex the narrow vertical white stripes and the washed-out blue. (*The Sunday Times,* Feb. 20, 1955.)

butcher's bill (p. 114) occurs 'way back in 1829, as a Naval term: Fredk Marryat, *Frank Mildmay* (p. 68 of the 1897 edition), 'Having delivered his "butcher's bill", i.e., the list of killed and wounded . . .' Moe.

butcher's canary. A blowfly: Australian: since ca. 1925. Baker. It infests butchers' shops and buzzes loudly.

butcher's daughter, like the. A c.p. used as an elaboration of **dripping for it** (below): perhaps esp., but far from being only, Australian: since ca. 1910.

butcher's shop, the. The execution shed: prison officers': late C. 19–20. Ernest Raymond, *We the Accused,* 1935.

butt.—2. A buttery: Oxford and Cambridge undergraduates': mid-C. 19–20. (Marples, 2.) Also at certain schools, e.g. Dulwich.

butter-basher. A taxi-cabman employed during the 1913 taxicab strike: taxicab drivers': 1913. Herbert Hodge, *Cab, Sir?,* 1939. 'These new drivers, it was rumoured, were mostly unemployed shop assistants drawn mainly from the "grocery and provision" trade.'

butter boy.—2. (Usually in pl.) A sailor: Army: since ca. 1945.

butter in one's eyes, have no. To be clear-sighted, hence alert and shrewd: coll.: ca. 1810– 70. Alfred Burton, *Johnny Newcome,* 1818. (Moe.)

Butter-Nut (p. 115). 'The Confederate soldiers' clothes were often dyed with butternut bark' (Leechman).

butter-patter. A grocery or dairy shop assistant: C. 20. Often contemptuous. Cf. *butter basher*.

butter-slide (p. 115). Prob. ex the sense current ca. 1850–90, 'a mischievous trick of Victorian small boys who put a lump of butter down where their elders would tread on it and take a fall', Andrew Haggard, letter of Jan. 28, 1947.

butter-snout. 'An epithet hurled at people cursed with a nose oily in appearance': ca. 1890–1920. (Leechman, 'I first heard it at Gravesend in 1905'.)

butterboy; butter(-)boy. A novice taxi-driver: taxi-drivers': 'coined during the 1913 cab strike'. (Herbert Hodge, 1939.) Cf. **butter-fingers** (*Dict.*).

buttered eggs in one's breeches, make. To defecate through fear: mid-C. 17–18.

butterfly.—3. A coin that, when tossed, fails to spin: Australian two-up players': late C. 19–20. Baker.

butterfly, v., corresponds to *butterfly, n.,* 3.

butterfly cabman. A taxi-driver working only in the summer: taxi-drivers': since ca. 1910. Herbert Hodge, 1939.

buttinski (or **-sky**). 'The one-piece telephone used by P.M.G. linesmen' (B.P.): since ca. 1930. Ex sense 1 (p. 115).

buttock (p. 115) is, by James Dalton, in *A Narrative*, 1728, defined as 'One that dispenses her Favours without Advantage'—free of charge.

button.—4. Clitoris: low: C. 19–20.

button, off the. See **start off the button.**

button, win the. See **win the button.**

button B. Penniless; very short of money: since ca. 1938. I.e. *pushed for money* as Button B is in a telephone-booth when you want your money back.

button lurk, the. The 'dodge' whereby a plausible man removes from his coat a button to serve as a contraceptive pessary when a girl insists on protected coïtion: Australian since ca. 1915. Prob., as a correspondent has suggested, a Serviceman's trick.

button-tosser. A radio telegraphist: Australian Naval: since ca. 1925. (B., 1943.)

button (up) your lip! Stop talking (now)!; say nothing (later)!: Canadian c.p.: adopted, ca. 1935, ex U.S.

button your flap! Be quiet!—stop talking!: Naval: since ca. 1920. H. & P. In ref. to fly of male trousers: cf. **keep one's lip buttoned.**

buttoned has, since ca. 1940, often been used for:—

buttoned up. (Of a situation, a plan, a job) well in hand, all prepared: Services: since ca. 1935. *The English Digest*, Feb. 1941, Hector Bolitho. Admitting neither wind nor water. Cf. **laid on** and **teed up.**

buttons, damn (one's)! A (? mostly Naval) expletive: 1834, W. N. Glascock, *The Naval Sketch-Book*, II, 186, 'The slop-sellers d—n their buttons, and laugh in their sleeve'. (Moe.) Cf. **dash one's buttons** on p. 116.

buttons, get one's. To be promoted from Leading Hand to Petty Officer: Wrens' coll.; since ca. 1939. Granville, 'Given a set of brass buttons to replace the black ones on her uniform.'

butty (p. 116). Perhaps cf. the U.S. *buddy*.—2. Buttered bread: Liverpool: late C. 19–20.

butty-boat. A boat working in company with another; esp. a boat towed by a motor-boat: canal-men's: C. 20. L.T.C. Rolt, *Narrow Boat*, 1944. See **butty** (p. 116).

buturakie. To jump on a person and either rob him or beat him up: 'used in Fiji and understood in Auckland and Sydney along the waterfront where it was picked up from Fijian or part-Fijian sailors. The equivalent of the Australian *put the boot in*. From Fijian *buturaka*' (Edwin Morrisby, letter of Aug. 30, 1958).

buxed. 'Hard up'; without money: London schools': ca. 1870–95. A perversion of *busted*: cf. **broke** and **smashed up.**

Buxton bloaters. Fat men and women wheeled in bath-chairs, at Buxton: late C. 19–early 20. (R. G. Heapes, 1948.)

buy, as in 'a good buy'. A purchase: coll.: adopted, ca. 1956, ex U.S.

buy, v., 1 (p. 116) goes back to ca. 1800. It occurs in W. N. Glascock, *The Naval Sketch-Book*, I (p. 27), 1825. (Moe.)

buy a prop! Buy some stock!: stockbrokers' c.p.: from ca. 1885. B. & L. 'The market is flat and there is nobody to support it.'

buy and sell (someone), **able to.** To be much superior (orig., financially) to: coll.: since ca. 1920.

buy it. Usually *He bought it* (or *He bought a packet*), he was shot down: R.A.F.: 1939+. H. & P., both forms: Brickhill & Norton, *Escape to Danger*, 1946, the shorter. Ex *I'll buy it*, q.v. at **buy it**, p. 116, and **I'll bite.**—2. In the other Services: to become a casualty: 1940+. Both of these senses were, however, current during World War I; more in the Navy and the R.F.C.-R.A.F. than in the Army.—3. '"Oh, no! I won't buy that!" I'll not accept that as an excuse or an argument' (Leechman): since ca. 1930. Cf. **buy it, I'll**, on p. 116.

buzz, n., 3. Adopted, ca. 1937, by the R.A.F (H. & P.)—4. Hence, news: Naval (—1940). Michie & Graebner, *Their Finest Hour*, 1940, p. 118.

buzz, n.—5. The n. corresponding to sense 1 of the v. (p. 116): mid-C. 19–20. 'It's your buzz' = It's time you filled your glass. (Marples, 2.)—6. A pickpocket: c.: C. 18–early 19. James Dalton, *A Narrative*, 1728, 'They might defy all the *Buzzes* in *London* to *haul the Cly*'—i.e. to steal their purses.

buzz, v., 1 (p. 116): much earlier in Anon., *Tyburn's Worthies*, 1722.

buzz about, or **around, like a blue-arsed fly.** To be—or appear to be—excessively or officiously busy: late C. 19–20.

buzz-merchant. A constant spreader of rumours: Australian Naval: 1939–45. (B., 1943.)

buzzard.—2. See **old buzzard.**

buzz-box (p. 116): esp., a noisy taxicab: 1939, Herbert Hodge, *Cab, Sir?*

buzzer.—6. A telephone, esp. on a house telephone system: Services: since ca. 1939. H. & P.—7. That workman who 'puts wet yarn or cloth under hydro-extracting machines' (*The Evening News*, Sept. 28, 1955): industrial: C. 20. Also coll. *slinger* or *swisser* or *whizzer* or *wuzzer*. All are echoic; all, originally, were s. (or dial. > s.); ever since ca. 1940, they have been semi- or entirely official.

buzzing. Law-copyists' s., dating from ca. 1870, as in Edwin Pugh, *Harry the Cockney*, 1912, 'They were both writing swiftly and beautifully the words that McGuffney dictated, this arrangement being known as "buzzing" from the use of the word "buzz" to indicate the end of a line.'

buzzing about like a blue-arsed fly. Ostentatiously active: Cockney (C. 20) and Army and R.A.F. (1939–45).

by Christchurch, hooya? Juvenile c.p.: New Zealand: C. 20. B., 1941. Euphemistic and Maorified form of 'By crikey, who are you?'

by hand, adj. (in the predicate), as in *church by hand*, improvised: Naval: since ca. 1910.

by the (bloody) centre or **left!** Military oaths, slightly euphemistic: C. 20. Ex the Manual of Instructions.

by the great god Bingo! A c.p. sort of asseveration: since ca. 1962. Satirical of the craze for the game.

***byce.** See **bice.**

bye-bye for just now!, frequently preceded by **well—.** Blaker, referring to the latter half of 1916, though it was still used early in 1917: 'An infantry phrase of the moment.'

by(e)-lo. A bed; to sleep: children's: C. 20. A variant of **by(e)-bye(s)** (*Dict.*).

byoke. See 'Prisoner-of-War Slang', 7.

C

C or K or M or O. One's, or the, *C.B.E.*—
Knighthood—*M.B.E.*—*O.B.E.*: Civil Servants'
hence clubmen's; C. 20.

C. and E. Such Church of England (*C. of E.*)
members as go to church only at Christmas *and*
*E*aster: jocular since ca. 1945. (A. B. Petch,
April 1966.)

C.B.—2. Sir Henry Campbell-Bannerman (1836–
1908), who was Prime Minister during the last three
years of his life: mostly political and journalistic:
from ca. 1895; ob.

C.D.F. Common sense: Naval lower deck:
since ca. 1930. For Naval '*common dry fuck*',
common sense.

C.G.I. or Corticene-Grabber's itch. A strong
desire to throw oneself upon the ship's deck
during a dive-bombing attack: Australian Naval:
1940–5. (B., 1943.) A cork floor-covering.

C.O. bloke. A Public Carriage Officer: taxi-
drivers': since ca. 1918. Herbert Hodge, *Cab,
Sir?*, 1939.

C.P.R. strawberries. Prunes: Canadian railwaymen's: since ca. 1918–40. (Priestley.)

cab, n.—6. A cabbage: Shelta: C. 18–20.
B. & L.—7. A motor-car: Naval: since ca. 1920.
(P-G-R.)—8. A lavatory: Felixstowe Ladies'
College: since ca. 1925. Perhaps ex sense 4 of
caboose.

cab-moll.—2. 'A prostitute in a brothel': low:
ca. 1840–1910. Ibid.

cab-rank. 'A destroyer "trot" or a line of motor
launches, motor torpedo boats, etc.' (P-G-R.):
Naval: since ca. 1925.

cab-rank technique. 'A number of aircraft
raiding in line, one after the other' (P-G-R.):
Air Force coll., verging on j.: 1940 +.

cab-ranker. A cheap cigar: C. 20. Gilbert
Frankau, *Peter Jackson, Cigar Merchant*, 1920.
Prompted by cabbagio perfumo and punning on
rank, evil-smelling.

cab-talk. Taxi-cabmen's cab-shelter gossip,
sometimes contemptuously called *cabology*: taxi-
drivers' coll.: resp., since ca. 1910, 1925. Herbert
Hodge uses both terms in, *Cab, Sir?*, 1939.

cabbage, n.—9. A bomb: R.A.F.: since 1939.
Jackson, 'Thus, "And then we sowed our cab-
bages". (See "egg", "cookies", "groceries".)'
—10. Lettuce: Cranbrook School: C. 20.—For
additional information on sense 1 of the n. and the
v. (p. 118) see kibosh below.—11. Paper money:
Canadian c. (C. 20) >, ca. 1950, (low) Canadian s.

Cabbage Gardens, the (p. 118). Also Cabbage
Garden Patch, whence *cabbage-gardener* or *-patcher*,
a Victorian. (B., 1943.) In 1959 B. notes the
derivative *The Cabbage Patch*.

cabbage-leaf.—2. The tiny bronze oak-leaf worn
on medal ribbon, to indicate a mention in despatches: Services': 1914–18, and decreasingly
since. (V. M. Yeates, *Winged Victory*, 1934, at p.
259.)

cabbage leaves. See who's smoking cabbage
leaves?

Cabbage-Stalks, the. See Ox-Tails, the.

cabbage tree!, my. An Australian exclamation:
? ca. 1920–50. (B., 1943.)

cabbagio perfumo; flor di cabbagio. A cheap,
rank cigar; jocular: late C. 19–20. Ex *cabbage* +
the Sp. suffix *-o*.

Cabby. A fairly common nickname of men
surnamed Harris: C. 20. Why?

cabin-boy's breeches, the. Southern nautical,
esp. around Chatham and Rochester, from ca. 1870,
as in Neil Bell, *Crocus*, 1936, '"Dog's nose [q.v.]
with a squirt of rum," Delfontaine replied;
"called round here, the cabin boy's breeches and
up in the north Devil's rot-gut."'

cabology. See cab-talk.

caboose.—4. An office; a small cabin or compartment: Naval: C. 20. Cf. *caboose*, 1 (p.
119).—5. 'Brake van. Used especially of uncomfortable box tacked on back of liner train for
ornamental purposes only (W R)': railwaymen's:
since late 1940's. *Railway*, 3rd.

cache. A private store or reserve, esp. of
under-the-counter goods: coll.: since ca. 1910;
by 1950, S.E.

cackle-berry (p. 119). Also, since ca. 1943 (ex
U.S. servicemen), Australian. D'Arcy Niland,
The Shiralee, 1945.

cackle one's fat. 'To brag; to express self-
opinionated, esp. if contradictory, point of view'
(Laurie Atkinson, noting its use on April 29, 1960):
low: since late 1940's.

cackler's ken. See cackler, 3 (*Dict.*).

cacky. Human excrement: mostly children's
and, domestically, women's coll.: since ca. 1880.
Ex cack (p. 119).

cacky, adj. Of or like excrement, hence yellow-
ish-brown; hence, filthy, malodorous: coll.,
mostly children's: late C. 19–20. Ex cack on p.
119.

cacto. *Cactoblastus* (an insect): Australian
coll.: C. 20. B., 1942.

cactus, in the. In an awkward situation: Australian and New Zealand: since ca. 1925.

cad, 2 (p. 119): rather, since ca. 1820, for it
occurs in Wm Maginn, *Whitehall*, 1827.—8. A
private tutor: Eton: ca. 1810–60. *Spy*, 1825.
Cf. sense 1 (p. 119).

[cadaver!, by my. A Cockney oath: from ca.
1880; ob. Pugh (2).]

Cadborosaurus (affectionately, Caddie) is 'a
mythical (?) sea monster . . . often reported
near Victoria, B.C. Named after a local bay—
Cadboro Bay, where it was first reported. Cf.
Ogopogo' (Leechman): Canadian: C. 20.

caddee (or caddy). To the entry on p. 119, add:
—Baumann is prob. right. Note that in Jon Bee,
A Living Picture of London, 1828, we have these
two senses: (1) a fellow that hangs about the

yards of an inn and, for a shilling or two, procures, for the landlords, 'customers from other inns': inns' and taverns': ca. 1820–60; (2) such a hanger-on, who permits himself to pass counterfeit money: c.: ca. 1820–80.

Caddie. See **Cadborosaurus**.

*cadee smasher. A professed tout to innkeepers, but one who occ. acts as a 'smasher' (sense 4): c.: ca. 1810–70. Here *cadee = cadet*, inferior.

cademy. Academy: lower-class coll.: late C. 19–20. W. L. George, *The Making of an Englishman*, 1914.

cadger.—3. 'Slangily applied to cabmen when they are off the rank soliciting fares, or to waiters who hang about and fawn for a gratuity': ca. 1870–1910. B. & L.

Cadogan Light Horse, the. 'The Special Constables mounted on the horses from Smith's riding school in Cadogan Square, London, during the general strike of 1926. Ex a cavalry officer on leave from India at that time who was specially enrolled for this "force"' (Peter Sanders): 1926; then historical.

Cads' Bar. The junior officers' corner in any favourite 'pub': Naval: since ca. 1914. (P.G.R.) Cf.:—

Cads' Corner. That corner of the Ward Room in which the junior officers gather: Naval: since ca. 1914. (P-G-R.)

cad's (or cads') crawlers. Suède shoes: since ca. 1930. Cf. **brothel creepers**.

Caesar. A Caesarian section or operation: medical coll.: C. 20.

cafe, occasionally written *kayf.* A café, a small restaurant: low, esp. London: since ca. 1920. Simply *café* without the accent.

café au lait, adj. or n. (A half-caste) with a touch of colour: since ca. 1920.

caff (p. 120). Recorded earlier in Desmond Morse-Boycott, *We Do See Life!*, 1931.

caffy avec. Coffee and rum; coffee-and-chicory mixture with a little cognac: coll.: late C. 19–20, the former; 1914–18, the latter. Ex the Fr. coll. *café avec,* short for *café avec du rhum* (or *du cognac*).

*cafishio. See **Creolo**.

cag (see p. 120) is by Granville spelt *kagg* and defined as 'a naval argument in which everybody speaks and nobody listens. A "branch-kagg" means talking shop.—*Kagg, to.* To "argue the toss."'

cage (see p. 120).—6. A caboose: Canadian railroadmen's: C. 20.—7. Goal-net: ice-hockey players': since ca. 1938.

cage of ivories. See **ivories, box of** (*Dict.*).

cagey. 'Up-stage'; conceited: since ca. 1935; ob. Recorded in Addenda of 2nd ed., 1938.—2. Much more usual, since 1940, has been the sense 'cautious; suspicious of others; unforthcoming, reserved', a sense that, ca. 1946, > coll. Ex animals in cages.

cahootchy. Indiarubber: Glasgow: C. 20. Ex *caoutchouc.*

Cain. Short for *Cain and Abel:* C. 20.

cake.—4. A pile of currency or bank-notes: (low) Cockney: C. 20. Cf. **wad,** 2 (*Dict.*).—5. A gold nugget: Australian: C. 20. B., 1942.—6. A prostitute: low Australian: since ca. 1910. Baker, 'Whence "cake shop", a brothel'. Euphemism for *cat,* etc.—6. But probably suggested by *tart,* 1 (p. 866).

cake, take the. 'I seem to remember, in 1882 or 1883, a lyric which told us that, "For rudeness to the Grand Old Man, Lord Randolph takes the cake"' [Lord Randolph Churchill]: Professor Ernest Weekley, in *The Observer,* Feb. 21, 1937.

cake-hole. The mouth: R.A.F.: since ca. 1936. H. &. P. Adopted ex Yorkshire s., where current at least as early as 1914.

cake is getting thin, the. One's money is running short: (low) Cockney: C. 20. See **cake,** 4 (Supplement).

cake-shop. See **cake,** n., 6.

caked up. Well provided with money: low: since ca. 1940. (Norman.)

cakey bar. See **bar,** n., 3.

calaboose (p. 120) has, since ca. 1895, been occasionally used in Australia. (Sarah Campion, *Bonanza,* 1942.)

Calathumpian. One who claims an imaginary religion: jocular: since ca. 1920. Perhaps cf. the U.S. *callithump,* a boisterous, or a burlesque, parade or serenade, hence *callithumpian,* a practitioner, or a supporter, of such goings-on.

Calendar, The. *The Racing Calendar:* from ca. 1820: turf coll. >, by 1900, S.E. Established in 1773.

calf-dozer. A small *bull*-dozer: since ca. 1940.

calf-licked. (Of human hair) hanging in a quiff: North Country coll.: C. 20. Bernard Hesling, *Little and Orphan,* 1954.

calf's head.—2. 'A white-faced man with a large head': lower classes': from ca. 1860. B. & L.

Calies, the. The *Caledonian* Association Football Club: sporting: C. 20. *The Daily Telegraph,* Nov. 24, 1937. More usually spelt *Callies.*

California.—2. A 'spot in Barnsbury, which rarely yields a fare,' Clarkson & Richardson, *Police!,* 1889: cabmen's: ca. 1860–1905. Ironic upon the Californian gold-fields. *California* 'is often pronounced *Californi-ay* in five syllables; facetious' (Leechman): mostly Canadian: since ca. 1945.

call a cab. 'A jockey is said to "*call a cab*" when he waves one arm to balance himself crossing a fence' (John Lawrence in *The Sunday Telegraph,* Aug. 13, 1961): racing: since late 1940's.

call a go (at **call it a day:** p. 121) is also, in C. 20, usually *call it a go.*

call-bird. In *The Observer,* Jan. 5, 1958, the writer of 'Call-Bird at the Sales' explains the term as the name shopkeepers 'give to extraordinary bargains as lures for the sale-minded': East-End Londoners': late C. 19–20. Ex Ger. *Lockvogel,* a decoy-bird, probably via Yiddish. (Atkinson.)

call for a damper. To break wind: Naval: C. 20.

call-girl. A prostitute, esp. one who advertises by shop-window announcement of services as socalled model: since ca. 1945. Adopted from the American—hence, by 1944 at latest, also Australian—*call-girl,* a prostitute available only by telephone-*call;* a use that, by 1950, is coll.

call me—or you can call me—anything (you like), so (or as) long as you don't call me late for breakfast. A c.p. used by one who has been addressed by the wrong name: mostly Australian: C. 20. (B.P.)

call-out. A summons: coll., esp. Londoners': late C. 19–20. (Jane Brown, *I Had a Pitch,* 1946.)

call-party. A party 'given in hall by students

called to the bar in the Middle Temple': law coll.: from ca. 1860. B. & L.

call the game in (p. 121): also Australian. B., 1942.

Callao ship. 'One in which the discipline is free and easy,' Granville: Naval: C. 20. At Callao, the principal seaport of Peru, things seem, to a naval rating, to be free and easy. Hence, *Callao routine*, one that is free and easy. (P-G-R.)

callee. Curry: pidgin: mid-C. 19–20. B. & L.

calliante-stroke, the. A rather clumsy method of boat-pulling that, adopted from the Italian Navy, results in many broken oars: Naval: since ca. 1918. (P-G-R.)

callibisters. See **male-mules**.

calligraphy is frequently misused, i.e. it is a catachresis, for 'handwriting': C. 20. E.g., n. David Frome, *Mr Simpson Finds a Body*, 1933, 'The calligraphy expert'.

Cally, the: Cally Market. The Caledonian Market: Londoners': late C. 19–20.

calonkus. A stupid person: Irish-Australian: late C. 19–20. (Ruth Park, *Poor Man's Orange*, 1950.) Arbitrary.

cambra. A dog: Shelta: C. 18–20. B. & L.

Camcreek. Cambridge: undergraduates': since ca. 1920.

Camden Town (p. 122). Also a penny. Since ca. 1920, used mostly by buskers. (Franklyn, *Rhyming*.)

came over with the onion boat. Often said with the usual British insularity and contempt for foreigners. From the Breton onion-vendors. Sometimes used as: 'You don't think that I came over with the onion boat, do you?' Sometimes 'cattle boat' is used, ex the boats from German ports. Of Italians it is sometimes said: 'Came over with an ice-cream barrow.' Other similar expressions, used facetiously, are, 'Came over with the Mormons', or 'Come over with the morons' (Albert B. Petch, letter of Sept. 5, 1946): coll.: C. 20; *morons*, not before 1930.

came up with the rations, it or **they.** An Army c.p. that, both in 1914–18 and in 1939–45, was applied to medals easily won. (P-G-R.)

Camel to Consumer. 'C. to C.' (Cape to Cairo) cigarettes, sent to the troops in North Africa by kindly South Africans: ca. 1940–3. (P-G-R.)

camelies! Muster the camels!: Australian pidgin: late C. 19–20. Archer Russell, *A Tramp-Royal in Wild Australia*, 1934. Cf. the Australian *camaleer*, a camel-driver: not 'unconventional', but S.E., on analogy of muleteer.

Camerer Cuss. A bus: London: since ca. 1925. Arthur Gardner, *Tinker's Kitchen*, 1932. Rhyming. Ex the name of a well-known London firm.

camp, adj.—4. Homosexual; Lesbian: theatrical: since ca. 1920; by 1945, fairly general. Ex sense 3 (p. 123).—5. Hence, characteristic of homosexuals, as in 'camp words, phraseology, signs, greetings'.

camp. A Station with or without an airfield—a unit's or a detachment's location—a training school—a depot—a landing ground; even if it (any of them) is situated in a town: R.A.F. coll. (since ca. 1920) >, by 1943, j. Jackson. The ubiquity of *Camp Commandant* and the versatility of *camp commandants* have been operative.

camp, n.—2. Whether in reference or in address,

Camp Commandant: Army coll. late C. 19–20. 'Oh, you had better ask Camp; he deals with such things.'—3. A short sleep, a rest, a sleep for the purpose of rest: Australian coll.: since ca. 1890 (Vance Palmer, *Golconda*, 1948.)—4. Effeminate esp. homosexual mannerisms of speech and gesture: mostly Society: since ca. 1945. 'The momentary absence of the customary "camp" once again calmed Elizabeth's hostility' (Angus Wilson, *Hemlock and After*, 1952).

camp, v.—4. To be a male, or a female, homosexual: theatrical: since ca. 1945. Ex the adj., senses 3 and 4.—5. (Of a shearer) to go slow, in order to leave a difficult sheep for another shearer: Australian shearers': since ca. 1910. (B., 1943.) Ex *camp*, v., 2: p. 122.—6. To act in a characteristically (male or female) homosexual manner, esp. if showily: since the late 1930's. Cf. senses 3 and 4 of the adj. (*The Lavender Lexicon*, 1965.)

camp, look for a. To seek a room, esp. a bedroom: Australian coll.: late C. 19–20. (B., 1943.)

camp about. 'To pirouette and gesture eloquently' (Robin Cook, 1962): since ca. 1945. Cf. **camp it up**, 1, below.

camp as a row of tents, as. Extremely homosexual; also, very histrionic and affected in speech and gesture, manners and movements: c.p.: since ca. 1960. John Gardner, *Madrigal*, 1967, at p. 155.

camp comedian. A Camp Commandant: Army & R.A.F.: since ca. 1930. Jackson.

camp it up. To render unnecessarily effeminate the part one is playing: theatrical: since ca. 1935. Ex *camp*, adj., 3, on p. 123.—2. To have a homosexual affair; to spend a 'queer' week-end together: homosexuals': since ca. 1945. Cf. **camp**, v., 4, above.

camp-master. See 'Tavern terms', § 6.

Camp of the Tartars, the. 'From the rapacity of the shop-keepers in the wooden galleries, this part of the *Palais Royal* has been nicknamed the "Camp of the Tartars",' David Carey, *Life in Paris*, 1822: Anglo-French: ca. 1815–40. Ex the late-medieval armies of victorious Tartars.

*Campo (or **c.**), **the.** The country, i.e. all that part of the Argentine which is not Buenos Aires: white-slavers' c.: from the 1890's. (A. Londres, 1928.) Direct ex Sp.

can, n.—4. A simpleton: military: ca. 1890–1930. Prompted by **mug**, 5 (*Dict.*).—5. Esp. *in the can*, in lock-up or prison: Australian: adopted ca. 1944, ex U.S. (Dick.)—6. Always *the can*, the w.c., esp. and orig. 'an outdoor privy with a *can* or other receptacle under the seat' (Leechman): Canadian: C. 20.—7. Mostly in pl. *cans*, 'the ear-phones used by technicians in radio and television' (Leechman): Canadian: since ca. 1950.

can, v. To decide not to use an article or pamphlet: Public Relations Directorate, the Air Ministry: since ca. 1943. I.e. to put into the swill-can.—2. Usually *be canned*, to be taken out of service: Canadian railroadmen's (— 1931). But *can*, to discharge (an employee), existed in British Columbia at least as early as 1910. (Leechman.)

can back, carry the (*Dict.*), is usually a vbl n., *carrying . . .*, 'accepting the blame for your own or another's error' (H. & P.), and common to all three Fighting Services. Hence, *the can-back king*, one who is very good at it: Feb. 1941, Hector Bolitho in *The English Digest*.

can I do you now, sir? A c.p., adopted from 'Itma' and dating since 1940. In that B.B.C. radio programme, the 'gag' was spoken by 'Mrs Mopp' (Dorothy Summers) to Tommy Handley. Cf. **it's that man again,** q.v.

can of oil. A boil: rhyming s.: late C. 19–20.

can-opener. A tank-busting aircraft (e.g. Hurricane): R.A.F.: 1940–5.

Canadian Adolescents' Slang in 1946. 'Mother! Do you want to be able to converse easily with your teenagers? Here is the glossary: Ameche, telephone: alligator, swing fan: blitz-buggy, automobile: bone-box, mouth: crumb-hunting, house work: dazzle dust, face powder: dig the drape, buy a new dress: droolin with schoolin, a grind: fag hag, a girl who smokes: give with the goo, explain in detail: in a gazelle, I'm feeling good: junior wolf, kid brother: make like a boid, go away: pucker paint, lipstick: Red Mike, a woman hater: riffs, music: slab, sandwich: slide your jive, talk freely: square, a person who doesn't dance: snazzy, smooth: ticks, moments: twister to the turner, a door key: watch works, brains: whing ding, head covering: you shred it, Wheat, you said it: zoon bat, funny looking.' (A Toronto newspaper, Oct. 24, 1946.) *Teenagers* = *teen-agers* = those in their teens.

'Practically all this is now obsolescent or obsolete' (Leechman, May 1959).

canagger. A Canadian canoe: Oxford undergraduates': since the 1880's; rare after 1940. (Marples, 2.) Cf. *canadar* on p. 123.

canal boat, the. The 'tote' (totalisator): rhyming: C. 20.

canaries. Bananas: since ca. 1930. Ex Canary Island bananas.—2. Squeaks in the bodywork of one's motorcar: motorists': since ca. 1950. Cf. **flatter** below.

canary.—11. A girl singer with an orchestra: Canadian (and U.S.): since ca. 1945. Cf. sense 8 (p. 123).—12. 'A mouse is a young lady. So is a *slick chick, duck, canary, pig, beast, head, sun* or *sunflower,* or *doll*.)' Beatnik s., dating from the late 1950's. Anderson. But also Australian—since ca. 1930. (Lawson Glassop, *Lucky Palmer,* 1949.)

canary ward, the. The V.D. ward in a Naval hospital: lower-deck: C. 20. Ex its predominant colour. (P-G-R.)

candle. Short for **candle-sconce** below. Franklyn 2nd.

candle-basher. A spinster: low: late C. 19–20. Outmoded by 1967. The connotation is of masturbation.

candle money. Fire-insurance paid out: police and underworld: C. 20. (Maurice Proctor, *Man in Ambush,* 1958.) Ex candle purposely left burning.

candle-sconce. A prostitute's protector: low rhyming s. (on *ponce*): since ca. 1920. Jim Phelan, 1943.

candy boy. See **bumper-up,** 2.

cane, v.—4. To coït with (a woman): C. 20. Cf. **bang,** v., 3 (p. 31).—5. To defeat, esp. as vbl n., *caning*: 'a beating, a defeat': since ca. 1918.

cane nigger. A happy-go-lucky fellow: West Indian coll.: from ca. 1870. B. & L.

caner. A young woman carrying a cane: Society: 1886, then only historical, there having been a vogue lasting only that summer. Ibid.

*canfinfiero. See **Créolo.**

caning. See **cane,** v., 4 (above).

*canke is Randle Holme's spelling (1688) of **cank** (*Dict.*).

canker. See **kanker.**

canned. Tipsy: since ca. 1910 in Britain and ca. 1938 in South Africa. (Prof. W. G. Mackie in *The Cape Argus,* July 4, 1946.) Adopted from U.S.: cf. **tanked** (p. 864).

canned music. Music from phonograph or gramophone: adopted, ca. 1925, from U.S.

*cannon.—2. A pickpocket: c.: from ca. 1920. (*The Evening News,* Dec. 9, 1936.) Prob. suggested by *gun*, n., 4 (q.v. in *Dict.*).

cannon fodder. 'Those soldiers whose destiny was to do or die, not to reason why. A newspaper or political agitator's phrase occasionally used by the troops' (P-G-R.): derisive: 1939–45. 'Cf. the Ger. coll. *Kanonenfutter*' (Ramsey Spencer).

canny Newcassel. Newcastle-upon-Tyne: North Country: late C. 19–20. Newcastletonians also call it 'The Pride of the North'.

canoe inspection. Service women's weekly V.D. inspection: Canadian Army: 1939–45.

canov. Short for **can of oil** above. Franklyn 2nd quotes "E's gotta lovely canov on 'e's nick, ain' 'e?'

can't claim (a) halfpenny. A c.p. indicative of 'a complete alibi which is carefully concocted when one is about to face a charge,' H. & P.: Services, esp. Army: since ca. 1930.

can't-keep-still. A treadmill: rhyming s.: ca. 1850–90. (Franklyn, *Rhyming*.)

canteen cowboy. A ladies' man: R.A.F.: since 1940. Jackson, 'The origin is in the American expression, "drug-store cowboy" . . . (See "Naafi Romeo" and "Poodle-faker").'—2. Hence, orderly corporal on duty in a Station Institute: 1941 +. Atkinson.

canteen damager. See **damager,** 3.

canteen medal, 1 (p. 125): also, since ca. 1919, R.A.F. (Jackson.)—3. A fly-button undone: Army: since ca. 1917.

canteen open—mind yer fingers!—canteen closed. A Naval c.p. spoken by a seaman offering cigarettes to a group of messmates: since ca. 1920. Wilfred Granville, *A Dictionary of Sailors' Slang,* 1962.

Canterbury Bell(e). An 'unmarried wife' receiving an allowance from a Fighting Service. 'When conscription was introduced in April 1939, it was decided that such women could qualify for a wife's allowance. The story goes that the Archbishop of Canterbury objected to "unmarried wife" and so it was changed to "unmarried dependant living as wife" or popularly "Canterbury Belle"' (Peter Sanders): Forces': mid-1939 †. A pun on the flower named *Canterbury bell* and (Archbishop of) *Canterbury,* as well as on *belle,* a pretty girl, and *Belle,* a girl's name.

cantilever bust. Large female breasts seeming to defy the laws of gravity: Australian: since ca. 1950. They do so, but only with the help of **structural engineering,** q.v. below.

canty. (Of persons) disagreeable; irritable: Australian: since ca. 1920. B., 1942, 'From cantankerous'.

canvas or **canvass.** Human skin, pelt: pugilistic: ca. 1810–70. *Boxiana,* III, 1821.

cap at, set one's (p. 125). Variant: *cock one's cap at,* as in W. N. Glascock, *Sailors and Saints,* 1829, II, 145. Moe.

cap badge; flit gun. A 25-pounder; a 3.7 gun: medium gunners' (Army): 1940 +. Both are satirical.

cap on three hairs. 'A sailor's cap worn flat-a-back' (Granville): Naval: since ca. 1910.

cap one's lucky. See **lucky** . . .

cap-struck. Besotted with a girl or a woman: Naval: C. 19; † by 1890. *Cap*, a woman's cap, was, in Naval circles, often used fig. of a (desirable) female: see Wm Nugent Glascock, *The Naval Sketch-Book*, 2nd Series, 1934, at II, 73 and 74.

cap-tally. A sailor's cap-ribbon bearing the name of his ship: Naval coll.: C. 20.

cap-tally drink and **collar-band pint.** A short measure pint: C. 20: resp. Naval and civilian. (P-G-R.)

capabarre (p. 125) occurs in 1818: Alfred Burton, *Johnny Newcome*. (Moe.) Variant *capper-bar* in W. N. Glascock, *Sailors and Saints*, 1829. (Moe.)

cape. See 'Guard-Room in Army Slang'.

Cape. Short for **Cape of Good Hope** (p. 126). Franklyn 2nd.

caper, n.—3. (Ex sense 1: p. 126.) 'Game' or trick, as in 'You can shove that caper' (Slatter): New Zealand and elsewhere: since ca. 1920.

capite. See 'Tavern terms', § 9.

Cappo. A Capstan cigarette: Australian: since ca. 1918. B., 1942.

captain.—5. See 'Nicknames'.—6. The 'leader' of a drinking group, esp. if he buys the drinks: Australian jocular: since ca. 1945. (B., 1953.)

Captain Cook; occ. shortened to **Cook** (or **cook**) (p. 126). Also *Captain Cooker.* B., 1941.—3. A cook: Australian rhyming s.: C. 20. B., 1942. —4. A look: Australian rhyming s.: since ca. 1948. (B.P.) Cf. **give a cook** below. It occurs in Nino Culotta, *Cop This Lot*, 1960, '"Let's have a Captain Cook"'.

Captain Criterion. A racing sharp; mostly London theatrical and smart Society: ? ca. 1880–1905. Ex a music-hall song:

'I'm Captain Criterion of London,
Dashing and never afraid.
If ever you find a mug's been well done,
Be sure that it's by our brigade.'

The Criterion Theatre and Restaurant (founded in 1874) obtained an injunction against the singer, and the song was suppressed.

captain is at home, the (p. 127), probably lasted throughout C. 19.

Captain Kettle. To settle (vigorously), v.t.: rhyming s. of ca. 1899–1950. Ex the famous character of fiction: Cutcliffe Hyne's stories were published over the years 1893–1938. (Franklyn, *Rhyming*.)

captain of a foot company. See 'Tavern terms', § 6.

Captain of the Heads. See **Heads, the, 2.**

captain's blue-eyed boy. 'The officer most in favour at the moment,' Granville: Naval coll.: C. 20.

captain's tiger. A boy that waits upon the captain (and him alone) at table: nautical, esp. on ocean-liners: late C. 19–20. Cf. **tiger, 3** (p. 885).

capture the pickled biscuit. 'Take the biscuit': Australian: ca. 1925–50. B., 1942.

car knock, car toad, car tonk, car whack or

whacker. A car repairman: Canadian railroadmen's (— 1931).

Carab. An occasional form of *Carib.* (P-G.R.)

carb. See **bicarb.—2.** Carburetter: motorists' coll.: since ca. 1910.

carbie or **carby.** A carburettor: Australian: since ca. 1920. (B.P.)

carbolic naked is a punning, not very common, C. 20 variant of **starbolic naked.**

cardboard foc'sle. 'The peak on the cap worn by officers and petty officers (and "men not dressed as seamen")': Naval lowerdeck: since ca. 1930. 'Just because you wear a cardboard foc'sle, don't think you can come it with the troops!' (Wilfred Granville, letter of July 24, 1963.)

Cardiganise. To destroy (a cannon): ca. 1855–1900. Surtees, *Plain or Ringlets*, 1860, 'Talk of the courage of facing an enemy, or Cardigan-ising a cannon.' D.N.B., Epitome: 'The seventh Earl of Cardigan commanded the light cavalry brigade in the Crimea, and destroyed it in the famous "charge", 1854.' (I.e., The Russian guns.)

care a pin . . . a fig, not to (p. 128): rather, since ca. 1820 or even earlier. (Wm Maginn, *Whitehall*, 1827.)

careen is, in Canada (imitating the U.S.), misused for 'to career', to go wildly and rapidly, esp. of a motor-car: in Canada, frequent only since ca. 1935.

career boy. One who, in a combatant Service, puts self-success before the public, esp. the nation's, welfare: R.A.F. s. (1942) >, by 1944, all three Services' coll. Cf. **back-room boy.**

careless talk. (A stick of) chalk: mostly dartsplayers': since ca. 1945. Ex a famous warslogan. (Franklyn, *Rhyming*.)

Careys. A coll. ellipsis of *Mother Carey's chickens*: 1829, W. N. Glascock, *Sailors and Saints* (I, 179). Moe.

Carib (or **c-**). A member of the *Carabinieri*: prisoners-of-war in Italy: 1942–44, then historical. (Michael Gilbert, *Death in Captivity*, 1952.) Influenced (*C-*) by *Carib*, one of a Caribbean tribe and (*c-*) by *cannibal.* Cf. *Carab.*

carmes or **carnes.** Flattery; blandishments: rather low: ca. 1860–1910. Ex Romany. B. & L.

carn. A carnation: flower-sellers': late C. 19–20. Richard Llewellyn, *None But the Lonely Heart*, 1943.

Carney. A hypocrite: Naval: C. 20. Ex a certain captain friendly ashore, devil aboard: Granville.

carney, n. (p. 128). Earliest (?) in *The London Guide*, 1818.—2. A lizard: Australian: C. 20. (Dal Stivens, *The Gambling Ghost*, 1953.)—3. A *carnival* show; hence, a man employed there: Canadian: adopted, ca. 1930, ex U.S.

carni (pron. *carnee*) **guy.** Any fellow connected with a carnival: Canadian s.: C. 20. Adopted ex U.S.

carob. To cut: Shelta: C. 18–20. B. & L.

carol singer. Police car with loud-speaker: Brisbane, Australia: since ca. 1930. B., 1942.

*****carpet, n.** This term (see p. 128) is an abbr. of *carpet bag*, rhyming s. on **drag** in same sense.—2. A carpet snake: Australian coll.: late C. 19–20. Archer Russell, *In Wild Australia*, 1934.—3. The sum of £3: spivs' c.: since ca. 1942. (*Picture Post*, Jan. 1954.)—4. But in Australia, according to B., 1943, a £1 note: ? since ca. 1925.—5. Odds of 3 to 1: racing: esp. bookmakers': C. 20. (*The*

Sunday Telegraph, May 7, 1967.) Ex sense 1 on p. 128: a prison sentence of three months. Cf. **double carpet** below.

carpet-biter; carpet-biting. One (usually male) who gets into a fearful rage, a visibly very angry man; a distressing exhibition of uncontrollable rage: coll. since ca. 1940. Ex the stories of Hitler biting carpets in his insane rages.

carpet tom-cat. An officer often with and very attentive to the ladies: military: ca. 1875–1910. B. &. L.

carpet-trade. See **carpet-man** (*Dict.*).

carpurtle esp. in 'It won't carpurtle', work, function, act: R.A.F.: ca. 1940–4. Arbitrary.

carra or **carrer.** A motor caravan: Australian: since ca. 1925. B., 1942. Cf. **chara** (p. 140).

carrier.—2. A Bren-gun carrier: Army coll.: 1940 +. (P-G-G.)

carrion.—3. Draught cattle: Australian: since ca. 1860. 'Tom Collins', *Such is Life*, 1903. By humorous depreciation, but with a ref. to the grim potentialities of severe and widespread drought.

carrion-case (p. 129). In, e.g., *Sinks*, 1848.

carrot. 'Tobacco, done up in a similar but larger shape than **salt's pricker**, q.v. below, was an important trade item in the fur-trading days of Canada, and was called a *carrot*' (Leechman): mid C. 18–19.

carry, v. At cricket, to continue to bat: Australian schooboys': since ca. 1930. 'Last man doesn't carry.' Short for *carry on*, to continue. (B.P.)

carry (someone) **around** or, usually, **round.** 'To do a man's job for him until he knows the routine' (P-G-R.): Services' coll.: since ca. 1910.

carry ballast. To hold one's drinks well: Naval: C. 20. Granville.

carry both ends of the log. To do all the work, esp. in a complementary pair: Australian coll.: C. 20. 'Rann Daly' in 1924.

carry both sheets aft. See **aft** . . .

*carry (someone) **in one's heart.** 'If the "sky blue", languishing in prison, considers that he has been framed by one of his previous cronies (variously known as chummies, pallie blues, or beans) he will "carry him in his heart" until he can . . . get his revenge,' *The Cape Times*, May 23, 1946: S. African c.: C. 20.

carry milk-pails. 'Presently a gentleman, "carrying milk-pails", as the [London street] boys called it—that is, with a lady on each arm—advanced up the colonnade,' Augustus Mayhew, *Paved With Gold*, 1857: ca. 1830–80. Cf. **milkshop** in *Dict.*

carry on, London. A public-spirited c.p., used in 'the London blitz' of Aug. 1940–May 1941 and again in the V.2 blitz of July–Dec. 1944.

'This was the "sign-off" of a B.B.C. radio weekly magazine programme, "In Town To-night", which ran for many years.

'In the interests of historical accuracy, may I amend the phrase "again in the V.2 blitz of July–Dec. 1944"? The V.1 (flying bomb) blitz on London was from 13 June–6 Sept 1944, thereafter reduced to a sporadic trickle as the launching sites were overrun. The V.2 (rocket) blitz started on 8 Sept 1944 and lasted until March 1945 (Churchill, "The Second World War"). I was personally in charge of a special Intelligence Reporting team set up at Headquarters, Air Defence of Great Britain (better, and more proudly, known by its

1939–43 name Fighter Command) in June 1944 to record hour by hour the launchings and fall, or successful interception by our defences, of the V. weapons. Having then been posted to London in Aug 1944, I witnessed (at varying distances) a great number of the V.2's, including the original "flying gas main" (p. 1125) on 8 Sept.' (Ramsey Spencer, 1967.)

carry-over, n. A 'hang-over' in which one is still slightly tipsy: coll.: since ca. 1912. (J. B. Priestley, *Three Men in New Suits*, 1945.)

carry the banner. 'To support or praise some movement, often one of the not so popular type' (Petch): coll.: since ca. 1950. Ex *banner-carrying* at protest meetings or on protest matches.

carry the can has, since ca. 1945, been the usual form of *carry the can back* (see **can back, carry the,** above, and cf. **take the can back** on p. 863).

carry the can back. See **can back,** above.

carry the knot. To 'hump a bluey' or go on tramp: Australian: since ca. 1930. (B., 1943.)

carry the mail. To stand drinks: Australian: C. 20. Baker.

carry the stockwhip. (Of a domineering wife) to be 'the boss': N.T., Australia: since ca. 1930. (Ernestine Hill, *The Territory*, 1951.)

carry the torch for (somebody; hence for a cause). To be amorous of; to be devoted to: Canadian: adopted, ca. 1945, ex U.S. Perhaps ex U.S. torchlight processions in honour of a political, or a local-government, candidate. (Leechman.)

carrying all before her. (Of girl or woman) having a well-developed bust, or being obviously pregnant: raffish jocular: since ca. 1920.

carrying weight. 'Loaded with depression' (Anderson): beatniks': since ca. 1959. A broken.

*carser is an occ. variant of **casa,** 2 (*Dict.*).

carsey.—3. A w.c.: low Cockney: from ca. 1870. Cf. **case,** n., 9 (*Dict.*).—4. A public-house: parlyaree: since ca. 1860. (P. H. Emerson, *Signor Lippo*, 1893.)

cart, traverse the. See **traverse the cart.**

cart off or **out.** See **cart away** (*Dict.*).

cart out with. As 'He's carting out with Liz' = he's courting her: Cockneys': since ca. 1880. Ex, not 'he's carting her out', but 'he's carting himself out with her.'

cartload of blancmange. *Carte blanche*: facetious: since ca. 1950.

cartload of monkeys and the wheel won't turn! A children's c.p., 'shouted after a crowd of people cycling, or riding, slowly past, or sitting in a bus, or a coach, awaiting departure' (Peter Ibbotson, letter of Feb. 9, 1963): since late C. 19; by 1960, slightly ob.

*carve. To slash (a person) with a razor: c., and low (esp. Cockneys'): C. 20.

carve oneself a slice is a Cockney synonym of *have a cut* . . ., q.v. at **cut off the joint** below.

carve up, v.—4. (Cf. 1.) To spoil the chances of (a person), in business: London commercial and taxi-drivers': from ca. 1910.—5. A *carve-up* is also a fight or even a war: mostly Cockney: since ca. 1905.

carv d out of wood. See **cedar,** 3.

carsey (p. 129). Sydney Lester, 1937. A variant spelling and pronunciation of **carzey.**

Cas, the. The Chief of Air Staff: Air Ministry, and the higher R.A.F. formations: since ca. 1930. Jackson.

casa.—4. A ladies' man, a masher: Australian Naval: 1939–45. (B., 1943.)

cascade, v. (p. 130). It dates rather from the early 1660's. Pepys once 'cascaded' at the theatre.

case, n., 6 (a love-affair) is actively extant in S. Africa: Prof. W. S. Mackie in *The Cape Argus*, July 4, 1946.—14. 'A Baudy-house' (James Dalton, *A Narrative*, 1728): c.: C. 18 and prob. C. 19 also.

case, v.—3. To weep: Marlborough College: since ca. 1920.

case, v.—4. To reconnoitre (a building to be robbed): Australian police: adopted, ca. 1918, ex U.S. (Vince Kelly, 1955.)

*case a joint. To make a reconnaissance of, before robbing, a house or other building: Canadian, since ca. 1925; English by 1930, as in Nicholas Blake, *The Whisper in the Gloom*, 1954.

cased-up, be. To be in a brothel: low: C. 20. Herbert Hodge, 1939. Cf. cased-up with (p. 130).

caseo.—2. A full night in bed with a prostitute: low: since ca. 1930. (*The New Statesman*, May 10, 1947.)

caser (p. 130). Also low Australian: late C. 19–20.—2. A careless variant of casa, 2 (p. 130).—3. One who 'cases' buildings, houses, etc., for burglars: c.: since ca. 1950. Ex U.S.

cases. Boots: military (esp. the Guards): C. 20; ob. by 1945. *John o' London's Weekly*, Nov. 3, 1939. Cf. trotter-cases (*Dict.*).

casey.—2. A variant of *carsey*, 1 (p. 129).

cash and carried. Married: rhyming s.: late C. 19–20. Cf. *cut* or *dot*, *and carried*.

cash on the knocker. Cash down: Australian: since ca. 1925. (B.P.) Paid at the door?

cash-up.—2. To earn or make money; often as *get cashed up*, to earn and save money: Australian coll.: C. 20. D'Arcy Niland, 'But I thought the idea would be to work on here for a bit longer . . . Get cashed up a bit, then move' (*Call Me When the Cross Turns Over*, 1958).

casher. 'A "good casher" is a driver whose average taximeter-money is high; a "bad casher", one whose average is low,' Herbert Hodge, *Cab, Sir?*, 1939: taxicab owners' and drivers' coll.: since ca. 1910.

*caso. A prostitute that takes a man for the night: c.: C. 20. Ex *case*, n., 8.—2. A brothel: since ca. 1910. Herbert Hodge, *Cab, Sir?*, 1939. Variant of caseo (p. 130), itself dissyllabic.

caso, go. See go caso.

cassie. 'Wrinkled, stained, or outside sheets of paper': printers': mid-C. 19–20. B. & L. Cognate with Fr. *cassé*, broken.

cast-iron or bullet-proof. Irrefutable: Services, resp. coll. and s.: since the 1920's. H. & P.

cast off. To unbind; to set free: nautical: C. 19. *The Dublin University Magazine*, March 1834 (p. 252), '''Cast him off!'' *............* * Unbind him.' (Moe.)

cast one's skin. To strip oneself to the buff: low: ca. 1815–80. *Sinks*, 1848. See also cap one's skin (p. 125).

castle, the. The stumps: cricketers': since ca. 1925. (Ian Peebles in *The Sunday Times*, May 31, 1959.) The batsman defends them from the bowler.

castor.—2. (Always pl.) A bicycle: see cads on castors (*Dict.*).

castor, adj. and exclamation. All right: excel-

lent: Australian: from ca. 1905. Suggested by 'dinkum *oil*'.

castor with, be on the. To be popular with or well regarded by: low Australian: since ca. 1930. (Kylie Tennant, *The Joyful Condemned*, 1953.)

casual. 'A casual payment of "something on account" to an officer or a rating whose pay documents are still in his last ship' (Granville): Naval coll.: C. 20.

Cat.—2. A Catalina aircraft: 1943. H. & P.

cat, n. Sense 1 survived until ca. 1910 as 'a drunken, fighting prostitute' (B. & L.).—11. A gossiping woman: upper-middle class: since ca. 1927. (Angus Wilson, *Such Darling Dodos*, 1950.) A back-formation from S.E. *catty*, spiteful.—12. (Usually in pl.) A lion or a tiger or a leopard: circusmen's: C. 20. Also, *the big cats*, all of these collectively.—13. A catamaran: boating coll.: since ca. 1955.—14. A *cat*erpillar tractor: orig., Canadian: since early 1930's.—15. An hydraulic catapult on an aircraft carrier: Fleet Air Arm: since late 1930's. John Winton, *H.M.S. Leviathan*, 1967.

cat, not room enough to swing a (p. 132). The reference is to the cat-o'-nine-tails.

cat, pinch the; gen. be pinching . . . This proletarian phrase has, from ca. 1880, been applied to a man that, hand in pocket, palps his genitals.

cat, shoot the.—2. 'To sound the bugle for defaulters' drill': infantrymen's: from ca. 1880. B. & L.

cat, whip the.—4. See cat, shoot the in the *Dict.*

cat cuff. A sly punch: Australian sporting: C. 20. B., 1942.

cat-heads. Female breasts: Naval, mostly lowerdeck: late C. 18–mid-19. *The Night Watch* (II, 89), 1828, but also, much earlier, in John Davis, *The Post Captain*. Ex nautical j. In W. N. Glascock, *The Naval Sketch-Book*, II, 1826, it seems to mean 'falsies'.

cat house. A brothel: Canadian: adopted, ca. 1925, ex U.S. (Cf. *cat*, n., 1: p. 131.)

cat in hell's chance. Only a very slight chance; *not a* . . . , not even that: c.p.: since ca. 1930. (Laurie Atkinson, Sept. 11, 1967.)

cat-lap is applied also to milk: C. 19–20.

cat-lick (and a promise) is a contemporaneous variant of lick and a promise (*Dict.*).

cat-skinner. Driver of a caterpillar tractor: Canadian lumbermen's: since ca. 1930. A blend of *cat*erpillar + mule-*skinner*. 'No longer restricted to lumbering. Any man who drives a "cat"' (Leechman, April 1947).

cat-walk.—2. See cat's walk.

cat-whipper. One who 'cries over spilt milk': Australian: since ca. 1930. (B., *Australia Speaks*, 1953.)

catastrophe (p. 133) survives in Anglo-Irish: witness James Joyce, *Ulysses*, 1922, the Falstaffian phrase.

catch, n., 1 (p. 133) occurs in, e.g., W. N. Glascock, *Sailors and Saints* (II, 145), 1829. Moe. —3. 'A sheep taken by a shearer from his catching pen' (B., 1959): Aus. rural coll.: C. 20.

catch a cold. 'To get oneself into trouble by being too impetuous.' H. & P.: Services: since ca. 1930. Cf. catch cold; prob. ex the earlier:— 2. To 'get the wind up' (become or feel afraid): Army: 1914–18. Ex that chilly feeling.

catch a horse; or, go and catch . . . To urinate:

Australian: C. 20. B., 1942. Cf. *water one's nag* (at nag, p. 549).

catch afire. To set fire to: Cockney coll.: mid-C. 19–20. Edwin Pugh, *A Street in Suburbia*, 1895, 'It blazed up in the pan an' caught the chimley afire almost.'

***catch (bang to) rights.** See **rights, catch (bang) to.**

catch cold. 'I told her if she did not give it me again she would *catch cold*, meaning she would repent of it' (rather, get into trouble, be 'for it'): 1775.

catch hand. A 'casual workman who moves from job to job, esp. at commencement of new jobs, to get more favourable rate and conditions, and who has no intention of staying on one job until the end' (Laurie Atkinson, Sept. 11, 1967): urban labourers' coll.: since ca. 1950.

catch on the fly. To board a train while it is moving: Canadian, orig. hoboes': C. 20. (Frederick Niven, *Wild Honey*, 1927.)

catch one's death. To catch a very bad cold: coll.: late C. 19–20. Elliptical. (G. B. Lancaster, *Sons o' Men*, 1904.)

catch the boat up. To get V.D.: Naval: since ca. 1930.

catch under the pinny. See **pinny** . . .

catch (someone) with his trousers down. See **caught with** . . .

catchee (p. 134) means also 'to get or obtain; to find out; to hold, to win'.

catching flies, n. or predicative adj. Gaping: coll.: C. 19–20.

catching the bird, ppl. and n. Cruising in one's car, persuading a girl to go for a drive, finally intercoursing with her: Australian raffish: since ca. 1930. Cf. **bird,** n., 8, on p. 54.

catchpole rapparee. See 'Constables'.

Caten (or c-) **wheel.** A Catherine wheel; a fig. cartwheel: London streets' illiteracy: mid-C. 19–20. Augustus Mayhew, *Paved with Gold*, 1857.

caterpillar.—4. Habitual drunkard: Australian: C. 20. B., 1942. A caterpillar crawls; so does a pub-crawler.

catheter. See **piss out of, take the.**

Cat's (p. 134). The Cambridge seat of learning has long been St Catharine's College.

cats, fight like Kilkenny (p. 134). 'The origin of this expression as I have heard is this. Cromwell's soldiers in Ireland used to amuse themselves by tying two cats together by their tails and hanging them over a clothes line. Of course the wretched animals clawed each other to death.' (Andrew Haggard, letter of Jan. 28, 1947.)

Cats, the. The Canadian Auxiliary Territorial Service: mostly Canadian: 1939–45.

cat's breakfast. A very common Scottish and North Country variant since ca. 1920—of **dog's breakfast** (p. 231).

cat's eyes. Usually in pl., *cats' eyes*, 'the pilots to our night-fighter squadrons', H. & P., 1943. Orig. a journalistic term, it was jocularly adopted by R.A.F. flying-crews; by Jan. 1945, however, it was already ob.—2. (Or hyphenated). Marbles thus coloured: children's coll.: late C. 19–20.

cat's head cut open. Pudendum muliebre: low: C. 20.

cat's mother, 'She' is a. See **'She' is a cat's mother** (*Dict.*).

Cat's nouns! See 'Ejaculations'.

cat's pyjamas; cat's whiskers (p. 134): still, in 1965 anyway, 'far from dead in Australia' (B.P.).

cat's walk; occ., **cat-walk.** 'The long plank on bomber aircraft stretching between cockpit and tail,' H. & P.: R.A.F.: since ca. 1938. Cf. **cat-walk** (*Dict.*), its imm. origin. This form has, since late 1950's, been far less common than *cat-walk*, itself >, by 1960 at latest, S.E. Soon after World War II, *cat-walk* came to mean a gangway in a building and at theatrical and mannequin shows.

'This goes back to World War I, not in connection with bombers, but with zeppelins and later with our own large rigid dirigibles. In "The Wonder Book of Aircraft" (1919), a work full of illustrations now of almost historic value, are two photographs showing inside the envelope of a zeppelin the "cat-walk" (vide caption) whereby the crew could move from one gondola to another.' (Ramsey Spencer, March 1967.)

cattie or **catty,** n. A catapult: schoolchildren's: late C. 19–20.

cattle, v. To coït with: low Cockney: C. 20. Cf. **bull,** v., 1 (p. 104).

cattle(-)banger. A cattle-station hand; a milker: Australian: since ca. 1910. B., 1942. Cf. **stockbanger.**

cattle-boat, came over with the. See **came over** . . .

cattle truck; since ca. 1945, always shortened to *cattle*. To copulate with, also fig.: (esp. racing): rhyming, s.: C. 20. Franklyn 2nd. On *fuck*. 'The favourite was well cattled when he fell at the last fence.'

cattley man. A cattleman: Australian coll.: since ca. 1880. Archer Russell, *A Tramp Royal in Wild Australia*, 1934.

Catts or **Catt's** is a mere variant of **Cat's** (*Dick.*).

caught short. Experiencing the onset of menstruation when no pads are available: feminine coll., esp. in Australia: since middle 1930's. On analogy of **taken short** below.

caught with one's trousers down. Taken unawares; unready; Services: since ca. 1920; gen. since 1940. H. & P. Cf. **stand on one leg,** q.v.

Cauldron, the. That part of the Knightsbridge battlefield (North Africa) where the movement of numerous tanks raised clouds of dust and helped to create the effect of a seething cauldron: Army (and Air Force) in North Africa in World War II.

'No! This is a notorious journalistic mistranslation of standard military Ger. "Kesselschlacht", a battle of encirclement; although by itself "Kessel" *does* mean a cauldron, in hunting "Kesseltreiben" means driving game into an enclosed killing-ground. Cf. driving wild elephants into the Keddah enclosure where they are captured and tamed. At Knightsbridge our armour suffered severe losses in just this way (v. "The Second World War", by Sir Winston Churchill). In Normandy, Falaise was a not-quite-successful "Kesselschlacht", with the Allies as the hunters.' (Ramsey Spencer, March 1967.)

cauli (p. 135). Recorded earlier in W. L. George, *A Bed of Roses*, 1911.

cauliflower.—8. A locomotive with a crested front: railwaymen's: since ca. 1910. (*Railway*.)

Cauliflower Alley; Tin-Ear Alley. The boxing world: boxing journalists': since ca. 1935.

cauliflower and mashed. A c.p. description of a

boxer's face: since the 1930's. Cauliflower ears and mashed nose.

cauliflower top. An upper deck full of passengers: busmen's (esp. London): since ca. 1935.

caulk, n., 1 (p. 135): prob. since very early C. 19. It occurs in, e.g., *The Night Watch* (II, 117), 1828, thus, 'Wrapped up in a pea-jacket for a caulk in the waist' (of the ship). Moe.

caulk, v., 1 (p. 135). 'Caulking—napping on the deck', Captain Glascock, *Land Sharks*, 1838. And even earlier in Alfred Burton, *Johnny Newcome*, 1818. (Moe.)

caulk a few seams is a C. 20 elaboration of the preceding. (P-G.R.)

caulk off. A variant—mostly Canadian—of **caulk,** v., 1 (p. 135): C. 20. (Leechman.)

caulker, 1 (p. 135), has, in C. 20 Australia, the nuance 'a stiff brandy to end an evening's potations' (B., 1943).

caulker.—3. 'A stranger, a novice' (*Spy*, 1825): Eton: ca. 1815–60. *Spy* spells it *cawker*. **—4.** 'A greatcoat or blanket for sleeping on deck during a "make and mend",' Granville: Naval: late C. 19–20. Ex **caulk,** n., 1, and v., 1 (p. 135).

caulks to (someone), **put the.** See **logger's smallpox.**

causey, causy; cawsey, cawsy. Latrines: low: late C. 19–20. Brendan Behan, *Borstal Boy*, 1958 (*cawsy*). Ex one or other of the secondary meanings of dial. *causey*, causeway, highway, street, perhaps influenced by c. *carsey*.

caustic. An acoustic mine: Naval: 1939 +.

caustic, old; or capitals. 'Nickname for a surly or querulous type of man' (Granville): Naval: C. 20.

caution.—3. (Ex sense 1.) A person mildly bad: from ca. 1880. E.g. 'Dad's a bit of a caution when he's had too much to drink.'

cavalry. See **dirty face.**

cavalry are coming, or are here, the. Help is coming, or has arrived: c.p.: late C. 19–20. Ex the lit. military sense.—Cf. the American c.p., *the marines have landed*, occasionally completed with *and the situation is well in hand*: C. 20.

cave-board. A creaky board or stair-step: Public Schools': since ca. 1880. Ronald Knox, *Double Cross Purposes*, 1937. One that cries 'Cave!'?

cavity gremlin. A mole-like gremlin that digs large holes just before and where the pilot is about to land: R.A.F.: 1940–5. (P.G.R.)

cavy.—2. A caged rabbit; rabbit fanciers': mid-C. 19–20. Josephine Bell, *Death on the Borough Council*, 1937. A corruption of *cag(e)y*. The corruption may have been in part due to S.E. *cavy*, a kind of guinea-pig, as Mr Ramsey Spencer has (1967) suggested.

cawbawn or **cobbon.** Big, large: Australian (mostly Queensland) coll.: from ca. 1860; ob. B. & L. Ex Aboriginal.

cawsey or **cawsy.** See **causey** above.

*caz.—2. An easy dupe: c. mid-C. 19–20; very ob. Ibid.

cazo. A Service casualty: Australian servicemen's: 1939—45. (B., 1943.) That is, *casualty* + the Australian *-o*.

cedar.—A simpleton, a dupe: Australian: since ca. 1930. B., 1953, adduces the synonymous *log* and *mahogany* and (someone) *carved out of wood.*

cellar-flap (p. 136). Prob. short for 'tap dance': therefore rhyming s. Cf.:—2. To borrow: C. 20. Rhyming on *tap*, and often shortened to *cellar.*

cement. 'A very frequent U.S. and Canadian sol. for concrete. "Cement sidewalks", "cement piers" and so forth' (Leechman): since ca. 1920 (?).

cement-mixer; esp., *have a cement-mixer*, 'to have a ball or dance' (Anderson): beatniks': since ca. 1959.

cements. Stock Exchange shares: since ca. 1935. 'Often jocularly, as "Cements are hardening"' (A. B. Petch, Sept. 1946). Stock Exchange j. 'to *harden*' originated the term.

censor. A blue-pencilled comma that should be a semi-colon: journalists' and printers' since ca. 1915.

[**Centre, the.** Orig. half j., half c., it has, since ca. 1925, been j. for the organisation that sends girls and women out to the Argentine to become courtesans or prostitutes. Albert Londres, 1928.]

centre man, the. A synonym of *boxer*, the organizer and arbitrator of a two-up game: Aus.: C. 20. (B., 1959.) See **boxer,** 1, above.

century. With sense 1 (p. 136) cf. the Canadian railroadmen's (— 1931): a 100-dollar bill: a sense adopted from U.S. c. See esp. *Underworld.*

certified. Certified as insane: C. 20: coll. rather than euphemistic. Ironically as a virtual c.p., *time you were certified*, to a person acting the fool or having been exceptionally stupid.

Ces, the. The Cesarewitch, run in mid-October: sporting coll.: late C. 19–20.

cess. 'Extreme rails of track' (*Railway*, 3rd): railwaymen's: since ca. 1930 (?). Origin? Perhaps *excess.*

Chad. 'The British Services' counterpart of Kilroy . . . is known variously as Chad, Flywheel, Clem, Private Snoops, the Jeep, or just Phoo. His chalked-up picture is always accompanied by the theme song: "What no . . .?"': a newspaper cutting of Nov. 17, 1945. The same cutting informs us that '*Kilroy was here*, chalked up by American pilots and air crews all over the world, originated in the fact that a friend of Sergeant Francis Kilroy thought him a wonderful guy and scrawled on the bulletin board of a Florida air base: "Kilroy will be here next week." The phrase took the fancy of army fliers and it spread across the world'—often in the form, *What, no Kilroy?* But see **Kilroy was here** below.

Chad is mostly R.A.F., whereas *Private Snoops* is Army; in the Navy he is *The Watcher.*

chaff.—3. Money: low Australian: C. 20. Kylie Tennant, *Foveaux*, 1939, 'He'—a barrowman—'gave money its rightful designation of "chaff", "sugar" or "hay".'

chaff, v., 1 (p. 137) occurs in *Boxiana*, III, 1821, rather in the sense 'to rebuke': 'Wood . . . was severely *chaffing* Randall for interference'. Perhaps by confusion with S.E. *chide.*

chaff-cutter. A typewriter: Australian: since ca. 1920. B., 1942. Ex the noise it makes.

chaffer, 2 (p. 137). In *Boxiana*, III, 1821, the nuance is 'throat'; thus, 'Cool their *chaffer* with a drop of *heavy wet*'; sense 1, by the way, occurs in the same work, some thirty years earlier than the *Dict.* recording.

chaffy.—3. '. . . Slang current sixty years ago when I was a boy at Christ's Hospital: a slap on the face was a fotch, bread a krug and butter flab. A fag was a swab. Chaffy meant pleased—"I'm awfully chaffy"' (A.B.S. in correspondence columns of *The Sunday Times*, Sept. 8, 1963). Cf. **chuffed** below.

chai. See **chy.**

chain and crank. A bank: rhyming s.: C. 20. (Cf. *rattle and crank*.)

chain-breaker (p. 137). And, of course, shorts.

chain-gang.—3. Those waiters who, not on saloon duty, perform the odd jobs: passenger ships': Dave Marlowe, 1937.

Chain Gang, the. Aircrafthands, General Duties: R.A.F.: since ca. 1930. Partridge, 1945, 'The R.A.F.'s maids of all work.' Perhaps imm. ex **chain-gang**, 2 (p. 137).

chain gang, the.—4. A bus-running inspector: busmen's, esp. in London: since ca. 1930.

chain up a pup. See **tie up a dog.**

chair-borne divisions, the. Those members of the Force who work in offices: Air Force (mostly R.A.F.): since 1942. Ironically ex *Airborne Divisions.*—Also called *chair-borne types.*

chair-marking (p. 137) is, among taxi-drivers, an illicit marking of their licences by their employers: Herbert Hodge, *Cab, Sir?*, 1939.

chal droch. A knife: Shelta: C. 18–20. B. & L.

chalk, adj. To the *Dict.* entry add F. & H.'s explanation: 'From the practice at race-meetings of keeping blank slides at the telegraph board on which the names of new jockeys can be inscribed in chalk, while the names of well-known men are usually painted or printed in permanent characters . . . The public argued that [the latter] were incompetent, being unknown.'

chalk! Silence!: tailors': mid-C. 19–20. B. & L.

chalk and talk; also *chalk-and-talker.* A schoolteacher: Australian: since ca. 1920. B., 1942. He or she uses much chalk, more talk.

Chalk Farm (p. 138) was, by the late 1920's, ob. and by 1960, virtually †.

chalk jockey. 'One who rides too seldom to have his name printed on the notice board' (it's chalked up, instead): racing: since ca. 1935. (John Lawrence, 1963.)

chalkie. A schoolteacher: Australian: since ca. 1930. (B., 1953.)

chalks. Legs: low: ca. 1825–70. *Sinks*, 1848.

chalks, do the. To write the score at darts, esp. in match-games: dart-players': since ca. 1945. With chalk on a board.

chamber-music. The sound made by a chamberpot being used: jocular domestic: late C. 19–20.

chamfer up. To tidy up, make things tidy: Naval: C. 20: Granville. Ex the stonemasonry and carpentry senses.

chammy. See **cham** (*Dict.*).

Champagne Charley. Any noted drinker of champagne; hence, any dissipated man: mostly Londoners': from 1868; ob. B. & L., 'The name of a song which appeared in 1868. . . . The original *Charley* was a wine-merchant that was very generous with presents of champagne to his friends.'

champagne-glass.—A Hampden (or less frequently a Hereford) aircraft in the plan view: R.A.F.: ca. 1940–3, then ob. Partridge, 1945. Resemblance.

Champaigne Country. Dining and wining; champagne drinking: Oxford and buckish: ca. 1810–40. Pierce Egan, *Life in London*, 1821.

champers. Champagne: since ca. 1920. Oxford undergraduates' ('the Oxford-*er*'); hence, since ca. 1950, also among the smart young set. (Gilderdale, 2.)

chance, v. (p. 139). 'Some would "chance" everything to be transported,' Anon., *A History of Van Diemen's Land*, 1835.

chance one's mitt. To make an attempt; to risk it, take a chance: Army: 1914–18. Cf. **chance your arm** on p. 139.

chancer.—2. 'One who tries it on by *telling the tale*; or one who just takes chances' (H. & P.): Services: since the 1920's. See **chance your arm** in the *Dict.*—3. Hence, one not too smart in appearance or at drill: Army: since ca. 1930.— 4. An expensive motor-car, oldish and of unusual make: motor trade: since ca. 1920. The dealer 'takes a chance' when he buys it.—5. A bluffer: Anglo-Irish: C. 20. (Desmond O'Neill, *Life Has No Price*, 1959.)

chancery, v. To put 'in chancery': pugilistic: ca. 1815–50. *Boxiana*, III, 1821. Ex **chancery, in** (*Dict.*).

chancery (or **C-**) **practice.** Habit of putting opponent's head 'in chancery': pugilistic: ca. 1815–60. *Boxiana*, II, 1818.

change the record! See **record!, change the,** below.

changes, ring the.—4. To muddle a tradesman over the correct change to be received: c.: from ca. 1880.

Channel crossing. Bread-and-butter pudding: Marlborough College: since ca. 1920.

Channel fever (p. 139). Laurie Atkinson, in a note dated Sept. 11, 1967, defines it as 'the nervous state that overcomes some sailors as their ship nears home after long absence or relatively long abstinence'.

Channel fleet. A street: Irish rhyming s.: C. 20. Franklyn, *Rhyming.*

Channel (or **channel**)-**groper;** cf., on p. 139, **Channel-groping,** which, occurring in Smyth, 1867, prob. goes back to early C. 19. 'In the course of time, the ship and her convoy arrived safe and sound in Portsmouth harbour, and we became one of the "channel-gropers" (as they dignified ships on the home station)': Fredk Chamier, *The Life of a Sailor*, at II, 66. Colonel Moe records its use by Marryat in *The King's Own*, 1830 (p. 88 of the 1896 edition).

Channel swimmers, the. The fighting man's self-description, March–April 1918, as a result of Haig's famous order, during the Spring retreat, 'to fight it out with our backs to the wall': British troops', not Dominion troops'. Those who couldn't swim called themselves 'the *non*-Channel swimmers'. (A. B. Petch.)

chant the poker!, don't. See **sing it!, don't.**

chanticleer. Penis: literary and cultured: mid-C. 19–20; ob. Punning *cock.*

chanting slum. A music-hall: fast life: ca. 1830. Anon., *The New Swell's Guide to Night Life*, 1846. Cf. **chanting ken.**

character.—2. A character part: theatrical coll.: late C. 19–20. Leonard Merrick, *Peggy Harper*, 1911.—3. Whereas the R.A.F. speaks of *types* and the Navy and the Army imitate, the

Royal Navy speaks of *characters* and the other two services imitate: since ca. 1925.

'So widely was this Swordfish known
That characters could not be found
To drive it. It remained unknown—
Un-airborne, wholly hangar-bound,'
Commander Justin Richardson,
The Phoney Phleet, 1946.

Indeed, since ca. 1945, the term has become increasingly popular everywhere and now means simply 'fellows' or 'guys'.

characters. One's references, as regards employment: Midland and North Country coll.: C. 20. (F. B. Vickers, *First Place to the Stranger*, 1955.)

charge, n.—2. Marijuana: c.: since ca. 1943. It contains a 'charge'—produces a 'kick'.—3. In hospitals, *the charge* is a Charge Nurse (esp. if male), i.e. one in charge of a ward or set of wards: coll.: C. 20.

charge. To run at full speed: Winchester College coll.: from ca. 1860. B. & L.

chariot.—2. A caboose; occ. a passenger car: Canadian railroadmen's (— 1931). Derisive.—3. (Also *wanking chariot*.) A bed: Army: since ca. 1940.—4. A motor car: jocular: since ca. 1945. Cf. sense 1 on p. 141.

charity dame or **for-free,** A prostitute undercutting the prices; an 'enthusiastic amateur': Australian c., esp. prostitutes': resp. since ca. 1930 and ca. 1944 (U.S. influence). B., 1953.

Charles his friend. The young man serving as foil to the *jeune premier*: theatrical: from ca. 1870. B. & L. Ex description in the *dramatis personae*.

Charles James.—2. A fox: hunting slang: late C. 19–20. Same origin as sense 1.

charley.—9. A gold watch: c. from ca. 1830. By pun ex sense 1.—10. Reveille: Naval: C. 20. Granville, 'The bugle call, to which the Navy has given these words:—

"Charley! Charley! get up and wash yourself!
Charley! Charley! lash up and stow!"'

—11. Short for *Charley Ronce*(?): mid-C. 19–20. *New Statesman*, Nov. 29, 1941.

charley (or -**lie**).—12. Esp. in 'your Charlie', your girl: Australian, esp. Sydney: since ca. 1945. (Lawson Glassop, *Lucky Palmer*, 1949.)—13. A male homosexual: since ca. 1945.—14. Afraid; 'windy': low: since ca. 1930. 'I was dead charlie' (Norman).—15. (A specialisation of 12.) A prostitute: low Australian: since ca. 1946. (B., 1953.)

charley or **charlie**—or **C**—.—16. A fool: C. 20 among Cockneys, but only since late 1940's at all general; esp. in *a proper charley*, a thorough fool. Short for **Charley Hunt** below.

Charley, hop the. See **hop the Charley.**

charley, turn. To turn coward or become frightened: low London: since ca. 1930.

Charley, turn. See **turn . . .**

Charley Brady. A hat: rhyming s. (on *cady*): late C. 19–20; by 1950, ob. (Franklyn, *Rhyming*.)

Charley Dilke. Milk: ca. 1880–1940. Franklyn, *Rhyming*.

Charley Fox. A politically minded seaman tending to harangue: Naval: ca. 1790–1815.

W. N. Glascock, *Sailors and Saints* (II, 186), 1829. Moe.

Charley Frisky. Whisky: navvies' rhyming s.: ca. 1860–1910. (D. W. Barrett, 1880.)

Charley Howard. A coward: rhyming: C. 20. James Curtis, 1936.

Charley (or **Charlie**) **Hunt;** often in C. 20 shortened to *Charley* (*Charlie*). The female pudend: rhyming s.: since ca. 1890. A variant of **Joe Hunt** (below)—cf. **Berkeley** (**Hunt**), q.v. on p. 48.—2. Hence, a 'softy', a fool: C. 20; in gen. use only since the late 1940's and increasingly in the shortened form.

Charley Lancaster (p. 141) fell into disuse ca. 1930.

Charley Mason. A basin: rhyming s.: since ca. 1880.

Charley More. See **act . . .**

Charley Noble is recorded earlier in 'Taffrail'.

Charley (or **Charlie**) **Orange.** Often merely *Charley* (etc.). The Commanding Officer: R.A.F.: 1939 +. W/Cdr Robin P. McDouall, April 12, 1945, 'From the phonetic alphabet'.

Charley Randy. Brandy: navvies' rhyming s.: ca. 1860–1910. (D. W. Barrett, 1880.)

Charley (or -**ie**) **Ronce.** A souteneur or prostitute's bully: late C. 19–20: rhyming s. on **ponce** (*Dict.*). Often shortened to *Charley* which, derivatively, = very smart, 'one of the boys'.

Charley Skinner. Dinner: navvies' rhyming s.: ca. 1860–1910. (Barrett.)

Charley Wheeler. A girl: Australian: C. 20. (S. J. Baker, *The Australian Language*, 1945; Dal Stivens, *Jimmy Brockett*, 1951.) Rhyming on *Sheila*.

Charley Wiggins. Lodgings: mainly theatrical rhyming s. (on *diggings* pronounced *diggins*): late C. 19–20. (Franklyn, *Rhyming*.)

charleys.—3. Testicles: low: C. 20. Perhaps ex sense 1 (p. 141).—4. (Mostly *Charlies*.) Sailors in general: Australian Naval: since ca. 1925. (B., 1943.)—5. Shoulders: North Country, esp. Yorkshire: C. 20. 'Straighten your charleys, lad' is said to a stooping boy.

Charley's coat. A Carley float: Australian rhyming s., mostly Navy and Air Force: 1942 +. (B., 1943.)

charley's fiddle. A watchman's rattle: fast life: ca. 1815–40. W. T. Moncrieff, *Tom and Jerry*, 1821. See **charley,** p. 141.

charmer. One's girl friend: Services': since ca. 1935. H. & P.

charming mottle. A bottle: Australian rhyming s.: ca. 1880–1910. *The* (Sydney) *Bulletin*, Jan. 18, 1902—cited by Baker, 1945.

charp. A bed: Regular Army and, since ca. 1920, R.A.F. regulars': late C. 19–20. Jackson, 'From the Hindustani, charpoy'.

charperer; or **charpering omee** (or **omer**). A policeman: parlyaree: since ca. 1860. P. H. Emerson, *Signor Lippo*, 1893. The shorter prob. derives from the longer term. Cf.:—

charpering carsey. A police station: parlyaree: since ca. 1870. In, e.g., P. H. Emerson, 1893. Cf. the prec. entry, where *omee* = a man; here, *carsey* = *casa* = a house. The dominant element, *charpering* = 'searching': ex It. *cercare*, 'to search (for)'.

charpoy-bashing. Sleeping; sleep: R.A.F. regulars' since ca. 1920. Gerald Emanuel, letter of

March 29, 1945. See **charp** and cf. **square-bashing**.

charrshom or **chershom**. A crown (coin): Shelta: C. 18–20; very ob. B. & L.

Chart and Evans. Knees: Naval: C. 20. (Granville.) A rationalized form of *chart an' 'eavens*, itself incorrect for *chart in 'eavens*. The semantic key is supplied by s. *benders*, knees— what you get down upon to say the Lord's Prayer, 'Our Father, *which art in Heaven*'—and strengthened by the second verb in the predominant construction and usage, 'Get down on your chart 'n eavens and *holy*stone the deck.'

charver (p. 142). Also spelt *charva*, as in *bona palone for a charva*, a good-time girl. (*John o'London's Weekly*, Feb. 4, 1949.)

charwallah.—2. 'In India this is a native servant who brings the early morning tea. In Gibraltar, a dining-hall waiter,' H. & P.: Services: since ca. 1930. (Gerald Emanuel, March 29, 1945.) Also used as an adj.; e.g. *charwallah squadron*, an Air Force squadron consisting of Indian personnel.

chase. 'To stand over and keep urging (someone) to do and get on with a piece of work': Services' coll.: since ca. 1920. H. & P.—2. To court (a girl): S. Africa: since ca. 1935. Prof. W. S. Mackie in *The Cape Argus*, July 4, 1946. But also Cockney since late C. 19.

chase-me-Charley. 'A radio-controlled gliderbomb used by the Germans': Naval: ca. 1940–5. Granville.

chase the hares; usually as n. or participle, *chasing the hares*. To run after women: C. 20. A pun on *hairs*.

chase the nimble pennyweight. To pick gold from a dish: Australian miners': C. 20, B., 1942. Journalistic in origin?

chase-up. A race; a speedy driving: since late 1940's. Peter Crookston, *Villain*, 1967, 'There were ten of us and we each stole a car from a carpark to have a bit of a chase-up.'

chaser.—2. A woman-chaser: Canadian coll.: adopted, ca. 1935, ex U.S. Cf. *chase*, v., 2.

chasing the red. (Of a flagman) going back with a red flag or a red light to protect a train: Canadian railroadmen's (— 1931).

chass, To chase; to harry: Naval cadets': since ca. 1880. 'Taffrail', *The Sub*, 1917. Cf. **chasse** (p. 142) and **chase**, 1 (above).

chasse. A drink after coffee: 1860, Surtees, *Plain or Ringlets*; † by 1920. Cf. **chaser** in *Dict*.

chat, n., 5 (see *Dict*.) is occ. extended to mean enterprise, esp. a criminal job: from ca. 1870. Pugh (2): 'The chat we're on is called The Observatory, an' it's got a sort of tower stickin' out o' the roof.'—10. (Usually in pl. *chats*.) A person: circusmen's: late C. 19–20. 'Fake the chats' = talk to the crowd to keep them quiet.— 11. 'The gift of the gab': low: since late 1940's. James Barlow, *The Burden of Proof*, 1968.—12. Language; way of speaking or writing; terminology: since ca. 1950. Laurence Henderson, *With Intent*, 1968, '"Says he's a nice fellow, likes hurting people, knocks girls about, sticks knives in people. An emotional pauper."—"How much?" —"That's college chat for a right bastard."'

chat, v.—3. Hence (?), to talk to or with (someone): since ca. 1920. 'Chatting a bogy', James Curtis, *The Gilt Kid*, 1936.—4. See **chat up**, 2, below.

chat marks. Quotation marks: mostly authors': C. 20. (Berta Ruck, *A Story-Teller Tells the Truth*, 1935.)

chat-up. The n. that corresponds to **chat-up**, v. (p. 142).

chat (someone) up. To bluff; to 'con': since ca. 1925. Robin Cook, *The Crust on Its Uppers*, 1962.—2. (Of a male) to talk to a girl, a woman, persistently and persuasively, esp. with a view to sexual dalliance: since ca. 1936. Also to *chat* (a girl). Ronald Harwood, *The Lads*, a television play shown on Aug. 15, 1963. (Laurie Atkinson.)

Chatham Dockyard . . . See **when Adam** . . . in *Dict*.

Chats. Sense 1 (p. 142) has, in the Navy, > 'the Chatham R.N. Barracks' (Granville): late C. 19–20.—2. Earlier in 'Taffrail'.

chatsby (p. 142): also in R.A.F. (G. Emanuel, March 29, 1945.)

chatterbox. A machine-gun: R.A.F. air-crews': adopted in mid-1940 from the American Eagle Squadron; ob. by 1946. *The Reader's Digest*, Feb. 1941. Also among Australians: B., 1942. The genuinely English form is *chatter-gun* (or one word), as in Brickhill & Norton, *Escape to Danger*, 1946, 'The chatter-guns opened up'.

chatterer. Slightly earlier in *Boxiana*, IV, 1824.

chatterers (p. 142). Slightly earlier in *Boxiana*, III, 1821.

chatty, n.—5. A louse: New Zealand: since ca. 1915. B., 1941. See **chat**, n., 7, and esp. **chati** (p. 142).

***chatty feeder**. A variant of **chattry feeder** (*Dict.*).

chauff. To act as chauffeur to: since ca. 1925. Gavin Holt, *The Murder Train*, 1936, 'Sorry, I'm chauffing Cynthia'.—2. To drive: since ca. 1925. Herbert Adams, *The Crooked Life*, 1931, 'Not fit to chauff a dust-cart'.

chauvering donna (or **moll**). See **chauvering** (*Dict.*).

chaw one's fat. A variant of *chew one's* or *the*, *fat*.

cheap and nasty. A pasty: Australian rhyming s.: C. 20. (A. A. Martin, letter, 1937.)

cheap at half the price! 'That's a very reasonable price': a c.p. used when one is satisfied with a price either asked or charged: since ca. 1920 (? much earlier).

cheat (p. 143) is probably related to '*chattel*'.

cheated the starter, they. A c.p., applied to a married couple whose first child arrives before it is formally due: since ca. 1910.

cheaters. See **daughters**. Dating from ca. 1910. (Esp. if with elastic leg-bands.)—2. Spectacles (glasses): Canadian: C. 20; originally, underworld; by 1935, s.—3. Foam-plastic bustforms ('falsies'): Australian: since ca. 1945. Lawson Glassop, *Lucky Palmer*, 1949, '"Cheaters," said Mrs Shendon, as if instructing a class of dull children, "make mountains out of molehills."' Cf. **falsies** below.

Sense 2 prob. went to Canada ex U.S., where it may or may not have orig. been c.: see, e.g., my *Underworld*. In Canada, moreover, it prob. > gen. s. by 1930 at latest; in U.S., it was certainly gen. s. by ca. 1920. (With indirect thanks to Mr R. W. Burchfield.)

check. 'To reprimand, to take to task, during the exercise of one's duty,' Partridge, 1945. Proleptic: it should check the recipient's evil ways.—2. The Artillery's *Check!* (As you were) came, in the Army and then in the other Services, to serve for 'I have checked', all is now well, all right, O.K.: coll.: since 1940. By 1950, *check!*, O.K., had become fairly common, and by 1955 very common, among civilians; but this civilian use was aided by adoption of American *check!*, O.K.

check up on. To eye amorously: since ca. 1936. To assess a woman's sexual charms.—2. A synonym of **keep tabs on** below: adopted, ca. 1960, ex Canada, where current since ca. 1920.

checker.—2. A homing pigeon: C. 20. H. U. Triston, *Men in Cages*, 1938.

checkerboard, a type of Fokker, and **red-nose**, another German fighter aircraft: airmen's: 1916–18. (Guy Fowler, *The Dawn Patrol*, 1930.)

chee, adj. Long: pidgin: from ca. 1870. B. & L. Abbr. *muchee*.

cheechako. A tenderfoot: Canadian (Yukon and N.W.): late C. 19–20; by 1949, ob. Note Robert W. Service, *Ballads of a Cheechako*, 1909. A Chinook jargon word, lit. 'new-comer': *chee*, new; *chako*, to come. (Leechman.)

cheek, n., 1: earlier in *Sessions*, June 1835.

cheeks (p. 144). Sense 1, 1. 5: for 'dresses' read 'skirts'.—3. 'Cheeks, an imaginary person; nobody; as in "Who does that belong to? Cheeks!"' (*Sinks*, 1848): low: ca. 1780–1870. *Sessions*, Feb. 1791 (p. 203).

cheeky possum. Cheeky fellow: esp., cheeky child (mostly boy): Australian juvenile: since ca. 1935. (B., 1953.)

cheer!, what. See **what cheer!**

cheer-chaser, -chasing; chase cheers. The agent, the verbal noun, the verb, for 'curry favour with the mob': Australian coll.: since ca. 1930. (B., 1943.)

cheer up (, cully), you'll soon be dead! A c.p. of C. 20. E.g. in W. L. George, *The Making of an Englishman*, 1914. It either comes from or, at the least, occurs in an early C. 20 music-hall song: 'I've got a motter "Always be merry and bright"'—rendered, Julian Franklyn tells me 'in a painfully miserable tone'.

cheerful giver. Liver (bodily organ): rhyming s.: C. 20. An allusion, not a designation; the designation is *bow and quiver*. See esp. Franklyn 2nd.

cheeri! Cheerio!: New Zealand: since ca. 1930. (Slatter.)

Cheeribye!, Good-bye, or au revoir: 1942 +. A blend of *cheerio + goodbye*. Cf. **cheerioski**.

cheerio.—3. Hence, tipsy: S. Africa: since ca. 1936. Prof. W. S. Mackie in *The Cape Argus*, June (? 29), 1946.

cheerioski. 'Cheerio!' ca. 1925–38. Phillip Macdonald, *The Rynox Mystery*, 1930.

cheers ! A toast that, arising ca. 1945, became very popular ca. 1950—and has remained so. Not s., of course, but a coll.

chees and chaws. The Italianate pronunciation of ecclesiastical Latin: British Catholics': ca. 1850–1900. See, e.g., Bernard Ward, *The Sequel to Catholic Emancipation*, 1915, and F. Brittain, *Latin in Church*, 1934. Ex *c* > *ch*, long *o* > *aw*, etc.

cheese, n.—3. Smegma: low: mid-C. 19–20.

cheese, v.—2, 3, 4 Morris Marples, in his excellent *Public School Slang*, 1940, records these senses: to study hard (Bradfield, since ca. 1917);

to smile (esp. broadly), at Oundle since ca. 1918, prob. ex *grin like a Cheshire cat* (see **Cheshire cat**, p. 145); to hurry, to stride out (Lancing since mid-1930's), perhaps ex 'go *flat* out, like a flat cheese'.

cheese and kisses. Wife: late C. 19–20. Rhyming on *missus*.

cheese-cutter, 4 (p. 144). Rather: since ca. 1840. *Sinks*, 1848.—5. A sword: Army: C. 20. H. & P.—6. A bicycle seat: Australian, esp. Sydney motor mechanics': since ca. 1950. (B.P.)

cheese down. 'To coil rope into neat spirals for a harbour stow' (P-G-R.): Naval coll.: late C. 19–20; by 1940, perhaps rather j. So to coil the rope that it assumes the shape of a large cheese.

cheese-eye (phonetic spelling); also **cheese-eyed** (inferior form). A pejorative intensive, as in 'that cheese-eye pusser': Naval, esp. on China-side: late C. 19–20. Ex Chinese? *Not* necessarily pejorative. 'Bartimeus' in his *A Tall Ship*, 1915, uses it neutrally when a character refers thus to his Captain's children—and he's speaking to their parents!

cheese-toaster (p. 144) occurs, as 'bayonet', in Fredk Chamier, *The Life of a Sailor*, 1832, at II, 104, as a Naval, esp. a Royal Marine, term. (Moe.)

cheesecake. A display, esp. in a smart magazine, of feminine beauty and physical charm: adopted, ca. 1944, ex U.S. Hence the complementary *beefcake*, a display of masculine muscle and good looks: adopted, ca. 1950, ex U.S. The display is of as much anatomy as the law will allow.

cheesed. Has, since 1941, been often used for the next. Jackson, 1943.

cheesed(-)off. Disgruntled: Liverpool boys' (— 1914); Liverpool troops' (1914–18); common in all Services since ca. 1935; but since 1940, esp. R.A.F.; and, since ca. 1950, general. Grenfell Finn-Smith, in list communicated in April 1942; H. & P., 1943; Partridge, 1945. Perhaps suggested by **browned off**, q.v., via the *brown* rind of *cheese*. Professor Douglas Hamer derives it ex the Liverpool boys' **cheese off!**, run away and don't be a nuisance, itself current since ca. 1890.

cheesy.—2. Smelly: (low) coll.: late C. 19–20. Ex the smell of strong cheese. B. & L.

Cheesy Gordons, the. The Gordon Highlanders: late C. 19–20. Perhaps ex *cheesy*, 1 (p. 145).

Chelt. A resident or frequenter of Cheltenham: sporting and fast life: ca. 1820–60. *Spy*, II, 1826. An abbr. of *Cheltonian*.

Cheltenham (Cold). Cold: rhyming: late C. 19–20. This is an intensive variant of *Cheltenham bold*. (Franklyn, *Rhyming*.)

chem, n. and adj. Chemistry, esp. as a subject of study; in or of chemistry: Australian students': since ca. 1910. (B.P.)

Chemist, the. Also, since ca. 1918, used by the Navy: Granville.

cherpin (*Dict.*) is a loose, almost sol., abbr. of **cherpin llowyer**, Shelta for a book: B. & L.

Cherries, the. Boscombe Association Football Club: sporting: since ca. 1950.

cherries, the. See **cherry hog** and **cherry oggs**, 2.

cherry.—2. A young man's virginity (physical): Canadian: C. 20.—3. The hymen: late C. 19–20. The origin of sense 2, as also of:—4. A girl's virginity: C. 20.

cherry, take the. To take the new ball: Australian cricketers'; since ca. 1950. (*The Observer*, June 21, 1953.) Ex the ball's redness.

cherry ace. A face: rhyming s.: only ca. 1940–55. (Franklyn, *Rhyming*.)

cherry-bounce. A charabanc: late C. 19–20. By perversion ex *char à banc*.

cherry-hog. A dog: mid-C. 19–20. Rhyming: In greyhound racing, *the cherries* = the dogs.

cherry(-)nose. Sherry: S. African low (? c.). C. 20. *The Cape Times*, June 3, 1946, article by Alan Nash.

cherry oggs. A game played with cherry-stones on the pavement: London children's: since ca. 1880.—2. Greyhound racing: rhyming s. (on *dogs*): since ca. 1920. Often shortened to *the cherries*.

cherry-picker. A pathic: Naval: C. 20.

Cherry Ripe. Centuripe, in Sicily: Army: 1944–5. By the process of 'Hobson-Jobson'. (P-G-R.)

Cherry Trees, the. H.M.S. *Rodney* and H.M.S. *Nelson*, because erroneously supposed to have been *truncated* by the *Washington* Treaty: Naval (ward-room): 1930's–very early 1940's.

chershom. See **charrshom.**

Chesby or **c-.** A good-natured fellow: R.A.F.: 1940 +; by 1960, ob. (P-G-R.)

chest, cock a. See **cock a chest.**

chest stooge. A junior detailed to keep a Cadet Captain's sea-chest tidy for him: R.N.C., Dartmouth: since 1939. Granville.

chesty or **a bit chesty.**—2. (Of a patient) coughing: hospital nurses' coll.: late C. 19–20. Ex sense 1 (p. 146).

Chev.—2. A Chevrolet truck: Army: 1939–45. (P-G-R.)

chew, n., 1 (p. 146): rather, since ca. 1820. It occurs in *The Dublin University Magazine*, Dec. 1835 (p. 616). Moe.—2. Food: South African schools': C. 20.—3. A 'camp' term: C. 20.

chew, v. To talk: New Zealand: since ca. 1920. Jean Devanney, *Riven*, 1929, 'Chewing about homely women and chasing the gay birds.' Ex *chew the fat* (as under).

chew (someone's) ballocks off. To rebuke or reprimand severely: Services', esp. the Army: C. 20. Cf. the synonym on p. 146.

chew (someone's) ear is a C. 20 Australian variant of **bite one's ear** (*Dict.*). B., 1942.

chew (someone) out. To reprimand severely: Canadian: C. 20. (Leechman.)

chew the fat. 'Taffrail', however, has *chew one's fat*, to argue.

chew the rag (cf. the entry at *chew the fat*, p. 146) has, since ca. 1920, predominantly signified 'to talk, to chat, to yarn'—with no undertone of grumbling.

chew up.—2. To savage; to mangle (the body of): C. 20. (Jean Devanney's *Travels*, 1951.)

chewies. Chewing gum: Australian, esp. juvenile: since mid-1940's. (Dick.)

chew(e)y. Chewing gum: Australian juvenile: since ca. 1944. (B., 1953.) Ex the habit rendered even more popular by the multiple and ubiquitous presence of U.S. servicemen in Australia in late 1942–5.

chi-chi, n. and adj. Half-caste (girl, rarely boy): Indian Army and Anglo-Indian coll.: C. 19–20. Ex Hindustani.

chi-chi, n. Unnecessary fuss; affected protests or manners: Society coll.: C. 20. Adopted ex

Fr. coll. Perhaps ex preceding term, but prob. an arbitrary formation.—2. Hence, excessive redtape: Army officers': since ca. 1939. (P-G-R.)

chiack is the predominant Aus. and N.Z. C. 20 form of *chiike*.

chib. A low Cockney corruption of the mainly dial. *jib*, mouth, lower part of the face: 1899, Clarence Rook, *The Hooligan Nights*, 'He slings a rope . . . round her chib, and fastens it to a hook in the wall. Then [she] can stand, but can no longer argue.'

Chicago-piano. A multiple pom-pom: Royal and Merchant Navy: since 1940. 'A rating . . . was crouched by the "Chicago-piano" (battery of A.A. pom-poms) amidships,' Major W. S. Murdock, in Allan Michie & Walter Graebner, *Lights of Freedom*, 1941.

Chicargot. Americanism: Naval officers': since ca. 1940. Granville. A blend of 'Chicago' and 'argot'. Mostly in 'to *talk Chicargot*', to use the argot of Chicago—American expressions.

chice a ma trice. Slightly earlier in *Boxiana*, III, 1821.

chick.—3. One's girl friend: dance-fanatics' and Teddy boys': adopted, ca. 1940, ex U.S. This is a specialisation of U.S. s. *chick*, a girl; cf. sense 1 on p. 146.—4. A male prostitute: prostitutes' and homosexuals': since ca. 1945.

chickaleary cove (p. 146): anticipated by *chickle-a-leary chap* in chorus of underworld song quoted by W. A. Miles, *Poverty*, 1839; more prob. has its origin in *cheeky* (impudent) and *leary* (see p. 474).

chickee. See **chickey**, 2, below.

chicken.—5. A boy homosexual: c., and low: C. 20. Cf. senses 1 and 2.

chicken! Coward!: 'a derisive cry hurled at one who shows signs of cowardice, or even of commendable prudence': Canadian teenagers': since ca. 1950. (Leechman.) Cf. *chicken*, on p. 146, and Michael Innes's novel, *Appleby Plays Chicken*, 1956.

chicken, adj. Cowardly: adopted, ex Canada, ca. 1946 in Britain. Cf. **chicken!**—2. Petty, insignificant; pettily cheating: Canadian: ca. 1910–40. The origin of sense 1. (Priestley.)

chicken-berries. Hen's eggs: Naval (lowerdeck): C. 20. (P-G-R.)

chicken-feed (p. 146). By 1937, also English.—2. Hence, a pittance (financial) or a bare minimum (of food): 1941 +.

chicken(-)fruit. Eggs: Naval: C. 20. Granville.

chicken out. To retire from fight, risk, adventure: Australian: adopted, ca. 1943, ex U.S. Cf. **chicken!** above. (B.P.) Current in R.A.F. since ca. 1950, and general R.A.F. s. since late 1950's. The R.A.F. usage has variant *go chicken*.

chicken-picker. A one-finger typist: Australian jocular: since ca. 1930. Ex plucking a chicken.

chicken-shit. Information from a superior: Canadian: since ca. 1920. But Canadian *have chicken-shit in one's blood* (since ca. 1930) = to be a coward.—2. Adj. Petty, insignificant; pettily cheating: Canadian: ca. 1910–30. The origin of **chicken, adj., 2** (above).

chickey.—2. (Often spelt *chickee* or *chickie*.) Any young girl: Australian teenagers': since ca. 1945. (Dick.)

chickster. Variant spelling of **shickster** (*Dict.*): 1848, *Sinks*.

chicky. A serviceman's girl friend or sweetheart: Australian soldiers': 1939–45. (B., 1943.) Cf. the U.S. *chick*, a girl.

chico. Used on R.A.F. Irak stations, ca. 1925–45, for 1, a bearer, a personal servant (esp. *bungalow chico*); 2, a child, a baby. Prob. ex. Sp. *chico*, 'small boy: lad: dear fellow'. (Atkinson.)

chief. A chief inspector: police coll.: late C. 19–20.

chief pricker. See pricker.

chief scribe, the. Chief Petty Officer, Writer: Naval: since ca. 1910. Granville.

chief stoker. 'A seagull said to be the incarnation of one' (Granville): Naval: late C. 19–20.

chiefie. A Flight-Sergeant: R.A.F.: since April 1918. Sgt-Pilot Rhodes, letter of Sept. 20, 1942. Ex the days when in the Royal Naval Air Service the corresponding man held the rank of *Chief* Petty Officer (3rd Class).

chïike (p. 147). Prob. etymology: a perverse reduplication of *hi* (as a call).

chïike, chiack, v. Sense 2—'to chaff (mercilessly)'—has been current in New Zealand since ca. 1890. (G. B. Lancaster, *Sons o' Men*, 1904, 'Feared o' the boys chiackin' yer?') In Australia, *chiack* has, in C. 20, predominantly meant 'to tease'—cf. sense 3 (p. 147)—and is sometimes used intransitively.

Childe Harold. Any male having the given-name *Harold* tends, in Australia, to be nicknamed *Childe Harold*: C. 20. Ex Byron's famous poem so titled. (B.P.)

children in the wood, the. 'Dice in the box' (Renton Nicholson, *An Autobiography*, 1860, at p. 64): gambling: ca. 1850–1900. Perhaps a pun on the Babes in the Wood.

Child's Guide, the. See Bible, the.

chiller. A 'thriller' that chills the blood: book world: since late 1950's. On the back of the jacket of Alistair Maclean's *Fear Is the Key*, 1961, his *Night without End* is described as 'A "chiller" by Alistair Maclean'. Elliptical for *spine-chiller*.

chilo. Child: pidgin: mid-C. 19–20. B. & L.

chime in with (p. 147), rather, since ca. 1800, to judge by a passage in *The Port Folio* of Nov. 1805. (Moe.)

*chiming. (See chime in *Dict.*) 'Praising a person or thing that is unworthy, for the purpose of getting off a bad bargain' (ibid.): c.: C. 19–20: ob.

Chimleyco. Pimlico: Londoners': from ca. 1860. Ibid.

chimmel; chimmes. Resp., a stick; wood, or a stick: Shelta: C. 18–20. Ibid.

chimney smoke, make the. See make the chimney smoke.

chimp (p. 147). Edward Lear, *Laughable Lyrics*, 1877, 'The wail of the Chimp and Snipe'.

chin, n. (p. 147). No! Prob. a shortening of chin-wag 2. (p. 148)—and current since late C. 19.—2. An actor: Australian: since ca. 1920. B., 1942, 'Cf. "blue-chin"'.

chin, take it on the. To 'take it hard', whether misfortune or disappointment: coll.: since ca. 1930. Ex boxing.

chin-food. A bore's conversation: Army and R.A.F.: since the 1920's. H. & P.—2. In the Navy: idle prattle (Granville): since ca. 1920.

chin-prop. A brooch: ca. 1820–80. Renton Nicholson, *An Autobiography*, 1860, at p. 256.

chin-strap. The buttocks: low Cockney: from ca. 1918. Derisive.

chin-straps, be on one's. To be utterly exhausted: Army: since ca. 1920. Ex come in on one's chin-strap (p. 147, foot).

china is also applied to a friend of the other sex.

China. This Cockney coll. dates from ca. 1870 and is defined by Mr Julian Franklyn as 'The whole world other than Europe and English-speaking lands. The place rich folk go to for their holidays. The place any person not wearing European dress comes from. Also distant-local, as in "Yeh sends that boy aht fer a errind an' 'e goes orf teh bleed'n Choina!"'

china, bring on one's (or the). To effect the orgasm: low: C. 20.

China bird (p. 148). Esp., 'one whose conversation is interlarded with "Chop Chops" and "Can do's".' Granville.

china plate (see china, p. 148); apparently since ca. 1870—witness D. W. Barrett, *Navvies*, 1880. —2. With *the*, the First Mate: Merchant Navy: C. 20. (Franklyn 2nd.)

China-side. The China station: Naval coll.: C. 20. Granville.

Chinaman.—2. An Irishman: English, esp. Londoners': late C. 19–20. Brendan Behan, *Borstal Boy*, 1958.—3. 'An unshorn lock on the sheep's rump, like the pigtail of Orientals' (*Straight Furrow*, Feb. 21, 1968): N.Z. shearers': C. 20.

Chinaman, I must have killed a. An Australian c.p. referring to a run of bad luck: since ca. 1905. (B.P.)

China's cow. The soya bean, abounding in the Far East: C. 20.

Chinese attack. 'A lot of noise and activity to delude the enemy that an attack was brewing in that spot, and to distract his attention from the real one' (P-G-R): Army, mostly officers', coll.: 1940 +.

Chinese burn. 'Cruelty perpetrated by grabbing someone's arm with both fists close together and twisting in opposite directions' (B.P.): Australian schoolchildren's: since ca. 1930. (B.P.) Variant: *Chinese burner*, as in Dick.

Chinese consumption. The possession of only one effective lung; hence also the so-called 'smokers' cough': Australian: since ca. 1935. A pun on *Wun Bung Lung*, one defective lung. (B.P.)

Chinese dominoes; Chinese Cement. See 'Hauliers' Slang'.

Chinese drive. See French drive below.

Chinese fashion. The sexual act performed with the partners lying on their side: Forces in the Far East, 1939–45. 'The Chinese fashion of writing at right angles to ours led the Far Eastern troops to assume that other things were at right angles to normal. Hence the female pudend was assumed to be transverse externally': thus a valued correspondent writing late in 1961.

Chinese fours. 'B.R. standard 4 freight locomotives' (*Railway*, 3rd): railwaymen's: since ca. 1945.

Chinese landing. A landing made with one wing lower than it should be: Canadian airmen's: since ca. 1917. A pun on *Wun Wing Low*. Dr Leechman heard it in W.W. I.

Chinese National Anthem. A loud expectoration: Naval: C. 20. Granville.

Chinese wedding-cake. Rice pudding: Naval:

C. 20. *Sunday Chronicle*, March 1, 1942. Ex rice as the staple food of China.

Chinkie (p. 148). 'Not ob.': Sidney J. Baker, letter of 1946.

Chinky. 'A rating who is always reminiscing about the good old days on China-side' (Granville): Naval: C. 20. Ex **Chinkie** (*Dict.*).

Chinky-toe-rot. A foot-complaint prevalent in the East (and in other tropics): Naval: C. 20. Granville. Unpleasant to see—or to smell.

chintz, bed-bug (p. 148). Far more probably ex Sp. *chinche*.

chip, n.—8. A quarrel: Australian: C. 20. 'We had a bit of a chip over one thing and another' (Kylie Tennant, *Lost Haven*, 1947).

chip, v.—3. To reprove: criticise adversely: Australian: C. 20. Baker.

chip back. To rebate, to discount; to reduce (a price) by a stated sum, as in 'I'd want some change out of that. Can't you chip me a tenner back?': secondhand-car dealers', esp. in London: since ca. 1945. (Anthony Cowdy in coloured supplement of *The Sunday Times*, Oct. 24, 1965.)

chip off the old block. The Australian form of *chip of . . .*, q.v. at **block, a chip of the old** (p. 65). B.P.

chip on one's shoulder, have a. To bear a grudge against the world: coll.: U.S., since ca. 1880; Canadian since ca. 1890; English, only since 1942, Australian and New Zealand since 1943 or 1944, all introduced by U.S. servicemen. Originally, lumbermen's, from chips falling on to the shoulders of men working beneath or very near a tree that is being felled. But Professor F. E. L. Priestly, in letter of Oct. 12, 1965, tells me that it 'comes from the American boy's method of challenge to a fight—putting a chip on his shoulder and daring the other to knock it off. . . . There are chips in the yard of every American farm where they burn wood. To go round with a chip on your shoulder is to be looking for a fight, constantly challenging all comers, and this is what the expression means in America.' This is the origin accepted by Craigie & Hulbert and by Mitford M. Mathews.

chip one off. To salute a superior officer: Naval: since ca. 1930. Granville.

chipper. A lively young fellow: 1821, Pierce Egan, *Life in London*; † by 1870. Cf. the adj. in the *Dict.*—2. A crisp blow or punch: pugilistic: ca. 1840–90. Augustus Mayhew, *Paved with Gold*, 1857.

chippery. 'Chipping'; (an exchange of) banter: Cockneys': C. 20. Pugh, 'She hadn't 'alf got over that bit of chippery with the rozzer in the station.'

chipping.—3. See **chowing**.

Chippy.—2. A. G. Chipperfield, the N.S.W. and Australian general utility man, cool and classic batsman, guileful spinner of leg breaks, and magnificent fielder in the slips: cricketers' and Australian cricket-enthusiasts': from 1934. C. B. Fry in *The Evening Standard*, Nov. 21, 1936, 'If "Chippy", why not "Birdy" [on this responsive wicket]?' (See **Birdy**, 2.)

chippy, n. A variant of **chips**, 1 (*Dict.*), 'carpenter': Services: since ca. 1918. H. & P. But also builders' s., C. 20, for either a carpenter or a joiner.—2. A fish-and-chips shop: Merseyside: C. 20.—3. A semi-professional prostitute: Australian and Canadian: adopted, ca. 1942, ex

U.S. (B., 1943.)—4. Hence, since ca. 1950, any girl: Australian. (B., 1953.)

chippy, adj. Cheap: Canadian (— 1949).

chippy chap (q.v. in *Dict.*) occurs earlier in 'Taffrail'; see also **wood-spoiler** in these Addenda.

chippy rigger. A Carpenter Rigger: R.A.F.: since ca. 1930. Jackson. Cf. **chippy**.

chips.—6. Knees; esp. *on one's chips*, exhausted: R.A.F.: since ca. 1930.—7. Cipollata sausages, the very small sausages flavoured with herbs: lower and lower-middle classes: since ca. 1950. (Anthony Burgess, Nov. 15, 1967.) *Via* the careless English pronunciation *chip-oh-lah-ta*.

chips, cash—or **throw in**—**one's**. To die: Canadian: adopted, ca. 1880, ex U.S. Ex the S.E. sense, to stop gambling, esp. at cards, notably poker.

chips, give (someone) **full; (his) chips are high.** Both expressions signify approval: Royal Indian Navy: ca. 1939–45. Here, a *chip* is a rupee: cf. *chip*, n., 7 (p. 148). P-G-R.

chips, have had (sometimes **got**) **one's**. To have died, to be dead: since ca. 1917. Adapted from U.S. *pass in one's chips*, itself from the game of poker.

Chips, the. A train that takes office workers in Sydney to the towns in the Blue Mountains: Australian: esp. N.S.W.: since late 1940's. Prompted by 'the **Fish**' below. (B.P.)

chirrup and titter. A bitter (beer): mostly theatrical rhyming s.: late C. 19–20. (Franklyn, *Rhyming*.)

chise.—2. A variant of **chice** (p. 146): *Boxiana*, IV, 1824.

chisel-mouth. A sheep with teeth in good condition: Australian: C. 20. (B., 1943.) Contrast *gummy*, n., 7.

chisler (loose but usual for *chiseller*). A young fellow: Anglo-Irish (— 1951). Rarely offensive.

chit.—4. A pill: showmen's: late C. 19–20. *Night and Day*, July 22, 1937. Hence, *chitworker*, a fellow who sells pills on the markets. 'A "crocus" would say, "I'm grafting chits"' (Phillip Allingham, in letter, 1937).—5. See *have a good chit*.

chit, give (someone) **a good**—**a bad.** To speak well, or badly, of someone: Army: C. 20. See **chit**, 1 (*Dict.*).

chit-up. To seek (someone) through the head of his department: Naval officers': since ca. 1940. (P-G-R.) Ex **chit**, 1 (p. 149).

chitty.—2. A chit: Naval: since ca. 1935. (P-G-R.) Hence, also an Army term, since at least as early as 1945.

*****chiv**, n., 1, is, in C. 20, applied esp. to a razor-blade set in a piece of wood and used as a weapon in the underworld.

*****chiv-man.** A criminal that is a professional knifer: c.: C. 20. (*The Pawnshop Murder.*) See **chive-fencer** in *Dict.*

*****chive**, v. 'To cut with a knife' (James Dalton, *A Narrative*, 1728): c.: C. 18–20. Cf. **chiv**, v., on p. 149, and also at p. 8, '"I'll chive him."'

*****chivey; chivvy.** (Gen. as ppl. adj., *chiv(v)ied*.) To slash (a person) with a knife: c.: C. 20. Ex **chivey**, n., 1 (*Dict.*).

chivoo or **chiveau.** See **shevoo**.

chivver. A variant—since ca. 1920—of **chiv-man** above. (John Gosling, 1959.)

chivvy, 3 (p. 149): esp. among Cockneys, as, e.g., in A. Neil Lyons, *Clara*, 1912: late C. 19–20. n.—5. A moustache: London, mostly low but not c.: since ca. 1940. (Hank Hobson, *Mission House Murder*, 1959.) Ex sense 4 on p. 149.

chivvy, v.—6. To keep (someone) up to the mark by word and gesture: Army: late C. 19–20. Ex sense 2 of the v. on p. 149.

chizz. To cheat or swindle: Public and Grammar Schools': since ca. 1880; by 1950 at latest, archaic. From 'to *chisel*'.—2. Hence n., as in 'What a chizz!' (What a nuisance): C. 20.

chizzer. A 'chiseller': (preparatory) schoolboys': C. 20. Nicholas Blake, *A Question of Proof*, 1935. Cf. **swiz** (*Dict.*).

chizzle (see **chisel**, p. 149): 1848, *Sinks*.

chizzy wag. A charity boy: Christ's Hospital: late C. 18–19. The reference in Leigh Hunt's *Autobiography* is valid for 1795 (Marples).

Chloe, blind as; drunk as Chloe. Utterly drunk. The former, ca. 1780–1860, occurs in *The New Vocal Enchantress*, 1791; the latter dates from ca. 1850 and, though (1948) slightly ob., is very far from †. The origin is lost in the mists of topicality.

Chloe, do a. See **do a Chloe** below.

chlorhin. To hear: Shelta: C. 18–20. B. & L.

chobey shop. A second-hand shop: circus hands': late C. 19–20. Perhaps cf. *chovey* (p. 151).

choc.—2. A militiaman (also *choco* and *chocolate soldier*): Australian: 1939–45. (B., 1943.)

choc-absorber. 'A girl or woman who can consume all the chocolates some fool of a man can supply her with. Derived from S. E. *shock-absorber*' (A. B. Petch, April 1966): since ca. 1955.

chock-a-block. Crammed full; as full as may be: coll., orig. nautical, esp. Naval: C. 19–20. In, e.g., Fredk Chamier, *The Life of a Sailor*, 1832, at I, 23, 'I was ushered into the larboard berth thus:—"Here, my lads, is another messmate . . ." —"What another!" roared a ruddy-faced midshipman of about eighteen; "he must stow himself away, for we are chock-a-block here."' Ex the lit. S.E. Sense. (Moe.)

chocka. A variant of **chocker**.

chockablock with. Full of: Australian coll.: since ca. 1880. Brian Penton, *Inheritors*, 1936, ' "Chockablock with skite," he growled.' Cf.:—

chocker, adj. Disgruntled, 'fed up': Naval lower-deck: since ca. 1920. H. & P. Ex *chockful*; corresponding to the Army's *browned off*. A 1939–45 Naval variant was *at chocker stations*. (Mr H. R. Spencer.) The simple *chocker* reached the R.A.F. by 1943 at latest.

chocks away! Get on with it!: R.A.F.: since ca. 1935. H. & P., 'Remove the wooden chocks and let the 'planes get off the ground'. Short for *pull the chocks away*.

choco. A conscientious objector: Australian: 1939 +: Lawson Glassop, *We Were the Rats*, 1944.—2. See **choc**, 2.

chocolate occurs in certain arbitrarily varied phrases implying sycophancy: Services (esp. R.A.F.): since ca. 1930. The semantic clue lies in **brown-nose** and **brown-tongue**.

chocolate, get a bar of. To receive praise from a senior officer: Naval: since ca. 1941. Granville.

chocolate gale. A strong wind blowing from the N.W. of the Spanish main: Naval coll.: mid-C. 19–20. (Bowen's *Sea Slang*.)

chocolate soldier. See **choc**, 2.

D

Chocolate Staircase, the. A road with forty hairpin bends, N. of Tiddim, Burma: Army: 1941–5. (P-G-R.)

choke, n.—2. Usually in pl.: *chokes*, Jerusalem artichokes: greengrocers': late C. 19–20.—3. A garotting: Australian c.: since ca. 1920. (B., 1953.)—4. A nervous shock; something grievous: low: since ca. 1945. (L. J. Cunliffe, *Having It Away*, 1965.) Ex sense 2 of:—

choke, v. A synonym of **strangle**, 2, below: racing: since ca. 1920. Dick Francis, *Dead Cert*, 1962, 'He said if I wanted a lesson in how to choke a horse I'd better watch him on Bolingbroke.'—2. To jolt or shock; to disgust: since ca. 1930.

choke-jade. 'A dip in the course at Newmarket a few hundred yards on the Cambridge side of the running gap in the Ditch,' B. & L.; turf: from ca. 1860. It 'chokes off' inferior horses.

choke-off, n. An admonishment: military (ex **choke off**, v., 2) and prison officers': since ca. 1914. (L. W. Merrow-Smith & J. Harris, *Prison Screw*, 1962.)

choke off.—2. To reprimand or 'tell off' or retort successfully upon: military coll.: late C. 19–20.

choke one's luff. To assuage (someone's) hunger; to keep (him) quiet (cf. *choke your luff* on p. 150): nautical: 1818, Alfred Burton, *Johnny Newcome*. (Moe.)

choke your luff! (p. 150) goes back to ca. 1810 or a decade earlier. It is implied in *The Night Watch*, II, 301), 1828.

choked, adj., predicative only, as in 'I was, *or* I felt, real *or* proper choked'—disgusted; 'fed-up' or 'browned off', disgruntled: since ca. 1945. Cf. **double-choked**, below.

chokey, 1 (p. 150). Recorded in Australia ca. 1840. (Sidney J. Baker, letter of 1946.)

choki or **chokie.** A variant of **chokey**, 1 and 3 (*Dict.*). Sense 3, by the way, dates back to ca. 1870.

chokker. Variant spelling of **chocker**, adj.

chooch hat. A Naval and Army variant (esp. in India) of *funny hat*: since 1920's; by 1960, ob. Urdu *chut*.

chook. A chicken; collectively, chickens: Australian and New Zealand coll.: mid-C. 19–20. Ex E. and Irish dialect.—2. A woman, esp. if an older one: Australian pejorative: since ca. 1935. (Culotta.)

chookie. 'A girl friend, a young woman' (B., 1942): Australian: since ca. 1925. Cf. **chuck**, n., 1 (p. 152).

choom (p. 150).—2. Cf. *Chooms*, Englishmen in general; *the C.*, a team of English cricketers or footballers: Australian: late C. 19–20; not very general before ca. 1919.

chop, n.—2. Wood-chopping contest: Australian and New Zealand coll.: late C. 19–20. B., 1942. It occurs in, e.g., K. S. Prichard, *Working Bullocks*, 1926.—3. A share: Australian: C. 20. (B., 1953.)—4. A swoop and the ensuing kill: N.E. Australian coll.: since ca. 1910. Jean Devanney, *Travels in North Queensland*, 1951, 'A school of large trevally in process of making what was known as a "chop".'

chop, v., 5. In nuance 'to move, come, go quickly, hurriedly, flurriedly': *Sessions*, Sept. 3, 1740.—6. To beat in a race: turf: from ca. 1860. Ex hunting j. (to seize prey before it clears cover). v.—7. To hit (a horse) on the thigh with the whip:

coach-drivers': C. 19. (W. O. Tristram, *Coaching Days* . . ., 1888. This author notes *fan*, to whip (a horse), *towel*, to flog it, and the nn. *chopping*, *fanning*, *towelling*.)

chop, get the. To 'go for a Burton' (see **gone for** . . .), esp. in 'die' sense: R.A.F. aircrews' (incl. pilots'): 1940 +. (W/Cdr R. P. McDouall, April 12, 1945.) Applied to aircraft, it = to lose them on a raid.

chop, not much. Worthless: late C. 19–20. Cf. **chop, no**, on p. 150.

chop-chop.—3. A meal: United Nations troops during the Korean War of the 1950's. Ex **chop-chop**, 1 (p. 150), influenced by *chop suey*, a favourite Chinese dish.—4. 'The green top [of sugar cane] isn't trash. That's chop-chop—horse feed—when it's chopped up' (Jean Devanney, *By Tropic Sea and Jungle*, 1944): Australian cane-cutters': since ca. 1910.

chop-chop! (p. 150) is recorded earlier in *The Chinese Repository*, IV (Jan. 1836) at p. 434, in the article headed 'Jargon spoken at Canton'. Moe.

chop to pieces. In fisticuffs or boxing, to defeat severely: Australian sporting coll.: late C. 19–20. (B., 1943.)

*chop-up. A division of plunder: Australian c.: C. 20. Baker.

Chopburg. Hamburg: R.A.F. (operational): 1941. (W/Cdr R. P. McDouall, April 12, 1945.) Obviously *ham* prompted *chop*. Another operational officer writes, in late 1961, thus, 'I always felt that Chopburg referred to the possibility of "getting the chop" over Hamburg rather than to any link between ham and a pork chop.' Both of these 'causes' were, I suspect, at work.

chopped. Killed, esp. by machine-gun fire: Army and Air Force: 1939–45. Perhaps cf. the U.S. underworld *chopper*, a machine-gun.

chopper.—3. A blow given from behind, esp. on the nape of the neck: Australian: since ca. 1915. (B., 1943.)—4. A sailor's broad-brimmed hat: Naval: ca. 1805–40. W. N. Glascock, *The Naval Sketch-Book* (II), 1826, 'I powders my pate, and claps on a broad-brimm'd chopper over all'. (Moe.)—5. A tail: mostly Cockney: late C. 19–20. 'Pleased as a dog with two choppers, 'e was, silly little bleeder,' Alexander Baron, *There's No Home*, 1950.—6. Penis: low: C. 20.—7. Usually in the pl. *choppers*, teeth, and *china choppers*, false teeth: Canadian (— 1949).—8. A helicopter: Fleet Air Arm: since ca. 1955. Ex a blade that could chop off your head.—9. A car taken in part exchange: secondhand-car dealers': since ca. 1955. (Anthony Cowdy in the coloured supplement of *The Sunday Times*, Oct. 24, 1965.) Cf. S.E. *chop and change*.

Sense 7 has also, since ca. 1950, been English, esp. in *National choppers*, provided by the National Health Service.

chopper, v. To convey by helicopter: orig. and mainly flying s.: since ca. 1960. (David Walker, *Devil's Plunge*, 1968.) Ex **chopper**, n., 8, above.

Chopping. Chopin, as in 'Oh, just something by Chopin'—'Um! Thought it was chopping.' Lower-middle and lower class jocularity: late C. 19–20.

chopping sticks. In the game of House, it = 6: rhyming s.: late C. 19–20. Michael Harrison, *Reported Safe Arrival*, 1943.

choppy, n. A choppy wave: Australian surfers'

coll.: since ca. 1950. (B.P.)

choppy. (Of a temperature chart) uneven, esp. of a fever patient: hospital nurses': since the 1920's. If even, it is *flat*.

chopsticks. Probably the original form of chopping sticks. (Franklyn, *Rhyming*.)

choss up. To wreck, esp. a vehicle: Army: since ca. 1946. Ex *chaos*?

chots. Potatoes: Cotton College: C. 20. In C. 19, the form was *chotties*: ex *teotties*, the latter being a deliberate (?) variant of *taties* or *taters*; cf. **totties.** Frank Roberts, in *The Cottonian*, Autumn, 1938.

chounter (p. 151): prob. ex Yorkshire dial. *chunter*, 'to grumble; mutter bitterly'.

chow, n.—4. A term of contempt for a person: Australian: C. 20. B., 1942. Due to association with *cow*?—5. Cabbage: Australian: since ca. 1920. (B., 1953.)

chow! Phonetic spelling of **ciao.**

chow-chow. From Colonel Albert F. Moe, U.S.M.C., Ret., of Arlington, Virginia comes the following summary of the English use of this term and its compounds. I give it *verbatim*.

chow-chow (food), on p. 151.

FANNING, Edmund, *Voyages Round the World*, N.Y.: 1832, p. 253. August 5th 1798 . . . At day-break, when the cable was hove in, their [Chinese fishermen's] net was found so entangled and wound around, that we were obliged to cut it into several pieces before it was cleared, (but it could not be avoided,) for now they could not procure any *chow-chow* (victuals) until the net was first taken on shore and mended.

W. W. Wood, *Sketches of China*, Philadelphia: 1830, p. 216.

*Chow-chow. This, in the slang of Canton [pidgin-English], means either food, or a collection of various trifling articles.

ROBERTS, Edmund, *Embassy to the Eastern Courts*. N.Y.: 1837, p. 65. (October, 1832) . . . Having stepped on board, the first words they uttered, were "Capetan me peloto—you wanty peloto?" . . . The "celestial" . . . not forgetting to ask, as is usual, for a bottle of samshew, (rum) which he snugly stowed away in his bosom. Scarcely had he taken half a dozen strides up and down the deck, and pointed to steer more to port, before he asked for chow, chow, meaning something to eat, which; to his astonished eyes, was furnished forthwith, in a lordly dish, on the quarterdeck.

chow-chow [food, general; pickles; preserves]

DOWNING, Charles Toogood, *The Fan-Qui in China in 1836–7*. London: 1848, I, p. 99.

(1838) *Chow-chow* is another favourite word with the Chinese. When applied to little dogs and tender rats, and other delicate articles of food, it is spoken with great gusto. . . . while a mixture of different pickles or preserves bear the same alluring title of chow-chow.

chow-chow (v. to eat). Charles de Montigny, *Manuel de Négociant Français en Chine, 1846*. Paris: 1846, p. 321.

chow-chow. Mixed, miscellaneous, mixed meats, to eat food.

chow-chow account [food account] Canton, November 2, 1830.

chow-chow amah [wet nurse] Hong Kong, 1886.

chow-chow basket [so-named from being divided

into compartments, not from carrying an assortment, miscellany or medley of knick-knacks or odds-and-ends].

DOWNING, *op. cit.*, I, p. 99.

Baskets, which are procured in Canton, with many compartments, are called chow-chow baskets. . . .

chow-chow cargo [assorted cargo], 1882.

chow-chow chop [chop = licensed lighter, chow-chow = odds-and-ends comprising the last lighter-load of cargo to complete the loading of the ship] [James Bannerman, ed.] *Dialogues and Detached Sentences in the Chinese Language*. Macao, 1816, p. 85. E[uropean]. That will do. Has the Country Ship sent down her Chow-chow Chop yet? MORRISON, Robert, *A Dictionary of the Chinese Language*. Macao, 1819. Part II, Volume I, p. 698/2.

. . . to send down the last boat load of goods to a ship, locally called the *Chow chow chop*.

chow-chow Joss [to place food offerings as a part of religious worship] 1886.

chow-chow man [dealer in all kinds of goods] 1878.

chow-chow water. DOWNING, *op. cit.*, I, p. 99. [1838] Where the river is troubled in particular parts near the shore by small eddies, that part of it is called chow-chow water.

chow line, the. A food queue in Naval Barracks: lower-deck: since ca. 1925. (P-G-R.)

chow miaow. 'A generic term (punning) for Chinese food': Australian: since ca. 1945. (Edwin Morrisby, Aug. 30, 1958.) Cf. *chow*, 1 (p. 151).

chowing or **chipping** is theatrical (from ca. 1870) for grumbling or incessant talking. B. & L.

Chowringhee star. See **Firpo star.**

chrissie. See **chryssie.**

Christ Almighty wonder. One who thinks very highly of himself; one who 'really has something', an exceedingly able person, some thing or event that is astounding or extremely surprising: late C. 19–20. 'He's a C.A.w. with cars'; 'It's a C.A.w. he's not run over twice nightly.'

christen.—6. To soil, chip, damage (something new or hitherto unmarked): late C. 19–20.

Christian poney or **pony.** A handcart man: Canadian, esp. in East: ? ca. 1860–1905. Canadian History Department's *Bulletin*, Dec. 1953. (Leechman.)—2. A sedan-chairman: late C. 18–early 19. (W. N. Glascock, *Sailors and Saints* (II, 89), 1829. Moe.) This makes better sense than Grose's (see p. 152).

Christmas, v.—2. Short for **Christmas Eve.** (*Dict.*)

Christmas card. A guard: mostly theatrical rhyming s.: C. 20. (Franklyn, *Rhyming*.)

Christmas comes but once a year—thank goodness (or God)! A c.p. dating from ca. 1945 and used by those who detest what Christmas has been turned into by the profiteers.

Christmas tree.—2. 'R.A.F. Intruder pilots' slang [1940–45] for the Luftwaffe's airfield lighting system: flare-paths, boundary-lights and, in particular, the "visual Lorenz" approach-path lights, which from the air looked like a stylised pine-tree.' (Ramsey Spencer, March 1967.)—3. 'The complex arrangement of pipes and valves at the head of an oil well to control the flow of oil' (Leechman): Canadian oilmen's: since ca. 1950. It occurs in, e.g., William Haggard, *The Telemann Touch*, 1958.—4. 'Colour [? coloured] light multi-

ple aspect gantry' (*Railway*, 3rd); railwaymen's: since ca. 1950.

chro. Short for **chromo,** 2: since 1930. (B.P.)

chromo.—2. A prostitute: Australian: since ca. 1925. B., 1942. Ex gay dresses.

chronic, n. 'Those pathetic figures called "chronics"—middle-aged men [students] who haunted medical schools for ten years on end and yet, somehow, never managed to become qualified,' Francis Brett Young, *Dr Bradley Remembers*, 1938: medical: since ca. 1870.

chryssie (loosely **chrissie**). A chrysanthemum: Australian: since ca. 1920. (B., 1953.)

chu-shung! You little beast (or, animal)!: pidgin: from ca. 1860. B. & L. I.e. Chinese *sheon-chu-shang*. 'Often used jestingly in conversation with flower-boat girls.'

Chuck. Charles: Canadian (and U.S.): mid-C. 19–20.

chuck, v.—8. 'We chucked everything we had at them' (shelled them heavily): Army: 1939–45. (P-G-R.)

chuck a charley. To have a fit: Australian: C. 20. B., 1942.

chuck a fit. To pretend to have a fit: (low) coll.: mid-C. 19–20. B. & L.

chuck a seven. To die: Australian: C. 20. Baker.

chuck a sixer. To have a figurative fit: Australian: late C. 19–20. Baker.

*****chuck a willy.** See **willy.**

chuck and chance it is an anglers' descriptive c.p. applied to rough-and-ready, artless fishermen: late C. 19–20. (H. A. Vachell, 1924.)

chuck and toss. Tossing for halfpence: proletarian coll.: mid-C. 19–20: ob. B. & L.

chuck-in. A voluntary subscription: Australian: late C. 19–20. Baker.

chuck one's hand in (p. 152) is, in the Navy, 'to refuse duty in order to state a "case" at the defaulter's table' (Granville).

chuck-out. A dismissal, esp. from a job: New Zealand coll.: late C. 19–20. (G. B. Lancaster, *The Tracks We Tread*, 1907.)—2. Closing-time at a public house: since ca. 1920. Ex **chuck out,** 1, on p. 153. Tommy Steele in a cinema interview, early Dec. 1963.

chuck the gab. See **bag.**

chuck-up.—2. Timely encouragement: a cheer (occ. ironical): Naval: since ca. 1920. Granville.

chuck up, v. To vomit. Australian: late C. 19–20. (B.P.)

chuck-wag(g)on. A cowboys' cook-wagon: Western prairies of Canada: since ca. 1910. Cf. *chuck*, n., 2 (p. 152).

chucking cabbage. (A bunch of) paper currency of low denomination: Australian journalists': adopted in 1942 or 1943 from U.S. Ex the predominant green of the notes or bills.

chucklehead. A stupid fellow: Newfoundland coll., adopted—ca. 1920—from U.S. Either American dial. *chuckle*, clumsy, stupid + head, or a pun n. The American chucklehead, the popular name of the *woolly-headed clover*. (L. E. F. English, *Historic Newfoundland*, 1955.)

chucks (a bosun) (p. 153): rather since ca. 1820: cf. Mr Chucks in Marryat's *Midshipman Easy*, 1836.

chuff, n. Food: Services, esp. Army: since

ca. 1930. H. & P. Ex *chow*, n., 1 (*Dict.*): *chow* >
chough > *chuff*.—2. Stimulation of male member
by lumbar thrust in coïtion: low: late C. 19–20.
In Durham dial., *chuff* = to cuff.—3. Hence, *chuff
chums*, male homosexual associates, a *chuff* being a
catamite; and *chuff-box*, pudendum muliebre;
C. 20.—4. Anus: Australian: C. 20. Also, since
ca. 1945, English.—5. Bottom, backside: New
Zealand: C. 20. Hence, *sit on one's chuff*, to sit
back and do nothing, as used by 'P.M.' Holyoake
on July 30, 1967 (*The Christchurch Star*, the next
day).

chuff, adj. Earlier in A. Neil Lyons, *Arthur's*,
1908.

chuff chum. A companion or 'pal': Services:
since ca. 1930. Ex **chuff**, n.

chuff-nuts; dingle berries. Fæcal nodules on
anal hair: Naval: C. 20. Cf. *chuff*, 4.

chuffed. Pleased, delighted; but also, displeased, disgruntled: Army: C. 20. If one
needed to distinguish, one used *chuffed to fuck* or
chuffed to arseholes or *chuffed pink* or *bo-chuffed*, in
the former, *dead chuffed* in the latter sense. Cf.
chuff, adj. (p. 153 and this page).—2. Flattered:
teenagers', esp. jazz-lovers': since ca. 1955.
'Janet Murray says: "I'd be chuffed" (current
"Cat" word for flattered). It's nice to think
someone fancies you"': *Woman's Own*, 1959.
Both of the main senses derive ex English dialect
chuff, which perhaps has two entirely different
origins.—3. Hence, *real chuffed*, excited: since late
1950's.

chum, n.—6. One of the Old Contemptibles:
Army: 1915 + ; but ob. by 1947.

chummy, n., 1 (p. 154), has, since ca. 1870,
signified an ordinary sweep. See *napper*, 7.—5. A
prisoner: jocularly euphemistic police term: since
ca. 1925. (*The Free-Lance Writer*, April 1948.)

Sense 2 (p. 154) prob. goes back to at least
twenty-five years earlier. Charles Clewearing,
Simon Solus, a one-act farce played and published
in New York in 1843, contains this passage:
'... Nicer fellows, stouter hearts, freer souls, than
some of my chummies just paid off.' As Colonel
Albert Moe, U.S.M.C., Ret., has remarked, 'As
American naval speech of that period was taken
almost entirely and directly from British naval
speech, I suggest that [this passage] represents a
British expression appearing in an American
publication': with so great an authority on
American naval speech, I gladly agree.

chummy, v. To 'go partners' (with someone);
work along with: Australian: since ca. 1870.
'Tom Collins', *Such is Life*, 1903, 'He chummied
for a few weeks with a squatter'.

chummy ship. 'A ship's next-door-neighbour in
an anchorage' (Granville): Naval: C. 20. See
chummy ships in *Dict.*

chunder. To vomit: Australian: since ca.
1925. (B.P.) Cf. English dial. *chunder*, to
grumble, an echoic word.

chunk, 3, appears in Thor Fredur, *Sketches from
Shady Places*, 1879.

chunka or **chunker.** A boss or 'head': Australian rhyming s.: C. 20. B., 1942. Short for
chunk of beef (late C. 19–20), rhyming on *chief*.

chup. Silence; mostly in *keep chup*, to keep
quiet: Army: late C. 19–20. Ex Hindustani.
(P-G-R.)

church, n. An endearment; esp. *my church*, my
dear: non-aristocratic: ca. 1870–1910. B. & L.

church (or **court** or **jail**), **I'll see you in.** A c.p.
used on departure: mostly Australian: since ca.
1910. (B.P.)

Church of Turkey. A non-existent religious
denomination: Naval: C. 20.

churcher. A threepenny piece: Cockneys': late
C. 19–20. J. W. Horsley, *I Remember*, 1912.

Churchill. A meal: taxi-drivers': late 1920's.
Winston Churchill gave the taximan the right to
refuse a fare whilst he is having a meal (newspaper
cutting, June 11, 1945).

chury (p. 155). No; Vaux was right. The
word comes from Welsh Romany *chury* (*čuri*); cf.
Hindi *chhuri*, itself of Sanskrit origin.

chut. See **chutty**.—2, 3. A variant of **chuff**, n.,
2, 3.

chute. A parachute: Air Force coll.: since
ca. 1930. Partridge, 1945.

chute, v. To throw away: Australian Naval:
since ca. 1930. (B., 1943.)

chute, up the. See **up the chute.**

chutney. See **Navy cake.**

chutty. Chewing gum: Australian: since ca.
1925. B., 1942. 'Whence "chutto", masticate
easily and pleasantly.' Ex *chew it.*

chy is merely a variant of *chai*, Romany for a
girl: a term heard occ. among tramps in mid-C.
19–20.

ciáo!—pron. *chow.* Common in the Espresso
bars of Britain, Australia and elsewhere. My
friend Nicolas Bentley, in a letter dated Oct. 13,
1961, writes, 'The Italian slang *ciaou!*—i.e. *ciáo*—
seems to be coming more and more into popular
use, particularly among teenagers, as a form both
of salutation and good-bye. I hear it frequently
among young friends of mine ... and fairly freely
at the Royal College of Art.' It arose in the late
1950's.

cigar. A Woodbine or Player's Weight or any
other similar cigarette, small but wholesome: from
ca. 1930 and mostly Cockneys'.

cigar-box. See **fish-horn.**

cigarette card, talk like the back of a. See **talk
like** ...

cigarette swag. 'A small swag carried by a
tramp when he comes into a city' (B., 1943):
Australian: since ca. 1930. Ex shape and
relative size.

cig(g)aboo. A cigarette: Australian, esp.
Sydney-siders': since ca. 1948. (Edwin Morrisby,
Aug. 30, 1958.)

Cigs. Chief of the Imperial General Staff:
Service officers': 1939–45. Ex the initials
C.I.G.S. (P-G-R.)

cinch (p. 155). But, since ca. 1910, the *c* has,
all over the world, been soft. Since ca. 1930, the
predominant sense, esp. in Australia, has been
'something (very) easy to do', as in 'Can you swim
the length of the pool?'—'Yes, it's a cinch.' (B.P.)

cinder cruncher. A switchman: Canadian railroadmen's (— 1931). Cf.:—

cinder shifter. A speedway rider: Australian:
1924 +. B., 1942. Ex cinder track.

Cinderella's coach; glass coach. A District
Engineer's coach; railwaymen's: since ca. 1920.
(*Railway.*)

cipher queen. See **Cypher Queen.**

circuit, the. 'The worn track round the
compound ... which kriegies "pounded" or
"bashed" (walked) ... to get away from their
own thoughts,' Paul Brickhill & Conrad Norton,

Escape to Danger, 1946: prisoners of war in Germany, 1940–5.

circuit and bumps. 'Exercise flights consisting of repeated take-offs and landings,' E. P., 'Air Warfare and Its Slang' in *The New Statesman*, Sept. 19, 1942: since ca. 1925.

circuit-and-bumps boy; usually in pl. A flying pupil: R.A.F.: since ca. 1930. Jackson. Ex the prec. entry.

circumference. See **radius**.

circus, it's a or **was a . . .;** or **. . . real circus.** It is, or was, very comical: soldiers': 1914–18.

Ciren (pron. as S.E. *syren*). Cirencester: local and railwaymen's coll.: late C. 19–20.

city bull-dog. See 'Constables'.

city slicker. A smart, smooth fellow from the city: Australian; adopted, ca. 1944, ex U.S. servicemen.—2. Hence, loosely, any city chap: since ca. 1950. (Jon Cleary, *Back of Sunset*, 1959.)

civil, do the. To do the civil—the polite—thing: coll.: C. 19–20; by 1960, slightly ob. (A. Trollope, *Barchester Towers*, 1857.)

civilian.—2. See 'Tavern terms', § 3, *d*.—3. 'The surgeon, purser, and chaplain, are commonly designated . . . civilians' (W. N. Glascock, *The Naval Sketch-Book* (I, 12), 1925): Naval: ca. 1800–60. Moe.

civvies (p. 156). Also in the Navy: C. 20. Granville, 'The term "mufti" is never used in the Royal Navy.'

civvy.—3. Hence, a recruit waiting to be issued with a uniform: Services: since ca. 1920. H. & P.

Civvy Street. The condition and status of a civilian; 'What did you do in Civvy Street?' was often heard, 1939–45, in the Services, where its use persists. H. & P. On the analogy of *Easy Street*, it was first used in ca. 1917 by the Army. See **civvy** in *Dict.*

cla. See 'Colston's'.

clacker.—2. Pie crust: Naval: C. 20. Granville, ' "Any gash clacker loafing?" means "Any more pie?" ' Echoic.

clackers; or **jam clacker** (cf. **clacker**, 2, above). 'Pastry, "duff," spread over with currants (or jam), prepared by men on small dish and which would be cooked by galley' (Laurie Atkinson, Sept. 11, 1967): Naval: C. 20. Cf. **clagger** in *Dict.*

clag. Cloud; a cloud: R.A.F.: since ca. 1935 (?). Ex dial, *clag*, clay.

claim, v., 2 (p. 156), is much earlier in sense 'catch hold of, seize, grasp (a person)': *Sessions*, Nov. 19, 1902, 'Tyler jumped out at the window—I *claimed* him and tustled [*sic*] with him.'

clamp down on (e.g. delinquents or malefactors). To apply the full severity of the law or the regulations: since mid-1940's: coll. >, by ca. 1960, S.E.

clamped down is an Air Force brevity for 'The cloud is now very low, or visibility bad': Flying-Officer Robert Hinde, letter of March 17, 1945: since ca. 1925. Cf. *clamp down*, v.i. to become foggy: Air Force: since ca. 1930. Cecil Lewis, *Pathfinders*, 1943.

clampers, often elaborated to **Harry Clampers** 'It's (Harry) Clampers' = It's non-flying weather: R.A.F.: since ca. 1930. Prob. ex **clamped down** (above).

clampy. A flat-footed person: Naval: since ca. 1925. Granville. Echoic; app. reminiscent both of *clatter* and *stamp* (about).

clanger. See **drop a ballock**.—2. A coward: Australian: since ca. 1940. (B., 1953.)—3. Diminutive of *double clanger*.

clanger, drop a. See **drop a ballock**.

clangeroo. A memorably bad misjudgement: mainly theatrical: since late 1940's. Terence Rattigan, in Introduction to Mander & Mitchenson's *Theatrical Companion to Coward*, 1957, '. . . Not just a floater but a real old-fashioned clangeroo'. Ex **clanger**, 1, q.v. at **drop a ballock** below. The *-oo* comes from the American suffix *-eroo*.

clap hands Charley (or **Charlie**), **do a.** To fly an aircraft in such a way as to cause the wings—or the rotor blades of a helicopter—to meet overhead: R.A.F.: since ca. 1945. (With thanks to an operational R.A.F. officer.)

clap-trap. Much talk: Londoners': C. 20. Perhaps ex S.E. sense of 'language designed to win applause'.—2. ? hence, mouth: low, esp. Londoners': from ca. 1910.

clapped out. (Of aircraft) unserviceable, worn out: R.A.F., esp. in Far East: 1942 +. I.e. the roof has been clamped down.—2. Hence, (of persons) exhausted: since ca. 1946; esp. among teenagers since ca. 1955. (Gilderdale.) Sense 1 is—esp. among racing drivers—derivatively applied to a car engine: since ca. 1946.

clapper.—4. (Ex 2.) A sandwich-board man: street s.: since ca. 1910. Desmond Morse-Boycott, *We Do See Life!*, 1931.

clappers. Testicles: mostly servicemen's: since ca. 1930. John Winton, *We Joined the Navy*, 1959, 'Don't let me hear you making another report like that again or I'll have your clappers for a necktie'. Cf. *clanger* at **drop a ballock**, below.

clappers, like the. 'Very fast, or very hard (e.g. "run like the clappers"; or "the clappers of hell").' Gerald Emanuel, letter of March 29, 1945: C. 20; since ca. 1925, much used by the R.A.F. As *clapper* suggests *bell*, so *hell* rhymes on *bell*: and *go like hell* is to run very hard indeed.

clappy. Strictly, infected with 'clap'; loosely, with either gonorrhoea or syphilis: Anglo-Irish: C. 20. Nicholas Blake, *The Private Wound*, 1968, ' "You son of a clappy whore." '

Clara and **Mona.** 'Mona and Clara, the air-raid and all-clear signals . . . the moaning of the warning sirens and a contraction of the welcome "all-clear" ', Berrey, 1940: since 1940.

claret, v. (Usually in passive.) To draw blood from, to cause to be covered with blood. 'Purcell's *mug* was clareted,' *Boxiana*, II, 1818. Ex **claret**, n.,—p. 157.

***clash.** A set battle, planned and announced, between two gangs of hooligans and/or near-criminals: Glasgow c. and lower-class s.: from ca. 1920. MacArthur & Long. It differs from a *rammy*, which is unarranged and may take place between two quite small groups.

clashy (p. 157). The Urdu *khlasy* has thus been corrupted.

***class, do a bit of.** To commit a crime that is, by criminals, considered notable or, at the least, not below one's abilities: c.: from ca. 1880. Clarence Rook, *The Hooligan Nights*, 1899.

classy, n.—2. A variant of **clashy** (*Dict.*).

clatter. 'He has just finished a "clatter", fourteen days in the compound,' R. Grinstead, *They Dug a Hole*, 1946: Guardsmen's: since ca. 1925. Echoic.

clayey or **clayie.** A home-made marble of sun-baked clay: Australian children's: ca. 1890–1945. (B.P.)

clean, v.—2. To scold severely: to chastise: (low) Cockney: late C. 19–20. 'I won' 'alf clean yer when I gits yer 'ome!' Ex the lit. sense of that threat.

clean, adv. (p. 157), in sense 'completely', is archaic S.E. rather than coll.: cf. '... until all the people were passed clean over Jordan' (*Joshua*, iii, 17).

clean job of it, make a. See **job of it** ...

clean potato.—2. 'A person of unblemished character' (B., 1943): Australian: ca. 1850–1910.

clean round the bend. See **round the bend.**

Clean-Shirt Day. Sunday: lower-classes' coll.: since ca. 1820; † by 1900. *Sinks*, 1848.

clean-skin. A person without a police record: Australian police: since ca. 1910. (B., 1943; Vince Kelly, *The Shadow*, 1955.) Ex sheep-farming: cf. *clean-skins* (p. 158).

Clean-Skins.—2. (Often in singular.) Persons of (esp. political) integrity: Australian: C. 20. B., 1942.

clean the slate. To pay all debts: non-aristocratic coll.: from ca. 1860. B. & L. (The *slate* on which, in public-houses, drinking debts are noted.)

clean up, v.—2. (Prob. ex sense 1: p. 158.) To defeat: Australian since ca. 1915, New Zealand since ca. 1916. Slatter.

clean-up. A victory; a rout: Australian: since ca. 1920. B., 1942. Ex the v.

clear one's yard-arm. See **yard-arm, clear one's** on p. 969.

clear-skin. An Australian variant of **clean-skin(s)** in all three senses: C. 20. (B., 1943.)

cleat. *Glans penis*: low: late C. 19—20.

cleek. 'A wet blanket (at a party)': beatniks': since ca. 1959. (Anderson.) Adopted ex American jazz s. for 'a sad or melancholy person' (Wentworth & Flexner).

Clem. See **Chad.**

Clem–Manny–Nye. Clement Attlee, Emanuel Shinwell, Aneurin Bevan: Labour familiarities of the 1930's–1950's; affected by the self-important.

clenchprop (see **clinchprop** on p. 158) seems to have gone underground for two or three centuries and then to have come again to the surface. Mr Spencer heard it applied, in July 1967, by a Mod to 'some typically repulsive Rockers' in the High Street, Camberley, Surrey.

Clerk of the Kitchen. See 'Tavern terms', § 5.

clever.—6. In good health; *not too clever*, ill: Aus.: C. 20. Baker, 1959.—7. Proficient: Aus.: C. 20. *Ibid.* Ex sense 1 on p. 158.

clever boys, the. Servicemen (or others) with only theoretical knowledge: Services: since 1940. Derisively: *the really clever boys*, 'people with positively academic knowledge' (H. & P.).

clever chaps these Chinese; sometimes **damned** (or **dead**) **clever these Chinese!** A Naval c.p., heard occasionally in the other Services: C. 20; by late 1940's, also fairly gen. among 'U' rather than 'non-U' civilians; used as a comment upon an explanation given about some device, especially if it hasn't been understood. A back-handed tribute to Chinese ingenuity. It occurs in, e.g., John Winton, *We Saw the Sea*, 1960, on p. 154.

clever Mike. A bicycle: C. 20. Rhyming on *bike*.

cleversides; clever Dick. Schoolchildren's (the former mainly North Country) coll.: synonym, often ironical, of *clever person*: late C. 19–20.

clew to ear-ring, (esp. **know**) **from.** In every detail, thoroughly: Naval coll.: late C. 19–20.

clew-up, v.i. To join another ship; Naval: since ca. 1895. H. & P., 'To fix one's hammock by the clew system.'—2. To finish a job: Naval: since ca. 1920. Granville, 'The original meaning was to draw the clews of the sail to the yard-arm for furling.'—3. To meet an old messmate: Naval: since ca. 1930. Granville, 'I clewed up with old Dusty Miller in the Smoke.'

*cleymans. A rare variant of **cleyme** (*Dict.*).

click, n.—5. (Cf. 2: p. 139.) A set, a group; somewhat pejorative: since ca. 1925.

click, v., 4 (p. 159), seems to have arisen before 1914; on the evidence of several dependables, I'd put it at ca. 1910.—5. (Of a cow) to become pregnant: Australian rural: since ca. 1919. (B., *Australia Speaks*, 1953.)

click, in the. See **crook, in the.**

Click, the. *The Clique*: booksellers' illiteracy: hence, educated booksellers' jocular coll.: C. 20.

clickety click (*Dict.*) is used also by darts players.

clicket(t)y-clicks. Rhyming s. on *knicks* = (female) *knickers*: C. 20. It occurs in one of Neil Bell's short stories—? *A Proper Beano*.

clicky. Cliquey: col.: C. 20. Cf. **click,** n., 2 (*Dict.*).

cliffhanger. 'A (silent) film shown in weekly serials; from the precarious predicaments in which the heroine'—so often played by Pearl White—'was left at the end of each part. Dates probably from before 1914 but has been revived to describe similar T.V. serials and extended to anything exciting and drawn out, e.g. a suspense novel' (Peter Sanders, in note of mid-1965).

clifty, to steal; **cliftying,** stealing, act(s) of theft: New Zealand: C. 20. (*Iddiwah*, July 1953.) Apparently an extension of the moribund *clift* (p. 159).

clifty wallah. A smart fellow, esp. a too smart man: Army: 1939–45. (P-G-R.) This *clifty* derives ex Arabic *klefti*, a thief—whence also, presumably, *clifty*, to steal.

climb the rigging. Earlier in 'Taffrail'.

climbing Mary. See **whistler,** 9.

climbing trees to get away from it! See **getting any?** below.

clinch.—2. A prolonged and passionate embrace: adopted, ca. 1945, ex U.S.

*clinched. Imprisoned: C. 20: Australian c. >, by 1940, low s. See **clinch** (p. 159).

cliner (p. 159): 'Practically obsolete,' says Baker, 1942. Ultimately ex Ger. *klein*, small.

clinic. A public-house: office- and shop-girls': ca. 1955–60. (Gilderdale.) There one finds exactly what the doctor prescribed.

clinker link. A lower-grade employee, engaged in furnace-cleaning: railwaymen's: since ca. 1920. (*Railway*.)

clip-joint. A night-club, or a restaurant, where the prices are high and the patrons are fleeced: Canadian: adopted, ca. 1930, ex U.S. Ex sheepshearing.

*clip-nit. See 'Rogues'.

clip-up, v.i. A Cockney coll. that, dating from ca. 1890 (or earlier), has no synonym in S.E. and should therefore, by this time, have been considered S.E. It is a schoolboys' 'method of casting lots by approaching each other from opposite kerbs, with a heel-to-toe step'. He who finds that the last gap is too small for the length of his foot is the loser.

clipped corner, the. The mark, on a discharge-paper, of a thoroughly bad character: Naval coll.: C. 20. Also called a *blanker* (see p. 61).

clipper.—3. '. . . "clippers", the police term for the professional store thieves' (Godfrey Winn, in *Woman*, Dec. 11, 1965): C. 20. Ex *clip*, to rob.

clippy. A girl conductor on bus or tram: since 1939. *The New Statesman*, Aug. 30, 1941. H. & P. Ex clipping tickets.—2. (Usually written *clippie*.) An employee checking and clipping tickets at railway stations: Australian: since ca. 1940. (B., 1953.)

Sense 1 was 'perhaps influenced by Messrs Lyons's waitresses, advertised by their employers in the 1920's and 1930's as "Nippies"' (Ramsey Spencer, March 1967).

clishpen. To break (a thing) by letting it fall: Shelta: C. 18–20. B. & L. Cf. Shelta *clisp*, to fall or to let fall.

cloak. To place (hat, coat, etc.) in a cloak-room: Australian: since ca. 1945. (B., *Australia Speaks*, 1953.) Rather, since ca. 1920, to judge by its use in Tom Ronan, *Only a Short Walk*, 1961.

cloak and dagger club, in the. See 'Prisoner-of-War Slang', 4. The phrase *cloak and dagger* was also, in 1939–45, used by Service officers for 'secret service' (work, etc.).

clob lout. A man very heavy on his feet: Army: C. 20. *Clob* is echoic.

clobber, v.—2. To re-decorate a (usually plain) piece of china to enhance its value; whence *clobbered china*: antique dealers': late C. 19–20. —3. To punch or strike; to assault: since ca. 1910: orig., low; by ca. 1945, fairly general. Echoic.

clobber with or **for.** To remember (someone) *with* or *for*, e.g. an onerous duty or an unwelcome burden.

clobbering. A heavy bombing: Air Force: 1941 +. Echoic. Ex **clobber, v., 3.**

clock, n., sense 4 (p. 160), continued. 'Then comes the "clock" in the taximeter. It has other names: the "ticker", the "kettle", "Mary Ann", and the "hickory". "Hickory" seems abstruse until you remember the nursery rhyme and add "dickory dock",' Herbert Hodge, *Cab, Sir?*, 1939. 5. Hence, an air-raid indicator: R.A.F.: since ca. 1930. Jackson.—6. (Also *round the clock*) A year's prison sentence: Australian c.: C. 20. B., 1942. As 12 hours, so 12 months.—7. A speedometer: coll.: since ca. 1920.

clock, v.—2. To punch, to strike (with one's fist): Australian: since ca. 1925. Baker. Cf. **dong** (p. 223).—3. To watch (someone) patiently: since ca. 1930. (Norman.) Ex sense 1, on p. 160. —4. To register on the speedometer; to attain a speed of (so many m.p.h.): since ca. 1925. Ex sense 7 of the n.—5. (A specialization of sense 3.) 'To "clock" someone is to follow someone and see what he backs. This is sometimes expressed as "Get on his daily"' (*The Sunday Telegraph*, May 7, 1967, anon. article on bookies' s.): racing: since ca. 1930.

Sense 2: also, since ca. 1930, English, as in 'I could have clocked him' or 'clocked him one'.

clock(-)basher or **watch(-)basher.** An instrument maker, instrument repairer, as an R.A.F.

'trade': R.A.F.: since ca. 1937. Jackson. See **basher, 6**.

clock captain. A captain that alters the bowling, not by a tactical but by a chronological calculation: cricketers' coll.: C. 20.

clock-in a beef. To make a 'regulation' complaint or a big fuss: Wrens': since ca. 1939. Cf. S.E. *put in a complaint* and *clocking-in* (punching the 'clock') at a factory.

clocky. A watchman: ca. 1820–70. *Sinks*, 1848. He makes his rounds at regular intervals.

clod, n.m 1 (p. 160). Rare in the singular, *clods = clod-hoppers*, rhyming s. on *coppers*, copper coins, dating from ca. 1870. Sydney Lester, *Vardi the Palarey*, (?) 1937.—2. Any non-Etonian: Eton: ca. 1800–60. *Spy*, 1825. *De haut en bas!*—3. At certain Scottish schools, a pupil: mid-C. 19–20.

clodhoppers. See **clod** above.

clod-skulled. See 'Epithets'.

Cloe. See **drunk as Chloe**, inadvertently omitted from the *Dict*.

clog. A clog-dancer: coll.: since ca. 1880. Josiah Flynt & F. Walton, *The Powers that Prey*, 1900 (p. 251).

Clog and Knocker (Railway), the. The old Great Central Railway running from Marylebone to Manchester: railwaymen's: C. 20; after ca. 1950, merely historical. (*Railway*.) Ex the clogs formerly much worn by Lancashire women. The *Knocker* element prob. derives ex 'that other Lancashire institution the knocker-up, who in pre-alarm-clock days used to do the rounds of the mill-hands' homes, waking them in time for work by knocking on bedroom windows with the pole which he carried' (Ramsey Spencer).

cloi. A cloister. Christ's Hospital: late C. 19–20. Marples.

close; more gen. **clo'es.** Clothes: sol.: C. 19–20. (Nevinson, 1895.)

close hangar, or **the hangar, doors!** Stop talking shop!: R.A.F.: since ca. 1936. H. & P. (shorter phrase); Jackson (longer).

close-poling. Two (trolley) buses running very close together: busmen's: since ca. 1935. Ex punting on the river? Perhaps rather ex the trolley-pole, as Ramsey Spencer suggests.

close stick; open stick. 'A stick of bombs dropped to explode in a small—a large—area': R.A.F.; j. rather than s. or coll. H. & P.

close your eyes and guess what God has sent—or **brought—you!** Often heard, in C. 20, as a jocular c.p.

clot. A fool, a 'stupid'; an incompetent: since ca. 1920: at the first, upper-middle class. Peter Chamberlain, 'The man's a bigger clot than I took him for.' By a pun on equivalent S.E. *clod*.

cloth-ears, he has (got) or **he's got.** A c.p. applied to one who doesn't wish to hear: Cockneys': C. 20. Ex caps with ear-flaps.

cloth in the wind (p. 161) goes back to ca. 1810 or earlier. 'I'd too many cloths in the wind'—glossed as 'drunk, in nautical slang': W. N. Glascock, *The Naval Sketch-Book* (II, 136), 1828. Moe.

clothes(-)peg. An egg: rhyming: C. 20.

cloud on the deck. 'A cloud base coincident with a sea or land surface,' E. P. in *The New Statesman*, Sept. 19, 1942. See **deck** (*Dict*.).

cloud-creep, mostly **be cloud-creeping.** To keep under cloud cover: R.F.C.–R.A.F.: 1916–18. 'Trying to get into position to attack some Huns that were cloud-creeping' (V. M. Yeates, *Winged Victory*, 1934, p. 92).

Cloudy Joe. Nickname for a Meteorological Officer: R.A.F.: 1940 +.

clout, v., 3: also Australian (with variant *clout on*): B., 1942. Prob. from U.S. See *Underworld*.—4. To palm cards dishonestly; often as n. *clouting*: Australian card-players': since ca. 1940. (B., 1953.)

clower. A basket: c.: ? C. 18–mid-19. B. & L. derive it ex Gaelic *cliah* (a basket). Open to suspicion, this entry!

clown; clown wagon. A switchman, a yard brakeman; a caboose: Canadian railroadmen's (— 1931). Humorously pejorative.

club, n.—6. A propeller: R.A.F.: since ca. 1925. H. & P. Ex shape.—7. A heavy cricket bat or lawn-tennis racket: Cranbrook School: C. 20.

club, put in the. Short, for **pudden club, put in the** (*Dict.*). Michael Harrison, *Reported Safe Arrival*, 1943.

club run, the. A routine convoy trip in wartime: Naval: 1939–45. Mostly officers'.

club-winder. A switchman, a brakeman: Canadian railroadmen's (— 1931). Rather, ca. 1880–1910. Ex a club used to 'wind' the brake. (Leechman.)

Clubs. Nickname for physical training instructor: Naval (lower-deck): since ca. 1910. Ex Indian clubs.

clucky. Pregnant: Australian low: C. 20. B., 1942. Ex hens.

clue. A girl, or young woman: Australian: since ca. 1930. Baker.—2. See:—

clue, have no; have you a clue? To be ignorant, have no information; have you heard anything, do you know anything?: mostly Army: 1942 +. Ex *clueless*.

clue up. To 'put (someone) in the picture', to brief, inform, instruct: since the middle 1940's. Cf. **gen up** below.

clued(-)up. Well-informed; alert: mostly Australian: since ca. 1941. (B.P.) Cf. **clue up** above and contrast **clueless** below.

clueless. Ignorant; esp. in *clueless type* (opposite of *gen wallah*) and, in answer to a question, 'I'm clueless': R.A.F., since ca. 1939; hence Army, since ca. 1941. Jackson. Ex crime-detection. Also, since ca. 1941, New Zealand airmen's and soldiers'. (Slatter.)

cluey, adj. and n. (One who is) well-informed or alert: Australian: since ca. 1900. Ex **clued-up** above. B.P. quotes 'He should be on T.V.; he's a real cluey' and 'Ask Bert, he's pretty cluey'.

clumsy as a cub-bear handling his prick. Very clumsy indeed: a low Canadian c.p.: C. 26.

clunk. A man; a chap: Australian low, esp. Sydney: C. 20. Ruth Park, *The Harp in the South*, 1948. Echoic.—2. Hence, since ca. 1950, predominantly a simple fellow, or even a fool. (B., 1953.)—3. An ill-bred or ill-mannered person: Canadian: since late 1950's. (Leechman.) Perhaps semantically 'a lump': cf. the *clunk, clunk-*, words in the E.D.D.

clunk!: intensively **ker-lunk!** Echoic of sounds deeper than those expressed by **boink** (above) and **doink** (below): late C. 19–20, but perhaps going back for centuries.

clunky. Ill-bred or ill-mannered: Canadian: since late 1950's. (Leechman.) Ex sense 3 of **clunk**, n., 3.

*cly. To haunt; molest: c. (— 1688). Randle Holme. Cf. **cloy**, v., on p. 162.

co, 2 (p. 162), is recorded in 1818. (Moe.)—Sense, 4. The phrase *in co*, 'in league with': earlier in *The New Monthly Magazine*, 1817 (article by Jon Bee).—6. Call-over: Rugby Schoolboys': from ca. 1880. Printed *C.O.* in the call-over lists.

co, join; co, part. To join (the) company; to part company: since ca. 1810—therefore **co**, 2, on p. 162, should be considerably back-dated. In *Sailors and Saints*, 2 vols., 1829, W. N. Glascock has 'Joining Co.' as title of Chapter 2 in Vol. I, and 'Parting Co.' as title of ch. 22 in II; earlier *The Port Folio*, Nov. 2, 1805 (p. 341), quotes ex a British song the words 'one King and Co' (the King of England and his subjects). Moe.

Co-Joe. The second pilot of a two-pilot aircraft: R.A.F.: since ca. 1945. Cf. **second dicky**, 2, below.

co-re. A co-respondent: Society: since ca. 1921. Cyril Burt, *The Case of the Fast Young Lady*, 1942.

co-respondent's shoes. Brown-and-white sports shoes: since ca. 1925.

coach-horses. The crew of the State or Royal Barge: late C. 18–19. John Davis, *The Post-Captain*, 1806. (Moe.)

coachers. Tame cattle as decoys to wild: Australian coll.: C. 20. Ion Idriess, *Men of the Jungle*, 1932.

coachman on the box. Syphilis: rhyming s. (on *pox*): from ca. 1870. In C. 20, **the coachman**.

coal, 2. Earlier in J. H. Horsley, *I Remember*, 1912. Prob. ex lost rhyming s. *coal-heaver*, a 'stever' (q.v. in *Dict.* at **stiver**).—3. Petrol: Army drivers': 1939–45. (P-G-R.)

coal, pour on the. The Canadian 'shape', adopted by all vehicle-drivers, of **coals on . . .** below: since ca. 1950. (Leechman.)

coal-box, 1 (p. 163): earlier in W. N. Glascock, *Sailors and Saints* (II, 119), 1829, ' "Now, my boys, reg'lar coal-box." ' Earlier in his *Sketch-Book*, II, 1826. (Moe.) It derives ex the din made by a coal-box being vigorously shaken.

coal-heaver (p. 163) probably rhymes on **stiver** (p. 833). Often shortened to *coal*; occasionally to *heaver*—cf. *heaver*, 4, below.

coal-scuttle (p. 163). The shorter form occurs in *Sinks*, 1848.—2. A Japanese heavy-mortar bomb: Army in Far East: 1942–5. (P-G-R.) Ex the heavy smoke.

Coalies, the.—2. The Coldstream Guards: Army: C. 20.

coals (and coke). Penniless: late C. 19–20. Rhyming on *broke*, it is a variant of **coal and coke** (*Dict.*).

coals on, put the. To increase speed: London busmen's: since ca. 1935.

coaly (p. 163). Rather, C. 19–20. *Boxiana*, II, 1818.

coast, v., 2. Esp. as vbl n. '*Coasting*. Walking near people in crowds,' Duncan Webb in *Daily Express*, Sept. 11, 1945: Black Market: 1943 +.

Coast, the.—2. The coast of British Columbia: Canadian coll., except, naturally, in the Eastern maritime provinces: C. 20. (Leechman.)

coast about. A synonym of *coast*, v. (p. 163): C. 20. (B., 1943.)

coast-crawling. Cruising along the coast of North Africa: Naval: 1940–5. (P-G-R.)

*coat.—2. To arrest (a person): c.: from ca. 1910. Gen. as ppl adj., *coated*.

coat, on the. (Of person) in—sent to—Coventry: Australian: since ca. 1930. B., 1942. Ex coat, v., 1 (*Dict*.)?

coat and badge (p. 163) is also gen. Cockney s. Len Ortzen, *Down Donkey Row*, 1938.

coat of arms. The rank badge of Warrant Officers, Class 1: Army: since ca. 1920. H. & P., 'When a man is promoted to this majestic rank he is said to "have his coat of arms up".' Humorous.

Coathanger, the. The Sydney Harbour Bridge: Melbourne, Australia: from 1932, when the bridge reached completion, until ca. 1940. (B.P.)

coating.—2. Hence (?), a thrashing: Army (esp. in the Guards): 1939 +. Gerald Kersh, *They Die with Their Boots Clean*, 1941, and *The Nine Lives of Bill Nelson*, 1942.

Cob or Cobb. 'Inevitable' nickname for man surnamed Webb: C. 20. A pun on S.E. *cobweb*. (A. B. Petch, March 1966.)

cob.—4. A roll of bread: prison c.: since ca. 1925. (Norman.)—5. A testicle: low: late C. 19–20. Brendan Behan, *Borstal Boy*, 1958. 'Now, no knee and nut stuff and no catching by the cobs.'

cob o' coal (p. 163): by 1960,†.

cob on, have a (p. 163), has, since ca. 1939, also been Naval. More probably ex dial. *cob*, a piece, esp. a large piece.

Cobar shower. A dust storm: Australian: C. 20. Baker, 'Other inland place-names are often used instead of Cobar'; Cobar is an inland town in N.S.W.

Cobb, by (p. 163). These coaches ceased to run in Aug. 1924.

cobber, 2 (p. 164). The Yiddish word itself comes from Hebrew.

cobber-dobber. 'One who betrays a friend' (B., 1959): Aus.: since early 1930's. Cf. dob-in below.

cobber-up. To become friends (*with* someone): Aus.: since ca. 1920. (B., 1959.)

cobbler, 2 (p. 164): also New Zealand sheepshearers': C. 20. *Straight Furrow*, Feb. 21, 1968.

cobbler's awls. Testicles: low rhyming s. (on *balls*): late C. 19–20. (Franklyn, *Rhyming*.) The effective origin of cobblers on p. 164. Cf. the variant *cobblers' stalls*.

cobbler's curls. See cobbler, 3 (*Dict*.).

cobblers' stalls. Human testicles: low rhyming: C. 20. Cf. orchestra stalls, q.v. in *Dict*.

cobbo is a familiar form of cobber, 2 (p. 164): since ca. 1920. B., 1942.

cobbon. See cawbawn.

cobweb rig, the. Some form of swindling: late C. 18–mid-19. In the anon. ballad (published ca. 1800) *The Rolling Blossom*, we find:

'The cobweb and the robbing rigs,
    I practise every day, sir.'

Cock. Cockfosters: London Transport Board employees': since ca. 1930.

cock, penis, appears earlier in N. Field, 1618. See quotation at standing . . .—7. Recorded by B. & L.; mid-C. 19–20.—13. Short for *poppycock*, nonsense: since ca. 1938. R. C. Hutchinson, *Interim*, 1945.—14. Cheek, impudence: Oundle: since late 1920's. Marples. Ex *cocky*.—15. A

cockle: mostly Welsh fishermen's: C. 20. (Wilfred Granville, March 17, 1967.)

cock, adj. Male: beatniks': since late 1950's. (Anderson.) Contrast hen, adj., below.

cock, all to. Awry; (of a statement) inaccurate; (of work) bungled: coll.: C. 20.

cock, hoist a. 'To win a regatta and display a silver or tin cut-out of a cock in the rigging of a winning ship' (Wilfred Granville, Aug. 10, 1962): Naval coll.: C. 20.

cock, hot; a lot of cock. (Utter) nonsense: Aus.: since ca. 1940. (B., 1959.)

*cock-a-brass. App. this c. term belongs to C. 18–19. B. & L., 'A confederate of card-sharpers who remains outside the public-house where they are operating. When they have left, *cock-a-brass* protects their retreat by misleading statements to the victim on the direction taken by them.'

cock a chest. To preen oneself; to put on 'side'; to brag: Naval: C. 20. Granville. Cf. chuck a chest, 2 and 3 (*Dict*.).

cock-a-wax, 2 (p. 164): dates from ca. 1820 or earlier. It occurs in Wm Maginn, *Whitehall* (p. 87), 1827, thus, 'What will you drink, my cock-of-wax, my Trojan, true as ever whistled'. Moe.

cock and hen. A man and wife (together): taxi-drivers': since ca. 1910.—Herbert Hodge, 1939.—4. Odds of 10 to 1: racing, esp. bookmakers': C. 20. (*The Daily Telegraph*, May 7, 1967.) Ex sense 2 on p. 164: ten.

*cock-broth. Nutritious soup: tramps' c.: C. 20. Esp. at the Brighton casual ward: see W. A. Gape, *Half a Million Tramps*, 1936.

cock-cheese. Smegma: low: late C. 19–20.

cock-eye, n. See cocky Bob.

cock-my-cap. Some kind of strong liquor fashionable in the 1720's. Anon., *The Quaker's Opera*, 1728.

cock on; usually as *cock it on*. To charge excessively; to exaggerate: since ca. 1910; by 1960, slightly ob. Perhaps ex haymaking.

Cock Robin(son). See 'Nicknames'.

cock-tail, 4 (p. 165): recorded in Australia in 1867. (Sidney J. Baker, letter.)

cock-tails, the. Diarrhœa: Australian: since ca. 1925. B., 1942.

cock-tax. Alimony: Australian: since ca. 1850. Ian Fleming, *You Only Live Twice*, 1964.

cock-tease, v.t. To excite sexually: low coll.: C. 20. (Angus Wilson, *A Bit off the Map*, 1957.)

cock up, v. To cane (a boy): Charterhouse (ca. 1870–1925) and St Bees (1915 +). Marples. —2. To make a mess of; hence, also n., as in 'He made a complete cock-up of his orders': Army: since ca. 1925. (P-G-R.)

cockatoo, 1 (p. 166) derives rather ex the fact that a farmer trying to live off a small piece of land resembles, in this, a cockatoo. (B.P.)

cockatoo, v.—2. (Ex the n., 2: p. 166). To act as look-out for a gang of crooks: Australian c.: since ca. 1910. Baker.

cockatoo's weather. Weather that is fine by day and wet at night; also, fine on weekdays but wet on Sunday: Australian coll.: since ca. 1925. (B., 1943.)

cocked-hat. An error in reckoning: Naval: C. 20: Granville, 'When pencilling a course on a chart, instead of the lines meeting, they cross and form a "cocked-hat".'—2. A Lord Mayor; a State Governor: Australian: C. 20. Baker. Ex hat worn on official occasions.

cocker. A cockroach: Australian: late C.
19–20. (Ruth Park, *A Power of Roses*, 1953.)
But also widespread nautical, as in Elleston
Trevor, *Gale Force*, 1956.—2. Also *me old cocker.*
Matey: a vocative between Cockney males: C. 20.

cockle. Short for:—

cockle-and-hen. A deformation (conscious?) of
cock-and-hen, 1–3, on pp. 164–5.

cockle to a penny, a. 10 to 1 the field: racing:
since ca. 1920. *Cockle = cock (and hen),* 10; and
penny = penny bun, 1. Rhyming s.

Cockney. 'WR staff name for MR lines and
trains, in South Wales. Also ER term for North
London train crews' (*Railway,* 3rd): railwaymen's:
C. 20.

[Cockney catch-phrases of derisory and/or provocative interrogation: **Do they have ponies down
a pit?; what was the name of the engine-driver?;
what does a mouse do when it spins?** These C. 20
c.pp. are used either to express boredom or to start
a discussion or a 'row'. The second derives ex the
trick of asking numerous questions concerning
speed, times, etc., etc. The third has the c.p.
answer, **because the higher the fewer!** And, by
the way, the third occurs perhaps more frequently
in the form, *Why is a mouse when it spins?,* with
the c.p. answer as given: so Mr Ramsey Spencer
tells me.]

[Cockney speech:—Edwin Pugh, one of the best
of all writers on Cockney life, wrote at the beginning of *Harry the Cockney,* 1912: 'There is no
such being . . . as a typical Cockney. But there
are approximations to a type. There are men and
women, the sons and daughters of Cockneys, born
and bred within sound of Bow bells, and subject
to all the common influences of circumstance and
training and environment that London brings into
play upon their personalities, who may be said to
be . . . typical. The average Cockney is not
articulate. He is often witty; he is sometimes
eloquent; he has a notable gift of phrase-making
and nicknaming. Every day he is enriching the
English tongue with new forms of speech, new
clichés, new slang, new catch-words. The new
thing and the new word to describe the new thing
are never very far apart in London. But the
spirit, the soul, of the Londoner is usually dumb.'

Considerable space is given in this work—both
in the *Dict.* proper and in the Addenda—to
peculiarities of Cockney speech, because it is in
itself important; it is important, too, for the
influence it has exercised on the everyday language
of Colonials—and, it must not be forgotten, that
of Americans. (See also the *Dict.*) Moreover, back
slang and rhyming slang were invented by Cockneys; they are still used widely by costermongers.
In 1908 Clarence Rook, in *London Side Lights,*
could say: 'I will back the costermonger . . . to
. . . talk to a Regius Professor of English for half
an hour, tell him the most amusing stories, and
leave that Professor aghast in darkest ignorance.'

One of the best-informed *aperçus* on the Cockney
is that on pp. 42–3 of Michael Harrison's *Reported
Safe Arrival,* 1943—a book containing many vivid,
and accurate, transcripts of the Cockney speech of
the 20th century.

But the best and most comprehensive study of
the Cockney and his speech is Julian Franklyn's
The Cockney, 1953, 2nd edition—revised—1954;
Andre Deutsch, London; the Macmillan Company,
New York.]

Cockney's luxury. Breakfast in bed and defecation in a chamber-pot; in the truly Cockney
idiom, *breakfast in bed and a shit in the pot,* which
is often added to—indeed, constitutes the original
form of—the c.p.: late C. 19–20. Dating from
the days of backyard privies.

cocko. In address, a variant of **cock,** n., 11 (p.
164): Cockney and Army: since ca. 1920.
Gerald Kersh, *The Nine Lives of Bill Nelson,*
1942.

cockroach.—1. (p. 166), occurs in Alex. Macdonald's *In the Land of Pearl and Gold,* 1907, at
p. 290.—2. A motor coach: rhyming s.: since
ca. 1946. (Franklyn, *Rhyming.*)

cockroach-crusher. A variant of crusher, 1 and
4 (*Dict.*).

cock's eggs. A cock's droppings: poultry-
keepers': C. 20.

cocksy fuss. 'Billing and cooing,' *Sinks*: ca.
1825–80 In *Sinks* it is spelt *coxy.*

cocktail route, be on the. To be drinking excessively: Society: ca. 1934–40. Horace Annesley
Vachell, *Quinney's for Quality,* 1938.

cocky, 3 (p. 166), is very much earlier than I had
thought. *Sessions,* 8th session of 1735, ' "Never
fear, Cocky," says the prisoner'; and as a nickname in *Sessions,* 1736.—5. Earlier in A. Bathgate, *Colonial Experiences,* 1874. (B., 1942.)—6.
Variant of **cockatoo,** n., 2 (*Dict.*): Australian c.:
C. 20. B., 1942.

cocky, n.—7. Also, of course, the bird *cockatoo*
itself. Australian coll.: mid-C. 19–20.—8. 'A
sheep which has lost some of its wool' (B., 1959):
C. 20. Cf. **parrot** and **rosella** below.

cocky, v. To farm: Australian: C. 20. Kylie
Tennant, *The Battlers,* 1941, 'A job "cockying"
for one of her uncles.' Ex sense 5 of the n.: p.
167.

Cocky Bob (Jon Cleary, 1954) or **Cock-eye Bob**
or **cock-eye bob** (Ion M. Idriess, *Forty Fathoms
Deep,* 1937). A coastal gale, a violent thunderstorm, in N.W. Australia: C. 20. Also in the
short form 'another cock-eye brewing': Idriess,
1937.

cockyolly bird.—2. An Australian trooper:
during the South African War. Ex the feathers
in his hat.

cocky's clip. Close-shearing: Australian: C.
20. B., 1942.—2. A (sheep) dip: Australian
rhyming s.: since ca. 1920. (B., 1945.)

cocky's coal. 'Corncobs used as fuel for a fire'
(B., 1959): Aus.: C. 20. By 1959, rare.

cocky's crow. Dawn: Australian: C. 20.
Baker. As in 'We have to be up at cocky's crow'.
Ex S.E. *cock's crow.*

cocky's string. Fencing wire: Australian: C.
20. (B., 1943.) 'Because, on farms, fencing wire
is used to repair things' (B.P.)

cocoa.—3. (Also *coco.*) The head: 1828,
George Godfrey, *History of George Godfrey.* Ex
coco-nut (p. 167).

cocoa (p. 167): by 1945, no longer c.; by 1965,
very common, esp. in the derisive 'I should
cocoa!'

Cocoa Press, the. *The Daily News,* and other
newspapers owned by Messrs Cadbury (chocolate
manufacturers): journalists': early C. 20. (Maisie
Ward, *G. K. Chesterton,* 1944.)

cod, n., 4 (p. 167). *Sinks,* 1848, defines it as
'haughty meddling fool'.—8. A foreman:
builders': late C. 19–20. Cf. *coddy.*

cod, adj. Burlesque; esp. *cod acting,* as in acting a Victorian melodrama as though it were a post-1918 farce or burlesque: actors': from ca. 1890.

cod(-)piece. 'In the latter half of the First World War it became a common practice with the front-line infantry to wear the entrenching tool in the leather cover across the front of the body, so as to protect the private parts. . . . Some of us called it the "cod piece", from the ornamental piece of clothing worn thus when men wore very tight hose' (A. B. Petch, April 1966).

codd. See cod, n., 6, in *Dict.*

coddy.—2. A builder's foreman: builders': C. 20. Cf. cod, n., 8.

codging job. A garment to repair: tailors': from ca. 1870. B. & L.

Codi. A codeine tablet: since late 1950's. (Roderic Jeffries, *A Traitor's Crime,* 1968.)

codology. The practice of chaffing and humbugging: Anglo-Irish: since ca. 1910. Alan Smith, letter of June 7, 1939.

cod's(-)wallop. ·Drivel, utter nonsense: C. 20; orig. low, but by 1930 general. With the phrase *a load of (old) cod's wallop,* a lot of nonsense, compare the synonymous *a load of (old) cobblers,* a lot of utter nonsense (*balls*). The testicular parallel of *cods* and *balls* may, of course, be accidental: but *is* it? Note also that there is a derivative variant, as in 'It's all cods' wallops', as if it were euphemistic for *cod's ballocks.* In S.E. *cod* = scrotum, and, loosely, *cods* = testicles: *cods* therefore may have suggested *ballocks,* with *cods-wallops* a tautologism, hence *cod's (or cods')* *wallop.*

coffee and cocoa; often reduced to *cocoa.* To say so: rhyming s.: C. 20. The longer form is occasionally varied to *tea and cocoa.* (Franklyn, *Rhyming.*)

coffee-bar Casanova. A dashing frequenter of coffee bars, one who seeks stimulation in coffee, dialectic, *amour*: since ca. 1955. Nina Epton, *Love and the English,* 1960.

coffee-grinder. A pedestal winch: Australian: since ca. 1945. Ex appearance. (B.P.)

coffee-pot.—2. 'That part of a barrage balloon winch from which the cable emerges,' Jackson: Balloon Barrage s.: 1939 +. Jackson. Ex its shape.

coffee-shop.—2. A coffin: proletarian: from ca. 1880; ob. B. & L.

coffee stall. A landing-craft kitchen, supplying meals to small craft off the Normandy beaches: nautical: 1944.

coffee stalls. Testicles: C. 20. Rhyming on *balls* and much less used than *orchestra stalls* or *orchestras.* (Franklyn 2nd.)

*coffin is Randle Holme's variant of **cuffin** (*Dict.*).—2. A serviceable but unreliable 'plane: R.A.F.: since ca. 1915. Jackson.—3. That posture in surf-board riding which consists in the surfer's lying flat on his back, with arms folded on chest: Australian surfers': since ca. 1960. (*Pix,* Sept. 28, 1963.) Like a corpse in its coffin.

coffin, put a nail in (a person's). See **put a nail** . . .

Coffin Company, the. A certain English insurance society: Cockneys': from ca. 1920. Ex the very large number of assurance policies taken out with it to ensure decent burial.

cog, v. 2 (p. 168). Extant, at least as late as 1930, among Liverpool undergraduates for any form of cheating. (Marples, 2.)—5. To understand: Australian low: C. 20. B., 1942. Ex sense 3 (p. 168).—6. To copy (another's composition or exercise): Cotton College: C. 20. *The Cottonian,* Autumn 1938. Cf. sense 2 (p. 168).

coggish. A variant of **coggage** (or **coggidge**) noted on p. 168.

coiler. A dead-beat that sleeps in parks and on wharves: low Australian: C. 20. B., 1942. He just coils up and goes off to sleep.

coiny cove. A man in funds: Australian low: since ca. 1920. B., 1942. Cf.:—

coiny-moneyed. Well-off: since ca. 1920. Cf. prec.

coke, n.,—2. (A drink of) *Coca*-Cola: adopted, ca. 1930, ex U.S.: s. until ca. 1950, then coll.—3. Hence any soft drink: soft drinks in gen.: Canadian: since ca. 1935. *The Evening News,* Jan. 9, 1940. Ex 'coca cola'?

cokes.—2. An eating-house: Liverpool: late C. 19–20. Ex *cocoa.* (Frank Shaw.)

cold, in the. Imprisoned, in gaol: Australian: since ca. 1910. (B., 1943.)

*cold biting. 'A straight-out request by a tramp or dead-beat for money,' B., 1941: Australian and New Zealand c.: since ca. 1920.

*Cold Blow, the. See **Rat's Hole, the.**

*cold botting. See **botting.**

cold enough to make a Jew drop his bundle. An Army variant (C. 20; ob. by 1945) of a ruder phrase for 'very cold'.

cold-meat box (p. 169). E. Sue, *The Mysteries of Paris,* vol. I, anon., translation, 1845.

cold-meat job. A case involving a corpse: police: late C. 19–20. (*The Free-Lance Writer,* April 1948.)

cold-meat train. The special carriage was also named *the larky subaltern's coach.*

*cold pigging. 'The practice of hawking goods from door to door' (B., 1942): New Zealand and Australian: C. 20. In this phrase and in **cold biting,** *cold* = cool = cheeky.

cold potato (pronounced *potater*). A waiter: theatrical rhyming s.: C. 20. (Franklyn, *Rhyming.*)

cold steel. A bayonet, Army: since ca. 1930. H. & P. With ironic humour ex journalistic *to use cold steel,* make a bayonet charge.

cold turkey. Door-to-door selling: travelling salesmen's, mostly Canadian: since ca. 1930. Ex a probably apocryphal story. (Leechman.) Cf. *cold-pigging.*

cole.—2. Incorrect spelling of **coal,** 2 (*Dict.*); cf. **coal,** 2, in these Addenda.

coll, 3 (p. 170), is also undergraduates'. Prob. mid-C. 19–20. As undergraduate s., it is prob. mid-C. 18–20; it occurs in *The Gentleman's Magazine,* May 1784 (p. 366), in 'A Familiar Epistle, paraphrased from Horace'. (Moe.)

collar and tie. A lie: rhyming s.: C. 20. Not very common. (Franklyn, *Rhyming.*)

collar-band pint. See **cap-tally drink.**

collar felt, get one's. To get, become, be arrested: low (but also police s.): C. 20. By a pun.

collared on, be. To be in love with: Australian: ca. 1860–1914. 'Tom Collins', *Such Is Life,* 1903.

collect, v.—5. 'To shoot down an aircraft. Thus "He was a sitting bird, I gave him a burst and collected",' Jackson: R.A.F.: 1939 +. Ex senses 1, 2, 4.

collect a gong. To be awarded a decoration: Army and Air Force officers': since ca. 1925. Partridge, 1945.

Colleen Bawn. An erection: rhyming s. (on *horn*): since ca. 1862. (Franklyn, *Rhyming*.)

college.—4. See 'Tavern terms', § 3.

college, v. To hit (a ball) high into the air: Cotton College: mid-C. 19–20. 'The height of the High House from the sloping Bounds [at Sedgley Park] was probably the origin,' Frank Roberts in *The Cottonian*, Autumn 1938.

college, go to. To go to prison: low: ca. 1720–1850. B. & L.

College Boys, the. 'With the departure of the R.A.F. from South Africa, it is now nearly forgotten that they were christened "The Blue Orchids" (1941) and "The College Boys" (1942),' Prof. W. S. Mackie in *The Cape Argus*, July 4, 1946: *blue* uniform; *orchids*: good looks; *College*: so many had recently left University or Public School.

college chum. An old acquaintance or companion: workers' facetious coll.: late C. 19–20.

college telegraph; often shortened to *telegraph*. A college servant given to telling tales: Oxford: 1815–60. *Spy*, 1825.

colley or **colly.** Columbine: theatrical: from ca. 1860. B. & L.

Colley thumper. A *thumping* good hand at cards: card-players': since 1881. In 1881, General Sir George Pomeroy Colley was defeated, and killed, by the Boers in the battle of Majuba Hill.

collie shangle (p. 170) should be *collieshangie*; but being Scottish dialectal, it has no business to be in this dictionary.

Collins.—2. A 'strong' drink; esp. *Tom C.*, made with gin, and *John C.*, made with rye whisky: since ca. 1860; by 1900, coll. See *John Collins* on p. 442.

colly. A written variant of **cauli** (p. 135).

colney. A match: mostly Cockney: C. 20. James Curtis, *You're in the Racket Too*, 1937. Short for *Colney Hatch* (*Dict.*).

Colney Hatch for you! You're crazy: a c.p. of ca. 1890–1914. Cf. *Winnick* (p. 961).

colo. Cold: pidgin: mid-C. 19–20. B. & L.

Colonel. A jocular form of address: Australian: since ca. 1945. (B.P.)

Colonel Barker; Colonel Barker's Own. A woman masquerading as a man: the Middlesex Regiment (a fighting term, so 'watch it'): since early 1930's. Ex the assumed name of a woman masquerader once prominent in the news.

Colonel Bogey; the Colonel. 'The number of strokes a good player may be reckoned to need for the course or for a hole' (O.E.D., Sup.): resp. golfers' s. (1893) >, by 1920, coll. >, by 1935, j.; and, hence, golfers' s. (1900) >, by 1925, coll. The former term is a personification of *bogey*, bugbear (of golfers).

colonel of a regiment. See 'Tavern terms', § 6.

Colonel Prescott; often shortened to *Colonel*. A waistcoat: rhyming s.: since ca. 1930. Cf. **Charley Prescott** (p. 141). The Colonel is a well-known sporting character.

colonel's cure, the. Cockney term of ca. 1870–1905, thus: 'I sent my yard-boy round for six-penn'orth o' physic, an' I took it all standing—one gulp, you know: what we useder call "the colonel's cure",' A. Neil Lyons, *Arthur's*, 1908.

colonial!, my. Short for *my colonial oath!*: 1895, Eric Gibbs, *Stirring Incidents in Australasia*; 1903, 'Tom Collins', *Such Is Life*, '"My bloody colonial!"' Ob. by 1940; † by 1960. (B.P.)

Colonial duck. 'A boned shoulder of mutton . . . stuffed with sage and onions' (B., 1942): Australian: C. 20. Contrast **Colonial goose** (p. 170). Rare, says B. in 1959.

colonial livery. A bloody nose and a black eye: Australian: C. 19. (B., 1943.) Cf. *Botany Bay coat-of-arms.*

colonist. A louse: ca. 1810–70. David Carey, *Life in Paris*, 1822. A neat pun.

colour.—2. Any oil paint: builders' coll.: since ca. 1870.—3. A colour-sergeant: Army coll.: late C. 19–20. (Patrick MacGill, *The Amateur Army*, 1915.)

coloured clothes. Civilian clothes: military coll. of ca. 1860–1914. B. & L.

Colston's School, Bristol, had in 1887–1922, and certainly for some years before 1887 and probably for some years since 1922, 'two popular types' of abbreviation, one in -*s*: e.g. *blots* (blotting paper), *detens* (detention), *impots*, *paps* (paper), *swifs* (soap); the other by omission of *s.*: e.g. *cla* (class), *gra* (grass). Marples.

column of lumps is the Canadian form, 1915 +, of:—

column of muck-up (or **fuck-up**). Column of route: Army: C. 20. Lewis Hastings, *Dragons Are Extra*, 1947. On a long march it tends to tangle.

column snake. Single file: Army in Burma: 1942–5. 'An old Standard Ger. word (C. 16, perhaps earlier) for an army on the march was "das Heerwurm"—lit., army-worm (or snake)': Ramsey Spencer, March 1967.

colundrum. A conundrum: music-halls': ca. 1885–90. Facetious.

colyum, ellum, fillum, are common Canadian solecisms (spoken only) for *column, elm, film*: C. 20, and probably much earlier. Nor are they unknown elsewhere—especially the 3rd, often the 2nd, occasionally the 1st.

com.—5. Commission: commercial: from ca. 1880. H. A. Vachell, *Quinney's*, 1914.—6. (Also **Com.**) A Communist: Australian: since ca. 1925. (Leonard Mann, *The Go-Getter*, 1942.)

comb down. To ill-treat; thrash: Australian coll.: from ca. 1860. B. & L.

comb out. 'To sweep over in formation, attacking ground targets with gun-fire. Thus, "We're combing out the North of France this afternoon,"' Jackson: R.A.F. coll. (1939) >, by 1944, j. Ex the military sense.

combine harvester. 'Class 9 goods locomotive' (*Railway*, 3rd): railwaymen's: since late 1940's.

combined operations. Marriage, with especial reference to sexual aspect: Services': since ca. 1942. Cf. *coöperation* below.

combined ops. Combined operations: Services' coll.: 1940 +. (P-G-R.)—2. Hence, a variant of the preceding entry.

combo. Short for **comboman** (p. 171): Australian: since ca. 1925. (K. S. Prichard, *Working Bullocks*, 1926; B., 1943; Sidney H. Courtier, *The Glass Spear*, 1951.) Hence, *go combo*, to cohabit—to live—with a gin, as in H. Drake Brockman, *Men Without Wives*, 1938.—2. A small jazz band: adopted, in late 1950's, ex U.S. Ex *combination*.

combo, v. (Of a white man) to live with an Aboriginal woman: Aus.: since ca. 1930. (B., 1959.) Ex sense 1 of the n.

come a clover. To tumble over: rhyming s.: ca. 1910–30. (Franklyn 2nd.)

come all over (someone). To thrash; defeat utterly: Australian: C. 20. B., 1942.

come-all-ye. Irish folk-songs and music; 'an old country song': Anglo-Irish: since ca. 1890. (P. W. Joyce, *English . . . in Ireland*, 1910.) Ex 'Come all ye faithful' and other such beginnings.

come aloft. To have an erection: coll.: ca. 1550–1840. Spenser, *The Faerie Queene*, 1590–96; Dryden, *The Maiden Queen*, 1668, 'I cannot come aloft to an old woman.'

come and get it. The cooks', or the orderlies', cry, amounting almost to a c.p., 'The meal is ready'; mainly Army: late C. 19–20. Since ca. 1945, general in Australia. (B.P.)

come at. To agree to (something); to agree to do (it): Australian: C. 20: s. >, by 1950, coll.: (H. Drake-Brockman, 1938; Gavin Casey, 1947; D'Arcy Niland, 1958.)—2. To try (to do) something: Australian: since ca. 1930; by 1960, coll. 'I wouldn't come at that if I were you'; 'I wouldn't come at eating frogs' legs'; 'I couldn't come at a prostitute'. (B.P.)

come-back, n. See **come-back, make a** (p. 172).—2. Redress; compensation: Australian coll.: since ca. 1930.—3. 'The progeny of a merino ram and a cross-bred ewe' (B., 1959): Aus.: C. 20.

come back.—2. To take back: Australian: since ca. 1920. Vance Palmer, *Seedtime*, 1957, 'Now I've put my foot in it—skin deep. Come back all I said.'

come back, make a (p. 172), occurs in *Punch*, April 11, 1934. (Dr D. Pechtold.)

come back to the field. See **field** . . .

come clean (p. 172). By 1939, it was s.

come Cripplegate (p. 172): W. N. Glascock, *Sketch-Book* (I, 209), 1825. Moe.

come-down, be on a. To be suffering from the diminishing effects of a drug: mostly teenagers': since ca. 1955. Cf. **come-down** on p. 172.

come down on a jump. (Of a docker) to turn up at a job on the chance of taking an absentee's place: Australian ports', esp. dockers': since ca. 1925. (B., 1943.) Perhaps cf. *jump the gun*.

come-from. Place of birth: lower-middle class: since ca. 1920.

come good. To make money; be in credit or in form; to be succeeding: Australian: since ca. 1930. (Jean Devanney, *By Tropic Sea and Jungle*, 1944; D'Arcy Niland, *The Shiralee*, 1955.)—2. Also, to 'turn up trumps', as in Jon Cleary, *The Climate of Courage*, 1954, 'I did a bit of smoodging to the wife of the pub owner in town, and she came good.'—3. Hence, to accede to a request for, e.g., a loan: Australian: since ca. 1940. (B.P.)

come-hither girl; come-hither look. A 'good time', money-seeking type of girl, a 'gold-digger'; a girl's inviting glance: resp., s., since ca. 1920; and coll. of C. 20.

come inside. 'A man who supplants another in any pursuit or design is said to "come inside him"' (P. W. Joyce, *English . . . in Ireland*, 1910): Anglo-Irish coll.: late (? mid) C. 19–20. To get on the *inside* track?

come it.—9. To be quiet, esp. in imperative: c.: from ca. 1880; ob. B. & L.

*****come it at the box—the broads.** To dice; to play cards: c.: from ca. 1860. Ibid.

come it over (p. 172) goes back to ca. 1820 or even earlier. John L. Gardner, *The Military Sketch-Book* (II, 30), 1829. Moe.

come-love tea. Weak tea; esp., tea made with leaves already used: Australian: since ca. 1930. (B., 1943.) Ex the mildness of 'Come, love'.

*****come on.** Swindler's 'bait' to dupe: Australian c.: since ca. 1925. B., 1942. Adopted from U.S. See *Underworld*. Usually hyphenated—and by 1945 no longer c.

come on, v. An extension—since ca. 1945—of **come**, v., 1 (p. 171): esp. among teenagers.

come on in out of the war! Take shelter!—during a bombing raid: civilians': a W.W. II c.p. A pun on 'come on in out of the rain'.

come on tally plonk (or **taller candle**)? How are you?: Army in France and Belgium: 1914–18. Hobson-Jobson for Fr. *comment allez-vous?*

come one's cocoa. (Of men) to experience an orgasm: low: C. 20. By alliteration. See **come**, v., 1, in *Dict*.

come one's guts. To 'spill' information: low Australian: since ca. 1920. (Kylie Tennant, 1953.)

come one's mutton or **turkey.** To masturbate: low: late C. 19–20.

come-out, adj. 'Execrable' (*Sinks*, 1848): low: ca. 1830–80.

come-out, n. Exodus of the audience after the show: circusmen's coll.: C. 20.

come out in the wash, it'll all. See **wash** . . .

come out of that hat—I can't see yer feet! A boys' c.p. cry to a man wearing a topper: ca. 1875–1900. (Mostly London.)

come right on the night, it will all. This—dating from ca. 1880—is perhaps the commonest c.p. of the theatre. Ex mishaps and mistakes that, happening at a—esp. at the dress—rehearsal, will probably not recur. (See esp. Wilfred Granville, *A Dictionary of Theatrical Slang*.) Since ca. 1920, often used in the world outside—when small things go wrong.

come round on the paint. (Of a racehorse) to take the turn on the inside: Australian sporting: since ca. 1935. (B., 1953.)

come the bag. See **bag, come the.**

come (the) blarney over (someone). To be very sweet to; to flatter: since ca. 1810 or a decade earlier. The shorter phrase occurs in W. N. Glascock, *Sailors and Saints* (I, 185), 1928. Moe.

come the bludge on. To sponge upon (someone): Australian: since ca. 1925. D'Arcy Niland, *Call Me . . .*, 1958, 'What's the big idea, coming the bludge on us?' Cf. *bludge*, n.

come the double (p. 172). Ex the sense recorded at **double, come the.**

come the gammon (over). To wheedle (someone): a C. 19 variant of **gammon**, v., on p. 314: cf. **gammon**, n., 1.

come the old soldier over (p. 173) occurs in 1818: Alfred Burton, *Johnny Newcome*. (Moe.)

come the old tin-man. To bluff: to flannel; make oneself a nuisance: Naval: C. 20. Granville.

come the raw prawn over. To swindle: Australian: since ca. 1935. (Cusack & James, *Come in Spinner*, 1951.)

come this side. Arrived here: pidgin: mid-C. 19–20. B. & L.

come to a sticky end. See *sticky*, adj., 4 (p. 831). To die murdered; to go to gaol: since ca. 1916.—2. To masturbate: low Australian: C. 20.

come to bat for. Tautological variant of **bat for.**

come to cues! Come to the point!: theatrical: late C. 19–20. Ex rehearsal practice of giving a hesitant actor the cue line only. (Wilfrid Granville, letter of April 12, 1948.)

come to grass; usually **coming** ... To come up to the surface of a mine: Cornish miners': mid-C. 19–20. (R. M. Ballantyne, *Deep Down*, 1869.)

come unbuttoned. See **unbuttoned, come.**

come-up, n. No. 11 punishment: Naval: since ca. 1930. The sufferers come up on deck to eat their meals.

come up! A variation of **get a number**: R.A.F.: since ca. 1930. Partridge, 1945.

come up for air! Take a rest!: Australian c.p.: since late 1940's. (B.P.) Ex pearl-diving?—2. 'To terminate a prolonged kiss' (Leechman): since ca. 1930.

Comedian, or **Camp Comedian, the.** The Camp Commandant: R.A.F.: since ca. 1930. H. & P.

comfort.—2. A sort of strong liquor in vogue ca. 1725–30. Anon., *The Quaker's Opera*, 1728. Cf. the liqueur known as Southern Comfort: C. 20. (Leechman.)

comfort for the troops. A catamite: Services': since ca. 1925.

comfortable, esp. in **Are you comfortable?** Have you been to the w.c.?: domestic (mostly feminine) euphemistic coll.: late C. 19–20.

comic cuts.—2. A comical fellow, esp. one who overdoes the funny stuff: since ca. 1920.

Comic Cuts. The confidential reports written on ratings' ability and conduct by Divisional Officers: Naval: since ca. 1945. (Wilfred Granville, *A Dict. of Naval Slang*, 1962.)

coming and going. (Of an aircraft) fitted with wireless: R.A.F.: since ca. 1938. H. & P.

coming on, be. To be learning the ways of the world, e.g. of women: coll.: mid-C. 19–20. Ex S.E. *coming on*, growing (up).

coming to town, they're. Enemy 'planes approaching: R.A.F. c.p.: 1940 +.

coming up on a lorry; often preceded by *it's*. A jocular c.p., dating since ca. 1910. in ref. to something small—a packet, a letter—that has not arrived when expected.

comings. Seminal fluid: low coll.: mid-C. 19–20. Ex the relevant sense of **come,** v., in *Dict.*

Commando tickle. A pinching of the thigh between thumb and forefinger: Forces': 1941 +.

commercial traveller. A person with bags under his eyes: from ca. 1930. Ex a music-hall joke. Cf. **bagman,** 1 (*Dict.*).—2. A swagman: Australian jocular: since ca. 1920. (B., 1943.)

commie. A Communist: since ca. 1943. Perhaps adopted from U.S.

*commissionaire. A better-class harlot in the Argentine white-slavers' c.: C. 20. (A. Londres.)

commo. A Communist: since ca. 1918. B., 1942; *Daily Express*, Dec. 20, 1946.

Commo. The *Combined Officer of Merchant Navy Operators*: nautical: 1940 +.—2. A Communist: Australian: since ca. 1925. (Dick.) A variant of **Commie.**

common as cat-shit and twice as nasty, as. A cockney c.p., applied either to a person regarded

as 'beneath' one or, less often, to an inferior article: since ca. 1920. Communicated by Julian Franklyn, Jan. 3, 1968.) Cf. **soft as shit and twice as nasty, as,** below.

common bouncer. Australian form (1897) of **common bounce** (p. 174). Sidney J. Baker, letter.

common John. A species of marble (in the game of marbles): children's: late C. 19–20. *The Manchester Evening News*, March 27, 1939.

commoner, 2 (p. 174). Rather, an inexpert boxer; an amateur. *Boxiana*, I–IV *passim*: 1818–24.

commono. A cheap marble: Australian children's: C. 20. (B.P.) Cf. **commoney** on p. 174.

commons, house of (p. 174). For origin, cf., however, **parliament,** 2.

commoray. A jocular 'French' pronunciation of *commodore*: Naval: since ca. 1925.

commugger. Communion: St Bees and Uppingham: since ca. 1905. Marples. By the Oxford *-er?*

*communion bloke. A religious hypocrite: prison c.: from ca. 1870. B. & L.

communionist. A Communist: jocular: since ca. 1919; by 1950, ob.; by 1960, †.

Communist (p. 174) returned to 'favour' ca. 1941, and **Bolshie** (p. 76) was, by 1943, archaic.

comp.—2. A newspaper competition: since ca. 1925.

comp list. Complimentary list (for free tickets): Australian: since ca. 1905. (Dal Stivens, 1951.)

comp number. See **compo,** 6.

[Comparative and superlative in illiterate speech. These consist mainly in the use of *-er, -est*, where literacy demands *more* or *most*. Thus, Nevinson, 1895, 'There ain't no skilleder sweep nor what I am this side eternity.']

compass-buster. See **basher,** 6.

compassionate. Compassionate leave: Services' (perhaps esp. Army) coll.: 1939–45. (P-G-R.)

comped. Matter set up or composed: printers': from ca. 1870. B. & L.

comping, n. Type-setting: printers' coll.: late C. 19–20. Ex *composing*. Cf. *comp* (p. 174).

complete and utter, n. Elliptical for 'complete and utter bastard': Australian: since late 1940's. 'You'll have trouble with him. He's a complete and utter.' (B.P.)

compo.—3. Compounding (e.g. an annuity for a cash payment): insurance: C. 20—4. A busman holding a licence both as conductor and as driver: busmen's: since ca. 1920.—5. Compensation: Australian workers': since the 1920's. (Dymphna Cusack, *Southern Steel*, 1953.)—6. Compensation allowance—in lieu of rations—to men ashore: Naval: C. 20. Such a job is a *comp number*.—7. See **compo rations.**

compo, on the. (Of workmen) in receipt of compensation: Australian: since ca. 1925. (B., 1943.) Cf. *compo*, 6. Since ca. 1950, usually *on compo*. (B.P.)

compo king. One who, to get workers' compensation, injures himself or malingers: New Zealand and Australian: since ca. 1925. B., 1941.

compo rations. A *composition* pack of one day's rations for fourteen men: Services' (mostly Army) coll.: 1939–45. (P-G-R.)

compound, v. (Of a horse) to fail, esp. to maintain speed or strength: racing: since ca. 1860.

The O.E.D. Sup. records it for 1876. Ex *compound*, to compromise.

compty. Deficient, as in 'What are you compty?': Army: late C. 19–20. (Ex Hindustani?)—2. Hence, mentally deficient: Army: since ca. 1920.

compul. Compulsory: Harrow School: mid-C. 19–20. Marples.

con, n.—5. A lavatory attendant: c., and low.: C. 20. ? abbr. *confidential.* Sense 1: at Eton = a friend. *Spy,* 1825.—6. A *con*sultation; a *con*ference: lawyers': late C. 19–20. (Collin Brooks, *The Swimming Frog,* 1951.)—7. As *the con,* it = confidence-trickery: Canadian: C. 20. Niven. 'I ain't a shark . . . trying to throw the con into you fellows'.

con course. A conversion course: R.A.F.: since ca. 1935. H. & P. For men remustering from one trade to another.—2. Hence, substitution of one type of armament for another on an aircraft: since ca. 1940. Partridge, 1945.

con depot. A convalescent (i.e., convalescence) depot: Army: 1940 +. Cf. the World War II **con camp** (p. 175).

*****con man** (p. 175). The English *locus classicus* is Percy J. Smith, *Con Man,* 1938.

Conan (Doyle). A boil: rhyming s.: C. 20.

concentric bird. See **oozlum bird.** With pun on concentric circles and eccentric flight.

concertina.—2. A side of mutton: Australian: since ca. 1925. (B., 1943.)—3. 'A sheep that is hard to shear because of the wrinkles in its skin' (B., 1959): Aus. rural: since ca. 1930.

concrete, the. The track: racing motorists' coll.: since ca. 1910. Hence, *take the concrete,* to go on to the racing track, whether in a race or for a practice run.

condenseritis. Leaking condensers (esp. in old destroyers): Naval officers': since ca. 1925. Granville. Caused by old age. 'You get salt water in the closed feed system: Condenseritis, it's called. Keeps Senior Engineers awake at nights': John Winton, *We Joined the Navy,* 1959.

condom (p. 175) and **cundum** (p. 197): by 1910, at latest, S.E.

condumble. See **your humble c.**

condys, the. Advice: Australian: since ca. 1920. Lawson Glassop, *We Were the Rats,* 1944. Ex the curative *Condy's fluid.*

*****confeck** is Randle Holme's spelling of **confect** (*Dict.*).

conference, in. Engaged, busy: jocular coll.: since ca. 1945. Running on the pretentious use of *conference* for any discussion or meeting, however trivial.

confetti. Machine-gun bullets: adopted in 1940 ex American airmen. *The Reader's Digest,* Feb. 1941.

confidence buck. A confidence trick: from ca. 1885; ob. B. & L.

confo. A conference: Australian: since ca. 1939. (B., 1953.)

Confucius he say. This c.p. introductory 'gag' is followed by the 'words of wisdom'—mostly of genuine or cynical homespun philosophy—couched in 'Chinese' grammar: since ca. 1920.

confused operations. Combined Operations: Naval officers': ca. 1941–3. Granville. Ex the viewpoint of the more conservative, the 100 per cent. service-minded officers: yet even they relented.

Cong. A Congregational chapel; (usually in pl.) a Congregationalist: C. 20.

Congo. A Congregationalist: Australian: since ca. 1925. (B., 1953.)

Conk. A lower-middle class nickname for a large-nosed person: late C. 19–20.

conk, n., 1: gen. of a big nose.—6. The head: Australian, esp. Sydney: since ca. 1920. (B.P.)

conk, v.—2. To hit: Australian: since ca. 1925. B., 1942. Echoic. Imm. ex:—. To punch (someone) on the nose: pugilistic: since ca. 1810; ob. *Boxiana,* III, 1821.

conk, go. To fail; to cease gradually, to peter out: Australian: since ca. 1920. Baker. Cf. **conk, v.,** 1 (*Dict.*).

conker (p. 176): 1821: *Boxiana,* III.—2. 'Internal user motor. Motor not licensed for road' (*Railway*): railwaymen's : since ca. 1910. Used for a pleasant, domestic sort of 'game'.

conkey, 1 (p. 167). Wellington was called *Conkey* at least a decade before 1815; *Old Conkey,* after 1815. Alternatively *Atty Conkey,* lit. 'Arthur the Long-Nosed'. During his campaigning years in Europe, his staff called him *The Peer,* from his aloofness. See esp. C. S. Forester's *Death to the French,* 1932.—3. Worthless; useless: Australian: since ca. 1925. B., 1942. Ex **conk, go.**

Connaught!, go to hell or. See **go to hell or Connaught** in *Dict.*

Connaught, the. 66 in the game of House: C. 20. Michael Harrison, 1943.

connect.—2. 'To make a buy' (*Hearings,* 1955) of narcotics: drug traffic: since ca. 1920. Cf. *connection,* one's contact.

conner.—2. Tinned food: Army: since late 1939. H. & P. Ex **Maconochie** (*Dict.*), the manufacturer's name, rather than an extension of sense 1.

Connie. A Constellation aircraft: since early 1950's. (Nino Culotta, *Cop This Lot,* 1960.)

connie or **conny.** A tram conductor: Melbournites': C. 20. (B., 1943.) As if a pet-form of *Constance.*—2. A cornelian marble: Australian children's: C. 20. (B.P.)—3. A convict: Aus. juvenile: C. 20. Ross Campbell, *Mummy, Who Is Your Husband?,* 1964.

conning, n. Generic for the confidence trick: C. 20: c. >, by 1930, also police s. Ex **con, v.,** 2 (p. 175).

connivering about. See **buggerizing about.** Perhaps ex S.E. *connive* + s. *bugger about.*

conny-onny. *Condensed* milk: Merseyside: since ca. 1920. A reduplication.

conque is a rare variant of **conk,** n., 1: *Boxiana,* III, 1821.

conrod. *Connecting rod* to piston: engineers' and mechanics': C. 20.

conservatory. Enclosed portion of an aircraft; sometimes the cockpit: R.A.F. since ca. 1935. H. & P., 'So called because of the "glass-roofing".'

consoo. Consul: pidgin: from ca. 1860.

constable, the. An unwanted companion; a burr that *will* stick: Services': since ca. 1930. H. & P.

[Constables. In the first quarter of the C. 18, the following terms occur in Ned Ward: *catchpole rap*[*p*]*aree* (1709), *city bull-dog* (1703; gen. in pl.), *cony-fumble* (1703), and *trap* (1703) or *town-trap* (1709); the watchmen are *hour-grunters* (1703) and bailiffs are *bums* (1703); lawyers are *tongue-padders* (1703).]

Constant. Constantinople (Istanbul): among Britons in E. Mediterranean and Near East: late C. 19–20; ob. by 1945, virtually † by 1960.

constant screamer (p. 177) is perhaps, as Franklyn suggests, rhyming s.; by 1950, †.

constitutional.—2. Gin and bitters: Australian: since ca. 1930. B., 1942.

contract. A hard task undertaken: Australian coll.: since ca. 1930. (In several of Vance Palmer's novels, e.g. *Golconda*, 1948.) Should be dated back to ca. 1910. It occurs also in Tom Ronan, *Vision Splendid*, 1954.

contract, mess up the (p. 177). More usually *bugger the contract*.

control. See **everything under control.**

conundrum.—3. Female pudend: ca. 1640–1830. App. earliest in R. W., *A Pill to Purge Melancholy*, 1652.

convalescent home. A place of work where conditions are 'good'—i.e. easy: jocular coll.: since ca. 1905.

convincing ground. 'The site for a grudge fight' (B., 1942): Australian: C. 20.

cony-wabble. See 'Dupes'.

cooee (p. 178), line 1. But the *oo* sound is onger; the *ee*, though long, is sharper.

cook, n. See **Captain Cook** above and **give a cook** below.

cook hot water for a barber, she couldn't. See **she couldn't . . .**

cook-off, n., and **cook off,** v. (To effect) a premature or accidental discharge of a firearm or a cannon: common during World War II, esp. in the Army. Ex the too-high temperature of the barrel. In, e.g., Gerald Pawle, *The Secret War*, 1956.

cook-shop. A kitchen on a station: rural Australian: C. 20, but not common. (B., 1943.)

cook up. To falsify (e.g. accounts): late C. 19–20. Variant of **cook,** 1 (p. 178).

cooked (p. 178). Rather, since ca. 1820. *Sessions*, 1825.

cookem fry. Hell: Naval: since ca. 1870. Granville. Presumably ex 'to cook and fry (in hell)'.

cookery. 'Many modern painters affect to despise the technique of their art, and deprecate attention to what they irreverently term "cookery",' Thomas Bodkin, *The Approach to Painting*, revised ed., 1945: artists': since ca. 1920.

cookery nook. A ship's galley; a shore station cookhouse: Naval: since ca. 1926. H. & P.

cookie. A heavy bomb: R.A.F.: 1940+. Jackson. Cf. *groceries*. 'In 1943–45, the 4,000 and then the 8,000 lb. bomb,' Partridge, 1945.

cook's last hope. 'A heavy steamed duff' (B., 1943): Australian Naval: 1939–45.

cook's tormentors, a cook's gig-forks (? big forks) —see **tormentors,** 2, on p. 901—occurs in *The Night Watch* (II, 88), 1828, and earlier in W. N. Glascock's *Sketch-Book*, 1825–26. Moe.

Cool and **Kal.** Coolgardie and Kalgoorlie: Australian (esp. Western Australia): late C. 19–20.

cool, adj.—4. (Of jazz) good and modern: jazz-lovers': since ca. 1945. (*The Observer*, Sept. 16, 1956.)—5. (Of a singer) slow and husky: since ca. 1948. (Ibid.)—6. Very pleasing or attractive or satisfactory: Canadian (esp. teenagers'): adopted, ca. 1955, from U.S. All these senses came from U.S.: 4 and 5 were adopted at

least five, perhaps ten, years earlier in Canada than in Britain. '*Cool* became a word of praise when *hot* ceased to be one; that is, when hot jazz went out of fashion, to be displaced by bop or bebop, a later—a "progressive" or "modern jazz".' (F. E. L. Priestley, in letter of Dec. 20, 1959.)—7. Self-possessed; *real cool*, devilishly self-possessed: jazz, beatnik, teenage: since ca. 1950. Cf.—in S.E.—'a *cool* hand' and '*cool*-headed'.—8. 'Not carrying illegal drugs' (Peter Fryer in *The Observer* colour supplement, Dec. 3, 1967): addicts': since early 1960's.

cool, play it. To take things calmly, or cautiously and moderately: since ca. 1955.

cool cat. An addict of modern jazz: jazz-lovers': since ca. 1945. (*The Observer*, Sept. 16, 1956.)—2. A rock-and-roller: adopted, 1956, from U.S.—3. (Ex. 1.) A fine fellow: Canadian: since ca. 1956.

coolaman. A drinking vessel: Australian coll.: from ca. 1870. B. & L. Ex Aborigine.

cooler.—5. A chilly glance: Australian: C. 20. B., 1942.

Coolgardie safe. A makeshift safe for keeping food cool in country districts: Aus.: since ca. 1920. Baker, 1959, 'The stress is on *cool* rather than on the place-name, *Coolgardie*' (in Western Australia).

coolie, 1 (p. 179). Ex Tamil for 'day labourer.'

cooloo, the whole. 'The whole lot' of whatever it is: since ca. 1935. Perhaps ex Am. *the whole caboodle*. But probably from Arabic *cooloo*, all: cf. *a cooloo*.

coon.—3. An aboriginal: Australian: since ca. 1920. (Jean Devanney, 1944.) Ex sense 2 (p. 179).

***coop,** a prison (p. 179), is very much earlier: *Sessions*, Sept. 1785.

cooper.—4. A bungling, or something bungled; a mistake: on borders between tramps' and Romany s.: C. 20. (Robert M. Dawson.) Cf. sense 3 on p. 179.

coöperation. Sexual play and intercourse with no implication of marriage: searchlight crews': 1939–early 40; in short, during 'the phoney war'— 'before Combined Operations had become a Staff concept' (H. R. Spencer). Contrast **combined operations** above.

Cooper's Snoopers. Social-survey investigators: 1940, then ob. Investigators proposed by the Rt Hon. Duff Cooper.

coosh. Good, comfortable, easy: Australian: since ca. 1919. Baker. Ex *cushy*.

cop, n., 2 (p. 179). 'What do you want to search me for, you have a good cop,' *Sessions*, Aug. 1886.

cop, v.—7. To catch on to; to notice, to detect: Australian: since ca. 1930. (Cusack & James, *Come in Spinner*, 1951.)

cop, be on a soft or **sweet.** To have an easy job; be on a 'good thing': Australian: since ca. 1925. (B.P.)

cop a chice (loosely **chise**). Variant of *catch a chice* (see **chice, n.,** 4). *News of the World*, Aug. 28, 1938.

cop a coronation. See **coronation** below.

cop a deaf 'un. To pretend not to hear or not to have heard: (c. and) low: since ca. 1920.

***cop bung!** 'A warning cry when the police make their appearance': c.: from ca. 1875. B. & L. See **cop, n.,** 1 (*Dict.*).

cop it.—2. To become pregnant: Australian

feminine (low): since ca. 1920. (Margaret Trist, *Now That We're Laughing*, 1944.)

cop on is the Northern equivalent of Southern **get off** (with a member of the other sex): late C. 19–20.

cop-out man. He who, in a crooked game, takes the winnings: Australian two-up players': since ca. 1920. (B., 1953.)

*****cop-shop.** Police station: Australian c.: C. 20. B., 1942.

cop that lot! Just look at those people or that scene or display or incident; with an implication of admiration or astonishment or derision: Aus. c.p.: since ca. 1930. Nino Culotta, *Cop This Lot*, 1960.

*****cop the drop.** (Of a policeman.) To accept bribes: c.: from ca. 1910. Cf. **drop**, n., 4, and **dropsy**, both in *Dict.*

*****cop the tale.** To swallow a confidence-trick story: c.: from ca. 1919.

cop this, young Harry! A c.p. used during horse-play (e.g. pie-throwing): Australian: since ca. 1950. (B.P.)

copasetic. All safe, wholly safe; all clear; excellent, most attractive: Canadian adaptation, ca. 1925, of U.S. *copesettic* (Berry & Van den Bark). For lack of an authenticated etymology, I provisionally accept the origin proposed by a witty and learned friend: 'able to *cope* and anti*septic*' Amerindian?

*****copbusy.** 'A thief handing over plunder to a confederate to escape the law' (B., 1942): Australian c.: C. 20. Ex the v.—see *Dict.*

cope. 'To do one's duty satisfactorily,' Grenfell Finn-Smith in list communicated in April 1942: Services (esp. Army officers') coll.: since 1935; adopted from Society s. (from ca. 1933), as in D. du Maurier, *Rebecca*, 1938. Short for *cope with things, cope with it*, etc. 'Can you cope?' is perhaps the most frequent form.

*****copman.** A policeman: Australian c.: C. 20. B., 1942. Ex **copper-man** (*Dict.*)?

copper, n., 1 (p. 179): earlier in *Sessions*, May 16, 1846.—4. (Ex 3.) A prison informer: c.: C. 20. (H. U. Triston, 1938.)

copper, sky a. See **sky**, v., 1, and **skying a copper,** both on p. 777.

copper-arse. 'A cabman who works long hours, that is, one who is able to sit on his cab longer than most. It is also applied to a man who is always cruising,' Herbert Hodge, *Cab, Sir?*, 1939. Cf. the nautical S.E. *copper-bottomed.*

copper(-)belly. A fat man: Cockneys': late C. 19–20. The *copper* being that used on washing day.

copper bolts. Excrement: low (? orig. artisans'): C. 20.

copper-bottom. 'A lorry driver who breaks the law by driving more than 11 hours in 24 to undercut other drivers. Also *day-and-night merchant*' (Peter Sanders): since late 1940's. In, e.g., *The Daily Telegraph*, Jan. 26, 1964.

copper Johns. See 'Money'.

Copper Knob. Nickname for red-headed person, esp. man: since ca. 1860; by 1960, slightly ob. (D. W. Barrett, *Navvies*, 1860.)

copper(-)knocker. A metal worker; in pl., the metal-workers' shop on an airfield: R.A.F.: since ca. 1925. H. & P.

copper-shop. A police station: police: since ca. 1910. Cf. *copper-house* (p. 180).

copper-tail (p. 180). Extant. Synonym: *bronzewing*: C. 20. B., 1942.

Coppers in Disguise. Members of the Criminal Investigation Department: jocular: C. 20.

coppers wore high hats, when. See **when coppers** . . .

coppist. A boy—or even a man—that, at level crossings, takes the plate numbers of railway engines: since ca. 1930. *The Daily Mirror*, Sept. 19, 1946. Ex *cop*, 'to catch; to take'.

copter. Helicopter: aviation: 1944 +.

copy-holder. See 'Tavern terms', § 9 (near end).

cor! chase me, winger, round the wash-(h)ouse. A c.p., expressing incredulity: Naval lower-deck: ca. 1947–57.

cor lummie (or **-y)!** A Cockney expletive: mid-C. 19–20. I.e. *God love me*: see **cor** (p. 180) and cf. **gorblimey** (*Dict.*).

coral. Money: 1841, W. Leman Rede, *Sixteen String Jack*; † by 1900.

'cordion or **c.** An accordion: coll., esp. Cockneys': from ca. 1890. Pugh. Cf. *'tina.*

cordite jaunty. 'Chief Gunner's Mate responsible for regulating duties at a Naval Gunnery School,' Granville: Naval: since ca. 1920.

cords. A pair of corduroy trousers; clothes of corduroy: from ca. 1880: lower classes' s., now verging on coll. (W. A. Gape, *Half a Million Tramps*, 1936.)

corduroy brigade. The workmen, plumbers, bricklayers employed by **Bricks:** since ca. 1930. H. & P.

corella. 'A sheep with patches of wool hanging loose' (B., 1959): Aus. rural: since ca. 1915. A *corella* is a kind of cockatoo: cf., therefore, **rosella** 2 below.

corey or **corie.** Penis: circus hands' and Cockney (and Kentish dial.): C. 20. Perhaps sadistic: cf. **coring mush** in *Dict.* More prob. ex Romany *kori*, a thorn, the penis.

cork. New bread: Cotton College: C. 19–20. Anecdotal—but almost certainly correct—origin (boys asking for cork received bread), *The Cottonian*, Autumn 1939, article by Frank Roberts.

cork, v. See **uncork!**

cork! Shut up!.: St Bees: since ca. 1914. Marples. I.e. *cork the bottle.*

cork, draw (p. 180). Usually *draw the cork of*, make an opponent's nose bleed. *Boxiana*, II, 1818.

cork eye (*at* someone), **have a.** To look hard and disapprovingly: Aus.: since ca. 1930. F. B. Vickers, *First Place to the Stranger*, 1955.

corkscrewed(-)up. Having Dutch courage after resort to the whisky or brandy bottle: applied to officers by Tommies: 1914–18. (A. B. Petch, April 1966.)

corn, earn or **be worth one's.** To be worth one's wages—one's keep: coll., orig. farmers': mid-C. 19–20.

corn fake; corn fake worker. A corn cure; a market-place or fair-ground chiropodist: showmen's: since ca. 1880. Cf. **nob fake.** Mostly a corn-plaster.

corn-holer. A pederast: low Canadian: C. 20.

corn off the cob, as in 'Don't give me that—it's corn off the cob'—i.e. 'corny' (see **corny,** 2, below): Australian: adopted, ca. 1944, ex U.S. (B.P.)

corn-snorter. The nose: low: ca. 1825–70. *Sinks*, 1848.

corn-yak. Corned beef: Merseyside: since ca. 1930.

Corncurer. H.M.S. *Conqueror*: Naval: C. 20.

corned.—2. Pleased; well content: tailors': from ca. 1870. B. & L.

corned beef. A thief: rhyming s.; C. 20. Hence the variant *bully beef.*—2. A Chief Officer in a British prison: rhyming s., orig. and still esp. in prisons. (Paul Tempest, *Lag's Lexicon*, 1950.)

Cornel Wilder. A hair-fashion (hair worn long) among Australian urban, esp. Sydney, youths: Australian: ca. 1950–9. (B., 1953.) Ex the American film star, Cornel Wilde (hair *not* excessively long).

corner, n., 4 (a share): by 1925, Australian low s.: Lawson Glassop, 1944. Prob. from U.S. rather than from England. (See *Underworld*.)

corner, go round the. To visit the lavatory: euphemistic coll.: from ca. 1890.

corner, on the. Out of work; on the dole: coll.: since late 1920's. F. D. Ommanny, *North Cape*, 1939, 'When he gets too old for job, he is "on the corner", one of a sad little crowd.'

Corner, the. See **corner,** n., 3 (p. 181).—2. The junction of the boundaries of Queensland, N.S.W., South Australia: Australian coll.: C. 20.—3. The Garden Island Naval Prison, Sydney: Australian Naval: since ca. 1930. (Senses 2 and 3: B., 1943.)

corner cove.—2. Earlier, hanger-on: pugilistic: ca. 1815–60. See quot'n at **Q-in-the-corner-cove.**

corner-ender (mostly in pl.). A loafer: since late 1920's. Cf. euphemistic **free,** 'out of a job'.

corner of the round table, on the. A c.p. reply to an inquiry where something may be found: lower-middle and upper working classes': from ca. 1890.

corner-shop. See 'Guard-Room in Army Slang'.

cornfield meet. A head-on meeting of two trains that are trying to use the same main line: Canadian railroadmen's (— 1931). Ex animal fights.

cornie or **corny.** A cornelian marble: Australian children's: C. 20. (B., 1943.)

Cornstalk (p. 181): ob. by 1945. 'Utterly unknown by people under the age of forty' (B.P., 1963). True also of **Sandgroper** (p. 726).

corny. Trivial: unimportant: Services': since ca. 1941. H. & P. Ex American *corny*, hackneyed, out of fashion.—2. Old-fashioned, hackneyed; sentimental, esp. in an outmoded way: adopted, ca. 1942, ex U.S. It was current among Canadian musicians as early as 1930. 'It implied old-fashioned and rural; belonging to the Corn Belt [of the U.S.] rather than to the city; also applied to jokes and humour' (Priestley).

coronation. A caning: esp., *cop a c.*, to receive a caning: Australian schoolboys': ca. 1910–40. Donald McLean, *Nature's Second Son*, 1954. Cf. **crown,** v., 4, below.

Corporal Cookie. The larger bomb mentioned at **cookie:** R.A.F.: 1944–5. (P-G-R.)

corporal of the field. See 'Tavern terms', § 6.

corpse.—2. Corporal—but not in his hearing: Tommies': ca. 1916–18. Applies esp. to an inferior type. (A. B. Petch, March 1966.)

corpse, v.i. To forget one's lines: drama school (since ca. 1950), hence smart young set (1956 +). Gilderdale, 2.

Corpse, the. A party of Marines: Naval: C. 20. Granville. By a pun on the Royal Marine Corps.

corpser. A contretemps as at **corpse,** v., 1 (*Dict.*): from ca. 1860. B. & L.

corpus (p. 182). An early record: *Sinks*, 1848.

Corpy. Belonging to, or concerning, the Corporation of the City: Liverpool: C. 20.

corral; round up. To get hold of, to acquire, as in 'I'll try to corral (*or* round up) a few drinks': Canadian, esp. in mid-West: since ca. 1920. (Leechman.) Ex cattle-herding.

Corridor, the. The '2 p.m. train from Euston, pioneer of corridor trains' (*Railway*, 3rd): railwaymen's: ? late C. 19–early 20.

corroboree, n. Sense 2—'a drunken spree'—is perhaps (Franklyn)—in part, at least—rhyming s. —4. (Ex 1, 3.) A discussion: Australian: C. 20. B., 1942.

corroboree, v.—2. To hold a discussion about something: Australian: C. 20. Baker.

corroboree water. Cheap wine: Australian: since ca. 1920. (B., 1943.) Perhaps ex **corroboree,** n., 4.

corsets. A soldier's bandolier: Australian military: 1939 +. B., 1942.

Corticene-Grabber's itch. See **C.G.I.**

corvette, a. A Wren addicted to Sub-Lieutenants. As the corvette (ship) chases 'subs', so does the 'corvette' (Wren).

cosh, n., 1. In the war of 1914–18 an 'offensive' stick carried by a man on night patrol: applied to the nape of a Teutonic neck, it made very little noise.

cosh, under the. (To have) at one's mercy: prisoners': since ca. 1945. Norman.

cosh-me-gosh. Sliced beef and vegetables: Naval (lower-deck): C. 20. (P-G-R.)

cosmography. See 'Tavern terms', § 3. *d.*

cossie (p. 182) is pron. *cozzie*—derives from *costume*—and was, by 1960, rare in speech, although still widely known. (B.P.)

Costly Farces. 'Self description of "Coastal Forces",' Granville: 1939–45.

cosy. All very snug and profitable; remarkably convenient: coll.: since ca. 1940. It attains its peak in the catch-word *cosy!*, that's very pleasant, that promises some very pleasant opportunities; esp., since ca. 1950, in Canada.

cotiva. A variant (Sydney Lester) of **catever** on p. 134.

Cottony, n. and adj. (A) Cockney: Cockneys': late C. 19–20

cough, v. i., as in 'Did he cough?' To confess: policemen's: since ca. 1910. (Lawrence Henderson, *With Intent*, 1968.) Ex gen. s. *cough it up*, to admit to something, to confess. Also cf. **cough it** below.

cough(-)and(-)sneeze. Cheese: rhyming 2.: since ca. 1880.

cough-drop.—2. An attractive girl: South Africa: 1942 +. Prof. W. S. Mackie in *The Cape Argus*, July 4, 1946.

***cough it.** To confess: c.: adopted, ca. 1945, ex U.S. Bournemouth *Evening Echo*, April 20, 1966, a crook *loquitur*, 'They have told me that the others have coughed it. That is their pigeon.'

cough-to-coffin. A 'cough-to-coffin cigarette', familiar to the Forces serving in the Near, the Middle, the Far East in World War II. Cf. **Camel to Consumer** above.

could eat the hind leg off a donkey. I am, you are, he is, etc., very hungry: coll.: C. 20. The

Canadian version (C. 20) is *could eat a horse, if you took his shoes off.* Leechman.

couldn't care fewer. An occ. variant of the next: ca. 1959–64.

couldn't care less, I or **he**, etc. A c.p. ('I'm quite indifferent') dating from 1940 and rampant ever since early 1948: originally, upper-middle class, but, by 1945, fairly general. On the pattern of *I couldn't agree (with you) more,* which, current ca. 1938–49, started in Society and was, by 1940, common among Service officers, but never so widely used as in the 'care less' inanity. (P-G-R.) In his *God Help America!* (1952), Sydney Moseley has 'Ordinary citizens "couldn't have cared less!"—to use a cant post-war phrase current in England.'

couldn't care less if the cow calves or breaks a leg, I or **he**, etc. A New Zealand extension, since ca. 1950, of the preceding. (Slatter.)

couldn't do it in the time, you. 'A sarcastic comment addressed to a person who threatens to fight' (B., 1942): Australian: since ca. 1910.

couldn't hit the inside of a barn (polite); **couldn't hit a bull in the arse with a scoop-shovel.** A Canadian c.p., directed at a bad marksman: C. 20.

couldn't organize a fuck in a brothel; occasionally ... *a piss-up* (drinking-bout) *in a brewery.* A derisive c.p., directed at an inefficient superior: low, esp. Services': C. 20.

Count No-Account. 'A facetious title for one who, lacking funds, claims an aristocratic background' (Leechman): Canadian: ca. 1895–1914.

counter.—2. An occasion of sexual intercourse (from the angle of the prostitute): prostitutes' and white-slavers' c.: C. 20. A. Londres, *The Road to Buenos Ayres,* 1928.

counter-skipper. See **counter-jumper** (*Dict.*).

country(-)boat. See **country-ship** (*Dict.*).

country chub; c. cokes; c. hick. See 'Dupes'.

coup (pron. *coop*). A coupon, e.g. for clothes: mostly women's: ca. 1940–5, then historical. (Monica Dickens, 1946.)

coupla.—2. Two coins that, tossed, fall 'heads': Australian: late C. 19–20. Baker.—3. 'A generality for several drinks, not necessarily two' (B., 1943): Australian: C. 20.

couple of bob. A damp swab: darts-players' rhyming s.: since ca. 1945. (Franklyn, *Rhyming.*)

couple of ducks. Synonymous with **two little ducks** or **duck in the** or **on a pond,** qq.v.

coupling bat. A shunter's pole: Kent and East Sussex railwaymen's: C. 20. (*Railway* 2nd.)

couranne. A crown piece: theatrical: from ca. 1860. B. & L. Via Fr. *couronne.*

course.—3. Because: Cockney coll.: C. 20. George Ingram, *Cockney Cavalcade,* 1935, ' "It's course he's got a 'cuddle' on for them." '

court, I'll see you in. (The law courts.) See **church, I'll** ... above.

court a cat. To take a girl out: Naval: since ca. 1925. H. & P. (By 1940 also R.A.F.—via the Fleet Air Arm.) Not in the least uncomplimentary.

court martial, n. A tossing in a blanket: schoolboys': from ca. 1870. B. & L.

court(-)short. A police-court paragraph (i.e. *short* news item): journalistic coll.: since ca. 1920.

Courtesy Cops. That section of the mobile police which on April 2, 1938, began, in England, to remonstrate politely with inconsiderate and to

instruct ignorant motorists: motorists': 1938, *The Observer,* April 3; *The Times,* April 4.

Courts, the. Steamers of the Ropner Line: nautical coll.: since ca. 1920. The ships bear such names as Errington or Wellington Court.

cousin Jack. A Cornishman: Canadian coll., esp. among miners: late C. 19–20. (Leechman.) Cf. *cousin Jon* (p. 184).

Cousin Sis, go on the. To drink heavily: low, since ca. 1925. Gerald Kersh, *The Nine Lives of Bill Nelson,* 1942. Rhyming on **go on the piss.**

covee. 'A variant spelling of *covey,* a man': *Boxiana,* IV, 1824. The term was ca. 1815–30 much applied to landlords of public-houses (Egan, 1821).

cover for, v. ' "Will you cover for me tonight?" meaning "Will you take my turn of duty?" Hospital internes and resident doctors' (Leechman): Canadian (ex U.S.): since ca. 1945; adopted, ca. 1950, in Britain.

cover(-)me(-)decent. A greatcoat: low: ca. 1825–70. *Sinks.* Cf. **decently** (*Dict.*) and:—

cover(-)me(-)properly. Fashionable clothes: low: ca. 1830–70. *Sinks.* Contrast:—

cover(-)me(-)queerly. Ragged clothes: low: ca. 1830–70. *Sinks.* Cf. prec. two entries.

*coving. 'Theft of jewellery by palming it as a conjuror does': c.: from ca. 1860. B. & L.

cow, 4. milk (p. 185). Also, since ca. 1920, common in Navy (lower-deck).

cow, three acres and a. See **three acres and a cow** in the *Dict.*

cow and calf.—2. A half: rhyming s., mostly racing men's: C. 20. (Franklyn, *Rhyming.*)

cow banger. A dairy-farm hand: Australian: C. 20. B., 1942. Cf. **cattle-banger.**

cow cage. A car or van for livestock: Canadian railroadmen's (– 1931).

Cow Cart Brigade, the. 'The Ossewa Brandwag (lit.: Ox-Wagon Sentinel), the Afrikaans Nationalist organization against whose activities British troops were warned' in World War II: 1940–45. (Peter Sanders.)

cow chilo; bull chilo. A girl child; a boy child; pidgin: mid-C. 19–20; ob. by 1890, † by 1920. B. & L.

cow cocky (p. 185): since ca. 1910, also New Zealand (Niall Alexander, letter of Oct. 22, 1939).

cow conductor. A bullock driver: Australian jocular: ca. 1925–50. (B., 1943.)

cow confetti. 'Bullshit': Australian: since ca. 1930. (Kylie Tennant, *The Honey Flow,* 1956.) B., 1942, has the less usual *cowyard confetti.*

cow-gun.—2. 'A 1½ pounder automatic gun fitted to the bows of a large R.A.F. flying boat, from ca. 1935' (Peter Sanders).

cow lick (p. 185). It looks as though a cow has licked it into shape.

Cow-shed, the. A certain ladies' club: London taxi-drivers': since ca. 1920. Herbert Hodge, *Cab, Sir?,* 1939.

cow spank; cow-spanker. To run a dairy farm; a dairy farmer: Australian: C. 20. Baker.

Cow Street or **Rue des Bitches.** The *Rue des Chats,* noted for its brothels: Tommies': W.W. I. Cf. **numbers, the,** below. (A. B. Petch, April 1966.)

cowabunga! 'Shouted as one makes down the face of a king wave' (*Pix,* Sept. 28, 1963): Australian surfers': since ca. 1961. Cf. *yabbadabba* below.

cowardy (occ. **cowardly**) **custard.** A child's taunt: coll.: C. 19–20. A custard *quivers*.

cowboy. A bow-legged man: since ca. 1950. Ex so much riding.

cowboys. Baked beans: Naval: since ca. 1920. Cf. **prairie rush.**—2. Policemen, the police: Teddy boys' and youthful gangsters': since ca. 1955. *The Observer*, May 15, 1960.

cowhide. Aware ('I'm cowhide to it'): Irish rhyming s.: C. 20. On *wide*. (Franklyn, *Rhyming*.)

cowie. A Western film: cinema-goers': since ca. 1955. Ex '*cowboy* film'.

cows. Short for **cow's calf** (*Dict.*): C. 20. *The New Statesman*, Nov. 29, 1941.

cow's breakfast. A farmer's large straw hat: Canadian: C. 20.

cow's udder. 'PVC sleeve for twin connections' (*Railway*, 3rd): railwaymen's: since ca. 1920 (?).

cowyard cake. A cake, or a bun, containing a few sultanas: Australian: since ca. 1925. (B., 1953.)

cowyard confetti. Empty talk; nonsense: Aus.: since ca. 1920. (B., 1959.) Cf. **bull-dust** above.

Coxey's army (p. 186) originated in 'General' J. S. Coxey's march, in April 1894, at the head of an 'Industrial Army' of the unemployed to Washington. The 'troops' deserted on the way to Washington, and Coxey himself entered the grounds of the Capitol—there to be arrested for walking on the grass! (With thanks to Mr I. O. Evans, editor of the 1967 British edition of Jack London's *The Road*; Jack London joined the Oakland contingent.)

coxon of the pram. A seaman's first-born: Naval (lower-deck) jocular: C. 20.

coze. An intimate talk; a comfortable friendly time together: 1814, Jane Austen, *Mansfield Park*, 'Proposed their going up into her room, where they might have a comfortable coze': ca. 1790–1860. Perhaps originally from Fr. *causerie*.

cozza (p. 186). Origin: Heb. *chazar*, a pig, hence pork and bacon. Cf. next.

cozzer, a policeman; **the cozzer,** the police, the Law: barrow-boys': since ca. 1930. Ex Hebrew *chazar*, a pig. Semantically cf. *pig*, n., 3 (p. 626) and phonetically and semantically **cozza** (p. 186).

crab, n., 6 (p. 186). Strictly a junior Midshipman. An earlier authority: 'Taffrail', 1910.—8. A police informer: Australian c.: since ca. 1925. (B., 1943.)—9. A telegraphist's badge: Australian Air Force: since ca. 1939. (B., 1943.)—10. A horse very unlikely to win a race: Australian: since late 1940's. (Culotta.) Ex tendency to run sideways—off the course? Cf. **goat,** n., 7, below.

crab, v.—2. (Usually as vbl n., *crabbing*.) 'Flying close to the ground or water' (Jackson), R.A.F.: since ca. 1925. Ex the habits of a crab: cf. also **crab,** n., 7 (p. 186). Robert Hinde, March 17; 1945, 'Orig., to fly with a large amount of drift; hence, to fly low because drift is more apparent near the ground—aircraft appear to fly diagonally'.

crab, adj. Perverse: C. 20. Short for *crabby*, ill-tempered. Atkinson.

crab along. To fly near the ground: R.A.F. since ca. 1920. H. & P. Cf. prec. entry.

Crab and Winkle Railway. 'Halesworth to Southwold. Former branch line of Great Eastern

Railway' (*Railway*, 3rd): railwaymen's: C. 20: by 1960.

crab-bat. (See its elements: **crab,** n., 4; **bat,** n. 3.) An Indian Army term, dating from the early 1890's; as in Richards, 'The Prayer-wallah spent his time in learning the "crab-bat" . . ., which was all the swear-words in the Hindoostani language and a few more from the other Indian dialects to help these out. He had picked up a fair knowledge of the crab-bat at Meerut but he now studied it seriously and used to curse the natives, whenever they deserved it, to such order that they looked upon him with veneration and praised him as the oldest of old soldiers.' But *crab* here perhaps = Hindustani *karob*, evil.

crab fat. Admiralty grey paint: Naval: since ca. 1910. Granville.—2. An airman: Army (mildly contemptuous): since ca. 1930. 'Ex Air Force blue uniform and the use of blue unction against "crabs"' (Atkinson).

crab on the rocks. Itching testicles: low: late C. 19–20.

crab station. A verminous station: R.A.F.: since ca. 1925. Atkinson. See **crab,** n., 2 (p. 186).

crab the act is the Canadian approximation to **cruel the pitch** (p. 194): adopted, ca. 1930, ex U.S. theatre. (Leechman.)

***crabs,** 1 (p. 186). Still current for 'boots' in Australia as late as 1898.—3. A certain type (Fowler 5 M.T.) of tender-engines: railwaymen's: since ca. 1920. (*Railway*.)

***crabs, move one's.** To run away: c.: mid-C. 19–20; virtually †. B. & L.

crack, n., 9. Cf. Shelta *crack*, a stick.—13. Esp., *have a crack at it.* An attempt: since ca. 1925. App. it was orig. a Service term. H. & P. Cf. 'have a *shot* at something'.—14. Short for *wisecrack*, a witticism: coll.: since late 1920's.

crack, v, 7 (p. 187): since ca. 1810. (W. N. Glascock, *Sketch-Book*, I, 1825.) Moe.—11. To change (money): used, by seamen, of cashing advance notes: mostly a Liverpool word: C. 20.

crack, cry a. To cry 'quits': Australian: C. 20. B., 1942. Perhaps ex *crack up*, to yield to strain.

***crack, good on the.** See **star, good on the.**

crack down. To shoot down (an enemy 'plane): R.A.F.: since 1940. H. & P.

crack down on. To suppress (lawless persons or acts); to reprimand: Services: since ca. 1935. H. & P.—2. Seize or make off with (something): Australian: C. 20.

crack down on the deck. To force-land on airfield or elsewhere on the ground: R.A.F.: since ca. 1930. H. & P.

crack it. (Of a male) to succeed, amorously: Australian: since ca. 1920. Baker.

crack mugs. '"Oh! I been crackin' mugs, Missisabella." "Crackin' mugs?" "Hitchin'-on to mugs at the races, miss, and tippin' winners at a bob a time"' (K. S. Prichard, *Kiss on the Lips*, 1932): low Australian: since ca. 1910.

crack one's egg. See **break one's egg.**

crack one's face. To smile broadly; to laugh: since ca. 1945. Mostly of a very serious person. (A. B. Petch, March 1966.)

crack up. 'An accident causing damage that can be repaired,' Jackson: R.A.F. coll.: since ca. 1925. Ex **crack up,** v., 2 (*Dict.*).

cracked.—5. See **wilderness, be in the.**

cracked up to be, (it's) not what it's. Falling short of its reputation: c.p.: since ca. 1910. Cf. **crack-up** on p. 187.

cracker.—11. (Nearly always pl.) A hair-curler: Cockneys': C. 20. Esp. of one's hair *in crackers*.—12. Karaka: New Zealand: since ca. 1860; by 1926, ob. B., 1941. By 'Hobson-Jobson'.—13. A £1 note: Australian: since ca. 1920. B., 1942.—14. A heavy punch: see **rammer** (?), 2. Cf. sense 5.—15. See **banger**, 6, above, and cf. sense 10 of **cracker** on p. 188.

cracker, not to have a. To be penniless: Australian: from ca. 1920. W. S. Howard, *You're Telling Me!*, 1934, 'What about money? . . . We haven't got a cracker.'

crackerjack. Synonym of **cracker-hash** (p. 188). Granville.

cracking, get. See **get cracking.**

crackling, n. See **crackle** (*Dict.*).—2. Usually *bit of crackling*, a girl, since ca. 1890. Cf. **bit of skirt, tart** (*Dict.*) and **crumpet**, 3.

cracky.—2. Crazy; senseless: Australian: since ca. 1925. (D'Arcy Niland, *Call Me . . .*, 1958.)

crafty. Skilful, clever, well judged, well planned, well timed, sly ('Just time for a crafty one'—a drink): R.A.F. coll.: since ca. 1920. Partridge, 1945.

crammer, 2. Earlier in *Sinks*, 1848.

crammer's pup (p. 188). Since ca. 1870. In, e.g., Rudyard Kipling's *Stalky and Co.*, 1899.

cramp in the kick, have. To be (very) short of money: from ca. 1880. Here, *kick* is one's pocket.

crank, n., 1. It survived until at least 1848 (*Sinks*).

crank file. Inventions department: mainly journalistic: C. 20. Office file kept for cranks' suggestions.

cranky, 1 (p. 189). Recorded by the O.E.D. for 1821.

cranky Fan. The bird known as the Grey Fantail: Australian: late C. 19–20. (B., 1943.)

crap. Rubbish; esp. 'It's crap', it's worthless: low: from ca. 1910. Cf. **crap, n., 4** (*Dict.*).

crap barge. See **shit barge** below.

crap on, get the. See **get the crap on.**

Crappo. The French, collectively, esp. seamen or warships: late C. 18–mid-19. (W. N. Glascock, *Sketch-Book*, I—published in 1825—at pp. 25, 27, 33. Moe.) Ex Fr. *crapaud*, a frog.

crappy. Afraid: low Glasgow: from ca. 1920. MacArthur & Long. Ex preceding.—2. Hence, of very poor quality: Sc.: since ca. 1925. Barry England, *Figures in a Landscape*, 1963.

crash, n.—4. A failure, a fiasco: policemen's and warders': late C. 19–20. Ernest Raymond, *We, The Accused*, 1935.

crash, v., 1 (p. 189). In *The English Digest*, Feb. 1941, Hector Bolitho says, 'It was first used by Paymaster Lieutenant Lidderdale in 1914.'—3. To sleep: Australian airmen's: 1939–45. (B., 1943.)

crash a party. To join one, uninvited, by guile or by force: coll.: since ca. 1928. Perhaps a back-formation ex **gate-crasher** (p. 318).

crash-box. A non-synchromesh gear box: Australian motorists': since ca. 1950. (B.P.)

crash down the swede. See **swede, crash . . .**

crash-draft. A sudden posting to another ship or station: Naval (? only Australian) coll.: since ca. 1930.

crash-hot. Very good; 'marvellous': Australian: since ca. 1950. Cf. **shit-hot** below.

crash into print. (Of a tyro writer) to get something published: since ca. 1920.

crash landing. A forced landing; a landing with undercarriage up: R.A.F. coll. (since ca. 1915) >, by 1940, j. Cf. **crash dive** and see **crash, v., 1**, both in *Dict.*

crash-lob; force-lob, v.i. To make a forced landing: R.A.F. s. and coll., resp.: since ca. 1930. Both occur in Paul Brickhill & Conrad Norton, *Escape to Danger*, 1946. Here, *lob* (ex cricket) = to arrive, to land.

crash-o! A Cockney term expressive of surprise, or wondering disgust, at a long bill to pay; used after the event: from ca. 1918. E.g. 'I had to pay a deaner; blimey, crash-o!' Cf. **thump!**, q.v. in *Dict.*

crash one's or **the swede.** To get one's head down on the pillow: Naval (lower-deck): since ca. 1920. *Weekly Telegraph*, Oct. 25, 1944.

crash (occasionally **flash**) **the ash**; or **lob the snout.** To offer a cigarette or, in a group, cigarettes: R.A.F. in Malta: ca. 1955–65. (Laurie Atkinson.)

crasher.—3. A crashing bore: since ca. 1945. (Noel Coward, *Pomp and Circumstance*, 1960.) 'The Oxford *-er*'.

*****crassing cheats** is a misprint for **crashing-cheats.**

crat; usually in pl. A bureaucrat: since ca. 1939.

crate.—2. Hence, an obsolescent aircraft: R.A.F.: since late 1917. Jackson. See **kite**.—3. A motor-car: 1937, F. E. Bailey, *Treat Them Gently*; slightly ob. Ex sense 1.

crawfords. 'Holding up one end of the mess table were the crawfords—steel, U-shaped supports forming legs' (*Daily Colonist*, June 19, 1960): Canadian Navy coll.: ca. 1910–25. Ex the manufacturer's name?

crawl, v. To cringe; Australian: since early C. 20. Ex **do a crawl** (p. 226)?

crawler.—4. A sheep; a shepherd: Australian: since ca. 1915. B., 1942.—5. A peaceable bullock or cow or calf: Australian rural: since ca. 1920. Baker.

crawling. Rotten: coll.: mid-C. 19–20. Short for *crawling with maggots*.—2. Verminous: Army and working-class's coll.: since ca. 1915. Short for *crawling with lice*.

crawling with it. Very rich: mostly Cockney: since ca. 1918. Cf. **lousy with** on p. 497.

crayfish, v. To act the coward or the low schemer: Australian: C. 20. (K. S. Prichard, *Haxby's Circus*, 1930.) Cf. **crayfish, n.**, on p. 190.

crazy.—2. Good; esp., very good: dance-fanatics': adopted, 1956, ex U.S. 'It's crazy—the most' = It's good—the best; 'the real crazy crew' = the really good musicians.—3. Hence, extraordinarily interesting; fascinating: Canadian dance-fanatics': since 1957. (*The Victoria Daily Colonist*, April 16, 1959, article 'Basic Beatnik'.)—4. Alert; progressive; 'with it': esp. among beatniks: since late 1950's. (Anderson.) Sense 2 had, by 1960, > gen. s. among drug addicts, hippies, Flower People. (*The Observer* colour supplement, Dec. 3, 1967, article by Peter Fryer.)

crazy mixed-up kid. A youth with psychological problems, esp. if unable to distinguish the good from the bad: adopted, in late 1940's, ex U.S.

Crazyman's Creek, the; often simply *the Creek*. The Straits of Messina: Naval: 1941–4.

cream.—2. Whiskey: mostly Australian: since ca. 1925. (B.P.)

cream in, v.i. 'To enter harbour "at the rate of knots",' Granville: Naval coll.: C. 20. Ex the creamy backwash.

creamy. A quarter-caste aboriginal, esp. a girl: Australian: since ca. 1920. (B., 1943.)—2. A palomino: Australian coll.: since ca. 1925. Jean Devanney, *Travels in North Queensland*, 1951, 'The breeding of Palominos—otherwise "yellow roses" or "creamies"—for show purposes . . .' (A south-western U.S. breed; *palomino*—American Sp. word.)

creamy do. A very special piece of luck: since ca. 1950. Cf. **creamy** on p. 190. (Laurie Atkinson).

crease. (Rare in singular.) Cress: sol., mostly Cockneys': mid-C. 19–20. Nevinson, 1895, ''E carried 'is groun'sel or creases or whatever green stuff it might be in an old sack slung over 'is shoulder.'

creased (p. 190). Prob. ex S.E. **crease**, to stun (a horse) by shooting it in ridge of neck.—2. Hence, exhausted: Services: since ca. 1930.—3. Hence, disgruntled, 'fed up': since ca. 1938. H. & P.

Creek, The. See **Crazyman's Creek.**

creep, n. An objectionable or unpleasant person; a dull, insignificant, unwanted person: adopted, ca. 1944, ex U.S. Cf. *creeper*, 1 (p. 190). In Canadian universities, a girl not voted into a sorority: ca. 1945–60.—2. Hence, a 'square': Canadian: 1957 +.

creep.—2. The coll. v. corresponding to **creeper**, 1 (p. 190). Sense 1, by the way, is often modified to = 'to be fined, not imprisoned'—as in James Curtis, *They Ride by Night*, 1938.—3. Only in *creep!*, go away: office- and shop-girls': ca. 1956–9. (Gilderdale.)—4. To rob 'on the creep': c.: since ca. 1920. (Norman.)—5. To dance, as in 'Come creeping with me': beatniks': since ca. 1959. (Anderson.) Ex the very slow types of dancing. Sense 4: 'Creep means to burgle when there's someone in the house': Peter Crookston, *Villain*, 1967.

*creep, on the. A variant (Norman) of *at . . .*, q.v. at *creep, at the* (p. 190).

creep into favour with oneself. To become self-conceited: ca. 1810–50. *Boxiana*, II, 1818.

creeper, 3 (p. 190), has become more general in sense and in distribution. In, e.g., Henri Fauconnier's *The Soul of Malaya*, 1931, it means any young (comparatively), inexperienced planter, and is thus used by many Far East planters.

creepers.—2. 'Gym' shoes: Naval: since ca. 1920.—3. 'Boots with thick rubber soles, worn by night-patrols in the desert': Army in North Africa: 1940–3. (P-G-R.)

creeping and weeping. The recovery of an errant torpedo during trials: Naval: since ca. 1910. Ship's boats 'creep' over—laboriously search—the potential area; if unsuccessful, the boats pull back—'weep'—and start again. (Wilfred Granville, letter of Jan. 7, 1947.)

Creeping Copulator, the. A variant of the **Flying Fornicator** below.

creeping Jesus (p. 190). Also, in Australia, an exclamation. (Sidney J. Baker, letter.)—2. In

billards, a long losing hazard played slowly: since ca. 1920.

creepy-crawly. An insect; a spider: mostly domestic and juvenile: mid-C. 19–20.

crenk. To offend; to irritate or annoy, as in 'It really crenked me!': mostly teenagers': since ca. 1950. Ex Yiddish *crenk*, to hurt; perhaps ultimately ex German *krank*, sick, ill. Mr Ramsey Spencer modifies my etymology thus: Ex Ger. *kränken* (pron. *krenken*), to hurt someone's feelings. 'Which is, of course, the same root as *krank*, ill.'

*Créolo. An Argentine that is a professional pimp: c. of the white-slavers: C. 20. Albert Londres, *The Road to Buenos Ayres*, 1928. He is also *canfinflero* (more familiarly *cafishio*); also, among the French, *le compadre*.

crew-cut hair, hence 'a *crew-cut*'. A man's hair cut short and *en brosse*, popular especially among athletes and the would-be manly: Canadian: adopted, ca. 1951, ex U.S. (Leechman.) By 1952, fairly common, and already coll., in Britain and Australia. Recorded by Berrey & Van den Bark in *The American Thesaurus of Slang*, 2nd edition, 1952, and by B., 1953. Perhaps because originally affected by 'rowing types' at Harvard and Yale Universities.

crew up, v.i. and v.t. To form, put into, a crew: R.A.F. coll.: 1939 +.

crib, n. Sense 1 ('food') is extant, as s., in Australia and New Zealand, esp. as 'prepared food, sandwiches for lunch, a lunch'. (K. S. Prichard, *Working Bullocks*, 1926; Jean Devanney, *Bushman Burke*, 1930; Dymphna Cusack, *Southern Steel*, 1953.)—8. Stomach: c.:? C. 17–mid-19. B. & L.—9. A grumble; a cause for grumbling: Services: since ca. 1920. H. & P. Ex *crib*, v., 8 (p. 191).—10. A caboose: Canadian railroadmen's (– 1931).—11. A brothel: low Australian: since ca. 1910. (B., 1943.) Perhaps cf. senses 3 and 4 (p. 190).

crib, v., 8. Also R.A.F.: 1919 +. The v.t. form is *crib at*, 'grumble or complain about' (something)—also *crib about*.—9. To eat, esp., to take a meal: Australian: late C. 19–20. K. S. Prichard, *Working Bullocks*, 1926, 'Be boiling the billy presently. Better come and crib with us, Red.' Ex the n., sense 1.

Cribby Islands (p. 191). Earlier in *Sessions*, 1774, 2nd session of E. Bull's mayoralty, 'Yes; there are many *cribby islands* about it', the ref. being to the thoroughfare from Cursitor Street to White's Alley.

cricket; usually in pl. A German night-fighter 'plane: R.A.F.: 1940–4. H. & P. Lively at night.—2. Both *the cricket* and *the football*, cricket news and football news, are coll.: C. 20.

cricket team. A (very) sparse moustache: Australian: since late 1940's. Eleven a side: eleven hairs on each side of the mid-lip dimple. (B.P.)

Cricklewood. Crich el Oued, Tunisia: Army in North Africa: World War II. (P-G-R.)

Crier of the Court. See 'Tavern terms', § 4.

crim. A criminal: Australian: since ca. 1925. (Kylie Tennant, *The Joyful Condemned*, 1953; Vince Kelly, *The Greedy Ones*, 1958.) A professional criminal: Australian: since ca. 1945. (Dick.)

Crimea. Beer: rhyming s.: ca. 1860–1910. (Franklyn 2nd.)

crimp. A swindler, a blackguard: Australian: C. 20. B., 1942. Ex lit. S.E. sense.

crimum. Sheep: Shelta: C. 18–20. B. & L.

*crinkle. Paper money: spivs' c.: since ca. 1942. (*Picture Post*, Jan. 1954.) It easily creases.

Crippen. See 'Ephemeral General Nicknames'.

cripple.—5. A defective car: Canadian railroadmen's (— 1931).

Cripplegate. See Bishopsgate.

Crisch. See 'Imperial'.

criss-cross. A cross-word puzzle; cross-words in general: 'since ca. 1935.

crit.—2. N. and v. To make an oral or a written critical report upon a fellow-student's work: training colleges': C. 20. In, e.g., Josephine Tey, *Miss Pym Disposes*, 1946.

crit sheet. That printed form which is attached to a report and on which the reader indicates the accuracy and value of the report: Services' and Civil service coll.: since ca. 1945. Cf. the preceding.

Criterion. See Captain Criterion.

critical. Dangerously ill or injured: coll., orig. and still mainly journalists': since ca. 1930. Ex 'be in a critical state'.

cro. A prostitute: low Australian: since the 1920's. (Kylie Tennant, *The Joyful Condemned*, 1953.) Origin? Loose for chro above.—2. A *c.r.o.* or cathode-ray oscilloscope: esp. in Australia: since ca. 1940. (B.P.)

cro or cros (pron. *cro*). A professional gambler: buckish s. of ca. 1810–40. In, e.g., J. J. Stockdale, *The Greeks*, 1817. Ex Fr. *escroc*, a sharper.

cro'-eyed. Cross-eyed: prob. mid-C. 18–19. A *cro'-eyed Jack* is a cross-eyed fellow, but often in the form *cro'-Jack(-)eyed*, as in Wm Nugent Glascock, *The Naval Sketch-Book*, 2nd Series, 1834; the dating of *cro'-Jack eyed* on p. 121 should therefore be altered. Cf. cross-jack below.

croaker.—7. A newspaper: Australian low: since ca. 1910. B., 1942. Cf. sense 3 (p. 192).

Croc. 'Short for *Crocodile*, a British flame-throwing tank': Army: ca. 1941–5. (P-G-R.)

croc, 2 (p. 192): in, e.g., Alexander Macdonald, *In the Land of Pearl and Gold*, 1907, on p. 205.

croci is used, occ., for *crocuses* by those who possess a smattering of Latin.

crock.—5. Earth they mar: navvies': ca. 1870–1910. (D. W. Barrett, 1880.)

Crocket(t)'s Folly. The Olympia cab-rank: London taxi-drivers': since ca. 1910. Herbert Hodge, *Cab, Sir?*, 1939.

crockus, variant of crocus (*Dict.*).

crocky, n. A crocodile: Australian (mostly juvenile): C. 20. (B., 1943.)

crocky, adj. Shaky and weak; groggy: Australian coll.: late C. 19–20; by 1900's ob. (K. S. Prichard, *The Black Opal*, 1921.)

crocodile.—3. (Both n. and v.) Applied to 'paint which has contracted during drying. . . . Resembling a crocodile's skin' (a master builder, Dec. 5, 1953): builders' and house-painters': C. 20.—4. A horse: Australian: since ca. 1930. (B., 1943.)

crocus, v. See crocussing below.—2. Hence, neutrally and widely, to sell medicines and toilet preparations to (the gathered customers): fairgrounds': C. 20. (W. Buchanan-Taylor, *Shake It Again*, 1943.) Cf. crocus metallorum on p. 192.

crocussing is the predominant form, in C. 20, of *crocussing rig* (p. 192).

Crombo. A. C. M. Croome, cricket correspondent of *The Times*: cricketers' and cricket journalists':

C. 20. Sir Home Gordon, *The Background of Cricket*, 1939.

cronk.—3. Hence, ill: C. 20.

cronker. A foreman: tailors': from ca. 1860. B. & L. Ex dial. *cronk*, either 'to croak; hence, grumble' or 'to sit; esp. sit huddled up' (E.D.D.).

cronky. 'Wonky' or unsound; inferior; not well: since ca. 1920. Cf. cronk (p. 192).

crook, adj.—3. (Ex 1.) Spurious: Australian: C. 20. B., 1942.—4. (Of, e.g., eggs) bad, rotten; Australian: ca. 1905. Gavin Casey, *It's Harder for Girls*, 1942.—5. (Of persons) objectionable: Australian: since ca. 1910. Gavin Casey, *Downhill is Easier*, 1945.—6. (Of land) poor, infertile: Australian: since ca. 1910. (Dal Stivens, *The Gambling Ghost*, 1953.)—7. Inferior: Australian: since early C. 20. A generalization of senses 1 (p. 192) and 3, 4. Culotta instances 'crook beer'.

crook, n., 2 (p. 192), goes back, in U.S., to the 1870's.

crook (or click), in the. In the act of cutting: tailors' coll.: from ca. 1860. B. & L.

crook and butcher. Cook & Butcher (a 'trade'): R.A.F.: since ca. 1935. Jackson, 'It is commonly believed that his sins go so often unpunished.'

crook up. To fall, to become, ill: Australian: since ca. 1910. (D'Arcy Niland, *Call Me When the Cross Turns Over*, 1958.) Ex crook, adj., 1, on p. 192.

crooked, adj.—2. Variation of crook, adj., 2 (p. 192), 'angry, annoyed': Australian: since ca. 1918. Lawson Glassop, *We Were the Rats*, 1944.—3. Esp., *crooked on*, as in '"That work," he said, "I'm crooked on that"' (Lawson Glassop, *Lucky Palmer*, 1949): Australian: since ca. 1930. This sense of *crooked* is pronounced as one syllable, not like the S.E. *crooked*, dishonest, criminal.

crooked as George Street West, as. Extremely crooked: Sydneysiders': late C. 19–20; by 1960 ob.—this street being now called Broadway. (B.P.)

crooked straight-edge or the round square, go and fetch the. C.pp. April Fool 'catches': carpenters': C. 19–20. Among warehousemen, it is *go and fetch the wall-stretcher*; in engineers' shops, *the rubber hammer*: both from ca. 1860.

croop. Stomach: lower-classes': mid-C. 19–20. B. & L. I.e. *crop*.

crople on. To take hold of, to seize: Australian: since ca. 1925. (B., 1943.) Ex *grapple*?

cropper, come a. Already in H., 2nd edition, 1860.

cros. See cro.

cross, n.—4. The tail of a two-up penny: Australian: since ca. 1920. (B., 1953.) Ex black cross painted on it to facilitate recognition.

Cross, the. The King's Cross district of Sydney: Sydney coll.: since ca. 1910. (Dymphna Cusack, 1951.)

cross (someone's) bows. To offend a senior officer: Naval: C. 20. Granville, 'It is a flagrant breach of manners for a junior ship to cross the bows of a senior ship.'

cross-buttock (p. 193) occurs earlier—1860—in H., 2nd ed. By 1920, this metaphor was virtually extinct.

cross-chopping. Argument: 1831, *Sessions*, 'There was a good deal of *cross-chopping* at the office as to whether it was on a Sunday': coll.: C. 19.

cross-cut. A Jewess: low: late C. 19–20. Ex the Gentile lower-class myth that she has to undergo an operation similar to her brother's.

cross-jack, adj. Squinting: C. 19. Fredk Chamier, *The Life of a Sailor*, 1832, at II, 230, 'He had a great advantage in both eyes and tongue, for he squinted so abominably, that you could not escape his cross-jack glance; and he had "a tongue to wheedle with the devil".' (Moe.)

cross-jack-eyed. Squint-eyed: ca. 1800–1870. *The Night Watch* (II, 88), 1828. Cf. **look Cro'Jack eyed** on p. 493. (Moe.)

cross-kid, n. 'Kidding', blarney; deception, imposition; irony: low: 1893, P. H. Emerson; † by 1920.

cross killicks. A Petty Officer's badge (crossed anchors): Naval (lower-deck): C. 20. (P-G-R.)

cross my heart! A c.p. of declaration that one is telling the truth: mid-C. 19–20.

cross (someone) **off one's visiting list;** usually *to have crossed* . . . 'This is sometimes used jocularly, mainly by working-class people who do not keep Books of Engagements' (A. B. Petch, March 1966): since ca. 1930.

Crosse and Blackwell's Regiment. The General Service Corps: Army; since late 1930's. Ex the similarity of its cap badge to Messrs Crosse & Blackwell's trademark. (Evelyn Waugh, *Put out More Flags*, 1942.)

crossers. Crossword puzzles in general, or one in particular: since ca. 1930. Ex *cross*word by 'the Oxford -*er*'.

Crosso, the. King's Cross, Sydney: Australian: C. 20. B., 1942.

crossword spanner. A pencil: Naval engineers': since ca. 1950. (Wilfred Granville, letter of April 22, 1962.)

crotch(-)rot. 'A form of skin fungus that attacks the area between the buttocks and around the groin. Extremely common affliction. One doctor told me "Everybody and his dog has it"' (Leechman): coll., mostly Canadian: C. 20.

crow, n.—4. A professional gambler: ca. 1805–40. (J. J. Stockwell, 1817.) Pun on S.E. *rook*.—5. A rating that's always getting into trouble: Naval: since ca. 1920. Granville. Prompted by **bird,** n., 7 (*Dict.*).

crow, draw the. To experience (an outstanding piece of) bad luck: Australian: since ca. 1910. Lawson Glassop, *We Were the Rats*, 1944.

crow, not to know (someone) **from a.** Not to know at all: C. 20. Variation of *. . . from Adam.*

crow-bait.—2. An aboriginal: Australian, coll. rather than s.: since ca. 1830. In, e.g., Brian Penton, *Landtakers*, 1934.

Sense 1 (p. 194): 'also used in Canada' (Leechman).

crow in working rig. A seagull: Naval: since ca. 1930. (P-G-R.)

crow-pee, at. At dawn: British Army in North Africa: 1941–3. 'English imitation of Australian slang, Western Desert' (Peter Sanders).

crowd, v. To verge on: Canadian coll.: adopted, ca. 1935, ex U.S. 'He must be crowding forty.' (Leechman.)

crowded space. Suitcase: since ca. 1930.: orig. c.; by 1940, low s. (Franklyn 2nd.)

crowder. A string: Shelta: C. 18–20. B. & L.

crown, v.—4. To cane: Australian schoolboys': ca. 1910–40. Donald McLean, *Nature's Second Son*, 1954. Cf. **coronation** above.

crown, adj. Very large: Australian coll.: since ca. 1920. Vance Palmer, *Let the Birds Fly*, 1955, 'If it's a crown fire we're gone a million'. Prompted by the *crowning* of, e.g., 'crowning glory'.

crown, to have got one's. To have been promoted to Flight-Sergeant: R.A.F. coll.: since ca. 1920. Partridge, 1945. See also **got his crown up** and the entry next but one.

[Crown and Anchor:—For the s. terms, see **puff and dart;** for a very clear description of the game, —a favourite of soldiers and sailors—see Richards, pp. 65–7.]

crown up, put one's. To be promoted to Company (or Battery) Sergeant-Major: Army coll.: since ca. 1905. H. & P.

crownie. 'A tram or bus inspector' (B., 1935): Australian: since ca. 1935. Ex the crown that indicates his rank.

crowning. A blow on the crown of the head: low: from ca. 1905. Ex **crown,** v., 3 (*Dict.*).

crowning him. Coupling a caboose to a train already made up: Canadian railroadmen's (— 1931).

crud. 'Equals turd as an expression of contempt for another person. "What a silly little crud Harry is!"' (Leechman): Canadian: since ca. 1930. Ex Canadian (and U.S.) dial., itself ex English dial., *crud,* a survival from late Middle English *crudde.* Also, since late 1930's, common in Australia. (B.P.)

crudget. The head: Australian: since ca. 1920. Prob. a corruption of **crumpet,** 1 [*Dict.*] (the head).

cruel. To spoil or ruin (e.g. a person's chances): Australian: since ca. 1910. (B., 1943.) Ex **cruel the pitch** (p. 194).

cruiser.—4. 'A taxi-cab that cruises the streets in search of fares' (Leechman): Canadian coll.: since ca. 1935; by 1960, S.E. Cf. the U.S. *cruiser,* a squad, or prowl, car.

cruity. A recruit: military: ca. 1850–1914. Robert Blatchford, *My Life in the Army*, 1910. Cf. **rooky** (*Dict.*), which superseded it.

cruize. To slip into the kitchen in order to cadge, or remove, food: Sedgley Park School and St. Wilfred's College: C. 19. I.e. to *cruise.* Its C. 20 derivative is *gooze,* which in the 1920's = 'to happen to get lost (in, say, the course of a general walk)'; and, in the 1930's, = 'to fail to report (to the Prefect of Discipline)'. Frank Roberts, in *The Cottonian,* Autumn 1938.

crumb act, put on the. 'To impose on another person' (B., 1959): Aus. low: C. 20.

crumb-hunting. See 'Canadian'.

crumbs.—2. Small change: mostly teenagers': since ca. 1950. Cf. **bread** above.

crummy, n. A caboose: Canadian railroadmen's (— 1931). Pejorative.

crummy, adj.—5. (Ex sense 4: p. 195.) Inferior; dull, as a *crummy joint* or dull night club: since ca. 1946.

crummy, the. Fat: sporting: ca. 1818–40. Tom Moore, *Tom Crib's Memorial,* 1819, 'To train down the crummy.' Ex sense 1 of the adj. (p. 195).

Crump Dump, the. The Ruhr: R.A.F.: late 1940–early 1945. *The New Statesman,* Sept. 19, 1942, E. P., 'Air Warfare and its Slang'. Ex the numerous bombs the R.A.F. dumped there; and see **crump,** n., 3 in *Dict.*

crump(-)hole. A bomb-caused crater: 1940, Berrey. Cf. preceding.

crumper.—3. A heavy crash, as in 'The Wimpey came a proper crumper' (Jackson): R.A.F.: since ca. 1925. Ex 1.

crumpet. Sense 2 follows ex:—3. Woman as sex; women viewed collectively as instruments of sexual pleasure: low: from ca. 1880. (James Curtis, *The Gilt Kid*, 1936.) Cf. **buttered bun,** 1, 2 (*Dict.*) and **crackling,** 2.—4. A 'softy' or a 'mug'; a dupe; a fool: Australian: since ca. 1920. Lawson Glassop, 1944. A crumpet is soft.—5. A female undergraduate: Durham male undergraduates' (— 1940). Marples, 2. Perhaps cf. sense 2 (p. 195).

crumpet, not worth a. (Utterly) worthless: Australian: since late 1940's. Ex sense 3 of **crumpet.** (B.P.)

crunch, the. The most severe—'the *real*'—test (of, e.g., strength, courage, nerve, skill, etc.): since ca. 1960. 'The crunch'll come when you have to go out and earn your living' (any irate father to teenage son); 'When it came to the crunch, his courage failed'; Bournemouth's *Evening Echo*, April 3, 1966. Of sporting origin, I think: prob. Rugby; perhaps boxing or all-in wrestling.

crupper, ride below the. To copulate with a woman: literary: mid-C. 17–18.

crush, n., 4 (p. 195). Read: U.S. (— 1903), anglicised in mid-1920's. Sylva Clapin, *Americanisms*, 1903, '"In college slang, a liking for a person."'—6. A narrow gateway in a mustering yard or paddock: Australian rural coll. (— 1938). (Dal Stivens, *The Courtship of Uncle Henry*, 1946.)

crush (bet). A bet that ensures one against loss: Australian sporting: C. 20. B., 1942, 'Whence, "crusher" (agent), "crushing" (action).'

crusher, 1. By extension, a Regulating Petty officer (equivalent to a Warrant Officer in Military or Service Police): Naval: since ca. 1920. H. & P.—See **crush (bet).**—6. A schoolmaster: Clifton College: C. 20. (J. Judfield Willis, letter.)

Crusoe, or Robinson Crusoe. R. C. Robertson-Glasgow, the Oxford and Somerset cricketer and, since ca. 1935, writer on cricket, brilliant wit and delightful stylist: cricketers': since ca. 1925. In, e.g., E. W. Swanton's report in *The Daily Telegraph*, May 16, 1948, and in 'Crusoe's autobiography, *46 Not Out*, June 19, 1948. Ex his initials and ex the approximation of *Robertson-Glasgow* to *Robinson Crusoe* (Defoe's famous novel, 1719).

crust.—3. A vagrancy charge: Australian c. (and police s.): since ca. 1935. (B., 1953.) A reference to 'lack of means of subsistence'.—4. Insolence: Canadian: since ca. 1910. 'Well, you've got a crust, I must say!' (Leechman.) Cf. sense 2 on p. 195.

crust of bread. The head: rhyming s.: C. 20. Usually shortened to *crust:* cf. *crust,* 1 on p. 195. (Franklyn, *Rhyming.*)

crusty or **-ie.** A crust: Cockneys': from ca. 1870. Pugh.

Crutch. Nickname of the school carpenter: Winchester: from ca. 1870. B. & L.

crutch. An experienced skater supporting a learner: skating rinks': since ca. 1935.

crutch, stiff as a. Penniless: Australian: C. 20. B., 1942.

crutch and toothpick parade, the. The old and doddery (usually, male): coll.: C. 20.

cry all the way to the bank, e.g. 'I'll cry . . .' or 'He cried . . .' A c.p., adopted in late 1950's ex U.S. and used by, or of, someone whose work is adversely criticized on literary or artistic or musical grounds, but who makes a lot of money by it.

cry (occasionally **say**) **Uncle.** To admit defeat; cry for mercy: Canadian: since ca. 1925. (Leechman.)

crying out loud!, for. A London phrase, from ca. 1930, used in the place of—and with more effect than—*for Christ's sake.* Prob. ex U.S., where euphemistic.

crypto. A 'secret' Communist; a sympathiser with Communism: Parliamentary: 1945 +. Tom Driberg in *Reynolds*, March 10, 1946. Gr. *kruptos*, hidden.

*C's, the three. The Central Criminal Court: prison c.: from ca. 1880. B. & L.

cu.—2. Cumulus cloud(s): R.A.F. (orig. meteorological) coll.: since ca. 1925. H. & P. Also, via R.A.F. Met. Officers on Divisional, Corps, and Army H.Q. Staffs, among Army officers since at least as early as 1940. Ex the official abbreviation.

cubby, short for **cubby-house.** A child's playhouse in the backyard: Australian coll.: since ca. 1925. (B.P.)

cube.—2. One who is squarest of the square: since ca. 1960. (Correspondence columns in *The Sunday Times,* Sept. 8, 1963.) Ex **square, n.,** 7, below.

cube of three!, the. See **three!, the cube of,** in *Dict.*

cubic type. A non-existent type-face that green apprentices are sent to find: printers': late C. 19–20.

cuckoo.—6. (Usually in pl.) A German bomber: 1940, Berrey. 'In allusion to the cuckoo's habit of laying its eggs in another bird's nest'; but not very gen. and never used by the Services. Cf. sense 5 (p. 196).

Cuckoo Line. 'Eridge to Polegate section (SR)': railwaymen's: C. 20. *Railway,* 3rd. These are two Sussex villages, the latter near Eastbourne.

cuddle, n. A rendezvous of boy and girl: low London: since ca. 1920. George Ingram, *Cockney Cavalcade,* 1935. Ex the v.; cf.—

cuddle and kiss. A girl: Cockneys': C. 20. Len Ortzen, *Down Donkey Row,* 1938. Rhyming on *miss.*

cuddle-pup. An over-dressed young officer: Waacs': 1915–18. (Anon., *W.A.A.C.,* 1930.)

cuddle-seat. One of the double seats provided in some cinemas for courting (or amorous) couples: Australian coll.: since ca. 1955. Perhaps ex the *cuddleseat*—a sling devised for baby-carrying. (B.P.)

cuddy, n.—3. *The cuddy* is the Captain's cabin: Naval: late C. 19–20. Granville. 'Taffrail', 1916.

cuds, in the. In the hills: R.A.F. in N.W. India: since ca. 1925. Jackson. Ex Hindustani *khud,* a steep hill-side.—4. A small, general-purpose horse: Australian: late C. 19–20. (B., 1943.) Ex sense 1 (p. 196).

Cud's bobs! See 'Ejaculations'.

cue-despiser. An actor that, careless in observing his cues, endangers the performance: theatrical coll.: from ca. 1870. B. & L.

cuff, on the. On credit: since ca. 1925: low >, ca. 1940, pretty respectable. In, e.g., F. D. Sharpe, *The Flying Squad*, 1938. Ex pencilling the debt on one's cuff.

cuffer, pitch the. To 'tell the tale': late C. 19–20. See **cuffer,** 1 (p. 197).

cufuffle. See the variant **gefuffle** below.—2. An amorous embrace: Anglo-Irish: late C. 19–20.—3. A row, a brawl, a disturbance: Canadian: since ca. 1930. (Leechman.)

cuke. A *cucumber*: Canadian greengrocers': since ca. 1910. (Leechman.) Cf. *cu* (p. 196).

culch. Inferior meat: odds and ends of meat: low, mostly London: ca. 1815–80. *Sinks*, 1848. Ex S.E. and S.W. English dial. *culch* or *culsh*, both in *Dict.*

culio. Curio: pidgin: from ca. 1880. B. & L.

cull.—4. A friend; a work companion: mid-C. 19–20. (Sydney Lester, 1937.) Cf. **rum cull,** 3 (p. 717).

culls, cullions (p. 197). Ex Fr. *couillons,* testicles.

***cully,** v. To dupe; to cheat or swindle: c. of ca. 1670–1800. Thomas Dangerfield, *Don Tomazo,* 1680; B.E., 1690. Ex the n.

culture vulture. A person avid for culture; esp., one who haunts exhibitions and lectures: adopted, in late 1950's, ex U.S. Of the same sort of American rhyming s. as *eager beaver.*

cumshaw (p. 197) prob. dates from thirty or forty years earlier than I suggested. It occurs in, e.g., John McLeod, *Voyage of His Majesty's Ship, Alceste,* 1818. Moe.

cundy. A small stone: Australian: late C. 19–20. (B., 1943.) Ex E. dial. *cundy,* a conduit, e.g. a small conduit made of stone-work.

Cunnamulla cartwheel. 'A big, broad-rimmed hat' (B., 1942): Aus., mostly Queensland and N.S.W.: ca. 1920–50. Cunnamulla is an out-west Queensland town.

cunnel. A potato: Shelta: C. 18–20. B. & L.

cunning as a Maori dog, as. Very cunning indeed: New Zealand: since ca. 1925. (Slatter.)

cunny.—2. As *the cunny,* it = the countryside: Merseyside: C. 20. Ex *country.*

cunt (p. 198) cannot be from the L. word but is certainly cognate with O.E. *cwithe,* 'the womb' (with a Gothic parallel); cf. mod. English *come,* ex O.E. *cweman.* The *-nt,* which is difficult to explain, was already present in O.E. *kunte.* The radical would seem to be *cu* (in O.E. *cwe*), which app. = quintessential physical femineity (cf. sense 2 of *cunt*) and partly explains why, in India, the cow is a sacred animal.—3. Anybody one dislikes: late C. 19–20. An objectionable fellow or an awkward thing: since ca. 1918. Perhaps influenced by **cunt!, silly** (p. 198). As a correspondent notes in 1963: '*Cunt* tends to mean "knave" rather than "fool". *Prick* tends to mean "fool" rather than "knave".' Cf. **cunt and a half,** below.

cunt, drunk as a. Extremely drunk: low: late C. 19–20. Prob. the commonest of all the *cunt* similes.

cunt and a half, he's a. A c.p. applied to an extremely objectionable youth or man: since the late 1950's. Cf. sense 3 of **cunt.**

cunt face is a low term of address to an ugly person: late C. 19–20. More insulting than the synonymous *shit face.*

cunt hat. See **fanny hat.**—2. (Also *cunt cap.*) A forage cap: Army: since ca. 1915.

cunt hooks. Fingers: low: C. 20. 'Keep your cunt hooks off my belongings!'

Cunts in Velvet (*Dict.*) was orig.—i.e. in the South African War—applied to the C.I.V.'s or City Imperial Volunteers. (*The Sunday Times,* Johannesburg, May 23, 1937.)

cup. Short for **cup of tea,** 2 (p. 198): since the late 1930's. Angus Wilson, *Hemlock and After,* 1952, 'Anyway, none of it would be your cup, darling.'

Cup, the. The Melbourne Cup (meeting or race): Australian coll.: late C. 19–20. B., 1942.

cup of tea. Sense 2 dates from ca. 1910 and is usually in the negative.—3. Ironically to a person (slightly) in the wrong—Cockneys', from ca. 1920—as in 'You're a nice ol' cup o' tea, now ain't yer?'

cupboard, adj. (Of the prospects of a house) no good, close-fisted: tramps' and Romanies' s.: C. 20. (Robert M. Dawson.) The inmates *keep* the food there.

cuppa. A cup of tea; esp., *a nice cuppa*: Australian: since ca. 1905; by 1940, coll. By abbreviation and ex the Australian addiction to 'nice cups of tea'.

Cupper (p. 199) has, since ca. 1920, been also a University of Cambridge word. The competition is *the Cuppers.*

curate.—2. A bar-tender: Anglo-Irish: late C. 19–20. James Joyce, *The Dubliners,* 1914. Ironic.—3. A grocer's assistant: Anglo-Irish: late C. 19–20. (P. W. Joyce, *English . . . in Ireland,* 1910.)

curate's egg, the. See **good in parts** (*Dict.*).

curbstone jockey. A street, or other unreliable, tipster: Australian: C. 20. B., 1942.

curdles one's milk, it. A c.p. directed at one who sours the milk of human kindness: since ca. 1925. Atkinson.

cure, the. A Canadian term of (?) ca. 1840–1900. Harry Guillod's 'Journal of a trip to Cariboo', 1862, in the *British Columbia Historical Quarterly,* July–Oct. 1965: 'It was good fun bathing here; the mosquitoes attacked us as soon as we undressed, and we had to bolt into the water, and when out again, to put our things on in no time, dancing "the Cure" without any exertion' (supplied by Dr Douglas Leechman).

curl-a-mo; curl the mo. See **kurl.**

***curler.** A sweater of gold coins: Australian c.: late C. 19–20. B., 1942. Cf. **curle** (*Dict.*).

curly.—3. Since ca. 1910, *Curly* has been predominantly used ironically for men almost entirely bald. Cf. **Tiny** (*Dict.*).—4. A story, an account: Cockney: since ca. 1910. Margery Allingham, *Coroner's Pidgin,* 1945.

curly, adj. Difficult, as in 'That's a curly one'—a question hard to answer: (? mostly) Australian: since ca. 1950. (The Sydney *Sunday Mirror,* Oct. 27, 1963.) Perhaps ex googly bowling in cricket, or, less prob., ex 'throwing a *curve*' in baseball.—2. But in New Zealand, e.g. as 'That was extra curly' (Slatter), it seems to mean 'excellent' or 'attractive' and to date since ca. 1935.

curly, chuck a. See **chuck a curly** (*Dict.*).

Curly Navy, the. The Royal Canadian Naval Reserve: Naval: since ca. 1939. H. & P., 'Variant of *Wavy Navy.*'

currant bun. The sun: Cockneys': late C. 19–20. Len Ortzen, *Down Donkey Row,* 1938. Rhyming.—2. *On the currant bun,* on the run from the police: since ca. 1920: rhyming s.—orig. underworld >, by ca. 1945, also police s. Often shortened to *on the currant*. John Gosling, *The Ghost Squad*, 1959.

current. In good health, esp. as in 'He is not current': Anglo-Irish, esp. Cork: late C. 19–20. (P. W. Joyce, 1910.)

curry, give (someone). To reprimand; reprove vigorously; vituperate: Australian: C. 20. B., 1942.

Curry, the. 'Cloncurry, generally called "The Curry", is the western Queensland base of the incomparable Flying Doctor Service' (Jock Marshall & Russell Drysdale, *Journey among Men*, 1962, at p. 21): Australian: C. 20.

curry and rice navy (p. 199). Better with capitals; since ca. 1930 the Royal Indian Navy.

curse, n. One's swag or 'bluey': Australian swagman's: C. 20. (Ion M. Idriess, 1934.)

curse, the. The menses: feminine euphemistic or jocular coll.: late C. 19–20.—2. A tramp's swag: Australian C. 20. B., 1942. Whence 'hump the curse', go on the tramp? Variant: *carry the curse*: B., 1959.

curse of Eve, the. The menses: domestic coll.: C. 19–20. (C. S. Forester, *Brown on Resolution*, 1929.) The origin of the preceding.

curse of the drinking classes, the. Work: c.p.: since late 1940's. A pun on the cliché, *the curse of the working classes is drink*. (A. B. Petch, March 1966.)

curse rag. A sanitary towel: Wrens': 1939 +. See **curse, the.**

cursed with (something), **(I) wish I was.** A Cockney formula, virtually a c.p. = I wish I were blessed with, I wish I had it: C. 20.

curtains. 'Paint running down surface and setting in drape-like pattern' (master builder, 1953): builders' and house-painters': C. 20.—2. Mostly in 'It's curtains for him', implying death or dismissal or 'the end': adopted, ca. 1944, from U.S. servicemen. Of theatrical origin.

cush, n.—2. Something easy to do or to endure: regular Army: since ca. 1918. Gerald Kersh, *They Die with Their Boots Clean*, 1941. Ex cushy (*Dict.*).—3. Female genitalia: among servicemen with Near East experience: C. 20. Ex Arabic.

cush, adj. Fair: honest, honourable: Australian: since ca. 1920. B., 1942. Cf. **coosh.**

custard bosun. A Warrant Cook: Naval: since ca. 1925. Granville. Jocular.

custards. Pimples: Australian: since ca. 1925. B., 1942. Ex colour.

customer. An enemy 'plane: R.A.F.: World War II. (Guy Gibson, *Enemy Coast Ahead*, 1946.) —2. (Usually in pl.) 'Do-gooders who visit patients in hospitals or elderly people in their homes, sometimes call them "customers"' (A. B. Petch, March 1966).

cut, n.—8. Hence (?), as in *get a cut* (at a station), a sheep-shearing job: Australian coll.: C. 20. B., 1942.—9. (Ex 7, 8.) 'Completion of a job,' Baker: Australian: since ca. 1910.

cut, v., 4 (p. 201) dates rather from ca. 1780. Charles Dibdin, 'Jack in His Element'—*The Britannic Magazine*, 1793 (I, No. 3), at p. 34—has 'She cut—I chac'd'. Moe.

cut, adj., dates back to before 1650: see 'Tavern terms', § 8.—2. Hence, stupid, silly; esp., *half-cut*: late C. 19–20. (B., 1943.) Cf. *half-cut* on p. 368 and here.

cut! Stop cameras and action: cinematic s., since ca. 1910; by 1930, coll.—Hence, esp. in Canada, 'used on other occasions and in other occupations' (Leechman): since ca. 1945.

cut, have one's. See **have one's cut.**

cut a rug. To 'jive' or 'jitterbug': dance addicts': adopted from U.S. soldiers in 1943. *John Bull*, Feb. 2, 1946.

cut about. To move smartly: Guardsmen's: since ca. 1930. Roger Grinstead, *They Dug a Hole*, 1946. Cf. **get cracking—get mobile—get weaving.**

cut and carried. (Of a woman) married: rhyming s.: C. 20. Franklyn, *Rhyming*.

cut and run (p. 201) prob. goes back to ca. 1810. It occurs in, e.g., *The Night Watch* (II, 99), 1828, 'I was sick of the ship and the sea and I again cut and run', and earlier still in Glascock's *Sketch-Book*, 1825–26, as *cut one's cable* and *cut cable and run*, and in his *Sailors and Saints* (I, 154), 1829, and seems to have had a nautical origin. Moe.

cut at, have a. To attempt: Australian coll.: late C. 19–20. (Vance Palmer, *Daybreak*, 1932.)

cut caper sauce. See **caper upon nothing** (*Dict.*).

cut down to size. To bring (someone) sharply back to earth in his estimate of his own worth; to reduce to a realistic opinion of (himself): coll.: adopted, ca. 1960, ex U.S. *Woman's Own*, Sept. 4, 1965, an advice-to-wives article headed 'Never Cut Him Down to Size . . . You may find there is nothing left but the pieces.' Elliptical for *cut down to true size*.

cut in; cut out. 'An automatic switch, such as a thermostat, is said to *cut in* when it makes a contact and *cut out* when it breaks it' (Leechman): electricians' coll.: since late 1940's.

cut of one's jib (p. 201): W. N. Glascock, *Sketch-Book*, I, 1825. Moe.

cut off a slice of cake. Synonymous with **chip one off**: Naval: since ca. 1930. Granville.

cut (him) off one. To salute one's superior: police: since ca. 1919. (*The Free-Lance Writer*, April 1948.)

cut off the joint, a. (From the male angle) copulation; esp., *have a . . .*: C. 20. Cf. **join, 3.** (*Dict.*).

cut off the nut, a. 'Used jocularly with regard to vegetarian menu, or to the lack of meat when dining out, as "I'll have a cut off the nut",' Albert B. Petch (Sept. 1946): since ca. 1942 for the latter, since ca. 1930 for the former nuance.

cut one's finger. To break wind: mostly lower-middle class: C. 20.

cut out, v., 3, is also Canadian: late C. 19–20. (Leechman.)—5. (Ex 3.) See **cut outs.**—6. Hence, to complete any job: Australian: since ca. 1905. Baker.—7. To depart: Canadian dance-fanatics': adopted, 1957, ex U.S. (The Victoria *Daily Colonist*, May 1958, 'Basic Beatnik'; *American Dialect Society*, April 16, 1959, 'Language of Jazz Musicians' by Norman D. Hinton.)—8. To cease; come to an end: Australian miners' coll.: late C. 19–20. Ion M. Idriess, *The Yellow Joss*, 1934, 'The gold was finished. It had "cut out".' This sense soon > widespread Australian coll.: cf. Tom Ronan, *Vision Splendid*, 1954, 'I'll hang around until this job cuts out.'

cut out to be a gentleman. Circumcised: C. 20. A neat, if inexact, pun.

cut out(s). 'The completion of shearing at a station'; *cut out*, v., to finish shearing: Australian coll.: C. 20. Baker. Specialized sense of **cut out**, v., 6.

cut saucy. 'To cut a garment in the height of fashion': tailors' coll.: from ca. 1860. B. & L.

cut snake . . . See **mad as a cut snake.**

cut the rough (stuff)! 'Stop it': Australian: c. 20. Baker.

cut-throat.—4. A 'cut-throat', or open-bladed, razor: coll.: late C. 19–20.

cut to waste. 'To cut up sheets of paper in such a way that some is wasted, either inevitably or intentionally' (Leechman): a widespread printers' coll.: C. 20.

*cut-up, n. 'A share-out of spoils': Australian c.: since ca. 1920. B., 1942.

cut up, v.—8. (Prob. ex 4.) See **cut and carve.**

Cutlers, the. See **Blades.**

cuts, 4, occurs earlier in 'Taffrail'.—6. A beating or caning: R.N.C. Dartmouth coll.: since ca. 1925. Also, since ca. 1910, Australian school-boys'. (B.P.)

cuts and scratches. Matches (ignition): rhyming: late C. 19–20.

cutsom. Custom: pidgin: mid-C. 19–20. B. & L.

cutting the job up. Working too hard, *making it bad for the other people*: Services: since ca. 1930. H. & P.

cutting the wind. Sword-drill: military: ca. 1850–1914. B. & L.

cuz.—2. A defecation; *the cuzzes*, the latrines: Cotton College: mid-C. 19–20. Said to derive ex Heb. *cuz*, a large metal refuse-container outside the temple at Jerusalem.

cylinder. Vagina: Australian, esp. mechanics': since ca. 1930.

Cyp. A Cypriot: mostly London: since late 1940's. Bill Turner, *Sex Trap*, 1968.

Cypher Queen. A Wren officer engaged in cypher duties ashore in wartime: Naval: 1940 +. Granville.

cysto. Cystoscopy: medical coll.: 1958 + (Leechman.)

D

D. Short for *Captain D*, officer commanding a Destroyer flotilla: Naval coll.: 1920 +. Granville.

'd.—3. Did: coll.: late C. 19–20. C. Bush, *The Monday Murders*, 1936, 'What'd Pole tell you?' Cf.:—

d'. Do: coll.: C. 19–20. E.g. 'What d'you know about it?'—2. Did: coll.: mid-C. 19–20. E.g. 'D'you know that?'

d.—5. Decent: girls' Public Schools': C. 20. (Nancy Spain, *Poison for Teacher*, 1949, 'I say, that's jolly d of you!'

D.A.L. 'Dog at large'—a humorous notation put on letters that cannot be delivered: postmen's: since ca. 1920.

D.C.D. A '*don't-care-a-damn*' or torpedo-boat destroyer: Naval: 1914–18.

D.C.M. 'Don't come Monday. One day's suspension' (*Railway*, 3rd): railwaymen's: C. 20.

D-Day Dodgers, the. The Army in Italy: mostly among men of that Army: June 1944–5. (D-Day, June 6; Rome captured, June 4.) Ex a widespread rumour that Lady Astor had called them that in a speech; subsequently denied, but not before a song had been composed, to the tune of *Lili Marlene*. One stanza goes:—

'We fought 'em on the mountains, we fought 'em
  on the plain.
We fought 'em in the sunshine, we fought 'em in
  the rain.
We didn't want to go and fight
In all the mud and all the shite,
We are the D-Day Dodgers, out here in Italy.'

D.F.s. Duty-free goods: Naval coll.: C. 20. (Granville.)

d.f.m. Short for *dog-fucked mutton*, scraps of food, mutton hash: mostly Forces': since ca. 1920.

d.h.f. (or capitals). A stupid fellow: cyclists': ca. 1885–1910. B. & L. Ex a cycling gadget knows as a double hollow fork.

D.S.O. Dick shot off: a smutty c.p. of 1914–18; rare in 1939–45.

D.X. (or DX) hound. A 'dial-twister'; a 'station-hunter'; i.e. one who, in a restless, senseless manner, tries station after station on the radio: wireless (radio) s.: since ca. 1927. J. J. Connington, *The Sweepstake Murders*, 1931. 'The essential point about D.X. is that it is the radio hound's abbreviation for "distance". In the early days of radio, hams tried for the most distant stations, at the antipodes if possible, and confirmed their triumphs by postcards to the sending stations' (Leechman, 1967).

D.Y.F.s. Officers under the age of thirty: Naval: since ca. 1914. Also **B.Y.F.s.** Damned and bloody young fools.

dab, adj., 2 (p. 203). Rather: since ca. 1845. See **doing dab**.

dab, says Daniel. A nautical c.p., applied to 'lying bread and butter fashion' in bed or bunk: ca. 1810–60. 'A Real Paddy', *Real Life in Ireland*, 1822.

dab(-)dab; dab(-)toe. A seaman: (Naval) stokers': C. 20. Granville. The seamen have so often to 'dab' about the deck in their bare feet.

dab out, v.t. To wash: lower classes': from ca. 1860. Perhaps ex dabbing the clothes out on the scrubbing-board.

dabblers and **lubbers** are black-marketeers in furniture: furniture trade: April 1, 1944, *John Bull*.

dabheno (p. 204). Earlier in Mayhew, I, 1851.

dabs, 2 (p. 204). By 1940, also police s.— Hence, *Dabs* (without *the*), the Finger-print Department of New Scotland Yard. (Ngaio Marsh, *Death at the Bar*, 1940.)

dacey (p. 204). The correct spelling of the Hindu word is *desi*. (Professor K. Appasamy.)

dachsie (or **-sy**). A dachshund: domestic coll.: C. 20.

dad.—4. A term of address to anyone ten-or-so years older than oneself, esp. in Australia: coll.: since ca. 1945. (B.P.)

Dad and Dave. To shave; a shave: Australian rhyming s.: since ca. 1930, when, approximately, the radio serial 'Dad and Dave' began to pleasure Australians. (Julian Franklyn, *A Dictionary of Rhyming Slang*, 1959.)

daddio. A teenagers' variant of **dad,** 4, above: Australian: since ca. 1950. (B.P.)—2. 'One of the most frequent words in early beatnik'—the 1950's. 'A title often conferred on the leader of a little beatnik coterie' (Leechman, April 1967).

daddle, v. See **dadle**.

daddler, 1. J. Horsley, *I Remember*, 1912, as *dadla*.—2. (Gen. pl.) A hand: low: from ca. 1870; ob. Pugh: 'If you put your daddlers on her again, I'll set such a mark on you.' Ex **daddle** (*Dict.*).

daddy.—6. (Cf. sense 2.) 'The comic old man of a company': theatrical: ca. 1860–1910. B. & L.

daddy, buy me one of those. An Australian variant of **oh, mummy . . .** (below): since ca. 1945. An allusion to **sugar daddy** (p. 846).

daddy of them all, the. The most notable; (of things) the largest: Australian coll.: C. 20. B., 1942.

dadla. See **daddler,** 1.

dadle; prob. more properly **daddle,** v.i. 'Cunnum contra sedem aut pueri aut puellae atterere; quod plus inter puellas quam inter feminas fieri solet': low: C. 19–20.

daff, v. (Ex **daffy,** n., 1: p. 204.) To wash: taxi-drivers': since ca. 1910. 'Furtively "daffing" the wheels with a mixture of water and paraffin ("Willy", he calls it)': Herbert Hodge, *Cab, Sir?*, 1939.

daffier. A gin-drinker: ca. 1820, 1820–60. *Boxiana*, III, 1821. Ex **daffy.**

daffodil. An effeminate and precious young man: since ca. 1945. Fred Bason's *Second Diary*, 1952.

Daffy. A Defiant fighter: 1941; by 1944, ob. Jackson. By 'Hobson-Jobson'. Also *Deffy.*

daffy; daffy it. To drink gin: ca. 1820–60. *Boxiana*, III, 1821. Ex the n.

daffydowndilly.—2. Silly: rhyming s., mainly theatrical: C. 20. (Franklyn, *Rhyming*.)

daft as a brush, as. Extremely stupid; very very silly: rural (mostly North Country):? mid-C. 19–20.

Dag, a shortening of **Dagger** (variant **Dugger**), **the.** The Dean: Oxford undergraduates': since the 1880's. Marples, 2.

dag, adj. Excellent: Australian: since ca. 1905. (B., 1943.) Ex **dag at . . .** (p. 204).

Dage (a hard-*g*'d monosyllable). A Dago: Australian: since ca. 1910. (Vince Kelly, *The Shadow*, 1955.)

dagga rooker. A scoundrel; a wastrel: South African low s.; since ca. 1910. Lit., a smoker of dagga (*Cannabis indica*); *rooker* is Afrikaans.

dagger. A jockey's general helper: Australian sporting: since ca. 1925. (B., 1953.) Perhaps ex **dag,** 1 (p. 204).

Dagger Div, the. The 14th Indian Division: Army: 1939–45. Ex its divisional sign. (P-G-R.)

dagger E; dagger G; dagger N. An officer with high specialist qualifications in engineering—gunnery—navigation: Naval Officers': since ca. 1925. Granville, 'In the Navy List a dagger appears against the names of such officers'; *E, G, N* are traditional abbreviations. Also a *dagger gunner*, a Gunner (W.O.) that has passed the advanced course in Gunnery.

dagmar (mostly in plural). A drachma (Greek currency unit): since ca. 1945. Ex *drachma* influenced by the female given-name *Dagmar.*

Dago (p. 204). 'Specifically an Italian, but loosely used by many Australians to refer to anyone from Europe, especially if dark-skinned' (Culotta, 1957).

dags, on the (p. 204). Since ca. 1925 it has usually been *on dags.* (P-G-R.)

daily.—3. Daily bread: coll.: since ca. 1925. 'Well, I must go and earn the daily.'

daily body. A daily help (servant): coll.: since ca. 1918. Phillip MacDonald, *Rope to Spare*, 1932.

daily-breader. A C. 20 variation of **daily bread** (p. 204): coll.: Ole Luk-Oie, *The Green Curve*, 1909, and Berta Ruck, *Pennies from Heaven*, 1940.

Daily Exaggerator or **Daily Suppress.** *Daily Express*: jocular: since ca. 1912.

Daily Mail, 1 (p. 205) was, by 1950, ob., as also the 2, 'ale' sense.—3. A, the, tale: C. 20. (Franklyn, *Rhyming*.)

Sense 2, also ob. by 1950.—4. Bail (legal): underworld, hence also police, rhyming s.: since ca. 1920. '"What about Daily Mail?" (bail)' occurs in John Gosling, *The Ghost Squad*, 1959.—5. A nail: carpenters' and joiners' rhyming s.: C. 20. (Franklyn 2nd.)

Daily-Tell-the-Tale. *Daily Mail*: jocular rhyming s.: since ca. 1920.

dainty digger. See **whistler**, 9.

Dairy Dot. See **whistler**, 9.

daisies, kick up. See **kick up daisies.**

Daisy is the inevitable nickname of men surnamed Bell: late C. 19–20. Ex a famous music-hall song. Cf. *Dolly* Gray in *Dict.*

daisy.—2. A chamber-pot: Midlands, esp. nursery: late C. 19–20. Probably ex floral design on the inner base.

daisy beat. To cheat; a cheat or swindle or minor crime: rhyming s.: late C. 19–20. Franklyn.

daisy-beaters (p. 205). Franklyn 2nd suggests that it 'rhymes' with s. *creepers*, feet. By 1960, †.

daisy chain. 'We used a device christened the "daisy chain", made from gun-cotton primers threaded on a five-foot length of prima cord. . . . Five primers went to each daisy chain spaced out and held in place by knots in the cord' (Vladimir Peniakoff, *Private Army*, 1950): military (North Africa): 1941–3, and afterwards elsewhere. Ex its appearance.—2. A circle of homosexuals engaged in collective sodomy: widespread homosexual term: since ca. 1950.

daisy-cutter.—5. A perfect landing: R.A.F.: since ca. 1930. Jackson. Ex cricket sense.—6. Sense 1 (p. 205) is extant in Australia in a modified nuance: 'Jim and Morgan were both "daisycutters", the bushman's term for those horses who drag their back hooves on the roadway in a scraping jog.' (Alan Marshall, 1940.)

Daisy Dormer. Warmer (adj.): theatrical rhyming s.: C. 20. Ex the famous music-hall artist. (Franklyn, *Rhyming*.)

daisy-picker. 'One who accompanies an engaged couple on a country walk. 'Brought to keep off gossip' (P. W. Joyce, *English . . . in Ireland*, 1910): Anglo-Irish: late C. 19–20. Cf. **gooseberry**, 2, on p. 344.

daiture. Ten: parlary: mid-C. 19–20. Cf. the quotation at **dewey** below.

Dak. A Dakota transport aircraft: Air Force: 1943 +.

dakes. Marbles: Australian schoolchildren's: C. 20. B., 1942. Corruption of *dukes*?

Dalmation pudding. That kind of boiled currant-pudding which is known as **spotted-dog** (p. 815): Naval: C. 20. Granville. A Dalmatian dog has black or blackish-brown spots on its coat.

dam, be on the. (Of a policeman) to be in trouble: police: since ca. 1920. (*The Free-Lance Writer*, April 1948.)

damager, 1 (p. 205). Perhaps originally rhyming s., as Julian Franklyn proposes.—2. A damaging punch: pugilistic coll.: since ca. 1815; ob. *Boxiana*, IV, 1824.—3. Manager of a N.A.A.F.I. canteen: Navy (lower-deck): ca. 1925. *Weekly Telegraph*, Oct. 25, 1941; Granville.

Dame's Delight. See **Parson's Pleasure.**

damfool or **damful,** v. To deceive: Army: 1914–18. Ex the n.: see p. 205.

Damnation Corner. A 'very sharp turn in the High Street', Windsor: Eton College: ca. 1840–1900. B. & L.

damnation take it! A coll. curse: C. 19 (? 18)–20.

damned!, I'll be; you be damned! A coll. exclamation and a coll. imprecation: C. 17–20.

damned clever these Chinese! See **clever chaps these Chinese** above.

damp.—3. An umbrella: jocular and not very common: since ca. 1950. A pun on the synonymous *gamp*. (A. B. Petch, March 1966.)

damp one's mug (p. 206). Rather: since ca. 1835. *Sinks*, 1848.

Dan.—2. A man in charge of a male public convenience: since ca. 1920. In, e.g., Neil Bell, *Many Waters*, 1954.

Dan Tucker (p. 206) was † by 1950, at latest.

dance a haka. To exhibit joy, 'dance with pleasure': New Zealand coll.: since ca. 1890. B., 1941. The *haka* is a Maori ceremonial dance, wild and impressive. Cf. the Australian **corroboree**, n. and v. (p. 182).

dance at your funeral, I'll or occ. **he'll, she'll.** 'An old slanging-match catchphrase' (Petch): late C. 19–20.

dancing on the carpet. Summoned to the superintendent's office for investigation or reprimand: Canadian railroadmen's (— 1931).

dander, have a. A malaudition of **gander**, 2.

dandy.—7. Homosexual (male), adj. and n.: mid-C. 19–20; since ca. 1900, mainly rural. Cf. *The Dandy Man*, a country song noted, in 1904, by Cecil Sharp. (James Reeves.)—8. 'A small tumbler; commonly used for drinking punch' (P. W. Joyce, *English . . . in Ireland*, 1910): Anglo-Irish: mid C. 19–20. Ex sense 2 on p. 207.

dandysette. A female dandy: fast life: ca. 1820–35. *Spy*, II, 1826. Also *dandizette* or *dandisette*.

dang, v. (p. 207), perhaps blends '*damn*' and '*hang*', as Dr Niels Haislund proposes.

danger light; danger signal. A red nose: mostly Cockneys': C. 20. Cf. **beacon** and **strawberry**, 2.

dangle from. A variation of *hang out of*: since ca. 1910.

dangler, 2, or **pup.** See 'Hauliers' Slang'.

danglers.—3. Medals: since ca. 1915.

Daniel, take one's. To depart or decamp: low: ca. 1860–1900. *Sessions*, Jan. 9, 1872.

dank, adj. See **ace**, adj., above. Since ca. 1945. Perhaps prompted by **wet**, adj., 7, on p. 945.

danner. A *dan*-laying vessel: nautical coll.: late C. 19–20. A *dan* is a small spar-buoy carrying a flag. (P-G-R.)

dannet is illiterate for *Daniel* in **sling one's Daniel.**

dap. To go; to potter: R.A.F., esp. in Irak: since ca. 1935. Esp. in *dap about—across—over*. (Atkinson.) Perhaps cf. Persian *dav*, 'a stroke at play; a wager'.

dapper was, at Eton ca. 1815–40, a gen. approbatory adj.: *Spy*, 1825.

darbs. (Playing) cards: rhyming s.: late C. 19–20. Ernest Raymond, *The Marsh*, 1937.

Darby or **Derby** (pron. *Darby*). A common nickname of men surnamed Kelly: C. 20. Ex the rhyming s. *Darby Kelly*, belly, as Julian Franklyn tells me this spring morning (5 April 1966).

Darby and Joan. A telephone: rhyming s.: very late C. 19–20.

Darby and Joan, on one's. Alone: rhyming s.: C. 20. Gerald Kersh, *Bill Nelson*, 1942.

dark as the inside of a cow (p. 208) has, in Canada (where the phrase is not merely nautical), the C. 20 extension, *tail down and eyes shut*. (Leechman.)

dark engineer. See 'Rogues'.

dark it (*Dict.*) goes back at least as far as 1880. B. & L.

dark 'un. See **dark horse** (*Dict.*).

darkened (p. 208). Cf. 'I threatened him, that, if he was severe upon them, we would darken him' (give him a black eye), D. Haggart, *Life*, 1821.

darkey. See **darky** (*Dict.*).

Darky. 'Inevitable' nickname of men surnamed *Knight*: C. 20. A pun on '*dark* night'.

darky.—7. (Usually as *darkie*.) A night shift: Australian: since ca. 1925. (B., 1953.)

darky (or **darkey**), **the,** noted on p. 208, is extant in itinerant entertainment. In composition, *bona darky!* = goodnight!; 'I left the rub-a-dub last darky'. (Sydney Lester.)

Darky Cox. A box: rhyming: C. 20. A theatrical box. 'Rarely used' (Franklyn 2nd).

darl. (Only in address and endearment.) Darling: Australian coll.: C. 20, but not general before ca. 1920. (K. S. Prichard, *Haxby's Circus*, 1930; Jon Cleary, *The Sundowners*, 1952.)

darling. Charming: 'sweet': feminine coll.: since ca. 1930. Monica Dickens, *The Happy Prisoner*, 1946, '"Isn't that darling of you!"' she exclaimed.'

darlings, the. The prostitutes of the King's Cross (Sydney) area: taxi-drivers', and the local residents': since ca. 1930. (B.P.)

dart.—3 'Dart is stuff (soil, sand, etc.) worth washing,' Wm Kelly, *Life in Victoria*, 1859.—4. 'A very quick try or last-minute effort,' H. & P.: Services': since ca. 1930. Cf. **stab at** (*Dict.*). —5. (Ex sense 2: p. 208.) An illicit activity, a racket: Australian: since ca. 1870. Sidney J. Baker, letter in *The Observer*, Nov. 13, 1938.

Darts. Naval officers trained at Dartmouth: Naval: C. 20.

dash, n.—5. Dash-board of a motor-car: motorists' coll.: since ca. 1910.

dash of the tar-brush. See **tar-brush**.

dash up the channel. A coïtion: English coastal fishermen's: C. 20. Mostly in the south, the English Channel being implied.

data is the L. pl.—not singular—of *datum*.

date, n., 1, occurs in W. L. George, *The Making of an Englishman*, 1914.—2. Delete the faulty entry on p. 208 and substitute:—The anus: Australian: low: late C. 19–20. This affords the origin of sense 2 of the v.—3. Ex sense 1: the person with whom one has a 'date': adopted, ca. 1944, ex U.S. Charles Franklin, *She'll Love You Dead*, 1950, '"You soppy date," she said. "You're nuts."'

dateless. (Of a girl) silly; foolish; 'slow': since ca. 1938. I.e. without 'dates' with boys.

David!, send it down (p. 209). To semantics, add: Wales is 'the Land of Leeks' (leaks): cf. **Urinal of the Planets** (p. 928).

Davy Crockett. A pocket: theatrical rhyming s.: since ca. 1956. (Franklyn.)

Davy Jones's locker (p. 209) occurs earlier in *The Journal of Richard Cresswell*, 1774–77 (pub. 1924; at p. 12), '"D-m my eyes," says he, "they are gone to Davy Jones's locker." This is a common saying when anything goes overboard.' Moe.

Davy Jones's shocker. Not a torpedo, as defined by H. & P., but (Granville) a depth charge. Punning his *locker*.

Davy Large. A barge: rhyming s.: late C. 19–20.

dawn hopper. An enemy raider 'plane using the uncertain light at dawn to slip away and get home: R.A.F.: 1940–5, then merely historical. H. & P.

day, that'll be the; or, that'll be the bloody day, boy! It is not very likely to occur or be done: c.p.: from late 1918. Prob. satirical on *der Tag*.

day and night. Light ale: late C. 19–20. Rhyming on *light*.

day-and-night merchant. See **copper-bottom** above.

day-mates (p. 209) should be back-dated to very early C. 19. The singular is common, as in Wm Nugent Glascock, *The Naval Sketch-Book*, 2nd Series, 1834, at I, 39 and 46. (Moe.)

day-on. 'Duty Boy' or officer-of-the-day: Naval: since ca. 1925.

day-opener. An eye; usually in pl.: pugilistic: ca. 1840–90. Augustus Mayhew, *Paved with Gold*, 1857. Cf. the much more gen. **daylights** (*Dict.*).

day the omelette hit the fan, the. The day everything went wrong. From U.S. c. 1966. Cf. **shit hits the fan, when;** above.

daymen. A synonym of **idlers.** Granville.

day's dawning. Morning: rhyming: C. 20. Superior form: *day's a-dawning.* (Franklyn.)

dazzle(-)dust. See Canadian.

deacon. A chimneysweep's scraper: chimney-sweeps': C. 19. George Elson, *The Last of the Climbing Boys*, 1900. Perhaps ex *degen*, a sword.

dead, n.—2. **the dead,** horses as dead certainties: turf: from ca. 1870; ob. B. & L.

dead, adj. Among tailors, it is applied to work that has been already paid for with a 'sub' in bad times and is being done in better times: from ca. 1870. Ex **dead horse,** q.v. in *Dict.*—2. (Of a horse) that is to be prevented from winning: low Australian: C. 20. (Dal Stivens, *Jimmy Brockett* 1951.)—3. Intensively: (*as*) *dead as mutton*: B., 1953.—4. 'Type matter that has been run off but is still standing; copy that has been set; hence, anything that may now be discarded' (Leechman): printers' coll.: late C. 19–20.

dead, adv. (p. 210), has, since ca. 1940, been increasingly popular, esp. among teenagers, in the nuances 'extremely', e.g. 'He's dead nice', and 'completely', e.g. 'Don't be dead stupid'. These usages apparently spring immediately ex such phrases as '*dead* tired' and 'to stop *dead*', as a very intelligent teenager has suggested in a letter dated March 25, 1965.

dead, making. Making a garment already paid for: tailors': late C. 19–20. Cf. *dead*, adj., 1.

dead, on the (p. 210).—2. Yet, ca. 1890–1910, it seems to have been applied to one who has actively ceased to be a teetotaller.

dead air-gunner. Spam: R.A.F.: 1940 +. Atkinson.

dead as dado, as. Completely, or long, dead: Australian: since ca. 1930; orig. a solecism for S.E. *as dead as the dodo*, but soon > coll. (B.P.)

dead as small beer. Quite dead; ancient: coll.: mid-C. 19–20; ob. B. & L. Cf. the **dead as a door-nail** entry in *Dict.*

dead beat, 2 (p. 210), goes back to ca. 1870. (*The Detectives' Handbook*, ca. 1880.)

dead-broker. A dead-beat: Australian: since ca. 1890. B., 1942.

dead centre. A cemetery: jocular: since ca. 1940.

dead chocker; dead chuffed. Utterly bored; delighted: coffee-bar set of teenagers: ca. 1955–9. (Gilderdale.)

dead clever these Chinese! See **clever chaps these Chinese;** above.

dead cop. A sure way to win, or to make money: sporting: from ca. 1870; ob. B. & L. Cf. **cop,** v., 5 (*Dict.*), which should be put back to ca. 1860.

dead-copper. An informer to the police: low Australian: since ca. 1920. (B., 1943.)

dead, dead, and (s)he never called me mother! (p. 210). It dates from the 1880's–90's, the hey-day of the melodrama of the Surrey-side, the so-called transpontine drama.

dead easy is a C. 20 Cockneys' coll. phrase to describe any such woman (other than a prostitute) as is ready to go home and sleep with a man.

Dead End Kids. Self-description of R.N.V.R. Lieutenants despairful of becoming Lieutenant-Commanders: 1942–5: Granville. Cf. **Abbeville Kids,** q.v.

dead-end street. The female pudend: Canadian: since ca. 1930.

dead fall. A Western stunt rider in motion pictures: cinematic: since ca. 1925.

dead from the neck up. Brainless; habitually tongue-tied: since ca. 1920. It occurs in, e.g., S. P. B. Mais, *Caper Sauce*, 1948.

dead hand. An expert: Australian: since ca. 1925. Baker.

dead handsome. 'Said of a circumstance that is fortunate and that turns, by whatever means, to one's advantage' (Laurie Atkinson, who first heard it on Nov. 10, 1959): since ca. 1955.

dead-head.—2. A locomotive that, not under power, is being hauled back in another train: Canadian railwaymen's: C. 20.—3. 'Railway personnel riding back without working. Also as verb' (Priestly): Canadian railwaymen's: since ca. 1910.

dead heat (p. 210). From at least as early as 1820. (Bee, 1823.)

dead horse. An Australian variant of **ride the dead horse:** A. Harris, *Settlers and Convicts*, 1847.—3. Sauce: Australian rhyming s.: C. 20. Baker.

dead lair. See **lair.**

dead loss. A person, place or thing that is decidedly 'dud' (dull; inefficient; without amenities): R.A.F.: 1940 +. (W/Cdr R. P. McDouall, letter of March 27, 1945.) Ex a 'plane no longer serviceable.

dead loss.—2. (Of a job, or a course of action) lacking prospects; unpromising: since ca. 1946.

dead low.—2. A very low barometer reading: Canadian scientific coll.: since ca. 1910. (Leechman.)

dead man.—4. A scarecrow; non-aristocratic coll.: from ca. 1870; ob. B. & L.—5. 'Why don't they tuck-in those dead-men out of sight'—glossed as 'the platted reef-points of the sails when carelessly hanging beneath the yard, when the sail is furled' (Glascock, *Sketch-Book*, I, 11, pub. in 1825): Naval: ca. 1790–1850. Moe.

dead man's effects. False teeth: Services': since ca. 1939. H. & P. Often the only thing he has to leave.

dead matter. Type that has been run and could now be 'dissed': Canadian printers' coll.: C. 20.—2. Hence, anything that, used or finished, can now be either returned to its place or discarded: Canadian coll.: since ca. 1920. (Leechman.)

dead-meat.—2. (Also *frozen meat*.) A prostitute,

as opposed to *fresh meat*, a non-prostitute: ow: late C. 19–20.

dead nail. See **nail**, n., 1 (*Dict.*).

dead nuts on. See **nuts on, be**, on p. 575.

dead on. See **dead steady.**—2. Absolutely right: since ca. 1945. Ex the R.A.F. sense 'right on the target'. Brendan Behan, *Borstal Boy*, 1958.

dead-pan (expression). Expressionless; impassive: adopted, ca. 1944, ex U.S. servicemen. Ex U.S. s. *dead pan*, an expressionless 'pan' or face (cf. the Eng. s. *dial*)—orig., theatrical.

dead pony gaff. A bad site: showmen's, esp. grafters': C. 20.

dead ring—or **spit**—**of, the.** Exactly, or almost, like: Australian: C. 20. (B., 1943.)

dead ringer. A spitting image: esp. Canadian: C. 20. Cf. the preceding.

dead set (p. 211). Cf. 'I have a dead set upon the Rogues,' Anon., *The Prison Breakers*, 1725.

dead spit and image, the. The exact facsimile: Canadian coll.: since ca. 1910. (Leechman.)

dead spotted ling of. Very much like, strikingly similar to: Australian: since ca. 1910. B., 1942. Rhyming on **dead ring of**, above.

dead steady or **dead on**. Applies to 'a good fellow': Guardsmen's: since ca. 1920. In, e.g., Roger Grinstead, *They Dug a Hole*, 1946.

dead stick is applied to the controls of an engine that has stopped: R.A.F.: since ca. 1925. Jackson.—2. See **sticking.**

dead thick. Wide-awake and cunning (or clever): low Glasgow: late C. 19–20. MacArthur & Long.

dead un.—5. A supernumerary that plays for nothing: theatrical: from ca. 1860; ob. B. & L.

dead uns, make. To charge not only for loaves delivered but also for loaves not delivered: bakers': mid-C. 19–20. B. & L.

deadener. A bully; one who, strong and quarrelsome, tends to resort to his fists: Australian: C. 20. Archer Russell, *Gone Nomad*, 1936.

deadhead. A brakeman: Canadian railroadmen's (— 1931).

deadly nightshade. See **nightshade.**

deado. See **dead oh!** (*Dict.*).

deads. Dead drunk; fast asleep (*dead to the world*): Naval: since ca. 1920. (P-G-R.)

Deaf and Dumb, the. The Ministry of Information: taxi-drivers': ca. 1940–5. *The Weekly Telegraph*, Sept. 13, 1941.

deaf as the mainmast (p. 211): W. N. Glascock, *The Naval Sketch-Book*, I, 1825. Moe.

deal, a.—3. (Always thus.) "I had a deal last night'—a successful crime: c.: C. 20. F. D. Sharpe, *The Flying Squad*, 1938.

Dean. A fairly common nickname of men surnamed *Swift*: late C. 19–20. Ex that Dean Swift who wrote *Gulliver's Travels*.

Dean and Dawson was Stalag Luft III's prisoner-of-war-in-Germany s. for their forgery department: 1942–5: Brickhill & Norton, *Escape to Danger*, 1946. Ex the fact that it handled passports, identity cards and other 'papers'; in short, a compliment to the well-known firm of travel agents.

deansea ville in B. & L. is an error. See **deuseaville** (*Dict.*).

dear John. A girl's letter telling a man in the Armed Forces she no longer loves him: American (1942–5) >, by 1945, Canadian >, by 1960, British.—2. Hence, a very friendly letter, begin-

ning with his first name and telling an officer that his services were no longer required, owing to the reunification of the Armed Forces: Canadian forces': 1965 +. (Leechman.)

dear Mother, it's a bugger! A military c.p., expressive of disgust with Service life: since ca. 1910. Atkinson.

dear old pals! 'A derisive chanted cat-call or song when boxers funk action or are in a clinch' (Petch): boxing spectators'; C. 20. Ex the song 'Dear old pals, jolly old pals'.

dear-stalker. A wealthy idler addicted to ogling and following pretty shop or office girls: C. 20; slightly ob. by 1940. H. A. Vachell, *Quinney's*, 1914. Pun on *dear, deer*.

death, in the. Finally; at last: since ca. 1945. (Norman.) Perhaps ex S.E. *in at the death*.

death adder. Machine gun: Australian soldiers': 1940 +. B., 1942.—2. (Mostly in pl.) A gossip; a cynic, esp. if old: Northern Territory (Australia): since ca. 1930. Ernestine Hill, *The Territory*, 1951.

death adder man. An eccentric solitary, more often called a *hatter*: mostly northern Australian: since ca. 1920. 'Some of them go under the name of death adder men, for it is reckoned they will bite your head off if spoken to before noon': Jock Marshall & Russell Drysdale, *Journey among Men*, 1962, at p. 56. (Cf. sense 2 of preceding entry.)

death adders in one's pocket, have. To be extremely mean with money: Australian: since ca. 1920. Baker.

death-hunting, n. The selling of 'last dying speeches': street vendors': ca. 1840–1900. Mayhew, I, 1851.

death or glory lads, the. The Commandos: Army: 1942–5.

death seat, the. The front seat, next to the driver: Australian motorists' coll.: since ca. 1945. The occupant is the most likely to be killed in an accident. (B.P.)

death-tally. An identity disc: Naval: C. 20. (P-G-R.)

death warmed up. See **feel like . . .**

death-warrant is out!, my (or **his** or **your**). A police c.p., dating from the late C. 19. Clarence Rook, *London Side-Lights*, 1908, 'When a constable is transferred against his will from one division to another, the process is alluded to in the force in the phrase, "His death-warrant is out." For this is a form of punishment for offences which do not demand dismissal.'

death watch. Attendance upon a man condemned to death: prison officers': C. 20. (L. W. Merrow-Smith & J. Harris, *Prison Screw*, 1962.)

deathy. A death adder: Australian coll.: late C. 19–20. (Sidney H. Courtier, *The Glass Spear*, 1951.)

deb.—2. A bed: back s.: since ca. 1845. Mayhew, I.

deb chick. A debutante beatnik: mostly beatniks': since late 1950's. (Anderson.)

debagged. Struck off the rolls: since ca. 1920. 'Sapper' uses it in *Bulldog Drummond at Bay*, 1935. Ex **de-bag** in p. 212.

debollicker. A small British mine that, trodden upon, fired a bullet upwards: Army: 1941 +. (P-G-R.) The *de-*connotes 'removal'; for the main element, cf. *ballock* (p. 29).

debuggerable. Disreputable: since ca. 1930.

Decanterbury pilgrims. Those who, during the

shortages in 1915–16, made the rounds in search of whisky: 1915–16, then historical (Reginald Pound, *The Lost Generation*, 1964). A pun on Chaucer's *The Canterbury Pilgrims* and on '*to decant*'.

decarb. To decarbonise: motorists' coll.: since ca. 1915. See **decoke** below.

decimal bosun. A Warrant Schoolmaster: Navy: since ca. 1930. Granville. Ex mathematics.

deck, 1 (p. 212): by 1945, common in England and Australia—and no longer low.—**4.** Also, since ca. 1925, *the deck* = the ground: R.A.F. (Jackson.) By 1945, general s.

decker.—**4.** A hat: Australian: C. 20. Baker. Ex 'top deck'.—**5.** A peaked cap: Liverpool: ca. 1900–50.—**6.** A glance, a look: Australian variant of *dekko*: C. 20. (Dal Stivens, *Jimmy Brockett*, 1951.)—**7.** A double-decker bus: Australian omnibus employers': since ca. 1935. (B. P.)

decoke has, since ca. 1945, everywhere superseded **decarb**.

decorate. To ride on top of a freight car: Canadian railroadmen's (— 1931).

decorate the mahogany. To put down—on the bar—money for drinks: Canadian: since ca. 1905: by 1959, ob. (Leechman.) This sort of jocularly verbose and pompous slang belongs chiefly to the years ca. 1890–1914 (July).—**2.** (Of a man) to lay the housekeeping money on the table: mostly lower-middle class: since ca. 1930.

decorators in, have the. A variant of *have the painters in*, q.v. at **rags on, have the**.

dedigitate. See **take your finger out**.

deed-pollers. Deed poll: since ca. 1930. (Nancy Mitford, *Don't Tell Alfred*, 1960.) The Oxford *-er*.

deep-noser. A pot of beer: Australian: since ca. 1920. (Arthur W. Upfield, *Murder Down Under*, 1937.) As the beer sinks, so does the drinker's nose into the pot.

deep-sea beef. Haddock: Naval (lower-deck): C. 20. (P-G-R.)

deep-sea tot. A short measure of rum, the shortness (supposedly) caused by the roll of the ship: Naval: C. 20. (P-G-R.)

defect. A prefect: Cranbrook School: C. 20.

defective. A detective (not the fictional detective): jocular: since ca. 1925.

Deffy. See **Daffy**.

deft and dumb. A c.p. denoting the ideal wife or mistress: since ca. 1940. Parodying *deaf and dumb*. ('A Girl in a Million', an English film of 1946, wasn't deaf, and only physically was she dumb.)

degen (p. 213). Sense 1 derives ex C. 17 Dutch *degen*, 'sword'. Prob., as Mr L. W. Forster has suggested to me, introduced into England by returned soldiers. Sense 2 follows from sense 1: cf. Middle High German *ein sneller Degen*, 'a brave knight', and the C. 17–18 Dutch *degen*, 'a brave soldier; an "old soldier".'

degger, n. Disgrace: Harrow School: late C. 19–20. Lunn. By 'the Oxford *-er*' ex *degradation*.

degommy (p. 213). Also, in 1939–45, Naval. Granville.

degra. Degradation; disgrace: Winchester: late C. 19–20. Marples. Cf. **degger**.

dehydrate. '"Let's have a drink, all this talking dries me—dehydrates me, to use the modern

slang,"' Manning Coles, *The Fifth Man*, 1946: since 1942, when dehydrated foods became fairly common.

dekkoscope was, among soldiers in India in World War II, a variant of **shaftiscope**. The short, thick variety (*dekkoscope, mark one*) was also known as a *pile-driver*; the long, thin variety as *dekkoscope, mark two*.

delible, n. A non-commissioned officer: Army, mostly officers', occ. men's, ever N.C.O.s': 1916–18. Ex the adj.: see p. 213.

*****delivered dodge.** A trick whereby one secures possession, without payment, of goods delivered to one's rooms: c.: mid-C. 19–20. B. & L.

delouse. 'His squadron was "delousing" Fortresses as they came back home out of Holland . . . liquidating such enemy fighters as still persisted in pestering the bombers,' Paul Brickhill & Conrad Norton, *Escape to Danger*, 1946: Air Force: 1940 +.—**2.** To remove mines and booby traps from (a terrain): Army; since ca. 1941.

Delphos. Incorrect for **Delphi**: mid-C. 16–20. Prob., as Mr G. G. Loane suggests, an accusative pl. taken as a nominative singular.

Deluge. A Delage car: Cambridge: since ca. 1925; by 1945, ob. By a pun.

delushious or **delushus.** (Esp. of a fruit dish) delicious: since the late 1940's. *Delicious* + *luscious*.

dem.—**2.** To demonstrate: fairgrounds': since ca. 1930. '"If you want to see this tool *demmed*," says Mr Pearson, meaning demonstrated' (W. Buchanan-Taylor, *Shake It Again*, 1943).

dem keb. A hansom: 'mashers'': ca. 1874–90. B. & L. Ex W. S. Gilbert's *Wedding March*, first played on Nov. 15, 1873.

demi-rep (p. 213) occurs earlier in *A Congratulatory Epistle from a Reformed Rake . . . upon Prostitutes*, 1728, at p. 8.

demmick. A soldier on the sick list; an article become unserviceable: Army: C. 20. H. & P., 'The derivation is probably "epi-demic-ked"'; probably.

demmy. A demonstrator: University of Leeds undergraduates': since ca. 1930. (Marples, 2.) Ex the official abbreviation, *dem*.

demo (p. 214). Also, since middle 1930's Army: *how* something is to be done.—**2.** A lowering of one's place in class; also as v.t., esp. in passive Charterhouse: from ca. 1919. Cf. **promo**.

demob, n. Demobilisation; hence *demob leave*, leave awarded on, and immediately following, demobilisation: Services': 1945 +. Cf. the v., noted on p. 214.

demobitis. See **funnel fever**.

demon.—**5.** A shilling: Australian: C. 20. B., 1942.

demon chandler. A chandler supplying ship's stores that are very inferior: nautical coll.: from ca. 1871. R. & L.

demon vino. Cheap Italian wine: Army in Italy: 1944–5. (P-G-R.) A pun on S.E. (revivalists') *the demon rum*.

Demons, the. Melbourne Club footballers: Melbournites': since ca. 1910. (B., 1943.)

Dempsey Press, the. The Kemsley Press: jocular: since ca. 1935. Ex its purchase of local newspapers and Jack Dempsey's heavyweight-boxing fame.

*****dempstered,** ppl. adj. Hanged: Scottish c.:

mid-C. 17–18. B. & L. Ex *dempster*, that official whose duty it was, until 1773, to 'repeat the sentence to the prisoner in open court'.

dems. 'All Naval personnel connected with "Defensively equipped merchant ships"': Navy: 1939–45. Granville. Also Army, because the Army had sometimes to supply the ammunition.

demur upon the plaintiff. See 'Tavern terms', § 4.

demure as a(n old) whore at a christening, as (p. 214) should be back-dated to ca. 1700, for it occurs in Captain Alexander Smith, *The Life of Jonathan Wild*, 1726, at p. 116, in the shorter form.

Den, the. The same as **Upper Tartary**: *Spy*, II, 1826.

denari. An occ. form of **denarly** (*Dict.*). Pugh. *Denari* has, since ca. 1910, been the predominant form: the only form adduced by Sydney Lester in *Vardi the Palarey*, (?) 1937.

Denim Light Infantry, the. The 2nd Corps Reinforcement Unit in Tunisia: Army in North Africa: 1943. (P-G-R.) A pun on the Durham Light Infantry, fighting in Tunisia at the same time.

dep.—4. A department (e.g. Physics): Imperial College, London: since ca. 1930. (Marples, 2.)

depending on what school you went to. 'A c.p. used by cowards who give two pronunciations of a rare, or a foreign, word' (B.P.): Australian: since ca. 1950.

depot stanchion. 'A rating who has been an unconscionable time in barracks or Shore Establishment,' Granville: Naval: since ca. 1930. Sarcastic.

depressed area. The abdomen: jocular: since ca. 1930. Claude Houghton, *Transformation Scene*, 1946. Ex the sociological sense.

depth charge; but nearly always in pl., *depth charges*, figs: Naval: since 1939. (H. & P.) By ca. 1941, R.A.F. for prunes: Jackson. Both are mild laxatives. (P-G-R.)—2. *Emissio in coitu*: low jocular: since ca. 1942, originally—like **combined operations**—a Services' witticism.—3. 'Prison "duff" ' . . . Anything heavy or stodgy, such as dumplings' (Paul Tempest, *Lag's Lexicon*): since ca. 1941; orig., prison c.; by ca. 1955, also (low) s.

derby, n.—5. Short for **Derby Kelly** (p. 214). Jackson.

Derby. See **Darby** above.—2. A railwaymen's colloquialism for the Midland Region: since ca. 1950. *Railway*, 3rd.

Derby, be in the. To be competing in the race for promotion, whether in the Wardroom or on the lower deck: Naval: since ca. 1940. (P-G-R.)

dermo. A New Guinea skin disease: Australian Army: 1942–5. (Jon Cleary, *The Climate of Courage*, 1954.)—2. Any skin affection: Services' and general: since ca. 1939. Ex *dermatitis*.

derrick. A nuance of sense 2 is: a casual ward: tramps' c.: late C. 19–20.

derriwag. Paper used for parsing: Harrow School (since ca. 1875) and Eton College (C. 20). 'Said to be a distortion of *derivation*,' as Marples records.

Derry and Tom. A bomb: rhyming s. (esp. Londoners'): 1940 +.

Derry-Down-Derry (or *d.-d.-d.*). Sherry: theatrical rhyming s.: C. 20. (Franklyn, *Rhyming*.)

dersie or **-y.** A variant—a loose—pron. of **derzy** (p. 214).

derv. Oil for Diesel engines: Army: 1940 +. From '*D*iesel-*e*ngined *r*oad *v*ehicle (fuel)'.—2. Hence, a *D*iesel-*e*ngined *r*oad *v*ehicle: since ca. 1950.

desert chicken. Bully beef: Army in North Africa: 1940–3. (P-G-R.)

desert drivers. 'Sand and water men' (*Railway*, 3rd): railwaymen's: since middle 1940's. An allusion to W.W. II service in North Africa.

desert lily. A circular or box-shaped funnel, adjustable—according to direction of wind—to a urine receptacle: R.A.F., esp. in North Africa: 1940 +. Atkinson.

desert loneliness. Horseplay, or suggestive chaffing, in the desert: coll, R.A.F. in North Africa: 1940–4. Atkinson.

Desert Rats, the. The Seventh Armoured Division in North Africa: self-bestowed 1941–3. Ex Mussolini's 'despicable desert rats'. (P-G-R.) The divisional flash worn on shoulder and shown on vehicles was the jerboa or desert rat.

desert rose. A urination-can let into the sand: Army in North Africa: 1940 +. Ironic. Cf. **desert lily.**

deserves a medal. See **beggar for work.**

desink. To de-synchronise (one's motors): R.A.F. aircrews': since ca. 1938. Michie & Graebner, *Their Finest Hour*, 1940 (p. 63).

destat. To get rid of the *stat*utory tenants from (a property): since ca. 1954. Cf. the quotation at **schwarz** below.

destroying. Serving, or a serving, in destroyers: Naval coll.: since ca. 1939.

det. A detonator: Combatant Services' coll.: since ca. 1910.

detec. A detective: ca. 1875–95. Capt. ——, *Eighteen Months' Imprisonment*, 1884. Superseded by **tec** (*Dict.*).

detens. See 'Colston's . . .'.

deuce.—4. The sum of two pounds (£2): London's East End: since ca. 1947. (Richard Herd, Nov. 12, 1957.)

Deuce, the. See **Musso.**

deucer. A double shift; double time: Australian (industrial) workers': since ca. 1910. Dymphna Cusack, *Southern Steel*, 1953.

Dev. De Valera: Anglo-Irish: since ca. 1930.

Deviation Dick. A compass-adjustor: R.A.F.: ca. 1940–5. Robert Hinde, letter of March 17, 1945. By personification, by alliteration and by ref. to the correction of compass deviation.

deviator; deviation. A crook; a crime: since ca. 1950: c. >, by 1965, s. (Robin Cook, 1962.) Ex euphemistic S.E. *devious*, 'shady' or crooked.

devil.—11. A coal brazier: railwaymen's: C. 20. *Railway*, 3rd.

devil, a or the (p. 125), prob. goes back to ca. 1800, to judge by a passage cited—in *The Port Folio*, Nov. 1809—from *Nolens Volens*, a play by Everard Hall. (Moe.)

devil-devil. 'Rough country broken up into holes and hillocks' (B., 1943): Australian s. (since ca. 1890) by 1930, coll. Ex Aboriginal pidgin.

devil-dodger, 1, is in C. 20 used, esp. in the Navy, for 'chaplain'. Granville.

devil's own (p. 217): W. N. Glascock, *Sketch-Book*, II (29), 1826, 'He led the boatswain the devil's own life'. Moe.

devil's rot-gut. See **cabin-boy's breeches**.

dew bit (p. 217). 'The harvesters' between-meals snacks were dew-bit, elevenses, fourses, and morn-bit,' Andrew Haggard, letter of Jan. 28, 1947.

dew-drop. 'I am going to knock off that "dew-drop", meaning the lock of the gas meter,' *Sessions*, Oct. 17, 1910: low: C. 20.—2. 'Right in the nose of a rigid airship is a large metal coupling known as the "dewdrop", for making fast to the mooring mast, when on the landing ground' (*The Airship*, III, No. 10, published in 1936): aviation coll.: since ca. 1933; by 1946, merely historical.

dewey. Two: parlary: mid-C. 19–20. (Cf. **dooce** on p. 234.) Sydney Lester, *Vardi the Palarey* (?) 1937, '"What's the bottle, cull?"—"Dewey funt, tray *bionk*, daiture soldi medza, so the divvi is otta bionk nobba peroon, and tray medzas back in the aris (Aristotle)", which in plain English would read: "How much have we taken, pal?"—"Two pounds, three shillings and tenpence half-penny, so we get eight shillings and ninepence each and put three-halfpence back in the box (bottle)".'

Dexies. See 'Minor Drugs'.

dexo. A dexamphetamine sulphate tablet: since ca. 1945, esp. in Australia. (B.P.)

dhobey day. Washing day: Naval: late C. 19–20. H. & P. See **dhob** in *Dict.*

dhobey (or dhobi) dust. Any washing-powder; any of the advertised detergents: Naval lower-deck: since the late 1940's.

dhob(e)ying firm. A partnership of ratings who —quite unofficially—do their messmates' laundry: Naval: C. 20. Granville. Also *dhobey firm*.

dhobi, etc.—3. One's laundry: Army: since ca. 1945. Ex senses 1 and 2 on p. 217.

di-da, di-da, di-da. 'Mocking burden to drawn-out explanation or, esp., complaint. Frequent in Geoffrey Cotterell, *Then a Soldier*, 1941' (Laurie Atkinson): since ca. 1930. Cf. **didah** below.

Dials, the.—2. In prison c. of C. 19–20 (but now almost †), 'members of the criminal class who live about the Seven Dials', B. & L.

diameter. See **radius**.

diamond-cracker. A fireman: Canadian rail-roadmen's (— 1931). Pun on *black diamonds* (coal).

Diana dip. A swim naked: girls' schools': late C. 19–20; by 1950, ob. Berta Ruck, *A Storyteller Tells the Truth*, 1935.

diary, the. See 'Prisoner-of-War Slang', 12.

dib. 'A portion or share': non-aristocratic: from ca. 1860; ob. B. & L. Prob. ex S.E. *dib*, a counter used in playing card-games for money.—2. Hence (?), a marble: Australian: C. 20. B., 1942. —3. In pl. *dibs*: the game of knuckle-bones: schoolchildren's: late C. 19–20.

dib(b)s, money (p. 218), occurs in *The Port Folio* of June 6, 1807, reporting a British source. (Moe.)

dibs, dics (Rugby) or **dicks, digs** (Shrewsbury), **dix** (Tonbridge); to **dick**. Prayers; to pray: Public Schools': late C. 19–20. Marples. Ex L. *dictare*, to say repeatedly, or *dictata*, lessons rather than precepts.

dibs and dabs. Body lice: rhyming s. on *crabs*: C. 20. (Franklyn 2nd.)

dice. To ride strenuously: Army mechanical transport: 1939 +. Cf. **dicing**.—2. To get rid of: Australian: since ca. 1920. Lawson Glassop, *We Were the Rats*, 1944, 'It's me name, but it's too cissy,

so I dices it and picks up "Mick".' Ex *discard*.

dicer. A hat: ca. 1800–40. Frequently in novels of Jeffrey Farnol.—2. A pilot undertaking a 'dicey' operation: R.A.F.: ca. 1940-5.—3. The sortie itself: R.A.F. 1941-5. Ex **dicing**, 1, below. (Peter Sanders.)

dicey. Risky; dangerous: R.A.F.: 1940 +; by 1946, common among civilians: cf. next entry. —2. Hence, esp. in 'It's a bit dicey', chancy and tricky: since early 1950's. (L.A. records hearing it on April 27, 1960.)

dicey on the ubble. 'Going thin on the top': Teddy boys': ca. 1955–60. (Gilderdale, 2.)

dicing, n. Flying; properly, operational flying: R.A.F.: 1940 +. Cynically and refreshingly jocular, in derision of the journalistic *dicing with death* (so often heard in Aug.–Oct. 1940). 'In a letter to *The Daily Telegraph* of 22 June '68, Mr W. A. H. Watts of Sunbury says that "dicing with death" was commonly used by motor racing enthusiasts long before 1939 and attributes it to the motor racing correspondent of one of the motoring journals of that era.' (Ramsey Spencer.) —2. Hence, a 'duel' between two drivers: car racing drivers' and the commentators': since ca. 1955.

Dick, man, is specifically pejorative; witness 'a dick' in *The English Rogue* and 'a desperate Dick in *The Verney Memoirs*.

dick, n.—1. on p. 218. No! The British usage prob. antecedes the American. The sense occurs in Wm Nugent Glascock, *The Naval Sketch-Book*, 2nd Series, 1834, at I, 206, and prob. goes back to early C. 19. (Moe.)—5. A perambulator: C. 20. A. Neil Lyon, *Moly Lane* 1916.—6. A detective: C. 20. Owes something to the 'Deadwood *Dick*' stories and to the '*Dick* Tracy' comic strip?

Dick (or **dick**), **have had the.** To be 'all washed-up' or finished, esp. financially or in one's career: Australian: since ca. 1920. Cf. **Richard, have had the**, below. (B.P.)

Dick Dunn. Sun: rhyming s.: C. 20. Sydney Lester derives it ex 'a famous bookmaker'.

Dick Turpin. 13: darts players': C. 20. Rhyming s. (*The Evening News*, July 2, 1937.)

dicken on that! Go easy!; Nothing doing. New Zealand: C. 20. (Slatter.)

Dick(e)y. Lord Louis Mountbatten: Naval (ward-room): 1939–45. (P-G-R.)

dick(e)y, n., 6 (p. 218): prob. goes back to ca. 1810 or earlier. (W. N. Glascock, *Sailors and Saints*, 1829, p. 23.) Moe.—10. A detachable name-plate (the name being false) on a van: low London: from ca. 1860. Ex sense 2.—11. (Cf. 9.) Word: C. 20.—12. The sailor's blue 'jean' collar: Naval: C. 20. Short for *dick(e)y birds*.

dick(e)y, adj.—3. Of plans or things: tricky, risky: C. 20.

dick(e)y birds.—5. (Often *dickey*.) Words: rhyming s.: late C. 19–20. Michael Harrison, *Reported Safe Arrival*, 1943, '"I give yer me dicky"'; Mark Benny, *Low Company*, 1936—the term in full.—6. See 'Prisoner-of-War Slang', 4.

Dick(e)y diddle. To urinate: Cockney juvenile rhyming s. variant of **Jimmy Riddle** (p. 439): C. 20. Franklyn, *Rhyming*.

dick(e)y dido.—2. The female pudend: low Canadian: C. 20; by 1960, slightly ob.

dickey pilot. A pilot flying with an experienced pilot for instructional purposes: Air Force: since ca. 1930. He occupied the dickey seat.

Dickie (or **-y**) **Bird.** See 'Nicknames'.

Dickie's. Dr Barnardo's Home at Kingston, Surrey: boys' and old boys': since ca. 1950. (*Woman's Own*, Oct. 2, 1965.)

dickory dock. A clock: rhyming s.: from ca. 1870. Ex the nursery rhyme.—2. Penis: rhyming s. on *cock*: C. 20. (Franklyn 2nd.)

dicky run. A quick dash ashore: Naval: C. 20. (P-G-R.)

dics. See **dibs.**

did I buggery—or **fuck**—or **hell!** See **fuck,** like.

did it hurt? 'This is heard in jocular use in several ways, as "Did it hurt?" when a chap has said that he had been thinking' (A. B. Petch, May 1966): c.p.: C. 20. The variant tense *does it hurt?* is less often heard.

did she fall or was she pushed? A c.p. applied to a girl 'in trouble' or shouted at an old-style actress in melodrama: C. 20. The late Thorne Smith used it as a punning title. See also **pushed?, did she . . .,** (*Dict.* and *Supplement.*)

didah. A radio telegraphist: Australian Naval: since ca. 1930. (B., 1943.)

didden. Didn't: sol.: C. 19–20. Very common in Australia—see, *passim,* Lawson Glassop, *We Were the Rats,* 1944.

diddle, n. 1. Earlier record: 1728, Anon., *The Quaker's Opera* (see quot'n at **bunter's tea**).

diddle, v.—6. To digitate sexually and successfully: Canadian: C. 20. Cf. senses 1, 3, 4, on p. 219.

diddle-diddle. See 'Miscellanea'.

diddleums. Delirium tremens: Australian jocular: since ca. 1925. (B., 1943.)

diddly pout (p. 219) perhaps derives rather—by elaboration—from **pouter** (p. 655); the latter could well be literal.

diddy.—2. A familiar diminutive of *didekei,* which strictly means a half-bred gypsy: among the folk of the road: late C. 19–20.

didn't ought. Port (wine): rhyming s.: late C. 19–20; ob. by 1950. (Franklyn, *Rhyming.*) Ex 'Oo! I didn't ought to.'

didn't oughter. Water: rhyming s.: ca. 1890–1920. (Franklyn 2nd.)

Dido. 'A girl who makes herself ridiculous with fantastic finery' (P. W. Joyce, 1910): Anglo-Irish: late C. 19–20. Ex Dido, the tragic queen.

*dido, v. 'To steal from carts in the street' (B., 1942): Australian c.: C. 20. Cf.:—

dido, act. To play the fool: Naval: C. 20. Granville. A variant of **cut a dido** (*Dict.*).

die is a rare variant spelling of **dee,** 2 (*Dict.*).—2. See **die the death.**

[**die, to.** Boxing synonyms of ca. 1810–60, recorded by Anon., *Every Night Book,* 1827, are: *go to see one's friends, mizzle, morris, muff it, not to be at home, snuff and toddle, step below, take it in.*]

die on it. To fail to keep a promise, or in an undertaking. Australian: since ca. 1918. Baker.

die the death. (Of a performer) to meet with a complete lack of response from the audience: theatrical, but esp. Variety, chiefly among comedians: since ca. 1940. Since ca. 1950, usually shortened to *die,* as in 'My gags didn't mean a thing (to the audience). I died!' (Richard Merry.)

*diener is a mainly Afrikaans-speakers' c. term for a policeman: C. 20. *The Cape Times,* May 23,

1946. Derisive of the fact that he is a public *servant:* cf. Ger. *Diener,* a male servant.

diet sheet. A Mess menu: Service officers' (esp. R.A.F.): since 1941. Jackson.

Dieu et mon droit (p. 219) often serves for the full c.p.; therefore, partly, rhyming s. (Franklyn.)

diff. A differential: since ca. 1920. It occurs in, e.g. Gavin Casey, *It's Harder for Girls,* 1942.

differ. Difference: New Zealand: late C. 19–20. (G. B. Lancaster, *Sons o' Men,* 1904.) Cf. *Differs.*

different ships, different cap-tallies. Synonymous with the entry on p. 219: C. 20.

differs. Difference: Anglo-Irish: C. 20. Desmond O'Neill, *Life Has No Price,* 1959, '"I don't suppose it'll make any differs, but," he said . . .' Perhaps via '*difference*'.

diffs (p. 220) occurs earlier in Renton Nicholson, *An Autobiography,* 1860, at p. 52, 'Soon after 1832, he got into "diffs", and his residence was divided between the King's Bench and the Fleet Prison.'

diffy. Deficient, as in 'He was diffy a hussif at the inspection yesterday': Army: since ca. 1939.—2. Difficult: Society: since ca. 1945; by 1960, almost †. Ngaio Marsh, *Swing, Brother, Swing,* 1949.

dig, n.—5. An (expedition for purposes of) excavation: (an expedition's) work on an excavation: archæologists' coll.: from ca. 1890. E.g. in Agatha Christie, *Murder in Mesopotamia,* 1936, 'He's the head of a large American dig' and 'Most of them were up on the dig.' Cf. **big dig,** 2.—6. Loss of privileges: Guards': since ca. 1930.—7. A reprimand: R.A.F.: since ca. 1925. Cf. sense 1 on p. 220.—8. (Ex sense 2: p. 220.) A New Zealand soldier in World War II: 1939 +. Also an Australian soldier therein: Australian: 1939–45, then historically. More used in address than in reference.—9. An injection: medical: since ca. 1910. (Warwick Deeping, *Mr Gurney and Mr Slade,* 1944.)—10. A loss of privileges: Army N.C.O.s: since ca. 1925. Perhaps ex 'a nasty dig' at one's self-esteem. (P-G-R.)—11. In cricket, a turn at batting: Australian schoolboys': since ca. 1930. (B.P.) An opportunity to 'dig in'?—12. A fisherman's stretch of water or other definite 'area': Aus. fishers' and anglers': since ca. 1920. Nino Culotta, *Gone Fishin',* 1963. Perhaps ex sense 5.

dig, v.—2. To irritate or annoy: Australian: since ca. 1920. 'The man was taken aback. "What's digging you?" he blustered,' D'Arcy Niland, *Call the . . .,* 1958. Semantically cf. 'What's got into you?'—3. To become aware of; look at and enjoy; to enjoy; to look at and understand; to understand and enjoy: jazz-musicians', hence also dance-fanatics': adopted, in Britain ca. 1945, in Canada ca. 1938, ex U.S. (*The Observer,* Sept. 16, 1956.) 'To get into and under the melody' (F. E. L. Priestley); ultimately from S.E. *dig into,* to investigate, to examine very closely. Cf. Norman D. Hinton's excellent 'Language of Jazz Musicians' in *The American Dialect Society,* Nov. 1958. 'Now [among teen-agers] means only "to enjoy or appreciate"': Miss Dinah Greenwood, March 25, 1965. As a schoolboys' word, it had, by mid-1963, reached the 7–10 age group: *New Society,* Aug. 22, 1963.—4. Among beatniks, 'to *dig* is to like, admire, understand or be at one with' (Anderson): since ca. 1957. Ex sense 3.

dig, full. See **full dig.**

dig in, v.i. To eat heartily: since ca. 1870 (?). Cf.:—

dig in (and) fill your boots! Eat as much as you like!: Naval: C. 20. Granville. Not only your belly but also your boots.

dig out. 'To work with a will' (Granville): Naval: C. 20. 'If anyone can do any better, let him ruddy well dig out, I'm chocker with the job' (quoted by Granville). Ex mining?—2. To tidy (a hut, etc.): Army in France, 1915–18, and Army since—as in Gerald Kersh, *Boots Clean*, 1941.

dig the drape. See 'Canadian'.

Digby chicken (q.v. at **Taunton turkey**) may well be B. & L.'s error for **Digby duck** (q.v. on p. 220). Smoked herring: Canadian: since the 1880's. Ex *Digby* in Nova Scotia. (Priestley.) More precisely, 'a small, smoke-cured herring'—not in error for Digby duck, but of independent origin. (Leechman.)

digger, 1 (p. 220). See also 'Guard-Room in Army Slang'.

diggers.—4. (Often **D . . .**) 'Idealist hippies undermining capitalist economies by giving away free clothes, washing machines to needy' (Peter Fryer, Dec. 3, 1967): hippies': since 1967.

digging a grave or **digging for worms, he is** or **they are.** A cricketers' c.p. for the spectacular process known as 'gardening' (q.v. in the *Dict.*): from ca. 1905.

digging one's grave with a (or **one's**) **knife and fork.** Gluttony: jocular coll.: late C. 19–20.

digit, remove the. See **take your finger out.**

dignity. A ball given by natives (among themselves): West Indies Europeans': mid-C. 19–20. B. & L. Ex the pompous formality there rife.

dike or **dyke.**—2. (Usually *dyke*.) A Lesbian: since ca. 1935; adopted ex U.S. Origin? Hardly ex sense 1 (p. 220).

dikey or **dykey, adj.** Lesbian: since the late 1930's. Ex preceding.

dikk.—2. A variant of **dick** v. (*Dict.*).

*dil or **dill.** A simpleton; a trickster's dupe: Australian c.: C. 20. B., 1942. Ex **dilly, adj.,** 2 (*Dict.*). By 1948, low s. (Gwen Robyns in *The Evening News*, Feb. 16, 1949.) By ca. 1955, no longer low. 'Popularly believed to be an ellipsis of *dill-pickle*, which also is used as a general term of abuse' (B.P.): C. 20.

dildo. A candle: Australian girls' boarding-schools': C. 20. Cf. their c.p., *lights out at nine, candles out at ten* (o'clock).

dill-pot; dillpot; also **dillypot.** A fool: Australian: C. 20. Ex the original sense, 'female pudend', itself rhyming s. for *twat* (p. 919), as Franklyn has suggested. The 'fool' sense may, however, rhyme on S.E. *pot.*

dillo namo (p. 220). Earlier in Mayhew, I, 1851 (*dillo nemo*).

Dilly, the. Piccadilly; as, among prostitutes, *on the Dilly*, working that area of London: C. 20.

dillybags of is an Australian elaboration of **bags of** (p. 27): B., *Australia Speaks*, 1953.

dillypot. See **dill-pot.**

dim as a Toc-H lamp. (Of a person) very dull: Services': since ca. 1925; by 1960, ob. Cf. *dim*, 2 (p. 221). Common in R.A.F. until past 1960.

dim bulb. A very dull person; adj. very dull: Canadian: ca. 1918–40. (Priestley.)

*dim(-)liggies. A police van: 'Wikkel, dim-liggies ([lit.] wobble, dim lights)': Alan Nash, in

The Cape Times, June 3, 1946: South African c.: C. 20. Ex Afrikaans.

Dim Sim. A reduplicating variant of **Sim,** 3, below: Australian c. and low: since ca. 1950. *Via* pseudo-Chinese. (B.P.)

dim type. A stupid fellow (or girl): R.A.F. (hence, W.A.A.F.): since ca. 1936. Jackson. See **type.**

dim view. See **take a dim view.**

dimmer. See **nicker,** 4.

Dimmo or **Dimo.** (Only in the vocative.) A Greek: Cockney: C. 20. Ex *Demo*, short for *Demosthenes*, a very common given-name among the Greeks. Usually pronounced *Jimmo*. (Franklyn.)

dimmocking bag. A bag for the collection of subscriptions in cash; an individual's 'savings bank' for the hoarding of money for, e.g., Christmas cheer: lower classes': mid-C. 19–20; ob. B. & L.

dimp. A cigarette-end: Army: 1939 +. *The Daily Mail*, Sept. 7, 1940.

dimple. A hole, esp. a small hole, made—by a torpedo—in the side of a ship: Australian Naval: 1939–45. (B., 1943.)

di'n or even **din.** Didn't: Cockney sol.: C. 19–20. (Pamela Branch, *The Wooden Overcoat*, 1951.)

din-dins. A meal, as in 'The din-dins were fab': teenagers': since ca. 1964. Ex **din-din** (p. 221).

Dinah (p. 221). Also, in early C. 20, Australian.

*dine. Spite; malice: c. (− 1688); † by 1820. Randle Holme. Origin?

Ding. An Italian: Australian: since ca. 1920. B., 1942. Perhaps from **Dings,** 2.

ding, n. 'A hole in the fibreglass sheath of the board' (*Pix*, Sept. 28, 1963): Australian surfers': since late 1950's. Perhaps cf. **ding,** v., 1 (p. 221). —2. The bottom of anything, esp. either the buttocks or a surf-board's base: Australian: since late 1950's. (B.P.)

Ding-Dong. Inseparable nickname—perhaps esp. in Australia—for men surnamed Bell: late C. 19–20. (S. H. Courtier, *Gently Dust the Corpse*, 1960.)

ding-dong, 2. No; actively current in other circles—witness, e.g., Charles Prior, *So I Wrote It*, 1937.—3. A party: music-hall and theatrical: C. 20. Ex. sense 2.

ding dong bell. Hell, as in 'What the ding dong bell does he think he's playing at?': rhyming s.: esp. in the R.A.F. of World War II: C. 20. (Franklyn 2nd.)

dingbat.—3. A thingummy: Canadian: since ca. 1920. (Leechman.)—4. A Chinese: Australian: since ca. 1925. (B., 1943.)—5. A crank; an eccentric: Australian since ca. 1930. (Culotta.) Ex **dingbats,** 1 (p. 221).

dingbat, go like a. To travel very fast: R.A.F.: since ca. 1920.

dingbats (p. 221): since ca. 1925, gen. and common. (B.P.)

dinge, n.—3. *The dinge*, the black-out: R.A.F. bombing crews': 1939 +.—4. A Negro: low s., adopted ca. 1944 ex U.S. (Robin Cook, 1962.) The American term derives ex S.E. *dingy*. With this sense, cf. sense 2 in *Dict.*

dinger.—2. A dingo: Australian coll.: since ca. 1830. Brian Penton, *Landtakers*, 1934.—3. (Pron. *dhing-er*.) A telephone; a bell-system: Services': since early 1930's. H. & P. Echoic.—4. Short for *humdinger*, 'anything excellent': Australian: since ca. 1920. B., 1942.—5. Anus: (low) Australian: since ca. 1935. 'Don't forget that he'll get more than a gentle tap up the dinger if something really goes wrong': A. M. Harris, *The Tall Man*, 1958, but dealing with Australians in Korea, 1953. Origin? Perhaps a pun on sense 4 ('humdinger') and on **hum**, v., 4, on p. 413, as Ramsey Spencer has (1967) suggested.

dinger, do a. To dodge work: Naval (lowerdeck): C. 20.

dinghy, 1 (p. 222), occurs in Alfred Burton's narrative poem, *Johnny Newcome*, 1818. (Moe.)

dingo, n. An armoured scout car: Army: 1940–5. The term soon > coll. and then, by 1945, j.—2. A coward; a mean-spirited person; a human jackal: Australian (rather allusive coll. than s.): C. 20. (Vance Palmer, *Golconda*, 1948.) —3. Hence, a treacherous person: since ca. 1900. (B., *Australia Speaks*, 1953.) Ex *dingo on.*—4. A batman: Australian soldiers' (esp. in New Guinea): 1942–5. Cf. *dingbat* (p. 221).

dingo, v. To shirk; to quit, back out of: Australian coll.: since ca. 1910. Jon Cleary, *The Sundowners*, 1952, 'I don't think he's dingoing the race'.

dingo on, v. To betray (someone); to fail (him): Australian: since ca. 1910. V., 1942.

dingus (see **dinges**, p. 222). By 1930 at latest, English too. K. R. G. Brown, *As We Lie*, 1937.

Dink. A Chinese: Australian: since ca. 1920. Baker in *The Observer*, Nov. 13, 1938. Perversion of *Chink* on *dinge*. Franklyn 2nd holds it to be rhyming s. on *Chink*.

dink, n. and v. See **double-dink.**—2, n. and adj. See **true dinkum.**—3. See **hammer**, 4.

dinker. Something (very) good: Australian: since ca. 1925. Baker. Cf. **dinkum** and **dinky die** (in *Dict.*).

dinkum (p. 222) prob. dates from ca. 1890: cf. S. B. Lancaster, *Jim of the Ranges*, 1940, '"Straight dinkum?" It was the old touchwood of their boyhood.' Hence, 'Are you fair dinkum?' = Are you telling me the truth? (Culotta.)

dinkum, the; the dinkum article. The genuine thing, the right person: Australian: C. 20. B., 1942. See **dinkum** (p. 222).

dinkum Aussie. A native Australian: Australian: late C. 19–20. (B., 1943.)

dinky, adj.—2. True; genuine: Australian: since ca. 1925. (B., 1943.) Ex:—

dinky, the. The truth: Australian: since ca. 1920. Baker. Short for **dinky die** (p. 222).

dinner for tea, be. To be easy, 'money for jam'; extremely pleasant or profitable: Cockney coll.: from ca. 1890. Pugh.

dinner pail, pass in one's. See **pass in one's dinner pail** and cf. **pass in one's checks** (*Dict.*).

dinnyhayser is the usual post-1930 form of **Dinny Hayes-er** (p. 222).—2. Hence, something notable: Australian: since ca. 1910. (B., 1943.)

dinting. 'Digging out old ballast (SR)': railwaymen's: C. 20. *Railway*, 3rd. Ex North Country dial. *dinting*, 'the taking up of the bottom of a colliery road, in order to enlarge the road' (E.D.D.).

Dinty. 'Inevitable' nickname for a male Moore: esp. in Services: C. 20. Cf. **Pony**(*Dict.*).

dip, n.—7. Diphtheria; a patient suffering from diphtheria; a case of diphtheria: medical, esp. nurses': C. 20. 'We had three dips in this

morning'; 'It's dip, you know.'—8. A sort of doughnut: Australian: since ca. 1910. (B., 1943.)—9. A simpleton: Australian: since ca. 1925. (B., 1943.)

Sense 1, on p. 223, may have, at first, been 'a pocket', for it is so defined by Renton Nicholson in his *Autobiography*, 1860, at p. 19. Sense 6, on p. 222, has a derivative nuance: 'melted bacon fat, usually a favourite with children when poured from frying-pan onto plate' (Peter Ibbotson, Feb. 9, 1963): late C. 19–20; in C. 20, no longer low.

dip, v.—6. (Ex sense 5: p. 222). Also *be dipped*: to be reduced in rank, for some misdemeanour: Naval: C. 20.—7. To fail, as in 'I dipped by five marks': Naval: since ca. 1930.

dip (or D.), the. The assistant purser: nautical, esp. ship's stewards': C. 20. Dave Marlowe, *Coming, Sir!*, 1937.

dip chick. A diver: Naval: C. 20. Granville, 'Corruption of Dabchick, or Little Grebe, a small diving bird'.

dip one's killick. (Of a Leading Hand) to be disrated: Naval: C. 20. Granville, '[Killick is] the anchor which symbolised his rate'—cf. the R.A.F. **props.**

dip one's wick; bury it. (Of the male) to have sexual intercourse: low: from ca. 1880, 1860 resp.

dip south. See **south, dip.**

dip the clutch. To de-clutch at the wrong moment: Army Mechanical Transport: 1939 +. (Peter Chamberlain, letter of Sept. 22, 1942.)

dipper!, in your. A New Zealand defiant c.p. of ca. 1920–40. R. G. C. McNab in *The Press* (Christchurch, N.Z.), April 2, 1938.

Dippy Street. Dieppe Street, West Kensington, London, W.14: locals': late C. 19–20.

dire. Unpleasant; objectionable; inferior: middle-class: since ca. 1930.

directly minute. Immediately; forthwith; this very minute: lower-class, esp. Cockney, coll.: from ca. 1870. W. Pett Ridge, *Minor Dialogues*, 1895, '"Oist me up on this seat, Robert, dreckly minute, there's a good soul.'

dirt.—5. Anti-aircraft fire: R.A.F.: since late 1939. H. & P. Cf. **shit.**—6. Bad weather: Coastal Command, R.A.F.: 1940 +. Flying-Officer Robert Hinde, letter of March 17, 1945.—7. Scandal: adopted ca. 1932 from the U.S.A. Cf. sense 4 and see **dirt?, what's the** (p. 223).—8. A mean or evil spirit or temper, in, e.g., a horse: Australian coll.: since ca. 1910. (K. S. Prichard, *Working Bullocks*, 1926.)—9. A trump card, esp. if unexpected ('He's put a bit of dirt on it'): cardplayers': since ca. 1945.

dirt, in the. In trouble: mostly R.A.F.: since ca. 1925. (P-G-R.)—2. adv. and adj. Derailed: railwaymen's: C. 20. (*Railway* 2nd.)

dirt, put in the; do dirt on. To act unfairly (towards someone): Australian: since ca. 1905, 1920, resp. B., 1942.

dirt and grease. Marine indications of a gathering storm: nautical: ? ca. 1800–50. (W. N. Glascock, *Sailors and Saints* (I, 184), 1829.) Cf. **greasy,** 1, on p. 351. Moe.

dirt (on), have the. To know some scandal (about someone): since ca. 1930. Cf. *What's the dirt?*, q.v. at **dirt . . . on** p. 223.

dirt on your tapes!, get some. Get some experience as an N.C.O.: Services: since ca. 1925. H. & P.

dirt-shoot. See **giggy**.

dirt's coming out, the. Now we're getting the truth: c.p., often with implication *in vino veritas*: since the late 1930's.

dirty, adj. Is—in low, and in semi-literate, English—often used as a mere intensive, not in the least pejorative: since ca. 1910 (perhaps from a decade earlier). 'He [Dante] meets another geezer down there called Virgil or something, and they make dirty great speeches at each other' (Norman). Cf. *dirty big* and *dirty great*.

dirty, do the.—2. Esp. *do the dirty on* a girl, to seduce her and then abandon her: since ca. 1913.

dirty barrel, have a. To have V.D.: Naval: late C. 19–20. Ex '*gun*-barrel'.

dirty big. A variant of **dirty great**: mostly Services': since ca. 1910. Among Australians, it has, since ca. 1920, tended to synonymise *bloody*: B., 1943.

dirty daughter. Water: rhyming s.: C. 20. (Franklyn 2nd.) Perhaps suggested by the words of a popular song: '. . . water,/In which you wash(ed) your dirty daughter'.

Dirty Dick's (or **Dicks**). The venereal ward in a military or other Service hospital: mostly Canadian: C. 20. A pun on s. *dick*, penis, and on a once-famous low London resort.

dirty dog. A lecher: coll., often jocular: since ca. 1880.

dirty dogs smell their own stuff first. A low Glasgow c.p.: C. 20. Cf. *foxes*.

dirty end, get—or be handed—the. To come off the worse in a deal or an encounter: coll. C. 20. ('Sapper', *The Third Round*, 1924, has the second form.)

dirty face?, who're you (or **who yer**) **calling.** Concerning the latter half of 1916, Richard Blaker, in his memorable War-novel (written from the viewpoint of the Artillery officer), *Medal without Bar*, 1930, remarks: ' "'Oo yer calling dirty-face?" ' became a standardised pleasantry in the light of a lantern held to a cigarette-stump, from drivers turned muleteer ("the cavalry", as the gunners called them).'

dirty great. A strong pejorative: Services: since ca. 1910. E.g. 'That dirty great bastard'.

Dirty Half-Mile, the. King's Cross Road, Sydney: mostly N.S.W.: since ca. 1925. (B., 1943.) Rough and tough.

Dirty Little Imps, the. The Durham Light Infantry: military: late C. 19–20. Punning on *D.L.I.*

dirty look. A look of contempt or strong dislike, as in 'He gave me a dirty look': coll.: late C. 19–20.

dirty money. Extra pay for very dirty work: labour coll.: C. 20.

dirty night at sea. 'A nocturnal drinking bout' (Baker): Australian: C. 20.

dirty old Jew. In the game of House, it means 'two': rhyming s.: C. 20. (Franklyn, *Rhyming*.)

dirty old man. A c.p., descriptive of or addressed to a middle-aged womanizer: C. 20.

dirty one. A bad wound: hence, a misfortune: Army: 1914–18, then ob. At first, of a wound that turns septic.

dirty 'ore. In House, thirty-four: rhyming s.: C. 20. (Franklyn, ibid.)

dirty sacks. Bedding: London Fire Brigade: C. 20. Ex sleeping bags?

dirty thing. Adolescent girls' term to, or for, a boy that becomes amorous: coll.: late (? mid) C. 19–20.

dirty water off one's chest, get the. (Of men) to obtain sexual relief by emission: low: C. 20.

dirty week-end. A week-end spent with one's mistress; jocularly, with one's wife but without the children: mostly (? orig.) Australian: since ca. 1930. (B.P.)

dis or **diss**, v.—3. Mostly as ppl. adj., **dissed**, disconnected: wireless s.: from ca. 1930. *The Wireless World*, Feb. 26, 1937, 'There's no warning whistle to tell [the wireless listener] the speaker is "dissed".'

Disappointments Board, the. The University Appointments Board: undergraduates' (esp. Oxford and Cambridge): since ca. 1950.

disaster (p. 223). Renewed by the Army in North Africa: 1940–43.

disc (or **disk**) **jockey.** A radio man whose job it is to play records and comment on them: adopted, ca. 1955, ex U.S.; by 1965, coll.

discip sergeant. A disciplinary sergeant: R.A.F. coll.: 1940 +.

disco. A repository for gramophone discs, i.e. a *discothèque*: music-lovers': since ca. 1955.—2. Hence, 'a club where music is provided by disc or tape as apart from a live = performing group' (*Woman's Own*, July 31, 1965): since ca. 1960.

discuss. A discussion: girls' Public Schools': since ca. 1925. (Nancy Spain, *Poison for Teacher*, 1949.)

disease. Weather erosion or chemical-fumes deterioration of statues or buildings: since ca. 1940. Ex the leprous appearance they assume.

disembark. Disembarkation leave: Services', esp. Army: 1939–45.

disguddy blusting. A transposition of *bloody disgusting*: schoolgirls': ca. 1935–50.

disgustigating. A playful deformation of *disgusting*: since ca. 1910.

dish, n.—2. A girl; (young) woman: adopted since ca. 1936 from U.S. James Curtis, *They Ride by Night*, 1938. For semantics, cf. **crackling**, **crumpet**, and—in *Dict.*—**tart**. Shakespeare adumbrates the term.—3. Hence, among Teddy boys, an attractive girl: since ca. 1953. Also *doll* or *tart*.—4. Buttocks, posterior: homosexual: since ca. 1954. Ex senses 2 and 3.—5. Any attractive person, of either sex: since ca. 1955. Ex senses 2 and 3. 'Screen dishes can be dark, fair, tall or tiny, but *never* tubby': *Woman*, Oct. 23, 1965. Of senses 2, 3, Ramsey Spencer writes on July 10, 1968, 'Since the early 1960's also applied by girls to men, in my hearing.'

dish, v.—2. To assault, to 'beat up', with variant *dish up*: Australian, mostly juvenile and teenage: since ca. 1945. (B.P.)

dish-down. A disappointment: C. 20. Logan Pearsall Smith, *Words and Idioms*, 1925. Cf. **dish**, n. and v. (p. 224).

dish it out. To be either physically or verbally severe towards others: since ca. 1925. Cf. the c.p. 'he can dish it out, but he can't take it' and **dish out** on p. 224.—2. To hand out punishment, information or, indeed, anything else, with ease and rapidity: Canadian, since ca. 1926; English, since ca. 1940. (Leechman.)

dish-lick. See **scissors-grinder**.

dish up. To wash up: Naval (cook's galley): since ca. 1920. (P-G-R.)—2. See **dish** v., 2.

dished.—2. Of a car's steering wheel: having its hub lower than its rim: Australian motorists': since ca. 1940. (B.P.)

dished up, look. To look 'washed up': Australian: since ca. 1930. (Margaret Trist, 1944.)

dishy. Attractive: since ca. 1960. Julian Rathbone, *Hand Out*, 1968, 'Dishy, I call him': Ramsey Spencer, letter of July 10, 1968. Ex dish, n., s.

dispense, n. A dispensary: since ca. 1910.

dispense with. To dispose of: catachrestic: C. 20. 'The moment he had dispensed with all the formalities . . ., he was not long in starting,' writes an able young novelist in 1935.

displace. See replace.

distance, go or last the full. See go the full distance.

district of sappers, the. 'Those who sap at [study hard] their quarto and folio volumes,' *Spy*, 1825: Oxford: ca. 1815–50.

dit.—2. A story, a yarn: Australian Naval: since ca. 1930. (B., 1943.) Ex nautical ditties.

ditch (last entry on p. 224). Strictly, to throw overboard: Granville.—2. To land (an aircraft) on the sea: R.A.F.: since ca. 1939.—3. (Ex sense 1.) To discard (something no longer useful): since ca. 1942: originally, R.A.F.

Ditch, the. Post-1920, also Houndsditch, London.—4. The Fleet Street taxicab rank: taxi-drivers': since ca. 1910. Herbert Hodge, *Cab, Sir?*, 1939. Ex that brook, the Fleet Ditch, which formerly ran, above ground, to join the River Thames south of Fleet Street.—5. The English Channel: Air Force: 1939–45. A specialisation of sense 2 (p. 225).

ditched, be or get. To come down into the sea: R.A.F.: since ca. 1938; by 1943, j. Either ex 'to be ditched' or, more probably, ex 'the Ditch' (sense 2, *Dict.*). After 1940 usually v.i.; as, e.g., in 'We had to ditch soon after we left the French coast'.

dithered. Tipsy: Australian: since ca. 1925. Baker.

ditto, smut. A variant (to a woman) of *ditto, brother smut!*, q.v. in *Dict.* at brother smut.

ditty box. 'A small wooden box . . . issued to seamen; displaced by the more convenient attaché case. . . . Believed to be a shortened form of "commodity box",' Granville: Naval: ca. 1890–1930.

div, n.—2. Division (military): Army: C. 20. Cf. divvy (p. 225).

dive, take a. To lose a boxing match—for a (considerable) bribe: sporting world: since ca. 1920. To the canvas.

Divi. Divinity as school or university subject: late C. 19–20.

diving suit. A condom: industrial Australia, esp. N.S.W.: since ca. 1945. A raffish pun.

divorced, be. To lose one's girl; (of a girl) to lose one's boy: Australian jocular, esp. teenagers': since ca. 1950. 'You'd better take her out more often, or you'll be divorced.' (B.P.)

divoteer. A golfer: Australian: ca. 1925–45; not very general. (B., 1943.)

divvi. Variant of divvy, 2 (p. 225); cf. quotation at dewey above.

divvy-hunter. One who joins a co-operative society merely to share in the dividends: since ca. 1910.

dix. See dibs.

dixie.—4. An ice-cream carton: Australian: since ca. 1919. Baker. Ex 2.

dizzy, adj.—2. Rather tipsy: 1791, *The New Vocal Enchantress* (p. 33); † by 1890.—3. Scatter-brained; wild; foolish: since ca. 1930.

dizzy blonde. 'A highly conspicuous blonde, both in appearance and in behaviour' (Leechman): Canadian: adopted, ca. 1935, ex U.S.; by 1956, fairly common in England. Cf. preceding, sense 3.

dizzy limit, the (p. 226) is, since ca. 1930, predominantly 'the final touch, the last straw' (B., 1943).

dlinkie. 'Facetious and pseudo-juvenile and pidgin for *drink*' (Leechman): Canadian: since ca. 1920.

do, n. Senses 2 and 4 are merged in the following quot'n from *Boxiana*, IV, 1824, 'How this particular course of lectures succeeded we do not find . . .; but the *spec* failed, as a generally profitable *do*.'—6. A gang fight: teenage gangsters': since ca. 1955. Cf. senses 4 and 5 on p. 266.

do, v., 1 (p. 226): occurs, in nuance 'to deceive', in W. N. Glascock, *Sketch-Book*, I (208), 1825. (Moe.)—11. To coït (with a girl): low: C. 20. Cf. senses 3 and 4 (p. 226).—12. To perpetrate sodomy upon: low: C. 20.

do a bitter; do a wet. See do a beer (*Dict.*).

do a Chloe. To appear in the nude: Australian, esp. Melbourne: late C. 19–20. A pre-1900 Melbourne Art Gallery reject of a nude painting of Chloe hangs in a well-known Australian hotel. (B.P.)

do a four-o-six (406). To make a routine inspection of vehicles: Army: 1939–45. Ex the relevant Army 'book'.

do a good turn to. To afford (a woman) sexual satisfaction: male coll., mostly jocular: C. 20.

do a job, 1. Orig., and still mostly, to commit a burglary; and English at first: *Sessions*, March 12, 1878.—2. To defecate: Australian, mainly: C. 20. B., 1942.—3 . To render a woman pregnant: Australian: C. 20. Baker.

do a job for oneself. To defecate: C. 20. Cf. sense 2 of preceding.

do a knock—or do a knock line—with. To be amorously interested in—and involved with—a member of the opposite sex: Australian: low: C. 20. Baker. Cf. knocking-shop (*Dict.*).

do a line with. To walk out with (a girl): originally and mostly Anglo-Irish: C. 20.

do a man over. See do over, 4.

do a Nelson. To withstand danger, or extreme difficulty, in a confident spirit: mostly Cockney: late C. 19–20. 'Knowing that whatever may befall, as upon Nelson on his column in Trafalgar Square, one will, like him, "be there" to-morrow' (Laurie Atkinson, July 1, 1948).—2. Hence, to be in irrepressibly good spirits: a 'London Blitz' word among Civil Defence on duty: late 1940–mid-1941, then at intervals until 1945.

do a never. See never.

do a Penang. To run away; to retreat ingloriously: Australian airmen's: 1942–5. (B., 1943.) Ex the British and Australian retreat down Malaya.

do a perish. Almost to die for lack of a drink: Australian: since ca. 1920. Baker.

do a rural (p. 226). Also *do an agricultural one*: C. 20.

do a rush. See **rush, do a** (*Dict.*).

do a tumble. See **do a spread** (*Dict.*).

do as you like. A bicycle: rhyming s. (on *bike*): late C. 19–20.

do-badder. An actively bad person: coll.: since ca. 1960. Prompted by **do-gooder,** 2, below.

do-do (pron. *doo-doo*). To excrete; excreta: school-children's: late C. 19–20. Hence, *do-do noise,* a fart.

do for, 3 (to kill), occurs so early as 1740. *Sessions,* July 1740, trial of Stephen Saunders.

do-gooder. An inveterate busybody, intent on reforming everybody's soul but his own: Canadian coll.: since ca. 1946. (Leechman.)—2. Hence, *do-gooders,* people who interest themselves in social work: English coll., became at all general only ca. 1957. (*The* Bournemouth *Evening Echo,* July 7, 1959.) Hence, since ca. 1960, the occ. *do-goodery.*

do hickey. See **hickey.**

do I ducks! 'Do I hell!'; I do *not!*: Cockney c.p.: C. 20. Euphemistic for *do I fuck!*

do I owe you anything? or **what do I owe you?** A c.p. addressed to someone staring rudely or reasonlessly at the speaker: late C. 19–20.

do in.—7. To steal: low: late C. 19–20. *Sessions,* July 1, 1905: A. Neil Lyons, *Sixpenny Pieces,* 1909.

do in the eye. To cheat: late C. 19–20. Ex idea of a nasty punch in the eye. Cf. *do,* v, 1.

do it. To coït: when not merely euphemistic, it is coll.: C. 18–20.

do it again, Ikey, I saw diamonds. Say it again, for it's a bit too good to be true: proletarian c.p.: ca. 1900–14. W. L. George, *The Making of an Englishman,* 1914.

do it now! (p. 227): still common in Australia. (B.P., 1965.)

do it on (someone). To swindle (v.t.), impose on: low: since ca. 1890. *Sessions,* Dec. 19, 1901.—2. Hence (?), to forestall, anticipate; get the better of, outdo, be too good for; since ca. 1905.

do it on the d.h. (damned head) is a variant of **do on one's head** (*Dict.*).

do it the hard way. A derisive c.p., shouted at an awkward workman struggling at his job; mostly preceded by *that's right!* and occasionally rounded off with *standing up in a hammock*: Canadian: since ca. 1910 (?). Leechman.

do-it-yourself. Masturbation: since ca. 1950. (Nicholas Monsarrat, *The Nylon Pirates,* 1960.)

do it yourself kit. 'Steam locomotives' (*Railway,* 3rd): railwaymen's: since ca. 1950. Ironic.

do(-)me(-)dag; usually pl., **do-me-dags.** A cigarette: low rhyming s.: late C. 19–20. Rhyming on *fag.*

do me good. A Woodbine cigarette: rhyming: late C. 19–20.—2. Timber: carpenters' and other workmen's rhyming s. on *wood*: late C. 19–20. (Franklyn 2nd.)

do one for the King. To be on a 24-hour guard: Army: 1902 +.

do one's cash. To spend, to lose one's money: Australian: C. 20. Baker.

do one's dags. Cigarettes: rhyming s. on *fags*: ca. 1890–1920. Franklyn 2nd.

do one's dough. To lose one's money: mostly Australian: since ca. 1925.

do one's fealty. See 'Tavern terms', § 9.

do one's luck. To be out of luck: Australian: C. 20. Baker.

do one's nut.—2. To explode with anger: since ca. 1945. Cf. **blow one's top** above.

do one's pegs is Australian and synonymous with *do one's block,* q.v. at *block, lose the* (p. 65). B., 1943.

do one's stuff (p. 227) is coll., rather than s.; is English, rather than American; and is very much older than I had supposed. George Fox, the Quaker, in his Journal for the year 1663 wrote: 'A while after, when the priest had done his stuff, they came to the friends again.' (With thanks to Alexander McQueen, letter of 1953.)

do others before they do you! A post-1920 c.p. variation of *do unto others as you would be done by.*

do over.—4. To *do the rank over* is to take position in a taxicab park other than one's usual: taxi-drivers': since ca. 1912. Herbert Hodge, *Cab, Sir?,* 1939. Prob. ex sense 3. But *do a man over* is to take a fare rightfully another driver's: Hodge.

do polly. See **polly, do.**

do-re-mi (pron. *dough-ray-me*). Money, esp. cash: Australian, adopted—ca. 1945—ex U.S.; but since late 1930's in Canada. An elaboration of **dough,** 2 (p. 237) and a pun on the tonic sol-fa.

do some good for oneself. (Of the male) to be amorously successful: Australian: C. 20. B., 1942.

do tell! Really?; you don't mean it: Canadian c.p., often ironic or sarcastic: since ca. 1950. (Leechman.) Adopted ex (the American) New England, where current since ca. 1920.

do the lot. To lose all one's money: coll.: C. 20.

do the spin. At two-up, to toss the coins: Australian: late C. 19–20. Baker.

do the tap. To win a game of cards; mostly as vbl n., *doing the tap*: Army: C. 20.

do they have ponies down a pit? See 'Cockney catch phrases . . .'

do things by penny numbers, i.e. by instalments or spasms: mid-C. 19–20; since ca. 1914, slightly ob. Ex novels so published ca. 1840–80.

do things to. See **make go all unnecessary.**

do what the steer did. To, at the least, try: Canadian: since ca. 1920. 'From the observed efforts of these underprivileged animals to lead a normal love-life' (Leechman).

do you know any other funny stories? A c.p., meaning 'Do you think I'm green?' or implying 'You're a leg-puller, or a liar': since ca. 1935.

do you spit much with that cough? A Canadian c.p. (of ca. 1910–30), addressed to one who has just broken wind.

do you think you'll know me again? or **you'll know me again, won't you!** A c.p. addressed to someone staring, esp. to a person one knows: C. 20.

do you want—or simply an abrupt **want—to buy a battleship?** A c.p., equivalent to 'Do you want to make water?'—often addressed to a man that one (what humour! what wit!) has playfully awakened: R.A.F.: 1940 +. Partridge, 1945. Elaboration of **pump ship,** 1 (p. 667), with an ironic veiled reference to flag days.

dob in. To inform on (someone): Australian, esp. teenage gangsters': since ca. 1930. 'He wouldn't dob me in, I knew that' (Dick). Ex the widespread English dial. *dob,* to put down heavily, to throw down.

dobash. A girl friend: Naval (lower-deck): since ca. 1925. (P-G-R.) She may—or may not —do a 'bash'.

dobbin.—3. A rum-container: Army in the East: 1942–5. (C. J. Rolo, *Wingate's Raiders*, 1944.) Ex the S.E. *dobbin*, a small drinking-vessel.

dobeying (see **dhobi**, 2, in *Dict.*): earlier recorded in 'Taffrail'.

dobs. The Sherborne shape of **dibs** (prayers): see above.

doby is a loose spelling of *dhob(e)y*: see **dhobi** (p. 217).

doc, 1. In Naval Wardrooms, the usual C. 20 address to the ship's surgeon. Granville. But, on the lower deck, *doc* always, in address, means a sick-berth attendant, the doctor himself being, in reference, *the quack*. Also, in Army from at least as early as 1939, a medical orderly.

dock, in. (Of motor cars) being serviced or re-paired: motorists': since ca. 1920.

docker.—3. A large sum of money; *go a docker*, spend much money: Australian: since ca. 1925. B., 1942. Origin?

dockers' ABC, the. *A*le, *b*accy, *c*unt: British docksides, mostly dockers' (esp. Liverpool): late C. 19–20.

dockie (or **-y**). A dock labourer: coll.: since ca. 1880. (Ernest Raymond, *The Marsh*, 1937.)

dockyard matey. A dockyard worker: Naval coll.: prob. since ca. 1810. Occurs in Kipling, *A Fleet in Being*, 1898; Captain Sherard Osborn, *ArcticJournal*, 1852, as Rear-Admiral P. W. Brock, D.S.O., tells me; and, very much earlier, in W. N. Glascock, *Sailors and Saints* (II, 115), 1829. Moe.

dockyarder. Earlier in *Sinks*, 1848.

docs. Documents, in the sense of a soldier's, sailor's, airman's official papers (attestation form, medical rating, classification, etc., etc., etc.): Services' coll.: C. 20. Jackson.

Doctor. See 'Tavern terms', § 3, *b*.

doctor, n.—14. See **magic doctors**, which it occ. shortens: rare after 1943.—15. A journeyman in collar and tie: tailors': C. 20.

doctor, v.—9. To dock (lambs): Australian: late C. 19–20. Archer Russell, *Gone Nomad*, 1936. Cf. senses 6–8 (p. 229).

Doctor Cotton. See **Johnny Cotton**.

Doctor Crippen. Dripping (the culinary n.): rhyming s.: C. 20.

Doctor Jim (p. 229). The derivative forms are obviously of the same origin as **cunt cap**.

Doctor Livingstone, I presume. This c.p., adopted from H. M. Stanley's greeting, 1871, in the African jungle, was originally (ca. 1900) a skit on Englishmen's proverbial punctiliousness, no matter what the circumstances; but, by ca. 1920, it was extended to almost any chance, or unexpected, meeting, whether between strangers or even between friends.

doctor's orders. 9 in the game of House; Army: C. 20. Michael Harrison. Ex the inevit-able 'No. 9 pill'. Also *doctor's favourite*.

doddering Dick. A Maxim gun; hence, any machine-gun: Naval: 1939–45. (P-G-R.)

doddle (p. 229). By 1940, fairly general, but low. (Norman.)—2. A 'walk-over': racing: since ca. 1920. Ex *dawdle*? or ex *toddle*?—3. Esp. in 'It's a doddle'—easy, simple: R.A.F., since ca. 1945; by 1955, widespread. Ex sense 1 (p. 229)?

Sense 2 was also, by the middle 1940's, gen. s., as in 'Pity you didn't come last night. It was a doddle' (Zoe Progl, *Woman of the Underworld*, 1964).

doddle, v. To 'walk it' or win very easily: racing: since ca. 1925. John Winton, *Never Go to Sea*, 1963, (of a filly) 'I think she started at even money but anyway she doddled it.' Ex sense 2 of the n.—unless it was the other way about.

Dodd's Sound. 'Where the candidate will have to acknowledge the receipt of a certificate em-powering him to float down Bachelor Creek' (i.e. to become a B.A.), *Spy*, 1825: Oxford University: ca. 1815–50. Ex a Vice-Chancellor's name?

***dodge, v.** To track (a person) stealthily: c.: from ca. 1830: ob. Dickens, *Oliver Twist*.

dodge the draft. See **draft-dodger**.

Dodger.—2. A fairly common nickname for men surnamed *Brown*: C. 20. Contrast sense 6 of **dodger** on p. 229.

dodger, 2. Earlier in J. Wright, *Mornings at Bow Street*, 1824.—10. Bread; food: Australian: since ca. 1918. Baker. (Ex sense 8.) n.—11. A leaflet: Canadian printers' and journalists': C. 20. (Leechman.)—12. 'A canvas screen on the bridge of small craft as protection against the weather.' (Naval colloquialism): C. 20. (P-G-R). —13. A shunting truck: railwaymen's, mostly Western: C. 20. (*Railway.*) It 'dodges about', all over the yard.

Sense 11 is, more precisely, 'a printed sheet, usually on coloured paper, and on one side only, for distribution from door to door advertising something or other' (Leechman, April 1967): since ca. 1910.

dodger, adj. First-class, excellent, fine: Aus-tralian: since late 1930's. (B., 1943; Dal Stivens, *The Gambling Ghost*, 1953.)

dodger, a hunk of. A slice of bread: Australian: since ca. 1920. (Culotta.) Cf. **dodger**, 10, above.

dodgy. 2. Hence, ingenious or neat: school-boys': late C. 19–20. Atkinson.—3. Difficult or complicated or tricky; risky; likely to become dangerous, esp. of a situation, a transaction, a concerted action: since ca. 1943. In, e.g., the film *Seven Days to Noon*, 1950; Norman. But foreshadowed in G. B. Shaw, *Mrs Warren's Pro-fession*, 1894.—4. Hence, stolen; esp. in *dodgy gear*, stolen property: since ca. 1955.

Doe. A Dornier 'plane: R.A.F.: 1939 +. Partridge, 1945. Ex the official abbr., *Do*.

doe. See 'Harlots'.—2. A girl, a woman: mostly University of Oxford: late C. 19–early 20. Compton Mackenzie, *Thin Ice*, 1956.

doesn't care what he (or **she**) **spends when he** (or **she**) **has nothing, he** (or **she**). A c.p. applied to one who, pockets empty of money, talks as if he had much: since ca. 1925.

doesn't know enough to pee down wind. 'A c.p. directed against a very stupid fellow' (Leechman): mostly Canadian: since ca. 1920.

dog, n.—9. A plain-clothes railway detective: Australian c.: C. 20. B., 1942.—10. A police 'shadow': Australian police: since the 1920's. (Vince Kelly, *The Shadow*, 1955.)—11. See **Malta dog.**—12. Food: Aus. rural: C. 20. (B., 1959.) Cf. **dogs**, 1, in *Dict.*—13. A drinking debt: Aus. urban: C. 20. Ibid.

dog. v.—3. See **wild-dog** below.

dog, tie up a. To book drinks in a bar, esp. at hotel: Australian: since ca. 1925. (B., 1943.)

dog, turn. See **turn dog** below.

dog act, the. See **blackfellows' act.**—2. Any such Act, or part of an Act, of Parliament as enables people to follow a profession even though they are not academically qualified to do so: Australian: since ca. 1955. (B.P.)

dog and bone. Telephone (mostly n.): rhyming s.: since ca. 1945. Franklyn 2nd.

dog-biscuit.—2. The staple biscuit issued to troops on active service: Army: 1914–18. Unsalted, unflavoured—and damned hard!

dog-box. A passenger carriage on rural railway services: Australian: C. 20. B., 1942. 'Refers only to carriages without corridors. Each compartment has its own door to the platform and its own w.c.' (B.P.)

dog-cart. A police car: Australian: since ca. 1920. Jocular. (Dick.)

dog-catchers. A train crew sent to relieve a crew that has become **outlawed**: Canadian railroadmen's (— 1931).

dog clutch. 'A disconnectable coupling,' H. & P.: R.A.F.: since ca. 1930.

dog-collar.—2. 'Broad necklace usually of small pearls worn tightly round the neck': Society: C. 20. Raymond Mortimer, in *The Listener*, March 10, 1937.—3. A tunic with collar hooking together at front (no shirt-collar or tie being worn): R.A.F.: ca. 1918–37, the present style being introduced ca. 1937.

Dog Collar Act, the. The Transport Workers' Act: Australian: B., 1942.

dog(-)dancing. 'Useless and exaggerated activity, such as a dog indulges in, capering with glee at the return of his master' (Douglas Leechman, July 31, 1967): orig. and mostly Canadian: since late 1966 or early 1967.

dog-end (q.v. in *Dict.*) is also low Cockney of C. 20: witness *The Evening News*, Dec. 21, 1936. It is prob. a corruption of *docked end*; a cigarette that is kept for another smoke has first been quenched or docked. The term has, since ca. 1927, been fairly gen., though it is still low.

dog-fashion, have it. To coït *à posteriori*: low coll.: C. 20. Cf. *dogways*.

dog-fight.—2. A regimental sergeant major's badge: Army: since ca. 1930. Cf. *fighting cats.*

dog-fight buttons. The buttons on a General Service overcoat: Army: since ca. 1930.

dog(-)house. A caboose: Canadian railroadmen's (— 1931).—2. See **fish-horn.**

dog-house, in the. In disgrace or bad odour: since ca. 1954. A man fallen out with his wife may say, 'I'm in the dog-house.' Ex dogs banished from house to kennel.

dog in a blanket (p. 230). No; prob. at least a decade earlier, for the term occurs in Edward Stirling's one-act play, *Mrs Coudle's Curtain Lecture*, 1845. (Moe.)

dog(-)leg. A good-conduct stripe: Services': since ca. 1925. H. & P., 'Shaped like a pair of legs'.

dog licence. 'A Certificate of Exemption to allow an aboriginal to buy a drink in a hotel' (B., 1959): since late 1940's.

dog list, be on the. To be debarred from drinking: Australian: since ca. 1920. B., 1942.

dog-napping. (The practice of) stealing pets: low: C. 20.

dog out. To keep watch: low: since ca. 1945. Maurice Procter, *His Weight in Gold*, 1966, '''You

can have Harry to dog out for you''' and 'Higgs left Wayman dogging out at the corner'.

dog-robbers. Civilian clothes (usually tweeds) worn by officers on shore leave: Naval: since ca. 1900. Granville. In, e.g., John Winton, *We Saw the Sea*, 1960 (p. 156).

dog-rough. Very unpleasant, hard: Services': since ca. 1920. (P-G-R.) Rough—even for a dog.

dog see the rabbit, let the. A c.p. in reference to one who wishes to do or see something: mostly in Services': C. 20. Atkinson.

dog-stiffener. A professional dingo-killer: Australian: C. 20. B., 1942.—2. Usually in pl., *dog-stiffeners*, leather leggings: Australian: since ca. 1910. Baker.

dog-tag. An identity disc: since ca. 1941, and after 1950 the commonest of all the Australian synonyms. (B.P.)

dog-walloper. A stick; a cudgel; a policeman's baton: Australian: C. 20. Baker.

dog-walloping. Picking up the ends of cigars and cigarettes: theatrical: ca. 1810–50.

dog(-)watch. esp. *on the dog-watch*, on night duty: Services': since ca. 1920. H. & P. Ex nautical j.—2. 'To say of a man that he hasn't been in the Service ''half a dog-watch'' is to imply that he is still in the green New Entry stage,' Granville: C. 20.

dog-whipper. 'Superintends work of pony drivers and leaders in metal mines' (*Evening News*, Sept. 28, 1953): industrial: C. 20.

dogger, 3; dogging. A *dogger* is one who practises *dogging*, the collecting, cleaning and selling of *dog*-end tobacco (cf. **dog-walloping**): 1941 +.

Dogger Bank Dragoons, the. The Royal Marines, esp. the commandos: Naval: since ca. 1914; slightly ob. (James Spenser, *The Awkward Marine*, 1948.)

doggers. 'Multi-coloured swim shorts' (*Pix*, Sept. 28, 1963): Australian surfers': since ca. 1960. Ex 'putting on *dog*' or 'side'.

doggery.—2. Nonsense: proletarian: mid-C. 19–20; ob. B. & L.

Dogget coat and badge. A variant of **coat and badge** (p. 163). Franklyn (*Rhyming*).

Doggie (or -y) Day. New Year's Day: Post Office officials': C. 20. Ex the dog-licences renewable then.

doggie, doggy. 5. For the second nuance, an earlier record is afforded by 'Taffrail'.

doggin (mostly in pl.). A cigarette-butt: New Zealanders': since ca. 1930. An adaptation—? rather a slovening—of **dog-end**. (J. H. Henderson, *Inglorious Gunner*, 1945.)

dogging. See **dogger** above.

Doggo. Nickname for a plain-featured person: Naval: C. 20. Granville.

doggy, n.—6. A 'hot dog': Australian: since ca. 1944. Ruth Park, *Poor Man's Orange*, 1950.—7. 'Platelayer. (ER)': railwaymen's: C. 20. (*Railway*, 3rd.) Possibly of mining origin, but more likely humorous.

dogman. That workman who travels with the load of a crane: Australian: since ca. 1930, (Robert Clark, *The Dogman and Other Poems*, 1962.)

dogs, 1. Post-1925, it tends to mean 'hot cooked sausages'. Short for *hot dogs*. E. C. Vivian, *Ladies in the Case*, 1933.—4. Feet: adopted, ca. 1935, from U.S. But *dogs that bite* seems to be an English elaboration, since ca. 1944, for sore feet.—5. In the Navy, *the dogs* are the Dog Watches: since ca. 1910. (P-G-R.)—6. As *the Dogs*, Footscray footballers: Melbournites': since ca. 1920. (B., 1943.)—7. The position achieved in mine-sweeping when two ships open out and finish stern to stern: Australian Naval: since ca. 1939. Ex two dogs breaking off relations.

dogs are barking it in the street, the. 'A c.p. used about something that is supposedly secret but is very widely known, an open secret' (B.P.): Australian: since ca. 1920.

dog's ballocks. The typographical colon-dash (:—): C. 20. Cf. **dog's prick.**

dog's body, 1 (p. 231), occurs rather earlier: Alfred Burton, *Johnny Newcome*, 1818. (Moe.)

dog's bottom?, is he (or it, etc.) **any.** Is he any good?: Australian: since ca. 1930. B., 1942.

dog's bird leg. Lance corporal's stripe: Australian soldiers': 1915 +.

dog's breakfast.—2. Confusion; turmoil: Australian: since ca. 1935. (B., 1943.)

dog's chance, not to have a. To have no chance at all: coll.: late C. 19–20.

dog's dinner. A shilling: Australian rhyming s.: C. 20. (B., 1945.) On *deaner* (p. 211).—2. See **dressed up like . . .** below.—3. Pejorative, as in 'Something-or-other was a dog's dinner'—bungled, no good: since ca. 1945.

dog's disease. Influenza: Australian: since ca. 1930. (B.P.)

dog's home, the. See 'Guard-Room in Army Slang'.

dog's licence. Seven shillings and sixpence: from ca. 1930. Ex the cost of that licence.

dog's nose.—2. Hence, from ca. 1850, a man addicted to whisky. B. & L.

dog's prick. An exclamation mark: authors' and journalists': C. 20.

dog's vomit.—2. Inferior food: Australian: C. 20. B., 1942. Ex sense 1 (p. 232).

dogun (p. 232). Since at least as early as 1920 the predominant Canadian form has been *dogan*. (Leechman.)

dogways, adv. and adj. (Of coïtion) like a dog, *à retro*: workmen's coll.: late C. 19–20.

dohickey. 'Now becoming common here [in New Zealand] as an alternative to "doings", [which is] now losing some of its novelty,' Niall Alexander, letter of Oct. 22, 1939.

doing! and doink! Variants of *boing* and *boink* above.

doing dab. Doing badly (in business): London low: since ca. 1845. Mayhew, I, 1851. Here *dab* is back s. for *bad*.

doing of, be. To be doing: illiterate coll.: C. 19–20. In, e.g., An Old Etonian, *Cavendo Tutus; or, Hints upon Slip-Slop*, forming the second part of his *The Alphabet Annotated*, 1853.

doings, the. (Ex sense 1: p. 232.) One's possessions or equipment: Australian: since ca. 1919. (Jean Devanney, *By Tropic Sea*, 1944.)

doldrums (p. 232). Perhaps, however, the more obvious derivation ex nautical *doldrums* is correct.

dole, the. Food handed out at a station to a tramp: Australian: since ca. 1925. B., 1942.

doley or dolee. A person on the dole: Australian coll.: since ca. 1930. Caddie, *A Sydney Barmaid*, 1953.—2. A soldier in an employment platoon: Australian: since ca. 1940. (B., 1943.)

doll, n. (p. 232). Augustus Mayhew, *Paved with Gold*, 1858, records that among London crossing-sweepers (of the 1850's–1860's) 'the insulting epithet of "doll" was applied to every aged female'—precisely as 'the rather degrading appellation of "toff" was given to all persons of the male gender'. n. But in Anon., *The New Swell's Guide to Night Life*, 1846, at p. 29, *doll* occurs, twice in sense 'a girl': 'soldiers and their Dolls' followed by 'another resort for soldiers and their girls'—a clear anticipation of U.S. 'guys and *dolls*'.—2. See *dish*, n., 3.—3. See *napper*, 7.—4. Any very attractive person of either sex: Canadian juveniles': adopted, ca. 1935, ex U.S. (Leechman.)—5. As in *a doll of a . . .*, an attractive (e.g. house, gown): since mid-1950's. Cf. sense 4.

dollar bosun. See **ledger bosun.**

dolled up like a barber's cat; usually **all . . .** Extravagantly fashionable in dress: Canadian: late C. 19–20; by 1950, slightly ob.

dollop, 2 (p. 232): but, after ca. 1935, coll. and widespread and respectable.

dolly, n.—11. A candle: tramps' c.: C. 20. Perhaps a corruption of **tolly,** n., 1 (see *Dict.*). Cf. sense 4 (p. 232).—12. A servant girl: chimney-sweeps': C. 19. (George Elson, 1900.) Cf. senses 1–3 on p. 232.—13. A girl, esp. an attractive girl: since ca. 1955. Cf. senses 1 and 3 on p. 232. —14. A small shunting engine: railwaymen's: since ca. 1920. (*Railway*.)—15. 'Dwarf Ground Signal (LMR)': railwaymen's: since ca. 1930. (*Railway*, 3rd.)

dolly, adj. Excellent: very attractive; very pleasant, as in 'Isn't that dolly?'; 'darling': an article published in *The Daily Telegraph*, coloured supplement, March 10, 1967; note the title of Alan Diment's novel, *The Dolly Dolly Spy*, 1967. Cf. **dolly,** n., 13, above.

Dolly Cotton. See **Johnny Cotton.**

***dolly up,** v.i. To heat water or tea with a candle: tramps' c.: from ca. 1905. Ex preceding.

dolly up, dolly down, dolly sick,—to play. (Of the male) to masturbate: low: C. 20. Cf. **dolly,** n., 6, on p. 232.

Dolly (Varden). A garden: rhyming s.: late C. 19–20.

dollypot. A simpleton: Australian: since ca. 1925. B., 1942. Cf. **dillypot.**

Domain cocktail (or **special**). Petrol and pepper; methylated spirits, boot-polish and Flytox: Sydney beggars' and dead-beats': ca. 1910–30. B., 1942.

Domain dosser. A beggar or a dead-beat frequenting the Sydney Domain: Australian: C. 20. Baker.

dome.—2; **doom.** The Sherborne shape of **dorm** (p. 235): since ca. 1880. Marples.

domino.—4. A false note played by the orchestra: theatrical: since ca. 1910. Ex **dominoes,** 2 (p. 233).

domino-walloper superseded **domino-thumper** (p. 233) since ca. 1930.

Doms, the. Members of the Order of Preachers (*Dominicans*): Australian Catholics': C. 20. (B.P.)

Don, the. See **Braddles.**

don, n.—4. A master: Winchester coll.: C. 19–20. Ex sense 2.

Don Freddie (or **Freddy**). See **Dutch fuck** below.

Don R. A dispatch rider: Services: since the 1920's. H. & P. In signalese, *don* = d.

dona (p. 233). The c.p. comes from a London Cockney song (? Gus Elen's), 'Never introduce your donah to a pal, for the odds is ten to one he sneaks your gal'; and the Australian use of *dona* (*h*) dates from ca. 1880.

dona Highland-flinger (p. 233): by 1940, †. (Franklyn.)

done thing, the. (See **done, it isn't:** p. 233.) Referring to July 1914, Wilfred Ewart wrote, in *The Way of Revelation*, 1921. 'Very young ladies were fond of calling young gentlemen by their christian names—it was rather "done" in their current idiotic phrase.'

done-up.—3. Beaten up; terribly manhandled: c.: from ca. 1920.

done-up, 1 (p. 233): to be back-dated to ca. 1820. See the quotation at **tub,** n., 3, below; it occurs also in Wm Maginn, *Whitehall*, 1827. (Moe.)

doner (p. 233): much earlier: as one fated to die shortly, it occurs in *Sessions*, Jan. 1838.

dong, n. A blow, a punch: Australian: C. 20. Ex the verb.—2. See **hammer,** 4.

donk.—2. Hence, a simpleton: mostly Australian: since ca. 1910. B., 1942.—3. See **double-dink.**

donkey.—5. *A regular donkey,* anything very long and big (as, e.g., a carrot).—6. And *a donkey's* = a large penis: low: late C. 19–20.—7. A transport mule: military: C. 20. Ex sense 4 (p. 233). —8. A '350 h.p. shunting locomotive' (*Railway* 2nd): railwaymen's: since ca. 1955. It does the '*donkey* work'.

donkey?, who stole the. 'Current as late as 1885 and probably much later too': Prof. Arnold Wall, letter of Aug. 1939.

donkey-drops and custard. Prunes and custard. Marlborough College: since early 1920's.

donkey-lick. Treacle; golden syrup: Australian rural: C. 20. (B., *Australia Speaks*, 1953.)

donkey-lick, v. To defeat easily, esp. in a horse race: Australian sporting: since ca. 1920. (B., 1953.)

donkey-rigged. Endowed with a large penis: low: late C. 19–20. Cf. **donkey,** 6.

donkey's breakfast, 3. Also, since ca. 1925, R.A.F.—via the old R.N.A.S. men. Jackson.

donkey's ears, 1. Earlier in *Sinks*, 1848, as 'a false collar'.

donk's dingbat. 'A soldier detailed to look after the mules' (Baker): Australian: soldiers': 1939 +. Ex **dingbat,** 1 (*Dict.*).

donner. 'I'll donner you' = give you a hiding: South African schools' esp. Milton Junior School, Bulawayo: since ca. 1925. Worth recording for its derivation ex the Dutch word for 'thunder' —via Afrikaans.

donny is a variant of **dona** (*Dict.*).

Donny John. Don Juan: jocular: late C. 19–20.

donnybrook. A fracas: Australian (esp. among soldiers): since ca. 1920. Ex *Donnybrook* Fair, famous for its free-for-alls.

donovan (p. 234): app. current since ca. 1830, at latest. It occurs in, e.g., Alex Harris, *The Emigrant Family*, 1849, and in *Sinks*, 1848.

don't act so daft or I'll buy you a coalyard. A jocular c.p.: since ca. 1956.

don't be auntie! Don't be silly; don't be a

spoilsport: Australian: since ca. 1935. (B., 1943.)

don't be funny! Don't be ridiculous; I'd never do such a thing: Canadian c.p.: since ca. 1930. (Leechman.)

don't be that way! Don't behave in that objectionable or unpleasant way: c.p.: adopted, ca. 1948, ex U.S.

don't do anything I wouldn't (do)! A c.p. of jocular advice: English and Australian since ca. 1910. Cf. **be good!** on p. 39.

don't do anything you couldn't eat! Don't take on anything you can't do: Australian c.p.: since ca. 1930. B., 1942. Via *bite off more than one can chew.*

don't excite. See **excite!, don't:** both in *Dict.* and in Addenda.

don't get your arse (or bowels or balls) in an uproar!; don't get your shit hot! Simmer down! Keep cool! low c.pp.: C. 20; the former, general; the latter, Canadian.

don't give me that! Tell that to the Marines: c.p.: since ca. 1920.

don't go down the mine, daddy. A fragment from a famous old sentimental song—in World War I a soldiers' chant—since ca. 1920, a c.p.

don't just stand there—do something! This exhortation has been so frequently employed that, ca. 1940, it became a c.p., both British and American, with either an allusive or a humorous connotation, as in the title of Charles Williams's delightful and exciting novel, *Don't Just Stand There*, 1966. It has even been reversed, thus, *don't do anything—just stand there!*

don't know which side his (or my) arse hangs, he or I. A low c.p., implying that the speaker is either bewildered or in a state of hopeless indecision: C. 20.

don't let your braces dangle in the shit! A workmen's and Servicemen's c.p., sometimes chanted: late C. 19–20.

don't look now, but I think we're being followed or **somebody's following us.** Since ca. 1933, a c.p.

don't make a fuss. A bus: rhyming: C. 20.

don't make a production of it!, often preceded by *all right!* 'Said to one making a big show of a simple affair' (Leechman, 1967): since late 1930's; common among servicemen in W.W. II; still (1969) often used. Ex movie makers' 'productions'; cf. **evolution** below.

don't make me laugh, I've got a split lip. A c.p.: C. 20; ob. by 1940. Leonard Merrick, *Peggy Harper*, 1911. Since ca. 1920, usually shortened to *don't make me laugh,* hence, since ca. 1925, *don't make me smile,* A jocular variant—since ca. 1930—is *don't make I laugh.*

don't shit the troops! See **you wouldn't shit . . .**

don't shoot the pianist!, with *he's doing his best* understood: c.p.: adopted, ca. 1918, ex U.S., where current—originally as a Wild West saloon-notice—prob. from ca. 1860. Another form of the plea is *don't shoot the piano-player; he's doing the best he can.* The original, according to Burton Stevenson's *Proverbs, Maxims and Familiar Phrases,* was *please do not shoot the pianist. He is doing his best:* and the gloss runs, 'Oscar Wilde, telling of a notice seen by him in a Western barroom during his American tour, in a lecture delivered in 1883.'

don't spend it all at one shop. See **here's a ha'penny.**

don't take any wooden nickels! Don't allow yourself to be cheated: Canadian: 'a c.p. of the last fifty years, and still heard occasionally' (Leechman: May 1959).

don't take it out, Chiefie: I'll walk off. A sailor's conciliatory jocularity to the Chief Petty Officer after a reprimand: Naval c.p.: since ca. 1930.

don't take me up till I fall! An Anglo-Irish, late C. 19-20, c.p., used 'when a person attempts to correct you when you are not in error' (P. W. Joyce, *English in Ireland*, 1910).

don't tell me. See **no, don't tell me.**

don't tell more than six! Don't tell anyone: Londoners' c.p.: June 1937–Aug. 1939.

don't wake it up! Don't talk about it!: Australian c.p.: since ca. 1920. Baker. 'Let sleeping dogs lie.'

(don't worry—) it may never happen. A c.p. addressed to the worried or the merely thoughtful: since ca. 1916.

don't worry your fat! Advice to someone who is worrying: c.p.: since ca. 1910.

doob. Penis: Australian schoolboys': since ca. 1950. Perhaps ex **dood**, 2, below, or ex **doodle**, n., 2 (p. 234).

dooby. Dowdy; old-fashioned: Aus., mostly feminine: since ca. 1950. (Ross Campbell, *Mummy, Who Is Your Husband?*, 1964.) Either a distortion of *dowdy* or an imperfect blend of *dowdy* + *booby*.

dood.—2. A pipe: Australian: since ca. 1910. B., 1942. Ex Aborigine?

doodad. A thingummy: Canadian: adopted, ca. 1930, ex U.S.—A word of fanciful formation.

doodah. A thingummy: since ca. 1910. 'Pass me the doodah.' Ex **ooja-ka-piv** (*Dict.*).—2. An air-raid siren: 1939–45.—3. A duodenal ulcer: since ca. 1945. Partly ex sense 1 and partly ex *duode*nal.—4. 'This has some use as a euphemism, in such ways as "Where's the doodah?" when somebody wants to know where the w.c. is' (A. B. Petch, March 1966): since late 1940's.

doodle, n.—3. Short for **doodlebug**, 3: since Aug. or Sept. 1944.—4. Corresponding to, and deriving from, sense 2 of the v.

doodle, v.—2. To write or draw aimlessly while one is listening to others at, e.g., a conference: since ca. 1930: coll. >, by 1950, S.E. Perhaps an arbitrary formation, but prob. ex dial. *doodle*, to waste time, to trifle. (E.D.D.)

doodle, adj. See 'Epithets'.

doodle-ally. Mentally deficient: since ca. 1940. Apparently a blend of *doodle* + doo*lally*-tap.

doodlebug.—2. Hence, 'utility truck, or light motor-van, as used by the Army. [Cf. jeep]': H. & P., 1943. The semantic ref. is to the 'squiggly bits' one doodles or absent-mindedly draws on a pad, etc.—3. A German flying-bomb (V.1): since mid-June 1944. Ex 1 or 2—or both. —4. A gremlin: Fleet Air Arm: ca. 1940-5. —5. A new-style locomotive: railwaymen's: ca. 1945-60 (*Railway*.) Ex sense 2 rather than sense 3.

doofah. Variant of **doofer**, 3, below. (John Winton, *We Joined the Navy*, 1959.)

doofer. A humorist, a wag: since ca. 1944. James Dunn in *World's Press News*, Nov. 21, 1946. Ex 'You'll *do* for me!'—i.e. I'll die laughing at you.—3. (Cf. sense 1, p. 234.) A gadget; anything not specifically named, any 'box of tricks': Forces', esp. R.A.F.: since ca. 1936.

Something that will '*do for* the time being'. Cf. *gubbins*, 4.—4. A partly smoked cigarette, extinguished so as to *do for* another smoke. Services': since ca. 1939.

'In the sense "humorist", might it derive from German s. *doof*, meaning "daft" or "crazy"?': H. R. Spencer. Yes, perhaps.

dooghene (p. 234). Earlier in Mayhew, I, 1851.

doohickey. Any mechanical device you can't find a name for: Services, esp. Navy: adopted, ca. 1940, ex Canada, which adopted it, ca. 1930, ex U.S.

dook, v. To give: Australian: since ca. 1910. D'Arcy Niland, *The Shiralee*, 1955.

dook on it, have one's. To seal a bargain with a hand-shake: Australian: C. 20. Baker.

dookering. See **dookin** (*Dict.*).

doolally. See **doolally tap** in *Dict.*—2. Hence, exceedingly drunk: Army: since ca. 1930. H. & P.

Doolally tap. The *Dict.* entry is rendered more correct, precise, and significant by the following passage from Richards: 'The trooping season began in October and finished in March, so that time-expired men sent to Deolalie from their different units might have to wait for months before a troop-ship fetched them home. . . . The time-expired men at Deolalie had no arms or equipment; they showed kit now and again and occasionally went on a route-march, but time hung heavily on their hands and in some cases men who had been exemplary soldiers got into serious trouble and were awarded terms of imprisonment before they were sent home. Others contracted venereal and had to go to hospital. The well-known saying among soldiers when speaking of a man who does queer things, "Oh, he's got the Doo-lally tap," originated, I think, in the peculiar way men behaved owing to the boredom of that camp. Before I was time-expired myself [in 1909] the custom of sending time-expired men to Deolalie was abolished: they were sent direct to the ports of embarkation, which in some cases meant weeks of travelling, but they got on the troop-ship the day they arrived at the port.' (This author's knowledge of s. in the Army ranks of the early C. 20 is prob. unrivalled.)

doolally-tapped. Knocked silly: low: from 1918.

doolan. A policeman: Australian: C. 20. (D'Arcy Niland, *The Big Smoke*, 1959.) Probably ex the Irish surname Doolan, there being so many Irishmen in the police force.

doom. See **dome**, 2.

Doomie. The R.A.F.'s nickname for the character adorning the 'Wot No——?' drawings: 1944 +.

doomie. 'Bodgie or widgie with criminal tendencies' (*The Sunday Chronicle*, Feb. 6, 1952): Australian: ca. 1950-60. All three terms are urban, raffish and confined mostly to Sydney.

door; usually in pl. '*Doors*. The lock gates on a canal,' Wilfred Granville, *Sea Slang of the 20th Century*, 1949. By humorous meiosis.

*door, work a. To ply prostitution by sitting or standing at the door of one's premises: Australian c.: since ca. 1920. (B., 1953.) Hence, loosely, *door*, a brothel.

door-knob (p. 235). By 1940, †. (Franklyn 2nd.)

door-knock. A door-to-door appeal for funds. Australian: since late 1950's. (B.P.)

door-knocker.—3. A feminine hair-style, two

long thick plaits bunched at the top: domestic: late C. 19–early C. 20.

door to door. Four; occasionally, where the context is clear, 24 or 34 or 44 or . . .: rhyming s.: C. 20. (Franklyn, *Rhyming*.)

dooser (or **D.**), **the.** The Second Steward: ships' stewards': C. 20. Dave Marlowe, 1937. I.e. *deucer!*

doover. Anything—any object whatsoever: Australian soldiers': 1939 +. Baker. Ex **doodah** above.—2. See 'Prisoner-of-War-Slang', 10.

dooverlackey; occ. dooverwock(e)y. An elaboration—since ca. 1945—of preceding. (B.P.)

dop down. See 'Verbs'.

dope, n.—9. In the South African underworld, it = dagga (*Cannabis Indica*): C. 20. (J. B. Fisher, letter of May 22, 1946.) A specialisation of sense 1 (p. 235).—10. Petrol (esp., if specially treated): since ca. 1930.

dope, n.—11. One's work: copywriters': since ca. 1930.

dope, v.—3. To smear: garage hands': since ca. 1905. Herbert Hodge, *It's Draughty in Front*, 1928, 'I soon acquired the knack, learning to "dope" the cylinders with petrol.'

dope up. To check (an aircraft's engines): R.A.F.: since ca. 1938. (P-G-R.)

dopey, n. A very dull or slow fellow; a fool: Army (1914–18), then general. Ex the adj.

doption. An adopted child: low, verging on c.: from ca. 1870. B. & L. I.e. *adoption.*

Dora (**Gray**). A threepenny piece: Australian rhyming s.: C. 20. On **tray**, 2 (*Dict.*).

Dorchester. See **gin palace.**

dork. A 'doorstep' (p. 235): lower classes': since ca. 1895. By 'telescoping' or conflation.

dorkum. A dumper (food): Australian: since ca. 1925. (B., 1943.)

dose, v.—2. To shell: Army: 1939–45. Hence, *dosing*, a shelling. (P-G-R.)

dose of salts, like a. Canada affords us, since ca. 1930, the very picturesque elaboration . . . *through a serpent girl.*

doser. A severe blow or punch: pugilistic: ca. 1840–90. Augustus Mayhew, *Paved with Gold*, 1857.

dosh. Money, esp. cash: Australian juvenile: since ca. 1944. (B., 1953.) Perhaps a blend of *dollars* + *cash*.—2. 'I dig dosh. Can you lend me a fiver?' is the Andersons' very free paraphrase: beatniks': since ca. 1950. I suspect that *dosh*, as in Eng. dialect. is a variant of *doss* and that the speaker is hinting that he needs money for bed and lodging.

doshed!, I'm. A variant, ca. 1870–1910, of *I'm dashed.* B. & L.

***doss, running.** See **running doss.**

doss(-)bag. A hammock: Australian Naval: 1939–45. (B., 1943.)

***doss in the pure.** To sleep in the open air: (mostly London) vagrants' c.: from ca. 1890; ob. Pugh.

dosser. A C. 20 tramps' nuance of sense 2 is: a regular old tramp.—4. The 50 ring, which counts as a double, there being no 25-ring double: darts players': since ca. 1930.

dossy.—2. Soft; daft: low: C. 20. '"Don't know what she ever saw in that dossy bastard"': Brendan Behan, *Borstal Boy*, 1958. Perhaps cf. North Country dial. *dossy*, soft, dull.

dot, n.—2. Anus: low Australian: C. 20. (D'Arcy Niland, *The Big Smoke*, 1959, 'Shove it up your black dot'—said to a Negro.)

dot, off one's. Recorded earlier by B. & L.

dot, on the.—2. At exactly the right time: coll. (English and Canadian): since ca. 1920. 'On the dot of nine.'

dot and carried. Married: rhyming s.: since ca. 1880. Cf. *cut and carried*. By 1925, †. (Franklyn 2nd.)

dot(-)and(-)dash. Cash: rhyming s.: C. 20. (Robin Cook, 1962.)

***dot-drag.** See **dot**, n., in *Dict.*

dottima; dottissima. Both are n. and adj. (An) eccentric (person), (a person) only slightly mad; *dottissima*, (one who is) completely mad: jocular medical: from ca. 1910. Ex **dotty** (*Dict.*) by mock Latin.

doub, occ. written dubb. A double, e.g. two crows with one shot: Australian: since ca. 1920. (Jean Devanney, 1951.)

doubite (p. 236) is, I suspect, a misprint in 'Matsell' and therefore a ghost-word: ? for *double.*

double, n.—6. A pimp's second woman: white-slavers' c.: from ca. 1902. Cf.—7. A pornographic picture of a man's and a woman's genitals: raffish coll.: since ca. 1920.

double, v.—4. (Of a pimp) to take a second woman: white-slavers' c.: C. 20. Albert Londres, 1928. (Gen., v.t.)

double, come the. To exercise trickery: Australian: since ca. 1880. (Sidney J. Baker, letter.)

double, make a. To repeat a line or a sentence: compositors' coll.: C. 19–20. B. & L.

double-bank. n. and v. See **double-banking.**—2. See **double-dink.**

double-banking, n. (The fact of) two lines of vehicles going in the same direction: Army coll. (1940) >, by 1945, j.

double carpet. Odds of 33 to 1: racing, esp. bookmakers': C. 20. (*The Sunday Telegraph*, May 7, 1967.) Ex **carpet**, n., 5, above.

double changer. The double chainwheel on a (racing) bicycle: cyclists: since ca. 1920. Ex 'the noise made by the chain shifting from one wheel to the other'. (W. Woodman.)

double-choked. Extremely disappointed or disgruntled; utterly disgusted: since ca. 1950. L. J. Cunliffe, *Having It Away*, 1965, 'The bogies knew he had had it away but just couldn't pin the job on him. Which meant he was laughing and they were double-choked.' Cf. **choked** above.

double-dink, v. and derivative n. 'To carry a second person on the top bar of a bicycle. It is also a noun. Exchangeable terms are "*dink*", "*donk*", and "*double-bank*", both as verbs and nouns,' B., 1942: Australian: since ca. 1925. Prob. the originating term is *double-bank*, and *dink* and *donk* are echoic variations.

double-distilled (p. 237). In Australia, 1840. (Sidney J. Baker, letter.)

double Dutch coiled against the sun (p. 237) occurs in Alfred Burton, *Johnny Newcome*, 1818. (Moe.)

double event.—3. Simultaneous defloration and impregnation: low: since ca. 1875. Cf. sense 1 (p. 237).

double fair! Goes one better than *fair enough!*: since ca. 1950. (Laurie Atkinson.)

double home turn. 'Train crew lodging over-night at terminus and returning next day' (*Railway*, 3rd): railwaymen's coll.: since ca. 1945 (?).

Double Hunts, the. 'New type of Hunt-Class Destroyers, twice the size of the old type,' Granville: Naval: since ca. 1940.

double-take; esp. *do a* . . . A second look, taken because one doesn't credit the first: since ca. 1948. Originally, film-producers' j.

double talk. Such speech, hence such writing, as deliberately misleads, orig. with the interpolation of meaningless syllables; hence, deliberately ambiguous and tendentious political matter: adopted, ca. 1959, ex U.S.: coll. >, by 1966, S.E.

double u. Variant of **w** (p. 934).

doubled over like a dog fucking a football. Doubled right over: Canadian soldiers': 1939–45.

doubt, toss it out,—when, occ. **if, in.** A pharmaceutical, esp. Australian, c.p.: C. 20. (B.P.)

Douche Can Alley. Palmer Street, Sydney, Australia, formerly a brothel district: Sydneyites': ca. 1910–60. A douche can is, in Australia, popularly supposed to be used only—or, at the least, mainly—by prostitutes.

dough, 2 (p. 237): also Canadian: since ca. 1870. (Niven.)

Dough or Die Boys, the. The American 'doughboys' (see **Doughboy** on p. 237): late 1917–19, then merely historical. The *dough* (money) reflects the Tommies' very natural reaction to comparative wealth. A pun on *do or die*.

Doughboy, 1 (p. 237). The 'large globular button' theory is perhaps correct, but, after exhaustive research, Colonel Moe has found no supporting evidence. The theory was originated by Mrs George A. Custer. The term is recorded as early as 1846.

doughy, adj.—2. Dull, stupid: Australian: C. 20. Kylie Tennant, *Lost Haven*, 1947.

Douglas. An axe: Australian: since ca. 1930 (?). (B., 1943.) Ex a famous axeman?

doul. A fag (boy): Shrewsbury: C. 19–20. Marples. Ex Gr. *doulos*, a slave.

dove is a common Canadian and U.S. sol. for 'dived': late C. 19–20.

dover. A re-heated dish: hotels': from ca. 1870. B. & L. I.e. 'do over again'.—2. A clasp knife: Australian: since ca. 1920. B., 1942. Ex *doover*? In 1959, B. declares it rare.

dovey, n. See **lovey-dovey.**

dovey or **dovy,** adj. Pretty; attractive; 'sweet': domestic, esp. feminine, coll.: from ca. 1890. Barry Pain, *Stories in Grey*, 1912, 'The very doviest white silk nightgown you ever saw.' Ex *lov(e)y-dov(e)y.*

Dowb, take care of. See **take care of dowb** in *Dict.* and **take care . . .** in Addenda.

down, n.—6. A move to open the game: Australian dominoes-players': C. 20. (B., 1953.)

down as a nail. A synonym of **down as a hammer** (p. 238): 1817, J. J. Stockdale, *The Greeks.*

down-haul. See **downhaul** below.

down in. Lacking in; short of: proletarian coll.: mid-C. 19–20. B. & L. E.g. 'down in cash'.

down in the forest something stirred. A c.p., referring to a consummated coïtion: domestic: since 1915, when Sir Landon Ronald's very famous song was published.

down in the forest something's turd. A Cockney c.p., dating from ca. 1920: evoked when a bird's

dropping lands on someone; uttered by either the victim or an onlooker. A pun on the preceding.

down on, get. To remove; appropriate; steal: Australian low s.: C. 20. B., 1942. Cf. **down on, be,** 2 (p. 238).

down the chute. In prison: Australian: since ca. 1920. Baker.

down the drain. See **drain, down the.**

down the drains. Brains: rhyming: late C. 19–20.

down the hatch! 'Bung ho! (*Pause.*) Down the hatch!': a drinking, esp. a toasting, c.p.: mid-C. 19–20; orig., nautical.

down the nick. See **nick, down the** below.

down the pan. See **pan, down the.**

down the plug. See **plug, down the** below.

down the slot. See **slot, down the** below.

downer.—5. A small unofficial strike: workmen's: since the early 1960's. *Sunday Citizen*, July 4, 1965: a news feature, 'He defends "downers".' Ex 'to *down* tools'.

downhaul. A greatcoat; a surtout: Naval ratings': C. 19; † by 1890. Wm Nugent Glascock, *The Naval Sketch-Book*, 2nd Series, 1834, at I, 51 (greatcoat) and 278 (surtout). Moe.

Downing Street. 10 in the game of House: C. 20. Michael Harrison, 1943. Ex No. 10, Downing Street—the Prime Minister's metropolitan residence.

downstairs, adv. See **upstairs.**

downy as a hammer. A variant of **down as a hammer** (p. 238); *Boxiana*, III, 1821.

downy (or **D.**) **Bible.** Douay Bible: tailors': from ca. 1860. Used as reference, like *according to Cocker.* B. & L.

dowsing. See **douser** (*Dict.*).

Dox, the. The Headmaster: Tonbridge: since ca. 1860. Marples. Ex *doctor* on L. *dux.*

doxy, 3 (p. 239). Augustus Mayhew, *Paved with Gold*, 1857, notes that among London crossing-sweepers—prob. it holds good for ca. 1840–80—*doxy* is a girl, a young woman, however respectable.

'dozer or **dozer.** A bulldozer: Australian: since late 1950's; orig., construction workers', but soon in gen. use. (B.P.)

dozy. Lazy; inefficient: Guards' Regiments' coll.: Lit., 'sleepy'. Cf. *idle.*—2. As a general coll., it means '(mentally) somnolent': C. 20.

drabs. 'A summer outfit of clothes' (B., 1943): Australian airmen's: 1939–45.

drack, n. A very plain female, esp. if lacking in personality: Australian: since ca. 1950. Perhaps ex the adj. and certainly at least influenced by it, but prob. = *Drac*(ula): cf. **Dracula,** 3, below.

drack, adj. Inferior; (of person) uninteresting, plain-looking: low Australian: since ca. 1930. (Ruth Park, 1950.) Yiddish? Cf. the Ger. *Dreck*, dung, muck (lit. and fig.). A *drack sort* is an unattractive person, opposite to *good* (superlative *extra*) *sort.*

Dracula.—2. A pathologist: hospitals': since ca. 1920. Ex the blood samples he takes. (Peter Sanders.)—3. A plain, esp. if uninteresting, girl: Australian: since ca. 1950. Ex the legend of Dracula. (B.P.)

draft-dodger is he who 'dodges the draft'—avoids being sent overseas: Services': 1939–45. (P-G-R.) Contrast the U.S. sense 'one who avoids conscription'.

drag, n.—13. A motor-car: c.: from ca. 1920.

An extension of sense 2.—14. A quick draw at a cigarette: Cockneys' and Services since ca. 1920. H. & P.—15. A long up-grade: Canadian lorry-drivers': since ca. 1915. Cf. sense 9.—16. A train; esp. a heavy freight train: Canadian rail-roadmen's (— 1931). With senses 1, 2, 13, 16, cf. 'The East Ender calls . . . all vehicles drags' (Richard Herd, Nov. 12, 1957): London: since ca. 1945.—17. 'Pull'—influence with the right people: Canadian: since ca. 1910.—18. (Ex sense 14.) A cigarette: mostly Services: since ca. 1925.—19. Anything boring or tedious: Canadian dance-lovers' (jazzmen's): since ca. 1950. (*The Victoria Daily Colonist*, April 16, 1959, 'Basic Beatnik'.) Also any person who is a bore: since ca. 1950, and English.—20. A marijuana cigarette: Australian: since ca. 1955. Ex sense 18. (B.P.)—21. Any act that requires a special effort: coll.: C. 20—22. A dance or ball: Canadian: ca. 1925–30. Also Australian teen-agers': since ca. 1950. (B.P.)—23. A particular kind of dance, as in the number entitled 'Doin' the Varsity Drag': Canadian: since ca. 1930. (Priestley.)—24. A casual female companion, as opposed to one's girl friend: Australian teenagers': since late 1950's.—25. That portion of winnings which one reserves for further play: Australian, esp. two-up, gamblers': C. 20. Ex **drag**, v., 3, on p. 240. (Tom Ronan, *Vision Splendid*, 1954, 'By the time I gave you the kip I had a few quid out of drags and showers'.)

Sense 10 has, since ca. 1910, predominantly signified 'female clothing as worn by men', esp. among homosexuals.

drag, v.—4. To challenge to, or to oppose in, a speed duel with cars: Australian teenagers' (esp. surfers'): since late 1950's. Cf. **drag strip** below.

drag, be in the. See '**dragged** or **dragged out**' (*Dict.*).

drag, flash the; go on the drag. See **drag**, n., 5, in the *Dict.*

drag on. (Of a man) *drag on a woman*, to marry her: Australian: since ca. 1910. B., 1942.—2. To undertake (a task): Australian coll.: since ca. 1910. (B., 1943.)

drag queen. A male homosexual addicted to transvestitism: since ca. 1930.

drag slicks. Racing-car wheels: Australian, esp. Sydney, motor mechanics': since ca. 1950. (B.P.)

drag strip. A short stretch (say a mile) of *road* on which teenagers try out or, esp., race their motorcycles or cars: Australian teenagers': since late 1950's. J. R. Westerway, 'The Rockers' in *The* (Sydney) *Bulletin*, April 6, 1963. Cf. **drag**, n., 13.

drag the chain. To be at the rear in a race or in a game (of, e.g., cribbage): New Zealand: C. 20. Niall Alexander, letter of Oct. 22, 1939, 'The ploughman's term to designate his slow horse that does not keep its chains tight'. Also Australian: B., 1943. Often of a slow drinker. (Slatter.)

dragging one's arse along the ground (so's you could cut washers off it). Utterly exhausted: Canadian soldiers': 1914 +.

dragon.—3. An old prostitute: since ca. 1959. Cf. sense 2 on p. 240.

Dragon, the. Robert Harley (1661–1724), 1st Earl of Oxford. Ca. 1700–40. See, e.g., *Swift's Letters*, ed. by F. E. Ball. Cf. **the Squire.**

Dragon-Slayers, hence Dragons, the. St George

footballers: Sydneyites': since ca. 1920. (B., 1943.)

dragon's teeth. A form of anti-tank obstacle: 1939–45, then merely reminiscent. H. & P.

drags on (someone), **put the.** To ask for a loan: Australian: since ca. 1910. Baker.

drain.—4. A melancholy, affectionate cadger of bed and board: beatniks': since ca. 1958. (Anderson.) A drain on one's provender and patience.

drain, down the. Lost; wasted: coll.: from ca. 1870.

Drain, the. The 'Waterloo & City Underground Railway under the Thames (SR)': railwaymen's: since ca. 1920. (*Railway*, 3rd.)

drain one's radiator. See **bleed one's turkey.**

drain one's snake. (Of men) to urinate: since ca. 1920. Not very common.

Drain Pipe or Snakey. Naval nickname for an excessively thin man: C. 20. Granville.

drain the bilge. To be extremely seasick: Australian Naval: since ca. 1915. (B., 1943.)

drammer. A partly sol., partly jocular, form of *drama*: late C. 19–20.

draped. Somewhat tipsy: Services officers': since 1939. H. & P. Draped about a friend or a lamp-post.

drapes; set of drapes. A man's suit of clothes: beatniks': since ca. 1958. (Anderson.) Adopted —and adapted—ex synonymous American *drape*.

draughters. Close-fitting, undivided knickers, the female counterpart of the male *cheaters*: since ca. 1920? They keep out the draught.

draw?, do you. Do you take your daily tot of rum?: Naval coll.: C. 20. Granville.

draw off. (Mostly of males) to make water: euphemistic coll.: C. 20.

draw pig on pork. See **pig on pork.**

draw the crow. See **crow, draw the.**

draw water. To weep: coll.: ca. 1820–90. Emily Brontë, *Wuthering Heights*, 1847.—2. In the late C. 19–20 Navy, it is used, as a coll., thus: 'He draws too much water for me'—outranks me.

drawback, the. Deliberate inhalation of cigar-ette smoke: smokers' coll.: since ca. 1930. In part, a pun.

drawing. A picture in water-colour: artists': from ca. 1870. B. & L.

drawing a pint. Using the controls of an air-craft: R.A.F.: since ca. 1939. H. & P., 'An action similar to that employed behind the public bars.' Cf. *beer-lever.*

drawing up the verbals. 'Det. Williams said it meant completely misinterpreting what a person said' (*Evening Standard*, Jan. 30, 1962): police: since ca. 1930. Ex the preparation of '*verbal* reports'?

dreadnoughts (p. 241): but also, 1940 +, an A.T.S. and Q.A.I.M.N.S. synonym of the Wrens' **E.T.B.s.** below.

Dreado. Earlier in 'Taffrail'. Because *nought* = 0.

dream.—3. Six months in prison: Australian c.: since ca. 1920. B., 1942.

dreg. One of the lowest of the low: Cranbrook School: C. 20. By back-formation ex S.E. *dregs.*

dress in, v.i. To dress ready to play in a game: Winchester: from ca. 1850. See **dress**, n., in *Dict.*

dress lodger (p. 241). 'The West End name for

prostitutes,' T. Archer, *The Pauper, the Thief, and the Convict*, 1865.

dress the nuts off. To reprimand (someone) severely: ? orig. Army: since ca. 1910. Cf. **chew the balls off** (p. 146).

dressed up like a dog's dinner. Wearing one's best uniform: Services, esp. Army: since ca. 1925. (P-G-R.)

dresser. Dress-circle: Oxford undergraduates' (— 1940). Marples, 2.

drift, on the. On tramp. Australian coll.: C. 20. B., 1942.

drill, v.—2. (Perhaps ex sense 1: p. 242.) *Subagitare feminam*: C. 18–20.

drill, the; occ., *the right drill*. The correct way to do anything: Army—by 1942, also R.A.F.—coll. (mostly officers): since ca. 1910. H. & P.; Jackson. A man that knows his drill *must* be good.

drill pig. A drill sergeant. Guards' Regiments': since ca. 1910. Gerald Kersh, *Boots Clean*, 1941.

drink, v.—2. To take water for the locomotive: Canadian railroadmen's (— 1931). Humorous.

Drink, the. The English Channel: R.A.F.: since ca. 1925. H. & P.

drink, the. Water: London Fire Brigade: C. 20. Cf. prec. entry.—2. The sea: mostly Air Force: 1939 +. (P-G-R.) Cf. *(the) Ditch*.

drink out of a nigger's clog. To be intemperate: Liverpool: since ca. 1945.

drinkite. Thirst: 1864, Surtees, *Mr Romford's Hounds*; † by 1900. Cf. **drinkitite** in *Dict*.

drip (p. 242). Senses 1 and 2 have, throughout C. 20 and perhaps from as early as 1890, been current at the Public Schools; sense 2 (see **wet dream**, 2) esp. in the nuances 'to be stupid; to be a terrible bore'.—3. Hence, a simpleton, a 'stupid', a bore: since ca. 1920.—4. To complain, to 'grouse': Naval: since ca. 1910. Granville.—5. 'Sloppy' sentiment; a person 'sloppily' sentimental: since ca. 1930. Berkeley Gray, *Mr. Ball of Fire*, 1946. Ex sense 1.

Answering to the v. of sense 4 is the n. *drip*, a complaint: since ca. 1910. (John Winton, *H.M.S. Leviathan*, 1967.)

drip-pan is a Naval variant (Granville) of **dripper**, 2. Ex prec.

dripper, a.—2. A bore or an inveterate 'grouser': Naval: since ca. 1930. H. & P.

dripping for it. (Of a woman) inflamed with lust: low: since ca. 1910.

drive, 1 (a blow or punch). Earlier in *Sessions*, May 1839.—3. See:—

drive, v. To irritate (someone) intensely: Australian teenagers': since ca. 1950. (Dick.) Perhaps elliptical for '*drive* mad' or '*drive* crazy' or '*drive* up the wall'.

drive, do a. To be (nearly) late for roll-call: Felsted School: since ca. 1880. Also simply *drive*. Marples.

drive blue. See **blue, drive**.

drive into. (Of the male) to coït with: low coll.: C. 19–20.

drive the train. 'To lead a number of squadrons,' Jackson: R.A.F.: since ca. 1938. Cf. **train driver**.

drive them home is the predominant C. 20 variation of *drive pigs to market*, to snore.

drive turkeys to market. See **turkeys to market** (*Dict*.).

drive (someone) **up the wall.** To send him mad (well, almost): since the mid-1940's.

driver.—3. A pilot: R.A.F.: since ca. 1929. Sgt-Pilot Rhodes, letter of Sept. 20, 1942; Partridge, 1945, 'Taken over from the R.N.A.S.': Jackson points out that it is an old Navy custom to refer to the captain of a ship as *the Driver*, and as W/Cdr R. P. McDouall tells me (March 17, 1945), '"Drivers, airframe" is what pilots are called by navigators.'

driver op. A wireless operator, capable also of driving: Royal Artillery: 1939–45. (P-G-R.)

droddum. Buttocks; breech: low: from ca. 1860. B. & L.

droggy, a hydrographic officer; **Droggy,** the Hydrographer of the Royal Navy; also as a nickname: Naval: since ca. 1910. The 2nd occurs in John Winton, *We Saw the Sea*, 1960. A conflation of '*hydrographer*'.

dromestoners. 'The men who clear the aerodromes before runways are laid down,' H. & P. R.A.F.: since ca. 1930.

drone. A rear-gunner: R.A.F.: 1939 +. Jackson. Except (what an except) during an attack he sits and sits.

drong. A shortening of **drongo**, 2.: Australian: since the late 1930's. (B.P.)

drongo. A new recruit: Australian airmen's (— 1943). Aboriginal? Immediately ex:—2. An ugly fellow; a 'bastard': low Australian, esp. Sydneyites': since ca. 1925. (Ruth Park, *Poor Man's Orange*, 1950.) Sydney's *Sunday Herald*, June 28, 1953, defined him as 'a lazy and usually undesirable human being'. 'Perhaps from a racehorse called Drongo, whose performances on the track were disappointing' (Sidney J. Baker); the horse got its name from the Australian bird called the *drongo*. Since ca. 1950, a widely used term of dislike. 'In Australian slang a drongo is a bit of a galah, a goat or a no-hoper . . . Drongo . . . raced on Melbourne tracks from 1924 to 1926. Drongo was a good galloper, but . . . second-rate. . . . Any who arouses the contemptuous disapproval of an Australian is apt to be described as a bloody drongo': Jock Marshall & Russell Drysdale, *Journey among Men*, 1962, at p. 91.

droob. A dull person: low Australian: since ca. 1944. (Ruth Park, 1950.) A blend of *drip* + *boob*.

drool, v. Often as vbl n., *drooling*. To loiter; to waste time: Australian: since ca. 1930. B., 1942. Ex S.E. *drool*, 'to dribble at the mouth'.

droolin' with schoolin'. See 'Canadian'.

droop-snoot, the. In March 1967 Mr Ramsey Spencer sent me the following note: 'There was in the late 1950's an experimental delta-wing supersonic aircraft flying at R.A.F. Farnborough, which, because its nose could be lowered at an angle to improve the pilot's field of view when landing, was known as "the droop-snoot"—and very odd it looked.'

drooper. A drooping moustache: Cockney coll.: from ca. 1880. (Pugh.)

droopers. Sagging breasts: Australian: since ca. 1930. Cf. the preceding.

drop, v., 4. Also Australian. By 1940, s. in both countries.—5. To get into trouble: Army: 1939–45. Short for *Drop in(to) the shit*.—6. To leave (a competitor) far behind: racing cyclists': since ca. 1945.—7. To knock (someone) down: coll., esp. in Australia: since ca. 1945. (Culotta.) —8. To give illicitly, to get rid of surreptitiously, e.g. a stolen cheque: since late 1940's. Cf. senses 1 and 4 on p. 242.

drop, a fabulous. A very attractive girl: Australian: since the late 1940's. (Culotta.) Cf. lay, n., 10, below.

***drop, cop the.** See cop the drop.

drop, not a bad. A good alcoholic drink: Australian: since ca. 1940. (B.P.)

***drop, take the.** To accept a bribe: C. 20: c.>, by 1930, taxi-drivers' s., as in Herbert Hodge, *Cab, Sir?*, 1939.

drop a ballock—banger—clanger—gooley. To blunder badly: Services: since ca. 1930. G. Kersh, *Bill Nelson*, 1942; H. & P. (*goolie* only). See goolies (*Dict.*).

drop a ballock for (someone). To let someone down; to fail him: Army: since ca. 1935. Gerald Kersh, 1942.

drop (one's) **anchor in the Levant.** To abscond: ca. 1815–60. David Carey, *Life in Paris*, 1822. A pun on synonymous S.E. *Levant*.

drop dead! Go away: adopted, esp. by English teenagers, ca. 1949, ex U.S. films. (Gilderdale.) General in Canada by ca. 1946.

drop heavy. 'To tip well is to "drop heavy",' Herbert Hodge, 1939: taxi-drivers': since ca. 1915.

drop it! Earlier in *Sessions*: May 1847, 'I told them several times to *drop it*.'

drop lullaby. A hanging: Australian low: C. 20. B., 1942.

drop of good. A glass—or even a bottle—of liquor: mostly workmen's: late C. 19–20.

drop of wet and warm, a. (a cup of) weak tea: lower-middle class domestic coll.: ? since ca. 1880.

drop off is coll. for *drop off to sleep*: late C. 19–20.

drop on, 2 (p. 243). In nuance 'to reprimand, to reprove': *Sessions*, April 1857.

drop on, have the. To have an advantage over (someone): Australian: adopted, ca. 1944, ex U.S. (B.P.) Semantically cf. *be quicker on the draw.*

drop on (also **shit on**) **from a great height.** To reprimand very severely: Army: 1939–45. Cf. *shat upon* . . .

drop one's, or the bundle. See bundle, drop one's on p. 108 and above.

drop one's flag (p. 243): W. N. Glascock, *Sailors and Saints* (I, 24), 1829, has *drop one's peak*. Moe.

drop one's guts. To break wind: low: C. 20. Cf. *shit bricks* (s.v. bricks . . .).

drop one's wax. To defecate: low: mid-C. 19–20.

drop-out. 'One who opts out of society' (Peter Fryer in *The Observer* colour supplement, Dec. 3, 1967): drug addicts', hippies', Flower People's: since ca. 1960.

drop the anchor. See anchor, drop the.

***drop the bucket (on).** 'To throw responsibility for an offence on to someone else' (B., 1959): Aus. c.: C. 20.

drop your tailboard. A 'camp' c.p. of late C. 19–20.

dropped. Born: Australian rural coll.: mid-C. 19–20. Brian Penton 1934, '"We weren't dropped yesterday, eh?"' Ex calving and lambing.

dropped magnets. Flat feet (? rather fallen arches): London busmen's: since ca. 1940.

***dropper.—3.** A passer of counterfeit, esp. paper money: c.: C. 20. H. T. F. Rhodes.

***dropperman.** A police informer: Australian c.: since ca. 1940. (B., 1945.)

dropping the anchor. Holding back a horse or merely not flogging it: turf: mid-C. 19–20. B. & L.

droppings. Porter; beer: low: ca. 1820–70. *Sinks*, 1848. Ex colour.

drops. Dropped handlebars, the two parts being below the rest: cyclists': since ca. 1930 Hence, to *ride on the Drops*.

dropsy, 3, is also c.: esp. as = hush-money. —4. (Prob. ex 2.) 'Tips are dropsy,' Herbert Hodge, 1939: taxi-drivers': since ca. 1910. A pun.—5. The habit of dropping things, of being butter-fingered: Australian: since ca. 1950. (B.P.)

Drover's Guide, The. See Bagman's Gazette above.

drown. To put too much water into whisky or brandy: jocular coll.: C. 20. 'Don't drown it!'

drozel. See 'Women'.

drube. A variant spelling of *droob*: B., 1953.

drug-store cowboy. Any lout that hangs about a corner drug-store, talks tough, gives the girls 'the glad eye': Canadian coll.: adopted, ca. 1935, ex U.S. (Leechman.) Cf. *Naffy Romeo*.

druid. A priest: Anglo-Irish: late C. 19–20. (Brendan Behan, *Borstal Boy*, 1958.)

drum, n., 6, is not † in *hump one's drum*: 1946. Sidney J. Baker, letter.—8. A tin for making tea, etc.: tramps' c.: from ca. 1890.—9. A racecourse tip: Australian sporting: C. 20. B., 1942. Also: any *tip* or *warning*.—10. Hence, information; 'the score' or true state of things: Australian: since ca. 1912. D'Arcy Niland, *The Shiralee*, 1955, 'If it's a fair question, what's the drum?' See esp. Sidney J. Baker's provocative, immensely readable *The Drum*, 1959.

drum, v.—3. To inform, tell: to 'put wise', to warn, tip off: low Australian: since ca. 1910. Lawson Glassop, *We Were the Rats*, 1944. Ex the n., 9. Note esp. Sidney G. Baker, *The Drum*, 1960.

drum, run a. In a race, esp of horses or dogs: to win a place: Australian sporting: since ca. 1945. (Culotta.)

***drum, stamp one's.** See stamp one's drum.

drum and fife. A wife: rhyming s., esp. in the Army: late C. 19–20.—2. A knife: Army rhyming s.: C. 20. (Franklyn, *Rhyming*.)

drum around. To prowl, as a thief does: police: since ca. 1910. Cf. *drum*, v., 2 (p. 243).

drum major. See 'Tavern terms', § 6.

drum up, n. (p. 243). Earlier in the Army (1914–18).

drum up, v., 2 (p. 243). Also, by 1920, gen. for 'to collect (a crowd, a quorum, etc.)'. B.P.

drummer.—6. A tramp: Australian: C. 20. B., 1942. Ex drum, n., 6.—7. A commercial traveller: adopted in Australia, ca. 1920, from U.S. Baker.—8. Slowest shearer in a shed: New Zealand shearers': since ca. 1890. Niall Alexander, letter of Oct. 22, 1939. Perhaps ex sense 1.—9. A yard conductor: Canadian railroadmen's (— 1931).—10. Anyone notorious for borrowing from his companions: Army: since ca. 1946.—11. (Ex sense 5, q.v. at drum, v., 2, on p. 243.) 'He chose the screwsman'—burglar— 'best fitted for the particular job. He sent with him a "drummer"—a man who had to make sure the coast was clear and help the screwsman with unskilled jobs, such as carrying the ladder' (John Gosling, *The Ghost Squad*, 1959): c.: since ca. 1910.

Drummond and Roce. (M. Harrison, *Reported Safe Arrival*, 1943.) *Drummond = drum and = drum and fife*, as above, sense 2; *Roce = roce = roast = roast pork*, a fork. (With thanks, for elucidation, to Michael Harrison.)

drunk and Irish. Fighting-drunk: military: ca. 1860–1920. Robert Blatchford, *My Life in the Army*, 1910.

drunk as a besom. Exceedingly drunk: coll.: ca. 1830–90. Cuthbert Bede in *Verdant Green*, 1853. Cf. **mops and brooms** in the *Dict.*

drunk as a fowl. Very tipsy: Australian: since ca. 1925. B., 1942, 'A variant of "*drunk as an owl*"'.

drunk as a newt. See **newt.**

drunk as a piss ant. Extremely drunk: Aus.: since ca. 1930. (B., 1959.) Cf. the terms immediately preceding and following this one.

drunk as a rolling fart. Very drunk: low coll.: from ca. 1860. Richards, 'In my old days it was a common sight by stop-tap to see every man in the Canteen as drunk as rolling f**ts.'

drunk as Chloe (loosely **Cloe**). Exceedingly drunk: from ca. 1815. Moore, 1819, has *like Cloe*, vigorously: a s. phrase † by 1890. It owes much of its Australian popularity to the painting mentioned at **do a Chloe** above. (B.P.)

drunk-up. A drinking bout: Australian coll.: C. 20. Baker. Cf. **beer-up.**

drunken sailor. A leaning type of chimney cowl, used to cure a smoking chimney: late C. 19–20.

drunok. Tipsy: from ca. 1930. A perversion of *drunk.*

druthers. 'One's choice or preference, from "I'd rather". Thus, "I'd rather go than stay"—I druther go than stay. Hence, "If I had my druthers, I'd go". Quite common in Canada and U.S.; mostly teen-agers and younger' (Leechman). Since ca. 1945.

dry, n. A 'drying-up' or being at a complete loss for one's lines: theatrical: C. 20. Hence, *dries*, instances of such loss. Ex 'to *dry* up' or forget one's lines. (Gavin Holt, *No Curtain for Cora*, 1950.)

dry, adj., is, in Australia, used with the low nn. of coition for rape and for homosexual intercourse: since ca. 1950.

dry, the. Desert; semi-desert; waterless country: Australian coll.: late C. 19–20. Boyd Cable in *The Observer*, Oct. 30, 1938. Cf. English dial. *dry*, a long period of rainless weather.—2. The dry season (winter) in N. and N.W. Australia: coll.: late C. 19–20. (B., 1942; Jean Devanney, 1944.)

dry as a sun-struck bone, extremely dry; **dry up like a sun-struck billalong**, to become so. 'Both similes are also used figuratively; "dry" suggesting irony, and "dry up" meaning to become silent or run out of words' (B., *The Drum*, 1959): Aus. coll.: C. 20.

dry bobbing; wet bobbing. Sport(s) on land; aquatics: Eton College: mid-C. 19–20: s. >, by 1875, coll.>, by 1900, S.E. B. & L. See **bob**, **dry and wet** in *Dict.*

dry dock (or hyphenated or one word); esp. *go*

into dry dock, to stay for a long time in hospital: Services: since ca. 1925. See **dock**, n., 2 (*Dict.*).

dry glasses without using a cloth. To 'booze': jocular: C. 20.

dry hash, 1, is used esp. as = one who will not 'shout' drinks: ca. 1870–1910. B. & L.

dry holy-stoning. A flogging: nautical: ca. 1800–70. *Boxiana*, II, 1818. Ex S.E. *holy-stones* (with which one cleans the deck).

dry list and **wet list.** Officers listed for shore service only, as opposed to the *w.l.*, listed for sea appointments: Naval: C. 20. (Wilfred Granville, Sept. 23, 1967.)

dry number, esp. in *to have dried one's number*, to have served for several weeks: Services': C. 20. See the **before you came up** entry in *Dict.*

dry old stick. An elderly person (esp. male) either boring or possessed of a very dry sense of humour: coll.: late C. 19–20. (Not only Aus. as B., 1959, seems to imply.)

dry run is the Canadian coll. equivalent, since ca. 1925, of **dummy run** (p. 248), but with the much wider connotation of 'experimental rehearsal'. (Leechman.)

dry-shave.—2. To annoy (a person) by vigorously rubbing his chin with one's fingers: lower classes' coll.: from ca. 1860. B. & L.

dry ship is the opposite of a *wet ship*: C. 20.

dry swim is synonymous with **grope**: R.A.F.: since ca. 1936.

dry up, v.—3. 'To slacken pace through exhaustion': turf: from ca. 1870. B. & L. Ex sense 1.—4. To cease work at lunch-time or at night; hence, leave a situation: printers': from ca. 1870. Ibid. Ex sense 1.

dry up and blow away! Go away: teenagers' (esp. the coffee-bar set): ca. 1957–59. (Gilderdale.) Cf. *dry up*, 1 (p. 244), and *blow*, v., 7.

dryknacking or **drynacking**, as in 'a spot of dryknacking', a little music-copying: Guards' Regiment musicians': since ca. 1920. It's *dry* work but rapidity therein is a *knack*.

dry-wipe. To win two legs straight off from (an opponent): darts players': since ca. 1930. Cf. **whitewash**, v., 3, below.

dual is coll. for 'dual-flying instruction': R.A.F.: since 1939 +. Jackson.

Dub. Dublin: Anglo-Irish: late C. 19–20. James Joyce, *Ulysses*, 1922.

dub, v.—2. To make (e.g.) British nationals speak (e.g.) French in films being shown in (e.g.) France: cinematic: since ca. 1935: by 1946, j.

***dub, go upon the.** 'To go upon a hou ebreaking expedition; to open or pick the lock or fastenings of a door': c.: late C. 17–mid-19. B. & L.

dub-dub. A complete failure: Army: C. 20; ob.

dub-snouted. See 'Epithets'. Prob., snub-nosed.

dub up, 2 (p. 245), apparently 'went underground'—existed without being recorded—for it is extant. 'Everybody in the nick had already been dubbed up'—locked in his cell—'for the night.' (Norman). It occurs also in, e.g., John Gosling, *The Ghost Squad*, 1959.

dubb. See **doub.**

dubby, the. The water-closet: children's: C. 20—perhaps late C. 19–20. Ex '*double*-u cee': *W.C.* (John A. Yates.)

Dublin tricks. (Rare in singular.) Bricks: rhyming s.: since ca. 1860; by 1940, ob. (D. W. Barrett, *Navvies*, 1880.)

dubs, n.—3. Marbles played in a ring: Australian school-children's: C. 20. B., 1942.—4. Hence (?), nipples of a girl's breasts: Australian: C. 20. Godfrey Blunden, *No More Reality*, 1935. Current among Southampton schoolboys before 1920, occ. in the form *dubbies* which suggests a deformation of **bubbies** (p. 99). On the other hand, *dubs* may have been influenced by S.E. *dugs* (in its 'nipples' sense).

duc. Ink-*ductor* or fountain regulating the amount of ink supplied for each impression on a machine: printers': from ca. 1860. B. & L.

duchess.—3. See:—

Duchess of Fife. Wife: rhyming s.: mid-C. 19–20; but by 1880, 'invariably reduced to *Dutch* ("my old Dutch"). It served as inspiration for Albert Chevalier's song of that title'—*My Old Dutch*—'and is by that immortalized': Franklyn 2nd.

Duchess of Teck. A cheque: rhyming s.: late C. 19–20. Often shortened to *duchess.*

duchesses. Female counter clerks in post-offices: mostly lower-middle class: since ca. 1948. Ex the airs so many of them give themselves.

duck, n.—9. An awkward-looking Japanese aircraft: Australian soldiers': December 1941–February 1942. (P-G-R.)—10. An amphibious vehicle: Services (esp. Army): 1942 +; by 1944, at least semi-official. Ex the factory serial initials *DUKW*. (P-G-R.)—11. A young lady; a girl: beatniks': since ca. 1959. Cf. list at **canary,** 12, above.

duck and dive. To hide: rhyming s.: C. 20.

duck (or goose) bumps. Gooseflesh; goose pimples: mostly Canadian, the latter sense jocular: C. 20. (Leechman.)

duck eggs. Coal ovoids: railwaymen's: since ca. 1945. (*Railway*.)

duck-house, v. To baffle, outwit, overcome (someone): Australian: since ca. 1925. B., 1942. Ex:—

duck-house, up against (someone's). (Something) that baffles, outwits, defeats, delays: Australian: since ca. 1910. 'I admit that this is one up against my duck-house.' Ex a game-score chalked on a duck-house wall or roof.

duck-house, upset one's. To upset someone's plan or calculations: Australian: since ca. 1920. (Miles Franklin, *Old Blastus of Bandicoot*, 1931.) Cf. *mind one's own duck-house*, to mind one's own business: ibid.

*duck in the green curtains. To 'sleep on the slopes of Table Mountain' (*The Cape Times*, May 23, 1946): South African c.: C. 20.

duck it. To 'waddle out as a lame duck', George Godfrey, *History of George Godfrey*, 1828: Stock Exchange: ca. 1815–70. Cf. **Duckery,** q.v.

duck-pot is a late C. 19–20 (ob. by 1940) variant of **duck,** n., 3. In, e.g., A. Neil Lyons, *Clara*, 1912.

duck-shovelling. 'Passing the buck': R.A.F.: since ca. 1960. (Sgt R. Farley, Feb. 16, 1967.) Origin ?

duck-shover, -shoving.—3. (Ex 1.) One who is over-sharp in business; unfair business methods: Australian: C. 20. B., 1942.

*duck the scone. See **bow the crumpet** above.

duck weather. Very wet weather: Australian: since ca. 1920. Ex **fine weather for ducks** (p. 276 and below). B.P.

ducker, 2 (p. 246). Already by 1878, current for some years. Before ca. 1860, the swimming pool had been known as the *duck-paddle* (Sir Sydney King-Farlow, letter to *The Times*).

Duckery, the. The disciplinary court of the Stock Exchange: Stock Exchange: ca. 1815–60. George Godfrey, 1828. Cf. **duck it** and **lame duck.**

duckets. Hat checks: Canadian railroadmen's (– 1931). Ex **Ducket** (p. 246).

Duckites; duckite. Girdlestone's 'house'; a member thereof: Charterhouse: C. 20. Ex Mr Girdlestone's *duck*-like walk. (Peter Sanders.)

ducks!, do I. See **do I ducks!**

ducks and doyleys. Pekin duck: among Britons on the China coast: C. 20. (*The Listener*, Dec. 8, 1949.)

duck's dinner. A drink of water, with nothing to eat: Australian: C. 20. Baker. Compare **duck's breakfast** (p. 246).

ducks in the pond (p. 246). Also *ducks on a pond* and a *couple of ducks*, usually pronounced *coupler ducks*, and:—

ducks on the water. 22 in the game of House: mostly military: C. 20. 'The two figures 2 are similar to a pair of ducks swimming side by side' (Lieutenant-General Sir J. R. E. Charles). Cf. **ducks in the pond** (*Dict.*).

ducky (p. 246): often, in Australia, used either sarcastically or jocularly by men: since early C. 20. 'She was wearing a ducky little pair of shorts.' (B.P.)

dud (p. 246). The adj. dates from mid-1890's in the nuance 'worthless': *Sessions*, Feb. 1898, 'I have it, it is a *dud* lot' (watch and chain).

dud up. To arrange (things) illicitly: serve short measure to (someone): Australian c.: since ca. 1925. Kylie Tennant, *Foveaux*, 1939. See **dud** (p. 246). Also 'Deliberately to misinform or mislead (someone). Whence, *dudder* and *dudder-upper*' (B. 1959).

dud weather. Weather unsuitable for flying: R.A.F. coll.: since ca. 1918. H. & P.

dudder(-upper).—3. See **dud-up.**

dudes is Randle Holme's (and others') spelling of *duds,* clothes.

Dudley. A water bottle: railwaymen's (E.R.): since ca. 1950 (?). *Railway*, 3rd.

duds.—4. Female knickers: late C. 19–20. A specialisation of sense 1 (p. 246).—5. In Australia —since ca. 1940, only trousers. (B.P.)

dufer. An occasional variant (Australian) of **doofer,** 1 (p. 234): B., 1943. Perhaps rather '*do for* after'.

duff, n.—3. Hence (?), a tin in which pudding is served; prison s. (not c.): C. 20. H. U. Triston, *Men in Cages*, 1938.

duff, v.—5. To render unusable; to ruin; to destroy: R.A.F.: since ca. 1935. Jackson. Cf. sense 3.

duff, adj. (p. 246), was, in 1939–45, applied by the Air Force to weather unsuitable to flying.

duff, a piece of. See **piece of dough.**

duff, up the. (Of a woman) pregnant: low Australian: C. 20. B., 1942. Cf. **pudden club** (*Dict.*), which prob. suggested it.

duff-bag. 'Formed in the sailor's black "silk" when the bight is tied in by the tapes of his jumper forming a loop just wide enough to hold two fingers,' Granville: Naval: since ca. 1910.

duff gen. Unconfirmed and improbable report;

unreliable news: R.A.F. since ca. 1930. See **duff,**
v., 1 in *Dict.* and **gen** in these Addenda. Partridge,
1945.

duffer, 1, has nuance 'a maker of spurious goods
esp. sham jewelry'; jewellers': ca. 1820–90,
Sessions, Oct. 1840 (p. 1037).—4. Occurs with
nuance 'an article of sham jewelry' in *Sessions,*
Oct. 1840 (pp. 1042–3).

duffie. A duffel jacket or coat: Australian
teenagers', es*ρ.* surfers': since the late 1950's.
(*Pix,* Sept. 28, 1963.)

duffman. Sick: rhyming s.: late C. 19–20.
In full: *Duffman Dick.* (W. Buchanan-Taylor,
Shake the Bottle, 1942.)

Duffoes. Ratings of the Plymouth Division:
Naval: C. 20. (P-G-R.) Perhaps ex **duff,** n., 2
(p. 246): cf. *Guzzle* (p. 364).

duffy, n., 2 (p. 247). No! *duffy* is valid: witness *duffy bottle,* a bottle of gin, occurring in *The
Port Folio* of May 16, 1807, reporting, at p. 247,
col. 1, a British source. (Moe.)—3. Esp. *have a
duffy,* to have a look: R.A.F. regulars': since ca.
1920. Ex **dekko** (*Dict.*).—4. But *have a duffy at* is
also general Services for 'have a try at': since ca.
1935. (P-G-R.)

duffy, v. To polish (e.g. one's buttons): R.A.F.:
since ca. 1930.

dug-in job. A safe job; a privileged job:
Army: since ca. 1917.

Duggie. Field-Marshal *Douglas* Haig: Army:
1916–18.

Duke. Cf. **Duke of Kent** below.—2. Inevitable
nickname for all males named Kent: since ca.
1930.—3. A navvies' nickname (ca. 1850–1910) for
a man with a large nose. 'Out of compliment to
the Great Duke' (of Wellington): D. W. Barrett,
Navvies, 1880.

duke.—7. A clay marble: New Zealand children's: C. 20. (Ruth Park, *The Witch's Thorn,*
1952.)

Duke of Kent (p. 247): often shortened to *Duke*
(or *duke*).

Duke of Teck. A cheque: rhyming s., mostly
theatrical: late C. 19–20. Cf. *Duchess . . .* above.
(Franklyn, *Rhyming*.)

Duke of York.—1 (p. 247), is also n.: a walk.
(D. W. Barrett, *Navvies,* 1880.)—4. Chalk:
Cockneys' rhyming: C. 20. Len Ortzen, *Down
Donkey Row,* 1938.

dukes (p. 247). In line 2, read 'Ex **Duke of
Yorks,** 2'. Another theory: 'Ex the rules of the
Duke of Queensberry'.

dukes, put up the (p. 247).—2. 'A variation of
meaning here is to hide something under one's
jersey, perhaps with arms folded. Glasgow, 19th
Century': Dr R. L. Mackay, M.D. (Confirmatory
evidence welcomed.)

duke's stove. See **Benghazi cooker.**

dukess. Duchess: sol.: C. 19–20.

Dumb Dick. See **Bob Short** above.

dumb squint. See **dumb glutton** (*Dict.*).

dumby (p. 248). Earlier in *Boxiana,* II, 1818.

dumfogged is an erroneous form of **dumb-fogged**
(*Dict.*).

dummestic dreamer. Domestic drama: proletarian sol.: C. 19. Mayhew I, 1851.

dummy. Sense 3 has in C. 20 the specific sense,
'wallet'.—9. A disc ground: railwaymen's: C. 20.
(*Railway*.)

dummy, v. To take up (land), nominally for
oneself, really for another: Australian: since ca.

1860. 'Tom Collins', *Such is Life,* 1903, 'Bob
and Bat dummied for ole McGregor'.

dummy chucker. A goods shunter: railwaymen's: since ca. 1945. (*Railway,* 3rd.)

dummy engineer. An engineer Midshipman:
Naval: since ca. 1920. (P-G-R.)

dummy run.—2. Hence, a rehearsal: Navy and
Air Force: 1943 +. By 1950, fairly gen. civilian;
by 1955, coll.; by 1960, among technicians and
scientists, j.

The Naval usage goes back to ca. 1910. '"Bartimeus" uses it, *à propos* preparations for a marriage service, in *Naval Occasions* (1914)': Ramsey
Spencer, 1967.

dummy week. Non-payment week: Naval:
C. 20. The ratings are paid fortnightly. It is
often called also *blank week*: Naval coll.: since ca.
1939. (Granville, Nov. 22, 1962.)

dump, n., 5 (see p. 248). Also Australian. B.,
1942.

dump, v., 2 (p. 248). In, e.g., W. L. George, *A
Bed of Roses,* 1911.—4. To press (wool) closely:
Australian: since ca. 1920. (B., 1943.) Perhaps
ex sense 2 (p. 248)—influenced by S.E. *tamp.*—
5. (Ex sense 2.) To abandon (e.g., stores):
Services: 1940 +; by 1945, civilian.

dumper. A heavy wave on a surfing beach:
Australian coll.: since ca. 1920. B., 1942. It
picks one up and dumps one down.—2. A
cigarette-end: Australian: since ca. 1925.
(B., 1943.) An object one 'dumps'. Hence a
dumper-dasher, one who picks up cigarette-ends
off the street and smokes them (B.).

dumplings. See 'Body' and cf. **dumpling-shop**
(*Dict.*).

dumps. Dumplings: cooks' and domestics':
C. 20.

Dun Territory. Like *Codrington's* (and
Mostyn's) *Manors, Dynasty of Venus, Fields of
Temptation, Land of Sheepishness, Plains of
Betteris, Point Nonplus, Province of Bacchus,
Pupil's Straits, River Tick* and *salt-pits,* it occurs
in Egan's *Goose,* 1823, and is thus recorded in the
Dict. Egan himself used all these terms two years
earlier in his *Life in London.*

Dunbar wether. A red herring: Scottish:
C. 19–20; ob. B. & L. (at *trout*). Cf. *Yarmouth
capon.*

dung, 3 (p. 249). Earlier in *Sessions,* April 17–
20 (trial of Wm Milbourn *et al.*), 1765. Blood, a
journeyman tailor, says, 'They that were agreeable to our rules we called *Flints* and those that
were not were called *Dungs.*'

dung it; esp. as vbl n., **dunging it.** To be a
traitor to the trade: tailors': mid-C. 19–20.
B. & L. Cf. the n. in *Dict.*

dunhead. An undesirable character: Australian: since ca. 1930. (D'Arcy Niland, *The
Shiralee,* 1955.)

dunk. To dip: Cockney-ex-Yiddish: mid-C.
19–20. (Julian Franklyn, communication of
Dec. 16, 1959.) For etymology, see **tunk.**
Current in Australia, 'but only for the practice of
dipping biscuits, etc., in tea' (B.P.). By 1945,
coll.

dunker. One who habitually 'dunks': mostly
Australian: since ca. 1930: s. >, by 1950, coll.
(B.P.)

Dunlop tyre (often shortened to *Dunlop*). A
liar: since ca. 1905. Rhyming: cf. the synonymous **holy friar.**

dunnaken. 'Used as an adj. at the R.M.A. Woolwich, 60 years ago to denote one's oldest uniform, in contradistinction to "spange" referring to one's best uniform,' as an eminent soldier writes in a private letter of April 3, 1937.

dunno. Don't know: Australian semi-literate: mid-C. 19–20.

*****dunnocker.** See **dunaker.**

dunnovan. A variant of **donovan** (*Dict.*).

Dunn's three-and-ninepenny. See **Lincoln and Bennett.**

dunny. A privy: Australian: since ca. 1880. Ex *dunnaken* (p. 249). John Cleary, *The Sundowners*, 1959. Mostly juvenile, it occurs in Norman Lindsay, *Saturdee*, 1933.

Dunsterforce. Synonymous and contemporaneous with **Noperforce** (*Dict.*).

[Dupes and fools receive many names in s.: here are those which Matthew lists as appearing in Ned Ward during the years 1700–24: *cod's head* (1703), *country chub* (1709), *golden chub* (1714), *gudgeon* (1703, prob. always S.E.); *bubble* (1703; but see *Dict.*), *coniwobble* (i.e. *coney-wobble*; 1703), *looby* (1703), *ninny-hammer* (1703; prob. always S.E.), *nisey* (1703), *Tom-doodle* (1703), *zany* (1709; prob. always S.E.); country fools being *buttered bun* (1715), *country cokes* (1709) or *c. hick* (1722) or *c. put* (1700). Those who resort to courtesans are *cullies* (1703), *rum cullies* (1709), *rum culls* (1709). Of debauchees, we hear of old *snufflers* (1709), young *fumblers* (1703) and *town-stallions* (1703).]

durry. A cigarette butt: low Australian: C. 20. B., 1942. Ex **durie** (*Dict.*)?—2. A cigarette: low Australian: since ca. 1910. (B., 1943.)

dussent or **dursn't.** A sol., mostly Cockney, form of **daren't**: C. 19–20. (Edwin Pugh, *Tony Drum*, 1898.)

dust.—3. Gunpowder: Australian coll.: mid-C. 19–20. Baker.—4. Flour: Australian: since ca. 1860. 'Tom Collins', *Such Is Life*, 1903.—5. Portland cement: builders': C. 20.

dust, v.—3. See:—

dust, get a. To receive severe disciplinary treatment; *to dust* (someone), to discipline severely: Army, esp. the Guards: since ca. 1920. (P-G-R.)

dust bin.—2. Gun position on the underside: R.A.F.: since ca. 1939. H. & P. It receives the *dirt*; also, pre-war bombers had belly turret-shaped like a dust-bin. Robert Hinde, letter of March 17, 1945.—3. Bridge in a motor torpedo (or gun) boat: Naval: since ca. 1938.

dust-bin lids. Children: rhyming s. on *kids*: C. 20. (Franklyn 2nd.)

dust-bin totting. Unauthorized removal of refuse from dust-bins: C. 20. *The Times*, April 25, 1940. See **tot,** n., 5 (p. 902). Also *d-b tatting.*

dust hole. See 'Guard-Room in Army Slang'.

dust of the Burma road. Bread: Royal Canadian Navy: 1942–5. (P-G-R.)

dust (someone's) **pants.** To spank: coll.: late C. 19–20. Cf. *dust one's cassock* (p. 250).

dust parade. 'Morning fatigue party for cleaning up,' H. & P.: Army: since ca. 1920.

dust-up.—2. A fall from a horse: Australian coll.: late C. 19–20. Archer Russell, *Gone Nomad*, 1936.

dust whapper (or **whopper**). A carpet beater: ca. 1815–70. George Smeeton, *Doings in London*, 1828.

dustbin seven. An old, cheap car: ca. 1925–55. Apparently suggested by *Austin Seven.*

dusted, adj. Beaten; worn out: Australian: since ca. 1930. (Dymphna Cusack, *Southern Steel*, 1953.)

dusters. Testicles: Army: C. 20; ob. by 1948. But extant in Navy and among Cockneys. Perhaps jocular, ex dust accumulated by shorts-wearers, esp. in India or in desert country.

dustie or **-y.** Sense 1: much earlier in Mayhew, II, 1851. To sense 3, add: Also *Dusty* Rhodes: late C. 19–20. Ex the phrase 'dusty roads'. Cf. *Knobby*. ('Taffrail' seems to constitute the earliest record for *Dusty* Miller.)

dustman, 2 (p. 250). In *Life in London* (1821) Pierce Egan cites the variant *to have met with the dustman*, to feel sleepy.

dusty, 3 (p. 250). But also for all men surnamed *Rhodes*: late C. 19–20.

dusty or **gritty.** Penniless: lower classes': from ca. 1870; ob. B. & L.

Dusty Miller. A coal-mine worker: miners' jocularity: C. 20.

dut. See **dutt.**

Dutch. See 'Tavern terms', § 3, *c*.

Dutch, in. In trouble; under suspicion: Australian: adopted ca. 1935 from U.S. B., 1942. Also adopted (ca. 1925) in Canada, with the additional nuance 'in disfavour' (Leechman).

Dutch auction (p. 252) occurs in Ruskin, *Unto This Last*, lectures delivered in 1859.

Dutch by injection. See **injection . . .**

Dutch cap. A type of female pessary: Londoners' and Forces': since ca. 1925. Ex the shape.

Dutch cheese.—2. The divisional sign of the 4th British Infantry Division: Army: 1939–45. (P-G-R.)

Dutch fuck. Lighting one cigarette from another: Forces': 1940 +. Prob. ex Territorial Army, where current from or before 1938. Also called *Don Freddie*, the Signalese for D.F.

Dutch kiss, n.; **Dutch-kiss,** v.i. Low coll. of C. 20, as in Auden & Isherwood, *The Dog under the Skin*, 1935, 'The boots and the slavey dutch-kissing on the stairs', it seems to mean indulgence, or to indulge, in sexual intimacies.

Dutch oven. The olfactory state of the bed-clothes after one has broken wind in bed: low: since ca. 1910, esp. in the Army.

Dutch pennants. Untidy ropes: nautical (Naval): mid-C. 19–20. Merely another of these little national amenities.

Dutch street, eat (or **lunch** or **dine**) **in.** To eat with someone, each paying his own bill: late C. 19–20. A Belfast newspaper, May 31, 1939. Rhyming *Dutch treat* (p. 251)?

Dutch uncle (p. 251). I have over-emphasized the severity: rather is the connotation that of 'didactic and heavy-handed, yet kindly'.

Dutchie.—2. In Australia, any Central European: coll.: C. 20. Baker.

Dutchman.—5. An irregular hard lump in brown sugar: late C. 19–20.

Dutchman's anchor (p. 251) occurs esp. in *alongside the Dutchman's anchor*, left behind: Naval: C. 20.

duties. Duty-free goods, esp. cigarettes: Naval: since ca. 1940. Short for *duty-frees*, itself a C. 20 coll.

dutt (or **dut**). A hat: North Country: C. 20. Ex a hatter named Dutton?

duty beauty. A W.R.N.S. duty officer: Naval (mostly ward-room): 1939–45.

duty boy. The officer of the Day or of the Watch: Naval officers': since ca. 1920. (P-G-R.)

duty dog. Duty Officer; loosely, Orderly Officer: Services: since ca. 1920. H. & P. Cf. **dog-watch.**

duty stooge. A Duty Corporal or Duty Air-man: R.A.F.: 1938 +. Gerald Emanuel, letter of March 29, 1945.

duty-sub, the. 'The duty sub-division of the watch, to be called upon to relieve pressure when needed' (Granville): Naval coll.: C. 20.

dwarf. A signal: railwaymen's: C. 20. (*Railway.*)

dwell on. To like very much, to long for (someone): Australian coll.: since ca. 1930. (Sarah Campion.)—2. 'Eagerly to await another's decision of action' (B., 1959): Aus.: since ca. 1930.

dwell the box. To be patient; to wait: low: since ca. 1930. (Norman.)

dyke; dykey. See **dike, dikey,** above.

dynamite, n.—2. Baking powder: Australian: since ca. 1920. B., 1942. It causes cakes, scones, etc., to rise—to 'blow up'.

dynamiter.—2. A car with a defective air-mechanism that inopportunely puts the brakes full on: Canadian railroadmen's (− 1931).

d'you know something? 'copied in Britain from American speech, may well be a Germanism . . . derived from *Weisst du 'was*: The point is that in conversational German *was* is used as a shortened form of *etwas*, meaning something, though its true meaning, as a word in its own right, is what. One assumes that German immigrants did not realize the existence of the traditional "D'you know what?" and quite unconsciously evolved "D'you know something?" on the strength of their native expression' (Brian Foster, *The Changing English Language*, 1968): in U.S. since ca. 1930, in Britain since ca. 1945. *D'you know what?* itself probably goes back to well before 1900—perhaps so far as 1850.

E

E-Boat Alley. 'Quite a sizable fleet . . . entered the Wold Channel, to which the war had given the name E-Boat Alley,' Humfrey Jordan, *Landfall and Departure*, 1946: nautical: 1939–45. (Off the Yorkshire Coast.)—2. Granville defines it as 'the stretch of coast between Great Yarmouth and Cromer and The Wash'.

'e dunno where 'e are! (p. 252) is from a music-hall song: 'Since Jack Jones come into a 'arf a' nounce o' snuff, 'E dunno where 'e are. 'E's got the cheek and impudence To call 'ee's muvver Ma.' (Julian Franklyn, 1962.)

E.T.B.s. A Wren's knickers: Naval (Wrens'): since ca. 1940. I.e. elastic top and bottom. Granville.

eager beaver. 'One who pitches right in, sometimes to the dismay of less highly geared colleagues, and sometimes none too intelligently' (Leechman): Canadian: adopted, ca. 1940, ex U.S. By imperfect reduplication: perhaps suggested by the U.S. (*as*) *busy*, or *industrious, as a beaver.*

eagle. A hole done in two strokes under bogey: golfers' s., adopted ca. 1922 ex U.S.; by 1930, it had > j. Prob. suggested by golfers' *birdie.*—2. A Stuka dive-bomber: Australian airmen's: ca. 1940–5. (B., 1943.)

eagle-eye. Locomotive engineer: Canadian railroadmen's (− 1931). He needs it. 'Ironic, and mostly used by non-drivers' (Priestley).

ear, on one's.—2. Tipsy: Australian: since ca. 1910. (K. S. Prichard, *Haxby's Circus*, 1930.)—3. Hence, *get on one's ear*, to get drunk. as in K. S. Prichard, *The Black Opal*, 1921 (p. 17).—4. *On one's ear* also means '(Of a task or undertaking) easily accomplished' (B., 1959). Aus.: since ca. 1920.

ear, pull down one's. To get money from (a person), esp. as a tip: Cockneys': from ca. 1870. Clarence Rook, *The Hooligan Nights*, 1899, 'Well, we couldn't pull down their ear for more'n 'alf a dollar.' Cf. *bite one's ear.*

ear, put on one's. To set on: low coll.: from ca. 1890. Pugh (2): '"An' I s'pose," said Deuce, looking puzzled, "that it wouldn't be quite the thing, would it, to put a tiggy"—detective—"on his ear?"'

ear-bash, n. A talk: Australian: since ca. 1925. Cf. next entry. (Jon Cleary, *The Sundowners*, 1952.)

ear-basher. One who is a bore: Australian: since ca. 1945. (*The Times*, Dec. 27, 1963.) Cf. **ear-bash** above and:—

ear-bashing, n., v., and occ. as adj. Conversation; talking, esp. fluently and at length: Australian soldiers': 1939 +. Lawson Glassop, *We Were the Rats*, 1944, '"You musta thought me a queer sorta feller with me French plays and me Bach fugues—ya know them things he's often ear-bashing about."'

ear-flip. A sketchy salute: Services: since ca. 1930. H. & P.

ear-guards. Small side-whiskers: Australian: C. 20. Baker.

ear-hole, v. To take a corner at an acute angle: motor-cyclists': since ca. 1925.—2. To eavesdrop, to listen in to someone's conversation: low: since ca. 1930. (Norman.)

ear-hole, on the. Also, by 1919, low s.—as in James Curtis, *You're in the Racket Too*, 1937.

ear-lugger. A persistent borrower; a 'scrounger': Australian: C. 20. Baker.

ear-mad. 'The thickened ear (in its upper portion) found in some cases of insanity': medical: from ca. 1870. B. & L. But is this not a misprint for *ear, mad,* the term surely being *mad ear,* which would be not s. but coll.; moreover, † by 1930. Dr M. Clement confirms me in this view and states that it is a lay, not a medical term; the medical term is 'degenerate ear'; *mad ear* refers, moreover, to the external ear. See, e.g., W. S. Dawson, *Aids to Psychiatry*, 1924; 3rd ed., 1934. Cf. **mad nurse.**

ear phones. Women's hair-style, with hair drawn to the side and clamped over the ears: since ca. 1930.

ear-wigging. A variant—? the original form—of **wigging,** n., on p. 958: C. 19. Wm Maginn, *Tales of Military Life*, 1829 (at II, 299), 'The effect of Sir Edward's petty tyranny, and the *ear-wigging*—as it is expressively termed in military life—were now apparent.' Moe.

earlies, the. The early days—old times—in Australia: Australian coll.: since ca. 1925. (B., 1943.) Or in Africa: since ca. 1910.

early bird. A word: rhyming s.: late C. 19–20. (Sydney Lester.) Cf. **dick(e)y birds,** 5, above.

early door. A whore: rhyming s.: late C. 19–20. (Franklyn, *Rhyming.*)

early doors. A pair of (female) drawers: rhyming: since ca. 1870.

early hour. A flower: rhyming: since ca. 1880.

early on; late on. Early in the morning; late at night: coll.: mainly North Country: late (? mid-) C. 19–20.—2. Hence (?), early—or late—in the proceedings; soon: coll.: C. 20.

Early Pullman. 'An imaginary architectural style marked by over-elaborate decoration like the first Pullman cars on North American railways' (Leechman): Canadian (ex U.S.): since ca. 1945. Cf. **North Oxford Gothic** and **Stockbrokers' Tudor** below.

early riser.—3. Blanket carried by a tramp: Australian: C. 20. B., 1942.

earn one's oats. To earn one's food; pull one's weight: Australian coll.: C. 20. (B., 1943.) Ex the upkeep of horses.

ears apart, I didn't ask what keeps your. A

counter to the rejoinder or comment *balls!* or *ballocks!*: low c.p.: since ca. 1940.

ears flapping, have—or keep—**one's.** To listen, esp. if closely: since ca. 1950.

ears from one's elbows, know one's. To be sensible or shrewd: coll.: mid-C. 19–20. Blaker. See quotation at **nor an 'un.** Perhaps a refined version of **arse from one's elbow** . . . (p. 18). Also, in the mid-1940's, 'He doesn't *know his brass* (or *bass*) *from his oboe*'.

earth-chasers. The Torpedo Officer's electric-light party; seamen torpedomen: Naval: since ca. 1920. Granville. *Earth* in its electricity sense.

earth stoppers (p. 252). Slightly earlier in W. T. Moncrieff, *Tom and Jerry*, 1821.

earwig, n.—3. 'A crony, or close friend' (*Sinks*, 1848): ca. 1830–70. Ex the mutual whispering. —4. An inquisitive person: from ca. 1880.

earwig, v. To detect; to understand: rhyming s. (on *twig*): C. 20.—2. Hence (?), to listen in on a radio telephone at sea: trawlers' and drifters': since ca. 1930. Cf. sense 2 of the n. (Granville.)

earwigger. An eavesdropper; a conversational interloper: Services: adopted, in 1940, from U.S. H. & P.—2. In pl. headphones: Services: since ca. 1941. H. & P.

ease one's arm; gen. imperative. To go steady: Cockneys': from ca. 1885; ob. Pugh (2): '"Ease your arm," growled Marketer. "You know me an' I know you, I reckon. If we can't couple up wi'out jibbin', I pass—that's all."'

ease oneself (p. 253). Prob. suggested by the S.E. sense, 'to defecate'.

East Enders, the. The Sussex County Cricket Club: cricketers': ca. 1885–1914. Sir Home Gordon, *The Background of Cricket*, 1939.

easy, n. A spell, a rest, as in 'I'll take an easy as soon as I can': coll.: late C. 19–20.

easy, adj. (Of a girl) easily picked up: coll.: from ca. 1890. (W. L. George, *The Making of an Englishman*, 1914.)—2. Esp. in 'I'm easy'—I don't mind one way or the other: R.A.F. coll.: since ca. 1938. Ex the R.A.F. c.p. of self-protecting acceptance: since ca. 1936.—3. Easily imposed upon: Canadian coll.: C. 20. (Leechman.)

easy as apple-pie, as. Very easy indeed: Australian coll.: since ca. 1920. (B.P.)

easy as taking money (or **toffee**) **from a child;** gen. preceded by **as.** Very easy (to do): coll.: late C. 19–20. The Canadian (and U.S.) version is . . . *candy from a kid.* (Leechman.)

easy as tea-drinking. Australian variant of prec.; coll.: C. 20. B., 1942.

easy mark. A girl easy to persuade into sexual intercourse: since ca. 1920. See **mark,** n., 3, 4, 5 (*Dict.*).

easy-meat. 'She's easy meat'—of a not invincible chastity: since ca. 1920.—2. (Of a thing) easy to obtain: (of a plan) easy to effect: since ca. 1925. 'Oh, that's easy meat!'

easy on! Steady!: Australian coll.: C. 20. B., 1942. Short for *go easy on it!*

easy to look at; easy on the eye. (Esp. of women) good-looking: the former, Anglicised, ex U.S., by 1930; the latter, derivatively ex the earlier, first heard by the editor in 1936. By meiosis.

eat, 1 (p. 253). Read: C. 20. Leonard Merrick, *Peggy Harper*, 1911, 'They ate the piece.'

eat one's toot. '*To eat toot* was the pioneer way of describing the period during which new immigrants settled down to the cold facts of New Zealand life. More correctly the expression was *to eat tutu,* for it was from the poisonous plant of that Maori name that the phrase was taken,' B., 1941: New Zealand coll. of ca. 1830–90. Baker records R. B. Paul, *Letters from Canterbury*, 1857, '. . . Which old settlers call *eating their tutu.*' Note: the correct pron. of the Maori word is 'toot', much as that of Lake Wakatipu is *Wakkatip.*

eat oneself stiff. To eat a hearty meal; to gorge: schoolboys': C. 20. Anthony Weymouth, *Temp Me Not*, 1937.

eat (someone) **out.** To reprimand severely: Canadian: since ca. 1930. (Leechman.) A variant of **chew out** above.

eat the wind out of a ship (p. 253) occurs much earlier in *The Dublin University Magazine*, Oct. 1834 (p. 400). Moe.

eating irons. Knife, fork, and spoon: Services coll.: since ca. 1920. H. & P. Weapons (cf. *shooting irons*) with which to attack the meal.

eau-de-Cologne, often shortened to **eau(-)de.** Telephone: rhyming s.: C. 20. 'Give me a blow on the eau de.' (Franklyn 2nd.)—2. A girl, a woman: itinerant entertainers' rhyming s. on the parlary *polone,* q.v. at **palone** below: late C. 19–20. (Sydney Lester.) Sometimes shortened to *eau-de.*

ebenezer. The Rev. A. K. Chignell writes: '*Ebenezer = stone of help* (Hebrew). Was there at Winchester some particular stone in the wall of fives' court that sent a ball heavenwards? This is the sheerest guess, but yet seems possible.' Mr F. W. Thomas settles it thus: 'Title of Nonconformist hymn, "Here I'll raise My Ebenezer." Hence the stone that makes a fives ball rise.'

eccer.—2. School homework: Australian schoolchildren's: C. 20. B., 1942. Ex the exercises forming so large a part of homework.—3. In the 1880's–1890's, Oxford undergraduates' s. for Association football. *The Times,* Oct. 12, 1938. Ex sense 1; cf. **soccer** (*Dict.*).

[Echoism in slang. Many of the most vivid slangy neologisms originate as echoic words, seen at their most immediate as nouns of impact, more or less synonymous with such exclamations as *smash!—crash!—bang!—whack!* Some of those nouns become or, at the least, give rise to nouns of enthusiastic approval. A long essay or even a monograph could very easily be written on the subject. This Supplement, however, is not in any sense, nor to any degree, a collection of essays, large or small.

The point can be illustrated, briefly yet perhaps adequately, with three passages from William Golding's masterpiece, *Lord of the Flies,* published in 1954 and dealing with a miscellaneous group of boys aged 6–13. (The edition used is the Faber paperback, 1962.)

'The great rock . . . leapt droning through the air and smashed a deep hole in the canopy of the forest. Echoes and birds flew, white and pink dust floated, the forest further down shook as with the passage of an enraged monster: and then the island was still.

"Wacco!"

"Like a bomb!"

"Whee-aa-oo!"' (p. 37)

'Jack was on his feet.

"We'll have rules!" he cried excitedly. "Lots of rules! Then when anyone breaks 'em—"
"Whee-oh!"
"Wacco!"
"Bong!"
"Doink!"' (p. 44)
'Immured in these tangles, at perhaps their most difficult moment, Ralph turned with shining eyes to the others.
"Wacco."
"Wizard."
"Smashing."
The cause of their pleasure was not obvious.' (p. 35)
'Again came the solemn communion of shining eyes in the gloom.
"Wacco."
"Wizard."' (p. 36)
Strictly, no comments are necessary. Yet perhaps one should note that *wacco* is better written *whacko* and that the echoic *bong* has the same root as *bonkers*, crazy, and that *doink* occurs, with its intensively echoic prefix *ger* or *ker*, in *gerdoying*, *kerdoying*, qq.v. at **kerdoying** below.]

Ecks. See **Ekes**.

ecnop. A prostitute's bully: low: C. 20. A back-s. synonym of **ponce** (p. 647).

edention. See **eclogue** (*Dict.*).

edge, n. Adjutant: Army: C. 20. Ex Cockney pron. of *adje.*—2. See 'Mock-Auction Slang' below.

edge, over the. Unreasonable; excessive; improper: Australian coll.: since ca. 1910. B., 1942.

edge against, have an. To dislike a person: Australian: since ca. 1910. Baker. Earlier as in 'Tom Collins', *Such Is Life*, 1903, 'Magomery's got an edge on you, Thompson, for . . . leavin' some gates open.'

edge it! Be quiet! Stop it!: Aus.: C. 20. Xavier Herbert, *Capricornia*, 1939. '"Hey—edge it, Mum!"'

edgy. Irritable; nervous: coll.: C. 20. Ex *nerves on edge*.

Edie. A cheap prostitute: Londoners', esp. police: since ca. 1945. 'From the point of view of the police, the best of the street-walkers, or "Toms" as they were called, was the Mayfair professional, and the worst the Edies of the East End, Piccadilly and the railway stations': John Gosling & Douglas Warner, *The Shame of a City*, 1960.

edjercation or **ejercation**. Education: sol.: mid-C. 19–20. (Nevinson, 1895.) Cf. **eddication** (*Dict.*).

Edna May, on (my, your, etc.). On one's way: rhyming s.: C. 20; since ca. 1930, predominantly theatrical. Ex the famous music-hall entertainer. (Franklyn, *Rhyming*.)

education has been sadly neglected, my or **your** or . . . A jocular c.p., esp. if the matter is unimportant: C. 20.

Edwardian. A Teddy boy: jocular; ca. 1956–64. Cf. **Teddy boy** below.

Edwards. King Edward potatoes (a very popular kind): growers' and sellers' coll.: since ca. 1910.

eejit. Idiot: Anglo-Irish sol.: C. 18–20.

eelerspee. A confidence trickster: Australian c.: since ca. 1910. (B., 1943.) Via *eeler sp*(ee), centre-s. of *speeler* or *spieler*, 1 (p. 808).

eff, v.; **effing,** vbl n. and ppl adj. To say *fuck*; foul-mouthed (swearing): C. 20. Michael Harrison, *Reported Safe Arrival*, 1943, '"They'd eff and blind till your ear-'oles started to frizzle."' At first euphemistic, it soon > jocularly allusive also.

effing and blinding, be. To be using bad language: C. 20. Cf. the preceding entry.

efforts. See 'Prisoner-of-War Slang', 10.

Egee Pete. Egypt: mostly Army: ca. 1880–1914.

Egg, or **Skating Rink.** Nickname for a bald-headed messmate: Naval: C. 20. Granville.

egg.—5. Head: C. 20. (Caradoc Evans, *Wasps*, 1933.)

egg, break or **crack one's.** See **break one's egg**.

egg-boiler. A bowler hat: Australian: since ca. 1920. (B., 1943.) Not because one could boil eggs in it but because, in torrid weather, one's own 'egg' (head) boils in it.

egg-bound. Slow-witted: Naval: C. 20. Eggs are very constipating; constipation renders 'heavy'.

egg-head. A scholar; an erudite person; anyone interested in intellectual matters: Canadian: adopted, ca. 1953, ex U.S.; by 1958, beginning to be used in Britain. Ex the high brow and the general shape of the scholar's head—in the popular misconception.

egg-laying. Dropping the second ball just behind the serving line when the first service has actually been 'in': lawn tennis: since ca. 1930. *The Daily Telegraph*, Aug. 7, 1937.

egg on, mostly in imperative. To get a move on, to hurry: low Australian: since the 1920's. (Kylie Tennant, *The Joyful Condemned*, 1953.) Probably ex S.E. *egg on*, to incite.

egg-shell blonde. Any bald person: Australian: since ca. 1945. (B., *Australia Speaks*, 1953.)

egg(-)whisk. An autogyro: R.A.F.: since ca. 1938. H. & P. Ex its rotatory motion. Cf. **windmill.**—2. A helicopter: Naval: since ca. 1948. Ex its appearance.

Egg Wiped. Egypt: Army: 1940–5. A rudimentary pun on *Eg-ypt*. (P-G-R.)

egged. A bus: Army in Palestine: ca. 1942–5. Ex the name of a Palestinian proprietor of a fleet of buses. (P-G-R.)

eggs, lay. See **lay eggs**.

eggs, off one's. Straying; hence, wide of the mark: Midlands: C. 20. (Dr R. L. Mackay, M.D., early 1967.)

eggy. Irritated; excited: Liverpool: C. 20. Ex dial *egg*, to tease, to irritate.

Egyptian Hall (p. 255). In sense 'dance'; † since ca. 1920 at the latest.

Egyptian medal, show an; esp. as c.p., *you're showing an E.m.* To have one's trouser-fly undone, to show a fly-button (or more than one): from ca. 1884; orig. military; slightly ob. Whence **Abyssinian medal** (*Dict.*).

Egyptian P.T. Synonymous with **studying for Staff College:** Army officers': since ca. 1925. Also, since ca. 1945, Naval. (Granville, Nov. 22, 1962.)

eh? to me! (why) you'll be saying 'arseholes' to the C.O. next! 'A c.p. of jocularly dignified reproof' (Atkinson): R.A.F.: since ca. 1930.

eighteen. Short for **eighteenpence** (*Dict.*).

eighteen bob in the pound, often preceded by **only.** (Of persons) not very bright: Aus.: since ca. 1920. Nino Culotta, *Gone Fishin'*, 1963.

Eighteen Imperturbables, the. A formation of eighteen Desert Air Force planes: Eighth Army officers': 1942–3.

Eighth, the. The Eighth Army: coll. (mostly Army): 1942–5, then historical.

eighty-eight, the. See fish-horn.

Eiley Mavourneen (p. 255). More usually *Kathleen Mavourneen*, which is the correct title of the song—written, not by Crouch but by Louisa Macartney Crawford. Cf. **Kathleen Mavourneen system** (p. 449).

Eine (dissyllabic). London: showmen's: since ca. 1870. P. H. Emerson, *Signor Lippo*, 1893. A parlyaree word: corruption of It. *Londra*.

Eisenhower Platz. Grosvenor Square (London), while it contained the American H.Q.: 1942–5.

either. Also, 4, it is used for 'any', 'any one': sol.: rare before C. 20. E.g. in Henry Holt, *Murder at the Bookstall*, 1934: ' "Did you notice anything peculiar about the manner of either of these three?" '

either piss or get off the pot! Either *do* the job or let someone else have a shot at it!: proletarian c.p.: C. 20. The chamber pot.

[Ejaculations of 1700–25, so far as they appear in Ned Ward, are these:—*'Ads-bleed* (1703) or *-flesh* (1709) or *-heart, -heart's-wounds*, both in 1703; *Cat's nouns* (God's wounds; 1703); *Cud's bobs* (1714); *Ud's bobs* (1714) or *bodkins* (1714) or *lidikins* (1714) or *niggers noggers* (1714) or *wountlikins* (1714); the shortenings, *bloody wounds* (1709), *nouns* (1706), and *wounds* (1703), all with *'Ads* or *Ud's* understood; *'zooks* (1706); non-*God* ejaculations are: *i'fecks* (1703), or *i'fackins* or *i'facks* (*ifacks*)—both in 1714 and all = *in faith*; and *sure as a gun*, 1715. Matthews.]

ekal. Equal: Cockneys' pronunciation (coll., not s.): C. 19–20. Edwin Pugh, *A Street in Suburbia*, 1895, ' "It's no good!" he said at length, very huskily. "I ain't ekal to it." '

ekat a torrac. See torrac in *Dict.*

Ekes (or Ecks), School of. London School of Economics: C. 20.

elbow in the hawse (p. 255) goes back to ca. 1810 or a decade earlier; it occurs in W. N. Glascock, *Sketch-Book*, I (16), 1825. Moe.

elbow-lifting. The n.-form of **lift one's elbow** (p. 481): C. 19–20.

elders. A woman's breasts: Australian: since ca. 1920. B., 1942. Either in ref. to an elder tree in full growth and leaf, or with an allusion to the story of Susanna and the Elders.

electric cow. A machine for the conversion of milk-powder and water into 'milk': Naval: since ca. 1940. Granville.

Electric Whiskers. Bergonzoli, an Italian general in N. Africa: Army: ca. 1941–3. Ex It. *Barba Elettrica*. (P-G-R.)

elementary, my dear Watson! An educated c.p. dating from ca. 1900. Ex Sherlock Holmes's frequent remark to touchstone Watson. Cf. **Sherlock Holmes!**, q.v.

elements embrocation. (Exposure to) rough weather that makes one's face red: since ca. 1925. With a pun on *Elliman's Embrocation*.

Elephant and Castle.—2. The anus: rhyming s. (on illiterate *ars'le*): late C. 19–20. Franklyn.—3. A parcel: rhyming s.: since ca. 1920. Often shortened to *Elephant*. John Gosling, *The Ghost Squad*, 1959.

elephant houses. Old forts at Dunkirk: Services: 1940: ob. H. & P.

elephant hut. A nissen hut: Services: since ca. 1919. H. & P. Appearance; cf. **elephant** in *Dict.*

elephant pistol or **gun.** An 'outsize weapon for firing parachute flares': P.B.I. coll.: 1914–18. (A. B. Petch, March 1966.)

elevenses occurs rather earlier in P. G. Wodehouse.

'Ell of a Mess. The London Midland and Scottish Railway: railwaymen's jocular: C. 20. (*Railway* 2nd.)

Ellen Terry. A chamberpot: rhyming s. (on *jerry*): rhyming s., mostly theatrical: C. 20. (Franklyn, *Rhyming*.)

ellum. See *colyum.*

Elsan Eddy (loosely **Eddie**). A latrine-cleaner ('sanitary wallah'); R.A.F.: since ca. 1940; ob. by 1950, † by 1955. A blend of *Elsan*, a proprietary name, and, by a pun, *Nelson Eddy*, the famous singer.

Elsan gen. Unreliable news: R.A.F.: since 1939. H. & P. Ex the excellent make of chemical lavatories on bombers.

Elsewicks (p. 256). Better *Elswicks*. Ex Elswick, a suburb of Newcastle-upon-Tyne.

Elsie.—2. 'A special searchlight adapted for use in the Maunsell Forts in the Thames Estuary': Londoners' (Services and Port of London Authority): 1939(?)–45. Ex *L.C.*, Light Control. (P-G-R.)

embark; usually in combination, as in 'go on embark leave': Services (esp. R.A.F.) coll.: 1939 +. Jackson.

Emma. Emmanuel College: Cambridge undergraduates': since ca. 1860.

emoh ruo. Suburbia; esp. in its smugness: Australian journalists' and publicists', hence others': since ca. 1950. The back-s. form of *our home.* Its use as a house-name—cf. *our home* itself and *chez nous*—led to its becoming generalized. (B.P.)

emote. To be or become emotional; to show excessive emotion: adopted, ca. 1950, ex U.S., where orig. theatrical: s. >, by 1960, coll. 'He is incapable of rational behaviour. He just reacts and emotes.' A back-formation ex *emotion.* (B.P.)

Emperor Augustus, the. See **Druriolanus** in the *Dict.*

empire. 'A large, esp. if unnecessarily large, department run with a view to obtaining promotion for those in charge, who thus become *empire-builders.* (Air Force)': 1944–5. (P-G-R.)

empty I can feel my (or me) backbone touching my (or me) belly-button, I'm so. A low c.p.: C. 20. Alexander Baron, *There's No Home*, 1950.

Emu. A member of the ground staff: R.A.A.F.: 1939–45. (B., 1943.) Cf. *penguin*, 1.

emu-bobbing, n. Picking up cigarette-ends: Australian soldiers': 1939–45. (B., 1943.) To do it, one bobs one's head as an emu does. Hence also *emuing.*

En Zed. New Zealand: N.Z., hence also Australian, troops: 1939–45. Common among N.Z. civilians since ca. 1910.

encore, get an; gen. as vbl n., **getting an encore.** To have to rectify a mistake in one's job: tailors': from ca. 1870. B. & L.—2. To have a second erection at one 'session' of love-making: raffish: C. 20.

end.—2. Glans penis; mostly in compounds: *bell-end, blunt end, red end*: esp. in Armed Forces: C. 20.—3. A net practice at cricket: Rugby School coll.: (?) late C. 19–20. 'The nets are situated at the ends of the field' (D. F. Wharton).

end, it's not my. It's no affair of mine: Naval: since ca. 1925. Granville. Ex Am. c.: see *Underworld*.

end-bit dobber. A tramp, or a beggar, collecting cigarette ends from gutters: Cambridge Town (*not* University): from ca. 1910.

end is (or end's) a-wagging, the. The end of a job is in sight: Naval: mid-C. 19–20. Granville, 'From sailing days when, after much "pulley-haulley", the end of a rope was in sight.'

end of the bobbin!, that's the. See **bobbin!, that's . . .**

Endacott, v.i. 'To act like a constable of that name who arrested a woman whom he thought to be a prostitute': journalistic coll.: ca. 1880–1900. B. & L.

ender. 'A dan buoy with a flag indicating a line of fishing nets or pots' (Granville): deep-sea fishermen's coll.: C. 20.

endless belt. A prostitute: Australian: since ca. 1925. B., 1942. Cf. **belt.**

enemy ships. The opposite of **chummy ships** (p. 154): Naval: late C. 19–20. (P-G-R.)

engineering pie. A special sort of pie served at lunch in the R.N. Engineering Shop at Dartmouth: Naval: since ca. 1930.

engineer's spanner. Sixpence: apparently at first, and perhaps still mainly, nautical, esp. Naval: since ca. 1920. Rhyming s. on *tanner*, sixpence.

Engines. Engineering (or Technical) Officer: R.A.F. coll.: since ca. 1925. Jackson.

English. See 'Tavern terms', § 3, *c*.

english. Spin on a ball, whether, as orig. and usually, in billiards or in baseball: Canadian: since ca. 1918. Mr D. S. Cameron, Librarian to the University of Alberta, has, in a private letter of Aug. 23, 1937, explained the stages of the origination thus:—'1. Language ekes out its own deficiency by gesture, hence, gesture equals "body English".

'2. By direct transference, any gesture or contortion (as in trying to do a difficult physical task becomes "body English").

'3. In a game (e.g. billiards), effect of effort on the ball becomes "body English" on the ball.

'4. By natural contraction, this becomes "English" on the ball or "spin". . . . Can be written with little "e".'

Mr Cameron adds that those who say *side English*, instead of *english* or *spin*, are merely being anti-English.

English, side. Whereas *english* >, ca. 1945, a technicality and part of the Standard language, *side English* has remained s., but was, by 1945, ob. See prec. entry. Then there's *bottom-english*, back spin plus side spin.

English as she is spoke (derivatively, occ. **broke** or **broken**). The broken English *spoken* by many foreigners: coll., virtually a c.p.: late C. 19–20. Cf. J. Y. T. Greig's *Breaking Priscian's Head*; or, *English as She Will Be Wrote and Spoke*, 1928.

enigmae is a catachrestic pl. (C. 19–20) of *enigma*,

as though it were of L. origin. (*Notes and Queries*, April 24, 1937.)

enin (p. 257). Earlier in Mayhew, I, 1851 (as *enina*).

Enoch Arden. A garden: ? originally (1942) among prisoners-of-war in the Far East; hence, since (but ? earlier), among civilians. B., 1953, quotes from *The* (Sydney) *Sun* of Sept. 22, 1945.

enough on one's plate, have. To have as much work as one can manage, or as much as one can do: Forces': 1939 +. Ex lit. domestic sense.

enough to give you a fit on the mat. Very amusing or laughable: non-aristocratic: C. 20; very ob. W. L. George, *The Making of an Englishman*, 1914. Cf. *enough to make a cat laugh*, the prob. origin.

ensign-bearer (*Dict.*) goes back to 1650: see 'Tavern terms', § 6.

enthusiastic amateur. See **amateur.**

*entjies. Cigarette-ends: South African c. (late C. 19–20) >, by 1940, low s. *The Cape Times*. June 3, 1946. Afrikaans in origin, *entjie* being the diminutive of *ent*, end.—2. Hence, short persons: S. African c.: since ca. 1920. (C. P. Wittstock, letter of May 23, 1946.)

envelope, n. A condom: coll.: late C. 19–20.

[Ephemeral General Nicknames. The names of the latest murderer (or murderess) and of certain film stars are, by children in the (esp. London) streets, shouted at persons having some sort of resemblance to the notoriety: prob. immemorial. A very few names—e.g. *Crippen*—have lasted more than a year or two; *Crippen*, indeed, is still to be heard frequently among Cockney children.]

[Epithets and adverbial phrases. Ned Ward, in 1700–25, has the following eligibles among epithets (mostly abusive):—*baker-legged* (1714), *brawny-buttock* (*jades*; 1714), *case-hardened* (1703), *clod-skulled* (1703), *cock-sure* (1712), *doodle* (foolish; 1708), *dub-snouted* (1709), *goggle-eyed* (1703), *jibber-nolling* (? nodding; 1715); *loobily* (1709; with caution), *lousie-look'd* (1703), *maggot-brained* (1703), *nitty* (lousy; 1703), *pat* (opposite; 1722), *peery* (suspicious-looking; 1703), *perdu* (hidden; 1709; more prob. S.E.), *sap-head* (*sot*; 1703), *smug-faced* (1703), *snotty* (1703), *swanking* (1709), *thumping* (great; 1703), *topping* (1703), *two-handed* (vigorous; 1714), and *tut-mouthed* (? dumb; 1714).

Adverbial phrases:—*hugger-mugger* (secretly; 1714; prob. always S.E.); *mutton fists* (1709; more prob. S.E.); *upon the tittup* (galloping; 1703; prob. always S.E.); *within an ambs-ace* (very nearly; 1703).]

Epsom. Inseparable nickname of men surnamed *Salt*. Ex 'Epsom('s) salt'.

equator. Waist: jocular: late C. 19–20; by 1960, slightly ob. In A. S. M. Hutchinson's best-seller *If Winter Comes*, 1921, we read, 'He'd make about four of me round the equator.'

er for *e* is a minor characteristic of Cockney speech: ? immemorial. E.g. *ernough* for *enough*.

Eras. Erasmus (as applied to certain divisions of the school): Christ's Hospital: late C. 19–20. Marples. Cf. **Grec.**

erg. 'In the R.N.A.S. at Mudros [in 1915] we called any member of a working party an "erg", i.e. the lowest unit of work,' S/Ldr. R. Raymond, letter of March 24, 1945. Ex Gr. *ergon*, work.

Eric, or Little by Little. A c.p. directed at shy

or sexually-slow youths: since ca. 1860. Ex the phenomenal popularity of Dean F. W. Farrar's novel of school-life, *Eric; or Little by Little*, 1858, the story of Eric, a boy that, little by little, went to the dogs and a pathetic end.

erk, 1 (p. 258). Perhaps ex 'a lower-deck rating' —the most probable explanation.—2. Hence (?), a recruit, an A.C.2 (the lowest of the low: I was one for 2 years 9 months, so *experto crede!*); occ. applied (Jackson, 1943) also to, but much resented by, an A.C.1: R.A.F.: since 1918. Prob. ex '*air*craftmen'. See esp. Partridge, 1945, both in introduction and in glossary; earlier in, e.g., E.P. in *The New Statesman*, Sept. 19, 1942, and H. & P., 1943. On March 9, 1945, W/Cdr F. J. H. Heading wrote to say, 'The term "Erk" was first used in the R.A.F. Depot, Uxbridge, in 1920. The origination . . . was brought about when I wrote the song "One of the Aircs", Aircs being an abbreviation of aircraftsmen. Through frequent use the term came to be pronounced Erk and I have no knowledge of the term being used in the R.F.C., R.N.A.S. or R.A.F. before the year 1920'; then on the 20th March, 'To me Air Mechanics of the R.A.F. were always known as Ack Emmas'. The weight of the evidence, however, shows that the song reinforced and hastened the growth of a term that was, in fact, already current.

Ermy One. H.M.S. *Hermione*: Naval (lower-deck): C. 20. Granville.

Ernie, the electronic brain that selects the numbers of the winners of Premium Savings Bonds, was never lower than coll. and very soon became the accepted name: since Oct. 1956, the month before the first bonds were issued. Ex the initials of the full technical and official name of the instrument.

Ernie Marsh. Grass: rhyming s.: C. 20.

Erroll Flynn; esp. *on the* . . ., on the chin: rhyming s.: ca. 1938–60. Franklyn 2nd.

erth. Three: back s.: since ca. 1845. A.W.S. in *The Evening News*, March 7, 1938, 'The inverted numbers, eno, owt, erth, and so on are sometimes used by card-players in the East End [of London].' Mayhew, I, 1851 has *erth*; 'threepence'.

erth pu. The game of Three-up: back s.: 1851, Mayhew, I.

ertia. The opposite of S.E. *inertia*: Australian jocular: since late 1950's. (B.P.)

esclop (p. 258). Earlier in Mayhew, I, 1851.

Eskimo Nell is an imaginary Naval heroine—the central figure in a ballad almost as long as it is bawdy. Late C. 19–20. Cf. **Ballocky Bill** (p. 29).

Essedartus. See 'Occupational names'.

essence of pig-shit, the. A luscious girl: Naval lower-deck: since ca. 1925, but never very general. Satirical of names for scents; but also allusive to *as happy as pigs in shit*.

estam. See **stam.**

estamint. The 'Hobson-Jobson' of *estaminet*: Army: 1914–18. (Ian Hay, *Carrying on*, 1917.)

et cet. Et cetera: trivial coll., mostly Australian: C. 20. C. E. McGill, 'With bags an' bottles, bones, et-cet, a bloke can make his pile, | An' knock about at rices then in real old Sydney style,' in 'Me Donah What's at Home', a poem (in *The Bakara Bulletin*, 1919) showing how strong is the Cockney influence on certain sections of Australian English. Cf. **rabbo,** q.v.

Eten Halen. See 'Prisoner-of-War Slang', 9.

eternal.—2. In C. 18 it occ. signified 'thorough; thorough-going', as in *Sessions*, 6th session of 1733, '"Kempton swore at me, *God damn your Blood and Liver, you eternal Bitch*"': cf. sense 1, on p. 258.

etsi-ketsi is a 1946 + variant of—and rather more disparaging (connotation 'wet') than—*allah keefik* ('couldn't care less'), whether comment or description. 'An *allahkeefik*—no! an *etsi-ketsi*—type, he was.' Perhaps from Modern Greek.

ettie or **etty.** A girl: low London: since ca. 1950. John Gloag, *Unlawful Justice*, 1962, '"Jimmy's no good to etties, see? Can't give what they take"' and 'Leader Lad going for this cute ettie'. Ex *Ettie, Etty*, a girl's name.

Europe morning, have a. To rise late from bed: Anglo-Indian coll.: from ca. 1870; ob. B. & L. In India one has to rise early in order to get a good day's work done, work being unhealthy in the middle of the day.

Evans, Mrs. See **Mrs Evans.**

evaporate (p. 259) goes back to ca. 1820 or perhaps a decade earlier still. William Maginn, *Tales of Military Life*, 1829 (at II, 257), '"By the powers, Major," exclaimed Miles . . .; "the Missus o' the house has frightened away that poor fellow; I suppose she put him in mind of his wife, that he evaporated with such alacrity."' (Moe.)

evasive action, take. 'To keep away from trouble' (Jackson, 1943): see **take evasive action.**

even blind Freddie. . . . See **blind Freddie . . .**

even Stephen (or **Steven**). Share and share alike: Canada and Australia: C. 20. B., 1942. Adopted from U.S. with ref. to **Stephen** (*Dict.*). By reduplication of *even*.

even terms. (To work) merely for one's keep: Australian coll.: since ca. 1910. Baker.

evening. See **Sunday.**

Evening, The. *The Evening News*: coll.: C. 20.

ever. An intensive coll. usage, adopted by non-cultured Canadians ca. 1940 ex U.S. 'In the Yukon, ca. 1950, I heard "Well, did Hard-Rock MacDonald ever tie one on!"' (Leechman.) Hence the Canadian teenagers' and (older) children's c.p., *was it ever!*, as in 'Was it a good dance, darling?'—'Was it ever!' Also as in 'Was he nice?'—'Was he ever!'

ever?, did you (p. 259) occurs in An Old Etonian, *The Alphabet Annotated*, 1853:

'Some exclaim, and think themselves so clever! Did you *ever*? (answer) no, I never!'

everlastings. Bare feet: Australian: ca. 1910–50. Ex **everlasting shoes** (p. 259).

ever-loving. One's wife: Australian: since ca. 1935. Elliptical. (B.P.)

every man Jack (p. 259) prob. goes back to ca. 1810 or perhaps even to late C. 18: it occurs in *The Night Watch* (II, 115), 1828. Moe.

every night about this time. An Australian c.p. referring to coition: since ca. 1955. Ex radio announcements. (B.P.)

every time! A c.p. of enthusiastic assent: since ca. 1935.

everybody's doing it, doing it, doing it. A c.p. of ca. 1912–14. (Robert Keable, *Simon Called Peter*, 1921.) Ex a very popular song, the reference being to the Turkey Trot, 'the rage' in 1912–13.

everything but the kitchen sink; esp. *throw in . . .*, applied notably to a bombardment: 1939–45; hence, since 1945, to an intense collective effort.

everything in the garden's lovely! An early record: G. B. Lancaster, *Jim of the Ranges*, 1910, p. 110.

everything is George. All is well, esp. for me: beatnik c.p.: since ca. 1959. (Anderson.)

everything that opens and shuts. Everything needed to make life comfortable: Australian c.p.: since ca. 1950. Ex household gadgets. (B.P.)

everything (or everything's) under control. A Services c.p., applied to a situation where things are 'ticking over' nicely: since ca. 1930. H. & P.; Granville.

everything's hunkey-dory. See **hunks.**

evo. Evening: Australian: C. 20. Baker. Cf. **afto.**

evolution, make an. 'To do anything with the maximum of fuss' (P-G-R): Naval officers': since ca. 1918.

ewif, five. Mayhew, I, 1851; where also *ewif yen(n)ep*, fivepence, and *ewif-gen*, five shillings (a crown).

ex.—2. Ex-wife or ex-husband: Society: since ca. 1920. Agatha Christie, *Towards Zero*, 1944, 'Leonard's new wife and his Ex'.

ex, v. To excise by crossing out: Australian coll.: since ca. 1930. (D'Arcy Niland, 1958.) To put a X through.

Ex, His. Also New Zealand, as is *the G.G* (B., 1941.)

exchange spits. To kiss: low: late C. 19–20.— 2. Hence (?), to coït: workmen's. C. 20.

excite!, don't. A much earlier reference is this: E. H. Hornung, *Raffles*, 1899, '"All right, guv'nor," drawled Raffles: "don't excite. It's a fair cop."'

Excitement (or e.), the. 'There were, in British Columbia, a number of gold rushes before the great strike in the Yukon in 1896. These events, of which the Fraser River gold rush of 1858 was the first, are still referred to as "the excitement". "Harry stayed on after the excitement" and so on' (Leechman, 1962): Canadian coll.: since ca. 1859.

excrementum cerebellum vincit. A jocularly erudite wartime c.p., 'translating' **bullshit baffles brains** (above): Army officers': 1939–45. Cf. **illegitimis non carborundum** below.

excuse me, the. The w.c.: rhyming s.: since ca. 1930.

excuse my abbrev; it's a hab. (I.e. abbreviation; habit.) A c.p. uttered by, or directed at, a person given to trivial abridgements: ca. 1910–12. Such abbr. were much more frequent ca. 1890–1912 than before—or since.

excuse the French! See **French!, pardon the.**

exec, esp. in *exec meeting*, an executive meeting: since late 1950's.

execution. A very large crowd drawn by a 'grafter': grafters': C. 20. *News of the World*, Aug. 28, 1938.—2. Hence, a large crowd around a market man: street market vendors': since ca. 1930. (Julian Franklyn, note of 1962.)

exercise P.U. A drinking-session: Naval officers': 1939–45. (P-G-R.)

Exhibish, the. Any notable Exhibition: Naval: C. 20.

exis, 1 (p. 260). Earlier in Mayhew, I, 1851; where also *exis yen(n)ep*, sixpence.

expat. An expatriate; applied esp. to a white man electing to earn his living in an Asian or East Indian or African state: since the late 1940's. In, e.g., John Slimming, *The Pepper Garden* (a novel about modern Sarawak), 1968.

expectations, not up to her. This innocent phrase has, among music-hall comedians and the lewd of the baser sort, come to have, since ca. 1927, an erotic implication.

expensive. Excellent; esp. in ref. to a very good party: Services (esp. Army) officers': since ca. 1938. (Communicated in April 1942, by Grenfell Finn-Smith.) Cf. American *ritzy*.

*export trade, the. The procuring of women and shipping them to the Argentine: white-slavers' c.: from ca. 1890. Albert Londres, *The Road to Buenos Ayres*, 1928.

express (train). In W.W. I 'we called large enemy shells this as we heard them passing over-head to the back areas. They made a noise like express trains' (A. B. Petch, March 1966): Army term.

extern. An external examiner: University: late C. 19–20.

extra-curricular activities. Adulterous sexual play and intercourse: cultured coll.: since late 1940's.

extra ducks. Additional waiters employed to serve at banquets: caterers': since ca. 1920. Ex their waddling gait.

extra early. First rate, very good, excellent: New Zealand: since ca. 1945.

extra grouse. Exceptionally well or attractive or meritorious: Aus.: C. 20. (B., 1959.) Cf. **grouse, the,** below.

extra sort (superlative to the positive *good sort*) is a person exceedingly attractive to the opposite sex; contrast *drack sort*: Australian: since ca. 1945. (B., 1953.)

extra two inches you're supposed to get after you're forty. A c.p. referring to an imaginary phallic compensation for the years that the locusts have eaten: Forces': 1939–45.

extract the urine from. To 'take the piss out of': Services' jocular euphemism: 1939 +. (P-G-R.)

extraordinar'. Extraordinary; extraordinarily: lower classes', resp. coll. and sol.: mid-C. 19–20. Nevinson, 1895, 'I've mostly been 'appy enough all my time . . . and at times I've been extraordinar' happy.' Common, too, in Scottish.

extry. Additional: sol. for *extra*: mid-C. 19–20. Ibid. (Also in dial.)

*eye. A look-out man: c.: from ca. 1925. *The Pawnshop Murder*.

eye, have in one's. To have in mind: coll.: ca. 1790–1860. 'To some true girl I'll be steering,/ I've got one in my eye'—from an unidentified British poem anteceding 1806 and quoted in an American magazine, *The Port Folio*, May 17, 1806, p. 304. (Moe.)

eye-hole.—2. *Introitus urethræ*: low: late C. 19–20.

eye—or arse—in a sling, get one's. To get into trouble: *eye*, C. 20; *arse*, since ca. 1930. The less respectable *arse* occurs in, e.g., Elleston Trevor, *The Freebooters*, 1967.

eye(-)lotion. Wine in small quantity: Services officers' since ca. 1925. H. & P. Cf. **lotion** and **gargle** in the *Dict*.

eye!, my.—2. But also as a simple exclamation, as in Wm Maginn, *Whitehall*, 1827 (p. 46), '"Bless us, there's the Dover coach again. My eye, she's setting down all her passengers at Holmes's".' Moe.

eye opened, have one's. To be robbed: ca. 1820–80. (Alexander Somerville, *Autobiography of a Working Man*, 1848.) Hence the n. *eye-opening.*

eye-opener.—2. A drink taken before going on early-morning patrol: R.F.C.–R.A.F. officers': since ca. 1916. (Guy Fowler, *The Dawn Patrol*, 1930.)

eye-picker. 'One who "picks the eyes out" of a grazing district by taking up the best land' (B., 1943): Australian: C. 20.

eyeful. An attractive girl or young woman: Australian: since ca. 1918. Baker. She takes the eye.—2. An accidental but fortunate glimpse of even the partial nakedness of a member of the opposite sex: C. 20. Cf. the next.

eyeful?, got your. Have you had a good look?: low: from ca. 1910. Cf. **eyeful** phrase in *Dict.*

eyes!, my (p. 261). Rather: ca. 1780–1910. In an English song (? Charles Dibdin's ?) reprinted in *The Port Folio* of Nov. 1, 1806 (p. 268), we find these lines:

'To Thompson let the bumbo pass,
  Grey, Parker, Walgrave, Calder,
Nelson, who took St. Nicholas,
  My eyes, why how he mauled her!'

(With thanks to Colonel Albert F. Moe.)

eyes and ears of the world, the. An Australian c.p., applied ironically to one who has all the latest information: since ca. 1950. Ex the motto of Gaumont British News. (B.P.)

eyes chalked!, get your. To one not looking where he is going, or to a clumsy person: North Country: late C. 19–20.

eyes for, have. To crave (a thing), be amorous (of a person): orig. (ca. 1955) and still mainly beatnik. 'What's the matter, man? You got eyes for Mary?'—'John's sure got eyes for that bottle!' (Leechman.)

eyes like cod's ballocks, have. To be pop-eyed: low: C. 20.

eyes like piss-holes in the snow. Deeply sunken yellow eyes: low coll.: C. 20. The Canadian form is . . . *two piss-holes* . . .

eyes of the ship, the. The bows of the ship; well forward therein. Naval coll.: C. 19–20. Granville, 'Chinese ships used to have eyes painted on the bows.'

eyes out, go. To make every effort: work exceedingly hard: Australian: since ca. 1820. B., 1942. On *cry one's eyes out.*

eyes stick out like chapel hat-pegs or **like organ stops**, e.g. his; the tense is adjustable. His eyes are (fig.) protuberant: coll.: since ca. 1910. These phrases could be classified as catch-phrases.

eyesight good, it does or **will do your** (or **my**, etc.). A c.p. applied to something well worth seeing: late C. 19–20.

eyesight in it, there's. That's evident or obvious: c.p.: since ca. 1935.

Eyetie. An Italian aircraft: R.A.F.: 1940 +. Jackson. See **Eyeties** (p. 261).

Eyeto. An Italian: Australian: 1940 +. B., 1942. Ex prec. on *Italiano.*

eyewash parade. A C.O.'s inspection: Army: 1914–18, and after. See **eyewash** (p. 261).

F

'f. Pron, rather as *v* and slurred into the preceding syllable, *'f* is a slovenly coll. (rare before C. 20) for *of*. E.g. Dornford Yates, *As Other Men Are*, 1930, in dialogue: 'About a quarter 'f a mile—that way.'

f for *th*. This process (see *Dict.*) is carried still further in the tendency observable since ca. 1920 for *th* to > *ff*, as in *broffer* (pron. *bruffer*) for *brother*.

F.H.B. occurs, e.g., in Ian Hay's *Safety Match*, 1911.

F.I.F.A.S. or **F.Y.F.A.S.** See **fyfas** below.

f.t.b. or **F.T.B.** A c.p. reply (lower-middle class) to 'Have you had enough to eat?': C. 20. I.e. **full to bursting.**

F.U. A 'fuck-up' or grave muddle: low (C. 20) and Forces' (1939 +). See e.g., **M.F.U.**

F.U.J. Fuck you, Jack! Also predicative, as in 'Oh, he's F.U.J.': indifferent to others' misfortunes: Forces': 1939–45.

fa. Father: upper classes' coll.: C. 20. Nancy Mitford, *The Pursuit of Love*, 1945.

fab, adj. Very good; successful; teenagers' (esp. the coffee-bar set): 1957–8. An ephemerid of 1958 was *fantabulous*, a blend of *fantastic* + *fabulous*.

fabulous. A verbal counter, meaning 'very— or merely—agreeable' or 'unusual' or '(very) interesting' or '(very) large' or 'distinguished' or . . .: coll.: since ca. 1945. After being theatrical s. of ca. 1945–50, it > gen. s. and, by 1962, something of a vogue word. Cf. **fab,** above, and **fantabulous** below.

face, n.—5. Personal appearance: Australian: since ca. 1925. B., 1942. Cf. American *front*.

face, v. To punch in the face: pugilistic: ca. 1815–50. *Boxiana*, III, 1821. Cf. **bellier** and **jawer**.

face, put on a. To change one's expression, usually to severity: coll.: C. 19–20. Cf. *what a face*: how severe or disapproving you look!: coll.: mid-C. 19–20.

face at half-past eight, with one's. Mournful; wry-mouthed: C. 20.

face at the window, the. A c.p. applied to someone looking through or even merely appearing at a window: late C. 19–20; little used since 1939. Originally, a 'thriller' or a melodrama— or both.

face-fins. Moustaches: orig. nautical: late C. 19–20. Frank Richardson.

face-fittings. A beard and/or moustache: Australian: C. 20. B., 1942. Cf.:—

face-fungus. Earlier in works of the late Frank Richardson (1870–1917).

face in a knot, get (or **tie**) **one's.** To become angry—or agitated—or bewilderingly excited: Australian: C. 20. Baker.

face-lifter. An uppercut to the jaw: pugilistic: since ca. 1925. Ex beauty-parlour treatment.

face like a coastguard station, have a. To look stony and grim: since ca. 1940. (Laurie Atkinson, Sept. 11, 1967.)

*face like a mountain goat('s), have a. To be an Irish, Scottish or Welsh dupe: c.: C. 20. With pun on **mug,** n., 1.

face like a scrubbed hammock, (have) a. To have) a pale sour-looking face: Naval: since ca. 1920. Granville. Contrast **face like a sea-boot** (p. 261), which Granville defines as 'a long-drawn "fathom of misery"'.

face like a sea-boot (p. 261). Since ca. 1930, however, it has predominantly denoted 'a long-drawn "fathom of misery"' (P-G-R).

face like a yard of pump-water. A 'long'—i.e. miserable or glum—face: coll.: C. 20.

face like the back of a bus, have a; occ. face that would stop a bus or **like the side of a house.** Of girls or women: to be very plain-looking: since late 1940's. A more brutal variant is . . . *like the rear end of a cow*.

face on the cutting room floor, the. An actor or actress cut out of a picture because, after the picture has been completed, it is found that the rôle is superfluous: filmland: since ca. 1920. See esp. Cameron McCabe's clever novel so titled, 1937.

face red?, is—or **was**—**my.** Am, or was, I embarrassed, or ashamed!—a c.p. dating from ca. 1954; by 1966, just slightly ob.

face-ticket is very ob. in its British Museum sense.—2. A season ticket: among those who travel by train or 'tube': coll.: from ca. 1920.

facer, 3 and 4 (p. 262). Cf. the earlier 'At the first facer Hume or Voltaire is grassed and gives in' (J. Wilson, *Noctes Ambrosianae*, I, 162, i.e. in 1822: O.E.D.).

facie is a mere variant of **facey** (*Dict.*).

facility is occ. misused for *faculty*. Thus, 'He had a remarkable facility for motor-racing.' The mistake (rare before C. 20) seems to be caused by confusing such locutions as 'There were, he found, excellent facilities for motor-racing' and 'He had a remarkable facility in motor-racing'; cf. too such a possibility as 'He had a facile faculty for motor-racing' and the implications of the Fr. *arrêt facultatif*, which is one of the municipal facilities.

*factory, the (p. 262).—2. Hence, *the factory*, the police station: late C. 19–20. F. D. Sharpe, *Sharpe of the Flying Squad*, 1938.—3. 'The model agricultural colony at Carroceto (Anzio bridgehead), a prominent landmark': Army: latter part of World War II. (P-G-R.)

fade, do a; take a powder. To disappear without paying rent: Canadian carnival workers': C. 20. The latter was adopted from U.S. and has, since ca. 1940, been general Canadian s. Ex the 'moving' powers of a laxative powder.

*fade, on the, adj. and adv. (By, in) evading

justice, dodging the police: Australian c.: since ca. 1920. B., 1942.

faded, have got (someone). To have someone at a disadvantage: Canadian: since ca. 1940. Esp. in relation to the dice game of craps—and perhaps from it. Dr Douglas Leechman has pertinently asked, 'Can this be ex *fated*?' I rather think it might. On the other hand, the Canadian sense derives ex the American: and the American is 'to have him matched or equalled'; the U.S. 'I've got him faded' = 'I can match any trick or threat of his with one just as potent', esp. at craps, as Mr Robert Clairborne of New York tells me.

fadger.—2. A farthing: Cockneys': late C. 19–20. J. W. Horsley, *I Remember*, 1912. By corruption.

fag, n.—6. (Ex 2.) A lawyer's clerk: Australian: C. 20. B. 1942. Jocular.—**7.** A bore, as in 'It's a bit of a fag', rather boring, rather a nuisance: C. 20. Perhaps cf. sense 3 of the v.

fag, v., 3 (p. 262), prob. derives ex the more gen. sense, 'to work hard, whether mentally or physically'—a sense app. current since ca. 1770 and almost certainly deriving ex Southern Scottish and Northern English dialect. *The Port Folio*, 30 May 1801, p. 175; *The Dublin Magazine*, March 1834, p. 246. (Moe.)

[**fag-end.** See 'Miscellanea'. But it has always, I think, been S.E.]

fag-end at Marlborough and Tonbridge = interruption; *fag-ends!* at Marlborough and *fag-end off!* at Durham = stop listening in!; at Durham *fag-ends* = eavesdropping; *fag-end*, v.t., and *pick up fag-ends* at Oundle = to overhear, or to interrupt: C. 20. Marples.—2. 'To have only a partial or muddled understanding of something that has been said' (Nicolas Bentley, 1961): since ca. 1955.

fag-hag. See 'Canadian'.

fag-hole. The mouth: contemptuous: since ca. 1945. Semantically cf. **cake-hole** above.

fagger.—2. A day with work periods in the afternoon: Marlborough College: since ca. 1880. Ex official *fag-day*.

fagging.—3. An exhausting experience or bout of work: late C. 18–20. Cf. **fag, v.,** 3, above.

fain I. Prob. ex † *feign*, to shirk or get out of.

faintest, the. The least idea; as in 'I haven't the faintest': coll.: since ca. 1910. I.e. *the faintest* (remotest) *idea*.

fair, intensive adj. and adv. ('That's a fair ol' coat'), characteristic of office- and shop-girls' of ca. 1956–9. (Gilderdale.)

fair crack of the whip, give (someone) **a.** To deal fairly with someone: Aus.: C. 20. (B., 1959.)

fair doo's (p. 263). Throughout C. 20, and earlier. Origin: *fair dues*, as in C. T. Clarkson & J. Hall Richardson, *Police*, 1889, 'Now then, fair dues; let everybody be searched, I have no money about me.' Since ca. 1930, more usually *fair doo's all round*.

fair enough. As a question it = 'Satisfied? Convinced? Agreeable to you?'; as a comment it = 'That sounds plausible enough' or 'I'll accept your statement'. Services (esp. R.A.F.) coll.: since the 1920's. R. M. Davison, Sept. 26, 1942 (letter). H. & P. point out that it is often used by instructors. Common in Australia by ca. 1940: Baker.

fair, fat and farty is a vulgar perversion—since ca. 1930—of the c.p. *fair, fat and forty*, itself current since ca. 1820. The c.p. occurs in, e.g., Anon., *The New Swell's Night Guide*, 1846.

fair few, a. A considerable number: Australian coll.: late C. 19–20. 'I have a fair few sheep in this paddock.' (B.P.)

fair go. A fight, esp. between two persons: Australian: late C. 19–20. Baker. As an interjection it = 'Be reasonable!'

fair meat. An easy dupe: c.: from ca. 1910.

fair skint. Very short of money or even entirely 'broke': mainly North Country: C. 20.

fair to middling. A jocular c.p. reply to 'How are you?': mostly Australian: since ca. 1945. (B.P.)

fairy glen. A lavatory: railwaymen's: since ca. 1945 (?). *Railway*, 3rd.

fairy powder. A mixture of potassium chlorate and sulphur: Australian schoolboys': since ca. 1930. 'Struck with a hammer, it makes a noise quite unlike a fairy (*lucus a non lucendo*)': B.P.

fairyland. A synonym of **Christmas tree,** 4, above.

fake, n.—5. (Ex sense 2, p. 263). Stuff used in patent medicines, a patent medicine; a (so-called) cure: showmen's: since ca. 1870. Wm Newton, *Secrets of Tramp Life*, 1886. Ex *corn fake*, corn cure, and *nob fake*, hair-restorer.—**6.** Make-up: theatrical: since ca. 1875. (B. & L.) Cf. **fake up** (*Dict.*).

fake, v. (Cf. sense 1 on p. 263.) To improvise; to play by ear: Canadian dance-bands': ca. 1920–36.

fake the marks. 'They're faking the marks'—footnoted 'the shares were changing hands at fictitious prices' (C. H. B. Kitchin, *The Cornish Fox*, 1949): stockbrokers': C. 20.

fakement.—5. Paint for the face: theatrical: from ca. 1870. B. & L.—**6.** Any letter; a note: 1826, *Spy*, II; † by 1910. Ex sense 1.

falderals, 'silly ideas' (p. 264), is very much older than I had suspected, for it occurs in a Charles Dibdin song quoted by *The Port Folio*, an American magazine, on Nov. 30, 1805 (p. 376, col. 2): 'He runs, while listening to their fal de rals,/Bump ashore on the Scilly Isles.' Moe.

fall down the sink. A, to, drink: rhyming s.: late C. 19–20. Since ca. 1930, usually *tumble . . .* (Franklyn, *Rhyming*.)

fall in the shit. See **shit.**

fall into a cart (or **dump** or **heap** or **load** or **pile**) **of shit and come out with a gold watch** (or **with a new suit on**). A C. 20 Cockney c.p., applied to an habitually lucky person, or to one who has been extraordinarily lucky on a specific occasion.

fall into (the) shit and come up smelling of violets. See **he could fall . . .**

fall off a Christmas tree, I didn't. A c.p., rejecting imputation of credulity: C. 20. (Atkinson.)

fall-out. 'Jocularly used regarding the danger of pieces falling out of an old car' (B.P.): Australian: since ca. 1955. Ex atomic *fall-out*.—**2.** The risk of breasts falling out of a scanty bra or a bikini swimsuit: Australian: since ca. 1960.

fall out of the boat. To become unpopular in a Naval mess: Naval: C. 20. (P-G-R.)

fall over backwards. To go beyond the normal and the expected in order to show how honourably disinterested or how honest or upright one is: since ca. 1945. 'He'll fall over backwards, just to prove that his friendship in no way influences him in your favour.' Cf. *two inches beyond upright*.

In Britain, however, much commoner is *lean over backwards*.

fall to pieces. (Of a woman) to be confined; to give birth to a child: Australian lower-middle class: C. 20. B., 1942.

fallen angel. A defaulter, a bankrupt: Stock Exchange: ca. 1810-70. *Spy*, II, 1826.

fallers. Windfall apples, pears, etc.: rural coll.: late C. 19-20. Perhaps on the S.E. *keepers*.

falling over oneself (to do something). Very eager: coll.: since ca. 1920.

falls, over the. Applied to a surfer 'trying to pull out of a wave too late' (*Pix*, Sept. 28, 1963): Australian surfers': since ca. 1961.

false, v. To tell dishonest lies: (orig. low) Australian: since ca. 1930. Lawson Glassop, *Lucky Palmer*, 1949, '"Perce," said "Lucky" earnestly. "You knew me well in Sydney. Have you ever caught me falsin'?"'

false flap. A bad cheque: N.T., Australia: since ca. 1930. Ernestine Hill, *The Territory*, 1951.

falsies. Imitation breasts, breasts artificially aggrandized: adopted, ca. 1944, from U.S. servicemen.

family, hold off. See **f.h.o.** in the *Dict*.

family prayers. See **prayers . . .**

family tree, the. The lavatory: mostly Services': since ca. 1930. (P-G-R.) Rhyming s. By 1960, †. (Franklyn 2nd.)

Famishing Fifty. See **Sinbad**.

famous crimes is a Naval synonym (since 1920) of **drip-pan**. Granville.

famous last words. 'A catch-phrase rejoinder to such fatuous statements as "Flak's not really dangerous". (Air Force)': 1939 +. (P-G-R.) Hence in the other Services and, since ca. 1945, among civilians. A jocular reference to History's 'famous last words'.

fan, n.—4. An aircraft propeller: R.A.F.: since ca. 1916. H. & P.—5. (also *whizzer*.) A ship's propeller: Naval: since ca. 1918.—6. Short for *fanny*, female pudend, as in 'her old fan': low: since ca. 1950.

fan-mail. Letters received from unknown admirers, esp. by a film star: adopted ca. 1925. ex U.S.; by 1936, it had > coll. Ex **fan,** n., 2 (*Dict*.).

fanad. None, nothing: Army: since the 1920's. H. & P. Short for 'Sweet Fanny Adams'.

fancy.—3. 'His father took a great deal to the fancy . . . it meant dealing in birds, and dogs, and rabbits,' J. Greenwood, *The Little Ragamuffins*, 1884: poor Londoners' coll.: from ca. 1860. B. & L.—Sense 1 appears earlier in one of Scott's letters, 1815.

***fancy house.** A brothel: prostitutes' c.: from ca. 1860. B. & L.

fancy man, 1 (p. 265), occurs earlier in Alfred Burton, *Johnny Newcome*, 1818. (Moe.)

fancy pants. Any male, esp. a child, 'dressed to the nines': Canadian: since ca. 1925. (Leechman.)

fancy piece (p. 265). An interesting sidelight is afforded by a slightly earlier recording: 1821, Pierce Egan, *Life in London*, 'Fancy piece . . . a sporting phrase for a "bit of *nice* game", kept in a preserve in the suburbs. A sort of *bird of Paradise*.'

fancy sash. A punch: Australian rhyming s.

(on *bash* or *smash*): ca. 1880-1920. B., 1945, cites *The* (Sydney) *Bulletin* of Jan. 18, 1902.

Fancy Tart, the. H.M.S. *Vansittart*: Naval (lower-deck): 1920's and 1930's. A 'Hobson-Jobson'.

fancy waistcoats, speak. To speak with the utmost accuracy: Naval: C. 20. Granville.

fancy work. Genitals, including the pubic hair, usually of the male parts: feminine euphemistic s.: C. 20. 'He must be a sexual maniac, he persists in showing his fancy work.'

fang or tooth, good on the. Applied to one who is a good trencherman: Australian: since ca. 1945. (Culotta.)

fang bo'sun; pill bo'sun. Dentist; doctor: Australian Naval: since ca. 1910.

fang(-)carpenter. Australian variant of:—

fang-()farrier. A dentist: Army: C. 20. H. & P. See **fang-chovey** in *Dict*.

fangs in, put the; v.t., into. To borrow money: Australian: C. 20. Baker.

Fanny.—8. Also the inevitable nickname of men surnamed Adams: late C. 19-20. Ex **Fanny Adams,** q.v., in *Dict*.

fanny, n. Sense 2: earlier in 'Taffrail'.—8. A large mess-kettle: Naval: since ca. 1925.—9. The backside: adopted, ca., 1930, from U.S. Noel Coward's *Private Lives*, 1930. Cf. sense 1 (p. 265, end).—10. A story: Guards regiments': since ca. 1935. Gerald Kersh, *Bill Nelson*, 1942. Ex senses 6, 7.—11. The knuckle-duster dagger used by Commandos: Army: 1942-5.

fanny, park one's. To sit down. Adopted from U.S. ca. 1939. See **fanny**, n, 9.

fanny a pitch. To 'spiel'—talk glibly—until enough people have gathered: showmen's: late C. 19-20. (*John o' London's Weekly*, March 4, 1949.) Cf. *fanny*, v., on p. 266.

Fanny Adams, 1, is predominantly, in the post-1910 Navy: stew. (Granville.)

fanny hat; cunt hat. A trilby: since ca. 1930. Ex the dent in the crown. (See **fanny,** n. 1: p. 265.) The latter term is regarded as low even in frank 'circles'.

fanny rag. A sanitary pad: low Australian: since ca. 1945. Cf. **fanny,** n., 1, on p. 265.

fantabulous. A blend of *fantastic* and *fabulous*: ca. 1961-4. It occurs in, e.g., John Winton, *Never Go to Sea*, 1963.

fantastic. Very good, or even merely good; excellent or almost so; attractive, unusual, esp. unusual and either good or attractive or both: since late 1940's. On a par with **fabulous** above; Anthony Lejeune indicted the pair in his witty 'Disc jockeys don't talk so good' in *The Daily Telegraph*, coloured supplement, March 10, 1967. Closely parallelled—and perhaps prompted by—**marvellous** on p. 511.

fantod, 2. 'The grogbibber is our highest authority on headaches, fantods, and bankruptcy,' 'Tom Collins', *Such is Life* (in Australia), 1903.

far and near. Beer: rhyming s.: late C. 19-20. Little used. (Franklyn, *Rhyming*.)

far away (p. 266). The origin of sense 1 is the hymn, 'There is a happy land, far, far away'.

far better off in a home, usually preceded by *you'd be*. A vague c.p.: since ca. 1920. The home is presumably institutional.

fardy. A farthing: (mostly London) street-vendors': C. 19–20; ob. Mayhew, I, 1851. Cf. **farden** (*Dict.*).

farewell do. A leaving of paybook, watch, rings, with someone not going into action when one is oneself going in: Tommies': W.W. I. (A. B. Petch.)

Farewell Jetty. 'Officially they call it South Railway Jetty, but all Portsmouth and the Navy's nearest and dearest have known it for decades as Farewell Jetty. It is down at the seaward end of the dockyard where warships lie their last night or two before leaving for abroad' (A Correspondent's article—'Outward Bound from Farewell Jetty'— in *The Times*, June 15, 1964): coll.: late C. 19–20.

*farm.—3. Hence, *the farm* is also loosely applied to the prison itself: c.: from ca. 1910.

*farm, at the. In prison: Australian c.: since ca. 1910. (K. S. Prichard, *Kiss on the Lips*, 1932.) Cf. preceding entry.

Farm, the. Warwick Farm racecourse and motor track: Sydneyites' coll.: since late 1940's. (B.P.)

Farmer Giles. Haemorrhoids: Aus. rhyming s. (on *piles*): C. 20. Mary Durack, *Keep Him My Country*, 1955, p. 351, 'This form of rhyming slang is . . . commonly used in the outback.'

Farmers, the. The Tank Corps: Australian soldiers': 1940 +. B., 1942.

Farmer's Bible, the. The mail-order catalogue of the T. Eaton Co.: Canadian: since ca. 1918.

Farmers' Strike, the. 'The Boer War was referred to as this, when comparing it to the 1914–18 War': W.W. I, esp. among soldiers. The latter war was, in turn, called the Bow and Arrow War when W.W. II got under way—of course, only by those who had had no experience of the first one': ca. 1940–45. (A. B. Petch, March 1966.)

farmyard nuggets. Eggs: Naval (lower-deck): C. 20. Granville.

Farrington Hotel. 'The Fleet Prison which is in Farringdon Street,' G. W. M. Reynolds, *Pickwick Abroad*, 1839: ca. 1825–70.

fart-arsed mechanic. A clumsy person: Londoners': from ca. 1925.

fart(-)catcher. A homosexual: low: since ca. 1930. John Gardner, *Madrigal*, 1967, '"Oh, bleeding hell . . . manager's a flaming pouve. A fart catcher."'

fart in a bottle, or colander, like a. See **pea in a colander.**

fart in a gale, like a. Utterly helpless: (West) Canadian: C. 20. Cf.:—

fart in a wind-storm, as much chance as a. No chance at all: Canadian c.p.: since ca. 1910. But *like a f. in a w.s.* is English for 'puny; ineffective; incommensurate': low: C. 20. (Laurie Atkinson, Sept. 11, 1967.)

fartarsing about or around. 'Moving (in a motor vehicle) without definite knowledge of one's exact location. Army from ca. 1940. There is a subtle difference between this and **swanning around** (below). If one was swanning around the blue (above: sense 13) one still *thought* one knew where one was.' (Peter Sanders.)

farthing dip. A piece of bread dipped in hot fat and sold by pork butchers: coll.: ca. 1820–80. Ex the candle so named.

farting, adj. A pejorative: low: C. 20. Angus Wilson, *Anglo-Saxon Attitudes*, 1956, 'Or some other farting nonsense.'

farting(-)clapper. The podex: mostly workmen's: late C. 19–20.

Farting Fanny. A German heavy gun operating in the Arras sector; its shell: military, esp. artillerymen's: 1915–16, then mostly historical. Blaker, 'The War was trundling on quite peaceably as they walked and jogged eastwards towards it, with the occasional clang of Farting-Fanny's arrival in cavernous Arras.'

farting shot. A vulgar way of showing contempt for the company (whether singular or plural) one is leaving, esp. after a quarrel: since ca. 1940.

fart's the cry of an imprisoned turd, a. This coarsely poetical c.p. satirizes the behaviour of one who, having just broken wind, might well, for more reasons than one, go to the water-closet. Apparently it dates from the 1930's; an allusion to 'a *bird* imprisoned in a cage'.

fast, adj.—5. (Mostly of animals.) Engaged in coïtion: C. 20. 'She would blush if she saw two dogs fast.' Cf. S.E. *fast colours.*

fast one. 'A remark giving rise for thought,' H. & P.: Services: since ca. 1935; ob. by 1946. H. & P. Ex Larwood fast-bowling at cricket.—2. Hence (or independently ex same origin), esp. in *pull a fast one*, to 'do the dirty', to malinger, to wangle something one is not entitled to, to evade a duty: Services: since ca. 1938. H. & P.

fat, n.—7. (Esp. of cattle, but also of sheep) a fat beast: Australian coll.: mid-C. 19–20. 'Tom Collins', *Such Is Life*, 1903.—8. Good luck: Regular Army: late C. 19–20. Cf. senses 4, 5. By ca. 1930, general lower-class s.: as in Pamela Branch, *The Wooden Overcoat*, 1951.

fat, adj.—4. See **ace**, adj., above: since ca. 1940. Cf. sense 3 on p. 267.

fat, fret one's. See **fret one's fat.**

fat-arse around. To waste time; to dawdle: New Zealand: C. 20. An elaboration of **fart about** (p. 267).

fat as a match. (Esp. of a person) very thin indeed: Aus.: since late 1940's. (B., 1959.)

fat as a porker, as; often corrupted to . . . **porcupine.** As fat as a pig: coll.: mid-C. 19–20.

fat as mud. See **mud-fat.**

fat-boy. 'Greases wagon axles and does odd jobs in a quarry' (*The Evening News*, Sept. 28, 1955): quarrymen's: late C 19–20.

fat cake.—2. A small fried (in fat) cake made of flour: Australian coll.: late C. 19–20; by 1940, Standard. (B., 1943.) Cf. *fatty*, 2.

Fat Jack. See **Bob Short** above.

fat-pated, -skulled, -thoughted, -witted. See **fat-headed** (*Dict.*).

fat show. No possible chance: New Zealand: since ca. 1930. Cf. the ironical *fat chance* and see **fat**, adj., 2 (p. 267).

fat woman, all behind like a. A c.p. in ref. to lateness or delay: C. 20. The Australian shape is . . . *like Barney's bull.*

father.—4. That boy who acts as guardian and instructor to a new boy during the latter's first fortnight at school: Charterhouse: mid-C. 19–20. In C. 20, rather j. than s.—5. Head of a common lodging house: low: since ca. 1840. *Sessions*, Dec. 1852.—6. The captain: Naval: since ca. 1954. 'Seems to be used mainly by pussers, but is coming into general use very fast': Wilfred Granville, letter of Nov. 22, 1962.

father and mother of a hiding (thrashing, beating,

etc.) or, esp., **of a row**, a tremendous or extremely vigorous thrashing or quarrel: Anglo-Irish coll.: C. 20.   An elaboration of **father of a** (p. 268).

Father Bunloaf.   A Catholic priest: Belfast: C. 20.   Pejorative.

Father Christmas.   A venerable old man: coll.: C. 20.

father keeps on doing it!   A c.p. in ref. to a man with a large family: since ca. 1920.   Ex a popular song.

father (something) **on** (someone).   To blame someone for something he did not do; to impute responsibility where it does not rest: coll.: since ca. 1910.   Ex fathering an illegitimate child upon the wrong man.

father's backbone, I was (e.g. *playing snooker*) **when you were running up and down your.**   A variant of **before you came up!**, q.v. in *Dict.*: Services, esp. Army: C. 20.   H. & P.

father's brother (p. 268) goes back to very early C. 19; it occurs in, e.g., W. N. Glascock, *The Naval Sketch-Book*, 2nd Series, 1834, at II, 34. (Moe.)

Fatso.   Common nickname for any fat person, esp. a fat youth: Canadian: adopted, ca. 1945, ex U.S.   (Leechman.)

fattened up, be.   The v.-form of **fattening for the slaughter** (p. 268).   Ian Hay, *Carrying On*, 1917.

fatty.—2. A damper-like cake: Australian: late C. 19–20.   B., 1942.   Ex the fat used.

favour, I could do that a (real).   'A c.p. tribute to the charms of an attractive woman, or a picture of one' (Laurie Atkinson): since ca. 1945.

favourite.   Excellent; the best; esp. in *This is* (or *That's*) *favourite*: Services: since ca. 1930. H. & P.

favvers is an Army shape of 'favours': Sept. 7, 1940, *The Daily Mail*.

fe.   Meat: chimneysweepers': C. 19–20; by 1930, ob.; by 1960, †.   Adopted from Shelta *fe*, itself ex Irish *feóil*.

fear God and tip the crusher! is a Naval motto (lower-deck): C. 20.   Cf. *crusher*, 1 and 3. (P-G-R.)

fear(-)not.   A greatcoat: ca. 1810–50.   Wm Maginn, *Tales of Military Life*, 1829, at I, 158. (Moe.)

fearnought.—2. A male pessary: Naval: C. 20. Cf. **dreadnought**, 1 (*Dict.*).

feather, in full, sense 2 (p. 269), prob. goes back to early C. 19, to judge by W. N. Glascock's *Naval Sketch-Book*, 2nd Series, 1834, at I, 149, 278—see quotation at **flying light** below.

In high feather often = 'in good form'.   A still earlier reference occurs in Wm Maginn, *Tales of Military Life*, 1829, at II, 282.   (Moe.)

feather, show the white (p. 269).   But it arose probably fifty years earlier, for in Grose, 1785, we find, at *white feather*, 'He has a *white feather*, he is a coward. . . .   An allusion to a game-cock, where having a white feather, is a proof that he is not of the true game breed.'   Has variant *show a feather*, as in Fredk Marryat, *Frank Mildmay*, 1829 (at p. 334 of the 1897 edition).   Moe.

feather and flip.   A bed; sleep: late C. 19–20. Rhyming **kip** (*Dict.*).   Often shortened to *feather*.

feather-bedding, n.   The practice of making things very easy for an elderly or indisposed member of a gang of, e.g., dockers: industrial: C. 20: s. >, by 1940, coll.

feather me!   A mild Aus. oath: since ca. 1930. Nino Culotta, *Cop That Lot*, 1960.

feather-plucker.   An objectionable fellow: City of London businessmen's euphemism, sometimes only mildly pejorative: since ca. 1945.   Rhyming on *fucker*.

feathers.—3. Head-hair; beard and/or moustache: Australian: C. 20.   B., 1942.

*****feathers, grow one's.**   See **grow one's feathers.**

February.   A brigadier: Australian soldiers': 1939–45.   (B., 1943: 'Seeing him always means 28 days' C.B.')

fed.   Short for **fed-up** (*Dict.*): Australian: since ca. 1919.   Baker.

fed at both ends . . .   (Of a slim bride) 'She should get a bit fatter, fed at both ends, as they say': a low c.p. (— 1958).

Federal case, esp. in 'Don't make a Federal case out of it!'—Don't exaggerate the urgency or desperateness—or, the importance—of the matter: a c.p., adopted ca. 1952, ex U.S., where prob. legal s. at first.

federating, vbl n.   Love-making: Australian: C. 20.   Baker.

feed a cold and starve a fever.   A misuse (C. 19–20) of the proverbial *feed a cold and you'll starve a fever.*

feed of jeelyreek.   A whiff of gelignite fumes: Scottish miners': C. 20.

feed one's face.   To eat: contemptuous or. at least, depreciatory: C. 20.

feed the brute!; always remember, or all you have to do or the great (or **main**) **thing or the secret is, to feed the brute.**   A feminine c.p., used either by wives, esp. if young, or by mother to daughters about to marry: late C. 19–20.   There is often a connotation of '*That*'ll keep him happy—and you too'.   This is one of the best known of all c.pp., and it arose in *Punch* (LXXXIX, p. 206) in 1886: witness *The Oxford Book of Quotations*.   It lies, therefore, on the borderline between c.p. and famous quotation.

feel, have a.   To take liberties with a member of the opposite sex: low coll.: mid-C. 19–20.

feel an awful heel, I.   A c.p., uttered to the accompaniment of a hand placed on the hearer's back: Australian juvenile: since ca. 1930.   (B.P.)

feel for (someone's) **knowledge box.**   To aim a blow at an opponent's head: pugilistic: ca. 1810–60.   Anon., *Every Night Book*, 1827.

feel (something) **in one's water;** often preceded by *be able to* or *can*.   To have a premonition: coll.: late C. 19–20.

feel like an ounce of uranium.   See **uranium** . . .

feel like death warmed up.   To feel very ill— half dead, in fact: (until ca. 1940 proletarian) coll.: C. 20.   'For hours and hours he had to stick to the controls [of his aircraft], feeling like death warmed up,' Paul Brickhill & Conrad Norton, *Escape to Danger*, 1946.   The earliest recording I've seen occurs in the anonymous little *The Soldiers' War Slang Dictionary*, published on Nov. 28, 1939.   Cf. S.E. *to look like a living corpse.*

feel no pain.   To be (very) drunk: since ca. 1945, esp. in Canada.   'How did Harry make out last night?'—'Well, he was certainly feeling no pain!'   (Leechman.)

feel of.   To feel, in nuance 'to touch': an American sol. that, by ca. 1945, was common also in Canada.   'He felt of his teeth'—to ascertain whether any had been dislodged.   (Leechman.)

feel rough. To feel unwell, indisposed, esp. after 'the night before': rather low: from ca. 1917.

feeler, 2 (p. 270), was, by 1890, low s.: witness, e.g., A. St. John Adcock, *East End Idylls*, 1897.

feelies, the. A cinema: Australian: since ca. 1945. On the analogies of *movies* and *talkies*; ex mutual petting.

But the Australian usage came from the England of the 1930's; the expression occurs in Aldous Huxley's satirical *Brave New World*, 1932, as Mr Ramsey Spencer has reminded me.

feelthy pictures (or pitchers). Pornographic post-cards, etc.: jocular and allusive: since ca. 1920. Ex the pictures offered by native vendors to troops and tourists in the Near and Middle East.

feet, off its. (Of typewriting) by a machine out of adjustment, one side of typewritten letters showing a faint or, at least, a light impression, the other side (of, e.g., a *w*) showing a strong impression: typists': since ca. 1910. J. J. Connington, *The Sweepstake Murders*, 1931. Ex:—2. Of type not standing square: printers': since ca. 1850. B. & L.

feet (or F.), the. The infantry; artillerymen's from ca. 1890, cavalry's from ca. 1840. Blaker.—2. The Royal Marine Light Infantry: Naval: late C. 19–early 20. The R.M.L.I. ceased, as a separate force, ca. 1920. (Wilfred Granville, Sept. 23, 1967.)—3. The Police Force: Naval: since ca. 1925. (W.G.)

feetesick walah or **Gunga wallah.** A male prostitute: Services' (esp. Army): C. 20. The former, ex Arabic; the latter, ex Hindustani.

feke.—2. A *feke* or *gimmick* is a conjurer's trick: magicians': the former since ca. 1890; the latter adopted, ca. 1930, from U.S. (*feke* ex *fake.*)

felican. A little boy: showmen's: since ca. 1870; by 1955, ob. Cf. *mosiqui* for sense and *feele* (p. 270) for form; a diminutive.

fellow-feeling (p. 270): † by 1960. Franklyn 2nd.

fellow P. 'A designation applied to each other by apprentices that have been bound to the same master or firm, whether in the past or in the present': printers' coll.: mid-C. 19–20. B. & L. I.e. fellow printers.

felon swell. A gentleman convict: Australian police and other officials': ca. 1810–60. J. W., *Perils, Pastimes and Pleasures*, 1849.

feloosh (p. 270) is also spelt *felooss* or *felous*.

Felstead School has a considerable body of slang. In *The Feldstedian* of December 1947, there appeared an excellent glossary of current slang, arranged by subject. I have re-arranged the material in alphabetical order, shortened the definitions, and omitted certain terms belonging to the main body of slang.

arge. A sergeant, e.g. a Gym Instructor. Amputated *sarge*.—Hence *argery*, mostly the gym.

bang-on or **bash-on.** Terms of approval, 'recent importations, but rapidly passing into common speech', as in 'It's absolutely bang-on'. From the Forces: *bang on the target.*

Billy boy; Billy man. A House boy, man.

blitch or **blotch.** Blotting-paper. The former is a thinning of the latter, and the later is proleptic.

bog. A bicycle. By a conflation (cf. *bike*) subjected to humorous perversion.

bumming. A caning, a beating. Ex **bum** (*Dict.*).

butch. A sturdy fellow; also in address. Cinematic influence.

cheery. Excellent; e.g. 'a cheery pudding'. By humorous transference.

cheese off. To annoy. Cf. **cheesed off.**

chigger. To cheat; *chigger notes*, notes used in cheating, or a crib; *chiggerer*, a cheat (person). By 'the Oxford -*er*'.

clothers. Clothes-room (?).

coffins. A particular set of deep and ancient baths in the main block.

Confirmaggers. Confirmation; *Confirmagger pragger* (prayers), a Confirmation class. By 'the Oxford -*er*'.

debaggers. A debate. By same process.

dip. A light; an electric bulb. Hence, *dips*, lights in general or 'Lights out!'.

Div (not *Divvers*). A Divinity period.

dockets. Cigarettes. By humorous euphemism.

drive, esp. in 'Am I driving?'—Must I hurry, and in *Drive in!*, Get a move on! Ex *drive*, energy.

Duck. Matron; *Under-Duck*, Under-Matron.

ex. Exercise, games. See **vol ex.**

fugs. A radiator; also *fug-pipes*; *under-fugs*, underpants.

grass. Lettuce; water-cress; any green salad.

Headman. Headmaster.

hook. To take—not necessarily to filch.

hot, as in *half-hot*, halfpenny; *six hots*, six-pence; *hots*, pennies, cash; *trav. hots*, travelling expenses; *hot ice*, an ice-cream costing a penny.

ipe. A rifle. Ex Army (*h*)*ipe*.

jack. As v.i. to cease; as v.t., to shirk.

knockers. Cigarettes.

Ma (e.g. *Smith*). A master's wife; a lady on the staff.

mooners. A man-servant that cleans class-rooms. Ex *moon about.*

new nip. A new *nip* or small boy, a new boy.

quagger-pragger. Choir practice. By 'the Oxford -*er*'.

razz up. To reprimand severely.

rollers. Roll-call. By 'the Oxford -*er*'.

shants. Lavatories.

Siggers. The J.T.C. Signals Hut. Oxford -*er*.

skiv. A maidservant. Short for **skivvy** (*Dict.*).

smut. A person one happens to dislike.

snitch. To take—not necessarily to filch.

stodge. A steamed pudding.

stooge. A School steward. Ex the Armed Forces' senses.

stub. To kick (a ball), esp. at Rugger.

swipe. To take—not necessarily to filch; cf. *hook* and *snitch.*

swot. A lesson period.

tabby. A bedside cupboard. *The Felstedian* proposes derivation ex *tabernacle.*

tolly mug. A tooth mug or glass.

tonk. To hit (a ball) with a stick, e.g. at hockey.

tough, a fight; **toughing,** fighting, fisticuffs.

toys. Desks with bookcase attached. Adopted from Winchester.

trav tie. A (too) smart tie, not worn in School. I.e. for travelling.

Tuckers. The tuck-shop. By 'the Oxford *-er*'.

Underling. Nickname for the under-butler. By pun on Ling, the butler.

uni (pron. *unny*). A uniform.

vic! A warning cry, in Lower school only and gradually going out of use.

Vill. Felsted village.

vol. 'An afternoon free from prescribed games'; *vol ex*, an afternoon when exercise—of one's own choice—must be taken.

wagger-pagger. A waste-paper basket. Short for **wagger pagger bagger** (*Dict.*).

Washes. The ablution rooms.

wasses. Lavatories. Ex Ger. *Wasser*, water.

wonker. A kipper.

The prevalence of 'the Oxford *-er*' is noteworthy.

fem.—2. A woman: Soho, London: late C. 19–20. (E. J. Oliver, 1948.) Ex Fr. *femme*: cf. *feme* on p. 270.

femlin. See **beach bunny** above.

fence, over the (p. 271). Since ca. 1910, also Australian. B., 1942.

***fend off.**—2. Hence, to steal: N.Z. c.: since ca. 1932. R. G. C. McNab, in *The Press* (Christchurch, N.Z.), April 2, 1938.

Ferdinand. Nickname for a German self-propelled assault gun: adopted, ca. 1942, by the British Army from the Russians. (P-G-R.)—2. A bull: mostly Australian: since ca. 1938. Ex a famous book, Munro Leaf's delightful *Ferdinand the Bull*, brilliantly illustrated by Robert Lawson; New York, 1936, and London, 1937.

ferret, n.—4. 'German security guard, usually in blue overalls,' Paul Brickhill & Conrad Norton, *Escape to Danger*, 1946: prisoners-of-war in Germany: 1940–5. Ex his sharp eyes and the colour of his overalls.

ferry, n. A prostitute: Australian: C. 20. B., 1942. She carries numerous men.—2. (*The Ferry*.) The Atlantic Ocean: nautical: C. 20. (Gibbard Jackson, *Sea Yarns*, 1931.)

ferv, n. and v. Divinity, as subject of study; chaplain;—to be religious: Cranbrook School: C. 20. Ex 'religious *fervour*'.

festering, adj. and adv. An intensive, as in 'You festering toe-rag' and 'It's festering hot': Glasgow: since ca. 1920. Euphemistic.

fetch.—Also n., 3: seminal fluid; and v., 6: to experience a seminal emission: coll.: late C. 19–20.—4. N., also v. (To commit) a haymaking stroke at cricket: cricketers' (and commentators'): since ca. 1950. (B.B.C.'s TV test-match commentary, July 27, 1963.) Perhaps ex sense 2 of the v. on p. 271.

fetch up, v.i. 'To recruit one's strength, to recover from some illness': coll.: mid-C. 19–20. B. & L. Ex S.E. sense, v.t., to make up (time, leeway).

fetch your bed and we'll keep you. A c.p. addressed to a too frequent visitor: C. 20. 'Sometimes among working-men to one who is always hungry and who can eat up any spare bait that is going around' (Albert B. Petch, Sept. 1946).

fetichist (or -shist). A person unable to resist the temptation to do a certain thing: psycho-analytical (verging on j.): since ca. 1920.

fettle. (Of a man) to coït with: North Country workmen's: late C. 19–20. Ex dial. *fettle*, to chastise, itself from a term in weaving.

fetus, tap the. See **fœtus, tap the** in the *Dict*.

fever time. 'The time when superannuated college prefects go for a fortnight into a sick-room in order . . . to give themselves up to hard study': Winchester: mid-C. 19–20. B. & L.

fez. A House cap; a boy entitled to one: Harrow School: from ca. 1890 (?). Lunn.

ff for *th*. See '**f for *th*'** at the head of this letter in this Supplement.

fi-fa (p. 272). Hence, as v., to issue this writ against someone: 1818, *The London Guide* (p. 202).

***fibre.** South African c. > by 1945, low s.: C. 20. C. P. Wittstock, letter of May 23, 1946, 'Pass the fibre . . . Pass the match-box'. (Wood fibre.)

fickle Johnny Crow. A man that does not know his own mind: West Indies coll.: mid-C. 19–20. B. & L.

fiddle, n.—10. A special commission paid by a jobber to a broker on important transactions involving no risk: Stock Exchange: ca. 1810–90. The broker *fiddles* one finger across another on these occasions. Also as v.: to pay such commissions.—11. A swindle: low (since ca. 1920) > by 1939, Services.—12. A maize-grater: Australian: C. 20. (B., 1943.) Ex shape.

fiddle, v.—7. To be a petty thief: c.: late C. 19–20. Ex senses 2, 3.—8. 'To purloin or obtain by a wangle. Thus *fiddler*, one who is expert in *fiddling*,' H. & P.: Services: since ca. 1910. Cf. senses 2. 3.—9. See **fiddle, n.,** 10.—10. V.i. and v.t., to cheat, swindle, be a swindler; to sell secretly or illicitly: low (since ca. 1912) >, by 1925, Services, and then, by 1945, common civilian s., esp. among 'spivs'.

fiddle, fine as a. (See **fiddle, fit as a,** p. 272.) Not merely dial. but coll. of late C. 16–19. In Haughton's *Englishmen for My Money*, acted in 1598. See:—

fiddle, fit as a—fine as a. Mr G. H. Hatchman has admirably summarised the evidence thus, in a private letter of Nov. 25, 1946, his researches completely superseding the entry on p. 272: *Fiddle, fit as a*. Excellent, most fitting or opportune: coll.: since ca. 1590: 1598, Wm Haughton; 1620, John Fletcher.—2. In good health, condition, form: coll. since ca. 1870: 1882, M. E. Braddon; 1883, R. L. S.; 1887, James Payn; 1922, E. V. Lucas.

Fiddle, fine as a. Excellent: coll. since ca. 1590: 1598, Wm Haughton. Very fine: U.S.: recorded for 1811–27.

fiddle and flute. A suit one wears: rhyming s.: late C. 19–20. (Lester.)

fiddle-arse about. To 'mess about'; to waste time: low Australian: since ca. 1920. (B., 1943.)

fiddled stick. A flag-staff: nautical, esp. Naval: ca. 1805–60. In, e.g., W. N. Glascock, *Sailors and Saints* (I, 21), 1829. Moe.

fiddler, 7. By 1939, at latest, also Services s.—as in **fiddle, v.,** 8. In Labour s. (since ca. 1925), thus '"Fiddler" (earns money on the quiet without telling labour exchange)': Hugh Massingham, *I Took Off My Tie*, 1936.

fiddler, fit as a. A mainly Australian (B., 1942), wholly C. 20, and not very gen. variant of *fit as a fiddle* (see **fiddle, fit as a**).

Fiddler's Green (p. 273) occurs in W. N. Glascock, *Sketch-Book* (II, 169), 1826, and prob. goes back to ca. 1800 or even 1790. (Moe.)

fiddley. A £1 note: Australian: since ca. 1920. Baker. In the pl., (?) *fiddleys* or *fiddlies*, it is generic for money. Lawson Glossop, 1944. Apparently short for *fiddley did*, Australian rhyming s. on *quid*. (B., 1945.)

field, v.i. To back the field: turf coll.: from ca. 1870. B. & L.—2. To be a bookmaker operating on the course: Australian racing: since ca. 1910. Lawson Glossop, *Lucky Palmer*, 1949. '"Well, boys," he said. "On Thursday I'll be fielding at Nerridale. I'm a licensed bookmaker now."'

field, come back to the. To return to earth: to cease being fanciful or romantic: Australian: since ca. 1910. Lawson Glossop, *We Were the Rats*, 1944. Ex straying animals.

Fiend, the. See **Terror, the.**

fierce, 1 (p. 273), was, however, current in South Africa at least as early as 1908 and perhaps late C. 19.

fiery snorter (p. 274). Rather; since ca. 1840. *Sinks*, 1848.

fifas or **FIFAS.** See **fyfas** below.

fife and drum. The buttocks: rhyming s. (on *bum*): C. 20. Franklyn, *Rhyming.*

fifteen-two. A Jew: an English adaptation, ca. 1945, of the American *fifteen-and-two*; cf. *five by two.*

fifty-one A.R. A liar: schoolchildren's. London: C. 20. I.e. LI + *ar.*

fig, n.—5. A numerical *figure*: lower-middle class: late C. 19–20. (Neil Bell, *Alpha and Omega*, 1946.)

fig, in full (p. 274) dates rather from ca. 1830. *The Dublin University Magazine*, April 1835 (p. 388), 'It was alleged by his shipmates that he was rather fond of arraying himself in "full fig".' Moe.

fig and post. Toast (bread): Army rhyming s.: 1939–45. (Franklyn, *Rhyming.*)

figgy-duff; figgy-dowdy. Suet pudding with (or even without) figs: Naval, general and (*dowdy*) West Country personnel: C. 20. Granville.

fight at the leg. 'To turn every event to good account,' Pierce Egan, *The Life of Hayward*, 1822: low: ca. 1810–50. Ex fencing or cross-stick?

fight cunning. To 'box clever' (see above): coll.: mid-C. 18–early 20. James Woodforde, *Diary*, Oct. 6, 1781.

fight for love. *Sessions*, 5th session, 1734, 'Agreed to *fight for Love*, as they call it': pugilistic s. >, by 1800, coll. >, by 1830, S.E.

fight like a threshing machine. To fight, esp. with the fists, very vigorously: Aus.: since ca. 1925. (B., 1959.)

fighter boy. Any operational member—but esp. a pilot—of Fighter Command: R.A.F. coll.: 1939 +. Jackson.

fighter type. Synonym of prec. entry: R.A.F.: since ca. 1940. John Brophy, *Target Island*, 1944.

fighting cats (Army) or **galloping horses** (R.A.F.). The coat of arms on a Warrant Officer's lower sleeve: since ca. 1920. H. & P.—2. Hence, a Warrant Officer: Army and R.A.F.: since ca. 1930. Sgt-Pilot F. Rhodes, letter of Sept. 20, 1942.

Fighting Eighth, the. The Navy's coll. for 'The 8th Destroyer Flotilla, which deservedly earned the sobriquet in the war of 1939–45' (Granville).

Fighting Mac.—2. General Sir Hector Macdonald: ca. 1883–1902. Now a legendary hero.

figlia. A child: *figlia homey*, a male child; *figlia polone* (or *poloney*), a female child: parlary: late C. 19–20. (Lester.) In the older parlary, *figlia* is strictly a girl: cf. **feele** on p. 270. In Italian, the m. form is *figlio.*

figure, take a. See **take a figure.**

figure man. 'The principal figure in a picture. In French artists' language, *le bonhomme*': studios': from ca. 1860; ob. B. & L.

figurehead. See **figure-head** (*Dict.*).

*file lay, the. Pickpocketry: c.: C. 18–early 19. Captain Alexander Smith, *The Life of Jonathan Wild*, 1726. See **file**, n., 1, and v., on p. 275.

fill, n. An artificial pneumo-thorax ('A.P.'): medical coll.: since the 1930's. (Dymphna Cusack, *Say No to Death*, 1951.)

fill in. To render (a woman) pregnant: Australian Naval: C. 20. But also gen. low Australian s. (Tom Ronan, *Moleskin Midas*, 1956.)—2. To thrash (lit.): Naval (lower-deck): since ca. 1925. 'Next time he says that to me, I'll fill him in.' (P-G-R.)—3. To inform or instruct (someone) in detail: since early 1940's. 'I've been away for a week now. Somebody had better fill me in.' (Leechman.)

fill one's pipe and leave others to enjoy it. To make a large fortune, which one's heirs or other relatives dissipate: 'a vulgar phrase,' says Pierce Egan in *Life in London*, 1821: coll.: ca. 1805–60.

fillers. Fill-up matter: journalistic: since ca. 1920. By 'the Oxford *-er*.' But Douglas Leechman tells me that the word goes back to early C. 20.

*fillet of veal, a prison, on p. 275, rhymes on *steel*, q.v. at **Steel, the.**

fillum. See **colyum.**

filly, 1 (p. 275), has, since ca. 1820, been, among the upper classes, a coll. and an entirely inoffensive word for a girl, a young unmarried woman. Pierce Egan the Elder, a very close observer of the speech of his day, glosses, in *Finish to Tom, Jerry, and Logic*, 1828, the phrase 'fillies of all ages', thus: 'This phrase is now so commonly used in a sporting point of view, without meaning any offence to the fair sex, that it would be almost *fastidious* to make any objections to it in this instance' (a race-meeting).

filth, the. The police, members of the police force: c. (among the bosses of crime) and low s.: since ca. 1950. James Barlow, *The Burden of Proof*, 1968.

filthy fellow. A mild endearment: coll.: C. 18. (H. C. K. Wyld in *The Spectator*, April 22, 1938.)

filthy lucre (p. 276) occurs in Mrs Gaskell, *Cranford*, 1853.

fin. 'A *fin* is a five-dollar bill, ex the large V (five) which marks it and looks like a fin. A ten-dollar bill is a *sawbuck*, from the X it bears.' (Leechman.) Also see **jive.**

final. 2. See **swing o' the door.**

find; on find. For both, see **on find.**

find, v., 2. Add: 'To "pick up" something which is needed by your section. Finding is generally less selfish than fiddling, and more silent than scrounging,' H. & P., *Service Slang*, 1943.

find fag. See **find**, n., 1 (*Dict.*).

find something. To obtain a job: coll.: mid-C. 19–20. 'Found anything yet?'

fine as a fiddle. See **fiddle, fine as a** and **fiddle, fit as a.**

fine as frog's hair. Fine, whether of dimension or of physical well-being: Canadian: since ca. 1910. (Leechman.)

fine fellow but his muck (or shit) stinks, (he's) a. He's only human after all: proletarian c.p.: C. 20.

fine Scot. A variant of **Scot,** 1, and, like it, current ca. 1800–50.

fine weather for ducks (p. 276) has, in Australia, the variants *great,* or *nice,* weather . . . (B.P.)

finger, n., 2 (p. 276): 'Possibly a mispronunciation of *figure* (a figure of fun)': Julian Franklyn, 1962.

finger and thumb, 2 (p. 277). Earlier in Mayhew, I, 1851.—3. A companion or 'mate': rhyming s.: since ca. 1930. On *chum.*

finger bowl. An outdoor cinema: Canadian: since ca. 1960. 'Ex U.S. sports arenas, the Rose Bowl, the Orange Bowl, etc.' (Leechman.)

finger-fuck. To caress (a woman) sexually: low: C. 20. Cf. **finger,** v., on p. 277.

*finger on, put the. To point (a wanted man) out to the police: c.: C. 20. Adopted from U.S.

finger out! A frequent shortening of *take your finger out!*

finger-tight, adj. and adv., as in 'Just make the nuts finger-tight and I'll follow you around with the spanner': Australian coll.: since ca. 1930. As tightly as possible with the fingers. (B.P.)

finger trouble; esp. in 'He has'—or 'He's suffering from'—'finger trouble': He's lazy; he is given to procrastination: R.A.F.: since ca. 1935. Gerald Emanuel, letter of March 29, 1945. Ex **take your finger out!**

finger up (or well in), have the. Synonym of prec.: mostly Army: 1940 +.

fingerer. One who, from sexual irritation, is constantly fingering him(her)self: coll.: late C. 19–20.

Fingers. Nickname for a pickpocket: c.: C. 20; by 1930, at latest, also police s. John Gosling, *The Ghost Squad,* 1959.

fingers crossed, keep one's. See **keep . . .** below.

Fingo. J. H. Fingleton, the New South Wales and Australian Test Cricketer: from ca. 1934. *The Evening News,* Sept. 30, 1936.

fings ain't wot they used ter (or to) be. A c.p., orig. Cockney, current since Frank Norman's *Fings Ain't Wot They Used t' Be* (lyrics by Lionel Bart), 1960.

finick. A finicky person: Australian coll.: since ca. 1925. (B.P.) Ex synonymous English dial. *fin(n)ick.*

finickerty. Finicky: Australian: since ca. 1935. (B.P.) A blend of *finicky* + pernick*ety.*

finicky Dick. A finicky person: Australian: since late 1930's. (B.P.) Perhaps orig. *finick Dick,* found too awkward to pronounce.

fink. An unpleasant, esp. if felt to be untrustworthy, person: Canadian: adopted, ca. 1965, ex U.S. (*Leechman.*) See *fink* in *Underworld.*

finkydiddle. Synonymous with—and prob. a variant of—**firkytoodle** (p. 278): late C. 19–20, but seldom heard after 1945.

finnie (or -y) haddock. Finnan haddock: Cockney coll. or sol.: C. 19. Mayhew, I, 1851.

Finsbury Park, often shortened to *Finsbury.* An *arc* light: cinematic technicians' rhyming s.: since ca. 1945. 'Cut the Finsburies!' (Communicated by Dallas Bower in 1956.)

fire, there's been a. A c.p. addressed to someone wearing a new suit: Londoners': late C. 19–20. Implying salvage.

fire a gun.—2. To take a (strong) drink: late C. 18–mid-19. George R. Gleig, *The Subaltern's Log-Book* (I, 208), 1828. (Moe.) Cf. **fire a slug** on p. 277.

fire-proof. Invulnerable; esp. in *fuck you, Jack, I'm fire-proof,* R.A.F. c.p.: since ca. 1930. Cf. the R.A.F. pun on the R.A.F. motto (*Per ardua ad astra*): 'Per ardua asbestos'. Partridge, 1945. An adaptation of the century-old Naval *fuck you, Jack, I'm all right.*—2, Hence, unimpeachable when trouble threatens: since ca. 1937.

fire-siders. Men that 'keep the home fires burning' (don't enlist): military: 1915–18.

fire-watcher. One who hugs the fire, the stove, etc., when duty calls him into the cold and the wet: Services, esp. Army: since ca. 1910. H. & P. Cf. **fire-spaniel,** which it superseded, and 'home-guard' as used by American tramps (see *Underworld*).

fire(-)water, p. 278, was perhaps so called because if one applied a match, the drink caught fire. 'The more sophisticated Indian tribes would not accept firewater that would not ignite with a match. 1800 on to ca. 1875.' (Leechman.)—2. See **bang-water.**

fireboy. A locomotive fireman: Canadian railroadworkers' (— 1931).

fire's gone out, the. The engine has stopped: Fleet Air Arm: 1940 +. (P-G-R.)

fireworks.—4. Hence, severe anti-aircraft fire: R.A.F., esp. among bomber crews: since 1939. Berrey, 1940; H. & P.—5. (Also ex 3.) A copious dropping of flares: R.A.F.: since 1940. Partridge, 1945.

firing line. See **in the firing line.**

firkin. A thingummy: R.A.F.: since ca. 1925. (Gerald Emanuel, March 29, 1945.) Ex the frequency with which one hears 'the fucking thing!' or, euphemistically, 'the firking thing!'

firm, n.—2. A criminal gang, of, e.g., burglars: c.: since ca. 1950. Peter Crookston, *Villain,* 'I blew a couple of peters for our firm.'

Firm, the. Messrs J. C. Williamson, who own and operate theatres in Australia and New Zealand; coll.; mostly there; and there in the world of entertainment: since ca. 1920. (B.P.)

firmed, well. See **well firmed.**

Firpo—or Chowringhee—Star. The 1939–45 Star: servicemen's (esp. R.A.F.), mostly among those with long service in India: 1945 +. 'Chowringhee is Calcutta's Regent Street, Piccadilly and Leicester Square; it houses Firpo's Restaurant' (R.A.F. correspondent).

first, n.—2. A First Lieutenant: Naval coll.: C. 19–20. Wm Nugent Glascock, *The Naval Sketch-Book,* 2nd Series, 1834, at I, 91, and 268. (Moe.)

first and first. First Class for leave and for conduct: Naval coll.: since ca. 1920. (P-G-R.)

first-chop, first-rate (see **chop,** n.: p. 150), occurs, e.g., in John Davis's *The Post-Captain,* 1806.

first-class rock. Naval Boy, 1st Class: Naval: since ca. 1920. (Granville.)

first fleeter (p. 278). Rather, a convict in the fleet of 1789: ca. 1789–1840, then historical. Marcus Clarke, 1874.

first of May (p. 278) is, as Julian Franklyn has shown, extant in its strict sense 'say' (firm speech, declaration) and is, of course, rhyming s.

first on the taxi-rank, be. To be the prime suspect: Australian: since ca. 1950. Ex the first taxi on a rank.

first on the top-sail (p. 278). The correct form is: *first at the topsail, last at the beef kid*; the *kid* is a wooden container for carrying beef from galley to mess-deck.

first pop. At the first attempt; on the first occasion: late C. 19–20. For *at the first pop*: cf. *pop, give it a*: cf. *pop, give a.*

first reader. Conductor's train book: Canadian railroadmen's (— 1931). With pun on school-children's *first reader* (or reading book).

first term too early, second term too cold, third term too late. Australian, esp. Sydney, under-graduates' c.p.: since ca. 1925. Cf. their *freshers work first term, nobody works second term, everybody works third term.* (B.P.)

first thing. Early in the morning or the day: coll.: mid-C. 19–20. 'The boss wasn't here first thing.'

first turn of the screw cancels all debts! 'Catch-phrase used when someone is worried about his dues ashore. A cheer-up from a messmate' (Wilfred Granville, Nov. 22, 1962): Naval: since late 1940's. The ship's screw, of course.

first up, adv. First time; at the first attempt: Australian: C. 20. B., 1942. Ex the game of two-up.

firty-free-fevvers on a frush's froat, occ. pre-ceded by *free fahsand free 'undred and.* 'The two-way dialect speech classic chaffing formula of and by Cockneys' (Laurie Atkinson): c.p.: since at least as early as 1930.

fish in names of P.O.W. dishes: see 'Prisoners-of-War Slang', 10.

fish, 7. Here 'fish' is euphemistic for 'flesh'.— 8. One who plays a game where he has no chance of winning: Canadian carnival s.: since ca. 1920. Ex U.S. c. for 'newcomer' (in a prison): see *Underworld.*—9. Short for **tin fish** (p. 887): Naval: since ca. 1918. Robert Harling, *The Steep Atlantick Stream,* 1946.

fish, clean (or **feed**) **the.** To 'skin' (or lead on) the victim: Canadian carnival s., since ca. 1920. See **fish,** 8.

Fish, the. This, the best-known train in Aus-tralia, serves the commuters between Sydney and the towns and townships of the Blue Mountains: Australian: since the early 1920's. Two or three of the first crew had 'fish' surnames. (B.P.)

fish-and-chip van. An old Sentinel steam coach: railwaymen's: ca. 1890–1940. *Railway 2nd.*

fish-eyes (p. 278) has the C. 20 variant *fishes' eyes* (Granville).

fish-fag (p. 278) should be dated ca. 1810–1910. Alfred Burton, *Johnny Newcome,* 1818. (Moe.)

Fish-Head Hall. At the R.N. Engineering College, at Manadon, Plymouth, a wing in which officers specialising in Marine Engineering are accommodated: Naval: since ca. 1946. (Gran-ville.)

fish-heads. 'Salthorse' officers—'those who go down to the sea in ships as opposed to going up in the air in jets' (Granville): Fleet Air Arm: since ca. 1945.

Fish-Hooks. Ficheux, a village in Northern France: military Hobson-Jobson: 1914–18. (Siegfried Sassoon.)

fish-horn. A soprano clarinet: Canadian musicians': since late 1930's. To the same group, place, period, belong *African harp,* a banjo; *bed springs* or *git-box,* a guitar; *cigar-box,* a violin; *dog-house,* a bass viol; *gob-stick,* a clarinet; *great-horn,* bass horn, or tuba—coll., rather than s.; *horn,* trumpet or cornet—not s. but coll.; *the ivories* or *the 88,* the piano; *slip-horn* or *slush-pump* or *tram,* a trombone; *wood-pile,* a xylophone. Professor Priestley, to whom (in 1949) I owe the list, adds: 'All these are current in a limited and jocular way among musicians in jazz bands; originally used by U.S. musicians ca. 1925; revised, extended and popularised in late 1930's, when swing became popular'.

On Oct. 12, 1965, Professor Priestley amends that passage (the errors were mine, not his) thus: 'The *fish-horn* is a soprano saxophone, not a clari-net. The wind bass is a *grunt-horn,* not a *great horn.' Horn* includes saxophones as well as trumpet and cornet. 'Among modern jazz players, "blow" means to play any instrument, as "He blows nice piano".'

fisherman. 'A trawler, drifter or other fishing craft' (Granville): Naval coll.: C. 20.

fisherman's daughter (p. 279) occurs in D. W. Barrett, *Navvies,* 1880.

Fisher's flimsies. Australian currency notes: Australian: ca. 1910–30, then historical. Ex Andrew *Fisher* (1862–1928)—Prime Minister and, esp., the founder of the Commonwealth Bank of Australia. (B.P.) Cf. **flimsy,** n., 1, on p. 287.

fishing? what shall we do, or go; or, **which shall we do,** or **go fishing?** What would you like to do?: c.p. since ca. 1920.

fishing expedition; esp. **on a . . .** Applied to one who is spying or 'pumping' others for informa-tion: jocular coll.: since ca. 1930. Ex Japanese fishing boats going into foreign waters in order to obtain information. This English nuance may well be independent of the American senses, even though the latter precede it.

fishing fleet, the.—2. Hence, 'women who fre-quent the Ladies' Lounge at the Union Club, Malta' (Granville): Naval: since ca. 1920. On the look-out for eligible Navy men.

fishmonger. A bawd: mid-C. 16–early 17. Barnaby Rich; Shakespeare, *Hamlet,* II, ii, 174. (J. Dover Wilson, *Hamlet,* 1934, pp. 170–1.) Prob. a corruption of *fleshmonger.* Hence:

fishmonger's daughter. A whore: late C. 16–early 17. Ben Jonson; Middleton. (J. Dover Wilson, *Hamlet,* 1934, p. 171.)

fisho, often written **fish-o.** A fisherman by trade; a fish-hawker: Australian: since ca. 1920. (K. S. Prichard, *Intimate Strangers,* 1937.) *Fisher*man + the ubiquitous Australian suffix *-o.*

*****fisno** (p. 279), a warning. Just possibly back-s. (with alteration) for 'the *office',* as Dr Leechman proposes.

fission chips. 'According to some, what sur-vivors will live on if there is ever a nuclear war' (A. B. Petch): since ca. 1955. A pun on *fish and chips,* that 'eternal' stand-by.

fist, make a good . . . (p. 279). Anglicized very much earlier than I had thought, and perhaps orig. British, for it occurs in W. N. Glascock, *Naval Sketch Book,* 2nd Series, 1834, at I, 280. '"Now, Ned, d'ye know, I doesn't think you'd make a bad fist yourself at a speech."' (Moe.)

fist it out. To fight it out: coll.: (?) ca. 1800–

60. In W. N. Glascock's *Naval Sketch Book*, 2nd Series, 1834. (Moe.)

fit, v., corresponds to **fit**, n., 1 (p. 279): New Zealand and Australian e.: since ca. 1930. B., 1942, records both v. and n. as Australian.

fit?, are you. Are you ready?: R.A.F. coll.: since ca. 1915. Partridge, 1945. Perhaps elliptical for 'Are you ready and fit?'

fit, chuck a. See **chuck a fit.**

fit as a buck rat (, as). Very fit and well: New Zealand: C. 20. (Slatter.)

fit as a fiddle. See **fiddle**, above.

fit like a purser's shirt on, or **upon, a handspike** goes back to 1806 (John Davis, *The Post-Captain*). Moe.

fit on the mat, a. See **enough to give you . . .**

fit the head, not. A C. 19 tailors' phrase, meaning that a garment, although faultless, is said by a customer to have some fault or other, the tailor then keeping it a while and sending it, untouched, back to the customer, who is thereupon delighted with it. *The Saturday Evening Post*, Sept. 28, 1822 (p. 4, col. 1)—reporting a trial held in London. (Moe.)

fit to be tied. 'Hopping mad'—furiously angry: Canadian: adopted, ca. 1908, ex U.S. (Leechman.) Cf. the Australian *ropeable*.

fit to go foreign. Ready for any and every undertaking: Canadian Naval: since ca. 1940. (Leechman.)

fit-up towns (p. 279). In *Showman Looks On*, 1945, C. B. Cochran uses *fit-ups* in same sense.

fit where they (e.g. trousers) **touch, they;** (of jacket, etc.) **it fits where it touches.** A jocular c.p., applied to loose, ill-fitting clothes: late C. 19–20. (Jack Lawson, *A Man's Life*, 1932.)

fitting. (Of a patient) having a fit: hospital nurses': since ca. 1935.

Fitzbilly, the. The Fitzwilliam Museum: Cambridge undergraduates': late C. 19–20.—2. Fitzwilliam House: Cambridge undergraduates': C. 20.

Fitzroy cocktail. An improvised drink with basis of methylated spirits: Australian: since ca. 1925. Baker. Ironic.

Fitzroy Yank is the Melbournites' equivalent of **Wooloomooloo Yank**: since ca. 1942. (B. 1953.)

five, n.—5. A Jew: since ca. 1930. Gerald Kersh, *They Die with their Boots Clean*, 1941. Ex from *five by two*.—6. A five-years' prison sentence: police and criminal coll.: late C. 19–20. (Norman.)—7. A sum of five pounds sterling: coll.: late C. 19–20.

five, v. To tout: drapery trade: C. 20. Origin? Perhaps ex **five-to-two's** (below), via Jewish shoe-shops; a Jew being, in rhyming s., a *five-to-two*: Julian Franklyn's suggestion, 1962.

five by five; often **Mr Five by Five.** A very short, fat man: Canadian: since ca. 1930. Leechman, 'Presumably 5 feet tall and 5 feet wide.'

five by two. A Jew: rhyming s. variant of **four by two:** since ca. 1925. Gerald Kersh, 1941.

five-acre farm. The arm: rhyming s. (London streets'): 1857, Augustus Mayhew, *Paved with Gold*; † by 1900. Cf. **Chalk Farm** (*Dict.*).

five-mile sniper. A gunner in the heavy artillery: infantrymen's: 1914–18.

five-letter woman, A 'bitch': since ca. 1925. Prompted by **four-letter-man** (*Dict.*).

five to two. A not very gen. rhyming s. term for 'Jew'. C. 20. Cf. **five by two.** Contrast:—

five-to-two's. Shoes: Cockney rhyming: C. 20. Len Ortzen, 1938.

fiver.—1 (p. 280), early occurs also in Renton Nicholson, *An Autobiography*, 1860 (at p. 63), for £5.—3. A fifth-columnist: since late 1939; by 1948, ob. Warren Stuart, *The Sword and the Net*, 1942.—4. (Cf. sense 1: p. 280.) Five thousand pounds, as in 'This house is worth a fiver': since ca. 1930.

fix, v.—4. To dog (very) cunningly an enemy aircraft: R.A.F. s. (1940) >, by 1944, coll. Partridge, 1945. Cf. next sense.—5. To 'settle a person's hash': coll.: since ca. 1920. 'I'll fix him!' is a frequent threat.—6. To bribe (someone): adopted, ca. 1939, from U.S.: c. > by 1946, low s. Hence *fixer*, a lawyer that bribes, e.g., officials: still c.—7. To prepare or plan; to arrange: Canadian (ex U.S.) coll.: since ca. 1910. 'I'm leery of Bill. He's fixing to shoot me!' (Leechman.)

The *fixer* of sense 6 need not be a lawyer; he may be, e.g., a political 'boss'.

fix, get a. To obtain the ship's or the aircraft's position: Naval and R.A.F.: since ca. 1939; by 1945, j. Granville.

fix (someone's) **clock.** To settle his hash: Canadian: since ca. 1940. (Leechman.) Here, *clock* perhaps = face.

fix (someone's) **duff.** Synonymous with the 'prompter', *settle his hash*: Army: since ca. 1930. (P-G-R.)

fix flint. See **flint.**

fix (someone's) **little red fire-engine.** To settle someone's hash: adopted in 1965 or, at latest, 1966 ex U.S. (Ramsey Spencer.)

fix the old gum tree. (Of a 'rolling stone') to settle down at last: Australian: C. 20. B., 1942.

fixer. An agent, esp. one who makes arrangements for 'pop' musicians: since ca. 1950.

fizz, n.—7. Synonymous with its source: *fizz-gig*, 2 (p. 280): Australian c. and police s.: since ca. 1953. (B., 1943.)—8. An erratic yet rapid movement; such motion: N.T., Australian: since ca. 1910. Ernestine Hill, *The Territory*, 1951.

fizz, v. A variant of *fizz out*. (H. Drake-Brockman, *Hot Gold*, 1940, 'Fizzed on you, didn't she? They're all the same.')

fizz-bang. An occasional variant of *whizz-bang*, 1 (p. 955): Army: 1914–18.

fizz out, n.; fizz out on, v. (To be) a thoroughly unreliable person (in respect of someone): Australian: since ca. 1919. Baker.

fizza is an Army variant (1914–18) of *fizzer*. Anon., *The Soldier's War Slang Dictionary*, 1939, defines it as barrack-room s. for 'parade ground'. Therefore *fizzer*, 3 (see next entry) may derive ex *defaulters on fizza*, doing pack-drill on the parade ground.

fizzer, 3. Esp. in *put on a* (or *the*) *fizzer*, to put someone's name on to a charge-sheet; loosely, *fizzer* may = guard-room, detention cell: Army since ca. 1920 and R.A.F. since ca. 1925. *Daily Mail*, Sept, 7, 1940; H. & P.; Partridge, 1945, 'Perhaps to (cause to) *fizz* with anger and resentment'.—5. A wild scrub bull or bullock: Australian: late C. 19–20. Cf. sense 1, 2 (p. 280).— 6. An adverse report against an employee:

busmen's: since ca. 1925. Ex sense 3.—7. A failure, esp. in *it's a fizzer*, 'the traditional c.p. when a mechanical device being demonstrated fails to work' (B.P.): Australian: since ca. 1920. Perhaps a slovening of *fizzler*, something that 'fizzles out'.

flab. Dripping (ca. 1840–1900); (also *flib*) butter (C. 20): Christ's Hospital. Marples. Ex its 'flabbiness'.

flabber is gasted. In, e.g., 'My flabber is gasted' —I'm flabbergasted: a jocular intensive: since ca. 1945.

fladge fiend. A masochist: low: from ca. 1920.

flag, n.—6. A bank-note: Australian: since ca. 1920. B., 1942. A blend of **flim** + **rag?**—7. In two-up, £1, whether sum or currency note. See **boxer.**

flag, v. To work under an assumed name: Canadian railroadmen's (— 1931), adopted from U.S. Ex *sail under a false flag.*

flag, the. The colour sergeant: military: ca. 1845–1914. Robert Blatchford, *My Life in the Army*, 1910.

flag-flapper. A signaller: Navy: late C. 19–20. H. & P. Cf. **flag-wagging** in *Dict.*

flag-flier is the agent in **flag-flying**, 3 (*Dict.*): 1927, *The Observer*, May 25 (O.E.D., Sup.).

*flagg is Randle Holme's spelling of *flag*, a groat.

flags, between the. See **between the flags.**

flags flying, she has—or **she's got**—**the.** A variant of **fly the flag**, 2 (p. 292): low: late C. 19–20.

flak. 'German anti-aircraft fire': 1939 +: prob. always j.; certainly j. by 1942. Ex the initials of the three-elemented compound name in German.

flak-happy. Not caring; reckless: R.A.F.: 1941 +. (W/Cdr R. McDouall, letter of April 12, 1945.) Cf. **punch-drunk**, but prob. an analogy of **slap-happy.** Contrast the Army's **bomb-happy.**

flake; flake out. (In full.) To go to bed, or merely to take a nap: Canadian: since ca. 1940. (Leechman.)—2. To fall asleep from exhaustion, or from ethyl alcohol: Australian: since ca. 1945. (B.P.) Cf. next.—3. To faint: since ca. 1940. '"I'm terribly sorry," he says, "but your shore leave is cancelled until further notice."' I all but flaked out': L. J. Cunliffe, *Having It Away*, 1965.

flaked out. Tired; listless; useless from drunkenness: Forces': 1939 +. Cf. *worn to a frazzle.*

Flakers. See **Harry Flakers.**—2. (Always *flakers.*) Half-drunk; mildly tipsy: Australian: since ca. 1945. (Elizabeth Lambert, *The Sleeping House Party*, 1951.) Ex **Harry Flakers.**

flame! or flaming hell! Expletive *hell*: C. 20, the latter; since ca. 1925, the former.

flamer. A target—esp. an aircraft or a vehicle —set on fire by the Air Force: R.A.F.: 1940 +. (P-G-R.) Ex sense 3 (p. 281).

flaming, 1 (p. 281): prob. from ten or twenty years earlier. 'The first time I saw the flaming mot/Was at the sign of the Porter Pot'—from a popular ballad titled *Fal de Ral Tit*, ca. 1800 or earlier.

flaming arsehole. A large red circle painted on side of Japanese aircraft: Australian airmen's: 1942–5. (B., 1943.)

flaming coffin. The D.H.4 aircraft: since ca. 1943.

flaming onions (p. 281). Add:—In 1939–45,

'tracer fire from the ground' (H. & P., 1943). Not all tracer fire, but only such as justifies this pertinently descriptive term.

flamp. To flatter; to wheedle: R.A.F.: since ca. 1937. (Atkinson.) Perhaps *flam* + *flannel.*

flange. *Corona glandis*: C. 20. Ex S.E. sense.

flanker, play a. See **play** . . . Also *work* or *pull a flanker*, to pass an unpleasant task to another: Army: 1939–45.

flannel, n. and v. (To speak or make) sweet things or small gifts to one's superiors in order to ask favours later on; to flatter, flattery: Services, esp. R.A.F.: since ca. 1935. *The New Statesman*, Aug. 30, 1941; H. & P. Cf. **flannel-mouth.**

flannel hammer or left-handed spanner. Imaginary tools, which an apprentice is sent to fetch: workmen's coll.: late C. 19–20.

flannel jacket. 'Merchant Navy Class 4–6–2 S.R.' (*Railway* 2nd): railwaymen's, esp. on the Southern Railway: C. 20. Perhaps rhyming s. 'for the first locomotive of the class "Channel Packet"' (ibid.).

flannel-mouth, in *Dict.* Hence, *flanneller* and *flannelling*, the corresponding agential and verbal nouns.

flannel through, v.i. 'To bluff one's way through an awkward situation': Naval: since ca. 1920. Granville. Ex **flannel.**

flannelette. 'The sailor's soft answer which occasionally succeeds in turning away wrath' (Granville): Naval: since ca. 1936. See **flannel.**

flap, n.—7. A cheque: c.: C. 20. (Ex 5 and 6.)—8. Great excitement; panic: Services: since ca. 1918. Berrey, 1940. Also, since ca. 1930, **flap on** (H. & P.). Whence *flapping*, undue or uncontrolled excitement: H. & P.

Flap, the. 'That great retreat from the battle of Sidi Rezegh (Western Desert) which ended at Alamein' (F-G-R): Army: middle of World War II. The apotheosis of **flap**, n., 8.

flap around. To rush about aimlessly: Services (esp. Naval): since ca. 1920. Granville. Cf. prec.

flap-dragon. See **flapdragon** (*Dict.*).—**flap-sauce.** See **flapdoodle** (*Dict.*).

flare-path. A petrol lighter: R.A.F.: since ca. 1935. *The New Statesman*, Aug. 30, 1941.

flare-up (p. 283). As 'spree', it occurs earlier in *Sessions*, March 7, 1842.

flash, n.—9. (Adj.) Fashionably smart: New Zealand and Australian: late C. 19–20. Jean Devanney, *Bushman Burke*, 1930, 'They [girls] think it's flash' to take strong drink; K. S. Prichard, 1932, 'Flash dame'.—10. One's personal appearance: low Australian: since ca. 1920. (B., 1943.) Cf. sense 6 on p. 283.—11. The Electrical Officer: Naval: since ca. 1940. (Granville.) Cf. sense 8 on p. 283.

flash, a show of. A slight, an affront, to a gang's tenets of proper behaviour: Teddy boys': since ca. 1950. (Clancy Sigal in *The Observer*, March 1, 1959.)

flash, cut the. To show off, make a display: Australian low: C. 20. B., 1942. Cf. **cut a dash** (or **splash**), p. 201.

flash as a Chinky's horse, as. (Very) high-spirited: Aus.: since ca. 1930. Baker, 1959.

flash gear. See 'Mock-Auction Slang' below.

flash Jack. A showy fellow; boaster: Australian: C. 20. Archer Russell, *A Tramp Royal in Australia*, 1934.

flash lot. A smart new taxicab: taxi-drivers': since ca. 1920. Herbert Hodge, *Cab, Sir?*, 1939.

flash-man, 1 (p. 284), should rather be dated 'late C. 18–19'. It occurs in the song *Fal de Ral Tit*, reprinted, from an unidentified British source, in an American magazine, *The Port Folio*, Jan. 9, 1808 (p. 31), 'I was a flashman of St Giles'. Also in the ballad *The Rolling Blossom*: see quotation at **nob the bib** below.

flash of light (p. 284) is rhyming s. on *sight* in nuance 'sorry sight'. Franklyn, *Rhyming*.

flash side, the. The 'knowing ones' or self-constituted judges: pugilistic: ca. 1810–50. *Boxiana*, I, 1818. See **flash**, adj., 2 (*Dict.*).

*flash the dicky. To show one's shirt-front: c.: from ca. 1820. B. & L.

flasher.—4. A stall-holder at a fair. C. 20. Ex **flash**, n., 6 (p. 283).

flashes, curse. See **curse flashes** (*Dict.*).

flashing, n. Signalling; also *flash*, v.i., to signal: Naval coll.: C. 20.

flat, n.—5. A prefect: Monkton Combe School, near Bath: ? ca. 1850–1914. *The Sunday Times*, correspondence columns, Sept. 8, 1963.—6. 'Worn part on wheel tyre due to skidding, or, in London Transport, due to excessive braking' (*Railway*, 3rd): transport workers' coll.: since late 1940's.

flat, adj. Penniless; short of money: low: from ca. 1925.—2. See **choppy**.

flat, adv.; **flat out.** At top speed; 'all out': motor-racers': resp. s., from ca. 1928, an abbr. of the second term; from ca. 1910, s. >, by 1930, coll. and now verging on S.E.; prob. ex a horse's pose at the gallop.

flat-aback. 'Cap worn on the back of the head to give a dégagé appearance' (Granville). Naval: C. 20.

flat-cap. See 'Women'.

flat-catcher.—2. Hence, 'an article to dupe the public', *Sinks*, 1848; ob.—3. Also applied to a horse that looks well and performs badly: ca. 1840–1930.

flat feet, go on one's or **its, own.** 'A man walking or a tank moving invariably went "on their own flat feet"' (P-G-R): Army: 1939–45.

Flat Feet, the.—3. (**flat feet.**) Naval seamen: bluejackets': late C. 19–20. 'Taffrail.'

flat-footer. See **frog-footed.**

flat-fuck. 'Fricatio mutua coniunctorum genitalium muliebrium': Lesbian coll.: C. 19–20. Also a v.

flat head or **flat-head** or **flathead.** A simpleton: Australian: since ca. 1910. B., 1942. Elaboration of **flat**, n., 1.

flat-iron.—2. A Monitor: Naval: ca. 1850–90. —3. A river gunboat: Naval: late C. 19–20. Cf. **flatiron gunboat** (p. 285).—4. Any large warship, esp. a battleship: Naval (mostly wardroom): C. 20.

flat out. See **flat**, adv.

flat out for. Strongly in favour of: R.A.F.: since ca. 1938. Jackson, Thus, 'I'm flat out for him having some leave.' Ex prec.

flat out like a lizard (1) **drinking** or (2) **on a log.** To lie on one's belly; but also, to work at great speed: Aus.: (C. 20. B., 1959.)

flat spin. See **go into a flat spin.**

flat to the boards. Synonymous with, and prob. the origin of, **flat (out)** above: since early C. 20. 'From the early days of motoring, when cars had wooden floor-boards. The car was at its maximum performance when the accelerator was pressed flat against the floor-boards' (B.P.).—2. Hence, fully extended; extremely busy: Australian: since ca. 1925. 'Can't you see that I'm flat to the boards?' (B.P.)

flat top. An aircraft carrier: Naval since ca. 1935. Granville.—2. Hence, a haircut similar to the crew cut but flat on the top: Australian: since ca. 1945. (B.P.)

flatch, 3. Earlier in Mayhew, I, 1851: therefore sense 1 is likewise earlier.

flatch enore, is a variant of **flatch yenork** (*Dict.*).

flathead. See **flat head.**

flatite. A dweller in a flat: Aus. coll.: since ca. 1925. (B., 1959.)

flats, 3, on p. 285, should be dated back to ca. 1780, for it occurs in Patrick Colquhoun, *A Treatise on the Police of the Metropolis*, 1796, at p. 120, and again in Maria & Richard Edgeworth, *Practical Education*, 1798.

flats yad. A day's jollification: tailors' back s.: from ca. 1865. B. & L.

flatter, n. 'The private motorist . . . knows that the squeaks in his bodywork are caused by "canaries" and that the tremendous speed he attains is due to "flatter" in his speedometer. When he "runs out of road", he gets severely "bent"' (Nigel Dennis, review 'Fancy Lingo', in *The Sunday Telegraph*, July 9, 1961): motorists' terms: resp. since ca. 1950, ca. 1950, ca. 1945, ca. 1930.

flatterback. The wearing of cap on back of head: Australian Naval: 1939–45. (B., 1943.)

flatters. A calm sea: Naval (mostly wardroom): since ca. 1920. By 'the Oxford *-er*'.

flattie, 2 (p. 285). Current well into C. 20, esp. among showmen, who (cf. sense 3) used *bobbin flattie* for a dupe, a simple fellow. *John o' London's Weekly*, March 4, 1949.

flatties. Flat heeled shoes: since ca. 1945. (John Boswell, *Lost Girl*, 1959.)

flatty.—8. A jam tart: St Bees: since ca. 1914. Marples.

flawed (*Dict.*) dates back to before 1650: see 'Tavern terms', § 8.

flaxies. Workers in a flax-mill: New Zealanders': C. 20. (Jean Devanney, *Old Savage and Other Stories*, 1927.)

flea. See **hot-plater.**

flea-and-louse (p. 285) has been † since ca. 1920. It went to the U.S.

flea-bag.—3. A dog; less gen., a cat: Australian: since ca. 1910. B., 1942.—4. (Ex 1 and 2: p. 285.) A seaman's hammock: Naval (lowerdeck): since ca. 1920.

flea-chariot. A flea-ridden palliasse: Anglo-Irish: since ca. 1920. (Patrick Doncaster, *A Sigh for a Drum-Beat*, 1947.)

flea-circus. A cheap cinema: Australian: since ca. 1925. Baker. Cf.:—

flea-pit.—2. A studio notorious for its low wages: glass-painters': from ca. 1880. *The* (Johannesburg) *Sunday Times*, May 23, 1937.—3. A second-rate, dirty cinema: since ca. 1918; by ca. 1939, also S. African. Cf. **bug-house**, n.—4. A sleeping-bag: Army (esp. officers): since ca. 1915. Cf. sense 2 of *flea-bag* (p. 285).

fleas(-)and(-)itchers, the. The cinema: Australian rhyming s. (on *pictures*): since ca. 1946. (B., 1953.) Probably influenced by **flea-pit**, 3.

fleeco. An Australian and New Zealand variant of the next term: C. 20. (Jean Devanney, *The Butcher Shop*, 1926.)

fleecy. That shearing-shed hand who picks up the shorn fleeces: New Zealand and Australian rural coll.: late C. 19–20. G. B. Lancaster, *Sons o' Men*, 1904; Baker.

Fleet Air Arm wallah. See **matlow**, 2.

Flemington confetti. Rubbish, nonsense, 'tripe', 'bulsh': Australian: since ca. 1920. B., 1942. Ex the appearance of Flemington racecourse at the close of a big meeting: paper everywhere. Cf. **Flemo**. 'More likely to be from the Flemington Saleyards in Sydney or Melbourne' (B.P.).

Flemish horse. 'A rope under the yard, on which the man at the extreme end of it stands to support himself in reefing or furling the topsail' (W. N. Glascock, *Sketch-Book* (I, 10), 1825). Moe.

Flemo. Flemington district (a north-west suburb of Melbourne) and race-course: Australian: C. 20. Baker.

fleshy, n.—2. A flesh wound: Australian soldiers': 1940 +. Lawson Glassop, *We Were the Rats*, 1944, '"Just a couple of fleshies. Be back again in a few weeks, dealing it out to old Jerry again."'

flib. See **flab**.

flick. A bioscope: Stellenbosch University, S. Africa: C. 20. Cf. Dutch *flikkeren*, to flicker.

flicking.—2. A corruption (from ca. 1910), orig. perhaps euphemistic, of **fricking**.

flicks.—3. Searchlights: Air Force: 1939 +. Jackson. Ex sense 2.

flicks, the, 1 (p. 286): still, in 1966, very common in Australia. (B.P.)

Flidget Sergeant. A Flight-Sergeant: R.A.F.: since ca. 1933. (Atkinson.) Prob. *flight* + *fidget*.

flies, up in the. Prosperous: theatrical: C. 20. W. L. George, *The Making of an Englishman*, 1914. Ex the *flies* of theatrical j.: the space over the proscenium.

flies' skating-rink. See **skating-rink** below.

Flight. In address (rarely otherwise): Flight-Sergeant: R.A.F. coll.: since ca. 1919. Jackson. It has never—at least by the Other Ranks—been so widely used as **chiefie**.

flight Louie. A Flight-Lieutenant: R.A.F.: since ca. 1930. Jackson. Ex *lootenant for* 'lieutenant'.

flight magician. A flight-mechanic: Air Force since ca. 1925. Jackson. Humorous.

flights. Hangars: Air Force: since ca. 1937. Jackson, 'Thus, "Down in the flights"': from the hangars the aircraft are moved preparatory to flying.

flim, 2 (p. 286). Also, since ca. 1942, common among spivs. (*Picture Post*, Jan. 2, 1954.)

flimping.—2. A 'rigging' of the weights on a pair of scales: barrow-boys': since ca. 1920. Cf. sense 1 (p. 287).

flimsy.—5. (Cf. sense 2.) An important message written on rice paper, which, if one is captured, can be swallowed without ill effects: Services: since 1939. H. & P.—6. A cheque: Australian: C. 20. B., 1942. Ex 1.—7. A train order: Canadian railroadmen's (— 1931).—8. 'Petrol-can, of the original British type, very easily broken': Army: ca. 1940–3. (P-G-R.) But Peter Sanders modifies my entry thus: 'More accurately a four-gallon

petrol can of tinplate (later ternplate) made in Egypt and used throughout the "Middle East". Egyptian industry was not capable of making a more substantial can. The ordinary British two-gallon can was an engineering marvel by comparison.'

fling for. See **rap**, v., 2, below. This is c. of C. 18–early 19.

fling one up is a variant (R.A.F.: since ca. 1930) of **throw one up**. Jackson.

flinking. Employed by youths to impress their friends that they are still 'he-men', not 'cissies', usually if women or strangers might overhear them: since ca. 1940. Ex S.W.-English dial. *flink*, 'to *fling* or toss', whence *flinker*, 'a proud woman'.

flint (p. 287). See **dung** (p. 249). I.e. one who is *true as steel*.

flint for, fix one's. To put a spoke in someone's wheel; to 'settle his hash': ca. 1850–1910. H., 2nd ed., 1860.

flint it out. To insist on full wages: workmen's: C. 19. B. & L.

flip, n., 3. Also in a motor-car: since ca. 1935. H. & P.—4. Earlier in A. Neil Lyons, *Clara*, 1912.—5. Short for **flip side** below: since late 1950's.—6. A chap, a fellow: Australian pejorative: C. 20. Ex sense 5 of v.

flip, v.—3. To approve wildly, to become deliriously elated: Canadian dance-lovers' and jazz musicians': adopted, 1957, ex U.S. (where originally *flip one's wig*).—4. To go literally mad: Canadian jazz musicians' and lovers': since 1956 or 1957. Cf. the U.S. *blow one's top*.—5. To masturbate: Australian male: late C. 19–20. Also *flip oneself off*.—6. To arouse enthusiasm: drug addicts', hippies', Flower People's: since ca. 1966. (Peter Fryer in *The Observer* colour supplement, Dec. 3, 1967.)

flip, adj. Flippant: American s., adopted ca. 1918 in Canada, ca. 1945 in Australia (Ruth Park, *The Good-Looking Women*, 1961); late 1940's in New Zealand; ca. 1950 in Britain.

flip-flaps or **flops**. Bouncing breasts: Australian: since ca. 1920.—2. Hence, girls with bouncing breasts, as in 'standing in Martin Place [Sydney] and watching the flip-flops go by': Australian: since early 1920's.

flip side. The reverse side of a record: teenagers', ex disc jockeys': since late 1950's.

flip (one's) top. To become extremely angry or excited, almost crazy: Australian: adopted, ca. 1950, ex U.S. (B.P.)

flip-wreck. Vaguely pejorative for a man: Australian: since ca. 1910. Cf. **flip**, n., 6, and v., 5, above.

flipped. Crazy: Australian: since early 1950's. Ex preceding. (B.P.)

flipper, 1 (p. 287). A year earlier in 'A Real Paddy', *Real Life in Ireland*, 1822.—4. A variant form of **flapper**, 5 (young harlot).—5. The controls of an aircraft: R.F.C.–R.A.F.: ca. 1916–25. (Guy Fowler, *The Dawn Patrol*, 1930.)—6. 'A top-spinner delivered by the bowler with an extra flip of the fingers' (Peter Sanders): cricketers': since ca. 1920.

flipping. A pejorative, usually intensive, adjective and adverb: proletarian: since ca. 1920. 'I sha'n't do the flipping thing'—'I don't flipping well know.' (The film, *Seven Days to Noon*, 1950.) Originally a euphemism. In S. P. B. Mais,

Caper Sauce, 1948, we find: "'No flipping Bovril about the Barley Mow, Aggie," said Lomax. "And I'll trouble you not to swear, Mr Lomax. There's ladies present."' Since ca. 1940 the commonest of all euphemisms for *fucking*, adj.

flit commode. A flight commander (not a rank but a function): R.A.F.: since ca. 1935. Jackson. Cf. **air commode.**

flit gun. See **cap badge.**

float, n.—3. That cash in the till which is there for ordinary trading: coll.: since the 1930's. Stephen Mogridge, *Talking Shop*, 1950. Perhaps ex sense 2 (p. 287).

float, v., 2 (p. 287): common, since before 1919, at Eton—where it is also a noun (= *faux pas*). Marples.—3. To go: from ca. 1910. Cf. **float up** (*Dict.*).

float around. To fly near by 'in a leisurely fashion for the fun of it or to kill time' (Jackson): R.A.F.: since ca. 1930.

floater, a *faux pas*, was in use at Oxford at least as early as 1913: witness Lunn (p. 78). Its essence is that it recurs.—7. Esp. in *floaters and mash*, sausages and mashed potatoes: R.A.F.: since ca. 1920. Jackson. Ex sense 1 ?—8. An employee always on the move: Canadian railroadmen's (— 1931). Also known as a *boomer.*—9. A departmental file that circulates for the information of the branch: Army officers': since ca. 1920.

floaters in the snow. Sausages and mashed potatoes: Naval (lower-deck): since ca. 1920. Cf. *floater*, 7.

floating one, vbl n. Passing a worthless cheque or arranging a loan without definite security: Services, esp. among officers: since ca. 1930. H. & P.

*****flock.** A bed: tramps' c.: C. 20. Ex the flock in a mattress.

flog.—2. (p. 288): but extant in Anglo-Irish until much later than 1910. (P. W. Joyce.)—7. (Ex 3.) 'To offer for sale (especially when financially embarrassed . . .),' H. & P.: Services: since ca. 1935.—8. To borrow without permission: Services: since ca. 1937. H. & P. (Cf. sense 5.)—9. To masturbate: low Australian: C. 20.

flog one's donkey. (Of a male) to masturbate: low (? orig. Cockney): late C. 19–20. Also *flog one's mutton*—a variant of **jerk** . . . Also *flog the bishop* (see **bishop** . . .).

flog the bung. To use a mallet instead of the regulation 'pricker' to draw the bung of a cask: Naval: mid-C. 19–20; † by 1930. Granville.

flog the cat.—2. To vent one's bad temper on someone: Naval: since ca. 1925. Granville.

flogging, adj.—2. (Also adv.) Objectionable; vaguely, yet strongly, pejorative: Australian: since ca. 1920. Ex **flog**, v., 9, above; semantically cf. the equivalent **flipping** above. It occurs in, e.g., Hugh Atkinson, *Low Company*, 1961, "'Down they come like the floggin' wool prices"' and 'They might land in the floggin' desert"'.

flogging, be. To be saving up one's money very carefully: proletarian: mid-C. 19–20; ob. B. & L.

floor, v., 1 (p. 288), occurs slightly earlier in W. N. Glascock's *Naval Sketch Book*, 2nd Series, 1834, at I, 207. (Moe.)

floor, on the (p. 288). By 1939, low s. Cf. familiar S.E. *down and out.*—2. Adj. and adv. Derailed: railwaymen's: C. 20. (*Railway* 2nd.) Cf. **dirt, on the**, above.

floor fuck. Copulation on the carpet: low Australian: since ca. 1910.

floor-polish. To prove (someone) to be utterly wrong; a severe defeat, in argument or in a contest: since ca. 1942. *John Bull*, Dec. 2, 1944. Ex 'to *wipe the floor* with someone'.

floorman, the; the top man. Drawing upon Messrs William Hill Ltd's diary for 1953, *The Sunday Dispatch* of Dec. 14, 1952 writes: 'Tic-tac is used chiefly to liaise between the big operators and the little bookmakers in the minor ring. The liaison man is usually to be found perched precariously in the main stand, and for that reason is called "The Top Man". He relays information to his partner, "The Floor Man", who stands down below on the rails.' The latter passes it on to the small bookmakers themselves. These terms go back at least as far as 1930.

floorman pitch-getter. One of those assistants at a mock or rigged auction who entice crowds into the auction room: mock-auction world: since ca. 1945. (*Sunday Chronicle*, June 28, 1951.) Strictly, only *pitch-getter* is slang and, in this 'world', very much commoner than the full expression.

floosie (or **-y**). A girl (as companion): Naval: since ca. 1940. Granville; *John Bull*, April 6, 1946. Adopted from U.S. s. For origin, cf. **Flossie.**

flop, n.—5. A bed: Canadian railroadmen's (— 1931). Adopted from U.S.: see *Underworld.*

flop, do a (p. 288).—3. To faint: current, esp. among V.A.D.'s, in 1914–18; extant.

flopper-stopper. A brassière: Australian teenagers': since ca. 1955. Cf. **flip-flops** above.

flopperoo. A spectacular 'flop' or failure: adopted, ca. 1960, ex U.S. Cf. **flop**, n., 3 (p. 288).

flor de cabbagio. A c.p. directed, ca. 1890–1914, at someone smoking a cheap cigar: cf. *cabbage*, n., 4 (p. 118) and **who's smoking . . .** below.

floricus is B. & L.'s error for *foricus*, q.v. in *Dict.* at **forakers.**

florid. Half-drunk; fuddled: ca. 1770–1830. See quot'n at **mops and brooms.** I.e. flushed with drink.

Florrie. Inseparable nickname of all *Ford(e)s*: C. 20. Cf. *Florrie Ford* (p. 289).

Flossie. A prostitute: South Africa: C. 20.

flossy or flossy up. To dress up (oneself); to furbish: Australian: since ca. 1935. (B., 1953.) Ex the S.E. adj.

flounder, n.—2. Short for *flounder and dab*—since ca. 1905, of a taxicab.

flounder-spearing. See **spearing flounders.**

flour-mixer. A Gentile girl: esp. Jewish Cockneys': C. 20. Rhyming s. on Yiddish *shiksa*, q.v. at **shickster** on p. 755. Franklyn 2nd.

Floury. The inseparable nickname of all *Bakers*: late C. 19–20.

flow, n. A 'travelling the bees' sojourn at a place where blossoms abound: Australian coll.: since ca. 1945. Kylie Tennant, *The Honey Flow*, 1956, 'You say nothing of what you did to get your honey, but tell wild lies of the flows you have been on, and how you took seven tins to the hive.'

Flower pot, the. Covent Garden (Market). London taxi-drivers': since ca. 1905. Herbert Hodge, *Cab, Sir?*, 1939. Ex the Flower Market there.

Flower power. 'Revolutionary philosophy akin to ideas of Young Liberals, e.g. Make Love Not

War' (Peter Fryer in *The Observer* colour supplement, Dec. 3, 1967): hippies', Flower People's: since early 1967. Ex 'the Flower (or Beautiful) People'.

flowers.—2. Orders, decorations, honours or degrees, indicated by letters after name: Forces': 1939 +. They look pretty. (Atkinson.)

flowers and frolics; fun and frolics. Testicles: Anglo-Irish rhyming s.: late C. 19–20. (Franklyn, *Rhyming*.)

flowery.—3. A cubicle: low: since ca. 1920. Ex *flowery* (*dell*), a prison cell. Brendan Behan, *Borstal Boy*, 1958.

fluey. Characteristic of, or characterized by, influenza, as '*fluey* weather': coll.: since ca. 1930. (A. B. Petch, March 1966.)

fluff, n., 5 (p. 289): esp. railwaymen's: late C. 19–20. (*Railway* 2nd.)—7. Nonsense, esp. 'That's all fluff': Australian: ca. 1935–40 (source as for **Bovril**).—8. A railway ticket: Australian low: since ca. 1920. B., 1942.—B., 1943.—9. 'A spoonerism or other vocal misadventure on the radio (wireless)': Canadian: since ca. 1945. (Leechman.)

fluff, v.—7. (Cf. sense 3 in *Dict.*) To 'foozle' a shot by hitting the ground just behind the ball instead of the ball: golfers': C. 20.—8, which should, chronologically, be sense 1. To disguise the defects of (a horse): 1822, David Carey, *Life in Paris*, 'He knew . . . when a *roarer* had been *fluffed* for the purpose of sale.'—9. To suspect; to understand; to guess or detect: Army, esp. the Guards: since ca. 1910. Gerald Kersh, *They Die with their Boots Clean*, 1941. Also *fluff to* (someone): to 'tumble to' him. Prob. ex sense 2.— 10. Break wind: Australian: since ca. 1919. B., 1942. Prob. ex sense 6.

fluffing, 2, or **quilling.** The selection, by off-duty employees, of rich passengers' luggage: railwaymen's: C. 20. (*Railway.*) Contrast and cf. **fluffing(s)** on p. 290.

fluffy ruffles. A girl in rustling petticoats and a feather boa: 1890's. Ex U.S. (and never very gen.), via the American illustrated periodicals.

flumdoodle. To humbug (someone): Australian C. 20. Baker. Cf. **flumdiddle** (p. 290).

flunk. A term of contempt for, usually, a male: Australian: since ca. 1910. Baker. Ex *flunkey*.

flunk, v.t. and v.i. To fail in an examination: Canadian universities: late C. 19–20. Adopted from U.S.; of hotly disputed—in short, of unknown—origin.

fluo tube. A fluorescent-lighting tube: Australian coll.: since ca. 1955. (B.P.)

flush, n. 'Those [convicts] with Army and Navy experience use the Maltese word for money, i.e. "flush",' H. Wicks, *The Prisoner Speaks*, 1938.— 2. A fellow with plenty of money, esp. if a free spender: Canadian carnival s.: since ca. 1910. Ex the adj.

flush of all four (aces). See 'Tavern terms', § 2.

flute.—4. See 'Tavern Terms', § 7 (near end).— 5. A, to, whistle: police and prison warders': C. 20. The n. in Axel Bracey, *School for Scoundrels*, 1934; n. and v. in Jim Phelan, *Murder by Numbers*, 1941.—6. A jockey's whip: Australian sporting s.: since ca. 1910. B., 1942.

fly, n.—9. (Ex 3.) Esp. *give* (it) *a fly*, *have a fly* (at it), to try it; to make an attempt: Australian: C. 20. Baker. K. S. Prichard, *Working Bullocks*,

1926, '"Might give him a fly," Red admitted.'—10. A shunting truck; hence *fly shunt*, 'uncoupled wagons diverted after engine has passed the points'. (*Railway*): railwaymen's: C. 20.

fly, do a (or **its**). Of a horse: to do a gallop: Australian: C. 20. (K. S. Prichard, 'Dark Horse' —in *Kiss on the Lips*, 1932.)

fly, give it a; have a fly (**at**). To attempt something: Aus.: since mid-1940's. (B., 1959.)

fly a desk. Of an aircrew member: to be grounded and doing an office job: R.A.F.: 1940– 5. Paul Brickhill, *The Dam Busters*, 1951.

fly a kite.—7. 'To tell a tall story' (Baker): Australian: C. 20.

fly-blow.—2. A flying-boat: R.A.F.: since ca. 1935. Jackson. By a pun on S.E. *by-blow.*

fly-blow, v. To separate (someone) from his money: Australian: C. 20. Baker. Ex **fly-blown,** 2 (*Dict.*).

fly-blown, 2. Also New Zealand. (B., 1941.)

fly-bog. Jam: Australian: ca. 1930–50, but never very general. (B., 1943.)—2. More general is the sense occurring in 'Sometimes you take a tin of fly-bog (treacle) with you as a luxury' (Jean Devanney, *By Tropic Sea and Jungle*, 1944): since ca. 1920.

fly boy. A Fleet Air Arm pilot or observer: among other branches of the Royal Navy and mostly officers': since ca. 1950; after 1965, only historical. (Wilfred Granville, *A Dictionary of Sailors' Slang*, 1962.) A pun on **fly,** adj., 1 (p. 291) and on S.E. '*flying*', adj.

fly-by-night. A transient boarder bilking his landlady: landladies' coll.: late C. 19–20.—2. Tipsy: rhyming s.: C. 20, but † by 1960. On synonymous *tight*. (Franklyn 2nd.)

fly by the seat of one's pants. To fly by instinct rather than by instruments: R.A.F.: since ca. 1930. Berrey: Brickhill & Norton, *Escape to Danger*, 1946, 'Only the line-shoot flying epics turned out by Hollywood could have produced the legend of the pilot who flew "by the seat of his pants".'—2. Hence, to essay a task (not necessarily aeronautical) and, although one is unfamiliar with it, to improve as one continues: originally (1942) and still (1960) mainly Air Force. (Atkinson.)

fly cemetery. A currant pudding: certain schools': since ca. 1945. (*New Society*, Aug. 22, 1963.)

fly-dusters. Fists: ca. 1880–1920. Arthur Binstead, *Mop Fair*, 1905.

fly flat.—2. A know-all; a 'smart Alec': low Australian: since ca. 1910. Cf.:

fly-gatherer. That workman who 'sweeps up and bags waste and "fly" (fibre dust) in spinning rooms' (*The Evening News*, Sept. 28, 1955): textile employees': late C. 19–20.

*fly gay. Intelligent dupe of a confidence trickster: Australian c.: since ca. 1920. Baker. On analogy of **fly flat** (p. 292). See **gay.**

fly jerks. 'Small pieces of cork suspended from the brim of a tramp's hat to ward off flies,' B., 1942: Australian: late C. 19–20.

fly my kite (p. 292): † since ca. 1920, at latest.

fly off the handle (p. 292). Probably ex the head of a tool coming loose and falling off.

fly-pitch (p. 292): esp. of 'a casual spot' (W. Buchanan-Taylor, *Shake It Again*, 1943).

Fly Speck, the. Tasmania: continental Australians': C. 20. (B., 1943.) Cf. *Speck, the*, on p. 806.

fly-swisher stew. Oxtail stew: Aus. rural: since ca. 1910. (B., 1959.) Cattle swish their tails to keep the flies away.

fly the blue pigeon.—2. To use the sounding-lead: nautical: from ca. 1870. Kipling, *Captains Courageous*, 1897.

fly-walk, the. The ridge on a loaf of bread: domestic: C. 20.

Fly Wheel. See **Chad**.

flyer.—10. A very fast start in a foot race: athletics coll.: C. 20.

Flying Angel (Club), the. The Mission to Seamen('s Club): seamen's: C. 20. 'From the flying angel on the blue ground of the Mission's flag, from *Rev.*, xiv, 6, "And I saw another angel fly in the midst of heaven . . ."' (Laurie Atkinson, Sept. 11, 1967).

flying arsehole.—2. Observer on a 'plane: R.A.A.F.: 1939–45. (B., 1943.)

Flying Cigar—**Flying Pencil**—**Flying Suitcase**—**Flying Tin-opener** (all preceded by **the**). Resp., the Wellington bomber (viewed laterally)—the Dornier (laterally)—the Hampden and the short-lived Hereford bombers (side view, forward section)—and the Hurricane tank-buster: R.A.F.: since 1940 (first three) and 1941 (the fourth). H. & P., 1943.

Flying Coffin, the. The Vengeance dive-bomber: R.A.F.: 1944–5. Cf. preceding entry.

***flying cove.** One who gets money by pretending to be able to supply robbed persons with such information as will lead to the recovery of the lost goods: c.: ca. 1860–1940. B. & L.

flying dhobey. A native washerman giving quick service: Army in India: late C. 19–20; ob. by 1950. Also 'the mysterious Arab who would turn up at every camp, . . . however far from civilisation, to provide a one-day laundry service' (Peter Sanders, 1967): Army in North Africa: 1940–43.

flying duck. A section insulator: railwaymen's: since ca. 1950. (*Railway*, 3rd.)

flying dustbin. A heavy mortar-bomb fired from a tank: Army: 1940–5. (P-G-R.) Ex its appearances. Peter Sanders again rescues me, thus: 'More accurately, the bomb thrown by an A.V.R.E. (Armoured Vehicle, Royal Engineers) for demolishing defences. ". . . a 12" spigot mortar, the Petard, which could throw a 25 lb H.E. charge (known as the 'Flying Dustbin') up to a distance of eighty yards . . ." From *The Tanks*, by B. H. Liddell Hart, 1959, vol. II, p. 324. Probably not widely used until 1944, as these vehicles were a secret weapon for the landings in Normandy.'

flying dustman. 'The defendant was what is termed a *Flying Dustman*, who . . . paying nothing to anyone, goes round the parish collecting all the ashes he can, to the great injury of the contractor,' says a witness in a trial of 1812 in *The New Newgate Calendar*, V, 519; J. Wight, *More Mornings at Bow Street*, 1827, for a most informative account: coll.: ca. 1805–70.

flying elephant; usually in pl. A barrage balloon: since 1939. Berrey, 1940.

flying-fish. A fish-shaped mortar shell: Army: 1915–18.

Flying Fornicator, the. The last express train home from London: in many English provincial

towns, esp. Oxford and Cambridge: C. 20. Also *the Fornicator*.

flying gas-main. A V.2 rocket: 1944–5. Jane Gordon, *Married to Charles*, 1950. An early report: 'A gas-main has exploded.'

flying handicap, the. An attack of diarrhœa: Australian sporting: C. 20. B., 1942. Cf. **Sheffield handicap**, 2.

Flying Horse; usually in pl. A Gloster Gladiator aircraft of the Fleet Air Arm: Naval: since ca. 1940. Granville.

flying kite (p. 292) is recorded in 1818: Alfred Burton, *Johnny Newcome*. (Moe.)

flying knacker. A horse-flesh butcher in a small way: Londoners': ca. 1860–1900. James Greenwood, *Odd People in Odd Places*, 1883.

flying light.—2. An earlier coll. nautical sense occurs in W. N. Glascock's *Naval Sketch Book*, 2nd Series, 1834, at I, 278, thus: 'Fell in with a full-feathered hearse—five mourning coaches—and a long line of carriages "flying light"' (with either no or only one passenger). Moe.

Flying Pencil. See **Flying Cigar**.

flying pig.—2. An aerial torpedo: 1940, Berrey. Ex appearance in the air.—3. A Vickers Vulcan aircraft of Imperial Airways: 1920's. (Wing Commander R. H. McIntosh, D.F.C., A.F.C., *Autobiography*, 1963.) Ex its pig-like appearance.

flying plumber. 'A Naval Engineering Officer borne for duty with the Fleet Air Arm' (P-G-R.): 1940 +.

flying sixty-six. A variant of **sixty-niner** below.

Flying Suitcase. See **Flying Cigar**. Also called a *Flying Tadpole*: Jackson.

Flying Tin-opener. See **Flying Cigar**.

fo-yok. Gunpowder: pidgin: from ca. 1860. B. & L. Lit., fire physic.

foaming at the mouth. See **ready to spit**.

***fob-diver.** A pickpocket: c.: from ca. 1880; slightly ob. (Binstead.)

***fob-worker.** A pickpocket specialising in the contents (esp. watches) of fobs: c.: from ca. 1890. (*The Evening News*, Dec. 9, 1936.) See **fob**, n., 2, in the *Dict.* Cf. *patch-worker*, q.v.

fog, n.—2. See **Scotch Mist**, 2.—3. Steam: Canadian railroadmen's (− 1931).—4. See **banger**, 6, above. Hence *fogging*, fog-signal duty: railwaymen's: since ca. 1930. (*Railway*.)

fog factory. 'A locality where fogs are plentiful,' Berrey: R.A.F.: since 1939.

fogles. A prize-fighter's colours: boxing: mid-C. 19–20. Ex **fogle**, 1 (p. 293).

fokesel (p. 294) has yet another variant: *folksel*, which occurs in W. N. Glascock, *Sketch-Book* (II, 30), 1826; and in Glascock's *Saints and Sinners* (I, 196), 1829, we find *folksle*. Moe.

fold, v. Elliptical for sense 2 of next.

fold up, v.i. (Of an aircraft) to crash: (of a person) to go sick unexpectedly or without warning: Services, esp. R.A.F.: since 1939. H. & P. Ex the 'to collapse' sense of the S.E. term; adopted from U.S.: perhaps, semantically, ex the 'action' of a defective parachute.—2. Hence, of a policy or a plan, of a business or a periodical: to fail, to collapse; to cease: since ca. 1945. Usually shortened to *fold*, as in 'This magazine is expected to fold before long'.

folding lettuce. Currency notes: beatniks': adopted, ca. 1958, ex U.S. (Anderson.)

follow the waterworks. To travel about the

country on reservoir jobs: navvies': since ca. 1920.

foo. A favourite gremlin: R.A.A.F.: 1941 +. Arbitrary, though perhaps with a pun on *F.O.O.*, a Forward Observation Officer. Baker, 1943, less precisely writes: 'A fictitious person to whom all lapses and bungling are attributed' and classifies it as general war slang: whence *fooism*, a saying, or an exploit, attributed to *Foo*. Perhaps ex a popular American cartoon strip called 'Smokey Storer': there, the 'hero' used it as a stop-gap name for anything for which he couldn't be bothered to find the correct word.

foo-foo. Talcum powder: pejorative: since ca. 1920. Perhaps ex **foo-foo barge.**

foo-foo band. A C. 20 synonym of **squeegee band** (p. 819). Cf.:—

foo-foo barge. A sewage boat on the Yangste River: Naval: C. 20. Granville, 'From "Phew, Phew!" perhaps?'; certainly with ref. to *Foo*, a common element in Chinese place-names.

foo-foo powder. 'Talcum powder, used a great deal by sailors in the tropics' (Granville): Naval lowerdeck: since ca. 1930. Cf. the preceding.

foo-foo valve. 'A mythical "gadget" that's always blamed for any mechanical break-down,' Wilfred Granville, letter of Jan. 7, 1947: Naval: since ca. 1910.

Foo was here! The Australian equivalent of **Kilroy was here:** since ca. 1940. Cf. **foo** above. (B.P.)

[Food in s. and coll. of early C. 18, as represented by Ned Ward, receives the following names: In gen., *belly-timber*. Trotters were *bullocks' pettitoes* (1703); sheep's heads, *nappers' nulls* (nolls), 1703; 'pigs' faces or the like' were *grunters' muns* (1703); butter-milk, *bonniclabber* (1709).]

food inspector. A tramp: Australian: C. 20. B., 1942. He goes about the country sampling food wherever he can get a 'hand-out'. By 1959, †: teste B., *The Drum.*

fool-rogue. 'Some officers . . . were what the men called "fool-rogues"—petty, stupid, spiteful martinets,' Robert Blatchford, *My Life in the Army*, 1910: Regular Army coll.: ca. 1860–1910.

foosch. See **Imperial.**

foot-back it. To go on foot, carrying one's pack: Australian coll.: Archer Russell, 1934. And see **footback.**

foot for thought. 'A kick in the pants, as a warning not to do it again' (A. B. Petch, April 1966): jocular: since ca. 1950. A .pun on '*food for thought*'.

foot it, (p. 295) goes back to ca. 1820 or even to very early C. 19. It occurs in Wm Maginn, *Tales of Military Life*, 1829, at III, 229. (Moe.)—3. To dance: coll.: late C. 18–19. W. N. Glascock, *Sketch-Book* (II, 135), 1826; and earlier in *The Port Folio* of May 23, 1805 (p. 158, col. 2) quoting a Charles Dibdin song. (Moe.)

foot on the floor, put one's; with one's. To accelerate; by accelerating: motorists': since ca. 1920.

foot-rotting, n. 'Kicking one's heels in idleness' (B., 1943): Australian: since ca. 1930.

foot scamper, the. Robbery on foot, esp. of coaches; 'footpaddery': c.: C. 18. James Dalton, *A Narrative*, 1728.

footback or **on footback.** On foot: Australian: since ca. 1920. Archer Russell, *A Tramp Royal*,

1934 (*footback*); B., 1943 (*on f-*). Punning *horseback*.

football.—2. See **cricket**, 2.

football feet, have. (Of an aircraft pilot) to make excessive use of the rudder: R.A.F.: since ca. 1930. H. & P.

footie. Football: Australian: since ca. 1920. (B., 1953.)

footle around, usually as vbl n., *footling around*, 'continuously circling over an area in search of a target or a landing-ground': E. P. in *The New Statesman*, Sept. 19, 1942. See **footle** (p. 295).

footprints, pair of. A pipe-wrench: Australian: since ca. 1930. 'Apparently so named because, when open, they are wide at the ends and narrow in the middle like a [human] footprint' (B.P.).

footsack! See **voetsak!** in *Dict.*

Footscray Alps, the. The higher parts of Footscray: Melbournites' irony: since ca. 1920. (B., 1943.)

footslogger. See **foot-slogger** (*Dict.*)

footy.—2. Futile: Society: since ca. 1934; ob. Margery Allingham, *The Fashion in Shrouds*, 1938.—3. As in '*footy* match', football match: Australian: since ca. 1920. (A. E. Farrell, *The Vengeance*, 1963.)

footy, play. To play feet: (mainly lower) middle-class coll.: late C. 19–20. Also *play footies*.

fop's alley (p. 295). Earlier *fop's corner* (nearest-the-stage corner of the pit): Wycherley, *The Country Wife*, 1675, in form *fop corner*. (With thanks to John Cannon, Esq.)

[Fops and gallants receive in the works of Ned Ward in the first quarter of C. 18 such various s. names as these: *butter-box* (1703), *crack* (1703), *Jack of Dandy* (1703), *pilgarlic* (1724), *skip-Jack* (1703), *sprag* (1709), *Tom Essence* (1703). Matthews, who notes that these terms are all pejorative: I doubt, however, this sense of *pilgarlic*.]

for 'Brighton' read 'tight 'un'. A c.p. directed at a drunk: R.A.F.: since ca. 1920.

for crying out loud! See **crying out loud!, for.**

*for free. See **charity dame.**

for free. Free: coll.: adopted, ca. 1954, ex U.S. 'I got it for free'. Tautology.

for king and cunt. A c.p. reply to 'What are *you* fighting for?': C. 20.

for the widows and orphans, it's; or as c.p., *all the money I take goes to the widows and orphans of* (such and such a group or class or profession): cheapjacks' and market grafters': C. 20; since ca. 1960, slightly ob. (A. B. Petch, April 1966.)

for what we are about to receive. A naval c.p.: C. 18–20. C. S. Forester, *The Happy Return*, 1937, '"For what we are about to receive——," said Bush, repeating the hackneyed blasphemy quoted in every ship awaiting a broadside.' Ex the Grace, 'For what we are about to receive, the Lord make us truly thankful.'

for you the war is over. A c.p. used by prisoners-of-war captured by the Italians (who thus addressed them on their arrival in Italy): 1940–4. (P-G-R.)

force, n. 'The ability of a sheepdog to control a mob of sheep, esp. without *legging*, i.e. leg-biting. A good dog is said to have *a lot of force*. Whence, *forcing dog*' (B., 1959): Aus. rural coll.: C. 20.

fore-and-aft, n. 'Field service cap, as distinct from dress service or peaked cap' (Jackson): R.A.F.: since ca. 1925.

fore and aft, adj. 'Descriptive of a sailor's

clothes, cut on the generous lines known to all,' H. & P.: Services, esp. Navy: C. 20. See **fore and aft rig** (*Dict.*). I.e. with plenty of freedom both in front and behind. Also *free and blowing*: H. & P.

fore-and-after, 2 (p. 296) is extant as Naval s. for 'officer's cocked hat with the peak in front' (Granville).

fore coach-wheel. See **coach-wheel** (*Dict.*).

forecourt, forehatch, forewoman. See **forecastle** (*Dict.*).

Foreign Legion, the. 'Men on loan' (*Railway*, 3rd): railwaymen's: since late 1940's.

foreign order. An Australian synonym of **foreigner** below: since early 1940's. (B.P.)

foreigner. An article—e.g. the model of an aircraft—made in the Service's time and with its materials: R.A.F.: since ca. 1941. H. & P. Adopted from civilian workers, who had used the term since at least as early as 1939.

forelo(o)per is a variant of **forlo(o)per**, q.v. in *Dict.*

foreman, near the door,—near the. See **near the foreman** . . .

foreman of the jury (*Dict.*) goes back to before 1650: see 'Tavern terms', § 4.

foretopman's lock. A quiff: Naval: late C. 19–20. 'Taffrail', *The Sub*, 1917.

Forever Amber or **f—a—.** A fixed distant signal: railwaymen's: since late 1940's. (*Railway*, 3rd.) Ex the title of Kathleen Winsor's famous popular novel, published in Britain in 1945—and the film two years later.

forget! . . . See **you'd forget** . . .

fork, n.—5. A jockey: Australian sporting: C. 20. B., 1942. He uses his fork so much.

fork, v.—5. To ride (a horse): Australian: C. 20. (D'Arcy Niland, *Call Me* . . ., 1958.) Cf. the preceding. (Occurs earlier in Tom Ronan, *Moleskin Midas*, 1956.)

fork and knife.—2. A wife: rhyming s.: C. 20. (Lester.) Far less common than **trouble and strife** (p. 912).

fork lifts. The two striped cushions placed in the rear window of a car: Australian raffish: since late 1950's. 'This is a status symbol, in that people with small cars or old cars with a small rear window have no room for the cushions' (B.P.) These cushions are reputed to facilitate rear-seat copulation, and there is a pun on the *fork* of the human body. In S.E., a *fork-lift* is 'a kind of industrial carrier that lifts goods by inserting a fork beneath a pallet stacked with goods'.

fork out (p. 297). Rather, since ca. 1815–20. W. T. Moncrieff, *The Collegians*, 1820, has *fork over*.

forks down, put one's. See **put one's forks down.**

form.—6. A reformatory: South African c.: late C. 19–20. *The Cape Times*, May 23, 1946.—7. A prison record, esp. if serious or recidivist: since ca. 1925. Norman, 'You can get at least a five and maybe even a neves for getting captured with a shooter especially if you've got a bit of form behind you.'—8. Situation, position, as in 'What's the form?' or 'It took me a couple of days to find out the form at H.Q.'—to ascertain how things were done and what the people were like: Services officers': since ca. 1930. (P-G-R.)

form, with. Having a police record: c. (and police s.): since ca. 1925. Peter Crookston,

Villain, 1967, 'They [the police] might check on everyone with form living within easy reach of the crime.'

form up (about it). To make a formal request or complaint to a superior officer: Army, mostly officers': 1939–45. (P-G-R.)

Formy. H.M.S. *Formidable*: Naval: since ca. 1930. Granville.

fornicating, adj. Lying; humbugging ('You fornicating sod!'): C. 20.

fornicating the poodle. See **fucking the dog.**

fornicator. 'He that passeth backward': trucks players': ca. 1650–1720. Charles Cotton, *The Compleat Gamester*, 1674.

Fornicator, The. See **Flying Fornicator.**

Fort. A Flying Fortress: coll. (R.A.F. and journalists'): 1941 +. Partridge, 1945.

Fort Bushy. The female pudend: Canadian: C. 20. Imaginary topography.

fortie. Variant (B., 1942) of **forty**, 2 (*Dict.*).

forty-acre field with her (or **him**) or **in her** (his) **hat** (**coat**, etc.), (**I,** etc.) **wouldn't be seen crossing** (or **dead in) a.** A c.p. of contempt or derision: mostly Cockneys': late C. 19–20. To a Cockney, 40 acres are a considerable area; *forty* is generic for a largish number.

forty-eight. A 48-hours' pass or leave: Services coll.: since ca. 1914.

forty-foot pole. See **wouldn't touch** . . .

forty-four. Door to door: rhyming s.: C. 20. (Franklyn, *Rhyming*.)

forty pounds of steam behind him, sometimes preceded by **with.** A Naval c.p. applied to someone who has received an immediate draft: since ca. 1900. Granville. At one time in the Navy's history, safety valves 'went off' at forty pounds pressure.

forty(-)rod; red(-)eye. Of illicit whisky going from Montana into Canada in 1889, Captain Burton Deane, *Mounted Police Life in Canada*, 1916, writes, 'The stuff itself was known as "Forty Rod", "Red Eye", "Rot Gut" and other similarly expressive names, and it was invariably of over-proof strength, so that it might be doctored by the retail vendors. In most cases it was little other than coloured alcohol': Canadian s.: since ca. 1885. In C. 20, *rot-gut* = bad beer. In 1914–18, the Army applied *red-eye* to rum. Mr Robert Clairborne reminds me that Mark Twain used it in *Huckleberry Finn*, 1884, and that the story is laid ca. 1850.

foss.—3. Generic for patent medicines and toilet preparations: fair-grounds': C. 20. (W. Buchanan-Taylor, *Shake It Again*, 1943.) Perhaps on *phosphorus*?

fotch. See the quotation at **chaffy** above. Perhaps cf. the North Country *fotch*, Sc. *foutch*, to challenge.

foul.—2. 'If the rank is full, and he "puts on" the tail end in the hope that the first cab will "get off" before a policeman catches him, he "puts on foul". When he has done so, *he* is "foul".' Herbert Hodge, *Cab, Sir?*, 1939: taxi-drivers': since ca. 1910. Ex the *foul* of sport, as in 'to play *foul*'.

Foul Weather Jack.—2. Hence, any person supposed to bring bad luck to a ship while he is on it: nautical coll.: late C. 18–20. B. & L.

found a nail. Round the tail: New Zealand sheep-shearers' rhyming s.: C. 20. B., 1941.

Foundling, the; pron. *fahnlin*. The Harmsworth Memorial Playground at Coram Fields: Cockneys': from ca. 1930 (?).

four-by-two, 2 (p. 298): but, by 1920, fairly common among users of rhyming s.

For sense 1 (p. 298), note that, strictly, this is the piece of flannelette within the loop at the end of the cord.

four F method, the. This is the lower-deck's allusive synonym (C. 20) of its sexual motto, *Find, feel, fuck and forget,* itself current since ca. 1890.

four(-)foot. '4 ft. 8½ in. gauge' (*Railway*, 3rd): railwaymen's coll.: C. 20.

four Johnny boys or **ladies** or **monarchs of the glen.** Quatorzes in picquet: C. 20. (Alan S. C. Ross.)

four-letter word. A 'rude word' of four letters: since 1929 (1st edition of *Lady Chatterley's Lover*: 1928): coll. >, by late 1950's, S.E. Usually reckoned as two or three, but there are at least ten of them: *arse, ball(s), cock, cunt, fart, fuck, piss, quim, shit, twat.*

four o'clock. A friar bird: Australian: C. 20. B., 1942. It's so diabolically matutinal!

four-ringed captain. 'A Captain R.N. as distinct from the captain of a ship who holds a junior rank' (Granville): Naval coll.: late C. 19–20.

four-stand flogger. '. . . As the ordinary whip made by an amateur is called' (Jean Devanney, *Travels in North Queensland,* 1951): Australian cattlemen's: C. 20.

fourble, adj. and—mostly in pl.—n. Quadruple: Australian juvenile: since ca. 1930. (B., 1953.)

fourpenny. An old ill-favoured whore: low London: ca. 1870–1910. Ex her tariff.

fourpenny one, get a. To be shot down: Air Force: 1940 +.—2. To receive a thrashing, get a hiding: since ca. 1910—the origin of sense 1.

fourteen penn'orth. An award of fourteen days in the cells: Naval: C. 20. Granville. Contrast the *Dict.* entry.

fourth, keep a. To the explanations at **fourth,** add this one: 1, Chapel; 2, breakfast; 3, pipe; 4, defecation. (This Cambridge interpretation dates back to at least as early as 1886.)

fourth, on one's. Very drunk: non-aristocratic: ca. 1870–1910. B. & L.

fowl-house, up against one's. A variant of duck-house . . ., q.v. Baker.

fowl-roost, start a. To assume a hyphenated surname: Australian: C. 20. B., 1942.

fowlo. A fowl: pidgin: mid-C. 19–20. B. & L.

fox.—7. To puzzle (a person)—e.g. with a flow of technicalities or of other erudition: Services' coll.: since 1939. H. & P. Ex sense 2.—8. (Ex sense 3.) 'To follow an enemy aircraft cunningly' (Jackson): R.A.F.: 1939 +.—9. To field (a cricket ball): Australian: since ca. 1925. Leonard Mann, *The Go-Getter,* 1942, 'You bowled it, you fox it.' To run to earth.

foxer. An apparatus used for foxing the *gnat* (German acoustic torpedo): Naval: ca. 1941–5.

foxes always smell their own hole first. A c.p. (ca. 1890–1914) uttered by the culprit in an endeavour (often serious) to shift the blame of a *flatus* on to the first complainant.

fox's paw (p. 299). Perhaps commoner is *fox's pass* as a lower-middle-class sol. for *faux pas*: late C. 19–20. **fox paw** (p. 299) 'has been brought

back to life in Australia. Not low here, but used mostly by university students' (B.P.)

frack. A noisy quarrel; an assault: Soho, London: since ca. 1920. (E. J. Oliver, *Not Long to Wait,* 1948.) Ex *fracas.*

***fragile.** (Of girls) exported under age to the Argentine: white-slavers' c.: C. 20. A. Londres, 1928.

fragment. A boy not good enough to play in the Peripatetics, the Etceteras or the Yearlings: Charterhouse: from 1926.

frail.—2. A courtesan: fast life: ca. 1830–70. Anon., *The New Swell's Guide to Night Life,* 1846. Cf. sense 1 on p. 299.

frames. Draught cattle: Australian coll.: late C. 19–20. B., 1942. Ex their large frames.

***franchucha.** A French prostitute in the Argentine: white-slave c.: late C. 19–20. (A. Londres, 1928.) In Argentine, a *Franchucha* was orig. 'Frenchwoman'.

Franklin teeth. Projecting teeth: Canadian: adopted, ca. 1920, ex U.S.; by 1935, †. Projecting, hence 'air-cooled': ex 'the air-cooled engine of the Franklin car. Became obsolete with the disappearance of the car in the Depression' (Priestley).

Frans, the. Members of the Friars Minor (*Franciscans*): Australian Catholics': C. 20. (B.P.)

frantic.—3. (Of a party) gay, lively: smart young set (esp. girls'): ca. 1955–60. Gilderdale, 2. Perhaps ex sense 2 (p. 300). Also (as in 'It's frantic' or good fun or exciting) Australian surfers', esp. teenagers': since late 1950's; by 1966, slightly ob. (*Pix,* Sept. 28, 1963.) Proleptic.

frarny (or **F-**). Rain: taxi-drivers': since ca. 1915. See **instalment mixture.** A very rare type of shortening from rhyming s.: *France and Spain.* Influenced by *parny* (see **parnee,** p. 606).

frat, n. Same as *fratter* in next entry: since late 1945. *John Bull,* June 8, 1946.

frat, v. To fraternise: Armed Forces': since May 1945. By back formation. Hence, *fratter,* a fraterniser. (North of the Brenner, the Allied Forces in 1945 referred to Austrian girls as *frats.*)

fraught. Risky or dangerous: smart set: since early 1960's. Andrew Garve, *The Long Short Cut,* 1968, '"Almost [no risks] in the early stages . . . The end could be a bit fraught."' Elliptical for 'fraught with danger'.

***frazzle,** v. To rob: Australian c.: C. 20. B., 1942 Ex. *done* (or *worn*) *to a frazzle.*

freak.—2. 'Trying to ring in a freak. . . . A double-header' (Vance Palmer, *Golconda,* 1948): Australian two-up players': since ca. 1910.

freak, v. To 'arouse or share collective enthusiasm (freak-out)': hippies' and then Flower People's: since late 1966 or very early 1967. Peter Fryer in *The Observer* colour supplement, Dec. 3, 1967. Cf. the next two entries.

freak-out, n. '. . . These curious way-out events, simulating drug ecstasies, which are known as "freak-outs", in which girls writhe and shriek and young men roll themselves naked in paint or jelly': Robert Pitman in the *Daily Express* of March 2, 1967—the day on which Anthony Burgess's review of D.S.U.E., 6th edition, appeared in *The Listener* and he animadverted upon my omission of the term; Peter Fryer in *The Observer* colour supplement, Dec. 3, 1967: since late 1966. Ex:—

freak out, v. To become a decided 'freak'—

temporarily crazy (hallucinated): Canadian drug addicts', since ca. 1965; > British, ca. 1966. *Daily Colonist*, March 29, 1967, 'Fred Sabine, 19, "freaked out" after taking the hallucinatory drug L.S.D., and said he encountered people who tried to bite his head off.' (Leechman.) Perhaps ex the S.E. adj. *freaked*, 'vivid with contrasting streaks of color occurring capriciously' (Webster); cf. preceding entry.

Fred Karno. 'A train made up of goods and passenger stock. In use among the L.M.S. employees ca. 1930. (As Fred Karno has not appeared on the halls for many years it is probably earlier)': J. A. Boycott, letter of Dec. 1938.

Fred Karno's Air Force. The British Air Force of World War I: ca. 1915–18. Prompted by his *Army* (p. 300).

Fred Karno's Army.—2. Hence, in the war of 1939–45, 'the Army on Home Service, and particularly the specialist branches regarded with a satirical eye' (H. & P.).

Fred Karno's Navy. 'Or *Harry Tate's Light Horse*. The auxiliary Patrol; terms . . . resuscitated in the Hitler War' (Granville): Naval: 1914 +.

Freddies. Orange Free State gold stocks and shares: Stock Exchange: C. 20.

Fred's. Fortnum & Mason's: Londoners': since ca. 1945. Cf. **Rod's.**

free and blowing. See **fore-and-aft.** Strictly worn by Petty Officers, E.R.A.'s, Accounts and Sick Berth ratings.

free chewing-gum. A chin-strap: Australian soldiers': 1939 +. B., 1942.

free expenses. A free dispensary: South African low s.: since ca. 1930. (C. P. Wittstock, letter of May 23, 1946.) A pun.

free gangway, a (p. 300), occurs in *The Navy and Army Illustrated*, Dec. 25, 1896. (Moe.)

free, gracious, (and) for nothing. A c.p. variant (only ca. 1885–1900) of **free, gratis and for nothing** (p. 300).

free gratis (p. 300) is to be dated from mid-C. 18. Thomas Bridges, *A Translation of Homer*, 1770, says, concerning *free gratis*, that 'the common people' always put these two words together. The longer *free, gratis and for nothing* occurs in W. L. Rede, *Sixteen String Jack*, 1841.

free-holder, 2, is recorded as early as 1650; see 'Tavern terms', § 9.

free issue. See **Froggie**, 3.

free object. A non-convict settler: Australian: ca. 1810–70. A. Harris, *Settlers and Convicts*, 1847. Punning 'free subject'.

free of sense as a frog of feathers, as; or . . . **from . . . from.** Complete fool: Australian: C. 20. Baker.

free school. See 'Tavern terms', § 3.

Freedom Corner. Marble Arch (but inside Hyde Park)—a spot famous for its orators: C. 20.

freeloader. 'One who crashes in on cocktail parties, luncheons, and other such affairs that are part of a publicity campaign, or otherwise accessible. The sin he commits is "freeloading"' (Leechman); the v., to *freeload*, is less common. Canadian: adopted, ca. 1955, ex U.S.

Freeman, Hardy and Willis. A synonym of, though much less used than, *Pip, Squeak and Wilfred* (p. 633): mostly R.A.F.: since ca. 1921. Jackson. Prompted by the older term and approximately equi-vocal with it.

Freemans is an Army shortening (C. 20) of *Harry Freeman's* (see **Freeman's . . .**, p. 300).

freeze, v.—2. To send (someone) to Coventry: Service officers': since ca. 1925. H. & P.—3. To stand stock still, e.g. when an enemy flare lights up the surroundings: coll.: C. 20. Ion M. Idriess, *The Desert Column*, 1932: Diary entry of May 30, 1915, 'When a blasted shell comes screaming . . . I don't move at all, just lie perfectly still and "freeze", waiting.'—3. (Usually of the wife.) To confine one's spouse to 'the dog-house': Australian: since ca. 1925. (B.P.)

freeze, do a.—2. Hence, to be ignored, neglected, overlooked: Australian: since ca. 1910. B., 1942.

freeze, the. A wife's deliberate withholding of sexual intercourse: Australian: since ca. 1930. 'Wives know that "the freeze" is their most potent weapon.' (B.P.) Cf. **freeze, v.**, 3.

freezer.—4 A C. 20 Salvation Army term. 'General Bramwell Booth was in the habit of putting too energetic officers into what was called the "freezer"—that is, sending them to remote and unexciting posts where their ardour would soon cool': footnote on p. 177 of Malcolm Muggeridge, *The Thirties*, 1940. William Bramwell Booth became the Salvation Army's chief organiser at the age of 26, in 1882; in 1912, he became its General.—5. A prison: Australian low: C. 20. B., 1942.

Fremantle doctor. A refreshing sea-breeze that, esp. in the evening, blows in to Fremantle and Perth: West Australian: since ca. 1920. (B., 1943.)

French, v. To perform an act of fellation upon: low: C. 20. 'She thought he was asleep, and Frenched him' (in a novel published ca. 1965). Cf. **French tricks** below.

French!, pardon (or excuse) the. Please excuse the strong language: non-aristocratic c.p.: from ca. 1916. Michael Harrison, *All the Trees were Green*, 1936, 'A bloody sight better (pardon the French!) than most.'

French by injection. See **injection . . .**

***French Consular Guard, the.** French prostitutes (Franchuchas) plying around the French Consulate at Buenos Aires: c., esp. white-slavers': C. 20. (A. Londres, 1928.)

French drive and **Chinese Drive.** A snick through the slips: cricket s., the former English, the latter Australian: since late 1940's. The former exemplifies 'the British tendency to ascribe anything irregular to the French' (Peter Sanders), the latter the Australian tendency to attribute anything odd to the Chinese.

French king, to have seen the. See 'Tavern terms', § 8.

French kiss (*Dict.*): lingual.

French letter.—2. A wind indicator: R.A.F.: since ca. 1925. Formerly, often called a 'windsock'. Ex shape.

French safe. A synonym of *French letter* (familiar S.E. for a condom): Canadian: since ca. 1910. (Leechman.)

French seventy-five (written **75**). A 'Tom Collins' mixed with champagne: since ca. 1918; ob. Alec Waugh, *Jill Somerset*, 1936. Ex its potency.

French tricks. Cunnilingism, penilingism: coll.: mid-C. 19–20.

Frenchman.—2. 'An Anglo-French printing machine': printers': from ca. 1870; ob. B. & L.

Frenchy.—2. (Also *Frenchie*.) A condom: Australian: since ca. 1910. Ex '*French* letter'.

fresh, 3 (p. 301). One year earlier in *Sessions*, 1828.—5. Uninitiated: c.: mid-C. 19–20. B. & L.

fresh and blood. 'Brandy and port wine, half and half,' *Spy*, 1825: Oxford University: ca. 1815–60.

fresh out of. Being short of; having no: Canadian coll., esp. among shopkeepers: adopted, ca. 1910, ex U.S. 'Sorry, sir, but we're fresh out of bacon.' (Leechman.)

freshen one's nip. To take a much-needed drink: nautical: C. 19. (W. N. Glascock's *Naval Sketch Book*, 2nd Series, 1834, at I, 283. Moe.)

freshen the hawse (p. 301) occurs earlier as *freshen hawse*, and bearing the sense 'to have an incidental drink', in *The Night Watch* (II, 117), 1828, 'After we had been mustered at quarters, and the hammocks down, I went and freshened hawse with a nip of Tom's grog.' Moe.

fresher.—2. A re*fresh*ment room, or a set of r. rooms: railwaymen's: C. 20. (*Railway*.)

freshers. Fresh air: Naval: C. 20. By 'the Oxford -*er*'.

freshers work first term . . . See **first term too early . . .** above.

freshgo, all. Al fresco: a sol. dating from ca. 1890. Esp. as in Edwin Pugh, *A Street in Suburbia*, 1895, 'It's nice ter be able ter take yer tea like this—all freshgo, ez the saying is.'

freshie (or -**ly**). A fresh-water crocodile: N. Queensland coll.: C. 20. (Jean Devanney, 1951.) Cf. *saltie*.

freshish. Verging on drunkenness, nearly tipsy: County s.: ca. 1819–60. P. Egan, *London*, 1821.

freshman's river. 'The Cam above Newnham Mill': Cambridge undergraduates': from ca. 1860. B. & L.

fret one's fat. To worry: low: from ca. 1880. Pugh (2). Cf. *fret one's giblets* in the *Dict*.

frey, v.i.: esp. as vbl n., *freying*, courting, courtship: South African: 1938 +. Professor W. S. Mackie in *The Cape Argus*, July 4, 1946, 'Simply an Anglicising of Africaans "vry" in its sense of "to court"—itself ex Dutch *vrijen*, "to court"—s. "To pet, to spoon."'

Friar Tuck. To coït; coïtion; an expletive: low rhyming s. (on *fuck*): late C. 19–20. (Franklyn, *Rhyming*.)

friar's balls. Friar's Balsam: Australian low jocular: since ca. 1930.

fricking. A s. euphemism for *fucking*, adj.: C. 20. On or ex *frigging*, adj.

Friday while (p. 302). Lieutenant Wilfred Granville, R.N.V.R., has neatly solved the origin: 'Leave from Friday noon to Monday. . . . The North Country *while*: "until". That is, "Friday until Monday."' A short weekend *Saturday while*.

fridge (p. 302) has, since ca. 1938 at latest, been the predominant form in Britain, Canada, Australia and elsewhere.—2. Prison: Australian low: since ca. 1910. Cf. **freezer**, 5.

fried. See **honkers**.

fried egg. A company sergeant-major's badge: Army: since ca. 1930.

fried eggs. Legs: Australian rhyming s.: C. 20. (A. A. Martin, letter, 1937.)—2. Underdeveloped female breasts: Australian male: since ca. 1930.

friend. The man who keeps a harlot as his mistress: (better-class) whores' euphemistic coll.: from ca. 1870. 'Oh yes, I have a friend.'—2. The ball-valve union one uses in blowing up a football: since ca. 1920. Ex advertisements?

friend, boy; girl friend. See **boy friend**.

friendies. A friend: Christ's Hospital: mid-C. 19–20. Marples.

friendly hostile. An enemy aircraft that doesn't attack: Naval: 1939–45. (P-G-R.)

friendly lead.—2. (Ex sense 1 on p. 302.) A 'passing the hat', a collection for someone in distress: C. 20.: coll.; by 1940, S.E.

frig, n.—3. 'Any military operation, from an exercise to a battle. "What time does the frig start?"' (P-G-R): Army: 1939–45. Perhaps ex 'a *frigging* nuisance or bore'.

frig, v.—3. Hence, in R.A.F. (since ca. 1935), to fix; e.g. fuses could be so 'frigged' that they would never blow.

frig around. Variant of *frig about* (p. 302): C. 20.

frig-up. A muddle, confusion: Australian: C. 20. Baker.

frighten the shit out of. To scare badly: low: late C. 19–20.

frightener. A scare: since ca. 1930. 'I'd been terrified . . ., but once I'd got over the first frightener I sort of liked it': L. J. Cunliffe, *Having It Away*, 1965. Cf.:—

frighteners on, put the. To scare (someone): low: since ca. 1930. (Norman.)

frightening powder. A stern warning: police: since ca. 1930. Robert Fabian, *London after Dark*, 1954, describes it as 'private police slang'. Cf. preceding entry.

frightfully (p. 302) dates rather from late C. 18, to judge by a passage (from *La Belle Assemblée*) in *The Port Folio* of June 1809. (Moe.)

frill, v. 'Partly to ring-bark a tree' (B., 1959): Aus. rural: C. 20.

frilled lizard. 'A man with a whisker-framed face' (B., 1942): Australian: C. 20. Family likeness.

fringer. One who wears side-whiskers only, or moustache and side-whiskers: beatniks': since ca. 1959. (Anderson.)

frippence. Threepence: sol., esp. Cockney: C. 19–20.

frippet; usually *a bit of frippet*. A young lady: military (officers'): from ca. 1933. Origin? Also among Leeds undergraduates for a townsman (or -woman): since ca. 1940. (Marples, 2.) 'Might this be a conflation of Lancashire *frip* ['anything worthless or trifling': E.D.D.]—cf. **fripping** below—and **snippet** below?': Ramsey Spencer. At the least, an influencing, I'd say.

fripping. Bickering; a more or less continuous irritation, petty quarrelling, esp. between husband and wife: Society and middle-class: since ca. 1919. In, e.g., W. Somerset Maugham, *The Circle*, 1921. Perhaps 'tearing things to tatters': Cf. C. 16–17 Fr. *fripon*, a rag, and Lancashire *frip*, something worthless.

'Frisco. San Francisco: a coll. contemned by the cultured: from ca. 1880.

frisk, v., 1 (p. 303), has, in Australia (late C. 19–20), the narrow sense, 'to examine (a person) by feeling *through the clothing* without searching pockets, etc.': B.P.

frisk and frolic. Carbolic: rhyming s.: ca. 1880–1920. Franklyn 2nd.

*frisk for. To take from (the person): c.: C. 20. W. L. Gibson Cowan, *Loud Report*, 1937, 'You have to keep your eye open for some cop who'll frisk you for a quid or threaten to take you up.' Ex frisk, v., 2.

frisking, n. Preliminary petting: Australian: since ca. 1930. Ex frisk, v., 1, above.

*fritter. Bacon-rind and/or bacon-fat wrapped up in rag to serve as a fire-lighter: tramps' c.: C. 20.

fritz, on the. See on the fritz.

Fritzkrieg. 'Facetious for a German bombardment,' Berrey: Sept. 1940–May 1941; thereafter hardly ever used, the strain on the air-raid victims causing facetiousness to wear thin. See Fritz (*Dict.*) and blitz (Addenda): Ger. *Krieg*, warfare.

frivols. Frivolities: since ca. 1920.

friz or frizz.—3. A female member of a show or carnival: Canadian carnival s.: since ca. 1920. Ex frizzed hair.—4. (Always *frizz*.) A 'flap', a panic: mostly theatrical: since ca. 1930. Noel Coward, *Pomp and Circumstance*, 1960.

*fro (or froe) file. A female pickpocket: C. 18. James Dalton, *A Narrative*, 1728, 'Fro Files, Women Pick-Pockets.' See *Dict.* for the separate terms.

frock and frill. A minor ill, esp. a *chill*: rhyming s.: late C. 19–20.

frock-hitcher. A milliner, esp. one in a small way: urban: ca. 1880–1915. Arthur Binstead, *Mop Fair*, 1905.

frocker. A frock coat: C. 20. By 'the Oxford -*er*'.

frog.—7. A £1 note: Australian: since ca. 1910. Vance Palmer, *Separate Lives*, 1931; B., 1942. A shortening of Australian rhyming s. *frog-skin = sovrin* = £1: late C. 19–20.—8. A condom: Australian: since ca. 1925. Prompted by Frenchy, 2 (above).

Sense 2 (p. 303): much earlier in *The Night Watch* (II, 299), 1828, and prob. going back to ca. 1790. Moe.

Frog-Eater (p. 303) should prob. be back-dated to late C. 18; it occurs in *The Night Watch* (II, 93), 1828. Moe. Moreover, the term is not ob. in Australia. (B.P.)

frog-footed; flat-footer. Resp. adj. and n. for a person going on foot: ca. 1870–1910. B. & L.

frog from (or of) feathers, as free of (or from) sense as a. See free of sense . . .

frog in the throat, have a. To have phlegm in the throat; hoarseness: coll.: (?) mid-C. 19–20.

frog it (p. 303). The military usage was adopted from the language of showmen, who used it before —and after—P. H. Emerson, *Signor Lippo*, 1893. The origin is prob. frog and toad (p. 303).

frog-skin. See frog, 7.—2. A condom: Australian: since ca. 1925. (B., 1943.)

frog-spawn. Tapioca pudding: Public Schoolboys': since ca. 1890. (F. Spencer Chapman, *The Jungle Is Neutral*, 1949.)

Froggie (or -gy).—3. A 'French letter': Naval: since ca. 1910. Also Naval: *free issue* and *froth bugle*: since ca. 1920.

frog's eyes. Boiled sago: Australian: since ca. 1910. (B., 1953.)

from clew to ear-ring. See clew to . . .

from here to breakfast-time. A polite variant, since ca. 1920, of *from arse-holes to breakfast-time*, q.v. at arse-holes to . . . above.

from over yonder. From Ireland: tailors' coll.: mid-C. 19–20. B. & L.

from there on in. From this, or that, point forward: coll., perhaps mostly Canadian, but not unknown elsewhere: since ca. 1925. 'I'll get the thing set up for you, and you can play it from there on in.' (Leechman.)

fromage! Hard cheese!: ca. 1890–1905 at the Royal Military Academy. B. & L. The pun being on Fr. *fromage*, cheese.

front, n., 1: since ca. 1930, also Australian. B., 1942.—2. The scene of a thief's operations: c.: anglicised ca. 1929 from U.S. Julian Franklyn, *This Gutter Life*, 1934. Ex shop-*fronts*.—3. As *the front*, it = the main road or street of a Teddy-boy gang's district: Teddy boys': since ca. 1947. (*The Observer*, March 1, 1959.)—4. A large diamond tie-pin or ring (usually genuine) worn by vaude-villians to indicate prosperity: Canadian: since ca. 1930.

front, v., 1, is not ob. in Australia. Sidney J. Baker, letter, 1946.—3. To go in front of (someone), to be reprimanded (by him): Australian coll.: since ca. 1930. Kylie Tennant, *The Joyful Condemned*, 1953.—4. (V.i.) To appear in public, esp. if conspicuously; to turn up: Australian teenagers': since late 1940's. (*Pix*, Sept. 28, 1963.)—5. To *front* a band, esp. in the big-band era of the 1930's, is—'often with little skill, but with a winning personality'—to be, or to be made, leader of a band: Canadian jazz-men's: since the late 1920's. (Priestley.)

front, adj. Angry; vexed: Winchester (the school): from ca, 1860. B. & L. Ex *affronted*.

front, show a. To turn out in haste, and as best one can, for a short-notice parade: military: from ca. 1870; ob. Ibid.

Front, the. Piccadilly: male prostitutes' & homosexuals': since ca. 1945. (See, e.g., Anne Sharpley's 'London's Hidden Problem' series in the *Evening Standard*, July 20–24, 1964. Cf. (the) Dilly above.

*front man or psyche man. He who lures the victim into a crooked game of cards: Australian c.: since ca. 1935. (B., 1953.) Also, by ca. 1940, English c. and, by 1950, police s. (John Gosling, *The Ghost Squad*, 1959.)

front stuff. A smart appearance designed esp. to impress either prospective dupes or one's companions: low: since ca. 1930. See 'front' in *Underworld*.

front suspension. A brassière: Australian, esp. mechanics': since ca. 1930.

front the bull. To face a charge: Australian soldiers': 1939–45. (B., 1943.) Cf. *front*, v., 3.

front up. 'Mr Rudling said part of his duty'— at a mock-auction—'was to front up at the "hinting gear" table for the purpose of getting people into the shop'; *hinting gear* occurs thus, 'The selling was done by gathering an audience. There was a table put inside the shop on which was what was called "hinting gear". To passers-by it was said that alarm clocks were going at a shilling each or even sixpence. Among the "hinting gear" were such things as electric shavers and musical boxes'; 'articles sold for sixpence or a shilling were called "nailers" and were such things as after-shave lotions and ornamental poodle dogs' (the Bournemouth *Evening Echo*, Feb. 18, 1960): mock-auctioneers': since the late 1940's.

front-wheel skid. A Jew: rhyming s. (not very general): since ca. 1920. Franklyn, *Rhyming*.

frontsman. See 'Mock-Auction Slang'.

froom or **frume**, adv. In an orthodox (religious) manner: Jewish coll., almost sol.: late C. 19–20. Ex the adj., q.v. in *Dict*.

frosty face.—2. 'Harsh, white hairs covering the face' of a sheep: Aus. rural: C. 20. B., 1959.

frosty Friday. 'A most unusual day. "What? Go out with him? That'll be a frosty Friday!"' (Leechman): Canadian: since ca. 1940.

froth bugle. See **Froggie**, 3.

frothblower. A certain type (Fowler Class 5 M.T.) of tender-engine: railwaymen's: since ca. 1925 (?). *Railway*.

froust, n.—4. An armchair: Universities' and Public Schools': C. 20. (John Galsworthy, *Caravan*, 1927, and *On Forsyte 'Change*, 1930.)

frouster or **frowster.** A wearer of warm clothes in the summer: Naval cadets': since ca. 1880. 'Taffrail', *The Sub*, 1917. See **frousty**, n. and v., in *Dict*.

frozen on the stick. Stricken with fear: R.A.F.: since ca. 1925. Jackson. See **stick**, n. 13.

*fruit. A 'pouf': c.: anglicised, ex U.S., in 1937. (See esp. *Underworld*.)—2—2. A term of address among Teddy boys: since ca. 1954. Gilderdale, 2: 'Anyone may be a fruit, though it often denotes class. One Ted told me: "To a City chap—all stuck with his umbrella—we call out 'ello, me ol' lemon."'

fruit machine. An anti-aircraft predictor: A.A. crews': since ca. 1939. H. & P. Ex its appearance.—2. See **gooseberries**, 3.—3. An electrical calculator used in radar: mostly R.A.F.: ca. 1942–6.—4. In the Royal Navy, esp. among submariners, it designated, in World War II, any prediction device, esp. (Geoffrey Jenkins, *A Twist of Sand*, 1959.)

fruit salad. 'A large collection of medal ribbons which runs to three or more rows,' H. & P.: Services, esp. the R.A.F.: since ca. 1919. As worn on the left breast, where they made a colourful display.

fry, v.—2. 'If the "mike" should begin "frying" or picking up camera noises, "Sound" in his "ice box" (so called because it is usually very hot inside the glass-fronted booth) would soon protest to the "slinger" (or microphone operator)': *The Evening News*, Nov. 7, 1939: cinema: since ca. 1930.

fuck (p. 305). Certainly not ex the Gr. or L. word mentioned in the *Dict*.; almost certainly cognate with the Latin v. *pungere* and n. *pugil*, both ex a radical meaning 'to strike'; semantically, therefore, *fuck* links with **prick**, 3 (p. 659).

fuck, create. In protesting, to display annoyance or anger: low: since ca. 1920. Cf. **create** (*Dict*.).

fuck!, like. Expressive of extreme scepticism or aversion; 'certainly not!': low: late C. 19–20. Synonyms: *like buggery!* and *like hell!* Also in form *did* (or *will*) I (etc.) *buggery* or *fuck* or *hell!*, I certainly didn't or won't.

fuck, to. A low intensive, as in 'Get to fuck out of it!': late C. 19–20. Here, *fuck* is apparently n.

fuck a day, a. See **shit a day . . .** below.

fuck about. To play the fool: low: mid-C. 19–20. Brendan Behan, *Borstal Boy*, 1958.

fuck all. A low variant of *damn all*: nothing: late C. 19–20.

fuck anything with a hole in it, he'd, I'd, etc.; **fuck anything on two legs, he'd, I'd,** etc. A low c.p. of satyriasis or of extreme randiness: C. 20.

fuck arse. A low term of contempt: C. 20.

fuck 'em all! A c.p. expressive of (usually cheerful) defiance: since ca. 1920. In the song *Bless 'Em All* the orig. words were *fuck 'em all*.

fuck like a rattlesnake. (Of the male) to coït vigorously: low Australian: from ca. 1895. As there are no rattlesnakes in Australia, the phrase would seem to be of North American origin, as Robert Clairborne has rightly mentioned. Cf. **mad as a cut snake**, q.v.

fuck me gently or **pink!** Exclamations of surprise or wonderment: since ca. 1920, 1910, resp.

fuck me! said the Duchess more in hope than in anger. A c.p., current since ca. 1910. Cf. **'hell!' said the Duchess.**

fuck my or **your luck!** Oh, what a pity: Forces': since ca. 1940.

fuck my old boots! A c.p. connoting astonishment: Londoners' (C. 20), hence R.A.F. (1918 onwards). A humorously euphemistic variant is *seduce my ancient footwear!*

fuck-pig. A thoroughly unpleasant man: low Cockney: from ca. 1870.

fuck-up of, make a. To fail miserably at; to spoil utterly: low coll.: C. 20.

fuck you, Jack, I'm fire-proof! See **fire-proof**.

fucked, adj. Extremely weary; (utterly) exhausted: late C. 19–20. Ex **fuck**, v. (p. 305). Here, the German origin—*ficken*, 'to strike'—is clear. Compare the low-American-slang terms recorded by Henry Leverage in *Flynn's*, Jan. 24, 1925:—'fick, v. To fight; to beat. ficked, adj. Beaten; exhausted. ficker, n. A fighter; a rough.'

fucked!, go and get; go and fuck yourself. Run away and stop bothering me!: low: mid-C. 19–20. Cf. **get joined!** and **get stuffed!**

fucked by the fickle finger of fate. Down on one's luck; done for: Canadian Army officers': 1939–45.

fucked more times than she's had hot dinners, she's been. A low c.p. of late C. 19–20.

fucked-up and far from home is a variant, prob. the orig. (for it dates from 1899), of **fucked and far from home**, q.v. in *Dict*.

fucker soldiers. 'From Pukka Soldiers, who were the men of the Regular Army and who had a poor opinion of Kitchener's Army. From what we saw of them, they seemed to be more interested in women and wine than in anything else' (A. B. Petch, March 1966): 1915–18.

fucking the dog; occ. elaborated to *fornicating the poodle*. Irritating and senseless occupation: Canadian soldiers': C. 20. Cf. *picking gooseberries* (p. 625).—2. Hence, the avoidance of work by appearing to be busy at a useless task: Canadian: since ca. 1920.

fucks like a mink, she. She is amorous and promiscuous: Canadian c.p.: since ca. 1920.

fuddle, on the. Engaged in drinking; on a drinking bout: coll.: C. 19. *Sessions*, May 1845 (Surrey cases).

fuddle, out on the. Out on a day's drinking: (low), coll.: mid-C. 19–20. B. & L. See **fuddle, n.,** 3 (*Dict.*).

fuddy-duddy, esp. 'an old . . .'; **fuddy-dud.** A fussy, old-fashioned, narrow-minded person; an 'old woman': coll.: adopted, ca. 1944, ex U.S.— The latter term, mostly Australian, arose derivatively ca. 1955. *Fuddy-duddy* may blend *fussy* + *fogey*, influenced by s. *dud*, an insufficient person; or it may be an altered reduplication of that *dud*.

fudge, n.—4. 'Late News' column: journalists': since ca. 1920. David Hume, *Requiem for Rogues,* 1942. Often the type is blurred, the ink not having had time to dry.

fug, n.—3. (Prob. ex sense 1; cf. sense 2.) A prefect: Marlborough College: mid-C. 19–20. (Communication, Feb. 13, 1939, from Mr Peter Bomford, to whom I owe all Addenda terms from the College.)

fug-footer. An informal game played with a small ball: Harrovians': from ca. 1880. Lunn.

fug out. To clean or tidy (a room): Rugby School: since ca. 1880. To take the *fug out* of it: see **fug, n.,** 1 (p. 305).

fug pants. Thick winter underwear: Naval: since ca. 1925. Granville.

fug trap. A ventilator above a study door: Marlborough College: since ca. 1870. See **fug, n.,** 1 (p. 305).

fugger. A waste-paper basket: Tonbridge: late C. 19–20. Marples. Smell, musty.

*fugleman. The strong-arm man of a gang or of a racket; a petty gangster: Australian c.: since ca. 1945. (B., 1953.) Ex S.E. *fugleman,* that soldier from whom the others take their time in drill movements. (Ramsey Spencer.)

Fuhrer's boys, the. The German armed forces: Naval officers': 1939–45.

full as a boot. Dead-drunk: Australian: since ca. 1925. (D'Arcy Niland, *The Shiralee,* 1955.)

full as a bull (, as). Very drunk: New Zealand: C. 20. (Slatter.)

full as an egg.—2. In Britain it also applies to food: C. 20: coll. rather than s.

full as a goog. Completely drunk: Australian: since ca. 1925. Baker.

full as a tick, 2 (p. 306): also British and, as in James Joyce's *Ulysses,* 1922, Anglo-Irish.

full bore. At full speed: R.A.F. coll.: since ca. 1925. Jackson, 'Thus, "I went after him full bore"'; Brickhill & Norton, *Escape to Danger,* 1946 (*passim*). Ex motoring coll. (dating from ca. 1918).

full dig. 'Full allowance of pay' (B. & L.): low classes': from ca. 1870; very ob.

full distance. See **go the full distance.**

full frame, have a. To have obtained regular employment after being a temporary hand: printers': from ca. 1860. B. & L.

full hand, a. Syphilis and gonorrhœa simultaneously: Australian: C. 20. B., 1942.—2. A life sentence: low Australian: since ca. 1920. (Kylie Tennant, *The Joyful Condemned,* 1953.)

full house.—2. A mixed grill: Naval: since ca. 1930. Granville.

full jerry. To understand completely—in every detail and implication: Australian low: C. 20. B., 1942. See **jerry, v.,** 1, in *Dict.*

full(-)mouth. An eight-teeth sheep: Aus. rural coll.: C. 20. (B., 1959.)

full of piss and vinegar. Robust in health, and full of energy: low Canadian: C. 20. In Canada, as in U.S., *vinegar* has a sexual connotation.

full on.—3. A bookmaker that is 'full on' a horse is one who has so many bets placed on that horse that he risks losing much money to the betters: 1868, *All the Year Round,* June 13.

full private. An ordinary Tommy: Army: since ca. 1910.

full quid. Having all one's faculties: Aus.: since ca. 1920. B., 1959, adds: 'A person . . . *ten bob in the quid* or any smaller sum down to *tuppence in the quid,* is held to be stupid.' Also, since ca. 1925, N.Z., esp. in 'He's *not the full quid*', mentally defective. (Harold Griffiths.)

full to the guards. Dead drunk: nautical: C. 20. (W. McFee, *North of Suez,* 1930.) Ex nautical j.: lit., full to the top of a vessel. Cf. **full to the bung** in the *Dict.*

full togs. Full dress, esp. of uniform: Naval: C. 19. In, e.g., W. N. Glascock's *Naval Sketch Book,* 2nd Series, 1834, at I, 229. '*Sam.* Our captains also appeared in full uniform. . . . *Ned.* The skippers seldom wear full togs for nothing.' (Moe.)

fuller's earth (p. 307).—3. Hence, a *Fuller's* = a vaudeville show: New Zealand coll.: ca. 1910–30. (Ruth Park, *Pink Flannel,* 1955.)

[***fumbles.** Gloves: c.: mid-C. 19–20. B. & L. A suspect term. Almost certainly an error for **famblers,** q.v. in *Dict.*]

Fuming Freddie. Fiumefreddo, a Sicilian township, a Calabrian village: Army in Sicily and Italy: 1943–5.

fumtu. Frigged *up* (= messed about) *more than usual:* Army: 1940–5. (P-G-R.)

fun, have; mostly as vbl n., *having fun,* (a being engaged in) a raid, an attack: Army officers': 1941 +. Suggested by **party,** 2.

fun and frolics. See **flowers and frolics.**

fun and games. A (very) agreeable time: middle-class coll.: since ca. 1921.—2. Hence, 'any sort of brush with the enemy at sea' (P-G-R): Naval officers': 1939–45. Cf. preceding entry.—3. Love-making, esp. intercourse: since ca. 1925. A special application of sense 1.

fun of Cork, the. A very 'good time': Australian: C. 20. B., 1942. Adopted from Irish immigrants.

funnel fever is the demobitis (1945 +)—or restlessness—of soldiers overseas: Army: perhaps not before 1946. The funnels of the homebound troopship.

funnies, the. The comic strips in a newspaper: since ca. 1946.—2. But, in the Army of ca. 1942–5, *funnies* were 'armoured vehicles used for purposes which had hitherto been unorthodox' (P-G-R).

funniment. A tasty dish made up from bits and pieces: Cockneys': C. 20.

funny, n. (p. 308). 'The origin is probably Japanese *fune,* a boat. Purchas, 1625, "The funnies or toe-boats came out to meet us,"' E. V. Gatenby, letter of Oct. 16, 1938.—2. In filmland, the comic man is called *the funny:* since ca. 1910. Cameron McCabe, *The Face on the Cutting Room Floor,* 1937.—3. A comic (magazine or newspaper): Canadian: since ca. 1920. *The Evening News,* Jan. 9, 1940. Usually as the *funnies.* Cf. sense 1 above.—4. A joke; a funny story: mostly Aus.: since ca. 1950. Ian Hamilton, *The Man with the*

Brown Paper Face, 1967, '"What makes you say that?" "Nothing. Just trying to make a funny."'

funny, get or **turn.** To feel—esp. to show that one feels—offended: coll.: C. 20. See **funny,** 1 (*Dict.*).

funny-face. A jocular term of address: coll.: late C. 19–20. Cf. **face-ache** (*Dict.*).

funny fellows (or **-ers**). Policemen, esp. the College-trained ones: London, esp. children's: since ca. 1935. (Mrs C. H. Langford, letter of July 29, 1941.)

funny-looking article, a. A c.p. applied to an odd-looking person: C. 20. Originally, shop-keepers'.

funny peculiar or **funny ha-ha?** A c.p. comment upon, e.g., 'Something funny happened to-day': since ca. 1924. Aspic-in-amber'd by Ian Hay Beith in *Housemaster* (Act III), 1938.

funny thing happened on the, my, way to the . . ., a, as in John D. Macdonald, *One Fearful Yellow Eye,* 1966, 'A funny thing happened to me on my way to the hotel room.' Since ca. 1960 and ex the film, *A Funny Thing Happened on the Way to the Forum,* 1966, itself an elaboration of the very much older 'A funny thing happened (when or while) . . .'; and '*Funny,* odd'—not '*Funny,* ha ha!'

funt. A pound sterling (£1): a Yiddish word incorporated into parlary: mid-C. 19–20. (Sydney Lester, *Vardi the Palarey,* ? 1937.) Ex German *Pfund.*

Furibox. The aircraft carrier *Furious*: Naval: 1939–45. Granville.

furph. A shortened from of **furphy**: since ca. 1925. (B., 1943.)

furphy (p. 308). Perhaps rather ex the tall stories told by Joseph Furphy (1843–1913), the 'Tom Collins' who wrote *Such Is Life,* 1903.

fusilier. Dating from ca. 1860, it is, in the main, an Army term and is now ob.; *Crimea,* by the way, had > † before the end of the G.W. Thus in Richards, writing of the beginning of C. 20: 'A good deal of rhyming-slang was used in those days . . . Beer was "pig's ear" or "Crimea" or "Fusilier", but if a Welshman went into a pub where a Highland soldier was, of the regiment whose square was once broken by the Mahdi's dervishes in the Sudan, he would sometimes ask for a "pint of 'broken-square'". Then he would have his bellyfull of scrapping.'

Fusilier, you're a. A contemptuous c.p. from one Rifleman to another: Regular Army: ca. 1890–1920.

fuss-arse. A fussy person: rural coll.: from ca. 1880. Cf. **fuss-pot** (*Dict.*).

fuss-up. A fuss: Australian coll.: since ca. 1920. (H. Drake-Brockman, 1938.)

fussy, not. Not particularly keen: Canadian coll.: since ca. 1920. 'Wear your evening things to-night, Harry.'—'All right. But I'm not fussy about it.' (Leechman.)

fusters! A claim to 'have *first* go' in a game: Cockney school-children's: from ca. 1870.

future at all, no; no future in it or **in that.** Of these catch-phrases (Services', esp. R.A.F.), the former implies danger in the sortie concerned, whereas the latter either does the same or merely hints that the job concerned is a thankless one: since 1939. *The Observer,* Oct. 4, 1942 (both phrases); H. & P., *no future in it* ('particularly hazardous'); Jackson, *no future in that* ('Implies a thankless job') and *no future at all* ('Implies a dangerous job'). Ex civilian pre-September-1939 familiar English *There's no future in it*—or *in it at all*—as applied to love affairs.

fuzz, n.—2. Collective for 'policemen': Canadian jazz-lovers': since ca. 1956. (*The Victoria Daily Colonist,* April 16, 1959, 'Basic Beatnik'.) By 1966, common among British hippies and, by early 1967, among the Flower People. Peter Fryer in *The Observer* colour supplement, Dec. 3, 1967.

Fuzzgug, Mr or **Mrs.** John or Jane Doe: Australian: since ca. 1930. (B.P.) Arbitrary.

Fuzzy-Wuzzy.—2. A Papuan: Australian: since ca. 1918. Ex sense 1 on p. 309; cf. the next.

Fuzzy-Wuzzy Angels. New Guinea natives carrying Allied wounded to safety over the Owen Stanley Mountains: mostly Australian: 1942–5.

fyfas, often written **fifas**; or with capital letters. *Fuck yourself for a start* (or *starter*): a certain British unit, during the latter half of W.W. II. (Communicated to me, on Dec. 26, 1967, by Edmund Wilson, who got it from Philip Merivale, the actor.) Mostly, of course, in conversation—esp., to open one.

G

g for *x* is a mark of illiteracy, esp. among Cockneys: C. 19–20 and prob. from much earlier. Seen best in *eg(g)spec(t)*, expect. This is merely one aspect of that dulling of sharp consonants which characterises illiterate speech.

g'. Good; esp. in *g'day, g'morning, g'night* as greetings: coll., mostly proletarian: C. 19–20, and prob. longer.

G five. 'A beard cut to resemble that of King George V' (Granville): Naval: since very soon after date (1910) of his accession to the throne; by 1960, slightly ob.

G.G., the. The Governor-General: New Zealand and Australian coll.: late C. 19–20. B., 1941.

g.i. or **G.I.** A birthday, a 'beano', apprentice's attaining journeymanship: tailors': mid-C. 19–20. B. & L. Not, as is sometimes stated, 'great independence' but 'general indulgence'.—2. An American soldier (not an officer): adopted in 1943 from U.S. Ex 'general issue' as applied to clothes and equipment.—3. A variant of **geographically impossible** below.

G.I.B. See **good-oh** (adj.) below.

G.O.F. Good Old Friday: schoolteachers' c.p.: C. 20.

G.O.K. God only knows, for a doubtful diagnosis: Canadian Army doctors': 1914–18. (Leechman.)

G.O.M., the. This is the nicknominal form of **the Grand Old Man**, q.v. (*Dict.*). To his political intimates, Gladstone was known as *Mr G.*; but *Mr G* is ineligible.

G.P.I. Eccentricity; (extreme) folly: medical students': C. 20. Ex its lit. sense, General Paralysis of the Insane.

g.p. on, have a. To be much in love with (someone): ca. 1905–15. I.e. *grande passion*.

G.R. navvy. See **navvy**, 2.

G.S. Keen; esp., excessively keen: Army: 1939 +; by 1960, slightly ob. Lit., *G*eneral *S*ervice.

G-string. See 'Prisoner-of-War Slang', 13.—2. *Frenulum preputii*: low: C. 20.

gab, n.—3. Gaberdine; London clothes-dealers': C. 20. Mark McShane, *The Straight and Crooked*, 1960.

gab, chuck the. To talk fluently or well; to 'tell the tale': low: C. 20. Frank Jennings, *Tramping with Tramps*, 1932. Ex **gab**, n., 2 (*Dict.*).

gabby, n. Water: Australian: mid-C. 19–20. B., 1942. Aboriginal.

gaberdine! Excellent!: Londoners': since ca. 1918. It is prob. a pun on Fr. *très bien!*

gaberdine swine. 'Staff officers in Cairo, so christened by forward troops in the Western Desert' (P-G-R): ca. 1941–3. With a pun on Biblical *Gadarene* swine.

gadabout (p. 310) appears, in American usage, in *The Port Folio*, March 2, 1805 (p. 60, col. 1), thus 'The pert and flippant gad-a-bouts [*sic*], whose chief employment is to parade the streets': females. Moe.

*gadgy. A man: c.: from ca. 1910. Of North Country origin.

gaff, n.—13. Synonymous with **gaffer**, 12. Canadian carnival s.: C. 20.—14. A concert: Regular Army: late C. 19–20; by 1950, slightly ob. (*Chambers's Journal*, July 1949.) Ex senses 5 and 6 (p. 310).—15. A brothel: c. and low s.: since ca. 1920. (*The New Statesman*, May 10, 1947.)—16. Home: c.: since ca. 1920. '"Come to my gaff (home) at three o'clock, pinch him and get him out of the way"' (John Gosling, *The Ghost Squad*, 1959). Cf. sense 10 on p. 310.

*gaff, one's. One's place of abode: c.: C. 20. Cf. **gaff**, n., 10 (*Dict.*).

gaff joint. A game of chance where there is no chance of winning: Canadian carnival: C. 20.

Gaff Street Theatreland; more generally, the West End: London taxi-drivers': since ca. 1920. Herbert Hodge, *It's Draughty in Front*, 1938, where also: 'Before the theatres broke—or, as we say: the "gaffs burst".'

gaffer.—11. The man who runs a gambling game or device: Canadian carnival s.: C. 20.—12. Hence, the brake with which he stops the wheel, etc., at any desired number: id.: id.—13. (As *the gaffer*.) The officer commanding an H.M. ship: since the 1920's. Cf. sense 4 on p. 310.—14. 'A boy, a young chap' (P. W. Joyce, *English . . . in Ireland*, 1910): Anglo-Irish: mid C. 19–20. Ex senses 2 and 3 on p. 310.

gag, n.—8. (Cf. 3.) A handbill: sporting: ca. 1810–60. *Boxiana*, III, 1821.

gag, v., 3 (p. 310). As 'to gird, to nag, (*gag at*) to scold': earlier in *Sessions*, Sept. 1837.

gaga (*Dict.*), according to a French scholar, came into use, ca. 1875, in the theatrical world, and it is derived ex Fr. s. *gâteux*, an old man feebleminded and no longer able to control his body, itself ex Standard Fr. *gâter*, to impair, damage, spoil.

gagarino, n. 'A melodrama performed by professional actors, usually of the lower ranks, in which the general outline of the plot is so familiar that it is not necessary to write a concrete play at all, everything being "gagged" impromptu. Before C. 20.

'I first encountered this in the Yukon in about 1950. A professional old-time one-man-show man told me he had often played in them as a boy in a strolling group of players in the north of England. His name was Crowhurst or something like that, and he had come to the Yukon to see the land of Robert Service.' (Douglas Leechman, note of 1962.) Ex **gag**, n., 4 (p. 311) + comic suffix *-arino*.

gage, 1 (p. 311), is, in C. 20, often 'a drink of

1152

beer'—esp. among tramps and Romanies. (Robert M. Dawson.)—6. A C. 18 variant of **gager** (*Dict.*).

gaggle. A number of aircraft; 'a gaggle of Jerries': Naval: 1939–45. Ex 'a *gaggle* of geese'.

gain. To obtain deviously or questionably: Leeds undergraduates' (— 1940). Cf. *win* (p. 959). Marples, 2.

gajit is a rare (mainly C. 20) spelling of **gadget**.

gal, 1 (p. 312) app. began rather lower in the scale: J. Wight, *Bow Street*, 1824, 'Gal—cockney for girl'.

gal, I'll have your. See **I'll have your gal!**

gal nymph. A housemaid: Winchester College: from ca. 1880; very ob.

galah. A chap, fellow, 'bird': Australian: C. 20. H. Drake-Brockman, *Hot Gold*, 1940. Lawson Glassop, *We Were the Rats*, 1944. An Australian cockatoo.—2. A simpleton, a fool: Australian: since ca. 1930. (B., *Australia Speaks*, 1953.) It prob. derives 'from the old bush saying, "As mad as a treeful of galahs"': Jock Marshall & Russell Drysdale, *Journey among Men*, 1962, fn. on p. 91. A galah is 'a big pink-and-grey coekatoo' (ibid.).

galee. Bad language: Anglo-Indian: from ca. 1860. B. & L. Ex Hindustani *gali*.

galinipper. See **gallinipper** (*Dict.*).

gall (p. 312) occurs, however, in W. N. Glascock, *Sketch-Book* (II, 244), 1826, and should, therefore, be back-dated to ca. 1810 or even earlier. (Moe.)

gallanty show. See **galanty show** (*Dict.*).

galley growler (p. 312) follows naturally ex *galley politician*, as in W. N. Glascock, *Sailors and Saints* (II, 185), 1829: a term app. existing ca. 1790–1850 or so. (Moe.)

galley packet. A Naval rumour: Naval: ca. 1790–1860. W. N. Glascock, *Sailors and Saints* (I, 190), 1829, '. . . Unauthenticated rumour; or, as sailors term it, "*a galley packet*".' Moe. See **galley-yarn** (p. 312), sense 2: 1818, Alfred Burton, *Johnny Newcome*. (Moe.) Also **galley-yarn** below.

galley slang. A landsman's attempts at Naval jargon and slang: Naval: since ca. 1925.

galley-slave.—2. A proof-reader: C. 20. Mostly jocular.

galley slaves. 'Cockroaches in the Sunday plum-duff; they turn white when cooked, and are not unpalatable' (Ramsey Spencer, July 10, 1967): Merchant Navy: C. 20.

galley-yarn, 2 (p. 312). The *galley-packet* variant occurs in W. N. Glascock, *Sketch Book* (I, 22), 1825, and therefore goes back to ca. 1810 or a decade earlier. On I, 19, there is the further variant, *galley-story*, but in sense 1 of *galley-yarn*. Moe.

Gallipoli gallop (other ranks'); **G. riot** (officers'). Dysentery, entailing frequent running to the latrines: military: 1915. John Hargrave, *The Suvla Bay Landing*, 1964.

galoot, 2, on p. 313, occurs slightly earlier in W. N. Glascock's *Naval Sketch Book*, 2nd Series, 1834, at II, 58, where it is footnoted as 'new re-cruit'. (Moe.)

gallop, raise a; esp. *unable to.* To have—esp. to be unable to have—an erection: mostly work-men's: since ca. 1930. Ex horses.

gallop one's antelope or **one's maggot; jerk one's mutton; pull one's pudding.** Synonyms of **pull one's wire** (*Dict.*): low: resp. C. 20 Cockneys',

mid-C. 19–20; gen., from ca. 1870; gen., from ca. 1890. The second seems to have been prompted by **get cockroaches** (*Dict.*); the fourth may have originated **pull one's wire;** the first occurs in J. Curtis, *They Ride by Night*, 1938.

gallopers. A variant of *goon bag*.

galloping horses. See **fighting cats.**

galloping irons. Spurs for riding: Canadian jocular: since ca. 1930.

Galloping Jack. Brigadier-General J. R. Roy-ston: military: late C. 19–20. He served dash-ingly in the South African War; his reminiscences were published, under that title, in 1937.

galloping knob-rot, a touch of the. A phallic itch; a phrase often used 'in palliation of attempted alleviation' (correspondent, 1967): R.A.F., Malta: ca. 1955–67.

gallows, adv. (p. 313), goes back to late C. 18. On Aug. 24, 1805 (p. 261, col. 3), *The Port Folio* quotes an anon. English song, Dust-man Bill:

'Why, jealous girls, 'tis all my eye,
Besides 'tis gallows silly'.   (Moe.)

gallowses. Braces: Sedgley Park School: ca. 1800–60. *The Cottonian*, Autumn, 1938. With a pun on hanging. Cf. the synonymous U.S. *galluses*.

gallumph. See **galumph** (*Dict.*).

galluptious is a variant spelling of **galoptious** (*Dict.*).

galoot (p. 313), an inexperienced seaman, occurs as early as 1818. (Moe.)

gam, n.—5. A sanitary tampon or pad: Aus-tralian girls': since ca. 1950. Because applied between the 'gams' or legs? Cf. **gam,** n., 2, on p. 313.

gam, v. To have a yarn, esp. with one's oppo-site number on another ship: nautical: late C. 19–20; by 1945 slightly ob. Ex *gamenon*, v., 1 (p. 314).

gam on, as in 'He's gammin' on dumb' (he's pretending to be dumb), is a C. 20 corruption of **gammon,** v., 2 (*Dict.*).

gamahoosh. Variant of *gamaroosh* (p. 313).

Gamaliel. There is some confusion here; obviously *Acts* xviii. 12–17, refers to Gallio.

gamble, go the. To make a bet: sporting: from ca. 1880. B. & L.

game, n.—7. *Gameness*; courage: pugilistic: ca. 1810–50. *Boxiana*, I, 1818 (concerning Tom Crib), '. . . is *game* or *gluttony* exhibited in every one of his conquests'.—8. One's work or occupa-tion: mostly Australian: since ca. 1920. (B.P.) Cf. sense 5 on p. 314.

game as Ned Kelly, as. Extremely brave; willing to tackle heavy odds: Australian: late C. 19–20. B., 1942. Ex the famous bushranger (1854–80), who held out against the police for two years. In 1959, B. notes the synonymous *game as a pebble* or *game as a piss ant*.

game ball, adj. (predicatively). In good health or spirits or form: Anglo-Irish: since ca. 1940.

game sewn up, have the. To be in a position where one cannot lose; to have a monopoly; to be on a 'good thing': mostly Australian: since ca. 1925. Ex games in which one side can hardly lose. 'Anyone who does not know this one is not an Australian' (B.P.).

gammon the draper. 'When a man is without a shirt, and is buttoned up close to his neck, to make an appearance of cleanliness, it is termed "gammoning the draper",' Pierce Egan, *Life in London*, 1821: ca. 1810–50.

gammy, adj. lazy; idle; navvies': ca. 1860–1900. (D. W. Barrett, 1880.)

gammy arm; gammy-eyed; gammy leg. See **gammy**, adj., 4 (*Dict.*).—**gammy ville.** See **gammy**, adj., 3 (*Dict.*).

gamo or, phonetically, **gammo.** 'Gamaroosh' (see p. 313): since ca. 1915.

gander, n.—2. (Also v.) A—to—look through the mail or over another's shoulder at a letter or a newspaper: Services, esp. R.A.F.: since 1941. H. & P. Adopted ex U.S. (cf. Am. *rubberneck*); the gander is a long-necked bird.

Gandhi's revenge. Matches that, made in India, would, when struck, either ignite explosively or lose their heads: R.A.F.: ca. 1935–48. The Mahatma Gandhi (1869–1948) preached a passive resistance.

gandy dancer. 'A section hand on the railway; the "gandy dance" is the vigorous exercise indulged in when tamping ties—that is tamping ballast under the sleepers with a spade or shovel. U.S. and Canadian railwaymen's; 1908 +.' (Leechman.) Ex U.S. c., of unknown origin.

gandy month. A proletarian form of **gander-month** (*Dict.*).

gang-bang or **-shag; pig-party.** One girl serving many males in succession: British (1st and 3rd) and Australian (all three): mostly teenage gangsters' and mentally retardeds': since ca. 1950. The 1st and 3rd occur in an article published by *New Society*, July 2, 1963; the 2nd was adopted ex U.S.

Also *gang-fuck*: ?mostly Canadian: since ca. 1920. Cf. **back-up**, 1, above.

gaol, there are worse in. See **worse in gaol** (*Dict.*).

gaol-bait; usually *jail.* A girl under 16 (the age of consent): Canadian: adopted, ca. 1940, ex U.S.

gap, n.—3. The gap between the female breasts: Australian motor mechanics' and car fanatics': since ca. 1945. Ex the gap of a spark plug.

gap. To make gaps in (wire obstacles): Army coll. (since ca. 1939) >, by 1945, j. (P-G.R.)

gapeseed. See **gape-seed** (*Dict.*).

garbage cans. Metal containers for the keeping or despatch of spools or reels of motion pictures: cinematic: since ca. 1955. A scathing reference to 'rubbish'.

garbo. A garbage man: Australian: since ca. 1930. (B., 1953.)

Garbo, do a. To avoid Press reporters and photographers and other publicity: journalists' and publicity men's, also film-world's: since ca. 1925. Ex Greta Garbo's often-expressed wish 'to be alone'.

garden, n.—2. A freight yard: Canadian railroadmen's (— 1931). Ironic.

garden!, I beg your. I beg your pardon: modified rhyming s., not at all general: since ca. 1920. Michael Harrison, *Reported Safe Arrival*, 1943.

garden gate.—3. A First Officer: Merchant Navy occasional rhyming s. (on *mate*): C. 20. Franklyn 2nd.—4. Eight: (mostly underworld) rhyming s.: C. 20. (Ibid.)

garden gates. Rates (and taxes): rhyming s.: C. 20. Franklyn, *Rhyming*.

gardening.—2. Mine-dropping from aircraft: Bomber Command: 1940–5.

gardie (or **-y**) is a phonetic variant of **guardy** (p. 359).

gargle, n.—2. Strong drink: 1872, Edward Lear, *More Nonsense*,

'There was an old man of the Dargle
 Who purchased six barrels of Gargle';

extant. Ex sense 1.—3. Hence, beer: Australian: C. 20. (B.P.)

gargler. Throat: Cockneys': from ca. 1890. Clarence Rook, *The Hooligan Nights*, 1899, 'There was the little bleeder gettin' black in the face froo its night-dress bein' tied too tight round its gargler.' Cf. *gargle*, liquor.

garotte; garotting. See **garrotte, garrotting** in the *Dict.*

garters.—2. 'The streamers jumped by the lady rider,' Edward Seago, *Sons of Sawdust*, 1934: circus: late C. 19–20.

gas, n.—4. Fun, amusement, a good time: Anglo-Irish: since ca. 1935. Ex '*laughing* gas'?—5. Hence, a joke, a jest; a very amusing situation: since ca. 1945. Nicholas Blake, *The Sad Variety*, 1964, 'That's spy stuff, isn't it? What a gas!'

gas, adj. Wonderful: Australian: since ca. 1955. (B.P.) Ex **gas**, n., 4.

gas!, or out goes the. See **or out . . .**

gas, taking the. (Of a patient) having a pneumothorax treatment: hospital nurses': since ca. 1935. *Nursing Mirror*, May 7, 1949.

gas (or **G.**), **the.** A person representing the Gas Company: coll.: C. 20. E.g. in David Frome, *Mr Simpson Finds a Body*, 1933.

Gas and Water Socialists, the. The Fabian Society: political: since ca. 1910. Ex their obsession with the social services.

gas boat.—2. Any small craft driven by gasoline: Canadian coll.: since ca. 1920. (Leechman.)

gas-cape stew. See 'Prisoner-of-War Slang', 10.

gas(-)face. A synonym of **gas-bag**, 3 (p. 317); but not before 1939: Services. H. & P.

gas man, the. 'Used jocularly in reference to insurance men and canvassers who waste the time of housewives. From the gas-meter reader or collector' (A. B. Petch, May 1966): c.p.: since 1940's.

gas-pipe. See **gaspipe** (*Dict.*).

gas-pipe cavalry (p. 317). Current in 1914–18, esp. among the Regulars.

gas round.—2. To chat idly with anyone available: Canadian: C. 20. (Leechman.)

gash, n.—3. '"Is there any gash around?" Are there any willing girls in the vicinity? Early C. 20 and current' (Leechman, April 1967). Ex sense 2 on p. 317.

gash, adj. A shortening of **gashion** (p. 317); often—'spare' or 'available': Naval: since ca. 1915. Robert Harling, *The Steep Atlantick Stream*, 1946. Cf.:

gash, the. Waste food; an over-issue; anything surplus: Services (mostly Naval): since ca. 1910. H. & P. Cf. **gash**, 1 (*Dict.*), but imm. ex **gashion** (ibid). Hence also, since ca. 1939, Australian: B., 1953.

gash-boat; -hand; -shoot. A stand-by duty boat; a rating temporarily idle; refuse chute: Naval: since ca. 1920. Granville. All three, so

named because 'over' or 'spare': See prec. pair of
entries.

As 'waste', *gash* occurs in such other combinations as *gash-barge, -bin, -bucket*, the 1st of which is
recorded by John Winton in *We Joined the Navy*,
1959.

gashions. Extra rations: Naval: since ca.
1920. Granville. See **gash** and, in *Dict.*, **gashion.**

gasp and grunt. A variant of **grumble and
grunt** below. (Franklyn 2nd.)

gasser. A cigarette: Australian, esp. Sydney:
since ca. 1945. Perhaps a slovening of the
synonymous *gasper*.—2. Something wonderful,
very exceptional, extraordinarily successful:
Australian: adopted, ca. 1955, ex U.S.; adopted,
slightly earlier, in Canada. Perhaps ex American
gasser, a gas-propelled oil-well that needs no
pumping. (B.P.)—3. See 'Jazz Slang'.

gassy, n. A gas-meter: Midlands and Northern:
since ca. 1950.

gastro. Gastro-enteritis: medical coll. (C. 20)
> gen. ca. 1940. Throughout the British
Commonwealth; it is recorded by, e.g., B.,
Australia Speaks, 1953.

gat.—3. (Ex 2.) Hence, a machine-gun:
R.A.F.: since ca. 1936. Jackson.

gate, n.—5. A switch: Canadian railroadmen's
(— 1931). Jocular.—6. See 'Jazz Slang'.

gate, go through the. To open the throttle—
hence, fly at full speed: R.A.F.: since ca. 1925.
H. & P. Not quite synonymous with *turn up the
wick*, for *go through the gate* is to open the throttle
in an emergency, whereas in the other there is no
implication of urgency. See also **go through the
gate.**

gate, on the. (See the *Dict.*) Perhaps the explanation of the last sense is that the names of
persons on the danger-list are left with the porter
at the gate.

gate and gaiters. Naval allusion to 'severe
discipline': C. 20. Granville, 'Originated at
Whale Island, the Naval Gunnery School and
hot-bed of discipline. Gunnery instructors are
noted for the resonance of their voices, and the
gaiters they wear are symbolic of much squad-
drill.'

gate(-)fever. That restlessness which affects
long-term prisoners due to be released fairly soon:
prisons': since ca. 1920. (Norman.)

gates of Rome. Home: rhyming: C. 20. An
off-shoot from the obsolescent **Pope of Rome** (p.
649). Franklyn, *Rhyming*.

gate's shut, e.g. *my* or *his*. I'll say no more:
Australian coll., verging on c.p.: since ca. 1920.
D'Arcy Niland, *Call Me . . .*, 1958, '"No," she
insisted. "I want to know."—"No good prodding me. My gate's shut."'

gathering the mush, n. Potato-picking: tramps'
and Romanies': C. 20. (Robert M. Dawson.)

'gator (usually without the apostrophe). A
crocodile: Australian coll.: late C. 19–20. Cf.
sense 1 on p. 318. 'Ex the belief, now fading,
that our crocodiles are alligators' (B.P., mid-
1963).

gats. See **gat** (*Dict.*).

gaucho; usually in pl. 'When the Ashkenazim
(Jews from North and Central Europe) are dis-
cussing the Sephardim (Jews from Spain and
Portugal) they sometimes refer to them as the
Gauchos,' Julian Franklyn, letter of Sept. 13, 1946:
since ca. 1936. *Gaucho*, a cowboy of the pampas

and a notable horseman, is of mixed Spanish and
Indian descent; the Spaniards used to be notable
horsemen (caballeros); *gaucho* prob. derives ex
Araucan *cauchu*, 'wanderer' (Webster's); the
Sephardim came from *Sepharad*, credibly identified
with Spain (O.E.D.).

Gaw (or **Gawd**) **cast me, don't ask me!** 'An
expression by a racing chap, such as "Gaw-cast-
me-don't-ask-me" means blood pressure soaring.
It usually denotes a fancied horse has fell over or
something—says Danny' (Anon. article in *The
Sunday Telegraph*, May 7, 1967): a racing c.p.:
since the late 1940's.

Gawd Aggie! and **Gawd love-a-duck!** Australian
elaborations of exclamatory use of *Gawd* (cf.
Gawd on p. 319): C. 20. (B.P.)

gawdelpus. A helpless person: Cockney: late
C. 19–20. A. Niel Lyons, *Clara*, 1912. I.e. a
God-help-us.—2. 'I have also heard it with the
meaning of sad, or woebegone, distressed, "What's
the matter with you? You look like twopenn'orth of gawdelpus!" Before 1908.' Leechman.

gawdfer. A corrupted shortening of **God forbid**
(*Dict.*): C. 20.

Gawdsaker. 'Marjorie cried: "What is a
Gawdsaker?" "Oh," said Trafford, "haven't you
heard that before? He's the person who gets
excited by an deliberate discussion and gets
up . . . screaming, 'For Gawd's sake, let's do
something now!' I think they used it first for
Pethick Lawrence."' Thus H. G. Wells, in
Marriage, 1912. Arising ca. 1905, it was, by 1945,
ob.; by 1960, virtually †.

***gay,** n. A dupe: Australian c. (esp. prosti-
tutes' and confidence-tricksters'): C. 20. Kylie
Tennant, *Foveaux*, 1939. Cf. **gay**, adj., 1 (p.
319).

gay, adj., 1 (p. 319) occurs in John Davis, *The
Post-Captain*, 1806. (Moe.)—4. Homosexual: C.
20. Homosexuals 'use an argot and a phraseology
meaningless to the heterosexual but fraught
with significance for the fellow homosexual.
For instance . . . "Are you married?" Other
words in the language are "camp" and "gay"
(both synonyms for "homosexual"), and "rent",
the slang for a male prostitute [for men]': homosexuals': since ca. 1930—if not much earlier.
John Gosling & Douglas Warner, *The Shame of a
City*, 1960. The anon. *Lavender Lexicon*, 1965,
says that the word 'must be defined as belonging
to or characteristic of that element of society, pre-
dominately homosexually oriented, who make up a
"night life" or a society of some continuity based
on common acceptance of each other's sexual expressions'.

gay!, that's all. A Cockney c.p. of agreement:
ca. 1900–15. Pugh, '"There, that's all gay," he
broke off, pacifically.' Ex **all gay** (*Dict.*).

gay, turn. To become a prostitute: since ca.
1870. (A. Neil Lyons, *Clara*, 1912.)

gay and hearty. A party: rhyming s.: since ca.
1920.

gay as a goose in a gutter (, **as**). Very gay indeed: coll.: late C. 18–mid-19. (W. N. Glascock,
Sketch-Book, 1826, at II, 30.) Moe.

gay boy. A homosexual: Australian: since ca.
1925. (Elisabeth Lambert, *The Sleeping House
Party*, 1951.) Cf. *gay*, 1 (p. 316).

gay-cat (p. 319). Also Canadian: C. 20.
(Niven.)

gay deceivers. 'Falsies' or foam-plastic bust-forms: Australian raffish: since ca. 1950.

gay girl; gay woman. A prostitute: non-aristocratic: mid-C. 19–20; ob. B. & L. See gay, 1 (*Dict.*).

gazebo; gazook. A foolish fellow: Australian: mid-C. 19–20. Brian Penton, *Landtakers*, 1934 (the former); Brian Penton, *Inheritors*, 1936 (the latter). Cf. **gazob** (*Dict.*). Also cf. the American s. *gazebo*, a gawky or awkward fellow—the prob. origin of the Australian, sense. Mitford M. Mathews derives it ex Spanish *gazapo*, a shrewd fellow; I'd derive it ex 'to *gaze*' or 'gazer' (gawper) + the comic suffix *-ebo*.

gazelle, in a. See 'Canadian'.

gazinta. A division sum in arithmetic: Elementary schoolchildren's: C. 20. Ex a slovenly pronunciation of *goes into*. Cf. **guzunder** below.

gazoomphing. Swindling: mock-auctions': C. 20. A variant of:—

gazumph (and derivatives). Variant of **ge-zumph** (p. 326). *News of the World*, Aug. 28, 1938.

gear, n.—3. Any narcotic, but esp. marijuana: (mostly teenage) drug addicts': since the late 1940's. Euphemistic?—4. '"Got a load of gear (stolen property) for you, John," he'd say' (John Gosling, *The Ghost Squad*, 1959): c.: since ca. 1930.

gear, adj. Homosexual: rhyming s. (on *queer*): only since ca. 1930. Franklyn, *Rhyming.*—2. Excellent: teenagers': 1961–64, then ob. (D. F. Wharton, Oct. 24, 1965.) Ex:—

gear, the. (Always predicatively; e.g. 'That's the gear', q.v. in Dict.) Very good: low, but also Liverpool ordinary: late C. 19–20. Popularized by the Beatles, to mean 'something that is unique and extra good' (*News of the World*, Nov. 19, 1963).

gee, n., 1, a horse (p. 319), occurs earlier in the Major-General's song in Gilbert & Sullivan's *The Pirates of Penzance*, 1879, 'They'll say a finer Major-General has never sat a gee.' With thanks to Mr Leonard Goldstein, letter of March 27, 1967. —2 (p. 319): cf. 'A *gee* is a *rick* (stooge) who stands among the audience (*hedge*) and *slings gees*— praising the goods and saying audibly how satisfied he is' (W. Buchanan-Taylor, *Shake It Again*, 1943). Cf. 'Mock-Auction Slang' below. For **rick**, see p. 696.—4. Derived from and synonymous with *gen box*, a complicated instrument used, operationally, by the R.A.F.: since ca. 1942. W/Cdr R. P. McDouall, letter of March 27, 1945. See **gen, the**.

gee, v. 3 (p. 320): esp. as a grafter's assistant: showmen's: See **gee-men**.

gee, adj.; esp. a *gee fight*, a catchpenny bout that is not a true contest: boxing: since ca. 1930. Cf. **gee, put in the**, on p. 320.

gee-gee dodge, the. Earlier in James Greenwood, *Odd People in Odd Places*, 1883: esp. butchers': app. since ca. 1860.

gee, lookit! A Canadian children's c.p. of astonishment or great interest: adopted, ca. 1950. ex U.S. (Leechman, who, in May 1959, adds, 'I read recently the next step: "Oh, lookit at that!"')

gee-man or **micky finn.** Australian showmen's variant and synonym of gee, n., 2. (*Dict.*): C. 20. Kylie Tennant, *The Battlers*, 1941, 'In the show world a "gee-man" or "micky finn" was socially on the level of a duck's feet.'

gee(-)up. A spree; a jollification: Australian,

esp. Sydney: since ca. 1920. Ruth Park, *The Harp in the South*, 1948.

gee up, v.—3. To pull someone's leg: c.: since ca. 1940. (Norman.) A variant of *gee*, v., 3.

gee whiz!; occ. variant, **gee whillikens!** Juvenile exclamations, orig. euphemistic for *Jesus Christ!*: C. 20.

geebung. An old settler: Australian: since ca. 1870. B., 1942. Aboriginal word.

geek. A (long) look: Australian: since ca. 1920. 'Gis'—give us—'a geek at that book.' Barry Prentice derives it ex German *gucken*, to peep or peek; perhaps influenced by Cornish dial. *geek*, to look intently at.

geezer (p. 320). Note, however, that Wellington's soldiers may, ca. 1811, have picked up Basque *giza*, man, fellow, and changed it to *geezer*. (Hugh Morrison, Perth, W.A.)—3. A fellow prisoner: c.: since ca. 1930. (Norman.)

gefuffle. A to-do, a fuss; a 'flap': R.A.F.: since ca. 1939. (W/Cdr Robin P. McDouall, letter of April 12, 1945.) Partly echoic and prob. reminiscent of such terms as *fluster* and **waffle** (v., 5); the *ge* perhaps implies stammering.

As for *cufuffle* above and *kerfuffle* below, the immediate origin lies in Scots *curfuffle*, n., ex *curfuffle*, v., based on Sc. *fuffle*, to throw into disorder, whence the n. *fuffle*, violent effort, fuss. The *cur-* may, as *The O.E.D.* suggests, be Gaelic *car*, to bend or twist or turn about. (With thanks to Mr R. W. Burchfield.) The modern s. usage arises, naturally enough, in the dialectal, and the *cu(r)-, ge(r)-, ke(r)-* element has been influenced—perhaps even superseded—by the echoic *ge-* or *ke(r)-* indicative of effort or noise (cf. **kerplunk** below).

geggie. A 'penny gaff'; a cheap vaudeville show: Glasgow: C. 20. Ex *gag*? Also spelt *geggy*. Not restricted to Glasgow: fairly common among showmen. Cf. **gagger**, 3, on p. 311.

gelly. An occ. variant of **jelly**, 3, below.

geloptious is an occ. variant of **goloptious** (*Dict.*).

gelt (p. 320). Rather ex Dutch *gelt*, 'money'.

gemman. An early recording: 1828, P. Egan, *Finish to Tom, Jerry and Logic*.

gen, 'genuine': not ex *genuine* but either ex the n. or, more prob., ex the combination *pukka gen*, Not very general: since ca. 1941. Partridge, 1945.

gen, the. Information: whether *pukka gen*, trustworthy, or *duff gen*, incorrect, or *phoney gen*, doubtful or unreliable: R.A.F.: since ca. 1929, but widely used only since 1939. Recorded by, e.g., an R.A.F. Flight Sergeant, article 'I bombed the Ruhr', in Michie & Graebner, *Their Finest Hour*, 1940, 'Operations room where I got my Gen (R.A.F. slang for information, instruction)'; myself in article in *The New Statesman*, Sept. 19, 1942; H. & P., 1943; and esp. Partridge, 1945. Ex the consecrated phrase 'for the *general information* of all ranks' or '. . . of all concerned'. *Pukka* is Hindustani, whereas *duff* and *phoney* are from the underworld: see *Dict.* and, for fuller information, *Underworld*.—2. Hence, notes on procedure; notes for a test; notes taken during a course: R.A.F.: since 1938. Partridge, 1945.

gen book. A note-book (for useful scraps of information): R.A.F.: since early 1930's. Jackson. See **prec.**

gen box. See **gee, n., 4.**

gen file. A general file (general to a particular department: policy, procedure, etc.): R.A.F. clerical: since ca. 1939. Partridge, 1945.

gen king. One who is well supplied with trustworthy information: R.A.F.: since ca. 1939. H. & P.

gen man has, since 1938, been rather more usual than its synonym, *gen wallah*. In, e.g., R. M. Davison, letter of Sept. 26, 1942, and in Brickhill & Norton, *Escape to Danger*, 1946.—2. An Intelligence Officer: R.A.F.: 1939 +. (P-G-R.)

gen up, v.i. and v.t. To learn (esp., quickly), to swot, to study: R.A.F.: since ca. 1933. Jackson. Ex **gen, the.**

gen(-)wallah. Anyone conversant with Service procedure or with Service 'occurrences' (postings, promotions), esp. an Orderly Room Sergeant or Corporal: R.A.F.: since ca. 1935. Jackson. See **gen, the.**

General, the. A general post-office: coll.: C. 20.—2. The yardmaster: Canadian railroadmen's (— 1931). Humorous.

General Schools. General School Leaving Examination: schools' coll.: from ca. 1920. W. L. Gibson Cowan, *Loud Report*, 1937.

General Weatherall (or Wetherall, etc.) in command. See **Wetherall . . .**

genned(-)up. Well supplied with information: R.A.F.: since ca. 1934. Partridge, 1945. Ex **gen up.**

gens.—2. 'Also used for General Quarters' (Granville): Naval: C. 20.

Gentleman Jackson (p. 321) was a native, not of Australia but of the West Indies.

gentleman of a company. 'Tavern terms', § 6.

gentleman outer. See 'Rogues'. Perhaps a c. term, as prob. is **gentleman of the nig** ('Rogues').

gentlemen, the. Members of the Royal Australian Air Force: Australian: 1940 +. B., 1942.

gentlemen present, ladies!, usually preceded by *there're.* A jocular, yet satirical, variation (1945 +) of (*there are*) *ladies present, gentlemen!*

gents', the. A men's convenience: coll.: C. 20.

genuffel, v.i. To flirt: South Africa: 1938 +. Professor W. S. Mackie in *The Cape Argus*, July 4, 1946, 'Though it has a German or Dutch appearance, its origin is unknown.' Mr Ramsey Spencer asks, 'Could this be a case of back-slang? "A form of loving", in fact?' Not impossibly.

genuwine. A jocular intensive of *genuine*, via the mispron. *genu-ine*: since ca. 1918.

geo-graphy (p. 322) occurs, as *ge-ography*, in W. N. Glascock, *Sketch-Book*, 1825–26, and therefore goes back to ca. 1810 or earlier. (Moe.)

geog (pron. *jog*). Geography: Public Schools': mid-C. 19–20. Marples.

geographically impossible. A girl rendered, by the distance of her home from Sydney, inconvenient to see for long, esp. in the evening and, above all, to take home: Sydneysiders': since ca. 1945. (B.P.)

geography. Female genitals: cultured: from ca. 1920. C. Isherwood, in *New Country*, 1933, 'He'll get a bit of geography with luck. She's only a teaser.' I.e. to the *exploring* hand.

Geological Survey, the. A stony stare: Naval officers': since ca. 1930. Granville.

Geometer. A Jesuit: ca. 1660–1720. Jane Lane, *England for Sale*, 1943, in ref. to the 1680's. Perhaps because, the Society of Jesus being a pre-

dominantly missionary order, its members may not be inaptly described as 'earth measurers'.

geometrician. See 'Tavern terms', § 3, *d.*

Geordie or **geordie.**—5. (Ex sense 1: p. 322.) A townsman, esp. a working-man: Durham University and School: late C. 19–20. (Marples, 2.)—6. A N.E. Railway employee: railwaymen's: C. 20, after ca. 1950, any employee in that region. (*Railway.*) Ex sense 1 on p. 322.

George.—10. An automatic pilot: since 1928. Jackson; H. & P., 'The saying "Let George do it" may well have suggested the name.' In ref. to sense 9 (p. 322), *Joe* has, since ca. 1920, been gradually superseding it: Jackson.—11. A common vocative to a Negro whose name is unknown: Canadian: since ca. 1920; by 1960, slightly ob.—12. Defecation: Naval: C. 20. John Winton, *We Joined the Navy*, 1859. '"Bowles, I'm going to have my Morning George now. . . . Bowles, always have your George in the *morning*"' (Captain to midshipman). Personification.

George Bohee. Tea (the beverage): rhyming s.: C. 20; by 1945, ob.—by 1960, †. Ex the name of 'a famous Banjoist', says Sydney Lester; but obviously influenced by the Chinese tea named *Bohea* (pron. *Bohee*) *tea.*

George Gerrard. A gross exaggeration: Australian: C. 20. B., 1942. Ex an Australian 'character'.

*George Robey; esp. on the George Robey. The road, or tramping; on the road, or a-tramping: tramps' rhyming c. (on *toby*): from ca. 1910.

George the Third. A variant of **Richard the Third** (p. 696): C. 20. Franklyn 2nd.

George's wrecks. See **gorgeous wrecks.**

ger along or **on!** Get on or, as is gen., Get out!; i.e. don't be silly!: illiterate coll.: C. 19–20. Nevinson, 1895, has both.

geranium.—2. A brigadier-general: Army officers': late C. 19–20. (Gilbert Frankau, *Peter Jackson*, 1920.)

gerbera. A Yarborough (in the game of bridge): Australian: since ca. 1930. B., 1942. Merely *Yarborough* in an Aboriginal shape. B.P., however, thinks that *gerbera* has been chosen because it is the name of a plant that, although imported, is extremely common in Australia.

gerdoying. See **kerdoying.**

Gerines (p. 322) has long been †. Perhaps ex 'the *jolly* m*arines*' (Colonel Albert F. Moe, formerly of the U.S. Marine Corps); perhaps ex mar*garines*, 'substitutes' for sailors + soldiers (E.P.). If the term did not arise until ca. 1870, the latter origin is the more plausible, for Mège-Mouriés, the inventor and namer of margarine, patented his invention, for France, in 1867 or 1868, and, for Britain, in 1869.

German bands (p. 322) was occasionally used in the singular, but has been † since ca. 1920.

German by injection. See **injection . . .**

Germs. German soldiers: 1914 +, but never common. Boyd Cable, *Between the Lines*, 1915.

gerswinty or geswinty. Hurried; engaged on an urgent job: Jewish Cockney tailors': C. 19–20. 'He can't stay for another pint—having been late this morning, he's a bit gerswinty.' Ex Yiddish. (Julian Franklyn.)

Gert and Daisy. Two Messerschmitts familiar to troops in the Green Hill area of Tunisia: ca. 1942–3. Ex the music-hall comediennes, 'Gert and Daisy' (Doris and Elsie Waters). P-G-R.

gertcha! Don't pull my leg!: Cockneys': late C. 19–20. '"Gertcha!" said Jimmy, "I ain't interested in women."' A corruption of *get out with yer!*

Gertie. See **whistler**.

Gertie Gitana. Banana: rhyming: C. 20. Ex a music-hall star of Edwardian days; by 1950, ob. (Franklyn, *Rhyming*.)

Gestapo, the. The Service (later R.A.F.) Police: R.A.F.: since ca. 1938. Sgt-Pilot F. Rhodes, letter of Sept. 20, 1942, 'Service police are "Gestapo" much more often than "snoops".' But also Army: witness Gerald Kersh, *They Die with their Boots Clean*, 1941. Humorous on the name of the German Secret Police of the Third Reich.

get, v., 12 (p. 323). Read: mid-C. 18–20. *Sessions*, mid-September 1759 (trial of John Mayland), 'The prisoner got jumping about, telling him he had won the twopence'.—14. To get the mastery of: pugilistic: ca. 1810–60. *Boxiana*, III, 1821.

get, n.—5. A chump, a fool: Army: since ca. 1930. *The Daily Mail*, Sept. 7, 1940. Ex the S.E. sense, 'bastard'.

get a bag! A cricket spectators' c.p., addressed to a fielder missing an easy catch: esp. in Australia and New Zealand: late C. 19–20. The implication is that he would do better as twelfth man, who carries the bag, but also that, if he held a bag open, he might succeed.

get a barrage. See **barrage, get a.**

get a blow. See **blow**, n., 4 (*Dict.*).

get a bottle. See **bottle.**

get a broom! Cancel it!: R.A.F.: since ca. 1930. Jackson. Cf. **scrub**, 4. I.e. 'sweep it away!': cf. familiar S.E. *wash out*, 'to cancel'.

get a bun on. See **bun on . . .**

get a capture. To be arrested (c. and) low: since ca. 1945. (Norman.)

get a fair crack of the whip, not to. To receive a disproportionately heavy share of duties: R.A.F.: since ca. 1936. (Atkinson.)

get a hand on. See **hand on, get a** in *Dict.*

get a hat. See **hat, get a** in *Dict.*

get a heave on (someone). To treat severely or unpleasantly: Army: since ca. 1930. (P-G-R.)

get a knob. To catch a venereal disease: low, ? esp. Army: C. 20. (Leslie Thomas, *The Virgin Soldiers*, 1966.) Cf. **knob**, n., 6, below.

get a load of that! Just look at that: since ca. 1944. Cf:

get a load of this! Listen to this!: adopted, ca. 1942, from U.S.

get a load on. To become tipsy: Australian: C. 20. Vance Palmer, *Golconda*, 1948. The *load* comes ex Canada, where current since late C. 19. (Niven.)

get a marked tray. To catch a venereal disease: Canadian hospitals' (perhaps orig. a euphemism): since ca. 1910. (To avoid infection.)

get a number! is a variant of *before you came up!*, q.v. at p. 44: since ca. 1925. H. & P.—2. Synonymous with **get joined**.

get a set on. To make a dead set against (a person): Australian: ca. 1880–1920. B. & L. Cf. **get a pick on** (*Dict.*).

get a squeak. (Of police) to become suspicious: police: since ca. 1910. (*The Free-Lance Writer*, April 1948.) Cf. **squeak**, n., 2 (p. 819).

get a wiggle on. (Mostly in imperative.) To get a move on; to look lively: Naval: C. 20. (P-G-R.)

get (food) **about** (one). To 'get outside of', to eat: Aus.: since ca. 1920.

get among it. To be making a lot of money: Australian: since ca. 1910.—2. To 'have a woman' from time to time: Australian: since ca. 1915. (Dal Stivens, *Jimmy Brockett*, 1951.)

get an encore. See **encore, get an.**

get at, 4 (p. 324): should rather be dated late C. 19–20. The American David Belasco was prob. borrowing it when he used it in *Naughty Anthony* (II, i), 1849. (Moe.)

get (someone) **at**—intensively, **right at**—**it.** To make fun of; to jeer at; to make a fool of: low: since ca. 1940. (Norman.)

get back to taws. Ex the technical or S.E. sense, 'to go back to the base-line' in the game of marbles, comes the sense, 'to (have or prefer to) start again', of which B.P. remarks, 'I believe that this is the best known c.p. of Australian origin.'

get bumbed. See **bumped.**

get cracking—get mobile—get skates on—get stuck into it—get weaving. To respond (immediately) to an order; to get a move on: Services (the 2nd, 3rd, 4th, general; the 1st, orig. Army and then gen.; the 5th, R.A.F.—see separately at **weaving**): since ca. 1925, except *stuck* (ca. 1916) and the last, q.v. All usually in the imperative. Origins: whip-cracking at the mustering of cattle; *mobile* and *skates*, obvious refs. to speed (cf. a *mobile* column); *stuck*, perhaps ex dough-kneading but prob. ex ditch-digging, road-making, mining; see **weaving**.—2. Hence, to think or plan seriously; to take the steps necessary to achieve an end: since ca. 1940. Cf. **organised, get.**

get dizzy: earlier in 'Taffrail'. Cf. *dizzy*, n. (in *Dict.*).

get down. To depress mentally; to exasperate or irritate: coll.: late C. 19–20.

get down in (*Dict.*). Also Australian: B., 1942.

get down on (p. 324) is also Australian: B., 1943.

get down to it. To coït: coll.: C. 20.

get fell in! Fall in: c.p. among N.C.O.s: C. 20. Originally, Army, then the other Services. (P-G-R.) A sol. that became consecrated.

get (one's) **fingers nipped.** To get into trouble for some misdeed: coll.: late C. 19–20. Perhaps suggested by S.E. *get one's fingers burnt.*

get his. To receive a wound, an injury, esp. a fatal one: Army: since ca. 1914. Ronald Knox, *Double Cross Purposes*, 1937; Gerald Kersh, *The Nine Lives of Bill Nelson*, 1942. Cf. **get it** (p. 324) and **cop**, v., 3 (p. 179).

get (someone) **in.** To put a story over on, to deceive with a story: Australian: since ca. 1925. D'Arcy Niland, *Call Me . . .*, 1958, 'Old Ted Proctor . . . the greatest liar God ever put breath in—even he could get you in.'

get in bad with. See **bad with.**

get in, knob, you're posted. See **knob**, n., 6, below.—2. Hence, a c.p. uttered when, having been posted to another district, one is determined to have a final fling, usually sexual: R.A.F.: 1939–45, then mainly historical.

get it, as in 'He's got it': Much less usual than **get his** (above).

get it in the neck (p. 324) was orig. American. It occurs in J. Flynt & F. Walton, *The Powers that Prey*, 1900.

get it on the whisper. 'To buy on hire purchase (because at one time you didn't tell the neighbours you couldn't afford to pay cash)': lower and lower-middle class: since ca. 1920. (John Gosling, 1959.)

get joined or **knotted!** Go and 'play trains'!: Services: since 1930. Coïtional.

get knackered or **knotted** 'have come to mean, innocently enough, "go to hell"' (*New Society*, Aug. 22, 1963, article 'From the Blackboard Jungle'): cf. **knackered** below.

get knocked. To be punched, or knocked out: Australian sporting coll.: late C. 19–20. Baker. —2. Hence, to suffer a set-back: Australian coll.: since ca. 1930.

get knotted! See **get joined!**

get Laurence. See **Laurence.**

get lost! Oh, run away!: adopted, ex U.S., ca. 1950 in Britain, ca. 1944 in Australia.

get marched. See **marched.**

get me, Steve? See **got me, Steve?**

get mobile. See **get cracking.**

get off, v., 3 (p. 325). Much earlier in George Godfrey, *History*, 1828.—9. (Of a taxicabman) to pick up a fare: taxicabmen's: from ca. 1919. Ex sense 5.

get off my back! Leave me alone! or Stop being a nuisance!: Australian c.p.: since ca. 1940. (B., 1953.)

get off my neck (p. 325). Orig. form (ca. 1905): *Oh, Gertie, get off my neck.*

get off one's bike. See **bike . . .**

get off with.—2. (Ex sense 1 on p. 325.) To have a good time together, including sexual play and intercourse: since the late 1930's, esp. among teenagers.

get off your knees! A Services c.p. addressed to one whose job seems to be too much for him or who is lazy: Sgt-Pilot F. Rhodes, letter of Sept. 20, 1942: since ca. 1920. H. & P., 1943, 'You're *not* beaten to your knees.' A rare R.A.F. variant, ca. 1940–5, was *get off your cap-badge.*

get on (someone's) **daily.** See **clock,** v., 5, above.

get on it; n., **getting on it.** To go on a drinking-bout; such a bout: Australian: since ca. 1920. (Dymphna Cusack, *Say No to Death*, 1951.)

get on (someone's) **wick.** To exasperate someone: low: since ca. 1920. Here, *wick* = **Hampton Wick** (p. 370).

get on (someone's) **tit.** To annoy or irritate: low: Aus.: C. 20. (B., 1959.)

get on to.—2. To question: coll.: C. 20.—3. To reprimand: coll., mostly North Country: C. 20.

get on toast. See **toast, get on.**

get on (someone's) **tripe.** To get on his nerves: Aus.: since ca. 1930. (F. B. Vickers, *First Place to the Stranger*, 1955.)

get on (someone's) **works.** To annoy—even to infuriate: Australian: since ca. 1925. B., 1942. Adaptation of **get on one's wick** above?

get one's arse, or **eye, in a sling.** See **eye in a sling** above.

get one's blood back. See **blood back.**

get one's end in. (Of the male) to achieve copulation, to copulate: low: since ca. 1910. Leslie Thomas, *The Virgin Soldiers*, 1966, 'It was the place in the town for getting one's end in, they said, and it was naturally very crowded.' See **end,** 2., above.

get one's feet under the table. To establish friendly relations; esp., of servicemen in homes of residents local to barracks or camp: coll.: since ca. 1925. (Atkinson.)

get one's head down. To lie down and sleep:

Services (esp. R.A.F.) coll.: since ca. 1920. (Gerald Emanuel, March 29, 1945.)

get one's head sharpened. See **I'm going to get . . .** below.

get one's leg across. To achieve mastery of (a woman): low coll.: late C. 19–20.

get one's monkey up (p. 529) should be back-dated to ca. 1810.

get one's one. See **one, get one's.**

get organised! See **organised, get.**

get-out. (See *Dict.*) An earlier example, though in the nuance 'an escape from a difficult or dangerous position', occurs in E. H. Hornung, *Raffles*, 1899. The term now verges on S.E.

get out and push! A derisive c.p. directed at a motorist whose car keeps on stopping: since ca. 1925.

get out and walk. To use one's parachute: aviators' and Airborne Divisions': 1939 +.

get out of the shine! Get out of the light!: since ca. 1925.

get out one's mad. To become (very) angry: Australian: since ca. 1920. (B., 1943.)

get past oneself. See **past oneself, get.**

get pipped. See **bumped.**

get rooted! or **go and . . .!** (Go and) get fucked!: low Australian: late C. 19–20. (B., 1953.)

get roused on is a variant (B., 1943) of *rouse on,* q.v. at **rouse,** 2 (p. 709): since ca. 1920.

get scrubbed. See **scrubbed.**

get set.—2. To 'get someone set' is to bear him a grudge: Australian: since ca. 1880. B., 1942. Ex *have a set against.*

get shit of. See **shit of . . .**

get slopped out. To empty one's slops: prison coll.: late C. 19–20. (Norman.)

get some flying hours in. 'To get some sleep' (Jackson): R.A.F.: since ca. 1935.

get some service in! Synonymous with **get a number!:** since ca. 1925. H. & P. Also *get some time in*; often simply *get some in!:* Partridge, 1945.

get some straight and level in. To obtain some sleep: R.A.F.: since ca. 1939. Robert Hinde, letter of March 17, 1945.

get some time in! See **get some service in!**

get stuck into. See **get cracking.**—2. To 'get stuck into someone' is to fight someone with one's fists: Australian: C. 20. Baker.—3. To coït with a woman: workman's: C. 20.—4. To abuse verbally: Aus.: C. 20. (B., 1959.) Ex sense 2.

*get stuff on the mace. See **mace . . .**

get stuffed! Oh, run away and 'play trains'!: low: late C. 19–20. Cf. **get joined!**

get that across your chest! Eat that: C. 20.

get the bird. See **bird,** n., 5, and **bird, get the,** both on p. 54. Mr S. H. Ward, in letter dated May 8, 1967, tells me of a letter written by John Fabian—contained in the Lansdowne MSS, vol. 22—and dated by the British Museum as ca. 1576. Of the sentence 'Some after deride me and de-maunde, what I have p[ro]fited thereby, saying that I have spounde a faire thread, have beaten the bushe, but after have gotten the birde . . .,' Mr Ward says, 'The tone of the whole letter is one in which the modern sense of "getting the bird" would suit very well. Bewailing that his work has not brought the reward to which he believed him-self entitled.'

get the cat to lick it off! or **try a piece of sand-paper!** A piece of c.p. advice (C. 20) to youths with down on cheeks or upper lip.

get the chop. See **chop, get the.**

get the crap on. To be afraid, 'get the wind up': low Glasgow: from ca. 1919. MacArthur & Long. Ex that loosening of the bowels which often results from fear.

get the gate. See **gate, get the.**

get the go. The complement of *give the go.* (G. B. Lancaster, 1910.)

get the hoof. See **hoof, get the.**

get the lead out. A variant of *take . . .*: mostly Canadian: since ca. 1940.

get the length of one's foot. See **foot, know the length of one's** in *Dict.*

get the message. See 'Jazz Slang' (at *message, get the*).

get the needle. See **needle, cop the** in both *Dict.* and Addenda.

get the picture. To understand: mostly Australian: since ca. 1945. Cf. **put in the picture** below. (B.P.)

get the run. See **run, get the.**

get the shits up. To panic: low: C. 20. Elleston Trevor, *The Freebooters*, 1967, 'If it's a false alarm they'll know I've just got the shits up'. Cf. *get the wind up*, q.v. at **wind up** both in *Dict.* and below.

get the spear. To be dismissed from a job: Australian: since ca. 1920. (B., 1943.)

get the stick. See **stick, get the,** below.

get the white ants. See **white ants.**

get them.—3. *He's got them,* he's mad: since ca. 1910.

get through.—4. To copulate with (a woman): low: late C. 19–20. But orig. and strictly, to take a girl's virginity.

get to. To begin to (do something): coll.: from ca. 1870. Nevinson, 1895.

get to wind'ard of. See **wind'ard of, get to.**

get-together. A (usually informal) meeting or assembly: coll.: since ca. 1925. Sydney Moseley, *God Help America!*, 1952.

get tonked. To be punched; to be defeated: Australian: since ca. 1920. Baker. Ex **tonk,** 1 (*Dict.*).

get tore! Get a move on!: Services: since ca. 1930. (P-G-R.)

get tossed. To lose money on a horse-race: Australian sporting: C. 20. (Lawson Glassop, 1949.)

get under (someone's) **neck.** To beat or outwit or circumvent (someone): Australian: since ca. 1930. (B., 1953.) Lit., to get in front of him; ex horse-racing.

get up, n.—4. A 'framing', a 'frame-up' (a trumped-up case): c.: since mid 1940's. Peter Crookston, *Villain*, 1967, '"I can't really get annoyed when the police have a get-up against Harry."' Ex coll. *get up a case*, to prepare one.

get up, 5 (p. 326). This coll. goes, as v.t., much further back: in John Aubrey's *Brief Lives*, written in 1679–96, we hear of Sir Walter Raleigh 'getting up one of the mayds of honour'.—6. (Of a horse) to win: Australian racing: C. 20. Lawson Glassop, *Lucky Palmer*, 1949.

get up and go, n. A person's energy, initiative, courage; a car's acceleration, a lawn mower's reliability, etc.: Australian: since ca. 1930. (B.P.)

get up them stairs! A c.p. to a man (esp. if married) going on leave: Services (perhaps mostly R.A.F.): since ca. 1940. Before the phrase gained widespread and broadcast renown, i.e. before 1942, it used often to be preceded or, more often, followed by *Blossom,* generic for a woman's name.

get up to, as in 'What's he getting up to?'— What mischief is he doing or planning?: coll.: late C. 19–20.

get weaving. See **weaving.**

get weighed off. See **weighed off.**

get worked! A low Australian expletive: C. 20. (Dal Stivens, *Jimmy Brockett*, 1951.)

get you (emphatic *yew*) or **he's got ten bob each way on himself.** Female teenagers' c.p. directed at a conceited young man: ca. 1957–9. (Gilderdale.)

get—or go and get—your brain(s) examined! A disparaging, or a derisive, c.p.: since ca. 1920.

get your ears dropped! Your hair needs cutting: facetious Canadian c.p.: since ca. 1955. (Leechman.)

get your knees brown! See **knees.**

get your knickers untwisted!; often preceded by *you want to.* Among men: Clarify your ideas!; elude an impasse: since ca. 1950.

get your steel helmets (or tin hats)! The Army's (1940–5) 'answer' to the R.A.F.'s line! 'Often accompanied by the gesture of handle-turning, like that of a street organist, to the tune of da-dĭ-dĭ-da' (Bebbington).

getaway. See **get away** (*Dict.*).

getaway, make a. The invariable v. form of **getaway** (n.) on p. 324.

getaway man (coll., become semi-official); or **lucky Charlie** (s.). On a patrol, that man who, keeping in the rear, was detailed, in an emergency, to escape and report: Army coll.: 1940–5.

getting any?; also **getting any lately?** and **getting enough?** A c.p. used by men, mostly manual workers and esp. at meeting: Australian: since ca. 1930. Either ex angling, as B.P. proposes, or ex sex, as he fears; the latter is the more prob., as *getting enough?* seems to indicate. It does indeed imply 'Have you been amorously successful lately?': B., 1959. Baker records these 'formulas of reply': *climbing trees to get away from it!—got to swim under water to dodge it!—so busy I've had to put a man on (to help me)!*

Gezira Box, the. Base troops at Cairo: Army in North Africa: 1941–3. (P-G-R.) Ex the 'boxes' that formed the defence plan in the desert fighting. Cf. *Groppi's Light Horse.*

gezumph; loosely **gezump.**—2. To give (someone) short change: barrow-boys': since ca. 1935. Ex sense 1 (p. 326).

Ghan, the. 'The fortnightly train running from Adelaide to Alice Springs,' B., 1942: Australian: since ca. 1930. Aboriginal shaping of *go on?* No; short for *Afghan*: from those camel-trains which are so often conducted by the Afghan cameleers, as in, 'One old Ghan cameleer . . . had ridden from Alice Springs to Oodnadatta . . . 355 miles away without undue fatigue' (Archer Russell, *A Tramp Royal in Australia*, 1934): there, *Ghan* is a coll., dating since ca. 1890.

Ghardimaou Yeomanry, the. The 2nd Corps Reinforcement Unit, mobilised as infantry at the time of the German threat at Kasserine: Army in North Africa: World War II. This unit was stationed at Ghardimaou in Tunisia. (P-G-R.)

ghee factory. See **Rice Corps.**

ghost, n.—4. A Radio Officer: Services: since ca. 1939. H. & P.—5. An intrusive secondary image on a T.V. screen: since ca. 1950: television coll. >, by 1965, S.E.

ghost gun. A machine-gun operated from a distance by cable: Army in Italy: 1943–4.

ghost in goloshes, the. The B.B.C. time-signal: since ca. 1938.

ghoster. A full night's work preceded by a full day's work: builders': C. 20. (A master builder: Dec. 5, 1953.)

giant.—2. Dynamite: (esp. Canadian) miners': C. 20. A small stick has tremendous power. 'Giant was a trade mark for one brand of dynamite, and may still be' (Leechman, 1967).

giant-killer, the; tigers' milk. Whisky: Army officers': resp. from ca. 1910 and ca. 1890. Both occur in Blaker.—2. The latter occurs also as 'gin': 1850 (O.E.D.); † by 1890.—3. The latter, also as in George R. Gleig, *The Subaltern's Log-Book*, 1828, '"Will you take a glass of tiger's milk" (a pet name for brandy and water), I asked.' Moe.

Gib. An early record: 1869, A Merchant, *Six Years in the Prisons of England*.

gib, 3, is recorded as early as in B. & L.

gibber (p. 327) is pronounced *ghibber*. See, e.g., e.g., A. G. Mitchell, *The Pronunciation of English in Australia*, 1946.

gibbey is that variant of **gibby** (*Dict.*) which 'Taffrail' prefers.

gibby.—2. 'Naval word for a cap,' H. & P.: since ca. 1930. Granville precisions it, thus, 'A round cap worn by new entries in a training ship.'

giddy giddy gout. A child whose *shirt's hanging out*: Australian schoolchildren's: C. 20. Ex a schoolchildren's chant. (B.P.)

giddy goat. 'The tote' or totalisator: Australian rhyming s.: since ca. 1925. (B., 1945.)

giddy kipper, etc., survives in the Cockney c.p. **giddy little kipper** (or **whelk**) approvingly directed at one's get-up, esp. on some festive occasion.

giddy limit, the. The original form—English, esp. Cockney—of 'the *dizzy limit*' (p. 226 and above): since the 1890's. Julian Franklyn, letter of 1962, instances 'It is—you are—they are —the giddy limit'.

Gideon Force. Wingate's gallant little force in Abyssinia (1941). Biblical Gideon smote his enemies hip and thigh.

giever. A life-saving jacket sold by Messrs. *Gieves*, the Naval outfitters: Naval (ward-room): since ca. 1946.

gifted, adj. (Usually of men) homosexual, as in 'Is he gifted?': ? orig. Canadian: since ca. 1925. 'Presumably because so many of them are' (Leechman).

gig, n.—7. An engagement to play at a party for one evening: dance bands': since ca. 1935. In, e.g., Stanley Jackson, *An Indiscreet Guide to Soho*, 1946. Ex S.E. *gig*, a dance.—8. A young lady: Australian: since the 1920's. Perhaps ex *giggle*. (Kylie Tennant, 1953.)—9. A simpleton, a dupe: Australian: since ca. 1930. (B., 1953.) Whence 'to *gig*' or lure simpletons: B., 1953.—10. A shortened form of *fizz-gig*, 2 (p. 280): Australian c.: since ca. 1935. Hence the rhyming *Moreton Bay fig*, itself often shortened to *Moreton Bay*. (B., 1953.) 11. A detective: Aus.: since ca. 1935. (B., 1959.)—Sense 7 was, ca. 1966, adopted by hippies and, in 1967, by the Flower People: Peter

Fryer in *The Observer* colour supplement, Dec. 3, 1967.

gig, v.—2. To tease, make fun of (someone): Australian: since ca. 1945. B., *Australia Speaks*, 1953.—3. So to toss a coin that it does not spin: Australian two-up players': since ca. 1910. Also 'to *butterfly*' or 'to *float*'. (B., 1953.)—4. To stare (at someone): Aus.: since late 1930's. (B., 1959.)

gig!, it's a. See **it's a gig!**

giggle, n. A group or 'bunch', or crowd of girls: originating as a noun of assembly, it had, by ca. 1935, become a cultured coll. Berta Ruck, *Pennies from Heaven*, 1940, 'Picked her out of a giggle of society debutantes.' Ex *giggling*, as in 'a lot of giggling girls'.—2. 'When the show or party is fun—it's a giggle, or it's a screech' (Gilderdale, 2): smart young set (esp. girls'): ca. 1955–60. But also low s.: since ca. 1945, as in Norman. Cf. *giggle, no*, on p. 328.

giggle and titter. A bitter (beer): rhyming s., mainly theatrical: C. 20. Franklyn, *Rhyming*.

giggle-hat. Worn with a 'giggle-suit': Australian soldiers': 1939–45. (B., 1943.)

giggle-house. A lunatic asylum: Australian: since ca. 1925. D'Arcy Niland, *Call Me . . .*, 1958, 'Unless something's done he'll end up in the giggle-house. And that'll finish her.'

giggle-stick. The penis: low: C. 20. Cf. **joy-stick**, 2 (*Dict.*).—2. A stick, a spoon, used to stir a cocktail or other mixed alcoholic drink: Australian: since ca. 1920. B., 1942.

giggle-suit. Working dress; overalls: Australian soldiers': 1939 +. Lawson Glassop, *We Were the Rats*, 1944. Cf. a comic appearance.—2. Hence, prison clothes: Aus.: c.: since ca. 1945. (B., 1959.)

giggle-water. Champagne: since ca. 1910. Ex its effect.

giggling-pin. A variant of **giggle-stick** (penis): C. 20.

giggy; dirt-shoot. Anus: low Canadian: C. 20.

giggy!, up your. A low Canadian c.p. of contemptuous rejection: C. 20. Cf. preceding.

gilded ballocks, have. To be extremely lucky: Army: since ca. 1936. Cf. *golden ballocks*.

gilded staff, the. 'The staff on board a flag ship, the wearers of aiguillettes,' Granville: Naval officers': since ca. 1910.

gilderoy. A proud person: Newfoundland: C. 20. Cf. In Newfoundland simile (as) proud as *Gilderoy* or *Guilderoy*; both forms are recorded by L. E. F. English, *Historic Newfoundland*, 1955. *G(u)ilderoy* is here taken as the type of old, aristocratic Norman–English surname.

gill-ale. 'Physic-ale', says B.E., who, since a gill is only one-quarter of a pint, would seem to mean medicinal ale (? stout): coll.: ca. 1670–1750.

gilt, n.—6. A gilt-edged security: financial: since ca. 1915. W. B. M. Ferguson, *Somewhere off Borneo*, 1936.

gilt-edged (p. 328) goes back, in U.S., to ca. 1860. (*The Galaxy*, July 1867, on p. 278.) By 1890, Standard American English; by 1940, S.E. (Moe.)

gilt-tick is more closely defined by B. & L.: 'money as represented by gold coins'.

Gimracks, the. 'The big fir trees at the Governor's gate', esp. as a fighting ground: Sandhurst: from ca. 1826. Major A. F. Mockler-Ferryman, *Annals of Sandhurst*, 1900.

gimick. Variant of **gimmick.**

gimlet.—2. A gin and lime: Naval: since ca. 1930. Granville. Elaboration of blend.

gimmick. Synonym of **gaff**, n., 13, or **gaffer**, 12: Canadian carnival s.: since ca. 1920. Echoic. Adopted from U.S.—2. See **fake**, n., 2.—3. Hence, any device or plan or trick calculated to ensure success: since ca. 1946 in Britain, but since the middle 1930's in Canada.

gimp. A simpleton; a fool: Australian: since ca. 1925. B., 1942. A corruption of American *gink*, 'chap, fellow'?

gimp up, v.i. and v. reflexive. To dress oneself up smartly: Army: since ca. 1910. Ex North Country dial, *gimp*, 'to ornament with grooves, to put into scallops'.

gimpy. Lame in the leg: Canadian: adopted, ca. 1930, ex U.S. The adj. of c. *gimp*, a lame leg, hence a lame person. (Priestley.)

gin(-)and(-)fog. (Of the voice) hoarse with that peculiar quality of 'fruitiness' which spirituous indulgence causes: urban: since ca. 1930. In, e.g., Clifford Witting, *Let X Be the Murderer*, 1947.

Gin and Jaguar (or Stockbrokers') Belt, the. Any good—and very expensive—residential area near London, but esp. in Surrey: since ca. 1955.

gin-coaster. A pink gin with soda: British West Africa: since ca. 1880.

gin-jockey. A white man habitually consorting with aboriginal women (*gins*): Australian rural, esp. in the North: since ca. 1920. Margaret Henry, *Unlucky Dip*, 1960.

gin ken. A gin shop: low: late C. 18–19. See the quotation at **nab the bib** below.

gin palace.—2. 'Armoured Command vehicle or "Dorchester"' ... 'The nerve centre of the armoured brigades,' H. & P.: military: since 1940. Cf.: 3. 'Any impressive interior, such as that of a static A.A. Command Post,' H. & P.: since 1941. Ex the elaborateness and the apparent comfort.—4. 'Staff car. Any luxurious vehicle for the use of a superior officer' (Frank Roberts, letter of Sept. 28, 1946): Army: 1942 +. Ex 2.

Gin Palace, the. Earlier in 'Taffrail'.

gin pennant. A green-and-white flag run up by a ship as an invitation to all officers to come aboard for a drink: C. 20.

gin-spinner.—2. Hence, a wine-vault: 1821, Pierce Egan, *Life in London*; † by 1890.

gin up, v.i. 'To consume hard liquor'—esp. spirits—'before a party,' Jackson: Service officers': since ca. 1930. Cf. **ginned-up** (p. 329): *gin up*, however, means—not to get drunk but merely to induce the party-spirit.

ginch, elegance, smartness, esp. of skill or manner or clothing, or an instance of any of these exhibitions; adj., *ginchy*: Australian teenagers' (esp. surfboard riders'): since ca. 1960. *Pix*, Sept. 28, 1963, para. 1 of Dick Dennison's article, 'The Weird World of Surfies'.

ginchy. See preceding.—2. Hence (?), excellent, first-class: in the lower forms of Merseyside schools: ca. 1960–4.

ging. A catapult: Australian children's: C. 20. B., 1942. Echoic.

Ginge. Nickname, usually in vocative, for a ginger-haired person (mostly of men): since ca. 1880.

Ginger. Air Chief Marshall 'Bomber' Harris: R.A.F.: − 1939.

ginger, n., 5 (p. 329). Rather, since ca. 1815: sporting. *Spy*, 1825.—7. (Pronounced *ghing-er*.) A catapult: Australian juvenile: since ca. 1945. (B., 1953.) Ex **shot-ging?**—2. See next.

*****ginger**, v., **gingering**, n. To rob; robbery: Australian c. (prostitutes'): since ca. 1930. Kylie Tennant, *The Joyful Condemned*, 1953, '"gingering", or robbing prospective clients, was considered low taste, but after all, the man was a copper'. Hence the n., *ginger*, a prostitute that does this; also called a *ginger girl* or a *gingerer*: B., 1953. Hence also *work a ginger*.

ginger, knocking down. See **knocking down ginger.**

ginger beer.—2. Hence, *the Ginger Beers*, the Engineer Corps in the Australian Army: Australian soldiers': 1939 +. B., 1942.—3. A homosexual: rhyming s., since ca. 1920. On *queer*.

ginger one. See **back stick** above.

Ginger Smith. See 'Nicknames'.

*****gingerer.** See **ginger**, v., s.f.

Gingerless Pop. 'A name we gave to Poperinghe during the spring retreat of 1918. ... "Pop" was completely deserted and dead, and Talbot House was completely empty. ... It was nothing like the Poperinghe of 1917, always packed with troops and transport' and offering tea and soft drinks. (A. B. Petch, March 1966.)

ginnick. A Naval variant—since ca. 1950—of **gimmick.**

ginny. —2. Addicted to gin: coll.: C. 20. (Angus Wilson, *A Bit off the Map*, 1957.)

ginormous. Very large: R.A.F. and Navy: ca. 1940–5. (W/Cdr R. P. McDouall, March 27, 1945.) I.e. great + immense + enormous. Extant in R.A.F.

gin's flop. Synonymous with *honey-pot*, 2. (B., 1943.)

Gip. Garden Island Prison: Australian Naval: since ca. 1939. (B., 1943.)

gip, give, sense 1 (p. 330), was coll. by 1900 at latest, as in G. B. Lancaster, *Jim of the Ranges*, 1910—an Australian usage.—2. To cause pain to (someone), esp. a sudden pain: since ca. 1905.

gip artist. A confidence trickster: Australian: since ca. 1925. B., 1942. By American influence.

gippa. Gravy: Regular Army: C. 20. Cf. **Gip**, 3 and **gypoo**: in *Dict*.

gippo.—4. A cook; *master gippo*, head cook: Army: since ca. 1918. Ex sense 3: see **Gip**, p. 330 and:

Gippy.—3. Gravy: mostly R.A.F. regulars': since ca. 1925. Jackson. Ex **Gip**, 3 (p. 330), or ex *gippa* (above).

gippy.—4. (*G*.) An Egyptian cigarette: since ca. 1905.

Gippy tummy. Stomach-trouble in *Egypt* (hence also in *Libya*): Army: late C. 19–20. Perhaps commoner in form *Gippo tummy*.

Gipsy's warning. See **gypsy's warning.**

girl, n., 3, is also, in late C. 19–20, the white-slave term for a female in the service of 'the Centre'. Albert Londres, *The Road to Buenos Ayres*, 1928.

girl, v. (p. 330) is very much earlier than I had thought. 'The maid said two men were missing, and the others said, God d..n them, they are gone a-girling,' *Sessions*, Jan. 1787.

girl abductor. A tram conductor: Australian rhyming s.: ca.1890–1914. (*The* Sydney *Bulletin*, Jan. 18, 1902, cited by B., 1945.)

girl and boy (p. 330) fell into disuse by 1920, at latest.

girl friend, the. See **boy friend.**

girlie magazine. A magazine containing many pictures of female nudes or provocative seminudes: Australian, esp. teenagers', coll.: adopted, in late 1950's, ex U.S. (B.P.)

giro. A giraffe: big-game hunters': late C. 19–20. (Stephen Leacock, *Arcadian Adventures*, 1915.) After **hippo.**

git, n.—5. A fool; a useless fellow: mostly Cockney: since ca. 1920. A specialization of sense 2 on p. 323.

git-box. See **fish-horn.**

give (someone) **a bowler hat.** See **bowler hat** (p. 86).

give or **have** or **take a cook.** To take a look: rhyming s.: since ca. 1946. Ex Yiddish *guck.* (Franklyn, *Rhyming.*) The Yiddish v.i. itself derives from the coll. Ger. v.i. *gucken,* to look, to peep, inquisitively.

give (someone) **a fair crack of the whip.** To 'play fair' with: North Country miners': late C. 19–20. Hence also, since ca. 1910, Australian.

give (something) **a fly.** See **fly,** n., 9.

give (someone) **a go.** To give him a run for his money, to give 'something to think about'; Australian coll.: since ca. 1910. (H. Drake Brockman, 1947.)

give a good chit. See **have a . . .**

give a monkey's fuck, not to. Not to care a damn: low: C. 20.

give (someone) **a rap.** To reprove or reprimand: coll.: mid-C. 19–20; by 1890, S.E. B., 1941.

give (a woman) **a shot.** To coït with: low: C. 19–20.

give (a girl) **a thrill.** To coït: coll.: since ca. 1920.

give (someone) **a touch of 'em.** See **touch . . .**

give (a person) **a weight.** To assist in lifting a heavy weight: streets': from ca. 1860. B. & L.

give air. See **give the ball air** (*Dict.*).

give and take, sense 1 (p. 330). The O.E.D. records it for 1769.—2. A cake: rhyming s.: from ca. 1860.

give away, v. (p. 330). Senses 1 and 2 are, in C. 20, coll.—4. To abandon: Australian: C. 20. Jon Cleary, *Justin Bayard*, 1955, 'When I spoke to you . . ., you didn't say you'd given the idea away.' Cf. *give the game away.* Recorded earlier in Tom Ronan, *Vision Splendid*, 1954, and earlier still in Nevil Shute, *A Town Like Alice*, 1949, and Lawson Glassop, *Lucky Palmer*, 1949.

give beans.—2. To reprimand or scold (someone): Canadian: C. 20.

give (someone) **Bondi.** To 'give him hell': Australian: C. 20. (Dal Stivens, 1951.) Bondi beach: a lively place.

give (someone) **fits.** To scold thoroughly: Canadian: C. 20. (Leechman.)

give full chips. See **chips, give . . .**

give her twopence! 'A c.p. used on sighting a beautiful female child, i.e. Give her twopence to ring you up when she is sixteen' (B.P.): Australian: late 1945–1946–1947. The cost of a call rose to threepence, then fourpence.

give him a card! Just listen to him boasting: Naval: since ca. 1940. In the Near East, early in World War II, it was—so legend has it—customary to pass to anyone boasting of his exploits a card

bearing the words 'Carry on! I'm a bit of a bull-shitter myself.'

*****give in best.** To affect repentance: c.: from ca. 1860. B. & L.

give it a bone! A proletarian variant of **give it a rest** (*Dict.*): from ca. 1880. B. & L.

give it to, 2 (p. 331): in C. 18, coll., as, e.g., in *Sessions*, May 1739 (trial of Wm Kirkwood).

give me a pain . . ., you. See **you give me the balls-ache.**

give out. See 'Jazz Slang'.

give sky-high. To scold (a person) immoderately: proletarian: from ca. 1870; ob. B. & L.

give (someone) **something for** (his) **corner.** To make him 'sit up', to punish: North Country: C. 20. Ex boxing.

give (someone) **the brush-off.** To dismiss; to snub: Canadian (ex U.S.): since ca. 1925. Hence, English and Australian, since ca. 1943.

give (someone) **the business.** To inflict punishment, whether physical or mental, upon: Canadian: adopted, ca. 1945, ex U.S.

give (someone) **the freedom of the world.** To sack him: C. 20.

give the game away. 'To abandon interest in any activity or pursuit' (B., 1953): Australian: since ca. 1939. Ex **give away,** v., 4.

give the go. To reject (a suitor): New Zealand: late C. 19–20. (G. B. Lancaster, *Sons o' Men,* 1904.) For . . . *go-by.* Also *give the mitten:*—2. Also, to abandon (a country, a job): New Zealand and Australian: late C. 19–20. G. B. Lancaster 1904.

give the goo. See 'Canadian'.

give the gun (p. 331). Here, *the gun* = the accelerator.

*****give the heat.** To murder with a firearm: c.: anglicised, ca. 1932, ex the American usage (see Irwin). *The Pawnshop Murder.*

give (someone) **the length of one's tongue.** To reprove severely, to 'dress down': Londoners': C. 20.

give (one) **the shits.** To get on a person's nerves: low, esp. Londoners': C. 20.

give the sick. See **sick . . .**

give the slip; either with **us,** etc., or absolutely. To die: coll.: since ca. 1830. Emily Brontë, *Wuthering Heights*, 1847. Ex fox hunting.

give the works. See **works . . .**

give us a touch (usually with vocative *tosh*). Let me light my cigarette from yours, or from your pipe: National Servicemen's: since ca. 1947.

give your face a joy-ride! A c.p., addressed cheerily to someone looking mournful: since ca. 1930.

given away with a pound of tea. 'A Cockney c.p. of jocular disparagement, as in "Mum's new hat looks as if it was given away with a pound o' tea" and "Jack says his new bike was *not* given away with a pound o' tea"': late C. 19–20, but much less general since 1914 than before that date. Ex grocers' practice of giving away a pound of tea with a sizeable order. (Julian Franklyn.)

given the deep six (p. 331). No; but because at sea a body must not be buried in less than six fathoms of water.

giving the boys a treat. (Of girls) to show a lot of leg, whether unavoidably in a gusty wind or crossing a stile or getting out of a car: coll.: late C. 19–20. In late 1966 +, to make the best—or, if you prefer, the worst—of the numerous opportunities afforded by the mini skirt.

givo. A suit made not according to regulations: Naval (lower-deck): since ca. 1910. Granville. Perhaps ex *guiver*, adj.: see p. 360.

giz. 'To read a pal's letter to his girl friend,' H. & P.: Services: since ca. 1940. Either ex *inquisitive* or ex U.S. *kibitz*, to interfere, or *kibitzer*, busybody.

gizz, a face (p. 331). Perhaps influenced by *phiz*, but certainly derived from *guise* (a mask), of which it once formed a variant.

gizzard.—2. The solar plexus: low London: C. 20. E.g. 'Give a poke in the gizzard.'

gla. See 'Colston's.

Glad. A Gloster Gladiator fighter aircraft R.A.F. coll.: 1939–42. James Aldridge, *Signed with their Honour*, 1942.

glad. A gladiolus: flower-sellers': late C. 19–20. Richard Llewellyn, *None But the Lonely Heart*, 1943. Cf. **carn.**

glad, give the. To 'give the *glad eye*' (p. 331) since ca. 1930. (Angus Wilson, *Anglo-Saxon Attitudes*, 1956.)

glad-and-sorry system, the. Hire-purchase, since ca. 1910. (George Sava, *A Land Fit for Heroes*, 1945.)

glad eye (p. 331) occurs in *The Roussilon Gazette*, Jan. 1913, on p. 20. (S. H. Ward.)

gladdher (p. 332) derives either from Welsh Gypsy *glathera*, 'solder; pewter'—itself ex Shelta; or straight from Shelta. John Sampson, *The Gypsies of Wales*, 1926.

gladi, usu. in pl. *gladis.* A gladiolus: Australian: since ca. 1925. (B.P.)

glam. Glamour: film-world hangers-on: since ca. 1940.

glam, adj. Glamorous: mostly feminine: since ca. 1950. John Winton, *All the Nice Girls*, 1964, '"Her name's Maxine. She's rather glam, isn't she?"'

glamour. Hair-cream: Army: ca. 1939; by 1960, ob. (P-G-R.) Ex next.

Glamour Boys, the. The R.A.F.: Army and Navy: since 1937; ob. (E.P. in *The New Statesman*, Aug. 30, 1942, 'Glamour Boys—R.A.F., especially flying crews'.)

glamour gown. A khaki full-dress uniform: Australian soldiers': 1939–45. (B., 1943.)

glamour-pants. An attractive girl: since the late 1930's. In, e.g., Nicholas Montsarrat, *The Cruel Sea*, 1951.

glarney (or -**ny**). A corruption of *glassy* (q.v. at **glasser,** below): Cockney: late C. 19–20.

Glasgow boat. A coat: Anglo-Irish rhyming s.: late C. 19–20. (Franklyn, *Rhyming*.)

Glasgow Rangers; often shortened to **Glasgows.** (I spy) strangers: rhyming s.: since ca. 1920. Not, by the way, in Parliament, but at mock-auctions and other shady gatherings.

***glass.** An hour: c.: from ca. 1860; ob. B. & L. By abbr. of S.E. *hour-glass*.

glass, v. To hit with a tumbler or a wine-glass, esp. to cut a person with one: low: since ca. 1910. Mark Benney, *Low Company*, 1936. In Australia, since ca. 1920, it has borne the nuance, 'to slash a person with a piece of broken glass' (B., 1942.)

glass case. A face: rhyming s. (London streets'): 1857, Augustus Mayhew, *Paved with Gold*; app. † by 1914.

glass coach. See **Cinderella's coach** above. But this is coll. rather than s.

glass of beer. Ear: rhyming s.: since ca. 1880.

glass of something. An alcoholic drink: coll., orig. euphemistic: late C. 19–20. Elliptical for *glass of something strong*.

glasser; glassy. A glass marble with coloured centre: from ca. 1880: resp. Irish and London schoolboys'. The latter occurs also among New Zealand children: C. 20. (Ruth Park, *The Witch's Thorn*, 1952.) *Glassy* is also Australian schoolchildren's (B.P.) and usu. transparent.

glassy, n.—2. A smooth wave: Australian surfers': since ca. 1950. (*Pix*, Sept. 28, 1963.)

glaze, n., 1 (p. 332): still current 'on the road'. (Robert M. Dawson.)

glib-gabbed or -**gabbet.** 'Smooth and ready of speech': nautical: mid-C. 19–20; ob. B. & L.

gliding angle of a brick, usually preceded by **it has the.** It glides badly: R.A.F.: since ca. 1950. (R.A.F. officer, 1963.)

glim, v.—2. To look (*for* a taxicab): London taxi-drivers': since ca. 1905. Herbert Hodge, *Cab, Sir?*, 1939. Ex sense 1 (C. 20 nuance) of the n.: see p. 332.

***glim, on the.** (Adj. and adv.) A-begging: c., mostly tramps': C. 20. Cf. **glimmer,** 3, in *Dict.*

glim the devils. To light the coke fires: show-men's: since ca. 1870; by 1950, ob. (*John o' London's,* March 4, 1950.) Cf. *glim,* v., on p. 332.

glimmer.—4. (Prob. originating ex sense 3.) A match-seller (in the street): police s.: C. 20. Joseph F. Bradhurst, *From Vine Street to Jerusalem,* 1937. Cf. sense 1 (p. 333).—5. (Ex 3.) A teller of hard-luck stories: c.: since ca. 1920. Stanley Jackson, *Soho,* 1946.—6. (Ex 1.) A switchman's lantern: Canadian railroadmen's (— 1931).

glimmie glide, usually preceded by *far* or *other.* Side (of, e.g., the dog-track or street, etc.): Anglo-Irish rhyming s.: C. 20. Franklyn, *Rhyming.*

glint (at), take a. To have a look (at): C. 20. on familiar S.E. *take a squint at.*

glitch. A malfunction in a spacecraft, a Space 'gremlin': since 1964. (B.B.C. T.V.1: Oct. 20, 1965.)

globe, miss the. See **miss the globe.**

gloik. A simpleton; a fool: Australian: since ca. 1910. (B., 1953.) Ex Irish *gloichd*, an idiot.

glooms, the. A mood, a fit, of depression; gloominess, despondency: Anglo-Irish: late C. 19–20. James Joyce, *Ulysses,* 1922, 'I'm not going to think myself into the glooms about that any more.'

glop. An underwater explosion: depth-charge; mine; near-miss explosion: Naval: 1939 +. Echoic.

glorio. The pantry of the College servants ('scouts') at Christ Church: Oxford: ca. 1815-70. *Spy,* 1825. Prob. a corruption of *glory-hole*: cf. **glory-hole,** 5 (p. 333).

glorious sunset. Ham and eggs: Naval stewards': since ca. 1910. *Sunday Chronicle,* March 1, 1942.

glory. Death by accident; a string of empty cars: Canadian railroadmen's (— 1931).

glory be! A U.S. c.p. adopted by Canadians ca. 1910. Expressing astonishment. Short for *glory be to God!*

glory be to Pete! A Canadian c.p., expressing mild astonishment. 'Said to be confined to the Canadian prairies and to date from some time about 1925. My informant, James A. Dulmage, was living on a farm in Saskatchewan. His mother often used the c.p.: "Glory be!" and the farm hands and neighbours often said "For the love of Pete!" A central European working girl in their service, who spoke little English, combined the two phrases into "Glory be to Pete!" This so amused all concerned that they adopted the new c.p. and it still flourishes. (I have heard it myself.—I have bothered you with all this because it is so seldom that the origin of a c.p. can be determined precisely.)' Dr Douglas Leechman, May 1959.

glory-hole.—6. 'The bar of an R.A.F. sergeants' mess at Karachi was, ca. 1928–39, known as *the glory-hole*' (W/Cdr A. F. Wild, letter of Aug. 4, 1945); and prob. elsewhere.

gloss off, take the; gen. as c.p., **it takes** . . . It lessens the profit or the value: tailors': mid-C. 19–20. B. & L.

glossies. Glossy-paper magazines: adopted, ca. 1945, ex U.S.; by 1950, coll. Cf. the Canadian *slicks*.

glue-pot.—4. A convivial public-house: pub-frequenters': from ca. 1880; ob. Ex its 'fly-paper' attractiveness. (*The Sunday Times*, Johannesburg, May 23, 1937.)

gluttony. Willingness to take, fortitude in taking, punishment: pugilistic: ca. 1810–60. *Boxiana*, 1818 (see **game**, n., 7).

gnaff or **n'aff.** A low, irritating, no-account fellow, in averse from petty theft or from informing to the police: low Glasgow: mid-C. 19–20. Cf. Parisian s. *gniaffe*, a term of abuse for a man; prob. of same origin as **gonnof** on p. 341. (Communicated, as usage, by my friend Angus Scott, the black-and-white artist and portrait-painter.)

gnamma hole. A native (Aboriginal) well: Australian coll.: since ca. 1910. (B., 1943.) Aboriginal.

gnat. Naval s.: see **foxer.**

gnat's piss, have blood like. To feel (very much) afraid: low: C. 20.

go, n.—14. Coïtion, or rather an occasion thereof: low: mid-C. 19–20. Ex senses 5–7.—15. An iguana, via *goanna*: Australian rural: since ca. 1910. (B., 1943.)—16. A *near go* is an escape: Australian coll.: since ca. 1915. (H. Drake Brockman, 1947.) Cf. senses 5 and 6: p. 334.

go, v.—12. (Ex sense 5.) 'How do they go?' —as a character asks in Humfrey Jordan, *Roundabout*, 1935: How do they get along together?: upper class: late C. 19–20. Ex a pair of carriage horses.—13. To deal with; to find acceptable: English (? mostly Cockney) s., since ca. 1910; by ca. 1925, also Australian. '"I'll bet you could go a cup of tea, Sonny," I asked' (*Caddie, A Sydney Barmaid*, 1953).—14. To fight (v.i.) with one's fists: Australian: since ca. 1920. (Dick.) Cf. sense 11 on p. 334.

Sense 5 (p. 334) may have been current since ca. 1690, for in B.E., 1699, we find '*It won't Gee*, it won't Hit, or go'.

Sense 6 (p. 334), may, after all, have orig been English, for it occurs in *The Night Watch*, 1828, 'At grog-time there was nothing but wives and sweethearts going, and reckoning up our pay.' (Moe.)

go, all at one. Completed without interruption: coll.: from ca. 1880.

go, give a. See **give a go.**

go, no (p. 334): earlier in J. H. Lewis, *Lectures on the Art of Writing*, 7th edn, 1816; prob. dating from ca. 1810 at latest.

go, on the, 1 (see p. 334), survived until ca. 1850 in nuance '(of a tradesman) about to abscond': *The London Guide*, 1818, in form *upon the go.*

***go abroad.** To be transported: ca. 1825–1900: c. >, by 1860, low. B. & L. Cf. **abroaded** in *Dict.*

go-ahead. An advance agent: circus folk's: Nov. 16, 1861, *All the Year Round*; † by 1920.

go all out. See **all out,** 7, on p. 9.

go all the way. (Of a girl) to permit intercourse as well as 'petting': Canadian coll.: since ca. 1920.

go all unnecessary. See **make go . . .**

go along with you! A variant (mid-C. 19–20) of *get along with you!* (p. 324).

go and bag your head! A c.p. invitation to 'shut up' and go away: Australian: since ca. 1920. (B.P.)

go and bust yourself! 'You be blowed!': low: from ca. 1860; ob.

go and fetch the crooked straight-edge or **round square** or **rubber hammer** or **wall-stretcher.** See **crooked straight-edge.**

go and fuck yourself! A low equivalent of 'You be blowed!': from ca. 1880.

go and get cut! Go to hell: Australian: C. 20. B., 1942.

go and get your brains examined! A c.p.—since ca. 1925—addressed to someone arguing foolishly.

go and get your mother to take your nappies off!; or, **go and get your nappies changed!** Working-class girls' reply to callow youths' *does your mother know you're out?*: C. 20.

go and piss up a shutter! A low semantic variant of *go and jump in the lake!*, Run away!: since ca. 1910.

go and piss up your kilt! Rudely synonymous with 'No!': mostly Forces': since ca. 1939.

go and ride yourself! 'Go and take a running jump at yourself!': low c.p. (? esp. Merseyside): since ca. 1940.

go and scrape yourself! A contemptuous c.p. comment or reply: low: from ca. 1880; ob. Pugh (2).

go and see a taxidermist! See **taxidermist.**

go and take a crawling—or creeping—jump at yourself! A c.p., 'shouted derisively or in contempt to a crawler or a "creep"' (A. B. Petch, May 1966—'only rarely heard'): since ca. 1920. Adaptation of next.

go and take a run against the wind! Go away: Anglo-Irish c.p.: C. 20.

go and take a running jump at yourself! Go away!; Don't bother me!: c.p.: since ca. 1910.

go-ashore! Current at least as early as 1834. B., 1941.

go at. To deal vigorously with (something): ? late C. 18–mid-19. 'They can "go" at the bottle, and "stick" at the table till "all's blue"': John L. Gardner, *The Military Sketch-Book* (II, 28), 1831. Moe.

go away.—2. A train; a tram; a bus: Australian: since ca. 1920. Baker.

go(-)back, n. A reply; a retort: Australian: since ca. 1921. Lawson Glassop, 1944, '"You had a go-back?" I asked, "You didn't let him get away with it?"' Cf. *come-back.*

go back and cross the T's. A c.p. ironically directed at a helmsman that has 'written his name' by steering an erratic course: Naval: since ca. 1920. Granville.

go Ballarat. To drink alone: Australian: ca. 1890–1930. (B., 1943.)

go bang is the intransitive form of **bang,** v., 3 (p. 31): Australian: since ca. 1920.

go beyond. To be transported as a convict: Anglo-Irish: ca. 1810–70. Wm Carleton, *Rory the Rover,* 1845, 'You will *go beyant,* and no mistake at all' (i.e. beyond the sea).

go bush. To retire to the bushes in order to relieve nature: Canadian railway workers': from before 1909.—2, 3. See **bush, go,** above.

go-by (p. 335). Earlier in T. Fuller, *The Holy State,* 1642. (O.E.D.)

go by Walker's bus. To go on foot: non-aristocratic: from ca. 1870; very ob. B. & L. Cf. **Walker.**

*****go case with.** To go to bed with: since ca. 1910: c. that, by 1940, had > low s. (Norman.)

*****go caso.** To take a room or a flat and become a genteel prostitute: C. 20: c. >, by 1935, low s. 'He only married her for her money, and she got it going caso,' Gerald Kersh, *Night and the City,* 1938. See **caso.**

go chicken. See **chicken out** above.

go cold at. To reprove, blame, reprimand: Australian: since ca. 1925. (B., 1943.)

go cold on. To lose one's initial enthusiasm for (an idea, a plan, etc.): coll.: since ca. 1920.

go crawl up a hole! A dismissive c.p.: Australian, esp. Sydney: since ca. 1945.

go dog on. To fail (a person); to betray: Australian: late C. 19–20; by 1960 †. (G. B. Lancaster, *Jim of the Ranges,* 1910.) Cf. *dingo,* n., 2 and 3.

*****go down.** To rob (someone): since ca. 1880: c. until C. 20, then low s. *Sessions,* June 27, 1901, 'I was along with two men, and they *went down a man':* i.e. down into his pockets.

go down, v.i. To give birth to a child: C. 20. It occurs, e.g., in Ada E. Jones, *In Darkest London,* 1926, 'The girls who were with me waiting to go down.'

go down like a lead balloon; esp., *it will go,* or *it went, down . . .,* it won't, or it didn't, go down very well with him; he won't, or didn't, like that very much: R.A.F.: since the late 1940's.

go down on one's bended. To pray (on one's knees): coll.: since ca. 1925.

go for.—3. To act as; to become: coll.: since ca. 1920. Angus Wilson, *A Bit off the Map,* 1957, 'I'm well made all right. I could go for a model if I wanted.' Cf. sense 1 (p. 335).

go for a Burton—a shit. See **gone for** . . .

go for broke. To 'try to crash through the soup' (*Pix,* Sept. 28, 1963): Australian surfers': since ca. 1960. *Broke* = *broken* waves.

go for it. (Of a girl) to be extremely eager for sexual intercourse: Australian: since ca. 1925.

go for one's quoits. To run, to work, at one's fastest and best: Australian: since ca. 1925. (B., 1943.)

go for the doctor. To ride (a horse) fast: Australian rural: since ca. 1910; by 1960, slightly ob.

(B., *Australia Speaks,* 1953.)—2. To bet heavily on a horse in the expectation (? hope) of winning a lot of money: Australian sporting: since ca. 1930. (Lawson Glassop, *Lucky Palmer,* 1949.)

go for the lick of one's coit (? quoit). To run at top speed: Australian: since ca. 1920. (Jon Cleary, *The Sundowners,* 1952.) Origin?

go for to (do, etc.) on p. 335, occurs earlier in Thomas J. Williams, *A Cure for the Fidgets* (a one-act farce), 1867, 'My husband didn't go for to do it, sir' = didn't do it. It occurs even earlier in William Maginn, *Whitehall* (p. 46), 1827, 'You may go for to ax my character at Mr Robins'. (Moe.)

go for you in a big way!, I could. A between-men c.p., imputing effeminacy or softness: since ca. 1942.

go foreign. To go on an overseas commission: Naval officers': since ca. 1925. (P-G-R.)

go high. Same as **decorate.**

go-in.—3. A difference of opinion, a row: low Australian: since ca. 1920. (Kylie Tennant, *The Joyful Condemned,* 1953.)—4. An agreement, a partnership: Australian: since ca. 1930. (B., 1943.)—5. A run of bad luck, necessitating recourse to the central pool: Australian dominoes-players': C. 20. (B., 1953.)

go in a buster. See **buster, go in a.**

go into a flat spin.—2. Hence, *go or get into . . .,* to know not which way to turn, to become flustered: esp. in the Services and chiefly in the R.A.F.: since ca. 1937. *The English Digest,* Feb. 1941; H. & P. 'A flat-spin is very much harder to recover from than a nose-down one' (Flying-Officer Robert Hinde, letter of March 17, 1945).—3. Hence, to panic: Services': since ca. 1942.

go into cahoots with. Informally to get into touch with (someone): since ca. 1945. American influence.

*****go into smoke.** To go into hiding: Australian c.: C. 20.

go into the kitchen. See **kitchen, go,** . . .

go it, 1 (p. 336): earlier, in reference to two boxers fighting vigorously, in J. H. Lewis, *The Art of Writing,* 7th edn., 1816.

go it blind.—2. To drink heavily: Cockney: late C. 19–20. In, e.g., A. Neil Lyons, *Clara,* 1912.

go it, Ned. A Naval c.p. of (?) ca. 1810–40. It occurs in W. N. Glascock, *Sailors and Saints* (II, 117), 1829. Moe.

go lemony at. See **lemony.**

go like a bomb. See **bomb, go like a,** above.

go, man, go! A jazz c.p.: adopted, ca. 1948, ex U.S. '*Gone* is what logically becomes when one obeys the command "Go, man, go!"' (Atkinson.) Cf. '*Go!*—exhortation to dig, get with it, swing' (*The Victoria Daily Colonist,* April 16, 1959, 'Basic Beatnik'): Canadian, hence also English. See esp. Norman D. Hinton in *The American Dialect Society,* Nov. 1958.

go much on, not. Not to care much for; to dislike: New Zealand coll.: C. 20. (Jean Devanney, *Lenore Divine,* 1926.)

go mulga. To take to the bush; hence, to decamp, to seek solitude: Aus.: C. 20. (B., 1959.) Cf. **bush, go,** 2 and 3, above.

go muzzy. To bid *misère* in solo whist: esp. Merseyside: C. 20.

go off, v.—7. A horse either 'fixed' or confidently expected to win is said to 'go off': Australian sporting: since ca. 1910. B., 1942.—8. A hotel, a club, raided by the police for serving liquor after hours is said to 'go off': Australian urban: since ca. 1925. Baker.—9. To 'come' (sexually): coll.: C. 20.—10. To *go off* to prison, be sent to gaol: Australian: since ca. 1910. (Gavin Casey, *It's Easier Downhill*, 1945.)—11. Hence, merely to be fined, esp. for gambling, as in Lawson Glassop, *Lucky Palmer*, 1949.

go off at is the Australian variant (late C. 19–20) of **go off on** (*Dict.*). Baker.

go off the boil. Of a pregnant woman: to cease, temporarily, to feel the contractions and pangs of childbirth: medical students': since ca. 1910.—2. Of a woman: to lose, temporarily or momentarily, the desire for intercourse: raffish and mainly Australian: since ca. 1920.

go on about; be always on about. To complain of or about; (*be . . .*) to do this habitually: coll.: since ca. 1880. Cf. **on at.**

go on pump. To desert from the Foreign Legion: cosmopolitan: C. 20.

go on the box. See **box, on the.**

go on the bum. To go begging, esp. if habitually: adopted, ca. 1900, ex U.S. Cf. **bum,** n., 1 (p. 106).

go on the Cousin Sis. See **Cousin Cis.**

go on the piss. See **piss, go on the.**

go one's hardest. To do one's utmost: Australian coll.: C. 20. (D'Arcy Niland, *The Shiralee*, 1955.)

go out. To fight a duel: (? mostly Army) coll.: late C. 18–mid-19. George R. Gleig, *The Subaltern's Log-Book* (II, 214), 1828. Moe.

go over.—4. (Ex sense 1: p. 336.) To become a sexual pervert: Australian: since ca. 1910. B., 1942.

go over the side. To commit a first offence: police: since ca. 1918. Cf. *over the side* (p. 594).

go places. To travel extensively, or merely to gad about: coll.: adopted ca. 1938 from U.S. Often *go places and see things.*

go round the buoy is the full phrase; not—as on p. 110—*round the buoy.*

go round the corner. See **corner, go round the.**

***go sideways.** To engage in a criminal enterprise: c.: from ca. 1890; ob. Clarence Rook, *The Hooligan Nights*, 1899. 'Young Alf recounted this incident in his career, in order to illustrate his thesis that if you want to go sideways you have got to have your tale ready to pitch.'

go slumming. To mix with one's inferiors: jocular coll.: since ca. 1905. (Vernon Bartlett, *No Man's Land*, 1940.)

go snogging. See **snogging.**

go spare. To become distraught, esp. 'mad', with anger: Forces': since ca. 1935. (Atkinson.) By 1950, also fairly general civilian, as in Norman.

go steady. (Of juveniles) to be constantly together as boy-and-girl companions; to be a courting couple or one member thereof: coll.: Canadian: since ca. 1945. (Leechman.) By 1955, fairly common expression in England. Cf. *steady*, n., on p. 826 and in Addenda.

go take a flying fuck at, or **of, a galloping goose!** Beat it!: Canadian Army: 1939–45.

go tats. To go out (for an outing): children's, mostly Cockneys': C. 20. Ex **go ta-ta's** (*Dict.*).

go the bundle on. To support strongly; plump for; be enthusiastic concerning: naval: C. 20. Lit., go the whole lot on, stake one's all on; perhaps cf. *go nap on*, but prob. cf. **bundle,** n., 1—q.v.

in *Dict.* An early example occurs in 'Bartimeus', *A Tall Ship*, 1915. (Ramsey Spencer.)

go (or last) the full distance. To last the scheduled number of rounds in a contest: boxers' coll.: from ca. 1910; by 1940, S.E. (*The Times*, Nov. 24, 1936.)

go the gamble. See **gamble . . .**

go the knock on. To steal (something): low Australian: since ca. 1910. (D'Arcy Niland, *The Big Smoke*, 1959.)

go the knuckle. To fight—esp. if well—with one's fists: Australian: since ca. 1920. (Jean Devanney, *By Tropic Sea*, 1944; D'Arcy Niland, *The Shiralee*, 1955.)

go the limit. In courting or love-making, to achieve or permit coïtion: since ca. 1916.

go the whole pile. See **whole pile, go the.**

go through.—3. V.i., to abscond on bail: Australian c.: C. 20.—4. (v.i.) To give up, cease, desist: Australian: since ca. 1925. (Jean Devanney, *By Tropic Sea and Jungle*, 1944.)—5. To desert (from the Forces): Australian: since 1939. (B., 1943; Jon Cleary, *You Can't See round Corners*, 1949.)

go through for. '"He's going through for law": Canadian and U.S. Means he is taking a course of study in law (or medicine, or what else). Ex going through the university.' (Leechman.) Coll., not s.; since ca. 1935.

go through for the doctor. A variant of **go for the doctor** (sense 2) above. Lawson Glassop, *Lucky Palmer*, 1949.

go through on. To leave; give the slip to: see no more of (a person): Australian: since ca. 1920. Lawson Glassop, *We Were the Rats*, 1944. 'We'll go through on them two milk-bar sorts.'

go through the gate. To let the throttle full out, strictly in an emergency, with the use of *emergency power*: R.A.F.: since ca. 1937. E. P. in *The New Statesman*, Sept. 19, 1942; Robert Hinde, letter of March 17, 1945, 'This means literally to push the throttle through a small projection on the side of the groove in which it operates. Sometimes the gate takes the form of a breakable wire. Used only for emergency power, not synonymous with *turn up the wick*.'

go through the motions. To conform, whether in spirit or, esp., only in the letter, e.g. at church: since ca. 1950. (A. B. Petch, March 1966.)

go through without a water-bag. To be in a tremendous hurry: Australian: C. 20. (B., 1943.) In *The Drum*, 1959, B. records it as *the* not *a*, and declares it †.

go to a hundred feet. To sleep (very) deeply: submariners': since ca. 1939. (G. Hackforth-Jones, *Submarine Alone*, 1943.) Ex a submarine's submersion.

go to grass.—2. See **grass, go to,** in *Dict.*—3. To fall sprawling: pugilists': from ca. 1840; ob. B. & L.

go to Hell or Connaught! More precisely, 'Go where you like but don't bother me with where you're going!'

go to market. To kick up a fuss; cut a dash, let off steam: Australian coll.: C. 20. (K. S. Prichard, *Working Bullocks*, 1926: of a spirited stallion not yet fully trained to the saddle.)

go to see some friends. See **die.**

go to the movies. To go into action: R.A.F.: adopted in 1940 from American airmen. *The Reader's Digest*, Feb. 1941.

go to the top of the class! A c.p. remark to one who has made a quick and accurate answer: English and Canadian: since ca. 1948.

go tots. See **going tots.**

go up.—3. (Of a trotting horse) to change gait or pace: Australian sporting coll.: C. 20. B., 1942.

go up a gully. (Of a person) to vanish; get out of the way, make oneself scarce: Northern Territory, Australia: since ca. 1920. Ernestine Hill, *The Territory*, 1951.

go up a tree. See **ride up a gumtree.**

go up the Noo. To go on leave to Edinburgh— or to Scotland in general: Naval: C. 20. Granville.

go up the Smoke. To go on leave to London: Naval: C. 20. Granville. See **smoke,** n., 2.

go upon the dub. See **dub . . .**

Go When Ready. A railwaymen's nickname for the Great Western Railway: C. 20. (*Railway*, 3rd.)

go wide. See **wide, go.**

goalie (p. 337). Also in ice-hockey: Canadian: since ca. 1910.

goanna (*Dict.*). Note the following from *Australian Encyclopedia* (Angus & Robertson, 1927), Vol. I, p. 752: 'The Varanidae (monitor lizards) are in Australia popularly called goannas; this word is a corruption of "iguana", but—since the true iguana is not found in Australia—has been adopted as an independent name for Australian monitors.' *Goanna* therefore is no longer coll., as *iguana* is a mere misnomer. Rather a queer instance of change of status.—2. A piano: Australian rhyming s.: C. 20. B., 1942.

goanna, mad as a. Extremely stupid: Australian: since ca. 1910. Baker. Goannas are neither very spry nor very bright.

goat.—3. *Sinks*, 1848, s.v. 'stern', defines *the goat* as 'posteriors'—very much earlier than one had thought!—4. A fool: coll.: late C. 19–20. Cf. **nanny-goat** (p. 550).—5. Hence, a 'mug', a dupe: South African c.: C. 20. (J. B. Fisher, letter of May 22, 1946.)—6. A yard engine: Canadian railroadmen's (— 1931). Ex all the 'butting' it has to do.—7. A horse having no chance of winning: Australian sporting: since late 1940's. (Culotta.) Cf. **crab,** n., 10, above.

goat gunner. A mountain gunner: Regular Army, esp. in India: late C. 19–20; ob. by 1946.

goat-heads. See **blindy-eyes.**

goat's toe, be the. To be pre-eminent: Anglo-Irish: since ca. 1920. Applied, e.g., to James Stephens soon after his death in 1951. On the analogy of *the cat's whiskers* and with special reference to a mountain goat's sure-footedness.

gob, n.—4. An American sailor: adopted in 1940 from Canadians. H. & P. Ex sense 1?

***gob, the.** (Cf. **the wash.**) Theft from a man as he is washing at a public lavatory: c.: C. 20. Ex **gob,** mouth: the thief spits on the back of a man's coat, steers him to a lavatory, helps remove his coat and robs him of his wallet.

gob-shite. A fool; an easy dupe: Services: C. 20.

gob-spud. A lower-class term, dating from ca. 1870. Thus in Neil Bell, *Crocus*, 1936: ' "Not seen a gob-spud before, my boy?" went on the old man; "how d'y' think I shave with all m' grinders gone and no more suet to my chops than Welsh mutton?" He opened a cavernous mouth, popped in the potato and pointing to his now well-rounded cheek mumbled . . . "That's what a gob-spud's for, my boy." '

gob(-)stick. Sense 2 is also Canadian (ex U.S.). —3. A bridle: Australian rural: late C. 19–20. B., 1942.—4. A clarinet: Australian musicians': C. 20. Baker.

gobble, n.—4. Fellatio: low: C. 19–20.

gobble, v. To work overtime—esp., excessive overtime: printers': C. 20. Hence *gobbling,* n., (excessive) overtime.—2. To commit fellatio or penilingism: low: C. 18–20. Cf. **gobble-prick** in Dict., and sense 6 of **gobbler.**

gobble Greek. To study and/or speak Greek: Cambridge undergraduates': from ca. 1855; ob. B. & L. Pun on *gabble Greek.*

gobbler.—5. An 'ER tank engine 2-4-2' (*Railway*, 3rd): railwaymen's: post-W.W. II.—6. A fellator or penilingist: low, and homosexual: C. 19–20. Ex **gobble,** v., 2.

Gobbles. Goebbels: Army: 1939–45. Michael Harrison, 1943.

gobbling, n. See **gobble,** v., above.

god, 3 (p. 338). Also, since ca. 1935, a 'blood' at Lancing where *god-box* = House Captain's room. Marples.

God-Almighty.—2. Sir Douglas Haig: Tommies': 1915–18. To the rank-and-file he often seemed to be omnipotent. (A. B. Petch, March 1966.)

God bless the Duke of Argyle!: p. 338. 'The derivation of this as I heard it as a boy is that his Grace erected posts on certain large tracts of land belonging to him where there were no trees or boulders and where sheep, in consequence of having nothing to rub against, were always getting 'cast'. The shepherds who were not uncommonly verminous used these posts to scratch their backs against and when doing so blessed the Duke.' (Andrew Haggard, Jan. 28, 1947.)

God-box. A church; a chapel: atheists': since ca. 1880. Ernest Raymond, *We, the Accused,* 1935.

God-forbid.—2. A Jew: rhyming s. (on *Yid*): late C. 19–20.—3. A hat: rhyming s. (on *lid*): late C. 19–20. Franklyn, *Rhyming,* for both (2) and (3).

God in the box. A radio set: since ca. 1939. Anthony Armstrong, *Village of War,* 1941. Ex authoritarian news-announcements.

goddess Diana (p. 338) was † by 1920 at latest.

godfer (p. 338). For etymology, read *God-forbid.*

Godge. Godalming: Charterhouse: from ca. 1880 (?). The School is situated on Frith Hill overlooking Godalming in Surrey.

godma. Godmother: familiar coll.: since ca. 1825. (A. Neil Lyons, *Hookey,* 1902.)

godown.—2. A kitchen: Anglo-Indian: late C. 18–mid-19. (George R. Gleig, *The Subaltern's Log-Book,* 1828, at I, 247.) Moe.

gods of cloth. The greatest (contemporary) tailors: tailors': from ca. 1860. B. & L.

God's quantity. See **any God's quantity** above.

God's Wonderful Railway. The Great Western Railway: railwaymen's ironic: C. 20. (*Railway,* 3rd.) Cf. **Go When Ready** above.

goer.—2. A horse being honestly ridden to win: Australian sporting: since ca. 1910. (Lawson Glassop, 1949.)—3. A member of the gang; 'one of the boys': Teddy boys': since ca. 1947. (Clancy Sigal, article 'The Punchers' Night Out', in *The Observer,* March 1, 1959.)—4. One who enthusiastically seeks sexual satisfaction: since late 1940's. Ex sense 1 on p. 339.

goes to the (or their) tails (, it, etc.**).** Strong drink arouses men's sexual appetites: c.p.: since ca. 1910.

goffer, n.—3. A blow, a punch: low: ca. 1870–1910. *Sessions*, Feb. 11, 1886, 'Graham called out "Hop him, give him a *goffer*" . . . I then received a blow on my left shoulder.' Cf. **goffer,** v.—p. 339.

gog-eye. A catapult: Australian children's: C. 20. B., 1942.

goggle-box. A television set: since ca. 1958. Hence, **goggler,** a persistent viewer, and **goggling,** n., persistent viewing.

goggle-eyed. See 'Epithets'.

goggled goblin; usually in pl. A British night fighter: R.A.F. (jocular): since ca. Oct. 1940. H. & P. Cf. **cat's eyes.**

goggler.—3. See **goggle-box** above.

goggling, n. See **goggle-box** above.

Goggo. A Goggomobil car: Australian: since ca. 1955. (B.P.)

gogh'leen. See **r'ghoglin.**

gogs. A motorcyclist's goggles: since ca. 1940. Ian Jeffries, *Thirteen Days*, 1958, but dealing with the year 1948.

Gogs, the. The (golf-course at) Gog Magog Hills, near Cambridge: Cambridge undergraduates': since ca. 1880.

going and coming. 'The two-way radio telephonic system. Thus, "Had a word with him on the going and coming,"' Jackson: R.A.F.: since ca. 1935.

going for a walk with a spade. See **bending drill** above.

going home. Of an elderly person 'well on the way down the hill of life': coll. (not necessarily euphemistic): since ca. 1910. (Petch.)

going recce, a. A reconnaissance made to determine 'the going' in the country ahead: Army: since ca. 1940. (P-G-R.) Cf. **recce.** Also, esp. in North Africa, *going shufty*. (Peter Sanders, 1967.)

going spare. Available and easily obtainable or even stolen, esp. of things not strictly private property and even for unattached girls: since ca. 1940. 'She is not going spare': engaged and therefore not fair game. (A. B. Petch.)

going through 'L'. A c.p., 'used of learner drivers, since they have to stand a lot from instructors and the police' (Petch): since ca. 1950. A pun on *hell.*

going to see a man about a dog. See **see a man** (p. 742 and Addenda).

going to the Smoke—to the Noo. Going on leave to London—to Scotland. Naval (lower-deck): C. 20. (P-G-R.)

going tots. Trespassing on railway sidings: London schoolchildren: 1890's. See **tot,** n., 5 (*Dict.*).

gold braid.—2. 'Lowerdeck collective noun for officers; cf. *brass*,' Granville: Naval coll.: C. 20.

golden ballocks. Applied to a man lucky in 'love' and at cards: Forces': since ca. 1935. Contrast **grey ballocks.**

golden chub. See 'Dupes'.

golden duck = king duck. A batsman so unfortunate as to get out, first ball, in both innings of a cricket match: the former, schoolboys' s.—since ca. 1960; the latter, cricket commentators'—since early 1950's. (Peter Sanders, mid-1965.)

Golden Eagle sits on Friday, the; the golden eagle lays its egg(s). Next Friday is pay-day; by

itself, *the g.e.* = the paymaster: Army and R.A.F.: since early 1941. H. & P. Ex the eagle on the American dollar. Here, *sits* is prob. a euphemism, the American Army's c.p. being *the eagle shits on payday.* (Robert Clairborne.)

golden handshake. A large gift of money to a departing director or important employee: coll.: since ca. 1950. A *richly gilded* farewell handshake.

golden rivet, the. What a sky-hook is to an airman, *the golden rivet* is to the seaman (R.N.); the latter, however, concerns an unrepeatable piece of folk-lore. It probably goes back to ca. 1860. —2. Hence, *penis erectus*: Naval: since ca. 1910. Cf. *porthole duff.*

goldfish.—2. '"Termorrer," said Eddie, "we oughter have some goldfish." Goldfish were herrings,' Lawson Glassop, *We Were the Rats*, 1944: Australian soldiers': 1941–2 at Tobruk.—3. Hence, tinned fish: Australian: since ca. 1943. (B., 1953.)

Goldfish Gang, the. The Fleet Air Arm: Naval: since ca. 1937.

golf widow. A wife isolated by her husband's zeal for golf: jocular coll.: from ca. 1920. On *grass widow.*

gollion. 'A gob of phlegm' (B., 1942): Australian: C. 20. Perhaps cf. **gollop** (*Dict.*).

golliwog. A caterpillar: Australian: since ca. 1920. B., 1942. In ref. to the numerous very hairy caterpillars found in Australia and ex their resemblance to a golliwog doll.—2. A 'fence' or receiver of stolen goods: low (verging on c.): since ca. 1930.

golliwogs (or gollywogs), the. Greyhound racing: since ca. 1910. Rhyming on *the dogs.*

Golly. 'For the average Tommy, black or white, any local, be he Arab, Indian, or Somali, is a "Goliy"—a marginally less insulting retread of the old-fashioned "Wog"' (John de St Jorre, 'The End of the Affair' in *The Observer* supplement of June 11, 1967): since ca. 1950. See **wog,** 1, below.

golly (gum). Chewing gum: Australian: since ca. 1944. (B., *Australia Speaks*, 1953.)

golly pot. A spittoon: Australian: since ca. 1945. (B., 1953.)

goluptious. See **golopshus** (*Dict.*).

gomer, 2. Usually, *gomers*, going-home clothes, via 'go-homers'.

gone.—3. Pregnant, as in 'She's six months gone': coll.: mid-C. 19–20.—4. Jazz-ecstatic: adopted, ca. 1948, ex U.S.—5. Hence, excellent: Merseyside teenagers': ca. 1960–5.

gone-by. One who belongs to a recently gone-by period, a 'has been': coll.: C. 20.

gone for a Burton. (Of persons) dead or presumed dead; hence, (of things) missing and, occ., (of persons) absent: R.A.F.: app. not before 1939. '"He's had it" and "He's gone for a Burton" indicate that he's been killed,' Sgt-Pilot F. Rhodes, private letter of Sept. 1942; *The New Statesman*, Aug. 30, 1942; H. & P., 1943; C. H. Ward Jackson, *It's a Piece of Cake*, 1943; esp. Partridge, 1945. In popularity it belongs to the exalted group formed by **bind,** *(he's* or *you've)* **had it, piece of cake, that shook him.** Lit., for a glass of the excellent Burton ale, rather than for a suit made by Montague Burton. With the lit. sense, cf. **go west** (p. 337), and with the derivative (merely absent; missing) cf. **up in Annie's room** (p. 14).

gone for a shit (with a rug round him). An Air Force synonym (1939 +) of the preceding phrase. (R. M. Davison, letter of Sept. 26, 1942; Sgt Gerald Emanuel, letter of March 29, 1945.) Ex a 'common-form' practice in Service hospitals. Normally the longer phrase merely implies no more than a long absence, but the shorter usually implies 'missing on operations', 'dead': W/Cdr Robin McDouall, April 12, 1945.

gone for six. Missing, killed: R.A.F.: since ca. 1930. Jackson. Cf. **hit for six.**

gone native. A man that has gone native: coll.: from ca. 1920. Alec Waugh, *Thirteen Such Years*, 1932, 'He seemed equally at ease with Mexican half-castes, niggers from the Southern States, and "gone natives" from God knew where.'

gone off his dip. Crazy, mad: low: ca. 1885–1920. Arthur Binstead, *Mop Fair*, 1905. Cf. *Dippy*.

gone to lift his lying (or lying on) time. An Anglo-Irish c.p., applied to a labourer recently dead: C. 20. (In, e.g., Patrick MacGill.)

gone to Moscow. Pawned: Australian: since ca. 1918. B., 1942. With a pun on *mosk* or *moskeneer*, 'to pawn'.

gone to the pack (p. 340) is also common in Australia. (B.P.)

gone with the wind. Disappeared, e.g. money or spouse: since late 1930's. Ex the world-famous novel and film.

gong, v. To ring a bell for a waiter: late C. 19–20. H. G. Wells, *Twelve Stories and a Dream*, 1903, 'He had just gonged: no doubt to order another buttered teacake.'—2. (Of the mobile police) to strike a gong in order to stop a motorist: since ca. 1925.

Gong, the. Wollongong, Sydney, Australia: mainly Sydneysiders': since ca. 1925. (B.P.)

gong, the Naffy. See **Naffy gong.**

gong girl. A girl 'picked up' by a motorist for dalliance in a lonely spot: since ca. 1930. *The Evening News*, Aug. 19, 1937.

gong-ridden. Heavily be-medalled: R.A.F.: 1940 +. See **gong** (p. 340).

gong team. 'A Fleet Air Arm Albacore with both pilot and observer D.F.C.s' (P-G-R): Naval: ca. 1940–4.

gonga. Anus: Services: C. 20. Origin? (P-G-R.) Short for *gonga-pooch.* It sounds like a Regular Army perversion of some Hindustani word.

gongers, the. A police patrol in cars: since ca. 1935. Richard Llewellyn, *None But the Lonely Heart*, 1943, '"Gongers up," he says. "Right behind us."' Cf. **gongster** (*Dict.*).

gongoozler. An idle, inquisitive person that stands staring for prolonged periods at anything unusual: canal-men's: late C. 19–20. L. T. C. Rolt, *Narrow Boat*, 1944. Lakeland word (see E.D.D.): arbitrary: cf. **goon,** 2.

gonio. A goniometer—a device used in radar: R.A.F.: World War II. 'One had to keep turning a knob which controlled it. In the depths of an uneventful night-bind, an operator would often be heard to sigh, "Gonio, gonio, wherefore art thou gonio?"' (my **browned off** correspondent: 1949). For those who think that Shakespeare is a race-horse or a greyhound, that lament parodies 'O Romeo, Romeo! wherefore art thou Romeo?'

gonner. Going to: a coll. so slovenly as to be a sol.: rare before C. 20. Victor Canning, *Polycarp's Progress*, 1935, '"Gonner be a frost before sunrise," said the stall-man.'

gons. Money: Australian: since ca. 1935. B., 1942. It's soon *gone?* Rather, *'gone's* soon as it's got'.

goo, n.—3. Hence, any semi-liquid or viscous stuff: Canadian: adopted, ca. 1912, ex U.S. (Leechman.) Mathews, *Americanisms*, has suggested a derivation ex *burgoo* (as on p. 110). Since ca. 1930, common in Australia. (B.P.)

goo, v.; also *goob.* 'To spit a gob of phlegm' (B., 1942): Australian: C. 20. Cf. **goo,** n. in *Dict.*

good!—2. Thank you!: Australian non-cultured: since ca. 1930. (B.P.) Ex 'That's *good* of you'?—3. 'Esp. used by children, its senses embrace everything from passable to excellent, e.g., "How are you?"—"Good!" "How's work?" —"Good!" "How's school?"—"Good!" "How's your family?"—"Good!": B., 1959. Not, of course, s.; a coll., dating from ca. 1930 or earlier.

good and if you can't be good, be careful,—be. See **be good!** in *Dict.*

good books.—2. As the Good Books—a pun on *The Good Book*, the Bible—it means '(a pack of) playing cards': *The Night Watch* (I, 71), 1828. Cf. **books,** 1, on p. 79. (Moe.)

good chit. See **have a good chit.**

good Christmas! A euphemistic blasphemy: since ca. 1925.

good doer. One who knows his way about; a clever arranger: Australian: since ca. 1910. B., 1942.

good eating. (Of a girl, a woman) very attractive: Australian: since ca. 1921. Baker. 'Darling I could *eat* you!'

good egg! See **egg,** 1 (*Dict.*).—2. Hence, that's fortunate!: C. 20.

good evening, Mrs Wood, is fourpence any good? A c.p., dating since ca. 1910; by 1947, slightly ob.

good for a giggle, often preceded by *it's.* It's good for a laugh: a 'c.p. rejoinder to indignant protest to third person; also a general stop-gap reply' (Laurie Atkinson, Sept. 11, 1967).

good fun (predicative). Good company; amusing, entertaining: coll.: C. 19–20.

good goods! 'A c.p. addressed to one who has donned a new suit; said with Jewish intonation and an industrious feeling of the quality of the cloth' (Leechman): Canadian: since ca. 1950.

good guts, the. The true facts: Australian: since ca. 1930. 'That just about gives you the good guts of our end of the street' (Dick).

good guy. A 'disc jockey': 1964 +. (D. F. Wharton, Oct. 24, 1964.)

good-ho is a variant of **good-o(h).**

good hunting! Popularised—perhaps generated —by Kipling's *Jungle Book*, 1894 (2nd, 1895).

good ink (p. 342) is also Australian. B., 1942.

good iron. (Of things) good; agreeable, desirable: Australian: C. 20. Baker. Not just 'any old iron'.

good—or bad—marble, have a. (Of a racehorse). To have a good, or a bad, position at the starting barrier: Australian racing: C. 20; by 1960, ob. (*The Sydney Morning Herald*, Aug. 8, 1964.)—2. Hence, of a person, to be (dis)advantageously placed: since ca. 1920; by 1960, ob. (B.P.)

good mixer. See **mixer** (*Dict.*).

good morning! have you used Pears' soap? (p. 342). This slogan first appeared in the late 1880's and almost immediately became a c.p.; by 1930, it was moribund; by 1950, dead, except among the aged. Devised by Thomas W. Barratt, a well-known advertising man, later the chairman of the Pears' soap company. (With thanks to Alexander McQueen: 1953.) Cf. *since when* (p. 771 and below).

good murder, a. A detective novel with a strong murder-plot: circulating library subscribers' coll.: since ca. 1925.

good night!—2. Since ca. 1920, however, the predominant sense has been 'That's the end' or 'That's finished it'. A significant adumbration (cf. that in sense 1 on p. 342) occurs in Shakespeare's *I Henry IV*, I, iii, 191–4:

Worcester. 'As full of peril and adventurous spirit
　　　As to o'er-walk a current roaring loud
　　　On the unsteadfast footing of a spear.
Hotspur. 　If he fall in, good night!'

good night, nurse! See **good night!** in *Dict.*

good-o(h)! Excellent!: Australian coll.: C. 20. Cf. **whack-oh!** Hence also adv.: **well.**

good-oh, adj. Excellent: Australian: C. 20—2. Hence, esp. in variant *G.I.B.*, good in bed, a c.p. common in the late 1940's and the 1950's: since ca. 1910. (B.P.)

good old England and **terra firma.** Railwaymen's ironic c.pp., applied to 'off the railroad, at trap points' (*Railway*): since ca. 1920.

*****good on the crack** or **the star.** See **star, good on the.**

good on you! Good for you; excellent!: Australian coll.: C. 20. Cf. *good for him!* (p. 341).

good Sams, the. The Sisters of the Good Samaritan: Australian Catholics': C. 20. (B.P.)

good shit would do you more good, a. A low c.p., addressed to one who says that he 'could do with a woman': late C. 19–20.

good show. See at **show, bad.**

good skin. A decent fellow: ? mainly Liverpool: C. 20.

good soldier never looks behind him, a. A c.p. reply to a critic of one's shoe-heels: since ca. 1915.

good sort.—2. A beautiful girl: low: from ca. 1920. Esp. of one not remarkably reluctant.—3. As a person attractive to the opposite sex, it is the opposite of *drack sort* and has the superlative *extra sort*: these are Australianisms current since ca. 1939 but general throughout Australia only since ca. 1945. The Australian *good sort* arises partly from *sort*, 1, but mainly from *good sort*, 1 (p. 342), influenced perhaps by *good sort*, 2. Sidney J. Baker, in his fascinating *Australia Speaks*, 1953 (a supplement to his valuable *The Australian Language*, 1945), has concentrated overmuch on the Australian senses: both *sort* and *good sort* owe something to non-Australian sources and usages. Australia, by the way, owes much to this New Zealander who in the 1930's settled in Australia; but then, so does his native land.

good thing.—2. (Of a person) easy to exploit or to swindle: Australian: since ca. 1910. Baker.

good(-)time Charley. 'A man whose sole interest in life and especially in women is to have a "good time", often at no expense to himself' (Leechman): C. 20. Cf. **handsome Harry** below.

good to the poor. See **poor, she's (very) good to the.**

good value. Worth having: Australian and New Zealand coll.: since ca. 1920. J. H. Fullarton, *Troop Target*, 1943, 'Wavell's pretty good value.'

good wicket. A profitable transaction or venture: Australian: since ca. 1919. Baker. The phrase reflects the Australian passion for cricket. Always in (be) *on a good wicket*. (B.P.)

good-willer. A person of good will: since ca. 1930. Sydney Moseley, *Gold Help America!*, 1952.

good yunting! 'Employed jocularly by costermongers as a means of wishing next-stall neighbour (and some regular, understanding customers) a merry Christmas, a Happy New Year, a pleasant Easter, and so on' (Julian Franklyn, Jan. 3, 1968): c.p.: since ca. 1918. Influenced by *good hunting!*

goodness me, it's No. 3. One of the consecrated c.pp. of the game of bingo: since ca. 1955.

goody!, or **goody-goody!** Good!: coll.: adopted. ca. 1937 from U.S. But in Australia ca. 1927. (Mills Franklin, *Old Blastus*, 1931.)

goodying, n. Doing good of the kind practised by a **do-gooder,** 2, above: since ca. 1959. (A. B. Petch, May 1966.)

gooey, n. 'A gob of phlegm' (B., 1942): Australian low: C. 20. Cf. **gollion.**

gooey, adj. Excessively sentimental; fatuous; infatuated: Services (esp. the Navy) by 1936 and civilians by 1944. Granville, 'He's gooey over the dame.' Ex **goofy.** Rather ex sense 2. Viscous or semi-viscous: since ca. 1938. Ex **goo,** n., 3, above.

goof, v.—2. To blunder: since ca. 1950. Ex *goof,* n., 1 (p. 343).—3. To watch T.V. intently: Australian: since late 1950's. (B.P.)—4. Mostly *be goofing,* as in 'While you're goofing . . . Watching the flying. Anyone who watches the flying is known as a goofer. Where you're standing now is a goofing position' (John Winton, *We Joined the Navy,* 1959): The Royal Naval College, Dartmouth: since ca. 1950.

goof balls (rare in singular). Drugs that, in pill or tablet form and whether taken alone or in a drink, produce exhilaration; some are dangerous. Canadian: adopted, ca. 1945, ex U.S. (Leechman.)

goof box. A television set: Australian: since late 1950's. (B.P.) Cf. **goggle-box** above.

goofa; esp. in *on the goofa,* 'on the boat' (for home or for overseas): R.A.F.: since ca. 1925. Jackson. I.e. *go for.*

goofer. A bumboat: Naval: since ca. 1925. Granville. Cf. **goofa.**—2. One who, in 1940–4, gaped at enemy bombers instead of taking shelter. A blend of **goof,** 1 (p. 343) + *gaper?*—3. A 'cat walk' in an aircraft carrier: Naval: 1939–45.—4. See **goof,** v., 4, above.

goofy, n. A surfer riding with his right (*not* left) foot forward: Australian surfers', esp. teenagers': since ca. 1960. *Sun-Herald,* Sept. 22, 1963. In full: *goofy-footer.* Ex **goofy,** adj.

goofy. Stupid; dull-witted and almost crazy; wildly crazy; excessively sentimental; (*goofy about*) infatuated with: since ca. 1935. Ex **goof,** 1 and 2 (p. 343).

goog. An egg: Australian: C. 20. B., 1942. —2. A simpleton; a fool: Australian: since ca. 1943. (B., 1953.)

googly. The definition might well be amplified. A googly is 'a slow ball, pitched fairly high, which may break either way and often upsets the batsman's conjecture' (E. V. Lucas).—2. Hence, an awkward question: Australian: since ca. 1925. (B., 1943.)—3. A single bomb dropped from an aircraft: Australian airmen's: 1939–45. (B., 1943.) Cf. *bosie*, 2.

Gook. A Japanese: Australian: since ca. 1942. (Dymphna Cusack, *Say No to Death*, 1951.)—2. A Korean (cf. *Noggies*): United Nations troops': ca. 1951–5 in Korea. Perhaps influenced by **goon**, but probably derived from Korean *kuk* (pronounced *kook*), 'used to convey the idea of nationality; e.g., in *Popkuk*, France, *Chungkuk*, China, etc.' (*Iddiwah*, July 1953.)—3. During the Korean War (1950–3), it was applied also to Formosans. Note that sense 1 is rare, † by 1960, possibly catachrestic. Note also that, orig., *Gook* was American s.—derived from the *Gugus* of the Filipino Insurrection of 1899—for a Filipino and that, during World War II, the Americans applied it also to other friendly peoples of the Pacific. (With many thanks to Barry Prentice.)

gook, give or **have** or **take a.** See **give a gook.**

Gooly. An inevitable nickname for men named Ball: Services': since ca. 1920. Cf. *gooly chit.*

gooly. See **goolies** (p. 343).—2. A stone, a pebble: Australian: since ca. 1925. (B., 1943.) —3. A galah: Australian: since ca. 1910 (?). (B., 1943.)

gooly, drop a. See **drop a ballock.**

gooly chit is a variant of **blood chit.** Jackson, 1943. Ex *goolies*, low s. for 'testicles'. 'A common form of native torture consists in the excision of a man's testicles' (Partridge, 1945).

goomp. A pipe (tobacco): South African schoolboys': C. 20. (A. M. Brown, letter of Sept. 18, 1938.) Ex Dutch, via Afrikaans?

goon. A recruit: Services, esp. in the West of England: since 1940. (H. & P., 1943.) In Flying Training Command, R.A.F.: a pupil: 1941 +. Not a dial. word; prob. ex:—2. A gaper; a very stupid fellow: since 1938 or 1939. Perhaps it blends *goof* and *loon*; American origin. From Alice the Goon in the Popeye cartoons.—3. Hence, a German: prisoner-of-war s.: 1940 +. (W/Cdr Robin P. McDouall, letter of March 17, 1945.)

goon bag. A respirator case: R.A.F.: 1939–45. Ex *goon*, 1. Occasionally *gallopers*.

goon-stick. An officer's swagger cane: Australian soldiers': 1939–45. (B., 1943.)

goon suit. A flak apron: Royal Canadian Navy: 1939–45.

gooner, give—get—the. To dismiss; be dismissed: low: since ca. 1925. James Curtis, *You're in the Racket Too*, 1937. ? Ex *go on!*

goonskin. 'Observer's flying suit and parachute harness made in one piece,' Jackson: R.A.F.: since ca. 1939. Prob. ex **goon** (2) + *skin*.—2. Battledress: Army: since 1940. (Peter Sanders.)

goose, v., 1 (p. 343). Earlier in *Sinks*, 1848.—7. The predominant post-World War II meaning is 'to jab a finger *in ano*, in order to surprise or to annoy': Canadian: since ca. 1910; adopted, ca. 1944, in Britain and Australia.

goose and duck. A truck: rhyming s.: C. 20.

goose bumps. See **duck bumps** above.

goose girl. A Lesbian: since ca. 1918. Ex the synonymous Fr. s. *gousse*. Recorded by Sir Compton Mackenzie in the 1967 number of his serial autobiography.

goose hangs high . . . (p. 343). In full:

everything in the garden is lovely, and the goose hangs high.

gooseberries.—2. A gooseberry-shaped wire-entanglement: Army: 1914–18.—3. Also *fruit machine*: 'old freighters sunk end to end off the Normandy beaches to provide artificial shelter for small boats,' Gordon Holman, *Stand By to Beach*, 1944: Naval: 1944–5.

gooseberry.—6. Short for **gooseberry pudden** (*Dict.*).—7. See:

gooseberry tart. Heart: rhyming s.: from ca. 1860. Often abbr. to **gooseberry.** (*The Daily Herald*, Feb. 22, 1937.)

gooser.—5. A pederast: low Canadian: C. 20.

goose's. See **sausage, v.**

goose's neck. A cheque: rhyming s.: app. not before 1950. Franklyn 2nd.

gooze. See **cruize.**

goozie or **gozzie.** A gooseberry: Australian: late C. 19–20. B., 1942. Cf. **goosgog** in *Dict.*

gopher. Any fizzy drink: Naval: since ca. 1930. Granville. Some kind of blend: ? 'good fizzy water (or fizz-water)'. Hence *gopher firm*: unofficial purveyors thereof. Like *goffer* and the sol. *Gotha*, *gopher* is incorrect for *goffa*, properly *Goffa*, a trade-name.

Gor' damn (p. 344): † by 1960. Franklyn 2nd at *Gah-damn*.

gorblimey. The *Dict.* entry needs to be supplemented, thus: 'Colloquial for what was considered loud dress; until the late 1950's applied to men's wide cap, with big projecting peak and vivid, often check, pattern; later, from popular song, to dustmen's trousers, etc.': Laurie Atkinson, Sept. 11, 1967.

gorbling. A soft cap with 'dented' front, affected by young subalterns: Army: 1914–18. An officers' variant of **gorblimey,** 2 (*Dict.*).

Gordelpus, three ha'porth of. See **three ha'porth** . . . in *Dict.*

Gordon and Gotch. A watch: rhyming: C. 20.

Gordon Thailanders. See 'Prisoner-of-War Slang,' 15.

gorgeous wrecks. Mr F. W. Thomas has kindly corrected me: *G.R.* meant 'Government Recognition'; and the early form of the phrase was *George's wrecks.* Also *Grandfather's Regiment.*

gorgonzola, n. The Africa Star: Army: 1943 +. Ex its yellow and blue streaks.

gorgonzola, adj. (Very) good: Australian: since ca. 1920. B., 1942. A very rich cheese.

Gorillas, the. Fitzroy footballers: Melbournites': since ca. 1920. (B., 1943.)

gorm, v.—2. To stare, gape, look long (and greedily) *at*, e.g., second-hand books: since ca. 1910. Anthony Berkely, *The Piccadilly Murder*, 1929. Ex dial, *gaum*, to stare idly, vacantly or stupidly.

gormagon (*Dict.*) is more prob. a blend of *gorgon* + *dragon*.

gormless. Stupid; slow-witted and lacking in common sense: adopted, ca. 1935, ex dial., the predominant dial. form *gaumless* being adapted. Yet, in 1966, Cassius Clay was proclaiming himself to be precisely that.

gosher. A heavy blow or punch: Cockney: ca. 1890–1914. A. Neil Lyons, *Hookey*, 1902, '"On his snitch I gave him such a gosher."' Echoic.

goss. A Cockney term, dating from ca. 1870 (? earlier) and perhaps influenced by s. *goss*, a hat (worn on one's top); perhaps, too, influenced by Kentish dial, *goss*, a rockling (esp. a sea-loach or whistle-fish: small and flat); thus in Pugh, 'All the gels stuck the winkles' gooses, as we call 'em (you know, them hard, round, brown, scaly things on top), they all stuck 'em on their chins for beauty-spots.'

gossage. A barrage balloon: R.A.F.: since 1940. *The New Statesman*, Aug. 30, 1941; Jackson, 1943, 'Named after Air Marshal Sir Leslie Gossage, K.C.B., C.V.O., M.C., Air Officer Commanding Balloon Command'; Partridge, 1945, 'With a pun on *sausage*' (ex the shape).

gossip pint-pot (p. 345). Cf. 'Peace, good pint-pot' in Shakespeare, *I Henry IV*, II, iv, 438.

Gossy. Gosport: Naval: late C. 18-20. (W. N. Glascock, *Sketch-Book*, II, 1826.) Moe.

got 'em all on. Dressed up 'to the nines': domestic servants': C. 20. (Eric Horne, *What the Butler Winked At*, 1923.)

got his. See **get his.**

got his crown up—got his warrant—he's. He has been promoted to the rank of Warrant Officer from that of Flight-Sergeant: R.A.F. coll.: since ca. 1920. Jackson.

got it off—got it all off—got it all off pat. I or you have, he or she has, learnt the lesson: a schoolchildren's c.p.: since ca. 1920.

got me, Steve? (p. 346). Recorded earlier; in, e.g., W. L. George, *The Making of an Englishman*, 1914.

got to swim under water to dodge it! See **getting any?** above.

got your eyeful? See **eyeful.**

got your ladder. See 'Prisoner-of-War Slang'. 14.

Goth.—2. 'A fool, an idiot' (*Sinks*, 1848): ca. 1825-70.

Gottfordommer; pl. in *-s.* See 'Prisoner-of-War Slang', 9. (Also with one *t.*)

gouge or **gouger.** To seek (for opal); an opal miner or seeker: Australian coll.: late C. 19-20. Archer Russell, *Gone Nomad*, 1936. Ex manner of extraction.

gove or **guv.** Given: illiteracy: C. 19-20. In, e.g., B. Farjeon, *Grif*, 1870.

Government bad bargain. A pensioner drawing his money for an inordinately long time: C. 20. Cf. *bad bargain* (p. 25).

government house (p. 346) is, in the N.T. of Australia, applied to the homestead of a head station: *teste* Ernestine Hill, *The Territory*, 1951.

goy (p. 347), a Gentile. 'This goes back beyond Yiddish to the Hebrew *goy*, meaning "nation". This "goy" is exactly analogous to "gentile", from *gens*' (Leonard Goldstein, April 6, 1967).

gra. See 'Colston's . . .'

grab hooks. Fingers: Naval (lower-deck): since ca. 1910. Granville. Cf. **grabbing irons** (p. 347).

grab leather. 'A cowboy who takes hold of the saddle horn while riding a bucking horse is said to grab leather; this disqualifies him if he is in competition' (Leechman): Canadian (? ex U.S.): since ca. 1925.

grab oneself a ball. See 'Jazz Slang'.

grabben gullen pie. A scooped-out pumpkin stuffed with opossum meat and then baked as an outback delicacy: Australian: since ca. 1910. (B., 1943.) The two mysterious words are

Aboriginal, perhaps folk-etymologised with *grab'em* and *gullet.*

grabber.—4. A conductor: Canadian railroadmen's (— 1931).

grabbling irons.—2. Knife, fork and spoon: Army: C. 20. (P-G-R.)

Grable-bodied seaman. 'A boat's crew Wren—after Betty Grable, the film star' (Granville): Naval: 1940 +.

grace before meat. A kiss: domestic: late C. 19-20. A preliminary.

Gracie Fields. 'Rochdale to Manchester parcels train' (*Railway*, 3rd): railwaymen's: since ca. 1930. Miss Fields, the famous actress and singer, was born at Rochdale.

gracious!, 'pon my. Gracious me!: mostly Cockneys': from ca. 1890. Pugh.

grad. A graduate: rare, except at University of Durham: late C. 19-20. (Marples, 2.) After **undergrad** (p. 925).—2. 'Among Cambridge landladies, ca. 1925, it was used (mostly in the plural) to denote *undergraduates*' (H. R. Spencer).

graft, n.—4. 'Food and lodging. Thus *good graft*—comfortable living,' H. & P.: Services: since 1939. Ironically ex sense 1 (p. 347).

graft, v.—5. As a 'grafter'—see **grafter,** 4, on p. 347—to sell (something): fair-grounds': C. 20. 'He had grafted the tubed stickem for years': W. Buchanan-Taylor, *Shake It Again*, 1943.

grafter, 4 (p. 347). Also, a man skilled in extracting money from a difficult 'audience' at a mock or rigged auction: mock-auction world: since ca. 1945. (*Sunday Chronicle*, June 28, 1953.) At these auctions, the 'trick' is to sell inferior goods at top prices: cf. *top man.*

gram. Gramophone: C. 20—2. *The Gram*, the local grammar school: schoolboys': late C. 19-20. Bruce Hamilton, *Pro*, 1946.

grammar school. See 'Tavern terms', § 3.

grammarian. See 'Tavern terms', § 3, *d.*

gramo studio. A gramophone studio: filmland: since ca. 1910. Cameron McCabe, *The Face*, 1937.

gramophone. A telephone: Canadian railroadmen's (— 1931).

gramp, n. Grandfather: Cockney: mid-C. 19-20. (A. Neil Lyons, *Clara*, 1912.) I.e. 'grandpapa' slurred.

grampus, blow the, 1, on p. 348, occurs as early as 1818. (Moe.) The dating of both senses should read 'ca. 1790-1918'. *The Port Folio*, Aug. 4, 1804, p. 246. (Moe.)

grand, n.—2. 1,000 feet: R.A.F.: since 1940. Jackson. Ex American c., where it = 1,000 dollars (a *grand* sum to acquire).—3. £1,000: adopted, ca. 1940, from U.S. Alan Hoby in *The People*, April 7, 1946.

grand serientry. See 'Tavern terms', § 9.

grand strut (p. 348). Also, ca. 1840-80, either Rotten Row or Bond Street: *Sinks*, 1848.

Grand Walloper, the. 'King of all the *gremlins*—their director of operations,' H. & P.: R.A.F.: 1940 +.

grandfather; grandmother, 2. The former is a grandfather clock (watchmakers' and second-hand dealers' coll.: late C. 19-20); the latter, too, with some slight difference in the size (s.: C. 20).

Grandfathers' Regiment. See **gorgeous wrecks.**

grandstand, v.; esp. as vbl n., *grandstanding*, playing to the gallery: Australian: adopted, ca. 1944, ex U.S. (B.P.)

granite boulder. (One's) shoulder: rhyming s.: since ca. 1870.

Granite Jug, the. Dartmoor Prison: since ca. 1930 (*Reynolds News*, Aug. 16, 1953). With a pun on *jug*, n., 1 (p. 446).

Granny.—3. See 'Nicknames' on p. 560.—4. Also, *The Old Girl: The Sydney Morning Herald*: Australian: C. 20. B., 1942. Long established, very respectable.—5. A Granny Smith apple: mainly Australian: since ca. 1920. 'Australia's most popular apple' (B.P.).

granny, n.—4. Nonsense, rubbish: Australian: ca. 1860–1914. 'Tom Collins', *Such Is Life*, 1903. Ex 2.—5. See **grandmother** (in *Dict.*).

grape—a toby—on, have a. To be ill, well, disposed towards: Australian: since ca. 1925. (Alan Marshall, *These Are My People*, 1946.) Perhaps ex sour grapes and toby-jugs full of beer. Cf. the next.

grape on the business, a. (Of a person that is) a 'wet blanket' on cheerful company; a bluestocking; a 'wallflower': Australian: since ca. 1925. B., 1942. Since the grape is usually and rightly regarded as a cheerful influence, *grape* is perhaps a perversion of *gripe*: cf. 'He gives me a pain in the belly' and *bellyful*.

grape-vine (p. 349). Julian Franklyn doubts its authenticity. (*Dict. Rhm. Sl.* – 1960.)

*****grapevine, the.** A secret means employed by the chiefs of the underworld to ensure rapid and trustworthy transmission of important news: c.: adopted ca. 1920 from U.S., where orig. in form *the grapevine telegraph* and not c.—2. Hence, the mysterious source of rumours: Services: 1939–45. 'I heard it on the grapevine.' (P-G-R.)—3. That haphazard network of rumour-mongers in the Services, in factories, in offices, which through Unit or Staff, transmits advance knowledge—often not inaccurate—of policy and of administrative decisions: since ca. 1945: s. that, by 1955, had > coll. Also, in this sense, *the bush telegraph*, a term that has radiated from Australia, where current since ca. 1890.

grapple. To shake hands with: Naval: ca. 1790–1850. W. N. Glascock, *Sailors and Saints* (I, 138), 1829. (Moe.)

grasp and grunt. An occ. variant of **grumble and grunt** (below). Franklyn 2nd.

grass, n., 5, was, by 1930, taxi-drivers' s.: Herbert Hodge, *Cab, Sir?*, 1939.—7. Same as **greens**, 4 (p. 353): late C. 19–20.—8. '*Grass* was the normal "picture" seen on certain types of radar cathode-ray tube, as distinct from the signals produced by aircraft, etc. It looked like waving grass' (correspondent): R.A.F.: World War II.

grass, v., 2 (p. 349), occurs also in sense 'to baffle completely' and much earlier: 1822. See **facer**, 3 and 4. (O.E.D.)

grass, burn the. 'To urinate out of doors' (B., 1942): Australian: C. 20.

grass, go to. See **go to grass.**

grass, on. (Of ore) waiting to be removed to a smelting factory: Australian: since ca. 1910. (Vance Palmer, *Golconda*, 1948.)

grass, on the.—2. (Of a criminal) free; at large: Australian c.: since ca. 1925. (B., 1943.)

grass, out to. (Of person) retired: Australian: late C. 19–20. Baker. Ex retired horses.

grass, send to (p. 349), originated in the old prize-fights waged in a field and was, therefore,

orig. boxing s. (*The Galaxy*, Oct. 1868, on p. 557.) Moe.

grass, take Nebuchadnezzar out to (p. 349). Nebuchadnezzar ate grass: *grass* = (female) pubic hair.

grass-fighter. A slugger, a brawler, a bruiser; a fighter not a boxer: Australian: since ca. 1930. (D'Arcy Niland, *Call Me . . .*, 1958.) One who, in a field, fights to the finish.

grass-hopping, n. Low flying, designed to baffle and beat flak: Australian airmen's: 1940–5. (B., 1943.)

grass in the park. An informer to the police: rhyming s. (on *nark*): C. 20. (Franklyn 2nd.) Very prob. suggested by **grass**, n., 5, 6: a characteristic elaboration.

grass line. 'Coir rope which floats on the surface of the water,' Granville: Naval coll.: C. 20.

grass park. A shortening of **grass in the park** above: since ca. 1930. Franklyn 2nd.

grasser. An informer to the police: London's East End: since ca. 1945. (Richard Herd, Nov. 12, 1957.) Ex *grass*, v., 5 (p. 349).

grasshopper, 2 (p. 349). In C. 20 Australia, a waiter at a picnic. B., 1942.—4. An Italian one-man torpedo: Naval: 1940 +.—5. (Mostly in pl.) One of the 90 XX Class locomotives: railwaymen's: post-World War II. 'Tendency to slip' (*Railway*).

grave.—2. A cricket crease: cricketers': late C. 19–20. Cf. **grave-digger, the,** 2 (p. 349).

grave noddy. See 'Men'.

grave-trap; occ. abbr. to **grave.** 'A large oblong trap in the centre of the stage, so called because "the fair Ophelia" is supposed to be buried there. Every fugitive draught in the theatre rises from the cellar through this opening' (B. & L.): theatrical: mid-C. 19–20.

gravel(-)basher; gravel(-)bashing. (One who has to participate in) *square-bashing* or marching, esp. as a recruit at squad drill, on the parade ground: Services, esp. R.A.F.: since ca. 1936. H. & P. Contrast **swede(-)basher.**

gravel-crusher. A drill instructor; a physical training instructor. Services: since 1940. H. & P.—2. But also a recruit, drilling on the parade ground. He proudly spurns the gravel.

gravel-digger. 'A sharp-toed dancer' (*Sinks*, 1848): ca. 1840–80.

gravel-grinder.—2. (Usually in pl.) A gunner's mate: Naval: C. 20. Granville.

gravel-grinding. 'We crawled all round the park in bottom gear—"gravel-grinding", as we call it,' Herbert Hodge, *Cab, Sir?*, 1939: taxi-drivers': since ca. 1915.

graveyard flying. Dangerously low flying: R.A.F. coll.: 1939–45.

graveyard shift. A night shift: shipbuilders' and munition workers': since ca. 1915. (*John o' London's*, June 18, 1943.) Cf. the Canadian railroadmen's (– 1931) *graveyard watch*: 12.01 a.m. to 8 a.m.

graveyard watch. The middle watch (from midnight to 4 a.m.): Naval: C. 20. Cf. preceding entry.

gravy.—2. Petrol: R.A.F.: since ca. 1940. Partridge, 1945. The 'plane's nourishment.—3. Perquisites: adopted, ca. 1943, from U.S.—4. See 'Jive'. But older than jive.—5. Any tinned food: Australian children's, esp. in N.S.W.: since ca. 1947. Ex the cartoons of Emile Mercier. (B., 1953, at p. 111.)

Gravy, the. The Atlantic: R.A.F. pilots', esp. of Coastal Command: since 1939. Cf. **Pond** (p. 647).

*gray, 1. (p. 350): Ex Romany *gry*, a horse; *gray* being suggested by the synonymous *pony* (see **pony, 5,** in *Dict.*). B. & L. In two-up, properly a two-tailed penny. The nuance 'two-headed or -tailed penny' arose ca. 1870. It occurs in Renton Nicholson, *An Autobiography*, 1860, at p. 87.—4. (Or *grey*.) A 'middle-aged, conventionally dressed/minded person' (Peter Fryer in *The Observer* colour supplement, Dec. 3, 1967): hippies' (1965 or 66) and Flower People's (1967). Adopted ex U.S. Negro derogatory s. for 'a white person'.

Grays, the. (Or *Greys*.) The officers of the old Northwest Fur Company: Canadian coll.: ca. 1815–1900. Ex their grey uniforms; as opposed to the sky-blue of the Hudson's Bay Company. (Leechman.)

grease, n., **5.** Also margarine: mostly Services: since 1939. H. & P. At Dalton Hall, Manchester, it = either butter or margarine: *The Daltonian*, Dec. 1946.

grease, v., **4** (p. 350) >, in the Army of 1914–18, 'to get away' (esp. by running).

grease monkey. A mechanic: (non-Civil) engineers': from ca. 1910. Common also in Australia. (B.P.)

grease one's skates. To get ready to go—and go, promptly and speedily: Aus.: since ca. 1920. Mary Durack, *Keep Him My Country*. 1955.

Greasepaint Avenue. Brixton, London: ca. 1880–1914. Naomi Jacob, *The Lenient God*, 1937, 'Because all the music-hall people had lived there.'

greaser.—7. In the Services, 1939–45, 'one who angles for time off' (H. & P.).—8. An engineering student: Australian universities': C. 20. (B.P.) Cf. sense 2 on p. 351.—9. A teenage rowdy with long, greasy hair: since ca. 1962.

greasy, n. A butcher: Australian: C. 20. B., 1942.—2. A sheep-shearer: Aus.: since ca. 1920. F. B. Vickers, *First Place to the Stranger*, 1955, ' "When those five greasies get moving they'll shear a lot of sheep." ' Ex the greasy wool.

greasy, adj.—3. Dirty, as in 'greasy chap': Cranbrook School: C. 20.

greasy pig. 'A bet laid on tails after a long run of heads, or vice versa' (B., 1953): Australian two-up players': since ca. 1925.

greasy spoon. A railroad eating-house: Canadian (— 1931). Adopted ex U.S.—2. Hence, almost immediately any small, dirty restaurant: Canadian. (Leechman.) Ex the state of the cutlery.

great, n. A great, or a (very) famous, person: coll.: since late 1940's. Elliptical for '*great* man' or '*great* woman'.

Great Australian Bight, the. George Street, opposite the Sydney Town Hall: Sydneyites'. Also, the busier end of Queen Street, Brisbane: Brisbaneites'. Both, C. 20. (B., 1942.) One is apt to get *bitten* there. The Bight itself can be very rough.

Great Bore War, the. See **bore war, the.**

Great Brown Bomber. A Lockheed-Hudson: Australian airmen's: ca. 1942–5. (B., 1943.)

great divide (or capitals), **the.** The cleavage between the female breasts as revealed by a low décolletage: Australian: since ca. 1930. Ex the

Great Divide, the Blue Mountains, of eastern Australia. (B.P.)

great gun, 1. At Eton, ca. 1815–50, it = 'a good fellow, a knowing one' (*Spy*, 1825).

great guns. An intensive adv.: Naval: since ca. 1790; by 1940, ob. Cf. **blow great guns** on p. 67 and 'growling great guns' in W. N. Glascock, *Sailors and Saints* (II, 51), 1829.

Great Harry, the. Any battleship not—for security reasons—mentioned by name: Naval: 1914 +. Presumably suggested by Henry the Eighth's flagship (ca. 1540)—*the Great Harry*, so named, of course, in his honour.

Great Horatio, the. Horatio Bottomley, one-time editor of *John Bull*, his heyday being 1914–18.

great-horn. See **fish-horn.**

great Jehoshaphat! See **great Cæsar** (*Dict.*).

great pot. A tipster: turf: ca. 1870–1914. B. & L.

Great Profile, the. John Barrymore (1882–1944), the famous film-actor. The father, Maurice (d. 1905), John's brother Lionel, and sister Ethel were, ca. 1900–45, known as *the Royal Family of Broadway*.

Great Push, the. The sustained, wide-fronted attack, July–Aug. 1916, on the Somme: Army, whence journalistic, coll.: contemporaneous; then—mostly ironical (for it was one long blood-bath)—historical. Patrick MacGill, *The Great Push*, 1916. But, much more generally, *the Big Push*.

Great Silent, the. The Royal Navy: derisive, occasional self-name: 1939–45. Ex journalistic 'the Silent Service'. (P-G-R.)

Great White Chief, the. Lord Northcliffe: journalists': late C. 19–20.—2. A head of department: Civil Service: since ca. 1910.

greatest, the. The best; adopted, ca. 1961, ex U.S. Wallace Reyburn, in the colour section of *The Sunday Times* of July 8, 1965, 'The Americans snigger at the British when they use words and phrases like these: *bobby-soxer*, *in the groove*, *aw shucks*, *jive*, *baloney*, *you can say that again*, *what's cooking*, *the greatest*. To American ears they are all so dated.'

greb. A North Country schoolboys' term of abuse: since ca. 1930. (*New Society*, Aug. 22, 1963, 'From the Blackboard Jungle'.) Origin?

Grec is a late C. 19–20 shortening of **Grecian, 3** (p. 352). Marples.

Grecian; Greek. See 'Tavern terms', § 3, *c*.

Greco. A Greek: Army in North Africa: 1940–3. Adopted from the Italians.

greedy but he (or **you** or **. . .**) **like(s) a lot, he** (etc.) **is not.** A c.p., imputing greediness: late C. 19–20.

greefa or **grefa.** A marijuana cigarette: beat-niks': adopted, ca. 1958, ex U.S. drug addicts. (Anderson.) Either a rhyme on **reefer** (below) or a punning blend of S.E. *grief* and s. *reefer*.

green, adj., **2** (p. 352). This sense fell into disuse by 1930 at latest, *green* having long been the 'sign' for safety or 'Proceed'.

green, n. More prob. *the greengage* is simply rhyming s.—2. At Sedgley Park School, ca. 1780–1870, coll. for a *green linnet*.—3. See **red,** n., 4.—4. An inexperienced or unworldly person: coll.: ca. 1830–90. (Francis Francis, *Newton Dogvane*, 1859.)

green, take it. See **take it green.**

green-back.—3. A £1 note: C. 20.—4. A frog for re-railing rolling stock: Canadian railroad-men's (— 1931).—5. A dollar bill (anglice, note): Canadian: since ca. 1905. From U.S.; the colour.

green boys. 'A new type of highly efficient armour-piercing shell that was designed in 1917 to replace the inefficient shell used at the Battle of Jutland. The vastly improved new 15″ would carry their bursters through 10 to 12″ plates whereas at Jutland the shell broke up on impact. The new shells were termed *green* boys because they were painted green. But they did not reach the fleet until April 1918' (Wilfred Granville): naval: 1918 onwards, but soon only historical.—2. 'Variant of *green stripers*, the officers of the Special Branch of the R.N.V.R. in W.W. II. Ex the coloured bands of green between the gold stripes of rank' (Wilfred Granville, letter of Feb. 15, 1967).

green cart, the. That mythical vehicle in which people are conveyed to a lunatic asylum: Australian juvenile: since ca. 1920. (B.P.)

green coat, wear the. 'To act the innocent—a ruse tried by new entries who plead ignorance' (Granville): Naval: since ca. 1910. *Greenness* = inexperience.

green fingers, have. To be a successful gardener; to succeed, as an amateur, with one's flowers and vegetables: coll.: since ca. 1925. Coined by the late Mr Middleton, B.B.C. broadcaster and news-paper writer on gardening. Less usual: *a green thumb*. Perhaps the phrase was merely popular-ised by Mr Middleton, for various trustworthy correspondents place it at ca. 1910, at latest, but probably a generation earlier. 'I think the original was "a green thumb", probably by analogy with the miller's "golden thumb" (as in Chaucer)': Professor F. E. L. Priestley, 1965.

green-grocery (p. 352). More prob. ex greens, 4.

green lizards. Civilians in the Control Com-mission for Germany: Army: ca. 1945–8. Ex the green epaulets they used to wear.

Green Man, the. A urinal: pub-frequenters': C. 20. Ex urinals' often being painted green and ex *the Green Man* as a fairly common name for a public-house.

green rats, give (a person). See rats, give . . .

green rub, (get) a. To be reprimanded for another's fault: Naval: since ca. 1910. Granville. Ex the centuries-old metaphor, 'the rub of the green'.

green-striper. An officer in the Special Branch of the R.N.V.R.: Naval coll.: 1941 +. '(He) wears emerald-green braid between the gold lace on his sleeves.'

green suit or blouse suit. A suit of which one has no cards in a hand at bridge: Australian: since ca. 1925. B., 1942. An 'ungrown' suit.

green thumb, have a. See green fingers.

green un. A green envelope: Army: 1915 +; † by 1940.—2. 'A heavy sea that lands on the deck of a ship' (P-G-R): Naval coll.: late C. 19–20.

*Greenfields, Mrs; Mrs Ash-Tip or Ashtip. A 'bed' or a shelter in the open fields; one near a lime-kiln or a furnace: tramps' jocular c.: C. 20. W. A. Gape, *Half a Million Tramps*, 1936, '. . . Their lousy "kips". . . . I'd sooner have "Mrs Ashtip" or "Mrs Greenfields" any day.' Cf. sleep with Mrs Green (see the *Dict.*).

Greenfields, sit under Dr. 'To go for a rural walk rather than attend divine worship. In use among the older Nonconformists,' J. A. Boycott, letter of Dec. 1938. Cf.:

greenhouse.—2. Synonym of conservatory. H. & P., 1943; Partridge, 1945, 'From the per-spex on three sides of the pilot'. Perhaps prompt-ed by:—3. The transparent canopy that half covered the cockpit on the S.E. (a Sopwith): R.F.C.–R.A.F.: 1915–18. (W.G.)

greenie (or -ny).—5. A doping pill for a grey-hound: Australian (esp. Sydney) c., becoming low, esp. sporting, s.: since ca. 1946. (Lawson Glassop, *Lucky Palmer*, 1949.)—6. A smooth, un-broken wave (cf. glassy, n., 2, above): Australian surfers': since ca. 1950. (B.P.)

greens.—5. Short for greengages (p. 353): C. 20.

greeny, 1 (p. 353). Strictly: *Greeny* or *the greeny*: as in Pierce Egan, *Life in London*, 1821.

greeze (p. 353). Better *greaze*, and strictly applied only to the annual pancake-fight.

grego (p. 354): rather, since ca. 1800; recorded in 1806, John Davis, *The Post-Captain*. (Moe.)

gremlin, despite its appearance in H. & P., (early) 1943, and Jackson, (late) 1943, is S.E. for 'a mischievous sprite that, haunting aircraft, de-ludes pilots'. See esp. Jackson, and Charles Graves, *Seven Pilots*, 1943, for good accounts of the activities of gremlins: for the word itself, which is fanciful, see in *Words at War: Words at Peace*, the essay on the influence of the war of 1939–45. A fanciful explanation is that a gremlin is a *goblin* that lives in a *Fremlin* beer-bottle, the second *-lin* reinforcing the first.—2. A surfer lacking a board and sponging on his mates: Aus-tralian surfers': since ca. 1955. (B.P.)—3. (Also *gremmie.*) A boy of 12 or 13 aping his elders: Australian teenage surfers': since ca. 1960.—4. (Also *gremmie.*) 'A young and exuberant surfer, who is learning but still shows off' (*Pix*, Sept. 28, 1963): Australian surfers': since ca. 1960.

gremmie. The pet-form of gremlin 3 and 4. *The* Sydney *Bulletin*, March 30, 1963, and *Pix*, Sept. 28, 1963.

Grenadine Guards, the. 'Grenadine, a pinky, sickly syrup supposed to be made from pome-granates' (A. B. Petch): British soldiers in France: 1914–18. A pun on that famous regiment, *the Grenadier Guards*.

Grens, the. The Grenadier Guards: Army, but mostly Guardsmen's: late C. 19–20.

*grey, n. See gray above.

grey ballocks. Applied to a sour-tempered or sober-sided man: Forces': since ca. 1936. Con-trast golden ballocks.

Grey Funnel Line, the. The Royal Navy: mostly Naval: C. 20. By pun on 'the Blue Funnel Line'. (Granville.) Its ships are *grey-funnel liners*.

grey man, the. See Pinkie, 2, below.

grey matter. Intelligence: jocular coll.: from ca. 1895. Ex S.E. sense, 'the grey-coloured matter of which the active part of the brain is composed' (O.E.D.). E.g. 'Yes, a nice fellow, but quite deficient of any grey matter.'

greyback. See gray-back on p. 350.

greyhound or nipper. W. N. Glascock, *Sketch-Book* (I), 1825, defines the plurals as 'term applied to hammocks having a lean, or thin appearance, after having been lashed for stowage in the nettings upon deck': Naval: ca. 1790–1840. Moe.

grid, have (someone) **on the.** To have someone awaiting trial: police s.: since ca. 1930. (John Gosling, *The Ghost Squad*, 1959.)

Grid, the. The Grafton Club: clubmen's: from ca. 1870. B. & L.—2. The Central Electricity Board: commercial: since ca. 1920. Hence *Grids*, its stocks and shares.—3. (Also *the grid*.) An American Football field: Canadian: adopted, ca. 1925, ex U.S., where current since ca. 1915 and short for *gridiron*, itself current since ca. 1910. Ex the yard-marks. (Wentworth & Flexner.)

griddle, n. A violin: itinerant entertainers': ate C. 19–20. (Sydney Lester.) Cf. **bosh**, n., 3, on p. 82.

griddler.—2. A tinker: tramps' c.: from ca. 1860. B. & L.

griddling homey or **polone.** A violinist, male or female: partly parlary: late C. 19–20. Ex **griddle**, n., above.

gridiron.—4. 'The Stars and Stripes of the United States. Also called the "Stars and Bars"': nautical: from ca. 1860. Ibid.—5. A bicycle: Australian: since ca. 1925. B., 1942.—6. A public-house sweetheart: Anglo-Irish: ca. 1810–60. 'A Real Paddy', *Real Life in Ireland*, 1822.

gridiron, the whole. The whole party: non-aristocratic: from ca. 1860. B. & L. Perhaps suggested by *the whole boiling*, q.v. at **boiling** (*Dict.*).

Grids. See Grid, the, 2.

griff, n.—3. In the C. 20 Navy it = news, information (the equivalent of **gen**): H. & P. An abbr. of, and sense-development from, **griffin**, 8 (*Dict.*).—4. In Australia, trustworthy information: since ca. 1930. (B., 1943.)

griffin, 3 (p. 354), has the variant sense 'naval cadet', as on pp. 166, 174, 238, of C. J. R. Cook, *The Quarter Deck*, 1844: a sense app. current ca. 1820–90. On p. 135 of that book, the naval cadets are referred to as *the roaring griffins*—ex their neisiness. (Moe.)

Sense 1 dates from ca. 1810 or even earlier. It occurs in, e.g., Alfred Burton's *Johnny Newcome in the Navy*, 1818. (Moe.)

griggery-pokery. A pronouncement by Sir James *Grigg* concerning repatriation for troops in Burma: Army officers': 1944–5.

grim, on the. 'On the North-west Frontier of India. I believe Rudyard Kipling used the phrase,' Jackson: R.A.F.: 1919 +. There, life *is* 'grim'; and there, many a good man has lost it.

grim show. A (very) exhausting ordeal: the R.A.F.: since ca. 1939. A not unnatural sense-development of *grim*; see **show**, n., 2 (p. 765).

grimmer. An unpleasant person: Shrewsbury: since mid-1930's. Marples. Ex *grim* by 'the Oxford *-er*'.

grimpeur. A good hill-climber: cyclists': since ca. 1945. Sense-adapted ex Fr.

grin, the. A quizzing: low: 1821, Pierce Egan, *Life in London*; † by ca. 1860.

grin on the other side of one's face, esp. in some such context as 'You'll be grinning on the other side of your face when I have finished with you': coll.: late C. 19–20. (A. B. Petch, March 1966.)

grind, n.—10. Sexual titillation of a woman;

but also masturbation: since ca. 1935, esp. among teenagers. Very prob. ex sense 7 on p. 355.

grind, v.—7. To titillate a woman sexually, v.i. and v.t.: since ca. 1935, esp. among teenagers. Ex sense 5 (p. 355).—8. To masturbate: since late 1930's.

grinder. A small coin: Australian low: C. 20. Baker.—2. See **scissors-grinder**.

Gringo. An Englishman: used by Englishmen (and, of course, by the natives) in South America: C. 20. (Niall Alexander, letter of Oct. 22, 1939.) An American Spanish name, ex Sp. *gringo*, 'gibberish': to the Spaniards and to the Mexicans, the Englishman appears to speak gibberish. See esp. my *Name into Word*, 1949.

'May the "gibberish" derivation in fact perhaps be the other way round? In European coll. Span. "gringo" means "foreigner", and in the Argentine too the word is applied to *any* foreigner who is not S. American, Eur. Spanish or Portuguese, although in other parts of S. America, "gringos" are only Eng. or N. American. And I suggest that the apparent "gibberish" talked by these foreigners derives its name from the "gringos" who talk it. I have seen it stated that the Irish volunteers who flocked to support Bolivar and other liberators of the former Spanish S. American colonies after the Napoleonic wars liked marching to the song "Green grow the rushes, oh," which by Hobson-Jobson led to their becoming known as "gringos" by their S. Amer. paymasters and comrades. But I feel that the semantics may be rather strained.' (Ramsey Spencer, March 1967.)

grinning through. 'When undercoat or any previous coat is partly visible after finishing coat of paint has been applied' (master builder, Dec. 5, 1953): builders' and house-painters': late C. 19–20.

grip, v.—4. To bore (someone); hence *gripper*, a bore, and *the big grip*, one's military autobiography: Army, esp. officers': since ca. 1939. Perhaps suggested by the R.A.F.'s *bind* (p. 54 and Addenda).

gripe, v.—4. To complain, as in 'What are you griping about?': coll.: since ca. 1910, within my own knowledge; but probably late C. 19–20. Ex the pains of colic. Hence, although much less common, n., as in 'What's the, or your, gripe now?': since ca. 1915.

Gripes Hole. 'A hole close to the boat-house, thus called because the water there is very cold': Winchester College: mid-C. 19–20. B. & L.

grippo. A free entertainment; usually in pl. *grippos*: Naval: C. 20. It *grips* its audience—or is supposed to do so.

grips or **gripps.** A scene-shifter: filmland: since ca. 1920. Cameron McCabe, *The Face on the Cutting-Room Floor*, 1937.

Grips, the. The Hongkong Hotel, Hong-Kong: Far East: C. 20. C. S. Archer, *China Servant*, 1946.

gristle (*Dict.*); gen. **the**, occ. **one's.** A much earlier record is: 1665, R. Head, *The English Rogue*, ch. X; ob.

grit.—3. Food; Army, esp. R.A.: since ca. 1930. H. & P. Because of what gets into it.

gritty. See **dusty.**—2. In difficult, 'rugged', straitened circumstances or position, characterized by hardship and sociological handicap: since the late 1950's. Anthony Lejeune in *The Daily Telegraph*, colour supplement. March 10, 1967,

'The Prime Minister's sheep words range from "gritty" (meaning—well, what does it mean?) to the statesmanlike exhortation "Belt up".'

grizzle, n.—2. A (fit of) weeping: Cockney: late C. 19–20. In, e.g., A. Neil Lyons, *Arthur's*, 1908. 'Perhaps after *drizzle*, a light rain' (Leechman).

grizzle-pot (p. 356): since ca. 1920, common also in Australia, where (since ca. 1944—under American influence) *grizzle-puss* has > even commoner. (B.P.)

groan and grunt. A variant of **grumble and grunt** (below). Franklyn 2nd.—2. In full, *the groan and grunt game*, professional wrestling: sporting: since ca. 1950. (Leechman.)

Groat, the. *The John o' Groat Journal*: journalists' coll.: C. 20.

grob. Coarse, nasty: South African: since ca. 1945. Perhaps cf. the N.E. English dial. *grob*, 'to dig in soil or mud, as children do' (E.D.D.) and the S.E. v. *grub*. Cf. the Ger. *grob*, coarse, rough, unpolished.

grocer. An Equipment Officer: R.A.F.: since ca. 1925. Jackson, 'The suggestion that he has a nasty commercial attitude towards life.' Ex: 2. A Victualling Warrant Officer, R.N.: Naval: C. 20. (P.G.R.)

groceries, the.—2. Bombs: R.A.F.: 1930 +. Jackson. 'Thus, "We delivered the groceries."' Cf. **cabbage** and **cookie** and **gardening.**

grocer's hitch. 'A nondescript knot that won't come undone' (Granville): Naval: C. 20. Landlubberly.

grog, n.—6. Beer: Australian coll.: C. 20. (Dick.) Ex sense 3 on p. 356.

grog on. To drink heavily over a long period: United Nations troops in Korea: ca. 1952–5. But this verb 'is at least ten years older than the Korean War (1950–53)' and Australian. Hence, ca. 1945, the n. *grog-on*, a heavy-drinking party. (B.P.)

groin.—2. A finger ring: c.: C. 20. F. D. Sharpe, 1938. (See *Underworld*.)—3. Hence, a diamond: c.: since ca. 1940. John Gosling, *The Ghost Squad*, 1959.

groise. Grease: Haileybury: C. 20. Marples. By form-perversion.—2. At Uppingham, it = one who is over-efficient, one who curries favour by showing his efficiency: since the late 1920's. Cf. the Cheltenham *groise*, to curry favour; hence, *groiser*, one who does so: since ca. 1925. Marples.—3. A 'gorge' or 'spread' of edibles, etc.: Scottish Public Schools': since ca. 1870. Ian Miller, *School Tie*, 1935. Hence, *groisey*, greedy (Miller).

groise, v.i. To work hard; hence n., a 'swot': Harrow School: late C. 19–20. Lunn.—2. See **groise**, 2.—3. To 'fiddle'; to cheat in a petty way: Charterhouse: since ca. 1930. (Peter Sanders.)

groiser. See **groise**, 2.

grommet (pronounced *grummet*). A girl: Australian technicians' and mechanics': since ca. 1945. A grommet is a (usually rubber) ring, pushed into a hole in sheet metal. (B.P.)

groove, v. To 'make good progress, co-operate' (Peter Fryer in *The Observer* colour supplement, Dec. 3, 1967): jazz- and drug-addicts' and hippies': since ca. 1960. Ex the next two terms.

groove, in the, hence also **groovy.** Lost in jazz (swing-music) ecstasy: adopted, ca. 1940, ex

U.S. (*The Observer*, Sept. 16, 1956.) 'Like most jazz expressions, referred first to players, and only later to "fans". When the player suddenly hit his real stride, so that he improvised brilliantly and effortlessly, he was "in the groove".' (Priestley.) See also 'Jazz Slang'.

groovy.—2. Excellent: Australian teenage surfers': since ca. 1960; by 1966, slightly ob. (*Pix*, Sept. 28, 1963.) Cf. **groove, in the,** above.—3. Notably alert, progressive, well-informed, esp. in jazz music: beatniks': since ca. 1959. (Anderson.) By 1967, widely used by teenagers; on March 10, 1967, indicted by Anthony Lejeune in *The Daily Telegraph*, colour supplement.—4. Sexually attractive: jazz- and drug-addicts', and hippies': since early 1960's. Peter Fryer, as at **groove,** v., above.

grope. A *ground operational* exercise: R.A.F.: since ca. 1935. Jackson. Cf. **dry swim** and **tewt.**

Gropework, the. The Gourock Ropework Co. Ltd.: Scottish: C. 20—but † by 1960.

Groppi gong. See **Naffy medal.**

Groppi's Light Horse; Short Range Desert (or **Shepheard's) Group.** Combatant soldiers' names for Base troops at Cairo: Army: 1940–3. Sarcastic ref. to a famous tea-shop and a famous hotel in that city; the latter refers also to the Long Range Desert Group of aircraft. Also sometimes *Groppi's Hussars*. (Peter Sanders in *The Sunday Times* magazine, Sept. 10, 1967.)

Grosvenor Highlanders, the. The Gordon Highlanders: Army (mostly officers'): C. 20. Envious.

grot.—2. A hide-out: Australian c.: C. 20. B., 1942.—3. One's home or house or other residence: Naval: since ca. 1930. (John Winton, *We Saw the Sea*, 1960.) Ex sense 1 on p. 357.

grote. An informer (?): low s. or perhaps c.: ca. 1880–1920. W. L. George, *A Bed of Roses*, 1911 (one prostitute to another) '"What are you following me for?" she snarled. "If you're a grote, it's no go. You won't teach the copper anything he doesn't know."'

grotty. New, or newfangled, but useless; esp. in 'dead *grotty*': since ca. 1961. Ex '*grote*sque'.—2. (Very) inferior, bad—'crummy' or, in longer-established s., 'lousy': Liverpool s.: C. 20. Popularized by The Beatles and, by 1962, fairly gen. among teenagers. Origin presumably dialectal: ? *crotty*.

grouce, grouse, adj. First-class (e.g. hotel); excellent: Australian: since ca. 1920. B., 1942; Lawson Glassop, 1944. Cf. **grouse, the.**

grouce (or **grouse**) **sort** is a juvenile synonym of **good sort,** 3: since ca. 1940. (B., 1953.)

ground(-)loop. 'Aircraft crash' (Gerald Emanuel, March 29, 1945): R.A.F.: 1940 +. The last looping of the loop. 'An aircraft bursting a tyre on landing would swing (perhaps if the undercarriage collapsed) through 180°. This is referred to as a ground loop' (R.A.F. officer, late 1961).

ground-strafer; agent corresponding to next (both senses). Partridge, 1945.

ground-strafing. A low-flying attack on, e.g., transport: R.A.F.: since 1939. H. & P. See **strafe** (*Dict.*).—2. Hence, 'careless driving by servicemen', H. & P.: since 1940.

ground wallah. Synonymous with **penguin,** 1: R.A.F. coll.: since ca. 1918. Jackson.

Ground Walloper. That fat little gremlin who

is in charge of flying: R.A.F.: 1941 +. Perhaps a perversion of **Grand Walloper.**

grounded. Deprived of alcoholic and amorous adventure; applied esp. to a newly married man: R.A.F.: since ca. 1940. Partridge, 1945. Ex the technical sense, '(temporarily) affected to ground duties': he can no longer be a *fly*-by-night.—2. 'Stranded for lack of petrol' (Peter Sanders, 1967): Army in North Africa: 1940–43.

grounder.—4. (Cf. sense 2.) 'A ship that is liable to be run aground through bad seamanship': nautical coll.: from ca. 1860. B. & L.

grounders. 'Your "oppo's" entire tot of rum given to you as a very exceptional favour' (Granville): Naval: since ca. 1910. Perhaps cf. **grounder,** 2 (p. 357).

group-happy. Unreliable as a soldier, because his release (according to age-group) is near: Army: 1945–6.

grouper. 'An Officer on a Group Headquarters Staff,' Jackson: R.A.F. coll.: since ca. 1925.

groupie or **groupy.** Group Captain: R.A.F. coll.: since before 1930. H. & P.

grouse, adj. See **grouce.** Cf.:

***grouse, the.** (Only predicatively.) Very good: Australian c.: C. 20. Origin?

grout, n. Bread. Guards' Depot at Caterham: 1914–18, and decreasingly later. *John o' London,* Nov. 3, 1939.

grout-bag. One who studies hard: English schoolboys': since ca. 1880. (E. F. Benson, *The Babe, B.A.,* 1911.) Cf. *grout* (p. 357).

grouter. Cf. p. 357 and see **boxer.**—2. Hence, one who takes an unfair advantage; the unfair advantage itself: Australian: since ca. 1918. (B., 1943.)

grovel. Sherborne School s., from ca. 1890, as in Alec Waugh, *The Loom of Youth,* 1917: 'He led the "grovel" (as the scrum was called at Fernhurst), and kept it together.'

groves, the. The latrines: Lancing: since ca. 1920. Marples. Cf. Marlborough's **woods.**

grow on trees, it doesn't; or of currency and bank notes, *they don't* . . . A c.p., aimed at those who think money is easily got: late C. 19–20.

***grow one's feathers.** Gen. as *growing one's feathers,* 'letting one's hair and beard grow, a privilege accorded to convicts for some months before their discharge, that they may not be noticeable when free': prison c.: from ca. 1870. B. & L.

grow up? or **why don't you grow up?** Synonymous with **be your age!** above: c.p.: since late 1930's. (A. B. Petch, March 1966.)

growing pains. The difficulties and anxieties of getting settled down in life when one is young: coll.: C. 20. Ex the lit. *growing pains.*

***growl.** Female pudend: c.: from ca. 1890. Cf.:

growl and grunt. An occ. variant of **grumble and grunt** (below). Franklyn 2nd.

***growl-biter.** A cunnilingist: c.: late C. 19–20.

growler. Sense 1 may possibly have its origin in that conveyance which is known as a *sulky,* as B. & L. suggest, or perhaps ex **crawler,** 1 (p. 189). —3. A dog: Anglo-Irish: C. 19. 'A Real Paddy', *Real Life in Ireland,* 1822.—4. 'A low-lying mass of ice, frequently not showing up white like an iceberg, in the night-time not distinguishable from the surrounding sea' (and usually small): mostly nautical: since ca. 1910. Gibbard Jackson, *Twenty-Six Sea Yarns,* 1931.

grozzle, n. and v. 'This takes place at well-conducted tea-parties,' *The Daltonian,* Dec. 1946: Dalton Hall, Manchester: since ca. 1920. Perhaps a blend of *grub* + *guzzle.*

grub-stake, v. (p. 358), derives from the Western Canadian (and South-Western U.S.) practice whereby someone with capital provides a gold-prospector with food and, if necessary, equipment. Mitford M. Mathews (*Americanisms*) records it for 1863; it probably goes back to 1849 in California, and it could have reached Canada by 1851 or so. It had reached Australia by 1900 at latest; the term occurs in, e.g., Alexander Macdonald, *In the Land of Pearl and Gold,* 1907, 'The hotel-keepers "grubstake" men to work for them.'

grub-stakes. 'Grub' (food): non-aristocratic: from ca. 1890. Richards.—2. Food-supply: coll.: from ca. 1890. Ibid. Cf. **grub-stake,** n. and v. in the *Dict.*

grubber; grubbies; grubs. A tuck-shop: resp. Tonbridge, Wellington College, Bradfield: since ca. 1880. Marples. Ex *grub.*

grubbery.—5. An occ. variant of **grubber,** 2 (*Dict.*).

grubbing hall. The dining hall of any House: Winchester College: from ca. 1860. B. & L.

grubs. See **grubber.**

grue. Morbid; nervously upset or afraid; since ca. 1924; originally, Society. '"Well, I don't want to go all grue," said Woody, somewhat abashed' (Christianna Brand, *Green for Danger,* 1945). Ex S.E. *gruesome.*

gruesome twosome. 'Two young girls who are inseparable' (B.P.): Australian: adopted, ca. 1943, ex U.S.

grumble and grunt. Female genitals: C. 20. Mark Benny, *The Scapegoat Dances,* 1938. Rhyming on *cunt:* less usual than **Berkeley Hunt.**— 2. Hence, coïtion: C. 20. (Franklyn, *Rhyming.*)

grummet (or -it). Coïtion: nautical and low: mid-C. 19–20. The origin lies in nautical j.: sense 1, *b* or sense 1, *c* in the O.E.D.

grunt, make (a girl). To coït with her: low: C. 20.

grunt(-)horn. See the entry at **fish-horn** above.

grunter.—8. An officer: Royal Navy: since ca. 1915. A pun on *pig,* 11. (Atkinson.)—9. 'A baked suet roll to contain strips of pork or bacon' (Angus Wilson, *A Bit off the Map,* 1957): domestic: mid C. 19–20. Ex sense 1 (p. 359).

***gruntling.** A pig: c.: C. 18. Captain Alex. Smith, *The Life of Jonathan Wild,* 1776, at p. 179. Cf. **grunting cheat** in the *Dict.*

guacho (p. 359). Properly, no suggestion of 'half-breed' is intended.

Guard, the Old and **the Young.** A team consisting of the masters and one consisting of younger boys; the former also = the masters, in any connexion: Rugby School: C. 20. (D. F. Wharton, 1965.)

guard-rail critic. One who tenders overmuch advice and no assistance: Naval: since ca. 1920. Granville. He leans back against the rail while *you* work.

'Guard-room', in Army slang of late C. 19– early 20. *The Regiment* for 1900 noted *corner-shop, digger, mush;* that for 1898 had listed *cape, clink, dog's home, dust-hole, Marble Arch, net trap.* In detail: *cape* prob. derives from L. *capere,* to take; for *clink*, see p. 159; *corner-shop*, because often it stands at a corner of the barracks-square; *digger*, see p. 220; *the dog's home*, for 'lost' gay dogs; *dust-hole*, not because of dust, for usually it is spotlessly clean, but perhaps because it's a God-forsaken place for a soldier to be; *Marble Arch*, because within the Marble Arch itself there existed a small lock-up, for use by the police; *mush, the*, see p. 544, *mush*, 4; *the net*, catching all offenders; *trap, the*, for the unwary—cf. *trap*, 2 (p. 906).

guardo(-)chaps. 'The crew of a guard ship' (W. N. Glascock's *Naval Sketch Book*, 2nd Series, 1834, at I, 232, footnote): Naval: prob. late C. 18-mid 19. (Moe.)

guards, full to the. See **full to the guards.**

guard's bedroom. A brake van: railwaymen's: C. 20. (*Railway* 2nd.) Affording the opportunity of a quiet rest.

guardy or **-ie.** Earlier in Augustus Mayhew, *Paved with Gold*, 1857.

gubbins.—4. (Ex sense 3: p. 359.) Thin-gummy; anything one is too lazy or too forgetful to name: Services, esp. R.A.F.: since ca. 1918. Gerald Emanuel, letter of March 29, 1945. The transition from 3 is eased by the fact that in 1914–18 *gubbins* predominantly signified 'stores' or 'one's personal belongings'.

guddha. A metaphorical ass: Anglo-Indian: mid-C. 19–20. B. & L. Ex Hindustani *gadha*.

guernsey, get a. To receive due recognition; Australian (mainly in Victoria): since ca. 1930. A jersey as worn in Australian Rules football. (B.P.)

guess who's back! 'A c.p. uttered with one hand on hearer's back' (B.P.): Australian: since ca. 1950.

guff, n., 2 (p. 359)—impudence, impertinence—is also a Newfoundland usage: witness L. E. F. English, *Historic Newfoundland*, 1955.—3. Official, or other genuine and precise, information, esp. concerning the formal rules or the Service's regulations; mostly in *give* (someone), *the guff on* whatever the problem, etc., may be: chiefly in the Services: since ca. 1945. (Atkinson.)

guff, v. 'To romance, to humbug, to pitch yarns,' Jackson: R.A.F.: since ca. 1930. Ex **guff,** n., 1 (*Dict.*).

guffed. Summoned for infringement of 'guff rules' (**guff**, 2: p. 359): R.N.C. Dartmouth: since ca. 1912. Granville.

gugu (or **gu-gu**). See 'Prisoner-of-War Slang', 11.

guinea-dropper (p. 360) should be dated late C. 17–18; it occurs in B.E., 1699.

guinea-pig.—7. An evacuated Civil Servant: 1939 +. *The New Statesman*, Aug. 30, 1941. Cf. senses 3, 4. This included B.B.C. personnel to whom the Government paid one guinea a week towards their board and lodging.—8. One upon whom an experiment—or anything new—is tried: since ca. 1930: coll. >, by 1945, S.E. Ex guinea-pigs used in medical experiments.

guintzer. Fellow: Australian (urban): C. 20. Yiddish? Dal Stivens, *Jimmy Brockett*, 1951, 'I wanted to ask the old guintzer where all his bright boys were.'

guire cove is an error, astounding in B. & L., for *quire cove*, q.v. at queer cove (*Dict.*).

guiver, n., 2 (p. 360). 'Guyver: Make-believe, still used in Anglo-Jewish slang. It is Hebrew for

pride but has now come to mean pretence and is synonymous with . . . swank,' A. Abrahams in *The Observer*, Sept. 25, 1938.

gull in night clothes (p. 360): also *in night clothing* (Granville).

gully, n., 6. 'Any geographical indentation from a fair-sized drain to a grand canyon,' B., 1942: Australian coll.: C. 20.

gulpers. A sip (?) from a friend's tot of rum on (say) one's birthday: Naval: since ca. 1910. Granville. Ex *gulp* by 'the Oxford *-er*'.

gulph. See gulf, n. and v., in *Dict.*

gum(-)bucket. A pipe: Naval: C. 20. 'Taffrail', *Mystery at Milford Haven*, 1936, '"Can't I have even a suck at my old gum bucket?" He loved his pipe.'

gum(-)chum. An American soldier: 1942 +. Ex the constant request '(Got) any gum chum?'

gum-digger. A dentist: New Zealand and Australian: since ca. 1880. B., 1941 and 1942. Cf. **gum-smasher** (*Dict.*); there is a pun on the kauri-gum diggers of New Zealand.

gum leaves growing out of (one's or the) ears, have. To be a country bumpkin: Australian: since ca. 1920. B., 1942. The eucalyptus gum tree is much the commonest tree in Australia.

gum-puncher. A dentist: Australian: C. 20. Baker. Cf. **gum-digger.**

gum-tickler (p. 361) was perhaps adopted from U.S., where it is attested for the year 1810.

gum up the works. To spoil or upset things: since ca. 1918, when adopted from U.S. Georgette Heyer, *A Blunt Instrument*, 1938, 'That North dame's story gums up the works.'

gummer. A fighting dog now old and toothless: low London: mid-C. 19–20; ob. B. & L.

gummy, n.—7. (Ex 1: p. 361.) A toothless sheep: Australian: C. 20. Baker. It shows gums, not teeth.

gump.—2. Common sense: C. 20. Gladys Mitchell, *The Rising of the Moon*, 1945, '"Show a bit of gump."' Short for **gumption** (p. 361). 'Now current schoolchildren's slang' (Peter Sanders, 1965).

gun, n.—9. That injector on a locomotive which forces water from tank to boiler: Canadian (and U.S.) railroadmen's (— 1931).—10. An expert shearer: Australian: since ca. 1925. (B., 1943.) Also, since ca. 1930, N.Z. (*Straight Furrow*, Feb. 21, 1968.)

gun, get one's. To be promoted from lance-sergeant to full sergeant: Royal Artillery: C. 20. H. & P., 'On being promoted . . . an artilleryman wears a gun above his three stripes.'

gun, give her the. This metaphor is American and, in aviation = to accelerate.

gun, in the. (Of a person) about to be dismissed from job: Melbourne: ca. 1910–30. I.e. about to be *fired*.—2. Hence, in trouble: general Australian: since ca. 1920. (Dymphna Cusack, 1951.) Vance Palmer, *Legend for Sanderson*, 1937, has *get* (someone) *in the gun*, and earlier in his 'Rann Daly' novel, *The Outpost*, 1924.

gun-buster. An artificer (or *tiffy*) of the Royal Army Ordnance Corps: since ca. 1920. H. & P.

gun-fire (p. 362) probably arose ca. 1890. Cf. S. E. Burrow, *Friend or Foe*, 1912—a tale of the 1890's–early 1900's.

gun(-)fodder. Shells: Artillery: since 1940. The gunners *feed* the shells to the guns.

gun for, esp. **be gunning for**, someone. To seek

someone in order to cause him very serious trouble: adopted, ca. 1944, ex U.S. Ex hunting for, and shooting at, game.

gun speaker. A practised, proficient mob-orator: Australian political: since ca. 1920. B., 1942. Loud and rapid.

Gundaroo bullock. Koala meat cooked: Australian rural: C. 20. (B., 1943.)

Gunga Din. Gin (the drink): Australian rhyming s.: C. 20. Mostly in the combination *Gunga Din and squatter's daughter*, gin and water. Franklyn 2nd.

gunge. Grease; oily dirt, the opposite of *clag*, dry dirt: engineers': since ca. 1940. (D. F. ?harton, Oct. 24, 1965.)

gungineer. An *engineer* officer turned over to *gun*-mounting: Naval (ward-room): since ca. 1930.

gunk. 'Chemical compounds, especially those which provide solid fuel for space rockets' (Leechman): Canadian: 1958 +. A composite word? Now has a much wider application. Perhaps—as Douglas Leechman suggests—a blend of *goo* + *dunk*. Or, as Robert Clairborne suggests, of *goo* + *hunk*.

gunna. Going to: Australian sol.: mid C. 19–20. (Jon Cleary, *Just Let Me Be*, 1950.)

gunroom evolutions. 'Traditional "games" carried on in the Gunrooms (Midshipmen's Messes) of the Fleet,' Granville: Naval: since ca. 1910 if not earlier. Ironic on *tactical evolutions*.

guns. Also as a nickname: 'Taffrail'. Virtually the vocative of *Gunnery Jack*. See quotation at *pilot* (Addenda).

guntz, the. The whole lot, the whole way, etc., esp. in *go the guntz*: low. C. 20. Ex Yiddish; cf. Ger. *das Ganze*, all of it.

gunz. A drill sergeant: Rossall School: since ca. 1880. Marples. A Prussianising of *guns*?

gup.—3. (Also *guppy*.) A fool: Australian: since ca. 1925. B., 1942. Prob. ex sense 2.—4. (Ex senses 1 and 2: p. 362.) Information: Army: since ca. 1930. (P-G-R.)

guppy. See gup, 3.—2. Hence, adj., foolish, stupid, silly: since ca. 1930. Baker.

gurk.—3. In Australia, to break wind: C. 20. B., 1942. Ex sense 1.

gussie.—1 (p. 363), prob. goes back to ca. 1890: witness Miles Franklin, *My Brilliant Career*, 1901, 'I'm not a baby that will fall in love with every gussie I see.'—2. One of the Army's nick-names for the officers is (ex sense 1) *the gussies*: since ca. 1930. H. & P. By ca. 1940 also, occ., in R.A.F.: Jackson. Partridge, 1945, 'Familiar for Augustus, a "tony" name.'

Gussies. Great Universal Stores; stocks and shares thereof: commercial: since ca. 1940. —2. (Also *gussies*.) Women's lace panties: since ca. 1954. Ex 'Gorgeous Gussie' Moran, a picturesquely dressed American lawn tennis star.

gust-guesser. A meteorological officer of Im-perial Airways: 1920's. (W/Cdr R. H. McIntosh, D.F.C., A.F.C., *Autobiography*, 1963.) Gusts of wind, obviously!

gut like a crane, have a. To be very thirsty: Australian rural: C. 20. (K. S. Prichard, *Working Bullocks*, 1926.)

gut (or guts), one is a. One is greedy or a greedy person: Cockneys': C. 20.

Gut, the. A notorious street in Malta: Services (esp. the Navy): C. 20. Granville.

gut on, put a. To put on—gain in—weight: Australian: since ca. 1920. Culotta.

gut-rot. 'Unhealthy-looking food or strong drink' (B., 1942): Australian: C. 20. Cf. rot-gut (*Dict.*).

gut-spiller. A Ghurka soldier: Australian servicemen's: 1939–45. (B., 1943.) For *guts-spiller*.

gutbash. A bellyful of food; hence, a resultant bellyache: Services, esp. Navy: since ca. 1925. (P-G-R.)

gutbucket and **shipwreck chorus.** That part of a piece in which, at the end, all the instrumentalists join: jazz: ca. 1948–56. Professor F. E. L. Priestley, in letter of Oct. 12, 1965, tells me that *gutbucket* 'is not a special part of a jazz piece: it is a special kind of playing, especially of the blues; it is the most "dirty" or "low-down" sort of playing, with deliberately distorted tonalities, "growl" effects, and so on. The term [came into use] before 1930.'

gutless. Cowardly: coll.: C. 20. Cf. guts, 5 (p. 363).—2. Of motorcars: under-powered: Australian: since ca. 1945. (B.P.)

gutless wonder. A coward: coll.: since ca. 1910. Perhaps on the famous *boneless wonder*. —2. An under-powered car: Australian: since ca. 1945. (B.P.)

guts, n., 6 (p. 363). For a specialised Australian nuance, see boxer.

guts, v.i. and v.t. To eat; to eat greedily: Australian: since ca. 1890. Kylie Tennant, *Ride on, Stranger*, 1943, '"Gutsing again, Briscoe?" she reproved.' Ex the n.; cf. gutsy.

guts, drop one's. See drop . . .

guts, give the good. See good guts, the, above.

*guts, spew one's. To inform the police on one's friends: c.: from ca. 1930. Cf. spill the works (*Dict.*).

guts, spill one's. More usual than the synony-mous prec. phrase: adopted, ca. 1930, from U.S. into low British s. An interesting anticipation occurs in *Sessions*, July 1879, p. 442, 'Workman [accused of burglary] asked me to go to his wife . . . and tell her that he had been about Maudsley's job, and she must keep her "guts" what she knew about it.'

guts-ache. A contemptible person: Australian: C. 20. B., 1942.

guts for garters, have one's (p. 363). The dating should rather be 'C. 19–20'. The phrase must have 'gone underground' for a century or more: in Robert Greene's *James the Fourth*, III, ii, we find 'I'll make garters of thy guts, thou villain'. (With thanks to Mr E. Phillips Barker.)

guts up, v. To eat: Australian: since ca. 1840. Brian Penton, *Landtakers*, 1934.

gutser, n.—2. A 'greedy guts': New Zealand: since ca. 1910. (Jean Devanney, *Bushman Burke*, 1930.)—3. Four cards retained in the hope of making a straight: Australian poker-players': since ca. 1920. (B., 1953.)

gutser, v. To come a 'gutser' (p. 363); to fail badly: Australian: C. 20. D'Arcy Niland, *The Big Smoke*, 1959, 'You had your chance and you gutsered.'

gutser, come a (p. 363): also, since ca. 1916, New Zealand. (Slatter.)

gutsful of, have a. To have had too much of something: New Zealand: since ca. 1920.

(Slatter.) Cf. *have had a bellyful of*: see **belly-full** on p. 46.

gutsful of grunts. A disagreeable person: Australian: since ca. 1910. B., 1942. Cf. **gutsache.**

gutsy, n. A fat man: proletarian coll.: from ca. 1880.

gutsy, adj. Sense 2 should (p. 363) read: courageous.—3. Greedy; or merely very hungry: R.A.F.: since ca. 1920. Jackson. Ex **guts**, 1 (*Dict.*).

Gutta-Percha. A Victorian: Australian: ca. 1880–1920. Baker. Why? Perhaps there is a pun on *gum-trees*.

gutter.—3. 'Space in front of a race-course totalisator' (Baker): Australian sporting: C. 20. —4. A football scrum: Tonbridge: late C. 19–20. Marples.

gutter-crawler (hence **g-crawling,** 2). One of that flower of modern youth which specialises in driving its cars slowly along by the kerb in the expectation that some girl will allow herself to be 'picked up' (there always is): since ca. 1920.

gutty.—2. One who wolfs his food: St Bees: C. 20. Marples. Cf. **gutsy,** 3.

guv, v. See **gove.**

guv, adj. Expert: Oxford undergraduates': ca. 1820–60. Cuthbert Bede, *Verdant Green,* 1853.

Guv'nor, the. Robert Abel, Surrey batsman of 1881–1904, then a coach; also a maker of cricket bats: cricketers': from ca. 1895. He represented England in many Test matches. Almost blind in his later years, he died on Dec. 10, 1936, at the age of 77. (*The Daily Telegraph,* Dec. 11, 1936.)

guv'nor, the. The head of a Teddy boys' gang: Teddy boys': since ca. 1946. (*The Observer,* March 1, 1959.)

guy, n., 6 was anglicised by 1903, when it appeared in Binstead's *Pitcher in Paradise.* On July 15, 1860, J. M. Yale wrote from Colquitz Farm, Vancouver Island, to Sir George Simpson (see *blow-up* above), 'Thank God, we have got rid of all those damn drunken guys at last.' (Perhaps I might here mention that I'm coming to think that this sense of *guy* derives from Yiddish *goy,* a Gentile.)—10. Something to eat; esp., bread: South Africa, among the imported 'coloured' labour, esp. the half-caste Indians: C. 20. (Cyrus A. Smith, letter of July 17, 1946.) Prob. ex Hindustani.

guy-a-whack, adj. Incompetent; hence, n., a defaulting bookmaker: Australian low: C. 20. B., 1942.

guy out, v.t. and v.i. To make (the tents) secure by tightening the guy-ropes: circusmen's coll.: late C. 19–20.

guzinters. An animal's entrails: Australian rural: since ca. 1910. Baker. I.e. *guts + innards.*

guzunder. A chamber pot: Australian domestic: since ca. 1925; by 1960, ob. It *guzunder* the bed. (B.P.)

guzzump. A slovenly variant of **gezumph** (p. 326).

gwennie.—2. Hence, the gunner: Naval: since ca. 1918. (*The Weekly Telegraph,* Jan. 25, 1941.) —3. A gun: Naval: 1939–45. Not very general. (P-G-R.) Probably suggested by *gunnie,* diminutive of *gun.*

[**gyle hather; Gyles Hather.** Having the appearance of a (late C. 16–early 17) c. term, it is merely the name (or its perversion) of a noted rogue.]

gym cad. A gymnasium instructor: Royal Military Academy: from ca. 1870; very ob. B. & L.

gym nasty tricks. Gymnastics: (not Public) schoolboys': C. 20.

gynae. Gynæcology; also attributively, as in 'the famous gynæ-man': medical: late C. 19–20.

gynie or **gyno.** Australian variants of preceding, but also for a gynæcologist: since ca. 1920 and esp. among medical students.

gyp.—3. A thief: mid-C. 19–20: c. >, by 1900, low. B. & L. Abbr. *gypsy.*

gyp, v. (p. 365).—2. Hence, to rob: mostly Services': C. 20. 'Common also in Australia' (B.P.).

Gyppy tummy. See **Gippy tummy.**

gypsy (or **G.**). See **gipsy** (*Dict.*).

Gypsy. A nickname of men surnamed Smith: from ca. 1905. Ex 'Gypsy' Smith, the evangelist. Cf. **Darky** and **Shoey** in the *Dict.*

gypsy's warning. Morning: rhyming s.: mid-C. 19–20.

gyver. An occ. form (e.g. in E. Pugh, *Harry the Cockney,* 1912) of **guiver** (*Dict.*).

gyvo. Variant of **givo.**—Humbug: Australian: since ca. 1935. (B., 1953.) Ex **guiver,** 2 (p. 360).

H

H.B.'s. Human beings: jocular: since ca. 1930.

H.E. An 'H.E.' is a severe reprimand: Services: since late 1940. (H. & P.) Ex the abbr. of 'high explosive': cf. synonymous **blowing up** (p. 68).—2. A coll.—in reference only—for *His Excellency* (ambassador; Governor-General): late C. 19-20.

H.L.I. Richards, 'We'—The Royal Welch Fusiliers—'and the Highland Light Infantry were bitter enemies . . . Some say that it originated towards the end of last century during a final for the Army Football Championship of India when the H.L.I., having scored a lucky goal early on against our chaps, kept their advantage by delaying tactics—kicking wide intotouch whenever they had the ball. To this day, in the Battalion, these tactics are always greeted with the indignant cry of "H.L.I., H.L.I.!" and the expression has been adopted by other units and by civilians.'

H.T.W.S.S.T.K.S. Masonic initials sometimes interpreted, facetiously, as 'Hot-tailed Willie should stop tickling Katie's sex': Canadian: since ca. 1910 (?)

ha-ha. A defecation: nursery: late C. 19-20. Echoic of baby's instinctive grunting.

ha-ha pigeon. A kookaburra: Australian: C. 20. B., 1942. Widely known as *laughing jackass.*

habs-dabs, the (screaming). Better, and usually, *hab-dabs*, which, however, is less common than *ab-dabs*, q.v. above. Nervous irritation: mostly R.A.F.: since ca. 1937. (Atkinson.) Cf. **heebie-jeebies** on p. 385.

hachi, in *never hachi*, it never happened, i.e. bunkum: United Nations troops': ca. 1951-5 in Korea. Korean? Japanese?

hack, usually **hack down**. To shoot (*out* of the sky); to shoot *down*: R.A.F.: 1939 +. Brickhill & Norton, *Escape to Danger*, 1946, 'A couple of [the] 109's hacked two Hurricanes down near Montreuil on the 10th of June, 1940, and Eric jumped from his pranged kite and ran for it.' Prob. ex Rugby j. (for hearty work by the forwards): cf. **hack**, n. 3, on p. 365.

hack pilot; hack pusher. A taxi-driver; Australian: since ca. 1944. (B., *Australia Speaks*, 1953.) Suggested by perhaps confused with the U.S. s. synonyms *hackie* and *taxi-pusher.*

hackam; hackem. See **hackum** (*Dict.*).

Hackney is the inevitable nickname, though mostly among Londoners, of men surnamed Downs: late C. 19-20. Ex Hackney Downs, an open space in the borough of Hackney in the county of London.

Hackney Marsh. Glass: Londoners' rhyming s.: C. 20. Cf. **Khyber Pass.**

had it. See **have had it** (below).

had it in a big way, he's (or **I've** or **you've**.)

There's no chance whatsoever of that hope being fulfilled: since ca. 1944. An extension of *have had it*, 3.

had your penn'orth or do you want a ha'penny change? A c.p. addressed to someone staring: mostly Londoners': since ca. 1920. (Laurie Atkinson, Sept. 11, 1967.)

had your time. See **you've had your time.**

haddie. A haddock: Cockneys', esp. costermongers', coll.: C. 19. Mayhew, I, 1851. (Prob. independent of Scottish dial.)

hag, 2 (p. 366). At Haileybury, since ca. 1918, a housemaid or any other woman. 'At Charterhouse, now refers only to a house matron' (Peter Sanders, note of mid-1965).

haggis(-)basher. A Scot: R.A.F.: since ca. 1934. (Atkinson.) See **basher** in Addenda; *haggis*, one of the toothsome national dishes of Scotland.

hags, the. The nuns: Catholic priests' jocular: C. 20. Not, of course, ex the S.E. *hag* (although, naturally, there's an allusion), but from Greek *hag*iai, holy women.

hag's bush. A frequent synonym of **Sikh's beard** below.

hair, get in (someone's). To annoy or irritate: since ca. 1936. 'Like grit embedded in hair' (Atkinson). Adopted ex U.S. 'To irritate as lice in one's hair would irritate.' (W. & F.)

hair, tie one's. See **tie one's hair** (*Dict.*).

hair-cut. See **shave**, n., 7, in the *Dict.*

hair-do. Having one's hair dressed in a fashionable style: feminine coll.: since ca. 1920.—2. Hence, a style of coiffure: (feminine) coll.: since ca. 1925.

hair down, let one's. To let oneself go; to speak and act freely and intimately: coll.: since ca. 1930, but not very common before ca. 1950. Ex a number of girls talking together, esp. late at night.

hair off. To lose one's temper: Scottish Public Schools': C. 20. Ian Miller, *School Tie*, 1935, where it is spelt *hare*. Ex *get one's hair off.*

hair-restorer (p. 366). More prob. a play upon the words *fairy story.*

haircut with a hole in it. 'Jocular for barbering of bald man's tonsure' (Atkinson): C. 20.

hairing, adj. Tearing: furious: Scottish Public Schools': C. 20. Ian Miller, 'It was not worth risking a hairing great row.'

hairs, get or have by the short (p. 367), seems to have originated in the U.S.; at least, it occurs there, in form *get where the hair is short*, in George P. Burnham, *Memoirs of the United States Secret Service*, 1872.—2. (Only *have . . .*) Hence, to know a subject, a theme, very thoroughly: Australian: since ca. 1935. (B.P.)

hairy, adj., 5 (*Dict.*). Lunn's use, however, makes it clear that it dates back to ca. 1900 and that, even orig., it may not have been specifically Anglo-Irish.—6. Unpleasant: rough: Army:

since ca. 1935. 'We had a hairy time on patrol last night.'—7. Hence, dangerous, exciting; since ca. 1945. 'Applied esp. to wild, reckless driving in a race—to the limits of the car and safety' (David Mann, Jan. 10, 1963). Perhaps ex sense 5 of p. 367.

hairy, the. 'She was "one of the hairy"—a hatless slum girl conscious of her station in life'; Glasgow slum girls collectively: lower-class Glasgow: late C. 19–20. MacArthur & Long, 'In Glasgow, as in Rome, the hat is a badge of feminine quality.'

hairy-arsed. No longer young: low: late C. 19–20.—2. Mature and hirsute and virile: Naval: since ca. 1947. A young servicemen's term of the 1950's for a 'type' of rugged masculinity and maturity.

hairy-bottomed tromp. A term of abuse: Cambridge undergraduates': early 1930's. I.e. tramp with a jocular 'Dutch' twist.

hairy devil. A flying fox: Australian: late C. 19–20. B., 1942.

hairy dive. A dive made into a (very) fast and dirty current and with the diver hanging on to an anchor line: skin divers': since ca. 1950. Cf. hairy, adj., 7, above.

hairy goat, run like a. (Of a horse) to perform badly in a race: Australian: C. 20. Baker.

hairy mary (or **Mary**). 'The prickles that cover the cane' (Jean Devanney, *By Tropic Sea and Jungle*, 1944): Australian cane-cutters': C. 20.

hairy wheel. The female pudend: low Australian: from ca. 1860. Cf. hairy ring in *Dict.*—2. But also low English s. for the male genitals: since ca. 1870.

Hal, the. The Hallé orchestra: music-lovers': since ca. 1920.

half, n.—4. A half-holiday: schools' coll.: C. 20. (S. P. B. Mais, *A Schoolmaster's Diary*, 1918.)—5. A child travelling half fare: coll.: C. 20.—6. Implied in *anarf*, ten shillings.

half a (pint, mile, hour, million, etc.), **a.** Half a (pint, etc.): C. 20: Canadian sol. >, by 1955, non-educated coll. (Leechman.)

half a bar (p. 367). Recorded earlier in W. L. George, *A Bed of Roses*, 1911.

*****half a borde.** A variant of **half borde** (*Dict.*). Holme.

half a caser. Half a crown: Australian low: C. 20. B., 1942. See **caser** (*Dict.*).

half a couter. See **half a bean** (*Dict.*).

half a crown. See **bed and breakfast.**

half a cup of tea. Tea and whisky mixed: Covent Garden: C. 20. Partly rhyming s.

half a dog-watch, not. See **dog-watch, 2.**

half a grunter. Sixpence: low: C. 19. H., 2nd ed. Cf. grunter, 3 (*Dict.*), where the sense 'sixpence' is either loose or incorrect.

half a jiffy. See **half a crack** (*Dict.*).

half(-)a(-)stretch.—2. Odds of 6 to 1: racing, esp. bookmakers': C. 20. Ex sense 1 on p. 367: a prison sentence of *six* months.

half a surprise. A black eye: Londoners': ca. 1885–1905. B. & L. Ex a music-hall song. The chorus began, 'Two lovely black eyes,/Oh, what a surprise!'

half a tick. See **half a crack** (*Dict.*).

half a ton. See **ton, 3.**

half a tusheroon. See **half a bull** in the *Dict.*

half an hour. Flour: Australian rhyming s.: late C. 19–20. B., 1942.

half-arsed. (Of things) imperfect; (of persons) ineffective, indecisive: Canadian: late C. 19–20.

half-baked. An immature person: Australian: ca. 1890–1940. (G. B. Lancaster, *Jim of the Ranges*, 1910.) Cf. *half-baked*, 2., on p. 367.

half bar. Ten shillings: see **bar, n.**, in the *Dict.*

half-canned. Half drunk: since ca. 1925.

half-chat. An Indian Army term dating from ca. 1880, thus in Richards: 'Half-caste, or "half-chat" as the troops in my time [ca. 1901–9] contemptuously called them.' Also, C. 20, an Australian and Pacific Islands term, as, e.g., in Sydney Parkman, *Captain Bowker*, 1946.

half-colonel. A lieutenant-colonel: Army officers' coll.: C. 20.

half-crown battalion (p. 368). Also, in 1915 +, *half-crown brigade.*

half-cut.—2. Stupid: silly; foolish: Australian: late C. 19–20. B., 1942. I.e. with half one's virility and vigour removed.

Half-Dirties. 'Willesden men on dual steam and electric duties' (*Railway*, 3rd): railwaymen's: since ca. 1950.

half foolish. Ca. 1855–80: 'Ridiculous: means often *wholly* foolish,' H., 1st ed.

half-hard or **half-mast.** Semi-erect; not very intelligent: C. 20. (Atkinson.)

half-laugh and purser's grin (p. 368) derives ex the much earlier *half-and-half laugh and purser's grin* recorded by W. N. Glascock, *Sketch-Book*, II, 1826: Naval: ca. 1790–1880. (Moe.)

half-nicker (p. 368). Also Australian: B., 1942. The same for **half-pie** and **half-rinsed** (both on p. 368).

half-note. A ten-shilling note; hence its value: mostly Australian: C. 20. On the other hand, *half a note* = the sum of ten shillings. (B.P.)

half-ounce. To cheat (v.t.): rhyming s. (on *bounce*): late C. 19–20. (Franklyn, *Rhyming*.)

half-past two. A Jew: rhyming s.: C. 20. Franklyn, ibid.

half-pie.—2. Worthless: Aus.: since ca. 1925. (B., 1959.)

half-pie farm. 'A small nondescript holding' (Harold Griffiths): New Zealand: since ca. 1930. (Slatter.)

half-pint, adj.; Half-Pint. (Very) short; an often complimentary nickname for a short man: since ca. 1925. (*News-Chronicle*, July 13, 1954.) Also 'a term of endearment applied to a very small woman. Heard in 1938' (Leechman).

half-pint hero. A boaster, a swaggerer: R.A.F.: since ca. 1930. Jackson. The implication being that a half-pint of beer or ale will make him 'shoot a line'.

half-pissed. Mildly tipsy: low: C. 20.

half-ringer. See **ringer.**

half-rinsed. Tipsy: Aus.: since late 1940's. (B., 1959.)

half section, one's. One's friend: military: C. 20. Also, since ca. 1925, R.A.F., which, further, uses it for 'wife'.

half-shot. Tipsy: Naval: since ca. 1925. Granville. Ex **shot**, adj., on p. 763.

half-soaked. Only half-awake; slow; rather stupid: Midlands: C. 20. (Dr R. L. Mackay, M.D.; 1967.)

half-squarie. A prostitute: Australian low: since ca. 1920. B., 1942. Ironic.

half-stamp. A tramp (the person): rhyming s., orig. underworld: C. 20.

half your luck! A coll. ellipsis of 'I wish I had even a half of your good luck': Australian: since ca. 1915. B., 1942.

halfie or **halfy.** A half-caste Aboriginal: Australian coll.: since ca. 1910. (B., 1943.)

Halibag; Hallie or **Hally.** A Halifax bomber aircraft: Air Force: 1941 +. An analogy of **Stringbag.**

hall, n.—2. See 'Tavern terms', § 3.

Hall, the. Trinity Hall: Cambridge undergraduates' coll.: late C. 19–20.

hallelujah-hawking. Religious speaking; evangelism; esp., city-mission work: Australian: since ca. 1910. B., 1942.

hallelujah stew. Soup served at a Salvation Army hostel: C. 20. D. Crane, *A Vicarious Vagabond*, 1910.

haller. A hard biscuit—served in Hall: Marlborough College: C. 20.

Hallie (or **-y**). See **Halibag.**

halvers.—2. In Canada, an equal division of, e.g., supplies: coll.: late C. 19–20.

halves, go (p. 369). The dating should rather be 'since late C. 18'. Charles B. Burr, *Life and Letters of Joel Barlow* (New York, 1886, p. 294), quotes an imaginary dialogue by Joel Barlow, American poet and ambassador, familiar with Britain. (Moe.)

halves, on the. Sharing 50–50; e.g., in farming: Australian: since ca. 1925. (B., 1953.)

ham. (Gen. pl.) An amateur wireless transmitter: wireless s. adopted in late Sept. 1936 from the U.S. *The Daily Herald*, Sept. 19, 1936.—2. An (inferior) telegraph operator: Canadian railroadmen's (— 1931). Ex 1.

ham, v.: To be an inferior actor; esp., to act badly: adopted, ca. 1939, from U.S. Campbell Dixon in *The Daily Telegraph*, Nov. 18, 1946, 'After a deal of hamming'. Ex the n. in **hambone.** Also adj.: 'inferior': adopted ca. 1930.

ham! A warning cry when authority threatens to 'intrude' upon an unlawful activity: Cotton College (under other names): ca. 1860–1910. *The Cottonian*, Autumn, 1938. Origin?

ham(-)and(-)beef. A *chief* warder: prison rhyming s.: C. 20. Jim Phelan, *Murder by Numbers*, 1941.

ham(-)and(-)egg shift, the. A shift from 10 a.m. to 6 p.m.: British miners': late C. 19–20. 'Derived from former days—the ham was eaten before the shift began and the eggs in the evening at its finish' (*Toronto Globe*, Jan. 6, 1950).

Ham and High, The. 'The *Hampstead and Highgate* Express'—a weekly founded ca. 1860: London local and London journalistic. (Paragraphed by 'Peterborough' in *The Daily Telegraph* of Oct. 24, 1960.)

ham-bags. Female drawers: girls': ca. 1890–1914. Cf. **ham-frill.**

Ham-Bone. A Hampden bomber: R.A.F.: 1940 +; by 1945, ob., the 'plane having become ob. in 1942. Jackson. Ex 'Hampden' + its (vague) shape-resemblance to a ham-bone.

ham-bone. A greenhorn or an amateur among itinerant musicians: showmen's: since ca. 1880. P. H. Emerson, *Signor Lippo*, 1893. Whence, prob., the American *ham*, 'inferior actor', retransported to England ca. 1925; hence, ham, n., as above.—2. A sextant: Naval: C. 20. Granville. Ex the shape.

ham-fisted. (Esp. of pilot or mechanic) clumsy: R.A.F.: 1940 +. (W/Cdr R. P. McDouall, March 27, 1945.) Probably suggested by **ham-handed.**

ham-frill. A pair of female running shorts: (University) girls': from ca. 1925. H. H. Stanners, *At the Tenth Clue*, 1937.

ham-handed is the Navy's form of **ham-fisted**: since ca. 1925. Granville. 'Hands like hams' are usually clumsy—or look it.

ham it up. To act a part extravagantly; hence, to wreck (something) by ill-advised conduct: Canadian (ex U.S.): since ca. 1930; by 1945, English.

Ham Shank. See **Hamshank** below.

hammer.—4. Three Canadian terms for 'penis' —all current from before 1949 and all less vulgar than **prick**—are *dink, dong, hammer.*

hammer, v.—4. To shell heavily; to defeat severely: Army coll.: 1940–5. (P-G-R.)—5. See **hammer and nail** below.

hammer, at . . . (p. 369). The phrase *under the hammer* occurs much earlier in *The Port Folio*, Nov. 1, 1806, reporting, at p. 266, col. 2, a British source. Moe.

hammer, (right) on one's. (Right) on one's tail; immediately behind: Australian: since ca. 1920. Lawson, Glassop, *We Were the Rats*, 1944. Ex industrial j. Also *flat on one's*, or *its, hammer*: Jean Devanney, *Travels in North Queensland*, 1951.

hammer, under the.—2. (Of a train) 'accepted at caution' (*Railway*): railwaymen's: C. 20.

hammer(-)and(-)nail. To follow (someone, as a detective would): rhyming s. (on *tail*), orig., and still in 1966, mainly underworld: C. 20. Franklyn 2nd. Often shortened to *hammer.*

hammer and tack. A track, e.g. a metalled road: Australian rhyming s.: since ca. 1920. (Baker.)

hammered.—3. Married: metal workers': since ca. 1880. Ware.

hammock man (p. 370) occurs in *The Night Watch*, 1828. (Moe.)

hammy. A hamster: domestic: since ca. 1925.

Hamps, short for **Hampsteads** (p. 370): C. 20. *The New Statesman*, Nov. 29, 1941.

hams shrunk. 'Sides of trousers shrunk at thigh': tailors': from ca. 1820. B. & L.

Hamshank, or hyphenated. An American: rhyming s. (on *Yank*): since ca. 1944. (Mark McShane, *The Straight and Crooked*, 1960.)

han tun. One hundred: pidgin: mid-C. 19–20.

hand, 5, and **handful, 2.** Odds of 5 to 1: racing, esp. bookmakers': C. 20. The 2nd term comes ex sense 1 on p. 371: the number 5.

hand, bear a (p. 370): rather, since ca. 1720. It occurs in James Ralph's play, *The Fashionable Lady*, 1730, in Act I, scene 5, on p. 6. (Moe.)

hand, old.—2. An experienced settler (hence, farmer, drover, etc.) in the outback. Australian coll.: since ca. 1860. (B., 1943.)

hand, sign one's. See **name, bite one's.**

hand-Bible. A holystone: Naval: late C. 19–20. (P-G-R.)

hand gunner. A machine-gunner: Artillerymen's: ca. 1890–1920. (Gilbert Frankau, 1920.)

hand-in, give (someone) **a.** To help: Australian coll.: C. 20. B., 1942. As into tram or train.

hand in one's dinner pail. To die: since ca.

1920. (P. G. Wodehouse.) Suggested by **kick the bucket** (*Dict.*).

hand-jive. 'System of rhythmic hand-movements in time to music where floor is too crowded to allow people present to jive (dance), esp. as in coffee bars' (Atkinson): jazz-lovers': since ca. 1950.

hand like a foot, have a. To have a very bad hand of cards: card-players': C. 20; by 1950, ob., except in Canada. (Alan S. C. Ross in *The Sunday Times*, July 15, 1956.) Cf. **hand like a foot** in *Dict.*

hand-out (p. 371): but Canadian by late C. 19. (Niven.)

hand out the slack. To check a superior, be rude to a colleague: Services (esp. the Navy): since ca. 1925. H. & P. See **slack**, n., 3 (p. 778).

hand over fist (p. 371) goes back to very early C. 19. (W. N. Glascock, *Sketch-Book* (I, 23), 1825. Moe.)

hand over the baby. 'To pass on a responsibility no one particularly desires': coll.: C. 20. (*The Daily Express*, April 5, 1937.) Ex **holding the baby** (*Dict.*).

hand-reared. Phallically well-endowed: low: C. 20.

hand (someone) **the cold and frosty.** To snub; to treat coldly: since ca. 1920. Cf. **frozen mitt** (p. 304).

hand-to-hand. Hand-to-hand fighting: Army coll.: C. 20. Gerald Kersh, *Bill Nelson*, 1942, 'We done a bit of the good old hand-to-hand with the good old Wogs.'

hand-warmers. Female breasts: Australian raffish: since late 1920's.

handed to (someone) **on a plate,** (something) **was or has been.** A c.p. in ref. to easy acquisition: since ca. 1910.

*****handful.**—2. Hence, £5: c.: C. 20. See **hand**, 5, above.—3. Hence, also, a five-years' prison-sentence or -term: c., and London's East End s.: since ca. 1930. (Richard Herd, article in *The Evening News*, Nov. 12, 1957.)

handful of sprats. A sexual groping: low: late C. 19–20.

handies, play. To hold hands: jocular coll.: C. 20. Cf. *footy*.

handle, 1 (p. 371). The dating should read 'ca. 1790–1910'. *The Port Folio*, Dec. 29, 1804 (p. 413), quoting a British source, '. . . the *handle* of his face, ycleped the *nose*'. Moe.

handle the ribbing. To punch (someone) in the ribs: pugilistic: ca. 1830–70. *Sinks*, 1848.

handlebars. Moustaches resembling bicycle handlebars: since ca. 1910.

Handley Page. A stage: rhyming s.: since ca. 1920. 'Mainly theatrical' (Franklyn 2nd).

handraulic power. See **Johnny Armstrong**.

hands off cocks, feet in socks! A variant—mostly R.A.F.—of **rise and shine**: since ca. 1947.

hands to fishing-stations. The picking-up of dead fish after a depth-charge has been dropped at a test: Naval: since ca. 1938. (P-G-R.)

hands-upper. A surrendered Boer that eventually took (esp., fought on) the British side: 1900–2, then merely historical.

handshake. A 'backhander'—a tip, or a bribe, handed surreptitiously: since ca. 1930.

Handsome Harry. A 'gay Lothario' or ex-

ponent of the love-'em-and-leave-'em technique: feminine, esp. shop-girls' and office-girls': since ca. 1930.

handsomely . . . (p. 371). The nautical *handsomely!* has variant *handsomely, handsomely,* dating since ca. 1800 and occurring in, e.g., W. N. Glascock, *Sailors and Saints*, 1829, at I, 182, and II, 19. (Moe.)

handy Bill is a variant of **handy billy**, q.v. in *Dict.* 'Taffrail'.

handy Billy (p. 371) goes right back to ca. 1800. In W. N. Glascock, *Sailors and Saints*, 1829 (at I, 182), it is defined as 'Jigger-purchase, a small tackle so designated by seamen'. Moe.

hang a monkey. To buy a suit: proletarian (? mostly Liverpool): C. 20.

hang five—hang ten; hang eleven. To hang with one foot (five toes)—with both feet—over the *nose* or front of the board; 'ten toes and rider over nose of board': Australian surfers', esp. teenagers': since ca. 1960. (*Pix*, Sept. 28, 1963.)

hang it out. The *Dict.* sense prob. derives ex: 2. 'To "skulk" on a job—not to do justice when on time work': printers': from ca. 1870. B. & L.

hang on (p. 372) is current in Australia as *hang on!*, 'Don't be so hasty', or 'Be reasonable': coll.: mid-C. 19–20.—2. To wait: coll.: C. 20. Perhaps ex telephoning.

hang on that, Dook! Shake hands!: (non-aristocratic) Londoners': from ca. 1920. With a pun on **dook**, 1, 2 (*Dict.*).

hang—or tie—one on. To get (very) drunk: Canadian: adopted, ca. 1935, ex U.S.

hang one's hat up to is the v.t. form of **hang one's hat up** (*Dict.*). The nuance is often rather: to make pronounced matrimonial advances (to).

hang-out, n.—2. 'A feasting, an entertainment': Cambridge undergraduates': ca. 1845–70. B. & L.

hang out of. To coït with (a woman): Naval lower-deck: C. 20.—2. Hence, to commit sodomy: Naval (lower-deck): since ca. 1920.

hang-up, n.—2. Delay; frustration: Canadian jazz-lovers': since ca. 1956. *The* Victoria *Daily Colonist*, April 16, 1959, 'Basic Beatnik': '*Man*—Omnibus salutation extended to men, women, domestic animals—saves cool cat hangup of remembering names.'

hang up.—6. *Hanging it up*, cruising or dawdling near a given spot: taxi-drivers': since ca. 1910. Herbert Hodge, 1939.—7. See **phone, go for the**.

hang your number out to dry! A post-1920 variant of **before you came up!**: Services. H. & P.

hangar doors closed! A variant (Partridge, 1945) of **close hangar doors!**

hangashun or **hangava**, adv. Very: Australian children's: since ca. 1920. B., 1942. 'E.g., "hangashun good", very good, excellent. Cf. helluva.'

hangers. Female breasts: Australian raffish: since ca. 1930.

hanging on the slack. 'Waiting for something to happen' (Granville): Naval coll.: C. 20.

hangings. 'While the flogger was fixing me up [to the triangles] he said to me quietly, "Is there any hangings to it?" meaning had I anything to give him to lay it on lightly,' Louis Becke, *Old Convict Days*, 1897: prison warders' (esp. in Australia): ca. 1820–70.

hangover (one word) has, since ca. 1945, been preferred to *hang-over* (p. 372).

hangtelow. See **hanktelo** (*Dict.*).

hank, n.—2, 3. See **no hank**, 2 and 3.

hank, v. To hesitate, be diffident; also as ppl. adj., *hanking*: proletarian coll.: from ca. 1870. Nevinson, 1895, 'Lina's style, full of 'ankin' artful little ways'; 'Don't stand 'ankin' there; you're not the only person in the world.' Cf. S.E. *hank*, v.i., to hang, to hanker.

*****hank, on the.** On the look-out (for booty): c., and low Cockney: from ca. 1890. Clarence Rook, 1899.

hankie, occ. **hanky** (p. 373): much used also by women.

hanky-panky (p. 373). Julian Franklyn's suggestion (letter of 1962) is much more probable: a reduplication of *hanky*, handkerchief—the conjuror's handkerchief used 'to assist the quickness of the hand in deceiving the audience's eye'. —2. Hence, sexual caressing or intercourse, esp. in infidelity: C. 20.

Hannah. A Wren serving with the Royal Marines: 1939 +. 'From the famous Hannah Snell, who, disguised as a man, fought with the Marines on land and sea in the eighteenth century,' M.o.I.'s *News-Clip*, Feb. 16, 1944.

Hans Carvel's ring. Earlier in Urquhart's Rabelais, 1653.

Hans in Kelder (*Dict.*). For an interesting anecdote, see Thornbury's *London*, iii. 315.

Hansard. Messrs Hansard have for some years ceased to have the monopoly.

ha'penny.—2. The female pudend: feminine: C. 20.

Ha'penny Bumper, the. A horse-drawn tramcar that survived in Bermondsey long after the L.C.C. had electrified the rest of the system: Londoners': C. 20; now only historical.

ha'penny dip. A ship: Dockland rhyming s.: C. 20. (Franklyn 2nd.)

hap-harlot.—2. A woman's undergarments: C. 19. Also corrupted to *hap-parlet*. B. & L.

happen for (someone) **with** (something). '"I hope it may happen for her with this one" (meaning "I hope this one may be a success"' (Anthony Lejeune in *The Daily Telegraph*, colour supplement, March 10, 1967): since ca. 1965.

happening. A 'spontaneous eruption of feeling or display' (Peter Fryer in *The Observer* colour supplement, Dec. 3, 1967): jazz and drug addicts', and hippies': since ca. 1966. Cf. preceding entry.

Happy and Chatty (p. 374).—2. Hence, applied to any slack-disciplined, untidy ship: nautical: C. 20.

happy as a boxing kangaroo in fog time. Thoroughly discontented: Australian coll.: C. 20. B., 1942.

happy as a nun weeding the asparagus. Exceedingly happy: ? mostly Canadian: since ca. 1910. 'Uncommon but not rare' (Leechman). Erotic.

happy as Larry. See **Larry, (as) happy as**, on p. 470.

happy as pigs in shit, as. Completely happy: low: since ca. 1870. (Gerald Kersh, *Faces in a Dusty Picture*, 1944.)

happy days! A toast that has something of the quality of a c.p.: since ca. 1918. Rather since ca. 1910, for it occurs in 'Bartimeus', *Naval Occasions*, 1914, with the reply *Salue!*—either from Spanish *salud!* or, more probably, from the Fr. *salut!*

happy-ender. A story with a happy end: coll. (esp. in the book-world): late C. 19–20. Berta Ruck, 1935.

happy hours. Flowers: rhyming s., mainly theatrical: late C. 19–20. (Franklyn, *Rhyming*.)

happy in the Service? is the Navy's form of **are you happy in your work?** (Granville.)

Happy Valley.—2. (Cf. sense 1, p. 374.) Any city or locality, area, region, that is being (very) heavily bombed; esp. the Ruhr: R.A.F., esp. Bomber Command: 1941 +. H. & P.; Jackson. —3. A valley between Taungmaw and the Mankat Pass in Burma: Army: 1942–5.—4. (Usually lower-case.) Female genitals: C. 20.

harbour light, esp. **all . . .** (All) right: late C. 19–20; since ca. 1920, only in *all harbour*. (Franklyn.)

harch off. 'To abandon or leave' (B., 1953): Australian (originally Services'): since ca. 1940.

hard a-Gilbert. Hard a-port: Naval: late C. 19– mid C. 20. Presumably a corruption of *hard a-Gilbey*, a pun on Messrs *Gilbey*, wine-merchants to the Navy and noted for their excellent port wine. (P-G-R, 1948.)

hard-arse. A wooden chair: cf. *T.S.R. arse*, the effect of the hard chairs in Temple Speech Room: Rugby School: resp. since ca. 1910 and since ca. 1945. (D. F. Wharton.)

hard as a goat's knees. Extremely hard: Aus.: C. 20. (B., 1959.)

hard-faced. Impudent: Liverpool; half-way between coll. and dial.: late C. 19–20.

Hard-Faced Parliament, The. The one elected in 1919: coll.: ca. 1919–22, then merely historical. It contained many war-made millionaires. (Jack Lawson, 1932.)

hard-hat man. An inspector: railwaymen's: C. 20. (*Railway*.)

hard head. A 'hard case': Australian: since ca. 1910. (Caddie, *A Sydney Barmaid*, 1953.)

hard jack. Bully beef (in tins) and biscuits: Army: 1914–18, nor yet quite †. See **jack**, n., 21 (p. 429).

hard-lyers is the 1914–18 and 1939–45 form of **hard-lying money** (*Dict.*): 'Taffrail', *The Sub*, 1917; Granville, 1945.

hard neck. Impudence: Anglo-Irish: late C. 19–20. '"You had the hard neck to pass the time of day with him"': Brendan Behan, *Borstal Boy*, 1958. Cf. **neck**, n., on p. 554.

hard O'Brien, the. A complimentary remark: Anglo-Irish: since ca. 1925. Perhaps ex some famous Irish flatterer surnamed O'Brien.

hard put to it (p. 375) may well go back as far as to ca. 1690, for B.E., 1699, has the entry, '*Oxhouse*. . . . The Black Ox has not trod upon his Foot*, of one that has not been Pinch'd with Want, or been Hard put to it.'

hard scran! Hard luck!: Australian: mid-C. 19–20. B., 1942. Ex commiseration on hard fare. It occurs in, e.g., Norman Lindsay, *Saturdee*, 1933.

hard shot. A 'hard case' (p. 374): New Zealand: since ca. 1930. (Slatter.)

hard-skinned. (Of vehicles) armoured: Army: since 1940; by 1944, coll. (P-G-R.)

hard thing (p. 375) is also Australian: B., 1943.

hard (or **tough**) **titty!** Hard luck!: c.p., often

ironical: Canadian: since ca. 1930. Hard on the baby.

hard-up, adj., 1 (p. 375), occurs in Alfred Burton, *Johnny Newcome*, 1818. (Moe.)—4. Impeded; detained: Naval: ca. 1790–1850. W. N. Glascock, *Sketch-Book*, II, 1826. (Moe.)—5. (Of an engine) short of steam: railwaymen's: C. 20. (*Railway* 2nd.)

hard-up, n.—6. Tobacco from picked-up stumps of cigarettes: c., mostly vagrants': from ca. 1920. Ex sense 5.

hard wood, the. A useful 'tip' (information), a verbal warning: Anglo-Irish coll.: late (? mid) C. 19–20. 'They were planning to betray . . . me, but Ned gave me the hard wood, and I was prepared for them.' (P. W. Joyce, 1910.)

hard word on, put the (p. 375).—2. Of a man urging a woman to lie with him: Australian: C. 20. B., 1942. The phrase has, in Australia, long been applied to any request or approach difficult or unpleasant to make. (B.P.)

hardened tea-drinker. A person as fond of tea as a drunkard of his liquor: jocose coll.: since ca. 1910.

harder than pulling a soldier off your sister, it's or that's. A c.p., stigmatising circumstances in which compliance goes against the grain: low (mostly Naval): since ca. 1939.

hardware.—2. The basic arithmetical unit of a computer, as opposed to *software*, computer programmes and peripheral equipment: adopted, ex U.S., ca. 1960. (David Wharton, letter of 6 June 1966.)

hare, v. (p. 376). Hence, in the R.A.F., since ca. 1925: to fly at full speed. Jackson.

harem, the. The living-quarters of the Waafs or the Wrens (Waffery or Wrennery): Forces', mostly R.A.F. and esp. in the Near or the Middle East: 1939–45.

hark (usually **'ark**) **at her!** A derisive C. 20 c.p., directed at a man 'uttering supposedly well-meaning or high-sounding sentiments' (Atkinson). Evocative of back-street disputes.

[Harlots: C. 18 terms in the words of Ned Ward are these: *bang-tails* (1703), *belfas* (1703), *Blowzabellas* (1703), *blowzes* (1709), *bunters* (1709), *does* (1700; but in R. Head, *Proteus Redivivus*, 1675), *doxies* (1703), *drabs* (1715), *fire-ships* (1709), *frowes* (1703), *jilts* (1703), *lady-birds* (1703), *lechery-layers* (1703), *madams* (1703; prob. S.E.), *market dames* (1705), *nymphs of delight* (1703), *punchable nuns* (1709), *punks* (1703), *snuffling community* (1709), *still sows* (1709), *tickle-tail function* (1703), *trugmoldies* (1703), *trulls* (1703), *wag-tails* (1703). He calls bawds by three names: *madam* (1709), *Mother Knab-Cony* (1709) and *succubus* (1709: rare and prob. S.E.). With bawds he associates midwives, for whom his names are *groper* (1703) and *Mother Midnight* (1714). Matthews.]

harness.—3. Parachute straps: Air Force: since ca. 1935. Perhaps ex—certainly cf.—sense 2 (p. 376).—4. (Ex 2.) A passenger-train conductors' uniform: Canadian railroadmen's (— 1931).—5. Foundation garments: feminine coll., mostly Australian: since ca. 1930.

harness bull. A uniformed policeman: low Canadian: adopted, in 1930's, ex U.S., where originally underworld.

Harold Lloyd, often shortened to **Harold.** Celluloid, 'an instrument of housebreaking' (cf. **loid** below): rhyming s., dating from ca. 1917; orig.,

underworld; by 1940, also police s. (John Gosling, *The Ghost Squad*, 1959.) Ex the deservedly famous American cinematic comedian, whose heyday was ca. 1914–35.

Harpic. Mad, crazy; bomb-shocked: R.A.F.: since early 1930's; † by 1945: superseded by *round the bend.*

Harriet Lane. Also Naval: 'Taffrail'.

Harriet the Chariot. In Australia, any *Harriet* has, since ca. 1930, tended to be thus nicknamed. The nickname is derogatory—with *chariot*, semantically cf. **town-bike** below. '*Myrtle the Turtle* and *Harriet the Chariot* are so well known that any Australian male would veto the choice of such a name for his daughter. I have never heard of a Harriet, no matter how virtuous, who was not called *Harriet the Chariot*' (B.P., in a note written in June 1963).

Harry Blissington. See:

Harry Booters. See **boot-faced** above.

Harry Clampers. See **clampers** above.

Harry Crashers. Sleep; sleeping: Naval: since ca. 1940. (P-G-R.) Cf. *crash one's*, or *the*, *swede*.

Harry Flakers. One is 'Harry Flakers' when one is 'completely flaked out after a party' (Granville): Naval: since ca. 1918. *Harry* is predominant in s. phrases; cf. next two entries—also **flaked out.** Gilderdale, 2, concerning the smart young set, writes, on May 23, 1958, 'One verbal affectation (not new, but still in circulation) is the habit of saying "Harry" in conjunction with a host of words. Thus: Harry champers (champagne), Harry bangers (sausages), Harry redders (red wine), Harry spraggers (spaghetti), Harry blissington (absolutely wonderful).'

Harry Flatters. A calm, *flat* sea: Naval: C. 20. Granville.—2. Adv., 'flat out'—at full throttle: R.A.F.: since ca. 1958. (Peter Sanders.)

Harry Freeman's (or **Freemans**).—2. Free cigarettes: C. 20. From ca. 1925, often corrupted, mostly among Cockneys, to *Yenhams*.

Harry Hase. See **Henry Hase.**

Harry James. Nose; nostrils: low: since ca. 1940. 'There is plenty of dust floating about . . . which gets in your north and south and up your Harry James' (Norman).

Harry Jessell's gratitude, 'i.e., none at all—became a by-word' (C. Hindley, *Cheap Jack*, 1876): cheapjacks': ca. 1840–70.

Harry Lauder. A prison warder: rhyming s.: since ca. 1905.

Harry Roughers. See **roughers.**

Harry Screechers. See **screechers** below.

Harry Skinters. 'Skint' or penniless: since late 1950's, but 'not common' (Peter Sanders). By elaboration.

Harry Starkers. Stark-naked, or stark-mad: since late 1950's. (Sanders.) An elaboration of **starkers** (p. 825).

Harry Tagg. A bag: rhyming s., mostly theatrical: late C. 19–20. (Franklyn, *Rhyming*.)

Harry Tate.—4. Late: rhyming s.: ca. 1905–15. (Franklyn, *Rhyming*.)—5. First Officer: Merchant Navy rhyming s. (on *mate*): since ca. 1910. Franklyn 2nd.

Harry Tate's Light Horse. See **Fred Karno's Navy.**

Harry Tate's Navy (p. 377).—3. Hence, in 1939–45 (and after), the c.p. *what do you think this is—Harry Tate's Navy?*

Harry, Tom and Dick. Unwell: rhyming s.: C. 20. Cf. *Tom, Harry and Dick*.

Harry Wragg. A cigarette: rhyming s. on synonymous *fag*: since ca. 1930. Ex the famous ex-jockey and racehorse-trainer.

harumphrodite. A sol. form of *hermaphrodite*: ? from before 1880. Often for a person neither one thing nor the other. (More gen. —*fr*—; see **harumfrodite** in the *Dict*.) Wm McFee, *North of Suez*, 1930 (with debt to Kipling, *The Seven Seas*: 1896):

> ''E isn't one of the regular line
> And 'e isn't one of the crew—
> 'E's a sort o' giddy harumphrodite
> Soldier and sailor too.'

Harvest Moon. A racial term used, since ca. 1945, in the London docks. *The New Statesman*, Dec. 31, 1965.

Harvey. Short for **Harvey Nichol** (*Dict*.).

Harvey Nichol (p. 377) is 'pickle', trouble, predicament, not 'pickle', a condiment. The pl., however, does usually denote 'pickles', condiments. (Franklyn, *Rhyming*.)

has-beens. Greens: rhyming s., orig. and still mainly underworld: C. 20.

has everything, she. A c.p., applied to a—esp., physically—very attractive woman: since ca. 1945. Also *has two of everything*.

hash, n.—5. Hashish: teenage drug addicts': since early 1950's. By 1960, all addicts', as in Alan Diment, *The Dolly Dolly Spy*, 1963.

hash, settle one's. Thoroughly English; it occurs in Isaac Cruikshank, *Olympic Games*, June 16, 1803. (Thanks to Mrs M. D. George.)

hash-me-gandy. Station stew: New Zealand and Australian rural: since ca. 1920. B., 1942, suggests: ex Mahatma Gandhi's frugal meals. An elaboration of *hash*. 'Could the form of this word be based on S. E. *salmagundi*' (Ramsey Spencer)— a spiced dish of minced meat and eggs, hence a medley? It does indeed sound a plausible suggestion.

hashy. Clever: Charterhouse School: C. 20. Ex **hash pro** (*Dict*.).

hasn't had it so long, she or occasionally **he**; sometimes preceded by **but**. A c.p. reply to the frequently heard plaint, 'What has *she* (or *he*) got that *I* haven't got?': since late 1950's. (A. B. Petch, April 1966.)

hassle. A fuss, a disagreement, a row; a hullabaloo: Canadian: adopted, ca. 1860, ex U.S. Leechman, who proposes a blend of *haggle* + *tussle*; I, one of *haggle* + *wrestle*.

haste! 'Look out! Mainly used in criminal jargon. Whence *haste it!*, to cease some activity, equivalent of Stop it! Synonymous is *áce it!*' (B., 1959): Aus. c.: since ca. 1935.

haste, adv. Quickly; immediately: Australian: since ca. 1930. Kylie Tennant, *The Joyful Condemned*, 1953, 'So hand over the two quid and give it haste.' Probably ex S.E. *post-haste*.

hat.—7. Price: showmen's: late C. 19–20. *Night and Day*, July 22, 1937. Ex hat as offertory.

hat!, I'll have your. A street cry of ca. 1880–1905. B. & L.

hat, pass or **send round the** (p. 378). The *send* form is much the commoner and it goes back to ca. 1820 or even to ca. 1805. Wm Maginn, *Tales of Military Life*, 1829, at I, 64, 'Having "sent

round the hat"' for the benefit of the poor and half-petrified host.' (Moe.)

Hat, the. Medicine Hat, Alberta: Canadian: since ca. 1920. (Leechman.)

hat rack. Thin, scraggy horse or ox: Australian: C. 20. B., 1942.

hat trick (p. 378). Perhaps prompted by 'bowler hats': see article in *The Times*, Aug. 14, 1937.

hatch. A bomb hatch (a bomb-aimer's compartment): Air Force coll.: since ca. 1938.

hate against, have a. To dislike (person or thing) intensely: Australian coll.: 1918 +. B., 1942.

hate (someone's) **guts.** To hate someone intensely: adopted, ca. 1937, from U.S. Agatha Christie, *Towards Zero*, 1944.

hate oneself, as in 'You do hate yourself, don't you': ironic coll., applied to a person with a fine conceit of himself: since ca. 1938.

hatful of worms. See **silly as a hatful of worms** below.

hatter.—3. A pal, a mate, usually in a homosexual sense. C. 20.

Hatters, the. The Stockport Association football team: sporting: since ca. 1925. *Chronicles of the Chelsea Football Club*, Oct. 23, 1937.—2. Also the Luton A.F.C.: since ca. 1930. Hats are made in the town.

*haul a cly. To snatch a purse: c.: C. 18. James Dalton, 1728.

haul arse. To go off or away, often quickly: Canadian: since ca. 1930. 'Come on, Jack! Let's haul arse out of here.' (Leechman.)

*haul-cly. A pickpocket: c.: C. 18. James Dalton, *A Narrative*, 1728. Ex **haul a cly** above.

*haul cly, the. Purse-snatching: c.: C. 18. James Dalton, *A Narrative*, 1728. Ex **haul a cly** above.

haul down promotion. See **promotion.**

haul one's ashes. To coït: low Canadian: late C. 19–20.

Hauliers' slang. The British Road Services have a slang of their own: and much of it—that is, many of the printable terms—has been recorded in *British Road Services Magazine*, Dec. 1951.

Aberdeen booster. See *Scotsman's fifth.*

anchor. A brake: since ca. 1930.

Billy Bunter. A shunter: rhyming s.: since ca. 1925.

Chinese dominoes. A load of bricks: since ca. 1930.

Chinese gunpowder. Cement: since ca. 1930.

dangler or *pup.* A trailer: since ca. 1920.

hook, on the; *on the ribs.* On tow; very old; since ca. 1925 and 1920.

jockey or *pilot.* The driver of any heavy-load vehicle: since ca. 1925 and 1945.

load of wind. A light load: since ca. 1920.

monkey. 'Two-wheeled trailer used for carrying very long loads': since ca. 1930.

Mrs Greenfield's, staying at. See below.

pilot. See *jockey.*

pimple. A steep hill: since ca. 1925.

pipe. A telephone: since ca. 1925.

poodler. A small vehicle: since ca. 1935.

pup. See *dangler.*

ribs, on the. See *hook, on the.*

roller skate. A small, light waggon: since ca. 1945.

round the house. (Adj. and adv.) Of or for or in or by 'multiple delivery work': coll.: C. 20.

Scotsman's fifth or *Aberdeen booster*. Coasting (n.): since ca. 1930.

showboat. A large eight-wheeled van (Fisher Renwick type): since ca. 1946.

skull. A passenger: since ca. 1945.

smoke, up the, adj. and adv. Going to London: C. 20.

spud-basher. A lorry carrying potatoes: since ca. 1920.

staying at Mrs Greenfield's. Sleeping in the cab of one's vehicle: since ca. 1925.

track, up the, adj. and adv. Travelling along a depot's particular trunk route: since ca. 1940.

In *Drive*, a motorists' magazine, there appeared in 1968, at p. 113, an article that appears to 'catch up' and add to the list given above. The only new terms, including modifications, are these:—

bookie. A Scottish lorry-drivers' term for the office where he books in and receives his instructions and documents.

crime-sheet. A log-sheet.

gunpowder. Short for *Chinese gunpowder*.

junk pile. A lorry in exceedingly poor condition: a 'pile' fit only for the 'junk heap'.

quickie up the track. A return journey made during one night and along the usual route—cf. *track, up the*.

stiff 'un, the. A person given a lift: he just sits there while the driver does all the work and takes all the responsibility.

hava no and **hava yes**. (Mostly of persons, occasionally of events) to be ineligible or unattractive or inferior; to be very eligible or attractive; hence also n. and adj.: United Nations troops' (in Korea): ca. 1951–5. (*Iddiwah*, July 1953.) As it were, the 'have-nots' and the 'haves'; ex pidgin *hava*, to have.

Havannah, under a canopy of. 'Sitting where there are many persons smoking tobacco,' *Sinks*, 1848: ca. 1840–60.

have, n.—3. A disappointment, a 'let-down': C. 20. Ex sense 2 on p. 379.

have a baby. See **kittens, having.**

have a ball. To have a good time: among teenagers, since ca. 1945; among beatniks, since ca. 1957.

have a beat. To try; in cricket, to bat vigorously: since ca. 1925.

have a beat on. See **beat on . . .**

have a bit. See **bit, have a.**

have a bit off. See **bit off, have a.**

have a cook. See **give a cook.**

have a crack at. See **crack, n., 13.**

have a go.—2. To coït: late C. 19–20. Very general.

have a go, Joe, your mother will never know!; often shortened to *have a go, Jo.* A c.p. of encouragement to a reluctant man: Cockneys' and Forces': since ca. 1935. (Atkinson.)

have a good chit. To be well spoken, or thought, of: Army (mostly officers'): since ca. 1930. Ex **chit, 1, 2** (*Dict.*). Cf. **give** (someone) *a good chit*: to speak well of: Army officers': since ca. 1930.

have a roll!, usually preceded by *go and*. Go to the devil: Australian: since ca. 1925. (B., 1943.)

***have a tickle.** See **tickle, have a.**

have down the banks and **have high-ding-dong.** To have a 'row', a fight: Liverpool: late C. 19–20. '*High-ding-dong*, suggests a noisy fight; *the banks* refers to Canal banks, where fights often took place' (Frank Shaw, 1952).

have fifty (or a hundred) up. To coït with a girl: sporting: C. 20. Ex billiards.

have fun. See **fun, have.**

have had it.—3. Esp. in *You've had it*, You won't get it, you're too late, etc.: R.A.F.: since 1938 or 1939; current in Army since late 1940 or early 1941; >, in 1944, fairly general civilian. *The New Statesman*, Aug. 30, 1941; Grenfell Finn-Smith, in list communicated in April 1942; H. & P.; Jackson; Partridge. Ironic—perhaps short for 'Somebody else has (or, may have) had it, but you certainly won't.' See esp. Partridge, 1945.—4. '"He's had it" and "He's gone for a Burton" indicate that's he's been killed,' F. Rhodes (letter of Sept. 1942): R.A.F.: since late 1939. I.e. 'copped' it. This sense, according to Jock Marshall & Russell Drysdale, *Journey among Men*, 1962 (p. 17), 'originated in the Gulf Country of northern Queensland, where one of us heard it as early as 1929. Oddly enough, the phrase was never current in the populous south before the war. It was taken to Europe by Queensland troops or airmen and there, where lots of chaps were having it, so to speak, it came into general currency. It was circuitously from Europe, and not directly from the north, that the expression reached the southern parts of Australia.'

have (someone) in. To make a fool of: Aus.: since ca. 1940. Nino Culotta, *Cop This Lot*, 1960. A variant of *have on* (p. 380).

***have it away.** To escape: prison c.: since ca. 1940. (Norman.)

have it away on the hurry-up. To depart, to leave, smartly or hurriedly: since ca. 1945: c. >, by ca. 1955, low s. (Robin Cook, 1962.) An extension of the preceding.

have it away together. To copulate: mostly teenagers': since ca. 1950. Perhaps influenced by the sexual sense of **have it off** (below).

***have it away with** (something). To steal: since ca. 1925. Robin Cook, 1962.

have it in. To effect intromission: low coll.: late C. 19–20. Partly euphemistic.

have it in for (someone). To bear a grudge against: coll.: since ca. 1820. Alex. Harris, *The Emigrant Family*, 1849. Cf. **carry in one's heart.**

***have it off** (*Dict.*). It is the c. equivalent of *pull it off*. 'It is also used by a punter who has had a successful bet or by a man that has contrived to seduce a girl' (James Curtis, in a private letter, March 1937).—2. Hence, simply to copulate: low: since ca. 1940. In, e.g., Robin Cook, *The Crust on Its Uppers*, 1962.

***have it on one's toes.** A variant of **have it away**: prison c.: since ca. 1940. (Norman.) Cf. the S.E. *heel and toe it*, to walk in a race.

have it up. To copulate: low: late C. 19–20.

have kittens. See **kittens, having.**

have nothing on its feet. (Of a racehorse) to be either shoeless or to wear only light plates: Australian sporting coll.: since ca. 1925. (B., 1953.)

have on.—2. *To have someone on* is to be prepared, or actually, to fight: Australian: C. 20. B., 1942.

have on the stick. To make fun of, pull someone's leg: ca. 1870–1914. (William Westall, *Sons of Belial*, 1895.)

have one for the worms. See **worms**.

have one's back teeth awash (see **back teeth underground** in *Dict.*) is extant. Granville. The word *back* is sometimes omitted.

have one's ballocks in the right place. An approbatory c.p., applied to a well-set-up and level-headed man: C. 20.

have one's cut. (Of a male) to coït: low: late C. 19–20.

have the bird. To be sent about one's business: non-cultured: from ca. 1910. Edgar Wallace, *The Avenger*, 1926, 'In the vulgar language of the masses, I have had the bird.' Ex *get the bird*, q.v. in *Dict.* at **bird, give (one) the.**

have the goods on (p. 380) was also, by 1935, Australian and, by 1940, s. (B., 1943.)

*****have the needle**—intensively, **dead needle**—to (someone). To be (extremely) angry with: since ca. 1925; c. >, by 1940, low s.

have the painters in or **have the rags (on).** See **rags on . . .**

*****have (someone) well under the cosh.** To have someone completely in one's power: since ca. 1935. Cf. **cosh**, n., 1, on p. 151.

have (object)—**will** (verb), as in the 'Have gun— will travel' of advertisements in, e.g., *The Times* or in the jocular reassurance 'Have pen—will write': half a c.p., half a vogue phrase (cf. '*came the* dawn'): since ca. 1945; by 1966, slightly ob.

have you any kind thoughts in your mind? A c.p. preliminary to asking for a loan or other favour: since the 1920's.

have you any more funny stories? and **now tell me the one about the three bears.** Tell me another!: c.pp. of polite scepticism or boredom, esp. in Australia: since ca. 1930. (B.P.)

have you shit the bed? A low c.p. addressed to someone rising earlier than usual in the morning: late C. 19–20.

haven't his best friends told him? A jocular c.p.—based on the advertisements of a well-known deodorant—current since the late 1950's. Not necessarily in reference to body odour.

having a baby—having kittens. See **kittens, having,** near end.

having a good arm. A military c.p. (C. 20) applied to a man with numerous badges on his sleeve; e.g. 'marksman', 'farrier', 'Lewis gunner'.

having an easy. See **not off** below.

having fun? A c.p. addressed to someone in obvious difficulties: since ca. 1950. Cf. **are you happy in your work?** (above).

having kittens. See **kittens, having.**

Haw-Haw; in full, **Lord Haw-Haw.** William Joyce, broadcaster of propaganda from German wireless stations: 1939–45. Executed as traitor. Ex his tired and affected voice.

hawbuck (p. 380). Cf. John Masefield's novel, *The Hawbucks*, 1929, about fox-hunting people.

hawk it. To be a prostitute on the streets: low: late C. 19–20. Ex **hawk one's mutton** (*Dict.*).

Hawkesbury Rivers. The shivers: Australian rhyming s.: C. 20. B., 1942. Hence, *Hawkes buries.*

hawks. An advantage: London: ca. 1835–60. *Sinks*, 1848. Ex Fr. *haussé.*

hawse, come across one's (p. 381): goes back to ca. 1810 or even ca. 1800; it occurs in, e.g., W. N. Glascock, *Sailors and Saints*, 1829, at I, 82. (Moe.) The same work (I, 99) has also *cross one's hawse.*

hawse-holes, creep (or **come**) **in by the** (p. 381). Variant: *enter by . . .*, as in Fredk Marryat, *Frank Mildmay*, 1829 (p. 242 of the 1897 edition). Moe.

hay, n. See **chaff, 3.**

hay is for horses; occ.—with conversion of *hey* to *eh*—'ay is for 'orses. A c.p. used when someone says *hey!* or *eh?* for *I beg your pardon*: C. 18– 20. This, the oldest of all c.pp., is recorded in Swift's *Polite Conversation*, 1738: see esp. my *Comic Alphabets*, 1961, and commentary edition, 1963, of Swift's *Conversation.*

*****hay-tit** or **haytit.** A woman (*tit*) given to sleeping under haystacks; hence, a tramp prostitute: c., mostly tramps': C. 20. W. L. Gibson Cowan, *Loud Report*, 1937.

hay-wire; gen. **haywire.** Beside oneself with anger; crazy, very eccentric: anglicised, ex U.S., in 1936. (Ernest Weekley, in *The Observer*, Feb. 21, 1937.) For origin and American usage, see Irwin.

haybag, old. See **old haybag.**

haywire, go. To go crazy; of mechanisms, to get (completely) out of order: anglicised in 1936. Cf. **hay-wire.**

*****hazard drum;** or **h.-d.** A gambling den or house: c. (— 1860); ob. H., 2nd ed.

he bought it. See **buy it.**

he could fall into (the) shit (Canadian **a shit-hole**) **and come up smelling of violets.** A low c.p., directed at an exceptionally lucky fellow: late C. 19–20.

he-cups. Hiccoughs: mostly Cockneys': mid-C. 19–20.

he'd drink the stuff if he had to strain it through a shitty cloth. He's a hopeless drunkard: low Canadian c.p.: since ca. 1920.

He-Face. A Public Schools', esp. Harrovian, nickname for men surnamed Baker. Ex **he,** a cake (see the *Dict.*). For further details, consult my 'Inseparables' in *A Covey of Partridge.*—Hence, *He-Face Street*, Baker Street, London.

he-fo. A sky-rocket: pidgin: from ca. 1860. B. & L. In Cantonese, lit. rise-fire.

he has had it. See **have had it.**

he looks as if he'd pissed on a nettle. 'A c.p. evoked on seeing a doleful countenance' (Leechman): late C. 19–20. Ex **nettle, to have pissed on a,** on p. 556.

He, Me and You. 'Familiar German types (of aircraft) are summarised in the technical joke, "*He*, *Me*, and *You*", the Heinkel, Messerschmitt, Junkers', E. P., 'Air Warfare and its Slang', in *The New Statesman*, Sept. 19, 1942; earliest printed record, however, is a terse paragraph in *The Daily Express*, July 3, 1940.

he never does anything wrong! (p. 381): ex a Gaiety Theatre play wherein the 'Rajah of Bong' sings, 'In me you see the Rajah of Bong Who never, no never, did anything wrong.'

he never had no mother—he hatched out when his dad pissed against a wall one hot day. A low military c.p. of C. 20.

he thinks it's just to pee through! 'Said of an unsophisticated youth' (Leechman): c.p.: C. 20. He thinks his penis is for urination only.

he will shag anything from seventeen to seventy.

A c.p. applied to an inveterate womanizer: ate C. 19–20.

he wouldn't say 'shit' (even) if he had a, or his, mouth full of it. A low Canadian c.p., describing a man excessively mealy-mouthed: since ca. 1930.

head, n., 2, goes back to the early C. 18; it occurs, e.g., in Woodes Rogers, *A Cruising Voyage round the World*, 1708, and in Smollett's *Roderick Random*, 1748. (Moe.)—5. A racing sharp: c.: from ca. 1885–6. Hence, a professional gambler, e.g. at 'two-up': Australian c. and low: from ca. 1890.—6. A long-term prisoner: Australian c.: C. 20. B., 1942. Looked-up-to by his fellow convicts.—7. A girl, a young lady: beatniks': since ca. 1959. (Anderson.) Ex '*head* of hair'?

head, wear a. See **wear a head.**

head boy. Senior under-officer: Royal Military Academy: from ca. 1875. B. & L.

head bummaroo, the. A chief organiser; most important person present; manager: mid-C. 19–20; virtually †. A perversion of **bumper** (*Dict.*).

head down, get one's. To go to sleep: Services: since 1925. H. & P. One lays one's head down.

head hag. Headmistress: schoolgirls': C. 20. John Brophy, *Behold the Judge*, 1937.

head(-)lamp. An eye; usually in pl.: pugilistic: ca. 1840–90. Augustus Mayhew, 1857.

head like a sieve, have a. To be extremely forgetful: coll.: mid-C. 19–20.

head off, v.i. To begin a journey: Australian: since ca. 1925. 'Supposing that we get everything squared away, when'll you be ready to head off?': A. M. Harris, *The Tall Man*, 1958. Ex cattle-droving?

head on, have a.—2. To have a headache: coll.: C. 20.

head over tip. Head over heels: 1824, *Boxiana*, IV; ob. Cf. **arse over tip.**

head pin. The head brakeman: Canadian railroadmen's (— 1931). Cf. English *king pin*.

head screwed on right (or the right way), have one's. See **screw on right** (p. 738).

head-shrinker. A psychiatrist, esp. if a psychoanalyst: adopted, in late 1950's, ex U.S. In *Woman's Own*, Oct. 31, 1964, Monica Dickens writes, 'Deliver me from the head shrinkers, I have prayed.' An allusion to the shrinking of corpses' heads practised by certain South American tribes.

head them; heads-and-tails school. To play two-up; a two-up school: Australian coll.: resp. late C. 19–20 and C. 20. B., 1942.

***head-topper.** A hat; a wig: c.: mid-C. 19–20; ob. B. & L.

headache. A problem; a worry ('That's *your* headache!'): since ca. 1920: coll. >, by 1947, familiar S.E.

headacher. A severe punch on the head: pugilistic: ca. 1840–90. Augustus Mayhew, *Paved with Gold*, 1857.

headie. See **tailie.**

headlights. Spectacles: Australian: since ca. 1905. B., 1942.—2. Female breasts: Australian since ca. 1910. Baker.

headlines, make the. To get one's name into the headlines or on to the front page: journalistic coll.: since ca. 1925.

heads, the.—2. Seamen's latrines: Naval coll.: late C. 19–20. Granville, 'Right forward'. Hence *the Captain of the Heads*, the rating responsible for their cleanliness. It prob. goes back much further: W. N. Glascock, *Sketch-Book*, II, 1826,

has the variant *captain o' the head*, Naval s. of ca. 1790–1850. (Moe.)

heads-and-tails school. See **head them.**

heads on 'em like boils is an Australian two-up players' c.p., applied to coins that have yielded a long run of heads: since ca. 1930. (Lawson Glassop, *Lucky Palmer*, 1948.) Cf. the Australian card-players' *heads on 'em like mice*, applied to a very strong hand: since ca. 1935. (B., 1945.)

heap, n.—2. A person, a section, a detachment that is very slack and slovenly: Army: 1940 +. (H. & P.) Cf. **shower.**—3. An old car, esp. if owned by youths: Canadian: since ca. 1939. Ex '*heap* of old iron'. (Professor F. E. L. Priestley, who, 1949, writes: 'Displaces *jaloppy*, which barely survives, though still heard.')

heap, go over the. To relieve oneself: colliery surface workers': late C. 19–20. Ex using the slag heap for this purpose.

heap of coke. Much earlier in Mayhew, I, 1851.

heap of pot. A quantity—5 pounds in weight—of marijuana: drug addicts': since ca. 1960. (*The Times*, Feb. 19, 1964.)

hear from you!, let's. See **let's** . . . (p. 479).

hear (a pupil, a child) out. To test his knowledge: elementary schoolteachers' coll.: late C. 19–20.

hear (oneself) think, one cannot or **can hardly.** A c.p., directed at much, esp. if excessive, noise: since ca. 1916.

heard, or have you heard, the news? The squire—or the squire's daughter—has been foully —or most foully—murdered. A c.p. satirical of the old late Victorian and the Edwardian melodrama: since ca. 1905. For its use in the Army of 1914–18, see Brophy & Partridge, *Songs and Slang of the British Soldier*, 1930; Phillip MacDonald, *Rope to Spare*, 1932; 'Jokers still come on with it,' A. B. Petch, in letter of Sept. 5, 1946.

(have you) heard this one? A c.p., preliminary to a story: since ca. 1910.

hearse. An enemy submarine: Naval and R.A.F. on Western Approaches: from ca. 1941. Derogatory rather than macabre.

heart, have a. To have a weak heart: coll.: late C. 19–20.

Heart, the. A col. for *the Dead Heart* (of Australia), Central Australia: since ca. 1930. (B., 1959.)

heart . . ., you may have broke your mother's. See **you may have** . . . in the *Dict.*

heart bleeds for, usu. *my heart bleeds for you*, Although lit. 'I grieve for you', it is always ironic, often quite bitterly ironic: since the late 1950's. Probably by a wincing reaction against that gushing sympathy which is insincere and, indeed, hypocritical—and wouldn't part with a penny. A variant, c.p., more American than British, is *I weep for you*.

Heart-Break Corner. A store-room for postal matter wrongly or insufficiently addressed or too loosely tied: post office workers': since ca. 1935.

Heart-Break Hilda. Frau Sperling: lawn-tennis world: ca. 1931–39. (H. W. Austin, in *The Evening News*, June 29, 1937.) Ex her powers of retrieving and her steadiness in return: ineffectual, however, when playing against a Marble wall.

heart of oak. A variant (e.g. in Binstead's *Pitcher in Paradise*) of **hearts of oak** (*Dict.*).

heart throb. One's girl friend; occ. one's boy

friend: Cape Town University: 1940; ob. Prof. W. S. Mackie in *The Cape Argus*, July 4, 1946.—2. A glamorous film-star (either sex): 1945 +.

heart-to-heart. A heart-to-heart talk: coll.: C. 20.

heart-trouble. Euphemistic for 'fear' or 'cowardliness': 1940 +.

heart up, enough to have one's (p. 383) prob. goes back to ca. 1810 or even earlier, to judge by John L. Gardner, *The Military Sketch-Book* (II, 34), 1831, '. . . The rough sea had already almost "brought his heart up".' Moe.

hearth rug. A dupe, a simpleton: rhyming s.: since ca. 1910. On *mug*.—2. (Usually in plural.) A bug, esp. a bed-bug: rhyming s.: C. 20. Both senses, ob. by 1960. 'Never was so popular as **steam tug** (p. 827)': Franklyn 2nd.

hearts. Short for **hearts of oak** (p. 383): C. 20.

hearty.—4. (Slightly) tipsy: Anglo-Irish: late C. 19–20. (P. W. Joyce, 1910.) Cf. **happy** on p. 374.

*****heat.** A being wanted by the police: adopted, ca. 1936, from U.S. ('"The bleeding heat's on here for me,"' James Curtis, *They Ride By Night*, 1938) and >, by 1946, low s. See esp. *Underworld*.

*****heat, give the.** See **give the heat.**

heave, n.—2. An effort; display of energy: Guardsmen's: since ca. 1925. 'To tell us "to get a powerful heave" on our kits and lay them out neatly,' Roger Grinstead, 1946.—3. A thrower-out or bouncer: Sydneyites': since ca. 1943. (*The Evening News*, Feb. 16, 1949.)

heave, v.—3. To throw away; to discard: mostly Australian: since ca. 1920. Ex sense 2 on p. 384.—4. (V.i.) to vomit: Australian: since ca. 1925. (B.P.)

heavenly collar; heavenly lapel. A collar, or a lapel, that turns the wrong way: tailors': from ca. 1860. B. & L.

heavenly plan. A man: Australian rhyming s. of ca. 1885–1914. (B., 1945, citing *The* Sydney *Bulletin*, Jan. 18, 1902.)

heavens above. Love: rhyming s.: C. 20. Franklyn 2nd.

heaver.—3. (Gen. pl.) A person in love: low: ? C. 18–19. B. & L. Ex sense 2.—4. A coin of low value; a penny: C. 20. (A. E. Coppard, *Adam and Eve and Pinch Me*, 1921.) Ex being used in tossing-up? More likely to be a shortened form of the synonymous *coal-heaver* (p. 163).

heavy. For 1, 2, see **Heavies, the,** on p. 384.—3. (Ex, or at least cf., the artillery sense.) A heavy bomber or a large bomb: R.A.F. coll.: 1940 +. Jackson.—4. A serious actor: filmland's: since ca. 1915. Cameron McCabe, 1937.—5. A girl: Australian teenage surfers': since ca. 1960. (*Pix*, Sept. 28, 1963.)

For sense 6, note that *the heavy*, as in 'In recounting the incident, he made me the heavy'=he made me the villain of the piece. (Robert Clairborne, Aug. 31, 1966.)

heavy, v. To 'beat up'; to slash; to disfigure (a person): c. and low s.: since ca. 1955. James Barlow, *The Burden of Proof*, 1968.

heavy, the (p. 384). Slightly earlier in *Boxiana*, III, 1821.

heavy-handed. 'Said of one who makes his drinks, and those of others, too strong' (Leechman): Canadian coll.: since ca. 1955.

heavy line, the. Tragic or, at least, serious rôles: theatrical: ca. 1820–90. *Sessions*, Dec. 1840

(p. 286), 'He played various character . . . perhaps the King, in Hamlet he played what we call the "heavy line" of business.'

*****heavy mob, the.** The prison police: prison c.: since ca. 1944. (Norman.)

heavy petting. 'Petting' that is very passionate and stopping just short of coïtion: mostly teenagers': adopted, in late 1940's, ex U.S.

heavy sugar, the. 'The big money': low: since ca. 1925. Gerald Kersh, *Night*, 1938. See **sugar, n.,** 1 (*Dict.*).

*****heavy worker.** A safe-breaker: c.: C. 20. Because most safes are heavy.

Hebrew. See 'Tavern terms', § 3, *c*.

hedge, n.—2. A market stall: market-men's and showmen's: C. 20. Ex the fringe of greenery displayed, by many stall-keepers, at the front and sides of the stall.—3. The people gathered around a stall or a stand: fair-grounds': C. 20. (W. Buchanan-Taylor, *Shake It Again*, 1943.) Ex sense 2. Cf.:

hedge and ditch. Often shortened to *hedge*. A 'pitch' (stall; stand): rhyming s.: late C. 19–20.—2. Hence, since ca. 1910, a football, or a cricket, pitch. (Franklyn, *Rhyming*.)—3. The original of **hedge,** 3 (above): rhyming s. (on *pitch*): late C. 19–20. (W. Buchanan-Taylor, ibid.)

hedge-bottom attorney or **solicitor.** An unqualified or a disqualified attorney or solicitor doing business in the shelter of a proper solicitor's name: legal: mid-C. 19–20; ob. B. & L.

hedgehog. Veal: London streets': ca. 1840–1900. Augustus Mayhew, *Paved with Gold*, 1857. The two kinds of flesh, cooked, are not unlike.—2. An anti-submarine weapon: Naval coll.: since ca. 1940.

heebs, the. A post-1930 variation—and derivation—of **heebie-jeebies** (p. 385).

heef (p. 385). Orig., *heef* was military s., esp. in India, for '*beef* on the *hoof*'. 'The word heef became a parable for camping in the military areas and all its miseries,' Rudyard Kipling, 'The Army of a Dream' in *Traffics and Discoveries*, 1904: the n., therefore, was current ca. 1870–90. Unless, of course, Kipling 'invented the word, to flesh out his "dream" army with appropriate slang' (Robert Clairborne, Aug. 31, 1966).

heel. 'A fellow who seeks your company for the sake of a free drink.' H. & P.: Services, esp. among officers: since 1940. Adopted from U.S. airmen, ex the U.S. sense, 'hanger-on'. 'Thus *heeling*, paying a heel for something,' H. & P., 1943. —2. Ex U.S., ca. 1938, the sense 'objectionable fellow'—esp., 'one who is untrustworthy or treacherous'. You can't usually see your heel.— 3. Apparently it was at first a polite short form of *shit-heel*.

heel!, not a. See **not a heel!**

heel and toe. To operate the accelerator and heel brake simultaneously: Australian motorists': since late 1940's. (B.P.) A pun on heel-and-toe dancing.

heeler. A cattle dog: Australian coll., esp. in N.S.W.: late C. 19–20. 'They snap at the heels of the animals, they herd' (Dr J. W. Sutherland, letter of Jan. 21, 1940).

Heffer, the. 'A desk diary published by W. Heffer & Sons' (D. F. Wharton, Oct. 24, 1965): University of Cambridge: since ca. 1950.

hefty (p. 385), as 'big and strong', occurs in Rebecca Harding Davis's 'Waiting for the verdict' in *The Galaxy* (IV, 336), July 1867, 'This water's gettin' too hefty for me.' Moe.

heifer(-)dust. Airy or meaningless talk: Australian: since ca. 1930. B., 1942. It was probably adopted ex U.S.; certainly it was, at first, euphemistic for bull-shit (p. 105), also Canadian—but not common. Australia has the synonym *bull-dust*. (D'Arcy Niland, 1955.)

Heinz; (one of) the 57 varieties. A mongrel dog: since ca. 1925. A reference to the 57 varieties of tinned edibles and potables manufactured by Messrs Heinz, the American food-product manufacturers.—2. *Heinz varieties* = 57, in Bingo: since ca. 1955.

Hell.—2. The same as **Lower Tartary**, q.v.; see also **Upper Tartary**.

hell, like (p. 386) prob. goes back to late C. 18. 'Cutting them up like hell' (severely criticizing them): W. N. Glascock, 1826. (Moe.)

hell!, not a hope in. There's no hope at all: coll.: from ca. 1910. Oliver Onions, *Peace in Our Time*, 1923.

hell, the. *'To hell* and *the hell* are often confused in the U.S. and Canada. Apparently the abbreviated *Go t' hell* has been misapprehended, resulting in the ridiculous "Get the hell out of here!"' (Leechman): coll.: since ca. 1930.

hell and tommy (p. 386) occurs in John L. Gardner, *Sketch-Book* (II, 68), 1831. Moe. It is very much alive as an oath (*hell and Tommy!*) in Australia: witness, e.g., D'Arcy Niland, *Call Me . . .*, 1958.

hell around. To fly furiously 'all over the place': airmen's: since ca. 1915. Guy Fowler, *The Dawn Patrol*, 1930, 'He's been helling around the front since the start.'

hell-box and **hell-matter.** Among printers, the latter is strictly 'matter' set in type rescued from the *hell-box* or box for old battered type.

Hell-Fire is short for *Hell-Fire Pass*, which is soldiers' 'Hobson-Jobson' for Halfaya Pass in North Africa: 1940–3, then merely reminiscent. (See quotation at basinful, 2.)

Hell-Fire Corner. The Dover area, subject to shelling from German guns across the Channel, 1941–4; earlier (Aug.–Sept. 1940), S.E. England, conspicuous in the Battle of Britain.

hell hath—or **holds**—**no fury like a woman's corns.** A jocular c.p. (C. 20)—punning on the famous quotation, 'Heaven has no rage like love to hatred turn'd,/Nor hell a fury like a woman scorn'd' (Wm Congreve, *The Mourning Bride*, 1697).

hell of a note!, that's a. A grave situation: Canadian c.p.: adopted—ca. 1950—ex U.S. (Leechman.) Out of tune.

hell or Connaught!, go to. See **go to hell or Connaught** in *Dict.*

Hell over the Hill. R.M.C., Sandhurst: Wellington College boys': ca. 1850–80. Major A. F. Mockler-Ferryman, *Annals of Sandhurst*, 1900.

'hell!' said the Duchess (p. 387). No; the fuller form is prob. a ribald elaboration, for, as the reviewer of this book said in *The Times Literary Supplement*, March 20, 1937: 'The saga of the Duchess, "who had hitherto taken no part in the conversation," was on men's lips at least forty years ago.' Also *'hell!' said the Duke, pulling the Duchess on like a jack-boot*: C. 20. A Canadian variant is *'hell!' cried the duchess and flung down her cigar*. (Leechman.)

hellishun, adv. Very: Australian children's: since ca. 1920. B., 1942. Cf. **hangashun**, obviously a euphemism for adv. *hellish* or *hellishly*.

hello, baby! A teenagers' greeting to a girl: coll.: since the late 1940's. An adaptation of U.S. *hi, baby!*

hello, unconscious! A familiar greeting to a girl that is either 'sexy' or dumbly blonde: since ca. 1938.

hellova, helluva. Hellishly, i.e. extremely—or (no more than) very: low, esp. Glaswegian: from ca. (? earlier than) 1919. MacArthur & Long, '"They're looking hellova well too, aren't they?"' A natural development ex *helluva* = hell of a. Also, since ca. 1910, Australian.

hell's delight. 'She would kick up hell's *delight*,' *Sessions*, April 1835. See **hell, raise**: p. 386.—2. As exclamation it = hell!: since ca. 1880.

help in. To join in (a gang fight): Teddy boys' coll.: since ca. 1947. (*The Observer*, March 1, 1959.)

help me out?, can (or **will**) **you.** A polite request for a small loan of money: since late 1940's. In 1962, Julian Franklyn told me of a Soho café that had the notice, 'Of course I'll help you out. Which way did you come in?'

help! sharks! See **too late! too late!** below.

help yourself! Just as you please!; please yourself!: c.p.: from ca. 1917. Richard Blaker, *Enter, a Messenger*, 1926. 'Often said in reply to "Can I use your 'phone?"' (A. B. Petch, March 1967.)

helter-skelter.—2. An air-raid shelter: (mostly Londoners') rhyming s.: 1939 +. *The New Statesman*, Aug. 30, 1941.

hemp, n.—2. Marijuana: (mostly teenage) drug addicts': since ca. 1955. This drug is extracted from a plant resembling hemp, and the term is merely an ellipsis for American s. *Indian hemp*.

*hemp, stretch the. To be hanged: c.: mid-C. 19–20; ob.

Hempire, the. The British Commonwealth of Nations: C. 20: sometimes jocular; sometimes disparaging.

Hen. A Henschel 'plane (German): R.A.F. 1940 +. Partridge, 1945.

hen, adj. Female: beatniks': since ca. 1959. (Anderson.) Ex **hen**, 1, on p. 388.

Hen and Chickens, the. See **Queen's Arms**.

hen-cackle. A mountain easy to climb: New Zealand mountaineers': C. 20. B., 1941. Difficult enough to cause a cackle among the women. Cf.:

hen cackle, a mere. A trifle: New Zealand: C. 20. B., 1941. Ex prec.?

hen-convention or **-tea.** See **hen-party**.

hen-peck (or **henpeck**), n. A hen-pecked husband: domestic coll.: since ca. 1920.

hen-roost. That gallery in the old chapel (1872–1927) in which the masters' wives used to sit: Charterhouse (School): from ca. 1880; ob.

hen wife. See **old haybag**.

hence the pyramids! A c.p., applied to a *non sequitur* or uttered as an ironic jocular *non sequitur*: late C. 19–20. Ex the very rude, very droll recitation entitled *The Showman*, q.v. in John Brophy & E. P., *Songs and Slang of the British Soldier*, 3rd ed., 1931.

*Henry, look for. See **look for Henry**.

Henry Hase. A bank or currency note: 1820, W. J. Moncrieff, *The Collegians*: 'A twenty pound Henry Hase'. In *Boxiana*, IV, 1824, it occurs in a variant form, 'When to pass on the whip-hand makes his tender in *browns*, or *glistner*, *Henry Hase*, or *bender*.' Cf. **Abraham Newland** and **Bradbury**, both in *Dict.*

Henry Melville. Devil: rhyming s.: since 1887. Prompted—? originated—by 'Tottie', a Dagonet ballad written by G. R. Sims and published in *The Referee*, Nov. 7, 1887: 'What the Henry Melville/Do you think you're doing there?' Franklyn 2nd.

Henry Nash. Cash: rhyming s.: C. 20.

hens and bitches. Bends and hitches: Naval (R.N.V.R.) rhyming s.: 1914–18. (Gordon Maxwell, *The Motor Launch Patrol*, 1920.) Originally a spoonerism.

hen's fruit and hog's body. Bacon and egg(s): Naval stewards': since ca. 1925. *Sunday Chronicle*, March 1, 1942.

hens' teeth, as scarce as. Very scarce indeed: mostly Australian: late C. 19–20. (B.P.)

hep. In the know; having good taste: British jazz-lovers', since ca. 1945; ex Canadian jazz-musicians and -lovers, who adopted it, ca. 1925, ex U.S.—cf. next. (See also **hip**.) Ultimately ex the ploughman's, or the driver's *hep!* to his team of horses ('Get up'); the horses 'get *hep*'—lively, alert. In American, hence Canadian, rural dialect of late C. 19–20, 'He's mighty hep' = he's very shrewd.—2. Hence, alert and progressive and well-informed: beatniks' (as in 'hep doll') and others', esp. teenagers': since ca. 1957. Anderson.

hep cat. See 'Jive'. A jazz 'fiend' (swing music): adopted in Canada ca. 1925, in Britain ca. 1935, ex U.S.; ob. by 1950. (*The Observer*, Sept. 16, 1956.) Superseded by *hipster*.

her ladyship. See **his lordship** and cf. (at **my gentleman**) *my lady*. This is a working-class disparagement of a 'stuck-up' female: coll.: C. 20.

Her Majesty. 'A sneering reference to prudish and stand-offish girl or woman. A parody on *Her Majesty*' (Petch): late C. 19–20.

herbs. Oats: Australian racing: C. 20; by 1960, ob. 'When a horse became sluggish, it was given more "herbs"' (B.P.)—2. Hence, power of engine or motor: Australian motorists': since ca. 1930.

herder. An employee that, at a station, couples and uncouples rolling-stock: Canadian railroadmen's (— 1931). Ex ranching.

here and there. Hair: Australian rhyming s.: C. 20. (A. A. Martin, letter of late 1937.)

Here-before-Christ Company, the. 'The Hudson's Bay Company, ex initials and long presence in Canada' (Leechman): Canadian: since ca. 1910; by 1960, slightly ob. 'Here's an earlier quote: 1872, Johnson, R. B., *Very Far West Indeed*, "I calc'late 'H.B.C.' to mean 'Here before Christ'."'

here comes the bride! 'A jocular catchphrase, used when an engagement is announced' (Petch): since ca. 1920.

here endeth the first lesson. A (non-Catholic) c.p., used by the bored after a long speech or lecture or gratuitous exposition: since ca. 1870.

here goes! Sense 1 (on p. 388) occurs much earlier in *The Edinburgh Weekly Magazine*, Oct. 16, 1783, p. 77. (Moe.)—2. Hence a toast, equivalent to *here's how!*: *The Port Folio*, Sept. 6, 1806 (p. 144) reprints an unidentified British song, with the lines, 'So here goes what the world appals,/Old England and her wooden walls' (fighting ships). Moe.

here we come, mum—dad's on the axle. A schoolboys' c.p., current since ca. 1910 and expressing delight at speed on bicycle or scooter, hence at completion of some other activity.

here we go! or, implying repetition, **here we go again!** A c.p.: late (? mid) C. 19–20. (A. B. Petch, March 1966: as so often, reminding me that I had omitted the familiar and the obvious—which is shockingly easy to do.) Cf. **here goes!** on p. 388.

here's a couple of match-sticks. A mostly workmen's c.p., addressed to someone sleepy early in the day: late C. 19–20. To prop open his eyelids.

here's a five-pound note for you. A c.p. addressed to someone receiving mail obviously consisting of bill(s) and/or circular(s): C. 20.

here's a ha'penny—don't spend it all at one shop! A jocular c.p. to children: late C. 19–20. Or *a penny*.

here's hair on your chest! A fairly common Canadian toast: since ca. 1920. (Leechman.)

here he comes—the man they couldn't hang. An Australian c.p., directed at a man approaching a group of people: since ca. 1920. (B.P.)

here's looking! A toast: coll.: late C. 19–20. Short for *here's looking towards you!* (p. 388).

here's me head. See **here's my head** below.

here's mud in your eye! (p. 388) prob. dates from 1915, ex the muddy trenches of Belgium and northern France. The *here's* has often been omitted, even since very early days. One of the earliest written references is provided by H. V. Morton, *In Search of England*, 1927, on p. 71.

here's, my (or me) head, my (or me) arse is comin(g). A workman's c.p., dating from ca. 1895, but, owing to the lesser frequency of the female type, not much used since 1940: in ref. to a girl or woman that, wearing high heels, walks with the head and shoulders well forward and with posteriors (esp. if shapely or buxom) well behind. Originally, of any forward-sloping person. 'Oh, he's all *here's me head, me arse is comin*'—he walks very much head-forward: esp. the Midlands: late C. 19–20. (Richard Merry.)

here's Peter the Painter! See **Peter**.

here's where you want it!, with one's head touched or indicated. A c.p. = you must use your brains: since ca. 1910.

Herman Finck. Ink: theatrical rhyming s.: C. 20. (Franklyn, *Rhyming*.)

hermaphrodite brig. See **schooner orgy**.

hermaphy. A hermaphrodite: jocular diminutive, used in medical circles: C. 20.

herring-gutted.—2. 'Gutless' (lacking courage): coll.: mid-C. 19–20; by ca. 1960, slightly ob. Perhaps ex sense 1 on p. 389.

Herring Joker (p. 389) should be *Herring Choker*; the meaning, 'man or ship from New Brunswick' (Leechman).

he's a poet! and **who robbed the barber?** are c.pp. directed at a person whose hair is long: resp. C. 20 and from ca. 1880.

he's a prince. He's the best of good fellows: Canadian c.p.: since ca. 1930.

he's gone north about. See **north about . . .**

he's got it up there. See **this is where you want it.**

he's not so well since he fell off the organ. A jocular, communal c.p. addressed to a man present: C. 20. The reference is to the organ-grinder's monkey.

het-up; often **all het-up.** Excited; 'in a state': adopted (as a coll.), ca. 1935, from U.S. I.e. heated up. Contrast **steamed-up** (p. 827).

hetero, adj. and n. Heterosexual: coll.: since late 1940's. 'All kinds of fun and games, hetero and homo.'

hex; esp. in *put a hex on*, to lay a spell upon a person or, e.g., a machine: Australian: adopted, ca. 1950, ex U.S., where, orig., c., deriving, via Yiddish, ex Ger. *Hexe*, a witch—cf. *hexen*, to practise sorcery.

hey(-)diddle(-)diddle. A violin: late C. 19–20. Rhyming on *fiddle*.

hey, Mudder, give my brudder the udder udder! This Canadian c.p., used almost as a tongue-twister and clearly issuing from one, has been current since ca. 1930, although never—for rather obvious reasons—very general.

hey-nonny-no. Female pudend: ca. 1590–1750. E.g. in a ballad in John Aubrey's *Lives*.

hi! Of Canadian coll. usage, Dr Douglas Leechman, in May 1959, remarked: 'This is becoming almost the universal informal greeting. Juveniles use it, even when first introduced, and babes in arms will answer "Hi!" when spoken to.'

hi-de-hi, greeting, answered by **ho-de-ho** (Gerald Kersh, *They Die with Their Boots Clean*, 1941). *Hi there!*: ho (or *hullo*) *there!*

hi-fi. Of a gramophone recording, tape recorders, etc.: having *high fi*delity in tone and pitch: since the middle 1950's: coll. <, by 1960, S.E.

*****hi-jack**, v.t. (Of one criminal) forcibly to deprive (another criminal) of booty: c.: adopted ca. 1931 ex U.S., where orig. and mostly of one bootlegger's robbing another on the highway. *The Pawnshop Murder.* Whence:

*****hi-jacker.** One who acts as in the preceding entry: c.: adopted, ca. 1932, ex U.S. *The Pawnshop Murder.* For American usage and suggested etymology, see esp. Irwin.

hick, 2 (p. 389): common in Australia since ca. 1890.

hickaboo (p. 389). Perhaps rather an alteration of *peekaboo*? (Leechman.)

hickey (or **hike**): often elaborated to *do-hickey*. A 'thingummy': New Zealand: late C. 19–20. Perhaps ex a Maori word. B., 1941. n. The form *do-hickey* has long been common in the mid-west U.S.—2. An unsophisticated person: Australian: since ca. 1943. (Ruth Park, 1950.) Ex **hick**, 2 (p. 389).—3. A long, hard, 'suction' kiss that raises a blister; hence the blister so caused: Canadian: since ca. 1930 (?). Origin?

hickey(-)hockey. A jockey: Australian sporting rhyming s.: since ca. 1920. Lawson Glassop, *Lucky Palmer*, 1949.

hickory. See **clock**, n. 4.

hidden treasure. A landlady's husband that, rarely seen, does much work below stairs: jocular: C. 20.

hide, n.—3. A hide-out: coll.: since ca. 1910. In 1939–45, esp. a hide-out for vehicles—against enemy aircraft. (P-G-R.)

hide, v. (389). 'I was afraid to go back to my vessel as the captain would *hide* me for loosing my clothes,' *Sessions*, 1825.

hide, all. (Of cattle) mere skin and bone: Australian coll.: since ca. 1870. B., 1942.

Hide, the. The Covered Market: Caledonian Market pitch-holders': C. 20. (Jane Brown, *I Had a Pitch on the Stones*, 1946.)

*****hide and find.** That strap trick in which the gull is invited to put a pencil into the loop of a strap: c.: from ca. 1885. Anstey, *The Man from Blankley's*, 1901.

hide the snobbery. See **snobbery** (*Dict.*).

hide-up, n. A 'hide-out' (hiding place): Australian: since ca. 1920. B., 1942.

hidey (or **highdy** or **hidy**)! How are you?: Australian and elsewhere: since ca. 1935. B., 1942. Adopted from U.S., it = *how d'ye do*; cf. **hi-de-hi.**

hidey hole. A hiding-place: children's coll.: mid C. 19–20. A hole to hide in.—2. 'Also a place to hide things in' (Leechman): late C. 19–20.

high, n. A peak or record in, e.g., production or sales, the opposite being *low*: coll.: since 1940.

high, adj.—4. (Ex sense 1: p. 389.) Under the influence of an exhilarating drug: Canadian since ca. 1925, English since ca. 1930.—5. 'The bird'—girl—'might be high (high principled) in which case he would get no dice or merely "a bit of bazooka"'—petting' (correspondence columns in *The Sunday Times*, Sept. 8, 1963): since ca. 1960.

high as (occ. **higher than**) **a kite.** Extremely drunk: since ca. 1944. (Ex U.S.?) An elaboration of *high*, adj. (p. 389).

high as three pennyworth of coppers, about as. A c.p. (C. 20) applied to a short person.

high-ball. A signal to go: Canadian railway-men's: since ca. 1910. Hence, in general s. (since ca. 1925), give (someone) *the high-ball*, to approve, to sanction; hence also *high-balling*, n. and adj., travelling fast, succeeding.

high boost. See **boost, be in high.**

high boy or **H— B—.** 'A High Tory and Churchman, supposed to favour Jacobitism': C. 18. B. & L.

high-brow. See **highbrow** (*Dict.*).

high cost of dying, the. A trenchant c.p. parodying *high cost of living*: since ca. 1942.

high-falutin(g). See **highfalutin(g)** in the *Dict.*

high-fly, n. High-falutin; 'side': Cockney coll.: late C. 19–20. Pugh, 'She went in for so much style—sounding her "aitches", and all that kind of high-fly.'

high-grading, n. Stealing—or dealing in stolen —processed gold ore; illegal trading in gold from a mine: Canadian miners': since ca. 1918. (F. E. L. Priestley.)

high-hat, adj. 'Superior'; supercilious: since ca. 1930. Gerald Kersh, *Night and the City*, 1938; Oliver Onions, *Cockcrow*, 1940. Cf. the v.: p. 390.

high jinks, 2 ('a frolic'): earlier in Scott's notes to *Guy Mannering*, 1815.

high jump, take the. To be hanged: police: late C. 19–20. (*The Free-Lance Writer*, April 1948.)

high kick. A thrill obtained by taking a drug: drug addicts': since ca. 1940. John Gosling & Douglas Warner, *The Shame of a City*, 1960.

high line, the. A method of logging with high-boom transport: Canadian lumbermen's coll. (since ca. 1920), >, by 1950, S.E. (Priestley.)

high spots, hit the (p. 391) has, at least in Canada and since ca. 1925, meant rather 'to do something superficially' (Leechman).

High Street, China. Any remote place beyond one's ken: mostly R.A.F.: since ca. 1938. 'The underlying sense is that it is too remote to be taken seriously' (Atkinson).

high-tail. To make off speedily, as 'We high-tailed out of there': Canadian: C. 20; by 1950, coll. Ex a herd of cattle or buffalo suddenly taking off. Adopted from U.S.

*high-top(p)er. A 'swell' thief: c.: ca. 1850–1900. Burton, *Vikram and the Vampire*, 1870.

high-ups, the. Persons with high rank; politicians enjoying their brief authority 'on top of the world': coll.: since ca. 1937. (*John Bull*, Aug. 28, 1943, has *higher-ups*.)

> 'Among *Bazooka's* varied jobs
> She once conveyed to Bongo Bay
> Two high-ups, lordly ones, or nobs—
> Air-Marshal Bragg and General Fray,'
>   Commander Justin Richardson,
>   *The Phoney Phleet*, 1946.

high, wide and handsome. Going all out—swimmingly—very successfully: Canadian coll.: C. 20. (Leechman.) Also in the London Fire Brigade, of a building well alight: C. 20.

higher than a giraffe's toupet. Very 'high' on drugs: beatniks': ca. 1959–62. (Anderson.)

Highers. Higher School (or leaving) Certificate: schools': since ca. 1920.

highflier; highflyer. See **high-flyer** (*Dict.*).

Highland bail. See **high-kilted** (*Dict.*).

Highland frisky. Whisky: rhyming s.: since ca. 1870; by 1950, ob. (Franklyn, *Rhyming*.) Perhaps a blend of *Highland whisky* and *gay and frisky*.

Hightalian. An occ. variant of **Eyetalian** (*Dict.*). C. Rook, *The Hooligan Nights*, 1899.

highway surfer. One who 'rides highways with board on top of car but never surfs' (*Pix*, Sept. 28, 1963): Australian surfers': since ca. 1961.

*hijack; hijacker. See **hi-jack**.

hike, v., 1 (p. 391): Canadian coll.: late C. 19–20. (Niven.)—3. To arrest: low London: ca. 1860–1914. B. & L.

hike off, 1 (p. 392): much earlier in James Dalton, *A Narrative*, 1728, 'He *hyk'd* off with the *Cly*.'

hiki. See **hickey**.

Hill, the; the Plain. Harrow School; Eton College: Harrow School coll.: mid C. 19–20. (H. A. Vachell, *The Hill*, 1905.) The former comes from *Harrow-on-the-Hill*; hence, by contrast, the latter.—2. *The Hill*, among Londoners, is a coll. for the Notting Hill district: late C. 19–20. (Nicholas Blake, *The Whisper in the Gloom*, 1954.)

hill and dale. 'The tale' as practised by 'con men' and their like: orig., and still mainly, underworld rhyming s.: C. 20. Jim Phelan, *The Underworld*, 1953.

Hill (or hill) captain. A military officer that spends his summer leave in India in a Hill station in preference to spending it in some more manly way, e.g. in shooting: military, esp. Indian Army's: ca. 1890–1947. It implies undue addiction to feminine society.

Hill-parrot. (Gen. pl.) An Indian Army term, dating from ca. 1890 to ca. 1907, as in Richards: 'Some men managed to work it to be sent to the Hills every year with the first party, and to stay there the entire summer; these were sarcastically called Hill-parrots by the men who did not have the luck to go to the Hills at all. A year or two later the custom of one party relieving the other at the Hills was abolished.'

Hillite. A spectator 'barracking' from *the Hill*, an uncovered portion of the Sydney Cricket Ground: Australian coll.: since ca. 1920. (B.P.)

hills are closing in on him—(poor So-and-So,) the. He's becoming very odd, beginning to go mad: United Nations troops in Korea: ca. 1953–5. Ex the forbidding Korean hills and mountains. (Anon., 'Slanguage'—in *Iddiwah*, The New Zealanders' periodical of 1953–4.)

hinchinarfer (p. 392): 'Implying that her husband has but an inch and a half, hence her bad temper' (Julian Franklyn, 1962).

hinting gear. See **front up** above.

hinton. See 'Mock-Auction Slang' below.

hip. 'Equipped with enough wisdom, philosophy and courage to be self-sufficient, independent of society; able to swing on any scene' ('Basic Beatnik' in The Victoria *Daily Colonist*, April 16, 1959): Canadian jazz-lovers and musicians': adopted, 1956, ex U.S. A boppers' alteration of *hep*, which, in 1958, began to regain its virtue and its potency: see Norman D. Hinton, 'Language of Jazz Musicians' in *The American Dialect Society*, Nov. 1958. By 1961 (Anderson), it was old-fashioned among beatniks—cf., however, **hip duck** below.

Hip, the. The Hippodrome: London coll.: late C. 19–20. In, e.g., A. Neil Lyons, *Arthur's*, 1908. Cf. **Hipp, the.**

hip(-)disease. The habit of carrying a hip flask: Australian: since ca. 1925. B., 1942.

hip duck. A nice girl, i.e. an attractive or sympathetic one: beatniks': since ca. 1959. (Anderson.)

hip flask. A revolver: R.A.F.: 1939 +. *The Reader's Digest*, Feb. 1941, Michie & Waitt, 'Air Slanguage'; *The New Statesman*, Sept. 19, 1942, E. P., 'Air Warfare and its Slang'. Ex the position in which it is worn and its appearance in the case.

hip-hip-hurrahs. Engine-room artificers: Naval (lower-deck): since ca. 1920. Granville. Ex the initials **E.R.A.**

Hipp, the. The Hippodrome (anywhere): theatrical: since ca. 1880. Cf. *Hippo, the* (p. 392).

hipper. 'Something soft placed under the hip when sleeping on hard ground' (B., 1943): Australian tramps': C. 20.

hippy. 'The hippies, latter-day beatniks, along with the younger "teeny boppers", met in Stanley Park' (*Daily Colonist*, Victoria, B. C., March 28, 1967) & '. . . hippies, a latter-day beatnik type, some of them barefooted and waving flowers' (*ibid.*, April 16, 1967): Canadian: since 1966 or perhaps 1965. (Leechman.) By 1967, also British. In *The Observer* colour supplement, Dec. 3, 1967, Peter Fryer defines a hippy as a 'product of Haight-Ashbury district of San Francisco. Anarchic successors to Beat generation. Essential beliefs: protest, legalised drugs, opting out. Not to be confused with **plastic hippies**/most conventional youth who like to dress up at weekend.'

hipster. A jazz 'fiend' (modern jazz): adopted,

ca. 1950, ex U.S. (*The Observer*, Sept. 16, 1956.) A development from **hep cat**.

hire it done. To hire someone to do something: Canadian coll.: since ca. 1930. 'I never mow my own lawn. I hire it done.' (Leechman.)

his dibs is used concerning a wealthy man: since ca. 1925. By a pun on *his nibs* (cf. *nibs*, p. 559).

His Ex. See **Ex, His** in *Dict.*

his (or **his royal**) **highness.** My husband: feminine, either jocular or derisive: mainly lower-middle class: late C. 19–20. Cf. *his lordship*.

his lordship. He: derisive coll.: mid-C. 19–20. Feminine: *her ladyship*: same period. Cf. **my gentleman.**

his mother never raised a squib. See **squib, his mother . . .,** below.

hissy. The Tommy's 'Hobson-Jobson' for Fr. *ici*, 'here': 1914–18.

hit, n.—2. Also *hit-up*. A game of cricket or lawn tennis: Australian coll.: C. 20. B., 1942. —3. Only *hit-up*. A practice game; a few preliminary exchanges at lawn tennis: gen. sporting coll.: C. 20.—4. An attempted crime, esp. robbery or theft: c.: late C. 18-mid 19. In *The Rolling Blossom* (active prostitute), pub. ca. 1800 and reprinted in an American magazine, *The Port Folio*, Aug. 8, 1807 (pp. 125–6): 'To nimming Ned I went to bed,/Who look'd but queer and glumly,/ Yet every hit, he brought the bit,/And then we spent it rumly': where *bit* = booty, and *rumly* = excellently.

Hit and Miss. Hitler and Mussolini: since mid-1940; ob. by 1947.

hit (someone) **for six.** To rout decisively in argument or business or other battle of wits: since ca. 1920. Cf. **gone for six.** Ex cricket.

hit him where he'll feel it or **where it hurts him most.** See **knee,** v., below.

hit it with (someone). To get along well with: Australian: C. 20. B., 1942. A variant of **hit it off** (p. 393).

hit or miss (p. 393). Also, loosely, *hit and miss*.

hit that broad. See **broad.**

hit the deck. To land: R.A.F.: since ca. 1925. Jackson. See **deck.**—2. 'Also to sleep, cf. "*hit the hay*",' Robert Hinde, letter of March 17, 1945. —3. (Ex 1.) To crash-land: R.A.F.: since ca. 1940.

hit the hay (p. 393): but Canadian by ca. 1900. (Niven.)

hit the kellicks. To apply the brakes: Australian motorists': since ca. 1940. Cf. the synonymous *anchors*; *kellick* is an Australian form of S.E. *killick*. (B.P.)

hit the taps. To open the throttle: Air Force: 1939 +. Charles Graves, *Seven Pilots*, 1943.

hit the ties. To 'tramp the ties' or walk along the railway track: Canadian (? ex U.S.): since ca. 1905; by 1959 somewhat ob. (Leechman.) Here, *ties* = (transverse) railway sleepers.

hit the toe. To go: Australian rhyming s., esp. surf-board riders': since ca. 1958. (B.P.)

hit the white. To succeed: Australian sporting: C. 20. Baker. Ex games j.

hit-up, n. See **hit,** n., 2, 3.

hit up.—2. Hence, to charge (someone) unreasonably for a purchase, etc.: Australian: C. 20. Baker.

hit where one lives comes from U.S.: Artemus Ward (1834–67) uses it.

hitch, n.—2. A term of enlistment: Canadian Services': adopted, ca. 1935, ex U.S.

hitch-hike. To obtain a free ride on a walking tour, or, esp., to obtain a series of free rides, going on, or returning from, leave: coll.: adopted, ca. 1936, from U.S. The more English phrase is *to travel on thumb*: s.: since ca. 1925. Both mostly as verbal nn., *hitch-hiking* and *travelling . . .*

hitherao jildi! Come here, at the double!: Regular Army phrase: from ca. 1880. (*The Observer*, Sept. 20, 1936.) For *jildi* see the *Dict.*; hitherao is the Hindustani *idher ao* influenced by S.E. *hither*.

Hitsville. Success, as opposed to *Squaresville*, failure: since ca. 1960. (B.B.C. Light Programme, June 30, 1963.) The former elaborates **hit,** n. (p. 393); the latter, **square,** n., 6, below.

hive off. To depart: Australian: since ca. 1910. B., 1942. Ex bees.

ho gya, ho-gya, hogya. In trouble: nonplussed or stumped; failed: Anglo-Indians': mid C. 19–20. B. & L.

hobbs. A fad, an eccentricity: Tonbridge: since ca. 1880. (Marples.) Prob. ex a master's surname. Perhaps, however, from S.E. *hobby*.

hobson-jobson (p. 394) occurs earlier in George R. Gleig, *Log-Book* (I, 214), 1828. (Moe.)

*****hock.** A man that goes with 'poufs': c.: C. 20. A rhyme on *cock*.

hockey, the. See **hoggins.**

hockey stick. 'The hoist used for loading an aircraft with bombs,' Jackson: R.A.F.: since ca. 1938. Similarity of appearance.

hocus, v., 2. Earlier in *Boxiana*, III, 1821.

hod.—3. *A bit of hod*, a fast girl, a prostitute: teenagers': since late 1950's.

hodad. A 'non-surfing beach bum' (*Pix*, Sept. 28, 1963) or, alternatively, 'a surfer not loyal to one beach' (B.P.) or ephemerally (ca. 1962–64) 'a youth who has a surfie haircut and a rocker's clothes' (B.P.): Australian surfers', esp. if teenage: since ca. 1961. Origin obscure: possibly '*Who* [is that,] *dad*?' Dr Leechman, however, writes (April 1967): 'More likely, I feel, from "Who's that?"' In the U.S. Negroes are apt to enquire, on seeing a stranger, "Who dat?"'

hoddie. A hod-carrier, one who carries bricks: Australian: since ca. 1920. (B., 1953.)

hoddie-doddie (p. 395). Sense 1, read: ca. 1530–1900. Edward Lear, 1877, spells it *hoddy doddy*.

hoe into (a task). To work hard and diligently at (something): Australian: since ca. 1920. Agricultural metaphor. (B.P.)

hog, n., 1. Also, ca. 1860–1910, half a crown. B. & L.—7. A locomotive; hence, *hogger* or *hog-head*, a locomotive engineer: Canadian railroadmen's (— 1931). Ex U.S.—8. A hogget (a yearling sheep): Australian coll.: late C. 19–20.

hog-fat. (Of a person) a nuisance, useful-for-nothing, a parasite: Australian: C. 20. (K. S. Prichard, *Haxby's Circus*, 1930.)

hog-wash (p. 396) occurs earlier in B.E., 1699, thus: '*Toplash*, Wretched, sorry Drink, or Hog-Wash.'—3. See **ogwash.**

hoggers. 'Day •lreaming. (Perhaps not unconnected with the after-effects of Hogmanay ?)': H. & P., 1943: Services: since ca. 1930. Rather, I think, a sense-development ex *hogya* (see **ho gya**).

hoggin. See **oggin.**

hoggins or **oggins.** A due share, esp. in pleasure —e.g. sexual, i.e. 'hoggish', pleasures: low C. 20. 'Cf. *hoggins line* at darts' (Atkinson). *The (h)oggins line*, the line or position at which one stands to make the throw, has, since 1957 or 1958, been predominantly *the (h)ockey.*

hogya. See **ho gya.**

hoi (Rossall and Haileybury: C. 20), the lowest team, set, or game at Rugby football: **oips** (Haileybury: C. 20) and **hoips** (Christ's Hospital: C. 20), beginners at football; **hoy** (Bishop's Stortford: C. 20), a townsman, a 'cad'; **polloi** (Cheltenham: since ca. 1925), the lowest football team or set: all these terms come from the Greek *hoi polloi*, lit. 'the many', hence, 'the multitude, the masses, the common people'. Marples.

hoick, v., 4. Also Australian: C. 20. Baker. A corruption of 'to hawk'.

hoick off, v.i. To become airborne: R.A.F.: since ca. 1925. H. & P. An elaboration of **hoick,** v., 3 (*Dict.*).—2. Hence, to depart, to begin a journey, to be on one's 'way to somewhere' (H. & P.): since ca. 1930.

hoips. See **hoi.**

hoist, v.—4. To strike (someone) with one's fist: Australian low: C. 20 B., 1942. Cf. **lift,** n., 4 (*Dict.* and Addenda).—5. To discard: Australian: since ca. 1930. (B.P.)—6. To steal: Aus.: mid C. 19–20. (B., 1959.) A generalization of sense 1 on p. 396.

hoist in. To endure, tolerate; to accept: Naval: since ca. 1945. 'I explained, but he wouldn't hoist it in.'

*hoist merchant. A shoplifter: c.: late C. 19–20. Ex **hoist,** n., 3 (*Dict.*).

hoister, 1 (p. 396). Since ca. 1940, restricted to female operators.

hoity-toity, 2 (see **highty-tighty!** p. 391). Perhaps, rather, *hoity* comes ex *haught* and *toity* is a simple reduplication.

hokey-pokey, penny a lump, the more you eat the more you pump. 'It is often chanted derisively at children who have some ice cream, bought on the streets, by those who have none' (Albert B. Petch, Oct. 31, 1946): working-class children's c.p.: since ca. 1902.

Hokitika swindle. 'Hotel bar game played to create a jackpot from which payment for drinks may be made,' B., 1941: New Zealand: C. 20. of topical origin.

hold a spear. 'To take a very minor non-speaking part' (B.P.): Australian theatrical: since 1950; by 1965, coll.

hold a tangi. See **tangi, hold a.**

hold 'er, Newt! She's a-rarin'! This Canadian (esp. prairies) c.p. was adopted, ca. 1948, ex U.S.: 'pseudo-rural, with a tinge of contempt for the rustics' (Leechman). The 'she' naturally refers to an imaginary horse.

hold everything! See **hold your horses!**

hold it. To feel angry or resentful; to sulk or not speak: Cotton College: C. 20. Ex *hold one's backside* in angry desperation.

hold the baby (*Dict.* at **holding the baby**). See **sell a pup** (Addenda) for a note on both phrases.

*hold the bag. To be duped: c.: from ca. 1920. By 1940, at latest, it was general s., usually in the form *be left holding the bag.* Canadian has, since ca. 1950, used also an extended form: *(be) holding the nose bag,* 'left in a ridiculous position

after somebody has stolen the horse' (Leechman). 'Rather, I suggest, from the "snipe hunt", a practical joke current (among hunters, cowboys, etc.) in 1900 or earlier, in which the victim (usually a "greenhorn") is literally left holding the bag. Cf. under "snipe hunt" in Bernard Botkin, *A Treasury of American Folklore.*' (Robert Clairborne, Aug. 31, 1966.)

hold the fort. To mind the shop for someone while he's away (e.g. urinating): coll.: C. 20.

hold your horses! 'Hold the job up until further orders. [Comes from the Artillery],' H. & P.: since ca. 1890 in the R.A.; since ca. 1930, as a phrase common enough in also the R.A.F. and even the Navy. Variant (R.A.F.): *hold everything!*: coll. (1940) >, by 1944, j.

hold your water! Don't get impatient!: mostly Naval: C. 20.

hole, in the. (Of a compositor) that, being behindhand with his portion, is holding up compositors working on the same publication: printers': from ca. 1860. B. & L.

Hole, the. The Severn Tunnel: railwaymen's: late C. 19–20. (*Railway.*) A specialization of **hole,** n., 9 (p. 397).—2. The underground Operations Room at Fighter Command Headquarters, Bentley Priory, 1940–45: R.A.F.: after 1945, merely historical. (Ramsey Spencer.)

Hole below the Naval, the. A certain Piccadilly club: C. 20. Pun.

hole, or **hole out, in one.** To become pregnant as the result of one's first amour: Australian: since ca. 1910. B., 1942. Ex golf.—2. Often used at male parties just before the marriage of the guest of honour, in relation to first-night intercourse. 'A man who "does it the first night" is a "man". One who does not is a "mouse" and one who has already done it is a "rat"' (a valued correspondent): Australian: since ca. 1920.

hole-in-the-wall employer. A small employer of sweated labour: Labour coll. (almost j.): C. 20. Dorothy Sells, *The British Trade Boards System,* 1923.

Hole-Out-in-von Ribbentrop. Von Ribbentrop: ca. 1934–9. He was a very fair golfer, even before he acquired the *von.*

*hole up, v.; **hole-up,** n. To hide; a hiding place: Australian c.: adopted, ca. 1930, from U.S. (See *Underworld.*) B., 1942. In North Africa, 1940–2, Australian troops used *hole up* for 'to lie hidden'.

holiday, 1 (p. 398). Hence, especially among builders and house-painters: C. 19–20.—3. A transfer from a position to an easier one: c.: C. 20.

holla (or **holler** or **holloa**) **boys holla** (etc.); often shortened to **holla** (etc.) **boys.** A collar: rhyming s.: late C. 19–20.

holla, boys, holla. From an old Guy Fawkes Night chant.

hollow, n. (p. 398). Both this and its variant, *bit of hollow,* occur in Maginn's translation of *Memoirs of Vidocq,* III, 1829.

Holloway's Unfinished Symphonies. The Maunsell forts erected in the estuary of the Thames: World War II. Ex the contractor's name? (P-G-R.)

hols (q.v. in *Dict.*) is often treated as a singular. Thus Arnold Lunn, *Loose Ends,* 1919, 'Where are you going this hols?'; 'Did you have a good hols?'

holt, 1 (p. 398): by ca. 1940, no longer low, esp. in the phrase *in holts with*, at grips with.

Holy Boys, the. Another explanation is that the Spanish mistook the regimental crest—a figure of Britannia—for the Virgin Mary.

Holy City, the. St Albans: railwaymen's: C. 20. (*Railway*, 3rd.) A city with a very famous abbey.

Holy Communion. 'Rum collected by the Coxswain in a bottle and drunk quite illegally by the Chiefs' and Petty Officers' messes on Sundays, especially in small ships' (Humphry Osmond, formerly Surgeon Lieutenant, R.N., in a communication of late 1948): Naval: C. 20.

holy day. 'In well disciplined ships of war, many officers devote a certain day in the week, purposely, that the crew "may overhaul their bags", and repair their clothes—gloss, on *holyday*': W. N. Glascock, *Sailors and Saints*, 1829, at I, 97. (Moe.)

Holy Ghost. Toast (bread): rhyming s. (Army): 1939–45. Franklyn: *Rhyming*.

Holy Joe, 2. In Australia, a narrow-minded 'goody-goody': C. 20. B., 1942.

holy lance! See **holy show!** in the *Dict.*

holy mackerel! A mild oath, imported, ca. 1944, ex U.S.

holy nail. Bail (legal): mostly c.: late C. 19–20. (*Underworld*, 1961.)

Holy of Holies, the. The Admiralty, Whitehall: Naval: C. 20. Granville. Cf. **holy of holies** on p. 399.

Holy Rollers, the. Roman Catholics: since ca. 1920.

holy water. Water 'laced' with whiskey: C. 20.

Holy Week. Menstrual period: (Catholic) girls': late C. 19–20. Abstention from intercourse.

homage, to tender. See 'Tavern terms', § 9.

home, have gone. 'When an article of clothing, etc., ceases to be of service it is said . . . *to have gone home* . . . from the fact that many New Zealanders *go Home*—visit Britain—when they are old,' B., 1941: New Zealand: C. 20.

home?, what (or who) is that when it, he, she's at. See **what is that . . .**

home and dried, mentioned s.v. **home and fried** (p. 400), is itself coll.: late C. 19–20. In Australia, it has the nuance of 'easily done'. A common C. 20 elaboration is *home and dried on the pig's back*, as, for instance, in Vance Palmer, *The Passage*, 1930.

home-bug or **h.b.** A home-boarder, i.e. dayboy: at certain Public Schools, e.g. Harrow: from ca. 1880. Lunn.

Home for Lost Frogs, The. London; or England or even Britain: jocular: since ca. 1930. Punning *home for lost dogs.*

home, James! A c.p., dating from ca. 1870—if not earlier; *James* being the coachman, later the chauffeur. At first usually, and still occasionally, *home, James, and don't spare the horses.*

home with the milk, come or **get.** To reach home in the early morning: coll.: since ca. 1890.

homers. A 'home from home' in a port not one's own; a homely, comfortable place: Naval: since ca. 1925. By 'the Oxford-*er*'.—2. Homework: Public and Grammar schoolchildren's: since ca. 1930. The Oxford -*er.*

homework. Girls in gen., one's girl in particular: R.A.F. since ca. 1935, Naval since ca. 1940, Army since 1940 or 1941. Jackson. Also

piece of homework: Partridge, 1945. Cf. **knitting.**

homework, do one's. To do all the work necessary for the successful completion of any job, whether, for instance, detection or the writing of a book: since ca. 1955.

homey.—3. An Englishman: New Zealanders' and Australians': C. 20. B., 1941, 1942. Semantics as at **home, have gone.** For New Zealand use, cf. Jean Devanney, *Old Savage and Other Stories*, 1927, and John Mulgan, *Man Alone*, 1939.

homo, 1 (p. 400). An earlier example is: Pierce Egan, *Life in London*, 1821.

homo, adj. Homosexual: since ca. 1925. '"Mr Arkham's thinkin' very serious abaht the 'omo stuff,"' Michael Harrison, *Vernal Equinox*, 1939. Ex sense 2 of the n. (p. 400).

homo sap. A derisive alteration, virtually a c.p., implying that man (*homo*) is more of a 'sap' or fool than a wise man (*sapiens*): since ca. 1930; by 1965, ob.

Hon. An Honourable: upper classes' coll.: late C. 19–20. Nancy Mitford, *The Pursuit of Love*, 1945.

hon. 'Honey' (endearment): Australian coll.: adopted, ca. 1920, ex U.S. (Jon Cleary, *You Can't See round Corners*, 1949.)

honest. To the *Dict.* entry, there must be added: **honest?**, do you mean it?, or, are you speaking the truth? Both **honest!** and **honest?** arose ca. 1880.

Honest John.—3. (As *honest John*). An honest citizen: coll.: adopted, ca. 1943, ex U.S.

honest(-)to(-)dinkum. Australian variant of **honest-to-goodness** (*Dict.*).

honest trout. See 'Women'; cf. **trout** in *Dict.*

honestly! An expression of either disgust or unpleasant surprise: C. 20. (A. B. Petch, March 1966.)

Honey. An American Stuart tank: Army: 1943–45. (P-G-R.)

honey,—3. (Ex 1.) 'A shot you are pleased with is a "honey" or a "peach" or an "eagle"', *The Evening News*, Nov. 7, 1939: cinema: since ca. 1920.—4. Hence (?), anything choice or excellent: Canadian: since ca. 1945. 'Have you seen Jane's new hair-do? It's a honey.' (Leechman.)

honey!, it ain't all. See **it ain't all honey!**

honey-bun or **-bunch.** An attractive girl; also an endearment to one: Australian: adopted, ca. 1943, ex U.S. servicemen.

honey-do day. A man's odd, or unexpected, day off from his work, a day his wife will seize upon to urge him to 'Please *do* this, *honey*—please *do* that, *honey*': adopted, 1966, ex U.S. *The Daily Telegraph*, Oct. 8, 1966. (Owed to Mr Anthony Burgess.)

honey-pot.—2. A jumping into water with hands clasped around the knees: Australian children's: C. 20. B., 1942.

honey-star. One's sexual mistress: since ca. 1925.

honey thighs. A Canadian endearment to a girl: since ca. 1945.

honey-wag(g)on. A night-cart (only in outback towns): Canadian: C. 20. In the Canadian Army, 1914–18, the corresponding truck was called the *honey-cart.*

honeymoon salad. Lettuce: jocular: C. 20. '*Let us* alone!'

Hong-Kong dog. A tropical fever: Naval: C. 20. 'Taffrail.'

honk. A bad smell: Australian: since ca. 1925. B., 1953, suggests origin in Maori *haunga*, ill-smelling.—2. The nose: Australian: C. 20. (D'Arcy Niland, *The Big Smoke*, 1959.) Echoic.— 3. A wild party, with much drinking: English: since ca. 1945. (The 'William Hickey' column in *The Daily Express*, July 23, 1959.) Ex *honking* below.

honk, v. To vomit: Services', esp. R.A.F.: since ca. 1940. Echoic. (Sgt R. Farley, Feb. 16, 1967.)—2. To stink: Aus.: since ca. 1925. (B., 1959.) Ex **honk,** n., 1.

honk like a gaggle of geese. To stink very much indeed: Aus.: since ca. 1930. (B., 1959.) An elaboration of **honk,** v., 2.

honk one's ring up. To vomit violently: esp. R.A.F.: since ca. 1955. An elaboration of **honk,** v., 1; cf. the next. Here, *ring* = anus. (Sgt R. Farley.)

honk up one's tank (or **No. 6 tank**). To vomit after a 'beer-up': R.A.F.: since ca. 1940.

honked. Tipsy: servicemen's, esp. naval: since ca. 1950. John Winton, *We Joined the Navy,* 1959. Perhaps suggested by **stinking,** adj., 3, on p. 833, and below: cf. **honk,** n., 1.

honker. A (large) nose: Australian, esp. Sydney: since ca. 1910. Ruth Park, *The Harp in the South,* 1948. Ex the *honk* of a motor horn.

Honkers. Hong Kong: Naval (wardroom): C. 20. John Winton, *We Saw the Sea,* 1960. By the Oxford *-er.*

honkers, like **fried, jugged, sloshed,** is 'drunk' among office- and shop-girls—and presumably their companions—of ca. 1955-60, with one or two of these terms likely to last for another few years. (Michael Gilderdale's article 'Fugitives from Fowler: A Glossary for Our Times' in *The News-Chronicle*, May 22, 1958.) With *honkers,* cf. *honk,* 2, and *honking*; with *jugged,* cf. *jug,* n., 5, and v., 3; with *sloshed,* cf. *slosh,* n., 2.

Honkers was orig. and still is, R.A.F. s., in the nuance 'very drunk': since middle or early 1950's or late 1940's. (Sgt. R. Farley.) Cf. **honk,** v., above.

honking. 'A drinking session' (Granville): Naval: since ca. 1940. Cf. **toot,** v.

honkoe. A loafer; a seedy punter: Australian: since ca. 1930. (Dick.) Origin? Perhaps ex Australian s. *honk,* a bad smell.

honky-tonk (or one word). Jangling piano music; noisy jazz: adopted—? rather adapted— ca. 1950 ex U.S., where it predominantly means 'a low place of amusement, or a low burlesque show, esp. where strong drink is available'. Origin unknown. Perhaps either a rhyming reduplication of *honk,* to make a honking noise (cf. **honk,** n., 3, and **honking,** above), or related to N.W. England dial. *honk,* to idle about.

hoo. A fuss; perturbation: since ca. 1935. Ngaio Marsh, *Overture to Death,* 1939. Ex *hoo-ha* (p. 401).

hoo-ha. See **hoohah.**

hooch in quarters. '*Hooching in quarters.* Holding a party in one's room,' H. & P.: Services: since ca. 1940. See **hooch,** p. 401.

hooched. Tipsy: South Africa: since ca. 1939. Professor W. S. Mackie in *The Cape Argus,* 1946. Ex **hooch** (p. 401).

hoochie or **hoochy.** A temporary shelter serving as living-quarters: among United Nations troops in Korea: ca. 1951-5. Ex Japanese *uchi,* a house. (*Iddiwah,* July 1953.)

hood. A hoodlum: Canadian (— 1949); adopted from U.S.

hooer. See **hoor.**

hooey. Nonsense; 'eyewash': adopted, ca. 1937, from U.S. Short for *ballyhooey.*

hoof, get the. To be dismissed or turned out: proletarian: C. 20. W. L. George, *The Making of an Englishman,* 1914.

hoof it, 1 (p. 401): not low in C. 20 Australia, where it is used esp. by motorists temporarily and perforce pedestrian. (B.P.)—3. To decamp: c.: from ca. 1870. B. & L.

hoof the pad. To go on tramp; be a tramp: Australian: mid-C. 19-20; by 1930, ob. (G. B. Lancaster, *Jim of the Ranges,* 1910.) Cf. *hoof it* on p. 401.

hoofer. A dancer: Canadian: since ca. 1925. Cf. *hoof,* v., 2 (p. 401).—2. A chorus girl: Australian: adopted, ca. 1930, ex U.S. (John Cleary, *The Climate of Courage,* 1954.)

hoohah (or **hoo-ha**); sometimes **huhhah.** A water-closet: since ca. 1920. (Christianna Brand, *Death in High Heels,* 1941 (latter spelling).) Origin? 'I suggest as an origin the grunting *hoo!* of effort, followed by the *ha!* of satisfaction': Ramsey Spencer.—2. A two-tone warning horn: since ca. 1955. *The Evening Echo* (Bournemouth), April 21, 1966.

hook, n.—7. A shoplifter: c.: C. 20. A deviation from sense 2.—8. An anchor badge: Naval: C. 20. Also the anchor itself: nautical: since ca. 1890.—9. A chevron, usually in pl. *hooks*: Australian soldiers': since ca. 1910. (B., 1943.)— 10. A '7': Australian poker-players': since ca. 1920. (B., 1953.)

hook, v.—6. To punch (someone): Australian: since ca. 1925. (Dick.) Ex boxing—the punch known as *the hook.*

hook, off the. Out of a difficult or embarrassing situation: Canadian: since ca. 1945. (Leechman.)—2. (Of a married man) 'out with the boys': Australian: since ca. 1920. (B.P.)

hook, on the. See 'Hauliers' Slang'.

hook, sling one's.—3. (Ex. 1.) To die: since ca. 1860; ob.

hook it (p. 402): earlier in *Sessions,* Aug. 1835, 'Hobbs said, "Hook it, you b——s."'

hook, line and sinker. Completely, utterly: coll.: late C. 19-20. Ex fishing. (Roget's *Thesaurus,* edition of 1962.)

hook off.—2. To go away: Cockneys': late C. 19-20. 'Oi—'ook orf! 'op it!' (Julian Franklyn.)

hook one's bait (or **mutton**). To depart; to decamp, make off: New Zealand and Australian: C. 20. Baker. Elaboration of **hook it** (*Dict.*).

hook up (a horse) is applied to a jockey that prevents it from winning, usually by strong-arm tactics: Australian sporting: since ca. 1930. (B., 1953.) Lawson Glassop uses it in *Lucky Palmer,* 1949. By 1940, also British, as in 'The occasional horse will be "*stopped*" or "*hooked up*"' (John Lawrence, in *The Sunday Telegraph,* Aug. 13, 1961).

hook-up party. 'Men who, for some reason, avoid Divisions' (Granville): Naval: C. 20.

hook up with (p. 402). Dr Leechman thinks that Beames was perhaps confusing it with *lock* *horns with.* The predominant Canadian sense, since ca. 1910 at least, is 'to join forces with' or merely 'to encounter'.

hooked, adj. (Hopelessly) addicted to drugs: Canadian (from U.S.): since ca. 1925. Also, by 1945, English and Australian, esp. among drug addicts. (*The Times*, Feb. 19, 1964.)

hooked on, to be. (Of a woman) to be casually 'picked up': Australian: C. 20. B., 1942. Cf.— in *Dict.*—**hook on to** and **hooked up, 2.**

hooker.—5. A shunter: railwaymen's: C. 20. (*Railway*, 3rd.)

hooks, drop . . . off the (p. 403) prob. goes back to ca. 1800. John L. Gardner, *The Military Sketch-Book* (II, 17), 1831, 'The French, now at our right and left, opened fire on us, which knocked many a poor fellow off the hooks, and we fell back to the main body of our troops.' Moe.

hooks, off the, adj., 4. Earlier in W. M. Thackeray, *Vanity Fair*, 1848.

hooks, on. See **put the hooks on.**

hooks into, get her. (Of a female) to have a man in tow, or engaged, or married: since ca. 1920.

hookum (p. 403).—2. Hence, true information: Army: since ca. 1918.

hooky, n. A Leading Seaman: Naval: since ca. 1900. H. & P. 'Ex the anchor he wears as badge of office' (Granville).

hooky, do. To apply fingers and thumb contemptuously to one's nose: streets': from ca. 1860. B. & L.

hooler hoop. The ringed keel of a nuclear submarine of the Dreadnought type: Naval and dockyards': since ca. 1961. (Wilfred Granville.) A pun on S.E. *hula hoop.*

hooley. A spree: Anglo-Irish, probably originating among the Irish Guards: C. 20. Perhaps ex Hindustani *huli*, a festival. (Dr H. W. Dalton.)

hooligan. Too late for inclusion in the *Dict.* proper, I have found the following confirmation of the proper-name origin. Clarence Rook in his sociologically valuable *The Hooligan Nights*, 1899 —portions of it had been published early in the same year in *The Daily Chronicle*—writes thus: 'Good Americans . . . may be seen . . . eating their dinner at the Cheshire Cheese. I was bound on an expedition to the haunts of a more recent celebrity than Dr Johnson. My destination was Irish Court and the Lamb and Flag. For in the former Patrick Hooligan lived a portion of his ill-spent life, and gave laws and a name to his followers; in the latter, the same Patrick was to be met night after night, until a higher law than his own put a period to his rule. . . . My companion was one . . . who held by the Hooligan tradition, and controlled a gang of boys who made their living by their wits, and were ready for any devilry if you assured them of even an inadequate reward. . . . The dwelling-place of Patrick Hooligan enshrines the ideal towards which the Ishmaelites of Lambeth are working; and . . . young Alf's supremacy over his comrades was sealed by his association with the memory of a Prophet.'

At the beginning of Chapter II, he expatiates thus: 'There was, but a few years ago, a man called Patrick Hooligan, who walked to and fro among his fellow-men, robbing them and occasionally bashing them. This much is certain. His existence in the flesh is a fact as well established as the existence of Buddha or of Mahomet. But with the life of Patrick Hooligan, as with the lives of Buddha and of Mahomet, legend has been at work, and probably many of the exploits associated with his name spring from the imagination of disciples. It is at least certain that . . . he lived in Irish Court, that he was employed as a chucker-out at various resorts in the neighbourhood. . . . Moreover, he could do more than his share of tea-leafing, . . . being handy with his fingers, and a good man all round. Finally, one day he had a difference with a constable, put his light out, and threw the body into a dust-cart. He was lagged, and given a lifer. But he had not been in gaol long before he had to go into hospital, where he died. . . . The man must have had a forceful personality, a picturesqueness, a fascination, which elevated him into a type. It was doubtless the combination of skill and strength, a certain exuberance of lawlessness, an utter absence of scruple in his dealings, which marked him out as a leader among men. Anyhow, though his individuality may be obscured by legend, he . . . left a great tradition. . . . He established a cult.'

*hoon, whence the rhyming **silver spoon.** A procurer of prostitutes: Australian c.: since ca. 1935. (B., 1953.) The term occurs in Xavier Herbert's novel, *Capricornia*, 1939, '"You flash hoon," he went on, "Kiddin' you're white, eh?"'

hoop, n.—2. A jockey: Australian sporting: since ca. 1920. B., 1942. With a pun on race-course *ring.*

hoor; pronounced and often written **hooer.** An Australian and New Zealand pronunciation of fig. *whore*: (?) mid C. 19–20. (D'Arcy Niland, *The Shiralee*, 1955, 'Get out of here, you drunken hooer.')

hooray, 2 (p. 403), is also Australian, as in Leonard Mann, *Mountain Flat*, 1939, '"Good-bye, Jim, good-bye, Lottie." "Hooray, George," Jim answered.'

hooroo!—2. Good-bye: Australian: since ca. 1910. B., 1942.

hooroosh. A tremendous fuss or uproar or row, in, e.g., politics,: since ca. 1930. Cf. the North Country and Midlands dial. *hooroo*, an uproar (E.D.D.). Echoic. Immediately ex the W.W. I military sense, 'a hard-fought, a bloody, battle', ob.—not entirely †—in W.W. II. 'Often used in my battalion in France 1916–18': Dr R. L. Mackay, M.D., note of early 1967.

hoor's get or **hoorsget.** See **whore's get, 2** (Addenda).

hoosh.—2. 'Hoosh—corned beef prepared as a hash with potatoes' (*Daily Colonist*, Victoria, B.C., June 19, 1960): Canadian Navy: ca. 1900–25. Perhaps, therefore, a slangy variant of S.E. *hash.*

hooshing. Landing at great speed: R.A.F.: since ca. 1938. H. & P. Echoic.

hoot, 'money': B., 1942, thinks it arose in the early 1840's and proves its existence in the 1850's.

hoot, v. To stink: Australian low: since ca. 1920. B., 1942.

hoot him! A derisory and contemptuous c.p., roughly 'Look at him!' or, according to the context, 'Hark at him!': Aus. juvenile: ca. 1920–40. It often occurs in Norman Lindsay's novel about boys: *Saturdee*, 1933.

hooter.—2. Nose: low jocular: since ca. 1940.

hootin' Annie. A variant, partly jocular and partly folk-etymological, of the American *hootenanny*, an informal variety show held around a so-called camp fire: Australian surfers' coll., adopted ca. 1962. (*Pix*, Sept. 28, 1963.) *Hootenanny* is of obscure origin and, in 1963, was still mainly dialectal. At first, as in 'I don't give a hootenanny', I don't care a damn.

hoovering. 'The now famous "sweeps" by Fighter Command over Northern France. They get into all the corners!' (H. & P., 1943): R.A.F. Ex the Hoover vacuum-cleaner.—2. 'In use among Cockneys during the 1940 blitz: applied to the undulating note of the unsynchronized engines of the German Heinkel III bomber' (H. R. Spencer).

hooya! A children's derisive cry: Australian: C. 20. (B., 1943.)

hop.—3. Half: pidgin: mid-C. 19–20. B. & L. —4. (To) have: id.: id. Ibid.—5. A stage—the flying done in one day—of a long journey by air: R.A.F. coll.: since ca. 1925. Jackson.

hop, v. To get a lift on (a vehicle), as in 'I'll hop a lorry'; whence *lorry-hopping*. Services (originally Army): since ca. 1918; by 1946, civilian. (P-G-R.) Elliptical for *hop on to*.—2. Hence, simply to board, as *hop a tram* or *a bus*: coll.: since ca. 1945.

hop off.—2. To depart: coll. (? originally Cockney): late C. 19–20.

hop, skip and jump,—do with a. To do with ease: coll., mostly Cockneys': from ca. 1890.

hop Harry. A bowler hat: Australian: since ca. 1920. B., 1942. It'll just *bowl* along.

hop into. To attack (a person), tackle (a job), with alacrity: Australian: late C. 19–20. B., 1942. Ex a sprightly boxer's footwork. Cf. **hop-out** and **hop out** on p. 404.

hop on, v.i. (Of men) to coït: low: C. 20. George Ingram, *Cockney Cavalcade*, 1935.

hop the Charley (or -ie). To decamp: low: from ca. 1870; ob. B. & L. Ex *Charley Wag*.

hop the twig. Sense 2 (p. 404) had, among Air Force (esp. Canadian) pilots and aircrews in 1939–45, the particular nuance, 'to crash fatally': Partridge, 1945.

hop time. Leisure: pidgin: mid-C. 19–20. B. & L. Lit., half-time.

hope in hell!, not a. See **hell!, not a hope in.**

hope it keeps fine for you! A parting-phrase c.p., which may refer to prospects other than meteorological: since ca. 1915: often derisive. An occ. variant: *hope you have a fine day for it.*

hope your rabbit dies (p. 404). Orig., a curse, meaning 'I hope you lose your virility!': see **rabbit live,** on p. 682. Compare the eroticism of *pop goes the weasel.*

hophead. A wild fellow; a rash, foolish one: New Zealand: since ca. 1943. (Slatter.) Adapted ex U.S. sense.

***hopped up.** Under the influence of an exhilarating drug: Canadian c. (ex U.S.): since ca. 1935; by 1945, s.

hopper.—5. A bus inspector: Londoners': since ca. 1935. He keeps hopping on and off buses.

hopping pot, the. The lot; esp. 'That's the hopping pot', the end of the day's work: rhyming s. late C. 19–20.

hoppy Brum. A cripple: low: C. 20.

hops! (Acclamation for) a winning throw: darts players: since ca. 1930. 'A double thirteen

achieves this. If you get a single, you are said to be *split* or *cracked*, with two darts left and thirteen to make.' (Wilfred Granville.)

***hops, on the.** On a drinking bout: c.: from ca. 1920. On *on the beer.*

Horace. 'A jocular form of address, often used by men to boys in offices, etc.' (Albert B. Petch, Sept. 5, 1946): coll.: C. 20.

Horace—stop it! More gen. **stop it, Horace!**

horizontal, adj. Tipsy—very tipsy: Service officers': since ca. 1935. H. & P.

horizontal champion. 'One with an infinite capacity for sleep' (Granville): Naval: since ca. 1930. Ironic. Ex boxing.

horizontal exercise. Sexual intercourse: Naval (? Australian only): since ca. 1930.

horn, 4 (p. 405). Hence, *get* (or *give*) *cheap horn*, to be sexually excited by smutty talk or reading-matter: late C. 19–20.—6. n. See **fish-horn.**

horn in on. To intrude upon; to interfere in: Australian: late C. 19–20. (B.P.) Ex cattle.

horn pills. See **back-up pills** and cf. *horn*, 4 (p. 405).

Hornet's Nest, the. Heligoland Bight: R.A.F. Bomber Command: 1939–41. Ex multitudes of German fighters based near by.

horney, n.—4. A street horn-player: proletarian: from ca. 1880. Arthur Morrison, 1896. —5. A bull, steer, cow: Australian: C. 20.

horns. Cattle: Australian coll.: late C. 19–20. Archer Russell, *A Tramp Royal*, 1934, 'A mob of "horns" for the markets of the south.'

horny-steerer. A bullock driver: Australian: ca. 1920–50. (B., 1943.)

horrible. A larrikin: Australian: ca. 1925–55. (B., 1943.)

horrible man. 'Sergeant's sarcastic mode of address,' H. & P.: Army: since ca. 1930.

horrid, adj.—2. Tipsy: ca. 1780. See **mops and brooms** (*Dict.*).

horrorscope. A frightening horoscope-reading: since ca. 1930.

hors d'œuvre book. An order book: Australian jocular: since ca. 1950. (B.P.)

horse, n., 2 (p. 406). More explicitly: a day's rule, i.e. leave of absence, from the Fleet Prison: debtors': ca. 1815–50. Pierce Egan, *Life in London*, 1821.—9. A mud-bank, esp. in estuary waters: bargees': from ca. 1880. Why ?—10. A prostitute's customer: South African prostitutes': C. 20. (Communicated in May 1946.) Cf. **horse,** v., 1 (*Dict.*).—11. A vocative to a man whose name isn't known: Royal Navy: since ca. 1917. Cf. *old horse*, 2 (p. 584).—12. A practical joke: University of Alberta: since ca. 1930. Probably ex S.E. *horse-play.*—13. A prostitute: Naval lowerdeck: since late 1940's. Ex the pl. *whores.*— 14. Hence 'a casual girl friend, as opposed to a *party*, who is a more steady acquaintance' (W. Granville, Nov. 22, 1962): since ca. 1950. Sense 9 is also a yachtsmen's term and, as Julian Franklyn tells me, it arose 'because, if you *get astride* it on a falling tide, you must keep your seat until rescued by the next flood'.

horse, water one's. A variant of **water one's nag** (p. 549).

horse-and-buggy. Old-fashioned; antiquated: Canadian (? ex U.S.) coll.: since ca. 1925; by 1955, S.E.

Horse and Cart, the. The 'Wolverton to Willesden parcels train' (*Railway*, 3rd): railwaymen's: since ca. 1945 (?).

horse and horse. 'When shaking dice, best two out of three, if the first two throws result in a tie, the players have *a horse apiece*, or are *horse and horse*' (Leechman): Canadian: C. 20.

horse and trap. Gonorrhœa: since ca. 1870. Rhyming **clap** (*Dict.*).—2. To defecate: rhyming **s.**: C. 20. (Franklyn, *Rhyming*.) On *crap*, 1 (p. 189).

horse doctor. A medical officer: Forces': 1939–45. Never common.

horse lop. A pudding—or puddings—of plumless suet: military: from ca. 1870; ob. B. & L.

horse-marine (p. 407) occurs in W. N. Glascock, *Sketch-Book*, II, 1826. Moe.

horse marines, the.—3. Men that contract for the horse-traction of casual vessels: canal-men's (esp. in N.E. England): late C. 19–20. In e.g., L. T. C. Rolt, *Narrow Boat*, 1944.

horse on one, have a. When rolling best of three, to be one down: Canadian dice-players': since ca. 1925.

horse-painting. The disguising of racehorses: racing-world coll.: C. 20. (Margaret Lane, *Edgar Wallace*, 1938.)

horse(-)pug. A horse-driver on a labouring job: Australian: since ca. 1910. B., 1942. Rough on the horse's mouth.

horse-shoes, ringing the. See **ringing the horse-shoes.**

horse to a hen, a. Long odds: sporting coll.: ca. 1810–60. *Boxiana*, III, 1821.

***horsed.** Exhilarated with heroin: drug addicts': since ca. 1950. (Robin Cook, 1962.) Ex *horse*, c. for heroin—a term adopted, ca. 1945, ex U.S.

horses. Short for *galloping horses*, q.v. at **fighting cats**: R.A.F.: since ca. 1930. 'He's got his horses' = he's been promoted to Warrant Officer. (Bebbington.)—2. See **horse's hoof.**

horses, water the. See **water one's pony.**

horses and carts. (The game of) darts: rhyming **s.** mostly theatrical: C. 20. (Franklyn, *Rhyming*.)

horse's arse or **hoss's ass** is contemptuous for a person disliked and distrusted: Canadian (esp. soldiers'): C. 20. Jocular elaboration: (*the*) *north end of a horse going south*.

horse's hoof; often shortened to *horses*. A male pervert: rhyming s. (on *poof*): since ca. 1910. Cf. the commoner *iron* (*hoof*).

horse's neck. A drink of ginger ale and brandy: Public Schools' and Naval: since ca. 1925. Granville; *The Daily Telegraph*, August 14, 1956.—2. A polite form of *horse's ass*: Canadian: since ca. 1920.

horses sweat, men perspire and women glow. A c.p. directed, in mild (often jocular) reproof at a man saying he *sweats*, still more than a woman does: C. 20. By 1960, slightly ob.: nowadays, many women prefer to *sweat* or, at the worst, to perspire.

horseshoe. See **horse-shoe** (*Dict.*).

horsing around. The playing of practical jokes: Canadian Servicemen's: since not later than 1939. H. & P. Cf. S.E. *horse play*.

hose or **hosepipe**, v.i. and v.t. To spray liquid fire from a flame thrower: Army: 1941 +. (P-G-R.)

hospital bum. 'A young doctor who, having completed his medical training, cannot persuade himself to leave the hospital and enter general practice. This psychological block is so well known to the profession that those afflicted by it have become known as "hospital bums". I first heard it in October 1961' (Douglas Leechman). Canadian medical: since late 1950's.

hospital grounds. A flat, easy run: coach-drivers': C. 19. (W. O. Tristram, *Coaching Days* . . ., 1888.)

hospital sheep. Sick sheep that are segregated: Australian rural coll.: since ca. 1925. (B., 1943.)

hospitals, walk the. See **walk the hospitals.**

hoss's ass. See **horse's arse.**

hostel. See 'Tavern terms', § 3.

***hosteller.** A 'scrounger' and/or adventurer frequenting Work Aid Homes and such places: vagrants' c.: from ca. 1920. W. A. Gape, *Half a Million Tramps*, 1936.

hostie. An airline hostess: Aus.: since ca. 1955. Nino Culotta, *Cop This Lot*, 1960, '"That hostie's a slashin' line," Dennis said.'

hostile (p. 408): earlier in sense 'inimical, esp. to hoboes': Canadian tramps': late C. 19–20. (Niven.) Ex U.S.

hostile ord. An ordinary seaman enlisted for 'hostilities only': Naval: 1939 +. Granville.

Hostile Territory. Eastern Region: railwaymen's: since middle 1940's. *Railway*, 3rd.

hot, n.—2. 'I . . . had a pot of *hot*, which is beer with gin in it,' *Sessions*, March 1847: public-houses': ca. 1830–90.—3. A penny; *hots*, money: Felsted School: late C. 19–20.

hot, adj., 11 (p. 408), anticipates the sense 'recent or fresh' as applied to information, a sense adopted, ca. 1943, ex U.S.—12. Stinking; (e.g. of fish) stale: Australian traders': since ca. 1930. (B., 1953.) Probably influenced by **honk.**—13. Stolen: Canadian (ex U.S.), since ca. 1925; English and Australian, since ca. 1935. Originally c.; by 1945, at latest, s.—14. Hence, smuggled: Australian: since late 1930's. (B.P.)—15. Very much favoured; regarded as likely to win, as a candidate in an election: since ca. 1910. Ex senses 6 and 8 on p. 408.

hot and bothered, all. See **all hot and bothered.**

hot and cold. Gold: rhyming s.: C. 20. Franklyn 2nd.

hot and strong, I like—or he likes—my (his) **women.** An Australian c.p., dating from ca. 1945 and deriving from *I like my coffee—and my women—hot and strong* or some variant thereof.

hot-arsed. Earlier in Anon., *The Ten Pleasures of Marriage*, 1682–3. (Dr Niels Haislund.)

hot as a fire-cracker. Sexually hot-blooded and promiscuous: Canadian: since ca. 1910.

hot-bot. A highly sexed or over-sexed girl; often *Miss Hotbot* or *Lady Hotbot*: non-aristocratic, non-cultured: since ca. 1920.

hot-box. An overheated axle-bearing on a railway car: Canadian railwaymen's: C. 20.

hot cack. Good; very good: Australian low: C. 20. B., 1942. With a low pun on *go like hot cakes*. Mr Barry Prentice doubts the pun and thinks *hot cack* a semi-euphemism for **shit-hot** below.

hot cock. See **cock, hot,** above.

hot coppers (p. 408) occurs in 1806 (John Davis, *The Post-Captain*). Moe.

hot cross bun.—2. A Red Cross ambulance:

Army: 1914–18. Ex the marking.—3. On the run (from the police): rhyming s.: C. 20. (Franklyn, *Rhyming*.)

hot cup of tea, a. 'Hot stuff': ca. 1880–1914. William Westall, *Sons of Belial*, 1895.

hot dog. A Malibu board, i.e. a wide, not very large, board, made of 'foam' and sheathed with fibreglass: Australian surfers': adopted, ca. 1960, **ex** Hawaii. Hence, *hot-dogging* (n. and adj.), making 'fast turns and fancy stunts on waves' (*Pix*, Sept. 28, 1963): since ca. 1961.

hot drop, the latest. The latest fad or fashion; the latest craze of any kind: Australian: since ca. 1950. (B.P.)

hot fog. Steam: Naval (engineers'): since ca. 1930.

hot foot. To hasten; walk very quickly, to run; to decamp speedily: adopted ca. 1917 from U.S. (A. P. G. Vivian in *Fifty Amazing Stories of the Great War*.) But mostly *hot foot it*.

hot gen. Up-to-the-minute information: R.A.F.: 1939 +.

hot joint. 'A [taxicab] rank is a "mark", and the first position is the "point" or "hot joint",' Herbert Hodge, *Cab, Sir?*, 1939: taxi-drivers': since ca. 1920. Cf. the Army's **sweat on the top line** (*Dict.*).

hot line. A telephone line without a switchboard: coll., orig. political: since ca. 1960.

*****hot money.** Stolen notes of numbers known: c.: from ca. 1930. Ex U.S. Cf. **hot**, adj., 10 (*Dict.*).

hot mutton. See **hot meat** (*Dict.*).

hot pants (for someone), have. Esp. of women: to be very much in love: adopted, ca. 1938, from U.S. Peter Cheyney, *passim*. Cf. 'La rage de la culotte m'est passée,' Duplaix, letter of Oct. 4, 1738 (communicated by N. H. Prenter, Esq.).

hot-plater. 'A person who drives a car that is painted to look like a taxi and operates mainly at night to avoid detection' (B., *Australia Speaks*, 1953): Australian: since ca. 1945. Also called a *flea*.

hot pot. An 'engine emitting steam from safety valves' (*Railway*, 3rd): C. 20.

hot-potato (pronounced *potater*). A waiter: late C. 19–20. (Franklyn, *Rhyming*.) Also *cold potato*.—2. A political, or a sociological, problem too hot to handle comfortably: adopted, ca. 1954, ex U.S.; by 1965, coll.

hot rod. A very fast motor-car: Canadian motorists': 1948 +. Ex U.S. Cf. *jet job*. Also, since ca. 1950, Australian and, since ca. 1955, English.

hot roll with cream, a. Coïtion: low: late C. 19–20.

hot scone. 1. 2. See **scone.** Itself rhyming s. on synonymous *John*.

hot seat, hot squat, the electric chair, have been, ca. 1935, adopted from U.S.—but as allusive s. not as c. See *Underworld*.

*****hot seat—Irishman—second horse—split ace;** all preceded by the. The confidence trick: c.: the 1st and 4th from ca. 1919; the others from ca. 1905; the 1st, orig. U.S. Ex first (see *Dict.*): **hot seat mob**, confidence men, as in F. D. Sharpe, 1938.

hot seat, the, esp. *be in* . . . (To be) in a very difficult, or even a dangerous, position; to be in grave trouble: adapted, ca. 1950, ex U.S.

hot session. Coïtion: since ca. 1920.

*****hot spot;** esp. **be in a** . . . Trouble: c.: anglicised, ca. 1928, ex U.S.; by 1945, s.

hot stuff (p. 409). Senses 1 and 2 were remarkably anticipated in a song written by one of General Wolfe's officers, and sung by officers and men in 1759. It begins thus, 'Wolfe commands us, my boys; we shall give them'—the French— 'Hot Stuff.' Quoted by Edith & Alan Milles in *Canada's Story in Song*, Toronto, 1960. (Communicated by Dr Douglas Leechman.)

hot, sweet and filthy. See 'Prisoner-of-War Slang', 11. With a pun on the prescription, 'Coffee should be as *hot* as hell, as *sweet* as love, and as *black* as night.'

hot that broad. See **broad.**

hot 'un. Also, a severe punch or blow: pugilistic: mid-C. 19–20. Augustus Mayhew, *Paved with Gold*, 1857.

hot under the collar, get or **grow.** To become annoyed or angry: since ca. 1920.

hot(-)watcher. One who, at Winchester football, plays just behind the 'hot' or scrummage: Winchester College: since ca. 1870. E. H. Lacon Watson, *In the Days of His Youth*, 1935.

*****hotel barber.** A thief that lives in a hotel to rob it: Australian c.: C. 20. B., 1942. Ex **hotel-barbering** (p. 409).

Hotel Lockhart (p. 409). Ex the Lockhart chain of cheap eating-houses in London. By itself, *Lockhart* was a pejorative.

hotten up one's copper. To take warm food or a hot drink: New Zealand: C. 20. B., 1941.

hotter. A crumpet: Harrovians': from ca. 1895. Lunn. Ex *hot* (crumpets being only by idiots eaten other than ho t) by 'the Oxford -*er*'.

hotters. Hot water: Naval: since ca. 1920. By 'the Oxford-*er*'.

hottie.—2. A very tall story: Australian: C. 20. Baker.

hotty-watty bottles (or **b's**). Hot-water bottles: upper-middle class domestic s.: since ca. 1945. Sometimes abbreviated to **hotty.**

Houdini, do a. To escape, esp. from a seemingly inextricable position: mostly Australian: since ca. 1920. Ex the feats of the late Harry Houdini. (B.P.)

hour-grunters. See 'Constables' and cf. **yowlie,** q.v. in *Dict*. The term seems to have been unknown to Grose: it had prob. > † by 1870.

*****house.**—6. A brothel: c., and low: from ca. 1860.—7. A Naval Officer's cabin: Naval: C. 20. 'I'll drop the book in at your house when I pass.' (Wilfred Granville).

House, game of. See esp. the entry at **little Jimmy**—and B. & P.

house!, make yourself at our. See **make yourself at our house!**

house, on the. Free, as in 'It's on the house', esp. of a drink offered by the landlord: coll.: C. 20. Cf. **House,** 5, on p. 410.

house dog. House tutor: several Public Schools': from ca. 1880. Ian Hay, *Housemaster*, 1936.

house-keeper or **-piece.** See **house-bit** (*Dict.*).

house lighter. A lighter (boat) fitted with a cabin: canal-men's (esp. Fenland) coll.: C. 20. In, e.g., L. T. C. Rolt, *Narrow Boat*, 1944. On S.E. *house-boat*.

House of Corruption, the. 'The Glasgow Municipal Buildings were commonly known among [the city's slummies] as the "Chamber of Horrors" or the "House of Corruption"': C. 20. MacArthur & Long.

House of Lords, the. A urinal: Glasgow schoolboys': C. 20.

house that Jack built, the.—3. 'The Government Savings Bank, Sydney, opened in 1928,' B., 1942. Prompted by *jack*, n., 27.

house tic-tac. A 'tic-tac man' that acts for a group of small, subscribing 'bookies': race-course s.: C. 20. Robert Westerby, *Wide Boys Never Work*, 1937.

house to let.—2. A bet: late C. 19–20. F. D. Sharpe, *The Flying Squad*, 1938. Rhyming.

housekeeping. Housekeeping money: lower and lower-middle class coll.: C. 20. Gerald Kersh, *Slightly Oiled*, 1946.

housey, adj. (p. 410). Also *Housey*, Christ's Hospital: mid-C. 19–20 (W. H. Blanch, 1877).

houtkop. An aborigine: South African (C. 20) c. and low s. Afrikaans: *hout*, wood, and *kop*, head.

how! A coll. Australian salutation, adopted, ca. 1944, ex U.S. 'Often with right hand raised, palm forwards, and with an expressionless face. Ex Amerindian greeting' (B.P.)

how.—2. A patrol flight (?): R.A.F.: ca. 1939–41. James Aldridge, *Signed with Their Honour*, 1942, "'We're going on a how. Eleven hours," Hickey said.'

how are the troops treating you? A 1939–45, then merely allusive, finally historical, Australian c.p., used by women. (B.P.)

how are we? A jocular c.p. of greeting: C. 20.

how are you going? How are you? How do you do?: Australian coll.: since ca. 1930. (B.P.)

how come? How does that come about? or Why is that?: adopted, ca. 1943, ex U.S. servicemen.

how-d'ye-do. A shoe: rhyming s.: C. 20.—2. A fuss; mild excitement: since ca. 1910. (S. P. B. Mais, *Caper Sauce*, 1948.) Perhaps, as Franklyn (*Rhyming*) suggests, it rhymes on *stew*, perturbation.

how-d'ye (or **do you**) **do.** Add:—3. Hence, a source—or an instance—of trouble; a quarrel, a brawl: since ca. 1910; by ca. 1960, coll. 'A nice—or what a—how-d'you-do!' In, e.g., Eric Burgess, *A Killing Frost*, 1961.

how high is a Chinaman? A c.p. reply to a question either unanswerable or stupid: since ca. 1950. With a pun on a pseudo-Chinese personal name *How Hi*.

how long have you been in this regiment? See **regiment** . . .

how many times? 'I heard this on and off during the First World War. When a Tommy had got married while on leave, his chums would generally pull his leg and ask "How many times?" when he got back. They meant how many times had he made love to his bride on the first night' (A. B. Petch, May 1966): c.p.: 1914–18.

how nice and what a lot! A facetious c.p., expressive of pleasure: since ca. 1930.

how the other half lives. A c.p., dating since ca. 1930, and used as in "'Hobbes, go down to one of the section bases and see what's going on. It won't do you any harm to see how the other half lives'" (John Winton, *We Saw the Sea*, 1960). The original meaning is '(to see) how the poor live', and as such it was a literary allusion; but soon it came to mean little, if anything, more than 'other people' or even 'anyone else'.

how to do it and not get it; occ. with addition, *by one who did it and got it*. An Australian c.p.: since ca. 1950. A reference to books on marriage.

how to win friends and influence people, loosely, . . . **make friends** . . . Since ca. 1935 in U.S. and since ca. 1945 in Britain, a c.p.—often ironic and derisive. It is so embedded in both American and British English that it is often used allusively and flexibly, as in "'In this line of business I never tell anyone anything unless I think he can help me by having that knowledge."—"You must win an awful lot of friends and influence an awful lot of people," Swanson said dryly.—"It gets embarrassing"': Alistair MacLean, *Ice Station Zebra*, 1963 (p. 189). Ex a book so titled, written by Dale Carnegie (1888–1955) and published in 1936; he had, for many years before that, run a school for public speaking, toast-making, personal relationships in business.

how we apples swim! (p. 411). The longer form is probably the original, for it occurs in Ray's *English Proverbs*, 1670.

howling-box. A gas chamber: Australian airmen's: 1939–45. (B., 1943.)

howling-stick. A flute: low, mostly London: ca. 1840–90. Augustus Mayhew, *Paved with Gold*, 1857.

how's about? How about?: Canadian coll.: adopted, ca. 1953, ex U.S. 'How's about having a drink?' (Leechman).

how's biz? How's business: Australian c.p.: since ca. 1945. (B.P.)

how's it all going to end? A jocular c.p. (ca. 1906–10) based on a comic song current ca. 1906: 'Little Winston, little friend, | . . . . | How's it all going to end?'

how's the body? How are you—how do you feel?: Anglo-Irish: late C. 19–20. Brendan Behan, *Borstal Boy*, 1958.

how's the world treating you or **. . . been treating you?** A popular form of greeting, usually to someone not seen for some time: C. 20.

how's your dandruff? A jocular, vulgar, mostly lower-middle class greeting: since ca. 1950; by 1965, ob.

how's your dirty rotten form? or shortened to *how's your form?* 'This c.p. is not really a question, but is used when someone wins a lottery, passes an exam or gets a promotion. It is sometimes elaborated to . . . *dirty, rotten, stinking form?*' (B.P.): Australian: since ca. 1955.

how's your rotten form? An Australian c.p. dating from ca. 1941 in the Services and addressed to one who has shrewdly gained a personal success. (B., 1953.)

how's your sister? A pointless c.p.: since 1910. A friend writes: 'I believe this to be based on an anecdote. A punter, colliding with a barge, complained: "See what you've done? Broke one of my oars!" "Did I, lovey? Speakin' of oars, how's your sister?"'—This may be in [Robert Graves's] *Lars Porsena*, 1927.

howzat? How's that?, esp. in cricket: coll.: mid-C. 19–20.

hoy. See **hoi**.

hoy, v. To haul: Australian (? coll. rather than s.): since ca. 1920. (Jean Devanney, 1944.) Perhaps a blend of *hoist* and *haul*.—2. Hence; to take, as in 'I had to hoy myself down to Bega': Australian: since ca. 1920.—3. To discard:

Australian: since ca. 1930. (B.P.) Cf. **hoist,** v., 5, above.

Hoyle, according to. See **according.**

hubba! hubba! An Australian c.p., referring to a pretty girl: mostly teenagers': since ca. 1930. Cf. Cornish *hubba*, a fishing cry. (B.P.)—2. 'But also domestic and conventional when a young wife shows a new gown to her admiring husband' (B.P.): Australian: since ca. 1935.

hubshee. Applied in India to anyone, or to a pony, with woolly hair: coll.: from ca. 1850. A corruption of Arabic *Habashi*, Persian *Habshi*, an Abyssinian, an Ethiopian, a negro.

huckle. See 'Verbs'.

huddle, go into a. To go into secret or private conference; (of several people) to 'put their heads together': jocular coll.: since ca. 1930.

hue.—2. Hence, to belabour (a person) with a cudgel: c.: C. 19–20; ob. B. & L. Proleptic.

Huey. *The Police Gazette,* Melbourne: Australian: late C. 19–20. B., 1942. Short for *hue and cry* (cf. entry on p. 412).

huff-duff. See **shuff-duff** below.

huff of a boo, do a. To weep: Cockneys': C. 20. Pugh. A corruption of *hullabaloo.*

huffy, n. A Service girl that refuses one's invitation: Servicemen's: since 1940. H. & P. Cf. **toffee-nose.**

hug-booby. See 'Men'.

Huggers or **St Huggers.** St Hugh's College: Oxford undergraduates' (— 1922). Marples, 2.

huhhah. See **hoohah.**

hula hoop. See **hooler hoop** above.

hulk, n. A hulk-ship report on a convict: ca. 1810–70. Price Waring, *Tales,* 1897.—2. A severely damaged aircraft: R.A.F. coll.: since ca. 1925. H. & P.

hull down, or **turret down,** under cover, hidden, occurs esp. in *get . . .,* to take cover: Army: since ca. 1940; by 1960, slightly ob. Ex tank j. (P-G-R.)

hullo, beautiful! A male 'getting off' c.p. addressed to a girl: since ca. 1935.

hullo yourself (or **your own self**) **and see how you like it!** A lower-classes' c.p. of ca. 1890–1910. W. Pett Ridge, *Minor Dialogues,* 1895.

hum, n.—7. A professional sponger: Australian: since ca. 1920. (Caddie, *A Sydney Barmaid,* 1953.) He 'stinks'.

hum, v., 3 (p. 413): also, since ca. 1918, Aus. (B., 1959.)

hum-drum. See 'Occupational names'.

hum durgeon. See **humdudgeon** (*Dict.*).

human sausage-machine. A woman having a baby every twelve months: Australian coll.: since ca. 1930. (B.P.)

humble condumble. See **your humble condumble.**

humdinger. A fast aircraft or vehicle; a smooth-running engine: Services, but mostly R.A.F.: adopted in mid-1940 from American airmen. American s.: echoic: *hum* (speed) + *dinger* (something forceful).—2. Anything superlatively good: Australian: adopted, ca. 1945, ex U.S. (B.P.)

humid. Stupid: Naval: since ca. 1939. 'A pun on synonymous *wet*' (P-G-R).

hummer.—3. A 'scrounger': Australian: since ca. 1910. B., 1942.

hummerskew. A jocular perversion of

humoresque: Canadian: since ca. 1950. (Leechman.)

hummie or **hummy.** Bursitis (inflammation of a sac), caused by carrying weights: London dial. (See E.D.D.) >, ca. 1890, coll. Apparently an casing of *humpy*. Ex *hump*.

hump, v., 1, occurs in *Sessions,* 1769, Fifth Session.

hump it.—3. To depart: Cockney: late C. 19–20. (A. Neil Lyons, *Arthur's,* 1908.)

hump oneself (p. 415). Also, since ca. 1910, Australian, prob. influenced by *hump one's bluey*— see **hump,** v., 3, in *Dict.*

humped off. Noted for punishment by the Captain: Naval: C. 20.

humpey (or **-y**).—2. A hump-backed person: since ca. 1870. *Sessions,* June 30, 1885.—3. A camel: Australian: late C. 19–20. Archer Russell, *A Tramp Royal in Wild Australia,* 1934; B., 1942.

humpty-dumpty. A stretch of desert road that, with tarmac laid straight on to the sand, follows every ridge and hollow: Army in North Africa: ca. 1940–3.

Hun.—3. A German 'plane: R.F.C. and R.A.F. coll.: 1914 +. Partridge, 1945.

hundred-per-center. A thoroughly good fellow (or girl); one whole-heartedly devoted to a cause: coll.: since ca. 1930.

hung on. Very fond of and, to some degree, dependent on (another person): teenagers' and other young people's raffish s.: since ca. 1955. John Sherwood, *The Half Hunter,* 1961, defines it as 'emotionally dependent on' (Penguin edition, p. 86).

hung up, be.—2. To be (foolishly) involved or entangled; to be stalled or frustrated: Canadian jazz-lovers': since ca. 1956. (*The Victoria Daily Colonist,* April 16, 1959, article 'Basic Beatnik'.)— 3. Hence, annoyed; irritated, irritable: British jazz lovers', drug addicts', hippies': since ca. 1960. Peter Fryer in *The Observer* colour supplement, Dec. 3, 1967.

hunger-knock. A synonym of *bonk, the*: cyclists': since ca. 1945.

hungry. Close-fisted; selfish: Australian since ca. 1920. Baker.—2. Greedy: Australian: since ca. 1925. (Leonard Mann, *The Go-Getter,* 1942.)

Hungry, the. The Hungarian Restaurant: London taxi-drivers': since ca. 1920. Herbert Hodge, 1939.

hungry dog will eat dirty pudding, a. A c.p. —virtually a proverb—deprecating fastidiousness: mid-C. 19–20. Atkinson compares that other virtual proverb, *you don't look at the mantelpiece when you're poking the fire,* which by the way, is occ. used instead of the equally sexual proverb, *at night all cats are grey.*

hungry enough to eat the arse out of a dead skunk. Famished: low Canadian: C. 20.

Hungry Forties, the. The years 1940–5, when food was short: since ca. 1946; by 1951, merely historical. Ex Ireland's famine years, the 1840's.

Hungry Mile, the. Sussex Street, Sydney: Sydneyites': since ca. 1925. B., 1942.

hungry rock. 'Rock carrying little or no mineral' (Leechman): Canadian miners' coll.: late C. 19–20. (Cf. *hungry quartz* on p. 415.)

hungry staggers, the. Faintness or staggering caused by hunger: proletarian coll.: from ca. 1860. B. & L.

hunk, n.—2. A big man: Australian: since ca. 1920. Baker. Ex *hunk of beef*.

hunks or **hunky-dory;** esp. **everything's hunky-dory.** Predicatively, as in 'That's hunky-dory'—fine, just the thing: adopted ca. 1938 from U.S.

hunky, adj. Good: since ca. 1945. Ex preceding.

Huns. Cricklewood men (i.e., employees): London transport men's: since ca. 1920 (?). *Railway*, 3rd. Why?

hunt, v.—3. 'A compass needle (or similar indicator) is said to *hunt* when it oscillates about the true reading without coming to rest' (Leechman): scientific coll.: since ca. 1920.

huntaway. 'A sheepdog which drives sheep forward when mustering' (B., 1959): Aus. rural coll.: C. 20. Cf. **force,** n., above.

*****hunting.** In c., the pre-eminent mid-C. 19–20 sense is 'card-sharping'.

Hunts, the. The Hunt Class destroyers, named after famous packs (Pytchley, Quorn, etc.): Naval coll.: World War II. (P-G-R.)

hurdy-gurdy (p. 416). No; the 'barrel-organ' sense goes back to ca. 1800. It occurs in an 'Imitation of Ode XVI. Book II. of Horace', reprinted, from an unidentified British source, in *The Port Folio*, June 9, 1804, on p. 183:

'In London . . .
    .   .   .   .   .

The poor Savoyard, doom'd to roam,
In search of halfpence, sighs for home,
And spins his hurdy-gurdy.'

(With thanks to Colonel Albert F. Moe, U.S.M.C., Ret.)

hurdy-gurdy girls. 'In the Klondike gold rush of 1897–98 there were many dance hall girls, mostly German, who would dance for a fee, but stopped at that (except perhaps now and then). They were known as hurdy-gurdy girls and the references to them are numerous' (Leechman, April 1967). Ex Western American *hurdy-gurdy* (*house*), such a saloon.

hurrah, on the. With hustling and shouting: Australian Labour s.: since ca. 1930. B., 1942. 'The boss works us on the hurrah.'

hurrah for Casey! Splendid! Excellent! That's 'great'!: Australian: C. 20. Baker. Ex a political election.

hurriboys. Pilots and others operating Hurricanes: Air Force: 1940 +.

hurricane deck. Neck: theatrical rhyming s. C. 20. (Franklyn, *Rhyming*.) A Hurricane fighter aircraft: R.A.F.: since late 1939. E. P. in *The New Statesman*, Sept. 19, 1942 (1st); H. & P. (2nd, 3rd); Jackson, who adds the 4th, says, 'The first expression is the commonest'.

Hurry; Hurry-back or **hurryback; hurribox.**

A Hurricane fighter 'plane: R.A.F.: since 1940. But never very general.

Hurry boys. Pilots of Hurricane aircraft: mostly R.A.F.: ca. 1940–5. (P-G-R.)

Hurry-buster. A Hurricane aircraft employed as a tank-buster: R.A.F. and Army: ca. 1940–5. (P-G-R.)

hurry-scurry. A hack race: Australian sporting: since ca. 1920. (K. S. Prichard, 'Dark Horse of Darran'—in *Kiss on the Lips*, 1932.)

hurry-up, n. A hastener, esp. a shell or two fired to make the enemy hurry: Army coll.: since ca. 1941.

hurry up and take your time! A humorous exhortation: c.p.: C. 20.

hurry-up waggon. A 'black Maria': Canadian: since ca. 1945. (Leechman.)

husband. See **wife,** 4, below.

hush-hush. A caterpillar tank: Army: 1917–18. See **Hush-Hush Crowd** (p. 417).

hustler.—4. A peddler of peanuts, etc., at a fair: Canadian carnival s.: C. 20. Ex sense 2.—5. A prostitute; hence the n. *hustling*: Canadian: adopted, ca. 1925, ex U.S. She hustles for—briskly conducts—a living.

hut. A caboose; the cab of a locomotive: Canadian railroadmen's (— 1931).

hut-keep. 'To look after a hut in the bush or outback. Whence, "hut-keeper"' (B., 1943): Australian coll.: since ca. 1910.

hutch. (A sheep's) crutch: New Zealand shearers': C. 20. B., 1941. Rhyming s.

hyæna. A Society term of ca. 1770–80. Scott, *Diary*, May 9, 1828, in reference to Foote's play, *The Cozeners*, 1774: 'She had the disposal of what was then called a *hyæna*, that is, an heiress.'

hydro.—2. A hydroplane: coll.: since ca. 1930.

Hydromancy. See 'Tavern terms', § 3 *d*.

[**Hyphenation.** On this difficult subject, see esp. Fowler. The C. 20 tendency—an increasing tendency—is to do away with hyphens. The example of American English is potent; so are the inculcations of logic. But, as an examination of the O.E.D. will show, the English language has always been inconsistent in the matter of hyphens. Perhaps the safest rule (not that I follow it!) is to omit the hyphen wherever it is possible to do so without a loss of clarity or a blunting of nuance. Like punctuation, hyphens can often be used to ensure accuracy, as e.g. in compound epithets; often, too, they make for easier reading. See, my *You Have a Point There*, 1953.

hypo.—2. War-time sugar, hard and insoluble: St Bees: 1915–18. 'From its resemblance to photographic hypo,' Marples.—3. A hypochondriac; a valetudinarian; one who is both: Australian: since late 1930's. (B.P.)

I

i for ē is a minor characteristic of Cockney: dating from when? It occurs in only a few words. Above all in **sim(s)**, seem or seems; thus C. Rook, *The Hooligan Nights*, 1899, '"Sims to me what you start on you've got to go froo wiv."' Two other common instances are **bin** (been) and *sin* (seen).

I am (or **I'm**) **not here.** I don't feel inclined to work; or, I wish to be left alone: tailors' c.p.: from ca. 1870. B. & L.

I.B.A. Ignorant bloody aircrafthand: R.A.F.: since ca. 1930. Jackson, 'Aircrafthands are the jacks-of-all-trades of the R.A.F. . . . Officially, they are unskilled.' On the analogy of the I.R.A. and the **P.B.I.** (p. 596). Cf. **Ibach.**

I believe you, (but) thousands wouldn't. A c.p., tactfully implying that the addressee is a liar: late C. 19–20.

I.C., the. The officer, N.C.O. or senior man in charge of a squad, a detachment, a barrack-room, a hut, etc.: Service (esp. R.A.F.) coll.: since ca. 1930. Partridge, 1945, 'I must ask the I.C. about that; he's sure to know.'

I couldn't care fewer. A short-lived variant (1960–62) of *I couldn't care less*, q.v. at **couldn't care less** above.

I couldn't care less. See **couldn't care less** . . .

I couldn't eat that. I couldn't tolerate that female: lower- and lower-middle class c.p.: C. 20. Also general (with variant *cannot* or *can't*), as in 'I couldn't eat the last one' (a lodger), Pamela Branch, *The Wooden Overcoat*, 1951.

I.D.B.—2. Ignorant *D*utch *b*astard: Cockneys': since ca. 1920.

I.D. Herb? (Strictly *I.D., Herb!*) Hullo! How are you?: Australian: since ca. 1925. B., 1942. I.e. **hidey!** (q.v.) + generic *Herb.*

I didn't blow it out of my nose! '"I didn't do it offhand, or without trouble." Ex a French c.p., I believe. Heard in the last few years' (Leechman, April 1967): Canadian: since the late 1950's.

I didn't come . . . See **last bucket . . .**

I didn't come up with the last boat; or **I didn't fall off a Christmas tree.** I know my way about; I'm not to be fooled: c.p.: mostly, Services': since middle 1940's. (Laurie Atkinson, Sept. 11, 1967.)

I didn't get a sausage or **. . . so much as a tickle.** I got nothing, esp. in money: c.p.: since ca. 1945.

I don't want to be a sergeant-pilot anyway! A jocular c.p. in reference to masturbation: R.A.F.: since ca. 1935.

I don't go much on it. I dislike it: almost a c.p.: since ca. 1925.

I don't mind if I do. A c.p. (= Yes, please) that, in 1945, > fairly widespread and in 1946 almost a public nuisance. A Tommy Handley 'gag' in I.T.M.A. (E. P. in *The Radio Times*, Dec. 6, 1946.)

I have (or **I've**) **a picture of Lord Roberts.** 'A c.p. rejoinder to someone asking for something' (Atkinson): mostly Army and R.A.F.: since ca. 1918.

I haven't a thing to wear. The widest-spread and most popular female c.p.: late C. 19–20, and prob. very much earlier.

I haven't laughed so hard since my mother caught her (left) **tit in the wringer.** I haven't laughed so much for years: Canadian: C. 20. Cf. *'hell!' said the duchess* (p. 387 and Addenda).

I heard the voice of Moses say. See **roll on, my bloody twelve.**

I hope we shall meet in Heaven. A pious ecclesiastical convention (late C. 17–20) that soon acquired a wider currency, as in Swift, *Polite Conversation*, 1738, first dialogue, in the opening exchange.

I know and you know, but (the thing) **doesn't know,** where 'the thing' is usually a machine or a mechanical device: a mostly Australian c.p.: since late 1940's. Used mostly by workmen to justify, in part at least, some malpractice. (B.P.)

I like work: I could watch it all day. A witty Australian c.p., dating from early 1950's. (B.P.)

I Love You Only, Kid. See **keep off . . .** below.

I.M.F.U. An *M.F.U.* on an imperial scale: Services, esp. Army: World War II. (P-G-R.)

I must or **I'll bust.** I simply must go to the w.c.: a (mainly Australian) c.p.: since ca. 1925.

I need (or want) **a piss so bad my back teeth are floating** (or **I can taste it**); or **. . . a shit so bad my eyes are brown.** Low Canadian c.pp.: C. 20.

I quite agree with *you*! See **what do** *you* **think of it?**

I say! Prob. throughout C. 19. '"To the Bush Rangers?" "Yes; I say, you won't *blow* me?"': George Godfrey, *History*, 1828. A means of attracting attention: late C. 19–20.

I say, what a smasher! A c.p. dating from late 1945. Ex the B.B.C. radio programme, 'Stand Easy' (a post-war version of 'Merry-Go-Round'). Cf. **smashing.** E. P., 'Those Radio Phrases', in *The Radio Times*, Dec. 6, 1946.

I say, you fellows! A schoolboys' c.p.: since ca. 1947. In Frank Richards's Greyfriars School stories, the now famous character Billy Bunter is constantly using these words.

I suppose. I suppose so: coll.: rare before C. 20 and not, even now, very widespread. E.g. '"Will you be coming to town next month?" "Yes, I suppose."'

I weep for you (or him or her or . . .). An occ. variant of *my heart bleeds for you.*

I will work for my living. An underworld c.p., expressive of improbability, a preliminary *when that happens* being implied: since ca. 1950. (Communicated by Julian Franklyn, Jan. 3, 1968.)

I wish I had a man—I wouldn't half love

him! Servicewomen's c.p. of amorous longing: 1939 +.

I won't wear it! See **wear it!, I won't.**

I won't work. A c.p. applied since ca. 1912 to a member of the Industrial Workers of the World.

I work like a horse—(so) I may as well hang my prick out to dry! A c.p. palliation of accidental or ribald exposure: late C. 19–20.

I would (or I'd) rather sleep one night with her than three weeks with you! A c.p. approval of the charms of women: Forces': 1939 +.

I wouldn't be found dead in it! I certainly sha'n't wear that!: c.p.: C. 20.

I wouldn't bet a pound to a pinch of shit. A low c.p., implying lack of confidence: late C. 19–20.

I wouldn't give you the sweat off my balls or the steam off my shit. A low Canadian c.p. (C. 20), indicating detestation.

I wouldn't have—in reference, **her**; in address, **you—any other way.** A mainly Australian c.p., used in reference or address to one's wife: since ca. 1956. Often jocular as in: 'Do you realize that I'm just an unpaid servant? I get your breakfast, look after your children, entertain your friends. . . .'—(with demonstration of affection) 'I wouldn't have you any other way.' (B.P.)

I wouldn't know. (Occasionally '(S)he wouldn't know.) This originally American c.p. for the usual British 'I couldn't say' (= I don't know) came to Britain during the 1930's, and in a British film of 1940, Pimpernel Smith, Leslie Howard remarked, 'In the deplorable argot of the modern generation, "I wouldn't know."' This phrase has been much used ever since. Dr Brian Foster (The Changing English Language, 1968) thinks that it was a translation of ich wüsste nicht, taken to America by German immigrants. Therefore cf. **d'you know something?**

I wouldn't stick my walking-stick where you stick your prick! A c.p. common-reportedly spoken by physicians to men going to them with V.D.: C. 20. Or vice-versa, you stick . . . where I wouldn't . . . See also **put one's prick where . . .,** below.

iambi. Iambic verse(s): Harrow School coll.: mid-C. 19–20. (H. A. Vachell, The Hill, 1905.)

Ibach (short i, stressed; indeterminate a = ĕ). Ignorant bastard aircraft hand: R.A.F.: since ca. 1939. Also fibach, when f = fucking.

*ice. Diamonds; loosely, gems: c.: anglicised ca. 1925 ex U.S. The Pawnshop Murder. Ex the icy sheen of diamonds.—2. Impudence, effrontery: Society: from ca. 1927. Rebecca West, The Thinking Reed, 1936. Cf. cool, impudent.

*ice-box. A solitary cell: Australian c.: since ca. 1920. B., 1942. Adopted from U.S.: see Underworld and cf. **cooler,** 4 (Dict.).—2. See **fry,** v., 2.

ice-cream, short for **ice-cream freezer.** A person, usu. male; a fellow: since ca. 1920; c. >, by 1960, also low s. (Robin Cook, The Crust on Its Uppers, 1962.) Rhyming on s. geezer.

ice-cream barrow. See **came over** . . .

ice-cream freezer; usually shortened to **ice-cream.** A person; one of the crowd: rhyming s.: since ca. 1946. On geezer. (Jacob Jaffe.)

ice-cream suit. Except at Port Darwin and in the York Peninsula, ironic for the white tropical clothes worn by newcomers: Australian: C. 20. Baker. Probably adopted from U.S., where it isn't ironic and where it denotes 'men's summer garb, light in weight, cream or white in color' (Alexander McQueen), as also in Canada (Leechman).

ice-creamer. An Italian: since ca. 1955. A variant of—and obviously a derivative from—the preceding: 1916, 'A Post Mortem'—a University of Sydney song written in 1916 (and reprinted in The Company Song Book, 1918) and therefore presumably current from a few years earlier. (B.P.)

ice-o. An iceman: Australian: since ca. 1920. D'Arcy Niland, The Big Smoke, 1959.

iceberg. One who always goes swimming, no matter how cold the water: Australian: since ca. 1925. (B., 1943.)

I'd hate to cough. A c.p. spoken by one who is suffering from diarrhoea: late C. 19–20.

I'd like a pup off that. A c.p., indicative of covetous approbation: Services': since ca. 1930. (I.e. out of that bitch.)

I'd like to get you on a slow boat to China (starting from England). I'd like to have the time to gradually influence you: a nautical, usually jocular, c.p.: C. 20.

ideas about, have; get ideas into one's head. To have or get amorous ideas (about a girl): coll. mid C. 19–20.

identity, 2 (p. 419). 'It was current before [1862] . . . The anonymous writer of Otago, Its Goldfields and Resources, of 1862, declares that "the exclusive spirit of the old identity" was part of the curse of Dunedin,' Baker (1941), who indicates its prob. origin in 'the early settlers should endeavour to preserve their old identity'.—3. Hence, as adj., 'effete': New Zealand: ca. 1870–90. B., 1941.

idiot box and **idiot's lantern.** A television receiving set: since ca. 1955: the former (cf. **goggle box** above) is fairly general, the latter mostly Canadian. (Leechman.)

idle. Careless, slovenly ('an idle salute'—'Idle on parade'); dirty ('an idle cap-badge'): Guards Regiments': C. 20; hence, since ca. 1939, R.A.F. By ca. 1955, verging on jargon.—2. Hence, slow, as applied to, e.g., a batsman in a cricket match: since ca. 1960.

idlers, the. 'Officers or men who don't keep watch at sea, the Accountant Branch, for instance' (Granville): Naval: since ca. 1905. No! It goes all the way back to ca. 1790 or even 1780. The O.E.D. cites it for 1794, and it occurs in, e.g., W.N. Glascock, Sailors and Saints (I, 166), 1829, where it is glossed as 'Surgeon, Purser, &c. &c.' and in his Sketch-Book (I, 15, 16), 1825. Moe.

if omitted; gen. with omission of ensuing noun or pronoun: sol.: since when? See the quotation at **wipe round.**—2. See **ifs.**

if—a big if. A c.p. comment upon a startling hypothesis: C. 20; by 1960, slightly ob.

if and and. A band of (instrumentalists): rhyming s.: since ca. 1945. Franklyn 2nd.

if God permits. White Horse whisky: public-houses': late C. 19–20. This whisky has on its label the old coaching notice, 'If God permits'.

if he had the 'flu, he wouldn't give you a sneeze. A c.p., imputing extreme meanness: since ca. 1930.

if I stick a broom up my arse I can sweep the hangar at the same time. A c.p. uttered by one who has received a string of orders that will keep him very, very busy: R.A.F.: since ca. 1925.

if it moves, salute it; if it don't, paint (or **whitewash**) **it.** The R.A.F. 'motto' of the late 1940's and the 1950's.

if so be as how. If: coll., mainly rural: (?) mid C. 18–20. An elongation of *if so be*, if.

If that's nonsense, I'd like some of it. A c.p. rejoinder to a charge of talking nonsense, esp. if sex be involved: since ca. 1950. (Laurie Atkinson, Sept. 11, 1967.)

if they're big enough they're old enough. A cynical male c.p., referring to the 'negotiability' of *young* teenage girls: since ca. 1910 (? earlier). No nonsense about 'the age of consent'.

if you ask me. An introductory c.p., a feeble conversational make-weight: since ca. 1920. (Nobody has asked.)

if you can name it (or **tell what it is**)**, you can have it.** A c.p., referring to an odd-looking person or object: C. 20.

if you can't beat (Australian **lick**) **'em, join 'em.** A cynical c.p., dating since the 1940's. Origin, perhaps political: ? applying to areas where one party is predominant. (William Safire, *The New Language of Politics*, 1968.)

if you looked at him sideways, you wouldn't see him. A c.p. referring to a very thin man: C. 20.

If you see anything that God didn't make, throw your hat at it! A c.p. deprecating undue modesty: since ca. 1930. (L.A., 1967.)

If you vant to buy a vatch, buy a vatch, (but) if you don't vant to buy a vatch, keep your snotty nose off my clean window! A semi-jocular Jew-baiting phrase, C. 20; sometimes shouted by boys outside a jeweller's shop.

if your face fits. If you're in favour with the authorities: Services: since ca. 1930. (P-G-R.)

if your head was loose, you'd lose that too. A c.p., addressed mainly to children: late C. 19–20.

if you're going to buy, buy; if not, would you kindly take the baby's bottom off the counter! A Canadian c.p., addressed by butchers to customers, or even *vice versa*: since ca. 1920. (Leechman.)

iffy (incorrectly *iffey*). Uncertain: unsound, risky: coll., esp. in Australia: since ca. 1920. (B., 1942.)—2. Addicted to excessive *if's* in conversation: coll.: since ca. 1925.

ifs. (Rare in singular.) Spavins, etc.: horse-dealers': C. 20. They lead to doubts and queries.

igaretsay. A cigarette: Australian (urban): adopted, ca. 1944, ex U.S. serviceman. 'Centre slang and, as far as I know, the only example in use in Australia' (Edwin Morrisby, letter of Aug. 30, 1958). 'Surely not centre slang but rather Igpay Atinlay, or Pig Latin, which as you no doubt know is one of the most venerable of children's secret languages. *Ixnay* (= nix) is one of the few PL terms that penetrated the adult world': Robert Clairborne, who, Aug. 31, 1966, states that even *ixnay* is obsolescent.

iggri or **iggry**, n., esp. in *get an iggri on*, to hurry: Army: C. 20. (P-G-R.) Ex *iggri* on p. 419.

Ike. General of the Army Eisenhower: Services: 1943–45: adopted ex Americans. Then civilian.

Ikey, adj. Jewish: C. 20. James Joyce, *Ulysses*, 1922, 'Ikey touch that'. Ex the n. on p. 420.

ikey, play the. To play a sharp trick: Cockneys: from ca. 1880. V.t. with *on*. Also as in C. Rook, *The Hooligan Nights*, 1899: 'I don't think any

Lambeth boy'll play on the ikey like that wiv them girls again.' See **Ikey** in *Dict*.

ikona! No, you don't (or, won't)!: certainly not!: a c.p. current during the Boer War (1899–1901). Perhaps ex Zulu.

I'll be a monkey's uncle! A c.p. expressing astonishment: Canadian: since ca. 1945. Leechman, 'Not often heard.'

I'll be there. A chair: orig., and still mainly, underworld, esp. convicts', rhyming s.: C. 20. Franklyn 2nd.

I'll bite; I'll buy it. (See **bite** and **buy** in *Dict*.) 'I'll bite' is often said and understood as 'I'll buy it', which leads to the further c.p., **No. I'm not selling—serious!**, itself hardly before 1930.

I'll buy that. A Canadian c.p. = 'I'll agree to that plan or decision or explanation': since ca. 1930. Contrast *I'll buy it* in preceding entry.

I'll do (or **fix**) **you!** A c.p. threat, 'I'll settle your hash': often jocular: since ca. 1910 (*do*) and ca. 1920 (*fix*).

I'll eat my hat, head, boots, etc. See **hat, eat one's** (*Dict*.).

I'll go he! An exclamation of surprise = 'I'll be jiggered!': New Zealand c.p.: since ca. 1920. (Slatter.) Ex children's games.

I'll have your gal! 'A cry raised by street boys or roughs when they see a fond couple together': from ca. 1880; ob. B. & L.

I'll have your hat! See **hat!, I'll have your.**

I'll pay that one. I 'bought' that: a c.p. admission that one has been 'had': Australian: since ca. 1930. Kylie Tennant, *The Honey Flow*, 1956. Cf. *I'll bite.*—2. That's a good story or joke: Australian c.p.: since ca. 1950. (B.P.)

I'll push your face in; I'll spit in your eye and choke you. Working-class threats, often playful: c.pp.: late C. 19–20.

I'll saw your leg off! See **my word, if I catch you bending** (below).

I'll say! An enthusiastic affirmative: Australian since ca. 1930; by ca. 1965, slightly ob. (B.P.) Elliptical for *I'll say so!*

I'll tell your mother! A c.p. addressed to a young girl (or occ., one not so young) out with a boy: late C. 19–20.

I'll try anything once. A c.p., affected by the adventurous or the experimental, sometimes jocularly: since ca. 1925. Frank Clune's very readable autobiography—published in 1933—is titled *Try Anything Once.*

illegit. Illegitimate, n. and adj.: schoolboys': C. 20. Lunn, '"Was he a blooming illegit?" asked Kendal.'

*illegitimate. A free settler: convicts' (Australian): ca. 1830–70. B., 1942.

illegitimate glow-worm. A 'bright bastard' (as above): Australian pedantic: since ca. 1950. (B.P.)

illegitimis non carborundum. You mustn't let the bastards grind you down (—wear you down—get you down): Intelligence Corps (1939–45), hence (1940 +) a more general Army motto, esp. among officers. *Carborundum* (silicon carbide), being very hard, is used in grinding and polishing —and here the word serves as 'a mock-Latin gerund; lit., 'There is not to be any carborundum-ing—grinding with carborundum—by the illegitimate.' I wonder which Oxford 'Classic', exacerbated almost to desperation, coined this trenchant piece of exquisite Latinity? For lack of evidence

I suggest that it may have been my friend Stanley Casson, who, born in 1889, became Reader in Classical Archæology at Oxford, directed the Army Intelligence School early in World War II, and then went to Greece to lead the Resistance; he was killed in mid-April 1944, a gallant, learned, urbane and witty scholar, who has never received his due meed of praise. Had Casson lived a century earlier, Carlyle would, to *Heroes*, have added a chapter: The Hero as Scholar. B.P., in mid-1965, comments thus, 'This is general slang in Australia. It is by no means confined to those with a knowledge of Latin' and adduces the following Latin 'translations' or equivalents of gen. or Australian s.; *tauri excretio*, bullshit, and *belli bustum*, a 'belly-buster' (sense 2).

illumina. An abbr. of *illumination*: Winchester College: mid-C. 19–20. B. & L.

*****illywhacker.** A trickster, esp. a confidence man: Australian c.: since ca. 1930. (B., 1943.) Cf. *whack the illy.*

Ilyssus is a frequent error for *Ilissus*, the stream in Athens.

I'm a. An (over)coat: C. 20. Short for **I'm afloat** (*Dict.*). Sometimes written *I'm-a.* Lester.

I'm all right, Jack. See Jack policy, 2nd para.

I'm going to get my head sharpened. I'm going to get a haircut: R.A.F. c.p.: since ca. 1950.

I'm inboard—bugger you, Jack! Look after yourself!: Naval: C. 20. I'm aboard, so pull the ladder up. Cf. **I'm in the boat . . .** (p. 420).

im koy. You shouldn't: Canton pidgin: mid-C. 19–20. B. & L., 'Used politely in accepting or asking a civility'.

I'm not here. See **I am not here.**

I'm not out for chocolates, just had grapes! 'No thanks!' in an intensive, rather contemptuous form: c.p. of ca. 1905–14. W. L. George, *The Making of an Englishman*, 1914.

I'm off in a shower (or a cloud) of shit. Goodbye!: Canadian Army c.p.: 1939–45.

I'm so. Short for **I'm so frisky** (p. 420). Sydney Lester, 1937, 'A tumbler of some hot I'm-so.'

I'm so hungry I could eat a shit sandwich—only I don't like bread! 'A rather repugnant self-explanatory c.p., which is not used in vice-regal circles' (B.P.): Australian: since ca. 1950.

I'm sure! Certainly; certainly it is (or was or will be, etc.): lower-class coll.: from ca. 1870. Edwin Pugh, *A Street in Suburbia*, 1895, '"Ah, that was a funeral!" "I'm sure! Marsh Street ain't likely to see another for many a, etc."'

I'm telling you. A c.p. indicative of emphasis: since ca. 1920.

I'm willing. A shilling: rhyming s.: C. 20. Sydney Lester, *Vardi the Palarey*, (?) 1937.

I'm willing—but Mary isn't, with emphasis upon *I* and *Mary.* A c.p. used by a dyspeptic or other stomach-sufferer when some food is offered: C. 20.

ima(d)ge. Imagination: ca. 1905–20. A. Neil Lyons, *Simple Simon*, 1914.

imaginitis. A tendency to imagine things: coll.: since the late 1940's.

imbars bidbib. An Army 'motto', current in 1939–45 and composed of the initial letters of *I may be a rotten sod, but I don't believe in bullshit.*

*****imbo.** A simpleton; a dupe: Australian c.: since ca. 1935. (B., 1953.) Of Aboriginal origin?

imperial.—2. See **rocket.**

'Imperial Service College (1910 +) possessed three abbreviations of a curious type, *crisch* (= cricket), *foosch* (= football) and *hoosch* (= hockey), the last . . . failed to take root,' Marples. Otherwise, its two best-known terms have (since 1910) been **tramp,** 'a master'—ex former slovenliness?— and **topes** (q.v.).

impixlocated. Tipsy: from ca. 1932. A perversion of *intoxicated.* Also cf. **pixilated.**

impos. See **imposs** (*Dict.*).—2. Occ. variant (from ca. 1890) of **impot** (*Dict.*).

impots. See 'Colston's'.

impudence. Penis: lower-middle and lower-class women's: ca. 1760–1900. *Sessions*, July 1783 (No. VI, Part V, p. 723), Margaret Shehan, raped spinster, in evidence, '"He put his impudence . . ."—"What, do you mean his private parts?"—"Yes."'

impudent. Impotent: this C. 16–20 catachresis is noted as early as 1612 by Dekker in *O per se O.*

impurence. See **imperance** (*Dict.*).

Impuritans. People anything but puritanical: since ca. 1950. Ex *impurity* on *Puritan.*

in, adj.; esp. **be in,** to be accepted by, and a welcome member of, a group or a place: coll.: esp. Australian: since ca. 1920. 'Always written within inverted commas' (B.P.)

in, adv.—8. In to London: tramps' c.: C. 20. W. L. Gibson Cowan, *Loud Report*, 1937, 'Will you give us a lift in?'

in a pig's eye. See **pig's eye, 3.**

in a spot. See **spot, in a.**

in and out.—5. Tout: rhyming s.: C. 20.—6. The nose: rhyming s. (on *snout*): late C. 19–20.—7. Gout: rhyming s.: C. 20. (Nos. 6, 7: Franklyn, *Rhyming.*)—8. Copulation: raffish: late C. 19–20.—9. Continuous turns in (and out of) the trenches: Tommies' coll.: W.W. I. (A. B. Petch, April 1966.)

In-and-Out Club, the. The Naval & Military Club, London: C. 20. Granville. From the 'In' and 'Out' signs on the pillars of the forecourt. This expands the *In-and-Out*, q.v. at **in-and-out,** 3, on p. 421, a term that Julian Franklyn thinks originated among the cabbies and dating from years earlier.

in and out job. A passenger that returns to his point of departure: taxi-drivers': since ca. 1915. Herbert Hodge, 1939.

in-and-out man. An opportunist thief: London's East End: since ca. 1945. (Richard Herd, Nov. 12, 1957.) Quickly in and soon, or furtively, out.

in course (p. 422). Mayhew, I, 1851.

in dead trouble. See **in stook.**

in good arrow. See **arrow, in good.**

in it, be.—4. To be in trouble: coll.: from ca. 1880. B. & L.—5. To agree to (a suggestion); to share in (an undertaking): Australian: since ca. 1925. 'I put the hard word on him for a cut [a share, a commission], but he wouldn't be in it'; 'You've got to be in it to win it.'

*****in smoke.** Also, since ca. 1933, Australian. B., 1942.

in stook or **in dead trouble.** Very short of cash; extremely embarrassed financially: London's East End: since ca. 1945. (Richard Herd, Nov. 12, 1957.) Cf. *stook*, 2; the 2nd, illiterate for 'in deadly trouble'.

in the bag. See **bag, in the.**

in the blue. See **blue**, n., 13.

in the book . . . See **book all right . . .**

in the cuds. See **cuds, in the.**

in the death. Finally: since ca. 1945; by 1960, also s. (Robin Cook, 1962.) Perhaps a blend of '*in the* end' and 'at the *death*'.

in the firing line or **kept on the jump.** In danger of dismissal from one's job; since ca. 1917.

in the lurch. Church: Australian rhyming s.: C. 20. 'Left in the lurch, waiting at the church.'

in the mood. Desirous of sexual intimacies: euphemistic coll., mostly feminine ('I'm not in the mood'): late C. 19–20.

in the rattle. See **rattle, in the.**

in the wind (p. 422) is recorded in 1818: Alfred Burton, *Johnny Newcome*. (Moe.)

in the words of the Chinese poet. A c.p. expressive of disgust on hearing of bad luck or unpleasant instructions: Canadian: since ca. 1910. If a friend hears one say this, he is expected to ask, sympathetically, 'What Chinese poet?'—thus affording the opportunity for, 'Ah Shit, the Chinese poet.' By ca. 1919, also current in England, with the variant name *Hoo* (or *Who*) *Flung Dung*.

in the works. 'In preparation; being effected. "Your two weeks' leave? Oh, yes, it's in the works now. Come back for it at three."' (Leechman.) Canadian: since the middle 1940's.

in tow with, be. To be courting, as in 'John is in tow with Jane Sullivan' (P. W. Joyce, *English . . . in Ireland*, 1910): Anglo-Irish coll.: late C. 19–20. Ex shipping.

in waiting. On duty: Guards Regiments': C. 20. Ex performance of Palace guards. With a pun on *lady-in-waiting*? (P-G-R.)

Inbel. *I*ndependent *Bel*gian News Agency: journalists': since ca. 1935.

inboard, n. See **kicker**, 3 (Addenda): Canadian coll.: since ca. 1935.

inboard. See **I'm inboard . . .**

incident. 'There are no occasions, occurrences, or events in an airman's life. Anything that happens to him is an "incident" . . . why, nobody knows,' H. & P.: coll.: since 1938.

include me out! Leave me out: since late 1940's. Ex one of the few genuine Goldwynisms. 'Most of the zany cracks attributed to Sam Goldwyn are the work of Hollywood gagmen' (Petch).

income-tax. Those periodical fines to which they are subject for soliciting: prostitutes': since ca. 1930. (*The New Statesman*, May 10, 1947.)

increase. Another baby: bourgeois jocular: C. 20.—I.e. in (or of) the family.

Incubator, the. H.M.S. *King Alfred* (a shore establishment), 'where embryo R.N.V.R. officers are trained': Naval: since ca. 1939. Granville.

incy; pron. *insy.* An incendiary bomb: Services: since 1940. H. & P.

incypyent. See **incipience** (*Dict.*).

indentures, make (*Dict.*): for fuller form, see 'Tavern terms', § 8.

india-rubber gun. A German high-velocity gun, e.g. the ·77: Army: 1914–19.

Indian, he's a regular; he's on the Indian list A Canadian c.p., applied to habitual drunkards, esp. to one to whom it is illegal to sell liquor: since ca. 1925. It is illegal to sell liquor to Indians coming from any of the settlements or reserves. (F. E. L. Priestley.)

indigragger. Indignation: Aldenham School: C. 20. Marples. By 'the Oxford -*er*'.

indijaggers. Indigestion: Public Schools' (and Oxford undergraduates'): C. 20. (Nancy Spain, *Poison for Teacher*, 1949.) Also in, e.g., Dorothy Sayers, *Strong Poison*, 1930.

Indispensables, the; occasionally, **the Loyal Standbacks.** 'Those who, although fit and of military age, were kept at home working. This is from *The Fencibles*, name of the old militia. Another term used was *The Loyal Standbacks*' (A. B. Petch, May 1966), on the analogy of several regimental names: servicemen's: 1914–18.

indite, inscribe, invite. See **indict** (*Dict.*).

Indo. Indonesia; Indonesian, adj. and n.: Australian journalistic coll.: since late 1950's. (B.P.)

indorser (p. 423) goes back to ca. 1710. It occurs in James Dalton, *A Narrative*, 1728, at p. 34.

indulge, as in 'He doesn't indulge'. To take strong drink, whether habitually or incidentally: late C. 19–20; by 1930, coll.—2. To have sexual intercourse: Australian, jocular rather than euphemistic: since ca. 1930. (B.P.)

infanteer. An infantry man: Royal Artillery: C. 20.

infantile. Infantile paralysis: coll. : since ca. 1910; originally, medical; only since ca. 1945 at all general.

*****infor.** Information: C. 20: convicts' c. until ca. 1940, then gen. prison s. Jim Phelan, *Jail Journey*, 1940.

Ingee (p. 423) goes back to late C. 18. As n. and as adj., it occurs frequently in the works of William Nugent Glascock—e.g. *The Naval Sketch-Book*, 1825–26, and *Sailors and Saints*, 1829.

ingie-bungle. See **bungie.**

[**Inimitable, the.** Charles Dickens: from ca. 1840; ob. by 1890, † (except historically) by 1915. This, however, is rather a sobriquet than a nickname except when, and in so far as, it was used jocularly by his friends.]

injection, French (or **German** or **Dutch,** etc.) **by,** A Londoners' c.p. dating from ca. 1925 and applied to a woman living, as wife or as mistress, with a foreigner. Punning *by extraction* (or birth) and *copulation*.

Injer. India: sol., mostly Cockneys': C. 19–20. Nevinson, 1895.

ink, in. Journalistically occupied: journalists': since ca. 1910.

Ink-e-li. English: pidgin: C. 19–20. B. & L.

ink in one's pen is, since ca. 1910, a variant of *lead in one's pencil.*

inked. Tipsy: Australian: since ca. 1920. B., 1942. Cf.—perhaps ex—**inky,** 2 (p. 424).

inky fingers. The Accountant staff; one of them: Naval: since ca. 1920. (P-G-R.)

inland navy and **waterborne** were applied, by the Army, to British and Canadian troops using Ducks and Buffaloes for fighting in the flooded areas between Nijmegen and Cleve: 1944–5. (P-G-R.)

inn of court. See 'Tavern terms', § 3.

Inn of the Morning Star. See **at the Inn.**

innards.—2. The internal mechanism of any mechanical or electronic appliance: coll., esp. Australian: C. 20. (B.P.)

inner, the. 'The enclosure of a racecourse' (Baker): Australian sporting coll.: since ca. 1910.

inoc. An inoculation: Services coll.: since ca. 1930. Partridge, 1945.

inquest. A jocular variation, esp. among players at whist drives, of *post mortem* below: since ca. 1946.

***inquisitive.** A magistrate: white-slavers' c.: late C. 19–20. (A. Londres, 1928.)

insects and ants; often simply *insects*. Trousers; knickers: C. 20. Rhyming on *pants*.

***inside,** n.—3. In the innermost circle of the underworld: c.: from ca. 1910. *The Pawnshop Murder*: 'A man's got to be right on the "inside" before he'll get as much as a breath over the "grapevine".'—4. In pidgin (C. 19–20) it = 'within, in, interior; heart, mind, soul; in the country,' B. & L. Hence:

Inside, the. Central Australia: Australian coll.: late C. 19–20. Ex coll. *inside*, in the interior. Hence, *Insider*, one either born or long resident in this region. All three terms occur in the one or the other of Tom Ronan's *Vision Splendid*, 1954, and *Moleskin Midas*, 1956.

inside country; inside squatter. 'Well-populated country near or in coastal areas'; hence, a farmer or large landowner in such country: Aus. rural coll.: C. 20. (B., 1959.)

inside the mouth. 'Secretly in his mind, to himself, reserved': pidgin: C. 19–20. Ibid.

insinivating. Insinuating: Cockney: C. 19–20. Mayhew, I, 1851.

insinuendo. Usually in pl. (*-oes*). A coll. blend of *insinuation + innuendo*. Herbert Adams, *The Chief Witness*, 1940.

inspector of city buildings. One who, looking for work, hopes he won't find it: Australian: since ca. 1920. (B., 1943.)

inspector of manholes. A sanitary inspector: since ca. 1920.—2. A 'queer': low: since ca. 1930.

instalment mixture. 'Rain is "Instalment Mixture"—at least, to owner-drivers. The owner-driver is a "mush", and when still buying his cab, a "starving mush". Rain is sometimes referred to by journeyman drivers, therefore, as "Mush's Lotion". Otherwise it is simply "Frarny" (France and Spain),' Herbert Hodge, *Cab, Sir?*, 1939: taxi-drivers' terms: since ca. 1910.

instrument-basher. See **basher**, 6.

insult, the. One's pay: Naval (lower-deck): since ca. 1925. Granville.

insy. See **incy.**

intelligence department. The head: jocular: since ca. 1916.

intelligencer. See 'Tavern terms', § 6 end.

inter-uni. Inter-university: Australian coll.: C. 20. B., 1942.

intercom. Inter-communication telephonic system of an aircraft: R.A.F.: since ca. 1936. Allan A. Michie & Walter Graebner, *Their Finest Hour*, 1940 (p. 61): Jackson, 1943.—2. Hence, of a factory, a school, a business, a post office, etc.: coll.: since ca. 1946. Sense 1, by the way, has been common in the Navy since 1939.

interested in one thing only, men are. A cynical feminine c.p., dating from ca. 1925. Cf. **one-track mind** and contrast **it takes two** below.

interested in the opposite sex, not or **not much.** (Of either sex) homosexual: polite euphemism: since ca. 1925. Christopher Buckley, *Rain before Seven*, 1947—the longer form.

interflora. Love-making: among the Flower Boy and Girl 'hippies', esp. in London: 1967. *Inter*course between 'Flowers', with a pun on Interflora, the large firm of florists. (Communicated by Max Mack on Nov. 16, 1967.)

interrupter. An interpreter: jocular Canadian mispronunciation (Civil Service): since ca. 1910. (Leechman.)

introduce Charley (or **-ie**). Of the male: to coït: C. 20. The penis is frequently personified.

invalid fire. Enfilade fire: Army: 1915–18. It caused many casualties.

invisibles. Invisible exports: economic and financial circles' coll.: since ca. 1956.

invite (p. 426). Rather: coll. since ca. 1815. *Spy*, 1825.

Iodines, the. The Australian Army Medical Corps: Australian soldiers': 1939 +. B., 1942. Cf. **poultice-wallopers** (*Dict.*).

ipe. A rifle: Naval: C. 20. H. & P. Adaptation of *hipe* (*Dict.*).

Irian, South and **West.** Australia and Papua-New Guinea: Australian jocular: since ca. 1960. (B.P.)

Irish, n.—3. See 'Tavern terms', § 3, *c.*

Irish, three cold. See **Fenian** (*Dict.*).

Irish as Paddy's (or **Patrick's** or **Pat's**) **pig;** or, **Irish as Paddy Murphy's pig.** Very Irish indeed: coll.: from ca. 1890. Cf. **straight from the bog,** q.v.

Irish compliment. A back-handed, an oblique, compliment: C. 19–20; by ca. 1920, rather ob. Fredk Chamier, *The Life of a Sailor*, 1832, at II, 157. (Moe.)

Irish Confetti. Brickbats: C. 20. Gerald Kersh, *I Got References*, 1939.

Irish evidence (p. 426) should be dated 'late C. 17–mid 19': B.E., 1699, has '*Knight of the Post*, c. a Mercenary common swearer, a Prostitute to every Cause, an Irish Evidence'.

Irish harp. A long-handled shovel: Canadian railway-builders: since ca. 1905. (Leechman.) Cf. **banjo.**

Irish Mail. Potatoes: nautical, esp. Naval: C. 20. H. & P. So many potatoes are shipped from Ireland to Britain.

Irish man-of-war. A barge: Thames-side: late C. 19–20. Jocular.

Irish mile. A mile *plus*: coll.: late C. 19–20.

Irish pennants (p. 426) occurs in, e.g., W. N. Glascock, *Sailors and Saints*, 1829. Moe.

Irish rose. Nose: rhyming s.: C. 20. Franklyn 2nd.

***Irishman, the.** See **hot seat.**

Irishman's coat of arms. A black eye: mid C. 18–mid 19. 'Wednesday, 13 Aug. 1806. Goedike and La Rammer had a quarrel. The latter got an Irishman's coat of arms': the Journal of the fur-trading post of the North West Company at Dunregan, Canada. (Dr D. Leechman.)

irk. Incorrect form of **erk.**

iron, n.—5. (Always *the iron*). Also v. for both, see **iron horse.**—6. A bicycle: cyclists': since ca. 1925.

iron, v.—2. See preceding.—3. To kill: low: late C. 19–20. (Pamela Branch, *The Wooden Overcoat*, 1951.)—4. Hence, to attack or fight (someone) successfully: Australian: since ca. 1925. (B., 1953.)

iron compass; esp. *follow the . . . ,* to follow railway lines leading to a target area: R.F.C.–R.A.F.: since ca. 1917, but little-used during

World War II. (V. M. Yeates, *Winged Victory*, 1934.)

Iron Duke. A lucky chance: late C. 19–20. Rhyming on *fluke*.

iron face. Stern, obdurate, severe, cruel: pidgin: mid-C. 19–20. B. & L.

iron-fighter. A constructional engineer: master-builders' and engineers': since ca. 1930.

*****iron hoof.** A male prostitute: c.: C. 20. Rhyming s. and the real origin of **iron,** n., 4, q.v. in *Dict.*

iron hoop (p. 427): by 1960, †. Franklyn 2nd.

iron horse. (Of coins) a toss: late C. 19–20. 'Sometimes abbreviated to "the Iron" or "Iron-ing". ("I'll iron you for it"—"I'll toss you for it"),' F. D. Sharpe, *Sharpe of the Flying Squad*, 1938. Rhyming: in Cockney speech, *toss* is usually pron. *torse.*—2. A race-course: rhyming s.: C. 20. (Franklyn, *Rhyming*.)

iron lung. A Nissen hut: Barrage Balloon personnel's: since 1939. H. & P.—2. A shelter in the Tube: Londoners': 1940–5.—3. (*The Iron Lung.*) 'The new Underground line, running from Shoreditch to Essex, known to the criminal classes as the "iron lung"' (*The New Statesman*, Nov. 1950): c.: 1950 +; by 1960, rather ob. —4. A '2–8–0 ex W.D. locomotive' (*Railway* 2nd): railwaymen's: ? ca. 1940–50.

iron making. 'Occupying a berth or billet where money is to be put by': non-aristocratic: from ca. 1870; ob. B. & L.

iron man. A £1 note: Australian: sense-adapted, ca. 1944, ex U.S. *iron man*, a dollar.

iron (it) **out.** To put (it) right: perhaps originally Australian: since ca. 1930. Recorded by Gwen Robyns, article 'Holiday City' in *The Evening News*, Feb. 16, 1949. To remove the creases by ironing.

iron skull. A boiler-maker: Canadian railroad-men's (– 1931).

iron tank. A bank (for money): rhyming s.: since ca. 1918. Franklyn, *Rhyming*.

ironmongery department, the; His or **Her Majesty's School for Heavy Needlework.** Prison: cultured: since ca. 1945.

irons. A coll. shortening of **eating irons:** since ca. 1925. H. & P.

irons, in. 'A sailing ship is said to be "in irons" when she is head to wind and cannot pay off on either tack' (Granville): nautical: C. 20.

is used jocularly. See **'am** and **is'** above.

is all. That is all: Canadian coll.: adopted, ca. 1947, ex U.S. 'I'm tired, is all.' (Leechman.)

is it cold up there? A jocular c.p., to a tall person: late C. 19–20.

is that all? 'Still heard as a sarcastic exclamation, in reference to high prices, etc.' (A. B. Petch, May 1966): c.p.: C. 20.

is there room for a small one? A c.p. addressed to occupants of crowded vehicle: C. 20.

is there a proposal . . .? See **proposition,** n., 3.

is your journey really necessary, a war-time official slogan (1940 +), has, since as early as 1944, been used as a jocular c.p.; by 1960, slightly ob.

Isa, The. Mount Isa in western Queensland: Aus. coll.: C. 20. Jock Marshall & Russell Drysdale, *Journey among Men*, 1962.

Isabella (p. 427): † since ca. 1930.

Ish. Ismailia: British soldiers': late C. 19–20.

ish-ka-bibble! 'I should worry!': c.p.: ca. 1925–35. Ex U.S. Perhaps ex Yiddish *ich gebliebe.* In the U.S. it had a tremendous vogue ca. 1913. (Leechman.)

ishkimmisk. Drunk, tipsy: Shelta: C. 18–20. B. & L.

Island, the. Camp Hill, the prison on the Isle of Wight: police and criminal coll.: C. 20.

island, the. A battleship's, but esp. an aircraft carrier's, superstructure: Naval: since late 1930's (? earlier). John Winton, *H.M.S. Leviathan*, 1967, 'The flight deck and the island were scenes of continuous activity.'

island-hopping, n. The capture of one island after another: Allies in the Pacific: 1945. (P-G-R.)

Isle of Wight, adj. Right: rhyming s.: C. 20. (Franklyn, *Rhyming*.)

issue, the (p. 427): by 1919, also civilian.

I-sup. A shortening of **I suppose** (p. 419), as in 'She's got . . . a terrific I-sup (She has a beautiful nose)': Lester.

it. Sense 6 was adumbrated by Rudyard Kipling when, in his story of 'Mrs Bathurst', 1904, he wrote: ''Tisn't beauty, so to speak, nor good talk necessarily. It's just It.'

it ain't all honey! It isn't wholly pleasant: c.p. of ca. 1904–14. Cf. 'It ain't all honey and it ain't all jam, | Wheelin' round the 'ouses at a three-wheeled pram' in a music-hall song of Vesta Victoria's, ca. 1905.

it ain't gonna rain no more! A humorous c.p. (since ca. 1935), elicited by a downpour or by set-in rain. Ex a popular song.

it didn't fizz on me. This affair, this action, etc., had no effect on me: Canadian c.p.: since ca. 1945. It fell *flat.*

it happens all the time. A c.p. = it's **just one of those things:** since ca. 1925.

it isn't a hanging matter. Well, after all, it's not so very serious, is it?: c.p.: late C. 19–20.

it just goes to show. A conventional stop-gap of vague comment: since the 1920's.

it just shows to go. A nonsensical variant of the preceding: Australian: ca. 1960–65. (B.P.)

it only wanted a man on the job. A jocular c.p. (late C. 19–20) by a willing helper.

it shouldn't happen to a dog (let alone to a human being): c.p.: since ca. 1945: still mainly U.S., but by 1965 at latest, heard occasionally in Britain. Of Yiddish origin, according to Leo Rosten in *Encounter*, Sept. 1968.

it takes two to tango. Premarital coïtion, like the begetting of large families, requires co-operation between the sexes: a mainly feminine c.p., implying that either of these two activities is not operated only by selfish males: mostly Australian: since ca. 1935. 'Ex a popular song thus named' (B.P.).

it will all (or **it'll all**) **be put down in evidence against you.** A jocular c.p.: since ca. 1935.

Italian. See 'Tavern terms', § 3, *c.*

itchy back, have an. (Of women) to desire intercourse: Australian: since ca. 1920. 'Women in bed with dozing husbands reputedly ask them to scratch their backs. The resulting propinquity often has the desired effect' (a valued correspondent). Perhaps cf. the English *a bitch with an itch*, a lascivious woman: C. 20.

Ite. An Italian: 1940–5. Ex *Eye-tie.* (P-G-R.) Cf:

Ities is a variant spelling of **Eyeties** (p. 261). Michie & Graebner, *Lights of Freedom*, 1941.

it'll all be put down in evidence against you. See **it will all . . .** above.

it'll all be the same in a hundred years. A consolatory C. 20 c.p.; by 1940, verging on proverbial S.E.

it'll all come out in the wash. See **wash, it'll . . .**

it'll last my (or **our** or **your**) **time,** to which the cautious add **I hope.** A 'famous last words' c.p., dating since ca. 1945, but not in general use until ca. 1948. Nostalgic rather than cynical; and therefore not to be apprehended as synonymous with *après moi le déluge.*

it'll put hair on your chest! 'A c.p. urging someone to have a drink' (B.P.): mostly Australian: since ca. 1910.

it's a bastard; often **. . . proper bastard** or (Australian) **fair bastard.** A very common expression among workers and servicemen for anything difficult or exasperating: C. 20. Cf. the Australian *it's a fair cow:* late C. 19–20.

it's a breeze. It's easy: Australian (− 1945); almost a c.p. (B., 1945.)

it's a freak country. 'Sometimes heard in regard to the "sights" we see nowadays, like the dirty, long-haired teenagers. From the other expression, *It's a free country*' (A. B. Petch, March 1966): c.p.: since ca. 1960. The original *free* c.p. dates from late C. 19.

it's a gas—or a gasser! It's wonderful: Australian teenage surfers': since ca. 1961. (B.P.) Cf. **gas** and **gasser** above.

it's a gig! That's very nice—very nice indeed!: Australian c.p.: since ca. 1925. Cf. **gig**, n., 1 (p. 327).

it's a good game—(if) played slow (or slowly). 'Ironic c.p. evoked by repeated manual maladroitness, repeated inconvenience, idling, or imposed tedium of waiting, etc. (in use Services 1939–45)': Atkinson, 1959.

it's a little bit over. 'A phrase taught to every apprentice butcher in Australia. They'—butchers in general—'always sell you more meat than you ask for and excuse it with the above words' (B.P.): c.p.: late C. 19–20.

it's a piece of cake. See **piece of cake.**

it's a poor soldier who can't stand his comrade's breath. See **poor soldier . . .**

it's a sore arse that never rejoices. A c.p. uttered, when somebody breaks wind, by a member of one of those 'fraternities' of mighty wits in which public-houses abound: C. 20.

it's a way they have in the Army (p. 428) is a renewal; it has been current since ca. 1880 or even earlier. See, e.g., Kipling's *Stalky & Co.*, 1899. It derives from a popular song that opens thus.

it's all in a lifetime. It's no use grumbling: c.p.: (?) mid-C. 19–20.

it's all money. The c.p. reply to an apology for paying with small change, or with more small change than is either necessary or sensible: since ca. 1945.

it's all over bar (the) shouting. The game is virtually won or the job almost finished: c.p.: late C. 19–20. Ex sport: applause at end of a contest. It occurs earlier in A. L. Gordon's poem, 'How We Beat the Favourite' (1869), 'The race is all over, bar shouting'; earliest as '. . . but

shouting', in C. L. Apperley, *Life Sportsman*, 1842. (*The Oxford Dictionary of Proverbs.*)

it's all right for you. A coll. shortening of S.E. *it's all right for you to laugh*: C. 20. Atkinson, 'Deprecating another's "sitting pretty".'

it's all right if it comes off. A mostly Australian c.p., concerning an (apparent) attempt at a swindle: since ca. 1930. (B.P.)

it's always jam to-morrow . . . See **jam to-morrow . . .**

it's bad manners . . . See **bad manners . . .**

it's been known. It's not uncommon: c.p.: since the middle 1940's. Elliptical for 'It's been known to happen'.

it's Friday, so keep your nose tidy. A c.p., employed only on a Friday (a folklorishly unlucky day) and meaning either 'keep out of mischief' or 'mind your own business': non-aristocratic, non-cultured: late C. 19–20. Based upon the mispronunciation *Fridee.*

it's got a back to it. See **back to it . . .**

it's naughty but it's nice. A c.p., since ca. 1900, in ref. to copulation. Ex a popular song. In the U.S., Minnie Schult sang and popularised it in the 1890's.

it's nice to have a peg . . . See **peg to hang things on.**

it's not much if (or occ., **when**) **you say it quick!** A c.p. in ref. to a large sum of money or a very high price: since ca. 1910.

it's not right, it's not fair: (a certain film-star's) **left tit** or **Jack Johnson's** (or **Joe Louis's**) **left ballock** (or **testicle**). A mainly Forces' c.p. derisive of a complainant or his complaint: since ca. 1905.

it's not the bull they're afraid of—it's the calf. (Of girls) a c.p. implying that they fear, not the loss of virginity but pregnancy: Australian: C. 20.

it's on! A fight is starting: Australian: since ca. 1945. (B.P.)

it's only lent. 'A nonchalant acceptance of defeat, either physical or moral. It is sometimes embellished with the addition, "I'll get my own back"' (Julian Franklyn, 1962): c.p., mostly Cockney: since ca. 1920.

it's only money. 'Said to a reluctant spender or party-sharer': c.p.: orig. (? ca. 1945) Canadian; by ca. 1955, also British. (Leechman.)—2. 'A c.p. addressed to one'—including oneself—'suddenly confronted with an unexpected expenditure' (Leechman): since ca. 1945–50.

it's showery. See **shower!**

it's snowing down south. Your slip is showing: Australian feminine c.p.: since late 1940's. Perhaps an adaptation of English schoolchildren's *it's snowing in Paris*, current, since ca. 1919 and recorded by I. & P. Opie, *The Lore and Language of Schoolchildren*, 1959.

it's that man again! A c.p. dating from late 1939; during the bombing of Britain by the Luftwaffe, esp. in 1940–1, applied chiefly to bomb-damage, that man being Hitler. Ex Tommy Handley's scintillating B.B.C. radio-programme 'Itma' (Its That Man Again; as the traditional opening warns us).—Cf. **after you, Claude** and **can I do you now, sir?**: E. P. in *The Radio Times*, Dec. 6, 1946—reprinted in *Words at War: Words at Peace*, 1948.

it's the beer speaking. A public-house c.p. directed at one who breaks wind in public-house company: C. 20.

it's wonderful how they make guns, let alone

touch-holes! 'A c.p. used by women . . . to deflate male superiority, esp. about sex' (Laurie Atkinson, Sept. 11, 1967): late C. 19–20, esp. in military and naval circles. The erotic imagery of gunnery is involved: *gun*, penis; *touch-hole*, vulva.

It's your ball. The initiative lies with you: Canadian c.p.: since ca. 1946. (Leechman.) Ex ball-games.

I've done more sea miles . . . See sea miles.

I've something to do (that) nobody else can do for me. I must go to the 'Gents': c.p.: C. 20. (A. B. Petch, April 1966.)

ivories. For sense 3, see also fish-horn.—4. Checks and counters: card-players': from ca. 1860. B. & L.

ivory-snatcher. A dentist: from ca. 1880; ob. (G. B. Shaw, *You Never Can Tell*, 1897.) Cf. ivory carpenter in *Dict*.

ivory-turner. A skilful dicer: fast life: ca. 1820–40. *Spy*, 1825. Cf. ivories, 2 (p. 428) and 4 (above).

ivy cottage. An outside privy: a late C. 19–20 euphemistic coll. Formerly, often ivy-covered.

Ixta. Mount Ixtaccihuatl: British and American coll.: late C. 19–20. So too *Popo*, Mt Popocatapetl, also, since ca. 1930, *Popeye*. Malcolm Lowry, *Under the Volcano*, 1947.

J

J.—3. A Jesuit: Catholic coll.: mid-C. 19–20.
—4. Jesus: Anglo-Irish: late C. 19–20.

J. Arthur Rank. A bank (financial): rhyming s.: since late 1940's. 'Evolved when Mr Rank was making both films and news' (Franklyn 2nd). Mostly shortened to *Jay Arthur*.

J. C.'s area representatives (or **reps**). Dignitaries of the Church: R.A.F., but not very general: since ca. 1950.

J.P., the. Husband: at mothers' unions and meetings: since ca. 1935. *The People*, Oct. 14, 1945. I.e. junior partner.

Jaapies, the. 'These are Afrikaners,/The burly Jaapies, the Saray Marays', glossed thus, '"Jaapies" was a slang name for the South Africans, also known as "Saray Marays" from the title of the Afrikaans song they sang' (Hamish Henderson's poem, *Alamein, October 23, 1942*, written late in that year and revised for publication in *The Sunday Telegraph* of Oct. 22, 1967.

jab, n.—3. An inoculation: Services: since 1914. H. & P. Ex sense 1.

jabbed, be; get a jab. To be inoculated or vaccinated: Services: 1939 +. (P-G-R.)

Jabo Club, the. 'Any airman Just About Browned Off automatically qualifies,' Jackson: R.A.F. since ca. 1934. In India, in the 1930's, often *J.A.F.B.O.*, 'just about feeling (or fucking) browned off'. (W/Cdr A. J. Wild, letter of Aug. 4, 1945.)

jack, n. Sense 12, a privy, is also English: mid-C. 18–19. James Woodforde, *Diary*, Jan. 25, 1779, 'Busy this morning in cleaning my Jack, and did it completely.' This *Jack* or *jack* forms the effective origin of **john**, 8, a jakes.—14. The pl. *Jacks* is, in the Royal Navy of C. 20, generic for 'other ranks'. (Atkinson.)—15: since ca. 1689.—24. Money: low: adopted in 1937 from U.S.—25 (As *Jack.*) 'Familiar nickname for a kookaburra' (Baker, 1942): Australian: late C. 19–20. Ex 'laughing *jackass*'. Also *Jacko* (Baker).—26. A locomotive: Canadian railroadmen's (− 1931). Personification.—27. Syphilis: low Australian: C. 20.—28. Short for *black-jack*. a bludgeon: Australian coll.: C. 20. (Dal Stivens, *Jimmy Brockett*, 1951.)—29. A double-headed penny: Australian: C. 20. (B., 1943.) —30. Methylated spirit taken as an intoxicant: low: since ca. 1930. Gavin Lyall's article, 'Prison Saves the Jack Drinkers' in *The Sunday Times*, Aug. 13, 1961.—31. A policeman; a detective: Aus.: C. 20. (B., 1959.) Ex *John*, 4, on p. 442.

jack, adj. Mentally or morally tired or sick, esp. as *get jack of*, occurring both in Margaret Henry, *Unlucky Dip*, 1960, and in 'I'm getting jack of these holidays' (Dick): Australian: since ca. 1920. Cf. **jack up,** 3 (p. 431).

Jack(-)and(-)Jill.—2. A bill (account): since ca.

1910: c. >, by ca. 1955, s. Rhyming. (Robin Cook, 1962.)

jack-bit. Food: Army: 1939 +. *The Daily Mail*, Sept. 7, 1940.

Jack Club, the. See 'Prisoner-of-War Slang', 14.

Jack doesn't care. See **Jack loves a fight** below.

Jack Dusty (p. 430). In the R.N., esp. a Stores Assistant: late C. 19–20.

jack in is a variant of **jack up,** 3, to abandon: proletarian: since ca. 1910. But *jack* has, since ca. 1930, been commoner than either: cf. 'Jacked me for a civvy' in Alexander Baron, *From the City, from the Plough*, 1948.

jack in the box.—11. Syphilis: since ca. 1870. Often abbr. to *Jack*. Rhyming on **pox,** n. (p. 655.)

jack in the cellar (p. 430): prob. from late C. 17, for Wycherley in *Love in a Wood*, 1672, has *Hans en kelder*.

Jack in the dust (p. 430) occurs (as *Jack-i'-the-dust*) much earlier in W. N. Glascock, *Sailors and Saints* (I, 83), 1829, and should prob. be back-dated to ca. 1800. Moe.

jack-knife carpenter! 'A cry of derision hurled at a man, especially a carpenter, who uses a pocket knife in an emergency. Legend has it that all jack-knife carpenters end up in hell' (Leechman): Canadian c.p., dating since ca. 1910, but by 1960 ob.

Jack loves a fight and **Jack doesn't care** are C. 20 c.p.p., mostly Naval, referring to the seaman's love of a scrap and to his insouciance. (W. Kenneth Hubbard, March 22, 1968.)

Jack Malone, on one's. Alone: rhyming: C. 20. Jackson. Often abbr. to *on one's jack*, which also abbreviates *on one's Jack Jones*.

Jack-my-hearty. 'Boisterous "Jack's the boy" type of rating who makes himself a nuisance ashore,' Granville: Naval: since ca. 1895. Cf. **Jack Strop.**

jack of. Weary of or bored with: Australian: since ca. 1920. Jean Devanney, *By Tropic Sea and Jungle*, 1944, 'Maked you jack of it.' Ex *jack up*, v., 3 (p. 431).

It dates since ca. 1890 and occurs in, e.g., Edward Dyson, *The Gold Stealers*, 1901, '"Oh, well, Twitter's jack of it, an' I don't think it's much fun."'

Jack policy, or **Jack system, the.** An attitude—the habitual expression of—utter selfishness: Australian: since ca. 1945. (B., *Australia Speaks*, 1953.) 'Spontaneously combusted' ex *fuck you, Jack, I'm all right* (Naval, hence Army, hence general)—the peculiarly Naval . . . *I'm inboard*—and the specifically Air Force . . . *I'm fire-proof*: qq.v. on p. 305 and, in these Addenda, at *I'm inboard* and *fire-proof*. This attitude has, among civilians, and since ca. 1954, been widely expressed in the c.p. *I'm All Right, Jack*, as in the

1218

1959 film of that title: the Dishonourable Company of the Jacquerie has, since 1945, gained an increasingly large membership, with the result the freemasonic Men of Good Will have, unnoticed by the 'Jacks', quietly intensified their Resistance to the general rot.

Jack Portugoose. A Portuguese, esp. sailor: Naval: ? ca. 1810-60. In, e.g., W. N. Glascock's *Naval Sketch Book*, 2nd Series, 1834, at II, 137. (Moe.)

Jack Shalloo, 2 (*Dict.*). 'A corruption of John Chellew, who was a Naval Officer of the bon-homous, devil-may-care type' (Granville).

Jack Smithers. A drink taken by a man alone: Australian: ca. 1900-30. (B., 1943.)—2. Hence, a man drinking alone: Aus.: since ca. 1930. (B., 1959.) Cf. **Jimmy Woodser,** 1, on. p. 439.

Jack Sprat, 1 (p. 431), is perhaps, in its post-1850 career, rhyming s. on *brat*.—2. Fat (of meat): rhyming s.: late C. 19-20. Franklyn, *Rhyming*.

Jack Strop. 'A truculent "Jack-my-hearty"' (q.v.): Granville: since ca. 1900.

Jack Surpass. A glass (of liquor): beggars' rhyming s.: 1851. Mayhew, 1; app. † by 1910.

Jack Tar.—3. A bar (for drinks): rhyming s., mainly theatrical: C. 20. (Franklyn, *Rhyming*.)

jack the contract. To leave a job, esp. if difficult: Australian: since ca. 1910. (B., 1943.) A specialisation of *jack*, v., 3 (p. 431).

Jack trap. See **man-trap,** 5. below.

Jack the Ripper. A kipper: late C. 19-20. Rhyming.

jack up, 3 (p. 431), is also v.i. 'to abandon a job', was orig, navvies' and apparently rhyming s. on *pack up* (one's belongings): D. W. Barrett, *Navvies*, 1880.—4. To reprimand for slackness: Canadian: since ca. 1920. 'Harry's not doing his job. He needs jacking up.' (Leechman.)—5. To arrange: New Zealand: since ca. 1930. 'I'll get an early start tomorrow—I've jacked up a lift into town': Fiona Murray, *Invitation to Danger*, 1965. Ex 'to *jack up* a car'.

jackaroo, v.: earlier in Rolf Boldrewood, *Ups and Downs*, 1878.

jackass. A rowing boat that plies between ships and shore: Naval: ca. 1805 (? earlier)—1880. W. N. Glascock, *Naval Sketch-Book* (I, 140), 1825. Moe. Cf. the derivative sense in:—

jackass frigate (p. 431) perhaps refers to its structure, not to its speed, and is unrelated to *jackass*, a heavy rough boat used off Newfoundland. Colonel Moe cites from 'Scenes from the Life of Edward Lascelles, Gent.' in *The Dublin University Magazine* of March 1834 (p. 249), '. . . the Hesperus, being a frigate of the class denominated Jackass frigates, had no magazine forward'; elsewhere, the Hesperus is praised for its excellent sailing qualities.

jackdaw. The jaw: rhyming s. (London streets'): 1857, Augustus Mayhew, *Paved with Gold*; † by 1930.

jackdaw, v. 'To acquire dockyard paint or other materials with which to beautify your ship' (Granville): Naval: C. 20. Ex the jackdaw's acquisitiveness.

jackdaw and rook. A theatrical 'book of words': rhyming s. (theatrical): C. 20. Franklyn, *Rhyming*.

jackeen. 'A rascally boy' (L. E. F. English,

Historic Newfoundland, 1955): Newfoundland coll.: late C. 19-20.

Jacker. The Hon. F. S. Jackson: cricketers': since early 1890's. Born in 1870, he played for Harrow, Cambridge, Yorkshire, England: at his best, 1894-1910, he was a magnificent all-rounder: after retiring, one of the moguls of the game.

Jacket and Vest, the. The West End of London: rhyming s.: since ca. 1910. Charles Prior, *So I Wrote It*, 1937—cited by Franklyn, *Rhyming*.

jacketing (p. 432). In nuance 'a thrashing', it occurs earlier in *Sessions*, March 1848.

jacketing, n. Add:—2. A policeman's (very) severe report on a prisoner in the dock: police, and legal: since ca. 1920. Fredk P. Wensley, *Detective Days*, 1931, 'After I left the box the prosecuting counsel beckoned to me, "That was a pretty fierce 'jacketing'," he said. "I don't think you should have rubbed it in so hard."' Ex sense 1.

jackey or **jacky.**—3. A male Aboriginal, esp. in address (*Jacky*): Australian coll.: mid-C. 19-20 —4. A kookaburra: Australian: C. 20. (B., 1943; Jean Devanney, 1944.) Ex 'laughing *jackass*'.

Jackies. American sailors: 1942 +.—2. (Also **jackies.**) Aboriginals in general: Australian: since ca. 1930. (B., 1953.) Cf. *jackey*, 3.

Jacko.—2. See **jack,** n. (above). 3. A shunting engine, esp. in spoken reference: railwaymen's: C. 20. (*Railway*.)

jackpot, crack the. More common, in Australia, than the next. (B.P.)

jackpot, hit (sometimes **strike**) **the.** To meet with exceptionally good luck: adopted, 1943 in Britain and 1944 in Australia and New Zealand, from U.S. servicemen. Ex the game of poker.

Jack's alive, 1 (p. 432), perhaps goes back to early C. 19, to judge by its occurrence in W. N. Glascock's *Naval Sketch Book*, 2nd Series, 1834, at II, 38. (Moe.)—3. Hence, £5 note: low: C. 20. F. D. Sharpe, *The Flying Squad*, 1938. Rhyming *five*. Often shortened to *Jack's* (or *Jacks*),. as in 'I'll bet you a Jacks' (Norman).

Jack's come home. A slap-dash hotel or boarding house: theatrical: C. 20. Ngaio Marsh, *Vintage Murder*, 1938.

jacksharps. Sticklebacks: Liverpool: ca. 1945-55. Perhaps ex *Jack Sharp*, a nimble Association footballer.

jacksie (or **-y**). A brothel: Australian low: C. 20. B., 1942. Ex:—2. The posteriors: Army and Navy: late C. 19-20 (H. & P.) Cf. **jacksy-pardy** (*Dict.*).—3. Hence, rear of aircraft: R.A.F.: 1939-45.

Jacky.—3. A Turk: Army: 1915 +. Ex **Johnnie,** 8 (*Dict.*).

jacky or **Jacky.** See **jackey,** 3, 4.

Jacky, sit up like. To sit up straight; to be on one's best behaviour: Australian: C. 20; s. >, by 1930, coll. B., 1942. Like a monkey on a barrel-organ, Jacky or Jacko being a common nickname for a monkey. B., 1959, however, derives it ex **jackey,** 3, above.

Jacky Howe. A sleeveless shirt or singlet worn by shearers: New Zealand and Australian rural: late c. 19-20. B., 1941, 'After a noted shearer of that name'; B., 1942.

Jacky Raw. A 'new chum': Australian: late C. 19-20; ob. by 1930. B., 1942. Ex **Johnny Raw** (*Dict.*).

Jacky Rue. A squatter: Australian: C. 20.

Baker. Blend of **Jacky Raw** and *jackaroo*, perhaps.

*jade. A long prison-sentence: Australian c.: C. 20. B., 1942. There is probably an obscure pun on S.E. *sorry jade.*

Jafbo Club. See **Jabo Club.**

Jag. A Jaguar motor-car: coll.: since ca. 1946.

jag, n.—2. An injection: medical: adopted, ca. 1905, from U.S. Cognate with *jab*; indeed cf. **jab,** n., 3.—3. In Australia, 'a dose of a narcotic administered for purposes of addiction' and 'in any way whatsoever' and therefore having nothing to do with *jab*: since ca. 1945. (B.P.)—4. An 'organic solvent inhaled from a handkerchief' (B.P.): English: since ca. 1955. 'The child becomes dependent upon a regular "jag"' (*New Society*, June 20, 1963).

Sense 1 (p. 432): Canadian by late C. 19. (Niven.)

jag, v.—3. To depress; get on the nerves of: New Zealand: C. 19–20; by 1940, ob. (G. B. Lancaster, *Sons o' Men,* 1904.)

*Jag, the. The Turf Club races: South Africa (mostly Cape Town): c. and low s.: C. 20. *The Cape Times,* June 3, 1946. In Afrikaans, *jag* = hunt; cf. Dutch *jagen,* to hunt.

jag it in. To give up: Naval: since ca. 1945. John Winton, *H.M.S. Leviathan,* 1967, 'The messdeck dodger got discouraged and just jagged it in.'

Jagger. A Cornish rating: Naval (lower-deck): C. 20. An *-er* adaptation of the common Cornish surname *Jago.* (P-G-R.)

jagging, go. To make social visits, esp. in order to gossip: New Zealand: C. 20. B., 1941, who recalls *gad* and *on the jag.* Also, since ca. 1920, Aus. (B., 1959.)

Jago. A victualling paymaster: Naval (lower deck): C. 20. Granville, 'After the officer who introduced improved messing and victualling conditions in R.N. barracks'.

jags. Self: itinerant entertainers': C. 20. Always in combination, as *my jags,* I or me: *your jags,* you; *his* or *her jags,* he or she, him or her. 'Mind that your *jags* (self) keeps this book in your *skyrocket* (pocket) until you have mastered the lingo': Sydney Lester, *Vardi the Palarey,* (?) 1937. Perhaps an imperfect blend of *jills* and *nabs* used similarly.

Jail, the. That public playground which occupies the site of the demolished Horsemonger Lane jail: local London: late C. 19–20.

jail, there are worse in. See **worse in gaol** (*Dict.*).

jail-bait. See **bait,** 4, and cf. **gaol-bait,** both above.

jaisy. An effeminate and polite man: Midlands: C. 20. The Merseyside shape is *jessy.* Cf. *Jessy.*

jake, adj. (p. 432). In Australia, *we're jake* = we're all right; *she's jake* = it's jake, all is well. (Culotta.)

*jake-wallah. An addict to methylated spirits: c., esp. tramps': C. 20. W. A. Gape, *Half a Million Tramps,* 1936. Cf. **jake-drinker** in the *Dict.*

jakealoo. See **jake,** adj., on p. 432.

jaloppy. A cheap, or an old, motor-car: adopted, ca. 1950, ex U.S. (See *Underworld.*) The term always implies some degree of dilapidation.

jalouse. To infer; to guess: Scottish coll.: from ca. 1860.

jam, n.—10. Affectation: Australian: since ca. 1905. B., 1942. Remembered by E. P., ca. 1910–14.

jam, v.—3. To cancel: Naval: since ca. 1920. Granville, 'One's leave may be "jammed".' Rather since ca. 1910, for 'Bartimeus'—spelling it *jambed*—uses it in precisely this sense in *A Tall Ship,* 1915. (Ramsey Spencer.)

jam bosun. A victualling officer: Naval: since ca. 1920. Granville.

jam-buster. An assistant yardmaster: Canadian railroadmen's (— 1939). He disentangles the 'snarled-up' rolling-stock in a station yard.

jam clacker. See **clackers** above.

jam-jar.—2. Hence, an armoured car: Army and R.A.F.: since ca. 1938. Jackson.—3. An ordinary motor-car: rhyming s.: since ca. 1940.

jam on it (p. 433).—2. An (agreeable) surplus or addition: Services: since ca. 1920. 'D'you want jam on it?' = Aren't you satisfied? or Haven't you already got enough? (P-G-R.)

jam-strangling bastard. 'A man whose phenomenal luck suggests a degree of manoeuvering to ensure it, esp. R.N. sailor lucky in time and place of duties, privileges, etc.' (Laurie Atkinson, who records hearing it in 1951): Naval: since 1930's.

jam tart.—4. Heart: rhyming: C. 20.

jam to-morrow (but) never jam to-day, it's always. A c.p. synonymous with **pie in the sky when you die:** since ca. 1917. Its occasion was prob. the sugar shortage experienced during W.W. I, but its ultimate source is supplied by 'Jam yesterday and jam to-morrow, but never jam to-day' in Lewis Carroll's *Through the Looking Glass,* as Robert Clairborne reminds me.

Jamaica tea. See **rummy tea** below.

jamberoo. An Australian metathesis of **jam-boree** (p. 433): B., 1943.

jamborino. A jocular variant of S.E. *jamboree:* ca. 1910–40. (A. S. M. Hutchinson, *If Winter Comes,* 1921.)

James the First. The First Lieutenant in an H.M. ship: jocular Naval (officers'): since ca. 1920. Prompted by *Jimmy the One* (p. 439).

Jamie Duff. A professional mourner: mid-C. 19–20. Prob. ex the name of a firm that supplies them.

jammed like Jackson (p. 433) occurs in, e.g., W. N. Glascock, *Naval Sketch-Book* (II, 136), 1826, and *Sailors and Saints* (I, 182), 1829. Moe.

Jampans, the. The Japanese: among East African soldiers in Burma: ca. 1943–5. (P-G-R.)

Jan.—2. Frequent nickname of ratings with a Devon burr: Naval: C. 20. Hence, *Janner,* a West Countryman: Naval: since ca. 1910. (Wilfred Granville.)

*Jane, adj. Glasgow c., from ca. 1925, as in MacArthur & Long, 'Isobel was clearly a real "Jane bit o' stuff"—a girl of quality who wore a hat, without affectation, because she was accustomed to it.' Ex *jane,* a girl. Contrast **hairy, the,** q.v.

jane, 2 (p. 433). Also, since ca. 1918, in Canada.

Jane Shaw has, since ca. 1940, displaced **Jane Shore** (p. 433).

Jane Shore.—2. This goes back to mid-C. 19; the example in *The Ingoldsby Legends* may be merely euphemistic.

jank; janky. Impudence; impudent: Oundle: since mid-1920's. Marples. Perhaps *jank* is a back-formation ex *janky*, and *janky* may be a perversion of *jaunty*.

janker(-)wallah; rarely **jankers wallah.** An airman undergoing punishment: R.A.F.: since ca. 1920. Jackson. See **jankers** (*Dict.*).

Janner. See **Jan**, 2, above.

jannock (p. 433). Current in Australia since ca. 1880; in England, s. since ca. 1820 (*Sessions*, 1825 —as *jonnock*). In the Navy it has, since ca. 1925, meant 'in accordance with Service etiquette' (Granville).

*janusmug. An intermediary, esp. in shady arrangements or transactions: Australian c.: since ca. 1915. B., 1942. I.e. *Janus* (facing two ways) + *mug* (not necessarily a fool: merely small-town, insignificant).

jao!; jaw! See **jaw** below.

Jap-happy, often contracted to *Jappy.* Unduly afraid of, or subservient to, the Japanese: prisoners-of-war in Far East: 1942–5. Rohan Rivett, *Behind Bamboo*, 1946. **Jap-happies.** See 'Prisoner-of-War Slang', 13.

*japanned. (Of a criminal) converted by a prison chaplain: Australian c.: C. 20. B., 1942. Ex **japan** (p. 434).

jar, n.—2. A pint or 'handle' of beer: Australian: since ca. 1920. Baker.—3. A glass of beer: since ca. 1950.

jar of jam. A tram: Cockney rhyming: C. 20. Len Ortzen, *Down Donkey Row*, 1938.

*jargoon, v. To show (a person) a real diamond and sell him a paste: c.: C. 20. Ex the S.E. n.

jaro, give (p. 434)—recorded first by G. B. Lancaster (1873–1945) most probably, as to *jɪro*, derives from Maori *whaurau*, to scold.

jarrah-jerker. A West Australian timbergetter: Australian: since ca. 1920. (B., 1943.) The *jarrah* is an Australian hardwood.

jarred off. Depressed (and disgusted); 'fed up': Services (mostly Army): since ca. 1930. Gerald Kersh, *The Nine Lives of Bill Nelson*, 1942; H. & P., 1943.

java (p. 434) was only very rarely 'tea'—and never since ca. 1920.

jaw, v., 2 (p. 434). An early record: 1826, *Sessions* (trial of Leakes & Gould). To go: tramps' c.: from ca. 1860. B. & L. derive ex Romany *java*, I go, and cf. Anglo-India *jao* (or *jaw*)!, go, of mid-C. 19–20.

jaw, hold one's (p. 434) goes back to ca. 1780: it occurs in Charles Dibdin's 'Jack's Fidelity', published in *The Britannic Magazine* (I, No. 11, p. 345), 1793. Moe.

jaw-box, the. Journalism: C. 20. (Neil Munro, *The Brave Days*, 1931.)—2. The kitchen sink, with the constant chatter over the washing-up: Glasgow domestic: C. 19–early 20. 'Very common' (Dr R. L. Mackay, M.D.).

jaw-breaker (p. 434); Sense 1 occurs earlier in W. N. Glascock, *Sketch-Book* (II, 117), 1826. Moe.—3. (Usually pl.) A cheap, large, hard or sticky sweet: late C. 19–20.

jaw-breaking, adj. (p. 434). Earlier in Wm Maginn, *Tales of Military Life*, 1829, at III, 225.

jaw-mag. Talk: mostly Cockneys': from ca. 1880; ob. Pugh (2): 'He made her head ache, she declared, with his noisy jaw-mag.'

jaw-me-dead (p. 434) is extant, although, since ca. 1930, little used; an occasional late C. 19–20

pl. is *jaw-me-deaths.* Among Cockneys, the version is *jaw-me-dad* (father): late C. 19–20. (Julian Franklyn, 1962.)

jaw- or **jawing-tackle** (p. 434). Variant *jawing-tacks* in Glascock, 1826. Moe. It also has variant *jawing tacks aboard, haul one's,* as in W. N. Glascock, *Sailors and Saints* (I, 145), 1829. Moe.

jawer. A punch to the jaw: pugilistic coll.: since ca. 1810; ob. *Boxiana*, III, 1821.

jay-walker and **-walking** (p. 435): by 1960, S.E.

Jays, the. Members of the Society of Jesus: gen. Catholic coll.: C. 19–20. *The Jays* merely phoneticizes 'the J's'.

jaxy and **joxy.** Female pudend: prostitutes' (notably Liverpool): C. 20. Cf. **jacksie.**

jazz. Nonsense, 'baloney'; adopted, ex U.S., in 1960, but heard occ. in Britain as early as 1957. It occurs in *The Sunday Times* of Nov. 26, 1961, with its (? rhyming-s.) variant *razzmataz(z)*; and in *The Sunday Telegraph* of Dec. 3, 1961, in the almost consecrated phrase *all that jazz* (Ian Christie's article).

jazz, and all that. And all that sort of thing, esp., and all that nonsense: adopted, ca. 1960, ex U.S. See also 'Jazz Slang' at *all . . .*

jazz on, get a. To get a move on, esp. in imperative: mostly Army: 1939–45. (P-G-R.)

Jazz terms. An attempt has been made to include the best-known, mostly widely used British Commonwealth s. terms of jazz. Most of them come ultimately from the U.S. A sane, judicious article on the 'Language of Jazz Musicians', written by Norman D. Hinton, appeared in *The American Dialect Society*, Nov. 1958. For Canadian usage, I owe almost everything to Professor F. E. L. Priestley and Dr Douglas Leechman. Jazz Slang Current in May 1963:

In that month, Mr Rex Harris sent me a selected —and select—list of s. words and phrases popular and general at that time. Several, it will be noticed, were, well before that date, already used widely; and since, several others have gained a wide currency.

all that jazz. All that sort of thing: since ca. 1958, orig. jazz-lovers'.

bundle on, go a. To be wildly enthusiastic about (something): since ca. 1955, esp. among jazz-lovers.

gasser. Something quite breath-taking: adopted by jazz-lovers, in 1960, ex U.S.

gate.—6. A form of greeting, esp. in *Hiya, gate!*: adopted by jazz-lovers, in 1962, ex U.S.

get sent. See *sent, get*, below.

get the message. See *message, get the*, below.

get with it. See *with it, get*, below.

give out. To do one's utmost, esp. in playing a musical instrument: adopted, ca. 1960, ex U.S., by jazz-lovers. Elliptical for *give out one's best*?

grab (oneself) *a ball.* To have a very good time: adopted, ca. 1959 and orig. by jazz-lovers, ex U.S.

groove, in the.—2. 'Firmly established in the situation: musically integrated' (Rex Harris); adopted ex U.S., ca. 1955, by jazz-lovers.

jumping, adj. Moving, musically, in a fine, esp. an exciting, rhythm: jazz-lovers': since ca. 1959.—2. Hence, (very) successful, as in 'The joint is jumping'—the club, or the cafe, is happily excited: since ca. 1960.

message, get the. To understand the gist of

an argument, the point of a warning, a hint: since ca. 1957. Cf. the Fighting Services' j. *message received.*

out of this world. Very beautiful; wonderful; superlative; perfect; although heard occasionally since ca. 1956, it has been common only since 1960. Applied orig.—and, of course, still—to consummate playing by an instrumentalist or to consummate singing.

sent, get. To become *en rapport* with, or enthusiastic about, the music (esp. jazz) that is being played, whether one is listener or performer: jazz lovers': since ca. 1950.

solid.—6. Satisfactory; (solidly) good; since ca. 1960, orig. jazz-lovers'.

trad. 'Abbreviation of traditional (jazz)': since ca. 1961. Rex Harris.

way out. Of jazz music: 'extremely advanced; complicated; esoteric' (Rex Harris): jazz-lovers': adopted, ca. 1950, ex U.S.

with it, get. (Cf. **with it, be,** below.) To appreciate a situation or a quality: since ca. 1957, orig. among jazz-lovers.

jazz trains. '1920 suburban stock with coloured strips over doors denoting class of compartment (GER)': railwaymen's: 1920's. (*Railway* 2nd.)

jazz up. 'To modernize; to add decorative touches to; (jocularly of a book) to revise and augment' (B.P.): not only Australian: since ca. 1950. To enliven; esp., to convert classical music into 'pop': since ca. 1945.

jazzer. A 'K3 N.E.R. locomotive' (*Railway*): railwaymen's: ? ca. 1940–50.

jazzing. 'The rapid shooting and hauling of nets in the path of the incoming salmon' (Granville): trawlermen's: since ca. 1945.

jazzy. Loud-coloured; 'flashy': since ca. 1935. Michael Harrison, *Reported Safe Arrival*, 1943, 'He wore a blue jumper of that inarticulate boisterousness called "jazzy".'

Jean(-)Baptiste. A French Canadian: Canadian coll.: late C. 19–20. A common Fr., esp. Fr.-Canadian, pair of given names.

Jean Crappeau is an occasional variant of **John(ny) Crappo** (p. 443).

Jeanie boy is the North Country's equivalent of **Nancy boy** (see *Dict.*): C. 20.

Jeep. A member of the Royal Canadian Naval Volunteer Reserve: since ca. 1938. H. & P. Why?

jeep. A utility Service van or small truck: adopted by the Canadians in 1939, by the English Army in 1941, by the R.A.F. early in 1942, from the U.S. Army. H. & P., 1943. A *G.P.* (general purposes) vehicle.—2. Hence, a girl friend: Services: since late 1942.—3. A *junior production engineer*: B.B.C.: since ca. 1944. A vocalization of *j-p.*

Jeep, the. See **Chad.**

jeepable. (Of roads or tracks) usable by jeeps: Army coll.: 1944 +. (P-G-R.)

jeepers creepers, occ. merely **jeepers!** An exclamation adopted, ca. 1944, ex American servicemen. Euphemistic.

jeer, 2 (p. 436). Also low Australian: mid-C 19–20. (Ruth Park, *Poor Man's Orange*, 1950.)

Jekyll. 'Have a Jekyll. . . . Have a brandy and Coca Cola,' C. P. Wittstock, letter of May 23, 1946: South African: since ca. 1930. Ex 'Jekyll and Hyde'; the mild and the violent.—2. See:

Jekyll and Hyde. Crooked; spurious, counter-

feit: since ca. 1920; orig. and still mainly underworld, but, by 1940 at latest, also police s. It rhymes on **snide,** adj. (p. 793), and, esp. in the underworld, is often shortened to *Jekyll* (John Gosling, *The Ghost Squad,* 1959). A neat pun on R. L. Stevenson's characters.

jel. Jealous: girls' Public Schools': since ca. 1920. (Nancy Spain, *Poison for Teacher,* 1949.)

jell, n. A coward: Australian: since ca. 1950. (Dick.) Cf. the S.E. 'to tremble like a *jelly*'. Hence, *jell it,* to act like a coward. (Likewise Dick.)

Jellicoe Express, the. 'The all-Service train from London to Thurso (for Scapa Flow). Predominantly Naval. This train became famous in the 1914–18 war and was put back into service in the war of 1939–45': (P-G-R.)

jelly, 1, occurs also as **all jelly** (B. & L.)—3. Gelignite: Australian: since ca. 1918. B., 1942. By 1925, gen. British s.—4. See **put a jelly . . .**

jelly belly.—2. A coward: Australian: since ca. 1930. (B.P.) Hence the adj. *jelly-bellied*: since ca. 1935. Cf. **jell** above. The adj., in its lit. sense 'fat', occurs in Kipling's *Stalky & Co.,* 1899, and may safely be presumed to date since ca. 1870.

jelly-legged. (Of a boxer) groggy: sporting coll.: C. 20. Laurie Atkinson records hearing it in 1960.

Jem Mace (p. 435) fell into disuse ca. 1940.

jemima.—3. (Usually **J-.**) A dressmaker's dummy: domestic: since ca. 1880.

jemmy, n., 5, occurs in *Sinks,* 1848, as 'the head' (human or animal).—8. A sovereign (coin): 1857, Augustus Mayhew, *Paved with Gold,* 'Short for *Jemmy O' Goblin*': that term, therefore, must be dated back to ca. 1850.

*jemmy, v. To open (a door, a window, etc.) with a **jemmy** (n., 1: p. 435): late C. 19–20: c. until ca. 1910, then low and police s. In, e.g., J. V. Turner, *Homicide Haven,* 1933.

jemmy jessamy (p. 435). Ex Eliza Haywood's *The History of Jemmy and Jenny Jessamy,* 1753; the term, therefore, dates prob. from 1753 or 1754.

Jenkins is the journalistic nickname, ca. 1880–1910, for that person on the staff of *The Morning Post* who reports the doings of Court and Society. B. & L.

Jennies. See **Jenny Hills** below.

Jenny.—2. See **Jenny Wren.**

Jenny Darbies. Policemen: ca. 1830–70. Charles Martell, *The Detectives' Note Book,* 1860, 'Well, I joined the [police] force. . . . There was a good deal of animosity against us for a long while and all sorts of opprobrious epithets were bestowed upon us. We were "Bobbies", "Bluebottles", "Peelers", and "Jenny Darbies" (gens d'armes).'

Jenny Hills (p. 436) prob. dates from the late 1870's, for it was in the 1870's that Jenny Hill, the music-hall performer, was at the height of her fame. It occurs in, e.g., Sydney Lester, *Vardi the Palarey,* (?) 1937. Often shortened to *Jennies.*

Jenny Lea (or **Lee**).—3. A key: rhyming s.: C. 20.

Jenny Scribe. A Wren with Writer rating: Naval: since ca. 1940.

Jenny Wren; occ. **Jill tar** (or **Jiltar**). A Wren: since 1939. H. & P. By ca. 1942, however, *jenny* (Granville) was far commoner than either; *Jill tar* was never much used.

jer. You; thus *mindjer,* mind you: sol.: mid-

C. 19–20. (Pugh.) Only when the pronoun is unemphasised.

jere.—3. A male homosexual: low: C. 20. (Ex sense 2: p. 436.) Franklyn 2nd—but I doubt its being rhyming s.

Jericho (p. 436).—2. As a privy, it dates from ca. 1750 and has long been †, except among builders and masons. Parson Woodforde, *Diary*, April 26, 1780.—3. Extant among conservators of old Oxford University s. (John Betjeman.)

jerk, n.—3. A chap, fellow, 'guy'; usually with pejorative tinge: adopted in 1943 from American soldiers. Duncan Webb, in *Daily Express*, Sept. 11, 1945.—4. Custard: Australian soldiers: 1939–45. (B., 1943.)—5. Mostly in pl. *jerks*, elliptical for *fly-jerks*, 'small pieces of cork suspended from the brim of a tramp's hat to ward off flies' (B., 1943): Australian coll.: C. 20.

jerk, v., 1 (p. 436), occurs as early as 1773, in a letter from Charles Burney to his friend Twining.

jerk off (p. 436). Another variant is *jerk one's turkey*. *Jerk off*: occ. shortened to *jerk*. Whence *jerking(-)iron*, penis: mostly schoolboys': C. 20.

jerk one's mutton. See **gallop one's maggot.**

jerk the cat. A variant of *whip the cat*, q.v. at **cat, whip the** (senses 1, 2) on p. 132.

*****jerke** is Randle Holme's variant (1688) of *jark*, a seal. Also, he has *jerk't*, sealed.

jerrican. A petrol can captured from the Germans (*Jerries*); then any petrol can of similar ype: Army in N. Africa: 1940–3. (P-G-R.) Extant and, since ca. 1945, S.E.

Jerry (p. 436). There is much to be said for derivation from *jerry*, n., 3 (p. 436): the German soldier's large steel helmet did, in fact, look rather like a chamber-pot.—2. Ex sense 1 (p. 436) naturally comes ,the sense, 'a German aircraft': since ca. 1915 and current again in 1939–45; in 1940–1, frequently used by civilians (Berrey, 1940). —3. The inevitable nickname for anyone surnamed Dawson: C. 20. (*John o' London's Weekly*, Dec. 12, 1936.) Why?—4. *Jerry*, ex and synonymous with the *pot*, the headmaster: Cheltenham: resp. since ca. 1919 and since ca. 1890. Marples.

jerry, n., 3 (p. 436). A variant nuance, 'water-closet': *Sessions*, May 1850 (Surrey cases). It has the further nuance, 'a Jeroboam' of drink, as in 'The naval officer ... came into the Clarendon for a Jerry of punch': Wm Maginn, *Whitehall* (p. 140), 1827. Moe.

jerry, v., 1 (p. 437) occurs in New Zealand as *jerry to*, as in 'He hadn't jerried to it before' (Slatter): C. 20.

jerry, adj. Mostly in *be full jerry to* (someone), to be fully aware of his tricks or schemes or ulterior purpose: since ca. 1930. (Harold Griffiths, letter of Jan. 4, 1960.)

jerry-come-tumble. A water-closet: lower classes' (− 1860); † by 1920. H., 2nd ed. Ex **jerry**, n., 3, influenced by **jerry-go-nimble** or by **jerrycommumble** or by both (qq.v. in the *Dict.*).

jerry(-)diddle, or one word. 'A drink on the house' (B., 1942): Australian: C. 20. Cf. **Jerry Riddle.**—2. (Also *Jerry Diddle*.) A violin: rhyming s.: late C. 19–20. Franklyn, *Rhyming*.

Jerry O'Gorman. A Mormon: rhyming s.: C. 20.

Jerry Riddle (or **Riddell**), n. and v. Urination; to urinate: mid-C. 19–20. Rhyming in *piddle*.

jerrybuilder; jerrybuilding. See **jerry-builder** in *Dict*.

Jerry's Backyard. The Skagerrack and Kattegat: Coastal Command (R.A.F.): 1943–5. Communicated by S/Ldr Vernon Noble in Feb. 1945.

jersey. A red-headed person: Australian: ca. 1870–1920. B., 1942.

Jerusalem artichoke. A donkey: rhyming s.: ca. 1870–1930. (Franklyn 2nd.) On **moke**, 1: p. 526.

Jerusalem on Sea. A C. 20 variant of **Jerusalem the Golden** (*Dict.*).

Jerusalem pony. Often abbr. to *Jerusalem*. B. & L.

Jes (pron. *Jĕz*). A Jesuit: Catholics': C. 19–20.

jessie, give (someone), on p. 437. No; it almost certainly derives from *Isaiah*, xi, 1, 'There shall come forth a rod out of the stem of Jesse.' (Jespersen.)

Jessies. Custard: Naval (lower-deck): since ca. 1915. Semantics: custards quiver like Jessie's breasts. Cf. **bathing beauty.**

jessy. See **jaisy.**

Jesuit.—3. A member of Jesus College, Cambridge: Cambridge: late C. 19–20. Cf. sense 2 (p. 437).

jet, n. and v. A jet-propelled aircraft: R.A.F. (and aircraft engineers') coll.: mid-1944, by ca. 1960, S.E.; to travel by a jet aircraft: coll.: since ca. 1960.

jet job. An extremely fast racing car: Canadian motorists': 1948 +.

Jew chums. Jewish refugees from Germany and Central Europe: Australian: since ca. 1936, B., 1942. With a pun on *new chums*: cf. U.S. *refujews*.

Jew parade. Sunday cookhouse fatigue for those who dodge the church parade, whether they are Jews or not: Army: late C. 19–20.

jeweller's shop. A pocket of free (i.e. loose) gold in a shaft: Australian miners': since ca. 1910. It glitters so. (H. Drake Brockman, *Hot Gold*, 1940.)

Jewie. A Jew: Anglo-Irish coll.: late C. 19–20. James Joyce, *Ulysses*, 1922. Cf. **Jewy** below.

jewie. A jewfish; a jew lizard: Australian coll.: C. 20. (B., 1953.)

jewing. Earlier in 'Taffrail': 'To do "jewing" is to make or repair clothes.'

jewing firm. 'A tailoring concern run by one or more of the ship's company' (Granville): Naval: C. 20. See **jewing** (p. 438).

Jewish forest. Three threes: poker-players': C. 20. Ex the pronunciation *t'ree t'rees*. (Alan S. C. Ross.)

Jewish nightcap. Foreskin: low: late C. 19–20. With reference to circumcision.

Jewish pianola. A cash-register: Australian: since ca. 1925. (B., 1943.)

Jew's harp.—2. 'A shackle so shaped, used to join an anchor-chain to an anchor' (Granville): Naval: since ca. 1890 +.

Jew's Rolls-Royce. A Jaguar motor-car: since ca. 1938. Much chromium plating 'and all that'.

Jewtocracy. The art of hatching or developing mysteries: cultured: since ca. 1930. On *plutocracy*.

Jewy or **Jewey.** An inseparable nickname for Jews, esp. if surnamed Moss: from ca. 1890 (Pugh). Cf. **Ikey** in *Dict*.

jewy. Variant of *jewie*. (Cecil Mann, 1945.)

jib, n., 1 (p. 433) should be back-dated to late C. 18: it occurs in Charles Dibdin's *The Five Engagements*, cited by *The Port Folio*, Sept. 21, 1805 (p. 295). Moe.

jib, booze one's or the; booze up the jib (variant). See **booze the jib** (*Dict.*).

jib-and-staysail Jack. The seaman's name for an officer given, whether inexperienced or a martinet, to tormenting the men by constantly 'making and shortening sail' to keep the ship in station when it forms one of a fleet: Naval: late C. 18–mid-19. (W. N. Glascock, *Sketch-Book*, I, 1825.) Moe.

jib show. A show featuring only girls: Canadian carnival s.: since ca. 1920. Cf. **jig-a-jig** (p. 438).

jig is up, the.—2. 'The last line of type has been set and the forme can be locked and put on the press' (Leechman): Canadian printers': C. 20.

jigery pokery is B. & L.'s form of **jiggery-pokery** (*Dict.*).

jig(g)aree is a C. 20 variant—esp. Naval—of **jiggamaree** (*Dict.*). Granville.

jigger, n.—15. A bicycle: Army in France: 1914–18. Ex sense 12.—16. A man; esp., *silly jigger*: since ca. 1918. Orig. euphemistic for **bugger**, 2 (p. 103).—17. An entry; a passage between terrace-house backyards: Merseyside: late C. 19–20.

jiggery-pook is the Australian shape of **jiggery-pokery** (p. 439): since ca. 1910. B., 1942.

jiggle juice. Special fuel for racing cars: racing motorists': adopted, ca. 1955, ex U.S. (*The Autocar*, June 8, 1962.)

jiggy-jig. Variant (1914 +) of **jig-a-jig** (p. 438).

jildi. V.i., to be quick, move quickly or promptly: Regular Army: C. 20. Blaker (ex-Indian-Army sergeant *loquitur*): 'Come on. We'll catch 'im if we jildi.' Ex the **jildi** of the *Dict.* —3. As n., in *get a jildi on*, get a move on, hurry: Army, esp. in India: World War II. (P-G-R.)

jildi move, do a. To retreat hastily: Army: 1939–45.—2. Among tank men: to take evasive action: 1940–5. (P-G-R.)

Jill, hence also **jill**. A girl: since ca. 1945; not very common. Probably ex 'Every Jack has his *Jill*'.

jill (or J-) mill. Venetian shutters or blind: Anglo-Indian: mid-C. 19–20. B. & L.

Jillaroo or **j-**. A Land Girl: Australian war s. of 1939–45. (B., 1943.) A blend of *Jill*, a girl + *jackaroo*.

jillpots, his or **her**. He, she—him, her; that person: itinerant entertainers': C. 20. See quotation at **vardi**, 2, below. Often shortened to *his*, or *her*, *jills*. Sydney Lester, *Vardi the Palarey*, (?) 1937.

Jim. The sum of £1: Australian: since ca. 1910. (B., 1943.) Ex *Jimmy o' Goblin*, q.v. at **Jemmy o' Goblin** (pp. 435–6).

Jim Brown (p. 439): † by 1960. Franklyn 2nd.

Jim Crow.—2. A roof spotter of aircraft: civilian Services: 1939 +. H. & P.—3. Hence, one who keeps watch while, e.g., gambling is in progress: combatant Services: since 1940. H. & P.—4. A plate-layer: railwaymen's: since ca. 1945. (*Railway* 2nd.) He needs to keep a look-out for oncoming trains. Cf. senses 2 and 3.—5. Raci●

prejudice, esp. against Negroes: since ca. 1955. Cf. the song *Jim Crow Blues* sung by the American Negro folk-singer Huddie Ledbetter ('Leadbelly'), c. 1870?–1949.—6. A professional: itinerant entertainers': C. 20. Rhyming s. on **pro**, 2 (p. 661). Lester.

Jim Skinner! a C. 20 variant of **Joe Skinner** (*Dict.*). Len Ortzen, 1938.

Jiminy (or **Jiminiy**) **Crickets!** A widespread Canadian (ex U.S.) expletive: since ca. 1920. W. & F. suggest that it stands for *Jesu Domine*; Dr Douglas Leechman and I, that it is a euphemism for *Jesus Christ*.

Jimmies' Union. The First Lieutenants in a flotilla of destroyers, an informal association presided over by the senior 'Jimmy': Naval officers': since the 1920's. Cf. *watchkeepers' union*.

Jimmy. St James's Palace, London: mostly Regular Army: late C. 19–20. This and **Jimmy guard**: Gerald Kersh, *Boots Clean*, 1941.—2. See **Jimmy the One.**—3. (Or *jimmy*.) 'Piece of metal illicitly placed in blast pipe causing [= to cause] greater draught on fire and better steaming. Used in 1890–1930 period when drivers were paid a bonus for saving coal and oil and Railway Companies bought cheap coal' (*Railway*): railwaymen's, esp. among drivers and their mates. —4. See **Jimmy Grant** (p. 439 and below).

Jimmy Britts, often shortened to *Jimmies* and always preceded by *the*. Diarrhœa: Australian rhyming s. (on *the shits*): C. 20.

Jimmy Bungs (*Dict.*): by 1945, virtually extinct, Granville.

Jimmy Grant and **jimmy**, n., 2 (p. 439). The longer term was originally a New Zealand usage: 1845, E. J. Wakefield, *Adventure*: app. † by 1900 in New Zealand. (B., 1941.)

Jimmy Green. A sail set under the bowsprit: sailing ship nautical: ? ca. 1860–1910. (L. D. M. Roberts, June 27, 1951.)

Jimmy guard. Guard duty at St James's Palace: Army: C. 20. Cf. **Buck guard**.

Jimmy Prescott. Waistcoat: rhyming s.: C. 20. Lester.

Jimmy Rollocks. A C. 20 variant of **Tommy Rollocks** (below). (Franklyn 2nd.)

Jimmy the One. An earlier reference occurs in 'Taffrail': 'The first lieutenant (a lieutenant-commander as he usually is in these days [1916]) is "Jimmy the One".' Often simply **Jimmy** (Granville).

Jimmy Woodser.—2. Hence, a person alone, esp. an orphan: Australian: since ca. 1935. (D'Arcy Niland, *When the Cross Turns Over*, 1958.) Ex the nuance 'a person drinking alone' (since ca. 1910): B., 1959.

Jimmy Woods-ing, vbl n. Solitary drinking: New Zealand, esp. miners': C. 20. (Jean Devanney, *Down Below*, 1928.) Ex *Jimmy Woodset*, 1 (p. 439).

jing (or **J-**)**!, by.** A variant and derivative of *by jingo!*: C. 20. Philip MacDonald, *The Crime Conductor*, 1932. Imm. ex Scottish use, q.v. at **jings!** in the *Dict.*

jingbang (p. 440). Cf. *the whole shebang* at **shebang** (p. 752).

jingle, 2, is also Australian (since ca. 1925): B., 1942.

jingled. Tipsy: ca. 1910–30. Ward Muir, *Observations of an Orderly*, 1917.

*jingler (horse-courser) appears in early C. 17;

esp. in Dekker's *Lanthorne and Candlelight*, 1608-9.

Jingling Johnnie (or -y). A Turkish crescent, i.e. a noise-making instrument (a stick, with small *bells* depending from a crescent-shaped attachment): C. 19-20; ob. Percy Scholes, *The Oxford Companion to Music*. The *Johnnie* may be short for *Johnny Turk*, 'Turk'. The instrument was introduced into military bands when, late in C. 18, so-called Turkish music became popular in Europe.

jingling johnnies. 'We find shears called *jingling johnnies* and *tongs*,' B., 1942: New Zealand and Australian rural: since ca. 1870. Ex preceding term.

jings! (p. 440). The Aus. form—mostly juvenile—is *by jings!*, as, frequently, in Norman Lindsay, *Saturdee*, 1933.

jink, v.; **jinking**; **jinks**. Resp., 'To turn quickly and skilfully in the air to avoid enemy action; the activity or the practice of making these turns; the turns themselves. Also *jink away*, noun and verb,' Partridge, 1945; 1943, H. & P., the second and third; *The Reader's Digest*, Feb. 1941, the first, which dates from at least as early as 1937 in the R.A.F., whose use thereof is merely an application of S.E. (mainly Scottish) *jink*, 'to make a quick elusive turn' (O.E.D.).—2. To swindle (someone): Australian: since ca. 1920. Kylie Tennant, *Foveaux*, 1939.

jinker (p. 440) dates since ca. 1875. 'Tom Collins', *Such is Life*, 1903.—2. A variant of *junker*. (B., 1943.)—3. A bringer of bad luck: Newfoundland: since ca. 1920. A back-formation ex *jinx* (apprehended as *jinks*). L. E. F. English, *Historic Newfoundland*, 1955.

Jinties; the singular *Jinty* is rare. 'Class 3 0-6-0 tank engines (MR)': railwaymen's: ? ca. 1940. *(Railway.)*

*****jintoe**. A girl of poor reputation; a whore: South African (low s. and c.:) late C. 19-20. See *Underworld*.

jinx. A bringer, a causer, of bad luck: adopted, ca. 1936, from U.S. Walter Greenwood, *Only Mugs Work*, 1938, 'Lay off the dames, Mario, they're all jinxes.' Cognate with **jink** (above), the implication being that 'they are all twisters'. Hence, bad luck, as in, 'That's put a jinx on it.' More precisely: something that, midway between a devil *in* a thing and a curse *on* it, causes it to go repeatedly wrong, as in, 'This machine—this undertaking—has a jinx on it.'

jinx, v., corresponds to both senses of the n. and follows within a year or two; likewise adopted from U.S.

jip.—2. Energy: Australian: C. 20. (D'Arcy Niland, *Call Me . . .*, 1958.)

jirk-nod or **jirknod**. See **yerknod** (*Dict.*).

jitter-bug. A very nervous or *jittery* person: adopted in 1938 from U.S. Ex **jitters** (*Dict.*).

jitter party. A party of Japanese sneaking around a camp's perimeter and trying to cause alarm by making noises and throwing grenades: Burmese front: 1942 +.

jitterbuggery. The style of dancing known as *jitterbug*: Canadian adolescents' since ca. 1952.

jittery. On edge; very nervous: adopted in 1935 or 1936 from U.S. Somerset Maugham, *Theatre*, 1937, 'For two or three weeks she was very jittery'. Ex **jitters** (p. 440).

jive. To dance: Teddy boys': ca. 1955-9.

'In the palais [de danse] you don't dance. It is—care to jive, or, get terpsichorical (Terpsichore was the Greek muse of dancing)': Gilderdale, 2. Ex the n., itself probably of Negro origin (perhaps synonymous with *jazz*).—2. To talk: a talk: jazz fanatics': since ca. 1948. (*The Observer*, Sept. 16, 1956.) Ex the talking that accompanies, or ensues, upon dancing.

Jive and Swing Slang. This slang reached Britain from the U.S. in 1945; still in July 1947 was it very little known except among the *hep cats* or addicts of jive and swing, early called 'hot jazz'. All of it is American, most of it ephemeral. In mid-1947 Vic Filmer compiled a glossary of jive and swing. Almost the only terms that have the least importance and look at all likely to survive more than a year or two are these, culled from that glossary:

beat up one's chops. To be loquacious.

blow one's wig, to go crazy; hence, to act crazily. Prompted by that other Americanism, *blow ones' top*.

fin, £1 (sum or note); *mash me a fin*, give me one pound. See **finnif**, p. 277.

gravy, money. Hence, *get oneself some gravy for grease*, to obtain money for food.

neigho, pops!: no (or, nothing doing), pal! Ex *nay!*, no!

razz-ma-tazz! ordinary jazz, old-fashioned jazz, also called *ricky-tick* or *rooty-toot*.

twister, a key, esp. in *twister to the slammer*, a door key.

Writing on Oct. 12, 1965, Professor F. E. L. Priestley amends the foregoing paragraph thus, 'I have a record I bought ca. 1934, made by the Negro band-leader and pianist Fats Waller, with the title "Don't try your jive on me", which suggests that it did not then mean the same as jazz. May mean "tricks", whence *jive* as a "tricky" form of playing. When the term *jive* came in, it denoted the sort of music that jitterbugs danced to. This was a different style from the traditional "hot jazz". Jive and swing are not the same thing as what was before called "hot jazz".' He adds that *fin* and *gravy* are not, of course, jive talk; that *razz-ma-tazz* refers esp. to Cab Calloway's singing and conducting, ca. 1925-35; and that *ricky-ticky* (not *tick*) or *rooty-toot* is old-fashioned New Orleans jazz.

jive!, don't give me that. Don't talk such (utter) nonsense: jazz addicts': since ca. 1950. (L. Fordyce, letter in *The Observer*, Sept. 23, 1956.) Ex *jive*, 2, above.

jizzup is a Birmingham s. variant of **jossop** (p. 445): late C. 19-20. (Dr C. T. Onions, postcard of April 9, 1939.)

Jo-bag. A 'French letter': mostly Servicemen's: since ca. 1943. Ex U.S.?

jo-jo (pl. *jo-joes*).—2. 'A small grass-seed with a double-pronged head that sticks in the feet. Like a blindy-eye, only much smaller' (Edwin Morrisby, 1958): Australian: since ca. 1925. Either Aboriginal or imitative of Aboriginal. *Blindy-eye* is a rare variant of *bindy-eye*, itself app. an elaboration of *bindy* or *bindi*—a term belonging to S.E. (B.P.)

Joan of Arcs or **Joe Marks**. Sharks: Australian rhyming s. (— 1945.) B., 1945.

Joanna (p. 440): recorded earlier in A. Neil Lyons, *Clara*, 1912.

job, n.—6. A passenger: taxi-drivers': since ca.

1910. Herbert Hodge, *Cab, Sir?*, 1939.—7. An aircraft: R.A.F.: since ca. 1939. Jackson. Ex a *job of work*.—7. Hence, fig. as in *blonde job, blue job, brown job*. '"I saw a wizard job in the village this morning." . . . He had seen a beautiful girl.' Hector Bolitho in *The English Digest*, Feb. 1941; Jackson, 1943, 'Thus, "She's a blonde job"'; *et* (how many?) *alii*.—9. A drunk: Australian: since ca. 1939 at least. (B., 1943.)—10. In **make a job of** (someone).—11. An inferior worker; a fool; 'a bit of a mess': Australian: since ca. 1930. Cf. senses 5 (p. 440) and 9. Gavin Casey, *Downhill is Easier*, 1945 (p. 52).

job, v., 4; **lamp**, v. 'To lamp a bloke is to attack him with your bunch of fives (fists) or knives or razors. To job 'im means the same thing. A street corner fight is a bundle or a tole' (Gilderdale, 2): Teddy boys' since ca. 1954. Whereas *bundle* suggests **bundle up**, *tole* perhaps represents dial, *toll*, a clump (of, e.g., trees). Ex sense 3 on p. 440.

job, do a.—3. To defecate: both children's and adults': late C. 19–20. Euphemistic.

job, just the. See **just** . . .

job, on the. *In coitu*: low coll.: C. 20. Sexually at work.

job, on the, adv., hence also adj. (Engaged) in copulation; *be on the job*, to be copulating; *get on with the job*, to lose no time in beginning to copulate: coll.: C. 20. (Anthony Burgess, *Tremor of Intent*, 1966.)

job of it, make a clean. To do thoroughly: coll.: from ca. 1885. Anstey, *Voces Populi*, II, 1892.

jobbernolling. See 'Epithets'.

jock, 3, food; hence *jock tin*, a food container: railwaymen's: C. 20. (*Railway*.)

Jock, 2 (p. 441). Esp. *the Jocks*, the Scots Guards: Army: late C. 19–20. Gerald Kersh, *They Die with Their Boots Clean*, 1941, cites also *the Micks* and *the Taffs*, the Irish and the Welsh Guards.

Jock columns. Highly mobile bodies of troops in the Western Desert: Army coll.: 1942–3. Ex Brigadier *Jock* Campbell. (P-G-R.)

jocked off, be. (Of a jockey) to be deprived of an agreed mount: racing: since ca. 1930. Dick Francis, *Nerve*, 1964, 'I discovered that two of my three prospective mounts were mine no longer. I had been, in the expressive phrase, jocked off.' Ex **jock**, n., 2, on p. 441.

jockey, n.—5. A top boot: boot-makers' and repairers': 1851, Mayhew, II.—6. See 'Hauliers' Slang'.—7. A policeman: c.: since ca. 1945. (John Gosling, 1959.)—8. A pilot: R.A.F., Malta: since ca. 1950. Cf. sense 4 on p. 441 ('bus-driver').

jockey sticks; often shortened to *jockeys*. 'Two pieces of a flat stick, split lengthwise and fastened on to the two handles of a pair of shears to give a larger and softer grip,' B., 1942: Australian shearers': C. 20.

jockeys.—2. See **jockey sticks**.—3. A pole-roofing to keep bark of hut in position: Australian: C. 20. (B., 1943.) They 'ride' the hut.

jockey's whip, occasionally **jockeys**. A bed; (a) sleep: rhyming s. (on *kip*): since ca. 1940; by 1959, ob. (Franklyn, *Rhyming*.)

*****jocky**. 'A Man's Yard', Holme, 1688; whence **jock**, n. (see *Dict*.).

Joe, a marine (see **joe**, 3: p. 441), is recorded in *Fraser's Magazine*, Aug. 1875, as a 'household word'. (Moe.)

joe, n., 1 (p. 441), occurs in W. N. Glascock's *Naval Sketch Book*, 2nd Series, 1834, at I, 144, 'To avoid the appearance of official stiffness or dulness at dinner, relax in the recital of an occasional "*joe*".' Moe.—10. As *Joe*, it = an imaginary person, as in '"Who did that?"—"Joe"': ca. 1830–70. *Sinks*, 1848.—11. 'A name for anyone in the Service,' Jackson: R.A.F.: since ca. 1920. —12. Short for *Joe Soap*: R.A.F.: since ca. 1935. Gerald Emanuel, letter of March 29, 1945.—13. *Joe* has, since ca. 1935, but esp. since June 1941, denoted Joseph Stalin; by 1960, ob.—14. Short for **Joe Blake**, a snake: Australian: C. 20. The full term occurs in B., 3rd ed., 1943.—15. As *Joe*, the inseparable nickname of all men surnamed Beckett: since ca. 1919. Ex the English boxer so named.—16. As *Joe*, in such phrases as 'a *good Joe*', a good fellow, and 'an *honest Joe*', an honest man, it was, ca. 1944, adopted ex U.S.

*****Joe, rolling**. See **rolling Joe**.

Joe Blakes, the. Delirium tremens: Australian rhyming s. (on *snakes*): since ca. 1910. Ex *Joe Blake*, 2 (p. 442). Alan Marshall, *These Are My People*, 1946.

Joe boy; **Joe job**. One who is detailed for an unpleasant job (*Joe job*): Canadian soldiers': since ca. 1940.

Joe Brown. (A) town: rhyming s., ? orig. showmen's: 1893, P. H. Emerson, *Signor Lippo*.

Joe Buck. Coïtion: low Australian rhyming s., not very common: since ca. 1930. (B.P.)

Joe Cardboard. A synonym of *Joe Erk*, a softy, a constant dupe: mostly Services': since ca. 1950.

Joe Cunt is synonymous with the next: Services: since ca. 1920.

Joe Erk. 'A peculiar and ingenious combination of "Joe" (Canadian abbreviation of "Joe Soap"), "erk" (British) and "jerk", American for a dull-witted fellow,' Elgin Blair, letter of May 15, 1947: R.C.A.F.: 1939 +. Perhaps rhyming s. on U.S., hence Canadian, s. *jerk*. (Franklyn, *Rhyming*.)

Joe Goss. Boss: Australian rhyming s.: since ca. 1910. (Franklyn, *ibid*.)

*****Joe Gurr**. Prison: c.: since ca. 1930. F. D. Sharpe, *The Flying Squad*, 1938. Rhyming on **stir** (p. 833).

Joe Hook.—2. A book: since ca. 1930.

Joe Hunt. 'The man who gets all the dirty work to do,' H. & P.: Services: since ca. 1920. Rhyming with (*silly*) *cunt*.—2. Hence, a fool: C. 20. Franklyn.

Joe job. See **Joe boy**.

Joe Marks. See **Joan of Arcs**.

Joe Morgan is an Australian variant (B., 1945) of **Molly O'Morgan**.

Joe O'Gorman. A foreman: rhyming s.: late C. 19–20.

Joe Poke. A justice of the peace: lower classes': from ca. 1875. B. & L. By elaboration of *J.P.*

Joe Rocks. Socks: rhyming s.: C. 20. Suggested by **almond rocks** (*Dict*.).

Joe Ronce. A 'ponce': rhyming s.: C. 20. James Curtis, *The Gilt Kid*, 1936.

Joe Rook.—2. A crook: C. 20. Rhyming. Cf.:

Joe Rooks (singular very rare). Bookmakers, esp. those who ply on the course: racing rhyming s. (on synonymous *books*): C. 20. Franklyn 2nd.

*****Joe Rourke**. A thief, esp. a pickpocket: c.: mid-C. 19–20. F. D. Sharpe, 1938. Rhyming on **fork**, n., 1 and 2 (*Dict*.).

Joe Soap. An unintelligent fellow that is 'over-willing' and therefore made a 'willing-horse': Services (esp. R.A.F.): since ca. 1930. H. & P. Rhyming on **dope**, n., 6 (*Dict.*). Also as v.: 'Thus, "Yes, I'm always Joe Soaping for somebody"' (Jackson).

Joe'd, be. To be given the dirty work: R.A.F.: since ca. 1945. Ex the Joe of **Joe Soap** above.

joes, the.—2. Hence, (a state of) nerves: Australian: since ca. 1925. Vance Palmer, *Seedtime*, 1957, 'What I saw in the sugar country gave me the joes.'

Joey. A familiar form of **Joe Hunt**. Franklyn, *Rhyming.*—2. The senior Royal Marine officer in the wardroom: Naval officers': C. 20. (P-G-R.) —3. As in 'I'm having my Joey' or menstrual period: middle and upper-middle class feminine: C. 20.

joey. Sense 2 gen. has a capital. 'Taffrail': 'A Royal marine is a "bullock", "turkey", or "Joey", while a soldier is a "grabby" or "leather neck".'—8. A humbug: prison c.: mid-C. 19-20. Mayhew. Perhaps cf. **holy Joe** (*Dict.*).—9. Threepence: Cockneys': C. 20. Ex sense 1.—10. A hermaphrodite: a sodomite; an effeminate or foppish young man neither hermaphrodite nor sodomite: Australian low: C. 20. B., 1942. Perhaps ex sense 4, third nuance (p. 442).—11. An evasion; a small lie: low Australian: C. 20. (B., 1943.) Probably ex sense 8.—12. A worthless cheque: Australian (low; police): since ca. 1910. (B., 1943.)—13. A fake: Australian servicemen's: 1939-45. (B., 1953.) Ex senses 8, 11, 12.

Joey, it's. A call at knocking-off time: Midlands collieries: C. 20. (*The Manchester Guardian*, Aug. 19, 1954.)

joey, wood and water. An idler that hangs about hotels: Australian: C. 20. Baker. Ex sense 4 of **joey** (*Dict.*).

jogari homey or polone(y). Any instrumentalist or singer, resp. male (*homey*) or female: parlary: late (? mid) C. 19-20. (Sydney Lester, 1937.) A variant of **joggering omey** (p. 442)—cf. **jogger** (ibid.).

jogue (p. 442), a shilling, occurs in George Elson's *The Last of the Climbing Boys*, 1900, in form *jug*; the word, therefore, passed into chimneysweeps' s. and may have survived until very early C. 20.

John, 1. Major A. F. Mockler-Ferryman (*Annals of Sandhurst*, 1900) defines it as a cadet in his first two years and dates it from ca. 1860. Contrast **Reg.**—4. This sense may abbr. **John Hop.** —8. Short for **John Thomas**, 2 (p. 443): New Zealand: C. 20.—9. A kookaburra: Australian: C. 20. (B., 1943.)—10. See next entry.—11. An arrest: since ca. 1945: c. >, by ca. 1965, also low s. Short for *John Bull*, rhyming on s. *pull*, a or to arrest.

Sense 4 has, since ca. 1910, been common also in Canada—'I think, in this case, from John Darm (*gendarme*)': F. E. L. Priestley.

john, the. The water-closet: upper and middle class: C. 20. Less probably from Fr. *donjon*, a castle-keep, than a pun on dial. *Jack's house* or on *jack*, 12 (p. 429) or even on *Ajax* (p. 7).

John Bluebottle. A policeman: C. 20. Cf. **blue bottle** in *Dict.*

John Bull. See **John**, 11, above.

John Chinaman. A Chinese: C. 19-20; by 1940, ob.; by 1966, virtually †. John Hall, *Voyage to Loo-choo*, 1826 (p. 37), 'The seamen . . .

not caring whether John Chinaman, as they called him, understood them or not.' (Moe.)

John Dillon. A shilling: New Zealand rhyming s.: since ca. 1930. 'From the name of a famous racehorse' (Franklyn 2nd).

John Dunn; usually pl., *John Dunns*, policemen: Australian: since ca. 1920. B., 1942. For origin see **johndarm.**

John Hop. More prob. rhyming s. on *cop*: witness P. P., *Rhyming Slang*, 1932. Also English and South African and Australian.

John o' Groat. A coat; pl., *John o' Groats*, coats: rhyming s.: since ca. 1800.

John Thomas, 2. Not low but gentlemanly. In New Zealand at least as early as 1874 (A. Bathgate, *Colonial Experiences*): B., 1941. And in Australia as early as 1867 (Baker, letter).

John Trot. A bumpkin: upper classes': ? ca. 1710-70. (A letter, dated Dec. 17, 1733 and cited in *Lord Hervey and His Friends*, edited by the Earl of Ilchester, 1950.)

John Willie. A synonym of *John Thomas*, 2 (p. 443): since ca. 1930.

John Willie (or Willy), come on! A North Country c.p. of exhortation to a slow-witted or mentally deficient youth or man: late C. 19-20. Also, Julian Franklyn tells me, a London streets c.p. of ca. 1910: 'I believe from a song.'

johndarm (or J-). A policeman: London taxidrivers': since ca. 1917. Herbert Hodge, *Cab, Sir?*, 1939. Ex Fr. (*gens d'armes* >) *gendarme*.

Johnnie.—10. Short for *Johnnie Horner*, a corner: C. 20.—11. A Chinaman: Australian: since ca. 1905. B., 1942. Ex **John**, 5 (*Dict.*).—12. As *the Johnny*, the water-closet: C. 20. In, e.g., C. S. Archer, *China Servant*, 1946. Cf. sense 2 on p. 523.—13. An Arab: Army: 1939-45. (P-G-R.) —14. Penis: mostly feminine: late C. 19-20.—15. A kookaburra: Australian: C. 20. (K. S. Prichard, *Haxby's Circus*, 1930.)—16. A French letter: R.A.F.: since ca. 1950. Prompted by sense 14 ?

johnny bait (or one word). See **bait**, 4, above, and perhaps cf. **Johnnie**, 15, above.

Johnnie (or -y) Gallagher. A policeman: tramps' c.: C. 20.

Johnnie Hopper. A policeman: Australian rhyming s. (on *copper*): since ca. 1920. (B.P.)

Johnnie in the stalls. A (vapid) young man haunting the theatre stalls on account of the actresses: from ca. 1895. Leonard Merrick, *The Call from the Past*, 1910.

Johnnie (or -ny) Rann. A variant of **Tommy** O'Rann (p. 896). Franklyn 2nd.

Johnnie (or -ny) Rollocks. A variant of **Tommy Rollocks** below.

Johnnie Rutter. Butter: rhyming: C. 20.

Johnnie's or Johnny's. A doss-house: Australian servicemen's: 1939-45. (B., 1943.)

Johnny Armstrong (p. 443): 'the elementary motive power known as "handraulic"' (Granville): Naval: C. 20.

Johnny-come-lately. 'A nickname for a farm hand recently arrived from England,' B., 1942: New Zealand rural: since ca. 1910. Cf. **Johnny Newcome**, 2 (*Dict.*).—2. In Australia, any newcomer: C. 20. B., 1942.

Johnny Cotton. Rotten: rhyming s.: C. 20. Franklyn, *Rhyming.*

Johnny Crappo—see **John(ny) Crapose** on p. 443 —occurs in W. N. Glascock's *Naval Sketch Book*,

2nd Series, 1834, at II, 137. (Moe.) It also occurs as *Jean Crappeau* in Alfred Burton, *Johnny Newcome*, 1818. (Moe.)

Johnny Gurk. A Gurkha (soldier): 1915 +.

Johnny Haultaut (p. 443). Origin much more prob. in the lit. *haul taut*.

Johnny Newcome, 2 (p. 443), probably dates from late C. 18: cf. A. Burton, *Johnny Newcome*, 1818.

Johnny Randall. A candle: navvies' rhyming s.: ca. 1860–1900. (D. W. Barrett, 1880.)

***Johnny Ronce.** Variant of **Joe Ronce** (p. 442). Gerald Kersh, *Night and the City*, 1938.

Johnny Russell. A bustle: Australian rhyming s.: C. 20. B., 1942.

Johnny Skinner. A C. 20 variant of **Joe Skinner.** Franklyn, *Rhyming*.

Johnny Warder. An idler that hangs about public-houses in the hope of a free drink: Australian: ca. 1880–1920. B., 1942. Ex *John Ward*, the landlord of a low 'pub' in Sydney.—2. A lone drinker: Aus.: ca. 1910–40. (B., 1959.)

Johnny Woodser is a New Zealand and Australian variant of **Jimmy Woodser** (p. 439).

Johnson.—2. A prostitute's bully, esp. if a black: c., and low: from ca. 1910.—3. The penis: mid-C. 19–20; by 1950, ob. '. . . Neck frozen. Face ditto; thighs ditto; Johnson ditto, and sphincter vesicæ partially paralyzed': entry of Feb. 2, 1863 in *Cheadle's Journal of Trip across Canada, 1862–1863* (Ottawa, 1931). Communicated by Dr Douglas Leechman.

join!; join up! 'Get some Service in!': Services: since ca. 1925. H. & P.

join a brick wall. To crash into a wall: since ca. 1925. In 1939–45, young fellows thinking of volunteering for the Forces were sometimes told that they would do better to join a brick wall.

join the Army and see the world—the next world! A jocular gibe by disgruntled soldiers: since ca. 1948. Ex the poster carrying—without the last three words—that slogan.

join the back of the queue! A c.p. addressed to someone slow in the uptake: since ca. 1944. (A. B. Petch, March 1966.)

join the gang. To become a thief: low: from ca. 1860; ob. B. & L.

join ? When I get out of this (lot) they won't get me to join a Christmas Club: Forces' c.p.: 1939 +.

joined the R.A.F. we all knew one another, when I. R.A.F. regular's c.p., in 1939–45, to a 'duration only' man.

joint, 4 (p. 443) is app. Anglo-Irish in origin—and very much earlier in Ireland than in U.S. 'A Real Paddy', *Real Life in Ireland*, 1822, '*I slips the joint*' (ran away from the place—a boarding school).—8. A 'reefer'. *To roll a joint* is to make up a marihuana cigarette. This is the commonest synonym in current use among young people (1968).

With sense 6 of the n. (p. 443) cf. the entry at 'Mock Auction slang' below.

joke, it's no. See **no joke . . .**

joke over! or **when do we laugh?** A sarcastic c.p., directed at a feeble witticism: since the 1920's. The former is sometimes uttered by the joker himself when he sees that his wit has misfired.

joker (p. 443): very common in New Zealand since ca. 1890. 'A joker oughta bash ya' (Slatter.)

key. Funny: teenagers': since ca. 1955.

Nicholas Blake, *The Sad Variety*, 1964. '"Leake," I said, "your mind's as jokey as your clothes".'

joking, of course,—you're, he is, etc. A c.p. of modified optimism: since ca. 1955.

jol. To have fun: South African: C. 20. Adoption of Afrikaans (ex Dutch *jolen*, to make merry).—2. See **let's slaat . . .**

jollo. A festive occasion; a party: Australian: since ca. 1925. B., 1942. Ex *jollification*. Australian s. is fond of the jolly terminal -*o*.

jollop. 'Strong liquor, especially whiskey' (B., 1942): Australian: C. 20. Ex:—2. A laxative, a purgative: Australian coll.: late C. 19–20. A corruption of *julep*.

jolly, n., 7 (p. 444) goes back to ca. 1910: witness, e.g. Siegfried Sassoon's *Memoirs of an Infantry Officer*, 1930, 'a bit of a jolly' (in quotation marks); probably, at first, Public Schools'.

Sense 2 must antedate 1829: it occurs, in 1825, in W. N. Glascock, *Sketch-Book* (I, 14). Moe.

jolly, v.—5. (Cf. sense 3.) 'To impose upon, to act as an accomplice or abettor': c.: from ca. 1860. B. & L.

jolly boat, take the. To break out of barracks: Naval (lower-deck): since ca. 1920. (P-G-R.)

jolly d. 'Jolly decent': Public Schoolgirls: since ca. 1910. (Angus Wilson, *Hemlock and After*, 1952.) 'Not unknown in Australia' (B.P., 1963).

jolly Jack. Sailors' term for the civilian conception of (and illusions about) the seaman in the Navy: Naval coll.: since ca. 1920.

jolly stick. An occasional variant of *joy-stick*, 1 (p. 445). Virtually extinct by 1940.

jolly tit. See 'Men'.

jolly well. An intensive adverb: middle-class coll.: apparently since the 1880's. (The O.E.D. cites Rudyard Kipling, 1898.) It occurs, always with a verb, as in '"Sorry!"—"You jolly well ought to be!"' and 'You'll jolly well go there yourself, and not ask someone else to go.'

jolt, n. A drink, esp. of brandy and whiskey: Australian: since ca. 1920. Godfrey Blunden, *No More Reality*, 1935, '"Take another jolt, sport," said Clarrie with a grin.' Adopted ex Canada, where current since ca. 1900. (Niven.)

jolt, v.—2. To strike (someone): Australian: since ca. 1920. B., 1942.

jolt, pass (someone) **a.** To strike: Australian: since ca. 1920. (B., 1943.)

Jonah.—2. A frequent nickname for a man surnamed *Jones*: late C. 19–20. 'Lieut.-Colonel L. B. ("Jonah") Jones of the Rajputana Rifles,' Michie & Graebner, *Lights of Freedom*, 1941.

jonah, v. To bring bad luck to; to hinder: Australian coll.: C. 20. Baker.

Jonah Jones. See 'Nicknames' and **Jonah** above.

Jonah's whale. Tail: rhyming s.: 1887–ca. 1920. It first occurs in G. R. Sims's 'Tottie', a Dagonet Ballad published in *The Referee*, Nov. 7, 1887. (Franklyn 2nd.)

Jonas is a C. 20 coll. Naval lower-deck variant of ill-luck *Jonah*. Granville.—2. A kookaburra: Australian: since ca. 1910. Via *Johnass* ex **John**, 9 + laughing jack*ass*.

jonna: jonnop. Australian variants of *John*, John Hop, a policeman. (Sarah Campion, *Bonanza*, 1942.) The latter occurs in Xavier Herbert, *Capricornia*, 1939.

jonnick. See **jannock, 1,** on pp. 433–4. In 1959, B. declares its Aus. usage †.

Jonnup is the West Australian post-War pronunciation of **John Hop** (*Dict.*).

jonto. A fellow, a chap: East End of London: since ca. 1935. *The Evening News*, Nov. 27, 1947. Perhaps *ex jeune* (*homme*).

Jordan Highlanders, the. See **King's Own Schneiders** below.

jorrie. A girl: low Glasgow: late C. 19–20. MacArthur & Long. Origin?

Jose or Malts. A Maltese rating: Naval: since ca. 1925. Granville. Cf. **José** (p. 444).

josher.—2. A boat belonging to Messrs Fellows, Morton & Clayton, Ltd., canal carriers: canalmen's: C. 20. L. T. C. Rolt, *Narrow Boat*, 1944. The late Mr Fellows's name being Joshua.—3. A depraved old woman: Australian: ca. 1880–1910. B., 1942.

joss.—3. A synonym and derivative of **josser, 6** (*Dict.*).

joss-house man; joss-pidgin man. A priest; a missionary: pidgin: from ca. 1860. B. & L.

joss piece. A mascot: Naval: C. 20. (P-G-R.)

josser.—7. 'A synonym for a "prosser" or sponge': rather low: from ca. 1885; almost †. Ibid.

jossman. Plymouth gin: Naval (esp. on the China station): C. 20. Granville, 'From the picture of a monk on the bottle; all Holy men are "Jossmen" to the Chinese.'—2. (Also *Joss man*.) Police Chief Petty Officer; Master at Arms: Royal Navy and Royal Australian Navy: since ca. 1910. Ex his power. (Atkinson.)

jossop (p. 445). Also broth: Cockneys': C. 20. J. W. Horsley, *I Remember*, 1912.

jotter. A pad on which to take or make notes (*jotting pad*): secretaries' and typists' coll.: since late 1930's. (P. D. James, *A Mind to Murder*, 1963, 'Let's have a look at that jotter.')

journey, not one's. Not a successful day: turf: from ca. 1860; ob. B. & L., 'It is not his journey.' Ex Fr. *journée*.

journey's end. Prison: low: from 1929.

*jovah. Gaol: c.: from ca. 1870. Pugh (2): 'All I can say is, you never kept your brains clear while you was in jovah.' Perhaps a perversion of *jail* suggested by *chokey*.

jowl-sucking. Kissing, kisses: lower classes': from ca. 1865; ob. B. & L.

jowler. A lane between back-to-back houses: Liverpool: late C. 19–20. 'You pass cheek-by-jowl' (Frank Shaw).

joxy. See jaxy.

joy. Satisfaction; luck. Mostly in 'Any joy?' and 'No joy!': R.A.F. since ca. 1930; Naval since ca. 1935. Partridge, 1945; Granville; Brickhall & Norton, *Escape to Danger*, 1946, 'At 9.15 the workers had been down nearly forty minutes and still "no joy".'—2. Electrical current: R.A.F.: since ca. 1930. Gerald Emanuel, March 29, 1945. Cf. '"Is the W/T giving any joy?"—"Is the wireless working?"': Robert Hinde, March 17, 1945. Ex **joy stick**, 1 (p. 445).

Joy, the. Mountjoy Prison, Dublin: Anglo-Irish: late C. 19–20. (Desmond O'Neill, *Life Has No Price*, 1959.)

joy-bag.—2. A condom: mostly R.A.F.: since ca. 1950. Cf. **joy-stick**, 2, in *Dict.*

joy boy. A homosexual: undergraduates': C. 20; ob.

joy of my life. A wife: rhyming s., mostly

military: ca. 1880–1920. Richards. Prob. suggested by the much more gen. *trouble and strife*.

joy-prong (cf. *joy-stick*, 2: p. 445) is, like *mutton dagger and pork sword*, an adolescents' coy or facetious term for 'penis': since ca. 1920.

joy-stick, 1 (p. 445) derives immediately ex sense 2.—3. (Ex sense 2: p. 445.) Either of the two levers by which the steering of tanks and certain other tracked vehicles was controlled: Army: since ca. 1925. (P-G-R.)

Joynson Hicks. Six: theatrical rhyming s.: since ca. 1927. Ex a famous Home Secretary. Franklyn, *Rhyming*.

jubilee. Posterior, posteriors: sporting, and inferior society: 1887—ca. '97. B. & L.

judder. Engine noise: Air Force: since ca. 1925; by 1950, coll. Jar + shudder. (P-G-R.)

Judge Davis. Three tens: poker-players': C. 20. Ex a judge who mostly awarded '*thirty* days'.

judge of a circuit. See 'Tavern terms', § 4 (end).

Judy or, as Common Noun, judy.—4. A policewoman: Naval (lower-deck): since ca. 1930. Granville.—5. A Palestine Jew: Army, both in 1914–18 and in 1939–45. Ex Arabic *Yehudi*, 'a Jew'.—6. A duodenal ulcer: since ca. 1930. Ex '*duode*nal'. (Peter Sanders.)

Jug. A Jugoslav: since 1919 (the Peace Conference): orig., Civil Service; in 1940–5, Army. (Val Gielgud, *Fall of a Sparrow*, 1949.)

jug, n.—5. A can of beer: R.A.F. officers': since ca. 1930. (W/Cdr R. P. McDouall, March 17, 1945.)—6. See **jogue** (p. 442 and Addenda).—7. See **tea-pot**, 5, below.

jug, v.—3. To drink: R.A.F. since ca. 1930. Jackson. Ex the holding of a jug to one's mouth and drinking therefrom, also ex the idea of jugs of beer: cf. sense 5 of the n.

jug and pail. Prison: rhyming s. (on *jail*): C. 20. Franklyn 2nd.

jug(-)handle. See **Wagga grip** below.

jug up or scupper up. To drink liquor, esp. beer: office- and shop-girls': ca. 1955–60. (Gilderdale.)

jugged.—2. See honkers.

juggins has, in the sporting world, the nuance: 'An aspirant, usually young, and always more largely provided with money than with brains' (B. & L.).

juggler. An employee that has to find and remove part of the contents of a freight car: Canadian railroadmen's (— 1931).

jugs. Female breasts: low Australian: since ca. 1920. Ex '*jugs* of milk'.

juice, n., 4, in *Dict.* Also, dampness on, or of, a playing-field or a court: Charterhouse: C. 20.

juice, on the, adv. and adj. 'Running on electrified lines' (*Railway*): railwaymen's (esp. L.T.E.): since ca. 1955. Cf. juice, n., 6, on p. 446.

Juice, the. The North Sea: R.A.F. (aircrews'): since 1939. H. & P. Contrast *the Gravy*.

juice joint. A stand where refreshments are sold: Canadian carnival s.: C. 20.

juice money. Extra money paid for working on an electrified line: railwaymen's: since ca. 1920. Ex **juice**, n., 6 (p. 446).

juicy. (Of targets) either easy or profitable: artillerymen's: since ca. 1940. (P-G-R.)

juicy about. Aware of: Australian: since ca. 1925. B., 1942.

juke(-)box. An automatic record gramophone-player: adopted in 1945 from U.S.—2. See **jute box.** Sense 1 'applies only to coin-operated record-players' (B.P.).

Jumbo. Lieutenant-General Sir Henry Maitland Wilson: 1939 + (and before that date and rank).

jumbo, 6 (p. 447): esp. a Midland Railway locomotive, and over a longer period. (*Railway.*) —7. The backside: New Zealand: since ca. 1945. Simon Kay, *Sleepers Can Kill*, 1968, '"Parry for the high kick, or you'll land flat on your jumbo sir."' In many persons, the largest part.

jumbo-size, adj. Very large: commercial coll.: since ca. 1950. Notably in advertisements. (Ramsey Spencer, March 1967.)

jumbuck. See **jimbugg** p. 439. (By the way, *jumback* on p. 447 is a misprint.) Partially adopted in New Zealand: *teste* G. B. Lancaster.

jump, n.—6. A journey from one 'stand' to another: circus and fair-ground: late C. 19–20. (Eleanor Smith, *Satan's Circus*, 1931.)

jump, v.—9. To get a free ride on (train, lorry, etc.): Army coll.: C. 20. Short for *jump on to.* —10. To attack suddenly in the air: Air Force: since 1940. Short for *jump on.* (P-G-R.)—11. To understand, to deduce: Australian: since ca. 1910. (B., 1943.)—12. To forestall: cf. *jump the gun.*

jump, go for a. (Of a girl) sexually compliant or readily available: C. 20. See **jump,** n. and v., in the *Dict.*

jump-down, (p. 447) is, more precisely, Canadian.

jump down a person's throat (p. 447) dates from much earlier: 1806, John Davis, *The Post-Captain.* (Moe.)

jump off the dock. (Of a man) to get married: Naval: C. 20. Granville. Suicidal.

jump on (or **upon**) is also used as = punish severely; *jump down a person's throat* occ. = to snap at him: from the 1880's.

jump on the bandwagon. See **bandwagon** . . . above.

jump on the binders. To apply one's brakes: Canadian (and American) Services: since 1939. H. & P. Agricultural.—2. Hence, to brake hard: Air Force: since ca. 1940. (P-G-R.)

jump-out, the. The beginning: Australian: C. 20. B., 1942. Ex sport.

jump out (of) the window(s). To make a parachute descent from an aircraft: R.A.F.: since 1939. Allan A. Michie & Isabel Waitt in *The Reader's Digest*, Feb. 1941 (*jump out the windows*); Eric Partridge in *The New Statesman*, Sept. 19, 1942 (*jump out of the window*).

jump-rope, n. and v. A skipping-rope; to use one: Canadian coll.: adopted, ca. 1950, ex U.S. (Leechman.)

jump the gun. To be premature, act—esp., to publish 'news'—prematurely: journalistic: since ca. 1920. Ex athletics.

jump the queue. To get ahead of one's turn: coll.: since ca. 1943. Ex:—2. To cheat for a place in a queue: coll.: since 1940.

jump-up, n. 'A mixture of flour and water boiled into a paste with sugar added': Australian outback: since ca. 1910. (B., 1943.)

jumper, 7 (p. 447), is also a crude sled and, as Canadian, probably goes back to ca. 1830 or 1840; Mathews, *Americanisms*, records it for 1823.—8. A flea: ca. 1810–60. David Carey, *Life in Paris*,

1822.—9. A travelling ticket-collector: railwaymen's: since ca. 1920. *Railway*, 3rd.

jumping, adj. See 'Jazz Slang'. But by ca. 1960, also fairly gen. s., as in Zoe Progl, *Woman of the Underworld*, 1964, 'By the time I arrived the place was jumping.'

jumping Jinny. A mechanical stamper used in road-repairing: workmen's: from ca. 1920. *The Evening News*, Dec. 7, 1936.

jumping over the fat-pot. A stipulation that all players should assist in the old-fashioned pantomime, *The Man in the Moon*: theatrical of ca. 1830–80. B. & L. Ex flame from burning fat in the days before gas was in gen. use for lighting.

jumps.—4. (Cf. sense 2.) Excitement; craze: ca. 1885–1900. B. & L. 'He's got the Jubilee jumps.'

junc. Junction: transport-workers': late C. 19–20. E.g. *Clapham Junc.* Clarence Rook, *London Side-Lights*, 1908.

jungle. See 'Prisoner-of-War Slang', 10.

jungle. Wild, untamed; hence, rarely, angry: Army in Burma and India: 1942–5.

jungle juice. African rum: Liverpool: since ca. 1920.—2. Hence, any cheap, strong liquor: Services: 1939–45.

jungle telegraph, the. The way in which gossip and rumours are disseminated by men and women in public-houses: disparaging and jocular: since late 1940's. Ex preceding entry. (A. B. Petch, April 1966.)

jungle-wireless. Inside information; a rumour: Army: 1940 +. Cf. **latrine rumour** (*Dict.*) and **bamboo.** Also *jungle-telephone* (P-G-R).

junior Nelson. A Lieutenant-Commander: Naval (lower-deck): C. 20. Granville.

junior wolf. See 'Canadian . . .'.

junk.—3. Perique tobacco: Naval: C. 20. *The Weekly Telegraph*, Sept. 13, 1941.—4. Opium: Canadian drug-addicts': adopted, ca. 1925, ex U.S.; by 1930, also English—5. Any narcotic; narcotics in general: drug addicts': adopted, ca. 1945, ex U.S.

junker. 'A low four-wheeled vehicle used for transporting logs' (B., 1942): Australian coll.: C. 20. Ex *junk*, unvaluable stuff.

junket around. To waste time, play the fool: Australian coll.: C. 20. Baker.

junket bosun. A ship's steward: Naval: since ca. 1910. Granville.

junky, n. A drug addict: (esp. teenage) drug addicts': adopted, ca. 1955, ex U.S.

junky, adj. Pertaining to narcotics: drug addicts': since ca. 1950. Ex **junk,** n., 5, above.

jupper. Sexually 'up her': low Australian rhyming s. (rare): since ca. 1930. Cf. **skinner,** 8.

just as I feared. A beard: theatrical rhyming s.: C. 20. Franklyn, *Rhyming*.

just come up. Inexperienced, stupid: C. 20. '"Don't come that old caper on me. I ain't just come up,"' James Curtis, *You're in the Racket Too*, 1937. Ex plants very recently come up above the ground: green. But, among Londoners, it means 'just come up from the country for the day'.

just escaped, e.g. **he's.** A c.p., applied to someone who is acting strangely: C. 20. (From a lunatic asylum.)

just fancy that! A c.p., inviting the other party

either to admire, or to be astonished by, something or other: C. 20.

just my handwriting! A c.p.=I can do that very easily; that's 'right up my street': since ca. 1930.

just one of those things, it's or **it was.** A c.p., applied to something there's no explaining, or to something that, although inexplicable, simply has to happen: since the late 1930's. Nevil Shute, *The Chequer Board*, 1947, 'It wasn't his fault he got taken by the Japs. It was just one of those things.' This was the title of a Cole Porter song extremely popular in the 1930's.

just quietly (p. 448). In Australia, it = Just you and I. (B., 1942.)

just the job. Precisely what I need or wish: Services: since ca. 1935. H. & P.

just the job for my brother from Gozo. Try to get someone else; not for me: Naval: ca. 1860–1914. *Gozo*, one of the Maltese islands; many Maltese employed by Navy.

just the shiner. Precisely what was, is, needed: Australian: since ca. 1920. Baker.

just the shining. Perfect; a synonym of, and commoner than, the preceding. (B., 1943.)

just the shot. Exactly what is needed: Australian: since ca. 1918. (Jon Cleary, *Back of Sunset*, 1959.)

justass (p. 448) occurs earlier in Captain Alex. Smith, *The Life of Jonathan Wild*, 1726.

justice of the peace. See 'Tavern terms', § 4 (near end).

jute box or **jukebox.** A player-piano or pianola: Naval: since ca. 1916. Granville. Adopted from U.S.

juve. Juvenile; hence, a juvenile part or act: theatrical and music-halls': late C. 19–20. '"Trev's accustomed to leading child-juves"': Ngaio Marsh, *Death at the Dolphin*, 1967.

juvenile John. An actor of juvenile parts: theatrical: C. 20. (Communicated by Wilfred Granville, April 14, 1948.)

jyro. Horse-play; rough treatment: Cockneys': C. 20. Pugh, '"I'll prong yer!" she says. Then I give her a bit of jyro, till she squealed and bash'd my 'at in.' Origin? Prob. the same word (Cockney pronunciation) as **jaro** (*Dict.*) and cognate with dial, *jart*, to whip, or S.E. *jar*, a quarrel.

K

K. See entry **C-K-M-D.**

K.A. is a coll. shortening of H.M.S. *King Alfred*, Granville. See **Incubator.**—2. A 'know-all': Australian: since ca. 1950. (B.P.)

K Block. A building, a wing, a ward set aside for the (temporarily) insane: Naval: since ca. 1935. H. & P. I.e. for the **knuts** (*Dict.*) in the **nuthouse** (Addenda).

k.d. or **K.D.!** Say nothing about it!: printers' c.p.: from ca. 1860. B. & L. I.e. keep it dark.

K.G. *C*ommon Jew: 'used by "better-class" Jews. I first heard it ca. 1933' (Julian Franklyn). A pun on *K*night of the *G*arter.

K.G.V. See **Kay Gee Five.**

K.P. King's Parade: Cambridge undergraduates' coll.: since ca. 1880.—2. A common *p*rostitute: Australian low s.: since ca. 1945. (B., 1953.)

'k you (pron. *kwew*)! Thank you!: slovenly, not slangy: late (? mid) C. 19–20: not only Australian, although Mark Twain noted it while he was in the State of Victoria. (B.P.)

kadoova, off one's. Insane: New South Welsh: ca. 1870–1910. B. & L. Ex Aborigine.

kady. See **cady** (*Dict.*).

kaffir derives ex Arabic *kafir*, an infidel.

kaffir truck. 'General name for trade goods,' Archer Russell, *Gone Nomad*, 1936: Central and South African coll.: since ca. 1890.

kafuffle. A variant of *gefuffle*.

kag(g), n. and v. See **cag.**—2. (Only *kag*.) Tank crew's equipment and rations stored on the side of a tank: Army in Burma: 1943 +.

kahsi. Rectum; esp. in *up your kahsi!*, a gratuitous, usually humorous c.p., mostly on meeting or parting: Services': since ca. 1940.

kaifa. A girl, a woman, regarded sexually: R.A.F. in the Near and Middle East: since ca. 1930. Perhaps Hebrew via Yiddish.

kai-kai (p. 449) is also used in the simple form *kai* and, both, by Australian soldiers too.

Kaiser's War, the. The War of 1914–18: coll.: since ca. 1945. An avoidance of such question-begging labels as 'The Great War' and 'The First World War'.

Kal. See **Cool.**

kailed up, get. To become drunk: from ca. 1927. As though *alcoholied*. Perhaps cf. **canned**; note also **alc**, q.v.

kaloss. Finished: Australian and New Zealand troops in North Africa: 1940–2. Arabic word.

kanakas. Testicles: low Australian: C. 20. A pun on **knackers**, 1 (p. 459) and *Kanakas*, who formerly used to do the hard work on the sugar-cane fields.

kana(-)man. An artilleryman: pidgin: mid-C. 19–20. B. & L. Lit., cannon man.

kanga.—2. Short for:

kangaroo.—5. 'Harry was a Jew. In his own phrase: a "tin lid". Otherwise, a "four-by-two", a "kangaroo", or a "five-to-two",' Michael Harrison, *Reported Safe Arrival*, 1943: rhyming s.: since ca. 1930. *The Leader*, Jan. 1939.—6. A prison warder: rhyming s. (on *screw*), orig. and still mainly c.: since ca. 1920. Often shortened to *kanga* (*Underworld*, 2nd edn, 1961.)

kangaroo it. To have a 'kangaroo shit' (see next): Australian: since ca. 1920.—2. To make a *kangaroo start* in a car: Australian: since ca. 1946. 'A *k.s.* is caused by a faulty clutch or bad technique. The car shudders and moves off jerkily': itself Australian s.: since late 1930's. (B.P.)

kangaroo shit. A defecation from the haunch-sitting position: Australian: C. 20. B., 1942. —6. A pneumatic drill: labourers': since ca. 1935. It was soon shortened to *kanga*, which, indeed, has been predominant since ca. 1950. It's always jumping.—7. Mostly in pl. *kangaroos*, wild young cattle: Australian rural: since ca. 1920. (B., 1943.) They're always rushing and leaping.—8. A prison warder: Australian c.: since ca. 1925. (B., 1953.) Rhyming on *screw*, n., 2. Often shortened to *kanga*.

Kangaroo Valley. Earl's Court (London), an area popular among Australian expatriates: since ca. 1950. 'There is a Kangaroo Valley in N.S.W., but the term was probably coined by a newspaper.' (B.P.)

kangarooer; kangarooing. A kangaroo-hunter; kangaroo-hunting: Australian coll.: C. 20. (B., 1943.)

kangaroos in one's top paddock, have. To be crazy or very silly: Australian rural: since ca. 1910. Baker.

kangarooster. An eccentric—or very amusing —fellow: Australian: since ca. 1920. Baker.

kanker. A corruption of **kanga** (esp. in sense 2).

kaput (p. 449) was, in 1945, revived among soldiers and airmen serving in Germany.

Kate and Sydney. A steak-and-kidney pudding: rhyming s.: from ca. 1880. (W. L. George, *The Making of an Englishman*, 1914.)

Kate Karney (p. 449). Or *Carney*: in the 1890's there was a very popular comedienne named Kate Carney. *Three Pots a Shilling* was one of her songs (F. W. Thomas). Often shortened, esp. among World War II soldiers, to *Kate*, as in 'He's in the Kate'. Franklyn 2nd.

*kath (p. 449). Also Australian. B., 1942. Cf. **Kathleen Mavourneen system** (p. 449).

*Kathleen Maroon. A three-years' prison-sentence: Australian c.: C. 20. Baker. A corruption of sense 2 of:

*Kathleen Mavourneen (often corrupted to *Mavoureen*). An habitual criminal: Australian c.: since ca. 1910. For origin, see **Eiley Mavourneen.**—2. An indeterminate gaol-sentence: Australian: since ca. 1918. (B., 1943.) Cf. *kath*, 1

(p. 449).—3. Morning: (imperfect) rhyming s.: C. 20. Lester.

Kay Gee Five; usually written *K.G.V.* H.M.S. *King George the Fifth*: Naval: World War II. (P-G-R.)

keb. A cab: Cockney sol.: mid-C. 19–20. (Anstey, *Voces Populi*, I, 1890.)

kecks is the Liverpool shape (C. 19–20) of *kicks*, trousers (p. 453). Hence the 'camp' *punch up the kecks*; C. 20.

keel the goods. 'To code consigned goods for loading' (*Railway*, 3rd): railwaymen's: C. 20. Ex Sc. dial. *keel*, to mark with ruddle (E.D.D.).

Keeley. A water-can for cooling heated bearings: Canadian railroadmen's (— 1931). Ex the Keeley cure for drunkenness.

keen. Excellent; highly desirable: Canadian, esp. teenagers': adopted, ca. 1955, ex U.S. 'Seen Tom's new girl? Boy, is she ever keen!' (Leechman.)

keep a ten. To get back into college or one's rooms before 10 p.m., when fines start being levied at some colleges: Cambridge University: from ca. 1885.

keep a week than a fortnight. See **week than a fortnight.**

keep down. To retain, hold (a job) against difficulties: Australian coll.: C. 20. B., 1942. Variant of the S.E. *hold down.*

keep for a week . . . See **week than a fortnight.**

keep him (or it) in—he'll get pecking if let out. A low, ? mostly North Country, c.p., addressed to a man with his trousers-flap open: late C. 19–20. a pun on *cock.*

keep it. To pay heed: coll.: C. 20. Humfrey Jordan *Sea Way Only*, 1937. Ex *keep it in mind.*

keep it on the island! Keep the ball in play: Association Football spectators': from ca. 1895. 'That monotonous "Keep it on the island" when the ball is banged into the grand-stand to clear a dangerous position . . . I am told it was born on Whale Island, Portsmouth, back in the 90's, when teams of H.M.S. "Excellent" played on the officers' lawn. A lapse by the defenders resulted in the ball ending in the ferry, to loud yells of "Keep it on the island"' (Frank Butler, *Daily Express*, Jan. 17, 1944.)

keep nit (p. 450). Rather, late C. 19–20. A much earlier example occurs in Edward Dyson, *The Gold Stealers*, 1901.

Keep Off Young Ladies' Insides and, by reversion, **I Love You Only, Kid.** Punning nicknames of the *King's Own Yorkshire Light Infantry*: Army: since ca. 1910.

keep one's appointment, to be unable to—or **cannot.** To fail to come-to in time: pugilistic: ca. 1810–60. Anon., *Every Night Book*, 1827.

keep one's end up. To 'do one's bit': Australian coll.: since ca. 1925. (B., 1943.) Ex cricket.—2. Among Londoners, esp. Cockneys, it has a double meaning when the phrase is used by a man seeing a fellow out with yet another girl; thus, 'Keeps 'is end up, don't 'e!': since ca. 1910. Able to keep rising to the occasion.

keep one's (or the) eye down. To keep one's head down; to watch oneself, take care: Guardsmen's since ca. 1915.

keep (one's) fingers crossed. To 'pray' for success or merely to avert defeat or failure: coll.: C. 20, but, to me at least, uncommon before ca.

1925. A layman's modification of the ecclesiastical sign of the Cross.

keep one's lip buttoned. To maintain silence; to tell nothing: Cockney: since ca. 1910. Gerald Kersh, *Night and the City*, 1938, 'Pay, and I'll keep my lip buttoned.' Cf. **button your flap!**

keep one's tache on. See **tache on, keep one's.**

keep one's (or the) tail clear. (Of a pilot or his 'plane) to stay out of the sights of an enemy aircraft: R.A.F.: since 1939. Berrey.—2. Hence (?), to prevent a rear attack: 1940 +. Partridge, 1945.

keep (one's) wig cool. To remain calm: orig. legal, but soon gen.: since ca. 1910.

keep out of the rain. To avoid, evade trouble: Australian coll.: late C. 19–20. Baker.

keep sloom. To keep quiet: stock-cutting tailors': from ca. 1870. B. & L. Here, *sloom* is slumber; it is now Scottish, when not Northern dial, but was once S.E.

keep strum! Keep quiet: since ca. 1950. (I.T.V., Nov. 12, 1963.)

keep tabs on. To observe (someone) long and closely, in order to see what he's up to or how he's getting on: coll.: adopted, ca. 1958, ex Canada, which adopted it, ca. 1909 (Leechman), ex U.S. The U.S. phrase originally meant to keep a (tabulated) list of, e.g., winnings and losses, cards in and out, etc. (See esp. Mitford M. Mathews, *A Dict. of Americanisms*.) The phrase, however, was used 'in Cambridge ca. 1925 among fellow-undergraduates from Manchester Grammar School' (H. R. Spencer).

keep that in! That's worth repeating: theatrical c.p.: since ca. 1910. Ex the producer's instruction to an actor to retain in the script a spontaneous gag uttered at rehearsal.

keep the ball rolling. To keep things going: coll.: since ca. 1910. Ex Association football.

keep the line. To behave becomingly, decently: ca. 1815–50. Pierce Egan, *London*, 1821.

***keep the obs (or obbs) on** (someone). To keep under observation: since ca. 1945: c. >, by ca. 1950, also police s.

keep the party clean! No dirty stories or loose behaviour, please!: c.p.: since ca. 1930. A correspondent sends me this gloss:— But often does not quite mean it. '"Give me my hat and knickers," she said. "I thought you were going to keep the party clean."'

keep up one's end or **keep one's end up.** To do one's duty, one's share: coll.: C. 20. Ex cricket.

keep up one's frock. To keep (information, plan, etc.) secret: mostly Services (esp. Army): since ca. 1930. (P-G-R.)

keep up with the Joneses. To hold one's own in 'the rat race' of survival at a decent level: coll.: since ca. 1950.

keep your nose clean! A c.p. addressed—usually on parting—to a person one is warning to (1) keep out of trouble and, derivatively, (2) mind his own business: since ca. 1925 (within my own knowledge), at least.

keep your pecker up! Keep your spirits up: since ca. 1840. See **pecker**, 2 (p. 613).

keep your shirt on! Don't lose your temper!: Australian and New Zealand c.p.: C. 20. (B.P.)

keep yow. To keep watch: low Australian: since ca. 1925. (B., 1943.) Perhaps cf. *yowlie* (p. 973).—2. Hence, to act as an observer: Australian airmen's: 1939–45. (B., 1943.)

keeping, be on one's. 'A man is *on his keeping* when he is hiding away from the police, who are on his track for some offence' (P. W. Joyce, *English . . . in Ireland*, 1910): late C. 19–20. Elliptical for 'keeping out of the way'.

keeping the pot boiling; winding the chain. In R. W. Vanderkiste, *A Six Years' Mission among the Dens of London*, 1852, these two proletarian phrases are explained thus, 'They ran up stairs, jumped out of the window, up stairs again, and so on—called by them "Winding the chain", and "Keeping the pot boiling",—hordes of ruffians—men and boys': ca. 1830–80.

keet. A parakeet: Australian coll.: since ca. 1860. Archer Russell, *Gone Nomad*, 1936.

Kelly. A crow: Australian: C. 20. B., 1942. —2. An axe: Australian: Baker, '"On the kelly", engaged in axe work'. Ex a famous axeman. '*Kelly* is reputed to be from the name of a manufacturer of axes, rather than from that of an axeman' (B.P.).—3. A ticket inspector on the buses: Australian: since ca. 1945. Barry Prentice offers four possible origins: Ned Kelly; 'because often Irish'; *Kelly*, a 'crow' in its c. sense 'a spy'; and *Kelly*, axe: the 1st is vastly improbable; the 4th, unlikely; the 2nd, slightly more probable than the 3rd.

Kelly Gang. See **Ned Kelly**.

Kelly's legs. A C. 20, esp. military, variant of **legs eleven** (*Dict.*) in the game of House.

kelp. Hard-earned money; wages: workmen's: late C. 19–20. Opp. **bunce**, money for overtime work. Ex *kelp*, large seaweed.

ken.—2. Disraeli in *Venetia* uses it as = bed; this is almost certainly an error.—3. A boat: mostly Romany: C. 20. Ex sense 1 (p. 451)—perhaps via 'house-boat'.

Kennedy rot. Land scurvy: Aus. coll.: ca. 1850–1930. B., 1959.

kennetseeno. Earlier in Mayhew, I, 1851.

Kennington Lane. Pain: rhyming s.: C. 20. Franklyn 2nd.

keno. Lotto ('housey-housey'): Army: C. 20. Origin?

Kensington High (School). The University of New South Wales in the days when its name was the N.S.W. University of Technology (founded in 1949): Sydneysiders', esp. University of Sydney undergraduates'. Perhaps ex Kensington High School, London. (With thanks to Mr David Holloway.)

Kensingtons, the (p. 451). Earlier: at least as early as 1909.

Kenso. Kensington race-course, Sydney: Australian sporting: C. 20. B., 1942.

Kentish Town. An occ. variant of **Camden Town** (p. 122). Franklyn 2nd.

kept on the jump. See **in the firing line**.

kerb boy. A vendor of combs, elastic and other such things: London-street coll.: C. 20.

kerb-crawling, n. and adj. Looking out for a street prostitute: since ca. 1925.

Kerb Market, the. Very frequent for **Street, the** (p. 839).

kerbstone jockey. See **curbstone jockey**.

kerbstone mixture (or with capitals). Such tobacco for pipe or cigarettes as has been made up from fag-ends: C. 20. For sale among the very poor. Cf. *O.P.B.*

kerdoying or **gerdoying!** Crash!; wallop!: Air Force: 1939 +. 'He was cruising along, when —gerdoying!—he suddenly crashed.' (Communicated by S/Ldr H. E. Bates in Feb. 1945.) Echoic; cf. **kerdumf!** Sgt Gerald Emanuel, letter of March 29, 1945, notes the phonetic variant—the more exact form—*kerdoink* and defines the term 'interjection to indicate crash of aircraft, etc.' Cf. the Canadian *boing!* Often contracted to *kerdoing* or *kerdoink*.

kerdumf! Exclamation of surprise, amazement, etc.: R.A.F.: since ca. 1938. Jackson. 'Its origin is the crump of a crash-landed aircraft. Sometimes used as a verb, meaning to crash into' (Cf. **prang**, v.).

kerfuffle is perhaps commoner than **gefuffle**.

kero. Kerosene: Australian: since ca. 1920. (B.P.)—2. Beer: Australian: jocular: since ca. 1930. Xavier Herbert, *Capricornia*, 1939.

kerplunk, adv. Slap-bang: Australian: adopted, ca. 1944, ex U.S. (B.P.) Echoic.

kerr'b. To hit, strike, punch: Shelta: C. 19–20. B. & L.

kerridge. A carriage: Cockneys' sol.: C. 19–20. (Anstey, *Voces Populi*, II, 1892.)

ketchup. Beer: Australian: C. 20. Baker. Ex colour.

kettle.—4. See **cloak**, n., 4.—5. A locomotive: Canadian railroadmen's (— 1931).—6. A wristwatch: since ca. 1920: c. >, by 1930, fairground s. (Robin Cook, 1962.) A specialization of sense 3 on p. 452.

kettle brandy. 'Scandal water', i.e. tea: ca. 1870–1910. B. & L.

kettle on the hob; often shortened to *kettle*. A shilling: rhyming s. (on *bob*): late C. 19–20.—2. The pet-name *Bob*: rhyming s.: C. 20. Only very rarely the full term. Franklyn 2nd.

kettledrum (p. 452) goes back at least as far as 1850.

*key, n.—3. An habitual criminal: Australian c.: C. 20. B., 1942. To the police he is a 'key' suspect.—4. Detention under the Habitual Criminals Act (1905); hence, *key(-)man*, a prisoner under this Act: Aus. c.: since ca. 1910. B., 1959.

key-basher. A wireless-telegraphy operator: Army: 1939 +.

key of the door. In Bingo: 21. Since ca. 1955. Ex receiving key on one's 21st birthday. See **Little Jimmy**, near end.

keyholing, n. A singing, and a playing of musical instruments, at public-house doors: since ca. 1950. Laurie Atkinson notes having heard it in 1961.

Khaki Marines, the. The Royal Marine Commandos: Naval: 1940–5. (P-G-R.)

khaki patch. An Indian Army term, dating from the 1880's; thus in Richards: 'From our meat rations a small steak was cut for each man's breakfast. These steaks were called khaki patches, and a man's jaws would ache for hours after he had masticated one of them.' Since ca. 1940, merely historical.

khaloss. Exhausted; finished; dead: Australian soldiers in Palestine and North Africa: 1940–2. Lawson Glassop, *We Were the Rats*, 1944. Arabic.

khorosho is the more correct form of the **xaroshie** of the *Dict.*, for it is an adequate transliteration of the Russian word.

Khyber Pass. Glass: rhyming: since ca. 1885. Often merely *Khyber*.—2. Backside: late C. 19–20. Michael Harrison, *Reported Safe Arrival*, 1943,

'"Not knowin' wevver they was on their 'eads or their kybers."' Almost invariably in shorter form. Rhyming, of course, on *arse*.

kibitz, v. i. Corresponding to **kibitzer:** adopted ca. 1962 ex U.S. 'The Yiddish word "kibitz" is a valuable import because it has no equivalent in English': Anthony Lejeune in *The Daily Telegraph*, colour supplement, March 10, 1967.

kibitzer. A watcher, esp. if inquisitive, rather than a participant: adopted, ca. 1960, ex U.S., but not very gen. even by 1966. Ex German *Kibitz*, the lapwing—'the little bird very much an onlooker in life' (Wallace Reyburn in *The Sunday Times*, July 8, 1962).

kibosh (p. 464). Julian Franklyn (author of *The Cockney, A Dictionary of Rhyming Slang, Shield and Crest*) proposes a quite different origin: the heraldic *caboshed* (or *caboched* or *cabossed* or *cabaged* or . . .)—see the O.E.D.—and Scots hunting *caboche* or *cabage* or *cabbage*, to cut off a deer's head close behind the horns. This theory would also explain *cabbage*, n., 1, and v., 1, on p. 118. In short, a theory of considerable merit.

kibosh, n.—4. A prison sentence of 18 months: c.: C. 20. (John Gosling, *The Ghost Squad*, 1959.) Perhaps because it's enough to 'put the *kibosh* on' a man's activities.

kibosh on . . . From Yiddish, but ex Yiddish *kabas, kabbasten*, to suppress (B. & L.).

kick, n.—9. A thrill: coll.: since ca. 1943; adopted ex U.S. servicemen.—10. A trick; a 'line' or 'stunt': low: since ca. 1945. (Norman.) Sense 9: perhaps ex 'just for *kicks*'—see **kicks, just for,** below.

kick, v.—5. To dismiss (a man from a job): Aus.: since ca. 1925. (F. B. Vickers, *First Place to the Stranger*, 1955.)

kick, cramp in the. See **cramp in the kick, have.**

kick, make a. See **make a kick.**

kick a gong or **open up a tin.** To start a quarrel: Naval: since ca. 1910. (Wilfred Granville.)

kick-back. A *sub rosa* payment, esp. as commission on a more or less shady deal: adopted, ca. 1944, ex U.S. (B.P.)—2. That portion of a fee which, in the unethical practice of fee-splitting, is returned (or not collected): adopted, in late 1940's, ex U.S., perhaps via Canada.

kick her into a manœuvre. To take evasive action: R.A.F.: 1940–2. Berrey. Adopted from American airmen.

kick in the pants. (Not *on* as at **thump on the back**, p. 881.) Applied to any grave disappointment or set-back.

kick-off (p. 453). Earlier in *Punch*, Feb. 27, 1875. (O.E.D.)

kick off, v. To die: Aus.: C. 20. (B., 1959.)

kick out of, get a. To find that something is exciting or absorbing: coll.: since ca. 1925. Adopted from drug-addicts?

kick the arse off an emu, able to. Feeling very fit: Australian: C. 20. Baker.

kick-up.—4. A party: Aus.: mostly rural: ? mid C. 19–20; ob. b. 1960. (G. B. Lancaster, *Jim of the Ranges*, 1910.) Ex senses 2 (p. 453).

kick up a lark. To cause a commotion or disturbance: ca. 1810–60. Pierce Egan, 1821.

kick up Bob's-a-dying. To make the devil of a fuss (about something): since ca. 1810 (? earlier): by ca. 1910, ob.—and, by 1945, †. In, e.g., W. N.

Glascock's *Naval Sketch-Book*, 2nd Series, 1834, at II, 142. (Moe.) Cf.:

kick up Meg's devotion. To make a row, cause a disturbance: Naval: late C. 19–20. Some piece of Naval folklore; perhaps also a prompting by *commotion* or a pun on *diversion*.

kick up daisies. A variant (1914–18) of *push up daisies*. Graham Seton, *Pelican Row*, 1935. See **daisy-pushing** (*Dict.*).

kick up the backside. One jeep pushing another out of the mud: Army in Burma: 1942–5. Gerald Hanley, *Monsoon Victory*, 1946.

kick (someone) upstairs. To promote to a higher-sounding, but, in the fact, less important position: since ca. 1950: s. <; by 1965, coll.

kicker, 3 (p. 453). 'Now applied to portable outboard motors for small boats. An "inboard" is . . . a motor permanently installed inside the hull' (Leechman, 1959).—4. A small boy: Milton Junior School, Bulawayo: since ca. 1930. (A. M. Brown, letter of April 15, 1938.)—5. A triple valve that functions eccentrically: Canadian railroadmen's (— 1931).

kicks, just for. Just for the hell of it: adopted, ca. 1955, ex U.S., esp. among office- and shopgirls. (Gilderdale.) Since ca. 1960, often shortened to *for kicks*.

kicks than ha'pence, more (p. 453) has the early variant *more kicks than coppers*: W. N. Glascock, *Naval Sketch-Book* (II, 134), 1826. Moe.

kid, n.—9. A pretty young harlot: white-slavers' c.: C. 20. A. Londres, *The Road to Buenos Ayres*, 1928. Cf. sense 1.
Sense 7 (p. 454), in form *kid*, occurs in W. N. Glascock, *Naval Sketch-Book*, (I, 24), 1825. Moe.

kid, the. One's younger brother or sister; hence adj., as in 'my sister': mostly Cockneys': from ca. 1880.

kid brother or **sister.** One's (however slightly) younger brother or sister: coll.: adopted from U.S. ca. 1925. Cf. Cockney 'one's *kid*'—'brother' or 'sister' understood.

kid the troops; esp. as vbl n., *kidding . . .*, leg-pulling, 'telling the tale': Army: 1914–18 and occ. since.

kid-walloper (p. 454). Also Australian: C. 20. (Vance Palmer, *Golconda*, 1948.)

kidd. A variant (not very gen.) of **kid,** n., esp. sense 2, with the additional sense: swindler.

Kidder. Kidderminster: natives', inhabitants', regionals': mid-C. 19–20. (F. B. Brett Young, *The Far Forest*, 1936.)

kidder from Kidderville. An elaboration of *kidder*, 2 (p. 454): C. 20. (H. A. Vachell, *Quinney's Adventures*, 1924.)

kidderbunk. A youth, a boy: non-cultured: since ca. 1942. Elaboration of **kid,** n., 1 (p. 454).

kid(d)l(e)ywink, 3 (p. 454), needs to be modified. Used for a beerhouse—*any* beerhouse—it occurs as a footnote to p. 58 of G. B. H., *Teetotalism Unmasked*, 1845, in a song sung, at early teetotallers' meetings, to the tune of *Babylon Is Fallen*,

Kidley-winks must fall for ever
  At Teetotallers' powerful sound;
  Public-houses too must quiver,
  Landlords' signboards must come down.

(A note supplied by Mr Peter Fryer.)
—5. A loosely used, humorous word for a place, esp. a building, as in 'a sartain kidlie wink that is

called the "House of Commons"': J. H. Lewis, *The Art of Writing*, 7th ed., 1816. (Moe.)

kiddo (p. 454) is mostly Australian and New Zealand; an example of New Zealand usage occurs in, e.g., Jean Devanney, *Dawn Beloved*, 1928.

kiddy, 1 (p. 454), seems to be rather older—since ca. 1810, to judge by Alfred Burton's *Johnny Newcome*, 1818. (Moe.) Still earlier in J. H. Lewis, *The Art of Writing*, 7th ed., 1816. (Moe.)

kidger. A cadger: low Australian: late C. 19–20. (Ruth Park, *Poor Man's Orange*, 1950.)

Kidman's joy. Treacle: Australian: C. 20. B., 1942. Variation of **cockies' joy** (*Dict.*). The surname of a famous and very wealthy Australian pastoralist. Also known as *Kidman's blood mixture* (B., 1943).

kidney-pie (p. 455). Also Australian. Baker.

kidney punch. A, to, lunch: theatrical rhyming s.: C. 20. (Franklyn, *Rhyming*.)

kidney-wiper. Penis: low: C. 20. Ex a ribald song. Also *kidney-scraper*.

kidstakes. Pretence; nonsense; both, esp. in *cut the kidstakes!*, stop beating round the bush, or stop talking nonsense: Aus.: C. 20. (B., 1959.)

kie. A variant of **kye**.

kiff. Tea, coffee, cocoa: Christ's Hospital: since ca. 1870. Marples. Cf. **kiff, all** on p. 455.

kike. A Jew: low: adopted, ca. 1935, ex U.S. (Raymond Postgate, *Verdict of Twelve*, 1940.)—2. A cheque: c.: since ca. 1950. Bournemouth *Evening Echo*, April 20, 1966. Problematically: *cheque > chike > kike*.

kiko. To say so: low: C. 20. R. Llewellyn, *None But the Lonely Heart*, 1943. "'I should bloody kiko," says Slush. . . . "He's the Smasher, he is."' Rhyming on *sye* (Cockney for 'say') *so*. It is a Cockney alternative spelling of **cocoa** (p. 167). Franklyn, *Rhyming*.

Kildare, the. 'A major operation, with full outfit, masks, white overalls, etc. "Will it be a major op?"—"Yes, at 19.30 to-morrow; the full Kildare." Ex the T.V. programme *Dr Kildare*, a medical feature' (Wilfred Granville, March 17, 1967): medical: since ca. 1963.

kiley. A two-up 'kip': Australian: since ca. 1920. (B., 1943.) Ex the Aboriginal *kiley*, a boomerang.

kill, v.—3. (Gen, as p.ppl.) To ruin (a garment): tailors': mid-C. 19–20. Whence the n.—4. (Ex 2.) To get rid of: cinema: since ca. 1930. *The Evening News*, Nov. 7, 1939.—5. To destroy (aircraft or tanks); hence as n.: R.A.F. and Army coll.: World War II. (P-G-R.)

kill a snake. To 'see a man about a dog': Australian: C. 20. B., 1942. With a pun on *penis erectus*.

kill cobbler. Gin: ca. 1715–60. Anon., *The Quaker's Opera*, 1728. Contrast **kill grief**, below.

kill-cow.—3. An arrant boaster: lowest classes': C. 19–20: ob. B. & L.

kill grief. Some kind of strong liquor, prob. rum (cf. **kill-devil**: p. 455), fashionable in the 1720's. Anon., *The Quaker's Opera*, 1728.

kill-me-quick. 'We sat down to a dinner of rice, tinned meat, "kill-me-quicks" (a sort of fritter), jam, and tea' (Alex. Macdonald, *In the Land of Pearl and Gold*, 1907): Aus.: ca. 1880–1920.

kill the widow. 'As young journalists, we were horrified on being told to: "Kill that widow in

column three." (Don't be frightened—it merely meant "Alter the spacing so that there isn't a word all by itself in one line")': *Woman*, Dec. 19, 1964. Journalistic s.: C. 20.

Killarney is a synonym, more gen. as n. (madman) than as adj., of **lakes**, q.v. in *Dict.*, and likewise an abbr.: C. 20. Margery Allingham, *Flowers for the Judge*, 1936.

Killer. The Australian 'inevitable nickname' of all men named Caldwell: since ca. 1945. Ex 'Killer' Caldwell, famous war 'ace' of World War II. (B.P.)

killer. A 'lady-killer', as in 'He was a killer with the sheilas' (Dick): Australian: since ca. 1925.—2. (Also *whispering death*.) 'A Diesel unit' (*Railway*): railwaymen's: since ca. 1955. Ex its stealthy approach.—3. 'The final action or argument which means the end to whatever hopes have been held' (B., 1959): Aus.: since ca. 1945.

killerdiller. A wildly good time: beatniks' and teenagers': adopted and adapted, ca. 1959, ex U.S. s. *killerdiller*, any remarkable or attractive or successful thing or person or occasion (Wentworth & Flexner). A reduplication of *killer*.

killers.—2. 'Sheep for station mutton' (B., 1942): Australian coll.: late C. 19–20.

killick.—2. Hence, a Leading Hand: Naval: since ca. 1905. H. & P.; Granville, 'All wear the anchor as a badge of rank': cf. **props**.

killick scribe. A Leading Writer: Naval: since ca. 1900. Ex prec.

killing, make a. To win substantially from the bookmakers: Australian sporting: since ca. 1919. Baker. Also *make a kill*, current in English too.

killing a snake? A jocular golfing c.p., addressed to players taking many strokes in a sandtrap: Canadian: since ca. 1930.

killing match. A fierce battle: Army: 1940–5. (P-G-R.)

killings. 'The offals and heads of the animals killed for homestead use' (Jean Devanney, *Travels in North Queensland*, 1951): Australian cattlemen's and farmers' coll.: late C. 19–20.

***kilos,** 17* or *18* or *20*, etc. (Girls) aged 17 or 18 or 20, etc.: white-slavers' c.: C. 20. A. Londres, *The Road to Buenos Ayres*, 1928.

Kilroy was here. This c.p., which arose, early in World War II, as if by magic, was written on walls, etc., everywhere the British and American soldiers fought or were stationed. No satisfactory explanation has ever been made; hundreds have been suggested.

But the *San Francisco Chronicle* of Dec. 2, 1962 printed a short 'feature', *Kilroy Was Here*, in which a credible origin is proposed:

'Two days before the Japanese attack on Pearl Harbor, an unimposing, bespectacled, 39-year-old man took a job with a Bethlehem Steel Company shipyard in Quincy, Mass.

'As an inspector . . ., James J. Kilroy began making his mark on equipment to show test gangs he had checked a job. The mark: "Kilroy was here."

'Soon the words caught on at the shipyard, and Kilroy began finding the slogan written all over the installation.

'Before long, the phrase spread far beyond the bounds of the yard, and Kilroy—coupled with the sketch of a man, or at least his nose peering over a wall—became one of the most famous names of World War II.

'When the war ended, a nation-wide contest to discover the real Kilroy found him still employed at the shipyard.

'And last week, James Kilroy . . . died in Boston's Peter Bent Brigham Hospital, at the age of 60.'

(The cutting was passed to me by John Moore, author of *You English Words* and distinguished novelist, who had received it from an American admirer.)

kilted brickie (or **-y**). See **whistler, 9**.

kilter (p. 455) is also predominant in Canada. (Leechman.)

kilts, the. Kilted soldiers, esp. Highlanders: military coll.: C. 19. Wm Maginn, *Tales of Military Life*, 1829, at III, 250. Cf. **kiltie** on p. 455. (Moe.)

kilwack. 'A derogatory term for mixed European and Asian blood' (S. H. Ward): Royal Sussex Regiment: C. 20. *The Roussilon Gazette*, April 1911.

Kimberley. See **puff and dart**.

***kinchin lay**, according to the evidence of Pugh (2)—see quotation at **not much frocks**—was still extant in 1906.

kind. Friendly: North Country children's coll.: late C. 19–20. 'Are you kind again?'

kinder.—3. A kindergarten class in a school, but not a kindergarten itself: Australian: since ca. 1950.—2. Hence, a child in such a class: since ca. 1955. (B.P.)

kindness!, all done by. An ironical c.p.: C. 20. W. L. George, *The Making of an Englishman*, 1914.

kindness to, do a. To coït with (a girl): late C. 19–20: low Scottish >, ca. 1930, Society—esp. London Society.

King, 2 (p. 456). Hence, in the Services, the person in charge: e.g. *jankers king*: Regular Army: prob. since ca. 1910; in the R.A.F., since ca. 1920.—4. 'Someone who is good at a particular thing, e.g. Met king, Navigation king,' Robert Hinde, letter of March 17, 1945: R.A.F.: since ca. 1925.—5. Occ. a yardmaster but usually a freight-train conductor: Canadian railroadmen's (— 1931). Ex sense 2?—6. The leader of a *push* (or gang) of larrikins: Australian urban: ca. 1890–1940. (B., 1953.)

king, adj. Super-eminent or excellent: coll.: C. 20. See several phrases below.

King, The. The National Anthem: British Armed Forces' officers' coll.: C. 20. Now, of course, *the Queen*.

King Death. Breath: rhyming s.: mid-C. 19–20. In C. 20 only in abbr. form, *king*. Clarence Rook, *London Side-Lights*, 1908.

King Dick.—3. A leader, boss, overseer: Australian: C. 20. B., 1942.

King Dicky. A bricklayer: builders' rhyming s. (on *bricky*): C. 20. Franklyn 2nd.

king duck. See **golden duck** above.

king hit. As for prec.—2. A knock-out-blow: Australian sporting coll.: C. 20. Baker.

king-hit, v. To knock (someone) out with a punch: Aus. coll.: since ca. 1920. Jock Marshall & Russell Drysdale, *Journey among Men*, 1962 (p. 34).

king-hit merchant. A brawler; a bully: Aus-

tralian: C. 20. Lawson Glassop, *We Were the Rats*, 1944. Ex prec. Also *king-hit artist*: B., 1959.

king kong. A drink of methylated spirits mixed with lavender water: beatniks': since ca. 1959. (Anderson.) Deadly; ex the film *King Kong*.

King Lear.—2. Homosexual: rhyming s. on *queer*: since ca. 1940. Franklyn, *Rhyming*.

King Parnee is a late C. 19–20 showmen's variant of **parnee**, 2 (*Dict.*). *John o' London's Weekly*, March 19, 1937.

king-pin, the.—2. Airman in charge of a ground-crew gang: R.A.F.: since ca. 1940. Ex 1.

king pippin. An important, usually the most important, person; since ca. 1910. Cf. **king pin** (p. 456).

king-size. Very large: Australian: since ca. 1920, Canadian since ca. 1930, English since ca. 1945: by 1950, coll. (B.P.)

King Street Run, the. A tie awarded to those who successfully drink a pint of beer in each of the eight public-houses in King Street, without any form of physical relief and within two hours; a competition held twice a term and supposed to have been instituted by Ted Dexter; present record (D. F. Wharton tells me on Oct. 24, 1965), 28 minutes: Cambridge undergraduates': since early 1950's.

kingdom come. Rum (the drink): rhyming s.: C. 20. Lester.

kings (singular rare). Drivers: railwaymen's ironic: since ca. 1945. (*Railway* 2nd.)

King's Bench. A ship's galley: Naval: ca. 1790–1860. W. N. Glascock, *Sailors and Saints* (I, 130), 1829. Cf. **King's-Bencher** on p. 456 and the next entry.

King's Bench debater. A 'sea lawyer': Naval: ca. 1810–60. Captain Glascock. Cf. **King's Bencher** (*Dict.*).

King's Bencher (p. 456) goes back to late C. 18. (W. N. Glascock, *Sketch-Book*, II, 1826). Moe.

King's English, clip the (p. 456). In *The New-England Courant*, Sept. 10, 1722, Benjamin Franklin uses it for being drunk. (Moe.)

King's ex! Canadian equivalent (ca. 1918–40) of E. **fainits** (p. 263).

King's hard bargain (p. 456) goes right back to 1818 (Alfred Burton, *Johnny Newcome*). Moe. Also in Fredk Marryat, *Frank Mildmay*, 1829 (p. 350 of the 1897 edition). Moe.

kings on the roof; kings up. A pair of kings and a lower pair: Australian poker-players': C. 20. (B., 1953.)

King's Own Schneiders, the. In Viscount Samuel's delightful memoir *The Horseback Zionist* (published late in 1967 or early in 1968) we read, 'In the summer of 1918 . . . Dr. Weizmann returned to England and I was due to go back to GHQ. Inspired by the patriotic Jewish spirit I had found in Tel Aviv, I volunteered instead to join the so-called "Jewish Legion": I thought it was time I did a spot of fighting myself. Now, there were three Jewish (*Royal Fusilier*) Battalions then in the British Army. The first was the *38th Battalion*, raised in Whitechapel (and affectionately dubbed by British cockneys as the *King's Own Schneiders*). The second was the 39th Battalion, raised in the Bronx, which was said to have as its regimental motto: "No advance without security". These two battalions were already fighting in the Jordan Valley where they twice took part in raids across the river towards Amman and won many decorations for valor. The third Battalion (the *40th Royal Fusiliers*) was raised in Palestine itself and was known, not as "the Gordon Highlanders" but as "the Jordan Highlanders".'

King's parade, the (p. 456): earlier in, e.g., W. N. Glascock's *Naval Sketch Book*, 2nd Series, 1834, at I, 38. (Moe.)

king's peg. Champagne laced with brandy: late C. 19–20. (J. Symons, *The Gigantic Shadow*, 1958.) A much earlier reference is supplied by Kipling's *The End of the Passage*.

King's poor cousin. A synonym of **King's hard bargain** above: Naval: 1830, Fredk Marryat, *The King's Own* (p. 212 of the 1896 edition). Moe.

King's Proctor. A doctor: rhyming s.: C. 20. 'Never popular, and now obsolescent' (Franklyn 2nd).

kinifee. '"Yeah," said Ritchie, "they could get three months for carrying a kinifee." This was our bodgie slang word for a knife' (Dick): since early 1950's; by 1966, ob.

kink.—3. A fig., esp. a technical, 'wrinkle'; a smart idea: Australian: since ca. 1930. (B.P.)

kinker. (Usually in plural) A contortionist: circus and variety: C. 20.

kinky. A homosexual, whether male or female: semi-medical: since ca. 1920. (Neil Bell, *I Am Legion*, 1950.) Ex the coll. adj. **kinky**, eccentric, mentally twisted; itself ex the S.E. n. *kink*, a mental twist.

kinky, adj. See the n.—2. Hence, homosexual: since mid-1920's.

kinsman is a corruption of **kingsman** (*Dict.*): 1893, P. H. Emerson, *Signor Lippo*.

kip, n.—7. A job (employment): Anglo-Irish: late C. 19–20. James Joyce, *Ulysses*, 1922. 'I get paid this morning, Stephen said.—The school kip? Buck Mulligan said.' Perhaps ex sense 1 on p. 457.

kip in. To 'shut up': low: late C. 19–20. Brendan Behan, *Borstal Boy*, 1958. Ex *kip*, to go to bed (and sleep).

kip-in, adj. Easy: C. 20. '"It's only right that they should get the kip-in jobs when they're here longer than anyone else"': Brendan Behan, *Borstal Boy*, 1958. Ex *kip*, to go to bed.

Kipper. Occasional nickname for a man habitually sleeping in doss houses: C. 20. (A. B. Petch, April 1966.) Ex *kip*, v., 2, on p. 457.

kipper, n.—4. A serviceman, esp. a soldier, from Britain: Australian servicemen's, esp. soldiers': 1940–5. Of obscure origin: hardly that proposed by Baker, 1953.—5. 'I evaluate its firing power as eighteen torpedoes—I think Kipper is a distressing piece of naval slang—in thirty minutes' (Geoffrey Jenkins, *A Twist of Sand*, 1959): since ca. 1930. Suggested by *fish*, 9.—6. Of an English person, usually male, visiting Australia, being very nice about everything while he is there, and then, back in England, writing 'nasty little things that he failed to mention while among the people whose hospitality he accepted. This unlovable trait has led to the application of the expression *kipper* to a certain type of Englishman. A kipper, by virtue of the processing, has become two-faced with no guts': Jack Marshall & Russell Drysdale, *Journey among Men*, 1962, at p. 190. This sense, deriving ex sense 4, arose ca. 1945.

kipper, v. To ruin the chances of (a person):

from ca. 1920. Prob. ex *scupper* influenced by *cook one's hash.*

kipper kites. 'Aircraft engaged on convoy escort duties over the North Sea and casually giving protection to the fishing vessels,' H. & P.: esp., Coastal Command R.A.F.: since 1940. See **kite**, n., 5 (p. 458 and below).

kipper season, the. The period from Christmas to Easter: costermongers': late C. 19–20. 'No trade—the customers are kipping' (sleeping): Julian Franklyn.

kipper trip. An anglers' special train: railwaymen's: C. 20. (*Railway*.)

kippers, be unable to box. To be no boxer: low coll.: from ca. 1920. James Curtis, *The Gilt Kid*, 1936, 'You couldn't box kippers, you couldn't, talking about right hooks.'

kipping(-)house (often pron. *kippin' ahse*) is a low s. variant of **kip-house** (p. 457): C. 20. Eustace Jervis, *Twenty-Five Years*, 1925.

kipps. Bed; sleep: C. 20. Michael Harrison, 1943. On **kip**, n., 2, 4 (*Dict.*).

kipsey.—2. (Also *kipsie*.) A cheap lodging-house: Australian: since ca. 1910. Tom Ronan, *Vision Splendid*, 1954, and *Only a Short Walk*, 1961.

kish. More usual spelling of **kysh** (*Dict.*).

kish!; keep kish. Cave!; to keep watch: Scottish Public Schools': since ca. 1870. Ian Miller, *School Tie*, 1935. Ex *cave! + hist!* or *whish!*

kish, in one's. Quite at home and well pleased: tailors': from ca. 1860. Perhaps cf. **cushy** (*Dict.*).

kiss me, Hardy! An occasional, jocular c.p.: late C. 19–20. Ex Nelson's famous, and prob. mythical, last words. Some historians (?) have supposed that he said *Kismet, Hardy*—which I doubt.

kiss me, sergeant! An Army c.p. dating from ca. 1947 and satirising the mollycoddling of recruits. Cf. the entry on p. 457.

kiss my foot! Rubbish!: Australian: late C. 19–20. Baker. Also Canadian. But much commoner, everywhere, is **kiss my arse!** —see p. 457.

kiss of death, the. A fatal, or at the least very dangerous, contact: c.p.: since ca. 1950. Dr Brian Foster, in *The Changing English Language*, 1968, defines it as 'an apparently advantageous action which in reality will bring trouble or destruction' and adds that it 'seems to be a fairly new expression, current in speech for some time before it was met with in writing. A recent instance from the *Observer* supplement clearly illustrates the meaning. "Allying with Churchill was regarded as the political kiss of death even in 1939" (Sep. 18, 1966).' In his *The New Language of Politics*, New York, 1968, William Safire defines it as 'unwelcome support from an unpopular source'.

kiss of life, the. 'Used jocularly of the usual type of kiss between lovers' (A. B. Petch, March 1966): since ca. 1964. Ex mouth-to-mouth resuscitations.

kiss one's aircraft good-bye. To bale out: R.A.F. aircrews': since 1939. H. & P.

kiss the book on that!, you can. A coll. c.p. dating from ca. 1890 and = 'it's a dead cert!'

kiss the cross (? *Cross*). To be knocked out; in, e.g., boxing: Australian: since ca. 1925. (B., 1943.)

kiss the dealer! A c.p. used 'when four players throw down cards numbered ace, two, three and four of a suit on a single trick' (Baker): Australian: C. 20.

kisser.—3. A baby: Romanies' and tramps' s.: since ca. 1920. So many women kiss it.

kissing bug. A (young) man intent on kissing: Canadian: C. 20; by 1940, ob. 'Fifty years ago,' writes Leechman in May 1959, 'Canadian girls on a picnic might cry the warning, "There's a kissing bug about!"' With a pun on the true *kissing bug*, a blood-sucking insect of North America.

kissing cousins. Cousins sufficiently close or familiar to allow mutual kissing; hence, loosely, friends unrelated by either blood or marriage: Canadian coll.: late C. 19–20. (Leechman.) Also, in C. 20, Australian (B.P.) By 1940, at latest, S.E.

kisswosh. A thingummy: Regular Army: late C. 19–20. Ex service in the East.

kit.—4. (A special application of sense 2: p. 457.) Paint-kettle and -brushes: house-painters' coll.: late C. 19–20.

Kit has come. The monthly period is here: feminine: late C. 19–20. Cf. *(the) captain is at home* (p. 127 and Addenda).

kitch. Kitchen: mostly lower- and lower-middle class: since ca. 1920. (Norman.)

kitchen, go into the.' To drink one's tea out of the saucer': non-aristocratic: from ca. 1860. B. & L. Ex servants' tendency so to drink their tea.

kitchen, the. That part of the Monte Carlo casino which 'caters' for small-stakes habitués: C. 20. Mrs Belloc Lowndes, *The House by the Sea*, 1937.

kitchen range. Change (of scene or costume): theatrical rhyming s.: C. 20. Franklyn, *Rhyming*.

kitchen stoves (singular rare). Cloves: Australian rhyming s.: C. 20. Franklyn 2nd.

*****kitchin-coes** is Randle Holme's variant of **kinchin coes**.

kitchy-koo. The noise made by adults when tickling an infant: C. 19–20. Ex Irish dial. *kitchy, kitchy, kaw*, 'used to a baby when tossing it in the arms' (E.D.D.).

kite, n., 5 (p. 458). Modify thus: 'In the earliest days of aviation, aeroplanes looked like, and were called, box-kites. Early in the Great War (1914–18) design changed, and "box" was dropped. But kite was not generally used by the Royal Flying Corps till 1917–18, when "crate" came to be confined to obsolescent or obsolete types, "kite" taking its place. It has since been the most generally used slang-word for "an aircraft"' (Jackson). —6. Belly: low: mid-C. 19–20; ob.—7. See **bill, the.**—8. A ship's sail: nautical (mostly Australian): C. 20. Sydney Parkman, *Captain Bowker*, 1946.—9. See **barrow**, 2.

*****kite, fly a dodgy.** To issue a worthless cheque: since ca. 1945: c. >, by ca. 1950, also low s. (Robin Cook, *The Crust on Its Uppers*, 1962.) Cf. **kite**, n., 3, on p. 458.

kite-dropper. An issuer of worthless cheques: since ca. 1945. (Peter Sanders.) Cf. **kite**, n., 3, on p. 458.

kittens, having; very rare in any other form. Nervous, agitated; 'all hot and bothered': from ca. 1933. *The Times*, Feb. 15, 1937. Ex a cat's perturbation during this crisis. Since ca. 1938,

also *having a baby* and, among R.A.F. officers of ca. 1940–5, *having a set of metal jugs* (perhaps cf. *kitten* on p. 458).

kittens (or **like kittens**) **in a basket.** (Of two girls that are) very friendly to each other: W.A.A.F.: since early 1942. H. & P.

kitty.—5. (*The kitty*.) The female pudend: mostly card-players': late C. 19–20. Suggested by the synonymous *pussy*, q.v. at **puss**, 1 (p. 671).

Kitty. A Kittyhawk fighter aircraft (1941–2): Air Force coll.: Brickhill & Norton, *Escape to Danger*, 1946.

kitz. See **put on the kitz** below.

Kiwi.—2. A New Zealander: Australian coll.: C. 20. B., 1942.—2. 'New Zealanders have retained their national title from World War II and are widely known to other soldiers as "Kiwis"': *Iddiwah* (the New Zealand periodical in Korea), July 1953: United Nations troops: ca. 1951–5.

klepto. A kleptomaniac: since ca. 1920.

klina(h). See **clinah** (*Dict.*). A rare spelling.— 2. Adj. Very poor: Australian c.: C. 20. Ex Ger. *klein*, little.

Klondyker. A North Sea captain (or owner) that takes fish to Germany, where there was a profitable sale: North Sea fishing trade's s.: ca. 1930–9. With a pun on Klondyke mines and on 'gold-digging'.

klootch, an Indian woman of the Canadian Pacific Coast, is short for the synonymous *klootchman*, a Chinook jargon word ex Nootka Indian: Canadian: C. 20. (Leechman.)

knacker, v.—3. To geld, emasculate: Australian: since ca. 1860. Brian Penton, *Inheritors*, 1936. Ex **knackers** (*Dict.*).

knackered. Thwarted; in a predicament: low: C. 20. Ex **knackers** (p. 459): cf. **balls-up** (p. 29).

knave in grain (p. 459) goes back to late C. 17: it occurs in B.E., 1699, at *Pack of Knaves*.

knee, v. Short for *knee him in the balls*: low coll.: C. 20. Euphemistic variants: *hit him where he'll feel it* and *hit him where it hurts him most*, both dating from ca. 1930.

knee-high to a(n) . . . (p. 459). 'The common and almost exclusive phrase here is *knee-high to a grasshopper*' (Leechman): Canadian coll.: late C. 19–20.

knee-high to a daisy is the Australian version (C. 20) of **knee-high to a(n) . . .** as on p. 459 and above. (B.P.)

kneeling on it, you're. Your hair is too long: Guards' Regiments' c.p.: C. 20.

knees, on one's. Exhausted: jocular coll.: since ca. 1920. (Atkinson.)

knees brown, get your. 'Men with Overseas service to their credit tell Home Service chaps to do this,' H. & P.: Army and R.A.F.: since ca. 1925.

knicker. Incorrect for **nicker** (*Dict.*).

knife-edge. 'A sand-dune ridge in the desert': Australian soldiers' (N. Africa): 1940–2. (B., 1943.)

knight of the . . . (p. 460). *Sinks*, 1848, has . . . *awl*, a cobbler; . . . *hod*, bricklayer; . . . *brush and moon*, a drunken fellow.

knight of the cleaver (p. 460) should be back-dated to ca. 1830, to judge by *Spirit of the Times*, Nov. 23, 1839 (p. 446, col. 2): although an American publication, it implied a British source. (Moe.)—In the group, I should have included *knight of the cloth*, a tailor: ca. 1790–1860. *The Port*

Folio, quoting a 'London paper', records it on Dec. 31, 1803 (p. 422).

knight's service. See 'Tavern terms', § 9.

knit, n. Usually in pl. *knits*, knitted comforts, esp. garments, for Service men and women: feminine coll.: 1939 +.

knitting. Girls generally or one girl particularly: R.A.F.: since ca. 1930. Jackson. Also *piece of knitting* (Partridge, 1945). It belongs to the **homework** genus of metaphor.

knitting's out, often preceded by *her*. A Naval c.p. applied (1939–45) to a mine-sweeper with her gear over the side. (P-G-R.)

knob, n.—5. (Also *nob*.) A double-headed penny in the game of two-up: Australian, hence also New Zealand: late C. 19–20. Jean Devanney, 1928.—6. (Also *nob*.) Penis; *playing with one's nob*, male masturbation: low: late C. 19–20. With ref. to *glans penis*. Indeed, *knob* also = *glans penis*; cf. the Army c.p. at display of feminine flesh: *get in, knob, it's your birthday*. Sense 6 is, in both nuances, so very widespread that from it there has arisen the further c.p.: *you wouldn't knob it*, 'you wouldn't think, or realise, it' —with the implication that the speaker does know. Cf. **you wouldn't chuckle** and **you wouldn't knob it** below.

knob of a chair and a pump handle, a. A c.p. reply to an inquiry concerning what there is to eat; 'wait and see!': lower-middle class: from ca. 1890.

knobber-up; knobbing-up, n. A shunter operating points in a marshalling yard; the operation: railwaymen's: ca. 1910. (*Railway*.)

Knobby is the inseparable nickname (occ., loosely, **Nobby** by confusion with *Nobby* Clark) of men surnamed Cole: from ca. 1890. Ex the associations of the phrase 'knobby coal (or, coals)': cf. the associations in '*Happy Day*', '*Dusty* Rhodes', '*Smoky* Holmes'.

knobby, n. A knobby opal: Australian opal-miners' coll.: C. 20. (K. S. Prichard, *The Black Opal*, 1921.)

knobby nose. A friar bird: Australian: late C. 19–20. Baker.

knobsticked, be. To be beaten: railwaymen's: since ca. 1920. (*Railway*.)

knock, n., 1 (p. 460) recurs in low Australian s. of C. 20. 'I had caused him to miss out on a knock . . . with Elaine' (Dick).—4. Occurs earlier in Vance Palmer, *The Swayne Family*, 1934.—5. A synonym of *bonk, the*: cyclists': since ca. 1945. Short for *hunger-knock*.—6. A promiscuous, easy girl: low Australian: since ca. 1910. (Dick.)

knock, v.—7. (Also *knock back* or *knock over*.) To consume (a drink): C. 20. B., 1942 (all three). *The Eastbourne Herald* (England), May 6, 1939: *knockback*.—8. To wound; esp. *knocked*, wounded: Australian soldiers': 1939 +. Lawson Glassop, 1944.—9. To kill: Australian: C. 20. (Vance Palmer, *Legend for Sanderson*, 1937.)—10. To disparage: adopted ex U.S., ca. 1943 in Britain, and ca. 1944 in Australia.—11. To sell (a car) at a loss: secondhand-car dealers': since ca. 1950. (*The Sunday Times*, Oct. 24, 1965.)—12. To 'date', to flirt with (a girl): Aus.: since ca. 1920. Norman Lindsay, *Saturdee*, 1933—see quotation at **bum,** v., 6, above.—13. 'To get an article or meal on credit and not pay, or pay by bad check' (Robin Cook, 1962): since ca. 1945. Cf. sense 6 on p. 461.

knock, as an intensive adv. 'Will you lend me some money?'—'No, will I knock!' North Country grammar-school s., since ca. 1955. Cf. **thump!** on p. 880.

knock about, 1 (p. 461): should be back-dated to ca. 1810 or even 10–20 years earlier. It occurs in W. N. Glascock, *Sailors and Saints* (I, 16), 1829, 'Had you been served as I was—kept knocking about the North Seas. . . .' (Moe.)

knock along.—2. V.i., to move on: Army: C. 20; ob. by 1945.—3. To get on (with a person): coll.: since ca. 1910.

knock-back, 1 (p. 461): common also in New Zealand since ca. 1920. (Slatter.)—2. A participation in a 'back-up': Australian gangsters': since ca. 1945. (Dick.)

knock back, v. To cost (a person) so-much: C. 20. 'That knocked him back a fiver.'—2. To refuse; to reject: Australian: C. 20. Kylie Tennant, *Foveaux*: 1939. Cf. the n. (p. 461).—3. See **knock,** v., 7.—4. To fine: Cockney: since ca. 1910. Ex sense 1.

knock (someone's) **block off.** To punch him on the head; esp. as a jocular threat, *I'll k. your b. off*: since ca. 1870.

knock cold. To render (someone) unconscious by striking him; hence, to astound, to flabbergast: Australian: C. 20. Baker. Cf. **knock 'em cold.**

knock commission out of, e.g., a vehicle. To damage, by either misuse or over-use: Australian: since late 1940's. (B.P.) Cf. **out of commission,** 2, below.

knock corners off. See **knock off corners** (*Dict.*).

knock-down, n.—4. A loan: Australian: C. 20. (Dal Stivens, *Jimmy Brockett*, 1951.)

knock down, v., 3. Current in New Zealand as early as 1853. (B., 1941.)

knock down ginger, n. and v. The 'game' of knocking at doors and running away; to knock on a door and run away: South London school-children's: C. 20.—2. See **knocking-down ginger.**

knock 'em. To 'make a hit' or achieve success: C. 20. (H. A. Vachell, *Loot*, 1913.) Cf.:

knock 'em cold. To amaze 'them'; to have a sensational success: since ca. 1920. Ex boxing. A famous song of the 1890's was *Wotcher! or Knocked 'em in the Old Kent Road*, sung by Albert Chevalier.

knock for the loop. To astound: from ca. 1918. *The Pawnshop Murder*: 'Something had happened which had knocked even the imperturbable Wibley for the loop.' ? Ex aviation. It is more often . . . *a loop*, goes back to 1910 or earlier, therefore prob. 'antedates any reference to aviation' (Leechman).

knock (someone's) **hat off.** To astound: mostly Cockneys': since ca. 1940. 'It would knock your hat off if I told you.' As a result of a heavy blow on the head.

knock hell out of. To damage severely; to trounce: mostly Australian: late C. 19–20. (B., 1943.)

knock in, v., 3 (p. 461). Earlier in Diprose's *Book about London*, 1872.

knock into. To encounter: coll.: late C. 19–20. —2. To fight with (someone): Australian: since ca. 1910. Baker.

knock it off! Stop talking!: since late 1930's.

knock it on the head! Shut up!: Australian: since ca. 1920. (Dick.) Ex killing a snake.

knock-knock (usually in pl.—*knock-knocks*). An acoustic mine: Naval: 1941 +. Granville. Echoic.

knock! knock! A c.p., dating from the middle of Nov. 1936. Ex this phrase used effectively on the wireless (music-hall programme, Saturday night, Nov. 14, 1936. Wee Georgie Wood). Orig. ex U.S. It is used, esp. among busmen, by a person about to tell a dirty story or, esp., to make a pun, gen. in doubtful taste. Contrast **thump!** in the *Dict.*; also **whack!** 'It is possible that this derives from the Porter's scene in *Macbeth*, Act II, Scene iii? It looks uncommonly like it,' Alan Smith, letter of June 7, 1939.

knock me silly; usually shortened to *knock me*. A billy can: Australian rhyming s.: C. 20. (B., 1945.)

knock off.—7. As in 'I could knock off a pint': since ca. 1920. Cf. **knock back**, v., 3.—8. To kill: Army: 1939–45. (P-G-R.)—9. To seduce: low Australian: since ca. 1910. '"Remember the time old Ethel tried to knock off Terry?"' they would start' (Dick).—10. To coït with (a girl): mostly Australian: since ca. 1930. (B.P.) Sense 3 (p. 461) goes back to late C. 18. It occurs in the anon. song *Brick Dust Ben*, quoted by *The Port Folio*, Aug. 24, 1805 (p. 261, col. 2).

knock-out, n.—3 (p. 461). Rather, since ca. 1885. In 1892, Albert Chevalier, pride of the music-halls, was singing, 'Oh! 'e's a little champion, do me proud, well 'e's a knock-out'.—5. A division of spoils among illicit hangers-on at an auction: 1873, James Greenwood, *In Strange Company*. Ex sense 1, 2.—6. A knock-out competition (one in which a single defeat entails elimination): since ca. 1925: coll. <, by 1965, S.E.

knock-over, n. A considerable, esp. if surprising success: Australian: since ca. 1920. Baker.

knock over, v.—2. See **knock,** v., 7.—3. To kill (man or beast): Australian: C. 20. (D'Arcy Niland, 1958.)

knock (someone) **rotten.** To trounce; to defeat heavily: Australian: C. 20. B., 1942.

knock seven kinds of shit out of you (him, etc.), **I'll (he'll).** A low minatory c.p.: Naval: since ca. 1920.

knock(-)shop is a post-1910 variant of **knocking-shop** (*Dict.*).

knock the shit out of. To thrash; (of a job) to exhaust or strain: low coll.: late C. 19–20.

knock them in the Old Kent Road. See **knock 'em . . .**

knock three times and ask for Alice. 'A jocular c.p.—used, for example, to short-circuit someone else's long-drawn-out directions as to location' (Atkinson): C. 20: orig., Cockneys'; since 1939, mostly Forces'.

knock-up, n. 'An unpleasant device by which dealers conspire to rig the bidding at antique auctions' (*Evening Echo*, Bournemouth, April 17, 1966): antique dealers': C. 20.

knock up, as in 'He knocked her up'. To coït with: low: adopted, ca. 1944, ex U.S.

knock up a catcher.—2. Earlier is the Army sense, a more logical one; to be detected: 1914–18.

knock with, do a. To arrange a meeting with (one of the opposite sex): Aus.: since ca. 1920. Norman Lindsay, *Saturdee*, 1933.

knocked-knees and silly and can't hold his water. A pejorative c.p.: Public Schools': late C. 19–20.

knocked one's link out, to have. To be tipsy: ca. 1730–80. *The Proceedings on the King's Commission of the Peace . . . for the year 1754* (London, 1754, p. 176). Here, *link* = torch.

knocked to the wide. Utterly exhausted: Army: 1940 +. (P-G-R.)

knocker, 7 (p. 462). Earlier in the Army: 1914–18, commonly; among Regulars, since ca. 1890's—8. A man who knocks on the door to collect money for a street musician: vagrants' c.: C. 20.—9. A welshing bookmaker: Australian sporting: since ca. 1925. (B., 1953.) Cf. sense 7 on p. 462. Hence *take the knock on*, to welsh his clients: since ca. 1930. The phrase occurs in Lawson Glassop's Australian racing classic, *Lucky Palmer*, 1949.—10. One who consistently and persistently disparages or debunks: since ca. 1955. Ex *knock*, to criticize adversely.—11. A 'Class E freight train (M.R.)': railwaymen's: C. 20. (*Railway*.) Ex the noise it makes.

knocker, on the. On credit: Cockneys': from ca. 1930. *The Evening News*, Dec. 11, 1936. Perhaps suggested by *on tick*: cf. **knocker,** 7, in the *Dict.* More probably ex door-to-door salesmen.

knockers.—2. A Cockney mispronunciation of **knackers,** 1, q.v. in *Dict.*—3. Female breasts: low Australian: C. 20. By late 1950's, also English, as in James Kennaway, *Some Gorgeous Surprise*, 1967, 'She was slight . . . but with great little knockers—breasts being for mothers.'

knocking, the last. The late(est) fares: taxi-drivers': since ca. 1920. Herbert Hodge, *Cab, Sir?*, 1939.—2. *Be on the last knockings*, to be nearing the end of a job or an undertaking: since ca. 1925.

knocking company. A hire-purchase company: since late 1940's. (Robin Cook, 1962.) Perhaps ex **knock,** v., 12, above.

knocking-down ginger is a London street-boys' coll. (C. 20) for the game of follow-my-leader, during which boards and loose goods outside shops are thrown down. Cf. **knock down ginger.**

knofka. A variant of **nofgur** or **noffgur,** q.v. in *Dict.* B. & L.

knot.—3. The swelling (or shoulder) of the *glans penis*: coll.: mid-C. 19–20.

knot, carry the. See **carry the knot.**

knots. 'The status mark of the surfer—lumps on knees and top of foot from knee paddling' (*Pix*, Sept. 28, 1963): Australian (teenage) surfers': since ca. 1961.

knotted!, get. See **get knotted!**

Knotty, the. The North Staffordshire railway: railwaymen's: ca. 1890–1940. (*Railway*.)

know a thing or two or six; occ. **know a thing or six.** To be shrewd: a Cockney coll. elaboration, from ca. 1885 and now very ob., of *know a thing or two.* Both occur in Edwin Pugh: the former in *Harry the Cockney*, 1912; the latter in *The Cockney at Home*, 1914.

know all the answers. Applied to a person smart in repartee or in circumventing the cunning; often ironic or exasperated: adopted ca. 1939 from U.S.

know from a crow, not to. To have no idea what a person looks like: Australian: since ca. 1870. B., 1942.

know-how. Skill; the knack of doing something: coll., adopted, ca. 1943, from U.S.; by 1955, S.E. Short for 'the *know how* to do it'.

know how the cards are dealt. See 'Tavern terms', § 2. Cf. with the **know a great A** entry on p. 463.

know one thing and that ain't (or **isn't**) **two;** gen. **I know** . . . To know a thing for certain or emphatically: coll., esp. Cockneys': from ca. 1880. *Passim* in the Cockney stories and novels of Edwin Pugh (fl. ca. 1895–1925); e.g. 'But one think I do know, and that ain't two; he used to be very dirty.'

know one's age, not to. As in 'He doesn't'— or 'you don't'—'know his, or your, age', to be either stupid or very slow in the uptake. C. 20. (A. B. Petch, March 1966.)

know one's arse from a hole in the ground, not to. To be inordinately stupid: Canadian: since ca. 1910. (Leechman.)

know one's book. To be correctly informed: coll.: from ca. 1875; ob. by 1940. B. & L.

know one's ears from one's elbows. See **ears** . . .

know one's eccer. To be alert, (very) shrewd: Australian: C. 20. Baker. Ex **eccer,** 2.

know one's onions. To be well informed or smart or very wide-awake: Anglicised, ex U.S., by late 1936. (Ernest Weekley in *The Observer*, Feb. 21, 1937.)

know someone who knows someone. To be able to obtain an article wholesale: commercial (English and Australian): since ca. 1945.

know the difference between shitting and tearing his arse, he doesn't (or **don't**). He ignores the golden mean: Canadian c.p.: since the 1920's.

know the length of one's foot. See **foot, know** . . . in the *Dict.*

know the price of old iron—or **old rags.** To be knowledgeable, shrewd, alert: Cockneys': late C. 19–20.

know where he lives, he doesn't. A contemptuous c.p., applied to a futile person: since ca. 1920.

know whether one's Agnes or Angus, not to. 'A c.p. used in very cold weather or after swimming in cold water, by males only. "I'm so cold I don't know whether I'm Agnes or Angus!"' (Leechman): Canadian: since ca. 1930.

know whether one's Arthur or Martha, not to. Not to know which of two things one is: Australian: since ca. 1920. (D'Arcy Niland, *Call Me* . . ., 1958.)

know whether one's going or coming, not to. To be in a muddle; or, flustered, agitated: coll.: since ca. 1915.

Knowit of Knowall Park. See **Know-it of Knowall Park** (*Dict.*).

knowledge box (p. 463). In *Miss C.Y's Cabinet of Curiosities*, 1765.—2. Yardmaster's office: Canadian railroadmen's (— 1931). Jocular.

knows all about it now, or **now she knows** . . . A c.p. in ref. to a bride, the first night having elapsed: C. 20.

Knubs. German soldiers: 1939 +. Perhaps ex Ger. *Knabe,* a youth.

knuckle, n.—3. A fight (with fists): low: since ca. 1930. (Norman.)

knuckle, close to the. Slightly indecent: Aus. variant of **near the knuckle** on p. 463: late C. 19–20: coll. >, by 1930, standard.

knuckle-bleeders. Those spiky balls of the plane tree with which children hit one another over the knuckles: Cockneys': from ca. 1880.

knuckle(-)boy. A bare-fisted fighter: Australian: C. 20. (Dick.)

knuckle down to. To settle down to a task, esp. if arduous or tedious or disagreeable: Canadian coll.: C. 20. (Leechman.)

knuckle on, go the. 'To cheat, defraud, take down' (B., 1959): Aus. low: since ca. 1920.

knuckle up sky-high! A C. 20 Australian c.p., derived ex game of marbles. (B.P.)

koala. A motorist—e.g., a diplomat—immune from being booked for parking offences: Australian: since ca. 1945. (B., 1953.) A koala is a protected creature.

koala bear. A militiaman: Australian, mostly servicemen's: 1939–45. (B., 1943.)

koboko. An elaboration of *boko* (q.v. at **boco** in *Dict.*): ca. 1905–14. W. L. George, *The Making of an Englishman*, 1914.

komate. 'A dead or wounded soldier or horse (from the Maori *ka mate*),' B., 1941: New Zealanders': 1915 +.

***kone;** hence **koniacker.** Counterfeit money; counterfeiter: Australian c.: C. 20. B., 1942. Adopted from U.S. See *Underworld*.

konk is a rare variant of **conk,** n. (*Dict.*), esp. in senses 4 and 5. E.g. Henry Holt, *Murder at the Bookstall*, 1934, 'A konk on the head.'

kook. A clown; a simpleton: Australian (teenage) surfers': since ca. 1961. (*Pix,* Sept. 28, 1963.) Ex American *kook,* an odd person, a simpleton, in short anyone the speaker dislikes. Ex *cuckoo,* as in 'you silly cuckoo!'

kooka. A kookaburra: Australian coll.: late C. 19–20. B., 1942.

Kookaburras, the. The Australian Light Horse: Australian soldiers': 1939 +. Baker.

kopper is an occ., but long †, variant of *copper,* a policeman.

Korean War (words of ca.) 1951–5. During this war, the British Commonwealth troops, occasionally in collusion with the Americans, evolved a slang of their own. I owe all the examples given in these Addenda to Staff Sergeant C. R. O'Day of the Royal Army Educational Corps, four from his letter (Feb. 18, 1955) and the rest from 'Slanguage', an article in the New Zealand contingent's magazine, *Iddiwah,* issue of July 1953. These terms are: *bring on,* (?) *Britcom, bug out, chop-chop, Gook, grog on, hachi, hava no* and *hava yes, hills are closing in, hoochie, moose, Noggies, number one—ten—ninety-nine, sexy* (n.), *slickee-slick* and *slickee-slickee, skoshi, swan.*

Kortie. C. J. Kortright of Essex: cricketers': ca. 1890–1914. Sir Home Gordon, *The Background,* 1939.

Kozzie. Mt Kosciusco: Australian: C. 20. B., 1942.

Kraut. A German, esp. a German soldier: Army, mostly in Italy in 1944–5. 'It is the only building left standing in the village. The Krauts blew up the rest'; 'The Kraut will have to fall back': J. M. Scott, *The Other Side of the Moon,* 1946. Ex that favourite dish of the Germans: *sauerkraut.*

Kremlin, the. The headquarters of British Railways: railwaymen's: since ca. 1950. (*Railway.*)

kriegy. 'A prisoner of war (from the German "Kriegsgefangener"). *Kriegydom:* The world of kriegies, or, as the Germans put it so succinctly,

"Kriegsgefangenenschaft",' Paul Brickhill & Conrad Norton, *Escape to Danger*, 1946; Aug. 31, 1944, *World's Press News* (only *kriegy*): prisoners-of-war in Germany; 1940–5.

krug. See the quotation at **chaffy, 3,** above.

kurl or **kurl-a-mo.** Excellent: Australian: since ca. 1920. B., 1942. Fanciful.—2. Hence, *kurl the mo*, to succeed brilliantly or far beyond expectation; to win 'in a big way': since ca. 1925. (B., 1943.)

kushy. See **cushy** (*Dict.*).

kutcha. See **cutcha** on p. 202.—2. A mule; hence, mulish: Army: C. 20.

kweis(s). See **quis.** An occ. spelling is *kway-ess.*

kybo. A privy; a w.c.: low: C. 20. Ex **Khyber Pass, 2,** above.

kye.—3. Ship's cocoa of a rich and delicious consistency served during the Middle Watch (midnight to 4 a.m.): Naval: C. 20. H. & P.; Granville. Perhaps ex **kai-kai** (*Dict.*).—4. Chocolate: Australian Naval: since ca. 1930. (B., 1943.)

kye-boy; often simply **kye.** That member of the watch whose turn it is to make cocoa: since ca. 1910. Ex preceding.

kyfer. A girl, as in 'going after a bit of kyfer': low: C. 20. Hence *kyfer-mashing,* n.; courting a girl: still current in 1940, but † by 1967. (Ronald K. Rogers and Julian Franklyn.)

L

L.B.W. See **Leg before wicket.**

l.i. The offence known as '*loitering with intent*': spivs': since late 1940's. (Article on young spivs in *Picture Post*, Jan. 2, 1954.)

L.K., short for **L. K. Clark.** Mark: racing and underworld rhyming s.: C. 20. 'We get off the L.K. at nine' (o'clock): Franklyn 2nd.

l. of c. swine. Lines-of-communication troops: front-line troops': 1940–5. (P-G-R.)

la. A *lavatory*, a public convenience: Aus.: since ca. 1945. Bernard Hesling, *The Dinkumization and Depommification of an Artful English Immigrant*, 1963.

la-di-da.—5. A tramcar or motor-car: rhyming s.: C.20. Arthur Gardner, *Tinker's Kitchen*, 1932.

la-li-loong. A thief; thieves: pidgin: mid-C. 19–20. B. & L.

***label full of dents.** See **tune.**

Labour, the. 2. The, or a, Labour Exchange: working class coll.: since early 1920's.—3. Rhyming s., in shortened form (the original, the name of a famous entertainer, is never heard), for *syph*(ilis): since ca. 1930.

lac. Lacquer; lacquer work: antique-dealers': from ca. 1870. H. A. Vachell, *Quinney's*, 1914.

lace, n.—3. Beer: short for *lace curtain*, Burton beer, hence any beer; rhyming s.: since ca. 1930.

lace curtain. Foreskin: raffish; homosexual: C. 20.

lacks or lax. Lacrosse: schoolgirls': since ca. 1950. (Peter Sanders, 1965.)

lad (p. 465) a dashing fellow, is applied to also a humorous, or a saucy, girl, as in 'she's a lad'. Often as *a bit of a lad*.—2. 'A mischievous tricky fellow;—"There's no standing them lads."' (Gerald Griffin, quoted by P. W. Joyce, 1910). Anglo-Irish coll.: C. 19–20.

lad o' wax (p. 465) occurs in Wm. Maginn, *Whitehall* (p. 57), 1827. Moe.

ladder in a stocking: orig. (ca. 1830) coll.; by 1890, S.E.

ladder; ladder club; ladder job. See 'Prisoner-of-War Slang', 14.

laddie, -y (p. 465). In mid-C. 19–20, a coll. term among actors. Leonard Merrick, *Peggy Harper*, 1911.

Ladies', the. The women's lavatories: coll.: C. 20. (Monica Dickens, *The Happy Prisoner*, 1946.)

ladies of Barking Creek, like the. (Of women, esp. of girls still virgin) excusing themselves from intercourse on the grounds that they are menstruating: English since ca. 1910; adopted, ca. 1920, in Australia. Ex the well-known limerick about the ladies of Barking Creek, who have periods three times a week.

lady-and-gentleman racket men. Hen-and-chicken thieves: Australian low (? orig. c.): C. 20. B., 1942.

lady-bird.—3. A W.A.A.F. officer: R.A.F.: 1941 +. Jackson. Cf. **bluebird.**

lady-fender. It should be added that it is applied esp. to a woman giving herself airs and being too proud to assist with the housework.

Lady Godiva. A note or sum of five pounds sterling: C. 20. Rhyming on **fiver.**

Lady Hotbot. See **hot-bot.**

Lady in mourning. A Hottentot girl: ca. 1830–60. *Sinks*, 1848.

lady-in-waiting. A woman visibly pregnant: ? orig. and mainly Canadian: since early 1960's. (Leechman.) Adopted in Britain by 1965 at latest; it occurs in the Bournemouth *Evening Echo* of Feb. 24, 1966.

Lady Magger Hagger. Lady Margaret Hall: Oxford undergraduates' (— 1922). Marples, 2.

Lady Nevershit. A 'c.p. shock reproach to woman who seeks to opt away from fact seen as contaminating' (Laurie Atkinson, Sept. 11, 1967): C. 20. Cf. **they think . . .** below.

lady penguins. Nuns in general: Australian Catholics': C. 20. (B.P.) Ex their black-and-white habits.

lady's ladder (p. 466). Usually *ladies' ladders*, as in W. N. Glascock's *Naval Sketch Book*, 2nd Series, 1834, at I, 8. Moe.

lady's waist. A waisted glass in which beer is served; hence, the beer itself: Australian: since ca. 1920. B., 1942.

lag, n.—9. A prison-term of three months: Australian c.: C. 20. B., 1942. Ex second nuance of sense 5 (p. 466). A *lagging* is, in C. 20 Australia, a sentence of more than two years.

lage.—3. (Ex sense 1.) Weak liquor: C. 17–18. Brome, *A Jovial Crew*, 1652.

***lagging, fetch a.** See **fetch a lagging** (*Dict.*).

lagi. See 'Prisoner-of-War Slang', 6.

laid, adj. In pawn: Australian low: late C. 19–20. Baker. Ex **laid on the shelf**, etc.: p. 467.

laid on. See **lay on.**

laid on with a trowel. See **lie laid on with a trowel** (p. 480); but more usually applied, mid-C, 19–20, to flattery: coll. >, by 1910, S.E.

***lair.** 'A flashily-dressed man. "Dead Lair": one who overdoes this vulgar dressing—*lair-up*: To dress, esp. to don one's best clothes for a festive occasion. [Esp. *all laired-up*.]—*lairy*: Vulgar, flashily or showily dressed,' B., 1942. This *lairy* comes ex **leary, 2** (q.v.: p. 474), and it originates the n. and the v. See also the variant **lare.** In *Hot Gold*, 1940, H. Drake Brockman has 'a regular lare' (synonymous with 'dead lair') and 'lare around' (synonymous with 'lareup').—2. Hence a larrikin or young hoodlum, esp. if flashily dressed: since ca. 1935. Hence, since ca. 1946, such compounds as *mug lair*, *two-bob lair*, *ten-cent lair*, all pejorative. (B., 1953.)

lairize. To behave flashily; 'to act or dress as a lair' (B., 1953): Australian low: since ca. 1940. Kylie Tennant, *The Joyful Condemned*, 1953. Ex the preceding, sense 1.

***lairy.** See **lair** and cf. preceding entry.—2. Conceited: Teddy boys': since ca. 1954. (Gilderdale, 2.)

Lake Angels, the. South Melbourne footballers: Melbournites': since ca. 1920. (B., 1943.) Ironic.

laking; playing or **tromboning;** all, both n. and adj. (The) being out of work; (2nd and 3rd) being on half- or part-time: North Country, esp. Yorkshire: since ca. 1920 and (3rd only) since ca. 1931. Ex dial. *lake*, to play: *playing* (at a thing), by a pun; *tromboning*, by a musical pun. (John Hillerby: May 5, 1950.)

Lal Brough. Snuff: rhyming s.: C. 20. See esp. **Lally** in my *Underworld*.

lam, on the. On the run (from justice): in Britain, adopted, ca. 1944, from U.S. servicemen; in Canada, adopted ca. 1935.

lamb-fashion. Earliest (?) in *The London Guide*, 1818, 'Old harridans . . . dress out lamb-fashion, wear false curls, and paint a little'.

lambing-down shop. A public-house: Australian: late C. 19–20. B., 1942. Ex **lamb-down**, 2, on p. 467.

Lambra, the. 'The old Alhambra Theatre, Melbourne': Australian coll.: ca. 1880–1920. B., 1942.

lame duck, 1 (p. 467). Esp. a defaulter on the Stock Exchange: Stock Exchange: ca. 1760–1870. *Spy*, II, 1826.—3. A stockjobber: Australian: since ca. 1920. B., 1942. Cf. sense 1.

Lamington. A Homburg hat: Australian: since ca. 1910. B., 1942.

lammy.—3. A blanket: c.: from ca. 1885. B. & L. Ex nautical S.E. sense.

lamp, v. See **job**, v., 4.—2. To see, to espy: Australian c. and low s.: since ca. 1944. (Kylie Tennant, *The Joyful Condemned*, 1953.) Cf. *lamp*, n., 1 (p. 468).

lamp, light the. See **light the lamp.**

lamp, under the. Underhand; illicit: nautical: C. 20. With reference to an arrangement for payment. Cf. *under the rose* (at **rose** in *Dict.*).

lamp country. 'Walking out at night without money in one's pockets': military: from ca. 1880; virtually †. B. & L. I.e. when the lights are lit.

lamp-post navigation. Going from buoy to buoy: Naval: C. 20. (John Irving, *Royal Navalese*, 1946.)

lamper. A lamp-post; hence, a tall, thin person: since ca. 1920. By 'the Oxford-*er*'.

lamplighter. A species of cicada: Aus. coll.: late C. 19–20. (B., 1959.)

Lanc or **Lank.** A Lancaster bomber aircraft: R.A.F. coll.: 1942 +. Partridge, 1945.—2. A Lancashire man: navvies': since ca. 1870. (D. W. Barrett, 1880.)

Lancashire lasses. Spectacles: Manchester: C. 20. Rhyming on (*eye*)*glasses*. (Jacob Jaffe, April 4, 1959.)

lance. Lance-corporal: coll. late C. 19–20.

lance-comical. Lance-corporal: Army: since ca. 1946.

Lance-Corporal Towrope. A driver mechanic: Army: since ca. 1939. 'These "driver mecs" were not usually highly trained, and the tow-rope

was the tool they used most to get a broken-down truck to workshops. Not complimentary': Peter Sanders.

lance-knight (p. 468) prob. 'comes directly from S. German *Landsknechte*, the mercenary soldiers who looted and murdered all over Germany in C. 16–17, at a period when touring companies of English actors were popular over there' (H. R. Spencer).

lancepresado (*Dict.*) dates back to before 1650: see 'Tavern terms', § 6.

Lancy or **Lanky.** A Lancashire—hence, loosely, also a Yorkshire—employee: railwaymen's: C. 20. (*Railway.*)—2. A Lancaster bomber aircraft: mostly Canadian: W.W. II. Spelt *Lanky*, 'under the influence of a very popular radio serial entitled "L for Lanky"' (Leechman). Cf. **Lanc, 1,** above.

land, live off the. See **live off . . .**

land and sea. 'Last night, near Shepherd's Bush, I caught an airman, not from this Depot, eating "land and sea" (fish and chips)': T. E. Lawrence, *The Mint*, 1955, but dealing with the year 1922: airmen's: ca. 1918–40.

Land Crabs, the. See **Matelots** below.

Land of Hope. A variant of **Cape of Good Hope** (p. 126): C. 20. Franklyn 2nd.

Land of no Future. The Ruhr: Air Force: 1941–3. Cf. **future at all** and **Happy Valley, 2.** Communicated by S/Ldr John Pudney, in Feb. 1945.

landslip. A caterpillar tank: Army: 1917–18. Ex the landslides a tank may cause.

Lane, the, 5. See also **Petticoat Lane.—7.** *East Lane*, Walworth: local: late C. 19–20.—8. *Horsham Lane*: local London: late C. 19–20.

Langtries (p. 469).—2. Hence, during the same period, female breasts.

Languisher and Yawner, the. The Lancashire & Yorkshire railway: railwaymen's: ca. 1890–1925. (*Railway* 2nd.) Contrast **Lanky and York** (p. 469).

Lank. See **Lanc.** Also occasionally *Lanky*.

lannet. A slotted kip: Australian two-up players': since ca. 1910 (?). B., 1943. Origin?

lantern, hold the.—To relax while someone else does the work' (B.P.): mostly Australian: C. 20. Ex the song, 'I hold the lantern while my mother chops the wood'.

lantern-jaw. 'There are no set of men so badly used as the pursers . . . They are called *nipcheeses*, *lantern jaws*, with many other equally elegant cognomens on board': Fredk Chamier, *The Life of a Sailor*, 1832, at I, 174. (Moe.)

Lantun. London: pidgin: from ca. 1860. B. & L.

lap, under the. See **under the lap.**

lap-gunner. 'The member of a (Sherman tank) crew seated in the hull alongside the driver and firing a machine-gun' (B. A. Liddell Hart, *The Tanks*, 1959): Army: ca. 1943–45.

lap it up. To enjoy the fictions of novelists and film-producers: coll.: since ca. 1920. (Berta Ruck, *A Story-Teller Tells the Truth*, 1935.)

***lap up.** To flatter (a person): c.: C. 20. F. D. Sharpe, 1938. Ironically ex *lap it up*, to swallow flattery as a cat does cream: coll.: C. 20.

lapper.—3. A lap dog: late C. 19–20. W. N. Willis, *The White Slaves of London*, 1912.

lapping it up, be. To have a safe, or easy, time:

Guardsmen's: 1939 +. Roger Grinstead, *They Dug a Hole*, 1946.

laprogh. A goose: a duck; loosely, a bird of any kind: Shelta: C. 18–20. B. & L.

lard head. A fool; a very simple fellow: Australian: C. 20. B., 1942.

lardy-dardy toff. An effeminate 'swell': proletarian: from ca. 1885; ob. B. & L.

*lare. A loud-voiced, flashily dressed man: c.: C. 20. Cf.:

*lare up, v.i. To boast: c.: C. 20. Origin? Prob. ex:—2. To dress flashily: see entry at **lair.**

lare up.—2. A smart, shrewd fellow: Australian low: C. 20. Kylie Tennant, *The Battlers*, 1941. See also **lair.**

lareovers for meddlers (p. 470) has survived as *lay-over for meddlers.*

largey or **largo** (pron. *larjo*). 'Much, great, magnanimous, loud': pidgin: from before 1840.

lark, n., 1 (p. 470). Earlier in *Sessions*, April 1802 (p. 221).

larkin. A girl: Shelta: C. 18–20. B. & L.—2. 'A very strong spiced punch': Anglo-Indian: from ca. 1860. Ibid. Prob. ex concocter's name.

larking, n.—4. Theft: c., and policemen's s.: since ca. 1920. (Norman.)

larking, adj. (p. 470), prob. dates from early C. 19; it occurs in W. N. Glascock, *Sketch-Book* (II, 135), 1826. Moe.

larks in the night, the. A 'jocular c.p. for birds which are regarded as responsible for more births than the stork' (B.P.): Australian: since ca. 1930. A double pun: on **lark,** n., 1 (p. 470), and on **bird,** n., 8 (p. 54).

larn-pidgin. An apprentice: pidgin: mid-C. 19–20. Ibid. Lit., learn-pigeon.

larry. A familiar of **larrikin** (*Dict.*): from ca. 1875. Ibid.

larstin(g)s. Elastic-sided boots: Australian low: since ca. 1910. Baker. Sarah Campion, 1942. Blend of '*elastic*' + '*thing*s'? Or perhaps '*lastics,* from *lahstics* and 'softened' to *lahstins* or *larstins,* as Dr Douglas Leechman has proposed.

lary. Cheeky; 'cock-a-hoop': low: C. 20. Arthur Gardner, *Tinker's Kitchen,* 1923. Cf. **lare.**

lash, n.—2. Hence (?), a trick: Australian: since ca. 1920. B., 1942.

lash (at), have a. To try (v.i.); to attempt (v.t.): Australian: C. 20. B., 1942. Cf. *have a stab at* and similar phrases.

lash-out. 'A sudden burst of work on the approach of an officer' (Granville): Naval: since ca. 1905. Ex a (horse's or a) boxer's lashing out; cf. **lash,** n., 1 (*Dict.*).

lash-up. Anything makeshift: Naval coll. late C. 19–20. 'Taffrail', *Mystery at Milford Haven,* 1936, 'The boat . . . was what a bluejacket would have called a "lash-up", a thing of bits and pieces.' I.e. lashed together.—2. An informal social occasion, esp. an informal party: since ca. 1950. Desmond Bagley, *The Vivero Letter,* 1968.

lash up, v. To stand (someone) treat: Naval: since ca. 1905. Granville, '"I'll lash you up to a couple of pints when we have a run ashore", originated from lashing up a messmate's hammock.'

lash-up repairs. Rough-and-ready repairs: R.A.F. coll.: 1939 +.

lashool. Pleasant: Shelta: C. 18–20. B. & L.

*last, v. '"To last", derived from lashing a boat, meant that the man who actually got the money or cheque defrauded them of some part of their share' (Bournemouth *Evening Echo,* April 20, 1966): c.: since ca. 1930.

last bucket, I didn't come up in the. I wasn't born yesterday: Naval: C. 20. Granville.

last card of one's (or the) pack. The back: rhyming s.: 1857, Augustus Mayhew, *Paved with Gold.* Since ca. 1920, †.—2. Usually *last card in the pack,* a snack: theatrical rhyming s.: C. 20. Franklyn, *Rhyming.*

last of its tribe, the. An Australian variant of the **last of the Mohicans:** Australian: C. 20. 'Be careful with that chisel; it's the last of its tribe.' (B.P.)

last of the Barons, the. 'A nickname given to the "Baron of Exchequer" last appointed, since afterwards the Court of Exchequer was done away with': legal: ca. 1875–1910. B. & L. Pun suggested by the title of Bulwer Lytton's historical novel.

last of the Mohicans, the. A c.p. applied to the last of anything, e.g. a cigarette in a packet: C. 20; by 1950, ob. Ex Fenimore Cooper's famous novel.

last out, lousy! Children's (esp. Australian) c.p., mostly in games: C. 20. B.P.

last the full distance. See **go the full distance.**

last thing. Late at night: coll.: mid-C. 19–20. Short for *last thing at night.* Cf. **first thing.**

last three, one's. The last three figures of an airman's Service number: R.A.F. j. rather than coll.; and certainly not s. The last three figures are often used instead of the full number.

laster.—2. A large piece of toffee, designed to last a long time: Lancing: ca. 1890–1935. Marples.

lastins. Variant of **larstins.**

latch on, usually intransitive, as in 'He didn't latch on'. To understand: since ca. 1919. Ex dial. *latch,* to catch, to seize, to grasp.

Late and Never Early, the. The L.N.E.R. railway: railwaymen's: ca. 1890–1950. (*Railway* 2nd.)

Late Arrivals Club, the. Those aircrews who had, in the desert, been forced to walk back to their lines: R.A.F. in N. Africa: World War II. (P.-G.-R.)

late on. See **early on.**

Latin. See 'Tavern terms', § 3, *c.*

latrine wireless, the; a l.w. Rumour in general; a particular rumour: Australian soldiers' coll.: 1939 +. Lawson Glassop, *We Were the Rats,* 1944, 'Time was so short, the latrine wireless insisted that we would sail any day.' Adaptation of **latrine rumour** (p. 471); cf.:

latrino. A short form (1940 +) of:

latrinogram. Army officers' (1939 +) variant of **latrine rumour** (*Dict.*).

latter end (p. 471): earlier in Pierce Egan, *Finish to Tom, Gerry, and Logic,* 1928; perhaps rather fast life than pugilism.

laugh, n. The very common shortened form of **laugh and joke,** a smoke, on p. 471. Jim Phelan, *Tramp at Anchor,* 1954. 'A tiddley or a laugh (i.e. a drink or a smoke)'—footnoted thus, 'Rhyming slang. Tiddleywink—drink; laugh and joke—smoke. The last word is dropped for greater mystification.'

laugh, to complain. See **stop laughing!**

laugh and joke (p. 471). Also in Val Davis, *Gentlemen of the Broad Arrows*, 1939. Much earlier in D. W. Barrett, *Navvies*, 1880.

laugh like a Chief Stoker. To laugh a raucous 'belly laugh': Naval: C. 20. Granville, 'Ex the harsh cackle of a seagull, which is said to possess the soul of a departed Chief Stoker.'

laugh like a drain. To chuckle heartily: Naval wardrooms': C. 20. Granville. Water gurgles down a drain-pipe: babies gurgle with pleasure and a similar noise. The phrase has an intensive: *laugh like a row of drains* ('a jovial display of dentures, symbolized by the common iron grille over a kerbside drain, brings about this phrase': R.A.F. officer, April 10, 1962): since ca. 1950, and esp. in the R.A.F.

laugh of (someone), **have the.** To outdo, outwit someone: coll.: C. 20.

laughing, be (p. 471). Revived during the years 1939-45; extant.

laughing boy, the. A glum-faced man: Services' ironical: since ca. 1945.

laughing haversacks, I'll (he'll, etc.) **be.** A c.p. indicative of anticipated pleasure upon fulfilment of given conditions: Forces': since ca. 1930. Cf. **laughing, be**, in *Dict.* (Atkinson.)

laughing-side. An elastic-sided boot or shoe: Australian: since ca. 1920. Ruth Park, *The Harp in the South*, 1948. It stretches in, as it were, a grin. For sense, cf. **larsting.**

laughs, for. As a joke; for the fun of it: coll.: since ca. 1950.

laughy. A farce: filmland: since ca. 1925. Cameron McCabe, *The Face on the Cutting Room Floor*, 1937.

launching pad. A water-closet seat in a (moving) train: railwaymen's: since ca. 1962. (*Railway* 2nd.) Evacuation into outer space.

Lauras. Chocolates: Canadian: since ca. 1930. *The Evening News*, Jan. 9, 1940. The girls like them. 'Made by the firm "Laura Secord" [a name commemorating] a Canadian heroine of The War of 1812' (Leechman).

Laurence.—2. Also **get Laurence** (e.g. 'I've got Laurence') and **Laurence has got**, e.g., **me.**

lavatory (or **lavatorial**) **bombing.** 'The dropping of bombs from a great height. Army, World War II, generally referring to the Italian Air Force, which preferred staying out of the range of A.A. guns to accuracy. Cf. **pull the plug** (below) which is probably connected' (Peter Sanders).

Lavatory Lancers, the. The Westmorland and Cumberland Yeomanry: Army: C. 20.; † by 1930.

lavender, not all. Not all beer and skittles: coll. (mostly university?): ca. 1880–1914.

lavo. Lavatory: Australian: since ca. 1920. B., 1942.

lavvy. A Scottish, esp. children's, easing of *lavatory*: C. 20.

*law, v. 'The villainy [of posing as a policeman] became so widespread that the crooks' word for it went into their argot. They began to talk of "Law-ing" a man—robbing him in the guise of a policeman' (John Gosling, *The Ghost Squad*, 1959): c.: since late 1945.

Law, the. The police; a policeman: London's East End: coll.: since ca. 1945. (Richard Herd, Nov. 12, 1957; Norman, 1958.) Cf. the U.S. *John Law*. Also as in 'Two law came up to me and grabbed hold of me' (Norman).

[**Lawd** is unnecessary for *Lord*; moreover, it implies illiteracy where none exists.]

Lawk! (p. 472). The variant *lawk-a-daisy* (ibid.) is much earlier: in, e.g., *Sessions*, 5th session of 1734.

Lawn, the. The lawn at Ascot: sporting coll. from ca. 1860. B. & L.

lawners and **royallers.** Lawn tennis and royal tennis: Oxford and Cambridge undergraduates': C. 20. The Oxford-*er*.

lax, n. See **lacks** above.

lay, n.—10. A girl; esp. one who is usually compliant: low Canadian: since ca. 1945. Ex U.S. *lay*, to coït with (a girl). By 1955, also British, as in 'an easy *lay*'.

lay, v.—5. To coït with, usu. of a man with a woman: low: adopted, ca. 1944, ex American servicemen. '"But a dame's only a dame, Charlie-boy, you lay 'em and leave 'em"' (Douglas Warner, *Death of a Snout*, 1961).

*lay about.—2. A man that lives by cadging from thieves: c.: from ca. 1919.—3. (Ex sense 1 on p. 472.) 'There are always "layabouts"—out-of-works—hanging around [law] court buildings': police s. since ca. 1935; by ca. 1960, gen. s. John Gosling, *The Ghost Squad*, 1959.

lay an egg. To make a great fuss; esp. 'Don't lay an egg!'—stop worrying: Australian: since ca. 1920. (D'Arcy Niland, 1958.)—2. 'In show biz in Canada and U.S., to "lay an egg" is to put on a performance that fails to please the audience. This applies to a single actor or to the show as a whole' (Leechman): since ca. 1910 in Canada. The implication is that it's a *bad* egg.

lay-by, n. Money *laid by*, put aside, esp. out of housekeeping: Australian coll.: since ca. 1925. (Vince Kelly, *The Greedy Ones*, 1958.)

lay-down, n.—2. Hence, a (fortnight's) remand: c.: C. 20. In, e.g., F. D. Sharpe, 1938.

lay down one's ears. See 'Tavern terms', § 2.

lay eggs. 'To lay mines; *not* to drop bombs,' H. & P.: Naval and aerial: since 1939. See **egg**, 4 (p. 254). Cf. **gardening.**

lay of the last minstrel, the. A cultured c.p., applied to a particularly unattractive girl: Canadian: since ca. 1960. (Leechman.) An allusion to the famous poem by Sir Walter Scott, and a pun on **lay**, n., 10, above.

lay off with. To lie with—copulate with (women): Australian: C. 20. Lawson Glassop, *We Were the Rats*, 1944, '"Eddie," I said, "You like laying off with girls better than anything else in the world, don't you?"'

lay on; esp. in 'It's all laid on'—planned, arranged, assured: Army, since ca. 1930. E. P., 'In Mess and Field'—*The New Statesman*, Aug. 1, 1942. Adopted by the R.A.F., where it tends to be restricted to availability: Jackson, 1943. Also by the Navy: Granville. Cf. **plumbing.** Cf. the Army's synonym *tee up* and R.A.F.'s *organise* and:—2. To *lay* (someone) *on*, to put in the way of finding, as in 'He laid me on here' ('Tom Collins', *Such is Life*, 1903): Australian coll.: since ca. 1860; ob.

lay on air. To arrange for, obtain, provide, air support: Service: 1940 +. In, e.g., J. L. Hodson, *The Sea and the Land*, 1945.

*lay-out, n. A confidence-trickster's plan of action: Australian c.: since ca. 1925. Adopted from U.S.: see *Underworld*.

lay out,—2; more usually, **show out**. 'This is

a not uncommon practice in shipyards and works where men are mainly employed. When workmen are sitting talking, generally after a meal, one of the company will suddenly shout: "Let's show him out!" The victim, who is usually a boy or a youth, or sometimes a simple male who will not cause a "rough house", is pounced upon and exposed, his privates "annointed" with spit, grease, ashes, or anything handy. Women in works are not unknown to act the same. In a big shipyard on the Tyne, where I once worked, the boys were continually being warned by the men not to show their noses in the ropeworks near by, or the women employed there would show them out and tar them. A young man, unfit for war service, once told me that he was employed clearing a wood at a colliery for pit props. The only labour available was female, and they were not long on the job before they "showed Jimmy out". In telling the tale he always added with relish that he had his revenge on them individually' (communication made in 1946): coll.: mid-C. 19–20.

lay the dust. To take a drink of beer, spirits, etc.: since ca. 1910.

lazy is Navally applied to person or thing 'serving no particular purpose at the moment' (Granville): C. 20.

lazy-bed cooking. Cooking in the ashes of a camp-fire: Australian coll. C. 20. (B., 1943.) Practised by, and copied from, the Aboriginals.

lazy-dazy. Lazy: Australian: since ca. 1945. Cf. the Devonshire *hazy-dazy*. (B.P.)

lazy man's load (p. 473): 'in Australia, by no means ob.' (B.P., 1965).

lead, strike the. To be successful: Australian coll.: C. 20. B., 1942. Ex gold-mining.

lead from the duckhouse. To lead from lowest card of suit: Australian card-players': since ca. 1910. (B., 1953.)

lead in one's arse. Laziness; torpor: Canadian, esp. labourers': since ca. 1945. 'Shake the lead out of your arse!'

lead in one's pencil. Sexual vigour: C. 20. Hence, *put lead in one's pencil*, to render potent. Also used, derivatively, of women.

lead off, v. (p. 473). By ca. 1930, fairly general: cf. e.g., Roy Vickers, *Dead Ends*, 1949.

lead on, Macduff! A c.p. (late C. 19–20) based upon a frequent misquotation of 'Lay on, Macduff' in Shakespeare's *Macbeth* (V. vii. 62). The c.p. occurs in, e.g., Edward Burke, *Bachelor's Buttons*, 1912.

lead-pipe cinch. An absolute certainty: Canada: since ca. 1945. (Leechman.) Ex the effectiveness of a short length of lead-pipe as a weapon.

leaden fever, esp. in *die of l.f.*, to die from a bullet wound: late C. 18–mid 19. The phrase occurs in *The Rolling Blossom*, an anon. ballad of ca. 1800. (Moe.)

leader. A Leading Seaman: esp. in address: Naval coll.: since ca. 1934 (cf. sense 2: p. 474). In, e.g., C. S. Forester, *The Ship*, 1943.

leak, n.—4. A police informer: Australian: since ca. 1925. Vince Kelly, *The Shadow*, 1955.— 5. A trick, a dodge: Australian: since ca. 1930. Alan Marshall, *These Are My People*, 1946, '"I use Eno's Fruit Salts instead of baking powder," he said. "I know all the leaks."' A mere variant of **lurk**, 1, 2, on p. 500. (B.P.)

leak-house; leakery. A urinal: Australian,

mostly juvenile: since late 1940's. (B.P.) Cf. **leak**, n, 2, on p. 474.

lean and hungry. The markings on the ships' funnels of the Lampert & Holt Line: ca. 1900–40. The conditions have long since been improved.

lean over backwards. See **fall over backwards.**

leap-frog, v., whence the n. *leap-frogging*. To advance in successive waves, the second going through the first, the third through the second and so on: since 1941: Army coll. >, by 1945, S.E.

Leaping Lena. The train running between Darwin and Birdum: Australian (esp. N.T.): since ca. 1930. (B. 1953.)

leastest. Least: trivial coll.: from ca. 1890; ob. W. Pett Ridge, *Minor Dialogues*, 1895, 'If I have anything, it must be the leastest drop of claret-cup.'

leather, n.—4. A wallet: c.: C. 20. F. D. Sharpe, *The Flying Squad*, 1938, 'An inveterate pickpocket is sometimes called "A Leather Merchant".'

leather, your tongue is made of very loose. See **tongue is well hung** (*Dict.*).

leather-bottom; usu. in pl. A Civil Servant tied to his desk: C. 20. Compton Mackenzie, *Thin Ice*, 1956, 'It's worse than ever with these Colonial Office leather-bottoms'. Cf. **arse-polishing** above.

leather-head.—2. A swindler: Canadian: from ca. 1870; ob. B. & L.

Leather-Heads. Men of Stafford: London clubs': 1812–ca. 1850. (Charles Marsh, *Clubs of London*, 1832.) Attributed to R. B. Sheridan, who was rejected by them as their M.P. in 1812.

leather-jacket. See **rocker,** n., 2.

leather-neck. According to 'Taffrail', however, it is a bluejackets' name for a soldier: see quotation at **joey** (Addenda). Recorded first by B. & L.—1 (p. 475), seems to have, originally, been a British term, perhaps not ante-dating ca. 1880. As an American term, it is unrecorded before 1909; as a British, unrecorded before 1890. (Moe.)—2. A station 'rouseabout': Australian: since ca. 1910. Baker.

leatherhead. A friar bird: Australian: late C. 19–20. B., 1942.

leave an R in pawn (p. 475): Extant. Granville.

leave (someone) **for dead.** To be vastly superior to (him): Australian: since ca. 1930. Ex horse-racing. (B.P.)

Leave Nothing Loose. The Loyal North Lancashires: Army: late C. 19–20; † by 1940. Punning the initials *L.N.L.*

leave it for the cleaners! 'A c.p. often heard when someone drops small change on the floor' (B.P.): Australian: since late 1940's.

leave the deck to the last! An ironic shout greeting 'that hapless rating working aloft who has spilled paint onto the deck': C. 20. Wilfred Granville.

leave the lickings of a dog, not. 'Give a sound rating and leave one without a reputation. Often used in the North Country when there has been a row and one of those involved has had his past raked up,' Albert B. Petch, communication of Dec. 7, 1946: Northern England: late C. 19–20.

leave visiting cards. To bomb a locality: R.A.F. since 1939. Berrey, 1940, records *leave calling cards*, a variant among the Americans in the R.A.F.

leaver. A paroled convict: Australian: ca. 1840–70. B., 1942. One who is on ticket-of-leave.—2. A racehorse that won't eat enough: racing coll.: late C. 19–20. (John Winton, *Never Go to Sea*, 1963.) Obviously because it leaves its food.

leaves. Lettuce: beatniks': since ca. 1959. (Anderson.) Ex 'lettuce leaves'.—2. Dungarees: beatniks': since ca. 1960. (Anderson.)

lec. A lecture: Exeter undergraduates' (— 1940.) Marples, 2.

leccy or **lecky.** An *electric* tram: Liverpool: C. 20.

lech. A sexual attraction towards, or urge for, someone: since ca. 1918. (T. Washington-Metcalfe, *Aloysius O'Callaghan*, 1932.) A back formation ex *lechery*.

lechery-layer. See 'Harlots'.

ledger bosun or **dollar bosun.** A Warrant Writer in charge of pay accounts: Naval: since ca. 1925. Granville.

leeward, go to (p. 475) occurs early in W. N. Glascock's *Naval Sketch Book*, 2nd Series, 1834, at at II, 34. Moe.

lef.—2. As in 'the second lef', the second-lieutenant: Army: W.W. I. It occurs, e.g., in the song entitled 'The Conscientious Objector', part of the revue *Round the Map*, presented in 1916 or 1917. (Mr Stephen A. Burke.)

left and right. Variant of **read and write,** 1 (p. 690): late C. 19–20. Franklyn 2nd.

left-footer. A Catholic: Northern Ireland Protestants': C. 20. In Eire, 'they' say, farm labourers use a spade pushed into the ground with the left foot.

left forepart, it should be added, is tailors'.

left-handed spanner. See **flannel hammer.**

left hanging Judas. (Of a rope) left hanging over the side: Naval: late C. 19–20.—2. Hence (of a sailor) left in the lurch: Naval: C. 20. (P-G-R.)

left hook. An attack delivered from the left flank: Army coll.: 1941–5. Ex boxing. (P-G-R.)

left in the lurch. (A) church: rhyming s.: since ca. 1880.

left, right, centre. (Of bombs) dropped accurately upon the target: R.A.F.: 1939 +. H. & P.—2. Hence, as an injunction, Put your cap on straight!: R.A.F.: since 1940. H. & P.—3. 'In fact, to get everything just right,' H. & P.: R.A.F.: since 1940. (Not a v., but an adj. or an adv.)

left sucking the mop, be; or, **to have blown out.** 'When a cabman puts on a theatre or restaurant rank, and gets first just as the lights go out and the door shuts, he has "blown out" and is "left sucking the mop",' Herbert Hodge, *Cab, Sir?,* 1939: taxi-drivers': since ca. 1920. The lights have 'blown out', the driver is like a servant-girl out of a job, left with nothing to do but 'suck the mop'.

Lefty. A socialist or a communist: coll.: from 1936. In *Phœnix News-Progress,* Spring, 1937, we find the caption, 'COUNTERBLAST TO LEFTIES'. Ex S.E. *left wing.*

Lefty Wright. See 'Nicknames'.

leg, n.—6. 'A stage between landings on a long-distance flight' (Jackson): Air Force coll.: since ca. 1925. Cf. sense 2 on p. 476; perhaps rather ex cribbage.—7. Hence, a stage—a portion—of a journey; hence, of an undertaking: coll.: since ca. 1930; by 1960, S.E.

leg, get one's. To obtain a person's confidence: tailors': from ca. 1865. B. & L.

leg, have a. (Of a horse) to have an injured leg: racing, esp. steeplechase, coll.: C. 20. *The Sunday Telegraph,* Aug. 13, 1961, article by John Lawrence.

leg-bail, give.—2. To hoodwink (someone) or catch unawares: Australian: since ca. 1910. (B., 1943.)

leg before wicket, occ. **L.B.W.** A ticket: rhyming s.: C. 20. Note esp. 'That's the l.b.w.' —That's good. Franklyn 2nd.

leg in, get a.—2. Hence (?), to win on the first horse of a 'double': Australian sporting: C. 20. B., 1942.

leg over, have got a. To be under a misapprehension: Army (esp. Artillery officers'): C. 20. Ex horses getting a leg over the traces.

leg over, throw a. See **throw a leg over.**

leg-pull. A good-natured, innocuous hoax or deception: coll.: C. 20. Ex *pull* (someone's) *leg.*

leg-rope on, put the. To tame or master a recalcitrant person: Australian coll.: C. 20. (B., 1943.) Ex leg-roping cattle.

leg-up; esp. **give someone a leg-up,** to assist him: coll., esp. Australian: late C. 19–20. B. 1942.

leg-zeph. Short trousers; running shorts: St Bees: since ca. 1914. Marples, 'Apparently from the trade use of *zephyr*—a thin vest (through which the zephyrs blow).'

legal. A passenger that pays only the legal fare: taxi-drivers' coll.: since ca. 1910. Herbert Hodge, *Cab, Sir?,* 1939. Ex **legal, the:** p. 477.

legal beagle. A lawyer more than averagely keen, with a sharp nose for errors and omissions: Canadian, mostly journalistic: since ca. 1950. (Leechman.) Ex the ensuing entry.

legal eagle. A lawyer: adopted, in late 1940's, ex U.S. This sort of rhyming is very common in post World War II American s.: see esp. Wentworth & Flexner, Appendix.

leggy, n. See 'Prisoner-of-War Slang', 6. Another Far East P.O.W.—Mr R. H. Pantling—tells me (July 6, 1960) that 'its far more general use was for a second helping of our very inadequate rations. The frequent cry, towards the end of a meal, of "Any more leggies?" made pedantic scholars of Malay wince.'

Legion of the Lost, the. Those elderly or mentally infirm persons in homes or institutions who have been abandoned by relations and friends and who receive neither visits nor letters: coll.: since ca. 1925.

legit, adj. and, derivatively, adv. Legitimate(ly): low s., verging, at least orig., on c.: C. 20. '"I get my maggot [money] legit these days"': J. F. Straker, *Sin and Johnny Inch,* 1968.

legit joint. A game of chance where the genuine player has a chance of winning: Canadian carnival s.: C. 20. Contrast **gaff joint.**

legs on, put. To cause (a person) to hurry: from ca. 1880. Graham Seton, *Pelican Row,* 1935, 'That'll put legs on 'im.'

legs up to her bum, she's got. A mid-C. 19–20 c.p., addressed by men to boys in order to imply a common humanity: 'She has legs too, you know; just like you, son.'

*legsman. A race-course swindler that invites one to 'find the lady': c.: late C. 19–20.

lel or **lell.** To take, seize, arrest: low London s.

verging on c.: from ca. 1860. B. & L. Ex Romany.

lemon.—3. A Rugby football: sporting: from ca. 1895. H. G. Wells, *The New Machiavelli*, 1911, 'Naylor . . . negotiated the lemon safely home.' —4. A car that is hard to sell: motor trade: since ca. 1912. Ex sense 2.—5. A car that has many defects, discovered one after another: Canadian car-owners': since ca. 1945. (Leechman.)—6. See **lemon and dash** below.

lemon, hand (someone) **a.** To swindle, esp. in a business deal: commercial: since early 1920's. Ex **lemon**, 2 (p. 477).

lemon, the answer is a (p. 477) originated in a smutty story circulating very widely during the 1920's.

lemon and dash; often shortened to **lemon.** A *wash*-place (public lavatory): since ca. 1950: orig. and still mainly underworld. Franklyn 2nd.

Lemon Avenue. Spiritual home of 'wowsers': Australian: since ca. 1920. (B., 1943.)

lemon squash, n. and v. Wash: rhyming s.: C. 20.

lemon-squeezer. A peaked hat worn by New Zealand soldiers: New Zealand soldiers' (1939–45); adopted, ca. 1940, by Australian soldiers. (B., 1953.) Ex the shape.

lemonade turn, the. The shift from 2 to 10 p.m.: railwaymen's: since ca. 1920. (*Railway* 2nd.) The shift on which it is easiest to obtain refreshments.

lemonade wallah. A teetotaller: Army, esp. the Regulars: late C. 19–20; by 1940, slightly ob.

lemons, adv. With a will; vigorously: Australian: ca. 1860–1910. 'Tom Collins', *Such Is Life*, 1903, '"Grass up over yer boots, an' the carrion goin' into it lemons," he remarked.' Cf.:

lemony. Disgruntled, irritated, angry: Australian: C. 20. B., 1942, '*go lemony at*, to become angry, express anger towards someone'. A lemon is *sour*.

lend, n.—2. A person to whom one lends money: Australian: since ca. 1930. 'He was a safe lend all right' (Dick).

lend (or **loan**) **of, take a.** To impose on (someone); treat as a fool or a 'softy': coll.: since ca. 1910. Also *have a lend of.*

Lenin's tomb. That part of the Admiralty building—officially 'the Citadel'—which faces St James's Park and which, built during World War II, was regarded as impregnable: Naval officers': since ca. 1943. (Granville.)

lens louse. 'Bane of the news-reel cameraman is what he calls a "lens louse". They come in male and female species, publicity-hunters who never miss a chance of getting in front of a newsreel camera and hogging the scene as long as they can. There are the "anglers" . . . who have learned at which angle they photograph best, and always try to present that angle to the camera,' John Hall in *The Daily Mail*, May 24, 1950: since ca. 1945.

Leo, The. The Red Lion Inn: Cambridge undergraduates': late C. 19–20.

leopard's crawl. An allegedly noiseless approach towards sentries to be overpowered: Army (esp. in East): coll.: 1941–5. (P-G-R.)

lep. A leprechaun: Anglo-Irish: late C. 19–20.

lepper. A dog (esp. as runner): dog-racing: since ca. 1925. Robert Westerby, *Wide Boys Never Work*, 1937. Ex dial. *lepper*, lit. 'leaper'.

leprosy. Cabbage: Australian: C. 20. B., 1942.

Les. A Lesbian: Society: from ca. 1930. Since ca. 1950, fairly general.

Les be friends! 'A mixture of a bad joke'— *Les*, Lesbian, and *le's*, illiterate for *let's*—'and a catch-phrase . . . more generally used than one would expect' (a correspondent, March 25, 1965): since ca. 1963.

Lesbian (p. 478), not in the *Oxford* dictionaries by 1937, reached the Shorter in the middle 1940's.

Lesbo or **lesbo.** A Lesbian: Australian: since ca. 1935. Cf. **Lezo** below.

Leslie. A Lesbian: Australian: since ca. 1945. (B., 1953.) Perhaps by euphemistic elaboration of **Les.**

let down one's hair or **let one's hair down.** To enjoy oneself thoroughly, let oneself go; to be very friendly, or intimate; to be at one's ease: since ca. 1925. B., 1942. Australian; common in England too. Also in Canada and U.S.

let George do it! A journalistic c.p., dating from ca. 1910 and applied to the calling-in of an unnamed expert and putting the writer's own words into his mouth. Perhaps ex Fr. *Laissezfaire à Georges*, as Alexander McQueen has proposed.

let her go Gallagher! A c.p., equivalent to 'Let's begin!': Australian: C. 20. Baker.

let it slide! Let it go!; don't trouble!: coll.: C. 20. Leonard Merrick, *The Position of Peggy Harper*, 1911.

let it sweat! Let things now take their natural course; don't interfere any more: c.p.: since ca. 1920. Perhaps suggested by *sweat on the top line* (p. 853).

let me chat you! Take my advice!: New Zealanders' and Australians': 1915 +. B., 1941, 1942. Cf. **chat**, v., 3.

Let Me Sleep, the. The *L.M.S.* Railway: C. 20. *Railway*, 3rd.

let me tell you! A c.p.: 1944 +. As an emphatic tag, prob. since C. 18; but as c.p., only since the English Radio programme 'Happidrome' popularised it: Enoch, in every instalment, says at least once, 'Let me tell you, Mr Lovejoy . . .' (every word emphasised).

let-out, n. Exoneration; alibi: coll.: since ca. 1920. Ex **let out**, 5 (p. 478).—2. 'A spree, an entertainment' (P. W. Joyce, *English . . . in Ireland*, 1910): Anglo-Irish: late C. 19–20.

let out. Sense 2, on p. 478, occurs very much earlier in Fredk Marryat, *Frank Mildmay*, 1829 (at p. 296 of the 1897 edition). Moe.—6. v.i. To sing heartily: coll.: C. 20. (Eric Horne, *What the Butler Winked At*, 1923.)

let out at. To aim a blow at: Australian coll.: C. 20. (B., 1943.)

let the dog see the rabbit! Get out of the way or the light: dog-track frequenters' c.p.: since ca. 1938.—2. See **dog see the rabbit** . . .

let your braces dangle (**and let yourself go**)**!**, often preceded by *you want to*. Relax and enjoy yourself: c.p.: since ca. 1945.

letari. A variant of **lettary** (a lodging) on p. 479. Laura Knight, *Oil Paint and Grease Paint*, 1936.

letch, n. and v. (To have) an amorous feeling: since early 1920's.—2. Hence, to look, not necessarily amorously, at women: Army: ca. 1940–5. (P-G-R.)

letching-piece. A loose woman: low: C. 20. Cf. **letch-water** (p. 478).

lets. Bed and breakfast visitors: landladies' coll.: C. 20. Frank Vosper, *Murder on the Second Floor*, 1929.

let's appeal against the light! Let's object, just for the hell of it: Australian: c.p.: since ca. 1950. Ex cricket.

let's be having you! A foreman's call to start work; hence, the orig. form of **let's have you** below. C. 20.

let's call it eight bells! 'An excuse for drinking before noon' (Granville): Naval officers' c.p.: C. 20.

let's feel your pulse! A jocular c.p.: late C. 19-20.

let's go back to square one. Let's start again, let's go back to where we were: c.p.: since late 1940's. Ex the old B.B.C. football commentaries.

let's have you! N.C.O.s' c.p., addressed to men due to turn out for a parade or a fatigue: since ca. 1910. Cf. *let's hear from you!* (p. 479).

*let's slaat it out; let's jol. Let's 'beat it' (make off): South African c. (C. P. Wittstock, letter of May 23, 1946). Ex Afrikaans.

letters. Degree-letters after one's name: coll.: mid-C. 19-20.—2. Hence (?), service certificates: Canadian railroadmen's (— 1931).

letting one's little finger laugh. See **little finger laugh.**

leuc (or *leuk* or even *luke* or *Luke*), as in 'He's had a leuc', a leucotomy operation: doctors' and nurses': since ca. 1935.

level, v. To speak or act honestly and frankly: Canadian coll.: adopted, ca. 1950, ex U.S. (Leechman.)

level, one's. Esp. **do one's level,** do one's utmost: coll. esp. Cockneys': from ca. 1890. Clarence Rook, *The Hooligan Nights*, 1899. Ex **level best** (*Dict.*).

level money. '"Level money" means the most appropriate exact multiple of £100' (Anthony Cowdy in the coloured supplement of *The Sunday Times*, Oct. 24, 1965): secondhand-car dealers' coll. since ca. 1945.

levels on the splonk. Evens, as betting odds: racing, esp. bookies': C. 20. *The Sunday Telegraph*, May 7, 1967.

leven (p. 479). Earlier in Mayhew, I, 1851.

Leviathan, The. The Bank of Australasia: Australian journalistic nickname of ca. 1900-30. B., 1942.

Levy and Frank. (An instance of) male masturbation: low rhyming s. (on *whank*): from ca. 1880: often shortened to *Levy*: C. 20.

lewd infusion. Coïtion: low jocular: since ca. 1925.

Lewis & Witties. Breasts or nipples: Australian rhyming s.: since ca. 1890. (B., 1945.)

Lewo. Lewisham (a suburb of Sydney): Australian, esp. Sydneysiders': since ca. 1925. (B.P.)

Lexicon Bay. The language or phraseology of the undergraduates: Oxford: ca. 1815-40. Pierce Egan, *Life in London*, 1821.

Lezo or lezo. A Lesbian: Australian: since ca. 1925. B., 1942. Cf. the English **Les** and **Lesbo** above.

liaise. To get into touch (*with* someone); hence, to co-operate (*with*), confer (*with*): Army officers':

1938 +: by 1941 coll.: by mid-1943 j. E. P., 'In Mess and Field'—*The New Statesman*, Aug. 1, 1942. Ex *liaison* (as in Liaison Officer).

Lib. A Liberator aircraft: Air Force: 1943 +. (Gerald Emanuel, March 29. 1945.)

lib, n.—5. A liberty: trivial Cockney: from ca. 1895; ob. Pugh (2): '"Wust o' women." he said bitterly. "Treat 'em kind an' they take libs."'

Lib Lab. Any one of the Liberal-Labour alliances (ca. 1915-22) professing Radical principles: political: 1916 +; by 1925, merely historical.—2. 'A member of the Liberal-Labour Federation, 1899' (Keith Sinclair, *A History of New Zealand*, 1959): New Zealand coll.: 1899, then historically. Cf. *Red Fed.*

libb. An early variant of **lib, n.,** 1 and v., 1.

Libby. The pianist Liberace: 1958 +.

liberate. To gain illicitly or deviously; to steal: Army: 1944 (Italy) and 1945 (Germany). By humorous euphemism.

liberty!, on my. On my oath!: low coll.: C. 20.

liberty boat; liberty bus: boat taking leave-personnel ashore; free vehicular transport for men on leave: Canadian (1940), hence English (1941); adopted from U.S. Navy and Army: j., not coll.—much less, s.

library. A drinking school; a convivial club, meeting at a tavern: drinkers' or taverns': ca. 1640-90. Anon., *The Eighth Liberal Science*, 1650.—2. A book borrowed from a lending library: coll.: C. 20.

library cads. 'Two juniors who have to keep the library in order': Winchester College: mid-C. 19-20. B. & L.

lick, v., 2 (p. 479). *Boxiana*, II, 1818.

lick of the tar-brush (p. 480).—2. (also **a touch** ...). Applied to one who has a touch of coloured blood in his make-up: coll.: mid-C. 19-20.

licker (p. 480). Cf. the mid-C. 19-20 Cockney, *it's a licker to me*, I don't understand it. I.e. *it licks* (beats) me.—2. An ice-cream cornet: mostly children's: since ca. 1910.

lickerish all sorts. Strongly sexed: since ca. 1925. 'It takes *all sorts* to make a world.'—'Yes; and some are lickerish' (lecherous). Ex the well-known brand of confectionery, Liquorice All Sorts.

lickety-split. At full speed; in a tearing hurry: (mostly) juvenile: adopted ca. 1918 from U.S. Cf. **lick, at full** (p. 480).

lickings of a dog. See **leave the ...**

lie-down. A reclining and a rest: coll., mostly Australian and New Zealand: late C. 19-20.

lie down and I'll fan you! A c.p. reply to such request for service as the auditor thinks unjustifiable: R.A.F. (esp. among N.C.O. regulars): since ca. 1925. Ex the services of punkah-wallahs in India and with the implication that the requester must be distraught or feverish to make the request.

lie down on a, or the, job. To loaf: Australian: since ca. 1925. Dal Stivens, *The Scholarly Mouse*, 1958.

lie in state (p. 480). Recorded in *A Compleat Collection of Remarkable Tryals*, 1721: in vol. IV, p. 248.—2. To sleep protected by mosquito nets: Forces': 1939 +.

lie like a pig. To tell clever lies: Australian: C. 20. B., 1942.

life, n., 4 (p. 481). Current in Australia since ca. 1870. 'Tom Collins,' *Such is Life*, 1903.

life of Reilly, the; esp. *live the* . . ., to live a carefree and comfortable life: ? Anglo-Irish: C. 20.

Liffey water. Pórter (the drink): rhyming s.: late C. 19–20. before 1914, mostly Anglo-Irish. Franklyn 2nd.

lift, v.—7. To move stock overland from one place to another far away: Australian: late C. 19–20. Archer Russell, *Gone Nomad*, 1936.—8. To punch or strike (someone): Australian: C. 20. B., 1942. Cf. sense 4 of the n. and the S.E. *raise one's hand to* (a person).

lift one's little finger (p. 481) occurs, e.g., in Alfred Burton, *Johnny Newcome*, 1818. (Moe.)

lift your undercarriage! Get out!; Go away!: Australian airmen's: 1939–45. (B., 1943.)

*lifters. Hands: since ca. 1930: c. >, by ca. 1955, low s. (Robin Cook, 1962.) Ex the c. > s, *lift*, to steal, on p. 481; cf. s. *pickers and stealers* on p. 625.

lifting lines, vbl n.; rare as v.i. 'A young man earning a fairly good weekly wage by "lifting lines"—or acting as runner—to a baker in Bridgeton', MacArthur & Long. Low Glasgow s. of C. 20.

lifty, n. A liftman: mostly Aus.: since ca. 1930. Bernard Hesling, *The Dinkumization*, 1963.

light, adj.; gen. **very light.** Rather short of money: coll.: C. 20.—2. Also *light of*, which it shortens. Short of (something); 'I'm light a haversack': (mostly Forces') coll.: since ca. 1925.

light!, he (she, etc.) wouldn't give you a. He (she, etc.) is exceedingly mean: Cockney c.p.: late C. 19–20. I.e. a light (or match) for one's cigarette; possibly with a pun on **light,** n., 1 (*Dict.*).

light horseman.—2. 'A large species of ant' (B., 1943): Australian: C. 20. Swift.

light house.—4. A watch-house: Londoners': ca. 1805–40. Pierce Egan, *Life in London*, 1821. Cf. **pilot,** 2.

light master. A go-between to the landlord of a house of call and the workmen using it: printers': from ca. 1840. B. & L. Ex **light,** n., 1.

light of. See **light,** adj., 2.

light out (p. 482) was originally British, not American. It occurs, e.g., in John Davis's novel, *The Post-Captain*, 1806, as Colonel Moe reminds me.

light stags (p. 482). 'I have never heard this and suspect that Beames was under a misapprehension. Loggers and raftmen used to "stag" their trousers, by cutting off a few inches from the bottom, so that they came about half-way down the calves, clear of the top of the boots.—Mathews records it for 1902.' (Leechman.)

light the lamp. (Of a woman) to have sexual intercourse: rather literary: late C. 19–20. Albert Londres, 1928.

light the re-heat. 'More or less synonymous with **turn up the wick** (below). To light the afterburner of a jet engine: a phrase which obviously started as S.E. but is now used to denote rapid acceleration of any form of mechanical transport' (Peter Sanders): R.A.F.: since ca. 1960.

light up.—3. (V.i.) To reach—to experience —an orgasm: mostly teenagers': since ca. 1945.

lighters. 'The merest wetting of the lips in your pal's tot of rum' (Granville): Naval: since ca. 1905. Ex '*light* drinking'; by 'the Oxford *-er*'. Cf. **sippers.**

lightning-conductors. Naval officers' full-dress trousers: Naval: C. 20. They have broad gold stripes down the seams.

lightning jerker (or squirter). A telegraph operator: Australian: since ca. 1910. B., 1942. Among Canadian railroadmen the term is *lightning slinger*.

lights of Piccadilly Circus shining out of his arse-hole, he thinks he's got the; or **you think you've got . . . your . . .** A low c.p., satirical of someone's self-esteem: mostly Services': since ca. 1920. An elaboration and adaptation of the older and much more widely used *think the sun shines out of* (someone's) *arse* or *arse-hole*, to regard almost with idolatry: low coll.: late C. 19–20, for certain; and perhaps since late C. 16.

lightsome, the. Dancing: C. 20. Prompted by S.E. *the light fantastic*, but never very general.

like. '*Man* and *like* have'—in beatnik s.—'no actual meanings. They are code-signs, as in Morse or Semaphore, to show that communication has begun and ended' (Anderson): since ca. 1957. Adopted from general illiterate speech, as a tag— cf. **like,** adv., on p. 482.

like a . . ., like anything. It seems that *like be-damned* is slightly earlier than I thought. E. H. Hornung, *Raffles*, 1899, 'I'll show you the house when we get there, only drive like be-damned!'

like a fart in a bottle; like a pea in a colander. See **pea in a . . .**

like a pig, as in the common *sweat like a pig*, is a very frequent Australian coll. intensive: C. 20. (B.P.) Cf. **lie like a pig** above.

like bats out of (1) Hell or (2) a cave. In great haste, or with alacrity, esp. of departure: (1) mainly English; (2) mainly Canadian. (Leechman.) Since middle 1930's.

like beans; like billy-o; like boots; like bricks. See **like a . . .** in *Dict.*

like blazes. See **blazes, like,** p. 62 and above.

like Brown's cows, (we're) all together. (We're) alone: Anglo-Irish c.p.: C. 20. The anecdotal Brown possessed only one cow.

like buggery—like fuck—like hell. See **fuck . . .** (Add.) and **buggery . . ., hell . . .** (*Dict.*).

like Chloe (or Cloe). See **drunk as Chloe.**

like Christmas Day in the workhouse. Uncomfortable; niggardly; 'lousy': Army: since ca. 1910. Ex a famous soldiers' song, adapted from one of G. R. Sims's *Dagonet Ballads*, published in 1903.

like it or lump it. The sense of dislike comes ex 'a sort of block-acceptance, as if, not liking what was offered you, you anyhow swallowed it whole'. (Basil de Selincourt, in *The Manchester Guardian*, Feb. 19, 1937.)

like MacArthur I shall return. A c.p., mostly Australian, 'denoting that one's absence will be only temporary, esp. if it is suspected that one is trying to escape hard work' (B.P.): since 1942. Ex the famous promise of General Douglas MacArthur to the Filipinos. '(He promised to return and to liberate them from the Japanese)': B.P.

like mad; like shit to a shovel; like smoke; like thunder. See **like a . . .** in *Dict.*

like nobody's business. An adverbial intensive: c.p.: since ca. 1943.

like shit through a goose. Very fast: low Canadian: C. 20.

like sticks a-breaking. (Very) vigorously:

proletarian coll.: 1851, Mayhew, I: app. † by 1910.

like the man who fell out of the balloon (or **lifeboat** or **'plane**)—**he wasn't in it**. A c.p., orig. (ca. 1890), English, but, in C. 20, common throughout the British Dominions.

like the story of Pharaoh's daughter (who found Moses in a basket): 'a well-known Australian c.p.' (B.P.): C. 20. Cf. **you'll be telling me . . .**

like the wrath of God. See **wrath of God . . .**

like to meet (some person or animal) **in the dark, I** or **you** or **he**, etc., **would not**. A c.p., applied to any fearsome person or other creature: C. 20.

like which. The like of which: sol., esp. Cockneys': from ca. 1870. Edwin Pugh, *A Street in Suburbia*, 1895, 'It give me a' insight inter 'is character like which I wouldn't otherwise ha' got'.

*liker. A hobble or a halter: horse-copers' c. — 1914). Pugh. Prob. ex Fr. *licou*.

likes, not one's. Not one's wish: Cockney coll.: from ca. 1870. Pugh (2): '"Why have you not brought him with you?" '"Tain't my likes," said the man.'

likewise. I agree; I share the sentiment. Thus: 'Mr A. "Well, we must be off. We've had a wonderful time. Thank you so much!" Mrs A. "Likewise."' Canadian: since ca. 1965. (Leechman.)

*lil(l).—4. Hence, any bank-note: c.: C. 20.

lilac wonder. A day-return ticket: railwaymen's (M B): ? ca. 1920–50. (*Railway*). Ex its gay colour.

Lilian Gish. A fish: theatrical rhyming s.: since ca. 1920. Ex a famous film actress. (Franklyn, *Rhyming*.)

lilies. Floating runways for aircraft: Fleet Air Arm: 1939–45. John Irving, *Royal Navalese*, 1946.

Lill. Lillywhite, the famous English professional wicket-keeper (d., in 1874, aged only 48): cricketers': from ca. 1846; now only historical. (*The Observer*, Aug. 30, 1936.) He was the son of that still abler father who was mostly a bowler.

Lilley and Skinner.—2. A beginner: retail-trade rhyming s.: C. 20. Franklyn 2nd.

Lily Law (and **Inspector Beastly**). The police; the fuller form is intensive: London barrow-boys': since ca. 1930. Prob. of 'camp' origin.

lily-pond, the; or **sweet-pea ward**; or **male gynae ward**. A ward set aside for male pelvic-organs, and prostate-gland, patients: hospital nurses': C. 20. (Cf. 'The Pitfalls of Using Nursing Slang' in *Nursing Mirror*, May 7, 1949.)

lily-white.—3. A young pathic: late C. 19–20; ob. by 1940; virtually † by 1960.

lily-white, adj. Cowardly: Australian (teenage) surfers': since ca. 1960. *The Bulletin*, 30 March 1963.

Lily Whites, the.—2. Also, since ca. 1930, the Coldstream Guards (Gerald Kersh, 1941; Michael Harrison, 1943). Ironic on **coalies**.

limb.—3. Elliptical for *limb of the law* in its Australian sense 'a policeman': Australian: since ca. 1930. 'Carefully searching among the straw, the limb found nothing': Hay, *Hell and Booligal*, Melbourne, 1961. (B.P.)

limb, out on a. In a dangerous situation; hence, at a grave disadvantage: adopted, ca. 1945, ex U.S. Implying a precarious branch high up.

limby (p. 484). Also Australian. (B., 1942.)

lime, in the. Popular; much publicised: Australian: since ca. 1925. Baker. I.e. 'in the limelight'.

lime-juicer, in Wm Kelly, *Life in Victoria*, 1859 = an Englishman; an English sailor.—2. An English sailing-vessel: Canadian (ex U.S.): since ca. 1860; ob.

lime slime. See 'Prisoner-of-War Slang', 11.

Lime Tank, the. The Royal Naval Hospital, Haslar: Naval: since ca. 1920. Granville.

limers. Limejuice: Naval: since ca. 1930. John Winton, *We Joined the Navy*, 1959. By the Oxford *-er*.

limes. Limelight: theatrical: C. 20. Cf. **lime, in the** (above). Electric footlights are, of course, included.

limey.—2. Hence, esp., a Canadian name for a British seaman: since ca. 1925. (H. & P.) And a South African name for a Royal Navy rating: 1939 +. (Cyrus A. Smith: letter of May 22, 1946.)

limo-limo. See 'Prisoner-of-War Slang', 11.

limpet. A 'base-wallah'; a 'Cuthbert': Army: 1914–18. He clings to his job.

limping Annie. See **Annie . . .**

Limus (pron. *līm ŭs*). Limehouse, London: Cockneys': since ca. 1870. In, e.g., A. Neil Lyons, *Arthur's*, 1908.

Lincoln and Bennett (p. 484). Cf. *Dunn's three-and-ninepenny* for any cheap bowler hat, this make being the best of the lower-priced hats: coll.: late C. 19–early C. 20. (Alexander McQueen.)

Lincoln's Inn. A £5 note: racing rhyming s. on synonymous (orig. underworld) *finn*, q.v. at **finnif** (p. 277): late C. 19–20.—2. A hand: rhyming s. on **fin**, 1 (p. 276): late (? mid) C. 19–20. —3. Gin (the drink): rhyming s.: late C. 19–20. Cf. **Brian O'Linn** (p. 92). All three senses: Franklyn 2nd.

Lincolnshire gremlin. A sharp-toothed gremlin, fond of biting the control wires: R.A.F.: 1940–5.

line, n.—7. (Ex sense 5: p. 484.) A girl or a young woman, e.g. *nice line*, (not so) *good line*: Australian: since ca. 1920. B., 1942; Lawson Glassop, 1944. Since ca. 1950, esp. *a slashing line*, a very attractive girl. (Culotta.)—8. A special verbal approach, esp. from male to female: coll.: since ca. 1920. Ex the S.E. '*line* of goods (for sale)'.

line! Short for '(That's a) line-shoot': 1940 +. *The Observer*, Oct. 4, 1942.

line, go (for **a trip up the**). To go to prison: C. 20. F. Brett Young, *This Little World*, 1834.

*line, toe the. See **toe the line**.

line, up the. On leave: Naval: C. 20. Granville. Up the railway line from a Service port.

line book. See **lines book**.

line mob. An infantry regiment: Army: since ca. 1916.

line on, get a. To obtain information about: mostly Army: since ca. 1938. (P-G-R.)

line-shoot. A tall story; a boasting: R.A.F.: since 1940. *The Observer*, Oct. 4, 1942. H. & P. See **shoot a line**.

line-shooter. He who specialises in, or is addicted to, 'line-shoots'. Jackson. See **shoot a line**.

line-shooting is the vbl n. corresponding to **shoot a line**: since 1940. Jackson (by implication).

line up.—2. To arrange: since ca. 1920. Ex setting things or persons in an orderly line.

lined up. Synonymous with *sighted*: Royal Sussex Regiment: C. 20. (S. H. Ward.)

lined up, be. To stand, as a defaulter, before the Commander: Naval coll.: C. 20. Granville.

linen. Short for **linen-draper** (*Dict.*): late C. 19–20.

liner, 3 (p. 485): goes back to ca. 1810, prob. to 1800. It occurs in W. N. Glascock, *Sailors and Saints* (I, 15), 1829. Moe.

lines, on. 'Used by compositors to intimate that the companionship is in full swing': printers' coll.: from ca. 1860. B. & L.

lines, on his. Engaged in work paid according to scale: printers' coll.: C. 19–20. Ibid.

lines book. A book kept in the Mess for the recording of exaggerations by its members. 'Sometimes called a "Shooting Gallery". From the early 1920's' (Jackson). In *The Observer*, of Oct. 4, 1942, John Moore uses the occ. variant, *line book.* Cf. **line-shooter** and **shoot a line.**

ling. A stink: Australian: since ca. 1920. B., 1942. Cf. **ling-grappling** (p. 485).

linguist. A practitioner of cunnilingism: Australian: since ca. 1950.

linguistic exercise(s). Kissing: since ca. 1925.

link, n. A group of porters working under a foreman: railway 'porters': since ca. 1940. (*Radio Times*, Jan. 21, 1965.) A link—often somewhat tenuous—between staff and public.

link, to have knocked out one's. *Sessions*, 1754 (No. IV, Part iii), 'He said he supposed she had knocked out her link (meaning she was drunk)': Londoners': ca. 1730–80.

links of love. Sausages: Naval: since ca. 1925. *Weekly Telegraph*, Nov. 1942; Granville. Compare **stick and bangers, 2** (*Dict.*).

lintie; gen. pl. A sprite: theatrical: from ca. 1870; ob. B. & L. Prob. ex Scottish *lintie*, a linnet; perhaps influenced by Fr. *lutin*.

lion, v. To intimidate: Australian: since ca. 1930. B., 1942.

lion's lair. A chair: since ca. 1860. Rhyming.

lip, n., 1 (p. 485), is recorded in 1818: Alfred Burton, *Johnny Newcome*. (Moe.)

lipey is possibly ex Ger. *liebe*, 'beloved': B. & L.

lipish or **lippish.** Impudent: ca. 1835–70. *Sinks*, 1848. Ex **lip, n.,** 1 (p. 485).

lippy.—3. Lipstick: Australian: since ca. 1930. 'Not heard from women under forty' (B.P., 1963).

Lipton's orphan. A pig: ca. 1890–1914. Ex illuminated sign, advertising the bacon sold by Lipton's shops.

[Liquor named by language: see 'Tavern terms', § 3. *c*.]

liquorice legs! A schoolboys' cry directed at a schoolgirl wearing black stockings: Australian: 1950's. (B.P.) Obviously ex the colour.

liquorice stick. A clarinet: dance bands' (whether jazz or not): since ca. 1945. 'Obviously because (*a*) it is of black wood; and (*b*) it is sucked vertically to the lips' (Richard Merry).

lispers.—2. The lips: C. 18–mid-19. B. & L.

list, on the. In disfavour: coll.: from 1885; ob. Introduced in *The Mikado*, 1885. Abbr. S.E. *on the black list.*

listen, n. An act or period of listening: coll.: since ca. 1890. Usually *have a good listen* (coll.) or *do a listen* (s.), but also as in '"Out you'll go

. . . and give a good listen"': Christopher Bush, *The Case of the Green Felt Hat*, 1939.

listener (an ear). Rather: since ca. 1805. *Boxiana*, II, 1818.

*****lit, smack the.** To divide the booty: c.: ca. 1850–90. Burton, *Vikram and the Vampire*, 1870. (The term is suspect.)

Little Arthur. The A.R.P. Warden's pet name (1939–45), then (1941–5) used by the R.A.F., for arsenic gas: H. & P. By personification and by phonetic approximation.

Little Benjamin Our Ruler. 'The cane kept by the Sub-Lieutenant in charge of the Gunroom' (Granville): Naval: C. 20. The Gunroom is the Midshipmen's Mess.

little black book. The notebook in which bachelors are reputed to keep girls' telephone numbers: mostly Australian: since ca. 1930. (B.P.)

Little Bo-Peep. An occ. variant of **bo-peep,** 1 (p. 72). Franklyn 2nd.

little boy in the boat. A mostly Canadian variant (since ca. 1908) of *little man in the boat, 2.*

little boys'—little girls'—room, the. The men's —the women's—lavatory: euphemistic: adopted, ca. 1944, ex U.S. servicemen. The former occurs in, e.g. Angus Wilson, *A Bit off the Map*, 1957.

little brether. *Membrum virile*: low: mid-C. 19–20. On analogy of **little sister** (p. 487).

Little Brown Men. A variant of *Little* (*Yellow*) *Men*: B., 1943.

little bullshit goes a long way, a. It pays to flatter or to boast: Australian; c.p.: since ca. 1919. (B.P.)

little devils. Three '2' cards: Australian poker-players': since ca. 1920. (B., 1953.) A reference to children of two years.

little fields have big gates. A c.p.—? rather an unrecorded rural proverb—referring to the fact that many little women bear large families: (?) C. 19–20. The true reason is that they possess an invincible vitality.

little finger laugh, letting one's. Board-school girls' term, from ca. 1890, thus in W. Pett Ridge, *Mord Em'ly*, 1898: 'One of the most painful jibes that a girl could offer to another in school was to point her finger, and inflect it slightly—an act called "letting one's little finger laugh".'

little friend, one's. The menses: Canadian (a feminine euphemism): since ca. 1920. But also Australian; deriving mainly ex the fact that the menses are often welcome as a sign of *non-pregnancy.*

little green men. Mysterious beings alleged to have been seen emerging from flying saucers: Canadian c.p.: since 1957. (Leechman.)

little grey home in the west (p. 487): † by 1960. Franklyn 2nd.

*****Little Hell.** That part of Cow Cross, London, known thus to the inhabitants and as Jack Ketch's Kitchen to others; infested, at one time, with criminals: c.: ca. 1820–1900. B. & L.

little horrors; little monsters. Young children: mothers': perhaps orig. among those women who cook and serve Primary-school dinners: since the late 1940's.

little house (p. 487) is also Australian coll., as in Leonard Mann, *Mountain Flat*, 1939, '. . . Another yard in which were the pigsty, the henhouse, the tool-shed and what they called jocosely "the little house".'

little Jimmy. At House, good callers always called the nicknames for the following numbers:

No. 1—Little Jimmy, or Kelly's Eye.

No. 11—Legs Eleven. (The number resembles a pair of legs, and was given this extra syllable to distinguish it from Seven and avoid mistakes.)

No. 28—The Old Brags [q.v.] ...

No. 44—Open the Door.

No. 66—Clickety-Click.

No. 99—Top of the House, or, Top of the Bleeding Bungalow.

No. 13—Unlucky for some.

No. 16—Sweet sixteen and never been kissed.

No. 21—Key of the door.

Thus Richards. See also account in a novel by Michael Harrison: *Reported Safe Arrival*, 1943, p. 85. Cf. the entry at **puff and dart**, q.v.

Little Man, the. Lord Southwood (d. 1946), who did so much for the hospitals: colleagues' and journalists': since ca. 1925.

little man in a boat.—2. Clitoris: trivial: late C. 19–20. Also *little boy*.

Little (Yellow) Men. Japanese: coll., mostly in Army: 1942 +.

little monster. A child, especially if objectionable: Canadian c.p.: since ca. 1950. (Leechman.)

Little Moscow. Chopwell, County Durham: during the General Strike, 1926. It was the strikers' H.Q.—2. Mardy, a town in South Wales: *The Daily Worker*, Nov. 16, 1949.

little number, one's. What one wants: since ca. 1940. (Angus Wilson, *Hemlock and After*, 1952.)

little rabbits have big ears. A warning to speak more quietly or less frankly in front of children: Australian, partly c.p. and partly modification of the proverb *little pitchers* ... C. 20. (B.P.)

Little Rome. Liverpool (England): coll.: C. 20. Ex the large number of Catholics there. (A. B. Petch, April 1966.)

little shillings. 'Love money' (*Sinks*): ca. 1830–70.

little side (also written *littleside*). A game between teams from one house: Rugby School: mid C. 19–20. Complementary to **big side.**

little something. A dash of spirits: coll.: C. 20. 'Would you like a little something in it?'

little song and dance. See **song and dance.**

little terror. An extremely mischievous child: domestic coll.: late C. 19–20.

little tin god, as in 'He thinks he's a . . .': coll.: late C. 19–20.

little two shoes (or **T. S.**). See **two shoes** in the *Dict.*

little visitor, have a. To be undergoing one's period: Australian, esp. in Suburbia, and notably in the 1920's–1930's.

Little Willie.—2. A (small) boy's penis: Primary schoolchildren's (esp. girls) and teachers': heard in 1920's, but not very common before ca. 1945. A euphemism at once playful and sensible.

little wooden hill, the. The stairs: nursery coll.: mid-C. 19–20. Esp. in 'Now we'll go up the little wooden hill to Bedfordshire'; cf. **Bedfordshire** on p. 42.

littleish. Rather small: coll.: since ca. 1825. *Sessions*, 1832.

littly, before a surname at Christ's Hospital in C. 20, as in *Littly Smith*, corresponds to *minor* elsewhere.

live and let live! A c.p. addressed to a person head- or body-scratching, with implication of nits, fleas, lice: since ca. 1918.

live in one's boxes. Lacking a fixed abode, to move from place to place: coll.: C. 20. Ian Hay, *Carrying On*, 1917.

live in one's chest(s). (Of midshipmen) to sleep in a hammock in the gun-room; where one's chest is kept: Naval coll.: late C. 19–20. (P-G-R.)

live it up. To lead a gay extravagant life: coll.: since ca. 1960.

live off the land. To live the life of a tramp: Australian coll.: late C. 19–20. B., 1942. The tramp is non-productive.

live on the smell of an oilrag. 'To subsist on very little' (B.P.): Australian coll.: since ca. 1920. In, e.g., Cusack & James, *Come in, Spinner*, 1951. Adopted ex Anglo-Irish usage of late C. 19–20. 'A penurious miserable creature who starves himself to hoard up:—He could live on the smell of an oil-rag': P. W. Joyce, *English ... in Ireland*, 1910.

live stock.—3. House bugs: domestic: C. 20. Orig., and still mainly, euphemistic.

live up to one's blue china. To live up to or beyond one's means: from ca. 1860; ob. Cf.:

live up to the door (or **the knocker**). To live up to one's means: proletarian: mid-C. 19–20; ob. B. & L.

lively kid. 'A funny fellow, a brave man,' *Sinks*, 1848: coll.: not entirely † even by 1948.

liver-jerker. A tricycle: ca. 1890–1914. (G. & W. Grossmith, *The Diary of a Nobody*, 1894.)

liver-pad. A chest-protector, usually of flannel: ca. 1850–1905.

liver-shaker. A riding hack: late C. 19–20. ('Sapper' uses it in *The Lieutenant*, 1915.)

Lives of the Saints. *Crockford's Clerical Directory* established ca. 1871: Clerical: from ca. 1880.

livestock. See **live stock** (*Dict.*).

livid. Furiously angry; very much annoyed: since ca. 1920. Short for *livid with rage*.

living bloody wonder, a. A c.p. of ironic appreciation: Australian: since ca. 1930. (B.P.)

living doll. A very attractive girl: adopted, ca. 1945, ex U.S. Cf. **doll,** n., 4, above.

living end, the. The very end, 'the last straw': Australian ('not common': B.P.): since ca. 1950. Either *living* is ironic or it's an intensive—cf. its use in the preceding entry, where, however, it may = vital; hence, lively and attractive.—2. 'Perfection, the ultimate, the ideal. "But, Daddy, you should meet Harry! He's the living end!"' (Leechman): Canadian: since ca. 1955.

living in seduced circumstances. A jocular c.p., applied to a pregnant unmarried woman: since ca. 1920.

Liz; usually **Lizzie.** A Lysander aircraft: E. P., 'Air Warfare and Its Slang'—*The New Statesman*, Sept. 19, 1942. Partly ex *Lys*(ander), partly an allusion to *Liz(zie)*, a Ford motor-car.

lizard. A sheep-musterer: New Zealand and Australian rural: since ca. 1880. B., 1941, 1942. He has to move both slowly and quietly.

Lizzie.—4. H.M.S. *Queen Elizabeth*. 'Taffrail. Also *Big Lizzie*.—5. A Lysander plane: R.A.F. World War II. (P-G-R.)—6. A Lesbian: since ca. 1928. (Angus Wilson, *The Wrong Set*, 1949.) Ex *Lesbian*: cf. *Les*.—7. An L.M.S. Pacific locomotive: railwaymen's: since late 1940's. *Railway*, 3rd.

load, n.—3. See **get a load on.**

load, n.—4. A 'loafer' or idler; a lazy person: coll.: C. 20. Cf. sense 1.

load bummer. A 1941-4 variant of **line-shooter.** Partridge, 1945. Cf. **load of guff.**

load of, get a. To see, to perceive; understand: Australian: C. 20. B., 1942.

load of guff. 'A lot of humbug or nonsense,' Jackson: R.A.F. (mostly officers'): since ca. 1937.

load of old cobblers, a, esp. in 'That's a load . . .' —that's rubbish or nonsense: since ca. 1960. Often used by people ignorant of its origin in **cobbler's awls** (above). A comparison with **cod's wallop** (above) is unavoidable.

load of rabbits. See **trap.**

load of rough. A bus-load of pass-holders: London busmen's: since ca. 1930.

load of wind. See 'Hauliers' Slang'.

load or weight off one's behind. A defecation: low: since ca. 1925. Parodying:

load (but usually **weight**) **off one's mind.** A haircut: mostly in working-class barber-shops: since ca. 1920. Especially if the 'crop' is heavy.

loaded. (Cf. the note on p. 488.) Tipsy: adopted, ca. 1958 (and used esp. by beatniks), ex U.S.—2. Well-off; having plenty of money: since ca. 1945.

loaded with it. Over-sexed: beatniks': since ca. 1959. (Anderson.)

loafing, adj.—2. (Of gear) left lying about: Naval: C. 20. Granville.

loafing number. 'A nice easy job in depot' (Granville): Naval: C. 20. Ex prec.: cf. next.

loafing stations. Shore stations where men await drafting to ships: Naval: C. 20.

Loamshire dialect. Faulty dialect as used by ignorant writers: authors' coll.: C. 20. There being no such county, there is no such dialect.

Loamshires, the, as applied by novelists to an unspecified line regiment, has been so much used, and abused, that, though S.E., it verges on coll.: late C. 19-20.

loather. A cad: Rugby: since early 1920's. Ex *loathsome* by 'the Oxford -er'.

lob, n.—7. A haul of money: Australian c.: C. 20. B., 1942. Ex sense 1 (p. 488).—8. One's turn to 'lob out'—distribute or pay for—cigarettes and drinks at a convivial gathering: mostly Services': since ca. 1930. (Atkinson.)—9. As *the lob* it also means 'the w.c.': Londoners': C. 20.

lob, v.—**crash lob—force lob.** (Of pilot or aircraft) to land, crash-land, force-land: Air Force: 1939-45. All three occur in Brickhill & Norton's *Escape to Danger*, 1946.

lob in. To arrive; to call at a place: Australian: C. 20. H. Drake Brockman, *Men without Wives*, 1938. Ex sense 3 of **lob,** v. (p. 488).—2. Hence, to intromit (*inmissio penis*): low, mostly English: C. 20. Also, derivatively, *lop in.*

lob onto. To obtain or discover by a stroke of uck: Australian: since ca. 1925. (B., 1943.)

lob out. See **lob,** n., 8.

lob the snout. See **crash the ash** above.

lobscouse, as dialect, is recorded as early as Hone's *Every-day Book*, 1826; in 1706, Ned Ward, *The Wooden World Dissected*, the 'first inventor' of lobscouse was invited to go to the devil. (Ronald Hjort.)

lobster, 2 (p. 489), has also the derivative sense

'a marine', as, several times, in W. N. Glascock, *Sketch-Book*, I and II, 1825-26. (Moe.)

local, adj. Extremely eccentric; mad: South Africa: 1944 +. Professor W. S. Mackie in *The Cape Argus*, July 4, 1946. Corruption of American *loco.*—2. A local newspaper: coll.: since ca. 1910.

Lochinvar, (do) the. To catch, the catching of, Aboriginal women (lubras) to work cattle and perform other rough services: N.T., Australia: C. 20. Ernestine Hill, *The Territory*, 1951.

lock, on the. Attending to prisoners: prison warder's: mid-C. 19-20. B. & L.

lock, stock and barrel; bob, line and sinker. Whole; wholly; the whole lot or completely, entirely: Naval coll.: from ca. 1880. An elaboration of the S.E. idiom, *lock, stock and barrel.*

locket. A pocket: Australian rhyming s.: C. 20. Baker.

loco, adj. Insane; crazy: Canadian: adopted, ca. 1930, ex U.S. Ex the effects of the loco weed. The weed itself derives its name ex the Spanish *loco,* mad, which 'presumably reached N. America with the Jesuit missionaries in California, etc., in C. 17-18' (H. R. Spencer).

locus away (p. 489): Australia, 1893 (Sidney J. Baker, letter); England, 1831 (O.E.D.).

lodge and comp. Lodging-and-provision allowance granted to officers and men living ashore: Naval: C. 20. Granville. Cf. **compo** (p. 174). Short for 'Lodging and Compensation' Allowance.

lodger; gen. pl. Applied chiefly to head lice but also to all vermin—even rats and mice: mostly Cockneys': from ca. 1870.

lodgings. Prison: Australian: late C. 19-20. Baker.

Lofty. Nickname for any tall, thin man: mid-C. 19-20.—2. Ironically for any very short man: late C. 19-20. (P-G-R.)

log. Sense 2 (p. 490), has, since ca. 1920, been common also in Secondary Schools.—4. An energetic afternoon's exercise: R.N.C. Dartmouth: C. 20. Granville. Cf. nautical j. *a day's log.*—5. See **cedar,** 3.—6. A person without ability or brains or energy: Aus.: since early 1930's. (B., 1959.) Ex sense 5.

log, go up a. To hide: Australian: since ca. 1910. B., 1942. As snake or lizard does.

log, make up the. To note the wages: tailors': from ca. 1850. B. & L.

logger's small-pox is those markings on a man's face which are caused by a man's stamping on it with his spiked boots, an activity known as *putting the caulks to* (a man): Canadian loggers': C. 20 Gerald Kersh, *I Got References*, 1939 (p. 177).

logician. See 'Tavern terms', § 3, *l.*

***logue.** A variant of *loge* (p. 490).

loid. Celluloid: since ca. 1910. Hence, **the loid,** the art of using a piece of celluloid to slip open the latch of a door: mostly police: since ca. 1920. (Maurice Procter, *Man in Ambush*, 1958.)

loiner. A townsman: Leeds undergraduates' (— 1940). Marples, 2. Perhaps cf. either **oiner** (p. 581) or dial. *lointer,* to loiter.

Lola Montez. 'A drink of rum, ginger, lemon and hot water,' B., 1942: Australian: ca. 1870-1910. Hot and comforting, like that famous person.

lollipop.—5. See next entry.—Note that 1 (p. 470) occurs earlier in *The London Chronicle*, Jan. 17-20, 1784, p. 72: '. . . sweetmeats, called lolly-pops'. (S. H. Ward, who, by the way, was a descendant of Ned Ward's and a great authority on him.)—6. *Lots of local leave in place of Python* (leave due at end cf overseas service): Army: 1944–5.—7. A 'sugar daddy': shopgirls' and typists': ca. 1955–60.—8. To drop (e.g., a tip): rhyming s.: C. 20. Franklyn, *Rhyming.*—9. A policeman: rhyming s. (on *slop*): C. 20. Franklyn, ibid.—10. A 'shafted tool with iron ball for testing sleepers' (*Railway*): railwaymen's: C. 20. —11. One's girl friend: R.A.F.: 1939–45. A pun on '*sweet*heart'. (Ramsey Spencer.)

lollipop men. Traffic wardens shepherding children at street crossings: since ca. 1955.

Lollos. Female breasts, esp. if impressive and shapely: Australian: since ca. 1955. 'Not common. Probably originally journalistic. Ex the famous Italian film star, Gina Lollobrigida' (B.P.).

lolly, n., 3 (p. 490). Short for *lollipop*, rhyming s. for 'shop': C. 20.—4. Money: Cockney: C. 20. Michael Harrison, *Reported Safe Arrival*, 1943, 'Touches the Guv'ment for a nice drop of lolly.'— 5. Anything easy: Australian: C. 20. (Sidney J. Baker.)—6. An easy catch: cricketers': C. 20. (Hugh de Sélincourt, *The Cricket Match*, 1924.)— 7. A trickster's (easy) victim: Australian: since ca. 1910. (B., 1943.)—8. 'Soft ice beginning to form in harbours' (L. E. F. English, *Historic Newfoundland*, 1955): Newfoundland, C. 20.—9. A criminal either timid or half-hearted, esp. towards a coup: Aus. c.: since ca. 1920. (B., 1959.)

lolly, do one's. To get very angry: Australian: since ca. 1930. (Dick.)

lolly water; since ca. 1960, usu. written as one word. Soft drinks in general; a soft drink: Australian, esp. among those who prefer something stronger; since late 1940's. The implication is that lollies are more suitable for children than for adults.

The earliest printed record I have is Bernard Hesling, *The Dinkumization*, 1963, '"'Ave a lolly water," said the first stranger. "—Straw?" offered the second.'

London and Yorks. Navvies' bowgangs: navvies': ca. 1860–1910. The Rev. D. W. Barrett, *Life and Work among the Navvies*, 1880, derives the word ex the Great North Road (London to York).

London Closet-Cleaners. London County Council: Londoners': C. 20. By pun on the initials *L.C.C.*

London, Smashem and Turnover, the. The London, Chatham & Dover railway: railwaymen's: C. 20; after ca. 1955, only historical. (*Railway* 2nd.) An adaptation of **London Smash 'Em and Do for 'Em Railway** on p. 491.

lone, on one's. Alone: Australian coll.: late C. 19–20. (Vance Palmer, *The Passage*, 1939.)

lone wolf. 'Fighter pilot who leaves formation,' W/Cdr P. McDouall (letter of April 12, 1945): R.A.F.: mid-1940 +. Ex wild-life woodlore; cf. *lone wolf* in *Underworld.*

lonesome, all on cne's. Alone: coll.: since ca. 1890; by 1940, rather ob. W. L. George, *The Making of an Englishman*, 1914. Cf. **all on one's own** in *Dict.*

long blow, the. 'Paddy was beginning the longest cut, the "long blow", from the flank to the top of the head' (Jon Cleary, *The Sundowners*, 1952): Australian sheepshearers': late C. 19–20.

long-distance. 'Long service. Thus, a long-

distance medal' (Jackson): R.A.F.: since ca. 1930. Esp., also, *long-distance type*, a long-service airman: Partridge, 1945.

long drag, the. The 'uphill run from Carlisle to Settle' (*Railway*): railwaymen's: C. 20.

long drink of water. Unhappy-looking man: late C. 19–20.

Long Forties, the. Part of the North Sea, East of Aberdeen: nautical coll.: C. 19–20.

long grass, the. The Provinces: professional actors': C. 20. (Laurie Atkinson, 11 Sept. 1967.) Cf. **sticks,** 10, below.

long-hair. An intellectual; a highbrow: Australian: adopted, ca. 1944, ex U.S. (Dymphna Cusack, 1951.)

long-handled underwear. Men's 'extra-warm winter woollen underclothes, with long legs and sleeves' (Leechman): Canadian: since ca. 1950. Also *Long Johns.*

long-horn (p. 492). Only the Maurice Farman plane: it had a long, up-curving front projection carrying the elevator. (R. M. Inge.)

long in the arm. Addicted to theft: ca. 1870–1920. *Sessions*, Sept. 1893 (Surrey cases). Of one who *will* reach for things.

long-jawed. (Of rope) so strained and so far untwisted that it coils both ways; (of an eye-splice) badly tucked: Naval: late C. 19–20.

Long Johns. See **long-handled underwear** above.

long jump, the.—2. A being hanged: c.: from ca. 1921. Also *take the . . .*, to be hanged.

long-legs.—2. A hare: Australian: late C. 19–20. B., 1942.

*long lib. 'Long lying, last end', Randle Home, 1688. See **lib** (*Dict.*).

long neck. A camel: Australian: late C. 19–20. Archer Russell, *A Tramp Royal in Wild Australia*, 1934, 'He is the despised "humpie", the "filthy camel", the 'stinking old long neck', that 'mangy brute' of the traveller; but he is also . . . the great utility animal of the Inland.'

long-nosed chum. A horse: Army: late C. 19–20; ob. Cf. **long-faced chum** (*Dict.*).

long oats. See **ash beans.**

long paddock, the. The open road: New Zealand and Australian coll.: C. 20. B., 1941 (p. 40) and 1942.

long short'uns or short long'uns? A c.p. addressed to a man wearing trousers that fail to cover the ankles: Australian: since ca. 1930. (B.P.)

long slab. A tall, very thin woman: Londoners': C. 20.

long soup. See **short soup.**

*long-stopper. A look-out man: Aus. c.: C. 20. (B., 1959.) Ex cricket.

long streak of misery. A (very) tall, thin person, even if not miserable-looking: late C. 19–20.

long string of misery. A C. 20 variant of **streak of misery** (p. 838).

long-tail.—7. Treacle: Australian: C. 20. B., 1942.

Long Thinkers, the. The 7th Australian Infantry Division: 6th Division soldiers': 1941–2. Lawson Glassop, 1944. Cf. **Palestine Militia.**

long time dead, you'll be a. A c.p. addressed to someone failing to make the most of life: late C. 19–20.

long time no see. I haven't seen you for a long time: British and American c.p.: C. 20. In

British usage, it derives ex Far East pidgin; in American, either from the British phrase or from Amerindian pidgin. Perhaps the most widely used c.p. in the world.

Wilfred Granville thinks that it came to Britain via the Navy and says that it is a 'Chinaside locution akin to such phrases as *no can do, chop chop, no wanchee*, etc. Naval Officers used to greet "old ships" who'd been on China Station with "Hullo, old boy, long time no see"' (letter of Nov. 5, 1967). Douglas Leechman, however, supports a U.S.–Canadian origination, thus: 'It is based on an anecdote concerning an eminent citizen of some Pacific Coast city, Vancouver, Seattle, or San Francisco, who was showing the sights of Chinatown to a visiting tycoon. They were stopped by a ravishing Chinese girl, obviously of the profession, who cried in delight, "Why Hally. Wassa maller you? Long time no see!" I first heard it about 1910 and used it no later than last week. Very common out here.' (Letter written from Victoria, British Columbia, on Nov. 18, 1967.) Professor F.E.L. Priestley likewise thinks it of American origin—perhaps from the cinematic conception of Red Indian speech.

As for the printed record, the earliest I have is Harry C. Witever, *Love and Learn*, 1924, at p. 73. (Colonel A. F. Moe.)

long togs (p. 492) goes back to ca. 1810, perhaps to late C. 18: it occurs in, e.g., *The Night Watch* (II, 51), 1828, and W. N. Glascock, *Sailors and Saints* (II, 206), 1829. Moe.

long trot, to do the. To go home: low London: from ca. 1860; ob. B. & L.

long 'un. A tall person: coll.: mid-C. 19–20. Also as vocative.

long underwear. Highbrow music: beatniks': since ca. 1959. (Anderson.)

long 'uns. Long trousers: boys' coll.: late C. 19–20.

long-winded. Slow in doing something, not talk: coll.: late C. 19–20.

longer and linger. Finger: rhyming: C. 20.

longers. Fence-rails: Newfoundland: C. 20. (L. E. F. English, 1955.)

Lonsdale (Belt), give (someone) **the.** To dismiss, get rid of: low: since ca. 1940. (Norman.) An elaboration of *give the belt*.

loo. A lieutenant: Naval: ca. 1880–1914.

loo, the. The water closet: late C. 19–20. (Angus Wilson, *The Wrong Set*, 1949.) Ex Fr. *l'eau*. Or perhaps rather ex **gardy-loo** (p. 316).

loob. A cigarette: Plumtree School, Southern Rhodesia: since ca. 1920. Ex Dutch?

loobily. See 'Epithets'. It is more prob. the adv. of **looby** (*Dict.*).

look as if one has lost a pound and found (a) sixpence or occ. . . . **a shilling and found a ha'penny.** A coll. virtually a c.p.: C. 19–20.

look at every woman through the hole in one's prick. To regard every woman as a mere potential instrument of pleasure: low coll.: late C. 19–20.

*****look for Henry.** (Of a confidence-trickster) to look for a victim: c.: from ca. 1920.

look for one's swag-straps. See **swag-straps**.

look here! do me a favour, will you? Run away!; Stop talking: c.p.: since late 1940's.

look like a wet week. See **wet week** below.

look like death warmed up. To look seriously indisposed or even gravely ill: mostly Australian:

since ca. 1920. (B.P.) Adapted ex **feel like** . . . above.

look like the wrath of God. See **wrath of God.**

look marlinspikes. To 'look daggers': nautical, esp. Naval: ca. 1790–1860. *The Night Watch* (II, 119), 1829, 'Then comes the captain with the articles of war in his hand, looking marlinspikes, and calls for Paddy.' (Moe.)

look—no hands! A c.p. often applied to something cleverly done, but not conspicuously—if, indeed, at all—useful: since ca. 1910. Ex cycling.

look out for. 'To take over a shipmate's watch for a spell. "Look out for me for ten minutes, there's a good chap,"' Granville: Naval coll.: C. 20.

look-see. Sense 1 (p. 494) is used in the R.A.F. (1918 +) for a reconnaissance: Jackson.

look-see pidgin. Hypocrisy; mere pretence: pidgin: from ca. 1880. B. & L.

look up, v., 2 (p. 494). Earlier in *Sessions*, Jan. 1788 (p. 159).

look up nor-west-and-by-well. To look cheerful: Naval (? gen. nautical): late C. 18–mid 19. W. N. Glascock, *Sailors and Saints* (I, 210), 1829. '"Never mind that, boy," cried Cheerly, the captain's coxswain, "It can't be so bad with us either, for you see the skipper still looks up nor-west-and-by-well."' (Moe.) Perhaps 'by-all's-well'.

look upon a hedge. To urinate or defecate (in the open air): euphemistic coll.: C. 20. (E. Arnot Robertson, *Four Frightened People*, 1931.) An Elizabethan relic?

look what the cat's brought in! See **like something the cat has brought in** (*Dict.*). Also **see what the wind's blown in!**

looker. A pretty girl: coll.: since ca. 1920. Short for *good-looker*. 'I say, she's a real looker—oh, boy! what a smasher!'

looker-out. A cab-rank attendant: taxi-drivers' coll.: since ca. 1905. Herbert Hodge, *Cab, Sir?*, 1939.

looking all ways for Sunday. Bewildered; stupefied; stupid: North Country: late C. 19–20.

looking for a big penny for a little ha'penny. A North of England coll., almost a c.p., applied to those who always want the best of a bargain: late C. 19–20.

looking for maidenheads. A lower-class c.p. directed at people looking for something unprocurable or, at the least, very scarce: since ca. 1890.

looking up your kilts, here's. A facetious Australian toast. Since ca. 1919. B., 1942.

looks like a wet week-end. An Australian c.p., used—since ca. 1930—by girls menstruating at week-end, and, since late 1930's, by (mostly teenage) males to a girl carrying a parcel that may well, to judge by its size, contain a box or carton of sanitary pads.

loon-flat is B. & L.'s mistake for *loon-slate* (or *loonslatt*).

loony-bin (p. 494): 'very common in Australia' (B.P., 1965).

loop. A fool; a simpleton: Australian low: since ca. 1920. B., 1942.

loop, up the. Mad: military: from ca. 1870. Richards, 'The doctors were undecided as to whether he had lost his mental balance or not. A lot of us believed that he was really up the loop from having played at it so long.' Prob. by a fusion of *loopy* and *up the pole*.

*****loop off.** To run away: c.: C. 18. James

Dalton, *A Narrative*, 1728, 'To loop off with the *Cole*'. A corruption of **lope** on p. 495.

loop-the-loop. Soup: mostly Australian rhyming s.: since ca. 1910.

loose, let. To 'let fly' or express one's anger freely: Australian coll. (— 1939). Dal Stivens, *The Courtship of Uncle Henry*, 1946.

loose, on the. Earning money by prostitution: low coll.: from ca. 1860. B. & L.—2. Out of prison: proletarian: mid-C. 19–20; ob. Ibid.—3. On a drinking bout: Australian: C. 20. B., 1942.—4. On a quite innocent spree.

loose fish, 1 (p. 495) occurs earlier in an 'Anecdote of Garrick' re-told in *The Port Folio* of Oct. 11, 1806, at p. 219, and earlier still in the issue of Nov. 19, 1803, at p. 375. (Moe.)

loose off, v.i. and v.t. To fire a machine-gun or rounds therefrom: R.A.F.: since ca. 1938. Jackson. Of American origin.

loose (or **loosen**) **out.** To unspan a team (of, e.g., draught cattle): Australian coll.: mid-C. 19–20. In, e.g., 'Tom Collins', *Such Is Life*, 1903 (both forms). Cf. South African *outspan*.

loose screw, a. Variant of **a screw loose,** 1 (*Dict.*): 1821, Pierce Egan, *Life in London*.

loot, n.—3. 'Scottish slang for money received on pay day', H. & P.: Services: since ca. 1925. —4. Wedding presents, esp. those garnered collectively: Australian jocular: since late 1940's. (B.P.)

lop. A slight choppiness of the sea: Naval: late C. 19–20. Granville. Cf. North Country *lope*, v.i., 'to curdle'.—2. A wave that, in a choppy sea, is 'big enough to break inboard in a rowboat or dory' (Leechman): Newfoundland coll.: late C. 19–20.

lop in, adj. See **lob in,** 2.

loppy, n. A station 'rouseabout': Australian rural: since ca. 1910. (B., 1943.) Louse-infested; infected: Services: since ca. 1930. H. & P. Ex Yorkshire dial. *loppy*, 'flea-infested'.

Lord Aggie! A variant of **Gawd Aggie!** (above): Australian: C. 20. (B.P.)

lord and master. Husband, as in 'My lord and master will soon be home—and hungry': feminine jocular coll.: since ca. 1910. (B.P.)

Lord Doggo. Lord Keynes: the Treasury: 1942–5. His room was opposite Lord *Catto's*.

Lord Haw-Haw. See **Haw-Haw.**

Lord Mayor. To stare (?): racecourse rhyming s.: C. 20.

Lord Nelson. 1 cwt 1 qr 1 lb, or *three ones*: London warehousemen's: since ca. 1870. Of the same origin as **Three Ones.**

Lord Russell. An occ. variant of **Lord John Russell** (p. 495). Franklyn 2nd.

Lord's My Shepherd, the. The L.M.S. Railway: C. 20. (*Railway*, 3rd.)

lorry-hopping. 'Lorry-jumping' is inadequate: *lorry-hopping* was obtaining a ride in a lorry when one would otherwise have had to walk; gen. by stopping the driver and asking his permission, but occ. by clambering aboard as it is in progress; practised esp. on a pleasure-jaunt. From 1916 also as v., either *lorry-hop* (v.i.) or *lorry-hop it*; e.g. 'I lorry-hopped (it) to Amiens.'

*lorst, in the. Engaged in shoplifting: c.: ca. 1850–1900. Burton, *Vikram and the Vampire*, 1870. (The term is suspect.)

lose a meal. To vomit: Australian: C. 20. B., 1942. Jocularly euphemistic.

lose one's dash—one's punch. To lose one's energy and ability: since ca. 1880, 1900, resp.: coll. >, by 1930, S.E.

lose one's name. A post-1920 variant of *lose one's number* (p. 496).

losh! Lord!: C. 19–20. Cf. *gosh!*

loss(-)leader is the Canadian coll. equivalent, in C. 20, of *draw-boy* (p. 240). Leechman.

lot, n., 2 (p. 496). Or independently: 'I know the *lot* you mean, I was there,' *Sessions*, Feb. 17, 1902.—5. A taxicab: taxi-drivers': since ca. 1915. Herbert Hodge, *Cab, Sir?*, 1939. Ex the auction-room sense.—6. (With possessive pronoun—*his*, *your*, etc.) A man's genitals: feminine: late C. 19–early 20.

lot, v. To allot: lower-class coll.: 1914 +.

lot, do the. See **do the lot.**

lot of cock, a. See **cock, hot,** above.

lots. Many: coll.: late C. 18–20. *Boxiana*, IV, 1824, 'Hundreds were seen scampering . . .; *lots* looked like drowning rats.' See also **lot, a** (p. 496, col. 1).

Lot's Wife (p. 496). Also, in C. 20, a Regular Army term.

Lotta Girls, the. The Finnish Auxiliary Corps: 1939–40. Punning *Lotta*, a Continental girl's name, and *lot of*, 'many'.

loud one.—4. A severe wound: Army: 1914 +. Cf. sense 3 (p. 496).

loud pedal. An accelerator: Australian: motorists': since ca. 1940. (B.P.)

louie (pron. *looee*). A lieutenant: Forces: adopted ca. 1939 from U.S.

*lounge. 'The prisoner's box in a criminal court,' B., 1942: Australian c.: C. 20. Ironic.

lounge(-)lice. 'Lounge lizards': Australian: since ca. 1930. Baker.

lounge Lizzie. A (usually, female) writer of gossip for a newspaper: journalistic, mainly: since ca. 1920. Sydney Horler, *The Dark Journey*, 1938. Ex *lounge lizard*.

louse, three skips of a. See **three skips of a louse** (*Dict.*).

louse-bag.—2. A term of opprobrium or deep scorn for a person: C. 20. Gerald Kersh, *Bill Nelson*, 1942.

louse cage. A caboose: Canadian railroadmen's (— 1931).

louse-ladder.—2. A run in a woman's stocking: since ca. 1935. Ex sense 1 on p. 497: either a revival or a subterranean survival. (These words which go underground for a generation or a century or even longer provide one of the prettiest puzzles in the whole network of a language.)

louse-ladders. Side-whiskers: since ca. 1920. Contrast **louse-ladder** on p. 497.

louser. An objectionable person: Anglo-Irish: since ca. 1945. (Brian Moore, *The Luck of Ginger Coffey*, 1960.) One who *louses* things up. Rather, since ca. 1920, *teste* Nicholas Blake, *The Private Wound*, 1968, ref. the year 1939.

lousie-look'd. I.e. lousy-looking. See 'Epithets'.

lousy as a bandicoot. Very lousy indeed: Australian coll.: since ca. 1916. (B., 1943.)

Lousy Brown, the. The Rose and Crown (tavern or inn): rhyming s., esp. Londoners': C. 20. (Franklyn, *Rhyming*.)

love-bubbles. Female breasts of a pleasing contour: Army (not very common): since ca. 1930.

love 'em and leave 'em, adj. and n. Give not philandering; a philanderer: coll.: late C. 19–20.

love-in. 'A gathering associated with groovy scene' (Peter Fryer in *The Observer* colour supplement, Dec. 3, 1967): beatniks' and then hippies': since early 1960's. On analogy of the prototypal *-in* compounds *sit-in* and *teach-in*. Cf. **think-in** below.

love(-)truck. A 'small covered-in lorry,' *The New Statesman*, Aug. 30, 1941.

love-up, n. Intimate caresses; love-making: Australian low coll.: C. 20. Caddie, *A Sydney Barmaid*, 1953. '"Come on, what about a little bit of a love-up?" he went on.' Ex:

love up, v. To caress intimately, make love to: Australian: low coll.: C. 20. (K. S. Prichard, 'Two Men'—in *Kiss on the Lips*, 1932.)

lovely and . . . See **beautiful and . . .**

lovely bit of boy. A Servicewomen's c.p. in approval of a man: 1939 +.

lovely drop of. See **nice drop of.**

lovely grub! Very nice indeed!: Forces' c.p.: 1939 +. Transferred from food to anything else that looks gratifying.

lovely money. Good money; esp. plenty of money: Londoners': from ca. 1931.

lover boy. 'Man of age and appearance to be disposed to love: sometimes mock-affectionate or contemptuous': Laurie Atkinson, who, Sept. 11, 1967, adds that he first heard it in 1963 and that the expression had twice been used recently in two television plays, one being *Z Cars* on June 19, 1963: coll. rather than s., and app. dating from ca. 1960.

lover under the lap. A Lesbian: Australian: C. 20. Not very gen.

Lovers' code-initials. Mostly lower and lower-middle class, and widely used by Servicemen: C. 20; perhaps also late C. 19. Usually at the foot, or on the envelopes, of letters. The commonest of all is *S.W.A.L.K.*, sealed with a loving kiss; common also are *B.O.L.T.O.P.*, better on lips than on paper (set over against *X*, a 'paper kiss'), and *I.L.U.V.M.*, I love you very much. The next three occur in John Winton, *We Saw the Sea*, 1960, but are, of course, very much older: *I.T.A.L.Y.*, I trust and love you; *B.U.R.M.A.*, Be undressed ready, my angel (dating from W.W. II); *N.O.R.W.I.C.H.*, Nickers off ready when I come home (probably since W.W. I).

With thanks to Laurie Atkinson (Sept. 11, 1967), who cautiously adds that there are doubtless others. The phonetic element is worth noting. Also note the symbol ( ): an embrace.

lover's leap. 'The first early-morning train from London to Portsmouth' (Granville): Naval wardrooms': C. 20.

lovey-dovey (p. 497) may have been current throughout C. 18 as well, for *Sessions*, 1735, has '"Why; Dovee," says she . . .'

lovey-dovey stuff. 'Sentimental fiction published for the servant-girl type' (Albert B. Petch, Aug. 22, 1946): book-world coll.: since ca. 1925.

low, n.—2. See **high,** n.

low boost. See **boost, be in high** or **low.**

Low-Country soldier. See 'Tavern terms', § 2.

low heel. A prostitute: Australian: C. 20. B., 1942.—2. Hence (?), a dead-beat: Australian since ca. 1920.

Low Road, the. The 'Glasgow line via Dalry' (*Railway*, 3rd): C. 20. Ex a famous song.

Lower Tartary. See **Upper Tartary.** (Also called *Botany Bay* and *Hell*: Spy, II, 1826.)

lower than a snake's hips (or **belly**). An opprobrious c.p., esp. in the Armed Forces: 1939 +. (Atkinson.) Hence, since ca. 1945, the shortened form, *lower than a snake* and, since ca. 1947, the derivative *he'd* (or *he could*) *crawl under a snake's belly with a top hat on.* (Atkinson, 1959.)

lowerdeckese. The slang used by the lower-deck (non-commissioned officers and men): Naval officer's coll. (since ca. 1900) >, by 1945, S.E. (Granville.)

lowest form of animal life, the. A reporter: journalistic: since ca. 1925.—2. Hence, an A.C.2: R.A.F.: since ca. 1935.

lowest form of human life, the.—3. Hence, jocular for apprentices, trainees, office boys *et hoc genus omne*: since ca. 1945.

lowie. A prostitute: low Australian: since ca. 1930. Cf. *low-heel*, 1. (Kylie Tennant, *The Joyful Condemned*, 1953.)

lowze (occ. written *lowse*). A whistle indicating the end of a shift; knocking-off time: North Country miners': late C. 19–20. Ex *loose*?

Loyal Standbacks, the. The **Indispensables, the,** above.

lozenge (p. 498) occurs very much earlier, in sense 'rifle bullet', in John L. Gardner, *The Military Sketch-Book* (II, 17), 1831, thus, 'The French . . . opened fire on us, which knocked many a poor fellow off the hooks, and we fell back . . .; for we were only treating the enemy with a few steel lozenges.' (Moe.)

lubber. See 'Occupational names'.

lubbers. See **dabblers.**

lube. Lubrication, as in 'a *lube* job': motorists': since ca. 1920; by 1950, coll.—2. 'A drink, esp. of beer' (B., 1959): Aus.: since late 1940's. Lubrication of the throat.

lubra.—2. (In game of bridge) a Yarborough: Australian rhyming s.: since ca. 1926. B., 1942.

lubricate.—2. (Of the male) to copulate with: raffish London: C. 18-early 19. It occurs in, e.g., Boswell's *London Journey*.—3. To ply (someone) with drink: v.i., to drink: since ca. 1880; by 1940, ob.; by 1960, virtually †.

***luck, fuck, and a fiver!** A prostitutes' toast in first decade, C. 20. The 'fiver' is £5.

Lucky. Lieut.-General Sir Miles Dempsey: since 1944. He commanded the 2nd Army in Normandy in 1944–5.

lucky, cap one's. To decamp: Australian: C. 20. B., 1942. Ex **lucky, cut one's** (*Dict.*).

lucky, cut one's (p. 498). Rather, since ca. 1820: *make* . . . occurs in P. Egan, *Finish*, 1828.

lucky Charlie. See **getaway man.**

lucky for some. 13 in game of House: C. 20. Michael Harrison, *Reported Safe Arrival*, 1943.

lucky man, the. The bridegroom: coll.: late C. 19–20. Used by women, not by men.

Lucy and Mary (or vice versa). The *Lusitania* and the *Mauretania*: nautical: ca. 1912–40.

luff, 2 (p. 498), goes back to 1806 (John Davis, *The Post-Captain*); cf. also Alfred Burton, *The Adventures of Johnny Newcome*, 1818. (Moe.)

luffed in for, be. 'To be put in the way of something either pleasant or unpleasant. "We got luffed in for paint ship,"' Granville: Naval: late C. 19–20. Ex the S.E. senses—as, e.g., in *luff the helm.*

lufftackle. A lieutenant (? of marines): Naval

lowerdeck: late C. 18–mid 19. John Davis, *The Post-Captain*, 1806; W. N. Glascock, *Sailors and Saints* (I, 16), 1829. Moe. A lowerdeck pun.

lug, on the. 'On the borrow' or 'ear-biting' (seeking a loan): North Country: C. 20. Cf.:—

lug (someone's) **ear.** To ask for, to borrow, money from: Australian low: C. 20. B., 1942. Cf. **bite**, n., 8.

luke.—2. See **leuc.**

lulu. A very good show-place, where much money is made: Canadian carnival s.: since ca. 1925. Ex U.S. s. *lulu*, anything very attractive—or profitable. The American sense was adopted, ca. 1944, by Australians. (B.P.)—3. Always *the lulu* (or *Lulu*). A water-closet: upper classes': since ca. 1925. (Noel Coward, *To Step Aside*, 1939.) An elaboration of **loo, the,** above.

lumber, n.—3. 'Hide-out for stolen property,' F. D. Sharpe, *The Flying Squad*, 1938: c.: C. 20. Ex senses 1, 2 (p. 499).—4. Trouble: low: since ca. 1935. Peter Crookston, *Villain*, 1967, 'One night I got into a bit of lumber because I started giggling at the efforts of a fat lady who was a terrible singer.'—5. A resort of confidence tricksters, swindlers, thieves: c.: since ca. 1850; † by 1920. Renton Nicholson, *An Autobiography*, 1860, defines it as 'a place known to the "magsman"', generally a public-house or beershop kept by a friend of the "school"'. Ex sense 1 on p. 499.

lumber, v., 2 (p. 449), has survived in Australia: witness Kylie Tennant, *The Joyful Condemned*, 1953.—3. (As v.i.; but usually in form *lumbering*.) To court a girl: Teddy boys': since ca. 1954. 'Lumbering, mate. You know—courting. Going steady with a chick.'

lumber, be in.—2. To be in trouble, esp. as in 'I'm in dead lumber' (great trouble): orig.—ca. 1930 – c.; by 1950, low s.

lumber out. To eject (a person): Australian: C. 20. B., 1942. Cf. **lumber, v.,** 2 (p. 499).

lumbered.—3. Short of cash; financially embarrassed: London's East End: since ca. 1946. (Richard Herd, Nov. 12, 1957.)

lumbered, be or **get.** To get oneself 'landed' with, e.g., an unpleasant task or job: since ca. 1950.

*lumberer.—6. A brothel tout; one who lures men down alleys in order that others may rob them: Australian c.: since ca. 1920. See *Underworld*.

lump, n.—4. Short for **lump of lead** (*Dict.*): late C. 19–20.

lump, v., 2 (p. 499) has survived in Cockney (A. Neil Lyons, *Hookey*, 1902), though ob. by 1940.

lump into. To do (a job) with vigour: Cockneys': late C. 19–20. Esp. as adjuration, *lump into it!*

lump of, a. A large quantity; much: Australian coll.: late C. 19–20. 'Still a big lump of sea on down at the bar' (Kylie Tennant, *Lost Haven*, 1947).

lump of lead.—2. (Loaf of) bread: Australian rhyming s.: C. 20.

lumpy, 2 (p. 500). An early instance: *Sessions*, Nov. 28, 1833.

lunatic hat. A (very) wide-brimmed hat: Australian: since ca. 1930. (B., 1943.)

lunatic soup. Strong drink: New Zealand: C. 20. B., 1941, 'Lack of vigour or colour could not . . . be a charge levelled against such terms

for strong drink as *lunatic soup, Africa speaks, plonk, steam, red Ned,* or *sheep wash.*' In Australia it specifically = 'cheap, red wine' (B., 1942). Elsewhere (Michael Harrison, *Reported Safe Arrival*, 1943) we find the variant *lunatic's broth.*

lunch, n., 3 (p. 500), should be modified thus: '*Pace* Beames, not necessarily heavy, but used in the older sense of a "lump" at almost any time of the day, especially if it is, in some way, out of the usual run of events' (Leechman: May 1959).—4. 'What you become after a wipe out' (*Pix*, Sept. 28, 1963): Australian surfers', esp. teenagers': since ca. 1961.

lung. A drawbar: Canadian railroadmen's (– 1931).—2. The female bosom, as in 'Get a load of that doll! She's got plenty of lung' (prominent breasts): Australian low: since ca. 1955. 'Ex proximity of breasts to lungs?' (B.P.)

lung-disturber. Penis: low: C. 20. Ex the same ribald song as **kidney-wiper** above.

lurcher. A larrikin, a street tough: Australian low: C. 20. B., 1942.

lurid limit, the. The very limit: Australian: since ca. 1925. Baker. Cf. English *the ruddy limit.*

lurk, n., 1, is far from ob. in Australia in its nuance 'a racket' (Sidney J. Baker, letter in *The Observer*, Nov. 13, 1938).—2. (p. 500): by 1945, no longer low at all; mostly, since ca. 1920, in *up to all the lurks,* wide-awake, alert, and *a good lurk,* a smart plan, a good idea. (B.P.)—3. Direct ex Shelta: B. & L.—5. A hanger-on; an eavesdropper; a sneak: Australian low: C. 20. Baker.

lurked, be. To be chosen for a disagreeable duty one cannot avoid or evade: Services: C. 20.

lurker.—3. A petty crook: Australian low: C. 20. (B., 1953.)

lurkie (or **-ky**). A very wide-awake person, 'up to' all the 'lurks' or tricks: Australian: since ca. 1920. (B.P.) Cf. **lurk,** n., 1, on p. 500.

lurkman. A petty criminal: Australian: since ca. 1870; by 1920, †.—2. Hence, one who cheats at cards; a cardsharp: Australian: C. 20. (B., 1953.)—3. A racketeer or a 'shady' schemer. Also **lurk artist.**

lurkmanship. The art or the practice of the **lurk,** 1 and 2, above. (B., 1959.)

lurn. Scrotum: since ca. 1910. Origin? Perhaps a perversion ex 'to *lean*'.

lush, n., 4 (p. 500), is still common in Canada and owes something of its currency to the widespread use of the term in C. 20 U.S.

lush, adj.—3. As an extension of sense 1 it also = paralytic or half-witted: c.: C. 20.—4. Dainty: Eton: from ca. 1860; ob. B. & L.—5. (Of a girl) extremely attractive; esp. sexually: Services: since ca. 1915. An early use: 'a *lush* bint' (W.W. I). Granville, 'Rivals "smashing" in popularity on the lower deck.' Granville derives it ex *luscious* and he may be right. I propose, however, an extension of *lush* as in S.E. 'lush grass', where it = 'fresh and juicy': cf. **juicy,** 1 and 6 (p. 446).—6. (Of creature comforts) rich; appetising; plentiful: Services: 1939 +. Ex 5.

lush merchant. A drunkard: Australian: late C. 19–20. Baker.

*lush-roller. A pickpocket operating on drunkards, half-wits, paralytics: c.: C. 20. (*The Evening News*, Dec. 9, 1936, in an able essayette by Graveney Lodge.) See **lush** in *Dict.*

lush (someone) up. To stand someone a treat (of strong liquor); as v.i., *lush up,* to drink heavily: since ca. 1930.

lushings. Australian variant of lashings (p. 470): C. 20. Baker.

luxon, adj. *De luxe*: Christ's Hospital: C. 20. Marples. Ex *luxury one* or *de luxe one*?

Lyceum Charley. A (young) male entrant in, and for, the 'Mecca dancing' contests at the Lyceum Ballroom (formerly the Lyceum Theatre); or any youth in full evening dress, whether he intends to dance or not: Cockneys': since ca. 1960.

lyesken chirps. Fortune-telling; telling a fortune: Shelta: C. 18–20. B. & L.

lying in. See lie in (*Dict.*).

lyonch, gone to. A c.p. of ca. 1930–9 for 'gone to lunch' or anywhere else. James Street, *Carbon Monoxide,* 1937. (*Lyons* + lun*ch*.) Ex a famous Lyons advertisement.

M

M. See entry **C-K-M-O.**

M.B.; suffer from M.B. Tipsy; to be tipsy: Australian: since ca. 1930. Ex the well-known brand of beer, Melbourne Bitter. (B., 1953.)

M.F.U. Military 'fuck-up' or muddle: mostly Army: 1939–45. Cf. *S.A.M.F.U.*

M.I.K. Go ahead and eat it!: domestic c.p.: late C. 19–20. I.e. more in the kitchen: contrast **F.H.B.** (F. W. Thomas, private letter, 1939.)

M.Y.O.B. Mind your own business: C. 20. Also *M.Y.O.B.B.* (. . . bloody business).

ma.—4. One's wife: lower-middle-class term of address: mid-C. 19–20. Robert Eton, *The Bus Leaves for the Village*, 1936.

ma-in-law. Mother-in-law: humorous: late C. 19–20.

Ma State, the, on p. 502: † by 1959 (Baker, *The Drum*).

ma-ta. See **mata.**

maalish, adj. Indifferent; 'easy'; esp. 'I'm maalish'—I don't mind, either way; I'm agreeable: Army: since ca. 1920. Ex Arabic.

maalish or **maaleesh,** v. To be completely indifferent to or about; to ignore; to consign to the waste-paper basket: Army: since ca. 1925. Also an adj., as in 'He's dead maaleesh'. Both uses, ex the preceding.

Mabel. A girl friend: Australian soldiers': 1939–45. (B., 1943.)

mabsoot or **mabsut.** Happy: Services', esp. in World Wars I and II. Arabic.

Mac. McMaster University, Hamilton, Ontario: Canadian coll.: C. 20.—2. A non-cultured Canadian (? ex U.S.) form of address to a man of unknown surname: since ca. 1930.—3. The Rt Hon. Harold Macmillan, Prime Minister in 1957–63; also nicknamed **SuperMac,** on *superman*: mostly journalistic, esp. since 1957; the longer name, only since ca. 1960.

mac, 2 (p. 502). Nuance 'mud scraped or swept from *macadamised roads*': 1851, Mayhew, II.

macaroni, 3 (p. 502). Also, esp. in 1940–4, an Italian aircraft (Jackson).—5. A 'pony' (£25): C. 20. Ex sense 4.—6. Lengths of electric flex: cinematographic: since ca. 1925. Laurence Meynell, *The House in the Hills*, 1937.—7. Nonsense; folly: Australian: since ca. 1930. (B., 1943.)

Macaroni Boats or **Liners, the.** The Norddeutscher Lloyd vessels: nautical: ca. 1890–1914. They carried many emigrants from Italy to U.S.

macaroon. A new recruit: Australian Naval: 1939–45. (B., 1943.) Because he 'takes the biscuit' in awkwardness and ignorance?

macaroon, confiscate the. See **confiscate the macaroon** (*Dict.*). B. & L.: *monopolise the macaroon.*

MacDonald, do a. To desert one's party: Labour Leaders': since ca. 1930. Like most political gibes, this one is unfair.

*mace, get stuff on the; often as vbl n., **getting**

. . . To obtain goods by false pretences: c.: late C. 19–20. (*The Yorkshire Post*, latish May 1937.)

MacGimp. A pimp: low rhyming s.: adopted, ca. 1930, ex U.S. Franklyn 2nd, 'It is rarely used in Britain.'

MacGinnis (or **McGinnis** or **Maginnis**) **on, put the.** To render an opponent *hors-de-combat*: Australian: C. 20. B., 1942. Ex wrestling?—2. Hence, to put pressure on: since ca. 1910.

machin. A merchant: pidgin: from ca. 1830. B. & L.

Mack. A 10-ton lorry: Army: since ca. 1938. (P-G-R.)

Mackay, the real (p. 503). No; almost certainly the U.S. *McCoy* is a folk-etymologizing of *Mackay*; *the real Mackay* (see *From Sanskrit to Brazil*) dates from well before 1900, and was orig. a Scotch phrase. 'Tom Collins' Joseph Furphy's *Such Is Life*, 1903, contains 'There was an indescribable something . . . which made us feel that station aristocracy to be mere bourgeoisie, and ourselves the real Mackay.'

macker. A familiar form (Australian) of *macaroni*, a pony (horse). B., 1945.

macky. See **makki.**

Macready pauses! A theatrical c.p. applied to an actor that pauses too long: since ca. 1855. William Macready (1793–1873), the great mid-C. 19 actor, had a habit of pausing inordinately in any emphatic or dramatic speech. (Communicated by Wilfred Granville.)

mad; esp. in *this is mad,* that's excellent: South African: since ca. 1920.

mad, get out (one's). To become angry: Aus.: since ca. 1920. (B., 1959.)

mad as a cut snake. Very mad; exceedingly angry: Australian: from ca. 1890. Here, *cut* = castrated. Other Australian similes are *mad as a beetle*—*a Chinaman*—*a dingbat*—*a goanna*—*a gumtree full of galahs*—*a snake*: B., 1942. Also *silly as a curlew*—*a two-bob watch*—*a wet hen.* (B., 1959.)

mad as a maggot, with or without preceding *as.* Extremely eccentric: hence, egregiously foolish: New Zealand: C. 20. (Slatter.)

mad as a meat-axe. Utterly mad: Aus.: C. 20. (Nino Culotta, *Cop This Lot*, 1960.)

mad as a wet hen. Intensely annoyed: Canadian: since ca. 1920(?). Leechman. Ex the U.S. *mad,* angry.

mad dog.—2. 'An account which the debtor refuses to pay,' B., 1942: Australian: C. 20. See **tie up a dog.**—3. 'An unpaid score at a public-house' (Baker): Australian: C. 20.

mad ear. See **ear-mad.**

mad Fan. The bird Grey Fantail: Australian: late C. 19–20. (B., 1943.)

mad Greek. See 'Tavern terms', § 2.

mad haddock. A very eccentric, a crazy, or a very foolish person: Australian: C. 20. Baker.

mad house, up the, adv. and adj. 'Working trains into London (S.R.)' (*Railway* 2nd): railwaymen's: since late 1940's.

mad Mick. A pick: Australian: since late C. 19. B., 1942.—2. Penis: Australian rhyming s. (on *prick*): since ca. 1910. Franklyn, *Rhyming.*

mad mile, the. That part of the Perth–Fremantle road which runs through Claremont: W. Australian: since ca. 1920. Baker.—2. Hence, in the Australian Navy, the round made by a man either on draft, in or out of a depot, or in being demobilised: World War II.—3. In the British Army of the same period, the term denoted any such stretch of a road as was continually being shelled by the enemy.

mad minute. Bayonet drill, esp. in its finale: Australian soldiers': 1939–45. (B., 1943.)

mad money (p. 503) has, since ca. 1918, meant money that a girl carries as a precaution against any such quarrel with her boy friend as might leave her monetarily stranded, and been widely used also in Australia and Canada.

mad nurse. 'A nurse attending on insane patients' (O.E.D.): coll.: mid-C. 18–20; ob. (*The World*, 1753.)—2. A teacher, usu. female, in a school for mentally deficient children: mostly Primary schoolteachers': since ca. 1920.

madam, n. 1 (p. 503), has long borne also the well-known sense, 'proprietress, or manageress, of a brothel': coll.: C. 18 (? late C. 17)–20. James Dalton, *A Narrative*, 1728, p. 46, 'A Madam pick'd him up, and he being very much in Liquor, went along with his false Guide, who soon conducted him to a Baudy-House.' Sense 4 should be 3.—4. (Ex 1.) As *proper madam*, it=a girl with a bad temper; a *proper little madam*, a girl child with one: lower-middle and lower classes': C. 19–20.

*madam, v. To tell a tall story; 'pitch the tale': c.: from ca. 1930. In, e.g., F. D. Sharpe, *The Flying Squad*, 1938. Ex **madam,** n., 3.

madam, it's (or **that's**) **all.** It's all nonsense or bunkum or 'eye-wash': since ca. 1935: originally low, but by 1940 general.

madame, the. The owner or the manageress of a brothel: mid-C. 19–20. So often she is French. . . .

Madame Bishop. A drink (port, sugar, nutmeg): Australian: ca. 1880–1920. Baker. Ex a formerly well-known hotel-keeper. But 'the drink's attribution to a well-known Australian hotel-keeper may be coincidental' (Ramsey Spencer); in short, the Aus. term may be an extension of C. 18–19 S.E. *bishop*, 'mulled and spiced port' (O.E.D.). Note, however, that Ramsey Spencer, July 20, 1968, adds that Sir Arthur Bryant, in *The Age of Elegance* (1950), dates it firmly back to 1814, on the basis of contemporary menus.

Madame de Luce. Deceptive talk: rhyming s. (on *spruce*): late C. 19–20. (Franklyn, *Rhyming.*) Since ca. 1930, usually *madam*: cf. *madam*, 4, on p. 503.

madder. An unusual or eccentric boy: Harrow School: C. 20. Lunn. By 'the Oxford -*er*' ex *madman.*

made of money?, do you think I'm; or **you must think I'm** . . . A c.p. to a financial importunate: C. 20.

made up. Promoted (stages: L.A.C.–W.O.): R.A.F. coll.: since 1925. H. & P. Ex the social sense, 'painted and powdered'.

Mademoiselle from Armentiers has, from 1919 and esp. among Cockneys, been the female counterpart—occ. the companion—of **Ballocky Bill the Sailor** (*Dict.*).

madhouse! The call for three (one *plus* double one): darts players': since ca. 1930.

Madhouse, the. The Public Relations Office at Algiers: Army officers': 1943–4. (P-G-R.)

madman's broth. Brandy: Aus.: C. 20. Mary Durack, *Keep Him My County*, 1955. Cf. **Nelson's blood** on p. 556.

Mae West. A life-jacket worn by aircrews: R.A.F.: since 1937 or 1938. 'A pilot "goes to the movies" . . . wearing a "Mae West"—a lifejacket which bulges in the right places—in case he lands in the water,' Allan A. Michie & Isabel Waitt, 'Air Slanguage' in *The Reader's Digest* of Feb. 1941; Jackson, 1943, 'The film actress Mae West being especially notable for her buxom bosom thereby assuring for herself a place in the dictionary. Now used officially.'—2. Hence, a lifebelt issued to troops at sea: Army: 1940–5.—3. A breast: rhyming s.: since ca. 1930; by 1959, ob. (Franklyn, *Rhyming.*)

Mafeking is relieved! A c.p. used by shift workers on being relieved; also, vulgarly, by workmen after defecation: Australian: C. 20. (B.P.)

mafoo. A horse-boy; groom: pidgin: mid-C. 19–20. B. & L. Ex cultured Chinese *mah*, a horse.

mag, n.—9 (pron. *madge*). A magistrate; policemen's: since ca. 1870. Ernest Raymond, *We the Accused*, 1935.—10. In C. 18 c. and low s., a sodomite. James Dalton, *A Narrative*, 1726. Perhaps short for *Maggie.*

mag, v.—3. To talk to or at: Aus.: C. 20. '"You magged the poor boy into a daze. You and your silly stories"': H. D. Williamson, *Sammy Anderson*, 1959.

Magger of Bagger, the. The Master of Balliol: Oxford undergraduates' (— 1920). Marples, 2.

maggie or **Maggie.**—5. A Miles Magister elementary training aircraft: R.A.F.: since ca. 1938. (E. P., 'Air Warfare and its Slang' in *The New Statesman*, Sept. 19, 1942.) I.e. '*Mag*ister'.—6. A *mag*netic mine: Naval: 1939 +.—7. A machinegun nest: Army: 1940–5. (P-G-R.) *Maggie* is the diminutive of *Mag*: here we have *mag*, derived thus: *machine*-gun nest.—8. Mostly in pl. *Maggies*, matrons at Borstal institutions: since ca. 1930. *The Daily Telegraph*, June 4, 1967, 'Bacon Bonies, Joes & Maggies'.

Maggie Miller. That method of washing clothes which consists in towing them over the stern while the ship is under way: Naval: late C. 19–20. Granville, 'The origin, like that of most naval slang terms, is lost in obscurity': true; yet perhaps it is *Maggie* because that is a name common among washerwomen, and as for *Miller*—well, see **Andrew Millar** (p. 13). The Navy's washerwoman?

Maggie Moores, often shortened to *maggies*, is Australian rhyming s. for (women's) drawers: C. 20. B., 1942.

Maggies, the. The French *Maquis*: Army in France: 1944–5. (P-G-R.)

magging, n. (p. 504). In C. 20 Australia, 'chaffing, gossiping' (Culotta).—2. Confidencetrickery, swindling, mostly on a small scale: c.:

since ca. 1840. Renton Nicholson, *An Autobiography*, 1860, at p. 30.

maggot. Money: low s. and c.: C. 20. See quotation at **legit** above. Origin?

maggot, gallop one's. See **gallop one's maggot.**

maggot-brained. See 'Epithets'.

maggoty.—2, 'Angry, irritable, "snooty"' (Baker): Australian: since ca. 1920.

magic circle, the. 'The area within a quarter-mile radius of Piccadilly Circus,' Herbert Hodge, *It's Draughty in Front*, 1938: London taxi-drivers': since ca. 1920. Plenty of 'jobs'.

magic doctors. Ground-staff engineers: R.A.F.: ca. 1930–42, then ob. *The Weekly Telegraph*, Jan, 25, 1941.

Maginnis. See **MacGinnis.**

magnoon. A variant spelling of *maghnoon* (p. 504).

magpie.—7. A *Magpie*, a South Australian: C. 20. Baker.—8. An official that leaves State papers in a car or taxi: since ca. 1938.

Magpies, the. Collingwood footballers: Melbournites': since ca. 1910. (B., 1943.) Ex black-and-white jerseys.

magsman.—2. A talkative person, a chatterer: Australian: since ca. 1925. (D'Arcy Niland, *Call Me . . .*, 1958.)

Mah Jong slang terms.

A player writes, late in 1961: We have the White Dragon referred to as 'soup' (being a completely blank—or clean—tile). There are three suits commonly referred to as (*a*) woods, bamboos, sticks; (*b*) balls, circles; (*c*) characters, ricks or 'icks. These are numbered 1 to 9, and some have nicknames:

WOODS: 1. bird or shitehawk or hawk
          2. Long Annie
          3. tripod, hence tripe
          8. garden-gate, hence gate
          9. all the wood

CIRCLES: 1. plate
          2. dog's (for dog's balls)
          3. 'broker (for pawnbroker's three balls)
          4. taxi (four wheels or circles)
          5. spare wheel
          7. main crane
          8. scrubber
          9. all the balls.

RICKS: 1. Eric (from 'a rick')
       6. spew (from 'seasick' through 'six 'ick')

mahleesh. Hence also an adj., as in 'He's mahleesh'—fatalistic or indifferent.

mahogany.—5. See **cedar,** 3.

mahogany slosh. Cook-shop, or coffee-stall, tea: Cockneys': ca. 1870–1914. Ex the colour and the taste.

Mahogany Top. Nickname for a red-headed man: ca. 1860–1900. (D. W. Barrett, 1880.) Cf. *Copper Knob.*

maid, v. To act as maid to: theatrical coll.: C. 20. Somerset Maugham, *Theatre*, 1937, '"I'm young enough to dress 'er. And maid 'er."'

Maid tends, in Australia, to be prefixed to any girl named Marion: C. 20. Ex the *Maid Marion* of the Robin Hood legend. (B.P.)

maiden.—3. A maiden speech: Parliamentary

coll.: late C. 19–20.—4. Cloves; peppermint: Australian: ca. 1870–1920. B., 1942.—5. Probationary nurse that is paid less and does more work: Norland nurses': since ca. 1920.

Maidenhead maggot. A shirker: 1914–18. ('Sapper' in *The Lieutenant*, 1915.) Ex 'lounge lizards' disporting themselves at Maidenhead.

maidenheads. Parentheses: Canadian printers': late C. 19–20. Cf. *parentheses* on p. 606.

maiden's blush. Ginger beer and raspberry cordial: Australian: C. 20. Baker.

maiden's water. Any weak drink, esp. of beer: since ca. 1880. Whence, probably, *maid's water.*

maid's ring. The hymen: Cockney coll.: C. 19–20.

maid's water. Any weak drink; esp. of tea: Australian: late C. 19–20. Baker.

*****mail,** n. A liquor-carrier for an illicit grog-shop: South African c.: C. 20. *The Cape Times*, May 23, 1946. He carries important 'messages'.

mail run, the. Regular raids on Benghazi: R.A.F.: 1941–3.

maillhas or **mailyas.** Fingers: Shelta: C. 18–20. B. & L. Whence **mauley** (*Dict.*).

main-brace, splice the (p. 505). The definition should be: to give out a double ration of grog, to celebrate some special event. Also *splice of the main-brace*, a drink, orig. of rum, hence of any spirits, as in *The Dublin University Magazine*, 1835, May (p. 549). Moe.

main iron or **main stem; main pin.** A main track (railway line); an official: Canadian railroadmen's (– 1931).

main vein, the. The female pudend: to *stab in the m.v.*, to coït with (a woman): low, esp. among drug addicts: since ca. 1950.

maipan. A steward: (Canton) pidgin: mid-C. 19–20. B. & L. The Chinese word means 'buyer'.

Majesty's School for Heavy Needlework, Her or **His.** See **ironmongery department.**

major, the (p. 505). Usually, however, the Regimental Sergeant Major. Vocative: *Major.*

major domo. See 'Tavern terms', § 5.

Major Loder. Soda: rhyming slang: C. 20. 'From Major Eustace Loder (b. 1867), owner of the famous racehorse Pretty Polly' (Franklyn 2nd).

major operation. Cutting a person *dead*: since ca. 1935.

Major Stevens. Evens (in betting): rhyming: C. 20.

make, v.—6. Hence, to coït with (a girl): Canadian: since ca. 1918. Ex U.S. Since ca. 1944, common also in Australia. (B.P.)

make, on the.—2. (Of either sex) seeking sexual adventures: Canadian: since ca. 1920. Cf. the U.S. *make* (a girl), to coït.—3. (Of either sex) engaged in winning affection: Australian: since ca. 1925. (B., 1943.)

make a big feller (occ. **fellow) of oneself.** 'To give the impression that one is magnanimous' (B.P.): Australian: since ca. 1945.

*****make a blue with a rat.** To cause a dice to hit an obstruction: Australian gamblers': since ca. 1920. (B., 1953.)

make a bolt of it. To run away: decamp: coll.: from ca. 1850; slightly ob. B. & L.

make a box of. See **box of . . .**

make a break (p. 506): since late 1940's, ordinary s. in both New Zealand and Australia. See also **break** (p. 90).

make a clean job of it. See **job of it . . .**

make a (dead) bird of. See **bird of . . .**

make a go of (it). To succeed: since ca. 1920.

make a job of (someone). To thrash or trounce; to defeat severely: Australian: since ca. 1905. (B., 1943.) Cf. *job*, v., 3 (p. 440); 'a *good* job' is implied.

make a kick. To raise an objection: proletarian: from ca. 1860. B. & L. Cf. **kick**, n., 7 (*Dict.*).

make a long nose. See **long nose . . .** (*Dict.*).

make a loose. See 'Verbs'.

make a meet. See **meet, make a,** below.

make a monkey out of. See **monkey . . .**

make a noise. See **noise, make a.**

make a noise like a . . . See **noise . . .**

make a pass (at someone). See **pass at, make a,** below.

make a sale. To vomit: New Zealand and Australian low: C. 20. B., 1941 and 1943.

make and mend (p. 506) is recorded in 1899 (*The Navy and Army Illustrated*, Oct. 14). Moe.—2. Hence, off-duty hours: since ca. 1930.

make (someone) **go all unnecessary; do things to** (someone). To excite, esp. sexually; to arouse either passion or a mere momentary 'letch': since ca. 1930. 'She made him go all unnecessary, the hussy'; That girl does things to me, I don't know why.' The implications are functional.

make it. To succeed; to become prosperous: coll., adopted from U.S. ca. 1933. Ex **make**, v., 5 (*Dict.*).—2. Hence, to cope with anything: Canadian (hence English): adopted, ca. 1942, ex U.S.

make it a welter. See **welter, make it a.**

make it bad for other people. To set too good an example in one's work: Services: since ca. 1925.

make it fly. To spend money very freely; go on the spree: coll.: late C. 19–20. 'He's making it fly.'

make it, usu. **be making it, together.** To copulate: mostly teenagers': since late 1940's.

make like a boid. See 'Canadian . . .' '"Make like a bird" [the true Canadian, as opposed to U.S., form] is but one of many variants. "Make like" —almost anything, in fact. I've heard "make like an oyster" meaning "make no noise", and "make like a rich guy" meaning "pretend you're rich", and many others. From the Yiddish "mach wie . . ."' (Leechman, April 1967).

make mouths (p. 506). Read: late C. 16–20: S.E. >, ca. 1880, coll. (Shakespeare, *Hamlet*, IV, IV.).

make on. To make-believe, to 'pretend': children's: C. 20. 'Let's make on!'

make one, as in 'The Jerries are making us one', the Germans are making fools of us: Army: since ca. 1930. (P-G-R.)

make one's alley good. An Australian variant of **make one's marble good** (below).

*make one's expenses.** To gamble in the train: cardsharpers' c.: late C. 19–20.

make one's marble good. To improve one's position or status: Australian: since ca. 1925. (Kylie Tennant, 1956.) Ex the game of marbles.

make one's number. To get oneself acquainted in the right quarter: Army, mostly officers':

since ca. 1930. E. P., 'In Mess and Field'—*The New Statesman*, Aug. 1, 1942. Telephonic.

make passes at. See **pass at, make a,** below.

*make perde.** To cause trouble: South African c. (and, by 1940, also low s.): late C. 19–20. *The Cape Times*, June 3, 1946. Lit., *perde* is Afrikaans for 'horses': cf. Dutch *paarde*, a horse.

make rabbits. See **rabbits.**

make strange. (Of a child) to behave shyly: Canadian coll.: C. 20. 'See the nice lady? Don't make strange now!'

make the chimney smoke. To cause the female to experience the orgasm: low: mid-C. 19–20.

make the county. To become an accepted member of County society: since ca. 1945. (Angus Wilson, *A Bit off the Map*, 1957.)

make up. To promote. See **made up.**

make up the log. See **log, make up the.**

make with. To make: adopted, ca. 1959, ex U.S. '"Has he tried to blackmail you?" "Well, not exactly. But he sort of makes with sinister hints, you know."': Nicholas Blake, *The Sad Variety*, 1964. There are other nuances, esp. 'to use', the others more or less deriving therefrom. Of Canadian usage, Dr Leechman has, in April 1967, noted that '"Now, Fritz. Make with the fiddle!" and similar expressions are often heard. "Make with the accelerator!"' "Make with the beer!" From the Yiddish "mach mit der . . .".'

make yourself at our house! A jocular coll. variation, in C. 20, of S.E. *make yourself at home.* It is a c.p., now slightly ob.

makee. 'To make, do, cause, effect': pidgin: C. 19–20. B. & L.

makes one (esp. **you**) **shit through the eye of a needle,** to which is often added **without splashing the sides.** A low, mostly Cockneys' c.p. applied to any substance that causes diarrhœa: late C. 19–20.

makes you think (,doesn't it)! A humorous c.p. in the Services since 1939. H. & P.

making a trundle for a goose's eye or **a whimwham for a goose.** See **weaving leather aprons** (*Dict.*).

making dolls' eyes, or **putting spots on dominoes.** A c.p. reply to somebody asking what one does for a living: C. 20.

making one's will, be, as in 'He *or* she is making his *or* her will'. A c.p. applied to someone writing a letter or making notes or even merely filling in a form: jocular: C. 20. (A. B. Petch, March 1966.)

makings.—2. Cigarette-paper(s) and tobacco: coll.: C. 20.

makki (pron. *macky*). A machine-gun: infantrymen's: 1914 +; ob. by 1940. Ex '*machine*'.

makoo. (Predicative only.) Out of stock; gone; none: Army: 1914–18. Corruption of **napoo** (*Dict.*).

Malayan madness. 'Bloody-mindedness': Australian servicemen's: 1942–5. (B., 1943.)

Malcolm Scott. Hot: theatrical rhyming s.: C. 20. Franklyn, *Rhyming*.

male gynae ward. See **lily pond.**

male-mules; callibisters. (Human) testicles: C. 16–17. In Rabelais, *callistris* = the penis.

maleesh (p. 506): also much used by R.A.F. regulars since ca. 1918 (Partridge, 1945). See **maalish.**

mallee root. A prostitute: Australian rhyming: C. 20. B., 1942. With a pun on **root**, n., 3 (p. 705).

mallet, on the. 'Having goods on trust,' *Sinks*: low: ca. 1825–80.

malleted. Reprimanded (by an officer): Gibraltar servicemen's (since ca. 1930) >, ca. 1940 gen. servicemen's. H. & P. Forcible.

Malley's cow is an Australian c.p., applied to one who has departed traceless: C. 20. Ex Australian folklore. (B., *Australia Speaks*, 1953.)

mallum. 'Yes, mallum' = Yes, fair enough (or, that's good); interrogatively, *mallum* = Got that?; 'Use your mallum' = Use your common sense. 'A blank cheque of a word' (John Bebbington): Forces' (in the East): 1939–45.

Malt. A Maltese: mostly nautical: late C. 19–20. (John Davies, *See Naples and Die*, 1961.)

Malta dog; often simply *dog*. Diarrhœa; mild dysentery: Naval: late C. 19–20. Cf. the all-Services' *Gippy tummy*. John Winton, *We Joined the Navy*, 1959, 'There's a very awkward and unpleasant disease which people catch in the Mediterranean. It's a form of dysentery and it's known as the Malta Dog. Some people catch it because they're not used to the water . . . You can catch it from shellfish or from meat that's a bit too old . . . or from greens that have not been washed.'

Maltese lace, or **Spanish pennants**. Frayed edges of well-worn bell-bottomed trousers (Royal Navy); frayed shirt-cuffs, etc. (Royal and Merchant Navies): since ca. 1905. Wilfred Granville, *Sea Slang of the 20th Century*, 1949.

Malts. See **José.**

malty cove. A beer-drinker: low London: ca. 1825–80. *Sinks*, 1848.

mam.—3. A Lesbian: low London: since ca. 1945. John Gloag, *Unlawful Justice*, 1962, '"You're more than half a Lizzie, aren't you? I've met lady mams before: one of 'em kept a girl I wanted. It was easy for her: she had the lolly."'

mammoth. Huge: coll.: from ca. 1920. The reviewer of the 1st ed. in *The Times Literary Supplement*, March 20, 1937, 'If "demon" is an adjective, why not "mammoth"?' Ex circus- and show-men's hyperbole.—2. Hence, excellent: Naval: since 1938.

man, n.—8. A pimp: white-slavers' c.: late C. 19–20. (A. Londres, *The Road to Buenos Ayres*, 1928.)—9. See the note at **like** above. Adopted by the beatniks ex jazzmen's usage, itself taken from the very numerous Negro jazzmen.

man, dead.—2, 3, 4: see **dead man** (p. 210).

man, go out and see a (p. 507). The *out* is often —and since ca. 1940 usually—omitted; in full, *go (out) and see a man about a dog*.

man, old.—5. The penis: late C. 19–20.

man at the duff. See **duff, man at the** in *Dict.*

man-hunters. Women, esp. spinsters and widows: jocular coll.: late C. 19–20.

man in the box, the. The announcer of weather forecasts over the radio telephone: deep-sea fishermen's: since ca. 1946. (Granville.)

man-killer.—4. 'A piece of machinery geared to run so fast as to tire the men who feed it': Canadian: since ca. 1925. (Leechman, who in 1930, heard it applied to a concrete-mixer.)

man-mad. Of a girl or a woman: extremely sexy: since the early 1920's: coll. <, by 1955, S.E.

man(-)man. Gradually: little by little: pidgin: from ca. 1860. B. & L. Ex It. *mano mano* in same sense.

man of straw (p. 507), referred to **straw** . . . but not, in fact, treated there, is ineligible; it is S.E. Consequently, in the next entry (*man of the world), 'Ibid.' should read 'B. & L.'

*man of the world.** A professional thief: c.: from ca. 1870: ob. Ibid.

man outside Hoyts, the. 'A mythical person alleged to create rumours' (B., 1959): Aus.: since late 1940's. Cf. **furphy** (on p. 308) and **Tom Collins** below.

man-sized job. A difficult task: since ca. 1925: coll. >, by 1945, familiar S.E.

man-trap.—4. (Ex 1: p. 508.) Any attractive man-hunting female: C. 20. Eden Philpotts, *The Beacon*, 1911.—5. Also **Jack(-)trap.** 'Catch points to prevent unauthorized entry from siding' (*Railway*): railwaymen's: since ca. 1920.

man who brings home the bacon, the. The breadwinner: Canadian (and U.S.) and domestic coll.: C. 20. (Leechman.)

man with no hands, like a, adj. and adv. Miserly; in a miserly manner, esp. in *throw money around like a* . . . : Aus.: since ca. 1945. (B., 1959.)

man with the brass knackers, the. 'The boss': Canadian railroad labourers' (− 1910), hence general labourers' (− 1914).

manage it. To 'get off' with a fellow; to get married: feminine coll.: C. 20.

manager. The head of one's department at a H.Q.: Army officers': since ca. 1934. Ex **managing director** (p. 508).

manalive. See **man alive!** in *Dict.*

Manc. A native of Manchester; a pupil at Manchester Grammar School: Manchester: late C. 19–20. Ex *Mancunian.*

Manchester-bred (p. 508). Only one of several pejorative jingles; for instance, *Derbyshire born and bred* is common.

Manchester City. A variant of *Bristol City*, q.v. at **Bristols** above; mostly in pl. and shortened to *Manchesters*. Franklyn 2nd.

mandrake. A bugger (in the legal sense): among folk of the road: prob. since C. 17. In Nov. 1948, an octogenarian didekei was heard, in S.W. England, to remark of a certain man: "E's a bloody mandrake. 'E's a bugger, that's what 'e be, a bugger. Small boys and such.' (My distinguished informant wishes to be nameless.) See *mandrake* in the glossary of *Shakespeare's Bawdy*, in reference to 2 *Henry IV*, I, ii, 15, and esp. III, ii, 324–5 (Shakespeare Head edition). Yet, when that book appeared in 1947, several ivory-tower'd scholars accused me of seeing evil where none existed. I wonder what they'd do 'on the road'—yell for a policeman?—2. (Usually in pl.) A water-proof cape worn in the tropics: Australian soldiers': 1942–5. (B., 1943.)

mangle.—3. A bicycle: Australian: since ca. 1920. B., 1942.—4. A mangold wurzel: farm labourers': late C. 19–20. Via *mangol*, slovenly for *mangold.*—5. A manual drilling machine: railwaymen's: since ca. 1945. (*Railway*, 3rd.) A pun both on *manual* and on the effect it has on the nerves.

manhole cover. A sanitary pad: low male Australian: since ca. 1950.

manjaree. Variant of **mungaree** (p. 543 and Addenda).

mankie or **mank(e)y.** Rotten; very inferior: Cockneys': C. 20. Prob. ex Fr. *manqué.*

manner, all. See **all manner.**

manor, 1 (p. 508): by 1940, also police s. for a police Division.—2. See **team,** 2.—3. 'The area where one lives and is known' (Robin Cook, 1962) —whether 'Teddy boy' or not: since late 1940's.

man's a. A man-sized, esp. a large, *membrum virile:* low coll.: C. 19–20.

manual exercises. (Mostly male) masturbation: low: C. 20.

Maori is the original and correct form of **Mary,** 3.

Maori P.T. 'Taking it as easily as possible, i.e. resting when one should be undertaking physical training' (W. Colgan): New Zealand soldiers': 1939–45. Cf. *Egyptian P.T.*

map of England (occasionally **Ireland**). A stain on bed-linen: Forces', esp. R.A.F.: since ca. 1918. The latter occurs in T. E. Lawrence's *The Mint,* published in 1955 but dealing with 1922. Ex the outline.

marble. 'A word I have heard used in the Cape [Province], mostly from people attending Rhodes University College, Grahamstown, is *marble.* Examples are: "His marble is high"—he is "well in" (with such-and-such a person). "He is polishing his marble with so-and-so" = he is trying to ingratiate himself,' A. M. Brown of Bulawayo, letter of April 15, 1938.

marble, pass in one's. To die: Australian: C. 20. B., 1942. Variant of U.S. *pass in one's checks.*

Marble Arch. The Arco Philaenorum near El Agheila, N. Africa: Army: 1943.—2. See 'Guard-Room in Army Slang'.

marble orchard. A cemetery: Canadian: since ca. 1920.

marbles.—5. Money, cash; salary: mostly Londoners', esp. theatrical: since ca. 1950. 'The big marbles are not earned at the Festival Theatres or the Old Vic.'

marbles, have all one's. To be no fool; lit., 'to be all there': since ca. 1950.

marbles, have lost some of one's. To be not quite sane: Canadian (ex U.S.): since ca. 1930 (Leechman.) Contrast preceding.

marbles for old men. The game of bowls: jocular: since ca. 1930.

marbles to manslaughter, from. 'About the year 1831 or 1832, play [i.e. gambling] first became common. Harding Ackland, . . . an inveterate and spirited player at anything, "from marbles to manslaughter", as the saying is, opened the first shilling hell in the metropolis': (Renton Nicholson, *An Autobiography,* 1860, at p. 77): a London c.p.: ca. 1830–70.

marched, get. To make a formal complaint to the C.O.: Army coll., esp. among regulars: C. 20. One is marched in by an N.C.O.

marching money. Travelling expenses: Australian: since 1918–19. Baker. Also, since ca. 1945, English, as in Robin Cook's (1962) definition, 'small change to get from place A to B'. Influenced by the W.W. II Army.

mare, old or **silly old.** See **moo** below.

Maren or **marinette.** A *Marine* Wren: Naval: 1941 +. Granville, 'Employed at a Royal Marine Barracks . . . distinguished from their sisters by the Marine badge on their caps in place of the H.M.S. ribbon'.

marg or **marge** (p. 309). An early example: Ada E. Jones, *In Darkest London,* 1926.

margariny. Of or like margarine: coll.: C. 20. In, e.g., A. Neil Lyons, *Clara,* 1912.

Margery Jane. Margarine: lower-classes: ca. 1900–20. Mary Higgs, *Glimpses into the Abyss,* 1906. Cf. **marge** (*Dict.*).

*mari. A marijuana cigarette: since late 1920's: c. until ca. 1935, then s.

Maria Monk. Spunk, in all senses: rhyming s. late C. 19–20. Franklyn, *Rhyming.*

marine, 1 (p. 509) goes back to ca. 1810, perhaps to late C. 18. It occurs in W. N. Glascock, *Sailors and Saints* (I, 149), 1829. Moe.

Mariners, the. The Grimsby Town football club: sporting, esp. Association football: since ca. 1945.

marines, tell that to the (p. 509) is recorded in John Davis, *The Post-Captain,* 1806. (Moe.)

Marine's breakfast. Rare for '11' in the game of House: mostly Naval: C. 20. Michael Harrison, *Reported Safe Arrival,* 1943.

marinette. See **Maren.**

marionette. A minaret: Regular Army: mid-C. 19–20. By 'Hobson-Jobson'.

maritimes. Men of the Royal Artillery Marine Regiment, serving as A.A. gunners in merchant ships: Naval: 1939–45. (P-G-R.)

*Marjie. Marihuana: Australian c. (since ca. 1943) >, by 1950, low s. (B., 1953.)

mark, n.—9. A taxicab rank: taxi-drivers': since ca. 1910. Herbert Hodge, *Cab, Sir?,* 1939. —10. A humourist: mid-C. 19–20; by 1950, slightly ob. Probably ex *Mark* Lemon (1809–70), who helped to found *Punch* and was its first editor (1841).

mark, v.—2. See **mark it.**—3. To geld (lambs): Australian rural: C. 20. B., 1942.

mark, get a. (Of a publican) to be fined for illicit practice: Australian: C. 20. Baker. Short for *get a black mark.*

mark, work the. See **work the mark** (*Dict.*).

mark bad or **good.**—2. A general term of (dis)-approval: Australian: C. 20. (B., 1943.)

mark (someone's) **card.** To give him the information he needs; to put him right: barrow-boys': since ca. 1945. Ex the race-course.—2. 'To tell or warn him', with wider connotation and distribution: since late 1940's. (Robin Cook.)

Mark Foy. Boy: Australian rhyming s.: since ca. 1910. (B., 1943.)

mark it. To be careful: Cockney coll.: from ca. 1880. Pugh (2): '"Let's go," said Judith. "It's nearly twelve o'clock. Must be. I'll get the key of the street if I don't mark it."' I.e. 'watch one's step'. Julian Franklyn believes this to be a mis-print in Pugh, for *nark it*; on second thoughts, so do I.

mark of the beast. Add:—Ex:—3. See **M.B.** in *Dict.*

mark time on. To wait for: Army: 1939–45.

marker.—4. A rear-end signal: Canadian railroadmen's coll. (— 1931).

markers steady, be on. To be quite sober and without a tremor, esp. after a drinking-bout: Army: since ca. 1930. Ex the order 'Markers steady!' given to the N.C.O.'s (or others) acting as markers to the platoon or squads before a parade.

market, go to.—2. To become angry, complain bitterly: Australian: C. 20. B., 1942.

market, on the. (Of a girl) available for marriage: coll.: late C. 19–20. (Maud Diver, *The Great Amulet*, 1908.)

Marks. A Marks & Spencer store: coll.: since ca. 1925. Cf. **Timothy's** and **Woolly's**.

Marks and Sparks. An elaboration of preceding: since late 1940's. (*The Sunday Times*, April 5, 1964.)

marmalade is synonymous with **scrambled eggs**: R.A.F.: since ca. 1938. H. & P. Ex the gold-coloured braid.

Marquess of Lorn. An erection: rhyming s. (on *horn*): C. 20; rare. Franklyn, *Rhyming*.

married.—2. See **gay** above.

married but not churched. A living-together unmarried: almost a c.p.: late C. 19–20.

married crocks. An Army term dating from ca. 1885. Richards, 'Men and wives married on the strength of the Regiment were called the "married crocks". One had to have five years' service and be twenty-six years of age before one could get married on the strength. A regular number of married men were allowed in each regiment.'

married man's friend, the. The war-time black-out: 1939–45. It enabled him to take out other women without fear of being seen by 'friendly' neighbours.

married man's side. 'The left-hand half of the dart board, presumably because the "doubles" are found there' (Wilfred Granville): darts players': since ca. 1950.

married patch, the. Married quarters in permanent barracks: Army: C. 20. (P-G-R.)

marrieds. Married couples: Australian coll.: since ca. 1925. (D'Arcy Niland, *Call Me . . .*, 1958.)

marrowbone stage (p. 510) goes back to very early C. 19. It occurs for April 28, 1820, in *The British Columbia Historical Quarterly*, April 1937, at p. 120. (Leechman.)

marry poor blind Nell?, and did he. 'A rhetorical question asked about anything improbable. Also as a euphemism for *like fucking hell!* Ex the saga of *Poor Blind Nell*. (Cf. *Ballocky Bill the Sailor*, *The Bastard from the Bush*, etc.) As in "And did he marry . . .?"—"He did!—(*softly*) Like fuckin(g) hell!" *Poor blind Nell* itself is used to describe any simple girl who is over-trusting where men are concerned' (B.P.): Australian: since ca. 1910 or a little earlier.

marry up.—2. An expression often used by auctioneers, it means 'to put one lot with another'; often an article of little value that would be difficult to get a bid for by itself is 'married up' with something for which there is likely to be a good demand and the two articles sold as one lot: coll.: C. 20.

Mar's production. The manufacture of armaments: since ca. 1946. A pun on *Mars*, the Roman god of war, and '*mass production*'.

Marsel. Marseilles: Regular Army: C. 20.

marshall of the field. See 'Tavern terms', § 6.

marsingan. A machine-gun: Regular Army: C. 20.

Martin 'Enries. Reach-me-down clothes: Liverpool: late C. 19–20. Apparently ex a manufacturer's name, *Martin Henry*.

martins. The hands: low (and parlyaree?): ca. 1860–1914. P. H. Emerson, *Signor Lippo*, 1893. Ex It. *mani* (cf. Fr. *mains*)?

martyr to be smarter, a. A c.p. directed at

modern women in general or at some particular heroine: since ca. 1945. Ex fashionable masochism.

marv. Marvellous: teenagers': since the late 1950's. Cf. its original **marvellous**, on p. 511, and the much more popular **fab**(ulous).

marvelious (*mar-veé-li-us*). A jocular intensive of *marvellous*: since ca. 1925; virtually † by 1960.

Mary. Sense 1 (p. 511) not ob., Sidney Baker, letter of 1946, tells me.—2. The inseparable nickname of men surnamed Hook: C. 20. Why?—3. Air Marshal Sir Arthur Coningham: R.A.F.: 1939 +. A corruption of *Maori*: he came from New Zealand.—4. See **Balt.**—5. See **Lucy and Mom.**—6. '*Marys* . . . Post war suburban units' (*Railway*, 3rd): railwaymen's: since late 1940's. Why?

Mary Ann.—6. See **clock, n.**, 4.—7. The hand: rhyming s.: C. 20. Franklyn, *Rhyming*.

Mary Blane. A train: underworld rhyming s.: ca. 1880–1914.—2. Rain: rhyming s.: ca. 1860–1910.

Mary Ellen. 'If you are in Liverpool, stroll in the evening up the Scotland Road, and talk to the fascinating people you meet there, such as the "Mary Ellens"—the picturesque women who wear shawls over their heads, carry babies in their arms, work in the markets all day, and always have a good "tip" for tomorrow's race' (Robert Lynd, *Things One Hears*, 1945): Liverpool: since ca. 1910.

Mary Lou, bet on the. See **bet on the blue.**

maryanning. 'Cleaning, sweeping, polishing' (*Radio Times*, Jan. 21, 1965): railway porters': since ca. 1930. Ex *Mary Ann*, a type-name for a housemaid or a charwoman.

Marylebone kick. A kick in the belly: ca. 1820–80. *Sinks*, 1848.

masby. A motor anti-submarine boat (with an affectionate *y* added for euphony): Naval: since ca. 1940. (Granville.)

mash, n.—5. Hence, sentimental nonsense: Australian: since ca. 1920. B., 1942.

mash, v.—2. To study very hard: Australian R.M.C., Duntroon: since ca. 1920 (?). B., 1953.

mash-note. A love letter: Canadian: since ca. 1920. Cf. *mash*, n., 1, and v.: p. 511.

mash the tea. To stir the tea: coll.: C. 20. Stan Barstow, *A Kind of Loving*, 1960.

mashed. See **baked.**

mashed (the) potatoes for the Last Supper, he or **she.** 'Know him? Why, he helped me mash the potatoes for the Last Supper! Known him for years.' A Canadian c.p. dating since ca. 1940. (Leechman.)

masheen. A cat: Shelta: C. 18–20. B. & L.

Massey-Harris (p. 512). Hence also, by contacts made in 1915–18, Australian. (B., *Australia Speaks*, 1953.)

mast. A pin (in golf): trawlermen's: since ca. 1920. *The Daily Mail*, Aug. 16, 1939. Humorous.

master. A master-at-arms: Naval coll.: C. 20. —2. As *the master*, conductor of a train: Canadian railroadmen's (– 1931). Humorous.

Master, the. John Corlett, editor of *The Sporting Times* in the 1880's and -90's: sporting and social. It complements **the Mate** (*Dict.*).

Master Controller; Master Gunner. See 'Tavern terms', § 5, § 7.

master maniac; master mind. A master

mechanic; trainmaster or yardmaster or conductor or train-dispatcher: Canadian railroadmen's: C. 20.

Master of a ship. See 'Tavern terms', § 7.

Master of Art. See 'Tavern terms', § 3, *b*.

Master of ceremonies. That 'plane which hovers high over the target to direct a bombing raid: Air Force: 1941 +.

Master of Misrule—of the Ceremonies—of the Novelties—of the Ordnance—of the Wardrobe. See 'Tavern terms', § 5, § 5, § 5, § 6, § 5.

master's mate. See 'Tavern terms', § 7.

mat-boy. A professional wrestler: Australian: since ca. 1946. (Vince Kelly, *The Greedy Ones*, 1958.)

mata; occ. **ma-ta.** Mother: pidgin: C. 19–20. B. & L.

Matapan stew. A stew made of odds-and-ends: Australian Naval: 1942–5. (B., 1943.)

match and make a dispatch is a South African low s. variation of *hatch, match and dispatch column* (p. 378): C. 20. *The Cape Times*, June 3, 1946.

match-box. A troop-carrying glider: R.A.F. and Army: 1941–5. (P-G-R.)—2. A 57 XX locomotive: (Western) railwaymen's: ? ca. 1940–60. Ex its small pannier tank. (*Railway*.)

mate up. To become mates or companions: Australian coll. (? esp. West Australian): C. 20. (Tom Ronan, *Only a Short Walk*, 1961.)

Matelots, the. The London River Police: esp. among the other branches of the Metropolitan Police: since ca. 1945. The River Police return the compliment with *the Land Crabs*, all the other Metropolitan policemen. (B.B.C. T.V. service, 'No Hiding Place': Sept. 24, 1963.)

Maternity Home, the. 'The war-time nickname for the Liverpool Naval Base, whose headquarters were in the Liver Buildings, which had two storks or "livers" on the roof' (P-G-R): Naval: 1939–45. That the *liver* means a stork is a piece of folk-lore, because strictly *liver*, a back-formation ex *Liverpool*, represents—on the city arms—the eagle of St. John the Evangelist. (O.E.D.) 'There are no storks in the armorial bearings of Liverpool, nor (begging the O.E.D.'s pardon!) is there an eagle of St John the Evangelist': Julian Franklyn, who knows as much about heraldry as he does about Cockneys and their speech—which is saying quite a lot.

mat(e)y.—2. (Gen. in pl. and as *maties*.) A dockyard labourer: nautical: C. 20. 'Taffrail.'—3. A (hospital) matron, esp. in a workhouse: 1857, A. Mayhew, *Paved with Gold*; ob.

math. The Canadian (and American) schoolboys' form of **maths** (p. 512). Leechman.

matha; mathemat. Mathematics; mathematician: Christ's Hospital: since ca. 1870. J. S. Farmer, *Public School Word Book*, 1900.

matlow, 1 (p. 512). 'Taffrail' has pl. *matloes*.—2. Hence, like *Fleet Air Arm wallah*, a member of the Fleet Air Arm: Services (esp. R.A.F.): since ca. 1918. Partridge, 1945.

matrimonial (p. 512) is, an ethnographer communicates, known among English-speaking South Sea Islanders ('noted for their ingenuity in these matters') as *the missionaries' position*: late C. 19–20.

matspeak. 'Sixpence from everyone for the seats in the cathedral': church s.: ca. 1870–1900. B. & L.

maturing in the wood. A jocular c.p., applied 'to men whose heads are full of ideas that never get any further than their heads' (A. B. Petch, April 1966): since ca. 1950. A pun on liquor maturing in the cask, and a sly allusion to wooden heads.

Maud. A male prostitute: prostitutes' and homosexuals': since ca. 1940.

maul. A, or to, wrestle for the ball when, in Rugby football, it is 'held' over the goal-line. London schools' coll.: ca. 1875–1914.—2. 'Since ca. 1950, a coll. increasingly used by radio and press commentators to mean a wrestle for the ball in any part of the field. One even hears of "a loose maul", and a scrum has become "a set scrum"' (H. R. Spencer, 1963).

mauld is an occ. spelling of **mauled** (*Dict.*).

mauler, 'hand, fist' (p. 513): much earlier in W. T. Moncrieff, *The Collegians*, 1820, and in *Sessions*, 1832.

mauravalins is an Australian variant of *menovelings*, 2 (p. 516), Jean Devanney, 1944.

***maut** is an occ. C. 17–18 spelling of *mort*, q.v. Ned Ward has it in 1709. (Matthews.)

max (p. 513) prob. goes back to ca. 1710, for it occurs in James Dalton, *A Narrative*, 1728, thus: '*Max*, Geneva'.

maxi. A full-length skirt; reaction to the 'mini': mostly feminine: since Sept. 1967: by Jan. 1968, coll. See **mini** below.

May Blooms, the. The Hawthorn footballers: Melbournites': since ca. 1920. (B., 1943.)

may I pee in your cap (or **hat**)? A North Country working men's c.p., addressed to someone taken short: C. 20; by 1965, ob.

may your prick and (your) purse never fail you!; occ. *may his . . . him*. Half-toast, half-c.p. of C. 18–mid 19. James Dalton, *A Narrative*, 1728, 'They bid the Coachman drive on, and civilly saluted the Player, wishing *his—and Purse might never fail him*.'

mazuma (p. 514) became, ca. 1944 (via U.S. servicemen), also Australian, esp. in sporting circles. Lawson Glassop, *Lucky Palmer*, 1949.

McFluffer. See **Major McFluffer** (*Dict.*).

McGinnis. See **MacGinnis.**

Me. A Messerschmitt fighter 'plane: 1940, Berrey. See **He, Me and You** and cf. **Mess** and **Messer.**

meadow mayonnaise. Airy talk: worthless assurances: Australian: since ca. 1930. B., 1942. With a pun on *bull-shit* (found in meadows).

meal is dough, one's. See **cake is dough, one's** (*Dict.*).

mealy-back. A cicada: Australian: late C. 19–20. Baker.

mean, adj.—3. So good as to be unfair (*mean*): Canadian coll.: adopted, ca. 1910, ex U.S. 'He swings a mean bat!'—in baseball. (Leechman.)—4. Sly; crafty: Australian adopted, ca. 1944, ex American coll. senses. 'This job usually takes an hour, but I know a few mean tricks.' (B.P.)

mean as a Christian, as. Very mean: Jewish coll.: C. 19–20. Tit for tat.

mean he (or **she**) **wouldn't give anyone a fright, he** (or **she**) **is so.** A c.p. applied to a very mean, close-fisted person: C. 20. Variant: (*s*)*he wouldn't spit in your mouth if your throat was on fire*: since ca. 1915.

meanie or **-y.** A person reluctant to pay his share: Services: since ca. 1930. H. & P., 1943.

Diminutive of *mean*. Ex the more usual sense, a mean person: lower-middle class coll.: C. 20.

meant. (Of a horse) meant to win: turf: from ca. 1840; ob. B. & L. By cryptic abridgement.

measure (someone's) **daylights for mourning.** To give (him) a black-eye: boxing: ca. 1810–50. George Godfrey, *History*, 1828. Cf. **measured for** (*Dict.*).

meat and drink.—2. A cocktail in which an egg is beaten up: West Indian: from ca. 1870. B. & L.

meat and two veg. A man's sexual organs: low: C. 20. See **meat**, 2 (p. 514), and cf. **veg.**, (p. 931).

meat-drink-washing-and-lodging. A spirituous liquor, prob. gin: ca. 1720–50. Anon., *The Quaker's Opera*, 1728 (see quot'n at **bunter's tea**).

meat-mincer. The mouth: pugilistic: ca. 1840–90. Augustus Mayhew, *Paved with Gold*, 1857. The prototype of mechanical mincers.

meat-tag. An identity disc: Services', esp. Australian: 1939–45. Cf. *cold-meat ticket* (p. 169).

meat wag(g)on. An ambulance (flying or other): R.A.F.: since ca. 1925. Jackson. Cf. **blood wagon.**—2. A 'black Maria': policemen's and warders': since ca. 1930. (Norman.)

meaters. A dissection class; dissection as part of a medical course: medical students': from ca. 1910. Ex *meat* by 'the Oxford *-er*'.—2. Hence, esp. at Cambridge, the laboratory in which it is conducted: since ca. 1910. (Ramsey Spencer.)

mech. Mechanic; esp. in the old *air mech* of the R.F.C. and the current *flight mech* of the Air Force: coll.: since ca. 1912. Cf. **ack emma**, q.v.

mechanic. A dishonest card-player; a card-sharp: Australian: since ca. 1925. (B., 1953.)

Med, the. The Mediterranean: C. 20. Richard Llewellyn, *None But The Lonely Heart*, 1943. Hence *Med* as adjective.

medals, he (she, you) didn't win any (sol., no). He (etc.) profited nothing: Cockney c.p.: from late 1918.

Meddy, the. 'The Navy's alternative for *Med*' (P-G-R): since ca. 1910.

medical. An examination by a Medical Board: since ca. 1914: coll. >, by 1940, S.E.

medza or **medzer.** A halfpenny: parlary: mid-C. 19–20. Cf. **madza** on p. 503 and **medzies** on p. 515.

medzas. A variant (Sydney Lester, 1937) of **medzies** (p. 515).

meet has, since ca. 1919, been also English coll.—though non-aristocratic.

meet, make a. To meet the immediate seller of the drug (the connection): drug addicts': since ca. 1930, if not a decade earlier. (*Hearings*, 1955.) Cf. **meet**, 3, on p. 436.

meg. The cinematic variant of the next: since ca. 1912. Cameron McCabe, *The Face*, 1937.

megger. Megaphone: since ca. 1920. 'The Oxford *-er*.'

***megsmen.** 'North Country term for card-sharpers,' F. D. Sharpe, *The Flying Squad*, 1938: c.: late C. 19–20. Phonetic variant of **magsman** (p. 505).

meh-meh-meh . . . 'The bleat, repeated ad nauseam, of troops queueing for breakfast, dinner, tea and supper, for clothing, supplies, inoculation; flocking here and shepherded there. A World War II contribution by the ordinary man in uniform to philosophy and language' (Atkinson): Forces': 1939–45 and after.

Mei-le-kween-kwok. American: pidgin: mid-C. 19–20. B. & L. Via *'Melican.*

Melbourne Pier. Ear: Australian rhyming s.: since ca. 1930. (B., 1945.)

mell.—2. A smell: nursery: mid-C. 19–20. Ex baby-talk.

mellish (p. 516). Also, money in general: mainly pugilistic or, rather, sporting: ca. 1815–60. *Boxiana*, IV, 1824, 'The victor . . . handing him over a little Mellish; "Welcome sweetener of human ills",' the inner quotation suggesting that the etymology is Latin *mel*, 'honey.'

melon-head. A C. 20 elaboration of **melon**, 2 (p. 516). B., 1942.

melt, v.—6. To experience the sexual spasm: (slightly euphemistic) coll.: mid-C. 19–20.

melthog. A shirt: Shelta: C. 18–20. B. & L. Whence **mill-tag** or **mill-tog** (*Dict.*), q.v.

[Men. In the first quarter of C. 18, esp. in London, the following—culled by Matthews from the very representative Ned Ward—are the general s. and coll. names for men, apart from the Occupational and the Regional (qq.v.): Friends were *chaps* (1715) or *chums* (1722); a pleasant or a boon companion was a *merry grig* (1715), *merry snob* (1715), or *jolly tit* (1714); contemptuously, a married man was a *hug-booby* (1703) or *smug*[1] (1709); a chatterer was either a *prattle-box* or a *tattle-basket* (both in 1703); a miser, a *love-penny* (1703); a tell-tale, a *blab* (1714); an expert at games was thus early known as a *dab* (1715); *squabs* (1722) were fat people; a grumbler was a *grizzle* (1703) or a *grumbletonian* (1714); a mean, despicable or surly fellow was a *cuff* (1703), a *scab* (1715), a *swab* (1709), a *grave noddy* (1703) or a *muck-worm* (1703).]

menace. A person that is a bore or a general nuisance: coll.: since early 1930's.

mendic. Sick, ill: Australian: since ca. 1925. B., 1942. Ex '*mendicant*'? Many beggars look sick, many are ill.

mentioned in despatches. To have one's name appear in a newspaper, a parish magazine, or even on a notice-board: jocular: 1940 +.

Merchant, the. The Merchant Navy: nautical coll.: since late 1920's.

Merchant venturer. See 'Tavern terms', § 3, *d*.

Merchy. Merchiston: Scottish Public Schools': late C. 19–20. Ian Miller, *School Tie*, 1935.

mercy bucket (or **buttercup**)! *Merci beaucoup!*: Australian: C. 20. (B.P.) An instance of 'Hobson-Jobson'.

mercy launch. An air-sea rescue launch: Air Force: 1939–45.

mere. Foolish; inept; ridiculous: mostly Society: since ca. 1939. Perhaps ex '*merely* ridiculous'.

Meredith! we're in! A c.p. uttered when one succeeds in entering a place (e.g. a tea-shop) just before closing-time: from ca. 1910. C. F. Gregg, *Tragedy at Wembley*, 1936. Ex a music-hall turn.

merely fooling about, or with capitals. A Naval term of 1915, thus in W. McFee, *North of Suez*, 1930. '"Merchant Fleet Auxiliary . . ." " . . . They used to call them Merely Fooling About, but that's a libel. They're good men."' Cf. **Really Not A Sailor** (*Dict.*).

merino, pure (p. 517).—2. Hence, adj., 'of the

---

[1] Open to query: see **smug** (*Dict.*), n. 1.

best quality': Australian coll.: late C. 19-20.
B., 1942.

merkin. An artificial vagina for lonely men:
coll. (?, rather, S.E.): mid-C. 19-20. Ex the two
S.E. senses, 'female pudend' and 'artificial hair
for a woman's pudend'.

merp. A species of marble (as used in the game
of marbles): children's: late C. 19-20. *The
Manchester Evening News*, March 27, 1939. Ex
dial *mirk*, 'dusky, dingy, drab'?

Merry Andrew. The Royal Navy: Naval: late
C. 19-20. (P.-G.-R.) Cf. *Andrew* in both *Dict.*
and Addenda. A pun on the archaic S.E. *merry-
andrew.*

merry-go-round. A pound (£1): rhyming s.:
late C. 19-20.

merry grig; merry snob. See 'Men'.

merry heart or **merryheart.** A sweetheart: C.
20. Rhyming on *tart.*

merry-merry. Intoxicating liquor of dubious
origin, esp. in Gibraltar: Naval: C. 20.

Merry Widow, the. Champagne: since ca.
1906. Punning both the champagne '*Veuve
Clicquot*' and Franz Lehár's light opera *The
Merry Widow* (1905).

merry widows. 'Broad-gauge shearing combs
and cutter used by fast machine shearers' (B.,
1942): Australian rural: since ca. 1910. They
fairly dance over the sheep's body!

meshuga. (Tolerantly humorous in application.)
Crazy: Jewish coll.: mid-C. 19-20. Ex Yiddish;
cf. Hebrew *meshuga*, error (whence the Yiddish
word and sense). James Joyce, *Ulysses*, 1922,
'Meshuggah. Off his chump.'—2. 'There's a
further nuance. A Jew might say "I never look
at the moon through glass. That's my meshuga"
—my personal idiosyncrasy. I heard a Jewish
comedian say it only a few weeks ago' (Leechman,
April 1967).

Mespot.—2. Hence, 'letter from wife or sweetheart announcing unfaithfulness or break with husband or sweetheart serving in Forces overseas, esp.
R.A.F. Iraq and Middle East' (Atkinson, 1959):
since ca. 1919.—3. Hence, but usually *Mespot
piss-up*, 'ritual of group execration of unfaithful
wife or sweetheart, at which beer was drunk. On
this occasion a letter was written to the woman;
of which each of the injured man's hut-mates
wrote his unhampered part. The woman's
offending letter, pinned to the floor, was treated
to gestures of contempt. R.A.F. Habbaniya, and
current throughout Iraq 1940-5 and no doubt
earlier' (ibid.): app. since ca. 1925; by 1960,
slightly ob., R.A.F. links with Iraq virtually
ceasing in 1959.

Mess; Messer. A Messerschmitt (German
fighter aircraft): R.A.F.: since 1939. Jackson,
1943 (*Messers*); Partridge, 1945. Cf. **He, Me and
You.**

mess, n., 1 (p. 517). A shade earlier in *Sessions*,
Nov. 28, 1833.—3. Applied to a person either
objectionable or pitiably ineffectual: since ca.
1921. It occurs, e.g., in J. B. Priestley, *They
Walk in the City*, 1936.

mess, v.—2. (Of a married person) to go (sexually) with someone else: low: from ca. 1915.

mess, lose the number of one's (p. 518), is much
older: 1818, *Alfred Burton*, Johnny Newcome.
(Moe.) It also occurs in *The Dublin University
Magazine*, July 1834 (on p. 69). Moe.

mess-traps (p. 518) is far from obsolescent: it

occurs in C. S. Forester, *The Ship*, 1943, and in
Granville, 1945. The latter defines it as 'Mess
utensils, pots, pans, cutlery, etc.' It has to be
back-dated to very early C. 19, esp. as a Naval
term. See **traps**, n., 4, below.

message, 1 and 2. See next two entries.—3.
'"The message," he said impatiently, "you know,
the news. He was passing on the news. If we had
a fancied runner, he would tip off a professional
backer"' (Dick Francis, *Nerve*, 1964): racing:
since ca. 1920.

message, do a. To run an errand: North
Country coll.: late (? mid) C. 19-20. 'Heard as
"I want you to do a message for me", when somebody wanted a child to get something from a shop,
etc.': A. B. Petch, March 1966.

message, get the. See 'Jazz Slang' above.

message by wireless. See **wireless.**

messenger. A heaving-line: Naval, perhaps
coll. rather than s.: late C. 19-20. (P.-G.-R.)

Messer. See **Mess.**

***messer.**—2. A 'near' prostitute; an amateur
not above taking money or a present: prostitutes'
c.: from ca. 1915. Low also, though little used by
harlots, is **whore's robber**, dating from ca. 1916.—
3. A man, or a woman, that does not keep to one
lover: low: from ca. 1916.

Messerschmitt Alley. Any road subject to
attention from German aircraft; esp. the long,
straight stretch from Ghardimaou to Souk el Arba
in Tunisia: Army in N. Africa: World War II.
(P.-G.-R.)

mesty, mestee, mestez. A half-caste: Anglo-
Indian coll.: mid-C. 19-20; ob. B. & L. Ex
Spanish *mestizo*, a half-caste, itself ex L. *mixtus*,
mixed.

met. A weather report: Air Force: 1939 +.
Cf. :—

Met, the. The Meteorological Office: Services:
since ca. 1925. Hence, *Met man* or *Mets*, Meteoro-
logical Officer: Services: since ca. 1920. E. P.,
'In Mess and Field'—*The New Statesman*, Aug. 1,
1942; H. & P., 1943.—5. Enemy vehicles (not
tanks nor guns): Eighth Army: 1941-5. H. & P.
Ex *M.T.*, 'mechanical transport'.—6. Always *the
Mets*, the Metropolitan Police: police-officers':
C. 20. David Hume, *Toast to a Corpse*, 1944.—7.
Mets, 'trains, usually freight, operating over
Metropolitan widened lines section from King's
Cross to Southern Region' (*Railway*): London
railwaymen's: since late 1940's.

Met man. See prec.

Metaphysics. See 'Tavern terms', § 3, *d*.

meth. Methylated spirits: C. 20. Matt
Marshall, *Tramp Royal on the Toby*, 1933. Cf.
metho (in the *Dict.*).

metho.—2. A *Metho* is a Methodist: Australian:
since ca. 1920. B., 1942.—3. A methylated-
spirits addict: Australian: since ca. 1935. (B.,
1943.) Ex sense 1 on p. 518.

metho artist. Synonymous with **metho**, 2, above:
since ca. 1930. (B., 1959.)

Methody. A Methodist: (dial. and) semi-
literate coll.: mid-C. 19-20.

meths. Methylated spirits: mostly New
Zealand: C. 20.

methy. Methylated spirit. C. 20. Cf. *meth*
above and *metho* (p. 518).

mets or **Mets.**—2. See **Met, the**, 4, 5, 6, above.

mezzo brow. Middle-brow (of taste): cultured
coll.: since the late 1930's; by 1947, slightly ob.

mi. See **ma**, 3 (*Dict.*).

miaow! miaow! A cry uttered by a third party when two people are engaged in malicious gossip: since ca. 1925. Ex the fact that the gossip is *catty*.

mibbies. Marbles: Cockney schoolchildren's: late C. 19–20. Recorded by J. W. Horsley, *I Remember*, 1912. By affectionate 'thinning' of the predominant vowel-sound.

mic-a-mic. Scrub: New Zealand coll.: since ca. 1870. (G. B. Lancaster, *The Tracks We Tread*, 1907, Glossary.) Perhaps Hobson-Jobson for Maori *ukuiki*, scrub.

mice is a synonym of the pl. of **widgie**: Australian: ca. 1951–8. (B., 1953.)

Mick O'Dwyer. A fire: rhyming s.: late C. 19–20. Much less usual than *Anna Maria*.

mick.—3. Hence, a seaman's hammock: Naval lower-deck: since ca. 1920. H. & P.—4. The head of a penny: Australian two-up players': late C. 19–20. B., 1942. Cf. **harp** (*Dict.*).

mickey.—3. The penis: Anglo-Irish: late C. 19–20.—4. A pint flask of whiskey or other 'hard' liquor: Canadian (and U.S.): since ca. 1920. Leechman. Ex '*Irish* whiskey'.
Sense 3 occurs, *sub finem*, in James Joyce's *Ulysses*, 1922.

mickey at, take the. A variant of *take the mike out of*: since ca. 1950. Also absolutely, as in 'He's taking the—or, a—mickey'.

Mick(e)y Bliss. A rare variant of **Mike Bliss** below: C. 20. Franklyn 2nd.

Mickey Mouse. 'The bomb-dropping mechanism on some types of bomber aircraft is so called because it strongly resembles the intricate machinery portrayed by Walt Disney's [Mickey Mouse] cartoons,' H. & P.: R.A.F.: since 1939.—2. A motor mechanic: Naval: since 1939 or 1940. Granville. He does such very odd things, and there may be influence by **motor mech.**—3. A house: theatrical rhyming s.: since ca. 1930. (Franklyn, *Rhyming*.) Walt Disney began to produce the Mickey Mouse cartoons in 1928.—4. A small, wooden, inshore minesweeper used during World War II: Naval: since ca. 1940; since late 1940's, historical only. (Wilfred Granville, Nov. 22, 1962.)

Micks, the.—2. The Teaching (or Christian) Brothers: Catholic Australian schoolchildren's: late C. 19–20. 'The Brothers formerly came from Ireland' (B.P.). In general s., *the Micks* = all Catholics whatsoever.

Mickser. An *émigré* Irishman: since ca. 1950. (Patrick Campbell's column in *The Sunday Times*, April 12, 1964.) Ex *Mick*, an Irishman.

micky (or **M-**), 5; **mike** (or **M-**), 5. A casual ward: tramps' c.: late C. 19–20. By rhyming s. on **spike** (*Dict.*).

micky, do a. A C. 20 North Country equivalent of **mike, do a** (p. 520).

micky finn. See **gee-man**.

micky off. To decamp, run away: St Bees: since ca. 1910. (Marples.) At St Bees, *do a mike* is to break bounds (cf. entry on p. 520).

mid.—3. Middling, esp. as adv.: mostly lower-middle class: C. 20. Herbert Jenkins, *passim*.

*mid-day, a. Bread and cheese: tramps' c.: from ca. 1920. When he leaves a casual ward in the morning, a tramp receives an issue of bread and cheese.

midday. See **Sunday**.

midder.—2. A midwifery case. i.e. a childbirth attended by a doctor; physicians': late C. 19–20. A. Neil Lyons, *Sixpenny Pieces*, 1909, 'We get about seven "midders" every day.' This sense constitutes the imm. origin of sense 1 on p. 519.—3. A midwife: since ca. 1925. Ex '*mid*-wife' by the Oxford *-er*.

middie. (Also **middy**.) A 10-fluid-ounce beer glass: Australian: since ca. 1930. Culotta, 1957. (B.P.) Ex *middle*-weight or -size?

middle, n., 2, is found in Breton, *Court and Country*, 1613.

middle-age spread. Paunchiness coming in middle age: coll.: late C. 19–20.

Middle East has, since the late 1940's and even among those who are supposed to know better, been an astoundingly frequent and widespread sol. for the Near East. In the old days, we had the Near East—the Middle East—the Far East; now we have stupidity and confusion. Journalists and even commentators are the worst offenders; in their wake, naturally, flounder all the ignorant.
It would be sensible, and very much safer, to restrict *the Near East* to the Levant, Turkey, Iraq, Iran, Arabia: apply *the Middle East* to Afghanistan, India, Pakistan, Ceylon, Burma: the rest (Malaya, Thailand, China, Japan, the East Indies) being *the Far East*.

middle for diddle. The method of deciding who shall start a darts game: darts' players': since ca. 1920. Each side throws a single 'arrow'—and the side landing the dart nearest to the centre has first throw.

middle name, (something or other) **is his, my,** etc. A c.p. indicating that some quality or tendency forms a marked characteristic, as 'Gossiping is her middle name': C. 20. (I first heard it in 1920, but I'm sure it's much older—perhaps going back to ca. 1870.) 'One year, when I was doing field work in the Yukon, an entomologist appeared in Whitehorse. He was a nice lad and much admired for his intimate knowledge of the "bugs" he studied. As one incredulous old-timer said, "He knows every damn bug by his middle name".' (Dr Douglas Leechman, April 1967.)

middle-page spread. 'Matter printed over the centre of pages, not uncommon since paper shortage' (Albert B. Petch, Sept. 5, 1946): journalistic: 1941 +. Punning on *middle-age spread*: (above).

middle pie. That stomach: non-aristocratic: ca. 1870–1910. B. & L.

middle piece (p. 519). Rather, ca. 1800–70. *The Sporting Magazine*, 1817, 'A terrible blow in the middle piece' (O.E.D.). Head (1), trunk (2), legs (3).—2. *Sinks*, 1848, defines it as the stomach or belly. Perhaps the midriff is implied both in sense 1 and in sense 2.

middle-watcher (p. 519) prob. goes back to ca. 1810; it occurs in, e.g., W.N. Glascock's *Naval Sketch Book*, 2nd Series, 1834, at I, 48. (Moe.)

*middleman. One who, professionally, recovers property from the thief or thieves concerned: c.: ca. 1830–90. B. & L.

middling, adv., 2 (p. 519). The example is defective, for, there, *middling* is an adj. As an adv., it goes back to late C. 18, as in 'I did it pretty middling' (in a Charles Dibdin song written pre-1805 and quoted in *The Port Folio* of April, 13, 1805, p. 110, col. 2). Moe.

middling! I don't think so!; I don't believe you!: tailors': from ca. 1860. Ibid.

middy. Earlier in 'A Real Paddy'. *Real Life in Ireland*, 1822, and still earlier in Alfred Burton, *The Adventures of Johnny Newcome*, 1818. (Moe.) 'Taffrail' writes: 'We read in newspaper articles and boys' books of adventure of "middies". We sometimes even hear the term used in conversation round tea-tables ashore, but to call a present-day midshipman a "middy" to his face would make him squirm.' Granville, 'Mids = Midshipmen. Never "middies" in the Royal Navy.'—2. See **middie** above.

*midgic derives directly ex Shelta of C. 18–20. B. & L. (Also in Australia: B., 1942.)

Midnight Horror, the. A train running between Townsville and Cairns: Queenslanders': since ca. 1920. (B., 1953.)

midshipman's nuts (p. 519) occurs earlier in *The Night Watch* (II, 50), 1828. Moe.

midshipman's roll (p. 519) prob. goes back to ca. 1800 or a little earlier; W. N. Glascock *Sketch-Book* (I, 7), 1825, has it. Moe.

midwaaf or **midwaf.** A 'Waaf' N.C.O. 'very officious with her girls' (H. & P.): W.A.A.F. and R.A.F.: 1940 +. Punning *mid-W.A.A.F.* and *midwife*.

midwife's friend, the. Quinine contraceptive pessaries: since ca. 1925. Ex their unreliability. (*The Lancet*, 1935—on p. 1133.)

midzer. A half, as in *midzer caroon*, a half-crown: showmen's: since ca. 1860. Variant of *madza* (p. 503).

midzers. Money; esp., cash, coins: showmen's: late C. 19–20. (*John o' London's Weekly*, March 4, 1949.) Cf. *medzies*, p. 515.

miesli is an occ. form of **mizzle** (*Dict.*).

miffed, participial adj. Offended; annoyed: mostly Canadian: late C. 19–20. (Leechman.) Cf. *miff* and *miffy*, adj., on p. 519.

mike, n.—5. See **micky**, above.—6. A cup of tea: low Australian: since ca. 1925. (Ruth Park, 1950.) Perhaps ex sense 2 (p. 520).—7. See **Mike Bliss.**

Mike or **mike.**—5. See **Mike Bliss.**—6. (*Mike.*) A 'shunting yard engine (ER)': railwaymen's: C. 20. (*Railway* 2nd.)

Mike (Bliss), n. and v. Piss: rhyming s.: late C. 19–20.

mike-boom; mike slinger. 'To follow the players about, the "mike" [microphone] is moved across the floor on a long arm called a "mike boom", and its operator is a "mike slinger",' *The Evening News*, Nov. 7, 1939.

mike fright. (Extreme) nervousness in front of television, or news-reel, camera: radio and television operators': since ca. 1934. *The Daily Mail*, May 24, 1950.

mike out of, take a (or **the**). See **take a mike out of.**

mil-mil, v.t. To see: Australian pidgin: from ca. 1860. B. & L. Ex Aborigine.

mile, v. To ride on the Ladies' Mile in Hyde Park: Society: ca. 1870–1905. Ibid.

mileage yard. 'Station siding yard (WR)': railwaymen's coll.: C. 20. (*Railway*, 3rd.)

miles and miles and (bloody) miles of sweet fuck-all. A c.p. that is a ruefully jocular description of the African desert, esp. among soldiers (1914–18 and again in 1939–45) or of the Canadian prairies (1919 onwards).

miles away, be. To be either day-dreaming or lost in thought; coll.: since ca. 1910.

Miles' (or **Miles's**) **boy.**—2. 'A very knowing lad in receipt of much information': tailors': from ca. 1860. Ibid. Ex:

Miles's boy is spotted. A printers' c.p. ('We know all about *that*!') addressed to anyone who, in a printing office, begins to spin a yarn: from ca. 1830. Ex Miles, a Hampstead coach-boy 'celebrated for his faculty of diverting the passengers with anecdotes and tales'. (B. & L.)

milestones. Heavy seas breaking inboard when one is homeward-bound: Naval: C. 20. (Irving, *Royal Navalese*, 1946.) With a pun on *millstones*.

milk, v.—5. Hence (?), to remove spot-lamps, extra clocks, spare plugs, from second-hand cars and, 'on the quiet', sell them as accessories: motor trade: since ca. 1920. Often as vbl n., *milking*.—6. To stack a pack of cards: Australian card-players': since ca. 1920. (B., 1953.) Also 'to *build*'. The nn. *building* and *milking* are common.—7. To steal the petrol from (a car) by syphoning: ca. 1940–50, while petrol was short.—8. Hence, to syphon petrol (from tank of car) for legitimate purposes: since late 1940's. These two senses esp. common in Australia. (B.P.)

milk, come (or **get**) **home with the.** See **home with . . .**

milk, the. The milkman: lower-class coll.: 1895, W. Pett Ridge, *Minor Dialogues*.

milk bottles. Female breasts: Australian (not very common): since ca. 1930.

milk horse. 'A horse entered at a race to make money on, and always scratched before the affair comes off': turf: ca. 1865–1910. B. & L.

milk in the coconut (p. 520). Ex the U.S. phrase derives the Canadian c.p., *that accounts for the milk in the coconut, ah! that explains it*: late C. 19–20. (Leechman.)

*milk-jug, whence the variant **milkie.** A simpleton; a dupe: Australian c.: since ca. 1920. (B., 1953.) As 'dupe' it is also British and, of course, it rhymes on s. *mug*. (Franklyn 2nd.)

milk round. 'A run made fairly regularly by a squadron or a Force, if it returns to its station or base in the early morning.' Partridge, 1945: R.A.F.: 1940 +. Cf. *milk train*.

milk the bushes. To haul a small boat upstream by pulling on the bushes growing along the banks: N.W. Canadian, esp. the Yukon: since ca. 1910. (Leechman.)

milk train. The early-morning reconnaissance flight(s): R.A.F.: 1940 +. H. & P. Cf. prec. entry and **mail run.**

milkie, Australian variant (C. 20) of **milky** (p. 521). B., 1953.—2. See **milk-jug.**

milking.—2. The 'robbing' of a closely following bus of passengers: busmen's: C. 20.

milkman, go between the moon and the. See **moon and the milkman . . .**

milkman's horse. Bad-tempered; angry: rhyming s. (on *cross*): late C. 19–20. Franklyn 2nd.

milko has, since ca. 1955, been commoner in Australia than **milkie** (above). B.P.

Milky. The inevitable nickname of any man surnamed *Way* or *Waye*, *Wey* or *Weye*: late C. 19–20. Ex 'the *Milky Way*'.

milky, n.—2. A white marble: Australian children's: late C. 19–20. (B.P.)

mill, n.—8. A locomotive (also *mill kettle*); a typewriter: Canadian railroadmen's (— 1931).

mill, v., 2 (p. 521). Hence, *to mill a go*, to bring off a theft or a robbery, as in 'We have milled a precious go' (brought off a fine coup): *Fal de Ral Tit*, an English ballad of ca. 1790. Moe. 'For sense 3, cf. James Dalton, *A Narrative*, 1728, '*To Mill*, To knock down a Person.'

mill, ground and bolted.—I've been through the. I'm too experienced for that!: nautical: mid-C. 19–20; ob. B. & L. Cf. mill, go through the in the *Dict.*

mill, in the. (Imprisoned) in the guard-room: military: ca. 1880–1915. Ibid.

mill around. (Of tanks) to move about, either looking for targets or merely creating a dust: Army in N. Africa: 1942–3.—2. (Of aircraft) to fly in and out so as to cross paths: R.A.F.: 1943–5. Adopted ex U.S. Ex 'to *mill* (*around*), a cowboy term for corralled cattle going round in an ever-tightening circle' (Leechman).

mill kettle. See mill, n., 8.

mill the bowling. See mill, v., 7 (*Dict.*).

*mill the quod. See mill a quod (*Dict.*).

miller.—6. A housebreaker: c.: C. 17–mid-19. Ex *mill*, v., 1 (*Dict.*).—7. A cicada: Australian: C. 20. B., 1942. Cf. mealy back.

miller's thumb. See miller, drown the (*Dict.*).

Millibar Mike. A Meteorological Officer: R.A.F. (officers'): ca. 1940–5. Robert Hinde, letter of March 17, 1945. By alliterative personification and by ref. to millimetric readings. Specifically to the *millibar*, a unit of atmospheric pressure.

milling (around). High-speed flying in and out, and across one another's path; or 'flying in a defensive circle, with the nose of one aircraft a few yards from the tail of another' (Jackson): R.A.F.: 1940 +. Adopted from American airmen.

*milltag, milltog, milltug. See mill-tag (*Dict.*).

millwash. See mill-wash (*Dict.*).

mimming mugger. A buffoon mimic: theatrical: mid-C. 19–20; ob. B. & L. I.e. *miming* (corrupted) + mugger, 3 (*Dict.*).

Min. of Ag., the. The Ministry of Agriculture: since ca. 1930. Monica Dickens, *The Happy Prisoner*, 1946. By 1960, †. It was superseded by *Ag and Fish*.

minces. Short for *mince pies*, eyes: late C. 19–20. A C. 20 variant is *mincers*. Franklyn 2nd.

mincing machine, the. 'The marshalling area mechanism . . . must break up units and provide mixed loads for the various forms of sea transport,' Gordon Holman, *Stand By to Beach*, 1944: Naval.

mind-blowing, adj. 'Ecstasy-producing' (Peter Fryer in *The Observer* colour supplement, Dec. 3, 1967): 'jazz and drug addicts', and hippies': since ca. 1966.

mind how you go! A c.p., common only since ca. 1942 and addressed to someone either caught in traffic or slipping on, e.g., a banana skin; hence, since ca. 1945, also metaphorically.

mind me!, don't. See way?, are you in my.

mind one's own pigeon. To mind one's own business: New Zealand: C. 20. B., 1941.

mind your back! Get out of the way!: Cockneys' s.(— 1900) >, by 1920, coll. Cf. mind your eye! and mind the helm!—both in the *Dict.*

mind your nose, ducky! See nosey.

mind your own fish! Mind your own business!: Australian: C. 20. B., 1942.

mind your own interferences! A jocular 'mind your own business!': c.p.: since ca. 1910; by 1960, slightly ob.

mind your three S's! See three S's . . . in the *Dict.*

minder.—3. Hence, a 'con' man's assistant, who keeps the victim happy and unconscious: c. : C. 20. Cf. sense 2 (p. 522).—4. 'Occasionally he acted as "minder" to one of the top-class "stable" girls (that is, he was paid to keep an eye on the harlots to make sure that they were not molested by clients or rivals)': the world of prostitution: C. 20. (John Gosling & Douglas Warner, *The Shame of a City*, 1960).—5. A bouncer in a club or dance-hall or . . .: low: since late 1940's. James Barlow, *The Burden of Proof*, 1968.

mine, down the. 'Buried' by a heavy wave that collapses suddenly and violently: Australian surfers': since middle 1950's. (Culotta.) Perhaps ex the famous song, 'Don't Go Down the Mine, Daddy.'

miners' friends (or capitals). 'Royal Scots locomotives' (*Railway*, 3rd): railwaymen's: since ca. 1925 (?).

mine's up! See 'Prisoner-of-War Slang', 14.

Ming. Sir Robert Menzies: Australian: since ca. 1939. (B.P.) Ex the Scottish pron. of *Menzies*.

minge, 2 (p. 522). Also Services', esp. Army. Probably ex dialect.

minge, v.; minger; mingy. To prowl about in order to discover misdemeanours; one who does this; addicted thereto: St Bees: C. 20. Marples. Cf. dial. *minch*, to move stealthily.

mingy (p. 522). Prob. current throughout C. 20; cf. the Cockney sense, 'greedy', current ca. 1890–1915 and recorded by J. W. Horsley in *I Remember*, 1912.

mini. A mini(-) skirt: early, although not common until late, 1967, with multitudinous references, spoken and written, throughout 1967: coll.; by 1968, S.E. Hence, since (ca. Sept.) 1967, an adj., as in 'She was wearing the miniest of minis': s. The term *mini*(-)*skirt* stands for *minimum* (rather than *minimal*) skirt, ensuring the minimum of decency: you can't see her panties until the girl sits down or offers a rear view as she bends down. One of the most revolutionary fashions ever to enhance the gaiety of nations during a period when gaiety is rarer than gold. Usually, however, *mini* is short for the adjectival use of *miniature*: see F. Stuart's excellent article ('Mini-') in *Word Study*, Dec. 1967.

minions of the moon. 'Our night fighters and bombers,' H. & P.: journalistic, it was jocularly taken up by the R.A.F. in 1941–3. Ex the S.E. sense, 'moonlight-utilisers'.

Ministry of Fish and Chips, the. The Ministry of Agriculture and Fisheries: jocular political: since the 1930's.

Minnie. The *Ministry of Information*: since mid-Sept. 1939; ob. by 1946.—2. A *mini*car: motorists': since ca. 1960. Courtenay Edwards in *The Sunday Telegraph*, Sept. 24, 1961.

minnow. Usually in pl. A torpedo: Naval: since ca. 1937. Cf. mouldy (*Dict.*).

Minor Drugs: British slang names in 1963. Mandrake's 'Oxford: The Real Dope' in *The*

Sunday Telegraph, Oct. 20, 1963, speaking of undergraduate 'users', says:

'The demand for the minor drugs: Pot (marihuana), Purple Hearts and Blueies (Drinamyl), Black Bombers, Prels (Preludin), Bennies and Dexies (Benzedrine and Dexedrine) is almost unlimited. On the other hand, there is very little demand for Snow or the White Stuff (heroin or cocaine).'

mins. At several Public Schools, from ca. 1870 (?), as in Arnold Lunn, *Loose Ends,* 1919: 'Smith mins swears he said "damn".' I.e. *minor.*

mintie. See **without a mintie.**

miracles?, do you think (or **does he think**) **I can shit**; or **I can't shit miracles!** A c.p. addressed, not usually to the person imposing the task but to a third party: c.p.: from ca. 1920. (Mostly Londoners'.)

[Miscellanea: In the early C. 18, Ned Ward has —apart from the nn. listed here under 'Animals', 'Body', 'Burglars' tools', 'Dupes', 'Ejaculations', 'Epithets', 'Food', 'Fops', 'Harlots', 'Men', 'Occupational names', 'Personifications', 'Regional names', 'Rogues', 'Shortenings', 'Verbs', 'Weapons' and 'Women'—the following miscellaneous ones, all noted by Matthews: A bedroom, *snoring kennel* (1703); a privy, *boghouse* (1703) and *jakes* (1722). Talk was *padding*; chatter, *tittle-tattles* (likewise in 1703) or *prittleprattle* (1703); impudence, *bounce* (1703); a quarrel, *rattle* (1703); wind music, *tooting* (1703), and violin music, *diddle-diddle* (1703). Energy was *elbow-grease* (1709); kissing, *slip-slop* (1703); a jest, *flirt* (1709); *parchment dabs* (1709) were writs, leading to *Rat Castle* (1700), a prison; *razorridge* (1703), shaving; *fag-end* (1703), part near the end; *swag* (1703), swag (n.); *juggle* (1714, prob. always S.E.), a duping trick; *tag rag and bobtail* (1703; prob. always S.E.), rabble; *muckender* (1703), a swab; a hat was either *nab* (1703) or *mounteer* (1703), whereas pig-tails were *rat's tails* (1714); an object of name forgotten was a *thingum* (1703) or a *what-ye-call-'em* (1709).]

miserable. Close-fisted, stingy: Australian coll.: since ca. 1860. 'Tom Collins', *Such is Life,* 1903.

miserable as a shag on a rock. Very low-spirited: Aus.: since ca. 1920. (B., 1959.) Cf. **miserable as a bandicoot** in the *Dict.*

miserere seat. A seat so constructed that if the occupant fall asleep he falls off: ecclesiastical coll.: C. 19–20; ob. Cf. the slightly different Fr. *miséricorde.*

misery, be a. To be peevish; be a peevish person: lower classes', esp. Cockneys', coll.: from ca. 1880. Also *get the miseries,* to be peevish: id.: C. 20. '"I've got a misery" in Negro parlance means "I've got a pain" or an illness' (Leechman, April 1967).

mish.—3. A missionary: late C. 19–20. In, e.g., C. S. Archer, *China Servant,* 1946. Cf. sense 2 on p. 543.

mislain, miesli, misli. To rain: Shelta: C. 18–20.—2. To go: see *mizzle* (*Dict.*). B. & L.

misprint. A kiss that goes astray: bookworld: C. 20.

miss (p. 523). Earlier in W. Somerset Maugham, *Liza of Lambeth,* 1897.—2. 'An omission to lay on a sheet [of paper] in feeding a printing machine': printers' coll.: C. 19–20. B. & L.—3. 'She being taken to be the Earle of Oxford's *Misse,* as at this

time they began to call lewd women', *John Evelyn's Diary,* Jan. 9, 1662: Court and Society: ca. 1660–80.

Miss Fitch. A bitchy girl or woman: rhyming on *bitch*: C. 20. (Franklyn 2nd.)

Miss Hotbot. See **hot-bot.**

Miss Nancy, talk. To talk very politely: since ca. 1910. Wm. Riley, *Netherleigh,* 1916. With the implication that such politeness is effeminate.

miss not having is a Canadian (and U.S.) sol. for *miss having,* as in 'I miss not having a hammock' = I once had a hammock and now, in its absence, I miss it: since ca. 1920 (?). Leechman.

miss one's figure. To miss a chance; to make a mistake: non-aristocratic: from ca. 1860; ob. B. & L.

miss the globe. To miss the ball altogether: golfers': from ca. 1898. (W. B. Maxwell, *We Forget because We Must,* 1928.) With a pun on *globe,* a sphere, and on *globe,* the world.

missing. Courting, courtship: ca. 1830–70. *Sinks,* 1848.

missionary's or **missionaries' downfall, the.** A light rum; or—esp. Demerara—rum diluted: since ca. 1930. *Trader Vic's Book of Food and Drink,* 1946, p. 36, 'Don the Beachcomber of Hollywood and Chicago, th⌐ originator of such outstanding drinks as the Zombie and Missionary's Downfall': therefore perhaps of Am. origin. Cf. **bane, the,** above, and, on p. 535, **mother's ruin.**

'missioner (or without apostrophe). An agent bullying or seducing men into the Navy or, come to that, the Army: Naval coll. rather than s.: ca. 1770–1830. Short for *commissioner?* W. N. Glascock, *Sailors and Saints* (I, 82), 1829. (Moe.)

missy baba. A young lady: Anglo-Indian: mid-C. 19–20. B. & L., 'Borrowed from the natives, *baba* being meant for baby.'

Mister Bull. A typical Englishman: ? mostly Naval: ca. 1810–60. (W. N. Glascock's *Naval Sketch Book,* 2nd Series, 1834, at II, 244, and elsewhere.) Ex S.E. *John Bull.*

Mister Charlie. See **Pinkie, 2,** below.

Mister Middleton's Light Horse. 'A flotilla of flower-named corvettes. (After the late Mr Middleton, the B.B.C. gardening expert)': Naval, esp. officers': 1939 +. Granville.

Mister (or **Mr) Muggins.** Oneself regarded, esp. by oneself, as a dupe, a simpleton: Australian: late C. 19–20. (B.P.) Cf. **muggins** on p. 542.

mistura A.D.T. or, in full, **mistura any damn' thing.** A variant of next entry: medical and pharmaceutical: C. 20. (B.P.)

mistura God help 'em. A mixture of dregs and drugs administered as a last resort: medical: from ca. 1860; ob. B. & L.

mit, v. Might: Cockneys': since when? Clarence Rook, *The Hooligan Nights*: 1899.

mit, preposition. See **with or without?** below.

mit a. With a grain of salt—i.e. sceptically—as in 'I'd take that story mit a': Australian: since ca. 1950. This is the Ger. *mit,* with; 'possibly due to New Australian influence' (Edwin Morrisby, letter of Aug. 30, 1958).

mitney (p. 524). Also written *mitni.* More prob. ex either Romany or Shelta.

mitt.—3. Hand: adopted, ca. 1918, ex U.S.

mivey or **mivy.** A landlady: mostly Cockneys': from ca. 1870. B. & L. Prob. a sense variant of **mivvy, 1** (*Dict.*).

mivvy.—2. An adept; a very smart person: c.: from ca. 1870. Pugh (2): "'He's a mivvy at makin' things easy." "For himself. No doubt o' that.'" Perhaps ex *master* + *skilful*, but probably from S.E. *marvel.*—By 1900, low Cockney s., and by 1920, gen. Cockney s.

mix it.—2. *Mix it for*, to inform against (someone) to the police: low: C. 20. Mark Benney, *The Big Wheel*, 1940. Cf. **mix up** in *Dict.*

mix it; mix it up for; mix it with. See the next term, with which they are contemporaneous.

mix the red and the black, whence the synonymous *play roulette.* To assault an officer when brought before him on a charge: Army: since ca. 1925. (R. Wild, *The Rest of the Day's Your Own*, 1943.)

mixer.—2. One who makes mischief, esp. one given to mischief-making: Cockneys': from ca. 1912. E.g. 'He's a reg'lar mixer! He mixed it up for me with Joe, and he tried to mix it with Tom.'

mixing the breed! A c.p., employed either by someone using another's brush and comb or by a person (whether owner or not) watching this: noncultured: late C. 19–20.

mixing the breeds, mostly as n. 'It was a joke among the Tommies that German lice had black and white stripes, and ours were a dirty grey'; 'We sometimes got [additional] lice on us when we used German dugouts we had captured' (A. B. Petch): Army; 1915–18, then historical.

mizzle.—2. To rain: Shelta: C. 19–20. B. & L. Blend of *moan* and *drizzle.*—3. See **die, to.**—4. To complain: Australian: C. 20. Baker.

mizzle one's dick. To miss one's passage: nautical: since ca. 1880. John Masefield, *Sard Harker*, 1924. Cf. **mizzle**, p. 525.

mizzler, needy. See **needy mizzler** and cf. **rum mizzler**, both in *Dict.*

mo.—4. Coll. form of *Moses*: C. 18–20.—5. Nickname for very popular Australian comedian, Harry Van der Sluica: since ca. 1930. B., 1942. —6. A moustache: Australian: late C. 19–20. (Dal Stivens, *The Gambling Ghost*, 1953.)

moa, dead as a. Quite dead: New Zealand and Australian coll.: C. 20. Baker. The New Zealand moa—a very large bird—is as dead as the dodo.

moab.—3. A receptacle (e.g. a sink, a tub) for dirty plates: Haileybury: since ca. 1870. 'From Psalm LX. 8, "Moab is my wash-pot",' Marples. Cf. sense 1 (p. 525).

moan on, have a. To nurse a grudge, a 'grouse' esp. Services: since ca. 1915. See **moan** on p. 525.

moaner. A pessimist: Army coll.: C. 20, esp. 1914–18.

moaning Minnie. An occ. variant of *Mona* (see **Clara**).—2. A multi-barrelled German mortar: Army: 1941 +, Echoic.

mob, n., 5. As 'a party of men', it was whalers' s. of ca. 1820–1900. E. J. Wakefield, *Adventure*, 1845 (recorded by B., 1941).—7. survives, however, in sense 'a young woman' (B. & L.); ob.

mob, v.—3. See **ox up.**

mob up with. To join; to form two or more separate entities into a unit or whole: Regular Army: since ca. 1917. Ex **mob**, n., 6 (p. 525).

mobile.—3. A traymobile, i.e. a dinner waggon on castors or tyred wheels: Australian coll.: since late 1940's. (B.P.)

mobile, get. See **get cracking.**

mobs, adv. See:

mobs of. A large number, even a large quantity, of; e.g. *mobs of stones—birds—water*: Australian coll.: late C. 19–20. Ex **mob**, n., 5. This Australianism is explained by Arthur Russell, *A Tramp-Royal in Wild Australia: 1928–1929* (pub. in 1936), thus: 'So accustomed has the Inlander become to dealing in mobs—mobs of cattle, mobs of horses, mobs of sheep, mobs of camels, donkeys, mules, goats—that he has come to reckon in no other terms of measurement. . . . I asked Tuck a question . . . : did he think that the Finke River country . . . would give us better "going" than we had met with on the plains. "Oh, yes," he drawled, "mobs better . . . There'll be mobs of water on the track, we'll get mobs of beef at the runs, the stages'll be mobs shorter, an' there'll be mobs better camping grounds. And of course we'll be able to take it mobs easier."'

mocassin (or moccasin) telegraph, the. A frequent Canadian 'shape' of the **bush telegraph** and the **grapevine** (both above): since ca. 1910 at latest. (Leechman.)

mocassins. 'The shearer's homemade footwear, usually made in sacking or felt' (*Straight Furrow*, Feb. 21, 1968): N.Z.: since 1920.

mock. A halfpenny: Australian: C. 20. B., 1942. What a mockery!

Mock Auction slang. A few examples occur, scattered about the Dictionary and the Supplement; e.g. *front up, gezumph* (or *ga-*), *hinting gear, nailers*. But here is a passage reported, in the section headed 'Parliament' (dealing with the Mock Auctions Bill) in *The Daily Telegraph* of Feb. 25, 1961:

'Sir Tufton [Beamish] told members that he had been to mock auctions in Britain and America. He gave an example of the jargon used:

'The top man operates his joint by nailing the steamers among the plunder-snatchers in the pitch got by his frontsman, running out the flash gear or hinton lots as N.S. lots to ricks and gees or to hinton, and gazoomphing the sarkers with swag and plunder, while the raving Noahs are silenced with bung-ons and the bogies are smitzed to hinton to noise the edge. . . .

'He gave the translation:

'The mock auctioneer operates a stall by ensuring attendance until the end of the sale of those who are mugs rather than those who are just out for free gifts among the crowd collected by his men.

'He pretends to sell, as bait to his victims, genuine goods, which are in fact never sold, to accomplices among the crowd or to non-existent bidders at the back and tricking those of the mugs who have enough money to buy his cheap trash.

'Anyone who tries to warn the crowd is given a present. Dissatisfied customers who are likely to complain about previous sales are taken behind the rostrum to avoid trouble.'

The 'translation' is not a translation but a very free paraphrase. The following little glossary may help, even though, through my ignorance, I cannot render it either complete or 'watertight'.

bogies: dissatisfied customers. See **bogy**, n., 8, on p. 75.

bung-ons: gifts. Cf. **bung**, v., 2, on p. 109.

edge: see *noise the edge* below.

flash gear: showy, yet superior goods. Cf. **flash**, n., 6, on p. 283.

frontsman: that member of the gang who attracts the crowds.

gazoomphing: swindling. Cf. **gazumph** and **gezumph** above.

gees: auctioneer's accomplices—cf. **gee**, n., 2, on p. 319.

hinton-lots: goods offered as bait; usually genuine. What are also known as *hinting gear*.

joint: a stall; the room where the auction is held. See **joint**, n., 6, on p. 443.

nailing: successfully attracting—cf. **nailers** in this Supplement.

noise the edge: to avoid trouble: app. since ca. 1945.

pitch: the crowd around a stall or in the auction room. See **pitch**, n., below.

plunder-snatchers. Seekers after free gifts— and the real bargains.

raving Noahs: trouble-makers. (Noahs prophesying floods.)

ricks: accomplices. See **rick** on p. 696.

sarkers: ? those tending to be sarcastic, yet, for all that, 'mugs'.

smitzed: ? reduced to silence. Perhaps on 'smithereens', but prob. Yiddish ex German *schmitzen*, to lash, to whip.

steamers: simpletons (natural victims) or 'mugs'. See **steamer**, 2, on p. 827.

swag and plunder: cheap goods.

topman: auctioneer. See **top man**, 2, below.

mock (or **mocks**) **on, put the.** To upset the plans of (someone): Australian: since ca. 1925. (B., 1943.) To 'make a mock of'. Perhaps ex Yiddish 'wish the *mockers* on (someone)'—to wish him very bad luck, itself ex Hebrew (one of the Ten Plagues). Julian Franklyn. Ex **mocker on** . . . below.

mock turtle squadron. 'A fleet of dummy ships used in wartime to fox the enemy' (Granville): Naval officers': 1915 +.

mock up. To improvise; as n. (*mock-up*), a large- or a full-scale, although not usually a working, model: Services' coll. (1939), become, by 1942, j.

mocker. 'Clothes in general' (B., 1953): low Australian: since ca. 1920.—2. Hence, a woman's dress: New Zealand: since ca. 1935. Slatter, 'Have you seen that trot in the blue mocker?' Cf. **mockered up.**

mocker, esp. in *put the mocker on*, to lay a curse upon, to bring bad luck to: (low) Australian: since ca. 1925. (Lawson Glassop, *Lucky Palmer*, 1949.) The source of *put the mock* (or *mocks*) *on*, q.v. above at **mock on.**

mockered up. Dressed in one's best: low: late C. 19–20. Ironically ex **mockered on molled up** (both in *Dict.*).

mocking bird. A word: theatrical rhyming s.: C. 20. (Franklyn, *Rhyming*.)

mocks on . . . See **mock on** . . .

mod. A mechanical improvement or change in an aircraft: Air Force coll.: since ca. 1920. Jackson. Short for '*modification*'.—2. A teenager unable to afford a motorcycle, and doing his damnedest with a scooter: 1963 (+), partly in opposition to **rocker**, n., 2 (below). Short for *modern*. But Mr David Holloway, in his review (Feb. 23, 1967) of the 6th edition of this dictionary, writes: '"Mods" ride scooters because the

machines protect their clothes much better than the larger ones affected by "rockers" who wear leathers and jeans.'

mod con. (usually in pl., *mod cons*.) Modern convenience: jocular: since ca. 1945. Derisive of estate agents' jargon.

model, n. A working-men's hotel or lodging-house: Glasgow: from ca. 1920. MacArthur & Long.

model, v. To pose as a model: artists' and models' coll.: C. 20.

modern girl, 'from a proprietary brand of Chinese cigarette, was a common name for the particularly odorous dried fish we sometimes obtained in the rations': among Far East prisoners of war: 1942–45. (The aspersion is directed at the cigarette, not at the girl.)

modesties. Babies' pilchers: Australian euphemistic coll.: since ca. 1910. (B., 1943.)

*****moer!** or **your moer!** Go to hell: South African c. and very low s.: C. 20. See *Underworld* for elucidation.

moey.—3. A moustache: Australian: late C. 19–20. (Ruth Park, *Poor Man's Orange*, 1950.)

moff or **moph.** A hermaphrodite: working classes': C. 20. Ex illiterate 'her*moph*rodite'.—2. Hence, a dual-purpose farm wagon: rural: since ca. 1946. (John Moore in the *Bournemouth Daily Echo* of April 21, 1956.)

mog.—3. A lie: 1848, *Sinks*. Hence *no mogue* (**mogue,** p. 526) = *no mog*. The origin of *mog* and *mogue* is prob. the Fr.(*se*) *moquer* (*de*), for otherwise *-ue* is unexplainable.

mog; moggy. For additional information, see **moke.**

mogador. (Of persons) confused; depressed; all at sea: Cockneys': since ca. 1910. (Julian Franklyn, communication of 1939.) Cognate with **mogue** (p. 526)? Also *mogadored*, prob. the original form and therefore perhaps a perversion of *moidered*. The police have, since ca. 1940, used *magadored* of a suspect that, at an interrogation, is 'broken' to the state of giving facts. (Communicated by Laurie Atkinson, July 1, 1948.) Julian Franklyn, however, thinks *mogadored*, (fig.) floored, is rhyming s.

mogger. A cat: low: C. 20. Cf. **moggy** (*Dict.*).

moging is a variant of *moguing*, q.v. at **mogue** (*Dict.*).

mogue. See **mog,** 3, above.

mojo! A yell of approval or of excitement: rhythm-and-blues fans', esp. teenagers': ca. 1964–66. Ex an American Negro s. term of vague meaning (e.g. a spell, power).—But in American drug addicts' s. it = 'any narcotic': prob. a different word.

moke. The Gypsy *moxio* may well be an adaptation of the dial. *Mock*(*e*), a nickname for either a horse or an ass, precisely as *Moggy*, in several dial., is a nickname for cow, calf, or ass, and *Mog* is a cat. Since *Mog* (cf. *Meg*) and *Moggy* (cf. *Meggy*) and even *Moke* are diminutives of *Margaret*, perhaps via *Molly* (see my *Name This Child*), cf. with *Molly* the c. **miler** (q.v. in *Dict.*). We have, then, the interesting fact that both of the modern names for an ass represent diminutives: *donkey* of *Duncan*; *moke* of *Margaret*.

mokkered up. A variant of *mockered up*. (Cad lie, *A Sydney Barmaid*, 1953.)

moko, 1, may be a humorous perversion of *macaw* (B. & L.).

moldy is the Canadian spelling of **mouldy**, n., 2 (*Dict.*).

moleskin squatter. 'A working man who has come to own a small sheep run': New Zealand and Australian rural coll.: C. 20. B., 1941, 1942. Ex the moleskin trousers such farmers tend to wear.

moll, v.; **molling,** vbl n. To go—going—about with women; act—acting—effeminately: low: from ca. 1860; ob. B. & L. Ex the n.

*moll-buzzer. In C. 20, and more properly and gen. spelt *moll buzzer*, it has come to mean a female pickpocket. (*The Evening News,* Dec. 9, 1936.) Perhaps orig. influenced by **moll-tooler** (properly, unhyphenated), q.v. in *Dict.*

*moll hook. A female pickpocket: c.: ca. 1860–1920. B. & L. Cf. the preceding.

moll-rower, -rowing. See **molrower, molrowing** (*Dict.*).

*moll-slavey. A maid-servant: c. of ca. 1810–70. B. & L.

Molly! A variant of **Mary!**, q.v. in *Dict.*

molly, n.—4. A malingerer: Australian Naval: since ca. 1915. (B., 1943.) Ex S.E. *mollycoddle.*

molly, v.t. 'to bugger (someone)'; hence, adj. *mollying,* 'addicted to buggery'. *The Ordinary of Newgate's Account,* 1744, contains both—e.g. 'You mollying dog'. Ex sense 2 of the n.—see p. 527.

molly-dooker; whence **molly-dook.** A left-handed person, whence (the adj.) left-handed: Australian: since ca. 1920. (B., 1943.) Ex *molly,* 1 (p. 527) + *dook,* q.v. at *dukes* (p. 247).

molly(-)house. A resort of sodomites: esp. a house where men prostituted themselves to men: low: C. 18–mid 19. James Dalton, *A Narrative,* 1728, at p. 36.

Molly O'Morgan. An organ: late C. 19–20. Rhyming.

molo man. A Moor; negro: pidgin: mid-C. 19–20. Via It. and Sp. *moro.*

molocher. Variant of **molocker** (*Dict.*); B. & L., wrongly (I think), define it as 'a cheap hat'.

Molotov bread-basket. 'A bunch of incendiaries which blow out in a group as they drop to the ground.' H. & P.: 1940 +. Cf.:

Molotov cocktail. An anti-tank missile consisting of a bottle containing inflammable material and fitted with a fuse: 1939–45. H. & P. Like prec., ex the name of the Russian statesman. Adopted from Finnish usage.

Mona. A nickname for a female given to complaining, unless by chance it is her Christian name: Londoners': from ca. 1919. Punning *moaner.*—2. See **Clara** and cf. **wailing Winnie.**

monaker. B. & L. state that the It. word is *monarco,* king, and give the rare variant *monacher.* In a letter of April 4, 1959, Mr Jacob Jaffe suggests that the word might be back-s. for *ekename.* This theory presupposes that a back-form *emaneke* becomes, by aphesis, *maneke* (trisyllabic), varied to *moneke* (trisyllabic), whence *moneker,* *-iker, -aker,* etc. The chronologies of *ekename* and *monaker* do not preclude the possibility. But I prefer the derivation from *monogram.*

Monday, n. A very large hammer that can be effectually used by fit men only: railwaymen's: since ca. 1920. (*Railway* 2nd.) Men free of a week-end hangover.

[Money. In the period 1700–25, the following terms—for most of which, see the *Dict.*—occur in Ned Ward; Matthews lists them: Money in gen. was named *cole* (1700), *mumper's brass* (1709) and *rhino* (1700; spelt *rino*). A sixpence was *tester* (1709), *sice* (1715) or *Copper-John's* (1700; I'm not so sure about this term!); a guinea was a *Jacobus* or a *yellow boy* (both in 1700); a half-guinea, a *smelt* (1703); 'coppers' were *megs* (1703). Bribes or tips were *garnish* or *sweetning* (both in 1703); and the process of bribing was expressed in *grease a palm* (1703) and *drop* (a person so much: 1714).]

money.—3. Bubbles in a cup of tea: domestic: since ca. 1870.

money, in the. Receiving good wages or a large salary: coll.: since ca. 1934.

money(-)box. A 'Royal Mail train' (*Railway,* 3rd): C. 20.

money (or **toffee**) **from a child, (as) easy as taking.** See **easy as taking . . .**

money-maker or **-spinner.** See **money-box,** . . . (*Dict.*).

money to burn, have. To have plenty to spend; to be rich: col.: C. 20.

mong. A *mong*rel dog: Australian: since ca. 1910. B., 1942.—2. Hence, pejorative for any dog, even of the best pedigree: Australian: since ca. 1940. 'Get that bloody mong out of my yard!' (B.P.)

monish (p. 528). But also, ca. 1840–80, jocular, with a humorous imitation of Jewish pronunciation: *Sinks,* 1848.

monk.—5. A friar bird: Australian: late C. 19–20. Baker. A pun.

monk, da. A c.p. reference to an organ-grinder's monkey: C. 20. Ex Italian pronunciation.

monkery derives direct ex Shelta of C. 18–20: B. & L. For sense 5 (p. 528): also a district in which either tramps or beggars operate: C. 20.

monkey, n., 6. 'Not ob.,' Sidney J. Baker, letter, 1946.—13. A greatcoat: Naval: ca. 1810–60. Glascock, 1838. Cf. senses 3, 9.—14. 'In English vulgar speech the monkey is often made to figure as a witty, pragmatically wise, ribald simulacrum of unrestrained mankind. Of the numerous instances, "You must draw the line somewhere, as the monkey said, peeing across the carpet" is typical. The phrase ". . . as the monkey said," is invariable in this context' (Atkinson): esp. since ca. 1870. Cf. the **monkey** phrases on pp. 528–9.—15. See 'Hauliers' Slang'. —16. Short for *monkey strap:* B., 1943.

monkey, adj. '"Monkey" is diminutive in the Navy' (Granville): late C. 19–20. Cf. **monkey island** (*Dict.*). and **monkey jacket.**

monkey, cold enough.. . . (p. 528), has, in C. 20, been very common also in Canada, where, when it is necessary, to suit a more refined company, *the ears* is substituted. (Leechman.)

monkey, suck the (p. 528); or **tap the admiral.** The origin of the latter expression is interesting but ghoulish. 'A certain admiral whose name I cannot remember died while in the West Indies and as it was desired to bury him in England his coffin was filled with rum to preserve the body as was not uncommonly done in those days (about 1830–40). A guard was mounted over the coffin during the journey and this guard was frequently found drunk. Nobody could understand where the guard got the liquor until it was found that the admiral had been tapped!

'Incidentally it was not unknown for seamen to tap the alcohol used in certain compasses, to the great danger of the ship of course.' (Andrew Haggard, letter of Jan. 28, 1947.)

monkey(-)bite. A mark left—often on the shoulder—by amorous biting: Canadian: since ca. 1930.

monkey-cage.—2. The steel structure of a modern building: mostly Cockneys': C. 20.

monkey(-)crouch. An American 'seat in the saddle', introduced to English jockeys by a Negro jockey named Sims: racing coll.: since ca. 1925. Arthur J. Sarl, *Gamblers of the Turf*, 1938.

monkey-dodger. A sheep-station hand: Australian: C. 20. Baker. Ex monkey, 6 (p. 528).

monkey-farting, n. and adj. Applied to useless employment, waste of time, silly behaviour: Canadian (esp. soldiers'): C. 20.

monkey house. A caboose: Canadian railroadmen's (— 1931). Depreciative.

Monkey House, the. The Admiralty: Naval: since ca. 1890. Envious.

monkey(-)jacket. An officer's reefer coat: Naval: C. 20. Granville. Recorded by the O.E.D. as occurring in 1830, it seems rather to have dated since ca. 1810 or even earlier; it was of American origin (see esp. the D.A.E.); it appears in *The Saturday Evening Post*, March 16, 1822 (p. 1, col. 5). Moreover, it has been coll. since ca. 1890—and, indeed, S.E. since ca. 1920. (Moe.) An early English citation is supplied by *The Dublin University Magazine*, July 1834, at p. 63. Moe.

monkey oboe. A medical officer: Army: 1939–45. Ex the signals alphabet, for *M.O.* (P-G-R.)

monkey of, make a. To make someone look ridiculous: adopted from U.S. ca. 1930.

monkey on a gridiron. A cyclist: Cockneys': late C. 19–20. J. W. Horsley, *I Remember*, 1912. Hence the monkey on a gridiron, sit like a, of the *Dict.*

monkey on one's back, have a.—2. To be ridden by the drug habit: Canadian c.: adopted, ca. 1945, ex U.S.; by 1950, police and low s. (Leechman.)

monkey (out) of, make a; be made a monkey of. To use, be used, as a dupe, esp. as a cat's-paw: adopted, ca. 1943, ex U.S. servicemen.

monkey-parade. A lower-class Londoners' term of ca. 1895–1915. Pugh, 'A place where the elite of the beau-monde of [Cockney] suburbia meet nightly, for purposes of flirtation. It is generally a big main thoroughfare. The fellahs and the girls wink and smirk as they pass, and break hearts at two yards with deadly precision.'

monkey see, monkey do! A Canadian (and U.S.) c.p. 'addressed to one who imitates the actions of another, or as warning not to do such and such because someone (usually a child) might follow suit' (Leechman): since ca. 1925.

monkey shaft. 'A small trial shaft in a mine' (B., 1943): Australian miners': since ca. 1925.

monkey strap. 'A looped strap on the offside of the saddle pommel used by inferior roughriders in mounting and during the bucking of a horse' (Baker): Australian rural and rodeo: C. 20.

monkey suit. Uniform provided by carnival proprietor: Canadian carnival s.: C. 20.

monkey tail. A 'handle for opening doors on mineral wagons' (*Railway* 2nd): railwaymen's: C. 20.

*monkey tie. A gaudy necktie: South African c.: C. 20. *The Cape Times*, June 3, 1946. Suggested by zoo tie.

monkey-traps. Female finery, to 'catch' men: since ca. 1930.

monkey(-)tricks. Sexual liberties: non-aristocratic coll.: from ca. 1890. (W. L. George, *The Making of an Englishman*, 1914.)

monkey up, get one's (p. 529). As have one's *monkey up* it occurs in Benj. Webster's *The Golden Farmer*, 1833.

monkey up, put one's. Much earlier in Benj. Webster's *Paul Clifford*, 1833.

monkey up a (or the) stick, like a. Performing queer antics: coll.: late C. 19–20. Ex the popular toy.

monkey's allowance.—2. Short rations: Naval: late C. 18-very early 20. W. N. Glascock, *Sailors and Saints* (I, 166), 1829. Moe.

monkeys and parrots is perhaps more usual then **parrots and monkeys** (below).

monkey's fist. 'A knot at the end of a heaving-line to ensure its safe passage from a ship to jetty,' Granville: Naval coll.: late C. 19–20.

monkey's fuck, not to care a. Not to care a rap: low (esp. Naval): since ca. 1920.

monkey's tail, 1 (p. 529): earlier in *The Night Watch* (II, 130), 1828. Moe.

monopolise the macaroon. See **macaroon, confiscate the.**

mons, da. One of motor-trade s. terms for 'money' (others being, *bees and honey, gelt, kite, oats for the donkey, smash*): since ca. 1920. Jocular on Italian pron. of *money*.

Mont. A tramp or a beggar: Cockneys': late C. 19–20; ob. Origin prob. anecdotal—perhaps in a picturesque tramp named Monty.

Monte. Monte Carlo: a C. 20 coll. used mostly by those who have never been there. 'Christopher Quill' in *Books of To-Day and the Books of To-Morrow*, Oct. 1936.—2. Hence, the Monte Carlo Rally: motorists': since late 1940's.

month of Sundays (p. 530) occurs in Australia mostly in the form (*as*) *dull*—or *as slow*—*as a month of Sundays*. B., 1942.

month of Sundays, a, esp. in *with a face like a month of Sundays*, looking very glum or woebegone. Cf. the entry preceding this, as well as that on p. 530.

Monty. Field-Marshal Lord Montgomery: 1942 +.—2. A Naval patrol aircraft: 1939 +. B., 1942.

monty. A certainty: Australian: since ca. 1920. K. S. Prichard, *Haxby's Circus*, 1930; Vance Palmer, *Cyclone*, 1947, 'It's a monty there'll be a few skulls broken before it's settled.' Ex '*Monte Carlo*'?—2. Hence, a lie: Aus.: since ca. 1935. (B., 1959.)

montygram. A signal written by Field-Marshal Montgomery: Army officers': latter part of World War II. (P-G-R.)

Monty's foxhounds. The 40th (King's) Battalion, Royal Tank Regiment: 1942 +. See Monty, 1.

Monty's Own. Mine-sweepers clearing the fairway along the N. African coast for the 8th Army: Services: 1943. (P-G-R.) Ex *Monty*.

moo, old—silly—silly old; mare, old—silly—silly old. *Moo*, which shortens **moo cow** (p. 530) and is euphemistic for **cow,** 1, on p. 185, is virtually synonymous with *mare* as a mild Cockney pejorative of late C. 19–20. Whereas *old mare* and *old moo* are neutral and often affectionate, *silly mare* and *silly moo* connote silliness; more common than either of those pairs (so Julian Franklyn tells me on Aug. 11, 1967) are *silly old mare* and *silly old moo*; the last is the commonest of all and has moved out of the merely Cockney region to the social atmosphere wherein a young husband can, without fear of instant divorce, address his wife as *silly* (*old*) *moo*. With thanks also to Wilfred Granville, who recalls that, in the old Caledonian Market (see Stones, the, below), he often heard such admonitions as 'you silly moo, that was worth five bob more than you let him have it for', and has, then as since, heard it 'applied to kids returning from errands, "You stupid little mare, you've forgotten the tea"'. Addressed to females only, of course.

mooch.—n.—3. A dupe, esp. in respect of stocks and shares; *mooch man*, a good canvasser for the sale of (dud) shares; *mooch manna*, a (rich) business man too proud to admit that he has been victimised by share-pushers: commercial (under) world: since ca. 1925. *John Bull*, Jan. 21, 1939. The first, at least, has been adopted from U.S.— see *Underworld*.

mooch, v.—6. (Of a taxicabman) to 'coast': taxicabmen's: from ca. 1920. Ex sense 1.

moochers' mile. 'The Mecca of the suburbanites . . . along Piccadilly, through Piccadilly-circus to Leicester Square,' *The Daily Express*, June 12, 1944: since ca. 1930. Ex the sauntering.

*moody, adj. Simulated, faked, as in 'a moody ruck' or faked quarrel: prison c.: since ca. 1945. (Norman.)

*moody, the; the old moody. A psychiatrist's man-to-man, or even genial, approach to a prisoner: prison c.: since ca. 1945. (Norman.) A special application of the n. *moody* on p. 530. —2. Short for *Moody and Sankey* (now always *Moody*, hence *moody*)—rhyming s. on *hanky-panky*, itself perhaps an elaboration of *hanky*, handkerchief, that 'with which the conjurer employing the quick hand deceives an observing eye' (Franklyn 2nd).

moola or **moolah.** Money, esp. ready money: U.S., since early C. 20; by ca. 1910, also Canadian —*teste* Dr Douglas Leechman (Feb. 1, 1968). Origin unknown—? Yiddish. Both *The American Thesaurus* and Wentworth & Flexner record the word.

moon and the milkman, go between the. To 'shoot the moon': proletarian: ca. 1860–1910. B. & L.

moonlighter.—2. One who holds two paid positions at the same time; hence, moonlighting, the practice involved: Canadian: since ca. 1930. (Leechman.) As if working by moonlight as well as by daylight.

moose. 'An eligible female of Japan or Korea is known as a "moose", . . . from the Japanese word "musume"—girl' (*Iddiwah*, July 1953): United Nations troops' in Korea: ca. 1951–5.—2. (Also *regular moose* and *bull-moose*.) A huge, powerful fellow: Canadian coll.: C. 20. 'A moose of a man.'

moose milk. 'Any of various home brews concocted in the Yukon. One consists of Eagle Brand condensed milk laced liberally with rum': N.W. Canadian: since ca. 1920. (Dr Douglas Leechman, familiar with the Yukon territory.)

moosh.—2. Mate, companion: C. 20. Cf. mush, n., 7, on p. 544.

mooter. See 'Tavern terms', § 3, *d*.

mop, n.—5. (*Mop*.) 'A jocular form of *Ma* or *Mum*, used to rhyme with *Pop*' (A. B. Petch): since ca. 1955.—6. A horse whip: Aus. sporting: since ca. 1920. (B., 1959.)

mop-squeezer (p. 531): earlier in Anon., *A Congratulatory Epistle from a Reformed Rake*, '. . . From mop-squeezers, were promoted to Whores'.

Mope-Eyed Ladyship, her. See 'Personifications'.

mopey as a wet hen. Glum: New Zealand and Australian coll.: C. 20. B., 1941, 1942.

moph. See moff.

moppery. The head: 1821, Pierce Egan, *Life in London*; † by 1870. The site of one's *mop*.

moppie or **-y.** One of a cleaning-up party: Services: since ca. 1925. Ex the mop he wields so vigorously.

mopstick. See mop-stick (*Dict.*).

Morality. See 'Tavern terms', § 3, *d*.

more beef! A c.p., uttered when a heavy load or a hard task demands the help of one or two more men: Canadian: since ca. 1910. (Leechman.)

more curtains! 'Shouted by lary Cockney girls when a person clad in an evening frock passes by,' Julian Franklyn, communication in Feb. 1939: c.p. since ca. 1920; ob.

more firma the less terra, the. 'A c.p. used by those who distrust air travel' (B.P.): mostly Australian: since ca. 1950. A pun on L. *terra*, land, and *terror*.

more hair on your chest! Good for you!: Australian: C. 20. B., 1942.

more hair there than anywhere. Itself a c.p., it evokes the c.p. response, *on a cat's back*, but the implication is 'around girl's pudend': mostly Canadian: since ca. 1950.

more kid in him than a goat in the family way. An Aus. c.p., dating from ca. 1930. B., 1959.

more points (to one) than a porcupine, have. (Usually of a man) to possess many good points: Australian: C. 20. (B.P.) Partly jocular, partly raffish.

more power to your elbow! A c.p. of encouragement: late C. 19–20. Of Anglo-Irish origin.

more R than F. A c.p. applied, ca. 1860–1910, to one who is more rogue than fool; esp. to a servant that *seemed* foolish.

more than that! 'A Naval expression emphasising that their party, job or pay exceeds anything that you can put forward in competition', H. U: lower-deck c.p.: since ca. 1930. Granville, 'A fabulous amount. "Some lovely dames at the dance last night, lusher than that."'

morepork (p. 532): also a simpleton. Baker, 1959, implies that, as rural s., it was, at that date, extant.

Moreton Bay (fig.). See gig, n., 10.

Morgan's orchard.—2. In the game of poker, it is 9: C. 20. Anecdotally ex Morgan, a poker-player famous at end of C. 19 as being a character and as having a speech defect; he used to say 'tree trees' for 'three threes'. Hence, 9 = three trees. (I do not guarantee the authenticity of this.)

In cribbage, *orchard* arises from the fact that 4 contains two 2's—two pairs—two pears. (Professor F. E. L. Priestley.)

morgue, the. Obituary press-cuttings; obituaries kept ready for notabilities likely to die shortly: journalistic: C. 20. This 'department' also contains all the necessary information about anyone likely, for any reason at all, to become news.

Morgue, the. See **Pauper's Grave, the.**

morish. See **moreish** (*Dict.*).

morley (p. 533). Earlier in David Carey, 1822; see **slanger.**

Mormons. See **came over** . . .

morning. See **Sundays.**

morning prayers. See **prayers** . . .

morons, came over with the. See **came over** . . .

morris, v.—4. See **die, to;** cf. senses 1, 2 (p. 533).

Morrison mousetrap. A Morrison table shelter: 1941 +. Ex the sides of wire-work. Cf.:

Morrison time. Double British Summer time: coll.: 1940–5 (Minister of Home Security: the Rt Hon. Herbert Morrison).

mort.—4. An honest, old-fashioned person: Australian: since ca. 1961. Ex Fr. *mort*, dead. (B.P.)

mortallious. Very drunk: mostly lower classes': C. 19–20. Ex '*mortal* drunk'.

mortar and trowel. A towel: rhyming: since ca. 1870.

Mos (pron. *moss*) or **Mossey;** also **Moz** or **Mozzy.** A Mosquito aircraft: R.A.F.: 1943 +. Partridge, 1945, the *s* forms; W/Cdr Robin P. McDouall, letter of March 17, 1945, the *z* forms.

mos; esp. *show no mos.* Animosity: tailors': from ca. 1860. B. & L.

Moscow. Bayswater: Londoners': ca. 1815–70. *Spy*, II, 1826.—2. A pawnshop: Australian: C. 20. (B., 1943.)—2. Hence as v., to pawn: B., 1943. A folk-etymological alteration of *moskeener* (p. 534).

Moscow, gone to. See **gone** . . .

Moscow, in. In pawn: Australian: C. 20. (Caddie, *A Sydney Barmaid*, 1953.) Cf. *gone to Moscow.*

Moscow mule. "'Just add two ounces of vodka to a lager, and a couple of cubes of ice. . . . It should have a splash of lime juice as well'" (Andrew York, *The Co-Ordinator*, 1967): barrooms': since ca. 1950. *Moscow* refers to the vodka, *mule* to the 'kick'.

mosey off. See **mosey** (*Dict.*).

mosh game. An illegal game: low Australian: since ca. 1910. (Vince Kelley, *The Bogeyman*, 1956.)

mosiqui. A little girl: showmen's: since ca. 1870; ob. by 1950. (*John o' London's Weekly*, March 4, 1949.)

Moslem broker is a folk-etymological variant, since ca. 1930, of *mozzle and brocha*. Franklyn.

Moss Bross. Messrs Moss Brothers, Ltd, the firm from which so many people hire their formal (masculine) clothes: esp. Londoners': since ca. 1920.

mossie. A variant of *mozzy*, 2: B., 1943.

mossing, vbl n. Depositing things in pawn: mostly among Londoners: C. 20. Val Davis, *Phenomena in Crime*, 1941. A corruption of **mosk** (p. 534).

mossy.—2. (Of persons) hairy: C. 20.

most, the. The best, superlatively good, extremely attractive, as in 'He's the most': teenagers' and office- and shop-girls': since ca. 1957. (Gilderdale.) Adopted ex Canada, where current since ca. 1955. (Leechman.)

mostest, with the, adv. and adj. With—or having—every attraction: adopted, ca. 1959, ex U.S.: esp. among jazz-addicts and beatniks.

mote, v.—2. (Of vehicle, hence of athlete) to move speedily: Australian: C. 20. H. J. Oliver, July 1937 (see **Bovril**); B., 1942.—3. Hence, to walk: Australian: since ca. 1935. (Ruth Park, 1950.)

mothball fleet. A Reserve Fleet: Naval coll.: since ca. 1945. Its guns are in plastic covers.

mothballs. Tracer bullets: Australian servicemen's: 1939–45. (B., 1943.)

mother. Wife, if also a mother: Cockney coll.: from ca. 1880. E.g. 'I'll ask mother about that.' Ex the familiar S.E. *mother*, vocative to a wife and mother of one's children.

mother and daughter.—2. A *quarter* post: rhyming s.: C. 20. 'Used by Thames watermen with reference to the posts along London's river frontage at which a tug, a lighter, or other craft may be tied up' (Franklyn 2nd).

Mother Bunch.—2. Water: Cockneys': ca. 1590–1640. Dekker, *The Shoemaker's Holiday* (performed in 1599), IV, iv, Firk, 'Am I sure that Paul's steeple is a handful higher than London Stone, or that the Pissing-Conduit leaks nothing but pure Mother Bunch? Am I sure that I am lusty Firk? God's nails, do you think I am so base to gull you?' Mother Bunch was a well-known London ale-house 'hostess', as mentioned in *Pasquil's Jests*, 1604.

Mother Hubbard. A cupboard: rhyming s.: late C. 19–20.

mother-in-law.—3. (Cf. sense 2: p. 534.) A mixture of *stout* and *bitter*: Australian publichouse: C. 20. (B., 1953.) Since ca. 1945 also English.

Mother Knab (or **Nab**)-**Cony.** See '**Harlots**'.

mother of pearl. A girl: rhyming: since ca. 1870. But this very Cockney term occurs only in *my old mother of pearl*, my old girl, my wife; often shortened to *mother*—to the confusion of non-Cockneys. (Franklyn, *Rhyming*.)

motherer. A shepherd: Australian coll.: late C. 19–20. B., 1942.

mother's bright boy is a coll. C. 20 synonym of **mother's white-haired boy** (p. 535).

mother's milk, 2 (p. 535). Rather, since ca. 1840. *Sinks*, 1848, defines it as either strong drink or rum.

motor, n.—3. A motor car: coll.: since ca. 1920.

motor. To set going the motor (of boat or car): motorists' coll.: from ca. 1928. Peter Chamberlain, 'They'd started to motor the damn thing.'

motor mech. Motor mechanic: Naval coll.: C. 20. Granville.

motsa or **motser.** A large sum of money ('He made a motsa'): Australian: since ca. 1920. Yiddish. (B., 1943; Edwin Morrisby, 1958.) The Yiddish *motsa* is an outsize biscuit, about a foot in diameter.

mott. To look hard—or to stare—at (someone): Australian low, verging on c.: since ca. 1920. (B., *Australia Speaks*, 1953.) Perhaps ex sense 1 of *mot* (p. 534).

mouldering ruin. (Used predicatively.) Prehistoric; or merely very old: several British preparatory schools': since late 1940's.

mouldy, n., 2 was, via the old R.N.A.S., adopted by the R.A.F. in 1918. (Partridge, 1945.)

mouldy, adj., 2, is, in the Navy, 'miserable . . . "two blocks chocker"' (Granville): C. 20.

mouldy fig. A person even duller and more boring than a 'wet blanket': beatniks': since ca. 1959. (Anderson.) Ex the following sense.—2. 'Applied by the young supporters of the "new jazz", or "cool" or "progressive" jazz, to those who remained loyal to the old, "traditional", "New Orleans", or "hot" jazz. This was during the strong revival of hot jazz in the 1950's. The term, which had a limited circulation, became virtually obsolete by 1960.' (Professor F. E. L. Priestley, in letter dated Aug. 21, 1967.)

moulies. Copper coins: low Cockney: late C. 19–20. I.e. *mouldies*, ex the colour. Cf. **mouldy one** (*Dict.*).

mount, n.—6. '*The Mount.* One's bicycle,' H. & P., *Service Slang*, 1943: jocular: since ca. 1930.

*mount, do a. To give evidence in court: Australian c.: C. 20. B., 1942. Cf. **mount,** v., 4–6 (on p. 535).

*Mount, the. Montreal: Canadian tramps' c., hence gen. low s.: C. 20. W. A. Gape, *Half a Million Tramps*, 1936. 'Because one of its most notable topographical features, right in the city, is Mount Royal, or Mont Royal, an extinct volcanic peak, one of a number in that part of Quebec Province' (Leechman).

Mount Aldrich. Logic: Oxford University: ca. 1815–50. *Spy*, 1825. Ex a professor's name?

Mount Euclid. Mathematics: Oxford: ca. 1810–60. *Spy*, 1825.

Mount Misery (p. 535). For Bowen's reference, see **monkey island** (p. 529). 'Last night, when the fog kept you up on Mount Misery,' Frank Shaw, *Atlantic Murder*, 1932.

*mount the box. To give evidence in court: Australian c. (and police s.): since ca. 1930. (B., 1953.) Cf. **mount, do a.**

Mountain Devils. Tasmanians: Australian: C. 20. (B., 1943.) Ex the grotesque lizard so named—the *thorn-devil* or *Moloch horridus*—a native of Australia; with perhaps a reference to the *Tasmanian devil*.

mountain passes. Spectacles: rhyming s. (on *glasses*): C. 20; by 1959, ob. Franklyn, *Rhyming*.

Mountains, the. The Yorkshire moors: transport drivers': since ca. 1945.

Mountains of Mourne. Ash heaps: railwaymen's: C. 20. (*Railway*, 3rd.) Ironic.

Mountbatten pink. That shade of pink paint which was used on invasion craft: Services: 1943–5. 'Suggested by Lord Louis Mountbatten when he was Chief of Combined Operations,' Granville.

mounteer. See 'Miscellanea'.

mounter.—2. A peg-top of which the peg has, by constant play, been driven in until it is shorter than one's thumb-nail and must therefore be thrown away: London schoolchildren's: from ca. 1890.

Mounties, the, 1 (p. 536). Now the Royal Canadian Mounted Police. When first organized in 1873, the Northwest Mounted Police.

mournful Mary. A warning siren at Dunkirk: 1914–18. Gordon S. Maxwell, *The Motor Launch Patrol*, 1926. Cf. *moaning Minnie*.

mourning.—4. '"Aye, there she is—all in mourning for her fate," cried Brace, evidently affected by the tottering condition of every thing aloft . . .'—glossed thus, 'When a ship, or square-rigged vessel appears in mourning, the yards on each mast are alternately topped on end': W. N. Glascock, *Sailors and Saints* (I, 215), 1829. A Naval phrase, dating late C. 18–19.

mourning for the cat!, you're in. You have dirty finger-nails: non-aristocratic, non-cultured c.p.: C. 20. See **mourning** in the *Dict.*

mouse, n.—7. See the quotation at **hole (out) in one** (sense 2) above.—8. A young lady; a girl: beatniks': since ca. 1958. (Anderson.) Cf. the quotation at **canary,** 12, above, and contrast **mouse,** n., 5, on p. 536.

mouse-trap.—4. A submarine: R.A.F.: since early 1940. *The Reader's Digest*, Feb. 1941, 'Air Slanguage' by Allan A. Michie & Isabel Waitt. For the crew, that's what it is when caught on the surface by an aircraft.—5. Cheese: Naval (lower-deck): C. 20. Granville. Obviously because mouse-traps are baited with cheese.—6. A Morrison (i.e. an indoor) shelter: Aug. 30, 1941 *The New Statesman*.

mouth like a cow's cunt, (have) a. (To be) excessively talkative: low, mostly Cockney: late C. 19–20. (Communicated by J. F., Dec. 29, 1967.)

mouth like the bottom of a . . . (p. 537). A Services', esp. R.A.F., variant: *. . . of a baby's pram—all shit and biscuits*.

mouth-wash. A drink of liquor: since ca. 1930.

mouthful, say a (p. 537). Rather, English of ca. 1780–1880, then U.S., then again—from U.S.—English since ca. 1920. Clearly adumbrated in *Sessions*, Sept. 1790, 'I never said a *mouth full of ill against her* in my life'.

move, n.—2. A motion picture: since ca. 1935. Prob. short for **movie** (p. 537).

move in the blind. To 'shoot the moon' (q.v. at **moon, shoot the** in *Dict.*): low: ca. 1860–1910. B. & L. Here, *blind* = darkness.

move out, v.i. To expand; to bloom: New Zealand coll.: C. 20. (Jean Devanney, *The Butcher Shop*, 1926.)

move (or shift) your carcase! Get out of the way: Australian: since ca. 1920.

movies, go to the. See **go . . .**

movy. See **movie** (*Dict.*).

*mowat. A woman: c.: from ca. 1910. Of North Country origin. Cf. **gadgy.** Perhaps ex dial.: cf. N.E. and E. Anglian *mawther*, a big, lumbering girl. (Ramsey Spencer.)

mowing the lawn, n. and pple. Shaving with an electric razor: Australian: since ca. 1955. 'Hang on a jiffy, I'm mowing the lawn.' (B.P.)

Moz. See **Mos.**

moz, n. and v. See **mozzle,** v.

Mozart and Liszt, usu. shortened to *Mozart*. Tipsy: rhyming s., mostly racing: since ca. 1945. On s. *pissed*. (Franklyn 2nd.)

mozzle, n. Esp. as in '"My mozzle is out, Collins?" he said with an effort' ('Tom Collins', *Such is Life*, 1903), i.e. I've reached the end of my tether: Australian: ca. 1870–1910. Adopted from Yiddish *mozzle*, luck.

mozzle, v.; also the shortening, **moz.** To hinder, to interrupt (someone): Australian: since ca. 1920. Also n., as in *put the moz on* (someone), to inconvenience: B., 1942. Ex **muzzle.**

mozzle and brocha. (A door-to-door canvasser

or salesman) 'on the knocker': rhyming s.: C. 20. Yiddish: cf. preceding.

Mozzy. See **Mos.**

mozzy.—2. A mosquito; *mozzy net*, mosquito net: Australian (late C. 19–20) and R.A.F. Regulars' (since ca. 1925). B., 1942; Gerald Emanuel, letter of March 29, 1945. Cf. **mos.**

Mr Cochran's young ladies in blue. See **awful people.**

Mr Dunlop. An inner bicycle-tube filled with sand and used as a 'cosh': British prison-camps for Britons: 1915–18. (Private X., *War is War*, 1930.)

Mr Five by Five. See **five by five.**

Mr Nip. See **nip-cheese** below.

Mr Wood. See **Wood, Mr.**

Mrs Ashtip; Mrs Greenfields. See **Greenfields.**

Mrs Duckett.—2. As an expletive, 'Fuck it!': low rhyming s.: C. 20. (Franklyn, *Rhyming*.)

Mrs Evans. See **Evans, Mrs** (p. 259). For dating, read 'late C. 17–mid-19'. It occurs in the *Works*, 1704, of 'facetious' *Tom Brown*.

Mrs Gafoops. Any woman not specifically named: Australian: since ca. 1930. 'Are you going to make that dress yourself, or will you get Mrs Gafoops to run it up for you?' (B.P.)

Mrs Greenfield's, staying at. See *staying at* . . . in 'Hauliers' Slang'.

Mrs Kelly wouldn't let young Edward play with you! A derogatory c.p. addressed to a child either very dirty or very ill-behaved: Australian: since ca. 1925. The allusion is to Ned Kelly, the famous bushranger, who has, in Australia, become as legendary as Jesse James in the United States. (B.P.)

Mrs Murray, see. To go to the water-closet: Australian: late C. 19–20. B., 1942. With a pun on the Murray, the greatest river in Australia. The reference is esp. to a privy.

much! Short for the ironic *not much!*: Services (esp. R.A.F.) coll.: 1940 +. Partridge, 1945, ' "He never goes out with Waafs"— "Much!" ' (He very often does.)

muchee; intensified as **muchee-muchee.** Very: pidgin: mid-C. 19–20. B. & L.

muck, n., 4 (p. 538) occurs in D. W. Barrett, *Navvies*, 1880. Anti-aircraft fire: R.A.F.: 1940, Michie & Graebner, *Their Finest Hour*, 'I climbed to 12,000 feet, circling along the outside of the searchlights and all the muck [gunfire] that was coming up'.—11. (Very) dirty weather: R.A.F. pilots' and Army officers': since ca. 1938. H. & P. Also *shit*.

muck, v., 3 and 4, can be dated back to ca. 1840: *Sinks*, 1848, defines the v. as 'to clean out, to win all a person's money.'

muck, as. Exceedingly; as much as is possible: coll.: from ca. 1910. Esp. *sick as muck*, thoroughly disgusted or disgruntled or displeased, as in J. C. Masterman, *Fate Cannot Harm Me*, 1935, of a cricket match: 'He would be out any ball and poor old George would be as sick as muck.' Cf. **mad as mud** in *Dict.*

muck about, pron. *muck abaht.*—3. Usually *be mucked about*, to be messed about: Army: since ca. 1910. Orig. a euphemism for *fuck about*.

muck-arsing about. Larking about, esp. amorously: low: C. 20.

muck-bird. 'Dirty oil waste' (*Railway*): railwaymen's: since ca. 1930.

muck for luck! A c.p., addressed to one getting

befouled with excrement; usually applied to boots soiled with dog's excrement: late C. 19–20: by 1940, a proverb.

muck out. To clean out (the place)—to be a servant, esp. *for* someone: miners': C. 20. Ex cleaning out the stables down in the mines.

muck-rag. A handkerchief: low: C. 19. 'A Real Paddy', *Life in Ireland*, 1822.

muck-shifter. A navvy: navvies' coll.: ca. 1800–1910. (D. W. Barrett, *Navvies*, 1880.)

Muck, Sludge and Lightning, the. The Manchester, Sheffield and Lincolnshire railway: railwaymen's ca. 1890–1925. (*Railway* 2nd.)

muck(-)stick. A rifle: Naval: since ca. 1920. Granville, 'Muckstick drill, Rifle drill in Barracks'.

muck-sweat. Perspiration; orig. and properly if dust or dirt has accrued: proletarian coll.: since ca. 1830. *Sessions*, June 22, 1843.—2. Hence *be in a muck-sweat*, to be flurried or flustered; to be 'all hot and bothered': C. 20. (Atkinson.)

muck-up, v.—4. V.i., to play the fool: Australian: since ca. 1910. B., 1942.

muck-up, n. A 'mess', confusion, spoiling: late C. 19–20. Ex v., 2 (p. 539).

mucked. Short for **mucked out** (p. 539): 1848, *Sinks*; † by 1920.

muckender. See 'Miscellanea'.

mucker, n.—4. A friend, mate, pal: Army: since ca. 1917. Ex **muck in** (p. 539).

mucker(-)up and **mucking(-)up.** The agent and the action of **muck-up,** 4, above.

mucking-in spud. One's chief friend or companion: Army (and R.A.F.): since ca. 1930. H. & P., ' "Spud" is used in camps to denote "pal".' See **muck in** (p. 539).

Muckle Flugga Hussars, the (p. 539). For 'the most northerly of the Orkneys.' read 'the most northerly island of the Unst group in the extreme north of the Shetland Isles'.

mucko.—2. Hence, esp. a man detailed to serve food to troops aboard ship: Naval: since ca. 1910.—3. A seaman: Australian Naval: since ca. 1920. (B., 1943.)

mud.—4. Wet concrete: Australian builders and similars': since ca. 1920. (Culotta.)—5. Hence, thick, muddy coffee: Australian: since ca. 1930. (Culotta.)

mud, up to. See **up to mud.**

mud and blood. A mild and bitter, public-houses': C. 20.

Mud Bath, the. The Battle of Passchendaele: autumn and early winter, 1917, then historical. A pun on *the Blood Bath*, the 1916 Battle of the Somme. (A. B. Petch, who, like myself, attended at both of these ceremonies.)

mud chicken. A surveyor: Canadian railroadmen's (– 1931). He has a muddy job.

mud-fat. Exceedingly fat: Australian: since ca. 1925. B., 1942. Ex the C. 20 Australianism *as fat as mud*.

mud-hook.—3. Hence, for the board itself: Services: since ca. 1910. H. & P.—4. A hand: New Zealand and Australian: since ca. 1915. B., 1941, 1942.—5. A foot: Australian: since ca. 1920. Baker.

mud hop, or hyphenated or one word. A yard clerk: Canadian railroadmen's (– 1931). Cf. **mud chicken.**

mud in one's eye. A tie: rhyming s.: late

C. 19–20. *The New Statesman*, Nov. 29, 1941. But usually . . . *the eye*. (Franklyn 2nd.)

mud-lark.—12. Anyone who sings in the trenches: Army: 1914–18.

mud-pipes (p. 540). Prob. since early C. 19, for *Sinks*, 1848, defines the term as 'thick boots'.

mud-plunger.—2. From ca. 1860 and corresponding to **mud-plunging** (*Dict.*).

mud pup. An agricultural student, esp. if working on a farm: since ca. 1950. (Wilfred Granville.)

mud spring. A doughy damper: Northern Territory, Australia: since ca. 1925. Ernestine Hill, *The Territory*, 1951.

mud-walloper. One who is used to, or has to work in, mud: Army in Burma: 1942–5.

mudder. A horse that goes well on a wet track: Canadian sporting coll.: since ca. 1925.

Muddle and Go Nowhere, the. 'Peterborough to Yarmouth Line' (*Railway*, 3rd): C. 20. Among passengers, however, it was, up to 1939 anyway, 'the old Midland and Great Northern Railway, which meandered across North Norfolk from Norwich to Peterborough' (Ramsey Spencer, 1967).

Muddle East. An all-Services' name: 1941–4: for the Middle East.

muddled. Slightly tipsy: coll.: since ca. 1780. *The New Vocal Enchantress*, 1791.

Muddy. See 'Nicknames'.

muddy. A mud crab: Australian: since ca. 1920. (B., *Australia Speaks*, 1953.)

Mudros, Chios and chaos. A 1915 Services' c.p. alluding to the fact that the Mediterranean Expeditionary Force of that time had three separate authorities, or commands, and bases. (Captain C. R. O. Burge, D.S.O., R.N., letter of July 27, 1967.)

muff, v.—3. See **die, to.**

muff-diver. A cunnilingist: low Canadian: C. 20.

muffin-baker (p. 541). Franklyn, *Rhyming*, thinks that the term is restricted to the Cockney low s. *quaker*, excrement long retained.

muffy. A frill-necked lizard: Australian rural: C. 20. (B., 1953.) Ex its 'muff'.

mug, n., 4 (p. 541). 'Anyone not of the Underworld,' F. D. Sharpe, *The Flying Squad*, 1938: i.e. from the viewpoint, the angle, the 'slant' of the underworld itself. Cf. the American-c. use of 'honest John' (see *Underworld*). 'There is a whole range of talk which cannot be understood by the "mug", a word which describes *all* members of the public who attend fairs': W. Buchanan-Taylor, *Shake it Again*, 1943.

mug, v.—13. (Cf. sense 4, both nuances: p. 541.) '"Are you going to 'mug' us?"'... "What does 'mug us' mean?"'... "Are you going to stand me a drink?"': *Daily Mirror*, March 14, 1939.—14. To loaf: Australian: since ca. 1930. (Vance Palmer, *Seedtime*, 1957.) Cf. sense 4 on p. 541.

Note that sense 5 has narrowed to 'to garotte' and, as such, is actively extant in both Canada and U.S.

mug or mugged. Pleasant to look at: Winchester College: from ca. 1870. Cf. **mug, v.**, 8 (*Dict.*).

mug alec(k). Australian synonym of *smart alec*: since ca. 1930. Lawson Glassop, *We Were the Rats*, 1944.

*mug copper.** Variant of **mug John** (p. 541): Australian: since ca. 1920. B., 1942. Also *mug cop*: B., 1959.

mug lair. Variant of *dead lair*, q.v. at **lair**, 1, above. (B., 1959.)

mug-up, n. Lunch; a snack: 'a common expression in the [Canadian] far North, especially among fur-trade men and trappers: 1934 and earlier' (Leechman). Probably ex *mug up*, v., 3 (p. 541) or simply ex *mug up!*, bring up your mug.

mugger.—4. A punch or blow to or on the **mug** or face: pugilistic: ca. 1810–60. *Boxiana*, III, 1821.

Mugging Hall. The hall where the boys prepare their lessons: Winchester College: from ca. 1850. B. & L.

muggo. A tea break: London dockers': since ca. 1950. (B.B.C. T.V.1, July 15, 1965.) I.e. a '*mug o*' tea'.

mugs, cut. The singular *mug*, 'a grimace': 1821. Pierce Egan, *Life in London*, 1821.

mugs' alley. That bar along the edge of a rink along which learner-skaters feel their way: ice and roller skaters', esp. at Wembley: since ca. 1930.

mug's game. A silly—esp., an unprofitable—thing to do: late C. 19–20.

mugwump is now gen. used in a pejorative manner, to insinuate that he is, to repeat the President of Princeton's definition, 'a man with his mug on one side of the fence and his wump on the other'. —2. Hence, an unreliable voter: English: since the late 1920's.

Muke. A College passage leading to Big and Little Muke (rooms): Eton: late C. 19–20. Marples supports the derivation ex Gr. *mukhos*, a nook.

mulberry; usually in pl. A prefabricated harbour: Services: 1944, then ob. Ex *Operation Mulberry*, the erection of the two prefabricated harbours on the coast of Normandy in June 1944.

mulga madness. 'The "queerness" sometimes developed in lone bushmen or fossickers' (B., 1943): Australian coll.: C. 20. *Mulga* is an Australian tree that characterizes 'the outback'. Cf. **bushed**, 3, above.

mullarkey is the Australian adaptation—ca. 1944—of U.S. *mal(l)arkey*, 'blarney'. D'Arcy Niland, *The Shiralee*, 1955.

Muller. A German: Guards Regiments': 1939–45. Ex the common German surname *Müller*. (P-G-R.)

mullet. See **stunned mullet** and **prawn-headed mullet** below.

*mulliga stew.** A soupy sort of stew: Australian tramps': since ca. 1925. B., 1942. Ex U.S. *mulligan* (see *Underworld*), or, perhaps, from *mulligatawny* soup.

mulligans. Playing cards: Australian: C. 20. B., 1942. Why?

mullgrubber. Synonymous with and prob. deriving from **grub, n.**, 5 (p. 358): cricketers': C. 20.

Mullingar heifer (p. 542). The common Anglo-Irish expression is *beef to the heels, like a Mullingar heifer*.

mullock (p. 542): dates back to ca. 1852.—2. Hence, of an ignorant or otherwise worthless person: since ca. 1880. B., 1942, cites 'Rolf Boldrewood'.

multi (or **multy**) **cotiva.** A variant of **multee kertever** (p. 542). Sydney Lester.

multiples. Company shops, chain stores: commercial coll.: since ca. 1920; by 1946, S.E.

mum, n.—6. A chrysanthemum: flower growers' and sellers': C. 20.

mum, me bum's numb. A c.p., orig. (ca. 1910) North Country, but by 1920 very widely distributed; allusive to childish frankness and to dialectal pronunciation.

mum-tip. (A payment of) hush-money: ca. 1815–50. Pierce Egan, *Life in London*, 1821.

mumble-mumper. 'An old, sulky, inarticulate, unintelligible actor': theatrical: from ca. 1860; ob. B. & L.

mumble-peg (p. 543). In the old-fashioned wooden mole-trap still sometimes used, the mumble-peg is a peg which the mole loosens in his passage and thereby springs the trap.

mumbo-jumbo (p. 543). Read: Meaningless jargon: mid-C. 19–20; coll. >, by 1930, S.E.

mummery and millinery. 'Religious ritualism, mainly by those who do not approve of it or think that it is overdone' (A. B. Petch, April 1966): coll.: C. 20.

mump. See 'Shortenings'.

***mump, on the.** A-begging: vagabonds' c.: late C. 19–20. Pugh.

***mumper; mumping.** In C. 20 c., these terms have the specific senses: a tramp (person); tramping as a beggar. W. L. Gibson Cowan, *Loud Report*, 1937. Among Gypsies, it means a 'low-grade' Gypsy—one who has no van: C. 20.

mumper's brass. See 'Money'.

mun.—3. Money: C. 20. Michael Innes, *Appleby at Allington*, 1968.

muncher boy. A fellator: mostly Naval: since ca. 1950 (? earlier). Cf. *gobbler*, 6, above.

***munds.** See **muns** (*Dict.*).

mung. A look, a glance, a brief search: C. 20. (Percy F. Westerman, *The Terror of the Seas*, 1927.) Perhaps cf. *mung*, v. (p. 543).—2. A variant of *mong*.

munga. A smoke (or two) during a period of rest from work: New Zealand: C. 20. Maori? Cf. *smoko* (p. 789).—2. See **mungas**.

mungaree (p. 543) was, in form *mangaree* or *manjaree*, common among British soldiers in Sicily and Italy, 1943–5. (P-G-R.)

mungaree stuck. Penniless, esp. if temporarily: showmen's and grafters': C. 20. I.e. 'stuck for' —short of—**mungaree** (p. 543).

mungaria. Food: Army in N. Africa: 1940–5. The preceding word influenced by Arabic? (P-G-R.)

mungas or munja. Food; a meal, esp. lunch: New Zealand: since ca. 1919. Perhaps the Services' *mungy* (p. 544) given a Maori shape.—2. Also, among N.Z. soldiers of World War II, rations, as in 'the munja party' (Slatter).

munge.—2. A shortened form of **mungaree** (p. 543). Sydney Lester.

mungey. Food: mostly Army: C. 20. Ex Fr. *manger*. (P-G-R.)

munlee. Money: pidgin: C. 19–20. B. & L.

***muogh.** A pig: Shelta: C. 18–20. Ibid.

murder bag. A bag made of hide and containing all such equipment as is necessary in the investigation of a murder: Scotland Yard coll.: C. 20. *The murder bags are out*, 'a murder is being investigated'. Freeman Wills Crofts, *Fear Comes to Chalfont*, 1942.

murder on the mountain. Semolina pudding, (esp. if mound-shaped) splotched with (red) jam: schoolgirls': since ca. 1945.

murder suit. 'Get hold of a "murder suit". That's a long pair of overalls with deep pockets for carrying grenades, wire-cutters, and ammo. Nothing will shine if you wear that,' Lawson Glassop, *We Were the Rats*, 1944: Australian soldiers': 1940 +.

murky, n. An Aborigine: Australian: C. 20. B., 1942. Suggested by *darky*.

Murky Navy, the. The Merchant Navy: nautical: since ca. 1940. (TV, July 1, 1964; L. J. Cunliffe, *Having It Away*, 1965.) A pun on '*Merchant*'.

Murray. See **Mrs Murray**.

Murrumbidgee jam. 'Brown sugar moistened with cold tea and spread on damper' (B., 1943): Australian rural: C. 20. This rural s. term was † by 1959: B., *The Drum*.

muscateer. An addict of (very cheap) muscat wine: Australian: since ca. 1930. (B., 1943.) A pun on *musketeer*.

muscle factory. A gymnasium: mostly Army and esp. the Guards: C. 20. Gerald Kersh, 1941.

muscle in. To profit by another's advantage of good luck: Services: 1940 +. Partridge, 1945. 'From the language of the American underworld; via the cinema.' Current among civilians since ca. 1935, in the nuance 'to force oneself upon others (*muscle in on* them) in a criminal racket'—as in Anthony Weymouth, *Tempt Me Not*, 1937.

muscle merchant. A physical-training instructor: R.A.F.: since ca. 1940. Jackson.

mush, 2 (p. 544), is also Australian: C. 20. D'Arcy Niland, *The Shiralee*, 1955.—8. Hence, as in **instalment mixture**. Ex **mush man**.—9. Sentimentality: since ca. 1880: coll. >, by 1930, S.E. Cf. *sloppy*.—10. A scrum in Rugby football: *mush up!*, 'Push (in the scrum)!': London schools': ca. 1875–1900. Professor Arnold Wall, communication of Aug. 1939. This sense occurs also in Talbot Baines Reed, *The Fifth Form at St Dominic's*, 1907.—11. A man from somewhere else, e.g. a newcomer from Liverpool to Southampton: seamen's: since ca. 1910. Probably ex sense 7 ('a man').— 12. A companion, a pal: Army: 1939–45. (P-G-R.) Perhaps ex sense 7 (p. 544).

mush man. 'A driver who mounts his own cab': cabmen's: ca. 1880–1910. Clarkson & Richardson, *Police!*, 1889. His passenger is sheltered, as it were, by a *mush* or umbrella.

mush-rat (p. 545). Hardly a sol.: rather an archaic form.

musher.—2. A mushroom: market-gardeners' and greengrocers': late C. 19–20. (*The Bournemouth Echo*, June 29, 1944.)

mush's lotion. See **instalment mixture**.

Music. See 'Tavern terms', § 3, *d*.

musical bathtub. 'A motor-car, especially a small one, looked upon with little favour by professional drivers' (Leechman): mostly Canadian: since ca. 1960.

musical chair. 'A latrine consisting of a pole set over a trench' (P-G-R): Army: 1940–5.

muskie. A maskinonge (a large pike): Canadian: mid-C. 19–20. Gregory Clark, *Which We Did*, 1936. Short for the variant *muskellunge*.

muslin, 2, on p. 545, dates rather from ca. 1820. It occurs in, e.g., W. N. Glascock's *Naval Sketch Book*, 2nd Series, 1834, at II, 66. (Moe.)

Musso. Benito Mussolini: since ca. 1923. Gerald Kersh, *They Die with Their Boots Clean*, 1941. Also *the Deuce*, through mispronunciation (and misapprehension?) of *Il Duce*, which means, not 'the Duke' but 'the leader' (*Führer*).

must, n. Something that must be done, seen, heard, read, bought, etc., esp. if one is to keep up to date: coll.: since early 1950's, but not very gen. until late 1950's.

must have been drinking out of a damp glass or **mug** or **pot, he, you,** etc. A jocular c.p., either referring or addressed to someone who has caught a cold or who has a touch of rheumatism: C. 20.

mustard, keen as. See **keen as mustard** (*Dict.*).

musty. See **mesty.**

Mutt and Jeff.—2. Deaf: theatrical rhyming s.: C. 20. (Franklyn, *Rhyming.*) Also, by 1945 at the latest, gen. Cockney s.

mutt(-)eyes. Corn as food: Australian: since ca. 1935. (B., *Australia Speaks*, 1953.)

mutt(-)house. One's former school; preparatory school: Royal Naval College, Dartmouth: C. 20. Granville.

mutter and stutter. Butter (n. and v.): rhyming s.: C. 20.

mutton.—5. See **tug,** n., in Addenda.

mutton, jerk one's. See **gallop one's maggot.**

mutton-bird eater. Variant of **Mutton Bird** (p. 546). B., 1942.

Mutton Chops, the. The Royal West Surreys, also called *the Mutton Lancers*: Army: late C. 19–20. 'From emblem of lamb and flag' (Anon., *The Soldiers' War Slang Dictionary*, 1939).

mutton-fisted. Heavy on the controls of a 'plane: R.F.C. and R.A.F.: 1914 +.

Mutton Flaps. 'Japs' (the Japanese): prisoners-of-war in the Far East, 1942–5; then, to a limited extent, among civilians, mostly in Australia. (B., 1953.)

muttons.—3. 'When we speak of something being *our muttons* or *a person's muttons* we mean that we regard it with particular favour, that we like it especially well,' B., 1941: New Zealand and Australian: C. 20. Ex the excellence of New Zealand mutton.

***muzzling cheat.** A napkin: c. (— 1688); † by 1900. Randle Holme (*musseling c.*).

my. I; me; mine; occ., we, us, ours: pidgin: C. 19–20. B. & L.

my arse is dragging. I can hardly walk; I'm utterly exhausted: Canadian c.p.: since ca. 1916.

my blood! My bloody oath!: Australian: since ca. 1925. (Cf. **blood nose** above.)

my eyes and limbs! is an elaboration of *my eyes!* (see **my eye!** on p. 547) and was current ca. 1805–50. It may, orig. at least, have been nautical, for it occurs in W. N. Glascock, *The Naval Sketch-Book* (II, 107), 1826, and *Sailors and Saints* (II, 193), 1829. Moe.

my Gawd. A sword: rhyming s.: late C. 19–20. Occasionally *Oh* (or *O*) *my Gawd*. (Franklyn.)

my gentleman or **my lord; my lady.** He or she: derisive coll.: mid-C. 19–20. Cf. synonymous **his lordship.**

my goodness. A drink of Guinness: since late 1940's. Ex the variously illustrated slogan, 'My goodness, my Guinness!'

my granny! Nonsense!: coll.: C. 20. (James Stephens, *The Crock of Gold*, 1912.) Cf. *granny!* on p. 348.

my heart bleeds for you. As a c.p., it is ironic:

both British and American: since the late 1940's. In *Samantha*, 1968 (British edition), E. V. Cunningham makes his attractive Japanese detective say to his chief, '"With all respects to my esteemed boss . . . I am aware of his financial difficulties. My heart bleeds for the poverty of those who guard the wealthiest city in the world."'

Variant: *you're breaking my heart*, recorded in the same novel.

See **heart bleeds for.**

my hero! A c.p. 'that greets a diver who breaks surface with small green crabs or perfectly useless fish, such as wrasse' (Wilfred Granville, letter of March 11, 1964): skin divers': since ca. 1960. It prob. derives ex the ironic use of the phrase by girls satirizing the mushier films.

my king oath! An Australian variant of *my oath!*: since ca. 1910. Baker. Strictly, *'king*, short for *fucking*.

my mother told me there would be days like this, but she didn't say there'd be so many. A c.p. applied to a 'tough' time, esp. in the Army: Canadian soldiers': 1939–45. An oblique reference to menstruation.

my mother's away. The other day: Australian rhyming s.: since ca. 1890. (B., 1945.)

my name is Benjamin Brown, Ben Brown. 'Bend down, a formula pleasantry [uttered] when there is no inspiration [and] meant to be outrageous, but is merely tedious' (a correspondent): c.p.: since ca. 1950 (? much earlier). Homosexual implications.

my name is (or **name's**) **Simpson—not Samson.** A workmen's c.p. apropos of work too heavy for one: C. 20. Either originated by a humorist named Simpson or ex a scabrously witty limerick.

my name is Twyford. See **Twyford,** both in *Dict.* and Addenda.

my name is 'Unt not cunt. I'm not to be put upon, I'm nobody's fool: c.p., mostly R.A.F.: since middle 1940's. (Laurie Atkinson, Sept. 11, 1967.) Ex **Joe Hunt** above.

my part! 'I should worry!': c.p.: from ca. 1926; ob. Perhaps 'it's my part—to look after that'.

my tulip, vocative, was still extant in early C. 20: witness H. A. Vachell, *Quinney's*, 1914.

my very word. Exclamatory or emphatic form of 'my word!' (affirmative 'certainly'): Australian: since ca. 1945. '"Did he come good?"—"My very word!"' (B.P.)

my word—if I catch you bending! A semi-sexual c.p. of the London streets: ca. 1900–14; then more gen. in use and meaning. 'The answer is "I'll saw your leg off" (all from a song)' Julian Franklyn. Cf., therefore, the next.

my word, if you're not off! A c.p. of dismissal or of deterrence: ca. 1900–14. To which, during its last four or five years, was often added *I'll saw your leg off!*

Myall express. Natives showing the way; natives helping: N.T., Australia: since ca. 1910. Ernestine Hill, *The Territory*, 1951. Ironic reference to the leisureliness of the Myall tribe in these matters.

myrrh. Variant spelling of **mur** (p. 544).

myrtle. Sexual intercourse: Australian: C. 20. Baker. Why? It can hardly refer to that Myrtle who, in a famous limerick, failed to realize that 'the turtle was fertile', yet it's very odd that both *myrtle* and the synonymous *nurtle* (q.v.) should rhyme with *fertile*. Also cf. *turtle*, 2.

Myrtle the Turtle. The Australian nickname of any girl named Myrtle: since ca. 1910. (B.P.) Cf. both **Harriet the Chariot** (above) and the entry preceding this present one.

mystall crikey! Christ almighty: Australian: C. 20. (Dal Stivens, *Jimmy Brockett*, 1951.) Both a truncated spoonerism (become general) and a sort of back-slang, with words in reverse order and *mystall* (mīstall) a partial form. Cf. the next.

myst all critey! An Australian euphemistic oath: since ca. 1920. Baker. A reversal of *Christ Almighty*.

myxo. Myxomatosis: Australian: since ca. 1945. (B., 1953.) But, since ca. 1950, also current in Great Britain.

mzuri! All right!: Army in Burma: 1943 +. (Swahili word, adopted from African native troops serving in Burma.) 'Everything mzuri, chum?': Gerald Hanley, *Monsoon Victory*, 1946.

N

N.A.B.U. See **T.A.B.U.**

N.B. Penniless; temporarily without money: C. 20. I.e. 'not a bean': with a pun on *nota bene* (N.B.), note well.

n.e. or **N.E.**—2. **No** earthly [chance]: ca. 1900–14.

N.I., often written *N/I*. Not interested: R.A.F.: 1938 +. Jackson. On the analogy of the official abbr., *N.A.* (or *N/A*), 'not available'.

na-hop. Without, lacking, deprived of: pidgin: mid-C. 19–20. Lit., no have. B. & L.

nab, v.—8. 'To take something to which one is entitled, but which is not in plentiful supply' (B.P.): mostly Australian: late C. 19–20. 'The hall is filling up; I'd better nab myself a seat.' Also jocular, as in 'Nab your partners for the barn dance'.

nab the bib (p. 548); also **nab one's bib.** The latter dates from late C. 18 and occurs in a ballad, *The Rolling Blossom*, written prob. ca. 1800 and reprinted in an American magazine, *The Port Folio*, Aug. 8, 1807 (p. 125):

> 'At the new drop I nabb'd my bib,
>   While Will, my man, was swinging,
> At the gin ken I took a swig,
>   Reel'd home, blind drunk, a singing.'

(With thanks to Colonel A. F. Moe.)

nabu; sabu; tabu. Non-adjustable balls-up; self-adjusting balls-up; typical army balls-up: Army, esp. among New Zealanders and Australians in N. Africa: 1940–3. (J. H. Fullarton, *Troop Target*, 1943.) The Press, 1945 onwards, used the euphemistic *box-up* for *balls-up*.

nach. A variant of *natch*.

nadgers on, put the. (Of a co-worker supposed) to exercise, or to be exercising, an evil influence on equipment: R.A.F., Malta: since early 1940's. (Laurie Atkinson, who records hearing it on March 26, 1960.) Origin?

n'aff. See **gnaff.**

naff. Nothing: prostitutes': since ca. 1940. Origin? A shrewd and learnèd correspondent asks, 'Might the origin just possibly be "*rien à faire*"? Or perhaps "*not a fuck*"?' The latter is the more probable, yet far from a certainty.

Naffy, used as a pejorative adjective, connotes 'shirking': Services: since ca. 1940. Cf. the Navy's *Naffy rating*, a shirker. Here, the initials *N.A.A.F.I.* are interpreted as standing for '*No aim, ambition or fucking initiative*'.

Naffy gong. The 1939–45 star: Services. Partridge, 1945, 'For the semantics, cf. *rooty medal*. It is also called the *spam medal*.' Ex the resemblance of N.A.A.F.I. shoulder-strap colours to the ribbon colours. See **Naffy** on p. 548 and cf. **rooty gong** on p. 705.

Naffy medal; Groppi gong. Both mean 'the Africa Star', but the former belongs to the 1st Army, the latter (from the famous Cairo confectioners) to the 8th Army: 1943 +.

Naffy Romeo. A ladies' man: R.A.F.: since 1940. Jackson.

Naffy rumour. A baseless report: Forces: 1939 +.

Naffy sandwich, deal a. To deal a hand of 2 cards + one card + 2 cards: Services poker-players': since ca. 1930 Ex relative thickness.

Naffy time (or hyphen or as one word). The morning break: R.A.F. coll.: 1939 +. H. & P.

nag, n.—4. A Diesel shunting engine of 350 h.p.: railwaymen's: since ca. 1955. (*Railway* 2nd.) A pun on *nag*, a horse.

nag off! Shut up!: Rossall School: late C. 19–20. Marples. Via 'Leave off nagging!'

nags, the. Horseracing; the races themselves: racing coll., mostly Australian: C. 20. (B.P.)

nail, n.—4. A valve: motor-cycle racers': from ca. 1927. Peter Chamberlain.

nail, v., 2 (p. 549), occurs in *Boxiana*, III, 1821, as v.i., 'to charge extortionately'.—10. To attract (customers) successfully: fairgrounds' and mock-auctions': late C. 19–20. See 'Mock Auction Slang'.

nail!, no. I beg your pardon; sorry, but it's true!: printers': from ca. 1870. B. & L.

nail-can. A top hat: Australian: C. 20. B., 1942. Shape.

nail-groper. One who sweeps or scours the streets in search of nails, old iron, etc.: Londoners': ca. 1830–70. *Sinks*, 1848.

nail in one's coffin (p. 549). Pierce Egan, *Life in London*, 1821, 'A glass of spirits is termed, among the *we* ones, adding "another nail to the coffin"!'

nail on the ready. To catch someone in the criminal act: police s.: ca. 1830–80. *Sessions*, Feb. 1839. See **nail,** v., 3 (p. 549).

nailers. (Very rare in the singular.) A hold on prospective buyers: grafters': C. 20. Philip Allingham, *Cheapjack*, 1934, '"He's got his nailers out . . ." I enquired what he meant by "nailers". . . . "Well, you see," he explained "he's got their shillings and he hasn't given them anything yet. So he's sort of nailed them down. They can't walk away. He can hold them as long as he likes."'—2. See **front up** above.

naked, n. (p. 549) goes back to ca. 1810. It occurs in, e.g., W. N. Glascock, *Sailors and Saints* (II, 134), 1829. Moe.

Nalgo. The N.A.L.G.O., or National Association of Local Government Offices (or -ers): coll.: since ca. 1935.

name, bite someone's; or **sign one's hand** (or **name**). To eat a meal paid for by another: Australian: since ca. 1925. B., 1942.

name is Simpson, not Samson,—my. See **my name is Simpson.**

name is Twyford, my. See **Twyford** (Addenda as well as *Dict.*).

name of, by the (p. 550). Probably elliptical for *known by the name of*.

name on it, have one's (p. 550), was revived in World War II. (P-G-R.)

namesclop. Policeman: back s.: 1851, Mayhew, I; virtually † by 1910.

namma hole. Better *gnamma hole*, q.v.

nammas. A variant of **namm(o)us**, to depart hastily or speedily: Renton Nicholson, *An Autobiography*, 1860.

nammow (p. 550). Earlier in Mayhew, I, 1851.

nan, 2; nanna, 2; nanny, 5. Grandmother, both in reference and in address: lower classes' coll.: mid-C. 19–20. In **nanny**, 3, in the *Dict.*, the term is more accurately to be defined as '(a) nursemaid'.

nan-nan. A man's straw hat: Australian: ca. 1880–1914. B., 1942. Ex Aborigine?

nana.—2. (Ex sense 1: p. 550. A *soft* fruit.) Esp. *a right nana*, a real softy: low: since ca. 1930.

nana (hair-)cut. A womanlike hair-cut, the back of the head being shaved clean: Australian: since ca. 1920. B., 1942. Short for *banana* . . . ?

Nancy Dawson.—2. An effeminate, lackadaisical youth: ca. 1887–1910. B. & L. Cf. **Nancy boy** (*Dict.*).

Nancy homey. An effeminate man, esp. a homosexual: late C. 19–20. (Sydney Lester, 1937.) See **Nancy**, 1 and 2, on p. 550; *homey* is a parlary word.

nanna, nanny. See **nan** (above).

nanny.—5. (Or *nannie*.) A nannygai (or sort of fish): Australian: since ca. 1930. (B., 1953.) —6. The tote (see **nanny-goat**—3.)

Sense 3 (p. 550) goes back to early C. 19. Fredk Chamier records it in 1832 in *The Life of a Sailor* at I, 5, 7, 8. (Moe.)

nanny-goat.—3. Usu. *the nanny*. Totalisator: racing s.: Rhyming on *tote*.: since ca. 1925.—4. A boat: since ca. 1930; by 1960, slightly ob. (Franklyn, *Rhyming*.)

Nansen passports. Passports given by the League of Nations after the War of 1914–18, to persons without nationality. Ex the name of a famous explorer.

nant; non nant. A swimmer; a non-swimmer: Eton: mid-C. 19–20. Marples. Latin *nant*, they swim; *non nant*, they do not swim.

nantee (p. 550) is, in C. 20, usu. written *nanty*, as in 'Nanty, my jills, I'm whacked' = No, my friend, I'm exhausted. (Lester, 1937.)

nants. A variant of *nantee* (p. 550), as in Cockney and theatrical *nants for the dook*, no money for the rent (cf. *Duke of Kent*, p. 247). Cited by Christopher Fry in *The Sunday Times*, May 28, 1950.

nantwas. Nothing: prostitutes': since ca. 1930. Perhaps a filling out of **nants**.

nanty, n. Nothing: parlary: mid C. 19–20. (Sydney Lester.) See **nantee** on p. 550.

nap, n.—10. Blankets; sleeping bag: Australian: C. 20. Archer Russell, *A Tramp Royal*, 1934. Ex S.E. *nap*, (short) sleep.

nap, v.—9. To be 'nappy' (q.v.): sporting: C. 20.

nap, take the. To pretend to have been struck, 'by slapping the hands together unseen by the audience': theatrical: from ca. 1860. B. & L.

nap (or **knap**) **the slap.** To know how to receive a blow without being hurt in rough-and-tumble clownery: showmen's: from ca. 1860. Hindley, cited by B. & L.

napper, 4 (the head). Earlier in *Select Trials, from 1720 to 1724*, pub. in 1734: perhaps orig. c. —7. In *The News Chronicle* of March 15, 1954, C. H. Rolph—article 'Give Him a Napper'—notes the following chimneysweeps' terms: (*napper*) '"That's the brush you screw on the doll. Oh, the doll's what we call the set of rods. . . ." . . . A chummy is an ordinary sweep.'

napper, do on one's. A Cockney variant of **do on one's head.** Clarence Rook, *The Hooligan Nights*, 1899.

nappy, n. beer (p. 551) occurs as late as J. H. Lewis, *The Art of Writing*, 7th ed., 1816, in the form *nappy beer*. (Moe.)

nappy, adj.—2. 'A horse that refuses to answer to the hand or leg, tries to go the way home instead of the way you want, or plays other tricks, is spoken of as "nappy". It is very common speech with all who own horses': sporting: since ca. 1860. *Sessions*, Sept. 1880. It is often applied to persons if they are recalcitrant or unamenable. Ex *nab* (or *nap*) *the rust*.

nar-nar. Over-smart, esp. if effeminately so: Australian: ca. 1910–40. Colin MacInnes, *June in Her Spring*, 1952, 'You're not going to wear those nar-nar shoes to the gymkhana, are you?' Perhaps = *nah-nah* = the expostulatory, genteel *now, now!*

narang. Small: Australian pidgin: C. 19. John Lang, *The Forger's Wife*, 1855.

narangy. A 'swell': Australian: ca. 1870–1910. 'Tom Collins', *Such is Life*, 1903. Ex Aboriginal.—2. Hence, one who puts on 'side'; a social climber: since ca. 1910. B., 1942.

nark, n., 2 (p. 551): 'no longer low slang in Australia' (B.P., 1963).—7. An expert; e.g. *explosives nark*,' W/Cdr Robin P. McDouall, letter of April 12, 1945: R.A.F.: since ca. 1937. (Cf. sense 2: at foot of p. 551.)—8. 'A visiting senior officer on a tour of inspection' (P-G-R): R.A.F.: since ca. 1939.

nark it!—2. Hence (?), Stop it!: low (since ca. 1910) >, by ca. 1935, fairly gen.

narks, the; or **a dose of the narks.** That stupor which has been poetically described as 'the rapture of the depths' and is medically known as 'nitrogen narcosis': skin divers': since the late 1940's. (Wilfred Granville, Oct. 11, 1964.)

narky. Sarcastic: Cockney: C. 20. Michael Harrison, *Reported Safe Arrival*, 1943. Cf. **nark,** v., 4 (p. 552); but perhaps, in part at least, rhyming s. on *sarky*.—2. Ill-tempered: irritable: Australian: since ca. 1910. B., 1942. Ex **nark,** n., 2, on p. 551.

narp (p. 552) just possibly derives ex Fr. *nappe*.

*nase nab. A red nose; a drunkard: c. (— 1688); † by 1820. Randle Holme. See **nase** in the *Dict.*

nash, n. See **nosh.**

nasho. A National Service trainee: Australian: since ca. 1950. (B.P.) Cf. **Natios, the,** below.—2. (*Nasho.*) National Service Training: Australian: ca. 1945–60.—3. *The Nasho*, the National—later the Royal National—Park, near Sydney: Australian, mostly Sydneyites': since late 1940's. Hence, *a pash show at Nasho*, violent lovemaking at National Park. (B.P.)

Nasties, the. Germans: mid-1940 +. See **Old Nasty.**

nasturtiums, cast. To cast aspersions: jocular, mostly lower-middle class: C. 20; ob. By a kind of 'Hobson-Jobson' process.

nasty piece of work. An objectionable person: coll.: C. 20. Occ. *nasty bit.*

nat, in (all) one's. In one's life: Cockney: C. 20; ob. Pugh. Abbr. *in one's natural.*

natch! Of course!: Canadian: adopted, ca. 1945, ex U.S. Ex *naturally!* (Leechman.)

Nathans, the. The 'Jonathans', the Americans of the U.S.A.: Naval: ca. 1810–(?)40. *The Night Watch*, (II, 131), 1828, 'Our first trip was a regular-built *poser* to the Nathans. We landed on the banks of the Paxutent.' Also *Nathan* used collectively, as at II, 133, 'Nathan had Wellington's men to deal with.' (Moe.)

nation, adv. (p. 552): occurs, in U.S., earlier than 1788; e.g. in Anon., *The Trial of Atticus* (p. 26), 1771, 'He is a nation bawdy creature to talk' (Moe.)

National, the. National Assistance: coll.: since ca. 1946. 'He is doing well now—on the National.'

National Debt. A bet: theatrical rhyming s.: C. 20. (Franklyn, *Rhyming*.)

national exhibition. 'An execution at the Old Bailey; a term of the late Douglas Jerrold's, but now usual,' H., 3rd ed., 1864; † by ca. 1880.

Nationals, the. The so-called 'National' daily newspapers: coll.: mainly journalistic: since ca. 1920.

Natios, the. National military training: Australian: since ca. 1950. (Dick.) Cf. **Nasho** above.

native (p. 552). Earlier in *The London Guise*, 1818, where it is recorded only as a plural.

native leave. Leave granted to men whose homes are in, or near, the port at which a ship is lying: Naval coll.: C. 20. (P-G-R.)

natives were hostile, the. Anti-aircraft fire was heavy: R.A.F. c.p., usually referring to air-raids over Germany: 1940–5. (P-G-R.) A jocular allusion to this common statement in books of exploration and travel.

Nats, the (p. 552). Also in Australia: ca. 1916–18. (Dal Stivens, *Jimmy Brockett*, 1951.)

natter. To talk aimlessly, endlessly, irritatingly; to talk when speech is forbidden. Services, esp. R.A.F.: since ca. 1938. H. & P.; Partridge, 1945, 'Perhaps a blend of *nag* and *chatter*. Hence the frequent verbal noun, *nattering*.'—2. Hence, to grumble in a minor way: R.A.F.: 1939 +. Jackson.

natter can. A person, esp. a 'Waaf', prone to excessive speech: R.A.F. 1941 +. Partridge, 1945. Ex prec.

natter party. 'A Conference which leads nowhere,' H. & P.: R.A.F.: since 1939. See **natter.**

nattum. Sexual intercourse: Australian low: C. 20. B., 1942. Arbitrary? Perhaps ex 'do the *naughty*'. Perhaps back-s. on *mutton*: cf. *mutton, in her*, on p. 546.

natty, adj., 2 (p. 553): cf. the quotation at **twig**, below.

natural, n.—6. One who has an inborn gift, whether musician or painter or writer or gamesplayer 'or whatever'; a thing eminently suitable or adaptable (e.g. of a book: 'a natural for a film'): coll.: adopted, in early 1950's. ex U.S.—7. Mostly in plural *naturals*, 'non-hip people', 'squares': beatniks', then hippies': since early 1960's. (Peter Fryer, Dec. 3, 1967, in *The Observer*.)

Natural Philosophy. See 'Tavern terms', § 3, *d*.

nature of the beast, the. Eligible only when applied to things, not to animal life: coll.: since ca. 1910. 'This car tends to oversteer when cornered fast. It's the nature of the beast.' (B.P.)

nature run. A short leave ashore at night: Australian Naval: since ca. 1920.

Naughton and Gold. Cold (in the head): rhyming s.: since ca. 1945. Ex the famous music-hall pair. Franklyn 2nd.

naughty, n. A copulation: Australian: late C. 19–20. (D'Arcy Niland, *The Big Smoke*, 1959.)

naughty.—2. (Of an actor, actress) inferior: theatrical: late C. 19–20. Ngaio Marsh, *Vintage Murder*, 1938.

naughty, v. To coït with: Australian: C. 20. 'He naughties her.' Ex **naughty, do the** (p. 553).

***naughty!, it's.** It's dangerous!: c.p., c. and low: from ca. 1920.

nausea. A fuss; trouble: Royal Naval College, Dartmouth: since ca. 1950. John Winton, *We Joined the Navy*, 1959, 'I'd forgotten about the cap. I knew there'd be a nausea about it'; 'Keep this book up to date. It may save you a lot of nausea if you do.'

nauseate. To reprimand; to make life difficult for (someone): Navy: since ca. 1950. John Winton, *We Joined the Navy*, 1959, '"Have you tried the cable deck?" asked Michael. "He sometimes goes up there to nauseate the foc'sle men."' Cf. **nausea** above.

nauseous. Objectionable: coll.: C. 18–early 19. E.g. *nauseous toad*, often used as a mild endearment (cf. **filthy fellow**). Article by H. C. K. Wyld in *The Spectator*, April 22, 1938.

Naussie. A New Australian (esp. a recent migrant from Europe): Aus.: since ca. 1950. (B., 1959.) A blend of *New* + *Aussie*.

Nautics, the. The Royal Navy: R.A.F.: World War II. Slightly derogatory. (Paul Brickhill, *The Dam Busters*, 1951.) But in later, non-R.A.F. use, only very slightly if, indeed, at all derogatory.

nav.—2. A navigator: Naval and R.A.F.: since ca. 1920. Commoner than *navvy*, 2.

Nav House, the (p. 553). The definition should rather be: 'The Navigation School situated in H.M. Dockyard, Portsmouth' (Commander John A. Poland).

naval bank holiday. A day spent in coaling the ship: Naval: since ca. 1925. (P-G-R.) An ironic pun on *banking*, or heaping up, coal.

naval engagement. Sexual intercourse: Canadian naval officers', hence more gen.: since ca. 1940. Navel to navel.

navigator. See 'Tavern terms', § 3, *d*.

Navigators' Union, the. 'A select, most unofficial body which met in pubs anywhere near a Bomber Station.' (John Bebbington): R.A.F.: ca. 1940–5.

navvy, 2. Also, derivatively, an Air Force or a Naval navigating officer: since ca. 1920. Jackson (at *G.R. navvy*), 1943; Partridge, 1945; Granville.

navvy's (or navvies') piano. A pneumatic drill: roadmakers' and builders': since ca. 1925.

navvy's Prayer Book, the. A shovel: navvies':

ca. 1870–1910. (D. W. Barrett, *Navvies*, 1880.) Ex the prayerful attitude involved in its use.

navvy's wedding-cake. Bread pudding: Services, esp. the R.A.F.: since ca. 1925. H. & P. Jackson.

Navy cake and the commoner **Navy cut** (ex *Navy Cut* tobacco), like *chutney* and *port-hole duff*, are synonymous with *back-scuttle*: low Naval: C. 20. Cf. *golden rivet* and:

Navy cake, have a bit of. To indulge in sodomy: Army and R.A.F.: since ca. 1918. An unmerited aspersion.

Navy chicken. Corned beef: Naval: since ca. 1917. In 1939–45, it also designated spam.

Navy fish, n. and adv. A Naval beard, a beard worn in the Naval fashion: since ca. 1930.

Navy House. The Sailor's Rest, Chatham: Naval: C. 20. Granville.

Navy's here, the. In *The Daily Telegraph* of May 29, 1968, we read: 'Adml. of the Fleet Sir Philip Louis Vian, who will always be remembered as "Vian of the Cossack", has died at his home near Newbury, Berks, aged 73.

'The famous cry "The Navy's here!" with which 299 British seamen were freed from the German supply ship Altmark in Jossing Fjord, Norway, in February, 1940, became a national catch phrase.

'Sir Philip revealed in "Action This Day", his war memoirs, that the cry was made by the then Lieut. Bradwell Turner, who was the leader of the destroyer Cossack's boarding party. . . . Resistance was overcome, and the prisoners were found under locked hatches in the holds. When these had been broken open, Lt. Bradwell Turner called: "Any British down there?" He was greeted with a shout of: "Yes, we're all British." "Come on up, then," the lieutenant said. "The Navy's here!"'

This c.p., which was still extant in 1968, might well be compared with a U.S. c.p.: *the Cavalry's here* and the more recent *the Marines have landed*. Sometimes jocular, as when, for instance, addressed to or at a lone sailor entering a bar.

Nazi Goering. See 'Prisoner-of-War Slang', 6.

nazy (*Dict.*) derives ex Ger. *nass*, wet (B. & L.).

Neapolitan favour. Syphilis: euphemistic coll.: late C. 16–mid-17. Greene, *Notable Discovery*, 1591.

near enough. A variant of *nigh enough*. (Franklyn.)

near the foreman—near the door. A tailors' c.p. (mid-C. 19–20) verging on proverbial S.E. and implying that it is better to keep as far away from the foreman as possible. B. & L.

neat (p. 554). Cf. the Canadian teenagers' closely allied sense, 'very pleasing or attractive': since ca. 1956. (Leechman.)

neat but not gaudy (p. 554). A C. 20 elaboration is *neat but not gaudy, chic but not bizarre*.

neb.—2. A nebelwerfer (the German six-barrelled mortar): Army: 1940 (? 1939)–45. P-G-R. The German *Nebelwerfer*, lit. 'fog-thrower', has 'two distinct meanings: 1, a smoke-bomb mortar; 2, a cover-name (cf. "tank" as orig. used in English) for the multiple rocket-launcher (*not* a mortar), nicknamed "Moaning Minnie" by our Army, and similar to the Russian weapon called by them "Anooshka", and by the Germans "Stalin's organ"' (H. R. Spencer).

Nebuchadnezzar (p. 554), sense 1. 'Only—I

should think—it's a word-and-a-half just *asking* to be misused, as in "Nebuchadnezzar sold his wife for a pair of shoes"' (Julian Franklyn, 1962). This I accept, not as exclusive of, but as supplementary to, my origination.—3. Hence, a salad: Australian: C. 20. B., 1942.

necessaries, the or **one's.** The male genitals: raffish: since ca. 1940. Roderic Jefferies, *Exhibit No. 13*, 1962.

neck, n. Esp. *have a neck*, to be impudent, to make an outrageous request: Australian: C. 20. Baker.

neck, v.—4. To choke (a person): c.: mid-C. 19–20. Ex sense 1.

neck, get under (someone's). 'To outwit or anticipate a person' (B., 1959): Aus.: since ca. 1930.

neck, give one's. To give up; to become apathetic: English Midlands s.: C. 20. (F. B. Vickers, 1955.)

neck, lose or **win by a** (p. 554). The latter occurs in Bee, 1823, at p. 94.

neck, you give me a pain in the. See *you give me the balls-ache.*

neck and neck (p. 554). Also in E. Bulwer Lytton, *My Novel*, 1853.

neck-to-knees. A bathing costume covering the body from neck almost to knees: Australian coll.: since ca. 1925. (B., 1943.)

neck-warmer. The frill at the lower end of a nightdress: Australian: since the late 1940's. That's where—if still being worn at all—it tends to be found at the conclusion of conjugal love-making.

neckcloth. See **neck-cloth** (*Dict.*).

necker. A heavy fall: Australian: since ca. 1910. B., 1942.

necklace.—2. (Cf. sense 1.) A garrotter: Australian c.: C. 20. Baker.

ned.—3. Head: Australian: since ca. 1910. (Ruth Park, *Poor Man's Orange*, 1950.) Perhaps rhyming.

Ned Kelly. 'Any person of buccaneering business habits' (B., 1942): Australian coll.: C. 20. Ex the famous bushranger: whence also *Kelly Gang*, an unscrupulous firm or a tax-grabbing government: since ca. 1910. The actual Kelly Gang numbered four persons. See also **game as Ned Kelly.**—2. The belly: Australian rhyming s.: since ca. 1920. (Franklyn, *Rhyming.*)—3. A story of the 'Deadwood Dick' kind: Australian: since ca. 1925. (B., 1943.)—4. A poker machine: Australian: since ca. 1930. (B., 1943.)

Ned Kelly was hung—or **hanged—for less.** An Australian c.p. of gently jocular reproof or complaint, e.g. against taxation: since ca. 1945. The famous bushranger. (B.P.)

neddies, the. Racehorses; (almost) horse-racing in general: Australian: C. 20. (Dick.) Perhaps satirically ex **neddy,** 1, on p. 555.

need (something) like a hole in the head. To need it not at all: adopted, ca. 1950, ex U.S.

needle, n.—5. Short for **needle and pin** (*Dict.*). —6. A hypodermic injection: Australian coll.: since ca. 1918. (Jon Cleary, *Back of Sunset*, 1959.)

needle, v.—3. To 'winkle' or prize information from (someone): journalistic: since ca. 1940. *The New Statesman*, Jan. 12, 1946 (p. 1), '"Needled" from him by reporters.' Cf. sense 2 (p. 555).

needle, be on the. To be addicted to drugs requiring an injection: (esp. teenage) drug addicts': since ca. 1950. 'Implies a step from the theoretically non-addictive drugs to the more dangerous ones' (Dinah Greenwood). Cf. **needle,** n., 6, above—a sense that had, by ca. 1920, become fairly common in Britain.

needle, cop, get or **take the.**—2. (Only *get the needle*.) 'To lose much money at a game': card-players': from ca. 1870. B. & L.

needled. 'Inoculated before overseas service,' H. & P.: Services: since ca. 1930.

neg. A negative: photographers' coll.: C. 20.

neg driving. Negligent driving: (mostly Australian) motorists' coll.: since the late 1940's. (B.P.)

negateef! No!: R.A.F., hence other, personnel: since ca. 1955. A jocular alteration—prob. influenced by Fr. *négatif*—of *negative*. 'It's not uncommon for persons connected with flying to use "affirmative" and "negative" for "yes" and "no", this being R/T [radio telephone] procedure. Monotony is broken, and a feeling of "not on your Nellie" is implied by using "negateef"': an R.A.F. officer, late in 1961.

negro head is an occasional variant of *nigger-head*: B., 1943.

neigho, pops! See 'jive'.

neither buff nor bum. Neither one thing nor the other: proletarian coll.: from ca. 1860; slightly ob. B. & L.

Nell!, not on your. Not on your life!: since ca. 1950. Short for **not on your Nellie** (below). Franklyn 2nd.

Nellie or **Nelly.** Sense 2 is earlier in 'Taffrail'. —3. Any cheap wine: Australian: since ca. 1920. B., 1942.—4. (also *nelly*.) 'An effeminate, affected homosexual who makes public display of his homosexuality' (*Lavender Lexicon*, 1965): U.S.: partially adopted, ca. 1945, in Britain.

Nellie Bligh. An eye: English and Australian rhyming s.: C. 20.—2. A fly; in this sense usually *Nellie Bly* and mostly in plural: Aus. rhyming s.: since ca. 1910. Mary Durack, *Keep Him My Country*, 1955, '"Thanks, Stan. I never was one for drinking with the Nelly Blys."'

Nellie Duff!, not on your. Not likely!: a c.p.: 1939 +. *The New Statesman*, Aug. 30, 1941. *Nellie Duff* rhymes on **puff**, 4 (p. 665).

Nelly. See **Nellie.**

Nelly's death. Cheap red wine: Australian: since ca. 1930. (Dal Stivens, *The Gambling Ghost*, 1953.)

Nelson. One pound, one shilling and one penny: bank cashiers': late C. 19–20. Folklore derives it ex 'Nelson's one eye, one arm and one anus'.

Nelson stock. 'Driver's window on one side and an indicator's board on the other (SR)': railwaymen's: C. 20. (*Railway* 2nd.) An allusion to Lord Nelson's lost eye.

Nelson's blood (p. 556) is, specifically, Navy rum: Naval lore has it that Nelson's corpse was pickled in rum in order to preserve it on its passage to England. Also, in C. 20, Aus.

neo-barrack. A jocularly disparaging adjective applied to 'the barrack-like architecture so common to-day' (A. B. Petch, March 1966): since early 1950's. To be aligned with **North Oxford Gothic** and **Stockbrokers' Tudor** below.

nerts! Nonsense!: low, though not always apprehended as low: adopted ca. 1935 ex U.S., where it is polite for *nuts* = **balls** (q.v. in *Dict.*).

nerve, 2, seems orig. to have been Etonian and to date from ca. 1880. B. & L.

nerve war, a. The making of constant complaints in order to get things done: Australian soldiers': 1940–5. (B., 1943.)

Nervo and Knox. Socks: rhyming s.: since ca. 1940. Ex the famous pair of entertainers. Mainly theatrical, as Franklyn 2nd reminds me.

nervous Nellies. American isolationists: 1939–41. Perhaps ex *Nervous Nelly*, 'Nickname of U.S. Secretary of State Kellogg, who gave his name to the 1928 Pact outlawing war' (Ramsey Spencer, 1967).

Nessie. The Loch Ness monster, often revived during 'the silly season': dwellers on Loch Ness, hence journalists': since late 1933. (It was on May 2, 1933, that the newspapers announced that a giant marine creature had been seen in Loch Ness.)

nest.—2. A 'stick' of aerial bombs: R.A.F.: since 1939. H. & P. See **egg**, 3 (*Dict.*).—3. An aerodrome: Australian airmen's: 1939–45. (B., 1943.) To which all the little aircraft fly home.

nest, be on the. To enjoy the gratification of the marriage bed: C. 20.

nesting(-)box; usually in pl. A Wren's cabin: Naval: 1939 +. Granville.

net (p. 556). Sense 1 earlier in Mayhew, I, 1851, where also *net-gen*, 10 shillings.—3. See 'Guard-Room in Army Slang.'

net, be off. 'I'm a bit off net' = I don't quite get what you're trying to say: Army: 1941–5. The technical *off net* was applied to a wireless set not attuned to the collective needs of a unit. (P-G-R.)

net a load of rabbits. See **trap.**

neuc. '. . . Loading neuc boxes—which are the infant hives with one frame of brood and two stickies' (Kylie Tennant, *The Honey Flow*, 1956): Australian migratory bee-keepers': since ca. 1945. For '*nucleus*'?

neux, n. and **v.** A fag; to fag; Woolwich: mid-C. 19–20; ? †. (Dr C. T. Onions, postcard of Oct. 25, 1940.) Ex *new* (boy, lad, chap).

never a dull moment! An ironic c.p. in time of danger or excitement: Naval: since ca. 1939, Granville.

never country or **never land.** 'Desert lands or remote areas in the far outback of Australia' (B., 1959): Aus. coll.: since ca. 1920. Ex **never never,** 1, on p. 557.

never do a. To shirk work: Naval: since ca. 1900. Granville.

never greens. Eucalyptus: Australian: late C. 19–20. B., 1942. Ironic.

never had it so good, you've or **we've** or **they've** or **I've,** or **he's . . .;** in American usage, **you never had it so good.** So far as Britain is concerned, the original was 'Our people have . . .' (Prime Minister Harold Macmillan): *Nunquam id habuistis tam bonum,* as it was jocosely rendered in Latin. But 'the Americans were using this idiom by the end of the Second World War, and possibly long before that. In German it is old-established, while in modern German it is heard a dozen times a day.' This, adds Dr Brian Foster (*The Changing English Language*, 1968), seems to indicate that 'we are dealing with an idiom carried over into American English by the speech-habits of German immigrants'—cf. **I wouldn't know.**

In *The New Language of Politics*, 1968, William Safire records that it was 'the Democratic party slogan in the 1952 Stevenson campaign against Eisenhower'.

never let it be said . . . ! A lower-class genteel c.p.: C. 20. W. L. George, *The Making of an Englishman*, 1914.

never-mention-'ems (p. 557) is perhaps elliptical for, but more prob. the basic form of, *Oh-no-we-never-mention-'em*, which occurs on p. 59 of C. J. R. Cook, *The Quarter Deck*, 1844. (Moe.)

never stand still. A variant of *can't keep still*.

neves (p. 557). Rather, since ca. 1845. Mayhew, I, 1851, has it in sense 'sevenpence'.—2. A seven-years' prison-sentence: c.: late C. 19–20. (Norman.) Short for *neves stretch* (p. 557).

nevvy.—2. Hence, a schoolmaster's favourite: Tonbridge: late C. 19–20. Marples.

new boy. A new member of a ship's ward-room: Naval officers': 1939–45. (P-G-R.) Cf.

new chum.—2. A newly arrived officer: Army officers': 1939–45. (P-G-R.)

new-chum gold. Iron pyrites: Australian: mid-C. 19–20. Baker. Very deceptive.

new hand. Synonymous with **new chum** (p. 557): Australian coll.: late C. 19–20. (B., 1943.) By 1959 †: B., *The Drum.*

new jacks. Junior players in a football club: since ca. 1925.

new one on me, it's (or **that's**) **a.** First time I've heard of, or seen, that being done: c.p.: since ca. 1910.

New River Head (or **h-**), **the.** Tears: a London c.p. of ca. 1820–30. Bee, 'A watery head hath the wife, whose nob, like Niobe's, is a tears; sometimes termed "the New River head", after an elevated *back-water* near Islington.'

new tick. A new boy: certain Public Schools': from ca. 1880. George Orwell, *Burmese Days*, 1935. Prob. suggested by **new bug** (*Dict.*).

New Year revolution. A New Year resolution: Australian jocular: since ca. 1950. (B.P.)

New York nippers. Kippers: rare rhyming s.: C. 20. Franklyn, *Rhyming.*

Newgate gaol (or **jail**). A tale: mid-C. 19–20. Rhyming.

Newk. Newcastle: Durham and Newcastle undergraduates': C. 20. (Marples, 2.)

Newland (see **Abraham Newland** on p. 2) occurs in W. N. Glascock, *Sailors and Saints* (I, 21), 1829. Moe.

Newlicks. See **Noolucks.**

newly wed. A sergeant recently promoted to a lieutenancy: Australian soldiers': 1939 +. B., 1942.

news(-)hawk or **news(-)hound.** A reporter: journalistic: adopted, ca. 1925, from U.S.; by 1938, coll.

News of the World. A very long letter, containing nothing of note, from a woman: jocular: since ca. 1930.

newsie (or **-sy**), n. A newspaper seller: mostly Australian: C. 20. (B., 1953.)

newsy. Gossipy; full of news: late C. 19–20: coll. >, by 1940, familiar S.E.—2. Occ. euphemistically for *nosey*, inquisitive: since ca. 1930.

Newt. A *Neut*ral vessel: Naval: 1914–18, and since.

newt, drunk as a. Very drunk indeed: mostly Forces', esp. Army's: C. 20. Perhaps more often *tight as a newt*, ex the newt's tight, glossy skin. Cf. *tight as a drum* (p. 885).

Newton got him or **took him.** See **old Newton.**

Newton Heath. Teeth: Manchester rhyming s.: C. 20. (Jacob Jaffe, 1959.) Ex the industrial suburb so named.

Newts. Newtown footballers: Sydneyites': since ca. 1920. (B., 1943.)

Newy. Newcastle (N.S.W.): Australian: since ca. 1910. (B., 1953.)

newy.—2. A new one; a newcomer: Australian coll.: C. 20. (H. Drake-Brockman, *Hot Gold*, 1940; Cusack & James, *Come in Spinner*, 1951.)—3. (Also *newie.*) A new trick, as in 'That's a newy on me!': Australian: since ca. 1925.—4. A new story: Australian: since ca. 1930. (B.P.)

next time you make a pie, will you give me a piece? A man's c.p. suggestion to a girl that she should co-operate: Canadian: ca. 1895–1914.

next week, on for. A c.p. applied to a clock that is very fast: since ca. 1920.

Niagara Falls.—2. Balls (physiological): rhyming: C. 20. Michael Harrison, *Reported Safe Arrival*, 1943.

nib-like. See **niblike** (*Dict.*).

nibbets. A Canadian synonym, late C. 19–20, of *clinkers*, 2 (p. 160).

nibble, have a. 'To have the best of the bargain, or an easy, well-paid job' (B. & L.): tailors': mid-C. 19–20. See also **nibble, get a** in *Dict.*—2. To coït: low: C. 20. Ex **nibble**, v., 3 (*Dict.*).

nibbling. Taking out a girl fairly regularly, fairly often; courting: Services': since ca. 1925. H. & P. Cf. **nibble**, 4 (*Dict.*).

nice, n. See **piece of nice.**

nice as pie. (Of persons) very polite, very sweet and agreeable: coll.: since ca. 1910.

nice (or **lovely**) **drop of.** A coll. formula, dating since ca. 1935; e.g., *nice drop of work—sock—tie—jacket*, etc.; 'plurals are never employed in this phrase' (Atkinson).

nice pair of eyes, she has—or **she's got**—**a.** She has a shapely figure: c.p.: since ca. 1960.

nice work! A c.p. in approval of a favourable arrangement or of a good piece of work: since ca. 1930. Since ca. 1944, often extended to *nice work —if you can get it!*

nicely, thank you!, used as adj. for 'mildly exhilarated with liquor', as in 'He's nicely, thank you': Society: since ca. 1930; by 1950, slightly, and by 1960 very, ob. Ngaio Marsh, *Death in a White Tie*, 1938.

Nick. The inseparable nickname of men surnamed Carter: since ca. 1880. Ex the pseudonym *Nick Carter*, author of detective novels (1870 onwards).

nick, n., 6 (p. 559) seems to be very much older than I had supposed, for it is recorded in a song 'attributed to Ben Jonson', published by an American magazine, *The Port Folio*, April 14, 1804, at p. 120:

'Or else, unseen, with them I go,
   All in the nick
     To play some trick,
   And frolick it with ho, ho, ho!'

(Colonel Moe.)
—10. A winning throw at dice: gamblers':

ca. 1660–1750. Shadwell, *The Sullen Lovers*, 1668; Dryden, *An Evening's Love*, 1668; Otway, *The Atheist*, 1684. (Thanks to John Cannon, Esq.) Cf. sense 1 of the v.: p. 559.—11. Natal cleft at the fold of the buttock: low: late C. 19–20.

nick, v.—8. Also *nick off*. To depart, esp. if promptly or speedily: Australian late C. 19–20. B., 1942.

nick, do a. To decamp: Aus.: C. 20. (B., 1959.) Cf. the preceding entry.

nick, down the. (Of a locomotive) short of steam: railwaymen's: C. 20. (*Railway*.)

nick, in good. Physically fit: coll.: C. 20. (Very common in New Zealand.) Ex **nick**, n., 6, on p. 559.

nick, in the. In the nick of time: coll.: mid-C. 19–20.

nick off. See **nick**, v., 8.

nickels. Leaflets dropped: R.A.F.: 1939–40.

nicker, 3 (p. 560). Also Australian: B., 1942.—4. A cigarette-end: Liverpool: since ca. 1930. 'You nick it out on a wall.' (Frank Shaw, April 24, 1952; he compares the synonymous Cardiff *dimmer*.) Cf. *nicky*, 2 (p. 560).

Nicknames. To the list of 'inevitable' or inseparable nicknames on p. 560, add these (which I owe to Mr Albert B. Petch): *Cock* Robins, hence Robinson, ex the nursery rhyme: *Dickie* (or *-y*) Bird; *Foxy* Reynolds—an allusion to Reynard the fox; *Ginger* Smith (as well as Jones); *Jonah* Jones; *Lefty* Wright; *Peeler* Murphy, so many Irishmen being in the police force; *Rabbit* Hutchin(g)s, hence Hutchinson (a rabbit's hutch); *Sandy* Brown; *Taffy* Davies (Davis); *Tubby* Martin. And these, from Gerald Kersh, *They Die with Their Boots Clean*, 1941: *Captain* Kidd (from the buccaneer); *Iron* Duke, hence Dukes (of Wellington); *Muddy* Waters, hence Waterson; *Spider* Kelly (ex a boxer's nickname ?). And *Stitch* Taylor: G. Kersh, *Clean, Bright and Slightly Oiled*, 1946.

Nicknames of British Association Football teams.

A few—e.g. *Canaries, Gunners, Hammers, Magpies*—occur in the *Dict.* proper. Here is an incomplete list of others. All are preceded by *the*; all are s., except the few classified as coll. (I owe most of them to Mr Albert B. Petch.)

Addicks	Charlton Athletic
Borough	Middlesbrough
Cestrians	Chester
Dons	Aberdeen
Fifers	East Fife
Filberts	Leicester
Forest	Nottingham Forest: coll.
Gills	Gillingham
Glaziers	Crystal Palace
Grecians	Exeter City
Imps	Lincoln City
Latics	Oldham
Lions	Colchester (?)
Moorites	Burnley
Orient	Leyton Orient: coll.
Owls	Sheffield Wednesday
Paraders	Bradford (?)
Pilgrims	Plymouth
Rangers	Queen's Park Rangers: coll.
Reds	Manchester United
Robins	Bristol City
Saddlers	Walsall (?)
Seasiders	Blackpool
Tangerines	Blackpool (?)
Trotters	Bolton Wanderers
Villains	Aston Villa

niente — usually **nanty** — **crackling**. Female pudend: low: since ca. 1910. Cf. **crackling**.

niff. A sniff: Cockney: late C. 19–20. A. Neil Lyons, *Arthur's*, 1908.—2. An unpleasant odour: C. 20. Prob. ex the v. (see the *Dict.*).

niff-naff; esp. in Don't *niff-naff*, 'stop fussing and get cracking' (Jackson): R.A.F.: since ca. 1930. A variant reduplication of *niff*, which seems to combine *niggle* and *fuss*.

***nifty**; gen. **bit of nifty**. Sexual intercourse: c., and low: late C. 19–20.

nig, n., 4 (p. 561), can prob. be dated back to ca. 1840. (W. H. Blanch, *Bluecoat Boy*, 1877.)

nig pig. A native (of a coloured, i.e. non-white, race): R.A.F.: since ca. 1925. Jackson. Ex *nigger pig?*

nigger.—4. A member of a clique: Dalton Hall, Manchester: since ca. 1925. Hence, *niggery*, cliqueyness. *The Daltonian*, Dec. 1946.—5. A blackfish (a luderick): Aus. fishermen's: late C. 19–20. Nino Culotta, *Gone Fishin'*, 1963.

nigger, work like a. To work extremely hard: coll.: since ca. 1830 in U.S. and since ca. 1890 in Britain, where it began, ca. 1965, to > slightly ob.

nigger-head. 'An anthill-like peak of coral showing above water' (Baker): Australian pearlfishers' and sailors': late C. 19–20.

niggers in the snow is the usual post-1920 form of the 'prunes and rice' sense of **niggers in a snowstorm** (p. 561). Granville.

niggers' knackers. Prunes: R.A.F.: since ca. 1925. Cf. the preceding entry.

niggly. Bad-tempered, esp. about trifles: coll.: since ca. 1910. 'Oh, don't be so bloody niggly!'

niggly(-)gouger. A finicky, tiresome fellow: Naval: since ca. 1930. (Irving's *Royal Navalese*, 1946.) Ex preceding.

night(-)bind. A turn of night duty: R.A.F. (esp. N.C.O.s): since ca. 1930. Gerald Emanuel, letter of March 19, 1945. See **bind**.

night-fossick, n. 'To steal gold by night' (Baker): Australian: mid-C. 19–20. See **fossick** and **night-fossicker**, in *Dict*.

night hawk.—2. A thief; a prostitute: Australian: C. 20. B., 1942.

night owl. One who keeps late hours; one who works through the night: Australian coll.: since ca. 1920. (B.P.)

night starvation. Sexual deprivation, lack of sexual intimacy: since ca. 1938. By a pun on the advertisements that urge us to take a drink of this or that 'delicious beverage' before we go to bed.

night watchman. A (usually a second-rate) batsman sent into 'hold up an end' until the close of play: cricketers': 1946 +. *The Daily Telegraph*, May 6, 1948, in a report by E. W. Swanton.

nightshade or **deadly n.** 'A shameless prostitute of the very lowest class' (B. & L.): from ca. 1860; ob.

nighty night! Good night!: nursery—and jocular—coll.: since ca. 1910.

nignog. A fool: Army: late C. 19–20. Perhaps ex *nigmenog* (p. 562).—2. Hence, a raw recruit: Army: since ca. 1925. By 1960, fairly common general s.

nik, 'as a suffix is common in Yiddish slang.

It refers to a person of not much account and may follow a Yiddish word or its English equivalent, as in "He's a boozernik—or gamblernik—or spielernik". It is as old as all other Yiddishisms' (Julian Franklyn, letter of 1962). Cf. **Beatnik** above.

nine. See **niner, 3,** below. 'A nine-gallon keg of beer' (Culotta): Australian coll.: since ca. 1920.

nine-acre smile. A very broad grin, indicating supreme satisfaction: Canadian coll.: since ca. 1930. (Leechman.)

ninepence over the wall, 'nine days' C.C.': see **over the wall** and cf. **sevenpence over the wall.**

ninepennyworth. See **sixpennyworth.**

niner.—3. A woman nine months pregnant: Australian: since ca. 1920. (Dal Stivens, *Jimmy Brockett,* 1951.)

nineteen. In games, a score of nothing (nought): public-house: C. 20. At cribbage one cannot score 19.

nineteener. A swindler, sharper: an opportunist loafer: Australian c.: C. 20. B., 1942. A plausible talker 'nineteen to the dozen'.

ninety days' wonder. A newly commissioned Second Lieutenant: Army: since ca. 1946. Perhaps an adaptation of the U.S. *ninety-day wonder* (hence . . . *blunder*), applied during W.W. II to Second Lieutenants obtaining their position by passing a 90-days' course after being selected from 'other ranks', as Robert Clairborne thinks possible.

ninety-nine, a hundred, change hands! A scurrilous imputation of self-abuse: C. 20. (Cf. *change hands*: the number 50 in tombola: John Irving, *Royal Navalese,* 1946.)

ning-nog. See:

ning-nong. A nincompoop, a naturally foolish person: Australian: since ca. 1930; by 1963 (B.P.), ob. An assimilation of *nincom*(poop) and a variant of *ningnog,* itself a variant of **nignog** (above); perhaps influenced by **ning-nang** (p. 563).

ninon over Nanon. (Of a woman wearing) a silk nightdress with nothing under it: Australian feminine c.p.: since ca. 1925. A pun on *none on.*

nip, n.—5. A child: Australian: since ca. 1920. (Cusack & James, *Come in Spinner,* 1951.) Short for synonymous *nipper.*

nip, adj. Cheeky, impudent: Marlborough College: since ca. 1920. His speech nips.

nip-cheese (p. 563), a ship's purser, has the occ. variant *Mr Nip,* as in W. N. Glascock, *Sailors and Saints* (II, 168), 1829. Moe.

nip for it, make a. To try to escape at a run; e.g. from a train: Forces', but esp. prisoner-of-war: 1940–5. (Guy Morgan, *Only Ghosts Can Live,* 1945.) Cf. the civilian coll. *nip along,* to make haste.

nip in or **nip in smartly** or **nip smartly in.** To take advantage of an opportunity: Forces' (1939–45), hence general. Ex a drill formula.

nipper.—8. A prawn: Australian: late C. 19–20. Baker. Cf. senses 2, 3: p. 563.—9. That junior member of any gang who 'fags' for the others: railwaymen's: C. 20. (*Railway.*) Ex sense 2 on p. 563.—10. See **greyhound** above.

nippers.—6. 'Sound yarn taken from condemned cordage and marled together,' Granville: Naval: C. 20. Pinched or 'nipped' together.

nippy, adj. Fairly cold: coll.: late C. 19–20.

Cf. 'It's a bit nippy', as understatement of the fact that it's damned cold. Ex English dialect.

nippy with the weight. (Of a shopkeeper) giving short weight or, grudgingly, the bare weight: since ca. 1920.

Nips. Japanese: adopted, ca. 1941, from U.S. Ex *Nipponese.*

nishte. Nothing: low s.: since ca. 1918. (Robin Cook, 1962.) Via Yiddish ex Ger. **nichts.**

nit, n.—5. A simpleton, a moron, a fool: Australian: since ca. 1925. Baker. Short for *nit-wit.* Also, since ca. 1945, common in Britain.—6. Usually in pl. *nits,* whiskers: Liverpool: C. 20. Harbourage.

nit, v. As in '"Nit the jorrie (Leave the girl alone)!" he yelled. "Nark it! Nark it!"' MacArthur & Long: C. 20. Prob. ex *nix.*—2. To decamp: Australian low: C. 20. Baker. Perhaps ex **keep nit** (*Dict.*).

nit amang 'em! 'Nothing doing!': low Scottish: from ca. 1920.

nit-keep, v. and n. To keep watch; one who does this: Aus. c.: C. 20. (B., 1959.) Also **nit-keeper.** (B., 1942.)

Nitchie. A Prairies Indian: Canadian: since ca. 1910.

nitto! Stop! or Be quiet!: c.: since ca. 1940. (John Gosling, *The Ghost Squad,* 1959.) Perhaps cf. **keep nit** on p. 450.

nitty (p. 564) is Naval rather than merely nautical and it prob. goes back to ca. 1810 or even to ca. 1790; W. N. Glascock, *The Naval Sketch-Book* (I, 22), 1825, has it. Moe.

[**nitty,** adj. See 'Epithets'. Prob. always S.E.]

nitty. Idiotic: since late 1950's. Patricia Moyes, *Murder Fantastical,* 1967, 'If the girl was nitty enough to contemplate marrying him, she was only getting what she deserved.' Ex *nit,* short for *nit-wit.*

nix fish-tins. See 'Prisoner-of-War Slang', para 1.

nix on it! Stop that!: Australian low: C. 20. B., 1942. See **nix!** in *Dict.*

nixes! Don't do that!: Milton Junior School, Bulawayo: since ca. 1925. Cf. prec. entry.

nixies. A female's drawers: from 1933. Not ex S.E. *knickers* but ex **nix,** 1, as an advance on *scanties.*

nn for *nd* is a characteristic of Cockney: C. 19–20—and prob. older still. E.g. *unnerstand* and *wunnerful.*

no-bill. See **non-air.**

no bottle, as in 'It's no bottle'. No good: Services': C. 20.

no chance! An emphatic negative: coll., mostly Australian: C. 20. (B.P.)

no comment! 'A jocular catchphrase in imitation of politicians and prominent people who often say this when they are being pestered by reporters and TV interviewers' (Petch): since late 1950's.

no dice; no soap. The deal's off: Canadian: since ca. 1940. The latter, fairly common elsewhere in the British Commonwealth, probably rhymes on *no hope.*

no, don't tell me—I'll (or let me) guess! A c.p.: since ca. 1941. Sometimes *no* is omitted; occ., *now* is substituted for *no.*

no flies (p. 565). In sense 1, there is an Aus. variant: (*there are*) *no flies about* So-and-So: B., 1959.

no future . . . See **future at all.**

no go (p. 565) occurs a little earlier in *Boxiana*, IV, 1824. It prob. goes back to ca. 1800; it occurs in W. N. Glascock, *Sketch-Book* (I, 36), 1825. Moe.

no-go, n. A failure; something unfair or obstructive: Australian: late C. 19–20. B., 1942. Ex **no go** . . . (*Dict.* and Add.).

no good, a bit of. See **bit of** . . .

no good, do a bit of. See **bit of** . . .

no good to Gundy. (Very) unsatisfactory: Australian: C. 20. (B., 1943.) Who was Gundy? Also *no good to gundybluey* or to *gunty*: B., 1959.

no good to me! Won't satisfy me by far!: coll. c.p.: from ca. 1880. (Anstey, *Voces Populi*, I, 1890.)

no-gooder. A selfish, or a cynical, person given to adverse criticism of the 'do-gooders' and, indeed, all good-workers: coll.: since the late 1950's.

no guts! A derisive exhortation—a 'dare'—to do something dangerous: Londoners': since ca. 1920. Hence also, since ca. 1940, Forces'. Cf. **guts, without,** on p. 363.

no hank! See **hank,** n., in *Dict.*—2. At the end of a speaker's discourse, it = 'I am not deceiving you!'; as a question to the speaker at the end of his discourse, it = 'I hope you're not deceiving me?': Cockneys' s. (from ca. 1870) >, by 1920, coll. Either ex *hanky-panky* or, much less prob., ex **hank,** v. (see *Dict.*).—3. Hence, impudence; insolence: Cockneys': C. 20. 'Nah then, go orf teh bed, you young 'Arry—no 'ank!'

no harm in looking. 'The motto of husbands and boy friends whose eyes wander' (B.P.): esp. Australian: C. 20.

no hat brigade, the. A synonym of **the hatless brigade,** q.v., and indeed more common.

no hide, no Christmas box. An Australian c.p., referring to some specific example of 'hide' (impudence, excessive self-assurance) and meaning 'no hope of that!' or 'I certainly won't!': since ca. 1930. (B.P.)

no-hoper. A hopeless case: Australian coll.: since ca. 1915. Lawson Glassop, *We Were the Rats,* 1944, '"Is he bad?" I asked.—"A no-hoper, Mick. Copped two in the guts."'—2. An outsider, a horse with little, or no, chance: Australian racing s.: since ca. 1919. Lawson Glassop, *Lucky Palmer,* 1949.

no-hoping. Hopeless: Australian: since ca. 1920. 'Argles's youngest brother was a no-hoping ratbag. . . . He was a true bludger' (Dick). Cf. **no-hoper,** 1.

no joke, it's. It is far from being a joking matter: coll.: C. 20.

no joy. See **joy.**

no kidding! Truly; honestly; I'm (you're, etc.) not fooling: Canadian c.p.: adopted, ca. 1910, ex U.S. (Leechman.)

no lets. See **lets, no** (*Dict.*).

'no' man. The opposite of a **yes man** (p. 970): coll.: since ca. 1940.

no matter for. No matter: sol.: from ca. 1870. Nevinson, 1895, 'Some'ow she turned 'erself out neater nor the ordinary, no matter for what she 'ad on.'

no matter for that, you shall carry the rake. 'If you tax a Girl with playing the loose [i.e. being unfaithful], she shall immediately reply, *No matter* . . .,' Anon., *Tyburn's Worthies,* 1722: Essex c.p.: ca. 1715–40. A rural piece of sexual imagery:

'You shall have the raking, the harrowing' (compare the Lucretian *plough the fields of woman*).

no more chance than a snowball in hell, e.g. **he has.** (He has) no chance at all: c.p. C. 20.

no nail! See **nail!, no.—no object.** See **object, no.—no thanks.** See **thanks!, no.**

no rest for the wicked!, occ. preceded by **there's.** A c.p. uttered either by or about someone who isn't wicked at all but is being kept extremely busy: late (? mid) C. 19–20. Partly an ironic jocularity, partly ex several Biblical references.

no second prize! 'A c.p. used when someone makes an unoriginal suggestion' (B.P.): Australian: since ca. 1945.

no show without Punch, often preceded by **there's.** A c.p., applied to—or directed at—a ubiquitous person: mostly lower-middle class: late C. 19–20.

no soap. Not a hope: rhyming s. (on *no hope*): adopted, in early 1930's, ex U.S.

no tell. A frequent—indeed, a c.p.—assurance made by someone asked to keep a secret: since ca. 1945.

no wanchee. 'Pidgin English for "I don't want it, thank you"' (Granville): much used in the Navy, esp. on 'China-side': late C. 19–20.

Noah's ark.—5. A very dull, stupid, fellow: Australian: since ca. 1920. B., 1942, 'A rhyme on "nark".'

nob, n.—10. See **knob,** n., 5.—11. Linking with sense 4 is that of: an expert or a champion in sport, esp. in boxing: since ca. 1810. Thus, 'Several new *nobs* have made their appearance in the pugilistic hemisphere since April, 1818,' *Boxiana,* III, 1821.—12. See **knob,** n., 6.

nob, scuttle a (or **one's**). See **scuttle a nob.**

nob fake. Hair-restorer: showmen's: since ca. 1885. See **fake,** n., 6.

nobbet; esp. *n., round.* To collect the money; esp. in turn: itinerant minstrels' and tavernsingers': from ca. 1860. B. & L. Ex Romany but suggested by **nob,** v., 2.

nobbler, 1 and 3 (p. 566): prob. since ca. 1840. *Sinks,* 1848, defines it as a blow or a thump.—7. Current in England by 1856 (*Sessions,* June 19).

nobby, n. Sense 2: earlier in 'Taffrail'.—4. *Nobbie* (or -*by*), 'used when name of colleague is not known' (*The Evening News,* April 27, 1954): busmen's: since ca. 1940. Ex sense 2 (p. 566).

nobes, like. 'Like nobody's business'—very well indeed: Feb. 1941, *The English Digest,* Hector Bolitho's article; ob. by 1947.

nobody, that devil. A c.p. applied to the person causing an accident, or responsible for an error, when no one admits culpability: C. 20.

Nocky Knight (see *nocky,* 2, on p. 567) perhaps, as Mr Albert Petch has suggested, derives ex '*nocturnal*'.

*nod the nut. See **bow the crumpet** above.

noddy. A '100 h.p. diesel shunter 0–4–0' (*Railway,* 3rd): since late 1950's.

Noggies. Koreans: United Nations troops': ca. 1951–5 in Korea. (*Iddiwah,* July 1953.) Fanciful? Perhaps cf. *noggy* (p. 567). Also *Nogs*: B., 1953.

noggin (p. 567), the head, is 'still heard occ. in Britain and often in Australia' (B.P., 1965).

noise, make a. To break wind audibly: euphemistic coll.: C. 19–20.—2. (Of a horse) to be broken-winded: stables': mid-C. 19–20. Cf. *roar* in same sense.

noise like a —, make a (p. 567), dates from ca. 1908. Baden Powell, in his *Scouting for Boys*, instructed scouts in danger of detection to take cover and make a noise like a (say) thrush; P. G. Wodehouse brought out, with humorous illustrations, a skit on this particular piece of scout-craft, and the phrase took the public fancy. (Communicated by W. McFarlane, Esq.)

noise the edge. See 'Mock-Auction Slang' above.

nok, n. Nose: showmen's: mid-C. 19–20. Neil Bell, *Crocus*, 1936. Adopted direct ex Romany.

non-air or **no-bill.** A non-union railroad employee: Canadian railroadmen's (— 1931).

non-Aryan. See **Aryan.**

non compos. Not in one's right mind: coll.: mid C. 19–20. Elliptical for the legal *non compos mentis.*

non-flam (film). Non-inflammable: filmland: since ca. 1915. Cameron McCabe, *The Face*, 1937.

non-frat. Order(s) forbidding fraternization: Army: 1944–6 (? later). P-G-R. See **frat,** v.

non-nant. See **nant.**

Non-Skid. A Jew: low: C. 20. Richard Llewellyn, *None But the Lonely Heart*, 1943. Rhyming on **Yid**: cf. **tea-pot lid.**

nonch. Completely at one's ease; utterly relaxed: Teddy boys': ca. 1955–60. (Gilderdale, 2.) Ex *nonchalant.*

nong or **nong-nong.** A fool: Australian: since ca. 1945. 'The word *nong* probably Aboriginal; the reduplicated form has been influenced by Aboriginal names and such expressions as *woop-woop*' (Edwin Morrisby, letter of Aug. 30, 1958). Barry Prentice, however, states that *nong* is short for *nong compos*, an Australian assimilation of L. *non compos* and is no more an Aboriginal word than, say, the *Nullarbor* (L. *null' arbor*, no tree, hence, 'treeless') Plain. Cf. **ning-nong** above.

nonsense.—4. A fiasco: since ca. 1938. In, e.g., Peter Cheyney, *The Stars Are Dark*, 1943.—5. A piece of nonsense; an absurdity, e.g. a charmingly outrageous toque or hat; *make a nonsense*, to make nonsense, to make no sense, to mean nothing sensible: since early 1950's.

nonsense, stand the. See **stand . . .**

nonsense I'd like some of it!, if that's. 'A c.p. retort to reproof, for talking smut' (Atkinson): since ca. 1925.

noodles. Nickname for a *noodle*: Society: from ca. 1840; ob. B. & L.

nooky. Sexual intercourse: middle-class and almost polite; certainly a kind of baby-talk: late C. 19–20. Perhaps ex S.E. *nooky*, resembling a nook, characterized by nooks, but probably related to *nug*, v, and *nugging* (p. 573).—2. Hence, a girl, a woman regarded sexually: since ca. 1920.

Noolucks or **Newlicks.** An imaginary person: 1848, *Sinks*; † by 1890. Cf. **cheeks, 3,** and **joe, 10.**

nor an 'un. Thus Blaker: '"Nor an' un"' (this phrase was his masterpiece of thoughtful emphasis), 'nor an' 'un of us knows 'is ears from 'is elbows when it comes to learning' (vbl n.). This clarifies the too brief *Dict.* entry.

*Norfolk dumpling, the. The (practice of) sending convicts to Norfolk Island: Australian c.: ca. 1820–70. B., 1942. Conditions on Norfolk Island (800 miles east of Sydney) were appalling; Norfolk dumplings lie heavy on the stomach—fair

'settlers', as was a term on the Island. (See *Underworld.*)

norgies (mostly a feminine usage); **norgs** and rare **norkers** (both mostly masculine). Female breasts: Australian low: since ca. 1950. The *-g-* forms derive ex *norkers*, itself deriving ex those advertisements for *Norco* butter which show a copiously uddered cow. (B.P.)

norping, vbl. n. See **norp** (*Dict.*).

north about, he's gone. A nautical c.p. referring (from ca. 1860) to a sailor that has met his death by other than drowning. B. & L.

north and south (p. 569). No; prob. thirty years earlier. Augustus Mayhew, *Paved With Gold*, 1857.

north end of a horse going south, the. See **horse's arse.**

North Oxford Gothic. Bogus Gothic architecture: since late 1940's; by 1960, coll.; by 1966, almost S.E. Cf. **Stockbrokers' Tudor** below.

North Pole. Anus: since ca. 1870. Rhyming on *hole.*

North Sea Grunters. A flotilla of frigates doing patrol work in the North Sea during the Napoleonic Wars. Naval. (W. N. Glascock, *Sailors and Saints* (II, 115), 1829.) Moe.

North Sea pheasant. A kipper: nautical: late C. 19–20. Cf. **North Sea Rabbits** (p. 569).

Northern, the. King's Cross railway station: London taxi-drivers' coll.: since ca. 1905. Herbert Hodge, *Cab, Sir?*, 1939. The most important of the lines serving the North; also, it is in North London. Cf. **Western, the,** Paddington station: id.: id. Ibid.

Northern tike. See **Yorkshire tike** (*Dict.*).

northwester. A drink, a glass, of potent liquor: Naval: 1830, Fredk Marryat, *The King's Own* (p. 141 of the 1896 edition); app. † by ca. 1900. Moe.

Norwegian Towns. 'Hobson-Jobsoned' by the Army in 1940–1: Bergen > *Brummagem*; Lillehammer, *Littlehampton*; Oslo, *Oh-slow*; Steinkier, *Stinker.*

nose, n.—4. *The nose* = the front of a surfing-board: Australian surfers' coll.: since ca. 1950.

nose, v.—5. To hit (someone) on the nose: low: 1885, M. Davitt, *A Prison Diary*; by 1920, ob.; by 1940, virtually †.

nose, get up one's. To upset, annoy, irritate, render 'touchy'; since ca. 1935. Cf. **snuff, give** (p. 796).

nose, make a long. See **long nose, make a** (*Dict.*).

nose, on the.—2. Objectionable; no good: Australian: C. 20. B., 1942. Ex *have a nose on*, to dislike, bear a grudge against (someone): Australian: ca. 1860–1920: 'Tom Collins', *Such Is Life*, 1903.—3. Smelly: Australian: since ca. 1910. Kylie Tennant, *Lost Haven*, 1947; B., 1953.

nose and chin.—3. A win (on, e.g., the horses): bookmakers' rhyming s.: C. 20. Franklyn, *Rhyming.*

nose-ender, 1. Also in nuance 'a fall on one's nose; a punch that causes one to fall thus': 1901, Jerome Caminada, *Twenty-Five Years of Detective Life*, vol. II.

nose is bleeding, your. See **your nose is bleeding.**

nose is dirty, one's. See 'Tavern terms', § 2.

nose-scratch or **peek-a-boo.** A very sketchy salute: Services: since ca. 1938. H. & P.

*nosegent. See nose-gent. (*Dict.*)

noser-my-knacker. As *nosey-me-knacker* in Mayhew, I, 1851.

nosey (or nosy), n., esp. in *take a nosey around*, to take a look around, as a detective does at the scene of a crime: since ca. 1950. Ex nosey, adj. (p. 571); perhaps influenced by mosey (p. 533).

nosh, n. See the next. Among beatniks, this sense arose ca. 1958. (Anderson.) Orig., in Yiddish, of food eaten between meals.

nosh, v. To acquire furtively: children's: C. 19-20. (Atkinson.) Origin? Perhaps ex Ger. *naschen*, to eat on the sly, to nibble secretly; cf. Ger. *Nascherei*, a nibbling of dainties on the sly. Also spelt *nash*.—Hence, *nosher*, one who samples food before buying; a greedy person: mid C. 19-20. If ex German, it comes via Yiddish; 'In the 1960's this verb seems to have come to mean "to eat heartily and quite openly". I have frequently heard it used in this sense by radio comedians. As a noun, it seems now to mean just "food", "a meal"' (H. R. Spencer, communication of Sept. 17, 1965).

Nosh is properly 'to sample desirable food voluptuously, surreptitiously. . . . One eats breakfast or lunch, but one noshes in between': Guy Deghy, 'Leave Me the Noshers' in *The Observer*, Nov. 3, 1957. He also notes the frequent *noshing* used as noun.

nosh down. To eat a meal: beatniks': since ca. 1959. (Anderson.) Cf. nosh, v., above.

nosh-up. A bout of eating; a banquet: since ca. 1959. Ex nosh, v., above.

nosy, n. See nosey above.

not a bone in the truck, as in 'Ten o'clock, and not a bone in the truck', expressive of timewasting during working-hours: ? Australian and ? factories': C. 20.

not a heel! A mainly Cockney c.p. of 1880-1913. Edwin Pugh, *Harry the Cockney*, 1912, '"Seen anybody?" "Not a soul. And you?" "Not a 'eel." "That's odd."'

not a sausage. Not a 'plane in the sky; no luck: R.A.F.: since 1940. H. & P. Ex the phrase recorded as *sausage, not to have a.*

not a word to the vicar! 'Mum's the word'—'Keep it quiet!': c.p.: since ca. 1925; by 1966, slightly ob. (Richard Merry.)

not barmy!, let me out—I'm; also let me out —I'm barmy! A Forces' pantomimic c.p., expressing desire to be rid of service restrictions: 1939-45.

not half a one. A 'card' or 'character' ('You're not half a one!'): C. 20.

not *her—him—me—you*, it (just) isn't or wasn't. It doesn't—or didn't—truly suit her (etc.); it isn't or wasn't in character: c.p.: since ca. 1956. Apparently it originated in the smart fashion shops of Society.

not in these boots (or trousers)! See boots!, not in these in *Dict.*

not lost for it. 'Not at a disadvantage for lack of objective cheek. If Jack borrows Tony's bike without asking, he's *not lost for it*' (Franklin): Cockney: since late 1940's.

not me, Chief, I'm radar (or asdics or gunnery or . . .). A c.p. 'used by a rating when given to do something not connected with his usual job, or if volunteers are asked for' (Wilfred Granville, Nov. 22, 1962): Naval: since ca. 1946.

not much frocks. Socks: rhyming s. of ca. 1880-1910. Pugh (2): 'Never doin' no honest work out o' quod from the time when they was in not much frocks an' nickin' the baby's milk to when their poor ole shakin' legs got them lagged on the kinchin lay.'

not much you wouldn't! You certainly would: c.p. (notably Canadian): since the late 1930's. (Leechman.) Cf. *not half* (p. 571) and *much!* (above).

not nominated. Unlikely to win or to succeed: Aus.: since ca. 1930. (B., 1959.) Ex horseracing.

not of this world. 'Superlative in either direction, of both people and things. About 15 years ago [say 1947-48] it was *the* thing to say; now [1962] it is used with restraint' (Julian Franklyn). It forms the original of out of this world, q.v. below.

not off. '. . . A given horse was not intended to win'—cf. not meant on p. 571—'on a given occasion. When you hear that so and so'—a horse—'is or was "*not off*", "*not fancied*", "*on the arm*", "*having an easy*", or simply "*strong*". . .' (John Lawrence, in *The Sunday Telegraph*, Aug. 13, 1961): racing: prob. since ca. 1920.

not on your Nannie (or -ny) or nannie (or -y)! Not on your life!: Anglo-Irish: since ca. 1950. 'A very common expression in Dublin is "not on your Nannie!" Has this the same origin as "not on your Nellie"?': Dr Alan Bliss in letter of Dec. 8, 1961. Julian Franklyn thinks that *Nannie* is an arbitrary alteration of Nellie.

not on your Nellie! Not on your life: an intensive tag: since ca. 1940. (Norman.) Short for *Nellie Duff!* . . .

not Pygmalion likely! - Not at all likely; certainly not!; cultured c.p.: since 1912, when G. B. Shaw's *Pygmalion* appeared, containing that so delightfully shocking phrase, *not bloody likely!*

not quite. Mentally deficient: mostly Australian: since ca. 1920. For '*not quite* all there'. (B.P.)

not quite quite. Not quite suitable, respectable, moral, first-class: Society: from ca. 1923.

not selling! See I'll bite.

not sixteen annas to the rupee is the Regular Army version (late C. 19-20) of the more usual not sixteen ounces to the pound, not quite right in the head; from ca. 1870. *The Observer*, Sept. 20, 1936.

not so much lip! Be less impudent!: mid-C. 19-20.

not the full pound is the Australian version of shillings in the pound (below): since ca. 1920.

not to be at home. See die, to.

not to go much on (something). Not to like, not to be keen on, it: coll.: since ca. 1920.

not to know if one's coming or going. To be perplexed, bemused, befuddled or ignorant of what is happening around one: C. 20: coll. >, by 1945, familiar S.E.

not to worry! Don't worry; there's nothing to worry about: Services': C. 20. Suddenly, in 1957-8, it began to be generally and widely used. The Services based it upon a Maltese analogy; Italian scholars (and others) on, e.g., Italian *non tormentarsi*: I suggest that it merely truncates 'You are *not to worry*'—You mustn't worry, or There's nothing to worry you. On Nov. 5, 1967, Wilfred Granville writes: 'It is old hat. I first heard it, *ad nauseam*, in Admiralty about ten or twelve years ago when I was researching the R.N.V.R. book.' Peter Sanders tells me that the phrase was current in the War Office and Ministry of Defence at the time of the Korean War (1951). Colonel A. C. T. White, V.C., suggests that it may, in form, have been influenced by such French phrases as *ce n'est pas*—colloquially *c'est pas—à refuser*; but is it not rather from Italian *non tormentarsi*, don't worry!, and brought to England by Army officers returning from the Italian campaign, and British occupation of Italy, 1944–45? Dr Douglas Leechman thinks it goes back to ca. 1935—which does not, of course, rule out an Italian origination.

not today, baker! A c.p., refusing an offer or a suggestion: Canadian: since ca. 1945. Connoting 'Oh, no! you don't catch me like that!' (Leechman.)

not to-night, Josephine! A c.p. used—or said to be used—by husbands, lovers, boy friends, refusing a request for sexual intercourse: late C. 19–20. Apocryphally attributed to Napoleon refusing Josephine.—2. Hence, in other circumstances, and regardless of sex; since ca. 1920. 'Care for a drink?'—'Not to-night Josephine.' (B.P.) Hence the loose variant *not to-day, Josephine!*, a c.p. of emphatic refusal.

not up. Inferior; bad, very poor in quality: Australian: since ca. 1930. B., 1943. 'Not up to standard.'

not worth a cracker. Worthless, valueless: Aus. coll.: C. 20. Also *not worth a cupful of cold water* or . . . *a pinch of shit.* (B., 1959.)

notch.—2. A pocket: Australian low: C. 20. B. 1942.

note, n.—2. A state of affairs; a happening: since ca. 1925. James Curtis, *You're in the Racket Too*, 1937, 'It would be a hell of a note if he was to be knocked off [i.e. arrested] to-night.' Ex music. —3. A £1 note; hence, the sum of £1: (esp. Australian) coll.: since ca. 1870. 'Tom Collins', *Such Is Life*, 1903.

nothing!, you can always pick up. See **you can** . . .

nothing below the waist. A c.p., referring to girls permitting breast-fondling but no other intimacies: mostly Australian: C. 20.

nothing for nothing and very little for tuppence-ha'penny, often preceded by **you get.** A c.p., originated by George Bernard Shaw: since ca. 1910.

nothing on the clock. Of an aircraft that is out of control: R.A.F.: since ca. 1938.

nothing startling, adj. (predicative only). Unimpressive: coll.: C. 20. 'Oh, it's nothing startling.'

notice to quit (p. 572). To *receive a notice to quit*, 'be destined to die shortly': 1821, Pierce Egan, *Life in London.*

noticing, adj. Given to noticing everything; observant (and censorious): non-cultured coll.: C. 20. (Raymond Postgate, *Verdict of Twelve*, 1940.)

notionable. Sensible: shrewd: coll., mostly Cockneys': from ca. 1890. Pugh, 'Not a notionable idea to his conversation from beginning to end.' Contrast the Wiltshire *notionable*, having an inclination for something.

Nots and Dots, or Notts and Dotts. Nottingham (Notts) and Derby regiments: Army: late C. 19–20.

nought —. (In) the year nineteen hundred and (any figure from 1 to 9 inclusive): coll.: from 1902 or perhaps 1903. 'Taffrail', 'The little 3000-ton

Britisher, built in "nought five", carried only twelve 4-inch quickfirers.'

nought feet, at. (Of flying) very low: R.A.F. coll.: 1939–45.

nous, 1 (p. 572): academic s. >, by 1890, S.E.

nouvelle. New; stylish: smart society: ca. 1815–25. Passim in *Boxiana*, 1818–24; castigated by Jon Bee in 1823. An aping of the French *nouveau, nouvel, nouvelle*, new.

November, the. The Manchester November Handicap: racing coll.: C. 20.

now I've seen everything! An ironical, usu. good-natured c.p. of mock admiration or wonder: since the early 1950's. Cf. **this I must hear** (or **see**).

now, Mrs Rowbottom, *if* **you please!** I'm ready when you are: a Canadian c.p.: since ca. 1930. Leechman, 'Of anecdotal origin.'

now she knows. See **knows all about it.**

now then! Usually said sharply to a child one has just struck: Cockney coll.: since ca. 1860.

now then, me lucky lads! A workman's ironic c.p. in ref. to work: since ca. 1910. Ex the showmen's, three-card trickers', racing tipsters' invitation.

now what have you (got) to say for yourself? A c.p. of jocular greeting: since ca. 1920.

now you're asking! A variant of 'That's asking!': ca. 1900–15. Leonard Merrick, *Peggy Harper*, 1911.

nowler. A sheep that, its fleece covered with burrs and dirt, is hard to shear: Australian shearers': since ca. 1910. (B., 1943.) Origin? Perhaps *'n'owler = an 'owler = a howler*, a sheep that complains at the unavoidable tugging. (Julian Franklyn's suggestion.)

Nozmo. 'Inevitable' nickname for men surnamed King: C. 20. Ex a public character. (Atkinson.) Ultimately from '*No Smo-king*'.

nozzer; usually in pl. A new entry (i.e. a recruit) at Shotley Barracks (H.M.S. *Ganges*): Naval: C. 20. Granville. Ex the frequency of his 'No, Sir'?

nubbies. Female breasts: Australian low: late C. 19–20.

nucloid. 'Nucloids: Ships of the Reserve in peacetime which carry only a nucleus crew,' Granville: Naval: since ca. 1910.

nuddy, in the. Naked: Australian: since ca. 1945. (B., 1953.) Ex 'in the *nude*'.

nudged. '(Of a ship) slightly damaged by bomb shell or torpedo' (B., 1934): Australian Naval: 1940–5. By meiosis. 'In "The Dam Busters" (1951), Paul Brickhill quotes W/Cdr Tait (C.O. 617 Squadron) as saying, when returning from the raid that finally sank the "Tirpitz": "We gave her a hell of a nudge, anyway"' (H. R. Spencer).

nugget, n. —4. A very attractive girl, of whom it is hoped that she is not 'as good as gold': Australian: since ca. 1925. (B., 1943.)

number. —2. A person: adopted, ca. 1944, from U.S. servicemen. (Ngaio Marsh, *Swing, Brother Swing*, 1949.) Perhaps ex sense 1 (p. 573). —3. A dress: since ca. 1955. 'She put on that little black number.'

number, have (someone's). To have someone sized up or potentially mastered: since ca. 1910. Ex telephony.

number, make one's. See **make one's number.**

number, opposite. See **opposite number.**

number-catcher. A checker of goods wagons: railwaymen's: since ca. 1920. (*Railway.*)

number dummy, n. grabber. A yard clerk: Canadian railroadmen's (— 1931). —2. To report for duty: Services, mostly officers': 1939 +. (P-G-R.)

number nine—2. (*Number nines.*) Prunes: since ca. 1917. Reputed to be purgative—as, indeed, they are.

number one. Sense 4 is also used as a nickname: witness 'Taffrail'. See quotation at pilot in Addenda.—9. A boat owned by the boatman that works it: canal-men's: late C. 19–20. L. T. C. Bolt, *Narrow Boat*, 1944. Cf. senses 4 and esp. 1.

number one—ten—ninety-nine. 'The various degrees in the state of a soldier's feelings in Korea are seldom expressed in the well-worn favourites of World War II. He is rarely "browned off", "cheesed" or "brassed". No, sir. He's just "number one" to "number ten" and occasionally he may be "number ninety-nine" or "number hava no"' (*Iddiwah*, July 1953): United Nations troops fighting in the Korean War of the 1950's. For *hava no*, see that entry above.

number one piecee, adj. First Class: pidgin English: late C. 19–20. Used by the Navy, esp. on 'China-side'. Granville. Cf. **number one chow-chow** (p. 574).

number ones (p. 574): coll., not s., recorded earlier in Fredk Marryat, *Frank Mildmay*, 1829. Moe.

number seventeens. 'Any unofficial rig [clothing] of the day, for dirty work (Patrol Service slang),' Granville: Naval: 1940 +. Ironic, in ref. to the numbers designating the various official 'rigs' for sailors.

number(-)snatcher. A 'checker of goods wagons' (*Railway*, 3rd): C. 20.

number three. Sexual relief, whether normal or self-induced: low: C. 20. A development ex *number one*, sense 2, and *number two*, sense 1, both on p. 574.

numbers, the. The Red Lamp district of Dunkirk: Army: 1914–18.

number's still wet. See your . . .

nunk, nothing; **sunk,** something: Cockney: C. 20. Gordon Harker in *The Evening News*, March 31, 1938, 'I was familiar with suthink and som'ink, but "sunk for nunk" was a new one on me.' Strictly *n'unk* and *s'unk*, with a glottal stop.

nunky.—3. Also, a pawnbroker, whether Jewish or not: mostly Cockneys': C. 20.

nursemaid. 'A long-distance escort for bombers,' Jackson: R.A.F.: 1939 +.

nursery.—3. A training station for flying personnel: R.A.F. coll.: since ca. 1935. H. & P. Ex cricket nurseries.

nursery slopes, 'the easy targets allotted to beginners on bombing tests' (H. & P.). Ex skiing.—2. Hence (the singular is used in both 1 and 2), any easy target: like sense 1, R.A.F.: since ca. 1939.

nursing, n. An exceptionally slow collecting of fares: London busmen's: since ca. 1920.

nursing it. (Of a pregnant woman) holding her arms folded over her belly: lower-classes' col.: C. 20.

nurtle. Sexual intercourse: Australian low: C. 20. B., 1942. Cf. **myrtle.**

nut, n.—11. Rent for stall or side-show or stand at a fair: Canadian carnival s.: C. 20. Adopted from U.S.—12. A horse difficult to break in: Australian rural: late C. 19–20. Ex senses 4, 5

(p. 574). For 11 (especially) and probably for 12 and 4 (p. 574), note Alexander McQueen's explanation: 'Because rent is a nut to be cracked (paid) before reaching kernel (income).'—13. A 'nut case' (a mental case): since ca. 1944.

nut, v.—3. To butt (someone) with the head: public-house: since ca. 1920. *The Evening News*, Nov. 22, 1946.—4. To think, to 'use one's nut': Australian: C. 20. Dal Stivens, *Jimmy Brockett*, 1951, 'I did a bit of hard nutting.'

nut, give (someone) **the.** '"That's right, Paddy, give him the nut!" I was trying to pull his head back by the hair to hit him in the face with my head.' Anglo-Irish: C. 20. Also in Brendan Behan, *Borstal Boy*, 1958, is the variant **give** (him) **the loaf of bread.** Cf. **nut,** v., 3, above.

nut case. A mental case or patient (a 'nut'): adopted, ca. 1959, ex U.S. Xenia Field, *Under Lock and Key*, 1963, '"I'm not a nut case."'

nut on, put the, is the purely English equivalent of **nut, give the,** above: since ca. 1920. (Petch.)

nut out. To devise: Australian: since late 1930's. Ex *nut*, n., 1 and 2 (p. 574). D'Arcy Niland, 1955. Lit., 'to think out' (Culotta).

nut(-)splitter. A machinist: Canadian railroadmen's (— 1931).

nuthouse. A hospital, a wing, a ward set aside for the (temporarily) insane; an asylum for the insane: adopted, ca. 1925, from U.S. 'They're *nuts!*' Norman Lindsay, *Saturdee*, 1933, '"Whose old Aunt Beadle had to go to the nut-house?" roared Bill.'

Nuthouse, the. The R.N. Auxiliary Hospital at Barrow Gurney: Naval: 1939–45. Ex preceding.

nutmeg-grater. A beard: 1948, *Sinks*; † by 1900.

nuts! Nonsense: Canadian: adopted, ca. 1940, ex U.S. Partly a euphemism for *balls* (p. 29).

nuts and bolts; nuts and bolts with awning. Resp., a stew; a meat pie: Naval: C. 20. Granville.

nuts on, dead (p. 575): 1890 in Australia. Sidney J. Baker (letter).

nutter. A crazy person: low: since ca. 1945. (Norman.) 'Off one's *nut*' or head. Since ca. 1961, no longer low, but merely an alternative to **nut case** (above). Moreover, the 'low' tone of the word prob. arose from the London *milieu* to which it filtered from the Merseyside schoolchildren and teenagers. (See, e.g., *Woman*, Aug. 28, 1965.)

nutty, n. 'Chocolate, whether or not it contains nuts,' Granville: Naval: since ca. 1930. Ex senses 4 and 5 of the adj.—see p. 575.—2. Hence, candied sweets in general, as in 'the nutty ration': Naval: since ca. 1935.

nutty as a fruitcake. Insane: Canadian (probably from U.S.): since the 1930's. Cf. *nutty*, 2 (p. 575). Hence, since ca. 1943, English—partly via U.S. servicemen.

nutty-nutty. See 'Prisoner-of-War Slang', 11.

nymph. A charwoman: Haileybury: since ca. 1870. Marples. Ironic.

[**nymph of delight.** See 'Harlots'; either coll. or, more prob., S.E.]

nymph of the pave (p. 575) appears in the 1851 Census Return for Neithrop in Banbury, 'relating to the Occupation of two ladies lodging in a Beer House'. (With thanks to Mr Noel Blakiston.)

nympho. A nymphomaniac: since ca. 1910.

O

O. See entry **C—K—M—O.**

-o.—4. Ex sense 3 (p. 576) comes the Australian, esp. the Sydneyites', use of this ending, not only in, e.g., *afto* but also in such place-names as *Darlo* and *Kenso*. In June 1963 Mr Barry Prentice writes, 'We seem to have gone off "-y, -ie" except for women's terms. *Wharfie*, however, is very much alive.'

o or **O,** overseer, is recorded earlier in B. & L.

O.B. A term common, since ca. 1885, at several Public Schools. Ian Hay, *Housemaster*, 1936, 'The non-resident Staff—pithily described by the School as the O.B.'s, or Outside Bugs.'

O.C. Socks. A man detailed to collect the platoon's socks: Army: C. 20. Cf. **O.C. Grease** (p. 576).

O.D. Earlier recorded in 'Taffrail'.

*O for October. A swindle worked at races and at country fairs ca. 1870. Binstead.

O.K. To the *Dict.* entry it is pertinent to add the fact that Alfred Glanville Vance, 'the great Vance' of the music-halls (from the middle sixties to the late eighties, C. 19), used to sing:

The Stilton, sir, the cheese, the O.K. thing to do,
On Sunday afternoon, is to toddle to the Zoo.
Week-days may do for Cads, but not for me and you;
So dress'd right down the road, we show them who is who.

The chorus ran thus:

The walking in the Zoo—
Walking in the Zoo—
The O.K. thing on Sunday is the walking in the Zoo.

The expression was taken to England by Artemus Ward and was well acclimatized by 1880 at the latest. Dr Allen Walker Read, 'The Evidence on "O.K."'—in *The Saturday Review of Literature,* July 19, 1941, has conclusively dated it back to 1840 and to a semi-secret political society known as 'The Democratic O.K.', wherein the letters O.K. are used as a cabalistic symbol, perhaps for 'Old Kinderhook', the nickname of Martin Van Buren.

O.K. sheaf! All right!: Australian c.p.: since ca. 1930. B., 1942. 'A.N.S.W. advertising slogan that has won some currency. From Tooth's Sheaf Stout.' With a pun on *O.K.*, *chief*, although, in sense, it constitutes a mere elaboration of *O.K.*

O my Gawd. See **my Gawd.**

O.P.—5. Other people's: jocular coll.: C. 20. Esp. a borrowed cigarette: B., 1959. (Cf. **O.P.T.** on p. 577.)

O.P.B. Choice cigarette-ends: Australian: since ca. 1920. B., 1942, 'Old Picked Bumpers'. See **bumper,** 5. But also 'other *p*eople's *b*utts' or

cigarette-butts garnered from ash-trays: since ca. 1910. Cf. *kerbstone mixture.*

O.R.P.H.—orph! Off (you go)!; not worth considering (see **off,** 2, 3, in *Dict.*): lower-class c.p. of C. 20; slightly ob. W. L. George, *The Making of an Englishman,* 1914.

O.T., the. The overland telegraph, from Adelaide to Port Darwin: Australian coll.: since ca. 1930. B., 1942.

oak and ash. Cash: theatrical rhyming s.: C. 20. (Franklyn, *Rhyming.*)

oakie-doke is an occ. variant of **okey-doke.**

oakum-boy, when Adam was an. See **when Adam . . .** in *Dict.*

oats, have one's (p. 577), is also applied to women, as in 'Chrissie will not get her oats': George Simms, *Sleep No More,* 1967.

oats for the donkey. Money: motor trade: since ca. 1910. Rhyming (or almost).

oats from (a woman), **get ones.** To coït with: Australian: C. 20. B., 1942. Cf. **oats, feel one's** in *Dict.*

ob.—2. An objection: policemen's: C. 20. Grierson Dickson, *Design for Treason,* 1937.—3. An observation car, esp. on the Transcontinental: Australian: since ca. 1945. (Eric North, *Nobody Stops Me,* 1960.)

Obadiah.—2. A fire: rhyming s.: C. 20. Cf. **Jeremiah** (*Dict.*).

obie man. 'The obie man read obituaries. (The funeral will be at Wood Green on Tuesday and the house will be empty)': James Barlow, *The Burden of Proof,* 1968: c. and low s.: since ca. 1920.

object, no. E.g. 'distance no object' and, esp., 'price no object': catachrestic when = 'no obstacle' or 'not an objection'; mid-C. 19–20. The correct sense 'not a thing aimed at or considered important' has been vitiated by confusion with *no objection.*

oblige.—2. (Of a charwoman) to work for: charwomen's coll.: late C. 19–20. 'The lady I "oblige".'—3. (Of a woman) to make herself sexually available to: coll.: C. 20. 'She soon found that she'd never get promoted unless she were willing to oblige her boss.' (B.P.)

oboe, not to know one's brass (or **bass**) **from one's.** See **ears from one's elbow** above.

obs and sols. See **ob and sol** (*Dict.*).

obscene. Objectionable: upper classes': from ca. 1933. Nicholas Blake, *Thou Shell of Death,* 1936, '[At Christmastide] the shop windows are piled with that diversity of obscene knick-knacks' —actually of impeccable respectability—'which nothing but the spirit of universal goodwill could surely tolerate.'

observatory. The astrodome of an aircraft: R.A.F.: since ca. 1938. Jackson, '. . . Through which the navigator takes the observations of the stars'.

obstets. Obstetrics: nurses' and medical students': C. 20.

obstropulous occurs earlier in *Sessions*, 1736.

occabot. Earlier in Mayhew, I, 1851.

[Occupational names. Ned Ward, in 1700–24, has the following s. or coll. terms in addition to those at 'Constables', q.v.: sailors are *tar* or *lubber* (both, 1703); soldiers, *red-coat* (1703); fishmongers, *pull-guts* or *strip-eel* (both in 1700); parsons, *hum-drum* (1709), *pulpit-cackler* (1709 and *tubster* (1712), while Quakers are *Aminadab* (1709); scavengers are *Tom-Turd-man* (1703); *Tower-rook* (1703), a guide to the Tower; *Crispin* (1703), a cobbler—prob. always S.E.; a cook, *lick-fingers* (1703)—prob. S.E.; a butcher, *sheep-biter* (1703); *slab-dab*, a glover (1703); *Essedartus* (1703; rare), a coachman; a fiddler is a *cat-gut scraper* (1700); an astrologer, *hocus-pocus* (1703). Aldermen are *lob-cocks* (1703). Matthews.]

Occupied Territory, the. See **Resistance, the.**

ocean-dust. Salt: Naval: C. 20, but rare before 1914.

ocean-going grocers. 'Members of the N.A.A.F.I. staffs in H.M. Ships': Naval: 1939 +. Granville.

ocean rambler. A herring; a sardine: proletarian: C. 20. Cf. **ocean wanderers** in *Dict*.

Ocean Swell, the. Admiral Sir Bertram Ramsay (C. in C., Allied Naval Forces, invasion of France, June 1944): Naval officers': since ca. 1914. Ex his sartorial 'smartness'.

octu. An Officer Cadet's Training Unit: Services' coll.: 1939 + . Partridge, 1945.

octy. An octopus: Australian: since ca. 1925. (B., 1953.)

***odd**, n. A police detective: c.: since ca. 1935. Hence, *odd(-)lot*, a police car. (Both in Norman.) —2. A police station: c.: since ca. 1935. (Norman.)

odd, adj. Homosexual: partly euphemistic, partly coll.: ca. 1890–1940, then increasingly obsolescent. It occurs in, e.g., Compton Mackenzie, *Thin Ice*, 1956.

odd-ball, n., hence also adj. (An) eccentric: adopted, ca. 1950, ex U.S. Ex certain games, ? esp. golf.—2. (Often written *oddball*.) A—usu. male—homosexual: since ca. 1955.

odd bods and sods. Miscellaneous persons: Australian since ca. 1945. (B.P.) Cf. **odds and sods** on p. 579.

odd-come-shortly (p. 579). The unit is *one of these odd-come-shortlies*; the definition is 'one day soon'. Semantically: *one of these odd days shortly to come*, where *odd* = unspecified or, perhaps, unexpected.

odd-trick man. A hanger-on, for profit, at auctions: auctioneers': mid-C. 19–20. James Greenwood, *In Strange Company*, 1873. Ex cardplaying.

oddie; oddy is rare. A halfpenny: Australian: C. 20. Ex 'the *odd* halfpenny' in, e.g., 9½d.

odds. Odd volumes: publishers' and booksellers' coll.: late C. 19–20.

odds?, what's the (p. 579). App. earliest as *what odds?*: 1826, *Sessions*, 'I asked Jackson whose they were—he said, "What odds; they are mine."'

odds and sods.—3. In the Navy—since ca. 1925 —it means '"Hoi polloi"; the rank and file' (Granville).—4. Service personnel falling outside the main group or classification; hence esp. in

religion neither C. of E. nor Catholic, i.e. Other denominations, *O.D.'s*, from which the phrase is said to be derived.

odds it. To avoid it: low: since ca. 1945. (Norman.) Perhaps ex 'to bet against the odds'.

odds-on, n. An odds-on favourite: Australian racecourse coll.: C. 20. B., 1942.

odour. Either a misapprehension of, or a pun on, *eau-de*, q.v. at **eau-de-Cologne** above: C. 20. (Franklyn 2nd.)

ods. Policemen; the police. Teddy boys': since ca. 1948. (*The Observer*, March 1 1959.) Ex *odd*, n.

Odtaa. As comment or exclamation, it is a cultured c.p.—one damned thing after another: since publication of John Masefield's novel, *Odtaa*, 1926.

of omitted. A Canadian coll., general only since ca. 1945. 'Here, it's never "a new type of engine" but "a new type engine."' "He's just bought a new type lawn-mower"' (Leechman). The second example shows how the usage may have originated. 'Prob. U.S.–Jewish origin. "A nice type feller" and "A piece candy" are typical immigrant Jewish locutions, some of which . . . have passed into American speech (chiefly) through Jews in the entertainment industry' (Robert Clairborne, Aug. 31, 1966).

off, n. Start of a horse-race: sporting coll.: late C. 19–20. 'You can bet, on the course, right up to the off.' Ex the cry 'They're *off*'.

off-beat. Unconventional, but not unique nor unaccepted; (slightly) macabre: adopted, orig. by highbrows, ca. 1960 ex U.S. Cf. quotation at **shoe-string**, 2, below.

off caps! 'When naming anyone of eminence in the Navy or a departed shipmate, *off caps* is sometimes murmured' (P-G-R.): c.p.: C. 20.

off its feet. See **feet, off its.**

off of (p. 580); prob. since late C. 18 (J. Wight, *Mornings at Bow Street*, 1824).

off one's dot. See **dot, off one's** both in *Dict*. and in Addenda.

off one's eggs. See **eggs, off one's**, above.

off one's kadoova. See **kadoova**. In 1959, B. adduces also *off one's pannikin—off one's tile—off one's top*. Note also **mad as a cut snake** (and its synonyms) above.

off one's saucer. Off one's head: Australian: since ca. 1930. (B., 1943.)

off the back. A synonym of *dropped* handlebars, cyclists': since ca. 1945.

off the beam. See **beam** . . .

offer (someone) **out.** To challenge to a fight: Australian: late C. 19–20. B., 1942.

office, n., 3 (p. 580). Still in use, as, e.g., in *Their Finest Hour*, 1940, and Jackson, 1943, although Sgt-Pilot F. Rhodes, in letter of Sept. 20, 1942, remarks, 'This seems to be dying'.

Office, the. The Marble Arch public convenience: C. 20. A correspondent (1946) writes, 'Hyde Park orators, who are not allowed to take collections, sometimes say: "If anyone would like to speak to me after the meeting, they can see me at my office."'

office boy. A Pay Lieutenant acting as Assistant Secretary in the Captain's office: Naval: since ca. 1947.

officiate. To intrude, butt in: Christ's Hospital: C. 20. Marples. I.e. the S.E. *officiate*, but with the sense of 'to be officious'.

offsider.—4. A hanger-on: Aus.: since ca. 1925. (B., 1959.) Ex sense 1 on p. 580.

often trod but never laid. (Of women) often 'mauled' but never 'slept' with: c.p.: since late 1940's. *Trod* for '*trodden* on'; *lay* to copulate with.

ogg or og (p. 580). Also Australian. Baker.— 2. Usually in pl.: stones of fruit; e.g., *cherry-oggs*: non-aristocratic: mid-C. 19–20. Origin?

oggin, the; occ., hoggin. The sea: Naval (lower-deck): C. 20. Granville. The origin is obscure: perhaps a shortening of S.E. *noggin*, with a prompting by (the) drink; if *oggin* merely = unaspirated *hoggin*, then the semantics may be that, as hogs wallow, so do some ships.—2. Hence, a canal: spivs': since late 1940's. Cf. quotation at peep, n., below.

oggy. See tiddy-oggy.

Oggyland. Cornwall: Naval: C. 20. 'The home of the *tiddy-oggy*, beloved of the Janners in depot at Guzz' (Granville, Nov. 22, 1962). Cf. tiddy-oggy below and Jan, 2, above, and Guz (p. 364).

Ogopogo. 'A mythical lake-dwelling monster (cf. Loch Ness) believed (?) to inhabit Okanagan Lake in the southern interior of British Columbia' (Leechman): Canadian coll. or rather, folk-lore: late C. 19–20. The name is fanciful: cf. *Cadborosaurus*.

ogo-pogoing. 'Looking for unidentified aircraft,' H. & P.: R.A.F.: 1942–3, then ob. Fanciful, perhaps on '*go poking* about'. 'In the early 1920's there was a toy called the pogo-stick, as popular in its day as the hula-hoop in the 1950's. It was a straight stick, with foot-rests across the bottom end, and had a ferule embodying a strong spring. On it the expert could proceed in a series of kangaroo hops for considerable distances, gripping the stick with his (or her) knees. It somewhat resembled the old aircraft joystick, and may be the basis of this word. Such a mission, going up probably to no purpose, and then coming down again, might well suggest the hopping action of this toy.' (H. R. Spencer, Sept. 17, 1965.)

ogwash, i.e. hogwash. A variant of oggin, the sea, the ocean: Naval (lower-deck): C. 20. Recorded by *The Weekly Telegraph*, Nov. 1942. Also—prob. via the Fleet Air Arm—R.A.F.: since ca. 1945.

oh, after you! That'll do!; stop talking!: tailors' c.p.: from ca. 1870. B. & L. Ironic.

oh, come on, be a devil! See be a devil!

oh, dummy! Nonsense!; humbug!: tailors' c.p.: from ca. 1860. Ibid.

oh, Miss Weston. A c.p., expressing disapproval of strong language: Naval: since ca. 1910. 'Dame Agnes Weston was a great stickler for propriety' (P-G-R). Cf. *my oath, Miss Weston!* on p. 547.

oh, mummy! buy me one of those! A c.p. that, mostly Canadian and dating since ca. 1920, recalls the much older *one of those, I (really) must have* (p. 589). Leechman.

oh, my dear. Beer: rhyming s.: C. 20; since ca. 1950, ob. (Franklyn, *Rhyming*.)

oh, my Gawd. See my Gawd.

oh, oh, Antonio! A c.p. of ca. 1912–30. Ex the once famous song.

oh, swallow yourself! Hold your tongue!: don't bother!: proletarian: from ca. 1875; ob. B. & L.

oh, wouldn't it be loverlee! A teenagers' and shop- and office-girls' c.p. of 1958–9. Ex the title of one of Eliza Doolittle's songs, in *My Fair Lady*. (Gilderdale.)

oi for *i* occurs in Cockney (and illiterate American). Edwin Pugh, in *A Street in Suburbia*, 1895, has *noight, moight, woipe, woife*, etc.

oick or oik. A townee; a cad: at certain Public Schools in the North and the Midlands: late C. 19–20. See oickman and hoick, v., 4, in *Dict*.

oil, n., 4. By 1946, more Australian than New Zealand: Sidney J. Baker, letter.—7. Tea: Army: since ca. 1930. 'Due to the fat which often appears on top' (H. & P.).

oil, v.—2. V.i., to toady: Harrow School: late C. 19–20. In C. 20, also at Marlborough College. Lunn. Cf. oil up to, 2, and the corresponding sense of grease: qq.v. in the *Dict*.—3. To act in an underhand way; to obtain unfairly: Rugby School: from ca. 1880. Hence, oiler, one who does this.—4. To evade; an evasion: Winchester: late C. 19–20.—5. (Also *oil in*) to intrude: Oundle: 1930 + . Marples.—6. See 'Stonyhurst'.

oil, on the. On a drinking bout: Army: C. 20. Cf. oiled (p. 581).

oil out. To slip out or away: preparatory-schoolboys': from ca. 1920. Nicholas Blake, *A Question of Proof*, 1935.

oil-rag.—2. A fitter's mate: engineering trade's: from ca. 1910.

oil-spoiler; usually in pl. A stoker (in a turbine ship): Naval: since ca. 1925. Granville.

oil up. To advise; to 'tip off': Australian: since ca. C. 19–20. B., 1942. Ex oil, n., 4.—2. To enliven (a bullock) with blow or stroke: Australian: bullock-drivers': C. 20. (K. S. Prichard, *Working Bullocks*, 1926.)

oiled, oiled story, the. A c.p., referring to the drivel of the tipsy: since ca. 1950. A pun on 'the old, old story' and a reference to s. *oiled*, tipsy.

oiler.—4. See oil, v., 3 (Addenda).—5. A waiter in dining hall: Marlborough College: C. 20.

oily rag. A cigarette: C. 20. Rhyming on *fag*. Often shortened to *oily*.

oips. See hoi.

okay (or O.K.) by me, it's; O.K. by you? Virtual c.pp.; certainly coll.: adopted ex U.S.: ca. 1938 in Canada; ca. 1943 in Australia and New Zealand; ca. 1945 in England.

*okey. A wallet: c.: from ca. 1934. Prob. ex *okey-doke*, rhyming s. for *poke*.

okey-doke or -poke; okey-pokey. Perversions of O.K.: resp. 1934, 1935, 1936. The first occurs, e.g., in Michael Harrison, *All the Trees were Green*, 1936.—2. (*okey-doke*.) A wallet: (orig. and still mainly underworld) rhyming s.: since the late 1930's. (Franklyn 2nd.) On poke, n., 8, below.

Old. See Young.

old, n.—3. the old, the master: ca. 1860–1910. B. & L. Abbr. *the old man*.

Old age pension. In Bingo: 65. Since late 1950's.

old anchor. See anchor.

Old and Bolds, the. 'Naval officers brought back into the Service from the Retired List in time of war' (Granville): 1938 + . With an ironic ref. to Old and Bold on p. 582.

Old Annie. See Annie, 2.

old bag.—2. An elderly, slatternly prostitute, hence pejoratively of an unpopular younger one:

low: late C. 19–20. Franklyn 2nd proposes a rhyme on *old hag*, but I doubt this: cf. **bag**, n., 5, above.

old battle-axe. An old, or an elderly, woman that is resentful and vociferous, thoroughly unpleasant, usually arrogant, and no beauty: since the early 1920's, if not, indeed, since ca. 1910. Common to the U.S., Canada, Britain; nor unknown in Australia, New Zealand, South Africa.

old battleship or **old battle-cruiser.** A woman of the humorous mother-in-law type; a broad-shouldered, or stout, aggressive-looking woman: jocular coll.: since ca. 1914.

Old Ben. Newsagents' *Ben*evolent Association Fund: journalists': since ca. 1920.

Old Bill. 'An extraordinarily profitable fare,' Herbert Hodge, *Cab, Sir?*, 1939: taxi-drivers': since ca. 1917. Ex Bruce Bairnsfather's 1914–18 cartoons of benevolent-looking Old Bill.—2, 3. '"Old Bill" is either a rank outsider, or a policeman. It signifies something unknown' (*The Sunday Telegraph*, May 7, 1967): racing, esp. bookies': since late 1940's. In the latter sense, it occurs in Robin Cook, *The Crust on Its Uppers*, 1962, as fringe-of-the-underworld s., with variant *Uncle Bill*.

old black men. See **black chums**.

Old Blood and Guts. The late General George S. Patton, U.S. Army: 1944–5. A fire-eater.

*old boat. 'A house, usually in an untidy state, where old people live.' (Bournemouth *Evening Echo*, April 20, 1966): c.: since ca. 1930.

old boiled egg. An O.B.E.: since ca. 1925. Alec Waugh, *Fuel for the Flame*, 1959, 'He was not grumbling at a C.M.G.; the best he'd hoped for when he started was the old boiled egg they'd given him in the Middle East.'

old boy, 3 (p. 582), occurs in John L. Gardner, *The Military Sketch-Book* (I, 41 and 104), 1831, and earlier in W. N. Glascock, *Sailors and Saints*, 1829. Moe.

old boy (or **Old Boy**) **network, the.** That social and, esp. business, connexion between *old* (former) Public School *boys* which, the envious assume, operates from reciprocal advantage in the professions and which is, by outsiders, regarded as social bias—as if the same sort of thing didn't operate in the trades and in all social classes! It is, at all levels, at least based upon old and trusted standards. Not, of course, s. but coll. and dating from the early 1950's. Laurie Atkinson has recorded this remark, heard by him, on Oct. 4, 1959, 'The old boy network helps in getting jobs.'

Old Brown Cow. Any 'difficult' aircraft: airmen's: since ca. 1930. Ex a popular song so entitled; cf. *cow*, 5 (p. 185).

Old Brown Windsor. The anus: Australian: since ca. 1920. B., 1942. Ex the soap thus named.

old buck (p. 583) should be dated 'late—? even middle—C. 19–20' and it is perhaps of American origin, to judge by its occurrence in *The Saturday Evening News* of Dec. 8, 1821 (p. 4, col. 2); but it does occur as early as 1829 in W. N. Glascock, *Sailors and Saints* (II, 131) and therefore may, as a British natural usage, go back to ca. 1810 or 1800 or even 1790. (Moe.)—2. Impudence: back-answering: Services: since ca. 1935. H. & P.

old buffer. An old fellow: C. 19. It occurs in, e.g., W. N. Glascock, *Sailors and Saints* (I, 30),

1829, '. . . all for that old buffer on the hill'. Moe.

old buzzard. Contemptuous for elderly or old man: coll.: since ca. 1910. Orig., euphemistic for *old bastard*.

Old Caustic. See **caustic, old.**

old chaw. 'Old Harrovian, a term of affection': Harrow School: since ca. 1870(?). Lunn.

old China hand. One who has spent many years in China in commercial or civil service or as a missionary: coll.: since ca. 1910. By 1945, few of them remained, except in Hong Kong: and the term will necessarily become less and less a matter of usage, more and more a relic of history.

old chum (p. 583): by 1959, †, B. tells us.

old clanking irons. A constant grumbler: Naval: C. 20. (P-G-R.)

old clo! A c.p. applied to anything worn out, exhausted, behind the times: proletarian: from ca. 1860; ob. B. & L. Ex the street cry.

Old Close-the-Range. 'Admiral of the Fleet Lord Cunningham. From his habit of getting to close quarters' (P-G-R.): Naval: ca. 1940–5.

old cock (p. 583), as a term of address, occurs in Anon., *Parody of the Celebrated Alonzo the Brave . . .*, ante 1801 (for it appears, as a borrowing from Britain, in *The Port Folio*, I, No. 8, p. 64), thus: '. . . Cried poor Roger, I pray,/Aside your great coat, my old cock, you would lay,/And deign to partake of our cheer.'

old daddy. A Cockney 'prefix', as in *old daddy beer tonky—old daddy grumps—old daddy puddin'—old daddy tea-pot* (examples furnished by Julian Franklyn in 1962): C. 20, certainly; prob. since ca. 1870. Moreover, *old mother* is used in the same way.

Old Dart, the. An early record: Bart Kennedy, *A Sailor Tramp*, 1902. Also a New Zealand usage: B., 1941.

Old Davy, 1 (p. 583) goes back to late C. 18, to judge by an English song quoted, May 4, 1805, in an American magazine, *The Port Folio* (V, No. 17, p. 135, col. 3). Moe.—2. 'Davy Jones'—the spirit of the sea, hence the sea itself, as in Charles Dibdin's song, *The Five Engagements*, with its 'I've been rock'd on old Davy's rough bed': ca. 1780–1830. (Moe.)

old dog, 4, was orig. prison c.: B. & L.

old enough to know better. A mostly feminine c.p. reply to 'How old are you?': late (? mid) C. 19–20. Cf. **old as my tongue . . .** on p. 582.

Old Faithful. See **Annie, 2.**—2. Field-Marshal Montgomery's car in North Africa and Italy: Army: 1943–4. (P-G-R.)

*old fake. A criminal undergoing his second probation: Australian c.: ca. 1830–70. B., 1942.

old-fashioned look. A look, a glance, of quizzical disapproval: since ca. 1930.

Old Flash and a Dash, the. The Royal Welch Fusiliers: military: from ca. 1880. Rhyming s. on *flash*: 'They were the only regiment in the Army privileged to wear the flash . . . a smart bunch of five black ribbons sewed in a fan shape on the back of the tunic collar: it was a relic of the days when soldiers wore their hair long, and tied up the end of the queue in a bag to prevent it greasing their tunics' (Richards).

old four-by-two (p. 583). A four-by-two is not the pull-through itself but the size of the piece of flannelette attached thereto.

Old Freddies, the. (The consortium of) merchant banks: financial world: since late 1940's. *The Observer*, June 28, 1959, 'The Old Freddies quietly partition the City's vast business among themselves—which is why the City can put over a huge money deal in half the time it takes Wall Street—and the world is presented with a united front'. Cf. the **old boy network** above.

Old Frizzle. The ace of spades ('Old Mossy-face'): card players': late C. 19–20. (*Country Life*, Jan. 17, 1963.)

old fucky-off to Q.E. What's-his-name: Naval: since ca. 1950. The *Q.E.* is, of course, the *Queen Elizabeth*.

old girl (p. 534) prob. goes back to early C. 19, for in W. N. Glascock's *The Naval Sketch-Book*, 2nd Series, 1834, at I, 17, it is applied, Navally, to a ship. (Moe.)

Old Girl, the. See **Granny, 3.**

Old Glad-Eye. Mr Gladstone: Victorian prostitutes' nickname. Richard Deacon, *The Private Life of Mr Gladstone*, 1965 (p. 46).

old grabem pudden. 'Old women'—whether wife or mother: rhyming s.: since ca. 1870.

old hag, the. The matron: Preparatory Schools': late c. 19–20. Cf. *hag* in both *Dict.* and Addenda.

Old Harridan, the. See 'Personifications'.

old(-)hat.—3. Old-fashioned; out-of-date: since ca. 1945.

Sense 1 (p. 584) should be dated since late C. 17, for it occurs in B.E., 1699, at *top-diver*.

old haybag or **old henwife.** Disparaging for a woman: non-aristocratic: since ca. 1910.

Old Home Town, the. Cairo: Eighth Army: 1942–3. (P-G-R.)

old hoss. See **old horse** (*Dict.*).

old iron.—3. A bicycle; bicycles: since ca. 1925. H. & P.—4. 'Any copper coins which an airman will risk in a card game or raffle,' H. & P.: R.A.F.: since ca. 1930.

old Jamaica (p. 584): † by 1945. (Franklyn 2nd.)

old John, always on blob or **ready to spit** or **with a wet nose.** A low Naval c.p. of C. 20.

Old Kent Road. See **knock 'em . . .**—2. (*The.*) A long alleyway running, between decks, from bow to stern of H.M.S. *Kent*, the guided-missile destroyer, commissioned in 1963: Naval: 1963 +. (Wilfred Granville, letter of Oct. 28, 1963.)

old King Cole. The dole: rhyming s.: since the late 1920's. (Franklyn, *Rhyming*.) Since ca. 1950, the *old* has often been displaced by *Nat*, in deference to *Nat King Cole*, the American entertainer; since ca. 1955, usu. *Nat*, as in 'on the Nat'. (Franklyn 2nd.) Influenced by *National*?

old kohai. 'One who has long been out East and knows the ropes' (Jackson): R.A.F.: since the middle 1920's. Ex **qui-hi** (p. 679).

old lady, 4 (p. 584), occurs in American usage as early as late C. 18, to judge by *The Port Folio*, March 13, 1802 (p. 73). Moe.

Old Lady Five Fingers. Masturbation: low; mostly Canadian: C. 20.

Old Lady of the Bund, the. *The North China Daily News*, published at Shanghai ca. 1855–1950: among Britons in the Far East.

old lug. A term of abuse or of reproach: Army: since ca. 1930. (P-G-R.) Euphemistic?

old man, 3 (p. 584), has, in nuance 'commanding officer', been R.A.F. since 1918—indeed, it was used by the R.F.C. (Jackson).—5. This sense was perhaps adumbrated in B.E., 1699. Witness the entry: '*Backt*, dead, as *he wishes the old Man backt*, he longs to have his Father upon six men's shoulders'. But I doubt it. A genuine British example occurs in *The Dublin University Magazine*, Sept. 1834 (p. 271); but *A Dict. of American English* records it for 1792. (Moe.)—10. Recorded earlier in B. & L., 1890.—13. 'That part of a beer engine in which the surplus beer collects' (Dr H. W. Dalton, June 26, 1951): Anglo-Irish: C. 20.—14. All the 'commander' senses become crystallised and pinnacled in the very English coll. use of *the old man* for the head of a Service—a Ministry—a great institution—a profession, even the head of the State (e.g. the Prime Minister), the country: C. 20.—15. Owner of the circus: circus-men's: late C. 19–20.

old-man, adj. (p. 585): also 'Mature . . . extremely strong': B., 1959.

old mark, the. One's favourite taxicab rank: taxi-drivers': since ca. 1910. Herbert Hodge, *Cab, Sir?*, 1939.

Old Mick. Nauseated: rhyming s. (on *sick*): late C. 19–20. In an interview published in *Cinema*, early in Dec. 1967, Tommy Steele, 'Blimey, after you've got abaht twelve spoonsfulls down yer, on top o' Christmas dinner, yer don't half feel Old Mick.'

old moo. See **moo, old,** above.

old mother. See **old daddy** above.

Old Nasty. Adolf Hitler: mostly lower-middle and lower class: mid-1940 +; by Jan. 1947, slightly ob. Ex the Rt Hon. Winston Churchill's jocular pronunciation of *Nazi*.

old Newton (got him, took him, etc.), often shortened to *Newton*, refers to a pilot crashing, esp. if fatally: R.A.F.: since ca. 1925. *The Observer*, Oct. 4, 1942, John Moore, 'New R.A.F. Slang'. Gravity is an aircraft's implacable foe; Isaac Newton discovered the laws of gravity.

Old One-Eye is also **Ol'** (or **Ole) One Eye,** as in 'Taffrail'.

old pelt. 'Applied to old and worn-out pressmen—referring to the old ink pelts used in olden times by these individuals for distributing the ink' (B. & L.): printers': mid-C. 19–20; ob.

old pit, the. See **pit, 3.**

old pod. See **pod, old.**

old rip.—2. An old prostitute showing signs of age: low: late C. 19–20.

Old Rock, the. The Reformatory Training Ship *Cornwall*: C. 20. Netley Lucas, *My Selves*, 1934.

old rope. See **money for old rope** (p. 528).—2. (Very) strong or rank tobacco: Services: since ca. 1925. H. & P.; Granville. In the Navy, it specifies perique: *The Weekly Telegraph*, Sept. 13, 1941.

Old Sealed Lips. Earl, esp. when he was Mr Baldwin: since 1936. *The Fortnightly Review*, April 1937. 'My lips are sealed.'

old ship. See **ship, old** (p. 757).

*****old shoe.** Good luck: c.: C. 19. 'Prob. alluding to shoes and slippers thrown at a newly married couple' (B. & L.).

old six. 'Old ale at sixpence a quart' (ibid.): proletarian: ca. 1860–1914.

old so-and-so, that or **the.** A figurative bastard; jocularly euphemistic coll.: though heard ca. 1930, not gen. until ca. 1938.

old soldier.—4. See 'Tavern terms', § 6 (near

end).—5. A bad-tempered sort of ant: Australian: C. 20. B., 1942.

old soldiers, old cunts. A c.p. dating since before 1914; originally, Regular Army. Sometimes the exasperated sergeant or sergeant-major will add, 'You ain't even that; a cunt *is* useful.'

old son. My fine fellow: my dear chap: Australian coll.: from ca. 1870; ob. B. & L.

old squirt. An elderly passenger: (London) taxi-drivers': since ca. 1912. Herbert Hodge, *Cab, Sir?*, 1939, 'An affectionate term'.

old sticker. Army officers' s. of ca. 1810–50, as in John L. Gardner, *The Military Sketch-Book*, 1827, '"Good-tempered Old Stagers" and "Old Stickers", meaning thereby that they can "go" at the bottle, and "stick" at the table till "all's blue"'. (Moe.) Cf. **sticker**, 3, on p. 830.

old thing.—4. Female pudend: lower classes': mid-C. 19–20 (perhaps very much earlier). Orig., euphemistic.

old-tin man. See **come the old-tin man.**

old tin-whiskers is the more usual C. 20 form of **old whiskers** (p. 586).

old Tom.—2. A variant of **Tom**, 6 (*Dict.*); in C. 20, not necessarily of a masculine appearance.

old unspeakables, the. The silent films of the cinema: cultured; not at all general: mostly or, at the least, originally Canadian: since ca. 1945; by 1960, slightly ob. (Leechman.)

old vet. 'Pensioner called back to the R.N. with the Fleet Reserve' (Granville): 1939 +. I.e. 'old veteran'.

Old Whittle. The Whitley bomber aircraft: Air Force: 1940–3. The *old* is affectionate: the Whitley did much good work. (From S/Ldr Vernon Noble, Feb. 1945.)

old woman, 2 (p. 586). Perhaps, after all, orig. British, for it occurs in Fredk Marryat, *Frank Mildmay*, 1829 (on p. 47 of the 1897 edition). Moe.

Old Worser and Worser. 'The Oxford, Worcester and Wolverhampton railway before 1923 amalgamation' (*Railway*): ca. 1890–1923, then historical. A pun on *Worcestershire*.

oldie. An old trick or an old story; hence, an old film or play: coll.: since ca. 1925. (William Haggard, *The Telemann Touch*, 1958 (first nuance).—2. An old person: Australian: since ca. 1940. (B.P.)—3. An old song: coll.: since ca. 1945. Ex sense 1.

ole mal. (In address) old man: Australian: since ca. 1925; by 1950, ob. (Frank Arthur, *The Suva Harbour Mystery*, 1941.) Perhaps burlesquing pidgin English, or perhaps via *ol' pal*.

Oliver.—4. To *put the Oliver on it* is to handle or work something dishonestly: c.: since ca. 1910. F. D. Sharpe, *The Flying Squad*, 1938. Short for *Oliver Twist*, 'the Twist' (a dishonest practice).

olly, olly! An invitation to a schoolfellow to play with one or to accompany one on an errand; occ., a term of farewell: Cockney children's: ca. 1870–1920. Perhaps ex *ho there!* or ex Fr. *aller*—or ex both.—2. Hence among all Cockneys, 'a shout of greeting or recognition, usually with broad, rumbustious, freebooting lear to it' (Atkinson): C. 20.

olo piecee. Anything shabby, e.g. a cap: Naval officers': since ca. 1905. At first, genuinely China-side; since ca. 1946, either derisive or sentimental. Pidgin for *old piece*.

Olympic pool and **passion pit**. A drive-in cinema: Australian feminine: resp. since ca. 1960

and ca. 1955. Ex the petting, esp. the breast-stroking, that goes on there.

omee.—2. Hence, an inferior actor: theatrical: since ca. 1890. Ngaio Marsh, *Vintage Murder*, 1938.

omelette, make an. To blunder; commit *a faux pas*: since the late 1920's. *On ne fait pas d'omelette sans casser des œufs*; cf. *make a mess of it*.

ommi or **ommy** A variant of *omee* (p. 587). *John o' London's Weekly*, Feb. 4, 1949.

omnibus. An omnibus volume: since ca. 1920: book-world coll. >, by 1945, S.E.

on, adj., 4. Mayhew, I, 1851.

on, preposition, senses 5 and 6 (pp. 587–8), come under the meaning 'to the disadvantage of', as in 'It got away on me' and 'He did it on me'. Apparently esp. common in Canada.—7. 'Used for "at" in when applied to a gold-field. A miner was always "on Bendigo" or "on Ballarat", never "at" those places' (B., 1943): Australian coll.: mid C. 19–20. In short, 'on the field'. 6 (p. 588), originated, Professor Arnold Wall tells me (letter of Aug. 1939), in Erse idiom.

on phrases. See 'key-words'.

on and off, n. Lemonade on tap: Tonbridge: late C. 19–20. Marples.

on at, be. To nag (someone); reprove constantly: Australian coll.: late C. 19–20. Baker. Cf. *go on about*.

on boy, adj. and adv. On fag-duty: Harrow School: from ca. 1880 (?). Lunn: see the quotations at **slut about** and **on find**.

on doog. No good: 1851, Mayhew, I. Backslang.

on find. A Harrow term, now ranking rather as j. than as unconventional: from ca. 1890 (?). Lunn: 'Peter had a fortnight's grace before fagging began. These duties were by no means light. He was "on boy" once a fortnight, and "on find" one week out of three—sometimes more often. Two or three privs "found" together, that is, had breakfast and tea in their rooms. The fags attached to "the find" had to lay these meals and clear away. When "on boy" Peter had to stay in the House and answer prolonged shouts of "Boy-oy". He might be required to do anything, from lighting a fire to running a message.' See also **find**, n., 1, in the *Dict.*

on him (or **her** or **you**, etc.), **be.** Culotta defines as an 'exclamation, equivalent to "Just listen to him!" i.e. "He's talking nonsense"'.

on pleasure bent. A Canadian c.p., applied to a bow-legged female: since ca. 1950.

on the backs—down. Asleep: Army: since ca. 1930. On analogy of P.T. 'evolution' *on the hands—down*.

on the corner of the round table. See **corner of** . . .

on the Dilly. See **Dilly** above.

on the floor. Poor: rhyming s.: late C. 19–20. Franklyn, *Rhyming*. 2, 3. See **floor, on the**, above.

on the fritz; **on the bum.** Broken; out of order: since ca. 1934. 'Both expressions are quite widely acceptable in refined circles' (Professor F. E. L. Priestley, 1949). These Canadianisms have been adopted ex U.S.

on the juice. See **juice, on the**, above.

on the ooze. 'On the booze': rhyming s.: since ca. 1920. (Franklyn, *Rhyming*.)

on the sheep's back. Dependent on wool; 'a phrase often applied to the Australian economy' (B., 1959): Aus. coll.: C. 20.

on top. Bookmakers' s.: C. 20. See **rick**, adj., below.

on you! Hullo!: Australian: since ca. 1925. '"Hiya, Curly. Hi, Ronnie," I said . . . "On yuh, Terry," said Curly' (Dick). Perhaps for *good on you!*

on your bike! Off you go!; Run away!: c.p.: since ca. 1960. Anthony Burgess in *The Listener* of March 2, 1967.

once.—2. Short for **once a week** (*Dict.*).—3. A quick, shrewd glance: since ca. 1920. Edgar Wallace, *Elegant Edward*, 1928, 'You rumbles me. I saw you giving me the "once".' Short for **once-over** (p. 588).—4. One pound sterling: c.: since ca. 1935. (Norman.) Perhaps a slovening of *oncer*, 2 (p. 588).

once a week.—2. A magistrate: rhyming s. (on *beak*): mid C. 19–20. (Franklyn, *Rhyming*.)

once aboard the lugger and the girl is mine! A jocular c.p. late C. 19–20. Ben Landeck, *My Jack and Dorothy*, a melodrama produced at the Elephant and Castle theatre. Ca. 1889–90. (Julian Franklyn.)—A. S. M. Hutchinson's novel, *Once Aboard the Lugger—the History of George and His Mary*, 1908, merely reinforced the popularity of the phrase taken from a play that ran for many years.

once wounded, twice as windy (afraid or timorous). A Tommies' c.p. of 1915–18. On analogy of *once bitten, twice shy*. (A. B. Petch, April 1966.)

oncer.—3. Impudence: Cockneys': C. 20. Ex **once a week**, q.v. in *Dict.*—4. Something available, or occurring, only once: mostly Australian: since ca. 1925. (B.P.)

ondleton (pron. *wundletun*). At bridge, a singleton: Australian: since ca. 1925. Baker.

one.—Abbr. of **one and t'other** (*Dict.*): C. 20. *The* (Birmingham) *Evening Despatch*, July 19, 1937. —9. Short for Naval *Number One*: since ca. 1930. (P-G-R.)

one, v. To score two heads on a throw of the two coins: Australian two-up players': since ca. 1910. 'Joe, peering through the smoke . . ., called "And he's—one'd 'em!"': Lawson Glassop, *Lucky Palmer*, 1949.

one, get one's. To be promoted from A.C.2 to A.C.1: R.A.F. coll.: since ca. 1925 (Gerald Emanuel, letter of March 29, 1945).

one and a half. A prison-sentence or—term of 18 months (1½ years): London's East End: since ca. 1945.

one and eight. A plate: rhyming s.: C. 20. Uncommon. (Franklyn 2nd.)

one and elevenpence three farden. Garden; pardon: rhyming s.: since ca. 1870. Michael Harrison, 1943.

one another is an occ. variant of **one and t'other** (p. 588). Len Ortzen, *Down Donkey Row*, 1938.

one-armed bandit. A fruit machine, a slot machine: adopted, in late 1950's, ex U.S. Ex the main lever, resembling an arm, and ex the odds against the user.

one-er.—5. A clay marble all of one colour: London schoolchildren's: from ca. 1880. Opp. **twoer**, 4 (Addenda). Cf. sense 3 of **one-er** (*Dict.*).—6. 'An amusing or eccentric person' (B. 1959): mostly Aus.: C. 20. Ex sense 1 on p. 588.

One-Eyed City, the (p. 588). In full, *the o.-e.-c.* of *undiscovered crime*: while the city was very rapidly expanding, the city's police-force was constantly inadequate.

one-eyed milkman. The penis: Naval: C. 20.

one-finger exercise. Typing with one finger: jocular: since ca. 1925. Ex pianoforte lessons.— 2. Digital stimulation of the clitoris: raffish: since ca. 1920.

one five. Hand: low: ca. 1860–1910. B. & L.

one for his nob.—3. A shilling: street traders' rhyming s. (on *bob*): C. 20. Franklyn 2nd.

one for the bitumen. (Of a drink) one for the road: Australian drinkers': since ca. 1945. (B., 1953.)

one for the book!, often preceded by *that's*. A c.p., remarking upon 'a joke so funny or an event so extraordinary, that it deserves inclusion in "the book"'. Sc. "Joe Miller's" [Jest Book or] joke book' (Leechman): originally U.S., it was adopted in Canada ca. 1950; in Britain, ca. 1955. The phrase has, since the late 1950's in Canada and since ca. 1962 in Britain, had the variant *one for the record*, with reference to the record book.

But as an R.A.F. saying, it derives from **lines** (or **line**) **book**, q.v. above, and dates from late 1920's.

one for the gangway; one for the road. The last drink before the guest leaves the ship—before a journey (esp. by car): coll., by 1945 verging on S.E. Resp., Naval and general: C. 20. Granville.

one (or **and one**) **for the road.** See prec. entry and also **and one** . . .

one for the shelf; also **one for the old oak chest.** A share that, it is assumed, will handsomely repay holding for a long time: coll.—money market, esp. stockbrokers' and financial journalists': C. 20. (Laurie Atkinson, Sept. 11, 1967.) The latter is a special application of a very old, semi-humorous phrase employed of anything put aside for use in the more or less remote future.

one hand for the King (or **the Queen**) **and one for oneself.** A Naval motto: lower-deck: C. 20.

one in the box, have. To be pregnant: lower-classes': late C. 19–20.

one in the bush is worth two in the hand. A low Australian c.p., meaning that coïtion is preferable to masturbation: since ca. 1920. A jocular perversion of the proverbial *a bird in the hand* . . . and a pun on **bush**, n., 3, above. Cf. **push in the bush** . . ., below.

one Labour gain. 'A yellow light at a colour signal' (*Railway* 2nd): railwaymen's: since ca. 1945.

one-man band. A person that takes rather too much on himself: coll.: C. 20; slightly ob., as is *l'homme orchestre* supplying the origin.

one mother too many (, **have**). (To be) illegitimate: mostly lower-middle class: C. 20. Implying 'the child shouldn't have been born'.

one next door, it's number four, the. A Bingo 'set phrase' or c.p. since ca. 1955.

one O. A First Officer, W.R.N.S.: Naval since 1941. Granville. I.e. 1st (Officer).

one o'clock, often preceded by **it's.** A c.p. of warning ('You have one fly-button undone'): Canadian: since ca. 1910. (Leechman.) Also Australian, as in D'Arcy Niland, *Call Me* . . ., 1958.

one (or **two** or **three** or . . .) **o'clock at the waterworks.** A c.p. of warning that one or more of one's fly-buttons are undone: Australian: C. 20. (B.P.) Cf. **waterworks, 1,** on p. 941.

one of the bones. A member of a '*skeleton staff*': Canadian Civil Service: since ca. 1930. (Leechman.)

one of the mounted. A raffish c.p., dating from ca. 1945 and applied to a girl or woman successful in 'getting her man'. A punning reference to the old saying that 'the Mounties always get their man': cf. the entries at **Mounties**, p. 536 and above.

one of these fine mornings you'll wake up and find yourself dead. A jocular—or a derisive—Irishism: c.p.: C. 20.

one of those things, often preceded by *it's just*. A c.p. of resignation; used when the inexplicable ᵣ d annoying or baffling occurs: since ca. 1936.

one of us, he's. He is a homosexual c.p., perhaps at first euphemistic. Cf. *one of those* (p. 589).

one of your team is playing a man short, often prefaced with *I see* (*that*). A jocular c.p. addressed to a youth sporting an eleven-a-side moustache: since ca. 1920. Ex Association football rather than ex cricket.

one on! 'Train! Beware!' (*Railway*, 3rd): railwaymen's coll.: C. 20. On the line.

one or two, have had. To be slightly drunk: coll.: late C. 19–20.

one-out fight. A fist fight between two (usu. selected) individual members of rival gangs: Australian teenage coll.: since ca. 1925. (Dick.)

*****one-out man.** A 'lone wolf' cardsharp: Australian c.: since ca. 1920. (B., 1953.)

one over the odds is a variation of, and it arose slightly later than, **one over the eight** (*Dict.*).

one-pause-two course. An officer's initial-training course: R.A.F.: 1939 +. Jackson, 'From the left and right turn instruction . . ., when the instructor times the movement by saying, "one-pause-two."'

one-piece overcoat. A condom or 'French letter': since ca. 1950.

one side to his mouth, on. (Of a horse) that feels the bit on only one side of his mouth: turf coll.: from ca. 1850. B. & L.

one that got away, the. Orig. (early C. 20) a c.p. derisive of anglers boasting about the fish that escaped, a fish always remarkable for size or speed or cunning; then, since ca. 1945, applied to someone who has made a providential escape, e.g. a bachelor from a predatory female.

one them. To toss two coins that then fall head and tail: Australian two-up players': since ca. 1910. (B., 1953.)

one ton. 100: darts players': C. 20. Impressive number: impressive weight. (*The Evening News*, July 2, 1937.)

one toot and you're oot! Not a word from you, please: Australian c.p.: since ca. 1950. (B.P.) Australians, however, adopted it from England, where it has been a c.p. since ca. 1920, as Ramsey Spencer assures me in 1967.

one-track mind, have (or **have got**) **a;** occ. with elaboration **and that's a dirt track;** esp. in the c.p. **you've got a one-track mind,** an imputation of an excessive or, at the least, an absorbed interest in sex.

one-two; or **the old one-two.** Male masturbation: low, mostly Cockneys': late C. 19–20.

one up, have. To be a second lieutenant or a lance-corporal: Army coll.: late C. 19–20.

one up, put (someone). To give an advantage:

coll.: since ca. 1910. Ex golf? The extension *be one up on* occurs in *Punch*, July 11, 1933.

onedleton (pronounced *wun-del-tun*). In the game of bridge, a singleton: Australian: ca. 1925–50. (B., 1943.)

oner, do one's. To die; get killed: Australian since ca. 1918. Lawson Glassop, 1944. The one 'turn' one has.

onion, 3. An earlier reference occurs in 'Taffrail': '[The British cruiser] could not be relied upon to steam more than "twenty-one and an onion", as her own engineer lieutenant-commander expressed it.'—4. Occ. among civilians as pl., it = any anti-aircraft fire or shells: Berrey, 1940; ob.—5. A fool, a 'mug': Cockneys': from ca. 1920. 'I'm the onion'.

onion boat, came over with the. See **came over . . .**

onions, give (someone). To strike; assault, 'pitch into': *Sessions*, Nov. 1874; † by 1910. Ex their strong smell or ex their tendency to mak one's eyes water.

onions, know one's. See **know one's onions.**

onker (p. 589) derives ex the interminable *onk-urr onk-urr* of the windmill pumps carried by these old ships. many of them due to be broken up: Frank C. Bowen, *London Ship Types*, 1938. By 1950, ob.; by 1960, reminiscent.

onkey. Stinking; (e.g. of fish) stale: Australian: since ca. 1925. (B., 1953.) Cf. *honk.*

onkeypoo or **onkus,** adj. Crooked; out of order: Australian: since ca. 1925. Ex **onkey** above?

only a rumour! It's much worse than that!: Australian c.p.: since ca. 1919. Baker.

only another penny (needed) to make (up) the shilling! A c.p.; used, e.g., by persons collecting money: C. 20.

only birds can fornicate and fly. '"Just an old saying the unromantic R.A.F. had: only birds can fornicate *and* fly. And birds don't booze"' (Gavin Lyall, *Shooting Script*, 1966): W.W. II. 'Simultaneously' understood.

only eating a good soldier's rations. A c.p. applied, 1914–18, by soldiers to inferior soldiers.

only not. Except; always excepting: proletarian coll. verging on sol.: mid-C. 19–20. Nevinson, 1895, 'Mrs Simon would 'ave 'eaved at 'er 'ead whatever else she'd 'ad in 'er 'and, only not the baby.' Likewise, *nothing only* = nothing except; or, simply, nothing: as in Nevinson, 1895, 'But for all 'is bein' nothink only a stoker, the contractors would at whiles put 'im on for boss.'

only think! See **think!, only!** in *Dict.*

oo-er, occ. written solid. A children's exclamation of either surprise or disgust, or of both: C. 20. An intensification of *oo!* or *ooh!*, itself a variant of *oh!* 'I remember this from 1907. It was long drawn-out and marked by an extreme affectation of femininity or foppishness' (Leechman).

oo-la-la! A c.p. exclamation of pleasant surprise: Army: 1914–18. Ex the Fr. *ô la! la!*

oobyjiver. A what's-it, a thingammy: North Country grammar schools': since ca. 1945. Cf. **ooja-ka-piv** on p. 590.

oodle. Money in general: New Zealand and Australian: C. 20. B., 1941, 1942. Ex **oodles** (*Dict.*).

oodle, v. Fig., to drip, as in 'The book oodles with blood-curdling situations': since ca. 1940. Ex **oodles** (p. 589); punning *ooze.*

oodles (p. 589) occurs, since ca. 1920, mostly in *oodles of boodle*, lots of money.

Oodna. Oodnadatta: Australian coll.: late C. 19–20. Archer Russell, *A Tramp Royal in Wild Australia*, 1934.

ooey-gooey! A rhyming reduplication of **gooey** above, but used as a juvenile exclamation of disgust, esp. at something viscous: Australian: since ca. 1920. (B.P.)

oof (p. 589). Also Canadian: late C. 19–20. (Niven.)

oofle dust. 'The "secret magic powder" used on "fakes" or "gimmicks" that are not too new,' William Hickey in *Daily Express*, Nov. 26, 1945: magicians' (i.e. conjurers'). C. 20. An arbitrary, fanciful word, *oofle*: ? ex *spoof*. *Dust* in the eyes. Perhaps influenced by, or even derived ex, the now ob. U.S. Negro *goofer dust*, a magic powder alleged to be an aphrodisiac, as Robert Clairborne has suggested.

oojah. Sauce; custard: Services: since ca. 1938. H. & P. Ex **ooja-ka-piv** (p. 590).—2. An air-raid siren: 1939–45.

ooja(h)-pips. A woman's breasts: Public-School-men's: since ca. 1920.

oolala. (Of a girl; a woman) readily accessible; amorous: Services: since ca. Oct. 1939. I.e. the Fr. *ô la! la!* (expressive of sexual delight).

'Ooligan. An Oerlikon gun: Naval (lower deck) ca. 1941–6. By the honourable process of 'Hobson-Jobson'.

oomph; zing. Sex-appeal: adopted in 1941 and 1943, resp., from U.S. Echoic: the former distorts the bull's mating bellow; the latter 'rings a bell'. *Oomph* had a wonderful Press on Oct. 16, 1946.

oonshick. 'A person of low intelligence.' (L. E. F. English, *Historic Newfoundland*, 1955): Newfoundland: C. 20. Of Amerindian origin?

oont. Pejorative for 'fellow', 'chap'; a fool: low: since ca. 1920. Richard Llewellyn, *None But the Lonely Heart*, 1943, '''What's the matter with you, you big-headed oont, you?''' Cf. dial. *oonty* (empty) and the at least cognate *vont* or *hoont* (to want, to lack); paralleled by 'mental *deficient*'.—2. A camel: Australian: C. 20. Baker. Aboriginal? No; it has been adopted from Hindustani: cf. Kipling's poem 'Oonts' in *Barrack-Room Ballads*, 1892. (Niels Haislund.)

oony. Seasick: Australian: C. 20. Baker. Arbitrary formation, vaguely echoic of sufferer's groans.

oopizootics, the (p. 590). 'Not specifically Australian: and much earlier than 1916. Chorus of popular song about 1890:

> Father's got 'em, Father's got 'em,
> He's got the ooperzootics on the brain,
> He's running round the houses
> Without his shirt and trousis,
> Father's got 'em coming on again'
> (letter from F. W. Thomas).

oops! 'An exclamation of apology when two persons collide or when one accidentally enters a room where someone is dressing': since ca. 1930. (B.P.) Ex:

oops-a-daisy! A c.p. of consolation as one picks up a child that has fallen: late (? mid) C. 19–20.

oot. Money: Australian low: since ca. 1920. Lawson Glassop, *We Were the Rats*, 1944, '''Smash, dough, fiddlies, coin, tin, hay, oot, skekels, spon-

dulicks,'' said Gordon. ''Smash?'' asked Clive, ''What's that?''' Ex—perhaps, orig., illiterate for—**hoot** (p. 403).

Ooty Snooty Club, the. The Ootamacund Club (in the Nilgiri Hills), to which Naval officers serving in India were sent for recuperation or for leave: Naval: ca. 1940–5. 'Junior officers found the "Poona" element a little over-powering' (P-G-R); a punning rhyme on *Oota*—.

ooze, on the. On a drinking-bout: rhyming s. (on *booze*): from ca. 1930.

oozle, ouzle. In Australia also, the former has been current since ca. 1920. B., 1942.—2. 'To search for, capture, ambush, shoot or otherwise harry (bandits, rebels or other disturbers of the peace in Palestine): British Army in Palestine [1938 +]. E.g., ''D Company will send an oozling party.'' Ex Arabic *oozlebast* (''brigand''), in brief glossary of Arabic terms issued to ''the troops''.' (Letter of Nov. 15, 1939, from Earl Wavell.)

oozlum bird. 'A bird whose species you cannot recognize on sight,' Granville: Naval: C. 20. Granville compares the R.A.F.'s *concentric bird*; cf. **ooja-ka-piv** (*Dict.*).

op, n., 3 (p. 590): common, since ca. 1900, for any operation surgical (the earlier use) or military.

opaque (p. 590). Several years earlier in *The London Guide*, 1818.

***opcar.** A policeman: Australian c.: since the 1920's. (Kylie Tennant, *The Joyful Condemned*, 1953.) A modified centre s. on *copper*.

open a can of worms. 'To introduce an unsavoury subject into the conversation': Canadian: since ca. 1955. (Leechman: 'rare'.) Such a tin of worms as is purchased by a week-end fisherman.

open a tin. See **kick a gong** above.

open-and-shut. 'In Newfoundland, days of alternating sun and cloud are known as ''open-and-shut'' days' (Leechman): C. 20.

open slather. 'Open house' (free for all); open access: Australian: since ca. 1935. (B.P.) Cf. **slather** below.

open the door. See **little Jimmy**.

open the door, Richard! An Australian c.p., 'used when someone knocks on an unlocked door' (B.P.): since ca. 1930.

open the occurrence. To make, in the police-station books, an entry for a new case: policemen's: from ca. 1880. B. & L.

open the taps. See **taps**.

operate. To operate on: Canadian doctors' and nurses': since ca. 1930. At first a sol., it was by 1909, coll.—almost j.; but still to be deprecated. 'They operated her twice.' (Leechman.)

operation. 'Note to sub-editors and others: please co-operate in killing . . . the most overworked of current clichés—the whimsical application to a variety of topics of the military locution ''Operation——'',' T. Driberg in *Reynolds*, April 28, 1946: coll.: late 1945 +. Please!

Operation Park. Bondi Esplanade Park Sydney: Sydneyites': since ca. 1925. Baker. Erotic.

operator (p. 590). Still current in 1848 (*Sinks*).

opperore. See **uproar** (*Dict.*).

Oppo. Senior Officers in mess: Naval (lower-deck): since ca. 1920. Ex *operational*.

oppo. 'My oppo' is my chum, pal, usual companion: Royal Navy and Royal Marines (—1939) and R.A.F. (since 1940).—2. Hence, sweetheart (H. & P.) or even one's wife (Jackson).

opposite, n. The saloon bar: public-house coll.: late C. 19–20: † by 1940. A. Neil Lyons, *Clara,* 1912, 'You could come in—in Opposite, along of us.' *Opposite* the less 'superior' bar.

***opposite,** adj. Obscene (esp. of language): S. African c.: C. 20. *The Cape Times,* May 23, 1946.

opposite number, one's. 'The *opposite number* to a Brigade Intelligence Officer, for instance, is the Battalion Intelligence Officer on the one hand, the Divisional Intelligence Officer on the other,' E. P., 'In Mess and Field', *The New Statesman,* Aug. 1, 1942: Army: since ca. 1936: by 1942, it was j.

opposite tacks. Cross-purposes: nautical coll.: mid-C. 19–20. B. & L.

ops. Operations (activities): Services: since ca. 1915.—2. In R.A.F., Operations Room: Operations Officer: since ca. 1938. Partridge, 1945.

opt landing. Optional landing, there being, on a rainy day, no 'clear College': Royal Naval College, Dartmouth: C. 20. Granville.

or am I?—or are you?—or is (s) he or it? A c.p., added for effect: since ca. 1945. 'He's a great man—or *is* he?'

or out goes the gas! A c.p. 'threat to put an end to whatever is going on': ca. 1880–1905. B. & L.

or something. A vague, final tag, either to avoid full details or explanation or because the speaker doesn't know: coll.: late C. 19–20.

or what-have-you. A tag, indicative not of doubt but of a refusal to go into a catalogue: orig. (ca. 1942) and still (1960) a mainly cultured coll. This c.p. 'provides for any reasonable conceivable possibility appropriate to the context . . . For want of example, or as opening the sluicegates of possibility' (Atkinson, letter of July 1, 1948).

or would you rather be a fish? 'A c.p. quip after proposed line of action (the more at odds the better). To the response "Yes", the rejoinder is: "You haven't far to go"; rebutted by "No, it's too wet".' (Atkinson, March 1959.) This set of witticisms—cf. the 'chants' so common among servicemen in 1914–18—dates from ca. 1945 and springs from, indeed as an elaboration of, the c.p., *which would you rather—or go fishing?,* itself current at least as early as 1930, if my memory serves me aright. Indeed, it must date from ca. 1927: Dorothy Sayers used it in *The Nine Tailors,* 1929, as Ramsey Spencer reminds me.

orange. A long-distance call; esp., *give me an orange,* give me (put me on to) a long-distance exchange: telephone operators': since ca. 1939.

orange pip. An observation post: Artillery: 1939–45. *Orange* was signalese for *O, pip* for *P.*

oration, n. A noisy disturbance; a clamour, a din: low: ca. 1820–60. 'She kicked up such an *oration,' Sessions,* 1833. By a confusion of *uproar* and *oratorio* and *oration.*

oration box. The head: ca. 1815–60. *Spy,* II, 1826.

orbit. To circle: Fighter Command: 1939–45. It became official: cf. *angels* and *tally-ho.* Ex astronomy.

orchestra, 2 (p. 591). Cf. the Fr. C. 19–20 s. *violon,* gaol.

orchid (p. 591). See esp. 'Rouge et Noir', *The Gambling World,* 1898.

orchids to you, dear! A polite form of 'balls to you!': ca. 1935–55. Based upon an etymological pun; most users of the c.p. were ignorant of the testicular origin.

ord. Recorded earlier in 'Taffrail'.

order. 'A portion or helping of a dish or article of food served in a restaurant': coll.: U.S. (— 1906) anglicised by 1920. O.E.D. (Sup.). Cf.: —2. Pl., at Eton College, from ca. 1840, as in B. Richards, *Seven Years at Eton,* 'While we were in early school our . . . rooms [had to be] tidied; after that the orders, i.e. rolls, butter, and milk had to be served round.'

orderly buff. See **buff,** n., 5.

orderly dog (p. 591). In the R.A.F., it = Orderly Sergeant. (Jackson, 'The orderly officer's dog'.)

orderly pig. Orderly Officer: mostly officers': Army (— 1914) >, by 1939, R.A.F. Partridge, 1945. Cf. **orderly dog** in *Dict.*

orderly poodle is an R.A.F. N.C.O.'s variation of **orderly dog** as above. (G. Emanuel, March 29, 1945.)

orderly stooge. Orderly Officer: Orderly N.C.O.: Army: 1939–45. (P-G-R.)

orders is orders! A jocular c.p. (ex Army sergeants' use), 'we must obey orders': C. 20.

ordinar'. Ordinary: lower-class coll.: mid-C. 19–20. (Nevinson, 1895.) Also in Scottish; in England, until C. 19, it was S.E. Cf. **extra-ordinar'** (supra).

ordinary pursuivant. See 'Tavern terms', § 4.

[**orful** is an unnecessary spelling of *awful;* cf. *wot for what.*]

organ, play the. To copulate: Australian: C. 20. Prompted by the euphemistic *organ* (of reproduction), the penis.

organ bird. A magpie: Australian: late C. 19–20. B., 1942. Ironic.

Organ-Grinders, the. The Italians: a nickname in 1914–18, though not unheard either before or after. William McFee, *North of Suez,* 1930.

organ pipe.—2. In pl. it was, ca. 1840–90, used among boxers for the nostrils, as in Augustus Mayhew, *Paved With Gold,* 1857.

organise. To 'wangle' something; to get something deviously or illicitly; to obtain or arrange something (very) cleverly but not necessarily illicitly: R.A.F.: since ca. 1938. Jackson, 'Thus, "Leave it to me to organise some beer."' Flying Officer Robert Hinde, March 17, 1945, 'Used particularly in the sense "I must get organised with a girl in Town" or "with the C.O."' Cf. Ger. military s. *organisi(e)ren,* 'to win something'.—2. To avoid (an unpleasant duty), as 'I organised that fatigue all right': Army: 1939–45. (P-G-R.)

organise? You couldn't organise a piss-up in a brewery! Organisation certainly isn't *your* strong point: c.p.: since ca. 1939. Cf. *organise* above. Here, *piss-up* is a drinking bout.

organised, get. 'To arrange one's kit or the work to be done in order before starting the day,' H. & P.: R.A.F. coll.: since ca. 1930.—2. Hence, to so arrange work, or a plan, as to achieve one's purpose; he who has done this *is,* or *has got, organised:* since 1939. Partridge, 1945.

orgy. A party: mostly teenagers': since the late 1950's; by 1966, slightly ob.

orinoko, often **orinoker.**—2. A variant of **Oronoko** (p. 591), which itself may well have been influenced by Mrs Aphra Behn's *Oroonoko: or, The Royal Slave*. 1688: see the very interesting note on pp. 160–1 of Julian Franklyn's *Rhyming Slang*, 2nd edition.

orkneyitis or **scapathy.** That mental and moral depression which tends to ensue after one has been stationed for some time in the Orkneys: R.A.F.: since ca. 1939. H. & P. *Scapathy* deftly blends '*Scapa Flow*' and 'apa*thy*'.

orks. Short for *orchestras*, itself short for *orchestra stalls*, rhyming s. on *balls*, testicles: since ca. 1925.

ormolu. 'Wardroom adjective for anything ornate or expensive-looking' (Granville): Naval: since ca. 1917. No; since before 1914. It occurs in, e.g., 'Bartimeus', *Naval Occasions*, 1914. (H. R. Spencer.) Ex 'ormolu clocks'.

ornament. A station master: Canadian rail-roadmen's (— 1931). Derisive.

ornicle. 'A policeman, magistrate, or anyone in authority' (*John o' London's Weekly*, March 4, 1949): showmen's: ca. 1870–1930. 'Oracle? as having the last word—final' (J. o' L.).

Orokaivas. A tribe that, in N.E. Papua, speaks the Binandali language: catachresis: late C. 19–20. Sir Hubert Murray, *Papua*, 1912. Ex a word frequent in that language.

'orrible 'ole, the. The gun-room, 'home' of the midshipmen: Naval officers': since ca. 1925. (P-G-R.) Derivative of a typical Petty Officer's characteristic scorn.

orta recens. 'One who has either slept in or has had more sleep than the speaker. (*Orta recens . . .* form the first two words of the motto of New South Wales)': a c.p., dating from ca. 1955. (B.P.) But † by 1967, Mr Prentice tells me.

Oscar, n. A homosexual: coll. rather than s.: late C. 19–20; ob. Ex Oscar Wilde. Hence the v. —2. An annual award to the best film actor or actress of the past 12 months: cinematic: since ca. 1940. *John Bull*, Aug. 24, 1946. Ex the inaugurator's given-name.—3. A Japanese Army aircraft: R.A.F. in Far East: 1942 +. Barry Sutton, *Jungle Pilot*, 1946.

Oscar (or **o.**), v.t. To bugger: lower class: C. 20.

Oscar-Wildeing. Active homosexuality: lower class: C. 20. Cf. prec. two entries.

Oscarise, v.i. To be (an active) homosexual: C. 20. Cf. **Oscar,** n. and v.

ostrich. See **peninsula** below.

other half, the. See **swing o' the door.**

other place, the. Cambridge men speaking of Oxford; Oxford men, of Cambridge: coll.: mid-C. 19–20. Cf. **shop,** n., 3 (*Dict.*).

other side, the.—2. Australia: New Zealanders': since ca. 1880. B., 1941, 'The other side of the Tasman [Sea].'

otta. Eight (8): parlary: mid C. 19–20. Cf. the quotation at **dewey** above. (Sydney Lester.)

ounce.—2. A pound sterling: spivs' c.: since ca. 1942. (*Picture Post*, Jan 2, 1954.)

our. 'In the North of England and Scotland [but also among Cockneys], mainly working-class, "our" is nearly always used in referring to a member of the family, as "Our Billy" or "Our Mary Ann",' Albert B. Petch, letter of Oct. 31, 1946: coll.: C. 19–20.

our Bridge. Sydney Harbour Bridge; a Melbourne c.p.: since ca. 1925. Baker. Cf. **our 'Arbour** on p. 16.

Our 'Erb. The Rt Hon. Herbert Morrison: his London supporters': since ca. 1941.

our Glad. Gladys Moncrieff, an Australian musical-comedy star, whose career began in 1913: not only Australian: since ca. 1920. (B.P., 1963).

Our Marie. Marie Lloyd (1870–1922), the justly famous music-hall artist: ca. 1895–1920, then reminiscent. Cf. Naomi Jacob's biography, *Our Marie*, 1936.

Our Venerable Aunt. Catholic Church: Portestants': since ca. 1870.

out, n., 2. The terminal date should be 1910.— 6. An omission of part of matter to be printed: printers' coll.: mid-C. 19–20.—7. A walking-out together: lower-middle and lower class: since ca. 1920. Berta Ruck, *Pennies from Heaven*, 1940.— 8. An excuse; an alibi: adopted, ca. 1942, from U.S.

out, v., 1: much earlier in *Sessions*, Aug. 1857. —4. To dismiss from employment: late C. 19–20. A. Neil Lyons, *Hookey*, 1902, '"Yes, I shall be outed."' I.e. *to put outside.*—5. Hence, to eject from a meeting. Australian: C. 20. B., 1942.— 6. To suspend (a jockey or a professional games-player): Australian sporting: since late 1940's. (B.P.)

out, adj., 5 (p. 592), occurs much earlier in *The Night Watch* (I, 258), 1829, thus, '"What age is she?" asked Charlotte. "Twenty, or a little more; perhaps about your own age, though she has been out these two seasons; and, I am told, has had several advantageous offers in point of connexion."'

out-cry. See **outcry** (*Dict.*).

out goes the gas!, or. See **or out . . .**

out in the blue. Isolated—esp. in the desert: R.A.F.: since ca. 1930. Jackson. See **blue, into the,** 2 (p. 69).

out into the cold, cold snow. Half-way between a c.p. and a chant: C. 20. Ex a sentiment-ally melodramatic recitation.

out like a light. Unconscious drunk; very sound asleep: since ca. 1945.

out of commission.—2. Out of order; not running: coll.: since ca. 1920. 'We can't take the car; she's out of commission.'

out of register. (Of a drunken person) walking crookedly: printers': from ca. 1860. B. & L. A page *out of register* is a type-area not square on page or sheet.

out of the blue. A variant of **out in the blue.** (Partridge, 1945.)

out of the box. See **box, out of the.**

out of the wool. (Of sheep) 'that have just been shorn' (B., 1959): Aus. coll.: C. 20.

out of this world. See 'Jazz Slang'.

out on a limb. See **limb, out on a,** above.

out on its own—like a country shit-house. Excellent; unique: New Zealand: since ca. 1910. An elaboration of the coll.: *out on one's*, or *its, own* (p. 593).

out on one's ear; Australian, . . . **pink ear.** An intensive of *out*, as in 'Thrown out on one's (pink) ear': since ca. 1920. (B.P.)

out or down there (p. 593) occurs in 1818 (Alfred Burton, *Johnny Newcome*) as *out or down here*. Moe. The variant *out or down* occurs in W. N. Glascock, *Sailors and Saints* (I, 95), 1829. (Moe.)

out or in. '"Out or in" . . . is Queensland vernacular for dead or alive' (Alexander Macdonald, *In the Land of Pearl and Gold*, 1907): Queensland coll.: ca. 1880–1930.

out run. 'A sheep run at a considerable distance from the head station' (B., 1959): Aus. rural coll.: C. 20. But an *out station* is a sheep, or a cattle, station remote from the head station: coll.: C. 20.

out to it. Dead drunk: Australian: since ca. 1880. (B., 1942.)

out where the bull feeds. See **where** . . .

out with, 1 (p. 593). Earlier in *Sessions,* Dec. 1783 (p. 15): 'He *out* with the knife and shewed it me.'

outcast and **outcaste** (one who has lost caste or has no caste) have, from ca. 1880, been 'often confused', as Wyld has noted.

outdoor plumbing. An outdoor privy: (U.S. and) Canadian 'ironic, since there is no plumbing' (Priestley): C. 20.

outed. Dismissed from employment: Australian: since ca. 1925. (B., 1943.)

outer (p. 593). Hence, and much more usually '(of a racecourse) the section outside the enclosure' (B., 1942).—2. (*the outer.*) Outside coat pocket: c.: late C. 19–20. Cf. **bitch, safe, seat,** all in Addenda.

outfitter. An officer 'not fond of change from home to foreign service or from regimental to staff employment, and . . . always getting an "outfit" for the purpose': Royal Artillery officers': ca. 1885–1905. B. & L.

outlawed. Applied to a crew that has worked 16 hours, the statutory limit: Canadian railroadmen's (− 1931).

outs, run of. A succession of racing losses: Australian sporting: since ca. 1920. (Lawson Glassop, 1949.) Ex sense 5 of *out*, n.: p. 592.

outside, adv. In civilian life: Naval coll.: C. 20. Granville, '"I don't care what you were 'outside'; you're in the Andrew now, so don't forget it, or you'll be in the rattle," Petty Officer to recalcitrant New Entry.' Cf. the very much older coll. Canadian sense, 'in, or into, civilized parts'—as opposed to the backwoods. 'Trappers will spend the winter in the bush and then come "outside" to sell their catch. My earliest example is 1827' (Leechman, May 1959).—2. In Australia, however, *the outside* = unsettled parts or districts: coll.: C. 20. (B., 1943.)

outside bug. See **O.B.**

outside of (p. 594). But cf. Jane Austen, *Sense and Sensibility*, 1811, '"You think the little Middletons too much indulged. Perhaps they may be the outside of enough."'

outside (of), get (p. 594). Sense 1 occurs in U.S. in J. W. De Forest ('The Duchesne Estate'), writing in *The Galaxy*, June 1869 (p. 831), 'Don't let's get outside of more'n a bottle apiece, and that plain whiskey.' Moe.

Outside Old River. The Yangtse-Kiang: pidgin: mid-C. 19–20. B. & L.

outside tiffy; outside wrecker. A Naval artificer working 'outside': Naval: since ca. 1925. (Granville.) Strictly a submariners' term for 'an artificer working outside the hull or engine-room of a submarine' (Granville, Nov. 5, 1967). In *Down the Hatch*, 1961, John Winton remarks that 'Most of the machinery outside the engineroom was maintained by the man who was known by the traditional submarine title of the outside wrecker'.

outside view. A view of the target seen from the air: R.A.F. coll.: 1939 +. H. & P.

outsider.—5. 'A person living in the *outback*' (B., 1959): Aus.: C. 20.

outy. An outing, esp. for a pet animal: domestic: C. 20. (C. H. B. Kitchin, *The Cornish Fox*, 1949.)

over! A variant (− 1860) of **over the left shoulder!**, I don't believe you! H., 2nd ed. See **left, over the** (*Dict.*).

over backs; hence **overs.** Leap-frog: resp. Cockney coll. (mid-C. 19–20) and Cockney s. (from ca. 1890).

over-baked. Disappointed; 'fed up': Naval: C. 20. Cf. *browned off*. (P-G-R.)

over goes the show! A proletarian c.p. of ca. 1870–1900 referring to a disaster or to a sudden change. B. & L.

over-'omer. That kind of Englishman who talks constantly of how much better things are done 'over 'ome': Canadian: C. 20. Naturally, he's much resented.

over one's time. (Of women) having passed the date on which the period should have begun: mostly feminine coll.: mid C. 19–20.

over-rate it. To overdo one's part: theatrical: from ca. 1860; ob.

over the bun-house. See **bun-house** (*Dict.*).

over the Gilbert (p. 594) is explained by **hard-a-Gilbert** (p. 374).

over the mark. Tipsy: coll.: ca. 1820–80. In a letter written in 1846—from what is now Winnipeg—Robert Clouston, a Scot, remarks, 'Those not accustomed to dine at these parties will get over the mark (tipsy) before they have any idea of it.' (Communicated by Dr Douglas Leechman.)

over the top. See **top, over the.**

over the wall. 'In the guard-room, confined to camp. Thus, "9*d*. over the wall" means, "Nine days C.C."': Jackson. The phrase has been adopted from American c. (see *Underworld*): Services: since ca. 1935.

over the water (p. 595) is extant—but concerning Wandsworth Prison.

overgots book. 'Book showing credits in hand for which official debit not available. NER usage' (*Railway*, 3rd): coll.: C. 20.

overland, the. The back-country; remote, wholly or almost wholly unsettled districts: Australian coll.: since ca. 1910. (B., 1943.) Cf. *outside*. 2. Hence, *overland*, to travel in those parts, esp. to drive stock over them: coll.: since ca. 1920. (B., 1943.)

overlanded. Of goods 'arriving without invoice' (*Railway*, 3rd): C. 20.

overlander (p. 595). Morris's definition is suspect. In C. 20, at least, the sense has always been 'a drover of esp. cattle, chiefly over long distances': coll. >, by 1920 at latest, Standard Australian: so, too, the vbl n., *overlanding*.—2. A settler from another State: Australian: since ca. 1920. (B., 1943.)

overs. See **over backs** (above).—2. 'Shells and bullets that had passed their target' (P-G-R.): Army coll.: 1940–5.

overseas, adj. 'Half seas over' or half-drunk: since ca. 1930. By a reversal and a pun.

'Ow dare she? H.M.S. *Audacious*: Naval: since ca. 1930. Granville. By 'Hobson-Jobson'.

owe-forty. A lawn-tennis term of the late 1880's–early 90's. 'Every one with any pretensions to skill (and a good many with none) wore

long, thick, white blanket-coats. These were
called "owe-forty" coats—sometimes in reverence, occasionally in derision,' F. R. Burrow,
The Centre Court, 1937.

Owen Nares. Chairs: theatrical rhyming s.:
since ca. 1910. (Franklyn, *Rhyming*.) Ex a
very popular actor.

owl, n.—3. A blow or a punch, esp. on the head:
Christ's Hospital: since ca. 1870. Marples.
Proleptic.—4. An A.T.S. wireless operator: A.T.S.:
1940–5. Ex their wireless 'headgear', which gives
the wearer an owlish appearance.

owl, v., 1. Properly, to smuggle goods *out* of
the country.

Owl, the. The night train from Paddington to
Penzance: railwaymen's: C. 20. (*Railway* 2nd.)
A night bird for night birds.

Owlsville. Late-night London: 'with it' re-
vellers': since ca. 1961. (*Evening Standard*,
March 17, 1964; ? news item.)

owner, 1. Earlier authority: 'Taffrail'. 'The
captain of a ship [in the Navy] is invariably "the
owner", "old man" or "skipper", while . . . the
second in command . . . is "the bloke".'—3. The
captain of an aircraft: R.A.F.: 1918 +. Jackson. Ex sense 1.—4. *The Owner* is also the Commanding Officer: R.A.F.: 1918 +.
Sense 1 should rather be dated 'late C. 19–
20'.

Owners, the. The British public: Navy: since
ca. 1925. Granville. The B.P. owns it.

owner's scribe. The C.O.'s confidential clerk:
R.A.F.: since ca. 1930. Jackson. See **owner** 4.
—2. Hence, a Personal Assistant to an Air Marshal
or an Air Chief Marshal: since ca. 1940. Partridge, 1945.

ownsome, on one's. By oneself: lower-middle
class coll.: since ca. 1920. Michael Harrison, *What*

Are We Waiting For?, 1939. Ex *on one's own* =
lonesome.

owny-o, on one's (p. 595) or, as in James Joyce,
Ulysses, 1922, *ownio.*

owt. Mayhew, I, 1851.

ox. 'A large person or tough, esp. a clumsy one'
(Peter Bonford): Marlborough College (and upper-
middle class) coll.: late C. 19–20.

Ox, the. 'The old Oxford Theatre, Melbourne'
(B., 1942).

Ox-Tails, the; the Cabbage-Stalks. The Oxford
crew; the Cambridge crew in the boat race: ca.
1887. Mr Compton Mackenzie, broadcasting on
April 27, 1937.

ox up; knock up; mob. To promote (a pupil):
Christ's Hospital: resp. ca. 1840–80, 1850–1940,
1890 +. Marples.

Ox-Wag(g)on. An *Oxford* aircraft: airmen's,
esp. in S. Africa, where this craft was extensively
used in training: World War II.

Oxbridge. Oxford and Cambridge as = the
older English universities: journalistic coll.:
since ca. 1955.

Oxford '-er' (see p. 596). Mr Vernon Rendall,
himself an old Rugby School boy, rejects the
Rugby School origin; he is supported by Fischer
Williams (see 'Harrow Slang' on p. 376).

Oxford scholar.—2. Shirt collar: rhyming s.: C.
20; not very general. (Franklyn, *Rhyming*.)

***Oxo** (p. 596). Not quite correct, for it derives
ex '$O \times O$ (nought multiplied by nought) = O'
—an old schoolboys' joke. For date, read: late
C. 19–20.

Oxo cube. Tube (railway): rhyming: C. 20.

oxometer. An apocryphal instrument for the
measurement of '*bull*shit': Naval lower-deck:
1939 +. Granville.

ozzletozzle. See **uppardtizzle** below.

P

p. or **P.** A ponce: mostly Londoners': C. 20. Gerald Kersh, *Night and the City*, 1938.

P. & E., the. 'The Pike and Eel'—an inn on the Cam, hard by the finish of the bumping races: Cambridge undergraduates': since ca. 1880.

P.D.—2. Esp. in *caught P.D.*, 'caught with one's pants down', i.e. at a disadvantage: since ca. 1935.

P.F. man. See **pig-fucker.**

p.h. or **P.H.** See **purple heart** below.

p in swimming, silent—like the. A fairly common c.p., used in explaining a pronunciation. 'Her name is "Fenwick", but the "w" is silent, like the "p" in "swimming".' Since ca. 1914. (Leechman.) A pun on the **pee** recorded on p. 614.

P.M. A parlour maid: domestic servants' coll.: ate C. 19–20.

P.M.Y.O.B. *Please mind your own business*: c.p.: since ca. 1930. (Julian Symons, *The Gigantic Shadow*, 1958.) Also *P.M.Y.O.B.B.,...* your own bloody business. (Julian Franklyn, note of 1962.)

P.O. or **p.o.** is the shorter and probably the original form of **p.o.q.** (p. 596). Compton Mackenzie, *Sinister Street*, 1913–14, 'You can give me dinner and then I'll P.O.'—2. A coal wagon: railwaymen's: since ca. 1920. (*Railway*, 3rd.)

P.O. Prune. See **Prune, P/O.**

p.p., sense 2. This can be carried back to ca. 1830, for it appears in Surtees's *Ask Mamma* and Dickens's *Pickwick Papers*.

p.p.i. or **P.P.I.** Policy proof of interest: from ca. 1903. In its lit. sense, it is merely insurance j., but in pejorative allusion to speculative insurance policies, it is a commercial c.p., now slightly ob. (F. H. Collins, *Authors' and Printers' Dictionary*.)

p.t. or **P.T.** See **prick-teaser** in Addenda and **p.t.** in *Dict*.

p.y.c. Pay your cash: Australian coll.: C. 20. B., 1942.

P.Zs. 'Exercises in the Fleet at sea': Naval: C. 20. 'This flag-hoist used to be run up when the exercises began' (Granville).

*****pack.** A gang: c.: C. 17–mid-19. B. & L.

pack, v. To be ruined or spoilt; to become useless: motor-racers': from ca. 1920. Peter Chamberlain, 'Back-axles will pack before half distance anyway.' Ex **pack up,** q.v. in *Dict*.—2. To 'pack up', to desist, give up: cyclists': since ca. 1945. 'Where did you come?'—'Oh, I packed after fifty miles.'—3. To beat: to be superior to, or more enjoyable than: Aus.: since ca. 1920, Norman Lindsay, *Saturdee*, 1963, '"Fun o' the world, goin' with girls," said Peter, "By jings, you oughter try it on. . . . By jings, it packs football easy!"' And '"Oh, I'm pretty good," he said. "It takes a bit to pack me once I get goin'."'

Sense 2 was, by 1960, fairly gen.—as, e.g., in Alan Diment, *The Dolly Dolly Spy*, 1967.

pack, go to the (p. 598). Also Australian: B., 1942.

pack 'em. To be either timid or frightened: Aus.: since ca. 1930. (B., 1959.) Whence the vbl n. *packing 'em.*

pack in, v.i., is a synonym for **pack up,** v., 2 (below). W/Cdr R. P. McDouall, March 17, 1945.

pack it in; pack it up. To stop talking; to cease fooling or some foolish practice: Services (from Cockneys?): since ca. 1925. H. & P. Ex **pack the game in** and **pack up,** on p. 598.—2. Since the late 1940's, commoner than *pack it up*, to give up one's job: mostly manual workers', as in 'I'm packing it in, too much like hard work!'

pack the trail. To go on trail, whether on horseback or afoot: Australian coll.: since ca. 1870. Archer Russell, *A Tramp Royal in Wild Australia*, 1934.

pack-up, n., corresponds to the next: R.A.F.: since ca. 1937. (W/Cdr R. P. McDouall, letter of March 17, 1945.)

pack up, v.—2. Hence, (of a 'plane) to cease to function: R.A.F.: since ca. 1937. Partridge, 1945.

pack up one's awls and be gone (*Dict.*) occurs in *Eliz. Raper's Receipt Book* as *. . . alls . . .;* there also as **stuff up one's all.** (David Garnett, in *The New Statesman & Nation*, Feb. 20, 1937.)—The earliest record happens to be in the form **awls:** F. Kirkman, *The Unlucky Citizen*, 1673.

packed up, adj. in the predicate. Killed in warfare: Army: 1914–18. Ex **pack up** (p. 598).

packer. A pack-horse: Australian coll.: since ca. 1870. B., 1942.—2. A plate-layer: railwaymen's jocular: C. 20. (*Railway* 2nd.)

packet.—5. See *packet, cop a*, on p. 598. Also with variant *catch*, to be severely reprimanded: Services, esp. Army, since ca. 1925. (P-G-R.)

packet, three-op. See **three-op packet** (*Dict.*).

packet, buy a. See **buy it.**

packet of salts, like a. Variant of *. . . dose of salts* (p. 236).

packin(g) 'em. See **sterky.**

packet, take a. To reach the point at which effort is painful: racing cyclists': since ca. 1946. Cf. *packet, cop a*, on p. 598.

packs (rare in singular). Packhorses: Aus. coll.: late C. 19–20. Mary Durack, *Keep him My Country*, 1959.

pad, n.—9. A rough bush road or mere track: Australian coll.: late C. 19–20. (B., 1943.) Ex sense 1 (p. 599).—10. (Ex sense 6: p. 599.) 'Living quarters, often a bare room with a mattress on or near the floor' (*The Victoria Daily Colonist*, April 16, 1959, 'Basic Beatnik'): Canadian jazz-lovers' and musicians': adopted, in 1956 or 1957, ex U.S.—cf. *The American Dialect Society*, November 1958, Norman D. Hinton ('Language of Jazz Musicians'), '**pad,** *n.* A bed. Extended to mean bedroom, or even apartment. Occ[asional].'—11. 'A lot, "packet"' (Culotta): Australian: since late 1940's.

pad it (p. 599). Perhaps from as early as ca. 1690.

Padders. Paddington railway station: since ca. 1920. (*The New Statesman*, Feb. 5, 1965.) By 'the Oxford-*er*'.

Paddington Pollaky. See **pollaky** (Addenda, after *Dict.*).

paddle, n.—2. A semaphore signal: Canadian railroadmen's (– 1931). Ex shape.

*****paddler**, 2, and **walloper**, 3, are Australian c. terms for a policeman: since ca. 1945. (B., 1953.) Both are probably of sadistic origin.

paddles. Fleet: c. in C. 19 and low in C. 20. (Cf. **boats** in *Dict.*) Anon., *Autobiography of Jack Ketch*, 1836.

paddling. See **footing like a centipede** above.

Paddo. Paddington (N.S.W.): Sydneyites': since ca. 1920. (B., 1953.)

Paddy, 1 (Irishman): earlier in *Sessions*, 1748.— 2. In Australia with variant *Pat*, it = a Chinese: C. 20. B., 1942, has both; *Pat* occurs also in Sidney J. Baker's letter in *The Observer*, Nov. 13, 1938.—3. A 'colliery train from mine to railhead' (*Railway*): railwaymen's: C. 20.

Paddy Kelly. A policeman: Liverpool dockers': late C. 19–20; by 1960, slightly ob.

Paddy Quick.—3. A kick: rhyming s.: mid C. 19–20; by 1910. Franklyn, *Rhyming*.

Paddy rammer (p. 600): ob. by 1960. (Franklyn 2nd.) Clearly suggested by **panorama** (below).

Paddy wag(g)on. A van for the conveyance of prisoners: Australian: adopted, ca. 1955, ex U.S. (B.P.) Ex the prevalence of Irishmen in the police forces of the U.S.A.?

paddy-w(h)ack.—4. A smack; a smacking: Australian children's: late C. 19–20. Elaboration: *paddy(-)whack the drumstick*, as in 'You'll get paddy(-)whack the drumstick if your mother finds out'. The form *paddy(-)whack* is—obviously enough—partly echoic; it may also owe something to rhyming s. (B.P.)

Paddyland. See **Paddy Land** (*Dict.*).

Paddy's Goose (p. 600): earlier in *Sessions*, Dec. 1839.

Paddy's market. A market for the sale of second-hand goods, esp. clothes: coll.: mid-C. 19–20.

Paddy's pig . . . See **Irish as** . . .

Paddy's watch. Employed allusively, Irish ratings being (according to themselves) never off watch: Naval: since ca. 1920.

padhouse. One's bedroom or lodging: beatniks': since ca. 1958. (Anderson.) An extension of **pad**, n., 10 (above).

padre (p. 600) has app. been Naval since early C. 19, to judge by Fredk Marryat, *The King's Own*, 1830 (p. 215 of the 1896 edition). Moe.

pads, women: **married pads**, wives: Regular Army: late C. 19–20. Perhaps ex **pad**, n., 6 (*Dict.*).

pads, the. A padded cell, or the padded cells, in a lunatic asylum: esp. the attendants': since ca. 1925.

Paggers. St Peter's Hall: Oxford undergraduates': since ca. 1935. (Marples, 2.) After *Jaggers*.

paid out with spit. A c.p. applied to a small salary: U.S. theatrical >, ca. 1932, partly English theatrical.

pain in one's little finger (or toe), have a, esp. in the semi-c.p., 'He has a pain in his . . .': applied to the malingering type of serviceman or workman: C. 20. (A. B. Petch, April 1967.)

pain in the arm—arse—back—balls—neck (etc., etc.) **!, you give me a.** See **you give me the balls-ache.**

pain in the neck. A tedious or boring or irritating person: since ca. 1910. Ex *give one a pain in the neck* (see **you give** . . .). A low parody is *pain in the nick*: since ca. 1920.

pain in the penis, you give me a. You annoy me: a low 'educated' c.p.: since ca. 1930.

paint, v., 1 (*Dict.*). 'Alluding to a red nose caused by over-indulgence' (B. & L.).

paint a picture, 'vaguely to describe a situation or to outline a plan': Services: 1939–41. Rather j. than coll.: certainly not s. H. & P.

painters, have in the. See **rags (on), have the.**

pair of top ballocks. See **top ballocks.**

pair of white gloves, a. 'Safe return of all aircraft from a bombing operation': R.A.F.: 1939 +. Jackson, 'From the ancient legal custom whereby a judge is presented with a pair of white gloves if his calendar is free from crime.'

pakapu ticket, look like a. To be completely indecipherable: Australian (esp. Sydney) coll.: since ca. 1940. 'Pakapu is a Chinese gambling game, not unlike housie. A pakapu ticket, when filled, is covered with strange markings' (Edwin Morrisby, Aug. 30, 1958). B., 1959, spells it *pakapoo* and gives the variant *marked like a pakapoo ticket*, which he defines as 'confusedly or incomprehensibly marked'.

pakeha. But Keith Sinclair, 1959, defines it as 'Foreigner; (pop.) white man'; for probable etymology, see my *Origins*. Mr Sinclair notes *pakeha-Maori*, 'a European living with Maoris': N.Z. coll.: since ca. 1855.

Pal Police, the. The Palestine Police: since ca. 1946. Ian Jeffries, *Thirteen Days*, 1958 (period concerned: 1948). The adj. is *Pal Police*, as 'a Pal Police type' (not in Jeffries).

palace.—5. A caboose: Canadian railroadmen's (– 1931). Ironic.

Palace ends. Remnants of the candles put, on big occasions, in the chandeliers at Buckingham Palace: coll.: late C. 19–20. Removed by footmen and sold locally as perquisites.

palat, for **Palatinate purple,** is a Durham 'blue': C. 20. (Marples, 2.)

Palestine ache. See **wog gut.**

Palestine Militia, the. The 6th Australian Infantry Division: Australian soldiers': 1940–1. Lawson Glassop, *We Were the Rats*, 1944. Ex their long training in Palestine.

Pall Mall. A girl: rhyming s. (on *gal*): late C. 19–20, by 1950. Franklyn, *Rhyming*.

*****pallyard.** A C. 16–17 variant of **palliard** (*Dict.*).

Palm Beach. A cove at Tobruk: Army in North Africa: 1940–3. Much bathing there in quite unluxurious circumstances. The place referred to is not American but Australian; it was Australian soldiers who so named it from a resort in New South Wales.

palm-oil ruffian. An old-time trader on the West Coast of Africa: since ca. 1860. Buying oil and drinking gin.

Palmer's twister. (Gen. pl.) A strychnine pill: medical: ca. 1870–1910. B. & L. 'The medicine employed by Palmer of Rugeley in getting rid of Cooke.'

palo. A *Port Amenities Liaison Officer*: Naval: 1944–5. (P-G-R.)

palone; occ. **polone** (p. 646). Pron. *p'lone*, rarely *perlone*. It is, in short, the present shape of **blowen** (q.v.) by a common process of linguistic change. The erroneous *palore* or *polore* arises from a misreading and is very rare.

palsy-walsy. Jovially friendly: since ca. 1934. (C. Brand, *Death of Jezebel*, 1949.) Reduplication of *palsy*, itself ex *pally* + (*to be*) *pals*.

paltan. A platoon; loosely a battalion: ca. 1880–1913. A corruption of Fr. *peloton*.

pan, n.—6. Bread: Canadian Naval: C. 20. H. & P. I.e. Fr. *pain*.

pan, v.—2. V.t. (gen. as p.pple passive), to beg: tramps' c.: C. 20. W. L. Gibson Cowan, *Loud Report*, 1937.—3. To strike (someone) in the face: low (– 1943). H. & P. Ex the n., 5.—4. To criticize adversely; to disparage: Australian, adopted, ca. 1945, ex U.S. (B.P.)—5. '"To pan" is to punch just once, but "to ted up" or "to ted in" is to beat systematically, as in teddy boy' (or, rather, in its shortened form *Ted* or *ted*): North Country grammar school s., since ca. 1955. *New Society*, Aug. 22, 1963.

pan, down the. Too far behind; done-for: motor-racers': from ca. 1922. Peter Chamberlain. Perhaps suggested by *up the spout*; cf. also *down pin* (see **pin, be down**).—2. A Cockney equivalent of *down the drain*, ruined with no chances left: since the 1930's. (Julian Franklyn.) The pan is that of a water-closet.

pan-handler. A hospital orderly: military coll.: C. 20.

pandanny. Pandanus (a palm-like tree or shrub): Australian coll.: mid C. 19–20.

pane of glass. A monocle: Regular Army: since ca. 1870.

***panel-house.** See **panel-crib** (*Dict.*).

panic, v. 'To pick up cigarette butts and small debris in an army camp' (B., 1943): Australian soldiers': 1939–45.

panic bowler. A steel helmet: R.A.F.: 1939 +. Jackson, 'The R.A.F. never wear it unless there's a panic on.'

panic hat. A steel helmet: Australian soldiers': 1939–45. (B., 1943.)

panic helm. 'Erratic steering by "makee-learn" coxswain' (Granville): Naval: since ca. 1905.

panic merchant. A person given to panicking: Australian: since early 1940's. (*The Sydney Morning Herald*, Aug. 5, 1963.)

panic party.—2. The Navy's synonym of *flap on* (see **flap,** n., 7): since ca. 1925. H. & P.—3. Any rash move: Australian soldiers': 1939–45. (B., 1943.)

panic stations, be at. To be prepared for the worst: Naval: since ca. 1938. Granville.

panorama (pron. *panorammer*). A hammer: rhyming s.: since ca. 1870; by 1960 †. D. W. Barrett, *Navvies*, 1880.

pansy (p. 605) dates from the mid-1920's Hence, from late 1920's also an adj., as in Jean Devanney, *Riven*, 1929, ('a pansy voice')—occurring in New Zealand.

Pansy Patrol, the. Those officers who are sent by Scotland Yard to get evidence at a night club before the police raid it: mostly policemen's: from ca. 1930. They go in full evening dress and are usually chosen from the Public School members of the Force.

pansy up, v.i. and v. reflexive. (Of a man) to adorn oneself, to smarten oneself up sartorially, in an effeminate manner: since ca. 1932.

pantaloons. Knee-breeches, formerly worn as part of R.A.F. uniform: since ca. 1920; by 1940 merely historical. (Atkinson.)

pantechnicon. Sense 1 (p. 604) had > S.E. by 1920 at latest.—2. Hence, a Whitley bomber aircraft: R.A.F.: 1939–41. 'At one period it was our largest, with the biggest capacity' (Jackson).— 3. A large glider: R.A.F.: 1942 +, but ob. by the end of 1945.

panther-sweat. Surgical spirit and Italian vermouth mixed to form a potent drink: beatniks': since ca. 1959. (Anderson.) Adopted and adapted from American s. *panther-sweat*, raw inferior whiskey.

panther's piss. Strong liquor, esp. spirits: Australian: C. 20. B., 1942. Cf. **tiger's piss.** The term is prob. an adaptation of the U.S. *panther piss*.

pantry shelves. Female breasts: domestic: since ca. 1870; ob. by 1940.

pants.—5. Only in address to a pantryman: ship's stewards': C. 20. Dave Marlowe, *Coming, Sir!*, 1937.

panzer beetle. A large, hard-topped black beetle found in North Africa: Army: 1941–3.

Panzer Pete. A formidable liquor made by troops in New Guinea: Australian soldiers': 1942–5. (B., 1943.)

panzy.—2. Hence a burglar: Australian c.: late C. 19–20. B., 1942.

pape. Newspaper, mostly in newboys' cries: late C. 19–20. B., 1942.

paper-chewing. (Official) correspondence: Anglo-Indian: C. 20. George Orwell, *Burmese Days*, 1935.

paper-collared swell. A 'white-collar worker' (esp. a clerk): New Zealand: ca. 1860–1900. A. Bathgate, *Colonial Experiences*, 1874—cited by B., 1941.

paper end, the. 'The report, correspondence and documentary aspect of some matter as distinct from the matter itself,' Jackson: R.A.F. coll.: since ca. 1925. Cf. **paper-man** (p. 605).

***paper-hanger.** A passer of worthless cheques: Australian c.: adopted ca. 1925, from U.S. (Baker.) See *Underworld*.

paper war. 'Army red tape' (B., 1943): Australian soldiers': 1939–45.

paper yabber. Mail matter—newspapers sent through the post: Australian pidgin: C. 20. Archer Russell, *In Wild Australia*, 1934.

Papish, n. and adj., has from ca. 1870 been adjudged sol. when not genuinely dial.

paps. See 'Colston's'.

par for the course, that's (just) about. That's pretty normal; that's what, after all, you can expect. C.p.: since ca. 1920. Ex golf. (Leechman.)

para.—2. A *para*plegic (a spinal-cord paralytic): Canadian doctors and nurses': since ca. 1946. (Leechman.)—3. A member of Paratroops: Army: since ca. 1944.

paraboy, usually in pl. A member of a parachute regiment: Army: 1942–5. (P-G-R.)

paraffin. A smart appearance: lower-class Glasgow: C. 20. MacArthur & Long. In 1897–

1900, 'the word "paraphernalia" was much used by the working classes [of Glasgow] to describe anyone who was very much "got up" or over-dressed. It was pronounced "paraffinelly" . . . "There he was, dressed up wi' a' his paraffinelly" . . . My theory is that "paraffin" is simply a contraction of "paraffinelly" and is now used by a generation that knows nothing of its original meaning,' Norman T. McMurdo, in a letter of Aug. 30, 1937, and doubtless correctly.—2. Hence (?), a suit of clothes: (low) Glasgow: since ca. 1920. Kenneth Mackenzie, *Living Rough*, 1936.

Paraffin Pete. 'An Airfield Control Officer or N.V.O. . . . responsible . . . for ensuring that the flares are laid and lit at the right time and places; these forming the flare-path, guide . . . aircraft in darkness' (Jackson): R.A.F.: since ca. 1938.

paraffinelly. See sense 1 of **paraffin**: app. current ca. 1880–1905.

paralysed.—2. Jocularly (or ignorantly) for *analysed*: C. 20. 'Paralysed by the public anarchist.'

paralytic (p. 605). Rather: dead-drunk.

parapet Joe.—2. A soldier that is for ever exposing himself on the parapet: Army: 1914–18.

parcel.—4. A rolled blanket, with one's personal belongings inside: Australian tramps' coll.: since ca. 1910. (B., 1943.)

parcel, blue the. To spend all one's money; lose everything on a bet: sporting: since ca. 1910. Edgar Wallace, *Educated Evans*, 1924.

parchment dab. See 'Miscellanea'.

pardon me for living! 'An elaborate mock apology, used by one checked for some minor error' (Leechman): Canadian c.p.: since ca. 1945.

pardon the French! See **French!**, **pardon the.**

parish. A tin sconce: Rugby schoolboys': mid-C. 19–20. B. & L.—2. A battery's position in the front-line area: artillery officers': from mid-1916; ob. Hence *the rectory* (or *R.*), battery headquarters. Both terms are to be found in Blaker, resp. at p. 364 and p. 365.

park, v.—3. To do, to effect; e.g. *park or bath, a walk*, take, go for . . .; *park an oil*, do something (over-)smart: Oundle: since early 1920's. Marples.

park your stern here! Be seated!: since ca. 1925. Orig., nautical.

parker. 1. **parker from** (or **with**) **denarly.** To pay up: Parlyaree, esp. cheapjacks': from ca. 1870. Pugh, cheapjack *loquitur*: "'I like the Birmingham people," I said. "They are nice people, sensible people, and they 'parker from denarly' without fuss."' Lit., part from money; *parker* represents It. *partire*; for *denarly*, see the *Dict.*—2. To hand out (money): id.: id. Ibid., ' "If I'd a brighfull o'posh," she said, "I wouldn't parker no wedge to you."'

Parker trouble, have. To have one's conversation listened-to by an outsider: office- and shop-girls': since ca. 1945. (Gilderdale.) Ex *Nosey Parker*. The use of *trouble* in coll. phrases—e.g. *to have woman trouble*—was originally American.

parkering ninty. Wages: Parlyaree: since ca. 1860. (P. H. Emerson, *Signor Lippo*, 1893.) Cf. **part**, on p. 607.

parking. The use of a parked motor vehicle for love-making: Australian: since ca. 1945. (B.P.)

parlamaree. A 'gee' or that companion who starts a sale, or the donations, going: C. 20; by 1950, ob. Perhaps, as Franklyn, *Rhyming*, pro-

poses, ex *parlyaree* or *parlaree* (cf. *Parlyaree* below).

parlary. Slang: prostitutes': since ca. 1930. Ex the S.E. sense.

Parlary coinage. Sydney Lester, *Vardi the Palary*, (?) 1937, enumerates the coins thus: half-penny, *medza*; a penny, or (so many) pence, *soldi*; threepence, *tray-bit*, adopted from gen.—orig., low—s., and elaborated from **tray**, 2 (p. 998); six-pence, *say soldi*; a shilling, *bionk*; a florin, *dewey bionk*; a half-crown, *medza(-)caroon*; a crown (piece) or 5 shillings, *caroon*; 10 shillings, *daiture bionk* or *medza(-)funt*; £1, *funt*.

Parlary numerals. Sydney Lester cites: *una*, 1; *dewey*, 2; *tray*, 3; *quattro*, 4; *chi(n)qua*, 5; *say*, 6; *setta*, 7; *otta*, 8; *nobba*, 9; *daiture*, 10; *lepta*, 11; *kenza*, 12. For numbers over 12, see **daiture** above. The greatest deviation from the Italian originals are exhibited by *daiture*, *kenza*, *lepta*, which aren't Italian at all.

parliament.—2. Also *parliament house*. A privy: late C. 19–20. Because one sits there.

parlor. A caboose: Canadian railrcadmen's (— 1931). Ironic: cf. **palace**, 5. Cf.:

parlor man. Rear brakeman or flagman on a freight train: Canadian railroadmen's (— 1931).

parlour, in the. (Of a barge) 'on the hard gravel under the wharf' (Ernest Raymond, *The Marsh*, 1937): Thames-side nautical: late C. 19–20.

parlour pinks. Socialists not violent (*red*) but very moderate: political: adopted, ca. 1935, from U.S.

parly (or **Parly**) **train.** A 'daily passenger train compelled by Parliamentary Regulations' (*Railway*, 3rd): since ca. 1920.

Parlyaree (p. 606). In l. 3, read 'C. 18–20 actors', for a few terms (e.g. *letty*) survive among troopers and traditionalists.

In l. 10, *pargliare* is a misprint for *parlare*, which accounts for the *parlaree (-ry)* form; the *parlyaree* form has been influenced either by **palarie** (p. 601) or by, e.g., *parliamo*, 'let us speak'.

A full account of this Cinderella among languages appears in my book of essays and studies upon language, *Here, There and Everywhere*, 1949.

Parlyaree is both less general and less service-able than *Parlary* or *parlary*. In late C. 19–early 20, *palarey* or *palary* was very common, esp. among music-hall artists; after ca. 1945, *palary* is demotic, *parlary* hieratic. Sydney Lester's title for his glossary, *Vardi the Palary*, means 'Know Parlary'. Lester.

parnee or **parney.**—3. Tears (in the eyes): parlary: C. 20. Ex senses 1 and 2 (pp. 606–7).

parnee, v.i. To rain: showmen's and market-men's: C. 20. Ex the n.: see p. 606.

parrot. 'A sheep that has lost some of its wool' (B. 1959): Aus. rural: C. 20. Cf. **cocky**, n., 8, above, and **rosella**, 2, below.

parrots and monkeys. Goods and chattels; personal possessions: Army: since ca. 1930. Cf. the (1941 +) c.p. addressed to recruits, *All right! Pick up your parrots and monkeys, and get mobile.*

parsley. Nonsense: Cockneys': C. 20; ob. Pugh. Cf. **gammon and spinach** (*Dict.*).

parson's collar. Froth on a glass of beer: public-houses': since mid-1940's. (A. B. Petch, April 1966.)

Parson's Pleasure and **Dame's Delight.** The

two Oxford bathing places reserved for men and women respectively: mid C. 19–20 and C. 20: orig., s.; but, the former at least, accepted by 1920 at latest.

parson's wife. Gin: originally and properly Vickers Gin: Australian: since ca. 1925. (B., 1953.) *Vickers: vicar's.* 'And quite possibly *gin = Jin,* short for *Jinny,* a sort of collective for women' (Julian Franklyn, 1962).

parson's yeoman, the. 'The volunteer organist at Divine Service' (Granville): Naval: C. 20.

part co. To part company: ? orig. Naval: ? since ca. 1790; by 1850, ob.; by 1910, virtually †. It occurs in W. N. Glascock, *The Naval Sketch-Book* (II, 171), 1826, 'Thought it time to "cut cable" and run . . . "Parted co." from crowd.' (Moe.)

part up. An Australian variation of **part** (p. 607): late C. 19–20. B., 1942.

party.—2. A love affair: Society: ca. 1928–38. Alec Waugh, *Going Their Own Ways,* 1938.—3. An aerial combat; a bombing raid: R.A.F.: since early 1940. H. & P., 1943; Granville, 1945, of a commando raid or a naval operation, for it was also a Naval and an Army term; Brickhill & Norton, *Escape to Danger,* 1946, '"Oh, crumbs! Night fighter," he muttered. "What a b—— party!"' By nonchalant meiosis.—4. A very busy day: Services; esp. R.A.F. ground staff: since ca. 1940. H. & P. Ironic.—5. A girl friend: Navy: since ca. 1910. Granville. Ex sense 2. Cf. **horse,** n., 14 (above).

party in the attic. An elaboration of **party,** 3: R.A.F.: 1940 +. Partridge, 1945, '*Attic* because the fight takes place aloft.'

party pin. A working party in an aircraft carrier: Naval: 1939 +. (P-G-R.)

party-pooper. 'One who wrecks a convivial party by "pooping" it' (Leechman): Canadian: since ca. 1960. 'Water over the poop? Or "pooping", defecating, on it?'

pash.—3. A letter: Naval: since ca. 1930. H. & P., '*Number one pash* being a letter to one's best girl'. Ex sense 2.

pash, adj. Passionate; e.g. *pash pants,* non-regulation trousers affected by some officers: Canadian soldiers': 1914 +.

pash on; sex on. To indulge in sex, from petting to intercourse; Australian teenagers': since ca. 1950. *The Sydney Morning Herald,* Sept. 11, 1963.

pash show. A film that graphically shows love-making: Australian teenagers': since the late 1940's.—2. Hence, ardent love-making: Australian teenagers': since ca. 1950. (B.P.)

pash wag(g)on. A liberty bus: mostly Air Force: 1940–5. (P-G-R.) Cf. *passion waggon.*

pass a sham saint. See 'Verbs'.

pass at, make a. To attempt (a person's) virtue; to try to caress: U.S., anglicised ca. 1930. Cf. Dorothy Parker's famous couplet,

'Men seldom make passes
At girls who wear glasses.'

Usually of the male: to suggest sexual intimacies to: the nuance predominant in Britain since ca. 1945.

pass in one's dinner pail. To die: mostly Cockneys': ca. 1890–1914. Binstead, *Mop Fair,* 1905.

pass spark out. See **spark out** (*Dict.*).

pass the buck (p. 608). That sense was virtually † by 1945.—2. To pass on something one cannot trouble oneself with: Civil Service: since ca. 1938. An Americanism. By 1950, fairly general The expression derives from the game of poker.—3. But, in Canada, as Dr Leechman tells me in May 1959, 'again the general sense has changed. Now it means simply to evade responsibility, usually by passing the job on to someone else, but often by simply ignoring it. Used even in such senses as evading a difficult question in an argument.'

pass the can. A variation of *pass the buck,* to shift the blame: Army: ca. 1941–5. (P-G-R.)

pass the catheter. See **piss out of, take the.**

pass with a push; esp., it'll . . ., a c.p. of grudging approval: Australian: since ca. 1950. (B.P.)

passed-over; usually in pl. A Lieutenant-Commander that has failed to become a Commander: Naval coll.: C. 20. Granville.

passion-killers. The Service knickers worn by members of the W.A.A.F.: 1940 +. Jackson. By ca. 1950, fairly general Cf. **black-outs** and **twilights,** both of which terms are covered by 'passion-killers'.

passion(-)pit. See **Olympic pool** above.

passion(-)waggon. Transport for W.A.A.F. personnel: R.A.F.: 1941 +. Robert Hinde, letter of March 17, 1945.

passionate leave. Compassionate leave: R.A.F.: since ca. 1925.

passionate release. Compassionate release from W.A.A.F. because of pregnancy: R.A.F.: since ca. 1940.

passy (p. 608). For dating read: ca. 1790–1870.

past mark of mouth. See **mark of mouth** (*Dict.*).

past oneself, get. To be fractious or (very) excited: coll.: from ca. 1910.

paste away, v.i. To keep on punching: coll.: since ca. 1870. *Sessions,* Jan. 1882. See **paste,** v., 1 (p. 608).

pasteboard, . . . shoot one's. This form is recorded earlier by B. & L.

Pat, 1 (p. 609) occurs earlier in an anecdote drawn from an unidentified British source and repeated in an American magazine, *The Port Folio,* Oct. 11, 1806 (p. 221), thus, 'A company of honest Pats in the purlieus of St. Giles'. Moe.—2. Also Australian: see **Paddy, 2.** Also low English, esp. Londoners'.

[**pat.** See 'Epithets'. Prob. always S.E.]

Pat and Mick. A, or to, lick (lit. and fig.): Australian rhyming s.: C. 20.—2. Penis: Anglo-Irish: late C. 19–20. Rhyming on **prick,** 3 (p. 659).

patch.—5. A police area or district: Northern and Midland policemen's: since ca. 1920. '"Look, Ripley, my patch is the city. I'm not like you— a county officer. Your area is wide open"' (John Wainwright, *Death in a Sleeping City,* 1965). One's own 'cabbage *patch'.*

patch, on the. In trouble: Australian Naval: since ca. 1925. (B., 1943.) On the (patch of) carpet fronting the C.O.'s desk.

*patch-worker. A pickpocket specialising in outside pockets other than fob-pockets: c.: from ca. 1910. (*The Evening News,* Dec. 9, 1936.) Ex S.E. *patch-pocket,* defined by the O.E.D. Sup. as 'a pocket consisting of a piece of cloth sewn like a patch on to a garment'. Cf. **fob-worker.**

path. Pathology; pathological: late C. 19–20: medical s., now verging on coll.

pathfinder. An airman either very lucky or enviably judicious in finding women: R.A.F.: 1942-5. Ex the official sense of the term. (P-G-R.)

patriotic lance-corporal. An unpaid lance-corporal: Army: since ca. 1915.

Pats. See *Princess Pats* below.

patter, v., 5 (p. 610), has its corresponding n.: 'food': 1855, John Lang, *The Forger's Wife.*

*patter, in for. See in for patter and patter, n., 4, in the *Dict.*

Paul Pry. A 'giant searchlight': 1939–45; ob. by 1948. Berrey, 1940.

pauler. See pawler (p. 611) and below. Also, 'something very puzzling; a poser': as in Captain Glascock, *Land Sharks and Sea Gulls*, 1838. And earlier in his *Sketch-Book*, 2nd Series, 1834, at I, 206. (Moe.)

paup along. Bravely to make ends meet: middle and upper classes': ca. 1880–1920. (Edward Burke, *Bachelor's Buttons*, 1912.) By back-formation ex *pauper.*

Pauper's Grave, the; the Morgue. The smaller-print, brief reviews at back of *The Times Literary Supplement:* the world of books: resp. since ca. 1925 and 1920.

pavement, hit the. To be thrown out (of, e.g., a night-club); to be dismissed from one's job: since ca. 1936.

pavement pusher. A man selling goods on the kerb or anywhere in street or street-market: mostly Londoners': since ca. 1942. Duncan Webb in *Daily Express*, Sept, 17, 1945. Ex push the pavement.

pavy, the; gen. the P. The pavilion: Harrovian: from ca. 1880 (?). Lunn. Hence, at certain other Public Schools: C. 20.

pawler (p. 611) also means 'an unanswerable objection', as in W. N. Glascock, *Sailors and Saints* (I, 54), 1829, where it is spelt *pauler.* Moe.

pax-wax.—2. The *membrum virile*: C. 19–20.

pay, n. Also as nickname: witness 'Taffrail'.

pay for one's whistle. To pay excessively for one's fancy or whim: non-aristocratic: from ca. 1870; ob. B. & L.

pay-off.—2. Hence, the final settlement: Services: adopted, 1943, ex U.S.; by 1950, fairly general civilian s.

pay off, v.—2. (Of plans, ventures, attempts) to prove successful: Canadian since ca. 1940, English and Australian since ca. 1950. 'I put in for extended leave, but it didn't pay off.' (Leechman.) Ex gold-mining?

pay-off Gieves. 'It is an old Wardroom "crack" that anyone starting a sweepstake or a subscription does so in order to pay his outfitters . . . Gieves' (Granville): C. 20.

pay one's corner. To pay one's share, esp. for drinks: mostly in Lancashire and Yorkshire: late C. 19–20. (W. Sorley Brown, *T. W. H. Crosland*, 1928.)

pay one's relief. See 'Tavern terms', § 9.

pay the earth. To pay excessively: coll.: since ca. 1925.

pay the price of Admiralty. See price . . .

paybob is that form of pay-bob (*Dict.*) which is preferred by 'Taffrail'.

paybook!, he's been looking in your. A Forces' c.p. (1939–45) in reference to a third person's imputation of illegitimacy or other sexual irregu-larity. A Serviceman's paybook records many intimate details. (Atkinson.)

payola. Money: adopted, 1961, ex U.S., but already by end of 1964, slightly ob. and, by 1966, virtually †. Ex *pay* + *-ola*, a common, fanciful American s. suffix of Italian and Spanish origin. (Wentworth & Flexner.)

pazoo. Variant of Australian **razoo**: since ca. 1930. B., 1942.

pea.—3. A horse ridden to win, esp. in a field of doubtfuls: Australian sporting: since ca. 1920. (B., 1953.) Cf. sense 1: p. 612.

pea in a colander, like a. Flustered, agitated, jumpy: Services: C. 20. H. & P., 'Running round in small circles.' Just as common in the Services, who took it from civilians, is the late C. 19–20 low *like a fart in a bottle*, with which cf. *in and out like a fart in a colander* (mid-C. 19–20), used to describe restless and aimless movement. A Services' variant (since ca. 1920 at latest: probably since ca. 1890): *rushing round like a fart in a colander—doesn't know which hole to come out.*

pea-shooter. A rifle: Army's jocular irony: C. 20; esp. in 1914–18. Cf. sense 3.—2. A pea-shooter, says Berrey, is 'a pursuit 'plane' (a fighter). No; it is a machine-gun, or a light-calibred cannon on an aircraft (esp. if British): H. & P., 1943. Dating from 1939. By meiosis. —3. Also, a revolver: R.A.F.: since mid-1940. E. P. in *The New Statesman*, Sept. 19, 1942. But the term has existed in Australia since ca. 1900; it occurs in, e.g., Alex. Macdonald, *In the Land of Pearl and Gold*, 1907, at p. 247.

peace-time soldier. One who, in the Army, does the same work as he would do in civilian life: military: since ca. 1920. H. & P.—2. But also, in the predominantly civilian army of 1939–45, a Regular soldier. (P-G-R.)

peach-house. In the 1914–18 war and for some time afterwards at least, the Admiralty used to be known as *The Peach-House* on account of the remarkably high level of attractiveness of the girl clerks employed there.

peachy (p. 612) was, everywhere, ob. by 1959.

peacock, v.—3. Hence, to outwit, be too smart for (someone): since ca. 1910. B., 1942.

peacock engine is recorded earlier by B. & L.

peaking, n. Any behaviour unworthy of a courageous person; e.g. a facile complaint or 'bellyaching' or yelling if you're hurt: Australian coll.: since ca. 1920. (Kylie Tennant, *The Honey Flow*, 1956.) Ex the E. dial. *peak*, to squeak like a mouse; echoic.

peam(e)y. A seller of peas: ca. 1820–70. *Sessions*, 1833. A blend of '*pea-merchant*'.

peanut alley—p. gallery—p. row. The front row of stalls in a cinema: Australian urban juvenile: since ca. 1945. (B., 1953.) The 1st and the 2nd were adopted ex U.S.—more prob. ca. 1944, ex American servicemen. (Robert Clairborne.)

peanuts. A mere trifle; esp., a (very) small sum of money: Australian: since ca. 1930. Not necessarily ex U.S. (Morris West, *Gallows on the Sand*, 1956.)

peanutter. 'A person who grows peanuts' (B., 1959): Aus. coll.: C. 20.

pear-drop. An aerial bomb: 1914–18 aviators'. (William McFee, *North of Suez*, 1930.) Ex shape resembling that of the sweet so named.

pearl. Ale: Naval: ? ca. 1800–90. (W. N.

Glascock, *Sketch-Book*, 2nd Series, 1834, at II, 59, 'A pint o' pearl, a glass o' grog'.) Moe.

pearl; pearlier. Australian spelling variants of **purl, purler.** Baker.

pearl on the nail should be compared with **supernaculum**: both are in *Dict.*

pearlies.—3. Teeth: non-aristocratic: late C. 19–20. W. L. George, *The Making of an Englishman*, 1914.

pearling, adj. and n. 'Allowing the nose of the surfboard to slip under' (*Pix*, Sept. 28, 1963): Australian surfers': since ca. 1961.

peasant, usually in pl. One who is in the ranks, esp. an aircraftman: R.A.F. and R.A.A.F. jocular: 1939–45. (B., 1943.)

peavy (p. 613), better spelt *peavey*, perhaps derives from its deviser, a John or Joseph *Peavey*, was originally, as still, U.S., and, being Standard American, is quite out of place here.

peck, n.—2. A business or concern, as 'a racing peck' (P. H. Emerson, *Signor Lippo*, 1893): low: ca. 1870–1910. Perhaps ex sense 1 (p. 613).

peck, v.—3. 'To attack and break away quickly' (Jackson): R.A.F.: 1939 +.

pecker, 4 (p. 613), is still (1960) widely used in Canada.

Peckham. Short for **Peckham Rye** (*Dict.*).

pedal, v. To send (a message) by wireless transceiver: Australian coll.: since ca. 1936. Ex the obligatory pedalling on the generator pedals. (Tom Ronan, *Vision Splendid*, 1954.)

pedal; get the pedal or **be pedalled.** To dismiss —to get oneself, or to be, dismissed—from a job: motor and cycle trades: since ca. 1920. Robert Westerby, *Wide Boys Never Work*, 1937.

pedal-pushers. Three-quarter length, i.e. calf-length, pants suitable for female sports-wear: teenagers': adopted, ca. 1962, ex U.S.

peddle (her) **hips.** To be a prostitute: since ca. 1920. (Valtin, *Out of the Night*, 1941.)

pedestals. See 'Body'.

pedo. A patient with a pedicle: Australian (Services') hospitals': ca. 1942–6. Dal Stivens, *The Courtship of Uncle Henry*, 1946.

pee-hee, v. To ingratiate oneself with one's superiors: 1939 +; by 1946, ob. *The New Statesman*, Aug. 30, 1941. Echoic.

pee oneself laughing. To laugh very heartily and/or long: since ca. 1910. Gerald Kersh, *Clean, Bright and Slightly Oiled*, 1946. Also *piss . . .*

pee-warmer. See **piss-warmer.**

pee-Willy. An effeminate male: Canadian: since ca. 1925.

peechy.—2. (Ex sense 1: p. 614.) Hence, behind, both adv. and n. (backside): Army: C. 20. 'What are you doing, sitting on your peechy like a char-wallah?'—i.e. idling.

peek-a-boo or **peek(-)a(-)Bo.** See **nose-scratch.** —2. A girl's blouse with perforations: ca. 1880– 1914.—3. Any garment made from 'Swiss cotton' (*broderie anglaise*): Australian: since ca. 1950. (B.P.)

peeko. A glance; a quick look-about: since ca. 1910. (Belton Cobb, *No Last Words*, 1949.)

peel, n. A policeman: Australian: since ca. 1920. 'Unless this can be traced back to Mr, later Sir, Robert Peel, it is a shortening of **peeler**, 3 (p. 614)': Barry Prentice. The latter is the more likely.

peel-off, n. Illicit removal of part of a common booty: low s., police s., and underworld: C. 20.

'He wanted a lot more. He . . . indulged in a little "peel-off"' (Gosling, 1959). Contrast and cf.:

peel off.—2. To give money; esp. as 'He peeled off one', he gave me a pound: c.: from ca. 1925. I.e. to slip a (currency) note from a wad of notes.—3. To break away, esp. in a dive, from a formation: R.A.F. coll. (since ca. 1925) >, by 1941, j. Ex peeling off one's clothes.

Peeler Murphy. See 'Nicknames'. An alternative origin has been ingeniously suggested by Robert Clairborne, Aug. 21, 1966: 'a possible pun on "peel a Murphy"?

peelo. A pilot: R.A.F.: 1940 +; ob. by 1946. Jackson. Ex the French pron. of the English *pilot*; obviously not ex Fr. *pilote* (as occ. implied).

peenicker pawnee (or *-ie*). A frequent variant of **pinnicky pawnee.**

peep, n. A car belonging to a Command H.Q.: Canadian Army: ca. 1941–5. Suggested by *jeep*, 1.—2. A word: mostly spivs': since ca. 1945. '"One more peep out of you, Mister, and I'll get the boys to push you and your b— stall in the oggin"—which was a nearby canal': *Picture Post*, Jan. 2, 1954, article on young spivs.

peep-bo (p. 614) is recorded in 1818 (Alfred Burton, *Johnny Newcome*). Moe. It is 'still common in Australia' (B.P., mid-1963).

peeper, n., 5 (p. 614): late C. 19–20. In, e.g., A. Neil Lyons, *Arthur's*, 1908.

peeping Tom.—2. Hence, a pilot that is expert at flying in bad weather and at dodging from cloud to cloud: R.A.F.: since 1939. H. & P. His prey is less exciting and much more dangerous than that of Lady Godiva's peeping Tom.

Peer, the. See **conkey.**

*****peery**, n.—2. (Gen. in pl.: *peeries*.) A foot, c., and low: C. 20.

peewee. A small yellow marble: Australian schoolchildren's: C. 20. B., 1942.

Peg. Inseparable nickname of girls surnamed *Legge*: C. 20. Ex *peg-leg.*

peg, n., 5, is also Australian of C. 20.—10. Esp. in 'It's a peg!', it's first-class or -rate: Australian: since ca. 1930. (B., 1943.) Cf. sense 8: p. 615. —11. (Mostly in pl. *pegs*.) A signal: railwaymen's: C. 20. (*Railway*.)—12. (The sandbars and mudflats) 'have white posts on them, with a bit of tin pointing to deep water. . . . Well, they're called pegs' (Nino Culotta, *Gone Fishin'*, 1963): Aus. fishermen's: C. 20.

Sense 2, on p. 615, occurs earlier in James Dalton, *A Narrative*, 1728, '"I'll take him a Peg in the Face."'

peg, v.—8. (Ex sense 3 ?) To throw: Australian low: since ca. 1930. Baker, 'As in "peg a gooly", throw a stone.' v.—9. To starve (v.i.): Australian: late C. 19–20. Vance Palmer, *The Passage*, 1930, 'Damn it! I forgot that mare! She's come a long way, and must be pegging for a drink and a feed.' Ex *peg out*, to die.—10. To put (someone) on a charge: Army: since ca. 1910. (P-G-R.)

peg, put in the.—2. A loose variant of **peg, put** (oneself) **on the** in *Dict.*

peg, take down a. See **take down a peg**, which, in the *Dict.*, is wrongly referred to **peg.**

peg away (p. 615) occurs earlier in John L. Gardner, *The Military Sketch-Book* (II, 21), 1831. Moe.

peg-legger.—2. A variant of **peg-leg** (p. 615): C. 20. *The Bournemouth Echo*, Oct. 28, 1943.

peg out, 2 (p. 615), apparently comes from cribbage, where pegs are used to keep score; whoever pegs out first, wins. (Leechman.) "'My uncle's pegged out,'" he said. "'His game of cribbage is done".' Morley Roberts, *Maurice Quain*, 1897.

peg out. Sense 2 (p. 615) has early American occurrence in Joseph M. Field, *Job and His Children* (II, i), 1852. Moe.—3. To go to—and use—the w.c.: a certain Oxfordshire girls' school: (?) late C. 19–20. Ex the feminine posture involved and its resemblance to an old-fashioned clothes-peg.

peg to hang things on!, it's nice to have a. A c.p. said (C. 20) by such an inferior in business as bears the brunt of a superior's mistakes.

Peggy. A *Pega*sus engine—used on certain R.A.F. aircraft: R.A.F. coll.: 1943 +. Partridge, 1945.—2. A fairly common nickname of men surnamed Peters: since ca. 1910. Merely alliterative.

peggy.—5. A wooden leg: C. 20. Cf. **peg-legger.** —6. A man with only one leg: navvies' nickname: ca. 1860–1910. (D. W. Barrett, 1880.)

peggy, stand one's. To take one's turn in fetching food and cleaning the fo'c'sle: nautical: C. 20. In e.g., Norman Springer, *The Blood Ship*, 1923. See **peggy**, 3 (p. 615).

pegs, on the (p. 616): also, since ca. 1918, very common in the R.A.F.

pelf. Ill-gotten money: workmen's (— 1887). Implied by Baumann. Ex S.E. *pelf*, money. Contrast **kelp.**

Pelican. A member of the Pelican Club: ca. 1880–1910. Binstead, *A Pink 'Un and a Pelican* 1898.

pelican. 'A non-flying officer with wings,' *The New Statesman*, Aug. 30, 1941. The term is suspect; if it did exist it was only very locally and briefly. See **penguin.**

pellets. Shells. Royal Artillery: 1939–45. A meiosis.

pelt, v.—3. Mostly *be*, or *get*, *pelted*, to get thrown from a horse: Australian rural: since ca. 1890. (Tom Ronan, *Moleskin Midas*, 1956.)

pelter, out for a. In a very bad temper: proletarian: from ca. 1860; ob. B. & L.

Pemma or **Pemmer.** Pembroke College (Cambridge): Cambridge undergraduates': C. 20.

pen, n., 3 (p. 616): Australian. B., 1942.—5. (Also v.) A, to, stink: low: late C. 19–20. The v. occurs in, e.g., James Curtis, *They Ride by Night*, 1938. Short for **pen and ink** (*Dict.*).—6. A prisoner-of-war cage: Army: 1941–5. (P-G-R.) Via Canadians; ex sense 2 (p. 616).

pen bait. An under-age girl that flirts with show boys: Canadian carnival s.: C. 20. Here, *pen* = *penitentiary*, the destination of men mistreating under-age girls.

Penang lawyer (p. 616): earlier in W. N. Glascock, *Sailors and Saints* (I, 145), 1829, where spelt *Panang lawyer*. Moe.

pencil, line the. 'To make a bee-line for anywhere. Dates from the time when Sir Percy (Guns before Ceremony) Scott introduced his "dotter",' Granville: Naval: C. 20.

penciller (p. 616). In Australia: also, the bookmaker himself: C. 20. B., 1942.

penguin (p. 616). But sense 1 survives in the nuance, 'a ground-staff, i.e. non-flying, member of the R.A.F.': since ca. 1925. H. & P. Cf. **kiwi.**—3. 'A cunning specialist who disposed of sand excavated from tunnels so that the ferrets' —see **ferret** in Addenda—'could not find it,' Brickhill & Norton, *Escape to Danger*, 1946: among prisoners-of-war in Germany, 1940–5.

penguin party. 'Those who go ashore every night but never go to sea . . . For these men there are shouts of derision: "Penguin Party, fall in!"' (correspondent, 1959): Naval: since 1946 or 1947. Cf. preceding entry.

penguin suit. A dinner jacket: since late 1950's. (B.B.C., Feb. 1, 1964.)

peninsula. A very inquisitive female, often with a long neck stretched out to *see*: jocular: since ca. 1955. Sometimes called an *ostrich*, esp. if seen peering over neighbours' hedges or fences. (Petch.)

pennal. Variant of **pinnel** (*Dict.*). Eustace Jervis, *Twenty-Five Years*, 1925.

penner or **penner-up.** 'A station hand who confines sheep in woolshed pens at shearing time' (B., 1943): late C. 19–20: originally coll., it was, by 1945 at latest, S.E.

pennies from heaven. Easy money: since ca. 1925: coll. >, by 1945, familiar S.E. Berta Ruck, *Pennies from Heaven*, 1940.

pennorth, take a, esp. in the imperative. To go away: Cockney: late C. 19. Of fresh air?

penn'orth of bread. Head: navvies' rhyming s.: ca. 1860–1910. (D. W. Barrett, *Navvies*, 1880.)

penn'orth (or **ball) of** chalk. A walk: late C. 19–20. F. D. Sharpe, *The Flying Squad*, 1938 (both); Axel Bracey, 1934 (**ball . . .**). Often shortened to *pennorth*.

Penny is, esp. in the Services, the inseparable nickname of men surnamed Singleton: since ca. 1945. Ex a woman film star—*Penny Singleton*.

penny.—2. See **penny the pound.**

penny? A coll. (late C. 19–20) shortening of *a penny for your thoughts*: W. L. George, *The Making of an Englishman*, 1914.

penny-a-mile. A hat: rhyming s. (on *tile*): from ca. 1870.—2. Hence, head: late C. 19–20. Neil Bell, *Crocus*, 1936.—3. A smile: rhyming s.: 20. Franklyn, *Rhyming*.

penny a pound; often merely *penny*. Ground: rhyming s.: late C. 19–20. (Franklyn, ibid.)

penny black. One of the early English postage-stamps: philatelists' coll.: C. 19–20.

penny bun. See **cockle to a penny** above.

penny packet; usually in pl. A small party of soldiers—smaller than a platoon—as seen aerially: R.A.F.: since early 1940. H. & P.

penny plain and tuppence coloured, originally (as in R. L. Stevenson's title for an essay published in 1880: O.E.D.) *a penny plain and twopence coloured*, has, since ca. 1890, been a c.p. that, since ca. 1950, is slightly ob. Meaning 'plain or fancy', the phrase seems to have, at first, referred to cheap fiction, costing one penny with plain jacket and, with coloured-picture jacket, two-pence.

penny steamboat. A ferry: jocular coll.: C. 20.

penny stinker. A bad cigar: mostly Cockneys': from ca. 1880; by 1946, †.

penny the pound. Ground: rhyming: C. 20. Arthur Gardner, *Tinker's Kitchen*, 1932. Also *penny a pound*. Often merely *penny*.

penny's dropped!; or **the penny'll drop in a minute.** 'A c.p. to mark the belated appreciation of humour' (Atkinson): since ca. 1930. Ex slot-payment in public lavatories.

pep.—2. Peppermint: C. 20.

pep pill. A stimulant (in tablet form) to a central nervous system: since the late 1940's. Cf. **pep** on p. 618.

pep talk. A talk or speech designed to improve morale: coll.: since ca. 1925. See **pep**, 1 (*Dict.*).

pepper, v.—4. To 'salt' a gold-mining claim. Australian: since ca. 1860. B., 1942.

Pepper Pot, the. 'The gallant *Penelope* which was so damaged by bomb splinters that she resembled one' (Granville): Naval: War of 1939–45.

peppered, be. To have laid a large stake: turf: from ca. 1870. 'He was peppered in one dangerous quarter alone to the extent of three or four thousand pounds,' quoted by B. & L.

peppermint in one's speech, have a. To stammer: coll., mostly Cockneys': from ca. 1890. Pugh.

peppermint rocks; often **peppermints.** Socks: rhyming s.: C. 20.

per.—2. Per hour: since ca. 1910. John Newton Chance, *Wheels in the Forest*, 1935, 'An average of eighty miles per.'

perc. A (coffee) percolator: Society: since ca. 1920. F. E. Bailey, *Fleet Street Girl*, 1934.

Perce. A Percival communication 'plane: R.A.F.: 1942 +. Partridge, 1945.—2. (Also *Percy.*) Penis: esp. in *point Perce at the porcelain*, to urinate: Australian: since ca. 1945. 'Perce the *piercer*'?—cf. Fr. *percer*, to pierce.

percentage. Profit; advantage: Army, since ca. 1940; civilian, since ca. 1945. 'There's no percentage in it'—nothing's to be gained by it. (P-G-R.)

percenter. One who works on a commission; one who does this and that, arranges this deal and that, for a percentage: business(-)world coll.: C. 20.

perch, on the. Handcuffed: police s.: since ca. 1925. '. . . A uniformed constable with his prisoner "on the perch"' (John Gosling, 1959).

percolator. '*To have a shake, rave or percolator . . . to have a party*' (Anderson): beatniks': since ca. 1959. Ex the coffee percolator that so often features as these affairs.

Percy, in the Royal Navy, has, since ca. 1925, meant an effeminate man; but since ca. 1940, also and esp. a studious, quiet, educated man as opposed to an uncouth 'tough'.—2. See **Perce**, 2, above.

***perde, make.** See **make perde.**

perf. A perforation: stamp-collectors' coll.: late C. 19–20.

perfectly good. Eminently satisfactory; trustworthy, dependable, reliable; (of things) sound, undamaged; (of persons) uninjured, in good health: coll.: since ca. 1930. 'A perfectly good reason or excuse'—'a perfectly good aircraft'—'perfectly good plan'—etc., etc., etc.

perfess. Short for *perfessor*, professor: Cockney (mostly): C. 19–20.

perform, 2 (p. 619), occurs in Miles Franklin, *My Brilliant Career*, 1901.—3. To swear vividly, to show a furious temper: Australian: since ca. 1925. (B., 1943.)

perhapser. A very risky stroke: Australian cricketers': since ca. 1930. Dal Stivens, *The Scholarly Mouse*, 1958.

perim. Perimeter track (encircling an airfield): R.A.F. coll.: since ca. 1937. Jackson.

period! Finally; without extension or modification, palliation or repeal: originally (ca. 1945), journalists', authors', broadcasters', perhaps typists': only since ca. 1955 has it been at all general. 'Dead as a door-nail? Just dead. Period!'

periscope potters. German snipers specialising in smashing British infantrymen's periscopes: 1915–18. (A. B. Petch, March 1966.)

perish, n. See *perish, do a,* senses 1 (p. 619) and 2. By 1900, sense 1 was general Australian; by 1910, *perish* was used as an entity, as in 'Their yarns of perishes on dry tracks' (Vance Palmer, *Golconda*, 1958).

perish, v.t. A low coll., prob. independent of the † S.E. sense, 'destroy'; thus in W. Pett Ridge, *Mord Em'ly*, 1898, 'Chrise, I'll perish you, if you ain't careful.'

perish, do a, 1 (p. 619): 'not confined to Western Australia' (B.P., mid-1963).—2. Hence, to be homeless; to sleep out at night in the parks: Australian: C. 20. B., 1942.

perisher, 3 (p. 619). A good early example: 'You bleeding little perisher,' *Sessions*, April 1898. 3 (fellow: p. 619). This sense probably goes back at least as far as 1850: cf. 'He had no name. In the thaw they buried him in the pass, and his epitaph was SOME POOR BLOODY PERISHER. 1864': Ruth Park, *One-a-Pecker, Two-a-Pecker*, 1958, concerning the Otago gold-rush of the 1860's.—6; **starver.** The former is less gen. than the latter, which is 'muvver's pet name for farver of a Sat'd'y, when 'e comes 'ome slewed wiv' 'alf 'is wages blued': Cockneys': C. 20. Esp. 'you blee'n ol' starver (or, perisher)!'

perisher, do a. To die from lack of water: Australian: C. 20. Archer Russell, 1934. A variant of **do a perish,** 1 (p. 619).

perisher, the. The C.O.'s course for submarine commanders: Naval: 1940 + .

perishing.—2. Very cold, as in 'I didn't 'ave no coat on, an' it were perishing': Cockneys': late C. 19–20. (Julian Franklyn.)

perishing track. An outback route affording no or very little water: Aus. rural: C. 20. (B., 1959.) Cf. **perish, do a,** above—and on p. 619.

perk, v. To vomit: Australian low: C. 20. B., 1942. A thinning of 'to *puke*'.—2. To percolate as in 'Coffee won't be long—it's perking nicely': since ca. 1955. Ex *percolator* rather than ex *percolate*.

perm (p. 619) had, by 1940, > merely a synonym for a 'hair wave': hence, since ca. 1940, *permanent perm*, jocular for a 'perm' (in its original sense). —3. A permutation: coll.: since the mid 1920's.

permanent spats. See **spats.**

pernicated dude. A swaggering dandy: Canadian: ca. 1885–1910. B. & L.

peroney (or **-nee**). For each man; hence, for each person: parlary, esp. among buskers: mid C. 19–20. Probably an 'easement' or, less likely, a deliberate distortion of *per omee,* per man (cf. *omee,* p. 587). Mr Herbert Seaman, learned in the ways of theatre, music-hall, side-show, tells me (letter of 23 July 1950) that 'Mr Dai Griffith, a singer, once sang to me this song, which he said was current among buskers.

Nantee dinarly; the omee of the carsey
Says due bionc peroney, manjaree on the cross.

We'll all have to scarper the letty in the morning,
Before the bonee omee of the carsey shakes his
doss.

The tune is simple, in 6/8 time, and should have a
guitar accompaniment.'

peroon. For each, apiece; hence, each: parlary: mid C. 19–20. Lit. 'for one': Italian *per
uno*. Cf. the entry preceding this and see the
quotation at **dewey** above.

perp(endicular)!, strike me. A Cockney asseveration: late C. 19–20; ob. Both forms are in
Edwin Pugh's 'The Honeymoon' in *The Cockney
at Home*, 1914.

perpetrate a nonsense. 'To issue an order
(Local A.A. slang),' H. & P.: ca. 1939–44.

Perry. A *Peregrine* engine: R.A.F. ground
crews': 1942 + . Partridge, 1945.

Persian Gulf. See **You know the . . .**
[Personifications in early C. 18: Ned Ward has
the Old Gentleman, Time (1703), and both *the Old
Harridan* (1700) and her *Mope-Eyed Ladyship*
(1703) for Fortune. Matthews.]

Perspiration Avenue, as in 'She lost weight
in . . .': the walking space between the lathes in
a large machine-shop, esp. a munitions factory:
factory workers': since ca. 1916.

persuader.—6. A crowbar: London Fire Brigade: late C. 19–20.

pertish. Fairly drunk: coll.: ca. 1760–1820.
Sessions, 1772, 4th session of Wm Nash's mayoralty.

Peru window. A one-way window that, in a
bedroom, enables a third party to watch coïtion:
low Australian: since ca. 1963.

perv, n. Corresponding to the adj.: Australian:
since ca. 1930. (B.P.) In nuance 'a male homosexual', it occurs in, e.g., Bernard Hesling, *The
Dinkumization and Depommification*, 1963.

perv, adj. Erotic: Australian: since the late
1920's. Lawson Glassop, 1944, 'Bluey brought a
perv book back from Cairo with him'. I.e. a
sense-perversion and shortening of *perverted*.

perv show. A strip-tease show: Australian:
since ca. 1930. (B.P.) Cf. **perv**, adj., above.

perve, v.i. To practise perversion; mostly
between women and esp. as in 'What about a
spot of perving?': Australian: since ca. 1930.
(Communication, June 9, 1941, from Melbourne.)
—2. Australian, since ca. 1930, as in 'Eddie was
. . . doing, as the boys expressed it, "a bit of
perving". He was looking at his gallery of nudes
and semi-nudes and trying, as usual, to reach
a decision about the one he would prefer to
sleep with,' Lawson Glassop, *We Were the Rats*,
1944. 'Its use here often involves no more than
watching a girl or woman in admiration. Whence,
to perve at (a girl), to extract pleasure from looking
at her, esp. if she is scantily dressed as on a beach'
(B., 1959).

pervy. Synonymous with **perv**: 1944, Lawson
Glassop.

pesi-pesi. See 'Swahili words . . .'

pest. To pester: Australian: since ca. 1930.
Margaret Trist, *Now that We're Laughing*, 1944,
'It's enough to have a hangover, without you
pesting me all the time.'

pest it!; pest it all! A Cockney imprecation:
since when? (Pugh).

petal. An effeminate: R.A.F.: since ca. 1938.
Partridge, 1945. Prompted by **pansy** (p. 604).

peted. (Very) weary; physically exhausted:
Canadian: since ca. 1860. Morley Roberts, *The
Western Avernus*, 1887. Ex **peter out** (p. 621),
Pete being the diminutive of *Peter*.

Peter.—2. Among schoolboys, in certain localities, it is a polite synonym of *prick*, penis: C. 20.
Alliterative; cf. **John Thomas**.

*peter, 2. among tramps, always means that bag
in which a tramp carries his belongings.—7.
Witness-box: Australian police: since ca. 1920.
(Vince Kelly, *The Greedy Ones*, 1958.) Cf. sense
4 on p. 620.—8. A prison cell, whether in gaol or
at a ccurt of law: c.: late C. 19–20. (B., 1943;
Norman.) Cf. sense 4: p. 620.—9. A prison:
Australian low: C. 20. (B., 1943.)—10. A cash-
register; a till: Australian c.: since ca. 1925.
(B., 1943.)

Sense 1 (p. 620) comes rather from *Peter*, a rock.

Peter Blobbs. Shirley Brooks of 'The Pink
'Un'. Cf. *the Pitcher* and *the Shifter*.

peter (or **Peter**) **boatman**; gen. pl. A river
pirate: ca. 1798–1840. Cf. **peter-man** (*Dict.*).

*peter school (p. 621). Also in Australia. B.,
1942.

Peter the Painter; usually **here's . . .**, a jocular
c.p. of ca. 1910–20. Ex the legendary figure
supposed to have taken part in 'the Battle of
Sidney Street' in 1910.

peters. Luggage: taxi-drivers': since ca. 1910.
Herbert Hodge, 1938. Cf. **peter**, n., 1 (p.
620).

petit sergeantry. See 'Tavern terms', § 9.

Petticoat Lane is now a coll.; has indeed been
a coll. ever since Petticoat Lane assumed respectability as Middlesex Street and Wentworth Street:
local London: C. 20.

pettitoes. See 'Body'.

petty (p. 621), 1, 2. Read *nighty*. The diminutive *-y* occurs frequently in women's names for
their clothes.

Peveril. Sir Walter Scott: from 1822, when his
Peveril of the Peak came out. Ex the fact that
Scott had a peaked forehead. Also **Old Peveril**,
q.v. in *Dict*.

pewter, n., 2. (Money): rather earlier in W. T.
Moncrieff, *Tom and Jerry*, 1821.

pewter, v.; **unload**. 'To drink porter out of a
quart pot' (*Sinks*): public-house: ca. 1830–70.

phagassies. 'Those gremlins which sit on the
wings and blow on the aileron and send it down'
(P-G-R): R.A.F.: 1940–5. Charles Graves, *Seven
Pilots*, 1943.

Phallic Symbol, the. The University Library:
Cambridge undergraduates': since ca. 1955. Ex
the shape of its tower.

phallic thimble. A sheath pessary: ca. 1920–
40. 'Low "educated" punning on "phallic
symbol"' (Ramsey Spencer).

phantom. A fraction: law-clerks': C. 20.
Edwin Pugh, *Harry the Cockney*, 1912, '"How
much more?" inquired Uncle Algernon, wearily.
"Three and a phantom," replied McGaffney.'

Phar Lap (p. 622). 'Term of address rather
than nickname,' Sidney J. Baker, letter, 1946.

Phar Lap gallop. A foxtrot: Australian: since
ca. 1932. (B., 1943.) Cf. *Phar Lap* (p. 622).

pharaoh (p. 622). In Belgium there was, as late
as June 18, 1938 (letter from François Fosca): a
beer named *faro*.

Pheeby. The sun: Army: C. 20. (P-G-R.)
Ex *Phoebus*.

phenobarb. Phenobarbitone: coll.: since ca. 1930.

phenomenal avoidance. 'A very narrow escape from crashing a car (Cambridge, 1930),' J. Judfield Willis, letter.

phi (p. 622) was probably coined by E. W. B. Nicholson, the eccentric and sarcastic Bodley's Librarian in 1882–1912. The semantics perhaps run something like this: 'Oh, fie! For shame! Fancy *you* wanting to read such a book!'

Phil, the. The Philathletic Club at: Harrow School: since ca. 1890 (?). Lunn.—2. A Philharmonic concert: C. 20. See **Philharmonic** in *Dict.*

Phil Garlick. Liverpool variant (C. 19–20) of *Pilgarlic* (p. 629).

Phil McBee. A flea: rhyming s. from ca. 1870. By 1940, †.

Philadelphia lawyer (p. 622) occurs earlier in W. N. Glascock, *Sailors and Saints* (I, 145), 1829. Moe.

Phineas (p. 622). 'No! The original Phineas McLino is still Catesby's'—as Julian Franklyn tells me in letter of 1962; he adds, 'A *copy* was presented to the U.C. students by Catesby's after they had taken police action.'

phizgig, n., is an Australian variant of *fizz-gig*, 2 (p. 280). Vince Kelly, *The Shadow*, 1955, and *The Greedy Ones*, 1958.

phizgig, v.i. To act as an informer to the police: Australian: since ca. 1920. (Vince Kelly, *The Shadow*, 1955.) Cf. preceding.

phone, go for—or use—**the.** To tic-tac: Australian racing: since ca. 1930. (B., 1953.) To cease doing so is to *hang up* (the phone).

phoney.—2. Hence, unreal, make-believe, as in *the phoney war* (Sept. 1939–March 1940), coined by the Americans late in 1939 and adopted by Englishmen early in 1940.—3. Applied to make-believe players in a gambling game: April 7, 1946, *The People* (article by Alan Hoby).

phoney gen. See **gen.**

phoney war, the. See **phoney,** 2 (above).

Phoo. See **Chad.** (Ex *phooey!*, nonsense! what do I care?)

phooey! An expression of utter disbelief or pronounced distaste or, even, contempt. Adopted, ca. 1959, ex U.S. Deriving ex the Yiddish form of German *pfui* and popularized by Walter Winchell during the 1930's. (Wallace Reyburn in the colour section of *The Sunday Times*, July 8, 1962.)

Phosgene. The Passive Defence Officer: Naval: 1939 + . Granville. Anti-*phosgene* and all other enemy gases.

photo finish; often reduced to *photo* (pronounced *photer*). A Guinness: rhyming s.: since ca. 1946. Franklyn, *Rhyming.*

Photo Freddie. 'Photo reconnaissance aircraft', Sgt G. Emanuel, letter of March 29, 1945: R.A.F.: 1942 + . *Freddie* is a frequent code-name or code-reference for a 'plane.

phys.—2. Physics: school's: late C. 19–20. (G. D. H. & M. Cole, *Scandal at School*, 1935.)

Physic(k). See 'Tavern terms', § 3, *d.*

Physio. Physiotherapy: physiotherapists', their patients', students': Australian: since ca. 1950.

pi squad (B. & L.) is prob. an error for synonymous **pi-squash** (*Dict.*). But, in the Army, *pi squad* is the regular term for a Bible class: C. 20.

piana. See **piano,** 3.

pianny. Tipsy: Regular Army: late C. 19–20. Ex **parnee** (p. 606).

piano, n. A chamber-pot: workmen's: C. 20. Echoic.—2. Ribs of beef: Cockney's: late C. 19–20. J. W. Horsley, 1912.—3. Often slovened to *piana*. A cash register: Anglo-Irish: since ca. 1920. It plays a merry tune.

***piano, play the.** To have one's finger-prints taken: c.: from ca. 1910. Contrast **playing the piano,** 1.—2. (Of a shearer) 'to run one's fingers over the backs of sheep to find the easiest to shear' (B., 1959): Aus. rural: C. 20.

pianola. At cards, a hand that almost *plays itself*: Australian: since ca. 1925. B., 1942.

piassa. A cleaning rod used on 4-inch Stokes mortars: Army: 1915 + . Ex **pisser,** 1 (p. 635).

Piccadilly bushman. Any wealthy Australian that lives in the West End of London: Australian: since ca. 1920. B., 1942.

Piccadilly commando. A London prostitute; since 1941, and orig. in the Forces; since 1946, increasingly ob. 'They certainly had the art of achieving a "kill" in the streets without creating a disturbance': the feeling comment made (in 1961) by a war-time R.A.F. officer.

Piccadilly daisy. A prostitute: ca. 1905–40. (Robert Keable, *Recompence*, 1924.)

Piccadilly Part II Orders. A certain Sunday newspaper (British) that profits by sex and sensationalism: ex-Servicemen's: 1946 + . On *Orders of the Day.*

piccolo and flute. A suit (of clothes): rhyming s.: since ca. 1870. Cf. *whistle and flute* (p. 953).

piccolos and flutes. / Boots: rhyming s.: since ca. 1930; not very general. Franklyn, *Rhyming.*

pice(-)money. 'Chicken feed' (small change): Army and R.A.F. in India: C. 20. Cf. **picey** in the *Dict.*

pick, c.pp. When a hostess, offering food, says 'Take your pick', some fatuous male can, in non-U society, be counted on to reply, either 'I don't think I'll need a pick' or 'I'll try a hammer and saw if a pick isn't enough': since ca. 1910.

pick, v.—2. To guess: lower-class Australian coll.: C. 20. D'Arcy Niland, *The Big Smoke*, 1959, 'I pick it right?' Ex *pick out*, to choose.

pick, come into full. As, e.g., of Brussels sprouts, to be ready for gathering: gardeners', esp. market-gardeners' coll.: late C. 19–20.

pick a bone with. To eat a meal with: jocular coll.: C. 20. (Sax Rohmer, *Grey Face*, 1924.)

pick and choose. Strong drink: rhyming s. (on *booze*): theatrical rhyming s.: C. 20. (Franklyn, *Rhyming.*)

***pick-me-up.**—3. A police van: South African c.: C. 20. *The Cape Times*, May 23, 1946.

pick off. To hit (a person) with a stone: Winchester College: mid-C. 19–20. B. & L.

pick on.—2. To find fault with: Canadian and (? hence) English coll.: since ca. 1910; this, since ca. 1930, has, indeed, been the predominant sense. (Leechman.)

pick-out job. 'A man with a smart new cab . . . is sometimes "picked out" by a passenger from the middle of the rank. He has, therefore, got a "pick-out job". They're not much cop, as a rule.' Herbert Hodge, *Cab, Sir?*, 1939.

pick the bones out of that!, let him; or he can . . . Let him try to retort, or retaliate, to that!: c.p. C. 20.

pick the eyes out of. See **eye picker.**

pick-up.—6. A ride in lorry or motor-car: tramps' c.: from ca. 1910. W. L. Gibson Cowan, *Loud Report*, 1937.—7. An arrest: c.: from ca. 1919. Ex sense 6 of the v.—8. *The* . . ., theft from unattended cars: c.: since ca. 1925. F. D. Sharpe, 1938.

pick up, v., 3 (harlot's nuance): very much earlier in report on trial held in 1721, in *Select Trials, from 1720 to 1724*, pub. in 1734.—6. To arrest (a wrongdoer): c.: C. 20. E.g. in *The Pawnshop Murder*. Ex senses 2, 3.—7. To obtain (esp. promotion): Naval coll.: C. 20. Granville, '"So-and-so hopes to pick up his half stripe next year."' Cf. **collect,** v., 3 (on p. 170).

Sense 2 and, in orig. nuance, 3 (p. 624) prob. date from ca. 1790 or even 1780. It occurs thus, 'I was a flashman of St Giles/And fell in love with Nelly Stiles . . ./. . . She picked up the flats as they passed by.' See *flash-man above.

pick up fag-ends. To listen to a conversation that does not concern one: Scottish Public Schools': from ca. 1910. Ian Miller, *School Tie*, 1935.

picked before he was ripe. (A person) 'under-sized or rawly innocent' (B., 1959): Aus.: since ca. 1920.

pickled monkey. 'A species of animal served by the Germans to prisoners-of-war. Its identity was never determined by the recipients,' Anon., *The Soldier's War Slang Dictionary*, 1939: P.o.W.s', 1914–18.

pickled pork. Conversations: since ca. 1890. *The* (Birmingham) *Evening Despatch*, July 19, 1937. Rhyming on *talk*.

pickling-tubs. 'Wellington, or top boots' (*Sinks*): low: ca. 1830–70.

picky. A pickpocket: policemen's: ca. 1880–1914. Arthur Griffiths, *Criminals I Have Known*, 1895.

picture, get the. To understand (esp. the general idea): coll.: since ca. 1935. Cf. **put in the picture** below.

picture, get one's. To 'get one's cards'—be dismissed from one's job: since ca. 1920. Richard Llewellyn, *None But the Lonely Heart*, 1943.

picture, paint a. See **paint.—picture, put in the.** See **put** . . .

picture gallery. A trench exposed to snipers: Army on the Western front: 1914–18. (Reginald Pound, *The Lost Generation*, 1964.)

piddle, v. Sense 1, also metaphorically of in-effectual writing. Scott, letter of Nov. 10, 1814, concerning a play: 'He piddles through a cullen-der.'

piddling. Trivial; insignificant: low coll.: C. 20.

pie.—4. 'Association of buyer at auction to buy at low prices and act as a monopoly' (B.P.): Australian coll., esp. 'the wool *pies*': since late 1940's. Ex 'to have a finger in every *pie*'.

pie, put into the. At book sales, to put into a large lot, to be sold at the end: auctioneers': from ca. 1860. B. & L.

pie and one. Son: rhyming s.: late C. 19–20.

pie-ard (see on p. 626). Straight ex the Hindu-stani comes the R.A.F. Regulars' nuance, '*any dog*' (Jackson). The Army in North Africa (1940–8) used *pie dog* of any desert dog.

pie at or **pie on, be.** To be very good at (some-thing): New Zealand and Australian: C. 20. B., 1941, 'It has been derived from the Maori *pai*, good.' Cf. **pie on** (*Dict.*).

pie eater. 'Someone of no importance' (B., 1959): Aus.: C. 20.

pie-eyed. Tipsy: adopted, ca. 1943, ex U.S., where it derives ex Standard American *pie-eyed*, having the eyes *pied*, i.e. disordered, unable to focus.

pie in the sky when you die, often preceded by *you'll get* or, occasionally and loosely, *there'll be*. A derisive, basically cynical American c.p., imply-ing that the hope of a happy hereafter is illusory. As an American c.p., it dates—according to Went-worth & Flexner—from ca. 1910, but there is reason to suspect that ca. 1907 would be nearer the mark, for either it originated as a taunt addressed by members of the I.W.W. (slogan: 'Workers of the world, unite') to non-sympathisers in general and to the conventionally minded in particular, and, as such, served to inspire Joe Hill's (but is it certain that it *was* Joe Hill's ?) song, *The Preacher and the Slave*, published in or about the year 1906, as *Webster's New International Dictionary*, 3rd edition, 1961, states, or the I.W.W. very promptly utilized the song or rather the one phrase *pie in the sky when you die*. The phrase caught on, and by ca. 1910 or, at latest, 1912, was addressed, no longer merely by the underprivileged to the privi-leged but by anyone to anyone sure of a coming Utopia or an eventual Heaven. By 1920, it was fairly common in Canada and in other American-affected parts of the world.

In his long-out-of-print *American Tramp and Underworld Songs and Slang*, the late Godfrey Irwin includes in the glossary this entry:—

PIE IN THE SKY.—One's reward in the hereafter. From that parody on the hymn, 'In the Sweet Bye and Bye', which declares in the refrain:

'You will eat, bye and bye,
In that glorious land in the sky;
Work and pray, live on hay,
You'll get pie in the sky when you die.'

In the selection of songs, Irwin gives the full text of Joe Hill's *The Preacher and the Slave* and thus identifies the parody with the song.

pie match. A cricket match after which the losing side pays for a feast: Rugby School: from ca. 1860. By 1966, †. (David Wharton, June 6, 1966.)

piebald pony. A half-caste (Aboriginal) child: Northern Territory, Australia: since ca. 1920. Ernestine Hill, *The Territory*, 1951.

piece, 1, has, in C. 19–20, been usually appre-hended as elliptical for *piece of tail.*—4. Patter: pitch-holders' in any open market, e.g. the old Caledonian, that in Portobello Road, the Sunday market in Petticoat Lane: late (? mid) C. 19–20.

piece, say one's. To say what one has intended to say, esp. in business or in moral duty: coll.: since ca. 1910. Ex obligatory recitation at, e.g., a party.

*piece-broker. A 'fence' specialising in stolen cloth: c.: mid-C. 19–20. B. & L.

piece of cake, a. 'A thing that is easy to handle or an unmistakable opportunity,' H. & P.: R.A.F.: since ca. 1938. 'A cakewalk, a snip' (H. & P.); or rather, perhaps, something as easy to take as a portion of cake. *It's a Piece of Cake or R.A.F.*

Slang Made Easy, by Squadron-Leader C. H. Ward-Jackson, 1943. For other festive or comestible terms, cf. **party** and **groceries, cookie** and **cabbage**.

piece of dough for the troops. A catamite: Forces': since ca. 1910.

piece of duff, a. An occ. variant of the prec. Jackson, 1943.

piece of homework—of knitting. See **homework** and **knitting**.

piece of nice. An attractive girl: R.A.F. and Navy: 1940 + . Partridge, 1945; Granville.

piece of piss. A 'piece of cake' (as above): R.A.F.: 1940 + . So often it turned out to be not quite so easy, not quite so pleasant as the 'It'll be a piece of cake' had led one to expect.

piece of pudding. A piece of good luck; a welcome change: proletarian: from ca. 1870; ob. B. & L.

piece of resistance (not *pièce de résistance*). Constipation: Australian: since ca. 1930. B., 1942. A pun!

piece of stray. A chance complaisant woman; a married man's mistress: mostly Forces': 1939 + .

piece of stuff. A woman: Naval: ca. 1790–1860. *The Night Watch* (I, 151), 1828. Moe.

piece of thick. A piece of pressed cake tobacco: non-aristocratic: from ca. 1860. B. & L.

***piece of toffee.** A 'toff': c. and low s.: since ca. 1920. (Nicholas Blake, *The Whisper in the Gloom*, 1954.)

piecee one. First rate: pidgin (mid-C. 19–20) > Naval (C. 20). Granville. Cf. **number one piecee.**

***pieces.** Money: c.: mid-C. 19–20; ob. B. & L. Perhaps, as Douglas Leechman has suggested, ex '*pieces* of eight'.

pieces, do one's. To go mad: Army: since ca. 1925.

pieces, the.—2. The ship's guns: Naval (officers') coll.: C. 20. Granville. The coll. revival of a Standard English term long obsolete.

pier-head jump. A wholly unexpected draft-chit: Naval: since ca. 1918. (P-G-R.) Cf.:

pier-head jumper is the agent of *pier-head jump, do a* (p. 626).

pierce. To peer: catachrestic: C. 20. *The Pawnshop Murder:* 'Beady eyes piercing around at all objects'.

Piermont Yank. Synonymous with *Woolloo-mooloo Yank:* B., 1943.

pig, n.—10. An elephant: circus: C. 20. Edward Seago, *Sons of Sawdust*, 1934.—11. Short for the singular of **pigs aft:** lower-deckese: since ca. 1912 (*Weekly Telegraph*, Oct. 25, 1941).—12. A rugby football: Australian rugby footballers': C. 20. B., 1942. Pigskin casing.—13. A locomotive; *pig mauler,* locomotive engineer; *pig(-)pen,* locomotive roundhouse: Canadian railroadmen's (− 1931).—14. An officer: Australian airmen's: 1939–45. (B., 1943.) Cf. sense 11.—15. A prostitute: low Canadian: since ca. 1930. (Brian Moore, *The Luck of Ginger Coffey*, 1960.)—16. A girl; a young lady: beatniks': since ca. 1959. (Anderson.)

pig, in. Pregnant: rural upper classes': since ca. 1870. (Nancy Mitford, *The Pursuit of Love*, 1945.)

Pig, the. The Blue Boar Hotel, Trinity Street, Cambridge: University of Cambridge, mostly undergraduates': C. 20. (David Wharton, June 6, 1966.)

pig and roast. Toast (bread): Army rhyming s.: ca. 1939–45. (Franklyn, *Rhyming*.)

Pig and Whistle, the. Also a certain college staircase: at Oxford (?): from ca. 1860. Perhaps connected with 'the Pig and Whistle', a coach mentioned in *Tom Brown's Schooldays*.

pig and whistle, the. A ship's canteen: nautical: C. 20. *The Pig and Whistle* is a popular inn-name.

pig at a tater, go at it like a. To act like a bull in a china shop: late C. 19–20; orig., Black Country dial.; by 1930, a gen. Midlands coll. (Richard Merry.)

Pig Bridge (p. 627). Note Ware's mistake of using the Oxford *quad* instead of the Cambridge *court.*

pig-fucker or, when there's company, *the P.F. man.* That man who, in a lumber camp, looks after the tools: Canadian lumbermen's: C. 20.

pig mauler. See **pig,** n., 13.

pig-mill. A canteen: industrial Australian: since ca. 1920. (D'Arcy Niland, 1958.)

pig on pork; esp. *draw pig on pork,* to draw post-dated cheques: commercial: ca. 1810–80. J. W., *Perils, Pastimes and Pleasures*, 1848.

pig pen. See **pig,** n., 13.

pig-sick, make (a person). To irritate (him): Cockneys': C. 20.

pig-sticker.—5. A cavalryman, or his lance: British infantrymen's: 1914–18.

pig-sticking. Sodomy: low Canadian: since ca. 1920.

pig-sty.—3. In the Navy, it is a lower-deck term (see **pigs aft**) for the Wardroom: since ca. 1914.

pig-sty.—4. A stye: Australian jocular: C. 20. (Ruth Park, *Poor Man's Orange*, 1950.) 'No longer jocular. It has become a solecism' (B.P., mid-1963).

pig-tail.—3. A roll of coarse tobacco: ? ca. 1780–1860. 'He answered, squirting a quid of pig-tail on the floor': Wm Maginn, *Whitehall*, 1827.

pig to be killed!, then comes a. See **then comes . . .** in the *Dict.*

pigeon, 6. (p. 628) should be back-dated by more than 100 years! It occurs in Basil Hall, *Voyage . . . to Eastern Seas, in the Year 1816,* published at Edinburgh in 1826, '"I come to see about your pigeon". . . . I afterwards learned that . . . "pigeon" in the strange jargon . . . spoken at Canton by way of English, means business. . . . "I am come to see about your business."' (Moe.)—7. In 1941–2, an airman was occ., in the R.A.F., called *pigeon.*

***pigeon-fancier.** A professional gambler: gamblers' c. of ca. 1800–50. J. J. Stockdale, *The Greeks*, 1817. Pun on **pigeon,** n., 5 (p. 628).

pigeon gremlin. A patronising gremlin, active only in hot weather: R.A.F.: 1940–5.

pigeon on. To drop (something) on to a person from above: Australian: C. 20. B., 1942.

pigeons and pigs. The boys of St Paul's and St Anthony's Schools were respectively called thus by each other: C. 16 and later.

piggies. Toes of baby or small child: domestic: late C. 19–20. Ex the nursery story, 'This little piggy went to market, this little piggy stayed at home.' (B.P.)

piggy. Pick-a-back: children's: C. 20. Short for *piggy-back,* pick-a-back.—2. A rating detailed to keep tidy a Petty Officers' mess; a messman: Naval (lower-deck): since ca. 1910. Mostly as a nickname. (P-G-R.)

pigs.—2. Small potatoes: farmers': C. 20. Cf. **pig,** n., 8 (*Dict.*).

pigs! A derisive or contemptuous exclamation: Australian: since ca. 1930. (B., 1943.) But prob. earlier: witness Norman Lindsay, *Saturdee*, 1933, '"Pigs to your old man."'

pig's. Beer: elliptical for **pig's ear** (p. 628 and below): C. 20. 'Nah, not a pint of pig's': Tommy Steele, the famous comedian, as reported in *Cinema* early in Dec. 1967.

pigs, Naval; pigs, small. Officers; Petty Officers: Naval (lower-deck): C. 20. (P-G-R.) Cf. *pig,* n., 11.

pigs aft. The officers regarded as drinking in the Wardroom: lower-deckese: since ca. 1910. Robert Harling, *The Steep Atlantick Stream*, 1946

pigs are up. 'The barrage balloons are up,' H. & P.: Services: since ca. 1939. Prob. with ref. to pork *sausages*.

pig's arse, in a. A low c.p. of dissent or disbelief: Australian: since ca. 1945. An adaptation of **pig's eye** (below)—which, by the way, had itself > Australian by 1945.

pig's back, on the (p. 628) occurs in James Joyce, *Ulysses*, 1922.

pig's ear (p. 628) occurs in D. W. Barrett, *Navvies*, 1880.—2. A 'side light colour signal' (*Railway*, 3rd): railwaymen's: C. 20.—3. A blunder: mostly middle-class: since ca. 1945. Elizabeth Hargreaves, *A Handful of Silver*, 1954, '"I've made a real pig's ear of it, haven't I?" said Basil, with an attempt at lightness.' (Laurie Atkinson, who asks, 'Rhyming s. for *smear*?')

pig's eye, 2, was, by 1959, dead. (Leechman.) —3. To convey an emphatic negative, thus: 'In a pig's eye, you could!': Canadian: adopted, ca. 1945, ex U.S. (Leechman.) The phrase *in a pig's eye* was orig. euphemistic for *in a pig's arse* or . . . *arse-hole*, as in a bawdy song current long before 1940. (Am. correspondent.)

pig's face. 'A nickname for the ice-plant' (B., 1943): Australian: C. 20.

pig's fry.—2. To try: rhyming s.: C. 20. Axel Bracey, *Public Enemies*, 1934.

pigs in shit; e.g., *as comfortable as* . . . The utmost comfort, utterly comfortable: low coll.: esp. in the Services: late C. 19–20.

pigskin artist. A jockey: Australian: since ca. 1912. B., 1942. See **pigskin** (p. 629).

pigtail. Navy perique tobacco: Naval: since ca. 1900. Granville. Cf.—and see—**prick,** n., 6.

pike, n., 1 (p. 629): earlier in *Sessions*, May 1839. —5. See **pyke.**

pike, hit the. To take to the road; to start travelling: Canadian (ex U.S.?): since ca. 1910. (Leechman.)

piker.—4. A man that habitually takes more than his share: low: from ca. 1931. Ex U.S.—5. One who ventures but timidly: Canadian (ex U.S.): since ca. 1930. Leechman.—6. Hence, a shirker: adopted, ca. 1943, ex U.S. and slightly adapted.— 7. A confidence trickster: Australian: since ca. 1935. (B., 1943.) In Australia the best-known sense is the 5th; it has 'killed sense 7' (B.P.). In New Zealand sense 6 has, since ca. 1943, been common. (Slatter.)—8. (Ex 5, 6, 7.) 'A mean, contemptible person' (Culotta): Australian: since ca. 1944.

Sense 3, on p. 629, is perhaps more accurately defined as 'a troublesome beast to muster' (Mary Durack, *Keep Him My Country*, 1955.)

piking, n. 'Sharp practice' (Culotta): Australian: since the late 1930's. Cf. **piker,** 7, above.

pile, have a. To have a difficult task, a hard time: Canadian coll.: late C. 19–20. W. A. Gape, *Half a Million Tramps*, 1936. I.e. a 'pile' of trouble.

pile-driver, (heavy punch). Rather: mid-C. 19–20. It occurs in Augustus Mayhew, *Paved with Gold*, 1857.—4. See **dekkoscope.**

pile o' mags. A conjurer: theatrical: ca. 1870– 1914. B. & L.

pile on the coals. 'To accelerate rapidly, to open the throttle of car or aeroplane' (Peter Sanders): since ca. 1950. Cf. **pour on** . . . below.

pile-up, n. See **pile-up,** 3 on p. 926.—2. (Hence?), a crash involving several cyclists: racing cyclists' coll.: since ca. 1945.—3. Hence, a motorway accident involving several cars: journalists' coll.: since ca. 1955; by 1965, fairly gen. (Ramsey Spencer, March 1967.) See also **pile up,** v., on p. 629.

pile up, v.i. (Of an aircraft) to crash-land: R.A.F.: since ca. 1930. The 'plane becomes a pile—a heap of useless material. Imm. ex **pile up,** 2 (p. 629).

pile up points. See **points** . . .

piled(-)in. (Of an aircraft) crashed: R.A.F.: since ca. 1930; ob. by 1946. Jackson.

pilgrims. A newcomer, whether persons or cattle: Western Canadian (and U.S.): late C. 19–20.

Pilgrims, the. The earliest settlers in Canterbury, New Zealand: N.Z. coll.: late C. 19–20. (B., 1943.)

pill, n.—10. A 'shot' of dagga (i.e. marijuana, *Cannabis indica*): S. African c.: C. 20. *The Cape Times*, May 22, 1946.

Pill Avenue. Harley Street: taxi-drivers': Sept. 12, 1941, *The Weekly Telegraph*. By 1948 (*The Daily Telegraph*, May 18) the name was *Pill Island*.

pill-bo'sun. See **fang bo'sun.**

pill-box.—7. (Ex senses 1, 2: p. 630.) A General Staff Daimler limousine: military: 1917 + .—8. A revolver: 1929, Edward Woodward, *The House of Terror*. Not much used.—9. A rocket-projector: Naval: 1939 + . Ex shape.

Pill Island. See **Pill Avenue.**

pillar and post. A ghost: 'the ghost' (monetary): theatrical rhyming s.: late C. 19–20. (Franklyn, *Rhyming*.)

pillar box. A rocket-projector: Naval: since ca. 1942. Ex the shape. (P-G-R.)

pillars to the temple. A woman's legs: Public Schoolmen's: late C. 19–20. Not so much euphemistic as playfully allusive.

pillocks; pillocky. 'He's talking pillocks' (nonsense) and 'Don't talk so pillocky' (so foolishly and nonsensically): Cockneys': late C. 19–20. Blends of *pill(s)*, testicles(s), and its synonym *ballocks*, adj. *ballocky*. (Julian Franklyn.)

Pills (cf. **pills,** 7) is also the inseparable nickname for men surnamed *Beecham*: C. 20. Ex the famous *Beecham's pills*.

pills, 1. Mostly as a nickname; in the Navy (since 1920, anyway), a Junior Medical Officer. Granville, 'The term is less popular than the more familiar "Doc".'

It occurs in 'Bartimeus', *A Tall Ship*, 1915, and may therefore have been current since ca. 1910 or even earlier.

pills!, all. Nonsense: Scottish Public Schools': C. 20. Ian Miller. Ex **pills,** 4 (*Dict.*). Note, however, that **pills!** or **all pills!** was gen. s. from as early as 1890.

pilot. Earlier in 'Taffrail'; also as nickname. 'Taffrail': 'The first lieutenant . . . is "Jimmy the One"; the gunnery and torpedo lieutenants, the "Gunnery Jack" and "Torpedo Jack" respectively, but, to their messmates in the wardroom, these three officers, with the officer borne for navigation duties, are usually "Number One", "Guns", "Torps", and "Pilot".'—2. A watchman: Londoners': ca. 1810–40. Pierce Egan, *Life in London,* 1821. Cf. **light-house,** 4.—3. See 'Hauliers' Slang'.

Pilot's Cockpit, the. The W.A.A.F.: airmen's since ca. 1946.

pimp, n., 3 (p. 630). Also Australian: B., 1942.—4. A police informer: Australian police: since ca. 1910. (Vince Kelly, *The Bogeyman,* 1956.) Prob. ex sense 1 (p. 630), pimps being reputed to 'tell all' if interrogated. Writing in mid-1963, B.P. notes that *pimp on* is very common among Australian schoolchildren in the innocent sense 'tell on' (someone).

pimp, v. 'To do little, mean, petty actions': University coll.: mid-C. 19–20; ob. B. & L.—2. To 'tell tales': Australian and New Zealand: C. 20. (B., 1943; Ruth Park, *Pink Flannel,* 1955.) —3. Hence, to inform the police: Australian: since ca. 1910. (B., 1943.)

pimp on. To inform against (someone): Australian low: since ca. 1910. Baker.

pimp-stick. A cigarette (low) Canadian: C. 20. (Niven.)

pimple.—4. A gun-position cover 'just visible above the fuselage of a 'plane'. H. & P.: R.A.F.: since ca. 1930.—5. A contemptible person: Marlborough College: since ca. 1930.—6. The nose: pugilistic: ca. 1815–60. 'A Real Paddy', 1822. —7. A baby's penis: women's: late C. 19–20.—8. Syphilis: Naval: C. 20. A jocular meiosis.—9. See 'Hauliers' Slang' and (on p. 630) cf. sense 3.— 10. A shunting hump: railwaymen's: C. 20. (*Railway* 2nd.)

pimple and blotch. Whisky (strictly Scotch): rhyming: C. 20.

pimple and wart. A quart: public-house rhyming s.: late C. 19–20; by 1960, virtually †. (Franklyn 2nd.)—2. Port wine: public-house rhyming s.: late C. 19–20; by 1960, very ob. (Ibid.)

pimple-coverer. The head; a hat: fast life: ca. 1815–40. Pierce Egan, *Finish of Tom, Jerry and Logic,* 1828. Cf. **pimple,** 2 (p. 630).

pin, n.—5. See **pinhead,** 3.

pin, v.—6. To coït with (a woman). C. 20. Cf. *prick,* 3 (p. 659).

pin back your ears or **pin your ears back,** Listen carefully: adopted, ca. 1937, from U.S.—2. Hence, *that'll pin your ears back,* that will constitute a set-back: mostly Forces': 1940 +. (Atkinson.)

pin for home. To go home: Canadian railroadmen's (— 1931).

pin-money spoof. Vague, pointless amateurish writing: journalistic: since ca. 1910.

pin-splitter.—2. Since ca. 1935, predominantly a golf-shot dead on the pin: golfers' col.

pin-up. An attractive girl, or her likeness: coll.: adopted, 1944–5, ex U.S. servicemen.

Extended, ca. 1955, to a handsome male, similarly 'honoured' by teen-age girls.

pin your ears back! See **pin back** . . .

pinch, n.—3. An arrest: low: late C. 19–20. (*The Pawnshop Murder.*) Ex **pinch,** v., 4 (*Dict.*). —4. 'Short, steep hill' (Sarah Campion, *Bonanza,* 1941): American coll.: late C. 19–20. Adopted from English dial.

pinch, on a (p. 631): earlier in W. N. Glascock, *Sailors and Saints* (I, 31), 1829. (Moe.) Prob. to be dated back to ca. 1800.

pinch-gut.—3. Hence (?), 'a niggardly victualling officer' (Granville): Naval: C. 20.

pinch it off! Get a move on!: Australian: since ca. 1925. B., 1942. Defecatory.

pinch the cat. See **cat, pinch the.**

pincher, 3, is recorded earlier by 'Taffrail.'

pine-apple.—4. See next.

pineapple chunk. A bunk (to sleep in): merchant seamen's rhyming s.: C. 20. Often shortened to *pineapple.*

pineapple cut. A 'basin crop': Australian: C. 20. Baker. Shaggy.

*piner. An axeman working on *pine* trees: Tasmanian coll.: late C. 19–20. Baker.

ping, n. An Asdic rating: Naval: since ca. 1935. Granville. He works the Asdic mechanism. Echoic.

ping! A synonym of **line!** above: R.A.F.: 1939–45. 'Echoic of the "line" rebounding from the wall like an asdic response?': Ramsey Spencer.

ping, get a. To receive a sound on the Asdic gear: Naval coll.: since ca. 1935. (P-G-R.)

pinger. The Asdic officer: Naval: since ca. 1936. Cf preceding entries.

pinhead.—2. A simple fellow; a fool: Australian: since ca. 1920. B., 1942. So small a head can contain but few brains.—3. (Also *pin*). A brakeman: Canadian railroadmen's (— 1931).— 4. Anyone with a very small head; esp., a very tall man with a head either really or apparently very small: since ca. 1945.

pining away, he (or she) **is**—or **you are.** A jocular c.p., referring or addressed to someone putting on weight: C. 20. (I remember hearing it ca. 1908.)

Pink or **Pinkie** (-ky). Inevitable nickname of any pink-eyed albino: late C. 19–20. In, e.g., John Gloag, *Unlawful Justice,* 1962.

pink, n.—5. An outstanding 'swell' or dandy: buckish: ca. 1815–40. Pierce Egan, 1821. Ex the adj., 1.—6. A caution card: Canadian railroadmen's coll. (— 1931). Ex its colour.

pink, adj.—4. Mildly Socialistic: C. 20. Prompted by *red,* Communistic.

pink-eye. An addict of 'pinky': Australian: C. 20. Baker.

pink fit, have a. Intensive of *have a fit,* to be much perturbed or alarmed: since ca. 1935.

pink lint. Penniless: racing circles' rhyming s.: since ca. 1920. On *skint.* Cf. **boracic lint** above. Franklyn 2nd.

Pink Palace, the. The Leander Club; its headquarters: oarsmen's: C. 20. Its colours are pink.

pink pills for pale people. A humorous c.p. interjected into talk about patent medicines or quacks' cure-alls: since ca. 1900. Ex the wording of an actual remedy, much advertised.

pink tea. 'A more than usually formal tea-party' (Leechman): Canadian: since ca. 1925. Leechman, 'Derisive.'

Pink 'Un, The.—2. *The Financial Times*, founded in 1913: businessmen's.

pinked, ppl. adj. Carefully and beautifully made: tailors': mid-C. 19–20. B. & L.

pinker. A blow that draws blood: pugilistic: ca. 1880–1914. Ibid.

pinkers. A pink gin: Naval officers': since ca. 1920. By 'The Oxford-*er*'.

Pinkie or **Pinky.** See **Pink** above.—2. A white man—less common—or woman: West African teenagers' (and others') in Britain: since late 1950's. *The Observer*, Sept. 10, 1967, 'By the time they leave school, whites have become "pinky", "the grey man" or—less common—"Mr Charlie".'

pinkie (or **-y**).—2. Red wine: since ca. 1890; ob. *Sessions*, March 10, 1897.—3. Methylated spirits coloured with red wine—or with Condy's crystals: Australian: C. 20. Archer Russell, *Gone Nomad*, 1936.—4. A Lesbian: low: since ca. 1925. Gerald Kersh, *Night and the City*, 1938. —5. An addict of methylated spirits: Australian: since ca. 1925. (B., 1943.) Ex sense 3.—6. A rabbit bandicoot: Australian rural: since ca. 1930. (B., 1953.)—7. A new hand: London dockers': since ca. 1945. (*The New Statesman*, Dec. 31, 1965.)

pinko.—2. Drunk on methylated spirits: Australian: since ca. 1925. (B., 1943.)

pinnicky pawnee (or **-ie**) and numerous other spellings. Drinking-water: mid-C. 19–30: Indian >, by 1900, gen Army s.: Blaker, concerning early 1915: 'This "rooti" and other words from the "bat" acquired in India were ancestors of the common speech of the army of coming years: "Rooti", "pinnicky pawnie", "dekko", "jildi", and the more ordinary "buckshee".' Ex Hindustani, in which *penee ka panee* is 'water of [*ka*] drinking', i.e. drinking-water.

pinny, catch (her) **under the.** To coït with a woman): C. 20.

pint-pot.—2. A one-pint tin can, used for boiling water: Australian rural coll.: late C. 19–20. (B., 1943.)

pinta. A pint of milk: since ca. 1962. Ex the slogan *Drinka pinta milka day.* Semantically and phonetically cf. *cuppa*, a cup of tea.

pioneer. An early convict in Australia: Australian ironic coll.: mid-C. 19–20. B., 1942.

pip off. To die: since ca. 1934. Ex the *pip-pip* of the radio. Cf. **pip out** (p. 633).

Pip, Squeak and Wilfred.—2. In the middle of a column of Palestine news, there appeared, on Friday, Oct. 2, 1936, in *The Evening News*, the following record of a phrase coined, in this connexion, late in Sept 1936:

Pip, Squeak, Wilfred.

The naval gun units known as Pip, Squeak, and Wilfred are being increasingly used in co-operation with the Army against the Arab rebels.

Pip is a two-pounder, Squeak is a three-pounder, and Wilfred is a searchlight. All are mounted on open lorries.— Reuter.

---

pip in. 'To clock in, to synchronise the time in an aircraft while in flight with the time at base in order that the navigational position may be fixed by radio,' Jackson: Air Force: since ca. 1936.

pip-squeak.—4. (Ex 2.) A rifle grenade: Army: 1914–18.—5. (Ex 1.) A toady: Australian: since ca. 1919. B., 1942.—6. 'Forgetting to switch off his "pip-squeak" (radio contactor), Nicky climbed thankfully out on to the wing,' Paul Brickhill & Conrad Norton, *Escape to Danger*, 1946. H. & P. 1943, 'Radio telephony set': R.A.F. (aircrews') since ca. 1935. Cf. sense 2. At short intervals, it goes *pip squeak.*

'"Radio-telephony set" is perhaps misleading. The pip-squeak was an automatic transmitter *only*, whose once-a-minute signals enabled ground direction-finding stations to fix the aircraft's position accurately for the benefit of the Fighter Controller in the Operations Room. But for those seconds when it was transmitting, ordinary radio-telephonic communication with the pilot was not possible. The Controller's occasional query: "Is your pip-squeak in (i.e. switched on)?" soon acquired sexual connotations.

'An equivalent equipment in homing bombers was I.F.F. (Identification, Friend or Foe), which, however, imparted a characteristic pulse to the visual echo on radar screens.' (Ramsey Spencer, March 1967.)

pipe, n.—7. *The Pipe* is the Underground: London taxi-drivers': since ca. 1930. See **rattler**, 6. See 'Hauliers' Slang'.

pipe, v.—6. To speak too loudly: Naval (lower-deck) coll.: C. 20. 'All right, Jack, don't pipe it. We can hear.' Ex the bosun's piping the routine calls.—8. To look at: Canadian (ex U.S.): since ca. 1930.

pipe, it's a. It's a certainty: filmland adopted, ca. 1925, from U.S. Cameron McCabe, *The Face*, 1937. 'Perhaps contraction of "lead-pipe cinch" = dead certainty, but possibly derived rather from *pipe-dream*—orig., from the opium pipe, which makes all things seem easy' (Robert Clairborne, Aug. 31, 1966).

pipe, take a (p. 633), seems to have a variant, as in

'I waited till the fruit was ripe,
  Then thinking to be thrifty,
I left the youth to stretch his pipe,
  I had nabb'd a bill for fifty'—

'I' being a prostitute and the lines occurring in *The Rolling Blossom*, a ballad of ca. 1800. (Moe.)

pipe, up your. A rude retort ('go and hang yourself'): Army: since ca. 1930. Also *up your gonga* (pron. *gong -ger*) *and up your jacksie.*

pipe line. An aerial: R.A.F.: 1939 +.

pipe-spoiler. A plumber: Naval (lower-deck): C. 20. (P-G-R.)

piped up, be or **get.** To be, or become, tipsy: since ca. 1925. Gavin Holt, *The Murder Train*, 1936.

pipers. Lungs: pugilistic: mid-C. 19–20; ob. B. & L.

pipes, 2, occurs in 1818 (Alfred Burton, *Johnny Newcome*). Moe.

pipes, open one's. See 'Verbs'.

pipi (p. 634). The forms *peppy, pippy,* are solecistic; but *pipi* is a 'Maori name for a bivalve-like cockle' (Sidney J. Baker, letter, 1946) and is therefore ineligible. But, Barry Prentice tells me in mid-1963, *pippy* is almost coll.: he adds that the Australian and the New Zealand *pipi* are quite different, the one from the other.

pipped, 'annoyed' (p. 634). An early occurrence: '"How's Leverton?"—"Rather pipped, thank you," replied Miss Disney,' A. Neil Lyons, *Simple Simon*, 1914.

pipped, get. See **bumped.**

pipped on (or **at**) **the post.** To fail or be circumvented after having been within reach of success or victory or one's goal: sporting (ca. 1892) >, by 1920, gen. (*The Daily Telegraph*, April 16, 1937.) Ex **pip,** v., 4 (*Dict.*). Also occasionally *pipped on the tape*, as in P. G. Wodehouse, *Ukridge*, 1924. See also **beaten at the post** above.

pipper. Something, esp. a play, that turns out to be very successful: theatrical: since ca. 1930. Anthony Berkeley, *Trial and Error*, 1937.

pippin, 2 (p. 634). An early record of *my pippin*, in address: 1821. W. T. Moncrief, *Tom and Jerry*.

pippish. Disgruntled; depressed: Cockney coll.: C. 20. Pugh. See **pip,** the corresponding n. in the *Dict.*

pippy.—3. Australian variation of **pipped:** since ca. 1925. B., 1942.

pirate.—2. (also v.) A man that picks up casual feminine company; *on the pirate*, watchful for such company: Australian: since ca. 1925. Baker.

pirate of the narrow seas. See 'Tavern terms', § 7.

pirates on the poop. 'Chaplain, marine officers, and midshipmen' (W. N. Glascock, *Sketch-Book*, 2nd Series, 1834, at I, 167). Moe.

piscatorial. Dubious: jocular: since ca. 1845, but never common. (Francis Francis, *Newton Dogvane*, 1859.) A word-play on *fishy*, 1 (p. 279).

Piscie. A member of the *Epis*copalian Church: Scottish Public Schools': C. 20. Ian Miller, *School Tie*, 1935. Cf.:

Piskey or **Pisky.** Episcopalian: Scottish: C. 20. Should prob. be dated mid C. 19–20.

piss, n.—2. Weak table-beer sold in France: Army: 1914 + .—3. Hence, weak English beer: 1919 + .—4. Hence, any drink of poor quality: since ca. 1920.—5. Beer: (low) Australian: since ca. 1925. (B.P.)

Sense 1, by the way, has, since ca. 1960, been regaining very fair respectability.

piss, go on the. To drink heavily: low: since ca. 1910. Much liquor, much urine.

piss, long streak of. Someone who overestimates his own ability or importance: low: C. 20.

piss, piece of. See **piece of piss.**

piss, take the. To make fun: low: since ca. 1925. Brendan Behan, *Borstal Boy*, 1958. '"Don't mind me, Kid," said Tubby. "I just can't help taking the piss."' Cf. **piss out of, take the** above.

piss-a-bed (p. 635). Cf. the Fr. *pisse-en-lit.*

piss about. To potter; fritter one's time away; to stall for time: low: C. 20.

piss and wind, as in 'He's all piss and wind!' Empty talk; unsubstantiated boast(s): low coll.: C. 20. He can urinate, not defecate.

piss-ant around. 'To waste time, dawdle, "mess about"' (B., 1959): Aus.: C. 20. 'For God's sake, stop piss-anting around!'

piss-arse about. To fool about, waste time:

Army: since ca. 1920. (P-G-R.)

piss-ball. A query to be answered: lower grades (male) of Civil Service: since ca. 1945. A 'stinker'.

piss-ball about. To act in a futile or an irritating manner: low: since ca. 1920.

piss down one's back (p. 635) survives in C. 20 in the slight variant *p. up one's back.*

piss hard-on, a. A matutinal erection caused by the desire, and need, to urinate; Canadian low: C. 20.

piss-head. An habitually heavy drinker: New Zealand low: since ca. 1930. Cf. *pissed* (p. 635) and, in form, *shit-head.*

piss in a quill (p. 635) was already current in C. 17; John Lilburne used it. (Jack Lindsay, communication of 1939.)

piss in (someone's) chips. To put an end to his hopes or plans: low; esp. in R.A.F.: C. 20; since ca. 1925. Ex wood-chips used as kindling.

piss in (someone's) pocket. To ingratiate oneself with him: (low) Australian: since ca. 1920. (B.P.)

piss oneself laughing. See **pee** ...

piss out of, take a. To laugh at (someone): low: C. 20. Cf.:

piss out of, take the. To pull someone's leg: low: C. 20. To deflate ?—2. To jeer at, deride: low: C. 20. Among the literary: *pass* (someone) *the catheter.*

piss out of a dozen holes. To have syphilis: low: late C. 19–20.

piss-poor. Penniless: low: since ca. 1925.—2. Hence, (of the weather) abominable: R.A.F. aircrews': 1939 +. Here, *piss* is a mere pejorative adverb.

piss-pot.—3. An objectionable fellow (a 'stinker'): late C. 19–20.

piss-pot emptier. A cabin steward: Merchant Navy: late C. 19–20.

piss-pot juggler. Chambermaid in hotel: Canadian: C. 20.

piss-taking, n., answers to **piss out of, take the,** above: low: since ca. 1930. Peter Crookston, *Villain*, 1967.

piss the bed waking. To do something avoidable or futile: lower-class coll.: late C. 19–20.

piss through it. To do something with ease: low: since ca. 1910.

piss-up. A drinking bout: low: C. 20. Cf. **pissed (-up)** in *Dict.*

piss-up in a brewery. See **couldn't organize** ...

piss-warm, adj. Distastefully tepid: low coll.: late C. 19–20. Contrast.—

piss (or **pee**) **-warmer.** A highly complimentary term for anything cordially approved: Canadian: C. 20. Also (—1952) *piss-cutter*, esp. in the Canadian Navy.

pissed (p. 635), tipsy, has the intensives *p. as a fiddler's bitch*, a variant of drunk as ... (p. 273); *as arseholes*; *p. as a cunt*: all low: all of C. 20.

pissed in the sea ... (p. 635): adumbrated in the proverbial saying, 'Everything helps, quoth the wren, when she pissed into the sea'—quoted by *The Oxford Dictionary of Proverbs* for the date 1623.

pissed on from a great height, he should be . He's beneath contempt: Naval (? only Australian) c.p.: C. 20.

pissed up to the eyebrows. Blind drunk: esp. R.A.F.: since late 1930's. (Laurie Atkinson.)

pisser.—3. A urinal: low coll.: late C. 19–20.—
4. A day of heavy rain: low, esp. Cockneys': since
ca. 1920. Ex the low *it's pissing down*, raining
heavily, itself of late C. 19–20. 'Cf. the Fr. coll.
"Il pleut comme trente-six vaches qui pissent"'
(Ramsey Spencer).

pisser, pull (someone's). To humbug: low:
C. 20. See **pisser**, 1, in *Dict*.

pisseroo. A ramp or a racket (?): since ca.
1955. Nancy Mitford. *Don't Tell Alfred*, 1960,
p. 143.

pisso. A drunkard; loosely and often, any
frequenter of public-house or hotel bars: low
Australian: since ca. 1930. (Wm Dick, *A Bunch
of Ratbags*, 1965.) Ex *pissed*, tipsy.

pissy-arsed. Prone to crapulous inebriation:
low: C. 20.

pissy pal. A public-house crony: mostly
Cockney: late C. 19–20. Ex their simultaneous
use of the urinal for the discharge of their heavy
cargo.—2. Hence, a bosom friend: Cockney commercial: C. 20. Thus, 'Go and see if you can't
get an order from old so-and-so, he's a pissy pal of
yours.'

piston (occ. **pistons**). '*Piston.* The nickname
for any Engineering Officer,' H. & P.: Services:
since ca. 1920.—2. (Also *piston-rod*.) Penis: engineers' and similars': C. 20.

piston job. See **blow job** above.

pit, 1, is extant for inside coat-pocket: 1938,
F. D. Sharpe, *The Flying Squad*.—3. One's bed:
R.A.F. regulars': since ca. 1925. Sergeant Gerald
Emanuel, letter of March 29, 1945. Cf. **flea pit**
(p. 285). Often in the form *the old pit*.

pit, shoot the (p. 636). The O.E.D. records it
as occurring in a letter written by Andrew Marvell
in 1675.

pit(-)circler. An occupant of the pit:theatrical:
ca. 1880–1910. B. & L.

pit-pat's the way! Go on!; don't stop!:
proletarian c.p.: ca. 1870–1914. Ibid.

pit-riser. 'A burst of powerful acting which
evokes an enthusiastic acclamation from the pit':
theatrical: from ca. 1814; ob. Ibid. Ex a saying
by Edmund Kean.

pitch, n., 4 (p. 636), is recorded for 1895 in
Australia (Sidney J. Baker, letter); I believe it
to have been current there since ca. 1870; see the
books by 'Tom Collins' (Joseph Furphy), *passim*.
—5. A camp: Australian: C. 20. B., 1942. Ex
'to pitch tents' or 'pitch camp'.—6. See 'Mock-
Auction Slang' above.—7. A plan; a 'game' or
trick: Canadian: since late 1940's. (Leechman.)
Perhaps cf. sense 2 on p. 636.

pitch, v., 2 (p. 636). Esp., among circus folk,
'To go on tour': prob. since ca. 1865. In, e.g.,
Thomas Frost, *Circus Life*, 1875. The word is,
among C. 20 fairground vendors, used esp. thus:
'A well-known drapery pitcher (one who sells
drapery by pitching it, i.e. telling a story about
each article offered) usually gagging in an entertaining way while describing, to keep the pitch
[crowd of customers or gogglers] interested': W.
Buchanan-Taylor, *Shake It Again*, 1943.

*pitch a game for a gay. To arrange a crooked
game of cards in order to rob an outsider: Australian professional cardsharps': since ca. 1930.
(B., 1953.)

pitch a woo. To commence a courtship: Services: since ca. 1930. H. & P.

pitch and toss, the. The boss: Australian gen-

eral (B., 1945) and English theatrical rhyming s.
(Franklyn, *Rhyming*): C. 20.

pitch-getter. See **floorman pitch-getter**.

pitch into (p. 636). Sixteen years earlier in
Sessions, 1827, 'Beddis . . . began to *pitch* into
Joseph Durden with his fists'.

pitch it mild. Usually in imperative. Don't
exaggerate: a Canadian coll. variant of *draw it
mild* (p. 241): late C. 19–20. (Leechman.)

pitch on. To nag at, to abuse, to reprimand:
Australian: C. 20. B., 1942. A confusion or,
perhaps a blend, of *pick on* and *pitch into* (a person).

pitch the cuffer. See **cuffer**.

pitch the fork; esp. as vbl n. *pitching the fork*.—
2. Hence, to put a penny on the counter for, say,
bacon and to receive both the bacon and the
penny: vagrants' c.: from ca. 1870. Thus the
tramp avoids a charge of mendicancy.

pitcher.—4. A street vendor: since ca. 1870:
s. >, by 1900, coll. William Newton, *Secrets of
Tramp Life Revealed*, 1886.—5. A chatterbox:
Australian: C. 20. B., 1942. Cf. **pitch**, n., 4
(p. 636). 6. A fairground vendor: fair-grounds':
C. 20. See quotation at **pitch**, v., 2, above.

Pitcher, the. Arthur Binstead (1861–1914) of
'The Pink 'Un' and various collections of stories
published from 1898 to 1909. I.e. *the tale-pitcher*,
this pseudonym > a genuine nickname.

pitching the plod. Greetings, talk between
miners coming on and going off shift: Australian:
C. 20. B., 1942. As they plod along.

pitiful objects. Petty Officers: Naval lower-
deck jocularity: since ca. 1930. (P-G-R.)

pitman's crop. A very close hair-cut, usually
among miners on account of the dirty nature of
their work: mining-towns' coll.: late C. 19–20.

Pitt Street farmers. Financiers interested in
farming: New South Wales, esp. Sydney: since
ca. 1950. (B.P.)

pitty. Pretty: nursery: C. 19–20. (Anstey,
Voces Populi, II, 1892.)

pity about you! A C. 20 derisive c.p. to a
boaster, self-seeker or irritating person. Also
to a person either constantly or excessively
complaining.

pity the poor sailor on a night like this! (p. 637).
Perhaps owing something to the Prayer Book's
'For those in peril on the sea'.

Piv, the. The Pavilion (theatre or music-hall,
esp. in a garrison town): Army: late C. 19–20.
(S. E. Burrow, *Friend or Foe*, 1912.)

Pivot City, the (p. 637). In C. 20, *the Pivot*
(Baker).

pixilated; often **pixolated.** Tipsy: since ca.
1930. Perhaps a blend of '*pixy-l*ed' and 'intoxicated'. Cf. *impixlocated*. 'Came into general
use with the release of the film "Mr Deedes
Comes to Town" (ca. 1930); in which, however,
it was used in the sense of "not right in the head"'
(H. R. Spencer).

pizz or, in full, **pizzicato.** Tipsy: since ca. 1930.
Ngaio Marsh, *Enter a Murderer*, 1935. Pun on
pissed.

place where you cough, the. The water-closet:
coll.: since ca. 1920. Ex coughing to warn an
approacher that it is occupied.

*placer. A woman in an official brothel, e.g. in
France: c., esp. white-slavers': from ca. 1895.
(A. Londres.)—2. A sheep that haunts one place:
Australian: C. 20. Baker.—3. A seller of stolen
or forged ration coupons: 'Many times we could

have picked up the "placers"—the men who actually sold the coupons—but this was no good to us' (John Gosling, 1959): since ca. 1940: orig. c., but by 1945 also police s.

plague.—2. *the plague* is a synonym of **the curse**, q.v.: women's: mid-C. 19–20.

plaguey. See **plaguy** (p. 637).

Plain, the. See **Hill, the**.

Plain and Gravy, the. The Navy: rhyming s.: late C. 19–20. A variant of **Soup and Gravy, the**, below.

plain and jam. A tram: rhyming s.: C. 20.

plain as a yard of pump water. Very plain: tailors': mid-C. 19–20. B. & L.

Plain City of the Queans, the. Bathurst, N.S.W.: Australian: C. 20. B., 1942. Derisive on the *Queen City of the Plains,* as sometimes it is rather ambitiously called.

plain-headed. Plain(-looking): Society: ca. 1880–1910. B. & L.

plain over (someone), **put the.** To search: Scottish (esp. Glasgow) policemen's: since ca. 1880; by 1940, ob. Ex-Inspector Elliot, *Tracking Glasgow Criminals,* 1904.

plain-turkey. A professional 'bush' tramp, always on the move, rarely working, old-fashioned, secretive: Australian: since ca. 1910. On pp. 26–7 of D'Arcy Niland's *The Shiralee,* 1955, occurs the *locus classicus* for description and characterisation.

plaintiff, demur upon the. See 'Tavern terms', § 4.

plank, whence **plonk, one's frame down.** To sit down: Aus.: C. 20. (B., 1959.)

plant, n.—11. (Cf. senses 4, 9: p. 638.) 'A "salted" gold-mining claim,' Baker: Australian: late C. 19–20.—12. An outfit (set of equipment + store of provisions): Australian miners' coll.: since ca. 1910. (Vance Palmer, 1948.)—13. A travelling herd of cattle: Australian rural: C. 20. '"'Oo's mob is it, Marty?"—"Should be one of the Lannigans. They're working two plants from Caroline Downs."' Thus in Tom Ronan, *Vision Splendid,* 1954. Also 'a plant of horses' (ibid.). Also, more generally, the herd and the drovers collectively (ibid.).

plant, v.—16. (Of a horse) to stand, or remain, still: Australian racing coll.: since ca. 1925. (B., 1943.)—17. To insert such an incident, etc., into a story as, although unnoticed at first reading, will eventually prove to influence the outcome: Canadian authors' and free-lance journalists': since ca. 1945. (Leechman.)—18. Robert Kennicott, *Journal,* 1869, 'When a sled can not keep up and take its proper place in the brigade at each spell, it is said to be "planted", which is considered something very disgraceful'—which Dr Douglas Leechman glosses thus: 'Dog travel in Northern Canada. Kennicott was a young naturalist, from the States.' Canadian: ca. 1850–1914.

*plant the books. To stack the cards: c.: mid-C. 19–20: ob. B. & L. See **plant, v.,** 11 (*Dict.*).

planting, n. A burial: Welsh: mid-C. 19–20. Cf. **plant, v.,** 5 (p. 638).

plaster, n.—3. An account or bill: Australian since ca. 1930. (Dymphna Cusack, 1951.)

plaster,—3. To flatter (a person): proletarian: from ca. 1860; ob. B. & L.—4. (Ex 2.) Often as vbl. n., *plastering*: to bomb from the air; bombing, a heavy raid: R.A.F.: since 1918. 'Jerry

is so annoyed about the plastering we've given him recently . . .', Flight-Sergeant in Allan Michie & Walter Graebner, *Their Finest Hour,* 1940.—5. To put (money) out on mortgage: New Zealand: C. 20. (Alan Mulgan, *Spur of Morning,* 1934.) Cf. *plaster,* n., 2 (p. 638).

plastic hippy. See the quotation from Peter Fryer at **hippy** above.

plat. A simpleton, fool, easy dupe: Australian: since ca. 1925. B., 1942. Ex Fr. *plat* (adj.), 'flat'.

plate.—2. See **plate of ham**.

plate, on a. A Cockney c.p. (C. 20) expressive of contempt for a person's stuck-up ways. As Julian Franklyn, *the* authority on current Cockney speech tells me, 'It comes from the Fish and Chips shop, where those who intend to eat on the premises add this phrase to their order, else they get the fish handed to them in paper.'

plate of beef. Borstal rhyming s. for a Chief (Officer): since ca. 1920 (? earlier, the first institution—at Borstal in Kent—dating from 1908). *The Daily Telegraph,* June 4, 1958. 'Bacon Bonces . . .'

plate of ham; often shortened to **plate:** a police term for *fellatio:* rhyming: C. 20.

plateful, have a; or, have too much on one's plate. To be desperately busy; hence, to feel 'browned off': Army 1941 +. Cf. **enough** . . .

plates and dishes.—2. Wife: C. 20. Rhyming on *missis(-us).*

platter. Broken crockery: lower-middle classes': from ca. 1865; ob. B. & L.

platty. A platman: Australian miner's coll.: since ca. 1910. (Gavin Casey, *It's Easier Downhill,* 1945.) He is the man who works a lift; *plat-* (form).

platypussery (or **-ary**). 'A pen or [other] specially prepared area in which platypuses are kept' (B., 1959): Aus.: since ca. 1930.

plausy or **plauzy.** 'When a person is smooth-tongued, meek-looking, over civil, and deceitful, he is *plauzy*' (P. W. Joyce, *English . . . in Ireland,* 1910): Anglo-Irish: late C. 19–20. Ex *'plausi*ble'.

play. —3. V.t., to tell (a 'mug') a story by which to get his money: c.: anglicised, ex U.S., ca. 1930.—4. To stay unnecessarily away from work: workmen's: C. 20.—5. V.i., to work in co-operation; to reciprocate; to agree: Services: since ca. 1930. H. & P. Short either for *play the game* (or *play fair*) or, more prob., for *play ball*.

play a flanker is an Air Force variant, since ca. 1925, of *work a flanker* (see **flanker, do a:** p. 282). Jackson.

play a hunch. To act on an intuitive idea: coll.: adopted, ca. 1945, ex U.S. *The Sunday Times* colour section, July 8, 1962, article by Wallace Reyburn.

play about, v.i. To waste money: C. 20.

play at hell and turn up Jack was a nautical elaboration (? ca. 1790–1860) of *play hell,* to cause a tremendous commotion or much damage. John Davis, *The Post-Captain,* 1806. (Moe.)

play ball. To co-operate: to reciprocate; to be helpful: coll.: since ca. 1937. Ex children's ball-games.

play board. The stage in Punch and Judy showmen's coll.: mid-C. 19–20. B. & L.

play fathers and mothers, late C. 19–20, coll.; **play mums and dads** or **dads and mums,** since late

1940's, s. To coït. The latter occurs in, e.g., John Gardner, *Madrigal*, 1967.

play footy. See **footy, play.**

play for time. To temporise: coll.: since early 1920's; by ca. 1945, familiar S.E. (Daphne Du Maurier, *Rebecca*, 1938.) Ex such games as football and cricket.

play hard to get. (Usually of girls) to resist amorous advances, all the while intending to acquiesce eventually: Canadian (and U.S.) coll.: since ca. 1925; by 1945, also English and Australian.

play hell and Tommy. See **hell and Tommy.** (*Dict.*).

play it close to one's chest. To hold one's cards close to one's chest so that nobody can see them: Canadian (and U.S.) poker-players' coll.: since ca. 1910.—2. Hence, to be secretive or 'cagey': Canadian (and U.S.) s.: since ca. 1925. (Leechman.)

play lively occurs mostly in the imperative. To 'get a move on', to bestir oneself: Naval: since ca. 1925. Granville, 'See "Smack it about!"'

play long. A golf-course is said to 'play long' when, owing to heaviness of ground and/or air, one has to hit the ball much harder than usual: golfers' coll.: from ca. 1920. *The Times*, Sept. 30, 1936.

play pussy. 'To take advantage of cloud cover, jumping from cloud to cloud to shadow a potential victim or avoid recognition,' H. & P.: R.A.F.: since 1939 or early 1940. Cat-and-mouse.

play roulette. Synonymous with *mix the red and the black*. (P-G-R.)

play the piano. See **piano, play the.**—2. To release bombs from an aircraft, one by one or in irregular numbers at irregular intervals: R.A.F.: 1939 +. Jackson. Contrast **pull the plug.**—3. 'To run one's fingers over the backs of sheep to find which are the easiest to shear,' B., 1941: New Zealand, hence Australian, orig. and mostly sheepshearers': C. 20. L. G. D. Acland, 'Sheep Station Glossary' in *The* (Christchurch) *Press*, 1933–4.

play tiddlywinks. To coït: partly euphemistic, partly trivial: C. 20.

play up, Nosey! A traditional London theatregallery cry: (?) mid-C. 18–20. Ex Cervette, that famous violoncellist of Drury Lane Theatre who, because of his big nose, was nicknamed *Nosey*. ('John o'London' in his *London Stories*, 1911–12.)

play war. To make a fuss; (*with*) to reprimand: North of England: since ca. 1918.

*****player.** One who 'plays' a dupe: c.: from ca. 1931. See **play** above.

playground.—2. A parade ground: R.A.F.: since ca. 1925. Jackson.

playing, adj. and n.—See **laking.**

playing hell with himself, he's. A c.p. applied to a man grumbling and muttering to himself: since ca. 1950.

playing the piano; gen. playin' the pianner. The shifting, by women, of rows of mineral-water bottles from a ship's hold into the baskets that are then hauled up by a crane on to the wharf: Thames-side workers': from ca. 1880; ob. Nevinson, 1895, 'By reason of the rows bein' so reg'lar and their 'ands jumpin' about on 'em so quick, same as when a man's vampin' on the black and white notes, and the singer keeps on always changin' 'is pitch.'—2. The vbl. n. of *play the piano*, q.v. at **piano, play the.**

please (something other than a person). To attract sensually, to excite, as in 'Please my prink and I'll . . .' (a railway train *graffito*): coll.: late C. 19–20.

please, teacher, may I leave the room? A jocular c.p., common among adult humorists: C. 20.

pleased as a dog with two choppers. Delighted: mostly lower-class: late C. 19–20. (Alexander Baron, *There's No Home*, 1950.) With two tails. Cf. the next.

pleased as a dog with two tails. Delighted: coll.: late C. 19–20.

pleased as Punch, as (p. 640). No; clearly not, after all, ex *Punch*, for the phrase occurs in *The Night Watch* (II, 126), 1828, 'The skipper was as pleased as punch'. Moe.

pleasure and pain. Rain: rhyming s.: C. 20. Franklyn, *Rhyming*.

pleasure-baulker. A petticoat: buckish: ca. 1810–40. David Carey, *Life in Paris*, 1822.

pleep. A German pilot that refuses combat: R.A.F.: 1939 +. H. & P. Ex echoic *pleep* as the sound made by, e.g., a frightened bird: cf. dial. *pleet*, a peevish cry.—2. A sleep: nursery, hence, adult jocular: Australian: since late 1940's. (B.P.) A childish rendering of *sleep*.

pleuro. Pleuro-pneumonia: coll.: late C. 19–20. 'Tom Collins', *Such is Life*, 1903.

plew or ploo. See **plue.**

plink. A shortened form, mostly Australian, of *plink-plonk* on p. 640. (B., 1943.)

plob. 'Hourly log kept by pilots, recording weather conditions on their patrols. (Coastal Command.) From *patrol-log observations*?' (P-G-R): since ca. 1941.

plod. Story: Australian, esp. miners': since ca. 1930. Gavin Casey, *Downhill is Easier*, 1945. '"I suppose he told you the whole plod?" I sneered. "What plod?" Sadie wanted to know.' Ex *plot*.

plonk, n., 1, 2. current in New Zealand also. —4. Inferior brandy sold in Italy: Naval: since ca. 1930. (Granville.) Prob. ex sense 3 (p. 640). —5. See **A/C Plonk.**—6. 'Any cheap handy form of drink' (Anderson): beatniks': since ca. 1958. Ex sense 3 on p. 640.

plonk, v.—2. To set, esp. in *plonk down*, to put, set, down, and *plonk out*, to set out—i.e. pay out, distribute—money: Australian: since ca. 1920. B., 1942. Variant of **plank** (p. 637).

plonk bar. A wine bar: Australian: since ca. 1935. Ex **plonk,** n., 3 (p. 640).

plonk-dot. 'A confirmed wine-bibber' (B., 1953): Australian: since ca. 1945. Ex *plonk,* n., 2 and 3 (p. 640).

plonk one's frame down. See **plank . . .** above.

plonk up. 'To hurry up and drink' (Anderson); to drink copiously: beatniks': since ca. 1959. Ex **plonk,** n., 6 (above).

plonker. A (cannon) shell: Australian soldiers': 1939 +. Baker. Ex **plonk,** v. (p. 640).—2. Penis: low: since ca. 1917.

plonkers. Feet: mostly Londoners' and esp. among policemen: since ca. 1920. (Laurence Henderson, *With Intent*, 1968.) Ex '*plonking*, or *planking*, one's feet down'.

plonko. A drunkard addicted to **plonk** (n., 3: p. 640). Australian: since ca. 1930. (Dick.) Cf. **pisso** above.

ploo. See **plue.**

plootered. Tipsy: Anglo-Irish: since ca. 1920. Ex Anglo-Irish *plouter*, to splash or wade in water or mire.

plotty is described by the O.E.D., quoting *Literature* (the early form of *The Times Literary Supplement*) for 1901, as a nonce-word. Rather is it literary coll., esp. if = full of intrigue, having an intricate plot, as in Edwin Pugh, *Tony Drum*, 1898, 'Novels of a common type, plotty and passionate, but gilt-edged with the proprieties.'

plough, v. (p. 640). 'In South Africa, he'—a student—'ploughs Latin,' Prof. W. S. Mackie, in *The Cape Argus*, July 4, 1946.

ploughed, 2, survived until ca. 1912.

plu. See **plue.**

pluck, n.—3. A stone: Aus.: C. 20. (B., 1959.) Origin ?

pluck, v. 'To fail (a candidate) in an examination' is familiar S.E.—not, as some tend to think, a coll.—2. To take out a part of one's winnings: Australian two-up players': C. 20. '"You've got forty quid in the guts, Sailor," said Stan. "Want to pluck some?"': Lawson Glassop, *Lucky Palmer*, 1949.

pluck a brand. 'To fake a new brand on stolen cattle or horses by pulling out the hairs around the existing brand' (B., 1942): Australian: since ca. 1860.

pluck a rose, 2 (p. 641), goes back to ca. 1600, perhaps even earlier. It occurs in, e.g., Beaumont & Fletcher, *The Knight of the Burning Pestle*, 1607.

plucky lot. An ironic 'bloody lot', i.e. 'not a bit', as in Kipling's 'Plucky lot she thought of idols when I kissed her where she stood'. Euphemistic. Cf. **plurry** below.

plue. Tea: Navy: C. 20. H. & P.; Granville, '"A cup of luscious plew."' Why? Perhaps a blend, '*pleasant* (or *pleasing*) brew': cf. **brew,** n. and v., on p. 92. Also used by Australian seamen. Note *wet the plue*, to make tea. (P-G-R.)

plug, n.—10. A small unimportant passenger-train: Canadian railroadmen's (— 1931). Ex sense 3 (p. 641). —11. A piece of publicity, a 'boost': since ca. 1935. Ex 'to *plug*' or 'boost': since ca. 1930: originally, advertising. Perhaps ex *plug away at*, to persevere with. —12. An objectionable fellow: Canadian (ex U.S.): late C. 19–20. (Niven.) Ex sense 3 on p. 641.—13. Cheese: Naval (officers'): C. 19. (W. N. Glascock, *Sketch-Book*, 2nd Series, 1834, I, 32: Moe.) It prob. shortens an assumed *plug-hole*, ex its constipating properties.

plug, v.—8. To kick (a person's) behind: R.M.A.: from ca. 1870; ob. B. & L.—9. To throw (a cricket ball): many preparatory schools': C. 20. Cf. sense 3 (p. 641) and sense 8.

plug, down the. (Of a tender) running short of water: railwaymen's: C. 20. (*Railway*, 3rd.) Short for . . . *plug-hole*.

plug along is a variant of **plug along** (see **plug**), v., 4: p. 641: late C. 19–20. H. & P.

plug hat. A bowler hat: Australian: C. 20. Baker. Because it is a *hard hitter*.

plug in. Fig., to 'switch on': jazz and drug addicts', and hippies': since ca. 1966. Peter Fryer in *The Observer* colour supplement. Dec. 3, 1967. Ex **switched on** below.

plug-tail (p. 641) occurs earlier in Ned Ward's *A Walk to Islington*, 1699.

Pluggeries, the. The Light Repair Squadron attached to the Long Range Desert Group in

N. Africa, 1942–3. A worthy unit of a fine formation. Their O.C. was Captain 'Plugs' Ashdown.

Plum.—2. H. C. O. Plumer (1857–1932), an Army Commander in World War I; later, Field-Marshal.

plum, n.—4. Usually *plums*, engines: Naval: since ca. 1930. Ex **plumber, 3.**

plum, v. See **plumb,** 2 (*Dict.*).

plum pud, good: **any plum?,** any good?: Australian rhyming s.: C. 20. B., 1942.

plum pudding.—3. (Whence 2.) A 'coach-dog (the dog with dark spots which runs after carriages)': Mayhew, II, 1851: † by 1910. Ex the markings; it is a sort of Dalmatian. Cf. **spotted dog** (*Dict.*).

plumb, n.—4. A plumber: Naval (lower-deck): C. 20. Ex sense 3 (p. 642). (P-G-R.)

plumber. An armourer: R.A.F.: since ca. 1925. E. P., 'Air Warfare and Its Slang' in *The New Statesman*, Sept. 19, 1942. Facetious.—2. *The Plumber* is the R.A.F.'s name (cf. coll. *Engines*) for an Engineering Officer: since ca. 1930. Jackson. Cf.: 3. '*Plumbers*': Generic term for Engineroom staff,' Granville: Naval: since ca. 1920.

plummy.—3. Dull; stupid: too respectable: low Glasgow: from ca. 1920. MacArthur & Long. Perhaps cf. Yorkshire *plum*, honest, straightforward; prob. influenced by U.S. *dumb*, slow.

plummy, adv. Well; 'nicely': Cockney: 1851, Mayhew, I; † by 1910. Ex adj., 1: see p. 642.

***plummy and slam.** All right: c.: ca. 1860–1910. B. & L.

plump, n.—3. An Anglo-Irish variant of **plum,** n., 1 (*Dict.*). 'A Real Paddy', *Life in Ireland*, 1822.

plumper.—4. Hence, all one's money, staked on one horse: turf coll.: from ca. 1881.

plunder.—3. (Cf. sense 2: p. 642.) One's equipment and personal belongings: Canadian: since ca. 1905. 'O.K.—grab your plunder and come along!' (Leechman.) It prob. derives ex Ger. *Plunder*, lumber, junk, rags. (Ramsey Spencer, 1967.)

plunder-snatcher. See 'Mock-Auction Slang' above.

plunger.—5. '"Plungers" is the name given to the men who clean the streets of the City [of London] with hoses and squeegees,' Rev. Eustace Jervis, *Twenty-five Years*, 1925: London: C. 20. They plunge about in the swirling waters.

plunk, n. An occasional, mostly Australian, variant of *plonk*, cheap liquor.

plunk, v. To strike (someone): Australian: since ca. 1918. B., 1942. Ex the n., 2 (p. 642).

plunk a baby; get plunked: get trubied: get karitanied. To go into a maternity home and have one baby's there; hence, to become pregnant: New Zealand: C. 20. B., 1941. The first (*plunked a baby*) refers to the Plunket Society, as obviously does the derivative second; the third refers to Sir Truby King, noted for sage advice upon, and sustenance for, the feeding of infants; the fourth comes ex Karitane Home.

plunk for. To plump for; support enthusiastically: coll.: C. 20. Cf. **plunk** (*Dict.*).

plurry. Bloody: orig. and still mainly (even though occ. jocular) euphemistic Australian: mid C. 19–20. Notably in *my plurry word!* and *no plurry fear!*. Ex Aboriginals' linguistically natural use of the word. (B.P.)

plus a little something. To the *Dict.* entry, it might be added that the company is Shell-Mex and B.P. Ltd.

plush, 2 (p. 642). The earlier sense is 'over*plus* of grog' and it occurs in W. N. Glascock, *The Naval Sketch-Book* (I, 24), 1825: Naval: prob. since ca. 1800. (Moe.)

pneumo. A pneumococcus: medica: C. 20. Gen. in pl. (*-os*).

pneumo, have a. To have artificial-pneumo-thorax treatment (*have an A.P.*: coll.): T.B. patients': since ca. 1930.

pneumonia blouse. A girl's low-cut blouse: since ca. 1920.

Pneumonia Bridge. A certain bridge that, at Gosport, is exposed to all the winds that blow: Naval: C. 20. Granville.

Pneumonia Corner. The junction of Putney Bridge and Lower Richmond Road: London policemen's: since ca. 1925. Many policemen on duty there end up by catching pneumonia.—2. The corner of Whitehall and Downing Street: Press photographers': since during the Munich crisis, Sept. 1938. Ex long, cold, wet waiting to 'snap' Ministers and other notables.

pneumonia rig. A set of tropical clothing: Naval: since ca. 1925. (P-G-R.)

pneumonia truck. 'Open lorry without doors or hood,' *The New Statesman*, Aug. 30, 1941: A.P.R. workers': 1940–5. Contrast **love-truck.**

P/O Prune. See **Prune.**

po-faced. 'A 1960's elastic word of disapproval, based on *po* (p. 643). It seems to equate with "square", "establishmentary", but also with "hearty". Debs' and book-reviewers'. Found in literary supplements and heard on radio' (Ramsey Spencer, Aug. 1967).
  'Of features bland or blank; set, socially correct, immobility of expression; the term implies social supercilious mask of a face that, unreasoning, claims deference by hauteur. One of the class brick-bats of the early 1960's, used in reflection i.e. disapproval, by and of upper classes' (Laurie Atkinson, Sept. 11, 1967.) Although heard less in late 1967 than in (say) 1962, it yet could not, at that time, be called obsolescent. In *The Guardian*, March 30, 1960, Mr Quintin Hogg referred to the Honourable Mr Wilson as 'po-faced', where the connotation seems to be rather that of 'poker-faced'. An early example occurs in Patricia Moyes, *Marriage à la Mode*, 1963.

poached egg. 'A yellow-coloured "silent cop" placed in the centre of intersections as a guide to traffic,' B., 1942: Australian: since ca. 1925.

pocket-billiards, to play, is the Public School synonym of **pinch the cat:** since ca. 1910.

pocket pistol. 'For a Pocket Pistol alias a dram bottle to carry in one's pocket, it being necessary on a journey or so, at Nicholl's pd 0.1.0' (paid one shilling): entry of June 29, 1763, in James Wood-forde's *Diary*: ? ca. 1740–1840. Ex shape. A late example occurs in Wm Maginn, *Tales of Military Life*, 1829, at I, 45. (Moe.)

pockies! That's mine; 'bags I!': Milton Junior School, Bulawayo: since ca. 1925. (A. M. Brown, letter of Sept. 18, 1938.) Worth recording as a variant of an enduring piece of folklore. I.e. *pockets I!*: cf. **bags I!** (*Dict.*).

pod.—3. Belly: C. 20. Mostly *in pod*, with child.—4. A marijuana cigarette; marijuana: Canadian jazz-lovers': since ca. 1956. (*The*

Victoria *Daily Colonist*, April 16, 1958, article 'Basic Beatnik'.)

pod, in. Recorded by B. & L.

pod, old. A big-bellied man: proletarian: from ca. 1860. Ibid.

poddy calf. Half-a-crown: Australian rhyming s.: since ca. 1910. (B., 1945.)

poddy-dodger. The agent corresponding to:—

poddy-dodging. 'The stealing of unbranded calves' (B., 1943): Australian rural: since ca. 1910. (B., 1943.)

poegah or **poegai.** Tipsy: South Africa: C. 20. *The Cape Times*, May 23, 1946 (latter form). Ex Afrikaans: cf. Dutch *pooier*, a tippler. Cf. **pogy** (p. 644).

poet, he's a. See **he's a poet.**

poet and didn't know it. See **that's a rhyme.**

Poetry. See 'Tavern terms', § 3, *d*.

pog. Face: Felsted School: since ca. 1880; ob. Prob. ex *physog* (see **phiz:** p. 622).

pog-top, pog-wag, poggle-top, etc. See **wog,** 3.

*poge-hunter. A thief specialising in the removal of purses: from ca. 1870. E.g. in Pugh (2). Ex **poge = poke =* a purse: mid-C. 19–20; ob.

pogy **aqua** (p. 644). For the etymology read 'Ex It. *poca aqua*'.

point, n.—5. (Perhaps ex sense 4: p. 644.) First place on a taxicab rank: taxi-drivers': since ca. 1910. See **hot joint.**—6. A smart, esp. a too smart, trick; an unfair advantage: Australian: C. 20. (Tom Ronan, *Vision Splendid*, 1954.) Ex **point, v.,** on p. 644.

point, v.—2. To malinger: Aus.: since ca. 1910. (B., 1959.) Ex sense 1 on p. 644.

Point Nonplus. 'Neither money nor credit' (*Sinks*): ca. 1820–70.

pointing. The n. corresponding to **point, v.** (p. 644): C. 20. B., 1943.

points, pile up. 'To curry favour. A person who draws attention to his "excellent qualities" with a view to advancement is said to pile up points,' Granville: Naval: since ca. 1925. Ex sport.

pointy. Pointed: coll.: C. 20. Gerald Kersh, *Slightly Oiled*, 1946, 'Where men wear pointy shoes.'

poison on armour plate. Beef tea and ship's biscuit: Naval (officers'): since ca. 1930. Well, perhaps the biscuits *are* a little hard . . .

poison(-)shop. A public-house: Australian: since ca. 1910. B., 1942.

poisoner. A cook: Australian: C. 20. Baker. Jocular.

poke, n., 2 (a punch, a blow): extant in Australia: B., 1942.—8. A purse: c.: mid-C. 19–20. —9. Horsepower: motorists': since ca. 1945. (R. T. Bickers, *The Hellions*, 1965, 'With all that poke under the bonnet')—10. A girl (notoriously) easy to have: low Australian: C. 20. 'I knew Elaine was a poke for the boys' (Dick). Ex sense 4: p. 644.
  For sense 7 (p. 644) cf. the quotation at **slag,** n., below. By 1940, fairly gen. s., as in 'It's a very satisfying feeling knowing you can put your finger on a bit of poke. (Which is slang for money: get it, poke, loot, poppy—any of them will do!'): L. J. Cunliffe, *Having It Away*, 1965.

poke, v.—4. To hit (someone): Australian: C. 20. Baker. Esp. as in 'Why don't you poke him one?' Synonymous with *take a poke at* someone.

poke Charley (v.t. demands *at*). To 'poke fun (at)', to be derisive—to deride: Naval: since ca. 1935. Granville. Ex the given-name of some noted humorist.

poke mullock at. See **mullock, poke,** on p. 542.

poke through on the rails. (Of a racehorse) to come through the field on the inside: Australian sporting: since ca. 1930. (B., 1953.)

poker!, don't chant the. See **sing it!, don't.**

pokey.—2. (Usually *the pokey.*) Prison: low Australian: late C. 19–20. (Ruth Park, 1950.) Ex '*poky* place'?—3. A poker machine: Aus. urban: since late 1930's. Jan Hamilton, *The Persecutor*, 1965. (Or **poky.**)

pokey-dice. Bluff poker: Regular Army: C. 20. Gerald Kersh, *Bill Nelson*, 1942.

poking drill. 'Aiming drill in the course of musketry instruction': military: from ca. 1870; ob. B. & L. Contrast **poky drill** in *Dict.*

*pola(c)k. A Pole, Russian or Czech dealing in Polish Jewesses: white-slavers' c.: C. 20. A. Londres, *The Road to Buenos Ayres*, 1928. A *Polack* is a Pole.

pole, v.i. To be an expense, obligation, nuisance: to 'scrounge': Australian: C. 20. In, e.g., Kylie Tennant, *Foveaux*, 1939. Cf. **pole, up the,** 6 (on p. 645).—2. To steal: New Zealand c.: since ca. 1930. R. G. C. McNab, in *The Press* (Christchurch, N.Z.), April 2, 1938. Also, since ca. 1935, Australian: B., 1943.—3. (Of the male) to copulate with, as in 'He poled the girl': Anglo-Irish: C. 20. Ex **pole,** n., 2, on p. 645.

pole, up the.—7. Pregnant: low, esp. Cockneys': from ca. 1908. Perhaps ex sense 3.—8. (Ex 6.) 'Wrong, worthless, stupid' (B., 1942): Australian: since ca. 1918.

pole on. To sponge on (somebody): Australian: C. 20. (Vance Palmer, *Daybreak*, 1932; Caddie, 1953.) Cf. preceding.

pole-pole. See 'Swahili words'.

poled (p. 645): also Australian. *The Drum*, 1959.

poler. A scrounger: Australian: since ca. 1930. (B., 1953.) Ex **pole** (v.i.), 1.

polers. 'Horses or bullocks harnessed alongside the pole of waggon or dray' (B., 1959): Aus. rural coll.: late C. 19–20.

policeman.—5. He who reminds a newcomer that he ought to pay footing: tailors': mid-C. 19–20; ob. B. & L.

policeman's helmet. *Glans penis erecti*: low: C. 20.

polio. *Polio*myelitis or infantile paralysis: coll., medical >, by 1958, general: since ca. 1930. (In, e.g., *Leader Magazine*, July 23, 1949.)

Polish Corridor, the. Cromwell Road (London, S.W.): taxi-drivers': 1945 +. *The Daily Telegraph*, May 18, 1948. Ex the many Poles resident there.—2. The passage leading from the front main hall to the Reading Room of the British Museum: B.M. habitués and attendants: since ca. 1940. but esp. ca. 1944–8. Ex a certain visitant and entourage.

polish one's arse on the top sheet. (Of men) to coït: low: late C. 19–20.

polish one's marble. See **marble.**

polish the apple. To curry favour, orig. of school-children polishing, on sleeve, an apple about to be presented to teacher: orig. (ca. 1920)

American, adopted in Britain ca. 1945. Hence, an *apple-polisher*, a toady—a term not yet (1966) very common in Britain.

*polisher. A gaol-bird: Australian c.: C. 20. B., 1942. Cf. **polish the King's iron** (p. 646).

politico. A politician either ambitious or unscrupulous or, esp., both: Australian: adopted, ca. 1955, ex U.S. (B.P.)—2. Hence, any politician: Australian coll.: since ca. 1960. Ex South American Spanish *politico*—or merely appearing to be?

poll, v.—4. To pollute: Christ's Hospital: ca. 1840–90. Marples.

poll up (p. 646). Semantically cf. *shack up.*

pollaky. To the *Dict,* entry add this information: Ignatius Paul Pollaky, Australian by birth: at an office in Paddington Green, he established 'Pollaky's Detective Agency' in 1862; in W. S. Gilbert's *Patience,* first performed on April 23, 1881, among the ingredients necessary to make a heavy dragoon is 'the keen penetration of Paddington Pollaky'; he frequently advertised in the agony columns of *The Times,* to which, in later life, he sometimes wrote over pseudonyms 'Ritter' or 'Criminalrath', letters of some length; and when at the age of 90, he died at Brighton, *The Times* gave him, on Feb. 28, 1918, an excellent obituary. (With thanks to the staff of *The Times.*)

polled up. See **poll up** (*Dict.*).

polloi. See **hoi.**

polly.—4. A prefect: Uppingham: since ca. 1870. Marples. By perversion.

*polly do. To pick oakum in jail: c.: from ca. 1860. B. & L. Cf. *mill doll* (q.v. at **doll, mill** in *Dict.*).

Polly Flinder. A window: Cockney rhyming s.: late C. 19–20. Cf. *Max Linder.*

Pollycon (or p-). Political Economy: undergraduates': C. 20. A blend.

polone. See **palone.** *Polone* is, in C. 20, the predominant form. The word goes back to ca. 1850 and is often used in combination as adj. 'female', as in *strill polone*, a female pianist. (Sydney Lester, *Vardi the Palarey*, 1937.)—2. A pony: circus and theatrical rhyming s.: C. 20. Franklyn 2nd.

pom.—2. Short for **pommy** (*Dict.*). Also written with a capital, as in Martin Boyd, *Day of My Delight*, 1965, 'The Poms have a kink on sex.'

pom-pom.—2. A French 75-mm. cannon: Army: 1914–18.—3. A multi-barrelled anti-aircraft gun: Services, esp. Naval, coll.: 1940 +. (P-G-R.)

pombi. See 'Swahili words'.

Pomme de Terre. A *Croix de Guerre*: Services': 1914–18; then only historical. (I never once heard it used during World War II.) Primarily rhyming s.; secondarily facetious. 'The Pomme de Terre was the only thing he'd earned, protecting a station-master's wife, he said' (V. M. Yeates, *Winged Victory*, 1934, p. 92).

pommy (p. 646). 'It is popularly believed that the term *pommy* . . . is a direct descendant of *jimmygrant* [see **Jimmy Grant,** both in *Dict.* and in Add.], via *jimmy-granate*: *pomegranate*, to *pommy*,' B., 1941,—which, fused with Jim Doone's theory, furnishes what is probably the correct explanation. Russell Braddon, however, in his preface to the English edition (1958) of Nino Culotta's *They're a Weird Mob*, thinks that the name is 'a compliment to your'—i.e. British—'complexions, because it comes from the French word *pommes*, which means apples'.—2. A Petty Officer *M*echanician (E): Naval: since ca. 1950. —3. Hence, any stoker Petty Officer: since ca. 1954. (Wilfred Granville, Nov. 22, 1962.)

Of sense 1, Jock Marshall & Russell Drysdale, *Journey among Men*, 1962 (p. 189), pertinently write: 'In colonial days the highly-coloured complexions of many Englishmen caused them to be called pomegranites [*sic*], a play on "immigrants" This was soon abbreviated to "pommy".'

pommy, adj. English: Australian: C. 20. Ex the n.—see p. 646.

Pompey 'ore, rarely **whore.** In the game of House, 24: rhyming s.: C. 20.

ponce. Prob. **pounce-spicer** should be **po(u)nce-shicer,** which occurs in B. & L. as a man living infamously upon an actress; both this and **pouncey** were † by 1920. For the etymology (p. 647), note the suggestion made to me by Michael Harrison in a letter of Jan. 4, 1947: 'Perhaps from Fr. *pensionnaire*' (boarder, lodger), conceivably with a pun on the English *pensioner*.—2. Hence, a young and dandified subaltern: Army (esp. Artillery): since ca. 1930.

ponce, v. To act as, to be a 'ponce' (p. 647): low: C. 20. G. Scott Moncrieff, *Café Bar*, 1932. Often as vbl n., *poncing*.—2. Hence, to sponge: low: since ca. 1915. James Curtis, *You're in the Racket Too*, 1937.—3. To obtain (money) by 'poncing': low: since ca. 1920. '"I don't ponce it orf 'em,"' Gerald Kersh, *Night and the City*, 1938.

ponce up, v.i. and v.refl; usu. *ponce oneself up* or *be ponced up.* To smarten up one's dress or appearance: Army: since ca. 1925. To put on one's best, esp. if flashy, clothes: since ca. 1950. (John Wainwright, *Death in a Sleeping City*, 1965.) On *dress up* but ex **ponce,** n., 2, and v., 1, above.

*poncess. A woman that supports a man by prostitution: c. from ca. 1870; ob. B. & L.

Pond-hopper. 'An R.A.F. Transport Command flight across the Atlantic. The routine is known in the Forces as "Pond-hopping"' (Laurie Atkinson): W.W. II and after. See **Pond, the,** on p. 647.

Ponderosa. 'Barking branch. Also Lake District' (*Railway*, 3rd): since ca. 1930 (?).

pong, n.—3. A Chinese: Australian low: C. 20. B., 1942. Ex *-ong* in Chinese monosyllabic names.

pongo, 3, 4 (p. 647), were very much alive in the war of 1939–45 also. (In, e.g., H. & P., Baker, and Granville.) Sense 3, in the R.A.F., was narrowed down to 'an Army officer': derogatory: 1939–45.—5. A *Pongo* = an Englishman, esp. an English serviceman: New Zealanders': since ca. 1943. (Slatter.) Prob. ex sense 2.

pongy. Evil-smelling: late C. 19–20. ('Taffrail', *Mystery at Milford Haven*, 1936.) Ex **pong,** n.: q.v. in *Dict.*

ponies, the. Horse racing: sporting coll.: C. 20.

ponk (see p. 647). As a New Zealand usage, however, it must be modified in the light of B., 1941: 'I suspect . . . that when we speak of an offensive stench as a *ponk* we are coupling the Maori *puhonga*, stinking, offensive, with the earlier English use of *pong*.'

Pontius Pilate in c.p. (R.A.F.): see **'way back when . . .**

Pontius Pilate's Guards occurs in a letter written from New York on Nov. 12, 1759, and printed in *The Public Ledger* of Jan. 15, 1760.

pontoon.—2. Hence, a twenty-one months' imprisonment: London's East End: since ca. 1925. (R. Herd, Nov. 12, 1957.) But also (Norman) of 21 years: c.: since ca. 1910. The latter is also an Army usage (P-G-R).

Ponty. A local coll. (C. 19–20) for any town named *Ponty*——, e.g. Pontypool, Pontypridd. —2. A Pontiac car: Australian: 1930's. (B.P.)

pony, 3 (p. 648). In *Sinks*, 1848, it = £50.—4. (Ibid.)—Earlier in *Sessions*, July 27, 1897.—5. For origin, see **gray.**—8. Short for rhyming s. *pony and trap*, to defecate: late C. 19–20. On *crap*, v. (p. 189).—9. A young girl's *pony tail* hair-style; coll.: since ca. 1960.

pooch, n.—2. A greyhound: Australian: C. 20. B., 1942. Origin? Probably ironically ex: 3. A dog, esp. if small or mongrel: Canadian: late C. 19–20. (Leechman.) Perhaps ex Ger. dial. *Butz*, a short thick animal. Canadian usage seems to antecede U.S. usage.—4. Hence, common for any dog: Canadian: since ca. 1920.

With sense 3, cf. the Ger. *Putzi*, 'a fairly common name given to a lap-dog' (Ramsey Spencer).

poochies. Insect and similar pests in Malaya: residents' and Army's: C. 20. Ex Malayan?

pood. An effeminate youth or man: Australian low: since ca. 1910. B., 1942. Cf. **poof.**

poodle-faker (p. 648), in a definition valid for the war of 1939–45 and for the cut-throat competition of the so-called peace: 'A payer of polite calls; a balancer of tea cups ashore' (Granville). *Poodle-faker* and *poodle-faking* antedate 1920 and prob. go back to 1910 or even earlier; 'Bartimeus' *A Tall Ship*, 1915, has the latter. It seems to be related to **dog-robbers** above. (Ramsey Spencer, 1967.)

poodle parade, the. The nightly parade of dog-owners exercising their dogs: coll.: since ca. 1920.

poodler. See 'Hauliers' Slang'.

pooey. See **poohy** below.

poof (p. 648). In Australia since ca. 1910. I definitely remember both *poof* and *poofter* as being used in the A.I.F. in 1915–18.

*poof-rorting (or **-wroughting**). Robbing male prostitutes with violence: c.: from ca. 1920. See **poof** and **rorty** in *Dict.*

poofter. A homosexual: Australian: C. 20. Cf. **poof** (*Dict.*).—2. Hence, a loud civilian suit: Naval (lower-deck): since ca. 1940. (P-G-R.) —3. (Ex sense 1.) An effeminate-looking man not necessarily homosexual: Australian: since ca. 1920. (B.P.)

poofter rorter. 'One who procures for a male homosexual' (B., 1959): low Aus.: since ca. 1935. Compare and contrast **poof-rorting** above. See **rorty** in *Dict.*

poofy. Smelly: children's: since ca. 1945 (? much earlier). 'I'd rather have a bath. I'm poofy': Nicholas Blake, *The Sad Variety*, 1964. Echoic of disgust: cf. the Scottish and North Country *poof!*, an exclamation of disgust. But perhaps imm. ex **poohy** below.

pooh. Anything smelly or disgusting, esp. *faeces*: Australian juvenile: since ca. 1930. (B.P.)

pooh, in the. In trouble: Australian: since ca. 1935. Lit., 'in the *shit*'. (B.P.) Ex preceding.

poohy, occ. written **pooey.** Lit. or fig., faecal; hence disgusting: Australian juvenile: since ca. 1935. Ex **pooh** above. (B.P.)—2. Hence, *poohy!* or *pooey!*, rubbish. Perhaps slightly influenced by U.S. *phooey!*

pool, v. To incriminate: to spoil the reputation or chances of someone *with* someone else: Australian low: since ca. 1910. Lawson Glassop, *We Were the Rats*, 1944, 'He pooled me with the Q.M. Just a top-off merchant, that's all he is.' By 1960, no longer low—and with a meaning less narrow.

Pool, the. Liverpool: C. 20.

pool(-)shark. One who is, or believes himself to be, exceptionally adept in the game of pool: Canadian: adopted, ca. 1925, ex U.S. (Leechman.)

poon, n. A lonely, loneliness-eccentric dweller in remote places: Australian: C. 20. B., 1942. Ex Aboriginal?—2. Hence (?), a simpleton; a fool; a gen. pejorative since ca. 1910. E.g. at Dulwich School since ca. 1930 (Marples).—3. A common shortening of **poontang** (below). Leechman.

Poona or **Poonah,** adj. Typical of the majors and colonels of the pre-1940 Regular Army: C. 20. 'He's very Poonah'—fiery, martinet, narrowly conservative, not excessively intelligent.

pooned up. Flashily dressed up: low Australian: since ca. 1930. (B., 1943; Dal Stivens, 1951.)

poontang. Copulation, esp. with a coloured woman: Canadian: C. 20. Supposedly of Chinese origin, there being such variants as *poong tai* and *poong kai.* (Whence *poontanger.*) Common also among homosexuals for 'sexual relations' (*The Lavender Lexicon*). The nuances 'copulation' and 'sexual relations' prob. derive ex the basic sense 'female pudend'.

poontanger. Penis: Canadian lumbermen's: C. 20. A logger's *tool*, more useful in town than in the woods.

poop, n.—5. A defecation; esp. in *do poop*: mostly children's: C. 20. Ex **poop,** v., 3, on p. 648.

pooped. Exhausted; very tired: since ca. 1890. 'Must stop for a bit; I'm pooped.' Probably ex the nautical S.E. v. *poop*: a sailing ship was temporarily disabled when a following sea came inboard from over the stern.

*****poor, she's (very) good to the.** A prostitutes' c.p. applied to a harlot known to be a price-cutter: from ca. 1910.

poor as a bandicoot. See **bandicoot.**

poor as piss (and twice as nasty), as. A Naval (lower-deck) pejorative: C. 20. Granville.

poor blind Nell. A girl wronged (i.e. seduced and abandoned): Australian: C. 20. Ex the well-known chant:

'Did he marry poor blind Nell?'
'He did. (*Pause.*) Like effing hell!'

Poor Man's Corner. A stand at an angle of Trafalgar Square: cabmen's: ca. 1870–1905. Clarkson & Richardson, *Police!*, 1889.

poor man's piano. A meal of (dried) beans. On account of the amount of wind in the bowels that it produces. Canadian slang, in use at the time of the construction of the Canadian Pacific Railway if not earlier.

poor soldier. A Noisy Friar Bird: Australian: C. 20. (B., 1943.)

poor soldier who can't stand his comrade's breath, it's a. A military c.p. proffered by the culprit when his companions complain of wind-breaking: from the 1890's. Contrast **foxes always smell** ...

poor view (of), take a. Transitive and intransitive synonyms of **take a dim view (of).**

poorboy. 'Something substantial and inexpensive, such as a big bottle of cheap wine' (*The Victoria Daily Colonist*, April 16, 1959, 'Basic Beatnik'): Canadian jazz-lovers': since ca. 1956.

pooty is a favourite mid-Victorian adjective meaning 'pretty'—of which, via *purty,* it is a perversion. 'A pooty little bit of money,' W. M. Thackeray, *Pendennis*, 1849–50. (Derek Pepys Whiteley, Esqre, letter of July 7, 1944.)

poove. A *poof* (p. 648): low: since mid-1940's. (*The New Statesman*, March 24, 1967.) Both *poove* and its rare variant *pouve* occur in John Gardner, *Madrigal*, 1967.

pop, n., 4 (p. 649). In full, *soda-pop*; since ca. 1910, all 'soft drinks'.—10. (Cf. sense 2: p. 649.) A popular song: song-writers' and publishers': since ca. 1920.—11. See **pop, a,** 2, below.—12. A bet, usu. at specified odds: Australian racing: since ca. 1920. '"Aeolus couldn't win it," said Lucky. "It'll be a fifty to one pop"': Lawson Glassop, *Lucky Palmer*, 1949.

Sense 10 came, ca. 1950, to mean also 'popular music, whether vocal or instrumental or both', as in 'The Capital of Pop' (Liverpool)—since early 1960's.

Pop. In address, any old or even, to the young, any middle-aged man: adopted, ca. 1944, ex U.S.

pop, a. Each time, or each, as in 'What did these set you back?'—'Five quid a pop': Australian: since ca. 1920. (B.P.)—2. An attempt, as in 'to have a *pop* at it': general, but perhaps esp. Australian: since ca. 1940.

pop, give a.—2. To *give it a pop* is to make an attempt at it; to make a bet: New Zealand: since ca. 1919. R. G. C. McNab, in *The Press* (Christchurch, N.Z.), April 2, 1938. In Australia, *have a pop (at)*: B., 1942: there it also means to engage (someone) in a fight. As 'an attempt', *pop* probably went to New Zealand and Australia from England: cf. J. B. Priestley, *The Good Companions*, 1929, 'I'll have a pop at it, of course.'

pop, let fly the. To fire the pistol: midway between c. and low s.: late C. 18–mid 19. See the quotation at **leaden fever.**

pop, not a fair. Not a fair chance: New Zealand: since ca. 1925. (Slatter.)

Pop-Eye or **Popeye.** See **Ixta.**—2. A ship's look-out man or an aircraft observer: since ca. 1938. H. & P. Ex 'Popeye the Sailor' in a famous series of comic cartoons (cf. **Wimpey**): anyone with such large eyes *must* have excellent eyesight.—3. The Pope: anti-papists' derogatory: since ca. 1945.

pop it on.—2. To make a bet: from ca. 1890. Anstey, *The Man from Blankley's* 1901.

pop of, be on the. To be about to: Anglo-Irish: late C. 19–20. James Joyce, *Ulysses*, 1922, 'He was on the pop of asking me to the night in the kitchen I was rolling the potato cake.'

pop-out. A mass-produced surfboard: Australian (teenage) surfers': since ca. 1961. *Pix*, Sept. 28, 1963.

pop-pimping. The spotting of theatrical talent: since ca. 1950. *The New Statesman*, Feb. 5, 1965; Competition.

pop the parapet. To 'go over the top': Army: 1915–18.

Pope of Fleet Street, the. Hannen Swaffer: 'Perhaps now more used than *The Bishop of Fleet Street*,' Albert B. Petch, letter of Dec. 18, 1946.

Pope's telephone number, the. 'Vat 69' whisky: since ca. 1905. Punning '*Vatican*'.

Poplar and Stepney Gurkhas, the. The Tower Hamlet Rifles: Army: 1914–18. (Letter to *The Daily Telegraph*, Sept. 26, 1963.) 'Presumably ex their area of recruitment' (Peter Sanders).

Popo. See **Ixta**.

poppery. A squall: ? mostly Naval: C. 19; † by 1890. (W. N. Glascock, *The Naval Sketch-Book*, 2nd Series, 1834, II, 177, 'Securin' the squadron in its old berth, and that too under another pelting poppery.') Moe.

popping?, how are you or how yer. How are you, as in '"How yer poppin' s'mornin'?"' (Norman Lindsay, *Saturdee*, 1933): Aus., mostly juvenile: since ca. 1910; by 1960, ob.

poppy, n. Money; esp., cash: Cockneys': C. 20.

Pops.—2. Popular Concerts: music-lovers': since ca. 1925. Cf. **Prom** (p. 661, end).

Popski. In reference to early 1941: 'I overheard him [Lieutenant-Colonel Prendergast, officer commanding the Long Range Desert Group in North Africa] mentioning on the phone someone named Popski and when he had done he turned to me, and, somewhat embarrassed, he said, "As you heard, we call you Popski. Nobody can understand Peniakoff on the phone. Do you mind?" I assured him I was delighted with my nickname and remembered that my namesake was the comical hairy littly bolshy in—was it the *Daily Mirror?*—comic strip. Whether I liked it or not, Popski I had become and Popski I have remained to this day,' Vladimir Peniakoff (Lieutenant-Colonel, D.S.O., M.C.), *Private Army*, 1950. Modelled on the tiny force he had already operated, *Popski's Private Army* (or *P.P.A.*) was formed late in October and thus christened early in Nov. 1942; after North Africa, it went to Italy. *Private Army*, quite the best 'Unit record' and perhaps the best autobiography of the war of 1939–45, is a fascinating and most notable book.

popsy (p. 650) may be written *popsey* or *popsie*; also R.A.F. and Naval (officers')—since ca. 1935—for 'a girl', not merely in address but also, and more usually, in reference. H. & P.; Granville.—2. A woman conductor: busmen's: since ca. 1945.

popular as a pork chop in a synagogue, as. Decidedly unpopular or unwelcome: since ca. 1950. Pork being forbidden to Jews.

population of China!, what's that—the. A c.p. 'deriding comparatively high service or regimental number' (Atkinson): Forces': 1941 +.

poque is an occ. Australian variant of **poke**, n., 8.

porangi. (Extremely) eccentric, crazy; (very) stupid: New Zealand coll.: late C. 19–20. B., 1941. Adoption of Maori word.

porc. A porcupine: Australian, coll. C. 20. (Ion Idriess, *Men of the Jungle*, 1932.)

Porcupine, H.M.S. H.M.S. *Penelope*: Naval: 1941 +. Ex holes plugged with protruding wooden pegs; cf. **Pepperpot**.

Pork and Lard, the. The 'St Ives to Ely line (closed)'—says *Railway*, 3rd, 1966. Railway-

men's: ? ca. 1930–65, then historical. Not St Ives, Cornwall, but St Ives, Huntingdonshire.

pork-knocker. 'A diamond prospector in the rivers and streams of British Guiana.—B.B.C. "Adventure" Mar. 16, 1964, but have seen it in print ca. 1961. ? from their diet of pork and beans' (Peter Sanders).

porky, adj. (p. 650), occurs earlier in *The Night Watch* (II, 105), 1828. Moe.

porn. Pornography: mostly photographers' and journalists': since late 1940's. Nicholas Luard, *The Warm and Golden War*, 1967, '"Porn or portrait they're all available."'

pornshop. Shop where pornography is sold. Witty pun on 'pawnshop'. Since about 1960.

porny. Bawdy (persons), smutty (talk, etc.): C. 20. Ex *pornographic*.

porous. A mild or polite form of **poor as piss**. (P-G-R.)

***porridge; esp. a bit of porridge.** Imprisonment; a term in prison: c.: since ca. 1930. (Norman.) Perhaps suggested, in part at least, by the semantics of S.E. **stir**, by a pun on **stir**, 2, a prison (p. 833).—2. 'Sludge removed from drains' (*Railway*): railwaymen's: C. 20. Of a similar consistency.

Porridge Box, the. The Royal Scot express: railwaymen's: since ca. 1920(?). *Railway*, 3rd.

porridge education. 'Sometimes when a knowledgeable chap is told that he must have had a college education, he says "*No*; I had a porridge education"—meaning that he was brought up in the Scottish manner, fed on little more than porridge and "educated" by some heavy-handed village dominie' (A. B. Petch, Jan. 1966): coll. C. 20.

port. A portmanteau: Australian: since ca. 1910. Ruth Park, *The Harp in the South*, 1948. Earlier in Vance Palmer, *Legend for Sanderson*, 1937. But also—and perhaps earlier—New Zealand, as in Jean Devanney, *Dawn Beloved*, 1928. 2. Porter, as term of address: C. 20.

port-hole duff. See **Navy cake**.

Port Melbourne pier. Variant of *Melbourne pier*.

Port Said garters. 'Any contraceptives worn by amorous (and prudent) soldiery': Army: ca. 1939–55.

port wine. Blood: pugilistic: ca. 1840–90. Augustus Mayhew, *Paved With Gold*, 1857. Much less gen. than **claret** (*Dict.*).

porter's knot. A large bob of hair worn by women at the back of the head in 1866: coll.: 1866 +; † by 1880, except historically. B. & L.

Portugoose (p. 651): prob. goes back to very early C. 19. (Glascock, 1834, as *Portegoose*.) Moe.

Portug(u)ee (p. 651). Much earlier. It occurs in, e.g., W. N. Glascock, *Sketch-Book*, 2nd Series, 1834, at II, 121. (Moe.)

Portuguese pumping (p. 651) is more usually *Portuguese pump* and it does mean masturbation.

posh, adj. (p. 651). The usual educated explanation—'*port outward bound, starboard home*' (sun-avoiding, hence the 'best', cabins on the England–India run in hot weather)—is ingenious and plausible; but, distrusting it, I prefer this: a contraction of *polish*, itself a slovened pronunciation of *polished*.—2. Hence, free, esp. if illicitly acquired: Regular Army: since ca. 1912.

posh, n.—4. Spit-and-polish: Army: 1914–18. Ex the adj.

posh, do the. To do things in style: to spend lavishly: Australian: since ca. 1920. B., 1942.

position is critical, the. See very grave.

possible sack. A Canadian coll., adopted, ca. 1895, ex U.S., but adapted from 'a bag for provisions and personal belongings' to 'a bag containing such articles sufficiently valuable to be deposited, as a pledge, with a pawnbroker'. (Leechman.)

*possodelux. A conman's victim (B., 1959): Aus. c.: since ca. 1930. See possum below.

possum.—2. A 'ring-in' (q.v.): low Australian: since ca. 1925. (B., 1943.)

*possum, with shortening poss. A simpleton; a dupe: Australian c.: since ca. 1925. (B., 1945.) —A very rich dupe is a posso-de-luxe. (B., 1953.)

possum up a gum-tree, like a. Entirely happy and contented; 'on top of the world': Australian coll.: C. 20. B., 1942.

post, n. A deferred examination: Australian university coll., esp. in N.S.W.: since ca. 1920. (B.P.)

post, v.—4. To promote (someone) to post-captain: Naval: ca. 1790–1850. (W. N. Glascock, Sailors and Saints, 1829, at I, 8. Moe.)

post a letter. To defecate: euphemistic: since ca. 1890.

post-and-rail. A wooden match as opp. a wax vesta: Australian: from ca. 1880; ob. B. & L. —2. A fairy tale, esp. a lie: Australian rhyming s.: since ca. 1910. (B., 1945.)

post and rails. 'Post and rail tea' (p. 652): Australian: C. 20.—2. Wooden matches: Australian: since ca. 1920. (B., 1943.)

post-and-rails tea is preferable, pedantically, to the form in the Dict.

post-mortem, as applied to discussion of a hand (or a game) at bridge after it has been finished, may orig. (1922: O.E.D., Sup.) have been bridge-players' s.; but it very quickly > S.E.—Lit., an after-death (examination).

Post Royal Tom. 'A wellknown shark in Jamaica' (W. N. Glascock, Sketch-Book, 2nd Series, 1834, II, 59): Naval: early C. 19.

post te.—2. Hence, forbidden or taboo, 'It's post te to do such a thing': Charterhouse: since ca. 1914.—3. Hence, to be privileged, a privilege: ibid.; since ca. 1918. Marples.

postchaise, postchay, postshay. See post-chaise and post-chay in the Dict.

postman's knock. A lock: burglars' rhyming s.: C. 20. Chubb's advertisement in The Daily Telegraph, March 5, 1962.

Postman's Park. A little 'square' within the G.P.O. block, London, E.C.4: Londoners': C. 20. Because this tiny square—the only square in the block—is nearly always filled with postmen that have come out for a breather.

pot, n.—15. Abbr. pot-hat: ca. 1890–1914. B. & L.—16. A china, or an enamel, mug: Services' coll.: since ca. 1925.—17. A paunch: esp. get a bit of a pot, to become fat-bellied: since ca. 1920. (Cf. sense 13: p. 652.)—18. A cylinder, esp. in one of the old rotary engines: R.F.C.– R.A.F.: 1914–18. They tended to split or to fly off. Hence, any aeroplane-engine cylinder: R.A.A.F.: 1939–45. (B., 1943.) 'Hence, a cylinder in any internal combustion engine, as in the phrase "hitting on all pots" = firing on all cylinders. Common in the 1930's.' (Peter

Sanders.)—19. A potentiometer: Australian and prob. elsewhere: since ca. 1950. (B.P.)—20. Marijuana: orig. and still mostly drug-addicts': adopted ex U.S., ca. 1945 in Canada, ca. 1947 in Britain, ca. 1950 in Australia (B.P.)

pot, v.—7. To stake a large sum on (a horse): turf: from ca. 1870.—8. To throw (e.g. a stone): Australian: C. 20. B., 1942. I.e. take a pot-shot —9. To put a baby on a chamber-pot: domestic coll.: C. 20.—10. To give (a pupil) an imposition: Public Schools': ca. 1880–1915. (Talbot Baines Reed, 1907.)—11. To inform upon, lay information against: Australian (low): since ca. 1920. Caddie, A Sidney Barmaid, 1943, 'To myself I said, "What dirty swine has potted me?"'

pot, on the.—2. In trouble; vexed: low: ca. 1840–80. Sinks, 1848.

pot and pan (p. 653). By 1925, far from rare. Len Ortzen, Down Donkey Row, 1938.

pot-gutted. Pot-bellied: Australian coll.: C. 20. Baker.

pot-hole. A shell-hole: military: 1914–18.

pot(-)mess. 'A stew made of bits and pieces too numerous for specification,' Granville: Naval coll.: late C. 19–20. Cf. pot, n., 12 (Dict.).—2. Hence, a complete mix-up: chaos: Australian Naval: since ca. 1910.

pot of honey. Variant of bees and honey (p. 43). Franklyn 2nd.

pot on, put (someone's). To inform on: Australian: C. 20. B., 1942.

pot on, put the. See put the pot on (Dict.).—2. To exaggerate: from ca. 1870; ob.—3. To overcharge: tradesmen's: mid-C. 19–20. B. & L.

pot scum. 'Bad or stinking dripping,' Sinks: domestic coll.: ca. 1825–1910.

Pot—the Princess of Tasmania. 'The vehicular ferry between the mainland and Tasmania' (B.P.): Australian: since ca. 1955.

pot to pee (or piss) in, doesn't (or didn't) have a. A Canadian c.p. (since ca. 1905) for extreme poverty.

Potash and Perlmutter. Butter: rhyming s.: since ca. 1910; by 1960, slightly ob. Montague Glass's play of that title 'was first produced in London at The Queen's Theatre, Shaftesbury Avenue, on April 14, 1914. The play was a huge success and the term may have come into use even before 1915' (Franklyn 2nd).

potato.—3. A girl, a (young) woman: Australian rural: since ca. 1925. (D'Arcy Niland, 1958.)

potato!, take a red-hot. A c.p. (ca. 1840–60) 'by way of silencing a person . . . a word of contempt,' Sinks, 1848. A very hot potato in one's mouth is a sharp deterrent from loquacity.

potato, the clean. A non-convict; a person of good character: Australian: ca. 1825–70. Baker.

potato-trap. See potato-jaw (Dict.).

potatoes in the mould, hence often potatoes whence taters. Cold (adj.): rhyming s.: late C. 19–20. Franklyn, Rhyming.

potch. '"Fire" or "live" opal was the most sought after; naturally being the rarest and most valuable, it was the least found. "Potch" or immature opal could be found by the ton,' Archer Russell, Gone Nomad, 1936: Australian opal-miners': late C. 19–20: coll. >, by 1930, j. App., potch is an English dial. variant of patch. The word occurs in K. S. Prichard, The Black Opal, 1921.

potential. A potential officer: Army coll.: since ca. 1940. (P-G-R.)

pothooks; Pothooks. See **pot-hooks** and **Pot-Hooks** in *Dict.*

pothouse; the Pothouse. See **pot-house** (*Dict.*).

pots; runners; straws. Potatoes; scarlet runner beans; strawberries: greengrocers' coll.: since ca. 1870.

pots.—2. A radio supervisor ('late *P.O.* Tel.'— Petty Officer Telegraphy): Naval: since late 1930's. 'Still in use, despite his new name' (Wilfred Granville, Nov. 22, 1962.)

pottage. The Book of Common Prayer: C. 17. Frequent in the less reputable writings of the time. Esau sold his birthright for a mess of pottage.

potted.—4. Snubbed; suppressed: non-aristocratic: from ca. 1880; ob. B. & L.—5. Tipsy: South Africa: since ca. 1938. Professor W. S. Mackie in *The Cape Argus*, July 4, 1946, 'A mere variant of "canned."'—6. Exhilarated by taking marijuana: drug-addicts': adopted, ca. 1956, ex U.S.

pottle.—2. An ice-cream carton (B., 1943): Australian coll.: since ca. 1925. Ex the S.E. *pottle*, a tiny basket for strawberries.

potty, n.—2. A chamber-pot, esp. a child's: nursery and domestic coll.: C. 20. Cf. **pot,** v., 9.

potwalloper; potwalloping. See **pot-walloper** and **-walloping** in *Dict.*

***pouf-wroughting.** See **poof-rorting.**

poufter. Variant of *poofter.*

poultice, n.—5. A mortgage: Australian: C. 20. (K. S. Prichard, *Kiss on the Lips*, 1932.)—6. A (large) sum of money; e.g. in wages: Australian: since ca. 1920. D'Arcy Niland, *Call Me . . .*, 1948, 'I got paid off, and it was a whacking big *poultice*.'—7. Hence, a bribe, esp. in *sling in a poultice*, to offer a bribe: Australian: since ca. 1925. (Culotta.)

Poultice, the. The taxicab rank outside the Middlesex Hospital: London taxi-drivers': since ca. 1910. Herbert Hodge, *Cab, Sir?*, 1939. Cf.:—

poultice plasterer, the. The Medical Officer: Navy: since ca. 1920. H. & P. Cf. the *poultice* combination on p. 654 and:—

poultice-walloper.—3. A nursing orderly: R.A.F. since ca. 1925. Jackson.

pounce.—2. A severe, esp. if written, criticism: book-world coll.: from ca. 1930. Ex **pounce, on the,** q.v. in *Dict.*

pouncer. See **whistler.** 9.

pound of lead; often shortened to *pound.* Variant of **lump of lead** (p. 499). Franklyn 2nd.

pound the stones. To walk a beat: police: C. 20. Via the coll. *pound the beat* (late C. 19–20).

pour on more coals. To open the throttle of either a piston or a jet engine: R.A.F.: since ca. 1950. Cf. *open the taps* at **taps** below.—2. 'Also used for accelerating in a motor car' (Leechman): motorists': since ca. 1955.

pouve. An occasional variant of **poove** above.

poverty. Some strong liquor that was in vogue in the 1720's. Anon., *The Quaker's Opera*, 1728.

Poverty Point. The junction of Park and Pitt Streets: Sydneyites': ca. 1890–1920. B., 1942. Cf. **poverty corner** on p. 655.

powder, take a. See **fade, do a.**

powder one's nose. To go to the lavatory: women's euphemistic: since ca. 1940.

powdered chalk. A walk: rhyming s. (not very common): late C. 19–20. The v. is *take a powdered chalk*, whence perhaps the U.S. *take a powder.* 'I believe the U.S. "take a powder" means take a

laxative, which will make you "go". In other words, "Get out of here"' (Leechman).

Powell it. To walk: sporting coll.: ca. 1810–50. *Boxiana*, II, 1818. Ex the name of a famous early C. 19 walker.

power.—2. Penis: low and rather rare: mid-C. 19–20. Prob. suggested by sexual *potency.*

pox doctor's clerk, like—or **got-up like—a.** In a very smart civilian suit: Naval: C. 20. Granville, 'Also "pox doctor's assistant" (lower-deck).'

pozzie. Variant (B., 1959) of **possy,** 1, on p. 652.

pozzy, 3 (p. 656). Also Naval (lower-deck) s., since ca. 1919. Granville.

prac. A practical test or examination: Australian students, esp. in Science or Medicine: since ca. 1925. (B.P.) Cf.:—

pracs. Practical classes: Reading undergraduates': since ca. 1920. (Marples, 2.)

pragger. A *practice* game: Rugby School: late C. 19–20. 'The Oxford *-er.*' (D. F. Wharton.)

Pragger Wagger, the (p. 656). But in the 1880's, the future King Edward VII. Marples, 2.

prairie rash. Baked beans: Naval (lower-deck): Sept. 13, 1941, *The Weekly Telegraph.* Ex **cowboys.**

prams. Legs: low Glasgow s., verging on c.: late (? mid-) C. 19–20. MacArthur & Long. Prob. a corruption of the old c. term, *gams.*

Prancing Queers, The. Ivor Novello's show, *The Dancing Years*: theatrical: late 1940's–early 1950's.

Prang; usu. in full, **Prang Bell.** A common nickname of men surnamed Bell: since ca. 1944. Cf. **prang,** v., 2, below.

prang, n. A crash; esp., a crash-landing: R.A.F.: since ca. 1937. H. & P. Ex the v.—2. A bombing raid: 1939 +. Partridge, 1945. Ex sense 2 of:—

prang, v. To crash-land an aircraft (usually v.t.): R.A.F.: since ca. 1935. Sgt-Pilot F. R. Rhodes, letter of Sept. 20, 1942; Jackson, 1943, 'To damage, destroy, wreck. . . . From the sound of the impact of a metal aircraft with the ground'; Paul Brickhill & Conrad Norton, *Escape to Danger*, 1946 (see quotation at **hack down**). Reminiscent of *bang.*—2. Hence (?), to bomb (a town, a factory, etc.): since late 1939. John Moore in *The Observer*, Oct. 4, 1942; Jackson, 'He pranged the target to blazes.'—3. (Ex 1 or 2—or both.) 'Sometimes applied to non-flying accidents, e.g., "Jones pranged his arm at rugger to-day,"' H. & P., 1943. —4. To coït with (a girl): R.A.F.: 1940 +. Cf. *bang,* v., 3 (p. 31) and *target . . .*

prannie or **pranny.** Female pudend: low: late C. 19–20. A term of contempt among men.

prat, v.—4. To speak, to talk, to someone: Australian low: since ca. 1918. B., 1942. Ex sense 2.

prat about. To potter, mess about: low: late C. 19–20. Cf. **prat,** n., 2, 3, and **prat,** v., 2: on p. 656.

prattle-box. See 'Men', and **prattling-box** (*Dict.*).

prawn, draw the raw. 'To get the worst part of an arrangement' (Culotta): Australian: since ca. 1930. Cf. the American colloquialism '*raw* deal'—but why *prawn*?

prawn-headed mullet. A very stupid fellow: Aus.: since ca. 1930. Nino Culotta, *Gone Fishin'*, 1963. Cf. *stunned mullet* below.

prawnie (or **-ny**). A catcher or a seller of prawns: Australian: since ca. 1920. (B., 1953.)

pray. 'No use to protest. To squeal, or to pray as they called it, might mean worse' (James Barlow, *The Burden of Proof*, 1968): raffish London, esp. teenage addicts': since ca. 1960.

prayers, morning or **family.** A daily Staff Conference at H.Q.: Army: 1939–45.

praying-mantis. 'A tail landing, whether accidental or intentional if the undercarriage fails to work,' H. & P.: R.A.F.: since ca. 1930. Ex that insect, *Mantis religiosa*, which holds its forelegs in a position suggestive of prayer: O.E.D.

pre.—2. A president of college: Oxford undergraduates': from ca. 1880.

pre-fab. A pre-fabricated house: 1945 +; by 1947, coll.

Pre Sci (pron. *sky*). *Preliminary science* examination, University of London: (mostly students') coll.: late C. 19–20.

'preciate. To appreciate: semi-literate coll., mostly Australian: C. 20. (Dymphna Cusack, 1953.)

precious, adv. (p. 657): earlier in W. N. Glascock, *The Naval Sketch-Book*, 2nd Series, 1834, at I, 209, 'We've taken a precious, precious wide yaw from our course'; and earlier still in Fredk Chamier, *The Life of a Sailor*, 1832, at II, 63 ('precious glad'). Moe.

precious few (p. 657) was perhaps adopted ex the U.S.A. It occurs in, e.g., *The Port Folio*, May 29, 1802, at p. 161, 'That we (precious few) who sometimes can think.' Contrast 'The skipper tucks in a precious lot of good things [victuals] under his belt': W. N. Glascock, *The Naval Sketch-Book* (II, 107), 1826. (Moe.)

pref. A prefect: Scottish Public Schools': since ca. 1870. Ian Miller, *School Tie*, 1935. Contrast **pre** (*Dict.*).

prefer room to company, as in 'She prefers my room to my company' and a hint, 'I prefer your room to your company': virtually a c.p.: late C. 19–20.

preggers. Pregnant: Oxford and Cambridge graduates': since ca. 1920. By male insensitivity out of Alma Mater tribalism. Cf. the next two.

preggy. Pregnant; hence, bulging: upper and upper-middle classes': since early 1920's. Ngaio Marsh, *Death in a White Tie*, 1938, 'There was your bag, simply preggy with bank-notes, lying there on the writing-table.'

Pregnant Duck. A Hudson bomber aircraft: R.A.F.: 1940–4. Ex appearance. (Communicated by S/Ldr John Pudney.)

pregnant scholar. See 'Tavern terms', § 3, *b*.

prego. Pregnant: Australian: since the 1920's. (Cusack & James, *Come in Spinner*, 1951.) The ubiquitous Australian suffix *-o*.

Prels. See 'Minor Drugs'.

premie (pronounced *premmie*). A *prematurely* born child: Canadian doctors' and nurses': since ca. 1925. (Leechman.) Also common in the Australian medical world. (B.P.)

prems. Premises (of property): trivial: from ca. 1890; ob. Pugh (2), ''E keeps no end o' bullion on the prems.'

prep, v. To prepare (a person; a limb, etc.) for operation: hospitals': C. 20. Josephine Bell, *Murder in Hospital*, 1937, 'Macdonald started to prep him' and 'She had finished prep'ing the leg'.

Presbo. A Presbyterian: Australian: since ca. 1925. (B., 1953.)

prescribe and **proscribe** confused: catachrestic: late C. 19–20.

present (p. 658). The white spot on the fingernail has a different meaning for each nail. Starting with the thumb the verse runs—'A gift, a friend, a foe; a letter to come, and a journey to go.'

present for a good girl. Jocular; sometimes with sexual innuendo; coll.: C. 20.

press and scratch, usu. in the pl. Variant of **cuts and scratches** (above). Franklyn 2nd.

Press Button. A Presbyterian: Australian: mostly Catholic: C. 20.

press on, regardless; press-on type. 'I must press on, regardless' = I have urgent work to do, I must finish this job. Ex lit. *press on*, to continue one's way towards the objective, despite damage or injury. Hence, *press-on type*, an energetic or very conscientious fellow: 1941 +; often derisive. (Communicated by S/Ldr Vernon Noble, Feb. 1945.)

Pressie, adj. and n. (A) Presbyterian: Australian: C. 20. (Colin MacInnes, *June in Her Spring*, 1952.)

pressing engagement. An appointment with a girl: jocular coll.: C. 20. With pun on *pressing*.

***pressure.** Police investigation; police interrogation: Australian c.: since ca. 1920. B., 1942. Ex *put pressure on*.

Preston Gild (or **Guild**), **every.** Rarely: Lancashire coll.: late C. 19–20. It is held only every twenty years.

pretend you're a bee—and buzz! A dismissive c.p.: Australian: since ca. 1950. (B.P.) Cf. **buzz,** v., 5 (p. 116).

pretty, n.—3. A pretty girl, a 'lovely': since ca. 1935. Ex: A domestic term of address to a girl child or adolescent, whether pretty or not: coll.: late C. 19–20.

pretty(-)boy. 'An effeminate young man' (B., 1942): Australian coll.: C. 20.

pretty-face (p. 658) is, more precisely, the whiptail kangaroo, which is smallish: the term is far from ob.: see esp. Jean Devanney, *Travels in North Queensland*, 1951, at pp. 118–119.

pretty much. Almost; to a large extent: coll.: since ca. 1860. E. Charles Vivian, *Tramp's Evidence*, 1937, 'Crandon'—a small country town— 'goes to bed with the dickey-birds, pretty much'.

pretty up. To 'make a mess of', to disfigure: Australian: since ca. 1920. D'Arcy Niland, *The Big Smoke*, 1959, 'I'll pretty up your face, boy.'

price of Admiralty; mostly *pay the . . .,* to be killed at sea: Naval (officers'): C. 20. Granville. A sarcastic euphemism.

'The source of this is "A song of the English" of the poems in Rudyard Kipling's "The Seven Seas" (1896). The line "If blood be the price of admiralty" is repeated cumulatively (an additional repetition in each succeeding verse), and produces an unintentionally hysterical effect that invites sarcasm from those who may be expected to pay it.' (Ramsey Spencer, March 1967.)

pricey or **pricy.** High-priced: 1944, *World's Press News*, Aug. 31. Also Australian and New Zealand, apparently since ca. 1910. It occurs in, e.g., H. Drake-Brockman, *Hot Gold*, 1940.

prick, n.—6. '*Perique*: Issue tobacco wrapped in canvas and lashed with spun yarn into a cylindrical shape tapered to a point,' Granville: Naval: since ca. 1890.

prick, v. To mark a course on (a chart): Naval officers' coll.: late C. 19-20. (P-G-R.)

prick, (standing about) like a (spare). Useless, unwanted, idle; esp. with hint of superfluity or of embarrassment: low: C. 20.

prick(-)farrier. A medical officer: R.A.F. regulars': since ca. 1928. Cf. **prick smith.**

prick for a (soft) plank (p. 659). Prob. throughout C. 19, for it occurs, as 'prick for the softest plank', in 'A Real Paddy', *Life in Ireland*, 1822.

prick-parade. A V.D. inspection. Services' coll.: C. 20.

prick(-)smith. Medical officer: Army: 1939 +. Ex the venereal inspection he administers.

prick-teaser. A late C. 19-20 variant of **cock-teaser** (*Dict.*). Often abbr. to *p.t.* or *P.T.*—2. Hence, a synonym of **p.t.,** 2, q.v. in *Dict.*

pricker, chief. A Chief Stoker: Naval: since ca. 1910. Granville.

pricker with (someone), **get the.** To take a dislike to: New Zealand: since ca. 1930. Slatter, 'Got the pricker with me'. Perhaps ex S.E. *prickly*, over-ready to take offence.

priest. A self-propelling field-gun: Eighth Army: 1941-5. H. & P.

prim, n.—2. (*Prim.*) A Primitive Methodist: Nonconformists': late C. 19-20.

Prin, the. 'The old Princess Theatre, Melbourne' (B., 1942): Australian: ca. 1890-1920.

Prince Alberts, 2 (p. 660). Add that the 'toe-rags' sense dates from ca. 1860. 'Tom Collins', *Such is Life*, 1903, 'Unlapping from his feet the inexpensive substitute for socks known as "prince alberts".' Cf. S.E. *albert*, a watch-chain: these rags are rolled about the feet.—3. Roughly made lace-up boots: Australian: since ca. 1920. (B., 1943.)

Prince Alfreds is the post-1910 variant of **Prince Alberts** (p. 660). Baker.

Prince of Wales. A locomotive's blowing-off of steam: railwaymen's: since ca. 1920. (*Railway.*) Perhaps rhyming s. on *gales* (of wind), unless it refers to King Edward the Eighth's refreshing outspokenness post-World War I, while, of course, he was still the Prince of Wales.

princess of the pavement. A prostitute: Australian: C. 20. Baker.

Princess Pats, the (p. 660). Also *Pat's Pets* and simply *Pats*: witness Jack Munroe, *Mopping Up!*, 1918.

Principal Secretary. See 'Tavern terms', § 5.

principle is a frequent misspelling for *principal*: prob. since C. 15. The following was perpetrated in 1936: 'The title-phrase, or the principle words of it, has generally been set in a conspicuous size of type'; a sophist but not a stylist could defend this error.

prink, n.—2. *The Prink* is the Principal, esp. of a women's college: girl undergraduates' and trainee teachers': since ca. 1905. Also *Prinny*.

prison. In the game of marbles, a hole placed farther from the taw-line than even third hole: Australian children's: C. 20. (B.P.)

Prisoner-of-War Slang. There is a valuable note on the prisoners-of-war-in-Germany slang at the beginning of Paul Brickhill & Conrad Norton, *Escape to Danger*, 1946: see entry at **kriegy.** All the terms mentioned in that book appear in these

Addenda. Guy Morgan's no less readable *Only Ghosts Can Live*, 1945, contains these additional terms: *big eats!*: How are you?—Ger. *wie gehts?*, how goes it?; *bunker*, solitary-confinement cell; *fish-paste?*, what time is it?—Ger. *wie spät ist es?*; *goon* (see separate entry), 'after that dumb top-heavy ham-handed race of giants in the "Pop-Eye" comic strip'; hence, *goon up!*—a warning that a German (soldier) is near-by or approaching; *millet*, 'porridge-like soup'; *nix fish-tins*, I don't understand—Ger. *nicht verstehen*; *stimmt*, genuine, true—from Ger. *alles stimmt*, all correct; *tiger-box*, a square box that, on a pole at each corner of the barbed wire, contained searchlight, machine-gun, telephone and a sentry.

2. For the P.O.W. slang of the Far East, there was published in a ship's news-sheet of late 1945, an excellent and delightful article by H. W. Fowler & I. P. Watt, who have generously allowed me to make full use of it. Here are some few of the terms they list; the quotations come from that article.

3. A rumour: *borehole* (ex a rough-and-ready latrine); *griff* (see **griff**, n., p. 354); and *latrin(e)o-gram* (Addenda).

4. 'Anyone thought to run a wireless set, or to have other sources of information, was "in the cloak and dagger club".' The word *canary* was officially suggested for 'radio' or 'wireless'; thence 'came "dicky bird", "birdsong" and "birdseed" . . . Trouble in getting batteries to work the sets was "trouble about birdseed".'

5. At Changi camp, the Sikh guards did not behave well: hence *sikhery*, 'brutality; bloody-mindedness'; *Sikh's beard*, a local tobacco, coarse, tough, wiry.

6. Terms from Malay were *go buso*, 'to turn septic'—from *busok*, 'rotten'; *lagi*, often mis-pronounced *leggy*, superseding the synonymous *baksheesh*; *Nazi Goering*, 'fried rice'—from *nasi goreng*; and a number of direct adoptions.

7. Japanese supplied *benjo*, lit. 'a convenient place'—a water closet or latrine; *byoki*, sick; *yasmé*, lit. 'rest', which did duty for 'rest'— 'sleep'—'holiday'—'peace'; camp headquarters being *Yasmé Villa*; and, remotely, *Nip*, a Japanese (Addenda).

8. From Australian slang, or from association with Australian soldiers, came *jokers*, 'chaps', 'fellows'; *bronzies* (Aussies, the "bronzed gods" of Singapore ballyhoo journalism)'; '*Bungs* (for Dutch half-castes), originally Australian slang for their own Aboriginals'.

9. Dutch yielded *eten halen*, lit. 'to fetch food', and *Got(t)fordommers*, from *Gott verdomme* (Dutch version of *God damn!*), both as nicknames for the Dutch themselves.

10. Some names for food were these: 'The staple stew, tasteless, meatless, . . . was dubbed "jungle stew"—anything bad was "jungle"— jungle sores, jungle camps, jungle fever, jungle bananas'; 'various types of dried fish . . . "Cheese fish"—"Bengofish"—"Picture-frame fish" or "Tennis-racket fish"'; the various disguises of rice were generically *doovers* (see **doover**; though perhaps ironically ex 'hors d'œuvre') or *efforts*, the latter having, at Changi, been a rissole. A *gas-cape stew* was a dried vegetable soup.

11. Canteen cries and names: *hot, sweet and filthy*, concerning coffee or for 'coffee'; *nutty nutty*, 'a local concoction of sugar, peanuts and

newspaper'; *lime slime*, a sweetened version of *gu-gu* (tapioca gruel); *limo-limo*, a hot lime drink.

12. Medical terms: 'Amputations were so frequent that two abbreviations, "amputs" and "stumpies", were required; and "amput cigarettes" were on sale'—rolled by those men who had had a limb amputated; *avit*, an avitaminosis patient; *the diary*, diarrhœa.

13. References to Japanese influence occur in *Jap-happy*, 'for those who were thought to "collaborate" in any way or to do well out of the Nips . . . coined early in Singapore. But it became current in Thailand when the lucky few were the recipients of Japanese clothing—rubber boots were "Jap-happies", and a loin cloth was a "Jap-happy" (or sometimes a "G-string").'

14. Phrases: Anyone who was in a constipated mental condition "had his finger up", and was expected to "pull it out"': see **take your finger out**. 'One phrase . . . stands out . . .; it will live to describe an aspect of human nature seen very clearly in the bad times, when selfishness and greed were matched by the envy and malice of the less fortunate, in the utter lack of privacy of the camps in Thailand. It was developed from the phrase "Pull the ladder up, Jack, I'm all right!" which had long been current, as had "fuck you, Jack, I'm all right!" It was abbreviated, however, by frequency of use to the P.O.W. forms "A Jack Club", "a ladder club" or "Ladder", "a ladder job", "Got your ladder", "Mine's up", and so on all to describe whatever was considered a "cushy" job for which the usual term could have been "administration" as opposed to "work". On the other hand, our officers spurred themselves to greater efforts in hut-building with the cry, "Up guards and atap!" (*Note*. All our huts were atap-roofed.)'

15. Miscellaneous: *Bangkok bowler*, a Thailander's bamboo hat; *bamboo presento*, a beating-up with a bamboo; *Gordon Thailanders*, Gordon Highlanders; *2359 (hours)*, a coloured officer—usually as a nickname—the time, on the very verge of midnight, when all is dark.

prissy. Effeminate: mostly women's: coll.: adopted, ca. 1943, ex U.S. servicemen. (Monica Dickens, *The Happy Prisoner*, 1946.) Perhaps a blend of *prim* + *sissy*, as Mitford M. Mathews has suggested. Hence a noun, as in Vincent Adrian, *End of a Summer's Day*, 1958.—2. Prudish: mostly men's: Australian: since ca. 1943. (D'Arcy Niland, *When the Cross Turns Over*, 1958.)

priv. A privilege: Public Schools': late C. 19–20. Marples.

private eye. A private detective: adopted, ca. 1944, ex U.S. servicemen, with the late Raymond Chandler intervening. A pun on 'private investigator', with esp. reference to the initial of the 2nd word.

private eyeful. A pretty girl or woman employed by a detective agency. Since ca. 1961. A pun on *eyeful* (p. 261) and on the term preceding this one.

private navy. Any detached Royal Navy unit working far from the surveillance of the C. in C.: Naval jocular: since ca. 1920.

private property. An engaged girl: (jocular) coll.: since ca. 1920.

Private Snoops. See **Chad**.

Private Tojo. A Japanese soldier: Army in the Pacific and Indian Oceans 'theatre': 1942–5. Ex the war-mongering Japanese Premier, Tojo. (P-G-R.)

privateer. A woman competing with prostitutes but not depending on prostitution for her whole livelihood: Society: ca. 1890–1914.

priver. A private school: Public Schools': C. 20. Arnold Lunn, *Loose Ends*, 1919.

privs, have one's. To have 'the privilege to fag and "whop",' Lunn. A late C. 19–20 Harrow term. Also in the singular, as in Lunn: a privilege; a privileged person: 'You couldn't go into a room without finding some fag smoking. And so the privs got rather fed up. It was jolly bad for the House footer. So they made it a four-year priv.'

privy. A preparatory school: Marlborough College: late C. 19–20. So many 'prep' schools are *privately* owned; cf. **privee** in *Dict*.

prize idiot. A (notable) fool: coll.: since ca. 1910. Suggested by *booby prize*?

pro, 1 (p. 661): This sense may well go back at least as far as 1750. It occurs in *The Gentleman's Magazine*, May 1784 (p. 366), 'Made Beadles, Pro's, and Proctors trun'. (Moe.) Cf. the Eton nuance, 'provost': C. 18–20. *Spy*, 1825.

pro-y. Professional; esp., of or like a professional prostitute: since ca. 1920. James Curtis, *You're in the Racket Too*, 1937, 'I always think those rooms at Paddington make it seem so pro-y.'

probably that. 'It is highly probably that I have interviewed him' comes from a 'thriller' published in 1934. This catachresis results ex a confusion of *it is probable that . . .* and *probably* (I *did something*).

proby. A probationer: Australian prison warders': ca. 1820–90. Louis Becke, *Old Convict Days*, 1899.

proctor (or **P-**). See 'Tavern terms', § 5.

Prod(d)o. A Protestant: Australian Catholics' C. 20. (B.P.) Cf. **Prot** below.

production of it, make a. See **don't make . . .** above.

productious. Productive: book-world: C. 20. (Berta Ruck, *A Story-Teller . . .*, 1935.)

profesh. Profession; esp. *the p.*, the stage: (lower-class) actors': from ca. 1885. Pugh.

professor. A professional: cricketers': C. 20. Sir Home Gordon, *The Background of Cricket*, 1939. —2. An Education Officer: R.A.F. (mostly officers'): since ca. 1938. Jackson.

proff, v. To profit (?): Naval: since ca. 1930. John Winton, *We Saw the Sea*, 1960, 'Except in a Leap Year, of course, when I proff and get no work at all.'

Prog. A Proctor aircraft: R.A.F.: 1943 + . Partridge, 1945. Cf. **prog**, n., 3 (p. 661).

proggins is recorded earlier by B. & L.

proggy book. A picture scrap-book, which the owner invited—usually for the fee of a marble or other small object—other children to prod with a pin: North Country children's: late C. 19–20; by 1950, slightly ob. Ex North Country dial. *prog*. to prod.

proggy mat. A mat, or a rug, made from cloth-cuttings, with a 'progger' (a type of cutting instrument): North Country coll.: late C. 19–20.

projie. A projectile: Australian Naval: since ca. 1930. (B., 1943.)

prole, n. Mostly *proles*, the proletariat: Australian Labour: since ca. 1925. Cf. and see:

prole, v. To educate the *prole*tariat to become conscious of themselves as Labour; *proling,* political speaking at street corners: Australian Labour: since ca. 1925. B., 1942.

promo, n. and v. To promote, a promotion, in class: Charterhouse: from ca. 1918.

promoss must be dated as arising a decade earlier.

promote. To borrow, or to scrounge, something; loosely, to steal: Australian soldiers': 1939–45. (B., 1943.) Euphemistic: cf. *organize* and *win.*

promotion, haul-down. 'Flag Officer's promotion on hauling down his flag on retirement,' Granville: Naval coll.: C. 20. But it was 'a promotion *by* a retiring flag officer, usually of his flag lieutenant, who might be his son or nephew. This injustice to many more experienced officers was very properly abolished in November, 1874, and so your date of 20 C. cannot be right' (Rear-Admiral P. W. Brock, R.N. (Ret.), C.B., D.S.O.: Jan. 10, 1963). Read, therefore: C. 19; after 1874, merely historical.

prong. A table fork: waiters': from ca. 1880. Anstey, *Voces Populi,* II, 1892.

pronounce judgment. See 'Tavern terms', § 4.

prop, n., 5 (p. 662). Rather earlier in *Sessions,* Dec. 1856.—9. Propaganda: journalists': since ca. 1939.

***prop game, the.** The gaining of useful information about, and access to, buildings, esp. to private houses, by posing as local government inspectors or as builders and later stealing from them: since ca. 1963. In 'Doctor Describes Widow's Injuries', an article in the Bournemouth *Evening Echo* of April 20, 1966, a detective sergeant stated that 'the "prop game" appeared to be . . . unique to Leeds, something that has cropped up in the last two and a half years': cf. **straight prop (man),** below, and **bowler-hat boys,** above.

proper article, the. Exactly what's needed; the real, or the best, thing: New Zealand coll.: since ca. 1910.

proper crowd, one's. One's personal friends; the circle or clique to which one belongs: Australian coll.: since 1920. B., 1942.

proper do. A very fine party or wedding-feast: working classes': since ca. 1910. See **do,** n., 4 (p. 226).

proper madam. See **madam.**

property. Any creative work; e.g. a book, play, song, not yet published: agents', book- and music-publishers', *et hoc genus omne*: coll. verging j., or *vice versa*: since ca. 1930.

prophets, the. Those Australian squatters who went to Canterbury, New Zealand, in 1851: Australian and New Zealand: ca. 1851–70. Baker.

proposition, n., 3, and v. To '*proposition*' a girl is to suggest sexual intimacy: hence the n.— cf. the c.p., or virtual c.p., 'Is this a proposal or a proposition?': Canadian (? ex U.S.) since ca. 1940, English and Australian since ca. 1943.

propping. The encouragement of a junior by addressing her by her Christian name: Lady Margaret Hall, Oxford: since ca. 1918. (Marples, 2.) Ex S.E. *prop,* to support.

props, esp. in *get one's props,* to become a Leading Aircraftman: R.A.F.: since ca. 1930. H. & P., 'The propeller-shaped badge worn on the sleeve.' See **prop,** n., 8 (*Dict.*).

pros, n.—2. A prostitute: variant spelling of

pross, n., 3 (p. 663); e.g. in *Sessions,* Feb. 8, 1905. —3. Proscenium: theatrical: since ca. 1910. (Gavin Holt, *No Curtain for Cora,* 1950.)

***prospector.** A confidence trickster: Australian c.: since ca. 1925. (B., 1953.) For mugs' gold.

pross about. To 'mooch' or hang about: low: from ca. 1890. Pugh (2), 'Afternoon I prosses about in 'Ampstead.' Ex **pross,** v., 1 (*Dict.*).

prossie. An Australian late C. 19–20 variant of **pross,** n., 3 (p. 663). B., 1942. But also English; it occurs in, e.g., Ada E. Jones (Mrs Cecil Chesterton), *Women of the Underworld,* 1931, at p. 164.

prosso. A prostitute: Australian: since ca. 1925. (Dick.) Cf. **prossie.**

prostitute, the. The twelfth man, or a *substitute,* in a cricket match: cricketers': ca. 1870–1914. Sir Home Gordon, *The Background of Cricket,* 1939.

Prot, n. and adj. (A) Protestant: Catholics': mid C. 19–20.

***protection, take** (a girl) **under one's.** To take care of a girl and send or accompany her out to the Argentine: (Polish) white-slavers' c.: C. 20. Albert Londres, 1928.

Protestant herring, a. A stale, a bad, herring; hence, any inferior provender, as in 'Oh, that butter is a Protestant herring' (P. W. Joyce, *English . . . in Ireland,* 1910): Anglo-Irish coll.: mid C. 19–20.

Prudential men, or **men of the Prudential.** Officers in the Special Branch of the R.N.V.R.: Naval: 1939–45. With a pun on the Prudential insurance company. (P-G-R.)

prune is short for *Prune, P/O.* John Moore, in *The Observer,* Oct. 4, 1942, '"Lost anybody?" "Some prune who thought he could beat up the searchlights"'; B., 1942.

prune, v. To adjust or otherwise tinker with (a ship's engines): Naval: since ca. 1930. (P-G-R.)

Prune, P/O; in speech, **Pilot Officer Prune.** 'A pilot who takes unnecessary risks, and generally loses his neck through his *prunery*' and '"P/O Prune" is the title bestowed upon a pilot who has several "prangs" on his record' (H. & P.): R.A.F.: since ca. 1935. He is a constant emblematic monitory figure in the pages of *The R.A.F. Journal.* Not unconnected with the impracticality of 'prunes and prisms'. Created, Jackson tells us, by S/Ldr Anthony Armstrong and L.A.C.W. Hooper ('Raff').

prune-juice. Hard liquor: since ca. 1935. (Richard Gordon, *Doctor and Son,* 1953.)

Prussian Guard. A flea: Army: 1914–18. 'Dignity and Impudence.'—2. In the game of House, a card: rhyming s.: C. 20.

psych. A 'psychological' bet, one made on a hunch: Australian two-up players': since ca. 1930. (Lawson Glassop, *Lucky Palmer,* 1949.)

***psyche man.** See **front man.**

psychedelia. 'Drugs, flashing lights, sound, colour, movies, dance—usually experienced simultaneously' (Peter Fryer in *The Observer* colour supplement, Dec. 3, 1967): drug addicts' and hippies': since early 1967. Ex *psychedelic,* (of a drug, e.g. LSD) inducing the taker to feel 'expanded' and to reveal his soul; an imperfect form, *psychodelic* (soul-revealing) being correct.

psycho. A psychopath: since ca. 1945.—2.

Hence, a lunatic or a very eccentric person or merely an egregious fool: since ca. 1955.

pub verandah push. Frequenters of the verandahs of country public-houses: Australian: C. 20. B., 1942.

public, n.—2. One who avails himself of the personal facilities of a public library: Canadian librarians': since ca. 1920. (Leechman.) He not only is a member of the general public but also makes a public convenience of the place. But also one who, although not a reader, applies to a library for assistance in a problem involving knowledge.—3. A pupil at a public (i.e., State) school in New South Wales: among N.S.W. children attending Catholic schools: since ca. 1920 (? earlier). B.P.

public convenience. A prostitute: C. 20.

Public Enemy Number One (or **No. 1**). Adopted in 1936, via the Press, ex U.S. journalese not only in its correct (the literal) sense but in extended applications; thus, among English lawn-tennis players, Von Cramm and Budge were, in June 1937, described as 'Joint Public Enemies Number One'.

public ledger (p. 664). The reference should be to that London commercial newspaper *The Public Ledger*, which, established in 1760, is still going strong.

public notary. See 'Tavern terms', § 5.

Public School slang is fairly well represented, both in the *Dict.* aud in these Addenda, the latter owing much to Morris Marples's excellent book, *Public School Slang*, 1940; the debts to him have been scrupulously indicated.

puce. Very bad, inferior: Charterhouse: from ca. 1920. Esp. 'Absolutely puce!' Perhaps suggested by *bloody* and *putrid* (qq.v.).

puckah is an occ. variant of **pukka** (*Dict.*).

pucker paint. See 'Canadian'.

puckerow (p. 665). Delete the problematic comparison with *pakaru*.

pud, n.—2. Pudding: lower-class and lower-middle class: late C. 19–20. Richard Llewellyn, *None But the Lonely Heart*, 1943, 'If you lot go to chokey, so do I, for harbouring. So we're all blackbirds in the same old pud.' Cf. **veg** (*Dict.*).

pud, v. 'To greet affectionately or familiarly': proletarian coll.: from ca. 1860; ob. B. & L. Ex **pud,** n.: see *Dict.*

pudden. A 'mess' or failure: Cockney coll.: late C. 19–20. 'Yes, he's made a pudden o' that job.'

pudden (or **pudding**)**!, beg your.** See **beg your pudding!**

pudden club, in the. Pregnant: low: C. 20. Cf. **pudding club** below.

pudding.—5. Weight; esp. *put (a bit of) pudding on,* to put on (a little) weight: rural Australian: C. 20. (D'Arcy Niland, *Call Me . . .*, 1958.)

pudding, piece of. See **piece of pudding.**

pudding, pull one's. See **gallop one's maggot.**

pudding about the heels (p. 665). Cf. *beef to the heels.*

Pudding and Gravy, the. The Royal Navy: rhyming s.: since ca. 1940. Franklyn 2nd.

pudding club, join the. To become pregnant: low: C. 20. Arthur Gardner, *Tinker's Kitchen*, 1932. Cf. the *Dict.* entry.

pudding house.—2. A workhouse: low: ca. 1830–70. *Sinks*, 1848.

pudding sleeves (p. 665). Earlier in Ned Ward's *The Delights of the Bottle*, 1720.

Puddle-Dock . . . in *Dict.* Until C. 19, always *Countess*; earlier record, T. Shadwell, *Epsom Wells*, 1673.

puddle-jumper. A small communications-aircraft: R.A.F.: 1942 +.

puddled. Very eccentric; insane: 1936, Wilfred Macarthney, *Walls Have Mouths.* Cf. **puddle,** v., on p. 665.

pudery. Pornographic books or prints: cultured: since ca. 1930. Cf. the L. *pudor*, shame.

puff, n.—5. A ladies' man: R.A.F.: since ca. 1935. Jackson. Prob. ex 'powder-*puff*'.

puff, v. To break wind: late C. 19–20.

puff-adder. An accountant: R.A.F. (mostly officers'): since ca. 1930. W/Cdr Robin P. McDouall, letter of April 12, 1945. Well, he *is* an adder of figures—and to some, as dangerous as that particular species of snake.

puff and dart, a beginning (see p. 665), has v. *make a puff and dart* and is recorded fifty years earlier in D. W. Barrett, *Navvies*, 1880.—2. In Crown and Anchor, 'These are the figures with their nicknames:

'Heart transfixed—Puff and Dart
Diamond   Kimberly
Club   Shamrock
Spade   Grave-digger
Anchor   Mud-hook
Crown   Sergeant-major, Richards.'

(Contrast the entry at **little Jimmy.**)
The first term is rhyming s. for *heart* and dates from ca. 1860; Kimberly is famed for its diamonds; the Club symbol in cards is a trefoil; for the last three s. terms, see the entries in the *Dict.*

puffickly. Perfectly: proletarian coll.: mid-C. 19–20. (Anstey, *Voces Populi*, II, 1892.)

puffler. A 'foreman or ganger' (*Railway*, 3rd): railwaymen's: C. 20. Adopted ex mining.

pufftaloonas. 'Hot fried cakes spread with jam, sugar or honey' (B., 1943): Australian: since ca. 1930. Much commoner is *pufftaloons*, applied also to fried scones (B.P., 1963).

Pug. General Sir Hastings Ismay: 1939–45. Short for *pugnacious*, he being a fighter for what he thought advisable.

pug, n.—10. 'Lancashire and Yorkshire [Railway] 0-4-0 clock saddle tank' (*Railway* 2nd): railwaymen's: C. 20.

pug, v. To hide: low: C. 20. Esp. of goods stolen by workmen, who 'pug it up' or 'pug it away' until they find it convenient to remove the article from the premises. Cf. Surrey dial. *pug*, 'to fill in a joint with softened clay', which seems to be a more likely origin than West County *pug*, to thrust. (E.D.D.)

pug Nancy. See 'Women'. Cf. **pug nasty** in *Dict.*

puggy.—4. A Great Central Railway employee: ca. 1890–1925. (*Railway.*)

pukaroo. To break (something), ruin (a plan), confuse an issue: New Zealand coll.: late C. 19–20. B., 1942. See **pakaru** (p. 601); not to be confused with *pukkaree* (see **puckerow,** p. 665).

puker.—2. An orange: preparatory schools': ca. 1870–1920.

pukka gen. See **gen** in Addenda and **pukka** in *Dict.*

puku, a pain in the. A stomach-ache: New Zealand coll.: late C. 19-20. B., 1941. *Puku*: a Maori word.

pull, v.—4. To do; commit: U.S., adopted ca. 1925. Cf. *pull off*, to achieve. E.g. Georgette Heyer, *Behold, Here's Poison*, 1936, 'If Rendall pulled the murder, Hyde's out of it.'—5. At Oxford, ca. 1840-80, it was coll. for 'to row a boat' or 'to row in a crew'. Thomas Hughes, *Tom Brown at Oxford*, 1861. (Marples, 2.)—6. To 'pull off', to achieve: Army: since ca. 1920. 'It was eighteen years before I pulled sergeant.'—7. To earn (as income), to make (a sum of money, e.g., by a sale): Australian: since ca. 1925. (B., 1943.)

pull, give (someone) **a**—esp. **a strong.** To speak severely to; to reprimand: c. and low s.: since ca. 1930. (Norman.) Cf. *to pull* (someone) *up sharply.*—2. Mostly *give it a pull*, to desist: Australian since ca. 1910. (H. Drake Brockman, *The Blister*, 1937.) A variant of *pull, take a* (p. 666).

pull a cluck. To die: low: ca. 1870-1920. Echoic.

pull a fast one. See **fast one.**

pull a flanker is the Army shape (since ca. 1925) of *work a flanker* (see **flanker, do a**: p. 282).

pull a horse's head off; esp. a vbl n., *pulling* . . . So to check a horse's progress that he does not win: turf: from ca. 1860. B. & L.

pull a pint (often as vbl n., *pulling* . . .). To operate the controls of an aircraft, to do a pilot's work: R.A.F.: since ca. 1930. H. & P. See **beer-lever.**

*****pull a stroke.** 'To be faster, smarter, quicker than your opponent' (Robin Cook, 1962): since late 1945: c. >, by ca. 1960, also low s. (Cf. the s. *pull a fast one.*)

pull down one's ear. See **ear, pull down one's.**

pull down the shutter. Butter: rhyming s.: late C. 19-20.

pull-guts; pulpit-cackler. See 'Occupational names'.

pull in the pieces. To make money; receive good wages: proletarian: from ca. 1860; ob. B. & L.

pull leather. 'A rider of a bucking horse in a rodeo is not allowed to "pull leather"—that is, to grab the saddle horn to steady himself, an act which would disqualify him' (Leechman): Canadian: since ca. 1920.

pull-off. A parachute jump from the wing of a 'plane: paratroops': since 1942. H. & P., 'A man opens his parachute and is then pulled off.'

pull on (a woman). To marry (one): Australian: C. 20. B., 1942.—2. To tackle, contend with; hence, to test: Australian: since ca. 1920. 'I'll pull on the Prime Minister himself if I can't get a permit for my business' (Edwin Morrisby, Aug. 30, 1958); B., 1953.—3. Elliptical for *pull a gun on*, to shoot at: ? mostly Dubliners': since ca. 1919.

pull on oneself, take a. See **take a pull** . . .

pull one out of the bag. To make a special effort; draw on one's reserve powers: from ca. 1920. An elaboration of **pull out,** 2 (*Dict.*).

pull one's pad. See **belt one's batter** above.

pull one's pudden. Cf. **pull one's wire,** p. 666.

pull one's pudding. See **gallop one's maggot.**

pull one's punches. To exercise moderation.

esp. in punishment or in blame: boxing coll, (since ca. 1930) become, ca. 1950, general coll.

pull oneself off. (Of the male) to masturbate: low: late C. 19-20.

pull out. 'Buying or selling for ready money,' *Spy*, II, 1826: Stock Exchange coll.: ca. 1805-1910.

pull out, v.i. To exaggerate: low: ca. 1830-80. *Sinks*, 1848. To 'stretch it a bit'.

pull (someone's) **pisser.** To 'pull his leg': Services', esp. R.A.F.: since ca. 1930.

pull (someone's) **Scotch** (often as vbl n.). To pull someone's leg: Services: since ca. 1930. 'Apparently a reference to the alleged lack of humour in Scotsmen,' H. & P.: no! *Scotch* is short for *Scotch peg*, a leg.

pull (someone's) **tit.** To pull someone's leg, to make a fool of—or to fool; to delude: low Australian: since ca. 1910. (Edward Lindall, *No Place to Hide*, 1959.) Also, by ca. 1920, New Zealand. Slatter, 'Is he pulling my tit?'

pull the chain! A c.p., expressing contempt at a feeble joke or a stupid remark: since ca. 1960; by late 1965, already ob.

pull the chocks away. To 'get going' (Jackson): R.A.F. coll.: since ca. 1918. Ex 'the process of removing the chocks beneath the wheels of aircraft before taxi-ing for the take-off' (Jackson): cf. **pull the chocks** (p. 667) and **chocks away!** (Addenda).

pull the ladder up, Jack, I'm all right! A late C. 19-20 variation of **fuck you, Jack** . . . (p. 305); see also 'Prisoner-of-War Slang', 14.

pull the monkey. To pull a rubber disc through a cess drain in order to clean the drain: railwaymen's: C. 20. (*Railway*.)

pull the pin. To resign; to quit a job: Canadian railroadmen's (— 1931). Ex bomb-throwing? But Dr Leechman, in May 1959, writes with that amicable courtesy which makes it a pleasure to be corrected by him: 'Not from bomb-throwing, but from the pins which, with a link, coupled cars together in the early days of railways. This rig was so dangerous that it was soon outlawed. Today few railwaymen know the origin of the term.'

pull the plug. To release all the bombs simultaneously: R.A.F.: 1939 +. Jackson. Cf. **play the piano.**

pull the string. To use all one's influence: tailors' coll.: mid-C. 19-20. B. & L.—2. To do well: proletarian: from ca. 1870; ob. Ibid.

pull the strings. To release the vacuum brake on a vehicle: railwaymen's: C. 20. (*Railway*.)

pull the weight. 'To meet a financial emergency' (Baker): Australian: since ca. 1910.

pull up one's socks (p. 667) has variant *pull one's socks up.*

pull up stakes. To depart: Australian: C. 20. Baker.

pull your finger out! Hurry up! or Get on with the job!: synonymous with *take your finger out!* (P-G-R.) Variant: *get your* . . .; see **take** . . . (below).

pull your head in! 'You're sticking your neck out'; be careful; stop talking wildly: Australian c.p.: since ca. 1930. Often *pull it in!*; an ephemeral Sydneyite variant of ca. 1948-51 was *pull your skull in!* (Sidney Baker, letter of Aug. 7, 1950; Kylie Tennant, *The Joyful Condemned* 1953.) Prob. ex 'the habit of army men sticking their heads out of troop trains and making smart remarks. The origin was "Pull your head in, or people will think it's a cattle train'" (B.P.).

pulling. A challenge from a gang, or from one of its members: Teddy boys': since ca. 1947. (Clancy Sigal in *The Observer*, March 1, 1959.)

pulling a—or the—cord, be. To be courting: Anglo-Irish: mid C. 19–20. Charles Kickham, *Knocknagow*, 1879; P. W. Joyce, 1910. Erotic ?

Pullman. A shunting truck: railwaymen's: C. 20. (*Railway*.) Ironic.

pulp magazines. The cheap, inferior (not the good) American magazines dumped on the English market: coll.: since ca. 1920. Fit only to be *pulped*. But more probably because printed on paper already used once and re-pulped. Dr Leechman modifies thus, 'These were so called because they were printed on pulp paper, which is the same (approx.) as newspaper'; orig., the paper was presumably wood-pulp paper.

pulpit.—2. A cockpit (in an aircraft): R.A.F.: since ca. 1935. H. & P. Ex next sense.—3. A B.E.9 aeroplane: R.F.C.–R.A.F.: World War I, then historical. (Duncan W. G. Milne, *Wind in the Wires*, 1933.) Ex the box-like ply-wood cockpit projecting from the front of the machine.

pulse.—2. The male member: workmen's: late C. 19–20.

pultan. See **puttun.**

Pulverizer, the. 'Nickname for the giant Stirling bomber, and very apt too,' H. & P.: R.A.F.: 1941–3, and ob.

pump one's pickle; jerk one's gherkin. Low Canadian variants of *gallop one's antelope*: C. 20.

pump(-)packing. Tough steak: Australian Naval: 1939–45. (B., 1943.)

pump water, plain as a yard of. See **plain as a yard . . .**

pumpkins of oneself, think. To think well of oneself: 1897, Ouida, *The Massarenes*; ob. by 1940, † by 1950. Cf. *pumpkin*, 1 (parenthesis), on p. 668; cf. *potatoes, small*, on p. 654.

punce (p. 668). 'Especially in Australia,' Sidney J. Baker, letter, 1946.—2. The female pudend: Australian: C. 20. B., 1942. n.—3. An effeminate; a homosexual: low Australian: since ca. 1925. (B., 1943.) Perhaps ex *ponce*.

punce, v. To kick (someone) with one's clogs: Lancashire: late C. 19–20. (*The Manchester Guardian*, May 2, 1950.) Ex S.E. *punch* and s.

purr.

Punch—2. A short, thickset man: navvies' nickname: mid C. 19–20. (D. W. Barrett, *Navvies*, 1880.)

punch, v.—4. To drive (sheep) forcibly uphill or when they are tired: Australian: C. 20. Baker.

punch-drunk. Slap-happily crazed from the punching he's received: boxing coll.: since ca. 1925. *Answers*, Nov. 30, 1940. By ca. 1942 it was S.E.

punch the breeze. See **take it in the neck** below.

punch-up. A fight with bare fists: low coll.: since ca. 1920. (Norman.)

punch up the bracket. To give (someone) an uppercut to the nose: since ca. 1950.

punchable nun. See 'Harlots' and cf., in *Dict.*, **punchable.**

puncher; punchy. A boxer; punch-drunk: low: since ca. 1930. (Both in Norman.)

punctured.—2. Vaccinated: Services: since ca. 1920. H. & P.

pungo, go (p. 668). Earlier in Rudyard Kipling, 'The Horse Marines' (1910), reprinted in *A Diversity of Creatures*, 1917, as Rear-Admiral P. W. Brock has reminded me.

punisher.—4. A long-winded bore: Australian: since ca. 1925. (B., *Australia Speaks*, 1953.)

Punjab head, have a. To be forgetful; *Punjab head*, forgetfulness: Anglo-Indian, esp. Indian Army's: from the 1880's. An allusion to the (supposed) fact that service in the Punjab saps the memory.

punk, n.—4. A young fellow that, having just started to work for a carnival, thinks he knows everything: Canadian carnival s.: since ca. 1910. Adopted from U.S. See *Underworld*.

punny. Punishment: Manchester Grammar School: since ca. 1870. Marples. Cf **pun, n., 1** (*Dict.*).

punt at, take a. See **take a . . .** (below).

punter.—6. A pickpocket's assistant: New Zealand c.: C. 20. B., 1941. Ex sense 1.—7. 'The "punters" (dealer-buyers) who promenade the Street' (Warren Street, centre of the London secondhand-car dealers): the secondhand-car business: since ca. 1945. *The Sunday Times* coloured supplement, Oct. 24, 1965, article by Richard Cowdy. (Prob. ex sense 3 on p. 669.)—7. 'Someone with money looking for a scheme to put it into and ignorant of the ways of the morrie world [underworld and its fringes]. An extreme case would be called "a mug punter" or "a half-wide mug"' (Robin Cook, *The Crust on Its Uppers*, 1962): since ca. 1945: c. >, by ca. 1960, also low s. Ex the racing sense.

Sense 2, on p. 669, occurs earlier, in the gen. sense 'better' or 'gambler', in Renton Nicholson, *An Autobiography*, 1860, 'No 14, Park Place, St James's Street, was an elegant gambling-house, frequented by the highest class of "punters".'

pup, n., 1 (p. 669), is, in the R.A.F., a pupil pilot (Jackson); also *pups* (Charles Graves, *Seven Pilots*, 1943). Cf. **pup's Bible.**—3. A paid-up policy: insurance world's: C. 20.—4. See *dangler* in 'Hauliers' Slang'.—5. Mostly in *the night's (only) a pup*, it's still early: Australian, at least mainly: C. 20. (Kylie Tennant, *Lost Haven*, 1947.) Suggested by the (familiar) S.E. *the night's still young*.

pupe.—3. A pupil pilot: R.A.F.: 1939–45. (P-G-R.) Cf. *pup*, 1, above.

puppies, the. See **yappies, the,** below.

puppy-dog corner. 'The corner of Collins and Swanton Streets, Melbourne,' B., 1942: Australian: C. 20. Where the gay young dogs congregate.

puppy(-)fat. Fattiness that, acquired from eating starchy food, lacks substance: coll.: since ca. 1910.

puppy-hole. A late C. 19–20 variant of **pupe, 1** (p. 669). Marples.

pup's Bible, the. *The Flying Training Manual*: R.A.F.: since ca. 1925. Jackson.

*pure, doss in the. See **doss in the pure.**

pure merino, adj. See **merino, pure.**

purge. 'A newly arrived batch of kriegies from . . . the Luftwaffe interrogation centre. From this, also, the passive verb, "to be purged",' Paul Brickhill & Conrad Norton, *Escape to Danger*, 1946: prisoner-of-war in Germany, 1940–5.

Satirical ref. to the German purges and 'blood-baths'.—2. 'A concentrated complaint or moan from a well-known source is called "a purge-on by So and So". An habitual grumbler is called by this name in many places,' H. & P.: Services: since 1939.

purl, n., 2; **purler,** 2; **purter.** Something exceptionally good: Australian: since ca. 1910. B., 1942.

purple empire. An establishment in which many of the executive officers are Engineering Officers (wearing a purple stripe between their gold bands): Naval officers': since ca. 1945.—2. Hence, Fleet Air Arm officers, there being numerous Engineering Officers in this branch of the Service: Naval officers': since ca. 1946.

purple heart. A dexedrine pill used narcotically: teenage drug-addicts': since ca. 1960. One of the minor drugs.

purr, n. 'A rushing-in, Lancashire fashion, with the head against the opponent's guts,' Bee, 1823: pugilistic: ca. 1810–50. It causes the opponent to *purr* or grunt.

purr, v. To strike (a person): Lancashire: late C. 19–20. Eustace Jervis, *Twenty-Five Years*, 1925. 'He had . . . sent them . . . to Strange-ways Prison for "booting" their "missus", or "pur-ring" the "copper" with their clogs.' Rather, to kick violently.

purser's. Short for **purser's name** below: C. 19. In, e.g., W. N. Glascock, *The Naval Sketch-Book*, 2nd Series, 1834, at II, 64. (Moe.)

purser's dagger (*Dict.*): see **pusser's dagger** below.

purser's dip (p. 670) occurs earlier in Fredk Marryat, *Frank Mildmay*, 1829, as 'a farthing candle'. Moe.

purser's grin (p. 670) occurs in Alfred Burton, *Johnny Newcome*, 1818. (Moe.)

purser's name (p. 670). In, e.g., Captain Glascock, *Landsharks and Sea Gulls*, 1838. An early example occurs in *The Night Watch* (II, 82), 1828. Moe.

purser's pump. 'The midshipman's cant [i.e. slang] term for a spy-glass' (W. N. Glascock, *Sketch-Book*, 1834, at I, 45): Naval: Naval: C. 19; † by 1890. (Moe.)

purser's shirt on a handspike (p. 670). An early occurrence: 1821, P. Egan, *London*. Also in W. N. Glascock, *The Naval Sketch-Book*, II, 1826.

purter. See **purl,** n., 2.

Puseyite. A coll. term of general abuse at Oxford ca. 1840–60. (Cf. R. S. Surtees, *Mr Sponge's Sporting Tour* (ch. xxi), 1853.)

push, n., 4, on p. 670: an early Aus. example occurs in Alex. Macdonald, *In the Land of Pearl and Gold*, 1907, at p. 202.

push about the bottle. To drink heavily: Naval officers': ca. 1790–1870. (Moe.) Cf. **push the boat out** below.

push-bike, n. (p. 671. 'A pedal-bike' in contra-distinction, i.e. not a motor-bike' (Leechman).

push-bike. (Gen. v.i.) To ride on a bicycle: from ca. 1910. S. P. B. Mais, *A Schoolmaster's Diary*, 1918, 'I "push-biked" the eight miles into Lewes.' Ex the n.: see *Dict.*

push in the bush is worth two in the hand, a. A working-men's parody of the proverb *a bird in the hand is worth two in the bush*: since ca. 1925. Erotic. See also **one in the bush . . .,** above.

push in the truck, n. Coïtion: low: C. 20.

James Curtis, *They Drive by Night*, 1938, '"I ain't had a push in the truck since I came out of the nick."' Rhyming on **fuck.**

push off, 1 (p. 671). *Sessions*, May 1740 (trial of Eliz. Pooley), 'He . . . heard somebody cursing and swearing and a woman . . . say, *d—n it, push off,* or *go off*.'

push one's own barrow. To boast; to look out for oneself only: Australian coll.: since ca. 1910. (Vance Palmer, *Golconda*, 1948.)

push over. Something easy to do; a girl easy to 'make': Australian: adopted, ca. 1925, from U.S. Lawson Glossop, *We Were the Rats*, 1944, 'I've got a couple of smashing lines who've come from Sydney for the Mayoral Ball. They're a couple of pushovers.' By 1945, also English. Since ca. 1940, mostly written *pushover*.—2. A 'mug' or a 'softy': since ca. 1940; orig., Aus-tralian (B.P.).

*****push powder.** To sell narcotics: adopted, ca. 1955, ex U.S.

push-pudding. A bachelor: low: C. 20. A reference to self-abuse.

push the boat out. To be generous, act gener-ously, with money: low: C. 20. James Curtis, *You're in the Racket Too*, 1937.—2. To pay for a round of drinks: Naval officers' since ca. 1924. Granville. (Also Army officers'.)

push the knot. To be on tramp: Australian: C. 20. B., 1942.

push the pavement. To sell goods in the street: Black Market: since ca. 1941. Duncan Webb in *Daily Express*, Sept. 17, 1945.

*****push up for.** To approach, as a pickpocket his victim: Australian c.: C. 20. B., 1942.

pushed. Late: Army since ca. 1930. Ex 'pushed for time'. See quot'n at **tripe, in.**

pushed?, did she fall or was she (p. 671). This catch-phrase dates from approximately 1908 and arose from a newspaper headline, probably in the *Daily Mail*. A woman named Violet Charles-worth was found dead near Beachy Head at the bottom of the cliff. Suicide was at first presumed, but later a suggestion of foul play was made and the newspaper headline appeared 'Did she fall or was she pushed?' The innuendo caught the pub-lic fancy and for a long time the phrase was used on every possible and impossible occasion. I have never heard it used in particular as applied to a person stumbling. (Andrew Haggard, Jan. 28, 1947.) See also **did she fall . . . ?,** above.

pusher.—8. A rifle: Guards Depot at Caterham: 1914–18. *John o' London*, Nov. 3, 1939.—9. One who 'pushes' or sells drugs to others (rather than taking them himself): drug addicts': adopted, ca. 1955, ex the underworld.

*****pusher-up.** A variant of **pusher,** 7 (p. 671). since ca. 1920. Stanley Jackson, *Soho*, 1946.

*****pushing-up** is the n. (B., 1943) corresponding to *push up for.*

pushite. A member of a gang of larrikins: Australian: C. 20. B., 1942.

pushover. See **push over** above.

pushy. Pushful; thrusting: Anglo-Irish coll.: since ca. 1925. Ex *push*, energy, thrustfulness.

puss, 2.—Also *pussy*: ca. 1820–60.—3. A hare: late coll.: C. 19–20.

Pusser. Fairly common nickname of men sur-named Hill: since ca. 1910. Why exactly?

pusser. Sense 1 occurs earlier in 'Taffrail'.

pusser, be. 'To be one hundred per cent.

Service' (entirely Service minded): Naval: C. 20. Granville. See **pusser** (*Dict.*).

pusser-built. Thoroughgoing, as in 'a pusser-built bastard': Australian Naval (lower-deck): since ca. 1910. Cf. preceding entry.

pusser ship. A very smart, severely disciplined ship: Naval: C. 20. (P-G-R.)

pusserpock (p. 671). The second sense ('a fur') belongs to **pussy**, not to **pusserpock**.

pusser's cow. Tinned milk: Australian Naval: since ca. 1915. (B., 1943.)

pusser's crabs. Heavy service-issue boots: Naval: C. 20. (P-G-R.)

pusser's dagger. Earlier in 'Taffrail'.

pusser's dip. A candle: Naval: late C. 19–20. (P-G-R.)

pusser's dirk (see **purser's dirk** on p. 670): also Canadian Navy. *Daily Colonist*, June 19, 1960, article on p. 33, 'Use Your Dirk!'

pusser's duck. A Supermarine Walrus aircraft. Naval: 1940 +. Granville. Contrast **pregnant duck**.

pusser's grey. Admiralty grey paint: Naval coll.: C. 20. Granville.

pusser's hard. Naval soap: Naval: since late 1950's. 'Now used exclusively in preference to the old term, *pusser's yellow* or *pusser's Vinolia*' (Granville: Nov. 22, 1962). And *hard* it is!

pusser's issue. Clothing, food, tobacco, etc., provided by the Admiralty: Naval coll.: late C. 19–20.

pusser's lisle. Regulation black-lisle stockings issued to Wrens: Naval (Wrens'): since ca. 1940.

pusser's tally. A Naval Patrol: Naval: C. 20. (P-G-R.)

pusser's Vinolia or yellow. Navy soap: Naval: since ca. 1920. (P-G-R.) Ex a well-known brand; from the colour.

pusser's wag(g)on. A warship: Australian Naval: since ca. 1930. (B., 1943.)

pusson. See **ss**.

pussy.—1. is that at **puss**, 1 (p. 671). Sense 2: see **pusserpock**, 2 (p. 671)—and correct by the note at sense 1 above.—3. A rabbit: Australian: C. 20. Baker.—4. Usu. in pl. *pussies*, as in 'When a crook speaks about "the pussies" he's talking about furs—or women. They go together. Furs, to the thieves, are the product of "cats"; and women are cats, as every crook knows' (Gosling, 1959): c. and low s.: C. 20.

pussy Nellie (or **-ly**). A male homosexual: mostly Naval: since ca. 1910.

pussy-pelmet. A very short mini-skirt: since late 1966. A neat pun on *pussy*, the female pubic hair (and pudend).

pussy-struck. (Of a male, esp. a youth with a much older woman) infatuated: low: C. 20. Although low, it is yet, in a measure, euphemistic for **cunt-struck** (*Dict.*).

put, 3, on p. 671, occurs in Fielding's skit, *Shamela*, 1741. Shamela exults over the fine clothes she had got 'of the old put my mistress's'. (With thanks to Miss Elizabeth MacAndrew, Columbia University.)

put, stay (p. 671).—2. To remain, in time of emergency (e.g. invasion), where one lives: 1940 + by 1942, familiar S.E.

put a bit of hair round it for you?; in full, **shall I . . .?** A Canadian c.p. (C. 20)—directed at any workman having trouble inserting something into

something. Cf. *don't look down* . . . on p. 234. 'The conventional response is "Yes, if you've got the right kind"' (Leechman).

put a cross—or an X—on the wall! 'A c.p. addressed to someone who has done something out of character, or when something strange and un-expected happens' (B.P.): Australian: since late 1940's.

*****put a down on** (a person). See **down on, put a** (*Dict.*), of which the period is C. 19–20; ob.

put a jelly on the ashcan (or **on the baby**). 'Fix a gelatine diffuser in front of an iron-cased lamp,' *The Evening News*, Nov. 7, 1939: cinema: since ca. 1930.

put a knife through (the) money. To share-out illicit winnings: Australian two-up players': since ca. 1920. (B., 1953.) Cf. *cop-out man*.

put a nail in (a person's) **coffin.** To talk ill of: tailors': mid-C. 19–20. B. & L.

put a roughie (or **-y**) **over.** See **roughy**, 2.

put a squeak in. To complain to a superior: Services: since ca. 1935. H. & P. Adopted from cant, where it = 'to inform to the police' (see *Underworld*).

put a stone in the pot with 'em, and when it's soft they're cooked. Australian c.p., mostly rural, applied to food that remains tough. C. 20. Jean Devanney, *By Tropic Sea and Jungle*, 1944, 'The old saying applied to them [galahs] . . .'—2. 'This is also [British—] a famous recipe for cooking porcupine. *In extenso*, When it's soft, throw the porcupine out and eat the stone' (Leechman): late C. 19–20, and presumably the origin of the Australian phrase.

put a streak into it. To hurry; to 'get a move on': Anglo-Irish: C. 20. Nicholas Blake, *The Private Wound*, 1968, 'Through the pandemonium cut a megaphone voice, adjuring the laggards in some class to "put a streak into it! Numbers 3, 7 and 16, we're waiting for you."'

put an X on the wall! See **put a cross** . . . above.

put-and-take. Sexual intercourse: mostly Londoners' (somewhat raffish): C. 20. The male puts, the female takes, it in.

put another record on! See **record!, change the,** below.

put away proper. To give a good funeral: lower-classes' coll.: late C. 19–20.

put (someone) **crook with** (a third party). To reduce one's standing in the eyes of someone else: New Zealand: since ca. 1930. 'You wouldn't put me crook with him, would you ?' (Harold Griffiths, communication of Dec. 12, 1959.) A variant appears in 'Got a snitch on me and put me in crook with the boss' (Slatter).

put dots on (someone). To weary or bore him: Army: C. 20. Ex 'to dot every *i*'?

put down, v.i. To land: R.F.C. and R.A.F. pilots' coll.: since ca. 1916. Richard Hillary, *The Last Enemy*, 1942.

put down, v.t.—3. To fire (shells), project (smoke): Artillery coll.: 1939–45. (P-G-R.)—4. To reject; to belittle (e.g. someone's playing): Canadian jazz-lovers': adopted, in 1956, ex U.S. jazz musicians.

put 'em up (p. 672): also **put 'em up** (or **stick 'em up**) **or shut up!** (B.P.)

put her along. See **put along** (*Dict.*).

put her face on. To make up (apply cosmetics): since ca. 1930. 'I'll just go upstairs and put my face on.'

put in.—3. To '*put* somebody *in*' is to involve
or embroil him; to get him into trouble: Australian: since ca. 1925. D'Arcy Niland, *Call Me…*,
1958, 'Don't put me in. Don't try to hang anything on me.'

put in a declaration. See 'Tavern terms', § 4.

put in the leather. 'Others … "put in the
leather",' Jim Phelan, *Letters from the Big House*,
1943: to kick: low: C. 20. Cf. leather, the
(p. 475).

put (someone) in the picture. 'To give you, as
a newcomer, an idea of what is happening . . . and
so enable you to play your part in it,' H. & P.:
Services coll.: since ca. 1935. Cf. paint a picture.

put (someone) in with (someone else). To
blacken someone's name in the mind of a third
party, to put him in his bad books: Australian:
since late 1920's. (Often in Margaret Henry,
Unlucky Dip, 1960.) Elliptical for *put* (someone)
in wrong with (another).

put it on.—3. To 'show off': late C. 19–20.
Prob. short for *put on airs*.—4. To make a suggestion—a proposition—to (someone): Australian:
since ca. 1925. Lawson Glassop, 1944, 'I'll have
a pint at the Royal tomorrer and put it on the
blonde' (an invitation).—5. To put on 'side':
British and Australian: C. 20. Ex sense 3.

put it where the monkeys . . . (p. 672): more
commonly *monkey* and perhaps orig. *nut-shells*
(as in Niven, p. 242).

put legs on. See legs on, put.

put (someone) off the walk. To kill him:
Anglo-Irish, esp. County Meath: ca. 1880–1940.
(P. W. Joyce, *English . . . in Ireland*, 1910.)

put on, n.—3. A nondescript frock for afternoon
wear: women's: since ca. 1925; ob.

put on, v. (p. 672), prob. goes back to ca. 1870.
It occurs in Conway Edwardes's play *Heroes*, 1876,
'Put on a smoke'.—2. See trap.—3. To initiate (a
person): coll.: from ca. 1860; ob. B. & L.—4.
'The mail attests that the men . . . thoroughly
enjoy dressing up in women's clothes. I assure
you these people are not putting me on'—kidding
me. 'They are strictly for real.' (*Daily Colonist*,
Victoria, B.C., on April 18, 1967.) Canadian:
since ca. 1945. (Leechman.)

put on, well or better or best. See well put on.

put on foul. See foul.

put on one's ear. See ear, put on one's.

put on the kitz. To put on one's best clothes:
since the late 1930's. Ex Yiddish.

put on the long rank. To cruise: taxi-drivers':
since ca. 1912. Herbert Hodge, 1939.

put on the rattle (or the whizzer). To report a
policeman to his superior: police: C. 20. (*The
Free-Lance Writer*, April 1948.)

put one or two on the floor. To fire a few rounds:
Artillerymen's: 1939–45. (P-G-R.)

put one's balls in a knot; put one's tits in a
tangle. Low equivalents of S.E. *put one's nose out
of joint*: Australian: since ca. 1930.

put one's bones up; put up one's forks. To be
prepared to fight: proletarian: from ca. 1865.
B. & L.

put one's feet up. To lie in one's hammock;
to sleep: Naval: C. 20. *Weekly Telegraph*, Oct.
25, 1941. Mother does this to rest her weary feet.

*put one's forks down. To pick a pocket: c.:
mid-C. 19–20; ob. B. & L.

put one's hand down. To pay; to stand one's
turn: C. 20. Cf. put down south in *Dict*.

put one's name into it. See name into it . . .

put one's prick where another wouldn't put his
walking-stick. Among physicians, esp. Fighting
Services medical officers, almost a c.p., as in 'Some
of you fellows'd put your prick where I wouldn't
put my walking-stick' (as I heard an Australian
M.O. say, in 1915, to a company of infantrymen
paraded for a 'talk' before they were let loose in
Cairo); and in 1959, John Winton, *We Joined the
Navy*, 1959, records it of a Naval M.O. addressing
a group of midshipmen and saying, 'Tomorrow
we'll be getting to Gibraltar . . . and I've no
doubt that some of you'll be putting your private
parts where I wouldn't be putting my walking-
stick.' It prob. dates from late C. 19.

put one's snout in the trough. To drink (beer
or ale rather than wine or spirits): mainly public-
house: since ca. 1945.

put one's time in. To occupy one's time: coll.:
late C. 19–20.

put one's tits in a tangle. See put one's balls . . .
above.

put out.—2. V.i., (of a girl) to permit, even to
invite, sexual liberties: Canadian: adopted, ca.
1950, ex U.S. 'Millie? Oh, she'll put out, all
right.'

put (someone's) pot on.—2. Hence (?), to detect
in a misdeed; to settle his hash: New Zealand:
since ca. 1945. (Fiona Murray, *Invitation to
Danger*, 1965.)

put the acid (or the squeaks) in. To tell-tale; to
make mischief by causing a bias against one in
another's mind: orig. and mostly Cockneys': from
ca. 1910, ca. 1918, resp.

put the bee on. To borrow money from: Australian: since ca. 1935. (B., 1953.) Either 'to
sting' or ex the next two (*bite*).

put the bit on. An Australian variant of the
next: since ca. 1920. (D'Arcy Niland, 1958.)

put the bite on. To ask someone for a loan of
money: Canadian: since ca. 1910; by 1940, also
English. (Leechman.)

put the blocks to. To coït with (a woman): low:
C. 20; by 1950, it was somewhat ob., by 1960,
archaic. Ca. 1900, there was a Canadian lumbermen's ballad, with the pertinent lines, 'Some were
fiddling, some were diddling, some were lying on
the floor,/I was over in the corner putting the
blocks to the Winnipeg whore'. (Robert Clairborne, Aug. 31, 1966.)

put the caulks to. See logger's small-pox.

put the cleaners through (someone) is a variant
of *put* (someone) *through the cleaners*, to get the
better of, to swindle: Australian airmen's: 1939–
45. (B., 1943.)

*put the finger on. See finger on, put the.

put the hooks on; more usually put (someone)
on the hooks. To put (someone) on a charge:
R.A.F.: since ca. 1920. R. M. Davison, letter of
Sept. 26, 1942; Jackson, 1943. Cf. hooks, catch
(*Dict*.).

put the kibosh on. See kibosh on . . .
(*Dict*.).

put the lid on. To close (a hotel bar) at the
legal time: Australian: since ca. 1925. (B.,
1943.)

put the mocker on. To bring bad luck to, put
a hoodoo on: Australian sporting: since ca. 1935.
Lawson Glassop, 1949. Apparently ex the next,
mocker being prob. a back-formation ex *mockers*,
which almost certainly comes ex Yiddish *makkes*,

itself ex the Hebrew word for 'a plague'. *Mockers* has variant *mokkers*. (Dr Mark Burke, letter of Feb. 25, 1961.)

put the mockers either **in for** or **on** (someone). To tell tales to authority in order to get someone into trouble: Naval: since ca. 1930. Perhaps for *muckers*; perhaps cf. next. See the etymology proposed near end of preceding entry.—2. To delude, to befool, someone: low: since ca. 1935. Frank Norman, *Stand on Me*, 1959.

put the mocks on. See **mock on, put the.**

put the pot on.—2, 3. See **pot on, put the.** 'Up came the trout . . . The fish was making for its haunt. Newton "put the pot on", as it is called, and turned him, and in due time he visited the basket' (Francis Francis, *Newton Dogvane*, 1859): anglers': since ca. 1930.

*put the skates on; usually as vbl n., *putting . . .*: c.: since ca. 1925. F. D. Sharpe, *The Flying Squad*, 1938. Cf. **skates put on . . .** in *Dict.*

put the skids under (someone). To dismiss from a job, a course, etc.: since ca. 1940: Army, then—by 1944—gen. Forces' s.—2. Hence, to speed or hurry (him) along: Forces': since 1945.

put the weights on. To seek a loan from or ask a favour of (someone): Australian sporting: since ca. 1910. B., 1942. Ex horse-racing.

put them in a field and let them fight it out! Let the Heads of State fight it out among themselves and thus prevent millions of innocent men and women from getting killed: servicemen's (and others') c.p.: W.W. I—and again in W.W. II.

put through Stubbs. See **Stubbs . . .**

put up a black. See **black.** Probably 'derived from the Naval custom of putting up two black balls at the masthead when the ship is out of control' (Surgeon-Lieutenant H. Osmond, Dec. 1948).

put up one's forks. See **put one's bones up.**

put up (one's) **third.** To put up one's third star, i.e. to become a captain: Army coll.: C. 20. (P-G-R.)

put (someone's) **weight up.** To declare—to disclose—his (illicit) activities; to 'pimp on': Australian miners': since ca. 1925. Gavin Casey, *It's Easier Downhill*, 1945.

put years on me, you (or **he** or **it puts . . .**). A c.p. of disparagement: late C. 19–20.

put you where the rooks won't shit on you, I'll. A jocular c.p. for 'I'll kill you' (humorous threat): Army: since ca. 1935.

put your back up!, that'll. That will render you sexually desirous: since ca. 1920. Ex cats' fighting: cf. familiar S.E. *fighting fit.*

put your skates on! Hurry!; go away quickly; get out of the way if you wish to avoid duty!: Army: since ca. 1910.

putting his oof down. A c.p. dating from ca. 1950 and applied to 'poor old Dad', forking out the *oof* or money, instead of putting his *'oof* down.

putting spots on dominoes. See **making doll's eyes.**

puttun in the *Dict.* is an error for **pultan** (or **-on** or **-un**), which derives directly ex Hindustani.

putty, n., 3 (p. 673): esp., in the Navy, as *be on the putty*, 'to be aground' (lit. and fig.). Granville. —4. Steam: Canadian railroadmen's (— 1931). Ex colour.

putty, on the. High-and-dry on a falling tide: Naval: C. 20. (P-G-R.) Cf. *putty*, 3, on p. 673, and here.

putty and soap. Bread and cheese: low. ca. 1830–80. *Sinks*, 1848.

putty wallah. A messenger or orderly attached to an office: Bombay: mid-C. 19–20. B. & L.

puv. A field: chimneysweeps': C. 19. (George Elson, *The Last of the Climbing Boys*, 1900.) Ex the synonymous Romany *phuv*, itself related to Sanskrit *bhumi*. With thanks to my late friend Gerald Hatchman, who in 1949 contributed two articles on chimneysweeps' s. to *Notes and Queries*.

puzzle the monkey. A coll. variant, since ca. 1880, of S.E. *monkey-puzzle* (the *Araucaria imbricata*).

Pygmalion. See **not Pygmalion likely.**

pyke; occ. **pike.** A civilian that stands an impecunious soldier a drink: military: ca. 1870–1910. B. & L. ? ex Fr. s. *pékin*, a civilian.

Pyrmont Yank. A synonym of **Woolloomooloo Yank** below.

pyrotechnic. A reprimand: R.A.F.: since ca. 1938. Jackson. Cf. **rocket,** which suggested it.

Q

Q. Sir Arthur Quiller-Couch: from ca. 1890; in 1887 had appeared *Dead Man's Rock*, in 1888 the fame-bringing *Troy Town*, both under the pseudonym *Q.*—2. A homosexual: theatrical, whence also Army: since ca. 1930. For **queer**, n., 7, below.

Q, Old. See **Old Q.**

Q, the. Short for **the quarter bloke** (p. 675): Army: since ca. 1925. H. & P.

Q.B.I. (Of flying condition) deplorable: aviation c.p.: ca. 1937–9. *The Times*, March 3, 1938. Lit. quite bloody impossible.

Q bloke, the. Same as *Q, the.*

Q-in-the-corner cove. A keen (and cautious?) follower of boxing: pugilistic: ca. 1815–60. *Boxiana*, IV, 1824, 'Great doubts have been expressed by the "Q-in-the-corner coves", whether Randall is *actually well*, or only "patched up".' Here, *Q* app. = 'query' or 'question'.

Qantas (p. 674) is no longer eligible; 'has for many years been the official name' (B.P.: mid-1963).

quack, n.—3. (Ex sense 1: p. 674.) In the R.A.F., *the quack* is frequently used for the Medical Officer: since ca. 1918. (Gerald Emanuel, letter of March 29, 1945.)

quad.—7. 'A *four*-wheel drive tractor used for towing field guns,' H. & P.: Army: since ca. 1930; by 1942, coll.; by 1944, j. Short for *quadruple?*

quadding. A triumphal promenade of the 1st XV round the cloisters: Rugby schoolboys' coll.: mid-C. 19–20. B. & L.

Quagger, the. Queen Victoria: Oxford undergraduates': 1890's. (Marples, 2.)

quailer. A stone: Aus.: C. 20. (B., 1959.) Origin ?

Quaky Isles, the. New Zealand: Australian coll.: C. 20. (B., 1943.) Earthquaky.

qual. See 'Shortenings'.

*quandong. A prostitute: Australian c.: C. 20. Kylie Tennant, *Foveaux*, 1939. 'After the fruit: soft on the outside, a hard centre,' Sidney J. Baker, letter of Aug. 3, 1946. Although blue-coloured and cherry-sized, it is also known as 'native peach'; the word is of Australian Aboriginal origin.

quart-pot tea (p. 675) is strictly tea made, over an open fire, and only in a quart pot. A billy may be of any size! In C. 20 Australia, *quart-pot* is often shortened to *quart*, which thus > a coll., as in 'We'll . . . boil up the "quarts",' Archer Russell, *A Tramp Royal*, 1934.

quarter flash and three-parts foolish. A fool with a smattering of wordly knowledge: c.p.: ca. 1815–50. Pierce Egan, *London*, 1821. Cf. **fly flat** (p. 292).

quarter to one or three. See **what's the time?**

quarter(-)to(-)ten. A 9·45-inch trench-mortar: Army: ca. 1915–18.

quarter to two. A Jew: rhyming s.: C. 20. Franklyn, *Rhyming*.

quean up; mostly as (*all*) *queaned up*, 'carefully, not necessarily effeminately, dressed': Australian: since ca. 1920. B., 1942. See **quean** and cf. **doll up** (both in *Dict.*). Also *queen up*. (B., 1959.)

queanie, adj. Effeminate; soft: Australian: since ca. 1910. Baker. Ex the n.: see p. 676.

queen, 1, q.v. at **quean** on p. 676, is still common. Among homosexuals, it means 'an ageing passive homosexual', with adj. *queeny*, as in 'He's very queeny'.—2. In combination, a girl: R.A.F.: 1940 +. Jackson, 'Thus, "I'm going to the flicks to-night with one of the ops room queens".' Humorous.

Queen At, the. 'A Chief Commander of the A.T.S.,' H. & P.: Services: since 1939 or 1940. See **At** and cf.:

Queen Bee, the. 'The Director of the Women's Auxiliary Air Force; or the senior W.A.A.F. officer on a station,' Jackson: W.A.A.F. and hence R.A.F.: since 1940 or 1941. Cf. prec. entry.

queen bee. 'A 'plane used for anti-aircraft firing practice, having no crew and controlled by radio from the ground. (Not a new invention),' H. & P., 1943: R.A.F.: since ca. 1935; by mid-1942, at latest, it was j.

Queen Mary. A long, low-loading, articulated vehicle for the transportation of aircraft by road: R.A.F.: since ca. 1938. Jackson. An occ. synonym is *artic* (Jackson.)—2. 'The basement under the new House of Commons where the secretaries and typists work . . . (From its appearance and general decorative scheme.) The term is in pretty general use now, I gather,' Oct. 13, 1953, in letter from Wilfred Granville.—3. A very large goods brake van: railwaymen's: since the middle 1940's. Ex sense 1; in full, *Queen Mary brake van*. (*Railway*.) **queen up**, q.v. **quean up** above.

Queen's Arms, The; or The Hen and Chickens. Home: commercial travellers': from ca. 1890. It comes into conversations concerning hotels; thus: '"Where do you stay in York?" "Oh, at The Queen's Arms (or, The Hen and Chickens)."' With punning reference to wife or to wife and children.

Queen's Park Ranger. A stranger: Londoner's rhyming s.: C. 20. Ex a London 'soccer' team: cf. *West Ham Reserves*.

queeny, adj. See **queen**, and cf. **queanie**, both above.

queer, n.—6. A simpleton; a fool: Australian: since ca. 1925. B., 1942. Ex sense 7 of its adj.

queer, n.—7. A male homosexual: since ca. 1920. (Angus Wilson, *Hemlock and After*, 1952.) Ex sense 8 of the adj.

*queer, adj. See, esp. for its relation to **rum**, the essay entitled 'Neither Cricket nor Philology' in *A Covey of Partridge*, 1937.—8. Homosexual C. 20, ex U.S.: rather coll. than s. *The Listener*,

1354

March 10, 1937.—9. Roughly 'any', but vaguely intensive, in, e.g., 'the queer thing' (thingummy) and 'old queer man' (what's-his-name): Army: late C. 19–20. From several dial. uses (adj. and adv.), themselves vaguely intensive.

queer and; *queer* nearly always pronounced *quare*. An intensive of the adjective preceding, as '*quare and* hot', very hot, or '*quare and* sick', very sick; Northern Ireland coll.: C. 19–20. (P. W. Joyce, *English in Ireland*, 1910.)

queer as a three-dollar bill. Very odd (or strange) indeed: Canadian: late C. 19–20. 'There are no $3 bills' (Leechman).

queer belch. Sour beer: low: ca. 1825–70. *Sinks*, 1848.

queer fella, the. The person that happens to be in command: Regular Army: late C. 19–20.

queer hawk. An eccentric person: mostly Army: since ca. 1930. Cf. **queer bird** (p. 677).

queer put. 'An ill-looking, foolish fellow' (*Sinks*): low: prob. ca. 1800–60.

queer start. A strange business: ca. 1820–80: low >, by 1860, gen. Anon., *Autobiography of Jack Ketch*, 1836. See **start**, n., 3 (p. 825).

queer the job. A theatrical variation of **queer the pitch** (*Dict.*). Leonard Merrick, *Peggy Harper*, 1911.

Quego. A Pacific Islander (native): New Zealand: C. 20: Ex Fijian *ko iko*, you (in calling to a person). Edwin Morrisby (Aug. 30, 1958) compares the Australian C. 20 use of *boong* for an Aboriginal, as recorded by B., 1942, with occasional variant *bong*, themselves borrowed from Aboriginal. *Bo(o)ng* is also employed as adj.

querier (p. 678). Rather, since ca. 1845. Mayhew, II, 1851.

qui-es kateer (p. 697) is properly *quiess kateer*, lit. 'well, very', i.e. 'very well'—the answer to 'How are you?' Soldiers' Arabic, perhaps deduced from 'Enta [or, Inta] quiess [or, *kwaiss*]?'— 'You well?' It occurs in G. W. Steevens, *With Kitchener to Khartoum*, 1896: 'the earliest printed use'—as a phrase familiar to British regular soldiers—'I have seen' (H. R. Spencer); or I.

quick. Dapper and clever: Society: 1870's and 1880's. B. & L.

quick quid has, since ca. 1925, been the Australian answer to the American *fast buck*. (B.P.)

quick(-)shits, the. Dysentery: Army in North Africa: 1940–43. (Peter Sanders in *The Sunday Times* magazine, Sept. 10, 1967.)

quick squirt. A (sudden and) brief burst of machine-gun fire from one aircraft at another: R.A.F.: since 1939 +. H. & P.

quick sticks. The phrase *in quick sticks* (see sense 1 on p. 679) occurs in *The Dublin University Magazine* of April 1835 (p. 391) and should be dated back to at least as far as 1830. Used by J. B. Priestley in *They Walk in the City* in 1963; by 1960, slightly ob. (Moe.)—2. As *quick sticks!* it is Australian domestic coll.—addressed to children—and synonymous with 'Come quickly!': C. 20. (B.P.)

quicky.—3. (Usually *quickie*.) A rapid burst of machine-gun fire at close range: R.A.F. (mostly): since 1939. H. & P. Ex prec.—4. A drink, esp. 'a quick one'; Service officers' (esp. R.A.F.): 1940 +. W/Cdr Robin P. McDouall, letter of March 17, 1945.—5. Sexual intercourse hurriedly effected: since ca. 1945.—6. A brief bawdy story

told at the break-up of a party: since the late 1940's.

Quid, the Tiddle. H.M.S. *Royal Sovereign*: Naval: World War II. A pun on *quid*, £1. (P-G-R.)

quid-box. A snuff box: ? 1790–1850. (Wm Maginn, *Whitehall*, 1827, at p. 53.)

quidlet, l (p. 679). An early record: J. W. Horsley, *I Remember*, 1912.

quids, for. For anything at all, as in 'He wouldn't miss a [race] meeting for quids' (Slatter): New Zealand: since ca. 1920.

quids in. Applied to a state of things when one is doing well; 'I'm quids in!': Army (C. 20); by 1919, it was gen. Short either for *quids in the till* or for *in, to the tune of quids* (pounds).—2. Hence, *be quids in* is to accomplish something with plenty of time, effort, etc., to spare; to do it easily or comfortably: since ca. 1935. Perhaps ex the result of a highly successful wager.

quiet mouse. A synonym of **lone duck**, q.v. in *Dict.* B. & L.

quiff.—4. The female pudend: low: C. 20. Perhaps cf. sense 3 on p. 679.—5. A hint; a piece of advice: since ca. 1920. Netley Lucas, *The Autobiography of a Crook*, 1925, 'I'll give you one quiff, right now . . . Never touch the dope, it's hell.' Ex sense 2 on p. 679.

quilling. The carrying of (rich) passengers' luggage and getting a tip for doing so: railwaymen's, esp. porters': C. 20. Semantically = favour-currying. See also **fluffing**, 2, above. *Railway*, 3rd, modifies the definition by confining the practice to off-duty employees.

quim (p. 680). More prob. ex Celtic *cwm*, a cleft, a valley.

quin. See **quim** (*Dict.*).

quince. A soft, an effeminate person; a softly stupid person: low Australian: since ca. 1920. B., 1942.

quince, get on (someone's). To annoy, irritate, exasperate someone: low Australian: since ca. 1920. Baker. Cf. 'These bloody trees are getting on me quince!': A. E. Farrell, *The Vengeance*, 1963.

quint. 'Any one of a set of quintuplets; common in Canada since the birth of the Dionne children in 1934 in Calendar, Ontario' (Leechman). Cf. next.

Quints, the. The Canadian shape of the *Quins* (p. 680). Leechman.

quirk, l (p. 680), was revived in the R.A.F. of 1939–45. (Jackson.)

quirley. A cigarette: Australian: since ca. 1930. (B., 1953.) Cf. *twirly*.

quis (pron. *kwyce*); occ. **kweis** or **kweiss**. Usually as exclamation: 'good' or 'capital' or 'O.K.!': Regular Army's and R.A.F. regulars': C. 20. Partridge, 1945. Direct ex Arabic.

quisling. A tell-tale, esp. one who curries favour with the C.O. by acting as tale-bearer: Services: since mid-1940. H. & P. Ex Vidkum Quisling (1889–1946), the Norwegian Army officer turned traitor. (See, esp., my *Name into Word*, 1949.)

quit by proclamation. See 'Tavern terms', § 4.

quite, adj. 'Quite the thing'—somebody first-class, very well—better—or—mannered, etc.: since ca. 1920. (H. Drake Brockman, *Men Without Wives*, 1938, 'There is a polite fiction current that once he went to Oxford, and he isn't "quite", and everybody knows this, in the strange way that everybody does know these things.'

quite a bit. Fairly often; a fair amount (n.), rather (adv.): coll.: late C. 19–20. 'It hurts quite a bit.'

quite too nice. Nice: female æsthetic Society: 1880's and 1890's. B. & L.

quius kius! Hush!; cease: theatrical c.p. of ca. 1880–1910. Ibid. The *kius* reduplicates *quius* ex *quietus.*

quizzy. Inquisitive: Australian: C. 20. (D'Arcy Niland, *The Shiralee*, 1955.)

quoit. A simpleton; a fool: Australian: since ca. 1930. (B., 1943.) Why? 'Probably because a quoit is a hollow ring—nothing in it' (Julian Franklyn, 1962).

quoits. Buttocks: Australian: since ca. 1925. B., 1942. Ex roundness.

quoits, go for one's. To go for one's life; to travel very fast: Australian: since ca. 1920. Baker.

*****quondong.** Variant of **quandong.**

quoniam (p. 680). Sense 2 must be even ear-lier, for in the Wife of Bath's prologue (lines 607–8), in *The Canterbury Tales*, Chaucer caused her to say:

> And trewely, as mine housebonds tolde me,
> I hadde the beste *quoniam* might be.

(With thanks to L. F. Masters, Esq.) The pun, therefore, is probably also on L. *cunnum*, the acc. of *cunnus.*

quot is a variant spelling and pron. of **cot** (*Dict.*). B. & L.

quota quicky. A short British film made as quickly and cheaply as possible, and put on a cinema programme to fulfil the regulation concerning the quota of British films to be used, in Britain, in proportion to foreign (including American) films: cinema world: 1936. (It doesn't matter how short the films are; a nasty reflection on British films.)

quoz (p. 681) is the subject of an entire song in *The New Vocal Enchantress* (a song-book), 1791, at pp. 32–4. Also occ. as diminutive *quozzy:* ibid.

R

R in pawn, leave an. See leave . . .

R. J. Knowles. Holes: theatrical rhyming s.: since ca. 1892.

r.o. lollies. Run-out money: mock-auction world: since ca. 1945. (*Sunday Chronicle*, June 28, 1953.)

R.O.T.F.B. To the entry at roll on that boat, add: 'I.e. roll on that effing boat'.

Rab. The Rt Hon. Richard Austen Butler: political and journalistic: since early 1930's; ob. by 1967. Ex his initials *R.A.B.*

*rab, the. The till: c.: C. 20. F. D. Sharpe, *The Flying Squad*, 1938. With a pun on *Rab*, the Scots form of *Rob*.

rabbit, n.—7. A bottle of beer: Australian: C. 20. B., 1942.—8. A young girl: Australian: since ca. 1920. Baker.—9. A native born Australian: Australian: since ca. 1925. Baker.—10. (Ex 5.) Any 'scrounged' article: Naval: since ca. 1920.—11. See rabbit and pork.—12. A short-journey passenger: busmen's and trammen's: since ca. 1910. Also, since ca. 1912, railwaymen's. (*Railway*.) Mostly in plural.

rabbit, v.—2. '(In football) to collar a player by the ankles when he is running with the ball,' Baker: Australian sporting: C. 20.—3. To chat: low: C. 20. (Norman.) Short for *rabbit and pork*.—4. Hence, to grumble and mumble: low: C. 20.—5. To borrow or 'scrounge' (something): Australian Naval: since ca. 1920. (B., 1943.)

rabbit, live (p. 682). Cf. dial. *rabbit*, 'to coït'—as in John Masefield, *Reynard the Fox*, 1919, '"I'll larn 'ee rabbit in my shed!"'

rabbit, run the. See run . . .

rabbit and pork. A, to, talk: rhyming: C. 20. Often shortened to *rabbit*. (Gerald Kersh, *Boots Clean*, 1941.)

Rabbit Hutchin(g)s or Hutchinson. See 'Nick names'.

rabbit-killer. A punch on the nape of the neck: Australian: since ca. 1925. Cf. rabbiter, 1, on p. 682.

rabbit-o. 'An itinerant street seller of rabbits': Australian: C. 20. Ex his cry. (Caddie, 1953.)

Rabbit-o's, the. South Sydney footballers: Sydney sporting: since ca. 1925. (B., 1943.)

rabbit-pulling. A variant of baby-pulling above; cf. *rabbit-catcher* at rabbit, 1, on p. 681.

Rabbits. Railwaymen's nickname for the 'Leicester to Birmingham parcels train' (*Railway*, 3rd): since ca. 1945.

rabbits. A customs officer: Naval: late C. 19–20.—2. Hence, perquisites, gifts: Naval C. 20. Cf. *rabbit*, n., 3 (p. 682) and 10. (Frank Shaw.)—3. Hence(?), plunder, loot; esp. contraband goods smuggled ashore: Naval: since ca. 1920.—4. See *white rabbits*.

rabbits, make. To indulge one's hobby, esp. in making things, e.g. gifts for children: Naval coll.: C. 20.

rabbit's food. Vegetable salad: Naval: C. 20. *The Birmingham Mail*, Feb. 24, 1939. Among civilians: *rabbit meat*, since ca. 1920.—2. Hence, esp., lettuce: Forces': W.W. II and after.

rabbit's paw; often shortened to *rabbit*. Conversation: rhyming s. (on *jaw*): since ca. 1930. Cf. rabbit and pork above. Franklyn 2nd.

rabbo. A rabbit; rabbits considered collectively; *rabbo!*, the street-cry of a rabbit-meat vendor: lower-class Australian, esp. Sydneyites': late C. 19–20. C. F. McGill, 'Me Donah What's at Home' in *The Bakara Bulletin*, 1919, 'I've been a thinking what to do fer me an' my gal Flo; | I think I'll buy a barrer an' sell the good rabbo.' (This short poem shows, very clearly, the influence of C. J. Dennis's *The Sentimental Bloke*.)

race for the steward's basin, n. and v. (To experience) sea-sickness: jocular: C. 20. Parodying the race-course *race for the Stewards' Cup*.

racehorse. A long, slim cigarette: Australian: since ca. 1930. (Kylie Tennant, *The Joyful Condemned*, 1953.)

*races, be at the. To walk the streets as a prostitute: c., and low: C. 20.

rack, on the. Always on the move: Canadian coll.: from ca. 1860. B. & L.: abbr. of '*racket*, a Canadian snow-shoe'.

racket, 1 (p. 682): since ca. 1930, jocular for one's trade or profession. 'What racket are you in?' or 'What's your racket?'

racket, stand the, 2 (p. 682). Rather: since ca. 1830 or 1840. *Sinks*, 1848.

racket(t)y. (Of places) low, 'shady': Cockney: ca. 1840–90. Mayhew, I, 1851. Ex racket, 1 (p. 682).

radar king, the. The senior Radar officer: Naval: since ca. 1940.

Raddie. An Italian: low: C. 20. F. D. Sharpe, 1938. Ex the *raddled*-seeming complexion of many Southern Italians; but cf. Reddy.

raddie. A radical in politics: since ca. 1930. Eric Parr, *Grafters All*, 1964, '. . . He discovered that his acquaintance was a bit of a raddie at heart.' A pet-form of rad, 1, on p. 682.

radge. Silly: low: C. 20. Prob. ex *rage* via 'mad'. Cf. Northern dial. *radgy*, mad.

radical; Hunt's breakfast powder. Roasted corn: ca. 1820–60. *Sinks*, 1848. Prob. at first *radical Hunt's* . . ., then divided into a pair of synonyms. This was 'Orator' Hunt the Radicals's favourite breakfast dish.

Radio Catch-Phrases. See, e.g., after you, Claude—it's that man again—steady, Barker!; and E. P., 'Those Radio Catch-Phrases' in *The Radio Times*, Dec. 6, 1946, reprinted in *Words at War: Words at Peace*, 1948.

radius, diameter, circumference are often confused one with another; catachrestic: C. 19–20. *The Pawnshop Murder*: 'Objects which came within the radius lit by her torch.'

Rafer. See **Raffer.**

Raff, the. The Royal Air Force: R.A.F. coll.: 1918 +. Partridge, 1945.

Raffer; rare in singular. A person in the R.A.F.; not usually applied to officers: civilian: 1939 +.

Rafferty's rules. Variant (B., 1959) of **Rafferty rules** on p. 683.

Raffles, properly a gentleman or Society thief, esp. burglar, has, in C. 20, been frequently misused to mean almost any burglar. (E.g. in *The Daily Mirror*, Dec. 16, 1936.) E. W. Hornung's *Raffles, the Amateur Cracksman*, appeared in 1899. It was followed up by *The Shadow of the Rope*, 1902; *A Thief in the Night*, 1905; and *Mr Justice Raffles* in 1909. These four books have been assembled in an omnibus-volume entitled *Raffles*.

raft. 'A number of wagons during shunting' (*Railway*): railwaymen's: since ca. 1945. Ex U.S. s. *raft*, a large number or quantity.

rag, v., 1 (p. 683), in nuance 'to scold': a century and a half earlier! *Sessions*, June 1739 (trial of Samuel Bird and Suzannah Clark), 'On Monday night Bird and Clark came to their House to *ragg* (scold) her Grandfather for what he had talk'd of concerning them.'

rag-and snatcher man. A rag-and-bones man: chimneysweeps': C. 19. (George Elson, 1900). Here, *snatcher* apparently = a bone; if so, it probably comes ex dogs *snatching* bones.

rag bramah. A rag-and-bones merchant: police: since ca. 1925. (*The Free-Lance Writer*, April 1948.)

rag-time girl (p. 684). For dates read '1908 or 1909'.

rag-time routine is that which obtained in the Auxiliary Patrol, World War I: Naval: 1914–18. Cf. *rag-time*, 2 (p. 684).

ragged.—4. Unwell; tired and unwell: Australian coll.: late C. 19–20. (D'Arcy Niland, *Call Me . . .*, 1958.) Cf. *rough*.

rags, in the. In trouble or disgrace; in a dispute: tailors': from ca. 1860. B. & L.

rags, the.—6. A bookmakers' term for the horses that ran, esp. those which 'also ran': since ca. 1920.

rags (on), have the. To be having one's period: women's low coll.: from ca. 1860. Whence, prob., *have the painters in*, gen. as c.p., *she's got the painters in*: C. 20. Also, *wear rags*: coll.: mid C. 19–20.

ragsooker. See **rag-sooker** (*Dict.*).

rahzo. Phonetic variant of **rarzo.**

rail. A railroad employee in transportation service: Canadian railroadmen's (— 1931). Short for *railroadman*.—2. Edge of a surfboard: Australian (teenage) surfers': since late 1950's; by 1963, coll. (B.P.)

railings is the modern (since at least as early as 1910) form of *front*, or *head*, *rails*, teeth.

rails.—4. (Cf. 3: p. 684) 'The "Rails" are railway stations, as distinct from the Underground,' Herbert Hodge, *Cab, Sir?*, 1939; taxidrivers': since ca. 1919.

[Railway slang. A feature to note is the deliberate mispronunciation of place-names, e.g. **Carliss-lee**, Carlisle, and **Cree-wee**, Crewe: C. 20.]

rainbow, 6 (p. 685). Hence, in 1939–45, applied to various late-comers or those who, relatively, came late; as, e.g., by the 6th to the 7th Australian Infantry Division (Lawson Glassop, *We Were*

the Rats, 1944).—7. A gay young spark: ca. 1835–70. *Sinks*, 1848.

raise, v.—2. To complete (a form): R.A.F. coll.: since ca. 1935: by 1943, j. Jackson, 'Thus, "You want a vehicle? O.K., raise a Form 658 and push it into the Adj."' Perhaps ex 'to raise all relevant points and deal with them'.

raise a gallop. To have an erection: low (mostly Services'): since ca. 1930.

raise hell (q.v. at *hell, raise,* on p. 386) has, in Western Canadian since ca. 1908, existed also with the extension *and slip a shingle* (or *a shim*) *under one corner* (or *under it*). Leechman.

raise the colour. To find gold: Australian coll.: mid C. 19–20. (B., 1943.)

raise the wind. To raise money, esp. to obtain a loan: coll., perhaps orig. nautical: 1789 (*OED*); 1830, Fredk Marryat, *The King's Own*.

Rajrifs, the. See at **Burrifs.**

rake, n.—2. A (timber) train on a narrow-gauge line: Australian: C. 20. (K. S. Prichard, *Working Bullocks*, 1926.) Probably a pun.—3. A 'complete set of coaches' (*Railway*): railwaymen's: since ca. 1910. Cf. sense 2.

rake it in. To make money fast: coll.: late C. 19–20. 'He's simply raking it in!'

rake-out. A fill of tobacco: Cockneys': from cq. 1890; very ob. Pugh.

raker, go a. To fall heavily; fig., to come a 'cropper': Australian: C. 20. B., 1942. See **raker,** 2, on p. 685.

ral. 'A disorderly fellow' (L. E. F. English, *Historic Newfoundland*, 1955): Newfoundland: C. 20. Origin? Perhaps ex Irish *ralac*, huge, monstrous.

ram, n.—3. A confidence trickster's accomplice: Australian c.: C. 20. B., 1942. A battering-ram?

Ram, the. The *Ramillies* (ship of the line): Naval: ? ca. 1800–1815. (W. N. Glascock, *The Naval Sketch-Book*, I, 1825, '. . . 'twixt the *Ram* and the *Rion*' (Orion). Moe.

Ram Corps, the. The Royal Army Medical Corps: Army (mostly officers'): since ca. 1915.

ram in or **ram on.** To put one's name down for, e.g., an outing: Shrewsbury: late C. 19–20. Marples.

ram-rod, 2, and **rammer,** 3, are mid-C. 19–20 low for a penis.

ram-skin (or one word). A bailiff: Anglo-Irish: C. 19. 'A Real Paddy', *Real Life in Ireland*, 1822. 'He would take even a mat made of a ram's fell.'

ram-struck mutton. 'Tough meat from old ewes past breeding' (Baker): Australian: late C. 19–20.

Ramasammy (p. 685) occurs, as *Ram Sammee* (or *Sammy*), in George R. Gleig, *The Subaltern's Log-Book* (I, 292; II, 233), 1828. Moe.

rambler. A whore: C. 17. In, e.g., *The English Rogue*.

rammer.—2. The leg: pugilistic: ca. 1840–80. Augustus Mayhew, *Paved With Gold*, 1857, 'Jack got a "cracker on his nut" which knocked his "rammers" from under him.' *Cracker*, as 'a heavy punch', occurs earlier—in, e.g., *Boxiana*, IV, 1824.—3. See **ram-rod,** 2, above.

rammies. Trousers: Australian: since ca. 1925. (B., 1943.)

*rammy. A sudden fight between gangs: Glasgow c.: C. 20. MacArthur & Long, '[The police] knew that evidence about a rammy is always

conflicting, never reliable and frequently perjured.'
Ex Scottish *rammish*, violent, untamed. Contrast
clash, q.v. above and cf.:—

rammy, big; rammy, little. A battle; a trench
raid: Argyll & Sutherland Highlanders': 1914–18.
(Dr R. L. Mackay, M.D., who, early 1967, comments, 'Many recruited in Glasgow.') Genuine
s. rather than dial.

ramp, n.—10. A public-house: c.: since ca.
1925. *Daily Express*, March 25, 1935. Ex sense
9 (p. 686), the bar being likened to a counter.
But more usually a public-house counter, as in
John Gosling, *The Ghost Squad*, 1959. Therefore
cf. sense 9 on p. 686.

rampage, on the. Storming about: coll.: since
ca. 1880. (E.D.D.)

*****ramping.**—2. 'Calling at the houses where
parcels [have] just been delivered from tradesmen
to customers, and obtaining possession of them
under various pretences': c.: from ca. 1870.
B. & L.

ram's head. The wooden rudder post of a canal-
boat: canal-men's: late C. 19–20. L. T. C. Rolt,
Narrow Boat, 1944. Usually bound with pipe-
clayed *Turk's Head* knots.

Ramsay Mac. James Ramsay Macdonald (d.
1937): mostly Labour: C. 20.

ranch. A cookhouse: North Queensland (coll.
rather than s.): since ca. 1910. Jean Devanney,
By Tropic Sea and Jungle, 1944.

randy (p. 686). Perhaps influenced by Hindustani *randi*-baz, a lecher. (S. H. Ward.) 'Now
becoming almost respectable': Peter Sanders,
mid-1965.

randy Rupert. See **Rupert**.

ranger.—3. A bushranger: Australian coll.:
late C. 19–20; by 1940, ob. (B., 1943.)

Rangers, the. The Queen's Park Rangers:
Association football coll.: C. 20.

rank outsider. 'A vulgar fellow, a cad': from
ca. 1880: coll. >, 1910, S.E. B. & L. Ex the
turf.

rantan, on the (p. 647): still common in New
Zealand. (Slatter.)

rap, n., 3 (p. 687). This sense goes back to ca.
1710, to judge by James Dalton, *A Narrative*, 1728,
'*Rap*, Swearing against a Person.'

rap, v., 2 (p. 687). This sense should be back-
dated to ca. 1710, for it occurs in James Dalton,
1728, 'The Whores are our Safeguard; for when
we *fling for a Cly* [go for a purse], if we are taken
on Suspicion, they'll *rap* for us.'

rap, get the. To get into trouble: Australian
low: adopted, ca. 1925, from U.S., B., 1942.
(See *Underworld*.)

rap give a. See **give** . . .

rap up. To praise, speak highly of: Australian:
since ca. 1930. D'Arcy Niland, *Call Me* . . .,
1939, 'They could rap him up enough then.'

rapless. Penniless: coll.: from ca. 1880: very
ob. Binstead.

rapper.—2. A dealer that raps at doors to find
out whether there is anything worth buying:
secondhand (e.g. curio) dealers' coll.: late C. 19–20.
H. A. Vachell, *Quinneys*, 1914.

Rarey-fying (a horse). Taming it: sporting:
ca. 1855–95. Cf. **rarefied** (*Dict.*).

rarzer.—2. The Army Other Ranks' form of
raspberry, 4 (below): since ca. 1925. E. P. in
The New Statesman, Aug. 1, 1942.

rarzo (or **rahzo**). A red-nosed man: Cockney':s.

late C. 19–20. 'Whatcher, rarzo!' Ex *raspberry*
colour, whence also **razzo** of the *Dict*.

ras. See **rarzer** (*Dict.*).

ras(-)class bastard. A first-class bastard or
thoroughly objectionable fellow: among West
Indian immigrants at Wolverhampton: since
1962. (Dr R. L. Mackay, M.D., 1967.) Here, *ras*
is perhaps a blend of *arse + first*.

rasher and fingers. A rasher of bacon and
potato-chips: low eating-house: C. 20. Frank
Jennings, *Tramping*, 1932.

rasher-splasher. A mess cook: Naval: since
ca. 1925. Granville. Reduplicatory.

rasp, n.—3. A shave: C. 20. (Brendan
Behan, *Borstal Boy*, 1958.)

rasp, v.—2. V.i., corresponding to **rasping**, adj.,
2.

rasp away, v.i.; esp. in present participle. To
make coïtal movements: Australian, esp. mechan-
ician fitters' and turners': since ca. 1925. Ex the
movements of a *rasp* (a coarse file) being used.
Cf. **rasp**, v., 1, on p. 687.

raspberry.—4. (Ex 1.) A reprimand: Services
(esp. Army) officers': since ca. 1925. E. P., 'In
Mess and Field'—*The New Statesman*, Aug. 1,
1942. Cf. **rocket**.

Raspberry-Landers. Tasmanian: Australian
coll.: C. 20. (B., 1943.)

rasper.—5. A (very) noisy breaking of wind:
low: C. 20. Anticipated by Swift in one of his
improper poems (a bridal night).

rasping, adj.—2. (of a stockbroker) 'giving
greater turns to the jobbers than those regulated
in the market,' *Spy*, II, 1826: Stock Exchange:
ca. 1810–70. Also as n.

rass. A variant of *ras*, q.v. at **rarze(r)** on
p. 687.

rat.—10. Short for *rat and mouse*, a louse: C. 20.
F. D. Sharpe, *The Flying Squad*, 1938.—11. '. . .
Rats, the man who sneaked into the men's mines
when they were on good stuff, and took out their
opal during the night.' (K. S. Prichard, *The Black
Opal*, 1921): Australian opal-miners': C. 20.—12.
Hence, any opal-thief, and the n. *ratting*. Cf. *rat*,
n., 8, on p. 688.—13. See the quotation at **hole
(out) in one**, sense 2, above.

rat, v., 1 (p. 688). Also Australian: since ca.
1918. (Vance Palmer, *Seedtime*, 1957.)

rat, have a. To be insane: Australian: since
ca. 1910. B., 1942.

rat and mouse. A house: rhyming s.: C. 20.
(Sydney Lester.)

rat-bag. An ill-disposed person: Australian: C.
20. Baker.—2. An eccentric: Australian: since
ca. 1910. (Vance Palmer, *Golconda*, 1948.) Cf.
rats, get, 4, on p. 688. Hence *ratbagging*, a display
of eccentricity; eccentric activities: since ca.
1930. (B., *Australia Speaks*, 1953.)—3. A worthless person, esp. if young and with near-criminal
tendencies and habits: Australian: since ca.
1940. The *locus classicus* resides in William Dick's
scarifying novel, *A Bunch of Ratbags* (1965),
where, on p. 27, he postulates an origin to which I
prefer the probability that it simply = a bag in
which to carry rats, hence the rats themselves,
hence a single *rat* or thoroughly objectionable
person.
In all senses, it has always, since ca. 1960, been
written *ratbag*.

Rat Castle. See 'Miscellanea'.

rat-catcher (p. 688) is also written *ratcatcher*.

Rear-Admiral P. W. Brock, R.N., C.B., D.S.O., comments (Jan. 10, 1963) thus: 'In "The Horse Marines" (1911), Kipling writes, ". . . After he'd changed into those rat-catcher clothes . . ." Two very different people whom I have tried have both said that to them "rat-catcher" implies a rough shooting-rig, e.g. knickerbocker trousers with stockings and a Norfolk jacket, and a date considerably before 1931.—I suggest that "rat-catcher" was once used for a purpose even more plebeian and much more countrified than the "dog-robbers" dealt with in your addendum, at much the same period, and was far less dressy than any hunting kit, though it may have arrived at this by 1931.'

Rat Hole, the. The 'Camden short tunnel' (*Railway*, 3rd): London Transport workers': since late 1940's.

rat-house. An asylum for the insane: Australian: since ca. 1910. B., 1942.

rat-office. See **rat-firm** (*Dict.*).

rat on. To fail (someone); to betray: Australian: adopted, ca. 1925, from U.S. Sidney J. Baker, letter in *The Observer*, Nov. 13, 1938. Mostly, to inform to the police about (someone); also Canadian. (Leechman.)

rat race, the. Fierce competition to make a living, esp. in the professions: coll.: since ca. 1945.

rat-shop. Recorded by B. & L., it dates from ca. 1875.

rat-trap.—4. A balloon barrage: civilian: since 1939. Berrey, 1940.—5. In the R.A.F., a submarine: since 1939; but since ca. 1915 in the Navy. E. P., 'Air Warfare and Its Slang' in *The New Statesman*, Sept. 19, 1942. Also *mouse-trap* (less usual). The crew being doubly *rats*.

ratbagging (see **rat-bag**, 2, above) is, as Barry Prentice tells me in mid-1963, a 'ghost word'; he adds, 'It should be *ratbaggery*'.

ratcatcher's daughter. A rare variant of fisher-man's daughter (above). Franklyn 2nd.

rate is the rank of *the Rate*, a Leading Rate (or Leading Hand) in any branch of the Royal Navy: Naval coll., esp. lower-deck: late C. 19–20. (P-G-R.)

rate of knots, at the. Very fast: Naval coll.: mid-C. 19–20. Granville. Current also in Australia and New Zealand since ca. 1860: see, e.g., 'Tom Collins', *Such Is Life*, 1903, and G. B. Lancaster, *Sons o' Men*, 1904.

rather! (p. 688). During the very approximate period 1890–1910 and especially among schoolboys and schoolgirls, the word was often emphasised by stressing the second syllable (-*ther*). The practice is far from dead.

rather keep a week than a fortnight. See **week than a fortnight**.

rather-nicers. 'A term of contempt stigmatizing ladies who pottered about sale rooms applying substantive and adverb to "gems" which they had no intention of purchasing' (H. A. Vachell, *Quinney's Adventures*, 1924): sale rooms': C. 20.

rations king. Catering Officer; a messing clerk: R.A.F.: since ca. 1930. Jackson.

rats and scabs. Rupees: Regular Army': C. 20.

rats, be in the. To have *delirium tremens*: Australian: C. 20. (D'Arcy Niland, 1955.) Cf. *rats*, 3 (p. 688).—2. Hence, to be insane: Australian: since ca. 1920. (D'Arcy Niland, *Call Me . . .*, 1958.)

rats, give a person green. To backbite (him): proletarian: from ca. 1860; ob. B. & L.

rats, in the. Suffering from delirium tremens: low and military: from ca. 1880. Richards. Ex *rats*, 3 (*Dict.*).

rats and mice. Dice: rhyming: since ca. 1860. —2. Cards of '3' and '2' in one hand: Australian poker-players': since ca. 1920. (B., 1953.)

rat's head. A fool: low: C. 20.

Rat's Hole, the. 'Victoria Station is the "Vic", King's Cross the "Northern", Paddington the "Western", St Pancras the "Cold Blow", and Charing Cross Underground the "Rat's Hole",' Herbert Hodge, *Cab, Sir?*, 1939: London taxi-drivers': since ca. 1905.

rats' tails. See 'Miscellanea', near end.

rattle, n., 2: earlier in 'Taffrail', thus: 'A "bird" is a man who is always in the rattle", i.e. defaulter.' Cf.: **rattle, in the**.

rattle, have a. (Of men) to coït: low: C. 20.

rattle, in the. Under arrest, in detention; on a charge: Naval: C. 20. H. & P. Cf. **rattle, be in the** (p. 689), and:

rattle, score a. To get oneself put on the list of defaulters: Naval: C. 20. Granville.

***rattle, work the.** See **work the rattle**.

rattle and clank. Bank (for money): rhyming s.: C. 20. Franklyn 2nd.

rattle-blanket. A great-coat: Regular Army's: C. 20. (Atkinson.) Often used as a blanket, a greatcoat has buttons, etc., that clink.

rattler.—6. 'The Underground used to be the "Rattler" but has lately become the "Pipe",' Herbert Hodge, *Cab, Sir?*, 1939: London taxi-drivers': ca. 1905–30. Ex sense 3.—7. (Of men) an assiduous amorist: since ca. 1920.

rattlesnake, fuck like a. See **fuck like a rattle-snake**.

ratty.—3. Silly; stupid: New Zealand, hence also Australian: since ca. 1890. G. B. Lancaster, *Sons o' Men*, 1904; B., 1942. Hence, *ratty on*, infatuated with; also *ratty over* (B., 1943).

rave.—3. An enthusiastic notice in the Press: theatrical: since ca. 1920; in the world of books, since ca. 1945.—4. 'At a rave, blast or orgy—all synonyms for party—a guy (never a boy) meets a bit of hod, or tart (whether or not she is)'—to quote from 'Cool Culture' in the correspondence columns of *The Sunday Times*, Sept. 8, 1963: teenagers': ca. 1961–65. Also a dance. Cf. sense 1 on p. 689.—5. Among beatniks, a bottle party: since ca. 1957; by 1963, ob.

raver. A confirmed party-goer: beatniks': since ca. 1958. (Anderson.) Ex *rave*, n., 5, above; cf. **ravist** below.

ravers. Raving mad: since ca. 1925; by 1960, slightly ob. (Ngaio Marsh, *Death in a White Tie*, 1938.)

raving Noah. See 'Mock-Auction Slang' above. Since the late 1940's.

ravist. A party-goer, esp. if habitual: office-and shop-girls': ca. 1956–9. (Gilderdale.)

raw, in the; esp. *sleep in the raw*, to sleep naked: adopted ex U.S., ca. 1943 in Britain, ca. 1944 in Australia.

raw, on the. Adj. and adv.: roughing it: Australian coll.: since ca. 1920. (Jean Devanney, *By Tropic Sea and Jungle*, 1944.)

raw chaw. A dram of spirituous liquor: low s.: ca. 1810–60. Captain Glascock, *Land Sharks and Sea Gulls*, 1838.

raw deal and **rough spin**. Unfair treatment: English, adopted ca. 1930 ex U.S.; Australian, dating since ca. 1910, and deriving ex games in which a coin or a disc is spun.

raw lobster.—2. (Gen. pl.) A sailor dressed in blue: ca. 1800–55. B. & L. Contrast **boiled lobster** (*Dict.*).

raw prawn. See **prawn, draw the raw,** above.

raw tea. Tea without milk or sugar: jocular coll.: since ca. 1925.

rawg. A waggon: Shelta: C. 18–20. B. & L.

rawhider. A conductor, a driver, hard on men or locomotives: Canadian railroadmen's (— 1931). Adopted from U.S. and perhaps ex 'a *rawhide* whip.'

rawniel or **runniel.** Beer: Shelta: C. 18–20. B. & L.

raws, the. Bare fists (cf. **raw 'uns** in *Dict.*).: coll.: from ca. 1895. In 1899, Clarence Rook says of the hooligan that 'He has usually done a bit of fighting with the gloves . . . But he is better with the raws, and is very bad to tackle in a street row.'

ray. An X-ray (photograph): medical coll.: since ca. 1905. (Dymphna Cusack, 1951.) Cf.:

rayed. X-rayed: hospital coll.: since ca. 1910.

raz, in the. In the nude: Australian: since the late 1940's. A jocular alteration of **raw, in the,** above.

razoo (p. 690). A farthing; any very small sum: Australian: from ca. 1920. W. S. Howard, *You're Telling Me!*, 1934, 'Haven't got a razoo left. Gave me last two bob to the wife': heard mainly in the negative phrases *I haven't a razoo* or . . . *a brass razoo*, for . . . no money at all, B., 1941.

razor. To slash (a person) with a razor: Glasgow lower-class coll., obviously destined to > S.E.: from ca. 1920. MacArthur & Long, 'There's been some hooligan who has razored poor Frank and very near done him in awthegither.'

razor-backs. 'Cattle that are lean and scraggy' (B., 1943): Australian coll.: late C. 19–20.—2. 'In the U.S. and, to a less extent, in Canada, a razorback is a pig, semi-wild and of no ascertainable ancestry' (Leechman): late C. 19–20. Both senses are occ. used in the singular.

razor gang, the. 'Economy men from Headquarters' (*Railway* 2nd): railwaymen's: since ca. 1930.

razor-grinder. See **scissors-grinder.**

***Razor King, the.** The Glasgow hooligans' and gangsters' name for one who, using as weapons a razor in each hand, is recognised as the head of a gang of hooligans: from ca. 1920. The 'hero' of MacArthur & Long's damning book is a 'razor king.'

razorridge. See 'Miscellanea'.

razz, n. A good talking-to, an harangue; esp. by a master to a boy: Eton: C. 20. Ex *raspberry.* (J. D. R. McConnell, *Eton: How It Works,* 1967 (p. 61).)

razz. To jeer at (someone): Australian: since ca. 1920. Baker. Pron. *rarze,* is a variant of the *raz* noted at **rarze(r)** on p. 687. (Lester.) 'To *razz*' occurs as early as ca. 1890, to judge by Jack Lawson—Lord Lawson—*A Man's Life,* 1932.—2. See **razzle.**

razz-ma-tazz. See 'Jive'. Perhaps as Franklyn, *Rhyming,* has suggested, it is rhyming s.—2. Nonsense or 'boloney'. See **jazz** above.

***razzle.** To steal: Australian c.: C. 20. Baker. Often shortened to *razz.*

razzo (p. 690). Usually applied to a red nose. For origin, see **rarzo** above.

razzo. 'At the Park'—Sedgeley Park School—'a thin slice of bread was a *razor*'—a thinned form of *razzor,* 'and slices cut lengthwise from a long loaf were splithers' (doubtless from *splinters*): ca. 1790–1870. Frank Roberts, article in *The Cottonian,* Autumn 1938.

re-bushed. 'Men's egotism applied to woman who is thought to be no longer of attractive physique: "She'd have to be rebushed—put a ham in and pull the bone out."' Noted about 1962' (Laurie Atkinson, Sept. 11, 1967): since ca. 1940, prob. originally among artificers in the R.A.F.

read.—3. V.t., 'to try to ascertain by the expression of a man's features what his intentions are', B. & L.: Stock Exchange: from ca. 1880.

read, have a. To read: coll.: late C. 19–20.

read and write, 1. Also n.: C. 20.

readers. Reading-glasses: coll.: since ca. 1925.

ready, n.—3. A swindle, a conspiracy: Aus.; C. 20. (B., 1959.) Oftener *ready-up.*

***ready, work a.** To effect a swindle: Australian c.: C. 20. B., 1942. Ex **ready-up** (*Dict.*).

***ready thick'un.** A sovereign (coin): c.: from ca. 1860.

ready to spit; foaming at the mouth. Upon the point of *urethrorrhœa ex libidine:* low: C. 20.—2. (Only *foaming . . .*) exceedingly angry: coll.: since ca. 1910.

ready-up, n.—2. A swindle: low Australian: C. 20. (B., 1943.)

ready up, v.—2. Hence, to produce or procure ready money: Australian: since ca. 1910. Baker. —3. To 'put someone wise' or 'tip off': Australian: since ca. 1912. (B., 1943.)

real, adj. 'The most basic of all basic beat-age words is *real.* This really covers everything. Whatever else they may be, all beat-agers are real. Everything they do, or think they do or not, is *real.* Everything they say is *real*' (Anderson): beatniks': since ca. 1958. Hence **really** below.

real Air Force, the. Flying personnel: the others': 1939 +. Jackson.

real cool. See **cool,** adj., 7, above.

real Mackay, the. See **Mackay . . .**

real money. A large sum, or large sums, of money as opposed to 'chicken feed': coll.: since ca. 1955. (A. B. Petch, April 1966.)

real nervous, dad; commoner, **'way out.** Adjectivally admirative: jazz-lovers': since ca. 1950. (*The Observer,* Sept. 16, 1956.) Perhaps ex 'It makes me real nervous [excited], dad' and ex ''way out in front of the rest'.

real turned on. Very 'high' (drug-exhilarated): beatniks': since ca. 1959. (Anderson.)

really. A beatnik, male or female: beatniks', hence among those on the fringe: since ca. 1959. The Andersons exemplify it four times on p. 2 of their witty and informative article. Ex **real** above.

really! You don't say so!; well I never! coll. tag: late C. 19–20.

Really Not a Sailor (p. 691). In l. 2, for 'Squadron' read 'Service'. The c.p. originated (1915) in the Royal Navy and > a Merchant Service expression only after April 1, 1918, the date on which the R.N.A.S. and the R.F.C. merged to form the R.A.F. (Wilfred Granville.)

reaper. A submarine: Naval: since ca. 1940. Ex the U-boats' 'reaping' of merchant vessels.

rear, rears, the (p. 691). Perhaps of military origin: a man 'taken short' is told to 'fall out to the *rear*'.

rec. See **wreck.**

rec, the (p. 691) goes back to at least ca. 1890, several reputable correspondents have assured me.

rec-space, the. 'The men's recreation space for games, etc.' (Granville): Naval coll.: C. 20.

recap. Recapitulation: schools' (late C. 19–20) and authors' (C. 20) and B.B.C. (since ca. 1938) coll.—2. A synonym of **retread** below: Australian: since ca. 1939. (B.P.)

recce, pron. and occ. written *recky*. Reconnaissance in gen., a reconnaissance in particular: Services: since ca. 1920: orig. coll., it was, by 1941 at latest, j. In the 1939–45 war every Army division had a Recce Battalion.—2. Hence, as v.i., to go on a reconnaissance, and as v.t., to reconnoitre: since ca. 1935 in Army and by at least as early as 1939 in the R.A.F.: coll. >, by 1942, j. —3. A reconnaissance 'plane: since ca. 1936: R.A.F. coll.>, by 1942, j. H. & P.

recco. A reconnaissance flight: R.A.F.: 1939 +. Jackson. Ex prec.

reccy. A variant spelling of *recce*.

receive what one gets. To receive only what one modestly expects; especially, to count on nothing until one gets it: c.p.: C. 20. (Patrick MacGill, *The Great Push*, 1916.)

receiver-general, 2 (p. 691). Much earlier in *Boxiana*, III, 1821.

recep. Reception by an audience: theatrical and music halls': late C. 19–20. '"Did you hear my little recep?" he cried ecstatically,' W. H. Lane Craufurd, *Murder to Music*, 1936.

reckon. To count as worth-while; to esteem: London's East End: since the late 1940's. Always negative, as 'I don't reckon him' = I don't think he's much good. (*The Evening News*, Nov. 12, 1957, article by Richard Herd; Norman.) Elliptical for '*reckon* to be worth much'.

reckon oneself. To be conceited: since mid-1940's. (Laurence Henderson, *With Intent*, 1968.) Ex '*reckon oneself* to be important or to be something'.

reckon up. To talk of, maliciously or even slanderously: non-aristocratic: from ca. 1870; ob. B. & L.

recliner; usually in pl. A Crown issue armchair: Naval officers': C. 20. Granville. By 'the Oxford *-er*' ex *recline*.

record!, change the; also put another record on! A c.p. addressed to a nagging spouse or to anyone else 'going on about something': C. 20. 'Heard as "For God's sake, put another record on, will you?"': A. B. Petch, April 1966.

Recs, the. The Records and Fingerprints Department: police coll.: C. 20.

Red, 1 and 2. See **Reds** below.

red, n.—3. Short for **red Ned** (*Dict.*): B., 1942. —4. The port side of a ship; it shows a red light; cf. *green*, the starboard side, which shows a green one: nautical coll.: late C. 19–20.—5. Gold: C. 20: orig. c.; by 1950, low s. Therefore cf. sense 1 on p. 691.

Sense 1 (p. 691) occurs in James Joyce, *Ulysses*, 1922.

red, in the. Having failed to make one's expenses: Canadian carnival s.: C. 20. *Red* indicates debit.—2. A general coll. phrase for 'in debt': British Commonwealth: since ca. 1920.

Its much less used complement, *in the black*, hardly antecedes 1945.

red, put in the. Bankrupt; penniless: trade and commerce: C. 20. *Red*, in book-keeping, indicates debt.

red 'Arry. A £10 note: Aus.: since ca. 1930. (B., 1959.)

red arse. A recruit: Guardsmen's: C. 20. Roger Grinstead, *They Dug a Hole*, 1946.

red Biddy (p. 692). The term soon spread: witness, e.g. Michael Harrison, *Reported Safe Arrival*, 1943.—2. Methylated spirit as a drink: c., esp. tramps': from ca. 1910. Also **jake** (*Dict.*).

red cap.—2. The penis: since ca. 1918.

red centre, the. The inland: Australian coll.: C. 20. Baker. Ex the red soil: see *passim* Archer Russell's *A Tramp Royal*, 1934.

red-currant jelly. (Not as n., but as adj. in the predicate.) 'He's red-currant jelly' is Country s., of ca. 1840–1900, applied to a tradesman or merchant that, retiring to the country, out-Counties the County. Usually, however, simply *currant jelly*. (A staple produce on the shop-keeper's shelves.)

red devils. Little tin-encased Italian hand-grenades: North Africa, British Army in: 1941–3. —2. (Or capitals.) 'Midland Compound Locomotives' (*Railway*, 3rd): railwaymen's: since ca. 1950 (?).

red eye. See **forty-rod.**

Red-Fed. 'A member of the ("Red") Federation of Labour, 1909' (Keith Sinclair, 1959): New Zealand coll.: 1909; then historical.

red flannel.—2. Collective for high-ranking officers: Army (not officers'): 1939–45. (Alan Moorehead, *African Trilogy*, 1944.) Ex the red bands on their hats and their red gorget patches. (P-G-R.)

red-herring, 1 (p. 692): earlier in John L. Gardner, *The Military Sketch-Book* (I, 30 and 312), 1827. Moe.

red herrings. Red-tabbed staff officers: Army: late C. 19–20.

red-hot poker. Penis: feminine: C. 19–20.

red-hot poker, wouldn't touch it with a. Indicative of extreme aversion: Australian coll.: C. 20. B., 1942.

red-hots, the. Trotting races: Australian rhyming s. (on 'the *trots*'): since ca. 1920. (B.P.)

red-ink.—2. Blood: pugilistic: ca. 1840–90. Augustus Mayhew, *Paved With Gold*, 1857.

red inside (allee) same as Queen Victoria. A c.p., used of—and reputedly by—dark-skinned races: late C. 19–20. I.e. a dark skin does not preclude moral merit.

red lead. Tomato juice: Royal Navy: since ca. 1925. Ex colour. Herrings in tomato sauce: Naval (lower-deck): C. 20. Granville.

Red Legs, the. The Melbourne Club football team: Melbournites': since ca. 1920. Also called *The Red Demons*. (B., 1943.)

Red Light News. See **Whore's Gazette.**

red lioner. Variant of **red liner** (*Dict.*). Augustus Mayhew, 1857.

red Lizzie (cf. **red Biddy**). 'About once a month he used to get drunk on Red Lisbon—a deadly and incalculable wine concocted of the squeezed-out scrapings of rotted port casks and laced with methylated spirits—a terrible drink . . ., which smites the higher centres as with a sandbag. It is otherwise known as Lunatic's Broth or Red

Lizzie,' Gerald Kersh, *I Got References*, 1939: low: since ca. 1930.

red lobsters. The original Metropolitan Police: Londoners': ca. 1830–60.

red mare. See **red steer.**

Red Mike. See 'Canadian'.

red Ned. Also in New Zealand. (B., 1941.)

red one.—2. A town where the show has made a large profit: circusmen's: C. 20. Contrast **bloomer,** 2.

red onion. A railroad eating-house: Canadian railroadmen's (— 1931). Rough—and smelly.

red pottage of Esau. 'Lentils cooked into a porridge-like mess' (A. B. Petch, Dec. 7, 1946): domestic: C. 20. Ex the Biblical Esau's 'mess of pottage'.

red rag, 1 (p. 692): earlier in Robert Dixon, *Canidia*, 1683.

red-ragger. A Communist: Australian: since ca. 1930. (Dymphna Cusack, *Southern Steel*, 1953.)

red recommend. 'A recommendation in red ink on a Service Certificate, much coveted by ambitious and zealous ratings,' Granville: Naval lower-deck coll.: C. 20.

red ribbon (*Dict.*) seems to have survived until ca. 1910 and, from ca. 1850, to have been c.

Red Shield, the. Generic for clubs, particular for a club, conducted by the Salvation Army: Services' coll.: 1939 +. H. & P. Ex the sign displayed.

***red shirt.** A back scarified with the cat-o'-nine-tails: Australian c.: ca. 1820–70. B., 1942.

red steer, the. A bush fire: Australian rural: late C. 19–20. Baker. Also *red mare*: B., 1943. 'Cf. the Standard German *der rote Hahn* (the red cockerel), meaning "fire", usually in a phrase translatable as "putting the red cock on someone's roof"' (H. R. Spencer).

red 'un.—2. A red-tipped match: low eating-houses': C. 20. Frank Jennings, *Tramping*, 1932.

Redbrick, generic for the provincial English (i.e. not **Oxbridge;** q.v. above; or London) universities and university colleges, founded before W.W. II; also adj., as in 'the *Redbrick* universities': journalistic coll., dating from the late 1940's and, by 1955, S.E.

redders. Red wine: Oxford undergraduates', since ca. 1920; then also, since ca. 1950, among the smart young set. (Gilderdale, 2.) By 'the Oxford-*er*'.

Reddy. An Italian: c., and low: C. 20. Prob. ex red Italian wine; yet cf. **Raddie.**

Redfern, get off at. To practise *coïtus interruptus:* Sydneyites': since ca. 1950. Redfern is a railway station immediately before Sydney Central. (B.P.)

reds.—3. Fleas: Australian: C. 20. B., 1942. —4. Full-dress uniform: Army coll.: ca. 1860–1914. (S. E. Burrow, *Friend or Foe*, 1912.)

Reds, the. The Redemptorists: Catholics', esp. in Australia: C. 20.—2. The Russians: since 1917 or 1918.

reduce. To take (someone) down a peg: Shrewsbury: 1938 +. Marples.

reef.—2. Hence, simply to steal: Australian: C. 20. Lawson Glassop, *We Were the Rats*, 1944.

reef it off in lumps. ''To extract large sums of money from someone' (B., 1959): Aus.: since ca. 1920. An elaboration of:—

reef off. To take (money) from (a person):

Australian racing: since ca. 1910. (Lawson Glassop, 1949.) Cf. preceding.

reefer. Sense 1 (p. 693) occurs in Alfred Burton, *Johnny Newcome*, 1818.—2. 'A pickpocket's accomplice' (Baker): Australian c.: since ca. 1910. Ex *reef* (*Dict.*).—3. A cigarette drugged with marihuana: c.: adopted ex U.S. ca. 1935.—4. A *refrigerator* car: Canadian, esp. railroadmen's (— 1931). Adopted from U.S.—5. (Or **Reefer,**) An inhabitant of—or one who is familiar with— the Great Barrier Reef: Australian coll.: since ca. 1925. (Jean Devanney, *Travels in North Queensland*, 1951.)

reefer, have a. To smoke a drugged cigarette, esp. marijuana: since the late 1930's. Cf. **reefer,** 3.

reeler; esp. *cop a reeler*, to get drunk: low: since ca. 1920. James Curtis, *You're in the Racket Too*, 1937.

reely. Tipsy: coll. (— 1933); not at all common. (William Juniper, *The True Drunkard's Delight*, 1933.)

Reemy or **Reemee.** The Royal Electrical and Mechanical Engineers (formed in 1942): Services' (esp. Army) coll. of 1942–3, then j. Ex the initials *R.E.M.E.* Also the *R*oyal *C*anadian *E*lectrical and *M*echanical *E*ngineers: Canadian coll. > j. 'In spite of the *C*' (Leechman).

***reesbin** more prob. comes direct ex Shelta.

ref, n.—4. A refectory: mostly religious Orders': mid-C. 19–20.

ref, v. To referee (a match): coll C. 20. Ex the n., 2.

refained or **refayned.** Excessively refined and genteel: cultured coll.: since ca. 1920. Ex a 'refained' pronunciation of *refined*.

refec. Refectory: Birmingham undergraduates' (— 1940). Marples, 2.

reffo. A refugee from Europe: Australian: 1939 +. B., 1942. Cf. the American *refujew*, refugee Jew.

refill, have a. To have an inflation, in the artificial-pneumothorax treatment of T.B.: patients': since ca. 1930. Cf. **have a pneumo.**

Reg. A senior cadet: Sandhurst: from ca. 1860. Major A. Mockler-Ferryman, *Annals of Sandhurst*, 1900. Opp. **John,** a junior; ex *Reginald* with pun on L. *rex*, a king.

reg, n. A stickler for discipline: Army: C. 20. P-G-R.—2. See **regs.**

reg., adj. Regular; according to regulations: Guardsmen's: since ca. 1920.

***reg rooker.** A fine fellow: South African c.: C. 20. (C. P. Wittstock, May 23, 1946.) See **rooker;** with *reg*, cf. Dutch *regaal*, 'royal'.

regent. 'Half a sovereign' (coin): ca. 1820–60. *Sinks*, 1848. By a not despicable pun.

Reggie. The *Regimental* Sergeant Major: since ca. 1919. 'Watch it!, here comes Reggie.' Not in his hearing. For a fine 'portrait' of an R.S.M., see Hugh Kimber, *Prelude to Calvary*, 1938.

reggie. A *registered* customer: civilians': 1940 +. *The New Statesman*, Aug. 30, 1941.

reggie or **reggy** (hard *g*'s), adj. Regimental; intensively, *dead reggie*: R.A.F.: since ca. 1930.

regiment, chum?—how long have you been in this. How long have *you* been in the Navy?: Naval (lower-deck) c.p.: C. 20. Granville.

regimental or **regulation.** A 'mess'; a signal failure: Londoners': from 1919. 'Oh, I made a regimental [or a regulation] of the whole bloody thing.' Ex **regimental, 1**: see *Dict.* Short for *regimental (or regulation) fuck-up*: C. 20.

regimental fire. A volley of cheers: military: from ca. 1860. B. & L. rightly confine it to some particular but unspecified regiment.

region of rejoicing, the. 'Joy attendant upon success in the schools,' *Spy*, 1825: Oxford University: ca. 1815–60.

[Regional names current in the first quarter of the C. 18, as represented by Ned Ward, are *Bog-Lander* and *Teague*, both in 1703; *Sawney* in 1709; *Taffy* in 1714; *Tike* in 1703; and *Butter-Box*, a Dutchman, in 1700. Matthews.]

Register (or **r-**). See 'Tavern terms', § 5.

register, out of. See **out of register.**

rego (soft *g*). Registration of a motor vehicle: Australian: since ca. 1945. 'The rego is up'—expired—'next month.' (B.P.)

regs. Regulations, as in *King's Regs*: Services, orig. and mainly Army: since ca. 1870.

regular, n.—3. One who quits a pleasure party at 11 or 12 at night: ca. 1830–65. *Sinks*, 1848. With a sneer—or perhaps a laugh—at regular, sober habits.

regular nuisances or, oftener, **pests.** Time-expired Regular Army men: Kitchener's Army: W.W. I. 'Many of these ex-regulars worked as Base wallahs or on lines of communication' and, among non-regulars, tended to throw their weight about. A pun on *Regular* Army and *regular*, thoroughgoing. (A. B. Petch, May 1966.)

regular tradesman. Anyone thoroughly understanding his business or occupation: proletarian coll.: mid-C. 19–20; ob. B. & L.

regulation. See **regimental** above.

rehab. A rehabilitation ward or department in a hospital: since ca. 1945. Ex the official abbreviation *rehab.*—2. A rehabilitation loan: New Zealand servicemen's: since ca. 1944. Slatter, 'Rehab was the caper, you jokers'.

reign, n.—2. The period during which the spinner operates: Australian two-up players': C. 20. (B., 1953.)

relation. A pawnbroker: Londoners': ca. 1845–1900. Mayhew, II, 1851. Suggested by synonymous **uncle** (*Dict.*).

relish all waters. See 'Tavern terms', § 2.

remember a name and I always forget a face, I never. 'A c.p. used when people are discussing their inability to remember names and faces' (B.P.): Australian: since the late 1940's. Ex 'I never remember a name but I always remember a face'.

remember Pearl Harbour!, often preceded by *don't panic* (with jocular variant *don't picnic*): the Australian World War II equivalent of **remember Belgium!** (p. 694). B.P.

remember the girl who went out to buy a knick-knack and came back with a titbit. A low-punning Canadian c.p. of ca. 1935–55.

remish. Remission (of sentence): prisons': since ca. 1920. Norman.

remit. A remittance (dispatch) of money: Australian: late C. 19–20. (W. Sorley Brown, *The Life and Genius of T. W. H. Crosland*, 1928; cited as a word often used by Phil May, who died in 1903.)

*remount; gen. pl. A woman for export as a harlot, esp. to the Argentine: white-slave traffickers' c.: C. 20. (A. Londres, *The Road to*

Buenos Ayres, 1928.) Hence *on remount service*, (of a white-slaver) engaged in procuring fresh women.

rent.—4. (Also *renting*.) Blackmail: since ca. 1920; by 1965, slightly ob. (Compton Mackenzie, *Thin Ice*, 1956.)—5. See **gay** above. A male always, or nearly always, charging for his homosexual services: homosexual: since ca. 1930 (? much earlier). He earns his rent in this way. Hence, and usu., and adj., as in 'Be careful of that one, he's rent' (he will ask payment). Contrast **trade.**

rent guardsman. A soldier—hence, any other man—consenting to homosexual practices for money: 'gay' society: since ca. 1950.

renter. One who, not a prostitute (female or male), sells casual sexual or homosexual favours for money or presents: low life: since ca. 1945. Cf. **rent**, 5, above. A much earlier date is provided by Max Beerbohm in a letter he wrote ca. 1895: see Lord David Cecil, *Max*, 1964, p. 122. (Mr C. E. Kemp.)

reo. Usually in pl. *reos*, reinforcements: Australian soldiers': 1939 +. Lawson Glassop, *We Were the Rats*, 1944. By abridgement and an unusual variety of conflation.

rep.—6. A politician, athlete, cricketer representing a State: Australian: since ca. 1920. B., 1942.—7. A reprimand: Regular Army (esp. N.C.O.s): C. 20. Gerald Kersh. *They Die with Their Boots Clean*, 1941. Cf. **severe.**—8. (Cf. 6) A trade-union representative: trade-unionists': since ca. 1920. (Vance Palmer, *Golconda*, 1948.)

repat, n. and **adj.** Repatriate, repatriation; repatriated: coll.: since ca. 1941. Brickhill & Norton, *Escape to Danger*, 1946, 'Typical of the repat boys was "Chuck" Lock.'

repeaters, the. (Of food) 'It gives me the repeaters': Australian coll.: C. 20. (Ruth Park, 1950.)

replace and **displace** are frequently confused. 'From the Post-Bag', *The Observer*, Sept. 20, 1936, contained this: 'May I call attention to a regrettable misuse of English perpetrated—of all places! —at the Journalists' Congress? The point under discussion was pressure alleged to be brought to bear on editors, with the result that "in more than one instance the correspondents have been replaced." To replace means, and can only mean, to put back in its place. Obviously the meaning was intended to be the opposite—to displace.— Stephen Tone, *Coventry*.'

report, in the. On the report (or charge) sheet: Navy coll.: C. 20. (P-G-R.)

res. A restaurant; as in *a British res*, one of the British Restaurants: since ca. 1945. (Josephine Bell, *The Summer School Mystery*, 1950.)

rescrub. To do (a job) over again: Naval: C. 20. Granville.

resin. 'Liquor given to musicians at a party' (B., 1942): Australian: C. 20. Cf.:

resin up (p. 695). Less vaguely: Ex resining a fiddle-bow.

Resistance, the. Harley Street: taxi-drivers': 1948. Ex the medical profession's opposition to the Aneurin Bevan health-plan. On the analogy of *La Résistance*, the Resistance Movement in France (1940–4).

Cf. *the Occupied Territory*, Bayswater (London): taxi-drivers': 1947–9. Ex the large number of foreigners there, and on *enemy-occupied territory*.

Both terms were recorded by *The Evening News* of March 19, 1948.—2. That part of West Hampstead which contains numerous Germans, whether residents or lodgers: since late 1930's, by which time many Germans had removed themselves from a 'Hitlerized' Germany they deplored.

reso. A residential, i.e. a boarding-house for permanent guests: Australian: since ca. 1950. (B.P.) *Res*idential + the ubiquitous Australian s. suffix -o.

rest, n.—2. A year's imprisonment: Australian c.: C. 20. Baker. Hence *resting*, (a person) 'in gaol'.

rest one's eyes. To have a short sleep: semi-jocular, usually evasive, coll.: C. 20. A clerk surprised sleeping, 'Sorry! I was just resting my eyes.' (A. B. Petch, March 1966.)

resurrection. See **resurrection-pie** (*Dict.*).

retired gremlin. It wears a yellow hat and a fancy waistcoat, and behaves in a Blimpish manner: R.A.F.: 1940–5. (P-G-R.)

retired to stud. (Of a woman who has) married: Australian jocular: since late 1940's. (B.P.)

retread (or **re-tread**). A 1914–18 soldier serving in 1939–45: Australian: since 1939. (B., 1943.) —2. A retired schoolteacher still teaching: Australian: since ca. 1950. (B.P.)

Retreat from Moscow, the. The exodus from Britain to Eire, in late 1946 and throughout 1947–8, in order to escape ruinous taxation, short rations and general totalitarianism. First used in Eire in March or April 1947, it 'caught on' in Britain on or about May 12th (1947). With an allusion to Napoleon's retreat in 1812 and to Russia's be-dazzlement of British Socialists.

return the other cheek. Instead of 'turning the other cheek' to return—or give—the other 'cheek' or impudence: since ca. 1955. (A. B. Petch, March 1966.)

Rev. Form of address to a clergyman: non-aristocratic, non-educated: C. 20. Richard Llewellyn, *None But the Lonely Heart*, 1943.

rev, v.—2. To pray: Cranbrook School: C. 20. Ex '*reverence*'?

reversed ear. That 'naval disease' which is caused by wearing 'dry' hoods, the pressure inside exceeding the pressure outside: skin divers': since ca. 1950. (Granville.)

revo. Revolution: Australian: since ca. 1945. (B., 1953.)

revolush, v.i. To revolt: South Seas lingua franca: mid C. 19–20. (*South Sea Bubbles*, by the Earl and the Doctor, 1872.) Ex *revolution*.

revved(-)up, often preceded by *all*. Very much excited; very tense: since ca. 1960. The opposite of *relaxed* (A. B. Petch, April 1966.) Of machines, esp. motor cars and bicycles.

reward. 'Dogs' or hounds' supper': kennels' s.: C. 19–20. B. & L. Ex S.E. sense, entrails given to hounds imm. after the kill.

r'ghoglin or **gogh'leen.** To laugh: Shelta: C. 18–20. B. & L.

rhetorician. See 'Tavern terms', § 3, *d*.

rheumatise. See **rheumatiz** (*Dict.*).

rhino, sense 1 (p. 693), 'money'. In Malaya, long ago, the rhinoceros was almost 'worth its weight in gold' to those opportunists who converted every part of a slain rhinoceros into aphrodisiacs and sold packets at very high prices, to Chinese mandarins, who placed great faith in them. —4. An outboard-engined raft: Combined Operations: June 1944.

rhino-arse. A large, long, tough bread roll having cheese in the middle and issued on O.T.C. field days: Rugby School: since ca. 1910.

rhodo. A C. 20 variant of **rhody** (p. 696), rhododendron.

rhubarb. Sense 1 (p. 696) perhaps derives from the illiterate pronunciation *rhubarb*, a 'sub' (or loan).—2. Genitals, male or, occ., female: low: late C. 19–20. E.g. 'How's your rhubarb, missis?' or 'How's your rhubarb coming up, Bill?'—3. See next entry.—4. A rumpus, a 'row'; a loud, confused noise; noises off, esp. those of the mob: theatrical: late C. 19–20. Alexander McQueen, an Englishman long resident in the United States, writes thus (on Aug. 31, 1953):

'Here's a genuine one that I've never seen recorded anywhere; I've been looking for it for half a century! It is the word "rhubarb" used as a theatrical term.

'When I was a boy (14–17 years old) I studied dramatic art under a pupil of the famous old actor Hermann Vezin. Although Vezin[1] had been born in Pennsylvania, he flourished in London for years, and studied and worked under Charles Kean, c. 1852. Kean had received traditions from other actors, and they from others, all the way back to Davenant and Shakespeare. They all took a pride in passing down the genuine Shakespearian acting traditions and "business". One of these was to do with "rhubarbing". When a few actors gathered backstage and represented the "noise without" made by a mob, they intoned the sonorous word "rhubarb". The action was called "rhubarbing", the actors "rhubarbers". (Try the word yourself; it really DOES produce an effect if only two or three work at it.)

'I have only met one old-time actor in the United States who knew about this custom; and he was from England.'

'In *Holy Deadlock*, 1934, Sir Alan Herbert describes a stage rehearsal with the chorus "rushing about excitedly and muttering 'Rhubarb'"' (Ramsey Spencer).

rhubarb (pill). A hill: rhyming: late C. 19–20.

rhyme if you take it in time, a. See **that's a rhyme . . .**

Rhyming and Alliterative Nicknames, Australian.

'Most of these are inevitables,' says Barry Prentice, who has—in June 1963—supplied the ensuing list. Several of them come from the U.S. and are known also in the other Dominions and in Britain.

Den(n)is the Menace. Ex U.S.

Even Stephen (or *Steven*). Ex U.S. *even-Steven*, evenly or fairly.

Flo the Chro. See **chro** (ex **chromo**) above.

Giggling Gertie.

Hairy Mary.

Harriet the Chariot. See separate entry.

Harry the Horse. Ex the character created by Damon Runyan.

Merv the Perv. Cf. **perv** and **perve** and **pervy** above.

Myrtle the Turtle. See separate entry. Occ. invested with a Brooklyn pronunciation: *Moitle the Toitle.*

Nola the Bowler. Ex 'Nola Dekyvere, the social

---

[1] Hermann Vezin (1829–1910).

leader of Sydney' (B.P.) But † by end of 1967, B.P. tells me.

Peter the Poof.
Phil the Dill. Cf. **dill** above.
Roger the Lodger.
Slapsie Maxie. Ex Maxie Rosenbloom.
Terry the Ferry.
Tizzie Lizzie. Cf. **tizzy** below.

Rhyming Slang: to the entry on p. 669, add this, 'It is erroneous to affirm—as so many "Philologists" do—that the slang-rhyme is always shortened to its initial element. . . . "Army" is always "Kate Carney" and "dinner" "Lilley and Skinner",' Michael Harrison, letter of Jan. 4, 1947.

The entire question of rhyming s. has, for the first time, been adequately treated by Julian Franklyn in *Rhyming Slang*, 1960: a history and a study, a glossary and even a 'reverse' glossary. This book covers Great Britain and Ireland, Australia and the U.S. (*A Dictionary of R.S.*)

rib, v. To make fun of; pull someone's leg: Cockney and Canadian since ca. 1925. Michael Harrison, *Reported Safe Arrival*, 1943.—2. To swindle: Australian c.: since ca. 1930. B. 1942.

ribbing, n., corresponds to **rib**, v., esp. in sense 1.

***ribby** (p. 696). Earlier in George Ingram, *Cockney Cavalcade*, 1935. By 1939, low London s. —2. Hence, (of things) inferior; (of conditions) unsatisfactory: mostly lower-class London: since ca. 1939.

ribs, on the.—3. See 'Hauliers' Slang'.

ribuck! (p. 696): 'From the Hebrew Reivach, meaning profit or good business,' A. Abrahams in *The Observer*, Sept. 25, 1938.

Rice Corps. Royal Indian Army Service Corps: 1939–45. Any of its units tended to be called a *ghee factory*, because of their predilection for *ghee* (Indian butter).

rice-pudding, he couldn't knock the skin off a. A contemptuous c.p.: C. 20.

rich friend is 'an universal phrase with the girls of the town for "their keepers"', Pierce Egan, *Life in London*, 1821: euphemistic coll.: ca. 1805–70.

Richard, have had the. (Of persons) to have been dismissed; (of things) to have been superseded; to be 'all washed up' or finished: Australian: since ca. 1930. Cf. **Richard, get the**, on p. 696.

Richard the Third.—2. A word: rhyming: C. 20 —3. A turd: rhyming s.: late C. 19–20.—4. A girl: rhyming s. (on synonymous *bird*): since ca. 1920. Often shortened to *Richard.*—5. A bad reception, a hissing: theatrical rhyming s. (on *bird*, n., 5: p. 54): C. 20. (Paul Tempest, *Lag's Lexicon*, 1950.)

rick, adj. Spurious: low racing: since ca. 1950. 'If you are standing near a bookie's joint, undecided, and a merchant dashes in and places a bet, such as "Seventy pounds to forty. On top," don't take a blind bit of notice. The give-away is the "On top". It's a rick bet. It don't mean nothing. It don't even go in the book. It's sole object is to push or goad you into making your bet': *The Sunday Telegraph*, May 7, 1967, Anon., 'A punter's guide to the bookie's secret lingo.' Ex *rick*, a cheapjack's, hence a mock-auctioneer's, accomplice whose job it is to boost sales.

rick, v. To remove one testicle of (usually a horse): Australian: C. 20. Ex S.E. *rick*, to wrench or sprain. 'That horse was ricked and Sammy Hall' = It was rendered unitesticular. *Sammy Hall* is Cockney and Australian (esp. Sydney rhyming s. on *ball*, testicle, the reference being to a song very popular in mid-C. 19 and still heard occasionally 'where men are men'. (Edwin Morrisby, letter of Aug. 30, 1958.)

rick-rack. A policeman's whistle: Manchester children's: ca. 1860–80. Jerome Caminada, *Detective*, II, 1901. Echoic.

ricket. A mistake: low (? originally c.): since ca. 1930. 'You've made a bit of a ricket' (Norman). Used in the B.B.C.'s account of the Great Train Robbery Trial, Aug. 23, 1963.

Ricky. Rickmansworth (Hertfordshire): Hertfordshiremen's: from ca. 1920.

ricky. A ricochet; to ricochet: Army: since ca. 1925. (P-G-R.) Cf. *ricko* on p. 696.

ricky-tick. See 'Jive'.

ride, find a. To be given a car to drive in a race: motor-racing s.: from ca. 1925. (Peter Chamberlain.)

ride below the crupper. See **crupper, ride below the.**

ride on the cushions. 'Engine men travelling as passengers' (*Railway*): railwaymen's: since ca. 1920. Cf. Canadian *ride the cushions*, q.v. at **ride plush** below.

ride one's stripes or **tapes.** (Of an N.C.O.) to be over-strict or officious: Army: C. 20.

ride out. To depart: London teenagers': ca. 1957–9. (Gilderdale.)

ride plush. To travel illicitly free on a train: Australian: adopted, ca. 1920, from U.S. B., 1942. Cf. the Canadian hoboes' *ride the cushions*: late C. 19–20. (Leechman.)

ride shotgun. 'An extraordinary survival of the stage-coach days. When gold or other valuables were carried, or a hold-up apprehended, a man, armed with a shotgun, rode on top of the coach with the driver. In the speech of the period, this man "rode shotgun". It is still [1963] used, sometimes in the sense of "Quis custodiet . . .?"' Douglas Leechman. Only is the derivative sense eligible, and then as a coll.

ride the dead horse. See **dead horse** and **work a dead horse.**

ride up a gumtree or **go up a tree.** To fall off one's horse: Australian: since ca. 1910. (B., *Australia Speaks*, 1953.)

riders. A synonym of **jockey sticks!** Australian shearers': since ca. 1910. B., 1942. By a pun.

ridge, n. By 1940 it was general Australian s.

***ridge**, adj. Good; valuable: Australian c.: late C. 19–20. Ex *ridge*, gold.—2. Hence, genuine: c.: since ca. 1930; becoming, ca. 1945, low sporting s.: in Australia. Lawson Glassop, *Lucky Palmer*, 1949.

ridgy-didge. Honest; genuine: Australian: since ca. 1938. (B., *Australia Speaks*, 1953.) Ex preceding. Also *ridgey-dig.*

ridgy-dite. All right; trustworthy: Australian low rhyming s.: since ca. 1925. (Kylie Tennant, *The Joyful Condemned*, 1953.)

riding his low horse. A jocular c.p., referring to a tipsy, or a half-tipsy, fool either boasting or making a fool of himself: since ca. 1930. Not very common. (A. B. Petch, May 1966.)

Riff Raff, the. The R.A.F.: 1930 +. Partridge, 1945, 'A jocular—sometimes a contemptuous—elaboration of *Raff*.'

riffs. See 'Canadian'.

rift. Energy, speed; esp. *get a rift on*, to move or work quickly, energetically: Guards Regiments': since ca. 1920. Gerald Kersh, *They Die with Their Boots Clean*, 1941. Perhaps a blend of *rush + shift*.

rig, run a (p. 697). The phrase *run one's rigs* occurs in *The Port Folio* of June 26, 1802, at p. 193. Moe.

rig-of-the-day, the. The Service dress to be worn on the day concerned: Naval coll.: since ca. 1880. (P-G-R.)

rigger.—5. 'A quart of draught beer in a square-faced gin bottle' (B., 1942): Australian: since ca. 1918.

rigger mortis. 'A good-for-nothing airman' (Jackson): R.A.F.: since ca. 1938. Ex the pre-1939 official *rigger* (now flight mechanic 'A'), with a pun on *rigor mortis*: as Jackson neatly puts it, 'a dead type' (dead above the ears).

riggers. Clothes made to look like new: low: ca. 1820–80. *Sessions*, Oct. 1840 (p. 1044). Ex **rig**, v., 2, with pun on **rig**, n., 5.

right, adj.—3. Safe: Australian coll.: C. 20. (Vince Kelly, *The Shadow*, 1955.) Cf. the *right*, all entries on p. 698.

right, she's. That, or it, is satisfactory; it's all right (= don't mention it): Australian coll.: since ca. 1925. (Culotta.) Cf. **she** below.

right bastard, a. A thoroughly mean-spirited, bloody-minded man: coll., mostly Naval: since ca. 1925.

right cool fish. 'One who is not particular what he says or does,' *Spy*, 1825: Eton: ca. 1810–90.

right down, adv. Wholly, quite: coll.: Jan. 1835, *Sessions*, 'I was *right down* certain that the money was bad'; ob. by 1920.

right drill. See **drill, the.**

right-(h)o.—2. That's enough! Break it down!' (B., 1959): Aus.: since ca. 1920. Ex sense 1 on p. 698.

right into one's barrel. Precisely what one needs or desires: Australian: C. 20. B., 1942.

right man. 'The workman who makes the right forepart, and finishes the coat': tailors' coll.: mid-C. 19–20. B. & L.

right oil, the. Correct information: Australian: since ca. 1920. Baker. A variant of 'the dinkum oil'.

right up one's alley (see **alley**)—**street** (see **street . . .**, p. 838, end). Intensives of **up . . .**

righteous. An adj. applied, in the 1920's and early 1930's, by musicians to good jazz and to those who recognised it: Canadian (ex U.S.). 'A good hot chorus would be greeted with cries—from other members of the band—of "Righteous, brother! Righteous!"' (Professor F. E. L. Priestley, in letter dated Dec. 20, 1959.)

*rights, catch (bang) to. To catch (a person) doing something he ought not to do: c.: from ca. 1860. Cf. **rights, be to** in *Dict.*

righty-o. Right-o: since ca. 1905; by 1960, ob.

rigid, adv. Only in *bind rigid*: see **bind.** Substitution for 'to (bind) *stiff*'. Whence:

rigid bind. One who bores you stiff: R.A.F.: since ca. 1938. H. & P.

*rim. To bugger (a woman): c.: C. 20. Also **bottle**, likewise v.t. Both, brutally anatomical.

rimp. To sprint; a sprint, a turn of speed:

Christ's Hospital: late C. 19–20. Marples, 'From the Homeric adverb *rimpha*, swiftly.'

ring, n.—5. See **rings.**—6. Anus (also *ring-piece*): low: late C. 19–20. Hence, *ring-snatcher, snatching* sodomite, sodomy: C. 20.

ring, lose one's. To lose one's virginity: coll.: C. 19–20. Cf. *ring*, n., 1 (p. 699), and *ring, cracked in the* (ibid.).

ring a bell; ring the bell. 'That rings a bell': That brings something to mind; that sounds familiar: coll.: adopted, ca. 1925, from U.S. and derived earlier ex the striking of a clock or ex: 2. *To ring the bell*: 'to hit the target; to hit the nail on the head; to win an argument by proving one's statement,' H. & P.: Services' coll.: since ca. 1920. Ex the fairground game.

ring-chaser. An officer seeking promotion: R.A.F., mostly officers': 1939–45. (P-G-R.)

ring-conscious. (Of an officer) manifestly conscious of recent promotion; also, of an officer excessively officious: R.A.F. coll.: since ca. 1925. Cf. **rings.**

ring-dang-do. A spree: Australian: since late 1940's. A. M. Harris, *The Tall Man*, 1958 (events of 1953), 'They've earned a bit of a ring-dang-do'.

ring-in. A horse, a dog, etc., entered for a contest either under a false name or 'in disguise': Australian sporting: C. 20. B., 1942. Ex **ring in**, v. (p. 699).—2. A stacked pack of cards: Australian: since ca. 1910. (B., 1953.)

ring in a gray (or **grey**) or **ring in the knob** (or **nob**). 'To substitute a double-tailed penny for a genuine coin' (B., 1943): Australian two-up players': C. 20.

ring-neck. A jackaroo: Aus. rural: C. 20. (B., 1959.)

ring of roses. See **blue fever.**

ring one's tail. To cry quits; to give in: Australian: C. 20. Baker.

ring-tail.—2. A coward: Australian: C. 20. Baker. Ex prec. phrase. It also has the gen. sense 'a novice': Canadian: late C. 19–20, ex U.S. (Niven.)

ring the bell. To render a girl pregnant: since ca. 1910.—2. See **ring a bell, 2.**—3. To bring on an orgasm in one's female partner: since ca. 1920.

ring-twitch or **-twitter.** See **twittering ring-piece.**

ringer.—4. A crowbar: railwaymen's: C. 20. (*Railway*, 3rd.) Ex the ringing noise it emits on contact with metal.

ringer, half, Pilot Officer; **one ringer**, Flying-Officer; **three ringer**, Wing-Commander; **two ringer**, Flight-Lieutenant; **two-and-a-half ringer**, Squadron-Leader: Air Force coll.: 1919 +. Jackson. An Air Force officer's rank is denoted by rings on the cuff, not by stripes on the arm, nor by stars and what-have-you on the shoulder.—2. In the Navy *two-ringer* is 'lower-deckese' for Lieutenant: C. 20. Granville.

ringerangeroo. The female pudend: feminine: since ca. 1930. Origin ? Mr Ramsey Spencer tentatively suggests an origin ex **ring**, 1, on p. 699 + **ranger**, 1, on p. 686 + an ecstatic *oo*, the whole perhaps influenced by the simple game of 'ring-a-ring-o' roses'.

ringest, adj. Best: Australian teenage surfers': since ca. 1962; by 1966, ob. (B.P.)

ringie (p. 700). See also **boxer.**—2. The 'ringer'

or fastest shearer in a gang or team: N.Z.: C. 20. *Straight Furrow*, Feb. 21, 1968.

ringing, n. Milling-about of cattle: Australian rural coll.: late C. 19–20. (B., 1943.)

ringing the horse-shoes. 'A welcome to a man who has been out boozing' (B. & L.): tailors': mid-C. 19–20.

ringmaster. A Squadron Commander (function, not rank): R.A.F.: since ca. 1937. Jackson. Ex the circus ring.—2. A yardmaster: Canadian railroadmen's (– 1931). Humorous.

rings. 'Abbreviated reference to an Officer's rank, denoted in the Navy and R.A.F. by the number of rings on his sleeve,' H. & P.: since ca. 1890 in the Navy and since 1918 in the R.A.F.: coll. >, by 1930 at latest, j.

rings round, run (p. 700). Also . . . *around*.

rino is merely Ned Ward's spelling (1700) of **rhino.**

Rio Tinto, the. The 'Glasgow to Carlisle parcels train' (*Railway*, 3rd): since ca. 1950. Presumably ex the Portuguese or the Spanish town so named.

riot. A person, an incident, or a thing that is very amusing or very laughable: upper classes': from ca. 1931. E.g. 'That girl's a riot!'

Riot Act (to), read the.—2. To read the Fire Arms Act to prisoners about to be discharged: prisons': since ca. 1920. (Norman.)

riot good time, have—or **be having**—**a.** To have a riotously good time: since ca. 1950. (A.B. Petch, March 1966.) Cf. **riot** above. *Riot good time* is also a pun on *right good time*, a thoroughly good time.

rip, n.—4. A reproof indicated by a master's tearing of work shown up to him: Eton: C. 20. He tears the sheet or sheets of paper. (J. D. R. McConnell, *Eton: How It Works*, 1967, pp. 82–3; with synonym *tear-over*.)—5. 'A coarse ill-conditioned woman with a bad tongue' (P. W. Joyce, *English . . . in Ireland*, 1910): Anglo-Irish coll.: mid C. 19–20. Perhaps ex sense 1 on p. 700.

rip, v. To annoy intensely; to disgust: Australian: since ca. 1921. Lawson Glassop, *We Were the Rats*, 1944.

rip hell out of. To defeat severely (in a fight); to reproach, or reprove, bitterly: Australian: C. 20. B., 1942.

rip into. To attack, to fight, (someone) with one's fists: Australian: late C. 19–20. Baker.— 2. To defeat utterly in a fight; hence, to reprimand or reprove severely or bitterly: Australian coll.: since ca. 1910. (B., 1943.)

rip-rap, the; also 'to **rip-rap**'. A borrowing of, to borrow, money: rhyming s. (on *tap*): since ca. 1935. Franklyn 2nd.

rip-snorter. Anything exceptionally good; an eccentric or very entertaining person: Australian: since ca. 1910. Baker. Adopted from U.S.

rip-track, the. The repair-shops for cars (carriages): Canadian railwaymen's (– 1920).

ripe.—2. Complete, thoroughgoing, unmitigated; esp. 'a *ripe bastard*': Services: since ca. 1920. (P-G-R.)

ripped. With fly-buttons undone: C. 20. I.e. ripped open.

ripping, adj., 1 (p. 700): by 1930, slightly—by 1945, very—ob.; and by 1966 branding a user as antediluvian. Cf. the quotation at **top-hole** below.

rise, n. Sense 3 (p. 700) was current at Eton before 1880. An Eton Boy, *A Day of My Life*,

(before) 1880. (Dr Niels Haislund.)—4. A disturbance or commotion: low ca. 1840–70. *Sinks*, 1848.

rise, get a. To experience an erection: coll.: late C. 19–20.—2. To cause someone to 'bite': coll.: late C. 19–20. Ex angling.

rise and shine was, ca. 1919, adopted by the R.A.F.—esp. by its N.C.O. regulars. (Sergeant G. Emanuel, letter of March 29, 1945.)—2. Hence, jocularly applied to, or used by, father calling *son* in morning: 1945 +.—3. In the game of House: 49. Lewis Hastings, *Dragons Are Extra*, 1947.

rise in the world, give (someone) **a.** To kick in the behind: Australian: since ca. 1925. Baker.

rise to the occasion. To have an erection when desirable or suitable: raffish: since ca. 1920.

risk, take a. To risk venereal infection: euphemistic coll.: mid-C. 19–20.

risley. See **buffer**, 1, on p. 102 and above. In vaudeville a *risley* is 'a performance in which a man lies on his back on a special couch and juggles a boy or a small person with his feet' (Leechman): C. 20.

ritzy. Rich; stylish, fashionable: adopted ca. 1935 from U.S. James Curtis, *You're in the Racket Too*, 1937, 'Ritzy-looking dames with dogs.' Ex the various Ritz hotels in the great capitals, esp. that in London. (See my *Name into Word*.)

ritzy tart. Any upper- or middle-class woman or girl, esp. if she dresses well and speaks well: since ca. 1945. (Paul Tempest, *Lag's Lexicon*, 1950.)

river. 'An accidental effect produced in a page of type, when spaces occur in succeeding lines in such a way as to lie almost above each other, thus forming long thin lines (rivers), more easily observed when the page is held nearly level: printers' and publishers': from about 1910' (Leechman).

River Lea (p. 700). By 1959, sense (1) was ob.; sense (2), †. (Franklyn, *Rhyming*.)

***river ooze** or **River Ouse, the;** usu. simply **the river.** Strong drink: c.: since ca. 1910; by ca. 1950, also low s. (Robin Cook, 1962.) Rhyming on *booze*.

Riverina. A shilling: Australian rhyming s. (on *deaner*): since ca. 1920. (B., 1943.)

riveting. Revetting: mostly sol.: since ca. 1914.

rivets, 'money' (p. 701): goes back to ca. 1840. *Sinks*, 1848.

roach. A cockroach: Australian and New Zealand coll.: late C. 19–20. (B.P.)

road, on the. Out of work: Australian coll.: C. 20. B., 1942. Cf. **road, get the**, on p. 701.

Road, the. Charing Cross Road: booksellers' coll.: late C. 19–20.

road louse. A small car that, holding the road and proceeding, stately, at about 25 m.p.h., refuses, when hooted at, to move to the side: Cambridge undergraduates' (1930) >, by 1935, rather more general.

road-roller. A bushman; a 'hick': New Zealand: ca. 1910–45. (Jean Devanney, *Bushman Burke*, 1930.)

roadster (p. 701). Not merely tailors'—fairly general.

roam on the rush. (Of a jockey) to swerve 'from the straight line at the finish [of a race] when the rush takes place': turf: from ca. 1870. B. & L.

roar.—2. (Of cattle) to low continuously,

whence the n. *roaring*: Australian coll.: late C. 19–20. (B., 1943.)

roar up.—2. (Of destroyers) to attack: Naval coll.: 1939–45. 'Roar in, roar up and roar out again.' (P-G-R.)—3. To scrounge; to find by hustling: Army: 1939–45. (P-G-R.)—4. To reprimand: Australian, mostly juvenile: since ca. 1940. (B., 1953.) Ex sense 1: p. 701.

Roarer, the. The Southern Au*rora*, a Melbourne–Sydney train: Australian: 1962 +. (B.P.)

roaring forties.—2. Hence, Lieutenant Commanders between 40 and 50 years of age: Naval: since ca. 1917; esp. in 1939–45. (P-G-R.)

roarin' horn. An urgent erection: low Australian: late C. 19–20. Cf. **roaring Jack** below.

roaring horsetails. The *aurora australis*: Australian: C. 20. B., 1942.

roaring Jack, have a. To have an urgent erection: low: late C. 19–20. Clamant—and cf. **Jack in a** (or **the**) **box**, sense 8, on p. 430.

roast-beef dress (p. 701). The term *roast-beef coat* occurs in Alfred Burton, *Johnny Newcome*, 1818. (Moe.)

roast pork. To, a, talk: rhyming s.: since ca. 1910. Often, as v., shortened to *roast*.—2. A table fork: rhyming s., since ca. 1930; esp. in the Army, 1939–45. Both: Franklyn, *Rhyming*.

roaster.—2. An extremely hot day; a heat wave: coll.: late C. 19–20.—3. A 'hot dog': since the late 1940's.

Rob Every Poor Soldier. The R.E., Postal Services: Army: since ca. 1922; † by 1940.

rob my pal. A girl: rhyming s. (on *gal*): C. 20. The modern version of *Bob my pal* (p. 73). Franklyn, *Rhyming*.

Rob Roy. Boy: rhyming: since ca. 1860. Since ca. 1930, †; apparently never at all general, says Franklyn.

Robbers, the. A variant—and derivative—of **Rob All My Comrades** (p. 702): 1914–18.

robbo. A cab or buggy plying for hire: Australian: ca. 1880–1910. Baker. Ex *robber*. Cf.:—

Robbo Park. Rosebery Park racecourse: Australian: C. 20. Baker. 'Now closed' (B.P., 1963).

Robert or **robert.**—2. A shilling; esp. in *accept Her Majesty's Robert*, to enlist in the Regular Army: military: ca. 1860–1901. Robert Blatchford, *My Life in the Army*, 1910.—3. A spell of watch below, or a short rest at any time: deepsea trawlers': C. 20. 'I've given the brats a Robert': L. Luard, *All Hands*, 1933.

Robert E. Lee. a quay: London dockland rhyming s.: C. 20.

Robertson & Moffat; usually **Robertson.** A profit: Australian rhyming s.: since ca. 1930. (B., 1945.)

Robin. Short for *Robin Hood*, good.

Robin Hood; Tarzan. G.H.Q. India nicknames for Brigadier Orde Wingate, leader of the Chindits in Burma.

Robin Redbreast (p. 702): earlier in W. N. Glascock, *Sailors and Saints* (I, 116), 1829. (Moe.)

Robinson & Cleaver. Fever: Londoners' rhyming: C. 20.

Robinson Crusoe. To do so: rhyming s.: late C. 19–20; by 1959, ob. (Franklyn, *Rhyming*.)

Robinson Crusoe, adj.: e.g., *travel . . .,* to travel alone: Australian teenagers', esp. surfers': since ca. 1962. *Pix*, Sept. 28, 1963.

rock, n.—6. A rock cake: coll.: C. 20.—7. A bunker (in golf): since ca. 1920. *The Daily Mail*, Aug. 16, 1939.

rock, v.—3. To startle (someone) with news or assertion: mostly R.A.F.: since late 1941. H. & P. 1943, 'A new version of *shake*.'

Rock, the (p. 702): prob. since early C. 19, for it occurs in Fredk Marryat, *Frank Mildmay*, 1829, at p. 115 of the 1897 edition. Moe.

Rock Apes. Personnel of the R.A.F. Regiment: R.A.F., Gibraltar,· whence also Malta: (?) since ca. 1940.

rock-bottom seats. Slatted seats in the buses of war-time construction: 1941 +.

rock cake. A bore; a nuisance: R.A.F. in India: ca. 1925–35. (G/Capt. Arnold Wall, letter of March 5, 1945.) Rhyming on **bake**, n. 3.

rock-creeper. A coastal ship: nautical: since ca. 1870. (Jack Lawson, *A Man's Life*, 1932.)

Rock Dodgers, the. Pilots and their aircraft flying to the Western Isles: R.A.F. Transport Command: 1944–5. They have to be! (Communicated by S/Ldr Vernon Noble, in April 1945.)

Rock-happy. Suffering from acute melancholia occasioned by too long service at Gibraltar: Naval: since ca. 1939. Cf. *Rock, the*, on p. 702.

rock-hopper. 'A person who fishes from rocks on a sea coast' (B., 1959): Aus.: since ca. 1930.

rock in. To accelerate or intensify; esp. *rock it in!*, hurry up: Australian: C. 20. B., 1942. Cf.:—

rock it in. To talk; to chatter: Australian low: C. 20. Lawson Glassop, *We Were the Rats*, 1944, '"Nearly all of 'em could speak English, an' they starts to rock it in about the war."' A fusion of three ideas: that of **rock**, v., 1 (p. 702) and that of **pitch**, n., 4 (p. 636) and that of **pitch in**, 1 (p. 636) Glassop, ibid.: '"We rocked it back"'—i.e. retorted.

Rock Scorpion (p. 702). 1. Also *Rock lizard*. In C. 20, often *Rock Scorp*, as in Percy F. Westerman, *The Terror of the Seas*, 1927. The word is much older than one had supposed; in 1818, Colonel Moe informs me, it occurs in Alfred Burton's narrative poem, *Johnny Newcome*. 2. (Often *Rock Scorp*.) A Gibraltar policeman: Naval: C. 20. Granville.

*rock spider. A petty thief that robs amorous couples sporting in parks or by the seashore: Australian c.: since ca. 1939. (B., 1953.)

rocker, n. A devotee of rock-and-roll: since ca. 1959; by 1966, ob.—2. A youthful motor-cyclist given to 'rocking' his machine as he rides and aspiring to be a 'ton-up' boy, doing 100 miles an hour: since ca. 1960.—3. Hence, a leather-jacketed non-surfer, esp. one of the *Rockers* gang; 'a youth who would formerly have been a motor-bike fiend' (B.P.): Sydney teenagers': 'not heard before 1962'.

rocker.—2. Hence, to understand: C. 20. Pugh (2), '"An' I must have 'em to go away with. Rokker?" "Yes, Chick," she faltered.' Ex Romany.

Rockers and Mods (both rare in singular). 'Teenagers today are split into two fairly even factions—the Rockers and the Mods. Their difference is simple: Mods are the fashion-conscious, with-it teenagers; Rockers are the old-fashioned, ton-up kids who think more of motor-bikes than themselves. Their only link lines are pop music and the fact that they are both young'

(Cathy McGowan's article 'Rockers and Mods' in *TV Times*, Nov. 29, 1963): since ca. 1960. The *Rockers* 'rock' their machines; the Mods tend to ride motor-scooters.

rocket. A severe reprimand (stronger than **raspberry**, 4, above): Army officers': since ca. 1934. 'To *stop a rocket*—receive a reprimand,' *The New Statesman*, Aug. 30, 1941; 'An exceptionally severe one is either an *imperial rocket* or an *outsize in rockets*,' E.P. in *The New Statesman*, Aug. 1, 1942; by late 1941, in fairly gen. use in the R.A.F. also—witness Jackson; and by 1942, in the Navy—witness Granville. It blows the recipient sky-high. Whence the variant **pyrotechnic**.

rocking horse. An 'oscillating guards van' (*Railway*): railwaymen's: late C. 19–20.

rocks.—2. Short for **rock of ages**, 1 (p. 702): C. 20.—3. Teeth: C. 20.

rocks, on the. (Of a strong drink) 'without water or soda, but simply poured over the rocks (lumps of ice)': Canadian: adopted, ca. 1945, ex U.S.; by 1958, also fairly general English. (Leechman.)

rocky, n. (p. 703). Granville, however, defines *rockies* as 'R.N.R., or R.N.V.R. officers' and implies that in both nuances the word was still current in 1945; it still is extant.—2. A rock wallaby: Australian: C. 20; by 1950, coll. (Jean Devanney, *Travels in North Queensland*, 1951.)—3. A rockmelon: Aus.: C. 20. (B., 1959.)

rod, n.—3. A revolver: c.: anglicised ca. 1931 ex U.S. *The Pawnshop Murder*. For American usage, see *Underworld*.—4. An overcoat or macintosh: c.: C. 20. In, e.g., F. D. Sharpe, *The Flying Squad*, 1938. Perhaps ex **rock-a-low** (*Dict.*).

rod in pickle.—2. A good horse that is being either reserved or nursed for a sure win: Australian sporting: since ca. 1930. (Lawson Glassop, 1949.)

Rodney (p. 703). A coll. until ca. 1905 or 1910; it occurs in, e.g., Jerome Caminada, *Detective Life*, 1895.—2. A South Wales railwaymen's nickname 'for last Saturday night trains from Newport and Cardiff for valley destination' (*Railway* 2nd): C. 20.

Rod's. Harrod's (London): Londoners': since ca. 1945. Cf. **Fred's**.

roger! or **wilco!** All right!; O.K.!: R.A.F. coll.: since ca. 1938. Strictly, the latter complements the former. From *Roger?*, All right?, and *Wilco* (Message understood and) *will* comply.

roger, v. (p. 703), goes back to well before 1750. In *The Secret Diary of William Byrd of Westover, 1709–1712*, ed. by L. B. Wright and M. Tinling, 1941 (Richmond, Virginia), this gentleman of Virginia was using *roger* for all his sexual relations with his wife, e.g. 'I rogered her lustily' (Dec. 26, 1711) and 'I lay abed till 9 o'clock this morning . . . and rogered her by way of reconciliation' (Jan. 1, 1712). With thanks to an American scholar.

Roger the Lodger. A c.p. directed at, or alluding to, a male lodger that makes love to the mistress of the house or apartment: since ca. 1925. Gerald Kersh, *Clean, Bright and Slightly Oiled*, 1946, '"Proper bloody Bluebeard." "Henry the Eighth," said Knocker White. "Roger the Lodger," said the Sergeant. "Breaking up homes," said the man in the next bed.' *Roger*, because it

rhymes with 'lodger'; there is, moreover, a pun on **roger**, n., 5, and v. (see p. 703).

roglan. A four-wheeled vehicle: Shelta: C. 18–20. B. & L.

rogue, n.—2. Short for **rogue and villain** (p. 703): Cockney and Australian: late C. 19–20.

rogue an' Dillon. A shilling: rhyming s.: late C. 19–20. Cf. **rogue and villain** (*Dict.*).

[Rogues and Beggars in C. 18. Ned Ward, during the period 1700–24, has the following terms. Beggars are *clapperdudgeons* (1709), *mumpers* (1703) or *mumps* (1709), and *strol[l]ers* (1709). Sodomites are *boretto-men* (1703), *buggerantoes* (1703), *Mollies* (1709), and *town-shifts* (1709). Highwaymen are *Gentlemen Outers* (1709), *light horse* (1700) and *pads and wods* (1709, in *The Secret History of Clubs*; the phrase is not very satisfactory). Cut-purses are **clippers* or *gentlemen of the nig* (1709); pickpockets, *divers* (1709). Rogues of various kinds are *canary-birds* (1703), *dark engineers* (1703; prob. a nonce-phrase), *Newgate birds* (1709), and *the sharping tribe* (coll. rather than s.; 1717). Dirty ruffians are **clip-nits* (1703). Various names for confidence-tricksters are *cadator*, *sweetner*, *tongue-pad* (1703, all three). Certain touts are *Long-Lane clickers* (1703). Horse-thieves are, in 1709, termed *snaffle-biters*. Matthews.]

rogue's yarn. 'Coloured thread found in the heart of government rope to prevent its being stolen' (Granville): Naval coll.: mid-C. 19–20. Rather does it date from very early C. 19, for it occurs in W. N. Glascock, *Sketch-Book* (II, 41), 1826. Moe.

roll, n., 2 (*Dict.*). This dates from at least as early as 1870 and occurs esp. in the phrase, *have a roll on*.—3. A fight: Naval: since mid 1940's.—4. Esp. in *have a roll*, to coït: since ca. 1950 (? rather since ca. 1920). Perhaps ex **roll in the hay** below.

roll, v.—2. To rob (a drunken person): nautical: since ca. 1810. Alfred Burton, *Johnny Newcome*, 1818. (Moe.) The word passed to the U.S. and became an underworld term; and, as c., was adopted, ca. 1920, in Australia. (B., 1942.)—3. To walk, stroll: Marlborough College: since ca. 1925.

roll!, go and have a. Go to the devil!: Australian: C. 20. B., 1942.

roll and rind. Bread and cheese: Australian hotel staffs': C. 20. B., 1942.

roll big enough to choke a bullock, a—a roll Jack Rice couldn't jump over—a roll that would choke an anteater; also **a wad that would choke a wombat.** A very large roll of money: Aus.: since ca. 1945. (B., 1959.)

roll, bowl, or pitch. Despite all obstacles: coll.: from ca. 1910. Peter Chamberlain, 'Whatever happens, roll, bowl, or pitch.' Cf. S.E. *rain or shine*. Immediately ex the coconut-shy pitch-holders' patter: 'Three balls a penny—roll, bowl, or pitch' (as Dr Leechman has reminded me).—The nuance is rather that of 'Come what may!'

roll 'em! Start filming: cinema: since ca. 1925. *The Evening News*, Nov. 7, 1939.

roll in the hay, n. A little love-making: C. 20: orig. rural, then loosely general.

roll-me-in-the-kennel. A spirituous liquor (? gin): ca. 1720–50. See quotation at **bunter's tea.**

roll on Death, Demob's too far away. A self-explanatory R.A.F. c.p. since ca. 1950.

roll on my bloody twelve (pause after 'on'). A Naval (lower-deck) c.p., indicative of the active-service ratings' longing that their twelve years of service should come to an end: C. 20. Granville. Cf. *roll on* . . . (p. 704) and *roll on that boat*. In full, *I heard the voice of Moses say, Roll on* . . . (P-G-R.)

roll on, pay-day! A workmen's c.p., uttered by one almost 'broke': since 1919. A c.p. also used by those who, 'fed up' with their job, are looking forward to the week-end: since ca. 1925.

roll on that boat (with a decided pause after 'on'). An R.A.F. overseas c.p. indicative of tedium and homesickness: since ca. 1925. Gerald Emanuel, letter of March 29, 1945, 'Also abbreviated to "roll on" and "R.O.T.F.B." The boat, by the way, has a name—it's "the good ship Tora Peechy" (from Hindustani "a little later").'

roll one's own. To make extemporaneously: Australian: since ca. 1930. Ex *roll one's own* cigarettes. (B.P.)

roll them in the aisle(s). Applied to a comedian that has his audience *(them)* roll, helpless with laughter, in the aisle(s)—or are in danger of doing so: theatrical, including music-hall: since ca. 1920.

roll(-)up, n.—4. A hand-rolled cigarette: since ca. 1920. (Norman.) Earlier in Paul Tempest, *Lag's Lexicon*, 1950.—5. Attendance, number of persons present: coll.: C. 20. Ex sense 2 on p. 704. —6. 'The roll-ups are those [customers] who have found the genuineness of the goods and walk into the "shop" for repeats' (W. Buchanan-Taylor, *Shake It Again*, 1943): fair-grounds': since ca. 1910. Cf. sense 2 on p. 704.

roll up, v.—3. To die: low: C. 20. Richard Llewellyn, *None But the Lonely Heart*, 1943.

roller skate. See 'Hauliers' Slang'.

roller skates. A tank, or tanks: R.A.F.: 1940 +. *The Reader's Digest*, Feb. 1941, Allan A. Michie & Isabel Waitt, 'Air Slanguage'. To the airmen overhead, a tank looks as if it moved on roller skates.

rolley. A vehicle: catachrestic: from ca. 1865. B. & L. In S.E. *rolley = rulley*, a lorry. It perhaps blends *roll* and *trolley*, as Julian Franklyn has proposed.

rollick. To make much fuss; become angry: Londoners': from ca. 1925.—2. As v.t., to 'tell off'; usually as vbl n., *rollicking*: low: since ca. 1920. F. D. Sharpe, *The Flying Squad*, 1938. It rhymes **ballock,** v.

rollies, with the *o* either long or short. Testicles: low: since ca. 1930. Ex *(Tommy) Rollocks*.

rolling billow. A pillow: rhyming s.: late C. 19–20; by 1960, ob. Franklyn 2nd.

*rolling Joe. A smartly dressed fellow: app. ca. 1830–90. B. & L. Cf. **rolling,** 1 (*Dict.*).

Rolling Motion Square. 'A square in Lisbon paved in alternate wavy lines of black and white cobbles. In walking across it one got the illusion of a rolling motion and it was said that it made some people feel sea-sick. I am told that it has long since been re-paved with concrete.' (Andrew Haggard, Jan. 28, 1947.) 'I was once told that it presented an almost impossible situation to any pedestrian with a few drinks aboard' (Leechman, April 1967).

rollocks. See **Tommy Rollocks.**

Rolls. A Rolls-Royce car: motorists' coll.: since ca. 1925.

Rolls-can-hardly. An old car: Australian youthful car-owners': since ca. 1950. '*Rolls* down a hill but *can hardly* get up the next.' Youthful Australian car-owners' synonyms: *bomb* (ironic), *jalop(p)y, tin-bitser*. (B.P.)

Rolls Royce, adj. 'Fancy'; expecting too much: Naval (esp. ward-room) coll.: since ca. 1918. 'A bit Rolls Royce in his ideas.'

Rolls Royce, n. Voice, esp. a very good one: theatrical rhyming s.; C. 20. (Franklyn, *Rhyming*.)

Rolly. A Rolliecord or Rollieflex camera: photographers': since ca. 1945.

roly-poly.—4. 'Miles of buckbrush or "rolypoly", cursed in the sheep country as a pest, but here [in Central Australia] regarded by the cattlemen as good cattle and camel feed,' Archer Russell, *A Tramp Royal*, 1934: late C. 19–20. Ex appearance.

rom.—3. A radar operator mechanic: R.A.F.: 1943 +. Sgt Gerald Emanuel, March 29, 1945. Ex the abbr. *R.O.M.* more fully *R. Op/Mech.*

Roman, the. Romano, proprietor of Romano's Restaurant (London): mostly Society: late C. 19– early 20.

Roman Candle. A Roman Catholic: mostly Army: late C. 19–20. Gerald Kersh, *Boots Clean*, 1941. Ex the use of candles.

Roman(-)candle landing; Roman candles. A bad landing (R.A.F., since ca. 1938: Jackson); a parachutist's fall to earth when his parachute has failed to open (paratroopers', since 1941: H. & P.). Ex the stars one sees on impact. Perhaps also ex the rapid fall of debris from fireworks of the rocket type.

romance. A person obviously in love: from ca. 1926. Ex influence of the cinema.

Rommel back another ten miles, that'll push or **that's pushed.** A c.p. of 1941–2, thus 'When in North Africa there was some extra bit of red tape or regimental procedure, we always used to say: "And that's pushed Rommel back another ten miles". Everybody said . . . "That'll push Rommel back another ten miles," ' Gerald Kersh, *Slightly Oiled*, 1946.

romp, n. A little light-hearted love-making: coll.: adopted, ca. 1945, ex U.S. Cf. **roll in the hay** above, whence the blend *romp in the hay*: since ca. 1950.

rompworthy. (Of a woman) sexually desirable: upper- and middle-class coll.: since ca. 1935. Cf. *bedworthy.*

Ronson. A 'ponce': very imperfect rhyming s., and showing the influence of high-powered advertising: since ca. 1954. (Franklyn, *Rhyming*.)

'roo, 2 (p. 705). This coll. occurs also as an adj.: late C. 19–20. 'A lump of 'roo steak,' K. S. Prichard, *Working Bullocks*, 1929; 'I know some good 'roo country,' Jon Cleary, *Back of Sunset*, 1959.

'roo, v.i. To hunt kangaroos: Australian coll.: C. 20. Hence the vbl n. *'rooing.* (K. S. Prichard, *Kiss on the Lips*, 1932.)

roof!, come off the. A non-aristocratic c.p. addressed to a person being high and mighty: from ca. 1890; ob. W. Pett Ridge, *Minor Dialogues*, 1895.

roof-spotter, usually in pl. An observer posted on a roof to watch for enemy aircraft: an all-Services and Civil Defence coll.: 1939–45. (P-G-R.)

roofer.—2. A hat: Australian: since ca. 1920. B., 1942. Cf. **tile** (*Dict.*).—3. (Orig., *hospitable roofer.*) A letter of thanks to one's host or hostess or both, after staying with them: mostly at the Universities of Oxford and Cambridge: since ca. 1925. By 'the Oxford *-er*' ex *roof* (over one's head).

rook, n.—5. A recruit: Regular Army: C. 20. Gerald Kersh, *Boots Clean*, 1941. Ex **rookey** (p. 705).—6. A swindle: Australian: late C. 19–20. Ruth Park, *The Harp in the South*, 1948. Cf. sense 2: p. 705.

*rooker. A dagga-smoker: South African c.: C. 20. Afrikaans (lit., 'smeller').

rookette. A female recruit: Services: 1940 +. Partridge, 1945. Never much used. Ex **rook(e)y** (p. 705).

rooky. For the n., see **rookey** (*Dict.*).—2. Adj., rascally: proletarian: from ca. 1860. B. & L.

room for a small one? See **is there room** . . .

*roon; though rare in singular. A mushroom: tramps' c.: late C. 19–20. W. L. Gibson Cowan, *Loud Report*, 1937. By perversion of Kentish *'room.*

Rooshians. See **Russians.**

roost, n., 2 (p. 705). Much earlier in *The London Guide*, 1818.—3. A city-dweller affecting a hyphenated name was, in the 1890's, stigmatised by the country-dweller thus: Robb-Smith became Roost-Smith; Carter-Jones became Roost-Jones; and so forth. B., 1942.

rooster.—5. Penis: low: C. 19–20. Orig. euphemistic for *cock*. Contrast sense 1 in *Dict.*—6. A roster: Services: late C. 19–20. (P-G-R.)

rooster tail. 'Wake of a board' (*Pix*, Sept. 28, 1963): Australian surfboard riders': since ca. 1961.

root, v.—2. (Of the male) to coït with: low Australian: C. 20. Ex **root,** n., 2 and 3, on p. 705.—3. 'To outwit, baffle, exhaust, utterly confound (someone)': Aus.: since ca. 1930. Baker, *The Drum*, 1959, adds: 'Whence, *to be rooted*, to be exhausted or confounded; *get rooted!*, Go to blazes!' This latter expression, however, derives more likely from sense 2. Cf. **get stuffed!; get joined!**

root for. To support ardently and esp. vocally: Australian—adopted, ca. 1945, ex U.S.—not common: **root,** v., 2, inhibits general use of *root for.* (B.P.)

roots. Short for **daisy roots** (p. 205): Australian: C. 20. B., 1942. The Cockney shortening is *daisies.*

rooty medal. See **rooty gong** (*Dict.*). Both of them were adopted ca. 1919 by the R.A.F.; cf. **Naffy gong.**

rooty-toot. See 'Jive'.

ropable. See **ropeable** in *Dict.* and below.

rope, have two penn'orth of. See **twopenny-rope** in *Dict.*

rope-yarn Thursday. 'The original "make and mend" day' (Granville): Naval coll.: late C. 19–20.

ropeable! In 'Tom Collins', *Such is Life*, 1903. Its predominant nuance is 'almost frantic with rage' (H. J. Oliver, July 1937—see **Bovril**). See **fit to be tied** above.

ropes. One who plays at half-back in football: schoolboys': from ca. 1880; ob. B. & L.

ropey. (Of a person) inefficient or dilatory or careless of appearance; (of an action, etc.) clumsy or inefficient; (of things, e.g. an aircraft, a meal) inferior: R.A.F.: since ca. 1930. H. & P.; Jackson; Partridge, 1945, 'Perhaps from rope-like smell of inferior tobacco; perhaps'—more prob., indeed—'from certain obsolete types of aircraft that carried an excess—or what seemed an excess—of ropes'.—2. (Whence, probably, sense 1.) Applied to 'paint drying out with a rope-like appearance' (a master builder, Dec. 5, 1953): builders' and house-painters' coll.: late C. 19–20.—3. Generally disliked; unpopular: Australian airmen's: since ca. 1939. (B., 1943.) Ex sense 1.—4. 'This is in current use among beatniks and teenagers, and any smelly member of a gang is called "ropey"' (A. B. Petch, April 1966): since ca. 1960. Ex sense 1 above.

rork (or **rorke**), **rorker.** A town boy, a 'cad': Tonbridge: since ca. 1870. Marples. Perhaps ex *raw.*

rort, n. A dodge, trick, scheme, racket: Australian c.: since ca. 1910. B., 1942.—2. A crowd; hence, showmen's patter: Australian low: since ca. 1912. Baker.—3. Something exceptionally good: Australian: since ca. 1920.—4. A wild party: Australian: since ca. 1930. Ex senses 2 and 3. (B.P.) Often 'a real rort', which leads B.P. to suggest that this sense may have been influenced by the almost synonymous *riot* ('The party was a *riot*').

rort, v. 'To be loudly argumentative' (Granville): Naval: C. 20. Cf. **rorty,** 1, 3 (*Dict.*).

*rorter. A professional swindler: Australian c.: since ca. 1910. Baker. Ex **rort,** n., 1.—2. Hence a hawker of worthless goods: since ca. 1912.—3. Variant of **rort,** n., 3.

*rorting. Confidence trickery: Australian c.: since ca. 1910. Baker. Ex **rort,** n., 1.—2. Hence, sharp practice: low: since ca. 1920.

rorty is derived by B. & L. ex Yiddish *rorität*, anything choice.—4. (Cf. sense 3.) 'Noisily drunk and argumentative' (Granville): Naval: C. 20.

rory, on the. Penniless: low: C. 20. F. D. Sharpe, *The Flying Squad*, 1938. I.e. *Rory o' More*, floor.—2. (Of a horse) fallen: racecourse rhyming s.: C. 20. Lit., 'on the *floor*'—rhyming s. *Rory o' More.*

Rory o' More.—4. See preceding.

rosaries all the way. A c.p. reference—when used by Protestants, as usually, it is disparaging—to Catholic processions: C. 20. A pun on S.E. *roses all the way* strewn at a triumphal procession. (A. B. Petch, April 1966.)

Rose Cottage. The V.D. quarters: Naval: C. 20.

rose in judgment. Turned up: tailors': from ca. 1860. B. & L.

rosebud. Mouth: Cockneys': late C. 19–20. Pugh.

rosella.—2. In Australia and New Zealand, since ca. 1910, it has been sheep-shearing s. for 'a sheep bare of wool on the "points" (hocks, head, foreleg, etc.) and consequently very easy to shear,' Niall Alexander, communication of Oct. 22, 1939.—3. A Staff officer: Australian soldiers': 1939 +. B., 1942. Ex his *red* tabs.—4. Hence, any high-ranking officer: Since ca. 1942. (B., 1953.)—5. 'A customer whose hair is easy to cut because of his partial baldness' (B.P.): Australian barbers': since ca. 1930. Partly ex sense 2.

Rosemary Lane to a rag shop. Heavy odds: coll.: ca. 1810–90. *Boxiana*, III, 1821.

Roses. Ordinary stock in the Buenos Aires & Rossario Railway: Stock Exchange: from ca. 1885. B. & L.

roses. A woman's period: Anglo-Irish: late (? mid) C. 19–20. James Joyce, *Ulysses*, 1920, 'Such a bad headache. Has her roses probably.' (Cf. **flowers** on p. 289, and esp. **reds**, 2, on p. 693; link, 'red roses'.

rosin, 2 (p. 707). Much earlier in *Select Trials, from 1720 to 1724*, pub. in 1734: 'Strong drink. A metaphor first used among Fidlers'.

rosin-back. A horse that has had its back rubbed with rosin in order to ensure a firmer seat for the bareback rider: circus coll.: late C. 19–20. (C. B. Cochran, *Showman Looks On*, 1945.)

rosiner or **rosner** or **rozner.** A very stiff drink with a hell of a kick: Australian: since ca. 1930. (H. Drake Brockman, *The Fatal Days*, 1947.) Cf. preceding, but esp. cf. *rosin*, 2, on p. 707.

rosy.—5. A (large) garbage-bin: ships' stewards': C. 20. Dave Marlow, *Coming Sir!*, 1937. Ironically ex 'A rose by any other name would smell as sweet'.

Rosy Lee (p. 707). Now (1960) used mostly in Dublin, as Franklyn, *Rhyming*, informs us. Also of course, *Rosie Lee* or, of course, *Lea*.—2. (Or *Rosy Lea*.) A flea: rhyming s.: C. 20. (Sydney Lester.)

Rosy (or **Rosie**) **Loader** or **Loder.** Whisky and soda: rhyming s.: C. 20. (Franklyn, *Rhyming*.)

rotary hoe, often shortened to **rotary.** A jocular variant of *righty-o* (or *rightio*): Australian: ca. 1960–5. (B.P.)

rots battleships, it; it rots your socks. Water, as opposed to beer, is harmful: public-house c.pp.: C. 20. (Atkinson.)

rotten.—3. (Of impression) weak; uneven: printers': from ca. 1870. B. & L.
Sense 2 has been adopted by Australians—cf. the next entry.

rotten, get. To get very drunk indeed: Australian: since ca. 1930. B., 1942. Ex **rotten**, 2 (p. 707).

Rotten Irish Rag-Times. The Royal Irish Regiment: Army: since ca. 1912; † by 1940.

Rotten Mess, the. That mess in which the venereals are quartered, on most ships No. 1 Mess: Naval: since ca. 1910. Rotten with disease.

Rotten Row.—3. (Cf. 1.) 'A line of ships waiting their turn to be broken up': Naval: C. 20. Granville.
2 (p. 707): † by 1960. (Franklyn 2nd.) Sense 3 existed nearly a century earlier, to judge by W. N. Glascock, *Sailors and Saints* (II, 75), 1829, thus, 'I should be cursed sorry to see our men-o'-war dismantled, and laid up in Rotten Row'. (Moe.)

rotter (*Dict.*) may orig. have been U.S., for it appears in Jonas B. Phillips, *Jack Sheppard*; or, *The Life of a Rotter*, 1839 (New York).—2. 'An expert or adept at any study or task' (B., 1943): Australian: since ca. 1930. Ironically ex sense 1.

Rotters' Rest, the. C. 20 Public School s., as in Arnold Lunn, *Loose Ends*, 1919: 'He was assigned to "Lower Field", a game [of football] more usually known as "The Rotters' Rest".'

rotto. Rotten: Anglo-Irish: C. 20. James Joyce, *Ulysses*, 1922, 'The father is rotto with money.' Cf. *lousy*—or *stinking—with money*.

roue is an occ. late C. 18–early 19 variant of **row** (n., 1: *Dict.*). H., 2nd ed.

rouf (p. 708). Earlier in Mayhew, I, 1851, where also *rouf yenep*, fourpence.—2. Hence a four-years' prison-sentence or -term: c.: late C. 19–20. (Norman.)—3. The sum of four shillings: London's East End: since ca. 1945. (*The Evening News*, Nov. 12, 1957.)

rouge, n. A force-down in Rugby football: London schools': ca. 1875–1900. Pun on *rough*?

rouge route, the. The 'red light' district of London: Londoners': ca. 1660–1700. William Boghurst's contemporary account of the Great Plague of London, in Payne's edition, 1894. The term shows the French influence of the Restoration Court.

rough, n.—2. Hence, an N.C.O. riding instructor: Royal Artillery: C. 20.—3. Short for *rough stuff*, esp. in *cut the rough stuff!*: Australian: since ca. 1925.

rough, v. To manhandle: Australian: since ca. 1925. D'Arcy Niland, *Call Me . . .*, 1958, 'They grabbed Shelton and roughed him outside into the rising wind.'

rough, a bit. Unfair, unreasonable; extortionate: Australian coll.: C. 20. (B., 1943.)

rough, feel. See **feel rough**.

rough as a bag or **rough as a pig's breakfast.** Uncouth: New Zealand and Australian: C. 20. B., 1941 and 1942. Cf. **rough as . . .**, p. 708.

rough as a goat's knees. Exceedingly rough: Aus.: C. 20.

rough-knot. A Marine: Naval: ca. 1780–1850. John Davis, *The Post Captain*, 1806 (p. 146 of the 1810 edition); W. N. Glascock, *Sailors and Saints* (I, 213), 1829. Moe.

rough neck.—2. Hence, one who, in a carnival, does the rough work: Canadian carnival s.: C. 20. —3. An oil-rig crewman: since ca. 1920.

rough off (a horse). To break-in without troubling about 'the fancy stuff', esp. for station work: Australian rural coll.: late C. 19–20. B., 1942.

rough on, 2 (p. 708). Recorded in Australia in 1878. Sidney J. Baker, letter.

rough on rats (p. 708). There was once a rat-poison called 'Rough on Rats'.

rough ride. To ride an unbroken horse; hence, to domineer over a person: Australian coll.: resp., late C. 19–20 and since ca. 1910. (B., 1943.)

rough spin. See **raw deal** above.

rough stuff. See **rough**, n., 2 and **cut the rough stuff**.

rough trade, the. The underworld of homosexual practices, esp. of homosexual prostitutes: low: since ca. 1950. *Evening Standard*, July 12, 1967, in a short review of Richard Chopping's novel, *The Ring*.

*rough 'un. (A 'bed' in) an improvised shelter: tramps' c.: C. 20. W. A. Gape, *Half a Million Tramps*, 1936.

rough-up.—3. A violent quarrel, a 'free for all': since ca. 1890. *Sessions*, June 22, 1896, 'There was a little rough-up, and I found myself stabbed in the arm.' In C. 20, also Australian: B., 1942.

roughers. A rough sea: Naval (mostly officers'): since ca. 1920. Occasionally personified as *Harry Roughers*: since ca. 1925. By 'the Oxford *-er*'.

roughing (*Dict.*) is interrupting a lecturer by rubbing the boot soles on the floor, as in a sand-dance. It carries no suggestion of physical violence.

roughneck. See **rough neck** (*Dict.*).

roughriding. See **bareback riding**.

roughy.—2. Esp. in *put a roughy over*, to 'pull a fast one on', to impose upon, to trick: Australian: C. 20. Kylie Tennant, *The Battlers*, 1941, in form *roughie.*—3. A story hard to believe: Australian (*roughie*): since ca. 1920. B.P.

round, adj.—2. (Of paint) needing to be thinned: builders' and house-painters': C. 20. Perhaps cf. Cumberland dial. *round*, coarse, thick.

round for *on* (preposition) is a characteristic of Cockney speech: coll.: mid-C. 19–20. Edwin Pugh, *Harry the Cockney*, 1912, '''If you don't gimme a bit . . . I shall punch you round the jaw.''' Cf. **wipe round**, q.v. below.

round box. An ephemeral variant (1957–58) of *square*, n., 6: Teddy boys'. (Gilderdale, 2.)

round heels, she has or **she's got.** She's sexually compliant: Canadian: since ca. 1925. A girl with heels so round that the least push will put her on her back.

round me houses, careless—indeed, incorrect—for *round the houses* (p. 709). Franklyn, *Rhyming.*

round shot. Peas: Services (mostly Army): C. 20. H. & P. Cf **bullet**, 3.

round square. See **crooked straight-edge.**

round the bend (p. 709): much used in the R.A.F. in 1939–45. (Robert Hinde, March 17, 1945.) It has since become much more general; quite common, indeed, among civilians. In 1957 the intensive *round the bend—and back again* was coined. Ex *Harpic*, a water-closet cleanser, advertised to '(clean) round the bend', whence the variant *clean round the bend*. Cf. *Harpic*. It has, since ca. 1957, had a second intensive: *round the bend—and half-way down the straight*, and also an occ. variant, *round the twist* (ca. 1957–63).

Round the Corner Smith. Sir C. Aubrey Smith (b. 1863), Cambridge and Sussex cricketer (1880's and 1890's) and, since 1930, G.O.M. of the films: cricketers': since ca. 1884. Ex 'his unusual run up to the wicket' (Sir Home Gordon, *The Background of Cricket*, 1939).

round the houses (p. 709). Earlier in Augustus Mayhew, *Paved With Gold*, 1857.—2. See 'Hauliers' Slang'.

round up, as in 'We'll try to *round up* a few males' or even 'some drinks': Australian coll.: C. 20. Ex cattle droving. (B.P.) But also Canadian—see **corral** above.

roundabout. See **round-about** (*Dict.*).

rounder.—3. A return journey: busmen's: since ca. 1920.

Roundheads and Cavaliers. The circumcised and the uncircumcised: Naval: C. 20.

roundhouse rangers. Fish that swim about the stern of a ship: Naval: C. 20. (P-G-R.)

roundyard. A harness cask: Australian rural: late C. 19–20. B., 1942.

rouse on; get roused on. To upbraid (someone); to reprove (him) forcibly: Aus.: C. 20. (B., 1959.) Cf. **rouse**, 2 and 3, on p. 709.

rouseabout. A member of the ground staff: Australian airmen's: 1939–45. (B., 1943.) Cf. *roustabout* on p. 709.

rouser.—3. 'A spring tonic, usually of shot-gun type: Eastern Canada: from before 1875' (Leechman).

rousie. A *roustabout*, or handy man at a shearing: Aus.: since ca. 1930. (F. B. Vickers, *First Place to the Stranger*, 1955 (p. 135).

roust on. Variant of **rouse on** above.

row, n. (p. 709). Sense 1 may orig. have been c., for it occurs in John Poulter, *Discoveries*, 1753.

row oneself on to (a person or a group). To attach oneself to: low: since ca. 1940. (Norman.)

rowdy, money (in *Dict.*). A reviewer has recalled 'Thackeray's (and C. Bede's) famous banking firm, Messrs Stump and Rowdy.'

rowing man. A spreester, fast liver: University: ca. 1875–1910. B. & L. Ex **row**, v., 2 and 3 (*Dict.*).

rows, the. The rows of hovels in the miners' section of a mining town: miners' (and their families') coll.: since ca. 1870. 'North Country miners call them *raas*' (A. B. Petch, Sept. 5, 1946).

roy. A townee, a 'cad': Christ's Hospital: since ca. 1870; ob. Marples. Ex *raucus*?

royal, adj.—2. Tipsy; hence, *royal row*, a drunken quarrel or brawl: Naval, mostly ratings': ca. 1805–60. Wm Nugent Glascock, *The Naval Sketch-Book*, 2nd Series, 1834, at II, 142, 'In course you knows it's never no more nor [= than] a reg'lar royal row . . . for I never gets royal myself, that I doesn't reg'larly get in a row'. (Moe.) Ex sense 1 on p. 709.

Royal Billy, The. 'The Royal William, said to have been 100 years old when broken up' (W. N. Glascock, *Sketch-Book*, 2nd Series, 1834, at II, 73): Naval: mid C. 18–early 19. Even earlier in Fredk Marryat, *Frank Mildmay*, 1829. (Moe.)

Royal Hearse Artillery. The gun support company of 2 Corps Reinforcement Unit: Army in North Africa: middle of World War II. A pun on *horse*. (P-G-R.)

Royal Light Foot, the. The Royal Marine Light Infantry: jocular Naval: mid-C. 19–early 20.

royal mail (or capitals). Bail (legal): rhyming s., orig. and still mostly underworld: C. 20. Franklyn 2nd.

royal order, the. Dismissal, e.g. from a job: mostly Australian: since ca. 1925. (B.P.) Ex the phrases noted at **order of the . . .** on p. 591.

Royal Repose, the. The Queen's Bench Prison: ca. 1837–80. G. W. M. Reynolds, *Pickwick Abroad*, 1839.

royal salute. 21 in the game of House: not Naval only: C. 20. Michael Harrison, *Reported Safe Arrival*, 1943. The Royal Salute is that from 21 guns.

Royal Sluice. Deuce; a Jack in cards: Australian rhyming s. (ex the famous Australian comedian, Harry Van der *Sluys*): since ca. 1940. (B., 1945.)

Royal Yachtsmen. Personnel serving in the Royal Yacht: Naval (mostly officers'): since ca. 1920.

Royalie (or **-y**) or **r.** An effeminate: esp., a catamite: Australian: C. 20; by 1944, ob.; by 1946, †. Ex *Rosalie*? Rather ex 'royal *quean*', with pun on 'royal *queen*', as a friend has suggested.

royallers. See **lawners.**

royals. Regular hands where the labour is mainly casual, orig. and esp. in shipyards: coll.: late C. 19–20. Ex *Royal Naval Shipyard*.—2. Always *the Royals* (or *royals*): members of the Royal Family of Britain, or of the royal families of the Continent: since ca. 1950: orig., sophisticated and upper-middle class s.: then, by the late 1950's, journalistic coll.; then, by 1960, fairly gen. coll.

roziner. Variant of **rosiner** above.

rozner. See **rosner.**

rub, n.—3. (Prob. ex sense 2: p. 710.) 'If a sailor wants to borrow his pal's brilliantine, he asks for *a* "*rub*" *of it*. A *rub* = "a loan" in the Navy, Granville: C. 20.—4. 'The rub is [a] cleaner or stain-remover' (W. Buchanan-Taylor, *Shake It Again*, 1943): fair-grounds': C. 20.

rub-a. Short for **rub-a-dub,** 2, public-house (p. 710): late C. 19–20. Sydney Lester.

rub-a-dub-dub (p. 710) is occasionally *rub-a-di-dub.*—2. A night club: rhyming s.: since ca. 1920. —3. A public-house: rhyming s.: since ca. 1925. (Nos. 2 and 3: Franklyn, *Rhyming*.)

rub-belly. Coïtion: low coll.: C. 18–20.

rub off on. (Esp. of money or good luck) to come one's way: since early 1950's. 'The lucky devil! Just come into a packet of money.'— 'Wish some of it would rub off on *me!*'

rub on. To make do, 'rub along': coll.: ca. 1870–1910. *Sessions*, Sept. 18, 1893.

rub-out.—2. To cut (a pattern): tailors': mid-C. 19–20. B. & L.—3. To disbar (person or horse): Australian coll.: C. 20. B., 1942.—4. To dismiss (a suggestion): Australian coll.: since ca. 1920. Baker.

rub-up, n.—2. A refresher course in a subject: Naval coll.: C. 20. Granville. With corresponding v.

rubbed down with the book (or **B.**), **be.** To be sworn on the Bible: London proletarian: from ca. 1880. Nevinson, 1895.

rubber, n.—3. A condom: low coll.: C. 20. Cf. sense 1.

rubber or **rubber at.** To gape (or stare) at: adopted ca. 1942 from U.S. Ex **rubber-neck,** v. (p. 711).

rubber cheque. A worthless cheque: adopted, ca. 1935, ex U.S.: by 1960, coll. It 'bounces'— like a rubber ball.

rubber firm. A mess-deck group of money-lenders: Naval lower-deck: since ca. 1925. Wilfred Granville, *Sea Slang of the 20th Century*, 1949. Ex **rub,** n., 2.

rubber hammer. See **crooked straight-edge.**

rubber heels. Long-range gun-shells: Army: 1917–18. One heard them—when they had arrived.—2. Hard fried eggs: Services: since ca. 1920. H. & P. The form *rubbers* denotes simply 'eggs' (P-G-R.)

rubber knackers. An impudent man: low: C. 20.

rubberdy or **rubbity** or **rubby.** A public-house: Australian low: since ca. 1920. B., 1942, 'Rhyming slang on "rub-a-dub-dub" for "pub".' In full, *rubberdy*—usually *rubbity*—*dub.* (Culotta.)

rubberneck car. An observation car: Canadian railroadmen's (— 1931). Ex **rubber neck** (p. 710, at foot). Originally U.S.

rubbish, v. To tease; to criticize adversely, to carp at: Australian: since ca. 1925. Ex 'treat as *rubbish*' and 'say *rubbish* about'.—2. Mostly in passive, as 'The fate the board rider dreads is the "wipe out". This is when he is "rubbished" or tipped violently off a wave' (*Sun-Herald*, Sept. 22, 1963), like so much rubbish: Australian surfies', esp. teenagers': since ca. 1961.

rubbling or **rubling.** Generic for oils used either medicinally or cosmetically: fair-grounds': C. 20. One *rubs* them in. (W. Buchanan-Taylor, *Shake It Again*, 1943.)

rubby, n. See prec. entry.

rubby-dub or **dubby.** A drinker of cheap spirits or wine: low Canadian: since ca. 1920. Originally and properly, a drunkard that drinks *rubbing* alcohol. (Leechman.) Commoner than the preceding term.

rubby-dubber. An old fellow that follows a carnival for what he can pick up and spends most of his money on drink: Canadian carnival s.: since ca. 1920.

rube.—2. Something exceptionally good or desirable; also as adj., 'fine excellent': Australian: since ca. 1925. B., 1942. Ironic ex sense 1 (p. 711)?

Rubies. Cigarettes of the at one time very widely distributed, free-issue, Ruby Queen brand: Tommies' coll.: 1915–16. (A. B. Petch, April 1966.)

ruby(-)dazzler or as one word. A synonym of **rube,** n., 2: since ca. 1930. Baker. A blend of *rube + bobby-dazzler.*

*$**ruby note.** A ten-shilling note: c., and low: from ca. 1920. Cf. **brown-back.**

ruby red (p. 711) was, by 1959, †. Franklyn, *Rhyming.*

***ruby wine.** Methylated spirits serving as liquor: c., esp. among tramps: C. 20. W. A. Gape, *Half a Million Tramps*, 1936.

ruck, n.—3. A heated argument; an angry fuss: low: C. 20. (Norman.) Ex the v., 2 (p. 711). 'Now fairly respectable. Used in a news item in *The Daily Telegraph*, Oct. 23, 1962. Perhaps ex U.S. *ruckus.*' (Peter Sanders.)

ruck, v.—3. Hence, to chide, nag at: low London: C. 20. George Ingram, *The Muffled Man*, 1936.

ruck, come in with the. 'To arrive at the winning-post among the unplaced horses' (B. & L.): turf: from ca. 1860.

ruck along dates from ca. 1890.

ruck on.—2. To go back on; to disown: Cockneys': late C. 19–20. Pugh (2), '"I don't care," said Deuce, defiantly . . . "I ain't goin' to ruck on Dad."'

rucking. A severe 'telling off', a reprimand: mostly prisons': C. 20. (Norman.) Ex *ruction.*

rudder. A quadruped's, esp. a dog's, tail: mostly jocular (cf. *stern*, backside): C. 20.

rude noise, make a. To break wind: euphemistic: mid-C. 19–20.

Rude to Officers (or in lower case). An Army officers' c.p. concerning an *R.T.O.* or Railway Transport Officer: from 1915: ob. Blaker.

rudery. A rude remark; risky conversation; amorous gesture or behaviour: middle- and upper-class coll.: since the middle 1920's.—2. Hence, an air raid; a surface attack: Naval: 1939–45. Wilfred Granville, *Sea Slang of the 20th Century*, 1949.

Ruffin, the. The Bellerophon, a ship of the line: Naval: Napoleonic Wars. (W. N. Glascock, *Sketch-Book*, I, 1825.) Moe.

***ruffmans,** sense 1 (p. 712), was recorded by Harman in 1566.

rug. A £1 note: Australian: since ca. 1945. (B., *Australia Speaks*, 1953.) Semantically cf. *rag*, n., 3, on p. 683, and *rugs* made of rags.

rugged. Uncomfortable, characterized by hardship, 'tough': since ca. 1935. *News Chronicle*, Aug. 30, 1946, 'The first night was a bit rugged' —there being no bed, no conveniences in the hut occupied by 'squatters'. Ex the lit. S.E. *rugged*, 'rough, craggy'.

rule G. Thou shalt not drink: Canadian railroadmen's (— 1931).

rule over, run the.—2. To examine (someone) medically: coll.: since ca. 1914.—3. To interrogate (a suspect): police: C. 20. (*The Free-Lance Writer*, April 1948.) See also p. 712.

rules (or **Rules**). Australian Rules football: Australian coll.: since ca. 1910. (B.P.)

rullock (p. 712) occurs very much earlier in W. N. Glascock, *Sketch-Book* (I, 193), 1825, and again in *The Night Watch*, 1828.

***rum**, adj. See also 'Neither Cricket nor Philology' in *A Covey of Partridge*.—4. (Ex sense 2: p. 712.) 'A Naval word meaning "bad",' H. & P.: C. 20.

rum booze.—2. 'Flip made of white or port wine, the yolks of eggs, sugar and nutmeg,' *Spy*, 1825: Oxford University: ca. 1815–50.

rum bosun. He who 'dishes out' the rum: Naval: C. 20. (P-G-R.) Cf. *rum fiend*.

rum bowling is an incorrect form (as in B. & L.) of rumbowling (*Dict.*).

rum, bum and bacca. A variant of **beer, bum and bacca**: nautical: since ca. 1910. A summation of the sailor's pleasures.

Rum Corps, the; the Rum Hospital. The New South Wales Corps; Sydney Hospital: Australian: late C. 18–mid-19, then historical; mid-C. 19–20, but after ca. 1920, only historical Ex a rum monopoly granted by Governor Lachlan Macquarie. (B.P.)

rum customer (p. 713) was, in the pugilistic circles of ca. 1800–1850, a hard-punching, a skilful, attacking boxer, known also as a *swishing hitter*. (Moe.)

rum fiend. Such a rum-server as allows rum to drip over the brim of the measure into the 'save-all', the wastage being 'perks': Naval: since ca. 1910. (P-G-R.)

rum go (p. 713): perhaps orig. c.: in Oct. 1783 (*Sessions*, p. 952), a thief says, 'By God, this is a rum go.'

rum homee (or **homer**) **of the case.** See **omee** (*Dict.*).

rum rat. 'A rating very fond of his tot, and anyone else's if he can get it' (Granville, Nov. 22, 1962): Naval: since late 1940's.

rum-te-tum. See **rumtitum**.

rumble, n.—4. A gang fight, often carefully planned and esp. among teenagers: Canadian and Australian teenagers': adopted, ca. 1944, ex U.S. Cf. **clash** above.

rumble, v., 4. To experience stomachic gurgles, whether audible or inaudible: coll.: late C. 19–20.—5. To disturb, upset, irritate or anger (someone): Army: C. 20; by 1946, ob.

rumble-bumble. A shooting-up of targets on enemy coastline: Coastal Forces: 1940–4. Echoic.

rumble (someone's) **bumble** and the derivative **bumble** (someone's) **rumble** are punning elaborations of *run up* (someone's) *arse*, to collide with either a person or a motor-car (etc.): Cambridge undergraduates': ca. 1925–40. In the first phrase *bumble* elaborates *bum*, and *run* is rhymingly perverted to *rumble*.

rumbler.—4. Prison: low: Australian: ca. 1820–70. Brian Penton, *Landtakers*, 1934. Perversion of **rumbo**, n., 2.

***rumboile** or **rumboyle.** See **romboyle** (*Dict.*).

rumbowling (p. 715), often *rumbolin*, goes back to very early C. 19: it occurs in, e.g., W. N. Glascock, *Sketch-Book*, 2nd Series, 1834, at I, 203. (Moe.)

Rumford, or **Romford, lion** (p. 715): rather, late C. 17–mid-19, for it occurs in B.E., 1699.

rummy (or **Jamaica**) **tea.** Tea laced with rum, esp. when the tea has been made with chlorinated water: Tommies': 1915–18. (A. B. Petch, April 1966.)

rumour!, it's a (p. 715). Extant in Australia: B., 1942.

rump-sprung. 'Said of a woman's dress that, through much wear and a good deal of bending, has taken a permanent bulge over the rump. Knitted dresses are especially vulnerable. Canadian coll.; since ca. 1940.' (Leechman.)

Rumpety. A 'Maurice Farman "Shorthorn" aircraft of the Great War' (1914–18): R.F.C. and R.A.F. (Jackson.)

rumpty, adj. Excellent: Australian: since ca. 1910. Baker. Often elaborated to *rumptydooler*. Ex:

rumtitum (p. 716); often written *rum-ti-tum*. It survived until early C. 20. *Sinks*, 1848, has *rum ti tum with the chill off* (excellent), with a pun on the spirit *rum*. The term *rum-ti-tum* is an elaboration of *rum-tum*, a rhyming reduplication of **rum**, adj., 1 (p. 712). The Australian *rumpty* is a corruption of *rumti* (short for *rumtitum*).

run, v.—9. To desert (v.i.): Naval: late C. 19–20. Granville. Short for *run away*.—10. To *run a sheep* is 'to shear a sheep's fleece near the top, leaving the thick base wool intact' (B., 1959): Aus. rural coll.: late C. 19–20.

run, get the. To be discharged from employment: from ca. 1870. B. & L.

run, give the. To dismiss from employment: since ca. 1875. Prompted by prec. entry.

run, have a.—3. To get drunk; to go absent without leave: Australian Naval: 1939–45. (B., 1943.)—4. To desert ship: Naval: late C. 18–mid-19. (W. N. Glascock, *Sketch-Book*, II, 1826.) Moe.

run a skirt; frequent also as vbl n., *running* . . . To have a mistress: C. 20. (W. McFee, *North of Suez*, 1930.) See **run** and **skirt** in the *Dict.*

run-about.—2. Usually in pl. **run-abouts** (or one word), 'cattle allowed to graze freely': Australian coll.: late C. 19–20. (B., 1943.)

run about after (someone's) **arse.** To be obsequious or subservient to: low: late C. 19–20.

run-around, get or give the. To be treated, to treat, contemptuously or so as to serve a mere whim: Australian: since ca. 1910; by ca. 1945, coll. (B., *Australia Speaks*, 1953.)

run around like a hoo-hum-hah. To act as if one were hysterical or crazy: smart young set (esp. girls'): ca. 1955–60. Gilderdale, 2.

run away. See **toe-bitter**.

run big. More precisely, of a horse forced to race when too fat.

run-flat. A tyre that, if punctured, could be run-on flat for half a mile or so: Army coll.: 1939–45. (P-G-R.)

run for one's money, (get) a. 'Modern humorous reference to patent medicines like Kruschen's Salts' (A. B. Petch, Aug. 22, 1946): since ca. 1925.

run-in. Concerning thefts of bulk goods, 'The normal method was to hire a van from a small lorry-owner, run the van to the warehouse, break in, load the van, take the contents to a "run-in"—usually a shed or garage in the central London area—and return the van' (John Gosling, *The Ghost Squad*, 1959): since ca. 1920: c. >, by 1940, also police s.

run it fine (p. 716). Cf. *cut it close*, itself perhaps coll.

run off, have a. To urinate: Society and middle-class: since ca. 1930. Cf. the S.E. *to run off the bath water* and:

run out (at). To come to; to cost: coll., mostly Australian: since ca. 1920. 'How does this run out?'—'It runs out at six shillings a yard.' (B.P.)

run-out, have a. To urinate: C. 20. (Atkinson.)

run out of road. See **flatter**.

run out on.—2. To leave (someone) in the lurch: coll.: C. 20.

run straight. To remain faithful to one's husband: Society s. (from ca. 1870) >, by 1910, gen. coll. Ex the language of the stable.

run taper. See **taper, run**.

run the ferret. 'In Severn Tunnel, to descale the water main by inserting small propeller' (*Railway*): railwaymen's: C. 20.

run the rabbit. To obtain liquor, esp. if illicitly, after hours: Australian low: C. 20. B., 1942.

run the rule over. See **rule over**.

run up a lane. (Of a horse) to fail to get a place: Australian sporting: since ca. 1935. (B., 1953.) Also *run up lanes*, as in Lawson Glassop, *Lucky Palmer*, 1949.

run up (someone's) **arse.** See **rumble** (someone's) **bumble**.

run up the wall; make (someone) . . . To become bewildered or scared or crazy; to cause someone to do so: 1944 +, Army; 1948 +, general. Perhaps ex a famous exercise in Commando training. '(To have someone) climbing walls is a common and by no means new U.S. expression denoting a state of extreme agitation. A cat seeking to escape from an enclosure will do this' (Robert Clairborne, Aug. 31, 1966).

runabouts. 'Cattle allowed to graze freely' (B., 1959): Aus. rural coll.: late C. 19–20.

runcible. (Of women) sexually attractive: since ca. 1925. 'Rhyming' on *cuntable*; cf. also S.E. *runcible spoon*.

runner.—6. 'A vehicle that was in running order, as opposed to one that was off the road' (P-G-R): Army coll.: 1939–45. (P-G-R.)—7. A deserter from the Armed Forces: since ca. 1940: orig. and still mainly c. (John Gosling, 1959.) Cf. **blower**, 9, above.—8. A platform inspector: railwaymen's: C. 20. (*Railway*.)

runners. See **pots**.

runniel. See **rawniel**.

***running doss; running skipper.** That sleeping place which, on a damp night, a tramp obtains by kicking a cow and lying down on the warm, dry spot vacated by the animal: tramps' c.: C. 20.

running rabbit. Any small object hauled along a horizontal wire to enable trainee predictor-layers to get practice in following a target: Anti-Aircraft: 1938 +. H. & P. Ex 'the Dogs'.

***running ramp.** In *The Post Boy robbed of his Mail*, anon., 1706, it was—to reconstruct an apparent misprint—defined as 'formed of those Home-Beggers that scout for Weddings and Burials': c.: ? ca. 1700–1760.

***running rumble, the.** The practice of a 'running rumbler': ca. 1770–1830. B. & L.

running shoes, give (someone) **his.** To dismiss from office: New Zealand political: C. 20. B., 1941. Cf. **run, get the**.

running skipper. See **running doss**.

running writing. Cursive script: Australian schoolchildren's coll.: C. 20. (B.P.)

runny. A coll., dating from ca. 1910, and used as in Victor Canning, *Polycarp's Progress*, 1935, 'The ices had been runny with the heat.'

runs, the. Diarrhoea: perhaps esp. Australian and New Zealand: late C. 19–20. Ex the frequent and hasty visits to the water-closet.

runty. A dwarf signal: Canadian railroadmen's (– 1931). Adopted from U.S.

ruof.—2. Hence, four shillings: from ca. 1880.

Rupert (p. 717). Also *randy Rupert*: cf. *randy Richard* (s.v. **Richard**, 2: p. 697).—2. Hence, penis: Forces': since ca. 1908.

rush, n., 4, and v., 4. (Of cattle.) A, or to, stampede: Australian coll.: late C. 19–20.

rush, v.—4. See prec. entry.—5. To appropriate: Marlborough College: C. 20. Cf. senses 1, 3, on p. 717.

rush a brew. To make tea: Army officers': 1914–18. See **brew, n.**, 3 (p. 92).

rush of blood to the crutch, a. A sudden access of amorous desire: since ca. 1930. Cf. next two phrases. Also . . . **crotch**.

rush of brains to the feet. A bright idea: non-aristocratic jocularity: from ca. 1903. W. L. George, *The Making of an Englishman*, 1914.

rush of brains to the head, (s)he's had a. A c.p., deprecatory of a sudden bright idea: since ca. 1920.

rush of teeth to the head, a. Prominent teeth: facetious: since ca. 1925.

rush the bucket or growler. To send the printer's devil for a bucket of beer: Canadian printers': C. 20. (Leechman.) 'From the "growling" of the beer taps' (Robert Clairborne).

rushed job. A 'short time': low: C. 20.

rusher.—3. One who sets the pace for a gang of workers: Australian Labour: since ca. 1920. B., 1942.—4. A goat much given to butting: Aus.: late C. 19–20. Ex the corresponding v., as in Edward Dyson, *The Gold Stealers*, 1901, '. . . Billy's goat, Hector, a sturdy black brute much admired as the most inveterate "rusher" in the country. With the boys of Waddy a goat that butted or "rushed" was highly prized as an animal of spirit.'

rushing round like a . . . See **pea in a colander**.

Rusk; usu. in pl., *the Rusks*. The Russians: since ca. 1945. Ex *Russki*. In, e.g., Berkeley Mather, *The Springers*, 1968.

Russian duck (p. 718) was † by 1959 at the latest. (Franklyn, *Rhyming*.)—2. Copulation: low rhyming s.: since ca. 1942. Franklyn 2nd.

Russian Turk. Work: rhyming s.: ca. 1860–1910. (D. W. Barrett, *Navvies*, 1880.)

Russians or Rooshians. 'Wild horses, wild cattle' (Baker): Australian: late C. 19–20. A particularisation of **Russian** (p. 717); *Rooshian*: C. 20 only.

Russki (p. 718) was revived in World War II; again by the Army. (P-G-R.)

Rusty. Inseparable nickname for men surnamed *Adams*: Services (mostly the Army): C. 20. (P-G-R.)

rusty, adj.—2. Amorous; lecherous: Australian: late C. 19–20. (A. R. L. Wiltshire, letter of June 9, 1941.)

rusty ballocks. A red-headed man: mostly Naval: late C. 19–20.

Rusty Guts. H. M. S. *Restiguch*: Naval: 1939–45.

rusty rifle, get—or have—a. (Of men) to catch—to have—a venereal disease, esp. syphilis: mostly Services': since ca. 1925.

rutty. In a, leading to, consisting of a metaphorical rut, e.g. *rutty jobs*: coll: since ca. 1930. *Weekly Telegraph*, April 27, 1946.

rux, n. and v.: p. 718. Sense 2 of the n. as it stands should be under the v. The correct sense 2 of the n. is 'noise, fuss, etc.: R.N. College, Dartmouth slang': Granville.—3. In Public School s., *rux up the arse* = a, or to, kick: since ca. 1880. The ultimate source of all these senses is perhaps *rough-house*, n. (p. 708), as it is of U.S. and Canadian *ruckus*.

ry dates from ca. 1860. Brewer's anecdotal origin may just conceivably be correct. (p. 718.)

ryder derives more prob. ex Romany *ruder*, to clothe: B. & L.

ryebuck or rybuck. Usually ribuck (p. 696).

S

S.A.B.U. See **T.A.B.U.**

S.A.M.F.U. *Self adjusting military 'fuck-up'* (muddle): South African soldiers': 1940-5.

S.F.A. *S*weet *F*anny *A*dams, i.e. nothing: C. 20. Gerald Kersh, *Bill Nelson*, 1942. See **Fanny Adams** (p. 266).

S.N.A.F.U., usually solid (*snafu*). *Situation normal, all fucked up* (politely: . . . *fouled up*): Forces', originally and mainly Army: 1940 +. (P-G-R.) It spread to the Americans. Cf. the American derivative adj. **snafues**, bungled, chaotic, as in 'Everything snafues from the start' (Grover C. Hall, Jr, *1000 Destroyed*, 1961).

S.N.E.F.U., usu. written solid—*SNEFU* or *snefu*, or even *sneefoo*. 'Situation normal—everything fucked up': a Forces', esp. Army, mostly officers', c.p., dating from ca. 1941. A variant of **S.N.A.F.U.** above.

S.O.B. (p. 720) is also very common in Canada. Both countries adopted it ex U.S. Of the Australian use, B.P. says, 'It is very widely known but not very commonly used.'—2. 'Shit or bust' (see p. 758): since ca. 1925.

S.O.B.'s. *S*illy *O*ld *B*uggers, i.e. Wardroom officers over the advanced age of 39': Naval officers': since ca. 1914. (Granville.) Contrast **B.Y.F.'s.**

S.O.S.—2. A member of the Australian Signal Corps: Australian soldiers': 1939 +. B., 1942.

S.P. joint. A starting-price betting-shop: Australian sporting: C. 20. Baker.

S.P. merchant. A starting-price bookmaker: Australian sporting: since ca. 1920. (B., *Australia Speaks*, 1953.)

S.S.; P.P. 'Shimmy' showing; petticoat peeping: hortatory c.pp. from one girl to another, in ref. to dress disarranged: ca. 1895-1915. Petticoats have been discarded.

S.T.; esp. in plural S.Ts. *S*anitary *t*owel(s): feminine coll.: since ca. 1940.

S.U.E. See **servants' united effort.**

S.W.A.K. 'Sealed with a kiss' on the back of an envelope: coll.: late C. 19-20. Also *S.W.A.L.K.*, where *L.* = loving.

S.W.A.L.C.A.K.W.S. Humorous variant of preceding. 'Sealed with a lick 'cos a kiss won't stick.'

s.y.t. A 'sweet young thing' (girl): Australian: since ca. 1950. (B.P.)

sa soldi. Sixpence: see **sa** in *Dict.*

Sabrina. 'Prestwin silo wagon' (*Railway* 2nd): railwaymen's: since ca. 1925.

Sabu. See **Nabu.**

sac. A *s*accharine tablet: coll. (domestic, and small traders'): heard in 1917, but not gen. until 1942.

sack, n.—2. A hammock: Naval: C. 19. *The Night Watch* (I, 184), 1828. Moe.

sack, v., 2 (p. 720). An early record: *Chaplain's Twenty-Third Report of the Preston House of Correction* (in a prisoner's statement), 1846.

sack, get the. To be dismissed from employment: an early example occurs in *Sessions*, Aug. 23, 1843.

sack 'em up men. Resurrectionists: ca. 1830-70. Harvey Graham, *Surgeons All*, 1939.

sack of taters. A stick of (small) bombs, e.g. incendiaries: R.A.F.: 1939 +. H. & P. Humorous. Delivered like **groceries.**

sad.—2. 'Don't be sad . . . Don't be mean,' C. P. Wittstock, letter of May 23, 1946: South African: C. 20. I.e. don't be so serious that you can't be generous: cf. Dutch *sadie klass*, 'a dull dog'.

sad sack. A spoil-sport or a wet-blanket: Naval (lower-deck): adopted, in 1943, ex U.S. servicemen. But in U.S., a *sad sack* is 'the inevitable hopeless recruit or enlisted man, always a figure of fun'. (Orig., a blundering, unlikable youth—students' s., since ca. 1930; see W. & F.) 'In the U.S., almost a culture hero, and well-known in Canada.' (Leechman.)

sadogue. 'A fat, easy-going person'. (L. E. F. English, *Historic Newfoundland*, 1955): Newfoundland: perhaps coll. rather than s., or dial. rather than either: C. 20. A '*sad dog*' or gay fellow?

safack, properly **'safack.** It's a fact: Cockney sol.: C. 19-20. Michael Harrison, *What Are We Waiting For?*, 1939. Compare **sard.**

*safe. (Gen. *the safe*.) Inside waistcoat pocket: c.: late C. 19-20. Esp. among pickpockets.—2. A condom: Australian: since ca. 1925. Perhaps suggested by **safety** below.

safe as . . ., as (p. 721): *as safe as the bank* occurs in *Boxiana*, III, 1818: there, it is written . . . *Bank*, which implies *the Bank of England*, a phrase that, therefore, dates prob. from late C. 18.

safety. A condom: Australian: since ca. 1920. 'She said it was no go without a safety.' Orig. euphemistic?

Saff. *S*outh *A*frican *A*ir *F*orce: 1939-45. On analogy of **Raff.**

sag, n.; esp. have the sags, to lack energy: racing cyclists': since ca. 1945. Cf. 'the bonk'. Hence, **sag-wagon,** a van that, following a race, picks up exhausted riders.

sag, v.—2. To be illicitly absent from work: Liverpool: late C. 19-20: hence—3. To play truant: Merseyside: since ca. 1930. (*Woman*, Aug. 28, 1965.)

saha! Good-night!: Naval: late C. 19-20. (*Weekly Telegraph*, Nov. 1942.) Ex Maltese.

Sahara. 'Tall person . . . (miles and miles of blow all),' *The Cape Times*, June 3, 1946: South African: C. 20.

sail close to the wind has in the Royal Navy (late C. 19-20) a specific coll. sense: 'to take risks with Naval Law'. Granville.

sailer. A loose branch: coll.—a New Zealand

forestry term: C. 20. From a N.Z. cutting of late 1967. In a high wind, it tends to 'sail away'.

sailor is a Regular Army term of ca. 1855–1910. 'A "sailor" was the slang term for any person whose nature was so generous, and whose finances so sound, as to allow the quaffing of many cups at his personal charge,' Robert Blatchford, *My Life in the Army*, 1910.

sailor on a water-cart. Ineffective; inadequate: coll.: prob. C. 19–20. (Laurie Atkinson, Sept. 11, 1967.)

sailor's best friend, a. A hammock: Naval: C. 20. Granville records the pleasant tradition that, 'if properly lashed with seven regulation marline hitches', it 'will keep him afloat for twenty-four hours'. Cf. **sailor's friend** (p. 722). Prompted by **soldier's best friend**—see below.

sailor's cake. An occasional variant of *Navy cake*: Naval: since ca. 1940.

sailor's hornpipe. A Wren: Naval: since ca. 1941.

sailors on the sea; often shortened to *sailors*. Tea: rhyming s.: since ca. 1940, but not common. Franklyn 2nd.

sailor's prick. See **salt's pricker** below.

saint and sinner. Dinner: rhyming s.: late C. 19–20. Franklyn, *Rhyming*. Cf. *glorious sinner* (p. 333).

St Kilda Road Commandos. The staff of the Allied Land H.Q., Melbourne: Australian: 1939–45. (B., 1943.)

St Lubbock's Day should be 'August'—not 'a' —'Bank Holiday'.

St Martin's (le Grand). A hand: Londoners' rhyming s.: late C. 19–20.

St Pat. St Patrick: (mostly Anglo-Irish) coll.: C. 19–20.

St Peter's son (p. 723). Rather of ca. 1710–1850.

St Stephen's hell. Ware explains thus: 'When the Parnellite "split" took place, the Irish Nationalist members "discussed" in this chamber for many days—the noise resulting in the bestowal by the lower officials of this title upon the room in question.'

Saints (p. 723), 2. A more prob. etymology resides in the fact that the original name of the Club was Southampton *St Mary's* Football Club.

sal, 1 (p. 273): earlier in Anon., *A Congratulatory Epistle from a Reformed Rake*, 1728, p. 17, 'She's just down in a *Sal*.'

salam; salams. Incorrect for *salaam* (v.) and *salaams*, implying as they do a wrong pron.; the former occurs in Smyth's *Sailor's Word Book*, 1867.

sale, make a. To vomit: Australian low: C. 20. B., 1942.

Sale of Two Titties, A. Dickens's *A Tale of Two Cities*: an intentional spoonerism: since ca. 1925. Perhaps orig. Canadian. (Leechman.)

Salford Docks; sometimes merely **Salfords.** Rocks, esp. on a shore or coastline: rhyming s., esp. in Manchester: C. 20. Salford stands on the Mersey Ship Canal.

's'all or 'sall or even sall. It's, or that's, all: semi-literate coll.: late C. 19–20. Ruth Park, *A Power of Roses*, 1953, 'Everything sall right.'

Sallies.—2. As *the S.*, it = the Salvation Army: Australian: since ca. 1910. (D'Arcy Niland, *Call Me . . .*, 1958.)

Sally; Sally Ann. A Salvation Army hostel or canteen: C. 20. The short form occurs in James Curtis, *What Immortal Hand*, 1939.

Sally Fairy Ann! It doesn't matter!: Army: 1915–18. An occ. variant of san fairy ann (*Dict.*).

Sally Rand. H.M.S. *St Laurent*: Naval: 1939–45.

Sally Thompson. A shearer's cook: Australian rural: since ca. 1910. B., 1942.

*salmon.—3. A corpse fished from a river (esp. the Thames): water rats' c.: mid-C. 19–20. B. & L.

Salmon and Gluckstein. The *Scharnhorst* and *Gneisenau*, heavy German cruisers: R.A.F.: 1941–2. By 'Hobson-Jobson', on the well-known firm of tobacconists.

salmon and trout.—4. Stout (the drink): rhyming s.: C. 20. Franklyn, *Rhyming*.

salmon trout. Variant of **salmon and trout,** esp. in sense 3 ('gout'): C. 20.

salt, n.—3. Money collected at Montem: Etonians': from ca. 1790. *Spy*, 1825; B. & L.—4. 'Plain tobacco to mix with dagga', C. P. Wittstock, letter of May 23, 1946. South African c.: C. 20.

salt, v., 4 (p. 723) occurs earlier—in, e.g., Wm Kelly, *Life in Victoria*, 1859.

salt and batter. Assault and battery: partly s., partly illiterate: since ca. 1830. An Old Etonian, *Cavendo Tutus*; or, *Hints upon Slip-Slop*, being the 2nd part of his *The Alphabet Annotated*, 1853. Cf.:

*salt and rob. Assault and robbery: South African c.: C. 20. *The Cape Times*, May 23, 1946.

salt cat. A mess of 'old mortar, cumin seed, and wine' for birds to peck at: bird-fanciers': mid-C. 19–20. B. & L.

salt chuck, sea-water; *the s.c.*, the sea: Canadian: C. 20. Amerindian pidgin? 'Ex the Chinook jargon (*chuck*, water). Quite common in British Columbia.' Leechman.

salt eel (p. 724) has survived well into C. 20, although little used after ca. 1930. (P-G-R.)

salt junk (p. 724) occurs earlier in George R. Gleig, *The Chelsea Pensioners*, 1829, at II, 259, as a military term. (Moe.)

salta-di-banco is C. 17 erroneous for *saltimbanco*. O.E.D.

Saltash luck (p. 724): also *S. catch*: C. 20. Granville, 'A wet stern and no fish'.—There is a pun: 'salt(-wet) arse'.

saltie or **salty.** A man-eating crocodile of the coastal areas: N. Queensland coll.: C. 20. (Jean Devanney, *Travels in North Queensland*, 1951.)

salt's pricker (p. 774). The rolled leaf tobacco tightly bound with marline as put up by seamen in the R.N. was known to their friends ashore to whom they smuggled it as *sailors' prick*, ex the shape.

salvage (p. 724). Also gen. Australian: B., 1942.

Salvagger Agger, the. The Salvation Army: Oxford undergraduates' (− 1922). Marples, 2.

salvation. Station: rhyming s.: ca. 1870–1914. (C. Bent, *Criminal Life*, 1891.)

Salvation Navy, the. The Royal Navy: since ca. 1916. Ex 'Thank God, we've got a Navy!'

Salvo.—2. A Salvation Army officer; *the S.*, the Salvation Army: mostly Australian: since ca. 1917. (B., 1943.)—3. As *the Salvos*, it = the Salvation Army: Australian: since ca. 1910. (Jon Cleary, *The Sundowners*, 1952.)—4. (Ex senses 2 and 3.) Adj.: Salvationist: Australian: since ca. 1920. (H. Drake-Brockman, *The Blister*, 1937.)

salvo. 'A "snappy come-back" which in an argument, completely floors your opponent' (Granville): Naval officers': since ca. 1938. Cf. the R.A.F.'s **shoot down in flames.**

Sambo (p. 724) occurs in John Atkins, *A Voyage to Guinea, Brasil, and the West-Indies*, 1735. (Moe.)

same diff! The Australian form of the next: since ca. 1945. (B.P.)

same difference, it's the. A Canadian c.p.: since ca. 1940. Elliptical for 'It's the same thing; there is no difference'. (Leechman.)

same here; same there. What you say applies equally to me; to you: resp. from ca. 1880 and from ca. 1870, the latter being orig. a tailors' c.p. B. & L.—2. Either *same here* or *the same here*, I fully agree: Australian coll.: C. 20. (B., 1943.)

same old shit but (or **only**) **more of it.** The Canadian Army equivalent, 1939–45, of *S.N.A.F.U.*

Same Olds, the. Essendon footballers: Melbournites': since ca. 1925. (B., 1943.)

Sammy Hall. See **rick**, v.

[**sampsman** is B. & L.'s error for **scampsman** (*Dict.*).]

Samson. A combined magnetic and acoustic mine: Naval: 1940 +. Very powerful.

San Mig. 'San Miguel beer, famous in Hong Kong' (Granville, Nov. 22, 1962): Naval: since late 1940's.

sanakatowmer (p. 725) should be *sanakatowzer*, as in the next entry, which derives therefrom. It occurs in Rudyard Kipling's 'The Bonds of Discipline' (ca. 1902), collected in *Traffics and Discoveries*, 1904: 'a sanakatowzer of a smite with the flat of his sword'. (With thanks to Rear-Admiral P. W. Brock, R.N., C.B., D.S.O.)

sanakatowzer. Anything very big; e.g. 'a sanakatowzer of an apple': Milton Junior School, Bulawayo: since ca. 1925. An excellent example of arbitrary coinage that does yet evoke the idea of great size.

Sanctimoody. Sanctimonious and moody: mostly Nonconformists': C. 20. With a more than casual glance at the American evangelists, Ira David *Sankey* (1840–1908) and Dwight L. *Moody* (1837–99), who, at their meetings, used their own hymnals, *Sacred Songs* (1873) and *Gospel Hymns* (1875–91).

sandgroper (p. 726): by 1945, ob.; by 1960, †. (B.P.)

sand-happy. Odd or eccentric as a result of long service in the desert: Army: 1942–3. Cf. **bomb-happy.**

sand-hog. See **bends, the**, 2.

sand in one's hair, have. To be accustomed to the desert: Army in N. Africa, World War II. (P-G-R.)

sand in their boots. See **boots, blood in their.**

sand-rat. A moulder in a foundry: engineers': from ca. 1875. B. & L.—2. An Indian Army term, dating from ca. 1880. Richards, '. . . These native girls, who being in the last stages of the dreaded disease and rotten inside and out, only appeared after dark. These were the sand-rats and it was a horrible form of suicide to go with them.'

sand-scratch. 'To search for surface gold' (B., 1959): Aus. rural coll.: late C. 19–20.—2. (Hence

?) 'To be on the lookout for a feminine companion' (*ibid.*): Aus. low: since ca. 1930.

sand-scratcher (usually in pl.). A seaman rating: Naval: C. 20. (P-G-R.)

sand(-)vein. The notochord (*chorda dorsalis*), seen as a dark line down the back of a prepared shrimp: Canadian: ? coll., ? rather dial.: late C. 19–20. (Leechman.)

sandbag Mary Ann! It doesn't matter!: Army: 1915–18. A variant—cf. *Sally Fairy Ann* —of **san fairy ann** (p. 726).

sandgroping, n. Living in Western Australia: Aus.: ca. 1910–60. (B., 1959.) Ex **Sandgroper** on p. 726.

sandies. See **Sandy**, 2, in the *Dict.*

sandman. A footpad, a 'sandbagger': Australian: since ca. 1919. B., 1942.

sandy. A cute little surfing girl: Australian teenage surfers': since ca. 1962. *Pix*, Sept. 28, 1963.

sandy blight (p. 726). Since late C. 19, as Sidney J. Baker tells me. By 1940, Standard Australian.

Sandy Brown. See 'Nicknames'.

sandy hooker. A Nelson-born musterer of sheep: Canterbury and Marlborough shepherds' (New Zealand): late C. 19–20. B., 1941. Why?

Sandy McNab. A taxicab: rhyming s.: since ca. 1946. (Franklyn, *Rhyming*.)—2. A scab: Australian rhyming s.: since ca. 1920. (Jean Devanny; B., 1953.)

sane, n. The sum of ten shillings: low Australian: since ca. 1925. (B., 1943.) Origin? 'Seems to be derived from S. German numeral "zehn" (pron. *tsane*). Could it have been brought in by German immigrants, or conceivably by repatriated Anzac ex-POWs of World War I?' (H. R. Spencer): more prob. the latter; if so, the dating should rather be 'since 1919 or 1920'.—2. The sum of one pound: Aus. low: since ca. 1925. (B., 1959.)—3, 4. A prison sentence of ten months; 10 ounces of tobacco: Aus., the former, c.; the latter c. and low s.: since ca. 1930. B., 1959, adds that '10 years' jail or £10 is most commonly a *brick*'.

sanitary, the, as in 'Here comes the sanitary'. The Sanitary Inspector: coll.: since ca. 1946.

sanno. A sanitary inspector: Australian: since ca. 1930. (B., 1953.)

sanny. Sanatorium: Public Schools': C. 20.

Santa Claus. A 'sugar daddy' (rich elderly man keeping or assisting a young mistress): since ca. 1920.

sap-head, adj. See 'Epithets'. A coll. verging on S.E.

sap the tlas. A Cockney c.p. 'used when the drink does not go round freely': ca. 1880–1910. B. & L. Back s. for *pass the salt*.

Sarah Soo. A Jew: since ca. 1925: rhyming s., orig. underworld, >, by 1960, fairly common. John Gosling, *The Ghost Squad*, 1959.

Saray Morays, the. See **Jaapies** above.

sard, properly *'sard*. It's hard: Cockney sol.: late C. 19–20. Michael Harrison, *What Are We Waiting For?*, 1939, "'sard to say, boy"'. Compare **safack** and **sri.**

sardine tin.—2. A Bren Gun carrier: Army: since ca. 1938. H. & P. Humorous.—3. A torpedo-carrying 'plane: R.A.F.: 1939 +. Jackson. —4. A submarine: Naval (lower-deck): 1939 +. Granville. Cf. sense 1 (p. 727).—5. A minicar:

since early 1960's. (*Evening Echo*, Bournemouth, April 16, 1966.)

sarga (p. 727) was orig. an Arabic pronunciation, adopted by the Regulars.

sarker. See 'Mock-Auction Slang' above. Since late 1940's; (cf. **sarky** on p. 72).

sarm. Image: Australian: since ca. 1945. 'He's the dead sarm of his father.' This could derive ex a dial. pronunciation (*sahm*) of *same*; but probably Mr Edwin Morrisby's explanation, in letter of Aug. 30, 1958, is correct: Chinese *san* (pronounced *sahn*), the number 3, as used in the game of fan-tan, where 3 is said to be the 'safest' number on which to bet.

sarnies. Sandwiches: Army: C. 20. Hence, since ca. 1925, Liverpool s.

sarse; occasionally **sarspidilly.** Sarsaparilla: Australian: since ca. 1925. (B., 1953.)

s'arvo. This afternoon: low Australian: since ca. 1910. (B., 1953.) This *arvo* (see **arvo** above).

sass, get too much. To become 'too bold, or powerful, or wicked': 'English negro s.' of the West Coast of Africa: from ca. 1870. B. & L. I.e. 'sauce'.

Sasso, the. The Senior Air Staff Officer: R.A.F. coll.: 1936 +. Partridge, 1945. Ex the initials by which he is usually referred to: *S.A.S.O.*

satchel-arsed fellow; satchel-arsed son of a whore. A man fitted by Jon Bee's indictment in 1823: 'Some chaps put on certain habiliments in a very bag-like manner': † by 1900.

Sat'd'y; Sat'day. Saturday: illiterate: C. 19–20. (Pugh.) The Cockney pronunciation is *Sa'dee*: short *a*, followed by a glottal stop.

Saturday-afternoon sailor. A Naval reservist: Australian Naval: 1939–45. (B., 1943.)

Saturday afternoon soldiers. The Home Guard: Army: 1940–5. Cf.:

Saturday night sailors. 'Lower-deck pre-1939 view of the Royal Naval Volunteer Reserve' (Granville). Compare the R.A.F.'s **Week-End Air Force.**

Saturday-night security. A steady boy friend: Australian: since ca. 1945. He ensures that she doesn't have to stay at home on Saturday nights—a condition truly to be deplored. (B.P.)

Saturday while. See **Friday while.**

saucepan. A (young) boy: Australian: since ca. 1920. (B., 1953.) Short for *saucepan lid*, 3.—2. Short for **saucepan lid**, 1.

saucepan lid. £1: C. 20. Rhyming on *quid*.—2. A Jew: rhyming s. (on *Yid*): late C. 19–20. Franklyn, *Rhyming.*—3. A child: rhyming s. (on *kid*): late C. 19–20. Ibid.—4. A mild deception, a 'leg-pulling'; hence also v., as in 'Now you're saucepan-lidding me': rhyming s. (on *kid*): late C. 19–20. *Ibid.*—5. As a collective plural, it = money, esp. in coin: C. 20. Franklyn 2nd adduces *heap of saucepan lids*, lots of money.

saucer, off one's. Not in the humour; indisposed: Australian: ca. 1860–1910. B. & L.—2. Crazy: Australian: C. 20. B., 1942.

*sauney. A variant of **sawney,** 2 (*Dict.*).

sausage, n.—4. A draught-excluder placed at foot of a door: domestic coll.: C. 20. Ex shape.—5. A dog in heat: since ca. 1945. A pun on *hot dog.*—6. Short for *sausage and mash,* money in cash: since ca. 1870.—7. See **sausage roll** below.

sausage, v. To cash; esp. *sausage a goose's,* to

cash a cheque: low: from ca. 1920. Abbr. *sausage and mash,* rhyming s., to cash, itself dating from ca. 1870. Moreover, *goose's = goose's neck,* rhyming s. (late C. 19–20) for a cheque.

sausage, not to have a. To be penniless, esp. temporarily: from ca. 1927. (Peter Chamberlain.) See prec. entry.

sausage and mash, n. See **sausage, n.,** 6, and **sausage, v.,** both above.—2. A collision: rhyming s. (on *crash* or *smash*): since the late 1950's. Franklyn 2nd.

sausage dog. A dachshund: Australian: since ca. 1930. (B.P.)

sausage game. A German game: billiards-players': from ca. 1870; ob. B. & L.

sausage machine, the. A synonym of **mincing machine.**

sausage roll, or capitals; often shortened to *sausage* (or *S.*). A Pole: rhyming s.: prob. since 1939, ex Poland's fate in World War II. John Gosling, *The Ghost Squad,* 1959; Franklyn 2nd.

sausages. Fetters: low: ca. 1820–65. *Sinks.* 1848. Shape: string of sausages = a chain.—2. Side whiskers: mid-C. 19–20.

sav. A saveloy: low: C. 20. (James Curtis, *The Gilt Kid,* 1936.)

savages. Men able to claim 'native leave', granted to those whose homes are in or near the port where their ships are lying: Australian Naval: 1939–45.

save one's bacon. See **bacon, save one's** (*Dict.*).

saved by his clergy. See 'Tavern terms', § 4.

saved by the bell. Saved by a lucky intervention: coll.; often as a c.p.: late C. 19–20. Ex the bell signifying the end of a round in a boxing match.

saveloy. A boy: rhyming s.: C. 20. Franklyn 2nd.

Saveloy, the. The Savoy Hotel: London taxi-drivers': since ca. 1910. Herbert Hodge, 1939.

savings, take up. See **take up.**

savoy, v. (p. 728). The form *sabe* should rather be dated 'since ca. 1820', for it occurs in, e.g., *The Dublin University Magazine* of Aug. 1834 (p. 145) as 'No sabe dat pigeon'.

saw-off. 'A tie; one wins on this deal and loses on that, it's a saw-off' (Leechman): Canadian: since ca. 1910.

saw off a chunk or **a piece.** To coït: Canadian: since ca. 1920. Semantically cf. the phrases cited at *slice, take a,* on p. 781, and *tear off a piece* below.

*saw them off. To snore; to sleep soundly: C. 20 c. >, ca. 1940, low s. John Worby, *Spiv's Progress,* 1939. Ex the noise made with a saw clumsily handled.

saw-tooth edged beanie. See **beanie.**

sawdust bloke. A circus rider: circus coll.: from ca. 1860. B. & L.

Sawdust Caesar, the or **that.** Benito Mussolini, the Italian dictator: since ca. 1925; after 1945, merely historical. *Sawdust Caesar* was the title of a biography published ca. 1937.

sawdust lurk, the. 'Stuffing the differential of an old car with sawdust to get a better price for it' (B.P.): Australian secondhand-car dealers': since ca. 1920. Cf. **speedo lurk, the,** below.

sawed off. Short: the Canadian form of **sawn off** below, as in 'Look at that sawed-off little runt' (instanced by Leechman).

sawn. A softy, a 'dope': low Australian: since ca. 1920. (Kylie Tennant, *The Joyful Condemned*, 1953.) Ex *sawney.*

sawn off. (Of a person) short; small; Services (esp. R.A.F.) coll.: since ca. 1920. H. & P. I.e. truncated.

sawn off at the waist, should be. An R.A.F. c.p. applied to a 'dumb' girl since ca. 1930.

sawyer. 'The repulsive grasshopper called *weta* by the Maoris,' B., 1941: New Zealand: since ca. 1880.

sax.—2. Sixpence: Australian: since ca. 1920. B., 1942. Cf.:—

saxa. A saxophone: Australian: since ca. 1920. (K. S. Prichard, *Haxby's Circus*, 1930.) Cf. *sax*, 1, on p. 729.

saxpence!, bang goes (p. 729). Rather, re-popularised by Lauder; originated by Charles Keene in *Punch*, Dec. 5, 1868.

say, 1 (p. 729). Earlier in Mayhew, I, 1851.

say it again! I heartily agree with you: tailors' c.p.: from ca. 1870. B. & L.

say one's piece. See **piece.**

say-so. A leader or chief; a boss: Australian: since ca. 1930. B., 1942. '*I* say so, *do* it!'

say when you're mad! 'Tell me when you're ready to lift': Canadian workmen's c.p. as from one to another: since ca. 1930. (Leechman.)

saying one's prayers, be. To be scrubbing the floor: jocular domestic: late C. 19–20.

scab, n.—4. A scarab: mostly Public and Grammar Schools': since ca. 1925. Nicholas Blake, *Head of a Traveller*, 1948.—5. See **rats.**

scab, v.—2. V.t., to treat as 'scabs': from ca. 1906. Francis E. Brett Young, *Pilgrim's Rest*, 1922, '[The rioting strikers] went away, saying they'd come back again and scab us to-night.'

scabby.—5. Hence, a non-Union worker: Australian: since ca. 1910. B., 1942.

scads. Much; e.g. 'scads of money': adopted, ca. 1935, from U.S. esp. by would-be 'slick' thriller-writers.

scalawag (see *Dict.*) is prob. cognate with, or a survival of, the † Scottish *scurryvaig*, a vagabond: itself perhaps ex L. *scurra vagas*, a wandering buffoon (O.E.D.).

scald, n. Very hot tea (the beverage): Naval ratings': C. 19. Wm N. Glascock, *Sketch-Book*, 2nd Series, 1834, I, 53, 'a cup of scald', and 56, 'Half an hour was the time allowed to the discussion of the "scald".' (Moe.)

scalded-cat raids. German air-raids of 1943 and earlier half of 1944: that period. Fearing invasion, the Germans were jumpy; they made numerous tip-and-run raids.

scale, v.—5. Hence, to swindle: Australian: since ca. 1920. B., 1942.—6. Hence (?), to ride illicitly free on train, tram, bus: Australian: since ca. 1920. Baker.

Scale 'em Corner. 'A George Street corner, near Central Station, Sydney'—where appointments are not kept: since ca. 1920. Baker.

scale on. To treat (someone) sarcastically: Shrewsbury: since mid-1930's. Marples.

scaler.—2. Hence (?), a thief, a swindler: Australian low: since ca. 1920.—3. One who rides illicitly free on train, bus, etc.: Australian low: since early 1920's. B., 1942. Ex sense 6 of the v. **scale.** *Not* low, B.P. assures me.

scales. An epaulette: Australian Naval: since ca. 1935.

scaling, vbl n. The practice of illicitly riding free on a bus: Aus.: since ca. 1920.

scallywagging, n. Guerilla warfare: military: since 1940. Peter Fleming, *Invasion 1940*, 1957. Cf. **scalawag** on p. 729. Prim—or jocular—disapproval?

scalp ticket. Return half of a train or bus ticket: Australian: since ca. 1920. Baker.

scaly, n. A crocodile: Australian: since ca. 1910. (B., 1943.)

scaly-back.—2. A Naval pensioner: Naval: since ca. 1910. (P-G-R.)

scammel. A breakdown vehicle: Army coll.: 1939–45. Ex the firm of engineers. (P-G-R.)

***scamper,** n. See **foot scamper, the,** above.

Scan. 'A Scandinavian printing machine invented by a native of Stockholm': printers': from ca. 1870; ob. B. & L.

scan. 'Common U.S. and Canadian sol. for *skim*. "I was too busy to do more than scan the paper"' (Leechman): C. 20.

Scandinoogian. An occ., mainly nautical, form of **Scandihoofian** (*Dict.*). William McFee, *Sailors of Fortune*, 1930.

scanty. Allowance of bread (ca. 1870–1905): a small loaf for study tea on Sundays (since ca. 1905): Rossall School. Marples.

Scapa Flow is a folk-etymological elaboration of *scarper*, 1 (p. 731), as if rhyming s. on 'to *go*': since ca. 1918.

scapali is a variant of *scaparey*, q.v. at **Johnny Scaparey** (*Dict.*).

scapathy. See **orkneyitis.**

scarce, make oneself (p. 731). Grose, 1785, is the earliest authority, for the supposed Smollett quotation occurs, as the O.E.D. has shown, in Malkin's translation, 1809, of *Gil Blas.*

scare the shit out of; scare shitless. To scare very badly indeed: low: late C. 19–20. A variant (C. 20) of **frighten . . .** above.

Scarecrow Patrol, the. Coastal Command's patrol by Hornet Moths and Tiger Moths in Sept.–Dec. 1939: Coastal Command: 1939; ob. Ex their pathetic inadequacy to the immensity of the task.

scared fartless. Admittedly much afraid: Canadian: C. 20. Since the late 1930's, also English. A|'cleaned-up 'variant arose ca. 1942: *scared spitless.*

scared shitless. Scared to death: mostly Canadian: C. 20. Cf. **frighten the shit out of,** but imm. ex **scare shitless,** both noted above; cf. also **scared fartless** above.

scaredy. A timorous person: a frightened one: Anglo-Irish: since ca. 1910. (Patrick Doncaster, *A Sight for a Drum-Beat*, 1947.)

scarlet-runner, 3 (p. 731). Also *scarlet-runners*, the old-fashioned red-jacketed uniform: same period. (Gilbert Frankau, *Peter Jackson*, 1920.)

scarlet slugs. Tracer-fire from Bofors anti-aircraft guns: Services (esp. R.A.F.): 1939 +. H. & P., 'Apt name'.

scarve. A finger-ring: parlary: late C. 19–20. Sydney Lester, *Vardi the Palarey*, (?) 1937. Not from any Italian word, but app.—this is a mere guess—a parlary'd shape of an English term: *scarf*-ring.

scat. But as *scram,* q.v. in *Dict.*, is an abbr. of S.E. *scramble,* so prob. is *scat* an abbr. of S.E. *scatter*; likewise v.i.—2. In the R.A.F. (1939 +), to take off in a hurry. Partridge, 1945.

scatter.—2. To make water: proletarian: from ca. 1860. B. & L.

scatters, the. Diarrhœa; *get the scatters*, to feel very nervous: Naval: C. 20. 'Taffrail', *The Sub*, 1917.

scatty (p. 731). Earlier in J. W. Horsley, *I Remember*, 1912. In W. H. Davis, *Beggars*, 1909, the sense appears to be rather that of 'short-tempered', as if from **scotty** (p. 735).

scavenge.—2. To cadge money, or to thieve in a petty way: Australian: since ca. 1925. B., 1942.

scene. 'Something that's happening or the place where it's happening' (*The Victoria Daily Colonist*, April 16, 1959, 'Basic Beatnik'): Canadian jazz-lovers' and musicians': since ca. 1955. Adopted, ca. 1962, in Britain by jazz musicians and devotees, by drug addicts, by beatniks and then hippies, for the 'world' comprised by those three classes or for 'any specific part of it' (Peter Fryer in *The Observer* colour supplement, Dec. 3, 1967). In the underworld, the scene of a crime, the set-up of a burglary or a hold-up: by 1964 at latest. (James Barlow, *The Burden of Proof*, 1968.)—2. Hence, the performers, the active participants: raffish London: since ca. 1964. (James Barlow, *ibid.*)

scent, on the. On the road; travelling about: show- and circus-men's: from ca. 1865. B. & L.

*****schfatzer.** A fellow, a chap: c.: since ca. 1930. (Norman.) 'Refers esp. to an old or, at the least, elderly man and is a misshapen form of the Yiddish word for "father"' (Julian Franklyn). Ramsey Spencer, on the other hand, writes (March 1967): 'This appears to come from Standard German "Schwatzer"—chatter-box, bore, gas-bag, blatherskite.'

schill. See **shill**.

*****schip.** Wine: South African c.: C. 20; by 1945, low s. 'Prob. from a brand of sherry—"Ship Sherry",' C. P. Wittstock, letter of May 23, 1946.

schitz or **schiz** or **skitz** or **skiz.** A schizophrenic: since the late 1920's. (Zenia Field, *Under Lock and Key*, 1963.) Cf. next entry.

schizo. A schizophrenic: psychologists', esp. psychiatrists' coll.: since ca. 1925. Nigel Balchin, *Mine Own Executioner*, 1945.

schlemihl. A booby: Jewish coll.: late C. 19–20. Ex Yiddish.

*****schlent.** An impostor: c.: from ca. 1921. *The Pawn-shop Murder*. Ex:

*****schlent,** v.i. To double-cross; to be evasive for illicit ends: c.: from ca. 1920. Ibid. Ex **schlenter** (*Dict.*).

schlepper-in. A barker (see **barker**, 3, in *Dict.*): orig. and mainly Jewish: C. 20. Via Yiddish ex Ger. *schleppen*, to tug, haul, hence to tout for customers. (Ramsey Spencer.)

schlog (or **slog**) **it on.** To raise the price extortionately: Australian: since ca. 1925. B., 1942. A literal translation of Standard Ger. *auf den Preis schlagen*—clap the price on, hence push the price up' (Ramsey Spencer).

Probably from *schlock* (Yiddish) = shoddy, overpriced. '"It's the biggest schlock house on Seventh Avenue"—J. Weidner, *I Can Get It for You Wholesale*, c. 1940': Robert Clairborne, Aug. 31, 1966.

schmal(t)z, n. and adj. (Something) entirely satisfactory, notably if it exhibits panache and esp. of a performance, as in 'Gee, that's schmalz!': theatrical, mostly in Variety: adopted, ca. 1957, ex U.S., but drastically adapted from the orig. sense of the n., which means 'sweetly sentimental music or song or performance'—a sense current, since ca. 1955, in Britain also. (Richard Merry.) Ex Yiddish *schmaltz*, 'chicken fat, used for cooking, hence greasy, slick' (Wentworth & Flexner). Hence the adj. *schmal(t)z*, sweetly and excessively sentimental.

Schmitter. A Messerschmitt aircraft (a German fighter): Services: 1939–45.

schmock. A fool: c. and low s.: since ca. 1910. 'Yiddish for "fool", is used in a particularly derogatory way, and has variant *schmuck*' (Julian Franklyn); its lit. Yiddish meaning is 'female pudend'—cf., therefore, the low 'you silly cunt!' Note that Yiddish *schmuck*, orig. 'jewel' or 'ornament', has been adopted from German *Schmuck*. (Leonard Goldstein, April 6, 1967.)

schmo(e). A foolish or very naïve person, hence anyone objectionable to the speaker: adopted, ca. 1959, ex U.S. It seems to be a contrived word; mock-Yiddish. (Wentworth & Flexner.) Perhaps, however, ex Yiddish *schmok*, a fool. Cf. the preceding.

'Ca. 1950 in the U.S., there was a comic strip featuring small, armless, pear-shaped bipeds called Schmoos. They were simple, amiable, and everlastingly "put upon"' (Ramsey Spencer, March 1967).

schmuck. See **schmock** above.

schnifter, a drink, is a variant of **snifter** (*Dict.*), in sense 1. E.g. in Henry Holt, *Murder at the Bookstall*, 1934.

schnozzle and its elaboration **schnozzola,** the nose, are Canadian adoptions, ca. 1940, of American terms.

School for Heavy Needlework, Her or **His Majesty's.** See **ironmongery department**.

School of Wind, the. The R.N. School of Music: Naval: since ca. 1920. (P-G-R.)

schoolie (or **-y**).—3. An Education Officer: Army and R.A.F.: since ca. 1890 in the Army, where coll. for '(Army) schoolmaster'; since ca. 1920 in the Navy, says Granville; and since ca. 1930 in the R.A.F. (Partridge, 1945.)—4. Any schoolteacher: Australian: since ca. 1925. (B., 1953.)

schoolie, v.t. To inflict a prefects' beating on (a boy): Scottish Public Schools': C. 20. Ian Miller, *School Tie*, 1935. Ex n., 2 (*Dict.*).

school's (or **the school's**) **out.** A c.p., referring to a sudden crowd: C. 20.

schooner on the rocks (p. 732). Earlier in 'Taffrail'. An occ. variant is *schooner on a rock*, as in *The Birmingham Mail*, Feb. 24, 1939.

schooner orgy; hermaphrodite brig; bastard brig. A coaster: nautical, esp. Naval: from ca. 1860. B. & L.

schuffle-hunter. See **shuffle-hunter**.

schwarz, p. schwarzes. A coloured person, esp. a West Indian: landlords' and property speculators': mostly in London: since ca. 1954. Via Yiddish ex German *schwarz*, black. 'Put in the schwarzes and de-stat it'—rid the property of *stats* or statutory tenants: *The Sunday Times*, July 7, 1963.

schwaya or **shwaya.** Small or insignificant; as n., a small quantity, a little: Army in N. Africa: 1940–3. 'He's a schwaya job'—'Give me a schwaya more char'. Ex the Arabic *suqair*. (P-G-R.) See also *shwaiya*.

scissor-grinder. Recorded earlier by 'Taffrail'. **scissors-grinder** or **razor-grinder** or merely **grinder**; occasionally, **dish-lick.** The bird known as the Restless Flycatcher: Australian: late C. 19–20. (B., 1943.)

sciver. A shoemaker's knife: shoemakers': from ca. 1890. A corruption of **chiver** (*Dict.*).

scoach. Rum: Regular Army: late C. 19–20. Why?

scobolotcher. 'An undergraduate walking round a quadrangle hands in pocket and deep in thought' (John Moore, as reported in the *Bournemouth Daily Echo*, April 21, 1956): since ca. 1925. Origin?

The word is at least 300 years old. As *scobberlotcher* it occurs in Aubrey's 'Life' (1697) of Dr Ralph Kettell (1563–1643), President of Trinity College, Oxford. Dr Kettell applied it to undergraduates acting in this way, but also counting the trees in 'The Grove'. (With thanks to Mr H. R. Spencer.) The O.E.D. attempts no etymology, but does compare the North Country and East Anglian *scopperloit*, *scoppoloit*, a time of idleness or of play, and the rare *scoterlope*, to wander aimlessly.

scoff, v.—5. To kill or otherwise dispose of: Army: C. 20. (P-G-R.) Ex senses 1 and 4 (pp. 732–3).

sconce, do one's. To become extremely annoyed or angry: New Zealand servicemen's: since ca. 1944. Slatter, 'I'll do my sconce properly'. Cf. **sconce,** n., 1 and 2, on p. 733, and semantically **do one's nut** on p. 227.

scone (pron. *skon*). A detective: Australian low: since ca. 1920. B., 1942. Also *hot scone.*—2. See **sconer.**—3. The head: Australian: since ca. 1930. Often *go off one's scone*, as in D'Arcy Niland, 1958.—4. Odds of 20 to 1: racing, esp. bookmakers': since ca. 1910. (*The Sunday Telegraph*, May 7, 1967.) Why? Or is it merely a printer's error for *score*?

scone, v. To hit (someone) on the top of the head: Australian: since ca. 1935. Ex **scone,** n., 3. (B.P.)

scone-hot, adj. and adv. An intensive, whether favourable ('He's scone-hot at cricket'), unfavourable ('unreasonable; extortionate'), or neutral ('Go for someone scone-hot'—vigorously): Australian: since ca. 1925. Baker. Newly baked scones are both hot and delicious.

scone in!, suck your. Pull your 'scone' in!— Stop talking nonsense: Australia: since ca. 1950. (Culotta.) Cf. **scone,** 3, above.

sconer. 'Any skull-threatening bumper,' Ray Robinson, *Between Wickets*, 1946: Australian cricketers': since ca. 1925. Ex Australian s. *scone*, the head (C. 20).

scoop the pool. To make a 'killing': financial coll.: C. 20. Ex gambling.

scoot, get on the. To go on a drinking-bout: Australian: since ca. 1930. (Dal Stivens, *The Courtship of Uncle Henry*, 1946.) Also *on the scoot*, engaged in a drinking bout, as in H. Drake Brockman, *Sydney or Bust*, 1948. The phrase *on the scoot* has, since ca. 1940, been common in New Zealand. (Slatter.)

scooter.—3. A single-deck bus; a driver-only bus: busmen's: since ca. 1945.

scope.—2. A telescope; a periscope: since ca.

1910; by 1940, coll.—3. An oscilloscope: technicians': since ca. 1940. (B.P.)

scorched earth. Destruction of everything that might be useful to an advancing enemy: 1940 +: coll. >, by 1943, S.E.

scorchy. Discoloured: Christ's Hospital coll.: since ca. 1840. Marples. Ex *scorched*.

score, n.—4. 'The number of drinks consumed or the bill to be paid,' H. & P.: Services coll.: since ca. 1915. Ex sense 1.—5. See **what's the score.**

scotch.—3. (Usually in pl. *scotches*.) A police —esp. a C.I.D.—detective: c.: since ca. 1945; hence, also, since ca. 1950, police s. (John Dickson Carr, *Patrick Butler for the Defence*, 1956.)

Scotch bed, make a. To fold blankets into the form of a sleeping-bag: Forces': since ca. 1918. Economical conservation of heat. (Atkinson.)

Scotch by absorption. Not of Scottish extraction, yet fond of Scotch: since ca. 1930.

Scotch, or Scots, Greys (p. 734). Strictly, body lice. (John Hargrave, *The Suvla Bay Landing* 1964.)

Scotch mist.—2. A sarcastic c.p. of the Services (esp. the R.A.F.), implying that one is either 'seeing things' or failing to see things he ought to see: since ca. 1925. H. & P., 1943; Partridge, 1945. '"Can't you see my tapes? What do you think they are—Scotch mist?" Sometimes *fog* is used instead of *Scotch mist*.'—2. Hence, of noise: R.A.F.: 1940 +. 'A bomb falls. "What was that?"—"Well it wasn't Scotch . . . mist".' W/Cdr R. P. McDouall, letter of March 17, 1945.

Scotch mist, adj. Tipsy: racing rhyming s. (on *pissed*): since ca. 1920.

Scotch Mist, the. The Scottish Church canteen at Abbassia (Cairo): Army in N. Africa: ca. 1940–3. (P-G-R.)

Scotch peg.—2. Occ. for 'egg': rhyming: C. 20.

Scotch prize (p. 734) goes back to 1818 (Alfred Burton, *Johnny Newcome*). Moe.

Scotchy (p. 735). More prob., C. 19–20. My earliest 'confirmation', however, is *Sessions*, July 9, 1856.

Scotland Yarders. New Scotland Yard: late C. 19–20. By 'the Oxford *-er*'.

Scotsman's fifth. See 'Hauliers' Slang'.

Scottish (p. 735) is defined in *Sinks*, 1848, as 'savage, wild chagrined'.

scouce or **scouse** or **scowse.** See **skowse. scouse** (p. 735) is clearly a survival from a general Naval use going back to ca. 1820 or even earlier, for it occurs in *The Night Watch*, II (p. 116), 1828.

Scouse. A native of Liverpool: late C. 19–20. Ex dialect.

Scouseland. Liverpool: nautical and (Liverpool) dockers': late C. 19–20. Cf. **scouse** (p. 735).

scousy or **scowsy.** Mean, stingy: Christ's Hospital: since ca. 1860; ob. Marples. 'Perhaps *scabby* + *lousy*'.

scout, n.—5. 'A reproachful name for a bold forward girl' (P. W. Joyce, *English . . . in Ireland*, 1910): Anglo-Irish: late (? mid) C. 19–20.

scow, v. To be illicitly absent: mostly Liverpool: late C. 19–20. Short for *scowbank* (p. 735).

scowbanker (p. 735). *The Bukman Mercantile Papers* (New York Historical Society) show, in letters dated Nov. 18, and Dec. 4, 1750—Feb. 14, 1752—Nov. 30, 1764, that the word was orig. American. (Moe.) Perhaps of Irish origin. 'In the sense of an idler, this word recalls **scrimshanker** (p. 738), one who does scrimshaw work in his idle time. Are they both merely facetious inventions?': Leechman.

Scowegian. A seaman of any Scandinavian country: C. 20. Granville. Cf. **Scandinoogian.**

scrag, v., 4, 'to manhandle': earlier in *Sessions*, May 1835.—5. To scratch (an entry, an event): Shrewsbury: since ca. 1936. Marples.

scram is also short for the official *scramble*, wrongly classified in *The Reader's Digest* of Feb. 1941 as s.: (of aircraft) to take off: R.A.F.: since 1939. Article by E. P. in *The New Statesman*, Sept. 19, 1942.

scram bag. See **steaming bag.**

scramble, n. A **dog-fight** (p. 230): R.A.F.: 1939 +, but never very much used. Berrey; Jackson.

scramble, v. To use the *scrambler*, an apparatus for distorting telephone conversations: Army: 1939 +.

scrambled egg (R.A.F.: since ca. 1930) is the wearer (mentioned by Jackson) of:

scrambled eggs. 'The ornate gold oak leaves on the peak of an Air Commodore's cap [actually on that of any officer from Group-Captain upwards] are called "scrambled eggs",' Hector Bolitho in *The English Digest*, Feb. 1941: R.A.F.: since ca. 1925.

scran, adj. 'A Naval word meaning "good",' H. & P.: since ca. 1920. Prob. ex **scran,** n., 2 and 4, 5 (*Dict.*). But *this* is an adj. only by implication, as in 'That's *scran!*' = that's real *scran* (food). In short, the original Addenda entry is strictly a 'ghost' entry, retained only as a horrible warning.

scrap merchants or dealers. Souvenir hunters: Tommies': W.W. I. (A. B. Petch, April 1966.)

scrape, 'a predicament', is not—despite many people's impression—unconventional; it is (familiar) S.E.

scrape the bottom of the barrel. To use, or to approach in order to enlist, anyone at all to do something, esp. to fill a vacant position: coll.: since ca. 1945. After ca. 1955, often simply *scrape the barrel*.

scrape the kettle. To go to confession: lower-middle-class and proletarian Catholic: late C. 19–20.

scraper, 3 (p. 736) is recorded exactly ten years earlier (Alfred Burton, *Johnny Newcome*). Moe. Esp. Naval of ca. 1790–1840; W. N. Glascock, *The Naval Sketch-Book* (I, 34), 1825, defines it as a 'gold-laced cocked hat'. Moe.

scraper ring. 'The middle or half-ring on the cuffs of a Squadron-Leader's tunic'; R.A.F.: since ca. 1920. Jackson, 'In a piston there is a compression ring, an oil-retaining ring and a middle, or scraper, ring.'

scrapper goes back to fifty years earlier: B. & L.

scrappo. A scrap or fight: Australian (mostly youthful): since ca. 1925. (B., 1943.)

scratch, n.—4. A housemaid: Christ's Hospital: since ca. 1890. Marples.—5. The Captain's Secretary: Naval: C. 20. Granville. Also *Sec.* John Winton, *We Joined the Navy,* 1959.

scratch, v. To go fast, travel rapidly: Australian: since ca. 1920. Baker. Like a sprinter from the scratch-mark?

scratch!, have a. A 'c.p. of satirical encouragement to someone at a loss for answer or informa-

tion' (Atkinson): C. 20. Ex advice to a man stirring uneasily as if at the bite of a flea.—2. A Cockney c.p. of contemptuous dismissal, as in 'Oi, goo-orn! 'Op it! Go and 'ave a scratch!': since ca. 1910. (Julian Franklyn.)

In sense 1, 'Is this not a suggestion that the puzzled one should scratch his head in bewilderment?': Leechman.

scratch-cat. A sour-tempered female: New Zealand feminine: ca. 1910–50. (Jean Devanney, *Riven,* 1929.)

*****scratched, have one's back.** See **back scratched.**

scratcher, n.—3. (p. 737). Also in the Army: 1939 +.—4. A toe: Anglo-Irish: C. 29. 'A Real Paddy', *Life in Ireland,* 1822.—5. Usually pl., *scratchers.* The hand (*Boxiana,* IV, 1824): ca. 1815–60.—6. A slow driver: busmen's: since ca. 1925. He 'scratches about'. Contrast **slasher** 3.—7. A small ship: Merchant Navy: late C. 19–20. 'It scratches the dock wall in entering at ebb tides' (Frank Shaw).—8. Any scratching tool; also, the person operating it: fair-grounds': C. 20. (W. Buchanan-Taylor, *Shake It Again,* 1943.)

scratching, be. To be in a dilemma, a quandary: Australian: since ca. 1910. B., 1942. Like a hen, scratching about for food.

scratching one's balls (or **ballocks**), **be** or **sit.** Instead of being either active or alert, to sit or loll in idleness and vacancy: low coll.: late C. 19–20.

scratching rake. A comb: proletarian: from ca. 1870; ob. B. & L.

scream, n.—2. An uproar; a tremendous fuss, e.g. in the Press: since ca. 1925. (Norman.)

scream, v. Sense 1 derives ex: 2. (Of a thief, robbed by another) to apply to the police: c.: from ca. 1885. Whence:

scream like a wounded eagle. 'Said of one who makes a terrific fuss about something' (Leechman): Canadian: since ca. 1955.

*****scream the place down.** To go to Scotland Yard to report one's loss: c.: from ca. 1900. Esp., to report a burglary, a sense that >, ca. 1935, gen. urban s. (Nigel Dennis in *The Sunday Telegraph,* July 9, 1961.)

screamer.—6. A whistling bomb: civilians and Services: Sept. 1940 +. H. & P. A 'terror bomb' with a scream-producing device.—7. A man very obviously homosexual: since ca. 1950. In, e.g., John Gardner, *Madrigal,* 1967. A 'roaring queer'.

screamer over the target. A man that sees danger everywhere—and is constantly drawing attention to it: R.A.F.: 1940 +.

screamers, the. An intense dislike of operational flying: R.A.F.: 1940–5. (P-G-R.)

screaming downhill, vbl n. 'Making a power dive in a fighter aircraft,' H. & P.: R.A.F.: since ca. 1938. A whistling noise is caused by the wind and perhaps by the propeller.

screaming hab-dabs, the. See **hab-dabs** above.

screaming shits, the. Diarrhoea: Forces': since ca. 1939.—2. Hence, *give* (one) *the s.s.,* to get on the nerves of: Forces': since ca. 1940.

screech.—2. See *giggle,* 2, and cf. *scream* (p. 737). —3. (Cf. sense 1: p. 737.) Wine obtained by 111 Fighter Squadron, R.A.F., from the White Fathers at Thibar in Tunisia: 1943.

screechers, occ. **Harry Screechers.** Screeching drunk; hysterical: since late 1950's. Not common. (Peter Sanders.)

screw, n.—12. A glance, a look; esp. **take a screw at**, q.v.—13. A tight-fisted person: coll.: ca. 1820–90. 'He would call her an old screw, or skinflint' (*Hogg's Instructor*, Nov. 55, 'Memoranda by a Marine Officer').

screw, v.—4. To scrutinize (a person); to eye, accusingly, up and down: mostly delinquent teenagers': C. 20. (Laurie Atkinson, Sept. 11, 1967.) Cf. **screw**, n., 12, above.

screw (a woman's) back legs off, (he'd). A c.p. that credits a man with satyriasis: mostly Services' esp. Naval: C. 20.

screw-driver. A hammer: carpenters' and joiners' jocularity: late C. 19–20.—2. A drink of vodka (or gin) and orange juice: since late 1940's. (David Wharton, June 6, 1966.)

screw the arse off (a woman). To coït with, vigorously and often: low: C. 20. Peter Crookston, *Villain*, 1967. Cf. **screw back legs off** above.

screw up (someone's) **ogle.** To punch so hard in the eye that it closes: boxing: ca. 1805–40. *The Plymouth Telegraph*, early 1822. Moe.

screwball, adj. and n. (An) eccentric: Canadian: adopted, during the 1930's, ex U.S. Perhaps from billiards or snooker. 'More likely from baseball, in which the screwball is a recognized pitch, but heavily influenced by **screwy**, 4 (*Dict.*)': Robert Clairborne, Aug. 31, 1966.

screwed.—2. Broken-up with hard work: Australian: C. 20. B., 1942. Cf. *screw*, a worn-out horse?

screwed up.—3. (Utterly) spoilt; wrecked; fouled up: Canadian: since ca. 1930. (Leechman.) Euphemistic for *fucked-up*.

Screws of the World. See **Whore's Gazette.**

screwy, 4 (p. 738). But in New Zealand since ca. 1910. (Ruth Park, *Pink Flannel*, 1955.) By the early 1960's, quite common in Britain, but as a reinforcement derived ex **screwball** (above), itself not unknown there since 1962.

scribe.—4. A forger: c.: C. 20. F. D. Sharpe, *The Flying Squad*, 1938.

scrigger. Scripture: Christ's Hospital: since ca. 1905. Marples. By 'the Oxford -er'.

scrimshank, n.—2. A hesitation—in order 'to avoid an issue' (L. E. F. English, 1955): Newfoundland: C. 20. Cf. **scrimshanker** on p. 738.

scrimshaw (etymology: 739, top). 'Perhaps connected with **scrimshank**, that is, work done or a hobby pursued during leisure hours on board ship. The old whalers' logs often had an entry "All hands at scrimshanking"' (Leechman).

***scroof**, v.i. To sponge or live on a person; v.t., *scroof with*: c.: ca. 1840–1910. B. & L. Perhaps ex **scroof**, n. (*Dict.*). Whence **scroofer**, a parasite: same status and period.

scrounge (p. 739).—2. In 1939–45 the soldiers used it to mean 'to avoid a fatigue'. (P-G-R.)

scrousher. An old, esp. if broken-down, goldprospector or digger: New Zealand: since ca. 1862; long, merely historical. (Ruth Park, *One-a-Pecker, Two-a-Pecker*, 1958.) Perhaps an imitative word.—2. Hence (?), a prostitute: low Australian: late C. 19–20. (D'Arcy Niland, *The Big City*, 1959.)

scrub, n.—3. A small (dirty or slovenly) boy: Christ's Hospital: since ca. 1860. Marples. Cf. sense 1 (p. 739).—4. (Cf. **scrub-bull** at **scrubber**, 4: p. 739.) An inferior bull or cow: Canadian rural: since ca. 1920. (Leechman.)—5. A low-class

prostitute: C. 18. James Dalton, *A Narrative*, 1728, at p. 17.

scrub, v.—4. Esp. in *scrub it!*, cancel it!; forget it!: Services (esp. R.A.F.): since ca. 1910. H. & P. I.e. wash it out (as e.g., with a scrubbing brush).—5. To reprimand: Naval: late C. 19–20. —6. To dismiss or give up or abandon (someone): Australian: since ca. 1935. (D'Arcy Niland, 1958.)—7. 'To assist in a surgical operation. "Will you scrub with me tomorrow?" I.e., will you scrub your hands (for asepsis) and follow me and assist?': Leechman. Canadian surgeons': since ca. 1945.

scrub cockie. A small farmer working land mainly covered with trees, or other rough land: Australian coll.: C. 20. B., 1942.

scrub-dashing, n. 'Riding through bush or scrub, esp. after strayed cattle or brumbies' (B., 1943): Australian coll.: C. 20.

scrub-happy. Suffering from nervous exhaustion resulting from service in outback regions, hence in the tropics: Australian soldiers': 1940–5. (B., 1943.)

scrub out. V.i., to cease to be friends: low: from ca. 1919. I.e. to wash it (friendship) out.

scrub round. To agree to forget; to omit, to cancel, ignore: Services: since ca. 1935 +. ob. H. & P. Elaboration of **scrub**, v., 4. Also *scrub all round*.—2. To take evasive action: 1939 +: R.A.F.: Jackson. Not general, because of confusion with sense 1. In the Navy, however, the term is frequently used (Granville, 1945).

scrubbed, get.—2. To be severely reprimanded or punished: Naval: C. 20. 'Taffrail', *The Sub*, 1917. Cf. sense 1 at **get scrubbed** (p. 325).

scrubber.—6. An other-ranker: Army: since ca. 1920. Cf. senses 3 and 4 (p. 739).—7. A low woman: mostly Army: since ca. 1925. In Liverpool (C. 20), a prostitute.—8. 'Any weedy or unpleasant person' (B., 1943): Australian: since ca. 1925. Ex sense 4 (p. 739).—9. A girl not at all glamorous: since ca. 1955.—10. 'An unwashed female teenager' (Robin Cook, 1962): since ca. 1945: c. >, by ca. 1955, also low s. Ex sense 7?

scrubbers! That's finished, exists no longer: R.A.F. c.p.: since early 1930's. Jackson. Ex **scrub**, v., 4, prob. via *scrub 'er!*

scrubbing-brushes. Loaves of bread containing more bran and chaff than flour: Australian: ca. 1880–1930. (B., 1943.)

scruff, v.—2. To manhandle; to attack: Australian coll.: late C. 19–20. B., 1942. I.e. take by the scruff of the neck.—3. To seize (esp. a sheep): Australian abattoirs' coll.: C. 20. (Dick.) Cf. sense 2.

Scruff, the. 'The Desert Airforce (a combination of *scruffy* and *R.A.F.*). Eighth Army used to think that men of the Desert Airforce were dirtier and scruffier than themselves. A debatable point.' Thus Peter Sanders, *à propos* the war in North Africa in 1940–43; in *The Sunday Times* magazine, Sept. 10, 1967.

Scruffy Kings, the. The Liverpool Regiment: Liverpool: C. 20.

scrum, n.—2. Hence, a crowd or a 'rag': Rugby School: from the 1880's.—3. A threepenny bit: Australian: C. 20. Baker.

scrum, adj. Wonderful, excellent: schoolgirls': C. 20; by 1945, virtually †. Ex *scrumptious*.

scrunch. Food; esp. sweets (lollies): Australian: since ca. 1920. Baker. Cf. **scruncher** (*Dict.*).

scrutch. To *scratch* the *crutch*: Australian: since ca. 1930. (B., 1943.)

scud, n.—3. A travelling ticket inspector: railwaymen's: since ca. 1920. (*Railway* 2nd.) He works fast.

scud, v. Of persons: to run: Naval: late C. 18–mid-19. (W. N. Glasock, *Sketch-Book*, II, 1826. (Moe.) Ex the nautical S.E. sense.

***scue.** Randle Holme, 1688, lists this as a variant of **skew** (*Dict.*).

scuffer. A policeman: Liverpool: C. 20. Ex dial. *scuff*, to strike. (Frank Shaw.) Cf. *scufter* (p. 740).

scuffle. To 'get by' or barely manage to exist: beatniks': since ca. 1959. Anderson, 'Some scuffle on leaves and coke' (lettuce and Coca-Cola).

***scull about.** To seek something easy to steal: c.: since ca. 1910. (*The Free-Lance Writer*, April 1948.) Cf. *sculling around* on p. 740; in 1939–45, *sculling about* was a variant. (P-G-R.)

sculling around (p. 740). Earlier in 'Taffrail', *The Sub*, 1917.

scum, n. A 'fag'; *new scum*, a new boy: Shrewsbury: C. 20. Marples.

scungy or **-ey.** 'A pejorative currently'—June 1963—'popular in Sydney and Melbourne undergraduate circles' (B.P.). Perhaps ex Scottish and Northern Irish *scunge*, to slink about, and Scottish *scunge*, a sly or vicious fellow; or, as B.P. suggests, ex Australian *scungy*, scabby, itself perhaps s.— dating from ca. 1920. Cf. the archaic S.E. adj. *scurvy*.

scupper up. See **jug up.**

scurf, adj. (Of labour) cheap: Cockneys': ca. 1845–90. Mayhew, II, 1851. Cf. the n., 2 (p. 740).

scurze. 'Generic term for the whiskered' (Granville): Naval: since ca. 1925. There is a ref. prob. to *furze*, perhaps to *scythe*.

scut.—3. A female servant: Tonbridge School: C. 20. Also *skiff*.—4. 'A dirty, mean person' (L. E. F. English, *Historic Newfoundland*, 1955): Newfoundland: C. 20. A specialisation of sense 2 (p. 741).

scutcher. Anything very large or, esp., very good; adj., excellent: Australian: since ca. 1910. B., 1942. ? *scotcher* something, 'killing' (to *scotch* a snake).

scuttle, v.—8. To disappear: R.A.F. coll.: since ca. 1938. H. & P. Cf. senses 1 and 5.—9. To fail (a candidate): Cape Town University: ca. 1940–5.—10. v. reflexive, to make oneself scarce: ibid.: ca. 1940–5. Prof. W. S. Mackie, in *The Cape Argus*, July 4, 1946.

scuttle, to carry tales; **scuttle-cat,** a sneak: Christ's Hospital: since ca. 1870. Marples. Cf. the U.S. Naval s. *scuttlebut*, a rumour.

scuttle, do a back.—2. But also to coït dorsally: low: C. 20.

'se.—2. Am: children's coll.: C. 19–20; perhaps from C. 15. Also dial.

se for *ths* is a characteristic of Cockney speech. Thus in W. Pett Ridge, *Mord Em'ly*, 1898: 'I was in the orspital for monse and monse.'

sea attorney. Synonymous with **sea lawyer** (*Dict.* and above): Naval: since ca. 1810. Fredk Chamier, *The Life of a Sailor*, 1832, at II, 17. (Moe.)

sea-coal. Smuggled spirits: mid-C. 18–mid-C. 19. (S. R. Crockett, *The Raiders*, 1894.)

sea-cook, son of a (p. 741), is recorded in 1806: John Davis, *The Post-Captain*. (Moe.)

sea daddy. A staid rating: Naval: since ca. 1900. Granville, 'Usually a badgeman who acts as mentor to new entries'. 'Taffrail' uses it in *Pincher Martin*, 1916.

sea-flea. 'A very fast motor boat that skips and bounces over the ocean like a flea on a sheet' (Leechman): mostly Canadian: since ca. 1950. Perhaps ex the U.S. s. *sea-flea*, an outboard motor boat (W. & F.).

Sea-Gallopers' Society, the. The Imperial Maritime League, set up (ca. 1901) in opposition to the Navy League.

sea-gull. See **seagull** (*Dict.*).

sea(-)lawyer should be dated back to ca. 1820, for it occurs in *The Canton Register*, July 4, 1837 (p. 112), in a letter written by a British sea captain, Christopher Biden, and in W. N. Glascock, *Sailors and Saints* (I, 18), 1829. Moe.

sea miles than you've had (or **eaten**) **pusser's peas, I've done** (or **had**) **more.** A boast of comparatively long service at sea: Naval: since ca. 1917. (*Pusser*, purser.) Cf. the Army's and R.A.F.'s *get your knees brown!* (hot-country service) and *get some in!* (general).

seabees. R.A.F. men serving with the Navy: 1944–5. Gordon Holman, *Stand by to Beach*, 1944.

seagull on. Synonym of **pigeon on:** Australian: C. 20. B., 1942.

seamer. A medium- or a fast-medium-paced ball delivered with a skilful use of the seam: cricketers': since ca. 1948. By 1960, coll.

Seasiders, the. The St Kilda footballers: Melbournites': since ca. 1910. (B., 1943.)

seat.—2. *the seat* is the hip pocket: c.: late C. 19–20. I.e. in pickpocketing. Cf. **outer,** q.v.

seat-of-the-pants flyer. One of the pioneers of air transport over the unmapped Canadian North during the 1920's and 1930's: Canadian coll.: at first, modestly among themselves; then, admiringly by journalists: since ca. 1925; after ca. 1950, mostly historical 'They flew, with few instruments, over practically uninhabited country, to land on small lakes or rude airfields' (F. E. L. Priestley).

seats. Buttocks: partly humorous and partly euphemistic; and, in the main, middle-class domestic: since ca. 1945. 'She has prominent'—or 'a prominent pair of'—'seats'.

secko. A male pervert: low Australian: since ca. 1925. (Ruth Park, *Poor Man's Orange*, 1950.) Ex *seek*? No! Either ex Italian *secco*, dry, or ex French *sec* with anglicized spelling + the Australian suffix *-o*.

second, n.—2. (Also adj.) Second-hand; *seconds*, second-hand goods: dealers' coll.: C. 19–20.

second-class buff. A Stoker, 2nd class: Naval: C. 20. (P-G-R.)

second dicky.—2. Hence, Reserve pilot in an aircraft: Air Force: since ca. 1938. Jackson. (Don't give yourself away by speaking of a 'first dicky'—the term does not exist.)

second eleven, the. The Commander and the deputy heads of department, as opposed to the Captain and the heads of department, on board a capital ship. Naval: since ca. 1940. Ex cricket.

second-hand daylight. The light of another world: non-aristocratic: ca. 1890–1910. B. & L.

Ex a music-hall song. Cf. **second-hand sun** in *Dict.*

second horse, the. See **hot seat**.

seconds, the. Nervousness: since ca. 1930. (Nicholas Blake, *The Whisper in the Gloom*, 1954.) Perhaps ex '*second* thoughts'.

secret works. Automatic air-brake application: Canadian railroadmen's (— 1931). Ironic.

seduce my ancient footwear! See **fuck my old boots** above.

sedulous ape. A writer that, aiming at a certain periodical, imitates the style, arrangement, etc., of its articles: authors' coll.: since ca. 1890. Ex a famous passage in Robert Louis Stevenson, who speaks of having, in his essays, 'played the sedulous ape' to such as Montaigne and Hazlitt.

see! or you see. A conversational tag among those who possess a meagre vocabulary: late (? mid) C. 19–20.

see a man (p. 742): **see a man about a dog.**—2. Often, too, in answer to an inconvenient question about one's destination: C. 20, also = to go to the lavatory (to urinate only): men's: late C. 19–20.

see anything, as in 'Have you seen anything?' —'Have you had your monthly courses?': a lower and lower-middle class feminine euphemism: mid-C. 19–20 >, 1910, coll.

see (someone's) **arse for dust, you couldn't.** He departed in a tremendous hurry: c.p.: late C. 19–20.

see-ers-off-ers. 'R. N. drinking gradations, when drink is shared: allowed to drink the whole of (the rest of) a tot' (Laurie Atkinson, Sept. 11, 1967): C. 20.

see it, cannot (or **be unable to**). To see one's way to doing something; to concur or agree: coll.: mid C. 19–20. '"Get up, my man, and let us go on," said the stranger, almost throttling Cracroft. That worthy gentleman, however, "could not see it", as we now say in modern slang. With a struggle he stammered that he had lost the wager': Renton Nicholson, *An Autobiography*, 1860, at p. 67.

see Mrs Murphy. See **Mrs Murphy**.

see-o. See **seeo** (*Dict.*).

see off (p. 742): Much used in the Navy. Granville.—2. To defeat (in, e.g., a boat race): Naval: C. 20. Granville. Current among Cambridge undergraduates at least as early as 1930, as in 'I had an affair with a Buick near Reading, but as he can't corner, I saw him off through that esses bend' (passed him in his despite).—3. Hence, to outwit: Naval: since ca. 1920.—4. To attend to (a task, an emergency) effectually: since ca. 1940.

see (somebody) **over the side.** To accompany someone to the door in saying *au revoir*: Canadian: since ca. 1945. Ex the Navy. (Leechman.)

see the shine by moonlight. To take a night walk with a female companion: Australian: since ca. 1925. Baker. The shine on the water of sea or river or billabong. (More poetic than most Australian s.)

see (a newspaper) **to bed.** To set the presses in motion for the print of an edition: journalistic: C. 20.

see ya! A post-1945 English, esp. London, shape of the next.

see you! Au revoir!: Australian coll.: since ca. 1930. Baker. I.e. I shall see you: cf. *I'll be seeing you!*

see you later, alligator! Au revoir!: Canadian c.p.: ca. 1948–60. The c.p. response is *in a while,*

crocodile! This sort of rhyming c.p. was, ca. 1953–7, a vogue, current also in advertising; it has left a meagre residue of a very few phrases, which, after their heyday, strike one as being even more moronically painful than they were when popular.

seed tick. 'The larval stage of the cattle tick' (B., 1959): Aus. rural coll.: C. 20.

seeing you! A variant—and obviously a derivative—of *I'll be seeing you*, q.v. at **see you!** above.

seen the French king, to have. See 'Tavern terms', § 8.

segarney. A loose Australian variant of *sirgarneo*: C. 20. (Vance Palmer, *Cyclone*, 1947.)

segs on the dooks. Work-callused hard skin, or callosities, on the hands: Services, esp. Army: since ca. 1939. H. & P., 'Very popular amongst transport drivers.' See **dukes** (*Dict.*); *seg* or *segg* is North Country dial., ? ex Fr. *sec*, 'dry'.

sei-cordi box. A guitar: parlary: since ca. 1945. Lit., a *six-strings* box: a guitar usually has six strings. Like most parlary terms, it comes from Italian.

seksion. A section: Regular Army sol.: ca. 1880–1912.

Selborne's Light Horse. Recorded earlier in 'Taffrail', who makes the nickname clearer: 'The "C.I.V.'s" or "Selborne's Light Horse"' . . . are . . . the names given to the temporary service ordinary seamen who entered the Navy for five years while Lord Selborne was First Lord of the Admiralty. The scheme was brought in soon after the South African War, hence the names.'

seldoms, the. Money, esp. cash: mostly Naval: ? ca. 1810–50. In *The Night Watch*, II (p. 88), 1828, we find 'To save the seldoms, (you know what I mean, Wad? the dibbs, the shiners, ye rascal!) they sent their daughter to service.' (Moe.) Because seldom come by, hard to get.

sell a pup and **hold the baby** (both in *Dict.*) are both, perhaps rather fortuitously than significantly, anticipated in this refrain of a late C. 17 or early C. 18 ballad (Roxburghe, xxxi, 8):

'This Lady of Pleasure she got all my treasure, Adzooks! she left me the dog to hold.'

sell out, v.i. To vomit: Australian: C. 20. B., 1942.—2. To betray a cause, one's country, etc.: coll.: adopted, ca. 1945, ex U.S. Ex selling out one's business to a competitor, esp. if unexpectedly or after loud assurances to the contrary.

selling!, not. See **I'll bite.**

s'elp me, Bill Arline!; s'elp me tater! Synonyms of s'elp me Bob!: proletarian: resp. ca. 1870–1910 and from ca. 1855 (ob.).

s'lp me Bob! Earlier in Benj. Webster, *The Golden Farmer*, 1833.

semi. A semi-detached house: suburban coll.: since ca. 1930. Ruby Ferguson in *The Queen's Book of the Red Cross*, 1939; J. Symons, *The Gigantic Shadow*, 1958. Also in Australia (originally an estate-agents' term): B., *Australia Speaks*, 1953.—2. A semi-final: sporting, esp. Australian since ca. 1930; by 1965, coll. (B.P.)

send. To afford much pleasure to, as in 'His music doesn't send me': Canadian (? ex U.S.): since ca. 1935. Perhaps elliptical for '*send* into ecstasies'. (Leechman.) Also, to excite. Both nuances were, ca. 1960, adopted by British s., esp. among jazz-lovers.

send along. To send to gaol; esp., to cause to

be arrested: Australian coll.: since ca. 1870. Tom Ronan, *Moleskin Midas*, 1956.

send her down, Hughie! An Australian c.p., expressing an urgent desire for rain: late C. 19–20. During World War I, the 'Diggers' used *send her down, Steve!* (B., *Australia Speaks*, 1953.) See **David!**, **send it down** (p. 209).

send it down, Davy lad! A Regular Army variant of **send it down, David**: p. 209.

send me! (p. 744). Also used by Birmingham schoolboys as early as 1890. 'I think it must be from God send . . ., i.e. "grant",' Dr C. T. Onions, postcard of June 13, 1939.

send (someone) **to** (his, etc.) **long account.** To kill, or cause to be killed: coll. (? orig. Naval): C. 19–20. Fredk Marryat, *Frank Mildmay*, 1829 (p. 294 of 1897 edition), 'He was one . . . whom you sent . . . to his long account; and it was fortunate for you that you did; . . . that man would have compassed your death.' (Moe.) The final accounting.

send up.—3. To blow sky-high, esp. with heavy shells: Artillery: 1914–18. (Ian Hay, *Carrying On*, 1917.)

sender (p. 744). Much earlier; it occurs in *Boxiana*, II, 1818, as pugilistic s. and it prob. dates from ca. 1805 or a few years earlier.

sengwich. Sandwich: Cockney sol.: from ca. 1870. (Anstey, *Voces Populi*, II, 1892.) 'But not now! As near as one can get, it is *senwich* or *sanwidge* or *samwidge*—the last is suburban' (Julian Franklyn, 1962).

Senior. The senior Engineer Lieutenant of the Engine-room: Naval officers' coll.: C. 20. (P-G-R.)

senior scribe, the. The N.C.O. in charge of the Orderly Room: R.A.F. (mostly officers'): since ca. 1930. Jackson. Humorous. Cf. **owner's scribe.**

sensitive plant. The nose: pugilistic c.: ca. 1815–60. *Boxiana*, II, 1818; III, 1821; IV, 1824.

sent, get. See 'Jazz Slang' above.

serf. A fag (at school): Cranbrook School: C. 20.

sergeant.—4. See 'Tavern terms', § 4.—5. A Commander or a Head of Department in a battleship or an aircraft carrier: Naval wardrooms': since ca. 1935. (Cf. **sergeants' union** below.)

Sergeant of the Coif. See 'Tavern terms', § 4.

sergeant's (or **sergeants'**) **run.** 'A run ashore given by the Heads of Departments (fellow Commanders—wearers of three stripes) to a departing Commander on the eve of his leaving to take up an appointment elsewhere. If [he is] a popular messmate, members of the sergeants' union give this traditional gin-up at the favourite pub in the port to which the ship is attached' (Wilfred Granville, Sept. 23, 1967): Naval: since ca. 1920 (? earlier).

sergeants' union, the. The Commanders aboard an H.M. ship: Naval: since ca. 1920. Ex their three stripes. Cf. *Jimmies' Union* and *watchkeepers' union*.

Seringapatam. Ham: rhyming s.: late C. 19–early 20. (J. Redding Ware, *Passing English*, 1909.)

Serps, the. The Serpentine: low London: C. 20. James Curtis, *You're in the Racket Too*, 1937.

servants' united effort. Lemonade: R.M.A., Woolwich: from ca. 1920. By indelicate allusion to the colour of the fluid. Gen. abbr. to **S.U.E.**

serve out slops (p. 745) prob. goes back to ca. 1790. It occurs in W. N. Glascock, *Sketch-Book*, I, 1825. (Moe.)

served with his papers. 'Being dealt with as an habitual criminal,' F. D. Sharpe, *The Flying Squad*, 1918: police: C. 20.

service-stripes. 'Broad diamond bracelets, as collected by experienced *cocottes*': Naval and military, hence Society: from ca. 1918. Raymond Mortimer, in *The Listener*, March 10, 1937. They resemble Service *galons*.

sesame. A pass word: since ca. 1930. Ex the *open sesame!* of the Arabian tale.

sesh. Session, as in 'A "rug-cutting" sesh at the local dance-hall' (private letter of Oct. 16, 1947).

sesquies, the. 'The 150th anniversary celebrations of Sydney and Parramatta . . . in 1938,' B., 1942.

set, n.—2. An accident: taxicab-drivers': from ca. 1925. Ex set-up, 7 (*Dict.*).—3. Full beard and moustache: Naval: C. 20. Granville.

set, have. Sense 1 (p. 746): since ca. 1890. (Sidney J. Baker, letter.)

set (one's) **child a-crying.** (Of a watchman) to spring or sound one's rattle: fast life: ca. 1810–40. *Spy*, 1825.

set 'em up in the other alley. 'A c.p. used when a task is accomplished. "O.K. So that's that. Now set 'em up in the other alley." In other words, "Well, that's done. What's next?"' (Leechman.) Mostly printers': C. 20.

set on, get a. See **get a set on**.

set to rights. To set right: coll.: C. 19–20. (Glascock, *Sketch-Book*, II, 1826.) Moe.

set-up.—2. 'A place setting at the dining table: knife, fork, spoon, plates, etc. "How many set-ups for the Smith banquet?" "Oh, let's say a hundred and twenty."' (Leechman.) Canadian restaurateurs' and caterers' coll.: since ca. 1950.

set up (one's) **stall.** To settle down on an easy wicket and make a big score: since ca. 1930. 'The ball came off the turf and unhurried . . . It was par excellence the sort of pitch on which, in the cricketer's phrase, a batsman can "set up his stall",' E. W. Swanton in *The Daily Telegraph*, Oct. 26, 1946.

settle-us powders. Seidlitz powders: (mostly) Australian; partly jocular and partly folketymological: C. 20. (B.P.)

settlement. A cemetery: Australian: late C. 19–20. B., 1942. 'Oh, lucky Jim . . .'

settler's clock; settler's matches. A kookaburra; readily inflammable strips of bark: Australian coll.: since ca. 1870. Baker.

seven, throw a. To die: Australian: late C. 19–20; ob. by 1940. (Dr J. W. Sutherland, letter of Jan. 21, 1940.) A die has no '7'. B., 1942, notes the variants . . . *six, sixer, willy.*

Robert Clairborne, however, says, 'More likely, I think, from craps, where to throw a seven (when one is trying to make a point) is to lose—to "crap out", itself occ. used in U.S. as synonym for "die" (more commonly, to depart, to withdraw).'

seven and six, was she worth it? A Bingo c.p.: since ca. 1955.

seven-bell. Tea at 3.30 p.m.: Naval officers' coll.: since ca. 1910. Granville. Hence:

seven-beller. A cup of tea: Navy: since ca. 1920. H. & P. Ex nautical *seven bells*.

Seven Bob Beach. Seven Shilling Beach, Sydney: Sydneyites' coll.: C. 20. B., 1942.

seven-pennorth.—3. A rest-day when one should be working: London busmen's: since ca. 1930.

'sevening. This evening: Australian semiliterate: late C. 19–20. (Kylie Tennant, *Lost Haven*, 1947.)

sevenpence over the wall. Seven days' confinement to camp: R.A.F.: since ca. 1925. Jackson. See **over the wall**; the abbr. 7*d.* for 'seven days'. has been apprehended as 'seven pence'—and vice versa. See *Underworld* (at 'sevenpence' and 'ninepence').

sevens and elevens, everything is or **was** or **will be.** Everything is (or was or will be) perfect: Canadian c.p.: since ca. 1910. 'From shooting dice, where sevens and elevens are desirable scores' (Leechman).

seventeener. A corpse. Australian low: C. 20. B., 1942. Why?

[Seventeenth-century drinking terms. See 'Tavern Terms . . .']

seventy-two. A 72-hours' pass or leave: Services' coll.: since ca. 1914.

severe. A severe reprimand: Regular Army (esp. N.C.O.'s) coll.: C. 20. Gerald Kersh, *Boots Clean*, 1941.

sewed up. Sense 7 (tipsy) occurs earlier in Alfred Burton, *Johnny Newcome*, 1818. (Moe.) —9. (A specialisation of sense 4: p. 747.) In the game of pool, (to have been) put into such a ball-position that it is difficult to play: Canadian: since ca. 1925. (Leechman.)

sewer press, the. The gutter press (newspapers careless of morals, negligent of truth, but very, very wide-awake to profit): coll.: since ca. 1943.

sewer-rats. 'Description of passengers in 2*d.* tube by indignant bus-drivers when the Oxford Street Tube opened in 1900': 1900–ca. 1902.—2. 'L.T.E. motormen' (*Railway*, 3rd): London Transport employees': since ca. 1945 (?).

sewn up. A variant of **buttoned up**, q.v.: Services: since ca. 1936. H. & P. By 1946, quite common, esp. in 'Everything's sewn up' or organized, arranged, settled.

sex-appeal bombing. Air-raid(s) directed against hospitals, schools and, in short, against civilians: R.A.F.: 1930 +. Jackson. Ironic.

sex-appeal Pete. A *semi*-armour *p*iercing shell: Naval: 1939–45. (P-G-R.)

sex-kitten. A (young) girl addicted to making the most of her sexual attractions in order to gain masculine admiration and attention: coll.: since late 1950's. It used, ca. 1960, to be very freely applied to Brigitte Bardot and, since ca. 1965, to her imitators.

sex on. See **pash on** above.

sexing-piece. Penis: since ca. 1925. Cf. S.E. *fowling-piece.*

sex-pot or **sexpot.** A very desirable female: adopted, ca. 1960, ex U.S.

sex(-)up. To render a manuscript (more) sexually exciting: authors' and publishers': since ca. 1945.

Sexton Blake.—2. Cake: rhyming: late C. 19–20. Often shortened to *Sexton.*

sexy (or **sexie**). A Korean girl generous in her favours: United Nations troops in Korea: ca. 1952–5.

sexy, adj. Agreeably efficient; simple and neat and efficient: Australian, esp. Sydney: since the

late 1950's. 'Have you seen the automatic choke in that car?'—'Yes, rather sexy, what!' (B.P.)

shack.—2. A brakeman: Canadian railwaymen's: since ca. 1900. (Frederick Niven, *Wild Honey*, 1927.)

shack, go. To share a parcel with one's schoolfellows: Felsted: since ca. 1875; ob. Cf. Christ's Hospital *shag*, a share: ? *quelquechose pour chaque personne* (or . . . *pour chacun*).

shack off. To abuse; to reprimand: Oundle: since mid-1920's. Marples. Origin?

shack up. To live together although unmarried: Canadian: adopted, ca. 1945, ex U.S. By ca. 1955, also British, esp. Londoners. Also as in 'They've been shacked up for some months' (Mark McShane, *The Straight and Crooked*, 1960). Perhaps ex 'to live together in a *shack*'.

shackie. A white girl living with a coloured man: low London: since ca. 1950. Cf. the U.S. *shacked up*, living together although unmarried.

shackle, n. and v. A, to, 'rag': Dalton Hall, Manchester: since ca. 1935. *The Daltonian*, Dec. 1946.

***shackle up,** v.i. To cook odds and ends of meat, etc., by the side of the road: tramps' c.: C. 20. Ex **shackle-up,** n.: in *Dict.*

shade, v.—2. To be superior to or better than: Australian coll.: C. 20. Semantics: 'to overshadow'. D'Arcy Niland, *Call Me . . .*, 1958, 'Her figure's no better than mine; in fact, I'd shade her a bit, I'd say.'

shaded, ppl adj. Reduced in price: commercial and trade: since ca. 1920.

shadow.—2. A woman watching 'dress-women' prostitutes: C.: ca. 1860–1910. James Greenwood.

shadows—the singular is rare. Members of the Opposition's 'Shadow Cabinet': political and journalistic coll.: since ca. 1964.

Shady. A common nickname of men surnamed Lane: C. 20. Contrast *Dusty* Rhodes.

shaft, v. To copulate with (a girl): low: since late 1940's. Perhaps prompted by **pole**, v., 3, above.

shaftable. (Of a woman) bedworthy: low: since ca. 1950. Ex preceding.

shafti (or **-y**). See **shufty.**

shag, it's a bit of a. It's a bore, a nuisance: certain Public Schools': C. 20.

shag, miserable as a. Very miserable indeed: Australian coll.: late C. 19–20. B., 1942. Cf **wet as a shag** (p. 748). Cf.:

shag-bags. A dirty pair of flannel trousers: Cranbrook School: since ca. 1920. Perhaps ex *shag-bag* (p. 743).

shag labourer. A labourer (or almost) member of the beatnik clan: beatniks': since ca. 1960. Anderson, 'Partial to a particularly powerful blend of shag' (tobacco).

shag-nasty. An unpopular man: C. 20.

shag off. To go away: low: late C. 19–20. Prompted by *fuck off.*

shag on a rock, standing out—occ. **sitting**—like a; or . . . **like a lily on a dirt-tin;** or, rarely, . . . **like a beer bottle on the Coliseum.** These picturesque Australian similes, dating from, resp., ca. 1930, 1935, 1945, bear three distinct senses: Lonely, as in 'He shot through and left me sitting like a shag on a rock'; conspicuous, as in 'It stood out like a lily on a dirt-tin'; incongruous, as in 'He was as out of place as a beer bottle on the

Coliseum'. (B.P.) The first occurs in Nino Culotta, *Cop This Lot*, 1960, "'Shootin' through ter bloody Italy and leavin' me here like a shag on a rock.'"

shag one's lugs off. (Of the male) to coït vigorously and enthusiastically: Naval: C. 20.

Shagbat. A Walrus aircraft: R.A.F. (esp. Coastal Command) and Naval: since ca. 1940. H. & P.; Partridge, 1945, 'A bat flies; *walrus* whiskers are shaggy'; Granville.

shagged, adj. Weary, exhausted: Army: 1940 +. Cf. **shag,** adj. (*Dict.*). Army use adopted ex Public Schools' s. of C. 20. Ex the next?

shagged out. Exhausted, utterly weary: Clifton College: late C. 19–20. Of same origin as **shag,** adj. (q.v. on p. 748); cf. **shagged.**

Shagroons. Australian settlers that went, *en masse*, to Canterbury, New Zealand, in 1851–2: Australian and New Zealand: ca. 1851–70. B. 1942. With a pun on *shagreen*, the rough skin of *sharks*. But Keith Sinclair, *A History of New Zealand*, 1959, writes: 'Term used in Canterbury for Australian stockdrovers. (Derived from Irish *Shaughraun*, Saxon [hence, foreigner]?)'

shags, go.—2. To go shares: Public Schools': late C. 19–20. (Ernest Raymond, *Tell England*, 1922.)

shags-pot. A term of abuse for a man, but esp. for a fellow schoolboy: Clifton College: C. 20. I.e. a 'pot' (chap) that 'shags' (v., 2).

shah. A tremendous 'swell': mostly Cockneys': ca. 1880–1910. B. & L.

Shaiba blues, the. Homesickness among air-men overseas, originally at the R.A.F. Station, Shaibah, on the Shatt-el-Arab in the Persian Gulf: R.A.F.: since ca. 1925. (C. H. Ward Jackson, *Airman's Song Book*, 1945.)

shake, n., 5. Also, esp. among Cockneys: (*in*) *two shakes of a donkey's* (or *a monkey's*) *tail*: from ca. 1910. The *lamb's tail* form has, since ca. 1905, taken also the form, *in two shakes of a dead lamb's tail*.—9. A 'slur' on a printed sheet, the slur being caused by an uneven impression: printers' coll.: mid-C. 19–20. B. & L.—10. See **shake, the.**—11. A throw of the dice to decide who is to pay for drinks: Australian coll.: C. 20. B., 1942.—12. A party: beatniks': since ca. 1958. Anderson. Cf. the quotation at **rave,** 4, above.

shake, v.—8. See **that shook him.**—9 To bor-row money (a person): Australian: since ca. 1910. Baker.—10. To stir up (the sluggards): Services, esp. Naval, coll.: since ca. 1920. (P-G-R.)

*****shake, the.** Pick-pocketing: c.: C. 20. Cf. **shake,** v. 3, 4, in *Dict.*

shake a cloth in the wind.—2. Gen. as ppl adj., **shaking . . .** To be slightly intoxicated: nautical: from ca. 1865. B. & L. A much earlier use of the phrase occurs in W. N. Glascock, *The Naval Sketch-Book* (II, 33), 1826. Moe.

shake a toe. To dance: ca. 1820–80. *Sinks,* 1848.

shake and shiver. A river: theatrical rhyming s.: late C. 19–20. (Franklyn, *Rhyming*.)

shake-bag.—2. Prostitute: ca. 1730–1890. Smollett, *Humphrey Clinker*, 1771, 'I would pit her for a cool hundred (cried Quin) against the best shake-bag of the whole main.' Cf. sense 1 on p. 749; sense 1, therefore, may go back to early C. 18.

shake(-)book. A notebook that, kept by the quartermaster of the watch, contains the names of the men to be roused during the night: Naval: C. 20. Granville.

*****shake-down** or **shakedown.** Blackmailing of bookmakers: c.: C. 20. In Australia, violent threats; a 'rough house': B., 1942, as *the shake-down.*

shake hands with an old friend; shoot a lion; spend a penny. To urinate: euphemistic: since ca. 1880. A Forces' (1939–45) variant of the first is: *shake hands with the bloke one enlisted with* (Atkinson) . . . A general variant (C. 20) is *shake hands with Mr Right* or *with him*, which bears the additional sense (low: C. 20), to masturbate. As 'to urinate', there is a further variant: *shake hands with one's wife's best friend*, as in Nicholas Monsarrat, *The Nylon Pirates*, 1960.

shake the lead out of your arse! Get a move on!: Canadian workmen's c.p.: since ca. 1930.

shake-up. An unnerving experience: coll. late C. 19–20.—2. Strenuous 'gym' for a large class: Royal Naval College, Dartmouth: C. 20. Granville.

shaker.—5. Any rickety vehicle: Australian: late C. 19–20. B., 1942. Cf. sense 3 (p. 749).

Shakers, the. Bury Association Football Club: sporting: C. 20. They've 'shaken' many strong teams.

shakings. Litter, e.g. fragments of paper or thread: Naval: ca. 1800–50. W. N. Glascock, *Sailors and Saints* (I, 143), 1829. Moe.

shaky do. A mismanaged affair, e.g. a bungled raid, work badly done, something that has—or very nearly has—serious consequences; also, 2, a risky, haphazard raid necessitated by general policy; 3, a dangerous raid, esp. a very dangerous one: R.A.F.: the first (H. & P.), since ca. 1935; the second, since late 1939 (Brickhill & Norton, *Escape to Danger*, 1946); the third, since late 1940, as in James Aldridge, *Signed With Their Honour*, 1942, and in Robert Hinde, letter of March 17, 1945. See **do,** n., 2 (*Dict.*).—4. Hence, an arrange-ment or agreement or contract that, apparently fair, is, in the fact, one-sided: since ca. 1945.

Shaky Isles, the. New Zealand: Australian coll.: C. 20. (B., 1943.) Ex numerous earth-quakes, esp. in the North Island.

shaky tot. Synonymous with *deep-sea tot.* (P-G-R.)

shall us? Let's. A c.p., esp. among juveniles: ca. 1895–1914. Perhaps it originates in the Cockneys' *shall us?* for *shall we?* (Suggested by the article 'Cockneyism Vindicated' in *La Belle Assemblée*, New Series, No. 148 (April 1821), on p. 176.)

shalloming, n. Doing something one wishes or likes to do: Army: since ca. 1925. Ex emphatic *shall?* 'Can Hebrew "shalom" (peace) be involved?' Dr Leechman pertinently asks. Well, it does seem possible.

shallow, n., ('hat'), on p. 749, survived until ca. 1870. Renton Nicholson, *An Autobiography,* 1860, at p. 87.

sham-Abraham seems to be the predominant C. 19 Naval ratings' form of **Abraham-sham** on p. 2. (W. N. Glascock, *Sketch-Book*, 2nd Series, 1834, at I, 291, and II, 272.)

Sham Berlin. The Rt Hon. Neville Chamber-lain: lower and lower-middle classes': Sept. 22,

1938–Aug. 3, 1939. Ex his propitiatory visits to Hitler.

Sham saint, pass a. See 'Verbs'.

shambles. Uproar; confusion; 'mess': Services (mostly officers'): 1939 +; by 1945, also civilian. Brickhill & Norton, 1946, 'While the new camp was in the shambles of moving in and settling down' and 'Everything was in a shambles'. Ex the definition of *shambles* as, e.g., 'bloody confusion'.

shambling, n. Ragging the authorities: Royal Naval College, Dartmouth: since ca. 1930. Granville. Creating a 'shambles'.

shame!, it's (or **it's only**) **a.** Variation of rumour!, it's a. B., 1942.

shame on your shimmy! Shame on you!: lower-middle class c.p.: since ca. 1930.

shame to take the money, (it's) a. That's money very easily come by: c.p.: late C. 19–20.

shampoo. See **shave,** n., 7, in *Dict.*

shamus. A private detective: adopted, ca. 1944, from U.S. servicemen. (Cf. *private eye*.) Ex the Irish name *Seumas*, there being so many Irishmen in America, and so many of them connected with police work. Julian Franklyn, however, suggests that the word may represent *the shamos*, the sexton or caretaker of a synagogue. Hence, anyone who takes care of somebody else's problems for a fee. 'Assuming this was originally c., as seems likely, it would be consistent with the incorporation of other Yiddish terms into c. (e.g., "gun-moll" from "goniff-moll")': Robert Clairborne, Aug. 31, 1966. ('Seumas' is, in fact, a very uncommon name among Irish Americans.)

shandy man. Electrician: circus: since ca. 1910. Edward Seago, *Sons of Sawdust*, 1934. He causes things to sparkle.

shaney is a variant of **shanny** (*Dict.*).

shanghai, v.—2. To detail (someone) for special duty: Naval: since ca. 1925. (P-G-R.)

Shanghai'd (or **shanghaied**). Tossed from a horse: Australian: C. 20. B., 1942. Ex Australian *shanghai*, to shoot with a catapult.

shangie. A catapult: Australian, esp. juvenile: since ca. 1930. (B., 1953.) Ex *shanghai*.

shant.—2. A particular (alcoholic) beverage, '"Thought you'd go for top-end shants—cocktails or sherry"' (John Gloag, *Unlawful Justice*, 1962): C. 20. Ex sense 1 on p. 750.

sha'n't play!, I. I'm annoyed!; I don't like it: Australian c.p.: from ca. 1885; ob. B. & L. Ex children's peevishness in games.

shanting, n. The drinking of alcoholic liquor: low London: since ca. 1910. In, e.g., John Gloag, *Unlawful Justice*, 1962; cf. preceding entry.

shanty, 1 (p. 760): in New Zealand since before 1862. (B., 1941.)—5. A caboose: Canadian railroadmen's (— 1931). Derisively ex senses 1, 2.

shape, v. To shape up to, to (offer to) fight someone: Australian: C. 20. Baker.

share. A female easily accessible, esp. in 'a bit of share' (copulation): low: since the 1920's. Shared out?

***share-certificate.** A pimp's prostitute: whiteslavers' c.: from ca. 1910. A. Londres, *The Road to Buenos Ayres*, 1928.

shark, n., 4 (p. 751): earlier in an unidentified British song antedating 1806, the year in which, on May 17 (p. 304), it appeared in an American magazine, *The Port Folio*. Moe.

—8. A ticket inspector: railwaymen's: C. 20. (*Railway*, 3rd).

shark-bait. Variant of **shark-baiter** (p. 751). K. S. Prichard, *Intimate Stranger* 1937.—2. Hence, 'Pickets supplied by a military unit to a town' (Baker): Australian soldiers': 1939 +.

Shark Parade. Bedford Row (many solicitors' offices): taxi-drivers': since ca. 1920. Cf. **Thieves' Kitchen,** 3.

sharkerie, better **-y.** Financial sharp-dealing or shameless exploitation of others: Australian coll.: since ca. 1925. B., 1942.

Shark(e)y. The almost inevitable nickname for men surnamed *Armstrong*: Services: C. 20. (P-G-R.)

sharks, esp. **box of.** (A tin of) sardines: nautical: C. 20. (P-G-R.)

sharonsed. Nonplussed: Newfoundland (? dial. rather than s. or coll.): C. 20. (L. E. F. English, *Historic Newfoundland*, 1955.) Ex Gaelic *saraich*, to distress, to overcome.

sharoshie. See **xaroshie** (*Dict.*).

sharp, adj. Rather too smartly dressed: Canadian: since ca. 1940. A *sharp set of drapes* = a too smart suit. Hence, by ca. 1944 (? ex U.S. servicemen), English.

sharp end, the. The bows of the ship: Naval jocular upon landlubbers' ignorance: C. 20. Granville. Cf. **blunt end.**—2. Hence, *at the sharp—the blunt—end*, well forward (at the front), well behind the lines: Army: 1940–5. (P-G-R.)

sharpies. That band, or gang, of rivals to the bodgies which lasted only about a year: Australian, esp. Melbourne, teenagers': mid-1950's. 'I guess you could say they were square-bodgies' (Dick). Ex their 'sharp' bodgie clothes.

sharping tribe, the. See 'Rogues.'

sharpshooter (activity: **sharpshooting**). 'A person who mingles with a crowd round a bookmaker's stand, holds out his hand, and demands a ticket for a non-existent bet' (B., 1953): Australian sporting: since ca. 1930.

shat or **shat-off,** adj. Very angry; very much annoyed: low Australian since ca. 1945. (B.P.)

shat on from a great height. Reprimanded by someone of much higher rank: Services', esp. Canadian: 1939–45.

shat upon!, I won't be. I won't be 'squashed': c.p.: since ca. 1930. By a pun on *sat upon* and *shit upon*.

shatter, out on a. Engaged in making a heavy raid: R.A.F. bombers': April 17, 1943, *John Bull*.

Shaun Spadah. A motor-car: rhyming s. (? Dockland only): C. 20. Ex the name of a ship?

shauri, shauria. See 'Swahili words . . .'

shave, a shilling, and a shove ashore, a. Short leave: Naval: C. 20. Cf. **soldier's three-penn'orth.**

shave off! An exclamation of surprise or amazement: Naval: since ca. 1920. Perhaps ex *shave off!*, an order issued to those who, after a probationary period, are refused permission 'to grow' (a beard).

shave off, v.i.; shave off at (someone). To deliver a severe reprimand (to someone): Naval since ca. 1920. (Wilfred Granville, letter of Aug. 10, 1962.) John Winton, *We Joined the Navy*, 1959, '"He shaved off at *me* this morning before I'd even had a chance to get a grip on things."'

shawk. An Indian kite: Anglo-Indian: from

ca. 1870. A blend of *shit-hawk*: in allusion to the scavenging characteristics of this bird.

shawly,—2. A shawl-wearing working-class woman: Anglo-Irish: C. 20. (Patrick Doncaster, *A Sigh for a Drum Beat*, 1947.) Ex sense 1 on p. 752; cf. the Anglo-Irish *shawl*, a prostitute, as in James Joyce, *Ulysses*, 1922, 'Fornicating with two shawls and a bully on guard.'

she.—4. Penis: Londoners': C. 20. Partly euphemistic, partly proleptic.—5. Used for *it* in impersonal constructions: Australian coll., based upon a practice common in the dialects of Ireland, Scotland, the North Country: late C. 19–20. Australian examples, extant in the 1960's: *she's apples—jake—right*. It's all right, or All's well. (B.P.)

she couldn't cook hot water for a barber. A c.p. (from ca. 1880) applied to a poor housekeeper, esp. to a girl unlikely to be able to 'feed the brute'.

she is, or was, so innocent that she thinks, or thought, Fucking is, or was, a town in China. A Londoners' c.p.: since ca. 1940. (Chinese *Fukien* is a S.E. maritime province.)

she walks like she's got a feather up her ass. A Canadian c.p. (C. 20)—applied to a woman with a mincing, self-conscious gait.

she'll die wondering. An Australian, c.p. (C. 20) —applied to a virgin spinster. Hence, *at least she won't die wondering*, applied, since ca. 1920, to a spinster marrying late and badly. (B.P.)

she would take you in and blow you out as bubbles. A c.p., used between men: low: C. 20. Aimed to deflate amorous bombast.

she wouldn't know if someone was up her. A low c.p., referring to a very stupid girl: mostly Australian: since ca. 1910.

shears, off the. (Of sheep) very recently shorn: Australian coll. (late C. 19–20) >, by 1940, S.E. B., 1942.

sheary. (Of a painted surface) drying out un-evenly: builders' and house-painters': C. 20. Perhaps cf. Lincolnshire dial. *sheary*, sharp, cut-ting, (of grass) coarse. (E.D.D.)

sheckles! A s. Cockney expletive of late C. 19–20; ob. Pugh (2). Perhaps cf. *shucks!*

shed, n. A hangar: R.A.F. coll.: since ca. 1925. Jackson. By humorous depreciation.—2. Chapel: St Bees: since ca. 1910. Marples.—3. A common Australian conflation of **shithead** (below), itself Australian as well as New Zealand: since ca. 1925. Cf. **shouse** below. B.P.

sheebing. 'Black-market racketeering and pro-fiteering in Germany. From the German *schieben* . . . "to push or shunt", the racketeer gangs mak-ing a practice of uncoupling a goods wagon from a train and shunting into a siding,' Albert B. Petch, Dec. 18, 1946: British Army of Occupation and officials in Germany since late 1945.

sheen.—2. Hence, money: Australian low: c. C. 20. Baker.

sheeny, 1 (p. 752). In 1.3, for 'C. 20' read 'C. 19' and note that, to most people, the term has always been somewhat offensive. To be noted is this passage from Richard Llewellyn, *None But the Lonely Heart*, 1943, '''Well, there's sheenies and Sheenies you know . . .'' he says. . . . ''Then there's Yids and Non Skids. to say nothing of the Shonks. Then there's Three Be Twos, and Jews.''' (See also my article, on Jews' nicknames, in *Words at War: Words at Peace*, 1948.)

Sense 1 arises earlier than the date noted on p. 752, for it occurs in J. H. Lewis, *Lectures on the Art of Writing*, 7th ed., 1816. (Moe.)

sheep-biter. See 'Occupational names'.

sheep-dodger; sheep-dodging. A sheep hand; 'sheep mustering and droving' (Archer Russell, *Gone Nomad*, 1936): Australian: C. 20.

sheep in wolf's clothing. A boy looking like a 'wolf', but so timid as to ask permission to kiss a girl: teenage girls': since ca. 1950.—2. 'A clergyman (not wearing his clericals) who tries to appear a man of the world' (Leechman): since ca. 1930.

sheep-pen. (?) Midshipmen's quarters: Naval: early C. 19. Fredk Marryat, *Frank Mildmay*, 1829 (at p. 202 of the 1897 edition), 'Reflecting, as I returned to the "sheep-pen", that I had nearly lost my promotion.' Moe.

Sheep-Shaggers, the. The Black Watch: Scot-tish military nickname: mid-C. 19–20.

sheep-sick. (Land) grazed too long by sheep: Australian rural coll.: C. 20. (B., 1943.)

sheep-wash, n.: Australian and New Zealand: C. 20. Inferior liquor. B., 1941, 1942. Some 'poison'!

sheepo. A shepherd: Australian and New Zealand: C. 20. Jean Devanney, *The Butcher Shop*, 1926.—2. As *sheepo!*, it is the call 'for the rousie (rouse-about) to fill the catching pen' (*Straight Furrow*, Feb. 21, 1968): N.Z. shearers': C. 20.

sheep's back, on the. Dependent upon wool: Australian coll.: C. 20. B., 1942, 'Australia's economic existence'.

sheet or two in the wind, a. Half-drunk: nauti-cal, esp. Naval: 1832, Fredk Chamier, *The Life of a Sailor*, at I, 239. (Moe.) Perhaps the im-mediate source of **sheet in the wind, a**, on p. 753.

sheet short, have a. To be mentally deficient: Australian: since ca. 1910. B., 1942.

Sheffield handicap.—2. In C. 20, it = a defeca-tion: sporting s.

sheikh; loosely but usu. **sheik.**—3. (Ex senses 1 and 2.) Any attractive and/or smartly dressed young man: from ca. 1931.

The entry on p. 753 needs to be modified. Miss Hull's novel, *The Sheik*, appeared in England in 1919; in U.S., 1921. The s. term arose in America in 1921 and soon 'caught on' in Britain. Cf. the entry at **shoot a line** below.

sheik(h), v. Esp., *go sheik(h)ing*, to seek femi-nine company: Australian: since ca. 1925. B., 1942.

Sheldogger, the. The Sheldonian Theatre: Oxford undergraduates' (– 1922). Marples, 2.

***shelf,** n.—2. A pawnshop: Australian c.: since ca. 1930. Baker. Ex sense 1; so many pawnbrokers turn informer.—3. As *the shelf* it = the dress circle in a cinema: Australian juvenile: since ca. 1945. (B., 1953.)

shelf, v. To inform upon: Australian: since ca. 1920. Vince Kelly, *The Shadow*, 1955.

***shelfer** (p. 753). Also Australian. Baker.

shell, in one's. Sulky: not inclined to talk: tailors' coll.: mid-C. 19–20. B. & L.

shell down. See **shell out** (*Dict.*).

shell-happy. Suffering from shell-shock: Army since 1940. (P-G-R.)

shell-out, n. The counterpart of sense 1 of the v. (p. 753): coll.: C. 20. B., 1942.

***shell-shock** is by tramps applied only to casual-ward tea.—2. A drink of spirits: Australian low: since ca. 1919. B., 1942.

shellback. See **shell-back** (*Dict.*).

shemozzle (*Dict.*) is a corruption of Ger. *schlimm* and Hebrew *mazel*; lit. and orig., 'bad luck'.

Shepheard's Short-Range Group. 'G.H.Q., Cairo; especially when it was moved forward' (P-G-R): Army: 1940-3. Ex Shepheard's hotel; cf. *Groppi's Light Horse.*

shepherd, n.—2. A miner holding but not working a gold mine: Australian miners': since ca. 1870. B., 1942.

shepherd, v.—4. To act as a 'shepherd' (see prec. entry): Australian miners': since ca. 1880. Baker.

shepherds. Short for **shepherd's plaid** (*Dict.*).

shepherd's clock. Another synonym of **bushman's clock**; cf. **settler's clock**: Australian coll.: late C. 19-20. Baker.

shepherd's friend. The dingo: Australian ironic coll.: late C. 19-20. B., 1942.

shepherd's plaid (p. 754) was apparently † by 1950.

Sherlock Holmes! A c.p. directed at detection of the obvious: from ca. 1898; very ob. Obviously with reference to Conan Doyle's famous detective. Often abbr. to *Sherlock!*

sherrick, v.t.; **sherrickin(g),** vbl n. To scold severely, or to show up, in public; such a scolding or showing up: low Glasgow coll.: C. 20. MacArthur & Long, 'That strange and wild appeal to crowd justice and crowd sympathy which Glasgow describes as a "sherricking"'. Ex Scottish *sherra-, sherry-, shirra-* or *shirrymoor,* a tumult or a 'tongue-banging' (E.D.D.).

Sherwood Forest. 'The two rows of Polaris missile tubes which run along each side of a submarine's interior. They resemble the trunks of trees in a forest glade' (Wilfred Granville, letter of Aug. 25, 1961): Naval: since 1960.

she's got her run on. A senior Public School girls' c.p.: applied to a period: C. 20.

she's right! Everything's all right: New Zealand c.p.: since ca. 1925. (J. H. Henderson, *Gunner Inglorious,* 1945.)

she's (very) good to the poor. See **poor, she's . . .**

she's wet. See **brew,** n., 3.

shevoo (p. 755). 'A "Chiveau", or merry dinner,' Jon Bee, *A Living Picture of London,* 1828. The word occurs as *shiveau* in A. Harris, *The Emigrant Family,* 1847: an Australian usage. B., 1942, uses the form *shivoo.*

*****shice, the.** Welshing: c.: C. 20. F. D. Sharpe, 1938. Ex **shice,** n., 1, 4 (*Dict.*).

shicer, 2 (p. 755). In Australia, often uncompromisingly used for 'a crook'. B., 1942.

*****shicey.** A variant of **shice,** adj., esp. in sense 1. B. & L.

shick, n. A drunken person: Australian: since ca. 1920. (B., 1943.) Ex the adj. (p. 755).

shicked, adj. Tipsy: low Australian: since ca. 1910. Baker. Cf. **shick** (p. 755).

shicker, on the. (Of a person) drinking heavily: Aus.: C. 20. (B., 1959.)

shickered (p. 755). 'This is pure Hebrew,' A. Abrahams in *The Observer,* Sept. 25, 1938.—2. Bankrupt; very short of money: c.: since ca. 1945. Robin Cook, 1962.

shicksa. See **shickster** (*Dict.*).

shickster (p. 755) or **shi(c)ksa,** sense 2 ('a Gentile girl or woman'), was adopted from Yiddish; it is

the feminine of Yiddish *sheggetz,* a Gentile man; '*sheggetz* and, through it, *shicksa* come from the Hebrew *shecéts,* which means "detestable thing" or (ritually) "unclean animal".' Mr Leonard Goldstein, April 6, 1967, adds '"Shicksa" to-day is about as pejorative as its opposite term, "Jewess". . . . "Goy" has few opprobrious connotations, and can be used almost interchangeably with "gentile".'

shift, v.—6. To travel speedily: Australian coll.: late C. 19-20. Of a sprinter if is often said that 'He can shift!' B., 1942. But also, since ca. 1919, English.

shift, do a.—2. Synonym of prec. entry: Australian: C. 20. Baker.—3. To decamp: Aus.: C. 20. (B., 1959.)

shift, go on a. See **sod,** 5.

shift your carcase! A synonym of **move your carcase!** (above).

Shifter, the. W. F. Goldberg of 'The Pink 'Un'.

*****shill** or **schill.** A confidence-trickster's confederate: Australian c.: since ca. 1925. B., 1942. Cf:

shill or **stick.** One who plays or bets in order to encourage the genuine customers: Canadian carnival s.: C. 20. See *Underworld.*

shilling. 'Circular hammer-mark on wood—the sign manual of a poor carpenter' (Leechman): Canadian: C. 20.

shilling in the pound; e.g. *eighteen* or, say, *twelve and six,* to indicate slight mental dullness or mild insanity; 'He's only twelve and six in the pound': New Zealand: since ca. 1925. Niall Alexander, Oct. 22, 1939.

shimmy (p. 756). The *shimmey* form occurs earlier in *Sessions,* March 5, 1850.

shimmy, v. To oscillate or vibrate, esp. of the front wheels of a small motor-car: Canadian: ca. 1924-39. (Leechman.) Ex the *shimmy-shake* dance.

shin, v.—2. (Also *shin off* and *do a shin.*) To depart in a hurry or at speed: Australian: C. 20. B., 1942. Cf:

shin off. To depart: mostly Cockney: since ca. 1870. (A. Neil Lyons, *Arthur's,* 1908.) And see, **shin,** v., 2.—2. Hence, to decamp in haste: Aus.: C. 20. (B., 1959.)

shin out. To pay up (v.i. and v.t.): proletarian: from ca. 1860; ob. B. & L.

shin-plaster. A cheque; a bank-note: ca. 1870-1910. Ibid.—2. A Canadian 25-cent bill (note): Canadian: late C. 19-20; but, since ca. 1930, merely historical, the issue ceasing in 1923. (Leechman.) Both 1 and 2 owe much to the U.S. sense, '(doubtful) paper currency' of late C. 18-19: see esp. Mitford M. Mathews's fascinating *Dictionary of Americanisms.*

shin up. To climb (v.i.): C. 19-20. (W. N. Glascock, *Sailors and Saints,* 1829, at I, 21.) Moe.

shindig. An altercation, a violent quarrel, a tremendous fuss: late C. 19-20. Ex *shindy,* 3 (p. 756).—2. A dinner party; a large (and lively) party: Australian: since ca. 1925. *The Sydney Morning Herald,* Aug. 18, 1963.

shine, n., 1: earlier in *The Individual,* Nov. 8, 1836.—5. A glossy paint; enamel: builders' coll.: C. 20.

shine, v., 3, occurs in C. 20 Australian in nuance, 'to show off'. Baker.

shine, adj. (p. 756). Hence also Australian. B., 1942.

[shine-nag, ruin the. B. & L.'s incorrectness for shine-rag, win the.]

shine to, take a (p. 756). By 1910 at latest, also English, as, e.g., in H. A. Vachell, *Quinney's*, 1914.

Shiner. 8. Earlier in 'Taffrail'.

shiner, 4 (p. 756). Australian nuance, 'one who shows off; an exhibitionist': Baker.—9. A black eye: Naval: since ca. 1920. In, e.g., C. S. Forester, *The Ship*, 1943.—10. A French-polisher; a window-cleaner: builders'. resp. coll. and s.: C. 20.

Shiney.—3. Inevitable nickname of men surnamed White or Wright: Naval: late C. 19–20. 'Taffrail'. Cf. Shiner, 8.

Shiney (or Shiny) Bob, the. One who thinks very well of himself: Australian: since ca. 1925. B., 1942.

shingle-merchant. A doctor: Naval: since ca. 1820; app. † by 1890. Fredk Chamier, *The Life of a Sailor*, 1832. Ex S.E. *shingle*, a small signboard. (Moe.)

shingle short, be a. The New Zealand shape (1862 +) of 'have a shingle short' (p. 757). B., 1941.

shining time. Starting-time: Canadian railroadmen's (— 1931). At rise of the shining sun.

Shinners. Sinn Fein leaders and adherents: Anglo-Irish coll.: since ca. 1917. (H. A. Vachell, *Quinney's Adventures*, 1924.)

shiny-bum, v.; shiny-bumming. To have a desk job; the occupant;—the occupancy: Australian: 1939–45. The v. and the verbal n. occur in Cusack & James, *Come in Spriner*, 1951; the n. *shiny-bum*, in Cusack, *Southern Steel*, 1953.

shiny ten. In the game of House, '"Ten" is always "Shiny Ten"—by analogy with the nickname of the Tenth Lancers: The "Shiny Tenth".' Michael Harrison, *Reported Safe Arrival*, 1943: late C. 19–20.

ship, n.—4. An aircraft (any sort—not only a flying ship): R.A.F.: 1939 +. Jackson.—5. A bus: Sydney busmen's: since ca. 1944. Jocular.

ship, v.—5. To obtain promotion: Naval: C. 20. Granville, 'An A.B. who is rated Leading Seaman "ships his killick".' Ex S.E. sense, 'to take aboard'.—6. To assume (an expression): Naval: since ca. 1900. Granville, '"Unship that grin, my lad!"'

ship, three-island. See three-island ship (*Dict.*).

ship a bagnet. To carry or wear a bayonet: Naval: late C. 18–mid-19. (W. N. Glascock, *Sketch-Book*, I, 1825.) Moe.

ship a swab (p. 757) occurs much earlier in W. N. Glascock, *Sketch-Book*, I, 1825, where, on p. 113, it = to be a fully qualified captain. (Moe.) To *ship an epaulette* occurs in Glascock's *Sailors and Saints*, 1829, at II, 14; at I, 5, occurs *ship swabs*, thus 'Boy's shipping swabs* before they shave'— glossed as 'Mounting epaulettes, which in his day denoted a captain'.

ship under sail. A begging or a confidence-trick story: rhyming s. (on *tale*): C. 20. Jim Phelan, 1939.

Shipka Pass. See Western Front.

shipment. An imposition: Shrewsbury: late C. 19–20. Marples. Ex ship, v., 2 (*Dict.*).

shippy. A shipkeeper: coll.: since ca. 1885. Arthur Morrison, *To London Town*, 1899.

ship's.—2. Sodomy; esp. *have a bit of ship's*, to commit it: low: C. 20.

ship's husband (see ship husband, p. 757) is extant in the Naval sense, 'Captain who is inordinately proud of his ship's appearance and "puts his hand in his pocket" to keep her "tiddley"' (Granville): late C. 19–20.

ships that pass in the night. 'A regular's term for wartime serving airmen and officers' (Jackson): R.A.F. coll.: 1939 +. Ex the cliché started by the famous novel so entitled (see my *A Dictionary of Clichés*). This novel, by Beatrice Harraden, published in 1893, itself drew its title from Longfellow's *Poems*, 1873.

shipwreck chorus. See gutbucket.

shiralee (p. 757). But still extant in D'Arcy Niland, *The Shiralee*, 1955.

shirking party, the. An occasional P.B.I. name for the Royal Engineers supervising work done by Infantrymen: W.W. I.

shirt-buttons, go on. (Of clock or watch) to be erratic: since ca. 1920. (Atkinson.) Ex shoddy works.

shirt collar (p. 758) occurs also as *shirt and collar*. (Franklyn, *Rhyming*.)

shiser. Variant of shicer (*Dict.*).

shit (p. 758), always common in earthy speech, seems to be particularly so in that of Canada, esp. in C. 20, if I judge correctly from the evidence supplied, over a period of many years, by a number of Canadians—most of them, well-educated men; all, exceptionally knowledgeable. These Addenda omit some of the very numerous compounds and phrases containing the term. For Addenda phrases not listed here, see give the . . ., knock the . . ., . . . miracles, so thin . . ., and think one's . . .

shit.—7. 'Bad weather is always invariably "shit",' Sgt-Pilot F. Rhodes, letter of Sept. 20, 1942: R.A.F.: since ca. 1918. Cf. dirt, 6.—8. Short for *bull-shit* in senses 'hot air; blarney': Canadian soldiers': 1939–45. 'Don't hand'—or 'feed'—'me that shit' = I don't believe you.

shit, v.—3. To disgust, as in 'It shits me' (Dick): low Australian: since ca. 1930.

shit, fall in the. To get into trouble: low coll.: since ca. 1870.

shit, happy as a pig in. 'Happy, even if lacking in grace' (Atkinson): non-aristocratic coll.: late C. 19–20.

shit a brick. To defecate after a costive period: low: late C. 19–20. Cf. bake it (p. 27).

shit a brick! An expletive of annoyance: Australian: since ca. 1925.—2. *Yeah, you could shit a brick*, Like hell, you could: Canadian: since ca. 1930.

shit (or fuck) a day keeps the doctor away, a. An Australian c.p., dating since ca. 1925. After the proverbial *an apple a day* . . .

shit a top-block. To become excited or angry or both: shipyard workers', then rather more gen.: C. 20. 'Get that straightened—if the boss sees it, he'll shit a top-block.' *Top-block* is a shipbuilding term.

shit and corruption; shit and derision. Bad weather, with rain and flak; clouds, with rain: R.A.F. aircrews': 1940–5. (P-G-R.)

shit and sugar mixed. A low c.p. reply to a question concerning ingredients: C. 20.

shit-ass luck. Extremely bad luck: Canadian: C. 20.

shit-bag.—2. An unpleasant person: low: late C. 19–20. Also **shite-hawk**: low: C. 20.

shit barge; also **crap barge.** A ship lacking efficiency and discipline, and generally known to be such: Naval: resp. C. 20 and since middle 1940's. (Wilfred Granville, Sept. 23, 1967.)

shit, esp. be shitting bricks. To be really worried: low Canadian: C. 20.—2. To be thoroughly frightened: Army: 1939–45.

Shit Creek. See **up Shit Creek.**

shit-disturber. See **shit-stirrer.**

shit-eh? (or !). 'Isn't that just *too* bad!': Australian c.p.: since ca. 1945.

shit-face is a low, late C. 19–20 term of address to an ugly man. W. L. Gibson Cowan, *Loud Report*, 1937. Cf. *cunt face.*

shit fish. Fish caught around sewage outfalls: fishermen's: C. 20.

shit-head. An objectionable person: New Zealand low: since ca. 1918.

shit hits the fan, when; and **then the shit'll hit the fan.** 'A c.p. indicative of grave or exciting consequences': Canadian: since ca. 1930. 'Wait till the major hears that! Then the shit'll hit the fan!' Douglas Leechman, who adds that 'the allusion is to the consequences of throwing this material into an electric fan'.

shit-hot. Unpleasantly enthusiastic; e.g. 'He's shit-hot on spit and polish': Canadian soldiers': 1914 +.—2. Very skilful, cunning, knowledgeable: low: since ca. 1918.

shit-house.—2. A commode: mostly among furniture-removers: late C. 19–20.—3. A hospital (or a hospital ward) or a home for very old people who have lost control of their natural functions: hospital staffs': C. 20.

shit-house in the fog, stands out like a. A low Canadian c.p.: C. 20.

shit-house luck. Very bad luck indeed: low Canadian: C. 20.

shit in it! Stop it; shut up: Naval (lower-deck): since ca. 1930. Emphatic.

shit-locker. Bowels: Naval (lower-deck): since ca. 1910.

shit! mother, I can't dance. A low, jocular Canadian c.p., 'just for something to say': since ca. 1920.

shit not far behind that, there's. A workmen's c.p., evoked by a noisy breaking of wind: late C. 19–20.

shit of, get. A very gen. variant of 'get **shut of**': C. 20.

shit official, in the. In serious trouble: Army, mostly officers': 1942–5. Intensive of *shit, in the* (p. 758).

shit on. To impose on, use shamelessly: low: late C. 19–20. Cf. **do it on, 1.** 'He's shitting on you.' Cf. **shat upon . . .**

shit on from a great height. (Of one who has been) landed in great trouble by others: low (esp., since ca. 1925, R.A.F.): C. 20.

shit on your own doorstep, you don't. You don't 'foul your own nest': c.p.: late C. 19–20.

shit—or shit in—one's own nest. A low variant of S.E. *foul one's own nest.*

shit or bust.—2. *Be shit or bust*, to be given to trying desperately hard; to do a thing and damn the consequences: non-cultured coll.: since ca. 1910. 'I set out in direct disobedience of orders.

. . . My batman was delighted. . . . "I like you, sir," he said. "You're shit or bust, you are,"' Keith Douglas, *Alamein to Zem Zem*, dated 1946 but pub. in 1947. But 'I'm shit or bust' was, in 1939–45, very often used ironically, to mean 'I'm completely indifferent'.

shit or get off the pot! A Canadian c.p. (1939–45), directed at a dice-player unable to 'crap out'. 'In U.S. usage (still current) it has the broader meaning of "Either do it or get out of the way and let someone else try" or simply "Make up your mind"' (Robert Clairborne, Aug. 31, 1966). So, too, in English s. since ca. 1945, as Laurie Atkinson has (Sept. 11, 1967) reminded me.

shit order, in; or simply **shit order.** A dirty barrack room, hut, dress, equipment, etc.: Regular Army: C. 20.

shit-pan alley; euphemistically, **bed-pan alley.** Dysentery ward in a hospital: Army: since ca. 1915.

'shit!' said the king, often elaborated to . . . **and all his loyal subjects strained in unison** or . . . **and ten thousand loyal subjects shat.** An Australian c.p.: C. 20. Of the same order as **'hell!' said the duchess** (above and on p. 387).

shit-scared. Extremely scared: low, esp. R.A.F. since ca. 1935.

shit, shave and shove ashore. Naval lower-deck term (C. 20) for a matlow's evening-leave routine. Here, *shove* = copulation.

shit, shave, shower, shoe-shine and shampoo, I've had (or **I had**) **a.** A Canadian c.p., since ca. 1930, but esp. among Canadian soldiers in 1939–45; referring to or implying a 'heavy date'.

shit, shine, shave, shampoo and shift. A British variant—? the source—of Canadian **shit, shave . . .** (above).

shit, shot and shell. The ammunition in the anti-aircraft 'rocket' barrage, first used in the Portsmouth area: Naval (lower-deck): 1942 +. Granville. Even nails and bits of old iron were used.

shit-stirrer. One who, by his actions, causes everybody unnecessary trouble: low: late C. 19–20. The Canadian form is **shit-disturber.**

Shit Street, be in. To be in extreme difficulties: New Zealand low: since ca. 1920. Common also in Australia: B.P., 1963.

shit through the eye of a needle. See **makes one . . .**

shit through the eye of a needle, I could. A low c.p., uttered 'on the morning after': C. 20.

shit(-)wallah. A sanitary man: Army: late C. 19–20. (P-G-R.)

shit weighs heavy! A low Canadian c.p., directed at a boaster: late C. 19–20.

shite(-)hawk. See **shit-bag.**—2. The badge of the 4th Indian Division: Army: 1940 +.—3. A vulture: British Army in India: ca. 1870–1947.

Shite-hawk Soldiers, the. The R.A.F. Regiment: Army: since ca. 1945.

shite-poke. The bittern: Canadian: since ca. 1880. 'From popular belief it has only one straight gut from gullet to exit, and has therefore to sit down promptly after swallowing anything' (D. E. Cameron in letter of Aug. 23, 1937). But Dr Leechman says that the *shit-* or *shite-poke* (euphemistically *shy-poke*) is a bird of the heron family and that it is so named because 'it habitually defecates on taking flight when alarmed'. He adds that the bittern is, in Canada, called the *thunder-pump*, 'from the noise it makes'.

shits, the. An evident dislike of operational flying: R.A.F. Bomber and Fighter Commands: 1940 +. (Communicated by S/Ldr H. E. Bates.) Ex the mid-C. 19–20 coll. sense 'diarrhœa'.

shitten look, have a. To look as if one needed to defecate: workman's coll.: late C. 19–20.

shivaree is the Canadian shape of **shivaroo** (*Dict.*): from ca. 1870.

shiveau, shivoo. See **shevoo.**

shiv(e)y. (Of wool) 'carrying small, fine particles of vegetable matter' (B., 1959): Aus. coll.: C. 20. Perhaps ex Yorkshire dial. *shivvins*, 'fragments of wool, rough yarn, &c. in woollen matter' (E.D.D.).

shnide. A variant of **snide**, n., 3 (p. 793). Norman. Since the late 1950's, it has been the pronunciation current among teenagers, esp. in 'a shnide remark'. (H. R. Spencer.)

shobbos of, make. To set in good order; to tidy up: Jewish: late C. 19–20. To make clean and neat as if for the *Shobbos* or Sabbath.

shock-a-lolly. See **wally.**

shocker.—2. Also *complete shocker*: 'A hopeless individual or object—simply terrible,' H. & P.: Services: since ca. 1920. See **shocking**, adj. (p. 759).—3. A shock-absorber: motorists': since ca. 1925.—4. (Cf. sense 2.) A thoroughly unpleasant fellow: Army (mostly officers'): since ca. 1925. (P-G-R.)

shod. 'Colloquially applied to motor vehicles. A car with good tyres is described as *well shod*' (B.P.): Australian: since ca. 1945.

*shoddy-dropper (p. 759). Also Australian. B., 1942.

shoe. A sanitary pad: Australian feminine: since late 1940's. Ex shape.

shoe-string; esp. *operate*, or do it, *on a shoe-string*. A small sum of money, esp. as working capital: coll.: adopted, in late 1950's, ex U.S. (See W. & F.)—2. Hence the adj. *shoe-string*, operating on a (very) small capital; 'run' very economically: coll.: since ca. 1960. 'Acting in *Scruggs*, an off-beat, shoe-string movie' (*Woman*, Oct. 23, 1965).

shoe the wild colt (p. 759). Part of initiation ceremony, 'Swearing on the horns', performed at the Gate House, Highgate, at least as late as 1900.

shoful (p. 760) occurs, spelt thus, in *Sessions*, 1828; eleven years before the *Dict*. recording.

shog. To amble along, as on—or as if on—horseback: Australian: C. 20. B., 1942. Perhaps a blend of *shamble* (v.i.) + *jog*. It comes ex English dialect and is coll. rather than s.

shoke. A hobby; a whim: Anglo-Indian: mid-C. 19–20. B. & L.

shong. A catapult: Australian, mostly juvenile: since ca. 1925. (B., 1943.) Ex synonymous *shanghai*.

shonky, n.; **shonk.** A Jew: low: mid-C. 19–20. *The Leader*, Jan. 1939 (the former); Matthews, *Cockney*, 1938 (the latter). The former is the diminutive of the latter which derives (ex American) ex Yiddish *shonnicker*, 'a trader in a small way, a pedlar'.

shonky, adj. Mean; money-grubbing: late C. 19–20. Ex the n.

shont. A foreigner: Cockneys': ca. 1880–1915. J. W. Horsley, *I Remember*, 1912. Cf. **shonk.**

shook him, that. See **that shook him.**

shook on (p. 760). Sense 1 has, since ca. 1945, been only jocular; sense 2 is very common, esp. in the negative *not much shook on*. (B.P.)

shooken, 1 (p. 760), is also New Zealand—and applicable to either sex: cf. Jean Devanney, *The Butcher Shop*, 1926, 'Being "shook" on a man.'

shoosh. Silence: Australian, esp. among two-up players: since ca. 1925. Lawson Glassop, *Lucky Palmer*, 1949, '"Gents," he said plaintively, "a bit of shoosh, please, gents. Just a little bit of shoosh. We don't want no coppers breakin' in on us."'

shoot, v.—5. To experience the sexual spasm: low: mid-C. 19–20. Whence sense 1.—6. V.i., to quote a man a close price even at the risk of loss: stockbrokers': ca. 1870–1910.

shoot! Euphemistic for expletive *shit*: Canadian: C. 20. Current in U.S. much earlier. 'It appears, e.g., in *Tom Sawyer* [1876], though probably *not* as a conscious euphemism': Robert Clairborne, Aug. 31, 1966.

shoot, do a. To fire the guns: artillerymen's coll.: since ca. 1910. (P-G-R.)

shoot on early. Beginning work at 6 a.m.: London labourers': from ca. 1920. *The Evening News*, Nov. 13, 1936.

Shoot, the.—2. Also, ca. 1900–10: Walthamstow, which, then, was—in part—a dump of undesirables.

shoot a card. To leave one's card at a house: Society: ca. 1910–40. ('Sapper' in 1924—*The Third Round*.)

shoot a—rarely **the—line.** To talk too much, esp. to boast: R.A.F. since ca. 1928, Army officers' since 1940. List from Grenfell Finn-Smith, April 1942; Richard Hillary, *The Last Enemy*, 1942 (also *line-shooter*); Sept. 20, 1942, Sgt-Pilot F. Rhodes (private letter), '"Shooting a line", for boasting, probably the most characteristic of all R.A.F. phrases'; H. & P., 1943; Partridge, 1945. Jackson notes that in the 1920's the R.A.F. used *shoot a line of bull*, which they soon shortened; the longer phrase may combine the theatrical *shoot one's lines* (declaim them vigorously), and **bulsh** (p. 106), and the American *shoot off one's mouth*, as Jackson has suggested. The phrase perhaps dates from as early as 1919, for *line-shooter* occurs in a song sung at Christmas, 1925: witness C. H. Ward-Jackson, *Airman's Song Book*, 1945. Perhaps, as Professor F. E. L. Priestley has suggested, reminiscent of the fact that in the early 1920's every 'sheik' (see p. 753) had a special verbal approach—or 'line'—with the girls.

shoot a lion. See **shake hands.**

shoot down—**shoot down in flames**—**shoot down from a great height.** 'To defeat in an argument; to be right on a question of procedure, dress, drill, etc.': R.A.F.: resp. since ca. 1938, 1939, 1940. Grenfell Finn-Smith, in list sent to me in April 1942 has the first, as has H. & P.; the latter records also the second; E. P. in *The New Statesman*, Sept. 19, 1942, has the first and second; Partridge, 1945, 'The first—though far from colourless—is the weakest; the second connotes a victory that utterly routs the opponent—as does the third, with the added connotation of calm and/or great intellectual superiority in the victory.' Obviously ex aerial warfare; compare the Navy's **salvo.**—2. Only *shoot down*: '*Shot down*. Pulled up for not saluting or for being improperly dressed,' H. & P.: R.A.F.: since 1939. In gen., 'to reprimand a subordinate' (R. Hinde, March 17, 1945). Of same origin as 1.

shoot off. To depart hastily or very quickly: New Zealand: since ca. 1919. (Jean Devanney, *Bushman Burke*, 1930.)

shoot on the post. To catch and pass an opponent just before the tape: sporting: from ca. 1870; ob. B. & L.

shoot one's neck off. 'To talk loudly and self-assertively' (P-G-R.): mostly Services: since ca. 1920.

shoot the bones. To throw dice: gamblers': since ca. 1942. Duncan Webb in *Daily Express*, Sept. 11, 1945. Also *shoot craps*, adopted from U.S. in ca. 1940.

shoot the shit. To chat; tell tall stories: Canadian Army: 1939–45.

shoot the tube. See **tube, in the,** below.

shoot through. To go absent without leave: Australian: since ca. 1940. (Dymphna Cusack, 1951.) Cf. *go through*, 4.

shoot through like a Bondi tram. To travel very fast (and not stop): Sydneyites': since ca. 1935. (B.P.)

shoot up. 'To dive on to' (an enemy 'plane): aviators': from 1917. (*The New Statesman and Nation*, Feb. 20, 1937.) Ex the shooting that follows.—2. 'To "shoot up" a place or a person is to make a mock diving attack,' Sgt-Pilot F. Rhodes, Sept. 20, 1942: R.A.F.: since late 1939. Jackson, 1943, 'The origin is American gangster slang meaning to attack with gun-fire.'

shoot white. To ejaculate: low: from ca. 1870 Whence a Boer War conundrum.

shooting a ruby, n. A hæmotypsis, i.e. a spitting of blood: hospital nurses': since ca. 1935. *Nursing Mirror*, May 7, 1949.

shooting double-headers. 'We would use both nets, so that the whole of a large area [of water] would be encircled. This is called "shooting double headers"' (Nino Culotta, *Gone Fishin'*, 1963): Aus. fishermen's: since ca. 1920. Ex the game of two-up.

shooting for, be. 'Recently, in hospital, I saw a very old man tottering about and discovered that he was 93 . . . "and shooting for 100".' Aiming at, hoping to reach.' (Leechman.) Mostly Canadian: since ca. 1920.

shooting gallery. See **lines book.**

shooting-iron. A rifle: mostly marksmen's: adopted, ca. 1918, from U.S.

shooting stick. A gun: ca. 1825–1900. E. J. Wakefield, *Adventure*, 1845.

shop, n. Sense 2 occurs rather earlier in Thomas Surr, *Richmond*, 1827, 'The office, or *shop* as he called it.'—13. (Cf. sense 4.) A public-house: buckish: ca. 1810–40. Pierce Egan, *London*, 1821.—14. As *the Shop* it is Melbourne undergraduates' s. for the University: since ca. 1910. (B., 1943.)

shop, v.—8. To punish severely: pugilistic: ca. 1870–1910. B. & L.—9. To deliberately get (someone) into trouble: Services: since ca. 1930. Ex sense 3.—10. To shop at: Canadian advertisers' and radio coll.: since ca. 1957. 'Shop Eaton's' for 'Shop at Eaton's' affords a good example. (Leechman.)

Sense 3 (p. 761) occurs earlier in J. H. Lewis, *The Art of Writing*, 7th ed., 1816. Moe.

shop, two-to-one. See **two-to-one shop** (*Dict.*).

shop-door. Trouser-fly: from ca. 1890. Also *your shop-door is open!*

shop lobber. A dandified shop-assistant: ca. 1830–70. *Sinks*, 1848.

shoplift; shoplifter. See **shop-lift, shop-lifter:** *Dict.*

shopping, participle, hence also n. Looking around for a wife or, *vice versa*, a husband: since late 1940's: by 1965, coll. In, e.g., *Woman's Illustrated*, Jan. 2, 1960 ('Does Your Date Rate as a Mate?'). Also *shopping around*.

shorders. A Cockney variant of *shorters* or drinks in short measures: C. 20. (Franklyn.)

shore loafer. Earlier authority: 'Taffrail.'

shore-side. Retirement; life as a civilian: Naval coll. of late C. 19–20. Ex pidgin. Granville. Cf. **China side.**—2. The shore or beach; ashore: Naval: C. 20. 'Are you coming shore-side this afternoon?' (P-G-R.)

short, n.—4. A short circuit: electricians' coll.: C. 20.

short, v. Of a selection committee: to short-list (a candidate): esp. Civil Service: since ca. 1930.

short, adj.—4. Not very 'bright'; stupid: Australian: C. 20. B., 1942, 'Esp. "a bit short".' Ex 'a **shingle short**'.

short, taken. See **taken short.**

short and curlies, the. The short hairs, used fig. ('He got me by the short and curlies'—caught me properly): Army: since ca. 1935. (P-G-R.)

short-arm has, since 1916, been the usual form of *short-arm inspection* (p. 762).

Short Arse. 'Inevitable' nickname of men surnamed Longbottom: C. 20.

short-arse. A short person: coll., mostly Cockneys': from ca. 1890. Ex:

short-arsed. (Of a person) that is short: coll.: from ca. 1870. Cf. **duck's disease** (*Dict.*).

short of a sheet. See **sheet . . .;** sometimes *short of a sheet of bark.* Baker.

Short Range Desert (or **Shepheard's**) **Group.** See **Groppi's Light Horse.**

short, or long, soup. A soup with short, or one with long, noodles in it: Australian coll.: since ca. 1920. (Edwin Morrisby, letter of Aug. 30, 1958.)

short(-)weight. (Of a person) rather simple; mentally, a little defective: C. 20.

[Shortenings were, in the first quarter of C. 18, very common; they were satirized by both Addison and Swift. Ned Ward has these, culled by Matthews: *blab*, a blabber, 1714; *bub*, 'bubble' or liquor, 1715; *cit*, citizen, 1703; *fiz*, a face, 1700; *mob*, n., 1703; *mump*, a mumper, 1709; *non-com-schools*, 1709; *non-Con*, Nonconformist, 1709; *qual*, the quality or gentry, 1715; *rep*(utation), 1715; *skip*, skipper, 1715; and *strum*, a strumpet, 1712.]

shorters. See **shorders.**

Shorty.—2. And of men surnamed Little: late C. 19–20. 'Taffrail'.—3. Also of short men in general: C. 20—4. A nickname for tall persons, esp. if male: mostly Australian: since ca. 1925. (B.P.)

shot, n.—11. (Cf. 9.) An injection: medical: adopted, ca. 1920, from U.S.

shot, be.—3. To be exhausted: Aus.: since ca. 1920. F. B. Vickers, *First Place to the Stranger*, 1955, 'Another man turned on the water and out it gushed. But only for a minute, then it spluttered, then it dribbled. "She's shot," the man at the hose shouted.' (Cf. she, 5, above.)

shot, that'll—or that would—be the. That will —or would—be most satisfactory: Australian: since ca. 1945. (Culotta.) Cf.:

shot, that's the. That's the idea: Australian, and almost a c.p.: since ca. 1945. (A. M. Harris, *The Tall Man*, 1958.)

shot at, have a. To attempt: coll.: late C. 19–20.—2. To make a fuss of: Aus.: since ca. 1930. Nino Culotta, *Cop This Lot*, 1960.

shot down. Crossed in love: since early 1940's. (Nevil Shute, *Pastoral*, 1944.) Ex sense 2 of:

shot down in flames. See shot down.—2. Hence, crossed in love; jilted: R.A.F. aircrews': 1940 +. Partridge, 1945.

shot for less, in (the currently most unpopular country) people are. 'A c.p. (often jocular) implying that the bearer is lucky to be living in such a tolerant country' (B.P.): Australian: since the late 1940's. 'You're reading my book. In ——, people are shot'—or 'being shot'—'for less'. Cf. Ned Kelly was hanged—or hung—for less above.

shot full of holes. Tipsy: New Zealanders' (1915 +) and Australians' (since ca. 1918). B., 1941, 'An elaboration of shot.'

shot-ging. A catapult: Australian, mostly juvenile: since ca. 1925. (B., 1943.) Suggested by *shanghai* + *shot* + *gun* + *sling*.

shot himself! A c.p. applied to someone breaking wind in or near a company of men, often with the c.p. comment, *if he's not careful, he'll shit himself*: late C. 19–20.

shot in the (or one's) locker, have still (or still have) a. To be still potent: late C. 19–20.

shot in the locker, not a (p. 763). Much earlier, in a positive form, in an unidentified British song reprinted in *The Port Folio* of May 17, 1806, at p. 304:

'Then with shot in my locker, a wife and a cot,
    Tobacco, grog, flip, and no purser,
I'll sit down contented with what I have got,
    And may each honest tar do no *worser*.'

It occurs also in W. N. Glascock, *The Naval Sketch-Book* (I, 207), 1825; but earliest of all in George Brewer, *Bannian Day* (a farce), 1796, Act I, sc. iii, p. 12, 'I've always got a shot in the locker.' (All three references from Colonel Moe.)

shot of (p. 763): earlier in *Sessions*, Oct. 1836.

shot on a hand. Beaten by a better hand: Australian card-players': since ca. 1918. (B., 1953.)

shot to (e.g. you)! You score there: a c.p. 'aimed at indifference or complacent cocksureness at lucky chance or when sharp practice has triumphed' (Atkinson): Forces': 1939 +.

shot up; shot to ribbons. Very drunk; as drunk as one can possibly be: R.A.F.: since late 1939. Partridge, 1945. Ex aerial warfare: Cf. shoot up.

shot up the arse (more politely, back). Rendered *hors de combat* by some witticism; detected, found out: Army: C. 20.—2. (Of aircraft) shot-up from the rear: R.A.F.: 1939–45.

shotgun mixture. A pharmaceutical mixture containing numerous ingredients, any one of them prob. efficacious: C. 20.

shoulder, 1 (p. 763). Earlier in *The London Guide*, 1818.

shoulder-knot. A bailiff: ca. 1825–80. *Sinks*, 1848. Ex hand clapped on to victim's shoulder.

shouse. A conflation of shithouse (p. 758): Australian: since ca. 1925. Cf. shed, n., 3, above. (B.P.) It occurs in, e.g., Nino Culotta, *Cop This Lot*, 1960.

shout, n., 1 and 2 (p. 764): earlier; as, e.g., in Wm Kelly, *Life in Victoria*, 1859.—3. A summons (to duty): nautical, esp. stewards', coll.: C. 20. 'He'd asked me for an early shout,' Frank Shaw, 1932.—4. An alarm: fire brigades': since ca. 1880.

shout and holler. A collar: rhyming s.: C. 20. (Lester.)

shouted, be. To have one's wedding banns proclaimed: since ca. 1860. (Williams Westall, *Sons of Belial*, 1895.)

shouter.—2. He who shouts the numbers at Housey-Housey: Army coll.: C. 20. (P-G-R.)

shouters. The (school) house's shouting in support of its rowing crew: Public Schools': late C. 19–20. By 'the Oxford *-er*'.

shove, v.—4. (Of cabmen) 'to adopt unfair methods to obtain fares,' Baker: Australian: ca. 1880–1920.—5. To stop; to forget: low Australian and New Zealand: since ca. 1910. Slatter, 'You can shove that caper'. Ex the next.

shove along, v.t. Sense 1 (p. 764) occurs in James Joyce, *Ulysses*, 1922.—2. To cause sailing ships to make as much speed as possible: Naval coll.: late C. 18–19. (W. N. Glascock, *Sketch-Book*, I, 1825.) Moe.

shove-along, in. In echelon: soldiers' and sailors': late C. 18–mid-19. (Glascock, I, 1825.) Moe. By the process of 'Hobson-Jobson'.

shove it! Run away and play trains!: Australian low: C. 20. Cf. stick it!

shove it up your anal canal (often with *canal* rhyming *anal*). A low Australian c.p.: since ca. 1930.

shove of the mouth is a variant of shove in the mouth (*Dict.*).

*shove the flogging tumbler. Randle Holme's variant (1688) of shove the tumbler (*Dict.*).

shove under. To kill; mostly in passive, *be shoved under*: Australian: C. 20. Archer Russell, *A Tramp Royal in Wild Australia*, 1934. Ex *shove underground*, to bury: itself a coll., dating since ca. 1870, but English as well as Australian and New Zealand.

shovel. To pass, hand, give: South African low s.: since ca. 1925. C. P. Wittstock, letter of May 23, 1946, 'Shovel us a burn . . . Give me a light': jocular on shove, v., 1.

shovel, put up one's. To cease work: workmen's coll.: from ca. 1890; slightly ob.

shovel and broom. A room: rhyming s.: since ca. 1910; by 1959, ob. (Franklyn, *Rhyming*.)

shovel and tank. A bank (for money): rhyming s.: C. 20. Franklyn 2nd.

shovelling is a form of bullying at Sandhurst, ca. 1830–55: coll. 'Spread-eagling the victim on the table and beating him with racquet-bats and shovels,' A. F. Mockler-Ferryman, *Annals of Sandhurst*, 1900. Cf. ventilating, q.v.

shoving money upstairs. 'When a man is worrying about going bald, someone tells him banteringly it must be with "shoving money upstairs",' Albert B. Petch, Aug. 22, 1946: c.p., mainly North Country: C. 20. Instead of putting it into a bank—where it's safer.—2. Spending money on useless 'cures': Londoners': since ca. 1920. (Julian Franklyn.)

show, n.—5. See **show, the.**—6. A (gold) mine: Australian: C. 20. B., 1942.

show, v. Sense 2 (p. 765), is, after all, extant, although at a lower social level, as in 'I asked him . . . if my bird had shown' (turned up).—4. To surrender, give up, desist: coll.: from ca. 1930. In the j. of cards, 'to show' is to throw in one's hand. *The Daily Telegraph*, April 16, 1937.—5. (Cf. senses 1 and 3: p. 765.) To gain a place: horse-racing coll.: C. 20. (Julian Symons, *The Thirtyfirst of February*, 1950.)

show, bad; good show. Phrases expressive of disapprobation and approval or praise: Services (mostly officers'): since ca. 1925. H. & P., 'Oh, good show!' Cf. **show,** n., 2 and 4 (p. 765).

*****show, the; showing out.** Signs by which three cardsharpers, who have a 'mug' in tow, tell one another how to play: c.: C. 20.

show a front. See **front, show a.**

show a leg, 2, at **shew . . .**: p. 755, is recorded for 1818 (Alfred Burton, *Johnny Newcome*: Moe). Originally to make sure that the occupant of the bed was male—not an illicit female bed-warmer.

show an Egyptian medal. See **Egyptian medal.**

show-box, the. The theatre: theatrical: from ca. 1870; ob. B. & L.

show-down. A test of the real strength and backing of two persons, parties, peoples: adopted ca. 1930 from U.S.: coll until ca. 1940, then S.E. Ex bluff poker.

show hackle. See **hackle** (*Dict.*).

show like a shilling on a sweep's arse, v.i. To be extremely conspicuous: low: C. 20. Barry England, *Figures in a Landscape*, 1968.

show-off, n. One who 'shows off': Australian coll.: late C. 19–20. Godfrey Blunden, *No More Reality*, 1935. '"MacKissock's a 'show-off'"'. Ex the v.

show-out, n. 'Another cardinal rule in making contact with a snout [= informer] was that the detective never made the first move. When you entered the rendezvous and saw your man you waited for the "show-out"—a brief nod—before you joined him' (John Gosling, *The Ghost Squad*, 1959): police s.: since ca. 1920.

show out. See **lay out.**

showboat. See 'Hauliers' Slang'.

shower. A large number: Air Force: 1939–45. 'A shower of Messerschmitts.' (P-G-R.)—2. See *What a shower!* below.—3. Short for *shower tea*, a bride's trousseau-showing: Australian: since ca. 1950. (B.P.)—4. See the quotation at **drag,** n., 20, above. A contribution from players to operators: Australian two-up gamblers': C. 20. (Tom Ronan, *Vision Splendid*, 1954.)—5. 'A dust storm—as in *Cobar shower, Bedourie shower, Darling shower, Wilcannia shower*, etc.' (B., 1959): Aus. rural: late C. 19–20. The 3rd occurs on p. 208; the 1st, above.

shower!, what a; it's showery. A c.p. 'addressed to one who has just made a bad mistake,' Partridge, 1945: R.A.F.: since ca. 1930. Either the ref. is to the cold douche he'll receive from his superior, or *what a shower!* is short for *what a shower of shit* (as several experienced R.A.F. 'types' have hastened to inform me)—and *it's showery* is derivative.—2. *What a shower!* has, since 1919, been used by the Army as a c.p. directed at

members of another unit; and here the reference is indubitably defecatory. Cf. 'Some of the lousiest showers of rooks you ever saw,' Gerald Kersh, *Bill Nelson*, 1942.

shower bath. Ten shillings: rhyming s. (on *half* a sovereign); usually *shower*, esp. in pl., as *shahs to a shillin'*, odds of 10 to 1: sporting rhyming s.: C. 20. (Franklyn, *Rhyming*.)

showie or **showy.** A handkerchief worn 'for show only': Aus.: since ca. 1950. Ross Campbell, *Mummy, Who Is your Husband?*, 1964.

showing next week's washing? Your shirt is showing (at the flap): non-cultured c.p.: C. 20.

shows, the. A fair with sideshows and round-abouts: Scottish and North Country coll.: late C. 19–20.

shrewd. In *Picture Post*, Jan. 2, 1954, there was an article on youthful 'spivs'. It began thus: 'The word "Spiv", it seems, is out of date. The new word, we are reliably informed, is "Shrewd" —and it is used as a noun, adjective and verb. The "shrewd" is not an American by-product. He is home-bred and thoroughly English, in style and slang.' With the word itself, compare *shrewdy*, a cunning person—see *Dict.* at p. 765.

shriek.—4. A call at nap; e.g. 'It's your shriek' (or turn to call): card-players' (at Cambridge): from ca. 1890.

shrieks of hysterical laughter. A c.p., used when someone has advanced an untenable proposition or made a ludicrous suggestion: mostly Australian: since ca. 1950. 'I'm going to sell this car. Should get about eight hundred for it.' —'Shrieks of hysterical laughter.' (B.P.) Cf.:

shrieks of silence was the stern reply. There was no reply: Australian c.p.: since the early 1950's. (B.P.)

Shrimp, the. H. D. Leveson-Gower: cricketers' and Surrey spectators': late C. 19–early 20. Small man with big heart, he captained Oxford in 1896 and Surrey in 1908 onwards.

shroff up; buff up. To smarten up: Naval: C. 20. Resp., Urdu *shroff*, a banker (who judges the quality of coins); cf. *buff*, v., 3 (p. 102).

Shroppie, the. The Shropshire Union Canal: canalmen's: late C. 19–20. (Wilfred Granville, June 3, 1966.)

shtibbur. See **stiver** (*Dict.*).

shtoom (or **shtum**), keep; properly, *stoom* (*stum*). To keep quiet; to 'act dumb': low: mostly East End of London: C. 20. Probably cf. *stumer*, 1 (p. 843). 'Simply the anglicized phonetic spelling of S. German "stumm"—dumb, silent. Presumably it reached England through Yiddish' (H. R. Spencer).

shucks! (p. 766). Hence, Darn it!: Canadian: adopted, ca. 1910, ex U.S.

shuff-duff; orig., **huff-duff.** 'The super high frequency d.f. gear' (Granville, Nov. 22, 1962): Naval: since ca. 1955. Echoic.

shuffle-hunter. A Thames longshoreman: nautical: *temp.* George IV.

shuffler.—2. Usually in pl. (*shufflers*), the feet: pugilistic: ca. 1840–90. Augustus Mayhew, *Paved With Gold*, 1857. The old-time boxer used to shuffle about on his feet; it was Jim Corbett who introduced—or at least popularised—'ballet dancing' in the ring.

shufti bint. A (Moslem) woman willing to reveal her charms: R.A.F. regulars': since ca. 1930. See **shufty.**

shuftiscope. Instrument used by a doctor for research in cases of dysentery: Army: since ca. 1930.—2. Hence, 'a long metal probe with a light on it used by Customs officers for probing into cars and baggage' (Sanders): since ca. 1945. *The Times*, April 12, 1962, news item. Cf:—

shufty, usually in imperative, 'look' or 'watch': R.A.F.: since ca. 1925. Jackson, 'The origin is Arabic'. Also *shafty* (or *-y*) or *sharfty*: W/Cdr R. P. McDouall, letter of April 12, 1945. Also as n., as in 'Let's have a shufty'. As 'a look', it has, since ca. 1944, been New Zealand servicemen's. Slatter, 'We had a good shufti.'

shufty, going. See **going recce** above.

shufty-hatch. 'A trap door in the cab of some trucks through which a passenger could keep a lookout for enemy aircraft' (Peter Sanders, Sept. 10, 1967): Army in North Africa: 1940–43.

shufty-kite. A reconnaissance aircraft: Air Force, esp. in N. Africa and Burma. 1940–5. (P-G-R.)

shufty-truck. A scout car: Army in North Africa: 1940–43. (Peter Sanders.)

shuftyscope. Variant of *shuftiscope.*—2. A telescope; a periscope: mostly Army: since ca. 1935. (P-G-R.)

shug; sug. Money: Australian low: since ca. 1920. B., 1942. The second is pron. as first: short for **sugar,** n., 1 (*Dict.*).

shunt, v.—4. To **shunt a horse** is to start it in a race 'with no intention of winning . . ., to induce the handicapper to reduce the horse's weight as if it were a bona fide loser' (Baker): Australian racing: C. 20.—5. Also *shunt off.* To get rid of peremptorily, to dismiss (someone): Australian: since ca. 1910. Baker.

shunter.—3. A Railway Traffic Officer: Army (mostly officers'): late C. 19–20. *The Green Curve,* by 'Ole Luk-oie', 1909.

shunting. A switch engine: Canadian railroadmen's (— 1931). Depreciatory.

shut, n. A shutter: since ca. 1780. In, e.g., *Sessions,* Jan. 1789 (p. 184).

shut-eye, 2 (p. 766), is recorded in John Stockholm's 'A Day on the Lower Deck' in *The Navy and Army Illustrated,* Dec. 1899. (Moe.) Moreover, it had > general Australian s. before 1921, when K. S. Prichard used it in *The Black Opal.*

shut of, get (p. 766). Cf. the U.S. variant *get shed of.*

shut(-)out, have (got) a. (Of the goal-keeper) to have no goals scored against one: at ice-hockey: from 1936. Wireless commentator, Feb. 17, 1937; *The Evening Standard,* Feb. 25, 1937. Cf. S.E. *lock-out* and s. *put up the shutters.* Immediately ex the jargon of baseball, where 'to *shut out*' = to hold scoreless in an entire game. (Robert Clairborne.)

shut up, v., 2. Earlier in *Sessions,* July 1850.

shut your face . . . ! (p. 766): also, *shut your trap!:* low: late C. 19–20. (Dr R. L. Mackay.)

shutter(-)bug. An amateur photographer: Australian: adopted, ca. 1945, ex U.S. (B.P.)

shutters against, put up the. To debar, or to black-list, someone: coll.: since ca. 1925. Sydney A. Moseley, *The Truth about a Journalist,* 1935.

shwaiya. A little; esp. *stana shwaiya,* wait a moment: Army, hence Air Force, in Arabic-speaking lands: since ca. 1925. (Atkinson.) Also written *shwaya* and *schwaya* (q.v.)

shy, n., 2 (p. 766). Slightly earlier in *Boxiana,* III, 1821.

shy, adj., 2 (p. 766), is also late C. 19–20 Canadian, where, instead of *shy of,* often simply *shy,* as in Frederick Niven, *Wild Honey,* 1927, 'The queer fellow with the jacket on his shoulder, shy his blankets.'

Sense 1 was early applied to things other than money, as in W. N. Glascock, *Sketch-Book* (II, 142), 1826, 'As there was eight . . . of us lock'd by the legs, the duty'—the duty roster—'looked shy in the ship.' (Moe.)

shy(-)cock, 2 (p. 767). It does occur later than 1825: in *The Night Watch,* I (p. 232), 1828. Moe.

shy for (someone), **have a.** To search for: Australian: since ca. 1920. Baker. Ex **shy,** v., 1 and 2 (p. 766).

***shy of the blues.** Anxious to avoid the police: c.: from ca. 1870; ob. James Greenwood, 1883.

shy pook. A sly-grog shop: Australian low: C. 20. B., 1942.

shypoo, adj. Inferior, cheap, worthless: Australian low: since ca. 1920. Baker. Ex prec. entry.—2. Hence, n.: Australian beer: since ca. 1920. Baker. Hence:

shypoo joint. An inferior public-house: Australian low: since ca. 1925. Baker.

shypoo shop. 'A place where you bought beer and wine, but nothing stronger' (Tom Ronan, *Only a Short Walk,* 1961): Australian: C. 20. Cf. the two entries preceding this.

shyster.—3. A worthless mine: Australian: late C. 19–20. (Baker.) I.e. **shicer,** 1 (p. 755), influenced by **shyster,** 1 and 2 (p. 767).

sick, n. Mostly in *give* (someone) *the sick,* to disgust: low coll.: ca. 1840–1930. *Sessions,* Nov. 1849, 'If I have many such markets as this, it will give me *the sick.*'

sick, adj.—3. Without trumps: Australian card-players': from ca. 1870. B. & L.—4. Silly, stupid; extremely eccentric, (slightly) mad: Australian: C. 20. B., 1942. Orig. euphemistic.—5. As applied to humour: morbid—esp., gruesomely morbid; mentally or morally unhealthy; callous; viciously unkind; callously or sadistically unkind: but often too unreal, or even too ludicrously morbid, to carry a deadly sting: coll.: adopted, ca. 1959, ex U.S.; by 1965, S.E. (Cf. sense 4.) An example of the 'sick' joke of the most objectionable kind:

'Mummy! Why do I go round in circles all the time?'—'Shut up, or I'll nail your other foot to the floor.'

Sense 1 (p. 767) occurs in an unidentified British song reprinted in *The Port Folio,* May 17, 1806, at p. 304, thus, 'Of the sport I got sick, so threw up the game'. (Moe.)

Sick and Tired. 'Signal and Telecommunications Department' (*Railway,* 3rd): railwaymen's: since ca. 1955 (?).

sick as a blackfellow's dog. 'Extremely ill' (B., 1959): Aus.: C. 20.

sick as muck. See **muck, as.**

sick-bay cocktail. A dose of medicine: Naval: since ca. 1925. (P-G-R.)

sick-bay goose, a bed-pan; hence, *gooseneck bos'un,* a Warrant Wardmaster: Naval: C. 20.

sick-bay loungers. Fellows that go to Sick Bay to avoid Divisions or studies: Royal Naval College, Dartmouth: C. 20. Cf. **sick-bay moocher** (*Dict.*).

sick-bay shackle. A safety-pin: Naval: since ca. 1939. (*The News-Chronicle*, Nov. 4, 1954.)

sick-bay tiffy. A medical orderly in the sick-bay: Naval: since ca. 1920. Cf. *tiffy.*

sick bunk. A hospital bed: Army coll. (regimental aid-posts'): 1940–5. (P-G-R.)

sick market. A market 'in which sales of stock are difficult to place': Stock Exchange coll.: from ca. 1860. B. & L.

sicker, as in *sixpenny,* or *shilling, sicker,* a seaside pleasure-boat: C. 20. (Warwick Deeping, 1944.)—2. A sick-room, an infirmary: preparatory and Public schools: since ca. 1910. 'The Oxford *-er.*'

sickie. A day off, allegedly because of sickness: Australian: since ca. 1930. (B.P.)—2. A day of one's '*sick* leave', esp. 'to *take a sickie*'—a day of such leave of absence: Australian: since the late 1940's. (B.P.) Hence, attributively, as in 'a *sickie* conscience': *The Sydney Morning Herald,* Sept. 8, 1963.

Sid Walker gang. A crash-landing salvage party (from a salvage and repair unit): R.A.F.: 1939 +. Jackson, 'From the Cockney comedian of that name famous for his broadcast song "Day after day, I'm on my way, Any rags, bottles or bones?"' This philosophic fellow, who died before the war of 1939–45 ended, has, by posing problems and asking, 'What would you do, chums?' generated a c.p.

side, v.i. Harrovians' s., from ca. 1890, as in Lunn: 'He'll side to his kids about when he was at school with us'. Cf. and ex the n.: see the *Dict.*

side, v.—2. To hide away: police: since ca. 1920. (Maurice Proctor, *Man in Ambush,* 1958.)

side! The origin is more prob. 'I *side* with you': B. & L.

side, A and **B.** The main song and the secondary song on a record: gramophone-record lovers': since ca. 1959. The latter is also called the *flip side.*

side, on the. In addition; not downright illegally, yet dubiously, in unacknowledged commissions, tips, bribes: coll.: late C. 19–20.

side-kick (p. 768) was, in 1939–45, common in the British Army as a whole. P-G-R.

side of his mouth, on one. See **one side of his mouth.**

side out (a matter); mostly, **side it out.** To settle an argument; to discuss a matter and come to a decision; apparently mostly Naval, and ratings', at that: C. 19; ? † by ca. 1890. Wm Nugent Glascock, *The Naval Sketch-Book,* 2nd Series, 1834, at I, 24, '"Don't mind him," says Sal, 'leavin Tom and the captin-o'-the-top to side it out', and 225, '. . . to settle the score in the reg'lar way, and to side it out in the bay below'.

side wind. A bastard: Naval: ? ca. 1780–1850. (W. N. Glascock, *Sailors and Saints* (I, 17), 1829. Moe.) Mr Ramsey Spencer neatly suggests a nautical pun on S.E. *by-blow.*

sideburns. Side whiskers: form-adopted, ca. 1945, ex U.S., and sense-adapted. A variant of *burnsides,* named after the famous General A. E. Burnside (1824–81), who affected them.

sidedoor Pullman. A box car: Canadian railroadmen's (— 1931). Adopted ex U.S.

sidelights. See **side-lights** (*Dict.*).

sidewalk, superintendent—or supervisor—of the. A pedestrian standing, esp. if habitually standing, on the sidewalk (or pavement or footpath and what-have-you) and gazing up at a new building in the course of construction: Australian: adopted, ca. 1956, ex U.S. (B.P.)

sideways. Of a sum of money: split each way, i.e. winner and place: racing s.: C. 20. Mark McShane, *The Straight and Crooked,* 1960, 'Saucepan, sideways, Lanternjaw' = One pound, half to win, half for a place.

sideways, go. See **go sideways.**

sidies. Side whiskers: mostly Naval: C. 20. Cf. **sideboards** on p. 768. (Wilfred Granville, Sept. 18, 1967.)

Sifton's pets. Eastern European, esp. Ruthenian and Galician, immigrants: Canadian (esp. Manitoba): ca. 1900–10. Brought in under the immigration scheme of the Hon. afterwards Sir, Clifford Sifton (1861–1910), at that time Minister of the Interior. (Roger Goodland, letter of June 4, 1938.)

sig.—2. A signature: Harrow School: late C. 19–20. Marples.

sight, give a. Variant of *take a sight* (**sight,** n., 5: p. 768): *Sessions,* April 6, 1847.

sighted. 'Singled out for attention as a possible candidate for a disciplinary charge': Royal Sussex Regiment: C. 20. *The Roussilon Gazette,* April 1911. (S. H. Ward.)

sign one's hand (or **name**). See **name, bite someone's.**

signal basher, usually in pl. A signaller: Army: since ca. 1930. (P-G-R.)

Signalman Jimmy. The figure of Mercury in the Royal Corps of Signals badge: R.S.C.: since ca. 1939 (P-G-R.)

*Signs of the Zodiac, the. (Members of) the Christchurch Club: Canterbury, New Zealand: C. 20. 'When the Christchurch club was started by twelve squatters . . . there were never more than two of the twelve visible at the same time,' L. G. D. Acland, 'Sheep Station Glossary'—in *The* (Christchurch) *Press,* 1933–4 (cited by B., 1941).

sigster. A short sleep: low: ca. 1830–60. *Sinks,* 1848.

sikhery; Sikh's beard. See 'Prisoner-of-War Slang', 5.

Silas Hocking. A stocking: theatrical rhyming s.: late C. 19–20. Silas Hocking's very popular novels appeared over a period of fifty years or more, beginning in ca. 1879.

silence in the court, the monkey wants to talk. An Australian juvenile c.p.: C. 20. (B.P.) Cf. **silence in the court . . .** on p. 769.

silent cop. A traffic dome: adopted, in late 1920's, ex U.S.; by 1955, coll.; by 1966, verging on S.E. 'About 100 times as common as **poached egg**' (above): B.P., mid-1963.

silent death. An electric train: railwaymen's: since ca. 1950. (*Railway,* 3rd.)

silent hours, the. From 11 p.m. to 5.30 a.m. (ship's bells not sounded): Naval coll.: since ca. 1910. (P-G-R.)

silent like the p in swimming. See **p in swimming** above.

silly, v. To stun: coll.: ca. 1850–1900. *Sessions,* May 10, 1859, 'I felt great pain from the blows . . . it half *sillied* me at the time.'

silly as a hatful of worms; also . . . a bag . . . 'Extremely silly or stupid' (B., 1959): Aus.: since ca. 1930. For other Aus. *silly* similes, see **mad as a cut snake** above (at end of entry). Cf:—

silly as a two-bob watch. Extremely silly: N.Z.: since ca. 1920. (Harold Griffith.)

silly as a wheel, as. (Of persons) extremely silly: Australian: since ca. 1930. (Dick.) Silly *all round* or in every way.

silly buggers, play. To indulge in provocative horse-play; hence, to feign stupidity: low: since ca. 1920. By itself, *s.b.* denotes an imaginary card-game: since ca. 1910.

silly kipper. A mild term of disapproval; affectionate address to a child: non-aristocratic: C. 20.

silly moo. See **moo, old,** above.

silver plate! Please: jocular: since ca. 1916. A 'Hobson-Jobson' of French *s'il vous plaît*.

silver saddle. A bed-pan made of stainless steel: since ca. 1950. '"They call them silver saddles in the Air Force," he said': Leslie Blight, *Love and Idleness*, 1952. (With thanks to L.A.)

silver sausage. A barrage balloon: 1938 +. H. & P. Ex its shape and, in the sun, its colour.

*silver spoon. See **hoon.**

silvertail.—2. Hence, an affected person, one who puts on airs, a social climber: since ca. 1910. B., 1942.—3. A better-class prisoner in gaol: Australian c.: since ca. 1930. (H. C. Brewster, *King's Cross Calling*, 1944—cited by B., 1953.)

Sim.—3. (Usually *sim.*) A confidence-trickster's dupe: Australian c.: C. 20. B., 1942. I.e. a simpleton.

Similes. It is difficult to record all the eligible similes: they so easily slip through the linguistic net. Most of the important ones have been caught, to be exhibited at the appropriate counter. But here are a few that I had missed and that I owe to the pertinacious scholarship of Mr Laurie Atkinson. (The datings are mine.)

(as) *drunk as a kettlefish* (late C. 19–20); cf. *pissed as a newt* (C. 20) or, R.A.F. in Iraq (1920–45), *pissed as a piard*.

(as) *dry as a basket*, very thirsty (since ca. 1930).

eyes like a cod's ballocks, pop-eyed (C. 20).

(a) *face like a milkman's round*, long and dreary (since ca. 1910).

(as) *fit as a butcher's dog*, very robust (C. 20).

like a pregnant duck: ungainly (since ca. 1920); cf. **Pregnant Duck.**

like a rat up a drainpipe, with alacrity (late C. 19–20).

like a tit in a trance, dreamy, abstracted (low: C. 20).

like two of eels, nonplussed, at a loss (late C. 19–20).

(as) *peeved as arseholes*, offended, indignant (low: C. 20).

(as) *regimental as a button-stick*, punctiliously military (Army, C. 20; R.A.F. since ca. 1925).

(as) *rough as a badger's arse*, very rough of surface (low: late C. 19–20); cf. **rough as bags** (*Dict.*).

shag like a rattlesnake: shag the arse off: with immoderate vigour (low: late C. 19–20).

Simon Pure.—3. 'Simon Pures: Amateurs in the realm of sport,' Baker: Australian sporting: since ca. 1920. Sarcastic—and perhaps ironic.

simp (p. 770). Acclimatised, rather, by ca. 1910. In use at St Bees at least as early as 1915. (Marples.)

simple sailor, a. 'The Naval Officer's self-description' (Granville): c.p.: C. 20. How 'simple' he is appears very clearly in the novels of William McFee, C. S. Forester (see esp. that magnificent book, *The Ship*), Humfrey Jordan—and others. Often 'I'm a simple sailor' serves a very useful purpose.

simply throwing up buckets. See **throwing up buckets.**

Simpson not Samson, my name's. See **my name is Simpson . . .**

sim(s). See '**i for *ē*'.**

sin-bin. Penalty box: ice-hockey players', commentators', journalists': since ca. 1946. The penalty against an offending player is a two-minutes' 'rest' there. Some 'crimes', however, attract a more than two minutes' penalty.

sin bosun, the. The ship's chaplain: Naval: since ca. 1925. Granville. There are numerous *bosun* compounds—e.g. **custard bosun.**

sin-shifter. A Catholic priest: Australian: since ca. 1930. Jock Marshall & Russell Drysdale, *Journey among Men*, 1962, at p. 7. An allusion to Confession.

Sinbad (p. 770) has, since the 1890's, been 'the Wardroom name for a Royal Naval Reserve Officer. Dates from the time when the first batch of R.N.R. officers joined the Royal Navy from the Mercantile Marine. These were known somewhat unkindly as "the Hungry Hundred". Later a small batch arrived who were called "the Famishing Fifty",' Granville.

Sinbad the Sailor. A tailor: rhyming: late C. 19–20.

since Auntie had her accident. For a very long time, as in 'I haven't been to Melbourne since Auntie had her accident': Australian c.p.: since ca. 1920. (B.P.) The accident is that which is so poignantly described at **'hell!' said the duchess** (p. 387 and above).

since Nelly had her operation. 'A burlesque c.p., marking banteringly a certain lapse of time' (Atkinson): since ca. 1910.

since Pontius was a pilot, as in 'He's been in that mob since . . .': R.A.F. c.p., testifying to long service: since ca. 1944. A pun on *Pontius Pilate*: cf. *Pontius Pilate's Bodyguard* (p. 647). Of the same semi-erudite order, and dating from ca. 1946, are: *since the Air Ministry was a tent* and, referring to Air Ministry Orders, *since A.M.O.s were carved on stone*.

since the battle of Crecy. Since long ago: coll.: late C. 19–20.

since when I have used no other (p. 771) dates from the 1890's and the original painting was by Phil May. For 'twenty years' read 'two years'. (Alexander McQueen, letter of 1953.)

since Willie died. '"We haven't had so much fun since Willie died"—said in approbation of a good time' (Leechman): Canadian: since ca. 1910. Cf. **since Auntie . . .** above.

sine. A House team, exclusive of Colours (*sine coloribus*): Eton: since ca. 1870. Marples.

*sing. To inform to the police: Australian c. and low s.: adopted, in 1943 or '44, ex U.S. servicemen.

sing a bone is the Australian Aboriginal practice of *pointing the bone* at someone under a curse: the former is s., the latter is S.E.: *sing a bone*, late C. 19–20. (B., 1942.) For the practice, see Archer Russell, *A Tramp Royal in Wild Australia*, 1934.

sing it!, don't; or don't chant the poker! Don't exaggerate!: proletarian c.p. of ca. 1870–1910. B. & L.

singe. See shave, n., 7, in *Dict.*

Singers. Singapore: Naval: since ca. 1930. (Granville, Nov. 22, 1962.) By 'the Oxford -*er*'.

singlet, up one's, with *have* either expressed or implied: Australian: since ca. 1935. (B., *Australia Speaks*, 1953.)

singleton, 2 (p. 771). 'Could a singleton nail be one of a size that once sold at a penny each?' a correspondent asks. Rather, a nail *one*-inch long; if *sixpenny nail*, *sevenpenny nail*, nails 6 and 7 inches long. (Julian Franklyn.)

Singular instead of Plural.

'The use of plurals as if they were singular is common in the Unites States and Canada. I have heard and read: a rapids, a scissors, a suds, a stairs, a scales, and even (God save the mark!) a trousers.' Leechman.

This solecism, arising at some time in C. 19, has steadily increased in use—and in acceptance.

sinister, bar (p. 771). The noted heraldist Julian Franklyn corrects me thus: 'Not incorrect for *bend sinister* nor for *baton* (which is always *sinister*). Simply a crass vulgarism—a kitchen or scullery way of referring to a bastard.' He adds that 'there is no special mark for a bastard— various marks are used at various periods'.

sink, down the. Lost, wasted; squandered, misspent: C. 20. Cf. *down the drain* and the *pan*.

sink 'er. To intromit the penis: low (? orig. nautical): C. 20.

sink-hole. The throat: low: ca. 1830–90. *Sinks*, 1848. Cf. **sink, fall down the,** p. 771.

sink the boot in. To kick (someone) brutally: low Australian: C. 20. (B., 1953.)

sink the soldier. (Of the male) to copulate: low: C. 20. Cf. *dip the wick*.

sinker.—4. A suet dumpling: Naval: C. 20. Cf. sense 2 on p. 771. (P-G-R.)

sinner.—2. Affectionately for a person (usually male), as in 'You old sinner!' or 'The old sinner should arrive any moment'; coll.: late C. 19–20. Cf. the affectionate use of *scamp*, *scallywag*, *bastard*, etc.

sipper.—2. A tea spoon: low: ca. 1810–90. *Sinks*, 1848.

sippers. 'A sip from the "tot" of each member of the mess, allowed to the Leading Hand who measures the rum' (Granville): Naval: since ca. 1900. By 'the Oxford -*er*' ex *sip*.

sir. One's teacher: Elementary schools': C. 20. 'I'll tell sir.' Ex the *sir* of respectful address.

Sir Berkeley. Female genitals; hence, sexual intercourse (from the male angle): late C. 19–20. James Curtis, *They Drive by Night*, 1938, 'The quick-lime was burning him up now. No more of the old Sir Berkeley for him.' Short for *Sir Berkeley Hunt*: mid-C. 19–20 variant of **Berkeley Hunt** (*Dict.*).

Sir Garny. A Cockney variant dating from ca. 1890, of **Sir Garnet** (*Dict.*). E. Pugh, *Harry the Cockney*, 1912.

Sir Oliver is an ephemeral fast-life variant of **Oliver,** 1 (p. 587): P. Egan, *Finish to Tom, Jerry, and Logic*, 1828.

Sir Roger Dowler. Suraj-ud-Dowlah, who (d. 1757) permitted 'the Black Hole of Calcutta': military: C. 18. B. & L. (*at Upper Roger*).

sis.—2. An Australian shortening of **sissie** (p. 772): since ca. 1935. (Dymphna Cusack, 1953.)

siss (or **ciss**). A shortening of **sissie** (p. 772): Australian: since ca. 1920. (B.P.)

sissified. Effeminate: coll.: since mid-1920's. Ex **sissie** (or -**y**): p. 772.

sit, n.—2. Esp. *have a sit with* (a girl, a boy): Aus., mostly teenagers': since ca. 1920. Norman Lindsay, *Saturdee*, 1933.

sit, v.—2. To sit for, to take (an examination): middle-class coll.: C. 20. (Angus Wilson, *A Bit off the Map*, 1957.)

sit a buckjumper. To ride a buckjumping horse: Australian coll.: since ca. 1880. B., 1942.

sit-down. A sit-down meal: Canadian (ex U.S.) hoboes' coll.: late C. 19–20. (Frederick Niven, *Wild Honey*, 1927.)

sit down.—2. To settle (at or in a place); to take up land: Australian: C. 20. Baker.

sit on a draft-chit, esp. *be sitting . . .*, about to be transferred to another ship: Naval (lower-deck): since ca. 1920. P-G-R.

sit, or be sitting, pretty. To be in a very advantageous position: since ca. 1920. Ex sitting hens?

sit up and beg. 'He can make it sit up and beg' indicates that a man has become extremely proficient in working some material, e.g. a metal: c.p.: since ca. 1930. Ex teaching a dog to do so.—2. But 'it sits up and begs' (or 'it is sitting up and begging') is at least a generation older—and it refers to an *erectio penis*: low: late C. 19–20.

sit up like Jacky. See **Jacky . . .**

sit-upon.—3. One's posterior: euphemistic: late C. 19–20. Cf. *sit-me-down* (p. 772).

sitter.—5. An easy target: artillerymen's coll.: since ca. 1910. (P-G-R.)—6. A regular drinker of alcoholic liquor: Australian, esp. Sydneyites': since ca. 1940. (Gwen Robyns in *The Evening News*, Feb. 16, 1949.) He sits and sits—and drinks and drinks.

sitter, for a. See **sitter,** 4 (*Dict.*).

sittiwation is, if I remember rightly and am reminded by Mr Ralph Thompson (of New York), a Sam Wellerism and should, therefore, be dated back to the 1830's—and indeed further than that.

Sitz, the. The 'phoney war' of late 1939–early 1940: coined, 1940, in retrospect and as a pun on the German 'blitz' invasion of N.W. and N. Europe; by 1946, ob. (Gunbuster, *Battledress*, 1941; P-G-R, 1948.)

siwash (p. 773)—dating back to ca. 1840—is 'a corruption of the Fr. *sauvage*, wild, savage. Common on the Pacific Coast of North America. I've heard it since 1910' (Leechman).

siwash, v. To put on the 'Indian list' of those to whom intoxicants may not be served: Canadian: C. 20; by 1959, ob. (Leechman.) 'The Siwash list is by no means obsolete, but only a few old-timers so refer to it. The expression would be understood by most people, however' (Leechman, April 1967).

six, gone for. See **gone . . .**

six, hit for. See **hit . . .**

six or sixer, throw a. See **seven, throw a.**

six-and-eight. Honest: rhyming s. on *straight*: since ca. 1930. (John Gosling, 1959.)

*****six doss in the steel.** Six months' imprisonment: Australian c.: C. 20. B., 1942. See the elements **doss** and **steel** in the *Dict.*

six foot. '6 ft 5½ in. space between tracks' (*Railway*, 3rd): railwaymen's coll.: C. 20.

six foot of land—that's all the land *you*'ll get!

A c.p. addressed to one who expresses a desire to 'own a bit of ground (land)': C. 20. See **land-owner**, p. 469.

six months hard. A card in the game of House: rhyming s.: C. 20. (Franklyn, *Rhyming*.)

six o'clock swill. 'The rushed drinking before 6 p.m. in hotel bars. Mainly Victorian, since ten o'clock closing was introduced into N.S.W. some years back' (B.P.): Australian: since ca. 1930. Also New Zealand, as in 'New Zealanders . . . vote to-day on whether to end their "six o'clock swill"': *Daily Mail*, Sept. 23, 1967.

six quarter, get. To be dismissed from employment: commercial: ca. 1860–1910. B. & L. Origin?

six(-)to(-)four. A prostitute: low: C. 20. James Curtis, *What Immortal Hand*, 1939. Rhyming on *whore*.

six-water grog (p. 773): earlier in W. N. Glascock, *Sketch-Book*, II, 1826. (Moe.)

six-wheeler (usually in pl.) A draught horse: cavairymen's: late C. 19–20; by 1945, ob. (Anthony Armstrong, *Captain Bayonet*, 1937.)

sixer.—6. A Christian girl: East End of London: late C. 19–20. Ex Yiddish *Shicksa* (same sense). —7. A scout with six younger boys in his charge: Boy Scouts' coll.: since ca. 1910.

sixer, chuck- or **throw-a.** To be startled or completely nonplussed: Australian since ca. 1910. (Dal Stivens, *Jimmy Brockett*, 1951.) Ex cricket.

sixpenny (p. 773) takes its name from the junior cricket club founded in 1830 and known as the Sixpenny Club, the subscription being sixpence; the name applied only in the summer.—2. The chocolate-coloured, white-ringed cap awarded as a 'colour' for junior cricket at Eton: mid C. 19–20.

sixpennyworth; ninepennyworth. A prison-sentence or term of *six*, of *nine*, months: London's East End: since ca. 1945. Richard Herd, article in *The Evening News*, Nov. 12, 1957.

sixteen annas, at full speed; esp. *go sixteen annas*, to go flat out, as in steeplechasing: Anglo-Indian: C. 20.

sixteen annas to the rupee or **ounces to the pound not.** See **not sixteen annas . . .**

sixty-miler. A collier transporting coal from Newcastle to Sydney: Aus., esp. N.S.W., coll.: C. 20. (B., 1959.)

sixty nine! 'The shearers' code-warning that ladies or visitors are approaching and bad language is "out of order"' (*Straight Furrow*, Feb. 21, 1968): N.Z.: C. 20.

sixty-niner; occ. variants, flying sixty-nine and **swaffonder** or **swassander.** The sexual practice known in France—and in Britain and the Dominions—as *soixante-neuf*, 69: Naval ratings': since ca. 1940. See **soixante-neuf**, below.

Sixy; gen. **Sixy Smith.** Smith, the Middlesex fast bowler and mighty hitter: cricket-lovers': ca. 1935–39. Usually in reference and in the longer form.

size, n. Jelly (to eat): London street s.: ca. 1840–90. Augustus Mayhew, *Paved With Gold*, 1857.

sizzler. An exceedingly fast ball, race-horse, etc.: coll.: late C. 19–20. Cf. the familiar S.E. sense, a broiling hot day.—2. 'A restaurant steak served on a metal plate . . . so hot that the meat sizzles vigorously when it reaches the table' (Leechman): coll., mostly Canadian: since ca. 1945.

skate (p. 773). Because often 'in the rattle': roller-skates rattle along. More accurately, *skate* is a rating addicted to shirking.

skate, v. To 'act Jack-my-hearty; to go in search of wine, women and song' (Granville): Naval: since ca. 1925.—2. (Also *skate off* or *do a skate*.) To depart hurriedly: Australian low: since ca. 1925. B., 1942.

*skate-lurker. See **skates lurk** (*Dict*.). Prob. the 'dodge' is *skates lurk*, the impostor *skate-lurker*.

skates. 'Wire shoes issued to the Infantry in Sinai and speedily condemned as worse than useless,' *The Soldiers' War Slang Dict.*, 1939: Army: 1917–18.

skates on, get. See **get cracking.**

skating, adj. Drug-exhilarated: raffish: since ca. 1955. 'She had nearly half a bottle—and, boy, was she skating?' 'Hardly a question, but rather an exclamation of delighted astonishment, therefore ". . . was she skating!"' (Leechman.)

Skating Rink. See **Egg.**

skating rink. A bald head: jocular: since ca. 1910. Wm Riley, *Old Obbut*, 1933. Short for *flies' skating-rink* (C. 20).

sked. A *scheduled* time or programme: radio: since ca. 1930. (F. Spencer Chapman, *The Jungle Is Neutral*, 1949.)

skeletons fucking on a tin roof, a noise like—it rattles like—two (or **a pair of**). This Canadian and American c.p., not unheard in Britain and Australia since ca. 1940, dates from the 1920's—if not, indeed, from at least a generation earlier.

skerrick.—2. Hence, *have not a skerrick:* to be penniless: Australian: C. 20. B., 1942.

sketch, v. To deal with (someone) in a disciplinary way: Army: since ca. 1939.

*skew. Sense 1 derives ex Low L. *scutella*, a platter, a dish: cf. the Welsh Gypsy *skudela* in the same sense (Sampson).

skewer.—2. An Aboriginal throwing-spear: Australian: since ca. 1860. Archer Russell, *In Wild Australia*, 1934.—3. A sword: ca. 1840–1900. *Sinks*, 1848.

ski. A taxi: Australian, esp. bodgies': since ca. 1950. (Dick.) Rather ex *taxi* than by rhyming s.

skib. A house-painter: builders': C. 20. Cf. the Warwickshire dial. *skibbo*, a house-painter, a whitewasher. (E.D.D.) The variant *skiv* (ca. 1920+) was probably suggested by **skivvy.**

skid kids. Boys racing, speedway fashion, on ordinary bicycles: 1945+. A factual rhyme.

skid lid. A crash helmet: since late 1950's. (David Wharton, June 6, 1966.) Cf. preceding entry, and s. *lid*, a hat.

Skid Road. 'That part of town where the hopeless down-and-outs congregate. Derived from a logging term, *the skid road*, a logging road down which logs were skidded to the river or other water for driving to the mill. When a logger had blown his stake and was ready to return to work, he waited at the end of the skid road, hoping for a lift back to camp. Hence, any place where penniless men congregate. Almost invariably, and quite mistakenly, rendered as *Skid Row*' (Dr Douglas Leechman): U.S. and Canadian: late C. 19–20 and C. 20 (*Row*). It isn't definitely known whether Canada or the United States originated the term; it may have arisen simultaneously in the two countries.

Skid Row. A notoriously depressed street in a city: Australian: esp. Melbourne and Sydney: adopted, ca. 1955, ex U.S. (B.P.) See the preceding entry.

skids, as in 'The skids are under him', he has been dismissed from a job: Army: 1940+. (P-G-R.)

Skies. Italians: Australian: since ca. 1910. (B., 1943.) Perhaps cf. *Sky,* 1 and 2 (p. 777). No! It is rhyming s. on *Ities* or *Eyeties.* (B.P.)

skiet-skop-en-donder film. A blood-and-thunder film; a Western: South Africa: since ca. 1930. 'The words are from the Afrikaans: *skiet,* shoot; *skop,* kick; *en,* and; *donder,* fight.' Cyrus A. Smith (letter of July 17, 1946). Also *thud and blunder* (film): *The Cape Times,* June 3, 1946 (Alan Nash).

skiff, n.—2. See **scut,** 3.

skiff, v.t. To upset, to spill: Christ's Hospital: C. 20. Marples.

skikster is an occ. C. 20 Australian variant of **shickster,** 1, 2. B., 1942.

skilly and toke. Anything mild or insipid: proletarian: from ca. 1860. B. & L. See **skilly,** 1, and **toke,** n., 1, in *Dict.*

skilly-pot. A teapot: H.M.S. *Conway:* late C. 19–20. Cf. **skilly,** 3 (p. 775).

skimisher. A public-house, an inn, esp. if rural: tramps' and Romanies' s.: C. 20. (Robert M. Dawson.) Ex **skimish** on p. 775.

skimmer. A broad-brimmed hat: Sedgeley Park School: ca. 1800–65. Frank Roberts in *The Cottonian,* Autumn 1938. One could send it skimming into the air.—2. (Also *skimming dish.*) A fast planing motor-boat: Naval: since ca. 1935. (P-G-R.) It skims along.

skin, n., 1 (a purse): 'Until ca. 1895 or later in Australia' (Sidney J. Baker, letter). Also, in C. 20, Australian for 'a horse' (B., 1942).—6. Foreskin: coll.: mid-C. 19–20.—7. Women in general, girls in particular: as in 'a taut drop of skin', a shapely female: Naval: C. 20.—8. A person: Anglo-Irish: late C. 19–20. 'He was known far and wide as a decent old skin': Brendan Behan, *Borstal Boy,* 1958.

skin, a bit of. A girl: low Anglo-Irish: C. 20.

skin, get under (someone's), with complementary **have under one's skin.** To irritate; to be constantly irritated: since ca. 1925.

skin, go on the. To save money by rigid economy over a period: military, esp. in India: from ca. 1885; ob. Richards. Cf. **skin,** v., 1 and 2, in *Dict.*

skin, have a. To possess (overmuch) self-assurance: Naval: since ca. 1920. Granville. Short for *thick skin.*

skin a turd, he'd. He is parsimonious: low Canadian c.p.: late C. 19–20.

skin diver. A naked diver: Australian pearldivers' coll.: since ca. 1865. (Ion M. Idriess, *Forty Fathoms Deep,* 1937.)

skin dog. A male 'sexual athlete': low Canadian: since ca. 1950.

skin-game.—3. Facial plastic surgery as practised on would-be glamorous women: since ca. 1935.

skinful, have got a.—2. To have received more than enough: low coll. (— 1915). Graham Seton, *Pelican Row,* 1935. Cf. **bellyful** (*Dict.*).

skinful, have had a. To have had too much to drink; hence, to put up with: mostly Army: since ca. 1939. (P-G-R.)

skinner.—5. A hanger-on for profit at auctions: auctioneers': mid-C. 19–20; ob. James Greenwood, *In Strange Company,* 1873. Cf. **odd-trick man.**—6. A very successful bet, or 'book', on a horse-race: Australian: since ca. 1910. (Jon Cleary, 1949.)—7. An appointment deliberately missed: Australian: since ca. 1925. (B., 1943.)—8. Sexually 'in her': low Australian rhyming s. (not common): since ca. 1930.

Sense 7 has also, since ca. 1920, been common in Britain. (*The Sunday Times,* Oct. 3, 1965: of a very successful day for the 'bookies'.)

skinny, n. A girl or young woman: Australian: C. 20. B., 1942. Ex frequent thinness.

skinny Liz. Any elderly woman: St Bees: C. 20. Marples.

skint (p. 776): by 1945, fairly general.

skip, v.—3. (Ex sense 1.) To abscond on bail: c.: C. 20.

skip it! Don't trouble! Forget it!: coll.: adopted ca. 1939 from U.S.

skip-jack. See 'Fops'.

skip-stop. A train that 'skips' every second station: Australian: since ca. 1925. (B.P.)

skip the gutter! Houp la!; over she goes!: proletarian: ca. 1865–1910. B. & L.

skipper, n., 5 (p. 776), occurs in 1818 (Alfred Burton, *Johnny Newcome*). Moe. Also, since 1917 or 1918, the commander of an aircraft in flight: R.A.F. coll.—7. A mode of address, as in 'What's the time, skipper?': since ca. 1920.

skippy. A logger (?): Australian miners': C. 20. (Gavin Casey, *It's Easier Downhill,* 1945.)

skips. The ship's captain: Naval (lower-deck): since ca. 1925. Familiar for *skipper.* (P-G-R.)

skirt, v. To skirt-dance: coll., mostly Cockneys': from ca. 1880. Nevinson, 1895, 'I've seed the Sheenies step-dancin' in the Lane, and I've seed the sisters Toddles skirtin' at the Cambridge, but I never see dancin' as was a patch on Lina's that night.'

skirt, run a. See **run a skirt.**

Skirt-Chasers, the. The Royal Army Service Corps: Army: since ca. 1940. A pun on 'R.A.S.C.'

skirt patrol is a Service (esp. R.A.F.) variation, since ca. 1938, of **skirt-hunting** (p. 776). H. & P.

skite, go on the. To go drinking: Army: since ca. 1920. (P-G-R.) Cf.:

skite, on the. Having a terrific binge: Scottish Public Schoolmen's: C. 20.

skitey. Boastful: New Zealand: since ca. 1925. ex *skite,* to boast.

skits. A schizophrenic: since ca. 1930, but not common before ca. 1960. Ex **schizo** above.

skitsy. Afraid, timorous: Milton Junior School, Bulawayo: since ca. 1920. Cf. *skittish* (horse).

skitter. An Australian variant of **scutter** (p. 741): C. 20. Ruth Park, *Pink Flannel,* 1945. The origin of **skitters, the.** (B.P.)

skitterbug. A Bren-gun carrier: Australian soldiers': 1940–5. (B., 1943.)

skitters, the. Diarrhœa: Services: since ca. 1930. (P-G-R.) Cf. *squitters,* p. 821.

skittle.—3. To knock down; to kill: mostly Australian: late C. 19–20. B., 1942. Ex the game of skittles.

Skittles. Nickname of a famous London prostitute in 'the Langtry period' (1881–99).

skittling. The feminine practice of washing stockings, handkerchiefs and 'smalls' in the bedroom or bathroom wash-basin: hotel-keepers' and hotel-staffs', esp. in Scotland: since ca. 1920.

skitz. See **schitz** above.

skiv.—2. Short for **skivvy** (p. 776): since ca. 1925. Marples.—3. See *skib.*—4. A bookmaker's runner or tout: the racing-world, esp. at Epsom: late C. 19–20. Cf. *skiver.*

skive, n. An evasion; a loafing: low: since ca. 1925. (Norman.) Ex the v.

skive, v.—2. Hence, v.t., to evade (a parade): since ca. 1918. Gerald Kersh, *Slightly Oiled*, 1946. Sense 1 (p. 776) may derive ex Fr. *esquiver.*

skiver. A shirker, 'schemer': Army: since ca. 1915. Gerald Kersh, 1941. Ex **skive** (p. 776).

skivvy (p. 776). An early example in W. L. George, *The Making of an Englishman*, 1914. It occurs in James Joyce's *Ulysses*, 1922.

skivvy! (p. 776). Ex Japanese *sukebei*, 'bawdy, lecherous'. (E. V. Gatenby, letter of Oct. 16, 1939.)

skiz. See **schitz** above.

skolfuring, n. Trading stores or equipment to civilians: Regular Army: C. 20; virtually † by 1939. Origin?

***skolly.** A non-European delinquent or loafer or criminal: S. African c. and police s.: C. 20. *The Cape Times*, May 23, 1946. Via Afrikaans ex Dutch *schuilen*, to lie low.

skookum. Satisfactory ('Everything's skookum'): Canadian West Coast: late C. 19–20. Chinook jargon; lit., 'strong'. Cf.:

skookum house, often preceded by *strong*. A gaol: West Canadian: C. 20; slightly ob. by 1952. (Leechman.)

skoshi. A little (Fr. *un peu*): United Nations troops': ca. 1951–5 in Korea. (*Iddiwah*, July 1953.) A Korean word? Or Japanese?

skowse or scouce or scouse or scowse. A Liverpool-born rating: Naval: C. 20. Granville derives it ex **scouse** (p. 735), 'thin meal peculiar to the district'.

skulker (p. 777) is recorded as early as 1748: Smollett, *Roderick Random*. (Moe.)

skull. See 'Hauliers' Slang'.—2. The head of a two-up penny: Australian: since ca. 1910. Lawson Glassop, *Lucky Palmer*, 1949, where the nuance is 'a two-up penny turning up heads'. (B., 1953.)

***skull-dragging, n.** 'Pulling a victim downstairs by his feet so that his head is painfully battered' (B., 1953): Australian c.: since ca. 1930.

skul(l)duggery. Underhand practices; villainy: coll., orig. jocular: C. 20. An extension of the mostly American senses (malversation of public money; obscenity), spelt *skullduggery*, of the Scottish *sculduddery*, in C. 19–20: also *sculduggery* (or *sk-*), itself of obscure origin.

skun. Skinned: sol: C. 19–20. *The Pawnshop Murder*. On *spin*: spun.

skunk, v.—3. To defeat (an opponent)—in cribbage, by a large score; in other games of chance, to nil: Canadian: adopted, late C. 19, ex U.S. (Leechman.)

Sky.—3. An Italian; usually in pl., *Skies*: Australian: since ca. 1930. Leonard Man, *Mountain Flats*, 1939.

sky, n.—3. In *have a sky*, have a look, to glance around: ? mostly Liverpool: since ca. 1920. Matutinal meteorology.—4. Whisk(e)y: Australian: since ca. 1950. (B.P.) Ex whisky.

sky, v.—5. Of a horse: to throw (its rider) high

into the air: Australian, mostly rural: mid C. 19–20. (Tom Ronan, *Moleskin Midas*, 1956.) A special application of sense 1 on p. 777.

sky(-)artist. A psychiatrist: Naval (lower-deck) and Army: 1940 +. Granville; Michael Harrison, 1943. By 'Hobson-Jobson'—and wit.

sky-blue.—3. A long-term prisoner: South African c.: C. 20. *The Cape Times*, May 23, 1946. Ex the blue jacket he wears.

sky-blue pink. Jocular c.p. for colour unknown or indeterminate: since ca. 1885.

Sky-Blues. 'Officers of the Hudson's Bay Company, so called from the colour of their uniform (no longer worn). My earliest reference is 1821.' (Leechman): Canadian coll.: since ca. 1815; by 1940, ob.

sky farmer.—2. A farmer either without, or with very little, land: Anglo-Irish (esp. Southern): mid (? early) C. 19–20. J. W. Joyce, *English . . . in Ireland*, 1910.) Perhaps ex sense 1 on p. 777, but prob. of independent origin.

sky-hacking (or one word), n. Back-biting; slander: Australian: since ca. 1925. Baker.

sky-high. To scold (a person) excessively: proletarian: from ca. 1880. Ex **give sky high**, q.v.

sky-hog. An airman that flies low over houses: 1945 +. On **road-hog**.

sky-hook. 'A useful, but mythical, piece of apparatus which enables an airman to hover over one spot. Can also be used for any difficult job of lifting,' Gerald Emanuel, letter of March 29, 1945; R.A.F., esp. among the regulars: since 1918. But Dr Douglas Leechman vouches for its use, in Canada (esp. among loggers), as early as 1909.—2. The D.A.6, a World War I trainer aircraft: since 1915. Also called a *clutching hand*, as on p. 162. In, e.g., P. R. Reid, *Winged Diplomat*, 1962.

sky-lodging. See **sky-parlour** (*Dict.*).

sky-topper dates back to ca. 1880: in B. & L.

sky wire. A radio aerial; an antenna: Australian radio hams': since ca. 1955. (B.P.)

skylark, v., and **skylarking**, vbl n. (p. 778). Perhaps orig. s.; earlier in *Sessions*, April 1803.

skylight. A 'daylight' or unliquored interval at top of one's drinking glass: 1816, Peacock; ob. by 1880; † by 1920. O.E.D. Suggested by *daylight*.

skypiece. 'Smoke trails of sky-writing,' H. & P.: R.A.F.: since ca. 1930. Ex painting.

***skyser** = *skycer* = **shicer**, q.v. in *Dict.*

skyte.—2. A fool: Scottish Public Schools' coll.: mid-C. 19–20. B. & L.

slaat. See **let's slaat**.

slab.—4. A slice of bread and butter: streets': C. 20. E. C. Vivian, *Ladies in the Case*, 1933.—5. A long paragraph: journalists': since ca. 1910. —6. See 'Canadian'.

slab, on the. On the operating table: R.A.F. aircrews': 1940 +. (Atkinson.)

slab dab. See 'Occupational names'.

slack, n., 3 (p. 778), occurs as early as 1818 (Alfred Burton, *Johnny Newcome*), Colonel Moe points out; again in *Boxiana* (IV), 1824.—5. A 'depression in rail level' (*Railway*): railwaymen's coll.: late C. 19–20. Ex the *slack* in a rope.

slack, the. The slack period or off season: Australian coll.: esp. among sheep-shearers and cane-cutters: C. 20. (Jean Devanney, *By Tropic Sea and Jungle*, 1944.)

slack bobs. The small minority of boys excused from rowing and cricket, but allowed to play tennis: Eton: C. 20. (J. D. R. McConnell, *Eton: How It Works*, 1967.) Cf. **dry bobs** and **wet bobs** in the *Dict*.

slack in stays (p. 778) goes back to 1806 (John Davis, *The Post-Captain*). Moe.

slack party. Punishment for defaulters: Royal Naval College, Dartmouth: C. 20. Granville. Ironic; cf. **slack in stays** (p. 778).

Slackers. Halifax, Canada: Royal Canadian Navy: 1939–45. (P-G-R.) Ex the slight slackening of discipline after arduous convoy work. See also **Squibbley** below.

slag.—4. One who looks at the free attractions but avoids the paying shows: showmen's: since ca. 1880. (Hence, prob., sense 3: p. 778.)—5. (Ex sense 3.) 'A man, never less than 35, who has often been in trouble with the police and who, more often than not, is liable to be sentenced to preventive detention when he next gets into trouble' (A. T. Roeves, letter in *The Manchester Guardian*, Sept. 11, 1958): low, mostly London: since ca. 1945. Probably ex: 6. A figurative bitch or a ditto bastard: since ca. 1930. Both in Norman.—7. Rubbish, nonsense: Australian: since ca. 1910. Vance Palmer, *Golconda*, 1948. —8. A prostitute: but rare except in *old slag*, an old prostitute: low: since the late 1950's. Perhaps ex **slagger** on p. 778.—9. Collective for 'young third-rate grafters, male or female, unwashed, useless' (Robin Cook, 1962): since ca. 1945: c. >, by ca. 1960, also low s. Also, *ibid.*, such an individual: cf. senses 5 and 6.—10. Females collectively: low: since ca. 1950. 'Suburban slag filling in time' (James Barlow, *The Burden of Proof*, 1968).

Sense 1 (p. 778) is glossed thus in W. Buchanan-Taylor, *Shake It Again*, 1943: 'It seemed slaggy to me. (A *slag* is a person who is not much *bottle*—not much good; a person for whom you have no respect, even if he or she is holding a *poke* (plenty of money) . . .' Sense 7 has, since ca. 1950, been much less common in Australia than sense 6. (B.P.)

slag, v. To expectorate or spit (v.i.): low Australian: C. 20. ' "Hell," muttered Richie, "he's slaggin' on me car!" ' (Dick.) Ex Scottish dial. *slag*, to moisten, to besmear.

slaggy is the adj. of n. **slag** (p. 778 and above). See quotation at **slag**, n., above.

slam, v.—3. To strike or punch (someone): since ca. 1910. In, e.g., Dave Marlow, *Coming, Sir*, 1937.

slang a dolly to the edge. 'To show and work a marionette on a small platform outside the booth' —as a means of attracting customers for the play shown inside: showmen's: ca. 1875–1940. (*John o'London's Weekly*, March 4, 1949.) The phrase shows that **slang**, v., 2 (p. 779) was current well into the 20th century.

slanger of one's mauleys (or **morleys**). A boxer: one who excels with his fists: 1822, David Carey, *Life in Paris;* † by 1890. (Carey spells it *morleys*.) I.e. *slinger*.

slanging, adj. Performing, as *slanging buffer* (dog) and *slanging pig* (elephant): circus: late C. 19–20. (Laura Knight, *Oil Paint and Grease Paint*, 1936.) Cf. **slanger** and **slanging**, n., 1, on p. 779, and also **buffer** and **pig**, n., 10, both above.

slanging match. An altercation: since ca. 1860: coll. >, ca. 1910, S.E.

slant, n.—4. (Cf. 2.) An opportunity: Australian: since ca. 1870. 'Tom Collins', *Such is Life*, 1903.

slap. 'A slap-up meal' (Anderson): beatniks': since ca. 1959. Anderson, 'Others have the folding-lettuce for slap.'

slap, knap (or **nap**) **the.** See **nap the slap.**

slap a few on the deck. To fire a few rounds: artillerymen's: 1939–45. (P-G-R.)

slap and tickle, a; esp., *have a bit of slap and tickle.* 'Necking', to 'neck'; but, since late 1950's, usu. to make love: the former, since ca. 1910, the latter since ca. 1920; since ca. 1950, both are coll. The former occurs in, e.g., Somerset Maugham, *The Lion's Skin*, ca. 1924.

slap-bang in the middle. Right in the middle: Australian coll.: C. 20. (B.P.)

slap-dash. To do something happy-go-luckily or carelessly: Australian coll.: since ca. 1920. B., 1942.

slap-happy. Very—strictly, boisterously—happy; esp., recklessly happy: coll.: adopted in 1942 from U.S. (see quotation at **stream-lined**). Jackson. I.e. back-slappingly happy.—2. A synonym of *punch-drunk*: since ca. 1945. (*Evening News*, Oct. 27, 1950.)

slap in, v.i. To make a request, e.g. for leave: Naval: since ca. 1930. (P-G-R.)

slap in the belly with a wet fish, better than a. See **better than a slap . . .**

slap of the tongue. A reprimand or a sharp reply: Anglo-Irish: late C. 19–20.

***slash,** n.—2. A urination: c., and low: C. 20.—3. Hence (?), a drink: low London: since ca. 1930. Arthur La Bern, *Pennygreen Street*, 1950. For the semantics, cf. *piss-up*, a drunken bout.

slash, in the. Fighting: tailor's: from ca. 1860. B. & L.

slasher.—3. A fast driver: busmen's: since ca. 1925. Contrast **scratcher**, 6.—4. A hockey stick: Cranbrook School: since ca. 1920. Proleptic.

slasheroo. Excellent, most attractive: Australian: since ca. 1944. (B., 1953.) The suffix *-eroo* was adopted from U.S. servicemen; *slashing* + *-eroo*.

slashers. Testicles: low: C. 20. (Barry England, *Figures in a Landscape*, 1968.)

slate, n.—4. A quarrel: from ca. 1880. Ibid.

slather. (Rights of) access: Australian: since ca. 1930. (D'Arcy Niland, *The Shiralee*, 1955.) Perhaps ex Irish *slighe*, craft; a way; access.

slathered. Tipsy: Australian: since ca. 1920. (B.P.) Prob. ex North Country dial. *slather*, to spill, to rain, to slobber.

***slaughter-house.**—6. A low brothel: white-slavers' c.: C. 20. Albert Londres, 1928. Ex sense 3.

slave. An aircraftman or aircraftwoman: R.A.F. (since ca. 1939) and W.A.A.F. (1941 +). Jackson. Humorous.

slaver. (p. 781.) Orig. coll., it was, by 1946, almost S.E.

slavey market. An employment bureau for domestic servants: C. 20. (Eric Horne, *What the Butler Winked At*, 1923.) A pun on S.E. *slave market*.

***slaving gloak.** A servant: c.: C. 19. B. & L.

sleazy. Grimy or dilapidated—or both; (cheap and) inferior: adopted, in late 1950's, ex U.S. A blend of *slimy* and *greasy*.—2. Hence, in Britain,

garish and disreputable: since ca. 1959. 'Half
the wardroom were in some sleazy night club that
was raided' (John Winton, *We Saw the Sea*, 1960).

sleep at Mrs Green's. An Australian variant of
sleep with Mrs Green. (K. S. Prichard, *Kiss on the
Lips*, 1932.)

sleep black. To sleep unwashed: chimney-
sweeps' coll.: mid C. 19–20; by 1950, ob.

sleep the caller. To lose a shift by failing to hear
the caller: miners' (esp. North Country) coll.:
late C. 19–20. I.e. to *oversleep* (*by failing to hear*)
the caller.

sleep tight, mind the fleas don't bite. A children's
bed-time c.p.: late C. 19–20.

*****sleep-walker.** A sneak thief: Australian c.:
C. 20. B., 1942.

*****sleep with Mrs Green** (p. 781). Hence, also
Australian. (Baker).

sleeper.—2. A delayed-action bomb: 1940 +.—
3. 'Second man on diesel' (*Railway*, 3rd): railwaymen's: since late 1950's.—4. A gramophone record
that, released a long time, suddenly becomes a
'hit': since ca. 1950. Ex sense 2. (David
Wharton, June 6, 1966.)

sleepers. Sleeping pills: since late 1920's.
The agential *sleeper*, a soporific.

sleever.—2. A drinking straw: New Zealand:
C. 20. B., 1941, compares Australian (*long*) *sleever*, a long drink.

slew. To defeat, baffle, outwit: late C. 19–20.
Implied in **slewed**, 2 (p. 781); since ca. 1930,
predominantly Australian. Baker.

slewed.—3. (Ex sense 2—see p. 781). Lost in
'the bush': Australian: late C. 19–20. Boyd
Cable, letter in *The Observer*, Oct. 30, 1938, 'The
man who (on tramp,) loses the track and gets
"bushed" or "slewed" may easily die of thirst
or "do a perish".'

slice, take a. Extant as *take* (or *help yourself
to*) *a slice off the loaf*, as in Arthur J. Sarl, *Gamblers
of the Turf*, 1938 ('You could safely help yourself
to . . .').

Slice of Cheese, the. 'The monument erected
by Mussolini west of Tobruk. It was wedge-
shaped' (Peter Sanders in *The Sunday Times*
magazine, Sept. 10, 1967): Army in North Africa:
1940–43.

slice of ham. A variant of *plate of ham.*

slice of pie. The Army's variant (since 1940) of
piece of cake. (P-G-R.)

slick, adj. See next, s.f.—2. Neat or smooth;
attractive, desirable: Canadian: adopted, ca. 1946,
ex U.S. 'Boy, look at Jane! There's a slick
chick.' (Leechman.)

slick chick. A girl; esp., a young lady: beatniks' (and teenagers'): adopted, ca. 1958, ex U.S.
(Anderson—cf. the quotation at **canary,** 12,
above.)

slicked down. (Of male head-hair) plastered
down with brilliantine, etc.: coll.: adopted ca.
1930 from U.S.

slickee-slickee, n., and **slicky-slick,** v. Theft;
to steal; not in a big way: United Nations troops
in Korea: ca. 1951–55. (*Iddiwah*, July 1953.) By
pidgin English out of *slick*, not-quite-honestly
smart, itself adopted, ca. 1918, ex U.S.—as coll.,
not s.

slicks. Magazines printed on glazed stock:
Canadian journalists', printers', publishers', news-
vendors': since ca. 1930. (Leechman.) Cf.
glossies.

slide, n. Butter: Naval: since ca. 1930. 'Pass
the slide!' Ex its greasiness.

slide!, let it. See **let** . . .

slide and glitter. Toast and marmalade: Naval
(lower-deck): Sept. 13, 1941, *The Weekly Telegraph*.—2. But strictly butter and marmalade:
lower-deck.

slide your jive. See 'Canadian . . .'

slieveen. A deceitful person: Newfoundland
coll. (? dial.): late C. 19–20. (L. E. F. English,
Historic Newfoundland, 1955.) Ex Gaelic *sligh-
each*, sly.

Sligger. Francis Urquhart (d. 1935), a Balliol
don for forty years: Oxford undergraduates': late
C. 19–20; † except among graduates. See esp.
Cyril Bailey, *Francis Urquhart*, 1936, and Harold
Nicolson's review thereof in *The Daily Telegraph*,
Nov. 6, 1936.

Slim. 'The Navy's ironic nickname for a fat
man'. (P-G-R): since ca. 1920.

slim-dilly. A girl or young woman: Australian:
since ca. 1920. B., 1942. Cf. **skinney.**

slime, n. Semen: low: C. 19–20.

sling, n.—2. A bribe: Australian c.: since ca.
1930. Kylie Tennant, *The Joyful Condemned*,
1953.—3. A tip (of money): Aus.: since ca. 1935.
(B., 1959.) Ex sense 3 of the v. on p. 782.

sling, v.—10. To fire (shells): Army: 1939–45.
(P-G-R.)—11. (Of a horse) to throw (its rider):
Australian: since ca. 1910. (B., 1943.)

sling 'em out. The c.p. of *the dhobey firm*:
Naval: C. 20. (P-G-R.)

sling it. To leave one's work or one's job:
Australian coll.: since ca. 1910. (K. S. Prichard.)
Cf. *sling up*.

sling off.—3. To depart; to make off: Australian: since ca. 1925. B., 1942.

sling one up. A variant (Army and R.A.F.) of
throw one up. Jackson.

sling one's bunk. To depart: ca. 1860–1910.
B. & L. I.e. sling up one's hammock (and
go).

sling one's Daniel. Earlier in *Sessions*, Nov.
1866, 'One of the constables said, "Sling your
dannel."'

sling one's hammock (p. 782) is defined by
'Taffrail' in *The Sub*, 1917, as 'to be given time
to settle down in new surroundings'.

sling one's hook. See **hook** . . .

sling round. 'To air-test an aircraft,' Jackson:
R.A.F., and civilian test pilots': since ca. 1930.
The pilot does aerobatics.

sling tail. Pickled pork: low: ca. 1825–90.
Sinks, 1848.

sling the hatchet (p. 782). In nuance 'tell a
pitiful tale': 1893, P. H. Emerson, *Signor Lippo*.

sling the tip. See **tip, sling the.**

sling to. To pay out (esp. protection) money to;
to bribe: Australian: since ca. 1920.

sling (esp. *it*) **up.** To abandon (job, country,
talk, action, etc.): Australian: late C. 19–20.
G. B. Lancaster, *Jim of the Ranges*, 1910. 'I've
sling her [Queensland] up. Give her the go, the
old Jade.'

slinge. To play truant; to stay away from
work: Newfoundland coll.: C. 19–20. (L. E. F.
English, *Historic Newfoundland*, 1955.) Ex Irish
and Sc. Dial *slinge* to skulk.

slinkers in for (someone), **put the.** To hint
adversely to authority about (someone): since
ca. 1950. (Laurie Atkinson, who notes hearing

it 'about 1960'.) To *slink* evokes an impression of craftiness and slyness.

slinter. A trick, esp. if unfair; mostly in *work a slinter*, to effect a mean trick, tell a false story: Australian low: since ca. 1920. B., 1942. Cf. **slant**, n., 4 (Add.) and **slanter** (*Dict.*) and **schlenter** (*Dict.*).

slip, n.—4. A slipper: domestic: since ca. 1880. Daphne Du Maurier, *Rebecca*, 1938.—5. Baked custard: middle-class: since ca. 1860. Slippery stuff.—6. A small sum given by the operators to a loser now penniless, to enable him to get home: Australian two-up players': since ca. 1920. (B., 1953.) They slip it to him.

slip a joey. (Of a woman) to have a miscarriage; but also, to give birth to a child: Australian low: C. 20. B., 1942. Ex **joey**, 4 (p. 442).

slip (her) a length. To coït with (a woman): low: late C. 19–20.—2. Hence, *slip him a length*, to reprimand: Army: since ca. 1925.—3. Of a man, to have homosexual relations with: Australian low s.: late C. 19–20. Construction: *slip a length into*. (Colin MacInnes, *June in Her Spring*, 1952.)

slip-horn. See **fish-horn.**

slip in the gutter. (Bread and) butter: rhyming s.: C. 20. (Franklyn, *Rhyming*.]

slip into.—3. To have sexual connexion with: low: from ca. 1870.

slip it. To decamp, make off: ca. 1880–1920. J. W. Horsley, *Prisons and Prisoners*, 1898. Cf. S.E. *to slip away.*

slip it about (a woman). To coït with: C. 20. Cf. **slip into**, 3.

slip it across (someone).—2 To punch or strike: Army: C. 20. Also *push* . . .

slip off (height). To fly lower esp. by rapid descent: aviators' coll.: from ca. 1925. *The New Statesman and Nation*, Feb. 20, 1937.

slip oneself. To let oneself go; make the most of a thing or opportunity: Cockney coll.: from ca. 1890. Edwin Pugh's Cockney stories, *passim.*

slip-slop. See 'Miscellanea'.

slip-stick. A slide-rule: Canadian engineers' and architects': since ca. 1940. (Leechman.) Cf. the Naval *look-stick* (p. 494).

slip-up. An appointment or rendezvous intentionally failed: Australian: C. 20. B., 1942.

slipped his trolley (sc. 'he has'). Crazy: since late 1940's. Ex *slipped off* his trolley, or *lost* it? Perhaps orig. trolley-bus or tram-drivers' s., as Ramsey Spencer has suggested; if so, then dating from ca. 1925 or earlier.

slipper.—2. A male urine-bottle: hospitals': C. 20. Ex shape. Rather: a slipper-shaped bed-pan for both sexes and both purposes: hospital coll.: late C. 19–20.

Slipper-Slopper...(p. 783). Ex a nursery rhyme.

slipper Sam. A gambling card game: late C. 19–20.

slippery.—2. Clever; (very) skilful or adroit: lower-class: since ca. 1930. Peter Crookston, *Villain*, 1967, 'Some of the old blacksmiths very very slippery.'

*slipping, be. To be dying: white-slavers' c., applied to a prostitute (working for a pimp): C. 20. A. Londres, 1928.

slips. In theatre or cinema, the sides of a gallery: Australian: since ca. 1920. Baker.

slips his braces, he. Said of a man complaisant to homosexuality: coll.: C. 20.

slit, the female pudend. When not a euphemism it is a low coll.: C. 17–20.—2. Clitoris: raffish: since ca. 1920.

slither, n.—3. Short for *slither and dodge*, a lodge (of, e.g., Oddfellows): late C. 19–20. *The New Statesman*, Nov. 29, 1941.

slither, v. (p. 783), is also Australian: B., 1943.

*slitherum. A counterfeit coin: c.: C. 20. (*The Yorkshire Post*, latish May 1937.) Ex **slither**, n., 1 (*Dict.*); lit., a 'slither' one.

*slithery. Sexual intercourse: c., and low: C. 20.

slittie. A slit trench: Army (other ranks'): 1940–5. (P-G-R.)

slob. A 'softy', a fool, a (stupid) lout: in New Zealand, Australia, England: C. 20. (Ruth Park, *Pink Flannel*, 1955.) Ex the Anglo-Irish *slob*, 'a soft fat quiet simple-minded girl or boy:—"Your little Nellie is a quiet poor slob": used as a term of endearment' (P. W. Joyce, *English . . . in Ireland*, 1910).

slobber, n., 2 (p. 783). A Cockney term; earlier in W. Somerset Maugham, *Liza of Lambeth*, 1897.

slog, v., 1 (p. 783). Earlier in *Sessions*, Sept. 1824, 'One of them said, "Go back and *slog* him"'; also in H. D. Miles, *Dick Turpin*, 1941, ' "Slog her, Nan; that's the cheese." '

slog it on. See **schlog** . . .

slogged, get. To be charged an excessive price: Australian: C. 20. B., 1942.

slogger, 4 (p. 783). Much earlier in *Boxiana*, IV, 1824; and sense 2 occurs also in *Sinks*, 1848, as a boxer.—6. A quick worker: proletarian coll.: from ca. 1860; slightly ob. B. & L.

sloo. 'To get out of the way' (L. E. F. English, *Historic Newfoundland*, 1955): Newfoundland coll.: C. 20. An adaptation of E. *slew* or *slue* (v.i.), to swing round.

sloom. See **keep sloom.**

slop, n.—4. A prisoner's overcoat: Dartmoor c.: C. 20. H. U. Triston, *Men in Cages*, 1938. Ex *slops*, old and very cheap clothes.

slop back. To drink freely, as in Slatter, 'Slopping back the suds': New Zealand: since ca. 1925. Cf. **slops**, 1, on p. 784.

Slop Carriers, the. The Australian A.S.C.: Australian soldiers': 1939+. B., 1942.

slop chest. See **slops, 4.**

slop-chit. A 'form made out by the Supply rating, which enables a man to buy "slops" in the stores' (Granville): Naval coll.: C. 20.—2. Hence, as in 'I can't do that job, I've enough on my slop-chit already' (cited by Granville): since ca. 1900.

Slop House, the. The House of Commons: journalistic: since ca. 1910. Sydney Horler, *The Dark Journey*, 1938. Ex the amount of 'slop' talked there.

slop over; slop over (in) one's talk. 'To exhibit exaggerated effusiveness of manner and words': from ca. 1870; coll. >, by 1900, S.E. B. & L.

Sloperies, the. 99 Shoe Lane, London, E.C.4, the publishing address of *Ally Sloper's Half-Holiday*: ca. 1884–90.

sloppy.—2. Slack, careless, negligent: C. 20.

slops.—4. Sailors' clothes: Navy: C. 20. H. & P., 'The slop chest is their Clothing Stores.' Ex the 'sloppy', i.e. loose, make.—5. Ca. 1930–42, the Service Police: R.A.F. Ex *slop*, n., 1 (p. 783, at end).—6. Beer: Australian: since ca. 1920. (B.P.)

slosh.—3. Beer: Naval (lower-deck): since ca. 1910. Echoic.

slosh, n.—5. (Ex 1.) Boiled rice: Christ's Hospital: C. 20. Marples.—6. Coffee: Australian: since ca. 1920. (B., 1953.) Ex senses 2 and 3: p. 784.

slosh, v. (p. 784). 'I sloshed him one,' *Sessions*, Dec. 13, 1904; ''Im what I sloshed for readin' my letters,' A. Neil Lyons, *Clara*, 1912.

slosh and mud. A collar stud: theatrical rhyming s.: late C. 19–20. (Franklyn, *Rhyming*.)

sloshed. See **honkers.**—But also in more general use (late C. 19–20). Ex *slosh, n.*, 2 (p. 784).

slot (strictly **'s'lot**)! Thank you very much: Australian: since ca. 1945. Obviously 'thank*s* a *lot*'. (B.P.)

slot, down the. (Of a slow train) diverted to allow faster trains to pass: railwaymen's: since ca. 1910. (*Railway*.)

slother. A sol. blend (from ca. 1880) of *slither* and *slosh*; thus in Nevinson, 1895, 'Slotherin' about Shadwell in the cold and wet.'

*****slotted kip.** A two-up 'kip' in which, to hold a two-headed penny, a slot has been cut: Australian two-up gamblers' c.: C. 20. B., 1942.

slotted job. A woman: low, orig. in the Armed Forces: since ca. 1940.

slouch, no (p. 784): also Canadian of late C. 19–20. (Frederick Niven, 1927.)

Slow and Dirty, the. The Somerset and Dorset railway: railwaymen's: ca. 1890–1925. (*Railway*.)

slow as a wet week, as. (Of persons) very slow; esp., unenterprising, mostly in sexual matters: late C. 19–20.

Slow, Easy and Comfortable, the. The South-Eastern and Chatham railway: railwaymen's: C. 20. (*Railway* 2nd.)

Slow Starvation and Agony. A jocular interpretation of the initials of the Shaw Savile and Albion shipping line: since ca. 1910; by 1965, ob.

sludge. Beer: office- and shop-girls': ca. 1955 –60. The variant *plasma* lasted less than the year 1958. (Gliderdale.)

slug, n., 2 (p. 785): earlier in Smollett's play, *The Reprisal* (II, viii), 1757. Moe.—4. An Eton Fellow: Windsor townsmen's: 1825, *Spy*; † by 1890.—5. A heavy bill: Australian: C. 20. B., 1942. Ex 3.—6. A small shell (projectile): Army: 1940 +.—7. An armour-piercing shell or shot: artillerymen's: 1940–5. (P.G.-R.)—8. 'A horse lacking vitality': Australian coll.: C. 20. (B., *Australia Speaks*, 1953.) Probably not a transferred sense of S.E. *slug* but a back-formation ex S.E. *sluggish.*—9. A nugget of gold: Australian miners': C. 20. (K. S. Prichard, 1932—see *speck, v.*, 3.)

slug, v.—2. To smoke: South African children's: since ca. 1930.—3. To charge (someone) as a price: Australian: since ca. 1920. (B.P.) 'He slugged me a quid.'—4. To drink: Anglo-Irish: mid C. 19–20. (P. W. Joyce, 1910.) Ex sense 2 of the n. on p. 785.

Slug, the. R. P. Lewis, noted Oxford wicket-keeper: cricketers': late C. 19.

*****slug-up.** A 'frame-up' (fraudulent charge or victimisation) Australian c.: since ca. 1910. B., 1942.

slugged, get. Synonym of **slogged** . . .; cf. **slug, n.**, 4 (above).

sluggers. Sloe gin, 'always a popular Navy drink' (Granville): Naval officers': C. 20. Ex *sloe* by the process of 'the Oxford *-er*'.

sluicery (p. 785). A shade earlier in J. Burrowes, *Life in St George's Fields*, 1921, and in Pierce Egan's *Life in London*, 1821.

slum, n.—12. Cheap prizes esp. for children: Canadian carnival s.: C. 20. Cf. sense 10.

slum, v.—10. (Cf. senses 6–8 on p. 785.) Applied to those members of the Government who, disapproving a policy, sit among the back-benchers: Parliament: since ca. 1920.—11. The cheap jewellery, watches, etc., given as prizes: fairgrounds (carnivals): late C. 19–20. (Cf. senses 4 and 8.)

Slump Alley. Carey Street, where the Bankruptcy Court is situated: mostly Londoners': since ca. 1930.

slums, act in. To act in very small towns or in low plays: theatrical: ca. 1865–1910. B. & L.

slunch. Eton pudding: C. 20. Also *slunching*.

slung, get. To be tossed by a horse: Australian: C. 20. B., 1942. Short for the Australian coll. *get slung off* (mid-C. 19–20).

slurge. 'A very *ropey* recruit,' H. & P.: Services: since ca. 1935. A corruption, or a perverted blend, of *slack + splayed*, influenced by *sludge*.

slush, 2, is by tramps, applied only to tea.—4. 'To work and toil like a slave: a woman who toils hard' (P. W. Joyce, 1910): Anglo-Irish: late C. 19–20.

slush bucket and **slush fund.** Resp. s. and coll. for 'a secret fund raised by a political party from dubious sources' (B.P.): Australian: the latter, adopted ca. 1930 ex U.S.; the former, dating since ca. 1950.

slush-pump. A trombone: musicians' (esp. in theatres): C. 20. Ex saliva tending to gather in instrument: Cf. the entry at *fish-horn*.

slut about, v.i. To go about working: coll., esp. at Harrow School: C. 20. Lunn, 'They [the 'swots'] groise their horrid eyes off and get out of fagging in a term or two, while we poor devils [the 'hearties'] have to slut about "on boy" for three years'.

sly-bag (or one word). A cunning person: Australian: since ca. 1930. (B., *Australia Speaks*, 1953.) Suggested by *sly-boots* (p. 786).

sly-grog. A sly-grog shop: Australian: since ca. 1930. (B., 1953.) Cf.:

sly-groggery. A sly-grog shop: Australian coll.: since ca. 1920. B., 1942.

smack calfskin. To kiss the Bible: low: C. 19.

smack in the eye. A rebuff, refusal; severe disappointment; set back: coll., esp. in Australia: C. 20. B., 1942.

smack it about! Get a move on!: Naval: C. 20. Granville, 'From the vigorous smacking about of brushes when painting the ship's side.'

*****smack the lit.** See **lit, smack the.**

smack up, v. To attack— 'go for'—a person: Australian: since ca. 1919. Ex the n. (p. 786), which, since ca. 1918, has also been Australian.

smacker, 2 (p. 786) 'is used of large sums only; *two smackers* would not be used': B.P.—3. A dollar bill (note): Canadian: adopted, ca. 1925, ex U.S. (Leechman.)—4. A boy; a youth: Australian: since ca. 1930. Dal Stivens, *Jimmy Brockett*, 1951.

small beer of, think (p. 786). Cf. 'Thinking no pale ale of himself' in Francis Francis, *Newton Dogvane*, 1859.

small bull's-eyes. The odds and ends, the smouldering remains, of a fire: London Fire Brigade: C. 20. They glow like a bull's eyes. Or, rather, 'they are *targets* for the jet' (of water from the hose). Julian Franklyn, a Volunteer Fireman during World War II.

small fry (p. 786) is S.E. and therefore ineligible.

small go. 'A reasonable night out with everybody happy and nobody drunk,' H. & P.: Services: since ca. 1930.

small pigs (rare in the singular). Petty Officers: Naval (lower-deck): C. 20. As opposed to *Naval pigs*; cf. the Guards Regiments' *drill pig* (Granville).

small world! A c.p. of greeting to an acquaintance met unexpectedly: since ca. 1920. Ex the full *it's a small world*.

smalley. Small, little, *smalley porsh*, a small portion, esp. of food: Naval: since ca. 1940.

smalls. Underclothes, men's or women's: coll.: C. 20. Ex S.E. *smalls*, 'small clothes, breeches'. —2. Small advertisements, esp. those in classified lists: mainly journalistic coll.: since ca. 1910.

smarm (p. 787). The old spelling *smalm* suggests to Dr Leechman the—to me—probable solution: *smear* + *balm*.

smart Alec.—2. (Usually . . . *alec*.) A train conductor: Canadian railroadmen's (— 1931). Ex sense 1.

smart-arse. An obnoxiously—not a cleverly— smart person: Australian: since ca. 1910. Perhaps the origin of **smarty-pants** (below), which B.P. says he has never heard used by an adult male.

smarten up one's parade. To work more efficiently; to make oneself smart: Army and R.A.F. regulars': since ca. 1925. (Atkinson.)

smarty-pants. A smart person: perhaps orig. Australian: since ca. 1920. (Jon Cleary, *Just Let Me Be*, 1950; Nicholas Blake, *The Whisper . . .*, 1954.) Cf. **fancy pants** above.

smash, n.—6. A drink of brandy in iced water: Australian: ca. 1920–30. B., 1942.—7. A fearsome person: Australian: since ca. 1910. Jean Devanney, *Paradise Flow*, 1938—of a man violent in drink. Proleptic.—8. Money; wages: low Australian: since ca. 1920. Kylie Tennant, *The Joyful Command*, 1953, 'Giving her his smash on pay-night.'

smash, v.—8. To commit a smash-and-grab raid on (a ship, etc.): c.: since the late 1940's. Peter Crookston, *Villain*, 1967, 'When you're driving away from a jeweller's you've just smashed . . .'

smash a pass. To overstay one's leave: military: 1914–19. E. W. Mason, *Made Free in Prison*, 1918

smash-ankle. Deck hockey: Naval: C. 20.

*smash the tea-pot. To lose the privilege of tea: prison c.: from ca. 1880. B. & L.—2. To kill someone: mostly Canadian: C. 20. (Leechman.)

smashed. Tipsy: since ca. 1960. Jimmy Sangster, *Foreign Exchange*, 1968, 'Getting smashed on airline champagne.'

smashed(-)up. Penniless: low: ca. 1830–1900. Mayhew, I, 1851. Suggested by **broke** (p. 95).

smashing, adj., 1, had in the war of 1939–45, a phenomenal popularity in the R.A.F.; *smashing job* might be 'a very fine aircraft; a task excellently performed; a girl exceedingly easy on the eye' (Partridge, 1945). On Feb. 4, 1850, Harry (later

Sir) Burnett Lumsden said, 'When our cloth arrives we shall be the most smashing-looking regiment in India' (*Journal of the Society for Army Historical Research*, xxxi, Autumn 1953, article by Sir Patrick Cadell, 'The Beginnings of Khaki'). The adj. caught on among post-1945 civilians; after ca. 1957, it began to lose popularity, except among schoolchildren, teenagers, lower-middle class. This sense may have originated in boxing: cf. 'Bartlett and Peacock had a *smashing set to* for three hours! during which time no less than 72 rounds were fought' (*The Plymouth Telegraph* early 1822). Moe.

smashing, adv. Intensive—'very' or 'much' or 'extremely' or 'notably': C. 20. Gerald Kersh, *The Nine Lives of Bill Nelson*, 1942, 'He'd done . . . a smashing hot job' (extremely expert and artistic piece of tattooing). Ex **smashing**, adj., 3 (p. 787 and above).

smashing line. A beautiful girl: low: from ca. 1920. Cf. **smasher**, 1, in *Dict.*

smear, n.—3. See **tumour**.—4. A murdered person: Australian c.: since ca. 1925. (B., 1943.)

smear, v. To defeat heavily at fisticuffs: Australian low: since ca. 1925. B., 1942. Cf. *make a mess of*.

smear-gelt (p. 787). More prob. ex the long-established Yiddish *schmiergeld*. (L. W. Forster.)

smear it with butter and get the cat to lick it off! See **bum-fluff**.

smell, n. A boastful, conceited or otherwise objectionable boy; Sedgeley Park School (now Cotton College): ca. 1800–65. Provost Husenbeth, *History of Sedgeley Park*, 1856. Cf. the C. 20 use of *stinker*.

Smell Burn, or as one word. Melbourne: Australian rhyming pun, rather than rhyming s.: C. 20. (B., 1943.)

smell my finger! A low male c.p. with an erotic implication: late C. 19–20.

smell of bread and butter. To be tied to nursery ways: Public Schools' coll.: late C. 19–20. (H. A. Vachell, *The Hill*, 1905.)

smell of gunpowder, there's a. Someone has broken wind: Army: late C. 19–20.

smell of the barman's apron, he's had a. A c.p. applied to one who easily gets drunk: since ca. 1920. For *smell*, *sniff* is occ. substituted.

smeller.—An objectionable fellow: New Zealand: late C. 19–early C. 20. See quotation at *straight wire*: cf., semantically, the fig. *stinker*.

smelly, n. A film, or a play, in which scents or sprays are used to create a realistic effect: since ca. 1958.

smice. To depart; make off: Australian low: since ca. 1925. B., 1942. Yiddish? 'Yes; it means "to smack"' (Julian Franklyn).

smiddy. A blacksmith's section (technically, 'bay') in a marine-engineering works: such Scottish workmen's coll.: from ca. 1885. Lit., the Scottish form of *smithy*.

smig. A sergeant-major instructor in gunnery: Army: since ca. 1920. H. & P.

smigget(t). 'Lower-deck term for a good-looking messmate' (Granville): Naval: since ca. 1925. Origin?

smiggins (p. 788), in nuance 'cold meat hash', survives in C. 20. Australian. (B., 1943.)

smile - please run. A photo-reconnaissance flight' (Jackson): R.A.F.: 1939 + . Ex the photographer's stock phrase.

smiler.—2. Boiled beef: Cotton College: ca. 1860–1914. Ex a horse named Smiler. (Frank Roberts in *The Cottonian*, Autumn 1938.)

smite, n. An infatuation, a passion: Society: ca. 1932–40. Mrs Belloc Lowndes, *The House by the Sea*, 1937. Cf. **crush,** n., 4 (*Dict.*).

Smithy. 'The late Sir Charles Kingsford Smith' (B., 1942), the celebrated Australian aviator.

smitz. See 'Mock-Auction Slang' above. Since ca. 1930.

smoke, n.—5. A railroad fireman: railroadmen's (–1931). Ex the nature of his job.

smoke, v., 5. Rather: mid-C. 19–20.

*****smoke,** go into. See **go into smoke.**

smoke, up the. See 'Hauliers' Slang'. Cf. *smoke,* n., 2, on p. 788.

smoke!, watch my. See **watch my smoke!**

smoke and oakum, like. An early C. 19 Naval form of *like smoke,* q.v. at **smoke, like** on p. 789. (W. N. Glascock, *Sketch-Book,* I, 1825.) Moe.

smoke 'em. An illicit yet frequent method of getting from one station to another—by moving along slowly and watching for the smoke of an approaching, or an overtaking, train: Canadian railroadmen's (— 1931).

smoke-ho.—2. Hence, a cup of tea, orig. one drunk during a rest: Australian coll.: since ca. 1920. (Sarah Campion).—3. Cups of tea, collectively; a pot, a billy, of tea: Australian coll.: since ca. 1925. (Margaret Trist, 1946, 'I'll just trou the men's smoko over.')

smoke-jack. A steamship; esp. a steam warship: Naval: ca. 1830–90. Fredk Chamier, *The Life of a Sailor,* 1832, at II, 16. (Moe.) Cf. **smoke-stack** on p. 789.

smoke off. (Gen. in imperative.) To cease blushing: Scottish Public Schools': from ca. 1890. Ian Miller, *School Tie,* 1935. Prompted by *smoke-on,* q.v. at **smoke,** n., 4.

smoked haddock, the. The paddock: racecourse rhyming s.: C. 20. Franklyn 2nd.

smoker.—6. A black-headed cuckoo-shrike: Australian: C. 20. B., 1942.—7. See **smokes . . .** —8. A locomotive: Canadian railroadmen's (— 1931). Cf. **smoke,** n., 5.—'Driving home at night in his "smoker" (car that a trader is using for himself) or just whatever car is left over' (Anthony Cowdy in the coloured supplement of *The Sunday Times,* Oct. 24, 1965): secondhand-car dealers': since late 1940's. Ex a *smoker* or smoking carriage, or compartment, on a train.

smokers. Smoked salmon: since ca. 1925. By 'the Oxford *-er*'.

smoker's tickers. 'Shag tobacco; any coarse dark tobacco' (B., 1943): Australian: since ca. 1925.

smokes, she; she's a smoker. A c.p. directed at a female (harlot or not) that performs oral perversions: low: C. 20.

smokestick. A rifle: Australian soldiers': 1939 +. B., 1942.

Smokey. Nickname—whether in address or in reference—of a railway fireman: ? mostly Canadian: C. 20. Cf. **smoke,** n., 5. above.

smoking next, you'll or he'll be. See **you'll be smoking next.**

Smoky Joe. 'A Fleet Class minesweeper. This type being coal-burning' (Granville): Naval: 1939–45.

smooch, v.i. To caress amorously: Canadian: C. 20. Akin to *smoodge* (p. 789); cf. *smooze.*—2.

Hence (?), to flirt or (v.i.) to court: beatniks': since ca. 1959. Anderson, 'Come smooching with me, real-ly' (cf. **really** above).

smoocher. A gold-digger without a licence: Australian: ca. 1851–1900. Eric Gibb, *Stirring Incidents in Australasia,* 1895. Cf. *smoodger* (s.v. **smoodge** in *Dict.*).

smoodge (p. 789). 'Smoodge: to flatter or fawn. Still used in Anglo-Jewish slang and pronounced shmooze . . . from the Hebrew's shmoo-os, meaning news or hearsay. Later came to mean gossip, flattery,' A. Abrahams in *The Observer,* Sept. 25, 1938. It 'is now used only in jocular fashion. Even when we use it in sense 2, our mind is half on sense 1. If a man is said to be smoodging with a girl, he is more likely to be trying to make amends for forgetting her birthday than planning to make an attack on her virtue. "Stop smoodging!" is said to young couples holding hands, etc.' (B.P., mid-1963.)

smoodge up to. Variant of *smoodge,* 1 and 2, p. 789. (B., 1943.)

smooth as a baby's bottom; like a b.b. Smooth-shaved; (second only) expressionless: coll.: since ca. 1925.

smoothie (or **-y**). A ladies' man; (among non-dancers) a good dancer: R.A.F.: since ca. 1920. H. & P. Ex his smooth ways and manners.—2. A smooth-spoken person, esp. if male: since ca. 1925. (Nicholas Blake, *The Whisper in the Gloom,* 1954.)

smooze (vbl. n. *smoozing*) 1., is a New Zealand variant of *smoodge,* v., 2. (p. 789). Jean Devanney, *The Butcher Shop,* 1926.

smother, n.—3. (p. 789): also, by 1925, common in the underworld and its fringes.—4. Hence, a macintosh: c.: since 1920. F. D. Sharpe, 1938.

smother, v. Also Australian: B., 1942.

smother a parrot (p. 789). Probably direct from the synonymous Fr. *étrangler un perroquet.* (Leechman.)

smother (up). To secrete a part of (the accumulated stakes and winnings): Australian two-up players' and esp. operators': C. 20. Tom Ronan, *Vision Splendid,* 1954, 'Darcy [the cash-holder] was too shaky with laudanum. He couldn't smother up the money. We had to leave it all in sight and just let you spin for our win.' Cf. **smother,** v., on p. 789.

Smouchy. A Jew: Jewen: 1825, *The Universal Songster,* I, 172. Ex *smouch.*

Smouge. 'Nickname for all surnamed Smith' (Granville): Naval: C. 20. Cf. **Smudger** (*Dict.*).

smous or **smouse,** v.—2. Hence, to pet, to flirt: ' "There are two of them smousing in that room," ' cited as of 1938, by Prof. W. S. Mackie in *The Cape Argus,* July 4, 1946: S. African.

Smudge. Synonymous with *Smudger* (p. 790) and *Smouge.*

smudger. An inferior street photographer: photographers': C. 20. Cf. **smudge** (p. 789).—2. An engine cleaner: railwaymen's: C. 20. (*Railway.*)

[**smug-faced.** See 'Epithets'. Prob. always S.E.]

Smuggins. A variant of **Smudger** (p. 790): since ca. 1920. (Peter Sanders.)

Smuggling, n. Bringing harlots into College: Oxford: ca. 1815–60. *Spy,* 1825.

smugs! Bullies running away with all the marbles at the end of a game used to call *smugs!*:

Australian schoolchildren's: ca. 1900–1950. (B.P.)
Ex smuggings (p. 790)—or perhaps ex **smug,** v.,
1, ibid.

smut-hound. A man with a marked predilection for bawdiness: coll.: C. 20.

Smutty is the inevitable nickname of all men named *Black*: since ca. 1880. In, e.g., John Newton Chance, *Wheels in the Forest,* 1935.

snack.—3. A certainty; hence, a thief's or a swindler's dupe: Australian c.: C. 20. B., 1942.
—4. Hence, something easy to do; esp., 'it's a snack': Australian: since ca. 1920. (B.P.)

snack up. To have a (hurried) meal: Army: C. 20.

***snaffle-biter.** See 'Rogues'.

snafu or **Snafu.** See **S.N.A.F.U.**

snag, n.—2. A jagged tooth: Australian: since ca. 1910. (Ruth Park, *Poor Man's Orange,* 1950.)
—3. A sausage, usually in pl. *snags*: Australian: since ca. 1918. (B., 1942 (pl.); R. Park, 1950 (sing.).) They are mysteries of 'snags'.—4. An aircraft apprentice with one small chevron (*snag*): R.A.F., Halton: since ca. 1939.

snagger. A proletarian: Clifton College: since ca. 1910. 'The College ran [in 1915] a *Saint Agnes* mission for poor children' (J. Judfield Willis, letter).—2. A clumsy or inexperienced shearer; a cow-milker; a cow hard to milk: Australian rural: since ca. 1910. (B., 1943.)

***snaggling.** See **snaggle** (*Dict.*).

snags. False teeth: ? mostly Naval: ca. 1800–50. It occurs in W. N. Glascock, *Sailors and Saints* (I, 183), 1829. (Moe.)—2. Sausages: Aus.: since ca. 1910. (B., 1959.)

snail(-)pie. Rice pudding: Guards Depot, Caterham: 1914–18. *John o' London,* Nov. 3, 1939.

snake, n.—2. A lively party: R.A.F.: since ca. 1925. Jackson, 'Thus, "Out on the snake"—out on a party.' Perhaps cf. **snake-juice** (p. 791) and certainly cf. **snake-charmers.**—3. A switchman: Canadian railroadmen's (— 1931).

snake, v.—2. 'To wriggle about in the air by constant jinking when taking evasive action,' Jackson: R.A.F.: since ca. 1938; by 1944, j. Cf. the American *snake-* (or *snaky*) *hips.*—3. (Also *snake off*.) To go quietly; slip along quietly: Anglo-Irish: C. 20. Brendan Behan, *Borstal Boy,* 1958, uses both terms—as exact synonyms. To move silently, as a snake does.

snake, the. The hose: London Fire Brigade: C. 20.

snake, about. To take evasive action: R.A.F. aircrews' coll. (1939) >, by 1943, j. Ex **snake,** v., 2.

snake-charmers. A dance band: R.A.F.: since ca. 1930. Jackson. Ex snake-charming by music, and cf. **snake,** n., 2. There may be a reference to 'Snake Hips' Johnson, the dance-band leader.
—2. Plate-layers: Australian railwaymen's: C. 20. B., 1942.

Snake Gully (course). A country race-course: Australian sporting: since ca. 1925. (B., 1953.) Imaginary country-town.

snake-headed. Spitefully angry: vindictive: Australian: since ca. 1925. (B., 1943.)

snake-hips. 'Ironic for man with middle-age spread' (Atkinson): mostly R.A.F.: since ca. 1935. Cf. sense 1 of prec. entry.

snake in your pocket?, a—or got a ...? or, in full, **have you got a ...?** An Australian c.p.,

addressed to one who is slow to 'shout' his friends to a round of drinks: since ca. 1920. (B.P.) The implication being that the snake will bite him if he puts his hand in his pocket to get at his money.

snake-juice.—2. Hence, bad liquor: Australian: since ca. 1920. B., 1942.

snake-juicer. An addict to bad liquor: Australian: since early 1920's. Baker. Ex prec.

snake off. To slip quietly away: Australian coll.: since ca. 1910. (H. Drake Brockman, *The Fatal Years,* 1947.)

Snake Pit, the. The haunt mentioned at **Fishing Fleet:** Naval: C. 20. Granville.—2. Hence (probably), the Maymo Club lounge: Burma: ca. 1925–41.

snake yarn. A tall story: Australian juvenile: since ca. 1935. (B., 1953.)

snakes, bag of. A girl, esp. a very lively one: Canadian: since ca. 1955. (Leechman.)

snake's hiss. Urine; to urinate: Australian rhyming s.: C. 20. (Franklyn, *Rhyming.*)

Snakey. See **Drain Pipe.**

Snak(e)y. Bad-tempered: Australian: C. 20. Kylie Tennant, *The Battlers,* 1941. Apt to bite.—2. Jealous: Australian: since ca. 1939. (Cusack & James, *Come in Spinner,* 1951.)

snap, n.—6. Packed food; hence, *snap tin,* a container for a packed meal: railwaymen's: since ca. 1920. (*Railway.*)—7. 'An ampoule of amyl nitrate sewn into cotton-wool pads': drug addicts': since ca. 1950. Because 'broken with a sharp sound under the nose and inhaled'. (Robin Cook, *The Crust on Its Uppers,* 1962.)

snap-jack. A pancake: Australian: late C. 19–20. B., 1942.

snap out of it!—2. Wake up!; realise the truth!; 'be your age!': adopted ca. 1933 from U.S.

snapper.—3. 'A railway ticket inspector, so called because he "snaps" holes in tickets' (Culotta): Australian: since ca. 1930.

snappy undercut; or merely **undercut.** A smart sexually attractive girl: butchers' (C. 20) >, by 1935, fairly gen.

snaps. Handcuffs: policemen's: ca. 1870–1910. Jerome Caminada, *Twenty-Five Years of Detective Life,* 1895. Ex the sound they make on being closed about the arrested person's wrists.—2. (Or *Snaps.*) A Naval photographer: Naval: since ca. 1940. (Granville, Nov. 22, 1962.)

snare, v.—2. To cheat; hence, *snare sheet,* a slip of paper with notes for use in an examination: Marlborough College: C. 20.

snargasher. A training aircraft: Canadian airmen's: 1939 +. H. & P. A corruption—perhaps rather a deliberate distortion—of 'tarmacsmasher'.

snarl, v. To steal; acquire illicitly—or even lawfully: circus: since ca. 1920. Edward Seago, *Sons of Sawdust,* 1934. Perhaps ex American *snarl,* a tangle.

snarler. A bad discharge: Australian Services': since ca. 1919. 'Services *no longer required.*' (L. D. M. Roberts.)

snart. A cigarette: Army: since ca. 1925.

snatch. The pick-up, by a towing 'plane, of a glider: Air Force coll. (1943–4); by 1945, official. Gerald Hanley, *Monsoon Victory,* 1946.

snatch-box. The female pudend: low: C. 20. Elaboration of **snatch,** 2 (p. 791).

***snatch game, the.** Kidnapping: c.: from ca. 1920. John G. Brandon, *The 'Snatch' Game,* 1936.

snatch one's time. To resign from a job: Australian: since ca. 1920. (B., 1943; Gavin Casey, *Downhill Is Easier*, 1945.) Hence also *snatch it* (Alan Marshall, 1946).

snatched (car or cab). A car taken back from an owner-driver that has failed with his payments: taxi-drivers': since ca. 1925. Herbert Hodge, 938.

snatcher.—2. A young and inexperienced thief: c.: from ca. 1860. B. & L.—3. An assistant conductor: busmen's: since ca. 1945.

snatchers. Handcuffs: Glasgow policemen's: since ca. 1890. Ex-Inspector Elliot, *Tracking Glasgow Criminals*, 1904. Cf. synonymous c. **snitchers.**

snavel.—3. To catch; to take: Australian: mid-C. 19–20. Vance Palmer, *The Passage*, 1930, 'It's dead easy to make work. Dead easy, too, to snavel a few hours off if you use your head.' Ex sense 2 (p. 791).

snazzy. See 'Canadian . . .'

snazzy. Fashionable, smart: Australian: adopted, ca. 1943, ex U.S. servicemen. (Dymphna Cusack, *Say No to Death*, 1951, 'A couple of snazzy little cameras'; D'Arcy Niland, *The Shiralee*, 1955.) Also, by 1954, English s.—Perhaps a blend of *s*nappy + *ja*zzy.

snazzy chassis. A girl's good figure, esp. in *lassie with a snazzy chassis*: Australian: since ca. 1945. Cf. snazzy above; partly rhyming. (B.P.)

*sneak, go upon the (p. 792), should be back-dated to ca. 1710, for it occurs in James Dalton, *A Narrative*, 1728, at p. 31.

sneefoo. See S.N.E.F.U. above.

sneezer, 5, nuance 'gale' (p. 792), goes back to very early C. 19; it occurs in, e.g., W. N. Glascock, *Sketch-Book*, I, 1825. (Moe.)

SNEFU or **snefu.** See S.N.E.F.U. above.

Sneller. A student going to, and being at, the University of Oxford on a Snell exhibition: Oxford undergraduates' coll.: C. 9–20. See, e.g., Ernest Barker, *Age and Youth*, 1953.

*snelt. A sneak-thief; a term of abuse: New Zealand and Australian c.: C. 20. B., 1941, 1942. Yiddish?

snibbet. Sexual intercourse: low: C. 20. Probably ex Scottish and Northumberland dial. *snibbet* (or *-it*), a mechanical device involving an 'eye' and an insertion (E.D.D., *snibbit*, sense 1).

snibley, esp. *a bit of snibley*, as in "Ad a nice bit of snibley last night'. Sexual intercourse, mostly from the male angle: low: C. 20. A variant is **snibbet.**

snibs! A term of derision or defiance: late C. 19–20; by 1940, ob.

snick, n.—2. Esp. in *for a snick*, for a certainty: proletarian: late C. 19–20. J. J. Connington, *A Minor Operation*, 1937, 'Not a light showin' at any o' the windows—empty for a snick.' For the origin, cf. snip, n., 4, in *Dict*.

snicket, a bit of. A girl: since ca. 1945. (Richard Gordon, *Doctor at Sea*, 1953.) Ex Lancashire dial. *snicket*, a forward girl.

'The Lancashire dial. meaning, "a forward girl", contrasts with the W. Riding dial. meaning of *snicket*—a "passage-way" or "short cut between houses" (cf. W. Riding "ginnel"), apparently derived from *snick* v. (p. 792). Perhaps this Lancashire lass kept her assignments in Yorkshire back-alleys, unless the allusion is to a biological passage.' Cf. snippet below. (Ramsey Spencer.)

snide (p. 793), both the n., sense 2, and the adj. sense 1. 'The origin seems to be S. German "*aufschneiden*" (to boast, brag, show off, exaggerate, talk big), no doubt reaching English via Yiddish, as such words tend to do' (H. R. Spencer).

*snidey.—3. Bad; unfavourable: c., and low: from ca. 1870. Also *sniddy*.—4. Dirty: military: from ca. 1875. B. & L.

snidget. Excellent: Australian juvenile: since the 1930's. (B., 1953.) Cf. *snifter*, 2 (p. 793) and perhaps *sneezer*, 5 (p. 792).

snie (or **sny**), p. 793. Ex Canadian Fr. *chenal*, a canal-like watercourse. (Leechman.)

*sniff coke. To take drugs: c.: from ca. 1930. Ex U.S.

sniffer. The nose: pugilistic: ca. 1840–90. Augustus Mayhew, *Paved With Gold*, 1857.

sniftem. An inhalant: fair-grounds': C. 20. This *-em* is a characteristic (minor yet determinant) of fair-ground slang—cf. stickem below. Perhaps a variant or even a perversion of the mock-Latin *-um*; cf. the mock-Latin *-us* of *bonus* (p. 78) and *hocus-pocus* (p. 395).

snifty conner. Good food: Services (esp. R.A.F.): since ca. 1925. Jackson. See conner (p. 176).

sninny. A girl or young woman: Australian low: since ca. 1920. B., 1942. A perversion of synonymous Australian *skinny*.

snip, n.—7. A ticket collector: railwaymen's: C. 20. (*Railway*.)

snip, go. To go shares: coll.: mid-C. 19–20. B. & F.

snipe, n.—5. A trimmer (stoke-hold): Australian: since ca. 1910. (Dymphna Cusack, *Southern Steel*, 1953.)—6. A small poster glued—for political purposes—to a telegraph pole or a wall. Australian: since ca. 1945. (B.P.)

snipe, v., 2 (p. 793): also, since ca. 1920, low Australian s. (Tom Ronan, *Vision Splendid*, 1954.)

sniped, be; sniping. Terms in use among O.T.C. cadets in 1914–mid-1916, thus in Blaker: 'Men, so far, had gone off from Cartwright's Unit, gazetted to battalions by a process known among the Cadets as "sniping" . . . It was impossible to detect any system according to which groups or isolated individuals were "picked off" [as though by a sniper] and gazetted . . . [Cartwright's] name was not among the sniped".' The terms, Blaker makes clear, were also applied specifically to being ' "asked for" ' by some particular Colonel who was training a new battalion'.

sniper. 'A non-union wharf labourer' (B., 1943): Australian: since ca. 1930.

snipey or **snipy.** Crafty, esp. of a hiding-place: prison officers': C. 20. Jim Phelan, *Tramp at Anchor*, 1954.

snippet. The female pudend: Liverpool: late C. 19–20.—2. Hence, intercourse with a girl: Liverpool: C. 20.

snitch, n.—5. Synonymous with and perhaps ex **snitcher,** 5 (p. 794): New Zealand: C. 20. B., 1941. Perhaps suggested by 'to peach or snitch on someone' and 'a peach of a person or thing'.

*snitch, v.—4. To arrest (a person): c.: mid-C. 19–20; very ob. B. & L. Ex sense 2.

snitch, get a. To take a dislike, as in 'Got a snitch on me': Slatter: since ca. 1930. Perhaps cf. snitch, v., 2, on p. 794.

snitcher, adj. Excellent; attractive: Australian: since ca. 1930. B., 1942. Ex sense 5 of the n. (p. 794), which has also—*teste* Baker— > Australian.

snivel, do a. To tell a pitiful tale: tailors': from ca. 1865. B. & L.

snob, n., 2: earlier recorded in 'Taffrail'.—5. The last sheep to be shorn: Australian rural: C. 20. Prompted by **cobbler**, 2 (p. 164). B.P.

snob-stick. See snobstick (*Dict.*).

snobber (p. 794) is esp. a Naval nickname. H. & P.

snobbing, n. Boot-repairing: coll.: C. 19–20. See **snob**, n., 1, in *Dict.* Hence *snobbing firm*, group of ratings that repair their shipmates' boots and shoes: Naval: C. 20. Granville.

snodger, n. and adj. Excellent (person or thing), attractive (etc.): Australian: since ca. 1925. B., 1942. Arbitrary; yet cf. **snitcher** (above).

snog, n. A flirtation; a courting: esp. among beatniks: since ca. 1959. (Anderson.) Ex:

snog, v. To flirt, or to court, esp. in *be* or *come* or *go snogging*: beatniks', adopted, ca. 1959, ex general s. (Anderson.)

snogged up. Smartened up; 'all dressed up': R.A.F.: since ca. 1939. Cf. next.

snogging. The usual n. corresponding to the next.

snogging, be or **go.** To be—to go—courting a girl; to be, or go, love-making: R.A.F.: since ca. 1937. Partridge, 1945, '*Snog* is perhaps a blend of *snug* and *cod* (to flatter or "kid" a person).'

snogging session. A bout, an instance, of 'snogging': R.A.F.: since late 1930's. Ex preceding.

snook. To answer an examination paper throughout; to defeat (someone) in argument: Shrewsbury: late C. 19–20. Marples. Ex 'cock a snook'?

snooks. 'A term of endearment for a small child' (B.P.): Australian: since ca. 1925. (B.P.)

snooks—intensive, **dead snooks—on, be.** To be in love with: Australian: ca. 1900–40. (Miles Franklin, *Old Blastus of Bandicoot*, 1931.)

snooky. Critical; pernickety: Australian: since ca. 1910; by 1960, ob. Frank Clunes, *Try Anything Once*, 1933, 'There was a snooky guy up in the corner listening to all I had to say.'

snoop, v.—3. To be a Service policeman: R.A.F.: 1939 +. Partridge, 1945. Ex sense 1 (p. 794).

Snoops, the. Service (>, in late 1944, R.A.F.) Police: R.A.F.: since ca. 1939. E. P. in *The New Statesman*, Sept. 19, 1942. Short for *snooper*, ex snoop (*Dict.*)

snoot, n. A disagreeable, or a supercilious, person: Australian: since ca. 1930. B., 1942. Ex snooty (*Dict.*).

snootful, have a. To be tipsy: Canadian: adopted, ca. 1940, ex U.S.

snooze, n.—3. A three-months' sentence or imprisonment: Australian c.: C. 20. B., 1942. Cf **dream** and **rest** and the American *sleep*.

snooze, v. (pp. 794–5): but the word may simply be echoic—cf. **zizz.** Ramsey Spencer has suggested that the word is a blend of S.E. *snore* and *doze*—an attractive theory.

snoozer.—3. A baby: Australian: C. 20. Baker.—4. A Pullman sleeping-car: Canadian railroadmen's (– 1931).

*snoozey. See **snoozy** (*Dict.*).

snore. (A) sleep: low: since ca. 1920. James Curtis, *They drive by Night*, 1938, 'He had not had much snore the night before.' Extension of S.E. sense.

snore-bag. A sleeping-bag: Army officers': since ca. 1939. (P-G-R.)

snore-off. A short sleep: low Australian: C. 20. (Ruth Park, 1950.) Cf. preceding. Adopted, ca. 1925, by New Zealand. (Slatter.)

snore off, v. To have a short sleep: Aus.: C. 20. (Nino Culotta, *Cop This Lot*, 1960.)

snorer. The nose: pugilistic: ca. 1840–90. Augustus Mayhew, *Paved With Gold*, 1857.—2. Bed: Army: C. 20. Proleptic.

snoring, be. Thomas Skeats, barrow-boy (as in the *Daily Mail* of July 24, 1963), says, 'What you gotta watch is that your pears don't go "sleepy", as we say, in the 'eat. When it's very 'ot and they get real soft, we say they are "snoring" ': barrow boys': since ca. 1910. (*Sleepy* has long been S.E.)

snoring-kennel. See 'Miscellanea'.

snork.—4. A baby: New Zealand: C. 20. B., 1941. Perversion of baby-carrying *stork.*—5. Also *snorker*: a sausage: Australian: C. 20. B., 1941. Why? 'Uncooked sausages might convey a suggestion of babies' limbs (see sense 4)': Ramsey Spencer.

snorker. See **snork**, 5.

snort. A 'pull'—a drink—of spirits: Society: since late 1920's. In, e.g., P. G. Wodehouse, *Young Man in Spats*, 1936, 'He produced his flask and took a sharp snort.' Ex the snorting cough induced by a large 'pull' at a brandy, whisky, rum.

snorter, 2 (p. 795). In Australia, usually a very hot day. B., 1942.—3. Much earlier in *Boxiana*, II, 1818.

snorting-pole. A foot-brace at the end of a bed: Canadian lumbermen's: C. 20.

snot, n., 2 (p. 795). An early example: *Sessions*, Dec. 1816 (p. 43).

snot-condensing, n. Sleep: C. 20. Ex heavy breathing.

snot-rag (p. 795) occurs in, e.g., James Joyce's *Ulysses*, 1922.

snotties' nurse, the. 'The Sub-Lieutenant in charge of the Gunroom' (Granville): Naval: late C. 19–20. See **snotty**, n., on p. 795. 'The snotties' nurse was responsible for the midshipmen's instruction and training, vetting their journals, arranging courses . . . and generally doing everything possible to see that they got a fair run at the Seamanship Exam for the rank of lieutenant . . . He was usually a lieutenant-commander, certainly not more junior than a senior lieutenant' (Rear-Admiral P. W. Brock, R.N., C.B., D.S.O., in letter of April 20, 1963).

snotty, n. (p. 795), occurs in 1899: *The Navy and Army Illustrated*, Dec. 23. (Moe.)

snotty, 2. Earlier in *Sessions*, May 1847.

snotty. See 'Epithets'.

snout, n.—6. See **snout on.**—7. A cigarette: low London: C. 20. (Norman.) Since early 1950's, much used by Teddy boys.

snout, v.—3. To be an informer; to lay information: c.: since ca. 1925; by 1940 at latest, also police s. Ex **snout**, n., 4. Douglas Warner, *Death of a Snout*, 1961, 'Thereafter Ruskin snouted, and snouted good.'

*snout baron. In prison, a trafficker in tobacco:

since ca. 1930. (Robin Cook, 1962.) Cf. **baron**, 2, above, and **snout**, n., 2, on p. 795.

snout on, have a. To bear a grudge against (someone): Australian: since ca. 1920. B., 1942. Ex **snout**, v., 1 (p. 795).

snouty. Variant of **snout**, n., 2 (*Dict.*). F. D. Sharpe, 1938.

snow.—4. A white-coloured hair-cream: Australian, esp. undergraduates': ca. 1910–30. A song in *The Student Corps*, 1918, enshrines the heart-rending words, 'Gone are our blazers and creamy pants, Gone brilliantine and "snow".' Communicated by B.P., who confesses 'Unknown to me'.

snow again! or, in full, **snow again, I didn't get your drift.** Please repeat that, I didn't catch what you said (or meant): Canadian c.p.: since ca. 1930; by 1959, ob. Leechman.

snow-drop, v. To steal: low Australian: late C. 19–20. (Ruth Park, 1950.) Cf. *snow-dropper*, *-dropping*, on pp. 795–6.

snowball, v., usu. in passive. To return (a car) to its original owner: secondhand-car dealers': since ca. 1950. Ex the throwing of snowballs?

snowball hitch. A knot that easily loosens: Naval: C. 20. Granville. It comes *adrift*.

*****snowbirds.** Women that bring clients to dope-pedlars: c.: since ca. 1938. Ex *snow*, cocaine.

snowdrop. An American military policeman: 1942 +. *Daily Express*, June 12, 1944. Ex his white helmet and pipe-clayed equipment.

snowed in. 'The condition of the table or board when the shearers are working too fast for the shed hands to keep up' (*Straight Furrow*, Feb. 21, 1968): N.Z.: since ca. 1920. Ex the piles of fleeces.

snowed under; snowed up. Over-burdened with work; having a heavy back-log of work to attend to: coll.: since ca. 1930.

snozzler (p. 796). Also Australian. B., 1942.

snuff and butter (maiden). A Eurasian girl: Anglo-Indian: since early 1920's.

snuff-box.—2. A gas-mask: mostly civilians': 1939 +. *The New Statesman*, Aug. 30, 1941.—3. A newspaper's list of deaths; its obituaries: Australian journalists': since ca. 1920. Baker. A list of those who have 'snuffed out'.

snuffe and toddle. See **die, to.**

snuffle. The nose: low: ca. 1825–70. *Sinks*, 1848.

snuffler. See 'Dupes'.—**snuffling community.** See 'Harlots' and cf. *snuffler* at 'Dupes'.

snug as a duck in a ditch, as. Very snugly indeed: coll.: late C. 18–19. (W. N. Glascock, *The Naval Sketch-Book*, I (p. 117), 1825.) Moe.

snuggy. A public-house *snuggery*: public-houses': since ca. 1890; by 1940, ob. *Sessions*, Jan. 18, 1900.—2. A woman's muff: since ca. 1940. (Laurence Meynell, *The Lady on Platform One*, 1950.) It keeps one's hands snug and warm.

snurge, n. A Poor Law Institution: since ca. 1920. *Answers*, Sept. 21, 1940. Cf. the v.: p. 796.

so-and-so. Objectionable person, as in 'that old so-and-so': coll.: C. 20; but general and frequent only since ca. 1945. Euphemistic for *bastard* or *bugger* or *bitch*, as the context determines.

so busy I've had to put a man on! See **getting any?** above.

so crooked he couldn't lie straight in bed. A

c.p. used of a very unscrupulous man: Australian: since ca. 1925. (B.P.)

so fools say! A c.p. retort, esp. Cockneys', to a person asserting that one is a fool; occ. elaborated with, *You ought to know—you work where they're made*: from ca. 1890; ob. Edwin Pugh, *passim*.

so help me Bob, etc. See **s'elp** . . . (*Dict.*).

so long! (p. 796) is perhaps short for 'Good-bye. So long', elliptical for 'God be with you so long as we are apart'. Or perhaps ex Hebrew *shalom*, peace, used by Jews as a term of farewell: the most likely theory of all.

so lucky that if he fell in(to) the river, he'd only get dusty, he's. A c.p., implying exceptional luck: C. 20.

so mean (s)he wouldn't give anyone a fright. See **mean** . . .

so thin you can smell the shit through him. A low, mostly Cockneys' c.p., applied to an extremely thin man: from ca. 1880.

so well?; so what? That does not impress me!; Cockney c.p. (destined to > gen.): adopted, the latter, ex U.S., in 1936; the former arose also in 1936, prob. as a deliberate variation.

soak, n. A depression that, after rain, holds water—strictly underground (a foot or two down); loosely, on the surface: Australian coll. (since ca. 1860) >, 1940, S.E. Archer Russell, *A Tramp Royal in Wild Australia*, 1934, uses it, as would be expected, in its correct nuance: for it is water that has soaked into the soil. Occurring earlier in K. S. Prichard, *Coonardoo*, 1929.—2. A heavy fall of rain: Australian coll.: C. 20. B., 1942.—3. A drunkard: Australian and English: since ca. 1910.

soak, v.—8. (Also *soak it*.) Of the male: to linger over the sexual act; to delay withdrawal: low coll.: C. 19–20.

soak, put in. To pawn: late C. 19–20. Cf. **soak,** v., 3 (p. 797).

soakage. Synonymous with—and ex—**soak**, n., 1, above: Aus. coll.: late C. 19–20. (B., 1959.)

soaks. 'Folks' in the convivial sense: C. 20. Rhyming s., with pun on S.E. *soak*, a tippler.

soap, n.—5. A simpleton; a dupe: Australian c.: since ca. 1925. (B., 1953.) As soft as soap.

soap and flannel. Bread and cheese: Naval (lower-deck): C. 20. Granville.

soap and lather. Father: rhyming s.: late C. 19–20.

soap opera. 'Daytime radio serials for women. As in operas, the plot is less important than characters who attract emotional involvement. Often sponsored by soap manufacturers' (B.P.): coll.: Australian since middle 1950's, English since late 1950's. Adopted ex U.S.

soapy.—3. Silly, stupid; effeminate: Australian: since ca. 1920. B., 1942.

sob sister. A writer of articles for the more emotional, sensation-mongering newspapers, esp. a woman journalist replying to women readers' inquiries: journalistic, adopted ca. 1930 from U.S. Cf. **sob stuff** (p. 797).

sob story. A hard-luck story: C. 20: coll. >, by 1940, S.E.

sobbing sisters. German six-barrelled mortars: military: 1940–5. 'The bombs came over in broken volleys of six with a peculiar slow, sobbing wail' (V. Peniakoff, *Private Army*, 1950).

sober-water (p. 797) occurs earlier in C. Bede, *Verdant Green*, 1953–7.

soccage. See 'Tavern terms', § 9.

social tit. A 'poodle-faker': Naval: since ca. 1925. (P-G-R.)

sock, n., 4 (p. 797). Note that at Sedgeley Park (the original form of Cotton College), *socks* was, ca. 1805–45, any kind of confectionery and *sock*, derivatively, anything pleasant or agreeable. *The Cottonian*, Autumn 1938. In his *History of Sedgeley Park*, 1856, Provost Husenbeth derived it from *sucks*, long sticks of toffee.

sock, v.—9. To save up, put aside, deposit in the bank: Australian: since ca. 1930. Cusack & James, *Come in Spinner*, 1951, 'I bet he's socked a pretty packet away.' Ex a sock used as bank.— 10. To 'tip' (a schoolboy) with money: Public Schools': late C. 19–20. (Peter Sanders.) Ex sense 5 (p. 797)?

sock it to me (, baby)! A 'teenybopper' (q.v.) cult expression of vague meaning: 'liven things up!' Propagated to the point of absurdity by radio disc-jockeys: since 1967.

socks on!, leave the. Don't shear the 'socks' or wool between the sheep's knees and feet: N.Z. shearers': C. 20. *Straight Furrow*, 21 Feb. 1968.

sod, 2 (p. 798) must, like 1, be dated further back, for 2 appears in 'As he passed me he said the other was a bloody sod,' *Sessions*, June 1818 (p. 283). —5. *To go on a sod* or *to sod* is, at Cranbrook School in C. 20 (or prefects *et al.*), to try to catch someone doing wrong. At some schools the phrase is *go on a shift.*—6. Non-pejorative for 'chap, fellow' or even for 'girl, woman': English and Australian: late C. 19–20. 'Good on yer, Martha, yer old sod!': Elizabethan O'Connor, *Steak for Breakfast*, Sydney, 1962. (B.P.)

sod about. To play the fool, indulge in horse-play; to potter about, to waste time: low: late C. 19–20. Cf. *Dict.* entries at **arse about** and **bugger about.**

sod all. Nothing: mostly Naval: since ca. 1920. A variant of *bugger all.*

sod-buster. An agricultural (not a pastoral) farmer: Canadian (and U.S.): C. 20.

sod it! Low coll. expletive: since ca. 1880. Cf. **bugger it!**

sod off! Go away: low: C. 20. An exact semantic equivalent of *bugger off!*

soda. Something easy to do; someone easy to do': Australian low: since ca. 1925. Vance Palmer, *The Passage*, 1930, ' "Just one more guess, Lew ..." Lew chuckled. "Umph, that's a soda. Must be the old doctor." '

sodding, adj. A vague pejorative, as in ' "I've been in your sodding country" ' (Bernard Hesling, *The Dinkumization and Depommification*, 1963): late C. 19–20. Cf. *sod it!* above.

sodduk (p. 798): often spelt *soddick* (in, e.g., Granville).

sods' opera, the. 'An unofficial and extremely low concert, usually held in barracks' (Granville): Naval: C. 20. Hence, since ca. 1925, R.A.F. regulars' for 'the din of jollification; a drunken party' (Atkinson).

soft-arse. An arm-chair: Scottish Public Schools': late C. 19–20. Ian Miller, *School Tie*, 1935. Cf. the *Dict.* entry at **soft?, hard** . . .

soft as shit. Not physically nor morally tough; often applied by workmen to a man that can speak without filth and does occasionally think of something other than gambling, drinking, womanising: low coll.: late C. 19–20.

soft as shit and twice as nasty, as. A rural c.p. (the South of England) applied by country people to pasty-faced, loose-moralled visitors or residents from the city: late C. 19–20. (Heard by me in Kent, June 1932.) Cf. **common as cat-shit . . .** above.

soft bar. See **bar,** n., 3.

soft(-)belly. A wooden-frame car: Canadian railroadmen's (– 1931).

soft collar. A soft job; a very suitable locality; something easily obtained; something comfortable or agreeable: Australian coll.: ca. 1860–1920. 'Tom Collins', *Such Is Life*, 1903, ' "Soft collar we got here—ain't it?" ' Ex driving horses in buggy or bullocks in waggon.

soft ha'porth. A 'softy'; a person easily imposed upon or duped: mostly working-classes': C. 20.

Soft-nosed. Stupid: Naval: C. 20.

soft number (p. 798). Also, since ca. 1916, Naval. Robert Harling, *The Steep Atlantick Stream*, 1946.

soft roll. A girl easily persuaded to coït: since late 1940's. Easy to 'roll in the hay': *roll*, an act of coïtion from the male point of view, comes ex U.S.

soft-skinned vehicle. An unarmoured vehicle: Army coll. (1940) >, by 1944, j. As an apple is to a coconut, so . . .

soft-sop over is a variant (ca. 1875–1910) of **soft-soap,** v., in *Dict.*

soft sowder is a variant (e.g. in Carlyle) of **soft sawder** (*Dict.*).

soft spot for (someone), **have a.** To be either sentimentally or affectionately attached to: coll.: since ca. 1880. Cf. **soft on** (p. 798).

soft stuff. Unarmoured vehicles: Army s. (1940) >, by 1941, coll. (P-G-R.) Cf.—perhaps ex *soft-skinned vehicle.*

soft tack (see **soft tommy** on p. 799) occurs earlier in *The Night Watch* (II, 57), 1828. Moe.

soft tommy (p. 799) goes back to late C. 18, for it occurs in the English 'Bob Rousem's Epistle to Bonypart' quoted, Aug. 4, 1804, in an American magazine, *The Port Folio* (IV, No. 31, p. 246, col. 2), 'If you can't take care what you are about, you'll soon be afloat . . . in a high sea, upon a grating, my boy, without a bit of soft tommy to put into your lantern jaws.' The phrase *be afloat (up)on a grating* = to be in a dangerous situation. It occurs still earlier in George Brewer, *Bannian Day*, 1796, at I, i, p. 2. (Moe.)

softers. Figurative soft soap: Naval (mostly lower-deck): since ca. 1930. Ex '*soft* soap' by the Oxford *-er*'. (P-G-R.)

softie, softy (p. 799). By 1940 S.E.

soger, 2 (p. 799): earlier in W. N. Glascock, *Sailors and Saints* (I, 149), 1829. Moe.

soggy type. A dull-witted and slow-moving person: R.A.F.: since ca. 1937. Jackson. See **wet,** adj., 7 (p. 945), which prob. suggested it.— 2. One who drinks excessively: R.A.F.: since ca. 1938. Robert Hinde, letter of March 17, 1945.

soil. To tour in the country: theatrical: ca. 1750–1800. (*Theatrical Biography*, vol. I, 1772.)

soixante-neuf, adopted from French, is a term diagrammatically descriptive (69) of a reciprocal sexual act: late C. 19–20: orig., upper and middle classes', but by 1914 or 1915 fairly common in the Forces, esp. the Navy, as *swaffonder* or *swassonder*

(or *-ander*); by 1920, *soixante-neuf* was coll.—
and by 1960, virtually S.E.

soldier, n., 5 (see *Dict.*). An earlier record is
afforded by 'Taffrail'. But, as '(senior) Marine
officer', it goes back to very early C. 19, to judge
by W. N. Glascock, *The Naval Sketch-Book*, 2nd
Series, 1834, at II, 32 and 33. (Moe.)

soldier bold. A cold: rhyming s.: from ca.
1860; by 1940, †.

soldier's best friend. His rifle: late C. 19–20.
Often, by the soldier, used ironically.

soldier's joy.—2. Pease pudding: nautical: C.
19. Colonel Moe has found it at year 1818:
Alfred Burton, *Johnny Newcome*.

soldier's threepenn'orth, a. Short leave: military: C. 20. I.e. a shave, a shit and a shine.
Cf. the Naval *a shave, a shilling, and a shove ashore*.

soldiers' wind (p. 800) is recorded in Alfred
Burton, *Johnny Newcome*, 1818. (Moe.)

solemn; esp. in *give one's solemn*, 'to swear on
oath', 'give one's word': ca. 1890–1915. W. L.
George. *The Making of an Englishman*, 1914.
Short for *solemn word* (or *oath*).

solid, n. A road: tramps' and Romanies' s.:
C. 20. (Robert M. Dawson.)

solid.—4. Stupid: Naval: since ca. 1925.
Granville. Solid ivory above the ears.—5. Extortionate; unreasonable: Australian: since ca.
1918. B., 1942. Ex sense 2.—6. See 'Jazz Slang'
above.

solid dig. Copy that is to be set very close:
printers': mid-C. 19–20. B. & L.

sollicker, n. and adj. (Some thing or person)
very big or remarkable: Australian: since ca.
1920. B., 1942. Perhaps **sockdologer** (*Dict.*)
conflated.

Solly, like the more usual **Ikey**, means 'a Jew':
coll.: since ca. 1870. A very common Jewish
surname and given name.

solomon.—2. A hatter; one who cleans or
repairs toppers: Eton: C. 20. Ex a proper name.

solomon.—3. A job: navvies': ca. 1860–1910.
(D. W. Barrett, *Navvies*, 1880.) Julian Franklyn
proposes an ellipsis of 'Solomon and Job'.

Solomon, do a. To pretend to be very wise:
C. 20. Joan Lowell, *Child of the Deep*, 1929.

Solomon Isaac. A Jew: Canadian: ca. 1870–
1914.

some, and then. J. W. Mackail, in his *Æneid*,
1930, finds a parallel in viii, 487, *tormenti genus*.

some people (occ. **parents**) **rear** (occ. **raise**)
awkward children. A c.p., dating since ca. 1880
(? earlier) and directed at someone who has been
(very) clumsy. By 1960, on the verge of becoming a proverb.

some say good old (e.g., Smith)—**some, or I, say
blast**—or, vulgarly, **fuck**—**old** (Smith). A c.p.
dating from ca. 1919. Ex **some say . . .** on p.
801.

somebody's dropped his false teeth! A c.p.
apropos of a sudden noise, esp. a crash: since ca.
1925. In 1939–45, a Forces' c.p. in respect of a
bomb or a shell exploding in the distance.

some'ink. Something: sol., esp. Cockneys':
C. 19–20. (Edwin Pugh, 1895.) Cf. **sutthink**
(below). The predominant post-1920 Cockney
pronunciation of *something* is *sun'ink*. (Julian
Franklyn, author of *The Cockney*, 1953—a book
unfortunately out of print.)

something above the ears, have. To be intelligent: since ca. 1925.

something else. 'So cool [i.e. excellent; abreast
of contemporary music] it defies description' (*The
Victoria Daily Colonist*, April 16, 1959, 'Basic
Beatnik'): Canadian jazz-lovers': since ca. 1956.

something in socks. A bachelor, or what a girl
wants: jocular: since ca. 1910.

something nasty in the woodshed, to have seen,
esp. in the c.p. *He* (or *she*) *has seen something . . .*,
applied to 'a crazy, mixed-up kid': British and
Australian: since the late 1940's. Ironic of the
modern psychiatric tendency to explain evil by
adducing some such 'traumatic experience' as
having seen one's mother with a lover in the
woodshed. (B.P.)

'This c.p. was originated by Stella Gibbons in
her immortal *Cold Comfort Farm*, 1932, the satire
that put an end to a vogue for novels of rural
passions and dominant grandmothers' (Ramsey
Spencer, March 1959).

something-something!, what the. A euphemism
for *what the bloody* (or *the* effing) *hell!*: coll.: C. 20.

sometimes I wonder! A c.p., meaning—and
deriving ex—'Sometimes I wonder whether you
are right in the head *or* entirely sane *or* . . .': an
animadversion prompted by an inane remark the
unfortunate person has just made: C. 20. (B.P.)

son of a bitch.—2. 'A moustache and imperial
whiskers favoured by cattle-buyers and wool
inspectors in the 1890's,' B., 1942: Australian:
† by 1914.

song and dance; occ., as in H. A. Vachell,
Quinney's, 1914, *little* . . . Anyone's 'performance' in the course of doing his job: C. 20. A
salesman, e.g., reels off his patter.—2. A homosexual: rhyming s. (on *Nance*): since ca. 1910; by
1940, ob. and by 1960, †. (Franklyn, *Rhyming*.)
—3. A fuss; a commotion: coll.: late C. 19–20.

song of the thrush. A brush (lit. and fig.):
rhyming s.: C. 20. Franklyn, *Rhyming*. It
occurs in D. W. Barrett, *Among the Navvies*,
1880, and therefore prob. goes back to ca. 1860.
(Franklyn 2nd.)

sonk. A variant of **sonkey** (*Dict.*).

sonkey or **sonky,** adj. Silly, stupid; idiotic:
Australian low: C. 20. H. Drake Brockman,
1938, 'Mrs Abbott and her sonky ideas!' Baker.
Ex the n.: p. 801.

sonno. Son', fellow, lad; mostly in addressing
men: Australian: since ca. 1910. Baker. Cf.
boyo.

Soo. Staff Officer Operations: Naval: since
ca. 1914. In, e.g., 'Sea Lion', *The Phantom Fleet*,
1946. Ex the official abbreviation *S.O.O.*

soogan. A cowboy's bed-roll: adopted, ca.
1920, ex S.W. U.S. Apparently of Irish origin.

soogan. Add:—2. Hence, any bed-roll, but esp.
a transient worker's: Canadian: since ca. 1930.
As Dr Leechman has suggested, *soogan*, a blanket
roll, may have originated in the *soogun*, or hay
rope. once used to tie the roll.

soogey. To scrub, to scour: Naval: late C.
19–20. Granville, who adduces the derivative
soogey-moogey, 'a mixture of soap, soda and sundry
ingredients used for washing paintwork or scrubbing decks', says 'Derivation obscure.' But
perhaps cf. Scottish *sooch* (pron.—approximately
—*sooghk*, rather than *sook*), 'the sound of anything falling heavily into water or into soft mud';
an echoic word, the *moogey* being reduplicated,
though with a reminiscence of *mushy* in its literal
sense. More prob., however, *soogey* represents a

corruption of *squeegee*: and *moogey* simply rhyme-reduplicates it.

soogey the bulkhead. To go on a drinking bout: Naval: C. 20. Ex prec. entry.

soogun. A hay rope: Shelta: C. 18–20. B. & L.

soojey. Variant of *soogey*.

sook; sook(e)y. A coward; a timorous person; Australian: since ca. 1920. B., 1942. Cf. **sukey,** 4, on p. 846.—2. A calf: Australian: C. 20. (B., 1943.) Ex *suck*?

sookey, adj. Sentimental: Australian: since ca. 1925. (Dymphna Cusack, *Southern Steel*, 1953.)

sool.—3. To run: Australian juvenile: since ca. 1930. (B., 1953.) Ex sense 1 (p. 801).—4. *Sool after*, to pursue (a person, esp. of the opposite sex): Australian: since ca. 1935. (Gavin Casey, *It's Harder for Girls*, 1942.)—5. To wheedle; to bamboozle: Australian: C. 20. (Sarah Campion, *Bonanza*, 1942.) Hence, *soolin' sod*, a hypocrite (male): Australian: C. 20. Campion, 1942.

sooler. A war-monger: Capricornia, Australia: 1914–18. Xavier Herbert, *Capricornia*, 1939. Ex **sool,** 1, on p. 801.

sooner. Sense 1 (p. 801) is recorded as early as 1899. (Moe.) It is also Australian: B., 1942.—2. (Ex 1.) 'A jibbing horse (one that would sooner go backward than forward),' Niall Alexander, letter of Oct. 22, 1939: New Zealand: since ca. 1920. In Australia, not only such a horse but also a useless dog (Baker).—3. A swindler, a trickster: Australian: since ca. 1920. (Vance Palmer, *Separate Lives*, 1931.)

sooner (dog). A dog that would rather defecate indoors than outdoors: Canadian: since ca. 1908. (Leechman.)

sootie or **-y.** A dealer in soot: coll.: C. 19–20. *Boxiana*, II, 1818.

Sop. A Sopwith 'plane: R.F.C.–R.A.F.: 1916–18.

soppy, 1 (p. 801), arose a few years before 1919, to judge by H. G. Wells, *Joan and Peter*, 1918, 'What Joan knew surely to be lovely, Highmorton denounced as "soppy". "Soppy" was a terrible word in boys' schools and girls' schools alike, a flail for all romance.' (Dr Niels Haislund.)

sore, adj. Angry; disgruntled: coll.: 1830, Fredk Marryat, *The King's Own* (p. 143 of the 1896 edition)—prob. dating from rather earlier. (Moe.) Cf.:—

sore as a boil, as. Angry, resentful ('sore'): Australian: C. 20. (Kylie Tennant, *The Honey Flow*, 1956.)

sore as a snouted sheila. As resentful as a girl who has been 'stood up': Aus.: since ca. 1940. (B., 1959.)

sorry and sad. Bad: rhyming: C. 20.

sorry you spoke, aren't you? A c.p. dating from ca. 1905; ob. W. L. George, *The Making of an Englishman*, 1914.

sort. A companion of the opposite sex; thus, 'All the girls and their sorts are going to the pictures' (Baker): Australian: since ca. 1925. Sorts, good or bad, of people.—2. In England, a girl: low: since ca. 1945. (Norman.) Probable ex Australia, where this sense existed since ca. 1910: cf. Frank Chine, *Try Anything Once*, 1933, 'I've a great little sort to meet' (in 1911 or 1912).

sort, v. To shoot up; to attack fiercely: Army:

1940–5. 'We went to Div. H.Q., which had been well and truly sorted' (John D'Arcy Dawson, *European Victory*, 1946). Cf. *sort out*, 2 and 3.

sort of thing. A tag c.p. of late C. 19–20. Ernest Raymond *We, The Accused*, 1935, 'What he doesn't know about the law isn't worth knowing, sort of thing' and 'You've everything you want in here, sort of thing?'

sort out; also, **take on.** To tease; leg-pull (v.t.): Cockneys': C. 20. E.g. 'I took him on' or 'sorted him out'; 'Why are you taking *me* on, I'd like to know!'—2. To fight: low: C. 20.—3. To pick a quarrel with and use force upon someone: Services: since ca. 1934. H. & P. Cf. **sort-out,** n., on p. 802.—4. To choose (someone) for a job, esp. if it be unpleasant or arduous: Services (esp. R.A.F.): since ca. 1938. H. & P., 'Who sorted me out for this one?' Ex, e.g., wool-sorting.—5. In Australia, to reprove or reprimand (someone): since ca. 1930. B., 1942.

Sosh (long *o*). Socialism: political writers', mostly: since ca. 1918.

soul-driver (p. 802), still current in 1848 (*Sinks*), as a Methodist parson.

soul-hunter was, ca. 1900–14, a Cambridge undergraduates' term for 'a man intent on saving the souls of others' (Marples, 2).

soul-searcher. A drink: 1909, Phillip Gibbs, *The Street of Adventure*; † by 1920.

Soul-Trap, the. Whitefield's original chapel, built 1776, in Tottenham Court Road, London: ca. 1776–1914.

sound. Sound asleep: domestic coll.: C. 20.

sound card. See 'Tavern terms', § 2; cf. **sound egg** (*Dict.*).

sound (one's) **flute.** To blow one's whistle: police: since ca. 1925. *The Free-Lance Writer*, April 1948.

sound off. To become (very) angry about a particular topic or on a particular occasion: adopted, ca. 1955, ex U.S.

sound-spotting, n. Ascertaining position of enemy guns from the sound of firing: artillerymen's coll.: 1940–5. (P-G-R.)

soundings, in. Near the bottom of one's heap of sheets (in machining): printers': mid-C. 19–20. B. & L. Ex nautical j.

soup.—10. Bad weather: R.A.F.: since ca. 1915. Jackson. Ex soup, 4 (*Dict.*).—11. Short for **soup plate** below.—12. 'The broken part of a wave' (*Pix*, Sept. 28, 1963): Australian surfers'.

soup, in the (p. 803). Perhaps, after all, originally English, for Major C. E. Hare, in *The Language of Field Sports*, 1949, attributes it to that huntingfield mishap or a rider getting thown from his horse into a ditch of dirty water.

Soup and Gravy, the. The Navy: rhyming: C. 20.

soup plate. A taxicabman's badge: taxidrivers': since ca. 1910. Herbert Hodge, *Cab Sir?*, 1939.

soup-plate track. A small race-course: Australian: since ca. 1920. B., 1942.

souped, be. To get into trouble: Anglo-Irish: late C. 19–20. James Joyce, *Ulysses*, 1922, 'Luck I had the presence of mind to dive into Manning's or I was souped'. Ex **soup, in the,** on p. 803.

souped(-)up. (Of a car) supercharged: Canadian motorists': 1945+. Adopted, ca. 1957, by

Britain. Courtenay Edwards in *The Sunday Telegraph*, Sept. 24, 1961.

*sour-planter, however, is properly a *passer* of counterfeit coin. Likewise, **plant the sour** is to pass it.

sour(-)puss. A morose person: adopted in 1942 from U.S. *John Bull*, Aug. 14, 1943. Ex Am. *sour puss*, a sour face.

sourdough. An experienced old-timer in the northwest: Canadian: late C. 19–20. It arose during the Yukon gold-rush and refers to the sour dough carried for use in emergency. Robert Service's *Songs of a Sourdough*, 1907, popularised the term; by 1910, it was coll.

'The sourdough was, rather than for use in an emergency, used as a yeast in making bread. At each baking, a portion of the dough was retained and allowed to go sour or ferment. It was essential that the sour dough be kept warm and so the old timers took it to bed with them in cold weather.' (Dr Douglas Leechman.)

sous (p. 803). The phrase *not worth a sous* occurs in Charles Dibdin's 'Nautical Philosophy', pub.—app. in 1793—in *The Britannic Magazine*, I, 442. Moe.

souse, n.—2. A drunkard: Australian: since ca. 1925. B., 1942. Cf. the n. and v. on p. 803.

south, v. To put (something) into one's—esp. trouser—pocket: Aus.: since ca. 1920. Ex **south, dip,** on p. 803, an expression also Aus. (B., 1959.)

South, the. The South London Music Hall: London coll.: late C. 19–20. Cockneys pronounce it *Saarf.*

South Ken, the. The Victoria and Albert Museum, London: coll.: from ca. 1905. (Margery Allingham, *Sweet Danger*, 1932.) Situated in South Kensington.

South of France. A dance: rhyming s.: late C. 19–20.

Southend. See **bed and breakfast.**

southerly buster.—2. Hence, a cocktail or other mixed alcoholic drink: Australian: C. 20. B., 1942.

south-paw (p. 803). An American correspondent of Mr John Moore's has sent him this convincing explanation—'On regulation baseball fields, the batter faces East, so that the afternoon sun won't be in his eyes; the pitcher, therefore, must face West, which in the case of the left-hander puts his throwing arm and hand (or "paw") on the South side of his body.'

soutie. English sailor, soldier or, above all, airman serving in South Africa: South African: 1939 +. (Cyrus A. Smith, letter of May 22, 1946.) Ex Afrikaans *sout*, salt (ex Dutch *zout*).

sow. To lay (mines): Army coll.: 1940–5. P-G-R.

sow's ear, make a. To blunder: since ca. 1946. Ex the proverb 'you can't make a silk purse out of a sow's ear'.

space-pusher. An advertisement-canvasser working on a periodical: from ca. 1925.

spade (p. 804). But since ca. 1954, it has mostly designated a West Indian.

spade, go for a walk with a; take a spade for a walk. To defecate: Army in N. Africa, World War II. Ex the earthing-over in a latrineless land. P-G-R.

Spades. Coloured people, esp. Negroes and

West Indians: low, e.g. Teddy boys': since ca. 1947. (*The Observer*, March 1, 1949.) In cards, a 'dark' suit: cf. 'as black as the ace of spades'.

spadge (p. 804). Rather: since ca. 1780, not yet †. Ex L. *spatiare.* (Marples.)

spadger (p. 804). Perhaps cf. Ger. *Spatz*, a sparrow.

spag. 'Plastic tubing used to insulate wire in electronic equipment' (B.P.): radio s., esp. Australian: since late 1950's. Ex *spaghetti*—from the resemblance.

spaggers; loosely **spraggers.** Spaghetti: smart young set: ca. 1955–60. (Gilderdale, 2.) 'The Oxford *-er.*'

spam car. 'Q type locomotive (small pannier tank on WR)': railwaymen's: since early 1940's. *Railway.*

spam medal. See **Naffy gong.**

spandule. A gremlin that—but only at 9,999 feet—enjoys being tangled up with the air-screws: R.A.F.: 1940–5.

spangles. Acrobats: circus coll.: late C. 19–20. (C. B. Cochran, *Showman Looks On*, 1945.)

Spanglish. Writing from Argentina on May 26, 1960, Mrs Daphne Hobbs remarks, 'You would be quite interested in the sort of lingua franca spoken in Argentina—in Buenos Aires particularly—among the Argentine-born children of English parents. We call it "Spanglish". . . . The custom is to anglicize Spanish verbs and use them as if they were English—and also to do the same to some of the Argentine (Criollo) slang. For instance, "to iron" is *planchar* in Spanish and this becomes *planchate*, e.g. "I must heat the iron to planchate my dress." In Criollo slang, *canchero* means someone rather smart, good-looking, exciting, etc., so we get *canch*, meaning, roughly, "super" as the English schoolboy or -girl would use it. Again, in Criollo patois, we have *cacho*, a small chunk, and this becomes *catch*, meaning "a small piece" or even "slightly", e.g. "Now I understand a catch."'

Spanish.—2. A (large) Spanish onion: (lower-class) coll.: mid-C. 19–20. B. & L.—3. See 'Tavern Terms', § 3, *c.*

Spanish fly. Cantharides—an extremely potent aphrodisiac, taken in food or drink: C. 19–20: coll. until ca. 1910, then S.E.

Spanish football. See **blue fever.**

Spanish guitar. A cigar: rhyming s.: late C. 19–20. Wilfred Granville, *A Dictionary of Theatrical Terms*, 1952.

Spanish padlock prob. dates from C. 16.

spanjer; usually in pl. '*Spanjers.* Gremlins which live above 20,000 feet—anti-fighter types!' (H. & P.): R.A.F.: ca. 1940–5. Prob. ex dial. *spang*, 'with impetus, with a smack' (itself ex *spang*, 'to leap'): see **spang** (p. 804).

spank, up the. At—or, to—the pawnbrokers': East Enders': from ca. 1870. Nevinson, 1895. Perhaps ex *up the spout* on **bank.**

spank away. (Of a ship) to travel fast: Naval coll.: C. 19. Wm Maginn, *Tales of Military Life*, 1829—see quotation at **bone in the mouth** above.

spanners. A girl whose appearance is sexually exciting: Australian: since ca. 1950. A spanner tightens nuts; in s., *nuts* = testicles.

spare, adj.—2. Absent, esp. without leave, as in 'The Old Man turned down my compassionate, so I went spare': Army: 1939 +.—3. Angry, as in 'When the sarnt sees this, he'll go fucking spare':

Army: since ca. 1940.—4. Hence, crazy; (almost) mad: mostly teenagers': since late 1950's. 'They send me spare' = they drive me crazy.

spare, going. See **going spare** above.

spare a rub! Oblige me with some!; after you with it!: tailors' c.p.: from ca. 1860. B. & L.

spare boy. Treacle; golden syrup: Australian, mostly rural: since ca. 1920. (B., 1943.)

spare file and **spare wank.** A man with no definite job to do: Army: 1939–45. (P-G-R.)

spare prick. A useless fellow: Army: 1939 +. Cf. **prick,** 4 (p. 659) and **prick, standing about . . .** (Addenda). It shortens *spare prick at a wedding,* which gracefully emphasizes the superfluity.

spare whank (or **wank**). A spare man; (among gunners) a spare gunner: Army: since ca. 1930. Cf. prec. and see **wank.**

spark, v.—2. To send a wireless message to (ship or person): nautical and wireless operators': since ca. 1920. Frank Shaw, *Atlantic Murder,* 1932, 'If Scotland Yard . . . spark a ship that wanted people are aboard . . .'—3. To court (a girl): Canadian: C. 20; by 1959, ob. (Leechman.) Adopted ex U.S.

sparker. A telegraphist rating: Naval: C. 20. Granville. Cf. **sparks** (*Dict.*).

sparkle up. To hasten; be quick: proletarian: from ca. 1865; ob. B. & L.

sparkler, 1 (p. 805). In pugilistic s. of ca. 1805–60, any sort of eye, as in *Boxiana,* III, 1821, 'One of his *sparklers* got a little *damaged.*'—3. (Usually in pl.) A flare from an enemy aircraft: Naval: 1939–45. (P-G-R.)—4. An electric train: railwaymen's: since ca. 1939. (*Railway* 2nd.) Ex the sparks emitted from the live rails.

sparks, 1, 2 (*Dict.*): mostly in vocative. 'Taffrail'. 1917.—4. (Ex 1.) Electrical apparatus repairer in R.E.M.E.: Army: 1943 +.—5. An electrician: builders': since ca. 1945.

sparky, n. A wireless operator: Services: since ca. 1918. Cf. **sparker.**

*****sparring bloke.** A pugilist: mid-C. 19–20: c. >, ca. 1880, low. B. & L.

sparring partner, one's. One's companion or friend: coll.: C. 20. Ex pugilism. Wife; occasionally, husband: jocular domestic coll.: late C. 19–20.

sparrow.—5. 'A small weedy fellow' (B., 1942): Australian: C. 20.

sparrow-bill maker. A workman that 'forges wrought-iron nails from iron rod' (*The Evening News,* Sept. 28, 1955): industrial s. (C. 20) > industrial coll. >, by 1945 at latest, official jargon.

sparrow crow, at. A jocular Australian euphemism for 'at *sparrow fart*' (p. 805): C. 20. Baker.

sparrow-fart (or solid). A person of no consequence; a 'twerp': Anglo-Irish: C. 20. James Joyce, *Ulysses,* 1922, 'Miss This Miss That Miss Theother lot of sparrowfarts skitting around talking about politics they know as much about as my backside.'

sparrow's cough, at. At dawn: a polite English variant of 'at *sparrow fart*': since late 1930's. (Jane Gordon, *Married to Charles,* 1950.)

sparrow's ticket, (e.g.) **come in on a.** To gain an illicitly free admission to a match, contest, competition, show, what-have-you: Australian: C. 20. Baker.

spats (p. 806). 'If the wheels of a "spatted" 'plane do not retract, it is said to have permanent "spats",' H. & P.: R.A.F.: since ca. 1935.—2.

Slabs of bread and butter to assuage hunger about 4 p.m.: Marlborough College: C. 20.

spatted. See prec.

spatter. To strike (somebody); 'make a mess' of him: low: since ca. 1945. (Angus Wilson, *Anglo-Saxon Attitudes,* 1956.)

spawny. (Very) lucky: R.A.F.: since ca. 1930. Jackson. 'Thus, "You're spawny to get your promotion so soon."' Perhaps ex the near-cliché, *the best ever spawned.*

speak fancy waistcoats. See **fancy waistcoats.**

speak in (someone's) **knuckle.** To interrupt someone's conversation or story: North Country: C. 20. Ex the game of marbles, where the boy about to shoot may be 'advised' to do this or that and say 'I wish you wouldn't speak in my knuckle'.

speak proper. To talk in B.B.C English: Yorkshire coll.: since ca. 1930.

speak the same language. To have the same sort of upbringing, hence the same general ideas: coll.: since ca. 1930. (P-G-R.)

speak up, Brown! A jocular c.p., addressed to a noisy breaker of wind: Londoners' and Forces': since ca. 1930.

speakers. Rare outside of *on speakers,* on speaking terms (with someone): since ca. 1950. (Jessica Mitford, *Hons and Rebels,* 1960.) By 'the Oxford *-er*'.

speaking (or **talking**) **to the butcher, not to the block, be.** 'Putting 'em in their place! If the boy speaks up before the workman can frame a reply, or if Jack's missus joins in the (acrimonious) argument; but it *can* be used jocularly' (Julian Franklyn, 1962): Cockney: C. 20.

spear, get the. To be dismissed from employment: Australian: since ca. 1920. B., 1942.

spear, give (someone) **the.** To dismiss: Aus.: since ca. 1920. (B., 1959.)

spear a job. To obtain employment: Australian: since ca. 1910. Baker.

spear flounders. To conduct an orchestra: Australian: since ca. 1925. Baker, 'Whence, "flounder-spearing".'

spec, n., 3 (p. 806), goes back to early C. 19. It occurs in W. N. Glascock, *The Naval Sketch-Book,* 2nd Series, 1834, at I, 271,

'The ship's all alive—the ship's company crush
And crowd round the capsten on deck,
And all volunteer, in a regular rush,
To join in the *spree* and the *spec*'—

which makes me wonder whether this sense ('pleasant or memorable occasion') does not derive ex '*special* occasion'.

speccing on one's fez. Expecting to obtain one's cap: Harrow: late C: 19–20. Lunn. Cf. **speck,** v.: q.v. in *Dict.*

special. To act as a special nurse to (a person): nurses' coll.: from ca. 1910. 'She came to special me.' By abbr.

specilate. To invest money, in the hope of bringing good luck: Romanies', hence a few tramps', s.: since ca. 1930. (Robert M. Dawson.) Ex *speculate.*

speck, n. A place; a position: Liverpool: late C. 19–20. Ex S.E. *speck,* a spot. Hence *you're only in the meg specks,* lit. the halfpenny seats (cf. **meg,** n., 2, p. 516)—often used fig., connoting 'You are inferior in some respect, e.g. your school': Liverpool c.p.: C. 20. (Frank Shaw.)

speck, v.—2. 'To search for gold after rain. Whence, "specking"' (B., 1942): Australian miners': late C. 19–20. Rain-erosion may un-cover a lode, or a few specks of alluvial gold.—3. (V.t.) To discover thus: Australian miners': C. 20. (K. S. Prichard, '. . . Charley Beck . . . had specked a thirty-ounce slug, several smaller ones, and struck a reef . . .': 'Mrs Jinney's Shroud' in *Kiss on the Lips*, 1952.)

specking is the n. corresponding to preceding v., sense 2.

speckled.—2. 'Demoted': Rugby: since ca. 1916. Marples. To revert to a *speckled* straw hat.

specs, 1: coll. earlier in Pierce Egan, *Life in London*, 1821.

speed the wombats! Australian synonym of **stone the crows** (*Dict.*): since ca. 1925. B., 1942.

speedo lurk, the. The used-car dealers' trick of turning back the odometer: Australian dealers', hence also motorists': since ca. 1920. (B.P.) A *speedo* is strictly a speedometer.

speedy man. A messenger plying, on foot, between New College and Winchester College: New College, Oxford: ca. 1810–40. *Spy*, 1825.

speeler. See **spieler, 6**.

Speewa. 'A legendary station of doughty deeds (the orig. Speewa was near Swan Hill on the Murray River); a place of "great men and tall tales". Whence, *on the Speewa*' (B., 1959): Aus. coll.: C. 20.

spell-binder (p. 807). Adopted ca. 1910 from U.S., where it was earlier applied to Theodore Roosevelt.

spell for. To long for: proletarian: mid-C. 19–20. B. & L.

spell-oh (p. 807), 1. Much earlier in W. N. Glascock, *Sailors and Saints* (I, 215), 1829. Moe.

spend a penny. See **shake hands** . . . Strictly, to use the w.c. in a public convenience: mostly feminine. (Hilda Lewis, *Strange Story*, 1945.)

[**sperky** in Richards is a blend of *spunky* and *perky*; his *spryle* is a mistake for *funeral pyre*. These two personal unconventionalities are re-corded to illustrate one of the ways in which solec-isms and catachreses may arise.]

spew it. To leave one's job on a ship, go home, report again in the afternoon and try for another job, there or elsewhere: London docks': since ca. 1930. (*The New Statesman*, Dec. 31, 1965.) ' It' = the ship, hence also the job.

*****Spew one's guts.** See **guts, spew one's**.

spew one's ring up. To vomit violently: low: since ca. 1920. (The B.B.C. let this pass on March 1, 1963.) The *ring* = the anus.

spice, n.—2. Spicy sex-items in the newspapers: newsagents' coll.: C. 20. Cf.:

spicey or **spicy.** Usually in pl. *spicies*, spicy books or magazines: booksellers' and newsagents' coll.: since ca. 1910.

Spider. See 'Nicknames'.—2. Also of men surnamed Webb: since ca. 1910. Ex *spider-web* (for *spider's web*).

spider.—4. A wireless operator's badge: R.A.F.: since ca. 1935. Gerald Emanuel, 'From the shape'.—5. A light gig: Australian: since ca. 1910. B., 1942.—6. An inspector: navvies': ca. 1870–1910. (D. W. Barrett, *Navvies*, 1881.)

spiel, n.—3. Set or formal advice: Aus.: C. 20. (B., 1959.)—4. 'A wordy explanation' (B., 1959): Aus.: C. 20. (*Ibid.*) Cf. **spiel, v., 2**, on p. 808.

spiel, v.—4. To race 'all out'—at full speed: Australian sporting: C. 20. B., 1942.

*****spiel-ken.** A variant of **spell-ken** (*Dict.*).

*****spiel off.** To 'spout', utter plausibly: vag-rants' c.: C. 20. W. A. Gape, *Half a Million Tramps*, 1936, 'When my turn came I was not ready to "spiel" off the answers.'

spieler, 4 (p. 808). But also any room in which card-games are habitually played: London's East End: since ca. 1945. (Richard Herd, Nov. 12, 1957.)—6. A fast horse (usually *speeler*): Aus-tralian sporting: C. 20. B., 1942. Ex **spiel, v., 4**. —7. A welsher: Australian sporting: since ca. 1910.

Spike. Inseparable nickname of men surnamed *Hughes* (P-G-R.) or *Sullivan* (see p. 809: **spike, n., 6**).

spike, v.—2. To hit or strike; to knock (some-one) down: Australian low: since ca. 1920. Baker.

spiker. (Usually in pl.) A shark: nautical: late C. 19–20.

spill, n.—4. 'A declaration that all offices are vacant and that new elections will be held. Mostly in the Labour Party' (B.P.): Australian political: since ca. 1930; by 1950, coll.: by 1966, virtually S.E.

spill, v.—4. Used frequently in Australia by women when engaged in slander or in mere gossip: since ca. 1945. 'You know that I won't tell a living soul. Do tell! Spill!' Ex **spill the beans** (p. 809). B.P.

spill one's guts. See **guts, spill one's**.

spill over. That part of a newspaper or maga-zine contribution which has been deferred to the end of the periodical: journalistic coll. (for the S.E. *turn-over*): C. 20.

spin, n.—4. (also *spinnaker*). £5, whether note or sum: Australian: C. 20. Partridge, 1938; B., 1942. Used esp. in two-up: see *boxer*.

spin, v.—3. To tell a story: Naval: ca. 1790–1850. (W. N. Glascock, *Sailors and Saints*, 1829, at I, 177.) Moe.

spin a bender. See **bender, spin a**.

spin for. To court (a woman): Australian: since ca. 1930. Alan Marshall, *These Are My People*, 1946. Ex the game of two-up?

spin the bar. See **bar, 3**.

spin the dope. To tell a (good) story, e.g. in chiromancy: Australian: since ca. 1920. (K. S. Prichard, *Haxby's Circus*, 1930.)

spin the fanny. To 'tell the tale', to spin a good yarn or deliver a good, set 'spiel': fair-ground grafters': since ca. 1925. (Richard Merry.) Cf. **fanny, n., 7**, on p. 266.

spindle-prick. Vocative to a man deficient in energy: low: late C. 19–20. (Only mildly abusive.)

spine-bashing. Sleep; a rest on one's bunk: Australian soldiers': 1939 +. Lawson Glassop, *We Were the Rats*, 1944. Cf. **charpoy-bashing**.

spinnaker. See **spin, n., 4**.

spinner. £50: Australian low: since ca. 1910. B., 1942. Cf. **spin, n., 4**.—2. A parachutist with twisted rigging lines in his parachute: R.A.F.: 1939 +. Jackson. He spins as he descends.

spinnifax wire, the. A North Australian version of the bush telegraph: since c. 1930. (H. Drake Brockman, *Men without Wives*, 1938.) Hence, a *spinnifax wire*, a rumour, esp. if well-founded. (Ibid.)

spinning jenny. A prismatic compass, early model: Royal Artillery: ca. 1915–50. Ex the way in which the card spun.

spiny. The bird Spinebill; mostly as nickname: Australian rural: late C. 19–20. (B., 1943.)

spiral swallow. See **swallow, have a spiral:** *Dict.*

Spirit, the. A Melbourne–Sydney train: Australian coll.: 1962 +. Short for *the Spirit of Progress.* (B.P.) Cf. **Roarer, the** above.

Spirites, the. The Chesterfield 'soccer' team: sporting: from ca. 1930. The Chesterfield church has a crooked spire. (The Arsenal F.C. programme, Dec. 19, 1936.)

Spit. A Spitfire fighter 'plane: since 1938 in R.A.F.: since 1940 (Berrey) among civilians. Spitfires and Hurricanes saved Britain in Aug.–Sept. 1940.

spit, n.—3. A smoke (of a cigarette): low: C. 20. 'Some of them had bits of cigarettes, and asked us if we'd like a "spit"' (Brendan Behan, *Borstal Boy,* 1958).

spit a bone at. To 'point the bone at': Australian: C. 20. (B., 1943.)

spit and a drag, a (p. 810): since ca. 1920, gen. rhyming s.

spit and a draw, a (p. 810) is recorded much earlier in Alexander Paterson, *Across the Bridges,* 1911, and can prob. be back-dated to the 1890's.

Spit and Cough, the. The Athenæum Club: London taxi-drivers': since ca. 1910. Herbert Hodge, *Cab, Sir?,* 1939. Ex the high incidence of asthma and bronchitis among members?

spit and drag. See **spit and a drag** (*Dict.*).

spit and sawdust. A general saloon in a public-house: C. 20. Ex the sawdust sprinkled on the floor and the spitting on to the sawdust. (Peter Chamberlain.)

spit in the bag and stand up. (Of a bookmaker on the course) to occupy his stand and accept bets without the money to honour them if they are successful: Australian racing: since ca. 1925. Lawson Glassop, *Lucky Palmer,* 1949. He spits in his bag for luck.

Spit-in-the-Pew (Sunday). See **Gob Sunday.**

spit in your mouth. See **mean.**

spit-kid. A spittoon: Naval: since ca. 1900. C. F. Forester, *The Ship,* 1943; Granville.

spit o' my hand! A Cockney expletive, coll. ra her than s., dating from ca. 1880; slightly ob. Pu (2): '"Spit o' my hand! What I might ha' bin worth if it hadn't bin for this cursed stuff —bless it!" The liquor gurgled down his throat.' Cf.:

spit one's death. (See **strike one's breath.**) To swear solemnly, as in Pugh (2): 'An' I spit my death an' all, an I'll stick to it.' Cockney: late C. 19–20; ob. Perhaps on *may I die . . .!*

spit or get off the cuspidor. A refined Canadian c.p. for **shit or get off the pot** (above): since ca. 1940.

spitchered. Done for, 'sunk'; mortally wounded, etc.: Naval: since ca. 1900. Granville. Ex **spitcher** (p. 811). 'To *spitcher*' derives from Italianate Maltese *spizzia,* finished, done for, itself from It. *spezzare,* to break into small pieces.

spitfire. A contraceptive: Naval lower-deck: since ca. 1945. Effectual against the enemy.

Spitfire kitten. See **whistler, 9.**

Spitfires. 'Ration cigarettes with R.A.F. roundels on the packet. A fair description': Forces'

in North Africa: 1940–43. Peter Sanders in *The Sunday Times* magazine, Sept. 10, 1967.

Spithead pheasant. A bloater: Naval: C. 20. *The Birmingham Mail,* Feb. 24, 1939: Granville. —2. A kipper: since ca. 1950. (*The News Chronicle,* Nov. 4, 1954.) Cf. **Bombay duck** (*Dict.*).

Spitter is an occ. 1941–5 variant of **Spit.** H. & P., 1943. Partly because 'it just spits bullets'.

Spittoon, the; the Billiard Table. Two courts in Whewell's Court, Trinity College: Cambridge undergraduates': late C. 19–20. The former has cup-shaped base with central drain; the latter, six drains about a rectangular grass plot. Between these two courts lies a small garden (about 10 yards by 25) called *The Garden of Eden,* perhaps because of a large fruit tree growing in it. (With thanks to Mr D. F. Wharton.)

*spiv. One who lives by his wits—within the law, for preference; esp. by 'the racing game': c.: since ca. 1890; by 1940 low s. Lionel Seccombe, wireless-reporting the Foord–Neusel fight, Nov. 18, 1936; John Worby, *The Other Half,* 1937 (the 'locus classicus'); Alan Hoby in *The People,* April 7, 1946, '"Spivs"—the small town touts and racketeers'; a definition enunciated in June 1947 was 'One who earns his living by not working'. In *The Daily Telegraph* of July 29 and 30, 1947, Lord Rosebery and 'Peterborough' clearly established that the term had been in use by and among race-course gangs since the 1890's and had been known to a few police detectives since 1920 or so. Cf. **spiffing** in *Dict.,* for *spiv* may conceivably represent an abbreviation of *spiffing fellow.*

Indeed, *spiv* is of the same origin as *spiffing*: the dialectal *spif* or *spiff,* 'neat, smart, dandified; excellent'; compare Scottish and Northern *spiffer,* 'anything first-rate'. The adj. *spif* becomes a noun (compare **phoney**) and *spif* becomes *spiv* because the latter is easier to pronounce.—Whence *spivvish*: 'of or like a spiv': 1946 +.

See esp. 'Spivs and Phoneys' in *Here, There and Everywhere* (essays upon language), 1949.

spiv days (singular rare). Rest days: railwaymen's: since ca. 1945. (*Railway.*)

spiv-knot. 'The "Windsor" knotting of the tie: knotted double to emphasize the shoulders and waist of tie-knot. Of Cockney origin' (Atkinson): late 1947 +. See prec. entry.

splash, adj. (p. 811). Over fifty years earlier in W. H. Ainsworth, *Rookwood,* 1834, 'All my togs were so niblike and splash.'

splash (or slash), have a (Of men) to make water. C. 20. Probably ex the synonymous *splash one's boots* (or *shoes*).

splashing. Excessive or silly talk: proletarian: ca. 1870–1910. B. & L.

splattered, get. To lose heavily: racing, esp. bookies': since ca. 1920. *The Sunday Telegraph,* May 7, 1967.

splice, v., 1 (p. 811), is much earlier: 1710, John Shadwell, *The Fair Quaker of Deal.* (Moe.)

split, n.—12. (Cf. sense 10, 11.) Change (in money); small change: low: 1893, P. H. Emerson, *Signor Lippo.*—13. A safety match: Aus.: C. 20. (B., 1959.)

split, adj. See **wilderness, be in the,** below.

*split ace, the. See **hot seat.**

split-arse, adj. 'He's a pukka split-arse pilot' —i.e. stunt pilot: R.A.F.: since ca. 1915. Jackson. Ex the adv. (p. 812); cf. 'the splits' (ibid.).—2. Hence, addicted to stunting: R.A.F. since ca. 1920.—3. 'Used by the South Africans (in the Air Force) to indicate very good or very clever, e.g. "split-arse navigator",' Robert Hinde, letter of March 17, 1945.

split-arse cap (p. 812) has been kept alive by the R.A.F. for the field-service cap as distinct from the peaked dress-service cap. Jackson.

split-arse landing. A daring landing at speed: R.A.F.: since ca. 1925. Jackson.

split-arse pilot. A stunting pilot; a test pilot: R.A.F.: since ca. 1925. Cf. *split-arse merchant* on p. 812.

split-arse turn (*Dict.*): prob. from at least fifteen years earlier, perhaps from ca. 1917.

split-arsed one. A female (esp., baby): low: late C. 19–20.

split-arsing about. An elaboration of *split-arsing* (p. 812): since ca. 1916.—2. Hence, acting the fool in a dangerous way: all three Services': since ca. 1925. (P-G-R.)

split stuff. Women collectively: low Australian: C. 20. B., 1942. Physiological.

split the grain, enough to. Enough to make one drunk: coll.: from ca. 1880. Pugh (2): 'But . . . go easy with this . . . Jest enough to screw you up, y'know, but not enough to split the grain.'

split 'un. A bank-note split in two: Australian low coll.: C. 20. Baker.

split yarn, have everything on a. 'To be ready to carry out an evolution' (Granville): Naval coll.: C. 20.—2. Hence to have a plan worked out: Naval: since ca. 1925.

splithers. See razzor.

splits. Split peas or lentils: domestic and grocers' coll.: C. 20.

splitter.—2. A lawyer addicted to hair-splitting distinctions: ca. 1660–1750. Richard Head, *Proteus Redivivus*, 1675.

splodger.—2. (esp., in address) 'Codger': rhyming s.: 1856, H. Mayhew, *The Great World of London*; † by 1920.—3. A body-snatcher (?): ? ca. 1840–80.

'I'm Happy Jack the Splodger.
I'm as happy as I can be,
'Cos when I digs the bodies up,
The worms crawl over me.'
      The 'saga' of *Happy Jack*

Perhaps ex English dial. *splodge*, to trudge through dirt or mire (EDD).

splodgy. Coarse-looking; (of complexion) pimply: proletarian coll.: mid-C. 19–20. B. & L. Lit., splotchy.

sploshing it on, adj. or n. Betting heavily; heavy betting: racing, esp. bookies': since ca. 1920. *The Sunday Telegraph*, May 7, 1967.

Spode's law. 'If something *can* go wrong, it *will*'—esp. in scientific research: scientists', pharmaceutical chemists', technologists': since ca. 1930. (Ronald K. Rogers, Nov. 21, 1967.) Cf. the rather earlier scientific dictum about the mythical fourth general law of the physicists, 'the cussedness of the universe tends to a maximum'.

spodiodi. A 'mixture of cheap port and bar whisky' affected by the jazz world (*The Victoria Daily Colonist*, April 16, 1959, 'Basic Beatnik'): Canadian jazz-lovers' and musicians': since ca. 1955. Origin? Apparently arbitrary—perhaps after such a name as *asti spumante*.

spoffskins is more properly a courtesan willing to pretend to (temporary) marriage.

spoil dandy. A severe blow: pugilistic: ca. 1810–40. T. Moore, *Tom Cribb's Memorial*, 1819.

spon or **spons.** Money: Australian: since ca. 1920. B., 1942. Ex:

spondulicks (p. 813). A more prob. origin, I suggest, is Gr. *spondulikos*, adj. of *spondulos*, a species of shell very popular in prehistoric and early historic commerce; cf. the use of cowrie shells as money in ancient Asia and in both ancient and modern Africa.

Spongy. An inevitable nickname—as are **Doughy** and **Snowy**—of men surnamed Baker: late C. 19–20.

sponk. Infatuated. Public School girls': since late 1940's; by 1967, ob. John Winton, *We Saw the Sea*, 1960, "'I had a crush on my games mistress," Mary said. "I was absolutely *sponk* on her."' Less probably ex *spunk* + *bonk*ers than ex adj. *spank*ing + *bonk*ers.

spons. See spon.

spoof, n.—5. Confidence-trick swindle: low (– 1890); ob. B. & L.—6. Misleading or 'planted' information: Army, esp. Intelligence: since ca. 1940. (Peter Sanders.)

spook (p. 183). 'Perhaps because signallers occasionally practise at night with lamps' (Leechman).—2. A drug-addict: c.: since ca. 1943. (Norman.) Such addicts tend to look ghastly.

spook, v. To render (a horse or other quadruped) nervous: Canadian: since ca. 1930. 'Don't show him the whip, you'd spook him'— 'You'll never catch him now, he's spooked.' To cause to shy or to gallop away, as if at the sight of a *spook* or ghost. Perhaps of U.S. origin (cf. Wentworth & Flexner); Dr Douglas Leechman thinks not.

spoon, v., 2 (p. 813). Earlier in Trollope, *The Way We Live Now*, 1875. (Philip Gaskell.)—4. To make things easy for (a person, esp. for a pupil): Winchester College: since ca. 1880. E. H. Lacon Watson, *In the Days of His Youth*, 1935, 'You'd never have got your remove last half if Wray hadn't spooned you.' I.e. *spoon-feed*.

spoon in the wall, stick one's (p. 813) is recorded earlier in Matthew Todd's *Journal*, edited by Geoffrey Trease, 1968, but belonging to 1814.

Spoonerisms, intentional. In slang, there is a tendency to this sort of thing: *senal perviude* (p. 744) and, jocularly, *blazor rades* (razor blades) and *blubber roves* (rubber gloves).

spooney.—5. An effeminate youth or man: ca. 1825–80. Thackeray, *Vanity Fair*, 1848, 'Jim says he's remembered at Oxford as Miss Crawley still—the spooney.'

sport, n. (p. 814). *Be a Sport!* occurs in, e.g., *Punch* on May 21, 1913. As a term of address, it has been current in Australia since before 1914.

sport a toe. To dance: 1821, Pierce Egan, *Life in London*; app. † by 1870.

sportsman is at certain Public Schools a synonym for 'chap', 'fellow', 'man': from ca. 1890. (Arnold Lunn, *Loose Ends*, 1919.)

spot, n. Sense 5: A. Neil Lyons, *Clara*, 1912; † by 1940.—8. A guess: from ca. 1932. Gorell, *Red Lilac*, 1935, 'My spot is that after baiting his poor victim, he had a fancy for the melodramatic.' Perhaps abbr. *spot-light*.—9. £10: Australian low: since ca. 1930. B., 1942. Ex U.S. *ten-spot*, 10 dollars.—10. A spotlight: cinematic, since ca. 1925; T.V. since ca. 1945. By 1960, coll.

spot, v.—10. To set a box- or other freight-car in the right place for loading or unloading: Canadian railwaymen's since ca. 1905; by 1920, coll. (Leechman.)

Sense 7 (p. 815) is also, in C. 20, Aus. (B.), 1959.

spot, in a (p. 815). By 1939, s.; esp. in the Services. Partridge, 1945.

spot, off the. See **spot, on the**, in *Dict.*—2. Silly, imbecile: from ca. 1880; ob. B. & L.

spot below. Six (in game of House): mostly Army: C. 20. The Counter for number 6 has a spot below to distinguish it from 9 upside down.

spot of, 'a little' (see **spot, n.**, 2: p. 815, top), was adumbrated so long ago as in Wm Maginn's translation of *Memoirs of Vidocq*, III, 1829, 'He leads them to a *spot of work*'—a burglary; *spot of bother*, trouble: Army officers': since ca. 1914; *the recent spot of bother*, the war of 1914-18 or that of 1939-45.

spot(-)on. An occasional variant of **bang on**: R.A.F.: 1940-5. Via 'bang on the spot'. Since the late 1940's, the usual term in Australia. (B.P.)

spotter.—5. An employee assigned to watch the behaviour of other employees: Canadian railroadmen's (— 1931). Cf. senses 1-3 in *Dict.* Also on Canadian trams; by 1959, ob. (Leechman.)—6. A man on the look-out for military police: Army: 1939-45. (P-G-R.)

spout, n.—3. Penis: low: C. 19-20.—4. See **spout, up the** (*Dict.*).—5. A cannon: Woolwich Arsenal: C. 20. *The Daily Mail*, Aug. 16, 1939.

sprag. See 'Fops'.—2. A goods guard: Eastern Railway employees': ca. 1890-1925. (*Railway* 2nd.) Perhaps ex dial. *sprag*, to put a brake on something.

spraggers. Loose for *spaggers*.

sprarser or **sprarsey.** Sixpence. Variants of *spraser* (p. 816).

Sprat Day. Lord Mayor's Day: Cockneys': since ca. 1840; ob. Mayhew, I, 1851, 'Sprats . . . are generally introduced about the 9th of November.'

spread, n., 5 (p. 816). An early record: 1822, David Carey, *Life in Paris*.—With sense 6 (a dinner) cf. the nuance, 'any meal'—as in *morning spread*, breakfast: *Spy*, II, 1826.—11. A plasterer: builders': C. 20.—12. (Ex sense 3, 'butter': p. 816.) Jam, marmalade, or anything else that is spread upon bread: Canadian: late C. 19-20; by 1940, coll. (Leechman.)

spread, work the. See **spread, n.**, 10, in *Dict.*

spread-worker. A herbalist: showmen's: late C. 19-20. See **spread, n.**, 10 (p. 816).

spreader.—2. A blanket: whalers': C. 19. E. J. Wakefield, *Adventure in New Zealand*, 1845 (recorded by B.), 1941.

***spreaders.** A burglar's large pliers: c.: from ca. 1890. Pugh (2).

spree, n., 1 (p. 816): a little earlier in *Sessions*, Dec. 1798, p. 59.

spree man, or as one word. A junior permitted to work hard: Winchester College: from ca. 1870. B. & L.

spreeish, 2 (p. 816). Earlier in *Sessions*, April 1843.

sprey. An occ. spelling of **spree**; e.g. in *Sessions*, April 1822.

spridgy—sproggy—spudgy. Australian, esp.

juvenile, terms for a sparrow: C. 20. (B., 1953.) With the first, cf. the Scottish dial. *sprig*; with the second, cf. Scottish and N. Country dial. *sprog* (and *sprug*); with the third, cf. the Scottish and N. Country dial. *spug* and Sussex *spudger*; with all, cf. *spadger* on p. 804.

spring, v., 1 and 2: both senses anticipated by *Sessions*, 1832 (trial of John Robinson), 'You had better . . . hear the deal, for I think they will *spring* a little' (raise, increase, the price).—4. To see: Australian, esp. Sydneyites': since ca. 1945. 'I've never sprung him before.' (Edwin Morrisby, Aug. 30, 1958.)—5. To get a man released from prison, esp. on a technicality: Canadian: adopted, ca. 1935, ex U.S. (Leechman.)

spring his cattle. To rush the horses: coach-drivers': C. 19. (W. O. Tristram, *Coaching Days and Coaching Ways*, 1888.)

spring-sides. Elastic-sided boots: Australian: C. 20. B., 1942.

springer.—2. A physical-training officer: Naval (lower-deck): since ca. 1920. (P-G-R.)—3. A planner of a prison escape: since ca. 1960. Cf. the orig. c. *spring*, to get (someone) released from prison.

sprio. A sparrow: Sedgeley Park School: ca. 1780-1870. Frank Roberts in *The Cottonian*, Autumn 1938. Thus *sparrow > spro >*, by the principle of 'ease of pronunciation', *sprio*. Cf. **spug.**

sprog., n. A recruit: R.A.F.: since ca. 1930; by ca. 1939, also—via the Fleet Air Arm—used occ. by the Navy. H. & P. Origin obscure and debatable (see esp. Partridge, 1945); but perhaps a reversal of 'frog-spawn' (very, very green) or, more prob., the adoption of a recruit's *sprog*, a confusion of 'sprocket' and 'cog', a sprocket being, like the recruit, a cog in a wheel. In the Navy the term means an infant, 'Nobby Clark's gone on leave, his wife's just had a *sprog*': Granville, 1945.—2. Hence, an Aircraftman: Australian airmen's: since ca. 1939. (B., 1943.)—3. A child, esp. in relation to its parents: Fleet Air Arm, hence Naval: since the late 1930's.

Robert Clairborne has suggested that the word might conceivably be a distortion of S.E. *sprout*.

sprog, adj. New ('sprog tunic'); recently promoted ('sprog corporal'); recently created or become (' Two sprog fathers in the room in two days,' Brickhill & Norton, *Escape to Danger*, 1946). Ex the n.

sproggie. See **spridgey.**

spruce up. To clean and dress oneself to go out or to go on parade: Regular Army coll.: since ca. 1895. I.e. make oneself *spruce* or smart.

sprucing. n. Leg-pulling: Army: since ca. 1918. (P-G-R.) Ex the Australians?

spud, 1: earlier in E. J. Wakefield, *Adventure*, 1845.—3. A friend, chum, pal: Services: since ca. 1930. H. & P. See **mucking-in spud.**

spud barber: extant in the Navy. (Granville.)

spud-basher. 'A man on cookhouse fatigue for potato peeling,' H. & P.: Services: since ca. 1919. —2. See 'Hauliers' Slang'.

spud-bashing. Kitchen fatigue: Services: since ca. 1920. *The Daily Mail*, Sept. 7, 1940.

spud line, be in the. To be pregnant: Naval lower-deck: since ca. 1946.

spud locker, in the. Pregnant: Naval: C. 20.

spud-walloping. Variant of preceding: since ca. 1930. (P-G-R.)

spud(d)ler. An indirect cause of trouble: West Country railwaymen's: C. 20. (*Railway*.) Ex dial. *spuddle*, to 'mess about' or to 'make a mess of things'. More precisely, 'one who causes trouble indirectly' (*Railway*, 3rd).

spudgy. See **spridgey**.

spudoosh. 'Lower-deck "spudoosh", that dismal diet of many-eyed potatoes mashed with corned beef into a mockery of a meal,' Robert Harling, *The Steep Atlantick Stream*, 1946: Naval: C. 20. A blend of '*spuds*' + '*mash*ed potatoes', influenced by the *oes* of 'potatoes'.

spug. A sparrow: Cotton College: since ca. 1875. Adoption of dial. word.

spun in. Crash-landed ('plane or pilot): R.A.F.: since ca. 1930. H. & P.; Jackson, 'Failed to recover from a spin.'—2. Hence, applied to one who has committed a technical error: since ca. 1938. Partridge, 1945.

spun-yarn major (p. 817): strictly, any officer *above* that rank. Granville.

spun-yarn Sunday. A Sunday on which Church is voluntary: Naval: C. 20. (P-G-R.)

spun-yarn trick. 'An underhand method of achieving a desired end. From the use of spun yarn in effecting repairs' (Granville): Naval coll.: C. 20. Also, I'd say, in allusion to 'The Indian rope-trick'.

spunk, v.i. To ejaculate: low coll.: C. 20. The corresponding n., 2 (p. 817), is also coll. rather than s.

spunk-bound. (Of a man) lethargic; slow-witted: low: late C. 19-20. Cf.:

spunk-dust. 'A jovially abusive term of address between men' (Atkinson): low: C. 20. See **spunk**, 2, on p. 817.

spurge. An effeminate male: Australian low: since ca. 1920. B., 1942. Ex the rather weedy plant thus named.

squab. See 'Men'.

squab-job. A job for (young) girls: ca. 1910-15. Flora Klickman, *The Lure of the Pen*, 1919. A *squab* is a young sparrow.

squabbling bleeder. A Squadron Leader: R.A.F. rhyming s.: 1939-45, then mainly historical. Franklyn 2nd.

squadded, be. To be—on first joining up—put into a squad: Army col.: since ca. 1910. (P-G-R.)

Squadron, the. Headquarters of the Royal Yacht Squadron at Cowes, I.o.W.: Naval coll.: C. 20.

squadron bleeder. Squadron-Leader: R.A.F.: since ca. 1925. Jackson. By an entirely inoffensive pun.

Squadron-Leader Swill. Squadron-Leader 'A' (Administration) on a station: R.A.F. coll.: since ca. 1930. Jackson, 'The disposal of waste food-scraps . . . for use as pig-swill is one of [his] numerous responsibilities.'

squaff or **squoff** is a variant of **squo**. (W/Cdr P. McDouall, letter of April 12, 1945.)

squaler. A weapon consisting of an 18-inch cane surmounted with a pear-shaped piece of lead used for killing squirrels and deer in Savernake Forest: Marlborough College: ca. 1843-60. Either for *squirreller* or because it causes squirrels to *squeal*. But as *squailer* (see O.E.D.) it is an archæological technicality. The weapon is very old; by many archæologists and ethnologists it is known as a *rabbit stick*. (Dr Leechman.) 'Perhaps

the point should be made that it was thrown at the rabbit, not used as a club.'

squalid. A pejorative, synonymous with and prob. suggested by *filthy* (*Dict*.): upper classes': from ca. 1933. Nicholas Blake, *Thou Shell of Death*, 1936, 'Squalid fellow'.

squalid bleeder. A Squadron Leader: R.A.F.: 1939-45. 'An inoffensive pun' (Ramsey Spencer); cf. **squadron bleeder** above.

square, n.—4. A mortar-board: Cambridge undergraduates': late C. 19-20.—6. (See 'Canadian . . .') An old-fashioned person, esp. about dancing and music: dance-fanatics' and jazz-lovers': adopted, ca. 1938, ex U.S. *The Observer*, Sept. 16, 1956.—7. An honest citizen; anyone of conventional morals and habits: Canadian: adopted, ca. 1955, ex U.S.—8. Between sol. and coll. is the late C. 19-20 Army sense 'parade-ground' —whatever the shape.

Sense 7 was adopted by Britain ex Canada ca. 1958.

square, adj.—2. Corresponding to senses 6 and 7 of the n.: old-fashioned; esp., decent and honest; with connotation 'reactionary': since late 1950's. See **swinging**, below, and the adv. on p. 818.

square, run on the. To be honest or trustworthy: Society: from ca. 1880; very ob. B. & L.

square affair. One's legitimate sweetheart (girl): Cockney and Australian: ca. 1890-1914.

square away. To arrange: Australian naval, hence also military, coll.: since ca. 1940. See quotation at **head off**.

square back-down. A palpable shuffling: sporting: from ca. 1870.

square-basher is (C. 10) the victim of:

square-bashing. Drill, esp. by recruits on the parade ground: C. 20 Army and post-1930 R.A.F. H. & P. (at *gravel-bashing*). The recruits 'bash' their rifles down.

square-eyes. One who watches T.V. excessively: Australian: since ca. 1950. Ex reputed effect. (B.P.)

square Jane and no nonsense. A respectable, intensely self-respecting girl: Australian: since ca. 1925. Baker.

square-off, n. An apology; a concocted excuse: Australian: since ca. 1910. (B., 1943.) Ex sense 1 of the v.

square off.—2. (V.i. and v.t.) 'To make things ship-shape' (Granville). Naval coll.: C. 20.—3. To prepare to fight: Australian: C. 20. (B., 1943.)

square one! The shortened form of **let's go back to square one**.

square one's yardarm. To protect oneself in a manner inspectable by one's seniors: Naval (wardroom): C. 20.

square shepherd. An old-fashioned but essentially honest, decent, kindly person, esp. among the beatniks: beatniks': since ca. 1959. (Anderson.) An elaboration of **square**, n., 7, above.

square tack. A girl; girls in general: Guards': since ca. 1918. Roger Grinstead, *They Dug a Hole*, 1946.

square-toes. See **old square-toes**, which prob. dates from early in the 19th century; *young square-toes* occurs in Thackeray's *Vanity Fair*, 1848.

square up the job; often as n., **squaring up** . . .

To conclude an investigation by making an arrest: police coll.: since ca. 1910. (*The Free-Lance Writer*, April 1948.)

square wheels. 'Wheels with worn running surface' (*Railway*): railwaymen's: late C. 19–20.

squareface. See **square-face** (*Dict.*).

squarehead. See **square-head** (*Dict.*).—4. To prepare to fight, adopting the suitable stance: Australian: since ca. 1910. B., 1942.—5. A timid, or an amateurish, thief with a conscience: Australian low: since ca. 1920. (B., 1943.)—6. Hence, an unconvicted crook: Australian c.: since ca. 1945.

Squareville. 'The *fons et origo* of all "squares" and conventional people and conduct. "Him! Oh, he's strictly from Squareville!"' Canadian: adopted in 1960–1 ex U.S., where orig. it was jazz s. (Leechman.)

*****squarey.** A crook not yet convicted or not yet even interrogated: Australian c.: since ca. 1945. (B., 1953.)

squash, n.—2. A youth-movement gathering, many persons crowded into a small room: Church coll.: since ca. 1930.

squat, v. Medical s. of C. 20, as in C. Lillingston, *His Patients Died*, 1936, an agent to a young doctor: 'You may become someone's assistant . . ., or you may squat—put up your plate in a likely district and wait for patients.' Hence *squatter*, mentioned also by Lillingston. Ex land squatting.

squattage. A squatter's station; his homestead: Australian: since ca. 1930. (B., 1943.) A blend of *squat*ter + cot*tage*.

squatter.—2. See preceding entry.

squatter's daughter. Water: Australian rhyming s.: C. 20. (Baker.)

squatti. A loose variant of **swaddy** (*Dict.*).: Army: late C. 19–20.

squattocracy. Squatters, their life and customs, etc.: Australian coll.: since ca. 1920. (B., 1943.)

squawk, n. and v. A complaint; to complain: Canadian: adopted, ca. 1935, ex U.S.

squawk-box. An office intercommunication system: Canadian: since ca. 1945. (Leechman.) —2. 'Now applied to an intercom on an office desk, but specifically to the Admiralty desks' (Wilfred Granville, letter of July 24, 1963).

squeak, n.—3. A sergeant: Australian soldiers': 1939–45. (B., 1943.) Probably ex *pip-squeak*, 1 (p. 633).

squeak, get a. See **get a squeak.**

squeak, put in a. See **put in a squeak** (Addenda). But for *squeak, put in the*, see **squeak, n.**, 2 (p. 819).

squeaker, 2 (p. 819): 'a cross child' (*Sinks*, 1848).—12. In card-playing, either a low-value card that takes a trick or a trump that unnecessarily takes a trick: C. 20.

Sense 10 (p. 819) is also, in C. 20, Aus. (B., 1959.)

squeakers.—2. Boots; shoes: Australian rural: C. 20. (D'Arcy Niland, 1958.)

squeakies, the. The cinema: ca. 1931–5. E. C. Vivian, 1933. Cf. **talkies** (*Dict.*).

squeaks in, put the. See **put the acid** (or **squeaks) in.**

squeal, n.—3. A team of bullocks: Australian bullock drivers': C. 20. (K. S. Prichard, *Working Bullocks*, 1926.) Echoic.

Squealers, the. The Australian Provost Corps: Australian soldiers': 1939 +. B., 1942. Ex **squealer,** 1 (p. 819).

squee-pee. Nestlé's milk: Scottish Public

Schools', or at least at that of which Ian Miller writes in his notable novel, *School Tie*, 1935: from ca. 1905. Perhaps a reduplication of *squish* on *pee*.

'May I suggest an origin based on *squeezing* the punctured (not conventionally "opened") tin & thus producing a thin trickle (or jet, depending on the pressure applied) from the hole?' Ramsey Spencer.

squeegee, all. Very much askew: ca. 1860–1910. Perhaps by corruption.

squeegee band (p. 819) is recorded in 1896: *The Navy and Army Illustrated*, Oct. 3—article 'Fun on Board Ship'. (Moe.)

squeeze, n.—14. A woman's waist: Australian: since ca. 1925. (B., 1943.)—15. (Ex senses 8 and esp. 11: p. 819.) 'To threaten a thief with arrest unless he informed on his friends' (John Gosling, 1959): police s.: C. 20.—16. Economy, esp. *a credit squeeze*: since ca. 1958: coll. >, by 1966, S.E.

squeeze-box.—2. A concertina: 1914–18. (H. & P.)—3. A piano-accordion: 1939–45. (H. & P.) —4. A gas-respirator: Army: 1939 +. *The Daily Mail*, Sept. 7, 1940.

squeeze(-)gun. An anti-tank gun of small calibre: Army: 1941 +.—2. A gun with a slightly tapering bore: artillerymen's: ca. 1941–5. (P-G-R.)

squeeze off a fish. To fire a torpedo: Naval: since ca. 1939.

squeeze-pigeon or **-pidgin.** Blackmail: mostly Naval: since ca. 1910.

squeeze the teat (or **tit**). See **tit,** c.

squeeze up, v.i. To ejaculate: low: C. 20.

squeezer.—3. (Gen. pl.) One of a set of cards with index values shown in the corners: from ca. 1880.

squelch. A blunder, a *faux-pas*, a 'putting one's foot in it': Australian: since late 1950's. (B.P.)

squelcher.—2. Fig., e.g. in argument: from ca. 1890; ob.

squib.—8. One who backs out; a faint-heart: Australian: C. 20. Archer Russell, *Gone Nomad*, 1936.—9. A plan that fails: Australian: since ca. 1910. B., 1942. Ex a damp squib.—10. A small, weedy person: Australian: since ca. 1912. Baker.

squib, v. To be afraid; to be a coward: Australian: C. 20. (B., 1943.) Cf. sense 8 of the n.

squib, his mother never raised a. He is very brave: Aus. c.p.: C. 20. (B., 1959.) Ex **squib,** n., 8, above.

squib it. To turn coward, to 'chicken out': Australian: since ca. 1950. Cf. the fig. uses of *squib*, n. and v., in English dialect.

squib on. To betray (someone); to fail (him): Australian: since ca. 1910. Sidney J. Baker, letter in *The Observer*, Nov. 13, 1938. To go out, fail to explode, like a damp squib.

Squibbley. Esquimalt and Royal Naval College: Royal Canadian Navy: since ca. 1930. (P-G-R.) 'This distortion of the pronunciation of Esquimalt reminds me of Slackers, which I believe to be a distortion of Halifax, something like *Pompey* [for Portsmouth]. Two Navy types I have asked (but yesterday) say that they were not aware of any slackness while they were there. See also *Uckers*.' (Leechman, April 15, 1967.)

squiff. A drunkard: Australian: since ca. 1920. B., 1942. Ex **squiffy,** 1, 2 (p. 820).

squiff, on the. On a drinking-bout: Australian: since ca. 1925. (B., 1943.) Cf. the preceding.

squiff it. To die: Australian: since ca. 1945. (B.P.)

squiffy.—3. Hence, unwell: Australian: C. 20. Baker.—4. Silly; stupid: Australian: since ca. 1920.—5. Crooked; askew: Australian: since ca. 1920. Baker. Probably, as Ramsey Spencer suggests, a contraction of *skew-whiff*.

squinters (p. 820) may, however, have, orig., been Oxford University s. of ca. 1760–1860. It occurs in the poem 'A Familiar Epistle' on p. 367 of *The Gentleman's Magazine*, May 1784. (Moe.)

squinting. Being without a necessity or a requisite (e.g. food): tailors': from ca. 1860. B. & L.

squire.—2. Hence, a jocular term of address among men: coll.: C. 20.

Squire, the. Henry St John, Viscount Boling-broke (1678–1751): ca. 1710–70. See, e.g., *Swift's Letters*, ed. by F. E. Ball.

squirms, the; esp. in 'It'll give you the squirms' —horribly embarrass or irritate you: since ca. 1930.

squirt, n.—8. A quick burst of machine-gun fire: R.A.F.: since ca. 1937. H. & P. Cf. **quick squirt.**—9. A jet-propelled aircraft: R.A.F.: since May 1944; by 1950, slightly ob. A pun on *jet*. (P-G-R.)

squirter. A synonym of **squirt**, n., 1 and 2: from ca. 1920.

squiz, v. To regard; to inspect: Australian: since ca. 1910 (the n., dating since late C. 19: see p. 821). B., 1942. Ex the n.—2. Hence, to peep slyly: Australian: since ca. 1925. (Ruth Park, *Poor Man's Orange*, 1950.) With *squint—squiz*, cf. *swindle—swiz*.

squo. A Squadron-Officer (W.A.A.F. equivalent of S.Ldr): W.A.A.F. and R.A.F.: 1940 +. Jackson. Also *squoff*.

sri; strictly '*sri*. That's right: mostly Cock-ney (solecistic?) coll.: C. 20, '"It was two years last August: wasn't it, Fred?"—"Sri," said Fred,' Michael Harrison, *What Are We Waiting For?* 1931. I.e. 'that's right'.

ss is, in Cockney speech, the slurring of *rs*: C. 19–20. E.g. *passon*, common also in dial., and *pusson*, as in Edwin Pugh, *A Street in Suburbia*, 1895, 'An' you're the pusson as we've took the liberty with.' A better, because less obvious example, is *wuss* (worse).

stab, n.—2. An attempt, as in 'Let's have a stab at it!': Services: since ca. 1930. H. & P. Adopted from U.S.: J. Flynt, *The World of Graft*, 1901, has it. Cf. Fr. > S.E. *coup*.—3. A medical inoculation: Australian Services': 1939–45 (and after). B., 1943.

stable mate. 'A horse that develops such an affection for his stable companion that he will sicken if separated from him. Sometimes the affection is mutual. It can become a serious and difficult problem.' (Leechman, April 1967.) Coll.: late C. 19–20.

stable pea. The horse fancied by the members of its stable: racing: since ca. 1920. Arthur J. Sarl, 1938. With a pun on *sweet pea*.

Stable Yard, the. The Horse Guards, Whitehall: Londoners' and Army: ca. 1810–60. Richard Aldington, *Wellington*, 1946.

stack on a blue. To start a brawl or fight: Australian (mostly soldiers'): since ca. 1920.

Lawson Glassop, *We Were the Rats*, 1944. *Stack*: ex card-playing; *blue*, because the air is, with oaths.

stack on an act. A variant of **bung on an act** above. Since ca. 1925. (B., 1959.)

stack one's drapery. To place one's hat and coat on the ground prior to fighting: Australian: since ca. 1920. B., 1942.

stack-up. A synonym of **pile-up**, n., 2: racing cyclists': since ca. 1945.

stacked, esp. *well stacked*. (Of a girl) possessing large and attractive breasts: Canadian: adopted, ca. 1942, from U.S. Perhaps from playing-cards. The shorter form 'seems to have displaced *well stacked* in Australia' (B.P., mid-1963).

staff, n. (p. 821). Also a Colour Sergeant or a Quartermaster Sergeant: C. 20. (P-G-R.)

Staff College. See **studying for . . .**

staffy. A Staff Officer: Naval officers': C. 20.

stag, n.—9. A half-grown bull: Australian: C. 20. B., 1942.—10. 'An imperfectly castrated ram' (B., 1959): Aus. rural: C. 20.

stag, go. To go to, e.g., a party without a female companion: Canadian: adopted, ca. 1925, ex U.S. Cf. *stag-party* on p. 822.

stag, on. 'On sentry duty as a roving picket; on the prowl': Services (orig. Army): C. 20. H. & P. See **stag**, n., 8 (p. 821).

stag, the. Ny*stag*mus (a succession of involuntary eyeball-twitchings): miners': late C. 19–20.

stag or shag? Without or with female companion?: Australian c.p.: since late 1940's. Cf. **stag, go**, above, and **shag**, n., 1 (p. 748).

stage-dooring. Hanging about the scenes, or about doors reserved for actors: theatrical coll.: from ca. 1870. B. & L.

stagger juice. In the Royal Navy, it = Navy rum. Granville.

staggering Bob. A calf: Canadian and Australian: mid-C. 19–20. Ex Irish and North Country dial.; semantically cf. *quaking cheat* (p. 675).

staggering juice. See **stagger-juice** (*Dict.*).

Staggers. St Stephen's House: Oxford undergraduates': since ca. 1930. (Marples, 2.) Probably after **Jaggers.**

staggy. The adj. of **stag**, n., 9 and 10: Aus. rural: C. 20. (B., 1959.)

staining, n. An effusion of blood: hospitals' euphemistic coll.: C. 20. (Dymphna Cusack, *Say No to Death*, 1951.) Strictly, it is medical coll. for a slight discharge of blood.

stairs!, on the. A tailors' c.p. (from ca. 1860) when a job is called for. B. & L. Cf. *up in Annie's room*.

stake, n.—3. A (usually large) sum of money: Canadian coll.: late C. 19–20. 'He made a stake in gold-mining.'

stake, v. To give, or to lend for a long while, something to (someone): coll.: late C. 19–20, apparently Canadian before, ca. 1920, it became English. 'Will you stake me to a dinner?' As Dr Leechman notes, it orig. meant 'to supply someone (e.g., a prospector) with food and equipment on the understanding that a predetermined proportion of any finds shall go to the man doing the staking' (Leechman). Cf. the synonymous **grub-stake** above.

stale, adj. (Of freight) overdue: railwaymen's: since ca. 1920, but esp. since ca. 1940. (*Railway*.) Proleptic. Cf. **stinker**, 13, below.

stale drunk, adj. Having been drunk at night

and having taken too many spirit stimulants the next morning: from ca. 1860. B. & L.

Stalin's barrel organ. A Russian multi-barrelled rocket launcher copied by the Germans: Army: 1942–5. Ex the deafening noise it made. (Peter Sanders.)

*****stalk.** A tie-pin: c.: C. 20. F. D. Sharpe, *The Flying Squad*, 1938.—2. An erection: low: since ca. 1910.

stalk, the.—2. 'The flag is "the stalk" and to "do a stalker" is to carry a passenger without pulling the flag down. "Stalking a job" is doing the same thing,' Herbert Hodge, *Cab, Sir?*, 1939: taxi-drivers': since ca. 1910; since 1918 the phrases.

stalk a job. See prec.

stalker, do a. See **stalk, the,** 2.

stallion. A piebald horse: circusmen's: from ca. 1860. B. & L.—2. A prostitute's customer: prostitutes' c.: C. 20.

stam, short for *estam*, is an estaminet: Army: 1914–18.—2. Hence, short for *estaminet* (i.e. baseless) *rumour*: 1915–18.

stammer and stutter. Butter: theatrical rhyming s.: late C. 19–20. Franklyn, *Rhyming*. Recorded earlier in Sydney Lester, *Vardi the Palarey*, (?) 1937.

*****stamp one's drum.** To punch a hole in one's billy or kettle when it has become too old for further use; gen. as vbl n., *stamping* . . .: tramps' c.: late C. 19–20.

'Indians in western Canada and Eskimos usually punch a hole in the bottom or otherwise damage any goods left on a grave. Some say this is to release the spirit of the object and render it available for use in the next world, others (more mundane) say it is to prevent their being stolen. This may well have been a circumpolar custom.' (Dr Douglas Leechman, anthropologist and language-lover.)

stamping-ground. A field, a park, a by-way, notoriously frequented for amorous dalliance: British Empire: late C. 19–20. Ex the stamping and covering by stallions.

stamps. A person of no account, esp. of no relevant status: Naval: since ca. 1945. If, for instance, an assistant issues stores to another while the storekeeper himself is present, the storekeeper might well exclaim, 'What am I, stamps?' —usually 'fucking stamps'.

Stamshaw nanny-goat. See **Torpoint chicken.**

stana shwaya! Wait a moment!: soldiers' Arabic: late C. 19–20. See **shwaiya,** above.

stand, v., 1 (p. 823): earlier in W. N. Glascock, *Sailors and Saints*, 1829, at I, 85. Moe.—2 (p. 823). Earlier in *Sessions*, July 6, 1842.

stand a bar of, cannot. To dislike (someone) intensely: Australian: since ca. 1920. Dal Stivens, in a story written in 1944.—2. To refuse to tolerate (e.g. an act): Aus.: since ca. 1920. Mary Durack, *Keep Him My Country*, 1955.

stand and freeze. Stand at ease: military jocular, rather than rhyming s.: ca. 1895–1935. Franklyn 2nd.

stand at ease.—2. Fleas: rhyming s.: late C. 19–20.

stand at the peg. (Of racehorse) to be left at the starting-point: Australian racing: since ca. 1925. (B., 1953.)

stand-by. An optimistic air passenger in the habit of standing by, in the hope that a reservation

will lapse: Canadian air-travel coll., verging on j.: since ca. 1954. (Leechman.)

stand by your beds! A c.p., mimicking self-importance and pretending to stir occupants of room to (greater) activity: Forces': 1939–45. 'Ex disciplinary order of superior on entering barrack room' (Atkinson).

stand (surname) **down.** To cost: Australian coll.: since ca. 1925. H. Drake Brockman, *Hot Gold*, 1940, 'Only stand you down eighty quid.'

stand from under. Thunder: theatrical rhyming s.: late C. 19–20. (Franklyn, *Rhyming*.)

stand-in. A deputy; one who takes your turn of duty: Services coll.: since ca. 1925. H. & P. Ex:

stand in for. To take (someone's) turn of duty; to stand by for him: Services coll.: since ca. 1925. Partridge, 1945. Ex the theatre.

stand on a fag-paper! C.p. advice to one who cannot reach up to something: mostly Londoners': from ca. 1920.

stand on everything! Hold it!; Await further orders!: R.A.F.: since ca. 1938. H. & P., 'To put the brakes on'. Perhaps a development from 'Tread on everything', applied to the model-T Ford, with its rapid deceleration accomplished best by the driver pressing down all the foot controls.

stand on me! Take my word for it: a fringe-of-the-underworld c.p.: since ca. 1930. Frank Norman, *Stand on Me*, 1959.

stand (or **be standing**) **on one leg.** To be caught —*caught standing* . . . is the usual form—doing something unofficial in official hours; to be in an awkward position: Services: since ca. 1935. H. & P. Cf. **caught with one's trousers down.**

stand one's peggy. See **peggy** . . .

*****stand over** (a person). Menacingly to demand money from: c., and low: from ca. 1910.

stand the bears. See 'Verbs'.

stand the score is a Naval variant of **stand** (the) **shot** on p. 824: C. 19 (W. N. Glascock, *Sketch-Book*, II, 1826.) Moe.

stand-to-attention. A pension: rhyming s.: since ca. 1919.

stand up, v.,—3. To coït with (a girl), as in 'He stood her up three times in one evening': low: C. 20. Orig. of perpendicular conjunction.

stand up drinks. 'To set out drinks,' B., 1942: Australian coll.: C. 20.

standing dish. 'Any one who is constantly lunching, dining, or calling at a house': Society coll.: from ca. 1870; slightly ob. B. & L. Ex the j. of cookery.

standing ground. 'The bottom of a goldmine shaft which needs no timbering' (B., 1959): Aus. coll.: late C. 19–20.

standing prick has no conscience, a. (See *Dict.*) An eminent scholar points out that in Nathaniel Field's *Amends for Ladies*, 1618, there is this arresting adumbration: 'O man, what art thou when thy cock is up?'

standover, n. A piece of criminal intimidation: *standover man*, one who practises this sort of intimidation (for money): low Australian: since ca. 1920. Kylie Tennant, *Foveaux*, 1939. Ex **stand over.**—2. Short for **standover man:** Australian: since ca. 1920. B., 1942.

*****standover, work the.** To act as a **standover man:** Australian c.: since ca. 1920. B., 1942. See **standover,** 1, and cf. **stand over.**

*standover man. See standover, 1: Australian c. (since ca. 1920) >, ca. 1930, low s. Baker.

*standover merchant. Variant of preceding term: Aus. c.: since ca. 1925; by 1935, low s. (B., 1959.)

*star, good on the. (Esp. of a building) easy to open, i.e. burgle: c. (— 1812). Vaux. Also good on the crack. See *good in the *Dict.*

star and garter!, my (p. 824). Orig. ex dazzling breast-worn decorations. Dr C. T. Onions, postcard of April 9, 1939.

star-ballock naked. A loose variant of *stark-ballock naked.*

star-gazer, 4 (p. 824), goes back to early C. 19; it occurs in W. N. Glascock, *Sketch-Book,* 2nd Series, 1834 (at II, 64). Moe.

*Star Hotel, sleep in the (p. 825). Also, by 1935 at latest, Australian. B., 1942.

star in the East, a. A fly-button showing: Public Schools': since ca. 1915.

star-queller. 'An actor whose imperfect acting mars that of better actors': theatrical: ca. 1880–1910. B. & L.

star turn. The central or most important person: coll.: C. 20. Leonard Merrick, *Peggy Harper,* 1911. Ex the music hall.

starboard light. Crème de menthe: since ca. 1920. Philip Macdonald, *The Rynox Mystery,* 1930. Both are green.

starbolic naked. A corruption of *stark-ballock naked,* utterly naked: low (esp. Australian): since ca. 1870. Brian Penton, *Inheritors,* 1936, ' "Is it true he makes the miners strip starbolic naked in front of him to show they ain't pinching any of his gold?" '

starch out of, take the (p. 825). Probably there is an allusion to the *semen virile.* A valued correspondent writes, 'I suspect a double pun. With the "starch" taken out of him, he is no longer "stiff".'

starched collars. Game birds: poachers': since ca. 1920.

stare at the ceiling over a man's shoulder. (Of women) to coït: feminine, but jocular rather than euphemistic: C. 20.

stares, the. The 'fixed, glassy-eyed look of unwilling divers who realize what they have let themselves in for. They know that they have to go, but delay it to the last' (Wilfred Granville, March 11, 1964): skin divers': since the late 1940's.

starie chelevek. A Commanding Officer; anyone in authority: Regular Army with Eastern service: C. 20. Lit., old man.

stark-ballock naked. See starbolic naked.

stark-bol(l)ux. Stark-naked: Australian: since ca. 1890. Leonard Mann, *A Murder in Sydney,* 1937. Ex prec.

stars and bars. See gridiron.

star's nap. To borrow (money from): C. 20. Rhyming on tap for, v. p. 865. Mostly theatrical: Franklyn 2nd.

start, n., 3. See *queer start.*—5. A job, employment: Australian: since ca. 1920. B., 1942. Ex. 3.

start, v., 1 (p. 825), had, in the Navy of late C. 18–mid-19, the more drastic sense, 'to beat with a rope's end', as in W. N. Glascock, *The Naval Sketch-Book,* I (p. 121), 1825. (Moe.) The corresponding n. is *starting,* also in Glascock, I, 1825.—2. To start (i.e. begin) to complain or reprimand or abuse or boast or reminisce: coll.: C. 19–20. Thus ' "When I was your age I was up and about at six in the morning." "Now don't you start," said Paula,' Gerald Kersh, *Men Are so Ardent,* 1935.

start a fowl-roost. See fowl-roost . . .

start in. To start, to begin: Canadian sol. coll.: C. 20. 'Now, don't you start in worrying.' 'He's started in drinking again!' (Leechman.)

start off the button. (Of a car) to begin running immediately: motor trade: since ca. 1918. Press the button and off she goes.

start something, as, e.g., 'Now you've started something!' To set afoot, deliberately or unwittingly, something that will have important or exciting consequences, coll.: adopted (via the cinema) ca. 1938 from U.S.—2. To render a girl pregnant: raffish: since ca. 1940. (A. B. Petch, April 1966.)

starter, 2 (p. 825). Its opposite is *stopper,* an astringent. These two terms, orig. undergraduates', occur in Compton Mackenzie's *Gallipoli Memories,* 1929, and date back to the 1890's.—3. (Only *starter.*) One who frequently changes his occupation or his employer: ca. 1810–80. *Sessions,* Feb. 1823.

starter's orders, under. See under . . . below.

starting. A reprimand; a beating: proletarian: from ca. 1860; ob. B. & L.

starvation corner. That seat at (esp. the dinner-) table, whose occupant is served last: Army officers': from ca. 1885.

starve, do a (p. 826), is also Australian. (Kylie Tennant, *The Honey Flow,* 1956.)

starve the bardies! A W. Australian variant of stone the crows!: C. 20. B., 1942. A *bardy* is a wood-grub.

starve the lizards! An Australian expletive: C. 20. (Source as for Bovril.) Cf. stone the crows! on p. 834. Also *mopokes!* and *wombats!*: B. 1942.

starver. See perisher.—2. A saveloy: Australian: since ca. 1910. B., 1942.

starving mush. See instalment mixture.

stash (p. 826). For discussion of etymology, see *Underworld.*—4. To hide (something); to put money into a bank account: Canadian: adopted, ca. 1925, ex U.S. 'He's got thousands stashed away!' (Leechman.) Clearly influenced by 'to *cache*'.—5. Hence (?), to place: adopted, ca. 1944, ex U.S. Nicholas Blake, *The Sad Variety,* 1964, 'Well, Leake stashed the wheel in the car park.'

stat. A statutory tenant: landlords' and property speculators': since ca. 1954. See the quotation at schwarz above.

stat dec. A statutory declaration: Australian spoken, esp. legal and journalistic: since ca. 1940. (B.P.)

State of Independence. Variant of states of independence (p. 826): 1821, P. Egan, *Life in London.*

State secret, it's a. A c.p., used by someone refusing to disclose information, however, trivial: since ca. 1933.

station bicycle. A sexually generous girl employed on a R.A.F. station: R.A.F.: since ca. 1940. Cf. the Australian *town bike.*

station bloke and station master. The police officer in charge of a station: police: since ca. 1920. *The Free-Lance Writer,* April 1948.

stationmaster. Station Commander: R.A.F.: since ca. 1930. Berrey; H. & P. Ex the railway title.

stave-off. A scratch meal: coll.: from ca. 1880. Binstead.

stay a minute. An estaminet: Army: 1914–18. (Reginald Pound, *The Lost Generation*, 1964.) By the vivid process of 'Hobson-Jobson'.

stay home. To stay at home: Canadian coll.: since ca. 1920. (Leechman.)

stay-put. One who holds his ground ('stays put'): coll., esp. Australian: since ca. 1950. (B.P.)

stay-tape.—2. A dry-goods clerk or salesman: trade: mid-C. 19–20; ob. B. & L.

staying at Mrs Greenfields'. See 'Hauliers' Slang' and cf. *Greenfields* (, *Mrs*).

steady, n. (p. 826, end). In the Navy, 'a man's fiancée or "regular" girl friend' (Granville).

steady, adj. '"In the Guards, son, 'Steady' means 'Absolutely lousy'. If you want to sort of spit in a man's eye, call him Steady," ' Gerald Kersh, *They Die with Their Boots Clean*, 1941. An extension of S.E. nuance 'dependable but slow'.—2. Easy-going; 'decent': non-Guards units of the Army: since ca. 1939. (P-G-R.)

steady, Barker! A c.p. dating from ca. 1941. Adopted from the Navy's version of the B.B.C. radio-programme, 'Merry-Go-Round'. *Steady, Barker!* is an adaptation of that evergreen, **steady, the Buffs!**, q.v. in the *Dict.* (E. P. in *The Radio Times*, Dec. 6, 1946.)

steady, go. See **go steady**.

steady as a crock, as. Applied to someone hardly 'as steady as a rock': since ca. 1940. (A. B. Petch, March 1966.)

steady man. 'One who is so slow as to be practically useless,' H. & P.: Services: since ca. 1930. Sarcastic. Cf. **steady**, adj.

steak, two-eyed. See **two-eyed steak** (*Dict.*).

steak and bull's eyes. Steak-and-kidney pudding: low eating-house: C. 20. Frank Jennings, *Tramping*, 1932.

steak and kid. Steak-and-kidney pudding or pie: mostly eating-house employees' and their imitators': since ca. 1910.

Steak and Kidney. Sydney: Australian rhyming s.: C. 20. (B., 1945.)

steak and kidney pie. A theatrical (late C. 19–20) variant of *mince pie*, eye. (Franklyn, *Rhyming*.)

steam, n., 4. Also in New Zealand. (B., 1941.) By 1945, no longer low. (B.P.)—5. Hence, any wine: Aus.: since ca. 1945. Nino Culotta, *Cop This Lot*, 1960.

steam, v. To work hard and pertinently: R.A.F.: since ca. 1928. Jackson. To bring from 'steaming' to 'boiling'. Cf. next entry.

steam, v.—2. To work at high pressure; to hustle oneself: Naval: since ca. 1930.

steam, like. Fast, vigorously; easily; excellently: Australian coll.: since ca. 1920. Lawson Glassop, *We Were the Rats*, 1944, 'We reefed watches and rings off 'em like steam.'

steam, under one's own. Unaided: coll.: C. 20. Prob. ex locomotives not using a shunter. 'I have always thought this, as applied to ships or locomotives and, by extension, any moving or should-be moving object, meant "Damaged but still able to raise enough steam to proceed slowly"' (Leechman, April 1967).

steam boatswain is recorded earlier (in the shorter form) in 'Taffrail'.

steam chickens. Carrier-borne aircraft: Naval: 1943 +. (P-G-R.) 'Ex the British invented steam-propelled launching catapult above R.N. carriers?': Ramsey Spencer.

steam pig. Anybody—or, come to that, anything—either not defined or not easily definable: railwaymen's: since ca. 1930. (*Railway*.)

steam puncher. A steam-driven pinnace: Naval: late C. 19–20; ob. Granville.

steam radio. Radio (sound only): coined by the B.B.C. in 1958, as Mr Val Gielgud tells me; general since ca. 1961. In a sense, radio was outmoded by T.V., much as the steam engine was outmoded by the internal-combustion engine.

steamed-up.—2. Heated; angry: since ca. 1925; Australian by late 1920's (B., 1942).—3. Ready for sexual congress: Canadian: since ca. 1930.

steamer.—2. Mr James Curtis writes (March 1937): 'A steamer can, I think, be differentiated from a mug. A steamer wants something back for his money. He is a bookmaker's or a prostitute's client or a "con."-man's victim.'—3. A dish of stewed kangaroo, flavoured with pork: Australian: late C. 19–20.

steamer ticket. A master mariner's certificate valid only on steamships: nautical coll.: from ca. 1880; ob. William McFee, *Sailors of Fortune*, 1930. Punning a passenger's ticket on a steamer.

steaming, or scram, bag. A small bag, containing toilet and other necessary gear, drawn from the purser's stores by a sailor suddenly dispatched to a troopship where heavy gear is forbidden: Naval: since the middle 1940's. Probably *scram* = scramble; *steaming* perhaps refers to 'in a steaming hurry'.

steaming covers. Wren's knickers: Naval: since early 1940's. From the covers protecting guns when a ship is at sea in heavy weather.

steamy, n. A steam laundry: Glasgow s.—coll.: C. 20. Iain Crawford, *Scare the Gentle Citizen*, 1966.

steamy side of life, the. A housewife's or washer-woman's life in scullery or wash-house: jocular domestic: C. 20. On *seamy side*.

steel-chest. A fearless person; a hardened, courageous soldier: Guards': since ca. 1916. Cf. the cliché'd *hearts of steel*.

steel helmet. An Anderson shelter: esp. Londoners': late 1940 +. (Mrs C. H. Langford, letter of July 29, 1941.)

steel jockey. A train jumper: Australian: since ca. 1925. B., 1942. He *rides* free; *steel* wheels, etc., of the train.

Steele Rudds. Potatoes: Australian rhyming s. (on *spuds*): C. 20. (B., 1945.) Steele Rudd's *On Our Selection* and *Our New Selection* were famous in the Australia of ca. 1900–14 and, indeed, since.

steeler. A steel helmet: Army: 1914 +.

steelie or **-ly;** mostly in pl. *steelies.* 'Not real marbles, but large ball-bearings' (B.P.): Australian schoolchildren's: since ca. 1920.—2. A steel guitar: since ca. 1955. Ngaio Marsh, *Death at the Dolphin*, 1967.

steeped. Homosexual in practice or tendency: Society: ca. 1890–1905. *The Listener*, March 10, 1937. Ex *steeped in the higher philosophy*.

steeplechaser. 'A "ropey" landing, going across the airstrip in a succession of bounces' (John Bebbington): R.A.F.: since the middle 1930's,

*steer, v. To pick up (a 'mug'): c.: C. 20.

steer-decorating, since ca. 1945; bull-dogging, ca. 1910–45. A rodeo method of throwing a steer by grasping one horn and the muzzle and twisting the neck: Canadian.

steer small (p. 827) is much earlier: 1806, John Davis, *The Post-Captain*. (Moe.)

Stella. Egyptian beer: Services in N. Africa: World War II. Ex a well-known brand.

Stella by Starlight. Alliterative nickname for girls named Stella (L. *stella*, a star): Australian: since ca. 1925. (B.P.)

Stellenbosch; gen. be Stellenbosched. To relegate (a person) to a position where he can do little or no harm; esp. of an officer: military: 1900, Kipling in *The Daily Express*, June 16 (O.E.D.); very ob. Ex Stellenbosch as a base in the South African War.

stem jack (or J.) 'A small Union Flag flown in the bows of a battleship while the anchor is down' (Granville): Naval coll.: C. 20.

stenoggy. A stenographer: (esp. girl) clerks': since ca. 1925. (W. B. M. Ferguson, *London Lamb*, 1939.)

step, n.—4. See gradus (*Dict.*).

step!, mind your, has, since ca. 1940, been commoner than *mind the step*, q.v. at step, mind the, on p. 828. By 1960, *the* was virtually †.

step below. See 'Die'.

step-ins. Women's knickers that require no fastening: since ca. 1918: feminine coll. >, by 1940, S.E. Cf. pull-ons (*Dict.*).

step it. See step, v., 1, in *Dict.*

step out (p. 828) goes right back as far as 1806: John Davis, *The Post-Captain*. (Moe.)

*stepney. A white-slaver's fancy girl: white-slave c.: C. 20. (A. Londres translated, 1928.) Mr John Yeowell, in *The Daily Telegraph* of March 9, 1967, suggests that *stepney* perhaps = *Stepney*, short for a presumed *Stepney Green*, rhyming s. on *quean*, a prostitute. But Julian Franklyn, the authority on Cockney slang, thinks it comes from *stepney*, a spare wheel carried on a motor car. The latter seems to be the more probable.

stepper.—5. A smart, good-looking girl: mostly Cockney: C. 20; ob. by 1940. (A Neil Lyons, *Clara*, 1912.)

stepping it, vbl n. See step, v., 2, in *Dict.*

*steps, up the. At the Old Bailey: c.: late C. 19–20.—2. Hence, committed to Sessions or Assizes: c.: C. 20. F. D. Sharpe, 1938.

sterks, give (someone) the. To annoy, to infuriate; to render low-spirited: Australian: since ca. 1920. Prob. *sterks = sterics* = hysterics.

sterky. Afraid, frightened: Australian: since ca. 1939. Jean Devanney, *By Tropic Sea and Jungle*, 1944, 'He's a bit sterky, too'; B., 1953, says that it comes ex *stercocoraceous*, faecal; perhaps rather ex the preceding entry.

stern (p. 828) is applied also to a hound: hunting: mid-C. 19–20. (Sir W. B. Thomas, *Hunting England*, 1936.)

stern approach. *Venus aversa*: educated bawdy: since ca. 1945.

stern over appetite. Head over heels: Australian: since ca. 1930. Dal Stivens, *Jimmy Brockett*, 1951, 'I hit him on the chin and he went stern over appetite.'

stern-perisher. See bum-freezer, 2, which obviously suggested it.

stew, n.—3. A 'fixed' boxing match or horse race: Australian sporting: since ca. 1920. (B., 1943.)—4. Hence a case framed against a serviceman: Australian servicemen's: 1939–45. (B., 1953.)

stewed prune. A tune: rhyming: late C. 19–20.

stewkeeper. An Army cook: Australian soldiers': 1939–45. (B., 1943.)

stews. Fellows, chaps, strictly if crowded together or closely associated: Canadian: adopted, early in C. 20, ex U.S. From '*students*'. (Jack Munroe, *Mopping Up!*, 1918.)

stewy (of tea) that has stewed too long: Australian coll.: since ca. 1920. (Margaret Trist, 1944.)

stick, n.—13. Short for joy-stick, 1 (p. 445): R.A.F. coll.: since ca. 1925. Jackson.—14. (Ex sense 9: p. 828.) A wireless mast: R.A.F.: since ca. 1930. Sgt G. Emanuel, letter of March 29, 1945.—15. Short for sticky-beak (p. 831): Australian: since ca. 1930. B., 1942.—16. Short for *stick of bombs*, 'the entire load released in one operation so that the bombs hit the ground in a straight line' (Jackson): R.A.F. coll.: since ca. 1939.—17. See shill.—18. A small glass of beer: since ca. 1925. Cf. *finger* of spirits.—19. A ladder: builders': late C. 19–20. Jocular.—20. A log: Australian sawmills': late C. 19–20. K. S. Prichard, *Working Bullocks*, 1926; Kylie Tennant, *Lost Haven*, 1947, 'Great yokes of bullocks ... dragging the "sticks" from the forests'. Ex sense 9 (p. 828).—21. A column of newsprint: journalistic: C. 20.—22. A two-up 'kip': Australian: since ca. 1910. (B., 1943.)—23. Penis: (?) C. 17–20. Cf. the archaic Fr. *verge*.

Sense 9 (p. 828) occurs, along with the variant sense 'a spar', in W. N. Glascock, *Sailors and Saints*, 1829. (Moe.)

Of sense 21, Dr Leechman, in April 1967, writes: 'When I was setting type by hand (ca. 1910) a stick of type was about thirteen lines, which was all my composing stick would hold. When the stick was full the contents were transferred to a galley. An unimportant news item was quickly disposed of: "Don't give it more than a stick," the editor would say.'

stick, a bit of. A (heavy) shelling: Army: 1940 +. Cf. *stonk*.

stick, get the.—2. To receive a severe shelling, or to be otherwise 'punished': Army, esp. 'Kitchener's Army': W.W. I. Ex the schoolboys *get the stick*, to be caned. (A. B. Petch.)

stick, knock away a. To hit, with cannon fire, the masts or yards of an enemy ship: Naval officers': ca. 1800–40. Fredk Marryat, *The King's Own*, 1834, on p. 112 of the 1896 edition. (Moe.) Cf. stick, n., 9, in *Dict.*

stick, on the, adv. and adj. (Of a conductor) using the baton: musical coll.: C. 20.

stick, up the.—2. Pregnant: low, esp. Cockneys' and North of England, from ca. 1920. Cf. up the pole.

stick (someone) a length. To reprimand, or to punish, severely: Army: since ca. 1925. (P-G-R.)

stick (someone) for (a thing, a price or charge). To charge someone too much; make someone pay so much: C. 20.

stick in, v.i. To work steadily at one's job; to keep it: Glasgow coll.: C. 20. MacArthur & Long.

stick in it, with a (p. 829). 'To "put a stick"

in a soft drink is to add a slug of whisky or other hard liquor. I first met it in about 1910.' (Leechman.)

stick in the mud occurs as coll. nickname as early as: *Sessions*, 7th session, 1733, 'James Baker, alias, *Stick-in-the-Mud*'.

stick it!—2. A contemptuous exclamation to a person; 'Oh, buzz off!': low: late C. 19–20. I.e. up your anus. Also *stick it up your jumper!* and—a low Australian variant, addressed only to males—*stick it up your cunt!*: the former, since the late 1930's; the latter, since ca. 1935.

stick it into. To ask (someone) for a loan or other favour: Australian: since ca. 1910. (B., 1943.)

stick it, Jerry! An Army c.p. of ca. 1914–18. It has nothing to do with *Jerry*, 'a German (soldier)'; Lew Lake, the Cockney comedian († Nov. 5, 1939), originated a sketch, 'The Bloomsbury Burglars', featuring Nobbler and Jerry; as Nobbler, he would, as they hurled missiles at off-stage policemen, shout to his partner, 'Stick it, Jerry!' *Daily Express*, Nov. 6, 1939.

stick it in (p. 829). Earlier in W. T. Moncrieff, *Tom and Jerry*, 1821, in v.t. form (. . . *into*).—3. To work hard and fast: Australian: C. 20. B., 1942.

stick it on. To strike (someone): low (? originally c.): since ca. 1945. (Norman.)

stick like shit to a blanket. To be very sticky: low coll.: late C. 19–20.

stick one's neck out. To ask for trouble: since the early 1930's: perhaps originally Army. (P-G-R.) By exposing one's head.

stick out, 2 (p. 829), occurs in two Canadian similes that verge upon c.p. status: *he sticks* (or *stuck*) *out like a sore thumb* (polite) and . . . *like the balls on a bulldog*: since ca. 1920.

*****stick-slinger** (p. 829) is also late C. 19–20 Australian. (B., 1943.)

stick to.—2. To retain; hold (something) back: coll.: Feb. 7, 1845, *Sessions*.

stick-up, n.—2. A delay; a quandary: Australian: C. 20. B., 1942. Ex **stick up,** v., 5 (*Dict.*).—3. (Ex **stick up,** v.) A hold-up robbery; to hold up and rob: Canadian coll.: adopted, the v., ca. 1930; the n., ca. 1941; ex U.S. Also Australian: B., 1943.

stick up, as v. See **sticks, up,** in *Dict.*

stick up for (p. 830). Earlier example found in Anon., *A History of Van Diemen's Land*, 1835, at p. 271.

stick up goods. To obtain them on credit: Australian: since ca. 1910. Baker. Ex **stick-up,** v., 4 (*Dict.*).

stickem. Cement or gum: fair-grounds': C. 20. 'He had grafted the tubed stickem for years. (He had sold *a special cement in tubes*, used for sticking on rubber soles and dozens of other household repairs.)': W. Buchanan-Taylor, *Shake It Again*, 1943.

sticker.—10. A butcher: proletarian coll.: from ca. 1840. B. & L. Ex S.E. *sticker*, a slaughterman.—11. A small, sticky-backed poster: coll.: C. 20.—12. Usually pl. *stickers*, such goods in short supply as are slow in coming from manufacturers or wholesalers: trade: since ca. 1941.—13. (*Sticker*.) The Navy's nickname for anyone surnamed 'Leach' or 'Leech': C. 20. One of the inseparable nicknames.—14. A paperhanger: builders': late C. 19–20.—15. An awkward or

difficult question asked by a member of the public: Canadian librarians': since ca. 1920. (Leechman.)

sticking, or **dead stick.** A contretemps in which all the actors get muddled: theatrical: from ca. 1860; the former, very ob. B. & L.

sticks. Naval use of sense 8: earlier in 'Taffrail'.—10. (*The sticks.*) The outback: adopted, ca. 1945, ex U.S. ' "People will think that you come from the sticks" is often heard from parents admonishing their children' (B.P.). Cf. **bush,** n., 6, and **mulga madness,** both above. Dr Douglas Leechman, however, recalls that, 'When I was in south Wales, at Llanstefan, it was quite common for the people of the village to gather in the evenings to sing together in "the sticks", by which they meant a patch of trees just below the ruined castle. And that was some seventy years ago, but I can still hear them.'

Sense 3 (p. 830): earlier in W. N. Glascock, *Sailors and Saints* (I, 178), 1829. Moe.

sticks, (as) cross as two (p. 830): 'still common in Australia' (B.P., 1965).

sticks, knock all to. See **sticks, beat all to** (*Dict.*).

sticks and stones. One's household goods and possessions: proletarian coll.: mid-C. 19–20. B. & L.

sticks and whistles. A parade of warders coming on duty for the day: prison coll.: C. 20. They are inspected, to see whether they are carrying their batons and whistles. (Norman.)

sticky, n., 3 (p. 831): since late 1940's, usu. cellulose tape (Sellotape, Scotch tape, etc.).— 4. A 'sticky', i.e. damp and difficult, pitch: cricketers' coll., esp. Australian: C. 20.—5. A free pass on the buses: London busmen's: since ca. 1930.—6. A 'sticky beak': Australian: since ca. 1930. (B.P.)

sticky, adj.—6. Inquisitive: Australian: C. 20. B., 1942. Cf. **stick,** n., 15.

sticky, have a. To have an inquisitive lookround: Australian: since ca. 1935. (B.P.)

sticky, play. To hold fast to one's money or goods; esp. of one who has recently done well: since ca. 1920. Cf. **sticky,** adj., 3 (p. 831).

sticky-beak, v. To pry; to snoop: Australian: since ca. 1930. Margaret Trist, 1944, 'They only come to sticky-beak'. Ex the n. (on p. 831).

sticky-fingered. Thievish; covetous: proletarian: from ca. 1870. B. & L.

sticky on. See **sticky at** (*Dict.*).

stiff, n.—11. (p. 831). Earlier in 'Ouida', *The Massarenes*, 1897. (P. Gaskell.)—12. A nontipper: ships' stewards': C. 20. Dave Marlowe, 1937. Cf. sense 6.—13. A police summons: Australian low: C. 20. B., 1942. Cf. sense 1 (p. 831). On stiff paper.

stiff, adj.—6. Hard, severe towards someone: Australian: since ca. 1910. B., 1942.

stiff as a crutch. See **crutch** . . .

stiff blade. See 'Tavern terms', § 2; cf. the modern **stout fellow** (*Dict.*).

stiff-box. Obituary list in newspaper: Australian journalistic: since ca. 1915. B., 1942. Ex **stiff,** n., 5 (*Dict.*).

stiff for. Certain for, certain to win: Australian sporting: since ca. 1920. Baker. Ex **stiff,** adj., 3 (*Dict.*).

stiff-rump, n. (p. 831) is coll. rather than s. and the date should read 'late C. 17–early 19'; it is recorded, as an adj., in B.E., 1699.

stiff 'un.—3. A ticket already cancelled: busmen's: C. 20. Cf. sense 2 (p. 831).—4. An erection: schoolboys': late C. 19–20.

stiffen, v.—To swindle (someone); usually in passive: Australian: since ca. 1920. Baker.

stiffen the crows—lizards—snakes! An Australian exclamation: C. 20. Baker.

stiffened, get, is the usual passive of **stiffen**, 4: B., 1943.

stiffener.—2. A punch or blow that renders one unconscious: mid-C. 19–20.—3. A cigarette card: C. 20. Originally inserted to stiffen paper packets of cigarettes.—4. A (very) boring person: R.A.F. (mostly officers): since ca. 1937. Jackson, 'He bores you to death, i.e., stiff.'

stifficat or -cut. Certificate: sol.: C. 20.

stifler.—3. A dram of strong spirit: Anglo-Irish: C. 19. 'A Real Paddy', *Real Life in Ireland*, 1822. It takes one's breath away.

stift. One—usually a male—who won't work: Romanies' s.: since ca. 1920. (Robert M. Dawson.) Ex **stiff**, n., 7 and perhaps 8 (p. 831).

still alive and kissing. A c.p. applied to the sexy: since ca. 1955. A pun on *still alive and kicking*.

still in a bottle of stout, often particularized as *. . . a bottle of Guinness*. (Of a person) unborn: smokeroom wit: since ca. 1945. Ex the body-building virtues of good stout.

still running—like Charley's Aunt. A c.p., implying the durability of the evergreen and applied esp. to plays and films: C. 20. Ex the continuing popularity of that verdant farce.

still sow.—2. See 'Harlots'.

stimmt. See 'Prisoner-of-War Slang', opening paragraph.

sting, n. Penis: lowish: late C. 19–20. Cf. **prick**, 3 (*Dict.*).—2. Dope, esp. if by hypodermic, administered to a horse; hence *give* (it) a *sting*: Australian sporting: since ca. 1945.—3. Strong drink: Australian: C. 20. (K. S. Prichard, *Coonardoo*, 1920.) Ex *stingo*.

sting, v.—6. To inoculate with a hypodermic: Services s. (— 1930) >, by 1940, coll. H. & P.

stingah. An occ. spelling, the usual pronunciation, and the orig. form (ex Malay *setengah*, half) of:

stinger.—3. A small drink, at any time of the day: Singapore: from ca. 1890.—4. A brakeman: Canadian (and U.S.) railroadmen's (— 1931).

stink, 2, is also a fight.

stink-pot.—3. A motor-car: ca. 1898–1914. (Maxwell Gray, *The Great Refusal*, 1906.)—4. A small firework: Australian: C. 20. (B., 1943.)

stinker, 5 (p. 832), began as London, esp. boxing, s.: 1821, Pierce Egan, *Life in London*.—9. A sultry or very hot, humid day: Australian: C. 20. B., 1942. Also *stonkers*.—10. Mostly in pl., *stinkers*, R.A.M.C. laboratory workers: R.A.M.C.: since ca. 1915.—11. A police informer: low Australian: since ca. 1920. (B., 1943.)—12. The Blue-Winged Shoveller: Australian: since ca. 1910. (B., 1943.)—13. A delayed wagon 'remaining for several days in a marshalling yard' (*Railway*): railwaymen's: C. 20. Cf. **stale**, adj., above.

Sense 7 was 'used rather earlier by Kipling in "Regelus": "The next passage was what was technically"—read "slangily"—"known as a stinker"—hence, presumably in use in Kipling's schooldays, c. 1875' (Robert Clairborne).

Stinker, the. A fortune-telling device, often called 'the Mystic Writer' or 'the Gypsy Queen':

grafters': from ca. 1910. Philip Allingham, in *Cheapjack*, 1934, describes it at pp. 303–4.

stinkeroo. A poor show-place (town, etc.), with few customers: Canadian carnival s.: since ca. 1920. It 'stinks'. Contrast **lulu**.

stinkibus.—2. (Ex sense 1.) 'A cargo of spirits that had lain under water so long as to be spoiled,' John Davidson, *Baptist Lake*, 1896: smugglers': C. 19.

stinking, adj., 3 (p. 833). By 1939, general middle-class s.: cf. (e.g.) P-G-R. Also Australian: D'Arcy Niland, *Call Me . . .*, 1958.

stinking with (esp. money). Possessed of much (e.g. money): coll.: since ca. 1916. Cf. **lousy with** (*Dict.*).

stinko, n. Liquor; esp., wine: Australian: since ca. 1925. D'Arcy Niland, *Call Me When the Cross Turns Over*, 1958, 'This is a little bottle of stinko to go with it'. Cf. the adj.

stinko, adj. Exceedingly drunk: mostly clerks': from ca. 1928. Ex *stinking drunk* on *blotto*. Hence *stinko paralytico*, as in Evelyn Waugh's *Put Out More Flags*, 1942, and *stinko profundo*, as in Terence Rattigan's play *While the Sun Shines*, 1943. (Peter Sanders.)

stinks (p. 833). ' "Stinks" for chemistry is relegated to readers of mediocre school stories': *New Society*, Aug. 22, 1963, article 'From the blackboard jungle'.

stinksman. See **stinkman** (*Dict.*).

stinkubus. See **stinkibus** (*Dict.*).

stinky.—2. A cheap baked-clay marble: Australian children's: late C. 19–20. Baker.

stipe.—2. A stipendiary race-course steward: Australian sporting: C. 20. B., 1942. By 1930, also British. ' "Stipe" is short for stipendiary steward or stewards' secretary': John Lawrence, in *The Sunday Telegraph*, Aug. 13, 1961.

stir, n., 2 (p. 833). Also, since ca. 1920, Army s. for detention. H. & P.

stir-happy. Adversely affected by prison-life, whether at the time or afterwards: since ca. 1940 (see *Underworld*): orig. c., but by 1950 also police s. John Gosling, 1959.

stir it up!, often accompanied by a mime of stirring a huge cauldron. A third party's remark upon, and stimulation of, a quarrel either brewing or already in progress: c.p.: since ca. 1955. (Atkinson.)

stir shit out of. To scold bitterly: reprimand severely: New Zealand: since ca. 1940. 'Wait till I get hold of him! I'll stir shit out of him.'

Stitch. See 'Nicknames'.

stitch, n.—3. Elliptical for *stitch of canvas*: nautical, esp. Naval, coll.: since ca. 1790: by 1850, S.E. W. N. Glascock, *Sketch-Book*, I, 1825, 'Standing out on a wind, with every stitch they could crack.' Moe.

stitch, v. 'To overcome, to beat in a fight or contest' (B., 1953): Australian: since ca. 1930. Probably suggested by **sewed-up**, 5 (p. 747).

stitched. Tipsy: Services: since ca. 1925. H. & P.—2. Beaten, defeated: Australian: since ca. 1920. B., 1942. All sewn up.

stizzle.—2. To cane (a boy): Tonbridge: since ca. 1870. Marples, 'Origin obscure': ? a blend of *stick* + *sizzle*.

stoat. A virile person, esp. male and mostly in *fuck like a stoat*, frequently and athletically: low coll.: since ca. 1870.

stocious. Variant of **stotious**.

stock-sick is, in sense, a more general variant of *sheep-sick*: B., 1943.

stockbanger; stockbanging. A stockman; mustering (e.g. cattle): Australian: C. 20. Archer Russell, *In Wild Australia*, 1934. Cf. **cattle banger**.

Stockbrokers' Belt, the. See **Gin and Jaguar Belt** above. Also *stockbroker belt, the*.

stockbroker's taxi. A 'showy' motorcar, e.g. the Jaguar: since ca. 1960. *The New Statesman*, Feb. 5, 1965.

Stockbrokers' Tudor. Bogus Tudor architecture: since ca. 1950; by 1960, coll.; by 1966, virtually S.E. Cf. **North Oxford Gothic** above. ('eter Sanders.)

stocking-soles gun. A canon with high-velocity shell: Army: 1914–18. Cf. **stocking-foot** (p. 834).

stodge, n., 3: recorded earlier by B. & L.— Sense 5: ib., as c. This sense—also as 'extra food'—existed at Rugby School as early as 1880. As *the Stodge*, it = the School shop, where one can buy extra food: since ca. 1925. Ex **stodge,** n., 3. (D. F. Wharton, Oct. 24, 1965.)

stodger, 4 (p. 834). Also Tonbridge.

stodgery. See **stodger,** 2, in *Dict.*

stogy (p. 834). Since 1800, the preferred spelling of the place-name has been *Conestoga*.

stoked. Thrilled, as in 'He's stoked on [*or* about] surfing: Australian teenagers': esp. surfers': since the late 1950's. (*Pix*, Sept. 28, 1963.) Semantically 'hot and excited'.

stokehold bosun. Warrant Engineer of the Engine-Room: Naval: since 1925. Granville.

stokes. 'Anyone employed in the stoking side of the ship,' H. & P.: Navy: C. 20.

[*****stolen ken,** a broker's shop: old c., according to B. & L. But the whole entry is suspect. So is their **stomp drawers,** stockings.]

stom Jack. See **stomjack** (*Dict.*).

stomach, feel butterflies in the (or **one's**). To experience tremors, either of excitement or of apprehension—or of both: aircrews': 1940 +; by 1948, fairly gen.

stomacher. An apple that produces a stomach-ache: lower classes', esp. children's: C. 20.

stomp. To dance: Australian teenagers', esp. surfies': since ca. 1956. Ex U.S. dial. *stomp*, to stomp one's feet, walk heavily. Hence *stomping*, n. and adj., dancing. (In, e.g., *Sunday Mirror*, Sept. 22, 1963.) Hence also *stomp*, a dance; whence *stomp hall*, a dance hall.

stomping, n. and adj. See preceding.

stomping ground. A 'stamping ground'—one's habitat or district or *milieu*: Australian teenagers', esp. surfies': since ca. 1959. Cf. **stomp,** v., above.

stone, n.—5. A drug-taking, esp. of one of the less harmful drugs: addicts': since ca. 1955. (Alan Diment, *The Dolly Dolly Spy*, 1963.) Cf. **stones,** 2, below.

stone is a common Australian coll. intensive, sometimes adjectival and sometimes adverbial; as in *stone cert*, a dead-certainty, and its synonym, *stone moral*, and *stone motherless broke*, penniless and alone: late C. 19–20. (B., 1942–3.)

stone and a beating, give a (p. 834), probably arose a generation earlier: cf. G. Lawrence, *Sword and Gown*, 1859, 'I could give him 21 lb., and a beating, any day.' (Dr D. Pechtold.)

stone-blinder. A sure winner: horse-racing: since ca. 1910. Arthur J. Sarl, *Gamblers*, 1938. Cf. **stonge-ginger** (p. 834).

stone-bonker. A variant of **stone blinder:** since ca. 1945. 'Stone-bonker certainties' occurs in Leslie Frewin's editing, *The Boundary Book*, 1962.

stone-fence. A drink of whiskey with nothing added: ca. 1870–1910. B. & L., at *neat*; at *stone-fence*, however, it is defined as 'brandy and ale'.

stone finish, the. The very end: Australian coll.: C. 20. (Kylie Tennant, *Lost Haven*, 1947.)

stone frigates. 'Naval Barracks or Shore Establishments; . . . usually named after the old frigates' (P-G-R.): Naval coll.: late C. 19–20.

Stone House, the. Prison: since ca. 1930. (B.B.C., Sept. 22, 1963.)

stone-jug, 2 (p. 834): † by 1960. Franklyn 2nd.

stone me! An English variant, since ca. 1920, of **stone the crows!**

stone tavern. See **stone jug** (*Dict.*).

stone the crows! Prob. since mid-C. 19. Also, since ca. 1918, current in England, esp. among Cockneys, as in 'Cor, stone the crows!'

stoned. Very drunk: adopted, ca. 1950, ex U.S.—2. Drug-exhilarated: (mostly teenage) drug addicts': adopted, ca. 1960, ex U.S. Peter Fryer, in *The Observer* colour supplement of Dec. 3, 1967, defines it as 'very high on cannabis'.

stones, off the; on the stones. Outside London; in London: coll.: ca. 1830–80. Bulwer Lytton, 1841 (*off the stones*); Surtees, 1858, 'They now get upon the stones.' Ex the hardness of London streets.

stones, on the.—2. See *prec.*—3. Engaged in selling hired paintings from a pavement pitch or series of pitches: peddlers' and street vendors'; since ca. 1925 (prob. much earlier). Michael Fane, *Racecourse Swindlers*, 1936. Hence:—4. Selling goods laid out on the pavement, not from a stall: peddlers' and street vendors': since ca. 1910. 'Originally Caledonian market, now anywhere' (Julian Franklyn, 1962). Cf. the next.

Stones, the. The Caledonian Market, London: pitch-holders': late C. 19–20. (Jane Brown, *I Had a Pitch on the Stones*, 1946.) Ex the cobble-stones that characterized the Market, which closed ca. 1954.—2. 'A 20-mile belt of desert between Mechili and Msus entirely covered with boulders; the most uncomfortable "going" in Libya' (Peter Sanders in *The Sunday Times* magazine, Sept. 10, 1967): Army in North Africa: 1940–43.

Stoneyhurst slang. Marples lists *atramentarius*, a 'fag'; *bonk, bunker*, a cad; *cob*, to 'cop' (take); *crow*, a master; *haggory*, 'a garden used for discussion . . . from *agora*, market-place'; *heavy*, important (or self-important), impressive; *oil*, to take (a culprit) by surprise, and *oilers*, rubber-soled shoes; *pin*, to enjoy—hence *pinning* or *pin-nable*, enjoyable: *shouting cake*, a currant cake; *squash*, a football scrum; *stew*, to 'swot'; *swiz*, a crib; *taps*, a caning: *tolly*, an improvised cane.

stonies. Marbles made of stone: Australian children's coll.: C. 20. (B.P.)

stonk, n. A heavy shelling, as in 'giving 'em a stonk' (or 'a bit of stick'): Army: 1940 +. (P-G-R.; L. Marshland Gander, *After Many Quests*, 1949.) Cf.:

stonked, be. To be shelled (by artillery): Army: 1940 +. Echoic.

stonker. See **stinker,** 9.

stonkered, be.—2. Hence, to be outwitted: Australian: since ca. 1918. B., 1942.—3. Hence, to be in a fix, a dilemma: Australian and New Zealand soldiers': 1939–45. (J. H. Fullarton, *Troop Target*, 1942.) Now general throughout Australasia. (B.P., 1963.) But the v. *stonker* is also used actively, as in 'He stepped on a bloody mine. Stonkered the poor bastard properly' (Slatter): New Zealand: since ca. 1917.—4. To be dead drunk. Aus.: since mid 1940's. (F. B. Vickers, *First Place to the Stranger*, 1955.)

stony blind. Blind-drunk: Australian: since ca. 1920. Vance Palmer, *The Passage*, 1930.

stooge, n. A learner (as in 'Q learner') at a divisional or a corps H.Q. in the Army: since ca. 1935. E. P., 'In Mess and Field'—*The New Statesman*, Aug. 1, 1942. Either ex *student* or perhaps ex U.S. *stooge*, a comedian's butt or a conjurer's assistant, a 'feed', itself either ex *stool pigeon* via *studious* (mispronounced *stew-djus*) or ex *student*.—2. Hence, a deputy; a stand-in: since late 1940. H. & P.—3. Hence, 'an over-willing chap' (H. & P.): since early 1941.—4. 'A second-rater, one without importance,' Jackson: since late 1941. Ex sense 1.—5. (Ex sense 1.) 'One of our own sentries to warn escape workers whenever ferrets [**ferret** in Supplement] approached,' Paul Brickhill & Conrad Norton, *Escape to Danger*, 1946: prisoners-of-war in Germany: 1940-5.—6. 'A select social gathering in a study' (Marples): Lancing College: since mid-1930's. Perversion of *study*.—7. Hard work: Reading undergraduates' (– 1940). Marples, 2. Cf. sense 1.—8. A servile underling: Australian: since ca. 1945. (B.P.)

stooge, v. To fly over the same old ground as before; esp. to be on patrol: R.A.F.: since 1938. H. & P. Ex sense 1 of the n.

stooge, put in a. To act as a spare man (i.e. standing by) to a bomber crew: Air Force: since 1940. Cecil Lewis, *Pathfinders*, 1943. See **stooge,** n., 2.

stooge around. To 'hang about', waiting to land (1940 +); hence (also *about*), 'to idle about, on the ground, or in the air' (Jackson): R.A.F.: since 1940. *The Observer*, Oct. 4, 1942, 'We stooged about a bit above our target'. Cf. prec. entry and **stooge,** n., 4.—2. Also, with variant *stooge about*, a synonym of **stooge,** v.: since 1938 or 1939. Partridge, 1945.—3. As in **stooging.**

stooge pilot. A pilot engaged on flying-training 'planes carrying untrained navigators and/or gunners: R.A.F.: 1940 +, Robert Hinde, March 17, 1945.

stooging. 'General for non-operational flying,' Sgt-Pilot F. Rhodes, letter of Sept. 20, 1942.

stook.—2. Gen. *in stook*, in trouble: orig. and mostly Australian: from ca. 1920.—3. A cigarette: Australian R.M.C., Duntroon: since ca. 1920 (?). B., 1953. Ex shape.
Sense 2 is also London proletarian of late C. 19–20. 'From Yiddish, where it means "difficulties" and is pronounced *stooch*. "He took all the money and left Abe in stooch,"' (Julian Franklyn, 1962.)

***stook-buzzer** or **-hauler.** See **stook** (*Dict.*).

stool, three-legged. See **three-legged stool** (*Dict.*).

***stool-pigeon.**—3. A cardsharper's decoy: c.: from ca. 1880.

***stoolie.** An informer to the police: Australian c. >, ca. 1946, low. Adopted, ca. 1939, ex U.S. Ruth Park, *The Harp in the South*, 1948. Cf.:

***stoolie job.** An informer's or a spy's giving of information to the police: since ca. 1930: c. >, by 1940, low s. From U.S.: see 'stoolie' in *Underworld*.

stoop, n.—3. A petty thief: Australian c.: since ca. 1920. B., 1942.

***stoop-napper.** See **stoop,** n. (*Dict.*).

stooper. A cigarette-end picked off the street: London: since ca. 1930.

stop, v.—2. In a fisticuffs fight, to knock out; to kill (a quarry): Australian: C. 20. B., 1942.

***stop, on the.** 'Picking pockets when the party is standing still': c.: mid-C. 19–20. B. & L. Cf. **stop lay,** q.v.

stop a rocket. See **rocket.**

stop it, Horace! From ca. 1930, a c.p. 'shouted in a squeaky, semi-lisping, high-pitched voice after any refined-looking "delicate" young man: it does not mean Stop anything'. Prob. ex a 'gag' by George Robey.

stop it—I like it! A c.p., mostly in reference to giggling teenage girls pretending, not too long nor very convincingly, that they dislike their boy friends' caresses: since ca. 1920—if not a decade or two earlier.

stop laughing! Stop complaining! Australian ironic c.p.: since ca. 1920. (B., 1953; Jon Cleary, *Back of Sunset*, 1959.)

***stop(-)lay, the.** Pocket-picking by two confederates, of whom one stops the victim and engages him in conversation and the other robs him: c.: mid-C. 19–20. B. & L.

stop me if you have (or **you've**) **heard this one.** A c.p. by an imminent 'story'-teller: since ca. 1930.

stop off, v.t. To desist from, to cease doing or making: New Zealand: since ca. 1880. 'Stop that row, Tommy . . . stop it off.' G. B. Lancaster, *Sons o' Men*, 1904.

stop one.—2. To take a drink of liquor: Australian: C. 20. K. S. Prichard, *Coonardoo*, 1929. Archer Russell, *Gone Nomad*, 1936. Cf. **stop a pot** (p. 935).

stop-out, n. A person given to stopping out late at night: coll.: late C. 19–20. (B., 1942.)

stop out, v.—2. To go sick: Charterhouse: C. 20. (Peter Sanders.)

stop the show. To hold up the performance because of the loud, continuous applause for one's own acting: theatrical coll.: late C. 19–20.

Stop-the-Way Company, the. The Hudson's Bay Company: Canadian coll.: ca. 1840–90. Francis Francis, *Newton Dogvane*, 1959, but in a passage written in 1852. At one time, retrograde.

stop up. To study late: Charterhouse coll.: C. 20. (Peter Sanders.)

stop where you are. A friar bird: Australian: C. 20. Baker. Echoic.

stop your tickling (, Jock)! See **tickling . . .**

stopper. See **starter.** Sense 1 (p. 835): earlier in W. N. Glascock, *Sketch-Book*, I, 1825, 'He claps a stopper on all our proceedings.' Moe.

stopper with the dog. 'In bringing up a ship in bad weather, they'—seamen—'stopper with the dog' (W. N. Glascock, *Sketch-Book*, II (31), 1826: Naval: ca. 1790–1850. (Moe.)

stoppo. A 'spello'—or rest from work: C. 20. Jim Phelan, *Lifer*, 1938.

store, the. A branch store of a co-operative society: coll.: C. 20. Cf. **co-op,** 1 (*Dict.*).

store-basher. An Equipment assistant: R.A.F.: since ca. 1925. H. & P. Cf. **instrument-basher.**

store-basher's Bible, the. Air Publication No. 830, vol. 1 being *Equipment Regulations*; 11, *Storage and Packing*; III, *Scales of R.A.F. Equipment*: R.A.F.: since ca. 1930. Jackson; Partridge, 1945.

storm and strife. Canadian variant of **trouble and strife** (*Dict.*).

storm(-)stick. An umbrella: Australian jocular: since ca. 1925. B., 1942.

stormen. 'A hot member of society': Society: ca. 1880–1910. B. & L. Prob. ex *storm.*

*story with, do the. To copulate with (a woman): prostitutes' c.: C. 18. *Select Trials from 1720 to 1724*, pub. in 1734.

stotious. Late C. 19–20 (but very ob. by 1937), as in Robert Lynd, 'It's Good to Speak Slang' in *The News Chronicle*, Feb. 20, 1937: 'Slang also appeals to our elementary sense of humour, as when we say of a man who is drunk that he is "well-oiled", "stotious", "blind to the world", or "full up inside with tiddley".' An artificial word: cf. **goloptious** (*Dict.*).

stoush, v. See p. 836.—2. Hence, to hit, to punch: Australian: since ca. 1925. (B., *Australia Speaks*, 1953.)

stoush! also, derivatively, South African (C. 20), esp. as 'to hit, strike'.

stoush, put in the. To fight vigorously, spiritedly, esp. with the fists: Australian: since ca. 1910. B., 1942. See **stoush,** p. 836.

Stoush, the Big. World War I, Australian: since ca. 1919. (B., 1943.)

stoush merchant. A boxer; one good with his fists; a bully: Australian: since ca. 1918. Baker.

stout fellow (p. 836). Cf. *stout*, Eton s. for 'strong and expert' (e.g. a stout bowler): *Spy*, 1825.

Stove-Makers, or Stovies, the. 'Metters footballers, Sydney': since ca. 1925. (B., 1943.)

*stove up, v.; **stove-up,** n. To disinfect—the disinfecting of—clothes in a casual ward: tramps' c.: from ca. 1919. Also *bake up*, v., and *bake-up*, n. Ex the disinfector, which resembles a stove.

stow it! (p. 836): 'very much alive in Australia' (B.P., 1965).

stowaway. A pocket-sized magazine: book-world and newsagents': since ca. 1939.

*stomarket. See **stow magging** (*Dict.*).

strafe, n.—4. (Prob. ex senses 1, 2: p. 836.) An efficiency campaign: R.A.F.: since ca. 1930. 'The C.O. is going to have a gas-mask strafe.' (Robert Hinde, letter of March 17, 1945.)

Strafer. Lieutenant-General Gott, one-time commander of the 8th Army: 1939 +. Ex the song *Gott strafe England*. 'He was killed when the R.A.F. plane in which he was a passenger was shot down in 1943' (Peter Sanders).

straggling money (p. 836) goes back to ca. 1800. W. N. Glascock, *Sketch-Book*, II, 1826, 'The sogers were looking out sharp for their "straggling money".' Moe.

straight, adj.—7. (Of spirits) undiluted, neat: Canadian coll.: adopted, ca. 1880, ex U.S.; by ca. 1942, also English, 'I'll take mine straight, thanks.' (Leechman.)—8. *Not* homosexual: British and American homosexuals': C. 20.—9. Not using drugs: addicts' and hippies' and their like: since ca. 1960. Peter Fryer in *The Observer* colour supplement, Dec. 3, 1967.

straight, on the. See **straight, in the:** *Dict.*

straight and level. See **get some straight** ...

straight and narrow, the. The straight and narrow path of virtue or honour: coll.: since ca. 1925. 'Sometimes misapprehended as "the straight and narrow path between right and wrong"' (Leechman).

straight banana. A joke c.p. among greengrocers (re selling) and gardeners (re growing): mostly Cockney's: from ca. 1910.

straight from the bog. A c.p. applied, in late C. 19–20, to a crude Irishman.

straight from the horse's mouth. (Of information, news, etc.) genuine, authentic, correct: sporting s. (since ca. 1830) >, by 1900, coll. Ex **Stable Yard, the,** q.v. See Aldington's *Wellington*, 1946.

straight goer. A dependable—esp. an honest—person: Australian coll.: since ca. 1925. (Caddie, 1953.)

straight-hair. A convict: West Australian: ca. 1840–70. B., 1942.—2. A West Australian: since ca. 1870. Baker.

straight hooks. A butchers' joke, e.g., on April the First: from ca. 1860.

straight Navy, the. The Royal Navy: since ca. 1920. Prompted by 'the *Wavy Navy*' (p. 941).

straight oil. Variant of **dinkum oil,** influenced by **straight wire** (see *Dict.*): Australian: since ca. 1920. B., 1942.

straight prop (man). A genuine builder specialising in house-repair work: since ca. 1963. The Bournemouth *Evening Echo*, April 20, 1966. Cf. **prop game.**

*straight racket, on the. Living honestly: c.: from ca. 1885; ob. B. & L.

straight rush (p. 837) includes potatoes. In the Canadian Navy of ca. 1900–25 it was specifically 'the simplest preparation of a joint of beef, employed when time was short. The meat was placed in a baking dish, some fat spread over it, peeled potatoes placed round it, and the whole affair roasted. The dish got its name from the "straight rush" from the beef screen to the galley': *Daily Colonist*, June 19, 1960.

straight-striper. A Royal Australian Navy regular: Australian Naval: since ca. 1938. (B., 1943.)

straight up.—1. To *be s. u.*, up-to-date in one's work—2. *s. u.!*, honestly!: since early 1920's. (Atkinson.) Cf. S.E. *straight*, honest. Since ca. 1935, occasionally elaborated to *straight up on my eyesight!* (Norman.)—3. 'Precisely noon or midnight from the position of the hands of a clock. "It's twelve o'clock, straight up!": that is, exactly.' (Leechman.)

straight walk-in. An easy entry; esp. of a girl or woman easily 'made' or obviously wearing very little clothing: among would-be Lotharios, Lovelaces, Romeos, Don Juans: since ca. 1925.

straight wire, the (p. 837). The adj. and adv. are used *straight(-)wire*, recorded earlier for New Zealand than for Australia; as in ' "Walt, you are a smeller, straight wire" ': G. B. Lancaster, *Sons o' Men*, 1904.

straighten, 1 (p. 837): soon applied to other than policemen. (John Gosling, 1959.)—2. To defeat: Australian: ca. 1850–1910. Rolf Boldrewood, *The Miners' Rights*, 1890.—3. To set right: Australian coll.: since ca. 1910. (K. S. Prichard, *Kiss on the Lips*, 1932.) Ex 'put, or set, *straight*'.

—4. To avenge (an affront); to take revenge upon (a rival gang): Teddy boys': since ca. 1946. (*The Observer*, March 1, 1959.)

straightener. A fisticuffs fight between two rival gangs: Teddy boys', esp. in London: since ca. 1955. (*The Daily Mail*, Feb. 7, 1959.) It is fought in order to 'straighten things out' between them.

strange. Crazy; silly; stupid: Australian coll.: late C. 19–20. B., 1942.

stranger.—4. (Mostly in pl.) A wandering sheep: New Zealand and Australian sheep-farmers' coll.; since ca. 1870. B., 1941 and 1942.

strangle. To get something from (someone) for nothing: Naval lowerdeck: since ca. 1930. Mostly applied to 'runs ashore'. (Granville.)—2. To prevent (a horse) from winning: Australian racing: since ca. 1935. Lawson Glassop, *Lucky Palmer*, 1949. Strictly, to pull (a horse) back so strongly that it's almost strangled, as one of the 'dodges' employed by jockeys in order to lose a race, as in Dick Francis, *Dead Cert*, 1962, 'The general opinion among the jockeys was that Sandy had "strangled" a couple [of horses] at one stage, but not during the past few months.' Cf. **choke**, v., above.

strap, on the. Penniless: Australian: since ca. 1910. B., 1942. Cf. **strap**, n., 2 (p. 837).

strap up.—2. To obtain (goods; or drinks at an hotel) on credit: Australian: since ca. 1919. B., 1942. Cf. **strap**, v., 3, 4 (p. 837).

strapped.—2. Penniless: English and Canadian: late C. 19–20. (Leechman.) Probably ex rural *strap*, to strip (a cow), hence to draw (anything) dry, hence (London) to work to the limit.

strapper.—2. A stable lad: Australian racing: since ca. 1925. (Lawson Glassop, *Lucky Palmer*, 1949.)

straw, in the. (Of a woman) in childbirth: old S.E. > C. 20 Australian s., prob. influenced by cows lying in straw and about to calve. B., 1942.

straw-hat. See 'Women'.

Straw Plaiters, the. The Luton Association Football team: sporting: since ca. 1920. Hat-making is a predominant industry at Luton.

straw-walloper. In hayrick-making, the man that, standing at the head of the elevator, forks the hay, etc., to the stacker: Australian: since ca. 1910. Baker.

strawberry.—2. Hence, a red nose: Cockneys': C. 20. Cf. **beacon** and **danger light.**—3. A compliment, praise from a superior: Army Officers': since ca. 1930. H. & P. In contrast to **raspberry.**

strawing. Putting children on straw in front of seating stand: circus coll.: late C. 19–20. (C. B. Cochran, *Showman Looks On*, 1945.)

straws. See **pots.**

stray. A sausage: Australian Naval: since ca. 1930. (B., 1943.) Ex '*stray dog*'.

stray tup on the loose. See **tup**, n., 2, in *Dict.*

streak, n.—2. A 'locomotive Class A4 (N.E.)': railwaymen's: ? ca. 1940–60. (*Railway*.)

stream. A heavy raid; strictly the 'stream' of bombers delivering it: Air Force coll.: 1940 +.

stream, the. The fairway; an anchorage: nautical coll.: late C. 19–20.

stream-line, better **stream-lined, piece.** A very attractive girl: Naval: since ca. 1941. (P-G-R.)

stream-lined. (Of women) tall, slim, graceful;

(of clothes) neatly and closely tailored: coll.: since ca. 1940. ' "Yes," Jeffrey said, "slap-happy", and he laughed, but the colloquialism disturbed him. He was suddenly tired of all the new words—"stream-lined", "blitzed", "three-point programme", "blueprint",' John P. Marquand, *So Little Time*, 1943 (but written in late 1941–2). Ex aircraft stream-lined to reduce air-resistance.

street, bang (or right) up one's. That's just the sort of job one likes: since ca. 1920. (P-G-R.)

Street, the.—4. Archer Street, London, W.1. musicians' coll.: C. 20. Ex the agencies there.— 5. Wardour Street: film industry coll.: since ca. 1918.—6. In Sydney, since ca. 1920 or earlier, Macquarie Street: medical coll. (so many doctors); or Philip Street: legal coll. (so many lawyers); or Palmer Street: raffish coll. (so many prostitutes). B.P.

Street Walker & Co., working for. Out of work, walking the streets in search of it: Australian c.p.: since ca. 1920. B., 1942.

strell homey (or homie). A banjo player: parlary: late C. 19–20. Compare and contrast *strill homey*, q.v. at **strill**, 2, below.

strength?, what's the. What is the news?: Services, both combatant and protective: 1941, Allan A. Michie & Walter Graebner, *Lights of Freedom*. Cf.:

strength of it (p. 839). App. earliest in New Zealand: 1871, C. L. Money, *Knocking About in New Zealand*. B., 1941, 'Highly popular, throughout both New Zealand and Australia.'

strengthy. A gymnast: Christ's Hospital: late C. 19–20. Marples.

strepto. Streptomycin: medical coll.: since ca. 1940. (Dymphna Cusack, 1951.) Cf. *strep* on p. 839.

stretch, v.—3. To outstay an opponent, e.g. at fisticuffs: Anglo-Irish: C. 20. Nicholas Blake, *The Private Wound*, 1968, ref. the year 1939, ' "You're out of condition," Seumus told him. "If that fella'd persevered, he'd have stretched you." '

stretch off the land (p. 839), is, strictly, a short sleep. (P-G-R.)

*stretch the hemp. See **hemp, stretch the.**

stretcher case. A liar: since ca. 1942. Ex *lying.* Also 'because he is stretching the truth' (Robert Clairborne).

'Strewth! (p. 839) has long been pronounced, as a variant, in a drawl: *ster-ruth.*

strictly for the birds! See **that's for the birds!** below.

strides.—3. (Ex sense 1: p. 839.) 'Recent name for trousers worn by zoot-suiters' (Professor F. E. L. Priestley, letter of 1949): Canadian. Senses 1 (p. 839) and 3 were also, by 1930 at latest, common in the underworld and the near-under-world. (John Gosling, 1959.)

strike, n.—1 (p. 839) occurs 80 years earlier: *Memoirs of John Hall*, 1708.—5. Short for **strike me dead,** 2 (p. 840). Gerald Kersh, *They Die with Their Boots Clean*, 1941, in nuance 'bread-and-butter'.

strike, v.—7. To *strike a horse* is to feed it immediately before it runs in a race and therefore spoil its chance: Australian sporting: C. 20. B., 1942.—8. To go on strike at the location of: Canadian coll.: 1959 +. 'Four hundred men

struck the King Lumber Company this morning.'
(Leechman.)

strike! An Australian ejaculation: since ca.
1925. Baker. Short for *strike a light!* or *strike
me dead!*

strike a blow. To start work: Australian:
since ca. 1945. 'I must go now. It's half past
nine—and I haven't struck a blow.' (B.P.)

strike a bright.—2. 'To have a piece of good fortune': proletarian: from ca. 1880; ob. B. & L.

strike it down. To drink heavily, either on one
occasion or in general: Naval: since ca. 1920.
(P-G-R.)

strike-me. Bread: C. 20. 'I . . . had a quick
bite of strike-me and sweet evening' (bread and
cheese). S. Lester, *Vardi the Palarey*, (?) 1937.
Short for the next.

strike(-)me(-)dead. Bread: Cockney rhyming
s.: C. 20. Gerald Kersh, *Night and the City*, 1938.

strike me handsome! An Australian ejaculation
of the politer sort: C. 20. B., 1942. Cf. **strike!**

strike one's breath or **spit one's death** = to 'cross
one's heart' in assurance of one's truthfulness:
Australian coll.: late C. 19–20. Baker.

strill.—2. A piano: parlary: late C. 19–20.
(Sydney Lester.) Hence, *strill homey* or *strill
polone*, a pianist male or female. It app. derives
ex Italian *strillo*, a shrill cry, a piercing note, etc.;
cf. Italian *strillare*, to shriek, to scream.

Strine, despite Mr R. W. Burchfield's stricture,
'Australiana abound but *Strine* has escaped notice'
(*The New Statesman*, March 17, 1967, p. 376), has
nothing to do with slang: it doesn't mean 'Australian slang': it does concern the way in which
Australians, esp. the larger State capitals, run
words together—and mispronounce them—in
conversation; its true unit is not the word but the
colloquial group, usually a phrase. *Let Stalk
Strine*, Alistair Morrison's biting satire published
in 1965, mean's 'Let's talk Australian.'

String. Short for **String o' Beads** below. Mark
McShane, *The Passing of Evil*, 1961, 'Used to be a
good fight town, the old String.'

string, n.—4. The published material that, each
week, a writer 'on space rates' gets paid for. He
pastes 'clips' of all his published work in one long
'string' and is paid on this evidence: Canadian
journalists': C. 20. (Leechman.)

string, v. (p. 840): it occurs in *Sinks*, 1848, as
'to fool, deceive, humbug' (someone).

string along with . To go along with; agree with;
support: Canadian coll.: adopted, ca. 1930, ex U.S.

string and glitter boys. Men detailed for guard-
duty: Army: ca. 1905–20.

String of Beads. Leeds: rhyming s. (esp. in
Lancashire and Yorkshire): C. 20.

string of ponies. A 'stable' of prostitutes
'owned' by one man: white-slave traffic: since
ca. 1925. (B.B.C., Sept. 22, 1963.)

string up. To keep waiting: low: from ca.
1920. 'He strung me up.'

Stringbag. A Swordfish torpedo-bomber aircraft: R.A.F. and Fleet Air Arm: ca. 1939–43.
Sgt-Pilot F. Rhodes, letter of Sept. 20, 1942;
H. & P., 1943, rightly ex **'Stringbag the Sailor'.**
—2. Also, an Albacore aircraft: 1943–5. Jackson.

stringer.—3. A reporter paid for what is published: mostly journalists': since ca. 1925. Cf.
string, n., 4, above.

strings. Telegraph wires: Canadian railroadmen's (— 1931). Humorous.

stringy, usually in the pl. *stringies*. A stringy-
bark eucalypt: Australian coll.: late C. 19–20.
(B., 1953; Kylie Tennant, *The Honey Flow*,
1956.)

stringy-bark.—3. (Ex sense 2: p. 840.) Very
tough or hardy (persons); courageous: Australian: C. 20. (B., 1943.)

strip (someone's) **masthead.** To thrash: nautical: ca. 1760–1840. *Sessions*, 1786 (8th session).

strip-eel. See 'Occupational names'.

strip off . . . See **tear a strip off.**

***stripe.**—2. A long, esp. if narrow, scar: c.:
since ca. 1915. (Norman.)

stripes on the line, one's. One's N.C.O. stripes
in danger, as in 'Our stripes will be on the line for
this', heard in the TV programme,' Dixon of Dock
Green' on March 12, 1968. (A. B. Petch.)

stripey. A long-service A.B.: Navy: C. 20.
A. D. Divine, *Dunkirk*, 1944. Many service-
stripes, no promotion.

stripey or **stripy**, adj. Streaky; hence, patchy,
variable: New Zealand coll.: late C. 19–20.
(G. B. Lancaster, *Sons o' Men*, 1904, a snowstorm.)

stripper. Rare in singular: see **strippers** on
p. 840.—2. A strip-tease artiste: coll.: adopted,
in late 1940's, ex U.S.

strobe. A stroboscope (an electronic flash unit):
photographers': since ca. 1950. (B.P.)

stroke, n. 'To save detailing an officer to
supervise them, one of the men was chosen as
leader and made responsible for the general running
of the mess. Such leaders are called "strokes",
the word being taken from rowing parlance' (L. W.
Merrow Smith & J. Harris, *Prison Screw*, 1962):
prison officers': since ca. 1930.

stroll on! A c.p. comment on what seems very
hard to believe: Army and R.A.F.: since ca. 1950.
Willis Hall, *The Long and the Short and the Tall*, a
play, 1959, at pp. 20 and 29. (Laurie Atkinson.)
Pretend you haven't noticed!

strong.—2. See **not off** above.

***strong-arm**, v. To bully; to manhandle: Aus-
tralian c.: since late 1920's. B., 1942. Adopted
from U.S.: see *Underworld*.—2. Hence, to act as
bully to (a prostitute): c.: since ca. 1930. Baker.

strong as a drink of water. 'Used to describe a
weak man, or humorously to deride a man boasting
of his strength' (Albert B. Petch): C. 20.

***strong man.** A confidence trickster: Aus-
tralian c.: since ca. 1920. Baker. He 'comes it
strong'.

strong of, the. The truth; the essential point
or especial importance of, e.g., a message, instructions, news: Australian: since ca. 1910. Baker.
A variation of **strength of** (p. 839).

stroppy. Obstreperous: Naval: C. 20. Granville. Via *obstropolous* (see **obstreperous**: p. 578).
—2. Hence, 'to *get stroppy*' or become very angry:
general: since ca. 1946. (Gilderdale, 2.) Cf.
'You'll get me stroppy if you start bullying'
(Nicholas Blake, *The Sad Variety*, 1964).

struck comical. Much earlier in Jon Bee, *A
Living Picture of London*, 1828.

struggle and strife. Wife: rhyming s.: C. 20;
not very general (cf. *trouble . . .*). Franklyn,
Rhyming.

***Struggle Valley.** A collection of shacks where
tramps or beggars live: Australian tramps' c.:
C. 20. B., 1942.

struggling! 'A frequent answer to "How are
you going [*or* doing]?"': mostly Australian: since

ca. 1925. Either ex '*struggling* along' or ex '*struggling* to make ends meet'. (B.P.)

strull. Incorrect for *strut*, n.: C. 19–20. O.E.D.

strumil. See **strommel** (*Dict.*).

Stubbs, put (a person) **through.** To inquire from a financial agency whether a person's credit is good: commercial coll.: late C. 19–20. The firm of Stubbs was founded in 1836; since 1893, known as Stubbs Ltd.

*stubs. Teeth: c.: since ca. 1945. (Robin Cook, *The Crust on Its Uppers*, 1962.) Ex S.E. *stub*, a butt-end.

stuck in, get. Also, in New Zealand, applied to drinks: 'Don't wait—get stuck in!' The v.i. form of 'get **stuck into it**' (p. 842).

stuck into it, get. See **get cracking**—and **stuck into it!, get,** on p. 842.

stud. A virile man: Anglo-Irish: since ca. 1925. (Brian Moore, *The Luck of Brian Coffey*, 1960.) Short for S.E. '*stud* stallion' or 'stallion at *stud*'.—2. A mistress, esp. if available whenever required: Australian rural: since ca. 1920. (Tom Ronan, *Vision Splendid*, 1954, '. . . the boss's stud'. Short for S.E. *stud mare*.

stud book, in the. Of ancient lineage; esp. in Burke or Debrett; upper class: late C. 19–20.

studnsel (p. 842) has the further variant *studdensail*, which occurs in, e.g., W. N. Glascock, *The Naval Sketch-Book*, 2nd Series, 1834, at II, 64. Therefore back-date to very early C. 19.

studying for Staff College, be. To sleep in the afternoon, esp. in hot countries: Army officers': since ca. 1920.

stuff, n., 11 (p. 842): cf. ' "Does he suspect? Or is this chance and stuff?" ' in R. L. Stevenson, *The Wrong Box*, 1889 (communicated by Derek Pepys Whitely, Esq.).—14. Aircraft collectively, as in 'There's a lot of stuff going across (to, e.g., Germany)': R.A.F. coll.: 1940 +. Partridge, 1945, 'And in "Heavy stuff" (heavy bombers)': cf. sense 9 on p. 842.—15. A copulation: low Australian: C. 20. 'She's had more stuffs than you've had twins'—almost a c.p. Ex **stuff,** v., 4, below.

By late 1950, common—esp. as marijuana—among British addicts.

stuff, v.—4. (Of man) to copulate with: low: late (? mid-) C. 19–20. Ex upholstery. Hence the defiant c.p., *go and get stuffed.*—5. Hence, to defeat severely: New Zealand: since ca. 1920. Slatter, 'Wait till we clean up Otago [at Rugby Football]. We'll stuff 'em!'

*stuffed rat. In gambling, a loaded die: Australian c., since ca. 1930; by ca. 1945, low sporting s. Lawson Glassop, *Lucky Palmer*, 1949.

stuffy, n. A 'stuffy' person: since ca. 1950. Cf. **stuffy,** adj., 3 (p. 843).

stuffy.—4. (Ex 1–2.) Stand-offish; Services: since ca. 1926. H. & P.

stuggy. Thick-set: Public Schools': from ca. 1870. B. & L. Ex *stocky.*—Also Australian.

stuiver. See **stiver** (*Dict.*).

Stuka Valley. The plain around Souk el Khemis (Tunisia), notorious for the attentions of German *Stuka* dive-bombers: Army in N. Africa: 1942–3. (P-G-R.)

stumer.—7. Hence, a bankrupt; a defaulter; (of a plan or enterprise) a failure: Australian sporting and gambling: since ca. 1920. B., 1942. —8. A fool: Cockney: C. 20.—9. A deaf-mute:

Cockney: since ca. 1910. Like 8, it comes ex Yiddish. (Julian Franklyn.)

stumer, come a. To crash financially: New Zealand and Australian: C. 20. B., 1941 and 1942. See *stumer* on p. 843.

stumer, in a. In a 'mess' or hopeless confusion (He's in a 'stumer'): New Zealand and Australian: C. 20. Cf. prec. and:

stumer, on a. 'If they don't want a cab when he gets there, he's "been on a stumer",' Herbert Hodge, 1939: taxi-drivers': since ca. 1920.

stump, v., 2 (p. 843). The passive, *stumped* (for money), occurs in *Sessions*, Nov. 1834.—5. To pay: 1821, W. T. Moncrieff, *Tom and Jerry*; by 1860, superseded by **stump up** (p. 843).

stump jockey. A wicket-keeper: Australian: since ca. 1930; by 1960, archaic.

stump-jumper. A Stump Jump Plough: Australian farming coll.: C. 20. B., 1942, 'Whence, "stump-jumping": work with such a plough.'

stumped up. Penniless: Australian: C. 20. (B., 1943.)

stumpy, 1 (p. 843). A little earlier in W. T. Moncrieff, *Tom and Jerry*, 1821.—4. See 'Prisoner-of-War Slang', 12.

stun, on the. Engaged in drinking heavily: Australian: since ca. 1920. B., 1942. Cf.:

stung. Tipsy: Australian: since ca. 1920. (B., 1943.)

stung for, be. To be at a loss for: Australian: since ca. 1925. (B., 1943.)

stunned (p. 843). By ca. 1918, also Australian. Baker.

stunned mullet, like a. 'Stupid, silly' (B., 1959): since ca. 1930.

stunning, 1 (p. 843). Cf. France *épatant*, exact semantic parallel (L. W. Forster). Earlier in *Sessions*, Nov. 1847.

stunning, adv. Exceedingly: coll.: 1845, in 'The Stunning Meat Pie', in Labern's *Comic Songs*, was the line 'A stunning great meat pie'. See the adj. in *Dict.*

stunt, n., 2 (pp. 843–4) occurs in a letter of Feb. 17, 1878, from Samuel ('Erewhon') Butler to Miss Savage, 'It was a stunt for advertising the books.' (With thanks to R. M. Williams, Esq., letter of June 30, 1944.)

stupe (p. 844): revived, or perhaps re-invented, in Australia ca. 1950. (P.B.)

stupid as arse-holes (,as). Exceedingly stupid: low: since ca. 1925.

stupo. An Anglo-Irish variant of **stupe:** C. 20. James Joyce, *Ulysses*, 1922.

stute. An institute; a club: mostly proletarian: C. 20. By aphesis and conflation of *institute:* that is, *in* dropped, *stitute* is telescoped from two syllables to one.

stuyver, styver. See **stiver** (*Dict.*).

sub, n., 2 (p. 844). In the Navy: a Sub-Lieutenant: coll.: late C. 19–20. Wardroom term.—5. Also commercial and Naval: C. 20—10. A sub-machine gun (strictly a modified light machine gun): Army coll.: since ca. 1942. In, e.g., Elleston Trevor, *The Freebooters*, 1967.

sub, do a. To borrow money: proletarian: from ca. 1865; ob. B. & L. Ex **sub,** n., 7.

sub-sheriff. See 'Tavern terms', § 4.

subby.—2. A subaltern: military: ca. 1860–1910. Robert Blatchford, *My Life in the Army*, 1910.—3. A Sub-Lieutenant: Naval: C. 20. Granville, 'lower-deck'. Ex prec.

subcheese or **sub-cheese.** Everything, all there is, 'the whole shoot': Indian Army: Forces in India: mid-C. 19–20; 1939–45. From Hindustani. As in 'We saw a lot of Nips and gave 'em the sub-cheese' or, in a shop, 'Tighai, Mohammed, I'll take the sub-cheese' (All right, M., I'll take the lot). With thanks to John Bebbington, librarian. Here, *cheese* is probably Hindustani *chīz*, thing: cf. *cheese, the,* on p. 144.

subfusc. See **sub-fusc** (*Dict.*).

subject normal! An exclamatory c.p. in allusion to (esp. the resumption of) smutty talk: Forces' (1939) >, ca. 1945, general.

*submarine. See **torpedo.**

submarine, v.; mostly as verbal n. *submarining,* riding through tall grass: Northern Territory, Australia: since ca. 1942. Ernestine Hill, *The Territory,* 1951.

Submarine Lancers, the. A fictitious unit: 1914–18 and 1939–45. To an undersized would-be enlister, the recruiting sergeant might say, 'Try the . . .'

submariners. 'Officers and men of the submarine service; it rhymes with *mariners*' (Granville): Naval: since ca. 1941.

*subs, battle the. See **battle.**

subscribe to the Bookies' Benefit; esp., **be subscribing** . . . To throw money away by betting recklessly or haphazardly on horses: C. 20. (A. B. Petch, April 1966.) Cf. **for the widows and orphans** above.

subtle. See 'Tavern terms', § 8.

such another. Another such: sol.: mid-C. 19–20. Edwin Pugh, 1895: see quotation at **I'm sure.**

such as. What; so much as: catachrestic: C. 20. *The Pawnshop Murder:* 'Then he mooched to another window and surveyed such as was to be seen of the rear of the place from that point.'

such is life without a wife. A c.p. elaboration of the world-old, world-wide truism 'Such is life': C. 20. The addition bears little, if indeed any, relation to the facts.

suck, the v. denoting the act of fellation, is more gen. **suck off,** which is low coll.: C. 19–20. Not restricted—any more than *suck* is—to Lesbians.

suck-hole, v. To toady, as in 'He won't suck-hole to anyone'; hence, to cringe: low Canadian: C. 20.

suck-holer. A toady: New Zealand low coll.: C. 20. Cf. preceding.

suck it and see! A derisive c.p. retort current in the 1890's. After going underground, it has been revived, ca. 1945–60, by Australian children. (B., 1953.)

sucked that out of his (or **her** or . . .) **fingers, he** (etc.) **hasn't.** He hasn't thought of that by himself—that's not *his* idea—he has authentic (or mysterious) information: c.p., mostly Cockneys': late C. 19–20.

sucker.—6. (Gen. pl.) A sweet: dial (− 1823) >, by 1870, coll. (E.D.D.). Cf. **sucks** (*Dict.*).—7. A Lesbian; fellatrix: low coll.: C. 19–20.

sucking the hindtit. (Esp. in pool-rooms; but also general sporting.) Well behind or in arrears; low Canadian: since ca. 1930.—2. To have a low priority: since the late 1930's. (Nicholas Montsarrat, *The Cruel Sea,* 1951.)

suckster, suckstress (*Dict.*). The definition would more correctly read: fellator, -atrix.

suction raid. Such a bombing attack on enemy

concentrations just ahead of the Allied armies as was 'designed to create a vacuum and suck the *brown jobs* forward' (P-G-R.): Air Force: 1943–5.

sudden. Swift; efficient; esp., swift and efficient: Australian coll.: since ca. 1940. (B., *Australia Speaks,* 1953.) 'This use is pure Shakespeare. *Julius Caesar,* III, i, "Casca, be sudden, for we fear prevention".' (Ramsey Spencer.)—2. Hence, brutally drastic; brutal: Aus.: since ca. 1940. (B., 1959.)

sudden death.—6. A kind of plain boiled pudding: proletarian: from ca. 1880. B. & L.

sudden death on. Expert at (something); brutal or unnecessarily or extremely severe towards (someone): Australian: since ca. 1920. B., 1942. Ex **sudden death,** 1, 2 (p. 846).

suds.—2. Beer: Australian: since ca. 1930. (B.P.)

sue for one's livery. See 'Tavern terms', § 9.

suff. Enough: New Zealand: ca. 1880–1920. ' "I've 'ad suff o' you, Tommy. I'm goin' 'ome," ': G. B. Lancaster, *Sons o' Men,* 1904. Short for *sufficient.*

suffer a recovery. 'To recover from a drinking bout' (Baker): Australian jocular: C. 20.

sufferer (p. 846). Earlier in *Tom and Jerry,* 1821.—2. A sovereign (coin): 1848, *Sinks,* † by 1900. Cf.:

sufferin(g). A sovereign (coin): Cockneys': mid-C. 19–20. (Pugh.)

suffler (p. 846). Perhaps ex Netherlands High German *Suff,* 'the drink'. 'The N.H.G. word could well have been imported in the late 16th Century' (L. W. Forster, letter of June 17, 1938).

sug. See **shug.**

sugar, n.—6. Worthless banknotes: C. 20. Ex sense 1.—7. Inevitable nickname for men surnamed Cane, Kane, Cain: C. 20.—8. 'The ski-ing was quite excellent in granulated snow, what is sometimes called Sugar, formed by one day of hot spring sun' (David Walker, *Devil's Plunge,* 1968): skiers': C. 20.

sugar! A cry of triumph, uttered as one stands upon one leg and shakes the other up and down: ca. 1830–70. *Sinks,* 1848. Victory is sweet.—2. A euphemistic exclamation, used instead of *shit* or *bugger it,* and owing something to both: C. 20. Cf. **sugared!** on p. 846.

sugar(-)baby. A member of the Australian militia: Australian soldiers': 1940 +. B., 1942. No service overseas: perhaps imm. ex: 2. A child averse from going outside the house while it's raining: domestic: late C. 19–20.

sugar bag. (A nest of) native honey: water sweetened with it: Australian rural coll.: late C. 19–20. (B., 1943.)

sugar basin.—2. A marble mason: builders' and mason's rhyming s.: C. 20. (A master builder: Dec. 5, 1953.)

sugar bat. A sugar-cane cutter: Australian cane-cutters': since ca. 1910. (Jean Devanney, *Paradise Flow,* 1938.) Perhaps for 'sugar-batterer.'

sugar boat's in; sugar boat's been sunk. Naval c. pp., directed at the sweetness, or the non-sweetness of the tea: since ca. 1939. (P-G-R.)

sugar candy.—2. Adj., handy: rhyming: C. 20.

suicide.—2. In Australia the word has, to motorists, borne, since ca. 1945, the meaning treated by B.P. in this note, written in June 1963: 'The "cide" of a truck which should not be used for overtaking. In Australia and in Britain, this is the left. "Suicide" and "Passing Side" are often painted on the back of a truck. Also "Undertaker" on the left and "Overtaker" on the right. "Undertaker" is not used in Australia, but it is universally known. . . . Another motorists' phrase is, "Look out for the driver on your right and the fool on your left".'

suicide blonde. Dyed by her own hand: Australian jocular: since ca. 1950. (B.P.)

suicide brigade, the. Those fielders who stand very close to the man batting: cricketers': since ca. 1930. (Not, however, to Hammond, Constantine, Bradman, Compton, Nourse.)

Sullivanise (or -ize). To defeat thoroughly: sporting: late 1880's–1890's. Ex John L. *Sullivan* (1858–1918), that American who dominated the heavy-weights from 1882, when he won fame, until 1892, when Jim Corbett ended his career. In Oct. 1887 he visited England, where he was received by the Prince of Wales and idolized by the crowd. He battered his opponents into unconsciousness, the police often having to interfere.

summat short. The usual pron. of *something short*, q.v. at **short, something** in *Dict.*

summer cabbage. An umbrella; a parasol: fast life: ca. 1810–45. (P. Egan, *Finish*, 1828.)

sump oil. Hair oil: Australian, esp. Sydney, motor mechanics': since ca. 1940. (B.P.)

Sun. A Sunderland flying-boat: R.A.F.: 1939 +. Jackson.

sun. A short form of **sunflower** below. (Anderson.)

sun-dodger.—2. An extremely lazy tramp: Australian: since ca. 1910. B., 1942.

Sunday; morning; midday; evening. Newspaper (and vendors') coll. for a Sunday paper; one issued in the early morning, at noon, after noon: late C. 19–20.

Sunday dog. 'An indolent sheep or cattle dog,' B., 1941: New Zealand and Australian rural coll.: C. 20. Every day a Sunday.

Sunday face. Posteriors: late C. 19–20. Two-cheeked.

Sunday Graffiti, the. The *Sunday Graphic*, a pictorial newspaper: ca. 1945–60. This defunct newspaper was more reputable than its nickname would imply.

Sunday Punch, The. The *Church Times*: Clerical coll. nickname: ca. 1885–1900. Ex the wittiness of the 'answers to correspondents'.

Sunday sidings. 'Sidings compelling Sunday clearance' (*Railway*, 3rd): railwaymen's coll.: C. 20.

sundowner.—2. A drink taken at or about sundown: India, Singapore, the East Indies, Australia: late C. 19–20. (Geoffrey Gorer, letter of Dec. 4, 1938.)—3. (Ex sense 1.) A lazy sheepdog or cattle-dog: Australian: C. 20. Baker.

sunflower. A girl; a young lady: beatniks': since ca. 1959. (Anderson.) Perhaps 'flowering for the *sons*'.

sunk. See **nunk.**

sunk, adj. Ruined; 'finished': mid-C. 19–20: coll. >, by 1960, S.E.

Sunlight!, don't worry—use (p. 847). Alexander McQu τ ɪ., in letter of 1953, vouches for its use by, or slightly before, 1905.

sunny side up. 'An egg fried so that it is done on one side only, the yolk not broken, and not turned over' (Leechman): since ca. 1920: Cana-

dian restaurants >, by 1942, also English restaurants'.

Sunset Strip. The number 77 in the game of Bingo: bingo operators' and players': since ca. 1964; by 1968, already ob. (Anthony Burgess in *The Listener*, March 2, 1967.) Topical—ex a television programme.

sunshade. 'A superstructure on a tank to disguise it as a truck. It was "ditched" before going into action' (Peter Sanders in *The Sunday Times* magazine, Sept. 10, 1967): Army in North Africa: 1940–43. Humorous.

sunshine track, on the. On tramp in remote country districts: C. 20. Australian coll. >, by 1930, S.E. B., 1942.

super, n., 4. Current in New Zealand as early as 1853. (B., 1941.)—7. Superphosphate: farmers' and seed-merchants': C. 20.

super-duper (pron. *sooper-dooper*). An intensive of *super*, adj., 4 (p. 848): schoolgirls' and teen-agers': 1947 +; by 1957, slightly ob.

Super Mac. See **Mac**, 3, above.

super-master. Superintendent of the *supers*: theatrical: from ca. 1860. B. & L.

super sorrow. Very sorry, as in 'Oh! super sorrow': several British preparatory schools': ca. 1960–65.

supercharged (p. 848) has also, since ca. 1930, been common in the R.A.F. (Jackson.)

supering. See **super,** v., in *Dict.*

supernaculum dates from ca. 1640: witness 'Tavern terms', § 2.

Supply Chief. A Supply Chief Petty Officer: since ca. 1920: Naval coll.: by 1940, virtually j. Granville.

suppo. A suppository, whether anal or vaginal: medical and pharmaceutical coll.: since ca. 1935.

suppose, I. See **I suppose.**

Supreme Examples of Allied Confusion. South-East Asia Command (*S.E.A.C.*): coined by the Americans; adopted, 1944, by the Navy.

Supremo, the. Lord Louis Mountbatten: 1943 +. 'A handsome, romantic figure. Hence the Latin-sounding nickname' (*Daily Express*, July 6, 1944). Less prob. ex the Spanish dictator than ex 'El Supremo' in C. S. Forester's *The Happy Return*, 1937. (Peter Sanders.)

sure!, that's for. That's certain: New Zealand and elsewhere: adopted, ca. 1958, ex U.S.

sure!, you may be. See **sure!, be,** in *Dict.*

surface, v.i. To wake: Wrens' (? after submariners'): since ca. 1939. Ex a submarine surfacing.

surface raiders. 'Southern Railway electrical multiple units' (*Railway*, 3rd): since ca. 1946.

surfacing, n. 'Searching for gold on the surface of the ground': Aus. coll.: late C. 19–20. (B., 1959.)

surfie. A surfer, esp. a surfboard rider: 'not heard before 1961', says B.P., who, in mid-1963, adds that it's 'a term rarely used by genuine surfers'.

Surnames, truncated. 'Always in the plural, thus, "*The Partri*: The Partridges; *the Prenti*: the Prentices". This practice has some currency among schoolboys and undergraduates' (B.P.): Australian: since the late 1940's. I'd say that it originated as undergraduate wit, on the analogy of Ancient Roman *gens* (or clan) names ending in -*i*, reinforced by Latin plurals in -*i*, e.g. 'the *Gracchi*'.

Surro. 'Surry Hills (Sydney) and Surrey Hills (Melbourne)': Australian: since ca. 1930. (B., 1953.)

***sus,** adj. and adv. Suspicious(ly): c.: since ca. 1925. (Norman.)—2. (Adj.) suspect, esp. by the police: since ca. 1925; by 1960, also s. (Robin Cook, 1962.)

***suss.** To suspect: c.: from ca. 1920. Cf. **sus,** 2, in *Dict.*

suss out. To puzzle out, work out (an explanation of): mostly teenagers': since 1965 or 1966. *The Queen*, Sept. 28, 1966, 'Youth susses things out on its own'. Cf. **sus,** adj., above. (With thanks to Anthony Burgess.)

susso. The dole; esp. *on the susso*, 'in receipt of unemployment *sustenance*' (B., 1942): Australian: since ca. 1925.

sussy. Suspicious: since ca. 1940. L. J. Cunliffe, *Having It Away*, 1965, 'It seemed a bit sussy to me.'

sutler. See 'Tavern terms', § 6.

sutthink. Sol. for *something*: C. 19–20. (E. Pugh, 1895.) Via *somefink* or *somethink*. Cf. **some'ink.**

swab, n., 1 (p. 844) should be back-dated to 'since ca. 1780', for the derivative sense 'a naval officer' occurs in Charles Dibdin's 'Jack at the Windlass', appearing in *The Britannic Magazine* (I, 25), published in 1793, 'And there's never a swab but the captain knows the stem from the stern of the ship'; also in W. N. Glascock, *The Naval Sketch-Book*, II, 1826. Moe.—3. A dining-hall fatigue man: Army, esp. Guards': since ca. 1920. He swabs it out.—4. A fag: Christ's Hospital (Horsham, England): ? ca. 1840–1960. Perhaps the origin of sense 3.

swab, ship one's. (Of a Midshipman) to get promotion to Sub-Lieutenant: Naval: c. 20. Granville.

swab one's tonsils. To kiss passionately: low U.S., anglicised ca. 1920.

swabber. See 'Tavern terms', § 7.

Swaff. Hannen Swaffer, journalist, dramatic critic, publicist (b. Nov. 1, 1879): journalistic and theatrical: from ca. 1905.

swaffle; mostly as p.ppl. A sol. confusion (mid-C. 19–20) of *swaddle* with *muffle* as in Nevinson, 1895, 'They lay it, all swaffled up in the black skirt and other rags it 'ad on, upon a soot-bag in front o' the fire.'

swaffonder. See **sixty-niner** above.

swag, n.—6. 'Prizes offered at games of skill', B. Crocker in *John o' London's Weekly*, March 19, 1937: showmen's: late C. 19–20. Ex **swag,** n., 3 (*Dict.*).—7. A state, trend or tendency of the betting: sporting, esp. pugilistic: ca. 1810–50. *Boxiana*, III, 1821, 'The scene was now changed —the Cockneys are alive: the *swag* is now for London.' Prob. ex sense 3 (p. 850).—8. A 'packet' of money: Australian: since ca. 1925. Ex sense 3 (p. 850) Leonard Mann, *The Go-Getter*, 1942, 'I've got a chance to get a swag on commission.'

swag, adj. Worthless; gen. *it's swag*: low: from ca. 1860. Ex **swag,** n., 4.

swag, go on the. To become a tramp: Australian and New Zealand coll.: C. 20. B., 1941 and 1943.

swag and plunder. See 'Mock-Auction Slang' above and cf. both **swag,** n., 3 (p. 850) and **plunder,** n., 2 (p. 642); prob. since ca. 1945.

***swag-chovey; swag-shop.** A receivers' shop or store: c.: mid-C. 19–20. B. & L.

swag of, a. Many; much: New Zealand: since ca. 1930. 'There's a swag of them in this joint' (Slatter).

***swag-seller.** A pedlar: vagrants' c.: late C. 19–20. W. A. Gape, *Half a Million Tramps*, 1936.

swag-straps, look for one's. 'To consider leaving one's job in search of another,' B., 1941; New Zealand (mostly rural): late C. 19–20. In Australia, shearers' s.: C. 20: B., 1942.

swagger, n., 2 (p. 850): in Australia since ca. 1900; extant in New Zealand for 'a tramp.' B., 1941.

swaggering Bob. An impudent buffoon: theatrical coll.: mid-C. 19–20; ob. B. & L.

swaggering, n. Tramping, esp. in the outback: Australian coll.: late C. 19–20. Baker.

Swahili words used by the Armed Forces in E. Africa (and S. Africa) in 1939–45 include *pesi-pesi* (pronounced *pacey-pacey*), quickly, get a move on!, and *pole-pole* (pronounced *poley-poley*), slowly, take it easy; *pombī*, native beer, hence any brew obtained in the East; *shauri* or *shauria*, trouble, a row or fracas; *umgeni*, more, again, hence *amgenis*, 'afters'.

swain. Coxswain: Naval coll.: late C. 19–20. Granville.

swakking, n. Censoring Naval mail: Naval officers': 1939–45. Ex *swak* (p. 851). P-G-R.

swallow, n.—3. A quick draw at a cigarette: C. 20. Ex 'swallowing' the smoke and exhaling it through the nostrils.

swallow, v.—2. To cancel (an appointment or arrangement or plan): low, esp. Londoners': since ca. 1920. Arthur La Bern, *Night Darkens the Street*, 1947, 'We were all tired, so we decided to swallow it' (a visit to the racecourse).

swallow a hair. See 'Tavern terms', § 8, and cf. **swallow a tavern-token** (*Dict.*).

swallow (or swaller) and sigh. Collar and tie: theatrical rhyming s.: late C. 19–20. Ngaio Marsh, *Vintage Murder*, 1938.

swallow bobby. 'Some of the first "nobs" in the colony [of New South Wales] used to "swallow bobby" (make false affidavits to an enormous extent)': A. Harris, *Settlers and Convicts*, 1847: Australian: ca. 1810–90. Cf. **swallow the anchor** and **swelp me bob** (*Dict.*).

swallow it. 'Only a few weeks ago he told me he "had swallowed it"—got out of crime' (John Gosling, *The Ghost Squad*, 1959): since ca. 1920: orig. and still mainly c. On the analogy of *swallow the anchor*, q.v. at **anchor, swallow the** on p. 12; also cf. **swallow,** v., 2, above.

swallow the dictionary; esp. in *must have swallowed the dictionary*, applied to one who uses very long words: coll.: late C. 19–20.

swallow yourself!; oh, swallow yourself! See **oh, swallow yourself!**

swamp, v. To exchange or barter: Australian: C. 20. B., 1942. Perversion of *swap*?—2. To spend (money), esp. on drink: Australian: since ca. 1920. Baker. Perhaps ex the next.—3. The v.i. (with variant *swamp it*) of **swamper,** 1 and 2. *The Drum*, 1959.

swamp down. To swallow, gulp down (a drink): Australian: since ca. 1910. Baker. Cf. **swamp,** v. and **swamped.**

swamp one's way (with). To travel along (with someone), esp. in the outback: C. 20. Tom Ronan, *Only a Short Walk*, 1961. Cf. **swamp,** v., 1, above.

swamped. Tipsy: Services (little in Army): since ca. 1920. H. & P. Cf. American *tanked*.

swamper. A tramp; one who walks to his destination but has a teamster carry his 'swag': Australian rural: C. 20. B., 1942. Ex: A bullock-driver's assistant: Australian bullock drivers': C. 20. (K. S. Prichard, *Working Bullocks*, 1926, There we also find *swamp*, v.i., to be such an assistant.)—2. 'A man, often partially incapacitated, who keeps the bunkhouses clean (*swamped out*) in a logging camp or on a ranch' (Leechman): Canadian coll.: C. 20.

swamy-house is a variant of **sammy-house** (*Dict.*).

swan. 'The migratory habits of the swan have provided us with one of the most expressive of all Korean words. The act of "swanning" (going purposefully anywhere without a purpose) is one of the most favoured pastimes of the theatre. If one were to "swan" southward with the purpose of moving on from the enemy, the act would be called "bugging out"' (*Iddiwah*, July 1953): United Nations troops in and during the Korean War. Ex the next two entries.—2. Earlier, as used by the Army in France and Germany, 1944–45 and esp. in *a good swan*, a rapid advance. (Peter Sanders in *The Sunday Times* magazine, Sept. 10, 1965.) Ex **swan around** below.

swan about the blue. 'To drive about aimlessly, with more than a suspicion that one is lost' (Peter Sanders): Army: 1940–3, *the blue* being the desert; then loosely in, or concerning, regions other than North Africa.

swan around. (Of tanks) to circle about; (of persons) to wander either in search of a map-reference or aimlessly: Army: 1940 +. Ex the manœuvres of swans queening it on pond or stream. See esp. *Forces' Slang*, by Wilfred Granville, Frank Roberts, Eric Partridge, 1948. 2. To 'tour' unauthorised: Army: 1944–5. (P-G-R.)

Swank. Inevitable nickname for men surnamed Russell: Services: C. 20.

swank, v., 1 (p. 851). By extension in the Services: 'to dress in one's grandest attire; to prepare to meet a girl,' H. & P.: since ca. 1925. Cf. **swanks.**

swank, adj. (p. 851), is very much alive in Canada. (Leechman, 1959.) An early example occurs in James Joyce, *Ulysses*, 1922.

swank(e)y, n.—2. A conceited or pretentious person: ca. 1830–80. Edward Lancaster, *The Manager's Daughter* (a one-act interlude), ? 1837. (Moe.) Ex the adj. while that adj. was still dial.

swank(e)y swipes. Table beer: 1848, *Sinks*; † by 1920.

swanks. One's best clothes: Services: since ca. 1925. Cf. **swank, v.,** 1 (above).—2. Sausages: Army: since ca. 1940. P-G-R.: 'They pretend to be meat and are mostly bread.'

swanner. An unauthorised wanderer or tourist: Army: 1944–5. Ex **swan around.**

Swans, the.—2. South Melbourne footballers: Melbournites': since ca. 1920. (B., 1943.)

swap, get a. See **swap, n.,** 2 in the *Dict.*

swart pak, the. The police: South African c., mostly among Afrikaans-speakers: C. 20. *The Cape Times*, June 3, 1946 (Alan Nash). Lit., 'The Black Suit(s)'.

swassander or **-onder.** See **sixty-niner** above.

swatched. Tipsy: since ca. 1950. Perhaps cf.

Warwickshire dial. *swatched*, (of a woman) untidily dressed.

swatty is an occ. C. 20 (esp., R.A.F. regulars') variant of *swaddy*, 'a soldier' (*Dict.*).

swaying the main (p. 852). To *sway the main* also means 'to swagger; to assert oneself': Naval: C. 20.

swear and cuss. A bus: Cockney rhyming: since ca. 1910. Len Ortzen, *Down Donkey Row*, 1938.

Swears was suggested by the name of the firm of Swears & Wells. (p. 852.)

sweat(-)box.—2. 'A sluing or aligning jack requiring much human energy' (*Railway*): railwaymen's: late C. 19–20.

sweat it out. To keep on trying hard, esp. in order to 'survive', as in, say, cricket or football: coll.: C. 20.

sweat like a bull. See **bull, sweat like a.**

sweat machine. A bicycle: Australian, esp. Sydney, motor mechanics': since ca. 1945. (B.P.)

sweat on is short for *sweat* (or *be sweating*) **on the top line** (p. 853): 'The symptoms of one who anticipates promotion or posting are called "sweating on" . . . he is getting hot and bothered about it,' H. & P.: since ca. 1925. Cf.:

sweat on promotion. To make oneself conspicuous with a view to advancement: military: from ca. 1920. Ex **sweat on** (leave), q.v. in *Dict.*

sweat pads. Pancakes: Canadian: since ca. 1945. (Leechman.)

sweat the purser (p. 853) occurs earlier in Smyth's glossary, in Bowen's sense, which should be back-dated to ca. 1840. In George Brewer's farce, *Bannian Day*, 1796, at I, iii, p. 8, and II, iii, p. 25, it seems to mean 'to take an illicit or, at the least, a sly drink at the expense of the ship's purser'. Moe.

sweater girl. A girl, a woman, with a well-developed bust. Australian coll.: since ca. 1925. A sweater exhibits such a female to considerable advantage.

sweaty. Hard, difficult, severe: coll., esp. school-boys': C. 20. Arnold Lunn, *Loose Ends*, 1919, '"It's a sweaty house for new men." Cluff shook his head sadly. "Yes, it's a hard life for new men."' Also of persons, as in ibid.: 'These Blues [as schoolmasters] are sometimes rather sweaty. They think it lip if you cut your work for a man who's been a Blue.'

Swede. A fairly common nickname for men surnamed Harvey: since ca. 1930. Why?

swede, 1, as in *set the swede down* (p. 746), has, since ca. 1950, developed a separate existence, esp. in the R.A.F.—2. 'A raw recruit—i.e. one just from the country; or an airman with a rural, countrified manner,' Jackson: R.A.F.: since ca. 1930. Short for **swede-basher.** Hence, by 1945, in general use.

swede, crash down the. Variation (since ca. 1925) of set the swede down (p. 746). Granville. Sometimes shortened to *crash down.*

swede, crash the. See **crash . . .**

swede-basher. An agricultural labourer; a country bumpkin: Services: since ca. 1925. H. & P. He 'bashes about'—walks heavily—among the turnips.—2. Hence, since ca. 1930, the agent in:

swede-bashing. Field training, as opposed to *square-bashing* (parade work, drill): since ca. 1930. Army and R.A.F. Partridge, 1945, 'Field training . . . often takes recruits into the fields and hedgerows.' In the Navy *swede-bashing* means sleeping: Granville.

swede talk. Rural talk; countrymen's talk: Cockneys': late C. 19–20. Cf. **swede-bashing** above.

Swedeland. Country parts: since ca. 1950. (Laurie Atkinson, 11 Sept. 1967.) Ex **swede-basher**, 1, above.

swedey or **swedy.** An employee of the Great Eastern Railway: ca. 1890–1925. (*Railway*.) It passed through much agricultural country.—2. As *the Swed(e)y*, it = the old Great Eastern Railway.

sweedle. To trick with cajolery: from 1912; slightly ob. In Henry Arthur Jones's comedy, *Dolly Reforming Herself* (published in 1913), extravagant featherhead Dolly was played by Marie Lohr; her long-suffering husband accused her of 'sweedling' him, and the phrase caught on. Obviously a blend of *swindle* + *wheedle*.

Sweeney Todd, the. The Flying Squad: low London rhyming s.: since ca. 1925. F. D. Sharpe, *The Flying Squad*, 1938. Often shortened to *the Sweeny*, as in John Gosling, *The Ghost Squad*, 1959.

sweenies. Members of the Flying Squad: c., since ca. 1930; hence, since ca. 1940, also police s. (John Dickson Carr, *Patrick Butler for the Defence*, 1956.) Ex:

sweet, adj.—4. Arranged, settled; gen. *It's sweet*, all right because fixed: Australian: C. 20. —5. Hence, correct; in order: Australian: since ca. 1910. Lawson Glassop, *Lucky Palmer*, 1949. —6. Egregious; pejoratively, great, thorough: coll.: C. 19–20; by ca. 1930, slightly ob. 'The ship was at this time refitting, and . . . a sweet mess she was in.' F. Marryat, *Frank Mildmay*, 1829. (Moe.)

*sweet, adv. Without difficulty or trouble: c.: C. 20. F. D. Sharpe, *The Flying Squad*, 1938.

sweet, she's. Everything's all right: Aus.: C. 20. (B., 1959.)

sweet B.A. Nothing: low: since ca. 1940. 'You can do sweet B.A. about it' (Norman). Cf. *sweet F.A.* at *Fanny Adams*, 2 (p. 266) and esp. the exact semantic parallel, *sod all*.

sweet evening breeze. Cheese: rhyming s.: C. 20. (Lester.) Often shortened to *sweet(-)evening*: cf. quotation at **strike-me**, above.

sweet Jane (or **jane**). A complaisant girl: Teddy boys': since ca. 1948. (*The News of the World*, Sept. 26, 1954.)

sweet-meat. See **sweetmeat** (*Dict.*).

sweet-pea. Whiskey: Anglo-Irish: ca. 1810–70. 'A Real Paddy', *Life in Ireland*, 1822. Ex the colour of the resultant urine.—2. (Or without hyphen). Tea: rhyming s.: C. 20. Not at all common. Franklyn 2nd.—3. A 'pee' or urination: probably rhyming s.: mid C. 19–20. Used by and of both sexes; cf. **sweet-pea, do** or **plant a**, on p. 853.

sweet-pea ward. See **lily pond.**

sweet sixteen . . . See **Little Jimmy,** [near end.

sweetest thing, the. Very 'decent': coll.: from ca. 1902. W. L. George, *The Making of an Englishman*, 1914.

sweetie.—2. Also, since ca. 1945, in reference, e.g. 'He's been an absolute sweetie to me' (kind, considerate, generous).

sweetie (or **-y**) **pie.** In address: dear; 'sweet': since ca. 1930. In, e.g., Josephine Bell, *Trouble*

at *Wrekin Farm*, 1942. Elaboration of *sweet* (sweetheart).

sweetness and light. Whiskey: jocular Australian: since ca. 1910. (D'Arcy Niland, *Call Me . . .*, 1958.)

swell, n., 1 (p. 854) occurs in the nuance 'gentleman', a quarter of a century earlier than *Lex. Bal.*: in *Sessions*, Dec. 1786; also in Potter, 1797.—4. (Gen. pl.) One of those boys who, with special privileges, rule a house: Rugby School-boys': mid-C. 19–20.

swell head. A superintendent: Canadian railroadmen's (— 1931). Alluding to the *swelled* (or swollen) *head* of exhibited self-conceit.—2 (p. 854): prob. adopted ex U.S., where current at least as early as 1866, when it occurs in *The Galaxy* of Dec. 15 at p. 719. (Moe.)

swell mob, 1 (p. 854). Six years earlier in *Sessions*, 1830.

swell's lush. Champagne: Australian: ca. 1830–1900. In, e.g., *Sketches of Australian Life and Scenery* (by a Resident), 1876. See, in *Dict.*, the two elements.

swelp me ten men 'is a favourite Cockney version' of *swelp me bob*, etc., q.v. at **swelp** on p. 855. (Julian Franklyn.)

swerve, n. and v. (To stop at a) *coïtus interruptus*: Australian motorists': since ca. 1950. An evasive action to avoid a child.

*swi (p. 855). Also Australian: B., 1942, has *swy*. Hence, *swi-up school*: a two-up school: Baker.—2. A florin: low Australian: late C. 19–20. Also *swy*. Like sense 1, it derives ex Ger. *zwei*, two.—3. A sentence, or a term, of two years' imprisonment: Australian c.: since ca. 1925. (B., 1942.)

Swift or **Swifty.** 'Derisive nickname for slow-moving rating' (Granville): Naval coll.: late C. 19–20. Cf. **Curly,** 3 (Add.) and **Tiny** (*Dict.*).

swiftie (or **-ty**). An illegal trick: Australian: since ca. 1920. Caddie, *A Sydney Barmaid*, 1953, '"You didn't work a swiftie on them, did you?" I asked suspiciously.' Perhaps a semantic blend of *swift*, fast, and *fast one*. It is 'most commonly heard in the phrase *to pull a swiftie*' (B.P., mid-1963). Should be back-dated to ca. 1910: cf. its use in Tom Ronan, *Only a Short Walk*, 1961.

swiftly flowing. Going: Australian rhyming s.: late C. 19–20. B., 1945, cites *The* Sydney *Bulletin* of Jan. 18, 1902.

swill, n.—2. See **six o'clock swill** above.

swillery. A non-temperance hotel: Australian: since ca. 1945. (B., 1953.)

swimming market. A (very) good market: Stock Exchange coll.: from ca. 1860. B. & L. Opp. **sick market,** q.v.

swindle, n.—4. 'A cunning contrivance, a wangle' (Jackson): R.A.F.: since ca. 1930. Ex sense 2 (p. 855). Esp. in *tea swindle*, 'arrangement by section for co-operative purchase of tea and refreshments' (Sgt G. Emanuel).

swindle sheet. An expense sheet: Naval: C. 20. Humorous.

swine mixture. Mr Ramsey Spencer writes: 'At Bishop's Stortford College, between the wars, there was something called "swine mixture", composed of sardines mashed with cocoa and a minute tin of Nestlé's milk.'

swing, v.—5. To play 'swing' music: musicians': from 1936. E.g. 'Hear our Orchestra. They will swing for you', in an advertisement, seen in a MS. novel on July 1, 1937.—6. To postpone, put off, defer: Naval: since ca. 1925. Granville, 'Confronted with a pile of paper work, one occasionally "swings it till Monday".' Cf. **swing it** (p. 856).— 7. To boast about: Army: since ca. 1930. Esp. in *swinging one's service.* (P-G-R.)—8. (Cf. sense 5.) 'To get the feel of, to comprehend the truth or beauty of anything worth digging; to impart the same truth or beauty to others' (*The* Victoria *Daily Colonist*, April 16, 1959, 'Basic Beatnik'): Canadian jazz-lovers' and musicians': adopted, 1956 or 1957, ex U.S. In *The American Dialect Society*, Nov. 1958, Norman D. Hinton ('Language of Jazz Musicians') defines *swing* as 'to play well in all senses, technically and otherwise, but especially to have the basic feel for jazz rhythms'.—9. Hence, mostly as in 'These times are more swinging'— livelier: since ca. 1961.

*swing a bag (whence the n. **bag-swinger**). Of a prostitute: to walk the streets: Australian c.: since ca. 1925. (B., 1953.)

swing at (someone), **take a.** To punch (him): mostly children's and teenagers', esp. in Australia: since ca. 1925. (B.P.)

swing Kelly. See **swing Douglas** (*Dict.*).

swing o' the door. 'Publand . . . first round is known as "one", second as "the other half", third as "same again", fourth as "a final", fifth as "one for the road", sixth as "a binder", and seventh as "swing o' the door",' *Sunday Dispatch*, July 3, 1938.

swing on the ear; usually as vbl n., *swinging* . ., requesting a loan: Regular Army: C. 20.

swing one's tapes. See **tapes.**

swing round the buoy. To hold on to a soft job: Naval: since ca. 1920. Ex the Naval coll. sense 'to ride at anchor'. (P-G-R.)

swing that lamp, Jack! 'A shooter of lines is told to do this. A hint that he is being rather "bad form"' (Granville): Naval c.p.: since 1945.

swing the billy. To put the kettle on the fire in order to make a pot of tea: Australian: since ca. 1920. (D'Arcy Niland, *Call Me . . .*, 1958.)

swing the gate. 'From the New Zealand shearing sheds came those effective expressions *to drag the chain* and *swing the gate*, . . . applied to the slowest and the fastest shearer in the shed respectively,' B., 1941: New Zealand and Australian: C. 19–20.

swing the hammer. See **hammer, swing the** (*Dict.*).

swinge up. See **swinge off** (*Dict.*).

swinger.—6. A lame leg: low: ca. 1830–75. *Sinks*, 1848.—7. Short for *lead-swinger*, a malingerer: Australian: since ca. 1918. B., 1942.— 8. An unscheduled extra bus: London busmen's: since ca. 1925. It has been 'swung' on them.— 9. A fine or delightful person: Australian: since ca. 1925. (Jean Devanney, *Paradise Flow*, 1938.)—10. 'An additional train coach' (*Railway*): railwaymen's coll.: C. 20. At the end of the train, and esp. on a curve, it tends to swing. Cf. *tail-wag* below.

swingers. Self-supporting breasts that swing as the owner walks: Australian: since ca. 1930.—2. Hence, any female breasts: Australian: since ca. 1940.

swinging, adj. Lively and alert and progressive, with a connotation of success: since ca. 1963. Anthony Lejeune in *The Daily Telegraph*, colour supplement, March 10, 1967, 'The words "swinging" and "square" are like "progressive" and "reactionary", vague value judgements disguised as descriptions.' Perhaps ex *swinging along*—of, e.g., pedestrians.

swinging the copper. 'The rubbing of a copper coin on the back of the hand or on the arm to make it fester' (A. B. Petch, April 1966). Tommies': W.W. I. On the far better known *swinging the lead.*

swinjer (B., 1942). See **swinger,** 1: p. 856.

swipe, n.—4. A kind of jersey used for games: Marlborough College: C. 20.—5. An objectionable person: Australia and New Zealand: since ca. 1920. (Jean Devanney, *By Tropic Sea and Jungle*, 1944: Ruth Park, *The Witch's Thorn*, 1952.)

swipes, 2 (p. 856) app. goes back to late C. 18, to judge by an English song quoted in *The Port Folio* of Nov. 9, 1805. (Moe.)

swipey (p. 856). Rather earlier in Pierce Egan, *Life in London*, 1821.

swipington or **swippington.** A drunkard: Australian: C. 20. B., 1942. A confirmed consumer of **swipes** (p. 836).

swips. See 'Colston's'.

swish, v.—2. To beat, to cane: Clifton College: C. 20. Hence, *swishing*, a caning.—3. See:

swish or **swish-tail.** 'To check speed by a yaw before landing': aviators': from ca. 1920. *The New Statesman and Nation*, Feb. 20, 1937. Ex S.E. *swish-tail*, 'a long flowing tail which can be swished about' (O.E.D.).

swish, adj. (p. 857): much used in Australia. See, e.g., Kylie Tennant, *Foveaux*, 1939.—2. (Perhaps ex sense 1 on p. 857.) Effeminate: since the late 1930's and mostly theatrical. 'A male making "pansy" gestures is "swish"' (Richard Merry).

swishing hitter. See **rum customer** above.

Swiss. A pheasant: Oxford: ca. 1815–60. *Spy*, 1825.

switch. A chimneysweep's brush: chimney-sweeps' coll.: C. 19. (George Elson, 1900.)

switched.—2. 'Known in the [watchmaking] trade as a "switched" watch—with trashy works put into a case bought up for the purpose,' newspaper cutting of March 25, 1944: C. 20.

switched on. In the fashion; well-informed; 'with it': since ca. 1960. Ex electric lighting.

switchel. Cold tea: Newfoundland coll.: late C. 19–20. (L. E. F. English, *Historic Newfoundland*, 1955.) Ex U.S. *switchel*, molasses and water.

switching. A marriage: low: ca. 1840–1900. Mary Carpenter, *Juvenile Delinquents*, 1853. Ex **switch** (p. 857).

swivel-eyed (p. 857): earlier in Smollett, *The Reprisal* (II, xv), 1757. Moe.

swiz.—2. Abbr. **swizzle,** n., 1: mostly Cockneys': from ca. 1875; ob. B. & L.—3. (Also adj.) Something fine or excellent: Australian: since ca. 1925. B., 1942. A corruption of **swish,** adj. (p. 857).

swizzler. See **swizzle,** v., 3 (*Dict.*).

swog. See 'Miscellanea'.

swoman. A station warrant officer (S.W.O.) R.A.F.: since ca. 1925; slightly ob. since ca. 1955.

swopper; swopping. See **swapper** and **swapping** in the *Dict.*

sword. A bayonet: Army (other ranks') coll.:

late C. 19–20. Patrick MacGill, *The Amateur Army*, 1915. But note that in the Rifle regiments, *sword* is the correct term.

sword and medals. A ceremonial occasion: Naval officers' coll.: C. 20. Hence, adj., as in 'This will be a sword-and-medals "do"'. (Granville.)

sword swallowing. 'The practice of eating with one's knife' (Baker): Australian jocular: C. 20.

swottie. A soldier: Australian Naval: since ca. 1910. (B., 1943.) A slovening of **swaddy** (p. 850).

swy. See **swi**.

*sycher and **zoucher.** A contemptible person: c., and low: from ca. 1780; ob. B. & L.: '"Sich" is provincial for a bad man.'

Sydney blanket. A variant of *Wagga blanket*. (B., 1943.)

Sydney duck.—2. Any one of the numerous—many of them disreputable—Australians that rushed to California in 1849 ff.: mid-C. 19–20; in C. 20, mostly historical. Orig. an Americanism, it was adopted, ca. 1860, in Australia. B., 1942.

They sailed from Sydney; *duck* is ironic. (See esp. *Name into Word*.)

Sydney harbour. A barber: Australian rhyming s.: late C. 19–20. (B., 1943.)

Sydney or the bush, e.g. **it's (either).** A final choice or decision: Australian (esp. N.S.W.) c.p.: late C. 19–20. Edward Shann, *An Economic History of Australia*, 1930, '"Sydney or the bush!" cries the Australian when he gambles against odds.'

sync (pron. *sink*), n. and v. Synchronization; to synchronize: filmland: since ca. 1931. Cameron McCabe, *The Face on the Cutting Room Floor*, 1937, 'To get them synced' and 'Put them both in sync'. But, since ca. 1940, used in all technical fields. (B.P.)

synthetic. 'Often applied to news which is suspect, or to a person who seems to pretend to be something more than he really is,' H. & P.: Services: since ca. 1935. In the R.A.F. it is often applied to the theory as opposed to the practice of flying. For the semantics, cf. **ersatz girl** (p. 258).

sypho. Syphilis: Australian: since ca. 1920. (B., 1953.)

T

T.A. Tel Aviv: coll.: since ca. 1939. (Ian Jeffries, *Thirteen Days*, 1958.)

T.A.B.U.; S.A.B.U.; N.A.B.U. A *t*ypical *A*rmy *b*alls-*u*p; a *s*elf-*a*djusting *b*alls-*u*p; a *n*on-*a*djustable *b*alls-*u*p: Army: mostly officers' and esp. in N. Africa: 1940–5. (J. F. Fullarton, *Troop Target*, 1943.) Cf. *S.A.A.F.U.* and *T.A.R.F.U.* and *T.C.C.F.U.*

T. and O, (p. 858).—2. Taken and offered: racing coll.: C. 20.

t.b.—3. 'Two beauts' (large and shapely breasts): Australian: since ca. 1920.

T.C.C.F.U. Typical Coastal Command fuck-up: ca. 1941–4. In the R.A.F., permissible only to Coastal Command personnel: used by any other Command, 'Them's fightin' words, partner.'

T.M. A 'tailor-made'—i.e., ready made—cigarette: Aus.: since ca. 1935.

T.V. behind, you're getting. A c.p. addressed to a broad-beamed woman: since ca. 1956. The implication is that they spend too much time in sitting and watching T.V.

taa! See ta! in *Dict.*

tab, n., 3 (p. 859). Also, in C. 20, low London s. —as in John G. Brandon, *The Dragnet*, 1936.—8. See tabs, 2.—9. A sweetheart (female); one's girl; one's woman: Australian: since ca. 1910. B., 1942. Short for tabby, 4 (p. 859).

tab, keep a (p. 859). In Australian usage, *keep tab of*, 'for any record, esp. the bill at restaurants . . . for taxation purposes' (B.P., 1963).

Tab-socking, n. A boxing contest against Cambridge University ('the Can*tabs*'): Oxford University boxers': ca. 1895–1914.

tab (up) on. To 'keep tabs on' someone: Australian: since ca. 1930. Gavin Casey, *Downhill Is Easier*, 1945.

tabby party. See tabby, 3 (*Dict.*).

table, on the, adj. and adv. On the operating table: medical coll.: mid-C. 19–20. (Christianna Brand, *Green for Danger*, 1945.)

table, the. The pitch: cricketers': since ca. 1920. Ex the frequent description of Australian and South African pitches being 'as hard and smooth as a billiard table'.

table, under the, adj. and adv., applied to 'something given as a bribe' (F. D. Sharpe, *The Flying Squad*, 1938): low: C. 20. Cf. the commercial *under the counter* of 1941–8.

table-end man. A husband whose desires are so urgent that he cannot wait to go upstairs: domestic: late C. 19–20.

tabloid sports. A 'miniature' sports-meeting: Army officers' jocular coll.: ca. 1939–45. (P-G-R.)

tabs.—2. Curtains: theatrical: C. 20. Peter Fleming, *A Story to Tell*, 1942.—3. Feet: Army: since ca. 1930.

tabu. See nabu.

tache. See tash.

tache on, keep one's. To remain unruffled; 'keep one's hair on': Anglo-Indian: late C. 19–20. With a pun on *thatch* (head of hair) and with a reference to Tatcho, the hair-restorer. Ex Hindi *sac, sacca*: cf. Prakrit *sacca*, Sanskrit *satya*, true or genuine, and the Continental Gypsy *čačo*, Welsh Gypsy *tačo*, which have the same meaning (present in 'Tatcho'): witness Dr John Sampson in his *magnum opus*, 1926.

tack, n.—5. Gear (harness, etc.): hunting: late C. 19–20. (Joanna Cannan, *Murder Included* 1950.) Ex S.E. *tackle*.

tack or sheet (p. 859). Recorded earlier by B. & L. Rather, since early C. 19, for it occurs in W. N. Glascock, *Sailors and Saints* (I, 15), 1829. Moe.

tackline. A hyphen, as in a hyphenated name: Naval signalmen's: since the 1930's. A tackline 'joins' a set of flags.

tact, go on the. To 'go on the water-waggon': military: from ca. 1890; ob. Richards. Suggested by 'teetotal', perhaps; but imm., by corruption, ex tack, on the (q.v. in *Dict.*).

tadger. Penis: North Country, esp. Yorkshire: late C. 19–20. Perhaps ex *tadpole*.

Taff Davi(e)s. See 'Nicknames'.

Taffs, the. The Welch Guards regiment: Army: late C. 19–20. See Jock, 2. Ex taff, 2 (p. 860).

taffy horse. 'A chestnut with a much lighter (often silver) mane and tail' (B., 1942): Australian sporting and rural: C. 20. Ex the colour of toffee (dial. *taffy*).

tai-pai; tai-pan. See taipai.—tai-pay. See taipay.

tail, n.—6. A political following in the House of Commons: Parliamentary: late C. 19–20.—7. A rear gunner in an aircraft: R.A.F.: since ca. 1938. (P-G-R.) Cf. *tail-end Charlie.*

tail, v., 2. Recorded by C. L. Money in *Knocking About in New Zealand*, 1871. (B., 1941.)—3. See tail it below.

tail, get on (one's own). To grow angry—but also, to grow afraid: Australian: since ca. 1918. B., 1942. Perhaps cf. get on the tail of (p. 860): certainly tail is out (below).

tail, on (a person's). See tail, be on (*Dict.*).

tail arse Charlie is a confusion between arse-end Charlie and:

tail-end Charlie. The rear gunner on a bomber: R.A.F.: since ca. 1938. *The Weekly Telegraph*, Jan. 25, 1941; H. & P. A fellow at the rear.—2 . Hence, the rear 'plane in a formation: since ca. 1939. Jackson. Cf. arse-end Charlie.—3. (Ex senses 1 and 2.) A goods guard: railwaymen's: since ca. 1945. (*Railway*, 3rd.)

tail-feathers, -fence, -flowers, -fruit, -gap, -gate, -hole, -juice, -pike, -pin, -pipe, -tackle, -trading, -trimmer, -wagging, -water, -work. See tail, n., 3, in the *Dict.*

tail is out, one's. One is angry: non-aristocratic: from ca. 1860. B. & L.

tail it, occasionally merely *tail.* To die: c. and low s.: since ca. 1920. '. . . The old dear "tailed" meant the old lady died' (Bournemouth *Evening Echo*, April 20, 1966).

Tail Light Alley. A street frequented by amorous couples using parked cars at night: low Australian: since late 1940's. With a pun on **tail,** n., 2 (p. 860).

tail (strictly, **the tail) of my shirt looks like a french polisher's apron—all brown.** 'A typical would-be wicked pleasantry at the expense of a comrade': Naval: since ca. 1930.

tail of the cart, the. (Plenty of) manure: farmers' coll.: late C. 19–20. (*Daily Express*, Oct. 15, 1945.) Shovelled out freely, the cart-tail being down.

tail on fire. See **tail,** n., 3 (*Dict.*).

tail out of it. See **tail off** (*Dict.*).

*****tail-piece.** Three months' imprisonment: c.: ca. 1850–1910. James Greenwood, 1869.

tail up, 2 (p. 861) is in C. 20 Australia, however, not c. but rural coll., as in 'Sent out to "tail up" some horses that had strayed': Archer Russell, *A Tramp Royal in Australia,* 1934.

tail-wag. The motion of the rearmost coach or truck of a train: railwaymen's coll.: late C. 19–20. (*Railway.*)

tail-wagger. A dog: jocular coll.: C. 20. 'The "Tail-Waggers' Club" was started for publicity purposes by a manufacturer of "canine condition-powders" in, I think, the 1920's' (Ramsey Spencer, March 1967).

tailie; headie. A player consistently backing tails or heads: Australian two-up players': since ca. 1920. (B., 1953.) Both occur earlier in Lawson Glassop, *Lucky Palmer,* 1949.

tailor-made, adj. and n. (A) machine-made (cigarette): Naval: since ca. 1910. *The Weekly Telegraph,* Sept. 13, 1941. Fairly general by ca. 1920: current in New Zealand by 1925. (Jean Devanney, *Bushman Burke,* 1930.) Also Aus., since ca. 1925.

tailors. (Very rare in singular.) Machine-rolled cigarettes: Australian: since ca. 1920. B., 1942. Cf. prec. term.

tailor's Tarzan. A man whose bulk is manifestly emphasized by sartorial devices, e.g. padded shoulders: coll. (– 1947). Ex the 'beefcake' Tarzans of the films.

tainted money. Money belonging to a third party; or at least neither to the speaker nor to his 'audience': jocular: since ca. 1930. '*Taint* yours and '*taint* mine.

taipai or **tai-pai.** A large ticket; a boss: pidgin: from resp. ca. 1850, ca. 1870. B. & L. Also in second sense, *taipan* or *typan.*

taipay. A porter: Canton pidgin: mid-C. 19–20. Ibid.

taiteyoggy. A phonetic spelling of **tatie oggy.**

take, n.—2. A cheater at cards; esp. a professional cardsharp: Australian: since ca. 1930. (B., 1953.)—3. Esp. a confidence trickster: Australian c.: since ca. 1935. (B., 1953.)—4. A gross deception; a swindle: Australian: since ca. 1935. (B.P.) Ex sense 5 of the v.

take, v.—5. To swindle (someone): c.: since ca. 1920. (Gerald Kersh, *Slightly Oiled,* 1946.)—6. An Army, esp. a Guards, usage perhaps best exemplified by these examples from Roger Grinstead,

Some Talk of Alexander, 1943: 'It'll take you instead of me'—you, not I, will be on duty: 'It takes you for a casual day'—you'll be on this duty for a day, in addition to your usual work; 'Soon be taking us to storm the shores of France'—we'll soon be due to invade France.—7. To accept; to endure: see **take it** below.—8. To overtake: mostly motorists': since ca. 1950.

take a bend out of. To reduce the high spirits of; to quieten (beasts) by wearying: Australian: C. 20. (K. S. Prichard, *Working Bullocks,* 1926: Cf. brumbies.)

take a brush. To fight a bout: pugilistic and Naval: early C. 19. Fredk Marryat, *Frank Mildmay,* 1829 (p. 55 of the 1897 edition), 'I became a scientific pugilist, and now and then took a brush with an oldster.' Moe.

take a cook. See **give a cook.**

take a dim view of. To disapprove; think silly, inefficient, objectionable: Services: since ca. 1937. Communicated, in April 1942, by Grenfell Finn-Smith. Cf. **dim,** 2 (*Dict.*), and **take a poor view.**

take a figure. To appeal to the ballot instead of to tossing: printers': from ca. 1860. B. & L.

take a job off the blower. To receive a telephoned order for a cab: taxi-drivers': since ca. 1918. Herbert Hodge, *Cab, Sir?,* 1939.

take a lend (or loan) of someone. See **lend of.**

take a (or the) mike out of. To insult or annoy (a person) with a direct or an indirect verbal attack': Cockneys': C. 20.

take a piece out of. To reprimand or reprove (someone): Australian: since ca. 1925. B., 1942. Cf. **tear a strip off.**

take a piss out of. See **piss out of . . .**

take a poor view is slightly milder than . . . *dim* . . .: Services: since ca. 1938. Communicated by Grenfell Finn-Smith, April 1942; H. & P.

take a powder. See **fade, do a.**

take a pull on oneself, often shortened to *take a pull.* To take oneself in hand, to pull oneself together: Australian coll.: since ca. 1860. Brian Penton, *Inheritors,* 1936. '"Steady now . . . Take a pull or you'll cruel our pitch."'

take a punt at. To 'have a go' at, to attempt, something: Australian: since the late 1940's. John O'Grady, *Aussie English,* 1965. Cf. **punt,** v., 2 (p. 669).

take a red-hot potato! See **potato . . .**

take a run at yourself! Go to the deuce!: Australian: C. 20. B., 1942. Cf. *take a running jump.*

take a running jump at the moon! 'An instruction to depart': mostly Canadian: since ca. 1950. 'There are substitutes for *jump*' (Leechman)— very rude ones, at that!

take a screw at. To glance or look at: mostly Australian, but also low: C. 20. B., 1942.

take a snout. To take offence: low Australian: C. 20. (D'Arcy Niland, *The Big City,* 1959.)

take a stretch out of, (esp. a horse). To exercise: Australian coll.: late C. 19–20. (K. S. Prichard, *Coonardoo,* 1929.) To cause to stretch its limbs.

take a swab! Hold an investigation!—of any sort: Australian: since ca. 1950. 'Ex swab taken to detect drugs in the saliva of racehorses' (B.P.).

take a turn in the barrel or at the bung-hole. To sodomise: Naval, hence other Services', low: C. 20. Masked sodomy.

take a whirl at. See **birl**, latter part.

take care of Dowb (*Dict.*). 'The story goes that some high-placed person wished to look after an officer called Dowbiggin and sent to Lord Raglan in the Crimea the message "Take care of Dowbiggin." Communications broke down in the middle of the transmission of the message, so all that arrived was "Take care of Dowb . . ." and the receiver surmised that Dowb was some part of the Russian force or position. When the true meaning came out "Take care of Dowb" became current as a euphemism for jobbery of one sort or other.' (The late Professor A. W. Stewart, in a communication made in 1938.)

take coach. See **take horse** below.

take down, n.—3. The person 'taken down': Australian: since ca. 1920. B., 1942. Contrast sense 2 (p. 862).—4. The 'taker-down' or swindler; a thief (not a burglar): Australian: since ca. 1925. (B., 1943.)

take evasive action. To avoid a difficulty or a danger; to depart tactfully, or prudently escape: 1941, in Michie & Graebner, *Lights of Freedom*, Mary Welsh Monks: 'Fighter pilots' combat reports include "I took evasive action", and the W.A.A.F.s adopted it in describing their adventures on dates. It is heard in powder rooms everywhere now.' Since 1943 applied also to evasion of debt-payment and to non-performance of unpleasant tasks.

take felt. To be retired or superseded from the Service: Fighting Services: since ca. 1941. H. & P.—2. To be demobilized: mostly R.A.F.: 1945 +. Often as vbl n.: *taking felt.*

take-five (or ten)**!** Take five (or ten) minutes off: radio studios' coll.: since ca. 1945. 'The omission of *minutes* for short periods of time is becoming quite common' (B.P.) in Australia, as in 'I'll be back in about ten': coll.: since ca. 1945.

take for a ride. To abduct or entice someone to a lonely spot and there murder him: adopted, ca. 1937, from U.S.: c. >, by 1940, low s. (See *Underworld*.)

take gas. To get caught in the curl of a wave—its curved crest as it breaks—and lose one's board: Australian (teenage) surfers': since ca. 1961. (*Pix*, Sept. 28, 1963.)

take (one's) **hair down.** See **unpin** (one's) **back hair** below.

take his name and number!, with *sergeant* occasionally added. 'This had a vogue as a popular catchphrase after the First World War' (A. B. Petch, April 1966): ca. 1919–25.

take horse; take coach. 'She us'd much of the canting Language, saying, *Take Coach, take Horse*, and *mill the Gruntling*, by which she was meant, *Cut a throat, take a Purse*, and *steal a Pig*' (Captain Alex. Smith, *Jonathan Wild*, 1726, p. 179): c.: C. 18.

take in a cargo. To get drunk: ca. 1815–70. Pierce Egan, *Life in London*.

take in (a statement, a story, etc.) **like a dustbin.** To believe it all: North Country Grammar Schools': since ca. 1950. (*New Society*, Aug. 22, 1963.)

take it. To accept, endure, punishment courageously or cheerfully: boxing: since ca. 1933. Adopted from U.S.—2. Hence, since 1939: to endure trial and adversity without whining or cowardice.

take it away. (Usually in imperative.) To

drive off (one's car, the truck, one's aircraft, etc.): R.A.F. coll.: since ca. 1919. Gerald Emanuel, letter of March 29, 1945.

take it green. (Of a boat) to take water: oarsmen's: C. 20. *The Daily Telegraph*, April 4, 1938, 'The Oxford boat took it "green" and was half full of water.' Surface water is green.

take it in the neck and **punch the breeze.** Of hoboes sitting on a bar of a truck that supports the (railway) carriage, 'If you sit . . . facing ahead, that's called "punching the breeze". If you sit . . . looking back, it's called "taking it in the neck"' (Frederick Niven, *Wild Honey*, 1927): Canadian hoboes': late C. 19–20.

take it on. (Of an aircraft) to climb rapidly: R.A.F.: since ca. 1930. H. & P.

take it on the chin. See **chin** . . .

take it out in trade. To have sexual intercourse with the girl one entertains: Canadian: since ca. 1946. Jocular.

take (something) **lying down.** To submit tamely: coll.: C. 20. Either ex boxing or ex cowed dogs.—2. Esp., a feminine coll. for submitting to sexual intercourse—not necessarily passively: since the late 1940's; commoner in the 1950's than in the 1960's.

take me to your leader! 'A world-wide c.p. used by the **little green men**' (above): since ca. 1960. Ex cartoons depicting visitants from outer space. (B.P.)

take more water with it! A c.p., attributing clumsiness or incompetence or tipsiness: C. 20. Esp. and orig., a jocular c.p., addressed to a sober person happening to stumble or to sway: late C. 19–20.

take off! Run away!: Australian: since ca. 1945. Ex aircraft *taking off*. (B.P.)

take-off any minute now!, he'll. He's very angry—likely to 'hit the ceiling'; but more often, 'He's in a flap' (exceedingly excited): R.A.F. c.p.: 1938 +. (Atkinson.)

take-on, n. A fight, esp. with fists; a contest: Australian: since ca. 1920. B., 1942. Ex **take on,** v., 3 (p. 862).

take on, v.—4. See **sort out.**—5. To welsh (a person): turf: from ca. 1860; ob.—6. V.i., 'to complete time for a pension' (Granville): Naval: since ca. 1925. I.e. take it on again.

take (one) **down a peg.** To lower (a person's) pride: coll.: mid-C. 17–20. 'Hudibras' Butler.

take one's Daniel. See **Daniel, take one's.**

take one's hook (p. 862). Also, since ca. 1912, Australian. B., 1942.

take one's rouse. See 'Tavern terms', § 2.

take one's snake for a gallop. To urinate: R.A.F. regulars': since ca. 1925. Cf. **nag, water one's** (p. 549).

take oneself in hand. (Of man) to masturbate: nautical (— 1953). A low pun.

take out of winding. See **winding.**

take tea with. To associate (oneself) with (person or persons): Australian: since ca. 1910. B., 1942. Cf. 'She's not my cup of tea.'

take the benefit is tradesman's coll. for 'take the benefit of the Act for the relief of insolvent debtors': ca. 1810–90. *The London Guide*, 1818.

take the bent stick. 'Descriptive of a woman who, getting past the marrying age and having missed her chance with the man she wanted, decides to marry the elderly and faithful admirer who has been hanging around so long,' Alan Smith, June 28, 1939: since ca. 1910.

take the biscuit (p. 862) is prob. much older than *take the bun* († by 1950) and even *take the cake*, for its original seems to be late Medieval and early modern Latin. Wilfred J. W. Blunt, in *Sebastiano* (p. 88), records that the innkeeper's daughter at Bourgoin, a famous beauty, was present, in 1610, as a delegate at an International Innkeepers' Congress held at Rothenburg-am-Tauber. Against her name, the Secretary wrote, *Ista capit biscottum*, That one takes the biscuit. (Colonel W. G. Simpson, letter of July 16, 1956.) ML possesses *biscottus* or *biscottum*, a biscuit.

take the burnt chops. To work as a musterer of *sheep*: New Zealand rural: C. 20. B., 1941.

take the can back, 1 and 2 (p. 862). Also, since ca. 1919, R.A.F.

take the dairy off. To take the best of—or off— something: C. 20. Ex the late C. 19–20 coll. sense 'take the cream off the milk'.

take the gloss off. See **gloss off, take the**.

take the knock on. See **knocker**, 9.

take the map. See **map, take the.**

take the marbles out of your mouth! Speak more distinctly: a non-cultured c.p.: late C. 19–20.

take the piss out of. See **piss out of.**

take the weight off one's feet, mostly in the imperative. To sit down; properly, to put one's feet up: jocular: since ca. 1945.

take too much on one's plate. To act presumptuously: since ca. 1939. Cf. **enough** . . .

take up one's bed. To leave the shop for good: tailor's: mid-C. 19–20. B. & L.

take up savings (p. 863). 'Taffrail', *The Sub*, 1917, defines it as 'To go without, or not to do, a thing'. Ex savings, money drawn instead of 'certain items in the daily ration supplied by the Government'.

take water. To leave (esp. from a bar, a hotel) penniless after a 'spree': Australian: C. 20. B., 1942.

take (or **pull**) **your finger out!** A c.p. frequently addressed 'to a person who is slow or lazy', Sgt-Pilot F. Rhodes, letter of Sept. 20, 1942 (*take*): R.A.F.: since ca. 1930. Adopted by the Army in ca. 1942. *The Observer*, Oct. 4, 1942 (*pull*); Partridge, 1945 (*pull*), 'Among officers there is a variant: *Dedigitate!*' The semantics: 'Stop scratching your backside and get on with the job!' an R.A.F. officers' variant, 1939–45, was *remove the digit!* It has the variant *get your finger out!* An intensive and allusive form was current in the R.A.F. of World War II and until ca. 1950: *He's got his finger wedged*, with variant *He's got his finger concreted in.*

take your pipe! Take it easy; have a rest: North Country miners' and workers' c.p.: C. 20.

taken bad. See **bad, taken** (*Dict.* and Addenda).

taken short, be. 'To be pressed with the need of evacuation of faeces': coll. (— 1890). *Funk's Standard Dict.* Ex S.E. sense, 'to be taken by surprise'.—2. Hence, in such conditions to soil one's underclothes: coll.: C. 20.

taken to see the cups. Up before the superintendent: police: since ca. 1930. (*The Free-Lance Writer*, April 1948.) The cups that, won by the division, are displayed in the superintendent's room.

takes it, that (or **it** or **this story** or **incident**, etc.). A coll. variant, esp. in London, of **that takes the cake** (q.v. at **cake** in the *Dict.*): 1895, W. Pett Ridge, *Minor Dialogues.*

taking felt. See **take felt.**

taking money (or **toffee**) **from a child, (as) easy as.** See **easy as taking** . . .

talc, be on the. To be informed of strategy or tactics: Army officers: 1941 +. Ex **put in the picture.** Maps were protected with a talc covering.

'Military maps were (and are) not so much "protected" with a talc covering as given a convenient (talc) overlay on which dispositions, situations, movements, etc., can be quickly marked with coloured chinograph pencils, and just as quickly erased and amended at need. This saves time and makes for clarity—much more important than merely economising maps.' (Ramsey Spencer.)

tale. Showmen's patter: Australian: C. 20. B., 1942.

*****tale, cop the.** See **cop the tale.**

tale, tell the.—4. To be a confidence trickster: mostly Australian: since ca. 1910. Hence the verbal noun *telling the tale*, as in Vince Kelly, *The Shadow*, 1955.

Tale of Two Cities. Breasts (the two female): rhyming s., on *titties*: C. 20. Often spoonerized as *Sale of Two Titties*. Franklyn, *Rhyming.*

talent, the (p. 863). In Australia, however, it = the bookmakers' ring, bookmakers collectively: C. 20. B., 1942.—2. The underworld in general: Australian low: since ca. 1910. Baker. (See *Underworld.*)—3. The girls, as in 'Let's look into the Pally and see what the talent's like': raffish: since ca. 1930.

talk a bird's, dog's (etc.) **hind leg off.** See **talk the hind leg off** (*Dict.*).

talk bullock. To use much—and picturesque— bad language: New Zealand coll.: 1846, Charles R. Thatcher (cited by B., 1941). Both bullock-drivers and their beasts have much to put up with.

talk last commission. To tend to talk glowingly of one's preceding ship: Naval officers': C. 20. Granville.

talk like the back of a cigarette card. To speak pseudo-learnedly or with an unusual syntax: coll., non-aristocratic: from ca. 1931.

talk Miss Nancy. See **Miss Nancy.**

talk the leg off an iron pot. An Australian variant of **talk the hind leg off** . . . (above): C. 20. (B.P.)

talk turkey. To talk business; to talk sense: Canadian (ex U.S.) coll.: since ca. 1890; adopted, as coll., in England ca. 1930. Gerald Kersh, *Night and the City*, 1938. '"Just for the moment, let's talk turkey."' Also, since ca. 1935, Australian: B., 1942. The substantial and succulent part of a (Christmas) dinner.

talk wet. To speak sentimentally, foolishly; talk 'soft': from ca. 1910. 'Taffrail'. See **wet**, adj., 7, in the *Dict.*

talkee-talkee. Serious conversation or discussion on or of Service matters; a conference: Naval: C. 20. Ex pidgin English. (P-G-R.)

talking to the butcher, not the block, be. See **speaking to the butcher** above.

talking-Tommy (or **-tommy**). A comb-and-paper, serving as a musical instrument: secondary schools': C. 20. Michael Poole, *Revolution at Redways*, 1935.

talky. See **talkie** (*Dict.*).

tall poppy. A very important person, such as a senior Public Servant (English: Civil Servant): Australian: since early 1930's. Ex a savage threat made in the early 1930's by, and during the *régime* of, Mr J. Lang: taxation that would have 'cut off the heads of the tall poppies'. (B.P.)

tallie. A tall story: Australian: since ca. 1930. (B., 1953.)

tallow. Semen virile or spunk: low: C. 19–20.

tallowpot. A locomotive fireman: Canadian railroadmen's (– 1931). Ex his can of grease.

tally, n.—2. Hence, *cap tally*, name of ship on cap ribbon: Naval coll.: C. 20.—3. See **tallie**.

tally-ho, adj. and adv. In concubinage: low: late C. 19–20. Ex *live tally*, q.v. at **tally, live** in *Dict.*

tally-ho! Enemy sighted, the hunt is up: Fighter Command: 1939–45. It became official. Ex fox-hunting. In the fact, 'this was one of the prescribed code-words in signal procedure . . . already in official use when war was declared' (H. R. Spencer).

taliywhacker. Penis: C. 20. Ex *tallywag* (p. 864).

talosk. Weather: Shelta: C. 18–20. B. & L.

tamarboo. A hackney coachman: ca. 1840–60. *Sinks*, 1848. Ex a song thus entitled.

Tambaroora; in full, *Tambaroora muster*. A round-up of money to buy drinks: Australian: C. 20. B., 1942. Formerly Tambaroora, a township 30 miles N.W. of Bathurst, was a rich goldfield.

tambour. The drum in a Punch and Judy show: showmen's: mid-C. 19–20.

*****tame-cheater.** A cheater at cards: c.: C. 19–20; ob. B. & L.

tan, 1 (p. 864). In C. 20, of a quite mild beating: preparatory schools'.

tan-track. Rectum: proletarian: late C. 19–20.

tan-yard, the. See **tanyard, the:** in *Dict.*

tandum. See **tandem** (*Dict.*).

tangi, n. and v. *Tangi*, a Maori word for 'a tribal gathering at a funeral; a dirge': 'Now very commonly adopted here [New Zealand] by the upper classes, especially as an equivalent of the outmoded "beano". E.g., Harold and I were on the tangi (or were tangi-ing) last night; or there is a big tangi on to-night,' Niall Alexander, letter of Oct. 22, 1939; and earlier in Jean Devanney's novels.

tangi, holding a. Faced with a problem or a set-back: New Zealand: C. 20. B., 1941. Ex Maori *tangi*, 'a wake'. Cf. prec. entry.

tangle, or **get tangled, in the soup.** To become lost in a fog: R.A.F.: since 1939. Berrey (the former). Cf. **soup, in the,** on p. 803, and **pea-souper,** p. 612.

tangle-foot.—2. Hence, beer; bad liquor: Australian: C. 20. B., 1942.

tank, n.—4. An old, battered whore: Cockneys': from 1918 or 1919. Ex the appearance of tanks derelict on sodden plains.—5. A pint of beer: Australian: C. 20. Baker.—6. A locomotive tender: Canadian railroadmen's (– 1931).—7. A hammock: Australian Naval: since ca. 1925. (B., 1943.)—8. The head; *do one's tank*, to become extremely annoyed: Borstal: since middle 1940's. *The Daily Telegraph*, June 4, 1958, 'Bacon Bonces . . .'

tank, on a. On a drinking-bout: Australian: since ca. 1920. Baker. Cf. **tank up** (p. 864).

tank, on the. Engaged in beer-drinking, often with implication 'heavy drinking': British Army: since ca. 1890. Cf. *tank*, n., 3 (p. 864); probably the origin of the phrase preceding this. *The Regiment*, 1900 (vol. viii, p. 288). The early use, almost simultaneous in Britain and U.S., could have risen from joint service—e.g. in the Pekin expedition of 1900, with Americans adopting it from Britons.

tank-busting. Shooting up tanks, whether from the air or with field anti-tank guns: R.A.F. and Army coll.: 1940 +.

tanked, tipsy (p. 864), occurs in Ward Muir's *Observations of An Orderly*, 1917, in the form *tanked to the wide.*

tanked up. Tipsy: adopted, 1963, ex U.S. (Cf. **tanked** on p. 864 and above.)

tanker.—2. A heavy drinker: Canadian: C. 20. Ex **tank up** (p. 864).

Tanks. Shares in Tanganyika Concessions, Ltd: Stock Exchange: since ca. 1950.

tanky, 2, was, ca. 1938, superseded by sense 1 (p. 864); it had occurred in 'Taffrail'. Granville. —3. See **water jerry,** of which it is a C. 20 synonym. B., 1942.—4. A member of the Armoured Corps: Australian: 1939–45. (P-G-R.)—5. A seaman that helps the storekeeper (*Jack Dusty*) to handle his stores equipment: Naval: since ca. 1950. (P-G-R.) 'Now used almost exclusively for the seaman rating who helps the Supply Dept with daily issues and the rum. The rating responsible for the fresh-water supply is always from the engine-room branch, and is alluded to as the *fresh-water tanky*' (Wilfred Granville, Nov. 22, 1962).

tanner. For etymology, see esp. 'Neither Cricket nor Philology' in *A Covey of Partridge*, 1937, and *Adventuring among Words*, 1961.

tannercab; tannergram. See **tanner,** 2 (*Dict.*).

Tannhauser. Penis: cultured s. of ca. 1861–90. Wagner's opera *Tannhäuser* was enlarged with new Venusberg music in 1860–1.

tanyok. A halfpenny: Shelta: C. 18–20. B. & L.

tap, not to do a. A frequent post-1910 shortening of *not to do a tap of work*: see **tap of work**.

tap, on. 'Available at a moment's notice' (H. & P.): C. 20; much used by the Fighting Services in 1939–45. 'All modern conveniences, including h. and c.'

tap, the. Short for *doolally tap*: late C. 19–20.

tap for (p. 865). Among ships' stewards, used absolutely (i.e. *tap*, v.i.), it has the nuance 'to suggest or imply that one would not refuse a tip': Dave Marlow, *Coming, Sir!*, 1937.

tap in. 'R.A.F. slang in France [1939–40] for "have a good time",' Noel Monks, *Squadrons Up*, 1940. Perhaps 'to *tap* on the door, go right *in*, and make oneself at home'.

tap of work, not to do a. To do no work: Australian coll.: since ca. 1890. Ex carpentry.

tap run dry? or **tap-water run out?** A showmen's c.p. addressed to a quack doctor unoccupied or idling while his fellows are working: from ca. 1880. (Neil Bell, *Crocus*, 1936.) The implication being that most of his medicine consists of water.

tap the admiral. See **admiral** in *Dict.*

tap the boards. To be brought before the Officer Commanding: Army: since ca. 1925. Ex smart steps on the barrack-room floor. (P-G-R.)

tap the sling ! Get away with you: Rifle Regiments' c.p.: C. 20. Ex the salute given by the men when ordered to dismiss with the rifle at the shoulder.

tap up. Synonymous with *date*, v., 2 (p. 208): Naval: C. 20.

tape off. To set in order, put in place, prepare: Australian: since ca. 1920. B., 1942. Ex **taped** (p. 865).—2. To reprimand: Australian: since ca. 1925. Baker. To measure rightly: reduce to the correct size.

tape-worm.—3. A staff-officer: Army officers': from 1914. Blaker. Pejorative ex *red tape* and prob. suggested, in part, by the red tabs (see **red tab** in *Dict.*) indicating 'the nature of the beast'.—4. An airman expecting—or, at the least, hoping and working for—promotion: R.A.F.: since ca. 1935. Cf. *tapes*.

taper, run. (Esp. of money.) To run short: from before 1859; ob. H., 1st ed., at *mopusses*. See **taper**, adj., in *Dict.*

taper off (p. 865) has, since ca. 1945, been revived; by the late 1950's, indeed, it had > S.E. and is now used esp. of drink or of drugs.

tapes. Rank-stripes: Army and R.A.F. coll.: C. 20. H. & P. Hence, *get one's tapes*, to be promoted to corporal; *get one's third tape*, to be promoted from corporal to sergeant; *swing one's tapes*, 'to overdo one's N.C.O. authority' (Atkinson).

tapis, on the (p. 865). Earlier in *The Night Watch* (I, 147, and II, 228), 1828. Moe.

tapper.—4. A laster (one who affixes soles to uppers): shoemakers' coll.: from ca. 1880. Ex the noise made in the process.—5. A hard-hitting batsman: cricketers': C. 20. Sir Home Gordon, *The Background of Cricket*, 1939.—6. An habitual borrower: since ca. 1925. Ex **tap for** on p. 865.—7. 'A man who gives you false or useless information in return for a small loan' (John Gosling, 1959): police s.: since ca. 1930.—8. A 'carriage and wagon examiner' (*Railway*, 3rd): railwaymen's coll.: C. 20.

tappers. Overtime, as in, e.g., 'five hours' tappers': Post Office employees': C. 20. (Laurie Atkinson, Sept. 11, 1967.)

tapping, n. Asking for, or implying readiness to accept, a tip: ships' stewards': C. 20. See **tap for** above.

taps. 'The controls and gadgets of a modern aircraft,' H. & P.: R.A.F.: since ca. 1936. In *open the taps*, the sense is 'to open the throttle': since ca. 1940, usually *hit the taps*. The term 'probably originated in the old Bristol Fighter, where there were a multitude of taps in the petrol system that had to be manipulated to keep the feed system clear of air'—a certain R.A.F. officer, telling me (Nov. 25, 1949) of a collective opinion formed, appropriately in a R.A.F. bar, by a number of officers discussing the entry *taps* in Granville, Roberts and Partridge's *Forces' Slang*.

tar and maggots. Rice-pudding with treacle: girls' schools': late C. 19–20. (Berta Ruck, 1935.)

tar-brush, a touch of the, a trace of black blood, is S.E. in C. 20, but it was prob. s. at its origin (ca. 1850) and coll. from ca. 1880 until the end of the century. Occ. *a dash of the tar-brush*.

Taranaki top-dressing. Cattle dung: New Zealand (mostly the South Island): C. 20. Niall

Alexander, letter of Oct. 22, 1939; B., 1941. Taranaki Province is famous for its dairy cattle. 'Among the sheep-farming communities, Taranaki is usually referred to as a land of cows and cow cockies up to their knees in mud and cow dung' (N. Alexander, l.c.).

tardy (p. 866). At Eton, *tardy box*, a box for registering the names of boys that are late: late mid-C. 19–20. Marples.

TARFU. *Things are really fucked-up* (politely, *fouled up*): Army: 1942–5. P-G-R.

target, the. The fire or conflagration: London Fire Brigade: late C. 19–20. The water-jets are aimed at it.

target for to-night, one's. One's girl friend: R.A.F. (esp. aircrews'): 1939 +. Jackson.

tarp.—2. Tarpaulin: late C. 19–20.

tarradiddler. See **taradiddler** (*Dict.*).

tarry rope. 'A woman or girl who frequents the Sydney waterfront to consort with sailors' (B., 1942): Australian nautical and Sydney low: C. 20.

tarryin. A rope. Shelta: C. 18–20. B. & L.

tart.—3. See *dish* above and cf. *tart*, 1 (p. 866).

tartan, tear the. See **tear the tartan** (*Dict.*).

tartan banner. Sixpence: C. 20. Rhyming on *tanner*.

tarted(-)up. Dressed like a **tart** (sense 1: p. 866); very smartly (and brightly) dressed: since early 1920's. In, e.g., Christopher Buckley, *Rain before Seven*, 1947.

tarty. Of or like a prostitute (**tart**, p. 866): coll.: since ca. 1920. Angus Wilson, *The Wrong Set*, 1949.—2. (Of a girl) sexy: coll.: since ca. 1930. Marghanita Laski, *Love on the Super-Tax*, 1944.

Tarzan. See **Robin Hood**.

tash. Moustache: Services: since ca. 1920. H. & P. Also *tache*.

tashi shingomai. To read the newspaper: Shelta: C. 18–20. B. & L.

tassel.—3. A child's penis: lower-classes': C. 20. Ex **pencil and tassel** (*Dict.*).

tassels. 'Greasy locks of wool left on legs or brisket' (*Straight Furrow*, Feb. 21, 1968): N.Z. sheep shearers': C. 20.

Tassie, Tassy (p. 867): sense 2 occurs in Alex. Macdonald, *In the Land of Pearl and Gold*, 1907, and prob. goes back, as also prob. sense 1, to ca. 1860.

Taswegian. A Tasmanian seaman: Australian Naval: since ca. 1930. (B., 1943.) A blend of *Tasmanian* + *Norwegian*.

tata.—2. A silly person: since ca. 1920. An adult of the kind that would use such baby-talk as 'go (for) a *ta-ta*' or walk. (Frank Shaw.)

Tatar. See **tartar** (*Dict.*).

tatch is a variant of **tach** (*Dict.*) and **tattogey** (Supplement).

tater-pillin'. A variant of **potato-pillin** (p. 654). Franklyn 2nd.

tater-trap (p. 867): earlier in J. H. Lewis, *The Art of Writing*, 7th ed., 1816. (Moe.)

tatered. 'Fed up with having no luck or with unproductive patrols': R.A.F.: 1939 +. H. & P.; Partridge, 1945, 'A potato, though—like the patrol—exceedingly useful, can become monotonous.'

taters. See **sack of taters**.

taters in the mould. See **potatoes in the mould.**

tatie oggy. A Cornish pasty: Navy: C. 20. (*Weekly Telegraph*, Nov. 1942.) Prob. the origin of *tiddly oggy*: *tiddly* because so much appreciated: *tatie* ex potato ingredient.

tatogey. See **tat-monger** (*Dict.*).

tats.—2. Teeth: low: late C. 19–20.

tats, go. See **go tats.**

*tats, milky. See **tat**, n., 2, in the *Dict.*

tatt, n.—2. Odds and ends of (dress or furnishing) material: mostly theatrical: since ca. 1920. 'She turned out a whole mass of old tatt . . . to see what there was in the way of material. She found that old pair [of gloves] over there and a lot of old embroidery, silks and gold wire and some fake jewellery that was near enough for the props' (Ngaio Marsh, *Death at the Dolphin*, 1967).

Tattenham Corner (p. 867). At Epsom.

tatters in the mould. Variant of **taties in the mould** (p. 867). Len Ortzen, 1938.

tattics. Tactics: the Navy's traditional lower-deck pronunciation: mid-C. 19–20. (P.-G-R.) Cf. *taykle.*

tattle-basket. See 'Men'.

tattle water. A synonym of *scandal water*, q.v. at **scandal-broth** in *Dict.*: ca. 1865–1910. B. & L.

*tattler.—2. Hence, a dog that barks: c.: C. 19–20; ob. Ibid.

*tattogey. A player operating with loaded dice: c.: C. 19. Ibid. Ex *tattogey*, a dice-cloth.

Tatts. Tattersall's lottery, Tasmania: Australian coll.: C. 20. B., 1942. '"Take a ticket in Tatts": to take a chance. "Fair as Tatts": absolutely fair.' The English sense, Tattersall's horse-mart, London, dates from ca. 1870. Mr Barry Prentice thus sets me right: 'Tattersall's lottery is in Melbourne, *not* Tasmania. In Sydney, *Tatts* is more likely to refer to Tattersall's Club, where the "big-time punters" settle their debts on settling day.'

tatty. 'Fussy, especially as applied to clothes and decoration': C. 20. Raymond Mortimer, in *The Listener*, March 10, 1937.—2. Inferior; cheap: Australian: since ca. 1920. B., 1942. Ex **tat**, n., 2 (*Dict.*).—3. (Of persons) hopeless, or helpless, at something or other: certain Public Schools': since ca. 1925.—4. Of things, e.g. goods in a shop: trifling, insignificant: since ca. 1945.

Taunton turkey and **Digby chicken.** A herring: mid-C. 19–20. B. & L.

taut is a favourite adjective in the Navy. (Cf. *taut hand* on p. 867.) 'In "a taut drop of skin" or shapely female, the "taut" as applied to development of breasts and buttocks is a classic'— as I'm assured by a notably well-informed Naval correspondent.

Tavern terms, slangy and colloquial, of the C. 17.

1. In 1650 there appeared an anonymous pamphlet entitled *The English Liberal Science: or a new-found Art and Order of Drinking*. In addition to some general matter (introduction, comment, anecdote), there are groups of slangy and colloquial phrases used freely by tavern-frequenters of the time. Of these terms, a few will be found also in the body of the Dictionary; a few terms arose early in the C. 17, a few survived for long periods; but the majority, *qua* drinking-terms, belong to ca. 1640–90. Unfortunately I did not come upon this quite unknown book with its valuable and amusing list of terms—a list here reproduced complete— until June 14, 1937, or four months after the publication of the first edition and when the second edition was already in the press.

2. *The titles which they*—the drinkers—*give one to another.*

He is a good fellow.
A boon Companion.
A mad Greek.
A true Trojan.
A stiffe Blade.
One that is steel to the Back.
A sound Card.
A merry Comrade.
A Low-Country Souldier.
One that will take his rouse.
One that will drink deep, though it be a mile to the bottom.
One that knows how the Cards are dealt.
One that will be flush of all four.
One that will be as subtile as a Fox.
One that will drink till the ground looks blew.
One that will wind up his bottoms.
One that bears up stiff.
One whose nose is dirty.
One whom Brewers horse hath bitte.
One that can relish all waters.
One that knows of which side his bread is butter'd.
One that drinks Upse-Freeze.
One that drinks Supernaculum.
One that lays down his ears and drinks.
One that can sup of his Cyder.
He is true blew, &c.

3. The drinking-places and the orders of drinkers at the two Universities.

a. 'The Students or professors thereof call [a tavern with] a green garland, or painted hoop hanged out, a *Colledge*; a sign where there is lodging, man's meat, and horse meat [respectively] an *Inn of Court*, an *Hall*, or an *Hostle*; where nothing is sold but Ale & Tobacco, *Grammar School*: a red or blew Lettice'—i.e. a tavern with a lattice coloured thus—'*a free School* for all commers'.

b. '. . . In all Schools there are severall degrees to be attained unto, therefore they in their . . . profound Judgement, have thought it expedient to call,

A fat Corpulent fellow, *A Master of Art*.
A lean drunkard, *a Batchelor*.
He that hath a purple face, inchac't with Rubies . . ., *A Batchelor of Law*.
He that hath a Red-nose a *Doctour*.
And he that goeth to School by six of the morning and hath his lesson perfect by eleven, him they hold to be *a Pregnant Scholler*, and grace him with that title.'

c. 'Now before they go to study, at what time of the day or night soever, it is fit to know what language.'

English is the name for Ale.		
Dutch	„ „	Beer.
Spanish	„ „	Sack or Canary.
Italian	„ „	Bastard (a sweet Spanish wine).
Grecian	„ „	Rennish (Rhenish) or Palermo.
Irish	„ „	Usqueba'he (usquebagh).
Welsh	„ „	Metheglin.
Latin	„ „	Alligant (Alicante).
Greek	„ „	Muskadell (muscadel).
Hebrew	„ „	Hypocras (hippocras).

d. 'He that weeps in his cups, and is Maudlen drunk, is said to study *Hydromancie.*

'He that Laughs and Talks much, studies *Natural Philosophy.*

'He that gives good counsel, *Morality.*

'He that builds Castles in the Air, *Metaphisicks.*

'He that sings in his drink, *Musick.*

'He that disgorgeth his stomack, *Physick.*

'He that brags of his travels, *Cosmography.*

'He that rimes *ex tempore*, or speaks Play speeches, *Poetry.*

'He that cries Tril-lil boys is a *Rhetorician.*

'He that cals his fellow Drunkard, a *Logician.*

'He that proves his argument by a Pamphlet or Ballad, a *Grammarian.*

'He that rubs of[f] his score with his elbow, hat, or cloak, an *Arithmetician.*

'He that knocks his head against a post, then looks up to the Skie, an *Astronomer.*

'He that reels from one side of the channel to another, a *Geometrician.*

'He that going homewards fals into a ditch or chanel, a *Navigator.*

'He that looseth himself in his discourse, a *Mooter.*

'He that brawls or wrangles in his cups, a *Barrester.*

'He that loves to drink in hugger-mugger, a *Bencher.*

'He that drinks to all commers, a *young Student.*

'He that hath no money in his purse, but drinks on trust, a *Merchant venturer.*

'He that in his wine is nothing els but complement, a *Civilian.*

'He that drinks and forgets to whom, is said to study the *Art of Memory.*

4. Law terms.

'He that plucks his friend or acquintance into a Tavern or tipling-house perforce, is called a *Sergeant.*

'He that quarrels with his Hostesse, and cals her Whore, *Puts in his Declaration.*

'He that is silent or tongue-tied in his cups, is said to *Demur upon the Plaintiff.*

'He that ingrosseth all the talk to himself, is call'd *Foreman of the Jury.*

'He that with his loud talk deafens all the company, *Cryer of the Court.*

'He that takes upon him to make the reckoning, *Pronounceth Judgement.*

'He that wants money, and another man pays for, is *Quit by Proclamation.*

'He that gives his Host or Hostesse a Bill of his hand, is said to be *Sav'd by his Clergy.*

'He that is so free that he will pledge all commers, *Attourney General.*

'He that wears a night-cap, having been sick of a Surfeit, *Sergeant of the Coyffe.*

'He that is observed to be drunk but once a week, *An Ordinary Pursevant.*

'He that takes his rowse freely but once in a moneth, a *Sub-Sheriff.*

'He that healths it but once in a Quarter, a *Justice of the Peace.*

'And he that takes his rowse but twice a year, *Judge of a Circuit.*'

5. Terms in use among civilians (other than lawyers, ecclesiastics, University men); apparently, among Court officials and Civil Servants chiefly.

'He that is unruly in his cups, swaggers and flings pots and drawers down stairs, breaks glasses, and beats ye fidlers about the room, they call by ye name of *Major Domo.*

'He that cuts down signs, bushes or lettices— *Master Controuler.*

'He that can win the favour of the hostesses daughter to lie with her, *Principal Secretary.*

'He that stands upon his strength, and begins new healths, *M[aste]r of the Ceremonies.*

'He that is the first to begin new frolicks, *M[aste]r of the Novelties.*

'He that flings Cushions, Napkins, and Trenchers about the room, *M[aste]r of Mis-rule.*

'He that wanting mony is forc'd to pawn his Cloak, *Master of the Wardrobe.*

'He that calls for Rashers, pickle-Disters, or Anchova's, *Clerk of the Kitchin.*

'He that talks much, and speakes nonsense, is called a *Proctour.*

'He that tels tedious and long tales, *Register.*

'He that takes the tale out of another mans mouth, *Publick Notary.*

6. Soldiers' terms.

'He that drinks in his boots, and gingling spurs, is called a *Collonel of a Regiment.*

'He that drinks in silk-stockings, and silk-garters, *Captain of a Foot-Company.*

'He that flings pottle and quart pots down stairs, *Marshall of the Field.*

'He that begins three healths together to go round the table, *Master of the Ordnance.*

'He that calls first in al the company for a Looking-glasse, [i.e. a chamber-pot], *Camp-Master.*

'He that waters the faggots by pissing in the Chimney, *Corporall of the Field.*

'He that thunders in [the] room and beats the Drawers, *Drum Major.*

'He that looks red, and colors in his drink, *Ensign-Bearer.*

'He that thrusts himself into company, and hangs upon others, *Gentleman of a Company.*

'He that keeps company and hath but two pence to spend, *Lansprizado.*

'He that pockets up gloves, knives, or Handkerchers, *Sutler.*

'He that drinks three days together without respite, *An Old-Souldier.*

'He that swears and lies in his drink, *An Intelligencer.*'

7. Sailors' terms.

'He that having over-drunk himself utters his Stomack, in his next fellows Boots or Shooes, they call, *Admirall of the Narrow-Seas.*

'He that pisseth under the Table to offend their shoes or stockings, *Vice-Admirall.*

'He that is first flaw'd'—tipsy—'in the company before the rest, *Master of a Ship.*

'He that is the second, that is drunk at the Table *Masters-Mate.*

'He that slovenly spilleth his drink upon the Table, *Swabber.*

'He that privately and closely stealeth his liquor, *Pyrat of the Narrow-Seas.*

'He that is suddenly taken with the hitch-up, *Master Gunner.*

'He that is still smoking with the pipe at his nose, *Flute.*

'He that belcheth either backward or forward, *Trumpeter.*'

8. 'No man must call a Good-fellow Drunkard . . .: But if at any time they spie that defect in another, they may without any forfeit or just exceptions taken, say, He is Foxt, He is Flaw'd, He is Fluster'd, He is Suttle, Cupshot, Cut in the Leg or Back, He hath seen the French King, He hath swallowed an Hair or a Taven-Token, he hath whipt the Cat, He hath been at the Scriveners and learned to make Indentures, He hath bit his Grannam, or is bit by a Barn Weasel.'

9. 'Sundry Terms and Titles proper to their young Students.' (Nothing is said about lawyers but these terms would seem to be slang used by those practising or connected with the Law.)
'He that maketh himself a laughing stock to the whole company, is call'd a *Tenant in Fee-simple.*
'He that will be still smowching'—wheedling and caressing—'and kissing his hostesse behind the door, *Tenant in-tail special.*
'He that will be stil kissing all commers in, *Tenant in-tail general.*
'He that is three parts foxt, and will be kissing, *Tenant in-tail after possibility of Issue extinct.*
'He that is permitted to take a nap, and to sleep, *Tenant by the curtesie De Angliter.*
'If two or three women meet twice or thrice a week, to take Gossips cups, they are *Tenants in dower.*
'He that hath the disposing of a donative amongst his comrades, *Tenant in Frank-Almain.*
'He whose head seems heavier than his heels, holds in *Capite.*
'He whose heels are heavier than his head, holds in *Soccadge.*
'All Gentlemen-Drunkards, Schollers and Souldiers, hold in *Knights service.*
'He that drinks nothing but Sack, and *Acquavitae,* holds by *Grand serientry*'—sergeantry is properly a form of feudal tenure.
'He that drinks onely Ale or Beer, holds by *Petit serientry.*
'He that drinks uncovered, with his head bare, *Tenders his homage.*
'He that humbles himself to drink on his knee, *Doth his fealty.*
'He that h[a]unteth the Taverns, or Tap-houses, when he comes first to age, *Pays his relief*'—a fee.
'He that hath sold and mortgaged all the Land he hath, *Sueth for his Livery.*
'He whose wife goeth with him to the Tavern or Ale-house, is *A Free-holder.*
'He whose wife useth to fetch him home from the Library [tavern or ale-house], is a *Tenant at will.*
'He that articles with his hostesse about the reckoning, is a *Copy-holder.*
'He that staggering supports himself by a wall or a post, holds by the *Verge.*'

taxi. An aircraft that can carry a small number of passengers: R.A.F.: since ca. 1940. Jackson.

taxicabs. Bodylice: low s., on fringe of underworld: since ca. 1910. Frank Norman, *Stand on Me,* 1959. Rhyming on s. *crabs.*

taxi-driver. A staff pilot at a navigation school: R.A.F.: since ca. 1940. H. & P.

taxidermist!, go and see a. An R.A.F. variation (1943–5) of the civilian low c.p. 'go and get *stuffed'.* Partridge, 1945.

taxy. See **taxi** (*Dict.*).

taykle is the Navy's traditional pronunciation

of S.E. *tackle*: C. 19 (? earlier)—20. P.-G-R. Cf. *tattics.*

taz. A beard: Cockneys': C. 20. Whence the c.p. **taz been a fine day,** shouted by children at a passing 'beaver'.—2. An immature moustache; youthful down, wherever growing: mostly Cockneys': since ca. 1920. (Atkinson.) Ex *tache.*

Tazzie or **-y.** See **Tassy** (p. 867).

tea.—4. Marijuana: drug addicts': adopted, ca. 1945, ex U.S. (See esp. *Underworld.*)

tea, cup of. See **cup of tea** both in *Dict.* and in these Addenda.

tea and cocoa. See **coffee and cocoa.**

Tea and sugar, the. A supply train for the builders of the Transcontinental Railway: Australian: since ca. 1920(?).

tea-and-tattle. An afternoon tea; a minor social gathering: Australian coll.: since ca. 1925. B., 1942.

tea-boardy. (Of a picture) inferior: studio s.: from ca. 1870; ob. B. & L. Ex 'old-fashioned lacquered tea-trays with landscapes on them'.

tea boat, run a. To supply tea to one's messmates: Naval: C. 20. Granville.

Tea Cake. A Forces' nickname for a man named Smith: C. 20.

tea-cup and saucer (*Dict.*). The date should be ca. '1865–95'; the term is hardly fair to that dramatist.

tea for two and a bloater. A motor-car: derisive rhyming s.: since ca. 1905; by 1959, ob. (Franklyn, *Rhyming.*)

tea gardens. 'Somers Town goods yard' (*Railway,* 3rd): London railwaymen's: since ca. 1920 (?).—2. 'The cells or place of punishment' (*The Daily Telegraph,* June 4, 1958): Borstal: since ca. 1920. Ironic.

tea grout. A (boy) scout: rhyming s.: C. 20.

tea-kettle. An old, leaky locomotive: Canadian railroadmen's (– 1931).

***tea-leafing.** Thieving; esp. 'the picking up of unconsidered trifles', as Clarence Rook defines it in *The Hooligan Nights,* 1899: c.: from ca. 1890. Ex **tea-leaf** (*Dict.*).

tea-pot, n.—3. See **teapot lid.**—4. A Negro: ca. 1830–60. *Sinks,* 1848.—5. (Usu. written *teapot.*) A male baby: Australian domestic: since ca. 1930. A married woman loq., 'We want one with a spout next time'—cited by B.P., who comments thus, 'A male baby is called a "teapot" in such a conversation and a female baby is called a "jug"' (June 1963).

tea-pot, v. Short for **tea-pot lid**(ding) of p. 868. C. 20. *The New Statesman,* Nov. 29, 1941.

tea-pot, adj. A *spooned* stroke: cricketers': ca. 1885–1910. B. & L.

***tea-pot, smash the.** See **smash the tea-pot** (*Dict.* and Addenda).

tea-pot lid. A Jew: Cockney: C. 20. Rhyming *Yid,* often shortened to *tea-pot.*—2. A child: C. 20. Rhyming *kid.*

***tea-pot mended, have one's;** or **get it down the spout.** To be restored to the privilege of tea: prison c.: from ca. 1880; ob. B. & L. Cf. **smash the tea-pot,** q.v.

***tea-pot sneaking,** n. Theft of tea-pots and plate: c. from ca. 1860. Ibid.

***tea-pot soak.** One who does this: c.: from ca. 1860. Ibid. ? an error for *tea-pot sneak.*

tea squall. A tea party: ca. 1810–50. *The British Columbia Historical Quarterly* of April 1937

(p. 120) records it for April 28, 1820. (Leech-man.)

tea swindle. See **swindle**, n., 4.

tea trolley. Shell-hoist from magazine to gun in H.M. ships: Naval: since ca. 1916.

tea, two, and a bloater. A motor-car: rhyming: C. 20. See, **tea for two** . . .

teach. A teacher: adopted, ca. 1944, ex U.S. servicemen. (Norman.)

teacup . . . See **tea-cup** . . . in *Dict.*

teaich. Eight; eightpence: back s.: 1851, Mayhew, I.

teaks. Pieces of bread, served at table: Cheltenham College: C. 20. ex their dryness or hardness?

team. The pupils of a *coach* or a private tutor: Oxford and Cambridge: ca. 1860–1910. B. & L.—2. A gang: Teddy boys': since ca. 1947. The district where it lives is a *manor* (Clancy Signal in *The Observer*, March 1, 1959).

*teaman. See **tea-man** in *Dict.* and above.

teapot. See **tea-pot** (*Dict.*).

tear (teer). Gonorrhoea: Naval: late C. 19–20. Cf. *dripper* (p. 242).

tear, on the. Having a wildly enjoyable time, wining and wenching: Anglo-Irish: C. 20. (Liam O'Flaherty, *The Informer*, 1925.)

tear a strip off (someone); as v.i., usually *tear off a strip.* To reprimand: R.A.F.: since ca. 1938. Hector Bolitho in *The English Digest*, Feb. 1941, 'Hope that they won't have a strip torn off them'; Jackson, 1943, 'If you tear off a strip of cloth quickly and decisively, the noise caused thereby will not be unlike what has been referred to colloquially . . . as a raspberry'; Partridge, 1945, '"The 'Stationmaster' tore him off a strip for dressing in so slovenly a way." Off his self-satisfaction'; 1945, Granville records it as a Naval phrase—which it had, via the Fleet Air Arm, > as early as 1941.—2. In the Navy, *to tear off a strip* denotes sexual intercourse: World War II and after.

tear-arse.—4. Treacle; golden syrup: Australian rural: since ca. 1920. B., *Australia Speaks*, 1953.)

tear into. To attack vigorously, whether with fists or with words: Australian: C. 20. B., 1942.

tear-jerker. A very sentimental book or story or film: adopted, ca. 1954, ex U.S.

tear off a piece. To copulate with a woman: Australian low: late C. 19–20. Baker. Also Canadian and U.S.

tear off a strip. See **tear a strip off.**

tear-over. A synonym of **rip**, n., 4, above.

tear the name of God. See **tear Christ's body** (*Dict.*).

tear-up.—2. Deliberate destruction (often nerve-caused) of clothes and/or furniture: prison c.: from ca. 1870. B. & L.

tearaway. A would-be rough, esp. in *ladies' tearaway*, a man specializing in snatching handbags from women: low, verging on c.: late C. 19–20. (Norman.)—2. 'Bobby Twist, a tearaway (or strongarm man), now dead' (John Gosling, 1959): C. 20: orig. c., but by 1930 also police s. and by ca. 1960 fairly gen. s.—3. Anyone who, esp. with a criminal record, tends to violence: since ca. 1960.

tea's wet, the tea is ready; wet the tea, to make the tea: Naval coll.: since ca. 1910. (J. P. W. Mallalieu, *Very Ordinary Seaman*, 1944.) Cf. the Army's *brew up.*

teased out. Exhausted: R.A.F. (esp. aircrews') since ca. 1938. H. & P. Ex S.E. *teased* (out): 'with fibres pulled asunder'.

teaser.—6. A sixpence: ca. 1835–80. *Sinks*, 1848. Ex sense 1 (p. 869).—7. 'A castrated or partly castrated ram, which is placed in a ewe flock to identify ewes on heat' (B., 1950): Aus. rural coll.: late C. 19–20. (B., 1959.)

tec, n., 1 (p. 869). Earlier in *Sessions*, June 1879.

teck.—2. An occ. variant of **teek** (*Dict.*).

teckery. Detection of crime: coll. C. 20.

Ted; usually in pl. A German soldier: Army in Italy: 1943–5. Ex It. *Tedesco* (pl. *Tedeschi*), 'a German'—2. A Teddy boy: originally, among Teddy boys: since ca. 1954. (Gilderdale, 2.)

Ted, adj. Characteristic of a Teddy boy: mostly teenagers': since ca. 1956. (Anderson.)

Teddy. The law that no member of a train-crew shall work more than 16 hours at a stretch: Canadian railroadmen's (— 1931). Ex the given-name of its introducer.—2. A combination flying suit used by airship crews: aeronautical engineers' and airship crews': 1920's and 1930's. (Nevil Shute, *Slide Rule*, 1954.)—3. (Usually *teddy*.) A woman's garment, consisting of camisole and (loose) panties in one: Canadian, ex U.S.: ca. 1920–40. Named after 'Teddy' Roosevelt.

teddy bear (p. 869). The toy was named after Theodore ('Teddy') Roosevelt who, from one of his big-game hunting expeditions, returned with some baby bears for the Bronx Zoo. Hence, in 1939–45, an R.A.F. term for the fleece-lined jacket issued to aircrews.—2. A koala—the little native bear: Australian: since ca. 1919. B., 1942.—3. A flashily dressed man: Australian c.: since ca. 1930. (B., 1953.) Rhyming on *lair*.

Teddy boy. A youth imitating a garb (stove-pipe trousers and short jacket) supposed to characterize Edward VII's reign (1901–10): since ca. 1949; by 1960, coll.; by 1965, virtually S.E.

tedhi. See **thedi**.

tee-heeing. 'This currying favour with superiors—tee-heeing, as we call it,' Roger Grinstead, *They Dug a Hole*, 1946: Guards': C. 20. Ex *oui, oui*? But Mr Ramsey Spencer correctly supposes it to derive 'ex the sound of sycophantic sniggering'.

tee-ki! All right: mostly long-service men of the Indian Army: ca. 1910–45.

tee up; mostly as in 'It's (all) teed up' or fully arranged and virtually assured: Army officers': since ca. 1935. Ex golfing. Compare **lay on** and **organise.**—2. '*Tee up* . . . adopted in the R.A.F. to denote "Time to get ready" for a flight or for a parade' H. & P.: since 1940.—3. Among Australian soldiers (since 1940): to make arrangements: B., 1943. Hence, since ca. 1946, gen. s. (Culotta.)

teen-ager. A person aged from thirteen to nineteen, especially 15–17: coll.: adopted in 1945 from U.S., but not at all general until the latter half of 1947. Since ca. 1955, has usu. been written as one word—and, since ca. 1960, has been regarded as S.E.

teeny(-)bopper. A teen-age hellion, esp. as member of a gang: Canadian: since ca. 1965. *Daily Colonist*, Victoria, B.C., March 28, 1967, 'The hippies . . . along with the younger "teeny-boppers", met in Stanley Park.' (Leechman.) A *bopper* is one who *bops*, i.e. punches or otherwise uses violence, ex the echoic *bop*, to strike.

(See *Underworld*, 3rd edition, at **bop**.)—2. Hence, in Britain since ca. 1966, a young (11–16 years) jazz 'fan'. Peter Fryer, in *The Observer*, Dec. 3, 1967.

teesy-weesy. Very small: mostly feminine: since ca. 1930. (Angus Wilson, *Hemlock and After*, 1952.) Ex *teeny-weeny*, influenced by such locutions as *palsy-walsy*.

teeth, 2 (p. 870), occurs in John Davis's novel, *The Post-Captain*, 1806. (Moe.)

teething troubles. Such noises given out by a wireless set as indicate derangement: from 1935. *The Daily Telegraph*, Oct. 16 or 17, 1936.

Teetotal Hotel. Also *Her Majesty's Teetotal Hotel:* B. & L.

tekelite, 2 (p. 870). Ex Count Emeric Thokoly or Tokoly (1657–1705), spelt *Tekeli* (or *-ly*) or *Teckeli* (*-ly*) in England, where this great patriot, leader of insurrections against the Germanizing Habsburgs, 'was certainly the most talked-about, most praised and most abused Hungarian in 17th Century England' (Ladislas Orságh, formerly Professor of English in the University of Debrecen).

tel. A telegraphist rating: Naval: since ca. 1925. Granville.

tele, the. See **telly**.

telegram from arsehole: 'shit expected'. A variant of **it's a sore arse that never rejoices** (above): same milieu: since ca. 1910.

telegraph, n. See **college telegraph**.—2. Elliptical for *bush telegraph*: B., 1943.

telegraph, v. To tattle to: Eton: 1825, *Spy*, 'I have never telegraphed the *big wigs* in my life': Oxford: ca. 1815–60.

teliman. A tailor: pidgin: mid-C. 19–20. B. & L.

tell, v. To say, esp. in such locutions as 'Tell him good night' and 'Tell her good-bye': Canadian (and U.S.) coll.: mid-C. 19–20. (Leechman.)

tell a picture. To tell the story a film consists of: mostly Anglo-Irish coll.: since ca. 1930. (Brendan Behan, *Borstal Boy*, 1958.)

tell all. To tell everything; esp. in the imperative: Australian c.p.: since ca. 1945. (B.P.)

tell (someone) his fortune. To threaten with reprisal; to let (him) know what a bastard he is: ? esp. Forces': since ca. 1945. (Laurie Atkinson, Sept. 11, 1967.)

tell me about me (or **myself**), often preceded by *now*. A c.p. that is mainly a jocular courting expression: not general before ca. 1945.

tell me another! You don't expect me to believe that?: c.p.: C. 20. (W. L. George, 1914.)

tell me the old, old story (p. 870). Though very popular among Non-conformists, it appears also in No. 681 in The C. of E. Hymnary. Often heard at political meetings.

tell-tale. An indicator light (or lamp): Australian motorists': since ca. 1950. *The Open Road*, July 1, 1963.

tell that to the morons! A hecklers' c.p.: since ca. 1950. A pun on *tell that to the marines!*

tell (someone) where he gets off. To rebuke; to scold: since ca. 1930. Ex bus-conductors?

tellings! or **tellin's!** That would be telling!: mainly Aus. and mainly juvenile: late C. 19–mid 20. Edward Dyson, *The Gold Stealers*, 1901, '"Where is this reef?" . . . "Tellin's!" "But didn't you come to tell me?"' Ex *that's tellings*, q.v. at **tellings, that's**, on p. 870.

Telly, The. *The Daily Telegraph*: newsagents' and newsboys' coll.: late C. 19–20. Among Sydneyites, *The* (Sydney) *D.T.*: since ca. 1920. B., 1942.

telly, the. Television: non-cultured coll.: since ca. 1947. Properly but rarely *tele*, as in Angus Wilson, *Anglo-Saxon Attitudes*, 1956, 'I seen him on the Tele.'

temp. Temperature: doctors' and nurses' coll.: late C. 19–20. In, e.g., Winston Graham, *The Walking Stick*, 1967.—2. Temporary; coll.: since c. 1960.

temperament, throw; mostly **throwing temperament**. To lose one's temper: theatrical: from ca. 1930. *The Times*, Feb. 15, 1937. On *throw a party*.

temperance. A rating that does not draw his tot of rum: Naval coll.: C. 20. Granville. But among C. 20 Naval officers, it indicates 'a man who doesn't drink ashore but regularly takes his tot, the equivalent of three large rums ashore, in the middle of the forenoon' (Surgeon-Lieutenant H. Osmond: Dec. 1948).

temple of low men, the female pudend, is a late C. 19–20 jocular pun on the literary 'temple of *Hymen*'.

ten!, give her. Cox's or coaches' demand for a ten-stroke spurt: rowing coll.: since ca. 1880.

ten, keep a. See **keep a ten**.

ten A matches. Non-safety matches: Naval: late C. 19–20. 'The only matches allowed in H.M. Ships are "safeties" and in the old days anyone found with any other kind was given "Ten A" (now number eleven) punishment,' Granville.

ten(-)foot. 'Middle space between four rows of tracks' (*Railway*, 3rd): railwaymen's coll.: C. 20.

ten o'clock girls. Prostitutes: Londoners': since ca. 1930. (Sewell Stokes, *Court Circular*, 1950.) At that hour, a.m., they have to surrender to their bail in the Magistrates' Court.

ten stone eight. A '10' and an '8' in one's hand: Australian poker-players': since ca. 1920. (B., 1953.)

ten to two. See **what's the time?**—2. A Jew: rhyming s.: C. 20. Less usual than **four-by-two**. *The Leader*, Jan. 1939.

ten-ton Tessie. 'The R.A.F.'s latest and biggest bomb . . . yesterday . . . was used for the first time by specially equipped Lancasters . . . The new . . . bomb—the R.A.F. calls it "Ten-ton Tessie"— weighs 22,000 lb,' *Daily Herald*, March 15, 1945. The 4,000, 8,000, 12,000 pounders received the name *block-buster*. It was named after Tessie O'Shea, the famous variety artist.

ten up! A stockbrokers' c.p., directed at a broker whose credit is shaky: from ca. 1870. B. & L. Ex enforced deposit of 10%.

tenant (simple and compound) in C. 17 drinking terms: see 'Tavern terms', § 9.

tence; esp. in *false tences*, false pretences: C. 20. Jim Phelan, *In the Can*, 1939.

tender one's homage. See 'Tavern terms', § 9.

tenner, 1 (p. 871). Thirteen years earlier in *Sessions*, March 1848.

tennis, anyone? A c.p., by way of opening a conversation or, with a girl, a flirtation: ? mostly Canadian: since ca. 1956. But, in Britain, it 'goes back to at least the 1920's, being the hall-mark of that so familiar species of English "social comedy" where there are French windows upstage centre' (Ramsey Spencer, March 1967).

tennyrate. At any rate: Cockney sol.: mid-C. 19–20. A Neil Lyons, *Clara*, 1912, ' "It's a temp'rance drink . . . 'Tennyrate, it raises your spirits up." '

tenpence to the shilling (p. 871). In *Huntingtower*, 1922, John Buchan uses the variant *about tenpence in the shilling* only.

tent(-)peg. An egg: late C. 19–20: orig. and still tramps', by ca. 1925 also Cockney. (Jim Phelan, 1949; Julian Franklyn, 1961.)

[**Tenterden steeple is the cause of Goodwin Sands.** This proverb, which = 'any reason is better than none', is occ. used of a very weak or silly reason: C. 16–mid-19: rather S.E. than coll. Apperson.]

tenting. 'This is the word now in use among circus people to describe their mode of doing business in the country,' *All the Year Round*, Nov. 16, 1861: coll. >, by 1880, S.E. Thomas Frost, *Circus Life*, 1875, simply defines *tent* and the synonymous *pitch* as 'to go on tour.'

teotties. See **chots.**

term of endearment among sailors, it's a. A 'palliative c.p. for use of swear-word bugger. Unfair to the Navy, but sailors have had worse than that to bear; soldiers, airmen, and the French laugh it off too; *dirty bugger* is, however, meant to have a sting' (Laurie Atkinson, Sept. 11, 1967): C. 20.

termite. A political (esp. Labour) saboteur: Australian political: since ca. 1925. (B., 1943.)

terra firma. See **good old England.**

terri. Coal: Shelta: C. 18–20. B. & L.

Terries, the. See **Terry** (*Dict.*).—2. The Territorial Army: New Zealand: since ca. 1930. (Slatter.)

Terror, the. 'In 1888, . . . a very wet year in England, [Charles T. B. Turner] became known as "The Terror", and his fellow-bowler, J. J. Ferris, was called "The Fiend". In that season Turner took 314 wickets and Ferris 220, and they created almost a panic among English batsmen,' *The Observer*, Jan. 2, 1944.

terry. A heating-iron: Shelta: C. 18–20. B. & L.

tester, three slips for a. See **three slips . . .;** in *Dict.*

testicles to you! A 'polite' variation of **balls to you!** (*Dict.*): from ca. 1920.

tetra, additional, fine, 'splendid'; **go beyond the tetra,** to beat the record: Felsted School: ca. 1870–1920. Farmer, *Public Schools' Word-Book*, 1900. Perversion of *extra*? or ex Greek *tetra*, combining-form of *tessara*, 'four' (cf. *four-square*)?

tewt. Tactical exercises without troops: Army officers': from ca. 1934; by 1942, j. Also *toot*.

than for *other than* is a catachresis rare before the C. 19 but now more common than would, to the purist, seem possible. Thus the author of *London Symphony*, 1934, writes: 'He disliked the clash of personality, regarding any personality than his own as an intolerable intrusion.'

than that. See **more than that.**

thank God we have an army! A fleeting ironical c.p. of the Army when it heard the first official news of the Battle of Jutland (May 31, 1916).

thank you for nothing! I owe you no thanks for that, and indeed I scorn the offer: c.p.: C. 20.

thanks!, no. You don't catch me!: Society c.p.: ca. 1885–1905. B. & L.

thanks for having me! A c.p. uttered by boarder departing from seaside boarding-house: C. 20. Emphasis on *having*.

thanks for saving my life or **thanks! you've saved my life.** A jocular c.p. addressed to one who has just 'stood a drink': since ca. 1919.

thanks for the buggy ride! 'A c.p. expressing thanks for some small service; often ironical' (Leechman): Canadian: C. 20; by 1960, ob.

that. So far as: catachrestic: C. 20. *The Pawnshop Murder*: 'He found that it was unlocked; indeed, that he could see, [it] seemed to have no means of locking.'—2. Thus (manner)—not a very common usage; so (degree): app. orig. U.S.; then since the late 1930's (? earlier), Canadian; then, ca. 1945, British, Australian, New Zealand, etc.: even at its inception, coll. rather than s.—and, because of its brevity and expressiveness (it's elliptical for 'as—e.g., stupid —as all that'), it has, by 1969, almost attained the status of familiar S.E. As in these two examples cited by Dr Leechman in a communication of April 1967: 'I never knew he was that stupid', i.e. 'as stupid as that', and 'He's got money but he's not *that* rich'.

that adds up; that figures. That makes sense: c.pp.: the former, a British version, since ca. 1950, of the latter, itself adopted, ca. 1945, ex U.S.

that and this. A urination; to urinate: racing rhyming s. (on *piss*): C. 20. (Franklyn 2nd.) Contrast **this and that** below.

that devil nobody. See **nobody . . .**

that just shows to go. A jocular, mostly Australian, deliberate Spoonerism for the very gen. *that just goes to show*, itself verging on c.p. status: since ca. 1930. (B.P.)

that kind of money, as in 'I don't earn'— or 'have'—'that kind of money', I'm not well off: coll.: since the late 1940's.

that makes the cheese more binding! That's the stuff: Canadian c.p.: ca. 1945–55.

that makes two of us. A c.p., dating from ca. 1940 and addressed to someone who says that he doesn't understand what he has just heard or read.

that man. See **it's that man again.**

that remains to be seen, as the monkey said when he shat in the sugar-bowl. A Canadian c.p.: since ca. 1930. A facetious elaboration.

that shook him (or **me** or **. . .**). That astonished surprised, perturbed, perplexed, baffled, him: Services, esp. the R.A.F.: 1939 +. Sept. 20, 1942, Sgt-Pilot F. Rhodes (letter), 1943, H. & P. Short for . . . *shook . . . up*. Intensively: 'I was shaken rigid (or rotten).'

that side, there; **this side,** here: Pidgin: mid-C. 19–20. B. & L.

that there. See **this here.**

that there, a bit of. Sexual intercourse: low: C. 20.

that thing is wild. That aircraft is much faster than I thought: R.A.F.: 1939 +. H. & P.

that way, adj. Homosexual: since ca. 1920; by 1966 slightly ob. Compton Mackenzie, *Thin Ice*, 1956, 'She didn't want to believe the stories about Henry Fortesque being that way as he was obviously *épris* with his pretty sister-in-law.' Short for euphemistic *that way inclined*.

that will stop him laughing in church! That will take the smile off his face; that'll fix him: c.p.: since c.a. 1930. (Peter Sanders.) Cf. the (? mainly Public School) boys' *that will teach him to* *fart in chapel* or *that'll stop their farting in chapel*, that'll stop them from taking liberties: C. 20. (Laurie Atkinson, Sept. 11, 1967.)

that'll be the day! 'Expressing mild doubt following some boast or claim,' B., 1941: New Zealand: C. 20. See also **day, that'll be the.** Also, by ca. 1945, Aus., as in Eleanor Dark, *Lantana Lane*, 1959.

that's; in C. 17, occ. **thats.** That is: coll.: C. 17–20. Dekker, *Lanthorne and Candle-light*, 1608–9, 'They call a prison, a *Quier ken*, that's to say, an ill house.'

that's a bit under. A c.p. directed at a risqué joke or remark: office- and shop-girls': since ca. 1950. 'Not infrequently the "under" is dropped in favour of a dipping action with the elbow' (Gilderdale).

that's a rhyme if you take it in time is the c.p. directed at one who accidentally makes a rhyme; one replies, **yes, I'm a poet and I didn't know it.** Or **you're a poet and don't know it;** reply **Yes, that's a rhyme . . .** Mostly lower-middle class: from ca. 1870.

that's about it (or **right**). That's exactly right: Australian jocular coll.: since ca. 1920. (B.P.)

that's all was, ca. 1830–80, a much-used coll. intensive, as, e.g., in ' "When I'm in the army, won't I hate the French, that's all" '.

that's all I (or **we** or **you** or **they**) **need** (occ. **needed**). Ironic for 'That's the last thing I need or needed'; 'That's the last straw': c.p.: since ca. 1958.

that's all I wanted to know! A c.p. of confirmation of, and resentment against, disagreeable facts: since ca. 1936. (Atkinson.)

that's chummy or **ducky** or **just dandy** or **lovely!** An ironic c.p. = 'That's the last straw!': Australian: since ca. 1946, except *just dandy*, adopted, ca. 1944, ex U.S. servicemen. 'The petrol tank is empty.'—'That's chummy' or . . . (B.P.) The 2nd and 4th are common in England.

that's fighting talk! A jocular c.p., retorting upon a pretended affront: C. 20. (Atkinson.)

that's for sure! That's true; certainly: coll.: adopted in Britain and Australia, ca. 1945 and ex U.S.; by 1960, thoroughly naturalized.

that's for the birds! Tell that to the marines!: adopted, ca. 1950, ex U.S., with variant *that's strictly for the birds.*

'that's gone', as the girl said to the soldier in the park. A c.p. of ca. 1890–1910. Binstead.

that's him with the hat on! A humorous c.p. ref. to a person that is being pointed out and is standing near pigs, scarecrows, monkeys, what-have-you: orig. farmers'?: C. 20.

that's just too bad! A c.p., 'implying that an appeal to consideration or restraint, has failed' (Atkinson): adopted, ca. 1937, ex U.S.

that's my story and I'm stuck all round it. That is my excuse (or explanation) and I'm standing by it: Royal Engineers': since ca. 1930. H. & P.

that's not hay! That's big money: Canadian c.p.: adopted, ca. 1945, ex U.S. 'I sold my house for forty thousand dollars—and that's not hay!' (Leechman.)

that's one for you! That settles you: c.p.: C. 20.

that's the barber (at **barber**, p. 32). Earlier in George Parker, *A View of Society*, 1781.

that's the snuffler! Excellent; well done!:

c.p., ? mostly Naval: C. 19; †by ca. 1890—if not much earlier. Wm N. Glascock, *Sketch-Book*, 2nd Series, 1834, at I, 17.

that's the way the ball bounces or **. . . the cookie crumbles.** Such is life: Australian: both adopted, ca. 1944, ex U.S. servicemen. (B.P.)

that's up to you! A c.p. that caps a convincing argument: low: C. 20. Often accompanied by a coarse gesture.

that's what I say. A much overdone conversational tag that verges on being a c.p.: late C. 19–20.

that's your best bet. That's the best way to do it, to go, etc.: coll.: since ca. 1930. Ex horse-racing.

theatre, Irish. See **Irish theatre** (*Dict.*).

thedi or **theddy; tedhi.** Fire: Shelta: C. 18–20. B. & L.

them's the jockeys for me! A Canadian c.p., applied since ca. 1950 to anything delicious or desirable. (Leechman.) Of anecdotal origin.

then (or **and then**) **you woke up?** A c.p., implying disbelief in a tall story: late C. 19–20.

theolog. A student of Theology: Durham undergraduates': C. 20. (Marples, 2.)

Theory, the Sparks; the Stinks Theory. The theories that nerve impulses are transmitted electrically or (*Stinks*) chemically: medical coll.: since ca. 1940. (B.P.)

there is the door the carpenter made!; usually with *there* emphasised. You may go: lower middle-class c.p. of ca. 1760–90. *Sessions*, 1767, trial of Rebecca Pearce.

there she blows! A cheeky c.p. in ref. to a fat woman bathing: C. 20. It's the whaler's cry.

there you ain't! A proletarian, esp. Cockney, c.p. imputing or declaring failure: ca. 1880–1910. B. & L.

there you are!—2. A bar (for drinking): rhyming s.: C. 20. (Franklyn, *Rhyming*.)

there'll be blood for breakfast (**, let alone tea**). A cautionary c.p., esp. from N.C.O.'s: Forces' (− 1939) >, by 1943, gen.

there'll be pie in the sky when you die. See **pie in the sky . . .**

there's a war on. A c.p. of 1939–45: cf. *c'est la guerre* of 1914–18. During W.W. I, however, servicemen used the c.p. *they don't know there's a war on* of 'civvies' leading a safe and comfortable life—and, semi-jocularly, of Base wallahs. (A. B. Petch, March 1966.)

there's always something! A c.p., implying 'to bother or disappoint you': since the late 1940's.

there's no doubt about you! A c.p., expressive of admiration: Australian: since ca. 1925. B., 1942.

there's no future in it! See **future . . .**

there's nothing as (occ. **so**) **queer as folks.** A c.p., which = 'It's a queer world': since ca. 1910. Cf. the seemingly fatuous, really witty 'There's a lot of human nature in men, women and children'.

there's nothing like it. A c.p., often used with little—or no—relevance: C. 20.

there's one born every minute (**, they say**). A c.p. implying that one (self or other) has been duped: C. 20. By 1947, verging on the proverbial. 'Ex a saying attributed to P. T. Barnum [1810–91], the circus magnate, "There's a sucker born every minute" ' (Leechman).

thermos. An Italian bomb shaped like a thermos flask; hence *Thermos Bottle Flats*, an area where these bombs were dropped in large

numbers: Army in N. Africa: World War II.
(P-G-R.)

these and those. Nose; toes: Australian rhyming s.: C. 20.

they.—3. There: sol.: mid-C. 19–20. Pugh (2):
'I went where they was shops about.'

**they can make you do anything in the Air Force
except have a baby!** A 'c.p. tribute to authority
and discipline' (Atkinson): since ca. 1925.
Adopted from the Army's c.p. (1916 +); the
Army naturally says *Army*, not *Air Force*, and
often it adds, *and they'd have a bloody good try to
do that!*

they don't know there's a war on. See **there's a
war on** above.

**they don't yell, they don't tell, and they're very
grateful.** A 'young men's c.p. tribute to love of
good, mature women, and their supposed amorous
response' (Laurie Atkinson, who, on Sept. 11,
1967, records having heard it in 1959): since ca.
1920.

they got me!; occ. they've... 'A trivial c.p.,
uttered when one hears a peal of thunder or a loud
explosion' (B.P.): mostly Australian: since late
1940's. Ex the cry of the fatally injured or
wounded—in stories and films.

**they laughed when I sat down at the piano, but
when I started to play!** 'That old advertisement
has crept into the language as a standard cliché'
(Monica Dickens in *Woman's Own*, May 22, 1965):
not a cliché but a c.p.: since ca. 1920.

they think their shit doesn't stink. (Of would-
be) superior girls: c.p.: C. 20. (Laurie Atkinson,
who heard it used by a liftman on April 6, 1961.)
Cf. **Lady Nevershit** above.

they're eating nothing. They'll sell later: tradesmen's c.p.: C. 20.

they're off, Mr Cutts is a C. 20 New Zealand shape
(B., 1941) of:

they're off, said the monkey. The race has
started; or, applied to something that has come
loose: c.p.: late C. 19–20. Often enlarged thus:
...when he backed into the lawn-mower (with a
consequent loss of potency).

thick, n., 2 (p. 870). Also Anglo-Irish: late
C. 19–20. (Brian Moore, *The Luck of Ginger
Coffey*, 1960.) This *thick* may be for '*thick-
headed person*'. 6. A *thick* is a letter-card, a *thin*
a postcard: Post Office staffs': C. 20. First heard
by me on Oct. 31, 1947.

thick, adj.—6. Dull; slovenly; slack: Services:
since ca. 1935. H. & P. Cf. S.E. *thick-headed* and
thick, adj., 2 (p. 875).

thick, in the. In, esp. caught in, a thick fog:
R.A.F. (operational 'types'): since ca. 1930. (Cf.
shit, 7.)

thick, piece of. See **piece of thick.**

thick boot. A term of abuse: North Country
grammar schools': since late 1940's. *New Society*,
Aug. 22, 1963.

thick-legs (rare in singular). Navvies': ca.
1860–1910. (D. W. Barrett, *Navvies*, 1880.)

thick one, thick 'un.—2. (Always *thick 'un*.) A
slice of bread and butter: Cockney: late C. 19–20.
A. Neil Lyons, *Arthur's*, 1908.

thick 'un, do (somebody) **a.** To play a dirty
trick upon: mostly Londoners': since ca. 1920.
(Maurice Procter, *Man in Ambush*, 1958.)

thick upon one... (p. 875). With a pun on
this exact phrase in Shakespeare, *Henry VIII*,
III, ii.

thickening for something. Visibly pregnant:
since late 1950's. Ex S.E. *sickening for something*.
(A. B. Petch, April 1966.)

thickers. Strong mess-deck tea: Naval (lower-
deck): since ca. 1925. Ex *thick* by 'the Oxford *-er*'.
(P-G-R.)

Thicksides (p. 875). Also at Oxford ca. 1840–
90. It occurs in e.g., T. Hughes, *Tom Brown at
Oxford*, 1861. (Marples, 2.)

thieve, n. A theft: since ca. 1945. L. J.
Cunliffe, *Having It Away*, 1965, 'There was no
other way into the drum. (Which . . . is what
we call a thieve we've got in line for a thieve.)'

thieves' cat (p. 875): much earlier as *thief's-cat*,
in W. N. Glascock, *Sketch-Book*, 2nd Series, 1834,
at II, 59; prob. going back to very early C. 19.
(Moe.)

Thieves' Kitchen, the.—3. The London Stock
Exchange: taxi-drivers': since ca. 1920. (*Weekly
Telegraph*, April 6, 1946.)

thilly. A make-weight: Shelta: C. 18–20.
B. & L.

thimble and thumb. Rum: rhyming s.: C. 20.
Weekly Telegraph, April 6, 1946.

thin, n.; plural, *thin*. A thin slice of bread and
butter: Cockneys': ca. 1845–1910. Mayhew, I,
1851.—2. See **thick,** n., 6.

thin miner. 'A hewer working in thin seams of
coal' (*The Evening News*, Sept. 28, 1955): miners'
coll. (late C. 19–20) >, by 1945, official jargon.

thin(-)oil engine. A 'diesel locomotive, particularly during transitory period, when a driver may
have had to perform duties on either steam or
diesel locomotives' (*Railway*, 3rd): coll.: since
late 1950's.

thin on the ground. Sparse; sparsely: coll.,
middle and upper classes': C. 20. (But I cannot
remember hearing it before ca. 1930.) Of agricultural (or forestry) origin—cf. the S.E. sense,
'not dense, not bushy'? Or, less likely, of sport
(shooting). As applied to human beings, it was,
Professor Simeon Potter believes, used first by the
Higher Command, in W.W. I, of the disposition of
troops; Mr Oliver Stonor thinks it not later than
W.W. I and possibly of a fox's scent 'thin on the
ground'; my friends Alan Steele and 'Peter'
(J.A.) Cochrane knew it at the beginning of W.W.
II and believe that it was current in W.W. I ('At
the beginning of W.W. II all Service slang tended
to be based on that of W.W. I'): and Colonel
Archie White, a very distinguished V.C. of W.W. I,
confirms their opinion by telling me (Nov. 9, 1967),
that the phrase was 'applied in the 1914 war to
troops or dispositions in general'—and adds, 'But
most officers in that war had a country background,
and had already learned the phrase from sowing
of seeds, planting of young trees, etc.' Mr R. W.
Burchfield, editor of *The O.E.D. Supplement*,
remembers its use in W.W. II for troops 'thin on
the ground' and tells me that, on Oct. 4, 1967, the
only *O.E.D.* record was for 1964; Dr Ivor Brown
thinks it of hunting or shooting origin; Mr Peter
Sanders reminds me that, in Aug. 1942, Field
Marshal Montgomery, in an appreciation of the
desert campaign, referred to 13 Corps as being
'rather thin on the ground' (see General Brian
Horrocks, *A Full Life*, 1960.) My final guess is
that ultimately the phrase comes from the sowing
of seed.

thin red line, the. In *The Age of Elegance*,
Arthur Bryant quotes the 'thin red line of old

bricks' (staunch fellows), à propos the second Battle of the Nive, in Dec. 1813. (His exact source is unclear.)

thing.—4. Penis; pudend: when used not euphemistically but carelessly (cf. **affair**) or lightly, it is low coll.: C. 17–20.—5. A fad; a moral, or an intellectual, kink; an obsession: since ca. 1935. Ngaio Marsh, *Died in the Wool*, 1945, 'She hated bits on the carpet. She had a "thing" about them and always picked them up.' Prob. short for *thingummy*, used for 'obsession' or 'complex', words too learned for the commonalty of everyday speech.

thingo (pron. *thing-o*). An Australian equivalent —with the Australian suffix *-o*—of **thingummy** (p. 876).

things are looking up! A c.p., directed at some-one with a new suit or a new car: since ca. 1925.

things is crook in Muswell Brook and **things is weak in Werris Creek.** Australian card-players' c.pp.: since ca. 1920. (B., 1953.)

things to, do. See **make go all unnecessary.**

Things (will) happen (even) in the best-regulated families, these (occasionally **such**). An apologetic or an explanatory c.p., applied to a family quarrel or misfortune: domestic: late C. 19–20.

thingummybob. See **thingumbob** (*Dict.*).

thingy. Penis: C. 20. Ex the euphemistic, mindless *thingummy* (**bob**).

think (oneself). To be conceited: Australian: since ca. 1930. Margaret Trist, *Now That We're Laughing*, 1944, 'Thinks herself, that girl.' Elliptical for '*Think* well of (one)self'.

think, you can't. See **you can't think.**

think-box. The head: Australian: ca. 1890–1910. *The* Sydney *Bulletin*, Jan 18, 1902. (Baker.) Also *thinking-box*, as in Alex. Macdonald, *In the Land of Pearl and Gold*, 1907.

think-in. A poetry session or a discussion group: among the more intelligent jazz 'fans' and drug addicts and hippies: since ca. 1965. (Peter Fryer in *The Observer*, Dec. 3, 1967.) Cf.—and see—**love-in** above.

think (or do you think) I've just been dug up? Do you think me a fool?: c.p.: since ca. 1915.

think-piece. A serious article: journalists': since ca. 1946. It causes one to think, not merely to proliferate at the mouth. 'Also an article that the writer was able to "think up" out of his head without doing any research or "leg work"' (Douglas Leechman, 1960).

Think the lights of Piccadilly Circus (or the sun). See **lights of Piccadilly Circus.**

thinks his shit doesn't stink, often preceded by *the sort of bloke who* or *he*. A c.p. applied to a conceited fellow: non-aristocratic, non-cultured: ca. 1870. Often completed by *but it does, same as any other bugger's.*

Thirsty Island. Thursday Island, N.W. of Cape York Peninsula, Australia: late C. 19–20. It used to do a great trade in the sale of liquor to pearl-fishers.

thirteence. A shilling: since ca. 1920. '*Twelve pence*' > a baker's dozen.

thirty, but in form **30.** The end: Canadian journalists' and free-lance writers': since ca. 1910. 'I believe this to be one of the few remaining traces of a telegraphers' code (Phillips?) in which numbers stood for words or sentences, thus economizing space and time' (Leechman: May 1959).

Cf. *twenty-three.* In a note written a year later, Dr Leechman says, 'Two years ago, in the interior [of British Columbia], I dug up another remnant of this code: "73's"—which meant kind regards.'

thirty days. Three '10' cards: Australian poker-players': since ca. 1920. (B., 1953.)

*****thirty-first of May.** A simpleton: a dupe: Australian c.: since ca. 1925. (B., 1953.) Rhyming on *gay*, n.

this and that.—2. Mostly in the pl. *thises and thats*, spats, not sprats: rhyming s.: C. 20; by 1960, ob.—3. To bat (in cricket): rhyming s.: since ca. 1946. Franklyn 2nd.

this child (p. 877) was, by 1950, virtually dead.

this and that. A hat!: Australian rhyming s.: C. 20. A. A. Martin, letter, 1937; B., 1942.

this here. In *A Burlesque Translation of Homer*, 1770, Thomas Bridges writes, 'The inside of your this here church,' which somewhat exaggerated sentence he glosses thus, 'An elegant style much used by the cockneys, viz. That there wall, this here post, etc., etc.'

this I must see (or **hear**)! Partly ironic, partly deprecatory c.p. of amused intention: since ca. 1955. Cf. **now I've seen everything.**

this is better than a thump on the back with a stone. See **thump on . . .** in the *Dict.*

this is it! This is the end (lit. or fig.): Army c.p. of ca. 1940–5. Adopted ex American films. (P-G-R.)

this is mine! or **this is it!** Uttered when an approaching shell or bomb seems to indicate one's imminent death: Forces' c.p.: 1940 +. The latter was adopted from the U.S.

this is my day out. A c.p. used by one 'standing treat' in a public-house: since ca. 1930.

this is the weather we signed on for! A Merchant Navy c.p., applied, in C. 20, to agreeably warm, fine weather.

this is where I, or we, came in. We've come full cycle: a c.p. that, dating from ca. 1946, is taken from the experience of cinema-haunters.

this is where you want it, accompanied by a tap on one's own forehead. You need brains: c.p.: late C. 19–20. The same gesture accompanies the C. 20. c.p. *he's got it up there*, he's intelligent.

this savvy. This afternoon: Merseyside school-children's: late C. 19–20. A slovening of 'this *afternoon*'. Perhaps, rather, sol.

this should not be possible. A Naval, mostly wardroom, c.p.—used when the impossible has regrettably occurred: Naval: since ca. 1920. A quotation from the Gunnery Manual.

this training really toughens you: you get muscles in your shit. A Canadian Army c.p. of World War II.

this will give you the cock-stand. A male c.p. addressed to someone offered a drink or a special dish: since ca. 1910.

this won't buy Baby—or the baby—a frock (or a new dress, etc.)! But this is no good; I'm wasting my time, or being idle: c.p.: C. 20. Leonard Merrick, *Peggy Harper*, 1911 ('This won't buy baby a frock').

thises and thats. Sprats: rhyming s.: C. 20; by 1959, ob. (Franklyn, *Rhyming*.)

Thomas is a C. 19–20 variant of **John Thomas,** 2 (*Dict.*).

Thomas Tilling. A shilling; rhyming s.: C. 20. Michael Harrison, *All the Trees were Green*, 1936.

thomyok or **tomyok.** A magistrate: Shelta: C. 18–20. B. & L.

thora. A thoracoplasty: medical coll.: since ca. 1930. (Dymphna Cusack, *Say No to Death*, 1951.)

thou.—2. A thousandth of an inch: technical coll., mostly Australian: since ca. 1930. (B.P.)

Thou shalt not blab! An underworld 'commandment': late C. 19–20.

thoughtful, n. See **three and sixpenny thoughtful** (*Dict.*).

thousand-miler. A starched blue shirt with an attachable starched blue collar, worn by railroadmen in Canada: railroadmen's (– 1931). Good for 1,000 miles. Ex the much earlier U.S. synonym, *thousand-mile shirt.* (Robert Clairborne.)

thrash, n. A 'slog' or bout of hard-hitting, whether by one batsman or more: cricketers': since ca. 1960. Brian Close, England's captain at that time, in an interview reported in the *Daily Express* of Aug. 14, 1967.—2. A party, with drinks, supper, dancing: Naval: since late 1930's. (John Winton, *H.M.S. Leviathan*, 1967.)

thread, v. (Of the man) to coït with: Anglo-Irish: C. 20. (Brendan Behan, *Borstal Boy*, 1958.) Cf. *thread the needle* on p. 878 and below.

thread the needle (p. 878) is still active in Anglo-Irish; it occurs in, e.g., Brendan Behan, *Borstal Boy*, 1958.

three.—3. Three years' service: Services coll., among regulars: late C. 19–20. (P-G-R.)

three acres and a cow (p. 878). An ironic reference to the slogan coined by Joseph Chamberlain's henchman, Jesse Collings, who proposed that every smallholder should possess them; he became known as *Three Acres and a Cow Collings.* The slogan perhaps derived from a song popular so long ago as the 1880's. (A. McQueen.)

three bags full (or **three bagsful**). Much: coll.: from ca. 1890.

Three-Be (or, **By)-Two.** A Jew: low: C. 20. A variant of **four-by-two,** 2 (*Dict.*).

three B's.—2. (As in 1: *the.*) Bullshit baffles brains: R.A.F.: since ca. 1935.—3. Beer, bum (= copulation) and bacca (= tobacco): nautical: C. 20.—4. (*The* . . .) A c.p., embodying what every good bushwhacker ought to do with his rubbish, *Burn, bash and bury*: Australian: since ca. 1920. Cf. the very much longer-established c.p. used by bushwhackers: *the bigger the fire, the bigger the fool,* applied esp. to the fire made for the purpose of boiling a billy. (B.P.)

three cheers and a tiger. Three cheers and a very hearty additional cheer: adopted, ca. 1918, from U.S. A tiger is ferocious.

three-cornered horse. 'A scraggy, weedy, outlaw horse' (B., 1959): Aus. rural: late C. 19–20. (B., 1959.) Ex **three-cornered** on p. 878.

three-cornered pinch. A cocked hat, either a seaman's or resembling one: military: ca. 1800–50. John L. Gardner, *The Military Sketch-Book*, 1827. (Moe.) Cf.:

three-cornered scraper (p. 878) prob. dates from ca. 1810 or even earlier; it occurs in *The Saturday Evening Post* of March 16, 1822, on p. 1, col. 5.

*three C's, the. See **C's, the three.**

three-decker.—3. A three-volume novel: bookworld coll.: ca. 1840–1900, then historical.

three-figure man. One whose arrest comports a reward of £100: policemen's: mid-C. 19–20; by 1940, ob. John Lang, *The Forger's Wife*, 1855.

Three Graces, the. See **Graces, the Three** in *Dict.*

three hearty British cheers! 'Grudging praise for a minor accomplishment. "I passed that exam after three goes at it."—"Three hearty British cheers!"' (B.P.): British and Australian c.p.: since ca. 1930.

*three-kidney man. A pimp in whose service there are three women: white-slavers' c.: C. 20. Albert Londres, *The Road to Buenos Ayres*, 1928.

three months' bumps. (A course of) three months' flying training: R.A.F.: since ca. 1938. Jackson. Cf.—and see—**bump,** 1 and 2.

Three O. A Third Officer in the Wrens: Naval: since ca. 1939. (P-G-R.)

three of (e.g., whiskey). Three 'fingers' of, e.g. whiskey: public-house coll.: late C. 19–20.

three of the best. Three condoms: Australian: since ca. 1925. 'Gis [Give us] three of the best, mate.' In Australia, condoms are usu. sold in packets of three.

three on the hook, three on the book. Half-a-week's work: dockers': since ca. 1925. The *book* refers to the dole; the *hook* is a tool of the stevedore's trade.

Three Ones, the. Trafalgar Square: Londoner's since ca. 1860; ob. by 1920, but not yet †. The reference is to Nelson's column, Nelson having one eye, one arm and one anus.—2. (In lower case.) See **Lord Nelson.**

three-or-four-point drinker. 'A man who calls for 6*d.* gin with bitters, limejuice and soda,' B., 1942: since ca. 1925; by end of 1945, ob.

*three pennorth. Three years' penal servitude: c.: C. 20. F. D. Sharpe, *The Flying Squad*, 1938. See **penn'orth** (p. 617).

three pennorth of God help us. A weakling; a spiritless, unprepossessing fellow: Australian: C. 20. B., 1942.

three-pipper. A captain: Army: C. 20. Ex the three stars indicating his rank. (P-G-R.)

three-pointer is a variant (dating since ca. 1932 and, since 1940, more usual) of **three-pricker** (p. 878): R.A.F. coll. >, by 1944, j. Jackson.

three-ride business. 'The crack way of running over hurdles, in which just three strides are taken mechanically between each hurdle': athletics: from ca. 1870. B. & L.

three ringer. See **ringer, half.**

*three-rounder. A petty criminal; a small operator: since ca. 1950: c. >, by 1965, low s. (Douglas Warner, *Death of a Snout*, 1961.) Ex the three-round bouts of junior and novice boxing.

three screws. 'An aluminium box containing three condoms. Three Screws was the brand name' (Leechman): Canadian: since ca. 1920. A pun on s. *screw,* a copulation.

three sheets, short for *three sheets in the wind*: Sessions, Nov. 1857, 'He said, "A man will do anything when he is *tight,* or *three sheets*"—he had been drinking.'

three S's, the (p. 879). Since ca. 1920, it has tended to designate 'a *s*hit, a *s*have and a *s*hampoo'.

three-striper. See **striper** (*Dict.*).

three turns (p. 870). *Tom Cox's* (or *Coxe's*) *traverse* is recorded in 1806 (John Davis) and again in 1818 (Alfred Burton). Moe.

three weeks. A c.p., connoting a sexual experience either lasting or culminating at or near the end of that period: ca. 1907–14. A testimony to the vast popularity of Elinor Glyn's novel, *Three Weeks*, 1907.

three-year-old. A stone weighing 3 lb. and used as a weapon: Anglo-Irish: C. 19. Peter Cunningham, *Two Years*, 1827.

threepenny bits, the. Diarrhœa: C. 20. Rhyming on *the shits*. Often shortened to *the three-pennies*.—2. Hence, irritation, disgust, as in 'He gives me the *threepennies*': since ca. 1920.—3. The female breasts: rhyming s. (on *tits*): late C. 19–20.

threepenny dodger; t. Johnnie. A threepenny piece: Cockneys': C. 20. The former ex its elusiveness: the reference is to the silver coin.

thresh or **thresh-up.** A fight: Australian: since ca. 1930. (Dymphna Cusack, *Say No to Death*, 1951.)

threshing machine, fight like a. See **fight like a . . .** above.

thrifty. A threepenny piece: since ca. 1935, but esp. since the angular one came in.

thrill.—2. An orgasm; esp., *give one a thrill*: euphemistic coll.: since ca. 1910.

thriller merchant. A writer of 'thrillers': publishers' and authors': since ca. 1919. In, e.g., E. R. Lorac, *Death of an Author*, 1935. Ex **thriller** (p. 879) and **merchant** (p. 517).

throat-seizing, n. Naval s. of ca. 1800–90, as in W. N. Glascock, *Sketch-Book*, 2nd Series, 1834, at I, 15, 'As sure as the bell strikes four in the middle watch, he's always, *always* a throat-seizing ready for the man at the weather-wheel'—glossed as 'a glass of grog'. (Moe.)

throb. Such a person as, usually of the opposite sex, mightily appeals to someone: schoolgirls': since ca. 1945. Short for *heart-throb*. (Charles Franklin, *Escape to Death*, 1951.)

thrombosis. A traffic apprentice: railwaymen's: since ca. 1945. *Railway* 2nd records the witty professional definition, 'a bloody clot wandering round the system'.

throttler. A punch on the throat: pugilistic: ca. 1810–60. *Boxiana*, II, 1818. Ex S.E. *throttle*, jocular for 'throat'. 'Also, perhaps, because it half chokes him' (Robert Clairborne).

through, be. To have finished (a job, etc.): Canadian (and U.S.) coll.: since ca. 1910. (Leechman.)

through a side door, have come. To be illegitimate: coll.: from ca. 1860. B. & L.

through-put out of a mess, take the. To disentangle a 'mess': Naval ratings' coll.: C. 19. (W. N. Glascock, *Sketch-Book*, 2nd Series, 1834, at I, 215.) Moe.

through the gate. See **gate, through the.**

throw, v.—4. To castrate (an animal): Australian: late C. 19–20. B., 1942. Ex its being thrown to the ground for the operation to be performed.—5. To fail to extract the full meaning or emotional content out of one's lines as one might: theatrical coll.: since ca. 1945. Ex 'to *throw* away'. Cf. sense 2 (p. 879).—6. Hence, to deliberately fail in this; theatrical: since ca. 1950. —7. To disconcert; to upset: since ca. 1961. 'Your unexpected arrival threw him.'

throw, so much a. Such and such a price or charge at a time (each time), as in 'two bob a *throw*': New Zealand: since ca. 1956. Harold Griffiths, letter of March 28, 1962, 'From the old side-shows of the fair'.

throw a fit. To become very angry or agitated: C. 20: s. >, ca. 1930, coll.

throw a leg over. To coït with (the female): low coll.: late C. 18–20. Ex **leg on . . .**, q.v. in *Dict.*

throw a map. To vomit: Australian: since ca. 1925. (B., 1943.)

throw a rave—occ. a **shake** or a **percolator.** To give a party: beatniks': since ca. 1959. (Anderson.) Ex **throw a party** on pp. 879–880.

throw a seven. See **seven . . .**—2. To faint: Australian: C. 20. (Vince Kelly, *The Greedy Ones*, 1958.) On dice, the highest number of 'spots' is six.

throw a six is a variant (B., 1942) of:

throw a willy. See **willy . . .**

throw-away. A leaflet, esp. if of only one sheet: coll.: since ca. 1930. It is usually thrown away as soon as read—if not before. Cf. **dodger, 11,** above.

throw for a loop. See **thrown . . .**

throw him, would not trust him as far as I could. See **trust him . . .**

throw-in. Synonymous with **chuck-in:** Australian: C. 20. B., 1942.

throw it in. To give up, to desist: Australian coll.: since ca. 1910. 'They might be ready to throw it in': A. M. Harris, *The Tall Man*, 1958. Short for boxing *throw in the towel*.

throw it up against—or **at**—or **to** (someone) or **in** (his) **face.** To reproach: orig. (ca. 1870), low; by 1920, fairly general. Ex vomiting.

throw one up. To salute in a neat, efficient, regulation manner: Services: since ca. 1925. H. & P.

throw the baby out with the bath-water. To overdo something, carry it too far, e.g. a political measure or a commercial practice or a sociological activity, often as a warning to theorists 'Don't, throw . . .': since ca. 1946. 'Cf. the Ger. proverbial *Das Kind mit dem Bad ausgiessen*' (Ramsey Spencer).

throw the book at (someone). Of the police, a magistrate, a judge: to sentence to the full penalty of the law: adopted, ca. 1944, ex U.S. 'The book of rules' or 'the law book'.

throw up.—2. (Of the male) to experience the sexual orgasm: low: C. 19–20.—3. To vomit: coll.: late C. 19–20. 'I wanted to throw up' whether lit. or fig. used.

throw up a maiden. To bowl a maiden over: cricketers': from ca. 1880. B. & L.

throwing temperament. See **temperament, throw.**

throwing up buckets; gen. preceded by **simply.** Very vexed: exceedingly disappointed: Australian: ca. 1875–1910. B. & L. Suggested by sick, 3.

thrown for a loop. Startled; shocked: Air Force: 1939 +. 'That posting to the Med. threw me for a loop.' Ex aerobatics. 'Much earlier, I think, in U.S. I suspect from cowboy roping, but also influenced by "thrown for a loss" (U.S. football)': Robert Clairborne, Aug. 31, 1966.

throws his money about like a man with no arms, he. He is very mean with his money: humorous c.p.: C. 20. (Atkinson.) Sometimes: **. . . with no hands.**

thrum, n., survives in Australia for 'threepence'; 'threepenny piece'. B., 1942.

thruster, thrusting.—2. Hence, among motorists,

one who thrusts his car—thrusting one's car—ahead of others: coll.: since ca. 1910.

thud. A figurative fall: Australian: since ca. 1930. Gavin Casey, *Downhill is Easier*, 1945, 'You're heading for a thud with the yellow stuff, too.'

thud, v. To strike (a person) resoundingly: Australian coll.: since ca. 1919. (Ruth Park, 1950.) Echoic.

thud and blunder. See **skiet-skop-en-donder.**

thumb, v.—3. To ask (someone) for a 'lift' or free ride: coll.: 1940 +. Ex *thumb a lift from* (someone).

thumb, on the. Free; esp. in *travel on the thumb*, q.v. at **hitch-hike.**

thump, have a. To have one's chest finger-tapped; to be examined by the sanatorium doctor: TB. patients': since ca. 1920.

thunder and lightning, 2 (p. 881). Also *shrub and whiskey*: Anglo-Irish: C. 19. 'A Real Paddy', 1822.

Thunderbirds. See quotation at **trog.**

thunder-box. A commode: esp. in India: from ca. 1870; slightly ob. Cf. **thunder-mug** in *Dict.* Note, however, that it has, since ca. 1925, been common among submariners. (P-G-R.)

thunder-pump. See **shite-poke,** near end.

thunk. A facetious past participle of 'to *think*': Canadian: since ca. 1935. 'Who'd have thunk it?' (Leechman.)

ti-tri. See **ti-tree** in *Dict.*

tib, 1 (p. 881). Earlier in Mayhew, I, 1851.

tib and fib. Tibia and fibula: medical coll.: ate C. 19–20. (C. Brand, *Green for Danger*, 1945.)

tibby, n., 2 (p. 881). Rather since ca. 1810. *Sinks*, 1848; Jon Bee, 1823.—3. A 'tabloid' newspaper: Australian: since ca. 1930. (B., 1943.)

tibby, adj. Very eccentric; mad: Charterhouse School: C. 20.

Tic. A member of *the Tics* or Authentics' Cricket Club: Oxford: C. 20. (Marples, 2.)

Tich (p. 882) has also, since ca. 1925, been a nickname conferred by females upon a female.—2. Inseparable nickname of men surnamed *Little*: C. 20. Ex that famous comedian, *Little Tich*.

tick, n.—6. Esp. in *have a tick on,* to be monotonously or constantly complaining: Army: since ca. 1920. Ex **tick, v.,** 6 (p. 882). P-G-R.

tick, v.—8. To salute (a master): Rugby: since mid-1920's. Marples.

tick-jammer. The man that presses wool into bales: Australian: C. 20. B., 1942. I.e. sheep-ticks.

tick like fuck. To grumble like the very devil: Army: since ca. 1940. Cf. **tick, v.,** 6, on p. 882. 'The degrees of disgruntledness among troops of the 8th Army were, *brassed off, browned off, cheesed off*, and *ticking like fuck*' (a correspondent, May 1965).

*tick-tack, give the. To give the agreed word, or notice or warning: Glasgow c.: C. 20. Mac-Arthur & Long. Ex **tick-tack** and **give the tip**, qq.v. in *Dict.*

Tick-Tock. 'Inevitable' nickname of men surnamed Ingersoll: C. 20. (Dick Francis, *Nerve*, 1964.) Ex the name of a famous make of watch.

tick-tock. A clock: children's coll.: C. 19–20.

ticker, 2 (a watch). Earlier in *The Oracle*, 1800. —6. (Ex sense 2: p. 882.) A taxi-meter: taxi-drivers': since ca. 1910. See **clock, n.,** 4. 7.

One who is constantly, esp. if monotonously, complaining: Army: since ca. 1920. (P-G-R.) Cf. *tick*, n., 6.—8. A telephone: Army : since ca. 1930. (P-G-R.)

ticker is diving. A c.p. reference to a heart attack: since ca. 1930.

ticket, 1 (p. 882). Also an Air Force pilot's certificate: R.A.F.: since ca. 1919. Jackson. n. —4. A Trade Union contribution card: industrial coll.: since ca. 1910.—5. A playing card, usually in pl.: card-, esp. bridge-players': since ca. 1935.

ticket, v. To sentence (someone) to imprisonment: low: ca. 1880–1920. Fergus Hume, *Hagar of the Pawn Shop*, 1898.

ticket, get a. To catch a venereal disease: Australian: since ca. 1918. B., 1942. In World War I bad venereal cases were dismissed from the army.

ticket, on. On ticket-of-leave: police coll.: C. 20. Francis Carlin, *Reminiscences of an Ex-Detective*, 1927.

ticket, take a. To receive a 'ticket': Winchester College: since ca. 1870. E. H. Lacon Watson, *In the Days of His Youth*, 1935, 'A ticket . . . was a species of plenary indulgence, granted on the rarest of occasions by a prefect to whom an inferior had rendered some invaluable and unasked service. It meant, practically, immunity from any punishment for the next offence that came to the said prefect's notice.'

ticket, that's the (p. 883), prob. goes back to ca. 1800; it occurs in, e.g., W. N. Glascock, *Sketch-Book*, 2nd Series, 134, 'That's *you*, Ned—you has it—that's the ticket, bo.' (Moe.)

ticket-o(f)-leaver. A gen. term of abuse: coll.: ca. 1855–1900. Surtees, *Ask Mamma*, 1858.

ticket(-)snapper. A ticket collector: railway-men's: C. 20. (*Railway*.)

tickets for oneself, have. To be vain or conceited: Australian: since ca. 1925. (B.P.) Ex lotteries, raffles, sweepstakes, etc.

tickettyboo, all. 'Everything in the garden is lovely. No complaints,' Granville: Naval: since ca. 1925. All is 'the ticket' (p. 883, top); perhaps *boo* recalls Fr. *tout*. More prob. ex **tiggerty-boo.** Also simply *ticket(t)y-boo* (or one word), as in Shane Martin, *Twelve Girls in the Garden*, 1957, '"Capital,"' said Bloom [of the British embassy]. '"Tickety-boo, as we say."' Civil Service since ca. 1945.

tickeye. See **tig.**

ticking, adj. Disgruntled in the ultimate degree: Army in North Africa: 1940–43. (Peter Sanders in *The Sunday Times* magazine, Sept. 10, 1967.) Cf. **tick like fuck** above.

*tickle, n. A robbery; esp. a burglary: c.: since ca. 1920. (*Sharpe of the Flying Squad*, 1938.) A jocular meiosis.

tickle, 2 (p. 883). Also Australian (Sydney J. Baker, letter, 1946).—4. To ask (someone) for a loan: Australian: since ca. 1925. B., 1942.

*tickle, have a. To have (obtained) a haul of booty: c.: from ca. 1920. Cf. **tickle, v.,** 2, in *Dict.*

tickle (someone's) sneezer. To punch, even to break, his nose: pugilistic: ca. 1810–50. Anon., *Every Night Book*, 1827.

tickle-tail function. See 'Harlots'.

tickle the peter. To rob the till: Australian: adopted, and adapted, ex New Zealand in the middle 1930's. (B.P.)

tickle your fancy. A male homosexual:

rhyming s. on **Nancy,** 1, 2 (p. 550): C. 20. Franklyn 2nd.

tickled pink. Immensely pleased: late C. 19–20. 'I'll be tickled pink to accept the offer.' To the point of blushing with pleasure.

tickler.—10. A short poker used to save an ornamental one: domestic: from ca. 1870. B. & L.—11. A whip: proletarian: from ca. 1860. Ibid.

tickler's.—2. Tinned tobacco, whether for pipe or for cigarette: Naval: since ca. 1920. Cf. *tickler,* 4, 5, 6, 7, on p. 883.

tickling (, Jock)!, stop your. A C. 20 c.p., non-aristocratic. Ex Harry Lauder's song.

ticky (p. 883). The name holds good for the South African equivalent 2½-cent coin that has superseded the threepenny bit.

Tics. Peripatetics (a team within the School): Charterhouse: C. 20. By abbr.

tid. A drunkard: Australian low: since ca. 1925. B., 1942. Ex *tiddly.*—2. 'They'—an Invasion Day (June 6, 1944) convoy of tugs—'included the most powerful tugs in the world and also the "tids" (short for tiddlers)—prefabricated little fellows mass-produced in Yorkshire,' M.o.I.'s *News Clip,* Nov. 15, 1944.—3. 'Must be in a good tid, the W.O. No bellowing, no binding,' John Macadam, *The Reluctant Erk*: R.A.F.: since ca. 1935. Meaning 'temper, mood', *tid* may derive ex *tide*, 'time'.

tidapathy. Indifference: among Britons in Malaya: since ca. 1925. 'Tid' apa: it does not matter. Tidapathy' (Denis Godfrey, *A Tale That Is Told*, 1949). A punning blend: cf. *scapathy.*

tiddle. To make water: children's: C. 20. Cf. *widdle.*

tiddled. Tipsy: from ca. 1920. Cf. **tiddly,** adj. 2 (*Dict.*).

tiddler.—4. A £1 note: Australian: since ca. 1920. Baker. It tickles the fancy.—5. A midget submarine: Naval: 1942 +.—6. Any small fish: Australian: late C. 19–20. Cf. sense 1 on p. 883. (B.P.)—7. An easy, short putt: golfers': since ca. 1920. (Dominic Devine, *The Sleeping Tiger*, 1968.)

tiddler's bait. Late: rhyming s.: C. 20. (Franklyn, *Rhyming.*)

tiddley or **tiddly.** A threepenny piece: Australian: since ca. 1920. Baker. Ex its smallness.—2. A 'tailor-made' cigarette: Naval and Wrens': 1939–45.

tiddley and binder. See, in *Dict.*, **titley and binder.**

tiddley bull. 'Ceremony; Service etiquette; preparation to receive some exalted person on board' (Granville): Naval: since ca. 1930. Ex **tiddly,** 4 (p. 883, end) and **bull,** n., 12 (cf. **bull-shit,** 2, in Addenda).

Tiddly Chats. Earlier in 'Taffrail'.

Tiddl(e)y Dike (Railway), the. The Midland and South-Western Railway: railwaymen's: ca. 1890–1925. (*Railway.*)

tiddly oggy. A Cornish pasty: Navy: C. 20. H. & P. Ex **tiddly,** 3 or 4 (p. 883): see **tatie oggy.**

tiddly suit. 'Best shore-going uniform' (Granville): Naval: C. 20. See **tiddly,** 4 (*Dict.*).

tiddly wink, 3. (p. 884), occurs much earlier in D. W. Barrett, *Navvies*, 1880.

tiddlywinks.—3. See **play tiddlywinks.**

tiddy.—2. (Of clothes) pretty; pretty-pretty: Society: ca. 1930–9. Margery Allingham, *The*

Fashion in Shrouds, 1938. Ex *tiddyvated =* tittivated.

tiddy oggy is Granville's form of **tiddly oggy.** If this be the original, then the origin is *tidbit* (= tit-bit); *oggy* seems to be a fanciful arbitrariness.

tidemark. The dirty mark so many boys leave when they wash their neck: jocular: late C. 19–20. Hence, *I see the tide is high this morning*: domestic c.p.: C. 20.

tidgen, on. 'Working from 5 p.m. until midnight', *The Evening News,* Nov. 13, 1936. Prob. = on night; *tidgen* being back s. for *night.*

tie a noose. See 'Verbs'.

tie 'em down. To set hand-brakes: Canadian railroadmen's coll.: C. 20.

tie in with. To link up with (plans, or disposition of forces): Army coll.: since ca. 1930. P-G-R.

tie one on. See **hang one on.**

tie up a dog; occ. **chain up a pup.** To obtain credit for drinks at an hotel: Australian: resp. C. 20. and ca. 1905–20. B., 1942.

tied up.—5. Thoroughly prepared; in perfect order: Services: since ca. 1925. H. & P. Ex sense 1 (p. 884). Cf. **buttoned up** and **sewn up.**

tiers, mountains; *tiersman,* one living in the mountains: Tasmanian: late C. 19–20. B., 1942.

tiffed. Annoyed; angry: coll.: mid-C. 18–20. *Sessions,* May 31, 1856. See **tiff,** v., 3 (p. 884).

tiffle up. See 'Verbs'.

Tiffy. A Typhoon aircraft: R.A.F.: 1943 +.

tiffy.—3. An artificer of the Royal Army Ordnance Corps; applied loosely to a gun fitter of the Royal Artillery: Army: since ca. 1910. H. & P.

tiffy, sick bay. A sick-bay attendant: Naval: since ca. 1920. Granville. Humorous on **tiffy,** 1 or 2 (p. 885).

tiffy bloke. An engine-room artificer: Navy: C. 20. H. & P. An elaboration of **tiffy,** 1 (p. 885).

tig. All right (O.K.): Services': since ca. 1930. Short for *tickeye*, i.e. Hindustani *tighai* (O.K.): cf. *tiggerty-boo.*

tiger, 2 (p. 885). In Julia Byrne's *Red, White and Blue*, 1862, the term is applied to a soldier servant.—12. A Diesel locomotive: railwaymen's: since ca. 1960. 'Ex its roar of power' (Wilfred Granville, March 17, 1967).

tiger, on the. On a heavy drinking bout: Australian: since ca. 1910. B., 1942.

Tiger Bay.—2. A certain town on the West Coast of Africa: nautical: from ca. 1880. Ex the native prostitutes.—3. Cardiff also has one: ? since ca. 1870.

tiger-box. See 'Prisoner-of-War Slang', opening paragraph.

tiger in the tank, a. Since mid-1965, this seems to be well on the way to becoming a c.p., thanks to the oil companies', hence also the petrol stations', slogan.

tiger piss. 'Lower-deck name for beer sold on a certain foreign station. (From the picture of a tiger on the bottle)': Naval: since ca. 1930. Granville.

tigerism. See **tigerish** (*Dict.*).

Tigers, the.—4. Richmond footballers: Melbournites': since ca. 1920. (B., 1943.)

tigers' milk. See **giant-killer, the.**

Tigerschmitt. A Tiger Moth aircraft: Australian airmen's: since ca. 1940; by 1946, merely historical. (B., 1943.) A blend of *Tiger* + Mes-ser*schmitt.*

tiggerty-boo; esp. in 'Everything's all tiggerty-boo'—correct, arranged, safe, etc.: R.A.F. (regulars): since ca. 1922. Jackson, 'From the Hindustani *teega*'; Partridge, 1945, 'For the second element, cf. *peek-a-boo*' (s.v. **nose-scratch**).

tiggy. A detective: Cockneys': from ca. 1890; very ob. E. Pugh, *The Spoilers*, 1906.

tight, 3, close-fisted (p. 885), occurs in two very expressive Canadian c.pp. dating from the 1930's: *he's as tight as a bull's arse in fly-time* and *he's so tight he squeaks*.

tight-arsed. Money-mean: low: C. 20. 'Tight-arsed with his purse strings': Thorn Keyes, *All Night Stand*, 1966.

tight as a fart. Exceedingly tipsy: low: since ca. 1925.

tight as, or **tighter than, a fish's arsehole.** Exceedingly mean: low; C. 20: with **and that's watertight** sometimes added: low Australian: C. 20.

tight as a tick. Extremely drunk: low and Forces': C. 20. (Cf. *full as a tick*, p. 306.) 'Presumably from the appearance of a tick gorged with blood' (Philip Gaskell).

tight cunts and easy boots! A male toast, current ca. 1880–1914.

tight section. 'Water made rough and hard to ride by rips or cross-currents' (*Sun-Herald*, Sept. 22, 1963): Australian surfers' coll.: since ca. 1955.

tight-wad. A person mean with money: adopted, ca. 1934, from U.S. Gerald Kersh, *Night and the City*, 1938. I.e. he keeps his hand closed tight upon his wad of notes.

tigrish. See **tigerish** (*Dict.*).

tike.—2. A Roman Catholic: Australian: C. 20. B., 1942. A pun—or a rhyme—on *Mike*.

tike, Northern. See **Yorkshire tike** (*Dict.*).

tiker. See **tyker.**

Tikes, See **Tykes.**

Tilbury Docks. Socks: rhyming s.: late C. 19–20. (Franklyn, *Rhyming*.)

tilda. A tramp's swag: Australian: since ca. 1910. Baker. Short for *Matilda*. Dr Douglas Leechman suggests that in the Australian national song, *Waltzing Matilda*, the word *Matilda* is a corruption of 'waltzing my tilda'. '*Waltzing* is German tramps' for tramping, and his tilda goes waltzing with him.'

Tilden's hearthrugs. Of W. T. ('Big Bill') Tilden on his first visit to the Wimbledon lawn-tennis courts—1920, when he won the singles—F. R. Burrow, in *The Centre Court*, 1937, wrote: 'He wore some of the most remarkable sweaters that had ever been seen at Wimbledon. Their length and texture—"Tilden's hearthrugs", as they were commonly called—created quite a sensation.'

tile (p. 886). In l. 3, read *lum hat* (lit., chimney-pot hat). The term *tile*, which occurs two years earlier in D. Haggart, *Life*, 1821, may derive ex **pantile** (p. 604).

*****tile-frisking** lingered on until ca. 1910. B. & L.

tiled.—2. *To be tiled* is to be snug, comfortable: ca. 1815–50. Charles Dibdin, *Life in London*, 1882. With a *tiled* roof over one's head.—3. Detained by the police; locked up: fast life: ca. 1815–60. *Spy*, 1825, 'Safely *tiled* in.'

tilladumote. See **tilladum** (*Dict.*).

tiller. Steering wheel of a motor car: Australian motorists': since ca. 1930. (B.P.)

tillery (or **'t**); occ. **till'ry** or **tillry.** Artillery:

Army (not officers') coll.: from ca. 1890. Blaker.

tillikum. A friend: Canadian West Coast: since ca. 1930. Chinook; lit., 'people, friends'. (Leechman.)

tilly or, by personification, **Tilly.** A utility van or truck: Army: since ca. 1939. H. & P., 'See also *ute* or doodle-bug'. I.e. *utility*.

Tilly Bates. An illiteracy for **tiddler's bait:** C. 20. (Franklyn, *Rhyming*.)

tillywink(s). An illiteracy for *tiddly wink*, 3, and *tiddlywinks* (p. 884).

timber, 2, in the sense 'any human leg', is much earlier (prob. late C. 18): it occurs in Charles Dibdin's song—'The Five Engagements'—quoted in *The Port Folio* of Sept. 21, 1805. Moe.

timber! (with stress on the 2nd syllable, which is prolonged). An exclamation uttered when something is about to fall: Australian: since ca. 1920. 'Ex tree-fellers' use of the word when tree is about to fall' (B.P.). The word has long been 'in daily use in North American lumber camps' (Leechman), and the Australian usage may well have derived from that of Canada and the U.S.

timber-tuned. (Of a person) with a heavy, *wooden* touch on a musical instrument: musicians': from ca. 1870. B. & L.

timbers!, my . . . (p. 886). The phrase *shiver my timbers* occurs a year earlier in *The Dublin University Magazine*, July 1834 (p. 63). Moe.

time for *by the time that* is coll. and rather illiterate; it occurs mostly in Cockney speech: ? mid-C. 19–20. C. Rook, *The Hooligan Nights*, 1899, 'An' time I'd got a 'ansom an' put 'im inside, the job was worked.'

—time, as in 'I'll see you twelve o'clock time', at about 12 o'clock: coll.: C. 20. (Atkinson.)

time, in no (p. 886): earlier in W. N. Glascock, *Sailors and Saints* (II, 13), 1829. Moe.

time of day (p. 887). Sense 4: earlier in *The London Guide*, 1818, and in *Boxiana*, II, 1821.

time and tide wait for no man—neither do Beecham's Pills. A jocular c.p.: C. 20; little used since ca. 1940. A reference to a famous laxative.

time, gentlemen, please—haven't any of you got a home? 'Heard in pubs when the drinkers are reluctant to go' (a correspondent) c.p.: since ca. 1925.

timothy.—3. A brothel: Australian c.: since ca. 1930. (B., 1953.)

Timothy's. A branch of the Timothy White chain of stores in southern England: coll.: since ca. 1910.

timp. A *timpano* or orchestral kettledrum; usually the pl. *timps*, the timpani: musicians': C. 20. Cf. *tymp* on p. 923.

tin, n.—4. As *the tin* it = tin-mining country: Australian coll.: C. 20. (Jean Devanney, *By Tropic Sea and Jungle*, 1944.)

tin, adj. Light, short weight; hence, unconvincing (statement or story): pidgin: from ca. 1868. B. & L. I.e. *thin*.

tin-back, n. adj. Extremely lucky (person): Australian: since ca. 1920. Prompted by **tin-arsed** (*Dict.*).

tin(-)basher. A metalworker or coppersmith metalworker: R.A.F.: since ca. 1930. Jackson, 1943; Brickhill & Norton, *Escape to Danger*, 1946.

tin beard. A crêpe-hair beard that, unpainted at edges, has a metallic look: actors': late C. 19–20. (Granville.)

tin bitser. See **Rolls-can-hardly** above.

tin-bum. An habitually very lucky person: Australian: since ca. 1919. (D'Arcy Niland, *The Shiralee*, 1955.) Cf. *tin-arsed*, q.v. at *tinny*, adj., 2, on p. 888.

tin can. A destroyer, esp. one of the fifty obsolete American destroyers that came to Britain in 1940: Naval.

Tin-Can Alley. The London street that specializes in secondhand cars: since ca. 1955. A pun on *Tin Pan Alley*.

tin can (on wheels). An old, esp. if noisy, car: Australian, mostly teenagers': since mid-1950's.

tin-chapel, adj. Nonconformist, esp. Methodist: depreciatory coll.: late C. 19–20.

tin dog. Tinned meat: Australian: since ca. 1905. B., 1942.

tin ear. An eavesdropper: Australian: C. 20. Baker.—2. A fool; a simpleton: Australian: since ca. 1920. Baker.

Tin-Ear Alley. See **Cauliflower Alley.** Perhaps suggested by America's *Tin Pan Alley*.

tin ears, have. To be unmusical: since ca. 1945.

tinfish (p. 887), adopted by the R.A.F., ca. 1937. Jackson.

tin-fish or **tinfish,** v. To torpedo: Naval: 1939 +. Robert Harling, *The Steep Atlantick Stream*, 1946. Ex the n.

tin-fish man. A torpedo rating: Naval: since ca. 1917. Granville.

tin hare. The mechanical quadruped used in dog-racing: coll.: since late 1920's.

tin-hat, v. To show contempt for; to talk down to and at: Australian: since ca. 1919. B., 1942. Ex **tin hat on . . .** (p. 887).

tin-kettling. To celebrate a special occasion, the banging of tins or metal trays: Aus. coll.: since ca. 1930. (B., 1959.)

tin lid. A child: rhyming s. (on *kid*): C. 20. Cf. **God forbid** (*Dict.*).

tin off. 'The stuff [viz. honey] we sold was "tinned off" into four-gallon tins from a tap at the base of the tank' (Kylie Tennant, *The Honey Flow*, 1956): Australian coll.: since ca. 1920.

tin-opener.—2. A steel-cutting tool used in safe-breaking: Australian: C. 20. (Vince Kelly, *The Shadow*, 1955.)—3. A tank-destroying aircraft: Army: ca. 1944–5. (P-G-R.)

Tin Pan Alley. The Charing Cross Road district, where song publishers flourish: since ca. 1935. Often it implies 'the grave of the song writer's hopes'.

tin plate. A companion: rhyming s.: C. 20. Occasional variant of *china plate* (p. 148).

tin-pot, adj. (Of a place, a town, etc.) Small; insignificant: New Zealand coll.: C. 20. (Slatter.) Ex the S.E. sense, 'cheap, inferior'.

tin-scratcher, scratching. Tin-miner, -mining, Australian: C. 20. (Ion M. Idriess, *Men of the Jungle*, 1932.) Ex 'to scratch for tin'.

tin tack.—3. A racking track: rhyming s.: C. 20. Franklyn, *Rhyming*.

tin tack, get the. To lose one's job: C. 20. Rhyming on *sack*.

tin tack, the. Dismissal: rhyming s. (on 'the *sack*'): since ca. 1945. John Gardner, *Madrigal*, 1967.

tin titfa (or titfer or titfor). Steel helmet: nautical (esp. Naval): since ca. 1939. H. & P. A variant of **tin hat** (p. 887); *titfa = tit for (tat)*, rhyming s. for 'hat'.

tin trousers. Naval officers' full-dress trousers: Australian Naval: since ca. 1914. Cf. *lightning-conductors*.

'tina or **tina.** Concertina: mostly Cockneys': from ca. 1870. (Pugh.)

tingalairy. A hand-worked auger: railwaymen's: C. 20. (*Railway.*) Ex the West Yorkshire dial. *tingerlary*, a street organ. Echoic. Cf. **wimbler** below.

tingle. A 'tinkle' on the telephone: Australian: since ca. 1945. By assimilation of 'tin*k*le' to 'ring'. (B.P.)

tinhorn gambler. A petty gambler: Canadian since ca. 1912, Australian since ca. 1920, New Zealand since ca. 1922. Adopted from U.S.: for U.S., see *Underworld*; for Canada, see Michael Mason, *The Arctic Forests*, 1924.

tinies. Very small children: coll.: since ca. 1920. Ex *tiny tots*.

tinker's. Tinker's curse: Australian coll.: C. 20. Ruth Park, 1950, 'Nobody caring a tinker's.'

tinkle. A telephone-call; mostly *give* (someone) *a tinkle*, to telephone to them: trivial coll.: since ca. 1910. Also, since ca. 1925, New Zealand. (Slatter.)

tinkle, v. To urinate: children's, hence also nannies' and parents': since ca. 1920 (? much earlier). Ex the sound of urine falling into a light metal chamberpot. Dr Leechman compares the similarly echoic Ger. *pinkeln*, to pee.

tinman.—2. In the 1880's the turf and journalistic nickname of Archer, the famous jockey, was *the Tinman*.

tinned. Tipsy: since ca. 1940. Neil Bell, *Alpha and Omega*, 1946. A pun on *canned*.

tinned dog. Bully beef: Australian: since ca. 1920. (B.P.)

tinner. Afternoon *tea* and *dinner* combined: C. 20.

tinny, adj.—3. Cheap: Australian: since ca. 1925. Made of tin, not of iron, nor of steel.—4. Mean, close-fisted: Australian: since ca. 1935. (B.P.)

Tinsides. The *Martinsyde* aeroplane: W.W. I; then historical. (Wilfred Granville.)

*tiny dodge. Begging in the company of neatly dressed children (often borrowed for the purpose) and thus exciting sympathy: c.: from ca. 1860. B. & L.

Tip. A native, esp. if male, of Tipperary: New Zealand: the 1860's. (Ruth Park, *One-a-Pecker . . .*, 1958.)

tip, n., 1 (p. 888), occurs in *Boxiana*, III, 1821, in nuance 'entrance money'.

tip, booze one's or **the.** See **booze the jib** (*Dict.*), of which it is a variant cited by B. & L.

tip, miss one's. An earlier record of sense 2 is H., 2nd ed., 1860.

tip, sling the. To give a hint; impart information: proletarian: from ca. 1860. B. & L.

tip a stave (p. 889) is nautical, ? esp. Naval, in origin and it goes back to ca. 1790. It occurs in, e.g., W. N. Glascock, *The Naval Sketch-Book* (I, 120, and II, 34), 1825–6. Moe.

tip lark, the. A (racehorse) tipping business: the racing world: late C. 19–20. (Margaret Lane, *Edgar Wallace*, 1938.)

tip-off, n. A police informer: Australian police: since ca. 1915. Vince Kelly, *The Shadow*, 1955, 'Information supplied by underworld informers . . . variously known as "shelfs, tip-offs, stool-pigeons, phizgigs".' Immediately ex *tip-off*, a piece of information, itself current since ca. 1905 and derived from *tip off*, v., 4 (p. 889).

tip one's rags a gallop is a variant (W. T. Moncrieff, *Tom and Jerry*, 1821) of **tip one's legs ...**; † by 1870.

tip-sling, v.—whence **tip-slinging**, n.—is a backformation ex *tip-slinger* (p. 889): Australian: since ca. 1930. (B., 1953.)

Tip Street, be in. To be, at the time, generous with one's money: low: ca. 1815–50. Pierce Egan, *Life in London*, 1821, 'Jerry is in *Tip Street* upon this occasion, and the Mollishers are all *nutty* upon him, putting it about, one to the other, that he is a well-breeched Swell'.

tip the finger is a post-1920 variant of **tip the little finger** (p. 889). B., 1942.

tip them out. (Of railway officials) to clear a train of public passengers: railwaymen's, esp. underground railway guards': since mid-1940's. *The Daily Telegraph*, May 14, 1960, 'London Day by Day'.

tippery. Payment: non-aristocratic: ca. 1830–1910. B. & L. Ex **tip**, n., 1 and v., 4.

tippet.—2. 'A man ready to part with his money in treating others' (Renton Nicholson, *An Autobiography*, 1860, at p. 172): raffish, and fringe of the underworld: ca. 1820–80. A pun on *tip it*, give it.

tippy, 1, 2 (p. 890). Either the one or the other, the context being 'neutral', appears in *The New Vocal Enchantress* (a song book), 1791.

tippy, 2 (*the tippy*), on p. 890. *The London Chronicle*, June 29–July 1, 1784 (?), has: 'The beaver hat is now quite the *tippy* among the fair.' Cf. the quotation at **twig** below.

Tired Tim. See **Weary Willie.**

tish would seem to date from the late 1880's.

tishy. Drunk: ca. 1910–40. (Eric Horne, *What the Butler Winked At*, 1923.) A drunken pronunciation of *tipsy*.

tisket. A bastard, lit. and fig.: ca. 1940–50. Ex the popular song words, 'A tisket, a tasket, A little yellow basket', where *basket* euphemises *bastard*. Franklyn, *Rhyming*.

tissied up. Dressed up; smartly dressed: Australian: since ca. 1925. (S. H. Courtier, *A Corpse Won't Sing*, 1964.) Perhaps a blend of *titivated* + *sissified*.

tissue. A racing list: racing men's and racecourse workers': C. 20. Jack Henry, *Famous Cases*, 1942. Ex the flimsy paper used therefor.

tiswas. See **all of a tiswas** above.

tit.—6. A gun-button: R.A.F.: since ca. 1930. H. & P. Esp. in *squeeze the tit* (in firing a machinegun). See **tit**, 3 (p. 890).—7. Derivatively, any finger-pressed 'button' (of, e.g., an electric bell): R.A.F.: since ca. 1938. Jackson.—8. See **tit, look a.**—9. A female breast: low, esp. Australian, coll.: late C. 19–20. Ex sense 3 (p. 890). 'In Australia, *tit* always = breast, not nipple' (B.P.) —10. (Ex sense 7.) Any button-like or knobby protuberance that vaguely resembles a nipple: since ca. 1940; by 1955, coll.

tit, get on (someone's). To infuriate: Australian low: C. 20. B., 1942. In R.A.F., *get on one's tits*, to irritate; to antagonize: since ca. 1925.

tit, look a(n absolute). To look very foolish, or 'sloppy' and stupid: low: late C. 19–20. By itself, *tit* means a foolish, ineffectual man.

tit around. To potter uselessly or time-wastingly: low: C. 20. Cf. prec. entry.

tit-for-tat.—3. Usually pl., *tit for tats*, (female) breasts: Australian low: C. 20. Lawson Glassop, *We Were The Rats*, 1944. An elaboration of *tit* = teat, nipple.

tit-hammock. A brassière: sailors': since ca. 1920. By 1950, fairly gen. low s.

tit in a tight crack, have one's. To find oneself in an awkward and uncomfortable position, whether physical or emotional: low Canadian: since ca. 1920. Cf. '**hell!**' said the Duchess above.

tit(-)man. A male more interested in a woman's breasts than in her legs: low: since ca. 1910.

tit-show. A vaudeville act in which uncovered female breasts are to be seen: raffish coll.: since ca. 1930.

titbag. A brassière: low English and Australian: since ca. 1945.

titfa is a frequent variant of *titfer* (see **tit-fer**, p. 890).

title-page. The face: ca. 1830–70. *Sinks*, 1848. Cf. **frontispiece** (*Dict.*). Hence, 2, a type-face: printers': since ca. 1860. B. & L.

titoki. A shandygaff: New Zealand: C. 20. B., 1941. By perversion of sense of a genuine Maori word.

tittleback. See **tittlebat** (*Dict.*).

tittle-tat. A tittle-tattle; a tale-bearer: Australian juvenile: since ca. 1930. (B.P.)

titty.—6, 7. Synonymous with *tit*, 6 and 7. (P-G-R.)

titty, drop of. A drink from the breast: nursery: C. 19–20. See **titty**, 2. (p. 891).

titty-oggy or **tittie-oggie.** Irrumatio: low: late C. 19–20.

Tiv, the. The Tivoli Music Hall, London: late C. 19–early 20.

tiz up. See **tizz up.**

tizz. A shortened form of *tizzy*, 2: since ca. 1930. (Phœbe Fenwick Gaye, *Treen and the Wild Horses*, 1959.)

tizz (or **tiz**) **up.** To dress up, esp. flashily; to furbish or smarten (some object): Australian: since ca. 1938. (B., 1953.) Apparently ex *tizzy*, adj.

tizzy, n.—2. A 'state'; esp. *get into a tizzy*: C. 20. Perhaps ex S.E. *hysteria*.

tizzy, adj. Ostentatiously or flashily dressed: Australian: since ca. 1935. (B., *Australia Speaks*, 1953.) A thinning and a disguising of S.E. *tidy*. Or perhaps rather ex S.E. *tidy* + s. *jazzy*; or, more prob., ex *titivated* (see **titivate** on p. 890).—2. Hence, flashy, ostentatious, showy but cheaply made, as, e.g., an inferior Espresso machine: Australian: since ca. 1945. (B.P.)

tizzy-snatcher (p. 891). Earlier in 'Taffrail'. Ex the C. 19 Naval sense, 'a purser'.

*tjapan. A uniformed policeman: South African (esp., non-European) underworld: late C. 19–20. App. ex Malayan, as *The Cape Times* of May 22, 1946, states.

tlas. See **sap the tlas.**

to-an-froing. A constant moving-about; work that necessitates much getting-about: coll.: since ca. 1945.

to-and-from. A concertina: since ca. 1910. Ex the movements of the player's arms—2. An English serviceman: Australian prisoners-of-war in the Far East: 1942–5. Rhyming on *pom*, 2. (B., 1953.)

to coin a phrase. An ironic c.p., mildly apologetic for the immediately preceding or ensuing triteness (often a cliché): since ca. 1935, but general only since ca. 1949.

to hell with you, Jack, I'm all right! A euphemistic variation of *fuck you, Jack* (p. 305).

to-morrow, on for. (Of a clock) very fast: coll., almost a c.p.: C. 20.

to-night's the night! A c.p. indicative of the imminence of something important: since ca. 1916.

toad.—3. One who has done wrong yet is none the less popular: Marlborough College: since the late 1920's.—4. A mechanical derailer: Canadian railroadmen's (— 1931). Ex its shape.

toast, v. To blush: Shrewsbury: since mid-1930's. Marples.

toast, get on. To corner; *have got on toast*, have at one's mercy: from ca. 1895. Cf. **toast, (had) on** in the *Dict*.

toast-rack. A term applied, since ca. 1910, to the horse-trams at Douglas, Isle of Man. (Peter Chamberlain.)—2. 'One of the old-style footboard trams still used in Sydney' (B., 1943): Australian: since ca. 1920.

tobacco-box. A friar bird: Australian: C. 20. R., 1942. Ex colour?

tober-mush (p. 892).—2. Fair-ground official; collective for such officials: grafters': C. 20. *News of the World*, Aug. 28, 1938.

tobur is a rare variant of **tober** (*Dict*.).

toby, n.—9. A weak-witted, clumsy-handed, but very willing, obliging fellow: Australian: C. 20. B., 1942.—10. A dissolute girl or young woman: Australian low: since ca. 1920. Baker.—11. A man servant: Haileybury: since ca. 1920. Marples. Common-propertying of a familiar male given-name.

toby on, have a. See **grape on.**

toco for yam (p. 892). *Boxiana*, IV, 1824, 'Cabbage napt *toco* (a severe punch), and was sent down.' This has a variant *catch toko* (or *toco*): *The Night Watch* (II, 121), 1828—cf. the quotation at **blood-sucker** above. Moe.

Tod, on one's. Alone: since late 1930's; since ca. 1960, fairly common. Ex:

Tod Sloan, on one's. Rhyming 'on one's *own*' (alone): C. 20. Less usual than *on one's Jack* (*Jones*) or *on one's Pat* (*Malone*).

toddler. A walker—one who, on a given occasion, walks: coll.: ca. 1810–60. *Boxiana*, III, 1821.—2. See:

toddlers. Legs: ca. 1835–80. *Sinks*, 1848. Cf. prec. entry.

Toe, the. The tuck-shop erected in 1908 at Sherborne School. Alec Waugh, *The Loom of Youth*, 1917.

toe a line. To form a rank or line: Naval coll.: mid-C. 18–19, and perhaps rather earlier and rather later. It occurs in W. N. Glascock, *The Naval Sketch-Book* (I, 237), 1825, thus: 'The brigades of seamen embodied to act with our troops in America, as well as in the north coast of Spain, contrived to "*ship a bagnet*" [handle a bayonet] on a pinch, and to "toe" (for that was the phrase) "a tolerable line".' (Moe.)

toe-biter. 'If there is a long wait, without a job, the cabmen on the rank are "having a binder" —or, in cold weather, a "toe-biter". Some of them may decide to "run away"; that is, drive off without a job,' Herbert Hodge, *Cab, Sir?*, 1939; taxi-drivers': since ca. 1910.

toe-buster. An infantryman: cavalrymen's: ca. 1880–1905. (Atkinson.) Cf. the Fr. 1914–18 *pousse-caillou*.

toe-fug. A footpath: Tonbridge: since ca. 1870. Marples. Removal of smell.

toe(-)path. A running-board on a train: Canadian railroadmen's (— 1931). A pun on *tow(ing)-path*.

toe-pitch, be at. To be toeing the line at defaulters' table: Naval (lower-deck): C. 20. P-G-R.

toe-rag.—3. A term of contempt for a person: Australian: since ca. 1905. B., 1942. Ex **toe-ragger** (p. 893). But current in Glasgow University and schools in 1927 and probably for some years earlier.—4. A £1 note: Australian: since ca. 1925. (B., 1943.)

***toe-ragger.** 'A short-sentence prisoner in a jail' (B., 1959): Aus. c.: since ca. 1910. Ex sense 3 of preceding entry.

Toe-Rags, the. The Tuareg (Saharan tribesmen): Army: since ca. 1942. (Peter Sanders.) By the process of 'Hobson-Jobson'.

***toe the line.** To appear in an identification parade: c.: from ca. 1910.—2. To conform: coll.: C. 20. 'If you join the Army you'll have to toe the line.' Ex infantry drill.

toey. (Of a horse) speedy: Australian: C. 20. (B., *Australia Speaks*, 1953.)—2. But also: restive, unsettled: since ca. 1925. At first of horses, then also of persons. (B., 1953.)

toff, n., 1 (p. 893). A socially interesting comment and a colloquial variant are afforded by the quotation at **doll,** n.

toffed up, ppl adj. See **toff,** v., in *Dict*.

toffee.—2. (A stick of) gelignite: since mid-1940's. (B.B.C., 'Z Cars'—March 11, 1964.) Gelignite looks rather like soft toffee.

toffee!, don't give me that. 'Don't give me that wrapped up, glib explanation! (R.A.F., Malta, Feb. 1960)': c.p. since ca. 1950. Laurie Atkinson, Sept. 11, 1967.

toffee apple. A Very light, or a tracer bullet, fired as a guide to motor transport moving in the dark: 8th Army: 1942–3.—2. A cask of either asphalt or pitch: railwaymen's: since ca. 1945. (*Railway*, 3rd.) Ironic.

toffee (or **money**) **from a child, (as) easy as taking.** See **easy as taking** . . .

toffee-nosed (p. 893) was very popular, as was its variant *toffee-nose* (H. & P.), with the W.A.A.F. and R.A.F. in the war of 1939–45.

toffee ration. Marital sexual intercourse: Naval: since mid-1940's.

tog, v. (p. 893). Cf. 'Wait till I've togged my "round-the-houses",' Augustus Mayhew, *Paved With Gold*, 1857.

togey (p. 894).—2. Also, 'a rope's end used by senior cadets at Dartmouth for "chasing",' Granville, who spells it *toggie*: C. 20.

***toggy** (p. 894) probably dates from almost a century earlier (**tog,** n., 1, on p. 893, will therefore date from early C. 18)—to judge by James Isham's *Observations on Hudson's Bay 1743, and Notes*, published by the Champlain Society in 1949: '. . . a Beaver Coate or tockey which Reaches to the Calf of the Leg.' (With thanks to Dr Douglas Leechman.)

togs (p. 894). In C. 20 Australia, esp. a bathing suit. B., 1942.

togs, short. Short clothing: Naval (? also gen.

nautical): C. 19. In, e.g., W. N. Glascock, *The Naval Sketch-Book*, 2nd Series, 1834, at II, 179. (Moe.) Cf. **togs, long,** on p. 894.

Tojo. A variant of *Private Tojo*. (P-G-R.)

toko.—2. Praise; excessive praise; flattery, esp. if excessive: Australian: since ca. 1920. B., 1942. Perhaps ironically ex sense 1 (**toco,** p. 892).

tokus. A rare variant of **toco** (p. 892). H. D. Miles, *Dick Turpin*, 1841. This form either shows the influence of or, more probably, comes straight from Yiddish *tokus*, the backside.

tol, 2 (p. 894). Earlier in Mayhew, I, 1851.

tol-lollish.—3. 'Overbearing and/or foppish' (B., 1942): Australian: late C. 19–20.

tole. See **job,** v., 4.

toley. Excrement; esp., a turd: Scottish: C. 20. (? earlier). Alan Sharpe, *A Green Tree in Gedde*, 1967. Probably ex the Sc. dial. *toalie* or *tolie*, 'a small round bannock or cake' (E.D.D.).

toll-loll-loll-kiss-me-dear. A Middlesex finch: bird-fanciers': mid-C. 19–20. B. & L. Ex the bird's note.

tolly, n., 1 (p. 894), is, as 'a candle', extinct at Rugby School, where the word now occurs only in *the Tolly Church*. (D. F. Wharton, Oct. 24, 1965.)—3. A marble (as used in the game of marbles): children's: late C. 19–20. *The Manchester Evening News*, March 27, 1939. Cf. sense 2 (p. 894).—4. A cup or mug; a tin hip-bath: Marlborough College: since ca. 1870.

tolly(-)whacker. A roll of paper that, in the form of a club, is used by boys in rough play: Cockneys': from ca. 1920. Ex *tolly*, a candle.

tolo. 'A dance at which the girls pay the admission fee rather than the men' (Leechman): Canadian: since ca. 1955. Perhaps ex S.E. *toll*, a tax; perhaps, however, cf. the Newfoundland *tole*, to entice with bait.

*****tolsery.** A penny: c.: ? C. 18–19. Thus B. & L.: but the term is suspect.

Tom.—10. A hypocoristic variant of **Thomas:** low: mid-C. 19–20.—11. Any prostitute: police: C. 20. (*The Free-Lance Writer*, April 1948.) Cf. —and see—senses 5 and 6 on p. 895.—12. Jewellery: see **tomfoolery** below.

tom, v. (Of men) to coït with: North Country: late C. 19–20. Ex a tomcat's sexual activities.— 2. To be a prostitute: since ca. 1935. 'They were perfectly willing to go "tomming" on the streets to earn a few quid, but I never could': Zoe Progl, *Woman of the Underworld*, 1964.

Tom-and-Jerry gang. A noisy, riotous gang of fellows: ca. 1810–40. In J. H. Lewis, *The Art of Writing*, 7th ed., 1816, it is applied to the House of Commons. (Moe.) Cf. **Tom-and-Jerry days** on p. 895.

Tom and Jerry shop (see **Tom-and-Jerry days,** p. 895): earlier in *Sessions*, Feb. 1835.

Tom Beet. Feet: rhyming s., mostly itinerant entertainers': C. 20. (Sydney Lester, 1937.) Much less common than **plates (of meat).**

Tom Collins. A mythical person that figures in at least two Australian folk-tales: since ca. 1880. B., 1942. It's hardly s., nor even coll.—2. See **Collins,** 2.

Tom Essence. See 'Fops'.

Tom Fool's token. See **token, Tom Fool's:** in the *Dict*.

Tom, Harry and Dick. Sick: rhyming s., esp. busmen's: since ca. 1940. (*The Evening News*, April 27, 1954.)

Tom Mix. 6.: darts players': from ca. 1932. Rhyming s. (*The Evening News*, July 2, 1937.) From the name of a famous 'Westerns' film-actor.—2. A difficult situation: rhyming s. on **fix,** n. (p. 280): since ca. 1935. Franklyn 2nd.

Tom Mix in 'Cement' is a c.p. reply (ca. 1938–52) to 'What's on at the pictures?' A pun on 'to *mix cement*'.

Tom Pepper (p. 895) is much earlier: 1818, Alfred Burton, *Johnny Newcome*. (Moe.)

Tom Pudding or **Tompudding.** A 'compartment boat', worked in 'trains' with other such boats: canal-men's: C. 20. L. T. C. Rolt, *Narrow Boat*, 1944.

Tom Sawyer. A lawyer: rhyming s.: late C. 19–20.

Tom Tart. A (female) sweetheart: Australian rhyming s.: C. 20. B., 1942.

Tom Thacker (p. 895). By 1959, ob.—As also is **Tom Thumb** (*ibid*).

tom them up. Builders' s., 'roughly similar to putting up scaffolding' (Culotta): Australian: since ca. 1910.

Tom Tit (p. 895, end). Also a n.: Richard Llewellyn, *None But the Lonely Heart*, 1943.

Tom Tit on a round of beef. A children's c.p., shouted after someone wearing a cap, or a hat, too small; also 'used of anything small on anything big, e.g. of a lonely cottage on a hill' (Peter Ibbotson, letter of Feb. 9, 1963): C. 20.

tom(-)tits, n. Also used fig., as in 'You give me the tom-tits' = 'the shits'; you disgust me, or irritate me beyond endurance. But *get the tomtits* = to 'become demoralized with fear' (Culotta).

Tom Turdman (p. 896) should be dated 'from ca. 1690'. It occurs in B.E., 1699.

Tom Turd's field(s) or **Tom Turd's hole.** 'A place where the Nightmen lay their Soil,' *Sessions*, 1733 (11th session): low: C. 18.

Tomago!, go to. Go to hell: Newcastle, Australia: since ca. 1945. 'Tomago is a small town near Newcastle. Pronounced tommy-go' (Edwin Morrisby, Aug. 30, 1958). Cf. *hell and tommy* (p. 386) and *Jericho* (p. 436).

tomahawk. (Of a shearer) to cut a sheep: Australian rural: C. 20. B., 1942.

tomato. A girl: Australian: adopted, 1943, ex U.S. servicemen. (Ruth Park, 1950.) Luscious.

tomato-can tramp (p. 896) more probably derives ex the utensil being carried as a cooking-tin. (Leechman.)

tombola is the S.E. for **house** (p. 410, sense 3) or **housey-housey** (p. 410). See also **little Jimmy** and **puff and dart,** both in this Supplement. To all those entries, add the following 'table' furnished by Mr Laurie Atkinson:

'Eyes down, look in!' Call to attention on the game at the commencement or resumption of play. (See also paragraph next but one—i.e. immediately after the numbers.)

1: Kelly's eye
2: Dirty old Jew
   (The numbers two to ten are usually prefixed with the word 'number' except for 9, q.v., and 19 itself.)
3: —
8: Garden gate
9: Doctor's orders, or Doctor's favourite
10: Downing Street, or Shiny Ten

11: Legs Eleven
13: Unlucky for some, or simply Unlucky
17: Never been kissed, or Never had it
20: Blind twenty
21: Key of the door
22: Dinkie do, or All the twos
24: Pompey 'ore [Portsmouth whore]
26: Bed and breakfast; half-a-crown being
    evidently the accepted traditional charge
33: All the threes
34: Dirty 'ore
39: All the steps; from the title of the novel
    The Thirty-Nine Steps by John Buchan
44: All the fours
50: Blind fifty; Half-way house
55: All the fives
57: All the beans: from Heinz's well-known
    57 varieties
60: Blind sixty
66: Clicketty-click; sometimes All the sixes
70: Blind seventy
76: She was worth it; 7/6, 7s. and 6d. being
    the usual charge for a certificate of
    marriage issued by the Church of England
77: All the sevens
80: Blind eighty
88: All the eights
99: All the nines
100: Top of the house; Top of the ship; Top
    of the shop. Doubt as to this note is
    thrown by Lt-Comm. John Irving's
    Royal Navalese, 1946, under this heading,
    which gives 90 as the 'Top of the Grot'.

The call: 'Eyes down look in!'—as we have
seen—is usual at the commencement of a game.
After the call of 'House' for the claim of a won
game, the usual call is 'Eyes down for a check'.
For resumption after a trivial query, players are
warned of the resumption by 'Eyes down'.

Jildi five. Covering the first five numbers of the
'House' card.
NAAFI sandwich. Covering of, for example,
two in the top line of the card, one in the next
line, and two on the following line, or any
three lines in this order.
Officers' Mess sandwich. As in preceding, but
the 'middle term' is thicker, e.g. two, three,
and two.

tomboy. Female genitals: C. 17. Taylor (the
Water Poet), 'Playing the tomboy with her tomboy.'
tombstone, 2, dates back to ca. 1880.—3. Mess
menu: Naval (lower-deck): C. 20. Granville.—
4. A trade-union vote, recorded for a dead man:
Australian: since ca. 1910. (B., 1943.)
tomcat. A door mat: rhyming s.: C. 20.
Franklyn 2nd.
tomfoolery. Jewellery: rhyming s.: late C. 19–
20. Michael Harrison, *Reported Safe Arrival*, 1943.
Since ca. 1940, and esp. in the underworld, it has
often been shortened to *Tom*. John Gosling, *The
Ghost Squad*, 1958.
Tommy. See **tommy,** 4 and 6, on p. 896, and 7
and 8 here.—5. A Tommahawk fighter aircraft:
mostly airmen's 1944–5.—6. A 'Tommy gun'
(Thompson sub-machine gun): Australian: adopted, ca. 1940, ex U.S. (H. Drake Brockman, *The
Fatal Days*, 1947: concerning early 1942.)
tommy, n, 1 (p. 896). In Australia, 'bread

baked with currants and sugar': B., 1942.—7.
(*Tommy.*) Penis: rather low: C. 19–20; ob. Cf.
Thomas.—8. (*Tommy*). A feminine synonym of
the curse: late C. 19–20. By personification.—9.
Solder: silversmiths' and jewellers' (— 1877). G.
E. Gee, *The Practical Goldworker* (O.E.D.). Esp.
soft Tommy (or *t*—) as distinct from *hard Tommy*,
hard (or blowpipe) solder.—10. Short for **tommy
rot** (p. 896): since ca. 1905. (J. C. Snaith, *The
Sailor*, 1916.)—11. A bookmaker: Australian:
since ca. 1925. (B., 1943.)—12. Hence, his ledger:
since ca. 1930. (B., 1953.)—13. A 'small shunting
disc ground signal' (*Railway*): railwaymen's:
since ca. 1920.
Sense 6 is anticipated in *The Night Watch* (I,
204), 1828. Moe.
tommy, v.—2. To depart; to make off, decamp:
Australian low: C. 20. Baker.
tommy-axe. A tomahawk: Australian: C. 20.
B., 1942. By a pun.
Tommy Cornstalk. An Australian soldier.
1899–1902 (during the Boer War): coll. Baker.
Tommy Dodd.—2. God: rhyming s.: late C. 19–
20.—3. A sodomite: since ca. 1870. Rhyming on
sod. Since ca. 1890, often abbr. to *Tommy*.—4.
A small glass of beer: New Zealand and Australian: late C. 19–20. B., 1941, 1942.—5. A calling,
or a call, on a warning signal: railwaymen's:
since ca. 1930. (*Railway* 2nd.) Rhyming s. on
nod.
Tommy, get out and let your father in. Gin (the
drink): navvies' rhyming s.: ca. 1860–1900. (D.
W. Barrett, *Navvies*, 1880.)
Tommy of all trades. 'The ordinary infantry
Tommy who, apart from doing the "dirty work"
in the trenches, had to turn his hand to almost
anything when out "resting" or convalescing
from wounds or illness' (A. B. Petch, March 1966):
Army jocular coll.: W.W. I.
Tommy Roller. A collar: rhyming s.: since ca.
1880. (C. Bent, *Criminal Life*, 1891.)
Tommy Rollocks. Testicles: since ca. 1870.
Often abbr. to *rollocks*. Rhyming *ballocks*.
Tommy Tanna (or **Tanner**). Nickname for a
Kanaka working on a Queensland plantation: ca.
1880–1920. (B., 1943.)
tommy-toes; or as one word. Tomatoes:
London jocular: C. 20.
tommyato. A jocular perversion of *tomato*:
since ca. 1935.
tomyok. See **thomyok.**
ton. Sense 1 (p. 897) occurs, as an Australian
coll., in, e.g., Gavin Casey, *The Wits Are Out*, 1947,
'There was a ton to think of.'—3. £100; *half a ton*,
£50: gamblers' c.: since ca. 1940. Alan Hoby, in
The People, April 7, 1946.—4. A speed of 100
m.p.h.: motor cyclists': since ca. 1948.—5. A
score of 100 runs: cricketers', ex cricket reporters':
since ca. 1955.
tonge. Penis: low (esp. in R.A.F. of ca. 1930–
50): C. 20. Origin?
tongs.—2. See **jingling Johnnies.**
**tongue is hinged in the middle and one talks with
both ends, one's;** gen. *his* (or *her*) *tongue* . . . One
is extremely talkative: coll.: C. 20.
tongue-padder. See **tongue-pad, v.** (*Dict.*).—2.
A C. 18 sense is noted at 'Constables'.
tonguer. 'A native or white living in New
Zealand who assisted a whaling crew to cut up
whales and who also acted . . . [as] an interpreter.
These men earned their name not from the . . .

interpreting, but from the fact that they were given whale's carcass and tongue to dispose of as they wished.' B., 1945: New Zealand and whalers': C. 19.

tonic, 1 (p. 897): slightly earlier in Pierce Egan, *Life in London*, 1821.—2. In *Sessions*, Dec. 12, 1893.

tonight's the night! Rather since ca. 1913, when Miss Iris Hoey starred in a musical comedy of this name.—2. Hence, it 'often refers to coïtion in Australia' (B.P.): since ca. 1919.

tonk, n. A dude or fop: Australian: since ca. 1921. B., 1942. Perversion of *tony* (person) ?—2. A simpleton; a fool: Australian: since ca. 1925. Baker.—3. Hence, a general term of contempt: Australian: since ca. 1925, Baker. Sense 2 may perhaps be derived ex 'person *tonked* on the head'. —4. A term of abuse: North Country grammar schools': since ca. 1945. (Cf. senses 2 and 3.)

tonk, v.—3. (Ex 1 and 2: p. 897.) To punish, e.g. to cane: Australian: since ca. 1920. Baker.

tonked, get, is the usual passive of the preceding. (B., 1943.)

tonky, adj. Fashionable: New Zealand: since ca. 1935. Slatter, 'She's probably been to a tonky school.' Perhaps a blend of *tony* + swa*nky*.

tons. See **ton,** 1, in *Dict*.

tonsil-snatcher. A ship's surgeon: Naval: C. 20. (Granville.)

tonsil(-)varnish. 'Messdeck tea' (Granville): Naval: since ca. 1920.

too-a-roo! Good-bye!: Australian: ca. 1919–39. (Colin MacInnes, *June in Her Spring*, 1952.) Cf. **tootle-oo** on p. 899.

too Irish. See **too (bloody) Irish** on p. 897. The late Gerald Bullett, in letter of Aug. 22, 1950, proposed that *too bloody Irish* merely extends *too Irish* and that *too Irish* is short for *too Irish stew*, rhyming s. (? late C. 19–20) for 'too true'. He was probably right.

too late! too late! A C. 20 military c.p., always in high falsetto and with derisive inflection. Ex the story of the unfortunate who lost his manhood in a shark-infested sea after he had called for help. Also **help! sharks!** The first word is spoken in a normal voice, 'sharks' in falsetto.

too many for (p. 898) is perhaps of U.S. origin, for it occurs in *The Port Folio*, Feb. 14, 1801, at p. 52. Moe.

too mean to give you the time of day. Excessively mean: coll.: since ca. 1920.

too mean to part with (his) shit. Excessively miserly or close-fisted: low: late C. 19–20. Cf. **mean he** . . .

too much, adj.; always in predicate, as 'The tubes are too much' (excellent or wonderful): Australian teenagers', esp. surfers': since late 1950's. (B.P.) But also, by 1960, English, as in 'Isn't she too much?' (good at something or other) —as Anthony Lejeune noted in *The Daily Telegraph*, colour supplement, on March 10, 1967.

too old and too cold. 'Traditional domestic excuse by husbands for not being more "demanding"' (B.P.): c.p.: C. 20. Perhaps ex **not so old** . . . (p. 571).

too short for Richard, too long for Dick. 'Yorkshire expression for *N.B.G.*; said to have reference to Richard II, the Hunchback,' Earl (at that time Sir Archibald) Wavell, communication of Aug. 1, 1939: coll.: C. 19–20. But it was, of course, 'Richard III who was known as crookback.

Richard II was Tumble-Down Dick' (Ramsey Spencer, March 1967).

too thick to drink, too thin to plough. A c.p. referring to the Yarra river (flowing through Melbourne): common in New South Wales ca. 1900–40; then ob.: by 1963, almost †. (B.P.)

too (effing or sanguinarily) **true.** A c.p. of emphatic agreement or endorsement or corroboration: late C. 19–20. Cf. *too right* (p. 898) and *too bloody Irish* (p. 897) and *too Irish*.

toodle em buck.—2. Teetotum; to gamble with for cherry stones: Victorian (Australia) State-School children: ca. 1880–1910. (Guy Innes, March 1, 1944.)

tool, n.—6. (Ex sense 3 and v., 4.) In C. 20 c., it is that pickpocket who performs the actual theft. (*The Evening News*, Dec. 9, 1936.) Opp. **stall,** n., 1 q.v. in *Dict*.—7. A brush: studio s.: from ca. 1860. B. & L.—8. A one-inch paint-brush: builders' and house-painters': late C. 19–20. (A master builder: Dec. 5, 1953.)—9. A weapon: prison c.: since ca. 1942. (Norman.)

tool along. To fly without a fixed objective: R.A.F.: since ca. 1925. H. & P. See **tool,** v., 3 (*Dict*.).—2. Hence, to walk aimlessly: R.A.F.: since ca. 1938. Partridge, 1945.

tool check. A venereal inspection: R.A.F. mechanics': since ca. 1930. Cf. *tool,* 1 (p. 898).

tooled up. Equipped with weapons: Teddy boys': since ca. 1946. (*The Observer*, March 1, 1959.)

tools, 4 (p. 898) is also R.A.F.: since ca. 1935.

tooraloo! Goodbye for now!; I'll be seeing you: a mainly Anglo-Irish variant of **tootle-oo**, q.v. at p. 899 and below: since ca. 1910. James Joyce, *Ulysses*, 1922, '"Tooraloo," Lenehan said, "see you later."'

toot, n. 2 (p. 898). '*Pace* Beames, I've never heard this and doubt its authenticity. It doesn't ring true' (Leechman).—3. A variant of **tewt.** (H. & P.)—4. A complaint; a 'moan': Services: since ca. 1930. H. & P.—1. (Money: p. 898.) Prob. short for *whistle and toot*, rhyming on *loot*.— 5. A water-closet: Australian, orig. feminine: since ca. 1950. Ex *toilet*. (B.P.)

toot, v. To drink heavily (at one session): Naval: since ca. 1939. Granville. '*Exercise toot* is the Wardroom description of a mild "pub-crawl"; on the other hand, *Operation toot* is a monumental drinking party'. Cf.:

toot, have a. To have drink: since ca. 1930. Prompted by 'to wet one's *whistle*'.

tooter. 'One who "drinks between drinks", a seasoned performer' (Granville): Naval: since ca. 1930. Ex **toot,** v.

tooter the sweeter, the. See **toot, at the** (p. 898).

tooth, good on the. See **fang, good on the,** above.

tooth(e)y. A ship's Dental Surgeon: Naval Wardrooms': since ca. 1920. Granville.

toothpick, 1 (p. 899). In *Sinks*, 1848, it is an Irish watchman's shillelagh. Sense 3 (sword), has, however, survived in C. 20 Naval ward-rooms. (P-G-R.) Moreover, it dates back to ca. 1810 or even to ca. 1790. Wm Maginn, *Whitehall*, 1827 (p. 255). Moe.

Tooting. See **Tooting Bec.**

tooting. See 'Miscellanea'.

tooting!, too damn. Certainly: since ca. 1935. Perhaps ex *Tooting Common*, with a pun on *com-*

mon, usual, general. In Canada, *you're damn'*, or *darn'*, *tooting*, you're absolutely right: since ca. 1908. (Leechman.)

Tooting Bec. Food; a meal, esp. supper, rhyming s. (on **peck**—*Dict.*): since ca. 1880. *The* (Birmingham) *Evening Despatch*, July 19, 1937. Often abbr. to *Tooting*.

tootle-oo! (p. 899). Probably, as Mr F. W. Thomas has most ingeniously suggested, a Cockney corruption of the French equivalent of '(I'll) see you soon': *à tout à l'heure*.

top, over the.—3. 'Flying above the clouds or above the bad weather,' Jackson: R.A.F. coll.: since ca. 1939. Cf. the lit. S.E. *fly above the rooftops*.—4. 'Used by trans-Atlantic flyers to designate the Northern route by way of Greenland and Iceland' (P-G-R.): R.A.F.: since 1940; by 1946, also civilian.

top ballocks. Female breasts: military: late C. 19–20. E.g. 'a smashing pair of top ballocks' is a fine bust. Cf. **fore-buttocks** in *Dict.*

top brass. See **brass**, n., 5.

top buttocks. Female breasts: low: late C. 19–20. Cf. preceding entry.

top deck, the. The head: Australian nautical (C. 20) >, by 1925, gen. B., 1942.

Top End, the. North Australia; *Top Ender*, a resident there: Australian coll.: C. 20. Baker.

top-hat (p. 899) is, in C. 20, S.E. It prob. dates from ca. 1810; it occurs in, e.g., *The Saturday Evening Post*, March 16, 1822 (p. 1, col. 5). Moe.

top-hat on it, that's (or **this has) put the.** That's the finishing touch; that's the end: c.p. (mostly Liverpool): C. 20.

top-hole (p. 899): by 1945, decidedly ob.; by 1965, virtually extinct, except among those aged over 60. 'If somebody trying to take on the trappings of an Englishman were to use expressions such as *wizard prang*, *top-hole* and *ripping*, he would be a subject of ridicule': Wallace Reyburn's article 'This I don't Like' in *The Sunday Times* (colour supplement), July 8, 1962.

top hush. 'Top Secret': Service officers', esp. R.A.F.: 1939–45. (P-G-R.)

top-kick. A high-ranking officer: Australian servicemen's: since ca. 1939. (Kylie Tennant, *The Joyful Condemned*, 1953.)

top knot (p. 899, end). Much earlier: *Sessions*, April 1822 (p. 275).

top laddies. Senior officers of the Royal Navy; senior civil servants: wardrooms': since late 1930's. (Wilfred Granville, Sept. 23, 1967.)

top man. See **floor man**.—2. Auctioneer for a rigged auction: mock-auction world: since ca. 1945. (*Sunday Chronicle*, June 28, 1953.)

top of the bleeding bungalow. See **top of the house** (*Dict.*).

*top-off, n. An informer to the police: Australian c.: C. 20. B., 1942. By 1948, low s. (Park, 1950.)

top off, v.—4. (Ex 2, 3, p. 900.) To act as an informer to the police: Australian c.: C. 20. Baker.

top-off merchant. A low Australian variant of **top-off,** n. Lawson Glassop, 1944.

top people, the. Tic-tac men signalling from high in the stands: racing: since ca. 1920. *The Sunday Telegraph*, May 7, 1967, anon. article on bookies' s.

top ropes . . . (p. 900). In Australia, ca. 1850–

80, the phrase was 'carry on *top ropes*' (sense 1), as in Rolf Boldrewood, *The Miner's Right*, 1890.

top-sail. See **topsail** (*Dict.*).

top the officer is recorded in 1806: John Davis, *The Post-Captain*. (Moe.)

top 'uns'. Breasts: low: C. 20. (Norman.)

top up. To bring a liquid to the necessary level; hence, to fill a drinking-glass or a fuel tank: coll. (? originally Army): since ca. 1930. (P-G-R.)

Top Wop, the. Mussolini: ca. 1940–44, then historical only. 'Sir Alan Herbert, I believe, christened him thus.' (Ramsey Spencer.)

top your boom! (p. 900): earlier in W. N. Glascock, *Sailors and Saints* (I, 145, and II, 123), 1829. Moe.

topcoat warmer, a. Warmer by a topcoat, i.e. much warmer: coll.: since ca. 1930.

topes. Latrine: Imperial Service College: C. 20. Marples. Ex **topos** (p. 900).

topknot. See **top-knot** (*Dict.*).

toploftical; toplofty. See **top-lofty** (*Dict.*).

topnobber. Someone first-class or even pre-eminent: Anglo-Irish: C. 20. James Joyce, *Ulysses*, 1922.

topo. A topographical map: Australian: since ca. 1940. (B., 1953.)

topos (p. 900). As 'a latrine', it may have come from Rugby School. (Marples.) At Rugby School, always in the pl. *topoi*, except in *topos bumf*, toilet paper—a term current since ca. 1920.

topper, n.—9. An unamusing so-called 'funny story': since ca. 1950. (See, e.g., Romany Bain's column in the *Evening Standard* of July 20, 1963.) It '*tops* the lot'.

topper, v. (p. 900), prob. derives imm. ex: 2. To punch: pugilistic: ca. 1810–55. George Godfrey, *History of George Godfrey*, 1828, has the boxing phrase (current ca. 1815–45), *topper one's smellers*, to land a blow on one's opponent's nose.

*toppertjie. A cigarette-end: South African c.: C. 20. *The Cape Times*, May 23, 1946. It is an Afrikaans word, but used also by English-speakers: cf. **entjie**.

topping, n. A hanging: late C. 19–20. Cf. *topper*, 7 (p. 900), ex *top*, v., 4 (p. 899).

tops. Important persons; persons in the news: journalistic: since ca. 1925. Ex *top-liners*.

tops, adj. First-class: Army: 1944 +. Adapted from *tops, the*. (P-G-R.)

tops, the; as in 'He's the tops'—admirable, the best possible; most likeable: coll.: adopted, ca. 1943, from U.S.

*tops and bottoms. 'In his pockets were bundles of "tops and bottoms"—rolls of "notes" with genuine fivers on top and bottom and sheets of toilet paper or telephone directory pages, their edges trimmed to look like notes, in between' (John Gosling, 1959): C. 20; by ca. 1930, also police s.

topside.—2. Hence, in the air; airborne; flying: R.A.F.: since ca. 1918. Jackson.

topsider. A lazy dog: Australian: since ca. 1910. B., 1942. Prob. ex **topside** (p. 901).

topsides. Those at the head of a specialist corps or of a branch of the Service: Army: C. 20. E. P., 'In Mess and Field'—*The New Statesman*, Aug. 1, 1942. Ex **topside** (*Dict.*); it is a kind of pidgin English.

Topsy.—2. A term of address to any little girl whose name is unknown to the speaker: non-aristocratic coll.: mid-C. 19–20. Cf. *Tommy*, 6, in *Dict.*—3. 'All Turners are "Topsy" in the Navy' (Granville): C. 20.

topwire lizard. A boundary rider on large (sheep-) stations: Australian rural: C. 20. Baker. He often perches on the top wire of a fence; basks, lizard-like, in the sun; smokes; gazes around.

tore out. A small boat (up to about 15 tons T.M.) converted from cargo-boat to yacht: Essex-coast s. rather than Essex dial.: C. 20. I.e. *torn out* 'because the internals have been torn out' (J. A. Boycott, Dec. 1938).

tormentor of sheepskin (p. 901) prob. goes back to late C. 18, to judge by the synonym occurring in 'Police of London', reprinted by *The Port Folio* of May 16, 1807 (p. 312), where a drummer is referred to as 'this *tormentor of parchment*'. Moe.

tormentors, 2 (p. 901) occurs, in the singular, in C. J. R. Cook, *The Quarter Deck*, 1844. (Moe.)

torn off a strip. See **tear a strip off.**

torn thumb. An inferior form of *Tom Thumb* (p. 895). Franklyn, *Rhyming.*

torp. A torpedo: C. 20. Implied in **torps** (*Dict.* and Addenda); Berrey, 1940.

torpedo, v. To steal: Australian servicemen's (esp. Naval): 1939–45. (B., 1953.)

*****torpedo** and **submarine** are used by the South African underworld for 'a dagga, i.e. a marijuana cigarette'; a *submarine* is properly a large one (*The Cape Times*, May 23, 1946), *torpedo* a large, a medium or a small (C. P. Wittstock, letter of same date). Ex their effect.

torpedo-Jack. Earlier in 'Taffrail'. Cf.: **torps.**

Torpoint chicken; also **Stamshaw nanny-goat.** A very quick-tempered messmate: Naval: C. 20. Torpoint is that township which lies across from Devonport. Stamshaw is in the Portsmouth area. The chickens of the former were noted for their 'testiness', and the nanny-goats on Stamshaw Common, noted 'butters', usually attacked on sight. (Granville.)

torps. Earlier authority: 'Taffrail'. The vocative of *torpedo Jack.*

torrid. Rather tipsy: ca. 1780–1840. See **mops and brooms.** Amorous drunk?

Tosh. Sandhurst nickname for a man with a wooden leg: from ca. 1850. Major A. F. Mockler-Ferryman, *Annals of Sandhurst*, 1900. Perhaps ex the noisiness of the **tosh-can** (*Dict.*).—2. A coll. vocative to someone of unknown name: Cockney (C. 20); common in Army (1939 +). It occurred, e.g., in the film *The Blue Lamp*, 1950. (Philip Gaskell.)—3. As *the Tosh* it = the school swimming bath: Rugby School: C. 20. (D. F. Wharton, Oct. 24, 1965.) Ex **tosh,** n., 3, on p. 901.

tosh, n.—8. Sewage-refuse, esp. articles made of copper: sewage-hunters': since ca. 1830. Mayhew, II, 1851, where also **tosher,** 1, and **toshing** (p. 901). Cognate with—perhaps ex—East Anglian *toshy,* muddy, sticky.—9. See **tush** below.—10. A term of address, as in 'Wotcher, tosh!': since late 1930's: proletarian, much affected by spivs; but by 1945, fairly gen. Perhaps related to Scottish dial. *tosh,* neat, smart, whence the n.—a smart fellow.

tosh and waddle. Utter nonsense: Australian rhyming s. (on *twaddle*): since ca. 1950. Cf. **tosh,** n., 4, on p. 901. (B.P.)

tosh-room. A bathroom: Sandhurst: from ca. 1860. Mockler-Ferryman.

tosh-soap goes back at least a decade earlier than

the *Dict.* date. According to B. & L. it is esp. Charterhouse School s.; but it was † there by 1920.

toshing, n. See **tosher,** 1 (p. 901).

toss, v.—2. To throw away, esp. as useless or worthless: Australian: since ca. 1930. 'Do you want to keep this?'—'No, you can toss it.' (B.P.) Ex S.E. *toss away.*—3. In *toss a party,* to 'throw' (give) one: Australian: since ca. 1950. (B.P.)

Toss an' Joss. The T. and J. Harrison Steamship Company: H.M.S. *Conway:* C. 20. (Granville, Nov. 22, 1962.) *Joss* rhymes with *Toss; Toss* = *Thos.,* Thomas.

toss in the alley. A variant of **toss in the towel** (p. 901): since ca. 1920. B., 1942.

toss one's cookies. To vomit: Canadian: ca. 1920–55. (Leechman.)

tosspot. 'Used as a jocular affectionate term of address [to men] in Australia' (B.P.): Australian coll.: late C. 19–20. Ex the † S.E. *toss-pot,* a heavy and habitual toper.

toss-prick. A coarsely humorous vocative: C. 20.

total loss, a. 'He's a total loss', i.e. useless: R.A.F.: since ca. 1939. Ex aircraft thus classified.

total wreck. A cheque: Australian rhyming s.: C. 20. Baker.

tote, n.—4. A woman's large bag, used for carrying groceries or baby's napkins, etc.: Australian, coll. rather than s.: since ca. 1930. (B.P.) Ex **tote,** v., 2, on p. 902.

tote up. To add up: Australian: since ca. 1920. (B.P.) Ex *total.*

totem pole. 'An item of airfield lighting equipment, so called from its shape' (Jackson): R.A.F.: since ca. 1925. By 1943, jargon.

tother-sider.—3. A person from the Eastern States: West Australian. Also, a Tasmanian: Victoria. B., 1942.

tots. Old clothes: street-markets': since ca. 1870. Ex *tot,* n., 5 (p. 902).

tots, go. See **going tots.**

Tottie.—4. A girl, a young woman, esp. if of a compliant nature, but not a whore: Naval: C. 20. '"That mad pusser. Gone native. Shacking up with a Japanese tottie somewhere"' (John Winton, *We Saw the Sea*, 1960.) Ex sense 3 on p. 902.

Tottie (or **-y**) **fie.** A smart young woman given to 'throwing her weight about'; a prostitute or near-prostitute with such tendencies: Londoners', esp. Cockneys': C. 20. The *fie* is of exclamatory origin ('Oh my!'); see **Tottie,** 3 (*Dict.*). Hence, *Totty Fay* (pronounced *Fye*), alternatively *Tottie Hardbake,* a female assuming a haughty air: derisive Cockney: since ca. 1890. (Atkinson.)

totties. Potatoes: Regular Army: late C. 19–20. Perversion of *taties;* cf. the Cottonian **chotties.**

totting-up. See **tot,** v., 3 (*Dict.*).

touch, n., 3 (p. 903), applies, in C. 20, more esp. to cattle. (B., 1943.)—9. A simpleton; a dupe: Australian (originally c.): since ca. 1910. (B., 1953.) Soft to the touch: cf. sense 4 on p. 903.

touch, get a. 'To come into personal contact with a live rail' (*Railway* 2nd): railwaymen's: since ca. 1950. A pun on **touch,** n., 5 (p. 903).

touch-bottom. A forced landing, esp. a crash-landing: R.A.F.: since ca. 1925. H. & P. Also a v. (unhyphenated), 'to crash-land': since ca. 1925. Jackson. By meiosis.

touch down, v.i. To land: R.A.F. coll. (by 1944, j.): since ca. 1918. Jackson. Ex Rugby football.

touch of 'em (or **them**), **give** (someone) **a.** To irritate intensely; to get badly on the nerves; to disgust: Australian low: since ca. 1925. Lawson Glassop, *We Were the Rats*, 1944. Them = 'the shits'.

touch of the tar-brush. See tar-brush.

touch-up.—4. To borrow money from (someone): Feb. 1787, *Sessions*; by 1820, virtually superseded by **touch**, v., 3 (p. 903).

touch wood! A precautionary c.p., uttered in order to avert bad luck or a reversal of the good fortune or success of which one has just boasted, as in 'I've been lucky, so far—touch wood!': C. 20. Ex the proverbial *Touch wood, it's sure to come good* and the folklorish 'to *touch wood*', superstitiously to do so.

touchables, the. The corruptible; those open to bribes: since ca. 1939. Punning on India's *untouchables*.

touchy, 2 (p. 904), goes back to ca. 1840. Marples.

tough, a bit. Rather unreasonable or too severe or too expensive: Australian coll.: late C. 19–20. B., 1942.

tough as fencing wire. Extremely hardy or fit: Australian coll.: C. 20. B., 1942. Other Aus. similes are *tough as ironbark* or *as seasoned mulga*: C. 20. (B., 1959.)

tough titty. See hard titty above.

*tough-yarn. Slightly earlier in J. Burrowes, *Life in St George's Fields*, 1821. The hyphen is omitted by Burrowes—as it should be.

toughie. A tough: since ca. 1945. (Nicholas Blake, *The Whisper in the Gloom*, 1954.)

tour of miseries. 'The day's work when one is feeling down in the mouth.' H. & P.: Services (esp. Army): since ca. 1930. Ex military j. *tour* (as in *tour in the trenches, tour of duty*).

tour of the Grand Dukes, the. A tour of the fashionable *demi-monde* of Paris: ca. 1870–1914. B. & L.

tousle. A whisker worn bushy: proletarian: from ca. 1860; ob. B. & L.

tow-path. 'The runway or stretch of ground over which a glider is towed off by an engined aircraft or tug' (Jackson): R.A.F.: 1941 +. Cf. tug.

tow-row.—2. As **tow-row!**, it meant, among London crossing-sweepers of ca. 1840–80, 'Be careful, a policeman is coming!' Augustus Mayhew, *Paved With Gold*, 1858.

tow street. To be *in Tow Street* is to be 'decoyed or persuaded' (P. Egan, *London*, 1821).

towel up. Australian variation of towel, v. (p. 904): C. 20. B., 1942.

Tower-rook. See 'Occupational names'.

town, on the. Engaged in crime: 1818, *The London Guide*; 1822, Pierce Egan, *The Life of Hayward*; † by 1900.—2. Applied to 'a man of the World. A person supposed to have a general knowledge of men and manners,' Pierce Egan, *Life in London*, 1821: coll.: ca. 1815–60.—3. Applied to one who has gone into town in search of sexual or other entertainment: Canadian: since ca. 1920.

town-bike. A loose woman: Australian: since ca. 1920. (Dal Stivens, *Jimmy Brockett*, 1951;

D'Arcy Niland, *The Shiralee*, 1955.) So often and generally ridden.

*town shift. A sharper; a scoundrel living by his wits.: Londoners' c.: ca. 1660–1730. Because he so often changed his lodgings, says Richard Head, *Proteus Redivivus*, 1675. See also 'Rogues'.

town-stallion. See 'Dupes' and cf. town-bull (in *Dict.*).

town tabby. 'A dowager of quality' (*Sinks*): ca. 1830–80.

town-trap. See 'Constables'.

town(e)y.—6. *Townies*, men hailing from the same home town: Naval: C. 20. (P-G-R.)

toy.—2. A trainer aircraft: R.A.F.: since ca. 1930. Jackson. For the 'new boys' to play with.

toys.—2. 'The mechanical parts of a 'plane so beloved by the armourers and flight mechanics who care for the machine,' H. & P.: R.A.F.: since ca. 1920.—3. Equipment, vehicles, etc.; to a Gunner his guns: Army: since ca. 1925.

tra-la-la.—2. (Gen. pl.) One of 'the wealthiest and most extravagant class of dissipated men': mostly proletarian: ca. 1889–1900. B. & L.

trac. A Cockney variant of track, n., esp. 2 (*Dict.*). It would seem to be also a c. term for threepence, esp. a threepenny piece: late C. 19–20; ob. Pugh.

track, n.—3. 'Any outback road' (B., 1942): since ca. 1870: Australian coll. >, by 1920, S.E.—4. 'A warder who will carry contraband messages or goods out of or into jail for a prisoner' (B., 1959): Aus. c.: since ca. 1930. A *way* in or out.

track, go down the. To go down South on leave: Australian servicemen's: 1940–5. (B., 1943.) From Darwin.

track, (go) on the. (To go) tramping the back country in search of work: Australian coll: C. 20. (Caddie, *A Sydney Barmaid*, 1953.)

track, up the. See 'Hauliers' Slang'.

track mitts. Leather mittens: (racing) cyclists': since ca. 1930.

track square. To deal fairly (*with* a person): Australian: since ca. 1910. Baker. Cf. track with (p. 905).

tractor.—2. A motor car: since ca. 1950. (*The New Statesman*, Feb. 5, 1965.) Pejorative; cf. sense 1 (p. 905)—itself † since ca. 1930 and ob. since ca. 1920.

trad. Traditional or 'hot' jazz music: mostly teenagers': since ca. 1959, but not common until 1961. *The Sunday Telegraph*, Dec. 3, 1961. See also 'Jazz Slang'. Cf.:

trad rags. Traditional dress of a people: since ca. 1960. (Wilfred Granville, April 22, 1962.)

trade, n. Sense 3 was revived in World War II: P-G-R.—4. Booksellers' and publishers': book-world coll.: from ca. 1815. Lockhart, *Life of Scott*, 1837, 'Gentlemen of the *trade*, emphatically so called.'—5. In homosexual circles, it is the normal word for sexual commerce, as in 'Did you have any trade last night?': C. 20. (Correspondent.)

trade-in. A car 'traded in' as part of the purchase money for a new car. A motor-trade coll., esp. in Australia: since ca. 1930. (Gavin Casey, *The Wits Are Out*, 1947.)

tradesman, regular. See regular tradesman.

Tradesmen's Entrance, the. That entrance and narrow passage to the Grand Fleet anchorage at Scapa Flow which was used by destroyers and smaller craft: Naval: 1939–45; then semi-historical. (Wilfred Granville.)

traffic cop. A policeman controlling the traffic: adopted ex U.S., ca. 1935 in Canada, ca. 1945 elsewhere; by 1945 in Canada, by 1955 elsewhere, virtually coll.

traffique. See traffic (*Dict.*).

trag. A teralgon (a fish): Australian fishermen's coll.: since ca. 1920. (B.P.)

trail boss. A stationmaster: railwaymen's: since ca. 1935. (*Railway* 2nd.) Jocular, ex Western films.

train(-)detainer. A train-dispatcher: Canadian railroadmen's (— 1931). Jocular.

train(-)driver. 'The leader of a large formation (of aircraft)', H. & P.: R.A.F. since ca. 1938.

train(-)smash. Fried tomatoes: Naval (lower-deck): C. 20. *The Weekly Telegraph*, Sept. 13, 1941; Granville. Ex the colour of flowing gore, the aspect of mangled limbs. Thus do brave men deride their own secret dreads.

train-up, v.i. To hurry: proletarian: mid-C. 19–20. B. & L.

tram, n.—2. See **fish-horn.**

tram-driver. A coastal Command pilot on patrols: R.A.F.: 1940–5. Contrast **train-driver.**

tram-lined. (Of trousers) having a double crease: jocular coll.: since ca. 1925.

tram-lines.—2. 'The tram-lines are war-time convoy routes': Naval: 1939 +. Granville. Compare the R.A.F.'s **milk round.**—3. Parallel brush-marks: builders' and house-painters': since ca. 1910. (A master builder: Dec. 5, 1953.)

*****tram-walloper.** One who pickpockets on tramcars: C.: from ca. 1910. (*The Yorkshire Post*, latish May, 1937.)

trammy or **-ie.** A tram conductor or driver: Australian coll.: C. 20. (B., 1943; Margaret Trist, 1946.)

tramp, n.—2. See 'Imperial . . .'

*****tramp-major.** A tramp that, in exchange for his keep at a casual ward, helps the porter: tramps' c.: late C. 19–20. (From ca. 1930, he has been deprecated by the authorities.)

tramped, adj. (in predicate only). Dismissed from employment: Australian Labour: since ca. 1920. B., 1942. I.e. rendered a tramp.

trampolin (p. 906). That sense is ob. and was probably never worse than jargon.

trams. Legs: underworld (and 'fringe') rhyming s.: C. 20. On *gams*, pl. of **gam,** 2 (p. 313). Franklyn 2nd.

tranklements or **trollybobs.** Entrails; intestines: proletarian: mid-C. 19–20. B. & L.

tranko. 'The elongated barrel which a performer manages with his feet, and keeps up in the air while lying on his back': circusmen's s. verging on j.: mid-C. 19–20. Ibid. Origin? Cf. **risley** above.

trans. A translation: secondary schools': late C. 19–20. (Michael Poole, *Redways*, 1935.)

Trans, the. The train running between Adelaide and Perth, *trans* or across the Nullarbor Plains: Australian coll.: since ca. 1925. (B., 1953.)

transit is occ. (though very rarely before C. 20) used catachrestically for *transport* (or carriage).

trap, n.—8. See 'Guard-Room in Army Slang'.

trap, v.i. To obtain a fare: taxicabmen's: from ca. 1925. '''Did you trap off the Museum?''

"Yes, I puts on there and I traps in ten minutes."' This *put on*, v.i., is also cabmen's (same date): i.e. I put my car on the rank at ('the Museum' being the rank in front of the British Museum). Perhaps there is a reference to the old horse-busman's s. phrase *net a load of rabbits*, to get a load of passengers, of ca. 1860–1908.

trap, shut one's. See **shut your face!** above.

trap for young players. A c.p. applied to, e.g., marriage: mostly Australian: since ca. 1955. (B.P.)

trap-stick, 2 (p. 907), occurs much earlier in Addison's *The Spectator*, No. 599, published in 1714.

traps.—3. (Ex sense 1: p. 907.) *Cleaning traps*, one's cleaning-materials (polish, buttonstick, brushes, etc.): Army, esp. Artillery: C. 20.—4. Short for **mess-traps** (p. 518). In W. N. Glascock, *Sketch-Book*, 2nd Series, 1834, at I, 56. (Moe.)

trat. A pretty girl; an attractive harlot: proletarian: ca. 1880–1905. B. & L. Either a perversion or an anagram of *tart*.

travel, 1 (p. 907). By 1910 at latest, S.E.—3. To take stage properties and important accessories on tour: theatrical coll.: late C. 19–20. 'Theatrical people, on the road, may or may not "travel" all their "props" and accessories' (Leechman).

travel in the market. Applied to the way or extent in or to which a horse is betted on or against: turf: ca. 1870–1910. B. & L.

travel on the thumb. See **hitch hike.**

traveller.—9. A loafer: Australian: C. 20. B., 1942. Ex senses 2, 3 (p. 907).

travel(l)ing grunt; travelling man. A road foreman of engines; a travelling engineer or a travelling fireman: Canadian (and U.S.) railroadmen's (— 1931).

travelling scholarship (p. 907) has the variant *t. fellowship*, belonging to approximately the same period. On May 1, 1802 (p. 136), *The Port Folio* quotes from *The Rusticated Cantab*, an unidentified British source. Moe.

travelling the bees. Migratory bee-keeping; hence, *travel the bees*, to be a migratory bee-keeper: Australian coll.: since ca. 1945. Kylie Tennant's novel, *The Honey Flow*, 1956, forms the 'locus classicus' of the subject.

traverse the cart. To delay departure; be loath to depart: pedantic: ca. 1845–70. Thackeray.

tray-bit.—2. Hence, a term of contempt for an insignificant person: Australian: C. 20. B., 1942. —3. (Usually in pl.) A female breast: Australian c.: since ca. 1920. (B., 1963.) Rhyming on *tit*.

tray of moons. A three-months' prison-sentence: ca. 1870–1914. (Barry Pain, *The Memoirs of Constance Dix*, 1905.)

treacle, v. To flatter (esp. a superior): Services: since ca. 1930. H. & P., 'To administer soothing syrup'.

treacle, the. A hanger-on; one who is neither a constant nor an accepted member ●f a gang: Teddy boys': since ca. 1950. (*The Observer*, March 1, 1959.)

treacle toffee. Welsh coal: railwaymen's: C. 20. *Railway*, 3rd.

treaclemoon. Honeymoon: jocular (ugh!): C. 20.

treat, 1 (p. 908), occurs in *The Port Folio*—an American magazine, quoting a British source—of

Feb. 21, 1801 (p. 64), and therefore presumably goes back to late C. 18.

treat, give the boys a. See **give the boys . . .** above.

treat with ignore. To overrule (someone): Australian soldiers': 1939–45. (B., 1943.) To ignore someone's request.

tree frog. A Meteorological Officer in the German Zeppelin Service: R.F.C.–R.A.F.: 1915–18. (V. M. Yeates, *Winged Victory*, 1934.)

tree-hopping. An occ. variant of **hedge-hopping** on p. 385: R.F.C.–R.A.F. 1915–18, then historical. (V. M. Yeates, *Winged Victory*, 1934.)

*tree of knowledge. See **boom,** n., 3. (C. P. Wittstock, May 23, 1946.)

trees. Creases in carbon-paper: typists': since ca. 1910. Kate Stevens, *Typewriting Self-Taught*, 1942.

tremblers. Stairs: Anglo-Irish: C. 19. 'A Real Paddy', *Real Life in Ireland*, 1822.

Trenchard brat. An R.A.F. apprentice: 1920 +; by 1940, ob. Jackson, 'After Marshal of the Air the Viscount Trenchard who, in 1920, introduced the apprenticeship system into the Service.'

trendy, adj. Following the social or intellectual or artistic or literary or musical or sartorial or other trend; up-to-the-minute smart or fashionable: since 1966; by end of 1967, already verging on coll. *The New Statesman*, March 24, 1967.

trendy, n. One who is 'trendy': since 1967. Joan Fleming, *Kill or Cure*, 1968, '. . . the Chelsea Set . . . there are trendies and *personae non gratae* amongst them'.

trezzie. A threepenny piece: Australian: since ca. 1920. B., 1942. Ex *trey*: see **tray**, 2, on p. 908.

tri-car. A motor-car with only one wheel at rear: coll.: since ca. 1930.

trible, adj. and—usually in pl.—n. Treble: Australian juvenile: since ca. 1930. (B., 1953.) Cf. *fourble*.

trick.—3. A tour of duty; a turn at the wheel: Naval (late C. 19–20), Canadian railroadmen's (– 1931), and others'. Ex card-games.—4. A customer: prostitutes': adopted, ca. 1944, ex U.S. (where current since World War I); by 1960, also gen. low s. (Cf. sense 3.) Hence, *be on a trick* = to be 'entertaining' a customer.

trick cyclist. A psychiatrist: Army: 1943 +. By 'Hobson-Jobson'. In, e.g., Lewis Hastings, *Dragons Are Extra*, 1947. 'At least as early as 1938 in civilian slang. Also used as a verb in the Forces towards the end of the war [of 1939–45]. "He got himself trick-cycled out of the Army"' either legitimately or fraudulently: Peter Sanders.

trick up. To baffle; to get the better of: Australian: since ca. 1920. (Jean Devanney, *By Tropic Sea and Jungle*, 1944.)

trickle, n. Sweat: Scottish Public Schools': C. 20. Ian Miller, *School Tie*, 1935, has it also as a v.i. Whence *trickle-bags*. The sense 'to perspire' has been current at Harrow School since before 1913: witness Lunn.

trickle-bags. A coward: ibid.: id. Ian Miller, l.c.

tricks and mortar. A c.p. applied to jerry-building: since ca. 1930. A pun on *bricks*.

tricycle. 'An aircraft with a tricycle type under-carriage,' Jackson: R.A.F. coll.: since ca. 1930. That definition requires modification: 'A 'plane with a nose wheel instead of a tail wheel—all air-

craft have three wheels,' Robert Hinde, March 17, 1945.

tried it once, but I (or he) **didn't like it,** preceded by *I* or *he*. 'When used in the first person, it means that one is turning down an offer through preference rather than ignorance; when used in the third, it refers to a married person with an only child' (B.P.): Australian c.p.: since ca. 1920.

trier.—2. An unsuccessful thief: c.: C. 20.

trig, n.—4. A surveyor's pole or mark or station: Australian: C. 20. 'A flagpole . . . without a flag. "One of the border trigs", called Tuck from his camel . . . "Government surveyors built 'em up years ago when they ran the border line",' Archer Russell, *In Wild Australia*, 1934. Prob. ex *trigonometrical survey*.

trilbies. Feet: Australian: late C. 19–20. Ion M. Idriess, *The Yellow Joss*, 1934, 'Stony broke, tucker-bags busted, no smokes, corns on me trilbies, an' a thirst that'd swallow a brewery. What a life!'

trim-tram. In *Lord Hervey and His Friends*, edited by the Earl of Ilchester and published in 1950, there occurs, in a letter dated Oct. 23, 1731, this passage: 'There was a most magnificent entertainment, and everything that depended on his servants was in perfection. Whether it was trim tram, I know not, but can give a shrewd guess', the sense being either 'an absurdity' or 'absurd': upper-class: ? ca. 1700–70. A reduplication on *trim*.

trim your lamps, I'll. A threat to give someone a good hiding: c.p.: since ca. 1940. Perhaps the original sense was, 'I'll black your eyes': cf. *lamp* (p. 468).

trim your language! Cease swearing!: Australian: C. 20. B., 1942. I.e. render it less shaggy—less rough.

trimmer.—2. Anything excellent: (? mostly) Australian: C. 20. 'You little trimmer!' = 'You little beaut!': an Australian usage. (B.P.) Ex sense 1 on p. 909.

Trinco. Trincomalee, a seaport of Ceylon: coll.: late C. 19–20 nautical, 1942–5 Services'. (F. Spencer Chapman, *The Jungle Is Neutral*, 1949.)

Trindog. An undergraduate of Trinity College, Oxford: Oxford undergraduates': ca. 1890–1914. 'The expression "a hearty Trindog" was in vogue c. 1908' (Marples, 2): originated by Balliol?

trinkerman. A Thames Estuary fisherman: nautical: mid-C. 19–20. B. & L.

*trip, 1 (p. 910). Esp. as in '*Trips*: Women who decoy and rob drunken persons,' F. D. Sharpe, *The Flying Squad*, 1938.—4. An experience of drug-taking: drug addicts': since ca. 1966. *Daily Colonist* (Victoria, B.C.), March 29, 1967, 'A Vancouver youth who had a nightmare ride on an L.S.D. "trip", said Tuesday he never wants to make the journey again.' (Leechman.) By early 1967, also British: note Peter Fryer in *The Observer* colour supplement, Dec. 3, 1967.

trip up the Rhine, a. Sexual intercourse: Forces': 1945 +. Cf. the barmaids' *a bike ride to Brighton*: C. 20.

tripe.—5. Filth, dirt: Army, esp. in the Guards regiments: C. 20. Gerald Kersh, *They Die with Their Boots Clean*, 1941.—6. Hence, fig., as in **tripe, in** (below).—7. Very easy bowling: cricketers' coll.: since ca. 1920.

tripe, in. In trouble: Regular Army: since ca. 1920. Gerald Kersh, *The Nine Lives of Bill Nelson*, 1942, 'He was in tripe . . . and about forty hours pushed' (late). Ex prec.

tripe, up to. See up to mud.

tripe-hound.—3. A reporter: orig. and mainly newspapermen's: from ca. 1924. (In Dorothy Sayers's contribution to *Six against the Yard*, 1936.)—4. A sheep dog: New Zealand and Australian farmers': C. 20. B., 1941, 1942.

tripe medal is a C. 20 variant of *putty medal* (p. 693).

Tripe Shop, the. Broadcasting House, London: taxi-drivers': since ca. 1930. *Weekly Telegraph*, April 6, 1946.

Tripoli gallop, the. The advance towards Tripoli (N. Africa)—an advance that happened twice before the 8th Army captured it: Army: 1942-3. (P-G-R.)

trips. Triplets: mostly lower-middle class: since ca. 1910. Rose Macaulay, *I Would Be Private*, 1937.

*triss. An objectionable fellow: esp. a pathic: Australian c.: since ca. 1930. (Kylie Tennant, *The Joyful Condemned*, 1953.) Origin? A 'siss' or 'sissie' (see p. 772): rhyming s.; by 1950, no longer low.—2. A variant of **trizzie** below: Australian: since ca. 1925. (B.P.)

trizzer. A lavatory: Australian low: since ca. 1922. B., 1942. The charge for a wash and brush-up is a:

trizzie. A threepenny piece: Australian: since ca. 1920. Baker. See **trezzie.**

trog. 'We are "Trogs"—sort of "Mods" who go potholing. We were having a "do" at the "Thunderbirds"—they're a sort of "Rockers"': thus a youth of 20, as reported in *The Times* of June 8, 1965. Obviously ex S.E. *troglodyte*, a cave-dweller, it dates since ca. 1961.—2. A 'stuffy', old-fashioned person (a very cubical 'square'): since ca. 1950. (R. T. Bickers, *The Hellions*, 1965.) Ex the *Troglodytes* or Cave-Dwellers of the Ancient World.—3. A cadet: Royal Naval College, Dartmouth, and gen. R.N.L. since ca. 1950. John Winton, *We Joined the Navy*, 1959 (p. 65); a midshipman, a newly appointed officer, John Winton, *We Saw the Sea*, 1960, 'Now I must . . . introduce the rest of the trogs to the captain.'

trog boots. 'Especially heavy, cleated, rubber-soled boots used in bad-weather conditions by certain tradesmen and outdoor workers' (Sgt R. Farley, Feb. 16, 1967): R.A.F.: since ca. 1960. Ex S.E. '*Troglodyte*'?

Trojan.—4. A professional gambler: buckish: ca. 1805-40. J. J. Stockwell, *The Greeks*, 1817. Prob. ironic ex sense 2.

trolley and truck. Coïtion; to coït: low rhyming s.: since ca. 1910. (Franklyn, *Rhyming*.)

trolling, n. Streetwalking by a prostitute: prostitutes': since ca. 1930. I.e. *trawling*.

trollop (p. 911). Obviously it is an ironically humorous misuse of the S.E. sense: cf. **wench** (p. 945).

trollybobs. See **tranklements.**

trombone, the. The telephone: defective rhyming s.: since ca. 1930. (Douglas Warner, *Death of a Snout*, 1961).

tromboning, adj. and n. See **laking.**

tronker. A long-distance lorry driver: hauliers': since late 1950's. (*The Daily Telegraph*, Feb. 4, 1964.) Perhaps, as Peter Sanders has

suggested, ex *trunk*-route driver; prob., I'd add, influenced by French *tronc*.

troop.—2. To convey in a troop-ship: coll.: since ca. 1940. (Jane Gordon, *Married to Charles*, 1950.) —3. To cause (a defaulter) to be brought before a superior officer: coll., Armed Services', esp. the Navy: since ca. 1930. John Winton, *We Saw the Sea*, 1960.

trooper.—2. A prostitute: ca. 1830-90. *Sinks*, 1848.

troops, the.—2. 'The Ship's Company,' H. & P.: Naval: C. 20. 'Not quite correct, the truth being that this is the Wardroom's term for the lower-deck' (Granville).

troppo. 'Term used by men serving during World War II in the Pacific area = one who has had long service in tropical areas and, by inference, ought to be repatriated' (W. Colgan): New Zealand and Australian: since ca. 1941. (B., 1942, *troppo*; Dymphna Cusack, 1951, *half-troppo*, partly, or as if, crazy.) Ex '*trop*ical', with Australian suffix -*o*.—2. Hence, *go troppo*, to go crazy: since ca. 1942; by late 1940's, common throughout the Pacific: cf. 'He had the look of men Hurst had seen in the tropics, when they were going "troppo"—off their heads' in Elleston Trevor's *The Shoot*, 1966.

tros (p. 911). But *trosseno* occurs in Mayhew, I, 1851.

trossing, n. Walking: Post Office employees', esp. telegraph messenger boys': C. 20. (Laurie Atkinson, Sept. 11, 1967.) Ex S.E. *trudging*?

trossy.—2. (Cf. sense 1: p. 911.) Hence, shoddy, inferior; spurious: late C. 19-20.

trot.—7. A synonym of **twat, 1** (*Dict.*): low: C. 18-20.—8. A fellow, chap: mostly University: from ca. 1919. Nicholas Blake, *Thou Shell of Death*, 1936, Oxford don speaking: 'He's quite a decent old trot, but definitely in the Beta class.' Perhaps ironically ex † S.E. *trot*, a whore.—9. A sequence of bets, esp. *bad trot*: Australian racing: C. 20. Lawson Glassop, 1949. Cf. sense 4 (p. 911). By ca. 1955, no longer confined to the sporting and gambling world, but very widely used, in New Zealand also.—10. A woman: New Zealand: since ca. 1925. Cf. the quotation a **mocker, 2**, above.—11. A lavatory: R.A.F.: since ca. 1950. Cf. **trots, 3**, below.

trot, do a. To have a successful run: Australian two-up players': C. 20. (Vance Palmer, *Let the Birds Fly*, 1955.)

trot, on the. Gadding about: Society coll.: since ca. 1880. (Edward Burke, *Bachelor's Buttons*, 1912.)—2. In succession: Services' in 1939-45; then in general use. Cf. the familiar S.E. *running*.

trot(-)boat. 'A duty boat plying between ship and shore': Naval: C. 20. Granville. A *trot* is a line of buoys and the *trot-boat* serves ships moored on the *trot*.

trot-boat queen. 'Wren member of a trot-boat's crew' (Granville): Naval: 1941 +. Ex prec.

trot fob. The moving of submarines in the 'trot' alongside their parent ship to make way for a submarine that is to be victualled or ammunitioned: submariners': since ca. 1930. (P-G-R.)

trots.—3. As *the trots*, diarrhœa: mostly Canadian: since ca. 1910. Also, since ca. 1912, Australian (I heard it in Gallipoli in 1915.)—4. A horse-trotting meeting: Australian coll.: C. 20.

'Betting on the Harold Park trots' (B.P.). Perhaps the origin of sense 3.

Trotters, the. The Bolton *Wanderers* Association Football team: sporting: C. 20.

troub. A tram conductor: Australian: since ca. 1925. (B., 1943.) Ex *trouble* or perhaps *troublesome*.

trouble, n.—3. Short for **trouble and strife** (p. 912): C. 20.—4. Confinement (esp. of unmarried woman): euphemistic coll.: mid-C. 19–20.

Trouble, the. The Sinn Fein 'troubles' (1916–27): Anglo-Irish euphemistic coll.: since 1916; by 1930, merely historical.

trouble(-)box. Fuse in a mine or a bomb: Naval: 1939 +.

trouble-shooter. A public relations man: coll.: since late 1950's. A sense-adaptation of an American term; a word so useful that, by 1966, it has > S.E.

troubles!, my. An Australian equivalent of 'I should worry!': since ca. 1910. B., 1942.

trough. A school dinner: North Country grammar schools': since late 1940's. *New Society*, Aug. 22, 1963.

trouncer. A drink of strong liquor: (low) London: ca. 1820–70. *Sessions*, Feb. 1838.—2. Somebody extremely expert or capable; something excellent or astounding: Australian coll.: C. 20. B., 1942. Ex S.E. *trounce*, to thrash.

trousered; trousers. '*Trousers.* The streamline covering in which the undercarriage legs of some 'planes are enclosed; such planes being *trousered*. (Cf. *spats*),' H. & P.: Air Force: since ca. 1930.

*****trout, be all about.** To be alert or watchful: c.: since ca. 1945. (Robin Cook, 1962.) Origin?

troy school. A gambling school, ? esp. in two-up: Australian coll.: since ca. 1880. Jean Devanney, *By Tropic Sea and Jungle*, 1944, 'Tully'—in N. Queensland—'was full of gambling joints, poker schools, troy schools—all the trimmings'. Origin obscure: perhaps cf. S. W. English dial. *troy fair* and *troy town*, confusion, litter.

truckie (-ky). A railroad truck: Australian, mostly juvenile: since ca. 1920. (Dick.)—2. A truck (lorry) driver: Aus.: since ca. 1920. Bernard Hesling, *The Dinkumization and Depommification*, 1963.

trudge. A trudgen stroke (ex John Trudgen, British swimmer, † 1902): since ca. 1905. John Garden, *All on a Summer's Day*, 1949.)

true dinkum. A variant of **square dinkum** (p. 818): Australian: C. 20. B., 1942. Sometimes shortened to *true dink*: since ca. 1920.

true marmalade. See **marmalade** (*Dict.*).

true till death. Breath: theatrical rhyming s.: late C. 19–20. (Franklyn, *Rhyming*.)

true Trojan. See 'Tavern terms', § 2; and cf. **Trojan**, 2 (*Dict.*).

trugmoldies. See 'Harlots'.

trump, n.—2. A breaking of wind: mid-C. 19–20; ob. Ex **trump**, v. (*Dict.*).—3. A commanding officer: Australian soldiers': 1939 +. B., 1942. Ex card games. Cf. **trump of the dump** (p. 912).

trumpet, on the. Objectionable; disliked: Australian soldiers': 1939 +. B., 1942. Ex 'one who blows his own trumpet'?

trumpeter.—2. See 'Tavern terms', § 7 (end).

trumpeters. Convicts' 'irons which connected the ordinary leg-chains with a brazil riveter round each leg immediately below the knees,' Price Warung, *Tales of the Early Days*, 1894, in ref. to Norfolk Island ca. 1840; app. s. rather than c. They proclaimed the convict's presence if he so much as stirred.

trun. To run: University of Oxford s. of ca. 1760–1810. See quotation at **pro,** 1, above. Short for S.E. *trundle*.

trundle for a goose's eye, making a. See **weaving leather aprons** (*Dict.*).

trunk.—3. A trunk call: coll., among telephonists and constant telephone-users: since ca. 1920.

trunk(e)y or **T-.** Nickname for anyone with a prominent nose: Naval: C. 20. Granville. Suggested by 'elephant's trunk' and **conkey** (*Dict.*).

trunnions. 'Hair over the ears which curls over a sailor's cap' (Granville): Naval: since ca. 1920. Ex the lit. nautical S.E. sense.

trust him as far as I could throw him, I would not. A c.p. applied to an unreliable man: from ca. 1870. Dr Leechman, in April 1967, writes, 'I recently encountered "I wouldn't trust him as far as I could throw an anvil in a swamp"'—a Canadian variant.

trust him (or **her**) **with a kid's money-box, I wouldn't.** A self-explanatory c.p.: C. 20.

trust him with our cat, (I) wouldn't. A c.p. applied in C. 20 to a man with an unsavoury sexual record.

trusted alone (p. 913). Two years earlier in Pierce Egan, *Life in London*, 1821.

trut. A threepenny-piece: Australian: since ca. 1930. (B., 1943.) Origin? 'Perhaps from broad pronunciation of "trupenny bit"' (B.P.); with, I suggest, the *p* of 'trupenny' influenced by the *t* of 'bit'—in short, by assimilation.

try a piece of sandpaper! See **get the cat.**

try one on a wind. To take a chance: Naval coll.: C. 19. In W. N. Glascock, *The Naval Sketch-Book*, 2nd Series, 1834, at II, 67. (Moe.) Semantically, cf. *fly a kite*, 6, on p. 291.

try some horse-muck in your shoes! Workingmen's advice to undersized boys: c.p.: late C. 19–20. As manure to make them grow.

try the raw prawn act, v.t.: *on* someone. Variant of **come the raw prawn over** (above).

try this for size! A c.p. used in horseplay and accompanying a playful punch: variant, *how's that for centre?* (perhaps originally Army, ex markmanship): both, since ca. 1935. The former probably derives ex drapery salesmen's jargon.—2. Hence, but *try this for size* only, also—since ca. 1945—in contexts far removed from horseplay.

tse is incorrect for **tsetse**: mid-C. 19–20. O.E.D.

tu. Tuition: Public Schools': late C. 19–20. Marples.

tub, n. 7 (p. 914). By 1950, at latest, it had become busmen's: see **barrow**, 2.—9. A cathode-ray tube: R.A.F.: since ca. 1940. Sergeant G. Emanuel, letter of March 29, 1945, 'From "tube",'—10. A brake: railwaymen's: since ca. 1920. (*Railway* 2nd.)

The definition of sense 3 (p. 914) should be more precise: the term was applied to seatless carriages, also called *stand-ups*, on the early English railway trains. This sense derives ex that of 'a covered carriage of the sort called a *chariot*': s.: ca. 1815–40. *The New York Literary Gazette* of Nov. 12, 1805 (p. 145) app. quotes a British source in this passage: '"By Jove," languidly drew out Lord

Tubureux, "what!—the *steady fellow's* off at last [i.e., dead]. I wonder who gets his horses and his yellow *tub* (an impertinent term of contempt for his chariot); he had one *decentish* black horse, ha! ha! ha! (laughing.) Well, I'm glad that old sober sides is done up.'" (Moe.)

tubber; usually in pl. A difficult question asked in a *viva voce* examination: Naval: C. 20. Granville. It comes like a cold douche.

Tubby. The 'inevitable' nickname of men surnamed *Cooper*, even if not fat, the reference being to barrels: C. 20. (Peter Sanders.)

Tubby Martin. See 'Nicknames'.

tube, n.—4. A cigarette: Cambridge undergraduates': ca. 1925–40. Hence, 1940 +, among Leeds undergraduates. (Marples, 2.)—5. A submarine: Naval: since ca. 1918. Ex its torpedo-tubes.—6. Penis: Anglo-Irish feminine: late C. 19–20. James Joyce, *Ulysses*, 1922.

tube, v.; hence agent **tuber** and n. **tubing.** To toady; a toady; toadying: University of Alberta: ca. 1925–40.

tube, (ride) in a; tube, shoot the. This *tube* (n., 6) is, in *Pix*, Sept. 28, 1963, defined as 'a hollow piped wave'. The 2nd phrase occurs in *Pix*'s definition of *shooting the tube* as 'crouching on the nose of the board, shooting through the hollow portion of the curl'; the 1st phrase, in the *Sun-Herald* quotation (Sept. 22, 1963)—'Riding "in a tube" is the ultimate aim of all surfers—shooting along the tube formed by a perfect wave as its crest curls over.' An Australian surfers' term and phrases, dating from ca. 1961.

Tubes. Shares in Tube Investments, Ltd: Stock Exchange: since ca. 1950. (Sanders.)

tubs. Tubular tyres: cyclists' and motor-cyclists': since ca. 1935.

tuck, n.—4. The head: 1888, *The London Guide*; † by 1900. Cf. sense 1 of the v. (p. 914).

tuck in your tuppenny! Among boys playing leap-frog: Tuck in your head!: late C. 19–20. Rhyming s.: *tuppenny* (loaf of *bread*).

tuck on (a price). To charge exorbitantly: non-aristocratic: from ca. 1870; slightly ob. B. & L.

tucker, v. To eat one's tucker, to eat a meal: Australian: late C. 19–20. G. B. Lancaster, *Jim of the Ranges*, 1910, 'If I don't turn up before dinner time you come an' tucker, an' then go back.' Ex tucker, n., v (p. 914).—2. To provide with food: Australian: since ca. 1920. (Kylie Tennant, *The Honey Flow*, 1956.) Likewise ex *tucker*, n., 2.

tudgy yarn. Spun-yarn: R.N.C., Dartmouth: since ca. 1930. 'After a Seamanship Instructor of that name' (P-G-R.).

Tudorbethan (or **t-**), adj. Applied to a house possessing either no particular, or every, style: architecturally a 'mess': cultured coll.: since ca. 1950. (R. G. G. Price, *A History of Punch*, 1957.)

tug, n. Sense 3 (p. 915) is recorded earlier by 'Taffrail'.—5. An engined aircraft that tows glider-borne troops: since ca. 1941 or 1942: R.A.F. coll. >, by July 1944, j. H. & P. Sense 1, by the way, occurs as early as *Spy*, 1825, in forms *tug mutton, tug, mutton.*

tug-clothes and **tug-jaw.** See tug, adj., 2 (*Dict.*).

tug-mutton.—3. See tug, n. (above).

tug pilot. 'The pilot of the aeroplane towing a glider' (P-G-R.): Air Force coll.: since ca. 1942.

tuggery.—2. A variant of *toggery* (p. 894).

tugging, n. Dealing cards from the bottom of the pack: Australian card-players': since ca. 1920. (B., 1953.)

tuggy. A fireplace cloth: chimneysweeps': C. 19. (G. Elson, *The Last of the Climbing Boys*, 1900.) Cf. *toggy* on p. 894.

tulip, 2 (p. 915), occurs in, e.g., *Boxiana*, IV, 1824, 'A small number of Swells, Tulips, and Downey-coves'; ibid., 'Togged like a swelled tulip.'—3. A bomb dropped by a Zeppelin: 1916–18. Ironic.

tulips of the goes. 'Highest order of fashionables' (*Sinks*): ca. 1835–55.

tum-tum. A dog-cart: Anglo-Indian: from ca. 1860; ob.—2. See **tum** in *Dict.*

tumble, n.—3. '"Come and have a tumble" (from "Tumble down the sink", rhyming slang for "drink"),' F. D. Sharpe, *The Flying Squad*, 1938: since ca. 1912.—4. A rough sea: Australian nautical: since ca. 1915. In, e.g., Sydney Parkman, *Captain Bowker*, 1946. Proleptic. Recorded earlier in Sydney Lester, *Vardi the Palarey*, 1937.

tumble, v., 2 (p. 915). A little earlier in *Sessions*, March 1848.

tumble-down. Grog: Australian: ca. 1815–70. Peter Cunningham, *Two Years*, 1827. Proleptic. —2. Hence, alcoholic liquor: Australian: since ca. 1870; ob. B., 1942.

tumble to oneself, take a. The *to oneself* is often omitted. Used by 'Rolf Boldrewood' in 1891. (Sidney J. Baker, letter, 1946.)

tumble up, 2 (p. 915): prob. since late C. 18. (W. N. Glascock, *Sketch-Book* (I, 8), 1825.) Moe.

tumbler.—5. A printing machine: printers': from ca. 1880; ob. B. & L. Ex 'the peculiar rocking motion [of the cylinder]'.

tumour. A term of abuse, ca. 1930–4, at several Public Schools. Ian Hay, *Housemaster*, 1936, 'Smear is the very latest word here. Last year it was tumour.'

tune (p. 916) is, however, very much alive in South Africa c. and low s.: June 3, 1946, *The Cape Times* (article by Alan Nash), 'To hit back: Tune him, label him full of dents.'

tuniness. See **tuny** (*Dict.*).

Tunisgrad. 'The position the Germans ultimately found themselves in in Tunisia. (Tunisia + Stalingrad.)': thus Peter Sanders, Sept. 10, 1967, concerning the war in North Africa: 1943.

tunk. To dip (e.g. bread) in a liquid (esp. gravy or tea or coffee): coll.: adopted, ca. 1944, from U.S. servicemen. The U.S. coll. *tunk* comes ex the synonymous Pennsylvania German *dunke* (past p., *gedunkt*), a deviation from German *tunken*. See also *dunk*.

tunnel. A synonym of **tube**, n., 6 (above): since ca. 1961. *Pix*, Sept. 28, 1963.

tunnel motor. '0–6–0 Pannier tank fitted with condensing apparatus for working over the Inner Circle and Metropolitan lines' (*Railway*, 3rd): London railwaymen's: since ca. 1950.

tunny. See **turnee.**

tup. In sense 2, the phrase dates from before 1890. B. & L.

tup-three. 'Drill instructors' pronunciation of *two-three*, the pause between the stages of a movement' (P-G-R.): Army: since ca. 1880(?).

tuppence-ha'penny. A squadron-leader: R.A.F.

regulars': since ca. 1920. A pun on '*two-and-a-half* ringer'.

Turbot. A Talbot car: Cambridge undergraduates': ca. 1925–40. Pun.

turd.—2. A term of contempt, as in 'You are a turd': South African coll.: since ca. 1925. Cf. **shit**, 2, on p. 758.

turf or **turf up.** To throw up—abandon—a job: Australian: since ca. 1920. B., 1942. Cf. **pack it in** and **pack up** and **turn it in.**

turf it. To sleep on the ground with a tent-like canvas covering: 1883, James Greenwood, *Odd People*; ob. by 1919, virtually † by 1940.

turf it! Stow it!; Be quiet!: Australian: since ca. 1930. (B.P.) Cf. **turf** above.

turf out.—2. To throw out or away, to discard: mostly Australian: since ca. 1920. (B., *Australia Speaks*, 1953.) Ex sense 1: p. 916 at **turf**, v., 3.

Turk. 'An ill-natured surly boorish fellow' (P. W. Joyce, *English . . . in Ireland*, 1910): Anglo-Irish: late C. 19–20.

turk. A turkey: Australian: C. 20. B., 1942. Cf. **donk** and **monk.**

turkey. Earlier recorded in 'Taffrail'.—2. See *turkey-merchant*, 6 (p. 917)—which, obviously, should be *turkey*, 2.—3. A tramp's swag: Australian: C. 20. (B., 1943.) Common also in Canada and U.S. (Leechman.)

Turkey, Church of. Any 'fancy religion': Naval: C. 20.

turkey, talk. See **talk turkey.**

turkey off (p. 917). By ca. 1910, also Australian. Baker.

Turks. The Irish: Teddy boys': since ca. 1949. (*The Observer*, March 1, 1959.)

turn dog. To inform to the police: Aus.: mid C. 19–20, but ob. by 1930. Edward Dyson, *The Gold Stealers*, 1901, '"Tell me how you come to be in the Stream drive that night." Dick . . . answered nothing. "Come on, old man, I won't turn dog."'

turn in, 1 (p. 917). A slightly earlier nautical example occurs in *The Dublin University Magazine* of March 1834 (on p. 244). Moe.—3. To bring (someone) before the Officer Commanding: Army: since ca. 1930. Ex underworld. (P-G-R.)

turn it in.—2. In imperative, it = *turn it up* (see **turn up**, v., 1: (*Dict.*) = Shut up: C. 20. See **turn it in,** v., 2 (*Dict.*).

turn it on. To provide, to pay for, drinks, esp., to give a party: Australian: C. 20. B., 1942.—2. To fight—to begin to fight—with one's fists: Australian: since ca. 1920. Baker.—3. (Of a woman) to agree to coït: Australian low: since ca. 1920. Baker.

turn it up at that! All right, you may knock off now and call it a day: Naval c.p.: since ca. 1925. (P-G-R.)

**turn milky. See milky, adj., 2 (Dict.).

turn-on, n. A 'gag' or joke, a bogus jazz conversation intended to shock 'square' tourists: Canadian jazz musicians' and lovers': since ca. 1956. (*The* Victoria *Daily Colonist*, April 16, 1959, 'Basic Beatnik'.) *Turned-on* as if from a water-tap.

turn on, v.—2. To inspire (someone): Canadian jazz musicians' and lovers': since ca. 1955. (*The* Victoria *Daily Colonist*, April 16, 1959, 'Basic Beatnik'.) Esp., to excite, to thrill—a nuance that, ca. 1956, > popular among English teen-

agers. By 1960, also British.—3. To introduce to drugs; to supply with a drug: drug addicts' and hippies': since ca. 1961. Peter Fryer, *The Observer* colour supplement, Dec. 3, 1967.

turn on a cabbage-leaf. (Of a horse) to respond promptly to guidance: Australian coll.: C. 20. Baker.

turn on the waterworks. See **waterworks**, 2, in *Dict.*

turn-out, n.—2. A fight with fists: *Sessions*, Dec. 1816 (p. 43); not yet †.

turn out, v.—3. V.i., to become a bushranger: Australian coll.: ca. 1830–90. B., 1942.

turn(-)over, n.—5. A search of one's cell or belongings: prisons': since ca. 1920. (Jim Phelan, 1940; Norman.) Cf.:

turn over, v.—5. To raid (a building): Australian police: since ca. 1910. (Vince Kelly, *The Shadow*, 1955.)—6. To set upon and beat up: teenage gangsters': since ca. 1950. *The Observer*, July 15, 1962, reporting a fight between the 'Mussies' (Muswell Hill) and the Finchley Mob.

turn (oneself) round. To get used to one's job; to learn one's trade or profession: coll.: C. 19. Wm Maginn, *Tales of Military Life*, 1829, at III, 126. (Moe.)

turn up, v.t., sense 4: for '1890' read '1850'.

turn up the wick. To open the throttle: Air Force: since ca. 1920. Cf. **go through the gate.** Partridge, 1945, 'It's an easy transition from getting a better light to getting a better speed.' Since 1945, esp. of a jet engine.

**turned. Converted to an honest life: (prison) c.: from ca. 1870.

turned off. Married: Society: ca. 1880–1914. (Maxwell Gray, *The Great Refusal*, 1906.)

turned-on, adj. Having taken an exhilarating drug, esp. marijuana; hence, aware, 'with it': drug addicts', beatniks', hippies': since early 1960's. (Peter Fryer in *The Observer* colour supplement, Dec. 3, 1967.) Ex **turn on,** v., 3, above.

turned over, be. To be transferred from one ship to another: Naval coll.: late C. 18–mid- (? late) 19. It occurs in W. N. Glascock, *Sketch-Book* (I, 124), 1825. Moe.

turnee or **tunny.** An English supercargo: Anglo-Indian: mid-C. 19–20. B. & L., 'Sea-Hindu, and prob. a corruption of attorney.'

turnip, 1 (p. 918), occurs earlier in W. N. Glascock, *Sailors and Saints*, 1829; there it is glossed as simply 'a watch'. Moe.

turnip-bashing is a variant of **swede-bashing** q.v.: R.A.F.: 1940 +. Partridge, 1945. In the King's Royal Rifle Corps, however, *turnip-bashing* is ordinary drill and *turnip-bashers* is the name for County regiments, both because they are regarded as country bumpkins and because they bang their rifles on the ground, whereas the K.R.R.C. put theirs down quietly. (Peter Chamberlain, letter of Sept. 22, 1942.)

turnips, get (p. 918). The phrase *give turnips* occurs in Alfred Burton's *Johnny Newcome*, 1818. (Moe.)

Turpentine, the; often—cf. *turps*, p. 918—reduced to **Turps, the.** The Serpentine: Cockney rhyming s.: C. 20. (Franklyn, *Rhyming*.)

turps.—2. Beer: Australian: since ca. 1935. (B.P.)—3. 'Any alcoholic drink. Whence, *be on the turps* and *get on the turps*' (B., 1959): Aus.: since late 1930's.

turret down, esp. get . . . See **hull down.**

turtle.—2. A girl, a young woman, esp. regarded sexually; a (young) prostitute: Australian low: C. 20. B., 1942. Ex the billing-and-cooing of turtle-doves. But more prob. ex the tortoise-like creature: 'A turtle on its back is not unlike a girl in the same position, and they are both in a vulnerable state,' as a shrewd observer has remarked.

turtles. See turtle doves (*Dict.*).

tush or tosh. A half-crown: mostly showmen's: C. 20. *Night and Day*, July 22, 1937. Ex tosheroon and tusheroon (*Dict.*).—2. Money: Cockneys': late C. 19–20. J. W. Horsley, *I Remember*, 1912.

tut-mouthed. See 'Epithets'.

Tutbury Jinnie. 'Passenger train between Tutbury and Burton on Trent' (*Railway*, 3rd): railwaymen's: since ca. 1930 (?).

tute (loosely written *tut*). A tutorial: Universities': C. 20. (Marples, 2.)

tux. A tuxedo or dinner jacket: Australian: adopted, ca. 1945, ex U.S. (B.P.) For *tuxedo*, see esp. my *Name into Word*, 1949.

twack. 'To examine goods and buy nothing' (L. E. F. English, *Historic Newfoundland*, 1955): Newfoundland coll.: C. 19–20. Ex East Anglian dial. *twack*, 'to turn quickly; to change one's mind' (E.D.D.).

twaddle, v.i. To trifle: coll.: ca. 1770–1840. 'I have been twaddling enough to cut several slips from the most sacred *laurus*' (Earl of Mornington, letter of Feb. 15, 1791; in the Fortescue Manuscripts). Probably ex the n.

twaddy is a slang term fashionable in the 1780's:? 'characterized by twaddle'. In *The New Vocal Enchantress*, 1791, occurs on p. 32, a 'Song' beginning thus:

'Hey for buckish words, for phrases we've a passion,
Immensely great and little once, were all the fashion:
Hum'd, and then humbugg'd, twaddy, tippy, proz,
All have had their day, but now must yield to quoz.'

twam or twammy. The female pudend: low: C. 20. Perhaps a blend of '*twat*' + '*quim*', qq.v. in *Dict.*

*twang, n. Opium: Australian c.: C. 20. B., 1942. Ex a Chinese radical?

twanged, as good as ever; twanged, the worst that ever. See twanging, go off: in *Dict.*

twat. Also, as in *you silly twat!*, you fool!, and *that twat* in pejorative reference: late C. 19–20.

tweaker or tweeker. A leg-break spinner: cricketers': from ca. 1932. *The Times*, July 6, 1937, 'R. C. M. Kimpton came on with his "tweekers" at the Nursery end.'

twee. Small and dainty: Society and theatre: since mid-1930's. (C. Brand, *Death of Jezebel*, 1949.) A blend of *tiny* + *wee*.

*tweedle, n.—2. (Ex sense 1 on p. 919.) A trick involving dummy diamonds: c.: C. 20. '"A bloke's tried to pull a tweedle on me with a load of jargoons"' (John Gosling, *The Ghost Squad*, 1959).

tweedle, the. The selling of 'dud' diamonds: c.: C. 20. In, e.g., F. D. Sharpe, *The Flying Squad*, 1938. There is prob. no connection with S.E. *tweedle*; *tweedle* is a variant of *twiddle*, cognate with *twist*, and there is perhaps a humorous sideglance at *wheedle*. Cf. jargon.

*tweedler, agent, and tweedling, activity, can be applied to 'the tweedle' (above), 1 or 2.—3. Usu., however, a *tweedler* is a very minor, petty sort of 'con man'. John Gosling, 1959, 'The tweedler will flog you sawdust cigarettes or dummy diamond rings'—a nuance dating, like sense 1 (of which, clearly, it forms a mere extension), from early C. 20. 'The terms "conning" and "tweedling" cover virtually everything in the crime known as obtaining money by false pretences.' They derive, ultimately, ex tweedle on p. 919; cf. tweedle above.

twen-center. A modernist: early C. 20 († by 1914). H. A. Vachell *Quinney's*, 1914. Cf. twencent in *Dict.*

twenty-eight. The Yellow-Collared Parrakeet: Australian: C. 20. (B., 1943.)

twenty-seven. Three '9' cards: Australian poker-players': since ca. 1920. (B., 1953.)

twenty-three, but written 23. To depart; esp. in imperative, 'Get out!': Canadian journalists': since ca. 1910. Perhaps ex a telegrapher's code: see thirty. (Leechman.) This is the much-used shorter form of twenty-three, skidoo (or skiddoo)l, which is dated by Harold Wentworth & Stuart Berg Flexner, *Dictionary of American Slang*, 1960, as of ca. 1900–1910, said to be of male use, originally among students and youthful sophisticates, and described as 'perhaps the first truly national fad expression', still very widely known in 1960 and, oddly and ironically, associated by post-1950 writers with the 1920's and regarded as entirely characteristic of that crazy decade. They quote it also as *23 skid(d)oo* and class it as an expression of surprise or pleasure, but 'also used of . . . rejection or refusal, sometimes as = "Go away!" "Beat it!" or "I don't care"'. *The O.E.D. Supplement* cites its use, as *skiddoo*, by Neil Munro in *The Daft Days*, 1907, and notes its currency in Canada in 1910.

*twenty-two carat. Utterly trustworthy: since ca. 1930: c. >, by ca. 1950, also s. Robin Cook, *The Crust on Its Uppers*, 1962.

twibby. Ingenious: London schools': ca. 1875–95. (Prof. Arnold Wall, communication of Aug. 1939.) Arbitrary formation: *twiggez-vous?*—2. Funny, amusing: id. (Prof. A. Wall.) Heath-Robinsonishly funny?

twice, v. To cheat (somebody): low: C. 20. David Hume, *Five Acres*, 1940.

twice in a row. An ineptitude common among radio announcers and commentators since ca. 1945 and perhaps especially in Canada. At least three units are needed to form a row.

twice removed from Wigan. A disparaging c.p., applied to Lancashire (hence, loosely, also Yorkshire) people living permanently in the South of England: since ca. 1920.

twicer.—8. (Cf. 4, 5.) A twister; a crook: Australian: C. 20. G. B. Lancaster, 1910.—9. (Cf. 2.) A sycophant: Australian: since ca. 1918. Baker. Ex 'two-faced'.

Twickenham (p. 919). Messrs Thorneycroft once had, at Twickenham, a yard for building small Naval aircraft.

Twickers. Twickenham Rugby Football ground: sporting: since ca. 1920. *Twick*enham + the Oxford *-er*.

twict or twicst. See twicest (*Dict.*).

twiddler. A 'Penguin' or 'Pelican' or a 'Guild' paper-covered cheap edition: Naval: since Feb.

1940. *The Observer*, Aug. 18, 1940. One can twiddle them about in one's hands.

twig, n., 1 (p. 919), in the nuance 'fashion', goes back to before 1806, when *The Port Folio* of Sept. 6 (p. 143) quotes a Charles Dibdin song containing the lines:

> 'The wig's the thing, the wig, the wig,
> Be of the ton a natty sprig,
> The thing, the tippy and the twig'.

Sense 2 at top of p. 920 should be 3.—4. Mostly in pl. *twigs*, matches: Borstal boys': since ca. 1945. *The Daily Telegraph*, June 4, 1958, 'Bacon Bonces, Joes & Maggies'. Ex the rough, 'twiggy' quality of inferior safety matches.

twiggez-vous? (p. 920). 'I suspect that by the time it had filtered down to Kipling's schoolboys, it was rather *vieux jeu* in the metropolis. It may have originated in the song of Marie Lloyd, by whom it was first popularized in 1892' (Lindsay Verrier, M.R.C.S., letter of May 25, 1949).

twilight. Toilet: Universities' and Public Schools': ca. 1840–90. B. & L.

twilights. Summer-weight knickers worn by the W.A.A.F.: among W.A.A.F. and R.A.F.: 1940+. Jackson. Ex their pale-blue colour. Cf. **blackouts** and **passion-killers.**

twillies. Sympathy between twins: medical: since ca. 1920. Ex *twinly feelings*? The German for 'twins' is *Zwillinge* (from *zwei*, two), so prob. imm. ex Yiddish. (Ramsey Spencer.)

twillip. A 'twerp' (objectionable and/or insignificant person): Guards Regiments': since ca. 1935. Gerald Kersh, *They Die with Their Boots Clean*, 1941. A derisive perversion of **twerp.**

twim. Female pudend: low: C. 20. A blend of *twat* and *quim*.

twin-set. A two-bottle aqualung: skin divers': since ca. 1950. Ex the terminology of women's clothing.

***twine.** To grumble: c., and low: from ca. 1925.

twink. A moment: proletarian: C. 20. J. J. Connington, *A Minor Operation*, 1937, 'I just pressed the electric light switch for a twink—to make sure—an' the current was off.' Abbr. *twinkle* or *twinkling.*

***twirler.** A sharper with a *round-about* at a fair: c.: from ca. 1870. B. & L.

twirling. The dishonest substitution of a winning betting slip for a losing one: bookmakers': since ca. 1925. (*The Bournemouth Echo*, Aug. 18, 1960.)

twirly. A cigarette: Australian Naval: since ca. 1920. (B., 1943.) One twirls it in one's fingers.

twirp is a variant spelling of **twerp** (p. 919).—2. See:

twirt. (Also *twirp* or *twerp*.) A cheeky small boy: Shrewsbury: since mid-1930's. Marples. Cf. **twillip.**

twist, n.,—4. *The twist* is 'sharp practice, in gen. or in particular': c.: C. 20. F. D. Sharpe, *The Flying Squad*, 1938. Cf. **twist**, v., 3, and **twister**, 5: p. 920. As 'a *twist*' it = esp. 'a swindle', as in 'I thought the betting slip a twist'—a bookmaker's remark quoted by *The Bournemouth Echo*, Aug. 18, 1960.—5. An habitual criminal: Australian c.: since ca. 1910. B., 1942.—6. A girl: low Canadian: adopted, ca. 1940, from U.S.—as also were *bim, broad, frail*. All four

American terms originated in the underworld.—7. But *the twist* is the forcing of the arm up behind the back when a person is being arrested: coll.: since ca. 1860. (S. R. Crockett, *The Stickit Minister*, 1893.)

Of sense 6, Robert Clairborne, on Aug. 31, 1966, writes, 'This is rhyming slang: "twist-and-twirl"—one of the few bits of r.s. that ever became fairly gen. in U.S.: cf. E. E. Cummings, "To be a feller's twist-and-twirl". Now ob. here.'—4. A tale: Naval: C. 19. (W. N. Glascock, *Sketch-Book*.)

twist, v.—4. *Be twisted*, to be convicted of a crime: Australian low (? c.): C. 20. B., 1942.

twist, spin a (p. 920), goes back to ca. 1800 or perhaps 1790. In, e.g., W. N. Glascock, *Sketch-Book*, I (20 and 112), 1825. In Glascock's *Sailors and Saints* (I, 178), 1829, it has the variant *tip a twist*. Moe.

twist (someone's) **arm.** To persuade; strictly, to persuade forcibly, hence with lengthy argument: since the late 1950's.

twist joint. Any cheap dance hall for twist sessions: since ca. 1961; by late 1965, already slightly ob.

twister, 2 (p. 920), goes back to ca. 1800. In, e.g., W. N. Glascock, *The Naval Sketch-Book*, 2nd Series, 1834, at I, 235. (Moe.)

twister to the slammer. See 'Jive'.

twister to the turner. See 'Canadian'.

twisty. Odd, strange, esp. in 'a *twisty* look': low: C. 20. (Jim Phelan, *Fetters for Twenty*, 1957.) Semantically cf. *twist*, a strange turn of mood or bent of character.

twit, n. A contemptible—or a very insignificant —person: since ca. 1925. Eric Linklater, *Magnus Merriman*, 1934. A blend of *twerp* and *twat*.—2. A simpleton, a fool: Australian: late 1920's. B., 1942.—3. A term of abuse: North Country grammar schools': since late 1940's. (*New Society*, Aug. 22, 1963.) Ex sense 1.

twitch, n. A bout of nerves, esp. if noticeable by others: R.A.F.: since the late 1930's. (R. T. Bickers, *The Hellions*, 1965.) Cf. *twitchety* (p. 920), **twitters** (below) and 'Have you ever used that old service slang and said that someone has a "bit of a twitch on"? You don't mean it literally, of course. You're merely implying that the person concerned is in a highly emotional state and somewhat "het up" about something' (*Woman's Own*, Jan 16, 1965). Cf. **widow**, 7, below.

twitter. Short for *ring-twitter*. See **twittering ringpiece.**

twittering, n. Paying court to other sex: University of Alberta: ca. 1925–40.

twittering ringpiece; also **ring-twitter** and **ring-twitch.** A state of extreme nervousness: R.A.F.: since ca. 1939. Ex a physiological symptom.

twitters,' the. Nervousness: Scottish Public Schools': C. 20. Ian Miller, *School Tie*, 1935, 'I played my best game in the match v. the Academy, in spite of a bad attack of the twitters before going on to the field.'

two-acre back or **chest.** A massive woman wearing much heavy jewellery: jewellers': late C. 19–20.

two-and-a-half bloke. A Lieutenant-Commander: Navy: since ca. 1930. H. & P. A variant of **two-and-a-half-striper.**

two-and-a-half ringer. See **ringer, half.**

two-and-a-half striper. See **striper** (*Dict.*). Earlier in 'Taffrail': 'From the two thick and one thin stripes of gold lace he carries on his coat sleeves.' Ex the fact that the *half stripe*, like a *half ring*, is a band much narrower than the others.

two-and-eight. A fluster, a confusion, emotional state, attack of nerves: C. 20. Rhyming on **state**, 2 (*Dict.*).

two-and-from. A concertina: mostly Army: late C. 19–20; ob. by 1940. Ole Luk-oie, *The Green Curve*, 1909.

two bastards on spikes. See **two ladies on bikes** (*Dict.*).

two-bit. Insignificant: Canadian since ca. 1925. Australian since ca. 1945 but not very common. (B.P.)

two blocks chocker. See **blocks** and cf. **mouldy.**

two-bob. A blonde: Australian soldiers': 1939–45. (B., 1943.)

two-bob hop. A cheap evening's dancing: Australian since ca. 1920. (B.P.)

two bob lair is a particularly cheap **lair**, q.v. Lawson Glassop, 1944.

two-by-four. A whore: rhyming s.: since ca. 1870.

two cents' worth, my, his, etc. My opinion for what it's worth: Canadian c.p.; adopted, ca. 1945, ex U.S.

two crows for a banker. 'Code whistles exchanged between engine and second [or] banking engine when ready to move' (*Railway*): railwaymen's: since ca. 1920.

two dots and a dash. Fried eggs and bacon: army: 1914–18, then ob.

two draws and a spit. Smoking half a cigarette; hence, any short smoke at convenient intervals: mostly in factories and workshops: from ca. 1915. Cf. **spit and a draw** in *Dict.*

two-er. See **twoer** (*Dict.*).

two eyes of blue! Too true!: rhyming s.: since ca. 1925. Franklyn 2nd.

two eyes upon ten fingers. See **two upon ten** (*Dict.*).

two-fer. A cigarette: mostly Naval: since ca. 1950. 'For *two for a penny*'—the penny 'that one once put into a slot machine': Laurie Atkinson, who notes having heard it in Aug. 1967.

two-fisted, 2 (p. 921): earlier in W. N. Glascock, *Sailors and Saints* (I, 179), 1829. Moe.

two fools. See **two**, adj.: in *Dict.*

two, four, six, eight, bog in, don't wait! A secular grace before meals: Australian: since ca. 1920; perhaps much earlier. (B.P.) Cf. **bog in** above.

two ha'pennies to rub together, have not. To be very poor; occasionally, to lack any spare money whatsoever: coll.: C. 20. 'He hasn't . . .' (A. B. Petch, March 1966, reminds me that I had omitted this c.p.)

two i.c. (A spoken abbreviation.) A second in command or charge: Australian: since ca. 1945. (B.P.)

two inches beyond upright refers to 'falling over backards' in an excess of rectitude: Canadian: since ca. 1955. (Leechman.)

two Labour gains. 'Two yellow lights at a colour signal' (*Railway* 2nd): since 1945 or 1946. Cf. **one Labour gain** above.

two-legged calf. A gawky youth; a youthful country bumpkin as a wooer: rural: late C. 19–20.

two little ducks. The number 22 in game of House: late C. 19–20. Michael Harrison, 1943. Fancifully ex appearance of figure; also it is a 'duck' of a number.

Two O. A Second Officer in the Wrens: Wrens' and R.A.F.: since ca. 1939. (P-G-R.)

two of eels, (standing there) like. 'Abstracted, indecisive, at a loss' (Atkinson): C. 20.

two of fat and one of lean. The marking on the ships' funnels of The Harrison Line: nautical: C. 20.

two old ladies. The number 88 in houseyhousey: since ca. 1920.

two ones. At two-up, a 'head' and a 'tail' when two coins are used: Australian coll.: late C. 19–20. B., 1942.

two-peg. A florin: Australian: C. 20. B., 1942.

two-pence-ha'penny. See **tuppence ha'penny.**

***two penn'orth of rope, have.** See **twopenny-rope** (*Dict.*).

two pennorth of tripe, like. (Of something) contemptible or worthless: C. 20.

two-pipe scatter-gun. A double-barrelled shotgun: Canadian: from ca. 1870. (Sir Clive Phillipps-Wolley, *The Trottings of a Tenderfoot*, 1884.)

two-pipper. A First Lieutenant: Army: since ca. 1910. (P-G-R.)

two-ringer. See **ringer, half.**

two-shakes of a dead lamb's or **donkey's** or **a monkey's tail, in.** See **shake.**

two-six, do a. To do something very speedily and promptly, e.g. in bombing-up: R.A.F., esp. armourers': since ca. 1930. R. M. Davison, letter of Sept. 26, 1942, '"To do a two-six out of camp" (to leave camp immediately or very quickly)— "a two-six into a shelter".' Cf. a *one-two*, two quick, successive punches in boxing. But *two-six*, or *two*, *six*, also occurs alone, to urge speed or a spurt of energy, as in 'a spot of two, six'.

two-striper. Earlier in 'Taffrail'.

two-ten. A shopkeepers' code c.p.: C. 19–20. (George Seton, *A Budget of Anecdotes*, 1886.) 'Keep your *two* eyes upon his, or her, *ten* fingers.'

two-thirder. A printer's apprentice that has served two-thirds of his time; hence, loosely, someone fairly well-advanced in the trade: printers' coll.: C. 20.

two-thirty. Dirty: rhyming s.: late C. 19–20. Franklyn, *Rhyming*, 'It refers to grime, not to behaviour'.

two-three-five-nine; written **2359.** See 'Prisoner-of-War Slang', 15.

two-time, to double-cross (someone); **two-timer,** a double-crosser, or merely one who doesn't 'play the game': adopted, in 1939, from U.S.

two tin fucks (about it), I don't care or **worry.** To use a more polite c.p., which > popular in 1947–8, 'I couldn't care less': low c.p. of C. 20.

two-upper. A two-up player: Australian coll.: C. 20. (B., 1943.)

two ups, in. An Australian re-shaping of **two twos, in** (p. 922): C. 20. B., 1942.

two-water rum. 'The real "grog". Two parts water to one rum' (Granville): Naval coll.: mid-C. 19–20.

two-water tipple. A strong grog: Naval: C. 19. Wm N. Glascock, *Sketch-Book*, 2nd Series,

1834, at I, 74, 'The ship's company has already dined and the potent "two-water-tipple" was drained to the last drop.' (Moe.)

two-year-old, like a. An earlier record: *Punch*, June 19, 1912. (Dr D. Pechtold.)

twoer.—4. A clay marble with *two* coloured rings painted on: London schoolchildren's: from ca. 1880. Cf. **one-er,** 5 (Addenda).

twopenny burster. A twopenny loaf of bread: 1821, W. T. Moncrieff, *Tom and Jerry*: this puts **burster,** 1 (p. 112) back by nearly forty years.

twopenny dump, not to care a. To care not at all, not to care a damn: Australian: since ca. 1910. Cf. **twopenny damn** (on p. 922) and **dump,** n., 1 (p. 248). B.P.

twopenny fuck, not to care a. A variant of **monkey's fuck** . . . above: since ca. 1920. Both terms were, by ca. 1940, fairly common. In both, the offensive word is often omitted.

twopenny rope (p. 922) goes back probably as far as 1820 at least. It occurs in *The Pickwick Papers*, 1836–7, in ch. 16.

two's, the. The second floor: prison c. (and prison officers' s.): C. 20. Robin Cook, *The Crust on Its Uppers*, 1962.

twot, is a variant spelling, but the gen. pron., of **twat** (*Dict.* and Addenda).

Twyford, my name is. The true origin of this c.p. is given in *The New Statesman & Nation*, Feb. 20, 1937: 'Josiah Twyford, 1640–1729, learned a secret process in the manufacture of a glaze by persistently feigning stupidity and was thus . . . able to lay the foundation of the famous firm of sanitary potters' (David Garnett, acknowledging a debt to Mr Brian Guinness).

ty. Typhoid fever: Australian: C. 20. (K. S. Prichard, *Coonardoo*, 1929.)

tyker or **tiker.** A man who takes charge of dogs: from ca. 1860. B. & L.

Tykes, occ. **Tikes.** Australian Catholics' s. name for themselves: late C. 19–20. (B.P.)

typ. Typical: uncultured and trivial: since ca. 1930. (Margery Allingham, *More Work* . . ., 1948.)

typan. See **taipai.**—**typay.** See **taipay.**

type.—2. 'An officer whether of the R.A.F. or another service,' H. & P. (early 1943): R.A.F. since ca. 1920. Jackson (late 1943), however, does not confine it to officers: '*Type.* Classification of person. Thus, "He's a poor type, a ropey type, a dim type, a brown type." In the R.A.F. the word is universal in this sense, and derives from its common use in connection with aircraft. Used since the Great War' (1914–18). This 'etymology' is correct; I think, however, that there has been some influence by the French-slang use of *type* for 'chap, fellow'.—3. A typewriting machine: makers', dealers', repairers': since ca. 1920.

typed. (Of actors, theatrical or cinematic) kept in one type of role: theatrical and cinematic: since ca. 1937.

typewrite. To fire a Bren, or other, machine-gun in bursts: Army: 1939–45. (P-G-R.) Cf. *typewriters* on p. 923.

typewriters (p. 923). Rather, machine guns in action; *not* only New Zealanders'—witness Reginald Pound, *The Lost Generation*, 1964.

typo.—4. 'Astonishingly ugly and menacing insect' (Jean Devanney, *Dawn Beloved*, 1928). The taipo: New Zealand coll.: late C. 19–20. Strictly, *typo* is ineligible, for it is merely a folk-etymological spelling.

typogremlin. A 'gremlin' blamed for printer's errors: printers': 1942 +. See **gremlin.**

U

U.F.O. A hippy club: drug addicts' and hippies': since late 1966. For *unlimited freak-out* see **freak-out**, n., above. Peter Fryer in *The Observer* colour supplement, Dec. 3, 1967.

U.P., all (p. 923). Slightly earlier in *Boxiana*, III, 1821.

u/s or **U/S** or **u.s.** or **U.S.** (Of persons) unhelpful, helpless, useless: (of things) unavailable: R.A.F. coll.: since ca. 1935. Jackson, '"I'm in dock. I'm afraid I shall be u/s for some time"'; Partridge, 1945, 'From the official abbreviation, u/s (or U/S), "unserviceable"'—esp. as applied to aircraft or aircraft parts; Brickhill & Norton, *Escape to Danger*, 1946.

uck. To remove firmly, to heave, to hoist: Naval (lower-deck): late C. 19–20. For *huck*, a variant of dial. *hoick*, itself perhaps for *hoist*. This could—via *hack off*, remove (the 'men')—account for *uckers*.

uckers. The game of ludo: Naval (lower-deck): C. 20. Granville. Perverted back-slang: *ludo > udol > udlo >* (with some influence from 'the Oxford *-er*'?) *ucker >*, by a common process, *uckers*. Dr Leechman, in April 1967, writes, 'The proposed derivation reminds me once again of my hunch about **Slackers** and **Squibbley**'—in short, he thinks it an arbitrary alteration of the S.E. word. Certainly a much more 'natural' explanation than mine.

uckeye (p. 923). Julian Franklyn comments, 'But, I think, also connected with Scottish "och aye!" and perhaps with "O.K."'

uff, in *Sessions*, July 30, 1885, is a variant of **oof** (p. 589), which should be dated back to 1880 at the latest.

Ug. Uttoxeter: Cotton College: late C. 19–20. Article by Frank Roberts in *The Cottonian*, Autumn 1938.

ugly as sin (p. 923). Cf. 'His wife was as ugly as sin, and twice as nasty': *The Night Watch* (II, 88), 1828. Moe.

ugly customer. A vigorous boxer, not too scrupulous, but very difficult to knock out: pugilistic coll.: since ca. 1810. *Boxiana*, III, 1821.

uke. Ukelele: C. 20: musicians' >, ca. 1930, gen.

ukelele.—2. A locomotive, type J.39 (N.E.R.): railwaymen's: ? ca. 1900–25. (*Railway*.)

ultray (p. 924) dates from mid-C. 19 and is Parlyaree. Mayhew assigns it specifically to Punch and Judy showmen.

umbrella.—2. A parachute: Services, esp. R.A.F.: since ca. 1934. Partridge, 1945.

umbrella man. A parachutist: R.A.F. since ca. 1935, Army since ca. 1942. Jackson. Cf. **brolly**, 2.

umbrella regulations. 'The National Security Regulations—"they cover everything". (War slang.)': Australian: 1939–45. (B., 1943.)

umgeni, umgenis. See 'Swahili words . . .'

ump. An umpire: sporting, esp. cricketers': from ca. 1919. 'Ah, here comes the umps', heard in the Oval Pavilion on June 19, 1937.

umpie. Umpire: Australian: C. 20. (Vance Palmer, *Let the Birds Fly*, 1955.)

umpty. Indisposed, off colour: unsuccessful: since ca. 1916. Short for **umpty iddy** (p. 924). Gerald Kersh, *Night and the City*, 1938.

umpty iddy, feel (p. 924). Probably ex *umpty iddy* as the reverse form of signallers' *iddy umpty* (as on p. 419): 'all backwards', hence 'queer, ill'. (Leechman.)

umpty show. An inferior play, or inferior acting of a play: theatrical: since ca. 1917. Ngaio Marsh, *Vintage Murder*, 1938. Ex prec.

unbleached Australians. Aborigines: Australian jocular coll.: C. 20. B., 1942.

*unbridle. 'When he saw the thief he was to "unbridle" (take off his hat). Then it was up to us' (John Gosling, 1959): c.: since ca. 1925.

unbuttoned. Upset; unprepared: Army: 1939–45. (P-G-R.) Ex:

unbuttoned, come. To meet with disaster; be greatly perturbed, esp. if visibly: a Society jocular coll.: from ca. 1926. Dornford Yates, *As Other Men Are*, 1930, '"I don't want her to come unbuttoned," said Roger, musingly.' Cf. S.E. *burst with excitement*. Perhaps ex: 2. Of a good racing tip or of any reasonable expectation: to fail: sporting: from ca. 1910.

unc. A steward in the Merchant Navy: nautical: since ca. 1910. *The Bournemouth Echo*, Oct. 21, 1943.—2. Uncle, esp. in address: Australian coll.: C. 20. Alan Marshall, *Tell Us about the Turkey, Jo*, 1946, 'Wind slowly, Unc. The rope is rotten.'

uncle.—2. One's—esp. one's Hollywood—film agent: cinematic world: since ca. 1925.—3. A theatrical backer: since ca. 1925. (Sydney Moseley, *God Help America!*, 1952.)—4. Short for **Uncle Ned** (p. 924): C. 20. Sydney Lester, *Vardi the Palarey*, 1937.

uncle, keep your eye on—or watch your. A c.p. uttered by leader in banter, leg-pull, etc.: since ca. 1930.

Uncle Arthur. The late Rt Hon. Arthur Henderson: political: C. 20.

Uncle Ben. Rare for '10' in game of House: rhyming: C. 20. Michael Harrison, 1943.

Uncle Bert. A shirt: (not very common) rhyming s.: C. 20. Franklyn 2nd.

Uncle Bill. General Sir William Slim: Army in Burma (etc.): 1943–5.—2. The police: since ca. 1935: c. >, by ca. 1955, low s. (Robin Cook, 1962.) Cf. **Old Bill**, 2, 3, above.

Uncle Bob. A policeman: since ca. 1945. (L. J. Cunliffe, *Having It Away*, 1965.) Prompted by the synonymous *bobby*.

Uncle Charlie. A German long-distance gun

firing from Le Havre in June–July 1944: invasion forces': Humfrey Jordan, *Landfall Then Departure*, 1946. A 'Dutch' uncle.

Uncle Dick. Sick: rhyming s.: late C. 19–20. —2. Penis: rhyming s. (on *prick*): C. 20. Both are recorded by Franklyn in his *Rhyming Slang*.

Uncle George.—2. The late George Lansbury, the Labour politician and fine man: political: C. 20.

Uncle Joe. Joseph Stalin: since ca. 1942; after his death, merely historical.

Uncle Ned.—2. Occ., head: C. 20. Rhyming.

Uncle Tim's Cabin. The Vice-Regal Lodge of the Irish Free State during *Tim* Healy's governorship: Anglo-Irish: 1922–8. Timothy Healy: 1855–1931. Mrs H. B. Stowe's famous anti-slavery novel, *Uncle Tom's Cabin*, appeared serially in 1851–2, and in book form in 1852.

Uncle Willie.—2. Chilly: rhyming s.: since ca. 1920. Franklyn 2nd.

unconscious. A day-dreamer; a dreamy person: from ca. 1926. Cf. **romance**, q.v.—2. See **hello, unconscious!**

uncork!; cork! 'Decode'; 'Code'—as orders: Naval: since ca. 1920. (Occ. used in other grammatical moods.) Granville.

***under.** Also a bit of under.

under control. See **everything** . . .

under one's own steam. See **steam, under one's own,** above.

***under starter's orders, be.** To be, or to have been, arrested: since ca. 1945: orig. and still mainly c.; by ca. 1950, also police s. (John Gosling, *The Ghost Squad*, 1959.) Ex horse-racing.

under the arm. See **arm, under the,** above.

under the hammer. See **hammer, under the,** above.

under the influence.—2. Under an anæsthetic: since ca. 1925.

under the lamp. See **lamp, under the.**

under the lap? Confidentially: Australian: since ca. 1920. B., 1942.

under the rose. See **rose, under the** in *Dict.*

under the weather. Tipsy: nautical and Australian: mid-C. 19–20; by 1920, coll. B., 1942.— 2. Unwell: Canadian coll.: late C. 19–20.—3. Menstruating: Canadian (and U.S.): coll.: C. 20.

undercart. Undercarriage of an aircraft: Air Force: since ca. 1936. Jackson.

undercut. See **snappy undercut.**—2. Female pudend: low: C. 20.

underfug. An under-vest: C. 20. (Hugh de Sélincourt, *The Cricket Match*, 1924.)

underground fruit. Potatoes; hence, other vegetables: Naval lower-deck: since ca. 1925.

underground hog. A chief engineer: Canadian railroadmen's (— 1931). The labourers don't see much of him.

undergrounder. See **under-grounder** (*Dict.*).

underneath the arches. Sleeping, or virtually living, under arches: coll.: C. 20.

underneaths. Female legs: Welsh coll.: late C. 19–20. Caradoc Evans, *Taffy*, 1923.

underpants like St Paul's. Underpants very tight in the crutch: Australian: since late 1940's. (B.P.) Why, precisely? Perhaps 'It is better to marry than to burn'?

understandings, 2 (p. 925). In *The Port Folio*, May 30, 1801 (p. 165), we find the variant *understanding* used for 'a pair of legs'.

understumble. See **undercomestumble** (*Dict.*).

Undertakers, the. Two Melbourne bookmakers (ca. 1885–1905), 'because of their fondness for laying against *stiff uns* . . . horses that are certain not to win', the pun being on **stiff 'un,** 1 (*Dict.*). B. & L.

undertaker's job. A horse running *dead* (not intended to win): Australian sporting: since ca. 1930.

***underweight.** A girl under 21 sent out as prospective harlot to the Argentine: white-slave traffickers' c.: C. 20. (A. Londres, *The Road to Buenos Ayres*, 1928.)

undesertworthy. (Of a soldier) utterly useless: Army in North Africa: 1940–3. Ex vehicles and equipment classified *desertworthy* or *undesertworthy*, fit or unfit for use in the desert—jargon dating from 1938 or 1939. (Peter Sanders.)

undressing a sheep, n. Sheep-shearing: Australian (— 1953). B., *Australia Speaks.*

unflappable. Imperturbable: since ca. 1944. Ex **flap,** n., 8, above.

***unfortunate** and **vicious,** adj. In distress; already prostitute: white-slavers' terms for the two classes among whom they enlist their recruits: from ca. 1899. Albert Londres, *The Road to Buenos Ayres*, 1928.

unfrocked. One, usually an officer, who is unpopular with his branch of the Service: Naval: since ca. 1948. (Granville, letter of Nov. 22, 1962.) —2. 'Also of F.A.A. embryo pilots who fail their basic flying course' (Granville, *ibid.*): Naval: since ca. 1950.

unh unh. Sex appeal: since ca. 1940. Echoic of amorous utterance: cf. **oomph** and **yumph.**

unhook. To borrow (something) without asking the owner's permission: Naval: since ca. 1920. Granville. One merely takes it off the hook and strolls away.

unhorse. 'To deprive an owner of his car by means of long-drawn-out repairs' (B.P.): Australian motor trade: since ca. 1950.

Union (or **u.**), **the.** See **Bishopsgate.**

Univ.—2. University College, London: London undergraduates': C. 20. (Marples, 2.)

universal subject, the. (The subject of) smutty talk: Canadian coll., verging on S.E.: since ca. 1930. Cf. *subject normal*. By ca. 1935, fairly gen. coll.; by 1960, S.E. everywhere.

[University drinking terms of mid-C. 17. See 'Tavern terms', § 3, *a–d*.]

university of hard knocks, the. Experience: coll., esp. among those who haven't been to one: since ca. 1910.

unload.—2. See **pewter,** v.

unlucky for some. See **Little Jimmy,** near end.

unmentionables (p. 926): earlier in W. N. Glascock, *Sailors and Saints* (I, 12 and 132), 1829. Moe.

unnecessary, make go all. See **make go** . . .

unnerstand. Understand: sol.: (?) C. 16–20.

unpin one's back hair; take one's (back) hair down. To talk intimately, after a period of conventional politeness: coll.: the former, ca. 1930–50; the latter, since late 1940's. 'Although strictly applicable to women only, the phrases have, even in short-hair days, been used by men of themselves, or by either sex of men.' (Laurie Atkinson, Sept. 11, 1967.)

unprovoke, n. and v. Unprovoked assault; to commit one upon (esp. a warder): prison: since ca. 1920. Jim Phelan, *Letters from the Big House*, 1943.

unquote! Quotation ends here: U.S. journalistic coll. >, by 1951, Canadian and, by 1955, English. 'Now I quote: "Five thousand pounds each." Unquote,' with the emphasis upon *un*-. (Leechman.)

unshingling, n. Removing a man's hat and running away with it (and keeping it): Australian: ca. 1840–90. Marcus Clarke, *Stories of Australia in the Early Days*, 1897. Cf. *tile*, 'a hat'.

unship (e.g. a grin). To remove: Naval: since ca. 1910. Granville. Cf. **ship**, v., 6.

unspeakables. Men's trousers: coll.: ca. 1810–50. John L. Gardner, *The Military Sketch-Book* (II, 71), 1827. (Moe.) Cf. the collective entry at **unmentionables** on p. 926.

unstick.—2. To extricate (a vehicle) from the desert sand: Army coll. (N. Africa): ca. 1940–3; hence in other, although analogous, contexts. (P-G-R.)

unswallow. To vomit: euphemistic: 'current in the 30's, but (mercifully) not heard since' (Peter Sanders).

untidy as a Javanese brothel, as. Extremely untidy: Australian: brought back, ca. 1942, by servicemen. (B.P.)

unzymotic has, since ca. 1963, been a teenagers' synonym for s. *fab* (or *fabulous*). Mrs Verily Anderson, letter of Nov. 15, 1965. Cf. **zymotic** below.

up, v., 1 (p. 926). The *up and*—form occurs in *Sessions*, 1830, the earliest record of the v.—4. To copulate with (a woman): low: mid-C. 19–20. *Sessions*, April 8, 1874, 'The prisoner said, "I have *up*'d your old woman many a time, and I will up her again".'

up, adj.—2. Up to specifications; esp. *not up*, not up to specifications; hence, no good: Australian: since ca. 1925. B., 1942.—3. In the Services, *up* (as in *chai*—or *char*—*up!*) = the tea, etc., is made (or cooked) and ready to be served; or, others than cooks speaking, '(More) tea, etc., is wanted': coll.: mid-C. 19–20.—4. Up to date, conversant, well-informed, expert: undergraduate coll.: C. 20.

up a shade, Ada! An exclamatory appeal for more room ('Move up a bit there!'): R.A.F., esp. in Malta: since ca. 1950.—2. Hence applied also to a noisy collision between two persons.

up-and-a-downer, an. A variant of *up-and-downer*.

up and down. A rough-and-tumble fight: Cockney: C. 20. *Sessions*, June 9, 1902; George Ingram, *Cockney Cavalcade*, 1935. Ex **up-and-downer.**

up and down like a fiddler's elbow. Very restless: mostly lower-middle class: late C. 19–20. Contrast the North Country dial. phrase, *like a fiddler's elbow*, crooked.

up and down like a shit-house-seat. A Canadian Army c.p. (1939–45)—referring to a gambler's luck.

up and down like Tower Bridge. A Cockney c.p. (late C. 19–20), 'with scabrous innuendo, in response to *How goes it?*' (Atkinson).

up-and-down man. A coal-whipper: Londoners': since ca. 1840; by 1940, ob. H. Mayhew, *London Characters*, enlarged ed., 1874.

up-and-downer (p. 927) has, since ca. 1936, been much in Naval use (Granville) for 'a fierce argument'.—2. An unimaginative, usually medium-paced bowler of 'straight up-and-down stuff' (without break or swerve or spin): cricketers': since ca. 1925. Cliff Cary, *Cricket Controversy*, 1948.

*****up and up, on the.** Dependable; 'straight' in the crooks' sense: c.: from ca. 1919. Ex U.S.

up for office. On a charge; due to appear before the O.C.: Services, esp. Army, coll.: C. 20. (P-G-R.)

up guards and atap! See 'Prisoner-of-War Slang', 14.

up homers, as in 'He's up homers', applied to a rating welcome at home of a family in the port where he happens to be stationed: Naval: C. 20.

up in Annie's room.—2. A call for double-one: darts players': since ca. 1930. With a pun on a *double room*, or a room being used as one.

up King Street. Bankrupt; hence, in grave financial difficulties: Sydneysiders': C. 20. (B., 1943.)

up she comes and the colour's red! An exclamation at a favourable turn of events, esp. if the opposition suddenly collapses or the obstacle is unexpectedly removed: c.p.: since ca. 1945. Ex gambling?

up Shit Creek with a broken paddle is the usual form, since ca. 1950, of:

up Shit Creek—or **up the creek**—**without a paddle.** In trouble; esp., off the course, lost: C. 20. Naval and, by ca. 1920, R.A.F. Sgt-Pilot F. Rhodes, letter of Sept. 20, 1942, records the euphemistic form, as also H. & P., 1943. Also, occ., *in Shit Creek* or *in the creek*: Sgt G. Emanuel, March 29, 1945.—2. Hence, on a merry night-out: since ca. 1940. Partridge, 1945.

up stick(s), v. See **sticks, up,** in the *Dict*.

up the chute. Worthless; (persons and plans, acts, etc.) stupid; wrong: Australian: since ca. 1920. B., 1942.

up the dirt road. A low Canadian reference (— 1950) to sodomy.

up the Gulf. 'Serving in the Persian Gulf' (Granville): Naval coll.: since ca. 1915.

up the line or **go up the line.** To go on leave: Navy: since ca. 1916. H. & P. Ironic in military sense, 'to go into the trenches'.

up the mad house (or one word). See **mad house, up the,** above.

up the pole; *****up the steps; up the stick. See those nn.

up the rock. In detention: Services, at Gibraltar: late C. 19–20. H. & P. See **Rock, the** (p. 702).

up the Straits. On the Mediterranean Station: Naval coll.: late C. 19–20. Granville, 'Through the Straits of Gibraltar'.

up the wall, adv.; hence, occasionally, an adj. (in the predicate). Awry; (of supposed facts, calculations, premisses) fallacious; crazy: since ca. 1944, but general only since ca. 1950. 'It's'— 'He's'—'enough to drive'—or 'send'—'you up the wall.' Adopted, I suspect, from the slang of American drug-addicts and transmitted by American servicemen.

up the way (or **wop**). Of women: pregnant: Australian low: C. 20. B., 1942.

up there, Cazaly! A c.p. of encouragement: Australian, but mostly Melbournites': ca. 1930–50. 'Cazaly was a noted South Melbourne footballer, whose speciality was high marking' (B., 1943).

up to mud (or **tripe**). Worthless: mostly Australian: C. 20. B., 1942. Cf. **up to putty** (*Dict.*).

up to you for the rent! Synonymous with **upya!** below: Aus.: since ca. 1930. (B., 1959.)

up top. 'Flying at high altitude,' Jackson: R.A.F. coll.: since ca. 1925.—2. High ranked; among the high-ranked officers: adv. and adj.: Naval coll.: C. 20. (P-G-R.)

up topsides. 'On the upper-deck; aloft' (Granville): Naval coll.: C. 20.

up you! The original form of the next four entries: C. 19–20 (and prob. much earlier). This expression of rudest contempt forms the verbal equivalent of the world-wide extended-middle-finger gesture, indicating also derision and defiance.

up your ass, with a hard-wire brush (or **crooked stick** or **red-hot poker**)! A low Canadian c.p., uttered 'just for something to say; fellow doesn't mean anything uncomfortable when he says it' (Canadian correspondent, who adds the post-1945 variant . . . *with a charged condenser*): C. 20; common among Canadian soldiers of 1939–45.

up your gonga—jacksy—pipe! See **pipe, up your.**

up your jumper! A c.p. of either defiance or derision: Australian: since ca. 1920. (Jon Cleary, *Just Let Me Be*, 1950.)

up yours! Abbrev. of *up your arse*, etc. late C. 19–20. Still current c. 1967, often as semi-jocular expression of greeting or for lack of something to say. Cf. **up your ass, . . .,** above.

uplift. An auxiliary spring: Australian motorists': since ca. 1950. A reference to brassières. (B.P.)

uppard twizzle or, by deliberate alteration, **ozzletwizzle.** An upward—strictly, a vertical—climbing roll in flying: R.A.F.: since ca. 1950 at latest.

upped, ppl adj. Raped: lower: C. 20. W. L. Gibson Cowan, *Loud Report*, 1937. Cf. **up,** v., 4.

upper apartment. The head: ca. 1810–50. (J. H. Lewis, *The Art of Writing*, 7th ed., 1816.) Moe.

upper crust, (p. 927): rather, since ca. 1810. *Boxiana*, II, 1821.—3. Used in Australia as early as 1857. (Sidney J. Baker, letter, 1946.)

upper deck. (Female) bosom; breasts: mostly Australian: C. 20. Lawson Glassop, 1944. Cf. **upper works,** 2 (below).

upper garret (head; brains): Jan. 1790, *Sessions*. See **upper story** (p. 927).

upper Roger. A young king: Hobson-Jobson: mid-C. 18–20. Yule & Burnell. A corruption of Sanskrit *yuva-raja*, young king or heir apparent.

upper storey, gone in the. Crazy; mad: mid-C. 19–20; by 1940, ob. (T. Watters, at p. 79 of *The China Review*, Sept.–Oct. 1876.) Moe.

upper storeys, as an occasional variant of *upper storey* (p. 927), occurs in Keats's letters.

Upper Tartary. The Stock Exchange; *Lower Tartary*, non-members operating outside the Exchange: Stock Exchange: ca. 1810–50. *Spy*, II, 1926. The members are *Tartars* and *tartars* and *hellish* smart.

upper-ten push. 'Aristocratic' prisoners in gaol: Australian (prison s. rather than c.): C. 20. B., 1942.

upper works.—2. Female breasts: low: from ca. 1870.

upper yardman. 'Lower-deck rating who is a

candidate for a permanent R.N. commission' (Granville): Naval: since ca. 1930. *Yard* in the nautical sense, the implication being that he looks aloft.

uppers, the. The upper classes: coll., mostly lower-middle class: since ca. 1920.—2. Loafers aboard a warship: Australian Naval: 1939–45 (B., 1943.)

uppity. Above oneself; conceitedly recalcitrant or arrogant: since ca. 1910. (Nevil Shute, *The Checker Board*, 1947.) Either an arbitrary elaboration of **uppish** or a blend of *uppish* + *haughty*.—2. Hence, socially grand: beatniks': since ca. 1959. Anderson, '*He was carrying such weight at that uppity shake.* He was so bored by that grand reception . . .'

*upright. Highest: c. (— 1688); † by 1820. Randle Holme. Ex **upright man** (*Dict.*).

upright grand. Perpendicular copulation: Australian urban: since ca. 1925. B., 1942. 'Grand even though uncomfortable'? Perhaps in reference to the music one plays upon an upright grand (piano).

upside down in cloud. 'Abbreviated version of "There we were, upside down in cloud, fuck-all on the clock, and still climbing"—commonly used to check line-shooters,' W/Cdr R. P. McDouall, letter of April 12, 1945: R.A.F. operational: 1940 +. (See **clock,** n., 5.)

upsides of. See **upsides with** (*Dict.*).

upstairs, come or **go.** To ascend, to gain height: R.A.F.: since ca. 1935. An R.A.F. Squadron-Leader, '"Nasty Messerschmitts." And the answer came back, "Okay, pals, keep them busy. I'm coming upstairs,"' in Allan A. Michie & Walter Graebner, *Their Finest Hour*, Nov. 1940. In contrast, *downstairs* is in the air but near the ground or, at the least, at a low altitude, as in ibid., 'We were fighting upstairs and downstairs between 1,000 and 1,500 feet.'

upta or **upter.** Inferior; worthless, no good; contemptible: Australian: since ca. 1925. (Jon Cleary, *You Can't See Round Corners*, 1949: *upta*.) Perhaps ex '*up to no good*' or '*up to mud*'. *Upter* occurs in Caddie, *A Sydney Barmaid*, 1953, and in B., 1943. Perhaps rather ex '*up to putty*' (genteel) or '*up to shit*' (low), as a correspondent has proposed.

upya! or **upyer!** Oh, run away!; a fig for that, or for you!: low, contemptuous c.p.: Australian: C. 20. B., 1942. I.e. *up your—*: cf. entry at **up your gonga.**

uranium, feel like an ounce of. 'To feel "on top of the world". A recently born Royal Marine phrase,' Wilfred Granville, letter of Jan. 7, 1947: since mid-1946. Ex the use of uranium in the atomic bomb, which sends things sky-high.

urge. 'To hint (for something)': Australian coll.: C. 20. B., 1942.

urgent. Fast, speedy: catachrestic, mostly non-cultured: from ca. 1885. Nevinson, 1895, 'Eh, we was urgent in my old barge, almost as urgent as what steam is.'

urger.—2. Hence (?), a confidence-trickster's accomplice: Australian c.: since ca. 1920. B., 1942.—3. Tout for a brothel: Australian c.: since ca. 1925. Lawson Glassop, *We Were the Rats*, 1944.—4. A chap, a fellow: Australian ('not particularly pejorative': B.P.): since ca. 1940. 'What are you urgers up to?' Ex senses 1 (p. 928) and perhaps 2 and 3.—5. A sponger:

Australian: C. 20. (Tom Ronan, *Only a Short Walk*, 1961.) He urges you to stand him a drink. Prob. the earliest sense.

Sense 1 is amplified in Anthony Kimmins's Australian racing novel, *Lugs O'Leary*, 1960, thus: ' "An urger," explained Lugs patiently, " is a man who looks around for suckers like you— and tips each one a different horse. Someone's *got* to win." '

urky-purky (or **-perky**)! An Australian children's exclamation of disgust; also used attributively, as in 'I don't want to eat that urky-purky porridge': since ca. 1930. (B.P.) A defective reduplication of *dirty*—or, at the least, prompted by *dirty*.

urn, carry the. A Naval variant of *carry the can back*: jocular: since ca. 1925. (P-G-R.)

Ursa Major. See **Bear-Leader, the** in *Dict.* This term belongs rather to the sobriquets than to the nicknames; nevertheless it was indubitably a nickname among a cultured few—but not as a vocative.

use (pron. *yews*), **as per.** As usual: c.p. (non-aristocratic): from ca. 1902; very ob. W. L. George, *The Making of an Englishman*, 1914.

use frightening powder. 'The defending solicitor produced a recording machine at the lower court —a move which we call "using frightening powder" ' (John Gosling, 1959): police s.: since ca. 1935.

use one's loaf. To think (esp., hard or clearly); to be ingenious, exercise ingenuity: C. 20; esp. in the Services, 1939–45. H. & P. See **loaf**, 2 (p. 488).

used, with *would*. Not uncommon in illiterate speech of C. 19–20, as thus in Nevinson, 1895, 'Afore the year was out, the river was fair mad in love with 'er, and they'd used to watch for the white St George on the tops'l coming up be'ind

'em.' Here, *they'd used to watch = they used to watch*. Cf. 'She'd used to tell me we was so fond of each other through 'avin' been lovers a long time back.'

used-beer department. The latrine in a drinking establishment: Canadian: since ca. 1925.

used to was. Used to be: jocular c.p.: since ca. 1910; by 1960 very ob. ' "Losing y'r dash, Fin," grinned Ryan. "Not the family man yer useter was" ' (H. Drake Brockman, *Sydney of the Bush*, 1948; earlier in her play, *Men Without Wives*, 1938.)

useful, n. An odd-job man, a handyman: Australian: since ca. 1925. Frank Clune, *Try Anything Once*, 1933, 'I landed a job as a hotel "useful" '; *The Evening News*, Feb. 16, 1949 ('Holiday City'); Ruth Park, *Poor Man's Orange*, 1950; Caddie, *A Sydney Barmaid*, 1953.

useless as a third tit, as. Utterly useless; superfluous: Army: C. 20.

useless as tits on a bull (or **on a whore**). Completely useless: Canadian low: late C. 19–20. Also, since ca. 1945, ... *on a canary.*

usher. A Naval Instructor: Naval: C. 20. (P-G-R.)

ute. A utility truck (a light van): Army: since ca. 1936. H. & P. Also, since ca. 1945, common in Australia, as in 'Till You Come to a Green Ute' in Eleanor Dark's *Lantana Lane*, 1959.

utility. (Gen. pl.) A minor part for a beginner: theatrical: from ca. 1870; ob. B. & L.

utter. To speak; to make any vocal sound (e.g. of pain or pleasure): mostly Society: since ca. 1930. Ngaio Marsh, *Death in a White Tie*, 1938, '... If you stare like a fish and never utter,' Short for *utter a word* or *a sound*.

uxib. *Unexploded fire bomb*: Fire Services': 1940–45. (Julian Franklyn.) Cf. **incy** above.

V

v is gradually disappearing in Cockney speech in such words as *guv'nor*: a C. 20 process.

V. and A.—3. Anything worth stealing: R.A.F.: since ca. 1945. Ex stores marked 'V. and A.'—valuable and attractive, e.g. watches and cameras.

V.I.P., lit. 'very important person' (popularized during the latter half of World War II), has, since the late 1940's, often been used ironically, esp. of a self-important person.

vac.—2. A vacuum cleaner: Australian domestic: since ca. 1948. (B.P.)

[Vacant Letters (initially), or Aphæresis (see 'Aphæresis' in this Supplement). In addition to that noted and to the Supplement entries at **safack, sall, sri,** note esp. *kinell,* as an exclamation: short for *fuckin' 'ell!,* i.e. *fucking hell!,* very low but, in late C. 19–20, very common, it occurs, e.g., in John Prebble's fine war novel, *The Edge of Darkness,* 1947, in the sensible form, *'kinell!*]

vacc. Vaccination: medical world: late C. 19–20.

vack (rare after 1940); **vackie,** better **vacky.** A person, esp. a child, evacuated overseas or from city to country: since Sept. (ca. the 10th) 1939 *The Daily Telegraph,* Oct. 4, 1939 (*vack* and *vacky*); Berrey, Nov. 9, 1940 (the longer form). Ex *evacuee.*—2. (Only *vack.*) An old woman: Australian low: since ca. 1925. B., 1942. A corruption of '*vagabond*'?

vacuum cleaner. A sports car: Londoners': since ca. 1947. Used for *picking up* (p. 624) *bits of fluff* (p. 56).

vag, n. A vagabond: since ca. 1690. Edward ('Ned') Ward, *The Wooden World Dissected,* 1707 (p. 2), 'Its the New-Bridewell of the Nation, where all the incorrigible Vaiges are sent, to wear out Ropes.' (Admittedly the quotation constitutes a probability, not a certainty.)

vag, v. To charge (someone) under the Vagrancy Act: Canadian (late C. 19–20) and Australian (C. 20). B., 1942. Adopted from U.S.: see *Underworld.*

valise. A bed-roll: Army officers' coll.: C. 20. (P-G-R.)

Valpo. Valparaiso: nautical and S. American coll.: late C. 19–20.

valve. The female pudend: low: C. 19–20. Perhaps by confusion with *vulva.* 'Also, perhaps, because a valve is opened with a cock' (correspondent, 1966).

Vamosses. Portuguese soldiers: British Army in Spain, 1808–14. (Bernard Capes, *A Castle in Spain,* 1903.) Ex Sp. *Vamos!,* Let's go!

vampire. One who, in a hospital, draws off, for testing, a little of a patient's blood: Forces': 1940 +. Ex the activities of the traditional vampire. (Atkinson.)

van rooge. Red wine: Army: 1914–18. I.e. *vin rouge.*

vanboy. A conductor: busmen's: since ca. 1930.

vandyke (or **V-**). A privy: Australian: since ca. 1920. B., 1942. With a pun on *dike,* **dyke** (p. 220) and an allusion to the great painter Van Dyke.

Vandyke!, be no. To be plain-looking: C. 20. Applied esp. to men, in reference to the handsome fellows in Vandyke's portraits. Cf. prec. entry.

Vanity Fair. A chair: rhyming s.: since ca. 1870. Franklyn 2nd.

vap. A rather rare schoolboys' term dating from ca. 1905 and now ob. As in Arnold Lunn, *Loose Ends,* 1919: 'He distrusted the female sex because they seemed to indulge in an undue amount of "vap"—as he called it—chat which said one thing and meant another. Maurice hated "vap".' I.e. vapouring.

vardi.—2. Like *vardy,* it is a variant of **vardo,** v. (p. 930). Sydney Lester, *Vardi the Palarey,* (?) 1937, defines it as 'to see; know'; the context usually determines which of those two meanings it bears, as in 'Vardy his jillpots standing by the cain', glossed as 'See that chap standing by the table.'

vardy, v. To swear upon oath: showmen's: since ca. 1860. P. H. Emerson, *Signor Lippo,* 1893.

various veins. Varicose veins: pol.: C. 20. (Ruth Park, 1950.) Also *very coarse veins.*

varnish, n.—2. Sauce: coffee-stall frequenters: C. 20.

varnish one's cane. (Of the male) to coït: low Canadian: C. 20.

varnished wagons. Passenger-train cars: Canadian railroadmen's (— 1931).

Varsity occurs in *The Observator,* March 9, 1706. In sense 1 (p. 930), it has not been used since 1914 and was very little used during the preceding decade.

vastly. As a mere synonym of 'very' it is a coll. of C. 18–early 19. (H. C. K. Wyld in *The Spectator,* April 22, 1938.)

Vatican roulette. The so-called 'safe period' which immediately precedes menstruation and is regarded as a means of birth control: Catholics': 1960 (the date of a famous encyclical) and after. On the analogy of the dicing-with-death Russian *roulette.*

vaudevillian. A vaudeville 'villain': jocular coll.: since ca. 1930.

Vaux. A Vauxhall motor car: since ca. 1930. Elleston Trevor, *A Place for the Wicked,* 1968.

've (p. 931) occurs even at the beginning of a sentence, as in ''ve you done much?' (Neil Bell, *Alpha and Omega,* 1946), where *'ve you* is pronounced *view.*

vecle (strictly *ve'cle*) or **vekle.** A vehicle: illiteracy: since ca. 1830. James Grant, *Lights and Shadows of London Life,* I, 1840.

veegle. A motorcar: Australian jocular: since ca. 1950. (B.P.) Ex childish pron. of S.E. *vehicle.*

veg.—2. 'A sea-mine. (Bomber Command.) Short for *vegetable* in the same sense; *vegetable* was suggested by the fact that the mines were sown in areas known by such code-names as *Onions* and *Nectarine*' (P-G-R.): mostly R.A.F.: 1939–45.

vegetarian. A spinster averse from 'exchanging flesh': since ca. 1925.

vegy, adj. Vegetable: domestics': late C. 19– 20. H. A. Vachell, *Quinney's,* 1914.

velvet.—2. Elliptical for *black velvet,* any dark-skinned woman: in Australia, a lubra, a gin: C. 20. Tom Ronan, *Vision Splendid,* 1954, 'It was a case of black velvet or no material, and the pioneers took to the velvet.'

vent. A ventriloquist: mainly theatrical: C.20.

ventilating. That form of bullying at Sandhurst ca. 1830–55, by which 'the unfortunate was tied up to one of the ventilators . . . and then javelined with forks', A. Mockler-Ferryman, *Annals of Sandhurst.* Perhaps rather coll. than s. Cf. **Adamizing, bed-launching, shovelling.**

ventilator is rather earlier than the *Dict.* entry implies, for it is recorded by B. & L.

Vera Lynn. A (drink of) gin: rhyming s.: since ca. 1940. (*Weekly Telegraph,* April 6, 1946.) Often shortened to *Vera,* as in Robin Cook, *The Crust on Its Uppers,* 1962. Ex the singer immensely popular during W.W. II—and after.

Veranda(h), the.—2. An open exchange that, for mining shares, took place on the pavement: Melbournites': ca. 1855–1900. (B., 1943.)

[Verbs that are s. or coll. in Ned Ward—one of the most, if not the most, coll. of all C. 18 writers— are these, taken from his work of 1700–24: *brim* (1703; see *Dict.*), *tick* (to have credit: 1709), *pig in* (share quarters; 1703), *knock off* (to cease; 1708; prob. always S.E.), *mumble* (to chew; 1703; rather, S.E.), *tiffle up* (to dress up; 1709), *swop* (to exchange; 1703), *dop down* (*one's noddle*; to duck; 1703); *huckle* (to chatter; 1703).

Verbal phrases that are eligible: *make a loose* (to escape; 1709); *open one's pipes* (to sing; 1709), *pass a sham saint* (to be a hypocrite; 1709), *pay one's shot* (1722), *save one's bacon* (to escape; 1722), *stand the bears* (to suffer; 1703), and *tie the noose* (spelt *tye the nooze,* to marry; 1700). Matthews.]

verge. See 'Tavern terms', § 9 (end).

verites. But it ceased to be s. when, early in C. 20, it > official. (Peter Sanders.)

Vernon's private navy. A flotilla of five East Coast herring drifters—*Lord Cavan, Silver Dawn, Fisher Boy, Jacketa,* and *Fidget*: Naval: 1939 +. They were wooden ships, and so were used in the anti-magnetic mine operations of 1939. They also did excellent work bringing off troops from Dunkirk.

*verse, v.; verser. See **versing law** (*Dict.*).

very dead. Applied to a soldier, or to a quadruped, left unburied on the battlefield: a W.W. I c.p. Not so tautological as it sounds, the connotation being the squalor and the stink.

very grave. 'When finances are low you will often hear, in reply to a question, the words, "Very grave", or "The position is critical" . . . merely a polite way of letting the world know that you are broke,' H. & P.: Service officers': since June 1940. Ex the Allied military position in May–June 1940.

Very Little Water Society, the. 'A most informal and fluid group of North American anthropologists, who take their liquor "on the rocks". A play on the name of a real secret society of the Iroquois tribe, the "Little Water Society". Since ca. 1950' (Leechman): Canadian.

very tasty, very succulent! An Australian c.p. (ca. 1948–57), popularised by the Australian comedian known as 'Mo'. (B., 1953.)

very tasty, very sweet. A c.p. very popular during World War II and gradually dying ever since—indeed, † by 1965. Cf. the entry preceding this—a version manifestly elaborating the English one.

very, very. A ca. 1919–39 coll. equivalent of **too too** (see *Dict.*). 'That's very *very*' usually connotes blame, esp. for indecency. Short for, e.g., 'very *very* naughty'.

vestal. 'Ironical for an incontinent person,' *The London Guide,* 1818: app. ca. 1810–50. Short for *vestal virgin.*

vibrations. 'Atmosphere; reactions, with sexual overtones' (Peter Fryer in *The Observer* colour supplement, Dec. 3, 1967): jazz devotees', drug addicts', beatniks' and hippies': since ca. 1965.

Vic.—6. Victoria (the State): Australian coll.: since ca. 1870. 'Tom Collins', *Such Is Life,* 1903. —7. The *Vickers* '*Victoria*'—or the *Vickers* 'Valencia' troop-carrying aircraft: R.A.F.: 1940 +. Jackson—8. A V-shaped formation of aircraft: R.A.F.: since ca. 1940. (P-G-R.)—9. 'The old Victorian Hall, Melbourne' (B., 1943): ? ca. 1880–1920.

Vic and Alb, the. The Victoria and Albert Museum in South Kensington, London: arty: C. 20. (Ngaio Marsh, *Death at the Dolphin,* 1967.)

Vic C., the. The Victoria Cross: soldiers' coll.: late C. 19–20. (Gilbert Frankau, 1920.)

Vic Eddy. 'The night signal given on the headlights (if working) or horn by a truck "swanning" round a "laager" but unable to find it. The reply was anything recognisable as friendly' (Peter Sanders in *The Sunday Times* magazine, Sept. 10, 1967): Army in North Africa: 1940–43. Ex the Morse letters *V* and *E.*

Vicar of Bray. A tray; a 'trey' (the number 3): theatrical rhyming s.: late C. 19–20. Franklyn, *Rhyming.*

vicarage, the. The chaplain's cabin: Naval: since ca. 1930. Granville.

vice-admiral (or **V- A-**). See 'Tavern terms', § 7.

*vicious. See **unfortunate.**

vicky-verky. Vice versa: Merseyside: late C. 19–20. But perhaps sol. or dial. rather than s. or coll.

victim. A person very much in love: Society: ca. 1885–1914. B. & L.

Victor Trumper. A 'bumper' or cigarette-butt: Australian rhyming s.: since ca. 1905. (B., 1945.)

Victoria Monk. Semen: late C. 19–20. Rhyming on **spunk,** 2 (*Dict.*). Ex a character famous in pornographic fiction. Strictly, that character was *Maria Monk* and this, the original and still the commoner rhyming-s. form, became confused, in the popular mind, by the fame of *Victoria Monks* (with an -s), a very well-known music-hall singer, perhaps best remembered for her rendering of 'Won't you come home, Bill Bailey?'

Victoria the Great. Anna Neagle, the film actress: since ca. 1938. Ex her playing in that role.

victualled up, be. 'To have a good time ashore as guest of friends or relatives,' Granville: Naval: since ca. 1920.

vidiot. A constant, mindless looker-in at T.V.: Australian: since ca. 1960. A blend of *video* + id*iot*. (B.P.)

view. 'R.A.F. types do not "have an opinion", but instead "take a view". Thus, "He took a poor view when Bert snaffled his popsie",' Jackson: R.A.F. coll.: since ca. 1925. Ex the aerial view they get of things.

vig. Vigilance: Anti-aircraft: 1939–45. Allan Michie & Walter Graebner, *Lights of Freedom*, 1941, '"Special vig," says John. "That means keep a special vigilance," he explains to me.'

vile child. A mild Etonian pejorative of ca. 1875–90. B. & L.

*****Vill, the.** Pentonville (prison): c.: C. 20. Norman.

Village.—3. (*The V.*) Manley, N.S.W.: Sydneysiders': C. 20. (B., 1943.)

Village of Hate, the. Burgsteinfurt, a town in N.W. Germany: 1945–6. Ex the silent resentment shown by the inhabitants towards the occupying troops. (P-G-R.)

villain. A criminal; anyone with a criminal record: since ca. 1945. (*The Sunday Times*, July 14, 1963, 'Z Cars' competition.)

-ville. Adopted, ca. 1960, ex U.S. 'Beat- and, indeed, gen. American—jargon has crept in, including the habit of adding "ville" on the end of an adjective: "Cor, man, this prep"—see **prep,** 1, on p. 657—"is dead cinchyville" '—i.e. dead easy, a 'cinch': *New Society*, Aug. 22, 1963, 'From the blackboard jungle', a short article on North Country grammar school slang.

vingty. Ving-et-un: gamblers' coll.: C. 20. F. J. Whaley, *Trouble in College*, 1936.

vino. Italian wine: Army: 1942 +. It. *vino* 'any wine'.

violent evasive action; the v. being **take . . .** To avoid an undesirable task or a boring person: R.A.F.: 1940 +. (P-G-R.)—2. Hence, *coïtus interruptus:* Australian: since ca. 1943. (B.P.)

violet (1), 'onion': the usual term in the Navy (lower-deck): Granville.

vip. A very close-fisted, cheese-paring person: Australian: since ca. 1925. B., 1942. A thinning of *vipe* (short for viper)?

*****viper.** A marijuana-smoker: c.: adopted, ca. 1943, ex U.S. (Norman.—See *Underworld.*)

virgin. Excellent; very attractive; indeed, a

general superlative: Oxford undergraduates': late 1939—early 1938. Ex the idea of purity.

Virgin, the. The Petty Officers' Mess: Naval: C. 20. Screened off, at meal-times, from the vulgar gaze of the lower-deck.

virgin bride. A ride: Australian rhyming s.: since ca. 1890. (B., 1945, citing *The* Sydney *Bulletin*, Jan. 18, 1902.)

Virgin for short, but not for long. Humorous catchphrase applied to girls named Virginia: C.20.

vis. Visibility: esp. among skin divers: since ca. 1950. (Wilfred Granville.)

visit Lady Perriam. To go to the underground lavatory: Balliol College, Oxford: C. 20. Lord Bacon's sister, Lady Perriam, presented a new building to Balliol; on its site now stands this convenience. (Christopher Hobhouse, *Oxford*, 1939.)

visiting cards. See **leave visiting cards.**

Vital Spark, the. Sobriquet but also nickname for Jenny Hill, a famous music-hall performer of the 1870's.

vital statistics. A woman's bust, waist, hip measurements (e.g. 36, 23, 35 inches): since ca. 1945: jocular coll. >, by 1965, S.E.

Vits, the. A Licensed Victuallers' (Protective) Association: C. 20. In, e.g., *The Essex Chronicle*, March 17, 1939, where a caption reads, 'Rochford "Vits" '.

vive la différence! 'A c.p. used when someone has just said that there is hardly any difference between men and women' (B.P.): since ca. 1935. Ex the French toast.

vocab (p. 933) occurs also in *watch your vocab!*, mind your language!: Australian, orig. undergraduates': since ca. 1930. (B.P.)

vol. Volume (of a book): book-world coll.: late C. 19–20. Ex the abbr., as in 'Gibbon, vol. 2'.

Voluminous Prynne (*Dict.*) is, one sees on second thoughts, much rather a mere sobriquet than a genuine nickname.

voluntary. An involuntary and inartistic fall from one's mount: hunting s.: from ca. 1890.

Vosse's. A bell rung at 7 a.m.: Marlborough College: C. 20. Ex the name of that porter who first rang it.

vote for Boyle. 'Catch-phrase after the fall of Tunis [1943]. Hal Boyle, of the Associated Press, drove into Tunis chanting "Vote for Boyle, son of the soil; Honest Hal, the Arabs' pal". The Arabs, with their usual facility for picking up a phrase without knowing the meaning, puzzled the troops by greeting them with this cry, which they in turn adopted' (P-G-R.): Army: 1943–4.

vowels, three. See **three vowels** (*Dict.*).

W

W.C. A C.W. Candidate: Naval: C. 20. Granville, 'The C.W. Branch, Admiralty, deals with the awarding of "commissions and warrants"'.

W.O.S.'ers. Overseas British authors: authors': since ca. 1919. *The Writer*, May 1939. Ex 'the wide open spaces' + the agential *-er*.

Waaf. A member of the Woman's Auxiliary Air Force: since 1939: coll. >, by mid-1943, j. Ex the initials, *W.A.A.F.* Pronounced *Waff*, which is, however, to be regarded as an incorrect spelling.

waaf-basher. A male fornicator: R.A.F.: 1941 +. See **basher**, 8.

Waafery. 'The part of the camp frequented, or the billets occupied, by members of the W.A.A.F.,' H. & P.: R.A.F.: since 1939. See **Waaf.**

waafise. 'To substitute airwomen for airmen. I believe the term originated in Balloon Command, which was waafised in a big way,' Jackson: R.A.F. coll. (by 1943, j.): 1941 +. See **Waaf.**

waas or wass. To run; to hurry; to exercise oneself vigorously: Uppingham: since ca. 1912. Marples. Echoic.

wacker, n. A Merseyside term of address to a man: since ca. 1945. Perhaps ex Scottish and English dial. *whacker*, anything very large.—2. Hence, a fellow; esp., a poor sort of fellow: Australian: since ca. 1946. (Wm Dick, *A Bunch of Ratbags*, 1965.)

wacker or whacker, adj. Fine; excellent; wonderful: Australian, esp. Melbourne, children's: since ca. 1946. (Dick.) Cf. **whacker** on p. 946.

wacko! A variant of—and inferior to— *whacko!*

wacky. Unusual, out of the way, little known; esp. *wacky news*: adopted from U.S. by journalists ca. 1942. I.e. not ordinary 'straight' news.— 2. Also, in gen. use, since 1944, for 'incorrect, unreliable' (news) and 'eccentric' (persons).

Waco, Big and **Little.** The first two aircraft of the Long Range Desert Group: Air Force in North Africa: 1942-3. Ex **W**estern **A**ircraft **Co**rporation of Ohio.

wad.—5. Straw: proletarian: C. 19. B. & L. Abbr. *wadding.*—6. A drink of liquor: since ca. 1910. Humfrey Jordan, *Roundabout*, 1935. It comfortingly fills a void.—7. A (large) quantity of anything: Australian: since ca. 1920. B., 1942. Cf. sense 2 and **wadge** (p. 934).

waddurang. An old woman: Australian: mid-C. 19-20. B., 1942. Aboriginal.

waddy, v. To strike (someone) with a stick or club: Australian coll.: C. 20. B., 1942. Ex the n. (see p. 934).

Waff. See **Waaf.**—**Waffery.** See **Waafery.**

waffle, v.—4. (Of an aircraft) to be out of control (usually as vbl n. or participial adj. *waffling*, 'spinning, losing height'); to fly in a damaged condition and/or uncertainty: R.A.F.: since ca.

1930. H. & P.; W/Cdr R. P. McDouall (March 19, 1945), 'Waffling precedes spinning'; Brickhill & Norton, *Escape to Danger*, 1946.—5. Hence (?), to dither: Services (mostly officers'): since ca. 1930. H. & P. Cf. sense 2.—6. (Cf. 4, 5.) 'To cruise along unconcernedly and indecisively' (Jackson): R.A.F.: since ca. 1925.

waft; wafty. General madness or wildness, lack of tact and/or gumption; the corresponding adj.: Oundle: since late 1920's. Marples. Perhaps suggested by excessive *breeziness*.

wag.—6. As *the wag*, it designates the humorous *tail*-piece that appears at the end of a newspaper gossip-column: originally, and still mainly, journalistic: C. 20.

wag one's bum. (Of men) to copulate: mostly Services': C. 20. Contrast *wag one's bottom* (p. 935).

wages. Illegal or illicit or shady or disreputable income: as, e.g., thief's, race-gang's, whore's: c., and low (mostly Londoners'): from ca. 1925.—2. 'There is occasional use of this among Retired Pensioners, who, when they go to a post office to draw their pension, may say "I am going to draw my wages"' (A. B. Petch, May 1966): coll.: since late 1940's.

Wagga blanket. A rough bed-covering, used by tramps and made from sack or bag: Australian: late C. 19-20. B., 1942. Derisive of the N.S.W. town of Wagga-Wagga, small and genuinely rural.

Wagga grip. 'A leather strap or binding through the pommel D's of a saddle. Also called *jug handle* and *monkey*' (B., 1959): Aus.: C. 20. Cf. preceding term.

wagger. A truant: schools': from ca. 1870. (E. Pugh, *A Street in Suburbia*, 1895.)—2. Short for **wagger-pagger-bagger** (p. 935): Rugby and other Public Schools': C. 20. (D. F. Wharton, 1965.)

Wagglespear. Shakespeare: schoolboys': C. 20. Punning *Shake-speare*; cf. *Wagstaff.*

waggon.—4. A battleship: Naval: 1940 +. Granville. Short for **battle waggon.**—5. A cigarette: South African c. (C. 20) >, by 1945, also low s. (C. P. Wittstock, letter of May 23, 1946).

wags. Signallers: Australian airmen's: 1939-45. (B., 1943.)

wahine. A girl surfer: Australian surfers': since ca. 1962. Ex Hawaiian (and Maori) *wahine*, a female, a woman.

Wailing Winnie is synonymous with and echoically comparable to **Mona**: civilians only. E. P., 'Air Warfare and Its Slang' in *The New Statesman*, Sept. 19, 1942.—2. In the Royal Navy and the Merchant Navy, 'it is the broadcast system aboard ships' (H. & P.): since 1939.

wailo! is a mere variant spelling of **wylo!** in *Dict.*

waist tog. A waistcoat: Cockney: ca. 1840-1910. Mayhew, I, 1851. See **tog** (p. 893).

wait. Sense 1 occurs two years earlier (1836) in *Pickwick.*

1497

wait and see! To the *Dict.* entry, add this note sent by Mr Vernon Rendall: 'I am familiar with it in earlier literature and have an impression that it was a catchword in the legal chambers of Sir Henry (subsequently Lord) James, one of whose "devils" Asquith was' in the earlier 1880's; it was, however, in 1910 that *wait and see* > a gen. c.p. Asquith was himself, from 1910, often called *Old Wait-and-See.*

wait till (or until) you get it?,—will you have it now or. A c.p., addressed to someone either impatient or in a hurry: C. 19–20. (Dickens, *The Pickwick Papers*, 1936–7, ch. 10.)

waiter. A horse that, started in a race, is not meant to win: Australian race-courses': C. 20. B., 1942.—2. See:

waiters. As *full waiters* = men's full evening-dress, so *half waiters* = dinner jacket (a tuxedo): Society: since ca. 1930. Ex restaurant waiters' garb.

wake, v.i. To 'wake up' to a trick, a racket, etc.: Australian: since ca. 1925. Lawson Glassop, *Lucky Palmer*, 1949, ' "Lay off some of the others [= horses]," whispered Max. "I tell you, somebody'll wake." '

wake-up. A wide-awake person: Australian coll.: from ca. 1910. W. S. Howard, *You're Telling Me!*, 1934, 'Well, I'm a wake-up; they don't get nothing out of *me* !'

wake your ideas up! Pull yourself together: Services coll.: since ca. 1930. I.e. *wake up!*

waker (or W-). A sleeping train running between Paddington and Penzance: (mostly West Country) railwaymen's: since ca. 1910; by 1960, ob. (*Railway* 2nd).

Wakers. W. W. Wakefield, the International Rugby Union forward and English captain: Rugby-players': from 1920 (first 'cap'). By 'the Oxford -*er*'. (One of the classics of the game is *Rugger*, 1927: by W. W. Wakefield and Howard Marshall.)

wakey, wakey! Wake up: R.A.F. non-coms': since the early 1920's. Sgt Gerald Emanuel, letter of March 29, 1945. Ex nursery coll. (Perhaps I should add that these N.C.O.'s use it without tenderness and with a strongly emphasised irony, yet often with an innocuous sense of good clean fun.) Since ca. 1945, it has been very widely used, esp. fig.—that is, where the person(s) addressed merely seem(s) asleep or is extremely slow in getting something done or in moving along. An elaborated version (I myself never heard it in the Army, 1940–41, nor in the R.A.F., 1942–45) is *wakey, wakey, rise and shine*, which clearly combines *wakey, wakey* and *rise and shine* (p. 700)—*don't you know it's morning time?*

wakey-wakey watch, the. The watch from 4 to 8 a.m.: Naval lower-deck: C. 20.

waler.—3. (*Waler.*) An inhabitant of N.S.W.: Australian coll.: C. 20. B., 1942.—4. Short for *Murrumbidgee whaler*, q.v. at **whaler** (p. 947).

Wales, the. The Bank of New South Wales: Australian coll.: late C. 19–20. (B.P.)

walk, n. A postman's route or 'beat': Canadian coll.: late C. 19–20; since ca. 1940, virtually j. (Leechman.)

walk.—3. To be a prostitute on the streets: white-slavers' c.: C. 20. A Londres, 1928.—4. To disappear: mostly Army, as when a part of one's kit has disappeared: since ca. 1910.

walk (a girl) home. To accompany her back to her home: coll.: since ca. 1943. Ex U.S.?

walk it.—3. Ex sense 2 (p. 936): of a person, to win easily: since ca. 1930.

walk the barber (p. 936). Earlier in Mayhew, I, 1851.

walk the cart. See **cart, walk the** in the *Dict.*

walk the hospitals. To study medicine: medical coll.: from ca. 1870. For a pertinent comment, see the leading article in *The Times Literary Supplement*, Oct. 9, 1936.

walk the plank. An early variant of **walk the chalk** (p. 936): Naval: since ca. 1810 or earlier. It occurs in W. N. Glascock, *Sailors and Saints*, 1829, at I, 176, and II, 120. (Moe.)—2. To move up and down one's surfboard: Australian surfers': since ca. 1961. (B.P.) With a pun on the pirates' practice of making their victims walk the plank.

walk-up fuck; also simply *walk-up.* 'She's ... All you have to do is walk up and ask': low Australian: C. 20.

walkabout. A mid-C. 19–20 term as in a book-review in *The Times* of Sept. 8, 1936: 'Under the title "Walkabout"—the pidgin word for "journey" in the Western Pacific—Lord Moyne has written a book on his latest expedition in his yacht *Rosaura* to little-known lands between the Pacific and Indian Oceans.'—2. A walking tour, a riding (and walking) tour: Australian coll.: C. 20. Archer Russell, *A Tramp-Royal in Australia*, 1934. 3. An out-back road: Australian coll. C. 20. B., 1942.

Walker's bus. See **go by Walker's bus.**

walkie-talkie. 'A wireless set, carried by one man, with both receiving and transmitting equipment' (P-G-R.): Army: 1940–5; then civilian (e.g. police); by 1950, coll.

walking, go. To go rotten: C. 20. Mostly Londoners'. Ex the prospective maggots.

walking dry. A frequent variant of **dry walk** (*Dict.*).

walktalk. 'A conversational stroll' (B., 1942): Australian coll.: since ca. 1910.

wall, near the. Ill: Oxford University: ca. 1820–50. *Spy*, 1825. Ex Dr Wall, a celebrated surgeon.

wall fruit. 'Kissing against a wall' (*Sinks*): ca. 1830–80.

wall-stretcher. See **crooked straight-edge.**

wallaby. 'An outback track' (B., 1959): Aus.: C. 20. Perhaps immediately ex **wallaby, on the,** on p. 936.

wallaby, on the.—2. Hence, on an urban drinking-bout: Australian: ca. 1890–1910.—3. Penniless: Australian: C. 20. B., 1942.

wallaby-tracker. A tramp: Australian: C. 20. (B., 1943.) Ex *wallaby, on the,* 1: p. 936.

waller is a loose spelling of **wallah** (*Dict.*).

wallop, n., 4 (p. 937). Usually, beer; in the Services, always beer. H. & P.—5. Strictly, the proprietary Walpamur; 'but now [1953] often used for any washable distemper' builders' and house-painters' and -decorators'. (A master builder: communication of Dec. 5, 1953.)

wallop, get (or give) the. To be dismissed—to dismiss—from a job: Australian: since ca. 1920. B., 1942.

walloper.—3. See **paddler,** 2.—4. A dancer: itinerant entertainers': late C. 19–20. (Sydney Lester, *Vardi the Palarey*, 1937.) Perhaps influenced by It. *galoppo*, a lively dance, and *galoppare*, to gallop, and *galoppatore*, a galloper.

wallopers, the. The police: Aus.: since ca. 1950. Ian Hamilton, *The Persecutor*, 1965.

Walls have ices. A c.p. retort to 'Walls have ears': since ca. 1930. I.e. *Wall's have ices*, with reference to a well-known London firm of ice-cream manufacturers.

wally (pron. *wolly*); **shock-a-lolly.** Cockney terms (quite distinct one from the other) for cucumber pickled in brine, the second term being rare: from ca. 1880.

Walrus. Warlus, near Arras: military in G.W. Blaker. Cf. *Agony* (in Dict., s.v. agony, 2).

walrus. A large, bushy moustache; hence, its wearer: the former coll. (elliptical for '*walrus* moustache'); the latter, s.: since ca. 1917: virtually extinct by 1960.

Walter Joyce. Voice: rhyming s.: since ca. 1880. (G. R. Sims used it in a Dagonet Ballad published in *The Referee* of Nov. 7, 1887.) Franklyn 2nd.

waltz, do a (or **the:** see examples). To slide or skid: Cockneys': late C. 19–20. E.g. 'I was doing the waltz all the way'; 'In going along Russell Street, I done a waltz.'

waltz Matilda (p. 937). The phrase, recorded in 1893, long antedates the song (Sidney J. Baker, letter) and was—B., 1959, tells us—'to *walk* Matilda'. A jocularity.

wampo. Intoxicating liquor: R.A.F.: since ca. 1930. Jackson. Prob. ex Scottish **wampish**, 'to wave one's arms about'.

wampo coupons. Pound notes, regarded as fair exchange for liquor: R.A.F.: since ca. 1930; slightly ob. by 1960. Cf. preceding.

Wan. A member of the *W*omen's Royal *A*ustralian *N*aval Service: Australian Services': 1939–45.

wandering Willie. An 'escaped' barrage balloon: R.A.F.: since ca. 1938.

wang, n. Penis: C. 20. Better *whang*: cf. **whank.**—2. Hence, a cigarette: South African schools': C. 20. Ex shape.

wank, v.; **wank-pit; wanker.** See **whank**, etc.

wanks. Strong liquor: R.A.F.: since ca. 1930. Partridge, 1945. Perhaps because it causes one to feel 'wanky'.

wanky dates from before 1890: witness B. & L.

Wanstead Flats. Spats: Londoner's rhyming s.: since ca. 1920.

want down, in, off, out, up, etc. 'There is an extraordinary locution used here which omits "to get". "I want down" means "I want to get down". Cf. also "I want out, I want in, I want out of here, I want on (a tram), I want off"—and countless others.' Thus Dr Douglas Leechman, in May 1959, concerning a Canadian usage that was, ca. 1954, adopted ex the U.S. Probably a development ex the *want in; want out* treated on pp. 937–8.

want to buy a battleship? See **do you want . . .**

want to know all the ins and outs of a duck's bum. To be extremely inquisitive; esp. of one desirous of arriving at the underlying explanation: low: late C. 19–20.

want to make something of it? A threatening retort to criticism or insult: c.p.: since ca. 1925. (Atkinson.) Implying readiness for fisticuffs.

want to piss like a dressmaker. 'A Cockney figure of speech for urgent need, perhaps originating in sweated-labour days' (Atkinson): late C. 19–20.

want-to-was(s)er, on p. 938, is Dr Leechman assures me, very rare indeed and long out of use.

wappy. Idealistic; sentimental; 'soppy': since ca. 1950. Alan Sillitoe, *The Loneliness of the Long-Distance Runner*, 1959 (p. 18), '. . . Just like the governor of this Borstal who spouts to us about Borstal and all that wappy stuff.'

War Babies; War Babies' Brigade. A Junior Training Battalion: military: 1917–18. Ian Miller, *School Tie*, 1935. Cf. **war-baby**, 2 (*Dict.*).

War Box, the. The War Office: Army: since ca. 1919. Cf.:

War House, the. No; it dates back at least as far as the Boer War. (See the *Dict.*).

war-pot. See **war-hat** (*Dict.*).

[War Slang of 1939–45. As in 1914–18, so in 1939–45, war has considerably increased the vocabulary both of S.E. and of slang and other unconventional English: see esp. my *Words at War: Words at Peace* (1948), alike for general and for particular aspects of the subject, whether for 1914–18 or for 1939–45.

In this Supplement, Forces' slang of the latter period is richly—yet, inevitably, far from completely—represented; in Navy, Army, Air Force, there are so many arms or branches of each Service, and so many theatres of war involved, that it is impossible to glean everything from every harvest-field. For a conspectus, hence for a conspective view, the inquirer could do worse than consult *Forces' Slang: 1939–1945*, which published late in 1948, has been edited, with an introductory essay, by myself, and to which I have contributed the Air Force terms; the Navy's words and phrases being the privilege of Wilfred Granville, and the Army's being that of Frank Roberts, two men who know what they're talking about.

Wilfred Granville, by the way, is the author of *Sea Slang of the 20th Century* (published early in 1949), to which I have had the honour of writing the introduction and of supplying the etymologies: in that comprehensive work, he has assembled not only the Navy's slang and colloquialisms of both wars, and earlier and after, but also the Merchant Service's relevant terms, with the addition of yachtsmen's, trawlermen's, bargemen's, canalmen's and so forth. I have been fortunate in availing myself of Wilfred Granville's generosity: he has permitted me to draw upon this delightful book. (Note written in 1949.)]

warb. A badly paid manual worker: Australian Labour: since ca. 1910. B., 1942.—2. A simpleton or a fool: Australian: since ca. 1905. (B., 1943.) Ex next entry.—3. 'A dirty or untidy person' (B., 1959): Aus.: since ca. 1920.

warby. Silly, daft: Australian: C. 20. Kylie Tennant, *The Battlers*, 1941, 'Of all the warby ideas . . .' Ex Scottish *warback*, or obsolete *warbie*, 'a maggot': cf. **rotten** (*Dict.*).—2. Unwell; (of things) insecure: Australian: since ca. 1905. B., 1942.—3. Unattractive; inferior: Australian: since ca. 1910. (B., 1953.)

warco. A *war co*rrespondent: mostly journalistic: 1939 +.

wardo. Rare for **vardo,** n. (*Dict.*).

wardroom joint as messdeck stew is the predominant post-1930 shape of the *Dict.* entry, *ward-room joints as lower-deck hash*. Granville.

ware hawk! See **hawk!, ware** in *Dict.*

warm in winter and cool in summer. An Australian c.p., applied to women: since ca. 1945. (B.P.)

warm the bell. See **bell** ...

warorks! In hunting, it = 'Ware oxer'—look out for the stiff fence. See **oxer** (p. 595).

warrant, get one's. See entry at **got his crown up.**

warrigal.—2. Hence the adj., wild: Australian: late C. 19–20. (B., 1943.)

warriors bold, adj. and n. Cold, adj.; a cold: rhyming s.: C. 20. Cf. **soldier bold** above. Franklyn 2nd.

wart. For sense 2 an earlier authority is 'Taffrail', who, in his article on 'The Snotties', says: 'The newly-joined midshipmen are "crabs" or "warts", mere excrescences on the face of the earth.'

Warwick Farms. Arms: Australian rhyming s.: C. 20. (B., 1945.) An adaptation of **Chalk Farm(s),** as on p. 138.

Wasbees (or Wasbies), The. The Women's Auxiliary Service, Burma: 1942–6. (Disbanded in July 1946.)

waser or wasser. A girl: Cockneys: C. 20; ob. Fr. *oiseau,* a bird: cf. **bird,** 8 (*Dict.*).

wash, n.—6. In C. 20 c., *the wash* is the theft of money in public lavatories while the owner is washing. See **wash-up,** 2.

wash, it'll all come out in the. It will be discovered eventually; hence, never mind—it doesn't matter!: c.p.: from ca. 1902. W. L. George, *The Making of an Englishman,* 1914.

wash and brush-up tuppence. A c.p. uttered by the host when one was about to wash one's hands in a friend's house: ca. 1885–1915.

wash-boards (p. 939) is very much earlier: 1806, John Davis, *The Post-Captain.* (Moe.)

wash-deck, adj. Mediocre, as in 'wash-deck musician': Naval: C. 20. Granville.

wash-out (p. 939). In sense 2, l. 3, 'printing' is obviously a misprint for 'painting'.—3. Hence, a signal of cancellation, made by waving flags in a downward arc, completing a semicircle; at night, a lamp is swung in a wide, low semicircle: Canadian railroadmen's coll. (— 1931).

wash out is the v. corresponding to *wash-out,* n. (p. 939 and here): coll.: mid-C. 19–20. Like sense 1 of the n. (p. 939), it has, since 1919, been very widely used.

wash out one's mouth. Usually either *get your mouth washed out* or *go and wash out your mouth* (or *why don't you wash out your mouth?*—or *wash your mouth out?*), a virtual c.p. addressed to a dirty-tongued, foul-mouthed person: since ca. 1910.

wash-up.—2. 'Wash Up (the): Stealing from clothing hung up in wash-houses. A thief engaged in this sort of crime would be ... "at the wash" or "at the wash-up",' F. D. Sharpe, *The Flying Squad,* 1938: c.: since ca. 1910.—3. A post-exercise analytical discussion attended by officers during Fleet exercises: Naval: since ca. 1950. (Wilfred Granville, Nov. 11, 1965.)

washers. Playing to an almost empty tent: circus- and show-men's: from ca. 1920. *John o' London's Weekly,* March 19, 1937 (B. Crocker). Perhaps ex *wash-out.*

washerwoman. 'A type of cicada' (B., 1959): Aus., mostly rural'. C. 20.

washup, your. See **wushup** (*Dict.*).

wass. See **waas.**

wasser. See **waser.**

watch. To guard against; refrain from: lower-class: C. 20. W. A. Gape, *Half a Million Tramps,* 1936, 'They're jealous because we won't use their lousy "kips"'. I'll watch getting lousy and paying eightpence for it too.'

watch, chain and seals. See **watch and seals** (*Dict.*).

watch(-)basher. See **clock basher.**

watch-dropper. One who uses a cheap watch in a version of the ring-dropping game: Australian: late C. 19–20. B., 1942.

watch how you go! Look after yourself—take care: a c.p. of parting: general only since ca. 1950, but common in the Services since ca. 1935.

watch my smoke! Just you watch me!; you won't see me for dust!: a nautical coll. that is virtually a c.p.: late C. 19–20. Ex the smoke of a departing steamer.

watch on—stop on. Watch-and-watch **or** a double turn of duty (eight hours instead of four): Naval coll.: late C. 19–20. P-G-R.

watch the dicky-bird! 'Photographers' c.p. used when photographing children, so that they will be gazing at the camera lens with a bright, expectant look' (B.P.): late C. 19–20. (I clearly remember it being successfully directed at my brothers and myself in the year 1901.)

watch-works. See 'Canadian'.

watch your pockets, lads! A humorous c.p., directed at someone who has just arrived: workmen's and Tommies': C. 20.

watcher! What cheer!: mostly Cockney: C. 18–20; at first illiterate, then—by (say) 1900—coll. As Dr Leechman reminds me, we read, in Hakluyt's *Voyages* (XII, p. 206), the date being 1578, 'They hailed one another according to the manner of the sea, and demaunded what cheare? and either party answered the other, that all was well.'

watchie or -y. A watchman: coll.: ca. 1810–40. W. T. Moncrieff, *Tom and Jerry,* 1821 (-y).

watchkeepers' union, the. Junior Officers of the Watch: Naval: since ca. 1920.

water, v.—3. To paint in water-colours: artistic: since ca. 1920. (Ngaio Marsh, *Death at the Bar,* 1940.)—4. To spray (e.g. a road, a restricted locality) with shells or machine-gun bullets: Army: since ca. 1910.

water, on the. 'The machinery is on the water' —will arrive soon: Australian coll.: C. 20. (B.P.) Arriving by ship.

water(-)boiler. A fireman: railwaymen's: C. 20. (*Railway,* 3rd.)

water bonse. A cry-baby: Cockney's: late C. 19–20; ob. J. W. Horsley, *I Remember,* 1912.

water carnival, the.—2. 'The weekly orgy of hosing, scrubbing and general "chamfering-up" which takes place on Saturday in order that the ship may be "tiddley" for Captain's inspection and Sunday Divisions,' Granville: Naval: since ca. 1920.

water-cart. 'A 15-cwt truck, fitted with a tank for bringing water from the waterpoint to the unit' (P-G-R.): Army coll.: ca. 1940–5.

water fag. That boy who, from 7 until 7.40, calls out the time at regular intervals and at 7.40 opens the dormitory windows: Marlborough College: mid-C. 19–20.

water horse. 'Salt fish just washed from a vat' (L. E. F. English, *Historic Newfoundland*, 1955): Newfoundland: C. 20.

water jerry. At a harvesting, he who looks after the water-tank: Australian: C. 20. B., 1942.

water-lily. A flat punt: Oxford undergraduates': ca. 1840–90. (Marples, 2.)

water one's pony is a late C. 19–20 Anglo-Irish variation of **water one's nag** (*Dict.*); *water the horses*, a C. 20 Australian variant (B., 1942); *water one's horse*, a C. 20 English and New Zealand variant.

water-plant. An umbrella: fast life: ca. 1810–45. Pierce Egan, *Finish*, 1828.

water-rat. See **black beetle.**

water-works. See **waterworks** (*Dict.*).

water wren. 'A Wren member of a boat's crew' (Granville): Naval: 1940 +.

waterbag. A teetotaller; a temperance fanatic: Australian: since ca. 1920. B., 1942.

waterborne. See **inland navy.**

water's wet, the. A jocular c.p., addressed to someone trying the temperature of the water with his toes: late C. 19–20.

Watson. See **obvious, my dear Watson!**

wattle, n. 'A dirty or untidy person. Truncated from *wattle and daub*, rhyming sl. based on *warb*' (B., 1959): Aus.: since ca. 1950. Cf. **warb,** 3, above.

wattle, v.i. To drink (an intoxicant): C. 20. Ex 'What'll you have?' A certain Oxford college has its Watling Club.

Waussie. A female member of any of the Australian fighting Services: Australian: 1940–5. (B., 1943.) A blend of *women* + *Aussie*.

Waves. Volunteer 'Wrens' of the American Navy: since early 1942. H. & P. Ex the initials.

Wavies, the. R.N.V.R. personnel: mostly Naval: since ca. 1918. Ex 'the *wavy navy*': p. 941. (Granville.)

wavy navy, the (p. 941); better with capitals. Granville, 'When the first uniform was issued to the Reserve, the three white tapes on the jean collar were wavy to distinguish them from the Active Service rating. To-day, only R.N.V.R. officers have wavy lace on their sleeves.'

wax, n.—2. An impression in wax: coll.: since ca. 1870. *Sessions*, Aug. 1879.

*wax, v. To have one's eye on; to spy out: c.: from ca. 1890. Clarence Rook, *The Hooligan Nights*, 1899, cracksman *loquitur*: 'There's a 'ouse I've 'ad waxed for about a week.'

wax (something) **up.** To 'mess' up: low Cockney: 1899, C. Rook, *The Hooligan Nights*, ' "Didn't I never tell you", he said, "how we waxed things up for that butcher . . .?" '

wax-borer. A long-winded bore: Australian: since ca. 1935. (B., *Australia Speaks*, 1953.) The wax is that of the auditors' ears.

waxer. A little drink: Merchant Navy: C. 20. Perhaps from 'a drop of *wax*'.

Waxies. Wellingborough men: railwaymen's: C. 20. (*Railway*, 3rd.)

waxy.—4. Short for **waxy-homey** (p. 941), which prob. dates since ca. 1880. (P. H. Emerson, 1893.) —5. Hence, an equipment repairer: Army: 1939 +.

waxy homey. A minstrel: partly parlary: late C. 19–20. Sydney Lester, *Vardi the Palarey*, (?) 1937. Why *waxy*? Perhaps because he uses wax on the instrument he plays.

way. In horse-racing, a double—a bet on two races: Australian sporting: since ca. 1930. (B., 1953.) Perhaps ex 'two-*way* bet' as opposed to 'each-*way* bet'.

way?, are you in my. A c.p. reminder of egotistical obliviousness' (Atkinson): since ca. 1925.

*way, that (sense 1 in *Dict.*); **this way.** Crooked; criminal, engaged in crime: c.: from ca. 1910.

'way back when A.M.O.s—Air Ministry Orders were chiselled on slabs of rock; when I joined the R.A.F., Pontius Pilate was (still) at I.T.W. (Initial Training Wing, where *pilots* do their elementary course): R.A.F. c.pp., signifying '(It was) a long time ago': both since ca. 1935.

way of life, the (p. 942). Earlier in *The London Guide*, 1818.

way out; way out with the birds. Living in a world of fantasy; hence, extremely eccentric: resp. jazz-lovers' (esp. teenagers') and beatniks': since ca. 1954 and, the latter, since ca. 1959. The beatnik phrase is recorded in Rachel & Verily Anderson's *Guide to The Beatniks*; for the jazz phrase, cf. the entry at 'Jazz Slang'.

way out, on the. (Of a person) due for retirement or, esp., for dismissal: coll.: since ca. 1935. —2. Hence, (of things) wearing out, coming to end of useful 'life': coll.: since ca. 1939.

way to London, that's the—or **is that the?** A c.p. question disguising a nose-wiping with back of hand or on sleeve: mostly children's, and occasionally an adult jocularity without a wiping, but always 'non-*U*': C. 20.

way, up the. See **up the way.**

ways, as in 'a long *ways*': Canadian coll.: adopted, late C. 19, ex U.S.

wazzums; or **w., then.** Were you [e.g. hurt], then?: jocular: C. 20. Ex baby talk. Cf. **diddums** in *Dict.*

we didn't come here to talk, as the man (or **the sailor**) **said to the girl in the park.** An Australian c.p.: since ca. 1940. 'Let's get on with it!'

we do get them! See **if you can tell me . . .**

we had one and the wheel came (sol. **come**) **off.** I don't know what on earth you're talking about: lower-middle and lower-class—c.p.—perhaps mostly Liverpool—of C. 20. Common also in Australia. (B.P.)

we must press on regardless. A c.p. form of **press on regardless.**

we want eight and we won't wait! A c.p. of 1909 when eight dreadnoughts were demanded for the Royal Navy.

we was robbed (in Australia, occ. **rooked**)! A jocular c.p. used when one has been tricked: since the late 1940's. Ex the indignant and usu. bogus claim of illiterate boxers when the referee has declared them to have lost. Often *we wuz robbed.*

wea-bit. See **Yorkshire way-bit** in the *Dict.*

weak. Tea: coffee-stalls' and low coffeehouses': from ca. 1860. B. & L.

weak eyes—big tits. A c.p. expressing a piece of fallacious folklore: Australian: since ca. 1920. 'Also worded in other ways' (B.P.).

weakie (or **-ky**). A weak person; esp., a coward: Australian, mostly juvenile: since ca. 1920. (Dick.)

weapon. Penis; esp. among workmen: late

C. 19–20. It has the best of precedents: see my *Shakespeare's Bawdy*.

[Weapons in early C. 18, as represented by Ned Ward: A gun was a *kill-devil* (1703); a sword a *rip* (1700; spelt *ripp*). A blow was called a *wherret* (1703). Matthews.]

wear, v.—2. 'The verb *to wear* is used in extraordinary senses in the U.S. and Canada. Women *Wear* perfume, cripples *wear* a cane, and sandwich men *wear* placards.' Thus Dr Douglas Leechman, in May 1959.

This coll. usage—by 1955, Standard in U.S.; by 1960, virtually Standard in Canada—originated in the U.S. and began to affect Canada during the 1930's. Note, however, that '*wear* a cane' derives from the idea implicit in '*wear* a sword'. In April 1967 he adds: 'I caught an even better one some years ago. Margaret Mead, the anthropologist, spoke of a woman "wearing a baby on her back".'

wear a head. To be intelligent; to possess much sense: ca. 1815–60. *Boxiana*, III, 1821.

wear (someone's) **balls for a necktie.** 'To inflict a most drastic punishment or revenge. "You pull that trick again and I'll wear your balls for a necktie."' (Leechman.) Mostly Canadian: since ca. 1920.

wear it!, I won't. I won't tolerate (or, suffer) it!: Cockneys': C. 20. In the Services, esp. in 1939–45, *wear it* = to agree to, to accept it. Jackson. Ex wearing—or refusing to wear—shoddy clothes.

wear one's hair out against the head of the bed. A jocular explanation of 'thinness on top': C. 20. Implication of abundant sexual intercourse.

*wear the gaiters. To be a convict: c.: C. 20. F. D. Sharpe, *The Flying Squad*, 1938, 'Convicts wear breeches and cloth gaiters, while short-term prisoners wear trousers.'

wear the kilt. To be the passive partner in male perversion: euphemistic: C. 20.

Weary Willie and Tired Tim. Two tramps, esp. if they resemble the famous cartoons: since ca. 1902. Created by artist Tom Browne (1870–1910).—2. Hence, lazy, loafing males: coll.: since ca. 1935.

weasel. A tip: railway porters': since ca. 1945. (*Radio Times*, Jan. 21, 1965.) Perhaps ex 'to *weasel* (something) out of somebody'.

weasel(l)ing, adj. and n. 'Extracting tips' (*Railway*, 3rd): since ca. 1945. Cf. the preceding entry.

weather, under the. See **under . . .**

weather-breeder (p. 942). Still in daily use in Sussex, meaning a fine day leading undoubtedly to a wet one. Reference in Kipling's *Puck of Pook's Hill*, 'The Conversion of St Wilfrid'; F. W. Thomas, letter of 1942.

weather Moses. To (try to) keep alive by getting a favourable deal with the pawnbrokers: Naval ratings': C. 19. (W. N. Glascock, *Sketch-Book*, 2nd Series, 1834, at II, 34. (Moe.) Cf.:—

weather out of. To rob (someone) of (something); esp., by sly, unfair means: Naval (? also gen. nautical) coll.: C. 19. Wm Nugent Glascock, *The Naval Sketch-Book*, 2nd Series, 1834, at I, 225, 'Tom took his stand on the folksel, an' the right *honourable* Mister Varmint Vaux in front of the prop, levellin' at his shipmate's life after tryin' all his soft, sinnuvating [= insinuating] ways to weather him out of his wife.' (Moe.)

Weatherall (or -ell). See **Wetherall . . .**

weaver, I'm a doll's eye. See **weaving leather aprons** (*Dict.*).

weaving, get. (Usually in imperative.) Since 1939, if H. & P.'s explanation be correct. See **get cracking.** 'Refers to the 'planes which circle round a formation to protect the rear from surprise attack,' H. & P.; Jackson, ' "Weaving" is a flying expression meaning a formation or flight in which the aircraft weave in and out of each other's paths': if this explanation be the right one (and I think it is), then prob. the phrase dates from the 1920's.

web. A foot: Liverpool: late C. 19–20. Cf. the S.E. *web-foot* and s. *webs* (p. 942).

web foot.—2. Hence (?), 'any rating whose port Division is Devonport,' Granville: Naval: C. 20.

webbing. Web equipment: Army coll.: C. 20. (P-G-R.)

Wedding Cake, the. 'The Victoria Memorial (in front of Buckingham Palace),' Herbert Hodge, 1939: London taxi-drivers': since ca. 1910. Shape and ornament.—2. Hence, the Vittorio Emanuele monument in Rome: since ca. 1944.

wedding kit. Genitals: mostly Army and Air Force: since ca. 1918.

wedge, n.—4. A sandwich: Naval: since late 1930's. (Wilfred Granville, 23 Sept. 1967; John Winton, *H.M.S. Leviathan*, late 1967.) The Navy's answer to the Army's *wad*.

wedge, v. To hit (someone) hard: North Country miners': C. 21. Ex driving-in a wedge.

*wedges. Cards cut narrower at one end than at the other, for the purpose of cheating: card-sharpers' c.: from ca. 1880. (J. N. Maskelyne, *Sharps and Flats*, 1894.)

wedgies. Wedge-heeled shoes: since ca. 1945. (John Boswell, *Lost Girl*, 1959.)

wee, n. A 'wee-wee' (p. 943): Australian nursery coll. and adult jocular: since ca. 1920. 'It's the Australian practice to use only the first element of reduplications' (B.P.).

wee Danny. A glass of Aitkin's ale: Falkirk: since ca. 1930. Ex Mr *Dan* Robertson, J.P., for many years the head brewer of Messrs James Aitkin, The Falkirk Brewery.

Wee Ellen. The Rt Hon. Ellen Wilkinson († 1947): since ca. 1935.

wee Georgie. See **any wee Georgie.**

wee-poh. Among 'children of Welsh descent in Canada, ca. 1912, the penis' (Leechman): C. 20; by ca. 1950, ob. Cf the nursery *wee-wee*, a euphemism for 'to *pee*'.

weed, bitter. See **bitter weed.**

weed on, have a. To have a 'grouse'; to be grumbling: Naval: since ca. 1920. Granville.

weedy chizz. Injustice: several British preparatory schools': since ca. 1945.

weejee. See **wee-jee** (*Dict.*).

weejie. A variant of *widgie*; the form preferred by B., 1953.

Week-End Air Force, the. The Auxiliary Air Force: R.A.F. coll.: since 1925 (year of its inception). Jackson. Only at week-ends could most of these selfless fellows do their flying.

week-ender.—3. Hence, a week-end cottage or shack: Australian coll.: C. 20. B., 1942.

week than a fortnight, rather keep you (for) a. A c.p. formula directed at a hearty eater: since ca. 1870.

weekers. A week-end: since ca. 1925. By 'the Oxford *-er*'. (Peter Sanders.)

weekly accompts (p. 943) occurs in 1806: John Davis, *The Post-Captain*. (Moe.)

weeno. Wine: Canadian carnival s.: C. 20. I.e. a blend of '*wine*' + It. '*vino*' (pron. '*veeno*'). 'In Australia, this is undergraduate jocularity': B.P., who, prob. rightly, thinks the Australian use of *weeno* originates in the L. *in vino veritas* pron. *in weeno veritas*.

weep and wail. A begging tale: rhyming s., often shortened to *weep*: since ca. 1870; by 1959, ob. (Franklyn, *Rhyming*.)

weepie, weepy. A sentimental moving-picture: coll.: from ca. 1930. Cf. **weeper, 3** (in *Dict.*).

weeping willow (p. 943) occurs forty-five years earlier in D. W. Barrett, *Navvies*, 1850.

Weetabix Junction. Burton Latimer, in Northamptonshire: railwaymen's: since ca. 1950. (*Railway*, 3rd.)

weevil bo'sun. The same as **jam bo'sun.** Granville.

weigh in with (p. 943), ll 5–6. Note that the jockey *weighs in* after, not before, the race.

weigh into (someone). To attack; to punch vigorously: Australian sporting: since ca. 1910. B., 1942. Ex the boxers' *weighing-in* before a fight.

*weigh off. To sentence (someone) to imprisonment: c.: since ca. 1920. *Daily Express*, March 25, 1938. Cf. next entry.—2. (Of the prison governor) to reprimand (a prisoner) and sentence (him) to the solitary cell: prisons': since ca. 1930. The process, from the receiving end, is known as *getting weighed off.* (Both in Norman.)

weighed off, get. To be punished or severely reprimanded: Naval: since ca. 1910. H. & P. Occ. shortened to *get weighed* (W/Cdr R. P. Mc-Douall, March 17, 1945).—2. To be received into prison: prison c.: since ca. 1925. (Norman.)

weight, give a. See **give a weight.**

weight?, have you got the. Do you understand?: Naval c.p.: since ca. 1930. Granville.

weight off one's behind—mind. See **load off** . . . (two entries).

weirdy. A very odd person; an eccentric; since ca. 1947 'The Chelsea set' of 1959 was—at least, then—described as 'the weirdies'.—2. Hence, a beatnik: journalists' and teenagers': since ca. 1959. (Anderson.)—3. (Also *weirdie*.) 'One who affects weird dress, such as a beatnik; often found in company with beardies' (Leechman, April 1967): mostly Canadian: since ca. 1950. Note that, in this sense, it is predominantly male.

well-bottled. Tipsy: Services (mostly officers') since ca. 1920. H. & P.

well-breeched. Rich: ca. 1810–60. See quot'n at **Tip Street** . . .

well-cemented. Well-off, rich: Australian: since ca. 1945. (B., *Australia Speaks*, 1953.) Probably suggested by the U.S. coll. *well-fixee.*

well-endowed. (Of a woman) having well-developed breasts: coll., often jocular: since ca. 1925.—2. (Of a man) equipped with ample genitals: since late 1920's. Nicholas Montsarrat, *The Cruel Sea*, 1951. (Ramsey Spencer.)

well firmed. 'Perfect in the "business" and words': theatrical: from ca. 1870. B. & L.

well-gone, in the 'infatuated' nuance (p. 944): Australian by ca. 1920. B., 1942.

well-heeled. Rich, either temporarily or permanently: Canadian: adopted, ca. 1910, ex U.S. (Leechman.)

well-hung. But extant in Canada.

well in.—2. (Ex sense 1: p. 944). Engaged in profitable business: Australian coll.: C. 20. (B., 1943.)—3. (Of a person) popular: coll.: C. 20.

well, Joe, what do you know? A derisive c.p. addressed to anyone named *Joe*: common in the Forces, ca. 1939–46. Ex **well, what** . . . (below).

well put-on. (Of a male person) well turned-out; well-dressed: lower-class Glasgow coll.: from ca. 1890. MacArthur & Long, 'Perhaps there may be some association of ideas between slumland's passion for smoothed and glistening crops [of hair] and its general term for a smart appearance.' Also in comparative and superlative.

well-sprung. Tipsy: ca. 1910–40. Ward Muir, *Observations of an Orderly,* 1917.

well, what do you know! A c.p. expressive of incredulous surprise: New Zealand (and elsewhere): since ca. 1918. B., 1941, 1942.

wellies. Wellington boots (in the modern, i.e. rubber, form): domestic: C. 20.

Wells Fargo. 'Old Pullman coaching stock named after the Television Western Programme' (*Railway* 2nd): railwaymen's: since ca. 1960; by 1966, slightly ob. Ex the *Wells Fargo* coaching company of the U.S.

Welly B. Wellington Barracks: Regular Army: late C. 19–20. Andrew Sinclair, *The Breaking of Bumbo,* 1959.

Welsh.—2. See 'Tavern terms', § 3, *c.*

Welsh Wizard, the. A C. 20 nickname of the late Rt Hon. David Lloyd George.

welt, n.—3. A self-awarded period of loafing or absence: Liverpool labourers': C. 20.—4. A large penis: Forces': C. 20. Sadistic?

welt, v. To punch or strike (someone): Australian: C. 20. B., 1942. Ex n., 2 (p. 945).

welter, make it a. A variant (as in D'Arcy Niland, *Call Me* . . ., 1958) of:

welter of it, make a. To go to extremes or to excess: Australian: since ca. 1905. (Jon Cleary, *The Sundowners,* 1952.)

Welwyn. Nickname for a slow or lazy fellow: R.A.F.: 1941 +. Cf. **take your finger out.** The relevant finger is *well in.*

wem. A wireless and electrical mechanic (as a 'trade'): R.A.F.: since ca. 1935. Sgt Gerald Emanuel, letter of March 29, 1945. Ex the abbr. *W.E.M.* or *W/E/M.*

went to night school and he (or she) can't spell in the daytime, he or she. A c.p. applied to a bad speller: not solely Australian: C. 20. (B.P.)

Wentworth Falls; Wentworth's Balls. Testicles: Australian rhyming s., not widely used: since 1920. Wentworth Falls is a resort, near Katoomba, in the Blue Mountains of New South Wales. (B.P.)

we're winning. We are getting on well: c.p.: 1942 +. Also as 'an evasive stock answer to "How're we getting on?" or "How goes it?"' (Atkinson).

were you born in a barn? A c.p., addressed to one who leaves a door open: mostly in Britain and in Canada, yet hardly rare in Australia and New Zealand: mid-C. 19–20, and probably much earlier. Of the same order as *was your father a glazier?* (q.v. at *glazier* on p. 332): in short, semi-proverbial.

Wessy. A London North-*Western* employee: railwaymen's: C. 20. (*Railway.*)

West Ham reserves. Nerves: Londoners' rhyming s.: C. 20. 'That sod gets on me West Hams.' Cf. *Queens Park Ranger*.

West(-)Ingee, the. The West Indies: Naval lowerdeck coll.: late C. 18–mid 19; hence, *West-Ingee man*, a West-Indiaman (ship). In W. N. Glascock, *The Naval Sketch-Book* (I, 115; II, 135), 1825–26. Moe.

Western. An American cowboy film or novel: coll.: since ca. 1910; by 1940, S.E. The action takes place in the south-west of the U.S.

Western, the. The Atlantic Ocean: nautical coll.: late C. 19–20. W. A. Gape, *Half a Million Tramps*, 1936. See Western Ocean relief in the *Dict.*

Western Front, all quiet on the; all quiet in the Shipka Pass. C.pp. resp. of 1917 + and 1915–16. The former arose ex journalistic comment on official communiques, but was suggested by the latter, which alludes to Verestchagin's cartoons of a Russian soldier's being gradually buried in falling snow.

Westminster Abbey; often merely *Westminster*. Shabby: rhyming: since ca. 1880.

Westminster's Palace of Varieties. 'Sarcastic name given to the Admiralty by officers serving in sea-going ships,' Granville: Naval: C. 20.

Westralia; Westralian. Western Australia; Western Australian: Australian coll.: late C. 19–20. B., 1942.

wet, n., 3 (p. 945). Rather, late C. 19–20, at the Public Schools; so, too, for the adj., 7.—4. A sip. esp. of rum: Naval: late C. 19–20. (Granville.) Ex sense 3 on p. 945.

wet, adj.—8. (Excessively) sentimental: since ca. 1930. Partly ex sense 7 and partly ex the idea of 'tearfully sentimental'.

wet, all (p. 945). Also, by 1935, Australian; the predominating Australian sense is 'very foolish, or very stupid': B., 1942. Ex wet, adj., 7 (*Dict.*): also, since ca. 1920, Canadian. (Leechman.)

wet,—is, (p. 946). Cf. *wet 'n' warm*, tea or coffee or cocoa, used in the same way and from well before 1900. (Alexander McQueen.)

wet, talk. See talk wet.

wet, the. The rainy season, esp. in N.W. Australia but also in N. Queensland: coll.: late C. 19–20. Ion M. Idriess, *Man of the Jungle*, 1932 (N. Queensland); B., 1942; Jean Devanney, 1944 (N. Queensland); Jon Cleary, *Justin Bayard*, 1955, 'You know our work starts when the Wet finishes.' Contrast *dry, the*.

wet a stripe. To celebrate a messmate's promotion: Naval (Wardroom): C. 20. Granville. But Naval *wet one's commission* is a coll. that goes back to ca. 1700; it occurs, e.g., in Shadwell's *The Fair Quaker of Deal*, 1710. (Moe.)

wet arse and no fish, a. A fruitless quest or errand: coll. late C. 19–20.

wet as a scrubber. 'An incalculably stupid rating' (Granville): Naval: since ca. 1930. I.e. as a scrubbing-brush. In the Australian Navy, since the 1930's, such a rating would have been, would be, described as (*as*) *wet as piss*.

wet behind the ears (p. 946). But cf. the Fr. *avoir encore du lait derrière les oreilles*.

wet bobbing. See dry bobbing.

wet deck. A Canadian synonym of *buttered bun*, 2 (p. 115): late C. 19–20.

wet dream.—2. Hence, a dull, stupid person:

Public Schools': late C. 19–20. ' "He's a frightful wet; he's an absolute wet dream: he's so wet that he positively drips: oh him, he drips!" ' (Clifton, 1914, and I should think all schools since the beginning of time)': thus a valued correspondent.

wet fish, better than a slap in the belly with a. See better than a slap . . .

wet ha'porth. A person entirely insignificant or physically weedy: North Country: late C. 19–20.

wet list. See dry list above.

wet one. A loose breaking of wind: proletarian: late C. 19–20.

wet one's neck. See wet the neck (below).

wet one's props—one's tapes—one's third (tape). To celebrate promotion to Leading Aircraftman—Corporal—Sergeant—by buying drinks all round: R.A.F.: since ca. 1925. Sgt G. Emanuel, March 29, 1945. See wet, v., 2, on p. 945, and props and tapes.

wet one's stripes. Of N.C.O.s, to celebrate promotion: Army: since ca. 1910. (P-G-R.)

wet one's warrant. To celebrate one's promotion to the rank of warrant officer: Naval coll.: C. 19. (W. N. Glascock, *Sailors and Saints*, 1829, at II, 15.) The prototype of the other entries that, preceding this, exemplify the use of *wet* = to celebrate with a drink.

wet ship. 'A ship whose wardroom has a great drinking reputation,' Granville: Naval: C. 20.

wet shirt. A wetting: Naval: C. 20. Granville. Cf. Saltash luck (p. 724).

wet smack. A dull, ineffectual person, usu. male: low London: since ca. 1950. John Gloag, *Unlawful Justice*, 1962.

wet-suit. A plastic suit for protection against cold: Australian surfers' coll.: since ca. 1961. (B.P.)

wet the baby's head. To celebrate a child's birth: since ca. 1870. (B., 1942.)

wet the (or one's) neck (p. 946). Also, merely to take a drink of liquor: *Boxiana*, IV, 1824 (. . . one's . . .).

wet trance, in a. Bemused; abstracted: low: late C. 19–20. Ex wet dream (p. 946).

wet week, look like a. To look miserable or wretched: coll.: C. 20. Obviously because a wet week tends to cause people to look miserable.

Wetherall (or -ell) in command, General. A military c.p. applied to inclement weather's preventing a parade: from ca. 1880; extremely ob. B. & L.

wetter, 2 (p. 946). Also Public Schools'; indeed, orig. and still so.

Weymouth splashers. 'Paddle-steamers running pleasure-trips from Weymouth to adjacent ports' (Granville): coll.: since ca. 1925.

whack, n.—9. A pickpocket: Anglo-Irish c.: C. 19. 'A Real Paddy', *Life in London*, 1822. Cf. strike, v., 1 (p. 839).—10. 'Food, sustenance: —"He gets 2s. 6d. a day and his *whack*" ' (P. W. Joyce, *English . . . in Ireland*, 1910): Anglo-Irish: late C. 19–20. Perhaps ex—and certainly cf.— sense 3 on p. 946.

whack, out of. Not working properly; 'off colour': C. 20. 'His mind's out of whack'; 'Our wireless is out of whack'.

whack down. To put (e.g. money) down; to write (e.g. names) down, to note: coll.: C. 20.

*whack the illy. To trick or swindle someone:

Australian c.: since ca. 1925. (B., 1943.) Is *ill* for *silly*?

whack up, v.— 3. (Ex sense 3 of *whack*, v.: p. 946.) To increase the speed of (e.g. a ship): since ca. 1910. 'He heard . . . the skipper's voice . . . howling to somebody to "whack her up".' The tug seemed to leap suddenly forward,' Manning Coles, *The Fifth Man*, 1946. Rather since late C. 19; cf. 'Moorshead suggested "whacking her up" to 15 knots'—in *Their Lawful Occasions*.

Whacker. Nickname bestowed on men surnamed Payne: esp. in the Navy: C. 20. Granville.

whacker.—2. A friend: since ca. 1940. One 'goes *whacks*'—shares—with him: cf. *whack*, n., 3 and v., 4 p. 946.—3. A Liverpudlian: since ca. 1945.

whacking, adj. (p. 946), occurs as early as 1806: John Davis, *The Post-Captain*. (Moe.)

whacko! Splendid! Good!: Australian: since ca. 1920. B., 1942. Hence, since ca. 1930, an ordinary adj., as in 'a whacko time'. (Cusack). Sarah Campion, 1940. By 1945, at latest, also English—popularized by Mr Jimmy Edwards.

whacko-the-diddle-o. (Of a girl) extremely attractive: Australian (esp. Sydney) youth's: since ca. 1938. Ruth Park, *Poor Man's Grange*, 1950. An elaboration of *whacko!*, perhaps aided by the refrain of some Irish or dial. song.—2. Indeed, 'an elaboration of *whacko* in all its senses' (B.P.): Australian: since ca. 1940.

whacky dates from the 1880's and is recorded by B. & L.

whale(-)belly. A type of coal car (= truck): Canadian railroadmen's (— 1931). Cavernous.

whale into. To attack, to punch, vigorously and spiritedly: Australian: C. 20. B., 1942. Perhaps ex (the idea behind) *whale of a* (p. 947).

whaler's delight is synonymous with *Murrumbidgee jam*. (B., 1943.)

wham, bang, thank you, madam! A c.p. applied to the rapidity of a rabbit's breeding activities: since mid-1940's: orig. Forces'. Slight adaptation of U.S. *wham bam (thank you, madam)* for rapid, unemotional copulation. (W. & F.)

whang, n.—2. A piece, portion, share: Australian low: since ca. 1918. B., 1942. Echoic: cf. **whack,** n., 3 (*Dict.*).—3. 4. See **wang.**

Whanger (p. 947): orig., Newfoundland s.; dating from ca. 1810 or earlier—it occurs in W. N. Glascock, *The Naval Sketch-Book* (I, 160, 164), 1825. Moe.

whank; loosely **wank.** V.i., to masturbate: low: late C. 19–20. Also *whank off*.

whank, spare. See **spare** . . .

whank-pit. A bed: R.A.F.: since ca. 1920. Ex **whank** (above) and cf. sense 2 of:

whanker (loosely *wanker*). A masturbator: low: late C. 19–20. Ex **whank.**—2. A bed: R.A.F.: since ca. 1925. Cf. **whank-pit.**

whanker's colic. An undiagnosed visceral pain: R.A.F.: since early 1920's.

whanker's doom. Debility: R.A.F.: since ca. 1925. It became, ca. 1945, fairly common, both in gen. low s. and esp. in prison s. (Paul Tempest, *Lag's Lexicon*, 1950.)

whanking(-)pit. The Army's form of **whank-pit:** since early 1920's. But used also by R.A.F.

whanking-spanner. An imaginary tool like a 'sky-hook': low: C. 20. Ex **whank,** v.—2. The hand: low since ca. 1920.

wharfie (or **-y**). A docker: Australian: since ca. 1920. (Alan Marshall, *Tell us about the Turkey, Jo*, 1946; Elizabeth Lambert, *The Sleeping House Party*, 1951.) Ex '*wharf*-labourer'.

what, as. As: coll. verging on sol.: mid-C. 19–20 (and perhaps from much earlier). E. C. Bentley & H. Warner Allen, *Trent's Own Case*, 1936, 'But that I did see, sir, as plain as what I see you now.'

what a face! See **face, put on a.**

what a funny little place to have one! A c.p. dating from ca. 1890; by 1960, slightly ob. The reference is to e.g., a mole or a pimple; often with suggestive undertones.

what a game (it is)! A humorously resigned c.p., referring to life's little ironies and not so little vicissitudes: since ca. 1910.

what a hope! See **what hopes!** in *Dict.*

what a life! (p. 947): often extended by the addition of *without a wife*.

what a long tail our cat's got! A c.p. addressed to—or at—someone boasting: Canadian, since ca. 1920. (Leechman.)

what a morgue! A variant, since ca. 1945, of **what a dump!,** itself current since ca. 1919. Cf. **dump,** n., 3, on p. 248.

what a shower! See **shower!**

what about it? If you're ready go ahead *or* let's get going: since ca. 1914. In *Carrying On*, 1917, Ian Hay numbers it among the 'current catch-phrases'.

what are you going to make of it? 'A c.p. inviting the hearer to fight' (B.P.): Australian: since late 1930's.

what can I do you for? A jocular c.p. variation of *what can I do for you*?: since ca. 1925.

what can we do you for? 'A c.p. forming a jocular inversion of *what can we do for you?* Often used by shopkeepers and other vendors' (B.P.): since ca. 1920.

what cheer! has been current in Yorkshire since ca. 1860: witness the E.D.D. 'The universal greeting of labourers and countrymen,' David Garnett in *The New Statesman & Nation*, Feb. 20, 1937. It is coll. It occurs very much earlier than I had supposed: James Isham uses it in *Observations and Notes*, 1743 (Hudson's Bay Record Society, XII, 54). Douglas Leechman. Also cf. **watcher** above.

what cheese is an occ. variant (ca. 1890–1910) of hard cheese (*Dict.*), as **fromage** was also.

what clock? See **what watch?**

what did Gladstone say in (date)**?** An electioneering c.p.: C. 20. No precise meaning.

what do I owe you? See **do I owe** . . .

what do you expect me to do—burst into flames? A c.p., deprecating excitement: R.A.F.: 1940 +. (Atkinson.) Ex aircraft bursting into flames.

what do you know?; what's the form? Army officers' greetings: coll. or c.ppl.: 1939 +. The former is also Australian, but not restricted to officers nor yet to servicemen. (B., 1943.) Hence, *what do you know!*, 'an exclamatory phrase of approval, mainly used ironically' (B., 1959): mostly Aus.: since ca. 1945.

what do *you* think of it? A c.p. of the 1880's and, less the –90's. An elaboration of **what do you think** (see the *Dict.*). The reply was **I quite agree with you.**

what do you think that is? (or what's that?)—

for (or **Scotch mist**)**?** See **Scotch mist**. Jackson records the form *what's that—fog?*; Partridge, 1945, the double longer.

what does a mouse do when it spins?; what was the name of the engine-driver? See 'Cockney catch-phrases . . .'

what does that make me? A c.p., expression of disinterest or of refusal to participate or to be implicated: since ca. 1937. (Atkinson.)

what-d'yer-call-it; whatcher-call-it. A 'thing-ummy': coll. and semi-literate coll.: late C. 19–20.

what gives? What's happening?: c.p.: since ca. 1945. Via U.S. ex German *was gibt's?*

what gives out? What is happening?: R.A.F. in North Italy: 1945.

what is that when it's at home?; who is he (or she) **when he** (or she) **is at home?** I've never heard of it, him, her!: c.p. of C. 20. Pugh. See also **when it's at home** in *Dict.*

what is there in it for me? What do I get out of it?: c.p.: late C. 19–20.

what it takes. Esp., courage, fortitude, per-severance; ability; (in Australia) money: coll., adopted ca. 1935 from U.S. B., 1942. Lit., what the situation requires.

what makes (someone) **tick.** (His) chief interest in life, his driving-force: since ca. 1930. 'I've never discovered what makes him tick.' Ex watches and clocks.

what odds? is the usual post-1920 form of coll. (late C. 19–20) *what's the odds?*, what difference does it make?

what say? What do you think?; what do you say to the idea, plan, what not?: Cockney c.p.: from ca. 1880. W. Pett Ridge, *Minor Dialogues*, 1895; Edwin Pugh, *Harry the Cockney*, 1912.

what say you? The gen. form of the preceding: c.p.: late C. 19–20; by ca. 1940, slightly ob.; by 1967, very ob.

what-shall-call-'um. A light woman: euphem-istic coll.: ca. 1800–70. Scott; *Redgauntlet*, 1824.

what shall we do, or go fishing? (p. 948) is also Australian: B., 1943, 'A rather pointless elabora-tion of . . . "What shall we do?"'

what the fucking hell! A very common lower-class expletive: mid-C. 19–20.

what the Llanfairfechan hell! A euphemism for 'what the effing hell!': since the 1920's.

what watch?; occ., **what clock?** What's the time?: Australian (rare, says B.P.): since ca. 1950. Cf. the German *wieviel Uhr?*

what would you do, chums? A c.p. dating since ca. 1938. Syd Walker, 'The Philosophic Dustman', with these words propounded various droll problems in the B.B.C. radio-programme entitled 'Band Wagon'. Syd Walker died of appendicitis during the 1939–45 war. (E. P. in *The Radio Times*, Dec. 6, 1946.)

what you say goes—all over the town. A c.p. addressed to gossips and rumour-mongers: since late 1940's. (A. B. Petch, April 1966.)

whatcher-call-it. See **what-d'yer-call-it** above.

what(d)jer. What do you?; what did you?: low coll.: mid-C. 19–20.

what's all this in aid of? The usual post-1945 form of *what's this in aid of?*, q.v. at **aid of? . . .** (above).

what's cooking? What is happening?: Ser-vices (esp. R.A.F.): since mid-1940. Jackson, 1943; Partridge, 1945, 'From "What is that smell

—what's cooking?"': asked so very often by so many husbands'. Adopted from U.S. In 1942–6, often amplified to *what's cooking, good looking?*

what's it in aid of? What's the reason, the purpose of it all—of this, etc.?: coll.: since ca. 1925, esp. in the Services. Jackson. In what respect, or way, does it help?

what's new? What's the news?: Army coll.: 1939 +. (P-G-R.)

what's(-)o'clock. A *wattle* bird: Australian: C. 20. B., 1942.

what's on your mind? What is your difficulty, or what is the query?: coll. c.p.: since ca. 1930. Ex the S.E. sense, 'What's worrying or pre-occupying, you?'

what's that—fog? See **what do you . . .** (above).

what's the drill? How do you do it?—What are the arrangements?—What's the 'form'?: Ser-vices (orig., Army): since ca. 1920; but general only since 1939. See **drill, the.**

what's the form? See **what do you know?**

what's the score? What sort of weather is it?: R.A.F. pilots': 1939 +. Ex sport.—2. Hence, what is the latest 'gen' (information): Air Force: 1941 +.

what's the strong of it? What is the truth? the gist of it?: Australian: since ca. 1910. Baker.

what's the time? A juvenile c.p., dating from the 1880's (but by 1940 rather ob.) and directed, from cover, at a man whose feet are wide-spread as he walks. The posture is variously described as *ten to two* (o'clock), (a) *quarter to three* and (a) *quarter to one*, this last being in the *Dict.* and requiring to be dated back to ca. 1885.

what's this blown in? Whom have we here?: contemptuous c.p.: from ca. 1905. W. L. George, *The Making of an Englishman*, 1914.

what's this—bush week? A jocular Australian c.p., directed at men making a noise and fuss: since ca. 1930. (B., 1943.) Also *what do you think this is? bush week?* An entirely imaginary week: see, esp., B., *Australia Speaks*, 1953. The commonest form of this c.p. is *What do you think this is—Bush Week or Christmas?* (B.P., 1963.)

what's this in aid of? See **what's it in aid of?**

what's up? What is the matter? What's wrong?: coll.: late (? mid) C. 19–20. A c.p. rejoinder is 'The sky'—or, now and then, 'Prices'. (A. B. Petch, March 1966.)

whatsie. A shortened form of **whatsiname** (p. 949): Australian: since ca. 1950. (B.P.)

wheat belt. A prostitute: Australian: since ca. 1920. B., 1942. With an erotic pun on harvest-ing.

wheel, n.—3. A motor car: since ca. 1959. Nicholas Blake, *The Sad Variety*, 1964, '"The Leake character gave us a ride in his wheel."'—4. Someone important, esp. in an enterprise, whether licit or illicit: Canadian: adopted, in late 1940's, ex U.S. *Daily Colonist* (April 16, 1967), 'Poor old Robin Hood may have been a wheel in Sherwood Forest, but he would have had to call it quits [nowadays]'—'because,' as Dr Leechman remarks, 'of the cost of modern first-rate archery tackle'.

wheel him in! Show him in: c.p.: since late 1950's.

wheel it on! Bring it on, or in; let's have it: originally (ca. 1939) R.A.F.; by 1950, fairly general. In reference to aircraft.

wheel up. To bring (someone) before the Officer Commanding: Army: since ca. 1935. (P-G-R.)

wheelbarrow. 'A bullock waggon laden with supplies for convicts working in the bush or country.' B., 1942: Australian: ca. 1820–70.

wheelbarrows is a coll. synonym of *travelling piquet* (p. 907): mid-C. 19–20.

wheeler.—3. A landing on the front wheel: R.A.F.: since ca. 1938. (P-G-R.)

wheels, your tongue runs on. See **tongue is well hung** (*Dict.*).

wheels down! Get ready; esp., ready to leave train, tram, bus: R.A.F.: since ca. 1937. H. & P. 'Taken from the lowering of the undercarriage . . . necessary to enable a modern 'plane to make a good landing.'

wheels up, land. To slip, lit. or fig.: R.A.F.: since ca. 1941. (Wheels unlowered.)

wheeze, n., 1 (p. 949). The nuance, 'a circus clown's joke': Nov. 16, 1861, *All the Year Round*.

*wheeze, v., dates from ca. 1880; it is in B. & L.

wheeze, crack one's. To speak one's patter: circus clowns': mid-C. 19–20. Source as for **wheeze** n., 1.

when coppers wore high hats. A long while ago: Cockney coll.: C. 20; ob. I.e. policemen.

when do we laugh? See **joke over!**

when do you shine? What time have you been called for?: Canadian railroadmen's (— 1931).

when donkeys wore high hats. A long time ago: Londoners': since ca. 1920. Cf. **when coppers . . .** above.

when I come into my Yorkshire estates. See **Yorkshire estate** (*Dict.*).

when I joined the R.A.F. . . . See **'way back when . . .**

when my wife is here, she's my right hand; when my wife is away, my right hand is my wife. A c.p. applied to masturbation: C. 20.

when Pontius was a pilot (and Nero was his navigator). A long time ago: R.A.F.: since ca. 1935. Cf. **'way back when . . .**

when roses are red (significant pause). An elliptical c.p., meaning that when girls attain the age of sixteen, they are no longer too young for sexual intercourse: mostly Australian: since ca. 1925. Ex the—in Australia—very widely known couplet:

When roses are red, they are ready to pluck;
When girls are sixteen, they are ready to fuck.

Cf. the C. 20 c.p. familiar to English-speakers all over the world: *if they are big enough, they are old enough.*

when (name of person) **suffers, everybody suffers.** 'A c.p. used when a person with a cold, etc., makes everyone else miserable' (B.P.): Australian c.p.: since ca. 1930.

when you dance in France, the last drop always goes down your pants. A low Australian c.p., dating from ca. 1955 and having three 'operative words' pronounced *dahnce—Frahnce—pahnts* in derision of those who say *dahnce* and *Frahnce*, regarded by most Australians as affected, even though they say *bahstard* and *cahstrated.* (B.P.) 'An American (U.S.) artist gave me this version ca. 1925: "No matter how much you may wiggle and dance/The last drop invariably falls in your pants." There was nothing of the long "a" in his version.' (Dr Douglas Leechman, April 1967.)

when you were wearing short (or, intensively, three-cornered) pants. When you were still a boy

(or a baby): Australian c.p.: since ca. 1920. (B.P.) Ex the **before you came up** group on p. 44.

when you're on a good thing, stick to it! A self-explanatory c.p., dating from ca. 1920. That is the sole form in the British Dominions; in Britain itself, *on to* or *onto* is much commoner than *on*.

when (or **while**) **you're talking about me, you're giving somebody else a rest.** A c.p. (— 1949), implying slander: mostly Canadian.

when(d)jer. When do you?; when did you?: low coll.: mid-C. 19–20. Cf. **whatdjer** and **wheredjer.**

where do flies go in the winter time? A c.p. of ca. 1910–30. Ex a popular song.

where do you think you are—on Daddy's yacht? A c.p. reproof to a sailor complaining about conditions or discipline, or both, aboard ship: Naval: since ca. 1946.

where I (or we) came, in this is; or which is where we came in. We've gone full circle; I'm beginning to repeat myself; I, or we, have heard or seen this before: c.p.: dating since ca. 1953, but not very general before 1956. Ex cinemagoers realising that a film has reached this point.

where (or out where) the bull feeds (or gets his bleeding, or bloody, breakfast). In the outback—remote country districts: Australian c.p.: C. 20. B., 1942

where the deception took place. A c.p., applied to courtship and marriage: C. 20. A jocular reference to '. . . where the *reception* took place'. (A. B. Petch, May 1966.)

where the dirty work's done. 'Office, workshop or room where any work or business is carried on. Mostly used jocularly,' Albert B. Petch, Dec. 18, 1946: coll.: since ca. 1919.

where the monkey shoves (occ. **puts**) **its nuts!, you can shove** (occ. **put**) **it or them.** A c.p. retort to one who refuses to give a share or hand over something: low: late C. 19–20. Cf. **stick it!,** 2.
Also in the past tense (*where the monkey put the nuts*). James Joyce, *Ulysses*, 1922, has the variant *where Jacko put the nuts.*

where the sergeant put the pudding!, put it. 'You know what you can do with it': low c.p.: late C. 19–20.

whereabouts. Men's underpants: Australian: since ca. 1920. B., 1942. A pun on *wear-abouts.*

where(d)jer. Where do you?; where did you?: low coll.: mid-C. 19–20. Cf. **whatdjer.**

where's the fire? Jocular c.p. (C. 20) to a person in a tearing hurry.

where's your violin? An Australian c.p., implying that a haircut is needed: since late 1940's. (B.P.) Ex tradition that male musicians wear their hair long.

wherry-go-nimble (p. 950). Not 'senseless', for *wherry* is—or was—a Cockneyism for 'very'.

which way one is playing, not to know; to ask which . . . Not to know, to ask about, the accepted procedure or the agreed arrangements: mostly Services': since ca. 1935. Ex 'soccer'?

which would you rather—or go fishing? See, above, **or would you rather be a fish?** and cf. next entry.

which would you rather be—or a wasp? London schoolchildren's c.p. of ca. 1905–14. Julian Franklyn compares **or would you rather be a fish?** (above) and adds, 'So far as I remember, there was no standard reply.'

whid (a word: see *Dict.*) prob. derives ex. O.E. *cwide*, a word, though influenced by *word* itself. Cf. the debased American *woid*, which orig. represented a Jewish pronunciation. Scholarly opinion has, since ca. 1945, strongly opposed the Jewish origination of *woid*. (Robin Clairborne, Aug. 31, 1966.)

whiff. A signal from a ship in convoy to the commodore: Naval: 1832, Fredk Chamier, *The Life of a Sailor*, at II, 51. (Moe.)—2. (A whiff of) oxygen: R.A.F. coll.: since ca. 1935. Jackson.

whiff. (A whiff of) oxygen: R.A.F. coll.: since ca. 1935. Jackson.

whiff out. To cause (e.g. a room) to stink: mostly Aus.: since ca. 1920. (Ross Campbell, 1964.)

whiffled. Tipsy: since ca. 1930. Origin?

whim-wham for a goose, making a. See weaving leather aprons (*Dict.*).

whingding. See 'Canadian'.

whinge, whinger, whinging. See winge.

whingey (inferior -gy). See wingey.

whiny. Given to whining: New Zealand coll.: late C. 19–20. (Ruth Park, *The Witch's Thorn*, 1952.)

whip, n.—4. Rum, the drink: Aus.: since ca. 1920. Nino Culotta, *Gone Fishin'*, 1963.

whip, v.—4. (Ex sense 3: p. 951.) To steal: since ca. 1917. Gerald Kersh, *Slightly Oiled*, 1946.

whip (someone) a cripple, as in 'The C.O.'ll whip him a cripple all right', pass a heavy sentence on: Army: since ca. 1930. Proleptic. (P-G-R.)

whip the cat.—8. To cry over spilt milk: Australian: since ca. 1910. (B., *Australia Speaks*, 1953.)

whip up a smart one. To salute smartly; merely to salute: mostly R.A.F.: since ca. 1925. (Atkinson.)

whip with a wet boot-lace. To apply an antidote to recalcitrance of the flesh: men's low: C. 20.

whipperginnie, or whip her Ginny or whip-her-ginny. Term of abuse for a woman: late C. 16–early 17. (O.E.D.) One who merits 'whip her, Jinny!'

whippy. In the game of hide-and-seek, the starting-out point: Australian, esp. children's: late C. 19–20. Origin?

whips (p. 952): recorded earlier in Alex. Mac-donald, *In the Land of Pearl and Gold*, 1907, '"There is good feed an' whips of water up that way."'

*whipster. 'A sly, cunning fellow' (B. & L.): c.: C. 19–early 20. A deviation ex † S.E. *whip-ster*, a mischievous fellow.

whirl, give it a. To 'have a go'. Canadian and English: C. 20. Cf. the synonymous Australian *give it a burl*, q.v. at *burl* above.

whirl!, have a. An insulting c.p. = have a banana (p. 30) or take a carrot (p. 129): Australian: since late 1940's. Here, *whirl* refers to a *whirling*-spray. (B.P.)

Whirligig. A Whirlwind fighter aircraft: R.A.F.: since 1941. H. & P. By affectionate depreciation.

whirling spray. A Wirraway aircraft: Australian airmen's: ca. 1940–5. (B., 1943.) By the process of Hobson-Jobson; also cf. the next entry.—2. A long-winded bore: Australian: since ca. 1940. (B., *Australia Speaks*, 1953.)

A fanciful elaboration of the idea informing *drip*, 3.

whirly-bird or whirlybird. A helicopter: Canadian (Air Force, and commercial air-lines): since ca. 1950. (Leechman.) By the late 1950's, also British, esp. in R.A.F.—2. A 'Matisa tamping machine' (*Railway*, 3rd): railwaymen's: since late 1950's.

whisker.—2. A girl or young woman: Austra-lian: since ca. 1921. B., 1942. Antiphrastically, but also because 'she's the *cat's whiskers*'.

whiskers down to here, have. Usually 'He has...': a low c.p.: C. 20. Simultaneous with the utterance of *here* is the placing of the hand upon trousers flap.

whisk(e)y. The Yellow-Tufted Honey-Eater bird: Australian rural: C. 20. (B., 1943.)

whisk(e)y drinker. 'A type of cicada' (B., 1959): Aus., mostly rural: C. 20.

whisk(e)y MacDonald. A whiskey and ginger-wine: mostly Scottish: since ca. 1920. 'And by the 1960's, almost invariably abbreviated to whisk(e)y Mac' (Ramsey Spencer, Aug. 1967).

whiskey racket, the. The offer of printing machinery (and accessories) without the pro-duction of bona fides: printers': 1945 +. *World's Press News*, Jan. 10, 1946. So often made over a whisky offered by a crook.

whisper, get it on the. See get it ... above.

whisperer.—2. A racing tipster: Australian race-courses': C. 20. B., 1942.

whispering death. See killer above.

whispering gill. A variant of whisper syl-slinger (*Dict.*).

whispering death. See killer above.

whisticaster, a variant of whister-clister (p. 952), occurs in *The Night Watch* (II, 338), 1828. Moe.

whistle, n.—4. Penis, esp. a child's: domestic: late C. 19–20.

whistle. 'To hurry away, to scram' (Jackson): R.A.F.: 1940 +. Ex the speed of the going.

whistle and toot. Money, esp. cash: rhyming s. (on *loot*): C. 20. Usually shortened to *toot*—see toot, n., 4, above. (Franklyn 2nd.)

whistle-punk. That boy who conveys signals from loggers to donkey-engineer: Canadian lumbermen's: since ca. 1920.

whistle-stop. A very small town: Canadian coll. (ex U.S.): since ca. 1925.

whistle up. To send for (esp. reinforcements) in a hurry: Army coll.: since ca. 1925. (P-G-R.)

whistlecocks. Aboriginals: Australian: since ca. 1880. B., 1942.

whistled. Tipsy: upper classes': since ca. 1920; then Services (esp. R.A.F.) since ca. 1925. G. March-Phillipps, *Ace High*, 1938; Jackson. Cf. whistle-drunk (p. 953): perhaps ex the cheerful whistling that is characteristic of the drunk.

whistler.—7. 'A high-explosive bomb as it des-cends': civilian (1940) and Services (1939). H. & P. Cf. screamer, 6.—8. As in the following quotation from *The Weekly Telegraph*, Feb. 28, 1942: 'The war has brought into being many nicknames, which often mystify the uninitiated. Thus, women railway porters are known as "whistlers", female bus conductors as "Annie Lauries", women van drivers as "Gerties", girl munition workers as "Spitfire kittens", female "milk-roundsmen" as "dairy dots", women window-cleaners as "climbing Marys" and women fire-watchers as "pouncers", while land-girls are known as "dainty diggers" and women employed in the building trade as "kilted brickies".'

whistling Toms. 'Well, there was your whistlin' Toms—your twenty-four and forty-two pounders —flyin' athwart your folksel and crossin' your poop on opposite tacks' (W. N. Glascock, *Sketch-Book*, 2nd Series, 1834, at II, 175): Naval: late C. 18– early 19. Cf. **long-winded whistler** on p. 493. (Moe.)

Whit.—3. Whitsuntide: coll.: late C. 19–20. In, e.g., *The North Wales Pioneer*, May 19, 1939.

white, n.—4. A white waistcoat: coll.: since ca. 1860. *Sessions*, Sept. 1871.—5. A £5 note: low sporting: William Hickey in *Daily Express*, March 20, 1946. Ex the white paper.

white-ant, v. To sabotage; to undermine: Australian Labour: since ca. 1920. Hence, *white-anter*, a saboteur, and *white-anting*, sabotage. B., 1942. White ants are wood-destructive.

white ants, have the. To be exceedingly silly, or insane: Australian: C. 20. B., 1942, 'Also "in one's attic".'

white ants in the billy (, have). (To be) crazy: N.T., Australia: since ca. 1920. Ernestine Hill, *The Territory*, 1951. (The billycan.) Applied originally to men gone crazy or, at the least, eccentric through isolation. Also *get the white ants*, as in H. Drake Brockman, *Men Without Wives*, 1938, ' "Get the white ants"? What do you mean?—Go ratty. Mad. Get our senses eaten away till only a shell is left.'

white-bearded boys, the. 'People who establish unintelligible principles and prove them, like the ballisticians of Woolwich,' H. & P.: Services (mostly Army): since ca. 1938. Cf. **really clever boys, the.**

white blackboard. An instructional film: school-teachers': since ca. 1930.

white blow. Semen: literary or cultured: C. 20.

white bottle. A bottle of medicine coloured white: coll. among female surgery-habituées: late C. 19–20.

white boy. A C. 17 term of endearment-reference: coll. Cf. **white-haired boy** in *Dict.*

White City, the. The military hospital at Helles (Gallipoli): 1915.

white face. Gin (the liquor): Australian: ca. 1820–80. J. W., *Perils, Pastimes and Pleasures*, 1849.

white feather, show the.—2. See **feather, show the white,** on p. 269 and in Addenda.

white fustian. See **fustian** (*Dict.*).

white-haired boy (p. 954) is common also in C. 20, Canada.

white hope. A heavy German shell, esp. the 5·9: soldiers': 1915–18. (Vernon Bartlett, *No Man's Land*, 1930.) Prompted by *Jack Johnson* (p. 430).

***white it out.** To serve a prison sentence: Australian c.: C. 20. B., 1942.

white jenny (*Dict.*) occurs in B. & L.

white lady. Methylated spirits drunk as an intoxicant: Australian: since ca. 1920. (B., 1953.)

White Maori. Tungstate of lime: New Zealand miners': since ca. 1875. B., 1941. Ex appearance.

white mice. Lice: low Australian rhyming s.: C. 20. (K. S. Prichard, 'Kiss on the Lips'—a story in *Kiss on the Lips*, 1932.)—2. Dice: English

spivs': since late 1940's. *Picture Post*, Jan. 2, 1954.

white money. Silver money: low: C. 20. Stanley Jackson, *An Indiscreet Guide to Soho*, 1946. Cf. **whites** (*Dict.*).

White Paper candidate. A candidate for a temporary commission in the R.N.V.R.: Naval: 1940 +. Granville.

white rabbits! or simply **rabbits!** A South of England greeting on the first day of every month: late (? mid- or even earlier) C. 19–20. 'Good luck!' In Southern folklore, however, it is 'a strictly female invocation to the new *month*, and must be uttered on the 1st of the month before speaking to anyone else. . . . Also a feminine incantation on first seeing the new moon, regardless of date; apparently with sexual implications' (Ramsey Spencer, March 1967).

white rat. 'A sycophant; a tale-bearer': Naval: since ca. 1925. Granville. Cf. the c. use of *rat*, esp. for 'informer'.

***white sheep.** A c. term dating from ca. 1880. Clarence Rook, *The Hooligan Nights*, 1899, 'The young man who walks out with [the servant], and takes a sympathetic interest in her employer's affairs, rarely takes a hand in the actual [burglary]. He is known as a "black cap" or a "white sheep" and is usually looked upon as useful in his way, but a bit too soft for the hard grind of the business.'

whitewash, v.—2. To coït with (a woman): C. 20.—3. To beat (an opponent) before he has scored an opening double: darts players': since ca. 1930.

whither or no, Tom Collins, 'is a phrase among sailors, signifying, whether you will or not' (W. N. Glascock, *Sailors and Saints*, 1829, at II, 7). A variant—perhaps rather the original—is *Tom Collins, whether or no*, occurring in Alfred Burton, *Johnny Newcome*, 1818. (Moe.)

whizz, n. See **whiz,** 2, in *Dict.*—3. Energy, 'go': Australian: since ca. 1910. (Dal Stivens, *Jimmy Brockett*, 1951.)

whizz-bang.—3. 'A Fighter on the tail of an enemy aircraft,' H. & P.: R.A.F.: 1939 +.—4. R.A.F.: 1940–5. (P.G-R.)

Whizzbang. 'Major-General Sir F. de Guingand, on Montgomery's staff, is known to his soldiers as "Whizzbang",' *Daily Express*, July 6, 1944.

whizzer. See **whizz-man** (*Dict.*).—2. See **fan,** n., 5.—3. See **put on the rattle.**—4. Anything superlative, whether good or bad: since ca. 1945. Elleston Trevor, *Gale Force*, 1956, ' "Rather windy."—"I'll bet it's a real whizzer on deck." '

whizzo, ess. as exclamation. Splendid: mostly children's: since ca. 1944. Ex the adj. *wizard*. (Nicholas Blake, *The Whisper in the Gloom*, 1954.)

whizzuck; usually in pl. 'Whizzucks. Gremlins which live on the outskirts of enemy aerodromes,' H. & P., 1943. Echoic. See **gremlin.**

'who are you shoving (or pushing)?' said the elephant to the flea. A jocular c.p., uttered by a big—or, at the least, a noticeably bigger—man jostled, or knocked into, by a small man: since ca. 1920. (A. B. Petch.)

who boiled the bell? and **who hanged—or hung— the monkey?** On the Clyde these are derisive C. 20 c.pp. (Peter Sanders.)

who do you think? See **think?, what do you:** in *Dict.*

who(-)done-it; usually *whodunit*. A murder

story; a detective novel; a murder-story cartoon: coll.: adopted in 1942 from U.S. where current since ca. 1934. *The Writer*, Jan. 1944. Ex the gaping curiosity and inquiries of the illiterate.

who hung the monkey. A derisive c.p., mainly North Country: C. 20. Ex a Hartlepool incident.

who is 'She'? a cat's mother? is a variant of 'She' is a cat's mother.

who kicked your kennel (or pig-sty)? Mind your own business: lower-middle class: since ca. 1910.

who let you out? 'When a person shows himself very cute and clever another says to him "Who let you out?"'—an ironical expression of fun: as much as to say that he must have been confined in an asylum as a confirmed fool' (P. W. Joyce, *English . . . in Ireland*, 1910): Anglo-Irish c.p.: late C. 19–20. Occasionally heard elsewhere; by 1940, slightly—by 1960, very—old-fashioned.

who robbed the barber? See **he's a poet.**

who stole the monkey? See **monkey, who stole the** (*Dict.* and Addenda).

whoa, anchors! See **anchors!** above.

whole —, the. All the —; e.g. 'the whole three of them': incorrect coll.: mid-C. 19–20.

whole box and dice, the. The whole lot, everything; (of persons) all: Aus.: since ca. 1930. Mary Durack, *Keep Him My Country*, 1955, 'The boys tossed it in . . . and the whole box and dice clears out to Jericho.'

whole caboose, the. The whole lot; everyone and everything: Australian: since ca. 1930. (B., 1943.) Perhaps ex:

whole kit and caboodle, the. The lot; everything: Canadian: adopted, ca. 1920, ex U.S. (Leechman.)

whole pile, go the. 'To put all one's money on a solitary chance': gamesters', anglicised ca. 1885 ex U.S. B. & L.

whole shebang, the. See **shebang** on p. 752.

who'll sell his farm and go to sea? A Naval officers' c.p. either directed at or alluding to someone who is feeling liverish: since ca. 1910. (P-G-R.) But more commonly **who'd sell . . .,** for 'the implication is regret rather than proposition' (Ramsey Spencer).

whoosh. To move rapidly, emitting a dull, usually soft, always sibilant sound; eligible only when used fig.; coll.: since ca. 1920. 'He whooshed through the house without even saying goodbye.' Ex the lit., echoic S.E. sense, as in 'Miserable passengers huddled back against the wall while passing vehicles "whooshed" through the inches-deep roadway puddles' (*The Sydney Morning Herald*, Aug. 30, 1963—with thanks to B.P.). The lit. sense is admitted by *Webster's International* without comment; in British—esp. Scottish—dialect, it has long been common as an interjection expressive of a dull, rushing, hissing sound, as noted by the E.D.D.

whopcacker or **wopcacker.** Anything astounding, notable, excellent; hence as an adj.: Australian: since ca. 1925. B., 1942. With *whop-*, cf. **stunning** (p. 843).

whopping, n. (p. 956) occurs in, e.g., W. N. Glascock, *Sailors and Saints*, 1829, at II, 132. Moe.

whore.—3. A semi-affectionate term (cf. *bastard*) for a man: Anglo-Irish: C. 20. Desmond O'Neill, *Life Has No Price*, 1959, 'Brian was one of the best—the cute whore.'

whore-shop. A brothel: coll.: C. 19–20.—2. Hence, a house or flat where behaviour is dissolute: C. 20.

Whores' Canteen, the. A certain Plymouth public-house frequented by soldiers, sailors, and prostitutes: from the 1880's. Richards.

Whore's Gazette—Red Light News—Piccadilly Part Two Orders—Screws of the World. National Servicemen's names, all in common use, for a famous newspaper: since ca. 1947. The 1st and the 2nd were common in the Services in 1939–45, and presumably date from much earlier. Affectionate, not (except very rarely) derogatory.

whore's get.—2. A white-slaver: c., and low: C. 20. Gen *hoorsget*.

whore's musk. Scented cosmetics; esp., their odour when advertising the presence of women: military coll.: C. 20.

whore's robber. See **messer.**

who's hoisting my pennants? Who's talking about me?: Naval (lower-deck) c.p.: C. 20. P-G-R.

who's milking this cat? An Aus. variant, recorded by B., 1959, and dating from late 1940's, of:—

who's robbing this coach? Mind your own business!: Australian c.p.: since ca. 1880. B., 1942. In humorous allusion to bushranging. Hence 'Let me get on with the job!': a jocular Australian c.p., dating since ca. 1890. (B.P.) 'The anecdote from which this phrase derives: The train robbers were robbing the passengers and threatening to rape the women. An altruistic passenger cries, "Spare the women!" An elderly lady turns on him, exclaiming, "Who's robbing this train anyway?"' (Leechman, April 1967.) Therefore of American & Canadian origin.

who's smoking cabbage leaves? A c.p. to a person smoking a cigar, esp. if rank: mostly Londoners': late C. 19–20. Cf. **cabbage, 4,** in *Dict.*

whosermybob or **whosermyjig.** 'Whatsit' or 'thingummy(bob)' or 'whatsiname': Australian: since ca. 1930. (B.P.)

why buy a book when you can join a library?; (2) **you don't have to buy a cow merely because you are fond of**—or **like** or **need**—**milk.** These male c.pp. jeers at marriage are (1) Australian, since ca. 1920, and (2) general, late C. 19–20. In the 2nd, Australians say *just*, not *merely*, and prefer the interrogative *if you like milk, why buy a cow* or *why buy a cow just because you like milk?* (B.P.)

why curls leave home. A c.p., referring to baldness: since ca. 1950. A pun on *why girls leave home*, which, by the way, has, since ca. 1910, been a c.p. derisive of a good-looking 'ladies' man'. (Petch.)

why keep a dog and bark yourself (or *. . . do your own barking?*)? A self-explanatory c.p.: C. 20.

whyfor (erroneously **-fore**)? Why: Australian: C. 20. (B.P.) Cf. *for why*, which, however, means 'because'.

Wi-Wi (p. 956). Earlier in R. G. Jameson, 1842. (B., 1941.)

wick, dip one's. See **dip one's wick.**

wick, get on (a person's). To annoy; to get on someone's nerves: low, Cockney and Naval: C. 20. *Wick* = **Hampton Wick** (*Dict.*). Cf. 'give (one) a pain in the belly' (U.S.: 'to gripe').

wicked.—2. Hence, expensive: not upper-class: late C. 19–20. Robert Eton, *The Bus Leaves for the Village*, 1936. Esp. 'a wicked price'.

wicked enemy, the. The Germans; esp. German aircraft (sing. or plural): ca. Sept.–Dec. 1940. Hector Bolitho in *The English Digest*, Feb. 1941, 'Fashionable for a time.' Ex the Press.

wicked lady, the. The cat-o'-nine tails: London's East End: since ca. 1945. (Richard Herd, Nov. 12, 1957.)

wicked sod. A liar: proletarian: C. 20.

Wid; usually in pl. *Wids.* A member of the *W*omen's *D*ivision of the R.C.A.F.: Canadian airmen's: 1942–5.

widdle. To make water: children's: C. 20. Ex *wee-wee* + *piddle.*

wide, n., is elliptical for *wide boy:* since ca. 1940.

wide, adv. Outside the harbour: Sydney anglers': since ca. 1930. 'Have you been fishing wide?' (B.P.)

wide, go. To spend money freely: military: ca. 1860–1905. Robert Blatchford, *My Life in the Army*, 1910. I.e. to spread oneself.

wide boy. A man living by his wits: C. 20: c. > by 1935, s. See **wide**, 2 (p. 957).

wider the brim, the fewer the acres, the. An Australian c.p., corresponding to **lunatic hat** (above), but implying a lack of intelligence: since ca. 1935. (B.P.)

widgie (or **-gy**). 'Girl with horse-tail hair-do and bobby-socks, also playing juke-box in milk-bar' (*The Sunday Chronicle*, Jan. 6, 1952): Australian: ca. 1950–60. Cf. *bodgie.* Ex **wigeon** below.—2. Esp. *have* (*got*) *a widgy on*, to be in a bad temper: Naval: since ca. 1950. (Laurie Atkinson records it for April 1961.)

*****wido,** n. A hooligan: Glasgow c. and low s. late C. 19–20. MacArthur & Long. Prob. ex the adj. **wido** (in *Dict.*).

widow.—7. A single word in the top line of a page: printers': late C. 19–20. Printers think it unsightly.

widows and orphans. A railwaymen's c.p., applied to the suicidal practice of walking along a railway line with one's back to the approaching traffic: C. 20. (*Railway.*)

wids, adj. (p. 957). Extant, esp. in London. Robert Greenwood, *The Squad Goes Out*, 1943.

wife.—2. A pimp's favourite harlot-mistress: white-slavers' c.: late C. 19–20. A. Londres, *The Road to Buenos Ayres*, 1928.—3. Fiancée; one's girl; one's mistress: Services (esp. R.A.F.): since ca. 1930. Partridge, 1945. Cf. **bride.**—4. The passive member of a homosexual partnership: homosexuals': late C. 19–20. Complement: **husband.** (Anon., *Lavender Lexicon*, 1965.)

wife-in-law. A girl belonging to a 'stable' of prostitutes: the world of prostitution: since ca. 1920. (John Gosling & Douglas Warner, *The Shame of a City*, 1960.) An extension of **wife**, 2, above.

wife-preserver. A rolling pin: jocular: C. 20. (Petch.) A pun on S.E. *life-preserver.*

wig, n.—4. A scene, an act; such playing as will render the audience ecstatic: Canadian jazz-lovers' and musicians': since ca. 1956. (*The* Victoria *Daily Colonist*; April 16, 1959, 'Basic Beatnik'.) Cf. the U.S. jazzmen's *flip one's wig* (later *flip*), to approve ecstatically (Norman D. Hinton in *The American Dialect Society*, Nov. 1958).

wig, v., 1 (p. 957): slightly earlier in George R. Gleig, *The Subaltern's Log-Book* (II, 31), 1828, 'You rise often in a hurry, fearing that you may be too late for parade, and get "wigged" by the

Major for not coming in time to inspect your company on the private parade'. (Moe.)—3. (V.i.) 'To post a scout on the route of flight in a pigeon race with a hen pigeon, to attract the opponent's bird and retard his progress': pigeon-fanciers': from ca. 1860. James Greenwood.

wig-block (p. 957). Much earlier, prob.—as pugilistic s.—since ca. 1840. In, e.g., Augustus Mayhew, *Paved With Gold*, 1857.

Wigan. Derisive reference is made also to **Wigan Pier:** a fact alluded to in a book by George Orwell, 1937.

wigeon. An endearment for a little girl or a female teenager or a young woman: Australian: since ca. 1946. This—the source of **widgie** above —derives ex S.E. *pigeon* (used occ. as endearment) + piggy-*wiggy* (see **piggy-wig** on p. 628), as B.P. informs me.

wigga-wagga. A flexible walking-cane: ca. 1895–1912. Ex **wiggle-waggle.**—2, Hence, penis: low: C. 20; slightly ob. Perhaps influenced by an early C. 20 popular song, 'With my little wigga-wagga in my hand', the protagonist being represented as walking down the Strand: cf. Harry Randall's gag, 'There *is* such a thing as love at first sight, but, young man, if you meet it in the Strand, *walk on!*'

wigging.—2. See **wig**, v., 3 (Addenda).—3. Short for *earwigging:* see **earwig.**

wigster. See **wigsby** (*Dict.*).

*****wikkel.** See **dim-liggies** (more fully in *Under-world*).

Wilcannia shower. See **shower,** 5, above.

wilco. See **roger!** above.

wild cat.—3. In the petroleum industry, since ca. 1910, thus, 'Indications are sought of [geological] structures which might act as oil traps, and the most promising of these are tested by the drilling of deep wells, known in the industry as "wild cats",' Colonial Report No. 1930, *State of Borneo*, 1938 (pub. in 1940).—4. Elliptical for *wild-cat strike*, an unofficial strike: industrial coll.: since ca. 1959. Perhaps ex sense 2 on p. 958.

wild-dog, v.i. To hunt dingoes: Australian coll.: late C. 19–20. Archer Russell, *A Tramp-Royal in Wild Australia*, 1934. Often shortened to *dog:* Russell, *op. cit.*

Wild Irishman, the.—2. The tumatakuru (a New Zealand plant): New Zealand coll.: late C. 19–20. B., 1941.

Wilderness, the. See **Woods,** 2 (below).

wilderness, be in the. To be in need of 99 points: darts players': since ca. 1930. Also the adjj. *cracked* and *split.*

wilds, the. Esp. in **give** (someone) **the wilds,** to make angry, to depress: Australian: ca. 1860–1920. 'Tom Collins', *Such Is Life*, 1903. Cf. **willies** (*Dict.*).

Wilfred. A teetotaller: mostly proletarian: ca. 1865–1910. B. & L.: 'This reference to Sir Wilfred Lawson [1829–1906], M.P., the great teetotal champion.'

Wilfred Pickles, do a. To 'have a go': ca. 1947–60. An allusion to the famous radio star's most famous programme.

Wilkie is a City nickname for men surnamed Collins: late C. 19–20. Ex Wilkie Collins the novelist (1824–89). See also **Lottie** (*Dict.*).

Wilkie Bard. Also, in racecourse rhyming s., a race card: C. 20. (Mr Clive Graham—'The Scout'—via Julian Franklyn.)

will, making a. See **making one's will** above.

will I buggery!—or **fuck!**—or **hell!** See **fuck, like.**

will you shoot? Will you pay for the drinks?: Australian hotel bars': since ca. 1920. B., 1942. A pun on **shout,** n., 1 (p. 764).

William.—3. An occ. synonym of **John Thomas,** 2 (*Dict.*): low: mid-C. 19–20.

William Powell. A towel: convicts' rhyming s.: since ca. 1935. (Franklyn 2nd.) Ex the famous American film star.

Willie.—2. For this garage-hand's term, see **daff,** v.—3. A way*bill*: Canadian railroadmen's (— 1931).—4. A supply of betting money: Australian sporting: since ca. 1935. (Lawson Glassop, *Lucky Palmer,* 1949.)

willy. See **willy-willy.**—2. A ball: Shrewsbury: since mid-1930's. Marples, 'Perhaps *pill, bill, willy*'.—3. See **Willie.**

willy, chuck or **throw a.** To throw a fit: Australian: C. 20. B., 1942. Cf. American *whingding.*

willy, throw a. See prec. entry and also **seven, throw a.**

Willy Lee. A flea; mostly in pl. *Willy Lees*: Australian rhyming s.: since ca. 1925. (B., *Australia Speaks,* 1953.)

Willy Wag or **W.w.** or **w.w.** A swag: Aus. rhyming s.: C. 20. Mary Durack, *Keep Him My Country,* 1955.

willy-willy. A whirlwind: Australian: late C. 19–20. Archer Russell, *A Tramp-Royal,* 1934. Thus: *whirlwind > whirl > wil > willie* (or *-y*) *> willy-willy*. Often shortened to *willy*: B., 1942. By 1945 at latest, it > S.E.

Wilson's den; in full, **W.-d., number ten.** In Bingo: 10: since late 1964. The Rt Hon. Harold Wilson; No. 10 Downing Street—the Prime Minister's London residence.

wimbler. A hand-worked auger: railwaymen's coll.: C. 20. (*Railway.*) Ex S.E. 'to *wimble*', itself ex the n. *wimble.*

wimp (p. 959). Current among Cambridge undergraduates as early as 1909 (R. M. Williamson, letter, 1939).

Wimpey. A Wellington (bomber 'plane): R.A.F.: since 1938 or 1939. *The New Statesman,* Aug. 30, 1941; E. P. in *The New Statesman,* Sept. 19, 1942. Ex J. Wellington Wimpey, Popeye the Sailor's esteemed partner, in a very popular series of comic cartoons.

win(-)on, v.i. To 'get off' with a girl: Australian: since ca. 1945. (Dick.)

win the button. To be the best: tailors': from ca. 1860. B. & L. Here, *button* = medal.

winching, n. An Army variant of **winchin'** (p. 960): since the 1930's. Perhaps contaminated, purposely, by '*winching* a vehicle'.

winco or **winko.** Wing Commander: R.A.F.: since before 1930. Allan A. Michie & Walter Graebner, *Lights of Freedom,* 1941 ('winko'); Jackson, 1943. Ex *Wing Co,* a frequent abbreviation.

wind.—2. A strong liquor, prob. rum or gin: ca. 1715–50. Anon., *The Quaker's Opera,* 1728. See the quot'n at **bunter's tea.** Because it catches the breath.—3. A wind instrument: musicians': C. 20: coll. >, by 1945, S.E.

wind-bagger. A deep-sea sailor: nautical: since ca. 1880. Bart Kennedy, *London in Shadow,* 1902.

wind(-)hammer. A pneumatic riveter: Naval: since ca. 1930. Granville.

wind in your neck! 'A polite way of asking someone to close a door,' H. & P.: Services (esp. R.A.F.): since ca. 1936. Cf. the entry at **wood in it** (p. 963); contrast **wind your neck in!**

wind-jammer. Sense 2 dates back to the 1870's. B. & L.

wind of, get. See **get wind of** above.

wind of change, the. 'An inexorable current not under control of leaders' (William Safire, *The New Language of Politics,* 1968): Prime Minister Harold Macmillan used it in a speech made on Feb. 2, 1960. But public opinion 'changed all that' and when, in 1966, he published his memoirs, 'he accepted the editing of common usage that changed his "wind of change" to "winds" and called his book *The Winds of Change*' (Wm Safire). It is, indeed, *the winds* . . . which became, ca. 1961, a c.p.

wind-sock is an aviation term mentioned by *The New Statesman & Nation,* Feb. 20, 1937, and dating from ca. 1928: coll. for a hollow wind-indicator.

wind-splitters. 'Lean and scraggy cattle' (B., 1943): Australian rural: C. 20.

wind-sucker. A horse with the heaves: stablemen's: from ca. 1865. B. & L.

wind up. Pinned up; hence taut: rhyming s.: ca. 1870–1929. Franklyn, *Rhyming.* Association with the next is extremely doubtful.

wind up, get the (p. 960). Professor Arnold Wall, in his review (*The Press,* Christchurch, N.Z.) of the 3rd edition of this dictionary, relates that, having long thought about the origin of the phrase, he is at last convinced that it arose thus: 'A favourite marching tune in the Army was "The British Grenadiers", of which a rude parody had been made [perhaps soon after the Peninsular War] . . . and the marching soldiers would sing it right up to the time of the war of 1914–1918. One verse ran: "Father was a soldier, at the battle of Waterloo, The wind blew up his trousers, and he didn't know what to do." It was natural that when a man was flustered . . ., he was said to have "got the wind up his trousers", later shortened to "got the wind up". This bears the obvious stamp of truth. . . . The wedding of the words to a well known tune doubtless aided the vitality of the expression.' Professor Wall is probably right.

wind up one's bottoms, vbl phrase. See 'Tavern terms', § 2.

wind your neck in! Stop talking!: R.A.F.: since ca. 1937. Robert Hinde, letter of March 17, 1945. Cf. **winding, take out of.**

wind'ard of, get to. To get the better of (a person): nautical, esp. Naval, coll.: late C. 19–20. 'Taffrail'. I.e. windward.—2. Also, to get on the right side of someone: Naval: since ca. 1900. Granville.

winding, take (someone) **out of.** To silence; to nonplus: Australian: since ca. 1920. B., 1942.

winding the chain. See **keeping the pot boiling.**

windmill. An autogyro: R.A.F.: since ca. 1935. H. & P. Cf. **egg-whisk,** q.v.—2. A propeller: R.A.F.: since ca. 1938. Jackson.

windy, 2 (p. 960). Recalled, as current since ca. 1909 in the Royal Sussex Regiment, by S. H. Ward, Esq., who adduces the evidence ('Winde Expert') afforded by the *Roussillon Gazette* (The Regiment's journal) of July 1911 (p. 87). 3 (p. 960). See next entry.—4. (Ex sense 2: p. 960.) Of officer or N.C.O.: fussy: Army: since ca. 1917.—5. (Of matter or of type) set very open: Australian printers' (— 1950). B., 1953.

Windy Corner. Northern Germany, esp. the coast near Kiel: R.A.F. pilots': since 1939. Allan Michie & Walter Graebner, *Their Finest Hour*, 1940 (p. 63). Cf. **windy,** 3 (*Dict.*). The date 1916 given for the various 'Windy Corners' of World War I 'suggests that they took the name from that notorious Windy Corner at the Battle of Jutland through which Beatty's depleted Battle Cruisers and the Fifth Battle Squadron had to make their turn North to rejoin the Grand Fleet, under the concentrated fire of the German High Seas Fleet' (Ramsey Spencer, March 1967). But the phrase was in Navy use as early as 1900, when it was employed of the approach to the attack on the Taku Forts during the Boxer Rising; attested by Geoffrey Bennett in *Coronel and the Falklands*, 1962, as Mr Spencer tells me.

wing her. To set the brakes on a moving train: Canadian railroadmen's (— 1931). Ex sportsmen's S.E. 'to *wing* a bird'.

wing of a woolbird. See **wool-bird** (*Dict.*).

wingco is a variation of **winco**.

wing'd. Tipsy: ca. 1840–90. (William Juniper, *The True Drunkard's Delight*, 1933.) Cf. *wing, hit under the* (p. 961).

winge, v. To complain frequently or habitually: Australian: since ca. 1910. Sidney J. Baker, letter in *The Observer*, Nov. 13, 1938. A perversion—or perhaps merely a corruption of—*to wince*. Also *whinge*. Hence, *winger* or *whinger*, a grouser, and *w(h)inging*, grousing (*g* pron. *dj*). But also English—esp. Lancashire and Yorkshire—dial.; whence presumably the Australian usage.

winger.—3. An assistant; a 'pal': Naval: since ca. 1939. Granville. Cf. **side-kick** (*Dict.*). —4. See **winge.**—5. *The Winger*: the Commander (Flying): Fleet Air Arm: since ca. 1920.—6. (Also *wings* and *wingsy bash*.) Mate, chum, pal: Naval: since, resp., ca. 1925–1930–1940.—7. A ship's steward, or a sailor, habitually allowing himself to be used passively: homosexuals': since ca. 1930. Cf. sense 1 (p. 961) and esp. 5.—8. Hence, fig., as in 'She seems to think she's the admiral's winger' = He thinks a lot of himself: since ca. 1935: orig., Naval; by ca. 1950, fairly gen. homosexual.

wingey or **whingey**; inferior forms in *-gy*. Querulous; cantankerous: Australian: since ca. 1930. (B., *Australia Speaks*, 1953.) Ex *winge.*

wingless wonder. An officer on ground duties: R.A.F.: since ca. 1930. Gerald Emanuel, letter of March 29, 1945. Cf. **kiwi** and **penguin.** There may be a ref. to Winston Churchill's description of Ramsay MacDonald as 'the spineless wonder'.

Wings. Wing Commander: R.A.F.: since ca. 1935. Robert Kee, *A Crowd Is Not Company*, 1947. Cf. **winco.**—2. In the Royal Navy, a Commander in the Fleet Air Arm: since ca. 1925. (Granville.) Cf. *winger*, 5.—3. Hence, Commander (Air) 'responsible for the flying routine or operations in an aircraft carrier' (Wilfred Granville, Sept. 23, 1967): Naval: since late 1930's.

wings, get one's. To complete one's flying training and qualify as an operational pilot: R.A.F. coll. (— 1939) >, by 1943, j.

wingy, n. (p. 961) was orig. a navvies' nickname for such a man. (D. W. Barrett, *Navvies*, 1881.)

wingy, adj. See **wingey.**

wink, n.—3. A housemaid: Marlborough college: since ca. 1870. See **Winkery.**—4. A sixpence: Australian: since ca. 1920. B., 1942, 'One and a wink'.

wink in one's eye, have a. To feel sleepy: Australian coll. of ca. 1850–1910. W. W., *The Detective's Album*, 1871. (Baker.)

winkers.—3. Spectacles: Australian: C. 20. (Caddie, *A Sydney Barmaid*, 1953.) Ex sense 1 on p. 961.

Winkery, the. The maidservant's dormitory: Marlborough College: late C. 19–20. Ex **wink,** n., 3 (above), which that excellent scholar Leonard Forster holds to be a doublet of *wench* (used at the College for a maidservant) and not, as I flippantly suggested, to derive from the winks she saucily bestows upon 'the young gentlemen'.

winking at you—is. A c.p., directed at some specified feature of the body's innocent or unabashed exposure: C. 20.

winkle, n. Penis: children's; (young) schoolboys': late C. 19–20.

winkle barge. An anti-aircraft ship, esp. a Landing Craft (Flak): Naval: ca. 1941–5. (P-G-R.)

winkle out; winkling. To hunt out, house by house or 'fox-hole' by 'fox-hole', esp. with rifle and bayonet: bayonet exercises: resp. since 1940 (military) and ca. 1930 (Naval). The latter: Granville. The former: *The People*, Oct. 31, 1943.—2. *Winkling*: attacks by Typhoon aircraft on small enemy strong-points, 500-or-so yards ahead of the troops: R.A.F.: 1944–5.

winkle-pickers. 'Winkle-picker' shoes—shoes with very pointed toe-caps: since ca. 1959.

winko. See **winco.**

winks (p. 961): Mayhew, I, 1851.

Winnick (p. 961). The place-name is written *Winwick*, pronounced *winnick*.

Winnie.—2. The Rt Hon Sir Winston Churchill, K.G.: since ca. 1914, but esp. since April 1940: wholly affectionate. In 1940–5, mostly Army.

wino. A drunkard on wine: Canadian: adopted, ca. 1925, ex U.S. (Leechman.)

*****Winter Headquarters.** Devon and Cornwall: tramps' c.: C. 20. W. A. Gape, *Half a Million Tramps*, 1936.

*****wipe,** n., 2 (p. 961), should be back-dated to ca. 1700, for it occurs in Captain Alexander Smith, *The Life of Jonathan Wild*, 1726—see **wipe lay, the,** below. (Then sense 3, to which add: Very common in Anglo-Irish: P. W. Joyce, *English in Ireland*, 1910; he instances 'He gave him a wipe on the face.')—3. A blow, hit, punch: low: from ca. 1875. B. & L.

wipe, v.—2. To refuse (a loan): c.: from ca. 1921. Perhaps ex **wipe out** (*Dict.*).—3. To do without, dispense with: Australian: since ca. 1920. B., 1942. I.e. 'wipe off the plate'.—4. To have nothing to do with; to refuse to see or to speak to (someone): Australian: since ca. 1940. (Jon Cleary, *Back of Sunset*, 1959.)—5. Hence, to ignore (someone) coldly; to snub severely: Australian: since the middle 1940's. Culotta, 1957, adduces 'He got wiped' and 'I've wiped him'.

wipe (a person's) **eye for** (something). To rob him of it: Army: since ca. 1930. P-G-R.

wipe hell out of (someone). To thrash, or defeat soundly: Australian: C. 20. B., 1942.

***wipe lay, the.** Handkerchief-stealing: C. 18–19. Recorded by Captain Alexander Smith in 1726: see **wipe,** n., 2, above.

wipe-off, n. A dismissal: Australian: since ca. 1930. (H. Drake Brockman, *Hot Gold*, 1940.) Ex:

wipe off. To say a final good-bye to; to decide to see no more of (e.g. a locality): Australian coll.: since ca. 1925. (D'Arcy Niland, *The Shiralee*, 1955.) Probably elliptical for *wipe off the slate.*

wipe-out. A violent dumping of a surfer by a wave: Australian surfboard riders': since ca. 1960. *Sun-Herald*, Sept. 22, 1963; *Pix*, Sept. 28, 1963.

wipe round. To hit on: Cockney: 1895, E. Pugh, *A Street in Suburbia*, 'Garn! I'll woipe yer rarned the marth, talk ter me . . .'

wipe up, 1 (p. 961). Also police s.: *The Free-Lance Writer and Photographer*, April 1948.

wire, n.—3. A wire-haired terrier: dog dealers': from ca. 1890. (*The Evening News*, July 2, 1937.) —4. Penis: low: since ca. 1925. Ex *pull one's wire* (p. 666).—5. A reprimand: Australian: since ca. 1930. (B., 1943.)

wire, give (someone) **the,** as on p. 962. Hence, in World War II, to give advance information: mostly Army. (P-G-R.)

Wire, the. The wire fence built by Mussolini on the frontier of Libya and Egypt: Army coll.: 1940–3. 'It kept out nothing but the gazelles' (Peter Sanders, Sept. 10, 1967).

wire at (e.g. Loos)**, on the.** A variant of **hanging on the barbed wire** (p. 373).

wire-puller. A Royal Engineer: Army: C. 20. They're forever handling wire.—2. An electrician: ca. 1900–25.

wire-worm. A man that collects prices to *wire* to country clients: Stock Exchange: from ca. 1890. B. & L.

wired for sound. (Of a person) wearing an ear-piece of any kind: Australian: since late 1950's. (B.P.) Ex radio mechanics' jargon.

wireless or **message by wireless.** A baseless rumour, a report without ascertainable origin: since ca. 1925.

wires, on. Jumpy; nervous: coll.: late C. 19–20. Prompted by S.E. *highly strung.*

Wise Boy's Paradise, the. 'This very apt term is used in the services to describe the *unimportant* jobs which seem to keep so many eligible men out of uniform, and the places overseas to which men have gone to avoid conscription,' H. & P. (early 1943): since 1939. A list should be published of all those actors, artists, authors, *et al.*, who put themselves far (and long) before their country: 'Wise guys? huh!' The loss of a creative life is unfortunate and deplorable; loss of the nation's, nay civilization's, opportunity to create, tragic and unthinkable.

wise-crack now, as for some time since in U.S., has a pejorative connotation.

wise up (p. 962): but Canadian by 1905 at latest. 'You've got a little way to hike alone . . . and you're not wised up in everything': Frederick Niven, *Wild Honey*, 1927.

Wiselion. A Wesleyan: Welsh: late C. 19–20. 'Draig Glas,' *The Perfidious Welshman*, ca. 1911.

wish I had yer job! I work much harder than you do: Cockney c.p.: C. 20.

wish I may die! An asseverative tag: Cockney: mid-C. 19–20.

wish in one hand and shit in the other and see which (hand) gets full first! A c.p. retort on the expression of any wish whatsoever: low, mostly Cockneys': C. 20.

wish (a person) **on** (occ. **upon**). To recommend a person to another: rare before C. 20. Many knowledgeable persons think (and several have written to tell me so) that this term should be included: but at lowest it is coll. and I myself believe it to be familiar S.E. E.g. 'That officer was wished on us by the —— Brigade.' 'Ulti-mately, I think, from the Witch Doctor's ability to transfer evil wishes from his client to his client's enemy, and it prob. comes into English slang via the Colonial Service' (Julian Franklyn).

wished on, as in 'I had this job wished on me', i.e. foisted upon me: coll.: late C. 19–20. Ex prec. entry.

wiskideon. A waistcoat: since ca. 1945. Fanciful; ex the now dial. pronunciation, *weskit.*

wisty(-)castor or **wistycastor** (or **-er**). A blow; a punch: pugilistic: ca. 1815–40. *Boxiana*, III, 1821, 'This round was all fighting, and the *wisty-castors* flew about till both went down.'

witch-piss. An inferior, or an unpopular, beverage, ranging from 'Naffy' tea to thin beer: R.A.F.: since ca. 1940; by 1960, ob.

witch tit (or **teat**), adj. (Of weather) very, esp. if bitterly, cold: since ca. 1960. (Wilfred Gran-ville, Nov. 21, 1962.) With pun on *witch* and *which.*

with a face like yesterday. Glum- or sulky-looking; ill-favoured: non-aristocratic: from ca. 1903; ob. W. L. George, *The Making of an Englishman*, 1914.

with a five-franc note in one hand and his —— in the other. A soldiers' c.p. (1914–18), applied to those who, as soon as they received their week's pay, dashed off to a brothel.

with it, be. To understand and appreciate and enjoy music: jazz-lovers': since the late 1930's. (*The Observer*, Sept. 16, 1956.) This perhaps derives from the Canadian (and U.S.) carnival employees' to *be with it*, to be one of carnival or fair-ground crew. C. 20. (Leechman.)—2. Hence, to be alert or well-informed and up-to-date: since ca. 1959. Cf. the quotation at **Rockers** . . . (above). 'Even "with-it" might be acceptable as a kind of sociological onomatopoeia, an expres-sion with overtones which match the thing des-cribed': Anthony Lejeune in *The Daily Telegraph*, colour supplement, March 10, 1967.

with it, get. See 'Jazz Slang'.

with one's trousers down, caught. See **caught** . . .

with or without?; positive: **with** or **without.** 'Often heard in cafés and snack bars. The server at the counter, where sugar is put in tea at the counter, will say "With or without?" The person ordering often asks for tea and adds "With" or "Without". People who have heard German or Swiss say "mit" sometimes use this. They seldom say "With sugar"' (A. B. Petch, April 1966): coll.: since ca. 1920.

without a mintie. Penniless: Australian sport-ing: since ca. 1920. (Lawson Glassop, 1949.) I.e. without a *minted* coin.

without a word of a lie. A c.p., emphatic for 'honestly!': late C. 19–20.

witter. To annoy (someone) by talking nonsense: Leeds undergraduates' (— 1940). Marples, 2.

wiv no error is a Cockney variant (slightly ob.) of **no error**, indubitably. Clarence Rook, *The Hooligan Nights*, 1899.

wizard (p. 962) was immensely popular in the R.A.F. (and the W.A.A.F.) in 1939–45: witness, e.g., Mary Welsh Monks in *Lights of Freedom*; Hector Bolitho's article in *The Listener*, late 1940; H. & P.; Jackson, who postulates R.A.F. currency before 1930; Partridge, 1945. Via the Fleet Air Arm, it > popular in the Navy by 1942 (Granville). The term became general civilian s.; after ca. 1952, however, it was little used except by schoolchildren and—such things reach them after they've reached everyone else—by the lower-middle class.

wizard prang. A spectacularly successful raid on an enemy target: R.A.F.: since ca. 1940; by 1955, ob.

*wizz, the. Variant of **whiz(z)**, n., 2 (p. 955). F. D. Sharpe, *The Flying Squad*, 1938, where also occurs *wizzer* for *whizzer* (see **whizz-man**: p. 955).

wizzer or **wizzy.** Urination: Scottish children's: late C. 19–20. Echoic.

wizzo, usually exclamatory: splendid!: R.A.F.: 1942 +. Partridge. Ex **wizard** (*Dict.* and Spp.).

wobbegong. Anything notable or excellent: Australian: since ca. 1920. B., 1942. Ironic ex *woebegone?*—2. A 'thingummy': Australian: since ca. 1925. Baker.

wobbie or **-y.** A member of the International Workers of the World: Canadian workers': from ca. 1920. W. A. Gape, *Half a Million Tramps*, 1936. In U.S., it is **wobbly** or **wabbly**.

wobbler.—6. 'A soldier toadying for stripes' (B., 1942): Australian soldiers': 1939 +.

wobbles, the. In horses, a sickness caused by eating palm leaves: Australian coll.: since ca. 1880. Baker.

Wobblies. Members of the International Workers of the World: since ca. 1910.

Woff. A member of the Women's Auxiliary Australian Air Force: Australian Services': 1939–45. (B., 1943.) Cf. the English *Waff*.

wog. Any Indian of India (not merely as on p. 963); an Arab; 'A native. Someone once called enlightened natives "Westernised Oriental gentlemen" and the name caught on' (Jackson), via the initials: R.A.F.: since ca. 1930. But Gerald Emanuel goes nearer the mark, I think, when (letter of March 29, 1945) he asks, 'Surely the derivation is from "golliwog"?'—with ref. to the frizzy or curly hair; *wog*, indeed, is a nursery shortening of *golliwog*.—2. A germ or parasite; anything small (e.g. tea-leaf floating on cup of tea): Australian: C. 20. B., 1942.—3. A baby; a very young child: Australian nursery: C. 20. Also *pog-wog*, *poggy-wog*, *pog-top*, *poggle-top*, etc. Baker. Of the *diddums* (p. 219) variety of affectionate idiocy.

wog, the. Tubercular infection: Australian: since ca. 1920. (Margaret Trist, *Now That We're Laughing*, 1945.) A specialisation of **wog**, 2.—2. Hence, *wog*, a person with tuberculosis: since ca. 1925. (Dymphna Cusack, *Say No to Death*, 1951.) Cf. sense 2 of preceding entry.

'I have made extensive enquiries and everybody agrees with my belief that *the wog* is used of tuberculosis only by those in sanatoria or during

a discussion concerning tuberculosis. Ten million Australians regard *the wog* as influenza, or loosely as a heavy cold with aches and pains, running nose, headache, etc.': Barry Prentice, in a communication of mid-1963. Therefore: 3. Influenza: loosely, a heavy cold: Australian: since ca. 1925. Ex sense 1.

wog gut; or **Palestine ache.** (Acute) diarrhœa: Australian soldiers: mostly in 1940–2. Lawson Glassop, *We Were the Rats*, 1944. Ex their training period in Palestine; see **wog**.

wog pub. A public-house that admits coloured people and therefore loses—or tends to lose—its best white customers: since ca. 1955. (*The Times*, Jan. 23, 1965.) By extension of **wog**, 1, above.

woggery. An Arab village: Army and Air Force: since ca. 1930. (P-G-R.)

woggling. Waggling one's club for a long time before making the stroke: golfers' coll.: since ca. 1920. Bernard Darwin, *Golf Between Two Wars*. Ex *waggle* + *jog*.

wogs, white. British and Continental European residents in Near and Middle East countries: Army and R.A.F.; since ca. 1930. Cf. sense 1 of preceding entry.

wolf. A philanderer: adopted, ca. 1944, ex U.S. servicemen. One of the linguistic consequences of the American occupation of London during 1943–5. Cf. S.E. *wolfish*, predatory.

'The word "wolf" has softer meanings in Australia, particularly when used by girls, as in "I don't trust your father, he's a wolf"' (B.P.).

Wolf of Tuscany. An Italian soldier: British Army in North Africa: 1940–43. Peter Sanders, in *The Sunday Times* magazine, Sept. 10, 1967, adds that 'one of the Italian formations in the desert was the Wolves of Tuscany division'.

Wolver. Penis. Midland and Northern English rhyming s.: since ca. 1945. Short for *Wolverhampton*, clearly an elaboration of *Hampton*, itself elliptical for **Hampton Wick** on p. 370. (Ronald Hjort, Nov. 16, 1967.)

wom. A wireless operator (mechanic): R.A.F.: since ca. 1935. E. P. in *The New Statesman*, Sept. 19, 1942. Ex the initials *W.O.M.* Distinct from **wop**.

woman. In tossing, the Britannia side of the penny: from ca. 1780. Grose (at *harp*).

woman of the world. A married woman: coll.: ca. 1580–1640. Shakespeare, *As You Like It* and *All's Well*.

[Women receive the following s. names in the writings of Ned Ward in the first third of C. 18. A girl: *drozel* (1714), *giggler* (more usually of a wanton), *hussif* (1703; gen. of a married woman and perhaps always S.E.), *Malkin* (1706; spelt *Maukin*; prob. always S.E.), *petticoat* (1709; ditto), *pug* (1706) or *pug-Nancy* (1703); in 1712 he applies *blowze* to a shrew, and in 1709 *honest trout* to a respectable woman (? who is 'a good sort'); Billingsgate fishwives he refers to in 1703 as *Flat-Caps* and *Straw-Hats*. Matthews.]

women and children first. A jocular c.p. on an occasion of non-emergency: since ca. 1914.

womming. A 'GW/GC joint line expression for rail turning' (*Railway* 2nd): ca. 1890–1925. Ex dial. *wamble* or *womble*, to revolve.

wong. A catapult: Australian: since ca. 1920. (B., 1943.) Echoic?

Wong-Wong. The German Gotha bombing

plane of 1918: R.A.F. and A.A.: 1918, then historical. (Sholto Douglas, *Years of Combat*, 1963.) Ex the sound issuing from its twin engines.

wonk (p. 963): since ca. 1930, predominantly a junior midshipman. Granville.—2. An Aus. Aboriginals' pejorative for a white person—cf. the Aus. white's use of *boong* for an Aboriginal: C. 20. (B., 1959.)

won't have it, I (or **he**, etc.). I don't believe it; or, I won't admit it: coll.: mid-C. 19–20.

woo, n. A 'petting session', a bout of mild love-making: New Zealand: since ca. 1930. Slatter, 'Having a woo with some joker.' Directly ex S.E. 'to *woo*'.

Wood. Collingwood, a suburb of Melbourne: Melbournites' coll.: C. 20. B., 1942.

Wood, Mr. A truncheon: police: C. 20. (*The Free-Lance Writer*, April 1948.)

wood-and-water Joey. A parasite hanging about hotels: Australian: ca. 1880–1910. B. & L.

Wood in front, Mr and Mrs (p. 963). In *Showman Looks On*, 1945, C. B. Cochran has *Wood family in front* and implies late C. 19–20.

wood merchant. A seller of lucifer matches: London streets': ca. 1875–1912. Ibid. Superseded by **timber merchant** (*Dict.*).

wood on, have the. 'To have an advantage over someone' (B., 1941): Australia and New Zealand: since ca. 1920. Either rhyming *have the goods on* or more probably ex the game of bowls.

wood-pile. See **fish-horn.**

wood-spoiler is in the Navy applied rather to the carpenter's mate, who is also termed *chippy chap*: witness 'Taffrail'.

Woodbine, 1 (p. 963): revived in 1939–45. (B., 1943.)

Woodbine Willie. The Rev. William Studdert Kennedy: military in 1914–18; hence gen. Contrast **Teddy Woodbine** in *Dict.*

wooden, v. See **would'n.**

wooden ears on, have, as 'I had wooden ears on', I couldn't hear: since ca. 1920. Cf. *cloth ears* and **tin ears.**

wooden fit is recorded earlier by B. & L.

wooden hill, the. The stairs; esp. (*go*) *up the wooden hills to Bedford(shire*): lower-middle and upper working classes': mid-C. 19–20.

wooden out. To floor (someone), esp. with a punch: New Zealand: since ca. 1925. Slatter, 'You bloody piker. A man oughta wooden you out.' Ex the idea of 'wooden *floors*'.

wooden pegs. Legs: rhyming s.: C. 20. An occ. variant of *Scotch pegs*, q.v. at **Scotch peg** on p. 734. Franklyn 2nd.

wooden set-too. Anglo-Irish (C. 19) for **wooden surtout** (*Dict.*): Wm Carleton, *Rory the Rover*, 1845.

Wooden Shoes. Those who favoured either Pretender, hence France: ca. 1665–1750. With a pun on *sabots.* 'Here in England, two hundred years ago, when the "Jew Bill" was before Parliament, the walls were chalked with the words "No Jews.—No Wooden Shoes" . . . rhyming slang. . . . Wooden Shoes implied "foreigners"—people who wore sabots,' Julian Franklyn in *The Leader*, Jan. 1939. The Bill was passed in the year 1753: see Cecil Roth, *A Jewish Book of Days* (1931), p. 92.

'After the honeymoon of the 1660 Restoration was over, the slogan was: "No popery—no wooden shoes"; Charles II's wife, Catherine of Braganza, was Catholic, & so was his brother, later James II and father of the Old Pretender; both surrounded themselves with priests, native and foreign. The Fire of London itself was put down to papist action, and it was rumoured that French and Dutch spies helped to spread it. The traditional English distrust of foreigners (wooden shoes) has been repeatedly linked with whatever was the immediate bogy of the period.' (Ramsey Spencer.)

wooden swear. An ill-tempered slamming of a door: C. 20.

wooden tenpenny cases. Sabots: Anglo-French: ca. 1815–50. David Carey, *Life in Paris*, 1822. Here, *cases* = encasers.

woodener of five. A fist: Australian low: since ca. 1910. B., 1942. Cf. **bunch of fives** (p. 108).

woodie. An 'old wood-panelled station wagon' (*Pix*, Sept. 28, 1963) or 'an old car, partly constructed, or reconstructed, of wood' (B.P., mid-1963); hence, 'any old car having surfboard racks' (B.P., late 1963): Australian; the latter, surfers': since ca. 1950, 1961, resp.

woodman.—2. A prison sentence of one month: c.: C. 20. 'From the fact that years ago in prison you slept on wooden boards for the first month' (John Gosling, *The Ghost Squad*, 1959).

Woods.—2. *The Woods* (or *the w-*). The lavatories: Marlborough College: since ca. 1870. 'The lavatories were originally by the Mound behind the College, in the part now known as "the Wilderness"' (L. W. Forster).

Woody. A Wild Woodbine cigarette: since ca. 1915. Cf. *Woods* (p. 964).—2. P. G. Wodehouse, the novelist: bookmen's: since ca. 1920.

woof. 'To eat fast (from "to wolf"),' Jackson: R.A.F.: since ca. 1925.—2. Hence (?), 'to open the throttle quickly' (ibid.): since ca. 1930.

woof run. A hash-house; a cheap restaurant: Australian Naval: 1939–45. (B., 1943.) Probably ex preceding.

woofits, the; esp. *get the woofits*, to be moodily depressed: from ca. 1916; ob. ? = *woeful fits.*

wool, have (someone) **by the.** By infatuation to control: Australian: C. 20. Baker.

wool, in the; out of the wool. (Of sheep) about, or soon, to be shorn; having only just been shorn: Australian coll.: C. 20. B., 1942.

wool, tie one's. See **tie one's hair** (*Dict.*).

wool(-)barber. A sheep-shearer: Australian jocular: C. 20. Tom Ronan, *Only a Short Walk*, 1961.

wool-bug. 'He pictured the shearers, the "wool-bugs", in their dirt and grease' (Jean Devanney, *The Butcher Shop*, 1926): New Zealand: ca. 1890–1940.

wool-classer. A sheep-biting dog: Australian jocular: since ca. 1910. Baker. A wool-classer 'pecks at' the wool he classifies.

wool-grower. The head: pugilistic: ca. 1840–90. Augustus Mayhew, *Paved With Gold*, 1857.

wool-hawk. A skilful shearer: Australian: C. 20. Baker. Ex the habits of that bird.

wool is up; wool is down. Times are good; times are bad: rural Australian c.pp. (coll., not s.): from ca. 1880; slightly ob. B. & L. In reference to the price of wool, which is the staple product of Australia.

wool, or woollen, king. A sheep 'king' or owner of a very large sheep-station or of numerous stations: Australian: since ca. 1920. (B., 1943.)

wool shorn, have one's. To have or get a haircut: Australian: since ca. 1925. (B.P.)

Woolies. A Woolworth's store: urban Australian: since ca. 1930. (H. C. Brewster, *King's Cross Calling*, 1944—cited by B., 1953.) Cf. *Woolly's* below.

Woollies. See **Woolly's**.

woollies. Woollen underwear: domestic coll.: late C. 19–20.

Woolloomooloo Frenchman; – Yank. A Sydney youth that apes the French or the Americans: Sydneyites': 1940 +. B., 1942 and 1943.

Woolly. 'Woollongong (popularly pronounced Woollen-gong)': Australian: since ca. 1920. (B., 1953.)

woolly, n.—2. A sheep: Australian: late C. 19–20. B., 1942.

woolly-headed, go at. To attack furiously, most vigorously, very rashly: Australian: C. 20. Baker.

woolly-headed boy. A favourite: tailors': from ca. 1860. B. & L. Cf. **white-headed boy** (*Dict.*).

Woolly's or **Woollies.** A Woolworth's store: since ca. 1910. Cf. **Marks**.

Woolwich and Greenwich. Spinach: (mostly green-grocers') rhyming s.: late C. 19–20. Franklyn 2nd.

Woolwich Arsenal or, in full, **make way for Woolwich Arsenal!** A c.p. applied by satirical, not unkindly onlookers, at the P.B.I., more heavily loaded than a Christmas tree (see *Christmas tree order* on p. 152): 1915–18. As an 'Anzac', I never, at the time, heard the expression; as a Tommy, Albert Petch knew both phrases.

Woolworth carrier. A merchant ship converted into an aircraft carrier: Naval and R.A.F.: ca. 1940–5. (P-G-R.)

Woolworth marriage or **wedding.** A fictitious one, as feigned by the week-end couples that buy a 'wedding-ring' at 'Woolly's': coll.: since ca. 1925.

wooney or **woony.** Mother; darling: nursery and young children's: (?) mid-C. 19–20. (Atkinson.) Prob. a two-year-old's attempt at *mother*.

woop. See **woop woop**, 2 (p. 964).

woopknacker. A decided 'hard case': New Zealand: since ca. 1920. Slatter, 'He's a hard shot. Yeah, he's a woopknacker all right.' Arbitrary?

woop woop.—3. As *Woop Woop*, it is 'the hypothetically most rustic of all rustic townships in Australia' (B., 1959): Aus.: since ca. 1930. Ex sense 1 on p. 964.

woop-woop pigeon. A kookaburra: Australian: since ca. 1920. B., 1942. See **woop woop** (p. 964).—2. A swamp pheasant: Australian: since ca. 1925. (B., 1943.)

Wop (p. 964). Rather, since the early 1920's. It occurs in W. L. George, *The Triumph of Gallio*, 1924. Ex Sp. *guapo*, 'a dandy'—via Sicilian dialect. In A. Train, *Courts, Criminals and the Camorra*, 1912, we read, 'There is a society of criminal young men in New York City, who are almost the exact counterpart of the Apaches of Paris. They are known by the euphonious name of "Waps" or "Jacks". These are young Italian-Americans who allow themselves to be supported by one or two women, almost never of their own race . . . They form one variety of the many gangs that infest the city.'—2. Hence, in Australia, an Italian prostitute: since ca. 1925.—3. Hence, any prostitute: since ca. 1930, but never very general. Whence *wop-shop*, a brothel, ob. by 1960. (B., 1953.)

wop. A wireless operator: R.A.F.: since ca. 1930. Sgt-Pilot F. Rhodes, letter of Sept. 20, 1942. Ex the abbr., *W/Op*.

wopag. 'An airman of the trade of wireless operator/air gunner,' Jackson: R.A.F.: ca. 1937–43, then ob. Ex the unofficial abbr. *W.Op/A.G.*, the official one being *W/O/AG*.

wopcacker. See **whopcacker**.

woppidown. A damper (cake): Australian: since ca. 1910. (B., 1943.) Ex *whop it down*?

word up. To warn, advise, 'tip off': Australian: since ca. 1925. B., 1942.

work.—5. To steal: c.: mid-C. 18–20. B. & L. Ex sense 2.—6. V.i., to ply one's trade of prostitution: white-slavers' c.: C. 20. Albert Londres, 1928.

work a dead horse (New Zealand): **ride the dead horse** or **work off the dead horse** (Australian). Variants of *work for a dead horse*, q.v. at **dead horse** (p. 210).

*****work a door.** See **door, work a**.

work a flanker. See **flanker, play a**.

*****work a ginger.** See **ginger, v., s.f.**

*****work a ready.** See **ready, work a**.

work a slinter. To play a mean or illicit trick; tell a false story: Australian low: C. 20. B., 1942. See **schlenter**, 3 (p. 732).

work a swindle. To accomplish something by devious or irregular means: R.A.F.: since ca. 1930. Jackson. See **work**, 2 (p. 964), and **swindle**, 4.

work like a bastard. To work very hard: low coll.: C. 20. (Atkinson.) Here, *like a bastard* merely connotes an expletive energy.

work off.—3. As *work oneself off*, to masturbate: low coll.: perhaps since C. 16; certainly old.

work one's bot. See **bot**.

work over, v.; a work(ing)-over. To beat up; a beating-up: low: since ca. 1930.

work Pompey. A variant (since ca. 1920) of *dodge Pompey* (p. 229).

work the pea. 'To swindle one's employer by skilfully appropriating small sums off the takings at the bar of a public-house, alluding to a conjuror's trick': barmen's: from ca. 1860. B. & L.

*****work the rattle.** (Gen. as vbl n. or as ppl adj.) To operate, as a professional thief, on the trains: c.: from ca. 1890. (*The Yorkshire Post*, latish May 1937.)

work the spread. See **spread, n.**, 10, in *Dict.*

work things. To achieve something, not necessarily though usually dishonest or, at best, dubious: coll.: late C. 19–20. Cf. *work*, sense 2, on p. 964, and *work the oracle* on p. 965.

work up. (Of men) to effect carnal union with: low coll.: late C. 19–20. Variant: *work oneself up*.

worker. A draught bullock: Australian coll.: since ca. 1870. B., 1942.

working by. Work on the wharves or from wharf to ship: stewards' coll.: C. 20. W. A. Gape, *Half a Million Tramps*, 1936.

workingman's solo. A Solo Whist hand (almost) impossible to beat: Australian card-players': C. 20.

*****workman.** A professional gambler: gamblers' c.: ca. 1800–50. J. J. Stockwell, *The Greeks*, 1817,

works, get on (someone's). To irritate, to infuriate: Australian low: C. 20. B., 1942.

*works, give the. To beat up; to kill: c.: adopted ca. 1930 from U.S. Gerald Kersh, 1938. (See *Underworld*.)—2. Hence, to address a political meeting: tub-thumpers': since ca. 1936. Perhaps, however, ex '*fireworks*'. Note that sense 1 is probably short for *give the whole works*, i.e. everything, the ultimate—death.

*works, the. A convict establishment: prisoners' c.: from ca. 1870. B. & L. Contrast **the** **Works** (*Dict.*).

Works and Bricks. The Air Ministry Works Directorate: Air Force coll.: since ca. 1920. Jackson. A variant is *Bricks* (*and Mortar*).

worm-eater dates from the 1880's and is recorded by B. & L.

worms.—3 (Mostly as nickname.) That rating who, in a Naval Establishment, attends to the gardens: since ca. 1910. Ex the worm-casts. (P-G-R.)

worms, give (someone) **the.** An Australian synonym of *works, get on*. Baker.

worms, have one for the. To take a drink of liquor: since ca. 1880. J. J. Connington, *Truth Comes Limping*, 1938. Ex jocular pretext of medicinal use. 'Compare Spanish *matar el gusano*—to kill the worm—applied to the first drink of the day, particularly if spirituous' (H. R. Spencer).

worret. See **worrit** (*Dict.*).

worried as a pregnant fox in a forest fire, as. A Canadian c.p., dating from ca. 1920. (Douglas Leechman.)

worry, not to. See **not to worry.**

Worry and Grumble. A taxicab company (W. & G.): from ca. 1910; †.

worry and strife. A wife: rhyming s.: C. 20. (Len Ortzen, *Down Donkey Row*, 1938.) Much less used than *trouble and strife*, which it varies.

worse things happen at sea. A vaguely consolatory c.p.: since ca. 1910.

wors'n. See **worsen** (*Dict.*).

worthy. Trustworthy and honest and good-natured, but rather dull: middle- and upper-class coll.: since ca. 1944.

Worst End, the. The West End (London): among those who (e.g. waiters, taxicabmen, 'con' men, whores) go there for profit rather than pleasure: from ca. 1928. I.e. worst for the pleasure-seekers.

Wosby. The *War Office Selection Board*: Army: World War II. Adopted by civilians, as in *spiritual Wosby*, an extended interview and tests for intending clerics.

wotcher! is the predominant Cockney shape, in C. 20, of *what cheer!* as a greeting: coll.

would followed by *used*. See **used.**

would you rather do this than work? A jocular c.p., addressed to someone working manually in his leisure, or even to someone at work: since ca. 1920.

would'n, pronounced and, since ca. 1945, often written *wooden*. Wouldn't: sol., esp. Cockney: (?) C. 16–20.

wouldn't be in it, I or he, etc. I, he, wouldn't take part: Australian c.p.: since ca. 1945. (B.P.)

wouldn't it! Short for *wouldn't it make you sick?*, angry: Australian c.p.: since ca. 1925. B., 1942.—2. But it is also an Australian c.p. that, dating from the 1930's, is elliptical for 'wouldn't

it make you laugh?' Jon Cleary, *The Climate of Courage*, 1954, 'Asking your wife if you can write to her. Wouldn't it?'

Barry Prentice glosses the phrase thus: '[It] is an expression in its own right, but I personally wouldn't extend it as you have done. *Wouldn't it give you the pip—the shits—the tom-tits—a touch of them*, or *wouldn't it rock you* or *rotate you*, are all more likely in this case.' All these expressions are recorded in either the *Dict.* or the *Supplement.*

wouldn't it make you spit chips (Australian) or **blood** (English) or **. . . rot your socks** (Australian). A c.p. of disgust: since, respectively, ca. 1920—ca. 1910—ca. 1930. (Partly B.P.)

wouldn't it rock you!; wouldn't it rotate you! New Zealand servicemen's, esp. soldiers': resp. 1941–5 and 1942–5. (J. H. Henderson, *Gunner Inglorious*, 1945.) The latter c.p. merely elaborates the former and the former elaborates, as it arises from, *rock*, v., 3.

wouldn't read about it, you—but occ. **he** or **she** or **they.** It would amaze—it amazes—you (or him or . . .); it 'beats the band': New Zealand c.p.: since ca. 1935. Slatter. Also Aus., as in Mary Durack, *Keep Him My Country*, 1955, '"Blimey!" Wilde exclaimed. "You wouldn't read about it."'

wouldn't touch (it—her—him—you—etc.) **with a forty-foot pole.** A c.p. that, mostly preceded by *I*, indicates the uttermost distaste or contempt: C. 20. Not solely Australian, *pace* B.

woune is Randle Holme's form of *won*, stolen.

wowser (p. 966). Adopted, ca. 1925, by New Zealand. (R. G. C. McNab in *The Press*, Christchurch, New Zealand, April 2, 1938.)—2. (Ex sense 1: p. 966.) Since ca. 1945, the sense has tended to > narrowed to 'teetotaller'—as in Culotta, 1957.—3. 'A blue-stocking' (B., 1959): Aus.: since late 1940's. Most unfair to blue-stockings, many of whom are anything but wowsers.

wowsery. Puritanical: Australian coll.: since ca. 1925. (B., *Australia Speaks*, 1953.) Ex *wowser* (p. 966).

wrap rascal (p. 966). Half a century earlier in *The London Evening Post*, 1738.

wrap up, usually in imperative. To cease talking; also, stop making a row or a noisy fuss: Services: since ca. 1930. Grenfell Finn-Smith, in list communicated in April 1942; H. & P., 1943. Prob. ex *wrapping up* preparatory to cold-weather departure.—2. See **wrapped-up** (below).—3. To crash-land (an aircraft): R.A.F.: since ca. 1938. Jackson, 'Thus, "I'm afraid I've wrapped her up, sir".' I.e. to cause to *fold up*.—4. (Contrast sense 1.) Only as *wrap up!*, 'a cry of despair at the imbecility of one's superior or at one's own state of boredom' (P-G-R.): Army: since ca. 1935.—5. To thoroughly understand: Australian airmen's: since ca. 1939. (B., 1943.) Probably ex:

wrapped(-)up.—2. Carefully arranged; carefully prepared; entirely in order: Services: since ca. 1935. H. & P. 'Don't worry; it's all wrapped up!' Often shortened to *wrapped*. Cf. **buttoned up** and **sewn up.**

wrapper. An overcoat, a top coat: fast life: ca. 1810–45. P. Egan, *Finish*, 1828. Cf. **wrap-rascal.**

wrath of God, like the. 'The wrath of God . . . To my children it is just a phrase, like "nothing on earth". I hear Christine and her friends saying that a dress or a play is "like the wrath of God" [i.e. terrible]. It seems to me to be one of the catch-words of 1936,' Stephen McKenna, *Last Confession*, 1937: Society c.p., † by the end of 1939. Still common in Canada at least as late as May 1959. (Leechman.) Nor, even in Britain, did it quite disappear in 1939; have myself heard it, occasionally, during the 1950's.—2. Feeling very ill, esp. if from a bad hangover: since ca. 1950. (Peter Sanders.)

wreck. A recreation ground: Cockneys': C. 20. A deliberate perversion of **rec**, q.v. in *Dict.*—2. A 'dud' boy: Public Schools': since ca. 1925. Marples. Ex *total wreck*.

Wrecker's Retreat, the. The R.N. School of Navigation: Naval: C. 20; since 1941, merely reminiscent. Granville, 'This building, perhaps the oldest in Portsmouth Dockyard, was destroyed by enemy action during the Hitler War.'

wren, 2 (p. 966): since 1930 at latest, it has been j.

Wrenlin (or w). A Wren 'gremlin': Fleet Air Arm: 1940–5. (P-G-R.)

wrennery. Quarters or billets of the Wrens: Services (esp. Navy and W.R.N.S.): since 1920. H. & P. See **wren,** 2: *Wren*, by the way, has long been the official term.

wren-pecked. Wren - beset; Wren - harrassed: Naval: 1940 +. Granville. Poor, *poor* fellow!

wriggle like a cut snake. To be evasive, shifty; to toady: Australian: C. 20. B., 1942.

wring one's sock out. (Of men) to urinate: jocular rather than euphemistic: C. 20.

*****wring oneself.** To change one's clothes: c.: from ca. 1860; ob. B. & L. Ex *wring (out) one's clothes*.

write-off. 'A crashed 'plane; equipment beyond repair' (Partridge, 1945): since ca. 1930: R.A.F. coll. >, by 1944, j. Ex its orig. sense, 'something beyond repair which must be written off the station inventory' (H. & P.).

write oneself off. To get killed, esp., through carelessness or impetuousness: R.A.F.: since 1939. Jackson. Cf. prec. and *written off*.

write to 'John Bull' about it, or ... **'The Times'** ... If you wish to complain, write to the newspapers: c.p.: resp., ca. 1910–30 (before *John Bull* turned genteel) and late C. 19–20.

write-up. A eulogistic paragraph or 'feature' or article: journalists' coll.: since ca. 1945.

write (an account) **with a fork.** To charge three times as much: N.T., Australia: since ca. 1925. Ernestine Hill, *The Territory*, 1951. Ex a fork's three tines.

written off. (Of aircraft) damaged, esp. crashed, beyond repair; (of a person) killed, esp. as in prec. entry: R.A.F., resp. coll. and, for persons, s.: resp. ca. 1930 and ca. 1939. Jackson. Cf. **write-off.**

wrong. Silly, foolish; extremely eccentric, or slightly mad: Australian: since early 1920's. B., 1942, 'I.e., wrong in the head'.

wrong, get (someone). To mistake his spoken meaning or unexpressed intentions: coll.: since the early 1920's. 'Don't get me wrong, I mean you no harm.'—2. To render a girl pregnant; also v.i.: North Country: C. 20. Mostly among women and girls, as in 'Don't do that, or you'll get me wrong' (render me pregnant).

wrong side of the hedge when the brains were given away, (he) was on the. He is brainless, or stupid, or at the least very dull: c.p.: ca. 1810–80. In late C. 19–20, the form is *on the wrong side of the door when (the) brains were handed out.*

wrong 'un (p. 967).—5. Hence, esp. in *tip a wrong 'un*, to prophesy wrongly, make a bad guess. as in Howard Spring, *Rachel Rosing*, 1935, concerning a promising actress, 'Hansford has never been known to tip a wrong 'un.'

wrought. An Australian spelling-variant of *rort*.

W's, between the two. Between wind and water: ca. 1830–70. *Sinks*, 1848.

wuff. To shoot (a person) dead; to blast with gunfire: Guards': 1940–5. Roger Grinstead, *They Dug a Hole*, 1946. Echoic.

wuffler. A guinea-piece; a Sovereign: late C. 19–20; ob.

wulla or **wuller!** There you are: Army: 1914–19. Ex Fr. *voilà*.

wurley. A hut: Australian coll.: late C. 19–20. B., 1942. Ex Aboriginal.

wuss. See **ss.**

wusser dates from the 1880's, if not indeed earlier. (B. & L.)

wust. Worst: rather illiterate coll., mostly Cockneys': C. 19–20. Cf. **wuss** (*Dict.*).

Wyckers. Wycliffe Hall, Oxford: undergraduates' (— 1940). Marples, 2.

X

*X, adj. Annoyed, irritated: since ca. 1945: c. >, by 1960, also s. (Robin Cook, *The Crust on Its Uppers*, 1962). By a pun on S.E. *cross*, n., and *cross*, irritable, angry.

X-chaser (p. 967). Since ca. 1905. 'Taffrail', *The Sub*, 1917. The *x* is that *x* which figures so disturbingly in mathematics.—2. Hence, an ardent mathematician: Naval: since ca. 1910. Granville.

X-ray art. 'A form of aboriginal bark and cave painting which shows internal parts of human and animal anatomy' (B., 1959): Aus. artists' and art-critics' coll.: since ca. 1950. Technically known as *mimi art*.

X.Y.Z.—2. A hack of all work: literary: ca. 1887–1905. B. & L. Ex an advertiser in *The Times*: using this pseudonym and offering to do any sort of literary work at unprofessionally low prices.

xaroshie. See khorosho.

Y

Y, the. The Y.M.C.A.: Services: 1939–45. (Jackson.) Used elsewhere since ca. 1919: see, e.g., C. S. Archer, *China Servant*, 1946. Short for **Y.M.** (p. 968).

ya. You are: Australian illiteracy: mid-C. 19–20. Lawson Glassop, *We Were the Rats*, 1944, ' "Mick," he said, "ya me mate." ' But *ya* for 'you' is a world-wide illiteracy, as in ' "I've lived with ya an' I've fought with ya",' ibid.

yabbadabba doo! A cry of exaltation: Australian surfers': since ca. 1961. (B.P.) Cf. **hubba dubba!** above.

yabber.—2. (Ex sense 1: p. 968.) To chatter: Australian: C. 20. (Culotta, 1957.)

Of sense 1 (p. 968), B.P. remarks that 'although perhaps influenced by some such Aboriginal word as *yabba*, the word prob. derives ex synonymous S.E. *jabber*'.

yabby, v. To fish for fresh-water crayfish: Australian coll.: C. 20. In, e.g., Kylie Tennant, *The Battlers*, 1941. Ex **yabbie** (p. 968), which, by the way, occurs in, e.g., 'Tom Collins', *Such Is Life*, 1903.

yack, n. Food, esp. in *hard yack* (= hard tack): Australian: since ca. 1955. It is, indeed, correct for **yakker,** 3 and 4, as B.P. has pointed out.

yack, v., often **yak;** in full, **ya(c)kety-ya(c)k.** Both n. and v.: voluble talk; to talk volubly and either idly or stupidly or both: adopted, in the late 1950's, ex U.S. Clearly echoic of idle chatter: *yack-yack-yack*.—2. Hence, a or to talk, or even a, or to, lecture: since ca. 1962. Early in 1964, the late Nancy Spain, in a *News of the World* article, said, 'I was to yak'—deliver a talk —'in Spennymoor (or some such place) that night.'

yackum. Human excrement: low: late C. 19–20.

yair. Yes: Australian illiterate: C. 20. 'The vowel sound is a definite diphthong' (B.P.).

yak; yakety-yak. See **yack,** v., above.

yakker.—3. Food: Australian: C. 20. B., 1942.—4. Talk: Australian: C. 20. Baker. These two senses are loose, perverse, corrupt.—5. Hence, a contract: Australian rural: since ca. 1925. (Sarah Campion.)

yam, n., dates from before 1890. It is, e.g., recorded by B. & L.

yamen or **yaman.** 'A mandarin, a prefect's residence': pidgin: mid-C. 19–20. Ibid.

Yank.—2. An American motor car: esp. in the secondhand-car business: since ca. 1945. (Anthony Cowdy in the coloured supplement of *The Sunday Times*, Oct. 24, 1965.)

yank; yankee shout. A drinking bout or party or rendezvous at which everyone pays for his own drinks: Australian: 1940 +. B., 1942.

Yankee is Australian coll. for *American* in its nuance 'equal for all', as in *Yankee tournament*: since ca. 1930. (B., 1943.)

yankee particular. A glass of spirits: Austra-

lian: ca. 1820–80. J. W., *Perils, Pastimes and Pleasures*, 1849.

yankee shout. See **yank** above.

yankee tournament. An American tournament (everyone playing everyone else): sporting coll.: since ca. 1930. Baker.

Yanking. 'Popular expression to describe the activities of girls who specialize in picking up American soldiers' (or, come to that, sailors or airmen): since 1943; by 1966, slightly ob. Paul Tempest, *Lag's Lexicon*, 1950.

Yanks. Cheap American magazines flooding British bookstalls ca. 1930–9: coll.: since ca. 1930.

yap. 'To retort angrily' (L. E. F. English, 1955): Newfoundland coll.: late C. 19–20. Cf. sense 2: p. 969.

yapper. A Bofors gun: Army and Civil Defence: 1940 +. It barks very loudly.

yappies, the; or **the puppies.** 'The dogs'— greyhound racing or coursing: Australian: since ca. 1946. (B.P.)

yard, v. To 'corral' or 'round up', to get hold of: Canadian: since late 1950's. 'We yarded Harry and Alice and tooled off to the dance'—adduced by Dr Douglas Leechman, who remarks, 'First heard by me 3rd Dec. 1961.'

yard goose: usually pl., *yard geese*, yard switchmen: Canadian railroadmen's: adopted, before 1931, ex U.S.

yard of tripe. A pipe: rhyming: 1851, Mayhew, I; ob.

yarker. Ear: Cockneys': late (? mid-)C. 19–20. Atkinson. I.e., *harker*, that with which one hearkens.

yarm. A rare form of **yarrum** (*Dict.*).

Yarmouth (p. 969) occurs esp. in *go* (above all *have gone*) *Yarmouth*, to go—chiefly, to have gone— mad.

Yarmouth bloater.—2. A motor-car: rhyming s.: since ca. 1910. Franklyn, *Rhyming*, 'Merely a contracted and less derisive form of *tea for two* and . . .'

yarra. Stupid; eccentric or even crazy: Australian: since ca. 1910. (B., 1943.) Ex Aboriginal. The intensive is '*stone yarra*, completely mad' (B., 1959).

Yarra-bankers. Loafers and down-and-outs idling on the banks of the Yarra River: Melbourne coll.: C. 20. B., 1942.—2. Melbourne soap-box orators: Melbournites': since ca. 1914. (B., 1943.) On the banks of the Yarra river.

yarraman (p. 969). Obsolete by 1942 (Baker).

yasmé. See 'Prisoner-of-War Slang', 7.— **Yasmé Villa:** ibid.

yawner. A very wide brook: hunting: since ca. 1830. (Rolf Boldrewood, *My Run Home*, 1897, at p. 360.)

ye'. See **yeh** (*Dict.*).

yea. 'About "yea" high, or "yea" long, or

1521

broad, with appropriate gestures, meaning about "so" high, etc. Heard in the last 4 or 5 years' (Leechman, April 1967). Canadian.

year dot, in the. A long time ago: mostly Londoners': C. 20. At that point in historical times which lies between the last year B.C. and the first year A.D.

yearling. A boy that has been at the School for three terms: Charterhouse: C. 20. There, a new boy is a **new bug** (q.v. in *Dict.*); a boy that has been at the School for a term is an *ex new bug*; for two terms, an *ex ex new bug*: the second and the third are rather j. than eligible.—2. Simply a boy in his first year: Charterhouse: C. 20. (Peter Sanders.)

Yeddan; Yeddican. Variants (ca. 1880–1910) of **Yid** (*Dict.*). B. & L.

Yehudi; usually in pl. A Jew: Army officers' (esp. in Palestine): since ca. 1941. Ex a frequent Jewish given-name.

yell. Beer: 1848. *Sinks,* 'A pint of yell'; † by 1900. Short for its *yellow* colour.—2. A (tremendous) joke: mostly theatrical: since late 1950's. '"Of course Harry made it sound a bit of a yell"' (Ngaio Marsh, *Death at The Dolphin,* 1967).

yeller feller. An Aboriginal half-caste: Aus.: late C. 19–20. Xavier Herbert, *Capricornia,* 1939; B., 1959.

yellow, n.—3. A punishment at Greenwich College: ca. 1820–60. *Sessions,* 1831, where also *be yellowed,* to undergo punishment there.—4. (Pl. *yellow.*) A pound sterling: c.: from ca. 1910. *The Pawnshop Murder*: 'Five hundred "yellow" to pay for it.' Ex the colour of a sovereign.

yellow, v.—3. See **yellow, n.,** 3 (above).

yellow Admiral (p. 970). Since ca. 1925, it has predominantly signified 'Captain promoted, upon retirement, to Rear Admiral' (Granville): Naval.

yellow-back.—2. 'A gob of phlegm' (B., 1942): Australian low: C. 20.

yellow belly.—4. A coward: low: from ca. 1925. Ex U.S.—5. (Cf. 2.) A Central American: British and Americans in C. America: late C. 19–20.—6. A Japanese: Australian: 1942–5, then historical. Dymphna Cusack, *Southern Steel,* 1953.—7. A Yorkshire and Lancashire Railway tank engine: railwaymen's: ? ca. 1910–25. (*Railway.*)

yellow Bob. The Yellow Robin: Australian: late C. 19–20. (B., 1943.)

yellow doughnut. The small collapsible dinghy carried by modern aircraft: Air Force: since ca. 1936. H. & P., 'It looks like a doughnut from the air.'

yellow feller. A half-caste Aboriginal: N. Australian coll.: late C. 19–20. (Jean Devanney, *Travels in North Queensland,* 1951.)

yellow fever.—3. Spy mania: Singapore: ca. 1930–41. How enthusiastically we Britons succeeded in shutting our eyes to the obvious danger!

yellow jack (p. 970) occurs a year earlier in W. N. Glascock, *The Naval Sketch-Book,* 1834, at p. 231. And two years earlier still in Frederick Chamier, *The Life of a Sailor,* 1832. (Moe.)

yellow-jacket (p. 970) is common also in U.S.

yellow Monday and **yellow Tuesday** are only two of the numerous Australian folk-names for various kinds of cicada. The second is analogous with the first; the element *Monday* folk-etymologises *mundee,* as heard, by the early settlers, in the speech of the Port Jackson natives, as also does yellow for the first part of the Aboriginal name.

See S. J. Baker, *Australia Speaks,* 1953, at p. 110.

yellow mould. A sovereign: tailors': from ca. 1860; slightly ob. B. & L.

yellow peril.—2. A trainer aircraft: R.A.F.: since ca. 1940. (A proper 'plane, not a Link Trainer.) Jackson, 1943. Ex its colour—also ex the 'yellow streak' it may display if carelessly handled.—3. 'Navy cake'—slab cake, yellowish and not notably edible, sold in the canteen: Naval: 1939 +. Granville.—4. A haddock: Naval (— 1950).

yellow silk (p. 970): ob. by 1960. Franklyn 2nd.

*****yellow stuff.** Gold: c.: mid-C. 19–20. B. & L.—2. Hence, gold stolen by miners from the company's mine they're working: Australian miners': C. 20. (Gavin Casey, *Downhill Is Easier,* 1945.)

yellowback. See **yellow-back** (*Dict.*).

yells, bells and knells. An Australian variation of **hatch, match and despatch column** on p. 378.

yelper.—3. A whining fellow: coll.: ca. 1830–90. *Sinks,* 1848.—4. The Red-Necked Avocet: Australian: late C. 19–20. (B., 1943.) Ex its distinctive call or note.

yelper, get the. To be discharged from employment; proletarian: ca. 1870–1910. B. & L.

Yen, the. *The Yorkshire Evening News:* journalists': since ca. 1933. Cf.:

yen. A passion; intense craving; esp. in *have a yen for*: U.S.: adopted in England ca. 1931. (See *Underworld.*) The etymology is obscure: there has been much 'talk about it and about'. My own guess, for I cannot prove it, is that it is a thinned form of *yearn*. But *Webster's New International Dictionary* convincingly adduces Chinese (Pekin dialect) *yen,* 'smoke; hence, opium'.

Yenham's. See **Harry Freeman's,** 2.

yennep; yennep flatch (p. 970). Earlier in Mayhew, I, 1851.

Yeos, the. The Yeomanry: Army: late C. 19–20.

yer blood's worth bottling! An Australian c.p., either of very warm approval or of hearty congratulation: since ca. 1950. 'To Nino Culotta, therefore, in thanks for this book, I say: "Thanks, mate. Yer blood's worth bottling"': conclusion of Russell Braddon's Preface to the English edition (1958) of *They're a Weird Mob,* 1957.

yes, all day. See **all day** above.

yes—but in the right place. A fast girl's c.p. rejoinder to 'You're cracked' or 'You must be cracked': late C. 19–20. I first heard it, in 1922, from a man-about-town.

yes, but not the inclination. A c.p., in jocular reply to 'Have you the time?': C. 20.

yes, she's with us! A c.p. reply to **does your mother know you're out?** (p. 230): since ca. 1920.

yes, teacher; or **yes, doctor.** A jocular yet ironic c.p. addressed to someone who is fond of airing his knowledge on general matters or esp.— the latter form—on medical ailments and cures: since ca. 1910. (A. B. Petch.)

yes(-)girls. Girls very easily persuaded to participate in sexual intimacy: since ca. 1960. After **yes man** on p. 970.

yessir! See **yes'm** (*Dict.*).—**yesman.** See **yes man** (*Dict.*).

yesterday, with a face like. See **with a face . . .**

yet to be. Usually, costing nothing; occ., unrestrained: rhyming s. (on *free*): C. 20. Franklyn 2nd.

yeute. No; not: Punch and Judy showmen's: mid-C. 19–20. B. & L.

Yid (or **yid**); **half a yid.** A sovereign, £1; a half-sovereign, 10 shillings: Australian: C. 20. (Dal Stivens, *Jimmy Brockett*, 1951.) Rhyming on *quid* (£1).

Yiddified. Anti-Semitic: Jewish: since 1934. I.e. Yiddish *Yiddenfeint*, itself = *Yid* + Ger. *Feind*, an enemy. Therefore, lit., inimical to the 'Yids'. Possibly in ironic contrast with the usual sense.

Yiddisher fiddle. A minor cheating or illegality: since ca. 1925; by 1960, ob. (Franklyn 2nd.) An elaboration of **fiddle** n., 12, above.

Yiddisher piano. A cash-register: Cockney street-boys': from ca. 1910.

yiesk. (A) fish: Shelta: C. 18–20. B. & L.

yike. A hot argument; a quarrel; a fight: Australian low: since ca. 1920. B., 1942. A perversion of *fight*?

yikes! An exclamation of surprise or excitement or shock or pain: Australian, adopted, ca. 1945, ex U.S., and common esp. among children. Ex *yoicks!*—or is it a euphemism for *Christ* (cf. **crikey** on p. 191)?

Yim, Yoe and Yesus. Three knaves: Australian poker-players': since ca. 1930. (B., 1953.)

yimpkin. 'Perhaps. Expressive of extreme scepticism. "When Tunis falls, we're all going home, yimpkin!"': Army in North Africa, 1943. Peter Sanders in *The Sunday Times* magazine, Sept. 10, 1967. Arbitrary.

Ying-gen. An Englishman: pidgin: from ca. 1930. B. & L.

yippee! An exclamation of delight: since ca. 1930. Allan A. Michie & Walter Graebner, *Their Finest Hour*, 1940.

yiu. A street: Punch and Judy showmen's: mid-C. 19–20. B. & L. ? ex Fr. *rue*.

ynork. Mostly in *flatch ynork*, a half-crown: back s.: 1851, Mayhew, I.

yo-yo, up and down like a. Applied mostly to a person bobbing up and down, hence also to, e.g., statistics: Australian: since ca. 1930. (B.P.)

yob.—4. 'A raw recruit; a very much countrified airman (cf. *swede*),' Partridge, 1945: R.A.F.: since ca. 1937. Earliest dictionary-recording: Jackson, 1943. Ex senses 1 and 3 (p. 971). Sense 3, by the way, occurs in A. Neil Lyons, 1908.
Sense 3 (p. 971), a lout, an oaf: by ca. 1930, fairly gen. London s.

yob-gab. Boys' talk or 'ziph' (q.v. in *Dict.*): coster's s., and c.: mid-C. 19–20. B. & L.

yobbo. A post-1910 variant of **yob**, 3 (*Dict.*). In, e.g., *The Evening News*, March 7, 1938, and in Herbert Hodge, *Cab, Sir?*, 1939.—2. Hence, an arrogant and resentful, loutish and violent Teddy boy: low, mostly London: since ca. 1948. An extension of *yob*, as Anglo-Irish *boyo* is of S.E. *boy*; cf. *yob*, 3, on p. 971. (*The Manchester Guardian*, Sept. 11, 1958—a letter from A. T. Reeves.)

yock, 1, is also c. of mid-C. 19–20. B. & L.—3. In Shelta (where also spelt *yok* or *yoke*), a man: C. 18–20. B. & L.—4. See:

yog (p. 971), a gentile: 'Pronounced *yock* for euphony,' *The Leader*, Jan. 1939.

yoke. An apparatus; almost any gadget:

Anglo-Irish: since ca. 1925. In *The Student Body*, 1958, Nigel Fitzgerald applies it to a revolver.

yonnie. A pebble, small stone: Australian: late C. 19–20. B., 1942. Aboriginal?

Yorkshire, n.—2. Yorkshire pudding: coll.: late C. 19–20. Esp. in 'roast and Yorkshire'.

Yorkshire tike.—2. (Often shortened to *Yorkshire*.) A microphone: since ca. 1945. Rhyming on s. *mike*. (Communicated by Dallas Bower in 1957.)

Yorky. A Yorkshireman (or -woman): coll.: C. 19–20. *Boxiana* II, 1818; James Curtis, *They Ride by Night*, 1938.

yorter. You ought to: Australian semi-literate coll.: late C. 19–20. Jock Marshall & Russell Drysdale, *Journey among Men*, 1962, p. 117, '"I tell yer, fellas, yorter go there."'

you. Short for **you and me** (p. 971): since ca. 1910. Gerald Kersh, 1941.

you and me.—2. A pea: Australian rhyming s.: C. 20.—3. A urination: rhyming s. (on **pee**): C. 20. —4. A flea: rhyming s.: ca. 1880–1914. Franklyn 2nd.

you—and who else?; Australian, **you and whose army?** A c.p. of derisive defiance addressed to a belligerent opponent: since, resp., ca. 1920 and 1944. 'I reckon I can fight you any day.'— 'Yeah, you and whose army?' (B.P.)

you beaut! A c.p., indicative originally and predominantly of approval, hence occasionally of derision: Australian: since ca. 1925. (B., 1943.)

you can always stoop and pick up nothing! A c.p. remark made by a friend after a 'row' or by a parent concerning a child's intended husband (or wife): mostly Cockneys': C. 20.

you can hear them change their minds. A c.p. that, dating from ca. 1946, satirizes the thinness of the walls in post-war flats and council houses.

you can put a ring around that one. That's one thing you *can* be sure of: a New Zealand c.p.: since ca. 1925. (Slatter.) To 'ring' it so that it stands out on the page.

you can say that again! A c.p. expressive of heartfelt agreement: adopted, ca. 1930, ex U.S. Cf. **say it again!** above.

you can say that in spades! A c.p. of heartfelt agreement: since ca. 1945. 'He saw me properly then for the first time . . . "You look bushed. You need a drink."—"You can say that in spades," I said': John Welcome, *Beware of Midnight*, 1961. Cf. the preceding entry.

you can take it from me! You may accept it as true: c.p.: since ca. 1910.

you can't do that there 'ere! and **'ere, what's all this?** C.pp. that originated in derision at the illiteracy of the old-style police constable: C. 20.

you can't fly on one wing. A c.p. invitation to one more drink before departure: Canadian: since ca. 1945. (Leechman.)

you can't take it with you! A C. 20 c.p. directed at one who, saving money, loses happiness. In, e.g., S. P. B. Mais, *Cape Sauce*, 1948.

you can't think. You cannot imagine it; to an incredible degree: non-aristocratic, non-cultured c.p.: from ca. 1890. W. Pett Ridge, *Minor Dialogues*, 1895, 'She took up such a 'igh and mighty attitude, you can't think.' This *you can't think*, coming at the end of a phrase or sentence, derives naturally ex that *you can't think!* (see, in *Dict.*, at **think!, only**) which precedes a sentence.

you can't win. A Canadian c.p., dating since ca. 1950 and 'expressing the impossibility of coming out on top and the futility of kicking against the pricks' (Leechman). Was it Ring Lardner who said, approximately, 'The odds are 6–4 against life'? But then, no spirited person would refuse such odds.

you can't win them all; in England, often . . . **'em all.** You can't *always* succeed: an American c.p., adopted ca. 1960, yet hardly acclimatized before ca. 1964. You can't win every game or battle—or girl.

you could piss from one end of the country to the other. A c.p., in reference to the small size of England: since ca. 1910.

you couldn't be more right! A c.p. of entire agreement: Australian: since the late 1930's. (B.P.) A variant of *I couldn't agree more*, q.v. at **couldn't care less** above.

you couldn't blow the froth off a pint or **knock a pint back; you couldn't fight (or punch) your way out of a paper bag.** C.pp. addressed, in C. 20, to a man boasting of his strength or of his fist-fighting ability; the third is mainly Australian.

you couldn't throw your hat over the workhouse wall! You have many illegitimate children in there: a Cockney c.p. of C. 20. To retrieve one's hat thrown over the wall would be to expose oneself to the risk of recognition.

you don't have to buy . . . See **why buy . . . ?**

you don't know whether (*a*) **you want a shit or a haircut,** or (*b*) **your arse-hole's bored or punched.** These low C. 20 c.pp. are used, the former to impute befuddlement, the latter to undermine an argument.—2. With substitution of *won't* for *don't*, both of these c.pp. are, in reaction to insult or to horse-play, intended to deter or to intimidate: since ca. 1910. (Atkinson.)

you don't look at the mantel-piece when (or while) you're poking the fire. A c.p. (verging on the proverbial) in reference to sexual intercourse: late C. 19–20.

you don't say! A c.p. indicative of astonishment: C. 20. Short for *you don't say so!*

you fasten on! Go on!; proceed: non-aristocratic: from ca. 1870; ob. B. & L.

you get nothing for nothing . . . See **nothing for nothing** above.

you give me the balls-ache!; or **you give me a pain in the arm—arse—back—balls—neck—etc.,** etc. I disagree with your point of view; or, I disapprove of your behaviour: c.pp., the first, third, fifth being low; mostly Londoners': C. 20.

you have (usually, you've) been doing naughty things. A bourgeois c.p. addressed, C. 20, to a young couple when, obviously, the wife is pregnant.

you have it made or **you've got it made.** You're on the point of succeeding: Australian c.p.: adopted, ca. 1944, ex U.S.

you haven't a dirty pound note or two (that) you don't want, have you? (or, **I suppose?**) A borrower's 'touch'—which may be merely playful: since ca. 1925.

you haven't got the brains you were born with! A derisive c.p.: C. 20.

you kill me! You're so funny!: ironic c.p.: since ca. 1935. Also, since ca. 1942, *you slay me!*

you know. This stop-gap, almost meaningless phrase ranks as coll. and dates from at least as early as C. 18.—2. Hence, in the Services, its use, as a coll., in contradiction. Thus: 'I'm just off to the flicks.'—'You're not, you know. You're duty stooge.' Apparently it arose in the 1920's and perhaps it originated in the R.A.F.

you know the old saying: the Persian Gulf's the arse-hole of the world, and Shaiba's half-way up it. A depreciatory c.p.: R.A.F. and Army: since the 1920's. At Shaiba—properly, Shu'aiba—there was, for many years, a transit camp. (Atkinson.) This distinction has, since the middle 1920's been claimed by the R.A.F. for such unpopular stations as Aden, Basra, Freetown, Shaiba (in Iraq), Suez.

you know what (? or !) An introductory c.p.: a mere announcer of a phrase or of a statement: mid-C. 19–20; perhaps going back to late C. 17.

you know what thought did! See **thought did!** . . . in the *Dict.* 'The pert Cockney boy's response is, "No, 'e never! 'E only thought 'e did!"' (Julian Franklyn, Jan. 3, 1968): C. 20.

you know what you can do! or **what to do with it!** or **what you can do with it!** *I* don't want it, *you* can 'stick it' (in the anatomical nuance): since ca. 1925: adopted by the Services. Partridge, 1945.

you make a better door than a window. A C. 20 New Zealand c.p., addressed to a person getting in the light. B., 1941. Cf. **glazier? . . .** in the *Dict.*

you make I laugh! A derisive variation of the contemptuous *you make me laugh!*: lower-middle class c.p.: ca. 1905–40.

you may have broken your mother's heart, but you bloody well won't break mine! A drill instructors', esp. drill sergeants', c.p.: dating from ca. 1870—or earlier (? during the Napoleonic Wars).

you must be joking! See **are you kidding?**

you never did. You never did hear the like of it; you've never heard anything so funny: Cockney coll.: from ca. 1870. A. Neil Lyons, *Matilda's Mabel*, 1903, 'My dearest Tilda. Such a go you never did! Mr Appleby proposed to me this afternoon!'

you never get a satisfied cock without a wet pussy. A low c.p.: C. 20. 'The crude and the undeniable in juxtaposition are a frequent astringent herb of popular speech': Laurie Atkinson, Sept. 11, 1967.

you never know! You never know what may come of it: c.p.: late C. 19–20.

you never know your luck! A C. 20 c.p.; probably elaborating the preceding.

you pays your money and you takes your choice. Except when literal, it is a c.p.: C. 20.

you play like I fuck. You're a poor card-player: Canadian Army c.p.: 1939–45.

you ring the bell. You're accepted by the chaps: Services (esp. R.A.F.): since 1939. H. & P. See **ring a bell.**

you see! At **see!** above.

you shock my mahogany! A silly c.p. (you offend my morals) among the empty-headed: since ca. 1935; by 1948, ob.

you should pay for them! A jocular c.p., addressed to the wearer of squeaky boots or shoes: late C. 19–20. The wearer sometimes forestalls the witticism by saying (*I*) *haven't paid for them yet.* (They squeak in protest.)

you shouldn't have joined! A Forces' c.p. directed in 1939–45 at a complaint against the Service. (Atkinson.)

you shouldn't have joined if you can't take a joke.

A c.p. addressed to one complaining among workmates, esp. of being put upon: since ca. 1945: ? orig. servicemen's.

you shread it, Wheat. See 'Canadian'. With pun on *said it* and *shredded wheat*.

you slay me. See **you kill me**.

you stick your prick . . . See **I wouldn't . . .**

you still wouldn't like it on your eye for a wart. A low c.p. 'retort to imputation of undersized penis, but, even more, with boring suggestiveness and knowing wink when anything is thought not big enough' (Laurie Atkinson, Sept. 11, 1967): C. 20.

you talk like a halfpenny book. You talk foolishly: a Liverpool c.p.: late C. 19–20; by 1955, rather ob.

you (or **you'd**) **want to know all the ins-and-outs of a nag's arse!** You're very inquisitive: Cockney: late C. 19–20.

you want your head read! You need a phrenologist: a c.p. addressed to someone who has done or said something exceptionally stupid: since ca. 1920. (B.P.)

you were born stupid—you've learnt nothing—and you've forgotten (even) that. A c.p., not only Australian, current throughout C. 20. B.P., who adds that 'it is known in Austria and Germany'.

you weren't born—you were pissed up against the wall and hatched in the sun. This c.p., prompted by, e.g., 'before I was born', is a piece of stock wit beloved by the unfastidious male section of the proletariat.

you won't know . . . See **you don't know**.

you won't know yourself, as in 'Try on this overcoat—you won't know yourself': c.p.: C. 20.

you won't melt! A c.p. addressed to a child objecting to going out—esp. to running an errand —in the rain: C. 19–20 (? even older).

you wouldn't chuckle. You wouldn't think so: Forces' c.p.: since ca. 1938.—2. You bet I would: Forces': since ca. 1940. Cf.:

you wouldn't fuck it (or **rob it**). 'Signifies the complete positive to a question or a statement. "It's cold this morning." "You wouldn't rob it" (or "fuck it"),' R. M. Davison, letter of Sept. 26, 1942: R.A.F. c.p.: since ca. 1925. It = S.E. 'And that's no lie.'

you wouldn't knob it, q.v. at **knob,** n., 6 (above), has, esp. in the R.A.F., the further meaning, 'You bet I would!'

you wouldn't read about it. See **wouldn't read . . .** above.

you wouldn't shit me; or **don't shit the troops.** A Canadian Army c.p. (1939–45): I don't believe you.

you'd be (or **get**) **killed in the rush.** A low c.p., addressed to a girl who has just said 'I wouldn't marry you (even) if you were the last man in the world': C. 20. Ex various ribald and scabrous anecdotes.

you'd forget your head if it wasn't screwed on (properly, often preceded by **forget!** A C. 20 c.p. addressed to a forgetful person.

you'd have been taller if they hadn't turned up so much for feet. A Canadian c.p.: since ca. 1930.

you'd have died. You'd have died of laughing: c.p.: since ca. 1920.

you'd only spend it. A c.p. reply to someone saying that he'd like to have a lot of money: late C. 19–20.

you'd soon find it if there was hair round—or all around—it! A drill sergeants' c.p. to very new recruits learning their rifle drill and forbidden to look what they're doing: C. 20, or prob. since ca. 1870.

You'll be smoking next! What a dissipated fellow—or fast girl—you are: a jocular c.p., commenting upon an act very much more audacious or improper: since ca. 1955. Based upon the story of a young boy who has been interfering with, or playing sexually with, the girls of his age or a little older and whose neighbours have complained to his father, who, promising to deal suitably with this grave matter, calls the lad before him and says, 'I hear you've been fooling round with the girls. What a young devil you are! Dammit, you'll be smoking next!' Occasionally allusive, as in 'Why! he'll be smoking next *or* soon'.

you'll be telling me like the girl that you've fahnd (or **found**) **a shilling.** An 'anecdotal c.p. expression of derisive incredulity' (Atkinson): Cockneys': C. 20. Also, *you come home with your drawers torn and say you found the money?*

you'll do yourself out of a job. A jocularity addressed to someone working hard: c.p.: since ca. 1910.

you'll get something you don't want. A C. 20 c.p. When addressed to a man, it implies a venereal disease; to a girl or a young woman, pregnancy.

you'll know me again, won't you! See **do you think . . .**

you'll wake up one of these mornings and find yourself dead. An Anglo-Irish c.p. of late C. 19–20; not much heard since 1945.

Young is a nickname applied in contrast to *Old* to a Moore younger than another man thus surnamed: late C. 19–20. Ex *Old Moore's Monthly Messenger,* a prophetical periodical usually called *Old Moore's* for short.

young bear. A young midshipman very recently come to his first ship: Naval: ca. 1810–60. *The Night Watch* (II, 71), 1828; *The Dublin University Magazine,* Sept. 1834, p. 243, 'I found my brother middies on the whole very agreeable, and as a mark of kindness to the "young bear", I was invited to dine in the gun-room with the officers.' (Moe.)

young doc, the. The Junior Medical Officer: Naval: since ca. 1925. Granville.

young gentlemen, the. The midshipmen: Wardroom ironic coll.: C. 20. Granville. But it goes back to ca. 1810 or perhaps even earlier. It occurs in *The Dublin University Magazine,* Sept. 1836 on p. 263, and, in the singular (' "Young gentleman! pray where's your bed?" '), in Alfred Burton's narrative poem, *The Adventures of Johnny Newcome in the Navy,* 1818. (Moe.)

young one. 'I have been making a *young one* this morning . . . I have been making a truss of hay,' *Sessions,* April 9, 1845: farmers': since ca. 1829. In comparison with a rick of hay.

young student. See 'Tavern terms', § 3, *d.*

your ass-hole's sucking wind. You don't know what you're talking about: low Canadian c.p., common in Army of 1939–45. Note also the low Canadian c.pp. (since ca. 1925): *your ass is sucking blue mud* or *your cock's out a foot,* both meaning 'You are in error'.

your cough's getting better. A c.p. addressed

to one who coughs (not badly): since ca. 1910. Also *you're coughing better*.

your feet won't touch (the ground: cf. next entry). Very quickly; in no time at all: Army c.p.: since ca. 1925. 'Any more of that, my lad, and your feet won't touch'—you'll soon be up before the C.O. (P-G-R.) Cf. *your heels . . .* below.

your guess is as good as mine. A c.p., current since ca. 1943, for a situation where neither party knows the facts. Adopted ex U.S.

your heels won't touch the ground! A minatory c.p., intended to deter or intimidate, esp. as a retort upon insult or horse-play: since ca. 1920. (Atkinson.)

your humble condumble. Your humble servant; I (myself): C. 18. Scott, in letter of Dec. 30, 1808, 'Every assistance that can be afforded by your humble condumble, as Swift says.' By rhyming reduplication. Recorded as early as Swift's *Polite Conversation*, 1738.

your knees aren't brown. A variant of *knees brown . . .*

your lip's bleeding! What big words you're using!: Australian juvenile: since ca. 1945. (B., 1953.) `On the analogy of *tongue-twister*.

your mother does it. An Australian c.p., dating from ca. 1920 and designed to overcome virginal reluctance.

your nose is bleeding. Your trouser-fly is un-done: c.p.: from ca. 1885; slightly ob.

your number's still wet. A variant (ca. 1918 +) of the theme at *before you came up* (p. 44).

you're a big lad for your age. A jocular c.p., addressed to an apprentice or other youthful worker: esp. in factories: late C. 19–20.

you're a poet and don't (or **didn't**) **know it.** See *that's a rhyme . . .*

you're all about—like shit in a field. You're alert and efficient—I *don't* think!: c.p.: C. 20. First, a compliment (see **all about**); then a significant pause; finally a jeer.

you're all mouth and trousers, euphemistic for **you're all prick and breeches.** A c.p. addressed to a loud-talking, blustering man: since ca. 1950, ca. 1920, resp. Laurie Atkinson records hearing the former on TV, July 1, 1964.

you're as much use as tits on a canary. A 'c.p. hurled at inefficient player in baseball, or other field sport' (Leechman): Canadian: since ca. 1945.

you're breaking my heart. See **my heart bleeds for you.**

you're fond of a job. A c.p. to someone doing another's work or unnecessary work: C. 20.

You're getting a big boy—or occasionally **girl**—**now.** To a boy, a mild reproof for petulance or bad manners; to a girl, for (usually accidental) immodesty: c.p.: late C. 19–20.

you're holding up production. You're wasting time (own or other's): R.A.F. (mostly): since 1940. Partridge, 1945.

you're jealous! A jocular c.p. in retort to 'You're drunk': since ca. 1920.

you're not on; occ. **you're on next.** I want nothing to do with you; you don't convince me; you've failed: a Liverpool c.p., dating since ca.

1945. Ex boxing: 'You've been waiting, and expecting to substitute for an absentee—but you're not needed.' (Communicated by Frank Shaw.)

you're on my hook. You're getting in my way: Australian c.p.: ca. 1946–55. Ex angling.

you're selling tea! A facetious variant of *you're telling me!*: ca. 1945–55.

You're so full of shit your eyes are brown. A Canadian Army c.p. (1939–45)—expressing a violent dislike.

you're so sharp you'll be cutting yourself! A late C. 19–20 c.p., addressed to a 'smart' person.

you're the doctor! Whatever you say, (for) *you're* doing it; you're the authority or the expert or the man in charge—and the responsibility is *yours*: c.p., Canadian and English: since ca. 1945. (Leechman.)

yours and hours (p. 972), flowers, is probably a mistaken form of the synonymous *yours and ours*, current among Covent Garden porters and street vendors since ca. 1850. (Based upon Franklyn, *Rhyming*.)

you've a bad cough; occ. **that's a bad cough you have.** A c.p., addressed to one who breaks wind: since ca. 1910.

you've been. Your promised trip (esp. in an aircraft) has been cancelled: R.A.F.: since ca. 1936. H. & P. Cf. **you've had it.**

you've fixed it up nicely for me! No, you don't!; do you think I'm green?!: proletarian c.p.: ca. 1880–1910. B. & L.

you've forgot(ten) the piano! Sarcastic c.p. (C. 20) addressed to one with much baggage; often witheringly by bus conductors.

you've got a smile like a can of worms. A Canadian (? originally fishermen's) c.p., expressing dislike: since ca. 1925.

you've got a swinging brick. Your heart is like stone, you have no emotions: c.p.: North of England: since late 1950's. (David Wharton, June 6, 1966.)

you've got eyes in your head, haven't you? A disparaging c.p.: late C. 19–20.

you've got it all round your neck. A c.p., stig-matizing confusion, esp. inability or hesitancy to complete an explanation: since ca. 1945.

you've got something there. You're on to something good; there's much to be said for it: c.p.: since ca. 1910.

you've had it! See **have had it.**

you've had your time. You're finished, you're 'through'; you're too late: R.A.F.: 1940 +. Gerald Emanuel, letter of March 29, 1945.

you've picked a bad apple. You've chosen badly: c.p.: since ca. 1920.

*****yow, keep.** To stand guard; act as look-out man: Aus. c.: since ca. 1930. B., 1959.

yum-yum (p. 973) is recorded by B. & L., 1890. —2. Hence, as n.: love-letters: Navy: since ca. 1920. H. & P.; Granville.

yunk. A piece, a portion; a lump: Australian: since ca. 1910. (B., 1943.) Ex Aboriginal?

yunk of dodger. A slice of bread: Aus.: since ca. 1919. (B., 1959.) Cf. preceding.

Z

zac is Culotta's spelling of:

zack. Sixpence: New Zealand and Australian: since ca. 1890. This dictionary, 2nd ed., 1938. Perhaps a perversion of *six*; but cf. Dutch *zaakje*, 'small affair'.—2. Hence, a six-months' prison sentence: Australian c.: C. 20. B., 1942.

zack, not worth a. Utterly worthless: Australian C. 20. Ex zack, 1, above.

zambuk. 'A first-aid man in attendance at a sporting contest' (B., 1943): Australian: since ca. 1925. Ex a famous embrocation.

zanth. A chrys*anth*emum: market-gardeners' coll.: late C. 19–20. (Gerald Kersh, *Faces in a Dusty Picture*, 1944.)

Zarp (*Dict.*) is not an anagram but a simple initials-word.

zeck. A variant (B., 1942) of zack (above)—in sense 2.

zift. No good; inferior; ineffectual: Army: C. 20. Arabic for 'pitch, tar, dirt'. (Atkinson.) Perhaps the E. *zift* contracts Ar. *zefut*, weak. (A. McQueen.)

zigzag (p. 973), also zig-a-zag.

zigzig, n. and v. Copulation; to copulate: Services': late C. 19–20. A word known and used throughout the Near and Middle East, and in the Mediterranean. Ultimately, probably echoic. Commoner is jig-a-jig, q.v. on p. 438.

zilch. Nothing: R.A.F.: since ca. 1948. Just possibly ex zero + nil + German nichts.

zing. See oomph.—2. Earlier, however, it had been current in the Guards Regiment for 'vigour, energy'. Gerald Kersh, *They Die with Their Boots Clean*, 1941, records it as having been used in 1940 by a P.T. instructor, 'I'll soon get that paleness off your faces and put some zing into those limbs.'

zippy.—2. Hence, fast, speedy: since ca. 1930. 'My idea . . . was to get a zippy load into Richon, and then move on to T.A.': Ian Jeffries, *Thirteen Days*, 1958.

zizz, n. A rest period: Services: since ca. 1925. H. & P. Echoic ex the hissing and whistling noises made by those who fall off to sleep; or perhaps coined by regulars with service in tropical countries, where, at night, they had so often heard the mosquitoes going 'zizz-zizz-zizz . . .'.

zizz, v. To sleep: mostly R.A.F.: since ca. 1930. Ex the n. By 1940, via the Fleet Air Arm, it was fairly common in the Navy. (Granville.) It may, however, derive ex the fact that newspaper cartoons (e.g. Felix) have long used a string of z's issuing from the mouths of their somnolent characters.

zizz-pudding. A heavy suet-pudding: Naval: 1940 +. Granville, 'Because of its sleep-inducing properties.'

zizzer. A bed: Services, esp. R.A.F.: since ca. 1930. Ex zizz, v.

zob. Very nice: Plumtree School, Southern

Rhodesia: since ca. 1920. (A. M. Brown, letter of Sept. 18, 1938.) Arbitrary?

zobbit. An officer: R.A.F. lower ranks': since ca. 1965. (Sgt R. Farley, Feb. 16, 1967.) Ex S.E. zombie?

*zol or aap (or arp); esp. *make an aap* or *a zol*, to make a dagga cigarette: South African c.: C. 20. (C. P. Wittstock, letter of May 23, 1946.) The nouns are Afrikaans words, the former phrase meaning, lit., 'make a monkey'.

Zombie. A Canadian 'Home Guard' not allowed to serve outside North America: ca. 1940–5. 'After the Voodoo cult which insists that dead men can be made to walk and act as if they were alive,' *Daily Express*, Sept. 16, 1943 (cable from Austin Cross).

zombie. A conscript: Canadian Army: 1939–45. He has a lost appearance: cf. the sense of S.E. *Zombie*.—2. (Rare in singular.) *Zombies*, policewomen: c., since ca. 1949; then, since ca. 1952, also police s. (John Dickson Carr, *Patrick Butler* . . ., 1956.)

zombies. Basutoland and Bechuanaland companies of Pioneers in E. Africa and Near East: Army: ca. 1940–6.—2. See prec., sense 2.

Zone, the. 'The coveted promotion zone, the goal of the two-and-a-half striper. If one is outside the zone one is said to have "been",' Granville: Naval officers': since ca. 1925. Compare the Army's sweat on the top line (p. 853).

zoo.—3. Zoology: schoolboys' and -girls': since ca. 1925.—4. As *the zoo*, it was the 29th Armoured Division's name for 'funnies' (see *funny*, n., 4): ca. 1942–5. (P-G-R.)—5. *The zoo*, the barbed-wire entanglements: Army in France: 1915–18. (Reginald Pound, *The Lost Generation*, 1964.)

zoo box. A messing van: railwaymen's: C. 20. (*Railway*.)

zoo tie. A gaudy necktie: South African: C. 20. Alan Nash in *The Cape Times*, June 3, 1946. Afrikaans *zoot*.

zooks. Sweets: schoolchildren's, esp. in West Country: late C. 19–20. Ex dial. form of *sucks* = *suckers*, sweets.

zoom, v.i., to 'make a hit'; v.t., to boost by publicity: since ca. 1944. Ex Air Force zoom (p. 974).

zoomer. A member of an air crew: Australian airmen's: 1939–45. (B., 1943.) Ex *zoom* (p. 974).

zoon(-)bat. See 'Canadian'.

zoot canary. A fashion model (the person): beatniks' and teenagers': since ca. 1959. (Anderson.) Cf.:

zoot suit. A flashy suit of clothes: adopted, ca. 1950, from U.S. Here, *zoot*, is perhaps Dutch *zoet*, sweet. Dr Douglas Leechman comments thus: This is a bit complicated. In the first place, the New York ruffians corresponding to the Teddy boys pronounce 'suit' as 'soot', rhyming with 'boot', not as we do, rhyming with 'cute'. When zoot suits became fashionable, it was 'the thing' to duplicate words, thus the 'zoot soot', which had a fashionable 'drape shape'.—2. 'Special wind- and water-proof clothing which, issued to the crews of armoured vehicles in Europe in Nov. 1944, could also be used as sleeping bags' (Peter Sanders): late 1944-45. (Major-General G. L. Verney, *The Desert Rats*, 1954.)

*zoucher. See **sycher** (Addenda) and cf. **zouch** (*Dict.*).

Zowie. 'A new import from San Francisco, meaning hippy language' (Peter Fryer in *The Observer* colour supplement, Dec. 3, 1967): hippies': since (? May) 1967. In Am. s., since ca. 1945, *zowie* has signified 'energy' or 'zest' or the two combined (W. & F.); itself ex the exclamatory *zowie!, biff!* or *bang!*

Zozo. A metropolitan Frenchman: late C. 19-20: 'a term with little currency in Australia but quite widespread in the New Hebrides and New Caledonia among Australians. From Pidgin '*mens-aux-o*reilles' (ear-men) because the French offered a bounty on the ears of New Caledonian natives during the revolt of 1878' (Edwin Morrisby, letter of Aug. 30, 1958).

zubrick. Penis: Australian: since ca. 1941. Perhaps a rhyming-s. elaboration—on **prick,** 3 (p. 659)—of the synonymous Arabic *zab.* (Edwin Morrisby, Aug. 30, 1958.)

Zulu. 'An emigrant outfit', esp. a train for either emigrants or immigrants: Canadian railroadmen's: adopted, before 1931, ex U.S. Perhaps ex anglers' *zulu*, a gaudy fly.

zyders. The washing places: Felsted School: since ca. 1925. Marples, 'Probably from Zuyder Zee.'

zymotic, whence the even slangier *zymy*, 'Lousy': teenagers': since ca. 1963. (Mrs Verily Anderson, letter of Nov. 15, 1963.) Contrast **unzymotic.**